ANNUAL STATEMENT STUDIES

Financial Ratio Benchmarks

2007
2008

RMA
Annual Statement Studies®
Copyright, Ordering, Licensing, and Use of Data

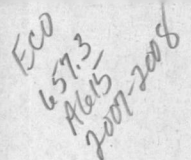

TABLE OF CONTENTS

*General Industries Format means that a valid construction NAICS was assigned to the subject companies contained in the sample; however, the financial statements were prepared using a general or traditional manufacturing or service industries presentation of results versus using a percentage-of-completion method of accounting. Industries found in the percentage-of-completion presentation follow the presentation used by RMA in the past.

4

THE RISK MANAGEMENT ASSOCIATION (RMA)

Founded in 1914, the Risk Management Association is a not-for-profit, member-driven professional association whose sole purpose is to advance the use of sound risk principles in the financial services industry. RMA promotes an enterprise approach to risk management that focuses on credit risk, market risk, and operational risk.

Headquartered in Philadelphia, Pennsylvania, RMA has 3,000 institutional members that include banks of all sizes as well as nonbank financial institutions. They are represented in the association by 18,000 risk management professionals who are chapter members in financial centers throughout North America, Europe, and Asia/Pacific. Visit RMA on the Web at www.rmahq.org.

RMA ACKNOWLEDGES AND THANKS THE FOLLOWING MEMBER INSTITUTIONS, CONTRIBUTORS TO THE 2007 RECORD-BREAKING STATEMENT STUDIES DATA SUBMISSIONS PROGRAM.

ALABAMA
Compass Bank
Regions Financial Corp.

ARIZONA
First National Bank of Arizona
Mohave State Bank

ARKANSAS
Malvern National Bank
Metropolitan National Bank
Simmons First National Bank

CALIFORNIA
Affinity Bank
Bank of Agriculture & Commerce
Central Valley Community Bank
Citizens Business Bank
City National Bank
Community Bank
Desert Community Bank
Exchange Bank
Farmers & Merchants Bank
    Central CA
First Commerce Bank
Medway Co-operative Bank
Mizahi Tefahot Bank Ltd.
Presidio Bank
Rabobank N.A.
Service 1st Bank
Tri Counties Bank
Valley Community Bank
Wells Fargo Bank N.A.
Westamerica Bank

COLORADO
American National Bank
CoBank
Colorado Business Bank N.A.
Farmers State Bank of Fort Morgan

CONNECTICUT
Chelsea Groton Savings Bank
Dime Bank
Milford Bank
Naugatuck Savings Bank
Northwest Community Bank
People's Bank
Webster Bank

DELAWARE
Delaware National Bank
Wilmington Trust Co.

FLORIDA
Bank of Tampa
Capital City Bank
Seacoast National Bank

GEORGIA
Citizens Trust Bank
Cohutta Banking Co.
Columbus Bank & Trust
First American Bank & Trust Co.
Georgia Bank & Trust Co.
Heritage Bank
Northwest Georgia Bank
Security Bank of Bibb County
SunTrust Banks, Inc.
Wachovia Corporation

HAWAII
American Savings Bank
Bank of Hawaii
Central Pacific Bank
Finance Factors Ltd.
First Hawaiian Bank

ILLINOIS
Albany Bank & Trust Co. N.A.
Alpine Bank of Illinois
American National Bank DeKalb
    County
Amerimark Bank
Busey Bank
Cole Taylor Bank
Des Plaines National Bank
First National Bank
First National Bank of La Grange
Glenview State Bank
Harris Nesbitt
JP Morgan Chase
LaSalle Bank N.A.
National Republic Bank Chicago
Northern Trust Company
Resource Bank N.A.
The National Bank & Trust Company

INDIANA
1st Source Bank
Campbell & Fetter Bank
Irwin Union Bank & Trust Co.
Lafayette Bank & Trust Co.
Lake City Bank
Old National Bank
STAR Financial Bank

IOWA
American Trust & Savings Bank
Farmers State Bank
First National Bank
Heartland Financial USA
Security National Bank
Wells Fargo Bank Iowa N.A.

KANSAS
Bankers Bank of Kansas
Citizens National Bank
Cornerstone Bank
Emprise Bank
Fidelity Bank
First Bank
First Bank of Newton
First State Bank Kansas City
Intrust Bank
Legacy Bank
Midland National Bank
Sunflower Bank
Verus Bank N.A.

KENTUCKY
Central Bank & Trust Co
Citizens Commerce National Bank
Community Trust Bank, Inc.

LOUISIANA
Bancorp South
Capital One Banking Segment
Jeff Davis Bank & Trust Co.
Omni Bank
Progressive Bank
South Louisiana Bank
Whitney National Bank

MAINE
Gardiner Savings Institution FSB
Gorham Savings Bank

Kennebunk Savings Bank
TD Banknorth N.A.
The First N.A.

MARYLAND
Annapolis Banking & Trust Co.
Bank of Glen Burnie
Citizens National Bank
Farmers & Mechanics Bank
Frederick County Bank
Hagerstown Trust Company
K Bank
OBA Federal Savings Bank
Peoples Bank of Elkton
Provident Bank of Maryland
Susquehanna Bank

MASSACHUSETTS
Beverly National Bank
Boston Private Bank & Trust Co.
Bristol County Savings Bank
Commonwealth National Bank
Eastern Bank
Enterprise Bank and Trust Co.
Fall River Five Cents Svgs Bank
Flagship Bank & Trust Co.
Legacy Banks
North Middlesex Savings Bank
Peoples Savings Bank
Randolph Savings Bank
River Bank
Slade's Ferry Trust Co.
South Shore Savings Bank
Sovereign Bank
The Bank of Canton
The Milford National Bank and Trust
Webster Five Cents Savings Bank
Westfield Bank

MICHIGAN
Capitol National Bank
Citizens Bank F&M
Citizens National Bank
Comerica Bank
Commercial Bank
CSB Bank
Honor State Bank
Huron Community Bank
Mercantile Bank of Michigan
United Bank & Trust
United Bank of Michigan

MINNESOTA
AgriBank FCB
American Bank of St. Paul
Anchor Bank Heritage

BankCherokee
Beacon Bank
Bremer Bank N.A.
Citizens Independent Bank
Community Bank Corporation
Crown Bank
Fidelity Bank
First Minnetonka City Bank
First National Bank Cannon Falls
Home Federal Savings Bank
KleinBank
Lake Elmo Bank
Merchants Bank N.A.
North Shore Bank of Commerce
Northeast Bank of Minneapolis
Roundbank
StearnsBank N.A.
TCF National Bank
US Bank National Association
Western Bank

MISSISIPPI
BanCorp South Bank
Merchants & Farmers Bank
Peoples Bank
Renasant Bank
Trustmark National Bank

MISSOURI
Cass Commercial Bank
Commerce Bank N.A.
Exchange National Bank Jeff City
First Bank
Jefferson Bank of Missouri
Renasant Bank
Royal Banks of Missouri
Triad Bank

MONTANA
American Bank
First Interstate Bank

NEBRASKA
First National Bank & Trust Co.
First National Bank of North Platte
First National Bank of Omaha
Fremont National Bank
Washington County Bank

NEW HAMPSHIRE
Connecticut River Bank
Ledyard National Bank

NEW JERSEY
Commerce Bank N.A.
Peapack-Gladstone Bank

Skylands Community Bank
Sun National Bank
The Bank
Union Center National Bank
Yardville National Bank

NEW MEXICO
Charter Bank
Citizens Bank of Las Cruces
Western Commerce Bank

NEW YORK
Adirondack Bank
Adirondack Trust Company
Alliance Bank N.A.
Bank of Castile
Canandaigua National Bank
Chemung Canal Trust Co.
Community Bank N.A.
Elmira Savings Bank FSB
Glens Falls National Bank
HSBC Bank USA, National
    Association
National Union Bank of Kinderhook
NBT Bank N.A.
Partners Trust Bank
State Bank of Long Island
Steuben Trust Co.
Suffolk County National Bank
Tioga State Bank

NORTH CAROLINA
Bank of America
BB&T
First Charter Bank
First Citizens Bank & Trust Co.
Lexington State Bank

NORTH DAKOTA
Alerus Financial N.A.
Bank of North Dakota
Bremer Bank N.A.
Community Bank of the Red River
    Valley
State Bank & Trust

OHIO
Buckeye Community Bank
Fifth Third Bank
First Financial Bancorp
FirstMerit Bank N.A.
Home Savings & Loan Co. of
    Youngstown
Huntington National Bank
Key Bank
Liberty Savings Bank FSB

National City Corp.
North Side Bank & Trust Co.
Second National Bank
Sky Bank

OKLAHOMA
Bank of Oklahoma N.A.

OREGON
Pacific Continental Bank
People's Bank of Commerce
West Coast Bank

PENNSYLVANIA
Bryn Mawr Trust Co.
Community Bank
Community Banks
County National Bank
Dollar Bank
Fidelity Bank PA SB
Fidelity Deposit & Discount Bank
First Columbia Bank & Trust Co.
First Commonwealth Bank
First National Bank of Chester
    County
First National Bank Pennslyvania
Firstrust Bank
FNB Bank
FNB Corp.
Fulton Bank
Harleysville National Bank
Jersey Shore State Bank
Lafayette Ambassador Bank
Luzerne National Bank
Mellon Bank N.A.
National Penn Bank
Northwest Savings Bank
Orrstown Bank
PNC Bank
Portage National Bank
Somerset Trust Company
Sterling Financial
Swineford National Bank
Univest National Bank & Trust Co.
Washington Federal Savings
Woodlands Bank

RHODE ISLAND
Bank Rhode Island
Citizens Financial Group

SOUTH CAROLINA
Carolina First Bank
CommunitySouth Bank & Trust
Conway National Bank
First Citizens Bank

Greer State Bank

SOUTH DAKOTA
BankWest
First National Bank in Sioux Falls
First National Bank South Dakota
First Premier Bank
Home Federal Bank

TENNESSEE
American Security Bank & Trust
Bank of Nashville
Cumberland Bank
First Farmers and Merchants Bank
First Tennessee Bank N.A.

TEXAS
Amarillo National Bank
Bank of the West
Extraco Banks N.A.
First Financial Bank, N.A. Abilene
Frost National Bank
Southside Bank
State National Bank

UTAH
Bank of Utah
First Utah Bank
Zions First National Bank

VERMONT
Chittenden Bank
Community National Bank
Merchants Bank
National Bank of Middlebury

VIRGINIA
Bank of Lancaster
First Community Bank N.A.
First National Bank
Freedom Bank of Virginia
Monarch Bank
Old Point National Bank
TowneBank
United Bank
Virginia Commerce Bank
Virginia National Bank

WASHINGTON
Bank of the Pacific
Banner Bank
Columbia State Bank
Northwest Farm Credit Services
    (ACA)
Security State Bank
Skagit State Bank

Washington First International Bank
Washington Mutual
Washington Trust Bank
Whidbey Island Bank

WEST VIRGINIA
First Century Bank N.A.
Progressive Bank N.A.
United Bank
Wesbanco Bank Wheeling

WISCONSIN
Anchor Bank, FSB
Associated Bank Green Bay N.A.
Bank of Elmwood
Bank of Sun Prairie
Bremer Bank N.A.
Community Business Bank
Fidelity National Bank
First Bank Financial Centre
First Bank of Baldwin
Grafton State Bank c/o Merchants &
    Manufacturers Bancorp
Horicon Bank
Johnson Bank
M&I Bank
Oak Bank
Park Bank
TCF National Bank
The Business Bank

WYOMING
Jackson State Bank

Introduction to
Annual Statement Studies: Financial Ratio Benchmarks, 2007-2008
and
General Organization of Content

The notes below will explain the presentation of *Annual Statement Studies: Financial Ratio Benchmarks,* show clearly how the book is organized, and answer most of your questions.

- **The Quality You Expect from RMA:** RMA is the most respected source of objective, unbiased information on issues of importance to credit risk professionals. For over 88 years, RMA's *Annual Statement Studies®* has been the industry standard for comparative financial data. Material contained in today's *Annual Statement Studies* was first published in the March 1919 issue of the *Federal Reserve Bulletin.* In the days before computers, the *Annual Statement Studies* data was recorded in pencil on yellow ledger paper! Today, it features data for over 740 industries derived <u>directly</u> from more than 265,000 statements of financial institutions' borrowers and prospects.

- **Data That Comes Straight from Original Sources:** The more than 265,000 statements used to produce the composites presented here come directly from RMA member institutions and represent the financials from their commercial customers and prospects. RMA does not know the names of the individual entities. In fact, to ensure confidentiality, company names are removed before the data is even delivered to RMA. The raw data making up each composite is not available to any third party.

- **Data Presented in Common Size:** *Annual Statement Studies: Financial Ratio Benchmarks* contains composite financial data. Balance sheet and income statement information is shown in common size format, with each item a percentage of total assets and sales. RMA computes common size statements for each individual statement in an industry group, then aggregates and averages all the figures. In some cases, because of computer rounding, the figures to the right of the decimal point do not balance exactly with the totals shown. A minus sign beside the value indicates credits and losses.

- **Includes Most Widely Used Ratios:** Nineteen of the most widely used ratios in the financial services industry accompany the balance sheet information, including various types of liquidity, coverage, leverage, and operating ratios.

- **Organized by the NAICS for Ease of Use:** This edition is organized according to the North American Industry Classification System (NAICS), a product of the U.S. Office of Management and Budget. At the top of each page of data, you will find the NAICS, plus cross-references to the Standard Industrial Classification (SIC) codes. A NAICS code may correspond to more than one SIC, so there may be several SICs listed. If a NAICS code maps to more than three SIC codes, only the first three SICs will be listed at the top of the page, with all corresponding SIC codes found in the NAICS description index.

- **Twenty Sections Outline Major Types of Businesses:** To provide further delineation, the book is divided into 20 sections outlining major lines of businesses. If you know the NAICS number you are looking for, use the NAICS-page guide provided in the front of this book. If you know the SIC number you are looking for, refer to the SIC-page guide also provided in the front of the book. In general, the book is arranged in ascending NAICS numerical order. For your convenience, full descriptions of each NAICS are presented in this book. In addition, you will find a text-based index near the end of the book.

- **If You Do Not Know the NAICS or SIC Code You Are Looking for...** If you do not know the precise industry NAICS/SIC you are looking for, contact the Census Bureau at 1-888-75NAICS or naics@census.gov. Describe the activity of the establishment for which you need an industry code and you will receive a reply. Another source to help you assign the correct NAICS/SIC industry name and number can be found at www.census.gov/epcd/www/naics.html.

- **Can't Find the Industry You Want?** There are a number of reasons you may not find the industry you are looking for (i.e., you know you need industry xxxxxx but it is not in the product). Many times we have information on an industry, but it is not published because the sample size was too small or there were significant questions concerning the data. (For an industry to be displayed in the *Annual Statement Studies: Financial Ratio Benchmarks,* there must be at least 30 valid statements submitted to RMA.) In other instances, we simply do not have the data. Generally, most of what we receive is published.

- **Composite Data Not Shown?** When there are fewer than 10 financial statements in a particular asset or sales size category, the composite data is not shown because a sample this small is not considered representative and could be misleading. However, all the data for that industry is shown in the All Sizes column. The total number of statements for each size category is shown in bold print at the top of each column. In addition, the number of statements used in a ratio array will differ from the number of statements in a sample because certain elements of data may not be present in all financial statements. In these cases, the number of statements used is shown in parentheses to the left of the array.

- **Presentation of the Data on Each Page-Spread:** For all non-contracting spread statements, the data for a particular industry appears on both the left and right pages. The heading Current Data Sorted by Assets is in the five columns on the left side. The center section of the double-page presentation contains the Comparative Historical Data, with the All Sizes column for the current year shown under the heading 4/1/xx-3/31/xx. Comparable data from past editions of the *Annual Statement Studies: Financial Ratio Benchmarks* also appears in this section. Current Data Sorted by Sales is displayed in the five columns to the far right.

- **Companies with Less than $250 Million in Total Assets:** In our presentation, we used companies having less than $250 million in total assets—except in the case of contractors who use the percentage-of-completion method of accounting. *The section for contractors using the percentage-of-completion method of accounting contains data only sorted by revenue.* There is no upper limit placed on revenue size for any industry. Its information is found on only one page.

- **Page Headers:** The information shown at the top of each page includes the following: 1) the identity of the industry group; 2) its NAICS number and its SIC number; 3) a breakdown by size categories of the types of financial statements reported; 4) the number of statements in each category; 5) the dates of the statements used; and 6) the size categories. For instance, 16 (4/1-9/30/06) means that 16 statements with fiscal dates between April 1 and September 30, 2006, make up part of the sample.

- **Page Footers:** At the bottom of each page, we have included the sum of the sales (or revenues) and total assets for all the financial statements in each size category. This data allows recasting of the common-size statements into dollar amounts. To do this, divide the number at the bottom of the page by the number of statements in that size category. Then multiply the result by the percentages in the common-size statement.

- **Our Thanks to CFMA:** RMA appreciates the cooperation of the Construction Financial Management Association (CFMA) in permitting us to reproduce excerpts from its *Construction Industry Annual Financial Survey*. This data complements the RMA contractor industry data.

- **Recommended for Use as General Guidelines:** RMA recommends you use *Annual Statement Studies: Financial Ratio Benchmarks* data only as general guidelines and not as absolute industry norms. There are several reasons why the data may not be fully representative of a given industry:

  1. **Data Not Random**—The financial statements used in the *Annual Statement Studies: Financial Ratio Benchmarks* are not selected by any random or statistically reliable method. RMA member banks voluntarily submit the raw data they have available each year with no limitation on company size.

  2. **Categorized by Primary Product Only**—Many companies have varied product lines; however, the *Annual Statement Studies: Financial Ratio Benchmarks* categorizes them by their primary product NAICS/SIC number only.

  3. **Small Samples**—Some of the industry samples are small in relation to the total number of firms for a given industry. A relatively small sample can increase the chances that some composites do not fully represent an industry.

  4. **Extreme Statements**—An extreme or outlier statement can occasionally be present in a sample, causing a disproportionate influence on the industry composite. This is particularly true in a relatively small sample.

  5. **Operational Differences**—Companies within the same industry may differ in their method of operations, which in turn can directly influence their financial statements. Since they are included in the sample, these statements can significantly affect the composite calculations.

  6. **Additional Considerations**—There are other considerations that can result in variations among different companies engaged in the same general line of business. These include different labor markets, geographical location, different accounting methods, quality of products handled, sources and methods of financing, and terms of sale.

For these reasons, RMA does not recommend using the *Annual Statement Studies: Financial Ratio Benchmarks* figures as absolute norms for a given industry. Rather, you should use the figures only as general guidelines and as a supplement to the other methods of financial analysis. RMA makes no claim regarding how representative the figures printed in this book are.

DEFINITION OF RATIOS
INTRODUCTION

On each data page, below the common-size balance sheet and income statement information, you will find a series of ratios computed from the financial statement data.

Here is how these figures are calculated for any given ratio:

1. The ratio is computed for each financial statement in the sample.

2. These values are arrayed (listed) in an order from the strongest to the weakest. In interpreting ratios, the "strongest" or "best" value is not always the largest numerical value, nor is the "weakest" always the lowest numerical value. (For certain ratios, there may be differing opinions as to what constitutes a strong or a weak value. RMA follows general banking guidelines consistent with sound credit practice to resolve this problem.)

3. The array of values is divided into four groups of equal size. The description of each ratio appearing in the *Statement Studies* provides details regarding the arraying of the values.

What Are Quartiles?

Each ratio has three points, or "cut-off values," that divide an array of values into four equal-sized groups called quartiles, as shown below. The quartiles include the upper quartile, upper-middle quartile, lower-middle quartile, and the lower quartile. The upper quartile is the cut-off value where one-quarter of the array of ratios falls between it and the strongest ratio. The median is the midpoint—that is, the middle cut-off value where half of the array falls above it and half below it. The lower quartile is the point where one-quarter of the array falls between it and the weakest ratio. In many cases, the average of two values is used to arrive at the quartile value. You will find the median and quartile values on all *Statement Studies* data pages in the order indicated in the chart below.

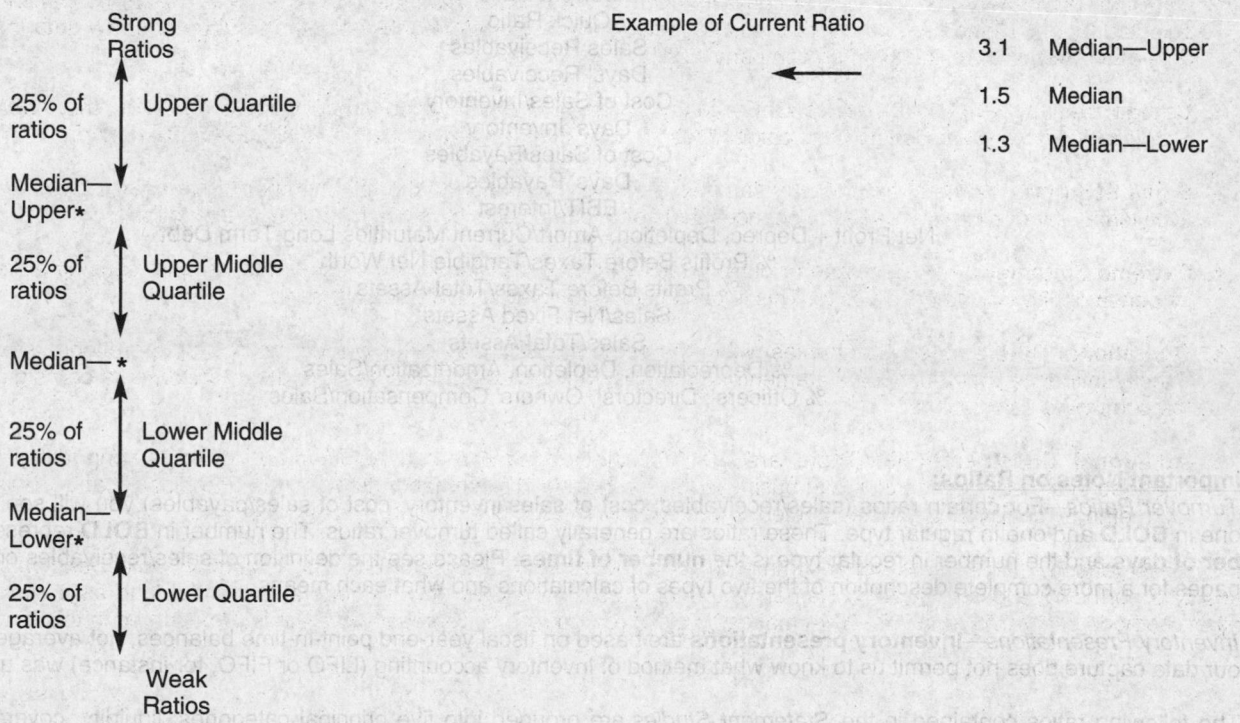

		Example of Current Ratio	
Strong Ratios		3.1	Median—Upper
25% of ratios — Upper Quartile		1.5	Median
Median—Upper*		1.3	Median—Lower
25% of ratios — Upper Middle Quartile			
Median—*			
25% of ratios — Lower Middle Quartile			
Median—Lower*			
25% of ratios — Lower Quartile			
Weak Ratios			

Why Use Medians/Quartiles Instead of the Average?

There are several reasons medians and quartiles are used instead of an average. Medians and quartiles eliminate the influence an "outlier" (an extremely high or low value when compared to the rest of the values). They also more accurately reflect the ranges of ratio values than a straight averaging method.

It is important to understand that the spread (range) between the upper and lower quartiles represents the middle 50% of all the companies in a sample. Therefore, ratio values greater than the upper quartile or less than the lower quartile may begin to approach "unusual" values.

Non-Conventional Values:
For some ratio values, you will occasionally see an entry that is other than a conventional number. These entries are defined as follows:

(1) <u>UND</u>—This stands for "undefined," the result of the denominator in a ratio calculation approaching zero.

(2) <u>NM</u>—This may occasionally appear as a quartile or median for the ratios sales/working capital, debt/worth, and fixed/worth. It stands for "no meaning" in cases where the dispersion is so small that any interpretation is meaningless.

(3) <u>999.8</u>—When a ratio value equals 1,000 or more, it also becomes an "unusual" value and is given the "999.8" designation. This is considered to be a close enough approximation to the actual unusually large value.

Linear versus Non-Linear Ratios:
An array that is ordered in ascending sequence or in descending sequence is linear. An array that deviates from true ascending or true descending when its values change from positive to negative (low to high positive, followed by high to low negative) is non-linear.

A specific example of a non-linear ratio would be the Sales/Working Capital ratio. In other words, when the Sales/Working Capital ratio is positive, then the top quartile would be represented by the *lowest positive* ratio. However, if the ratio is negative, the top quartile will be represented by the *highest negative* ratio! In a non-linear array such as this, the median could be either positive or negative because it is whatever the middle value is in the particular array of numbers.

Non-Linear Ratios

Sales/Working Capital
Fixed/Worth
Debt/Worth

Linear Ratios

Current Ratio
Quick Ratio
Sales Receivables
Days' Receivables
Cost of Sales/Inventory
Days' Inventory
Cost of Sales/Payables
Days' Payables
EBIT/Interest
Net Profit + Deprec, Depletion, Amort/Current Maturities Long-Term Debt
% Profits Before Taxes/Tangible Net Worth
% Profits Before Taxes/Total Assets
Sales/Net Fixed Assets
Sales/Total Assets
% Depreciation, Depletion, Amortization/Sales
% Officers', Directors', Owners' Compensation/Sales

Important Notes on Ratios:
Turnover Ratios—For certain ratios (sales/receivables, cost of sales/inventory, cost of sales/payables) you will see two numbers, one in **BOLD** and one in regular type. These ratios are generally called turnover ratios. The number in **BOLD** represents **the number of days** and the number in regular type is the **number of times**. Please see the definition of sales/receivables on the following pages for a more complete description of the two types of calculations and what each means.

Inventory Presentations—**Inventory presentations** are based on fiscal year-end point-in-time balances, not averages. In addition, our data capture does not permit us to know what method of inventory accounting (LIFO or FIFO, for instance) was used.

The following ratios contained in the *Statement Studies* are grouped into five principal categories: liquidity, coverage, leverage, operating, and specific expense items.

LIQUIDITY RATIOS

Liquidity is a measure of the quality and adequacy of current assets to meet current obligations as they come due. In other words, can a firm quickly convert its assets to cash—without a loss in value—in order to meet its immediate and short-term obligations? For firms such as utilities that can readily and accurately predict their cash inflows, liquidity is not nearly as critical as it is for firms like airlines or manufacturing businesses that can have wide fluctuations in demand and revenue streams. These ratios provide a level of comfort to lenders in case of liquidation.

1. Current Ratio

How to Calculate: Divide total current assets by total current liabilities.

$$\frac{\text{Total Current Assets}}{\text{Total Current Liabilities}}$$

How to Interpret: This ratio is a rough indication of a firm's ability to service its current obligations. Generally, the higher the current ratio, the greater the "cushion" between current obligations and a firm's ability to pay them. While a stronger ratio shows that the numbers for current assets exceed those for current liabilities, the composition and quality of current assets are critical factors in the analysis of an individual firm's liquidity.

The ratio values are arrayed from the highest positive to the lowest positive.

2. Quick Ratio

How to Calculate: Add cash and equivalents to trade receivables. Then, divide by total current liabilities.

$$\frac{\text{Cash \& Equivalents + Trade Receivables (net)}}{\text{Total Current Liabilities}}$$

How to Interpret: Also known as the "acid test" ratio, this is a stricter, more conservative measure of liquidity than the current ratio. This ratio reflects the degree to which a company's current liabilities are covered by its most liquid current assets, the kind of assets that can be converted quickly to cash and at amounts close to book value. Inventory and other less liquid current assets are removed from the calculation. Generally, if the ratio produces a value that's less than 1 to 1, it implies a "dependency" on inventory or other "less" current assets to liquidate short-term debt.

The ratio values are arrayed from the highest positive to the lowest positive.

3. Sales/Receivables

How to Calculate: Divide net sales by trade receivables.

$$\frac{\text{Net Sales}}{\text{Trade Receivables (net)}}$$

Please note—In the contractor section, both accounts receivable-progress billings and accounts receivable-current retention are included in the receivables figure used in calculating the revenues/receivables and receivables/payables ratios.

How to Interpret: This ratio measures the number of times trade receivables turn over during the year. The higher the turnover of receivables, the shorter the time between sale and cash collection.

> For example, a company with sales of $720,000 and receivables of $120,000 would have a sales/receivables ratio of 6.0. This means receivables turn over six times a year. If a company's receivables appear to be turning more slowly than the rest of the industry, further research is needed and the quality of the receivables should be examined closely.

Cautions—A problem with this ratio is that it compares one day's receivables, shown at statement date, to total annual sales and does not take into consideration seasonal fluctuations. An additional problem in interpretation may arise when there is a large proportion of cash sales to total sales.

When the receivables figure is zero, the quotient will be undefined (UND) and represents the best possible ratio. The ratio values are therefore arrayed starting with undefined (UND) and then from the numerically highest value to the numerically lowest value. The only time a zero will appear in the array is when the sales figure is low and the quotient rounds off to zero. By definition, this ratio cannot be negative.

4. Days' Receivables

The sales/receivables ratio will have a figure printed in bold type directly to the left of the array. This figure is the days' receivables.

How to Calculate the Days' Receivables: Divide the sales/receivables ratio into 365 (the number of days in one year).

$$\frac{365}{\text{Sales/Receivable ratio}}$$

How to Interpret the Days' Receivables: This figure expresses the average number of days that receivables are outstanding. Generally, the greater the number of days outstanding, the greater the probability of delinquencies in accounts receivable. A comparison of a company's daily receivables may indicate the extent of a company's control over credit and collections.

Please note—You should take into consideration the terms offered by a company to its customers because these may differ from terms within the industry.

> For example, using the sales/receivable ratio calculated above, 365 ÷ 6 = 61 (i.e., the average receivable is collected in 61 days).

5. Cost of Sales/Inventory

How to Calculate: Divide cost of sales by inventory.

$$\frac{\text{Cost of Sales}}{\text{Inventory}}$$

How to Interpret: This ratio measures the number of times inventory is turned over during the year.

High Inventory Turnover—On the positive side, high inventory turnover can indicate greater liquidity or superior merchandising. Conversely, it can indicate a shortage of needed inventory for sales.

Low Inventory Turnover—Low inventory turnover can indicate poor liquidity, possible overstocking, or obsolescence. On the positive side, it could indicate a planned inventory buildup in the case of material shortages.

Cautions—A problem with this ratio is that it compares one day's inventory to cost of goods sold and does not take seasonal fluctuations into account. When the inventory figure is zero, the quotient will be undefined (UND) and represents the best possible ratio. The ratio values are arrayed starting with undefined (UND) and then from the numerically highest value to the numerically lowest value. The only time a zero will appear in the array is when the figure for cost of sales is very low and the quotient rounds off to zero.

Please note—For service industries, the cost of sales is included in operating expenses. In addition, please note that the data collection process does not differentiate the method of inventory valuation.

6. Days' Inventory

The days' inventory is the figure printed in bold directly to the left of the cost of sales/inventory ratio.

How to Calculate the Days' Inventory: Divide the cost of sales/inventory ratio into 365 (the number of days in one year).

$$\frac{365}{\text{Cost of Sales/Inventory ratio}}$$

How to Interpret: Dividing of the inventory turnover ratio into 365 days yields the average length of time units are in inventory.

7. Cost of Sales/Payables

How to Calculate: Divide cost of sales by trade payables.

$$\frac{\text{Cost of Sales}}{\text{Trade Payables}}$$

Please note—In the contractor section, both accounts payable-trade and accounts payable-retention are included in the payables figure used in calculating the cost of revenues/payables and receivables/payables ratios.

How to Interpret: This ratio measures the number of times trade payables turn over during the year. The higher the turnover of payables, the shorter the time between purchase and payment. If a company's payables appear to be turning more slowly than the industry, then the company may be experiencing cash shortages, disputing invoices with suppliers, enjoying extended terms, or deliberately expanding its trade credit. The ratio comparison of company to industry suggests the existence of these or other possible causes. If a firm buys on 30-day terms, it is reasonable to expect this ratio to turn over in approximately 30 days.

Cautions—A problem with this ratio is that it compares one day's payables to cost of goods sold and does not take seasonal fluctuations into account. When the payables figure is zero, the quotient will be undefined (UND) and represents the best possible ratio. The ratio values are arrayed starting with undefined (UND) and then from the numerically highest to the numerically lowest value. The only time a zero will appear in the array is when the figure for cost of sales is very low and the quotient rounds off to zero.

8. Days' Payables

The days' payables is the figure printed in bold type directly to the left of the cost of sales/payables ratio.

How to Calculate the Days' Payables: Divide the cost of sales/payables ratio into 365 (the number of days in one year).

$$\frac{365}{\text{Cost of Sales/Payables ratio}}$$

How to Interpret: Division of the payables turnover ratio into 365 days yields the average length of time trade debt is outstanding.

9. Sales/Working Capital

How to Calculate: Divide net sales by net working capital (current assets less current liabilities equals net working capital).

$$\frac{\text{Net Sales}}{\text{Net Working Capital}}$$

How to Interpret: Because it reflects the ability to finance current operations, working capital is a measure of the margin of protection for current creditors. When you relate the level of sales resulting from operations to the underlying working capital, you can measure how efficiently working capital is being used.

Low ratio (close to zero)—A low ratio may indicate an inefficient use of working capital.

High ratio (high positive or high negative)—A very high ratio often signifies overtrading, which is a vulnerable position for creditors.

Please note—Sales/Working Capital ratio is a nonlinear array. In other words, an array that is NOT ordered from highest positive to highest negative as is the case for linear arrays. The ratio values are arrayed from the lowest positive to the highest positive, to undefined (UND), and then from the highest negative to the lowest negative. If working capital is zero, the quotient is undefined (UND).

If the Sales/Working Capital ratio is positive, then the top quartile would be represented by the *lowest positive* ratio. However, if the ratio is negative, the top quartile will be represented by the *highest negative* ratio! In a non-linear array such as the sales/working capital ratio, the median could be either positive or negative because it is whatever the middle value is in the particular array of numbers.

Cautions—When analyzing this ratio, you need to focus on working capital, not on the sales figure. Although sales cannot be negative, working capital can be. If you have a large, positive working capital number, the ratio will be small *and* positive—which is good. Because negative working capital is bad, if you have a large, negative working capital number, the sales/working capital ratio will be small *and* negative—which is NOT good. Therefore, the lowest positive ratio is the best and the lowest negative ratio is the worst. If working capital is a small negative number, the ratio will be large, which is the best of the negatives.

COVERAGE RATIOS

Coverage ratios measure a firm's ability to service its debt. In other words, how well does the flow of a company's funds cover its short-term financial obligations? In contrast to liquidity ratios that focus on the possibility of liquidation, coverage ratios seek to provide lenders a comfort level based on the belief the firm will remain a viable enterprise.

1. Earnings Before Interest and Taxes (EBIT)/Interest

How to Calculate: Divide earnings (profit) before annual interest expense and taxes by annual interest expense.

$$\frac{\text{Earnings Before Interest \& Taxes}}{\text{Annual Interest Expense}}$$

How to Interpret: This ratio measures a firm's ability to meet interest payments. A high ratio may indicate that a borrower can easily meet the interest obligations of a loan. This ratio also indicates a firm's capacity to take on additional debt.

Please note—Only statements reporting annual interest expense were used in the calculation of this ratio. The ratio values are arrayed from the highest positive to the lowest positive and then from the lowest negative to the highest negative.

2. Net Profit + Depreciation, Depletion, Amortization/Current Maturities Long-Term Debt

How to Calculate: Add net profit to depreciation, depletion, and amortization expenses. Then, divide by the current portion of long-term debt.

$$\frac{\text{Net Profit + Depreciation, Depletion, Amortization Expenses}}{\text{Current Portion of Long-Term Debt}}$$

How to Interpret: This ratio reflects how well cash flow from operations covers current maturities. Because cash flow is the primary source of debt retirement, the ratio measures a firm's ability to service principal repayment and take on additional debt. Even though it is a mistake to believe all cash flow is available for debt service, this ratio is still a valid measure of the ability to service long-term debt.

Please note—Only data for corporations with the following items was used:

(1) Profit or loss after taxes (positive, negative, or zero).

(2) A positive figure for depreciation/depletion/amortization expenses.

(3) A positive figure for current maturities of long-term debt.

Ratio values are arrayed from the highest to the lowest positive and then from the lowest to the highest negative.

LEVERAGE RATIOS

How much protection do a company's assets provide for the debt held by its creditors? Highly leveraged firms are companies with heavy debt in relation to their net worth. These firms are more vulnerable to business downturns than those with lower debt-to-worth positions. While leverage ratios help measure this vulnerability, keep in mind that these ratios vary greatly depending on the requirements of particular industry groups.

1. Fixed/Worth

How to Calculate: Divide fixed assets (net of accumulated depreciation) by tangible net worth (net worth minus intangibles).

$$\frac{\text{Net Fixed Assets}}{\text{Tangible Net Worth}}$$

How to Interpret: This ratio measures the extent to which owner's equity (capital) has been invested in plant and equipment (fixed assets). A lower ratio indicates a proportionately smaller investment in fixed assets in relation to net worth and a better "cushion" for creditors in case of liquidation. Similarly, a higher ratio would indicate the opposite situation. The presence of a substantial number of fixed assets that are leased—and not appearing on the balance sheet—may result in a deceptively lower ratio.

Fixed assets may be zero, in which case the quotient is zero. If tangible net worth is zero, the quotient is undefined (UND). If tangible net worth is negative, the quotient is negative.

Please note—Like the sales/working capital ratio discussed above, this fixed/worth ratio is a nonlinear array. In other words, an array that is NOT ordered from highest positive to highest negative as a linear array would be. The ratio values are arrayed from the lowest positive to the highest positive, to undefined (UND), and then from the highest negative to the lowest negative.

If the Fixed/Worth ratio is positive, then the top quartile would be represented by the *lowest positive* ratio. However, if the ratio is negative, the top quartile will be represented by the *highest negative* ratio! In a nonlinear array such as this, the median could be either positive or negative because it is whatever the middle value is in the particular array of numbers.

2. Debt/Worth

How to Calculate: Divide total liabilities by tangible net worth.

$$\frac{\text{Total Liabilities}}{\text{Tangible Net Worth}}$$

How to Interpret: This ratio expresses the relationship between capital contributed by creditors and that contributed by owners. Basically, it shows how much protection the owners are providing creditors. The higher the ratio, the greater the risk being assumed by creditors. A lower ratio generally indicates greater long-term financial safety. Unlike a highly leveraged firm, a firm with a low debt/worth ratio usually has greater flexibility to borrow in the future.

Tangible net worth may be zero, in which case the ratio is undefined (UND). Tangible net worth may also be negative, which results in the quotient being negative. The ratio values are arrayed from the lowest to highest positive, to undefined, and then from the highest to lowest negative.

Please note—Like the sales/working capital ratio discussed above, this debt/worth ratio is a nonlinear array. In other words, it is an array that is NOT ordered from highest positive to highest negative as a linear array would be. The ratio values are arrayed from the lowest positive to the highest positive, to undefined (UND), and then from the highest negative to the lowest negative.

If the debt/worth ratio is positive, then the top quartile would be represented by the *lowest positive* ratio. However, if the ratio is negative, the top quartile will be represented by the *highest negative* ratio! In a non-linear array such as this, the median could be either positive or negative because it is whatever the middle value is in the particular array of numbers.

OPERATING RATIOS

Operating ratios are designed to assist in the evaluation of management performance.

1. % Profits Before Taxes/Tangible Net Worth

How to Calculate: Divide profit before taxes by tangible net worth. Then, multiply by 100.

$$\frac{\text{Profit Before Taxes}}{\text{Tangible Net Worth}} \times 100$$

How to Interpret: This ratio expresses the rate of return on tangible capital employed. While it can serve as an indicator of management performance, you should always use it in conjunction with other ratios. Normally associated with effective management, a high return could actually point to an undercapitalized firm. Conversely, a low return that's usually viewed as an indicator of inefficient management performance could actually reflect a highly capitalized, conservatively operated business.

This ratio has been multiplied by 100 because it is shown as a percentage.

Profit before taxes may be zero, in which case the ratio is zero. Profits before taxes may be negative, resulting in negative quotients. Firms with negative tangible net worth have been omitted from the ratio arrays. Negative ratios will therefore only result in the case of negative profit before taxes. If the tangible net worth is zero, the quotient is undefined (UND). If there are fewer than 10 ratios for a particular size class, the result is not shown. The ratio values are arrayed starting with undefined (UND), then from the highest to the lowest positive values, and finally from the lowest to the highest negative values.

2. % Profits Before Taxes/Total Assets

How to Calculate: Divide profit before taxes by total assets and multiply by 100.

$$\frac{\text{Profit Before Taxes}}{\text{Total Assets}} \times 100$$

How to Interpret: This ratio expresses the pre-tax return on total assets and measures the effectiveness of management in employing the resources available to it. If a specific ratio varies considerably from the ranges found in this book, the analyst will need to examine the makeup of the assets and take a closer look at the earnings figure. A heavily depreciated plant and a large amount of intangible assets or unusual income or expense items will cause distortions of this ratio.

This ratio has been multiplied by 100 since it is shown as a percentage. If profit before taxes is zero, the quotient is zero. If profit before taxes is negative, the quotient is negative. These ratio values are arrayed from the highest to the lowest positive and then from the lowest to the highest negative.

3. Sales/Net Fixed Assets

How to Calculate: Divide net sales by net fixed assets (net of accumulated depreciation).

$$\frac{\text{Net Sales}}{\text{Net Fixed Assets}}$$

How to Interpret: This ratio is a measure of the productive use of a firm's fixed assets. Largely depreciated fixed assets or a labor-intensive operation may cause a distortion of this ratio.

If the net fixed figure is zero, the quotient is undefined (UND). The only time a zero will appear in the array will be when the net sales figure is low and the quotient rounds off to zero. These ratio values cannot be negative.

They are arrayed from undefined (UND) and then from the highest to the lowest positive values.

4. Sales/Total Assets

How to Calculate: Divide net sales by total assets.

$$\frac{\text{Net Sales}}{\text{Total Assets}}$$

How to Interpret: This ratio is a general measure of a firm's ability to generate sales in relation to total assets. It should be used only to compare firms within specific industry groups and in conjunction with other operating ratios to determine the effective employment of assets.

The only time a zero will appear in the array will be when the net sales figure is low and the quotient rounds off to zero. The ratio values cannot be negative. They are arrayed from the highest to the lowest positive values.

EXPENSE TO SALES RATIOS

The following two ratios relate specific expense items to net sales and express this relationship as a percentage. Comparisons are convenient because the item, net sales, is used as a constant. Variations in these ratios are most pronounced between capital- and labor-intensive industries.

1. % Depreciation, Depletion, Amortization/Sales

How to Calculate: Divide annual depreciation, amortization, and depletion expenses by net sales and multiply by 100.

$$\frac{\text{Depreciation, Amortization, Depletion Expenses}}{\text{Net Sales}} \times 100$$

2. % Officers', Directors', Owners' Compensation/Sales

How to Calculate: Divide annual officers', directors', owners' compensation by net sales and multiply by 100. Include total salaries, bonuses, commissions, and other monetary remuneration to all officers, directors, and/or owners of the firm during the year covered by the statement. This includes drawings of partners and proprietors.

$$\frac{\text{Officers', Directors', Owners' Compensation}}{\text{Net Sales}} \times 100$$

Only statements showing a positive figure for each of the expense categories shown above were used. The ratios are arrayed from the lowest to highest positive values.

Explanation of Noncontractor Balance Sheet and Income Data

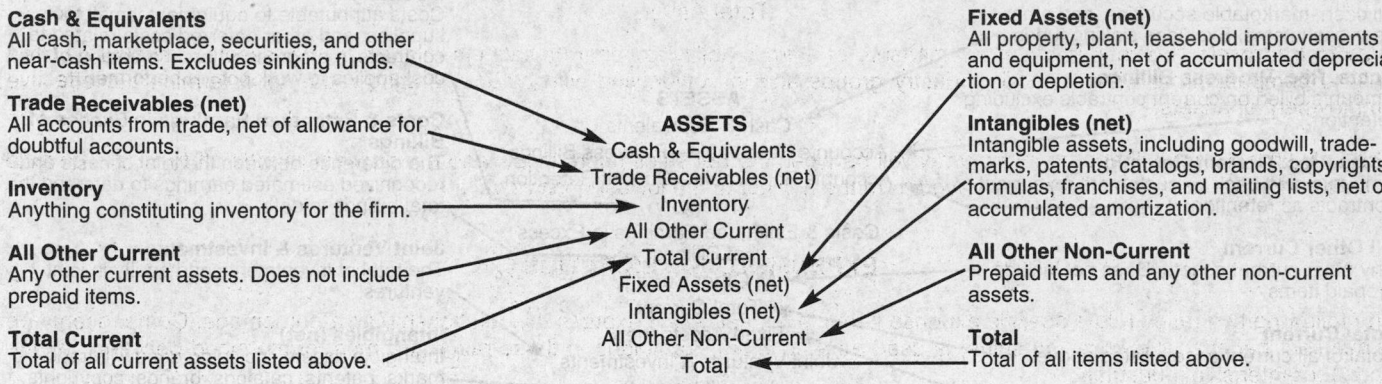

Cash & Equivalents
All cash, marketplace, securities, and other near-cash items. Excludes sinking funds.

Trade Receivables (net)
All accounts from trade, net of allowance for doubtful accounts.

Inventory
Anything constituting inventory for the firm.

All Other Current
Any other current assets. Does not include prepaid items.

Total Current
Total of all current assets listed above.

ASSETS
Cash & Equivalents
Trade Receivables (net)
Inventory
All Other Current
Total Current
Fixed Assets (net)
Intangibles (net)
All Other Non-Current
Total

Fixed Assets (net)
All property, plant, leasehold improvements and equipment, net of accumulated depreciation or depletion.

Intangibles (net)
Intangible assets, including goodwill, trademarks, patents, catalogs, brands, copyrights, formulas, franchises, and mailing lists, net of accumulated amortization.

All Other Non-Current
Prepaid items and any other non-current assets.

Total
Total of all items listed above.

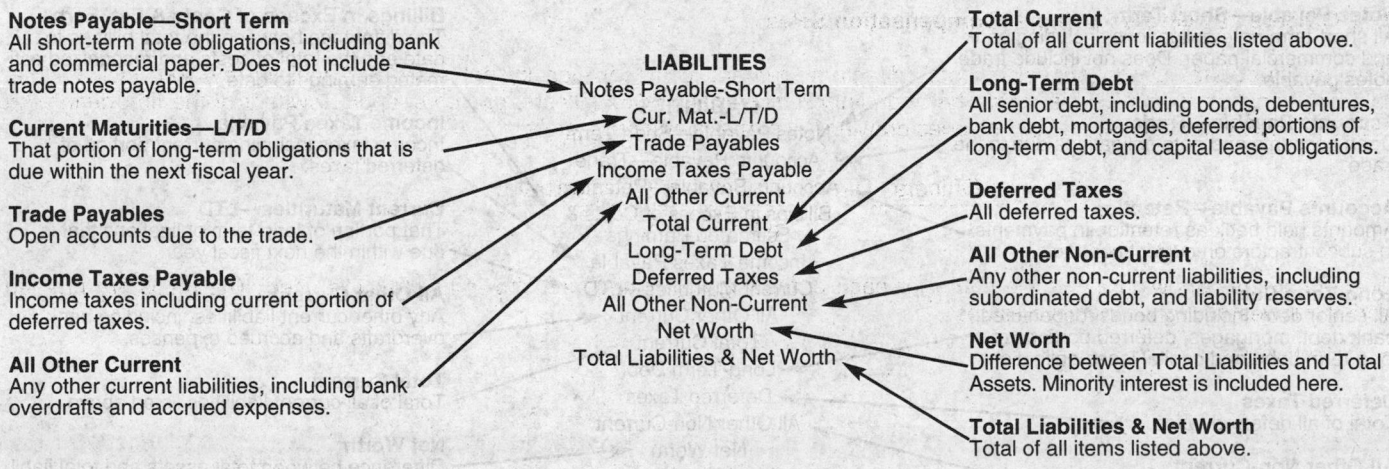

Notes Payable—Short Term
All short-term note obligations, including bank and commercial paper. Does not include trade notes payable.

Current Maturities—L/T/D
That portion of long-term obligations that is due within the next fiscal year.

Trade Payables
Open accounts due to the trade.

Income Taxes Payable
Income taxes including current portion of deferred taxes.

All Other Current
Any other current liabilities, including bank overdrafts and accrued expenses.

LIABILITIES
Notes Payable-Short Term
Cur. Mat.-L/T/D
Trade Payables
Income Taxes Payable
All Other Current
Total Current
Long-Term Debt
Deferred Taxes
All Other Non-Current
Net Worth
Total Liabilities & Net Worth

Total Current
Total of all current liabilities listed above.

Long-Term Debt
All senior debt, including bonds, debentures, bank debt, mortgages, deferred portions of long-term debt, and capital lease obligations.

Deferred Taxes
All deferred taxes.

All Other Non-Current
Any other non-current liabilities, including subordinated debt, and liability reserves.

Net Worth
Difference between Total Liabilities and Total Assets. Minority interest is included here.

Total Liabilities & Net Worth
Total of all items listed above.

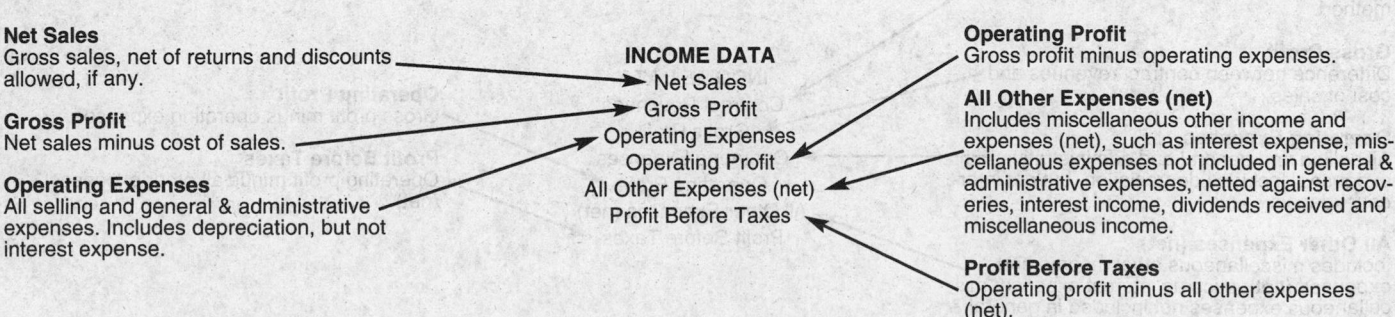

Net Sales
Gross sales, net of returns and discounts allowed, if any.

Gross Profit
Net sales minus cost of sales.

Operating Expenses
All selling and general & administrative expenses. Includes depreciation, but not interest expense.

INCOME DATA
Net Sales
Gross Profit
Operating Expenses
Operating Profit
All Other Expenses (net)
Profit Before Taxes

Operating Profit
Gross profit minus operating expenses.

All Other Expenses (net)
Includes miscellaneous other income and expenses (net), such as interest expense, miscellaneous expenses not included in general & administrative expenses, netted against recoveries, interest income, dividends received and miscellaneous income.

Profit Before Taxes
Operating profit minus all other expenses (net).

Explanation of Contractor Percentage-of-Completion Basis of Accounting
Balance Sheet and Income Data

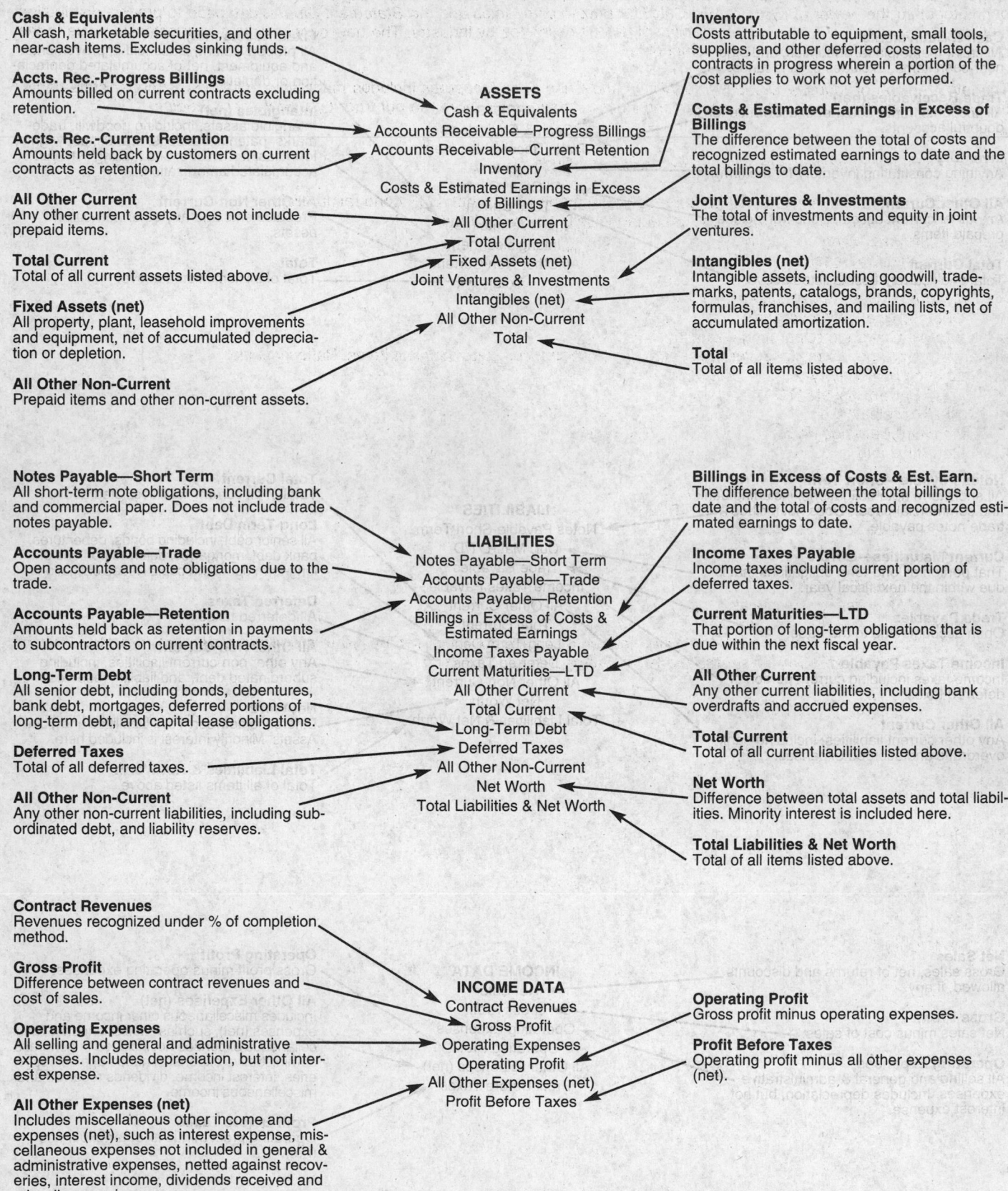

Cash & Equivalents
All cash, marketable securities, and other near-cash items. Excludes sinking funds.

Accts. Rec.-Progress Billings
Amounts billed on current contracts excluding retention.

Accts. Rec.-Current Retention
Amounts held back by customers on current contracts as retention.

All Other Current
Any other current assets. Does not include prepaid items.

Total Current
Total of all current assets listed above.

Fixed Assets (net)
All property, plant, leasehold improvements and equipment, net of accumulated depreciation or depletion.

All Other Non-Current
Prepaid items and other non-current assets.

Inventory
Costs attributable to equipment, small tools, supplies, and other deferred costs related to contracts in progress wherein a portion of the cost applies to work not yet performed.

Costs & Estimated Earnings in Excess of Billings
The difference between the total of costs and recognized estimated earnings to date and the total billings to date.

Joint Ventures & Investments
The total of investments and equity in joint ventures.

Intangibles (net)
Intangible assets, including goodwill, trademarks, patents, catalogs, brands, copyrights, formulas, franchises, and mailing lists, net of accumulated amortization.

Total
Total of all items listed above.

ASSETS
Cash & Equivalents
Accounts Receivable—Progress Billings
Accounts Receivable—Current Retention
Inventory
Costs & Estimated Earnings in Excess of Billings
All Other Current
Total Current
Fixed Assets (net)
Joint Ventures & Investments
Intangibles (net)
All Other Non-Current
Total

Notes Payable—Short Term
All short-term note obligations, including bank and commercial paper. Does not include trade notes payable.

Accounts Payable—Trade
Open accounts and note obligations due to the trade.

Accounts Payable—Retention
Amounts held back as retention in payments to subcontractors on current contracts.

Long-Term Debt
All senior debt, including bonds, debentures, bank debt, mortgages, deferred portions of long-term debt, and capital lease obligations.

Deferred Taxes
Total of all deferred taxes.

All Other Non-Current
Any other non-current liabilities, including subordinated debt, and liability reserves.

Billings in Excess of Costs & Est. Earn.
The difference between the total billings to date and the total of costs and recognized estimated earnings to date.

Income Taxes Payable
Income taxes including current portion of deferred taxes.

Current Maturities—LTD
That portion of long-term obligations that is due within the next fiscal year.

All Other Current
Any other current liabilities, including bank overdrafts and accrued expenses.

Total Current
Total of all current liabilities listed above.

Net Worth
Difference between total assets and total liabilities. Minority interest is included here.

Total Liabilities & Net Worth
Total of all items listed above.

LIABILITIES
Notes Payable—Short Term
Accounts Payable—Trade
Accounts Payable—Retention
Billings in Excess of Costs & Estimated Earnings
Income Taxes Payable
Current Maturities—LTD
All Other Current
Total Current
Long-Term Debt
Deferred Taxes
All Other Non-Current
Net Worth
Total Liabilities & Net Worth

Contract Revenues
Revenues recognized under % of completion method.

Gross Profit
Difference between contract revenues and cost of sales.

Operating Expenses
All selling and general and administrative expenses. Includes depreciation, but not interest expense.

All Other Expenses (net)
Includes miscellaneous other income and expenses (net), such as interest expense, miscellaneous expenses not included in general & administrative expenses, netted against recoveries, interest income, dividends received and miscellaneous income.

Operating Profit
Gross profit minus operating expenses.

Profit Before Taxes
Operating profit minus all other expenses (net).

INCOME DATA
Contract Revenues
Gross Profit
Operating Expenses
Operating Profit
All Other Expenses (net)
Profit Before Taxes

For further analysis, please refer to *Industry Default Probabilities and Cash Flow Measures*

If you think *Financial Ratio Benchmarks* is a valuable resource, wait until you see its companion study. Now in its seventh year and bigger than ever, *Industry Default Probabilities and Cash Flow Measures* is a major expansion of our *Annual Statement Studies*. It brings together the power of Moody's RiskCalc® for private companies and the *Statement Studies* database to provide distribution statistics on one-year and five-year probability of default estimates by industry. The new benchmarks add substantial value to the critical analysis of cash flow for private companies.

The latest edition of *Industry Default Probabilities and Cash Flow Measures* includes many new industries, stronger statements, five years of historical data sorted by assets and sales… In short, it is more like our traditional *Statement Studies*.

Industry Default Probabilities and Cash Flow Measures includes:

- Probability of default estimates on a percentage scale, mapped to a "dot" EDF bond rating scale.
- Cash flow measures on a common-size percentage scale. Ratios include:
  - Cash from Trading
  - Cash after Operations
  - Net Cash after Operations
  - Cash after Debt Amortization
  - Debt Service P&I Coverage
  - Interest Coverage (Operating Cash)
- Change in position, normalized, year over year, for eight financial statement line items. Ratios include:
  - Change in Inventory
  - Total Current Assets (TCA)
  - Total Assets (TA)
  - Retained Earnings (RE)
  - Net Sales (NS)
  - Cost of Goods Sold (CGS)
  - Profit before Interest & Taxes (PBIT)
  - Depreciation/Depletion/Amortization (DDA)
- Trend data available for the past three years.
- Other ratios.
  - Sustainable Growth Rate
  - Funded Debt/EBITDA
- Data arrayed by asset and sales size.

Please see the inside back cover for more information, or you can set up your standing order for *Industry Default Probabilities and Cash Flow Measures* today by calling 1-800-677-7621!

NAICS CODES APPEARING IN THE STATEMENT STUDIES

NAICS Codes	Page	NAICS Codes	Page	NAICS Codes	Page
111140	98-99	238190	212-213	315299	322-323
111150	100-101	238210	214-215, 1600	315999	324-325
111199	102-103	238220	216-217, 1601	316110	326-327
111211	104-105	238290	218-219	321113	328-329
111219	106-107	238310	220-221, 1602	321114	330-331
111310	108-109	238320	222-223, 1603	321211	332-333
111331	110-111	238330	224-225, 1604	321214	334-335
111332	112-113	238340	226-227	321911	336-337
111411	114-115	238350	228-229	321912	338-339
111421	116-117	238390	230-231	321918	340-341
111920	118-119	238910	232-233, 1605	321920	342-343
111998	120-121	238990	234-235, 1606	321991	344-345
112111	122-123	311119	238-239	321992	346-347
112112	124-125	311211	240-241	321999	348-349
112120	126-127	311330	242-243	322121	350-351
112210	128-129	311411	244-245	322211	352-353
112310	130-131	311412	246-247	322212	354-355
113110	132-133	311421	248-249	322213	356-357
113310	134-135	311423	250-251	322221	358-359
114111	136-137	311511	252-253	322222	360-361
114112	138-139	311513	254-255	322223	362-363
115111	140-141	311520	256-257	322232	364-365
115112	142-143	311611	258-259	322291	366-367
115114	144-145	311612	260-261	322299	368-369
115210	146-147	311615	262-263	323110	370-371
211111	150-151	311712	264-265	323112	372-373
212111	152-153	311811	266-267	323113	374-375
212312	154-155	311812	268-269	323114	376-377
212319	156-157	311821	270-271	323116	378-379
212321	158-159	311919	272-273	323117	380-381
213111	160-161	311920	274-275	323119	382-383
213112	162-163, 1584	311930	276-277	323121	384-385
221111	166-167	311941	278-279	323122	386-387
221122	168-169	311942	280-281	324110	388-389
221210	170-171	311999	282-283	324121	390-391
221310	172-173	312111	284-285	324191	392-393
236115	176-177, 1585	312112	286-287	324199	394-395
236116	178-179, 1586	312120	288-289	325188	396-397
236117	180-181, 1587	312130	290-291	325199	398-399
236118	182-183, 1588	313111	292-293	325211	400-401
236210	184-185, 1589	313210	294-295	325311	402-403
236220	186-187, 1590	313221	296-297	325314	404-405
237110	188-189, 1591	313311	298-299	325320	406-407
237120	190-191	313320	300-301	325411	408-409
237130	192-193	314110	302-303	325412	410-411
237210	194-195, 1592	314129	304-305	325510	412-413
237310	196-197, 1593	314912	306-307	325520	414-415
237990	198-199, 1594	314999	308-309	325611	416-417
238110	200-201, 1595	315211	310-311	325612	418-419
238120	202-203, 1596	315212	312-313	325620	420-421
238130	204-205	315222	314-315	325910	422-423
238140	206-207, 1597	315228	316-317	325991	424-425
238150	208-209, 1598	315233	318-319	325998	426-427
238160	210-211, 1599	315239	320-321	326113	428-429

If more than three SIC codes map to one NAICS code, then only the first three SIC will appear at the top of the page listed above. For a complete listing of the SIC codes, see the Description of Industries beginning on page 35.

NAICS CODES APPEARING IN THE STATEMENT STUDIES

If more than three SIC codes map to one NAICS code, then only the first three SIC will appear at the top of the page listed above. For a complete listing of the SIC codes, see the Description of Industries beginning on page 35.

SIC NUMBERS APPEARING IN THE STATEMENT STUDIES

See pages 23-27 for corresponding NAICS look-up table.

SIC NUMBERS APPEARING IN THE STATEMENT STUDIES

SIC No.	Page	SIC No.	Page	SIC No.	Page
2514	706-707	2951	390-391	3443	510-511, 584-585
2515	706-707, 720-721	2992	392-393	3444	512-513, 514-515, 518-519, 584-585
2519	710-711	2999	394-395		
2521	714-715	3052	444-445	3446	516-517
2522	716-717	3053	746-747	3448	506-507
2531	712-713	3061	446-447	3449	508-509, 516-517
2541	704-705, 718-719	3069	300-301, 448-449, 740-741, 742-743	3451	528-529
2542	712-713, 718-719			3452	530-531
2591	722-723	3081	428-429	3462	500-501
2599	712-713, 724-725	3082	430-431	3465	686-687
2611	350-351	3083	434-435	3469	502-503
2621	350-351	3084	432-433	3471	536-537
2652	356-357	3085	438-439	3479	534-535, 736-737, 738-739
2653	352-353	3086	436-437	3491	538-539
2657	354-355	3087	424-425	3492	540-541
2671	358-359	3089	430-431, 432-433, 440-441	3494	544-545, 550-551
2672	360-361	3111	326-327	3495	522-523
2673	362-363	3172	738-739	3496	524-525, 610-611
2675	368-369	3211	452-453	3498	548-549
2676	366-367	3231	454-455	3499	518-519, 520-521, 544-545, 550-551, 684-685, 718-719
2677	364-365	3251	450-451, 458-459		
2679	352-353, 360-361, 368-369	3271	458-459	3519	688-689
2711	1084-1085	3272	460-461, 462-463, 468-469	3523	516-517, 552-553, 606-607
2721	1086 1087	3273	456 457	3524	554-555
2731	1088-1089	3281	466-467	3531	556-557, 608-609, 694-695
2732	380-381	3291	464-465	3532	558-559
2741	1086-1087, 1088-1089, 1090-1091, 1092-1093	3292	468-469	3533	560-561
		3299	468-469	3535	606-607
2752	370-371, 376-377	3312	394-395, 470-471, 474-475	3536	608-609
2759	372-373, 374-375, 376-377, 382-383	3315	476-477, 524-525	3537	610-611
		3316	474-475	3541	588-589
2761	378-379	3317	472-473	3542	590-591
2771	370-371, 372-373, 374-375, 382-383	3321	488-489	3544	586-587, 592-593
		3322	488-489	3545	504-505, 594-595
2782	378-379	3325	490-491	3548	612-613, 664-665
2789	384-385	3341	478-479, 486-487	3549	596-597
2791	386-387	3354	480-481	3552	566-567
2796	386-387	3356	484-485	3554	564-565
2819	396-397, 426-427	3357	482-483, 484-485	3555	568-569
2821	400-401	3363	492-493	3556	570-571
2833	408-409	3364	494-495	3559	552-553, 562-563, 572-573, 578-579
2834	410-411	3365	496-497		
2835	410-411	3369	498-499	3561	602-603
2841	416-417	3398	532-533	3562	546-547
2842	418-419	3399	470-471, 474-475, 478-479, 486-487, 524-525, 536-537	3563	604-605
2844	416-417, 420-421			3564	580-581
2851	412-413	3412	518-519	3565	614-615
2869	396-397, 398-399, 426 427	3421	504-505	3566	598-599
2873	402-403	3423	504-505	3567	616-617
2875	404-405	3429	520-521, 530-531, 550-551, 608-609	3568	600-601
2879	406-407			3569	582-583, 618-619
2891	414-415	3432	542-543, 544-545	3571	620-621
2893	422-423	3433	582-583	3577	622-623
2899	398-399, 412-413, 426-427	3441	508-509	3578	622-623
2911	388-389	3442	512-513	3585	584-585

See pages 23-27 for corresponding NAICS look-up table.

SIC NUMBERS APPEARING IN THE STATEMENT STUDIES

See pages 23-27 for corresponding NAICS look-up table.

SIC NUMBERS APPEARING IN THE STATEMENT STUDIES

SIC No.	Page	SIC No.	Page	SIC No.	Page
5113	834-835	5599	910-911	6289	1154-1155, 1156-1157
5122	836-837, 954-955, 956-957	5611	964-965, 970-971	6321	1158-1159
5131	838-839	5621	966-967, 972-973	6324	1158-1159
5136	820-821, 840-841, 964-965	5632	970-971, 972-973	6331	1160-1161, 1164-1165
5137	820-821, 842-843, 966-967	5651	968-969	6351	1160-1161, 1164-1165
5139	844-845, 974-975	5661	974-975	6361	1162-1163
5141	846-847, 940-941	5699	970-971, 972-973	6371	1150-1151, 1168-1169, 1174-1175
5142	848-849	5712	916-917		
5143	850-851	5713	918-919	6399	1164-1165
5144	852-853, 944-945	5719	920-921	6411	1166-1167, 1168-1169
5145	854-855, 948-949	5722	922-923	6512	1180-1181
5146	856-857	5731	924-925	6513	1178-1179
5147	858-859, 944-945	5734	926-927	6514	1178-1179
5148	860-861, 946-947	5736	982-983	6515	1184-1185
5149	862-863, 998-999	5812	0, 1440-1441, 1480-1481, 1482-1483, 1484-1485, 1486-1487, 1488-1489	6517	1184-1185
5153	864-865			6519	1184-1185
5154	866-867			6531	1178-1179, 1186-1187, 1188-1189, 1190-1191, 1192-1193, 1522-1523
5159	868-869	5813	1490-1491		
5162	870-871	5912	954-955		
5169	872-873	5921	952-953	6541	1224-1225
5171	874-875, 1010-1011, 1012-1013	5932	996-997	6552	194-195, 1592
		5941	978-979	6553	1522-1523
5172	876-877	5942	984-985	6719	1292-1293
5181	878-879, 952-953	5943	992-993	6722	1170-1171
5182	880-881, 952-953	5944	976-977	6726	1174-1175
5191	882-883, 938-939	5945	980-981	6732	1538-1539
5192	884-885, 984-985	5947	994-995	6733	1150-1151, 1154-1155
5193	886-887, 938-939	5961	1004-1005, 1006-1007	6792	1218-1219
5194	888-889	5962	1008-1009	6794	1218-1219
5198	890-891	5963	1014-1015	6798	1172-1173
5199	838-839, 844-845, 870-871, 892-893, 994-995, 998-999	5983	1010-1011	6799	1144-1145, 1148-1149
		5984	1012-1013	7011	1472-1473, 1474-1475
5211	928-929	5992	990-991	7032	1478-1479
5231	930-931	5995	958-959	7033	1476-1477
5251	932-933	5999	894-895, 956-957, 998-999, 1002-1003	7041	1472-1473
5261	936-937, 938-939			7211	1526-1527
5271	1000-1001	6019	1132-1133	7212	1526-1527
5311	986-987	6021	1122-1123	7213	1528-1529
5331	988-989	6022	1122-1123	7215	1524-1525
5399	988-989	6091	1154-1155	7216	1526-1527
5411	940-941, 942-943, 960-961, 1014-1015	6099	1136-1137, 1138-1139, 1144-1145	7217	1326-1327
				7219	1516-1517, 1528-1529
5421	944-945	6111	1128-1129, 1130-1131	7221	1282-1283
5431	946-947, 1014-1015	6141	1122-1123, 1124-1125, 1126-1127	7231	1518-1519
5441	948-949			7251	1534-1535
5451	950-951	6153	1124-1125, 1132-1133, 1136-1137, 1148-1149	7261	1520-1521, 1522-1523
5461	266-267, 1484-1485			7299	1288-1289, 1332-1333, 1532-1533, 1534-1535
5499	950-951	6159	1124-1125, 1128-1129, 1130-1131, 1132-1133		
5511	900-901			7311	1268-1269
5521	902-903	6162	1128-1129, 1138-1139	7312	1272-1273
5531	912-913, 914-915, 988-989	6163	1134-1135	7319	1022-1023, 1272-1273, 1276-1277, 1278-1279
5541	960-961, 962-963	6211	1140-1141, 1142-1143, 1148-1149, 1156-1157		
5551	908-909			7322	1306-1307
5561	904-905	6221	1144-1145, 1146-1147	7331	1090-1091, 1274-1275
5571	906-907	6282	1150-1151, 1152-1153	7334	376-377, 1304-1305

See pages 23-27 for corresponding NAICS look-up table.

SIC NUMBERS APPEARING IN THE STATEMENT STUDIES

SIC No.	Page	SIC No.	Page	SIC No.	Page
7335	1284-1285	7832	1098-1099	8361	1416-1417, 1418-1419, 1422-1423, 1424-1425
7336	1242-1243	7841	1202-1203		
7342	1320-1321, 1322-1323	7911	1358-1359	8399	1540-1541, 1542-1543
7349	1322-1323, 1328-1329	7922	1440-1441, 1448-1449	8412	1450-1451
7352	1204-1205, 1216-1217	7929	1442-1443	8611	1546-1547
7353	1212-1213	7933	1466-1467	8621	1548-1549
7359	1200-1201, 1206-1207, 1208-1209, 1210-1211, 1212-1213, 1214-1215, 1216-1217	7941	1444-1445, 1448-1449	8631	1550-1551
		7948	1446-1447	8641	1542-1543, 1544-1545, 1552-1553, 1564-1565
		7991	1464-1465		
7361	1252-1253, 1300-1301	7992	1458-1459	8661	1536-1537
7363	1302-1303	7993	1454-1455, 1468-1469	8699	1314-1315, 1544-1545, 1546-1547, 1552-1553
7371	1244-1245	7996	1452-1453		
7372	1094-1095	7997	1022-1023, 1458-1459, 1464-1465, 1468-1469	8711	1234-1235
7373	1246-1247			8712	1230-1231
7374	1118-1119	7999	1448-1449, 1456-1457, 1460-1461, 1464-1465, 1468-1469	8713	1236-1237
7375	1116-1117			8721	1226-1227, 1228-1229
7377	1214-1215			8731	1264-1265
7378	926-927, 1508-1509	8011	1366-1367, 1368-1369, 1390-1391	8732	1266-1267, 1280-1281
7379	1118-1119, 1246-1247, 1248-1249			8733	1264-1265, 1266-1267
		8021	1370-1371	8734	1238-1239, 1286-1287
7381	1316-1317	8031	1366-1367, 1368-1369	8741	1296-1297
7382	1318-1319	8041	1372-1373	8742	1250-1251, 1252-1253, 1254-1255, 1256-1257
7384	1530-1531	8042	1374-1375		
7389	1118-1119, 1236-1237, 1240-1241, 1276-1277, 1278-1279, 1288-1289, 1304-1305, 1306-1307	8043	1380-1381	8743	1270-1271
		8049	1376-1377, 1378-1379, 1382-1383	8744	1298-1299
				8748	1232-1233, 1234-1235, 1258-1259, 1262-1263, 1362-1363
7513	1198-1199	8051	1414-1415, 1416-1417, 1420-1421		
7514	1194-1195			8811	1554-1555
7515	1196-1197	8052	1414-1415, 1416-1417, 1420-1421	8999	1102-1103, 1260-1261, 1288-1289
7519	1198-1199				
7521	1532-1533	8059	1414-1415, 1420-1421	9111	1558-1559
7532	1500-1501	8062	1406-1407, 1408-1409	9121	1560-1561
7533	1496-1497	8063	1410-1411	9131	1562-1563
7534	442-443, 1506-1507	8069	1410-1411, 1412-1413	9199	1566-1567
7536	1502-1503	8071	1394-1395, 1396-1397	9224	1568-1569
7538	1494-1495	8072	734-735	9411	1570-1571
7539	1498-1499, 1506-1507	8082	1398-1399	9431	1572-1573
7542	1504-1505	8092	1388-1389	9511	1574-1575
7549	1062-1063, 1502-1503, 1506-1507	8093	1382-1383, 1384-1385, 1386-1387, 1392-1393	9531	1576-1577
				9532	1578-1579
7622	924-925	8099	1384-1385, 1402-1403, 1404-1405		
7623	1512-1513, 1514-1515				
7629	1508-1509, 1510-1511, 1514-1515	8111	1222-1223		
		8211	1348-1349		
7631	976-977, 1516-1517	8221	1352-1353		
7692	1512-1513	8222	1350-1351		
7694	666-667, 1512-1513	8243	1356-1357		
7699	978-979, 1508-1509, 1510-1511, 1514-1515	8249	1356-1357		
		8299	1354-1355, 1356-1357, 1358-1359, 1360-1361, 1362-1363		
7812	1096-1097				
7819	1100-1101, 1216-1217, 1262-1263	8322	1426-1427, 1428-1429, 1430-1431, 1432-1433		
7822	828-829	8331	1434-1435		
7829	1100-1101	8351	1436-1437		

See pages 23-27 for corresponding NAICS look-up table.

DESCRIPTION OF INDUSTRIES INCLUDED IN THE STATEMENT STUDIES

AGRICULTURE, FORESTRY, FISHING AND HUNTING

MINING

MINING

CONSTRUCTION-GENERAL

CONSTRUCTION-GENERAL

CONSTRUCTION-GENERAL

MANUFACTURING

MANUFACTURING

MANUFACTURING

MANUFACTURING

NAICS #

MANUFACTURING

MANUFACTURING

MANUFACTURING

MANUFACTURING

MANUFACTURING

MANUFACTURING

MANUFACTURING

MANUFACTURING

MANUFACTURING

MANUFACTURING

NAICS #

WHOLESALE TRADE

WHOLESALE

423140 Motor Vehicle Parts (Used) Merchant Wholesalers. This industry comprises establishments primarily engaged in the merchant wholesale distribution of used motor vehicle parts (except used tires and tubes) and establishments primarily engaged in dismantling motor vehicles for the purpose of selling the parts. (SIC: 5015)   762-763

423210 Furniture Merchant Wholesalers. This industry comprises establishments primarily engaged in the merchant wholesale distribution of furniture (except hospital beds, medical furniture, and drafting tables). (SIC: 5021)   764-765

423220 Home Furnishing Merchant Wholesalers. This industry comprises establishments primarily engaged in the merchant wholesale distribution of home furnishings and/or housewares. (SIC: 5023)   766-767

423310 Lumber, Plywood, Millwork, and Wood Panel Merchant Wholesalers. This industry comprises establishments primarily engaged in the merchant wholesale distribution of lumber; plywood; reconstituted wood fiber products; wood fencing; doors and windows and their frames (all materials); wood roofing and siding; and/or other wood or metal millwork. (SIC: 5031, 5039) . .   768-769

423320 Brick, Stone, and Related Construction Material Merchant Wholesalers. This industry comprises establishments primarily engaged in the merchant wholesale distribution of stone, cement, lime, construction sand, and gravel; brick; asphalt and concrete mixtures; and/or concrete, stone, and structural clay products. (SIC: 5032)   770-771

423330 Roofing, Siding, and Insulation Material Merchant Wholesalers. This industry comprises establishments primarily engaged in the merchant wholesale distribution of nonwood roofing and nonwood siding and insulation materials. (SIC: 5033)   772-773

423390 Other Construction Material Merchant Wholesalers. This industry comprises (1) establishments primarily engaged in the merchant wholesale distribution of manufactured homes (i.e., mobile homes) and/or prefabricated buildings and (2) establishments primarily engaged in the merchant wholesale distribution of construction materials (except lumber, plywood, millwork, wood panels, brick, stone, roofing, siding, electrical and wiring supplies, and insulation materials). (SIC: 5039)   774-775

423410 Photographic Equipment and Supplies Merchant Wholesalers. This industry comprises establishments primarily engaged in the merchant wholesale distribution of photographic equipment and supplies (except office equipment). (SIC: 5043)   776-777

423420 Office Equipment Merchant Wholesalers. This industry comprises establishments primarily engaged in the merchant wholesale distribution of office machines and related equipment (except computers and computer peripheral equipment). (SIC: 5044)   778-779

423430 Computer and Computer Peripheral Equipment and Software Merchant Wholesalers. This industry comprises establishments primarily engaged in the merchant wholesale distribution of computers, computer peripheral equipment, loaded computer boards, and/or computer software. (SIC: 5045)   780-781

423440 Other Commercial Equipment Merchant Wholesalers. This industry comprises establishments primarily engaged in the merchant wholesale distribution of commercial and related machines and equipment (except photographic equipment and supplies; office equipment; and computers and computer peripheral equipment and software) generally used in restaurants and stores. (SIC: 5046)   782-783

423450 Medical, Dental, and Hospital Equipment and Supplies Merchant Wholesalers. This industry comprises establishments primarily engaged in the merchant wholesale distribution of professional medical equipment, instruments, and supplies (except ophthalmic equipment and instruments and goods used by ophthalmologists, optometrists, and opticians). (SIC: 5047) . .   784-785

423460 Ophthalmic Goods Merchant Wholesalers. This industry comprises establishments primarily engaged in the merchant wholesale distribution of professional equipment, instruments, and/or goods sold, prescribed, or used by ophthalmologists, optometrists, and opticians. (SIC: 5048)   786-787

423490 Other Professional Equipment and Supplies Merchant Wholesalers. This industry comprises establishments primarily engaged in the merchant wholesale distribution of professional equipment and supplies (except ophthalmic goods and medical, dental, and hospital equipment and supplies). (SIC: 5049)   788-789

RETAIL

RETAIL TRADE

RETAIL

TRANSPORTATION

TRANSPORTATION AND WAREHOUSING

INFORMATION

INFORMATION

FINANCE

FINANCE

REAL ESTATE AND RENTAL AND LEASING

PROFESSIONAL SERVICES

PROFESSIONAL, SCIENTIFIC, AND TECHNICAL SERVICES

PROFESSIONAL SERVICES

PROFESSIONAL SERVICES

PROFESSIONAL SERVICES

ADMIN & WASTE MANAGEMENT SERVICES

MANAGEMENT OF COMPANIES AND ENTERPRISES

ADMINISTRATIVE AND SUPPORT AND WASTE MANAGEMENT AND REMEDIATION SERVICES

ADMIN & WASTE MANAGEMENT SERVICES

EDUCATIONAL SERVICES

HEALTH CARE

HEALTH CARE AND SOCIAL ASSISTANCE

HEALTH CARE

HEALTH CARE

ENTERTAINMENT

ARTS, ENTERTAINMENT, AND RECREATION

ACCOMMODATION AND FOOD SERVICES

OTHER SERVICES

OTHER SERVICES (EXCEPT PUBLIC ADMINISTRATION)

OTHER SERVICES

PUBLIC ADMINISTRATION

CONSTRUCTION—PERCENTAGE OF COMPLETION

CONSTRUCTION-% OF COMPLETION

AGRICULTURE, FORESTRY, FISHING AND HUNTING

Current Data Sorted by Assets

Comparative Historical Data

0-500M	500M-2MM	2-10MM	10-50MM	50-100MM	100-250MM	Type of Statement	4/1/02-3/31/03 ALL	4/1/03-3/31/04 ALL
1	4	6	7	3	5	Unqualified	7	2
4	4	9	8	2		Reviewed	6	7
2	7	14	4	2	1	Compiled	14	10
13	20	10	1			Tax Returns	12	12
4	15	22	16	6		Other	34	37
34 (4/1-9/30/06)			150 (10/1/06-3/31/07)					
20	50	61	36	11	6	NUMBER OF STATEMENTS	73	68
%	%	%	%	%	%	**ASSETS**	%	%
29.6	13.1	10.7	8.3	18.4		Cash & Equivalents	9.9	6.8
10.0	19.7	20.6	18.3	12.6		Trade Receivables (net)	11.5	15.3
11.6	9.1	21.1	17.8	15.6		Inventory	14.8	17.0
2.2	1.9	3.0	6.1	2.5		All Other Current	6.3	6.2
53.3	43.8	55.4	50.5	49.1		Total Current	42.5	45.3
35.4	48.7	36.5	32.2	42.3		Fixed Assets (net)	37.1	32.4
3.7	4.0	1.5	9.2	3.8		Intangibles (net)	3.9	5.0
7.5	3.6	6.7	8.1	4.7		All Other Non-Current	16.5	17.3
100.0	100.0	100.0	100.0	100.0		Total	100.0	100.0
						LIABILITIES		
17.5	6.8	16.3	17.4	8.0		Notes Payable-Short Term	12.2	21.3
10.8	3.8	2.4	2.9	1.8		Cur. Mat.-L.T.D.	3.4	3.0
9.3	8.6	10.1	7.7	9.8		Trade Payables	9.3	9.4
.0	.6	.1	.3	.1		Income Taxes Payable	.2	.5
15.0	11.9	11.3	9.2	7.0		All Other Current	8.7	7.9
52.7	31.6	40.2	37.6	26.7		Total Current	33.8	42.1
28.7	28.6	18.8	18.9	30.8		Long-Term Debt	33.9	18.4
.0	.0	.1	.7	.7		Deferred Taxes	.0	.1
2.7	10.5	4.1	2.6	4.2		All Other Non-Current	2.6	7.4
16.0	29.2	36.8	40.1	37.5		Net Worth	29.6	31.9
100.0	100.0	100.0	100.0	100.0		Total Liabilities & Net Worth	100.0	100.0
						INCOME DATA		
100.0	100.0	100.0	100.0	100.0		Net Sales	100.0	100.0
						Gross Profit		
95.2	91.5	87.3	84.4	88.8		Operating Expenses	89.1	88.6
4.8	8.5	12.7	15.6	11.2		Operating Profit	10.9	11.4
.7	3.9	5.0	4.2	3.1		All Other Expenses (net)	4.9	4.6
4.1	4.6	7.7	11.5	8.1		Profit Before Taxes	6.0	6.9
						RATIOS		
3.3	2.3	2.1	1.9	3.3		Current	2.5	1.8
1.1	1.3	1.3	1.2	1.6			1.2	1.1
.7	.6	1.0	1.0	1.5			.8	.8
1.6	1.7	1.9	1.7	1.9		Quick	1.0	.7
.8	1.0	.8	.6	1.3			.7	.4
.3	.4	.2	.3	.9			.2	.1
0 UND	0 UND	3 112.8	1 262.3	7 50.2		Sales/Receivables	0 UND	0 UND
0 UND	23 16.2	26 14.0	29 12.5	44 8.3			18 20.4	18 20.9
23 16.0	51 7.2	56 6.5	60 6.1	60 6.1			42 8.8	50 7.3
						Cost of Sales/Inventory		
						Cost of Sales/Payables		
10.7	6.3	5.8	4.3	4.1		Sales/Working Capital	5.1	5.3
341.7	22.1	19.6	12.3	5.3			30.4	33.2
-36.6	-24.5	172.1	NM	41.8			-18.8	-19.2
7.1	6.4	10.9	4.2	20.0		EBIT/Interest	5.5	5.5
(14) 1.7	(43) 3.4	(45) 3.4	(29) 2.9	(10) 8.2			(58) 1.8	(55) 3.2
-6.2	1.6	1.6	1.7	4.1			.7	1.1
		9.3				Net Profit + Depr., Dep.,		
	(10)	5.0				Amort./Cur. Mat. L/T/D		
		1.8						
.5	.6	.2	.3	.4		Fixed/Worth	.3	.3
2.4	1.6	.8	.9	.9			.9	.7
-2.2	-18.6	1.5	2.3	-359.9			14.5	5.2
.8	.7	.6	1.0	.5		Debt/Worth	.5	.6
15.7	2.8	2.0	2.5	1.8			1.4	1.7
-9.3	-19.8	5.7	6.3	-394.7			23.2	22.7
636.9	68.5	60.8	71.7			% Profit Before Taxes/Tangible	20.1	30.8
(13) 33.1	(37) 24.8	(55) 24.7	(32) 23.0			Net Worth	(59) 5.7	(54) 7.3
-23.8	4.9	2.9	5.4				-2.8	.5
84.8	17.5	13.2	12.1	15.2		% Profit Before Taxes/Total	6.8	9.0
8.3	6.9	5.7	5.7	8.7		Assets	2.8	3.7
-38.0	-.1	1.1	2.8	3.8			-.4	-.2
182.0	14.2	30.2	31.5	28.4		Sales/Net Fixed Assets	25.8	26.0
18.3	4.2	7.3	10.7	4.1			4.0	6.0
4.0	1.1	2.1	1.7	1.3			.7	1.0
8.4	3.2	3.0	2.6	3.0		Sales/Total Assets	3.2	2.9
4.4	1.8	1.7	1.1	1.3			1.2	1.1
2.1	.8	.5	.4	.6			.3	.3
.7	1.1	.9	.9			% Depr., Dep., Amort./Sales	1.5	1.3
(15) 3.5	(40) 3.7	(49) 2.1	(31) 1.8				(60) 5.2	(55) 3.5
9.1	11.6	5.6	6.8				12.4	13.6
	.8	1.4				% Officers', Directors'	3.2	1.8
	(19) 3.0	(24) 2.1				Owners' Comp/Sales	(20) 7.8	(20) 3.1
	4.5	5.7					13.3	6.5
22808M	124814M	544075M	1134036M	1373076M	1800234M	Net Sales ($)	1297854M	852801M
4320M	59598M	280027M	792689M	793670M	1195886M	Total Assets ($)	613071M	549436M

M = $ thousand   MM = $ million
See Pages 11 through 21 for Explanation of Ratios and Data

Comparative Historical Data   Current Data Sorted by Sales

	Hist 1	Hist 2	Hist 3		0-1MM	1-3MM	3-5MM	5-10MM	10-25MM	25MM & OVER
Type of Statement										
Unqualified	16	27	26		3	4		3	4	12
Reviewed	10	16	21			3	2	3	8	5
Compiled	16	25	30		3	2	9	5	7	4
Tax Returns	27	31	44		19	13	4	5	2	1
Other	48	68	63		11	14	8	5	10	15
	4/1/04-3/31/05 ALL	4/1/05-3/31/06 ALL	4/1/06-3/31/07 ALL		34 (4/1-9/30/06)			150 (10/1/06-3/31/07)		
NUMBER OF STATEMENTS	117	167	184		36	36	23	21	31	37
	%	%	%		%	%	%	%	%	%
ASSETS										
Cash & Equivalents	11.7	14.6	13.4		12.3	15.7	13.6	20.2	8.7	12.4
Trade Receivables (net)	20.1	21.7	18.1		9.6	17.9	20.2	23.0	22.4	18.8
Inventory	15.7	19.0	15.7		5.7	9.7	19.7	20.2	14.4	27.1
All Other Current	4.2	4.6	3.2		1.6	2.6	2.6	3.2	5.7	3.4
Total Current	51.7	59.8	50.3		29.2	45.8	56.1	66.6	51.2	61.7
Fixed Assets (net)	36.5	29.2	39.5		63.5	42.7	35.8	27.1	28.6	31.5
Intangibles (net)	3.6	4.0	4.3		2.3	5.3	2.6	1.1	10.0	3.2
All Other Non-Current	8.3	7.0	5.9		5.0	6.1	5.4	5.3	10.2	3.6
Total	100.0	100.0	100.0		100.0	100.0	100.0	100.0	100.0	100.0
LIABILITIES										
Notes Payable-Short Term	13.9	13.5	13.2		13.9	9.9	12.8	16.8	10.6	15.9
Cur. Mat.-L.T.D.	2.5	2.2	3.8		7.4	3.8	2.4	3.0	2.3	2.9
Trade Payables	11.1	12.6	8.9		4.6	8.1	8.1	11.5	10.1	11.7
Income Taxes Payable	.3	.2	.3		.0	.8	.0	.0	.2	.3
All Other Current	10.1	12.6	11.4		5.4	15.6	11.2	12.5	13.2	11.2
Total Current	37.8	41.2	37.5		31.4	38.1	34.6	43.7	36.4	42.1
Long-Term Debt	25.3	22.3	23.4		36.9	24.2	23.1	15.9	20.2	16.8
Deferred Taxes	.2	.2	.2		.0	.0	.1	.1	.5	.6
All Other Non-Current	5.0	4.3	5.4		7.1	7.0	5.2	6.5	4.0	2.9
Net Worth	31.5	32.0	33.4		24.6	30.8	37.0	33.8	38.8	37.6
Total Liabilities & Net Worth	100.0	100.0	100.0		100.0	100.0	100.0	100.0	100.0	100.0
INCOME DATA										
Net Sales	100.0	100.0	100.0		100.0	100.0	100.0	100.0	100.0	100.0
Gross Profit										
Operating Expenses	87.5	88.5	88.8		82.2	88.6	92.1	90.9	89.5	91.8
Operating Profit	12.5	11.5	11.2		17.8	11.4	7.9	9.1	10.5	8.2
All Other Expenses (net)	4.8	3.3	3.8		11.4	2.2	2.2	2.4	2.9	.4
Profit Before Taxes	7.7	8.2	7.4		6.4	9.2	5.6	6.7	7.5	7.9
RATIOS										
Current	2.4	2.8	2.3		2.2	1.9	6.1	2.3	3.3	2.5
	1.3	1.4	1.3		.9	1.2	1.5	1.5	1.3	1.6
	.9	1.0	.9		.3	.7	1.1	.9	1.1	1.1
Quick	1.4	1.8	1.8		1.5	1.5	3.5	1.7	2.4	1.8
	.7	(166) .9	.8		.5	.9	1.1	.8	.9	.9
	.3	.3	.3		.1	.2	.5	.5	.4	.4
Sales/Receivables	0 UND	2 147.9	1 496.4		0 UND	0 UND	5 76.2	2 210.3	10 36.4	5 78.2
	21 17.7	30 12.3	23 16.2		1 257.0	10 35.4	27 13.7	32 11.3	43 8.6	33 11.1
	50 7.4	52 7.1	55 6.6		46 7.9	49 7.4	37 9.8	55 6.6	59 6.2	61 6.0
Cost of Sales/Inventory										
Cost of Sales/Payables										
Sales/Working Capital	4.4	4.8	5.7		6.7	5.8	4.1	6.5	5.8	5.5
	19.1	12.8	18.5		-77.4	32.6	10.1	15.4	13.0	12.3
	-42.3	-233.4	-70.7		-3.0	-34.2	32.1	NM	35.1	80.7
EBIT/Interest	7.9	10.5	8.5		4.3	15.1	8.6	21.6	5.9	11.9
	(93) 3.3	(124) 3.6	(146) 3.4		(23) 1.8	(29) 2.6	(21) 3.4	(16) 3.1	(23) 3.9	(34) 5.7
	1.1	1.5	1.6		.0	1.2	.4	1.4	1.4	2.6
Net Profit + Depr., Dep., Amort./Cur. Mat. L/T/D	4.3	5.1	6.8							
	(15) 1.5	(27) 2.0	(28) 1.9							
	.8	.6	1.3							
Fixed/Worth	.2	.1	.3		1.2	.5	.2	.1	.2	.3
	1.0	.7	1.1		1.8	1.2	.9	.6	.9	.9
	4.6	4.1	5.2		UND	-9.3	4.3	4.4	2.4	1.9
Debt/Worth	.6	.7	.7		.6	.5	1.0	.4	1.2	.8
	2.5	2.7	2.5		3.2	3.1	3.1	1.4	2.1	2.1
	8.6	12.6	15.1		UND	-12.1	15.9	33.6	4.5	5.4
% Profit Before Taxes/Tangible Net Worth	36.8	48.8	64.1		36.7	66.3	163.2	92.6	39.6	82.6
	(96) 15.2	(135) 23.5	(150) 23.7		(28) 12.0	(25) 9.9	(21) 40.1	(17) 51.2	(25) 19.5	(34) 31.6
	3.5	3.5	4.2		.6	.0	12.6	3.3	6.6	15.2
% Profit Before Taxes/Total Assets	10.6	15.5	15.1		11.0	21.9	13.8	24.3	12.2	18.5
	4.8	5.2	6.5		1.7	5.8	7.7	9.3	6.1	9.5
	.5	1.0	.7		-3.8	.0	-.3	.5	1.6	4.5
Sales/Net Fixed Assets	53.2	60.4	28.8		4.1	19.6	22.1	85.5	29.0	62.7
	7.7	16.0	6.5		1.1	4.4	8.8	11.3	13.3	11.0
	1.1	3.0	1.6		.2	1.5	4.8	4.4	3.5	2.7
Sales/Total Assets	2.9	3.1	3.1		1.9	2.4	3.2	3.6	3.4	3.4
	1.6	1.7	1.7		.7	1.3	1.9	3.0	2.0	2.3
	.4	.8	.8		.2	.6	.8	1.7	.8	1.2
% Depr., Dep., Amort./Sales	.8	.6	.9		3.8	1.3	1.0	.7	1.3	.2
	(86) 3.1	(129) 1.6	(145) 2.7		(27) 9.2	(28) 4.7	(22) 2.0	(15) 2.0	(23) 1.8	(30) 1.0
	9.2	4.6	7.1		19.2	9.1	4.3	3.1	3.8	3.8
% Officers', Directors' Owners' Comp/Sales	1.2	1.9	1.3		3.0	1.6	.9	1.2		
	(31) 4.4	(51) 3.8	(57) 2.7		(10) 7.0	(12) 4.1	(12) 2.1	(10) 3.1		
	11.0	10.6	5.7		10.9	14.2	4.4	4.5		
Net Sales ($)	2224252M	5054232M	4999043M		17504M	65267M	92565M	145900M	445196M	4232611M
Total Assets ($)	1977664M	2587005M	3126190M		56154M	108861M	91948M	91378M	468053M	2309796M

M = $ thousand   MM = $ million
See Pages 11 through 21 for Explanation of Ratios and Data

Current Data Sorted by Assets   Comparative Historical Data

Type of Statement	0-500M	500M-2MM	2-10MM	10-50MM	50-100MM	100-250MM		ALL 4/1/02-3/31/03	ALL 4/1/03-3/31/04
Unqualified		1	2	4					
Reviewed	1		5	2		1		4	2
Compiled		3	5	1				6	10
Tax Returns	3	8	8					2	9
Other	2	2	6					17	27
		6 (4/1-9/30/06)		49 (10/1/06-3/31/07)					
NUMBER OF STATEMENTS	6	14	26	8		1		29	51
ASSETS	%	%	%	%	%	%		%	%
Cash & Equivalents		1.6	3.4					7.5	6.2
Trade Receivables (net)		5.3	11.0					5.1	2.6
Inventory		18.9	18.5					16.8	15.7
All Other Current		6.0	8.5					4.8	5.3
Total Current		31.9	41.4					34.1	29.9
Fixed Assets (net)		65.1	51.6					44.4	49.6
Intangibles (net)		.2	.1					.0	.6
All Other Non-Current		2.8	6.9					21.5	19.9
Total		100.0	100.0					100.0	100.0
LIABILITIES									
Notes Payable-Short Term		16.1	26.4					25.3	24.7
Cur. Mat.-L.T.D.		5.6	3.1					1.4	2.0
Trade Payables		4.7	5.4					4.3	1.6
Income Taxes Payable		.0	1.3					.4	.1
All Other Current		.5	7.2					8.5	5.3
Total Current		26.9	43.4					39.8	33.9
Long-Term Debt		27.9	30.8					16.8	22.1
Deferred Taxes		.0	.3					.0	.2
All Other Non-Current		1.8	1.4					3.9	4.4
Net Worth		43.4	24.1					39.4	39.4
Total Liabilities & Net Worth		100.0	100.0					100.0	100.0
INCOME DATA									
Net Sales		100.0	100.0					100.0	100.0
Gross Profit									
Operating Expenses		79.8	89.4					86.5	88.1
Operating Profit		20.2	10.6					13.5	11.9
All Other Expenses (net)		4.6	8.6					3.1	4.4
Profit Before Taxes		15.5	2.0					10.5	7.4
RATIOS									
Current		1.6	1.8					1.7	2.3
		.9	1.1					1.3	1.4
		.0	.6					.9	.8
Quick		.4	.9					.5	.8
		.1	.2					.3	.2
		.0	.0					.1	.0
Sales/Receivables	0 UND	0 UND					0 UND	0 UND	
	0 UND	0 UND					6 57.0	0 976.7	
	2 189.8	44 8.3					34 10.8	22 16.2	
Cost of Sales/Inventory									
Cost of Sales/Payables									
Sales/Working Capital		5.3	4.1					3.1	3.3
		NM	14.5					9.4	8.5
		-3.8	-4.0					-22.9	-13.7
EBIT/Interest		13.6	5.7					4.3	7.5
	(13)	3.8	(21) 1.2				(26)	2.7	(46) 2.9
		1.4	.6					1.6	1.3
Net Profit + Depr., Dep., Amort./Cur. Mat. L/T/D									
Fixed/Worth		.6	.8					.6	.6
		1.2	2.5					1.0	1.0
		4.9	NM					1.3	2.0
Debt/Worth		.5	.5					.5	.4
		1.2	4.2					1.0	.9
		4.1	-11.9					2.0	2.8
% Profit Before Taxes/Tangible Net Worth		53.4	26.7					14.6	17.7
	(13)	11.7	(19) 4.3				(27)	7.2	(47) 5.1
		-2.1	-2.0					1.5	.8
% Profit Before Taxes/Total Assets		23.5	4.9					8.9	7.1
		7.7	.7					3.8	2.3
		.8	-2.1					1.1	.0
Sales/Net Fixed Assets		8.9	13.6					5.1	3.7
		1.0	1.3					1.2	1.2
		.3	.3					.4	.3
Sales/Total Assets		1.7	1.4					1.2	1.1
		.8	.6					.4	.4
		.3	.2					.2	.2
% Depr., Dep., Amort./Sales		2.8	2.9					4.2	4.8
	(13)	10.2	(17) 9.7				(26)	5.9	(47) 7.9
		14.5	16.2					15.3	13.3
% Officers', Directors' Owners' Comp/Sales									
Net Sales ($)	4534M	18516M	75346M	125134M		101807M		60720M	135061M
Total Assets ($)	1963M	16572M	101079M	137311M		100657M		99585M	223808M

M = $ thousand   MM = $ million
See Pages 11 through 21 for Explanation of Ratios and Data

Comparative Historical Data | Current Data Sorted by Sales

4/1/04-3/31/05 ALL	4/1/05-3/31/06 ALL	4/1/06-3/31/07 ALL	Type of Statement	0-1MM	1-3MM	3-5MM	5-10MM	10-25MM	25MM & OVER
4	4	7	Unqualified	2		2		2	1
4	10	9	Reviewed	1	3		2	2	1
5		9	Compiled	2	2	3	2		
13	11	19	Tax Returns	10	8	1			
19	17	11	Other	4	4	1		2	
				6 (4/1-9/30/06)		49 (10/1/06-3/31/07)			
45	42	55	**NUMBER OF STATEMENTS**	19	17	7	4	6	2
%	%	%	**ASSETS**	%	%	%	%	%	%
6.0	4.1	5.4	Cash & Equivalents	5.0	1.9				
10.4	12.0	9.2	Trade Receivables (net)	1.0	11.1				
14.2	16.7	18.6	Inventory	8.9	15.8				
3.5	5.5	8.1	All Other Current	5.1	11.1				
34.2	38.3	41.2	Total Current	20.0	40.0				
52.3	49.6	52.1	Fixed Assets (net)	75.4	48.9				
2.0	1.7	.1	Intangibles (net)	.1	.1				
11.6	10.5	6.5	All Other Non-Current	4.5	11.0				
100.0	100.0	100.0	Total	100.0	100.0				
			LIABILITIES						
24.3	22.8	26.5	Notes Payable-Short Term	30.3	23.7				
3.0	2.1	3.7	Cur. Mat.-L.T.D.	2.8	4.9				
2.9	4.3	5.7	Trade Payables	.8	.5				
.1	.3	.6	Income Taxes Payable	.0	1.9				
9.3	8.5	6.3	All Other Current	.7	6.4				
39.6	38.0	42.9	Total Current	34.6	37.5				
22.2	22.9	28.2	Long-Term Debt	30.3	36.5				
.6	.5	.4	Deferred Taxes	.0	.2				
2.9	3.9	1.6	All Other Non-Current	1.6	1.6				
34.7	34.7	26.9	Net Worth	33.5	24.1				
100.0	100.0	100.0	Total Liabilities & Net Worth	100.0	100.0				
			INCOME DATA						
100.0	100.0	100.0	Net Sales	100.0	100.0				
			Gross Profit						
85.1	87.4	88.5	Operating Expenses	82.2	90.0				
14.9	12.6	11.5	Operating Profit	17.8	10.0				
4.7	4.6	5.8	All Other Expenses (net)	9.9	5.5				
10.2	8.0	5.7	Profit Before Taxes	7.9	4.4				
			RATIOS						
1.8	1.7	1.8		2.0	1.6				
1.2	1.0	1.1	Current	.6	1.2				
.6	.8	.3		.1	.1				
.9	1.2	.7		.5	.9				
(44) .2	.3	.2	Quick	.1	.1				
.1	.1	.1		.0	.0				
0 UND	0 UND	0 UND		0 UND	0 UND				
3 134.0	24 15.0	0 UND	Sales/Receivables	0 UND	0 UND				
50 7.3	58 6.3	41 8.9		0 UND	70 5.2				
			Cost of Sales/Inventory						
			Cost of Sales/Payables						
4.1	4.6	4.6		3.7	4.6				
10.2	NM	13.2	Sales/Working Capital	-6.8	5.7				
-4.0	-10.8	-4.4		-2.7	-4.6				
7.0	4.2	5.4		6.2	4.8				
(42) 3.8	(37) 2.0	(47) 1.9	EBIT/Interest	(16) 2.0	(15) 1.2				
1.2	.6	.6		-.5	.6				
			Net Profit + Depr., Dep., Amort./Cur. Mat. L/T/D						
.7	.7	.5		1.0	.2				
1.2	1.4	1.4	Fixed/Worth	1.4	1.6				
3.1	6.2	5.5		5.5	NM				
.5	.5	.6		.4	.9				
1.4	2.4	2.3	Debt/Worth	.6	2.8				
34.7	13.0	15.0		4.6	NM				
25.2	34.9	30.2		25.6	28.7				
(35) 6.0	(35) 11.5	(43) 8.0	% Profit Before Taxes/Tangible Net Worth	(16) 2.8	(13) 4.3				
.7	.5	.2		-5.3	-1.1				
11.1	9.3	8.8		8.1	8.8				
4.0	1.4	1.8	% Profit Before Taxes/Total Assets	1.8	.9				
.5	-1.1	-1.3		-4.1	-1.8				
5.4	4.1	13.3		3.2	14.7				
2.0	1.8	2.0	Sales/Net Fixed Assets	.3	1.4				
.4	.7	.5		.1	.6				
1.9	1.5	1.8		1.8	1.1				
.6	.7	.8	Sales/Total Assets	.3	.6				
.3	.4	.3		.1	.4				
4.6	3.0	2.8		4.0	5.4				
(40) 8.5	(37) 5.5	(44) 6.4	% Depr., Dep., Amort./Sales	(17) 10.8	(12) 9.9				
13.8	14.2	13.3		16.2	14.0				
		2.2	% Officers', Directors' Owners' Comp/Sales						
	(11)	3.0							
		27.8							
186409M	251921M	325337M	Net Sales ($)	10274M	28421M	29308M	30485M	98932M	127917M
221436M	326399M	357582M	Total Assets ($)	42872M	48799M	24865M	22108M	93250M	125688M

M = $ thousand   MM = $ million
See Pages 11 through 21 for Explanation of Ratios and Data

Current Data Sorted by Assets   Comparative Historical Data

Type of Statement	0-500M	500M-2MM	2-10MM	10-50MM	50-100MM	100-250MM		6	8
Unqualified			4	5				6	8
Reviewed		7	2	1				7	5
Compiled	3	14	10	2				5	15
Tax Returns	8	9	3	12		1		7	17
Other	1							11	9
		13 (4/1-9/30/06)		71 (10/1/06-3/31/07)				4/1/02-3/31/03 ALL	4/1/03-3/31/04 ALL
NUMBER OF STATEMENTS	12	30	31	10		1		36	54

	0-500M %	500M-2MM %	2-10MM %	10-50MM %	50-100MM %	100-250MM %		6 %	8 %
ASSETS									
Cash & Equivalents	13.7	7.3	4.2	3.7				8.1	7.4
Trade Receivables (net)	4.4	5.9	5.3	17.9				19.2	11.1
Inventory	8.0	8.6	26.6	22.7				18.0	17.9
All Other Current	8.5	13.6	5.2	5.3	D			3.9	7.4
Total Current	34.7	35.4	41.3	49.5	A			49.2	43.9
Fixed Assets (net)	39.3	51.6	49.9	45.6	T			39.3	46.3
Intangibles (net)	4.2	.9	.2	1.0	A			1.2	1.2
All Other Non-Current	21.9	12.1	8.6	3.9				10.4	8.6
Total	100.0	100.0	100.0	100.0	N			100.0	100.0
LIABILITIES					O				
Notes Payable-Short Term	73.4	37.4	23.7	19.9	T			14.7	19.6
Cur. Mat.-L.T.D.	1.8	1.7	2.7	2.1				4.3	12.7
Trade Payables	.0	7.9	6.1	4.0	A			12.4	4.9
Income Taxes Payable	.0	.1	.1	.8	V			1.0	.2
All Other Current	12.8	4.6	10.0	15.2	A			10.3	4.7
Total Current	88.0	51.7	42.6	42.1	I			42.6	42.1
Long-Term Debt	18.7	29.9	17.5	18.2	L			40.6	31.9
Deferred Taxes	.0	.0	.2	.5	A			.0	.4
All Other Non-Current	11.5	3.0	1.2	.4	B			1.8	4.6
Net Worth	-18.2	15.4	38.6	38.8	L			15.0	21.0
Total Liabilities & Net Worth	100.0	100.0	100.0	100.0	E			100.0	100.0
INCOME DATA									
Net Sales	100.0	100.0	100.0	100.0				100.0	100.0
Gross Profit									
Operating Expenses	87.8	89.3	87.7	86.1				94.6	94.1
Operating Profit	12.2	10.7	12.3	13.9				5.4	5.9
All Other Expenses (net)	1.4	2.4	5.4	1.5				2.2	3.4
Profit Before Taxes	10.8	8.3	6.9	12.4				3.1	2.5
RATIOS									
Current	2.3	2.3	1.2	1.6				2.0	2.3
	.7	.9	1.1	1.1				1.1	1.1
	.1	.6	.7	.9				.8	.7
Quick	.9	.9	.3	.7				1.6	.8
	.2	.3	.1	.5				.6	.4
	.0	.1	.0	.3				.3	.1
Sales/Receivables	0 UND	0 UND	0 UND	14 26.1				6 65.2	0 UND
	0 UND	0 UND	1 589.2	49 7.5				30 12.3	7 50.1
	0 UND	7 53.8	11 33.7	84 4.3				99 3.7	31 11.7
Cost of Sales/Inventory									
Cost of Sales/Payables									
Sales/Working Capital	37.1	9.1	8.7	2.8				8.4	4.3
	-26.2	-59.8	45.9	NM				37.2	51.2
	-3.4	-3.6	-5.8	-22.7				-17.2	-17.4
EBIT/Interest	44.3	5.7	4.1					3.8	3.0
	(10) 4.5	(25) 1.7	(28) 2.5					(31) 2.2	(45) 1.2
	-1.7	.9	.3					.9	-4.3
Net Profit + Depr., Dep., Amort./Cur. Mat. L/T/D									
Fixed/Worth	.0	.6	.8	.8				.3	.5
	1.6	1.4	1.2	1.5				1.1	1.2
	15.9	NM	1.9	2.0				2.1	5.3
Debt/Worth	1.9	.6	.7	.6				.6	.4
	7.5	2.0	1.5	2.1				1.8	1.5
	NM	-100.9	4.9	5.1				6.7	10.3
% Profit Before Taxes/Tangible Net Worth		27.4	22.7	33.4				17.1	11.8
	(21) 14.6	(29) 8.6	2.5					(33) 5.1	(44) 2.8
	4.2	.7	-11.9					-1.7	-7.9
% Profit Before Taxes/Total Assets	33.4	13.7	7.0	12.0				8.9	5.3
	9.6	6.3	3.5	.9				2.9	1.0
	-.8	.3	-1.6	-2.9				-.1	-5.2
Sales/Net Fixed Assets	479.8	9.1	13.6	9.2				13.4	12.7
	14.6	2.2	1.4	3.7				4.8	5.4
	2.9	.7	.4	.7				.9	.7
Sales/Total Assets	8.2	2.8	1.5	2.0				2.7	2.9
	2.6	1.3	.6	1.1				1.3	1.2
	1.3	.5	.3	.4				.4	.5
% Depr., Dep., Amort./Sales		1.9	1.5	1.4				1.6	1.3
	(21) 4.6	(24) 7.3	4.7					(33) 4.8	(44) 4.9
	9.7	11.5	8.9					9.8	10.6
% Officers', Directors', Owners' Comp/Sales								1.3	1.5
								(14) 3.4	(20) 3.5
								21.2	6.2
Net Sales ($)	9672M	55884M	139263M	379844M		417177M		1305351M	996527M
Total Assets ($)	3085M	28969M	131665M	256624M		175505M		917211M	547539M

M = $ thousand   MM = $ million
See Pages 11 through 21 for Explanation of Ratios and Data

Comparative Historical Data | Current Data Sorted by Sales

14	9	9	Type of Statement		1	1	1	2	4
3	4	3	Unqualified / Reviewed	1			2		
13	12	22	Compiled	6	9	4	1		2
23	13	25	Tax Returns	9	13	2	1		
22	23	25	Other	11	6	2			2
4/1/04-3/31/05 ALL	4/1/05-3/31/06 ALL	4/1/06-3/31/07 ALL		13 (4/1-9/30/06) 0-1MM	1-3MM	3-5MM	71 (10/1/06-3/31/07) 5-10MM	10-25MM	25MM & OVER
75	61	84	**NUMBER OF STATEMENTS**	27	29	9	8	5	6
%	%	%	**ASSETS**	%	%	%	%	%	%
6.5	5.3	6.6	Cash & Equivalents	6.5	7.5				
11.0	9.8	7.3	Trade Receivables (net)	1.7	3.0				
17.9	25.1	17.2	Inventory	9.0	15.7				
2.7	4.1	8.6	All Other Current	5.7	9.5				
38.1	44.4	39.7	Total Current	23.0	35.7				
47.4	43.8	48.1	Fixed Assets (net)	58.1	51.2				
1.4	1.9	1.1	Intangibles (net)	2.4	.6				
13.1	10.0	11.1	All Other Non-Current	16.5	12.5				
100.0	100.0	100.0	Total	100.0	100.0				
			LIABILITIES						
22.6	28.8	35.4	Notes Payable-Short Term	38.2	47.5				
5.3	5.1	2.1	Cur. Mat.-L.T.D.	1.4	3.0				
6.2	7.6	5.9	Trade Payables	1.7	5.7				
.5	.2	.2	Income Taxes Payable	.1	.0				
5.2	9.1	9.0	All Other Current	6.8	2.4				
39.7	50.8	52.5	Total Current	48.2	58.7				
28.1	34.4	22.1	Long-Term Debt	20.0	28.8				
.2	.4	.1	Deferred Taxes	.0	.0				
3.8	.7	3.2	All Other Non-Current	5.2	3.1				
28.2	13.8	22.0	Net Worth	26.6	9.4				
100.0	100.0	100.0	Total Liabilties & Net Worth	100.0	100.0				
			INCOME DATA						
100.0	100.0	100.0	Net Sales	100.0	100.0				
			Gross Profit						
88.9	90.7	88.3	Operating Expenses	77.9	93.2				
11.1	9.3	11.7	Operating Profit	22.1	6.8				
3.6	1.5	3.2	All Other Expenses (net)	3.9	4.4				
7.4	7.8	8.5	Profit Before Taxes	18.2	2.3				
			RATIOS						
1.9	1.5	1.4	Current	2.2	1.1				
1.2	1.1	1.0		.9	.9				
.6	.4	.7		.2	.4				
.9	.7	.7	Quick	1.2	.4				
.3	.3	.2		.2	.1				
.1	.1	.1		.0	.0				
0 UND	0 UND	0 UND	Sales/Receivables	0 UND	0 UND				
4 81.8	3 116.5	0 UND		0 UND	0 UND				
41 8.8	24 15.2	23 16.2		6 65.2	0 UND				
			Cost of Sales/Inventory						
			Cost of Sales/Payables						
7.7	10.7	9.4	Sales/Working Capital	8.9	17.4				
30.6	26.5	-321.1		-18.2	-38.6				
-6.1	-8.2	-5.9		-2.0	-4.4				
7.4	8.3	5.4	EBIT/Interest	13.0	3.5				
(62) 2.6	(55) 2.9	(73) 2.3		(20) 5.1	(28) 1.6				
1.0	.8	.4		2.6	.3				
6.1			Net Profit + Depr., Dep., Amort./Cur. Mat. L/T/D						
(13) 3.1									
.9									
.5	.5	.7	Fixed/Worth	.7	1.0				
1.1	1.4	1.3		1.3	1.4				
3.1	31.1	2.6		1.9	19.9				
.6	1.0	.7	Debt/Worth	.5	1.0				
1.3	2.9	2.1		1.4	3.2				
18.5	-33.0	13.1		4.9	NM				
39.3	42.6	31.6	% Profit Before Taxes/Tangible Net Worth	38.8	20.3				
(60) 10.3	(45) 16.9	(70) 10.4		(24) 14.4	(22) 9.0				
2.4	2.5	.0		4.7	-.6				
9.6	16.8	9.1	% Profit Before Taxes/Total Assets	15.9	6.5				
3.3	5.7	4.3		7.4	2.5				
.0	-.7	-1.1		3.1	-3.7				
12.1	15.0	12.1	Sales/Net Fixed Assets	3.2	14.1				
3.2	4.3	2.5		.6	1.8				
.6	1.8	.7		.3	.7				
3.0	3.1	2.4	Sales/Total Assets	1.2	2.9				
1.2	1.4	1.1		.4	1.1				
.4	.8	.4		.2	.4				
2.1	1.2	1.5	% Depr., Dep., Amort./Sales	5.2	2.0				
(66) 5.9	(46) 4.0	(64) 6.2		(19) 8.4	(22) 7.4				
13.9	9.3	9.8		12.9	15.3				
1.3	1.5	1.6	% Officers', Directors' Owners' Comp/Sales						
(24) 2.6	(17) 3.2	(17) 4.2							
4.6	8.8	8.8							
1626742M	2582515M	1001840M	Net Sales ($)	11536M	51714M	35481M	60244M	86656M	756209M
1033108M	1094924M	595848M	Total Assets ($)	36298M	74067M	70340M	30195M	35875M	349073M

M = $ thousand   MM = $ million
See Pages 11 through 21 for Explanation of Ratios and Data

Current Data Sorted by Assets   Comparative Historical Data

0-500M	500M-2MM	2-10MM	10-50MM	50-100MM	100-250MM	Type of Statement	4/1/02-3/31/03 ALL	4/1/03-3/31/04 ALL
		1	6	1		Unqualified	2	7
		2	5			Reviewed	6	6
1	6	7	6			Compiled	9	16
1	5	2				Tax Returns	8	8
1	5	5	10		2	Other	8	6
	13 (4/1-9/30/06)		53 (10/1/06-3/31/07)					
3	16	17	27	1	2	NUMBER OF STATEMENTS	33	43
%	%	%	%	%	%	**ASSETS**	%	%
	11.5	8.9	2.1			Cash & Equivalents	5.8	2.8
	7.9	7.1	15.1			Trade Receivables (net)	13.6	15.3
	5.6	23.2	18.1			Inventory	16.0	14.8
	1.9	2.3	7.4			All Other Current	6.9	8.4
	27.0	41.5	42.7			Total Current	42.3	41.3
	51.1	50.7	42.0			Fixed Assets (net)	49.9	51.8
	3.6	.4	2.9			Intangibles (net)	.3	.7
	18.3	7.4	12.4			All Other Non-Current	7.5	6.2
	100.0	100.0	100.0			Total	100.0	100.0
						LIABILITIES		
	30.2	15.9	15.1			Notes Payable-Short Term	17.8	21.1
	26.6	7.3	4.7			Cur. Mat.-L.T.D.	9.6	9.7
	.2	4.0	6.8			Trade Payables	4.3	5.9
	.4	1.9	1.1			Income Taxes Payable	.7	.2
	3.4	4.3	7.8			All Other Current	11.1	8.3
	60.8	33.4	35.5			Total Current	43.4	45.3
	48.6	33.3	22.4			Long-Term Debt	40.3	37.8
	.0	.1	.1			Deferred Taxes	1.6	.9
	.6	1.7	6.3			All Other Non-Current	1.4	.9
	-9.9	31.5	35.7			Net Worth	13.3	15.1
	100.0	100.0	100.0			Total Liabilities & Net Worth	100.0	100.0
						INCOME DATA		
	100.0	100.0	100.0			Net Sales	100.0	100.0
						Gross Profit		
	91.1	86.8	84.0			Operating Expenses	90.9	97.8
	8.9	13.2	16.0			Operating Profit	9.1	2.2
	1.6	2.3	3.9			All Other Expenses (net)	2.6	1.8
	7.2	10.9	12.0			Profit Before Taxes	6.5	.3
						RATIOS		
	2.5	1.6	2.0				2.4	1.7
	.3	1.4	1.1			Current	1.1	1.1
	.1	.8	.8				.7	.6
	1.2	.8	.9				1.0	.9
	.2	.4	.3			Quick	.6	.3
	.0	.2	.1				.1	.0
0 UND	0 UND	0 UND	1 291.9				0 UND	0 999.8
0 UND	0 UND	16 22.5	32 11.3			Sales/Receivables	25 14.9	28 13.2
0 UND	0 UND	65 5.7	75 4.9				48 7.6	59 6.2
						Cost of Sales/Inventory		
						Cost of Sales/Payables		
	NM	3.6	3.4				4.2	5.1
	-5.9	8.8	23.3			Sales/Working Capital	25.3	177.5
	-2.4	-17.0	-57.2				-5.8	-11.1
	9.5	6.3	8.4				6.5	3.2
	4.5 (13)	3.1 (23)	2.9			EBIT/Interest	(32) 3.0	(40) 1.8
	1.3	1.9	1.6				1.5	-.8
						Net Profit + Depr., Dep., Amort./Cur. Mat. L/T/D		
	.6	.8	.7				.7	1.0
	2.9	1.1	1.5			Fixed/Worth	1.6	1.7
	-3.7	3.3	3.5				46.8	3.6
	.8	.9	.8				.8	.9
	3.3	1.4	2.4			Debt/Worth	2.1	2.9
	-7.3	4.0	7.8				73.7	13.5
	145.7	33.4	28.9				49.2	10.9
	(11) 48.2	(14) 15.5	(24) 14.1			% Profit Before Taxes/Tangible Net Worth	(27) 19.5	(36) 6.9
	12.4	10.1	4.1				6.0	-8.5
	25.4	15.6	9.5				13.2	5.0
	11.5	6.2	4.3			% Profit Before Taxes/Total Assets	8.1	1.5
	-2.0	1.9	1.1				1.8	-3.5
	9.2	2.8	5.3				5.1	7.4
	4.0	2.0	1.9			Sales/Net Fixed Assets	2.6	2.9
	2.8	1.1	.5				1.4	1.3
	3.2	1.3	1.1				2.0	2.6
	1.9	.9	.7			Sales/Total Assets	1.1	1.0
	1.2	.5	.4				.7	.7
	3.0	3.8	3.3				2.5	3.0
	(12) 7.2	(16) 5.6	(21) 4.8			% Depr., Dep., Amort./Sales	(32) 4.5	(38) 4.8
	10.5	7.5	6.2				6.2	8.1
								3.1
						% Officers', Directors' Owners' Comp/Sales		(11) 5.5
								7.9
1485M	42393M	88025M	925261M	90193M	202466M	Net Sales ($)	695707M	797728M
828M	17344M	95462M	629992M	71593M	448631M	Total Assets ($)	673286M	604860M

M = $ thousand MM = $ million
See Pages 11 through 21 for Explanation of Ratios and Data

Comparative Historical Data				Current Data Sorted by Sales					
.4	5	8	**Type of Statement**						
10	4	7	Unqualified		1	1	1	5	
13	15	20	Reviewed		3		2	2	
7	8	8	Compiled	4	2	3	5	5	1
6	12	23	Tax Returns	1	6		1		
4/1/04-	4/1/05-	4/1/06-	Other	5		4	4	2	4
3/31/05	3/31/06	3/31/07		0-1MM	1-3MM	3-5MM	5-10MM	10-25MM	25MM & OVER
ALL	ALL	ALL			13 (4/1-9/30/06)			53 (10/1/06-3/31/07)	
40	44	66	**NUMBER OF STATEMENTS**	10	12	8	14	10	12
%	%	%	**ASSETS**	%	%	%	%	%	%
4.3	5.1	6.4	Cash & Equivalents	12.3	9.9		8.9	2.5	2.2
9.6	9.6	10.5	Trade Receivables (net)	.6	11.5		6.7	11.5	25.3
20.0	17.5	15.5	Inventory	.0	13.0		17.9	18.7	18.3
2.4	3.5	4.3	All Other Current	.2	.5		6.0	11.4	5.9
36.3	35.6	36.7	Total Current	13.0	34.9		39.4	44.1	51.7
52.8	52.1	47.3	Fixed Assets (net)	61.2	52.6		43.3	44.6	30.3
.3	.6	3.4	Intangibles (net)	5.7	.0		.2	4.5	9.7
10.6	11.7	12.7	All Other Non-Current	20.1	12.5		17.2	6.8	8.3
100.0	100.0	100.0	Total	100.0	100.0		100.0	100.0	100.0
			LIABILITIES						
20.0	23.1	18.9	Notes Payable-Short Term	12.3	30.7		18.9	21.6	11.6
12.9	8.8	10.5	Cur. Mat.-L.T.D.	8.7	13.7		19.9	6.4	3.2
2.6	3.7	4.3	Trade Payables	.1	.2		1.3	9.1	12.1
.6	.8	1.0	Income Taxes Payable	.5	.0		2.2	.0	.0
9.6	5.0	5.9	All Other Current	1.3	3.4		4.5	2.6	18.8
45.6	41.4	40.5	Total Current	22.8	48.0		46.8	39.6	45.7
37.5	29.9	36.0	Long-Term Debt	59.0	52.2		38.9	19.3	19.7
.1	.5	.2	Deferred Taxes	.0	.0		.2	.0	1.0
4.8	1.4	4.7	All Other Non-Current	8.7	1.4		9.2	3.8	3.1
12.0	26.9	18.7	Net Worth	9.4	-1.6		5.0	37.3	30.5
100.0	100.0	100.0	Total Liabilties & Net Worth	100.0	100.0		100.0	100.0	100.0
			INCOME DATA						
100.0	100.0	100.0	Net Sales	100.0	100.0		100.0	100.0	100.0
			Gross Profit						
99.2	89.2	87.7	Operating Expenses	73.6	93.6		91.6	83.4	94.1
.8	10.8	12.3	Operating Profit	26.4	6.4		8.4	16.6	5.9
2.4	4.7	2.5	All Other Expenses (net)	9.0	.6		.9	4.2	.9
-1.6	6.1	9.8	Profit Before Taxes	17.4	5.8		7.5	12.4	4.9
			RATIOS						
1.7	1.4	1.7		2.8	3.8		2.1	1.9	1.6
1.0	.9	1.1	Current	.5	.9		1.5	1.1	1.1
.5	.4	.5		.1	.3		.7	.7	.9
.6	.8	.8		2.8	1.2		1.0	.9	1.0
.2	.2	.3	Quick	.5	.3		.3	.3	.6
.0	.0	.1		.1	.1		.0	.1	.2
0 UND	0 UND	0 UND		0 UND	0 UND		0 UND	0 UND	31 11.8
13 28.3	16 23.1	16 23.0	Sales/Receivables	0 UND	0 UND		2 162.7	35 10.4	38 9.7
45 8.1	71 5.1	60 6.1		0 UND	102 3.6		63 5.8	128 2.8	54 6.8
			Cost of Sales/Inventory						
			Cost of Sales/Payables						
5.0	6.3	4.2		15.4	2.2		4.8	4.2	7.7
NM	-102.8	61.1	Sales/Working Capital	-13.8	NM		47.0	NM	18.5
-5.0	-4.6	-5.9		-2.3	-2.9		-10.1	-7.8	NM
10.4	6.7	7.9			11.1		6.3	16.3	5.0
(35) 2.8	(36) 2.5	(55) 3.1	EBIT/Interest	(11) 2.8		(13) 3.0	2.8	(11) 3.0	
-.8	.4	1.6			.4		1.5	2.0	1.3
		5.8							
	(11) 3.3		Net Profit + Depr., Dep.,						
		1.3	Amort./Cur. Mat. L/T/D						
.7	.7	.8		1.0	.3		.7	.7	.8
1.4	1.3	1.5	Fixed/Worth	1.6	NM		1.6	2.4	1.6
7.2	7.0	9.8		NM	-1.6		3.6	NM	3.4
.8	.8	.9		.6	.5		.9	.6	1.6
1.7	1.9	2.0	Debt/Worth	1.6	NM		2.7	3.5	3.0
11.5	7.9	21.2		NM	-3.6		27.3	NM	14.5
15.7	29.0	36.3					30.8		35.5
(33) 5.9	(36) 5.2	(52) 17.0	% Profit Before Taxes/Tangible Net Worth				(12) 18.1	(10) 23.3	
-11.6	-1.6	6.7					4.5		2.3
5.7	8.9	13.7		10.9	25.1		16.3	15.0	10.1
1.6	1.7	5.9	% Profit Before Taxes/Total Assets	4.6	.5		5.6	7.8	7.0
-6.1	-1.5	1.2		1.2	-4.8		.9	3.6	1.4
4.9	4.0	5.2		2.4	5.5		7.7	5.3	20.2
2.3	2.3	2.7	Sales/Net Fixed Assets	1.4	2.8		2.7	2.4	5.0
.9	1.2	1.2		.1	1.1		1.0	1.5	2.6
1.6	1.9	1.8		1.4	2.0		1.7	1.2	3.7
1.0	1.1	1.1	Sales/Total Assets	1.1	1.2		.9	.8	1.4
.5	.5	.5		.1	.6		.4	.6	.8
4.1	4.0	3.5					3.6		2.6
(37) 6.6	(40) 6.1	(53) 5.2	% Depr., Dep., Amort./Sales				(13) 6.1	(10) 4.0	
11.8	7.9	7.7					7.7		4.9
		1.4							
	(16) 3.2		% Officers', Directors' Owners' Comp/Sales						
		6.4							
834215M	779955M	1349823M	Net Sales ($)	6435M	22069M	32512M	98745M	158819M	1031243M
562408M	610146M	1263850M	Total Assets ($)	59908M	36270M	45719M	145557M	218711M	757685M

© RMA 2007

M = $ thousand   MM = $ million
See Pages 11 through 21 for Explanation of Ratios and Data

Current Data Sorted by Assets   Comparative Historical Data

0-500M	500M-2MM	2-10MM	10-50MM	50-100MM	100-250MM	Type of Statement		
			5		2	Unqualified	12	7
		4	6	1		Reviewed	26	27
1	3	9	2			Compiled	23	18
1	8	3				Tax Returns	14	9
1	11	11	11	5		Other	17	22
	29 (4/1-9/30/06)		55 (10/1/06-3/31/07)				4/1/02-3/31/03 ALL	4/1/03-3/31/04 ALL
3	22	27	24	6	2	NUMBER OF STATEMENTS	92	83
%	%	%	%	%	%	ASSETS	%	%
	14.4	4.0	5.9			Cash & Equivalents	7.4	7.6
	19.2	21.7	15.6			Trade Receivables (net)	15.5	18.0
	5.3	12.9	24.7			Inventory	12.8	12.3
	9.0	3.5	8.5			All Other Current	7.2	8.3
	48.0	42.1	54.6			Total Current	42.9	46.2
	41.7	40.4	35.2			Fixed Assets (net)	44.5	41.5
	5.7	.1	.3			Intangibles (net)	.9	.5
	4.7	17.4	9.9			All Other Non-Current	11.6	11.8
	100.0	100.0	100.0			Total	100.0	100.0
						LIABILITIES		
	18.0	21.1	10.7			Notes Payable-Short Term	16.6	18.4
	2.0	2.6	2.2			Cur. Mat.-L.T.D.	5.3	4.2
	7.7	12.7	11.0			Trade Payables	9.7	11.0
	.0	.0	1.5			Income Taxes Payable	.5	.3
	5.0	6.9	7.3			All Other Current	7.1	5.4
	32.8	43.3	32.6			Total Current	39.0	39.3
	23.8	19.1	10.1			Long-Term Debt	32.1	20.4
	.0	.7	.7			Deferred Taxes	.7	1.3
	1.8	.9	3.0			All Other Non-Current	2.0	3.7
	41.6	36.0	53.6			Net Worth	26.2	35.3
	100.0	100.0	100.0			Total Liabilities & Net Worth	100.0	100.0
						INCOME DATA		
	100.0	100.0	100.0			Net Sales	100.0	100.0
						Gross Profit		
	91.7	92.7	95.4			Operating Expenses	92.7	94.6
	8.3	7.3	4.6			Operating Profit	7.3	5.4
	1.1	1.9	-.3			All Other Expenses (net)	2.5	1.2
	7.2	5.4	4.9			Profit Before Taxes	4.8	4.1
						RATIOS		
	6.2	1.5	2.9				2.4	1.8
	2.3	1.0	1.6			Current	1.3	1.3
	.8	.5	1.1				.7	.9
	3.5	1.0	1.4				1.3	1.2
	1.1	.5	.6			Quick	.6	.6
	.3	.2	.2				.2	.2
	0 UND	11 32.4	6 56.4				1 313.9	1 277.7
	1 537.0	30 12.0	30 12.3			Sales/Receivables	27 13.3	32 11.5
	28 13.0	59 6.2	58 6.3				48 7.5	59 6.2
						Cost of Sales/Inventory		
						Cost of Sales/Payables		
	7.3	13.4	4.5				5.8	5.5
	25.2	211.3	8.9			Sales/Working Capital	19.2	13.2
	-16.3	-12.8	36.4				-16.0	-34.1
	19.3	6.9	18.0				11.0	13.3
	(17) 1.8	(24) 3.8	(21) 5.7			EBIT/Interest	(84) 3.5	(77) 3.1
	1.2	.3	.1				1.3	1.1
						Net Profit + Depr., Dep.,	7.6	6.0
						Amort./Cur. Mat. L/T/D	(17) 1.5	(18) 2.2
							.5	-1.3
	.2	.5	.4				.5	.5
	1.2	1.1	.6			Fixed/Worth	.9	1.0
	NM	2.1	1.1				2.6	2.8
	.2	.8	.4				.6	.8
	1.1	2.0	1.1			Debt/Worth	1.3	1.8
	-16.2	4.6	2.0				4.5	3.7
	48.6	59.2	43.7			% Profit Before Taxes/Tangible	32.1	26.8
	(16) 23.6	(26) 24.0	10.6			Net Worth	(81) 14.2	(78) 12.8
	1.1	-5.1	-6.8				3.6	-.4
	28.1	21.2	17.9			% Profit Before Taxes/Total	13.2	11.0
	8.9	5.1	4.1			Assets	6.1	4.2
	1.1	-2.9	-3.5				1.2	-.7
	35.2	9.9	10.4				9.1	11.1
	10.4	5.8	4.8			Sales/Net Fixed Assets	4.2	4.3
	3.5	2.5	2.8				2.2	2.1
	5.3	3.3	2.4				3.1	2.6
	3.5	1.9	1.7			Sales/Total Assets	1.7	1.3
	2.2	.8	1.2				.7	.8
	.8	1.7	1.8				1.6	2.2
	(17) 2.5	(23) 3.0	(21) 3.1			% Depr., Dep., Amort./Sales	(88) 3.2	(75) 3.4
	6.2	5.6	4.0				5.1	6.3
						% Officers', Directors'	1.3	1.2
						Owners' Comp/Sales	(25) 3.2	(24) 2.6
							7.1	4.7
3777M	85434M	282260M	942394M	471871M	352411M	Net Sales ($)	2096052M	1588551M
861M	25523M	126350M	520921M	409571M	353938M	Total Assets ($)	1253450M	1161488M

M = $ thousand   MM = $ million
See Pages 11 through 21 for Explanation of Ratios and Data

Comparative Historical Data | | | Current Data Sorted by Sales

			Type of Statement						
5	16	7	Unqualified		2			2	5
22	19	11	Reviewed		4			4	7
12	18	15	Compiled	1	4		4	4	1
19	13	12	Tax Returns	2	4	2	2	2	
25	28	39	Other	1	11	4	4	8	11
4/1/04-3/31/05	4/1/05-3/31/06	4/1/06-3/31/07			29 (4/1-9/30/06)			55 (10/1/06-3/31/07)	
ALL	ALL	ALL		0-1MM	1-3MM	3-5MM	5-10MM	10-25MM	25MM & OVER
83	94	84	NUMBER OF STATEMENTS	4	17	9	10	20	24
%	%	%	**ASSETS**	%	%	%	%	%	%
8.0	8.5	7.0	Cash & Equivalents		9.7		15.4	7.5	2.5
16.5	18.4	17.5	Trade Receivables (net)		15.3		22.3	19.2	14.6
11.6	13.3	15.4	Inventory		5.5		3.2	21.2	27.0
6.0	4.1	6.6	All Other Current		1.5		10.8	6.2	8.5
42.1	44.3	46.5	Total Current		31.9		51.6	54.1	52.6
44.7	39.0	40.7	Fixed Assets (net)		51.5		38.0	34.9	38.5
1.9	.8	1.7	Intangibles (net)		5.8		.0	.1	.7
11.3	15.9	11.1	All Other Non-Current		10.9		10.3	11.0	8.2
100.0	100.0	100.0	Total		100.0		100.0	100.0	100.0
			LIABILITIES						
19.3	18.7	17.1	Notes Payable-Short Term		17.0		25.1	20.2	12.2
4.8	3.2	2.5	Cur. Mat.-L.T.D.		4.3		2.0	2.7	2.5
7.7	11.2	9.8	Trade Payables		4.2		10.9	11.9	12.7
.5	.5	.4	Income Taxes Payable		.0		.0	.4	1.1
8.2	10.3	6.5	All Other Current		6.5		6.6	4.9	8.0
40.4	44.0	36.3	Total Current		31.9		44.7	40.1	36.1
25.3	22.4	19.5	Long-Term Debt		33.5		4.7	15.8	19.6
.9	1.2	.6	Deferred Taxes		.0		.0	1.0	1.3
5.4	6.1	3.7	All Other Non-Current		.1		5.9	.9	2.9
28.0	26.4	39.9	Net Worth		34.5		44.8	42.2	40.2
100.0	100.0	100.0	Total Liabilties & Net Worth		100.0		100.0	100.0	100.0
			INCOME DATA						
100.0	100.0	100.0	Net Sales		100.0		100.0	100.0	100.0
			Gross Profit						
93.4	92.4	93.0	Operating Expenses		95.4		95.8	91.6	96.8
6.6	7.6	7.0	Operating Profit		4.6		4.2	8.4	3.2
1.3	2.0	1.3	All Other Expenses (net)		.1		-.8	.2	1.6
5.3	5.6	5.6	Profit Before Taxes		4.4		5.0	8.2	1.6
			RATIOS						
2.1	1.9	2.7	Current		3.1		6.2	8.5	2.7
1.3	1.2	1.2			1.2		1.7	1.2	1.4
.6	.7	.9			.1		.7	.9	1.1
1.4	1.4	1.2	Quick		1.6		5.3	1.1	.7
(82) .6	.7	.5			.3		1.4	.5	.5
.2	.2	.2			.1		.4	.3	.2
0 UND	0 UND	0 999.8	Sales/Receivables		0 UND		0 UND	12 30.6	9 39.1
28 13.2	28 12.9	27 13.5			0 999.8		26 14.3	30 12.0	30 12.3
54 6.7	43 8.5	47 7.8			50 7.3		36 10.1	55 6.7	39 9.4
			Cost of Sales/Inventory						
			Cost of Sales/Payables						
5.2	7.5	6.2	Sales/Working Capital		5.7		13.3	4.9	4.8
26.2	28.9	21.5			35.4		22.3	18.8	11.9
-22.0	-26.8	-51.8			-5.5		-15.7	-51.8	127.2
9.4	13.5	11.8	EBIT/Interest		5.1		23.4	18.1	10.3
(72) 2.5	(80) 3.2	(72) 3.0			(13) 1.5		8.9	(19) 4.6	(21) 2.4
.2	.9	.4			-1.4		-3.6	.6	-.8
5.0	7.7	7.7	Net Profit + Depr., Dep., Amort./Cur. Mat. L/T/D						
(13) 2.4	(19) 2.3	(14) 2.9							
1.2	.9	1.7							
.5	.5	.5	Fixed/Worth		.4		.4	.4	.6
1.2	1.0	.9			1.5		.7	1.0	.9
4.8	2.9	1.9			7.3		NM	2.0	1.3
.5	.5	.5	Debt/Worth		.4		.2	.3	.7
2.1	1.6	1.4			2.4		1.0	1.7	1.4
8.8	6.1	4.6			7.4		NM	5.3	2.9
31.4	34.3	50.0	% Profit Before Taxes/Tangible Net Worth		40.0			66.3	36.1
(69) 14.7	(83) 12.7	(75) 15.1			(14) 23.6			(19) 35.3	(23) 6.5
-.6	.6	-.2			-14.9			15.1	-6.1
11.0	14.6	21.6	% Profit Before Taxes/Total Assets		22.7		75.7	28.0	11.2
3.0	4.8	4.2			3.6		14.9	9.7	2.2
-1.6	.0	-1.9			-2.7		-11.6	.7	-4.9
11.2	16.3	11.1	Sales/Net Fixed Assets		17.3		68.5	12.8	9.5
5.5	5.3	5.1			3.2		9.6	6.5	4.9
2.0	2.8	2.5			2.3		5.9	3.6	2.3
3.1	3.7	3.3	Sales/Total Assets		3.2		5.1	3.2	2.6
1.7	1.9	2.0			1.9		3.9	2.1	2.0
.8	1.2	1.2			.9		2.8	1.5	1.2
1.6	1.3	1.8	% Depr., Dep., Amort./Sales		2.6			1.3	2.1
(73) 3.6	(80) 3.0	(69) 3.0			(13) 5.6			(17) 2.7	(21) 2.6
6.4	5.0	4.7			8.0			4.5	3.9
1.5	.7	1.1	% Officers', Directors' Owners' Comp/Sales						
(25) 3.3	(25) 1.7	(23) 3.0							
7.7	8.0	5.0							
1886764M	3086065M	2138147M	Net Sales ($)	1823M	39544M	37010M	67617M	347622M	1644531M
1299126M	1811315M	1437164M	Total Assets ($)	12196M	27209M	25927M	50745M	203822M	1117265M

M = $ thousand   MM = $ million
See Pages 11 through 21 for Explanation of Ratios and Data

Current Data Sorted by Assets   Comparative Historical Data

	0-500M	500M-2MM	2-10MM	10-50MM	50-100MM	100-250MM		4/1/02-3/31/03 ALL	4/1/03-3/31/04 ALL
Type of Statement									
Unqualified			1	1	1	2		16	17
Reviewed				2				15	9
Compiled	1	5	3	4				19	20
Tax Returns	2	2	1	1	1			23	10
Other	1	1	1	2		1		8	4
	19 (4/1-9/30/06)			14 (10/1/06-3/31/07)					
NUMBER OF STATEMENTS	4	8	6	10	2	3		81	60
	%	%	%	%	%	%		%	%
ASSETS									
Cash & Equivalents				12.4				8.5	7.3
Trade Receivables (net)				7.1				6.5	10.4
Inventory				8.3				6.5	9.1
All Other Current				4.0				4.5	12.2
Total Current				31.9				26.1	39.1
Fixed Assets (net)				49.7				58.4	47.8
Intangibles (net)				.3				1.6	1.4
All Other Non-Current				18.2				13.9	11.7
Total				100.0				100.0	100.0
LIABILITIES									
Notes Payable-Short Term				9.5				10.8	14.3
Cur. Mat.-L.T.D.				2.7				4.4	2.7
Trade Payables				4.6				3.8	5.0
Income Taxes Payable				.1				.1	.1
All Other Current				5.6				12.4	10.8
Total Current				22.4				31.4	33.0
Long-Term Debt				41.2				32.6	32.8
Deferred Taxes				.0				.8	.8
All Other Non-Current				7.8				4.2	4.7
Net Worth				28.6				31.0	28.7
Total Liabilities & Net Worth				100.0				100.0	100.0
INCOME DATA									
Net Sales				100.0				100.0	100.0
Gross Profit									
Operating Expenses				84.4				94.4	95.0
Operating Profit				15.6				5.6	5.0
All Other Expenses (net)				2.6				4.0	3.6
Profit Before Taxes				13.0				1.6	1.4
RATIOS									
Current				3.6				2.1	2.7
				1.3				1.0	1.1
				.6				.4	.7
Quick				2.7				1.1	1.1
				.6				.5	.4
				.5				.1	.1
Sales/Receivables				0 UND				0 UND	0 UND
				43 8.5				3 133.7	5 79.6
				82 4.5				22 17.0	27 13.4
Cost of Sales/Inventory									
Cost of Sales/Payables									
Sales/Working Capital				2.6				8.1	4.7
				9.9				-480.9	65.0
				-5.8				-5.9	-9.0
EBIT/Interest				11.7				5.8	4.0
				2.1				(67) 2.1	(51) 1.2
				1.2				.5	-.5
Net Profit + Depr., Dep., Amort./Cur. Mat. L/T/D								4.3	
								(12) 3.5	
								.1	
Fixed/Worth				.8				.8	.7
				1.3				1.3	1.5
				NM				16.4	-270.9
Debt/Worth				.9				.5	.6
				1.8				1.4	3.0
				NM				23.0	-365.6
% Profit Before Taxes/Tangible Net Worth								25.3	20.2
								(63) 9.3	(44) 1.5
								.1	-9.3
% Profit Before Taxes/Total Assets				14.7				9.2	8.2
				2.5				1.9	.9
				.9				-1.3	-2.2
Sales/Net Fixed Assets				2.6				5.9	8.3
				.8				2.0	2.7
				.4				.6	.6
Sales/Total Assets				.7				2.4	2.4
				.4				1.1	1.1
				.3				.3	.3
% Depr., Dep., Amort./Sales								3.1	2.8
								(76) 6.1	(54) 6.4
								11.3	11.9
% Officers', Directors' Owners' Comp/Sales								1.5	
								(20) 2.5	
								5.4	
Net Sales ($)	15196M	40314M	23715M	91260M	56763M	132320M		971767M	1123498M
Total Assets ($)	1502M	10072M	34192M	196474M	138812M	375105M		1306677M	1450367M

© RMA 2007

M = $ thousand   MM = $ million

See Pages 11 through 21 for Explanation of Ratios and Data

Comparative Historical Data   ## Current Data Sorted by Sales

			Type of Statement	0-1MM	1-3MM	3-5MM	5-10MM	10-25MM	25MM & OVER
11	13	5	Unqualified				1	2	3
8	6	2	Reviewed				2	1	1
5	7	13	Compiled	1	7	1	2	1	1
14	7	7	Tax Returns	2		2	1	1	
9	10	6	Other	1		2		1	
4/1/04-3/31/05	4/1/05-3/31/06	4/1/06-3/31/07			19 (4/1-9/30/06)			14 (10/1/06-3/31/07)	
ALL	ALL	ALL		0-1MM	1-3MM	3-5MM	5-10MM	10-25MM	25MM & OVER
47	43	33	NUMBER OF STATEMENTS	4	7	5	6	6	5
%	%	%	**ASSETS**	%	%	%	%	%	%
12.6	15.1	14.9	Cash & Equivalents						
7.6	9.4	6.1	Trade Receivables (net)						
8.1	10.2	5.6	Inventory						
1.6	2.6	4.3	All Other Current						
29.9	37.2	31.0	Total Current						
57.7	49.4	51.3	Fixed Assets (net)						
1.5	4.5	.6	Intangibles (net)						
10.8	8.9	17.1	All Other Non-Current						
100.0	100.0	100.0	Total						
			LIABILITIES						
9.2	11.2	11.2	Notes Payable-Short Term						
3.3	5.4	3.1	Cur. Mat.-L.T.D.						
2.8	5.5	3.3	Trade Payables						
.1	.5	.1	Income Taxes Payable						
18.0	11.9	8.0	All Other Current						
33.3	34.5	25.8	Total Current						
38.0	32.9	52.8	Long-Term Debt						
.8	.7	.0	Deferred Taxes						
4.4	3.6	5.2	All Other Non-Current						
23.4	28.4	16.2	Net Worth						
100.0	100.0	100.0	Total Liabilities & Net Worth						
			INCOME DATA						
100.0	100.0	100.0	Net Sales						
			Gross Profit						
90.4	89.4	86.9	Operating Expenses						
9.6	10.6	13.1	Operating Profit						
1.7	2.6	1.9	All Other Expenses (net)						
7.9	8.0	11.2	Profit Before Taxes						
			RATIOS						
2.5	2.4	3.3	Current						
1.2	1.7	1.2							
.7	.6	.6							
1.6	1.9	2.2	Quick						
.8	.6	.6							
.2	.3	.2							
0 UND	0 UND	0 UND	Sales/Receivables						
5 76.2	9 40.2	7 55.0							
36 10.3	39 9.4	69 5.3							
			Cost of Sales/Inventory						
			Cost of Sales/Payables						
4.1	3.1	3.6	Sales/Working Capital						
30.3	9.7	99.4							
-8.1	-6.3	-6.1							
3.7	7.3	6.7	EBIT/Interest						
(38) 2.5	(36) 3.6	(28) 2.8							
-.5	1.2	1.3							
			Net Profit + Depr., Dep., Amort./Cur. Mat. L/T/D						
.8	.8	.8	Fixed/Worth						
1.3	1.3	1.8							
5.5	9.7	UND							
.7	.7	.8	Debt/Worth						
1.5	1.5	2.3							
8.4	20.3	UND							
28.0	36.2	58.4	% Profit Before Taxes/Tangible Net Worth						
(40) 6.5	(35) 12.8	(25) 29.6							
-2.0	.8	4.6							
8.5	14.0	15.1	% Profit Before Taxes/Total Assets						
4.2	4.4	5.4							
-1.7	.0	1.1							
3.4	7.4	5.6	Sales/Net Fixed Assets						
1.1	1.8	1.2							
.6	.5	.5							
1.6	2.4	1.6	Sales/Total Assets						
.7	.9	.5							
.3	.3	.3							
4.0	2.3	5.3	% Depr., Dep., Amort./Sales						
(40) 6.6	(37) 6.1	(26) 7.5							
13.8	12.4	11.8							
1.6			% Officers', Directors' Owners' Comp/Sales						
(10) 2.7									
5.4									
1227542M	910241M	359568M	Net Sales ($)	1304M	15147M	17845M	40829M	86324M	198119M
1522643M	1261290M	756157M	Total Assets ($)	2360M	65085M	36663M	62101M	114303M	475645M

© RMA 2007

M = $ thousand   MM = $ million
See Pages 11 through 21 for Explanation of Ratios and Data

Current Data Sorted by Assets							Comparative Historical Data	
						Type of Statement		
		1	3			Unqualified	2	3
1		3	3			Reviewed	13	11
1		11				Compiled	9	10
4	5	1				Tax Returns	8	9
	3	1	1		1	Other	2	6
	7 (4/1-9/30/06)		32 (10/1/06-3/31/07)				4/1/02-3/31/03	4/1/03-3/31/04
0-500M	**500M-2MM**	**2-10MM**	**10-50MM**	**50-100MM**	**100-250MM**		**ALL**	**ALL**
6	8	17	7		1	**NUMBER OF STATEMENTS**	34	39
%	%	%	%	%	%	**ASSETS**	%	%
		2.8		DATA NOT AVAILABLE		Cash & Equivalents	12.9	11.9
		8.8				Trade Receivables (net)	12.4	11.0
		28.5				Inventory	7.2	9.6
		2.1				All Other Current	4.5	2.4
		42.2				Total Current	36.9	34.9
		50.1				Fixed Assets (net)	53.5	57.4
		.2				Intangibles (net)	.4	.7
		7.6				All Other Non-Current	9.2	7.0
		100.0				Total	100.0	100.0
						LIABILITIES		
		14.9				Notes Payable-Short Term	13.1	23.6
		1.9				Cur. Mat.-L.T.D.	4.2	4.9
		2.1				Trade Payables	5.7	6.1
		.0				Income Taxes Payable	.1	.2
		3.3				All Other Current	7.8	5.1
		22.2				Total Current	30.9	40.0
		25.1				Long-Term Debt	35.2	19.8
		.1				Deferred Taxes	.4	.4
		.8				All Other Non-Current	4.7	2.2
		51.8				Net Worth	28.8	37.7
		100.0				Total Liabilties & Net Worth	100.0	100.0
						INCOME DATA		
		100.0				Net Sales	100.0	100.0
						Gross Profit		
		80.8				Operating Expenses	93.7	93.5
		19.2				Operating Profit	6.3	6.5
		.8				All Other Expenses (net)	8.2	3.1
		18.4				Profit Before Taxes	-1.9	3.4
						RATIOS		
		3.7					2.5	2.1
		1.7				Current	1.5	1.3
		1.1					.7	.6
		1.4					2.1	1.4
		.8				Quick	.8	.6
		.0					.3	.3
		0 UND					0 UND	0 UND
		11 34.0				Sales/Receivables	26 14.1	22 16.8
		49 7.4					52 7.1	53 6.8
						Cost of Sales/Inventory		
						Cost of Sales/Payables		
		2.0					4.4	4.1
		7.9				Sales/Working Capital	9.3	75.7
		46.2					-10.2	-16.6
		14.5					3.1	7.9
		(15) 5.1				EBIT/Interest	(31) 1.1	(36) 2.7
		2.3					.1	.5
						Net Profit + Depr., Dep., Amort./Cur. Mat. L/T/D		
		.6					.7	.8
		1.2				Fixed/Worth	1.4	1.2
		2.0					9.8	1.9
		.3					.8	.5
		.6				Debt/Worth	1.3	1.0
		2.4					13.8	2.5
		42.3					21.6	29.1
		32.3				% Profit Before Taxes/Tangible Net Worth	(29) 2.4	(36) 14.0
		17.4					-7.7	2.2
		25.6					7.6	13.4
		14.6				% Profit Before Taxes/Total Assets	.7	4.7
		4.1					-2.9	-.5
		2.4					5.0	5.1
		1.4				Sales/Net Fixed Assets	1.9	2.6
		1.1					1.0	.9
		1.3					2.2	2.7
		.7				Sales/Total Assets	1.2	1.1
		.5					.6	.6
		4.4					3.6	2.2
		(14) 5.2				% Depr., Dep., Amort./Sales	(32) 5.2	(35) 4.5
		6.6					9.9	8.6
							1.2	2.3
						% Officers', Directors' Owners' Comp/Sales	(11) 2.4	(13) 3.0
							10.8	9.0
8559M	19759M	87306M	297394M		143079M	Net Sales ($)	402127M	560486M
1436M	9156M	90409M	216420M		199450M	Total Assets ($)	461357M	534703M

M = $ thousand MM = $ million

See Pages 11 through 21 for Explanation of Ratios and Data

Comparative Historical Data | Current Data Sorted by Sales

			Type of Statement						
4	1	4	Unqualified		1			1	2
9	3	7	Reviewed	1		2	1	2	1
10	8	12	Compiled	1	5	2	4		
4	4	10	Tax Returns	4	4	1	1		
9	14	6	Other			2	2		2
4/1/04-3/31/05 ALL	4/1/05-3/31/06 ALL	4/1/06-3/31/07 ALL		0-1MM	7 (4/1-9/30/06) 1-3MM	3-5MM	32 (10/1/06-3/31/07) 5-10MM	10-25MM	25MM & OVER
36	30	39	NUMBER OF STATEMENTS	6	10	7	8	3	5
%	%	%	ASSETS	%	%	%	%	%	%
6.2	3.8	7.5	Cash & Equivalents		9.3				
12.9	9.9	9.2	Trade Receivables (net)		3.7				
17.6	17.4	19.3	Inventory		29.3				
2.5	5.7	5.0	All Other Current		1.2				
39.2	36.8	41.0	Total Current		43.5				
52.6	53.9	47.1	Fixed Assets (net)		42.7				
.3	.2	.2	Intangibles (net)		.4				
7.8	9.0	11.6	All Other Non-Current		13.4				
100.0	100.0	100.0	Total		100.0				
			LIABILITIES						
8.5	16.4	12.6	Notes Payable-Short Term		26.5				
3.5	2.9	6.5	Cur. Mat.-L.T.D.		7.7				
8.4	7.7	5.0	Trade Payables		.6				
.0	.1	.0	Income Taxes Payable		.0				
6.1	10.4	12.9	All Other Current		7.8				
26.5	37.3	37.0	Total Current		42.5				
19.9	22.2	37.6	Long-Term Debt		35.1				
.1	.3	.2	Deferred Taxes		.0				
2.2	.7	3.5	All Other Non-Current		3.4				
51.3	39.5	21.6	Net Worth		19.0				
100.0	100.0	100.0	Total Liabilties & Net Worth		100.0				
			INCOME DATA						
100.0	100.0	100.0	Net Sales		100.0				
			Gross Profit						
94.0	91.1	84.3	Operating Expenses		84.9				
6.0	8.9	15.7	Operating Profit		15.1				
1.6	1.7	3.4	All Other Expenses (net)		.7				
4.5	7.2	12.3	Profit Before Taxes		14.4				
			RATIOS						
3.1	3.4	2.5			1.8				
1.5	1.6	1.3	Current		1.1				
.7	.6	.9			.8				
1.5	2.0	1.3			.6				
(35) .6	.5 (38)	.6	Quick		.3				
.3	.0	.1			.0				
3 129.3	0 UND	0 UND		0 UND					
26 13.8	14 25.8	11 34.0	Sales/Receivables	0 UND					
49 7.4	41 8.8	45 8.2		13 27.8					
			Cost of Sales/Inventory						
			Cost of Sales/Payables						
2.8	2.4	3.5			2.4				
8.7	15.1	25.2	Sales/Working Capital		43.3				
-24.9	-9.5	-21.5			-8.0				
8.1	5.5	9.0							
(30) 2.9	2.1 (27)	4.3 (35)	EBIT/Interest						
.9	.1	1.6							
			Net Profit + Depr., Dep., Amort./Cur. Mat. L/T/D						
.6	.7	.8			.8				
1.1	1.2	1.4	Fixed/Worth		1.6				
1.5	4.5	4.2			NM				
.4	.5	.6			.6				
1.0	1.1	1.9	Debt/Worth		2.3				
1.7	8.5	8.2			NM				
26.2	27.5	44.5	% Profit Before Taxes/Tangible Net Worth						
(34) 11.9	6.8 (26)	31.8 (31)							
1.2	-1.7	13.9							
12.8	9.4	21.7	% Profit Before Taxes/Total Assets		23.3				
5.9	1.8	14.3			6.2				
.8	-1.4	3.9			2.3				
6.1	3.3	6.0			8.3				
1.7	1.9	1.9	Sales/Net Fixed Assets		1.4				
1.1	.9	1.1			1.0				
2.3	1.7	1.9			2.7				
1.1	.9	1.0	Sales/Total Assets		.6				
.7	.6	.6			.5				
2.8	3.6	3.2	% Depr., Dep., Amort./Sales						
(32) 4.6	5.8 (28)	5.0 (34)							
7.6	7.9	6.6							
1.9			% Officers', Directors' Owners' Comp/Sales						
(11) 3.7									
11.9									
899815M	2121737M	556097M	Net Sales ($)	2725M	18934M	27226M	59362M	52722M	395128M
688130M	600128M	516871M	Total Assets ($)	1963M	25576M	28604M	50432M	67674M	342622M

© RMA 2007

M = $ thousand   MM = $ million
See Pages 11 through 21 for Explanation of Ratios and Data

Current Data Sorted by Assets   Comparative Historical Data

0-500M	500M-2MM	2-10MM	10-50MM	50-100MM	100-250MM	Type of Statement	4/1/02-3/31/03 ALL	4/1/03-3/31/04 ALL
2		4	1	1	2	Unqualified	5	1
	1	5	3	4		Reviewed	18	19
1	4	5	1			Compiled	15	7
3	8	7	1			Tax Returns	15	16
3	3	12	5	3		Other	27	21
	8 (4/1-9/30/06)		71 (10/1/06-3/31/07)					
9	16	33	11	8	2	**NUMBER OF STATEMENTS**	80	64
%	%	%	%	%	%	**ASSETS**	%	%
	15.0	6.3	6.8			Cash & Equivalents	6.1	5.5
	8.2	9.7	14.2			Trade Receivables (net)	12.1	11.7
	4.6	10.3	5.1			Inventory	6.6	5.1
	8.5	3.1	3.0			All Other Current	3.8	8.5
	36.3	29.4	29.2			Total Current	28.5	30.8
	53.8	62.0	57.8			Fixed Assets (net)	61.4	58.6
	1.7	.3	.1			Intangibles (net)	1.0	.8
	8.1	8.3	13.0			All Other Non-Current	9.2	9.8
	100.0	100.0	100.0			Total	100.0	100.0
						LIABILITIES		
	10.3	11.1	6.8			Notes Payable-Short Term	14.3	15.1
	4.2	3.5	.7			Cur. Mat.-L.T.D.	4.0	3.7
	1.8	1.6	3.9			Trade Payables	3.9	4.2
	.0	.0	.0			Income Taxes Payable	.3	.1
	4.2	3.0	1.6			All Other Current	5.8	4.0
	20.6	19.2	13.0			Total Current	28.3	27.2
	51.9	39.4	29.1			Long-Term Debt	42.2	40.2
	.0	.1	.6			Deferred Taxes	.2	.0
	6.8	5.3	1.0			All Other Non-Current	4.4	5.0
	20.8	36.0	56.2			Net Worth	24.9	27.6
	100.0	100.0	100.0			Total Liabilities & Net Worth	100.0	100.0
						INCOME DATA		
	100.0	100.0	100.0			Net Sales	100.0	100.0
						Gross Profit		
	89.5	90.6	88.6			Operating Expenses	86.2	90.9
	10.5	9.4	11.4			Operating Profit	13.8	9.1
	5.3	7.8	3.3			All Other Expenses (net)	7.9	8.0
	5.2	1.7	8.2			Profit Before Taxes	5.9	1.1
						RATIOS		
	4.0	4.1	10.4				2.3	3.2
	2.1	2.0	2.1			Current	1.2	1.4
	.8	.5	1.6				.6	.7
	3.4	2.9	7.8				1.6	2.3
	1.1	.7	1.4			Quick	.8	.8
	.1	.1	.9				.2	.2
0 UND	0 UND	32 11.3					0 UND	0 UND
0 UND	36 10.2	53 6.9				Sales/Receivables	36 10.2	27 13.5
89 4.1	146 2.5	103 3.5					124 2.9	127 2.9
						Cost of Sales/Inventory		
						Cost of Sales/Payables		
	2.4	1.9	1.7				4.1	2.5
	9.0	3.7	5.7			Sales/Working Capital	41.2	7.1
	NM	-12.3	12.4				-7.8	-12.1
	18.6	4.2					5.7	6.2
	(14) 1.5	(25) 1.4				EBIT/Interest	(63) 2.7	(51) 1.8
	.6	-.7					.9	-.1
						Net Profit + Depr., Dep., Amort./Cur. Mat. L/T/D	1.8	5.1
							(15) .5	(12) 2.4
							-1.8	.6
	.5	.9	.4				.9	1.0
	2.0	1.1	1.0			Fixed/Worth	2.1	2.1
	NM	NM	3.5				12.7	66.9
	.6	.5	.2				.9	.6
	2.6	.9	.6			Debt/Worth	2.2	2.4
	NM	NM	3.8				15.6	69.3
	35.5	20.5	11.6			% Profit Before Taxes/Tangible Net Worth	42.5	31.1
	(12) 10.5	(25) 7.6	1.6				(65) 10.2	(49) 8.7
	-18.4	-7.8	-8.2				-4.2	-8.5
	13.9	9.0	8.7			% Profit Before Taxes/Total Assets	14.6	7.4
	1.4	.3	1.3				3.2	.6
	-3.3	-5.1	-3.4				-3.7	-4.8
	4.5	1.4	5.5			Sales/Net Fixed Assets	4.3	3.3
	1.2	.7	.9				1.1	.8
	.8	.5	.4				.5	.5
	.9	.9	1.9			Sales/Total Assets	1.4	.8
	.7	.5	.5				.6	.5
	.5	.3	.3				.3	.3
	4.3	4.6	2.0			% Depr., Dep., Amort./Sales	3.8	4.8
	(11) 6.9	(31) 10.1	4.2				(71) 8.1	(57) 11.3
	16.9	15.6	19.6				15.9	19.8
						% Officers', Directors' Owners' Comp/Sales	3.0	4.4
							(13) 4.6	(12) 7.2
							11.6	10.4
5813M	17462M	115754M	378926M	316312M	212560M	Net Sales ($)	1009107M	633557M
2571M	19428M	166220M	325879M	583961M	277428M	Total Assets ($)	1165442M	784067M

Comparative Historical Data / Current Data Sorted by Sales

5 yrs	4 yrs	10 yrs		Type of Statement	0-1MM	1-3MM	3-5MM	5-10MM	10-25MM	25MM & OVER
5	4	10		Unqualified	2	1	1	1	3	2
16	16	13		Reviewed	2	1	2	1	5	2
7	12	11		Compiled	3	6		1	1	
20	19	19		Tax Returns	8	6	2	1	1	1
24	33	26		Other	8	8	2	3	1	4
4/1/04-3/31/05 ALL	4/1/05-3/31/06 ALL	4/1/06-3/31/07 ALL			8 (4/1-9/30/06)			71 (10/1/06-3/31/07)		
72	84	79		**NUMBER OF STATEMENTS**	23	22	7	7	11	9
%	%	%		**ASSETS**	%	%	%	%	%	%
9.2	10.3	7.5		Cash & Equivalents	5.3	13.1			1.4	
9.4	10.1	11.1		Trade Receivables (net)	9.2	13.3			13.6	
7.2	5.6	10.5		Inventory	11.1	8.6			13.0	
5.6	5.0	4.8		All Other Current	7.6	5.8			4.0	
31.4	31.1	34.0		Total Current	33.2	40.8			32.0	
58.8	57.8	55.2		Fixed Assets (net)	60.4	50.9			53.8	
1.3	.9	1.9		Intangibles (net)	.5	.9			4.5	
8.5	10.2	8.9		All Other Non-Current	6.0	7.5			9.7	
100.0	100.0	100.0		Total	100.0	100.0			100.0	
				LIABILITIES						
15.6	11.8	13.1		Notes Payable-Short Term	11.2	22.6			17.7	
5.4	3.6	2.8		Cur. Mat.-L.T.D.	4.0	3.8			1.6	
2.5	2.8	3.8		Trade Payables	3.1	5.6			2.2	
.0	.0	.0		Income Taxes Payable	.0	.0			.0	
5.8	2.5	3.9		All Other Current	6.8	.8			6.2	
29.3	20.6	23.5		Total Current	25.1	32.8			27.7	
43.3	43.1	39.0		Long-Term Debt	46.7	47.2			36.1	
.0	.0	.2		Deferred Taxes	.0	.0			.7	
4.5	7.2	4.7		All Other Non-Current	7.8	1.3			2.1	
22.9	29.0	32.7		Net Worth	20.5	18.7			33.3	
100.0	100.0	100.0		Total Liabilities & Net Worth	100.0	100.0			100.0	
				INCOME DATA						
100.0	100.0	100.0		Net Sales	100.0	100.0			100.0	
				Gross Profit						
88.5	83.5	90.4		Operating Expenses	92.2	86.2			98.2	
11.5	16.5	9.6		Operating Profit	7.8	13.8			1.8	
7.1	5.8	5.8		All Other Expenses (net)	8.9	5.4			9.1	
4.3	10.8	3.8		Profit Before Taxes	-1.1	8.4			-7.2	
				RATIOS						
2.8	5.4	4.1		Current	4.1	5.0			3.0	
1.5	2.2	2.0			1.8	1.3			1.6	
.5	.7	.8			.6	.5			.9	
1.9	4.3	2.3		Quick	2.3	4.7			1.1	
.8	1.1	.9			.5	.6			.8	
.2	.2	.2			.1	.1			.7	
0 UND	0 UND	0 UND		Sales/Receivables	0 UND	0 UND			36 10.2	
24 15.1	20 18.6	32 11.3			32 11.3	1 592.6			103 3.5	
107 3.4	108 3.4	120 3.0			135 2.7	156 2.3			249 1.5	
				Cost of Sales/Inventory						
				Cost of Sales/Payables						
3.4	2.2	1.9		Sales/Working Capital	1.5	2.3			1.9	
9.4	5.7	5.7			5.5	5.2			5.7	
-7.2	-28.1	-17.0			-13.6	-6.9			-9.8	
5.0	6.4	4.7		EBIT/Interest	2.6	6.9				
(60) 1.6	(64) 1.8	(62) 1.9			(15) 1.1	(20) 3.8				
.5	.6	.5			-.5	.9				
	9.8	5.1		Net Profit + Depr., Dep., Amort./Cur. Mat. L/T/D						
	(11) 7.0	(15) 1.8								
	3.3	.5								
.9	.7	.6		Fixed/Worth	.9	.4			.7	
1.9	1.6	1.2			2.7	1.1			1.7	
13.7	5.3	10.0			12.7	-228.2			6.3	
.8	.4	.5		Debt/Worth	1.1	.6			1.0	
2.5	1.6	1.7			2.9	2.1			2.3	
38.3	8.7	13.4			16.0	-8.5			12.2	
25.8	31.5	20.4		% Profit Before Taxes/Tangible Net Worth	21.1	43.7			9.5	
(55) 11.8	(69) 16.6	(62) 6.5			(18) 2.9	(14) 18.5		(10) 2.0		
-2.6	-.3	-7.8			-11.9	-8.8			-34.2	
10.8	13.7	12.2		% Profit Before Taxes/Total Assets	5.9	16.2			3.1	
2.1	2.9	1.8			1.1	5.2			.3	
-1.6	-1.8	-3.5			-7.6	-3.4			-4.3	
3.7	3.7	4.8		Sales/Net Fixed Assets	2.3	4.0			4.9	
1.0	1.2	.9			.7	.9			.6	
.6	.6	.6			.3	.7			.4	
1.3	1.2	1.0		Sales/Total Assets	.8	1.0			.8	
.6	.6	.6			.4	.6			.3	
.4	.4	.4			.3	.4			.2	
5.5	3.8	3.6		% Depr., Dep., Amort./Sales	5.8	5.5			2.0	
(63) 9.0	(68) 7.3	(68) 7.2			(19) 10.5	(17) 10.1			4.7	
16.6	16.2	13.9			18.3	14.4			21.0	
1.5	3.7	3.2		% Officers', Directors', Owners' Comp/Sales						
(16) 4.4	(19) 6.0	(19) 7.5								
6.3	8.2	9.8								
718878M	1019113M	1046827M		Net Sales ($)	13790M	33527M	25548M	53265M	167152M	753545M
1176549M	1614507M	1375487M		Total Assets ($)	45110M	58501M	42456M	77436M	461325M	690659M

M = $ thousand   MM = $ million
See Pages 11 through 21 for Explanation of Ratios and Data

Current Data Sorted by Assets							Comparative Historical Data	
						Type of Statement		
		1	1			Unqualified	3	5
		3	3			Reviewed	4	4
	6	4	2			Compiled	2	15
4	3					Tax Returns	2	1
	3	4	3	2		Other	1	5
	9 (4/1-9/30/06)		30 (10/1/06-3/31/07)				4/1/02-3/31/03 ALL	4/1/03-3/31/04 ALL
0-500M	500M-2MM	2-10MM	10-50MM	50-100MM	100-250MM			
4	12	12	9	2		**NUMBER OF STATEMENTS**	12	30
%	%	%	%	%	%	**ASSETS**	%	%
	2.3	.7			D	Cash & Equivalents	.7	2.2
	30.2	31.3			A	Trade Receivables (net)	23.8	20.3
	14.6	17.5			T	Inventory	11.6	13.3
	1.7	2.7			A	All Other Current	9.0	7.2
	48.9	52.2				Total Current	45.2	42.9
	46.7	40.9			N	Fixed Assets (net)	42.9	48.8
	.0	1.3			O	Intangibles (net)	1.8	2.2
	4.4	5.6			T	All Other Non-Current	10.1	6.1
	100.0	100.0				Total	100.0	100.0
					A	**LIABILITIES**		
	11.3	8.3			V	Notes Payable-Short Term	8.6	6.9
	10.0	4.8			A	Cur. Mat.-L.T.D.	4.7	4.9
	21.5	24.7			I	Trade Payables	16.1	12.4
	.0	.5			L	Income Taxes Payable	.1	.4
	3.0	7.9			A	All Other Current	3.6	2.9
	45.8	46.2			B	Total Current	33.3	27.6
	26.7	29.4			L	Long-Term Debt	31.7	36.4
	.0	.4			E	Deferred Taxes	.7	1.1
	5.6	5.9				All Other Non-Current	.0	2.6
	21.9	18.1				Net Worth	34.4	32.4
	100.0	100.0				Total Liabilties & Net Worth	100.0	100.0
						INCOME DATA		
	100.0	100.0				Net Sales	100.0	100.0
						Gross Profit		
	96.1	99.6				Operating Expenses	96.2	93.9
	3.9	.4				Operating Profit	3.8	6.1
	-.3	1.2				All Other Expenses (net)	.8	3.0
	4.2	-.8				Profit Before Taxes	3.1	3.1
						RATIOS		
	2.0	1.5					2.1	2.5
	1.2	1.2				Current	1.1	1.6
	.5	1.0					.9	1.1
	1.3	.9					.9	1.4
	.7	.7				Quick	.7	.7
	.1	.4					.4	.5
	0 UND	34 10.7					21 17.1	25 14.8
	28 13.1	40 9.1				Sales/Receivables	27 13.3	31 11.7
	44 8.3	51 7.1					31 11.8	48 7.6
						Cost of Sales/Inventory		
						Cost of Sales/Payables		
	12.2	17.5					13.2	5.8
	127.2	39.5				Sales/Working Capital	104.2	17.0
	-22.4	NM					-47.0	67.2
	4.2	2.0					5.7	8.4
	(10) 2.6	(11) 1.0				EBIT/Interest	(11) 2.4	(28) 3.8
	1.1	-1.8					1.8	1.3
						Net Profit + Depr., Dep., Amort./Cur. Mat. L/T/D		
	.3	1.3					.6	.8
	1.5	1.5				Fixed/Worth	1.7	1.4
	5.7	8.9					3.9	3.8
	1.3	1.9					.9	.9
	2.4	4.0				Debt/Worth	2.5	1.5
	15.2	NM					9.4	5.2
	82.6						54.8	32.4
	(10) 9.7					% Profit Before Taxes/Tangible Net Worth	(11) 14.8	(25) 15.4
	.6						11.8	7.7
	13.5	2.4					8.7	14.7
	5.2	.0				% Profit Before Taxes/Total Assets	5.0	4.9
	.8	-7.3					2.4	1.3
	218.5	8.7					13.1	7.9
	12.9	6.4				Sales/Net Fixed Assets	7.1	3.4
	3.3	3.3					2.7	1.9
	8.7	3.4					5.3	2.5
	5.3	2.2				Sales/Total Assets	2.1	1.8
	2.1	1.5					1.6	1.0
	.7	1.7					1.7	2.0
	(10) 1.9	(11) 3.1				% Depr., Dep., Amort./Sales	3.1	(28) 3.9
	5.0	4.8					5.0	7.4
						% Officers', Directors' Owners' Comp/Sales		
9093M	73484M	169251M	405383M	130241M		Net Sales ($)	450685M	826799M
1160M	14710M	63115M	180831M	122912M		Total Assets ($)	206899M	488503M

M = $ thousand MM = $ million

See Pages 11 through 21 for Explanation of Ratios and Data

Comparative Historical Data | Current Data Sorted by Sales

Hist 4/1/04-3/31/05 ALL	Hist 4/1/05-3/31/06 ALL	Hist 4/1/06-3/31/07 ALL	Type of Statement	0-1MM	1-3MM	3-5MM	5-10MM	10-25MM	25MM & OVER
4	3	2	Unqualified			1	1	1	1
5	6	6	Reviewed		2		3	2	2
10	10	12	Compiled		2	1	1	4	2
11	11	7	Tax Returns	1		2			
8	4	12	Other	1	2	1	3	1	5
					9 (4/1-9/30/06)			30 (10/1/06-3/31/07)	
38	34	39	NUMBER OF STATEMENTS	2	6	5	8	8	10
%	%	%	**ASSETS**	%	%	%	%	%	%
4.3	3.3	2.1	Cash & Equivalents						.6
16.7	20.3	25.9	Trade Receivables (net)						33.9
10.9	11.6	13.7	Inventory						7.6
3.2	2.5	3.0	All Other Current						3.3
35.1	37.6	44.7	Total Current						45.3
52.1	49.0	44.6	Fixed Assets (net)						38.2
3.1	1.1	3.0	Intangibles (net)						5.6
9.7	12.3	7.7	All Other Non-Current						10.8
100.0	100.0	100.0	Total						100.0
			LIABILITIES						
17.6	7.7	8.1	Notes Payable-Short Term						7.6
16.1	16.3	10.8	Cur. Mat.-L.T.D.						6.2
8.9	12.9	18.6	Trade Payables						21.0
1.7	.4	.2	Income Taxes Payable						.2
6.1	6.8	6.9	All Other Current						8.3
50.4	44.2	44.6	Total Current						43.2
37.7	37.8	28.9	Long-Term Debt						29.6
.2	1.0	.7	Deferred Taxes						2.1
4.6	4.7	5.6	All Other Non-Current						1.0
7.2	12.3	20.1	Net Worth						24.1
100.0	100.0	100.0	Total Liabilities & Net Worth						100.0
			INCOME DATA						
100.0	100.0	100.0	Net Sales						100.0
			Gross Profit						
98.8	98.8	95.8	Operating Expenses						100.4
1.2	1.2	4.2	Operating Profit						-.4
1.0	.9	.5	All Other Expenses (net)						-.2
.1	.3	3.6	Profit Before Taxes						-.2
			RATIOS						
1.4	1.8	1.5	Current						1.2
1.1	1.1	1.1							1.1
.6	.5	.8							.8
1.1	1.0	.9	Quick						1.0
.6	.5	.7							.7
.1	.0	.2							.5
0 UND	0 UND	13 27.3	Sales/Receivables						36 10.3
15 24.3	24 15.4	35 10.3							41 8.9
31 11.9	36 10.2	46 7.9							46 8.0
			Cost of Sales/Inventory						
			Cost of Sales/Payables						
31.5	19.1	11.3	Sales/Working Capital						16.9
261.0	90.8	57.5							107.3
-33.3	-19.7	-27.7							-27.7
6.6	5.5	3.2	EBIT/Interest						1.9
(33) 1.5	(30) 2.5	(34) 1.1							.8
-1.3	-.5	.2							-3.2
			Net Profit + Depr., Dep., Amort./Cur. Mat. L/T/D						
1.0	.8	.9	Fixed/Worth						1.5
3.6	1.4	1.6							2.1
UND	6.8	11.0							3.9
1.7	1.5	1.8	Debt/Worth						3.6
6.1	2.5	4.2							4.7
UND	9.1	21.4							9.1
70.6	36.4	31.0	% Profit Before Taxes/Tangible Net Worth						7.9
(30) 29.3	(27) 14.7	(31) 2.5							-12.1
-1.5	5.8	-17.3							-42.4
12.6	12.8	7.9	% Profit Before Taxes/Total Assets						2.0
3.4	3.7	.4							-.7
-5.2	-2.8	-3.1							-5.0
24.3	17.9	13.7	Sales/Net Fixed Assets						14.1
8.4	9.4	7.5							6.1
3.6	4.0	2.9							3.4
7.9	7.8	6.2	Sales/Total Assets						4.5
3.5	3.4	2.9							2.7
1.7	2.0	1.2							1.1
1.1	1.2	1.3	% Depr., Dep., Amort./Sales						1.1
(34) 2.8	(29) 2.4	(35) 2.5							1.9
4.9	3.6	4.9							5.1
1.3	1.3	.9	% Officers', Directors' Owners' Comp/Sales						
(16) 2.2	(17) 1.9	(14) 1.6							
4.0	5.3	1.8							
755585M	666853M	787452M	Net Sales ($)	1052M	11926M	19985M	61845M	110955M	581689M
455646M	267000M	382728M	Total Assets ($)	2412M	7325M	19455M	35860M	38291M	279385M

Current Data Sorted by Assets   Comparative Historical Data

	0-500M	500M-2MM	2-10MM	10-50MM	50-100MM	100-250MM		ALL 4/1/02-3/31/03	ALL 4/1/03-3/31/04
Type of Statement									
Unqualified		1	2	8	4	2		12	16
Reviewed		3	13	7	1	1		16	17
Compiled	5	10	15	2	1			28	43
Tax Returns	13	7	5					18	14
Other	4	16	14	19	1	2		31	38
	36 (4/1-9/30/06)			120 (10/1/06-3/31/07)					
NUMBER OF STATEMENTS	22	37	49	36	7	5		105	128
	%	%	%	%	%	%		%	%
ASSETS									
Cash & Equivalents	13.3	12.3	7.1	3.8				8.1	6.4
Trade Receivables (net)	2.4	14.4	16.0	12.8				12.7	13.5
Inventory	22.3	13.4	24.1	39.4				31.6	28.4
All Other Current	3.9	1.5	2.9	2.9				1.9	4.5
Total Current	41.8	41.6	50.1	58.9				54.3	52.8
Fixed Assets (net)	46.8	49.4	41.8	30.8				36.7	37.5
Intangibles (net)	2.0	2.5	1.1	2.8				1.4	2.8
All Other Non-Current	9.4	6.5	7.0	7.5				7.6	6.9
Total	100.0	100.0	100.0	100.0				100.0	100.0
LIABILITIES									
Notes Payable-Short Term	48.2	10.3	9.5	14.4				17.3	15.9
Cur. Mat.-L.T.D.	3.5	1.9	3.6	4.5				4.2	4.3
Trade Payables	3.9	8.3	9.1	10.5				8.1	8.3
Income Taxes Payable	.2	.2	.7	2.3				1.2	1.1
All Other Current	12.6	17.1	6.8	6.6				8.2	5.7
Total Current	68.3	37.8	29.6	38.3				39.1	35.2
Long-Term Debt	37.3	23.7	21.2	18.1				16.7	23.5
Deferred Taxes	.0	.9	1.1	1.4				1.1	1.0
All Other Non-Current	23.3	5.3	6.1	4.2				7.2	11.2
Net Worth	-28.9	32.3	41.9	38.0				35.9	29.1
Total Liabilities & Net Worth	100.0	100.0	100.0	100.0				100.0	100.0
INCOME DATA									
Net Sales	100.0	100.0	100.0	100.0				100.0	100.0
Gross Profit	50.5	49.2	36.1	42.1				39.2	40.4
Operating Expenses	48.1	45.8	29.2	35.5				34.4	35.3
Operating Profit	2.3	3.4	6.9	6.6				4.8	5.1
All Other Expenses (net)	2.3	1.4	1.4	2.9				1.7	1.9
Profit Before Taxes	.0	2.0	5.5	3.7				3.0	3.2
RATIOS									
Current	2.1	2.8	4.3	4.0				3.5	3.8
	1.0	1.6	1.6	1.6				1.6	1.7
	.3	.9	1.0	1.1				1.0	1.1
Quick	1.2	2.0	1.7	.7				1.1	1.2
	.4	.8	.9	.3			(104)	.6	.5
	.0	.3	.2	.2				.2	.2
Sales/Receivables	0 UND	2 237.3	4 87.5	16 23.3				2 173.2	4 102.2
	0 UND	13 27.3	20 18.7	31 11.7				25 14.9	22 16.5
	5 74.3	34 10.9	53 6.9	49 7.4				44 8.2	44 8.2
Cost of Sales/Inventory	0 UND	0 UND	0 UND	44 8.4				10 38.3	1 571.2
	29 12.7	26 13.9	57 6.4	171 2.1				123 3.0	97 3.8
	99 3.7	63 5.8	195 1.9	382 1.0				241 1.5	194 1.9
Cost of Sales/Payables	0 UND	0 UND	0 UND	17 21.7				3 134.7	2 222.2
	0 UND	10 36.9	18 20.5	43 8.5				19 19.6	16 22.8
	15 25.1	37 9.7	45 8.0	99 3.7				47 7.8	48 7.6
Sales/Working Capital	15.6	7.9	3.6	2.0				2.9	2.9
	NM	13.2	11.0	4.7				9.7	8.2
	-5.3	-62.2	-178.1	40.7				419.2	61.0
EBIT/Interest	4.4	9.6	11.2	5.7				5.6	6.9
	(19) 1.6	(34) 1.7	(46) 3.3	(34) 2.3			(97)	2.5	(124) 2.4
	-2.7	.5	1.0	.7				1.0	.2
Net Profit + Depr., Dep., Amort./Cur. Mat. L/T/D			3.3	3.6				4.3	4.5
		(10)	2.2	(11) 2.1			(24)	3.0	(33) 1.7
			1.1	.8				1.0	.5
Fixed/Worth	.8	.6	.4	.3				.4	.4
	11.9	1.2	1.1	1.0				.8	.9
	-1.2	7.9	3.3	2.1				2.3	3.4
Debt/Worth	1.8	.5	.4	.8				.7	.7
	14.0	1.7	1.2	1.5				1.4	1.5
	-5.8	13.1	5.8	6.1				4.1	6.0
% Profit Before Taxes/Tangible Net Worth	76.3	65.1	30.5	21.9				23.1	28.5
	(12) 22.6	(32) 17.9	(44) 13.5	(32) 10.7			(90)	12.6	(105) 12.4
	.5	-2.1	3.8	-.1				1.7	1.0
% Profit Before Taxes/Total Assets	16.9	14.4	10.9	7.5				10.9	9.8
	2.9	6.4	5.7	2.7				5.1	4.1
	-23.8	-2.3	-.1	-1.3				-.3	-1.3
Sales/Net Fixed Assets	23.3	11.5	9.1	9.6				9.2	10.1
	8.6	6.2	4.5	4.4				5.9	5.3
	4.3	3.0	2.8	2.0				3.3	3.1
Sales/Total Assets	6.6	5.0	2.5	1.8				2.8	2.8
	3.2	2.5	1.7	1.0				1.5	1.5
	1.8	1.5	.9	.6				.8	.9
% Depr., Dep., Amort./Sales	.8	2.2	1.4	1.6				2.3	2.1
	(20) 2.9	(31) 3.7	(46) 3.0	(34) 3.3			(95)	3.5	(116) 3.3
	6.8	5.8	4.2	4.2				5.1	4.7
% Officers', Directors' Owners' Comp/Sales	3.6	1.8	1.7					2.4	1.3
	(14) 9.8	(22) 2.5	(20) 2.5				(47)	4.4	(51) 2.9
	14.1	6.8	6.1					8.8	6.2
Net Sales ($)	24204M	131879M	459361M	996413M	1633182M	659022M		1139476M	2341667M
Total Assets ($)	6232M	41284M	247797M	756973M	508007M	780378M		920089M	1946643M

M = $ thousand   MM = $ million
See Pages 11 through 21 for Explanation of Ratios and Data

Comparative Historical Data | Current Data Sorted by Sales

Current Data time periods: **36 (4/1–9/30/06)** for 0-1MM ; **120 (10/1/06–3/31/07)** for 1-3MM through 25MM & Over.

4/1/04-3/31/05 ALL	4/1/05-3/31/06 ALL	4/1/06-3/31/07 ALL	Type of Statement	0-1MM	1-3MM	3-5MM	5-10MM	10-25MM	25MM & OVER
17	15	17	Unqualified			2	2	3	10
30	23	25	Reviewed		1	4	9	7	4
35	26	33	Compiled	3	9	6	10	4	1
30	26	25	Tax Returns	8	8	2	5	2	
44	45	56	Other	7	8	9	11	10	14
156	135	156	**NUMBER OF STATEMENTS**	18	23	23	37	26	29
%	%	%	**ASSETS**	%	%	%	%	%	%
5.5	7.6	8.2	Cash & Equivalents	10.9	10.9	8.3	9.5	8.7	2.4
13.3	12.4	12.7	Trade Receivables (net)	2.6	8.4	12.3	15.9	17.4	14.3
28.9	26.5	26.1	Inventory	16.8	24.2	22.5	29.1	20.7	37.2
3.4	2.5	2.5	All Other Current	4.8	.6	1.6	4.2	.5	3.0
51.1	49.1	49.5	Total Current	35.1	44.1	44.7	58.7	47.3	56.9
37.8	39.7	41.4	Fixed Assets (net)	51.7	47.0	47.5	34.4	41.5	34.7
2.4	2.5	2.0	Intangibles (net)	1.3	3.9	1.5	.5	4.3	1.2
8.8	8.8	7.0	All Other Non-Current	11.9	5.0	6.3	6.4	6.8	7.2
100.0	100.0	100.0	Total	100.0	100.0	100.0	100.0	100.0	100.0
			LIABILITIES						
16.4	15.1	16.4	Notes Payable-Short Term	45.7	9.5	19.2	11.0	8.1	15.6
4.3	3.8	3.3	Cur. Mat.-L.T.D.	1.4	2.8	3.3	3.4	3.2	4.9
8.9	8.0	8.5	Trade Payables	2.5	5.3	7.4	9.4	9.8	13.1
1.0	1.0	1.2	Income Taxes Payable	.0	.7	.0	.9	1.2	3.5
6.0	7.0	10.0	All Other Current	10.9	8.6	20.7	7.1	7.4	8.0
36.6	34.8	39.3	Total Current	60.5	26.9	50.6	31.7	29.7	45.1
23.5	27.7	23.7	Long-Term Debt	43.6	23.1	28.7	19.0	19.3	17.6
.7	.7	.9	Deferred Taxes	.0	1.3	.0	1.5	.9	1.2
8.7	9.0	7.5	All Other Non-Current	9.6	5.1	21.9	5.5	3.7	2.6
30.5	27.7	28.7	Net Worth	-13.7	43.5	-1.2	42.3	46.5	33.5
100.0	100.0	100.0	Total Liabilities & Net Worth	100.0	100.0	100.0	100.0	100.0	100.0
			INCOME DATA						
100.0	100.0	100.0	Net Sales	100.0	100.0	100.0	100.0	100.0	100.0
42.6	42.3	42.9	Gross Profit	61.7	47.4	49.9	36.3	40.3	32.8
37.5	36.8	37.2	Operating Expenses	57.5	41.5	45.1	29.6	34.8	26.7
5.1	5.5	5.7	Operating Profit	4.3	5.9	4.9	6.7	5.5	6.1
1.7	1.3	2.0	All Other Expenses (net)	3.7	1.5	3.5	1.0	1.9	1.7
3.4	4.2	3.7	Profit Before Taxes	.6	4.4	1.4	5.7	3.5	4.5
			RATIOS						
3.9	4.0	3.2		7.0	4.2	3.6	4.0	3.5	2.1
1.5	1.4	1.5	Current	1.3	1.6	1.4	1.8	1.6	1.5
.8	1.0	.9		.3	.9	.7	1.0	.9	.9
1.1	1.5	1.5		1.2	1.6	1.7	1.5	2.2	.7
.4	.5	.5	Quick	.3	.7	.5	.8	.6	.3
.2	.2	.2		.0	.3	.3	.3	.2	.2
2 157.8	1 343.1	2 156.7		0 UND	0 UND	2 194.2	4 96.9	13 27.6	15 24.8
19 19.5	17 21.1	17 21.3	Sales/Receivables	0 UND	9 42.3	17 21.5	19 19.1	27 13.5	30 12.1
43 8.4	40 9.1	47 7.8		8 43.0	27 13.6	45 8.1	52 7.0	51 7.2	58 6.2
13 28.9	0 UND	0 748.1		0 UND	0 UND	0 UND	0 UND	0 UND	33 11.2
83 4.4	75 4.9	59 6.1	Cost of Sales/Inventory	50 7.3	52 7.0	41 8.8	63 5.8	40 9.1	166 2.2
176 2.1	165 2.2	196 1.9		138 2.6	128 2.9	198 1.8	367 1.0	168 2.2	333 1.1
1 332.6	2 146.8	0 UND		0 UND	0 UND	0 UND	0 UND	6 61.8	12 31.4
21 17.2	16 23.4	18 19.9	Cost of Sales/Payables	0 UND	12 30.7	22 16.6	21 17.5	24 15.5	42 8.7
51 7.1	46 7.9	48 7.6		7 49.6	40 9.2	49 7.5	39 9.4	85 4.3	63 5.8
4.1	5.0	3.9		4.6	5.2	5.1	1.7	3.7	3.4
11.5	16.3	11.1	Sales/Working Capital	30.4	12.4	12.4	8.3	11.1	8.3
-44.3	-90.1	-112.9		-4.0	-462.0	-34.6	-224.0	-105.8	NM
6.3	8.1	6.8		3.3	14.1	4.0	9.6	13.5	4.3
(141) 2.5	(125) 2.7	(145) 2.5	EBIT/Interest	(16) 1.5	(22) 1.8	(20) 2.1	(34) 4.8	(24) 2.4	2.4
.6	.7	.7		-1.2	.5	-.5	1.4	-.4	.9
7.6	5.8	3.7					3.1		5.6
(34) 2.5	(28) 2.1	(29) 2.1	Net Profit + Depr., Dep., Amort./Cur. Mat. L/T/D				(12) 2.2		(10) 2.2
1.3	1.4	1.1					.7		.8
.4	.5	.6		.8	.6	.6	.3	.5	.6
1.1	1.1	1.1	Fixed/Worth	12.8	1.2	2.1	1.0	.9	1.0
3.9	4.8	4.7		-3.9	7.9	73.0	2.5	2.1	2.1
.6	.6	.6		1.1	.4	1.0	.4	.4	1.0
2.2	1.8	1.6	Debt/Worth	17.0	1.7	4.5	1.2	.9	1.5
12.6	13.2	8.8		-7.9	7.3	97.3	5.8	3.0	5.7
29.4	36.0	35.5		46.7	38.7	43.3	32.0	34.0	22.7
(130) 11.8	(110) 13.4	(131) 15.8	% Profit Before Taxes/Tangible Net Worth	(11) 2.2	(20) 17.9	(18) 15.2	(34) 17.6	(22) 15.3	(26) 13.6
.4	2.0	1.3		1.3	-2.3	-3.2	2.8	2.3	2.8
8.6	13.6	11.6		13.4	15.0	11.1	12.2	9.8	9.6
3.6	4.5	5.1	% Profit Before Taxes/Total Assets	1.1	6.4	5.0	5.9	5.7	4.4
-1.3	-1.3	-1.3		-7.2	-2.6	-7.3	.9	-1.5	-.6
11.9	11.1	10.0		10.6	19.3	7.7	12.1	8.7	10.0
5.9	6.1	4.8	Sales/Net Fixed Assets	3.4	5.6	5.2	5.2	3.8	4.5
2.9	3.3	2.7		1.0	3.1	1.5	2.9	2.1	2.8
2.8	3.0	2.9		2.2	3.4	3.4	2.8	2.9	2.5
1.7	1.8	1.8	Sales/Total Assets	1.2	2.5	2.3	1.8	1.7	1.5
.9	1.0	.9		.8	1.6	.9	.9	1.0	.8
1.9	1.6	1.6		2.4	1.1	1.9	1.2	2.0	1.3
(135) 3.3	(116) 2.9	(141) 3.1	% Depr., Dep., Amort./Sales	(13) 5.1	(21) 3.0	(21) 3.1	3.0	(22) 3.5	(27) 2.9
5.7	4.3	4.8		9.3	7.4	5.6	3.7	4.7	4.1
1.3	1.4	1.9			2.4	1.9	1.0		
(63) 3.1	(61) 3.1	(63) 2.8	% Officers', Directors' Owners' Comp/Sales		(16) 5.1	(12) 3.7	(10) 2.0		
9.8	8.8	7.9			9.1	5.9	3.7		
3155457M	4175213M	3904061M	Net Sales ($)	9214M	40156M	86587M	270813M	414756M	3082535M
2023805M	1983995M	2340671M	Total Assets ($)	8585M	23241M	75227M	221587M	337980M	1674051M

M = $ thousand   MM = $ million
See Pages 11 through 21 for Explanation of Ratios and Data

Current Data Sorted by Assets   Comparative Historical Data

Type of Statement

						Type of Statement	4/1/02-3/31/03	4/1/03-3/31/04
1	1	3			1	Unqualified		
	6	3				Reviewed		4
3	6	7				Compiled	27	20
6	4					Tax Returns	13	9
	4				1	Other	19	15
	8 (4/1-9/30/06)	5	37 (10/1/06-3/31/07)				3/31/03	3/31/04
0-500M	500M-2MM	2-10MM	10-50MM	50-100MM	100-250MM		ALL	ALL
10	15	18			2	NUMBER OF STATEMENTS	59	51

0-500M	500M-2MM	2-10MM	10-50MM	50-100MM	100-250MM		4/1/02-3/31/03 ALL	4/1/03-3/31/04 ALL
%	%	%	%	%	%	**ASSETS**	%	%
29.3	7.0	5.7	D	D		Cash & Equivalents	9.2	9.8
8.1	11.7	12.1	A	A		Trade Receivables (net)	15.3	15.0
1.6	8.0	14.5	T	T		Inventory	10.1	12.7
10.3	8.7	6.1	A	A		All Other Current	6.7	8.8
49.4	35.4	38.5				Total Current	41.4	46.4
42.4	52.2	55.3	N	N		Fixed Assets (net)	47.9	35.3
.0	2.3	.0	O	O		Intangibles (net)	3.1	3.3
8.2	10.0	6.2	T	T		All Other Non-Current	7.6	14.9
100.0	100.0	100.0				Total	100.0	100.0
			A	A	**LIABILITIES**			
82.2	36.6	24.2	V	V		Notes Payable-Short Term	45.4	32.6
28.9	7.2	2.8	A	A		Cur. Mat.-L.T.D.	5.1	4.7
3.2	2.2	2.7	I	I		Trade Payables	5.6	6.9
1.7	.0	.0	L	L		Income Taxes Payable	.1	.1
3.4	16.6	3.3	A	A		All Other Current	8.4	8.0
119.5	62.6	33.0	B	B		Total Current	64.6	52.3
48.8	24.0	13.3	L	L		Long-Term Debt	18.2	24.8
.0	.4	.0	E	E		Deferred Taxes	.3	.0
.0	.0	1.6				All Other Non-Current	4.8	1.4
-68.3	13.1	52.1				Net Worth	12.1	21.5
100.0	100.0	100.0				Total Liabilties & Net Worth	100.0	100.0
					INCOME DATA			
100.0	100.0	100.0				Net Sales	100.0	100.0
						Gross Profit		
92.6	85.0	92.9				Operating Expenses	84.7	88.0
7.4	15.0	7.1				Operating Profit	15.3	12.0
3.6	6.4	3.3				All Other Expenses (net)	4.3	2.4
3.8	8.7	3.8				Profit Before Taxes	10.9	9.6
					RATIOS			
1.3	1.2	1.7					2.3	1.9
.7	.7	1.2				Current	1.3	1.2
.4	.1	1.0					.5	.4
1.0	.9	1.2					1.6	1.2
.5	.4	.7				Quick	.7	.4
.1	.0	.1					.2	.1
0 UND	0 UND	0 UND					0 UND	0 UND
0 UND	0 UND	18 20.3				Sales/Receivables	23 15.7	10 35.0
0 UND	61 6.0	92 4.0					108 3.4	44 8.3
						Cost of Sales/Inventory		
						Cost of Sales/Payables		
122.4	50.8	5.3					4.0	4.8
-354.8	-4.5	29.1				Sales/Working Capital	18.7	40.5
-2.8	-1.6	NM					-5.9	-7.9
	1.9	3.7					9.0	8.0
	(12) 1.1	2.0				EBIT/Interest	(54) 4.2	(40) 5.3
	-.6	-.4					1.6	1.5
						Net Profit + Depr., Dep., Amort./Cur. Mat. L/T/D		
.5	1.3	.6					.6	.2
2.5	2.0	1.0				Fixed/Worth	1.5	.8
-.4	-9.0	1.3					5.5	2.8
.9	1.6	.4					.6	1.0
NM	4.3	.8				Debt/Worth	1.8	2.4
-1.7	-10.1	4.9					12.8	53.8
	73.0	18.3					57.5	89.4
	(11) 13.0	2.0				% Profit Before Taxes/Tangible Net Worth	(46) 25.3	(41) 28.5
	.5	-7.6					9.4	10.6
74.1	15.6	6.1					17.7	19.2
9.1	.5	1.5				% Profit Before Taxes/Total Assets	9.0	10.6
-15.4	-2.0	-4.2					1.4	1.7
40.3	4.0	3.2					13.9	159.7
8.3	2.2	1.2				Sales/Net Fixed Assets	2.0	7.3
5.1	1.4	.4					.9	1.7
8.2	1.7	1.4					1.8	2.6
2.7	1.1	.7				Sales/Total Assets	.9	1.5
2.0	.5	.2					.5	.7
	5.9	2.2					2.1	.6
	(13) 8.4	(14) 5.6				% Depr., Dep., Amort./Sales	(50) 4.8	(34) 4.5
	14.1	13.7					9.5	8.4
								1.5
						% Officers', Directors' Owners' Comp/Sales	(10)	6.8
								13.3
10217M	20021M	81383M			553035M	Net Sales ($)	474573M	757917M
2773M	15185M	70818M			356314M	Total Assets ($)	496748M	321031M

© RMA 2007

M = $ thousand   MM = $ million
See Pages 11 through 21 for Explanation of Ratios and Data

Comparative Historical Data				Current Data Sorted by Sales					

Type of Statement

			Type of Statement						
5	8	5	Unqualified		2		1		2
4	5	4	Reviewed		1	2	1		
18	15	16	Compiled	8	6	1	1		
12	5	10	Tax Returns	5	4	1			
19	11	10	Other	3	6				1
4/1/04-3/31/05 ALL	4/1/05-3/31/06 ALL	4/1/06-3/31/07 ALL		8 (4/1-9/30/06)			37 (10/1/06-3/31/07)		
				0-1MM	1-3MM	3-5MM	5-10MM	10-25MM	25MM & OVER
58	44	45	NUMBER OF STATEMENTS	16	19	4	3		3
%	%	%	ASSETS	%	%	%	%	%	%
12.7	9.8	11.6	Cash & Equivalents	14.2	13.2				
14.0	12.0	11.3	Trade Receivables (net)	1.0	11.5				
14.3	16.9	10.4	Inventory	2.4	9.5				
5.6	2.9	7.9	All Other Current	10.4	4.4				
46.5	41.6	41.2	Total Current	28.0	38.6				
42.0	45.8	50.0	Fixed Assets (net)	60.6	53.6				
1.7	.4	1.0	Intangibles (net)	1.0	1.1				
9.8	12.3	7.8	All Other Non-Current	10.4	6.8				
100.0	100.0	100.0	Total	100.0	100.0				
			LIABILITIES						
27.0	25.9	40.9	Notes Payable-Short Term	25.1	58.4				
4.0	5.1	10.0	Cur. Mat.-L.T.D.	21.7	5.0				
5.1	6.4	3.1	Trade Payables	1.6	2.6				
.1	.1	.4	Income Taxes Payable	1.1	.0				
7.5	7.9	8.0	All Other Current	4.8	7.6				
43.7	45.4	62.5	Total Current	54.4	73.5				
24.0	22.7	24.8	Long-Term Debt	36.3	26.2				
.0	.1	.2	Deferred Taxes	.3	.0				
3.8	2.5	.7	All Other Non-Current	.0	.2				
28.5	29.3	11.8	Net Worth	8.9	.1				
100.0	100.0	100.0	Total Liabilties & Net Worth	100.0	100.0				
			INCOME DATA						
100.0	100.0	100.0	Net Sales	100.0	100.0				
			Gross Profit						
89.5	89.0	90.3	Operating Expenses	82.1	96.2				
10.5	11.0	9.7	Operating Profit	17.9	3.8				
2.4	1.1	4.3	All Other Expenses (net)	9.1	1.8				
8.0	9.9	5.4	Profit Before Taxes	8.8	2.0				
			RATIOS						
1.9	2.3	1.4		1.4	1.4				
1.2	1.3	1.0	Current	.6	1.0				
.7	.4	.5		.2	.7				
1.3	1.3	1.0		1.0	1.0				
.5	.5	.6	Quick	.2	.6				
.1	.0	.1		.0	.1				
0 UND	0 UND	0 UND		0 UND	0 UND				
9 41.2	11 31.8	0 UND	Sales/Receivables	0 UND	25 14.3				
56 6.5	43 8.5	58 6.3		0 UND	91 4.0				
			Cost of Sales/Inventory						
			Cost of Sales/Payables						
4.2	7.1	10.2		166.7	7.6				
19.0	36.2	194.5	Sales/Working Capital	-2.7	-999.8				
-17.2	-4.9	-2.8		-1.1	-4.5				
11.5	18.4	4.5		4.2	4.6				
(56) 3.7	(40) 5.7	(41) 1.8	EBIT/Interest	(13) 2.2	(18) 1.1				
1.5	1.9	-.5		-.7	-9.2				
			Net Profit + Depr., Dep., Amort./Cur. Mat. L/T/D						
.4	.4	.7		1.0	1.0				
1.0	1.1	1.3	Fixed/Worth	1.8	1.3				
4.3	3.0	3.6		-2.6	3.7				
.7	.6	.6		.6	.5				
2.0	1.2	1.7	Debt/Worth	3.2	1.3				
15.9	6.5	11.9		-4.8	8.7				
49.3	45.1	31.7	% Profit Before Taxes/Tangible Net Worth	12.2	38.3				
(48) 16.9	(37) 21.6	(36) 8.4		(11) 7.8	(15) 1.1				
5.0	9.4	-7.1		-2.2	-7.9				
15.7	19.9	11.8	% Profit Before Taxes/Total Assets	9.7	15.6				
6.0	9.3	2.4		2.2	.5				
1.9	3.0	-2.7		-.7	-5.2				
12.0	9.9	7.7	Sales/Net Fixed Assets	5.5	4.4				
3.8	2.6	2.2		1.3	2.2				
1.4	1.2	1.0		.3	1.1				
2.1	2.6	2.1	Sales/Total Assets	2.0	2.3				
1.4	1.4	1.2		.5	1.1				
.8	.6	.5		.2	.6				
2.8	1.2	2.7	% Depr., Dep., Amort./Sales	3.9	2.9				
(41) 4.5	(35) 3.0	(38) 6.1		(15) 8.4	(15) 6.6				
10.3	7.1	11.0		24.6	10.4				
	2.1		% Officers', Directors' Owners' Comp/Sales						
	(10) 7.4								
	10.8								
531749M	860967M	664656M	Net Sales ($)	8101M	34249M	16578M	27388M		578340M
301833M	506672M	445090M	Total Assets ($)	21565M	38289M	11322M	14009M		359905M

(For the 3-5MM, 5-10MM, 10-25MM and 25MM & OVER columns in the ratio sections: "DATA NOT AVAILABLE")

M = $ thousand   MM = $ million
See Pages 11 through 21 for Explanation of Ratios and Data

Current Data Sorted by Assets | Comparative Historical Data

	0-500M	500M-2MM	2-10MM	10-50MM	50-100MM	100-250MM		Type of Statement	4/1/02-3/31/03 ALL	4/1/03-3/31/04 ALL
		1	4	2	3	3		Unqualified	18	21
	4	2	16	6	1	1		Reviewed	49	47
	6	13	25	13		1		Compiled	73	87
	22	39	24	3				Tax Returns	69	84
	16	23	23	15	2	4		Other	74	67
		49 (4/1-9/30/06)		223 (10/1/06-3/31/07)						
NUMBER OF STATEMENTS	48	78	92	39	6	9			283	306
ASSETS	%	%	%	%	%	%			%	%
Cash & Equivalents	14.0	8.9	4.0	9.7					7.2	7.3
Trade Receivables (net)	5.9	11.2	12.6	15.7					11.3	10.6
Inventory	10.7	6.4	12.5	15.9					14.6	13.2
All Other Current	9.5	3.0	5.4	3.8					6.2	6.7
Total Current	40.1	29.5	34.5	45.2					39.2	37.8
Fixed Assets (net)	47.3	58.4	55.6	46.3					51.3	50.8
Intangibles (net)	1.2	1.0	.9	.5					.8	1.3
All Other Non-Current	11.6	11.1	9.0	8.0					8.7	10.0
Total	100.0	100.0	100.0	100.0					100.0	100.0
LIABILITIES										
Notes Payable-Short Term	32.7	26.0	19.4	17.1					23.3	23.3
Cur. Mat.-L.T.D.	6.0	5.6	4.0	2.5					4.6	3.6
Trade Payables	4.4	4.5	5.3	4.3					5.5	5.2
Income Taxes Payable	.0	.1	.3	1.8					.2	.2
All Other Current	12.9	6.7	7.6	5.1					11.0	8.9
Total Current	56.0	42.9	36.7	30.7					44.7	41.2
Long-Term Debt	30.3	32.7	26.9	19.1					28.5	29.7
Deferred Taxes	.0	.0	.6	.7					.5	.4
All Other Non-Current	6.0	8.6	4.0	1.4					2.9	4.5
Net Worth	7.7	15.8	31.9	48.1					23.4	24.3
Total Liabilties & Net Worth	100.0	100.0	100.0	100.0					100.0	100.0
INCOME DATA										
Net Sales	100.0	100.0	100.0	100.0					100.0	100.0
Gross Profit										
Operating Expenses	90.5	92.5	92.9	82.9					91.2	90.9
Operating Profit	9.5	7.5	7.1	17.1					8.8	9.1
All Other Expenses (net)	2.2	3.0	4.2	3.1					3.7	3.7
Profit Before Taxes	7.2	4.5	2.9	14.0					5.2	5.4
RATIOS										
Current	5.0	2.3	1.8	1.7					1.9	2.1
	1.0	.7	1.1	1.3					1.2	1.1
	.2	.1	.5	.8					.6	.5
Quick	2.5	1.3	1.0	1.2					1.0	.9
	.4	.4	(91) .4	.4					(304) .4	.4
	.0	.1	.1	.2					.1	.1
Sales/Receivables	0 UND	0 UND	0 UND	6 60.3					0 UND	0 UND
	0 UND	0 UND	19 19.5	43 8.4					12 29.2	10 37.7
	0 UND	27 13.7	59 6.2	103 3.6					49 7.4	37 10.0
Cost of Sales/Inventory										
Cost of Sales/Payables										
Sales/Working Capital	11.8	9.5	5.9	2.6					5.9	5.4
	416.8	-73.6	52.0	9.0					31.2	38.1
	-4.7	-4.1	-5.2	-10.9					-6.7	-6.7
EBIT/Interest	5.6	4.5	3.9	6.0					5.6	5.0
	(41) 2.8	(71) 2.4	(86) 1.5	(34) 3.0					(254) 2.2	(272) 2.5
	.7	.8	.5	.9					.9	.9
Net Profit + Depr., Dep., Amort./Cur. Mat. L/T/D			6.1	3.3					5.2	4.2
		(10) 3.7	(18) 1.5						(47) 2.6	(35) 2.2
			1.4	.7					1.2	.9
Fixed/Worth	.6	.8	.8	.5					.7	.7
	2.4	1.6	1.6	1.0					1.4	1.4
	-1.5	-15.1	4.8	1.4					5.7	4.2
Debt/Worth	.5	.5	.8	.7					.7	.7
	16.7	1.5	1.7	1.1					1.8	1.6
	-5.6	-14.4	9.6	2.4					12.6	6.4
% Profit Before Taxes/Tangible Net Worth	146.8	25.8	19.8	21.6					29.9	27.8
	(30) 40.5	(55) 12.0	(80) 10.4	(38) 12.2					(236) 10.0	(255) 9.2
	-.1	1.2	-1.6	.3					.5	.9
% Profit Before Taxes/Total Assets	31.3	11.0	8.5	10.5					11.2	8.7
	10.6	3.3	2.3	5.2					3.5	3.3
	-.9	-.1	-2.5	.0					-.4	-.3
Sales/Net Fixed Assets	39.1	6.1	5.2	3.4					7.0	7.2
	6.0	2.6	1.3	1.4					2.4	2.6
	2.3	1.2	.6	.7					.8	.8
Sales/Total Assets	3.4	2.7	1.6	1.1					2.0	2.1
	2.3	1.3	.8	.5					1.1	1.0
	1.3	.8	.4	.4					.5	.5
% Depr., Dep., Amort./Sales	2.4	2.4	2.2	5.0					2.3	2.5
	(31) 5.4	(65) 5.3	(85) 6.6	(33) 6.3					(246) 5.2	(271) 5.9
	8.4	9.8	11.0	9.9					10.2	11.1
% Officers', Directors' Owners' Comp/Sales	1.9	1.9	1.1						1.9	1.3
	(17) 3.6	(33) 4.5	(27) 2.7						(80) 3.7	(97) 3.8
	9.0	6.1	4.7						6.9	9.4
Net Sales ($)	34761M	169341M	506217M	629347M	303942M	1876520M			3789698M	4313280M
Total Assets ($)	12885M	89654M	416217M	765235M	437539M	1275199M			3017050M	3237260M

M = $ thousand   MM = $ million

See Pages 11 through 21 for Explanation of Ratios and Data

Comparative Historical Data			Type of Statement	Current Data Sorted by Sales					
14	6	13	Unqualified	1		3	3	2	7
41	36	30	Reviewed	4	7	3	4	8	4
86	58	58	Compiled	8	16	11	13	6	4
102	68	88	Tax Returns	32	42	4	6	4	
70	109	83	Other	24	24	11	9		9
4/1/04-3/31/05 ALL	4/1/05-3/31/06 ALL	4/1/06-3/31/07 ALL		49 (4/1-9/30/06)			223 (10/1/06-3/31/07)		
				0-1MM	1-3MM	3-5MM	5-10MM	10-25MM	25MM & OVER
313	277	272	NUMBER OF STATEMENTS	69	89	29	35	26	24
%	%	%	ASSETS	%	%	%	%	%	%
7.0	8.5	8.1	Cash & Equivalents	9.1	9.2	3.9	9.7	4.3	7.5
7.1	10.7	11.3	Trade Receivables (net)	6.0	8.7	12.9	15.1	15.8	24.1
13.7	13.3	11.4	Inventory	8.1	5.7	18.3	17.2	17.6	18.5
4.1	5.5	5.2	All Other Current	7.6	3.8	6.4	4.9	3.0	5.2
32.0	38.0	36.0	Total Current	30.9	27.3	41.5	46.9	40.8	55.3
56.6	48.6	52.8	Fixed Assets (net)	58.8	61.3	48.5	41.6	47.9	31.1
1.5	1.0	1.2	Intangibles (net)	.9	.6	2.7	.9	.6	3.2
9.9	12.4	10.0	All Other Non-Current	9.6	10.7	7.4	10.6	10.7	10.4
100.0	100.0	100.0	Total	100.0	100.0	100.0	100.0	100.0	100.0
			LIABILITIES						
20.5	24.9	22.8	Notes Payable-Short Term	22.1	24.1	18.0	27.1	28.2	14.2
3.6	4.1	4.7	Cur. Mat.-L.T.D.	3.7	6.7	4.2	3.1	2.5	5.0
5.3	6.5	4.8	Trade Payables	2.7	3.5	4.9	7.7	6.4	9.2
.2	.2	.4	Income Taxes Payable	.1	.0	.1	.4	2.0	1.1
4.5	7.2	8.2	All Other Current	8.1	6.5	4.6	15.3	4.4	12.6
34.1	42.9	40.9	Total Current	36.7	40.9	31.8	53.5	43.5	42.2
30.1	29.6	27.4	Long-Term Debt	24.3	38.9	25.6	21.1	20.5	12.0
.5	.5	.4	Deferred Taxes	.0	.2	.4	.5	1.0	1.2
4.4	6.4	5.2	All Other Non-Current	5.5	7.1	6.5	2.4	1.2	4.8
31.0	20.6	26.1	Net Worth	33.5	12.8	35.7	22.5	33.7	39.9
100.0	100.0	100.0	Total Liabilities & Net Worth	100.0	100.0	100.0	100.0	100.0	100.0
			INCOME DATA						
100.0	100.0	100.0	Net Sales	100.0	100.0	100.0	100.0	100.0	100.0
			Gross Profit						
88.9	92.0	90.7	Operating Expenses	85.1	92.0	93.9	91.2	95.7	91.7
11.1	8.0	9.3	Operating Profit	14.9	8.0	6.1	8.8	4.3	8.3
3.8	2.9	3.2	All Other Expenses (net)	5.7	3.7	1.4	1.7	1.1	.6
7.3	5.1	6.1	Profit Before Taxes	9.2	4.3	4.7	7.2	3.1	7.7
			RATIOS						
2.1	1.9	1.9		2.5	1.8	2.2	2.1	1.5	1.5
1.1	1.1	1.1	Current	1.0	.7	1.4	1.1	1.2	1.3
.6	.5	.4		.2	.1	.9	.7	.8	1.0
.8	1.0	1.1		1.3	1.1	1.1	1.2	1.0	.9
(312) .4	.4 (271) .4		Quick	.4	.3 (28) .6		.4	.4	.8
.1	.1	.1		.1	.1	.2	.2	.2	.3
0 UND	0 UND	0 UND		0 UND	0 UND	0 UND	0 UND	6 59.7	18 20.5
0 UND	13 28.8	4 87.4	Sales/Receivables	0 UND	0 UND	31 11.8	21 17.4	35 10.4	41 9.0
35 10.3	43 8.4	48 7.6		0 UND	25 14.8	82 4.4	59 6.2	64 5.7	87 4.2
			Cost of Sales/Inventory						
			Cost of Sales/Payables						
4.0	5.2	7.2		5.6	10.8	4.2	6.3	8.5	4.3
27.5	56.2	54.0	Sales/Working Capital	308.0	-22.4	8.4	19.7	33.7	14.2
-7.7	-7.2	-5.8		-3.6	-3.3	-48.4	-10.5	-12.5	146.8
7.5	5.5	5.0		4.1	4.8	4.5	6.8	5.9	6.8
(286) 2.5	(248) 2.4	(245) 2.4	EBIT/Interest	(57) 1.4	(80) 2.0	2.7	(34) 3.2	(25) 1.9	(20) 3.8
1.1	1.0	.7		.3	.6	1.2	.1	.7	2.0
4.4	3.5	4.3	Net Profit + Depr., Dep., Amort./Cur. Mat. L/T/D		6.5				
(38) 1.9	(34) 2.3	(38) 2.1			(11) 1.8				
1.1	1.3	.9			.7				
.8	.6	.7		.8	1.1	.7	.3	.7	.5
1.4	1.4	1.4	Fixed/Worth	1.6	2.3	1.2	1.1	1.1	.9
4.6	8.5	6.5		21.7	-13.9	4.8	2.8	2.1	1.3
.5	.7	.6		.4	.8	.5	.7	.8	.9
1.5	1.8	1.7	Debt/Worth	1.1	3.4	1.5	1.6	1.4	1.6
7.5	81.3	16.3		35.6	-18.4	7.8	8.8	3.2	2.6
27.4	20.9	28.5	% Profit Before Taxes/Tangible Net Worth	31.8	47.7	17.9	37.7	24.8	29.5
(258) 8.8	(212) 8.3	(217) 12.9		(54) 8.3	(63) 12.3	(23) 11.2	(29) 19.5	(25) 7.5	(23) 20.0
1.6	1.7	.5		-1.9	1.2	3.9	5.8	-3.3	10.1
10.2	10.3	11.0	% Profit Before Taxes/Total Assets	11.1	14.1	8.4	12.4	10.0	10.9
3.7	3.2	4.0		2.7	3.9	3.0	5.7	2.5	6.5
.3	-.1	-.6		-1.6	-1.1	1.2	-3.5	-.7	3.1
4.9	8.5	7.1		6.0	4.8	5.8	11.9	11.1	25.0
1.5	2.2	2.3	Sales/Net Fixed Assets	1.5	1.8	2.2	3.6	2.7	5.9
.5	.9	.9		.4	.8	1.1	1.3	1.2	2.0
1.7	2.2	2.2		1.8	2.4	1.8	2.6	3.0	2.3
.7	1.0	1.1	Sales/Total Assets	.8	1.1	1.1	1.4	1.8	1.6
.3	.5	.5		.3	.5	.6	.6	.6	.8
3.5	2.5	2.8	% Depr., Dep., Amort./Sales	3.4	3.7	3.3	1.3	1.6	1.9
(273) 7.1	(240) 6.1	(225) 6.0		(50) 8.3	(74) 7.5	(25) 6.4	(34) 4.1	(25) 4.0	(17) 3.3
13.2	10.4	10.0		14.2	10.5	10.6	7.2	6.1	7.3
1.6	1.2	1.3	% Officers', Directors' Owners' Comp/Sales	2.8	1.7		.8		
(89) 3.6	(71) 3.0	(84) 3.3		(20) 4.9	(33) 3.6		(12) 1.8		
6.6	7.4	5.4		9.1	5.3		3.5		
2916148M	2510402M	3520128M	Net Sales ($)	33741M	159600M	111310M	253470M	420833M	2541174M
2422551M	2425968M	2996729M	Total Assets ($)	135802M	217386M	150254M	275379M	455778M	1762130M

M = $ thousand   MM = $ million
See Pages 11 through 21 for Explanation of Ratios and Data

Current Data Sorted by Assets   Comparative Historical Data

Type of Statement

0-500M	500M-2MM	2-10MM	10-50MM	50-100MM	100-250MM	Type of Statement	4/1/02-3/31/03 ALL	4/1/03-3/31/04 ALL
		1	4	3	2	Unqualified	6	8
	3	9	8			Reviewed	14	23
3	6	12	7	2		Compiled	14	22
8	19	11	1			Tax Returns	20	24
1	9	17	3		1	Other	40	32
	30 (4/1-9/30/06)		100 (10/1/06-3/31/07)					
12	37	50	23	5	3	NUMBER OF STATEMENTS	94	109

Financial Data

0-500M	500M-2MM	2-10MM	10-50MM	50-100MM	100-250MM		4/1/02-3/31/03 ALL	4/1/03-3/31/04 ALL
%	%	%	%	%	%	**ASSETS**	%	%
18.9	11.1	5.5	7.6			Cash & Equivalents	5.4	4.1
5.5	3.5	5.6	8.8			Trade Receivables (net)	4.1	5.4
17.3	22.5	32.8	40.3			Inventory	37.7	36.7
7.4	8.2	3.2	3.3			All Other Current	4.6	4.8
49.0	45.2	47.1	60.0			Total Current	51.8	51.0
39.6	48.7	42.9	33.0			Fixed Assets (net)	36.0	39.4
.1	.2	.5	.3			Intangibles (net)	.4	.2
11.3	5.9	9.5	6.7			All Other Non-Current	11.8	9.4
100.0	100.0	100.0	100.0			Total	100.0	100.0
						LIABILITIES		
29.8	32.7	24.3	37.9			Notes Payable-Short Term	41.3	35.7
8.8	2.9	2.8	1.4			Cur. Mat.-L.T.D.	3.7	4.2
1.3	1.5	4.0	2.4			Trade Payables	2.7	6.8
.0	.0	.6	.1			Income Taxes Payable	.4	.3
7.7	9.8	6.9	4.7			All Other Current	5.0	5.5
47.5	47.0	38.6	46.4			Total Current	53.1	52.5
20.3	26.5	23.4	16.4			Long-Term Debt	14.0	18.4
.0	.1	.6	.5			Deferred Taxes	.1	.1
12.0	3.8	3.5	3.2			All Other Non-Current	5.0	8.8
20.3	22.7	33.8	33.5			Net Worth	27.9	20.3
100.0	100.0	100.0	100.0			Total Liabilities & Net Worth	100.0	100.0
						INCOME DATA		
100.0	100.0	100.0	100.0			Net Sales	100.0	100.0
						Gross Profit		
93.1	89.4	91.6	95.3			Operating Expenses	99.7	94.7
6.9	10.6	8.4	4.7			Operating Profit	.3	5.3
4.1	2.9	5.6	2.7			All Other Expenses (net)	3.1	4.9
2.8	7.7	2.8	2.0			Profit Before Taxes	-2.8	.4
						RATIOS		
11.8	2.9	2.5	1.7			Current	1.7	1.7
.8	.9	1.2	1.2				1.2	1.1
.2	.6	.7	.9				.8	.6
5.2	.7	.5	.5			Quick	.4	.4
.3	(36) .2	.2	(22) .3				.1	.1
.0	.0	.0	.1				.0	.0
0 UND	0 UND	0 UND	1 264.0			Sales/Receivables	0 UND	0 UND
0 UND	0 UND	0 UND	5 67.5				0 UND	0 999.8
0 UND	0 UND	12 30.2	31 11.7				10 35.8	15 24.9
						Cost of Sales/Inventory		
						Cost of Sales/Payables		
3.2	5.1	3.0	2.9			Sales/Working Capital	5.0	5.7
-18.1	-24.6	20.1	10.2				18.0	19.5
-2.5	-3.8	-12.3	-21.6				-12.0	-6.2
4.5	4.5	4.0	2.4			EBIT/Interest	1.9	5.8
(10) .5	(28) 1.7	(43) 1.7	(22) 1.7				(92) .6	(92) 2.8
-2.9	.3	-.3	.7				-2.5	.4
						Net Profit + Depr., Dep., Amort./Cur. Mat. L/T/D	2.5	3.8
							(11) .9	(12) 2.4
							-1.7	1.3
.0	.6	.5	.2			Fixed/Worth	.4	.4
1.5	1.4	1.1	.7				.8	.9
UND	236.0	2.8	2.6				1.8	3.1
.3	.5	.9	.9			Debt/Worth	.5	1.0
3.6	2.2	1.9	2.3				1.8	2.7
UND	NM	4.4	6.3				9.7	12.5
	21.9	21.9	27.4			% Profit Before Taxes/Tangible Net Worth	8.8	32.4
	(28) 8.0	(44) 5.5	(21) 9.5				(77) -.5	(86) 11.7
	-.2	-3.9	1.5				-22.8	-2.2
19.3	12.8	7.4	4.9			% Profit Before Taxes/Total Assets	2.7	8.6
-.1	2.4	2.4	2.3				-.9	2.6
-9.4	-.6	-2.2	-.3				-10.4	-3.3
UND	13.2	24.3	24.1			Sales/Net Fixed Assets	15.5	26.7
3.0	1.9	3.1	5.7				3.7	4.0
1.1	.6	.6	1.5				1.0	1.0
2.3	1.7	2.1	1.6			Sales/Total Assets	1.9	2.2
1.2	1.0	1.1	1.1				1.0	1.1
.7	.3	.4	.5				.5	.5
	2.8	.7	.3			% Depr., Dep., Amort./Sales	1.6	1.0
	(26) 5.7	(40) 3.3	(21) 1.0				(77) 3.4	(86) 3.3
	15.0	7.1	10.3				9.5	16.7
		.5				% Officers', Directors' Owners' Comp/Sales	1.2	.8
		(10) 1.2					(24) 2.4	(18) 1.5
		5.9					7.1	2.8
4742M	78969M	658823M	751659M	1449423M	391888M	Net Sales ($)	1007960M	2567628M
3496M	40681M	241004M	530072M	310710M	509812M	Total Assets ($)	773756M	1364535M

M = $ thousand   MM = $ million
See Pages 11 through 21 for Explanation of Ratios and Data

Comparative Historical Data | Current Data Sorted by Sales

			Type of Statement		30 (4/1-9/30/06)		100 (10/1/06-3/31/07)		
				0-1MM	1-3MM	3-5MM	5-10MM	10-25MM	25MM & OVER
8	10	10	Unqualified	2	3	4	1	4	9
17	18	20	Reviewed	5	6	5	5	5	2
30	21	30	Compiled	23	9	3	3	1	6
29	24	39	Tax Returns	8	8	2	2	1	1
37	33	31	Other				6	2	4
4/1/04-3/31/05 ALL	4/1/05-3/31/06 ALL	4/1/06-3/31/07 ALL							
121	106	130	**NUMBER OF STATEMENTS**	38	26	14	17	13	22
%	%	%	**ASSETS**	%	%	%	%	%	%
5.4	7.7	8.4	Cash & Equivalents	9.7	11.6	4.3	5.2	9.8	6.8
6.1	7.6	6.5	Trade Receivables (net)	2.0	5.3	6.8	9.1	2.4	16.0
34.3	31.4	29.7	Inventory	15.4	23.1	35.3	37.4	47.0	42.4
3.7	5.3	4.9	All Other Current	5.4	6.1	2.8	2.1	4.2	6.7
49.6	52.0	49.6	Total Current	32.5	46.1	49.2	53.8	63.4	71.8
42.5	39.8	41.7	Fixed Assets (net)	55.7	50.4	44.9	30.9	28.9	21.1
.3	.5	.3	Intangibles (net)	.1	.1	.3	1.4	.2	.3
7.6	7.7	8.4	All Other Non-Current	11.8	3.4	5.7	13.8	7.5	6.8
100.0	100.0	100.0	Total	100.0	100.0	100.0	100.0	100.0	100.0
			LIABILITIES						
26.4	26.8	29.4	Notes Payable-Short Term	20.4	30.9	42.5	29.2	30.2	34.7
4.9	2.7	3.1	Cur. Mat.-L.T.D.	3.7	4.5	1.5	2.6	1.4	2.6
2.8	3.2	2.9	Trade Payables	1.1	1.3	3.5	1.3	5.1	7.2
.6	.7	.3	Income Taxes Payable	.0	.6	.1	.8	.2	.1
7.7	8.6	7.6	All Other Current	7.6	7.4	6.1	7.5	8.2	8.8
42.5	42.0	43.3	Total Current	32.9	44.7	53.7	41.4	45.0	53.4
23.3	24.9	22.7	Long-Term Debt	22.7	33.8	21.5	23.8	14.8	14.0
.4	.4	.4	Deferred Taxes	.1	.1	.3	1.5	.2	.8
6.2	4.6	4.2	All Other Non-Current	7.2	4.2	3.3	4.9	1.4	.9
27.6	28.1	29.4	Net Worth	37.2	17.1	21.2	28.4	38.7	30.9
100.0	100.0	100.0	Total Liabilities & Net Worth	100.0	100.0	100.0	100.0	100.0	100.0
			INCOME DATA						
100.0	100.0	100.0	Net Sales	100.0	100.0	100.0	100.0	100.0	100.0
			Gross Profit						
91.7	90.7	92.2	Operating Expenses	85.2	92.7	95.3	94.7	96.8	97.1
8.3	9.3	7.8	Operating Profit	14.8	7.3	4.7	5.3	3.2	2.9
2.4	3.3	3.8	All Other Expenses (net)	6.9	4.9	2.6	3.0	.2	.8
5.8	6.1	4.0	Profit Before Taxes	7.9	2.4	2.0	2.3	3.0	2.1
			RATIOS						
1.9	1.8	2.4	Current	3.8	3.0	2.5	2.2	2.0	1.8
1.2	1.2	1.2		.9	.9	.9	1.3	1.2	1.3
.8	.8	.6		.5	.6	.2	.9	.8	1.0
.8	.8	.7	Quick	.8	1.7	.4	.5	.4	.8
(120) .2	(103) .2	(128) .2		(37) .2	.4	.2	.2	(12) .2	.3
.0	.0	.1		.1	.0	.0	.0	.1	.1
0 UND	0 UND	0 UND	Sales/Receivables	0 UND	0 UND	0 UND	0 UND	0 UND	4 98.2
0 999.8	1 582.9	0 UND		0 UND	0 UND	0 UND	10 35.1	3 127.0	5 67.2
17 20.9	16 23.2	15 23.7		0 UND	30 12.1	27 13.6	24 15.3	12 30.2	21 17.0
			Cost of Sales/Inventory						
			Cost of Sales/Payables						
3.5	4.3	3.5	Sales/Working Capital	2.7	3.4	3.0	3.7	6.6	6.3
16.3	29.0	62.0		-31.2	-20.4	-47.7	14.8	20.7	32.3
-13.1	-9.4	-6.8		-2.9	-3.6	-3.1	-20.9	-13.4	125.4
8.6	6.0	3.6	EBIT/Interest	4.8	1.9	3.0	3.8	12.4	4.2
(96) 2.8	(89) 1.8	(110) 1.7		(27) 1.1	(19) 1.5	1.6	1.6	(12) 1.1	(21) 2.0
1.0	.9	.1		-.6	-.2	-1.0	.1	-.3	1.3
12.9	22.3	10.0	Net Profit + Depr., Dep., Amort./Cur. Mat. L/T/D						
(13) 5.7	(12) 4.2	(14) 4.6							
1.3	1.9	1.8							
.3	.4	.3	Fixed/Worth	.7	.5	.6	.4	.0	.2
1.1	.8	1.1		1.3	1.3	3.4	.7	.7	.4
6.1	2.7	3.4		6.6	133.2	-5.6	1.9	1.3	2.0
.8	.6	.8	Debt/Worth	.2	.6	1.7	1.1	.7	1.1
2.4	1.8	2.0		1.4	1.6	3.6	1.8	1.5	2.5
15.5	6.8	9.2		12.3	NM	-18.5	20.2	5.3	5.6
26.7	23.7	24.7	% Profit Before Taxes/Tangible Net Worth	23.5	10.0	22.3	25.9	36.4	41.6
(93) 12.4	(87) 8.9	(109) 6.5		(32) 6.0	(20) 3.1	(10) 6.4	(15) 12.9	(12) 7.9	(20) 13.3
1.8	.3	-1.1		-1.6	-9.9	-17.3	-1.3	-2.9	5.3
10.2	11.9	8.1	% Profit Before Taxes/Total Assets	6.1	12.3	8.0	8.9	9.2	10.9
3.9	2.8	2.4		.8	1.8	1.4	2.8	2.2	3.4
-.2	-.1	-1.5		-3.5	-3.3	-4.1	-3.7	-3.1	1.0
12.0	17.7	23.1	Sales/Net Fixed Assets	2.9	14.3	6.2	21.5	252.4	80.3
3.3	3.7	3.1		.7	1.8	3.1	3.2	13.9	20.4
.9	1.1	.7		.3	.5	1.1	2.2	2.2	8.5
1.8	1.9	1.8	Sales/Total Assets	1.1	1.7	1.4	1.9	3.4	5.6
1.1	1.1	1.1		.4	1.0	1.2	.9	1.9	2.5
.5	.6	.5		.2	.4	.6	.8	.6	1.2
1.4	.8	.8	% Depr., Dep., Amort./Sales	2.7	2.9	2.0	1.1	.1	.2
(102) 3.3	(90) 2.2	(103) 3.9		(26) 6.7	(19) 7.8	(13) 5.6	(14) 4.2	(10) .3	(21) .8
10.6	6.8	10.5		16.9	19.0	9.6	6.3	3.1	1.1
.6	.6	.5	% Officers', Directors' Owners' Comp/Sales						
(21) 2.3	(21) 1.7	(29) 1.5							
10.0	5.1	5.6							
2343731M	2357448M	3335504M	Net Sales ($)	17304M	46632M	53599M	123224M	210860M	2883885M
1515736M	985571M	1635775M	Total Assets ($)	49944M	113120M	62853M	135781M	227536M	1046541M

© RMA 2007

M = $ thousand   MM = $ million
See Pages 11 through 21 for Explanation of Ratios and Data

Current Data Sorted by Assets

Comparative Historical Data

						Type of Statement		
		1	21	10	7	Unqualified	39	52
	3	17	14	5	2	Reviewed	26	45
	9	15	12			Compiled	40	36
2	8	9	3			Tax Returns	14	10
3	2	20	26	6	6	Other	76	58
	51 (4/1-9/30/06)		150 (10/1/06-3/31/07)				4/1/02-3/31/03	4/1/03-3/31/04
0-500M	500M-2MM	2-10MM	10-50MM	50-100MM	100-250MM		ALL	ALL
5	22	62	76	21	15	NUMBER OF STATEMENTS	195	201
%	%	%	%	%	%	ASSETS	%	%
	3.4	3.6	5.4	2.7	1.6	Cash & Equivalents	3.8	4.9
	6.9	17.8	17.6	13.8	18.6	Trade Receivables (net)	17.6	15.9
	30.4	40.9	42.1	49.3	54.1	Inventory	36.6	37.7
	1.4	8.6	9.9	7.9	3.2	All Other Current	10.1	8.2
	42.2	70.8	75.1	73.7	77.6	Total Current	68.2	66.7
	39.4	22.1	17.3	14.9	16.6	Fixed Assets (net)	25.4	22.4
	.5	.2	.1	.5	1.1	Intangibles (net)	.2	.5
	17.9	6.9	7.6	10.9	4.7	All Other Non-Current	6.3	10.4
	100.0	100.0	100.0	100.0	100.0	Total	100.0	100.0
						LIABILITIES		
	24.2	31.0	41.2	40.8	43.1	Notes Payable-Short Term	41.0	32.8
	6.4	.9	1.0	.9	.9	Cur. Mat.-L.T.D.	1.9	2.5
	4.2	4.6	7.2	4.0	5.0	Trade Payables	7.2	8.5
	.1	.0	.9	.1	.0	Income Taxes Payable	.2	.4
	9.0	6.7	5.8	8.0	4.8	All Other Current	7.1	6.3
	43.9	43.2	56.1	53.8	53.9	Total Current	57.4	50.5
	25.7	14.0	7.3	5.5	9.6	Long-Term Debt	12.7	13.0
	.0	.2	.5	.4	.1	Deferred Taxes	.6	.6
	5.3	2.5	1.8	5.5	.8	All Other Non-Current	5.5	4.6
	25.2	40.1	34.3	34.8	35.6	Net Worth	23.9	31.3
	100.0	100.0	100.0	100.0	100.0	Total Liabilties & Net Worth	100.0	100.0
						INCOME DATA		
	100.0	100.0	100.0	100.0	100.0	Net Sales	100.0	100.0
						Gross Profit		
	86.4	94.5	95.7	97.0	97.7	Operating Expenses	98.1	93.3
	13.6	5.5	4.3	3.0	2.3	Operating Profit	1.9	6.7
	9.0	1.5	1.4	1.4	.4	All Other Expenses (net)	1.0	1.1
	4.6	4.0	3.0	1.6	2.0	Profit Before Taxes	.8	5.7
						RATIOS		
	1.5	2.9	1.6	1.6	1.6		1.7	1.9
	.7	1.5	1.2	1.2	1.4	Current	1.2	1.4
	.4	1.1	1.1	1.1	1.3		1.0	1.1
	.5	1.1	.6	.5	.4		.7	.6
	.2	(61) .4	.3	.2	.3	Quick	.3	.3
	.0	.1	.1	.1	.0		.1	.1
	0 UND	0 UND	2 188.6	9 39.5	4 82.3		6 58.7	3 140.5
	0 UND	13 28.6	22 16.6	30 12.1	24 15.3	Sales/Receivables	23 15.6	22 16.8
	21 17.2	63 5.8	65 5.6	53 6.9	105 3.5		63 5.8	50 7.3
						Cost of Sales/Inventory		
						Cost of Sales/Payables		
	7.7	3.2	5.0	4.8	4.1		5.4	4.8
	-26.3	8.9	8.2	10.0	5.2	Sales/Working Capital	12.2	8.7
	-5.1	29.1	29.8	14.2	6.3		60.1	33.9
	7.0	6.2	4.1	4.0	2.0		2.9	8.6
	(18) 1.7	(57) 1.9	(72) 1.9	(20) 1.2	1.3	EBIT/Interest	(182) 1.4	(187) 3.7
	-.7	1.2	.5	.3	.6		-.2	1.5
			6.9				2.2	7.6
		(11) 2.8				Net Profit + Depr., Dep., Amort./Cur. Mat. L/T/D	(36) 1.3	(34) 2.4
		1.1					.0	1.1
	.2	.1	.2	.2	.2		.3	.2
	1.3	.5	.5	.5	.4	Fixed/Worth	.8	.6
	19.8	1.3	1.1	1.1	.9		1.7	1.5
	1.0	.6	1.1	.9	1.4		1.3	1.0
	3.5	1.8	2.8	2.3	1.9	Debt/Worth	2.7	2.3
	39.8	4.5	4.7	4.4	2.7		7.2	5.3
	42.3	23.0	19.5	15.7	11.6	% Profit Before Taxes/Tangible Net Worth	21.0	34.4
	(18) 17.3	(59) 9.6	(75) 8.0	(20) 6.2	3.1		(177) 5.0	(185) 18.0
	-5.6	2.9	-2.9	-2.1	-2.9		-9.7	5.9
	13.2	8.8	7.4	5.9	3.9	% Profit Before Taxes/Total Assets	6.2	12.2
	2.1	2.6	2.3	.7	1.1		.9	5.6
	-4.1	.6	-.9	-2.1	-1.2		-3.5	1.3
	27.1	123.0	24.3	20.0	16.6	Sales/Net Fixed Assets	23.2	30.1
	5.7	10.9	10.5	9.1	7.6		8.6	10.9
	.7	3.8	5.6	6.5	5.3		4.2	3.8
	2.9	2.6	1.8	1.7	1.6	Sales/Total Assets	2.5	2.3
	1.4	1.8	1.5	1.4	1.2		1.6	1.6
	.5	1.0	.9	1.1	.7		1.1	1.0
	2.1	.9	.6	.7	.8	% Depr., Dep., Amort./Sales	.9	.8
	(20) 6.0	(45) 2.0	(70) 1.2	(19) 1.2	(13) 1.2		(166) 1.8	(173) 1.6
	14.5	2.9	1.9	2.4	1.6		3.1	3.3
	1.7	.3	.3			% Officers', Directors' Owners' Comp/Sales	.9	.9
	(11) 2.1	(14) 1.3	(16) 1.1				(56) 2.3	(43) 1.7
	8.3	4.2	3.0				4.3	3.8
5368M	38117M	1185476M	2898933M	2145238M	2965513M	Net Sales ($)	5994028M	8149332M
1729M	21907M	337315M	1730909M	1557605M	2394107M	Total Assets ($)	3679008M	4847434M

M = $ thousand MM = $ million

See Pages 11 through 21 for Explanation of Ratios and Data

Comparative Historical Data　　　　　　Current Data Sorted by Sales

4/1/04-3/31/05 ALL	4/1/05-3/31/06 ALL	4/1/06-3/31/07 ALL	Type of Statement	0-1MM	1-3MM	3-5MM	5-10MM	10-25MM	25MM & OVER
			Unqualified		1			6	32
54	47	39	Reviewed	3	2	3	5	15	13
40	34	41	Compiled	7	3	1	6	13	6
40	29	36	Tax Returns	3	7	3	6	3	
16	13	22	Other	4	2	5	5	14	33
52	59	63		51 (4/1-9/30/06)			150 (10/1/06-3/31/07)		
202	182	201	NUMBER OF STATEMENTS	17	15	12	22	51	84
%	%	%	ASSETS	%	%	%	%	%	%
4.5	4.9	4.2	Cash & Equivalents	2.5	5.0	4.2	5.0	6.7	2.7
17.3	12.8	15.8	Trade Receivables (net)	6.6	12.0	14.4	19.6	15.4	17.7
39.6	39.8	42.3	Inventory	17.8	46.6	33.5	33.4	47.2	47.1
9.4	9.9	7.6	All Other Current	1.0	1.6	7.7	14.5	6.9	8.6
70.7	67.4	69.8	Total Current	27.9	65.2	59.8	72.5	76.2	76.1
21.1	23.2	21.0	Fixed Assets (net)	50.2	26.6	25.0	16.6	16.7	17.2
.3	.5	.3	Intangibles (net)	.0	.0	.0	1.0	.0	.3
7.9	8.9	8.9	All Other Non-Current	21.9	8.2	15.2	9.9	7.0	6.4
100.0	100.0	100.0	Total	100.0	100.0	100.0	100.0	100.0	100.0
			LIABILITIES						
36.7	37.1	35.6	Notes Payable-Short Term	15.2	36.5	27.4	34.2	34.3	41.9
2.3	2.1	1.8	Cur. Mat.-L.T.D.	7.0	.9	7.6	.7	.9	1.0
6.8	6.3	5.5	Trade Payables	1.4	6.7	2.2	4.0	7.5	5.9
.3	.3	.4	Income Taxes Payable	.1	.0	.0	.9	.7	.2
6.6	8.4	7.2	All Other Current	9.4	12.1	2.9	6.9	6.4	7.0
52.8	54.2	50.5	Total Current	33.1	56.1	40.1	46.7	49.7	56.0
11.4	11.7	12.3	Long-Term Debt	44.9	13.6	20.9	11.1	6.3	8.3
.4	.3	.3	Deferred Taxes	.0	.0	.0	.1	.1	.5
3.7	4.7	3.3	All Other Non-Current	13.9	.4	8.5	1.5	1.5	2.5
31.7	29.0	33.6	Net Worth	8.2	29.8	30.4	40.7	42.3	32.7
100.0	100.0	100.0	Total Liabilities & Net Worth	100.0	100.0	100.0	100.0	100.0	100.0
			INCOME DATA						
100.0	100.0	100.0	Net Sales	100.0	100.0	100.0	100.0	100.0	100.0
			Gross Profit						
94.5	94.6	94.5	Operating Expenses	74.0	91.4	97.4	93.5	96.9	97.7
5.5	5.4	5.5	Operating Profit	26.0	8.6	2.6	6.5	3.1	2.3
.5	2.2	2.3	All Other Expenses (net)	14.5	6.6	1.8	.1	.9	.5
5.1	3.2	3.2	Profit Before Taxes	11.5	1.9	.8	6.5	2.2	1.8
			RATIOS						
1.8	1.8	1.8	Current	3.4	1.4	3.2	2.5	2.5	1.5
1.3	1.3	1.3		.6	1.2	1.2	1.4	1.3	1.3
1.1	1.1	1.1		.2	.8	.7	1.1	1.1	1.2
.7	.6	.6	Quick	.5	.5	.4	1.3	.9	.5
.3	.3	.3		.3	.1	.3	.5	.4	.3
.1	.1	.1		.0	.0	.0	.1	.1	.1
1　249.1	3　146.0	1　281.3	Sales/Receivables	0　UND	0　UND	0　UND	0　UND	1　385.2	4　87.3
20　18.4	17　21.8	17　21.4		0　UND	0　999.8	21　17.4	18　20.3	17　21.4	22　16.8
53　6.9	42　8.6	54　6.7		24　15.3	43　8.4	60　6.1	99　3.7	62　5.9	57　6.4
			Cost of Sales/Inventory						
			Cost of Sales/Payables						
4.7	5.1	4.6	Sales/Working Capital	3.1	5.3	2.6	3.3	3.6	5.1
9.8	10.1	9.0		-8.6	7.8	15.5	8.8	8.8	8.2
29.8	50.2	36.0		-2.4	-37.8	-15.8	22.2	23.3	19.0
8.6	5.5	4.3	EBIT/Interest	7.8	3.0	3.7	12.0	5.8	3.6
(180) 3.7	(167) 2.2	(186) 1.8		(12) 1.6	(13) 1.3	(10) 1.5	(20) 3.4	(49) 1.9	(82) 1.5
1.9	1.0	.7		-2.1	.0	.9	1.4	1.1	.6
9.3	4.1	5.7	Net Profit + Depr., Dep., Amort./Cur. Mat. L/T/D						9.8
(25) 4.8	(28) 2.3	(29) 2.2						(14)	2.2
2.2	.7	1.3							1.3
.2	.3	.2	Fixed/Worth	.2	.2	.1	.1	.1	.2
.6	.6	.5		3.3	1.0	1.3	.4	.4	.5
1.1	1.3	1.3		NM	2.8	31.3	1.1	.8	1.0
.9	1.0	1.0	Debt/Worth	2.2	1.0	.8	.5	.6	1.2
2.2	2.3	2.3		8.3	2.4	3.2	1.7	1.8	2.4
5.4	5.0	4.6		NM	9.5	177.3	6.1	4.5	4.3
33.2	20.5	21.2	% Profit Before Taxes/Tangible Net Worth	50.9	14.0	49.7	57.6	21.1	18.5
(183) 18.5	(165) 8.7	(190) 8.5		(13) 19.2	(13) 4.9	(10) 10.4	(21) 20.5	(50) 7.2	(83) 7.7
7.0	-.1	-1.0		-2.9	-5.4	1.1	3.7	.8	-2.9
9.8	6.9	7.8	% Profit Before Taxes/Total Assets	10.0	3.2	9.2	12.0	6.9	6.8
5.2	2.5	2.3		3.0	2.1	1.1	5.7	2.5	2.1
1.6	-.5	-.5		-6.9	-1.0	-2.0	2.3	.7	-1.1
31.6	26.9	29.1	Sales/Net Fixed Assets	6.1	63.3	113.7	31.0	43.7	24.8
10.2	8.3	9.5		1.2	11.2	18.1	9.9	11.0	10.3
4.5	4.2	5.1		.5	2.9	2.2	5.5	5.6	6.6
2.2	2.2	2.0	Sales/Total Assets	1.0	3.5	2.0	2.0	2.2	2.0
1.5	1.5	1.5		.5	1.7	1.1	1.3	1.6	1.6
1.0	.9	1.0		.1	.8	.9	.8	1.2	1.2
.8	.8	.8	% Depr., Dep., Amort./Sales	5.5	1.2		.5	.9	.7
(165) 1.7	(163) 1.7	(170) 1.5		(15) 10.4	(12) 2.4		(19) 1.2	(39) 1.7	(76) 1.1
2.8	3.1	2.6		19.7	6.1		2.9	2.4	1.7
.9	.6	.4	% Officers', Directors' Owners' Comp/Sales					.4	.1
(51) 1.5	(43) 1.2	(40) 1.5						(11) 1.0	(16) .5
3.6	3.7	3.8						1.3	1.6
7682009M	7535831M	9238645M	Net Sales ($)	8722M	33221M	47264M	162693M	852306M	8134439M
4788239M	4675648M	6043572M	Total Assets ($)	24669M	63302M	40773M	144379M	634923M	5135526M

M = $ thousand　　　MM = $ million
See Pages 11 through 21 for Explanation of Ratios and Data

Current Data Sorted by Assets

Comparative Historical Data

						Type of Statement			
1	1	106	3 131	3 7	2 1	Unqualified		4	9
5	10	37	14	1	1	Reviewed		256	300
7	6	11	3			Compiled		64	85
1	10	24	16	1	1	Tax Returns		19	22
	7					Other		36	31
	7 (4/1-9/30/06)		353 (10/1/06-3/31/07)					4/1/02-3/31/03	4/1/03-3/31/04
0-500M	500M-2MM	2-10MM	10-50MM	50-100MM	100-250MM			ALL	ALL
14	34	178	167	12	5	NUMBER OF STATEMENTS		379	447
%	%	%	%	%	%	ASSETS		%	%
5.8	4.5	1.9	2.0	2.5		Cash & Equivalents		1.4	1.5
4.2	6.8	6.2	7.0	6.2		Trade Receivables (net)		7.5	8.3
25.1	10.5	13.5	13.2	7.6		Inventory		13.2	11.6
.5	3.6	2.3	2.8	1.8		All Other Current		3.6	2.3
35.5	25.3	23.9	23.9	18.2		Total Current		25.7	23.8
51.8	66.0	64.4	66.1	68.7		Fixed Assets (net)		62.6	65.8
3.0	1.3	1.4	.6	.9		Intangibles (net)		.6	.9
9.6	7.4	10.3	9.4	12.3		All Other Non-Current		11.2	9.5
100.0	100.0	100.0	100.0	100.0		Total		100.0	100.0
						LIABILITIES			
17.6	22.2	15.9	14.9	11.3		Notes Payable-Short Term		19.3	17.8
5.0	3.1	6.0	5.2	2.6		Cur. Mat.-L.T.D.		5.9	6.3
8.8	6.2	4.6	3.3	2.8		Trade Payables		3.1	4.5
.0	.0	.0	.0	.2		Income Taxes Payable		.0	.1
11.5	2.2	2.8	2.1	4.5		All Other Current		3.3	2.4
42.9	33.6	29.3	25.6	21.4		Total Current		31.6	31.0
61.4	41.6	44.1	43.6	39.4		Long-Term Debt		36.1	40.0
.0	.6	.1	.2	.0		Deferred Taxes		.2	.1
6.4	9.1	3.5	2.3	.4		All Other Non-Current		2.3	2.3
-11.0	15.1	23.1	28.4	38.8		Net Worth		29.8	26.5
100.0	100.0	100.0	100.0	100.0		Total Liabilities & Net Worth		100.0	100.0
						INCOME DATA			
100.0	100.0	100.0	100.0	100.0		Net Sales		100.0	100.0
						Gross Profit			
92.9	94.5	98.9	98.5	92.4		Operating Expenses		95.7	95.3
7.1	5.5	1.1	1.5	7.6		Operating Profit		4.3	4.7
3.7	5.6	6.9	7.8	9.3		All Other Expenses (net)		6.1	5.8
3.4	-.1	-5.8	-6.3	-1.7		Profit Before Taxes		-1.7	-1.1
						RATIOS			
3.0	1.1	1.3	1.2	1.6				1.1	1.1
.9	.7	.8	.9	1.1		Current		.8	.8
.3	.3	.5	.7	.4				.6	.5
.7	.9	.4	.4	.6				.4	.5
.1	.2	.2	.3	.3		Quick		.2 (446)	.3
.0	.1	.1	.1	.1				.1	.1
0 UND	0 UND	15 24.5	18 20.4	26 14.0				16 23.0	17 21.4
0 UND	13 28.9	20 18.3	31 11.8	34 10.6		Sales/Receivables		28 12.8	29 12.4
9 42.7	21 17.8	34 10.9	54 6.8	51 7.2				56 6.5	49 7.5
						Cost of Sales/Inventory			
						Cost of Sales/Payables			
8.3	62.1	16.9	13.0	6.4				20.0	29.1
NM	-22.0	-14.0	-19.5	NM		Sales/Working Capital		-11.9	-15.1
-8.8	-4.4	-5.8	-6.8	-3.6				-5.3	-5.5
5.2	1.7	1.2	1.3	2.9				2.1	2.4
(12) 2.1	(29) .7	(173) .1	(165) .0	(11) 1.3		EBIT/Interest		(368) .7	(429) .8
.6	-.4	-1.3	-.8	-.2				-.7	-.7
			2.6					2.5	2.3
		(10)	1.4			Net Profit + Depr., Dep., Amort./Cur. Mat. L/T/D		(16) 1.4	(20) 1.4
			-.7					.0	.0
.7	1.2	1.4	1.5	1.3				1.2	1.4
3.6	3.0	2.8	2.5	1.7		Fixed/Worth		2.3	2.6
-8.3	-6.0	7.8	5.2	2.8				3.9	5.0
1.5	1.1	1.4	1.5	.9				1.3	1.3
6.1	4.0	2.9	2.7	1.6		Debt/Worth		2.5	2.7
-9.7	-9.2	9.0	6.3	2.6				4.6	6.2
	24.3	5.5	4.1	19.1				7.4	10.1
	(24) .0	(153) -9.5	(153) -8.3	-1.4		% Profit Before Taxes/Tangible Net Worth		(350) -1.2	(398) -1.2
	-14.1	-35.6	-24.3	-14.2				-16.7	-16.1
22.9	5.3	1.1	1.3	5.6				2.5	3.1
4.9	-.1	-3.0	-3.2	-.6		% Profit Before Taxes/Total Assets		-.6	-.7
-2.8	-6.9	-9.9	-6.6	-3.7				-5.0	-5.0
45.2	3.2	1.6	1.1	1.3				1.5	1.5
8.5	1.6	1.1	.8	.6		Sales/Net Fixed Assets		1.0	1.0
1.7	1.1	.8	.6	.4				.7	.7
4.4	1.8	.9	.7	.8				.8	.9
2.7	1.2	.7	.5	.4		Sales/Total Assets		.6	.6
1.0	.6	.6	.4	.3				.5	.5
2.2	3.0	7.8	9.4	8.8				8.3	8.2
(10) 6.6	(31) 10.1	(170) 10.7	(162) 12.2	12.8		% Depr., Dep., Amort./Sales		(364) 11.7	(427) 11.2
9.8	14.8	13.7	15.2	13.6				14.8	14.5
	2.3	1.0	.6					1.0	1.0
	(12) 3.4	(61) 2.2	(45) .8			% Officers', Directors' Owners' Comp/Sales		(109) 2.2	(120) 1.9
	21.6	3.7	1.3					6.9	4.0
15813M	69047M	833525M	1998770M	593519M	1329487M	Net Sales ($)		2502644M	3035797M
4281M	48043M	1025773M	3273629M	914895M	878072M	Total Assets ($)		3461909M	4388319M

M = $ thousand   MM = $ million
See Pages 11 through 21 for Explanation of Ratios and Data

Comparative Historical Data / Current Data Sorted by Sales

Comp 1	Comp 2	Comp 3	Type of Statement	0-1MM	1-3MM	3-5MM	5-10MM	10-25MM	25MM & OVER
6	5	9	Unqualified	1			1	3	5
274	279	256	Reviewed		39	41	102	63	10
86	77	64	Compiled	5	24	9	17	7	2
30	21	31	Tax Returns	9	11	6	1	3	1
42	44	50	Other	6	8	11	16	5	4
4/1/04-3/31/05 ALL	4/1/05-3/31/06 ALL	4/1/06-3/31/07 ALL		57 (4/1-9/30/06)		353 (10/1/06-3/31/07)			
438	426	410	NUMBER OF STATEMENTS	21	82	67	137	81	22
%	%	%	**ASSETS**	%	%	%	%	%	%
1.8	1.2	1.9	Cash & Equivalents	4.2	2.5	1.9	.7	2.0	4.2
9.2	8.2	6.6	Trade Receivables (net)	1.5	6.2	6.1	6.1	7.9	12.2
12.2	12.9	13.4	Inventory	7.1	13.1	12.6	15.2	12.8	13.5
2.4	2.5	2.5	All Other Current	4.8	.9	3.0	2.8	2.9	1.9
25.6	24.8	24.4	Total Current	17.5	22.7	23.6	24.9	25.6	31.8
64.0	64.7	64.8	Fixed Assets (net)	75.2	63.7	63.9	65.5	64.8	57.3
1.3	1.1	1.2	Intangibles (net)	.3	1.7	1.9	.9	.5	1.4
9.2	9.4	9.7	All Other Non-Current	7.1	11.9	10.6	8.7	9.0	9.5
100.0	100.0	100.0	Total	100.0	100.0	100.0	100.0	100.0	100.0
			LIABILITIES						
16.4	14.4	15.9	Notes Payable-Short Term	5.7	17.5	19.2	15.2	16.8	10.9
5.6	5.2	5.3	Cur. Mat.-L.T.D.	3.1	5.2	5.8	5.7	5.2	3.2
3.1	3.2	4.3	Trade Payables	2.9	5.0	3.5	3.8	4.5	8.0
.1	.1	.0	Income Taxes Payable	.0	.0	.0	.0	.0	.1
2.6	2.8	2.9	All Other Current	2.0	4.2	1.4	1.9	3.7	6.6
27.8	25.7	28.4	Total Current	13.7	31.8	29.9	26.7	30.1	28.9
39.0	41.9	44.0	Long-Term Debt	49.8	48.1	45.2	43.2	42.6	29.5
.1	.1	.2	Deferred Taxes	.0	.2	.0	.3	.0	.1
3.1	2.8	3.4	All Other Non-Current	6.3	5.1	2.7	3.3	2.6	.4
29.9	29.4	24.0	Net Worth	30.0	14.8	22.2	26.4	24.7	41.1
100.0	100.0	100.0	Total Liabilities & Net Worth	100.0	100.0	100.0	100.0	100.0	100.0
			INCOME DATA						
100.0	100.0	100.0	Net Sales	100.0	100.0	100.0	100.0	100.0	100.0
			Gross Profit						
84.6	87.0	97.8	Operating Expenses	83.6	97.7	101.3	99.5	97.3	93.1
15.4	13.0	2.2	Operating Profit	16.4	2.3	-1.3	.5	2.7	6.9
4.5	5.6	7.1	All Other Expenses (net)	8.9	6.5	6.1	8.5	7.1	2.3
10.9	7.4	-4.9	Profit Before Taxes	7.6	-4.2	-7.4	-7.9	-4.5	4.6
			RATIOS						
1.3	1.4	1.3	Current	5.5	1.1	1.3	1.2	1.2	1.6
.9	.9	.8		.4	.8	.8	.8	.9	1.3
.7	.6	.6		.2	.5	.6	.6	.7	.8
.6	.6	.5	Quick	.3	.5	.5	.4	.5	.9
(437) .4	.3	.2		.2	.3	.2	.2	.3	.4
.2	.2	.1		.0	.1	.1	.1	.1	.2
16 23.0	16 23.4	16 23.3	Sales/Receivables	0 UND	9 40.2	15 24.4	17 21.9	18 20.4	21 17.5
30 12.2	28 12.9	23 15.9		0 UND	18 20.1	25 14.4	25 14.9	27 13.4	30 12.0
53 6.8	52 7.0	36 10.1		16 23.1	34 10.8	36 10.2	37 9.8	59 6.1	36 10.1
			Cost of Sales/Inventory						
			Cost of Sales/Payables						
12.1	12.6	15.3	Sales/Working Capital	5.9	111.2	14.8	12.9	21.0	6.2
-74.6	-71.1	-17.6		-9.3	-17.1	-13.3	-15.3	-19.7	24.4
-8.8	-8.9	-6.6		-2.9	-6.6	-5.0	-6.6	-7.5	-17.7
7.4	4.5	1.4	EBIT/Interest	3.1	1.5	1.0	1.2	1.3	5.8
(422) 4.3	(415) 2.6	(395) .3		(14) .7	(79) .5	(66) .1	(136) -.3	(79) .5	(21) 2.3
2.2	1.3	-.9		-4.8	-1.0	-1.4	-1.1	-.2	1.3
7.0	4.2	3.9	Net Profit + Depr., Dep., Amort./Cur. Mat. L/T/D						11.1
(14) 1.9	(23) 2.2	(24) 1.6						(10)	5.2
1.0	1.5	.4							2.0
1.3	1.3	1.4	Fixed/Worth	1.2	1.5	1.3	1.5	1.6	.9
2.1	2.1	2.6		3.2	2.8	2.3	3.0	2.5	1.4
3.7	3.9	6.3		NM	7.9	8.4	6.2	5.1	2.2
1.1	1.2	1.4	Debt/Worth	.7	1.5	1.3	1.6	1.5	.9
2.0	2.1	2.8		2.5	3.0	2.7	3.5	2.7	1.6
4.2	4.3	7.4		NM	9.4	10.1	7.9	5.6	2.6
41.4	28.6	6.7	% Profit Before Taxes/Tangible Net Worth	24.2	11.0	1.4	3.3	3.7	23.0
(394) 26.0	(388) 15.5	(356) -6.6		(16) 6.2	(67) -3.7	(57) -14.5	(121) -11.4	(73) -7.1	7.9
14.6	5.0	-26.3		-2.2	-33.9	-29.3	-47.2	-20.7	3.3
13.7	9.3	1.8	% Profit Before Taxes/Total Assets	7.8	3.1	.0	.9	1.3	7.1
8.4	5.0	-2.6		2.0	-1.7	-3.7	-4.5	-2.2	3.4
4.0	1.1	-8.1		-2.5	-7.2	-9.5	-10.4	-5.1	1.3
1.8	1.6	1.5	Sales/Net Fixed Assets	1.6	1.9	1.5	1.3	1.4	8.2
1.2	1.0	1.0		.6	1.2	1.1	1.0	.9	1.6
.9	.8	.7		.2	.8	.7	.7	.7	.6
1.0	.9	.9	Sales/Total Assets	.8	1.1	.9	.8	.9	3.0
.8	.7	.6		.3	.7	.7	.6	.6	.8
.6	.5	.5		.2	.6	.5	.5	.6	.5
6.8	6.9	8.2	% Depr., Dep., Amort./Sales	6.7	8.2	7.9	8.9	8.1	1.7
(418) 9.3	(416) 9.7	(390) 11.3		(16) 10.2	(79) 11.5	(64) 10.5	(132) 11.6	(77) 12.0	5.4
12.1	12.6	14.6		25.0	14.9	13.5	14.8	14.6	12.2
.7	.7	.8	% Officers', Directors' Owners' Comp/Sales		2.1	1.8	.6	.6	
(138) 1.2	(128) 1.4	(126) 1.7		(26) 3.7	(23) 2.6	(41) .9	(24) .9		
3.0	3.2	3.5		11.0	3.5	1.3	1.7		
4089681M	4546514M	4840161M	Net Sales ($)	8532M	176334M	261457M	960735M	1193279M	2239824M
4773841M	5848813M	6144693M	Total Assets ($)	28115M	281431M	420419M	1605963M	2091964M	1716801M

© RMA 2007

M = $ thousand   MM = $ million
See Pages 11 through 21 for Explanation of Ratios and Data

Current Data Sorted by Assets   Comparative Historical Data

Type of Statement

Type of Statement	0-500M	500M-2MM	2-10MM	10-50MM	50-100MM	100-250MM		4/1/02-3/31/03 ALL	4/1/03-3/31/04 ALL
Unqualified		4	1	12	2	2		15	14
Reviewed	1	2	2	3				4	6
Compiled	1		8	3				16	10
Tax Returns	4	8	1	1				9	11
Other	1		9	12	6	1		23	19

15 (4/1-9/30/06)   73 (10/1/06-3/31/07)

	0-500M	500M-2MM	2-10MM	10-50MM	50-100MM	100-250MM		4/1/02-3/31/03 ALL	4/1/03-3/31/04 ALL
NUMBER OF STATEMENTS	7	18	21	31	8	3		67	60
	%	%	%	%	%	%	**ASSETS**	%	%
		3.3	4.2	2.8			Cash & Equivalents	3.4	4.0
		1.1	8.8	14.1			Trade Receivables (net)	4.4	5.7
		28.8	27.6	36.9			Inventory	30.3	25.4
		2.4	4.7	5.1			All Other Current	2.8	5.5
		35.6	45.3	58.8			Total Current	41.0	40.5
		62.8	48.5	31.6			Fixed Assets (net)	51.2	49.8
		.0	.6	.3			Intangibles (net)	.8	.8
		1.6	5.5	9.3			All Other Non-Current	7.0	8.8
		100.0	100.0	100.0			Total	100.0	100.0
							LIABILITIES		
		18.2	6.3	24.2			Notes Payable-Short Term	25.6	19.6
		4.2	5.1	2.4			Cur. Mat.-L.T.D.	6.6	4.5
		3.4	7.5	7.4			Trade Payables	5.4	4.8
		.1	.0	.2			Income Taxes Payable	.0	.2
		5.6	2.4	3.5			All Other Current	5.5	7.8
		31.4	21.3	37.7			Total Current	43.0	36.8
		41.6	26.6	18.2			Long-Term Debt	35.6	33.9
		.0	1.7	.2			Deferred Taxes	.3	.1
		3.0	3.5	7.0			All Other Non-Current	6.3	10.6
		24.0	47.0	36.9			Net Worth	14.8	18.6
		100.0	100.0	100.0			Total Liabilties & Net Worth	100.0	100.0
							INCOME DATA		
		100.0	100.0	100.0			Net Sales	100.0	100.0
							Gross Profit		
		96.5	94.5	93.5			Operating Expenses	97.5	96.5
		3.5	5.5	6.5			Operating Profit	2.5	3.5
		1.8	.4	2.4			All Other Expenses (net)	5.4	3.3
		1.7	5.1	4.1			Profit Before Taxes	-2.9	.2
							RATIOS		
		2.9	3.1	1.9				1.9	2.1
		1.1	1.8	1.5			Current	1.2	1.3
		.8	1.4	1.2				.7	.8
		.6	.9	.6				.3	.5
		(17) .1	.3	.3			Quick	(66) .1	(59) .1
		.0	.1	.1				.0	.0
		0 UND	0 UND	5 69.7				0 UND	0 UND
		0 UND	5 80.3	19 19.7			Sales/Receivables	4 95.5	7 53.8
		1 502.3	23 16.0	30 12.2				11 33.5	26 14.3
							Cost of Sales/Inventory		
							Cost of Sales/Payables		
		8.4	3.2	4.1				6.6	4.6
		50.5	7.4	6.4			Sales/Working Capital	22.3	14.3
		-9.1	17.0	21.9				-8.5	-22.3
		8.7	13.3	11.0				2.6	2.9
		1.6	(20) 3.7	(29) 3.3			EBIT/Interest	(63) 1.1	(55) 1.3
		-.1	2.5	.1				-1.5	-.8
							Net Profit + Depr., Dep., Amort./Cur. Mat. L/T/D		
		.9	.5	.2				.9	.8
		1.9	1.1	.7			Fixed/Worth	1.9	1.7
		27.7	2.1	2.1				-45.1	9.0
		1.3	.5	.5				.9	1.0
		2.4	1.1	1.5			Debt/Worth	2.5	2.1
		38.7	2.8	4.4				-92.5	NM
		37.7	43.1	25.7			% Profit Before Taxes/Tangible Net Worth	15.1	16.6
		(15) 7.7	19.1	(29) 14.8				(49) .6	(45) 3.2
		-5.7	8.9	-7.8				-17.3	-7.9
		14.4	13.4	12.4			% Profit Before Taxes/Total Assets	6.2	5.6
		2.3	8.5	4.6				.0	1.5
		-4.1	5.3	-5.1				-8.6	-4.1
		5.0	8.2	28.1				4.3	4.7
		1.7	3.2	4.7			Sales/Net Fixed Assets	2.0	2.3
		1.4	.8	1.6				1.0	.9
		1.8	1.8	2.0				1.5	1.7
		1.2	.9	1.2			Sales/Total Assets	1.0	1.0
		.9	.6	.6				.7	.6
		3.8	2.1	1.3				2.5	1.9
		(16) 7.1	(20) 5.1	(25) 3.4			% Depr., Dep., Amort./Sales	(57) 6.4	(52) 6.6
		17.3	12.1	7.2				10.9	18.0
							% Officers', Directors' Owners' Comp/Sales	1.1	1.2
								(19) 2.5	(12) 2.5
								8.1	11.3
	6883M	29065M	150559M	1022981M	708965M	688566M	Net Sales ($)	1530656M	1377349M
	2730M	21123M	95359M	706805M	681483M	549850M	Total Assets ($)	1463311M	1145587M

M = $ thousand   MM = $ million
See Pages 11 through 21 for Explanation of Ratios and Data

Comparative Historical Data   **Current Data Sorted by Sales**

4/1/04-3/31/05 ALL	4/1/05-3/31/06 ALL	4/1/06-3/31/07 ALL		0-1MM	1-3MM	3-5MM	5-10MM	10-25MM	25MM & OVER
			Type of Statement						
16	15	21	Unqualified	1	2	2		3	13
12	3	8	Reviewed	1	3	1			3
11	5	12	Compiled		2	4	4	1	1
8	14	14	Tax Returns	8	5		1		
15	21	33	Other	2	3	4	5	4	15
				15 (4/1-9/30/06)			73 (10/1/06-3/31/07)		
62	58	88	**NUMBER OF STATEMENTS**	12	15	11	10	8	32
%	%	%	**ASSETS**	%	%	%	%	%	%
6.1	3.2	3.2	Cash & Equivalents	3.1	4.1	5.2	1.8		2.3
5.9	6.7	8.7	Trade Receivables (net)	3.3	1.7	3.8	4.5		16.4
27.5	25.2	33.6	Inventory	17.4	30.4	33.5	39.2		40.9
6.1	5.6	5.0	All Other Current	2.9	4.9	4.7	4.5		5.3
45.6	40.8	50.5	Total Current	26.7	41.1	47.2	50.1		64.9
44.0	50.7	43.3	Fixed Assets (net)	71.3	57.5	39.7	44.5		27.3
.4	.5	.3	Intangibles (net)	.1	.1	.1	.1		.3
10.0	8.1	5.9	All Other Non-Current	1.9	1.3	13.0	5.4		7.5
100.0	100.0	100.0	Total	100.0	100.0	100.0	100.0		100.0
			LIABILITIES						
20.6	19.7	18.3	Notes Payable-Short Term	19.9	21.9	8.4	10.2		21.5
4.7	7.0	3.4	Cur. Mat.-L.T.D.	5.0	3.7	5.3	5.0		1.9
4.3	5.2	7.6	Trade Payables	9.9	5.0	6.3	6.6		8.9
.2	.0	.1	Income Taxes Payable	.0	.1	.0	.0		.0
5.0	4.8	7.1	All Other Current	20.7	10.4	3.1	3.1		3.9
34.7	36.7	36.5	Total Current	55.5	41.2	23.0	24.8		36.2
24.0	36.5	28.3	Long-Term Debt	42.8	39.1	29.3	22.1		22.3
.3	.0	.5	Deferred Taxes	.0	.5	2.4	.0		.2
8.8	7.5	5.1	All Other Non-Current	2.7	1.5	6.2	1.9		6.8
32.3	19.3	29.6	Net Worth	-1.0	17.7	39.0	51.2		34.5
100.0	100.0	100.0	Total Liabilities & Net Worth	100.0	100.0	100.0	100.0		100.0
			INCOME DATA						
100.0	100.0	100.0	Net Sales	100.0	100.0	100.0	100.0		100.0
			Gross Profit						
86.9	85.0	94.4	Operating Expenses	95.7	93.8	89.8	98.1		94.1
13.1	15.0	5.6	Operating Profit	4.3	6.2	10.2	1.9		5.9
2.5	3.5	1.8	All Other Expenses (net)	4.8	1.6	5.9	.6		.2
10.6	11.4	3.8	Profit Before Taxes	-.5	4.6	4.4	1.3		5.7
			RATIOS						
2.6	2.4	2.4		3.2	2.0	3.4	3.2		2.3
1.3	1.3	1.6	Current	.9	1.1	1.7	1.9		1.7
.8	.5	1.0		.2	.6	1.4	1.4		1.3
.5	.6	.6		.8	.6	.4	.4		.7
(55) .2	(87) .2	.3	Quick	(11) .1	.2	.3	.2		.3
.1	.1	.1		.0	.0	.1	.1		.1
0 UND	0 UND	0 UND		0 UND	0 UND	2 203.3	0 UND		6 59.2
2 146.9	0 999.8	7 54.2	Sales/Receivables	0 UND	0 UND	7 50.5	4 94.9		19 19.0
15 25.1	16 22.2	26 14.1		0 UND	1 421.3	10 35.6	28 13.0		34 10.9
			Cost of Sales/Inventory						
			Cost of Sales/Payables						
4.0	4.7	4.3		16.1	7.4	2.3	3.8		3.1
12.5	17.4	9.2	Sales/Working Capital	-25.1	52.4	3.8	7.0		7.6
-18.1	-12.5	72.0		-3.8	-7.0	6.7	11.7		22.2
12.8	10.0	9.5		4.2	5.0		25.5		10.2
(58) 5.3	(55) 4.2	(84) 3.3	EBIT/Interest	(11) 1.0	3.3		6.4		4.6
2.8	2.4	.8		-1.0	1.3		.3		1.1
			Net Profit + Depr., Dep., Amort./Cur. Mat. L/T/D						
.3	.8	.3		1.7	.6	.2	.5		.2
1.1	1.3	1.1	Fixed/Worth	3.1	2.7	.9	.8		.7
2.1	6.6	3.0		NM	6.3	1.4	2.1		1.7
.7	.8	.7		1.6	.6	.7	.3		.6
1.3	1.7	1.9	Debt/Worth	28.1	5.5	1.1	.9		1.7
5.0	7.9	5.9		NM	33.8	2.7	3.5		3.6
49.7	72.0	29.7			73.2	18.4	47.4		28.6
(55) 21.1	(46) 40.6	(78) 16.4	% Profit Before Taxes/Tangible Net Worth		(12) 21.5	(10) 11.2	10.6		(29) 23.8
7.7	14.3	2.8			8.1	8.5	-8.7		7.2
21.6	25.1	13.5		13.5	11.9	13.4	14.1		16.9
9.9	12.7	6.4	% Profit Before Taxes/Total Assets	-.1	5.5	5.5	6.5		8.5
4.3	4.0	-.4		-5.6	3.1	1.6	-3.2		.9
15.7	8.6	12.3		4.6	5.1	10.5	44.3		42.9
3.3	3.0	3.2	Sales/Net Fixed Assets	1.5	1.8	4.3	3.4		8.5
1.2	1.1	1.4		.5	.8	.8	.8		2.5
2.2	1.9	1.9		1.3	2.6	1.4	2.2		2.2
1.1	1.3	1.2	Sales/Total Assets	.9	1.3	.9	1.6		1.5
.7	.7	.7		.5	.6	.5	.6		1.2
1.4	1.6	2.1		2.8	4.2				.8
(55) 4.5	(50) 4.8	(72) 4.3	% Depr., Dep., Amort./Sales	(12) 9.4	7.9				(23) 2.1
11.2	15.2	8.9		20.5	13.0				4.2
1.2		.6							
(10) 2.8	(18) 1.7		% Officers', Directors' Owners' Comp/Sales						
5.1		5.0							
1064326M	1410368M	2607019M	Net Sales ($)	7656M	26175M	39649M	67430M	107933M	2358176M
779675M	1021404M	2057350M	Total Assets ($)	9722M	26232M	103370M	70764M	132844M	1714418M

M = $ thousand   MM = $ million
See Pages 11 through 21 for Explanation of Ratios and Data

Current Data Sorted by Assets   Comparative Historical Data

Date groupings: 16 (4/1-9/30/06) | 33 (10/1/06-3/31/07) | Historical: 4/1/02-3/31/03 ALL | 4/1/03-3/31/04 ALL

Type of Statement

	0-500M	500M-2MM	2-10MM	10-50MM	50-100MM	100-250MM	4/1/02-3/31/03 ALL	4/1/03-3/31/04 ALL
Unqualified	1		3	6	5	3	18	19
Reviewed			3	3	1		3	3
Compiled		3	3				5	6
Tax Returns	1	3	2				5	7
Other	1	4		3	2	2	13	12
NUMBER OF STATEMENTS	3	10	11	12	8	5	44	47

Assets (%)

	0-500M	500M-2MM	2-10MM	10-50MM	50-100MM	100-250MM	'02-'03 ALL	'03-'04 ALL
Cash & Equivalents		11.2	1.4	9.2			4.3	6.9
Trade Receivables (net)		8.3	16.1	13.5			14.1	13.1
Inventory		19.9	16.7	13.1			17.5	16.2
All Other Current		.2	3.8	6.9			5.9	3.8
Total Current		39.6	38.1	42.7			41.8	40.1
Fixed Assets (net)		55.7	55.5	47.4			44.6	51.0
Intangibles (net)		.6	1.1	.3			4.1	3.0
All Other Non-Current		4.1	5.3	9.6			9.6	6.0
Total		100.0	100.0	100.0			100.0	100.0

Liabilities

	0-500M	500M-2MM	2-10MM	10-50MM	50-100MM	100-250MM	'02-'03 ALL	'03-'04 ALL
Notes Payable-Short Term		15.4	14.8	6.8			12.5	14.1
Cur. Mat.-L.T.D.		2.9	7.7	3.9			4.5	4.4
Trade Payables		4.3	17.7	10.1			9.3	8.4
Income Taxes Payable		.0	.0	.6			.6	.9
All Other Current		1.2	4.6	2.5			7.5	5.7
Total Current		23.8	44.8	23.9			34.6	33.5
Long-Term Debt		42.6	29.0	19.6			23.3	27.5
Deferred Taxes		.0	.1	1.8			1.6	1.3
All Other Non-Current		1.9	8.0	4.1			3.0	6.4
Net Worth		31.7	18.0	50.6			37.6	31.3
Total Liabilities & Net Worth		100.0	100.0	100.0			100.0	100.0

Income Data

	0-500M	500M-2MM	2-10MM	10-50MM	50-100MM	100-250MM	'02-'03 ALL	'03-'04 ALL
Net Sales		100.0	100.0	100.0			100.0	100.0
Gross Profit								
Operating Expenses		99.7	100.7	100.3			97.3	92.9
Operating Profit		.3	-.7	-.3			2.7	7.1
All Other Expenses (net)		5.9	4.7	-.9			1.6	2.5
Profit Before Taxes		-5.6	-5.4	.5			1.1	4.6

Ratios

	0-500M	500M-2MM	2-10MM	10-50MM	50-100MM	100-250MM	'02-'03 ALL	'03-'04 ALL
Current		6.6	1.3	3.8			2.1	2.4
		2.9	1.0	1.9			1.3	1.5
		.9	.6	.9			.7	.8
Quick		4.4	.6	2.6			1.1	1.2
		1.8	.3	.8			.5	.5
		.4	.2	.4			.3	.3
Sales/Receivables		0 UND	15 23.7	20 18.1			20 18.1	16 22.3
		11 32.8	33 11.1	27 13.3			25 14.8	24 15.3
		47 7.7	48 7.6	33 11.1			33 10.9	31 11.7
Cost of Sales/Inventory								
Cost of Sales/Payables								
Sales/Working Capital		3.5	14.0	6.3			7.9	7.0
		7.5	111.7	14.3			23.5	14.9
		-18.2	-8.8	NM			-20.7	-28.7
EBIT/Interest			1.9				3.8	7.0
			(10) .2				(41) 1.3	(44) 3.2
			-1.7				-1.7	1.0
Net Profit + Depr., Dep., Amort./Cur. Mat. L/T/D							6.5	9.9
							(12) 2.7	(12) 3.8
							-.7	1.5
Fixed/Worth		.8	1.3	.5			.6	.7
		2.0	4.3	1.2			1.2	1.4
		-11.1	18.4	2.5			2.7	6.3
Debt/Worth		.6	1.5	.2			.8	.9
		1.6	4.6	1.2			1.7	1.6
		-13.1	38.3	3.9			4.4	8.0
% Profit Before Taxes/Tangible Net Worth			8.7	16.5			17.6	34.8
			(10) -8.1	2.0			(38) 3.7	(38) 16.0
			-160.5	-23.9			-20.4	1.6
% Profit Before Taxes/Total Assets		7.7	1.3	10.5			10.7	9.2
		-5.0	-3.1	.9			1.5	5.5
		-13.6	-7.9	-5.5			-6.0	.3
Sales/Net Fixed Assets		6.9	7.1	6.6			8.4	6.6
		2.0	3.7	3.8			4.0	3.1
		.5	1.1	2.4			1.9	1.9
Sales/Total Assets		2.2	3.3	2.1			2.7	2.6
		.9	1.2	1.7			1.7	1.7
		.3	.9	1.3			1.1	.9
% Depr., Dep., Amort./Sales			1.4	2.1			1.9	2.3
			2.1	(10) 3.6			(39) 3.7	(38) 4.3
			14.1	6.0			10.1	9.3
% Officers', Directors', Owners' Comp/Sales							1.1	
							(10) 4.4	
							10.0	
Net Sales ($)	4868M	18282M	111443M	583200M	639472M	608387M	1780762M	2203739M
Total Assets ($)	984M	12342M	66493M	328151M	596506M	667980M	1127485M	1387792M

M = $ thousand   MM = $ million
See Pages 11 through 21 for Explanation of Ratios and Data

Comparative Historical Data | Current Data Sorted by Sales

			Type of Statement	0-1MM	1-3MM	3-5MM	5-10MM	10-25MM	25MM & OVER
13	21	18	Unqualified	1		1	1	1	14
7	5	7	Reviewed				1	1	5
6	8	6	Compiled	1	1		4		
4	4	6	Tax Returns	3		3			
17	14	12	Other	3	2			2	5
4/1/04-3/31/05 ALL	4/1/05-3/31/06 ALL	4/1/06-3/31/07 ALL			16 (4/1-9/30/06)			33 (10/1/06-3/31/07)	
47	52	49	**NUMBER OF STATEMENTS**	8	3	4	6	4	24
%	%	%	**ASSETS**	%	%	%	%	%	%
10.5	9.4	8.3	Cash & Equivalents						8.1
17.6	15.5	11.6	Trade Receivables (net)						13.9
14.7	14.6	15.9	Inventory						15.2
4.9	4.9	3.4	All Other Current						2.5
47.8	44.4	39.2	Total Current						39.7
43.2	46.4	52.7	Fixed Assets (net)						50.2
3.8	1.2	1.8	Intangibles (net)						2.9
5.2	8.0	6.4	All Other Non-Current						7.2
100.0	100.0	100.0	Total						100.0
			LIABILITIES						
12.6	9.1	10.8	Notes Payable-Short Term						8.8
2.3	3.1	5.2	Cur. Mat.-L.T.D.						5.7
10.4	9.6	9.9	Trade Payables						11.5
.6	1.3	.2	Income Taxes Payable						.4
7.6	6.0	3.9	All Other Current						4.6
33.6	29.1	30.0	Total Current						31.1
23.1	20.9	30.4	Long-Term Debt						26.7
.6	.8	1.0	Deferred Taxes						1.8
2.3	5.9	4.1	All Other Non-Current						3.6
40.4	43.3	34.5	Net Worth						36.8
100.0	100.0	100.0	Total Liabilities & Net Worth						100.0
			INCOME DATA						
100.0	100.0	100.0	Net Sales						100.0
			Gross Profit						
90.1	99.5	98.9	Operating Expenses						99.6
9.9	.5	1.1	Operating Profit						.4
1.4	.9	3.2	All Other Expenses (net)						1.3
8.5	-.4	-2.1	Profit Before Taxes						-1.0
			RATIOS						
2.2	2.5	2.3							2.1
1.6	1.5	1.4	Current						1.3
1.0	1.0	.8							.8
1.5	1.7	1.5							.8
.8	.8	.6	Quick						.6
.5	.5	.3							.3
17 21.2	19 19.7	15 23.7						22	16.7
22 16.3	27 13.3	28 13.2	Sales/Receivables					29	12.7
34 10.6	37 10.0	40 9.1						41	9.0
			Cost of Sales/Inventory						
			Cost of Sales/Payables						
7.3	6.4	6.5							7.1
15.0	12.3	15.1	Sales/Working Capital						14.5
999.8	181.2	-17.5							-20.6
31.2	4.6	2.5							1.7
(42) 8.3	(46) -.3	(40) .9	EBIT/Interest					(22)	1.1
2.1	-4.9	-1.3							-1.2
7.9	5.6	2.6							2.2
(10) 5.7	(14) 1.9	(13) 1.2	Net Profit + Depr., Dep., Amort./Cur. Mat. L/T/D					(10)	1.1
2.6	-.3	.1							.2
.6	.4	1.0							1.0
1.2	1.2	1.6	Fixed/Worth						1.6
1.9	2.4	4.1							3.2
.6	.5	1.0							1.0
1.7	1.7	2.2	Debt/Worth						2.2
3.7	3.5	5.2							4.3
57.6	15.7	15.9							10.9
(44) 31.6	(50) -2.2	(43) 2.1	% Profit Before Taxes/Tangible Net Worth					(22)	2.6
8.0	-31.7	-24.4							-8.9
30.3	9.1	6.0							2.8
9.8	-.6	-.2	% Profit Before Taxes/Total Assets						.5
1.9	-13.6	-6.0							-5.0
10.9	11.0	5.0							4.7
4.2	3.5	2.4	Sales/Net Fixed Assets						2.6
2.6	1.5	1.5							1.9
2.8	2.5	2.1							2.0
1.9	1.6	1.3	Sales/Total Assets						1.5
1.0	.9	.8							.9
1.6	2.0	2.4							2.5
(38) 3.5	(43) 4.0	(43) 5.8	% Depr., Dep., Amort./Sales					(21)	5.4
5.5	9.3	11.6							9.6
			% Officers', Directors' Owners' Comp/Sales						
2751357M	2580487M	1965652M	Net Sales ($)	2671M	6529M	16890M	49480M	73627M	1816455M
1639319M	2028421M	1672456M	Total Assets ($)	13558M	4125M	10751M	37759M	45498M	1560765M

M = $ thousand   MM = $ million
See Pages 11 through 21 for Explanation of Ratios and Data

AGRICULTURE—Timber Tract Operations NAICS 113110 (SIC 0811)

Current Data Sorted by Assets
Comparative Historical Data

			3	9	4	1	Type of Statement		
	2	3	3	6			Unqualified	9	15
1	3	7		5			Reviewed	14	21
4	8	3					Compiled	28	23
3	7	15	11	3	3		Tax Returns	13	19
							Other	20	17
	13 (4/1-9/30/06)		88 (10/1/06-3/31/07)					4/1/02-3/31/03 ALL	4/1/03-3/31/04 ALL
0-500M	500M-2MM	2-10MM	10-50MM	50-100MM	100-250MM				
8	20	31	31	7	4	NUMBER OF STATEMENTS	84	95
%	%	%	%	%	%	ASSETS	%	%
	15.6	10.4	4.7			Cash & Equivalents	7.2	7.3
	16.0	9.7	10.1			Trade Receivables (net)	8.4	7.6
	19.8	15.7	14.0			Inventory	25.1	20.2
	1.3	7.2	6.5			All Other Current	2.6	4.8
	52.6	43.1	35.3			Total Current	43.2	39.8
	33.0	42.8	42.2			Fixed Assets (net)	39.1	41.8
	.1	.7	.4			Intangibles (net)	2.1	.4
	14.2	13.4	22.0			All Other Non-Current	15.7	18.0
	100.0	100.0	100.0			Total	100.0	100.0
						LIABILITIES		
	20.2	22.5	10.7			Notes Payable-Short Term	17.2	16.3
	10.9	6.5	7.7			Cur. Mat.-L.T.D.	3.7	7.1
	14.3	6.2	5.0			Trade Payables	4.9	3.9
	.1	.0	.0			Income Taxes Payable	.1	.2
	22.5	6.0	4.5			All Other Current	7.1	9.2
	68.0	41.3	27.9			Total Current	33.1	36.6
	27.8	27.4	29.4			Long-Term Debt	29.9	29.7
	.0	.0	.6			Deferred Taxes	.2	.5
	3.4	4.3	1.5			All Other Non-Current	2.5	2.6
	.8	27.0	40.7			Net Worth	34.4	30.7
	100.0	100.0	100.0			Total Liabilties & Net Worth	100.0	100.0
						INCOME DATA		
	100.0	100.0	100.0			Net Sales	100.0	100.0
						Gross Profit		
	95.1	77.3	83.6			Operating Expenses	85.8	90.5
	4.9	22.7	16.4			Operating Profit	14.2	9.5
	3.7	8.8	5.7			All Other Expenses (net)	3.7	2.5
	1.2	13.9	10.7			Profit Before Taxes	10.5	7.0
						RATIOS		
	2.8	2.6	2.4			Current	3.5	2.7
	1.0	1.0	1.1				1.5	1.2
	.4	.4	.6				.7	.6
	1.7	.6	1.1			Quick	1.8	.9
	.6	.3	.4				(83) .6	(94) .4
	.2	.2	.1				.2	.1
	0 UND	0 UND	4 83.9			Sales/Receivables	0 UND	1 477.5
	11 34.7	5 71.4	12 31.4				9 41.8	11 31.8
	41 8.8	26 13.8	22 16.8				22 16.4	25 14.3
						Cost of Sales/Inventory		
						Cost of Sales/Payables		
	16.3	5.9	4.0			Sales/Working Capital	4.1	5.4
	NM	402.6	18.6				21.0	26.6
	-4.0	-13.9	-4.3				-16.7	-12.1
	4.6	6.5	6.1			EBIT/Interest	8.5	9.3
	(18) 1.2	(27) 2.2	(25) 2.1				(74) 3.2	(84) 2.5
	-.7	1.8	1.1				1.3	1.2
						Net Profit + Depr., Dep., Amort./Cur. Mat. L/T/D		6.2
							(15)	3.2
								1.1
	.4	.3	.2			Fixed/Worth	.2	.4
	1.2	1.2	1.1				1.1	.9
	19.0	4.6	2.2				3.2	3.0
	1.9	.8	1.0			Debt/Worth	.5	.8
	7.0	2.3	1.6				1.6	2.7
	22.0	6.8	3.4				8.6	7.7
	70.6	72.8	26.8			% Profit Before Taxes/Tangible Net Worth	51.5	48.2
	(16) -.7	(27) 25.3	12.4				(74) 12.0	(84) 14.9
	-26.7	7.7	.0				3.7	2.6
	13.8	12.2	10.6			% Profit Before Taxes/Total Assets	12.4	12.1
	.6	6.4	2.8				5.4	4.4
	-6.1	2.8	.0				1.0	.5
	28.2	23.3	11.4			Sales/Net Fixed Assets	27.5	18.9
	10.8	4.8	2.7				8.1	4.3
	3.6	2.2	.7				.9	1.0
	4.2	3.8	1.3			Sales/Total Assets	3.9	3.1
	2.4	2.3	.6				1.4	1.4
	.9	.9	.3				.4	.5
	1.0	1.1	1.1			% Depr., Dep., Amort./Sales	.8	1.3
	(14) 3.8	(22) 2.4	(28) 3.1				(67) 3.2	(77) 4.3
	12.5	6.2	10.3				6.9	13.1
	1.1	.9				% Officers', Directors' Owners' Comp/Sales	1.3	1.0
	(11) 3.3	(12) 1.9					(22) 2.3	(32) 1.9
	8.2	3.6					3.9	6.4
23407M	80993M	337713M	756215M	297193M	413737M	Net Sales ($)	1115072M	1970782M
2487M	23053M	141996M	639759M	521211M	616815M	Total Assets ($)	1054879M	1993402M

M = $ thousand   MM = $ million

See Pages 11 through 21 for Explanation of Ratios and Data

Comparative Historical Data   Current Data Sorted by Sales

Historical columns: 4/1/04-3/31/05 ALL | 4/1/05-3/31/06 ALL | 4/1/06-3/31/07 ALL
Current columns under bands: **13 (4/1-9/30/06)** covers 0-1MM, 1-3MM, 3-5MM; **88 (10/1/06-3/31/07)** covers 5-10MM, 10-25MM, 25MM & OVER

4/1/04-3/31/05 ALL	4/1/05-3/31/06 ALL	4/1/06-3/31/07 ALL		0-1MM	1-3MM	3-5MM	5-10MM	10-25MM	25MM & OVER
Type of Statement									
12	9	17	Unqualified			1	5	4	7
15	16	11	Reviewed		4	3	1	1	2
27	22	16	Compiled	3	3		3	4	3
32	22	15	Tax Returns	4	6		2	2	1
24	32	42	Other	5	8	4	8	6	11
110	101	101	**NUMBER OF STATEMENTS**	12	21	8	19	17	24
%	%	%	**ASSETS**	%	%	%	%	%	%
9.5	8.6	9.7	Cash & Equivalents	16.0	9.1		15.4	6.5	6.8
9.2	10.2	10.2	Trade Receivables (net)	3.1	8.8		13.2	17.0	9.1
26.6	22.8	15.2	Inventory	13.5	14.0		16.9	22.1	15.0
3.4	4.8	4.7	All Other Current	.7	2.1		8.1	1.7	7.6
48.7	46.4	39.9	Total Current	33.5	34.0		53.7	47.3	38.5
39.2	41.1	44.3	Fixed Assets (net)	44.1	48.7		33.6	37.4	46.7
.8	.9	.4	Intangibles (net)	.0	.1		.9	.5	.3
11.3	11.6	15.4	All Other Non-Current	22.4	17.3		11.7	14.8	14.6
100.0	100.0	100.0	Total	100.0	100.0		100.0	100.0	100.0
			LIABILITIES						
18.4	17.3	14.8	Notes Payable-Short Term	12.7	14.3		7.2	23.9	14.1
7.7	6.8	7.3	Cur. Mat.-L.T.D.	7.1	11.0		3.9	4.8	7.7
5.5	5.3	7.2	Trade Payables	11.6	9.1		9.3	5.0	5.0
.3	.2	.1	Income Taxes Payable	.0	.0		.0	.1	.2
5.1	8.3	8.5	All Other Current	6.3	22.3		3.5	4.7	6.6
37.1	37.8	37.9	Total Current	37.7	56.7		23.9	38.5	33.5
33.5	28.9	32.0	Long-Term Debt	36.8	41.0		35.4	27.1	24.8
.2	.1	.3	Deferred Taxes	.0	.0		.3	.7	.4
4.1	1.9	3.6	All Other Non-Current	.5	8.3		5.2	2.3	1.0
25.0	31.2	26.2	Net Worth	25.0	-5.9		35.3	31.4	40.3
100.0	100.0	100.0	Total Liabilities & Net Worth	100.0	100.0		100.0	100.0	100.0
			INCOME DATA						
100.0	100.0	100.0	Net Sales	100.0	100.0		100.0	100.0	100.0
			Gross Profit						
89.4	84.7	84.9	Operating Expenses	66.1	86.8		76.8	94.0	92.5
10.6	15.3	15.1	Operating Profit	33.9	13.2		23.2	6.0	7.5
2.7	3.7	5.7	All Other Expenses (net)	25.4	5.0		2.4	2.5	1.3
7.8	11.6	9.4	Profit Before Taxes	8.5	8.3		20.8	3.5	6.2
			RATIOS						
3.2	2.5	2.7	Current	5.1	2.5		6.0	1.7	2.4
1.3	1.2	1.1		.8	.9		3.2	1.1	1.2
.8	.7	.5		.2	.2		1.1	.9	.7
1.4	1.2	1.3	Quick	4.6	1.4		2.1	1.2	1.0
.5	.4	.5		.3	.4		1.1	.5	.4
.2	.1	.2		.0	.0		.3	.2	.2
0 UND	0 UND	0 UND	Sales/Receivables	0 UND	0 UND		0 UND	3 130.4	5 72.4
8 48.1	8 43.2	9 39.6		0 UND	9 40.0		10 35.8	13 29.1	11 33.4
19 19.6	26 14.0	23 16.2		16 22.6	40 9.2		30 12.1	35 10.6	15 24.9
			Cost of Sales/Inventory						
			Cost of Sales/Payables						
6.0	7.1	5.6	Sales/Working Capital	1.3	9.8		2.7	7.6	8.7
34.3	23.2	46.2		-9.8	-30.0		5.5	75.1	55.9
-49.0	-12.1	-11.2		-.4	-4.3		16.2	-52.2	-61.7
8.0	7.8	6.9	EBIT/Interest		4.7		23.5	8.0	7.6
(102) 2.8	(91) 3.5	(85) 2.1			(18) 1.9		(17) 3.0	(16) 2.3	(23) 2.4
1.1	1.7	.8			-.7		1.3	1.4	1.2
7.4		21.5	Net Profit + Depr., Dep., Amort./Cur. Mat. L/T/D						
(16) 2.0	(11) 6.8	6.8							
1.0		.9							
.3	.3	.3	Fixed/Worth	.1	.6		.2	.5	.4
1.0	1.2	1.1		1.6	1.8		.7	.8	1.1
3.8	3.3	3.7		NM	-5.9		1.1	4.1	2.0
1.1	.8	.8	Debt/Worth	.7	1.4		.3	.5	.8
2.6	2.3	2.0		3.1	8.5		1.9	2.0	1.5
12.6	6.2	8.3		NM	-8.8		3.7	6.2	4.9
65.0	41.4	46.6	% Profit Before Taxes/Tangible Net Worth		38.9		73.5	71.2	44.7
(96) 17.3	(89) 22.6	(88) 12.6			(14) 11.5		(17) 28.9	(16) 17.6	23.5
2.7	5.2	-.9			-13.9		6.5	8.4	4.4
13.6	18.4	13.9	% Profit Before Taxes/Total Assets	4.8	15.9		34.8	10.9	13.9
4.0	8.5	5.3		1.3	6.6		7.9	5.3	7.1
.1	1.8	-.4		-1.2	-4.0		2.8	.5	1.3
24.6	19.5	18.5	Sales/Net Fixed Assets	27.1	18.4		23.6	25.7	51.8
9.0	7.4	4.6		4.7	4.1		4.8	6.4	5.6
2.4	1.3	1.1		.1	1.3		2.3	2.6	1.0
4.2	3.6	3.4	Sales/Total Assets	1.0	3.3		2.4	4.6	4.5
2.4	1.7	1.2		.2	1.4		1.8	2.9	1.2
.9	.5	.4		.1	.3		.5	1.2	.8
1.0	.9	1.3	% Depr., Dep., Amort./Sales		2.6		1.7	.6	.6
(85) 3.4	(83) 2.3	(79) 3.6			(14) 5.0		(14) 2.6	(15) 1.2	(21) 4.1
7.9	6.9	10.2			17.0		8.6	7.1	10.1
1.3	1.5	1.0	% Officers', Directors' Owners' Comp/Sales		1.7				
(45) 2.2	(29) 2.6	(28) 2.8			(10) 3.6				
8.7	6.5	6.1			7.0				
1962941M	2049263M	1909258M	Net Sales ($)	6065M	40460M	33453M	130483M	268840M	1429957M
1598293M	1888009M	1945321M	Total Assets ($)	37198M	80897M	192851M	164916M	193767M	1275692M

M = $ thousand   MM = $ million
See Pages 11 through 21 for Explanation of Ratios and Data

Current Data Sorted by Assets

Comparative Historical Data

Type of Statement

Type of Statement	4/1/02-3/31/03 ALL	4/1/03-3/31/04 ALL
Unqualified	9	18
Reviewed	25	29
Compiled	25	42
Tax Returns	36	31
Other	14	24

Current-period statement counts (by asset size):

Type of Statement	0-500M	500M-2MM	2-10MM	10-50MM	50-100MM	100-250MM
Unqualified		1		1		1
Reviewed	1	3	2	8	5	1
Compiled	5	17	12	12	2	
Tax Returns	12	21	10	7		
Other	2	11	7	7	4	1 / 2

26 (4/1-9/30/06) · 109 (10/1/06-3/31/07)

	0-500M	500M-2MM	2-10MM	10-50MM	50-100MM	100-250MM	4/1/02-3/31/03 ALL	4/1/03-3/31/04 ALL
NUMBER OF STATEMENTS	20	53	38	19	2	3	109	144
	%	%	%	%	%	%	%	%
ASSETS								
Cash & Equivalents	13.5	12.4	8.3	6.4			7.9	8.3
Trade Receivables (net)	10.2	10.4	9.9	8.6			10.2	10.8
Inventory	12.4	12.8	20.9	25.0			15.1	16.5
All Other Current	4.4	3.0	4.0	3.6			3.3	3.5
Total Current	40.6	38.6	43.1	43.6			36.5	39.1
Fixed Assets (net)	51.4	54.1	44.8	45.5			51.3	49.0
Intangibles (net)	3.3	.8	2.2	.0			1.2	1.2
All Other Non-Current	4.8	6.5	9.9	10.9			11.0	10.7
Total	100.0	100.0	100.0	100.0			100.0	100.0
LIABILITIES								
Notes Payable-Short Term	27.6	19.0	16.1	15.3			13.8	17.0
Cur. Mat.-L.T.D.	15.1	7.3	10.0	4.7			10.2	10.3
Trade Payables	6.9	5.4	6.9	6.7			6.4	5.4
Income Taxes Payable	.0	.2	.4	.5			.2	.1
All Other Current	9.7	2.7	4.5	5.5			4.9	4.4
Total Current	59.2	34.6	38.0	32.6			35.6	37.3
Long-Term Debt	51.6	36.2	24.2	21.9			32.5	26.6
Deferred Taxes	.0	.3	1.4	1.5			.6	.8
All Other Non-Current	4.8	4.2	3.9	5.0			5.9	4.2
Net Worth	-15.6	24.7	32.6	39.0			25.5	31.1
Total Liabilities & Net Worth	100.0	100.0	100.0	100.0			100.0	100.0
INCOME DATA								
Net Sales	100.0	100.0	100.0	100.0			100.0	100.0
Gross Profit	50.3	38.2	33.0	22.8			31.6	30.3
Operating Expenses	43.9	36.6	29.3	18.2			29.1	27.0
Operating Profit	6.4	1.5	3.6	4.6			2.5	3.2
All Other Expenses (net)	2.6	.3	1.2	1.3			1.6	1.5
Profit Before Taxes	3.7	1.2	2.4	3.3			.9	1.7
RATIOS								
Current	1.4	2.4	1.8	2.2			1.9	1.9
	.8	1.1	1.2	1.1			1.1	1.1
	.2	.4	.4	1.0			.5	.5
Quick	.8	1.6	1.3	1.6			1.1	1.0
	(19) .3	.7	.4	.5			.4	.4
	.1	.2	.1	.2			.2	.2
Sales/Receivables	0 UND	0 UND	6 61.9	5 68.2			0 UND	2 161.6
	0 UND	7 49.2	13 27.1	12 29.5			11 34.7	12 29.9
	1 278.5	23 16.2	23 15.9	23 15.7			21 17.2	25 14.5
Cost of Sales/Inventory	0 UND	0 UND	0 UND	7 49.1			0 UND	0 UND
	0 UND	9 40.9	20 18.1	47 7.8			14 25.5	13 28.5
	63 5.8	31 11.7	68 5.3	142 2.6			57 6.4	53 6.9
Cost of Sales/Payables	0 UND	0 UND	5 77.1	8 47.6			1 243.7	0 999.8
	0 UND	3 115.7	13 28.8	13 28.4			9 41.9	9 40.6
	12 31.4	22 17.0	34 10.8	33 11.0			19 19.1	19 19.3
Sales/Working Capital	29.7	10.2	10.5	5.5			13.3	9.4
	-31.6	150.4	41.7	73.0			69.2	123.3
	-8.8	-12.5	-11.3	999.8			-13.2	-12.6
EBIT/Interest	3.5	4.8	6.1	5.2			4.3	5.7
	(17) 1.5	(51) 1.9	1.6	(18) 2.1			(103) 1.6	(135) 2.2
	.6	.8	.9	1.0			.6	.5
Net Profit + Depr., Dep., Amort./Cur. Mat. L/T/D							1.9	2.3
							(19) 1.2	(25) 1.7
							.6	1.0
Fixed/Worth	.6	.8	.7	.4			.8	.5
	NM	2.0	1.6	1.1			1.7	1.4
	-1.0	17.5	4.9	3.7			7.2	5.0
Debt/Worth	2.5	.7	1.2	.3			1.0	.8
	NM	2.9	3.2	2.5			2.7	2.3
	-3.1	32.4	8.2	6.6			13.5	7.9
% Profit Before Taxes/Tangible Net Worth	145.8	51.0	27.6	17.7			22.7	35.2
	(10) 44.2	(43) 11.2	(36) 9.7	10.4			(86) 6.4	(122) 10.4
	-1.3	2.7	-11.2	.7			-3.4	-2.0
% Profit Before Taxes/Total Assets	30.5	14.0	8.9	7.7			8.6	9.3
	2.9	4.2	2.9	3.0			1.4	3.1
	-2.1	-.9	-.9	.2			-2.2	-2.3
Sales/Net Fixed Assets	27.2	10.8	23.0	7.9			10.9	14.1
	5.6	5.4	4.1	4.0			4.3	5.0
	2.4	2.2	2.3	1.5			2.0	2.1
Sales/Total Assets	5.5	3.8	2.8	2.0			3.6	3.6
	3.0	2.6	2.4	1.5			2.3	2.1
	1.5	1.5	1.4	.9			1.2	1.2
% Depr., Dep., Amort./Sales	4.9	3.8	2.2	1.4			2.6	2.1
	(13) 8.3	(47) 6.8	(34) 7.1	(17) 5.5			(98) 6.8	(131) 6.6
	18.0	11.9	12.8	10.2			11.8	10.9
% Officers', Directors' Owners' Comp/Sales		1.5	1.7				1.2	1.3
		(30) 3.5	(17) 2.9				(51) 2.6	(55) 2.5
		4.9	3.8				5.6	6.6
Net Sales ($)	13068M	198434M	387734M	724532M	86983M	394970M	2208381M	2575934M
Total Assets ($)	4361M	65844M	165651M	425596M	115021M	479205M	1059410M	1544913M

M = $ thousand   MM = $ million
See Pages 11 through 21 for Explanation of Ratios and Data

Comparative Historical Data | Current Data Sorted by Sales

Hist A	Hist B	Hist C	Type of Statement	0-1MM	1-3MM	3-5MM	5-10MM	10-25MM	25MM & OVER
11	10	13	Unqualified	1	1	1	2	3	7
16	27	21	Reviewed	1		1	7	10	1
44	34	34	Compiled	6	6	9	9	3	1
40	38	40	Tax Returns	10	14	7	8	1	1
18	21	27	Other	2	9	2	3	4	7
4/1/04-3/31/05	4/1/05-3/31/06	4/1/06-3/31/07			26 (4/1-9/30/06)			109 (10/1/06-3/31/07)	
ALL	ALL	ALL		0-1MM	1-3MM	3-5MM	5-10MM	10-25MM	25MM & OVER
129	130	135	**NUMBER OF STATEMENTS**	20	30	19	29	21	16
%	%	%	**ASSETS**	%	%	%	%	%	%
8.9	9.6	10.3	Cash & Equivalents	11.4	12.5	14.4	9.7	7.4	4.5
8.4	9.8	9.9	Trade Receivables (net)	13.1	7.3	8.0	9.4	12.0	11.0
17.5	16.1	16.6	Inventory	10.6	10.5	8.5	20.6	28.1	23.2
3.1	2.9	3.6	All Other Current	4.8	3.5	3.9	1.2	6.2	2.6
37.8	38.5	40.4	Total Current	40.0	33.8	34.9	40.9	53.8	41.3
50.7	52.2	50.1	Fixed Assets (net)	53.1	59.8	57.2	49.3	32.9	43.4
.4	1.0	1.7	Intangibles (net)	3.1	.6	1.6	.0	3.9	2.4
11.1	8.3	7.8	All Other Non-Current	3.8	5.8	6.4	9.7	9.4	12.9
100.0	100.0	100.0	Total	100.0	100.0	100.0	100.0	100.0	100.0
			LIABILITIES						
15.8	15.4	18.5	Notes Payable-Short Term	24.4	13.6	19.3	15.0	24.9	17.4
9.6	8.7	8.6	Cur. Mat.-L.T.D.	11.6	11.2	7.9	10.0	4.2	4.1
7.0	6.0	6.2	Trade Payables	6.1	5.5	5.9	4.5	8.9	7.8
.2	.2	.3	Income Taxes Payable	.0	.0	.8	.3	.1	.9
3.8	5.4	4.7	All Other Current	3.5	6.8	1.4	3.5	6.4	6.2
36.3	35.7	38.4	Total Current	45.6	37.1	35.3	33.3	44.4	36.4
37.6	33.3	32.7	Long-Term Debt	39.6	54.7	35.0	22.5	18.4	17.0
.9	.9	.8	Deferred Taxes	.0	.3	.3	1.0	1.5	2.0
5.2	3.3	4.2	All Other Non-Current	4.8	5.2	2.8	2.1	4.6	6.2
20.0	26.8	24.0	Net Worth	10.1	2.6	26.5	41.1	31.1	38.4
100.0	100.0	100.0	Total Liabilties & Net Worth	100.0	100.0	100.0	100.0	100.0	100.0
			INCOME DATA						
100.0	100.0	100.0	Net Sales	100.0	100.0	100.0	100.0	100.0	100.0
35.5	36.3	35.9	Gross Profit	51.2	49.7	36.5	35.1	15.6	17.8
31.1	33.0	32.2	Operating Expenses	45.8	48.6	32.9	30.4	13.5	12.0
4.4	3.3	3.6	Operating Profit	5.5	1.1	3.6	4.7	2.2	5.9
.8	1.4	1.1	All Other Expenses (net)	3.4	.1	.9	.7	.9	1.2
3.6	1.9	2.5	Profit Before Taxes	2.1	1.0	2.7	4.0	1.3	4.7
			RATIOS						
2.1	2.7	1.9		1.8	2.0	2.2	4.2	1.6	1.6
1.1	1.0	1.1	Current	1.0	1.0	1.0	1.3	1.2	1.1
.5	.5	.4		.3	.3	.5	.3	.7	.9
1.0	1.7	1.4		1.4	1.1	1.7	1.8	.8	1.0
(128) .5	(128) .5	(134) .5	Quick	(19) .3	.3	.5	.6	.4	.5
.2	.2	.2		.0	.2	.2	.2	.2	.2
0 UND	0 UND	0 UND		0 UND	0 UND	3 107.5	1 483.9	6 56.8	6 64.9
9 41.8	10 36.0	10 36.6	Sales/Receivables	0 UND	10 35.6	7 54.8	10 36.6	12 29.5	16 22.2
19 19.1	22 16.9	22 16.2		17 21.2	20 18.0	21 17.4	23 16.0	20 18.4	42 8.7
0 UND	0 UND	0 UND		0 UND	0 UND	0 UND	0 UND	10 35.6	12 29.5
13 28.1	9 38.8	15 24.5	Cost of Sales/Inventory	0 UND	5 67.0	5 76.9	0 UND	28 13.2	40 9.1
55 6.7	67 5.4	62 5.9		118 3.1	62 5.8	30 12.0	74 5.0	69 5.3	87 4.2
0 UND	0 UND	0 UND		0 UND	0 UND	1 477.7	0 UND	5 71.6	10 36.8
8 43.9	8 46.5	8 45.5	Cost of Sales/Payables	0 UND	6 57.3	9 40.1	5 75.1	10 38.1	16 22.2
25 14.7	17 22.0	24 15.1		0 UND	42 8.7	38 9.4	21 17.8	22 16.9	33 11.2
12.9	9.7	9.9		18.6	7.1	10.7	5.7	12.7	6.2
101.5	339.3	113.2	Sales/Working Capital	NM	NM	999.8	19.3	30.6	73.2
-14.1	-14.5	-13.4		-9.7	-9.9	-13.4	-9.7	-28.9	NM
5.9	5.5	5.4		3.2	5.0	6.1	12.2	4.1	7.1
(120) 2.3	(118) 2.6	(129) 1.8	EBIT/Interest	(17) 1.5	1.6	(18) 1.7	(27) 2.2	1.3	2.8
1.0	1.2	.9		.1	.3	1.0	1.4	.6	1.3
3.0	2.8	4.3	Net Profit + Depr., Dep.,						
(18) 1.5	(22) 1.2	(21) 2.0	Amort./Cur. Mat. L/T/D						
.9	.8	1.2							
.7	.6	.7		.5	1.8	.7	.6	.5	.5
2.3	1.8	1.8	Fixed/Worth	3.3	6.7	2.9	1.5	.9	1.2
13.7	11.0	8.5		-3.0	-16.0	5.8	3.2	6.8	2.3
1.2	1.0	.8		.8	2.0	.7	.4	1.3	.8
2.8	2.8	3.4	Debt/Worth	9.0	8.4	2.9	1.8	3.8	2.5
42.9	20.0	20.6		-5.3	-22.8	28.8	6.3	20.5	5.8
48.6	43.3	41.4	% Profit Before Taxes/Tangible	92.1	78.8	45.4	38.1	31.8	23.4
(102) 17.7	(106) 18.0	(113) 9.7	Net Worth	(12) 1.4	(21) 6.6	(17) 9.7	15.6	(18) 5.8	14.4
4.7	4.5	.6		-20.8	.5	1.6	2.4	-6.5	6.5
11.4	12.4	13.1	% Profit Before Taxes/Total	29.6	13.5	16.1	12.0	7.5	12.8
4.8	4.7	3.6	Assets	1.2	2.9	3.6	4.2	1.3	4.7
-.1	.6	-.2		-5.9	-5.1	.1	1.0	-.8	1.4
15.6	11.1	11.4		7.7	8.8	6.8	19.8	29.5	11.0
5.2	4.3	4.5	Sales/Net Fixed Assets	2.9	3.3	4.8	4.8	21.8	3.6
2.1	2.4	2.2		1.5	2.0	2.2	3.2	2.8	1.3
4.1	3.5	3.5		3.4	3.2	3.3	3.6	4.2	3.2
2.5	2.1	2.1	Sales/Total Assets	1.6	2.0	2.5	2.7	2.4	1.6
1.3	1.3	1.4		.9	1.4	1.6	1.4	1.6	.9
2.2	2.1	2.8		6.8	5.3	5.8	2.8	.9	1.0
(106) 6.5	(116) 6.4	(114) 6.9	% Depr., Dep., Amort./Sales	(14) 11.7	(24) 11.0	7.9	(27) 6.8	(18) 2.0	(12) 2.6
13.0	11.1	11.7		20.9	15.3	11.9	10.9	9.2	5.2
1.0	2.0	1.8	% Officers', Directors'	1.7	1.6	1.8			
(59) 2.6	(55) 3.9	(56) 3.3	Owners' Comp/Sales	(19) 4.0	(10) 3.0	(18) 3.0			
5.1	7.2	5.5		6.3	5.5	4.2			
3592341M	2868419M	1805721M	Net Sales ($)	9943M	57564M	76834M	201808M	354448M	1105124M
1369570M	1220349M	1255678M	Total Assets ($)	7145M	31411M	42217M	144701M	163407M	866797M

M = $ thousand   MM = $ million
See Pages 11 through 21 for Explanation of Ratios and Data

Current Data Sorted by Assets							Comparative Historical Data	
						Type of Statement		
		1	6	1	1	Unqualified	6	8
			2			Reviewed	2	2
	1	2				Compiled	8	8
	4					Tax Returns	17	14
3	5	8	5	1	2	Other	15	10
	8 (4/1-9/30/06)		34 (10/1/06-3/31/07)				4/1/02-3/31/03 ALL	4/1/03-3/31/04 ALL
0-500M	500M-2MM	2-10MM	10-50MM	50-100MM	100-250MM	**NUMBER OF STATEMENTS**	48	42
3	10	11	13	2	3			
%	%	%	%	%	%	**ASSETS**	%	%
	14.4	11.5	11.6			Cash & Equivalents	14.0	12.1
	3.0	13.7	8.0			Trade Receivables (net)	7.5	2.7
	2.6	1.8	16.3			Inventory	6.4	5.0
	8.1	3.0	2.7			All Other Current	3.7	3.1
	28.1	30.1	38.6			Total Current	31.5	23.0
	38.1	45.4	45.3			Fixed Assets (net)	52.3	60.6
	7.4	22.9	7.9			Intangibles (net)	3.1	4.6
	26.4	1.6	8.2			All Other Non-Current	13.0	11.9
	100.0	100.0	100.0			Total	100.0	100.0
						LIABILITIES		
	6.6	2.6	5.8			Notes Payable-Short Term	8.0	5.9
	4.2	5.8	2.9			Cur. Mat.-L.T.D.	11.6	10.7
	8.1	11.3	7.9			Trade Payables	4.5	6.6
	.0	.6	.4			Income Taxes Payable	.5	.2
	7.2	4.1	3.8			All Other Current	17.8	11.1
	26.2	24.4	20.6			Total Current	42.4	34.5
	58.2	33.7	31.8			Long-Term Debt	48.3	51.3
	.0	.0	.9			Deferred Taxes	.1	.4
	7.5	7.2	2.3			All Other Non-Current	7.1	12.6
	8.1	34.7	44.3			Net Worth	2.1	1.2
	100.0	100.0	100.0			Total Liabilities & Net Worth	100.0	100.0
						INCOME DATA		
	100.0	100.0	100.0			Net Sales	100.0	100.0
						Gross Profit		
	80.0	86.5	82.2			Operating Expenses	90.1	91.9
	20.0	13.5	17.8			Operating Profit	9.9	8.1
	2.8	1.5	2.0			All Other Expenses (net)	2.8	4.7
	17.2	12.0	15.9			Profit Before Taxes	7.1	3.4
						RATIOS		
	6.4	1.6	3.8				2.1	1.7
	1.7	.9	1.8			Current	.8	.7
	.4	.5	1.2				.2	.3
	2.2	1.3	1.8				1.7	1.0
	.9	.8	1.2			Quick	.5	.4
	.1	.5	.6				.2	.2
	0 UND	0 UND	3 139.2				0 UND	0 UND
	0 UND	0 999.8	20 18.6			Sales/Receivables	0 UND	0 UND
	0 UND	33 11.1	42 8.6				19 19.0	20 18.1
						Cost of Sales/Inventory		
						Cost of Sales/Payables		
	5.8	16.5	4.7				7.3	19.8
	67.1	-35.6	7.5			Sales/Working Capital	-86.8	-50.7
	-22.9	-21.7	22.0				-8.2	-7.0
	13.4	15.2	25.4				10.3	6.6
	8.3	6.6	4.3			EBIT/Interest	(44) 2.6	(39) 1.9
	1.8	1.7	2.7				.5	.2
						Net Profit + Depr., Dep., Amort./Cur. Mat. L/T/D		
	1.1	1.0	.6				1.1	1.3
	NM	2.8	1.0			Fixed/Worth	4.1	3.2
	-.5	-4.0	2.1				-3.7	-2.1
	1.8	1.6	.4				1.0	1.3
	NM	2.8	1.1			Debt/Worth	5.6	4.6
	-4.4	-6.6	4.7				-5.0	-3.4
			74.7				53.9	32.8
		(12)	39.8			% Profit Before Taxes/Tangible Net Worth	(27) 20.5	(24) 13.8
			16.6				9.8	3.8
	64.7	28.2	28.1				22.4	16.9
	23.8	13.8	7.2			% Profit Before Taxes/Total Assets	4.4	4.0
	1.7	2.8	5.5				-2.0	-4.1
	47.1	8.2	5.3				8.2	5.3
	9.0	6.0	3.7			Sales/Net Fixed Assets	3.2	3.0
	2.4	2.2	.6				1.6	1.6
	3.1	3.8	1.8				3.6	2.6
	1.8	1.9	1.2			Sales/Total Assets	1.4	1.6
	1.0	.7	.4				.9	.9
		2.2	1.6				3.9	5.4
		(10) 3.1	(12) 4.3			% Depr., Dep., Amort./Sales	(42) 6.7	7.1
		4.8	9.8				12.8	11.5
							3.8	
						% Officers', Directors' Owners' Comp/Sales	(12) 5.9	
							7.9	
2761M	21123M	132248M	339687M	150468M	553278M	Net Sales ($)	682671M	331408M
921M	9170M	61385M	280664M	147546M	472120M	Total Assets ($)	550981M	319516M

M = $ thousand   MM = $ million
See Pages 11 through 21 for Explanation of Ratios and Data

Comparative Historical Data / Current Data Sorted by Sales

Type of Statement	4/1/04-3/31/05 ALL	4/1/05-3/31/06 ALL	4/1/06-3/31/07 ALL	0-1MM	1-3MM	3-5MM	5-10MM	10-25MM	25MM & OVER
Unqualified	8	8	9			1	2		6
Reviewed	3	3	2					2	
Compiled	5	7	3		1	2			
Tax Returns	7	7	7	5	2				
Other	16	21	21	1	2	3	3	7	5
					8 (4/1-9/30/06)		34 (10/1/06-3/31/07)		
NUMBER OF STATEMENTS	39	45	42	6	5	6	5	9	11

ASSETS	%	%	%	%	%	%	%	%	%
Cash & Equivalents	13.6	10.2	11.1						6.5
Trade Receivables (net)	8.1	9.7	7.8						11.7
Inventory	7.3	8.6	10.4						29.4
All Other Current	7.7	7.2	4.2						4.6
Total Current	36.8	35.6	33.4						52.2
Fixed Assets (net)	48.8	50.0	42.3						31.4
Intangibles (net)	2.8	6.9	12.3						5.2
All Other Non-Current	11.6	7.4	12.0						11.1
Total	100.0	100.0	100.0						100.0

LIABILITIES									
Notes Payable-Short Term	4.5	6.5	7.4						8.2
Cur. Mat.-L.T.D.	7.5	5.3	4.3						3.4
Trade Payables	7.7	6.9	8.2						14.1
Income Taxes Payable	.4	.5	.3						.4
All Other Current	14.4	7.3	5.3						9.2
Total Current	34.4	26.6	25.5						35.4
Long-Term Debt	38.9	37.2	41.1						16.1
Deferred Taxes	.7	.2	.3						.7
All Other Non-Current	4.0	1.6	5.2						6.7
Net Worth	22.0	34.4	27.8						41.1
Total Liabilities & Net Worth	100.0	100.0	100.0						100.0

INCOME DATA									
Net Sales	100.0	100.0	100.0						100.0
Gross Profit									
Operating Expenses	91.4	88.5	83.9						89.2
Operating Profit	8.6	11.5	16.1						10.8
All Other Expenses (net)	5.0	1.3	1.9						.5
Profit Before Taxes	3.7	10.3	14.2						10.3

RATIOS									
Current	2.9	2.9	2.6						4.7
	1.2	1.3	1.5						2.2
	.6	.7	.7						1.2
Quick	1.5	1.7	1.7						1.7
	.8	.7	.8						.7
	.2	.3	.5						.4
Sales/Receivables	0 UND	0 999.8	0 UND					17	20.9
	6 58.1	11 33.5	8 44.3					22	16.7
	31 11.9	27 13.7	28 13.2					39	9.4
Cost of Sales/Inventory									
Cost of Sales/Payables									
Sales/Working Capital	5.7	6.9	5.3						4.9
	35.4	20.0	14.1						5.4
	-10.6	-35.9	-27.0						24.3
EBIT/Interest	12.6	15.1	14.6						21.7
	(37) 5.1	5.8	4.6						10.4
	.6	1.5	2.2						2.4
Net Profit + Depr., Dep., Amort./Cur. Mat. L/T/D									
Fixed/Worth	.7	.7	.7						.3
	2.0	1.7	1.8						.8
	-12.6	6.9	-3.9						1.0
Debt/Worth	.9	.6	.9						.4
	3.1	3.4	2.8						3.0
	-17.3	9.7	-16.2						5.5
% Profit Before Taxes/Tangible Net Worth	38.7	98.0	77.5						56.0
	(29) 25.9	(38) 48.6	(30) 36.3					(10)	31.4
	6.4	9.9	8.8						5.1
% Profit Before Taxes/Total Assets	15.6	31.2	27.5						24.4
	7.5	12.3	10.7						18.4
	-1.4	2.5	2.8						2.6
Sales/Net Fixed Assets	6.5	6.2	8.8						9.8
	2.8	3.7	4.8						4.8
	1.6	1.9	2.2						2.8
Sales/Total Assets	1.9	2.6	2.9						2.4
	1.4	1.6	1.5						1.6
	.8	1.0	.8						1.0
% Depr., Dep., Amort./Sales	3.1	3.1	2.0						1.0
	(37) 5.2	(42) 5.2	(36) 3.8					(10)	3.6
	7.0	8.7	8.7						5.6
% Officers', Directors' Owners' Comp/Sales			.5						
		(13)	1.5						
			6.0						
Net Sales ($)	526794M	1265028M	1199565M	4509M	8604M	24936M	38963M	147942M	974611M
Total Assets ($)	436940M	743899M	971806M	3579M	5634M	59700M	62175M	175797M	664921M

Current Data Sorted by Assets   Comparative Historical Data

0-500M	500M-2MM	2-10MM	10-50MM	50-100MM	100-250MM	Type of Statement	2 4/1/02-3/31/03 ALL	1 4/1/03-3/31/04 ALL
						Unqualified	2	1
2	1	4	2			Reviewed	5	3
5	2	3				Compiled	10	11
2	5	1				Tax Returns	16	9
	3	7				Other	6	5
							6 (4/1-9/30/06)	31 (10/1/06-3/31/07)
9	11	15	2			**NUMBER OF STATEMENTS**	39	29
%	%	%	%	%	%	**ASSETS**	%	%
	40.5	7.5	D	D		Cash & Equivalents	10.9	11.9
	14.3	23.6	A	A		Trade Receivables (net)	12.6	11.6
	.9	11.4	T	T		Inventory	14.1	9.4
	4.8	3.8	A	A		All Other Current	6.7	11.1
	60.5	46.4				Total Current	44.4	44.0
	30.0	44.2	N	N		Fixed Assets (net)	38.4	39.8
	6.9	1.2	O	O		Intangibles (net)	8.2	6.4
	2.6	8.2	T	T		All Other Non-Current	9.1	9.8
	100.0	100.0				Total	100.0	100.0
			A	A		**LIABILITIES**		
	9.1	14.5	V	V		Notes Payable-Short Term	13.2	18.9
	3.7	2.4	A	A		Cur. Mat.-L.T.D.	8.7	5.7
	1.9	14.7	I	I		Trade Payables	10.4	10.1
	.0	.0	L	L		Income Taxes Payable	.0	.8
	7.5	6.1	A	A		All Other Current	27.6	18.1
	22.2	37.8	B	B		Total Current	60.0	53.5
	23.1	16.2	L	L		Long-Term Debt	19.8	33.5
	.0	.0	E	E		Deferred Taxes	.7	.0
	2.5	2.6				All Other Non-Current	3.5	3.7
	52.2	43.4				Net Worth	16.0	9.2
	100.0	100.0				Total Liabilities & Net Worth	100.0	100.0
						INCOME DATA		
	100.0	100.0				Net Sales	100.0	100.0
						Gross Profit		
	93.7	91.6				Operating Expenses	91.9	91.5
	6.3	8.4				Operating Profit	8.1	8.5
	-.6	7.0				All Other Expenses (net)	.8	2.5
	6.9	1.3				Profit Before Taxes	7.3	6.0
						RATIOS		
	9.7	2.3					2.4	2.7
	3.2	1.3				Current	1.3	1.3
	2.0	.9					.5	.4
	9.7	1.5					1.5	1.3
	2.7	1.0				Quick	.5	.6
	1.8	.5					.2	.3
0 UND	0 UND						0 UND	0 UND
0 UND	20 18.4					Sales/Receivables	7 53.1	16 22.9
12 30.8	36 10.0					27 13.4	31 11.9
						Cost of Sales/Inventory		
						Cost of Sales/Payables		
	5.2	5.0					12.2	9.3
	9.8	21.3				Sales/Working Capital	61.7	28.0
	32.4	-61.6					-16.0	-17.0
		5.5					15.3	8.2
		(14) 3.0				EBIT/Interest	(35) 3.2	(26) 3.0
		-2.4					1.0	1.1
						Net Profit + Depr., Dep., Amort./Cur. Mat. L/T/D		
	.2	.6					.0	.7
	.6	.9				Fixed/Worth	1.0	1.4
	1.2	1.8					6.9	-1.9
	.2	.8					.7	1.2
	1.0	1.3				Debt/Worth	2.8	7.6
	3.6	4.0					-9.9	-5.5
	86.3	34.8					92.9	95.0
	(10) 60.0	10.5				% Profit Before Taxes/Tangible Net Worth	(28) 39.2	(19) 30.6
	16.3	-13.2					9.0	8.1
	36.6	10.1					25.2	26.1
	18.4	2.9				% Profit Before Taxes/Total Assets	7.3	8.0
	7.4	-9.2					1.0	.2
	77.2	36.4					111.8	20.6
	13.4	3.9				Sales/Net Fixed Assets	20.6	4.8
	8.0	.6					2.6	2.5
	8.4	4.6					3.7	3.4
	3.8	1.7				Sales/Total Assets	2.7	2.1
	1.9	.5					1.4	1.1
		.3					.6	.9
		(13) 2.8				% Depr., Dep., Amort./Sales	(27) 2.9	(24) 4.3
		6.8					12.0	7.7
							1.9	
						% Officers', Directors' Owners' Comp/Sales	(16) 2.5	
							9.3	
6364M	54831M	150259M	53515M			Net Sales ($)	469849M	271697M
1877M	11610M	60897M	70514M			Total Assets ($)	203870M	145882M

M = $ thousand   MM = $ million
See Pages 11 through 21 for Explanation of Ratios and Data

Comparative Historical Data   ## Current Data Sorted by Sales

4/1/04-3/31/05 ALL	4/1/05-3/31/06 ALL	4/1/06-3/31/07 ALL	Type of Statement	0-1MM	1-3MM	3-5MM	5-10MM	10-25MM	25MM & OVER
1			Unqualified				1		
5	3	7	Reviewed	2	3	1	1	3	2
7	5	7	Compiled		2	1		1	
19	9	11	Tax Returns	5	2			2	
10	13	12	Other	3	3	3	2	2	
	10					6 (4/1-9/30/06)		31 (10/1/06-3/31/07)	
42	**40**	**37**	**NUMBER OF STATEMENTS**	**10**	**8**	**4**	**6**	**7**	**2**
%	%	%	ASSETS	%	%	%	%	%	%
10.0	15.1	22.1	Cash & Equivalents	28.3					
8.9	10.9	14.1	Trade Receivables (net)	.2					
8.5	8.2	6.4	Inventory	.0					
4.3	2.8	3.1	All Other Current	1.1					
31.6	37.0	45.7	Total Current	29.6					
51.8	46.3	42.5	Fixed Assets (net)	63.3					
5.6	7.7	4.0	Intangibles (net)	.6					
11.0	9.0	7.8	All Other Non-Current	6.6					
100.0	100.0	100.0	Total	100.0					
			LIABILITIES						
10.8	9.0	9.0	Notes Payable-Short Term	.0					
3.3	2.9	3.1	Cur. Mat.-L.T.D.	3.4					
4.4	6.9	8.3	Trade Payables	.2					
.6	.0	.2	Income Taxes Payable	.0					
14.6	7.5	19.9	All Other Current	51.5					
33.7	26.4	40.5	Total Current	55.0					
31.3	34.4	20.3	Long-Term Debt	20.5					
.2	.1	.4	Deferred Taxes	.0					
2.6	1.3	4.2	All Other Non-Current	9.3					
32.2	37.8	34.6	Net Worth	15.2					
100.0	100.0	100.0	Total Liabilities & Net Worth	100.0					
			INCOME DATA						
100.0	100.0	100.0	Net Sales	100.0					
			Gross Profit						
90.6	90.3	92.5	Operating Expenses	86.5					
9.4	9.7	7.5	Operating Profit	13.5					
1.5	2.9	3.8	All Other Expenses (net)	10.3					
7.9	6.8	3.7	Profit Before Taxes	3.2					
			RATIOS						
2.4	2.4	3.3	Current	5.6					
1.0	1.5	1.7		2.8					
.2	1.0	.9		.0					
1.8	2.0	2.9	Quick	5.1					
.3	1.0	1.2		2.8					
.1	.5	.5		.0					
0 UND	0 UND	0 UND	Sales/Receivables	0 UND					
4 91.7	0 966.1	0 UND		0 UND					
25 14.7	28 13.1	25 14.8		0 UND					
			Cost of Sales/Inventory						
			Cost of Sales/Payables						
8.6	7.1	6.1	Sales/Working Capital	2.2					
NM	28.1	21.3		31.0					
-8.1	-277.4	-61.1		-1.5					
14.5	13.4	7.9	EBIT/Interest						
(41) 3.8	(37) 3.4	(32) 4.0							
1.1	1.7	1.6							
			Net Profit + Depr., Dep., Amort./Cur. Mat. L/T/D						
.7	.9	.5	Fixed/Worth	.9					
1.2	1.3	.9		1.4					
-16.6	6.3	2.2		NM					
.7	.8	.8	Debt/Worth	.6					
1.8	1.9	1.6		1.6					
-18.8	27.5	4.4		NM					
112.3	125.3	78.4	% Profit Before Taxes/Tangible Net Worth						
(31) 19.7	(33) 26.6	(33) 33.8							
9.4	5.5	6.7							
28.8	26.2	25.5	% Profit Before Taxes/Total Assets	49.9					
6.6	7.9	9.4		8.0					
.6	2.5	2.3		-5.1					
15.4	25.9	35.8	Sales/Net Fixed Assets	12.3					
3.9	4.7	8.0		1.7					
1.6	1.5	1.7		.3					
3.1	4.0	5.0	Sales/Total Assets	5.5					
1.9	1.8	2.1		1.4					
.9	.7	.8		.1					
2.5	.8	.7	% Depr., Dep., Amort./Sales						
(35) 5.5	(29) 3.8	(30) 3.9							
8.9	6.9	8.0							
3.1	1.3	.7	% Officers', Directors' Owners' Comp/Sales						
(15) 6.9	(17) 3.2	(17) 1.7							
11.7	7.9	6.7							
154252M	1992771M	264969M	Net Sales ($)	5365M	13315M	17172M	40489M	109671M	78957M
141317M	731205M	144898M	Total Assets ($)	7305M	10414M	14798M	20274M	47604M	44503M

M = $ thousand   MM = $ million
See Pages 11 through 21 for Explanation of Ratios and Data

Current Data Sorted by Assets   **Comparative Historical Data**

	0-500M	500M-2MM	2-10MM	10-50MM	50-100MM	100-250MM		4/1/02-3/31/03	4/1/03-3/31/04
Type of Statement									
Unqualified		7	17	1				36	27
Reviewed		2	8					6	7
Compiled			4					8	15
Tax Returns		4	2					4	
Other			3					7	4
		33 (4/1-9/30/06)		15 (10/1/06-3/31/07)				ALL	ALL
NUMBER OF STATEMENTS	13	13	34	1				61	53
	%	%	%	%	%	%		%	%
ASSETS									
Cash & Equivalents	D	15.6	8.8	D	D			10.9	10.3
Trade Receivables (net)	A	13.4	15.9	A	A			15.2	11.6
Inventory	T	9.3	12.4	T	T			7.7	5.9
All Other Current	A	7.0	5.5	A	A			3.8	10.2
Total Current		45.3	42.6					37.5	38.1
Fixed Assets (net)	N	40.1	48.7	N	N			51.8	51.2
Intangibles (net)	O	.4	.4	O	O			.2	.7
All Other Non-Current	T	14.2	8.3	T	T			10.5	9.9
Total		100.0	100.0					100.0	100.0
LIABILITIES	A			A	A				
Notes Payable-Short Term	V	8.0	8.3	V	V			7.0	7.3
Cur. Mat.-L.T.D.	A	5.5	3.5	A	A			4.3	9.5
Trade Payables	I	7.7	5.3	I	I			6.4	7.3
Income Taxes Payable	L	.3	.1	L	L			.2	.2
All Other Current	A	12.3	9.5	A	A			11.1	10.8
Total Current	B	33.8	26.6	B	B			28.9	34.9
Long-Term Debt	L	14.9	19.0	L	L			17.5	31.8
Deferred Taxes	E	.0	.3	E	E			.0	.0
All Other Non-Current		1.0	1.1					1.3	.9
Net Worth		50.3	53.0					52.3	32.3
Total Liabilities & Net Worth		100.0	100.0					100.0	100.0
INCOME DATA									
Net Sales		100.0	100.0					100.0	100.0
Gross Profit									
Operating Expenses		90.5	87.5					90.5	88.5
Operating Profit		9.5	12.5					9.5	11.5
All Other Expenses (net)		1.2	-.4					.3	2.9
Profit Before Taxes		8.4	13.0					9.2	8.6
RATIOS									
Current		3.2	2.4					2.0	2.0
		2.4	1.4					1.3	1.2
		.8	1.1					1.0	.7
Quick		2.0	1.3					1.4	1.4
		1.0	.9					1.0	.6
		.4	.5					.5	.2
Sales/Receivables	0	UND	11 32.4				7	52.4 2	164.4
	15	24.5	31 11.7				37	9.9 13	27.0
	39	9.4	71 5.1				91	4.0 78	4.7
Cost of Sales/Inventory									
Cost of Sales/Payables									
Sales/Working Capital		5.6	4.1					6.9	4.0
		10.1	9.2					15.8	17.3
		-30.6	32.2					-117.8	-9.2
EBIT/Interest		22.2	28.6					21.0	13.1
	(11)	9.2	5.2				(55)	5.4 (49)	4.7
		2.0	1.8					1.1	1.7
Net Profit + Depr., Dep., Amort./Cur. Mat. L/T/D			19.9					38.2	4.7
		(10)	4.0				(13)	7.5 (13)	2.4
			2.5					2.0	.6
Fixed/Worth		.4	.6					.6	.6
		1.1	.8					.9	1.1
		1.4	1.3					1.6	3.8
Debt/Worth		.4	.4					.4	.5
		.5	1.0					.7	.9
		1.8	1.7					1.7	4.7
% Profit Before Taxes/Tangible Net Worth		46.5	56.3					47.4	43.4
	(12)	20.9	(33) 12.2				(60)	18.5 (48)	10.0
		8.1	4.4					2.6	4.4
% Profit Before Taxes/Total Assets		23.2	28.5					21.1	12.4
		12.7	5.9					6.6	5.4
		6.0	2.1					1.5	1.1
Sales/Net Fixed Assets		12.9	4.7					4.9	5.0
		8.0	2.4					2.7	2.1
		2.6	1.4					1.1	1.0
Sales/Total Assets		2.9	1.4					1.7	1.5
		2.2	1.1					1.2	.8
		1.4	.7					.7	.6
% Depr., Dep., Amort./Sales		1.1	3.0					3.5	3.9
		3.1	5.2				(60)	5.4 (51)	6.1
		8.8	10.0					10.5	11.1
% Officers', Directors' Owners' Comp/Sales									
Net Sales ($)		33795M	217168M	30917M				238442M	242137M
Total Assets ($)		14852M	177602M	16982M				217958M	295007M

M = $ thousand   MM = $ million
See Pages 11 through 21 for Explanation of Ratios and Data

Comparative Historical Data | Current Data Sorted by Sales

Type of Statement	4/1/04-3/31/05 ALL	4/1/05-3/31/06 ALL	4/1/06-3/31/07 ALL	0-1MM	1-3MM	3-5MM	5-10MM	10-25MM	25MM & OVER
Unqualified	26	30	25	2	5	11	1	5	1
Reviewed	9	8	10		3	5	1	1	
Compiled	11	9	4			2	2		
Tax Returns	3	6	6		2	3		1	
Other	4	4	3			1		1	1
				33 (4/1-9/30/06)			15 (10/1/06-3/31/07)		
NUMBER OF STATEMENTS	53	57	48	2	10	22	5	7	2
ASSETS	%	%	%	%	%	%	%	%	%
Cash & Equivalents	11.2	10.3	10.5		13.8	10.2			
Trade Receivables (net)	12.9	13.3	15.1		13.1	12.9			
Inventory	7.8	12.3	12.4		4.5	9.8			
All Other Current	7.7	7.8	5.8		14.9	5.4			
Total Current	39.6	43.7	43.8		46.3	38.4			
Fixed Assets (net)	51.0	46.7	45.9		44.4	50.4			
Intangibles (net)	.2	.3	.4		.3	.6			
All Other Non-Current	9.2	9.3	9.9		9.1	10.6			
Total	100.0	100.0	100.0		100.0	100.0			
LIABILITIES									
Notes Payable-Short Term	7.9	10.7	8.8		8.1	10.5			
Cur. Mat.-L.T.D.	6.2	4.0	4.0		5.3	4.0			
Trade Payables	7.0	8.2	6.0		2.4	4.9			
Income Taxes Payable	.1	.2	.3		.1	.2			
All Other Current	11.6	15.8	10.1		12.5	8.4			
Total Current	32.8	38.9	29.3		28.3	28.0			
Long-Term Debt	16.8	26.1	17.8		5.7	25.9			
Deferred Taxes	.2	.4	.2		.5	.2			
All Other Non-Current	.7	1.6	1.1		.0	1.5			
Net Worth	49.5	33.1	51.6		65.5	44.4			
Total Liabilties & Net Worth	100.0	100.0	100.0		100.0	100.0			
INCOME DATA									
Net Sales	100.0	100.0	100.0		100.0	100.0			
Gross Profit									
Operating Expenses	83.6	88.5	88.5		85.6	90.7			
Operating Profit	16.4	11.5	11.5		14.4	9.3			
All Other Expenses (net)	1.3	.1	.0		-.9	.6			
Profit Before Taxes	15.1	11.4	11.5		15.2	8.7			
RATIOS									
Current	2.5	2.1	2.8		4.3	2.1			
	1.2	1.3	1.5		2.6	1.3			
	.8	.9	1.1		1.2	.9			
Quick	1.5	1.3	1.3		2.4	1.2			
	.8	.6	.9		1.0	.9			
	.4	.3	.5		.4	.4			
Sales/Receivables	9 42.7	5 69.1	8 43.3		0 UND	9 39.0			
	19 19.2	20 18.6	23 15.9		11 32.2	26 14.1			
	73 5.0	52 7.1	50 7.3		42 8.7	36 10.2			
Cost of Sales/Inventory									
Cost of Sales/Payables									
Sales/Working Capital	6.5	4.5	4.4		2.2	6.5			
	16.1	10.2	10.1		6.9	11.1			
	-25.6	-68.6	60.8		NM	-41.1			
EBIT/Interest	47.4	32.4	24.3			18.6			
	(52) 10.5	(54) 8.5	(46) 5.2			2.9			
	2.9	2.2	1.9			1.7			
Net Profit + Depr., Dep., Amort./Cur. Mat. L/T/D	9.4	5.3	10.5						
	(15) 4.4	(13) 2.5	(14) 3.3						
	2.3	1.4	2.1						
Fixed/Worth	.6	.6	.5		.5	.6			
	.9	.9	.8		.6	1.1			
	1.6	1.6	1.3		1.1	1.9			
Debt/Worth	.4	.5	.4		.2	.4			
	.8	1.1	.8		.4	1.3			
	2.3	2.9	1.8		1.1	2.4			
% Profit Before Taxes/Tangible Net Worth	61.0	51.6	50.3		56.7	43.3			
	(50) 29.4	(53) 23.2	(46) 18.6		15.7	(20) 11.5			
	13.9	6.2	4.8		6.4	1.4			
% Profit Before Taxes/Total Assets	24.3	24.1	24.9		41.3	14.7			
	12.4	8.3	6.8		9.7	5.3			
	3.4	2.6	2.4		4.3	.8			
Sales/Net Fixed Assets	5.7	6.4	7.4		5.0	6.4			
	2.3	2.9	3.1		2.4	2.4			
	1.3	1.5	1.6		1.6	1.0			
Sales/Total Assets	1.7	2.3	2.2		1.9	1.8			
	1.1	1.2	1.3		1.2	1.2			
	.8	.8	.8		.8	.7			
% Depr., Dep., Amort./Sales	3.4	2.0	2.7		4.8	3.6			
	(49) 5.8	(54) 4.2	4.7		7.1	5.2			
	9.4	6.7	9.5		11.0	10.9			
% Officers', Directors' Owners' Comp/Sales		1.2							
	(10) 2.5								
	9.8								
Net Sales ($)	215626M	754694M	281880M	1793M	21466M	85666M	28980M	82393M	61582M
Total Assets ($)	188076M	611171M	209436M	1710M	23999M	89180M	29144M	42604M	22799M

© RMA 2007

M = $ thousand   MM = $ million
See Pages 11 through 21 for Explanation of Ratios and Data

Current Data Sorted by Assets   Comparative Historical Data

							Type of Statement		
		1	4	3			Unqualified	7	8
		3	2	1	1		Reviewed	6	6
	2	6	7	2			Compiled	7	17
	10	14	4				Tax Returns	5	13
	1	1	1	1		2	Other	13	16
		21 (4/1-9/30/06)		45 (10/1/06-3/31/07)				4/1/02-3/31/03	4/1/03-3/31/04
	0-500M	500M-2MM	2-10MM	10-50MM	50-100MM	100-250MM		ALL	ALL
	13	25	18	7	1	2	NUMBER OF STATEMENTS	38	60
	%	%	%	%	%	%	ASSETS	%	%
	22.7	11.6	9.4				Cash & Equivalents	6.6	7.4
	7.8	18.3	17.3				Trade Receivables (net)	21.5	17.2
	5.2	5.9	24.4				Inventory	11.8	15.3
	16.3	2.0	3.6				All Other Current	5.0	5.4
	52.0	37.8	54.8				Total Current	45.0	45.2
	37.2	49.8	36.5				Fixed Assets (net)	43.7	44.5
	3.4	3.1	.6				Intangibles (net)	1.4	4.3
	7.4	9.3	8.1				All Other Non-Current	9.9	6.0
	100.0	100.0	100.0				Total	100.0	100.0
							LIABILITIES		
	24.2	16.1	18.0				Notes Payable-Short Term	14.2	21.0
	9.2	5.7	5.1				Cur. Mat.-L.T.D.	3.6	6.1
	9.5	9.0	16.3				Trade Payables	8.5	8.0
	.0	.1	.0				Income Taxes Payable	.3	.5
	6.2	6.2	7.6				All Other Current	8.3	6.5
	49.2	37.2	47.1				Total Current	34.8	42.0
	35.2	31.3	14.2				Long-Term Debt	24.7	34.6
	.0	.5	.1				Deferred Taxes	1.1	.5
	7.5	11.4	2.2				All Other Non-Current	2.0	1.7
	8.2	19.7	36.4				Net Worth	37.4	21.2
	100.0	100.0	100.0				Total Liabilties & Net Worth	100.0	100.0
							INCOME DATA		
	100.0	100.0	100.0				Net Sales	100.0	100.0
							Gross Profit		
	98.8	96.1	94.4				Operating Expenses	94.7	95.4
	1.2	3.9	5.6				Operating Profit	5.3	4.6
	1.0	.9	2.0				All Other Expenses (net)	1.5	1.0
	.2	3.0	3.6				Profit Before Taxes	3.8	3.6
							RATIOS		
	6.2	2.5	3.9					2.0	2.0
	1.0	.9	1.1				Current	1.2	1.4
	.5	.5	.7					.8	.9
	2.2	2.4	2.3					1.2	1.4
	.5	.7	.4				Quick	.8	.8
	.2	.3	.3					.5	.4
	0 UND	0 UND	13 27.2					8 47.3	9 41.1
	0 UND	13 29.1	18 20.5				Sales/Receivables	41 8.9	30 12.1
	11 32.1	54 6.8	46 7.9					80 4.5	61 6.0
							Cost of Sales/Inventory		
							Cost of Sales/Payables		
	7.5	9.6	5.2					7.1	6.9
	193.3	-53.0	58.0				Sales/Working Capital	24.0	20.0
	-19.3	-9.6	-12.3					-41.4	-38.3
	6.2	7.5	10.6					10.5	5.5
(10)	2.6	(23) 2.4	2.9				EBIT/Interest	(35) 2.3	(56) 2.6
	-.3	1.2	1.1					1.3	1.1
							Net Profit + Depr., Dep.,		6.8
							Amort./Cur. Mat. L/T/D	(16)	2.6
									1.8
	.2	.6	.4					.5	.5
	9.8	3.8	1.5				Fixed/Worth	1.0	1.8
	-2.1	-6.8	3.0					2.0	21.2
	.7	1.4	.4					.7	.8
	22.2	5.0	2.8				Debt/Worth	1.5	2.5
	-6.6	-9.5	6.7					2.9	49.0
		73.0	53.6				% Profit Before Taxes/Tangible	25.8	37.7
	(18)	23.3	(17) 26.8				Net Worth	(32) 6.8	(46) 14.4
		-3.1	1.7					2.4	2.7
	32.7	14.8	13.2				% Profit Before Taxes/Total	10.4	9.5
	16.2	2.7	6.0				Assets	4.8	5.1
	-.7	-2.3	.6					.6	.3
	108.9	10.3	17.4					11.1	11.4
	11.4	5.3	7.2				Sales/Net Fixed Assets	4.4	4.6
	6.0	2.2	4.2					1.9	2.4
	7.1	3.3	2.7					2.2	2.7
	4.6	2.5	2.2				Sales/Total Assets	1.6	1.9
	2.0	1.3	1.4					1.2	1.3
		3.4	1.5					1.9	2.3
	(22)	5.8	(17) 3.8				% Depr., Dep., Amort./Sales	(34) 4.2	(50) 4.9
		12.1	6.1					8.2	11.0
		3.7					% Officers', Directors'	4.6	2.9
	(13)	7.4					Owners' Comp/Sales	(10) 7.1	(18) 5.0
		9.9						13.9	17.0
	18012M	66790M	207375M	264808M	56119M	397962M	Net Sales ($)	435590M	813749M
	3784M	25041M	89110M	153788M	53255M	257585M	Total Assets ($)	307145M	607512M

M = $ thousand   MM = $ million
See Pages 11 through 21 for Explanation of Ratios and Data

Comparative Historical Data / Current Data Sorted by Sales

4/1/04-3/31/05 ALL	4/1/05-3/31/06 ALL	4/1/06-3/31/07 ALL	Type of Statement	0-1MM	1-3MM	3-5MM	5-10MM	10-25MM	25MM & OVER
7	11	8	Unqualified		2		1	2	3
3	5	7	Reviewed		2		1	2	2
17	11	17	Compiled	1	6	1	5	2	1
14	17	28	Tax Returns	9	12	2	2	2	
8	9	6	Other	1	1	3			3
				21 (4/1-9/30/06)		45 (10/1/06-3/31/07)			
49	53	66	**NUMBER OF STATEMENTS**	11	23	6	9	8	9
%	%	%	**ASSETS**	%	%	%	%	%	%
14.7	12.0	13.3	Cash & Equivalents	17.8	12.2				
13.0	14.3	16.2	Trade Receivables (net)	8.1	15.6				
13.5	14.9	14.0	Inventory	2.0	5.2				
4.9	3.9	5.3	All Other Current	6.4	7.9				
46.1	45.2	48.8	Total Current	34.4	41.0				
44.3	44.4	39.0	Fixed Assets (net)	54.0	46.7				
3.2	2.2	2.9	Intangibles (net)	6.6	2.4				
6.4	8.2	9.4	All Other Non-Current	5.1	9.9				
100.0	100.0	100.0	Total	100.0	100.0				
			LIABILITIES						
15.8	12.0	16.8	Notes Payable-Short Term	29.7	17.7				
6.6	5.6	5.7	Cur. Mat.-L.T.D.	6.2	7.3				
8.0	7.0	10.8	Trade Payables	8.2	9.8				
.3	.2	.2	Income Taxes Payable	.0	.1				
8.9	7.5	8.0	All Other Current	3.7	6.1				
39.7	32.4	41.6	Total Current	47.8	41.1				
34.2	25.5	23.8	Long-Term Debt	52.2	23.7				
.4	.4	.3	Deferred Taxes	.0	.6				
5.0	4.4	7.2	All Other Non-Current	6.6	9.7				
20.7	37.5	27.1	Net Worth	-6.5	25.0				
100.0	100.0	100.0	Total Liabilities & Net Worth	100.0	100.0				
			INCOME DATA						
100.0	100.0	100.0	Net Sales	100.0	100.0				
			Gross Profit						
97.8	97.4	95.5	Operating Expenses	97.4	95.6				
2.2	2.6	4.5	Operating Profit	2.6	4.4				
-.3	.1	1.1	All Other Expenses (net)	3.5	2.0				
2.5	2.6	3.4	Profit Before Taxes	-.9	2.4				
			RATIOS						
3.2	3.2	3.6	Current	2.4	4.6				
1.3	1.5	1.1	Current	.7	.9				
.7	1.0	.7	Current	.3	.5				
1.7	2.6	2.0	Quick	2.4	1.6				
.8	.8	.7	Quick	.7	.5				
.3	.4	.3	Quick	.1	.3				
0 UND	1 696.2	1 439.6	Sales/Receivables	0 UND	0 UND				
17 21.4	26 13.9	17 21.4	Sales/Receivables	0 UND	10 38.1				
52 7.0	54 6.8	46 7.9	Sales/Receivables	36 10.1	26 14.0				
			Cost of Sales/Inventory						
			Cost of Sales/Payables						
4.9	5.2	6.8	Sales/Working Capital	7.0	8.0				
18.2	14.2	38.8	Sales/Working Capital	-16.2	-53.0				
-24.8	-230.1	-15.5	Sales/Working Capital	-7.4	-5.6				
7.1	5.2	8.9	EBIT/Interest		7.5				
(43) 2.1	(47) 1.6	(60) 3.0	EBIT/Interest		(20) 2.0				
.5	.1	1.2	EBIT/Interest		1.0				
6.2	5.6	15.2	Net Profit + Depr., Dep., Amort./Cur. Mat. L/T/D						
(12) 3.1	(12) 1.8	(10) 5.1	Net Profit + Depr., Dep., Amort./Cur. Mat. L/T/D						
1.4	.8	2.3	Net Profit + Depr., Dep., Amort./Cur. Mat. L/T/D						
.5	.6	.4	Fixed/Worth	3.4	.4				
1.4	1.5	2.1	Fixed/Worth	18.1	3.6				
8.9	4.3	11.5	Fixed/Worth	-1.1	21.3				
.7	.6	.8	Debt/Worth	2.5	1.5				
1.7	2.1	4.0	Debt/Worth	29.2	4.0				
14.3	7.9	32.4	Debt/Worth	-3.2	52.8				
22.4	39.8	71.5	% Profit Before Taxes/Tangible Net Worth		88.0				
(40) 5.5	(49) 12.2	(54) 28.7	% Profit Before Taxes/Tangible Net Worth		(18) 24.3				
-1.4	-7.4	6.8	% Profit Before Taxes/Tangible Net Worth		3.4				
5.6	9.8	17.4	% Profit Before Taxes/Total Assets	14.8	20.9				
2.5	3.1	7.5	% Profit Before Taxes/Total Assets	1.3	2.9				
-.6	-2.2	.9	% Profit Before Taxes/Total Assets	-22.6	.1				
12.1	9.9	19.3	Sales/Net Fixed Assets	5.7	32.8				
5.7	5.9	7.6	Sales/Net Fixed Assets	2.8	6.7				
2.2	2.7	3.7	Sales/Net Fixed Assets	1.6	3.7				
2.9	2.6	3.2	Sales/Total Assets	1.9	5.0				
1.8	1.9	2.2	Sales/Total Assets	1.3	3.0				
1.3	1.3	1.5	Sales/Total Assets	.7	1.7				
2.7	2.6	1.7	% Depr., Dep., Amort./Sales	3.9	3.5				
(41) 5.3	(46) 4.6	(57) 3.9	% Depr., Dep., Amort./Sales	(10) 13.9	(17) 4.7				
12.5	7.1	7.2	% Depr., Dep., Amort./Sales	24.0	10.1				
1.6	2.1	2.5	% Officers', Directors' Owners' Comp/Sales	4.5	3.5				
(20) 5.9	(22) 6.9	(29) 5.0	% Officers', Directors' Owners' Comp/Sales	(10) 7.0	(10) 6.8				
18.8	14.6	8.8	% Officers', Directors' Owners' Comp/Sales	11.8	9.9				
427969M	1239572M	1011066M	Net Sales ($)	7107M	46691M	24287M	62495M	128650M	741836M
305144M	566282M	582563M	Total Assets ($)	6138M	22246M	16799M	24780M	73292M	439308M

M = $ thousand   MM = $ million
See Pages 11 through 21 for Explanation of Ratios and Data

Current Data Sorted by Assets   Comparative Historical Data

Type of Statement	0-500M	500M-2MM	2-10MM	10-50MM	50-100MM	100-250MM		4/1/02-3/31/03 ALL	4/1/03-3/31/04 ALL
Unqualified	1	1	14	27	9	9		35	50
Reviewed	2	3	26	22				58	52
Compiled	3	9	14	13	1	1		45	57
Tax Returns	6	8	4			1		19	24
Other	2	12	18	17	4	2		36	39
		106 (4/1-9/30/06)		123 (10/1/06-3/31/07)					
NUMBER OF STATEMENTS	14	33	76	79	14	13		193	222
ASSETS	%	%	%	%	%	%		%	%
Cash & Equivalents	18.3	8.5	6.7	6.2	4.9	6.7		8.3	9.1
Trade Receivables (net)	24.9	18.0	24.0	21.0	17.3	18.4		21.4	19.5
Inventory	10.6	12.3	22.5	26.9	19.4	18.2		13.8	15.5
All Other Current	7.5	6.0	5.6	6.4	7.9	5.7		6.1	6.4
Total Current	61.3	44.7	58.9	60.5	49.5	49.0		49.5	50.5
Fixed Assets (net)	26.6	44.4	32.3	32.2	34.4	42.6		41.9	39.4
Intangibles (net)	.0	1.6	1.4	.6	1.7	2.8		.8	1.1
All Other Non-Current	12.0	9.3	7.4	6.7	14.4	5.5		7.8	9.0
Total	100.0	100.0	100.0	100.0	100.0	100.0		100.0	100.0
LIABILITIES									
Notes Payable-Short Term	10.6	14.4	15.7	17.7	15.7	6.3		15.7	14.4
Cur. Mat.-L.T.D.	4.0	4.6	3.1	2.6	1.9	4.7		4.3	3.2
Trade Payables	37.8	7.0	19.5	16.4	9.3	17.1		13.3	11.9
Income Taxes Payable	.0	.0	.1	.3	.3	.1		.2	.3
All Other Current	12.8	10.6	10.2	10.0	9.5	9.6		9.2	12.7
Total Current	65.1	36.6	48.6	46.9	36.8	37.7		42.7	42.5
Long-Term Debt	42.5	26.3	14.8	16.9	13.3	27.0		21.4	21.5
Deferred Taxes	.0	.5	.5	.8	1.6	.9		.6	.4
All Other Non-Current	5.6	5.4	3.9	3.3	3.1	1.5		4.0	6.1
Net Worth	-13.3	31.2	32.3	32.1	45.2	32.9		31.3	29.5
Total Liabilities & Net Worth	100.0	100.0	100.0	100.0	100.0	100.0		100.0	100.0
INCOME DATA									
Net Sales	100.0	100.0	100.0	100.0	100.0	100.0		100.0	100.0
Gross Profit									
Operating Expenses	99.8	93.0	94.0	93.4	88.5	86.5		92.8	93.5
Operating Profit	.2	7.0	6.0	6.6	11.5	13.5		7.2	6.5
All Other Expenses (net)	.4	.3	.4	1.4	.2	7.1		1.2	1.5
Profit Before Taxes	-.1	6.6	5.5	5.2	11.3	6.4		6.0	5.0
RATIOS									
Current	2.4	2.8	1.6	1.7	1.8	1.7		1.9	2.0
	1.4	1.6	1.2	1.3	1.3	1.4		1.2	1.2
	.4	.7	1.0	1.1	1.1	.9		.9	1.0
Quick	1.9	2.0	1.0	.9	.9	.8		1.2	1.2
	.9	.8	.6	.6	.6	.5		.7	.7
	.3	.2	.4	.3	.4	.4		.4	.3
Sales/Receivables	0 UND	0 UND	14 26.1	21 17.4	21 17.6	28 13.1		13 28.4	9 38.5
	6 57.9	14 25.5	34 10.8	35 10.3	31 11.9	33 11.2		33 11.2	30 12.0
	22 16.7	35 10.3	69 5.3	62 5.9	50 7.3	48 7.6		53 6.8	52 7.0
Cost of Sales/Inventory									
Cost of Sales/Payables									
Sales/Working Capital	15.6	5.5	6.5	5.7	10.1	5.7		7.6	6.8
	144.5	16.2	23.8	13.0	19.0	22.1		20.3	19.5
	-30.9	-18.0	NM	50.8	NM	NM		-63.0	-141.2
EBIT/Interest	22.3	8.2	6.0	8.3	8.2	17.8		8.3	7.5
	(10) 2.7	(31) 2.9	(71) 2.4	(77) 3.0	(13) 3.6	6.1		(181) 3.2	(197) 3.1
	-10.9	1.0	1.2	1.4	2.5	1.8		1.1	1.0
Net Profit + Depr., Dep., Amort./Cur. Mat. L/T/D			9.1	9.1				4.4	4.3
			(23) 3.2	(29) 3.7				(55) 2.5	(55) 2.1
			1.1	1.3				1.2	1.0
Fixed/Worth	.0	.5	.5	.5	.4	.6		.6	.5
	.6	1.1	1.0	.9	1.0	1.2		1.1	1.1
	1.1	13.1	1.7	1.5	1.2	2.2		2.3	2.5
Debt/Worth	.5	.7	1.2	1.2	.7	1.0		.8	.8
	1.3	1.6	2.3	2.0	1.8	2.0		1.8	1.9
	-67.2	23.3	7.4	4.1	2.5	3.3		4.0	6.1
% Profit Before Taxes/Tangible Net Worth	68.1	95.3	34.1	31.0	33.9	39.6		39.9	28.6
	(10) 11.4	(27) 15.5	(75) 13.5	(74) 19.0	(12) 17.5	25.2		(169) 16.2	(193) 15.0
	-16.0	2.1	3.2	6.3	5.5	7.5		4.9	3.0
% Profit Before Taxes/Total Assets	49.8	14.3	8.3	12.4	13.6	14.2		13.1	10.6
	4.5	5.3	4.8	5.4	8.5	8.0		5.3	4.2
	-25.1	-.4	.6	1.2	3.2	3.6		.4	.1
Sales/Net Fixed Assets	314.8	12.7	14.4	14.4	13.3	8.3		12.7	11.8
	29.5	7.4	6.7	6.0	6.0	3.5		4.6	5.7
	11.4	3.5	3.4	2.6	2.8	2.4		2.0	2.1
Sales/Total Assets	15.9	3.9	2.8	2.9	2.7	2.6		2.8	2.9
	5.6	2.5	1.8	1.5	1.6	1.9		1.7	1.7
	3.0	1.3	1.0	.9	.9	1.2		.9	1.0
% Depr., Dep., Amort./Sales	.3	1.3	1.2	1.1	.6	1.4		1.3	1.2
	(11) .9	(29) 3.5	(72) 2.3	(73) 1.9	(10) 1.5	1.7		(181) 2.8	(202) 3.1
	1.8	6.0	4.0	4.4	2.7	5.2		6.5	6.0
% Officers', Directors' Owners' Comp/Sales		1.9	1.9		.4			1.5	1.0
		(13) 3.9	(21) 1.8	(12) 1.3				(48) 3.6	(54) 3.0
		8.5	2.8	3.1				7.0	6.1
Net Sales ($)	30690M	124636M	829709M	3052581M	1773094M	4469126M		6886829M	6118768M
Total Assets ($)	3832M	41046M	391829M	1630485M	944722M	2172555M		3857984M	3193478M

M = $ thousand   MM = $ million
See Pages 11 through 21 for Explanation of Ratios and Data

Comparative Historical Data   **Current Data Sorted by Sales**

Type of Statement								
Unqualified	56	41	61		3	2	9	10	37
Reviewed	52	46	53	1	3	5	7	20	17
Compiled	49	32	41	2	7	6	10	8	8
Tax Returns	22	12	19	5	4	8	1		1
Other	48	77	55	2	10	4	11	12	16

	4/1/04-3/31/05 ALL	4/1/05-3/31/06 ALL	4/1/06-3/31/07 ALL	106 (4/1-9/30/06) 0-1MM	1-3MM	3-5MM	123 (10/1/06-3/31/07) 5-10MM	10-25MM	25MM & OVER
NUMBER OF STATEMENTS	227	208	229	10	27	25	38	50	79
ASSETS	%	%	%	%	%	%	%	%	%
Cash & Equivalents	8.4	7.7	7.4	18.5	8.6	8.8	7.8	5.6	6.0
Trade Receivables (net)	20.4	19.4	21.5	7.3	20.5	20.9	19.2	23.1	23.8
Inventory	17.6	19.1	21.4	6.2	12.9	15.0	22.8	25.2	25.1
All Other Current	6.8	6.0	6.2	2.3	8.9	5.1	5.7	6.7	6.0
Total Current	53.1	52.1	56.4	34.2	50.7	49.9	55.5	60.7	60.9
Fixed Assets (net)	38.4	39.8	34.4	41.7	40.2	37.7	36.5	32.4	30.7
Intangibles (net)	1.7	1.6	1.2	.0	3.1	.5	.5	.9	1.3
All Other Non-Current	6.8	6.6	8.1	24.0	5.9	11.8	7.5	6.0	7.1
Total	100.0	100.0	100.0	100.0	100.0	100.0	100.0	100.0	100.0
LIABILITIES									
Notes Payable-Short Term	14.4	14.7	15.3	2.5	9.5	22.0	13.2	19.5	15.3
Cur. Mat.-L.T.D.	4.3	5.0	3.2	4.1	3.2	3.6	3.0	3.5	2.8
Trade Payables	14.5	14.2	17.0	38.6	10.4	11.2	18.2	15.9	18.5
Income Taxes Payable	.2	.3	.1	.0	.0	.0	.0	.2	.3
All Other Current	11.0	10.9	10.3	2.6	13.1	12.4	13.0	8.7	9.2
Total Current	44.4	45.1	45.9	47.9	36.2	49.2	47.5	47.8	46.1
Long-Term Debt	20.1	22.7	19.5	67.5	21.4	15.4	22.4	13.2	16.6
Deferred Taxes	.6	.6	.7	.0	.0	.9	1.0	.6	.8
All Other Non-Current	4.9	3.2	3.8	1.3	5.5	1.9	4.3	5.0	3.1
Net Worth	30.0	28.4	30.1	-16.7	36.9	32.6	24.8	33.5	33.4
Total Liabilities & Net Worth	100.0	100.0	100.0	100.0	100.0	100.0	100.0	100.0	100.0
INCOME DATA									
Net Sales	100.0	100.0	100.0	100.0	100.0	100.0	100.0	100.0	100.0
Gross Profit									
Operating Expenses	93.7	92.7	93.2	91.4	88.9	95.4	94.7	94.5	92.7
Operating Profit	6.3	7.3	6.8	8.6	11.1	4.6	5.3	5.5	7.3
All Other Expenses (net)	1.4	1.8	1.1	1.8	.7	2.2	.3	.7	1.5
Profit Before Taxes	4.9	5.5	5.6	6.8	10.3	2.4	4.9	4.8	5.7
RATIOS									
Current	1.8	1.7	1.8	2.8	2.6	1.8	1.6	1.5	1.7
	1.2	1.2	1.2	2.1	1.7	1.1	1.2	1.2	1.3
	1.0	1.0	1.0	.3	1.0	.9	1.0	1.1	1.1
Quick	1.1	1.1	1.0	1.9	1.8	1.0	1.0	.8	.9
	.7	.6	.6	1.0	.9	.6	.5	.6	.6
	.4	.3	.4	.3	.2	.3	.2	.4	.4
Sales/Receivables	12 30.0	7 52.0	14 26.1	0 UND	2 157.0	3 109.3	5 72.0	14 25.3	22 16.7
	31 11.7	29 12.4	32 11.5	0 UND	26 14.0	35 10.3	26 14.3	40 9.1	32 11.5
	48 7.6	47 7.7	54 6.7	15 23.9	42 8.7	92 4.0	54 6.7	75 4.8	48 7.5
Cost of Sales/Inventory									
Cost of Sales/Payables									
Sales/Working Capital	9.4	7.5	6.6	5.5	2.3	8.9	11.3	8.1	5.8
	21.9	21.4	17.3	13.3	7.7	57.8	21.0	18.0	16.7
	-156.8	-128.3	NM	-30.9	-36.4	-23.9	113.6	NM	101.1
EBIT/Interest	9.0	7.9	7.5		15.7	4.4	6.4	8.8	9.0
	(204) 3.2	(193) 3.5	(215) 2.9	(23) 4.4	(23) 1.6	(34) 2.6	2.6	(78) 3.5
	1.3	1.3	1.3		1.8	.8	1.7	1.1	1.6
Net Profit + Depr., Dep., Amort./Cur. Mat. L/T/D	5.3	3.9	9.1					6.6	11.4
	(59) 2.5	(59) 2.4	(71) 3.2				(14) 3.0	(34) 3.5
	1.0	1.7	1.3					.7	1.8
Fixed/Worth	.5	.6	.5	.0	.4	.6	.5	.5	.4
	1.1	1.2	.9	.9	.8	1.0	1.3	1.0	.9
	2.4	2.7	1.7	4.1	2.4	2.0	2.2	1.6	1.4
Debt/Worth	.9	1.0	1.1	.3	.6	.8	1.3	1.3	1.1
	2.3	2.2	2.0	.8	1.6	1.6	2.1	2.2	2.1
	5.7	8.9	4.7	NM	3.6	19.5	9.9	4.3	3.8
% Profit Before Taxes/Tangible Net Worth	41.2	42.8	32.8		32.5	23.3	38.6	43.1	35.1
	(202) 14.7	(181) 19.9	(212) 17.6	(22) 15.7	(22) 5.8	(37) 17.3	(48) 18.8	(75) 21.8
	3.3	6.2	4.8		5.3	-1.1	7.7	3.3	7.1
% Profit Before Taxes/Total Assets	11.0	12.9	12.4	11.5	18.3	5.7	10.8	11.1	13.9
	4.7	5.9	5.3	-5.7	8.9	.9	5.3	5.6	7.1
	.6	1.0	.8	-29.8	3.5	-1.3	1.8	.5	2.5
Sales/Net Fixed Assets	14.0	13.5	14.5	UND	11.1	12.5	13.2	13.0	16.3
	6.6	6.1	7.0	14.9	5.0	6.1	7.0	5.8	8.5
	2.3	2.4	3.0	1.0	1.6	3.5	2.8	3.0	3.4
Sales/Total Assets	3.1	3.4	3.0	8.0	2.8	3.3	3.1	2.6	3.5
	1.9	1.9	1.8	1.6	1.4	1.5	1.9	1.7	2.0
	1.1	1.1	1.0	.3	.6	1.0	1.0	1.0	1.3
% Depr., Dep., Amort./Sales	1.1	1.2	1.0		1.3	1.6	1.0	1.3	.6
	(204) 2.3	(184) 2.4	(209) 1.9	(24) 3.7	(24) 3.3	(34) 2.6	(46) 2.3	(73) 1.3
	5.2	5.5	4.2		8.2	4.3	4.7	4.7	2.5
% Officers', Directors' Owners' Comp/Sales	.9	1.0	1.1			1.9		.5	.5
	(51) 1.9	(46) 2.1	(53) 2.1	(10) 2.8		(13) 1.2	(13) 2.1
	4.6	4.6	4.3			8.2		1.9	3.5
Net Sales ($)	6968841M	8840560M	10279836M	5267M	50101M	99375M	282642M	780972M	9061479M
Total Assets ($)	3752501M	4349892M	5184469M	6800M	64420M	97493M	186844M	562792M	4266120M

© RMA 2007

M = $ thousand   MM = $ million

See Pages 11 through 21 for Explanation of Ratios and Data

Current Data Sorted by Assets							Comparative Historical Data	
	1	4	5	3	1	Unqualified	10	10
	2	3	2			Reviewed	12	3
4	6	4	1			Compiled	10	14
12	12	4				Tax Returns	14	15
2	4	1	3		1	Other	10	10
	20 (4/1-9/30/06)		55 (10/1/06-3/31/07)				4/1/02-3/31/03 ALL	4/1/03-3/31/04 ALL
0-500M	500M-2MM	2-10MM	10-50MM	50-100MM	100-250MM	NUMBER OF STATEMENTS	56	52
18	25	16	11	3	2			
%	%	%	%	%	%	**ASSETS**	%	%
19.4	11.7	5.6	7.1			Cash & Equivalents	11.7	8.9
18.4	21.0	21.5	13.5			Trade Receivables (net)	18.0	20.8
10.9	20.1	17.8	16.6			Inventory	21.7	18.6
3.6	1.4	1.8	2.7			All Other Current	4.5	4.6
52.2	54.2	46.8	39.9			Total Current	55.9	52.9
27.3	38.1	38.8	44.5			Fixed Assets (net)	32.5	38.0
3.9	2.5	.8	6.2			Intangibles (net)	3.0	2.3
16.6	5.2	13.6	9.4			All Other Non-Current	8.5	6.8
100.0	100.0	100.0	100.0			Total	100.0	100.0
						LIABILITIES		
22.3	9.7	12.6	9.2			Notes Payable-Short Term	15.4	11.9
6.4	1.4	4.4	1.1			Cur. Mat.-L.T.D.	3.4	3.2
9.9	9.1	15.1	10.7			Trade Payables	15.1	12.7
.1	.0	.4	.4			Income Taxes Payable	.0	.3
35.7	5.1	8.2	9.8			All Other Current	9.1	13.9
74.3	25.3	40.8	31.2			Total Current	43.0	42.1
41.8	22.7	18.0	11.9			Long-Term Debt	24.8	27.3
.0	.1	.0	.9			Deferred Taxes	.5	.2
8.6	4.0	2.3	1.2			All Other Non-Current	5.2	2.3
-24.8	47.8	38.8	54.8			Net Worth	26.6	28.1
100.0	100.0	100.0	100.0			Total Liabilities & Net Worth	100.0	100.0
						INCOME DATA		
100.0	100.0	100.0	100.0			Net Sales	100.0	100.0
						Gross Profit		
97.6	94.2	86.9	87.9			Operating Expenses	95.1	95.1
2.4	5.8	13.1	12.1			Operating Profit	4.9	4.9
2.2	2.8	2.4	.3			All Other Expenses (net)	2.0	1.5
.2	2.9	10.7	11.8			Profit Before Taxes	2.9	3.5
						RATIOS		
1.7	8.9	2.3	2.4				3.2	2.7
.8	1.8	1.0	1.4			Current	1.6	1.4
.2	.6	.7	1.3				1.0	.9
1.0	6.6	1.5	1.4				1.5	1.7
.5	1.2	.6	.8			Quick	.8	.9
.2	.3	.3	.3				.3	.2
0 UND	0 UND	16 22.9	2 195.5				3 106.4	4 82.1
2 170.2	22 17.0	36 10.3	20 17.9			Sales/Receivables	27 13.5	26 14.2
21 17.1	58 6.3	41 9.0	55 6.7				47 7.8	63 5.8
						Cost of Sales/Inventory		
						Cost of Sales/Payables		
9.1	4.3	5.2	3.0				5.3	5.4
-70.1	11.5	NM	5.4			Sales/Working Capital	12.1	16.6
-6.5	-15.0	-10.9	49.0				186.7	-25.0
12.3	7.7	7.8	19.7				7.0	5.5
(14) 1.8	(19) 2.9	(11) 3.4	5.6			EBIT/Interest	(45) 2.4	(41) 2.5
-2.8	1.7	1.6	2.3				.5	.7
						Net Profit + Depr., Dep., Amort./Cur. Mat. L/T/D		5.5
								(10) 2.7
								.3
.1	.1	.3	.5				.4	.5
UND	.7	1.2	.8			Fixed/Worth	.9	1.1
-.7	2.1	3.3	2.7				3.5	6.7
4.4	.4	.5	.3				.7	.8
UND	1.7	2.0	2.3			Debt/Worth	1.4	2.0
-3.4	3.2	13.1	3.6				10.0	11.8
	34.3	35.1	49.9				41.0	48.1
	(24) 11.3	(14) 15.2	18.5			% Profit Before Taxes/Tangible Net Worth	(49) 9.4	(43) 8.7
	1.9	3.8	9.4				-5.8	.0
12.6	11.0	14.5	11.9				11.2	16.8
5.1	4.2	5.4	9.5			% Profit Before Taxes/Total Assets	4.5	2.6
-23.1	1.2	1.5	4.0				-2.0	-.4
UND	24.8	14.6	7.6				20.6	15.9
28.7	8.3	4.6	-3.0			Sales/Net Fixed Assets	10.5	6.2
6.0	1.4	2.3	.7				3.0	2.3
6.6	2.8	3.3	2.7				3.2	3.3
2.8	2.0	1.7	.7			Sales/Total Assets	2.1	2.0
2.1	.8	.9	.4				1.3	1.1
.9	.3	1.4	1.7				1.4	1.6
(13) 1.4	(22) 2.9	(14) 2.4	5.3			% Depr., Dep., Amort./Sales	(50) 2.7	(41) 2.9
3.0	5.9	4.9	9.9				6.2	9.1
2.1	1.4						4.0	2.9
(12) 9.2	(12) 4.0					% Officers', Directors' Owners' Comp/Sales	(19) 6.2	(18) 5.0
16.6	12.8						17.1	9.7
21115M	97051M	123483M	499208M	366772M	784830M	Net Sales ($)	565441M	605596M
3870M	25910M	58311M	269562M	198368M	398612M	Total Assets ($)	355361M	394772M

© RMA 2007

M = $ thousand   MM = $ million
See Pages 11 through 21 for Explanation of Ratios and Data

Comparative Historical Data | Current Data Sorted by Sales

Type of Statement									
Unqualified	14	13	14	1	1		1	4	7
Reviewed	6	6	7		2	1	2		2
Compiled	16	11	15	6	6	3			
Tax Returns	24	14	28	12	7	4	2	2	1
Other	9	14	11	4	2	1			3
	4/1/04-3/31/05 ALL	4/1/05-3/31/06 ALL	4/1/06-3/31/07 ALL	20 (4/1-9/30/06)			55 (10/1/06-3/31/07)		
				0-1MM	1-3MM	3-5MM	5-10MM	10-25MM	25MM & OVER
NUMBER OF STATEMENTS	69	58	75	23	18	9	6	6	13
ASSETS	%	%	%	%	%	%	%	%	%
Cash & Equivalents	9.8	14.9	11.0	17.3	9.9				5.3
Trade Receivables (net)	21.3	18.7	19.5	7.5	31.1				21.1
Inventory	10.0	17.6	16.4	6.7	15.7				19.7
All Other Current	3.9	3.8	2.9	2.4	1.8				6.4
Total Current	44.9	55.0	49.8	34.0	58.7				52.5
Fixed Assets (net)	40.0	33.9	36.3	48.0	27.3				32.8
Intangibles (net)	3.6	2.8	3.4	3.0	2.8				8.1
All Other Non-Current	11.5	8.3	10.4	15.0	11.3				6.5
Total	100.0	100.0	100.0	100.0	100.0				100.0
LIABILITIES									
Notes Payable-Short Term	9.4	11.4	13.3	4.7	7.4				17.5
Cur. Mat.-L.T.D.	3.3	1.8	3.6	4.5	1.6				3.2
Trade Payables	8.8	12.2	10.9	6.4	9.6				10.2
Income Taxes Payable	.3	.4	.2	.0	.4				.5
All Other Current	16.1	10.5	13.9	23.7	10.7				7.7
Total Current	38.0	36.3	42.0	39.4	29.6				39.1
Long-Term Debt	34.2	19.3	24.5	47.7	11.2				13.8
Deferred Taxes	.6	.4	.2	.0	.0				1.0
All Other Non-Current	2.0	5.5	4.1	3.3	10.5				2.5
Net Worth	25.2	38.5	29.1	9.6	48.7				43.5
Total Liabilties & Net Worth	100.0	100.0	100.0	100.0	100.0				100.0
INCOME DATA									
Net Sales	100.0	100.0	100.0	100.0	100.0				100.0
Gross Profit									
Operating Expenses	93.7	92.3	92.6	90.6	91.0				94.7
Operating Profit	6.3	7.7	7.4	9.4	9.0				5.3
All Other Expenses (net)	1.2	1.1	2.0	6.6	.0				.0
Profit Before Taxes	5.1	6.6	5.4	2.8	9.0				5.3
RATIOS									
Current	2.0	4.0	2.8	2.8	8.7				1.8
	1.3	1.6	1.3	.6	1.7				1.3
	.8	1.0	.6	.1	1.1				1.0
Quick	1.5	2.4	1.6	1.0	7.3				1.0
	1.1	.9	.8	.5	1.3				.7
	.4	.4	.3	.1	.7				.4
Sales/Receivables	7 55.2	1 267.1	2 200.1	0 UND	20 18.7			16	23.1
	30 12.1	21 17.1	23 16.1	0 UND	34 10.8			27	13.3
	57 6.4	42 8.6	50 7.3	16 22.2	59 6.2			57	6.4
Cost of Sales/Inventory									
Cost of Sales/Payables									
Sales/Working Capital	6.9	5.3	5.4	7.1	3.6				6.2
	23.4	12.9	26.1	-20.0	6.2				27.5
	-37.6	-130.3	-13.4	-4.4	NM				NM
EBIT/Interest	10.4	15.9	8.0	5.3	10.7				13.0
	(58) 3.7	(44) 4.8	(60) 3.1	(16) 1.8	(12) 4.7				4.1
	1.3	1.3	1.6	-2.4	2.3				2.1
Net Profit + Depr., Dep., Amort./Cur. Mat. L/T/D	6.6								
	(13) 2.5								
	1.8								
Fixed/Worth	.4	.2	.3	.8	.1				.5
	1.2	.5	.8	3.4	.6				.6
	8.6	2.0	3.5	-7.0	1.7				2.3
Debt/Worth	.8	.4	.5	.4	.1				.7
	2.0	1.2	2.4	4.9	1.7				2.3
	10.2	4.6	10.2	-8.9	9.6				5.5
% Profit Before Taxes/Tangible Net Worth	50.6	32.2	49.9	78.9	64.0				67.9
	(56) 18.3	(51) 20.8	(63) 18.6	(16) 5.8	(16) 29.0				22.7
	4.5	2.2	4.5	.3	4.9				9.4
% Profit Before Taxes/Total Assets	14.6	14.8	11.6	8.5	20.3				15.1
	7.6	7.5	6.3	2.3	8.1				9.5
	.8	.9	1.4	-16.1	1.8				3.6
Sales/Net Fixed Assets	22.7	31.4	27.4	20.2	233.2				23.4
	6.8	9.8	6.6	4.0	10.8				6.6
	2.8	3.0	2.5	.9	3.2				3.7
Sales/Total Assets	4.1	4.0	3.1	2.4	3.0				5.2
	2.4	2.2	2.1	1.3	2.1				2.7
	1.3	1.2	.9	.4	1.0				1.5
% Depr., Dep., Amort./Sales	1.9	1.4	1.1	1.3	1.0				.6
	(58) 4.2	(49) 3.1	(63) 2.7	(20) 2.9	(14) 3.2			(11)	1.7
	6.9	5.6	5.5	8.5	6.6				4.8
% Officers', Directors' Owners' Comp/Sales	2.9	2.2	1.7	5.0					
	(27) 4.7	(19) 4.4	(35) 3.8	(11) 14.2					
	7.9	13.5	12.4	17.4					
Net Sales ($)	885728M	1837641M	1892459M	11666M	33211M	37616M	44679M	85309M	1679978M
Total Assets ($)	639105M	977870M	954633M	19421M	31833M	18154M	40464M	74858M	769903M

M = $ thousand   MM = $ million
See Pages 11 through 21 for Explanation of Ratios and Data

MINING

Current Data Sorted by Assets   Comparative Historical Data

Type of Statement

Type of Statement	0-500M	500M-2MM	2-10MM	10-50MM	50-100MM	100-250MM		4/1/02-3/31/03 ALL	4/1/03-3/31/04 ALL
Unqualified			6	18	12	29		73	59
Reviewed		2	2	5	1	1		11	12
Compiled	1	4	5	8		1		13	16
Tax Returns	1	6	5		14			5	9
Other	6	11	37	44		10		86	83
		27 (4/1-9/30/06)		202 (10/1/06-3/31/07)					
NUMBER OF STATEMENTS	8	23	55	75	27	41		188	179

Data Table

	0-500M	500M-2MM	2-10MM	10-50MM	50-100MM	100-250MM		4/1/02-3/31/03 ALL	4/1/03-3/31/04 ALL
	%	%	%	%	%	%	**ASSETS**	%	%
		22.1	11.0	10.4	10.5	5.1	Cash & Equivalents	7.9	11.2
		19.3	12.8	12.4	8.2	10.7	Trade Receivables (net)	11.3	12.6
		1.9	1.6	1.3	1.1	1.1	Inventory	2.1	2.5
		2.5	5.8	7.0	1.3	2.3	All Other Current	3.6	3.6
		45.7	31.3	31.1	21.1	19.2	Total Current	24.9	29.8
		34.5	56.7	56.9	68.2	74.6	Fixed Assets (net)	64.9	60.8
		.0	1.4	1.0	.8	2.1	Intangibles (net)	1.6	1.2
		19.7	10.7	10.9	10.0	4.1	All Other Non-Current	8.5	8.2
		100.0	100.0	100.0	100.0	100.0	Total	100.0	100.0
							LIABILITIES		
		16.7	9.5	4.6	1.7	1.5	Notes Payable-Short Term	4.1	7.7
		3.8	2.9	2.2	3.6	2.1	Cur. Mat.-L.T.D.	3.7	3.0
		11.9	11.0	11.5	7.9	10.9	Trade Payables	9.8	12.5
		.1	.2	.2	.2	.1	Income Taxes Payable	.3	.3
		8.2	7.8	6.8	5.6	4.4	All Other Current	8.0	7.4
		40.6	31.3	25.2	19.1	19.0	Total Current	25.9	30.8
		14.4	19.6	20.5	26.9	29.3	Long-Term Debt	31.0	21.7
		.3	.2	2.3	2.2	2.5	Deferred Taxes	1.7	1.7
		.4	2.4	4.3	5.7	8.8	All Other Non-Current	4.6	6.1
		44.3	46.4	47.7	46.1	40.3	Net Worth	36.8	39.7
		100.0	100.0	100.0	100.0	100.0	Total Liabilities & Net Worth	100.0	100.0
							INCOME DATA		
		100.0	100.0	100.0	100.0	100.0	Net Sales	100.0	100.0
		50.5	56.2	59.7	62.4	65.0	Gross Profit	52.2	55.0
		27.5	30.3	32.3	28.4	36.8	Operating Expenses	36.4	30.3
		22.9	25.9	27.4	34.0	28.2	Operating Profit	15.7	24.7
		1.4	1.0	1.2	3.2	4.3	All Other Expenses (net)	5.5	4.1
		21.5	25.0	26.2	30.8	23.8	Profit Before Taxes	10.2	20.6
							RATIOS		
		2.5	2.9	2.7	2.8	1.5		2.0	2.0
		1.5	.9	1.3	1.4	1.0	Current	1.1	1.1
		.4	.4	.7	.6	.7		.7	.6
		2.5	2.6	1.8	2.5	1.3		1.7	1.8
		1.3	.8	.9	1.1	.9	Quick	.9	.8
		.4	.3	.3	.3	.5		.5	.5
	0 UND	0 UND	15 24.5	18 20.4	40 9.1			18 20.8	12 30.2
	14 25.2	22 16.8	40 9.1	47 7.8	53 6.8		Sales/Receivables	51 7.1	42 8.8
	34 10.7	48 7.6	73 5.0	62 5.9	81 4.5			84 4.4	65 5.6
	0 UND	0 UND	0 UND	0 UND	0 UND			0 UND	0 UND
	0 UND	0 UND	0 UND	0 UND	0 UND		Cost of Sales/Inventory	0 UND	0 UND
	0 UND	0 999.8	3 114.2	6 59.8	3 118.4			6 65.6	4 81.7
	0 UND	1 578.0	21 17.2	35 10.3	84 4.3			17 21.8	18 20.3
	16 22.9	34 10.6	74 4.9	94 3.9	162 2.3		Cost of Sales/Payables	78 4.7	60 6.0
	55 6.6	91 1.9	195 1.9	199 1.8	478 .8			213 1.7	206 1.8
	6.5	7.5	3.5	6.4	13.0			7.7	7.1
	14.0	-122.2	13.8	19.9	-186.2		Sales/Working Capital	35.8	50.2
	-19.9	-5.8	-18.4	-7.8	-8.8			-9.5	-7.2
	48.4	110.2	48.5	30.5	16.2			9.6	23.7
	(15) 13.0	(44) 21.0	(62) 9.7	(20) 8.3	(36) 5.5		EBIT/Interest	(159) 3.1	(144) 6.7
	2.6	2.9	3.4	3.2	2.4			1.0	2.5
		173.2					Net Profit + Depr., Dep.,	22.2	10.9
		(13) 51.1					Amort./Cur. Mat. L/T/D	(21) 2.9	(27) 3.2
		2.9						1.4	1.3
		.3	.6	.7	.8	1.2		1.0	.8
		.6	1.2	1.2	1.3	1.8	Fixed/Worth	1.7	1.4
		1.8	2.5	2.3	4.7	3.3		3.4	2.8
		.2	.2	.4	.2	.5		.5	.5
		.7	1.1	1.0	1.1	1.4	Debt/Worth	1.6	1.4
		10.9	3.9	3.5	4.3	2.9		4.9	3.9
		78.5	85.6	46.4	47.8	40.4	% Profit Before Taxes/Tangible	30.9	51.6
	(20) 40.6	(49) 44.5	(69) 27.4	(26) 29.3	(38) 26.7		Net Worth	(172) 14.6	(164) 26.8
		20.1	15.7	15.9	18.9	9.4		.9	9.2
		39.0	42.9	22.5	19.5	19.3	% Profit Before Taxes/Total	11.6	21.6
		19.9	17.2	14.4	12.2	9.5	Assets	4.4	9.4
		3.4	5.9	6.2	5.5	3.4		.0	2.7
		39.3	4.2	2.6	1.6	.7		2.1	2.9
		4.9	1.8	1.0	.8	.5	Sales/Net Fixed Assets	.7	1.1
		2.0	1.0	.5	.4	.3		.4	.5
		3.6	1.6	1.2	.9	.6		1.1	1.4
		1.3	1.0	.5	.4	.4	Sales/Total Assets	.5	.6
		.6	.6	.3	.3	.3		.3	.4
		.9	3.8	4.3	7.9	9.9		6.5	3.9
	(16) 3.8	(40) 6.5	(59) 9.8	(25) 9.7	(19) 16.1		% Depr., Dep., Amort./Sales	(151) 17.2	(138) 10.7
		6.9	13.4	19.3	18.8	20.9		26.3	19.3
							% Officers', Directors'	1.2	.9
							Owners' Comp/Sales	(12) 3.5	(18) 2.4
								8.3	7.0
	5567M	81082M	430934M	2176280M	1546073M	5610793M	Net Sales ($)	7001634M	5460435M
	1661M	30058M	269032M	1812088M	1816398M	6662493M	Total Assets ($)	8699912M	7410580M

M = $ thousand   MM = $ million
See Pages 11 through 21 for Explanation of Ratios and Data

Comparative Historical Data   Current Data Sorted by Sales

Hist 4/1/04-3/31/05 ALL	Hist 4/1/05-3/31/06 ALL	Hist 4/1/06-3/31/07 ALL	Type of Statement	0-1MM	1-3MM	3-5MM	5-10MM	10-25MM	25MM & OVER
49	55	65	Unqualified		2	5	6	11	41
7	17	11	Reviewed		1		3	1	6
11	9	19	Compiled	1	3	3	6	3	3
7	8	12	Tax Returns	3	3	1	3		2
74	97	122	Other	9	23	10	22	29	29
					27 (4/1-9/30/06)		202 (10/1/06-3/31/07)		
148	186	229	NUMBER OF STATEMENTS	13	32	19	40	44	81
%	%	%	**ASSETS**	%	%	%	%	%	%
11.0	11.0	11.3	Cash & Equivalents	25.1	15.5	5.5	11.0	12.9	8.0
14.1	15.9	12.3	Trade Receivables (net)	.8	8.7	11.4	12.6	11.5	16.1
1.7	2.7	1.5	Inventory	2.5	.4	2.0	.6	1.7	2.1
2.4	3.1	4.8	All Other Current	5.6	5.2	7.2	4.5	7.8	2.5
29.2	32.7	29.9	Total Current	34.1	29.8	26.1	28.6	34.0	28.6
59.5	55.2	58.6	Fixed Assets (net)	46.8	53.1	65.8	57.9	55.0	63.3
1.4	1.0	1.1	Intangibles (net)	.2	1.1	.2	.0	1.3	1.9
9.9	11.1	10.4	All Other Non-Current	19.0	16.0	7.9	13.4	9.6	6.2
100.0	100.0	100.0	Total	100.0	100.0	100.0	100.0	100.0	100.0
			LIABILITIES						
11.2	5.5	6.7	Notes Payable-Short Term	30.6	10.7	2.4	9.0	1.9	3.7
2.3	2.5	2.6	Cur. Mat.-L.T.D.	.9	3.5	1.1	5.0	3.2	1.5
10.8	12.1	11.0	Trade Payables	10.0	11.3	10.7	5.4	11.3	13.6
.1	.1	.1	Income Taxes Payable	.1	.0	.1	.2	.1	.1
9.5	6.9	7.1	All Other Current	11.7	13.5	5.8	6.1	5.8	5.2
34.0	27.0	27.5	Total Current	53.2	39.0	20.1	25.8	22.3	24.1
22.6	20.2	21.7	Long-Term Debt	19.0	13.7	25.1	21.5	21.9	24.5
1.0	.8	1.6	Deferred Taxes	1.0	.5	.4	.3	3.6	1.9
4.4	5.4	4.5	All Other Non-Current	4.8	1.9	8.1	2.8	2.4	6.5
37.9	46.6	44.8	Net Worth	21.9	44.8	46.3	49.6	49.8	42.9
100.0	100.0	100.0	Total Liabilities & Net Worth	100.0	100.0	100.0	100.0	100.0	100.0
			INCOME DATA						
100.0	100.0	100.0	Net Sales	100.0	100.0	100.0	100.0	100.0	100.0
57.3	57.9	59.4	Gross Profit	82.2	60.5	57.9	56.7	63.1	55.1
33.6	29.3	32.4	Operating Expenses	55.4	35.5	34.9	29.8	26.5	31.4
23.7	28.6	27.0	Operating Profit	26.8	25.0	23.0	26.9	36.6	23.7
6.0	3.8	2.0	All Other Expenses (net)	3.8	1.3	3.1	.5	2.4	2.3
17.7	24.9	25.0	Profit Before Taxes	23.0	23.7	19.9	26.4	34.2	21.4
			RATIOS						
1.9	3.0	2.2	Current	1.6	1.9	2.1	3.4	3.7	1.7
1.0	1.3	1.2		1.0	1.0	1.3	1.1	1.5	1.2
.6	.7	.6		.2	.3	.9	.5	.9	.7
1.7	2.5	1.9	Quick	1.6	1.8	1.7	2.4	3.1	1.6
.9	1.1	.9		.5	.5	1.0	1.0	1.0	.9
.5	.5	.4		.1	.2	.5	.4	.4	.6
7 50.4	5 74.3	8 47.0	Sales/Receivables	0 UND	0 UND	0 UND	0 818.6	28 12.9	23 15.6
44 8.3	44 8.4	37 9.8		0 UND	19 18.9	46 8.0	28 13.1	51 7.1	46 8.0
76 4.8	79 4.6	62 5.9		11 34.2	45 8.1	81 4.5	53 6.9	72 5.1	65 5.6
0 UND	0 UND	0 UND	Cost of Sales/Inventory	0 UND	0 UND	0 UND	0 UND	0 UND	0 UND
0 UND	0 UND	0 UND		0 UND	0 UND	0 UND	0 UND	0 UND	0 UND
4 92.8	4 101.4	2 203.5		0 UND	0 UND	0 UND	1 434.4	4 81.1	6 62.0
10 37.2	6 56.6	15 24.4	Cost of Sales/Payables	0 UND	0 UND	0 UND	0 UND	55 6.7	29 12.5
65 5.6	52 7.0	72 5.1		42 8.6	55 6.6	50 7.2	21 17.5	101 3.6	91 4.0
266 1.4	206 1.8	197 1.9		270 1.4	228 1.6	181 2.0	53 6.9	253 1.4	220 1.7
8.7	7.0	6.4	Sales/Working Capital	3.9	7.5	3.8	6.3	2.2	10.4
-999.8	21.2	30.6		94.8	NM	14.5	30.9	9.9	62.4
-6.4	-13.3	-10.6		-.9	-2.0	-18.4	-9.2	-32.9	-19.7
23.8	27.2	44.8	EBIT/Interest		29.1	10.8	100.3	80.1	21.8
(124) 7.8	(149) 9.8	(183) 9.1			(23) 7.7	(15) 4.6	(35) 22.1	(37) 15.6	(66) 5.9
3.0	3.2	2.9			4.5	.6	3.4	5.9	2.8
12.0	100.0	373.2	Net Profit + Depr., Dep., Amort./Cur. Mat. L/T/D						495.0
(18) 3.4	(20) 3.6	(28) 35.8							(13) 116.3
2.2	2.3	2.7							3.2
1.0	.5	.7	Fixed/Worth	.5	.6	1.1	.6	.6	.8
1.5	1.2	1.3		1.3	1.1	1.3	1.0	1.1	1.3
3.2	2.3	2.8		15.8	2.8	3.7	2.4	2.8	2.5
.6	.4	.4	Debt/Worth	.5	.2	.3	.2	.4	.5
1.2	1.2	1.1		4.3	1.0	.9	.9	1.0	1.3
5.4	3.5	3.8		NM	5.1	4.8	3.4	2.4	3.5
44.2	56.8	58.9	% Profit Before Taxes/Tangible Net Worth	321.0	49.2	83.9	79.2	50.1	56.1
(128) 21.8	(171) 37.6	(208) 33.1		(10) 30.6	(27) 26.3	(17) 44.1	(35) 38.2	(42) 38.9	(77) 33.4
9.0	13.5	16.8		6.2	14.5	3.0	14.4	22.4	17.4
20.7	27.8	29.0	% Profit Before Taxes/Total Assets	22.8	24.1	37.5	41.4	22.5	24.7
8.9	12.5	14.4		4.8	14.1	6.5	16.6	16.6	13.2
3.2	4.0	5.1		-.7	4.8	-.8	6.0	10.2	5.0
3.7	6.3	3.4	Sales/Net Fixed Assets	12.3	3.9	1.8	4.8	3.1	5.7
1.1	1.5	1.1		1.1	1.9	1.0	1.7	1.3	.8
.5	.6	.5		.5	.6	.4	.7	.5	.4
1.6	2.1	1.4	Sales/Total Assets	2.4	1.3	1.2	1.9	1.1	1.7
.7	.7	.7		.4	.7	.4	.9	.5	.7
.3	.4	.3		.2	.3	.2	.4	.3	.4
3.9	2.4	4.2	% Depr., Dep., Amort./Sales		4.0	7.4	3.9	4.3	.8
(103) 9.8	(133) 8.1	(163) 8.6			(22) 7.7	(16) 13.2	(27) 6.0	(39) 9.2	(52) 9.3
17.2	16.0	17.9			16.0	21.1	13.7	19.3	17.6
.3	1.2	.7	% Officers', Directors' Owners' Comp/Sales						
(15) 2.2	(25) 3.0	(19) 3.0							
5.3	4.2	5.1							
6281456M	7188216M	9850729M	Net Sales ($)	5970M	57666M	77952M	269267M	696840M	8743034M
7014296M	7887246M	10591730M	Total Assets ($)	17566M	122325M	265236M	406463M	1406619M	8373521M

M = $ thousand   MM = $ million
See Pages 11 through 21 for Explanation of Ratios and Data

Current Data Sorted by Assets   Comparative Historical Data

Type of Statement	0-500M	500M-2MM	2-10MM	10-50MM	50-100MM	100-250MM		4/1/02-3/31/03 ALL	4/1/03-3/31/04 ALL
Unqualified			3	5	5	5		10	15
Reviewed		1	4	3				10	7
Compiled	2	1	9	4				4	6
Tax Returns		2	3					2	5
Other	1		4	8	10	3		14	18
	0-500M	500M-2MM	2-10MM	10-50MM	50-100MM	100-250MM			
			7 (4/1-9/30/06)	67 (10/1/06-3/31/07)					
NUMBER OF STATEMENTS	3	5	23	20	15	8		40	51
ASSETS	%	%	%	%	%	%		%	%
Cash & Equivalents			12.7	11.2	6.1			8.7	10.2
Trade Receivables (net)			19.7	9.2	12.6			15.5	15.7
Inventory			8.5	7.1	3.7			5.1	5.9
All Other Current			3.0	.8	3.4			3.9	3.8
Total Current			44.0	28.2	25.7			33.1	35.6
Fixed Assets (net)			38.1	50.5	57.3			52.5	48.8
Intangibles (net)			3.9	2.2	5.2			3.7	4.6
All Other Non-Current			14.0	19.2	11.8			10.7	11.0
Total			100.0	100.0	100.0			100.0	100.0
LIABILITIES									
Notes Payable-Short Term			6.5	4.9	1.6			4.1	3.9
Cur. Mat.-L.T.D.			7.8	8.6	4.3			9.6	7.6
Trade Payables			13.1	8.9	7.2			10.8	13.4
Income Taxes Payable			.0	.3	.0			.1	.1
All Other Current			11.7	3.9	11.0			7.1	6.8
Total Current			39.2	26.6	24.1			31.8	31.8
Long-Term Debt			21.4	32.2	27.4			30.5	21.7
Deferred Taxes			.0	.1	2.0			1.5	.5
All Other Non-Current			5.7	5.2	12.2			3.8	8.5
Net Worth			33.7	35.9	34.2			32.4	37.5
Total Liabilties & Net Worth			100.0	100.0	100.0			100.0	100.0
INCOME DATA									
Net Sales			100.0	100.0	100.0			100.0	100.0
Gross Profit			33.1	18.9	19.7			22.1	21.6
Operating Expenses			25.9	13.0	13.6			14.9	19.0
Operating Profit			7.3	6.0	6.1			7.1	2.6
All Other Expenses (net)			2.7	-.3	.9			.7	.4
Profit Before Taxes			4.6	6.3	5.2			6.4	2.2
RATIOS									
Current			1.8	2.2	1.3			2.2	2.2
			1.1	.9	1.1			1.2	1.1
			.7	.3	.7			.6	.6
Quick			1.5	1.4	1.2			1.3	1.6
			.7	.5	.7			.8	.7
			.4	.3	.5			.3	.4
Sales/Receivables			12 / 29.3	14 / 25.4	23 / 15.8			26 / 14.1	25 / 14.5
			23 / 15.8	21 / 17.0	29 / 12.5			36 / 10.0	33 / 11.1
			32 / 11.4	42 / 8.8	44 / 8.3			48 / 7.6	45 / 8.0
Cost of Sales/Inventory			0 / UND	2 / 192.4	0 / 999.8			0 / UND	0 / UND
			0 / UND	9 / 42.9	10 / 35.5			11 / 33.5	8 / 47.9
			25 / 14.7	49 / 7.5	24 / 15.1			31 / 11.7	29 / 12.8
Cost of Sales/Payables			13 / 28.7	17 / 20.9	13 / 27.8			14 / 26.0	20 / 17.9
			19 / 18.9	30 / 12.1	19 / 18.9			25 / 14.4	32 / 11.4
			40 / 9.1	40 / 9.1	39 / 9.4			46 / 7.9	49 / 7.4
Sales/Working Capital			13.1	6.4	28.2			5.7	8.0
			49.2	NM	63.0			31.9	36.9
			-17.0	-7.9	-10.0			-13.4	-8.7
EBIT/Interest			34.0	8.7	17.4			24.8	12.4
			(20) 4.8	2.8	(14) 3.0			(36) 3.8	(48) 3.6
			1.7	.7	.8			1.7	.6
Net Profit + Depr., Dep., Amort./Cur. Mat. L/T/D								2.3	
								(10) 1.4	
								.4	
Fixed/Worth			.3	.7	1.1			.8	.7
			1.1	1.7	2.3			1.6	1.5
			3.8	3.0	5.1			25.2	4.4
Debt/Worth			.7	.7	1.1			.5	.6
			2.0	1.8	2.6			1.9	2.2
			146.5	4.4	5.3			36.5	7.4
% Profit Before Taxes/Tangible Net Worth			127.8	39.0	61.8			41.2	31.1
			(19) 58.8	(18) 14.4	(14) 21.9			(32) 15.6	(44) 12.1
			14.1	1.4	4.9			.8	.1
% Profit Before Taxes/Total Assets			39.4	14.0	20.0			16.6	10.0
			12.2	4.9	4.8			8.4	5.8
			3.8	-.8	1.3			1.0	-1.5
Sales/Net Fixed Assets			14.4	4.3	3.7			6.1	4.9
			6.2	2.4	2.3			2.3	2.4
			3.0	1.8	1.5			1.1	1.4
Sales/Total Assets			3.8	1.6	1.8			1.9	2.2
			2.3	1.3	1.3			1.1	1.3
			1.2	1.1	1.0			.8	.8
% Depr., Dep., Amort./Sales			1.3	3.2	4.3			3.8	3.7
			(18) 4.1	(16) 6.2	4.8			(35) 6.8	(47) 7.5
			9.5	10.6	8.1			12.0	10.1
% Officers', Directors' Owners' Comp/Sales									1.6
									(10) 2.1
									5.4
Net Sales ($)	7779M	53010M	339357M	642416M	1540780M	1454960M		1865928M	2047972M
Total Assets ($)	911M	7570M	128400M	463435M	1068308M	1119689M		1707096M	1832869M

© RMA 2007

M = $ thousand   MM = $ million
See Pages 11 through 21 for Explanation of Ratios and Data

Comparative Historical Data | Current Data Sorted by Sales

Type of Statement	4/1/04–3/31/05 ALL	4/1/05–3/31/06 ALL	4/1/06–3/31/07 ALL	0-1MM	1-3MM	3-5MM	5-10MM	10-25MM	25MM & OVER
					7 (4/1-9/30/06)		67 (10/1/06-3/31/07)		
Unqualified	20	15	18		1		3	1	13
Reviewed	12	5	8		1	1	1	2	3
Compiled	9	8	16		1	1	4	5	5
Tax Returns	4	6	5			1	3	1	
Other	19	29	27	2			2	5	18
NUMBER OF STATEMENTS	64	63	74	2	3	3	13	14	39
	%	%	%	%	%	%	%	%	%
ASSETS									
Cash & Equivalents	11.2	10.7	10.0				14.5	10.6	9.4
Trade Receivables (net)	15.3	18.9	14.5				18.5	18.2	13.8
Inventory	5.2	7.4	6.1				5.4	6.5	7.1
All Other Current	4.5	2.8	5.0				8.3	2.7	2.8
Total Current	36.1	39.8	35.5				46.8	38.0	33.1
Fixed Assets (net)	44.5	40.1	47.4				39.7	34.1	51.9
Intangibles (net)	6.6	5.0	3.6				4.1	.5	4.4
All Other Non-Current	12.8	15.1	13.6				9.4	27.4	10.6
Total	100.0	100.0	100.0				100.0	100.0	100.0
LIABILITIES									
Notes Payable-Short Term	7.5	4.7	7.7				11.6	5.2	2.8
Cur. Mat.-L.T.D.	8.3	6.7	6.7				5.6	7.8	7.3
Trade Payables	15.1	15.6	11.3				16.4	12.8	9.5
Income Taxes Payable	.3	.3	.1				.1	.2	.1
All Other Current	10.3	9.6	13.7				6.5	12.3	9.9
Total Current	41.4	36.9	39.4				40.1	38.3	29.5
Long-Term Debt	24.8	26.5	29.5				16.2	14.4	29.6
Deferred Taxes	.3	.2	.7				.0	.1	1.2
All Other Non-Current	13.8	7.8	7.9				8.3	4.9	10.4
Net Worth	19.6	28.7	22.5				35.3	42.3	29.3
Total Liabilities & Net Worth	100.0	100.0	100.0				100.0	100.0	100.0
INCOME DATA									
Net Sales	100.0	100.0	100.0				100.0	100.0	100.0
Gross Profit	23.5	27.9	26.4				29.2	27.3	21.5
Operating Expenses	16.8	19.8	20.1				26.9	22.6	12.9
Operating Profit	6.8	8.0	6.3				2.3	4.7	8.6
All Other Expenses (net)	.7	.9	1.8				-.1	-.8	1.9
Profit Before Taxes	6.1	7.1	4.5				2.4	5.5	6.7
RATIOS									
	2.0	2.0	1.8				2.5	1.7	1.6
Current	1.0	1.2	1.1				1.5	.8	1.1
	.7	.7	.6				.7	.3	.7
	1.3	1.4	1.3				1.9	1.5	1.2
Quick	.7	.9	.7				1.1	.5	.6
	.4	.5	.3				.5	.2	.4
	15 23.9	19 19.2	13 29.0				15 24.1	2 150.9	15 25.0
Sales/Receivables	28 13.2	26 14.1	23 15.8				24 15.4	20 18.0	25 14.8
	40 9.1	42 8.6	39 9.3				45 8.1	40 9.1	39 9.4
	0 UND	0 999.8	0 UND				0 UND	0 UND	4 81.7
Cost of Sales/Inventory	8 48.5	12 30.9	5 75.6				0 UND	0 UND	10 35.5
	27 13.4	39 9.3	27 13.4				25 14.6	4 82.5	46 8.0
	19 19.2	19 19.4	13 27.8				13 27.2	13 27.9	13 27.8
Cost of Sales/Payables	28 13.2	27 13.3	22 16.7				33 11.2	26 14.0	20 18.0
	42 8.6	47 7.8	39 9.3				58 6.3	39 9.3	33 11.0
	9.8	11.0	13.1				5.2	11.3	15.9
Sales/Working Capital	235.9	58.1	75.1				20.2	-73.5	153.1
	-15.4	-15.1	-9.9				-29.0	-9.0	-10.0
	17.3	14.5	11.6				5.2	238.4	16.0
EBIT/Interest	(58) 5.3	(57) 4.2	(68) 3.9				(10) 1.4	(13) 3.8	(38) 4.0
	.5	1.0	.7				-3.9	1.1	1.3
	3.5	6.2	6.6						
Net Profit + Depr., Dep., Amort./Cur. Mat. L/T/D	(13) 1.7	(13) 2.3	(14) 1.3						
	1.2	1.1	.9						
	.8	.6	.7				.6	.0	1.1
Fixed/Worth	1.8	1.6	1.8				.9	.6	2.3
	44.5	9.9	20.5				3.7	2.5	5.7
	1.2	1.1	.8				.7	.5	1.2
Debt/Worth	2.2	2.9	2.6				1.1	1.2	2.7
	NM	65.5	81.3				15.5	38.6	11.7
	82.9	81.5	105.7				156.7	109.3	100.0
% Profit Before Taxes/Tangible Net Worth	(48) 34.5	(50) 28.4	(61) 28.1				(11) 58.8	(13) 23.2	(35) 38.0
	15.5	-1.4	6.6				-7.8	6.7	8.3
	23.6	23.3	24.0				29.3	27.6	27.6
% Profit Before Taxes/Total Assets	9.4	9.0	7.6				7.9	11.5	6.8
	-.4	.1	.0				-5.6	.7	1.5
	7.9	13.0	9.2				21.1	327.0	5.9
Sales/Net Fixed Assets	3.5	3.7	3.1				4.3	6.9	2.6
	1.9	2.2	1.8				2.8	2.2	1.6
	2.9	2.8	2.7				4.4	4.4	2.3
Sales/Total Assets	1.5	1.7	1.5				1.6	1.9	1.5
	1.0	1.0	1.0				1.1	1.3	1.0
	1.4	1.6	2.8				2.7	.4	2.9
% Depr., Dep., Amort./Sales	(57) 5.2	(52) 4.9	(56) 4.9				(10) 7.1	(10) 2.1	(30) 4.8
	8.1	7.7	9.8				14.1	10.1	8.4
	2.7	1.0	1.3						
% Officers', Directors' Owners' Comp/Sales	(11) 5.2	(13) 1.8	(11) 4.1						
	10.0	6.8	7.6						
Net Sales ($)	3232163M	4224387M	4038302M	1183M	6322M	12556M	99263M	245592M	3673386M
Total Assets ($)	2417672M	2738474M	2788313M	9773M	5347M	15055M	70606M	130282M	2557250M

© RMA 2007

M = $ thousand   MM = $ million
See Pages 11 through 21 for Explanation of Ratios and Data

Current Data Sorted by Assets   Comparative Historical Data

0-500M	500M-2MM	2-10MM	10-50MM	50-100MM	100-250MM		4/1/02-3/31/03 ALL	4/1/03-3/31/04 ALL
		2	14	3	3	**Type of Statement**		
		4	3	1		Unqualified	10	16
1	2	5		1	1	Reviewed	11	9
	2	3				Compiled	10	17
	1					Tax Returns	6	6
		8	11	3	4	Other	16	17
	8 (4/1-9/30/06)		63 (10/1/06-3/31/07)					
1	5	22	28	8	7	**NUMBER OF STATEMENTS**	53	65
%	%	%	%	%	%	**ASSETS**	%	%
		9.9	11.9			Cash & Equivalents	10.6	11.8
		19.6	14.2			Trade Receivables (net)	13.3	13.5
		8.6	13.9			Inventory	11.0	10.4
		2.7	2.4			All Other Current	2.8	3.4
		40.8	42.5			Total Current	37.8	39.2
		49.7	49.1			Fixed Assets (net)	49.3	49.6
		1.3	3.0			Intangibles (net)	1.9	3.7
		8.3	5.4			All Other Non-Current	11.0	7.6
		100.0	100.0			Total	100.0	100.0
						LIABILITIES		
		5.3	2.4			Notes Payable-Short Term	5.9	5.7
		3.1	4.9			Cur. Mat.-L.T.D.	5.8	6.4
		9.4	7.4			Trade Payables	7.7	7.8
		.1	.3			Income Taxes Payable	.1	.3
		6.0	8.1			All Other Current	6.4	4.7
		23.9	23.1			Total Current	25.9	24.9
		20.0	27.9			Long-Term Debt	21.0	20.2
		.0	.6			Deferred Taxes	.4	.5
		4.3	5.9			All Other Non-Current	3.6	8.2
		51.9	42.5			Net Worth	49.1	46.3
		100.0	100.0			Total Liabilties & Net Worth	100.0	100.0
						INCOME DATA		
		100.0	100.0			Net Sales	100.0	100.0
		34.3	22.8			Gross Profit	29.5	29.5
		21.2	10.4			Operating Expenses	19.8	19.4
		13.1	12.5			Operating Profit	9.8	10.1
		.8	2.2			All Other Expenses (net)	1.2	1.2
		12.3	10.3			Profit Before Taxes	8.5	8.9
						RATIOS		
		3.3	3.9				3.2	2.7
		1.9	1.8			Current	1.6	1.9
		1.1	1.4				1.0	1.0
		2.6	1.9				2.0	2.1
		1.5	1.1			Quick	.8	1.0
		.6	.7				.5	.5
		28 13.0	29 12.6				30 12.2	32 11.4
		46 7.9	41 8.9			Sales/Receivables	40 9.1	43 8.4
		57 6.4	53 6.9				51 7.2	55 6.6
		7 52.7	26 13.8				11 33.6	18 20.1
		18 19.8	47 7.7			Cost of Sales/Inventory	52 7.0	43 8.6
		58 6.3	79 4.6				78 4.7	71 5.1
		13 27.1	14 26.1				15 23.7	18 19.9
		27 13.6	25 14.7			Cost of Sales/Payables	26 13.8	29 12.6
		46 8.0	30 12.0				39 9.4	51 7.2
		3.6	2.9				4.0	3.7
		11.6	7.4			Sales/Working Capital	8.1	6.9
		290.6	14.9				465.9	-304.9
		32.7	27.2				9.9	11.4
		(18) 9.3	(24) 5.0			EBIT/Interest	(46) 3.3	(58) 3.9
		3.5	2.2				1.9	2.0
							5.7	3.4
						Net Profit + Depr., Dep., Amort./Cur. Mat. L/T/D	(12) 3.1	(18) 1.8
							1.8	1.4
		.5	.7				.5	.6
		1.0	1.1			Fixed/Worth	1.2	1.2
		1.9	1.6				2.8	2.5
		.2	.3				.2	.4
		1.2	1.0			Debt/Worth	.9	1.4
		2.2	3.4				4.5	3.2
		67.4	51.7				41.6	31.8
		(21) 30.1	(26) 21.0			% Profit Before Taxes/Tangible Net Worth	(48) 13.3	(59) 16.6
		17.5	11.1				4.0	8.7
		28.4	17.1				12.0	10.9
		15.2	7.8			% Profit Before Taxes/Total Assets	6.4	6.9
		4.7	4.0				2.4	3.2
		4.7	3.3				3.9	3.2
		2.9	2.0			Sales/Net Fixed Assets	2.3	2.1
		1.8	1.6				1.5	1.3
		2.0	1.5				1.4	1.3
		1.3	1.1			Sales/Total Assets	1.0	.9
		.9	.8				.8	.7
		3.7	3.5				5.0	4.9
		(21) 5.4	(27) 5.7			% Depr., Dep., Amort./Sales	(48) 7.7	(56) 7.8
		8.1	10.6				10.8	11.9
							1.3	1.5
						% Officers', Directors' Owners' Comp/Sales	(13) 2.7	(10) 2.9
							7.2	4.8
1307M	32441M	169985M	733345M	464436M	685150M	Net Sales ($)	855842M	1205958M
465M	6294M	104541M	666733M	541992M	1047085M	Total Assets ($)	1011095M	1611924M

© RMA 2007

M = $ thousand   MM = $ million
See Pages 11 through 21 for Explanation of Ratios and Data

Comparative Historical Data | Current Data Sorted by Sales

	4/1/04-3/31/05 ALL	4/1/05-3/31/06 ALL	4/1/06-3/31/07 ALL	Type of Statement	0-1MM	1-3MM	3-5MM	5-10MM	10-25MM	25MM & OVER
	16	19	22	Unqualified	1			2	7	12
	7	7	11	Reviewed	1	1	3	1	3	2
	12	7	8	Compiled			2	4	1	1
	2	4	4	Tax Returns		1	1		2	
	16	42	26	Other		2	2	4	8	12
					8 (4/1-9/30/06)			63 (10/1/06-3/31/07)		
NUMBER OF STATEMENTS	53	79	71		2	2	8	11	21	27
	%	%	%	ASSETS	%	%	%	%	%	%
Cash & Equivalents	11.5	11.5	9.9					9.4	14.4	7.5
Trade Receivables (net)	13.7	16.1	16.4					16.7	20.0	14.2
Inventory	9.1	11.1	11.1					7.7	10.9	13.1
All Other Current	4.3	3.9	2.4					1.7	2.1	2.0
Total Current	38.6	42.7	39.9					35.4	47.3	36.9
Fixed Assets (net)	49.3	43.4	49.0					58.2	43.7	50.2
Intangibles (net)	3.0	5.1	4.6					3.3	3.4	7.1
All Other Non-Current	9.1	8.9	6.5					3.1	5.6	5.8
Total	100.0	100.0	100.0					100.0	100.0	100.0
				LIABILITIES						
Notes Payable-Short Term	3.8	4.1	3.5					2.4	3.7	3.2
Cur. Mat.-L.T.D.	4.5	3.2	4.0					3.9	4.2	3.1
Trade Payables	7.9	7.2	8.0					10.1	7.4	7.6
Income Taxes Payable	.2	.2	.2					.2	.2	.1
All Other Current	5.3	8.0	8.3					10.3	11.5	7.0
Total Current	21.6	22.6	24.0					27.0	27.1	21.1
Long-Term Debt	27.2	25.7	26.5					44.0	21.4	24.6
Deferred Taxes	.8	1.5	1.0					.0	1.6	1.4
All Other Non-Current	1.8	4.3	4.1					13.5	3.0	1.9
Net Worth	48.5	45.9	44.4					15.5	47.0	51.0
Total Liabilities & Net Worth	100.0	100.0	100.0					100.0	100.0	100.0
				INCOME DATA						
Net Sales	100.0	100.0	100.0					100.0	100.0	100.0
Gross Profit	34.2	29.3	29.9					37.3	25.9	24.6
Operating Expenses	22.4	19.6	16.7					22.1	12.0	12.2
Operating Profit	11.8	9.7	13.2					15.2	14.0	12.4
All Other Expenses (net)	1.0	2.0	2.1					3.0	2.8	1.8
Profit Before Taxes	10.7	7.7	11.1					12.2	11.2	10.6
				RATIOS						
Current	2.7	3.6	3.3					2.6	3.7	3.3
	1.6	1.8	1.7					1.6	1.8	1.8
	1.2	1.3	1.2					.7	1.2	1.3
Quick	2.0	2.5	2.2					2.2	2.2	2.2
	1.1	1.2	1.1					1.4	1.3	1.1
	.5	.6	.7					.4	.8	.7
Sales/Receivables	(30) 12.1	(29) 12.5	(29) 12.7					(17) 21.1	(23) 16.1	(34) 10.6
	(38) 9.5	(43) 8.5	(41) 8.9					(42) 8.8	(39) 9.3	(43) 8.4
	(60) 6.0	(55) 6.6	(52) 7.0					(56) 6.5	(46) 7.9	(53) 6.9
Cost of Sales/Inventory	(12) 29.7	(21) 17.4	(18) 20.8					(0) UND	(12) 29.8	(35) 10.6
	(33) 11.1	(51) 7.1	(40) 9.2					(17) 21.5	(36) 10.1	(56) 6.5
	(73) 5.0	(97) 3.8	(72) 5.1					(64) 5.7	(83) 4.4	(81) 4.5
Cost of Sales/Payables	(20) 18.7	(15) 23.8	(17) 21.4					(14) 26.5	(14) 26.8	(18) 20.2
	(30) 12.2	(23) 15.7	(26) 13.9					(26) 14.3	(26) 13.9	(26) 14.3
	(48) 7.6	(38) 9.5	(38) 9.7					(52) 7.0	(30) 12.1	(38) 9.7
Sales/Working Capital	3.1	3.1	3.6					13.3	3.3	3.5
	6.9	6.5	10.4					14.7	7.6	7.6
	44.1	15.1	32.7					-14.5	57.9	17.7
EBIT/Interest	21.0	15.4	21.9						29.2	13.5
	(46) 4.7	(67) 3.5	(59) 6.4						(18) 4.7	(23) 8.4
	1.7	1.2	2.7						2.1	3.5
Net Profit + Depr., Dep., Amort./Cur. Mat. L/T/D	7.1	9.2	7.4							
	(11) 2.9	(18) 3.8	(12) 2.7							
	1.3	1.7	1.5							
Fixed/Worth	.5	.5	.7					.9	.6	.7
	1.2	1.0	1.1					2.2	1.1	1.0
	2.0	2.8	2.3					-2.2	2.1	1.6
Debt/Worth	.3	.3	.4					.4	.4	.4
	.9	1.1	1.3					1.7	1.6	.9
	2.4	4.0	3.8					-5.3	3.6	2.8
% Profit Before Taxes/Tangible Net Worth	29.1	30.3	53.3						58.7	55.2
	(46) 16.1	(68) 13.1	(64) 22.5						(19) 23.8	(26) 18.9
	3.9	4.5	13.1						11.3	12.4
% Profit Before Taxes/Total Assets	13.0	11.3	17.9					26.1	28.4	11.8
	7.5	6.9	8.8					14.7	6.8	8.1
	1.3	.6	4.9					3.0	4.0	5.1
Sales/Net Fixed Assets	3.2	4.3	3.9					4.1	5.0	2.8
	2.2	2.3	2.1					2.0	3.1	1.9
	1.2	1.3	1.4					1.3	1.7	1.3
Sales/Total Assets	1.3	1.4	1.6					1.9	1.7	1.5
	.9	1.0	1.0					1.2	1.2	.8
	.6	.7	.8					.9	.8	.7
% Depr., Dep., Amort./Sales	4.1	3.5	3.5						3.4	3.1
	(49) 7.0	(69) 6.6	(62) 5.8						(19) 5.1	(22) 7.7
	13.6	10.8	9.3						9.1	10.5
% Officers', Directors', Owners' Comp/Sales		1.5	1.7							
	(15)	3.5	(11) 3.0							
		5.6	15.5							
Net Sales ($)	941496M	1837997M	2086664M		1661M	3481M	33060M	75445M	377113M	1595904M
Total Assets ($)	1215128M	2366983M	2367110M		4006M	4213M	24807M	65183M	428633M	1840268M

M = $ thousand   MM = $ million
See Pages 11 through 21 for Explanation of Ratios and Data

Current Data Sorted by Assets

Comparative Historical Data

0-500M	500M-2MM	2-10MM	10-50MM	50-100MM	100-250MM		4/1/02-3/31/03 ALL	4/1/03-3/31/04 ALL
			7	1	1	Type of Statement Unqualified	15	8
		3	6			Reviewed	7	3
	1	3			1	Compiled	2	10
2	1	1				Tax Returns	1	1
	7	12	2	3	3	Other	11	7
5 (4/1-9/30/06)			49 (10/1/06-3/31/07)					
2	9	19	15	4	5	**NUMBER OF STATEMENTS**	36	29
%	%	%	%	%	%		%	%
						ASSETS		
		7.3	8.7			Cash & Equivalents	9.8	9.7
		15.3	18.4			Trade Receivables (net)	14.9	10.4
		20.5	11.7			Inventory	15.8	12.7
		5.1	2.4			All Other Current	4.7	11.4
		48.3	41.2			Total Current	45.2	44.1
		43.5	48.1			Fixed Assets (net)	44.8	43.4
		3.3	2.1			Intangibles (net)	.9	3.0
		4.8	8.5			All Other Non-Current	9.2	9.5
		100.0	100.0			Total	100.0	100.0
						LIABILITIES		
		12.0	1.2			Notes Payable-Short Term	5.6	8.4
		5.6	6.0			Cur. Mat.-L.T.D.	5.3	3.7
		8.4	9.4			Trade Payables	8.9	4.9
		.1	.5			Income Taxes Payable	.1	.1
		3.2	4.6			All Other Current	9.6	5.1
		29.4	21.8			Total Current	29.6	22.1
		22.3	16.8			Long-Term Debt	21.0	23.9
		.2	1.0			Deferred Taxes	.5	.6
		6.5	3.8			All Other Non-Current	4.3	6.5
		41.7	56.6			Net Worth	44.6	46.9
		100.0	100.0			Total Liabilities & Net Worth	100.0	100.0
						INCOME DATA		
		100.0	100.0			Net Sales	100.0	100.0
		32.5	20.9			Gross Profit	29.3	28.2
		25.8	13.4			Operating Expenses	22.3	22.9
		6.7	7.6			Operating Profit	7.1	5.3
		1.6	1.2			All Other Expenses (net)	1.7	1.6
		5.1	6.4			Profit Before Taxes	5.3	3.7
						RATIOS		
		2.6	3.8				3.0	5.7
		1.4	2.2			Current	1.8	1.7
		1.3	1.3				1.2	1.1
		1.6	1.8				1.8	2.1
		.9	1.3			Quick	1.0	.8
		.3	.9				.4	.4
		26 14.1	34 10.6				28 13.0	25 14.6
		34 10.8	44 8.2			Sales/Receivables	37 9.7	44 8.2
		54 6.8	60 6.1				58 6.3	58 6.3
		23 15.6	23 16.0				16 23.0	17 21.6
		42 8.6	50 7.4			Cost of Sales/Inventory	44 8.3	52 7.0
		131 2.8	87 4.2				103 3.5	86 4.2
		16 23.4	16 23.4				14 26.3	11 32.4
		22 16.9	25 14.8			Cost of Sales/Payables	24 15.3	18 19.7
		77 4.8	31 11.6				51 7.2	32 11.4
		4.6	3.3				3.4	1.9
		8.4	6.6			Sales/Working Capital	6.6	6.0
		19.1	12.6				28.6	44.8
		10.3	27.1				7.7	9.2
		(18) 4.6	8.1			EBIT/Interest	(31) 3.2	(25) 2.4
		.6	2.6				1.4	.1
							3.2	
						Net Profit + Depr., Dep., Amort./Cur. Mat. L/T/D	(15) 2.4	
							1.8	
		.5	.6				.6	.4
		1.0	.7			Fixed/Worth	.9	.8
		2.3	1.4				1.9	1.8
		.7	.2				.6	.3
		1.2	.4			Debt/Worth	.9	.9
		3.1	3.2				2.0	3.1
		57.6	30.4				30.3	21.5
		(17) 25.1	22.7			% Profit Before Taxes/Tangible Net Worth	(33) 10.6	(26) 10.5
		4.9	10.0				2.2	1.5
		15.2	16.7				11.5	11.1
		8.6	9.7			% Profit Before Taxes/Total Assets	4.3	4.5
		-.9	5.2				.1	-1.6
		6.9	4.7				5.3	5.1
		3.8	2.7			Sales/Net Fixed Assets	2.5	2.3
		1.8	1.8				1.7	1.6
		2.0	1.9				1.6	1.5
		1.3	1.3			Sales/Total Assets	1.2	.9
		.9	.8				.8	.7
		2.4	1.9				4.5	4.1
		(16) 4.2	(14) 4.8			% Depr., Dep., Amort./Sales	(33) 7.1	(23) 6.3
		7.9	7.6				11.9	10.4
							1.7	
						% Officers', Directors' Owners' Comp/Sales	(10) 2.7	
							6.0	
5063M	23039M	151840M	420181M	274258M	882643M	Net Sales ($)	623186M	609696M
492M	8576M	95786M	347953M	295779M	621637M	Total Assets ($)	643916M	809489M

M = $ thousand   MM = $ million
See Pages 11 through 21 for Explanation of Ratios and Data

Comparative Historical Data / Current Data Sorted by Sales

4/1/04-3/31/05 ALL	4/1/05-3/31/06 ALL	4/1/06-3/31/07 ALL	Type of Statement	0-1MM	1-3MM	3-5MM	5-10MM	10-25MM	25MM & OVER
					5 (4/1-9/30/06)			49 (10/1/06-3/31/07)	
9	7	9	Unqualified				1	2	6
3	12	9	Reviewed		1	2		1	5
1	1	5	Compiled		3	1			1
4	2	4	Tax Returns	1	1	1	1		
9	18	27	Other	2	6	1	1	7	6
26	40	54	NUMBER OF STATEMENTS	3	10	4	8	11	18
%	%	%	**ASSETS**	%	%	%	%	%	%
7.8	6.4	8.2	Cash & Equivalents		7.8			11.4	7.0
15.0	15.2	13.8	Trade Receivables (net)		10.7			16.8	15.1
14.8	15.7	16.1	Inventory		20.3			16.1	13.8
2.7	3.3	4.4	All Other Current		5.3			2.3	3.7
40.4	40.7	42.4	Total Current		44.2			46.7	39.6
49.6	49.1	48.5	Fixed Assets (net)		46.4			36.9	51.6
2.6	2.4	2.6	Intangibles (net)		3.6			6.2	1.7
7.4	7.8	6.5	All Other Non-Current		5.9			10.3	7.1
100.0	100.0	100.0	Total		100.0			100.0	100.0
			LIABILITIES						
6.2	5.6	6.1	Notes Payable-Short Term		7.1			4.2	3.4
7.6	7.2	5.4	Cur. Mat.-L.T.D.		6.2			7.7	2.3
6.8	8.8	8.4	Trade Payables		5.7			8.3	8.9
.1	.1	.2	Income Taxes Payable		.0			.2	.5
4.0	3.4	4.4	All Other Current		3.9			3.8	5.5
24.8	25.1	24.5	Total Current		22.9			24.2	20.6
30.9	18.1	27.5	Long-Term Debt		45.9			21.4	17.2
1.5	1.2	.7	Deferred Taxes		.1			.2	1.8
10.3	5.8	6.5	All Other Non-Current		10.0			3.0	7.8
32.5	49.8	40.9	Net Worth		21.2			51.3	52.6
100.0	100.0	100.0	Total Liabilties & Net Worth		100.0			100.0	100.0
			INCOME DATA						
100.0	100.0	100.0	Net Sales		100.0			100.0	100.0
28.3	24.6	31.9	Gross Profit		46.7			26.2	23.9
19.4	16.6	21.5	Operating Expenses		27.5			20.5	10.9
8.9	8.0	10.4	Operating Profit		19.2			5.7	13.0
2.1	.8	1.8	All Other Expenses (net)		2.1			2.1	1.4
6.7	7.2	8.6	Profit Before Taxes		17.1			3.6	11.6
			RATIOS						
3.0	3.1	2.7			2.8			3.2	3.1
1.6	1.6	1.7	Current		1.6			2.1	1.9
.9	1.0	1.3			1.2			1.3	1.6
1.6	1.6	1.6			2.0			2.1	1.6
.7	.8	1.0	Quick		1.1			1.1	1.0
.4	.5	.5			.3			.8	.5
14 25.5	28 13.2	14 25.2		0 UND			29 12.4	30 12.3	
38 9.7	41 9.0	35 10.5	Sales/Receivables	14 25.8			38 9.5	39 9.4	
59 6.2	54 6.8	52 7.0		37 9.9			54 6.8	53 6.9	
0 UND	20 18.0	16 22.5		0 UND			23 15.6	32 11.2	
26 13.8	45 8.1	43 8.4	Cost of Sales/Inventory	16 22.9			62 5.9	49 7.5	
61 6.0	91 4.0	85 4.3		125 2.9			94 3.9	71 5.2	
14 26.7	12 31.2	14 26.5		0 UND			16 23.4	16 23.2	
18 19.9	23 15.6	22 16.3	Cost of Sales/Payables	14 25.9			22 16.9	23 15.8	
42 8.7	44 8.2	42 8.6		33 11.1			31 11.6	42 8.6	
5.2	3.9	4.6			5.1			5.0	4.1
11.7	8.8	9.4	Sales/Working Capital		10.1			6.7	7.1
-27.8	137.1	19.6			256.1			10.8	15.1
12.3	15.3	13.6						14.6	26.2
(21) 3.1	(37) 4.3	(51) 4.6	EBIT/Interest					4.7	(17) 8.1
1.6	1.1	1.8						-.5	3.4
	12.5	17.2	Net Profit + Depr., Dep.,						
(14) 3.1	(10) 4.5		Amort./Cur. Mat. L/T/D						
1.5	3.0								
.7	.6	.7			1.1			.4	.6
1.6	1.0	1.1	Fixed/Worth		2.1			.8	.9
4.6	2.5	2.5			-1.5			1.2	2.1
.9	.3	.5			.5			.4	.4
1.9	1.0	1.2	Debt/Worth		2.1			1.1	.8
11.1	3.7	3.3			-5.1			3.2	2.4
39.3	28.5	62.8	% Profit Before Taxes/Tangible					32.6	66.1
(22) 19.5	(39) 17.4	(47) 25.8	Net Worth					18.9	(17) 28.5
10.6	2.7	10.0						-2.9	11.4
16.1	14.8	20.2	% Profit Before Taxes/Total		57.4			12.4	20.2
7.2	6.0	9.5	Assets		19.1			8.5	10.9
.7	.3	2.3			-3.4			-2.2	8.1
6.3	5.7	5.8			8.5			7.9	4.6
2.8	2.7	3.3	Sales/Net Fixed Assets		4.1			4.7	2.6
1.4	1.7	1.9			1.8			2.0	1.6
2.1	1.8	2.2			2.4			2.2	1.9
1.2	1.3	1.4	Sales/Total Assets		1.8			1.4	1.3
.8	.8	.9			1.0			.8	.9
3.3	2.8	2.4							2.0
(25) 4.8	(38) 5.2	(44) 5.4	% Depr., Dep., Amort./Sales					(15)	4.7
9.3	8.9	8.3							8.4
	1.5		% Officers', Directors'						
(11) 3.0			Owners' Comp/Sales						
4.9									
550143M	1052293M	1757024M	Net Sales ($)	2446M	20838M	15866M	60586M	160139M	1497149M
551591M	1006782M	1370223M	Total Assets ($)	4631M	14944M	8562M	49727M	145334M	1147025M

M = $ thousand   MM = $ million
See Pages 11 through 21 for Explanation of Ratios and Data

Current Data Sorted by Assets

Comparative Historical Data

						Type of Statement		
	1	5	19	3	6	Unqualified	29	27
1	5	24	9	1		Reviewed	31	42
4	15	16	3			Compiled	24	33
7	5	9				Tax Returns	17	13
1	8	18	14	4	2	Other	33	39
	31 (4/1-9/30/06)		149 (10/1/06-3/31/07)				4/1/02-3/31/03	4/1/03-3/31/04
0-500M	500M-2MM	2-10MM	10-50MM	50-100MM	100-250MM		ALL	ALL
13	34	72	45	8	8	**NUMBER OF STATEMENTS**	134	154
%	%	%	%	%	%	**ASSETS**	%	%
12.8	10.6	11.9	11.7			Cash & Equivalents	9.4	9.6
15.7	16.5	20.3	18.5			Trade Receivables (net)	15.4	16.3
1.7	15.7	8.0	8.2			Inventory	7.6	9.1
6.7	1.3	2.2	1.8			All Other Current	3.0	3.0
36.9	44.1	42.4	40.3			Total Current	35.4	38.1
58.7	45.9	51.3	49.4			Fixed Assets (net)	53.2	51.5
1.9	4.7	1.8	.8			Intangibles (net)	3.0	2.6
2.5	5.3	4.5	9.4			All Other Non-Current	8.4	7.8
100.0	100.0	100.0	100.0			Total	100.0	100.0
						LIABILITIES		
10.0	5.9	7.5	3.7			Notes Payable-Short Term	6.5	5.2
4.3	6.1	6.6	4.3			Cur. Mat.-L.T.D.	5.6	6.0
8.9	7.6	8.2	8.3			Trade Payables	6.4	8.5
.0	.2	.2	.2			Income Taxes Payable	.3	.2
2.7	10.7	4.7	5.8			All Other Current	6.2	7.0
25.8	30.4	27.2	22.4			Total Current	24.9	27.0
60.5	29.2	24.5	15.6			Long-Term Debt	27.5	26.6
.0	.1	.6	1.0			Deferred Taxes	1.1	.9
27.7	6.7	5.8	4.2			All Other Non-Current	4.3	3.1
-14.0	33.6	41.9	56.7			Net Worth	42.2	42.4
100.0	100.0	100.0	100.0			Total Liabilties & Net Worth	100.0	100.0
						INCOME DATA		
100.0	100.0	100.0	100.0			Net Sales	100.0	100.0
41.1	40.5	34.2	26.7			Gross Profit	36.2	35.6
32.1	30.8	24.4	15.5			Operating Expenses	28.4	28.3
9.0	9.7	9.8	11.1			Operating Profit	7.8	7.3
3.1	2.8	1.4	-.1			All Other Expenses (net)	2.3	1.6
5.8	7.0	8.4	11.2			Profit Before Taxes	5.5	5.7
						RATIOS		
2.0	3.3	3.0	3.6				3.1	2.6
1.6	1.9	1.5	2.0			Current	1.5	1.5
.5	.9	1.0	1.3				.9	.9
2.0	2.0	2.1	3.2				2.3	2.0
(12) 1.5	1.1	1.2	1.4			Quick	1.0	1.0
.4	.4	.5	.7				.5	.5
0 UND	19 18.8	28 13.1	35 10.4				25 14.4	28 13.1
13 29.0	38 9.7	41 8.8	46 8.0			Sales/Receivables	40 9.2	41 9.0
50 7.2	48 7.6	56 6.5	59 6.2				54 6.8	58 6.3
0 UND	0 UND	0 UND	3 125.8				0 UND	0 999.8
0 UND	37 9.8	11 32.8	20 17.8			Cost of Sales/Inventory	23 15.8	32 11.4
3 126.2	119 3.1	53 6.8	76 4.8				61 5.9	70 5.2
0 UND	11 32.3	12 30.7	17 21.5				10 35.5	13 28.6
9 41.8	27 13.7	24 15.1	24 15.2			Cost of Sales/Payables	20 18.1	27 13.6
36 10.1	44 8.2	41 8.8	31 11.8				42 8.7	53 6.9
10.3	4.3	4.4	3.6				4.0	5.1
49.6	7.8	15.9	9.6			Sales/Working Capital	12.3	11.0
-15.7	-32.5	-396.3	17.5				-75.8	-157.8
21.3	14.3	13.0	19.5				9.5	9.6
(12) 1.9	(30) 1.4	(64) 3.5	(41) 6.7			EBIT/Interest	(121) 3.1	(134) 3.4
-2.2	.0	1.7	2.6				1.0	1.5
		2.5	17.6				14.6	3.4
	(18) 1.4	(13) 3.5				Net Profit + Depr., Dep., Amort./Cur. Mat. L/T/D	(32) 2.6	(33) 2.2
		.7	2.2				1.5	1.1
1.3	.8	.8	.6				.6	.8
9.0	1.4	1.4	1.0			Fixed/Worth	1.2	1.2
-5.1	-221.6	2.5	1.4				4.0	2.9
3.5	.6	.6	.2				.5	.5
19.1	1.8	1.6	.7			Debt/Worth	1.3	1.4
-5.2	-648.9	3.7	1.8				5.5	3.8
	64.0	47.1	40.7				29.0	27.9
	(25) 23.5	(66) 24.5	(44) 22.0			% Profit Before Taxes/Tangible Net Worth	(117) 13.4	(135) 16.0
	.8	6.1	8.2				3.6	3.3
62.1	17.5	23.7	19.4				11.4	10.7
20.5	3.1	8.6	8.9			% Profit Before Taxes/Total Assets	5.7	5.8
-9.5	-2.6	1.7	4.4				.0	1.0
26.2	6.9	5.7	4.3				4.2	4.1
3.6	2.6	2.6	2.6			Sales/Net Fixed Assets	2.3	2.6
2.1	1.5	1.7	1.5				1.4	1.4
3.9	1.8	2.0	1.9				1.7	1.8
2.0	1.3	1.4	1.4			Sales/Total Assets	1.2	1.3
1.6	.7	1.0	.8				.8	.8
5.2	5.5	4.5	4.0				5.3	5.4
(11) 11.8	(30) 7.3	(67) 6.8	(40) 6.0			% Depr., Dep., Amort./Sales	(122) 8.5	(133) 8.3
21.5	13.5	10.8	10.2				13.2	12.1
	.7	1.8					1.9	1.0
	(13) 3.9	(35) 2.3				% Officers', Directors' Owners' Comp/Sales	(51) 3.6	(43) 2.8
	8.8	6.4					6.5	7.7
10512M	63099M	543175M	1365499M	689816M	1742976M	Net Sales ($)	1896569M	2577285M
3782M	45641M	343347M	1014015M	615039M	1416102M	Total Assets ($)	1779656M	2456683M

© RMA 2007

M = $ thousand   MM = $ million
See Pages 11 through 21 for Explanation of Ratios and Data

Comparative Historical Data / Current Data Sorted by Sales

			Type of Statement						
33	28	34	Unqualified		2	2	7	23
42	36	40	Reviewed	3	5	5	9	9	9
36	33	38	Compiled	8	13	6	6	4	1
15	25	21	Tax Returns	7	4	5	4	1	
35	56	47	Other	5	7	3	12	9	11
4/1/04-3/31/05 ALL	4/1/05-3/31/06 ALL	4/1/06-3/31/07 ALL			31 (4/1-9/30/06)		149 (10/1/06-3/31/07)		
				0-1MM	1-3MM	3-5MM	5-10MM	10-25MM	25MM & OVER
161	178	180	NUMBER OF STATEMENTS	23	29	21	33	30	44
%	%	%	ASSETS	%	%	%	%	%	%
9.5	10.7	11.3	Cash & Equivalents	12.3	12.5	8.3	13.1	9.7	11.4
17.9	17.7	18.5	Trade Receivables (net)	10.9	14.2	15.9	17.6	27.1	21.3
7.6	8.9	9.2	Inventory	11.2	17.2	7.9	5.0	5.6	9.1
2.8	3.1	2.4	All Other Current	.4	1.1	6.8	1.5	1.6	3.4
37.8	40.3	41.4	Total Current	34.8	45.0	38.9	37.3	44.0	45.1
51.0	50.9	49.4	Fixed Assets (net)	53.7	46.2	57.8	55.5	46.6	42.8
2.3	1.5	2.7	Intangibles (net)	3.3	3.8	1.4	2.8	.3	3.8
8.9	7.3	6.4	All Other Non-Current	8.2	4.9	1.9	4.4	9.2	8.3
100.0	100.0	100.0	Total	100.0	100.0	100.0	100.0	100.0	100.0
			LIABILITIES						
4.8	5.0	5.9	Notes Payable-Short Term	14.4	3.2	5.4	4.9	8.3	2.5
6.3	5.7	5.6	Cur. Mat.-L.T.D.	4.4	6.6	6.9	7.2	4.4	4.5
8.5	8.3	8.1	Trade Payables	5.2	7.4	6.0	7.0	11.5	9.8
.2	.3	.3	Income Taxes Payable	.0	.3	.0	.3	.1	.8
6.8	6.3	6.1	All Other Current	8.5	7.5	7.5	2.6	6.1	6.1
26.7	25.6	26.0	Total Current	32.4	24.9	25.8	22.0	30.4	23.6
29.0	26.2	26.8	Long-Term Debt	54.2	30.7	19.3	24.8	15.3	23.1
.9	.6	.8	Deferred Taxes	.1	.1	1.4	.7	.3	1.6
3.7	7.1	7.1	All Other Non-Current	15.9	10.5	1.4	4.8	5.0	5.9
39.7	40.5	39.3	Net Worth	-2.6	33.8	52.1	47.7	49.1	45.8
100.0	100.0	100.0	Total Liabilities & Net Worth	100.0	100.0	100.0	100.0	100.0	100.0
			INCOME DATA						
100.0	100.0	100.0	Net Sales	100.0	100.0	100.0	100.0	100.0	100.0
34.1	33.8	33.6	Gross Profit	47.6	37.9	34.0	38.3	25.9	24.9
26.1	25.7	22.8	Operating Expenses	35.6	30.2	24.0	26.1	16.1	12.8
8.1	8.1	10.8	Operating Profit	12.0	7.7	10.0	12.2	9.9	12.1
1.4	1.3	1.3	All Other Expenses (net)	5.3	2.3	1.6	.1	.0	.1
6.7	6.9	9.5	Profit Before Taxes	6.7	5.4	8.4	12.1	9.9	11.9
			RATIOS						
2.8	2.9	3.0		1.8	4.5	3.2	3.8	2.6	3.1
1.6	1.7	1.7	Current	1.1	2.1	2.0	1.6	1.5	1.9
1.0	1.1	1.1		.5	1.1	.9	1.0	1.1	1.4
2.1	2.2	2.1		1.8	2.1	2.0	2.9	2.0	2.3
1.1 (177)	1.1 (179)	1.2	Quick	.7	1.2 (20)	1.3	1.4	1.2	1.2
.5	.6	.6		.2	.5	.5	.5	.9	.7
29 12.7	28 13.2	28 12.9		4 94.0	17 21.4	26 14.0	27 13.4	34 10.8	37 9.8
41 8.9	43 8.4	42 8.8	Sales/Receivables	25 14.4	38 9.7	43 8.5	41 8.8	54 6.8	45 8.2
62 5.9	61 6.0	55 6.6		60 6.1	41 8.9	56 6.5	54 6.8	74 5.0	52 7.0
0 UND	0 UND	0 999.8		0 UND	9 42.7	0 UND	0 UND	0 UND	3 111.3
20 18.1	20 18.0	20 18.7	Cost of Sales/Inventory	3 141.3	66 5.5	41 9.0	8 44.0	15 25.0	31 11.7
54 6.7	66 5.5	62 5.8		343 1.1	110 3.3	61 5.9	54 6.7	25 14.4	50 7.3
15 24.2	12 29.8	13 28.0		0 UND	8 43.1	5 69.8	14 27.0	16 23.4	19 19.0
24 15.0	23 15.7	25 14.8	Cost of Sales/Payables	16 22.9	25 14.3	18 20.1	27 13.7	27 13.8	25 14.6
41 8.9	39 9.4	41 9.0		60 6.0	35 10.4	44 8.2	41 8.9	45 8.1	37 9.8
5.4	5.0	4.4		8.6	3.6	4.9	3.8	5.6	4.1
11.8	11.2	10.1	Sales/Working Capital	49.6	7.2	9.6	13.1	12.4	9.2
-114.0	78.6	84.4		-5.0	67.9	-120.9	-147.5	43.7	16.1
11.9	12.0	15.2		15.2	5.4	12.0	17.3	19.5	24.0
(143) 4.0	(162) 3.9	(163) 4.6	EBIT/Interest	(19) 1.0	(26) 1.8	(18) 5.0	(30) 7.1	(29) 5.4	(41) 6.3
1.7	1.7	1.5		-1.1	.3	1.4	2.2	2.1	2.4
5.3	4.8	4.7	Net Profit + Depr., Dep.,						35.4
(40) 2.0	(40) 2.1	(42) 1.9	Amort./Cur. Mat. L/T/D					(15)	3.9
1.4	1.3	1.2							1.6
.7	.7	.7		1.3	.8	.8	.7	.7	.5
1.3	1.2	1.2	Fixed/Worth	6.8	1.5	1.1	1.3	1.0	1.0
2.5	2.2	3.0		-4.3	NM	2.1	2.2	1.5	2.0
.5	.5	.5		2.6	.7	.5	.5	.4	.3
1.4	1.4	1.4	Debt/Worth	19.1	2.1	1.0	1.2	1.0	1.2
3.6	3.2	4.4		-4.8	NM	2.5	2.2	3.5	2.4
30.9	38.2	48.1	% Profit Before Taxes/Tangible	118.1	42.7	45.6	61.9	37.2	61.1
(142) 15.1	(163) 15.8	(153) 24.3	Net Worth	(13) 23.1	(22) 16.9	16.8	(30) 37.4	(29) 15.3	(38) 29.2
5.0	5.0	6.7		-13.5	-3.7	5.0	11.2	8.5	9.8
13.2	17.0	22.3	% Profit Before Taxes/Total	25.2	13.3	24.1	27.8	18.3	24.2
5.8	6.8	9.4	Assets	1.4	3.4	8.6	12.5	8.2	11.4
.9	1.7	1.9		-7.7	-2.2	1.8	3.1	2.9	5.2
4.8	4.8	5.1		5.1	7.4	3.3	4.5	6.2	6.0
2.7	2.5	2.7	Sales/Net Fixed Assets	2.1	2.6	2.1	2.4	2.8	3.2
1.4	1.4	1.7		.8	1.4	1.3	1.7	1.7	2.4
2.0	2.0	1.9		1.9	1.5	1.7	2.0	2.2	2.1
1.3	1.3	1.4	Sales/Total Assets	.9	1.2	1.3	1.4	1.5	1.6
.8	.8	.8		.4	.7	.9	1.0	.9	1.1
5.4	4.0	4.5		7.2	5.5	5.6	5.0	3.3	3.5
(146) 8.4	(160) 7.4	(159) 6.8	% Depr., Dep., Amort./Sales	(19) 11.8	(27) 7.4	(20) 8.4	(32) 7.3	(26) 5.0	(35) 4.7
12.4	11.7	11.5		18.6	14.5	13.4	10.8	8.1	7.5
1.5	1.1	1.8			1.7		1.1	1.0	
(42) 3.2	(52) 2.3	(50) 2.7	% Officers', Directors'	(13)	3.9	(16)	2.1	(13) 2.0	
6.7	5.7	6.4	Owners' Comp/Sales		6.5		3.1	3.3	
3134181M	3487517M	4415077M	Net Sales ($)	12904M	58382M	84250M	234261M	452980M	3572300M
2721432M	2836729M	3437926M	Total Assets ($)	19195M	57378M	75225M	192518M	393338M	2700272M

M = $ thousand   MM = $ million
See Pages 11 through 21 for Explanation of Ratios and Data

Current Data Sorted by Assets   Comparative Historical Data

Type of Statement

	0-500M	500M-2MM	2-10MM	10-50MM	50-100MM	100-250MM		4/1/02-3/31/03 ALL	4/1/03-3/31/04 ALL
Unqualified			1	4	3	1		11	9
Reviewed		6	6	4	1			2	5
Compiled		6	4	2				7	6
Tax Returns	3	5	2					6	7
Other		5	12	15	4	2		19	13

| | 7 (4/1-9/30/06) | | | 71 (10/1/06-3/31/07) | | |

Main Data

0-500M	500M-2MM	2-10MM	10-50MM	50-100MM	100-250MM	Item	4/1/02-3/31/03 ALL	4/1/03-3/31/04 ALL
3	16	25	23	8	3	**NUMBER OF STATEMENTS**	45	40
%	%	%	%	%	%	**ASSETS**	%	%
	13.0	15.6	9.9			Cash & Equivalents	13.4	8.6
	20.0	19.3	26.0			Trade Receivables (net)	18.3	26.0
	1.0	4.5	6.3			Inventory	1.9	1.1
	4.8	1.8	3.6			All Other Current	3.4	3.2
	38.7	41.1	45.8			Total Current	37.0	38.8
	49.9	45.0	44.9			Fixed Assets (net)	49.7	48.3
	.2	.9	3.3			Intangibles (net)	1.8	2.1
	11.1	13.1	6.0			All Other Non-Current	11.5	10.9
	100.0	100.0	100.0			Total	100.0	100.0
						LIABILITIES		
	3.5	5.6	8.0			Notes Payable-Short Term	5.1	6.3
	5.8	3.0	3.7			Cur. Mat.-L.T.D.	5.3	5.1
	5.2	9.2	13.3			Trade Payables	10.7	10.5
	.3	.0	.5			Income Taxes Payable	.4	.4
	4.9	11.6	16.7			All Other Current	7.5	8.6
	19.6	29.4	42.2			Total Current	28.9	30.9
	24.9	29.4	19.6			Long-Term Debt	21.5	24.0
	.0	.3	.3			Deferred Taxes	1.0	.9
	7.3	2.1	3.9			All Other Non-Current	3.9	2.3
	48.1	38.8	34.0			Net Worth	44.7	41.9
	100.0	100.0	100.0			Total Liabilities & Net Worth	100.0	100.0
						INCOME DATA		
	100.0	100.0	100.0			Net Sales	100.0	100.0
						Gross Profit		
	82.5	78.8	85.7			Operating Expenses	87.9	90.4
	17.5	21.2	14.3			Operating Profit	12.1	9.6
	.5	2.4	2.6			All Other Expenses (net)	1.2	-.2
	17.0	18.7	11.6			Profit Before Taxes	11.0	9.8
						RATIOS		
	2.7	2.8	1.9				2.4	2.7
	2.0	1.6	1.0			Current	1.2	1.2
	1.5	.6	.4				.8	.8
	2.3	2.6	1.5				2.3	2.6
	1.6	1.3	.8			Quick	1.1	1.0
	1.1	.5	.4				.7	.7
	1 408.9	**10** 37.3	**31** 11.9				**19** 19.1	**33** 11.1
	36 10.1	**40** 9.1	**62** 5.9			Sales/Receivables	**48** 7.6	**55** 6.6
	50 7.2	**62** 5.9	**78** 4.7				**67** 5.4	**91** 4.0
						Cost of Sales/Inventory		
						Cost of Sales/Payables		
	7.4	6.6	7.1				7.2	5.0
	10.6	13.1	211.5			Sales/Working Capital	18.8	28.8
	17.9	-7.8	-5.6				-20.7	-24.1
	18.8	43.8	19.8				11.9	16.4
	(14) 9.5	(21) 9.7	(22) 8.0			EBIT/Interest	(38) 3.6	(34) 6.2
	4.2	3.1	3.7				.9	2.3
						Net Profit + Depr., Dep., Amort./Cur. Mat. L/T/D		
	.3	.3	.3				.5	.6
	.9	.8	1.7			Fixed/Worth	1.1	1.1
	2.8	3.7	4.1				2.4	2.0
	.3	.3	1.1				.5	.4
	1.1	.9	2.2			Debt/Worth	1.5	1.3
	3.0	5.3	8.2				4.0	3.3
	110.7	101.6	80.9			% Profit Before Taxes/Tangible	45.3	47.0
	(15) 41.6	(23) 49.3	(21) 57.3			Net Worth	(42) 18.2	(35) 21.2
	12.8	24.4	22.0				4.4	6.8
	27.2	40.8	19.9			% Profit Before Taxes/Total	20.4	21.5
	15.1	12.9	10.6			Assets	6.2	7.4
	7.7	6.9	6.0				1.1	2.3
	7.2	8.8	9.6				5.7	6.9
	4.2	3.0	3.7			Sales/Net Fixed Assets	2.8	2.5
	2.1	1.5	1.7				1.2	.9
	2.7	2.2	2.1				2.2	2.0
	1.7	1.6	1.6			Sales/Total Assets	1.1	1.3
	1.2	.9	1.0				.7	.4
		2.6	1.8				3.3	3.3
	(18)	(18) 4.4	(20) 4.6			% Depr., Dep., Amort./Sales	(37) 8.0	(35) 6.6
		10.6	8.0				12.2	11.6
							1.3	1.1
						% Officers', Directors'	(14) 4.7	(11) 4.2
						Owners' Comp/Sales	8.2	14.2
4416M	30153M	252019M	702937M	673805M	610999M	Net Sales ($)	805149M	960550M
622M	16289M	122080M	439714M	515277M	512223M	Total Assets ($)	1010534M	929821M

M = $ thousand   MM = $ million
See Pages 11 through 21 for Explanation of Ratios and Data

Comparative Historical Data | Current Data Sorted by Sales

Type of Statement

Type of Statement	4/1/04-3/31/05 ALL	4/1/05-3/31/06 ALL	4/1/06-3/31/07 ALL	0-1MM	1-3MM	3-5MM	5-10MM	10-25MM	25MM & OVER
Unqualified	13	4	9					3	6
Reviewed	7	8	11		1	1	4	2	3
Compiled	12	7	10		4	3	1	1	1
Tax Returns	4	9	10	4	4		2		
Other	20	36	38	2	5	4	5	8	14

Right side spanning headers: 7 (4/1-9/30/06) for 0-1MM, 1-3MM, 3-5MM; 71 (10/1/06-3/31/07) for 5-10MM, 10-25MM, 25MM & OVER.

Number of Statements

	56	64	78	6	14	8	12	14	24

ASSETS (%)

	'04-05	'05-06	'06-07	0-1MM	1-3MM	3-5MM	5-10MM	10-25MM	25MM & OVER
Cash & Equivalents	11.4	11.7	13.1		16.1		14.4	13.1	10.0
Trade Receivables (net)	22.3	19.1	20.9		16.8		16.9	21.4	28.7
Inventory	.8	3.0	4.3		.7		4.0	9.1	5.6
All Other Current	4.5	2.3	3.3		5.4		1.8	3.0	4.2
Total Current	39.0	36.2	41.6		38.9		37.1	46.6	48.4
Fixed Assets (net)	49.1	49.6	47.6		45.4		48.2	46.3	42.5
Intangibles (net)	2.9	2.9	1.6		1.9		1.2	1.4	2.7
All Other Non-Current	9.0	11.4	9.2		13.8		13.5	5.8	6.4
Total	100.0	100.0	100.0		100.0		100.0	100.0	100.0

LIABILITIES

	'04-05	'05-06	'06-07	0-1MM	1-3MM	3-5MM	5-10MM	10-25MM	25MM & OVER
Notes Payable-Short Term	8.8	5.2	5.5		3.0		6.3	6.7	5.9
Cur. Mat.-L.T.D.	7.7	5.8	4.0		7.5		3.0	2.9	3.0
Trade Payables	9.8	7.6	8.9		4.0		7.7	12.1	12.4
Income Taxes Payable	.3	.3	.4		.3		.0	.1	1.0
All Other Current	9.8	11.3	11.1		8.2		12.6	14.2	12.4
Total Current	36.5	30.2	29.9		23.1		29.6	36.1	34.7
Long-Term Debt	20.8	19.2	23.0		19.2		26.3	17.4	12.9
Deferred Taxes	1.0	1.4	.3		.3		.0	.0	.8
All Other Non-Current	3.9	3.8	9.9		36.6		1.6	3.4	2.4
Net Worth	37.8	45.4	36.8		20.7		42.5	43.1	49.2
Total Liabilities & Net Worth	100.0	100.0	100.0		100.0		100.0	100.0	100.0

INCOME DATA

	'04-05	'05-06	'06-07	0-1MM	1-3MM	3-5MM	5-10MM	10-25MM	25MM & OVER
Net Sales	100.0	100.0	100.0		100.0		100.0	100.0	100.0
Gross Profit									
Operating Expenses	87.2	82.4	80.5		82.1		79.0	84.5	80.5
Operating Profit	12.8	17.6	19.5		17.9		21.0	15.5	19.5
All Other Expenses (net)	1.6	1.2	1.8		2.6		2.5	2.6	.4
Profit Before Taxes	11.2	16.4	17.7		15.2		18.5	12.9	19.1

RATIOS

	'04-05	'05-06	'06-07	0-1MM	1-3MM	3-5MM	5-10MM	10-25MM	25MM & OVER
Current	2.5	2.1	2.6		2.5		3.3	2.9	2.4
	1.3	1.4	1.6		1.8		1.6	1.2	1.6
	.6	.6	.8		1.2		.7	.8	.9
Quick	2.1	1.9	2.3		2.0		2.6	2.1	2.3
	1.1	1.1	1.2		1.4		1.4	1.0	1.1
	.5	.5	.7		.8		.6	.6	.8
Sales/Receivables	28 13.2	13 29.2	23 16.2		0 UND		0 UND	25 14.7	37 9.9
	54 6.7	54 6.7	46 8.0		37 9.9		39 9.4	48 7.6	50 7.3
	81 4.5	84 4.4	67 5.4		59 6.2		64 5.7	90 4.0	70 5.2
Cost of Sales/Inventory									
Cost of Sales/Payables									
Sales/Working Capital	5.6	5.9	7.2		8.9		6.2	5.5	6.5
	17.5	14.7	12.5		12.8		17.5	NM	10.0
	-15.4	-20.4	-25.4		NM		-13.0	-4.8	-102.5
EBIT/Interest	26.2	25.8	28.9		(13) 26.6		(11) 60.0	(12) 30.5	(22) 31.9
	(53) 7.3	(55) 8.5	(69) 10.1		13.0		7.8	11.6	15.2
	2.3	2.7	4.0		2.8		3.7	3.6	5.5
Net Profit + Depr., Dep., Amort./Cur. Mat. L/T/D	3.8	6.6	11.2						
	(10) 1.7	(10) 2.6	(12) 6.5						
	1.0	1.8	4.8						
Fixed/Worth	.7	.7	.4		.3		.4	.3	.3
	1.2	1.2	1.1		1.0		1.1	1.6	.9
	3.0	3.0	3.1		2.6		5.2	3.3	1.5
Debt/Worth	.6	.5	.4		.3		.2	.5	.3
	1.4	1.1	1.2		1.0		3.5	1.1	1.2
	4.1	4.1	4.6		2.4		7.7	6.0	2.2
% Profit Before Taxes/Tangible Net Worth	75.1	67.9	86.8		(13) 101.0		(11) 101.6	(13) 72.8	(23) 81.1
	(49) 23.7	(60) 41.0	(72) 49.5		30.3		76.9	57.3	48.5
	7.5	18.1	23.6		15.7		49.2	14.6	24.6
% Profit Before Taxes/Total Assets	19.8	32.3	31.5		25.5		41.0	30.0	32.5
	11.1	16.8	14.5		14.8		15.7	11.7	18.5
	2.3	5.6	7.4		7.4		7.2	3.8	11.2
Sales/Net Fixed Assets	8.3	7.3	8.6		8.3		7.8	23.2	19.0
	2.6	2.8	3.7		4.1		3.0	3.1	4.2
	1.6	1.4	1.5		1.4		1.8	.8	1.7
Sales/Total Assets	1.9	2.1	2.4		2.7		1.7	2.2	2.6
	1.2	1.4	1.6		1.4		1.6	1.2	1.8
	.7	.7	1.0		.8		1.2	.6	1.1
% Depr., Dep., Amort./Sales	4.0	2.7	2.5					3.8	1.2
	(44) 7.1	(52) 7.0	(58) 5.7					(11) 6.3	(21) 2.9
	12.2	10.9	9.6					9.7	7.4
% Officers', Directors' Owners' Comp/Sales	1.1	2.0	.7						
	(15) 7.0	(22) 4.6	(22) 2.7						
	17.3	12.7	6.1						
Net Sales ($)	1086779M	1201374M	2274329M	3671M	28468M	31205M	80617M	216683M	1913685M
Total Assets ($)	1248819M	1216817M	1606205M	3902M	30685M	32810M	56593M	264892M	1217323M

© RMA 2007

M = $ thousand   MM = $ million

See Pages 11 through 21 for Explanation of Ratios and Data

Current Data Sorted by Assets | Comparative Historical Data

Current data periods: 57 (4/1–9/30/06) covers 0-500M and 500M-2MM columns; 233 (10/1/06–3/31/07) covers 2-10MM through 100-250MM columns.

	0-500M	500M-2MM	2-10MM	10-50MM	50-100MM	100-250MM		4/1/02-3/31/03 ALL	4/1/03-3/31/04 ALL
Type of Statement									
Unqualified		1	10	26	9	13		42	41
Reviewed		4	15	5				25	31
Compiled	6	5	23	6	2			37	59
Tax Returns	7	5	6	2				12	23
Other	3	15	48	46	16	17		86	105
NUMBER OF STATEMENTS	16	30	102	85	27	30		202	259
	%	%	%	%	%	%		%	%
ASSETS									
Cash & Equivalents	26.6	15.1	8.6	7.4	11.1	6.8		10.2	10.8
Trade Receivables (net)	27.7	32.4	31.8	27.1	28.7	16.7		25.3	27.5
Inventory	1.4	3.4	7.1	6.4	9.3	9.0		8.2	7.8
All Other Current	8.7	8.1	5.8	3.6	7.9	4.9		4.7	4.5
Total Current	64.5	59.1	53.3	44.5	56.9	37.3		48.4	50.6
Fixed Assets (net)	25.0	35.4	39.4	43.8	33.3	47.6		41.9	39.1
Intangibles (net)	.0	1.9	2.4	3.9	6.5	12.2		2.9	3.1
All Other Non-Current	10.7	3.6	4.9	7.9	3.4	2.9		6.8	7.2
Total	100.0	100.0	100.0	100.0	100.0	100.0		100.0	100.0
LIABILITIES									
Notes Payable-Short Term	15.5	10.7	9.4	9.1	5.6	4.3		10.3	8.5
Cur. Mat.-L.T.D.	3.4	3.0	3.7	3.9	1.5	2.4		8.2	4.9
Trade Payables	11.1	10.4	12.0	11.4	12.9	6.8		10.3	11.1
Income Taxes Payable	.0	.3	.6	.8	.4	1.6		.9	.7
All Other Current	22.8	8.6	10.1	8.3	8.4	8.9		9.3	9.0
Total Current	52.8	33.0	35.9	33.6	28.9	23.9		39.0	34.1
Long-Term Debt	18.7	17.0	17.8	15.3	9.1	32.8		17.4	18.9
Deferred Taxes	.0	.0	.5	1.3	.6	2.5		1.1	1.0
All Other Non-Current	3.1	2.1	2.3	5.3	4.4	4.8		2.6	5.7
Net Worth	25.1	47.9	43.5	44.5	57.0	36.0		39.9	40.3
Total Liabilties & Net Worth	100.0	100.0	100.0	100.0	100.0	100.0		100.0	100.0
INCOME DATA									
Net Sales	100.0	100.0	100.0	100.0	100.0	100.0		100.0	100.0
Gross Profit									
Operating Expenses	92.2	86.9	85.8	81.7	82.0	76.7		92.9	90.7
Operating Profit	7.8	13.1	14.2	18.3	18.0	23.3		7.1	9.3
All Other Expenses (net)	.6	1.2	1.6	2.6	-.1	6.4		1.9	1.5
Profit Before Taxes	7.2	11.9	12.6	15.7	18.1	16.9		5.2	7.8
RATIOS									
Current	4.9	5.0	2.5	2.2	4.5	2.3		2.4	2.9
	1.2	1.7	1.6	1.3	2.1	1.7		1.3	1.6
	.6	1.2	1.0	.9	1.1	1.1		.9	1.0
Quick	4.9	4.1	2.1	1.8	3.3	1.4		1.7	2.3
	1.1	1.6	1.1	1.2	1.6	1.0		.9	1.2
	.5	1.1	.7	.6	.9	.6		.6	.7
Sales/Receivables	0 UND	0 UND	24 15.1	44 8.3	52 7.0	52 7.0		29 12.5	30 12.4
	27 13.5	42 8.7	53 6.9	64 5.7	67 5.4	70 5.2		50 7.4	51 7.1
	41 9.0	77 4.7	82 4.4	81 4.5	88 4.2	103 3.6		67 5.5	71 5.2
Cost of Sales/Inventory									
Cost of Sales/Payables									
Sales/Working Capital	7.2	6.8	5.8	6.3	2.3	3.3		5.9	5.3
	50.9	12.5	10.7	17.5	5.5	6.1		18.9	11.4
	-61.0	68.4	313.5	-26.8	15.7	27.9		-32.9	219.0
EBIT/Interest		22.0	26.7	41.5	283.0	8.0		9.3	14.4
		(23) 11.6	(92) 9.7	(75) 10.6	(21) 19.6	(21) 3.9		(174) 3.2	(216) 4.3
		6.0	2.9	3.6	6.6	2.3		1.0	1.4
Net Profit + Depr., Dep., Amort./Cur. Mat. L/T/D			6.2	17.8		40.2		5.8	8.6
			(20) 2.9	(26) 2.8		(13) 8.3		(38) 3.1	(47) 3.5
			1.4	1.1		2.4		1.4	1.5
Fixed/Worth	.0	.1	.4	.5	.1	.7		.4	.4
	.5	.7	.9	1.1	.5	2.7		1.0	.9
	42.8	1.4	2.1	2.0	1.0	7.7		2.1	1.9
Debt/Worth	.5	.5	.6	.6	.2	1.2		.6	.7
	1.9	1.1	1.5	1.3	1.0	3.2		1.4	1.5
	57.2	2.1	3.7	2.8	1.8	8.4		3.5	3.8
% Profit Before Taxes/Tangible Net Worth	109.8	89.6	80.9	65.8	64.2	50.3		38.5	47.7
	(13) 49.7	(28) 49.2	(96) 41.9	(79) 50.3	43.4	(25) 41.9		(184) 15.0	(237) 21.9
	12.0	16.7	16.2	13.5	25.9	23.9		2.4	3.9
% Profit Before Taxes/Total Assets	57.1	35.1	31.3	26.9	27.7	16.9		13.7	19.0
	11.4	24.0	15.2	15.8	18.5	9.4		5.2	7.8
	4.0	4.0	4.6	4.6	15.1	5.0		.2	.9
Sales/Net Fixed Assets	UND	75.6	13.8	8.7	36.9	6.8		13.4	17.1
	24.7	9.0	6.1	4.2	4.4	1.9		5.1	5.1
	15.0	3.2	2.8	1.6	2.2	.5		1.8	2.0
Sales/Total Assets	6.5	4.1	2.8	2.2	1.6	1.1		2.9	2.9
	5.2	2.8	2.0	1.4	1.2	.8		1.8	1.7
	2.1	1.7	1.3	.6	.8	.4		.9	1.0
% Depr., Dep., Amort./Sales		.4	1.4	1.6	1.6	2.0		1.9	1.9
		(20) 5.0	(83) 3.7	(75) 3.6	(19) 2.7	(22) 4.1		(173) 4.8	(214) 4.7
		6.5	6.4	6.3	5.2	8.7		10.4	9.3
% Officers', Directors' Owners' Comp/Sales			.9	1.5				3.0	2.3
			(30) 2.1	(15) 1.8				(59) 4.8	(60) 4.0
			8.6	4.1				9.3	9.4
Net Sales ($)	14167M	161543M	1450317M	3220668M	3192134M	4132279M		6624019M	8123355M
Total Assets ($)	3340M	32256M	489046M	1994374M	2040426M	4869511M		4401068M	5651535M

M = $ thousand   MM = $ million
See Pages 11 through 21 for Explanation of Ratios and Data

Comparative Historical Data | Current Data Sorted by Sales

			Type of Statement						
65	64	59	Unqualified			1	5	14	39
29	22	24	Reviewed		3	2	6	5	8
44	44	41	Compiled	4	9	3	10	10	5
24	15	21	Tax Returns	6	4	2	1	7	1
112	129	145	Other	8	13	14	24	30	56
4/1/04-3/31/05 ALL	4/1/05-3/31/06 ALL	4/1/06-3/31/07 ALL		0-1MM	57 (4/1-9/30/06) 1-3MM	3-5MM	233 (10/1/06-3/31/07) 5-10MM	10-25MM	25MM & OVER
274	274	290	**NUMBER OF STATEMENTS**	18	29	22	46	66	109
%	%	%	**ASSETS**	%	%	%	%	%	%
11.5	9.1	10.0	Cash & Equivalents	22.2	14.3	9.2	11.2	6.4	8.6
28.8	31.5	28.4	Trade Receivables (net)	16.4	19.7	37.1	30.9	28.8	29.7
7.0	7.4	6.6	Inventory	.9	2.0	1.6	7.1	6.1	9.8
4.4	4.2	5.6	All Other Current	6.7	6.9	6.6	5.3	4.1	6.0
51.7	52.2	50.6	Total Current	46.2	42.9	54.6	54.6	45.4	54.1
38.6	38.6	39.7	Fixed Assets (net)	38.7	48.4	41.4	37.5	44.5	35.3
3.3	3.9	4.0	Intangibles (net)	.0	2.9	1.1	3.2	3.4	6.3
6.5	5.2	5.6	All Other Non-Current	15.2	5.8	3.0	4.7	6.6	4.3
100.0	100.0	100.0	Total	100.0	100.0	100.0	100.0	100.0	100.0
			LIABILITIES						
8.4	8.2	8.9	Notes Payable-Short Term	15.9	14.7	10.4	7.8	7.2	7.5
6.3	4.7	3.4	Cur. Mat.-L.T.D.	2.4	3.9	2.0	4.4	3.9	2.9
11.5	13.9	11.2	Trade Payables	5.1	7.7	8.3	9.0	13.5	13.1
.6	.7	.7	Income Taxes Payable	.0	.1	.4	.6	.7	1.0
9.3	8.5	9.9	All Other Current	17.7	9.7	7.7	12.0	7.4	9.6
36.1	36.1	34.0	Total Current	41.0	36.1	28.8	33.8	32.6	34.2
20.0	21.5	17.8	Long-Term Debt	19.1	26.7	12.5	18.2	17.7	16.1
1.0	1.1	.9	Deferred Taxes	.0	.0	.0	.5	1.7	1.1
3.7	4.2	3.6	All Other Non-Current	4.6	3.2	1.0	2.9	4.7	3.8
39.2	37.1	43.7	Net Worth	35.0	34.0	57.6	44.6	43.3	44.8
100.0	100.0	100.0	Total Liabilities & Net Worth	100.0	100.0	100.0	100.0	100.0	100.0
			INCOME DATA						
100.0	100.0	100.0	Net Sales	100.0	100.0	100.0	100.0	100.0	100.0
			Gross Profit						
89.2	84.8	83.8	Operating Expenses	77.7	84.4	81.8	85.2	82.8	85.0
10.8	15.2	16.2	Operating Profit	22.3	15.6	18.2	14.8	17.2	15.0
1.4	2.5	2.1	All Other Expenses (net)	1.5	3.9	2.5	.8	2.1	2.3
9.4	12.7	14.1	Profit Before Taxes	20.8	11.7	15.7	13.9	15.1	12.7
			RATIOS						
2.6	2.3	2.7		23.1	2.8	5.2	2.7	2.4	2.5
1.4	1.4	1.6	Current	1.2	1.2	2.3	1.8	1.3	1.6
1.0	1.0	1.0		.3	.7	1.1	1.2	.9	1.1
2.0	1.9	2.0		22.2	2.2	3.6	2.3	1.8	1.9
1.1	1.1	1.2	Quick	1.0	1.1	1.8	1.4	1.1	1.2
.7	.7	.7		.2	.4	1.0	.8	.6	.8
28 12.8	41 8.9	35 10.4		0 UND	0 UND	35 10.3	30 12.2	43 8.5	44 8.4
53 6.9	62 5.9	58 6.2	Sales/Receivables	35 10.6	37 10.0	48 7.7	60 6.0	62 5.9	64 5.7
76 4.8	84 4.3	83 4.4		88 4.1	61 6.0	88 4.2	90 4.0	82 4.5	83 4.4
			Cost of Sales/Inventory						
			Cost of Sales/Payables						
5.3	5.3	5.3		1.9	6.7	5.5	4.9	6.2	4.2
15.9	13.0	10.8	Sales/Working Capital	20.2	30.0	8.6	8.4	19.0	9.9
-999.8	238.2	222.5		-3.1	-6.9	62.4	32.3	-45.1	68.4
19.7	23.2	30.7		38.6	14.7	35.5	25.0	49.5	32.4
(241) 7.7	(238) 8.6	(241) 9.6	EBIT/Interest	(10) 5.4	(21) 8.4	(19) 8.0	(42) 12.5	(61) 8.8	(88) 9.7
2.3	3.1	3.1		.9	1.5	2.6	3.6	4.0	2.9
7.1	6.0	10.1						4.7	19.0
(54) 2.5	(54) 2.8	(66) 3.4	Net Profit + Depr., Dep., Amort./Cur. Mat. L/T/D					(18) 1.4	(38) 5.8
1.4	1.5	1.3						.8	2.2
.4	.5	.4		.1	.5	.2	.4	.5	.3
1.0	1.0	.9	Fixed/Worth	.7	1.4	.8	.7	1.1	.8
2.4	2.4	2.0		15.8	7.5	1.2	2.1	2.1	1.7
.6	.8	.6		.2	.7	.3	.6	.7	.6
1.6	1.9	1.5	Debt/Worth	2.2	2.0	.9	1.3	1.6	1.5
4.5	5.3	3.5		66.9	22.6	1.6	3.9	3.5	3.2
64.5	69.1	69.8		82.1	99.3	65.5	89.1	66.7	64.2
(242) 31.4	(241) 41.5	(268) 43.8	% Profit Before Taxes/Tangible Net Worth	(16) 29.4	(24) 53.8	43.0	(44) 50.8	(63) 42.9	(99) 42.9
12.8	18.5	17.4		5.1	12.1	15.6	18.7	17.4	17.7
22.4	25.8	30.0		26.0	30.0	39.6	32.3	25.8	27.5
11.4	13.3	15.4	% Profit Before Taxes/Total Assets	8.2	9.6	22.6	17.5	15.4	15.8
3.0	5.6	4.9		1.1	2.4	6.3	5.7	5.3	5.9
19.4	16.6	14.9		54.5	12.7	20.8	13.7	10.0	18.2
6.1	5.3	4.8	Sales/Net Fixed Assets	9.8	3.1	4.5	5.1	4.5	5.5
2.2	2.0	2.1		.6	.6	2.9	2.7	1.4	2.2
3.2	2.7	2.7		5.5	2.8	3.3	2.6	2.5	2.8
1.9	1.7	1.7	Sales/Total Assets	1.2	1.4	1.9	2.0	1.7	1.6
1.0	1.0	.9		.2	.4	1.5	1.3	.6	.9
1.6	1.5	1.5			4.2	1.8	1.2	1.7	.9
(223) 4.6	(222) 3.9	(227) 3.7	% Depr., Dep., Amort./Sales		(18) 6.5	(18) 4.8	(36) 4.4	(58) 4.0	(88) 2.2
8.9	7.1	6.4			15.8	11.3	6.8	6.5	4.6
1.6	1.4	1.3					1.8	1.3	.2
(80) 3.6	(58) 3.9	(62) 3.1	% Officers', Directors' Owners' Comp/Sales				(14) 3.4	(19) 2.3	(10) .5
7.6	9.7	11.5					15.9	5.5	1.0
7868086M	11854338M	12171108M	Net Sales ($)	7439M	52883M	84390M	333870M	1075289M	10617237M
5430648M	7741562M	9428953M	Total Assets ($)	20594M	96143M	59754M	267225M	1355927M	7629310M

M = $ thousand   MM = $ million
See Pages 11 through 21 for Explanation of Ratios and Data

UTILITIES

Current Data Sorted by Assets							Comparative Historical Data	
						Type of Statement		
1		2	9	5	3	Unqualified	8	9
	2	1				Reviewed		1
		1				Compiled	2	2
						Tax Returns		1
1	1	1	6		2	Other	1	4
	9 (4/1-9/30/06)		26 (10/1/06-3/31/07)				1 4/1/02-3/31/03 ALL	4 4/1/03-3/31/04 ALL
0-500M	500M-2MM	2-10MM	10-50MM	50-100MM	100-250MM	**NUMBER OF STATEMENTS**	11	17
2	3	5	15	5	5			
%	%	%	%	%	%	**ASSETS**	%	%
			17.8			Cash & Equivalents	8.4	14.2
			5.0			Trade Receivables (net)	10.8	15.7
			.9			Inventory	1.3	5.3
			8.2			All Other Current	1.4	2.3
			31.9			Total Current	21.9	37.4
			61.4			Fixed Assets (net)	53.2	55.2
			1.3			Intangibles (net)	4.1	2.3
			5.4			All Other Non-Current	20.8	5.1
			100.0			Total	100.0	100.0
						LIABILITIES		
			1.4			Notes Payable-Short Term	.5	6.7
			2.3			Cur. Mat.-L.T.D.	3.4	3.1
			7.3			Trade Payables	5.3	13.8
			.0			Income Taxes Payable	.3	.0
			8.4			All Other Current	3.8	7.7
			19.4			Total Current	13.2	31.3
			29.7			Long-Term Debt	30.8	25.7
			.8			Deferred Taxes	.4	.1
			3.0			All Other Non-Current	2.2	1.7
			47.2			Net Worth	53.4	41.2
			100.0			Total Liabilties & Net Worth	100.0	100.0
						INCOME DATA		
			100.0			Net Sales	100.0	100.0
						Gross Profit		
			85.3			Operating Expenses	67.5	79.2
			14.7			Operating Profit	32.5	20.8
			5.3			All Other Expenses (net)	15.0	9.1
			9.4			Profit Before Taxes	17.4	11.6
						RATIOS		
			2.8				2.1	3.4
			1.4			Current	1.7	1.0
			1.0				.2	.4
			2.0				1.8	2.8
			1.4			Quick	1.1	.8
			.4				.2	.3
		3	132.3				6 57.1	23 16.0
		30	12.1			Sales/Receivables	29 12.4	29 12.4
		48	7.6				66 5.5	79 4.6
						Cost of Sales/Inventory		
						Cost of Sales/Payables		
			1.8				8.0	4.4
			16.8			Sales/Working Capital	9.9	76.3
			-91.6				-3.3	-4.5
			11.1					8.7
		(13)	3.2			EBIT/Interest		(12) 4.5
			2.4					1.1
						Net Profit + Depr., Dep., Amort./Cur. Mat. L/T/D		
			.8				.1	.4
			1.5			Fixed/Worth	1.3	1.1
			2.5				3.1	4.2
			.5				.1	.5
			1.6			Debt/Worth	1.2	1.7
			2.6				3.7	7.4
			17.4				18.0	24.9
		(14)	13.0			% Profit Before Taxes/Tangible Net Worth	11.9	(16) 8.6
			6.9				1.9	1.2
			6.0				11.6	9.6
			4.6			% Profit Before Taxes/Total Assets	3.0	4.2
			3.0				1.8	.2
			1.1				34.3	59.1
			.7			Sales/Net Fixed Assets	.5	.5
			.5				.2	.3
			.8				.8	2.0
			.6			Sales/Total Assets	.2	.4
			.4				.1	.2
			6.1				1.0	1.0
		(13)	8.3			% Depr., Dep., Amort./Sales	7.6	(14) 10.5
			12.9				16.3	14.5
						% Officers', Directors' Owners' Comp/Sales		
96M	7905M	12194M	291297M	565374M	573471M	Net Sales ($)	166547M	356986M
191M	3632M	22047M	489446M	410615M	1088446M	Total Assets ($)	300911M	732659M

Comparative Historical Data   Current Data Sorted by Sales

Hist 1	Hist 2	Hist 3	Type of Statement	0-1MM	1-3MM	3-5MM	5-10MM	10-25MM	25MM & OVER
9	5	20	Unqualified	1	1	1		7	10
1	2	3	Reviewed	2	1				
1		1	Compiled	1					
2	2		Tax Returns						
4	1	11	Other	1		2	3	2	3
4/1/04-3/31/05 ALL	4/1/05-3/31/06 ALL	4/1/06-3/31/07 ALL		9 (4/1-9/30/06) 0-1MM	1-3MM	3-5MM	26 (10/1/06-3/31/07) 5-10MM	10-25MM	25MM & OVER
17	10	35	**NUMBER OF STATEMENTS**	5	2	3	3	9	13
%	%	%	**ASSETS**	%	%	%	%	%	%
7.9	10.3	13.5	Cash & Equivalents						11.9
13.6	5.7	10.2	Trade Receivables (net)						10.5
6.7	1.2	2.7	Inventory						5.3
3.1	.1	4.3	All Other Current						6.6
31.4	17.3	30.6	Total Current						34.3
61.6	70.0	60.4	Fixed Assets (net)						57.6
1.5	2.2	1.8	Intangibles (net)						.9
5.6	10.5	7.1	All Other Non-Current						7.3
100.0	100.0	100.0	Total						100.0
			LIABILITIES						
7.5	.4	1.9	Notes Payable-Short Term						2.9
2.4	1.3	2.5	Cur. Mat.-L.T.D.						1.5
7.8	16.9	7.8	Trade Payables						12.9
.0	.0	.0	Income Taxes Payable						.0
7.4	3.7	8.0	All Other Current						6.0
25.2	22.4	20.4	Total Current						23.4
31.7	23.9	35.2	Long-Term Debt						24.7
.1	.0	1.6	Deferred Taxes						.2
2.7	3.4	3.8	All Other Non-Current						2.0
40.4	50.3	39.1	Net Worth						49.8
100.0	100.0	100.0	Total Liabilities & Net Worth						100.0
			INCOME DATA						
100.0	100.0	100.0	Net Sales						100.0
			Gross Profit						
83.7	83.3	85.9	Operating Expenses						90.7
16.3	16.7	14.1	Operating Profit						9.3
5.1	5.3	5.1	All Other Expenses (net)						1.6
11.2	11.4	9.0	Profit Before Taxes						7.7
			RATIOS						
2.6	4.8	2.5	Current						2.0
1.2	1.3	1.2							1.2
.8	.5	.8							.9
2.1	3.4	2.0	Quick						1.7
.8	1.2	1.0							.8
.5	.4	.5							.5
22 16.9	0 UND	20 18.5	Sales/Receivables					23 15.8	15.8
31 11.7	42 8.7	30 12.0						37 9.9	9.9
47 7.8	64 5.7	51 7.1						52 7.1	7.1
			Cost of Sales/Inventory						
			Cost of Sales/Payables						
4.6	3.3	4.1	Sales/Working Capital						9.2
25.4	40.4	22.2							25.8
-30.2	-10.5	-16.6							-54.1
29.2		6.4	EBIT/Interest						20.5
(13) 2.9	(30) 3.3	3.3						(12) 5.1	5.1
.9		2.2							2.3
			Net Profit + Depr., Dep., Amort./Cur. Mat. L/T/D						
.9	.9	1.0	Fixed/Worth						.7
2.1	1.1	1.8							1.2
3.3	9.7	2.5							2.0
.7	.1	.7	Debt/Worth						.4
2.4	.8	1.8							1.1
4.1	10.0	3.4							2.3
30.0		23.2	% Profit Before Taxes/Tangible Net Worth						21.3
(15) 5.7	(33) 9.8	9.8							9.5
.3		4.1							3.2
16.7	5.9	6.0	% Profit Before Taxes/Total Assets						11.1
3.0	4.3	4.5							4.5
.5	2.8	1.3							1.5
5.7	1.6	1.1	Sales/Net Fixed Assets						16.7
.7	.6	.7							1.0
.4	.4	.5							.6
3.2	.8	.8	Sales/Total Assets						1.5
.5	.4	.5							.8
.3	.3	.4							.5
2.1		3.5	% Depr., Dep., Amort./Sales						.9
(15) 8.3	(31) 7.4	7.4						(11) 5.3	5.3
14.4		12.4							6.5
			% Officers', Directors' Owners' Comp/Sales						
349772M	138347M	1450337M	Net Sales ($)	1760M	3857M	12511M	20187M	160918M	1251104M
703160M	379433M	2014377M	Total Assets ($)	6710M	4960M	23550M	44581M	369888M	1564688M

Current Data Sorted by Assets   Comparative Historical Data

						Type of Statement		
1	9	25	121	91	96	Unqualified	59	69
2	7	6	4	1		Reviewed	15	17
	4		2			Compiled	9	12
1	3	1				Tax Returns	5	4
2	4	8	11	8	6	Other	36	43
	107 (4/1-9/30/06)		306 (10/1/06-3/31/07)				4/1/02-3/31/03 ALL	4/1/03-3/31/04 ALL
0-500M	500M-2MM	2-10MM	10-50MM	50-100MM	100-250MM			
6	27	40	138	100	102	NUMBER OF STATEMENTS	124	145
%	%	%	%	%	%	ASSETS	%	%
	19.0	10.3	8.7	5.0	4.0	Cash & Equivalents	12.4	11.6
	22.2	21.9	9.3	6.6	5.7	Trade Receivables (net)	15.9	20.5
	5.9	3.0	2.1	2.1	1.5	Inventory	3.8	5.2
	6.7	3.8	2.1	1.4	2.4	All Other Current	4.2	5.8
	53.8	39.0	22.3	15.1	13.7	Total Current	36.2	43.0
	35.5	47.8	62.6	72.4	71.0	Fixed Assets (net)	49.1	45.4
	4.9	2.4	1.8	1.0	2.7	Intangibles (net)	3.9	2.5
	5.8	10.9	13.4	11.6	12.6	All Other Non-Current	10.8	9.0
	100.0	100.0	100.0	100.0	100.0	Total	100.0	100.0
						LIABILITIES		
	3.9	3.4	2.4	2.3	2.8	Notes Payable-Short Term	4.4	5.7
	4.1	3.3	2.1	1.9	1.7	Cur. Mat.-L.T.D.	6.2	3.5
	15.3	11.4	6.4	3.9	5.0	Trade Payables	12.3	11.9
	.5	.5	.4	.4	.3	Income Taxes Payable	.1	.3
	9.9	8.9	5.1	3.4	4.6	All Other Current	8.7	10.6
	33.8	27.5	16.3	11.9	14.4	Total Current	31.6	32.0
	32.7	33.0	31.1	38.0	45.3	Long-Term Debt	35.7	24.6
	2.0	1.8	1.1	.1	.8	Deferred Taxes	1.0	1.7
	4.3	6.8	5.3	4.7	5.2	All Other Non-Current	7.6	6.4
	27.3	30.9	46.2	45.3	34.3	Net Worth	24.0	35.4
	100.0	100.0	100.0	100.0	100.0	Total Liabilities & Net Worth	100.0	100.0
						INCOME DATA		
	100.0	100.0	100.0	100.0	100.0	Net Sales	100.0	100.0
						Gross Profit		
	88.7	87.0	88.8	92.5	90.9	Operating Expenses	86.1	89.3
	11.3	13.0	11.2	7.5	9.1	Operating Profit	13.9	10.7
	2.8	5.2	2.8	2.0	3.3	All Other Expenses (net)	4.7	3.3
	8.5	7.8	8.4	5.6	5.9	Profit Before Taxes	9.3	7.4
						RATIOS		
	3.2	2.0	2.0	1.7	1.3		1.8	1.9
	2.0	1.4	1.3	1.2	1.0	Current	1.3	1.2
	1.1	1.0	.9	.8	.7		.9	.9
	3.2	1.9	1.4	1.3	1.0		1.7	1.5
	1.2	1.2	1.0	.9	.7	Quick	1.0	.9
	.7	.7	.6	.6	.5		.4	.6
	21 17.3	24 15.1	29 12.6	28 13.0	25 14.5		25 14.4	27 13.5
	34 10.8	39 9.4	38 9.5	35 10.4	32 11.5	Sales/Receivables	37 10.0	40 9.1
	58 6.3	61 6.0	48 7.6	46 8.0	42 8.7		56 6.5	61 6.0
						Cost of Sales/Inventory		
						Cost of Sales/Payables		
	4.3	5.4	6.1	8.0	15.3		6.6	7.3
	10.7	19.9	16.2	34.2	NM	Sales/Working Capital	20.1	27.8
	78.3	79.9	-76.2	-18.1	-12.1		-43.9	-25.4
	13.3	5.1	5.1	3.3	2.8		7.7	6.3
	(21) 4.2	(32) 2.6	(128) 2.8	(98) 2.3	(100) 2.0	EBIT/Interest	(107) 2.9	(131) 3.3
	1.8	1.4	1.7	1.7	1.5		1.5	1.3
		3.1	14.6				4.1	9.1
		(13) 2.2	(22) 4.1			Net Profit + Depr., Dep., Amort./Cur. Mat. L/T/D	(16) 2.0	(31) 4.1
		1.4	2.6				.8	1.5
	.2	.8	1.0	1.3	1.8		.6	.5
	1.2	1.6	1.6	1.7	2.3	Fixed/Worth	1.4	1.5
	2.9	2.9	2.4	2.3	3.0		3.4	3.0
	.8	1.0	.7	.8	1.5		.7	.7
	1.4	1.9	1.3	1.3	2.0	Debt/Worth	2.2	1.9
	3.9	5.4	2.3	2.0	2.8		7.5	5.3
	65.9	35.3	13.2	8.4	12.1		31.9	35.7
	(23) 25.3	(37) 9.7	(135) 7.2	(99) 6.5	(100) 8.1	% Profit Before Taxes/Tangible Net Worth	(104) 13.4	(130) 11.3
	9.8	3.2	4.6	5.0	4.8		3.0	2.4
	32.8	11.0	4.9	4.5	3.4		11.1	10.7
	6.5	4.2	3.4	3.0	2.6	% Profit Before Taxes/Total Assets	4.2	3.9
	2.6	.7	1.8	2.0	1.6		1.4	.8
	40.0	15.0	1.1	1.0	.9		11.8	30.0
	9.2	1.3	.7	.7	.6	Sales/Net Fixed Assets	1.2	2.1
	.9	.6	.5	.5	.5		.6	.6
	3.3	2.4	.7	.7	.6		1.6	2.3
	2.3	.9	.5	.5	.5	Sales/Total Assets	.6	.9
	.5	.4	.4	.4	.4		.4	.5
	1.0	1.6	5.1	4.9	4.8		2.1	1.4
	(20) 4.0	(37) 5.8	(132) 6.9	(99) 6.2	(95) 6.3	% Depr., Dep., Amort./Sales	(105) 5.9	(118) 5.5
	8.6	12.7	9.2	8.3	7.4		11.5	8.1
							1.7	1.4
						% Officers', Directors' Owners' Comp/Sales	(20) 3.5	(27) 3.0
							6.9	5.9
13103M	79288M	634429M	2976774M	4347096M	10693519M	Net Sales ($)	3973897M	5791509M
1977M	35049M	209981M	3982739M	7126353M	16677573M	Total Assets ($)	5984585M	5899612M

M = $ thousand   MM = $ million
See Pages 11 through 21 for Explanation of Ratios and Data

Comparative Historical Data | | Current Data Sorted by Sales

			Type of Statement						
247	273	343	Unqualified	13	11	10	27	90	192
18	25	19	Reviewed	1	3	6	1	6	2
7	14	7	Compiled		3		1	1	2
8	4	5	Tax Returns		2	1	1		1
48	73	39	Other	4	2	6		7	16
4/1/04-3/31/05 ALL	4/1/05-3/31/06 ALL	4/1/06-3/31/07 ALL		107 (4/1-9/30/06)			306 (10/1/06-3/31/07)		
				0-1MM	1-3MM	3-5MM	5-10MM	10-25MM	25MM & OVER
328	389	413	NUMBER OF STATEMENTS	18	21	23	34	104	213
%	%	%	ASSETS	%	%	%	%	%	%
8.2	7.3	7.8	Cash & Equivalents	11.0	16.2	14.3	7.3	6.7	6.6
11.7	12.8	10.0	Trade Receivables (net)	7.3	15.5	15.9	6.1	8.9	10.2
2.6	2.4	2.3	Inventory	5.0	3.7	3.6	3.2	1.9	1.8
3.1	3.2	2.7	All Other Current	2.5	4.7	5.5	4.1	1.7	2.5
25.7	25.6	22.8	Total Current	25.8	40.1	39.3	20.7	19.2	21.1
60.7	61.3	63.3	Fixed Assets (net)	58.9	48.2	45.5	65.1	66.0	65.4
1.9	2.6	2.0	Intangibles (net)	2.1	4.9	.8	3.6	.9	2.2
11.7	10.6	11.9	All Other Non-Current	13.2	6.8	14.5	10.6	13.9	11.3
100.0	100.0	100.0	Total	100.0	100.0	100.0	100.0	100.0	100.0
			LIABILITIES						
3.0	2.7	2.7	Notes Payable-Short Term	3.3	4.2	1.8	2.2	1.6	3.3
2.7	2.5	2.2	Cur. Mat.-L.T.D.	3.1	4.0	3.2	1.8	2.0	2.0
7.6	9.0	6.5	Trade Payables	2.7	16.0	6.6	4.3	4.4	7.3
.3	.4	.4	Income Taxes Payable	1.2	.7	.3	.3	.5	.3
6.6	5.9	5.4	All Other Current	7.5	7.9	4.8	5.1	4.9	5.4
20.2	20.4	17.3	Total Current	17.9	32.8	16.6	13.8	13.4	18.2
35.6	36.4	36.3	Long-Term Debt	32.9	40.0	34.2	33.0	35.4	37.4
.7	.7	.9	Deferred Taxes	4.4	1.3	1.3	1.7	.8	.4
4.6	3.8	5.2	All Other Non-Current	6.3	7.6	6.0	5.4	4.2	5.3
38.9	38.7	40.3	Net Worth	38.5	18.3	42.0	46.1	46.1	38.7
100.0	100.0	100.0	Total Liabilities & Net Worth	100.0	100.0	100.0	100.0	100.0	100.0
			INCOME DATA						
100.0	100.0	100.0	Net Sales	100.0	100.0	100.0	100.0	100.0	100.0
			Gross Profit						
90.3	89.4	90.2	Operating Expenses	87.1	86.7	85.7	89.1	88.5	92.2
9.7	10.6	9.8	Operating Profit	12.9	13.3	14.3	10.9	11.5	7.8
3.3	4.0	2.9	All Other Expenses (net)	7.6	4.6	1.5	3.5	2.8	2.4
6.4	6.6	7.0	Profit Before Taxes	5.3	8.8	12.8	7.4	8.7	5.4
			RATIOS						
1.7	1.8	1.8		2.9	3.5	3.6	2.0	1.9	1.6
1.1	1.2	1.2	Current	1.0	1.8	2.3	1.3	1.3	1.1
.8	.9	.8		.6	.9	1.4	.9	.9	.7
1.4	1.5	1.4		2.9	2.3	2.9	1.4	1.5	1.3
.9	.9	.9	Quick	.6	1.2	1.7	.8	.9	.9
.5	.6	.6		.2	.8	1.1	.6	.6	.5
25 14.7	27 13.6	26 13.8		14 26.1	20 17.9	31 11.9	29 12.7	30 12.0	26 13.8
35 10.3	37 10.0	36 10.2	Sales/Receivables	29 12.8	26 13.8	39 9.4	40 9.2	39 9.2	34 10.8
49 7.5	50 7.3	47 7.8		52 7.0	45 8.0	58 6.3	48 7.6	51 7.2	44 8.3
			Cost of Sales/Inventory						
			Cost of Sales/Payables						
7.8	7.9	7.4		3.0	3.9	3.5	5.7	7.2	11.1
33.2	23.1	33.7	Sales/Working Capital	NM	5.1	7.5	20.7	18.9	65.3
-24.5	-36.8	-20.5		-3.4	-96.6	14.0	-62.8	-24.6	-17.5
4.7	4.3	3.8		4.0	4.5	12.6	3.7	4.6	3.4
(307) 2.5	(355) 2.4	(384) 2.4	EBIT/Interest	(13) 2.7	(18) 2.4	(18) 8.2	(31) 2.3	(100) 2.5	(204) 2.2
1.7	1.7	1.6		.8	1.5	4.7	1.6	1.6	1.7
4.9	5.2	6.8	Net Profit + Depr., Dep.,					6.1	7.0
(46) 2.9	(47) 2.7	(57) 3.3	Amort./Cur. Mat. L/T/D				(16) 3.2	(18) 4.6	
1.7	1.5	2.2						1.4	2.8
1.0	1.0	1.2		1.2	1.0	.5	1.0	1.2	1.3
1.7	1.7	1.8	Fixed/Worth	2.1	2.1	1.0	1.8	1.7	1.9
2.5	2.6	2.5		3.0	2.7	1.7	2.8	2.3	2.6
.9	.9	.9		.9	.9	.3	.6	.7	1.1
1.6	1.6	1.6	Debt/Worth	2.1	1.8	1.1	1.5	1.3	1.7
2.6	2.6	2.4		3.5	4.7	1.7	3.4	2.0	2.5
15.0	14.1	13.2	% Profit Before Taxes/Tangible	16.6	31.0	52.8	19.2	9.7	12.1
(310) 6.8	(368) 7.2	(399) 7.5	Net Worth	(16) 9.1	(18) 9.8	(22) 23.9	(33) 7.9	(103) 6.9	(207) 7.5
3.6	4.2	4.7		.9	3.5	7.0	3.0	4.5	5.1
5.2	4.8	4.9	% Profit Before Taxes/Total	4.2	10.1	23.7	5.6	4.9	4.5
2.9	2.9	3.1	Assets	1.6	4.6	9.9	2.5	3.4	2.9
1.5	1.5	1.7		-1.7	1.4	3.7	1.2	1.6	1.9
2.6	1.7	1.2		1.1	16.9	10.8	.9	.8	1.2
.8	.7	.7	Sales/Net Fixed Assets	.6	.9	2.4	.5	.6	.8
.5	.5	.5		.4	.5	.8	.4	.5	.6
1.0	.9	.8		.5	2.4	2.5	.5	.6	.8
.5	.5	.5	Sales/Total Assets	.4	.5	1.0	.4	.4	.6
.4	.4	.4		.3	.4	.5	.3	.4	.4
4.6	4.6	4.6		5.3	2.2	3.6	6.7	5.9	4.1
(307) 6.7	(360) 6.3	(386) 6.3	% Depr., Dep., Amort./Sales	(16) 8.1	(18) 9.8	(19) 6.7	(30) 9.1	(100) 6.8	(203) 5.6
8.8	8.8	8.6		13.8	13.6	9.1	12.7	8.9	7.0
2.0	1.7	2.0	% Officers', Directors'						
(23) 3.3	(28) 4.5	(10) 3.2	Owners' Comp/Sales						
6.4	9.7	5.6							
15201544M	19397955M	18744209M	Net Sales ($)	11151M	41911M	93237M	249340M	1689316M	16659254M
20389181M	25547502M	28033672M	Total Assets ($)	40142M	76952M	161991M	839644M	3662128M	23252815M

M = $ thousand   MM = $ million
See Pages 11 through 21 for Explanation of Ratios and Data

Current Data Sorted by Assets　　　　　　　　Comparative Historical Data

0-500M	500M-2MM	2-10MM	10-50MM	50-100MM	100-250MM	Type of Statement	4/1/02-3/31/03 ALL	4/1/03-3/31/04 ALL
3	2	14	23	12	21	Unqualified	50	47
	2	13	2	1		Reviewed	15	14
3	6	11	1			Compiled	11	14
3	9	2	1			Tax Returns	6	6
1	5	12	16	5	10	Other	36	29
	69 (4/1-9/30/06)		109 (10/1/06-3/31/07)					
10	24	52	43	18	31	**NUMBER OF STATEMENTS**	118	110
%	%	%	%	%	%	**ASSETS**	%	%
26.4	15.1	10.8	9.1	4.4	4.9	Cash & Equivalents	10.2	9.6
16.7	15.2	24.6	21.3	22.1	20.2	Trade Receivables (net)	18.5	21.9
22.8	10.8	10.2	6.8	11.3	10.4	Inventory	6.7	8.6
1.1	1.8	3.0	2.4	4.0	5.2	All Other Current	4.2	4.8
67.0	42.9	48.5	39.6	41.8	40.7	Total Current	39.7	44.8
24.8	40.4	41.6	47.0	41.8	44.9	Fixed Assets (net)	48.1	43.5
3.0	4.5	2.9	7.2	7.9	5.2	Intangibles (net)	5.2	4.3
4.9	12.2	7.0	6.3	8.5	9.3	All Other Non-Current	7.0	7.4
100.0	100.0	100.0	100.0	100.0	100.0	Total	100.0	100.0
						LIABILITIES		
5.5	5.9	9.9	6.1	4.0	7.0	Notes Payable-Short Term	9.1	6.6
2.3	7.6	3.5	3.1	1.8	1.9	Cur. Mat.-L.T.D.	3.0	3.4
13.3	17.4	19.6	14.8	13.9	19.8	Trade Payables	14.1	18.1
.4	.1	.2	.4	.3	.2	Income Taxes Payable	.4	.3
28.5	14.2	7.8	8.6	7.4	7.4	All Other Current	9.1	8.4
50.0	45.2	41.0	32.9	27.4	36.3	Total Current	35.7	36.7
49.3	30.1	19.6	24.8	19.3	20.5	Long-Term Debt	24.3	24.4
1.1	1.3	1.7	2.4	2.1	3.4	Deferred Taxes	2.0	1.9
2.5	8.7	2.3	2.6	9.2	5.9	All Other Non-Current	4.5	5.1
-2.9	14.8	35.4	37.2	42.0	34.0	Net Worth	33.5	32.0
100.0	100.0	100.0	100.0	100.0	100.0	Total Liabilities & Net Worth	100.0	100.0
						INCOME DATA		
100.0	100.0	100.0	100.0	100.0	100.0	Net Sales	100.0	100.0
						Gross Profit		
94.7	91.6	92.8	95.8	85.9	92.0	Operating Expenses	93.7	94.0
5.3	8.4	7.2	4.2	14.1	8.0	Operating Profit	6.3	6.0
1.0	2.3	2.6	.6	3.5	2.4	All Other Expenses (net)	1.8	1.8
4.3	6.2	4.7	3.5	10.6	5.6	Profit Before Taxes	4.5	4.2
						RATIOS		
3.4	2.0	1.6	2.0	2.2	1.5		1.7	1.7
1.3	1.2	1.0	1.2	1.4	1.2	Current	1.2	1.2
1.0	.4	.8	.8	1.1	1.0		.8	.9
1.8	1.2	1.4	1.3	1.6	1.0		1.3	1.3
.8	.7	.8	.8	.8	.8	Quick	.8	.9
.4	.2	.5	.6	.5	.5		.4	.4
0　UND	0　853.6	13　27.2	16　23.1	18　20.4	18　20.6		17　21.3	13　28.0
1　512.0	13　28.1	29　12.5	36　10.1	34　10.8	36　10.1	Sales/Receivables	31　11.8	28　13.1
21　17.3	35　10.4	51　7.2	48　7.6	67　5.5	49　7.4		49　7.4	48　7.6
						Cost of Sales/Inventory		
						Cost of Sales/Payables		
19.3	8.0	12.2	8.5	8.7	10.9		7.7	11.8
60.6	74.4	312.2	49.2	15.9	49.9	Sales/Working Capital	30.7	36.8
-881.2	-12.7	-22.4	-29.9	89.7	-150.8		-34.2	-62.0
	7.4	7.1	7.9	8.4	9.4		6.3	10.0
	(18)　3.5	(45)　3.3	(38)　2.4	(15)　3.5	(29)　3.0	EBIT/Interest	(104)　2.7	(95)　4.2
	1.1	2.1	1.7	1.7	1.2		1.6	1.5
			5.8				6.6	5.6
		(13)　2.6				Net Profit + Depr., Dep., Amort./Cur. Mat. L/T/D	(32)　2.9	(32)　2.7
		2.2					1.4	1.2
.0	.5	.3	.9	.5	.5		.7	.5
.5	2.0	1.3	1.5	1.3	2.0	Fixed/Worth	1.6	1.4
UND	-4.1	3.1	4.2	2.1	3.7		2.8	3.1
.6	2.1	.8	.9	.6	1.0		1.0	1.0
2.1	5.4	2.2	3.2	1.9	2.7	Debt/Worth	2.2	2.1
UND	-13.4	4.8	7.0	4.8	8.2		4.6	10.8
	72.2	35.8	40.5	26.9	44.4		31.6	33.8
	(16)　18.1	(46)　22.3	(37)　9.4	(16)　14.0	(29)　12.9	% Profit Before Taxes/Tangible Net Worth	(100)　13.9	(93)　17.2
	8.6	7.9	1.3	7.1	4.0		4.8	6.3
36.6	16.5	10.3	7.6	7.6	7.1		9.4	9.9
21.5	5.0	5.8	2.9	5.4	4.5	% Profit Before Taxes/Total Assets	4.3	4.9
6.0	-1.6	3.0	.5	3.7	.4		1.2	1.2
UND	40.6	32.4	18.9	44.4	164.0		19.4	30.3
655.0	5.3	4.2	2.7	2.2	1.4	Sales/Net Fixed Assets	2.7	4.6
16.0	2.5	1.7	1.3	.6	.8		1.0	1.1
53.6	3.7	3.9	3.0	2.6	4.5		2.7	4.4
7.7	2.4	1.7	1.4	1.3	.8	Sales/Total Assets	1.3	1.9
1.6	.9	1.0	.7	.5	.4		.6	.7
	.9	.9	1.2	2.4	.2		1.7	.9
	(21)　3.8	(45)　3.0	(38)　3.7	(16)　4.1	(28)　3.9	% Depr., Dep., Amort./Sales	(100)　4.8	(97)　3.2
	5.0	5.5	5.1	7.8	6.9		7.1	5.8
		.7					2.0	.4
	(10)　1.3					% Officers', Directors' Owners' Comp/Sales	(21)　4.3	(22)　2.4
	1.6						8.5	9.8
41789M	115270M	1075939M	2277397M	3942728M	13087114M	Net Sales ($)	8160243M	8537650M
1961M	29801M	290723M	1034778M	1323746M	5279905M	Total Assets ($)	5423885M	5173420M

© RMA 2007

M = $ thousand　　MM = $ million
See Pages 11 through 21 for Explanation of Ratios and Data

Comparative Historical Data | Current Data Sorted by Sales

	4/1/04- 3/31/05 ALL	4/1/05- 3/31/06 ALL	4/1/06- 3/31/07 ALL	0-1MM	1-3MM	3-5MM	5-10MM	10-25MM	25MM & OVER
Type of Statement					69 (4/1-9/30/06)			109 (10/1/06-3/31/07)	
Unqualified	59	43	75	2	8	4	5	12	44
Reviewed	21	17	18		2		2	7	7
Compiled	9	17	21	2	3		7	3	3
Tax Returns	3	5	15	3	4	3	3	4	1
Other	36	47	49	2	3	5	4	4	25
NUMBER OF STATEMENTS	128	129	178	9	18	14	21	36	80
	%	%	%	%	%	%	%	%	%
ASSETS									
Cash & Equivalents	9.5	9.5	10.1		10.1	9.2	12.7	8.9	8.9
Trade Receivables (net)	22.5	25.8	21.1		17.0	15.6	14.0	18.7	26.9
Inventory	7.4	9.7	10.3		8.5	7.0	12.6	13.9	9.6
All Other Current	4.4	4.1	3.1		2.8	2.2	1.8	2.7	4.0
Total Current	43.8	49.2	44.6		38.4	33.9	41.0	44.2	49.3
Fixed Assets (net)	44.6	40.5	42.4		53.3	49.2	43.3	41.9	39.2
Intangibles (net)	3.1	4.4	5.1		1.4	7.4	6.5	5.4	5.4
All Other Non-Current	8.6	5.9	7.9		6.8	9.5	9.2	8.5	6.1
Total	100.0	100.0	100.0		100.0	100.0	100.0	100.0	100.0
LIABILITIES									
Notes Payable-Short Term	7.2	10.8	7.1		2.0	5.2	8.4	12.4	6.5
Cur. Mat.-L.T.D.	2.6	3.1	3.4		4.0	4.7	3.7	4.6	2.6
Trade Payables	19.8	22.4	17.3		18.5	11.0	14.4	15.8	21.2
Income Taxes Payable	.4	.7	.3		.2	.1	.4	.1	.3
All Other Current	7.1	7.4	9.9		6.8	10.6	15.7	10.5	7.5
Total Current	37.1	44.4	37.9		31.5	31.6	42.7	43.4	38.2
Long-Term Debt	21.7	20.1	24.1		57.8	21.2	22.2	18.7	19.4
Deferred Taxes	2.1	1.8	2.1		2.6	2.0	2.1	2.1	2.2
All Other Non-Current	4.1	4.3	4.6		8.0	5.5	2.9	3.1	4.9
Net Worth	35.1	29.3	31.3		.2	39.7	30.1	32.8	35.4
Total Liabilities & Net Worth	100.0	100.0	100.0		100.0	100.0	100.0	100.0	100.0
INCOME DATA									
Net Sales	100.0	100.0	100.0		100.0	100.0	100.0	100.0	100.0
Gross Profit									
Operating Expenses	92.8	93.5	92.6		82.0	95.5	94.8	95.2	93.9
Operating Profit	7.2	6.5	7.4		18.0	4.5	5.2	4.8	6.1
All Other Expenses (net)	1.6	1.2	2.0		5.6	-.7	1.5	1.6	1.4
Profit Before Taxes	5.6	5.3	5.3		12.4	5.2	3.7	3.3	4.7
RATIOS									
Current	1.8	1.6	1.8		1.9	2.8	1.5	1.6	1.8
	1.2	1.2	1.2		1.5	1.0	1.0	.9	1.3
	.9	.8	.9		.9	.7	.7	.6	1.0
Quick	1.2	1.2	1.2		1.5	1.8	1.0	1.1	1.2
	.9	.9	.8		.9	.8	.6	.6	.9
	.4	.4	.5		.3	.5	.3	.3	.6
Sales/Receivables	19 19.7	17 21.3	15 24.3		2 210.7	17 22.0	1 514.8	15 24.8	17 21.9
	33 11.0	27 13.6	28 13.0		29 12.4	34 10.8	29 12.4	35 10.5	24 14.9
	51 7.1	52 7.0	46 8.0		50 7.2	47 7.8	53 6.9	52 7.0	44 8.3
Cost of Sales/Inventory									
Cost of Sales/Payables									
Sales/Working Capital	11.8	8.4	10.8		7.0	6.6	14.6	11.4	11.9
	37.8	38.2	53.1		38.9	NM	-525.2	-87.1	37.8
	-54.1	-48.4	-33.8		-23.4	-16.3	-13.5	-8.7	240.3
EBIT/Interest	11.4	11.0	7.4		6.4		6.8	4.6	9.5
	(110) 4.3	(116) 3.7	(151) 3.2		(16) 4.4		(15) 2.6	(32) 3.0	(73) 3.5
	1.9	1.8	1.6		2.5		1.7	.8	1.7
Net Profit + Depr., Dep., Amort./Cur. Mat. L/T/D	6.0	6.9	6.2						6.5
	(30) 3.2	(30) 2.1	(37) 2.9					(18)	3.8
	1.4	1.4	1.8						2.5
Fixed/Worth	.4	.4	.5		.8	.6	.4	.7	.4
	1.4	1.3	1.5		2.1	3.0	1.4	1.6	1.2
	2.9	3.5	3.8		UND	6.1	NM	4.1	2.6
Debt/Worth	.8	1.0	.9		1.3	.2	.8	.7	1.0
	2.1	2.5	2.5		2.4	4.7	2.2	2.2	2.7
	7.7	9.8	7.4		-5.0	10.0	-33.4	8.5	6.3
% Profit Before Taxes/Tangible Net Worth	40.6	49.2	43.9		44.6	32.0	48.5	45.0	46.2
	(113) 17.5	(113) 14.9	(152) 15.4		(13) 18.2	(12) 18.0	(15) 12.8	(30) 9.1	(73) 16.1
	6.2	4.7	6.5		13.5	.3	4.5	2.8	6.4
% Profit Before Taxes/Total Assets	9.2	11.9	10.2		10.9	10.8	16.8	8.1	9.8
	4.9	5.1	4.9		5.5	3.6	3.9	3.8	5.2
	1.6	1.7	1.0		4.1	-3.0	1.0	-.8	1.3
Sales/Net Fixed Assets	36.9	59.9	39.3		10.4	5.8	42.4	36.0	115.9
	3.3	6.3	3.8		1.8	4.0	5.2	3.3	5.4
	1.0	1.6	1.3		.9	1.6	1.7	1.2	1.4
Sales/Total Assets	3.4	5.0	3.8		3.2	2.3	4.8	3.6	5.9
	1.3	2.0	1.6		.9	1.8	1.8	1.5	1.9
	.7	.9	.8		.5	.8	.9	.7	.8
% Depr., Dep., Amort./Sales	1.5	.6	1.2		3.0	3.8	1.0	1.1	.3
	(108) 4.2	(106) 3.3	(151) 3.6		(13) 5.3	5.4	(16) 2.7	(33) 3.8	(70) 2.7
	6.2	5.5	5.4		6.2	10.2	9.8	4.9	5.0
% Officers', Directors' Owners' Comp/Sales	.8	.4	.6						
	(17) 1.8	(23) 1.2	(26) 1.0						
	5.0	2.6	2.5						
Net Sales ($)	10395634M	15200514M	20540237M	3753M	32750M	53372M	158413M	573943M	19718006M
Total Assets ($)	7019602M	6225734M	7960914M	6668M	44403M	61397M	333736M	741092M	6773618M

© RMA 2007

M = $ thousand   MM = $ million
See Pages 11 through 21 for Explanation of Ratios and Data

Current Data Sorted by Assets   Comparative Historical Data

Type of Statement

	0-500M	500M-2MM	2-10MM	10-50MM	50-100MM	100-250MM	Type of Statement	4/1/02-3/31/03 ALL	4/1/03-3/31/04 ALL
	1	12	27	43	12	19	Unqualified	65	67
	1	4	10	3			Reviewed	12	13
	2	4	7	2	1		Compiled	11	20
	8	2	5				Tax Returns	7	23
	3	7	19	24	4	1	Other	34	36
		58 (4/1-9/30/06)		163 (10/1/06-3/31/07)					
NUMBER OF STATEMENTS	15	29	68	72	17	20		129	159

ASSETS

	%	%	%	%	%	%		%	%
Cash & Equivalents	14.2	13.4	10.2	6.7	8.0	5.8		10.1	8.9
Trade Receivables (net)	18.2	11.7	11.2	3.5	4.0	1.3		6.0	8.0
Inventory	14.5	7.5	6.0	.9	.9	.3		1.6	2.6
All Other Current	6.4	3.1	2.4	.9	2.6	1.1		1.7	2.0
Total Current	53.2	35.7	29.7	12.1	15.6	8.6		19.4	21.5
Fixed Assets (net)	38.3	59.0	62.1	79.3	76.4	81.7		71.7	69.6
Intangibles (net)	.5	1.5	1.2	3.0	.4	2.5		1.8	1.5
All Other Non-Current	7.9	3.9	6.9	5.6	7.6	7.3		7.1	7.4
Total	100.0	100.0	100.0	100.0	100.0	100.0		100.0	100.0

LIABILITIES

Notes Payable-Short Term	19.2	9.2	3.2	1.1	1.6	1.6		3.4	4.0
Cur. Mat.-L.T.D.	10.9	2.6	2.5	2.1	1.2	1.0		3.6	3.8
Trade Payables	7.3	6.8	6.5	1.8	3.4	1.3		2.8	4.1
Income Taxes Payable	.1	.3	.3	.2	.1	.0		.1	.1
All Other Current	6.0	8.2	4.4	2.8	3.2	2.8		2.7	5.5
Total Current	43.4	27.1	16.8	8.0	9.5	6.7		12.6	17.4
Long-Term Debt	37.7	33.2	29.4	35.4	27.4	26.9		32.6	33.7
Deferred Taxes	.1	.4	.3	1.0	.6	3.9		.9	1.1
All Other Non-Current	12.4	8.7	8.5	10.7	4.3	13.9		6.2	9.8
Net Worth	6.3	30.6	45.0	44.9	58.2	48.6		47.7	38.0
Total Liabilities & Net Worth	100.0	100.0	100.0	100.0	100.0	100.0		100.0	100.0

INCOME DATA

Net Sales	100.0	100.0	100.0	100.0	100.0	100.0		100.0	100.0
Gross Profit									
Operating Expenses	79.9	86.6	83.9	78.0	79.1	72.8		82.8	84.5
Operating Profit	20.1	13.4	16.1	22.0	20.9	27.2		17.2	15.5
All Other Expenses (net)	2.1	5.3	5.3	8.4	5.6	4.5		7.5	5.6
Profit Before Taxes	17.9	8.0	10.9	13.7	15.3	22.6		9.7	9.9

RATIOS

Current	8.3	3.8	3.4	3.2	6.3	2.4		4.3	2.7
	1.7	1.5	1.8	1.6	2.2	.8		1.9	1.4
	.4	1.1	1.0	1.0	1.3	.5		.7	.6
Quick	2.7	3.6	3.1	2.8	5.4	1.8		3.3	2.3
	1.7	1.1	1.3	1.4	1.8	.5		1.6	1.0
	.2	.4	.7	.5	.9	.3		.5	.4
Sales/Receivables	0 UND	6 61.7	25 14.5	24 15.2	21 17.7	24 15.2		25 14.6	21 17.2
	12 29.5	35 10.5	36 10.1	34 10.8	37 9.8	31 11.7		34 10.8	34 10.8
	40 9.1	48 7.6	61 6.0	47 7.8	56 6.5	44 8.3		47 7.8	46 8.0
Cost of Sales/Inventory									
Cost of Sales/Payables									
Sales/Working Capital	6.8	1.9	2.6	2.3	1.5	3.6		1.5	3.0
	12.0	9.9	7.5	8.3	3.8	-14.6		7.1	11.9
	-18.1	40.5	116.3	138.2	98.3	-4.6		-25.9	-11.3
EBIT/Interest	12.0	4.5	7.6	4.4	6.8	6.0		4.0	5.9
	(11) 5.9	(28) 2.5	(59) 4.2	(58) 2.6	(13) 2.6	(17) 3.2		(118) 2.6	(127) 2.7
	2.3	.3	2.0	1.4	.8	2.3		1.5	1.0
Net Profit + Depr., Dep., Amort./Cur. Mat. L/T/D			10.1	11.1		12.8		8.6	5.3
			(12) 2.6	(13) 3.3		(10) 7.9		(28) 3.7	(24) 2.3
			.9	1.8		3.4		1.6	2.0
Fixed/Worth	.3	.8	.8	1.4	.9	1.1		1.1	1.1
	2.1	1.5	1.4	1.8	1.3	2.7		1.6	1.7
	-1.8	4.1	3.3	3.5	2.4	3.2		2.6	3.8
Debt/Worth	.8	.7	.5	.6	.3	.4		.5	.5
	3.6	1.7	1.1	1.2	.6	1.9		1.1	1.3
	-7.0	11.6	4.3	3.0	1.6	2.5		2.5	4.0
% Profit Before Taxes/Tangible Net Worth	409.1	22.9	32.1	10.7	6.4	13.5		16.1	14.6
	(11) 67.1	(25) 9.4	(65) 10.8	(65) 5.8	3.5	9.9		(122) 6.3	(139) 5.6
	42.7	2.6	2.8	1.6	1.4	1.7		1.6	.3
% Profit Before Taxes/Total Assets	107.1	9.2	8.9	4.4	3.7	6.1		5.1	5.4
	31.8	3.0	3.2	2.5	2.3	3.7		3.3	2.5
	10.7	-1.6	1.6	.8	.9	1.0		.5	-.1
Sales/Net Fixed Assets	30.1	12.2	3.3	.3	.2	.3		.7	1.5
	15.5	.6	.4	.2	.2	.2		.3	.3
	5.5	.3	.2	.2	.1	.2		.2	.2
Sales/Total Assets	5.7	2.1	1.3	.3	.2	.2		.4	.8
	2.8	.4	.3	.2	.1	.2		.2	.2
	2.1	.3	.2	.1	.1	.1		.2	.2
% Depr., Dep., Amort./Sales	1.7	3.0	3.7	11.9	12.4	11.8		8.2	7.9
	(12) 2.7	(27) 8.7	(64) 10.0	(70) 17.4	(16) 19.2	13.1		(124) 12.9	(149) 13.6
	7.9	15.0	14.1	23.3	21.6	16.4		19.6	19.4
% Officers', Directors' Owners' Comp/Sales			2.6					1.4	2.0
			(13) 4.1					(16) 3.2	(26) 4.6
			5.6					9.7	9.4
Net Sales ($)	12609M	49744M	279763M	509718M	305152M	551240M		944238M	884131M
Total Assets ($)	3823M	35398M	331729M	1701516M	1161683M	3100219M		3225802M	3660118M

M = $ thousand   MM = $ million
See Pages 11 through 21 for Explanation of Ratios and Data

Comparative Historical Data | Current Data Sorted by Sales

Type of Statement	4/1/04-3/31/05 ALL	4/1/05-3/31/06 ALL	4/1/06-3/31/07 ALL	0-1MM	1-3MM	3-5MM	5-10MM	10-25MM	25MM & OVER
					58 (4/1-9/30/06)		163 (10/1/06-3/31/07)		
Unqualified	108	105	114	22	33	15	16	15	13
Reviewed	14	13	18	5	3		4	5	1
Compiled	12	21	16	4	6	1	2	3	
Tax Returns	15	17	15	8	5		2		
Other	34	48	58	12	13	12	14	5	2
NUMBER OF STATEMENTS	183	204	221	51	60	28	38	28	16
ASSETS	%	%	%	%	%	%	%	%	%
Cash & Equivalents	8.9	9.0	9.2	10.0	12.1	7.0	7.4	7.8	6.3
Trade Receivables (net)	6.2	7.5	7.8	4.6	6.4	6.4	6.3	18.2	10.8
Inventory	2.6	4.0	4.2	2.7	3.1	.9	6.8	8.8	4.9
All Other Current	1.9	2.1	2.2	3.1	1.0	1.5	2.8	2.2	2.7
Total Current	19.7	22.7	23.4	20.5	22.7	15.8	23.2	37.1	24.7
Fixed Assets (net)	73.0	69.4	68.6	71.7	70.5	73.7	69.8	54.9	63.3
Intangibles (net)	1.2	1.4	1.8	1.3	1.5	3.2	1.0	1.7	5.0
All Other Non-Current	6.1	6.6	6.2	6.5	5.3	7.3	6.0	6.4	7.1
Total	100.0	100.0	100.0	100.0	100.0	100.0	100.0	100.0	100.0
LIABILITIES									
Notes Payable-Short Term	5.1	4.2	4.1	2.8	8.1	.5	2.6	4.2	2.7
Cur. Mat.-L.T.D.	3.4	2.6	2.7	4.3	2.7	2.0	1.8	2.0	2.1
Trade Payables	3.9	4.1	4.3	2.3	2.1	2.6	5.9	10.1	8.4
Income Taxes Payable	.1	.2	.2	.1	.2	.5	.3	.1	.1
All Other Current	2.4	5.2	4.3	3.3	4.1	3.3	5.6	4.7	5.3
Total Current	14.9	16.2	15.6	13.0	17.3	9.0	16.2	21.2	18.6
Long-Term Debt	34.2	28.6	32.0	43.2	30.0	33.5	30.5	22.2	22.3
Deferred Taxes	.7	.8	.9	.3	.2	1.5	.8	.7	5.0
All Other Non-Current	9.7	10.0	9.7	5.6	10.3	20.1	8.4	4.5	13.9
Net Worth	40.5	44.4	41.8	37.8	42.1	36.0	44.2	51.5	40.3
Total Liabilities & Net Worth	100.0	100.0	100.0	100.0	100.0	100.0	100.0	100.0	100.0
INCOME DATA									
Net Sales	100.0	100.0	100.0	100.0	100.0	100.0	100.0	100.0	100.0
Gross Profit									
Operating Expenses	81.6	81.5	80.7	80.4	80.0	79.5	85.2	79.3	77.6
Operating Profit	18.4	18.5	19.3	19.6	20.0	20.5	14.8	20.7	22.4
All Other Expenses (net)	7.5	6.3	6.0	6.8	6.7	8.4	5.8	2.6	3.4
Profit Before Taxes	10.9	12.2	13.3	12.8	13.2	12.1	9.0	18.1	18.9
RATIOS									
Current	3.9	3.0	3.4	5.4	4.0	3.9	2.3	3.5	1.8
	1.5	1.6	1.6	1.8	2.0	1.4	1.4	1.5	1.1
	.8	.8	.9	.6	1.1	.9	1.1	.9	.5
Quick	3.1	2.5	2.9	5.2	3.6	3.6	1.7	2.1	1.7
	1.2	(203) 1.1	1.3	1.7	1.7	1.1	1.1	1.0	.6
	.5	.5	.5	.4	.6	.6	.5	.6	.3
Sales/Receivables	25 14.6	19 19.1	20 17.9	0 UND	16 23.0	30 12.2	27 13.7	30 12.2	12 29.9
	33 11.2	33 10.9	34 10.7	31 12.0	33 11.1	34 10.7	36 10.2	39 9.4	26 13.9
	47 7.8	49 7.5	49 7.4	47 7.8	49 7.5	64 5.7	47 7.7	51 7.2	44 8.3
Cost of Sales/Inventory									
Cost of Sales/Payables									
Sales/Working Capital	1.9	3.0	2.4	1.7	2.3	2.5	3.2	3.7	5.3
	8.8	9.7	8.9	4.4	6.8	8.8	10.2	13.2	NM
	-15.4	-17.2	-52.0	-19.9	66.2	-49.4	38.7	NM	-6.1
EBIT/Interest	4.8	4.8	5.7	4.6	5.6	5.9	5.4	21.1	7.3
	(155) 2.4	(174) 2.6	(186) 3.0	(40) 2.6	(48) 2.7	(26) 2.3	(32) 3.0	(25) 4.2	(15) 4.4
	1.3	1.4	1.5	1.2	1.5	1.4	1.4	2.1	3.0
Net Profit + Depr., Dep., Amort./Cur. Mat. L/T/D	6.2	7.4	10.5						
	(41) 3.0	(47) 3.5	(44) 4.0						
	1.4	1.8	2.1						
Fixed/Worth	1.1	1.0	1.0	1.1	1.0	1.5	1.1	.4	1.0
	1.7	1.6	1.6	2.0	1.6	2.1	1.5	1.1	2.7
	3.6	3.1	3.3	4.5	3.7	4.0	2.7	2.1	3.3
Debt/Worth	.6	.5	.5	.7	.5	.7	.4	.5	.7
	1.4	1.2	1.3	1.7	1.0	1.5	1.5	.7	2.2
	3.3	3.0	3.6	4.7	4.2	3.4	4.0	2.5	4.0
% Profit Before Taxes/Tangible Net Worth	13.4	13.9	16.6	23.1	12.6	15.3	13.1	36.0	36.0
	(169) 5.1	(187) 6.0	(203) 8.3	(46) 9.7	(55) 5.9	(24) 8.6	(35) 4.2	(27) 12.1	13.7
	1.3	1.7	2.4	3.4	2.2	1.4	1.5	4.1	8.8
% Profit Before Taxes/Total Assets	4.8	5.3	6.7	7.7	6.1	5.9	4.4	19.2	8.4
	2.4	2.8	3.0	3.4	2.8	2.8	2.1	5.2	5.1
	.4	.7	1.1	.4	1.3	.7	.7	2.2	4.0
Sales/Net Fixed Assets	.6	.9	.9	.6	.8	.4	1.2	10.7	3.2
	.3	.3	.3	.3	.3	.2	.3	.6	.3
	.2	.2	.2	.3	.2	.2	.2	.2	.2
Sales/Total Assets	.4	.6	.6	.4	.6	.3	.7	2.1	1.1
	.2	.2	.2	.3	.2	.2	.2	.4	.3
	.1	.1	.2	.2	.2	.1	.1	.2	.2
% Depr., Dep., Amort./Sales	9.2	6.9	7.7	8.4	8.0	10.1	7.4	2.2	3.9
	(179) 14.6	(198) 12.0	(209) 12.5	(46) 12.8	(56) 12.6	14.2	(37) 12.1	(26) 11.7	11.2
	20.9	18.8	18.9	19.0	20.3	19.6	21.5	16.7	14.6
% Officers', Directors' Owners' Comp/Sales	2.0	1.6	1.9		2.6				
	(26) 5.0	(27) 3.0	(31) 3.7		(10) 4.2				
	12.9	6.7	5.7		9.9				
Net Sales ($)	1029652M	1254483M	1708226M	27333M	107430M	106074M	273673M	425840M	767876M
Total Assets ($)	4782255M	5781659M	6334368M	122491M	495012M	531128M	1478728M	1556610M	2150399M

© RMA 2007

M = $ thousand   MM = $ million
See Pages 11 through 21 for Explanation of Ratios and Data

CONSTRUCTION—GENERAL INDUSTRIES FORMAT*

Current Data Sorted by Assets   Comparative Historical Data

Type of Statement	0-500M	500M-2MM	2-10MM	10-50MM	50-100MM	100-250MM	ALL 4/1/02-3/31/03	ALL 4/1/03-3/31/04
Unqualified	1	6	35	52	34	26	118	178
Reviewed	10	36	113	108	27	17	199	343
Compiled	43	120	226	88	11	5	334	510
Tax Returns	284	539	536	146	6	9	422	1072
Other	86	233	525	287	58	26	450	736
	353 (4/1-9/30/06)			3,340 (10/1/06-3/31/07)				
NUMBER OF STATEMENTS	424	934	1435	681	136	83	1523	2839
ASSETS	%	%	%	%	%	%	%	%
Cash & Equivalents	22.1	9.6	7.0	7.2	9.1	8.2	9.7	9.9
Trade Receivables (net)	11.3	7.5	7.5	3.8	3.1	4.1	7.7	7.5
Inventory	27.2	55.3	62.4	70.1	70.5	63.0	56.2	56.4
All Other Current	7.2	5.9	5.6	4.7	2.6	2.7	6.8	5.6
Total Current	67.8	78.3	82.5	85.7	85.2	78.0	80.3	79.5
Fixed Assets (net)	21.5	13.9	11.1	7.7	7.3	11.8	11.0	12.2
Intangibles (net)	1.5	1.0	.6	.6	1.3	1.2	1.0	.9
All Other Non-Current	9.3	6.8	5.8	6.0	6.1	9.1	7.6	7.4
Total	100.0	100.0	100.0	100.0	100.0	100.0	100.0	100.0
LIABILITIES								
Notes Payable-Short Term	30.8	39.5	42.5	47.7	45.6	37.2	40.3	38.7
Cur. Mat.-L.T.D.	4.9	5.3	3.7	3.2	3.8	4.0	3.3	3.8
Trade Payables	11.9	7.9	7.8	7.0	5.9	4.1	8.8	8.8
Income Taxes Payable	.1	.2	.2	.1	.1	.1	.2	.2
All Other Current	17.8	10.2	12.1	11.1	8.1	7.6	13.1	12.3
Total Current	65.5	63.2	66.1	69.1	63.5	52.9	65.7	63.8
Long-Term Debt	22.4	13.8	12.4	10.3	11.7	19.4	9.9	11.7
Deferred Taxes	.0	.0	.1	.0	.0	.1	.0	.1
All Other Non-Current	7.8	3.8	2.6	3.1	3.7	3.5	4.1	4.3
Net Worth	4.3	19.2	18.8	17.4	21.1	24.2	20.1	20.1
Total Liabilities & Net Worth	100.0	100.0	100.0	100.0	100.0	100.0	100.0	100.0
INCOME DATA								
Net Sales	100.0	100.0	100.0	100.0	100.0	100.0	100.0	100.0
Gross Profit	24.4	17.9	17.3	17.9	19.8	23.3	18.3	18.9
Operating Expenses	19.5	12.9	11.6	11.4	11.5	12.7	13.5	13.6
Operating Profit	4.8	5.1	5.7	6.4	8.3	10.6	4.8	5.2
All Other Expenses (net)	1.0	1.2	1.0	1.1	1.4	2.1	.7	.5
Profit Before Taxes	3.8	3.9	4.7	5.4	6.8	8.4	4.1	4.7

RATIOS

Ratio	0-500M	500M-2MM	2-10MM	10-50MM	50-100MM	100-250MM	Comp 1	Comp 2
Current	3.1	1.8	1.6	1.4	1.6	2.2	1.7	1.7
	1.2	1.2	1.1	1.2	1.2	1.3	1.2	1.2
	.7	1.0	1.0	1.0	1.1	1.1	1.0	1.0
Quick	1.7	.6	.4	.2	.2	.5	.5	.5
	(422) .5	(929) .1	(1427) .1	(676) .1	.1	.1	(1515) .1	(2819) .1
	.1	.0	.0	.0	.0	.0	.0	.0
Sales/Receivables	0 UND	0 UND	0 UND	0 UND	0 UND	0 UND	0 UND	0 UND
	0 UND	0 UND	0 UND	0 999.8	1 654.1	0 999.8	0 999.8	0 UND
	7 54.4	4 82.9	8 43.3	3 106.9	4 83.0	7 52.6	8 46.0	7 53.1
Cost of Sales/Inventory	0 UND	0 UND	51 7.2	159 2.3	182 2.0	151 2.4	15 24.2	16 22.8
	0 UND	128 2.8	226 1.6	291 1.3	320 1.1	341 1.1	140 2.6	139 2.6
	69 5.3	284 1.3	407 .9	469 .8	484 .8	543 .7	271 1.3	264 1.4
Cost of Sales/Payables	0 UND	0 UND	0 UND	5 76.2	8 47.1	7 53.3	0 999.8	0 UND
	0 UND	1 244.4	10 35.1	15 23.8	16 23.4	17 21.1	11 34.4	10 35.2
	13 28.6	19 19.0	29 12.6	30 12.3	23 15.9	32 11.4	25 14.6	27 13.6
Sales/Working Capital	11.2	5.7	4.7	4.2	3.4	2.5	6.4	5.9
	48.7	19.8	13.8	10.8	7.2	5.2	16.1	15.7
	-33.5	-95.3	152.3	34.9	25.6	10.1	476.7	707.3
EBIT/Interest	14.6	15.5	19.0	20.5	13.7	9.9	17.1	20.4
	(315) 3.6	(691) 3.9	(1051) 4.8	(511) 5.1	(99) 4.9	(63) 4.6	(1173) 5.4	(2117) 5.8
	.9	1.1	1.5	1.7	2.0	1.7	1.7	1.7
Net Profit + Depr., Dep., Amort./Cur. Mat. L/T/D		5.4	6.6	18.3			8.7	7.7
		(23) 2.3	(65) 2.6	(27) 3.0			(127) 3.2	(171) 2.9
		.2	.7	.4			.9	1.1
Fixed/Worth	.0	.0	.0	.0	.0	.0	.0	.0
	.5	.3	.2	.1	.1	.1	.2	.2
	UND	3.7	1.3	.8	.5	.3	1.0	1.4
Debt/Worth	1.2	2.1	2.6	3.2	2.8	2.5	2.0	2.0
	6.1	6.7	7.3	7.0	4.7	3.5	4.7	5.2
	-14.1	64.2	26.9	16.8	9.4	7.3	19.0	22.6
% Profit Before Taxes/Tangible Net Worth	172.9	100.0	82.1	75.4	69.2	59.2	85.4	92.4
	(290) 71.6	(754) 39.8	(1257) 38.3	(627) 39.3	(128) 40.8	(80) 29.7	(1335) 37.9	(2453) 39.8
	15.9	9.0	10.8	12.3	20.3	11.3	11.0	11.9
% Profit Before Taxes/Total Assets	46.6	14.6	10.3	10.1	13.5	12.8	14.9	14.9
	11.7	5.3	4.2	4.2	7.3	6.7	6.3	6.1
	.0	.4	.8	1.0	2.4	1.4	1.1	1.1
Sales/Net Fixed Assets	989.4	720.2	729.6	353.4	233.9	385.8	254.5	289.9
	60.8	69.4	91.7	95.4	68.0	63.6	72.5	71.6
	17.2	16.5	17.6	22.6	22.5	11.2	21.9	20.1
Sales/Total Assets	9.0	3.2	2.1	1.6	1.5	1.5	3.1	3.1
	5.1	1.9	1.3	1.1	1.0	.9	1.9	1.9
	2.5	1.0	.8	.7	.7	.5	1.2	1.2
% Depr., Dep., Amort./Sales	.3	.2	.2	.1	.1	.1	.2	.2
	(217) .8	(498) .5	(783) .4	(397) .3	(74) .3	(44) .4	(1032) .4	(1701) .5
	1.7	1.2	.9	.5	.4	.7	1.1	1.2
% Officers', Directors' Owners' Comp/Sales	2.3	1.6	1.2	.7	.4	.3	1.4	1.5
	(227) 4.2	(475) 2.9	(656) 2.2	(260) 1.7	(30) 1.3	(18) 1.7	(703) 3.0	(1400) 3.0
	7.8	5.2	4.4	3.5	3.7	4.1	5.8	5.8
Net Sales ($)	627452M	2684825M	10839993M	18556120M	13413644M	18025836M	30597518M	59995076M
Total Assets ($)	111159M	1114391M	6844051M	14605613M	9556390M	13001156M	17867000M	27828950M

M = $ thousand   MM = $ million

See Pages 11 through 21 for Explanation of Ratios and Data

Comparative Historical Data | | | Type of Statement | | Current Data Sorted by Sales

			Type of Statement	5	6	6	12	28	97
163	157	154	Unqualified	5	6	6	12	28	97
290	282	311	Reviewed	6	25	27	59	74	120
481	487	493	Compiled	45	113	83	113	74	65
1220	1399	1520	Tax Returns	297	517	255	225	153	73
747	1101	1215	Other	107	259	179	230	238	202
4/1/04-3/31/05	4/1/05-3/31/06	4/1/06-3/31/07		353 (4/1-9/30/06)			3,340 (10/1/06-3/31/07)		
ALL	ALL	ALL		0-1MM	1-3MM	3-5MM	5-10MM	10-25MM	25MM & OVER
2901	3426	3693	**NUMBER OF STATEMENTS**	460	920	550	639	567	557
%	%	%	**ASSETS**	%	%	%	%	%	%
11.6	11.6	9.5	Cash & Equivalents	11.5	10.4	8.8	10.1	7.2	8.9
7.1	7.3	7.0	Trade Receivables (net)	4.8	5.6	7.0	8.2	8.3	8.5
55.3	55.8	58.3	Inventory	49.6	56.5	59.6	57.7	63.3	62.9
5.7	5.2	5.5	All Other Current	5.8	5.1	5.2	6.7	5.6	4.7
79.6	79.8	80.4	Total Current	71.8	77.5	80.6	82.7	84.4	85.0
12.5	12.2	12.3	Fixed Assets (net)	20.1	14.3	12.5	10.6	8.8	7.6
.5	1.0	.8	Intangibles (net)	1.3	1.2	.5	.4	.6	.9
7.4	6.9	6.6	All Other Non-Current	6.8	7.0	6.4	6.2	6.2	6.6
100.0	100.0	100.0	Total	100.0	100.0	100.0	100.0	100.0	100.0
			LIABILITIES						
40.2	40.9	41.3	Notes Payable-Short Term	38.1	43.0	40.4	40.7	42.9	41.3
2.9	3.1	4.2	Cur. Mat.-L.T.D.	6.2	4.4	4.9	3.1	3.5	3.1
8.5	7.9	8.0	Trade Payables	5.5	6.4	8.1	8.3	9.8	10.3
.2	.2	.1	Income Taxes Payable	.1	.1	.2	.2	.1	.1
13.0	12.4	11.8	All Other Current	12.7	11.9	11.8	11.7	12.3	10.8
64.8	64.5	65.5	Total Current	62.7	65.8	65.3	64.1	68.6	65.7
12.9	13.5	13.7	Long-Term Debt	21.9	15.6	14.0	12.3	9.4	9.3
.1	.0	.0	Deferred Taxes	.0	.0	.0	.1	.1	.0
3.9	4.3	3.6	All Other Non-Current	5.9	4.7	2.2	3.4	2.3	3.3
18.3	17.7	17.2	Net Worth	9.6	14.0	18.5	20.1	19.7	21.7
100.0	100.0	100.0	Total Liabilties & Net Worth	100.0	100.0	100.0	100.0	100.0	100.0
			INCOME DATA						
100.0	100.0	100.0	Net Sales	100.0	100.0	100.0	100.0	100.0	100.0
18.3	19.2	18.6	Gross Profit	26.8	19.2	16.6	16.6	15.8	17.8
13.2	12.7	12.8	Operating Expenses	20.9	13.5	11.9	11.0	10.2	10.7
5.0	6.5	5.8	Operating Profit	5.8	5.8	4.7	5.6	5.7	7.1
.4	.7	1.1	All Other Expenses (net)	2.6	1.3	.8	.6	.6	.8
4.6	5.8	4.7	Profit Before Taxes	3.2	4.5	3.9	5.0	5.1	6.2
			RATIOS						
1.7	1.8	1.7		2.6	1.9	1.8	1.7	1.5	1.5
1.2	1.2	1.2	Current	1.2	1.1	1.1	1.2	1.2	1.2
1.0	1.0	1.0		.9	1.0	1.0	1.0	1.0	1.1
.6	.6	.5		.8	.5	.5	.6	.4	.5
(2883) .1	(3414) .1	(3673) .1	Quick	(458) .1	(913) .1	(634) .1	(563) .1	(555) .1	.1
.0	.0	.0		.0	.0	.0	.0	.0	.0
0 UND	0 UND	0 UND		0 UND	0 UND	0 UND	0 UND	0 UND	0 UND
0 UND	0 UND	0 UND	Sales/Receivables	0 UND	0 UND	0 UND	0 UND	0 920.6	1 681.9
6 65.9	6 61.1	6 64.4		2 157.6	2 168.0	7 49.7	10 36.1	9 41.3	6 58.7
3 104.7	3 131.6	6 60.0		0 UND	0 UND	7 49.1	13 28.2	45 8.0	76 4.8
135 2.7	152 2.4	189 1.9	Cost of Sales/Inventory	218 1.7	176 2.1	187 2.0	167 2.2	193 1.9	219 1.7
269 1.4	304 1.2	376 1.0		699 .5	423 .9	340 1.1	326 1.1	351 1.0	354 1.0
0 UND	0 UND	0 UND		0 UND	0 UND	0 UND	0 999.8	3 139.8	7 49.9
8 44.4	9 40.7	9 42.7	Cost of Sales/Payables	0 UND	1 339.6	9 40.0	9 37.1	13 27.1	16 22.8
24 15.3	25 14.7	26 14.1		26 13.9	20 18.0	26 13.9	26 14.0	28 13.1	28 13.1
6.2	5.5	5.0		2.2	4.8	5.7	5.7	6.2	5.1
17.0	15.0	14.5	Sales/Working Capital	11.5	17.9	18.8	14.8	15.2	11.0
-999.8	999.8	705.0		-18.0	-53.5	-153.5	63.8	101.1	33.6
21.2	23.0	17.4		7.3	15.0	17.7	23.2	22.1	22.7
(2137) 5.9	(2524) 6.0	(2730) 4.5	EBIT/Interest	(304) 1.9	(658) 3.5	(422) 4.5	(485) 5.9	(429) 5.5	(432) 5.8
1.7	1.9	1.4		-.9	1.0	1.5	1.7	1.8	2.2
7.4	7.5	6.7			4.4	5.2	18.6	12.7	16.3
(161) 2.8	(166) 2.6	(133) 2.6	Net Profit + Depr., Dep., Amort./Cur. Mat. L/T/D	(17) .5	(21) 2.3	(30) 3.1	(27) 4.8	(36) 2.2	
.5	.9	.5		.2	.1	.6	1.8	.5	
.0	.0	.0		.0	.0	.0	.0	.0	.0
.2	.2	.2	Fixed/Worth	.4	.2	.2	.2	.2	.1
1.5	1.5	1.6		11.9	5.0	1.9	1.1	.9	.5
2.1	2.3	2.4		2.1	2.3	2.5	2.3	2.5	2.5
5.7	6.4	6.7	Debt/Worth	10.0	8.6	7.1	6.2	6.2	4.6
23.8	26.6	30.2		-63.3	255.3	29.1	24.3	16.2	10.1
93.7	97.3	88.3		84.7	97.6	91.7	88.2	87.6	76.1
(2501) 41.3	(2924) 47.8	(3136) 40.8	% Profit Before Taxes/Tangible Net Worth	(334) 20.6	(716) 39.9	(463) 39.9	(573) 43.4	(518) 43.8	(532) 44.4
13.0	18.0	11.8		-.1	8.6	12.9	14.7	15.8	19.1
14.8	15.3	13.0		10.7	12.8	11.3	13.2	13.4	15.0
5.8	6.8	4.9	% Profit Before Taxes/Total Assets	1.9	4.3	4.4	5.8	5.7	7.3
1.2	1.6	.8		-1.9	.4	.8	1.3	1.6	2.5
433.3	579.0	541.4		UND	999.8	597.5	464.2	450.5	319.6
79.2	87.3	82.2	Sales/Net Fixed Assets	32.8	70.3	82.2	83.1	108.3	95.5
20.0	20.0	17.9		5.6	16.9	19.5	20.5	28.5	27.3
3.1	2.8	2.6		2.0	2.8	2.6	2.7	2.6	2.4
1.8	1.7	1.5	Sales/Total Assets	.9	1.4	1.5	1.6	1.6	1.5
1.1	1.0	.8		.4	.7	.9	1.0	1.0	1.0
.2	.2	.2		.5	.2	.2	.1	.1	.1
(1641) .5	(1923) .4	(2013) .4	% Depr., Dep., Amort./Sales	(209) 1.4	(471) .5	(293) .4	(350) .4	(344) .3	(346) .3
1.1	1.0	1.0		3.4	1.2	.9	.8	.6	.5
1.4	1.2	1.3		3.6	1.9	1.4	1.2	.7	.5
(1352) 2.9	(1533) 2.6	(1666) 2.5	% Officers', Directors' Owners' Comp/Sales	(181) 6.8	(451) 3.2	(299) 2.3	(302) 2.1	(255) 1.4	(178) 1.3
5.4	4.9	5.1		10.6	5.5	4.3	3.5	2.8	3.4
46963562M	68446685M	64147870M	Net Sales ($)	269580M	1770247M	2162678M	4499102M	8897598M	46548665M
25725001M	38874576M	45232760M	Total Assets ($)	564540M	1921583M	1827004M	3846023M	6771702M	30301908M

© RMA 2007

M = $ thousand   MM = $ million
See Pages 11 through 21 for Explanation of Ratios and Data

Current Data Sorted by Assets   Comparative Historical Data

Type of Statement	0-500M	500M-2MM	2-10MM	10-50MM	50-100MM	100-250MM		4/1/02-3/31/03 ALL	4/1/03-3/31/04 ALL
Unqualified		2	14	24	3	5		29	37
Reviewed	2	15	28	12	1	1		33	48
Compiled	3	14	11	1	1	1		21	40
Tax Returns	16	32	38	10		1		47	78
Other	5	17	36	25	2	2		35	70
	44 (4/1-9/30/06)			278 (10/1/06-3/31/07)					
NUMBER OF STATEMENTS	26	80	127	72	7	10		165	273
	%	%	%	%	%	%		%	%
ASSETS									
Cash & Equivalents	16.3	9.1	10.8	8.7		10.7		13.2	14.5
Trade Receivables (net)	20.9	17.0	23.1	22.3		7.9		23.5	19.3
Inventory	29.6	35.7	33.1	36.2		38.1		24.6	28.6
All Other Current	6.6	10.1	10.0	8.0		.9		8.6	9.1
Total Current	73.4	71.9	77.0	75.3		57.6		70.0	71.5
Fixed Assets (net)	18.6	18.2	14.7	15.4		18.6		20.8	18.2
Intangibles (net)	.8	3.0	.9	1.5		.0		1.2	.7
All Other Non-Current	7.2	6.9	7.4	7.9		23.8		8.0	9.6
Total	100.0	100.0	100.0	100.0		100.0		100.0	100.0
LIABILITIES									
Notes Payable-Short Term	34.9	30.6	21.6	29.6		21.0		19.1	22.0
Cur. Mat.-L.T.D.	3.0	3.4	4.4	3.6		.7		7.1	5.1
Trade Payables	16.1	11.1	17.6	19.4		10.0		18.3	16.9
Income Taxes Payable	.0	.5	.3	.2		.0		.5	.3
All Other Current	22.9	13.7	15.8	13.8		14.5		15.1	15.4
Total Current	77.0	59.4	59.7	66.5		46.3		60.1	59.7
Long-Term Debt	16.5	12.0	11.1	9.7		13.0		12.6	12.3
Deferred Taxes	.0	.0	.1	.1		.0		.2	.2
All Other Non-Current	15.1	3.4	1.9	1.9		1.4		3.5	3.8
Net Worth	-8.7	25.2	27.2	21.7		39.3		23.5	23.9
Total Liabilties & Net Worth	100.0	100.0	100.0	100.0		100.0		100.0	100.0
INCOME DATA									
Net Sales	100.0	100.0	100.0	100.0		100.0		100.0	100.0
Gross Profit	31.4	19.6	18.6	15.8		26.3		19.1	19.5
Operating Expenses	26.9	12.1	11.8	9.4		15.2		15.0	14.8
Operating Profit	4.5	7.5	6.8	6.5		11.1		4.1	4.8
All Other Expenses (net)	1.7	1.5	.4	1.4		-.1		.4	.4
Profit Before Taxes	2.8	6.1	6.4	5.0		11.2		3.6	4.3
RATIOS									
Current	1.7	2.0	1.7	1.4		2.3		1.8	1.7
	1.2	1.3	1.2	1.1		1.3		1.2	1.3
	.8	.9	1.0	1.0		.6		1.0	1.0
Quick	1.2	1.2	1.2	1.0		1.0		1.2	1.2
	.4	.3	.5	.4		.4		(164) .7	(271) .6
	.1	.0	.1	.0		.1		.1	.1
Sales/Receivables	0 UND	0 UND	0 UND	0 UND		0 UND		0 UND	0 UND
	0 UND	2 146.5	17 21.3	4 99.8		1 549.1		10 37.3	6 62.7
	28 13.1	36 10.1	51 7.2	51 7.1		9 39.6		51 7.2	43 8.5
Cost of Sales/Inventory	0 UND	0 UND	0 UND	0 UND		0 UND		0 UND	0 UND
	3 138.5	23 15.9	8 44.7	40 9.0		177 2.1		0 UND	1 443.1
	119 3.1	178 2.0	259 1.4	303 1.2		405 .9		121 3.0	155 2.4
Cost of Sales/Payables	0 UND	0 UND	5 71.2	4 91.4		11 33.0		1 308.7	2 171.0
	4 89.8	7 56.1	20 18.3	21 17.0		20 18.4		17 21.6	17 21.0
	32 11.5	27 13.3	51 7.2	48 7.7		47 7.7		40 9.0	41 8.8
Sales/Working Capital	9.3	6.3	5.9	12.3		2.5		7.3	8.1
	33.9	14.9	16.4	25.8		11.3		23.5	18.0
	-29.6	-31.8	70.3	-200.3		-4.0		-503.6	-297.2
EBIT/Interest	18.4	20.7	23.2	55.3				27.3	24.5
	(18) 2.1	(54) 4.7	(89) 6.9	(53) 9.8				(131) 5.3	(214) 7.3
	-1.1	.9	1.7	2.3				1.2	2.1
Net Profit + Depr., Dep., Amort./Cur. Mat. L/T/D			4.8					7.2	5.9
			(15) 2.4					(26) 2.0	(30) 2.1
			1.2					.7	.2
Fixed/Worth	.1	.0	.0	.1		.0		.1	.1
	.6	.3	.2	.3		.2		.4	.3
	-2.2	2.1	1.0	2.8		.5		2.0	1.6
Debt/Worth	1.4	1.2	1.4	2.4		.4		1.4	1.3
	4.9	3.3	4.2	5.3		2.5		3.1	3.2
	-3.8	47.1	12.1	20.2		4.1		10.0	9.5
% Profit Before Taxes/Tangible Net Worth	153.8	84.4	71.5	68.8		47.3		73.2	78.4
	(16) 82.4	(66) 42.6	(116) 29.1	(61) 42.0		21.4		(142) 29.6	(243) 38.3
	-1.7	11.7	7.1	17.7		3.7		8.6	9.8
% Profit Before Taxes/Total Assets	35.2	19.0	16.5	16.9		11.9		15.3	17.1
	16.3	8.1	5.7	6.1		4.2		6.4	8.2
	-6.0	1.2	.6	2.8		2.5		1.0	2.0
Sales/Net Fixed Assets	561.2	542.8	317.0	337.0		152.3		126.2	174.1
	48.0	43.1	64.1	95.8		27.8		38.1	48.6
	15.7	10.2	14.6	7.5		1.2		10.5	10.8
Sales/Total Assets	11.5	3.8	3.2	3.4		1.4		4.3	4.1
	4.6	2.2	1.9	1.5		.7		2.6	2.3
	2.1	1.2	.9	.9		.3		1.5	1.5
% Depr., Dep., Amort./Sales	1.0	.5	.2	.1				.2	.2
	(13) 1.3	(43) .7	(83) .4	(50) .2				(127) .6	(187) .6
	3.2	2.9	1.1	.8				1.6	1.5
% Officers', Directors' Owners' Comp/Sales	3.9	1.4	.9	.6				1.6	1.4
	(14) 10.1	(31) 3.3	(55) 1.9	(19) 1.2				(70) 3.5	(106) 2.8
	13.4	4.9	3.2	2.8				5.9	6.0
Net Sales ($)	50330M	307362M	1426148M	3222150M	589578M	1958024M		8314765M	6208714M
Total Assets ($)	7548M	99467M	614235M	1584900M	518512M	1724029M		2166283M	3213264M

© RMA 2007

M = $ thousand   MM = $ million

See Pages 11 through 21 for Explanation of Ratios and Data

Comparative Historical Data   Current Data Sorted by Sales

41	29	48	Type of Statement						
51	44	59	Unqualified	2	1	1	9	7	30
34	41	31	Reviewed	9	9	7	9	15	17
107	115	97	Compiled	4	7	8	7	2	3
68	85	87	Tax Returns	18	29	19	16	11	4
4/1/04-3/31/05	4/1/05-3/31/06	4/1/06-3/31/07	Other	6	13	11	13	25	19
ALL	ALL	ALL		44 (4/1-9/30/06)			278 (10/1/06-3/31/07)		
				0-1MM	1-3MM	3-5MM	5-10MM	10-25MM	25MM & OVER
301	314	322	**NUMBER OF STATEMENTS**	30	59	46	54	60	73
%	%	%	**ASSETS**	%	%	%	%	%	%
12.5	11.8	10.3	Cash & Equivalents	9.5	9.0	7.5	9.4	10.0	14.4
19.9	20.3	20.7	Trade Receivables (net)	6.8	12.9	13.2	18.9	29.8	31.3
31.5	35.1	34.4	Inventory	55.4	38.5	36.9	38.8	28.2	22.6
7.6	6.7	8.9	All Other Current	.1	10.7	12.6	5.3	9.9	10.4
71.5	74.0	74.3	Total Current	71.7	71.1	70.2	72.5	78.0	78.6
17.9	16.6	16.2	Fixed Assets (net)	18.6	20.3	19.4	21.3	12.8	8.9
1.6	.9	1.5	Intangibles (net)	3.4	.5	1.7	.2	1.9	2.0
9.0	8.5	8.0	All Other Non-Current	6.2	8.0	8.7	6.1	7.3	10.5
100.0	100.0	100.0	Total	100.0	100.0	100.0	100.0	100.0	100.0
			LIABILITIES						
21.7	25.3	27.0	Notes Payable-Short Term	32.6	35.1	33.8	31.2	21.9	15.2
5.9	3.4	3.7	Cur. Mat.-L.T.D.	1.0	5.6	4.9	5.9	3.7	.7
14.9	14.9	15.9	Trade Payables	5.7	8.7	8.8	13.9	23.0	25.9
.3	.4	.3	Income Taxes Payable	.0	.3	.8	.3	.1	.3
13.8	12.3	15.3	All Other Current	19.4	12.3	17.2	11.0	13.2	19.8
56.7	56.4	62.2	Total Current	58.7	62.0	65.4	62.3	61.7	61.9
13.7	13.6	11.6	Long-Term Debt	15.8	15.5	13.5	9.1	12.4	6.9
.1	.1	.1	Deferred Taxes	.0	.0	.0	.1	.1	.1
4.7	5.0	3.3	All Other Non-Current	6.1	7.0	3.0	2.6	1.9	1.2
24.9	24.9	22.8	Net Worth	19.3	15.5	18.1	25.9	23.8	30.0
100.0	100.0	100.0	Total Liabilities & Net Worth	100.0	100.0	100.0	100.0	100.0	100.0
			INCOME DATA						
100.0	100.0	100.0	Net Sales	100.0	100.0	100.0	100.0	100.0	100.0
20.5	19.6	19.5	Gross Profit	23.2	22.7	22.9	19.2	18.3	14.5
14.7	13.6	12.6	Operating Expenses	16.3	15.6	15.6	12.2	10.4	8.7
5.8	5.9	7.0	Operating Profit	6.9	7.1	7.3	7.0	8.0	5.8
.3	.6	1.0	All Other Expenses (net)	3.7	1.5	.8	.8	.7	-.1
5.6	5.4	6.0	Profit Before Taxes	3.2	5.6	6.5	6.3	7.3	5.9
			RATIOS						
2.1	1.9	1.7		2.4	2.9	1.5	1.5	1.8	1.4
1.3	1.2	1.2	Current	1.1	1.3	1.2	1.2	1.2	1.2
1.0	1.0	1.0		.9	.9	.9	.9	1.0	1.1
1.3	1.2	1.2		.5	1.2	.6	1.2	1.2	1.2
(298) .6	.5	.4	Quick	.1	.2	.2	.2	.7	.8
.1	.1	.0		.0	.0	.0	.0	.1	.2
0 UND	0 UND	0 UND		0 UND	0 UND	0 UND	0 UND	0 UND	1 512.2
4 82.9	8 45.0	6 57.2	Sales/Receivables	0 UND	0 999.8	1 275.9	3 115.6	29 12.4	28 13.2
46 7.9	53 6.9	44 8.2		4 85.1	37 10.0	29 12.4	49 7.5	65 5.6	53 6.9
0 UND	0 UND	0 UND		33 11.1	0 UND	0 UND	0 UND	0 UND	0 UND
2 230.5	16 23.1	17 22.0	Cost of Sales/Inventory	474 .8	50 7.3	39 9.3	30 12.1	1 442.3	0 UND
154 2.4	228 1.6	258 1.4		1464 .2	256 1.4	259 1.4	296 1.2	178 2.1	188 1.9
1 614.7	0 770.2	2 166.2		0 UND	0 UND	2 183.7	8 45.0	8 44.9	13 27.1
16 23.4	16 23.3	16 22.8	Cost of Sales/Payables	0 UND	6 57.8	10 36.9	21 17.2	24 15.1	28 13.0
37 9.9	43 8.4	42 8.7		13 28.3	29 12.8	22 16.9	36 10.2	58 6.3	53 6.9
5.6	6.1	6.4		1.3	3.7	6.3	8.5	7.3	10.9
16.7	17.6	19.1	Sales/Working Capital	8.6	9.9	15.2	20.5	21.8	21.3
-432.7	288.4	-273.5		-11.1	-28.8	-231.7	-79.1	70.5	72.2
26.9	24.0	25.3		18.0	12.2	19.2	31.3	22.9	62.4
(237) 6.8	(233) 7.2	(225) 6.9	EBIT/Interest	(19) .7	(35) 3.1	(37) 4.7	(38) 5.8	(46) 7.2	(50) 14.4
2.2	2.2	1.6		-2.6	.1	1.4	2.3	2.1	3.7
9.7	10.9	5.1						11.7	
(31) 3.6	(39) 3.9	(33) 2.7	Net Profit + Depr., Dep., Amort./Cur. Mat. L/T/D					(12) 3.5	
1.5	.1	1.0						1.8	
.1	.1	.0		.0	.1	.1	.1	.0	.0
.3	.3	.2	Fixed/Worth	.1	.8	.3	.3	.3	.1
1.7	1.5	1.8		3.3	34.9	1.6	2.1	1.1	.5
1.3	1.6	1.6		2.4	1.3	1.5	1.8	1.6	1.6
3.4	3.8	4.3	Debt/Worth	8.3	6.6	4.3	4.2	4.4	3.2
17.9	14.3	16.4		-999.8	153.9	19.8	15.2	17.0	6.8
71.7	97.8	75.4		23.3	111.5	85.1	78.1	81.1	66.4
(263) 32.4	(285) 43.8	(276) 35.4	% Profit Before Taxes/Tangible Net Worth	(22) 8.0	(48) 31.0	(38) 37.6	(49) 37.1	(51) 38.8	(68) 40.9
11.9	14.6	9.5		-44.1	.9	7.4	14.0	12.1	20.4
17.0	17.1	18.5		7.4	18.5	16.6	17.1	23.3	19.8
6.6	7.2	7.0	% Profit Before Taxes/Total Assets	.1	7.4	7.7	7.1	5.9	9.5
1.7	2.0	1.1		-3.6	.9	-.9	2.0	1.8	3.6
251.6	216.1	318.4		UND	167.3	214.9	204.6	355.6	406.3
51.4	50.8	58.7	Sales/Net Fixed Assets	42.7	38.6	47.3	45.4	65.6	111.0
9.4	10.9	12.5		3.2	7.2	12.0	5.4	18.1	37.0
3.8	3.6	3.5		1.2	3.0	3.7	3.7	3.6	4.5
2.4	1.9	1.9	Sales/Total Assets	.7	1.5	2.0	1.9	2.4	3.1
1.2	1.0	.9		.2	.9	.9	1.0	1.4	1.4
.2	.2	.2		.9	.3	.2	.2	.2	.1
(202) .6	(212) .5	(201) .5	% Depr., Dep., Amort./Sales	(12) 3.1	(34) .8	(27) .7	(31) .5	(40) .4	(57) .2
1.7	1.8	1.4		4.1	2.1	1.9	1.4	1.2	.5
1.5	1.4	1.0			2.5	1.1	.9	.7	.6
(127) 2.7	(131) 3.1	(123) 2.3	% Officers', Directors' Owners' Comp/Sales		(26) 4.6	(20) 3.1	(25) 2.0	(22) 1.2	(21) 1.3
6.0	6.2	4.8			6.4	6.4	2.0	2.4	2.6
8618330M	7128865M	7553592M	Net Sales ($)	17171M	118103M	174547M	368975M	1009570M	5865226M
3673660M	3827843M	4548691M	Total Assets ($)	57858M	135163M	134312M	293039M	771560M	3156759M

© RMA 2007

M = $ thousand   MM = $ million
See Pages 11 through 21 for Explanation of Ratios and Data

Current Data Sorted by Assets   Comparative Historical Data

Type of Statement	0-500M	500M-2MM	2-10MM	10-50MM	50-100MM	100-250MM	4/1/02-3/31/03 ALL	4/1/03-3/31/04 ALL
Unqualified	2	2	10	12		6	16	21
Reviewed		7	20	18	4	5	7	30
Compiled	6	17	20	17	3	1	18	26
Tax Returns	15	41	35	16	1	2	15	44
Other	9	31	62	30	14	7	34	30
	40 (4/1-9/30/06)			373 (10/1/06-3/31/07)				
NUMBER OF STATEMENTS	30	98	139	91	34	21	90	151
ASSETS	%	%	%	%	%	%	%	%
Cash & Equivalents	17.3	11.0	7.0	5.5	6.9	9.9	12.3	13.8
Trade Receivables (net)	17.1	10.4	8.4	6.0	1.7	5.1	21.4	15.5
Inventory	36.9	43.9	60.1	67.0	65.3	61.5	32.0	38.8
All Other Current	2.3	11.9	6.6	5.1	3.3	2.1	10.1	6.1
Total Current	73.6	77.1	82.0	83.6	77.2	78.6	75.8	74.2
Fixed Assets (net)	18.2	17.0	11.6	11.1	5.8	9.1	17.8	15.9
Intangibles (net)	.9	.7	.4	.5	2.0	4.1	.8	1.3
All Other Non-Current	7.3	5.2	6.0	4.8	15.0	8.2	5.6	8.6
Total	100.0	100.0	100.0	100.0	100.0	100.0	100.0	100.0
LIABILITIES								
Notes Payable-Short Term	31.0	36.7	43.0	42.0	31.4	28.7	34.3	23.1
Cur. Mat.-L.T.D.	3.0	2.5	2.7	3.4	6.1	4.2	4.4	3.9
Trade Payables	6.6	10.1	9.9	7.1	6.4	6.5	13.3	14.4
Income Taxes Payable	.4	.3	.2	.1	.0	.4	.3	.3
All Other Current	13.5	12.5	13.2	12.2	8.6	16.1	11.0	15.6
Total Current	54.5	62.2	69.1	64.7	52.5	55.9	63.4	57.4
Long-Term Debt	11.7	13.1	10.0	14.0	13.1	13.6	8.8	10.3
Deferred Taxes	.0	.7	.0	.1	.2	.0	.3	.2
All Other Non-Current	6.9	5.0	4.6	2.5	4.4	4.2	5.2	6.3
Net Worth	27.0	19.0	16.3	18.9	29.8	26.3	22.2	25.7
Total Liabilities & Net Worth	100.0	100.0	100.0	100.0	100.0	100.0	100.0	100.0
INCOME DATA								
Net Sales	100.0	100.0	100.0	100.0	100.0	100.0	100.0	100.0
Gross Profit	25.8	18.4	19.1	17.7	25.5	24.7	20.5	19.6
Operating Expenses	20.7	14.2	12.2	10.9	13.2	13.9	16.1	14.4
Operating Profit	5.1	4.3	6.9	6.7	12.3	10.8	4.4	5.2
All Other Expenses (net)	.0	.5	.9	1.0	2.3	1.9	.5	.9
Profit Before Taxes	5.1	3.8	5.9	5.7	10.0	8.9	3.9	4.3
RATIOS								
Current	3.2	1.7	1.4	1.5	2.5	2.2	1.9	1.8
	1.3	1.2	1.1	1.2	1.3	1.2	1.2	1.3
	.9	1.0	1.0	1.1	1.1	1.0	1.0	1.0
Quick	1.3	.7	.3	.3	.4	.9	1.3	1.1
	.8	.2	(138) .1	(90) .1	.1	.1	.4	(150) .3
	.2	.0	.0	.0	.0	.0	.1	.1
Sales/Receivables	0 UND	0 UND	0 UND	0 UND	0 UND	0 UND	0 UND	0 UND
	0 UND	0 UND	0 999.8	0 805.8	1 584.7	1 268.9	10 36.9	2 234.5
	33 11.2	15 25.0	12 30.0	6 62.4	6 60.9	5 71.9	45 8.2	30 12.0
Cost of Sales/Inventory	0 UND	0 UND	25 14.3	144 2.5	118 3.1	238 1.5	0 UND	0 UND
	12 30.2	79 4.6	233 1.6	275 1.3	286 1.3	317 1.1	4 85.5	36 10.2
	101 3.6	302 1.2	415 .9	419 .9	463 .8	550 .7	199 1.8	259 1.4
Cost of Sales/Payables	0 UND	0 UND	0 999.8	4 89.4	8 47.7	3 112.6	3 118.3	4 94.9
	0 UND	6 60.8	11 33.1	12 31.4	19 19.1	25 14.3	22 16.8	22 16.9
	20 18.3	20 18.3	39 9.5	28 13.1	31 11.7	40 9.1	36 10.1	39 9.4
Sales/Working Capital	7.3	4.9	6.0	4.2	2.5	3.8	6.1	5.8
	30.8	18.1	17.0	9.5	4.5	7.3	16.5	14.4
	-41.2	-842.6	262.3	26.1	13.2	21.3	128.5	306.3
EBIT/Interest	12.0	11.9	28.7	17.9	52.3	16.6	25.8	19.0
	(22) 3.8	(70) 3.1	(110) 6.3	(71) 5.5	(30) 5.7	(16) 2.9	(68) 5.9	(114) 6.0
	-4.9	.8	1.6	2.6	2.0	1.8	1.3	2.0
Net Profit + Depr., Dep., Amort./Cur. Mat. L/T/D								3.8
								(18) 2.6
								1.4
Fixed/Worth	.0	.0	.0	.0	.0	.0	.1	.0
	.6	.3	.1	.1	.1	.1	.3	.2
	7.3	2.8	1.1	1.1	.3	.8	1.4	.9
Debt/Worth	.7	2.0	2.9	3.1	1.2	2.1	1.2	1.6
	3.1	5.9	5.9	5.5	5.0	5.4	3.9	3.7
	58.2	27.0	21.8	11.3	8.0	15.7	12.7	8.4
% Profit Before Taxes/Tangible Net Worth	124.5	84.8	96.3	74.6	61.5	62.4	78.7	68.8
	(25) 39.8	(80) 37.0	(122) 47.4	(89) 44.2	(32) 37.6	(19) 39.4	(80) 24.6	(135) 25.9
	1.1	6.2	12.5	20.0	11.2	13.3	3.2	7.0
% Profit Before Taxes/Total Assets	29.7	13.3	14.1	10.5	17.5	15.9	13.6	13.8
	14.9	4.8	5.0	6.2	7.1	7.6	5.6	5.4
	-3.3	.5	.9	2.9	2.7	2.2	.5	1.2
Sales/Net Fixed Assets	240.4	433.6	263.2	262.6	263.4	148.5	156.4	246.0
	57.4	43.9	67.6	106.1	92.5	64.1	31.1	51.2
	18.4	12.7	15.3	24.2	16.4	14.3	9.6	15.1
Sales/Total Assets	6.4	3.3	2.4	1.7	1.5	1.5	3.1	4.0
	4.2	1.7	1.3	1.2	1.0	1.0	2.0	2.1
	2.5	1.0	.8	.8	.8	.6	1.3	1.1
% Depr., Dep., Amort./Sales	.3	.3	.1	.1	.1	.1	.2	.3
	(18) .8	(60) .7	(77) .4	(55) .3	(22) .2	(14) .4	(56) .6	(100) .6
	1.8	1.2	1.0	.7	.5	1.5	1.6	1.5
% Officers', Directors' Owners' Comp/Sales	2.3	2.0	1.5	.5			1.8	1.1
	(20) 6.5	(44) 3.4	(52) 2.1	(34) 1.1			(34) 3.2	(61) 2.4
	8.5	6.9	4.8	2.4			6.4	5.9
Net Sales ($)	34843M	274295M	1305027M	2812690M	2751181M	4117246M	4031977M	4529103M
Total Assets ($)	8090M	117836M	741973M	2122374M	2472422M	3266375M	2311103M	2579921M

© RMA 2007

M = $ thousand   MM = $ million
See Pages 11 through 21 for Explanation of Ratios and Data

Comparative Historical Data | Current Data Sorted by Sales

			Type of Statement						
23	26	32	Unqualified	1		2	2		27
30	35	54	Reviewed		2	3	9	18	22
30	29	64	Compiled	1	12	14	12	15	10
61	62	110	Tax Returns	26	32	17	12	16	7
57	81	153	Other	16	38	9	24	25	41
4/1/04-3/31/05	4/1/05-3/31/06	4/1/06-3/31/07		40 (4/1-9/30/06)			373 (10/1/06-3/31/07)		
ALL	ALL	ALL		0-1MM	1-3MM	3-5MM	5-10MM	10-25MM	25MM & OVER
201	233	413	NUMBER OF STATEMENTS	44	84	45	59	74	107
%	%	%	ASSETS	%	%	%	%	%	%
11.8	11.6	8.5	Cash & Equivalents	9.7	11.2	5.1	8.0	7.6	8.2
13.1	15.1	8.2	Trade Receivables (net)	5.4	7.7	10.0	6.9	10.2	8.4
42.6	44.5	56.6	Inventory	54.0	51.2	47.4	61.7	57.9	62.0
6.4	5.9	6.7	All Other Current	5.9	10.7	10.8	3.2	6.4	4.4
73.9	77.0	80.0	Total Current	75.0	80.8	73.3	79.8	82.1	83.0
15.9	15.4	12.6	Fixed Assets (net)	16.4	14.3	18.5	15.6	10.1	7.5
1.5	1.6	.8	Intangibles (net)	1.1	.2	.6	.7	.1	1.8
8.6	6.0	6.5	All Other Non-Current	7.5	4.7	7.6	3.9	7.7	7.7
100.0	100.0	100.0	Total	100.0	100.0	100.0	100.0	100.0	100.0
			LIABILITIES						
31.1	28.3	38.7	Notes Payable-Short Term	50.6	33.8	39.8	41.9	41.7	33.5
3.6	3.5	3.2	Cur. Mat.-L.T.D.	1.8	3.6	4.9	1.7	2.6	3.9
12.6	14.5	8.6	Trade Payables	2.2	6.2	11.8	7.0	13.6	9.3
.2	.5	.2	Income Taxes Payable	.3	.2	.4	.1	.2	.3
13.5	14.3	12.6	All Other Current	7.1	16.0	13.1	13.9	11.3	12.1
60.9	61.0	63.4	Total Current	62.0	59.8	70.0	64.5	69.4	59.2
13.4	13.7	12.2	Long-Term Debt	15.5	13.6	12.0	11.2	9.0	12.5
.0	.1	.2	Deferred Taxes	.0	.8	.1	.1	.0	.1
5.0	4.1	4.3	All Other Non-Current	6.4	5.3	3.5	5.4	4.4	2.6
20.6	21.1	19.9	Net Worth	16.0	20.6	14.4	18.8	17.2	25.7
100.0	100.0	100.0	Total Liabilities & Net Worth	100.0	100.0	100.0	100.0	100.0	100.0
			INCOME DATA						
100.0	100.0	100.0	Net Sales	100.0	100.0	100.0	100.0	100.0	100.0
21.0	21.2	19.9	Gross Profit	28.7	21.3	16.9	16.7	18.2	19.4
15.0	14.2	13.2	Operating Expenses	21.2	15.2	14.8	9.9	11.3	10.8
6.0	7.0	6.7	Operating Profit	7.5	6.2	2.1	6.9	7.0	8.6
.8	.7	.9	All Other Expenses (net)	1.8	.7	.3	.6	1.8	.7
5.2	6.3	5.8	Profit Before Taxes	5.7	5.5	1.8	6.3	5.2	8.0
			RATIOS						
1.9	1.9	1.7		1.7	2.1	1.4	1.7	1.3	1.9
1.2	1.2	1.2	Current	1.2	1.2	1.1	1.2	1.2	1.2
1.0	1.0	1.0		.8	1.0	.9	1.1	1.0	1.1
1.0	1.0	.5		.5	.8	.4	.5	.4	.8
.2	.2 (411)	.1	Quick	.1	.1	.1 (58)	.1 (73)	.1	.1
.0	.1	.0		.0	.0	.0	.0	.0	.0
0 UND	0 UND	0 UND		0 UND	0 UND	0 UND	0 UND	0 UND	0 UND
1 469.8	2 237.1	0 999.8	Sales/Receivables	0 UND	0 UND	0 UND	0 742.8	1 538.6	1 284.3
21 17.1	29 12.6	9 39.6		3 145.5	9 41.4	14 25.4	14 26.1	10 36.2	8 45.3
0 UND	0 UND	8 46.2		0 UND	2 217.4	0 UND	34 10.9	2 191.9	52 7.1
99 3.7	98 3.7	212 1.7	Cost of Sales/Inventory	213 1.7	186 2.0	113 3.2	249 1.5	169 2.2	259 1.4
285 1.3	291 1.3	392 .9		537 .7	446 .8	345 1.1	420 .9	281 1.3	390 .9
2 204.1	3 131.5	0 973.5		0 UND	0 UND	0 999.8	1 504.7	2 210.0	5 72.3
20 18.6	17 22.1	11 33.5	Cost of Sales/Payables	0 UND	11 34.0	10 35.8	8 47.8	14 26.9	17 21.6
43 8.5	39 9.4	29 12.8		9 39.6	22 16.6	40 9.1	26 14.0	44 8.3	30 12.0
4.7	5.0	4.5		3.3	3.9	8.6	3.8	7.9	4.2
15.6	13.7	12.4	Sales/Working Capital	10.6	12.0	21.9	13.7	17.1	8.7
-93.4	212.4	82.2		-25.1	-999.8	-21.9	27.2	106.1	21.4
16.3	33.6	21.0		6.4	16.1	11.3	27.5	19.6	52.6
(138) 5.0	(177) 9.7	(319) 5.2	EBIT/Interest	(28) 2.2	(61) 6.3	(36) 2.1	(44) 5.4	(60) 4.3	(90) 8.8
1.6	2.7	1.5		-1.9	-.5	.5	1.6	2.1	2.8
17.4	12.0	10.4	Net Profit + Depr., Dep.,						10.4
(13) 4.5	(15) 7.2	(18) 4.6	Amort./Cur. Mat. L/T/D					(10)	5.0
1.8	2.5	1.4							1.4
.0	.1	.0		.0	.0	.1	.0	.0	.0
.2	.3	.1	Fixed/Worth	.1	.3	.3	.1	.1	.1
1.6	1.1	1.2		3.6	2.6	22.8	1.1	.7	.3
1.8	1.9	2.3		1.9	1.8	2.9	2.2	2.9	2.3
4.8	4.8	5.4	Debt/Worth	8.1	6.2	9.9	5.0	5.2	4.3
19.4	13.7	18.8		-389.0	31.3	71.4	14.7	14.3	8.3
64.1	93.3	84.6		59.3	100.0	59.5	94.6	92.1	83.1
(174) 33.6	(209) 42.2	(367) 43.3	% Profit Before Taxes/Tangible Net Worth	(32) 36.1	(73) 38.6	(35) 28.4	(55) 59.2	(71) 44.2	(101) 48.5
10.1	18.1	13.3		7.4	3.0	4.3	16.0	15.7	25.3
14.6	17.9	14.5		14.5	18.1	5.4	14.4	11.0	18.1
5.3	7.4	6.0	% Profit Before Taxes/Total Assets	3.2	4.9	2.3	6.9	5.4	8.9
1.7	2.8	1.0		-1.0	-1.1	-.4	2.3	2.1	4.0
309.6	222.8	263.0		UND	179.2	178.5	273.4	254.3	262.8
63.1	48.7	73.1	Sales/Net Fixed Assets	63.8	39.4	33.7	82.9	110.3	95.7
12.4	9.8	17.0		4.5	13.8	8.1	10.0	34.6	31.9
3.0	3.4	2.5		2.4	2.5	3.1	2.4	2.6	2.1
1.7	1.8	1.4	Sales/Total Assets	1.1	1.4	1.4	1.1	1.7	1.3
.9	1.0	.8		.4	.7	.9	.8	1.0	.9
.2	.2	.2		.7	.3	.2	.1	.1	.1
(115) .6	(154) .4	(246) .4	% Depr., Dep., Amort./Sales	(16) 1.4	(53) .5	(32) .7	(29) .1	(47) .3	(69) .2
2.0	1.2	1.0		2.8	1.5	1.0	1.1	.7	.7
1.5	1.5	1.3		5.2	2.0	2.0	1.8	1.0	.5
(72) 2.8	(90) 3.1	(163) 2.4	% Officers', Directors' Owners' Comp/Sales	(20) 7.4	(38) 3.4	(18) 2.5	(20) 2.5	(35) 1.7	(32) 1.1
5.6	6.0	6.3		13.0	6.5	3.8	4.7	2.5	2.3
4831229M	8659160M	11295282M	Net Sales ($)	28743M	158072M	180892M	424688M	1179567M	9323320M
3666908M	5509249M	8729070M	Total Assets ($)	58823M	158410M	171754M	428678M	1012041M	6899364M

M = $ thousand   MM = $ million
See Pages 11 through 21 for Explanation of Ratios and Data

Current Data Sorted by Assets

Comparative Historical Data

						Type of Statement		
						Unqualified		
		2	4	1 5		Reviewed	1	4
2		4	2	1		Compiled	2	6
14		14	8			Tax Returns	3	3
8		9	7	1	1	Other	3	4
		10 (4/1-9/30/06)					4/1/02-	4/1/03-
				73 (10/1/06-3/31/07)			3/31/03	3/31/04
0-500M		500M-2MM	2-10MM	10-50MM	50-100MM	100-250MM	ALL	ALL
24		29	21	8		1	NUMBER OF STATEMENTS	9	17
%		%	%	%	%	%	ASSETS	%	%
20.9		16.1	8.8				Cash & Equivalents		14.6
17.8		17.4	26.7				Trade Receivables (net)		29.9
15.3		21.3	24.8				Inventory		19.9
3.8		8.8	8.3				All Other Current		12.7
57.7		63.6	68.6				Total Current		77.1
24.2		23.5	21.7				Fixed Assets (net)		18.4
3.4		1.9	4.1				Intangibles (net)		.8
14.7		11.0	5.6				All Other Non-Current		3.7
100.0		100.0	100.0				Total		100.0
						LIABILITIES		
6.3		17.8	33.4				Notes Payable-Short Term		11.3
19.8		3.2	5.2				Cur. Mat.-L.T.D.		2.6
41.4		11.7	13.0				Trade Payables		15.6
.0		.1	.4				Income Taxes Payable		.9
15.1		16.9	10.5				All Other Current		10.6
82.6		49.6	62.5				Total Current		41.1
17.6		16.0	8.1				Long-Term Debt		22.7
.0		.0	.0				Deferred Taxes		1.4
11.0		6.8	1.5				All Other Non-Current		2.6
-11.1		27.5	28.0				Net Worth		32.3
100.0		100.0	100.0				Total Liabilities & Net Worth		100.0
						INCOME DATA		
100.0		100.0	100.0				Net Sales		100.0
32.5		28.5	26.5				Gross Profit		32.4
30.1		26.0	23.5				Operating Expenses		28.4
2.4		2.5	3.0				Operating Profit		3.9
.4		.7	.3				All Other Expenses (net)		.4
2.0		1.8	2.7				Profit Before Taxes		3.6
						RATIOS		
4.4		2.3	1.6						3.9
1.4		1.1	1.0				Current		1.9
.4		.9	.9						1.3
2.4		1.6	1.3						2.7
.6		.7	.6				Quick		1.6
.2		.1	.0						.2
0 UND		0 UND	0 UND					0 UND	
2 210.3		3 110.2	21 17.1				Sales/Receivables	26 13.9	
13 28.2		33 11.1	53 6.9					58 6.3	
0 UND		0 UND	0 UND					0 UND	
0 UND		0 849.5	19 19.7				Cost of Sales/Inventory	3 117.5	
3 105.6		176 2.1	124 3.0					40 9.2	
0 UND		0 UND	2 174.0					1 280.9	
5 68.4		15 24.0	13 29.1				Cost of Sales/Payables	17 22.0	
41 9.0		26 14.3	29 12.5					40 9.2	
17.5		10.3	8.4						7.1
61.4		32.4	94.4				Sales/Working Capital		11.3
-20.7		-24.7	-43.5						30.6
12.1		11.1	15.5						38.1
(16) 2.1		(23) 5.4	(16) 5.0				EBIT/Interest	(12) 2.1	
-1.3		1.2	2.3						-.6
						Net Profit + Depr., Dep., Amort./Cur. Mat. L/T/D		
.2		.3	.2						.0
.9		.9	.6				Fixed/Worth		.6
-6.0		13.9	4.4						2.5
.6		1.0	1.6						.8
3.3		5.4	5.0				Debt/Worth		3.2
-23.4		UND	19.6						5.5
137.5		57.7	89.2				% Profit Before Taxes/Tangible Net Worth		65.7
(16) 74.6		(23) 19.9	(19) 40.1					(15) 22.9	
4.3		4.7	10.1						-12.9
58.2		13.2	18.6				% Profit Before Taxes/Total Assets		27.1
8.1		3.9	10.0						3.6
-4.3		-.5	-.1						-3.5
151.6		50.2	54.4				Sales/Net Fixed Assets		163.3
65.7		23.9	29.3						27.1
17.8		15.4	9.7						9.4
14.2		4.8	3.4				Sales/Total Assets		4.4
5.7		2.7	2.7						3.6
3.5		1.1	1.1						2.9
.1		.4	.3				% Depr., Dep., Amort./Sales		.6
(14) 1.1		(22) .9	(14) .6					(13) 1.6	
2.2		2.1	1.0						2.9
2.8		2.7	2.3				% Officers', Directors' Owners' Comp/Sales		3.3
(12) 5.6		(19) 5.0	(14) 3.4					(12) 4.4	
14.5			7.3	7.3					9.2
42066M		82921M	232828M	239933M		544115M	Net Sales ($)	32698M	129926M
5317M		29519M	99384M	143102M		133734M	Total Assets ($)	11667M	38534M

© RMA 2007

M = $ thousand MM = $ million
See Pages 11 through 21 for Explanation of Ratios and Data

Comparative Historical Data | Current Data Sorted by Sales

H: 4/1/04-3/31/05 ALL	H: 4/1/05-3/31/06 ALL	H: 4/1/06-3/31/07 ALL	Type of Statement	0-1MM	1-3MM	3-5MM	5-10MM	10-25MM	25MM & OVER
2	8	1	Unqualified		2			1	
4	23	11	Reviewed	1	1	3	3	6	3
1	25	9	Compiled	16	6	7	4	1	
5	54	37	Tax Returns	4	10	2	3	3	1
3	44	25	Other					6	
				10 (4/1-9/30/06)		73 (10/1/06-3/31/07)			
15	154	83	NUMBER OF STATEMENTS	21	19	12	10	17	4
%	%	%	ASSETS	%	%	%	%	%	%
18.4	12.0	16.1	Cash & Equivalents	12.7	16.0	27.7	11.2	12.9	
30.9	12.0	19.0	Trade Receivables (net)	3.4	20.2	28.8	20.2	32.3	
14.1	46.6	21.3	Inventory	33.4	12.2	14.9	30.3	15.8	
9.1	4.8	7.5	All Other Current	3.8	10.8	3.7	4.4	13.3	
72.5	75.4	64.0	Total Current	53.3	59.2	75.1	66.1	74.3	
11.8	16.8	23.2	Fixed Assets (net)	35.5	16.9	18.6	18.2	18.6	
3.0	.9	2.8	Intangibles (net)	2.8	1.2	4.7	8.1	.3	
12.8	6.9	10.0	All Other Non-Current	8.4	22.7	1.6	7.6	6.7	
100.0	100.0	100.0	Total	100.0	100.0	100.0	100.0	100.0	
			LIABILITIES						
16.3	35.6	17.7	Notes Payable-Short Term	23.3	13.1	13.9	14.1	24.4	
5.5	3.0	8.2	Cur. Mat.-L.T.D.	23.9	4.3	4.5	1.3	1.5	
23.1	10.0	21.3	Trade Payables	12.9	38.0	17.6	27.2	14.8	
.7	.1	.2	Income Taxes Payable	.0	.0	.1	.0	.6	
22.9	17.2	13.6	All Other Current	10.8	17.8	16.9	17.0	10.4	
68.6	65.9	60.9	Total Current	70.9	73.2	53.0	59.6	51.8	
19.7	15.0	14.0	Long-Term Debt	17.7	21.8	9.3	3.3	8.2	
.0	.2	.1	Deferred Taxes	.0	.0	.1	.0	.5	
5.7	4.3	6.6	All Other Non-Current	12.8	.4	15.6	1.1	1.2	
6.1	14.5	18.5	Net Worth	-1.4	4.6	22.1	36.0	38.4	
100.0	100.0	100.0	Total Liabilities & Net Worth	100.0	100.0	100.0	100.0	100.0	
			INCOME DATA						
100.0	100.0	100.0	Net Sales	100.0	100.0	100.0	100.0	100.0	
23.8	19.5	29.3	Gross Profit	30.0	26.0	31.9	27.7	29.5	
19.4	15.4	26.0	Operating Expenses	30.0	23.3	29.9	22.9	23.0	
4.5	4.1	3.2	Operating Profit	.1	2.7	1.9	4.8	6.5	
-.1	.6	.4	All Other Expenses (net)	.9	1.0	.0	.2	-.3	
4.5	3.5	2.8	Profit Before Taxes	-.8	1.8	1.9	4.6	6.7	

RATIOS

H1	H2	H3	Ratio	0-1MM	1-3MM	3-5MM	5-10MM	10-25MM	25MM & OVER
2.0	1.6	2.4	Current	2.7	1.7	4.9	1.5	2.4	
1.3	1.1	1.2		1.0	1.1	2.0	1.0	1.6	
1.1	.9	.8		.4	.7	1.1	.7	1.0	
1.7	.8	1.7	Quick	1.6	1.2	4.4	1.1	2.3	
.9	.2	.7		.4	.4	1.6	.7	.8	
.3	.0	.1		.0	.2	.9	.1	.8	
16 22.8	0 UND	0 UND	Sales/Receivables	0 UND	0 999.8	0 UND	2 159.5	9 41.5	
30 12.0	0 999.8	8 47.4		0 UND	5 78.3	19 19.3	14 26.2	29 12.4	
48 7.6	18 20.3	31 11.6		2 150.3	26 13.8	61 6.0	26 14.0	70 5.2	
0 UND	0 UND	0 UND	Cost of Sales/Inventory	0 UND	0 UND	0 UND	0 UND	0 UND	
0 UND	96 3.8	0 UND		0 UND	0 UND	0 UND	13 28.5	0 UND	
49 7.4	228 1.6	59 6.2		494 .7	20 18.7	5 71.9	58 6.3	56 6.5	
2 146.8	0 UND	1 483.0	Cost of Sales/Payables	0 UND	0 UND	5 70.3	8 43.4	9 41.7	
19 18.8	9 41.9	14 27.0		0 UND	17 21.4	15 23.8	16 23.3	19 18.7	
55 6.7	26 14.0	30 12.1		19 18.9	41 8.9	25 14.8	36 10.3	35 10.6	
10.7	6.9	9.1	Sales/Working Capital	6.9	16.9	8.1	14.3	3.6	
19.0	21.9	49.7		-21.9	66.0	26.2	NM	12.3	
67.2	-77.2	-25.2		-6.0	-33.4	61.8	-22.8	NM	
32.2	18.6	12.2	EBIT/Interest	6.0	8.0			48.7	
(10) 7.4	(121) 5.1	(59) 4.5		(14) 1.7	(15) 2.2			(12) 5.0	
.4	1.1	1.1		-7.1	.3			2.6	
			Net Profit + Depr., Dep., Amort./Cur. Mat. L/T/D						
.1	.1	.2	Fixed/Worth	.0	.2	.4	.3	.1	
.5	.4	.7		6.0	.9	1.0	.4	.3	
-16.9	4.3	6.0		-17.3	6.3	-1.7	2.2	1.3	
1.3	1.9	.9	Debt/Worth	.5	1.2	.8	1.1	.7	
9.8	6.3	3.6		21.3	8.5	2.6	4.7	1.9	
-67.7	212.5	22.5		-20.8	27.4	-29.9	9.0	7.1	
81.6	89.0	100.0	% Profit Before Taxes/Tangible Net Worth	74.6	190.9		166.3	82.4	
(11) 57.0	(121) 40.1	(67) 34.6		(13) 17.5	(15) 40.7		29.1	42.5	
12.0	8.1	8.7		2.8	10.0		6.5	11.4	
23.3	18.0	19.2	% Profit Before Taxes/Total Assets	8.1	30.6	28.4	19.8	29.1	
7.4	5.5	7.6		1.4	4.0	4.0	12.2	12.4	
2.7	.5	.0		-3.2	-4.2	-.7	.8	3.9	
131.7	245.1	79.5	Sales/Net Fixed Assets	UND	101.8	47.9	86.4	59.4	
51.5	52.0	28.9		16.8	35.4	24.7	31.1	29.3	
15.4	13.0	14.4		1.8	20.9	18.2	17.2	9.7	
4.3	4.2	5.1	Sales/Total Assets	4.1	13.0	9.0	7.5	3.6	
3.8	2.1	3.2		1.5	4.7	3.5	4.3	2.9	
1.6	1.3	1.3		.3	2.0	2.4	1.1	1.5	
.4	.2	.3	% Depr., Dep., Amort./Sales	.3	.1			.3	
(11) .6	(108) .5	(56) .8		(10) 1.4	(14) .7		(14)	.5	
2.6	1.0	1.5		7.6	2.1			1.0	
	1.9	2.6	% Officers', Directors' Owners' Comp/Sales		1.9				
	(82) 3.0	(49) 4.0			(15) 3.6				
	5.9	7.2			5.9				
207563M	5402360M	1141863M	Net Sales ($)	9918M	41238M	49461M	65033M	272164M	704049M
86112M	1894690M	411056M	Total Assets ($)	17767M	12894M	15987M	38528M	117395M	208485M

M = $ thousand   MM = $ million
See Pages 11 through 21 for Explanation of Ratios and Data

Current Data Sorted by Assets | Comparative Historical Data

Type of Statement	0-500M	500M-2MM	2-10MM	10-50MM	50-100MM	100-250MM	ALL 4/1/02-3/31/03	ALL 4/1/03-3/31/04
Unqualified	1	16	78	90	16	17	213	204
Reviewed	5	51	133	35			218	234
Compiled	1	13	18	1	1		44	70
Tax Returns	33	43	19	4			27	59
Other	10	32	60	37	6	9	83	89
	151 (4/1-9/30/06)			578 (10/1/06-3/31/07)				
NUMBER OF STATEMENTS	50	155	308	167	23	26	585	656

ASSETS	0-500M %	500M-2MM %	2-10MM %	10-50MM %	50-100MM %	100-250MM %	ALL %	ALL %
Cash & Equivalents	26.0	16.5	20.0	18.6	17.8	13.4	21.1	21.2
Trade Receivables (net)	22.2	43.7	44.9	51.9	55.4	45.5	45.3	43.2
Inventory	2.5	6.4	4.5	1.9	4.3	1.1	2.6	2.8
All Other Current	12.1	7.6	10.4	8.9	12.1	9.0	9.1	9.0
Total Current	62.8	74.2	79.8	81.3	89.5	69.0	78.1	76.3
Fixed Assets (net)	25.0	16.5	12.6	13.0	6.8	22.5	14.0	15.4
Intangibles (net)	.0	.9	1.1	.9	.9	2.1	.7	1.0
All Other Non-Current	12.4	8.3	6.5	4.8	2.8	6.4	7.2	7.4
Total	100.0	100.0	100.0	100.0	100.0	100.0	100.0	100.0

LIABILITIES	0-500M	500M-2MM	2-10MM	10-50MM	50-100MM	100-250MM	ALL	ALL
Notes Payable-Short Term	18.3	10.8	6.5	3.4	6.9	.4	5.5	6.5
Cur. Mat.-L.T.D.	6.4	4.7	2.4	1.8	.7	2.4	2.3	2.5
Trade Payables	13.6	26.5	31.6	37.3	37.8	39.3	32.7	31.1
Income Taxes Payable	.3	.4	.5	.2	.3	.3	.5	.5
All Other Current	22.6	16.9	17.3	19.3	27.6	16.8	16.2	15.4
Total Current	61.1	59.4	58.2	62.0	73.3	59.2	57.1	56.0
Long-Term Debt	18.4	9.8	6.4	6.1	2.5	12.5	6.3	8.3
Deferred Taxes	.1	.4	.3	.3	.1	1.2	.3	.4
All Other Non-Current	6.3	2.3	1.8	1.5	.9	1.3	1.7	2.5
Net Worth	14.3	28.1	33.2	30.2	23.2	25.9	34.6	32.9
Total Liabilties & Net Worth	100.0	100.0	100.0	100.0	100.0	100.0	100.0	100.0

INCOME DATA	0-500M	500M-2MM	2-10MM	10-50MM	50-100MM	100-250MM	ALL	ALL
Net Sales	100.0	100.0	100.0	100.0	100.0	100.0	100.0	100.0
Gross Profit	32.1	22.4	14.7	11.1	12.2	11.1	14.4	16.1
Operating Expenses	29.8	17.3	10.9	7.4	8.4	7.1	12.7	13.9
Operating Profit	2.3	5.1	3.8	3.7	3.8	4.1	1.6	2.2
All Other Expenses (net)	.6	.5	-.3	-.4	.0	.2	-.1	.3
Profit Before Taxes	1.7	4.6	4.1	4.0	3.8	3.9	1.7	1.9

RATIOS	0-500M	500M-2MM	2-10MM	10-50MM	50-100MM	100-250MM	ALL	ALL
Current	2.7	2.0	1.7	1.5	1.3	1.3	1.8	1.8
	1.3	1.4	1.4	1.3	1.2	1.2	1.3	1.3
	.7	1.0	1.1	1.1	1.1	1.1	1.1	1.1
Quick	2.0	1.6	1.5	1.3	1.2	1.2	1.5	1.6
	1.0	1.2	1.2	1.1	1.1	1.0	1.2	1.2
	.4	.7	.9	.9	1.0	.8	1.0	.9
Sales/Receivables	0 UND	23 15.7	38 9.6	48 7.6	48 7.6	48 7.7	35 10.6	35 10.6
	11 32.9	46 8.0	53 6.8	63 5.8	63 5.8	62 5.9	52 7.1	51 7.1
	33 11.1	68 5.4	69 5.3	82 4.4	69 5.3	78 4.7	66 5.5	67 5.4
Cost of Sales/Inventory	0 UND	0 UND	0 UND	0 UND	0 UND	0 UND	0 UND	0 UND
	0 UND	0 UND	0 UND	0 UND	0 UND	0 UND	0 UND	0 UND
	0 UND	1 298.7	0 999.8	1 596.3	0 UND	5 73.8	0 888.6	0 937.5
Cost of Sales/Payables	0 UND	13 27.4	24 15.3	32 11.3	27 13.6	31 11.8	24 15.3	22 16.9
	4 100.8	28 12.9	41 8.9	49 7.5	45 8.2	53 6.9	39 9.3	41 8.9
	30 12.1	52 7.0	57 6.4	68 5.3	65 5.7	72 5.0	59 6.2	58 6.3
Sales/Working Capital	9.9	7.8	7.8	9.4	13.5	16.2	9.1	8.5
	40.7	18.2	15.0	18.6	20.8	23.4	17.4	16.2
	-43.3	-135.0	34.1	31.7	35.3	38.9	40.7	41.0
EBIT/Interest	8.5	19.6	44.5	67.8	103.7	84.0	26.6	25.8
	(35) 3.5	(131) 7.3	(248) 11.6	(134) 14.1	(17) 13.8	(22) 13.7	(452) 5.9	(511) 5.8
	1.0	1.7	3.1	5.5	6.9	3.1	1.2	.9
Net Profit + Depr., Dep., Amort./Cur. Mat. L/T/D		9.3	14.0	16.2			7.1	6.6
		(21) 2.6	(80) 4.8	(42) 5.4			(149) 2.6	(172) 2.3
		1.1	1.9	2.0			.8	.4
Fixed/Worth	.1	.2	.1	.1	.1	.2	.1	.1
	.7	.4	.3	.2	.1	.5	.3	.3
	UND	1.3	.7	.7	.4	1.5	.5	.7
Debt/Worth	.7	1.2	1.2	1.5	2.3	1.8	1.1	1.0
	4.6	2.2	2.3	2.7	3.9	3.9	2.3	2.2
	UND	17.2	4.4	5.1	6.1	5.8	4.4	4.3
% Profit Before Taxes/Tangible Net Worth	105.5	74.9	56.4	58.5	57.3	46.5	33.9	35.0
	(38) 58.9	(132) 40.3	(287) 27.8	(165) 30.9	40.0	(25) 34.2	(555) 14.2	(612) 12.3
	8.9	8.1	7.9	12.5	26.2	17.9	2.2	1.7
% Profit Before Taxes/Total Assets	49.6	22.6	16.6	15.8	11.9	10.3	10.2	10.4
	7.6	9.3	8.0	8.4	8.0	6.8	3.9	3.4
	-.4	1.2	2.2	2.6	4.4	3.8	.5	.3
Sales/Net Fixed Assets	231.2	95.9	123.5	144.1	440.2	89.8	106.2	90.8
	42.8	34.7	40.3	46.8	98.2	49.6	46.5	38.4
	12.7	15.7	16.4	13.4	43.2	5.2	17.8	15.0
Sales/Total Assets	9.2	4.7	3.9	3.7	4.2	3.4	4.2	4.1
	5.6	3.2	3.0	2.9	3.7	2.9	3.2	3.2
	2.9	2.2	2.2	2.2	2.8	2.0	2.4	2.2
% Depr., Dep., Amort./Sales	.4	.4	.2	.2	.1	.1	.3	.3
	(32) 1.0	(122) .7	(270) .5	(156) .4	(19) .3	(22) .3	(524) .6	(580) .6
	3.0	1.9	1.2	1.5	.6	1.3	1.4	1.6
% Officers', Directors' Owners' Comp/Sales	2.4	1.7	.9	.4			1.1	1.3
	(29) 4.2	(76) 3.2	(114) 2.0	(48) 1.1			(248) 2.1	(265) 2.5
	8.0	4.6	3.2	1.8			4.3	4.2
Net Sales ($)	62924M	715602M	4860675M	10901425M	5615300M	9606523M	21145869M	21005794M
Total Assets ($)	10803M	193264M	1585099M	3695247M	1573262M	3687576M	6778047M	6901728M

M = $ thousand   MM = $ million
See Pages 11 through 21 for Explanation of Ratios and Data

Comparative Historical Data | **Current Data Sorted by Sales**

			Type of Statement						
219	195	218	Unqualified	1	7	6	20	40	144
216	201	224	Reviewed	4	21	14	64	78	43
51	32	34	Compiled	2	6	7	9	6	4
56	67	99	Tax Returns	18	33	10	24	12	2
83	152	154	Other	6	21	16	21	34	56
4/1/04-3/31/05 ALL	4/1/05-3/31/06 ALL	4/1/06-3/31/07 ALL		151 (4/1-9/30/06)			578 (10/1/06-3/31/07)		
				0-1MM	1-3MM	3-5MM	5-10MM	10-25MM	25MM & OVER
625	647	729	NUMBER OF STATEMENTS	31	88	53	138	170	249
%	%	%	**ASSETS**	%	%	%	%	%	%
18.8	19.1	19.0	Cash & Equivalents	25.1	15.9	20.1	17.9	20.6	18.7
45.3	46.0	45.0	Trade Receivables (net)	15.9	30.9	31.9	44.8	50.2	53.1
3.8	3.2	4.1	Inventory	6.4	12.2	7.8	3.7	2.7	1.2
10.2	9.5	9.6	All Other Current	13.2	10.3	9.7	8.4	9.5	9.6
78.1	77.8	77.7	Total Current	60.6	69.3	69.5	74.9	83.0	82.5
14.0	14.8	14.6	Fixed Assets (net)	24.2	19.3	16.8	16.8	11.8	11.9
.9	.9	1.0	Intangibles (net)	2.0	.6	.3	1.5	.6	1.0
7.0	6.5	6.8	All Other Non-Current	13.5	10.8	13.4	6.8	4.6	4.6
100.0	100.0	100.0	Total	100.0	100.0	100.0	100.0	100.0	100.0
			LIABILITIES						
6.8	6.7	7.3	Notes Payable-Short Term	9.2	16.0	15.2	8.8	5.3	2.8
2.5	2.4	3.0	Cur. Mat.-L.T.D.	7.7	5.9	5.4	3.2	1.8	1.5
32.8	33.5	31.1	Trade Payables	9.3	17.3	20.7	27.3	35.9	39.6
.4	.4	.4	Income Taxes Payable	.0	.6	.2	.5	.4	.3
16.8	14.3	18.3	All Other Current	21.2	16.9	19.7	14.8	17.3	20.8
59.4	57.2	60.0	Total Current	47.5	56.8	61.2	54.6	60.7	65.1
9.0	7.4	8.0	Long-Term Debt	14.4	15.2	12.7	8.3	6.2	4.7
.3	.3	.3	Deferred Taxes	.0	.3	.4	.4	.3	.3
2.1	3.0	2.1	All Other Non-Current	7.2	3.4	3.5	2.1	1.4	1.2
29.2	32.1	29.5	Net Worth	31.1	24.3	22.2	34.5	31.5	28.7
100.0	100.0	100.0	Total Liabilities & Net Worth	100.0	100.0	100.0	100.0	100.0	100.0
			INCOME DATA						
100.0	100.0	100.0	Net Sales	100.0	100.0	100.0	100.0	100.0	100.0
14.7	15.0	16.5	Gross Profit	44.6	23.2	21.8	18.0	13.9	10.5
12.7	12.0	12.6	Operating Expenses	34.5	19.2	18.1	13.7	10.6	7.0
2.1	2.9	4.0	Operating Profit	10.1	4.1	3.7	4.2	3.2	3.5
.1	.0	.0	All Other Expenses (net)	1.3	.4	.2	.0	-.4	-.2
1.9	2.9	4.0	Profit Before Taxes	8.8	3.7	3.5	4.3	3.6	3.7
			RATIOS						
1.8	1.8	1.7	Current	3.0	2.3	2.3	2.0	1.7	1.4
1.3	1.3	1.3		1.2	1.5	1.4	1.4	1.4	1.3
1.1	1.1	1.1		.9	.9	.9	1.1	1.2	1.1
1.5	1.6	1.4	Quick	2.8	1.8	1.5	1.6	1.5	1.3
1.1 (646)	1.2	1.1		1.2	1.0	1.0	1.3	1.2	1.1
.9	.9	.9		.3	.3	.4	.9	1.0	1.0
34 10.8	36 10.0	35 10.3	Sales/Receivables	0 UND	5 68.8	6 65.6	32 11.3	39 9.2	46 7.9
53 6.9	55 6.7	54 6.8		0 UND	44 8.3	46 7.9	51 7.2	55 6.7	59 6.2
73 5.0	73 5.0	72 5.1		33 11.1	98 3.7	61 6.0	72 5.1	69 5.3	76 4.8
0 UND	0 UND	0 UND	Cost of Sales/Inventory	0 UND	0 UND	0 UND	0 UND	0 UND	0 UND
0 UND	0 UND	0 UND		0 UND	0 UND	0 UND	0 UND	0 UND	0 UND
1 659.4	0 999.8	0 972.9		0 UND	4 104.3	4 85.7	0 966.5	0 999.8	0 999.8
22 16.2	23 15.7	20 18.6	Cost of Sales/Payables	0 UND	3 106.0	12 31.7	17 21.0	28 13.0	30 12.0
41 8.9	41 8.8	39 9.4		2 209.0	26 13.9	25 14.8	32 11.3	43 8.5	46 8.0
61 6.0	62 5.9	58 6.3		11 32.5	65 5.7	50 7.3	51 7.2	60 6.1	64 5.7
8.9	8.4	8.7	Sales/Working Capital	7.8	4.7	6.7	7.1	8.4	12.5
17.7	17.0	17.7		37.0	14.4	13.4	15.2	14.5	21.5
42.2	37.2	42.3		-45.3	-40.6	-43.0	48.0	31.0	35.8
30.3	32.9	39.8	EBIT/Interest	10.8	13.1	14.4	27.1	54.4	69.8
(471) 6.9	(503) 8.1	(587) 9.7		(18) 5.2	(74) 4.5	(46) 4.7	(114) 7.8	(136) 10.1	(199) 20.3
1.4	2.5	3.1		2.0	1.0	1.5	2.5	3.2	6.0
8.2	8.2	14.8	Net Profit + Depr., Dep., Amort./Cur. Mat. L/T/D		6.9	23.3	11.4	14.3	20.3
(151) 2.8	(134) 3.2	(156) 4.8		(13) 2.4	(10) 6.4	(24) 2.4	(47) 5.6	(59) 7.5	
.9	1.2	1.9		.8	1.3	.8	2.2	2.3	
.1	.1	.1	Fixed/Worth	.0	.1	.2	.1	.1	.1
.3	.3	.3		1.0	.4	.4	.3	.3	.2
.8	.7	.8		47.0	4.1	3.6	.8	.6	.6
1.1	1.1	1.3	Debt/Worth	.2	1.0	1.0	.9	1.3	1.8
2.5	2.4	2.5		4.1	3.1	2.7	2.0	2.3	2.8
5.3	5.1	5.4		107.0	46.3	29.2	4.9	4.2	5.2
38.2	45.6	62.2	% Profit Before Taxes/Tangible Net Worth	106.3	67.0	72.7	59.3	53.0	62.7
(569) 14.0	(597) 21.6	(670) 32.7		(25) 57.9	(70) 31.2	(42) 19.9	(127) 28.9	(161) 28.0	(245) 36.8
1.2	7.0	11.0		5.7	5.7	7.0	6.1	8.1	14.0
10.9	13.5	17.4	% Profit Before Taxes/Total Assets	40.7	16.6	20.1	18.9	17.3	16.5
3.8	5.8	8.1		7.8	6.4	7.0	8.7	8.3	8.7
.4	1.8	2.3		.7	.0	.9	2.3	2.1	3.7
105.0	103.0	123.5	Sales/Net Fixed Assets	175.8	137.0	84.4	81.5	118.2	161.9
44.1	40.2	41.7		17.0	23.0	34.5	27.9	45.1	59.4
17.0	14.7	14.9		6.1	7.6	16.8	11.6	19.8	18.2
4.0	4.0	4.1	Sales/Total Assets	7.1	3.0	3.9	4.1	4.3	4.1
3.2	3.1	3.0		2.9	2.2	3.0	3.0	3.2	3.3
2.3	2.3	2.2		.8	1.5	1.9	2.2	2.5	2.6
.3	.2	.2	% Depr., Dep., Amort./Sales	.8	.4	.4	.4	.2	.1
(536) .6	(556) .5	(621) .6		(22) 2.0	(63) 1.1	(39) .7	(112) .8	(156) .5	(229) .3
1.4	1.3	1.5		3.6	2.7	3.0	1.7	1.0	.8
1.1	1.0	1.0	% Officers', Directors' Owners' Comp/Sales	4.2	2.4	1.1	1.6	.7	.3
(246) 2.2	(255) 2.0	(275) 2.2		(11) 9.6	(43) 4.2	(25) 2.5	(64) 2.7	(66) 1.5	(66) 1.1
4.2	3.8	4.3		14.9	6.7	4.9			1.8
23669917M	23391822M	31762449M	Net Sales ($)	14538M	168960M	211983M	1003707M	2856393M	27506868M
7490059M	7964001M	10745251M	Total Assets ($)	21680M	111602M	117049M	376435M	1013688M	9104797M

© RMA 2007

M = $ thousand   MM = $ million
See Pages 11 through 21 for Explanation of Ratios and Data

Current Data Sorted by Assets

Comparative Historical Data

						Type of Statement		
1	20	138	216	49	38	Unqualified	260	333
13	121	295	70	4	1	Reviewed	259	456
15	37	33	9			Compiled	54	137
52	59	39	6	1		Tax Returns	56	102
22	54	135	78	18	15	Other	133	181
	291 (4/1-9/30/06)		1,248 (10/1/06-3/31/07)				4/1/02-3/31/03	4/1/03-3/31/04
0-500M	500M-2MM	2-10MM	10-50MM	50-100MM	100-250MM		ALL	ALL
103	291	640	379	72	54	NUMBER OF STATEMENTS	762	1209
%	%	%	%	%	%	ASSETS	%	%
23.7	16.0	18.7	21.5	17.1	20.9	Cash & Equivalents	19.6	18.9
23.1	41.9	48.8	51.6	51.7	47.6	Trade Receivables (net)	46.6	44.5
5.2	5.6	4.1	2.3	3.5	4.1	Inventory	3.2	4.2
9.3	10.9	9.2	8.4	8.7	9.1	All Other Current	9.7	10.8
61.3	74.4	80.8	83.9	80.9	81.7	Total Current	79.2	78.4
25.1	17.6	12.5	11.6	12.8	12.2	Fixed Assets (net)	12.9	13.9
2.4	1.1	1.0	.9	.6	1.4	Intangibles (net)	1.0	.9
11.1	6.9	5.7	3.6	5.7	4.7	All Other Non-Current	6.9	6.8
100.0	100.0	100.0	100.0	100.0	100.0	Total	100.0	100.0
						LIABILITIES		
17.3	9.8	6.0	3.4	3.4	2.7	Notes Payable-Short Term	6.4	6.9
5.7	2.6	2.1	1.5	1.1	.7	Cur. Mat.-L.T.D.	2.0	1.9
17.7	27.2	33.6	40.0	44.3	41.2	Trade Payables	36.3	33.6
.1	.8	.7	.3	.3	.2	Income Taxes Payable	.6	.6
22.0	13.6	16.9	19.9	22.7	25.3	All Other Current	16.7	16.2
62.8	54.0	59.3	65.1	71.7	70.0	Total Current	62.0	59.1
19.7	10.1	6.2	5.9	8.1	6.8	Long-Term Debt	6.1	7.0
.0	.3	.4	.2	.1	.3	Deferred Taxes	.4	.3
7.2	4.8	2.0	1.6	1.4	1.9	All Other Non-Current	3.2	2.5
10.4	30.9	32.1	27.2	18.7	21.0	Net Worth	28.3	31.2
100.0	100.0	100.0	100.0	100.0	100.0	Total Liabilities & Net Worth	100.0	100.0
						INCOME DATA		
100.0	100.0	100.0	100.0	100.0	100.0	Net Sales	100.0	100.0
29.6	21.8	16.2	12.2	10.1	11.7	Gross Profit	13.8	15.4
26.2	17.2	12.1	8.0	7.2	7.4	Operating Expenses	11.7	13.6
3.3	4.7	4.1	4.3	2.9	4.3	Operating Profit	2.0	1.9
.6	.5	.2	.1	.3	.4	All Other Expenses (net)	.3	.1
2.8	4.2	3.9	4.1	2.6	3.9	Profit Before Taxes	1.7	1.8
						RATIOS		
3.2	2.1	1.7	1.5	1.3	1.2	Current	1.6	1.7
1.5	1.4	1.3	1.3	1.2	1.2		1.3	1.3
.6	1.1	1.1	1.1	1.1	1.1		1.1	1.1
2.7	1.7	1.5	1.3	1.2	1.1	Quick	1.4	1.4
(102) 1.1	1.1	1.2	1.2	1.1	1.0		(761) 1.1 (1208) 1.1	
.3	.8	1.0	1.0	1.0	.9		.9	.9
0 UND	22 16.3	38 9.6	46 7.9	52 7.0	45 8.0	Sales/Receivables	36 10.1	32 11.3
7 51.2	38 9.7	56 6.6	64 5.7	74 4.9	60 6.0		53 6.8	51 7.2
34 10.9	64 5.7	76 4.8	82 4.5	86 4.3	72 5.1		70 5.2	70 5.2
0 UND	0 UND	0 UND	0 UND	0 UND	0 UND	Cost of Sales/Inventory	0 UND	0 UND
0 UND	0 UND	0 UND	0 UND	0 UND	0 UND		0 UND	0 UND
0 UND	1 295.6	0 999.8	0 999.8	1 539.6	2 175.3		0 999.8	0 819.9
0 UND	15 23.9	24 14.9	32 11.4	41 8.9	45 8.1	Cost of Sales/Payables	27 13.5	23 15.8
5 71.3	29 12.4	43 8.6	51 7.2	61 6.0	58 6.3		44 8.2	43 8.4
20 17.9	49 7.5	60 6.1	71 5.1	87 4.2	73 5.0		63 5.8	61 5.9
10.7	7.8	8.2	10.4	13.7	16.2	Sales/Working Capital	10.0	9.5
48.6	16.9	17.4	17.7	24.5	27.3		20.7	18.1
-29.7	121.5	36.3	31.6	40.8	43.8		50.4	45.6
21.8	19.0	42.8	95.7	115.7	190.2	EBIT/Interest	25.7	28.4
(72) 5.0	(226) 5.9	(509) 10.2	(291) 21.8	(51) 19.6	(41) 35.4		(592) 6.4 (937) 6.9	
1.5	1.6	2.9	7.0	5.2	7.5		1.5	1.2
	7.0	9.5	24.4	17.3	35.2	Net Profit + Depr., Dep., Amort./Cur. Mat. L/T/D	10.9	9.5
	(52) 3.2	(147) 3.5	(81) 8.2	(17) 4.6	(19) 13.3		(194) 4.0 (284) 3.2	
	.8	1.4	2.5	2.6	9.9		.3	.6
.1	.2	.1	.1	.1	.1	Fixed/Worth	.1	.1
.6	.4	.2	.2	.3	.2		.3	.3
6.5	1.1	.6	.5	.7	.6		.7	.7
.7	.9	1.3	1.7	2.8	3.0	Debt/Worth	1.3	1.3
3.2	1.9	2.3	3.2	4.8	4.6		2.7	2.5
169.5	5.2	4.6	5.2	7.1	6.4		5.5	4.8
129.0	65.2	56.7	57.9	57.0	53.5	% Profit Before Taxes/Tangible Net Worth	40.3	37.5
(79) 44.8	(257) 29.8	(605) 30.0	(368) 33.5	(67) 32.8	(50) 36.9		(717) 16.5 (1140) 16.2	
10.1	7.4	9.8	15.8	16.8	24.4		3.4	2.0
36.4	22.0	18.1	14.8	10.8	9.8	% Profit Before Taxes/Total Assets	10.6	10.6
15.8	10.0	8.4	8.0	6.1	7.2		4.0	4.3
.7	2.4	2.3	3.1	1.8	5.1		.5	.2
276.1	83.6	121.9	185.7	161.5	126.7	Sales/Net Fixed Assets	118.3	113.3
41.0	34.7	48.0	76.9	68.4	67.7		48.3	47.8
15.9	13.2	18.6	22.7	17.3	30.8		19.2	17.6
10.8	4.8	4.1	3.8	3.5	3.5	Sales/Total Assets	4.3	4.2
5.8	3.6	3.2	3.1	3.0	3.1		3.3	3.2
3.5	2.2	2.3	2.3	2.2	2.5		2.5	2.4
.6	.4	.2	.1	.1	.1	% Depr., Dep., Amort./Sales	.2	.3
(57) 1.5	(226) .8	(561) .5	(338) .3	(60) .3	(50) .2		(678) .6 (1039) .6	
3.1	1.9	1.1	.7	.5	.5		1.2	1.3
2.0	2.1	1.0	.5	.3		% Officers', Directors' Owners' Comp/Sales	1.1	1.2
(51) 3.6	(146) 3.0	(257) 2.0	(114) 1.0	(14) .7			(298) 2.2 (493) 2.2	
6.2	4.7	3.4	2.1	1.6			4.5	4.5
208482M	1438744M	10123978M	24177710M	14884757M	22942297M	Net Sales ($)	35095042M	49600506M
26836M	370806M	3126452M	8001245M	5014158M	8163711M	Total Assets ($)	9983838M	14189112M

M = $ thousand   MM = $ million
See Pages 11 through 21 for Explanation of Ratios and Data

Comparative Historical Data   Current Data Sorted by Sales

Type of Statement	Hist 4/1/04-3/31/05	Hist 4/1/05-3/31/06	Hist 4/1/06-3/31/07	0-1MM	1-3MM	3-5MM	5-10MM	10-25MM	25MM & OVER
Unqualified	340	368	462	3	7	7	30	99	316
Reviewed	383	442	504	10	32	46	129	180	107
Compiled	69	87	94	8	21	13	27	23	2
Tax Returns	117	106	157	21	50	29	28	21	8
Other	186	284	322	16	29	23	58	80	116
	ALL	ALL	ALL	291 (4/1-9/30/06)			1,248 (10/1/06-3/31/07)		
NUMBER OF STATEMENTS	1095	1287	1539	58	139	118	272	403	549

ASSETS (%)

	Hist 1	Hist 2	Hist 3	0-1MM	1-3MM	3-5MM	5-10MM	10-25MM	25MM & OVER
Cash & Equivalents	18.6	19.1	19.2	15.2	16.5	18.8	16.5	19.8	21.3
Trade Receivables (net)	47.4	46.9	46.6	18.8	26.6	35.8	45.5	50.0	54.9
Inventory	4.2	3.9	4.0	14.2	8.2	8.0	4.7	2.6	1.7
All Other Current	8.9	9.5	9.3	7.7	12.3	8.0	10.4	9.2	8.6
Total Current	79.1	79.3	79.1	55.9	63.6	70.6	77.1	81.6	86.4
Fixed Assets (net)	13.0	13.7	14.1	30.1	25.3	20.3	15.2	12.0	9.2
Intangibles (net)	1.1	1.0	1.1	2.8	1.3	1.9	.9	1.2	.6
All Other Non-Current	6.8	6.0	5.7	11.2	9.7	7.2	6.8	5.2	3.7
Total	100.0	100.0	100.0	100.0	100.0	100.0	100.0	100.0	100.0

LIABILITIES

	Hist 1	Hist 2	Hist 3	0-1MM	1-3MM	3-5MM	5-10MM	10-25MM	25MM & OVER
Notes Payable-Short Term	7.5	6.5	6.6	17.7	16.7	11.6	7.5	4.9	2.6
Cur. Mat.-L.T.D.	2.3	1.9	2.2	5.4	3.2	3.6	2.4	2.2	1.1
Trade Payables	35.5	33.9	33.6	8.1	15.3	23.3	29.4	35.4	44.1
Income Taxes Payable	.5	.6	.5	.1	.2	1.2	.7	.8	.3
All Other Current	16.1	17.0	17.9	14.3	13.7	21.7	13.1	18.3	20.7
Total Current	61.9	59.9	60.9	45.7	49.1	61.5	53.2	61.5	68.8
Long-Term Debt	7.0	7.9	7.9	26.3	19.0	11.5	7.2	5.5	4.4
Deferred Taxes	.3	.3	.3	.0	.2	.1	.5	.4	.1
All Other Non-Current	2.6	3.0	2.8	3.5	8.8	2.4	2.7	2.7	1.3
Net Worth	28.2	28.9	28.2	24.4	22.9	24.4	36.5	30.0	25.4
Total Liabilities & Net Worth	100.0	100.0	100.0	100.0	100.0	100.0	100.0	100.0	100.0

INCOME DATA

	Hist 1	Hist 2	Hist 3	0-1MM	1-3MM	3-5MM	5-10MM	10-25MM	25MM & OVER
Net Sales	100.0	100.0	100.0	100.0	100.0	100.0	100.0	100.0	100.0
Gross Profit	15.2	15.3	16.7	41.6	28.8	22.1	19.2	15.1	9.8
Operating Expenses	12.6	12.1	12.6	32.7	23.7	17.4	14.9	11.0	6.6
Operating Profit	2.6	3.3	4.1	8.9	5.0	4.8	4.3	4.1	3.2
All Other Expenses (net)	.1	.3	.3	3.8	.9	.6	.1	.1	-.1
Profit Before Taxes	2.5	3.0	3.9	5.1	4.1	4.2	4.2	4.1	3.3

RATIOS

	Hist 1	Hist 2	Hist 3	0-1MM	1-3MM	3-5MM	5-10MM	10-25MM	25MM & OVER
Current	1.7	1.7	1.6	2.9	2.5	2.1	2.1	1.6	1.4
	1.3	1.3	1.3	1.2	1.5	1.3	1.5	1.3	1.2
	1.1	1.1	1.1	.6	1.0	1.0	1.1	1.1	1.1
Quick	1.4	1.4	1.4	2.2	2.0	1.7	1.8	1.5	1.3
	1.1 (1286)	1.1 (1538)	1.1	(57) .9	1.1	1.0	1.2	1.2	1.1
	.9	.9	.9	.2	.3	.5	.9	1.0	1.0
Sales/Receivables	35 10.5	36 10.2	34 10.7	0 UND	3 116.5	12 31.4	30 12.2	38 9.7	46 8.0
	56 6.5	55 6.6	54 6.7	13 27.3	27 13.7	37 9.9	52 7.0	56 6.5	60 6.1
	77 4.8	75 4.9	75 4.9	59 6.2	63 5.8	73 5.0	76 4.8	75 4.9	77 4.7
Cost of Sales/Inventory	0 UND	0 UND	0 UND	0 UND	0 UND	0 UND	0 UND	0 UND	0 UND
	0 UND	0 UND	0 UND	0 UND	0 UND	0 UND	0 UND	0 UND	0 UND
	0 999.8	0 999.8	0 999.8	18 20.7	2 200.1	8 47.1	2 234.3	0 UND	0 999.8
Cost of Sales/Payables	26 14.2	24 15.0	22 16.8	0 UND	3 104.5	9 42.0	19 19.5	25 14.9	36 10.2
	45 8.1	42 8.7	42 8.7	9 40.6	22 16.6	29 12.4	34 10.6	42 8.7	51 7.1
	67 5.5	62 5.9	62 5.9	30 12.0	50 7.3	49 7.4	55 6.7	61 5.9	70 5.2
Sales/Working Capital	9.4	9.0	9.3	3.6	5.9	7.4	7.6	9.7	12.4
	18.9	17.0	18.3	19.4	13.8	17.7	14.3	19.2	20.7
	51.6	37.6	41.1	-16.0	171.4	-140.5	37.3	42.2	34.4
EBIT/Interest	35.0	37.7	45.1	8.2	11.3	19.1	23.8	61.1	121.7
	(862) 8.4	(1017) 10.6	(1190) 11.3	(34) 3.5	(114) 4.0	(92) 5.2	(209) 7.2	(322) 11.0	(419) 27.1
	1.7	3.1	3.3	-.7	.2	1.6	2.7	3.5	7.6
Net Profit + Depr., Dep., Amort./Cur. Mat. L/T/D	14.4	13.2	13.9		3.1	10.2	7.0	9.7	24.5
	(243) 3.8	(284) 3.9	(320) 5.2		(15) .8	(19) 5.2	(57) 3.1	(100) 4.1	(125) 9.2
	1.1	1.7	1.8		-1.6	1.2	1.3	1.6	2.9
Fixed/Worth	.1	.1	.1	.0	.2	.1	.1	.1	.1
	.3	.3	.3	.6	.7	.5	.3	.3	.2
	.7	.7	.7	5.2	2.5	1.4	.7	.6	.5
Debt/Worth	1.4	1.3	1.3	1.0	.9	.9	.9	1.3	2.1
	2.9	2.7	2.7	3.3	2.2	2.2	1.8	2.6	3.4
	5.7	5.5	5.3	20.6	12.2	10.6	3.6	5.0	5.4
% Profit Before Taxes/Tangible Net Worth	41.4	49.9	58.9	72.9	64.0	64.0	55.3	63.0	58.0
	(1005) 18.2	(1204) 23.5	(1426) 31.9	(48) 23.6	(117) 20.6	(99) 33.2	(256) 26.6	(377) 30.1	(529) 35.4
	4.4	8.1	11.6	-.2	2.7	12.1	7.8	10.7	18.0
% Profit Before Taxes/Total Assets	11.3	13.5	18.0	19.5	21.2	22.1	20.8	19.1	14.6
	4.5	6.1	8.4	4.0	6.5	8.7	9.3	9.0	8.1
	.8	2.0	2.7	-3.0	.5	2.6	2.7	2.2	3.5
Sales/Net Fixed Assets	121.1	128.1	139.3	191.6	49.6	83.2	78.5	116.2	190.8
	50.2	50.4	49.3	18.5	18.6	29.2	35.9	50.9	85.0
	19.7	19.0	18.1	2.0	8.3	10.5	14.3	23.3	32.5
Sales/Total Assets	4.1	4.1	4.2	3.5	4.6	4.5	4.4	4.3	4.0
	3.2	3.2	3.2	1.4	2.5	2.9	3.2	3.3	3.3
	2.4	2.3	2.3	.6	1.6	1.9	2.1	2.5	2.7
% Depr., Dep., Amort./Sales	.2	.2	.2	1.1	.7	.4	.3	.2	.1
	(928) .5	(1112) .4	(1292) .5	(29) 3.7	(100) 1.5	(92) 1.0	(221) .8	(360) .5	(490) .3
	1.2	1.1	1.2	7.3	2.7	2.3	1.6	1.0	.5
% Officers', Directors' Owners' Comp/Sales	1.1	1.1	1.0	3.6	2.5	2.0	1.8	.9	.4
	(417) 2.1	(507) 2.2	(588) 2.1	(16) 6.1	(74) 3.6	(61) 3.0	(125) 2.5	(160) 1.7	(152) .9
	3.9	4.1	3.8	12.5	6.1	4.4	3.1	3.1	1.8
Net Sales ($)	42515074M	50327344M	73775968M	31259M	280810M	464786M	1969778M	6539903M	64489432M
Total Assets ($)	14283584M	17213635M	24703208M	71221M	239009M	219675M	806939M	2363932M	21002432M

© RMA 2007

M = $ thousand   MM = $ million
See Pages 11 through 21 for Explanation of Ratios and Data

Current Data Sorted by Assets | Comparative Historical Data

Type of Statement	0-500M	500M-2MM	2-10MM	10-50MM	50-100MM	100-250MM		4/1/02-3/31/03 ALL	4/1/03-3/31/04 ALL
Unqualified		5	54	49	8	7		103	110
Reviewed	1	33	94	19				128	158
Compiled	2	17	12	1				31	48
Tax Returns	10	14	7	1		1		21	34
Other	4	9	44	30	1	1		57	79
		102 (4/1-9/30/06)		322 (10/1/06-3/31/07)					
NUMBER OF STATEMENTS	17	78	211	100	9	9		340	429

ASSETS (%)

	0-500M	500M-2MM	2-10MM	10-50MM	50-100MM	100-250MM		ALL	ALL
Cash & Equivalents	25.7	12.4	13.8	15.6				13.9	13.2
Trade Receivables (net)	26.8	31.2	37.9	39.3				35.8	34.9
Inventory	5.4	3.3	2.5	2.2				2.0	2.5
All Other Current	4.6	4.3	7.3	9.7				8.5	9.1
Total Current	62.4	51.2	61.5	66.9				60.3	59.7
Fixed Assets (net)	28.1	40.3	33.2	27.2				31.6	32.6
Intangibles (net)	2.6	3.3	1.1	.8				1.2	1.5
All Other Non-Current	6.8	5.3	4.2	5.0				6.9	6.2
Total	100.0	100.0	100.0	100.0				100.0	100.0

LIABILITIES

	0-500M	500M-2MM	2-10MM	10-50MM				ALL	ALL
Notes Payable-Short Term	8.9	7.5	6.0	5.0				6.7	7.4
Cur. Mat.-L.T.D.	6.6	6.8	5.9	4.9				5.8	6.5
Trade Payables	12.6	15.9	16.5	20.6				17.4	17.2
Income Taxes Payable	.1	.6	1.4	.4				1.0	.8
All Other Current	5.3	7.7	11.4	14.5				10.7	9.4
Total Current	33.4	38.4	41.2	45.4				41.5	41.2
Long-Term Debt	25.8	24.7	13.6	11.0				13.2	14.2
Deferred Taxes	.0	.8	1.0	.7				1.0	1.1
All Other Non-Current	2.2	1.9	2.6	2.5				2.3	3.5
Net Worth	38.5	34.3	41.6	40.4				41.9	40.0
Total Liabilties & Net Worth	100.0	100.0	100.0	100.0				100.0	100.0

INCOME DATA

	0-500M	500M-2MM	2-10MM	10-50MM				ALL	ALL
Net Sales	100.0	100.0	100.0	100.0				100.0	100.0
Gross Profit	47.3	29.9	23.2	17.2				23.3	24.4
Operating Expenses	45.1	26.1	17.3	10.9				20.0	21.7
Operating Profit	2.2	3.8	5.9	6.3				3.3	2.7
All Other Expenses (net)	.8	.3	.4	-.2				.4	.5
Profit Before Taxes	1.3	3.5	5.5	6.5				2.9	2.2

RATIOS

	0-500M	500M-2MM	2-10MM	10-50MM				ALL	ALL
Current	5.5	2.2	2.1	1.9				2.1	2.1
	2.2	1.4	1.5	1.4				1.5	1.4
	1.1	1.0	1.2	1.2				1.1	1.1
Quick	4.5	1.9	1.8	1.7				1.8	1.7
	1.3	1.3	1.2	1.2				1.2	1.1
	1.1	.8	.9	.9				.9	.8
Sales/Receivables	0 UND	25 14.7	42 8.7	48 7.6				37 9.9	40 9.2
	26 13.9	39 9.4	60 6.1	68 5.4				57 6.4	58 6.3
	48 7.7	62 5.9	80 4.5	85 4.3				76 4.8	77 4.7
Cost of Sales/Inventory	0 UND	0 UND	0 UND	0 UND				0 UND	0 UND
	0 UND	0 UND	0 UND	0 UND				0 UND	0 UND
	30 12.0	6 59.9	3 140.2	1 407.9				2 159.8	5 78.3
Cost of Sales/Payables	0 UND	12 30.9	17 21.7	25 14.8				15 25.2	17 21.2
	18 20.1	24 15.1	31 11.9	40 9.2				29 12.4	32 11.5
	29 12.4	43 8.5	46 7.9	51 7.1				48 7.5	50 7.2
Sales/Working Capital	6.4	8.1	6.7	6.1				7.0	6.7
	15.2	17.3	11.9	12.0				12.9	12.7
	115.9	NM	29.7	20.9				47.0	65.8
EBIT/Interest	18.8	10.4	23.8	26.7				12.9	12.7
	(14) 5.7	(73) 4.0	(197) 7.3	(93) 10.0				(312) 4.1	(395) 4.2
	-1.1	1.4	2.7	3.5				1.0	1.0
Net Profit + Depr., Dep., Amort./Cur. Mat. L/T/D		3.7	5.1	5.9				5.0	3.4
		(18) 1.7	(69) 2.5	(38) 2.8				(112) 2.3	(137) 1.6
		1.1	1.7	1.7				1.3	.8
Fixed/Worth	.1	.5	.4	.4				.4	.4
	.6	1.1	.8	.6				.7	.7
	1.7	4.4	1.3	1.2				1.4	1.5
Debt/Worth	.5	.7	.8	.8				.7	.8
	1.6	1.7	1.4	1.7				1.6	1.6
	4.9	6.0	2.5	2.7				2.9	2.8
% Profit Before Taxes/Tangible Net Worth	42.3	78.4	47.8	42.5				33.9	28.4
	(15) 16.0	(68) 32.6	(207) 23.7	(98) 28.6				(325) 13.9	(410) 13.0
	-35.9	5.5	7.7	14.9				1.2	1.1
% Profit Before Taxes/Total Assets	45.8	19.4	18.6	17.8				13.3	10.8
	6.0	7.8	8.9	10.3				5.1	5.0
	-20.5	.6	3.3	4.7				.2	.0
Sales/Net Fixed Assets	64.2	13.5	14.3	17.4				14.1	14.2
	12.4	6.4	7.9	8.4				7.4	7.2
	6.3	3.7	4.4	5.5				4.9	4.4
Sales/Total Assets	6.7	3.5	2.9	2.6				3.0	2.8
	2.8	2.6	2.2	2.1				2.3	2.2
	2.0	1.8	1.7	1.7				1.7	1.7
% Depr., Dep., Amort./Sales		2.3	2.0	1.5				1.9	2.1
		(71) 4.5	(198) 3.4	(95) 2.4				(318) 3.6	(392) 3.8
		6.4	5.5	3.8				5.8	6.4
% Officers', Directors' Owners' Comp/Sales	5.8	2.6	1.6	.7				1.9	1.6
	(12) 7.3	(44) 4.5	(103) 2.9	(38) 1.1				(145) 3.6	(212) 3.5
	16.5	7.1	5.7	2.6				6.8	6.7
Net Sales ($)	20065M	265810M	2487732M	4128494M	1716831M	2601509M		7652515M	8232363M
Total Assets ($)	4511M	94673M	1075840M	1939387M	712247M	1313652M		3563400M	3967675M

M = $ thousand   MM = $ million
See Pages 11 through 21 for Explanation of Ratios and Data

Comparative Historical Data | **Current Data Sorted by Sales**

Type of Statement									
	4/1/04-3/31/05 ALL	4/1/05-3/31/06 ALL	4/1/06-3/31/07 ALL	0-1MM	1-3MM	3-5MM	5-10MM	10-25MM	25MM & OVER
Unqualified	136	116	123	1	3	6	12	39	62
Reviewed	119	107	147	1	16	24	47	38	21
Compiled	27	17	32	4	13	5	7	3	
Tax Returns	26	25	33	5	14	3	6	4	1
Other	60	84	89	3	9	3	20	27	27
				102 (4/1-9/30/06)			322 (10/1/06-3/31/07)		
NUMBER OF STATEMENTS	368	349	424	14	55	41	92	111	111
ASSETS	%	%	%	%	%	%	%	%	%
Cash & Equivalents	13.8	14.9	14.4	21.9	10.2	18.0	15.9	13.1	14.3
Trade Receivables (net)	36.4	38.0	36.4	14.4	29.9	31.9	34.0	41.0	41.6
Inventory	2.9	3.3	2.6	4.0	4.5	1.9	3.8	1.9	1.5
All Other Current	8.1	7.9	7.4	4.9	2.9	5.7	6.6	8.7	9.8
Total Current	61.2	64.1	60.8	45.2	47.5	57.5	60.3	64.8	67.2
Fixed Assets (net)	31.6	28.9	32.8	43.8	42.8	36.7	33.1	30.2	27.5
Intangibles (net)	1.3	1.3	1.5	4.0	4.4	.9	.8	1.1	1.1
All Other Non-Current	6.0	5.7	4.8	7.0	5.3	4.9	5.8	4.0	4.2
Total	100.0	100.0	100.0	100.0	100.0	100.0	100.0	100.0	100.0
LIABILITIES									
Notes Payable-Short Term	7.2	6.5	6.0	9.9	7.7	5.9	7.9	4.6	4.7
Cur. Mat.-L.T.D.	5.8	5.2	5.8	5.2	7.3	6.9	6.5	5.5	4.5
Trade Payables	18.4	18.4	17.2	6.9	14.4	14.0	15.8	17.3	22.1
Income Taxes Payable	.8	.7	.9	.1	.1	1.0	1.9	1.1	.4
All Other Current	11.2	12.2	11.4	7.3	7.7	9.5	9.1	13.3	14.7
Total Current	43.4	43.2	41.4	29.4	37.1	37.4	41.2	41.7	46.4
Long-Term Debt	15.2	12.2	15.4	31.7	29.8	17.5	12.5	12.9	10.4
Deferred Taxes	1.0	.8	.8	.0	.6	.6	1.2	.9	.8
All Other Non-Current	3.0	3.2	2.4	.1	2.9	2.8	3.3	2.4	1.6
Net Worth	37.4	40.6	39.9	38.7	29.5	41.7	41.8	42.1	40.8
Total Liabilities & Net Worth	100.0	100.0	100.0	100.0	100.0	100.0	100.0	100.0	100.0
INCOME DATA									
Net Sales	100.0	100.0	100.0	100.0	100.0	100.0	100.0	100.0	100.0
Gross Profit	22.5	22.5	23.8	40.3	37.1	29.7	24.4	20.6	15.8
Operating Expenses	19.1	17.5	18.2	42.4	32.0	23.9	18.8	14.2	9.9
Operating Profit	3.4	5.0	5.6	-2.1	5.1	5.8	5.6	6.4	5.9
All Other Expenses (net)	.2	.1	.3	.6	1.4	.2	-.1	.1	.2
Profit Before Taxes	3.3	4.9	5.3	-2.7	3.7	5.6	5.7	6.3	5.7
RATIOS									
Current	2.0	2.1	2.1	3.4	2.0	2.4	2.3	2.0	1.9
	1.4	1.5	1.4	2.0	1.3	1.7	1.4	1.5	1.4
	1.1	1.2	1.2	1.0	.8	1.1	1.2	1.2	1.2
Quick	1.7	1.9	1.8	2.7	1.6	2.1	1.9	1.8	1.6
	1.2	1.2	1.2	1.2	1.0	1.6	1.2	1.2	1.2
	.9	.9	.9	.8	.7	.9	1.0	1.0	.9
Sales/Receivables	44 8.3	43 8.5	40 9.2	0 UND	26 14.0	27 13.4	31 11.6	46 7.9	48 7.6
	59 6.2	60 6.1	58 6.3	20 18.4	42 8.7	59 6.2	54 6.8	62 5.9	63 5.8
	76 4.8	82 4.5	78 4.7	51 7.2	63 5.8	81 4.5	77 4.8	85 4.3	77 4.7
Cost of Sales/Inventory	0 UND	0 UND	0 UND	0 UND	0 UND	0 UND	0 UND	0 UND	0 UND
	0 UND	0 UND	0 UND	0 UND	2 215.5	0 UND	0 UND	0 UND	0 UND
	4 99.5	5 75.1	3 116.0	28 12.8	11 33.0	3 135.9	3 121.0	2 227.1	1 280.3
Cost of Sales/Payables	17 21.1	18 20.7	18 20.7	0 UND	14 26.5	12 30.8	16 23.2	19 19.7	26 13.8
	33 11.0	33 11.1	31 11.9	17 21.7	26 14.1	28 12.9	27 13.8	31 11.7	36 10.0
	52 7.1	50 7.2	48 7.6	34 10.6	55 6.6	52 7.0	41 9.0	46 7.9	50 7.3
Sales/Working Capital	7.1	6.0	6.8	5.7	8.1	5.5	6.9	6.8	6.9
	14.0	11.5	12.8	9.3	26.1	9.8	11.8	10.4	13.5
	46.4	28.7	33.4	NM	-43.8	28.0	30.2	23.6	30.9
EBIT/Interest	18.0	20.0	21.4	6.0	6.5	19.5	17.0	27.8	36.6
	(336) 5.1	(316) 7.2	(394) 6.9	(11) 1.3	(51) 3.6	(40) 3.9	(86) 6.9	(101) 11.4	(105) 9.7
	1.7	2.2	2.6	.7	1.5	1.7	2.9	3.6	3.1
Net Profit + Depr., Dep., Amort./Cur. Mat. L/T/D	5.4	5.3	5.3		2.3	5.0	4.6	5.9	6.2
	(115) 2.2	(108) 2.4	(135) 2.6		(11) 1.1	(12) 2.8	(33) 2.4	(32) 2.6	(45) 2.7
	1.2	1.2	1.6		.2	1.5	1.7	1.7	2.0
Fixed/Worth	.4	.3	.4	.3	.6	.4	.4	.4	.4
	.8	.6	.7	.8	1.7	.8	.7	.7	.6
	1.5	1.3	1.4	5.3	7.0	1.7	1.1	1.3	1.2
Debt/Worth	.9	.7	.8	.3	1.1	.6	.7	1.0	.8
	1.7	1.4	1.6	1.7	2.4	1.3	1.3	1.4	1.7
	3.3	2.7	2.7	32.2	13.7	3.8	2.4	2.6	2.7
% Profit Before Taxes/Tangible Net Worth	34.9	39.7	49.4	31.8	83.4	39.3	49.6	47.4	49.4
	(346) 17.5	(326) 19.9	(406) 26.1	(12) -.4	(46) 25.2	(39) 25.0	(90) 26.0	(109) 32.8	(110) 28.6
	5.1	6.4	9.2	-33.7	6.1	2.9	8.4	13.3	12.6
% Profit Before Taxes/Total Assets	13.1	16.6	19.0	7.1	19.9	18.6	18.0	20.6	19.5
	6.1	7.8	9.3	-.2	7.5	6.8	9.4	11.8	9.6
	1.4	1.9	3.1	-24.2	1.0	1.3	4.3	3.7	4.3
Sales/Net Fixed Assets	14.4	17.7	15.2	12.3	11.6	15.5	14.6	15.5	17.0
	7.8	8.7	7.9	4.7	5.2	6.2	8.0	7.9	10.4
	4.9	4.9	4.7	2.1	2.9	3.2	4.9	4.9	5.8
Sales/Total Assets	2.8	2.8	2.9	2.8	2.7	2.7	3.3	2.9	2.9
	2.2	2.2	2.2	1.6	2.1	1.9	2.4	2.2	2.4
	1.7	1.7	1.7	1.3	1.5	1.5	1.6	1.8	2.0
% Depr., Dep., Amort./Sales	2.0	1.6	1.8	3.2	3.9	1.9	2.2	1.6	1.5
	(331) 3.4	(312) 3.0	(386) 3.1	(10) 7.4	(43) 5.8	(39) 5.2	(86) 3.5	(108) 2.6	(100) 2.2
	5.3	4.8	5.3	9.2	8.9	6.6	5.3	4.8	3.4
% Officers', Directors' Owners' Comp/Sales	1.6	1.4	1.3		3.1	2.3	2.0	.9	.6
	(183) 3.4	(138) 3.3	(202) 2.9		(36) 4.8	(22) 5.2	(48) 3.5	(50) 2.0	(38) 1.2
	6.8	5.8	5.8		7.1	9.9	6.1	4.2	1.8
Net Sales ($)	10306531M	9996443M	11220441M	10110M	114206M	169911M	674432M	1807403M	8444379M
Total Assets ($)	4727966M	4682840M	5140310M	6402M	64795M	88798M	319916M	866956M	3793443M

© RMA 2007

M = $ thousand   MM = $ million
See Pages 11 through 21 for Explanation of Ratios and Data

Current Data Sorted by Assets   Comparative Historical Data

						Type of Statement	4/1/02-3/31/03 ALL	4/1/03-3/31/04 ALL
1	1	4	11	3	2	Unqualified	11	26
	1	6	3			Reviewed	5	11
			1			Compiled		1
2	1	2	7	1		Tax Returns		6
1	1	1				Other	6	11
							4/1/02-3/31/03	4/1/03-3/31/04
0-500M	**500M-2MM**	14 (4/1-9/30/06) 2-10MM	54 (10/1/06-3/31/07) 10-50MM	**50-100MM**	**100-250MM**	**NUMBER OF STATEMENTS**	**ALL 22**	**ALL 55**
4	9	23	23	4	5			
%	%	%	%	%	%	**ASSETS**	%	%
		14.9	9.2			Cash & Equivalents	14.5	11.9
		38.7	39.3			Trade Receivables (net)	32.1	33.3
		1.9	5.1			Inventory	3.9	3.8
		9.2	8.3			All Other Current	7.9	7.9
		64.7	61.9			Total Current	58.4	56.9
		32.1	31.2			Fixed Assets (net)	32.9	35.7
		.0	2.5			Intangibles (net)	2.1	2.5
		3.3	4.5			All Other Non-Current	6.6	5.0
		100.0	100.0			Total	100.0	100.0
						LIABILITIES		
		8.5	7.3			Notes Payable-Short Term	15.7	9.5
		4.0	4.4			Cur. Mat.-L.T.D.	4.3	4.5
		16.5	15.2			Trade Payables	17.4	15.7
		1.2	2.2			Income Taxes Payable	.0	.5
		16.3	10.6			All Other Current	14.0	14.0
		46.5	39.7			Total Current	51.5	44.2
		9.8	14.0			Long-Term Debt	15.4	17.6
		1.0	1.6			Deferred Taxes	1.5	1.7
		1.4	1.0			All Other Non-Current	4.4	4.5
		41.3	43.7			Net Worth	27.3	32.0
		100.0	100.0			Total Liabilties & Net Worth	100.0	100.0
						INCOME DATA		
		100.0	100.0			Net Sales	100.0	100.0
						Gross Profit		
		93.1	89.3			Operating Expenses	98.0	95.3
		6.9	10.7			Operating Profit	2.0	4.7
		.9	.6			All Other Expenses (net)	1.3	1.0
		5.9	10.1			Profit Before Taxes	.6	3.7
						RATIOS		
		2.0	2.2			Current	2.0	1.8
		1.3	1.7				1.2	1.3
		1.1	1.2				.9	.9
		1.7	1.9			Quick	1.7	1.6
		1.2	1.2				1.1	1.1
		.8	.9				.5	.7
		45 8.1	49 7.4			Sales/Receivables	25 14.7	27 13.7
		62 5.9	66 5.5				54 6.7	48 7.7
		72 5.1	87 4.2				64 5.7	66 5.5
						Cost of Sales/Inventory		
						Cost of Sales/Payables		
		7.8	5.9			Sales/Working Capital	8.5	10.9
		16.9	9.7				14.5	15.8
		55.8	21.3				-48.8	-54.7
		25.5	41.0			EBIT/Interest	17.9	15.0
		(18) 10.3	(21) 18.3				(21) 3.5	(51) 6.3
		2.4	5.2				.6	2.9
		8.9				Net Profit + Depr., Dep., Amort./Cur. Mat. L/T/D		4.8
		(11) 6.4						(17) 1.9
		2.0						.8
		.4	.4			Fixed/Worth	.3	.5
		.9	.7				.8	.8
		1.3	1.6				5.6	4.7
		.7	.7			Debt/Worth	.8	.9
		1.8	1.3				3.0	1.9
		3.1	2.7				9.4	10.4
		64.9	77.0			% Profit Before Taxes/Tangible Net Worth	24.8	41.8
		(22) 44.9	(22) 56.4				(20) 10.9	(49) 25.4
		13.2	40.3				-5.6	8.6
		22.2	41.1			% Profit Before Taxes/Total Assets	8.7	14.5
		14.6	22.2				3.0	8.7
		5.9	5.6				-3.9	2.4
		30.8	20.7			Sales/Net Fixed Assets	22.0	15.9
		11.3	7.3				8.5	9.0
		4.0	4.2				3.2	4.0
		3.7	3.0			Sales/Total Assets	3.2	3.1
		2.7	2.2				2.1	2.3
		1.6	1.9				1.2	1.8
		.4	.7			% Depr., Dep., Amort./Sales	1.1	1.3
		(20) 1.9	(22) 2.1				2.9	(47) 2.7
		4.3	4.0				7.2	4.2
		.7				% Officers', Directors' Owners' Comp/Sales		2.4
		(10) 1.1						(18) 4.8
		5.1						7.4
2147M	42602M	347568M	1102827M	424473M	1493503M	Net Sales ($)	564291M	2276112M
646M	8932M	126814M	438575M	299178M	779157M	Total Assets ($)	459677M	996615M

M = $ thousand   MM = $ million

See Pages 11 through 21 for Explanation of Ratios and Data

Comparative Historical Data

Current Data Sorted by Sales

4/1/04-3/31/05 ALL	4/1/05-3/31/06 ALL	4/1/06-3/31/07 ALL		0-1MM	1-3MM	3-5MM	5-10MM	10-25MM	25MM & OVER
			Type of Statement						
14	20	22	Unqualified	2			1	5	14
14	10	10	Reviewed			1	1	5	3
3	2	12	Compiled	2		2	2	4	2
4	7	3	Tax Returns	1			2		
7	18	21	Other		3	3	1	4	10
				14 (4/1-9/30/06)			54 (10/1/06-3/31/07)		
42	57	68	**NUMBER OF STATEMENTS**	5	3	6	7	18	29
%	%	%	**ASSETS**	%	%	%	%	%	%
12.4	12.9	11.8	Cash & Equivalents					10.6	10.3
35.7	31.9	36.6	Trade Receivables (net)					28.4	41.6
4.3	4.5	4.6	Inventory					3.1	6.3
5.5	6.8	8.0	All Other Current					7.7	9.9
57.9	56.1	61.0	Total Current					49.8	68.2
34.0	31.9	30.3	Fixed Assets (net)					42.0	22.9
3.1	4.0	4.1	Intangibles (net)					3.0	3.9
5.1	8.1	4.5	All Other Non-Current					5.3	5.0
100.0	100.0	100.0	Total					100.0	100.0
			LIABILITIES						
8.7	9.8	10.5	Notes Payable-Short Term					8.8	6.6
6.7	5.2	5.0	Cur. Mat.-L.T.D.					5.2	4.5
16.2	14.0	16.9	Trade Payables					12.7	17.2
.2	1.4	1.2	Income Taxes Payable					.6	2.2
15.1	12.3	14.2	All Other Current					9.4	17.0
46.9	42.7	47.7	Total Current					36.8	47.5
18.1	16.2	19.2	Long-Term Debt					18.5	10.8
.8	1.3	1.0	Deferred Taxes					2.2	.7
2.4	5.0	3.9	All Other Non-Current					1.4	.9
31.9	35.0	28.2	Net Worth					41.1	40.2
100.0	100.0	100.0	Total Liabilities & Net Worth					100.0	100.0
			INCOME DATA						
100.0	100.0	100.0	Net Sales					100.0	100.0
			Gross Profit						
95.3	91.5	93.2	Operating Expenses					92.9	90.9
4.7	8.5	6.8	Operating Profit					7.1	9.1
1.3	1.6	.7	All Other Expenses (net)					.8	.3
3.4	6.9	6.0	Profit Before Taxes					6.4	8.8
			RATIOS						
1.5	2.1	2.0						2.2	2.1
1.2	1.4	1.5	Current					1.8	1.5
.9	1.0	1.1						1.0	1.1
1.3	1.8	1.7						2.0	1.6
1.0	1.1	1.1	Quick					1.4	1.1
.7	.7	.8						.5	.9
40 9.1	34 10.6	35 10.5						26 14.0	39 9.3
54 6.7	54 6.7	59 6.2	Sales/Receivables					63 5.8	62 5.9
74 5.0	74 5.0	79 4.6						84 4.3	78 4.7
			Cost of Sales/Inventory						
			Cost of Sales/Payables						
12.3	7.9	7.0						6.6	6.9
19.9	15.4	12.6	Sales/Working Capital					13.6	10.3
-129.9	NM	54.6						63.7	45.9
7.1	25.4	24.9						16.4	36.2
(37) 3.8	(48) 5.2	(58) 8.7	EBIT/Interest					(15) 9.3	(27) 21.6
1.6	2.2	1.9						5.4	6.0
5.2	10.2	7.8							7.5
(15) 2.4	(18) 2.8	(22) 3.7	Net Profit + Depr., Dep., Amort./Cur. Mat. L/T/D					(12)	5.1
1.2	1.6	1.9							2.9
.4	.4	.4						.6	.2
1.2	.8	.8	Fixed/Worth					1.3	.6
2.4	3.1	1.7						2.3	1.2
1.3	.8	.8						.7	.8
2.4	2.2	2.1	Debt/Worth					1.8	2.2
5.2	4.4	3.7						4.2	3.1
54.2	70.1	76.3						71.7	78.7
(40) 17.7	(53) 30.0	(60) 47.7	% Profit Before Taxes/Tangible Net Worth					(17) 47.8	(27) 52.2
7.7	13.2	17.7						16.9	41.9
9.2	21.3	33.1						25.9	34.8
5.0	9.3	14.6	% Profit Before Taxes/Total Assets					12.4	20.6
1.6	3.3	4.1						5.9	8.9
21.7	24.0	30.2						9.7	43.8
7.6	9.1	9.6	Sales/Net Fixed Assets					5.4	17.8
4.3	4.7	4.5						2.3	7.0
3.5	3.2	3.4						2.8	3.5
2.3	2.3	2.2	Sales/Total Assets					2.1	2.6
1.8	1.5	1.6						1.1	1.9
1.4	.7	.7						1.1	.4
(41) 3.1	(50) 2.2	(57) 2.0	% Depr., Dep., Amort./Sales					(16) 3.4	(26) 1.1
5.1	5.2	3.8						5.4	2.2
1.8	1.4	.8							
(14) 2.9	(19) 3.5	(21) 1.4	% Officers', Directors' Owners' Comp/Sales						
4.1	8.0	3.9							
1509023M	4869011M	3413120M	Net Sales ($)	2612M	5123M	22262M	53445M	315567M	3014111M
828202M	1674534M	1653302M	Total Assets ($)	1433M	2818M	11623M	22645M	190885M	1423898M

© RMA 2007

M = $ thousand   MM = $ million
See Pages 11 through 21 for Explanation of Ratios and Data

Current Data Sorted by Assets

Comparative Historical Data

			6	8		1	Type of Statement	1	8
1	3		12				Unqualified	2	2
	2						Reviewed	2	2
3							Compiled	1	1
	5		6	9			Tax Returns	2	6
	8 (4/1-9/30/06)			48 (10/1/06-3/31/07)			Other		
								4/1/02-3/31/03	4/1/03-3/31/04
0-500M	500M-2MM		2-10MM	10-50MM	50-100MM	100-250MM		ALL	ALL
4	10		24	17		1	NUMBER OF STATEMENTS	8	19

0-500M	500M-2MM	2-10MM	10-50MM	50-100MM	100-250MM		4/1/02-3/31/03 ALL	4/1/03-3/31/04 ALL
%	%	%	%	%	%	**ASSETS**	%	%
	16.1	11.8	13.7			Cash & Equivalents		9.4
	34.4	38.4	40.3			Trade Receivables (net)		29.3
	2.6	4.3	3.8			Inventory		1.8
	8.2	6.9	13.5			All Other Current		6.4
	61.3	61.4	71.2			Total Current		46.9
	35.8	32.3	21.0			Fixed Assets (net)		35.7
	.0	.1	3.4			Intangibles (net)		11.1
	2.9	6.3	4.3			All Other Non-Current		6.1
	100.0	100.0	100.0			Total		100.0
						LIABILITIES		
	13.2	10.4	5.9			Notes Payable-Short Term		17.2
	5.7	5.5	4.3			Cur. Mat.-L.T.D.		4.3
	24.5	15.8	22.1			Trade Payables		15.2
	.0	.5	.4			Income Taxes Payable		.6
	19.0	9.4	14.0			All Other Current		10.2
	62.4	41.7	46.6			Total Current		47.5
	13.5	13.6	9.6			Long-Term Debt		17.8
	.0	.5	.3			Deferred Taxes		1.0
	1.0	1.2	4.9			All Other Non-Current		.7
	23.0	43.0	38.6			Net Worth		33.0
	100.0	100.0	100.0			Total Liabilities & Net Worth		100.0
						INCOME DATA		
	100.0	100.0	100.0			Net Sales		100.0
	34.0	20.1	15.8			Gross Profit		26.3
	30.5	14.5	10.3			Operating Expenses		24.4
	3.4	5.7	5.5			Operating Profit		1.9
	-.6	.4	.3			All Other Expenses (net)		1.8
	4.0	5.3	5.2			Profit Before Taxes		.1
						RATIOS		
	1.9	2.3	2.3					1.3
	1.4	1.5	1.5			Current		1.1
	.5	1.0	1.2					.7
	1.9	1.9	1.8					1.2
	1.0	1.2	1.2			Quick		.9
	.5	.7	.9					.5
	11 34.4	47 7.8	42 8.7				42 8.8	
	45 8.1	61 6.0	55 6.6			Sales/Receivables	65 5.6	
	62 5.9	70 5.2	78 4.7				73 5.0	
	0 UND	0 UND	0 UND				0 UND	
	0 UND	1 672.0	1 308.5			Cost of Sales/Inventory	0 UND	
	0 UND	10 37.8	8 47.0				6 64.8	
	7 49.0	20 18.5	19 19.0				17 20.9	
	33 11.0	30 12.3	40 9.2			Cost of Sales/Payables	25 14.4	
	49 7.5	38 9.5	54 6.8				60 6.1	
	7.6	6.4	6.2					5.5
	22.1	14.8	11.7			Sales/Working Capital		68.8
	-14.5	NM	20.5					-7.7
		17.8	16.7					2.9
		(21) 3.6	(15) 5.1			EBIT/Interest		(15) .7
		.6	2.2					-.9
		14.2						
		(10) 6.3				Net Profit + Depr., Dep., Amort./Cur. Mat. L/T/D		
		1.5						
	.3	.4	.4					.5
	1.4	.8	.7			Fixed/Worth		1.3
	-47.2	1.3	1.3					4.0
	1.0	.7	1.1					1.9
	2.7	1.2	2.3			Debt/Worth		2.9
	-72.9	2.7	4.2					6.7
		74.6	68.9					22.2
		30.1	(16) 38.3			% Profit Before Taxes/Tangible Net Worth		(15) 9.0
		.7	20.3					-13.9
	26.3	31.9	24.2					6.4
	13.3	8.2	11.1			% Profit Before Taxes/Total Assets		1.2
	-1.6	.5	3.8					-7.1
	26.8	10.5	31.1					7.1
	13.2	7.4	15.4			Sales/Net Fixed Assets		4.6
	6.9	4.6	5.9					3.7
	4.8	2.9	3.3					2.7
	3.8	2.5	2.4			Sales/Total Assets		1.4
	2.6	1.7	1.7					1.0
		1.7	1.1					3.6
		(23) 3.8	(15) 2.1			% Depr., Dep., Amort./Sales		(14) 4.9
		5.5	4.5					7.7
		1.3						
		(10) 2.7				% Officers', Directors' Owners' Comp/Sales		
		6.9						
3815M	43530M	242581M	1090370M		244775M	Net Sales ($)	92899M	101187M
730M	12109M	109638M	426661M	142320M		Total Assets ($)	38411M	85863M

M = $ thousand   MM = $ million
See Pages 11 through 21 for Explanation of Ratios and Data

Comparative Historical Data | Current Data Sorted by Sales

						Type of Statement							
	6		13		15	Unqualified					4	4	
	1		7		16	Reviewed	1		2		5	8	7
	3		1		2	Compiled	1		1				
	5		2		3	Tax Returns							
	2		7		20	Other	3		2		1		
	4/1/04-		4/1/05-		4/1/06-								
	3/31/05		3/31/06		3/31/07			8 (4/1-9/30/06)			48 (10/1/06-3/31/07)		
	ALL		ALL		ALL		0-1MM	1-3MM		3-5MM	5-10MM	10-25MM	25MM & OVER
	17		30		56	NUMBER OF STATEMENTS	3	3		5	14	16	15
	%		%		%	ASSETS	%	%		%	%	%	%
	17.7		16.9		15.7	Cash & Equivalents					17.7	12.3	10.2
	27.7		36.3		36.9	Trade Receivables (net)					40.4	36.7	40.5
	.6		2.2		3.5	Inventory					5.4	2.6	3.7
	10.7		8.4		9.4	All Other Current					1.4	12.9	12.7
	56.6		63.8		65.5	Total Current					64.9	64.5	67.1
	30.9		30.1		28.6	Fixed Assets (net)					29.6	29.0	24.6
	3.0		1.8		1.2	Intangibles (net)					.0	.1	3.9
	9.4		4.3		4.7	All Other Non-Current					5.4	6.5	4.4
	100.0		100.0		100.0	Total					100.0	100.0	100.0
						LIABILITIES							
	10.7		8.5		10.1	Notes Payable-Short Term					13.3	11.0	4.5
	3.8		4.6		5.6	Cur. Mat.-L.T.D.					4.3	5.6	5.0
	12.0		17.4		18.2	Trade Payables					16.3	19.2	21.5
	.3		.7		.3	Income Taxes Payable					.8	.1	.4
	8.9		11.1		12.3	All Other Current					8.8	14.0	10.5
	35.7		42.3		46.5	Total Current					43.6	49.7	41.9
	15.7		16.3		12.6	Long-Term Debt					9.1	14.6	11.5
	.1		.8		.3	Deferred Taxes					.5	.5	.3
	6.7		2.8		2.2	All Other Non-Current					.8	2.1	4.4
	41.8		37.8		38.4	Net Worth					46.1	33.1	41.9
	100.0		100.0		100.0	Total Liabilities & Net Worth					100.0	100.0	100.0
						INCOME DATA							
	100.0		100.0		100.0	Net Sales					100.0	100.0	100.0
	32.9		26.2		23.6	Gross Profit					22.6	18.1	15.9
	28.0		21.6		18.4	Operating Expenses					14.4	15.0	10.2
	4.9		4.6		5.2	Operating Profit					8.2	3.1	5.7
	.7		1.0		.2	All Other Expenses (net)					.6	.2	.3
	4.2		3.6		5.0	Profit Before Taxes					7.6	2.9	5.4
						RATIOS							
	3.0		2.2		2.3						2.4	1.9	2.8
	1.6		1.3		1.5	Current					1.7	1.3	1.5
	1.1		1.1		1.1						1.0	1.0	1.2
	2.6		1.6		2.0						2.2	1.6	2.0
	1.3		1.2		1.1	Quick					1.6	.9	1.0
	.8		.7		.8						.8	.7	.9
0	UND	43	8.6	40	9.0		46	7.9	40	9.2	45	8.1
46	8.0	63	5.8	54	6.8	Sales/Receivables	51	7.1	61	6.0	53	6.8
59	6.1	74	4.9	67	5.5		68	5.4	86	4.3	65	5.6
0	UND	0	UND	0	UND		0	UND	0	UND	0	UND
0	UND	0	UND	0	UND	Cost of Sales/Inventory	0	UND	1	261.9	1	574.3
0	UND	2	228.5	6	57.9		8	43.3	9	38.9	7	54.6
0	UND	13	28.7	17	21.2		8	46.7	26	14.0	17	21.3
21	17.7	31	11.9	29	12.5	Cost of Sales/Payables	22	16.4	37	10.0	27	13.3
34	10.9	61	6.0	42	8.7		37	9.8	58	6.3	47	7.8
	6.3		5.4		6.7			6.1		6.9		6.2
	18.8		18.4		13.1	Sales/Working Capital		13.0		15.8		12.2
	112.6		68.5		55.8			NM		-78.2		18.3
	87.4		29.3		15.8			20.3		8.6		29.4
(15)	6.8	(26)	6.0	(49)	5.1	EBIT/Interest		12.6	(13)	3.4	(13)	6.5
	-.6		1.0		1.3			2.9		-1.6		1.8
					13.1	Net Profit + Depr., Dep.,						
				(15)	5.2	Amort./Cur. Mat. L/T/D						
					1.8							
	.4		.3		.4			.4		.6		.3
	.7		.6		.7	Fixed/Worth		.6		.8		.7
	1.7		2.5		1.5			1.2		1.8		1.5
	.3		.8		.8			.7		1.2		.9
	1.3		2.0		1.8	Debt/Worth		1.0		2.3		2.3
	5.8		4.2		4.2			2.1		9.0		3.7
	48.4		56.7		74.6	% Profit Before Taxes/Tangible		66.8		109.6		69.9
(16)	23.5	(27)	26.3	(52)	38.3	Net Worth	(13)	43.3	(15)	30.7		38.8
	10.6		-.7		6.1			11.7		.4		13.6
	25.7		20.9		25.0			35.0		12.0		25.3
	8.9		7.7		11.9	% Profit Before Taxes/Total		20.7		6.3		14.5
	.5		-.6		1.0	Assets		5.7		-.4		3.8
	18.7		21.8		20.7			22.4		15.8		31.1
	11.4		8.6		8.5	Sales/Net Fixed Assets		8.4		7.7		14.8
	6.7		4.2		5.2			4.6		5.0		5.1
	4.8		2.7		3.5			4.1		2.5		3.3
	2.6		2.1		2.5	Sales/Total Assets		2.8		2.2		2.8
	1.9		1.6		1.8			1.8		1.6		1.7
	1.6		.9		1.2			.8		1.8		1.2
(13)	3.3	(27)	1.9	(47)	2.7	% Depr., Dep., Amort./Sales	(13)	1.6	(12)	3.7		2.3
	4.4		3.7		5.0			3.9		5.4		4.9
					1.8	% Officers', Directors'						
				(19)	5.6	Owners' Comp/Sales						
					8.3							
	1023316M		1095244M		1625071M	Net Sales ($)	1979M	5970M	18156M	97395M	219498M	1282073M
	461086M		661389M		691458M	Total Assets ($)	382M	2512M	5831M	38804M	113494M	530435M

M = $ thousand   MM = $ million
See Pages 11 through 21 for Explanation of Ratios and Data

Current Data Sorted by Assets   **Comparative Historical Data**

0-500M	500M-2MM	2-10MM	10-50MM	50-100MM	100-250MM	Type of Statement	4/1/02-3/31/03 ALL	4/1/03-3/31/04 ALL
	7	18	24	19	23	Unqualified	104	141
	10	22	31	14	11	Reviewed	82	103
9	32	61	24	5	1	Compiled	128	234
52	136	173	40	2	1	Tax Returns	228	397
19	61	151	120	28	20	Other	243	369
	73 (4/1-9/30/06)		1,041 (10/1/06-3/31/07)					
80	246	425	239	68	56	**NUMBER OF STATEMENTS**	785	1244
%	%	%	%	%	%	**ASSETS**	%	%
15.9	8.7	6.1	7.9	6.4	5.6	Cash & Equivalents	7.4	8.2
6.1	4.1	5.0	4.6	6.2	6.3	Trade Receivables (net)	4.9	5.3
23.9	34.8	42.8	45.1	46.7	34.3	Inventory	33.5	34.6
6.6	5.8	4.5	3.9	4.8	5.1	All Other Current	5.9	6.3
52.5	53.5	58.5	61.4	64.1	51.4	Total Current	51.7	54.3
29.3	34.1	28.9	22.5	20.5	33.6	Fixed Assets (net)	32.5	31.5
2.6	1.0	.8	1.3	1.2	1.0	Intangibles (net)	1.4	1.0
15.6	11.4	11.8	14.8	14.2	14.0	All Other Non-Current	14.4	13.2
100.0	100.0	100.0	100.0	100.0	100.0	Total	100.0	100.0
						LIABILITIES		
18.6	17.3	24.4	24.1	18.6	9.6	Notes Payable-Short Term	19.3	19.6
1.2	4.0	3.3	3.2	3.4	3.8	Cur. Mat.-L.T.D.	3.8	3.3
9.1	3.5	4.0	4.1	3.9	3.7	Trade Payables	4.8	5.4
.0	.0	.1	.0	.4	.2	Income Taxes Payable	.2	.1
18.1	9.9	9.5	11.1	9.3	8.0	All Other Current	10.4	11.4
47.1	34.7	41.3	42.5	35.6	25.3	Total Current	38.5	39.8
20.7	33.0	29.5	26.6	29.9	35.5	Long-Term Debt	29.9	28.8
.0	.0	.0	.0	.2	.2	Deferred Taxes	.2	.2
7.7	4.0	3.5	5.4	4.2	8.0	All Other Non-Current	6.6	5.2
24.5	28.3	25.7	25.5	30.0	31.1	Net Worth	24.8	26.0
100.0	100.0	100.0	100.0	100.0	100.0	Total Liabilities & Net Worth	100.0	100.0
						INCOME DATA		
100.0	100.0	100.0	100.0	100.0	100.0	Net Sales	100.0	100.0
						Gross Profit		
78.0	76.4	80.4	80.4	82.4	79.0	Operating Expenses	80.6	80.5
22.0	23.6	19.6	19.6	17.6	21.0	Operating Profit	19.4	19.5
4.7	8.0	8.3	4.7	1.9	6.3	All Other Expenses (net)	6.6	6.0
17.4	15.7	11.4	14.9	15.7	14.7	Profit Before Taxes	12.8	13.5
						RATIOS		
2.1	4.6	3.1	2.8	7.5	4.8		3.3	3.2
1.0	1.3	1.3	1.3	1.6	1.6	Current	1.3	1.3
.4	.6	.8	1.0	1.0	1.1		.7	.8
1.2	1.1	.8	.7	.8	1.0		1.0	1.0
.3	(245) .2	(423) .1	.1	.2	.4	Quick	(782) .2	(1237) .2
.1	.0	.0	.0	.0	.1		.0	.0
0 UND	0 UND	0 UND	0 UND	0 UND	0 UND		0 UND	0 UND
0 UND	0 UND	0 UND	0 815.0	4 89.4	1 395.4	Sales/Receivables	0 UND	0 UND
0 UND	5 79.7	6 56.9	15 23.9	35 10.4	23 15.6		10 38.0	10 35.6
						Cost of Sales/Inventory		
						Cost of Sales/Payables		
3.4	1.8	1.8	1.2	1.1	.8		2.3	2.0
247.0	11.6	9.2	4.2	3.2	3.8	Sales/Working Capital	10.3	7.4
-10.2	-6.6	-13.2	-128.1	427.6	19.9		-12.2	-14.3
15.6	17.3	12.6	21.3	29.8	18.1		12.7	16.4
(48) 3.5	(132) 3.9	(234) 3.5	(153) 5.3	(51) 4.7	(40) 4.2	EBIT/Interest	(506) 4.1	(841) 4.5
.9	1.2	1.4	1.3	1.9	1.8		1.5	1.6
			5.2				4.9	7.1
			(11) 2.9			Net Profit + Depr., Dep., Amort./Cur. Mat. L/T/D	(50) 2.7	(58) 1.9
			.4				.7	.6
.0	.0	.0	.0	.0	.0		.0	.0
.1	.5	.2	.2	.4	.8	Fixed/Worth	.5	.4
4.2	4.2	3.3	2.4	1.5	2.8		4.4	3.4
.4	.7	1.5	1.6	1.1	1.1		1.0	1.1
2.0	2.8	4.0	4.1	2.7	2.8	Debt/Worth	3.2	3.2
UND	22.9	17.8	14.7	12.7	5.2		15.6	12.5
126.9	76.0	63.9	63.7	44.7	29.3		57.3	64.9
(60) 39.7	(202) 26.8	(356) 25.4	(215) 28.2	(61) 28.5	(52) 18.5	% Profit Before Taxes/Tangible Net Worth	(661) 21.3	(1066) 26.2
15.6	3.5	4.6	5.6	11.6	5.3		4.9	7.3
41.7	17.7	12.2	12.9	12.2	10.5		13.0	15.4
10.5	6.2	3.8	4.6	6.1	3.7	% Profit Before Taxes/Total Assets	4.8	5.7
2.3	.5	.3	.7	1.3	1.1		.4	.9
UND	UND	UND	999.8	131.1	102.1		299.2	354.6
290.8	14.0	25.7	19.7	12.2	3.1	Sales/Net Fixed Assets	10.7	12.5
3.4	.6	.8	1.6	1.6	.6		.6	.7
5.6	1.5	1.2	.8	.9	.7		1.3	1.4
1.7	.6	.5	.4	.5	.4	Sales/Total Assets	.5	.6
.6	.2	.2	.2	.3	.2		.2	.3
3.0	.8	.3	.2	.2	.6		.6	.5
(25) 4.7	(108) 5.0	(212) 1.4	(138) .7	(43) .7	(41) 2.0	% Depr., Dep., Amort./Sales	(478) 3.1	(739) 2.6
13.5	17.8	11.9	3.5	3.3	7.1		13.2	12.1
2.5	2.3	1.2	1.1		.6		2.1	1.4
(16) 4.0	(47) 4.3	(84) 2.7	(44) 2.5		(10) 1.0	% Officers', Directors' Owners' Comp/Sales	(128) 5.1	(240) 3.3
5.0	10.9	5.7	5.1		4.9		11.9	9.4
66859M	352838M	1875007M	4032332M	3378451M	5066957M	Net Sales ($)	10519392M	18330375M
21968M	300540M	2119319M	5248490M	4983884M	9336196M	Total Assets ($)	14370913M	21306879M

M = $ thousand   MM = $ million
See Pages 11 through 21 for Explanation of Ratios and Data

Comparative Historical Data / Current Data Sorted by Sales

99 96 136 400 376	92 94 132 397 422	91 88 132 404 399	Type of Statement	8 13 47 171 86	7 7 22 122 93	7 7 16 41 55	11 10 22 43 52	19 15 20 24 58	39 36 5 3 55
4/1/04-3/31/05 ALL	4/1/05-3/31/06 ALL	4/1/06-3/31/07 ALL		73 (4/1-9/30/06)			1,041 (10/1/06-3/31/07)		
				0-1MM	1-3MM	3-5MM	5-10MM	10-25MM	25MM & OVER
1107	1137	1114	NUMBER OF STATEMENTS	325	251	126	138	136	138
%	%	%	**ASSETS**	%	%	%	%	%	%
8.1	8.2	7.8	Cash & Equivalents	5.2	9.0	7.5	8.5	9.5	9.3
4.8	5.4	4.9	Trade Receivables (net)	2.4	3.4	4.8	6.8	9.0	8.0
37.0	35.3	40.0	Inventory	31.1	38.4	46.3	45.9	49.4	42.7
4.4	4.8	4.9	All Other Current	5.1	5.2	6.5	3.8	2.8	5.3
54.4	53.8	57.6	Total Current	43.9	56.0	65.0	64.9	70.7	65.3
31.1	31.0	28.4	Fixed Assets (net)	43.0	27.8	20.8	19.3	18.3	21.3
1.2	1.4	1.1	Intangibles (net)	1.4	.9	1.1	1.1	.6	1.7
13.3	13.8	12.9	All Other Non-Current	11.8	15.3	13.1	14.7	10.4	11.7
100.0	100.0	100.0	Total	100.0	100.0	100.0	100.0	100.0	100.0
			LIABILITIES						
20.8	20.6	21.3	Notes Payable-Short Term	15.8	26.4	24.2	20.5	26.0	18.3
2.4	3.0	3.3	Cur. Mat.-L.T.D.	3.9	2.0	2.9	5.2	1.9	4.2
4.4	4.3	4.3	Trade Payables	2.4	3.6	4.0	5.4	5.8	7.4
.2	.1	.1	Income Taxes Payable	.0	.0	.0	.1	.1	.2
10.7	10.8	10.5	All Other Current	8.1	11.7	11.4	12.1	12.2	9.6
38.5	38.9	39.4	Total Current	30.2	43.7	42.6	43.3	46.0	39.7
29.6	28.6	29.3	Long-Term Debt	40.4	28.7	21.8	22.7	20.4	26.5
.2	.1	.1	Deferred Taxes	.0	.0	.0	.1	.1	.2
5.0	5.2	4.6	All Other Non-Current	3.6	3.5	7.5	5.2	5.2	5.0
26.7	27.2	26.7	Net Worth	25.7	24.0	28.1	28.8	28.4	28.6
100.0	100.0	100.0	Total Liabilities & Net Worth	100.0	100.0	100.0	100.0	100.0	100.0
			INCOME DATA						
100.0	100.0	100.0	Net Sales	100.0	100.0	100.0	100.0	100.0	100.0
			Gross Profit						
78.5	77.8	79.4	Operating Expenses	69.4	81.0	84.6	83.9	84.9	85.4
21.5	22.2	20.6	Operating Profit	30.6	19.0	15.4	16.1	15.1	14.6
5.2	6.3	6.7	All Other Expenses (net)	15.1	6.1	3.9	1.4	1.0	1.3
16.3	15.9	13.9	Profit Before Taxes	15.5	13.0	11.5	14.7	14.1	13.2
			RATIOS						
3.8	3.6	3.4	Current	4.4	3.1	4.0	3.4	2.8	3.2
1.4	1.3	1.3		1.1	1.3	1.4	1.3	1.5	1.4
.7	.7	.8		.3	.6	1.0	1.0	1.1	1.1
1.1	1.0	.9	Quick	.8	.9	.7	1.0	1.0	1.1
(1105) .2	(1135) .2	(1111) .2		.2	(249) .2	.1 (137)	.1	.2	.3
.0	.0	.0		.0	.0	.0	.0	.0	.1
0 UND	0 UND	0 UND	Sales/Receivables	0 UND	0 UND	0 UND	0 UND	0 UND	0 UND
0 UND	0 UND	0 UND		0 UND	0 UND	0 UND	1 500.1	1 261.5	3 125.2
8 45.7	12 30.7	9 38.9		1 698.0	5 70.9	12 30.6	21 17.6	18 20.8	30 12.3
			Cost of Sales/Inventory						
			Cost of Sales/Payables						
1.8	1.9	1.5	Sales/Working Capital	1.1	1.7	1.6	2.1	1.6	1.5
9.8	8.6	7.6		19.2	9.2	4.4	8.2	5.3	6.7
-11.6	-10.9	-14.7		-3.8	-9.0	-308.3	-392.4	34.3	41.6
17.5	20.9	15.9	EBIT/Interest	6.1	15.6	11.3	26.1	20.8	26.5
(734) 5.3	(719) 5.8	(658) 4.0		(127) 2.9	(156) 3.3	(82) 3.3	(97) 5.3	(91) 6.1	(105) 6.0
2.0	2.0	1.4		1.2	1.0	1.2	1.5	1.6	1.9
8.1	6.8	5.2	Net Profit + Depr., Dep., Amort./Cur. Mat. L/T/D						36.9
(43) 1.7	(46) 2.0	(34) 1.8						(15)	4.2
.8	.7	.4							.5
.0	.0	.0	Fixed/Worth	.0	.0	.0	.0	.0	.0
.5	.5	.2		1.1	.2	.1	.2	.1	.3
4.1	3.9	3.0		6.8	3.2	1.3	1.6	1.1	1.6
1.1	1.1	1.1	Debt/Worth	1.1	1.3	.9	1.2	1.1	1.4
3.4	3.4	3.6		4.0	3.6	3.2	4.1	3.1	3.0
12.5	14.2	17.4		42.3	15.9	23.9	13.0	13.4	6.6
85.1	72.8	64.0	% Profit Before Taxes/Tangible Net Worth	39.1	65.5	67.4	96.4	70.6	70.7
(963) 34.5	(960) 30.6	(946) 26.1		(260) 16.0	(209) 23.5	(105) 28.1	(125) 46.0	(120) 28.0	(127) 33.4
10.0	8.3	5.1		.9	3.9	4.7	12.5	11.4	18.9
19.2	17.2	14.2	% Profit Before Taxes/Total Assets	9.7	13.9	14.6	17.9	19.2	16.3
7.1	6.4	5.1		3.0	4.5	5.0	7.3	6.5	8.3
1.4	1.4	.6		-.1	.0	.5	1.4	1.2	2.9
682.2	511.0	UND	Sales/Net Fixed Assets	UND	UND	UND	373.7	UND	137.0
14.4	12.4	19.1		1.9	21.1	38.8	31.2	99.6	19.4
.9	.8	1.1		.2	1.2	2.3	3.8	5.0	2.9
1.5	1.3	1.2	Sales/Total Assets	.5	1.2	1.4	1.8	1.9	1.7
.7	.6	.5		.2	.5	.7	.9	.8	.8
.3	.2	.2		.1	.3	.3	.4	.4	.6
.4	.4	.3	% Depr., Dep., Amort./Sales	3.1	.5	.2	.2	.1	.2
(577) 1.8	(632) 1.6	(567) 1.4		(150) 14.2	(110) 1.3	(58) 1.0	(80) .5	(71) .4	(98) .7
10.8	9.2	9.3		22.2	8.2	5.6	3.1	1.6	2.5
1.4	1.5	1.3	% Officers', Directors' Owners' Comp/Sales	2.7	2.2	1.1	1.2	1.2	.5
(188) 3.0	(219) 3.2	(207) 2.8		(39) 4.6	(48) 4.0	(28) 2.5	(37) 2.8	(30) 2.2	(25) 1.0
7.6	7.8	6.0		9.1	6.7	5.9	3.8		2.1
17257436M	17974445M	14772444M	Net Sales ($)	144331M	474130M	486476M	986337M	2191249M	10489921M
18345723M	23053465M	22010397M	Total Assets ($)	762229M	1362766M	1275233M	2081098M	4120998M	12408073M

M = $ thousand   MM = $ million
See Pages 11 through 21 for Explanation of Ratios and Data

CONSTRUCTION-GENERAL—Highway, Street, and Bridge Construction NAICS 237310 (SIC 1611, 1622, 1721)

Current Data Sorted by Assets | Comparative Historical Data

Type of Statement	0-500M	500M-2MM	2-10MM	10-50MM	50-100MM	100-250MM	4/1/02-3/31/03 ALL	4/1/03-3/31/04 ALL
Unqualified	1	21	135	172	41	35	334	346
Reviewed	5	59	129	30		1	124	164
Compiled	7	20	13	3	1		33	87
Tax Returns	12	16	15	1			21	37
Other	3	21	57	58	21	11	117	138
	185 (4/1-9/30/06)			703 (10/1/06-3/31/07)				
NUMBER OF STATEMENTS	28	137	349	264	63	47	629	772
ASSETS	%	%	%	%	%	%	%	%
Cash & Equivalents	13.8	16.7	16.6	17.2	15.8	10.5	16.2	14.3
Trade Receivables (net)	23.5	31.0	34.1	32.9	30.5	27.2	29.4	30.9
Inventory	2.7	2.4	3.0	4.4	4.6	4.6	3.2	3.8
All Other Current	6.0	5.6	6.8	6.8	9.0	8.2	7.7	8.3
Total Current	46.0	55.7	60.5	61.4	59.8	50.5	56.5	57.4
Fixed Assets (net)	44.5	37.5	33.5	31.8	30.1	37.4	35.5	34.7
Intangibles (net)	3.4	.6	1.1	.5	2.4	4.1	1.2	1.2
All Other Non-Current	6.1	6.2	5.0	6.2	7.6	8.0	6.8	6.7
Total	100.0	100.0	100.0	100.0	100.0	100.0	100.0	100.0
LIABILITIES								
Notes Payable-Short Term	23.7	7.3	4.8	3.7	2.9	1.4	4.5	5.2
Cur. Mat.-L.T.D.	8.9	7.0	5.3	4.8	4.8	3.7	5.6	5.3
Trade Payables	11.3	14.0	15.9	17.2	17.7	13.4	17.1	17.6
Income Taxes Payable	.3	.5	.8	.6	.5	.6	.5	.5
All Other Current	8.4	7.2	9.5	13.3	16.1	15.2	10.3	10.6
Total Current	52.5	36.0	36.3	39.5	42.0	34.4	38.0	39.2
Long-Term Debt	27.7	16.7	13.6	15.0	16.5	16.7	16.0	15.1
Deferred Taxes	.0	1.0	1.4	1.1	1.2	1.7	1.3	1.3
All Other Non-Current	7.5	4.6	2.8	2.4	2.4	2.3	2.5	3.2
Net Worth	12.2	41.7	46.0	42.0	37.9	44.9	42.2	41.3
Total Liabilities & Net Worth	100.0	100.0	100.0	100.0	100.0	100.0	100.0	100.0
INCOME DATA								
Net Sales	100.0	100.0	100.0	100.0	100.0	100.0	100.0	100.0
Gross Profit	39.1	29.2	20.8	14.8	13.6	15.7	17.1	17.7
Operating Expenses	38.4	23.1	15.0	9.0	7.8	8.5	13.8	15.0
Operating Profit	.7	6.1	5.9	5.8	5.8	7.2	3.3	2.7
All Other Expenses (net)	1.1	.4	.0	.1	.0	.2	.3	.2
Profit Before Taxes	-.4	5.7	5.9	5.7	5.8	7.0	2.9	2.5
RATIOS								
Current	1.9	2.7	2.5	2.1	1.7	1.8	2.2	2.1
	1.2	1.6	1.6	1.5	1.4	1.5	1.5	1.5
	.2	1.1	1.2	1.2	1.2	1.1	1.1	1.2
Quick	1.6	2.2	2.0	1.7	1.4	1.5	1.8	1.7
	.8	1.3	1.4	1.2	1.1	1.1	1.2 (771)	1.2
	.2	.9	1.0	.9	.8	.8	.8	.8
Sales/Receivables	0 UND	17 20.9	33 11.0	36 10.2	41 8.8	40 9.1	30 12.2	31 11.7
	12 30.8	40 9.1	52 7.0	54 6.7	57 6.4	52 7.1	47 7.7	49 7.4
	43 8.5	63 5.7	71 5.1	73 5.0	80 4.6	70 5.3	64 5.7	72 5.1
Cost of Sales/Inventory	0 UND	0 UND	0 UND	0 UND	0 999.8	2 219.4	0 UND	0 UND
	0 UND	0 UND	0 UND	2 195.8	6 61.1	7 50.2	0 918.5	0 839.5
	11 34.6	2 201.6	5 75.7	11 32.1	13 27.8	22 16.9	8 48.5	9 40.9
Cost of Sales/Payables	0 UND	6 56.4	14 26.7	20 18.3	28 13.2	22 17.0	17 21.1	16 23.5
	13 28.5	19 19.0	25 14.5	30 12.1	40 9.2	30 12.1	29 12.4	31 11.8
	28 13.1	43 8.4	41 8.8	45 8.1	45 8.1	39 9.3	45 8.2	48 7.7
Sales/Working Capital	9.2	6.8	5.8	6.7	7.5	6.8	6.4	6.9
	101.5	14.7	10.2	10.7	11.5	10.9	12.8	12.9
	-13.2	63.6	25.5	20.4	20.2	30.8	38.1	32.4
EBIT/Interest	3.8	22.6	22.8	22.8	19.3	23.5	13.6	10.6
	(24) 1.8	(129) 6.0	(326) 7.5	(244) 7.4	(60) 7.1	(43) 8.2	(576) 4.1	(699) 4.1
	-3.8	1.9	2.6	3.1	2.4	3.2	1.5	1.2
Net Profit + Depr., Dep., Amort./Cur. Mat. L/T/D		6.5	5.7	6.0	4.7	5.1	3.7	3.4
		(31) 3.3	(127) 2.6	(103) 3.2	(26) 1.7	(11) 1.8	(202) 2.0	(247) 1.9
		2.0	1.5	1.6	.9	1.7	1.2	1.2
Fixed/Worth	.7	.4	.4	.4	.5	.6	.5	.4
	2.2	.9	.7	.7	.9	.8	.8	.8
	-2.2	1.8	1.2	1.2	1.5	1.4	1.4	1.4
Debt/Worth	1.1	.6	.7	.9	1.1	.9	.7	.8
	3.2	1.2	1.2	1.5	1.9	1.5	1.4	1.5
	-5.1	2.9	2.1	2.5	2.9	2.4	2.7	2.9
% Profit Before Taxes/Tangible Net Worth	114.6	56.3	43.9	45.2	47.5	46.6	28.8	26.6
	(19) 10.8	(128) 24.5	(340) 22.6	(261) 26.3	(62) 27.7	(46) 27.8	(604) 13.9	(733) 12.2
	-13.2	4.7	9.6	12.8	11.0	14.6	3.6	1.6
% Profit Before Taxes/Total Assets	13.4	25.4	19.8	18.8	16.3	15.8	12.0	11.4
	2.3	11.1	9.0	10.2	9.3	10.7	5.3	4.4
	-13.2	1.8	3.9	4.5	2.6	5.4	1.1	.3
Sales/Net Fixed Assets	23.5	15.6	13.4	12.1	10.7	8.3	12.0	12.1
	9.5	8.7	7.8	7.1	6.5	4.9	6.8	7.0
	4.6	4.3	4.8	4.5	4.5	3.1	4.2	4.1
Sales/Total Assets	7.6	3.6	3.0	2.6	2.4	2.3	2.8	2.8
	4.3	2.6	2.3	2.2	1.9	1.8	2.2	2.2
	1.8	1.8	1.8	1.7	1.5	1.4	1.6	1.6
% Depr., Dep., Amort./Sales	1.5	1.7	1.8	1.8	1.4	2.0	2.2	2.1
	(23) 3.7	(122) 3.1	(327) 2.8	(246) 3.0	(58) 2.8	(26) 2.8	(573) 3.6	(695) 3.7
	6.5	5.7	4.7	4.1	4.2	3.8	5.5	5.4
% Officers', Directors' Owners' Comp/Sales	4.8	2.2	1.3	.6		.4	1.1	1.2
	(14) 8.3	(70) 3.6	(144) 2.2	(59) 1.2	(13) .7		(209) 2.4	(263) 2.4
	13.2	5.5	4.7	2.3	3.3		4.5	4.3
Net Sales ($)	32502M	461993M	4348775M	13557181M	8378247M	13495046M	26195663M	28364203M
Total Assets ($)	7305M	164048M	1783808M	6274463M	4270949M	7502995M	12808966M	14343310M

M = $ thousand   MM = $ million

See Pages 11 through 21 for Explanation of Ratios and Data

Comparative Historical Data | **Current Data Sorted by Sales**

Hist 4/1/04-3/31/05 ALL	Hist 4/1/05-3/31/06 ALL	Hist 4/1/06-3/31/07 ALL	Type of Statement	0-1MM	1-3MM	3-5MM	5-10MM	10-25MM	25MM & OVER
385	395	405	Unqualified	1	8	17	39	100	240
169	158	224	Reviewed	9	28	31	64	61	31
40	42	44	Compiled	6	13	6	11	3	5
41	43	44	Tax Returns	10	11	6	11	5	1
143	195	171	Other	2	16	8	28	31	86
				185 (4/1-9/30/06)			703 (10/1/06-3/31/07)		
778	833	888	**NUMBER OF STATEMENTS**	28	76	68	153	200	363
%	%	%	**ASSETS**	%	%	%	%	%	%
14.6	15.7	16.3	Cash & Equivalents	15.3	16.5	17.9	14.8	17.1	16.3
31.8	32.0	32.3	Trade Receivables (net)	21.0	26.3	31.2	32.6	36.6	32.2
3.9	4.0	3.5	Inventory	7.0	2.1	2.1	3.4	2.8	4.3
7.5	7.6	6.8	All Other Current	4.4	6.0	5.8	6.8	6.5	7.6
57.7	59.3	59.0	Total Current	47.7	50.8	57.0	57.6	63.0	60.4
33.7	33.1	33.9	Fixed Assets (net)	45.8	40.6	35.1	35.5	31.7	31.9
1.2	1.0	1.2	Intangibles (net)	1.3	.9	1.7	1.0	1.0	1.3
7.4	6.6	5.9	All Other Non-Current	5.2	7.7	6.3	5.9	4.3	6.5
100.0	100.0	100.0	Total	100.0	100.0	100.0	100.0	100.0	100.0
			LIABILITIES						
5.4	4.8	5.1	Notes Payable-Short Term	18.8	8.7	8.6	5.6	4.1	3.1
5.4	5.6	5.4	Cur. Mat.-L.T.D.	4.4	8.1	6.7	5.8	5.1	4.6
17.4	17.6	15.8	Trade Payables	11.8	12.3	12.2	14.2	18.0	17.0
.6	.6	.7	Income Taxes Payable	.0	.3	.6	.8	1.0	.5
10.7	10.8	11.0	All Other Current	7.6	4.1	7.5	9.0	10.4	14.5
39.5	39.3	38.0	Total Current	42.6	33.5	35.6	35.4	38.7	39.8
15.3	15.5	15.3	Long-Term Debt	21.7	21.9	14.5	15.6	13.6	14.5
1.4	1.2	1.2	Deferred Taxes	.0	.6	1.4	1.4	1.2	1.3
3.2	3.2	3.0	All Other Non-Current	11.2	5.6	1.2	4.2	1.9	2.3
40.6	40.7	42.5	Net Worth	24.5	38.3	47.4	43.5	44.7	42.1
100.0	100.0	100.0	Total Liabilities & Net Worth	100.0	100.0	100.0	100.0	100.0	100.0
			INCOME DATA						
100.0	100.0	100.0	Net Sales	100.0	100.0	100.0	100.0	100.0	100.0
18.3	18.5	20.1	Gross Profit	37.5	35.6	24.5	24.6	17.6	14.2
14.8	14.5	14.3	Operating Expenses	34.4	27.2	18.3	19.2	12.1	8.5
3.4	3.9	5.8	Operating Profit	3.1	8.4	6.2	5.4	5.5	5.7
.1	.0	.1	All Other Expenses (net)	.5	.9	-.1	.2	.1	.0
3.3	3.9	5.7	Profit Before Taxes	2.7	7.5	6.3	5.2	5.4	5.7
			RATIOS						
2.1	2.2	2.2	Current	5.0	3.3	2.8	2.7	2.2	1.9
1.5	1.5	1.5		1.5	1.7	1.6	1.7	1.6	1.5
1.2	1.2	1.2		.3	1.0	1.2	1.2	1.2	1.2
1.7	1.8	1.8	Quick	2.6	3.0	2.4	2.2	1.9	1.5
1.2	1.3	1.3		1.1	1.3	1.4	1.3	1.4	1.2
.8	.9	.9		.1	.7	.9	.9	1.0	.9
33 11.0	32 11.3	31 11.6	Sales/Receivables	0 UND	17 21.4	21 17.4	29 12.4	38 9.7	34 10.6
51 7.1	50 7.4	52 7.1		23 15.8	44 8.3	42 8.6	52 7.1	54 6.8	53 6.9
71 5.1	73 5.0	71 5.1		86 4.3	64 5.7	72 5.1	68 5.4	71 5.2	73 5.0
0 UND	0 UND	0 UND	Cost of Sales/Inventory	0 UND	0 UND	0 UND	0 UND	0 UND	0 UND
1 631.1	1 538.5	0 883.1		0 UND	0 UND	0 UND	0 UND	1 601.6	3 141.7
9 41.2	10 35.7	8 43.2		22 17.0	2 164.4	1 358.7	6 61.3	7 48.9	11 33.1
18 20.5	16 22.6	15 23.6	Cost of Sales/Payables	2 228.6	8 43.9	6 57.6	10 36.3	17 21.1	21 17.7
31 11.9	29 12.5	28 13.0		22 16.3	20 18.1	19 19.3	23 15.5	28 12.9	31 11.8
47 7.7	47 7.8	44 8.3		57 6.4	51 7.2	36 10.1	44 8.2	45 8.2	44 8.3
6.7	6.3	6.4	Sales/Working Capital	3.8	5.1	6.2	5.3	6.4	7.1
12.1	11.9	11.3		16.1	11.7	10.4	11.2	11.1	11.4
33.0	25.9	27.5		-15.8	-97.0	41.5	35.2	24.4	21.5
16.5	17.0	22.1	EBIT/Interest	9.8	21.2	11.5	17.4	27.6	23.4
(707) 5.5	(770) 6.0	(826) 6.9		(22) 1.8	(74) 4.3	(61) 4.7	(144) 6.4	(188) 8.1	(337) 7.7
2.1	2.0	2.6		-3.4	1.6	2.1	2.0	3.1	3.1
4.1	4.3	5.7	Net Profit + Depr., Dep., Amort./Cur. Mat. L/T/D		4.9	7.5	5.8	6.4	5.1
(243) 2.0	(287) 2.2	(299) 2.7			(11) 2.9	(19) 2.8	(48) 2.4	(79) 2.7	(140) 2.6
1.2	1.3	1.6			1.6	2.1	1.8	2.0	1.4
.4	.4	.4	Fixed/Worth	.4	.4	.3	.4	.4	.5
.8	.8	.8		1.3	1.2	.6	.7	.7	.8
1.4	1.3	1.4		4.3	2.8	1.4	1.4	1.2	1.2
.7	.7	.8	Debt/Worth	.7	.5	.7	.6	.8	.9
1.5	1.5	1.4		1.8	1.2	1.1	1.2	1.4	1.5
2.9	2.8	2.5		8.2	6.5	2.1	2.6	2.1	2.5
30.2	38.3	46.0	% Profit Before Taxes/Tangible Net Worth	37.3	55.4	45.3	45.9	45.8	45.5
(741) 15.7	(792) 17.7	(856) 24.4		(23) 11.7	(66) 30.6	(67) 21.9	(145) 27.8	(197) 22.7	(358) 25.7
4.9	5.2	10.0		-14.3	6.2	4.3	10.2	10.5	12.2
12.3	14.5	19.1	% Profit Before Taxes/Total Assets	10.4	21.0	23.3	20.1	20.7	17.7
5.8	6.6	9.6		3.1	11.1	9.0	9.0	9.6	10.2
1.6	1.8	3.7		-10.3	2.6	1.9	2.4	4.1	4.2
12.2	13.5	13.0	Sales/Net Fixed Assets	13.6	12.9	16.0	13.2	13.6	11.4
7.1	7.6	7.5		4.8	5.9	8.7	7.6	9.1	7.0
4.1	4.4	4.5		2.0	3.1	4.2	4.4	5.3	4.6
2.9	3.0	2.9	Sales/Total Assets	3.8	3.2	3.4	3.1	3.0	2.7
2.2	2.2	2.2		1.5	2.2	2.2	2.2	2.2	2.2
1.6	1.7	1.7		.8	1.4	1.7	1.7	1.9	1.7
2.2	1.8	1.8	% Depr., Dep., Amort./Sales	2.6	2.6	1.7	2.2	1.6	1.8
(689) 3.6	(742) 3.2	(802) 2.9		(25) 6.1	(61) 4.4	(63) 2.8	(140) 3.4	(192) 2.5	(321) 2.8
5.2	4.6	4.5		11.8	7.3	5.0	5.7	4.0	4.0
1.3	1.3	1.2	% Officers', Directors' Owners' Comp/Sales	3.4	3.2	2.3	1.4	1.2	.5
(264) 2.3	(280) 2.5	(302) 2.4		(11) 6.4	(33) 5.4	(37) 3.7	(62) 2.5	(82) 2.0	(77) 1.3
4.1	4.2	4.8		10.1	9.3	4.7	4.5	4.7	2.5
30781163M	36337043M	40273744M	Net Sales ($)	17507M	156560M	268454M	1098836M	3340530M	35391857M
16146204M	17903441M	20003568M	Total Assets ($)	17618M	87697M	124702M	533164M	1432581M	17807806M

Current Data Sorted by Assets   Comparative Historical Data

						Type of Statement		
3	4	27	30	13	16	Unqualified	83	88
3	26	55	18			Reviewed	70	90
3	9	11	1			Compiled	17	41
19	14	13	1			Tax Returns	13	20
7	13	27	15	5	4	Other	39	70
	74 (4/1-9/30/06)		263 (10/1/06-3/31/07)				4/1/02-3/31/03	4/1/03-3/31/04
0-500M	500M-2MM	2-10MM	10-50MM	50-100MM	100-250MM		ALL	ALL
35	66	133	65	18	20	NUMBER OF STATEMENTS	222	309
%	%	%	%	%	%	ASSETS	%	%
22.1	10.3	12.0	16.6	14.3	12.9	Cash & Equivalents	12.3	12.2
21.6	37.7	37.8	37.2	35.7	37.8	Trade Receivables (net)	33.4	36.0
7.3	8.6	4.6	2.3	1.0	1.0	Inventory	4.2	3.5
5.0	3.4	7.9	6.5	13.9	12.3	All Other Current	8.3	8.3
56.0	60.0	62.4	62.7	64.8	63.9	Total Current	58.1	60.0
35.5	33.2	31.9	29.7	26.3	27.9	Fixed Assets (net)	33.4	31.9
2.0	.4	.8	1.1	1.2	3.9	Intangibles (net)	1.7	1.6
6.4	6.4	5.0	6.5	7.6	4.2	All Other Non-Current	6.8	6.4
100.0	100.0	100.0	100.0	100.0	100.0	Total	100.0	100.0
						LIABILITIES		
23.3	8.0	9.8	4.2	.8	2.9	Notes Payable-Short Term	6.9	6.8
3.3	4.8	5.7	5.9	2.2	3.0	Cur. Mat.-L.T.D.	4.9	5.5
16.2	17.3	16.2	18.0	18.7	19.9	Trade Payables	16.9	19.1
.0	1.3	1.4	.6	1.0	.4	Income Taxes Payable	.7	.7
24.6	10.4	11.6	13.3	22.5	20.0	All Other Current	12.0	13.1
67.5	41.7	44.9	42.1	45.2	46.2	Total Current	41.4	45.2
28.5	21.6	13.5	14.7	13.5	20.3	Long-Term Debt	14.2	14.3
.0	.9	1.0	.7	1.4	2.4	Deferred Taxes	1.3	1.2
3.2	2.0	.7	1.9	3.3	3.1	All Other Non-Current	3.6	3.0
.7	33.8	40.0	40.6	36.6	28.0	Net Worth	39.6	36.3
100.0	100.0	100.0	100.0	100.0	100.0	Total Liabilties & Net Worth	100.0	100.0
						INCOME DATA		
100.0	100.0	100.0	100.0	100.0	100.0	Net Sales	100.0	100.0
42.9	30.2	23.3	20.4	18.4	16.4	Gross Profit	22.9	22.6
38.7	25.3	16.8	13.2	9.9	12.8	Operating Expenses	18.7	19.2
4.3	4.9	6.5	7.1	8.6	3.6	Operating Profit	4.2	3.4
1.1	.8	.4	.3	.5	.6	All Other Expenses (net)	.7	.4
3.2	4.1	6.0	6.8	8.1	3.1	Profit Before Taxes	3.4	3.0
						RATIOS		
2.7	3.0	2.0	1.8	1.9	1.7	Current	1.9	1.8
1.4	1.4	1.4	1.4	1.5	1.5		1.4	1.3
.3	1.0	1.0	1.2	1.2	1.1		1.1	1.0
2.7	2.2	1.8	1.6	1.4	1.4	Quick	1.5	1.5
1.0	(65) 1.2	1.1	1.3	1.1	1.1		1.1	1.1
.3	.8	.7	1.0	.8	.9		.8	.7
0 UND	22 16.8	42 8.8	48 7.5	47 7.8	45 8.2	Sales/Receivables	37 9.9	38 9.6
15 24.1	48 7.6	61 5.9	64 5.7	61 6.0	72 5.1		55 6.7	57 6.4
43 8.4	68 5.3	79 4.6	84 4.3	85 4.3	87 4.2		75 4.8	82 4.5
0 UND	0 UND	0 UND	0 UND	0 UND	0 UND	Cost of Sales/Inventory	0 UND	0 UND
0 UND	0 UND	0 UND	0 UND	0 UND	2 204.7		0 966.0	0 UND
0 UND	14 26.6	3 114.8	4 94.0	4 98.5	4 99.1		9 41.3	6 60.0
1 661.0	7 51.3	14 25.6	24 14.9	19 19.5	28 13.3	Cost of Sales/Payables	18 20.1	16 23.1
15 23.9	23 16.1	32 11.4	37 9.9	40 9.2	40 9.1		33 11.2	33 11.0
54 6.8	48 7.6	46 7.9	59 6.2	56 6.6	54 6.7		50 7.3	54 6.8
8.4	8.1	6.5	6.0	6.1	7.1	Sales/Working Capital	7.4	7.8
37.0	18.2	12.8	11.3	9.7	10.1		15.0	15.8
-17.1	-355.2	119.3	31.3	13.7	63.9		47.8	231.5
15.3	20.1	19.5	25.7	19.3	22.6	EBIT/Interest	12.6	12.1
(29) 2.6	(58) 5.7	(123) 5.1	(62) 8.6	(17) 5.3	(19) 4.1		(197) 4.4	(282) 4.7
.9	1.6	2.6	4.1	2.2	2.5		1.4	1.2
	6.0	4.0	9.7		7.8	Net Profit + Depr., Dep.,	3.7	4.6
	(18) 2.2	(44) 2.2	(27) 3.3		(11) 3.2	Amort./Cur. Mat. L/T/D	(78) 2.2	(108) 1.9
	.9	1.5	1.3		1.7		1.3	1.0
.2	.3	.3	.3	.3	.4	Fixed/Worth	.4	.3
1.1	.8	.7	.6	.6	1.3		.8	.8
11.8	3.2	1.5	1.5	.9	2.3		1.6	1.9
.9	.9	.9	.9	1.0	2.1	Debt/Worth	.8	1.0
2.6	2.2	1.6	1.6	2.1	3.0		1.6	1.8
-8.0	7.1	2.9	2.6	3.6	4.9		3.0	4.0
100.9	74.1	49.4	47.1	34.6	49.0	% Profit Before Taxes/Tangible	29.1	34.1
(26) 33.6	(58) 36.9	(130) 26.4	(62) 26.3	(18) 16.5	34.9	Net Worth	(208) 16.2	(291) 16.3
2.7	8.5	10.6	18.4	6.0	22.1		2.5	1.4
37.7	19.7	20.6	17.9	10.4	15.1	% Profit Before Taxes/Total	10.8	12.1
17.9	9.8	9.7	10.4	3.9	7.4	Assets	4.6	5.4
.9	1.9	3.8	5.7	2.2	3.8		.8	.1
52.8	38.4	22.8	15.9	28.7	31.1	Sales/Net Fixed Assets	13.9	23.4
17.4	9.7	8.3	7.7	14.2	9.6		7.2	7.7
5.8	4.8	3.9	4.2	3.7	3.2		3.4	3.7
6.5	4.1	2.9	2.8	2.5	2.7	Sales/Total Assets	2.9	2.9
3.7	2.7	2.2	1.9	1.8	2.1		2.0	2.2
2.8	1.8	1.6	1.5	1.5	1.3		1.4	1.5
.8	1.1	.9	1.2	.8	.6	% Depr., Dep., Amort./Sales	1.7	1.2
(21) 2.5	(54) 2.8	(124) 2.6	(61) 2.9	(17) 1.5	(15) 1.4		(202) 3.9	(281) 2.9
6.5	5.2	5.6	5.5	4.5	3.2		6.9	6.2
3.5	2.0	1.1	1.1			% Officers', Directors'	1.9	1.4
(18) 6.1	(36) 4.5	(53) 2.2	(17) 1.6			Owners' Comp/Sales	(76) 3.0	(92) 2.4
9.2	6.9	4.1	4.2				5.7	4.3
37701M	240707M	1464388M	2983106M	2693940M	6409009M	Net Sales ($)	7499383M	11445548M
8805M	80906M	652058M	1370870M	1398834M	3107881M	Total Assets ($)	3407641M	5429380M

M = $ thousand   MM = $ million
See Pages 11 through 21 for Explanation of Ratios and Data

Comparative Historical Data | | | Type of Statement | Current Data Sorted by Sales | | | | | |

88 / 91 / 34 / 24 / 57	81 / 104 / 26 / 40 / 94	93 / 102 / 24 / 47 / 71	Type of Statement — Unqualified / Reviewed / Compiled / Tax Returns / Other	2 / 3 / 2 / 15 / 6	2 / 15 / 5 / 11 / 8	4 / 12 / 4 / 4 / 5	15 / 29 / 9 / 7 / 12	11 / 31 / 4 / 9 / 20	59 / 12 / / 1 / 20
4/1/04-3/31/05 ALL	4/1/05-3/31/06 ALL	4/1/06-3/31/07 ALL		74 (4/1-9/30/06)			263 (10/1/06-3/31/07)		
294	345	337	NUMBER OF STATEMENTS	0-1MM 28	1-3MM 41	3-5MM 29	5-10MM 72	10-25MM 75	25MM & OVER 92
%	%	%	**ASSETS**	%	%	%	%	%	%
12.1	13.6	13.7	Cash & Equivalents	19.3	10.1	12.2	15.3	10.3	15.8
36.0	38.1	35.9	Trade Receivables (net)	9.0	34.2	35.3	37.8	39.1	40.9
5.5	6.1	4.8	Inventory	13.0	7.3	5.2	3.8	5.1	1.8
8.4	8.0	7.1	All Other Current	5.9	2.8	3.3	7.5	7.9	9.5
61.9	65.7	61.5	Total Current	47.2	54.5	56.0	64.4	62.3	67.9
30.5	27.7	31.6	Fixed Assets (net)	47.5	35.6	37.1	30.2	30.7	25.0
1.3	.9	1.1	Intangibles (net)	.3	2.0	1.1	.3	1.3	1.4
6.2	5.7	5.8	All Other Non-Current	4.9	7.9	5.8	5.0	5.7	5.8
100.0	100.0	100.0	Total	100.0	100.0	100.0	100.0	100.0	100.0
			LIABILITIES						
9.1	9.5	8.9	Notes Payable-Short Term	26.1	9.4	7.1	8.4	9.9	3.5
4.9	4.5	5.0	Cur. Mat.-L.T.D.	3.2	5.6	7.7	5.4	5.4	3.8
16.7	18.6	17.1	Trade Payables	5.7	19.7	14.7	18.3	16.3	20.0
.6	.8	1.0	Income Taxes Payable	.0	.9	1.2	1.6	1.4	.5
12.0	13.6	14.1	All Other Current	26.1	8.9	11.4	11.2	11.6	18.0
43.3	47.0	46.1	Total Current	61.2	44.5	42.0	45.0	44.6	45.8
15.0	14.0	17.3	Long-Term Debt	34.7	24.5	18.3	15.5	13.4	13.1
1.4	.8	.9	Deferred Taxes	.1	.9	.9	1.2	.8	1.0
3.0	3.4	1.7	All Other Non-Current	1.2	2.7	2.1	1.1	.9	2.4
37.3	34.9	33.9	Net Worth	2.8	27.4	36.7	37.1	40.3	37.7
100.0	100.0	100.0	Total Liabilities & Net Worth	100.0	100.0	100.0	100.0	100.0	100.0
			INCOME DATA						
100.0	100.0	100.0	Net Sales	100.0	100.0	100.0	100.0	100.0	100.0
24.2	23.0	25.4	Gross Profit	44.7	35.2	34.7	22.5	22.7	16.8
19.6	18.2	19.4	Operating Expenses	42.5	29.4	26.1	16.4	16.7	10.4
4.6	4.8	6.0	Operating Profit	2.2	5.8	8.5	6.1	6.0	6.4
.3	.5	.6	All Other Expenses (net)	1.9	.9	-.4	.6	.3	.5
4.3	4.3	5.4	Profit Before Taxes	.3	4.9	9.0	5.5	5.7	5.9
			RATIOS						
2.0	2.0	2.0	Current	3.6	2.6	2.5	1.9	1.9	1.8
1.4	1.4	1.4		1.5	1.4	1.4	1.4	1.4	1.5
1.1	1.1	1.1		.3	1.0	.8	1.0	1.0	1.2
1.6	1.6	1.8	Quick	2.7	2.2	2.4	1.7	1.6	1.5
1.2	1.1 (336)	1.2		(27) .6	1.1	1.1	1.2	1.1	1.2
.8	.8	.7		.2	.6	.7	.7	.7	1.0
40 9.0	39 9.2	37 9.9	Sales/Receivables	0 UND	22 16.9	34 10.6	40 9.2	41 9.0	45 8.2
59 6.2	63 5.8	56 6.5		5 70.1	52 7.0	53 6.9	53 6.9	61 5.9	66 5.6
80 4.5	85 4.3	79 4.6		30 12.0	70 5.2	87 4.2	77 4.7	79 4.6	85 4.3
0 UND	0 UND	0 UND	Cost of Sales/Inventory	0 UND	0 UND	0 UND	0 UND	0 UND	0 UND
0 UND	0 UND	0 UND		0 UND	0 UND	0 UND	0 UND	0 UND	0 UND
9 39.6	8 44.6	4 86.5		32 11.3	14 26.1	6 60.0	3 138.1	7 50.7	3 137.0
16 22.8	18 20.6	14 25.6	Cost of Sales/Payables	0 UND	7 51.7	5 71.3	14 25.4	18 20.6	23 15.8
32 11.5	37 10.0	32 11.5		7 53.8	26 14.0	31 11.9	25 14.7	30 12.0	38 9.6
48 7.7	56 6.5	51 7.1		54 6.7	53 6.9	56 6.5	47 7.8	44 8.3	53 6.9
6.2	6.6	7.0	Sales/Working Capital	3.7	8.2	7.3	6.3	7.2	6.6
11.7	12.5	12.8		18.5	15.4	26.2	14.2	12.8	10.5
40.4	57.7	99.9		-9.9	-297.5	-33.7	104.5	555.9	24.0
16.2	17.2	19.5	EBIT/Interest	4.9	12.6	41.5	14.4	19.3	32.8
(266) 6.8	(312) 5.5	(308) 5.5		(24) 1.8	(33) 4.1	(28) 10.8	(66) 5.1	(70) 4.6	(87) 9.3
1.8	1.7	2.5		-.6	2.0	2.8	2.7	2.5	4.0
3.6	4.4	6.2	Net Profit + Depr., Dep., Amort./Cur. Mat. L/T/D		3.4		6.7	4.0	9.0
(99) 2.3	(101) 2.4	(110) 2.6			(12) 2.7		(25) 2.1	(24) 2.4	(41) 4.4
1.2	1.2	1.3			1.1		1.2	1.3	1.8
.3	.3	.3	Fixed/Worth	.2	.4	.2	.2	.3	.3
.8	.7	.7		1.2	.9	.8	.7	.7	.6
1.6	1.6	1.6		8.1	13.6	3.0	1.5	1.5	1.2
1.0	1.0	.9	Debt/Worth	1.0	.7	.6	.9	1.0	.9
1.7	2.0	1.8		2.5	2.4	1.7	1.7	1.7	2.0
3.7	4.1	3.4		NM	35.7	4.3	3.3	2.8	3.2
44.4	45.5	54.2	% Profit Before Taxes/Tangible Net Worth	48.1	87.2	88.7	50.2	46.7	49.2
(279) 18.7	(324) 23.3	(312) 27.9		(21) 13.5	(33) 29.1	(27) 46.9	(69) 27.9	(74) 25.8	(88) 27.5
6.8	7.7	11.2		-3.9	7.0	29.5	13.3	10.7	16.5
13.5	15.3	19.3	% Profit Before Taxes/Total Assets	15.0	18.9	41.0	19.2	17.3	17.2
7.2	7.3	9.7		4.7	8.7	11.1	10.2	9.5	9.7
1.3	1.9	3.3		-4.4	1.3	6.5	3.8	3.2	4.5
29.3	27.0	27.0	Sales/Net Fixed Assets	25.2	25.9	46.0	30.6	19.4	27.8
8.1	10.4	9.5		6.0	7.5	8.1	9.6	8.4	12.7
3.8	4.7	4.3		2.9	4.3	3.1	4.2	4.4	5.6
2.8	3.0	3.1	Sales/Total Assets	4.4	3.7	3.6	3.0	3.1	2.9
2.2	2.2	2.3		2.2	2.4	2.1	2.2	2.4	2.2
1.5	1.6	1.6		1.0	1.7	1.8	1.6	1.6	1.6
1.2	1.0	1.0	% Depr., Dep., Amort./Sales	1.4	1.6	1.1	1.0	.9	.8
(249) 3.1	(305) 2.5	(292) 2.6		(20) 5.6	(31) 4.0	(24) 3.0	(65) 2.6	(68) 2.5	(84) 1.9
5.6	4.7	5.4		8.8	7.3	6.8	5.6	5.5	3.6
1.3	1.4	1.3	% Officers', Directors' Owners' Comp/Sales	4.0	3.6	1.6	1.4	.9	.7
(97) 2.3	(120) 2.5	(126) 3.2		(12) 8.8	(23) 5.1	(16) 3.0	(30) 2.9	(29) 1.6	(16) 1.1
4.7	4.6	5.6		12.6	7.2	5.4	2.7	2.7	4.4
11669061M	14213692M	13828851M	Net Sales ($)	16356M	79693M	116596M	508520M	1175025M	11932661M
5749478M	6305883M	6619354M	Total Assets ($)	9715M	43101M	63477M	247119M	558836M	5697106M

© RMA 2007

M = $ thousand   MM = $ million
See Pages 11 through 21 for Explanation of Ratios and Data

Current Data Sorted by Assets   Comparative Historical Data

	0-500M	500M-2MM	2-10MM	10-50MM	50-100MM	100-250MM	Type of Statement	4/1/02-3/31/03 ALL	4/1/03-3/31/04 ALL
	1	9	26	22	2	3	Unqualified	48	57
	2	33	67	24			Reviewed	85	120
	9	20	22	5	2	2	Compiled	52	98
	30	29	14	2		2	Tax Returns	25	54
	14	45	53	18	4	3	Other	64	56
		81 (4/1-9/30/06)		378 (10/1/06-3/31/07)					
NUMBER OF STATEMENTS	56	136	182	71	6	8		274	385

	%	%	%	%	%	%	**ASSETS**	%	%
	20.4	10.7	9.0	12.2			Cash & Equivalents	11.7	10.4
	20.2	42.2	43.9	37.0			Trade Receivables (net)	38.2	39.4
	3.2	2.2	3.4	4.1			Inventory	3.0	3.3
	4.7	4.2	6.1	5.9			All Other Current	5.9	6.2
	48.6	59.3	62.3	59.3			Total Current	58.8	59.3
	41.2	33.0	29.9	33.9			Fixed Assets (net)	33.1	33.0
	1.9	1.6	1.6	1.1			Intangibles (net)	1.4	1.6
	8.3	6.1	6.2	5.7			All Other Non-Current	6.6	6.1
	100.0	100.0	100.0	100.0			Total	100.0	100.0

	0-500M	500M-2MM	2-10MM	10-50MM	50-100MM	100-250MM	**LIABILITIES**		
	11.2	9.1	7.1	6.6			Notes Payable-Short Term	9.8	10.2
	6.2	5.0	5.1	5.4			Cur. Mat.-L.T.D.	6.8	5.8
	9.4	18.4	20.2	17.0			Trade Payables	16.1	17.7
	.0	.5	.5	.3			Income Taxes Payable	.6	.5
	17.3	6.4	9.4	11.5			All Other Current	9.6	10.3
	44.0	39.4	42.3	40.8			Total Current	43.0	44.5
	40.5	17.7	15.5	16.9			Long-Term Debt	18.4	19.6
	.0	.5	.7	1.1			Deferred Taxes	.6	.8
	8.4	4.7	2.6	3.8			All Other Non-Current	3.0	4.9
	7.0	37.8	39.0	37.5			Net Worth	34.9	30.2
	100.0	100.0	100.0	100.0			Total Liabilities & Net Worth	100.0	100.0

	0-500M	500M-2MM	2-10MM	10-50MM	50-100MM	100-250MM	**INCOME DATA**		
	100.0	100.0	100.0	100.0			Net Sales	100.0	100.0
	44.3	33.0	24.4	22.6			Gross Profit	26.1	26.2
	38.1	28.3	18.4	16.3			Operating Expenses	22.1	23.3
	6.2	4.7	6.0	6.3			Operating Profit	4.0	2.9
	.6	.4	.5	.8			All Other Expenses (net)	.7	.7
	5.6	4.3	5.5	5.4			Profit Before Taxes	3.3	2.1

	0-500M	500M-2MM	2-10MM	10-50MM	50-100MM	100-250MM	**RATIOS**		
	5.1	2.7	2.2	2.0			Current	2.3	2.1
	1.3	1.6	1.5	1.4				1.4	1.4
	.5	1.1	1.1	1.1				1.0	1.0
	3.7	2.4	1.8	1.8			Quick	1.9	1.8
	1.1	1.3	1.3	1.2				(273) 1.2	1.2
	.3	.8	.9	.7				.8	.8
	0 UND	24 15.1	39 9.4	39 9.5			Sales/Receivables	35 10.4	32 11.2
	0 UND	47 7.8	59 6.2	57 6.4				51 7.1	54 6.8
	40 9.2	73 5.0	83 4.4	83 4.4				73 5.0	73 5.0
	0 UND	0 UND	0 UND	0 UND			Cost of Sales/Inventory	0 UND	0 UND
	0 UND	0 UND	0 UND	1 362.7				0 UND	0 UND
	0 UND	2 208.9	6 61.7	8 43.8				5 67.7	6 66.3
	0 UND	7 55.0	18 19.8	16 22.8			Cost of Sales/Payables	11 33.6	12 31.3
	0 UND	25 14.8	31 11.8	33 11.0				25 14.3	27 13.4
	15 24.4	46 8.0	50 7.3	50 7.3				44 8.3	46 8.0
	12.8	9.2	6.3	7.3			Sales/Working Capital	7.9	8.0
	106.7	16.9	15.3	14.9				16.7	17.1
	-38.6	86.5	87.7	72.6				-800.0	216.7
	19.0	18.8	21.7	21.7			EBIT/Interest	11.5	10.1
	(47) 4.4	(124) 6.5	(171) 8.5	(64) 5.4				(242) 4.0	(354) 4.0
	1.0	1.7	2.2	2.0				1.3	1.0
		5.3	3.9	4.1			Net Profit + Depr., Dep., Amort./Cur. Mat. L/T/D	3.9	3.2
		(19) 2.2	(48) 2.2	(26) 2.0				(65) 1.9	(92) 1.4
		1.1	1.2	1.4				1.1	.8
	.5	.3	.3	.3			Fixed/Worth	.4	.4
	2.5	.8	.7	.8				.8	.9
	-4.2	2.2	1.9	2.1				2.6	2.5
	.8	.7	.8	.8			Debt/Worth	.7	.8
	3.0	1.5	1.5	2.3				1.7	2.1
	-7.4	4.5	4.1	3.8				5.3	6.2
	130.0	75.6	57.3	47.5			% Profit Before Taxes/Tangible Net Worth	41.6	44.4
	(36) 58.6	(120) 36.7	(171) 36.0	(70) 27.4				(242) 18.2	(341) 15.9
	26.0	10.8	12.1	12.1				4.1	2.3
	47.0	31.4	23.1	15.9			% Profit Before Taxes/Total Assets	17.2	15.0
	15.1	11.4	12.9	9.4				6.4	4.4
	3.4	2.2	3.9	3.8				1.2	.0
	45.8	30.7	24.0	24.5			Sales/Net Fixed Assets	21.4	21.9
	13.8	13.2	10.8	7.4				10.4	10.6
	6.6	5.7	5.4	3.3				5.2	5.4
	7.5	4.4	3.2	2.9			Sales/Total Assets	3.6	3.6
	4.9	3.2	2.5	2.1				2.6	2.6
	3.3	2.4	2.0	1.6				1.9	2.0
	1.1	1.2	1.3	.9			% Depr., Dep., Amort./Sales	1.4	1.6
	(37) 2.5	(106) 2.5	(163) 2.5	(66) 2.4				(248) 2.9	(332) 3.1
	5.2	5.1	4.4	4.5				5.1	5.5
	3.8	2.1	1.2	1.2			% Officers', Directors' Owners' Comp/Sales	2.2	1.9
	(31) 6.7	(64) 4.0	(83) 2.1	(19) 2.3				(148) 3.9	(191) 3.6
	10.3	6.8	4.2	3.8				6.6	5.6
	80973M	574816M	2446630M	3790477M	880003M	4768955M	Net Sales ($)	8226719M	6884049M
	13030M	163474M	898070M	1514086M	474947M	1184198M	Total Assets ($)	2473726M	2318159M

M = $ thousand   MM = $ million

See Pages 11 through 21 for Explanation of Ratios and Data

Comparative Historical Data | Current Data Sorted by Sales

Hist 4/1/04-3/31/05 ALL	Hist 4/1/05-3/31/06 ALL	Hist 4/1/06-3/31/07 ALL	Type of Statement	0-1MM	1-3MM	3-5MM	5-10MM	10-25MM	25MM & OVER
72	58	63	Unqualified		8	3	8	15	29
114	117	126	Reviewed	3	7	19	37	41	19
62	56	56	Compiled	5	11	11	14	8	7
73	69	77	Tax Returns	19	16	20	9	9	4
95	120	137	Other	5	25	19	30	34	24
					81 (4/1-9/30/06)		378 (10/1/06-3/31/07)		
416	420	459	**NUMBER OF STATEMENTS**	32	67	72	98	107	83
%	%	%	**ASSETS**	%	%	%	%	%	%
10.4	11.4	11.4	Cash & Equivalents	14.6	14.8	7.4	10.8	11.6	11.2
39.1	39.2	39.1	Trade Receivables (net)	19.4	30.7	43.5	41.6	40.2	45.4
4.0	3.1	3.1	Inventory	5.2	1.4	2.9	3.3	3.3	3.5
5.6	5.1	5.5	All Other Current	6.0	2.8	5.0	4.8	6.3	7.4
59.1	58.8	59.1	Total Current	45.2	49.8	58.8	60.5	61.5	67.5
33.4	33.1	33.0	Fixed Assets (net)	50.2	39.6	32.7	31.3	30.5	26.3
1.2	2.1	1.7	Intangibles (net)	.0	3.5	.7	1.9	.9	2.5
6.3	6.0	6.3	All Other Non-Current	4.6	7.0	7.8	6.3	7.1	3.8
100.0	100.0	100.0	Total	100.0	100.0	100.0	100.0	100.0	100.0
			LIABILITIES						
9.5	7.9	8.0	Notes Payable-Short Term	14.4	9.4	9.6	7.6	5.6	6.8
5.7	6.2	5.1	Cur. Mat.-L.T.D.	4.0	7.5	5.7	5.0	4.8	3.7
19.2	19.2	17.8	Trade Payables	9.7	12.7	19.5	18.0	19.1	21.9
.6	.5	.4	Income Taxes Payable	.2	.3	.2	.9	.3	.3
10.2	9.3	9.9	All Other Current	11.1	10.2	9.0	7.4	10.3	12.5
45.3	43.1	41.3	Total Current	39.4	40.2	44.0	38.9	40.0	45.3
21.5	22.3	19.7	Long-Term Debt	49.8	24.6	20.2	16.2	14.6	14.5
.9	1.0	.6	Deferred Taxes	.3	.2	.6	.9	.7	.8
4.2	3.6	4.1	All Other Non-Current	11.8	4.2	3.4	3.4	2.3	3.3
28.0	30.0	34.2	Net Worth	-1.4	30.7	30.0	40.8	42.4	36.2
100.0	100.0	100.0	Total Liabilities & Net Worth	100.0	100.0	100.0	100.0	100.0	100.0
			INCOME DATA						
100.0	100.0	100.0	Net Sales	100.0	100.0	100.0	100.0	100.0	100.0
26.8	27.8	29.2	Gross Profit	48.8	39.6	31.5	27.0	24.8	19.3
22.9	22.1	23.4	Operating Expenses	44.5	33.6	26.5	21.3	18.6	13.1
3.9	5.7	5.7	Operating Profit	4.4	6.0	5.0	5.7	6.3	6.2
.6	.6	.5	All Other Expenses (net)	1.3	.6	.4	.3	.6	.5
3.3	5.1	5.2	Profit Before Taxes	3.1	5.3	4.6	5.4	5.7	5.7
			RATIOS						
2.0	2.2	2.3		2.9	2.1	2.1	2.6	2.3	2.1
1.4	1.4	1.5	Current	1.1	1.3	1.4	1.6	1.5	1.5
1.0	1.1	1.0		.3	.8	.9	1.1	1.0	1.2
1.7	1.9	1.9		2.4	2.1	1.9	2.4	1.7	1.9
(415) 1.1	(419) 1.2	1.3	Quick	.9	1.2	1.2	1.3	1.3	1.3
.8	.8	.8		.3	.8	.8	.9	.8	.9
35 10.3	30 12.1	29 12.5		0 UND	10 36.1	38 9.7	34 10.8	36 10.1	38 9.5
51 7.1	51 7.2	50 7.3	Sales/Receivables	9 40.9	39 9.3	49 7.5	51 7.1	54 6.7	63 5.7
75 4.9	75 4.9	76 4.8		49 7.5	67 5.5	77 4.8	76 4.8	76 4.8	82 4.5
0 UND	0 UND	0 UND		0 UND	0 UND	0 UND	0 UND	0 UND	0 UND
0 UND	0 UND	0 UND	Cost of Sales/Inventory	0 UND	0 UND	0 UND	0 UND	999.8	1 508.3
8 47.7	5 73.1	5 76.4		0 UND	1 454.0	4 94.1	5 76.0	6 60.6	1 55.8
14 26.9	12 29.8	10 35.8		0 UND	1 485.0	11 33.4	14 25.5	14 26.2	15 23.6
29 12.7	26 14.0	28 13.3	Cost of Sales/Payables	0 UND	17 21.3	33 11.2	28 13.1	28 12.9	30 12.1
48 7.6	44 8.3	46 8.0		31 11.6	46 8.0	52 7.0	44 8.2	45 8.1	46 7.9
8.3	7.6	7.6		9.2	11.4	9.1	6.6	6.7	7.3
19.2	16.0	17.0	Sales/Working Capital	338.8	27.7	19.2	15.7	15.2	12.8
-590.4	135.3	386.0		-9.8	-33.3	-130.7	55.7	102.9	25.2
13.1	18.5	20.8		9.0	16.8	16.8	26.2	21.4	36.1
(376) 4.6	(386) 5.6	(418) 6.8	EBIT/Interest	(28) 2.9	(58) 3.9	(67) 3.7	(92) 8.1	(99) 8.5	(74) 8.7
1.7	2.1	2.0		-.4	1.7	1.9	1.7	2.5	3.7
3.5	4.9	4.4				4.6	3.7	5.4	6.9
(103) 1.9	(106) 2.2	(101) 2.2	Net Profit + Depr., Dep., Amort./Cur. Mat. L/T/D			(14) 2.1	(23) 2.0	(29) 2.2	(27) 2.6
1.0	1.1	1.3				1.2	1.0	1.3	1.8
.4	.4	.3		.6	.4	.4	.3	.2	.3
.9	.9	.8	Fixed/Worth	2.8	1.3	.9	.8	.6	.6
2.7	2.4	2.3		-5.3	13.4	4.9	2.2	1.6	1.7
1.0	.9	.7		.8	.7	.9	.6	.7	.8
2.3	2.0	1.8	Debt/Worth	3.0	2.1	2.0	1.6	1.4	2.1
7.1	6.1	4.8		-7.9	18.4	6.6	5.0	3.2	4.0
47.8	62.0	64.8		67.2	78.8	65.5	66.6	54.4	62.0
(360) 24.1	(365) 28.5	(409) 35.6	% Profit Before Taxes/Tangible Net Worth	(21) 29.0	(54) 53.1	(58) 32.8	(92) 36.4	(106) 34.2	(78) 37.9
8.3	13.9	12.9		6.1	16.2	9.9	9.9	12.9	22.5
15.2	24.4	25.5		25.5	33.2	24.5	28.6	22.9	25.7
6.5	9.4	11.5	% Profit Before Taxes/Total Assets	6.6	12.3	8.5	12.9	12.9	13.5
1.3	3.1	3.4		-12.2	3.7	1.6	2.2	4.4	5.2
23.2	25.6	27.9		15.1	35.6	25.9	22.3	28.3	33.3
10.7	11.1	11.2	Sales/Net Fixed Assets	8.8	8.6	11.3	11.4	11.3	12.5
5.2	5.4	5.4		3.8	4.2	5.7	5.6	5.4	5.7
3.7	3.9	3.9		5.4	4.5	4.0	3.5	3.4	3.6
2.7	2.8	2.8	Sales/Total Assets	3.3	2.9	3.0	2.7	2.6	2.7
2.0	2.0	2.1		2.0	1.9	2.1	2.2	2.0	2.0
1.4	1.3	1.2		1.9	1.3	1.2	1.4	1.1	.7
(350) 2.6	(363) 2.5	(384) 2.4	% Depr., Dep., Amort./Sales	(26) 3.7	(42) 4.2	(60) 2.4	(84) 2.7	(97) 2.4	(75) 1.5
4.9	4.5	4.8		8.4	7.3	5.7	4.5	3.7	2.9
1.9	1.7	1.6		4.4	2.9	2.6	1.3	1.1	.7
(191) 3.7	(195) 3.1	(201) 3.1	% Officers', Directors' Owners' Comp/Sales	(20) 9.3	(27) 4.9	(33) 4.9	(51) 2.6	(49) 2.0	(21) 2.0
6.4	6.1	6.4		16.5	8.1	4.6	3.3	3.3	3.7
11303801M	10119761M	12541854M	Net Sales ($)	17424M	132126M	275188M	707681M	1735393M	9674042M
3311610M	4185729M	4247805M	Total Assets ($)	9645M	57680M	107634M	285151M	769541M	3018154M

© RMA 2007

M = $ thousand   MM = $ million
See Pages 11 through 21 for Explanation of Ratios and Data

Current Data Sorted by Assets   Comparative Historical Data

0-500M	500M-2MM	2-10MM	10-50MM	50-100MM	100-250MM	Type of Statement	4/1/02-3/31/03 ALL	4/1/03-3/31/04 ALL
	3	17	27	1	5	Unqualified	25	28
1	11	32	14			Reviewed	45	57
2	13	8	2		2	Compiled	19	29
13	14	8				Tax Returns	6	18
5	10	16	11	2	2	Other	17	47
	45 (4/1-9/30/06)		172 (10/1/06-3/31/07)					
21	51	81	54	3	7	NUMBER OF STATEMENTS	112	179
%	%	%	%	%	%	**ASSETS**	%	%
13.4	12.2	10.9	12.7			Cash & Equivalents	8.9	9.9
41.2	45.5	50.7	48.0			Trade Receivables (net)	44.8	44.7
2.1	5.5	4.9	4.3			Inventory	3.2	4.6
8.2	8.2	7.9	9.1			All Other Current	10.9	8.6
64.9	71.4	74.4	74.1			Total Current	67.8	67.9
22.2	19.5	19.6	21.7			Fixed Assets (net)	22.7	23.3
1.6	2.1	.7	.7			Intangibles (net)	1.7	1.1
11.3	7.1	5.4	3.5			All Other Non-Current	7.9	7.8
100.0	100.0	100.0	100.0			Total	100.0	100.0
						LIABILITIES		
22.8	11.6	7.6	9.2			Notes Payable-Short Term	11.8	13.3
1.8	3.9	3.9	2.6			Cur. Mat.-L.T.D.	4.4	3.2
11.1	12.8	17.8	17.0			Trade Payables	16.1	17.0
.0	.6	1.0	.5			Income Taxes Payable	.8	.5
27.3	10.8	14.5	19.9			All Other Current	15.1	14.6
62.9	39.7	44.8	49.1			Total Current	48.1	48.6
31.4	15.0	10.8	12.8			Long-Term Debt	13.6	14.2
.0	.4	.8	.4			Deferred Taxes	.7	1.0
1.7	3.0	2.7	3.0			All Other Non-Current	2.5	3.8
4.0	41.9	40.8	34.7			Net Worth	35.0	32.5
100.0	100.0	100.0	100.0			Total Liabilities & Net Worth	100.0	100.0
						INCOME DATA		
100.0	100.0	100.0	100.0			Net Sales	100.0	100.0
33.5	32.0	22.1	18.4			Gross Profit	22.9	23.3
30.6	24.9	16.6	11.8			Operating Expenses	20.8	22.1
2.9	7.1	5.5	6.5			Operating Profit	2.2	1.2
.5	1.4	.4	.5			All Other Expenses (net)	.8	.5
2.3	5.6	5.1	6.0			Profit Before Taxes	1.4	.6
						RATIOS		
3.1	3.7	2.6	1.8			Current	2.1	2.1
1.2	1.9	1.6	1.4				1.5	1.5
.6	1.2	1.3	1.2				1.1	1.1
2.9	3.1	2.2	1.5			Quick	1.6	1.7
1.0	1.4	1.4	1.2				1.2	1.2
.2	.6	.9	1.0				.9	.8
0 UND	33 11.2	49 7.4	57 6.5			Sales/Receivables	43 8.5	46 7.9
38 9.6	64 5.7	67 5.4	83 4.4				61 5.9	68 5.4
61 5.9	86 4.2	88 4.1	94 3.9				93 3.9	96 3.8
0 UND	0 UND	0 UND	0 UND			Cost of Sales/Inventory	0 UND	0 UND
0 UND	0 UND	0 UND	2 184.8				0 UND	0 868.5
0 UND	13 29.1	14 27.0	13 29.1				7 52.4	10 36.8
0 UND	4 81.5	15 24.2	16 22.8			Cost of Sales/Payables	11 32.3	14 26.5
3 110.5	20 17.8	26 13.9	31 11.7				22 16.3	28 13.2
20 18.5	35 10.4	48 7.6	46 7.9				47 7.7	47 7.7
10.9	4.5	5.6	6.6			Sales/Working Capital	6.4	6.0
44.2	7.4	9.0	11.9				12.9	12.3
-39.2	26.1	16.4	18.8				40.8	52.9
23.2	36.6	26.3	27.9			EBIT/Interest	6.9	8.2
(16) 3.7	(43) 5.7	(69) 5.7	(50) 6.5				(99) 2.3	(157) 1.9
.4	1.9	2.2	3.0				-1.3	-2.6
		4.8	17.9			Net Profit + Depr., Dep.,	5.0	4.2
		(30) 2.8	(18) 7.0			Amort./Cur. Mat. L/T/D	(31) 1.8	(50) 1.4
		1.8	2.3				.3	.2
.1	.1	.2	.2			Fixed/Worth	.2	.3
.7	.3	.4	.5				.5	.5
-15.1	1.1	.8	1.2				1.0	1.5
.7	.5	.8	1.2			Debt/Worth	.8	.9
3.5	1.4	1.6	2.2				1.6	1.8
-14.3	3.4	2.9	4.0				3.5	4.6
321.7	68.4	62.1	61.0			% Profit Before Taxes/Tangible	26.8	27.7
(14) 60.0	(44) 29.8	(78) 28.8	(53) 38.1			Net Worth	(100) 10.5	(160) 7.0
17.7	9.0	6.7	17.5				-1.8	-12.2
45.3	30.0	21.4	19.7			% Profit Before Taxes/Total	11.4	8.0
13.6	12.7	9.9	10.8			Assets	2.5	2.2
-5.0	2.0	3.1	5.5				-2.7	-7.4
243.0	66.2	38.9	31.5			Sales/Net Fixed Assets	48.5	30.7
34.8	29.4	19.0	14.1				15.3	12.8
15.2	9.3	7.3	6.5				7.9	6.7
12.2	3.5	3.0	2.8			Sales/Total Assets	3.6	3.1
4.5	2.8	2.4	2.2				2.6	2.3
3.8	2.0	2.0	1.7				1.9	1.7
.6	.7	.6	.7			% Depr., Dep., Amort./Sales	.7	.8
(13) 1.0	(40) 1.3	(75) 1.2	(51) 1.1				(101) 1.7	(156) 1.7
2.5	3.2	2.6	2.7				3.4	3.3
	2.6	1.7	1.0			% Officers', Directors'	1.4	1.6
	(25) 3.9	(42) 2.6	(10) 2.6			Owners' Comp/Sales	(49) 4.4	(76) 3.4
	5.7	6.1	4.7				7.2	5.9
34459M	182167M	1025644M	2324444M	564728M	2406673M	Net Sales ($)	1548513M	3598920M
5450M	65101M	391039M	1016191M	227488M	1124543M	Total Assets ($)	785998M	1650075M

M = $ thousand   MM = $ million

See Pages 11 through 21 for Explanation of Ratios and Data

Comparative Historical Data / Current Data Sorted by Sales

Comparative Historical Data			Type of Statement	Current Data Sorted by Sales					
34	33	53	Unqualified		1	3	8	12	29
50	42	58	Reviewed		4	8	9	26	11
21	16	25	Compiled		6	8	5	4	2
15	15	35	Tax Returns	5	13	7	8	1	1
23	51	46	Other	1	7	8	7	8	15
4/1/04-3/31/05 ALL	4/1/05-3/31/06 ALL	4/1/06-3/31/07 ALL			45 (4/1-9/30/06)		172 (10/1/06-3/31/07)		
143	157	217	**NUMBER OF STATEMENTS**	6	31	34	37	51	58
%	%	%	**ASSETS**	%	%	%	%	%	%
9.0	9.3	11.6	Cash & Equivalents		15.1	9.6	10.5	14.8	9.1
49.4	50.0	47.9	Trade Receivables (net)		36.0	47.0	52.0	45.5	54.3
6.4	3.9	5.1	Inventory		5.5	6.2	4.2	4.4	5.9
7.3	9.5	8.3	All Other Current		8.5	8.3	8.5	8.4	8.7
72.1	72.7	72.8	Total Current		65.1	71.0	75.3	73.0	78.0
21.9	21.7	20.2	Fixed Assets (net)		23.0	17.6	20.0	20.7	17.9
1.3	1.4	1.2	Intangibles (net)		3.1	1.9	.0	.9	1.0
4.6	4.2	5.8	All Other Non-Current		8.8	9.5	4.7	5.4	3.1
100.0	100.0	100.0	Total		100.0	100.0	100.0	100.0	100.0
			LIABILITIES						
12.7	10.4	10.5	Notes Payable-Short Term		20.0	9.4	8.6	7.1	9.8
6.0	2.8	3.2	Cur. Mat.-L.T.D.		3.6	3.8	3.4	3.9	1.9
17.7	17.7	15.7	Trade Payables		11.4	15.9	12.4	19.9	18.0
.7	.6	.6	Income Taxes Payable		.4	.5	1.3	.8	.4
13.0	14.1	16.8	All Other Current		14.6	12.1	16.4	11.8	22.8
50.0	45.6	46.9	Total Current		49.9	41.7	42.0	43.5	52.9
11.3	13.0	14.3	Long-Term Debt		24.7	10.9	17.8	11.4	9.8
.6	.6	.5	Deferred Taxes		.1	.5	.4	1.1	.4
4.3	3.9	2.7	All Other Non-Current		3.5	3.2	1.9	3.2	2.3
33.7	36.8	35.6	Net Worth		21.8	43.7	37.9	40.8	34.5
100.0	100.0	100.0	Total Liabilities & Net Worth		100.0	100.0	100.0	100.0	100.0
			INCOME DATA						
100.0	100.0	100.0	Net Sales		100.0	100.0	100.0	100.0	100.0
21.2	21.5	24.4	Gross Profit		33.8	30.7	25.5	20.8	17.0
18.8	16.3	18.4	Operating Expenses		27.7	24.2	20.2	14.5	10.7
2.5	5.2	6.0	Operating Profit		6.1	6.5	5.3	6.3	6.4
.2	.6	.7	All Other Expenses (net)		2.1	.6	.1	.4	.5
2.2	4.6	5.3	Profit Before Taxes		4.0	5.9	5.3	5.9	5.9
			RATIOS						
2.2	2.3	2.5			3.3	3.3	3.5	2.5	1.8
1.5	1.5	1.5	Current		1.5	1.7	1.6	1.7	1.4
1.1	1.2	1.2			.9	1.3	1.2	1.3	1.2
1.7	1.9	2.0			2.4	3.2	2.9	2.0	1.5
1.2	1.2	1.3	Quick		1.1	1.4	1.5	1.4	1.2
.8	1.0	.9			.5	.7	.8	1.1	1.0
51 7.2	52 7.0	47 7.8			0 UND	41 9.0	48 7.6	51 7.2	56 6.5
76 4.8	73 5.0	68 5.4	Sales/Receivables		39 9.3	67 5.5	71 5.2	67 5.4	85 4.3
104 3.5	96 3.8	91 4.0			71 5.1	87 4.2	91 4.0	84 4.3	99 3.7
0 UND	0 UND	0 UND			0 UND	0 UND	0 UND	0 UND	0 UND
1 297.8	0 UND	0 UND	Cost of Sales/Inventory		0 UND	0 UND	0 UND	0 UND	3 104.7
13 28.7	8 44.5	12 29.7			13 29.1	20 18.4	17 21.2	11 32.5	14 25.2
14 25.8	15 24.2	11 32.8			2 226.7	9 42.6	10 37.3	16 22.6	19 19.2
27 13.5	27 13.7	25 14.6	Cost of Sales/Payables		15 24.5	21 17.5	23 16.2	27 13.5	30 12.1
48 7.5	48 7.5	44 8.2			26 14.1	49 7.4	38 9.6	59 6.2	44 8.3
6.2	5.7	5.8			5.8	5.0	4.6	5.3	6.8
11.0	10.2	10.5	Sales/Working Capital		15.3	8.9	7.7	8.8	12.9
42.4	21.2	21.7			-81.6	16.2	20.8	17.6	18.5
11.3	18.3	27.3			12.7	35.4	32.4	24.0	30.2
(127) 5.4	(148) 5.6	(188) 6.2	EBIT/Interest		(28) 3.6	(28) 9.9	(32) 4.9	(43) 5.7	(54) 9.5
1.5	2.0	2.4			1.3	2.6	1.8	1.6	4.1
4.4	9.1	9.0					3.6	6.3	17.9
(45) 2.3	(51) 3.1	(59) 4.2	Net Profit + Depr., Dep., Amort./Cur. Mat. L/T/D				(12) 2.8	(19) 3.2	(18) 7.0
1.1	1.8	2.2					2.0	1.8	2.3
.2	.2	.2			.1	.2	.1	.2	.2
.7	.5	.4	Fixed/Worth		.6	.3	.5	.4	.4
1.3	1.0	1.1			6.3	.8	1.6	.9	.8
.8	.8	.8			.5	.5	.5	.8	1.2
2.0	1.9	1.8	Debt/Worth		2.5	1.4	1.7	1.6	2.2
4.7	3.5	3.9			59.0	2.3	5.1	2.9	3.7
44.8	59.5	63.9			111.9	71.8	59.4	57.4	65.5
(129) 20.6	(146) 27.3	(199) 35.7	% Profit Before Taxes/Tangible Net Worth		(24) 38.4	(31) 43.3	(35) 29.0	(49) 26.7	(57) 46.6
1.7	8.2	12.7			10.9	8.7	5.3	7.9	22.0
15.1	20.0	21.7			30.3	33.0	19.4	21.4	19.8
6.3	8.1	11.8	% Profit Before Taxes/Total Assets		7.5	16.5	8.2	12.1	11.9
.5	2.2	3.3			.2	3.1	1.9	3.0	6.2
38.6	35.1	44.4			83.1	42.3	46.9	32.5	37.8
13.6	14.7	19.7	Sales/Net Fixed Assets		32.7	27.3	19.3	16.6	19.1
7.5	8.1	7.6			7.5	10.1	6.6	7.2	8.3
3.1	3.1	3.3			6.1	3.6	3.1	3.0	3.0
2.5	2.5	2.6	Sales/Total Assets		3.1	2.7	2.5	2.3	2.6
1.8	1.9	2.0			1.7	2.2	2.0	1.9	1.9
.9	.6	.7			.6	.6	.7	.6	.6
(130) 1.7	(146) 1.1	(187) 1.1	% Depr., Dep., Amort./Sales		(21) 1.6	(28) 1.1	(32) 2.1	(48) 1.1	(54) .9
3.1	2.1	2.6			4.5	2.3	2.8	2.4	1.7
1.6	1.3	1.8			3.1	2.3	1.8	1.6	.4
(61) 3.2	(61) 2.4	(87) 3.3	% Officers', Directors' Owners' Comp/Sales		(14) 4.7	(17) 3.6	(18) 2.5	(27) 2.6	(10) 2.2
5.2	3.6	5.9			9.2	5.2	5.4	5.4	5.1
3154830M	4666144M	6538115M	Net Sales ($)	3218M	53577M	139299M	275832M	799833M	5266356M
1461645M	2295996M	2829812M	Total Assets ($)	1766M	20582M	52572M	113773M	374816M	2266303M

M = $ thousand   MM = $ million
See Pages 11 through 21 for Explanation of Ratios and Data

Current Data Sorted by Assets | | | | | | **Comparative Historical Data**

Type of Statement

	0-500M	500M-2MM	2-10MM	10-50MM	50-100MM	100-250MM	4/1/02-3/31/03 ALL	4/1/03-3/31/04 ALL
Unqualified			1	1		1	1	3
Reviewed	4	4	3	4			9	6
Compiled	10	3	4			1	6	11
Tax Returns	3	1	5				4	5
Other		10	7	6		2	4	8
	16 (4/1-9/30/06)			54 (10/1/06-3/31/07)			24	33
NUMBER OF STATEMENTS	17	18	20	11		4	24	33
	%	%	%	%	%	%	%	%
ASSETS								
Cash & Equivalents	17.9	14.1	20.9	17.0			11.9	13.4
Trade Receivables (net)	20.9	39.1	38.4	36.4			51.3	38.5
Inventory	9.8	10.6	11.1	6.5			10.6	13.1
All Other Current	6.1	5.9	6.7	17.3			7.6	3.1
Total Current	54.6	69.6	77.1	77.2			81.5	68.1
Fixed Assets (net)	25.5	20.8	15.9	10.0			14.0	25.3
Intangibles (net)	7.0	4.5	.5	9.7			.5	1.3
All Other Non-Current	12.9	5.1	6.5	3.1			4.0	5.4
Total	100.0	100.0	100.0	100.0			100.0	100.0
LIABILITIES								
Notes Payable-Short Term	26.6	17.7	4.5	11.8			22.0	9.7
Cur. Mat.-L.T.D.	7.5	5.5	3.5	1.0			3.7	12.3
Trade Payables	16.8	15.0	16.0	16.6			24.9	16.2
Income Taxes Payable	.0	.4	.4	.2			.5	.3
All Other Current	15.8	19.5	19.2	18.2			9.7	23.5
Total Current	66.7	58.1	43.6	47.9			60.9	62.1
Long-Term Debt	18.9	17.8	9.8	3.5			9.3	18.9
Deferred Taxes	.0	.1	.2	.0			.1	2.0
All Other Non-Current	14.2	3.3	1.4	5.6			6.8	3.3
Net Worth	.2	20.5	45.0	43.0			23.0	13.7
Total Liabilties & Net Worth	100.0	100.0	100.0	100.0			100.0	100.0
INCOME DATA								
Net Sales	100.0	100.0	100.0	100.0			100.0	100.0
Gross Profit	43.3	28.8	36.8	17.7			20.6	24.5
Operating Expenses	39.9	27.8	33.2	13.4			16.6	22.9
Operating Profit	3.4	1.0	3.6	4.4			3.9	1.6
All Other Expenses (net)	-.1	1.0	.1	.4			.4	.5
Profit Before Taxes	3.5	.0	3.4	4.0			3.5	1.1
RATIOS								
Current	4.9	2.1	2.8	2.3			2.0	2.1
	.9	1.4	2.0	1.5			1.4	1.4
	.2	.8	1.2	1.4			1.1	.8
Quick	3.5	2.0	2.2	2.0			1.8	1.7
	.4	1.3	1.3	1.1			1.1	1.1
	.2	.5	.8	.8			.8	.6
Sales/Receivables	0 UND	21 17.7	17 22.1	26 14.2			25 14.6	10 35.2
	8 44.4	38 9.7	41 9.0	43 8.5			53 6.9	37 9.8
	19 19.3	65 5.6	62 5.9	57 6.4			74 4.9	70 5.2
Cost of Sales/Inventory	0 UND	0 UND	0 UND	0 UND			0 UND	0 UND
	0 UND	1 269.7	4 86.2	0 999.8			0 UND	2 203.2
	13 29.1	34 10.6	40 9.1	20 18.0			16 23.2	35 10.3
Cost of Sales/Payables	0 UND	10 36.8	7 52.4	5 79.5			10 35.4	8 46.6
	8 45.6	25 14.6	17 21.0	26 14.0			24 14.9	17 21.9
	29 12.5	35 10.5	50 7.3	37 9.9			42 8.6	36 10.2
Sales/Working Capital	19.6	7.7	4.3	7.9			7.4	9.0
	-161.4	30.1	11.5	8.6			23.8	18.9
	-10.8	-33.5	22.1	15.7			44.0	-46.2
EBIT/Interest	8.7	21.1	32.5	117.6			29.0	24.2
	(13) 3.4	(15) 7.8	(18) 6.1	8.9			(19) 11.4	(30) 3.5
	.4	2.0	1.9	2.8			.4	-1.1
Net Profit + Depr., Dep., Amort./Cur. Mat. L/T/D								23.4
							(10) 1.0
								-1.5
Fixed/Worth	.2	.2	.1	.2			.1	.2
	-8.6	.4	.2	.3			.5	.5
	-.3	NM	.9	.8			2.1	NM
Debt/Worth	.4	.6	.6	1.2			1.1	1.2
	-11.6	1.7	.9	1.5			3.2	2.8
	-3.6	NM	7.2	4.1			13.8	NM
% Profit Before Taxes/Tangible Net Worth		72.3	53.6	89.1			112.8	55.7
		(14) 29.9	(18) 22.9	(10) 25.3			(19) 47.5	(25) 12.1
		20.4	6.5	10.0			17.3	-5.7
% Profit Before Taxes/Total Assets	71.2	27.5	19.5	14.5			18.9	14.5
	20.5	10.9	5.7	6.4			10.9	3.3
	-2.7	4.7	.7	3.9			.2	-6.1
Sales/Net Fixed Assets	337.2	58.6	86.8	153.6			126.8	55.3
	43.6	34.6	30.4	36.0			42.9	33.3
	17.9	19.7	11.3	22.5			17.7	12.5
Sales/Total Assets	12.3	5.6	5.5	3.5			4.6	5.4
	5.6	3.3	3.0	2.9			4.0	2.7
	4.7	2.0	2.2	2.4			3.1	2.2
% Depr., Dep., Amort./Sales	.5	.5	.2	.2			.3	.4
	(11) 1.0	(12) 1.2	(16) .6	.8			(20) 1.0	(29) 1.0
	1.9	1.6	.9	.9			1.7	2.2
% Officers', Directors' Owners' Comp/Sales	2.7		.8				1.6	.8
	(11) 6.2		(13) 2.0				(12) 1.8	(14) 3.6
	13.7		3.2				4.0	6.0
Net Sales ($)	36048M	85922M	322220M	737418M		2178850M	279115M	367604M
Total Assets ($)	4641M	19599M	87984M	242356M		666737M	70032M	161555M

(The region for the 50-100MM and 100-250MM columns is marked: DATA NOT AVAILABLE)

M = $ thousand　　MM = $ million
See Pages 11 through 21 for Explanation of Ratios and Data

Comparative Historical Data   **Current Data Sorted by Sales**

4/1/04-3/31/05 ALL	4/1/05-3/31/06 ALL	4/1/06-3/31/07 ALL	Type of Statement	0-1MM	1-3MM	3-5MM	5-10MM	10-25MM	25MM & OVER
1	3	3	Unqualified		2			1	
8	10	11	Reviewed		4		1	2	4
8	6	11	Compiled	1	2	2	3	2	1
5	9	17	Tax Returns	2	4	2	2	4	3
9	14	28	Other	1	8	2	3	4	10
				16 (4/1-9/30/06)			54 (10/1/06-3/31/07)		
31	42	70	**NUMBER OF STATEMENTS**	4	20	6	9	13	18
%	%	%	**ASSETS**	%	%	%	%	%	%
14.6	16.9	17.8	Cash & Equivalents		12.9			21.9	19.6
42.6	40.5	32.5	Trade Receivables (net)		29.0			35.5	32.0
12.1	11.0	9.7	Inventory		13.1			6.0	6.8
10.1	6.3	7.8	All Other Current		7.5			9.1	12.3
79.5	74.7	67.9	Total Current		62.5			72.6	70.7
14.5	16.1	20.7	Fixed Assets (net)		21.3			19.8	20.6
1.4	3.5	4.5	Intangibles (net)		4.0			.2	6.3
4.6	5.7	6.8	All Other Non-Current		12.2			7.5	2.5
100.0	100.0	100.0	Total		100.0			100.0	100.0
			LIABILITIES						
14.3	13.9	14.5	Notes Payable-Short Term		19.0			3.1	10.4
3.1	3.6	4.5	Cur. Mat.-L.T.D.		4.0			4.3	1.0
20.5	20.3	15.5	Trade Payables		17.5			16.7	16.6
.5	.6	.2	Income Taxes Payable		.0			.1	.5
27.1	20.3	17.5	All Other Current		18.4			23.1	14.1
65.5	58.8	52.2	Total Current		58.9			47.3	42.6
11.1	12.7	13.7	Long-Term Debt		21.4			6.5	7.0
.0	.2	.1	Deferred Taxes		.2			.0	.0
2.2	3.9	6.3	All Other Non-Current		12.3			.6	6.4
21.1	24.4	27.6	Net Worth		7.2			45.5	44.0
100.0	100.0	100.0	Total Liabilities & Net Worth		100.0			100.0	100.0
			INCOME DATA						
100.0	100.0	100.0	Net Sales		100.0			100.0	100.0
18.9	21.8	33.8	Gross Profit		34.3			35.5	28.2
16.1	21.4	30.5	Operating Expenses		35.3			31.0	23.6
2.8	.4	3.2	Operating Profit		-1.0			4.5	4.5
.5	.2	.4	All Other Expenses (net)		.4			.5	.4
2.3	.1	2.8	Profit Before Taxes		-1.4			4.1	4.1
			RATIOS						
1.8	2.4	2.7	Current		2.7			2.4	2.7
1.4	1.3	1.6			1.1			1.6	2.0
1.0	.9	.9			.5			1.0	1.3
1.7	1.6	2.1	Quick		2.1			2.0	2.3
1.1	1.2	1.1			.6			1.0	1.4
.5	.6	.6			.2			.8	.8
16 22.2	14 25.6	12 31.2	Sales/Receivables		10 38.3			14 25.3	17 21.9
34 10.8	37 9.8	31 11.9			25 14.8			38 9.6	33 11.1
59 6.2	74 5.0	50 7.4			53 6.8			51 7.2	46 8.0
0 UND	0 UND	0 UND	Cost of Sales/Inventory		0 UND			0 UND	0 UND
1 575.4	0 UND	1 658.2			0 UND			2 222.8	1 523.2
25 14.6	27 13.6	31 11.8			47 7.8			52 7.0	21 17.4
10 38.0	1 304.0	6 62.5	Cost of Sales/Payables		10 36.1			3 114.2	5 80.9
17 22.1	22 16.5	18 20.6			22 16.2			13 28.2	19 19.5
28 13.0	51 7.1	36 10.2			41 8.8			37 9.9	37 10.0
12.7	8.6	8.2	Sales/Working Capital		6.8			9.7	7.9
20.5	25.5	15.4			NM			13.6	11.5
-258.4	-83.8	-76.7			-10.7			545.3	35.3
12.9	19.9	25.8	EBIT/Interest		8.6			47.9	44.0
(23) 7.7	(33) 3.1	(61) 6.6			(16) 2.8			(10) 6.1	10.7
2.2	-.4	2.1			-2.9			.9	3.0
			Net Profit + Depr., Dep., Amort./Cur. Mat. L/T/D						
.1	.1	.1	Fixed/Worth		.1			.1	.2
.3	.3	.4			.5			.2	.4
2.2	-4.3	6.2			-.7			1.0	1.2
.9	1.0	.6	Debt/Worth		.6			.5	.7
3.2	2.9	1.4			2.0			.9	1.4
9.7	-52.5	25.6			-3.1			7.1	4.2
84.1	81.5	76.1	% Profit Before Taxes/Tangible Net Worth		61.3			77.7	70.7
(25) 29.3	(31) 30.3	(54) 38.6			(12) 41.2			(12) 42.9	(16) 24.1
15.5	.3	16.2			20.3			10.5	15.7
20.1	18.9	30.2	% Profit Before Taxes/Total Assets		25.5			38.9	17.1
12.8	7.4	10.5			7.6			11.7	10.5
2.0	-2.3	3.6			-4.1			.9	4.0
166.6	207.7	74.7	Sales/Net Fixed Assets		69.3			135.6	105.9
40.3	41.6	33.8			33.0			30.1	28.7
16.7	16.0	13.3			11.8			13.9	10.6
6.0	6.3	5.6	Sales/Total Assets		5.4			5.6	4.2
4.2	3.5	3.5			3.4			3.6	3.4
3.3	2.5	2.5			1.9			2.5	2.5
.1	.2	.4	% Depr., Dep., Amort./Sales		.6			.2	.3
(25) .9	(29) .4	(52) .8			(12) 1.6			(10) .6	(15) .8
2.2	1.7	1.6			2.0			2.1	1.3
.8	1.3	1.8	% Officers', Directors', Owners' Comp/Sales		2.5				
(12) 1.6	(17) 2.4	(39) 3.1			(11) 6.2				
3.5	6.4	7.6			8.0				
563512M	824268M	3360458M	Net Sales ($)	2666M	36443M	24387M	64634M	207281M	3025047M
102596M	238650M	1021317M	Total Assets ($)	457M	13526M	8186M	16283M	57020M	925845M

M = $ thousand   MM = $ million
See Pages 11 through 21 for Explanation of Ratios and Data

Current Data Sorted by Assets   Comparative Historical Data

Type of Statement	0-500M	500M-2MM	2-10MM	10-50MM	50-100MM	100-250MM		4/1/02-3/31/03 ALL	4/1/03-3/31/04 ALL
Unqualified		2	13	9	2	1		21	21
Reviewed	2	24	75	6				62	103
Compiled	5	18	13	2		1		26	50
Tax Returns	21	17	6	1				15	32
Other	8	26	14	11		1		23	45
		54 (4/1-9/30/06)		224 (10/1/06-3/31/07)					
NUMBER OF STATEMENTS	36	87	121	29	2	3		147	251

ASSETS

	0-500M	500M-2MM	2-10MM	10-50MM	50-100MM	100-250MM		ALL	ALL
	%	%	%	%	%	%		%	%
Cash & Equivalents	24.8	14.3	11.2	13.5				12.5	11.8
Trade Receivables (net)	18.6	38.7	54.1	50.6				45.8	44.5
Inventory	4.6	6.3	4.3	2.0				3.6	4.5
All Other Current	5.2	5.5	8.2	10.2				8.6	8.1
Total Current	53.2	64.8	77.8	76.4				70.5	69.0
Fixed Assets (net)	34.4	27.3	15.6	17.8				22.4	22.9
Intangibles (net)	1.3	.3	1.9	.1				1.5	1.5
All Other Non-Current	11.1	7.5	4.6	5.7				5.6	6.6
Total	100.0	100.0	100.0	100.0				100.0	100.0

LIABILITIES

	0-500M	500M-2MM	2-10MM	10-50MM	50-100MM	100-250MM		ALL	ALL
Notes Payable-Short Term	16.4	11.2	7.9	8.5				10.5	13.0
Cur. Mat.-L.T.D.	3.5	4.3	2.6	1.5				3.6	3.8
Trade Payables	7.7	13.7	16.7	18.9				17.7	15.9
Income Taxes Payable	.0	.8	1.2	.6				.8	.9
All Other Current	15.8	9.6	16.8	18.7				15.5	14.7
Total Current	43.5	39.6	45.2	48.2				48.1	48.2
Long-Term Debt	44.3	14.3	7.1	7.9				13.1	10.9
Deferred Taxes	.0	.4	.6	.2				.5	.5
All Other Non-Current	10.4	3.5	2.8	1.3				3.9	2.8
Net Worth	1.8	42.1	44.3	42.4				34.5	37.5
Total Liabilities & Net Worth	100.0	100.0	100.0	100.0				100.0	100.0

INCOME DATA

	0-500M	500M-2MM	2-10MM	10-50MM	50-100MM	100-250MM		ALL	ALL
Net Sales	100.0	100.0	100.0	100.0				100.0	100.0
Gross Profit	41.4	30.2	21.3	21.1				24.0	24.6
Operating Expenses	34.8	24.4	15.1	13.6				21.8	22.2
Operating Profit	6.6	5.8	6.2	7.5				2.1	2.4
All Other Expenses (net)	.6	1.4	.4	.1				.2	.4
Profit Before Taxes	6.0	4.4	5.8	7.4				1.9	1.9

RATIOS

	0-500M	500M-2MM	2-10MM	10-50MM	50-100MM	100-250MM		ALL	ALL
Current	4.4	3.2	2.7	2.3				2.3	2.5
	1.7	1.6	1.8	1.6				1.5	1.5
	.8	1.1	1.3	1.2				1.2	1.1
Quick	3.6	2.9	2.4	1.9				1.8	2.1
	1.5	1.3	1.5	1.3				1.3	1.3
	.6	.9	1.0	1.1				.9	.8
Sales/Receivables	0 UND	24 15.4	55 6.6	45 8.1				41 8.8	37 9.8
	0 UND	48 7.6	74 5.0	69 5.3				63 5.8	59 6.2
	36 10.1	67 5.5	97 3.8	98 3.7				79 4.6	82 4.4
Cost of Sales/Inventory	0 UND	0 UND	0 UND	0 UND				0 UND	0 UND
	0 UND	0 UND	0 UND	0 UND				0 UND	0 UND
	0 UND	5 75.3	4 91.5	2 184.1				2 172.9	4 89.0
Cost of Sales/Payables	0 UND	6 64.5	14 26.6	16 22.9				10 36.8	10 36.6
	0 UND	16 23.3	23 15.8	26 13.8				21 17.1	21 17.0
	17 20.9	37 9.8	37 9.9	39 9.4				42 8.6	37 9.9
Sales/Working Capital	12.2	6.5	4.9	4.2				6.6	5.9
	45.0	11.7	7.8	9.6				13.9	12.3
	-194.8	56.5	16.8	24.2				38.2	125.0
EBIT/Interest	58.5	19.7	28.2	87.2				14.2	17.8
	(30) 10.1	(76) 5.8	(107) 10.8	(27) 14.4				(133) 5.2	(218) 5.1
	1.7	1.3	3.1	3.9				1.3	1.7
Net Profit + Depr., Dep., Amort./Cur. Mat. L/T/D		4.3	14.6					12.4	8.9
		(13) 3.3	(37) 6.0					(35) 4.2	(60) 3.1
		2.6	2.0					1.9	1.5
Fixed/Worth	.4	.2	.1	.1				.3	.2
	1.2	.5	.3	.4				.5	.4
	23.0	1.2	.6	.7				1.2	1.2
Debt/Worth	.3	.4	.6	.6				.7	.6
	3.6	1.3	1.2	1.4				1.5	1.5
	47.9	3.7	2.4	3.5				4.6	4.6
% Profit Before Taxes/Tangible Net Worth	258.8	56.5	51.4	62.4				42.9	38.8
	(28) 71.8	(79) 27.1	(115) 26.3	43.8				(134) 15.8	(228) 16.9
	12.0	11.1	9.9	16.5				3.2	4.0
% Profit Before Taxes/Total Assets	104.3	29.6	23.2	35.4				17.5	15.3
	26.1	11.2	11.2	10.0				4.5	5.4
	-.4	1.3	3.6	4.4				.1	1.3
Sales/Net Fixed Assets	45.5	40.3	41.0	46.9				29.2	35.6
	28.2	15.5	23.2	28.0				16.2	18.6
	13.1	6.9	14.1	9.4				10.0	10.3
Sales/Total Assets	10.6	4.1	3.3	3.3				3.7	4.0
	6.1	3.1	2.6	2.7				2.9	2.8
	3.3	2.3	2.1	2.0				2.2	2.0
% Depr., Dep., Amort./Sales	1.1	1.0	.6	.4				.9	1.1
	(27) 1.7	(66) 2.5	(114) 1.1	(25) 1.2				(137) 1.8	(215) 1.7
	2.6	3.5	1.9	2.1				3.3	3.0
% Officers', Directors' Owners' Comp/Sales	3.9	2.5	1.2					2.2	2.1
	(27) 6.8	(51) 4.5	(64) 2.8					(81) 4.0	(130) 3.6
	12.1	6.5	5.0					6.9	7.7
Net Sales ($)	62930M	354817M	1511726M	1537739M	314057M	1020185M		2592492M	3874119M
Total Assets ($)	9108M	97887M	557786M	531787M	125888M	587721M		549885M	1153690M

M = $ thousand   MM = $ million
See Pages 11 through 21 for Explanation of Ratios and Data

Comparative Historical Data | Current Data Sorted by Sales

4/1/04-3/31/05 ALL	4/1/05-3/31/06 ALL	4/1/06-3/31/07 ALL	Type of Statement	0-1MM	1-3MM	3-5MM	5-10MM	10-25MM	25MM & OVER
30	29	27	Unqualified		2		1	11	13
103	84	107	Reviewed	1	12	8	32	42	12
22	34	39	Compiled	3	10	11	8	5	2
32	49	45	Tax Returns	7	17	7	8	5	1
38	69	60	Other	6	12	10	13	10	9
				54 (4/1-9/30/06)			**224 (10/1/06-3/31/07)**		
225	265	278	**NUMBER OF STATEMENTS**	17	53	36	62	73	37
%	%	%	**ASSETS**	%	%	%	%	%	%
12.9	12.6	14.2	Cash & Equivalents	17.2	19.8	14.1	12.9	11.7	12.1
48.9	48.5	44.2	Trade Receivables (net)	25.3	25.2	43.2	47.5	54.4	55.2
4.1	3.6	4.7	Inventory	11.0	4.0	7.2	4.0	4.1	2.4
7.6	6.9	7.2	All Other Current	2.5	6.9	3.1	7.9	8.5	9.9
73.4	71.6	70.2	Total Current	56.0	55.9	67.6	72.3	78.8	79.7
19.9	21.5	21.8	Fixed Assets (net)	32.1	35.2	23.6	20.2	14.6	12.6
1.0	1.1	1.5	Intangibles (net)	2.7	1.9	.3	1.4	.7	3.4
5.7	5.8	6.5	All Other Non-Current	9.2	7.0	8.4	6.1	5.9	4.3
100.0	100.0	100.0	Total	100.0	100.0	100.0	100.0	100.0	100.0
			LIABILITIES						
12.1	13.5	10.0	Notes Payable-Short Term	12.6	13.0	14.1	8.9	7.2	7.6
3.8	5.3	3.1	Cur. Mat.-L.T.D.	.2	5.3	3.6	3.3	2.4	1.8
17.1	17.7	14.8	Trade Payables	9.8	8.5	13.5	15.3	16.3	23.5
.8	.7	.9	Income Taxes Payable	.0	.8	.8	1.5	.7	.7
13.8	15.1	14.7	All Other Current	18.1	10.1	6.4	14.2	19.6	18.7
47.6	52.3	43.4	Total Current	40.8	37.8	38.4	43.2	46.3	52.3
12.1	14.1	14.4	Long-Term Debt	50.7	25.0	12.6	10.7	7.0	5.5
.5	.5	.4	Deferred Taxes	.0	.4	.5	.6	.4	.2
4.6	4.6	4.0	All Other Non-Current	9.8	7.7	1.0	1.4	4.4	2.4
35.3	28.5	37.8	Net Worth	-1.3	29.1	47.5	44.1	42.0	39.6
100.0	100.0	100.0	Total Liabilities & Net Worth	100.0	100.0	100.0	100.0	100.0	100.0
			INCOME DATA						
100.0	100.0	100.0	Net Sales	100.0	100.0	100.0	100.0	100.0	100.0
23.7	26.9	26.7	Gross Profit	50.5	36.2	26.0	23.8	20.3	20.4
20.5	22.6	20.4	Operating Expenses	40.3	30.3	21.6	18.4	13.4	13.1
3.2	4.3	6.3	Operating Profit	10.2	6.0	4.4	5.3	7.0	7.3
.2	.2	.7	All Other Expenses (net)	5.4	.7	.4	.6	.1	.3
3.0	4.1	5.6	Profit Before Taxes	4.9	5.2	4.0	4.7	6.8	7.0
			RATIOS						
2.5	2.4	2.9	Current	4.0	4.3	4.2	2.9	2.6	2.2
1.6	1.6	1.7		1.7	1.6	1.7	1.7	1.7	1.6
1.2	1.1	1.2		.7	1.0	1.2	1.2	1.3	1.2
2.2	2.1	2.6	Quick	3.1	3.5	3.9	2.4	2.3	1.8
1.3	1.4	1.4		1.6	1.3	1.3	1.4	1.6	1.2
.9	.9	1.0		.5	.6	.9	1.1	1.1	1.0
40 9.1	36 10.0	32 11.3	Sales/Receivables	0 UND	0 UND	37 10.0	38 9.6	55 6.6	45 8.1
65 5.6	67 5.4	61 6.0		40 9.1	25 14.7	57 6.4	60 6.1	74 4.9	69 5.3
85 4.3	89 4.1	81 4.5		61 6.0	61 6.0	77 4.8	88 4.2	99 3.7	85 4.3
0 UND	0 UND	0 UND	Cost of Sales/Inventory	0 UND	0 UND	0 UND	0 UND	0 UND	0 UND
0 UND	0 UND	0 UND		0 UND	0 UND	0 UND	0 UND	0 UND	999.8
3 104.8	3 121.8	3 133.2		53 6.8	1 603.5	4 81.4	3 143.8	4 92.0	4 91.5
12 30.1	12 31.1	9 40.4	Cost of Sales/Payables	0 UND	0 UND	5 67.5	11 33.2	13 27.4	19 19.6
23 16.1	23 16.0	20 18.1		3 110.3	9 38.5	15 25.0	19 19.0	22 16.8	31 11.9
38 9.7	42 8.7	36 10.2		37 9.7	30 12.0	39 9.5	36 10.1	34 10.6	38 9.5
6.1	6.1	5.3	Sales/Working Capital	4.6	6.4	5.7	5.7	4.4	5.6
11.0	10.7	10.1		12.1	18.7	9.6	10.3	7.7	12.6
28.3	49.0	35.2		-46.8	NM	29.8	24.3	17.2	33.4
16.8	22.2	28.9	EBIT/Interest	20.0	24.5	20.7	18.9	42.0	87.2
(202) 4.6	(234) 6.3	(245) 8.6		(11) 7.9	(48) 7.0	(32) 6.5	(57) 8.5	(62) 11.3	(35) 19.0
1.3	1.5	2.2		-1.1	2.0	1.5	1.6	2.8	5.2
6.0	8.3	11.3	Net Profit + Depr., Dep., Amort./Cur. Mat. L/T/D				9.1	20.2	9.7
(54) 2.8	(51) 2.7	(62) 4.6					(18) 3.7	(21) 8.7	(12) 6.8
1.0	1.1	2.1					1.0	4.1	2.1
.2	.2	.2	Fixed/Worth	.1	.2	.2	.2	.1	.1
.4	.4	.4		.8	.7	.5	.3	.3	.3
1.0	1.3	.9		-5.7	2.5	1.0	.9	.6	.6
.8	.8	.6	Debt/Worth	.4	.3	.3	.6	.7	.7
1.6	1.6	1.3		1.1	1.6	1.2	1.2	1.3	2.0
4.2	5.3	3.7		-10.3	6.5	3.7	2.5	2.7	4.1
38.6	66.0	64.2	% Profit Before Taxes/Tangible Net Worth	71.8	79.2	44.8	56.3	64.8	89.0
(198) 16.0	(233) 27.4	(254) 29.4		(11) 15.3	(45) 34.9	(35) 20.7	(57) 27.2	(71) 30.2	(35) 45.9
2.1	8.3	11.0		.0	10.0	10.8	8.2	10.1	19.0
17.1	26.4	30.1	% Profit Before Taxes/Total Assets	29.4	33.6	21.4	26.4	29.0	35.0
5.7	9.5	11.8		.7	13.9	11.0	11.1	12.2	11.1
.7	1.5	2.9		-3.3	1.4	2.5	2.0	4.6	7.3
43.0	40.5	43.4	Sales/Net Fixed Assets	37.3	35.0	24.1	43.3	51.4	62.9
20.0	21.4	21.7		7.2	15.2	16.4	23.7	23.3	36.3
12.1	11.9	10.8		5.2	6.9	8.7	13.2	14.8	16.4
3.9	4.2	3.8	Sales/Total Assets	4.4	6.2	3.9	4.0	3.4	3.7
2.8	2.9	2.9		2.2	2.8	2.9	3.0	2.8	3.0
2.2	2.2	2.2		1.2	2.3	2.2	2.3	2.2	2.5
.8	.8	.7	% Depr., Dep., Amort./Sales	2.2	1.1	1.0	.7	.6	.4
(191) 1.6	(224) 1.5	(235) 1.3		(13) 3.5	(43) 2.3	(28) 1.9	(54) 1.2	(66) 1.0	(31) .7
2.4	2.5	2.5		5.9	3.9	3.1	2.5	1.6	1.4
1.8	1.9	1.5	% Officers', Directors', Owners' Comp/Sales		3.6	2.2	1.3	.8	.6
(124) 3.9	(144) 3.4	(153) 3.8			(34) 5.1	(24) 5.0	(39) 3.2	(36) 1.5	(11) 1.5
6.5	6.1	6.4			7.2	8.0	7.3	3.7	3.4
3713277M	4830600M	4801454M	Net Sales ($)	10024M	111305M	139941M	430746M	1066593M	3042845M
1348556M	1366063M	1910177M	Total Assets ($)	5722M	40635M	50617M	161166M	413579M	1238458M

M = $ thousand   MM = $ million
See Pages 11 through 21 for Explanation of Ratios and Data

Current Data Sorted by Assets   Comparative Historical Data

Type of Statement	0-500M	500M-2MM	2-10MM	10-50MM	50-100MM	100-250MM		ALL	ALL
Unqualified		1	3	1		1		5	6
Reviewed		10	29	2				25	43
Compiled	3	10	10					11	27
Tax Returns	8	8	2					19	22
Other	3	13	11	3	1	1		16	21
		30 (4/1-9/30/06)		90 (10/1/06-3/31/07)				4/1/02-3/31/03	4/1/03-3/31/04
NUMBER OF STATEMENTS	14	42	55	6	1	2		76	119

ASSETS	%	%	%	%	%	%		%	%
Cash & Equivalents	15.4	12.1	9.5					12.3	11.5
Trade Receivables (net)	17.8	51.2	53.7					46.3	48.1
Inventory	7.3	11.8	11.9					9.7	11.2
All Other Current	1.9	5.0	8.3					5.0	6.8
Total Current	42.5	80.2	83.4					73.3	77.6
Fixed Assets (net)	25.6	12.9	12.2					19.3	14.4
Intangibles (net)	7.5	1.1	.3					2.6	2.8
All Other Non-Current	24.5	5.8	4.1					4.7	5.2
Total	100.0	100.0	100.0					100.0	100.0

LIABILITIES									
Notes Payable-Short Term	11.8	10.2	12.7					12.3	13.7
Cur. Mat.-L.T.D.	8.5	3.1	1.8					3.2	2.5
Trade Payables	15.4	23.2	21.6					21.5	20.7
Income Taxes Payable	.1	.5	1.1					.4	1.0
All Other Current	30.2	9.8	15.5					15.0	15.1
Total Current	66.1	46.9	52.8					52.5	53.1
Long-Term Debt	12.2	6.4	5.3					13.3	6.7
Deferred Taxes	.0	.2	.2					.4	.2
All Other Non-Current	14.5	3.6	3.6					3.0	5.4
Net Worth	7.1	42.9	38.2					30.9	34.6
Total Liabilties & Net Worth	100.0	100.0	100.0					100.0	100.0

INCOME DATA									
Net Sales	100.0	100.0	100.0					100.0	100.0
Gross Profit	41.1	30.9	27.6					32.4	30.9
Operating Expenses	36.4	25.5	22.7					29.1	28.5
Operating Profit	4.7	5.4	4.9					3.2	2.5
All Other Expenses (net)	1.4	.4	.6					.3	.4
Profit Before Taxes	3.3	5.0	4.3					2.9	2.1

RATIOS									
Current	1.3	2.8	2.1					2.0	2.4
	.6	1.7	1.6					1.3	1.5
	.3	1.3	1.3					1.1	1.1
Quick	1.0	2.2	1.7					1.6	1.8
	.4	1.3	1.2					1.1	1.2
	.2	1.1	.8					.7	.8
Sales/Receivables	0 UND	43 8.4	59 6.2					32 11.2	42 8.6
	6 57.1	55 6.6	79 4.6					56 6.5	60 6.0
	27 13.4	67 5.5	90 4.1					84 4.3	81 4.5
Cost of Sales/Inventory	0 UND	7 54.5	1 556.5					0 UND	1 678.4
	1 567.5	17 21.1	11 32.6					7 52.8	10 36.0
	19 19.0	30 12.2	36 10.1					27 13.6	28 13.2
Cost of Sales/Payables	0 UND	20 18.5	24 15.5					17 21.0	17 21.9
	1 408.8	37 9.9	39 9.4					33 11.1	35 10.4
	37 9.8	53 6.9	55 6.7					53 6.9	53 6.8
Sales/Working Capital	28.7	6.5	5.9					7.6	5.9
	-67.2	9.4	9.2					15.9	11.5
	-22.3	16.7	15.8					57.5	46.5
EBIT/Interest	64.8	15.0	18.2					19.5	16.5
	(12) 5.1	(33) 5.3	(52) 6.6					(67) 6.4	(101) 3.8
	-3.4	2.8	2.2					1.7	1.2
Net Profit + Depr., Dep., Amort./Cur. Mat. L/T/D			14.4					19.4	7.9
		(25) 5.1						(20) 4.0	(25) 4.5
			2.2					2.8	1.4
Fixed/Worth	.8	.1	.1					.2	.1
	5.4	.2	.3					.4	.4
	UND	.7	.5					1.1	.8
Debt/Worth	1.4	.8	.9					1.0	.8
	14.3	1.8	1.8					2.2	1.7
	UND	2.8	4.1					4.8	4.8
% Profit Before Taxes/Tangible Net Worth	UND	93.1	53.0					52.8	35.0
	(11) 758.5	29.8	26.4					(65) 22.0	(101) 16.4
	42.6	10.8	10.4					4.7	4.1
% Profit Before Taxes/Total Assets	110.9	25.9	16.2					16.0	12.5
	24.7	10.3	8.5					6.5	5.0
	-14.8	3.9	2.8					1.6	.7
Sales/Net Fixed Assets	107.2	78.5	70.6					45.6	50.4
	42.9	33.2	41.5					25.5	28.9
	24.7	17.2	12.2					14.3	16.1
Sales/Total Assets	13.6	4.1	3.3					4.3	3.7
	6.4	3.1	2.7					3.1	2.8
	4.2	2.4	2.2					2.3	2.2
% Depr., Dep., Amort./Sales	.5	.4	.4					.6	.6
	(10) .9	(34) .8	(51) .8					(69) 1.2	(104) 1.0
	2.0	1.3	1.4					2.4	1.9
% Officers', Directors' Owners' Comp/Sales		2.1	2.4					2.7	3.0
		(26) 4.4	(27) 3.2					(50) 4.5	(64) 5.0
		8.7	4.8					8.7	9.6
Net Sales ($)	26525M	171713M	664994M	249165M	143700M	808520M		517218M	2650843M
Total Assets ($)	3754M	48696M	243441M	89760M	61200M	301769M		180366M	509882M

M = $ thousand   MM = $ million

See Pages 11 through 21 for Explanation of Ratios and Data

Comparative Historical Data | Current Data Sorted by Sales

10	8	.6	Type of Statement		1	2	1	2
49	44	41	Unqualified	3	8	13	13	4
19	13	23	Reviewed	7	5	6	5	
15	14	18	Compiled	9	1	4		
22	29	32	Tax Returns	4				
4/1/04-	4/1/05-	4/1/06-	Other — 1	5	6	8	5	7

3/31/05 ALL	3/31/06 ALL	3/31/07 ALL		0-1MM	1-3MM 30 (4/1-9/30/06)	3-5MM	5-10MM 90 (10/1/06-3/31/07)	10-25MM	25MM & OVER
115	108	120	NUMBER OF STATEMENTS	5	24	21	33	24	13
%	%	%	ASSETS	%	%	%	%	%	%
10.4	9.4	10.8	Cash & Equivalents		12.4	9.5	11.3	10.6	8.2
50.9	51.8	48.9	Trade Receivables (net)		38.0	49.3	54.3	55.1	53.4
10.7	11.8	11.4	Inventory		9.5	10.7	11.1	11.6	16.1
6.1	5.0	6.2	All Other Current		3.9	6.5	8.9	6.6	4.1
78.0	78.1	77.2	Total Current		63.8	76.0	85.6	83.9	81.7
14.6	13.8	14.2	Fixed Assets (net)		14.7	13.1	12.4	12.1	13.9
2.5	1.9	1.6	Intangibles (net)		4.8	1.2	.4	.2	2.0
4.9	6.2	7.0	All Other Non-Current		16.8	9.7	1.6	3.9	2.4
100.0	100.0	100.0	Total		100.0	100.0	100.0	100.0	100.0
			LIABILITIES						
15.4	13.0	11.4	Notes Payable-Short Term		10.3	15.3	10.6	11.5	10.3
3.1	2.4	3.0	Cur. Mat.-L.T.D.		6.7	2.9	2.1	2.2	1.6
21.3	22.3	21.3	Trade Payables		21.4	22.4	21.3	24.2	17.7
1.1	.8	.7	Income Taxes Payable		.5	.5	1.4	.8	.1
14.0	13.0	16.0	All Other Current		12.7	8.0	17.2	15.4	23.0
55.0	51.5	52.4	Total Current		51.6	49.1	52.6	54.0	52.7
12.6	8.6	7.0	Long-Term Debt		5.8	9.2	5.9	4.8	9.4
.2	.3	.2	Deferred Taxes		.1	.3	.2	.1	.0
3.0	4.9	4.8	All Other Non-Current		10.6	3.0	1.4	3.5	2.2
29.2	34.7	35.5	Net Worth		31.9	38.4	37.4	37.6	35.7
100.0	100.0	100.0	Total Liabilties & Net Worth		100.0	100.0	100.0	100.0	100.0
			INCOME DATA						
100.0	100.0	100.0	Net Sales		100.0	100.0	100.0	100.0	100.0
30.4	29.7	30.1	Gross Profit		33.1	30.7	30.7	24.2	26.8
28.6	25.6	25.1	Operating Expenses		27.8	25.7	24.7	20.6	22.5
1.8	4.1	5.0	Operating Profit		5.2	5.1	6.0	3.6	4.3
.4	.4	.6	All Other Expenses (net)		.4	.6	.7	.2	.3
1.4	3.7	4.4	Profit Before Taxes		4.9	4.4	5.3	3.4	4.0
			RATIOS						
2.4	2.1	2.2			3.0	2.1	2.1	2.1	2.9
1.5	1.5	1.5	Current		1.5	1.4	1.7	1.5	1.3
1.2	1.2	1.2			.8	1.2	1.3	1.2	1.2
1.8	1.7	1.7			2.3	1.6	1.8	1.6	1.7
1.2	1.2	1.2	Quick		1.4	1.1	1.3	1.3	1.1
.8	.8	.8			.5	.8	.9	.9	.7
41 8.9	39 9.4	39 9.4			9 40.2	44 8.2	57 6.4	43 8.6	33 11.1
62 5.9	62 5.9	63 5.8	Sales/Receivables		39 9.4	65 5.6	80 4.6	66 5.5	68 5.4
83 4.4	88 4.1	84 4.4			64 5.7	88 4.1	97 3.7	81 4.5	91 4.0
1 424.2	1 363.2	1 482.3			0 780.2	7 48.9	0 999.8	1 472.7	1 566.1
10 37.5	11 34.6	13 27.2	Cost of Sales/Inventory		10 37.3	18 20.0	9 38.8	13 27.4	17 17.3
32 11.6	30 12.1	33 11.0			20 18.1	34 10.9	31 11.6	26 13.9	45 8.1
17 21.0	20 17.9	18 20.4			10 37.0	22 16.4	26 14.3	15 24.3	12 29.2
33 11.1	35 10.6	36 10.2	Cost of Sales/Payables		28 13.2	45 8.2	37 9.8	29 12.4	21 17.8
53 6.9	55 6.6	53 6.9			50 7.2	55 6.6	57 6.4	52 7.1	54 6.7
6.8	7.1	6.3			7.3	6.3	5.9	7.8	5.5
11.4	11.3	10.0	Sales/Working Capital		13.1	11.2	9.0	11.1	9.6
29.3	26.2	27.2			-58.3	25.2	13.2	18.2	43.1
14.1	17.1	15.9			18.5	9.9	20.3	20.2	11.1
(98) 3.7	(98) 6.2	(106) 5.9	EBIT/Interest		(18) 4.7	(17) 4.7	(30) 8.3	8.1	(12) 5.4
-.4	2.2	2.4			2.5	2.7	2.1	3.1	2.8
8.5	9.4	11.7					14.6	18.9	
(40) 3.7	(35) 3.4	(36) 3.7	Net Profit + Depr., Dep., Amort./Cur. Mat. L/T/D				(12) 7.2	(12) 4.9	
.8	2.0	1.7					2.6	1.7	
.2	.2	.1			.1	.1	.1	.1	.3
.4	.3	.3	Fixed/Worth		.3	.2	.3	.3	.5
.8	.8	.7			1.1	.8	.7	.6	.6
.9	1.0	.9			.6	1.0	1.1	.8	1.1
1.9	2.0	2.0	Debt/Worth		2.0	1.8	1.8	2.4	2.2
5.3	4.4	4.6			5.1	3.3	4.1	4.3	4.9
38.0	58.4	73.6			240.3	69.7	62.8	63.3	65.3
(96) 14.2	(99) 33.2	(117) 34.6	% Profit Before Taxes/Tangible Net Worth		(22) 37.5	28.7	35.7	26.3	40.6
-1.3	7.6	11.3			11.4	9.3	10.8	9.3	9.3
15.3	17.6	22.3			39.7	27.8	22.0	21.5	16.0
5.9	8.6	9.5	% Profit Before Taxes/Total Assets		10.8	10.9	8.5	9.0	11.2
-1.0	2.2	3.0			3.3	3.4	3.2	2.8	4.6
60.1	66.3	72.8			105.8	50.7	75.3	84.1	60.7
29.4	30.7	35.0	Sales/Net Fixed Assets		41.3	26.5	45.6	48.5	20.5
17.0	17.2	18.2			22.9	12.7	12.8	19.9	18.7
4.1	3.9	3.9			5.6	3.6	3.1	3.8	4.5
3.0	2.9	3.0	Sales/Total Assets		3.7	3.0	2.7	3.2	3.2
2.3	2.4	2.3			2.6	2.2	2.0	2.6	2.2
.6	.5	.4			.5	.5	.4	.4	.5
(95) 1.0	(95) .9	(104) .8	% Depr., Dep., Amort./Sales		(17) .9	(17) .7	(30) .7	(22) .7	1.0
1.8	1.5	1.4			1.9	.8	1.4	1.8	1.3
3.0	2.1	2.3			3.5	2.1	2.0		
(63) 5.4	(61) 3.8	(63) 3.6	% Officers', Directors' Owners' Comp/Sales		(13) 7.3	(13) 3.8	(23) 2.8		
8.6	7.3	6.6			11.2	7.8	5.2		
3888452M	1176774M	2064617M	Net Sales ($)	4137M	50851M	82339M	245235M	369602M	1312453M
630864M	469992M	748620M	Total Assets ($)	1781M	14182M	31177M	104939M	117205M	479336M

M = $ thousand   MM = $ million
See Pages 11 through 21 for Explanation of Ratios and Data

Current Data Sorted by Assets

Comparative Historical Data

Type of Statement	0-500M	500M-2MM	2-10MM	10-50MM	50-100MM	100-250MM		ALL	ALL
Unqualified	1	4	17	7	1	1		34	49
Reviewed	13	69	90	7	1			133	168
Compiled	7	29	12	1				35	63
Tax Returns	26	16	5			1		25	44
Other	13	33	34	10	1	1		55	67
		73 (4/1-9/30/06)		327 (10/1/06-3/31/07)				4/1/02-3/31/03	4/1/03-3/31/04
NUMBER OF STATEMENTS	60	151	158	25	3	3		282	391

ASSETS	%	%	%	%	%	%		%	%
Cash & Equivalents	17.6	10.7	12.5	9.3				12.4	10.2
Trade Receivables (net)	26.3	46.6	48.6	44.5				45.8	47.4
Inventory	7.0	9.3	5.9	5.4				7.6	7.8
All Other Current	8.4	6.8	8.3	12.5				8.2	7.2
Total Current	59.3	73.4	75.3	71.7				74.0	72.7
Fixed Assets (net)	27.6	17.9	14.3	16.7				17.5	17.9
Intangibles (net)	2.4	2.4	2.8	2.6				2.0	1.9
All Other Non-Current	10.8	6.3	7.6	9.0				6.5	7.4
Total	100.0	100.0	100.0	100.0				100.0	100.0

LIABILITIES	0-500M	500M-2MM	2-10MM	10-50MM				ALL	ALL
Notes Payable-Short Term	14.8	11.6	9.5	8.0				12.6	13.3
Cur. Mat.-L.T.D.	6.4	3.6	2.9	3.4				3.5	3.3
Trade Payables	22.5	20.5	18.1	17.8				21.1	21.4
Income Taxes Payable	.3	1.1	.7	.9				.6	.7
All Other Current	15.7	13.5	14.1	16.4				14.3	13.6
Total Current	59.7	50.2	45.3	46.5				52.2	52.3
Long-Term Debt	28.3	10.2	9.3	8.6				8.1	11.7
Deferred Taxes	.0	.7	.4	.3				.3	.4
All Other Non-Current	14.9	3.4	2.6	1.9				2.4	3.0
Net Worth	-2.9	35.5	42.4	42.6				37.0	32.7
Total Liabilties & Net Worth	100.0	100.0	100.0	100.0				100.0	100.0

INCOME DATA	0-500M	500M-2MM	2-10MM	10-50MM				ALL	ALL
Net Sales	100.0	100.0	100.0	100.0				100.0	100.0
Gross Profit	37.3	29.2	25.9	23.9				26.5	26.9
Operating Expenses	34.0	24.6	20.0	17.8				24.2	24.4
Operating Profit	3.3	4.6	6.0	6.1				2.3	2.5
All Other Expenses (net)	.4	.4	.5	-.1				.2	.4
Profit Before Taxes	2.9	4.2	5.5	6.2				2.1	2.1

RATIOS

Ratio	0-500M	500M-2MM	2-10MM	10-50MM				ALL	ALL
Current	2.7	2.2	2.2	2.0				2.0	2.1
	1.1	1.5	1.6	1.6				1.4	1.4
	.6	1.1	1.3	1.3				1.1	1.1
Quick	2.2	1.9	1.9	1.5				1.6	1.6
	.8	(150) 1.2	1.3	1.2				1.1	1.2
	.4	.8	1.0	.8				.9	.8
Sales/Receivables	0 UND	33 11.0	45 8.2	44 8.3				33 11.0	38 9.6
	14 25.7	49 7.4	63 5.8	68 5.3				54 6.7	57 6.4
	32 11.5	70 5.2	82 4.5	73 5.0				78 4.7	81 4.5
Cost of Sales/Inventory	0 UND	1 470.3	1 303.2	1 551.7				1 377.4	1 683.0
	0 UND	7 55.4	7 54.4	4 104.0				6 61.2	6 65.0
	5 76.3	23 15.8	14 26.9	22 16.8				16 23.5	18 20.1
Cost of Sales/Payables	0 UND	14 25.7	16 23.2	20 17.9				16 23.5	16 23.4
	13 28.2	24 15.3	30 12.3	27 13.5				28 12.9	29 12.7
	28 13.2	41 9.0	45 8.1	51 7.2				44 8.2	47 7.8
Sales/Working Capital	12.7	7.3	6.2	6.6				7.8	7.8
	545.4	15.4	9.7	9.3				13.9	13.7
	-29.3	45.9	22.0	20.8				59.6	49.7
EBIT/Interest	13.7	15.5	32.9	53.2				14.2	14.6
	(53) 2.9	(131) 3.8	(145) 7.2	(23) 10.4				(247) 3.8	(344) 4.4
	.0	1.2	2.6	4.5				.7	1.1
Net Profit + Depr., Dep., Amort./Cur. Mat. L/T/D		4.6	10.4					5.4	5.4
		(38) 2.8	(50) 3.6					(81) 2.3	(95) 3.0
		1.1	1.2					.8	1.3
Fixed/Worth	.2	.2	.2	.1				.2	.2
	1.2	.5	.3	.3				.4	.4
	-12.1	1.4	.6	1.0				.8	1.0
Debt/Worth	1.5	.7	.7	.8				.8	.9
	4.0	1.7	1.5	1.4				1.6	1.8
	-11.7	4.4	3.0	3.8				3.5	4.0
% Profit Before Taxes/Tangible Net Worth	99.9	62.9	56.0	77.3				42.8	41.2
	(42) 40.9	(134) 19.6	(149) 27.9	33.4				(257) 17.3	(349) 16.7
	3.9	6.0	12.6	18.3				1.6	2.8
% Profit Before Taxes/Total Assets	36.1	20.3	21.8	27.5				14.7	16.2
	11.1	6.8	11.3	9.2				6.0	5.2
	-1.4	1.0	3.3	5.4				-.6	.4
Sales/Net Fixed Assets	97.6	45.3	43.7	42.1				45.0	41.8
	29.9	23.6	25.5	20.2				23.6	22.5
	14.4	13.3	15.3	9.0				14.0	14.1
Sales/Total Assets	8.3	4.4	3.4	3.4				4.0	4.1
	5.5	3.3	2.8	2.5				3.1	3.1
	3.0	2.6	2.2	1.8				2.5	2.4
% Depr., Dep., Amort./Sales	.5	.7	.7	.5				1.0	.8
	(39) 1.4	(132) 1.3	(139) 1.1	(22) .9				(248) 1.5	(328) 1.4
	2.4	2.0	1.8	1.3				2.3	2.1
% Officers', Directors' Owners' Comp/Sales	3.3	2.3	1.6					2.3	2.3
	(35) 5.9	(81) 3.7	(79) 3.0					(151) 4.1	(209) 4.4
	7.8	6.1	4.9					7.0	6.8
Net Sales ($)	113285M	646161M	1870128M	1301977M	552055M	2769916M		6182290M	6848714M
Total Assets ($)	17265M	184808M	662967M	484131M	191990M	517195M		1450807M	1862930M

M = $ thousand   MM = $ million
See Pages 11 through 21 for Explanation of Ratios and Data

Comparative Historical Data | Current Data Sorted by Sales

Current data periods: 73 (4/1-9/30/06) and 327 (10/1/06-3/31/07)

Type of Statement	4/1/04-3/31/05 ALL	4/1/05-3/31/06 ALL	4/1/06-3/31/07 ALL	0-1MM	1-3MM	3-5MM	5-10MM	10-25MM	25MM & OVER
Unqualified	33	35	31	2	2	1	8	8	10
Reviewed	156	145	180	5	27	32	60	46	10
Compiled	37	45	49	1	17	11	13	6	1
Tax Returns	46	46	48	5	20	12	6	4	1
Other	73	111	92	6	16	16	23	20	11
NUMBER OF STATEMENTS	345	382	400	19	82	72	110	84	33
ASSETS	%	%	%	%	%	%	%	%	%
Cash & Equivalents	11.6	11.1	12.3	11.8	15.6	12.5	12.0	11.0	8.8
Trade Receivables (net)	45.7	46.4	44.1	26.4	35.1	42.2	48.1	52.0	47.8
Inventory	7.5	8.6	7.3	5.4	9.4	7.2	6.9	6.9	5.9
All Other Current	8.0	8.7	8.0	12.1	6.2	7.1	7.7	8.8	11.4
Total Current	72.8	74.9	71.8	55.7	66.3	69.0	74.6	78.7	74.0
Fixed Assets (net)	17.0	16.9	17.9	25.9	22.8	18.1	16.2	14.5	15.3
Intangibles (net)	1.6	1.6	2.7	.7	3.2	4.4	2.5	1.2	3.2
All Other Non-Current	8.5	6.6	7.6	17.7	7.7	8.6	6.7	5.6	7.4
Total	100.0	100.0	100.0	100.0	100.0	100.0	100.0	100.0	100.0
LIABILITIES									
Notes Payable-Short Term	11.6	10.9	11.0	9.1	15.0	11.5	10.5	8.5	9.1
Cur. Mat.-L.T.D.	3.1	3.4	3.7	2.4	4.3	5.8	3.4	2.5	2.3
Trade Payables	22.3	21.5	19.5	20.4	17.8	20.1	20.7	18.9	20.1
Income Taxes Payable	.8	.7	.8	.0	1.2	.5	.8	.8	.8
All Other Current	14.5	13.3	14.3	29.2	9.0	16.0	13.2	14.9	17.5
Total Current	52.4	49.8	49.3	61.2	47.3	53.9	48.6	45.6	49.8
Long-Term Debt	9.6	12.7	12.6	32.4	17.0	13.5	11.1	5.8	11.0
Deferred Taxes	.4	.4	.4	.0	.2	.9	.4	.6	.3
All Other Non-Current	3.2	4.2	4.7	15.5	9.6	1.9	3.3	2.9	2.2
Net Worth	34.5	32.9	32.8	-9.1	25.9	29.8	36.7	45.1	36.8
Total Liabilities & Net Worth	100.0	100.0	100.0	100.0	100.0	100.0	100.0	100.0	100.0
INCOME DATA									
Net Sales	100.0	100.0	100.0	100.0	100.0	100.0	100.0	100.0	100.0
Gross Profit	27.1	28.1	28.7	35.2	35.4	28.5	28.1	23.1	24.7
Operating Expenses	23.8	24.3	23.6	29.8	31.8	24.1	22.1	17.5	19.1
Operating Profit	3.3	3.8	5.1	5.4	3.7	4.4	5.9	5.6	5.7
All Other Expenses (net)	.5	.6	.4	-.1	.5	.4	.5	.4	.2
Profit Before Taxes	2.8	3.2	4.7	5.5	3.2	4.0	5.4	5.2	5.5
RATIOS									
Current	2.2	2.3	2.2	7.0	2.9	2.1	2.1	2.4	2.0
	1.4	1.5	1.5	1.1	1.5	1.3	1.5	1.7	1.6
	1.1	1.2	1.2	.5	.9	.9	1.3	1.3	1.3
Quick	1.7	1.7	1.9	5.7	2.4	1.7	1.8	2.0	1.6
	1.2	1.2 (399)	1.2	.6	1.1 (71)	1.1	1.2	1.4	1.2
	.8	.8	.8	.2	.7	.6	.9	1.0	.8
Sales/Receivables	36 10.1	33 11.0	31 11.7	0 UND	16 23.4	24 15.2	39 9.4	43 8.5	43 8.4
	54 6.7	57 6.4	52 7.0	16 22.4	34 10.7	55 6.7	56 6.5	61 6.0	63 5.8
	78 4.7	80 4.6	74 4.9	69 5.3	54 6.8	77 4.8	70 5.2	88 4.2	72 5.0
Cost of Sales/Inventory	0 UND	0 999.8	0 UND	0 UND	0 UND	0 UND	2 206.2	0 UND	1 551.7
	5 73.1	6 57.6	5 72.6	0 UND	4 91.4	6 61.9	7 49.9	6 64.7	4 91.7
	16 22.2	19 18.9	16 23.2	0 UND	25 14.8	16 22.9	16 22.6	14 26.9	16 23.4
Cost of Sales/Payables	16 22.9	16 22.2	13 27.1	0 UND	9 40.2	14 24	16 23.5	14 26.5	19 19.0
	30 12.0	31 11.7	25 14.8	12 30.0	22 16.4	25 14.7	27 13.4	28 13.0	27 13.5
	49 7.4	51 7.2	42 8.7	24 15.0	38 9.5	52 7.0	42 8.8	43 8.6	49 7.4
Sales/Working Capital	7.8	7.2	7.1	2.5	8.3	7.1	7.7	6.1	7.6
	14.0	11.9	12.8	48.5	16.1	18.3	12.8	9.2	10.1
	48.1	31.1	39.3	-21.2	-453.8	-64.7	24.5	17.2	27.4
EBIT/Interest	18.8	18.5	21.7	6.4	13.2	10.0	27.8	57.0	41.8
	(309) 6.3	(330) 6.0	(358) 5.0	(13) 1.2	(71) 3.0	(66) 3.7	(102) 5.6	(75) 11.4	(31) 11.0
	1.8	2.0	1.8	-2.1	-.4	1.7	2.6	2.6	3.7
Net Profit + Depr., Dep., Amort./Cur. Mat. L/T/D	6.9	11.0	8.2		6.1	3.4	10.1	10.8	8.6
	(83) 3.2	(89) 3.6	(103) 3.2		(13) 2.2	(16) 2.5	(34) 3.6	(22) 5.0	(17) 3.0
	1.4	1.4	1.3		.7	.5	1.6	.9	2.0
Fixed/Worth	.2	.2	.2	.0	.2	.2	.2	.1	.1
	.4	.4	.4	.4	.7	.4	.4	.3	.3
	1.0	.9	1.2	-9.2	2.7	2.8	.8	.6	1.0
Debt/Worth	.9	.8	.8	1.1	.6	.8	.8	.6	.9
	1.9	1.9	1.7	3.6	2.9	1.9	1.7	1.2	1.6
	4.4	4.3	4.5	-11.4	21.7	11.0	3.6	2.4	4.1
% Profit Before Taxes/Tangible Net Worth	53.5	56.6	64.3	90.7	46.7	74.8	56.9	61.0	80.3
	(311) 20.6	(337) 25.3	(354) 24.5	(13) 24.4	(68) 13.5	(61) 21.4	(100) 28.1	(82) 26.1	(30) 52.8
	4.4	7.8	8.8	1.8	-5.8	6.1	14.2	12.7	19.1
% Profit Before Taxes/Total Assets	16.1	18.6	22.0	23.5	20.0	20.3	21.9	24.4	30.2
	6.9	9.0	9.3	2.1	6.6	7.5	11.9	11.1	9.5
	1.2	1.9	2.5	-7.6	-4.0	1.8	3.6	3.1	6.4
Sales/Net Fixed Assets	43.7	46.0	48.1	UND	43.1	57.5	42.8	50.1	53.1
	24.4	25.4	25.1	15.4	20.6	28.4	23.9	28.9	24.7
	14.5	15.1	14.3	6.8	11.0	15.1	14.8	17.6	16.7
Sales/Total Assets	4.1	4.2	4.3	6.1	4.8	4.4	4.1	3.9	3.7
	3.1	3.1	3.1	2.4	3.3	3.1	3.1	3.1	2.8
	2.4	2.3	2.4	1.7	2.5	2.4	2.5	2.3	2.3
% Depr., Dep., Amort./Sales	.8	.7	.7	1.4	.8	.7	.8	.6	.6
	(294) 1.2	(314) 1.2	(337) 1.2	(10) 2.4	(69) 1.3	(58) 1.4	(98) 1.3	(72) .9	(30) .8
	2.0	1.9	1.9	3.4	2.4	2.0	2.0	1.3	1.2
% Officers', Directors', Owners' Comp/Sales	2.1	2.3	2.0		3.1	2.2	2.0	1.2	
	(182) 3.5	(188) 3.7	(201) 3.5		(47) 5.4	(42) 3.6	(59) 3.4	(40) 2.2	
	6.2	6.0	6.5		7.9	5.2	5.7	3.8	
Net Sales ($)	5980274M	4873217M	7253522M	10502M	171567M	290042M	770965M	1294812M	4715634M
Total Assets ($)	1664649M	1868893M	2058356M	4944M	57016M	94329M	271130M	447176M	1183761M

M = $ thousand   MM = $ million
See Pages 11 through 21 for Explanation of Ratios and Data

Current Data Sorted by Assets   Comparative Historical Data

							Type of Statement		
		4	1	1			Unqualified	1	1
	1	4	1				Reviewed	3	4
	4	1					Compiled		1
5	1	1	1				Tax Returns	3	1
1	5	2		1			Other	1	
	5 (4/1-9/30/06)		28 (10/1/06-3/31/07)					4/1/02-3/31/03	4/1/03-3/31/04
0-500M	500M-2MM	2-10MM	10-50MM	50-100MM	100-250MM			ALL	ALL
6	11	12	3	1			NUMBER OF STATEMENTS	8	7
%	%	%	%	%	%		ASSETS	%	%
	11.1	6.3			D		Cash & Equivalents		
	32.7	52.3			A		Trade Receivables (net)		
	5.6	14.6			T		Inventory		
	2.4	4.8			A		All Other Current		
	51.9	77.9					Total Current		
	25.2	18.9			N		Fixed Assets (net)		
	2.3	1.2			O		Intangibles (net)		
	20.6	1.9			T		All Other Non-Current		
	100.0	100.0					Total		
					A		LIABILITIES		
	9.7	10.2			V		Notes Payable-Short Term		
	2.4	4.1			A		Cur. Mat.-L.T.D.		
	16.3	18.5			I		Trade Payables		
	.7	.7			L		Income Taxes Payable		
	8.2	19.1			A		All Other Current		
	37.4	52.6			B		Total Current		
	12.7	13.6			L		Long-Term Debt		
	.4	.7			E		Deferred Taxes		
	4.6	4.2					All Other Non-Current		
	44.9	28.9					Net Worth		
	100.0	100.0					Total Liabilities & Net Worth		
							INCOME DATA		
	100.0	100.0					Net Sales		
	44.3	20.2					Gross Profit		
	37.5	15.0					Operating Expenses		
	6.8	5.2					Operating Profit		
	1.1	.8					All Other Expenses (net)		
	5.7	4.4					Profit Before Taxes		
							RATIOS		
	4.0	2.1							
	1.6	1.6					Current		
	.8	1.2							
	3.1	1.9							
	1.3	1.2					Quick		
	.6	.9							
13	28.6	45	8.1						
37	9.9	75	4.9				Sales/Receivables		
53	6.9	107	3.4						
0	UND	0	UND						
0	UND	5	69.1				Cost of Sales/Inventory		
10	35.4	27	13.4						
7	50.1	9	39.1						
13	28.6	26	14.2				Cost of Sales/Payables		
99	3.7	38	9.5						
	8.5	7.4							
	12.0	9.6					Sales/Working Capital		
	-121.2	32.5							
		16.4							
	(11)	4.0					EBIT/Interest		
		1.5							
							Net Profit + Depr., Dep., Amort./Cur. Mat. L/T/D		
	.1	.3							
	.4	.7					Fixed/Worth		
	.8	1.2							
	.5	1.1							
	1.0	3.2					Debt/Worth		
	3.0	8.0							
	96.4	47.8							
	(10) 53.8	32.7					% Profit Before Taxes/Tangible Net Worth		
	12.8	-13.0							
	32.2	19.7							
	22.6	7.2					% Profit Before Taxes/Total Assets		
	2.8	1.1							
	52.3	27.2							
	16.9	16.8					Sales/Net Fixed Assets		
	5.7	9.5							
	4.5	3.0							
	3.3	2.6					Sales/Total Assets		
	2.6	2.0							
		.7							
	(11)	1.5					% Depr., Dep., Amort./Sales		
		2.9							
							% Officers', Directors' Owners' Comp/Sales		
8539M	51151M	165563M	135543M	273732M			Net Sales ($)	77574M	68384M
2008M	13723M	63467M	73245M	58906M			Total Assets ($)	31163M	24440M

M = $ thousand MM = $ million
See Pages 11 through 21 for Explanation of Ratios and Data

Comparative Historical Data / Current Data Sorted by Sales

4/1/04-3/31/05 ALL	4/1/05-3/31/06 ALL	4/1/06-3/31/07 ALL	Type of Statement	0-1MM	1-3MM	3-5MM	5-10MM	10-25MM	25MM & OVER
2	3	6	Unqualified				1	2	3
2	13	6	Reviewed		1	1		3	1
1	13	5	Compiled		1	3			
2	23	7	Tax Returns		4		1		
3	17	9	Other	2	1	2	1	3	
				5 (4/1-9/30/06)			28 (10/1/06-3/31/07)		
10	69	33	NUMBER OF STATEMENTS	2	7	6	6	8	4
%	%	%	ASSETS	%	%	%	%	%	%
12.2	9.5	9.8	Cash & Equivalents						
25.7	41.9	37.2	Trade Receivables (net)						
8.5	8.5	10.1	Inventory						
2.8	6.5	3.5	All Other Current						
49.1	66.4	60.5	Total Current						
38.1	21.1	24.7	Fixed Assets (net)						
7.6	4.9	5.4	Intangibles (net)						
5.1	7.6	9.4	All Other Non-Current						
100.0	100.0	100.0	Total						
			LIABILITIES						
11.0	14.9	8.4	Notes Payable-Short Term						
6.5	4.4	2.9	Cur. Mat.-L.T.D.						
11.3	17.7	17.0	Trade Payables						
.1	.7	.7	Income Taxes Payable						
7.5	13.6	14.9	All Other Current						
36.4	51.5	43.9	Total Current						
14.0	16.9	20.0	Long-Term Debt						
.8	.2	.4	Deferred Taxes						
10.9	5.3	6.5	All Other Non-Current						
37.8	26.2	29.2	Net Worth						
100.0	100.0	100.0	Total Liabilities & Net Worth						
			INCOME DATA						
100.0	100.0	100.0	Net Sales						
38.1	33.0	35.0	Gross Profit						
31.7	27.2	29.8	Operating Expenses						
6.5	5.8	5.1	Operating Profit						
.9	.5	1.1	All Other Expenses (net)						
5.6	5.3	4.0	Profit Before Taxes						
			RATIOS						
1.9	2.3	2.3	Current						
1.6	1.4	1.6							
1.2	1.0	1.1							
1.6	1.9	2.0	Quick						
1.4 (68)	1.1	1.2							
.8	.7	.7							
0 UND	28 13.1	22 16.8	Sales/Receivables						
60 6.1	55 6.6	39 9.5							
82 4.4	72 5.1	76 4.8							
0 UND	0 UND	0 UND	Cost of Sales/Inventory						
0 UND	0 UND	3 126.0							
35 10.3	17 21.5	17 21.1							
0 UND	10 37.5	9 40.9	Cost of Sales/Payables						
21 17.4	28 12.8	24 15.3							
55 6.6	48 7.6	39 9.3							
7.1	9.2	8.1	Sales/Working Capital						
17.8	19.0	12.0							
77.3	NM	44.7							
	23.2	14.6	EBIT/Interest						
(58)	5.3	(28) 3.9							
	2.4	1.4							
	5.7		Net Profit + Depr., Dep., Amort./Cur. Mat. L/T/D						
(11)	2.7								
	1.3								
.5	.2	.3	Fixed/Worth						
1.2	.7	.8							
3.4	4.6	2.7							
.7	1.2	1.0	Debt/Worth						
2.0	3.4	2.7							
5.3	32.2	9.0							
	99.9	74.4	% Profit Before Taxes/Tangible Net Worth						
(54)	44.0	(28) 38.7							
	11.4	17.5							
22.0	27.3	24.4	% Profit Before Taxes/Total Assets						
10.4	10.5	9.8							
1.4	4.6	.7							
24.2	55.5	35.9	Sales/Net Fixed Assets						
8.0	18.0	13.3							
2.9	9.7	7.0							
4.3	4.3	4.4	Sales/Total Assets						
2.4	3.2	2.8							
1.1	2.3	2.2							
1.8	.8	1.1	% Depr., Dep., Amort./Sales						
3.0 (53)	1.5 (25)	2.2							
5.1	3.4	3.8							
	2.0	2.7	% Officers', Directors', Owners' Comp/Sales						
(35)	4.3 (17)	4.9							
	6.2	8.4							
64107M	716938M	634528M	Net Sales ($)	1165M	13849M	24168M	46208M	108702M	440436M
29817M	237823M	211349M	Total Assets ($)	342M	4634M	9011M	23468M	44369M	129525M

M = $ thousand   MM = $ million
See Pages 11 through 21 for Explanation of Ratios and Data

Current Data Sorted by Assets   Comparative Historical Data

Type of Statement	0-500M	500M-2MM	2-10MM	10-50MM	50-100MM	100-250MM		4/1/02-3/31/03 ALL	4/1/03-3/31/04 ALL
Unqualified	4	14	77	81	12	6		133	153
Reviewed	11	142	264	34				285	388
Compiled	40	62	29	2	2	1		88	160
Tax Returns	68	86	28	1	3	7		60	96
Other	35	74	130	50				100	152
		298 (4/1-9/30/06)		965 (10/1/06-3/31/07)					
NUMBER OF STATEMENTS	158	378	528	168	17	14		666	949
ASSETS	%	%	%	%	%	%		%	%
Cash & Equivalents	17.1	13.2	11.1	11.3	7.6	9.0		12.4	12.0
Trade Receivables (net)	35.3	50.6	55.3	56.2	48.9	40.1		49.9	48.7
Inventory	7.5	7.2	4.8	3.1	.3	6.1		5.2	6.1
All Other Current	5.0	6.8	9.9	11.2	15.8	10.5		9.2	9.6
Total Current	64.9	77.8	81.0	81.9	72.6	65.7		76.7	76.4
Fixed Assets (net)	26.0	15.2	12.8	11.3	18.3	22.3		16.5	16.3
Intangibles (net)	2.0	1.3	1.4	1.7	.5	7.4		1.5	1.6
All Other Non-Current	7.1	5.7	4.7	5.2	8.6	4.5		5.3	5.7
Total	100.0	100.0	100.0	100.0	100.0	100.0		100.0	100.0
LIABILITIES									
Notes Payable-Short Term	30.2	11.3	9.0	5.4	2.8	5.6		12.4	12.8
Cur. Mat.-L.T.D.	5.9	3.7	2.3	2.1	4.0	2.3		4.1	3.0
Trade Payables	17.4	20.1	20.1	20.8	19.0	12.7		18.5	18.6
Income Taxes Payable	.1	1.1	.8	.4	.1	.3		1.1	.7
All Other Current	17.7	11.9	17.3	24.1	32.3	30.0		15.7	14.5
Total Current	71.3	48.1	49.4	52.9	58.2	50.9		51.8	49.6
Long-Term Debt	26.7	9.5	7.0	6.3	14.5	12.8		9.8	9.3
Deferred Taxes	.1	.4	.6	.2	.2	.5		.4	.5
All Other Non-Current	6.9	4.9	2.8	3.0	14.9	16.6		2.8	4.1
Net Worth	-4.9	37.0	40.2	37.5	12.2	19.2		35.2	36.4
Total Liabilities & Net Worth	100.0	100.0	100.0	100.0	100.0	100.0		100.0	100.0
INCOME DATA									
Net Sales	100.0	100.0	100.0	100.0	100.0	100.0		100.0	100.0
Gross Profit	38.5	29.2	22.3	16.9	22.1	27.1		24.7	24.6
Operating Expenses	34.4	25.1	17.6	11.6	17.7	22.1		22.4	22.9
Operating Profit	4.2	4.1	4.7	5.3	4.4	5.0		2.3	1.7
All Other Expenses (net)	1.5	.4	.4	.2	.2	1.2		.5	.4
Profit Before Taxes	2.7	3.7	4.3	5.1	4.2	3.8		1.8	1.3
RATIOS									
Current	2.3	2.7	2.2	1.9	1.7	1.6		2.2	2.3
	1.1	1.7	1.6	1.5	1.4	1.4		1.6	1.5
	.5	1.2	1.3	1.3	1.1	.9		1.2	1.2
Quick	1.8	2.2	1.8	1.6	1.3	1.3		1.9	1.9
	.9	1.4	1.3	1.3	1.1	1.1		1.3	1.2
	.4	.9	1.0	1.1	.8	.6		.9	.9
Sales/Receivables	0 UND	39 9.5	53 6.8	61 6.0	58 6.3	42 8.7		46 8.0	44 8.3
	29 12.7	55 6.6	74 5.0	74 4.9	75 4.9	76 4.8		63 5.8	63 5.8
	50 7.3	75 4.9	90 4.1	92 4.0	89 4.1	97 3.8		83 4.4	81 4.5
Cost of Sales/Inventory	0 UND	0 UND	0 UND	0 UND	0 UND	0 UND		0 UND	0 UND
	0 UND	3 123.1	2 171.7	1 347.3	1 722.9	2 218.1		2 173.4	2 134.4
	8 44.6	16 22.5	11 33.8	4 87.3	1 492.2	13 27.4		10 36.2	13 28.3
Cost of Sales/Payables	0 UND	15 24.6	19 19.5	21 17.5	21 17.4	4 81.2		15 24.6	15 24.4
	15 24.0	27 13.4	30 12.3	31 11.8	26 14.0	28 13.2		26 14.3	27 13.6
	33 11.0	42 8.6	45 8.1	45 8.1	39 9.4	46 7.9		43 8.5	41 8.8
Sales/Working Capital	14.6	6.3	5.9	6.9	7.6	8.3		6.6	6.2
	105.1	11.3	9.6	10.1	9.6	12.5		10.8	11.3
	-20.8	27.3	16.9	15.6	33.8	-54.3		23.9	27.0
EBIT/Interest	13.7	19.0	23.8	36.5	46.8	15.3		15.9	12.8
	(142) 4.6	(344) 5.7	(474) 7.7	(147) 13.4	(16) 22.6	(13) 8.5		(582) 3.9	(827) 3.7
	1.0	1.7	2.3	3.9	13.3	2.9		1.0	.7
Net Profit + Depr., Dep., Amort./Cur. Mat. L/T/D		5.6	13.5	34.0				6.1	3.5
		(79) 3.2	(147) 4.4	(60) 7.1				(194) 2.2	(242) 1.7
		1.6	1.7	2.4				.6	.5
Fixed/Worth	.3	.1	.1	.1	.1	.2		.2	.2
	1.6	.3	.3	.2	.3	.7		.3	.4
	-1.3	.9	.6	.4	.5	-1.6		.9	.9
Debt/Worth	1.1	.7	.8	1.1	1.5	1.8		.8	.8
	11.6	1.4	1.6	1.9	2.2	2.8		1.6	1.8
	-4.6	3.6	2.9	3.1	3.9	-5.8		3.5	3.9
% Profit Before Taxes/Tangible Net Worth	179.4	55.4	47.6	48.1	58.1	52.3		36.6	32.1
	(98) 46.2	(330) 21.9	(506) 25.2	(163) 29.6	(15) 34.9	(10) 26.4		(618) 14.1	(867) 10.3
	17.0	4.8	8.4	14.4	21.9	14.2		.4	.4
% Profit Before Taxes/Total Assets	32.0	20.4	18.5	16.8	22.6	11.5		12.4	11.6
	11.9	9.2	8.9	10.7	12.5	6.4		4.7	3.5
	.0	1.7	2.4	4.5	6.8	4.9		.5	-.9
Sales/Net Fixed Assets	113.0	55.2	57.1	91.6	62.7	54.2		49.5	49.5
	32.1	28.2	31.9	40.9	42.3	20.5		25.2	25.3
	13.6	15.3	17.2	17.3	25.3	10.7		14.0	13.7
Sales/Total Assets	9.2	4.2	3.5	3.4	3.6	2.9		3.6	3.7
	5.0	3.2	2.8	2.8	2.9	2.4		2.9	3.0
	3.4	2.5	2.2	2.3	2.4	2.0		2.3	2.2
% Depr., Dep., Amort./Sales	.7	.6	.5	.3	.3			.7	.6
	(97) 1.4	(306) 1.1	(479) .8	(161) .6	(14) .5			(612) 1.2	(824) 1.2
	2.8	1.9	1.4	.9				2.1	2.1
% Officers', Directors' Owners' Comp/Sales	3.4	2.8	1.5	.6				2.5	2.3
	(103) 6.2	(231) 4.5	(251) 2.8	(52) 1.6				(309) 4.7	(502) 4.0
	10.8	8.1	4.8	3.4				8.0	7.0
Net Sales ($)	263943M	1574072M	6910498M	9596471M	7022120M	6210778M		13458024M	17816474M
Total Assets ($)	40970M	455390M	2450234M	3340837M	1228803M	2098659M		4381238M	5385119M

© RMA 2007

M = $ thousand   MM = $ million
See Pages 11 through 21 for Explanation of Ratios and Data

Comparative Historical Data / Current Data Sorted by Sales

			Type of Statement						
163	170	194	Unqualified	3	7	7	23	52	102
397	383	451	Reviewed	7	39	73	143	144	45
99	85	133	Compiled	15	53	27	24	11	3
104	120	186	Tax Returns	27	67	44	22	21	5
196	276	299	Other	15	44	41	53	81	65
4/1/04-3/31/05 ALL	4/1/05-3/31/06 ALL	4/1/06-3/31/07 ALL		298 (4/1-9/30/06)			965 (10/1/06-3/31/07)		
				0-1MM	1-3MM	3-5MM	5-10MM	10-25MM	25MM & OVER
959	1034	1263	NUMBER OF STATEMENTS	67	210	192	265	309	220
%	%	%	**ASSETS**	%	%	%	%	%	%
11.2	12.0	12.4	Cash & Equivalents	17.0	13.1	14.0	12.9	11.4	9.8
52.1	51.0	51.2	Trade Receivables (net)	30.4	44.7	47.3	52.2	58.0	56.7
6.0	5.7	5.6	Inventory	11.2	7.6	6.4	5.4	4.1	3.6
8.2	9.2	8.6	All Other Current	7.4	4.9	7.5	8.7	10.0	11.5
77.5	77.8	77.9	Total Current	66.0	70.4	75.3	79.1	83.5	81.5
15.2	15.3	15.1	Fixed Assets (net)	24.3	20.6	16.5	13.9	11.7	12.1
1.5	1.5	1.6	Intangibles (net)	1.2	2.3	1.6	1.8	.8	1.9
5.8	5.4	5.4	All Other Non-Current	8.4	6.8	6.6	5.2	4.0	4.5
100.0	100.0	100.0	Total	100.0	100.0	100.0	100.0	100.0	100.0
			LIABILITIES						
12.8	12.2	11.7	Notes Payable-Short Term	23.8	19.3	13.1	9.5	9.4	5.7
3.2	2.9	3.1	Cur. Mat.-L.T.D.	8.6	3.7	3.9	3.1	2.1	2.0
20.0	20.1	19.7	Trade Payables	16.9	16.7	18.8	21.1	21.3	20.6
.7	.7	.8	Income Taxes Payable	.0	.7	1.1	1.0	.7	.5
15.1	16.1	17.0	All Other Current	21.6	11.6	12.8	14.0	19.1	25.1
51.8	51.9	52.4	Total Current	71.0	51.9	49.7	48.6	52.5	53.8
9.9	9.7	10.3	Long-Term Debt	28.7	17.3	9.4	9.4	5.5	6.5
.4	.4	.4	Deferred Taxes	.2	.3	.5	.5	.4	.2
4.6	4.6	4.3	All Other Non-Current	8.3	6.1	2.7	4.5	2.8	4.7
33.3	33.3	32.6	Net Worth	-8.2	24.4	37.7	37.0	38.7	34.7
100.0	100.0	100.0	Total Liabilities & Net Worth	100.0	100.0	100.0	100.0	100.0	100.0
			INCOME DATA						
100.0	100.0	100.0	Net Sales	100.0	100.0	100.0	100.0	100.0	100.0
23.7	25.2	25.7	Gross Profit	44.7	34.7	27.8	25.0	20.6	17.5
21.2	21.3	21.2	Operating Expenses	38.2	30.7	23.1	20.4	16.5	12.8
2.5	3.9	4.5	Operating Profit	6.5	4.0	4.6	4.6	4.1	4.7
.3	.4	.5	All Other Expenses (net)	2.4	.9	.3	.4	.2	.2
2.3	3.5	4.0	Profit Before Taxes	4.1	3.1	4.3	4.2	3.9	4.5
			RATIOS						
2.3	2.3	2.3		2.5	2.9	2.6	2.5	2.1	1.9
1.5	1.6	1.6	Current	1.1	1.5	1.6	1.7	1.5	1.5
1.2	1.2	1.2		.5	1.0	1.1	1.3	1.3	1.3
1.9	1.9	1.9		1.8	2.5	2.1	2.1	1.8	1.5
1.3	1.3	1.3	Quick	.7	1.2	1.3	1.4	1.3	1.3
.9	.9	1.0		.3	.8	.9	1.0	1.0	1.0
48 7.6	46 7.9	43 8.6		6 63.3	33 11.0	39 9.5	45 8.2	52 7.0	56 6.5
66 5.5	66 5.5	64 5.7	Sales/Receivables	25 14.6	51 7.2	57 6.4	65 5.6	73 5.0	72 5.1
86 4.3	86 4.3	85 4.3		57 6.4	76 4.8	79 4.6	79 4.6	91 4.0	88 4.2
0 UND	0 UND	0 UND		0 UND	0 UND	0 UND	0 UND	0 UND	0 UND
3 143.3	2 211.7	1 245.1	Cost of Sales/Inventory	0 UND	1 339.0	3 112.1	2 180.2	2 240.5	1 341.4
12 31.1	12 30.8	10 35.8		50 7.3	22 16.2	14 26.0	11 33.5	8 45.1	4 87.2
17 21.6	17 21.3	16 22.9		0 UND	10 36.3	16 23.1	18 20.6	19 19.6	19 19.0
28 12.9	29 12.4	28 13.1	Cost of Sales/Payables	20 18.1	25 14.9	27 13.6	30 12.2	29 12.7	28 12.9
44 8.3	45 8.1	43 8.5		45 8.1	44 8.4	44 8.4	45 8.2	44 8.3	41 9.0
6.6	6.3	6.5		6.4	6.1	6.0	6.0	6.5	7.8
11.2	10.6	11.1	Sales/Working Capital	72.5	14.8	11.8	10.4	10.4	10.3
24.2	23.0	25.0		-9.8	-230.2	39.5	18.8	18.0	17.2
15.9	19.8	22.5		12.6	11.8	19.3	25.7	22.7	33.6
(827) 4.6	(911) 6.1	(1136) 7.1	EBIT/Interest	(56) 2.7	(190) 4.9	(173) 6.0	(242) 7.5	(278) 7.6	(197) 13.3
1.0	1.8	2.1		.5	1.1	2.0	2.3	2.2	4.6
6.8	7.2	12.5			4.2	6.3	9.2	14.3	36.9
(243) 2.5	(261) 3.0	(303) 4.4	Net Profit + Depr., Dep., Amort./Cur. Mat. L/T/D	(28) 2.1	(45) 2.8	(64) 3.7	(87) 6.1	(75) 8.6	
1.1	1.4	1.8			.8	1.6	1.7	1.7	3.4
.1	.1	.1		.2	.1	.1	.1	.1	.1
.3	.3	.3	Fixed/Worth	1.7	.6	.3	.3	.3	.2
.9	.8	.8		-3.3	9.5	.9	.6	.6	.4
.9	.8	.8		.8	.6	.7	.7	.9	1.2
1.8	1.7	1.8	Debt/Worth	6.2	2.1	1.4	1.4	1.8	1.9
3.7	3.7	3.6		-7.3	UND	3.8	3.0	3.1	3.0
36.0	43.0	53.3		72.2	74.6	55.1	50.6	49.2	52.3
(861) 13.7	(932) 19.4	(1122) 26.3	% Profit Before Taxes/Tangible Net Worth	(43) 25.5	(160) 22.9	(170) 23.4	(238) 23.7	(301) 27.1	(210) 30.9
1.9	5.5	8.6		3.3	4.0	5.6	6.6	8.8	16.0
13.0	16.9	20.3		25.0	21.5	21.0	22.6	18.0	18.3
4.6	7.1	9.3	% Profit Before Taxes/Total Assets	4.7	9.2	7.9	9.2	9.6	10.7
.1	1.7	2.4		-.7	.4	1.7	2.2	2.8	5.7
58.4	58.3	64.7		75.4	71.8	45.4	65.4	64.8	83.3
28.4	29.0	31.7	Sales/Net Fixed Assets	21.5	24.0	24.7	34.1	35.7	41.9
15.7	14.9	16.3		9.4	13.1	13.8	16.7	20.5	21.4
3.8	3.6	3.8		5.3	4.7	4.0	3.8	3.7	3.5
3.0	2.9	3.0	Sales/Total Assets	3.1	3.2	2.9	3.1	3.0	3.0
2.4	2.3	2.4		2.0	2.5	2.2	2.4	2.4	2.5
.6	.5	.5		1.1	.6	.7	.5	.5	.3
(819) 1.1	(894) 1.0	(1066) .9	% Depr., Dep., Amort./Sales	(46) 2.2	(146) 1.3	(161) 1.2	(222) .9	(286) .8	(205) .6
1.9	1.7	1.6		4.2	2.4	2.0	1.5	1.3	.9
1.8	1.9	1.9		7.0	3.3	2.5	2.1	1.4	.8
(466) 3.4	(486) 3.4	(644) 3.6	% Officers', Directors' Owners' Comp/Sales	(36) 10.2	(136) 5.4	(112) 4.0	(141) 3.7	(151) 2.5	(68) 1.9
5.9	6.5	6.8		13.6	8.6	8.0	5.9	4.8	3.4
18690166M	25525914M	31577882M	Net Sales ($)	41014M	413684M	761473M	1912229M	4828532M	23620950M
5629092M	7630230M	9614893M	Total Assets ($)	30383M	153040M	285482M	678298M	1722389M	6745301M

© RMA 2007

M = $ thousand   MM = $ million
See Pages 11 through 21 for Explanation of Ratios and Data

Current Data Sorted by Assets   Comparative Historical Data

						Type of Statement		
2	11	54	69	8	4	Unqualified	128	148
7	102	229	37			Reviewed	316	370
24	72	43	8		3	Compiled	130	210
108	69	35	4	5	4	Tax Returns	93	141
30	69	88	46	3	7	Other	144	215
	246 (4/1-9/30/06)		895 (10/1/06-3/31/07)				4/1/02-3/31/03	4/1/03-3/31/04
0-500M	500M-2MM	2-10MM	10-50MM	50-100MM	100-250MM		ALL	ALL
171	323	449	164	16	18	NUMBER OF STATEMENTS	811	1084
%	%	%	%	%	%	ASSETS	%	%
21.0	13.1	12.7	13.2	8.9	12.0	Cash & Equivalents	12.5	12.4
26.6	44.9	53.0	56.1	42.9	27.1	Trade Receivables (net)	48.7	46.6
9.7	10.1	6.0	5.4	7.3	3.5	Inventory	7.6	7.7
4.1	5.4	9.0	9.2	4.7	5.4	All Other Current	6.6	7.8
61.4	73.5	80.6	83.9	63.8	48.0	Total Current	75.5	74.5
29.0	17.9	12.7	9.5	17.0	23.3	Fixed Assets (net)	17.3	17.9
3.0	3.3	1.7	1.5	9.4	19.1	Intangibles (net)	1.5	1.5
6.5	5.4	5.0	5.1	9.7	9.6	All Other Non-Current	5.7	6.0
100.0	100.0	100.0	100.0	100.0	100.0	Total	100.0	100.0
						LIABILITIES		
14.5	10.1	7.4	6.1	4.6	3.9	Notes Payable-Short Term	10.3	10.7
4.9	3.1	2.1	1.7	2.2	4.1	Cur. Mat.-L.T.D.	3.2	3.8
16.3	22.9	22.7	23.4	25.8	14.4	Trade Payables	23.7	22.4
.0	.7	.9	.6	.1	.1	Income Taxes Payable	.7	.6
17.2	12.8	18.3	26.2	27.6	13.2	All Other Current	16.1	15.9
53.0	49.6	51.4	58.1	60.3	35.7	Total Current	54.0	53.4
28.8	13.2	6.8	5.5	22.4	33.3	Long-Term Debt	9.7	11.1
.0	.2	.5	.3	1.0	.0	Deferred Taxes	.4	.5
6.4	3.6	2.5	2.5	2.5	14.1	All Other Non-Current	3.0	3.5
11.9	33.4	38.7	33.6	13.9	17.0	Net Worth	32.8	31.5
100.0	100.0	100.0	100.0	100.0	100.0	Total Liabilties & Net Worth	100.0	100.0
						INCOME DATA		
100.0	100.0	100.0	100.0	100.0	100.0	Net Sales	100.0	100.0
42.3	31.9	23.4	19.6	21.9	39.3	Gross Profit	25.8	26.9
37.2	27.3	18.5	15.0	17.9	32.0	Operating Expenses	23.5	24.7
5.0	4.6	4.9	4.6	4.0	7.3	Operating Profit	2.3	2.1
.7	.7	.2	.1	1.0	1.8	All Other Expenses (net)	.3	.3
4.4	3.8	4.7	4.5	3.0	5.5	Profit Before Taxes	2.0	1.8
						RATIOS		
2.6	2.4	2.1	1.7	1.6	2.2		2.1	2.0
1.5	1.5	1.5	1.4	1.3	1.3	Current	1.4	1.4
.8	1.1	1.2	1.2	1.1	.9		1.1	1.1
2.0	1.9	1.7	1.4	1.3	1.9		1.7	1.7
(170) 1.0	1.2	1.3	1.2	1.0	(17) 1.0	Quick	1.2	1.1
.5	.8	1.0	1.0	.8	.4		.9	.8
0 UND	28 13.3	47 7.8	57 6.4	23 15.7	0 UND		37 9.8	33 11.0
13 27.7	46 7.9	67 5.4	76 4.8	48 7.6	28 13.3	Sales/Receivables	58 6.3	54 6.8
35 10.4	68 5.4	87 4.2	97 3.8	71 5.1	59 6.1		78 4.7	76 4.8
0 UND	0 999.8	0 999.8	0 999.8	0 UND	0 UND		0 UND	0 UND
1 393.3	9 41.9	4 94.8	2 204.6	5 80.5	0 UND	Cost of Sales/Inventory	4 87.6	4 83.6
17 21.0	21 17.2	12 29.8	8 44.8	15 24.3	13 27.2		15 24.5	15 23.7
0 UND	17 20.9	21 17.7	25 14.6	12 29.6	8 43.5		20 18.6	18 20.5
11 33.9	29 12.6	32 11.5	35 10.5	30 12.3	14 26.0	Cost of Sales/Payables	32 11.4	30 12.2
30 12.2	47 7.8	48 7.5	50 7.3	42 8.8	65 5.6		48 7.6	45 8.0
12.4	7.6	6.6	7.3	10.7	11.4		7.9	7.9
36.4	14.1	11.1	11.1	15.8	39.5	Sales/Working Capital	13.7	15.3
-70.2	61.0	21.2	17.6	213.3	-48.4		39.6	48.8
15.7	16.5	32.6	38.6	19.9	19.9		15.8	14.0
(143) 5.0	(291) 6.4	(387) 8.7	(141) 10.4	(15) 6.5	(16) 5.6	EBIT/Interest	(701) 4.7	(938) 4.0
1.3	1.6	2.9	5.1	1.7	1.3		1.4	.2
	14.9	10.5	13.4				5.9	5.5
	(52) 5.2	(128) 3.9	(54) 3.9			Net Profit + Depr., Dep., Amort./Cur. Mat. L/T/D	(217) 2.4	(264) 2.2
	1.5	2.0	2.2				.9	.7
.2	.2	.1	.1	.2	.9		.2	.2
1.1	.5	.3	.2	.6	-1.0	Fixed/Worth	.4	.4
-4.8	1.8	.6	.5	750.6	-.2		1.0	1.0
.8	.9	.9	1.2	1.3	1.4		.9	.9
3.6	2.2	1.8	2.2	3.4	-16.7	Debt/Worth	1.9	2.0
-11.3	6.9	3.6	3.5	NM	-2.2		4.2	4.4
133.9	65.3	53.4	51.4	48.4			37.3	36.9
(118) 54.4	(281) 31.4	(429) 31.0	(157) 33.1	(12) 19.5		% Profit Before Taxes/Tangible Net Worth	(737) 15.9	(966) 13.3
15.6	8.1	11.3	15.7	12.6			4.0	.4
45.1	22.0	20.1	16.7	14.7	30.8		11.9	12.7
13.2	9.5	9.9	9.4	8.6	10.1	% Profit Before Taxes/Total Assets	4.8	4.1
.6	2.1	3.5	4.8	2.9	4.2		.8	-.9
86.6	51.6	69.1	75.8	59.0	62.3		46.5	46.7
29.8	27.2	34.1	35.8	28.0	25.2	Sales/Net Fixed Assets	26.4	25.6
13.6	14.7	19.3	18.8	16.3	10.2		15.0	14.9
9.9	4.5	3.6	3.3	8.1	4.9		4.0	4.2
5.7	3.5	3.0	2.6	3.1	3.1	Sales/Total Assets	3.1	3.3
3.9	2.7	2.3	2.2	2.3	2.2		2.6	2.6
.7	.6	.5	.3				.7	.7
(117) 1.3	(263) 1.1	(401) .9	(151) .6			% Depr., Dep., Amort./Sales	(732) 1.3	(914) 1.2
2.6	1.9	1.4	1.0				2.1	2.1
4.2	2.5	1.4	1.0				2.2	2.4
(124) 6.8	(194) 4.3	(214) 2.7	(51) 1.9			% Officers', Directors' Owners' Comp/Sales	(441) 3.9	(589) 4.3
11.2	5.9	5.1	4.4				7.4	7.3
300806M	1419319M	6182092M	9513589M	7431078M	10358058M	Net Sales ($)	12086690M	23658090M
42739M	381475M	2064639M	3285152M	1097194M	2728816M	Total Assets ($)	4066949M	6186611M

M = $ thousand   MM = $ million
See Pages 11 through 21 for Explanation of Ratios and Data

Comparative Historical Data

Current Data Sorted by Sales

			Type of Statement						
124	133	148	Unqualified	1	2	8	13	43	81
371	340	375	Reviewed	5	24	47	119	130	50
140	136	150	Compiled	9	41	33	28	25	14
145	169	225	Tax Returns	41	81	35	35	19	14
182	293	243	Other	10	42	28	51	51	61
4/1/04-3/31/05 ALL	4/1/05-3/31/06 ALL	4/1/06-3/31/07 ALL		246 (4/1-9/30/06)			895 (10/1/06-3/31/07)		
				0-1MM	1-3MM	3-5MM	5-10MM	10-25MM	25MM & OVER
962	1071	1141	NUMBER OF STATEMENTS	66	190	151	246	268	220
%	%	%	ASSETS	%	%	%	%	%	%
11.5	12.1	14.1	Cash & Equivalents	24.9	15.1	13.7	13.5	13.7	11.4
49.4	48.5	46.6	Trade Receivables (net)	22.8	34.7	45.4	49.1	52.8	54.6
7.5	8.3	7.6	Inventory	9.8	9.9	9.8	8.3	5.1	5.6
7.2	7.6	7.2	All Other Current	3.0	4.4	5.9	8.3	8.5	8.7
75.6	76.4	75.4	Total Current	60.5	64.0	74.8	79.2	80.1	80.3
16.4	15.8	16.4	Fixed Assets (net)	30.3	24.8	16.9	14.2	12.8	11.3
1.9	2.1	2.7	Intangibles (net)	3.6	4.9	2.0	1.9	1.9	3.0
6.0	5.7	5.5	All Other Non-Current	5.5	6.3	6.3	4.7	5.2	5.4
100.0	100.0	100.0	Total	100.0	100.0	100.0	100.0	100.0	100.0
			LIABILITIES						
10.3	11.2	8.9	Notes Payable-Short Term	12.5	12.7	9.9	9.5	6.3	6.5
3.1	3.1	2.8	Cur. Mat.-L.T.D.	3.7	3.6	3.6	2.6	2.4	2.1
23.3	23.5	21.8	Trade Payables	13.8	18.3	21.5	23.6	23.0	23.8
.8	.7	.7	Income Taxes Payable	.1	.3	.9	.9	.8	.5
16.2	15.8	17.8	All Other Current	13.6	13.2	16.0	15.9	18.8	25.0
53.6	54.3	52.0	Total Current	43.8	48.2	51.9	52.5	51.4	57.9
12.5	12.0	12.4	Long-Term Debt	27.2	23.8	13.5	8.5	6.3	9.0
.3	.4	.3	Deferred Taxes	.0	.1	.3	.3	.5	.3
2.7	4.8	3.6	All Other Non-Current	5.8	5.6	4.0	2.9	2.2	3.4
30.9	28.5	31.8	Net Worth	23.2	22.3	30.2	35.8	39.6	29.4
100.0	100.0	100.0	Total Liabilties & Net Worth	100.0	100.0	100.0	100.0	100.0	100.0
			INCOME DATA						
100.0	100.0	100.0	Net Sales	100.0	100.0	100.0	100.0	100.0	100.0
25.4	26.5	28.3	Gross Profit	47.3	38.8	28.9	26.8	22.6	21.8
23.1	23.4	23.5	Operating Expenses	38.7	34.1	24.9	22.5	17.7	16.9
2.3	3.2	4.8	Operating Profit	8.6	4.7	4.0	4.3	4.8	4.8
.3	.2	.4	All Other Expenses (net)	2.0	.7	.3	.3	.2	.4
2.0	2.9	4.4	Profit Before Taxes	6.6	4.0	3.7	4.0	4.7	4.5
			RATIOS						
2.1	2.1	2.1		3.9	2.8	2.2	2.2	2.1	1.7
1.5	1.5	1.5	Current	1.6	1.6	1.6	1.5	1.6	1.4
1.2	1.2	1.2		.8	1.0	1.1	1.2	1.2	1.2
1.7	1.7	1.8		3.1	2.0	1.9	1.8	1.7	1.4
(961) 1.2	1.2 (1139)	1.2	Quick	1.1	1.1	1.3 (245)	1.2	1.3 (219)	1.2
.9	.8	.9		.5	.6	.8	.8	1.0	.9
38 9.6	35 10.3	31 11.7		0 UND	13 27.8	28 13.2	35 10.5	45 8.2	46 8.0
57 6.4	57 6.3	56 6.5	Sales/Receivables	15 24.5	34 10.8	49 7.4	60 6.1	64 5.7	69 5.3
78 4.7	80 4.6	79 4.6		44 8.2	59 6.2	77 4.7	79 4.6	85 4.3	89 4.1
0 UND	0 UND	0 UND		0 UND	0 UND	0 UND	1 576.8	0 999.8	0 UND
4 88.6	4 84.0	4 93.7	Cost of Sales/Inventory	0 UND	7 50.1	6 57.5	6 64.7	3 107.7	2 200.2
15 23.9	16 22.8	15 24.3		25 14.8	22 16.6	22 16.3	18 20.6	10 37.5	8 43.3
18 20.2	20 18.7	17 21.7		0 UND	6 56.8	15 23.9	19 19.5	20 18.0	22 17.0
31 11.8	32 11.5	29 12.5	Cost of Sales/Payables	13 28.4	24 15.1	27 13.3	32 11.5	30 12.3	34 10.7
48 7.7	50 7.3	47 7.8		39 9.4	47 7.8	45 8.1	48 7.6	45 8.1	49 7.5
7.8	7.7	7.6		7.6	8.2	6.5	7.0	7.3	9.2
13.5	13.3	13.2	Sales/Working Capital	23.1	17.9	11.6	13.8	12.0	12.6
33.3	35.8	36.5		-65.1	-390.7	48.9	38.2	22.5	24.0
18.4	19.0	22.7		13.0	14.7	14.5	25.5	40.7	28.7
(842) 4.8	(962) 6.2	(993) 7.7	EBIT/Interest	(45) 3.0	(170) 5.5	(130) 6.4	(217) 6.8	(237) 11.9	(194) 9.2
1.1	1.8	2.4		.5	1.4	1.5	2.2	3.6	4.6
7.3	7.8	11.1			17.3	17.0	11.4	14.3	8.1
(252) 2.5	(256) 2.7	(245) 3.9	Net Profit + Depr., Dep., Amort./Cur. Mat. L/T/D		(13) 2.6	(25) 5.5	(58) 3.8	(82) 4.7	(65) 3.4
.8	1.3	1.8			-.6	1.5	1.4	2.3	1.9
.2	.2	.1		.1	.2	.2	.2	.1	.1
.4	.4	.4	Fixed/Worth	.7	.4	.4	.3	.3	.3
1.0	1.1	1.1		-29.4	111.3	1.4	.8	.6	.6
1.0	1.1	.9		.4	.8	.8	1.0	.8	1.4
2.0	2.1	2.1	Debt/Worth	2.6	3.1	1.8	2.1	1.6	2.4
4.6	5.6	5.0		-20.6	UND	5.0	4.7	3.1	4.3
39.0	54.8	64.2		71.1	89.5	56.6	65.6	53.2	59.1
(858) 16.1	(932) 26.0	(1005) 32.9	% Profit Before Taxes/Tangible Net Worth	(47) 31.1	(144) 36.7	(127) 31.5	(232) 30.7	(255) 31.6	(200) 35.6
2.6	7.0	11.5		7.1	12.3	8.3	8.6	13.1	16.8
13.5	17.8	22.0		31.9	24.1	23.5	22.5	20.7	17.8
5.0	7.5	9.9	% Profit Before Taxes/Total Assets	8.0	10.6	9.5	8.4	10.3	9.7
.1	1.7	3.2		.0	1.7	1.8	2.7	4.8	4.6
53.6	59.5	63.3		86.7	44.3	56.5	62.9	72.3	75.8
28.2	30.5	31.4	Sales/Net Fixed Assets	25.6	19.5	28.5	34.5	34.7	36.5
15.8	16.9	16.6		7.5	11.3	15.8	20.4	19.3	21.0
4.2	4.1	4.3		7.9	5.7	4.5	4.1	3.8	3.7
3.2	3.2	3.2	Sales/Total Assets	3.8	3.6	3.3	3.3	3.1	3.0
2.5	2.5	2.5		1.8	2.5	2.5	2.4	2.5	2.4
.6	.5	.5		.7	.8	.6	.5	.5	.3
(833) 1.1	(906) 1.0	(950) .9	% Depr., Dep., Amort./Sales	(42) 1.4	(141) 1.6	(124) 1.1	(217) .8	(240) .8	(186) .6
1.8	1.7	1.6		3.1	2.7	1.9	1.4	1.4	1.0
2.0	1.7	1.9		7.4	4.2	1.9	1.2	1.2	1.0
(508) 3.6	(504) 3.0	(595) 4.0	% Officers', Directors' Owners' Comp/Sales	(37) 11.5	(135) 5.5	(84) 4.3	(137) 3.1	(132) 2.6	(70) 1.9
6.5	6.1	6.5		16.2	8.4	5.8	5.1	4.6	5.4
16571432M	29702232M	35204942M	Net Sales ($)	41009M	366112M	600892M	1787528M	4254053M	28155348M
5726947M	7361791M	9600015M	Total Assets ($)	14716M	121689M	204030M	603952M	1442665M	7212963M

M = $ thousand   MM = $ million
See Pages 11 through 21 for Explanation of Ratios and Data

Current Data Sorted by Assets

Comparative Historical Data

Type of Statement	0-500M	500M-2MM	2-10MM	10-50MM	50-100MM	100-250MM		4/1/02-3/31/03 ALL	4/1/03-3/31/04 ALL
Unqualified	1	1	10	7	5	1		9	12
Reviewed	2	12	39	6				25	30
Compiled	9	13	8	1				12	23
Tax Returns	18	12	7					5	13
Other	8	18	16	5				12	21
		31 (4/1-9/30/06)		168 (10/1/06-3/31/07)					
NUMBER OF STATEMENTS	38	56	80	19	5	1		63	99
ASSETS	%	%	%	%	%	%		%	%
Cash & Equivalents	16.9	10.8	14.0	8.2				13.9	12.5
Trade Receivables (net)	33.0	42.3	43.6	46.5				43.2	41.4
Inventory	10.6	15.2	7.6	9.2				7.3	8.2
All Other Current	1.9	4.3	9.8	9.0				8.0	8.9
Total Current	62.5	72.6	74.9	72.9				72.3	71.0
Fixed Assets (net)	27.1	17.1	17.7	19.8				20.4	20.0
Intangibles (net)	2.2	4.2	1.1	2.6				1.0	2.1
All Other Non-Current	8.3	6.1	6.2	4.7				6.2	6.9
Total	100.0	100.0	100.0	100.0				100.0	100.0
LIABILITIES									
Notes Payable-Short Term	18.8	11.8	10.1	11.5				11.5	15.8
Cur. Mat.-L.T.D.	4.7	3.4	3.2	2.2				3.1	3.5
Trade Payables	21.0	16.2	14.9	17.0				15.4	20.9
Income Taxes Payable	.3	.3	.4	.3				.4	.4
All Other Current	14.6	17.4	14.8	17.6				15.7	16.2
Total Current	59.3	49.1	43.5	48.7				46.0	56.8
Long-Term Debt	24.9	12.6	9.1	9.1				11.8	12.3
Deferred Taxes	.1	.5	.4	.7				.6	.3
All Other Non-Current	20.7	4.5	3.1	4.3				1.8	5.5
Net Worth	-4.8	33.3	43.8	37.3				39.9	25.0
Total Liabilties & Net Worth	100.0	100.0	100.0	100.0				100.0	100.0
INCOME DATA									
Net Sales	100.0	100.0	100.0	100.0				100.0	100.0
Gross Profit	40.8	31.6	25.4	23.2				28.3	27.4
Operating Expenses	38.6	27.3	19.4	16.4				27.3	25.4
Operating Profit	2.2	4.3	6.0	6.8				1.0	2.0
All Other Expenses (net)	.5	.6	-.2	.7				.1	.9
Profit Before Taxes	1.7	3.7	6.2	6.1				.9	1.1
RATIOS									
	2.6	3.3	2.7	1.8				2.5	2.0
Current	1.5	1.6	1.6	1.3				1.6	1.3
	.7	1.0	1.3	1.2				1.2	1.0
	2.1	2.6	2.2	1.4				1.8	1.6
Quick	1.0	1.2	1.3	1.0				1.3 (98)	1.0
	.3	.7	.9	.9				.9	.7
	6 65.5	25 14.6	42 8.7	61 6.0				44 8.3	33 11.0
Sales/Receivables	26 14.2	53 6.9	62 5.9	74 4.9				71 5.1	56 6.5
	45 8.1	75 4.9	87 4.2	87 4.2				86 4.2	75 4.9
	0 UND	0 UND	0 UND	0 UND				0 UND	0 UND
Cost of Sales/Inventory	3 114.1	10 37.0	2 161.5	3 145.0				4 83.2	1 273.5
	16 23.2	48 7.7	16 22.2	22 16.5				31 11.9	24 15.5
	1 360.2	4 103.5	12 30.4	16 23.4				12 29.5	14 26.2
Cost of Sales/Payables	14 26.6	18 20.8	25 14.5	31 11.7				25 14.6	32 11.5
	43 8.5	33 11.1	37 10.0	49 7.5				46 7.9	52 7.0
	10.7	5.6	5.3	6.0				5.9	7.8
Sales/Working Capital	49.1	11.2	8.8	15.1				11.0	13.2
	-33.8	805.4	16.5	20.5				24.3	770.0
	11.7	17.3	40.8	52.7				12.4	9.5
EBIT/Interest	(27) 3.2	(49) 5.2	(66) 6.7	7.2				(56) 3.7	(90) 2.1
	-.2	1.4	2.4	2.2				.3	-1.1
Net Profit + Depr., Dep.,			5.3					3.7	3.3
Amort./Cur. Mat. L/T/D		(15) 4.4						(17) 1.4	(16) 1.6
			1.7					.8	-.5
	.2	.1	.2	.2				.2	.2
Fixed/Worth	1.3	.5	.3	.4				.3	.7
	-1.6	1.8	.7	1.2				1.0	5.6
	.9	.6	.6	1.1				.7	1.2
Debt/Worth	3.4	1.8	1.5	2.5				1.6	2.4
	-3.8	9.9	2.9	5.5				3.2	21.9
% Profit Before Taxes/Tangible	76.7	48.8	56.0	62.8				28.1	32.5
Net Worth	(23) 40.0	(46) 22.7	(77) 29.9	33.7				(59) 9.0	(78) 7.7
	12.4	7.6	11.1	16.7				-.8	-12.5
% Profit Before Taxes/Total	21.6	17.1	22.6	20.2				9.7	12.2
Assets	10.5	7.9	11.9	9.5				3.3	1.6
	-7.9	.4	4.7	4.0				-3.1	-3.6
	49.3	63.0	45.2	34.3				39.2	44.4
Sales/Net Fixed Assets	32.1	24.7	22.3	13.4				20.6	22.1
	15.8	12.3	8.6	9.5				8.0	10.0
	7.2	3.8	3.2	3.2				3.3	3.9
Sales/Total Assets	5.4	3.0	2.5	2.2				2.6	2.7
	3.5	2.3	2.0	1.7				1.9	2.1
	.7	.6	.6	.4				.9	.6
% Depr., Dep., Amort./Sales	(32) 1.3	(42) 1.1	(70) 1.0	(16) 1.0				(60) 1.7	(84) 1.4
	3.1	2.4	1.9	2.2				4.1	2.3
% Officers', Directors'	5.3	2.2	1.8					2.8	2.2
Owners' Comp/Sales	(20) 8.0	(33) 4.1	(40) 3.1					(32) 4.6	(43) 4.1
	14.5	7.1	5.7					7.3	8.4
Net Sales ($)	51015M	204937M	851293M	993340M	758062M	242452M		3962584M	1506092M
Total Assets ($)	9131M	67224M	330449M	431090M	381855M	115131M		566980M	652416M

M = $ thousand   MM = $ million
See Pages 11 through 21 for Explanation of Ratios and Data

Comparative Historical Data | Current Data Sorted by Sales

Type of Statement									
Unqualified	11	22	25	1	1	1	1	8	13
Reviewed	25	34	59		5	4	30	14	6
Compiled	15	28	31	7	7	8	5	3	1
Tax Returns	16	17	37	10	17	3	3	4	
Other	34	45	47	3	14	11	8		4
	4/1/04-3/31/05 ALL	4/1/05-3/31/06 ALL	4/1/06-3/31/07 ALL	31 (4/1-9/30/06) 0-1MM	1-3MM	3-5MM	168 (10/1/06-3/31/07) 5-10MM	10-25MM	25MM & OVER
NUMBER OF STATEMENTS	101	146	199	21	44	27	47	36	24

ASSETS

	%	%	%	%	%	%	%	%	%
Cash & Equivalents	12.3	12.2	12.9	15.3	14.6	13.5	11.1	12.8	10.7
Trade Receivables (net)	43.8	43.1	41.1	28.5	32.5	43.6	51.8	39.7	46.3
Inventory	8.4	10.5	10.7	9.6	14.1	13.0	7.5	10.1	10.5
All Other Current	7.1	6.2	6.5	1.0	4.6	5.2	8.2	9.4	8.7
Total Current	71.7	72.0	71.3	54.3	65.8	75.3	78.6	71.9	76.2
Fixed Assets (net)	19.5	19.8	19.8	24.9	24.7	17.0	14.7	22.8	15.3
Intangibles (net)	2.2	3.4	2.5	8.7	2.5	2.3	.8	.8	3.6
All Other Non-Current	6.5	4.8	6.4	12.2	6.9	5.4	5.9	4.5	4.9
Total	100.0	100.0	100.0	100.0	100.0	100.0	100.0	100.0	100.0

LIABILITIES

Notes Payable-Short Term	13.0	13.6	12.4	17.4	13.9	15.0	12.1	5.7	13.2
Cur. Mat.-L.T.D.	3.2	4.2	3.4	3.4	3.3	3.1	4.0	4.5	1.1
Trade Payables	20.2	17.1	16.6	19.4	14.8	17.7	16.4	15.2	18.9
Income Taxes Payable	.4	.6	.3	.1	.3	.1	.6	.5	.2
All Other Current	16.0	16.9	15.6	28.6	12.4	11.3	14.2	16.1	17.1
Total Current	52.9	52.2	48.4	68.9	44.7	47.1	47.2	42.1	50.4
Long-Term Debt	15.6	17.2	13.2	25.7	21.4	10.0	6.0	12.4	6.1
Deferred Taxes	.4	.4	.5	.0	.5	.2	.4	.9	.6
All Other Non-Current	4.9	3.3	7.0	6.5	16.5	4.4	4.9	1.5	5.1
Net Worth	26.3	26.9	31.0	-1.0	16.9	38.3	41.5	43.1	37.7
Total Liabilties & Net Worth	100.0	100.0	100.0	100.0	100.0	100.0	100.0	100.0	100.0

INCOME DATA

Net Sales	100.0	100.0	100.0	100.0	100.0	100.0	100.0	100.0	100.0
Gross Profit	32.1	31.2	29.8	43.8	35.9	31.8	25.0	25.0	20.9
Operating Expenses	29.4	27.0	24.9	41.6	31.3	28.4	19.4	18.6	14.9
Operating Profit	2.7	4.2	4.9	2.2	4.5	3.4	5.6	6.3	6.0
All Other Expenses (net)	.3	.8	.4	1.4	.3	-.2	-.1	.4	.9
Profit Before Taxes	2.4	3.4	4.5	.8	4.2	3.6	5.8	5.9	5.1

RATIOS

Current	2.1	2.2	2.6	2.8	4.4	2.4	2.7	2.6	1.8
	1.5	1.5	1.5	1.1	1.4	1.8	1.7	1.5	1.4
	1.1	1.1	1.1	.4	1.0	1.1	1.2	1.3	1.2
Quick	1.9	1.8	2.2	2.7	3.3	1.9	2.2	2.2	1.4
	1.1	1.1	1.3	.8	1.2	1.2	1.5	1.3	1.2
	.7	.7	.7	.3	.5	.7	.9	.9	.7
Sales/Receivables	38 9.7	30 12.1	30 12.0	0 UND	7 53.5	37 9.8	52 7.0	32 11.5	55 6.6
	56 6.5	56 6.5	54 6.8	34 10.7	29 12.6	54 6.8	70 5.2	55 6.7	68 5.4
	81 4.5	83 4.4	77 4.7	65 5.6	56 6.5	76 4.8	88 4.1	73 5.0	85 4.3
Cost of Sales/Inventory	0 UND	0 UND	0 UND	0 UND	0 UND	1 615.4	0 UND	0 UND	0 UND
	4 98.2	5 72.5	4 88.4	0 UND	6 65.4	10 35.6	4 103.2	3 114.3	2 174.0
	28 12.9	24 14.9	22 16.5	31 11.8	33 11.1	50 7.3	20 18.6	16 23.0	33 11.1
Cost of Sales/Payables	10 35.3	11 34.0	10 36.0	0 UND	0 UND	13 28.3	13 27.6	12 29.5	12 30.6
	32 11.4	24 15.0	21 17.6	12 30.0	14 26.9	18 20.7	25 14.5	26 14.1	27 13.5
	53 6.9	46 7.9	36 10.1	50 7.3	32 11.5	36 10.1	36 10.2	33 11.2	50 7.3
Sales/Working Capital	8.4	6.9	6.2	10.7	6.3	5.4	5.1	6.4	6.3
	12.3	13.0	12.0	64.9	18.8	8.5	9.7	13.0	10.4
	52.4	73.1	94.9	-3.9	-172.6	82.8	17.4	19.7	18.1
EBIT/Interest	21.9	24.3	21.4	10.8	17.0	15.3	29.7	73.1	50.9
	(89) 4.4	(132) 5.2	(166) 5.2	(14) 1.8	(35) 4.6	(24) 3.5	(42) 6.8	(30) 10.2	(21) 7.2
	1.1	1.8	2.0	-.3	.7	1.6	3.0	3.2	2.2
Net Profit + Depr., Dep., Amort./Cur. Mat. L/T/D	7.5	7.6	6.3				5.3	16.7	
	(18) 2.4	(36) 2.0	(35) 2.6			(11) 2.7	(10) 3.0		
	1.3	1.0	1.7				1.8	1.3	
Fixed/Worth	.2	.2	.2	.2	.2	.1	.1	.2	.2
	.4	.5	.4	8.4	.6	.4	.2	.3	.3
	3.2	2.1	1.4	-.3	4.3	1.5	.8	1.0	1.0
Debt/Worth	1.0	.9	.7	.9	.6	.5	.7	.6	1.1
	2.1	2.3	1.7	164.7	2.0	1.6	1.5	1.6	2.2
	7.2	13.2	5.8	-2.0	NM	6.2	3.1	3.5	4.6
% Profit Before Taxes/Tangible Net Worth	41.7	62.5	53.8	137.7	73.2	47.3	53.3	56.8	43.7
	(83) 19.1	(120) 31.9	(171) 29.9	(12) 53.7	(33) 30.0	(23) 21.7	(44) 24.8	(35) 39.4	29.9
	3.6	12.0	11.6	3.8	6.5	7.7	10.9	13.7	18.1
% Profit Before Taxes/Total Assets	14.2	21.3	20.2	18.5	21.2	16.1	19.6	26.2	15.7
	5.6	9.3	10.2	4.6	10.0	7.4	11.5	12.4	11.0
	.2	1.6	2.5	-13.7	-1.6	1.6	5.7	5.2	4.1
Sales/Net Fixed Assets	68.7	53.3	46.0	64.1	47.1	37.8	46.1	49.5	53.2
	24.9	24.0	23.9	17.2	25.4	22.2	24.3	25.3	26.8
	9.7	10.6	10.8	9.1	10.9	14.7	11.9	7.0	10.6
Sales/Total Assets	4.1	3.9	3.8	4.5	5.6	5.2	3.4	3.6	3.3
	2.9	3.1	2.9	3.4	3.3	2.7	2.5	3.1	2.5
	2.3	2.2	2.1	1.9	2.2	2.0	2.1	2.2	1.8
% Depr., Dep., Amort./Sales	.6	.5	.6	1.1	.7	.5	.6	.7	.4
	(77) 1.4	(123) 1.0	(166) 1.1	(17) 2.1	(33) 1.4	(24) .9	(39) 1.0	(31) 1.0	(22) 1.0
	2.9	2.3	2.5	3.9	3.6	1.8	1.9	3.6	2.1
% Officers', Directors' Owners' Comp/Sales	4.1	2.6	2.0		3.0	2.8	1.9	1.6	
	(38) 5.0	(64) 4.7	(98) 4.1		(23) 5.3	(21) 4.6	(25) 3.4	(16) 2.6	
	8.8	7.9	7.5		7.7	8.1	5.4	5.2	
Net Sales ($)	1309315M	3263332M	3101099M	12476M	90969M	104067M	344748M	541038M	2007801M
Total Assets ($)	558872M	1541697M	1334880M	6971M	38493M	43050M	138607M	209019M	898740M

M = $ thousand   MM = $ million
See Pages 11 through 21 for Explanation of Ratios and Data

Current Data Sorted by Assets / Comparative Historical Data

						Type of Statement		
2	1	15	19	4	1	Unqualified	36	41
1	27	69	13			Reviewed	92	134
10	29	24	2		1	Compiled	40	78
25	19	16				Tax Returns	25	55
4	24	37	9		1	Other	38	73
	74 (4/1-9/30/06)		279 (10/1/06-3/31/07)				4/1/02-3/31/03 ALL	4/1/03-3/31/04 ALL
0-500M	500M-2MM	2-10MM	10-50MM	50-100MM	100-250MM			
42	100	161	43	4	3	NUMBER OF STATEMENTS	231	381
%	%	%	%	%	%	ASSETS	%	%
18.3	8.2	9.0	7.9			Cash & Equivalents	10.3	10.8
32.5	55.3	58.8	62.3			Trade Receivables (net)	52.7	51.4
5.5	7.2	6.5	3.9			Inventory	5.8	5.0
5.3	6.0	8.3	11.1			All Other Current	9.1	8.5
61.7	76.8	82.6	85.2			Total Current	77.9	75.6
23.6	17.2	10.5	9.1			Fixed Assets (net)	12.7	15.6
.2	1.5	1.9	.4			Intangibles (net)	3.2	2.1
14.6	4.5	5.0	5.3			All Other Non-Current	6.1	6.7
100.0	100.0	100.0	100.0			Total	100.0	100.0
						LIABILITIES		
21.4	15.8	12.3	9.6			Notes Payable-Short Term	12.8	14.3
5.3	3.9	2.2	1.7			Cur. Mat.-L.T.D.	2.4	2.9
12.9	20.2	18.5	14.4			Trade Payables	14.8	16.7
.8	.6	.9	.4			Income Taxes Payable	.8	.3
21.3	12.6	16.9	27.6			All Other Current	17.3	15.1
61.7	53.0	50.8	53.6			Total Current	48.1	49.3
26.5	9.9	5.3	4.2			Long-Term Debt	8.4	10.2
.0	.4	.5	.1			Deferred Taxes	.6	.5
7.5	3.8	3.7	6.3			All Other Non-Current	3.4	3.7
4.3	32.9	39.8	35.8			Net Worth	39.6	36.4
100.0	100.0	100.0	100.0			Total Liabilties & Net Worth	100.0	100.0
						INCOME DATA		
100.0	100.0	100.0	100.0			Net Sales	100.0	100.0
38.0	27.4	21.3	18.7			Gross Profit	23.3	23.0
33.4	22.7	16.4	12.4			Operating Expenses	20.2	20.5
4.6	4.7	4.9	6.3			Operating Profit	3.1	2.4
-.3	.7	.3	.1			All Other Expenses (net)	.1	.2
4.9	3.9	4.6	6.2			Profit Before Taxes	2.9	2.2
						RATIOS		
2.9	2.3	2.7	1.9			Current	2.5	2.5
1.2	1.6	1.7	1.6				1.7	1.6
.5	1.0	1.2	1.3				1.2	1.2
2.7	2.0	2.2	1.7			Quick	1.9	2.0
.9	1.3	1.3	1.4				1.4 (380)	1.3
.3	.7	1.0	1.0				1.0	.9

Sales/Receivables

0	UND	39	9.3	45	8.0	56	6.5			42	8.8	40	9.1
11	34.4	57	6.4	69	5.3	78	4.7			64	5.7	60	6.0
61	5.9	81	4.5	90	4.1	98	3.7			81	4.5	83	4.4

Cost of Sales/Inventory

0	UND	0	UND	0	UND	0	859.3			0	UND	0	UND
0	UND	2	164.8	2	197.0	3	119.5			2	147.0	1	374.1
1	550.7	20	18.3	11	32.3	7	52.2			12	31.4	9	42.4

Cost of Sales/Payables

0	UND	10	37.8	11	32.0	15	23.7			10	35.1	10	36.1
8	45.6	19	18.8	21	17.0	20	18.6			17	21.5	20	18.4
29	12.5	45	8.1	35	10.5	27	13.7			26	13.9	34	10.7

0-500M	500M-2MM	2-10MM	10-50MM	50-100MM	100-250MM		Hist	Hist
14.8	7.6	6.2	6.2			Sales/Working Capital	6.3	6.2
162.1	13.2	10.1	9.3				11.7	11.8
-24.1	213.1	21.9	13.8				30.9	36.6
35.5	13.8	35.0	43.7			EBIT/Interest	19.3	15.2
(32) 7.4	(92) 4.8	(149) 7.5	(40) 13.6				(203) 4.7	(329) 5.0
.9	1.8	2.1	3.9				2.0	1.0
	7.2	16.0	24.6			Net Profit + Depr., Dep., Amort./Cur. Mat. L/T/D	8.5	9.1
	(20) 3.2	(40) 4.1	(12) 7.2				(57) 2.6	(78) 2.8
	.9	1.9	4.0				1.1	.9
.1	.2	.1	.1			Fixed/Worth	.1	.1
.7	.5	.2	.2				.2	.3
UND	3.9	.6	.4				.7	.9
1.1	.8	.8	1.1			Debt/Worth	.8	.7
4.1	1.7	1.6	1.7				1.5	1.6
-15.2	11.2	3.6	3.4				3.5	4.4
426.3	81.6	56.7	58.1			% Profit Before Taxes/Tangible Net Worth	39.8	36.6
(30) 67.8	(84) 30.6	(151) 26.8	(42) 38.7				(211) 16.7	(338) 14.4
19.2	12.3	6.4	23.5				4.6	.3
57.3	24.4	19.7	21.1			% Profit Before Taxes/Total Assets	16.8	14.6
20.4	9.2	9.2	12.8				6.5	4.9
.0	2.1	2.3	7.8				1.7	-.1
268.2	73.6	96.9	108.1			Sales/Net Fixed Assets	73.0	74.3
66.3	31.4	41.4	51.3				39.2	35.7
20.2	14.8	25.4	29.4				19.3	19.2
9.2	4.9	4.1	3.6			Sales/Total Assets	4.1	4.3
5.2	3.5	3.2	3.1				3.2	3.3
3.5	2.6	2.5	2.4				2.6	2.5
.3	.5	.3	.3			% Depr., Dep., Amort./Sales	.5	.4
(27) .8	(82) .8	(136) .6	(38) .4				(207) .9	(320) .9
1.9	1.5	1.0	.9				1.4	1.7
2.3	2.2	1.4	1.7			% Officers', Directors' Owners' Comp/Sales	2.4	2.0
(31) 4.1	(65) 3.8	(70) 2.3	(11) 2.8				(138) 4.1	(217) 3.6
11.9	6.8	4.9	4.3				6.7	6.3
67633M	428654M	2307060M	2385475M	590101M	2158484M	Net Sales ($)	6802635M	11675681M
9533M	113878M	684641M	802606M	272277M	466579M	Total Assets ($)	2014541M	2519499M

M = $ thousand   MM = $ million
See Pages 11 through 21 for Explanation of Ratios and Data

Comparative Historical Data | Current Data Sorted by Sales

39 / 117 / 47 / 43 / 73	37 / 116 / 58 / 47 / 85	42 / 110 / 66 / 60 / 75	Type of Statement Unqualified Reviewed Compiled Tax Returns Other	2 / 2 / 2 / 10 / 2	1 / 6 / 22 / 17 / 8	/ 16 / 6 / 7 / 14	3 / 34 / 18 / 15 / 17	8 / 34 / 14 / 10 / 23	28 / 18 / 4 / 1 / 11
4/1/04- 3/31/05 ALL	4/1/05- 3/31/06 ALL	4/1/06- 3/31/07 ALL		74 (4/1-9/30/06) 0-1MM	1-3MM	3-5MM	279 (10/1/06-3/31/07) 5-10MM	10-25MM	25MM & OVER
319	343	353	**NUMBER OF STATEMENTS**	18	54	43	87	89	62
%	%	%	**ASSETS**	%	%	%	%	%	%
9.5	9.4	9.8	Cash & Equivalents	18.9	11.1	11.9	8.5	9.1	7.4
51.8	55.5	54.6	Trade Receivables (net)	33.8	40.8	52.1	61.0	59.3	58.5
6.0	5.8	6.2	Inventory	6.9	8.1	6.9	7.0	4.3	5.6
8.6	7.1	7.9	All Other Current	7.4	4.7	6.6	6.3	10.1	10.6
75.9	77.8	78.4	Total Current	67.0	64.7	77.5	82.7	82.9	82.1
15.5	14.1	14.2	Fixed Assets (net)	22.9	21.7	16.7	11.9	10.9	11.5
2.0	1.9	1.4	Intangibles (net)	.3	1.3	1.2	1.9	1.6	1.0
6.6	6.3	6.0	All Other Non-Current	9.9	12.3	4.7	3.6	4.6	5.5
100.0	100.0	100.0	Total	100.0	100.0	100.0	100.0	100.0	100.0
			LIABILITIES						
15.3	15.6	14.0	Notes Payable-Short Term	34.3	15.0	14.3	14.4	11.4	10.1
2.6	3.2	2.9	Cur. Mat.-L.T.D.	8.9	4.8	2.2	2.7	1.9	2.0
16.9	17.9	17.8	Trade Payables	14.3	13.6	21.3	19.3	18.5	16.8
.6	.5	.8	Income Taxes Payable	.1	1.1	.5	.8	1.0	.4
16.0	15.2	17.5	All Other Current	15.4	16.8	13.6	15.3	18.3	23.6
51.3	52.4	53.0	Total Current	73.0	51.1	52.0	52.5	51.1	52.9
9.8	10.0	9.2	Long-Term Debt	11.0	14.5	13.5	10.5	4.9	5.3
.5	.4	.3	Deferred Taxes	.0	.1	.7	.4	.6	.1
3.4	3.6	4.4	All Other Non-Current	6.7	3.5	5.2	5.0	3.3	5.0
35.0	33.6	33.0	Net Worth	9.3	30.7	28.6	31.6	40.1	36.7
100.0	100.0	100.0	Total Liabilities & Net Worth	100.0	100.0	100.0	100.0	100.0	100.0
			INCOME DATA						
100.0	100.0	100.0	Net Sales	100.0	100.0	100.0	100.0	100.0	100.0
22.4	22.0	24.9	Gross Profit	46.2	34.8	25.5	23.7	19.1	19.8
19.8	18.2	19.9	Operating Expenses	43.8	28.4	19.6	19.5	14.3	14.5
2.7	3.8	5.0	Operating Profit	2.4	6.4	5.9	4.2	4.7	5.3
.3	.3	.3	All Other Expenses (net)	-1.4	.7	.9	.4	.1	.3
2.4	3.4	4.6	Profit Before Taxes	3.8	5.7	5.0	3.8	4.6	5.0
			RATIOS						
2.4 1.5 1.2	2.4 1.6 1.2	2.3 1.6 1.1	Current	2.0 1.0 .4	2.2 1.3 .8	3.2 1.8 1.0	2.4 1.7 1.1	2.2 1.7 1.2	1.9 1.5 1.2
2.0 1.3 .9	2.1 1.3 .9	1.9 1.3 .8	Quick	1.7 .9 .2	1.9 1.1 .6	2.9 1.7 .7	2.2 1.3 1.0	1.9 1.3 1.0	1.7 1.3 .9
40 9.1 62 5.9 83 4.4	41 8.9 61 6.0 84 4.3	39 9.4 65 5.6 85 4.3	Sales/Receivables	0 UND 11 33.2 68 5.4	21 17.4 49 7.5 78 4.7	45 8.0 71 5.2 89 4.1	47 7.8 67 5.5 94 3.9	40 9.2 65 5.6 84 4.4	40 9.1 72 5.1 84 4.3
0 UND 3 143.5 13 27.9	0 UND 2 195.3 10 37.8	0 UND 2 224.9 10 34.9	Cost of Sales/Inventory	0 UND 0 UND 0 UND	0 UND 3 135.6 29 12.4	0 UND 2 228.4 20 18.0	0 UND 1 309.8 17 22.0	0 UND 2 224.9 7 54.9	0 999.8 3 123.2 10 34.9
11 32.8 19 18.8 32 11.5	11 31.8 19 18.7 31 11.8	11 35.2 20 18.7 34 10.7	Cost of Sales/Payables	0 UND 13 29.2 51 7.2	5 75.9 17 22.1 42 8.7	13 28.1 23 15.8 49 7.4	10 35.1 22 16.6 40 9.1	10 35.6 20 18.5 28 13.1	13 27.5 20 18.6 27 13.4
7.1 11.8 33.6	6.9 12.1 38.9	7.1 11.6 41.7	Sales/Working Capital	9.8 NM -13.0	7.8 20.4 -51.0	4.7 8.8 259.9	6.8 11.6 36.6	7.3 10.3 21.0	7.5 10.8 29.6
18.4 (276) 6.1 1.6	19.3 (313) 5.7 2.1	29.6 (320) 6.5 2.1	EBIT/Interest	35.2 (12) 2.1 -1.5	28.0 (51) 5.1 1.4	14.9 (37) 4.8 2.5	18.3 (78) 4.9 1.7	41.1 (84) 11.7 2.4	35.4 (58) 11.8 4.4
8.0 (67) 2.9 1.0	9.9 (81) 3.4 1.1	12.0 (78) 4.4 1.8	Net Profit + Depr., Dep., Amort./Cur. Mat. L/T/D		7.4 (11) 1.0 .6		7.2 (17) 4.0 1.1	33.3 (25) 5.6 2.5	12.7 (18) 5.2 3.6
.1 .3 .9	.1 .3 .9	.1 .3 1.0	Fixed/Worth	.0 .5 UND	.1 .4 3.0	.1 .4 2.1	.1 .3 1.0	.1 .2 .5	.1 .2 .4
.8 1.7 4.6	.9 1.9 5.1	.9 1.8 4.5	Debt/Worth	.7 7.4 -5.0	.9 2.0 7.2	.6 1.6 10.4	.8 2.0 5.5	.9 1.5 3.1	1.1 1.8 3.4
45.4 (284) 17.5 1.9	59.0 (302) 25.9 9.5	65.3 (314) 31.6 12.9	% Profit Before Taxes/Tangible Net Worth	866.1 (12) 35.3 16.7	96.8 (48) 30.4 7.4	52.6 (35) 28.4 14.9	71.9 (75) 32.0 6.2	61.0 (84) 28.4 9.8	55.5 (60) 33.1 22.1
16.2 5.6 .6	20.8 7.6 1.9	24.3 10.7 2.6	% Profit Before Taxes/Total Assets	34.0 7.1 -9.5	32.2 9.8 1.6	22.7 9.3 4.6	24.2 11.6 1.7	23.4 10.1 2.4	19.8 12.4 6.9
83.4 34.3 17.3	87.9 39.6 19.7	97.2 41.4 21.7	Sales/Net Fixed Assets	UND 57.9 16.6	81.4 22.0 13.2	76.2 40.4 17.6	88.8 37.9 25.6	100.1 51.1 27.3	109.6 51.4 29.1
4.3 3.2 2.5	4.4 3.4 2.6	4.4 3.4 2.6	Sales/Total Assets	7.4 4.9 3.0	4.7 3.3 2.6	4.3 3.1 2.2	4.4 3.4 2.6	4.5 3.5 2.8	4.1 3.3 2.7
.5 (254) .8 1.6	.3 (280) .7 1.3	.3 (287) .7 1.1	% Depr., Dep., Amort./Sales		.7 (43) 1.2 1.9	.4 (35) .7 1.0	.3 (72) .7 1.1	.3 (75) .6 1.0	.2 (53) .4 .7
1.9 (174) 3.7 6.3	1.8 (100) 3.5 5.8	1.8 (177) 3.3 6.8	% Officers', Directors' Owners' Comp/Sales	1.0 (11) 10.7 19.9	2.5 (40) 4.9 6.9	2.5 (25) 5.3 8.7	1.3 (40) 2.5 4.5	1.4 (45) 2.8 4.5	1.4 (16) 2.4 5.5
8840039M	5916581M	7937407M	Net Sales ($)	9086M	105023M	167847M	636032M	1420982M	5598437M
2142510M	1951022M	2349514M	Total Assets ($)	5701M	36537M	59906M	207530M	431527M	1608313M

© RMA 2007

M = $ thousand   MM = $ million
See Pages 11 through 21 for Explanation of Ratios and Data

	Current Data Sorted by Assets							Comparative Historical Data	
Type of Statement	0-500M	500M-2MM	2-10MM	10-50MM	50-100MM	100-250MM		4/1/02-3/31/03 ALL	4/1/03-3/31/04 ALL
Unqualified		4	14	4	1			15	27
Reviewed	5	21	41	3	1			54	78
Compiled	9	14	6	1		1		26	54
Tax Returns	21	13	6					22	38
Other	7	10	7	5	1			14	57
		36 (4/1-9/30/06)		158 (10/1/06-3/31/07)					
	0-500M	500M-2MM	2-10MM	10-50MM	50-100MM	100-250MM			
NUMBER OF STATEMENTS	42	62	74	13	3			131	254
	%	%	%	%	%	%		%	%
ASSETS									
Cash & Equivalents	18.7	12.2	14.1	8.3				12.8	12.3
Trade Receivables (net)	31.7	44.1	53.8	47.1				42.5	43.0
Inventory	1.5	4.2	1.6	2.6				4.6	3.4
All Other Current	7.5	7.9	11.5	15.3				6.8	9.1
Total Current	59.4	68.4	81.0	73.2				66.7	67.8
Fixed Assets (net)	27.6	24.2	13.8	10.3				23.3	23.6
Intangibles (net)	.6	3.3	.8	3.2				2.1	1.4
All Other Non-Current	12.4	4.1	4.4	13.3				7.9	7.2
Total	100.0	100.0	100.0	100.0				100.0	100.0
LIABILITIES									
Notes Payable-Short Term	18.3	10.4	9.8	9.1				11.7	16.0
Cur. Mat.-L.T.D.	4.1	3.7	2.2	.7				4.1	3.8
Trade Payables	11.2	15.3	14.2	15.2				13.7	14.6
Income Taxes Payable	.3	.4	1.0	.2				.5	.5
All Other Current	16.1	8.8	16.4	19.2				14.9	15.9
Total Current	50.0	38.6	43.5	44.4				44.8	50.8
Long-Term Debt	31.1	13.4	6.5	3.7				13.0	12.3
Deferred Taxes	.0	.3	.5	.6				.3	.7
All Other Non-Current	1.1	1.3	1.3	4.1				5.3	6.7
Net Worth	17.9	46.3	48.3	47.1				36.5	29.5
Total Liabilities & Net Worth	100.0	100.0	100.0	100.0				100.0	100.0
INCOME DATA									
Net Sales	100.0	100.0	100.0	100.0				100.0	100.0
Gross Profit	49.1	34.3	23.4	24.4				29.9	32.2
Operating Expenses	42.5	28.8	18.1	18.3				27.6	29.3
Operating Profit	6.6	5.5	5.3	6.1				2.2	3.0
All Other Expenses (net)	.8	.7	.3	-.1				.8	.7
Profit Before Taxes	5.7	4.8	5.0	6.1				1.4	2.3
RATIOS									
Current	3.1	3.5	2.8	2.5				2.7	2.4
	1.5	1.8	1.9	1.5				1.6	1.5
	.6	1.2	1.4	1.2				1.1	1.0
Quick	2.5	3.2	2.4	2.1				2.3	2.0
	(41) 1.2	1.6	1.6	1.2				1.3	1.2
	.6	.9	1.1	.8				.9	.8
Sales/Receivables	0 UND	27 13.6	52 7.1	38 9.7				36 10.3	33 11.2
	18 19.7	55 6.7	77 4.8	79 4.6				59 6.2	58 6.3
	50 7.3	77 4.7	105 3.5	91 4.0				82 4.5	82 4.4
Cost of Sales/Inventory	0 UND	0 UND	0 UND	0 UND				0 UND	0 UND
	0 UND	0 UND	0 UND	0 887.8				0 UND	0 UND
	2 213.9	4 94.8	1 249.0	5 75.7				10 36.0	6 64.5
Cost of Sales/Payables	0 UND	3 112.8	14 26.6	18 19.8				8 45.3	9 39.9
	14 26.0	18 19.8	22 16.3	27 13.5				19 19.6	20 17.8
	30 12.1	36 10.1	40 9.2	42 8.7				34 10.7	42 8.6
Sales/Working Capital	8.7	5.6	5.1	5.4				6.2	6.2
	26.6	9.5	7.4	10.6				11.6	13.9
	-86.7	45.1	11.6	19.1				79.9	122.5
EBIT/Interest	14.3	16.3	40.7	61.7				10.0	11.0
	(37) 5.3	(51) 6.1	(66) 11.9	(12) 16.8				(119) 3.9	(223) 3.4
	1.7	1.4	3.2	3.3				.5	.2
Net Profit + Depr., Dep., Amort./Cur. Mat. L/T/D			20.8					10.1	5.5
		(17) 9.7						(29) 3.1	(58) 2.3
			2.0					1.4	.9
Fixed/Worth	.2	.2	.1	.1				.2	.2
	1.0	.5	.2	.2				.5	.6
	-2.6	.8	.5	.3				1.3	1.5
Debt/Worth	.8	.5	.5	.5				.6	.7
	5.2	1.2	1.1	1.7				1.5	1.6
	-12.2	3.2	1.9	2.5				4.4	4.8
% Profit Before Taxes/Tangible Net Worth	150.1	61.5	44.0	59.3				27.1	39.6
	(30) 76.6	(54) 24.8	(71) 20.2	19.6				(114) 10.1	(222) 12.2
	21.5	6.0	7.2	12.4				1.2	.1
% Profit Before Taxes/Total Assets	41.3	26.9	19.9	17.0				12.9	14.8
	22.6	8.9	9.9	9.2				4.5	4.2
	4.4	1.4	2.9	6.3				-1.5	-1.7
Sales/Net Fixed Assets	119.4	37.3	68.5	113.7				34.3	35.9
	32.9	16.7	28.6	28.5				16.4	16.2
	14.7	8.8	11.5	12.9				9.0	8.8
Sales/Total Assets	8.6	4.0	3.2	3.1				3.9	3.7
	4.7	3.0	2.6	2.6				2.7	2.8
	3.0	2.3	2.0	1.2				2.0	2.0
% Depr., Dep., Amort./Sales	.5	.7	.5	.4				.8	.9
	(27) .9	(49) 1.3	(67) 1.1	.8				(119) 1.7	(217) 1.8
	2.9	2.0	2.3	1.2				3.1	3.4
% Officers', Directors' Owners' Comp/Sales	4.7	2.5	1.8					2.4	3.0
	(26) 6.3	(40) 4.8	(37) 3.9					(70) 5.4	(140) 6.5
	12.7	8.1	6.3					8.7	10.2
Net Sales ($)	61275M	229571M	830439M	472585M	335164M			1701834M	3597976M
Total Assets ($)	10326M	68515M	312132M	205874M	211320M			422281M	1033318M

© RMA 2007

M = $ thousand   MM = $ million
See Pages 11 through 21 for Explanation of Ratios and Data

Comparative Historical Data / Current Data Sorted by Sales

Type of Statement

Type of Statement	4/1/04-3/31/05 ALL	4/1/05-3/31/06 ALL	4/1/06-3/31/07 ALL	0-1MM	1-3MM	3-5MM	5-10MM	10-25MM	25MM & OVER
Unqualified	15	18	23		4	2	7	6	4
Reviewed	51	50	70		15	7	21	24	3
Compiled	35	20	31	3	15	4	5	3	1
Tax Returns	31	31	40	11	12	7	7	3	
Other	44	52	30	4	6	3	7	4	6
				36 (4/1-9/30/06)		158 (10/1/06-3/31/07)			
NUMBER OF STATEMENTS	176	171	194	18	52	23	47	40	14

Data

	4/1/04-3/31/05 ALL	4/1/05-3/31/06 ALL	4/1/06-3/31/07 ALL	0-1MM	1-3MM	3-5MM	5-10MM	10-25MM	25MM & OVER
ASSETS %	%	%	%	%	%	%	%	%	%
Cash & Equivalents	10.9	13.3	14.2	18.2	15.4	12.7	13.8	13.9	9.0
Trade Receivables (net)	48.4	45.6	45.1	24.1	42.1	41.8	48.0	53.6	55.3
Inventory	3.5	4.0	2.5	4.9	3.4	.4	1.7	2.5	1.7
All Other Current	7.7	6.3	9.6	9.9	6.3	13.3	9.1	12.3	9.0
Total Current	70.4	69.2	71.4	57.2	67.2	68.2	72.7	82.3	75.1
Fixed Assets (net)	20.6	21.8	20.2	27.4	26.1	20.7	20.1	11.2	13.7
Intangibles (net)	1.5	2.0	1.7	.8	1.0	4.9	1.7	.6	2.8
All Other Non-Current	7.5	7.1	6.7	14.6	5.7	6.2	5.5	5.9	8.4
Total	100.0	100.0	100.0	100.0	100.0	100.0	100.0	100.0	100.0
LIABILITIES									
Notes Payable-Short Term	16.7	10.1	11.9	27.6	11.4	10.2	8.1	10.0	14.9
Cur. Mat.-L.T.D.	3.9	3.5	2.9	4.7	3.8	4.2	2.4	1.7	.9
Trade Payables	15.5	12.9	14.0	10.9	10.7	13.0	17.2	15.3	18.4
Income Taxes Payable	.9	.6	.6	.4	.1	.9	1.2	.5	.2
All Other Current	12.4	13.8	14.1	15.0	8.6	8.5	16.6	19.6	18.2
Total Current	49.5	40.8	43.6	58.4	34.6	36.8	45.5	47.1	52.7
Long-Term Debt	14.3	13.5	13.8	26.1	20.8	18.7	10.1	4.5	3.4
Deferred Taxes	.4	.2	.3	.0	.1	.7	.7	.3	.0
All Other Non-Current	2.7	2.7	1.5	2.5	.6	.8	1.2	1.5	5.6
Net Worth	33.1	42.7	40.8	13.1	43.9	42.9	42.6	46.7	38.3
Total Liabilities & Net Worth	100.0	100.0	100.0	100.0	100.0	100.0	100.0	100.0	100.0
INCOME DATA									
Net Sales	100.0	100.0	100.0	100.0	100.0	100.0	100.0	100.0	100.0
Gross Profit	32.0	32.4	32.7	59.9	39.0	31.3	25.1	25.7	21.8
Operating Expenses	28.5	27.1	27.0	50.0	32.9	27.1	20.3	20.4	16.6
Operating Profit	3.5	5.3	5.7	9.9	6.2	4.3	4.8	5.3	5.2
All Other Expenses (net)	.4	.7	.5	1.6	.7	.6	.6	-.5	.9
Profit Before Taxes	3.0	4.6	5.2	8.3	5.4	3.7	4.2	5.8	4.3
RATIOS									
Current	2.5	3.0	3.2	2.0	4.7	3.1	3.6	2.6	2.1
	1.6	1.7	1.7	1.1	2.1	1.7	1.7	1.8	1.5
	1.1	1.2	1.2	.4	1.4	1.2	1.2	1.4	1.2
Quick	2.2	2.3	2.6	1.8	4.3	1.8	3.0	2.3	1.6
	1.4	1.4	(193) 1.6	.9	1.7	1.3	(46) 1.6	1.6	1.3
	.9	1.0	.9	.3	.9	.9	1.6	1.1	1.0
Sales/Receivables	33 10.9	35 10.6	29 12.5	0 UND	23 15.8	27 13.4	34 10.8	45 8.2	49 7.5
	65 5.6	63 5.8	58 6.3	10 36.5	49 7.4	43 8.5	72 5.1	70 5.2	69 5.3
	93 3.9	89 4.1	86 4.2	51 7.1	78 4.7	76 4.8	102 3.6	94 3.9	87 4.2
Cost of Sales/Inventory	0 UND	0 UND	0 UND	0 UND	0 UND	0 UND	0 UND	0 UND	0 UND
	0 UND	0 UND	0 UND	0 UND	0 UND	0 UND	0 UND	0 UND	0 UND
	3 126.0	4 102.3	3 137.2	2 184.0	7 50.1	2 198.4	1 356.4	3 131.3	3 124.2
Cost of Sales/Payables	9 41.5	8 44.0	7 49.8	0 UND	2 188.4	1 543.6	10 35.9	15 24.8	15 23.8
	21 17.1	19 18.9	20 18.4	6 64.8	15 24.2	19 19.3	21 17.0	23 15.7	26 14.1
	36 10.1	36 10.2	36 10.1	52 7.1	30 12.0	33 11.1	49 7.5	39 9.4	52 7.1
Sales/Working Capital	6.3	5.4	5.6	7.9	5.3	9.0	4.7	5.5	7.6
	11.3	8.6	9.1	114.6	8.9	11.9	7.5	8.4	9.7
	38.1	40.5	31.6	-14.9	30.7	44.5	23.7	16.3	20.9
EBIT/Interest	18.4	19.8	22.9	9.4	19.2	22.5	20.3	55.0	65.0
	(154) 5.7	(147) 4.8	(169) 8.0	(15) 5.3	(42) 7.9	(22) 7.1	(41) 6.1	(35) 21.3	10.3
	1.8	1.5	2.3	1.5	1.7	1.4	2.0	4.8	2.8
Net Profit + Depr., Dep., Amort./Cur. Mat. L/T/D	14.9	6.4	12.2					30.9	
	(27) 4.7	(27) 3.5	(32) 5.2					(10) 14.8	
	2.2	1.8	2.2					2.3	
Fixed/Worth	.1	.1	.1	.6	.2	.2	.2	.1	.1
	.4	.4	.4	1.4	.5	.5	.4	.2	.3
	1.3	1.0	.8	-1.1	2.5	.7	1.0	.4	.4
Debt/Worth	.6	.5	.5	1.5	.2	.6	.4	.6	.8
	1.5	1.1	1.3	4.1	1.0	1.2	1.1	1.2	2.0
	4.4	3.7	3.8	-15.2	6.9	3.9	2.8	2.1	2.6
% Profit Before Taxes/Tangible Net Worth	48.5	50.8	55.7	197.1	94.8	50.4	42.3	47.7	47.9
	(156) 14.4	(156) 19.0	(171) 24.7	(13) 74.4	(44) 30.9	(20) 20.7	(42) 24.3	(39) 19.6	(13) 22.9
	4.4	3.9	9.6	11.0	9.0	3.3	7.0	12.3	16.3
% Profit Before Taxes/Total Assets	17.2	22.3	25.7	39.4	30.3	25.6	18.9	23.8	15.6
	5.4	7.4	11.2	17.9	15.5	7.2	11.4	10.5	8.3
	1.5	1.2	3.1	2.7	3.6	.6	2.6	3.7	4.9
Sales/Net Fixed Assets	60.0	56.3	69.5	196.0	67.5	47.4	46.0	100.2	99.4
	21.1	22.5	24.2	23.1	17.1	20.5	18.3	35.4	28.9
	11.8	9.1	11.3	7.1	8.0	12.5	10.4	22.1	12.4
Sales/Total Assets	4.2	3.8	4.0	4.6	4.6	5.4	3.3	3.9	3.9
	3.0	2.9	3.0	3.0	3.3	3.6	2.7	3.0	2.7
	2.2	2.0	2.2	2.2	2.3	2.5	2.2	2.3	1.9
% Depr., Dep., Amort./Sales	.6	.5	.5	.6	.8	.5	.5	.4	.3
	(147) 1.3	(141) 1.2	(159) 1.2	(10) 1.6	(40) 1.7	(17) 1.3	(42) 1.2	(36) .8	.6
	2.2	2.3	2.1	3.5	3.3	2.1	2.9	1.2	1.2
% Officers', Directors' Owners' Comp/Sales	2.8	2.8	2.3		4.5	2.1	2.8	1.3	
	(98) 5.3	(91) 5.7	(107) 4.0		(32) 6.0	(14) 3.9	(28) 4.1	(22) 2.1	
	8.2	9.9	8.8		10.0	8.3	6.4	4.5	
Net Sales ($)	1287892M	1480198M	1929034M	9617M	101840M	94119M	329512M	606708M	787238M
Total Assets ($)	491998M	603255M	808167M	3760M	36212M	31239M	132321M	237408M	367227M

M = $ thousand   MM = $ million
See Pages 11 through 21 for Explanation of Ratios and Data

Current Data Sorted by Assets | Comparative Historical Data

Type of Statement	0-500M	500M-2MM	2-10MM	10-50MM	50-100MM	100-250MM		4/1/02-3/31/03 ALL	4/1/03-3/31/04 ALL
Unqualified			4	4				2	3
Reviewed	2	14	31	12				38	36
Compiled	12	20	5					19	32
Tax Returns		4	4					19	31
Other	11	22	16	5	1	1		26	41
		21 (4/1-9/30/06)		147 (10/1/06-3/31/07)					
NUMBER OF STATEMENTS	25	60	60	21	1	1		104	143
	%	%	%	%	%	%		%	%
ASSETS									
Cash & Equivalents	22.9	8.2	5.5	5.2				10.7	10.1
Trade Receivables (net)	34.7	49.2	54.6	54.0				48.6	49.3
Inventory	9.6	18.5	14.6	19.5				14.9	13.1
All Other Current	1.8	3.7	7.9	4.8				5.2	4.9
Total Current	69.0	79.6	82.6	83.4				79.3	77.4
Fixed Assets (net)	25.0	14.7	13.5	9.0				14.8	14.1
Intangibles (net)	1.1	1.2	.9	1.5				.8	2.2
All Other Non-Current	5.0	4.5	3.0	6.0				5.0	6.3
Total	100.0	100.0	100.0	100.0				100.0	100.0
LIABILITIES									
Notes Payable-Short Term	15.6	18.3	14.3	22.2				17.8	17.7
Cur. Mat.-L.T.D.	9.3	1.3	1.8	1.5				4.0	3.3
Trade Payables	14.9	20.0	17.7	13.6				17.9	20.1
Income Taxes Payable	.0	.6	.4	.4				.4	.5
All Other Current	16.2	12.2	11.8	19.8				12.6	10.1
Total Current	56.0	52.4	46.1	57.4				52.7	51.6
Long-Term Debt	32.2	9.1	6.7	6.8				7.1	8.4
Deferred Taxes	.0	.0	.4	.2				.1	.1
All Other Non-Current	3.5	3.5	3.1	1.8				3.4	6.3
Net Worth	8.4	34.9	43.6	33.9				36.6	33.6
Total Liabilties & Net Worth	100.0	100.0	100.0	100.0				100.0	100.0
INCOME DATA									
Net Sales	100.0	100.0	100.0	100.0				100.0	100.0
Gross Profit	37.0	26.2	24.8	26.1				30.6	28.3
Operating Expenses	31.0	23.7	20.3	22.3				27.5	25.6
Operating Profit	6.0	2.5	4.5	3.8				3.2	2.7
All Other Expenses (net)	.9	.3	.4	.7				.4	.3
Profit Before Taxes	5.1	2.3	4.0	3.1				2.7	2.4
RATIOS									
Current	3.3	2.5	2.4	2.0				2.3	2.2
	1.3	1.7	1.8	1.3				1.5	1.5
	.8	1.2	1.3	1.2				1.2	1.2
Quick	3.3	1.8	2.0	1.5				1.7	1.7
	1.3	1.4	1.2	1.1				1.1	1.2
	.5	.8	1.0	.8				.8	.8
Sales/Receivables	0 UND	26 14.3	43 8.5	40 9.0				31 11.8	32 11.5
	17 21.4	42 8.6	66 5.5	60 6.1				53 6.9	57 6.4
	46 8.0	68 5.4	81 4.5	90 4.1				71 5.1	74 5.0
Cost of Sales/Inventory	0 UND	2 174.8	4 93.8	5 76.3				2 232.7	3 130.4
	2 229.7	13 27.3	13 28.6	23 16.0				11 33.2	12 30.8
	15 24.1	27 13.3	28 12.8	48 7.6				35 10.3	27 13.4
Cost of Sales/Payables	0 UND	9 39.5	13 28.4	16 23.5				13 29.1	12 29.3
	6 62.2	23 16.1	24 15.1	21 17.7				21 17.5	25 14.7
	28 13.1	35 10.3	41 8.8	30 12.4				37 9.8	39 9.4
Sales/Working Capital	10.5	7.4	5.7	8.0				7.4	8.5
	54.6	13.2	9.0	13.7				12.4	12.7
	-50.6	32.6	14.2	31.1				29.0	47.3
EBIT/Interest	14.1	15.5	24.0	11.4				12.6	14.9
	(17) 4.3	(55) 4.2	(57) 4.4	(20) 3.2				(92) 4.3	(123) 4.0
	-1.6	1.7	1.9	1.9				2.0	1.2
Net Profit + Depr., Dep., Amort./Cur. Mat. L/T/D			14.3					9.3	5.1
			(20) 9.2					(18) 4.5	(24) 1.4
			2.1					1.3	.2
Fixed/Worth	.2	.1	.1	.2				.1	.1
	.9	.3	.2	.3				.3	.3
	-1.3	1.0	.4	.4				.8	1.0
Debt/Worth	.2	1.0	.8	1.3				.8	.8
	2.9	1.7	1.4	2.1				1.7	2.0
	-3.5	4.3	2.7	4.9				3.3	5.3
% Profit Before Taxes/Tangible Net Worth	204.4	55.4	42.5	50.9				50.6	51.2
	(17) 55.9	(53) 24.7	(59) 25.2	29.5				(95) 21.7	(126) 19.2
	25.3	11.5	10.8	10.0				5.4	4.6
% Profit Before Taxes/Total Assets	76.1	20.3	21.3	18.7				24.9	18.3
	29.3	9.1	8.4	7.5				7.0	5.6
	-5.5	1.7	2.3	2.5				1.5	.5
Sales/Net Fixed Assets	96.9	113.7	89.0	68.3				93.2	88.1
	37.1	42.3	48.1	55.7				40.7	39.9
	14.5	19.8	14.5	26.6				18.4	21.3
Sales/Total Assets	10.1	5.6	3.8	3.9				4.8	4.6
	6.1	3.9	3.2	3.1				3.6	3.5
	4.0	2.9	2.5	2.7				2.9	2.8
% Depr., Dep., Amort./Sales	.5	.3	.3	.3				.4	.3
	(14) .8	(41) .5	(51) .5	(20) .5				(96) .7	(116) .6
	1.6	1.2	.9	.7				1.4	1.4
% Officers', Directors' Owners' Comp/Sales	2.0	1.7	1.7					2.8	2.5
	(14) 4.6	(33) 2.3	(27) 3.4					(65) 4.7	(85) 4.3
	9.5	4.8	4.7					7.4	6.8
Net Sales ($)	48226M	318225M	783702M	1160125M	217616M	801703M		1999633M	1659716M
Total Assets ($)	7425M	74677M	247738M	355943M	70776M	115071M		552589M	496552M

M = $ thousand   MM = $ million
See Pages 11 through 21 for Explanation of Ratios and Data

Comparative Historical Data / Current Data Sorted by Sales

					Type of Statement						4	4
	6		9		8	Unqualified						
	38		48		57	Reviewed	1	3	6	15	18	14
	27		27		27	Compiled		6	8	7	6	
	30		25		20	Tax Returns	3	7	2	7	1	
	50		49		56	Other	2	12	9	14	9	10
	4/1/04-3/31/05 ALL		4/1/05-3/31/06 ALL		4/1/06-3/31/07 ALL			21 (4/1-9/30/06)		147 (10/1/06-3/31/07)		
							0-1MM	1-3MM	3-5MM	5-10MM	10-25MM	25MM & OVER
	151		158		168	NUMBER OF STATEMENTS	6	28	25	43	38	28
	%		%		%	ASSETS	%	%	%	%	%	%
	10.3		7.1		9.0	Cash & Equivalents		13.1	8.9	7.1	6.6	4.6
	49.6		51.1		49.3	Trade Receivables (net)		35.0	49.9	51.7	58.9	52.9
	13.9		12.9		15.9	Inventory		17.1	19.2	16.7	10.8	19.8
	5.4		6.9		5.1	All Other Current		3.2	2.1	5.2	8.2	5.2
	79.2		78.1		79.3	Total Current		68.4	80.2	80.7	84.6	82.5
	14.2		14.9		15.3	Fixed Assets (net)		26.4	13.5	14.1	11.4	11.0
	1.3		2.1		1.2	Intangibles (net)		1.4	2.2	1.0	.3	1.6
	5.3		4.9		4.2	All Other Non-Current		3.8	4.1	4.2	3.7	4.9
	100.0		100.0		100.0	Total		100.0	100.0	100.0	100.0	100.0
						LIABILITIES						
	17.2		16.9		16.9	Notes Payable-Short Term		20.2	14.2	14.4	18.8	20.4
	1.9		2.4		2.8	Cur. Mat.-L.T.D.		4.0	.6	1.5	1.8	2.6
	19.3		19.0		17.4	Trade Payables		16.6	15.5	17.9	21.2	14.5
	.3		.7		.4	Income Taxes Payable		.5	.6	.6	.1	.4
	12.0		11.1		13.9	All Other Current		12.8	13.8	11.8	10.6	19.3
	50.7		50.1		51.6	Total Current		54.1	44.6	46.1	52.5	57.2
	10.0		10.4		11.3	Long-Term Debt		18.2	8.6	7.8	6.1	6.4
	.1		.3		.2	Deferred Taxes		.0	.0	.6	.1	.1
	7.5		4.3		3.2	All Other Non-Current		9.2	1.9	1.6	2.3	2.6
	31.6		35.0		33.8	Net Worth		18.5	44.9	44.0	39.1	33.7
	100.0		100.0		100.0	Total Liabilities & Net Worth		100.0	100.0	100.0	100.0	100.0
						INCOME DATA						
	100.0		100.0		100.0	Net Sales		100.0	100.0	100.0	100.0	100.0
	28.3		28.3		27.5	Gross Profit		32.6	28.8	24.4	23.4	26.9
	24.4		23.5		23.5	Operating Expenses		31.9	23.7	20.9	19.1	22.8
	3.9		4.8		3.9	Operating Profit		.8	5.1	3.5	4.3	4.0
	.1		.4		.5	All Other Expenses (net)		.8	.0	.4	.3	.6
	3.8		4.4		3.5	Profit Before Taxes		.0	5.0	3.1	4.0	3.4
						RATIOS						
	2.5		2.6		2.4			2.5	2.6	2.5	2.3	1.9
	1.6		1.5		1.6	Current		1.2	1.7	1.9	1.6	1.3
	1.2		1.1		1.2			.8	1.3	1.4	1.2	1.2
	1.9		1.9		1.8			1.8	2.1	1.9	1.8	1.5
	1.1		1.1		1.2	Quick		1.0	1.5	1.5	1.3	1.1
	.9		.8		.8			.4	.8	.9	.8	.7
33	11.0	37	9.8	30	12.1		8 47.7	26 14.3	31 11.7	42 8.7	40 9.1	
53	6.9	54	6.7	49	7.4	Sales/Receivables	36 10.1	47 7.7	50 7.2	62 5.9	59 6.2	
75	4.9	75	4.8	74	4.9		48 7.6	81 4.5	77 4.7	76 4.8	80 4.5	
3	118.6	1	652.3	2	178.4		0 UND	0 UND	2 162.8	6 63.5	4 85.4	
13	27.0	9	38.8	13	28.9	Cost of Sales/Inventory	9 42.6	16 22.3	11 34.3	12 29.4	23 15.6	
34	10.6	29	12.8	27	13.5		43 8.5	37 9.8	27 13.6	23 16.1	49 7.4	
11	32.3	12	29.4	10	35.1		2 154.8	7 53.2	11 34.4	12 30.0	16 22.5	
23	15.8	23	16.1	21	17.4	Cost of Sales/Payables	26 14.0	20 18.6	17 21.0	25 14.8	21 17.3	
38	9.5	38	9.6	34	10.7		35 10.5	33 10.9	35 10.3	41 9.0	28 12.9	
	7.3		7.5		7.1			11.0	7.0	6.7	5.6	8.5
	12.6		12.4		12.2	Sales/Working Capital		43.9	8.7	9.4	10.3	13.5
	36.9		45.0		34.0			-74.0	20.5	20.2	41.1	32.7
	16.7		17.2		17.1			12.9	34.2	17.3	38.1	11.3
(131)	5.7	(139)	6.6	(151)	4.2	EBIT/Interest	(23) 2.2	(22) 11.5	(39) 4.4	(37) 4.3	(27) 3.8	
	2.9		3.0		1.7			-1.6	2.6	2.0	1.7	2.2
	10.5		14.8		13.0	Net Profit + Depr., Dep.,					15.0	14.3
(23)	3.9	(29)	6.0	(35)	4.0	Amort./Cur. Mat. L/T/D				(14) 5.0	(12) 5.8	
	1.5		2.5		1.2						1.4	.8
	.1		.1		.1			.3	.0	.1	.1	.2
	.3		.3		.3	Fixed/Worth		1.4	.2	.2	.2	.3
	.8		.9		.9			-7.6	.5	.4	.6	.6
	.7		.9		.8			.7	.6	.8	.8	1.4
	1.9		1.9		1.7	Debt/Worth		5.3	1.7	1.1	1.6	2.5
	5.9		5.1		3.9			-10.9	2.3	2.2	4.0	4.3
	66.5		81.3		62.0	% Profit Before Taxes/Tangible		138.1	82.1	43.2	57.5	56.1
(137)	35.6	(143)	38.7	(152)	28.0	Net Worth	(20) 35.2	(24) 33.2	(41) 20.9	(36) 27.9	34.6	
	11.3		14.4		11.5			9.1	10.7	6.3	14.5	17.4
	21.9		25.6		24.1	% Profit Before Taxes/Total		49.3	32.0	18.3	27.2	20.4
	10.4		12.6		9.4	Assets		3.9	17.2	9.1	7.8	8.4
	2.9		4.2		2.0			-12.9	5.5	2.4	2.1	4.0
	144.8		101.3		91.9			59.0	467.5	95.4	114.8	65.4
	55.1		48.7		42.4	Sales/Net Fixed Assets		22.4	43.5	48.5	52.5	44.6
	21.3		17.7		18.5			10.8	21.3	30.8	19.7	23.4
	4.7		4.7		4.9			6.1	5.5	5.4	4.4	4.2
	3.5		3.6		3.6	Sales/Total Assets		3.8	3.8	3.4	3.6	3.2
	2.7		2.7		2.7			2.6	2.8	2.8	2.6	2.8
	.3		.2		.3			.5	.2	.2	.3	.3
(115)	.5	(124)	.5	(127)	.5	% Depr., Dep., Amort./Sales	(19) 1.2	(15) .5	(30) .4	(32) .5	(26) .5	
	1.1		1.1		1.0			2.6	1.0	.8	.8	.9
	2.1		2.0		1.7			1.6	1.7	1.6	1.5	
(74)	3.7	(70)	3.9	(79)	3.2	% Officers', Directors' Owners' Comp/Sales	(14) 3.6	(10) 2.4	(25) 2.9	(19) 2.4		
	6.5		6.5		5.2			6.6	5.8	4.6	4.7	
	1781374M		4405279M		3329597M	Net Sales ($)	3513M	54392M	97673M	307905M	545299M	2320815M
	539777M		1374365M		871630M	Total Assets ($)	1339M	16652M	29919M	88067M	157643M	578010M

© RMA 2007

M = $ thousand   MM = $ million
See Pages 11 through 21 for Explanation of Ratios and Data

		Current Data Sorted by Assets							Comparative Historical Data	
							Type of Statement			
	2	1 6	1 9	3		1	Unqualified		6	5
	2	3	2				Reviewed		9	14
	16	3	3				Compiled		2	6
	6	13	8	2	1		Tax Returns		4	10
		7 (4/1-9/30/06)		75 (10/1/06-3/31/07)			Other		7	10
									4/1/02-3/31/03	4/1/03-3/31/04
	0-500M	500M-2MM	2-10MM	10-50MM	50-100MM	100-250MM			ALL	ALL
	26	26	23	5	2		**NUMBER OF STATEMENTS**		28	45
	%	%	%	%	%	%	**ASSETS**		%	%
	22.1	5.3	11.0				Cash & Equivalents	D	11.2	12.4
	30.5	42.0	44.0				Trade Receivables (net)	A	38.8	38.0
	2.4	11.0	20.6				Inventory	T	16.0	15.0
	8.0	9.1	6.0				All Other Current	A	6.8	3.7
	63.1	67.5	81.7				Total Current		72.9	69.2
	29.5	24.7	12.1				Fixed Assets (net)	N	18.5	21.3
	2.9	1.0	.4				Intangibles (net)	O	1.2	1.0
	4.5	6.8	5.8				All Other Non-Current	T	7.5	8.5
	100.0	100.0	100.0				Total		100.0	100.0
							LIABILITIES	A		
	9.0	14.8	10.6				Notes Payable-Short Term	V	8.6	18.4
	3.2	2.5	1.9				Cur. Mat.-L.T.D.	A	3.2	3.4
	16.5	16.3	14.6				Trade Payables	I	14.9	17.8
	.2	.8	1.4				Income Taxes Payable	L	.3	.3
	16.3	13.3	18.0				All Other Current	A	19.7	14.8
	45.2	47.8	46.5				Total Current	B	46.7	54.8
	22.3	21.8	8.1				Long-Term Debt	L	12.1	14.0
	.0	.0	.1				Deferred Taxes	E	.1	.3
	6.8	4.2	1.6				All Other Non-Current		4.9	6.7
	25.7	26.2	43.6				Net Worth		36.2	24.2
	100.0	100.0	100.0				Total Liabilties & Net Worth		100.0	100.0
							INCOME DATA			
	100.0	100.0	100.0				Net Sales		100.0	100.0
	40.9	34.5	27.5				Gross Profit		33.3	33.0
	36.8	30.7	19.4				Operating Expenses		27.9	26.8
	4.1	3.8	8.1				Operating Profit		5.4	6.3
	.4	1.7	.4				All Other Expenses (net)		.7	.5
	3.8	2.1	7.7				Profit Before Taxes		4.6	5.8
							RATIOS			
	6.8	2.2	2.4						2.1	2.0
	1.9	1.3	1.8				Current		1.6	1.6
	1.0	1.0	1.3						1.1	1.2
	5.3	1.6	1.9						2.0	1.5
	1.6	.9	1.0				Quick		1.0	1.2
	.7	.6	.8						.7	.7
1	644.3	24 15.5	38 9.5					31	11.8	18 20.7
20	18.0	43 8.6	56 6.5				Sales/Receivables	59	6.2	40 9.0
35	10.4	76 4.8	85 4.3					79	4.6	73 5.0
0	UND	0 UND	1 388.4					3	121.1	4 100.1
0	UND	8 48.2	23 16.0				Cost of Sales/Inventory	12	29.7	16 22.7
3	136.5	27 13.6	84 4.4					55	6.7	36 10.0
0	UND	10 37.2	16 22.3					12	31.0	9 38.6
8	45.3	25 14.8	23 15.6				Cost of Sales/Payables	27	13.4	30 12.3
33	11.1	52 7.0	41 8.9					51	7.2	49 7.5
	12.8	6.6	5.0						6.0	8.3
	21.7	19.1	7.7				Sales/Working Capital		9.5	14.2
	UND	NM	12.4						36.1	36.8
	32.3	12.9	36.7						14.2	28.4
(20)	8.9	(24) 2.6	(21) 13.1				EBIT/Interest	(23)	4.9	(38) 7.8
	2.0	.7	4.4						-.4	3.0
							Net Profit + Depr., Dep.,			4.6
							Amort./Cur. Mat. L/T/D	(11)		1.6
										1.1
	.3	.1	.1						.1	.2
	.8	.5	.2				Fixed/Worth		.6	.5
	NM	UND	.5						1.8	.9
	.2	.8	.7						.8	1.0
	2.0	2.6	1.4				Debt/Worth		1.9	1.4
	NM	UND	2.6						4.7	3.4
	190.4	103.8	58.3				% Profit Before Taxes/Tangible		79.2	91.7
(20)	71.5	(21) 42.2	(22) 35.9				Net Worth	(25)	15.4	(40) 36.3
	12.1	9.3	26.8						.5	10.2
	46.6	19.8	25.5				% Profit Before Taxes/Total		17.5	26.3
	22.7	5.0	18.6				Assets		6.1	14.8
	5.5	.9	8.3						-.4	3.7
	63.8	76.5	69.0						58.2	52.0
	29.6	22.9	35.8				Sales/Net Fixed Assets		14.6	24.7
	14.5	7.1	17.0						8.0	10.0
	8.2	4.0	3.0						3.4	4.3
	5.3	3.0	2.6				Sales/Total Assets		2.7	3.1
	4.2	2.2	2.0						2.2	2.3
	.4	.3	.4						.9	.7
(18)	.7	(19) .8	(16) .8				% Depr., Dep., Amort./Sales	(24)	1.1	(35) 1.3
	1.7	2.4	1.1						1.8	1.8
	3.9	1.3					% Officers', Directors'		2.6	2.3
(12)	5.6	(12) 2.5					Owners' Comp/Sales	(15)	7.7	(26) 3.6
	7.0	3.3							9.3	7.1
	44250M	96188M	295194M	205561M	718568M		Net Sales ($)		351477M	354305M
	6733M	31982M	118334M	93105M	161197M		Total Assets ($)		161279M	128646M

© RMA 2007

M = $ thousand   MM = $ million
See Pages 11 through 21 for Explanation of Ratios and Data

Comparative Historical Data / Current Data Sorted by Sales

Type of Statement	Hist 1	Hist 2	Hist 3		0-1MM	1-3MM	3-5MM	5-10MM	10-25MM	25MM & OVER
Unqualified	6	5	3			1				2
Reviewed	13	17	20			1	4	6	7	2
Compiled	4	9	7			4	2	3	1	
Tax Returns	17	21	22		8	8	3	3	5	
Other	17	14	30		2	9	7	5	4	3
	4/1/04-3/31/05	4/1/05-3/31/06	4/1/06-3/31/07			7 (4/1-9/30/06)		75 (10/1/06-3/31/07)		
	ALL	ALL	ALL							
NUMBER OF STATEMENTS	57	66	82		10	23	14	16	12	7
ASSETS	%	%	%		%	%	%	%	%	%
Cash & Equivalents	12.4	10.0	12.4		14.7	17.0	9.4	10.1	6.1	
Trade Receivables (net)	41.7	34.9	38.7		34.3	25.8	55.9	34.7	49.7	
Inventory	11.4	16.8	11.3		1.6	4.9	14.0	20.7	20.6	
All Other Current	3.8	2.5	7.8		11.4	10.4	4.1	6.4	6.1	
Total Current	69.3	64.3	70.2		62.1	58.1	83.4	71.9	82.5	
Fixed Assets (net)	20.2	26.3	21.9		35.4	32.3	11.5	19.8	10.8	
Intangibles (net)	.7	.2	1.4		.0	3.3	1.8	.5	.0	
All Other Non-Current	9.8	9.3	6.6		2.5	6.3	3.3	7.8	6.7	
Total	100.0	100.0	100.0		100.0	100.0	100.0	100.0	100.0	
LIABILITIES										
Notes Payable-Short Term	11.4	12.3	11.8		10.3	9.9	11.9	10.8	20.2	
Cur. Mat.-L.T.D.	2.4	2.5	2.5		.3	5.0	2.4	1.6	1.8	
Trade Payables	16.5	18.4	15.6		9.4	17.9	17.5	17.3	16.9	
Income Taxes Payable	.4	.3	.8		.0	.2	.4	2.7	.4	
All Other Current	13.5	10.6	16.1		3.0	18.1	15.6	21.4	11.6	
Total Current	44.3	44.1	46.8		23.0	51.1	47.8	53.8	50.9	
Long-Term Debt	15.0	15.5	17.7		21.6	34.3	7.4	10.3	6.8	
Deferred Taxes	.1	.2	.1		.0	.0	.0	.1	.1	
All Other Non-Current	6.1	5.3	4.0		9.1	2.3	5.3	6.2	.7	
Net Worth	34.6	34.9	31.4		46.3	12.3	39.5	29.6	41.5	
Total Liabilities & Net Worth	100.0	100.0	100.0		100.0	100.0	100.0	100.0	100.0	
INCOME DATA										
Net Sales	100.0	100.0	100.0		100.0	100.0	100.0	100.0	100.0	
Gross Profit	34.9	33.8	33.7		53.6	41.0	26.7	27.3	25.0	
Operating Expenses	30.3	27.9	28.4		53.2	34.7	23.1	20.9	18.7	
Operating Profit	4.6	5.9	5.3		.4	6.3	3.6	6.3	6.2	
All Other Expenses (net)	.5	.5	.8		1.5	1.2	.5	1.1	.4	
Profit Before Taxes	4.1	5.4	4.4		-1.2	5.1	3.1	5.3	5.8	

RATIOS

Ratio	Hist 1	Hist 2	Hist 3		0-1MM	1-3MM	3-5MM	5-10MM	10-25MM	25MM & OVER
Current	3.5	2.3	2.3		13.1	2.2	3.6	2.1	2.0	
	1.7	1.4	1.5		3.2	1.3	1.9	1.6	1.4	
	1.1	1.1	1.1		.9	1.0	1.2	1.0	1.2	
Quick	2.9	1.8	1.9		6.1	1.8	3.6	1.3	1.9	
	1.2	.9	1.1		2.9	1.1	1.5	.9	1.0	
	.9	.6	.7		.7	.5	.8	.5	.8	
Sales/Receivables	29 12.6	20 17.9	21 17.1		0 UND	1 321.8	32 11.4	22 16.7	43 8.5	
	48 7.6	37 9.9	39 9.4		30 12.2	22 16.7	65 5.6	33 10.9	65 5.6	
	79 4.6	63 5.8	79 4.6		47 7.8	41 9.0	87 4.2	57 6.4	104 3.5	
Cost of Sales/Inventory	0 UND	0 UND	0 UND		0 UND	0 UND	0 UND	0 847.0	0 755.8	
	7 51.1	8 46.1	5 73.9		0 UND	0 UND	7 55.7	10 37.3	25 14.6	
	38 9.7	71 5.1	27 13.7		6 56.6	10 35.5	29 12.7	101 3.6	51 7.1	
Cost of Sales/Payables	7 54.3	5 78.0	6 58.4		0 UND	1 353.7	1 373.6	13 28.7	20 18.1	
	22 16.3	28 12.8	23 16.2		3 124.0	25 14.5	20 18.1	23 15.6	27 13.6	
	40 9.2	53 6.9	43 8.5		43 8.5	61 6.0	48 7.5	43 8.4	35 10.4	
Sales/Working Capital	7.1	8.4	6.6		4.9	13.4	5.1	6.4	6.2	
	11.2	16.0	13.7		18.0	22.2	15.2	9.9	10.3	
	49.6	55.9	34.9		-122.3	UND	28.7	245.3	19.7	
EBIT/Interest	28.0	36.6	19.1			20.2	64.1	27.9	13.5	
	(48) 6.9	(60) 6.9	(71) 5.8			(22) 4.1	(13) 6.0	(14) 7.3	(11) 5.8	
	1.6	3.0	2.2			1.6	-.2	3.8	2.5	
Net Profit + Depr., Dep., Amort./Cur. Mat. L/T/D		6.3								
		(10) 3.7								
		1.7								
Fixed/Worth	.1	.2	.1		.2	.4	.0	.1	.1	
	.4	.6	.4		.8	1.0	.2	.6	.3	
	1.0	2.3	1.8		-63.3	UND	.6	2.1	.5	
Debt/Worth	.6	.9	.8		.1	.9	.4	1.0	.9	
	1.6	2.2	1.9		1.1	4.6	1.4	1.6	1.6	
	3.5	5.1	6.6		-90.6	UND	4.0	10.0	3.0	
% Profit Before Taxes/Tangible Net Worth	82.9	74.3	85.8			317.6	73.6	90.3	68.1	
	(50) 37.2	(60) 37.0	(70) 40.2			(18) 125.4	(13) 36.6	(13) 36.6	36.1	
	4.9	16.7	17.5			9.6	-2.7	29.3	26.5	
% Profit Before Taxes/Total Assets	29.4	23.3	28.7		21.0	48.9	35.0	22.0	21.9	
	13.1	11.6	14.3		9.3	20.2	11.0	16.1	13.6	
	1.0	5.6	3.2		-6.6	2.9	-5.0	7.7	6.4	
Sales/Net Fixed Assets	58.9	38.5	66.1		74.1	47.0	390.4	55.6	76.4	
	25.7	14.1	27.9		14.2	23.3	32.1	35.7	32.9	
	12.1	6.7	12.8		5.0	8.2	15.9	12.9	20.5	
Sales/Total Assets	4.1	3.9	4.9		5.6	6.9	4.9	4.6	3.3	
	2.9	3.1	3.1		4.1	4.3	3.2	3.1	2.4	
	2.3	2.2	2.2		1.8	2.5	2.4	2.3	2.1	
% Depr., Dep., Amort./Sales	.7	.7	.4			.4		.2		
	(36) 1.0	(53) 1.1	(60) .8			(18) .8		(13) .5		
	2.4	1.9	1.6			1.6		1.5		
% Officers', Directors', Owners' Comp/Sales	2.5	1.8	2.1			3.0		1.4		
	(27) 5.0	(38) 3.7	(34) 3.3			(12) 5.2		(10) 2.9		
	7.1	7.3	6.0			5.8		5.6		
Net Sales ($)	429822M	866250M	1359761M		5554M	45018M	53579M	121195M	203179M	931236M
Total Assets ($)	159256M	417983M	411351M		3073M	13579M	17677M	45028M	80931M	251063M

© RMA 2007

M = $ thousand   MM = $ million
See Pages 11 through 21 for Explanation of Ratios and Data

Current Data Sorted by Assets · Comparative Historical Data

Type of Statement	0-500M	500M-2MM	2-10MM	10-50MM	50-100MM	100-250MM		4/1/02-3/31/03 ALL	4/1/03-3/31/04 ALL
Unqualified			3	1		1		5	9
Reviewed	1	9	27	3				24	35
Compiled	4	10	8					19	27
Tax Returns	14	14	6	1				14	16
Other	13	11	11	5	1			28	32
		21 (4/1-9/30/06)	122 (10/1/06-3/31/07)						

	0-500M	500M-2MM	2-10MM	10-50MM	50-100MM	100-250MM		4/1/02-3/31/03 ALL	4/1/03-3/31/04 ALL
NUMBER OF STATEMENTS	32	44	55	10	1	1		90	119
	%	%	%	%	%	%	**ASSETS**	%	%
	14.6	12.4	8.6	14.2			Cash & Equivalents	11.5	11.2
	23.0	35.6	44.9	44.5			Trade Receivables (net)	39.4	36.4
	9.5	12.8	16.7	11.8			Inventory	12.2	14.5
	1.4	5.1	8.2	9.2			All Other Current	4.9	6.4
	48.5	66.0	78.5	79.6			Total Current	67.9	68.5
	35.6	23.7	15.3	10.9			Fixed Assets (net)	19.5	19.6
	1.3	3.1	.5	3.9			Intangibles (net)	2.9	1.8
	14.4	7.3	5.7	5.6			All Other Non-Current	9.7	10.1
	100.0	100.0	100.0	100.0			Total	100.0	100.0
							LIABILITIES		
	16.2	8.3	9.7	10.3			Notes Payable-Short Term	13.6	15.9
	5.4	3.2	3.6	2.7			Cur. Mat.-L.T.D.	3.6	3.5
	7.1	15.8	21.3	30.4			Trade Payables	16.5	17.7
	.1	.3	.3	.2			Income Taxes Payable	.3	.4
	14.1	16.4	16.0	17.4			All Other Current	13.0	13.0
	42.9	44.0	50.8	61.1			Total Current	47.0	50.5
	28.3	19.3	11.5	6.9			Long-Term Debt	10.3	13.6
	.0	.3	.1	.5			Deferred Taxes	.2	.3
	4.2	5.7	2.0	.1			All Other Non-Current	5.8	3.9
	24.6	30.7	35.6	31.4			Net Worth	36.7	31.7
	100.0	100.0	100.0	100.0			Total Liabilities & Net Worth	100.0	100.0
							INCOME DATA		
	100.0	100.0	100.0	100.0			Net Sales	100.0	100.0
	45.4	32.2	25.6	20.7			Gross Profit	30.7	28.3
	39.5	27.6	20.3	15.6			Operating Expenses	27.4	25.5
	5.9	4.5	5.4	5.1			Operating Profit	3.3	2.8
	.8	1.2	.4	.2			All Other Expenses (net)	1.1	.6
	5.1	3.3	5.0	4.8			Profit Before Taxes	2.2	2.2
							RATIOS		
	3.1	2.9	3.0	1.6				2.5	2.1
	1.4	1.3	1.5	1.2			Current	1.4	1.4
	.6	1.1	1.1	.9				1.0	1.1
	3.1	2.5	1.7	1.4				1.8	1.6
	.9	1.1	1.0	1.0			Quick	1.1	1.1
	.3	.6	.7	.5				.7	.7
	0 UND	19 19.3	33 11.0	16 23.5				21 17.2	21 17.7
	11 34.6	34 10.6	45 8.1	60 6.1			Sales/Receivables	40 9.2	43 8.5
	43 8.5	68 5.4	73 5.0	74 5.0				66 5.5	60 6.1
	0 UND	0 UND	0 UND	0 UND				0 UND	0 UND
	0 UND	11 34.5	17 21.5	0 UND			Cost of Sales/Inventory	14 25.6	7 54.8
	22 16.8	36 10.3	47 7.7	11 33.2				29 12.6	37 9.9
	0 UND	10 35.6	10 35.2	20 18.3				8 47.1	6 63.4
	4 103.4	24 14.9	21 17.2	40 9.1			Cost of Sales/Payables	20 18.2	20 18.4
	24 15.1	38 9.7	49 7.4	62 5.9				37 10.0	40 9.1
	8.3	6.8	6.2	11.3				7.9	7.8
	38.9	17.9	13.4	28.8			Sales/Working Capital	16.3	15.8
	-69.7	66.3	36.2	-27.9				83.6	111.7
	33.4	21.9	23.5					10.8	15.2
	(27) 2.0	(35) 4.6	(50) 8.2				EBIT/Interest	(77) 3.7	(100) 3.5
	.3	.6	2.0					1.2	-.6
			6.7					7.1	7.7
		(13) 3.3					Net Profit + Depr., Dep., Amort./Cur. Mat. L/T/D	(18) 1.7	(22) 2.5
			2.3					.4	.3
	.3	.2	.2	.0				.2	.2
	1.4	.6	.4	.2			Fixed/Worth	.4	.5
	NM	2.1	1.8	1.2				1.1	1.8
	.7	.7	.6	1.6				1.0	1.0
	3.2	3.1	2.1	2.9			Debt/Worth	2.3	2.1
	NM	10.4	9.0	10.9				4.6	8.1
	170.9	84.1	78.6					56.1	63.4
	(24) 66.2	(37) 35.9	(50) 28.9				% Profit Before Taxes/Tangible Net Worth	(83) 21.0	(100) 22.5
	25.7	9.5	14.6					2.7	3.2
	57.2	27.2	22.5	19.7				15.9	18.5
	15.6	8.7	12.5	13.5			% Profit Before Taxes/Total Assets	7.3	7.1
	-2.8	-1.7	2.6	5.9				.6	-.6
	63.8	59.7	77.2	278.0				64.5	58.3
	18.1	18.4	26.9	113.4			Sales/Net Fixed Assets	22.8	22.7
	7.2	8.5	12.4	18.3				11.8	11.4
	7.9	4.0	4.2	3.8				4.5	4.6
	4.0	2.9	3.1	3.0			Sales/Total Assets	3.3	3.0
	2.5	2.4	2.5	1.8				2.4	2.3
	.7	.9	.5					.5	.5
	(20) 1.7	(31) 1.6	(49) .9				% Depr., Dep., Amort./Sales	(80) 1.3	(94) 1.2
	3.2	3.7	1.3					2.5	2.2
	4.4	2.7	1.6					2.2	1.8
	(18) 8.4	(26) 4.3	(26) 2.4				% Officers', Directors' Owners' Comp/Sales	(51) 3.8	(63) 3.6
	12.0	7.0	6.7					8.0	8.4
	37088M	148236M	883201M	526902M	243811M	134356M	Net Sales ($)	974653M	1630228M
	7696M	47074M	250130M	192688M	75062M	156925M	Total Assets ($)	293220M	624457M

M = $ thousand   MM = $ million
See Pages 11 through 21 for Explanation of Ratios and Data

Comparative Historical Data | Current Data Sorted by Sales

Type of Statement

4/1/04-3/31/05 ALL	4/1/05-3/31/06 ALL	4/1/06-3/31/07 ALL	Type of Statement	0-1MM	1-3MM	3-5MM	5-10MM	10-25MM	25MM & OVER
5	7	5	Unqualified	2	1	8	12	2	3
35	29	40	Reviewed		4	9	1	13	6
22	21	22	Compiled	11	13	4	2	5	1
38	39	35	Tax Returns					4	1
27	39	41	Other	7	10	7	3	8	6
				21 (4/1-9/30/06)		122 (10/1/06-3/31/07)			
127	135	143	NUMBER OF STATEMENTS	20	28	28	18	32	17

ASSETS

%	%	%		%	%	%	%	%	%
11.3	11.5	11.4	Cash & Equivalents	11.9	15.2	10.5	8.9	11.8	8.1
39.8	38.4	37.1	Trade Receivables (net)	17.4	21.8	44.9	47.0	45.1	46.7
12.4	15.0	13.9	Inventory	8.5	21.7	8.2	16.9	15.7	9.8
6.2	6.2	5.8	All Other Current	4.0	1.3	5.6	4.7	9.5	9.9
69.7	71.0	68.2	Total Current	41.8	60.1	69.3	77.4	82.2	74.5
20.7	21.0	22.0	Fixed Assets (net)	42.8	26.9	19.8	17.0	13.7	14.0
1.3	1.0	1.7	Intangibles (net)	.9	3.5	1.9	.5	.6	2.8
8.3	7.0	8.1	All Other Non-Current	14.3	9.5	9.0	5.1	3.6	8.7
100.0	100.0	100.0	Total	100.0	100.0	100.0	100.0	100.0	100.0

LIABILITIES

12.2	13.0	10.6	Notes Payable-Short Term	20.5	9.7	6.2	12.1	10.6	6.3
3.4	4.9	3.8	Cur. Mat.-L.T.D.	2.9	4.1	5.0	2.6	4.1	3.4
18.7	18.4	17.1	Trade Payables	4.6	7.1	21.0	21.4	20.7	30.1
.6	.2	.2	Income Taxes Payable	.0	.2	.4	.4	.1	.3
16.2	16.1	15.8	All Other Current	17.8	14.0	16.0	15.7	14.4	18.9
51.2	52.6	47.6	Total Current	45.9	35.1	48.6	52.3	49.9	59.0
12.5	16.8	17.5	Long-Term Debt	27.6	30.0	15.1	10.3	11.3	8.2
.2	.1	.2	Deferred Taxes	.0	.0	.5	.2	.0	.4
6.3	5.6	3.5	All Other Non-Current	5.3	3.7	6.3	1.1	2.0	1.7
29.8	25.0	31.3	Net Worth	21.3	31.2	29.6	36.1	36.9	30.7
100.0	100.0	100.0	Total Liabilities & Net Worth	100.0	100.0	100.0	100.0	100.0	100.0

INCOME DATA

100.0	100.0	100.0	Net Sales	100.0	100.0	100.0	100.0	100.0	100.0
30.4	31.7	31.6	Gross Profit	48.8	38.7	29.9	25.5	24.5	22.2
25.7	26.7	26.4	Operating Expenses	42.0	34.0	25.0	19.9	18.8	18.6
4.7	5.0	5.2	Operating Profit	6.8	4.7	4.8	5.6	5.7	3.6
.3	.7	.7	All Other Expenses (net)	2.1	.9	.6	.8	.1	.1
4.4	4.3	4.5	Profit Before Taxes	4.6	3.8	4.3	4.8	5.6	3.5

RATIOS

2.3	2.4	2.9	Current	2.8	5.0	2.3	2.9	3.6	1.9
1.4	1.5	1.4		1.2	2.1	1.3	1.7	1.5	1.2
1.1	1.0	1.1		.4	1.0	1.1	1.1	1.1	1.0
1.6	1.7	1.9	Quick	1.6	3.7	2.1	2.1	2.0	1.2
1.1	1.1	1.0		.5	1.1	1.1	1.1	1.0	1.1
.7	.7	.6		.1	.4	.7	.6	.8	.6
21 17.2	22 16.4	16 23.3	Sales/Receivables	0 UND	0 UND	26 14.0	31 11.7	32 11.5	15 24.7
37 9.7	42 8.7	38 9.7		5 69.8	18 19.8	42 8.7	73 5.0	44 8.3	45 8.1
61 5.9	65 5.6	64 5.7		43 8.5	46 7.9	79 4.6	87 4.2	62 5.8	66 5.5
0 UND	0 UND	0 UND	Cost of Sales/Inventory	0 UND	0 UND	0 UND	0 UND	0 UND	0 UND
8 43.8	12 30.7	9 41.6		0 UND	19 19.0	4 81.4	38 9.7	12 31.5	2 221.4
30 12.3	42 8.8	39 9.3		50 7.2	63 5.8	19 19.3	52 7.0	29 12.6	17 21.8
8 43.4	6 61.7	6 65.5	Cost of Sales/Payables	0 UND	0 UND	12 30.8	13 28.3	8 47.1	19 18.8
21 17.0	23 16.2	21 17.2		4 91.9	7 53.5	25 14.7	21 17.1	23 16.0	36 10.1
37 9.9	39 9.2	42 8.7		25 14.4	35 10.4	50 7.4	38 9.7	50 7.4	49 7.4
8.5	7.1	6.8	Sales/Working Capital	8.4	6.2	9.0	6.1	7.0	10.7
17.0	15.6	17.2		29.1	14.5	29.8	12.1	15.5	26.1
109.4	-135.6	195.9		-23.2	NM	47.8	78.1	33.2	-528.1
18.8	20.5	22.9	EBIT/Interest	10.3	27.9	22.8	30.4	22.8	38.7
(113) 6.8	(123) 7.0	(122) 6.0		(18) .8	(21) 2.0	(23) 6.1	(16) 4.8	(28) 7.8	(16) 18.1
2.1	1.6	1.5		-.7	.6	1.8	1.1	2.4	7.9
3.7	10.9	5.7	Net Profit + Depr., Dep., Amort./Cur. Mat. L/T/D						
(19) 1.8	(15) 4.8	(22) 3.2							
.7	1.4	1.9							
.2	.2	.2	Fixed/Worth	.6	.3	.1	.2	.2	.1
.5	.5	.6		1.9	.8	.5	.6	.4	.2
2.2	4.0	2.0		-2.4	2.5	1.8	2.0	1.4	1.3
.7	.9	.7	Debt/Worth	.5	.7	.7	.7	.7	1.7
1.8	3.3	2.7		3.2	3.3	3.3	1.7	2.2	2.7
7.6	13.3	9.2		-6.5	9.3	6.7	14.2	9.2	6.1
73.7	90.3	88.8	% Profit Before Taxes/Tangible Net Worth	112.0	97.3	107.1	73.8	88.0	75.5
(104) 28.9	(109) 39.2	(122) 36.2		(13) 27.8	(23) 63.9	(24) 47.0	(17) 29.6	(30) 36.2	(15) 27.4
8.8	17.3	14.6		-33.9	15.8	13.0	11.4	16.5	16.8
23.0	26.6	29.3	% Profit Before Taxes/Total Assets	40.1	38.4	38.6	29.6	22.1	17.9
10.6	11.4	12.4		1.6	13.6	10.2	13.1	13.8	12.4
2.1	2.8	1.6		-10.3	.9	2.6	1.8	2.3	4.9
68.6	49.2	77.2	Sales/Net Fixed Assets	25.3	63.8	78.1	65.4	98.7	121.3
25.9	23.5	22.1		8.6	17.5	21.6	26.1	27.3	55.4
11.3	12.6	9.8		3.1	6.4	10.6	11.3	16.1	17.1
4.9	4.6	4.5	Sales/Total Assets	5.2	4.7	4.5	3.6	4.5	5.2
3.4	3.2	3.2		2.5	3.5	3.2	2.9	3.1	3.4
2.5	2.3	2.4		1.5	2.0	2.6	2.3	2.5	2.9
.5	.5	.5	% Depr., Dep., Amort./Sales	1.2	.7	.8	.6	.4	.2
(97) 1.2	(113) 1.2	(110) 1.0		(13) 2.6	(20) 1.4	(18) 1.7	(17) 1.0	(26) .9	(16) .4
2.3	2.3	2.2		3.5	3.9	3.4	2.0	1.3	.9
2.6	2.0	2.0	% Officers', Directors', Owners' Comp/Sales	5.1	3.5	2.5		1.6	
(81) 5.5	(81) 3.9	(73) 4.5		(10) 8.4	(16) 7.3	(10) 3.8		(14) 2.0	
9.2	6.3	8.4		11.6	9.8	5.1		5.9	
2101606M	2215898M	1973594M	Net Sales ($)	10904M	55566M	105466M	134081M	495116M	1172461M
629419M	652642M	729575M	Total Assets ($)	5057M	21115M	32111M	44854M	175840M	450598M

M = $ thousand   MM = $ million
See Pages 11 through 21 for Explanation of Ratios and Data

							Type of Statement		
		2	**3**	**2**				**4**	**4**
1		**8**	**14**	**1**			Unqualified		**1**
1		**3**					Reviewed		**1**
6		**2**					Compiled		**1**
3		**2**	**8**	**2**			Tax Returns		**1**
		12 (4/1-9/30/06)		46 (10/1/06-3/31/07)			Other	4/1/02-3/31/03	4/1/03-3/31/04
0-500M		500M-2MM	2-10MM	10-50MM	50-100MM	100-250MM	NUMBER OF STATEMENTS	ALL	ALL
11		17	25	5				4	7
%		%	%	%	%	%	**ASSETS**	%	%
25.0		6.7	7.5				Cash & Equivalents		
16.7		54.4	44.9	D	D		Trade Receivables (net)		
6.2		6.0	9.7	A	A		Inventory		
1.8		5.9	6.3	T	T		All Other Current		
49.6		73.1	68.4	A	A		Total Current		
44.6		16.8	23.2				Fixed Assets (net)		
.6		5.1	2.5	N	N		Intangibles (net)		
5.0		5.1	5.9	O	O		All Other Non-Current		
100.0		100.0	100.0	T	T		Total		
							LIABILITIES		
32.5		11.6	8.0	A	A		Notes Payable-Short Term		
5.0		3.5	2.0	V	V		Cur. Mat.-L.T.D.		
10.5		24.2	18.9	A	A		Trade Payables		
.0		1.0	1.1	I	I		Income Taxes Payable		
9.4		11.2	13.8	L	L		All Other Current		
57.4		51.6	43.8	A	A		Total Current		
23.2		15.7	17.0	B	B		Long-Term Debt		
.3		.3	1.7	L	L		Deferred Taxes		
4.1		1.9	5.9	E	E		All Other Non-Current		
15.0		30.5	31.6				Net Worth		
100.0		100.0	100.0				Total Liabilities & Net Worth		
							INCOME DATA		
100.0		100.0	100.0				Net Sales		
56.2		32.1	25.3				Gross Profit		
50.9		28.4	21.1				Operating Expenses		
5.3		3.7	4.2				Operating Profit		
.8		.6	.2				All Other Expenses (net)		
4.4		3.1	4.0				Profit Before Taxes		
							RATIOS		
2.6		1.9	1.9						
1.3		1.5	1.5				Current		
.1		1.1	1.2						
2.4		1.7	1.5						
1.2		1.2	1.2				Quick		
.1		.9	.8						
0	UND	45	8.2	46	7.9			Sales/Receivables	
6	57.2	71	5.2	79	4.6				
29	12.8	91	4.0	101	3.6				
0	UND	0	UND	0	UND			Cost of Sales/Inventory	
0	UND	11	34.5	7	55.3				
10	34.9	28	13.0	20	18.6				
0	UND	19	19.4	21	17.6			Cost of Sales/Payables	
17	21.7	39	9.4	39	9.3				
48	7.5	71	5.1	59	6.2				
7.4		8.1	5.9					Sales/Working Capital	
59.4		11.7	9.6						
-7.8		74.2	23.6						
23.7		8.0	12.8					EBIT/Interest	
(10)	8.8	(15)	2.8	(23)	4.3				
-.6		1.2	2.2						
			12.7				Net Profit + Depr., Dep.,		
		(10)	3.3				Amort./Cur. Mat. L/T/D		
			1.7						
.7		.2	.2					Fixed/Worth	
15.7		.6	.5						
-20.0		1.5	1.4						
1.0		1.0	1.1					Debt/Worth	
16.7		3.0	1.7						
-36.4		6.7	5.3						
		66.7	37.9				% Profit Before Taxes/Tangible		
	(15)	11.2	(22)	13.9			Net Worth		
		2.4	9.1						
71.7		17.8	12.6				% Profit Before Taxes/Total		
15.3		3.8	4.5				Assets		
5.9		.3	2.6						
41.8		83.4	31.1					Sales/Net Fixed Assets	
18.2		16.6	16.4						
6.5		7.5	6.4						
9.8		4.0	2.8					Sales/Total Assets	
4.0		2.4	2.4						
2.7		2.0	1.4						
		.5	.6				% Depr., Dep., Amort./Sales		
	(12)	1.8	(24)	1.3					
		3.8	1.9						
			2.9				% Officers', Directors'		
	(13)	5.1					Owners' Comp/Sales		
		7.1							
15343M		59847M	274619M	180002M			Net Sales ($)	27519M	47578M
3178M		20878M	123559M	92341M			Total Assets ($)	9748M	21332M

M = $ thousand   MM = $ million
See Pages 11 through 21 for Explanation of Ratios and Data

Comparative Historical Data | Current Data Sorted by Sales

Type of Statement

	4/1/04-3/31/05 ALL	4/1/05-3/31/06 ALL	4/1/06-3/31/07 ALL	0-1MM	1-3MM	3-5MM	5-10MM	10-25MM	25MM & OVER
Unqualified	5	5	7		1		2	2	
Reviewed		14	24		4	6		7	1
Compiled		3	4		3		1		
Tax Returns	1	4	8	1	5	2			
Other	5	4	15	3	1	3			1
				12 (4/1-9/30/06)			46 (10/1/06-3/31/07)		
NUMBER OF STATEMENTS	**11**	**30**	**58**	**4**	**14**	**12**	**10**	**14**	**4**

ASSETS (%)

	4/1/04-3/31/05	4/1/05-3/31/06	4/1/06-3/31/07	0-1MM	1-3MM	3-5MM	5-10MM	10-25MM	25MM & OVER
Cash & Equivalents	5.7	9.3	10.1		13.7	11.5	8.5	6.9	
Trade Receivables (net)	36.4	47.5	42.1		43.0	37.1	52.3	47.3	
Inventory	4.7	9.8	9.7		5.7	7.9	1.1	19.0	
All Other Current	5.3	9.1	5.5		1.2	4.6	12.3	5.8	
Total Current	52.1	75.7	67.4		63.6	61.1	74.2	79.1	
Fixed Assets (net)	33.5	15.9	24.2		21.4	27.8	20.3	16.7	
Intangibles (net)	3.3	3.0	2.8		6.1	5.3	.6	.4	
All Other Non-Current	11.0	5.3	5.6		8.8	5.7	4.9	3.9	
Total	100.0	100.0	100.0		100.0	100.0	100.0	100.0	

LIABILITIES

	4/1/04-3/31/05	4/1/05-3/31/06	4/1/06-3/31/07	0-1MM	1-3MM	3-5MM	5-10MM	10-25MM	25MM & OVER
Notes Payable-Short Term	19.2	15.8	14.6		21.5	11.8	5.1	12.7	
Cur. Mat.-L.T.D.	6.9	13.0	3.6		4.0	3.4	1.6	1.7	
Trade Payables	23.3	22.2	18.3		13.9	24.3	21.6	20.4	
Income Taxes Payable	.0	.4	.9		.7	1.0	.2	1.4	
All Other Current	10.4	13.6	11.8		9.5	9.0	14.0	15.7	
Total Current	59.8	65.1	49.2		49.7	49.6	42.5	51.9	
Long-Term Debt	22.4	16.0	16.9		23.4	22.6	10.8	11.7	
Deferred Taxes	.2	.8	.9		.5	.8	3.3	.1	
All Other Non-Current	3.8	4.4	4.0		3.9	2.0	4.1	6.8	
Net Worth	13.8	13.7	29.0		22.6	25.0	39.3	29.4	
Total Liabilities & Net Worth	100.0	100.0	100.0		100.0	100.0	100.0	100.0	

INCOME DATA

	4/1/04-3/31/05	4/1/05-3/31/06	4/1/06-3/31/07	0-1MM	1-3MM	3-5MM	5-10MM	10-25MM	25MM & OVER
Net Sales	100.0	100.0	100.0		100.0	100.0	100.0	100.0	
Gross Profit	30.8	28.3	32.9		39.9	38.0	25.3	20.2	
Operating Expenses	33.3	24.1	28.4		33.7	35.3	21.0	15.9	
Operating Profit	-2.4	4.1	4.5		6.2	2.8	4.4	4.3	
All Other Expenses (net)	.2	.6	.6		1.1	.3	.0	.5	
Profit Before Taxes	-2.6	3.5	4.0		5.1	2.5	4.4	3.8	

RATIOS

	4/1/04-3/31/05	4/1/05-3/31/06	4/1/06-3/31/07	0-1MM	1-3MM	3-5MM	5-10MM	10-25MM	25MM & OVER
Current	1.6	2.3	2.0		2.2	1.7	2.0	2.2	
	.9	1.7	1.5		1.8	1.4	1.7	1.5	
	.6	1.4	1.1		1.1	1.1	1.4	1.1	
Quick	1.3	1.9	1.7		2.1	1.3	1.7	1.3	
	.7	1.4	1.2		1.7	1.1	1.4	.9	
	.4	.9	.7		.9	.8	1.2	.7	
Sales/Receivables	25 14.8	41 9.0	29 12.4		22 16.7	44 8.3	42 8.7	42 8.7	
	58 6.3	60 6.1	62 5.9		49 7.5	65 5.6	85 4.3	65 5.6	
	80 4.6	94 3.9	92 4.0		92 4.0	93 3.9	106 3.4	82 4.5	
Cost of Sales/Inventory	0 UND	1 583.4	0 UND		0 UND	0 UND	0 UND	0 UND	
	0 UND	7 55.1	7 52.1		8 46.6	11 32.1	0 UND	14 25.6	
	18 20.2	23 15.6	27 13.7		17 21.5	41 8.9	3 128.4	49 7.5	
Cost of Sales/Payables	23 16.1	16 23.2	16 22.8		9 40.4	40 9.1	16 23.5	23 16.2	
	40 9.1	35 10.5	32 11.5		19 18.8	60 6.1	35 10.4	30 12.3	
	59 6.2	49 7.4	56 6.6		59 6.1	70 5.2	67 5.4	40 9.2	
Sales/Working Capital	20.2	5.5	6.1		5.2	8.9	5.3	4.1	
	-70.2	10.6	10.5		9.4	11.7	8.7	10.5	
	-12.5	17.3	56.8		NM	58.5	14.6	77.5	
EBIT/Interest		22.5	12.9		13.2	5.5		11.3	
		(26) 9.4	(53) 3.8		(13) 7.0	(10) 2.1		(13) 3.1	
		2.8	2.0		1.5	.4		2.0	
Net Profit + Depr., Dep., Amort./Cur. Mat. L/T/D			7.7						
			(18) 4.1						
			1.6						
Fixed/Worth	.3	.1	.2		.0	.9	.1	.1	
	1.6	.3	.6		.7	1.5	.4	.4	
	-2.1	1.1	1.7		3.6	-2.7	.5	1.0	
Debt/Worth	1.3	.8	1.1		1.0	1.2	1.1	1.0	
	5.0	1.3	2.5		3.0	4.6	1.6	2.1	
	-4.5	4.9	7.8		42.1	-21.1	1.7	5.0	
% Profit Before Taxes/Tangible Net Worth		45.6	64.8		104.6		75.9	41.1	
		(26) 21.5	(50) 17.5		(12) 56.1		12.3	(13) 17.7	
		5.0	8.7		4.6		7.9	12.6	
% Profit Before Taxes/Total Assets	8.9	17.6	17.2		46.1	10.0	18.2	16.6	
	.8	8.2	6.0		15.7	2.9	5.0	5.1	
	-12.2	2.1	2.4		2.0	-1.0	3.0	2.7	
Sales/Net Fixed Assets	38.8	84.1	40.0		268.1	28.7	55.6	41.9	
	13.6	27.5	17.2		21.7	12.3	13.8	21.6	
	4.2	12.6	7.6		7.0	5.7	12.4	13.3	
Sales/Total Assets	4.7	3.9	3.4		5.3	3.5	3.2	2.9	
	2.3	3.0	2.5		2.9	2.2	2.5	2.6	
	1.5	2.0	1.8		2.0	1.3	1.9	1.6	
% Depr., Dep., Amort./Sales		.6	.6			.3		.5	
		(23) 1.0	(47) 1.3			(11) 1.8		1.3	
		2.1	1.9			3.6		1.7	
% Officers', Directors' Owners' Comp/Sales		2.4	2.9		2.9				
		(16) 3.8	(31) 5.1		(10) 5.1				
		7.9	7.9		7.8				
Net Sales ($)	48907M	1634802M	529811M	3056M	26906M	45736M	74323M	220337M	159453M
Total Assets ($)	22852M	340442M	239956M	942M	10001M	25441M	31501M	94289M	77782M

M = $ thousand   MM = $ million
See Pages 11 through 21 for Explanation of Ratios and Data

Current Data Sorted by Assets

Comparative Historical Data

						Type of Statement		
1	10	34	65	20	8	Unqualified	81	116
7	67	141	41		2	Reviewed	140	236
12	36	28				Compiled	53	106
53	49	17	3		2	Tax Returns	42	78
11	43	61	40	9	1	Other	69	74
	143 (4/1-9/30/06)		618 (10/1/06-3/31/07)				4/1/02-3/31/03 ALL	4/1/03-3/31/04 ALL
0-500M	500M-2MM	2-10MM	10-50MM	50-100MM	100-250MM			
84	205	281	149	29	13	NUMBER OF STATEMENTS	385	610
%	%	%	%	%	%	ASSETS	%	%
17.0	9.7	9.3	10.3	13.1	4.7	Cash & Equivalents	10.8	10.0
16.4	28.8	37.2	35.9	23.9	24.3	Trade Receivables (net)	31.2	31.5
3.0	3.0	2.4	4.7	8.7	8.8	Inventory	2.7	2.1
5.0	3.2	7.9	8.1	3.9	4.0	All Other Current	6.2	6.8
41.5	44.8	56.8	59.0	49.7	41.7	Total Current	50.9	50.3
47.6	47.8	37.8	35.6	43.4	51.6	Fixed Assets (net)	42.2	42.8
2.4	1.2	.6	.5	1.0	3.6	Intangibles (net)	1.2	1.0
8.4	6.3	4.8	4.9	5.9	3.0	All Other Non-Current	5.8	5.8
100.0	100.0	100.0	100.0	100.0	100.0	Total	100.0	100.0
						LIABILITIES		
19.0	8.5	5.5	6.1	7.4	10.9	Notes Payable-Short Term	7.1	7.3
12.0	7.7	6.6	6.3	7.7	17.8	Cur. Mat.-L.T.D.	7.6	8.5
6.9	14.2	17.4	16.2	10.5	8.2	Trade Payables	13.5	14.6
.1	.6	.7	.5	.3	.1	Income Taxes Payable	.9	.7
22.1	7.9	8.8	11.4	12.2	6.7	All Other Current	8.5	8.8
60.0	38.9	38.9	40.5	38.1	43.7	Total Current	37.6	39.9
44.4	26.2	18.5	18.8	27.3	31.2	Long-Term Debt	20.4	21.3
.1	.3	1.4	1.3	1.8	1.5	Deferred Taxes	1.5	1.2
5.6	3.1	1.2	1.9	2.4	5.5	All Other Non-Current	2.6	3.0
-10.0	31.5	39.9	37.5	30.3	18.2	Net Worth	37.9	34.5
100.0	100.0	100.0	100.0	100.0	100.0	Total Liabilities & Net Worth	100.0	100.0
						INCOME DATA		
100.0	100.0	100.0	100.0	100.0	100.0	Net Sales	100.0	100.0
46.7	36.9	24.9	20.1	25.1	32.7	Gross Profit	28.5	27.7
40.9	32.1	18.6	12.6	13.8	19.0	Operating Expenses	24.4	24.1
5.8	4.7	6.3	7.5	11.3	13.7	Operating Profit	4.1	3.6
1.6	1.1	.5	.4	1.7	3.8	All Other Expenses (net)	.7	.8
4.1	3.6	5.8	7.1	9.7	9.9	Profit Before Taxes	3.4	2.8
						RATIOS		
1.9	2.1	2.1	2.0	1.6	1.4		2.0	2.0
.9	1.2	1.4	1.4	1.3	1.1	Current	1.3	1.3
.3	.8	1.1	1.1	1.0	.6		1.0	.9
1.7	1.8	1.7	1.6	1.4	1.1		1.7	1.7
.8	1.0	1.2	1.2	1.0	.8	Quick	1.1 (609)	1.1
.3	.6	.8	.8	.9	.3		.8	.7
0 UND	19 19.4	45 8.0	50 7.4	41 8.8	36 10.2		35 10.5	32 11.3
0 UND	47 7.8	62 5.9	68 5.4	55 6.7	49 7.5	Sales/Receivables	55 6.7	57 6.4
33 11.1	67 5.5	85 4.3	88 4.1	75 4.8	77 4.7		78 4.7	79 4.6
0 UND	0 UND	0 UND	0 UND	0 UND	0 UND		0 UND	0 UND
0 UND	0 UND	0 UND	0 UND	0 UND	2 190.1	Cost of Sales/Inventory	0 UND	0 UND
0 UND	3 136.5	1 309.5	4 88.2	7 55.0	10 38.2		4 102.8	2 211.3
0 UND	4 81.2	18 20.8	23 15.6	22 16.7	0 UND		11 32.1	13 27.2
0 UND	21 17.0	33 11.2	33 11.0	27 13.7	19 18.8	Cost of Sales/Payables	27 13.7	29 12.8
24 15.5	56 6.5	56 6.6	48 7.5	40 9.1	42 8.6		46 7.9	48 7.7
22.6	10.4	6.7	6.1	5.2	9.6		8.1	7.6
-94.9	33.4	13.4	13.3	13.6	68.2	Sales/Working Capital	19.6	19.7
-18.6	-23.1	62.0	34.2	167.7	-8.6		NM	-77.7
8.6	10.1	17.0	25.0	27.9	6.4		9.1	9.4
(73) 2.4	(195) 3.7	(261) 5.7	(134) 6.3	4.1	(12) 3.4	EBIT/Interest	(351) 3.3	(570) 3.7
1.0	1.1	2.4	2.4	2.6	1.9		1.0	.8
	3.1	3.8	6.0			Net Profit + Depr., Dep.,	2.9	3.0
	(36) 1.7	(85) 2.0	(55) 2.4			Amort./Cur. Mat. L/T/D	(133) 1.8	(178) 1.7
	1.1	1.3	1.3				1.1	1.0
.7	.7	.5	.5	.6	1.5		.6	.6
6.7	1.5	1.0	1.0	1.6	2.2	Fixed/Worth	1.1	1.1
-2.7	5.1	1.7	1.7	2.8	9.0		2.0	2.3
2.3	.8	.8	1.0	1.4	2.6		.8	.8
9.8	2.3	1.5	1.9	2.8	3.6	Debt/Worth	1.6	1.7
-4.9	7.4	2.9	3.4	5.4	10.5		3.6	4.2
134.2	61.2	52.7	55.4	61.4	99.7	% Profit Before Taxes/Tangible	32.5	35.3
(52) 61.7	(171) 21.1	(271) 28.0	(146) 29.8	(28) 26.7	(11) 49.0	Net Worth	(354) 14.8	(549) 14.5
4.8	3.8	12.2	13.4	15.4	28.5		3.0	1.4
31.4	16.1	20.7	20.4	15.5	22.8	% Profit Before Taxes/Total	12.1	13.4
8.9	6.8	10.1	9.4	8.3	5.7	Assets	5.0	4.5
.0	.3	2.9	4.3	3.8	3.7		.0	-.3
19.8	10.2	11.5	9.9	6.2	8.9		9.2	9.9
9.9	4.5	5.7	5.7	4.3	4.1	Sales/Net Fixed Assets	4.9	4.9
4.0	2.8	3.3	3.6	2.0	3.2		2.9	2.9
7.1	3.0	2.7	2.4	2.1	2.8		2.5	2.7
3.3	2.2	2.0	1.9	1.5	1.9	Sales/Total Assets	2.0	2.1
2.3	1.5	1.6	1.4	.8	1.2		1.5	1.4
1.6	3.4	1.9	2.0	2.0		% Depr., Dep., Amort./Sales	3.2	3.1
(68) 4.6	(180) 6.4	(257) 4.0	(137) 3.5	(22) 3.6			(355) 5.7	(551) 5.6
8.2	9.5	6.5	5.8	6.2			9.3	9.2
4.2	2.3	1.3	.5			% Officers', Directors'	1.8	1.9
(50) 6.9	(119) 4.1	(118) 2.2	(47) 1.6			Owners' Comp/Sales	(175) 3.4	(282) 3.5
12.6	6.8	3.7	4.3				6.3	6.0
98094M	568423M	2966808M	6686948M	3378346M	4348335M	Net Sales ($)	5375492M	6647157M
21705M	237693M	1388321M	3373797M	2084359M	1970859M	Total Assets ($)	2699590M	3577696M

© RMA 2007

M = $ thousand   MM = $ million

See Pages 11 through 21 for Explanation of Ratios and Data

Comparative Historical Data | Current Data Sorted by Sales

Hist 4/1/04-3/31/05 ALL	Hist 4/1/05-3/31/06 ALL	Hist 4/1/06-3/31/07 ALL	Type of Statement	0-1MM	1-3MM	3-5MM	5-10MM	10-25MM	25MM & OVER
112	130	138	Unqualified	2	6	5	12	31	82
209	206	258	Reviewed	9	40	42	64	74	29
71	83	76	Compiled	16	29	13	11	7	
84	92	124	Tax Returns	36	48	16	15	5	4
101	165	165	Other	17	26	19	23	43	37
				(143) 4/1-9/30/06			(618) 10/1/06-3/31/07		
577	676	761	**NUMBER OF STATEMENTS**	80	149	95	125	160	152
%	%	%	**ASSETS**	%	%	%	%	%	%
11.6	11.1	10.5	Cash & Equivalents	11.5	11.8	9.2	10.3	9.9	10.5
32.2	32.8	31.7	Trade Receivables (net)	14.7	26.2	31.9	35.6	36.3	37.7
2.3	1.9	3.4	Inventory	3.2	3.9	4.0	2.3	3.2	3.8
6.3	6.1	6.2	All Other Current	4.5	3.4	4.5	6.8	8.7	7.5
52.4	52.0	51.8	Total Current	34.0	45.3	49.6	55.0	58.1	59.5
40.5	40.3	41.6	Fixed Assets (net)	55.0	45.9	43.5	39.1	37.8	35.1
.9	1.1	1.0	Intangibles (net)	2.5	1.7	.5	.6	.3	.9
6.2	6.6	5.6	All Other Non-Current	8.5	7.0	6.5	5.3	3.8	4.4
100.0	100.0	100.0	Total	100.0	100.0	100.0	100.0	100.0	100.0
			LIABILITIES						
8.2	7.0	8.1	Notes Payable-Short Term	11.0	12.0	10.3	5.8	4.4	7.2
6.8	6.5	7.6	Cur. Mat.-L.T.D.	8.5	9.8	7.6	6.3	6.8	7.1
14.2	14.9	14.7	Trade Payables	6.5	11.0	14.8	17.4	18.4	16.5
.8	.6	.5	Income Taxes Payable	.0	.8	.5	.7	.4	.5
9.3	10.6	10.6	All Other Current	19.2	8.6	6.5	10.8	9.1	12.1
39.3	39.6	41.6	Total Current	45.3	42.2	39.8	41.1	39.1	43.3
23.3	23.4	24.0	Long-Term Debt	43.6	29.0	22.5	20.5	19.1	17.9
1.0	1.0	1.0	Deferred Taxes	.2	.5	.6	1.8	1.0	1.3
4.0	3.6	2.5	All Other Non-Current	4.1	4.0	2.6	1.4	1.2	2.2
32.3	32.4	30.9	Net Worth	7.0	24.2	34.5	35.2	39.7	35.2
100.0	100.0	100.0	Total Liabilties & Net Worth	100.0	100.0	100.0	100.0	100.0	100.0
			INCOME DATA						
100.0	100.0	100.0	Net Sales	100.0	100.0	100.0	100.0	100.0	100.0
28.7	28.8	29.8	Gross Profit	50.8	38.8	32.1	24.5	22.5	20.3
23.5	23.3	23.4	Operating Expenses	43.2	33.4	27.4	19.2	15.6	12.2
5.2	5.5	6.4	Operating Profit	7.5	5.5	4.6	5.3	6.9	8.2
.8	.8	.9	All Other Expenses (net)	2.7	1.1	.4	.5	.4	.7
4.4	4.7	5.5	Profit Before Taxes	4.8	4.3	4.2	4.8	6.4	7.5
			RATIOS						
2.2	2.1	2.0	Current	2.3	2.3	2.0	2.2	2.1	1.8
1.4	1.4	1.3		1.0	1.2	1.3	1.3	1.5	1.3
1.0	1.0	1.0		.3	.8	.9	1.0	1.1	1.1
1.9	1.8	1.7	Quick	1.6	2.0	1.7	1.7	1.7	1.4
1.1	(675) 1.2	1.1		.6	1.0	1.1	1.2	1.2	1.1
.8	.8	.7		.2	.5	.7	.7	.9	.9
32 11.3	34 10.8	34 10.6	Sales/Receivables	0 UND	3 108.8	35 10.3	45 8.2	43 8.5	48 7.6
56 6.5	58 6.3	55 6.6		18 20.0	46 8.0	56 6.5	58 6.3	60 6.1	63 5.8
82 4.5	85 4.3	76 4.8		53 6.9	68 5.4	82 4.4	76 4.8	86 4.2	83 4.4
0 UND	0 UND	0 UND	Cost of Sales/Inventory	0 UND	0 UND	0 UND	0 UND	0 UND	0 UND
0 UND	0 UND	0 UND		0 UND	0 UND	0 UND	0 UND	0 UND	0 UND
1 249.9	1 298.3	2 156.2		0 UND	6 64.4	2 239.6	1 586.6	2 197.8	4 91.9
12 30.2	12 29.8	11 32.1	Cost of Sales/Payables	0 UND	0 UND	14 26.9	15 24.5	20 18.2	20 18.5
28 13.2	29 12.5	28 12.9		5 68.9	18 20.1	28 12.8	31 11.6	33 10.9	32 11.6
48 7.6	50 7.3	50 7.4		33 11.1	51 7.2	57 6.4	52 7.0	55 6.6	45 8.1
6.8	7.4	7.9	Sales/Working Capital	11.2	9.5	7.4	7.3	6.4	8.1
15.1	15.0	18.9		UND	26.8	21.2	19.0	12.0	15.1
549.7	-329.4	-193.3		-9.3	-24.7	-70.0	-316.5	56.6	43.5
11.9	12.7	13.5	EBIT/Interest	7.8	8.6	8.2	12.4	24.4	28.6
(533) 4.7	(621) 5.1	(704) 4.6		(72) 2.4	(136) 3.3	(89) 3.4	(117) 5.1	(150) 7.3	(140) 6.4
1.7	2.0	1.7		.7	.9	1.5	1.7	2.6	2.5
3.3	3.8	3.9	Net Profit + Depr., Dep., Amort./Cur. Mat. L/T/D		3.1	3.0	4.0	5.1	4.4
(152) 2.0	(197) 2.0	(189) 2.0		(21) 1.6	(15) 1.9	(46) 2.0	(44) 2.1	(55) 2.4	
1.2	1.2	1.2		.9	1.4	1.4	1.2	1.4	
.6	.6	.6	Fixed/Worth	1.0	.7	.6	.6	.5	.5
1.1	1.0	1.2		3.0	1.5	1.2	1.0	1.0	1.0
2.1	2.2	2.5		-292.0	41.9	3.2	2.3	1.6	1.8
.8	.9	.9	Debt/Worth	.9	.9	.8	.9	.9	1.1
1.8	1.8	2.0		4.0	2.7	1.7	1.9	1.6	1.9
4.1	4.1	4.7		-188.8	63.7	7.1	4.1	2.9	3.6
41.7	46.9	59.8	% Profit Before Taxes/Tangible Net Worth	74.6	63.2	57.1	53.3	51.9	65.1
(519) 20.6	(609) 21.4	(679) 29.0		(58) 28.0	(117) 18.1	(83) 23.0	(116) 25.0	(157) 31.7	(148) 37.7
4.9	7.0	10.1		-.3	2.5	5.9	11.8	15.3	18.3
15.8	17.0	20.7	% Profit Before Taxes/Total Assets	18.0	22.2	16.5	18.1	21.4	24.3
6.3	7.6	9.2		4.2	7.4	8.3	9.3	11.1	9.5
1.1	2.0	2.2		-1.5	.1	1.4	2.4	4.5	4.6
10.2	11.2	11.2	Sales/Net Fixed Assets	9.5	11.7	10.5	13.9	11.2	11.4
5.5	5.5	5.6		3.6	4.5	4.6	6.2	6.0	6.3
3.3	3.2	3.3		1.5	2.9	3.2	3.5	3.7	4.1
2.6	2.7	2.8	Sales/Total Assets	3.2	3.2	2.7	2.8	2.7	2.7
2.1	2.1	2.1		1.7	2.2	2.1	2.2	2.1	2.1
1.5	1.5	1.5		.9	1.5	1.5	1.6	1.6	1.6
3.2	2.8	2.1	% Depr., Dep., Amort./Sales	4.1	3.1	3.0	1.7	1.3	1.8
(514) 5.1	(596) 4.8	(668) 4.3		(68) 7.9	(125) 6.2	(86) 5.5	(115) 4.3	(149) 3.5	(125) 3.2
8.1	7.4	7.4		13.4	9.5	7.8	6.4	5.6	5.1
1.7	1.6	1.6	% Officers', Directors', Owners' Comp/Sales	5.2	2.9	2.0	1.6	.8	.5
(259) 3.3	(292) 3.3	(341) 3.5		(40) 7.8	(83) 4.9	(49) 3.6	(62) 2.7	(69) 1.7	(38) 1.0
6.1	6.1	6.1		13.3	7.3	5.5	4.3	3.7	2.9
8954613M	15637433M	18046954M	Net Sales ($)	47723M	298669M	376992M	918315M	2533438M	13871817M
4346733M	6887334M	9076734M	Total Assets ($)	37165M	169301M	218506M	497470M	1460179M	6694113M

M = $ thousand   MM = $ million
See Pages 11 through 21 for Explanation of Ratios and Data

Current Data Sorted by Assets   **Comparative Historical Data**

						Type of Statement		
1	17	45	42	10	7	Unqualified	82	85
9	87	154	25	1		Reviewed	158	223
33	73	40	2		1	Compiled	78	127
121	93	35	1		4	Tax Returns	65	124
64	96	93	28	9	4	Other	111	175
	176 (4/1-9/30/06)			919 (10/1/06-3/31/07)			4/1/02-3/31/03 ALL	4/1/03-3/31/04 ALL
0-500M	500M-2MM	2-10MM	10-50MM	50-100MM	100-250MM	**NUMBER OF STATEMENTS**	494	734
228	366	367	98	20	16			
%	%	%	%	%	%	**ASSETS**	%	%
18.3	12.0	11.8	10.6	11.5	17.7	Cash & Equivalents	11.9	11.1
21.4	37.8	41.8	39.9	45.0	36.3	Trade Receivables (net)	41.2	38.8
8.7	10.3	7.4	6.9	4.1	1.5	Inventory	8.4	9.0
4.1	5.5	7.2	6.6	6.5	6.9	All Other Current	7.4	6.5
52.5	65.7	68.3	64.1	67.1	62.3	Total Current	68.8	65.4
35.0	25.5	24.5	27.0	18.3	24.2	Fixed Assets (net)	22.7	25.1
2.5	1.8	1.6	5.2	8.9	10.4	Intangibles (net)	2.5	3.0
10.0	7.0	5.6	3.7	5.8	3.1	All Other Non-Current	5.9	6.5
100.0	100.0	100.0	100.0	100.0	100.0	Total	100.0	100.0
						LIABILITIES		
22.7	10.2	8.1	8.6	8.3	2.0	Notes Payable-Short Term	10.3	12.3
4.9	4.1	4.1	4.6	4.5	4.7	Cur. Mat.-L.T.D.	4.6	4.3
12.2	17.9	17.1	16.1	22.2	18.9	Trade Payables	18.1	17.8
.1	.6	1.1	.5	.5	.3	Income Taxes Payable	.7	.7
15.4	12.0	12.4	14.9	21.4	14.8	All Other Current	13.8	12.9
55.3	44.7	42.7	44.8	57.0	40.7	Total Current	47.6	47.9
26.0	18.1	12.5	13.4	8.3	29.5	Long-Term Debt	14.3	15.6
.0	.4	.7	1.1	1.5	.8	Deferred Taxes	.6	.6
5.9	3.4	3.5	3.8	3.1	5.7	All Other Non-Current	2.3	4.2
12.8	33.4	40.6	36.9	30.1	23.3	Net Worth	35.2	31.7
100.0	100.0	100.0	100.0	100.0	100.0	Total Liabilities & Net Worth	100.0	100.0
						INCOME DATA		
100.0	100.0	100.0	100.0	100.0	100.0	Net Sales	100.0	100.0
44.2	33.1	29.5	22.8	19.6	28.2	Gross Profit	30.5	31.3
39.8	29.1	23.2	16.8	12.8	22.0	Operating Expenses	26.9	27.7
4.4	4.0	6.3	6.1	6.9	6.2	Operating Profit	3.6	3.6
.5	.8	.7	.9	2.3	1.1	All Other Expenses (net)	.6	.8
3.9	3.2	5.6	5.1	4.5	5.1	Profit Before Taxes	2.9	2.8
						RATIOS		
3.1	2.5	2.3	1.8	1.8	2.1		2.2	2.3
1.3	1.5	1.5	1.4	1.3	1.5	Current	1.5	1.5
.6	1.0	1.2	1.2	1.0	1.2		1.1	1.0
2.4	1.9	1.9	1.6	1.4	1.8		1.8	1.8
1.0	1.1	1.2	1.1	1.0	1.4	Quick	1.2 (733)	1.1
.3	.7	.9	.8	.7	1.0		.8	.7
0 UND	20 18.0	36 10.2	43 8.6	53 6.9	24 15.2		31 11.7	28 12.8
6 57.1	43 8.6	58 6.3	62 5.9	72 5.1	53 6.8	Sales/Receivables	54 6.8	51 7.2
32 11.5	65 5.6	81 4.5	84 4.3	97 3.8	92 4.0		79 4.6	75 4.9
0 UND	0 UND	0 UND	0 UND	0 UND	0 UND		0 UND	0 UND
0 UND	2 182.1	1 266.1	1 364.6	3 142.5	1 448.8	Cost of Sales/Inventory	3 108.5	3 125.0
12 29.9	23 16.2	18 20.6	14 26.6	8 46.7	4 99.6		25 14.8	23 15.9
0 UND	10 36.5	14 26.4	19 18.8	16 22.5	18 19.8		12 29.9	12 31.6
4 95.2	24 15.3	28 12.9	28 12.9	33 11.2	32 11.4	Cost of Sales/Payables	27 13.6	27 13.6
26 13.8	45 8.0	46 8.0	48 7.6	60 6.0	54 6.8		48 7.6	48 7.6
13.6	8.0	6.2	6.9	7.5	7.1		6.7	6.8
58.4	15.1	11.1	13.5	17.9	11.7	Sales/Working Capital	13.1	14.1
-20.2	133.7	28.6	32.5	171.6	25.5		51.3	209.8
15.2	12.9	25.7	31.8	21.8	65.4		13.7	14.0
(189) 4.7	(334) 4.6	(330) 7.1	(90) 7.2	(17) 7.0	13.4	EBIT/Interest	(433) 4.8	(644) 4.2
1.0	1.5	2.2	2.1	2.8	1.9		1.1	1.2
	5.0	10.5	6.2			Net Profit + Depr., Dep.,	5.4	5.9
	(55) 1.9	(100) 2.8	(31) 3.4			Amort./Cur. Mat. L/T/D	(125) 2.7	(169) 2.7
	.6	1.3	1.8				1.3	1.2
.4	.2	.2	.3	.2	.3		.2	.2
1.5	.6	.5	.7	.5	.6	Fixed/Worth	.5	.6
-5.7	2.0	1.2	1.7	2.8	NM		1.5	2.0
.8	.8	.8	.9	1.6	2.3		.8	.9
3.3	1.9	1.5	1.9	3.5	3.7	Debt/Worth	1.7	2.0
-9.7	6.7	3.2	3.5	18.2	NM		4.1	7.0
160.2	71.8	58.9	52.8	88.1	61.1	% Profit Before Taxes/Tangible	46.3	47.3
(157) 65.9	(319) 26.4	(347) 31.0	(89) 28.8	(18) 39.0	(12) 48.0	Net Worth	(437) 19.8	(628) 18.4
20.8	6.2	10.6	11.9	25.6	41.1		2.8	3.6
46.8	21.3	24.0	17.4	14.2	21.5	% Profit Before Taxes/Total	16.6	17.0
13.6	8.0	11.1	9.1	10.2	10.6	Assets	6.5	5.8
.0	1.2	2.9	2.5	2.0	5.5		.4	.5
53.2	42.1	36.0	34.5	97.5	40.2		35.8	36.8
20.0	18.2	15.6	11.9	17.6	20.8	Sales/Net Fixed Assets	18.7	16.1
8.8	8.6	6.1	4.8	6.5	6.2		8.6	7.7
8.2	4.4	3.3	2.9	3.1	3.3		3.9	4.0
5.0	3.1	2.6	2.2	2.2	2.2	Sales/Total Assets	2.9	2.8
3.0	2.3	1.9	1.7	1.5	1.7		2.1	2.0
.8	.7	.7	.6	.4	.4		.9	.9
(152) 1.7	(302) 1.7	(330) 1.7	(87) 1.8	(17) 1.0	(11) 1.1	% Depr., Dep., Amort./Sales	(444) 1.7	(630) 1.7
4.8	3.3	3.9	3.9	3.7	2.5		3.2	3.7
4.2	2.5	1.5	1.1			% Officers', Directors'	2.6	2.3
(134) 6.1	(208) 4.3	(174) 3.1	(25) 2.3			Owners' Comp/Sales	(253) 4.8	(357) 4.3
9.3	6.9	6.8	4.9				8.6	7.5
347812M	1544382M	4419594M	5268553M	4111958M	8640087M	Net Sales ($)	7677416M	9651731M
60275M	436272M	1641621M	1868203M	1436354M	2555804M	Total Assets ($)	2740534M	4209845M

© RMA 2007

M = $ thousand   **MM = $ million**
See Pages 11 through 21 for Explanation of Ratios and Data

Comparative Historical Data | Current Data Sorted by Sales

Comparative Historical Data			Type of Statement	Current Data Sorted by Sales					
105	100	122	Unqualified	1	7	3	20	38	53
232	236	276	Reviewed	5	32	49	84	77	29
131	135	149	Compiled	15	45	29	39	18	3
141	207	254	Tax Returns	62	92	39	38	16	7
195	306	294	Other	24	68	56	58	50	38
4/1/04-3/31/05	4/1/05-3/31/06	4/1/06-3/31/07			176 (4/1-9/30/06)		919 (10/1/06-3/31/07)		
ALL	ALL	ALL		0-1MM	1-3MM	3-5MM	5-10MM	10-25MM	25MM & OVER
804	984	1095	NUMBER OF STATEMENTS	107	244	176	239	199	130
%	%	%	ASSETS	%	%	%	%	%	%
11.5	12.5	13.2	Cash & Equivalents	16.2	14.4	12.7	13.5	10.9	12.2
39.4	38.6	36.0	Trade Receivables (net)	16.2	30.1	37.9	39.8	42.8	43.6
9.4	8.0	8.5	Inventory	10.8	11.3	6.9	7.4	7.3	7.0
6.2	5.6	5.9	All Other Current	3.9	5.0	4.3	7.1	7.3	7.1
66.5	64.7	63.6	Total Current	47.1	60.8	61.8	67.9	68.3	69.9
25.1	25.9	27.1	Fixed Assets (net)	39.5	30.1	27.4	24.2	23.6	21.7
2.1	3.0	2.5	Intangibles (net)	3.9	1.7	2.1	1.6	2.7	4.5
6.3	6.4	6.8	All Other Non-Current	9.4	7.4	8.7	6.3	5.4	3.9
100.0	100.0	100.0	Total	100.0	100.0	100.0	100.0	100.0	100.0
			LIABILITIES						
12.5	11.3	11.8	Notes Payable-Short Term	22.3	14.1	13.4	8.1	8.8	7.8
4.7	4.5	4.3	Cur. Mat.-L.T.D.	4.0	4.9	4.1	4.0	4.6	3.9
17.8	17.6	16.4	Trade Payables	8.3	15.7	16.7	16.2	18.4	20.9
.7	.5	.6	Income Taxes Payable	.0	.4	.9	1.1	.6	.4
13.9	12.8	13.3	All Other Current	20.7	8.7	13.9	11.8	12.8	18.3
49.6	46.8	46.4	Total Current	55.3	43.9	49.1	41.3	45.3	51.4
17.5	17.1	17.4	Long-Term Debt	29.0	23.6	17.7	13.1	11.4	13.2
.6	.4	.5	Deferred Taxes	.0	.2	.5	.5	1.0	.7
3.9	4.2	4.0	All Other Non-Current	5.6	5.1	2.4	2.8	4.8	4.0
28.4	31.6	31.6	Net Worth	10.1	27.2	30.3	42.2	37.6	30.7
100.0	100.0	100.0	Total Liabilities & Net Worth	100.0	100.0	100.0	100.0	100.0	100.0
			INCOME DATA						
100.0	100.0	100.0	Net Sales	100.0	100.0	100.0	100.0	100.0	100.0
30.7	32.9	33.0	Gross Profit	48.4	40.4	32.9	30.3	26.5	21.3
26.7	27.3	27.8	Operating Expenses	44.1	36.0	27.8	25.1	20.4	15.7
4.1	5.6	5.1	Operating Profit	4.3	4.5	5.1	5.2	6.1	5.6
.6	.6	.8	All Other Expenses (net)	1.3	.7	.8	.5	.8	.9
3.5	5.0	4.4	Profit Before Taxes	3.1	3.8	4.3	4.7	5.3	4.8
			RATIOS						
2.4	2.3	2.4	Current	2.5	3.1	2.4	2.7	2.1	1.8
1.5	1.5	1.5		1.1	1.6	1.4	1.6	1.5	1.4
1.1	1.1	1.1		.5	1.0	1.0	1.2	1.2	1.2
1.8	1.9	1.9	Quick	1.9	2.2	1.9	2.3	1.6	1.6
(802) 1.1	(983) 1.2	1.2		.6	1.1	1.2	1.3	1.2	1.1
.8	.7	.7		.2	.6	.7	.8	.9	.8
26 13.9	24 15.3	19 19.5	Sales/Receivables	0 UND	6 58.5	27 13.8	26 13.8	34 10.7	35 10.5
50 7.3	51 7.1	44 8.2		9 40.3	29 12.5	46 7.9	48 7.5	54 6.7	58 6.3
78 4.7	79 4.6	71 5.2		38 9.7	55 6.6	76 4.8	76 4.8	72 5.1	82 4.4
0 UND	0 UND	0 UND	Cost of Sales/Inventory	0 UND	0 UND	0 UND	0 UND	0 UND	0 UND
3 139.6	1 562.9	1 632.0		0 UND	0 UND	0 878.1	0 995.2	2 179.8	1 284.8
21 17.1	19 19.6	18 20.7		20 18.4	24 15.0	17 21.3	19 19.5	15 24.3	13 28.3
11 33.5	11 33.9	7 49.9	Cost of Sales/Payables	0 UND	2 239.4	8 45.7	10 36.1	14 26.4	18 19.7
25 14.6	26 14.1	23 15.6		2 169.0	20 18.3	24 15.3	24 15.0	27 13.3	27 13.5
46 8.0	49 7.5	44 8.3		32 11.6	47 7.8	46 8.0	44 8.3	43 8.5	47 7.8
6.7	6.9	7.5	Sales/Working Capital	9.9	7.1	8.6	6.1	7.6	8.9
13.9	13.4	15.2		86.4	18.2	17.1	11.2	12.5	15.3
102.0	63.2	118.3		-11.5	999.8	999.8	45.6	30.0	34.4
15.1	18.0	19.3	EBIT/Interest	9.1	12.5	13.3	21.7	29.7	36.7
(708) 5.5	(868) 6.0	(976) 5.7		(81) 2.3	(221) 4.2	(159) 4.7	(214) 6.4	(185) 8.6	(116) 12.3
1.6	1.8	1.7		-.8	1.5	1.5	1.7	2.6	2.2
7.3	6.9	6.4	Net Profit + Depr., Dep., Amort./Cur. Mat. L/T/D		4.7	5.1	5.7	10.1	9.6
(199) 2.7	(194) 3.0	(205) 2.7		(26) 1.6	(21) 2.6	(55) 2.5	(64) 2.6	(37) 5.2
1.2	1.2	1.2			.4	1.5	.7	1.4	1.9
.2	.2	.2	Fixed/Worth	.5	.3	.3	.2	.2	.2
.6	.6	.7		2.0	.8	.7	.5	.5	.6
2.1	2.0	2.1		-4.8	5.5	2.0	1.3	1.3	1.7
.9	.9	.8	Debt/Worth	1.0	.7	.9	.7	.9	1.2
2.1	1.9	1.8		4.3	1.8	2.2	1.4	1.6	2.6
6.0	5.7	6.1		-9.4	22.7	6.8	3.2	3.1	5.4
55.2	71.7	71.9	% Profit Before Taxes/Tangible Net Worth	120.3	94.0	80.0	54.8	59.8	72.3
(690) 25.7	(849) 32.8	(942) 32.5		(70) 41.4	(198) 35.7	(150) 25.3	(222) 28.0	(187) 33.9	(115) 40.5
6.1	9.6	10.0		3.0	9.0	6.4	6.8	13.9	22.5
18.8	23.0	24.0	% Profit Before Taxes/Total Assets	22.1	28.4	23.7	23.9	22.8	23.3
7.7	10.3	10.4		4.8	11.2	8.0	11.1	11.6	11.0
1.2	1.9	1.9		-9.5	2.1	.9	2.1	3.4	4.0
40.6	41.5	42.4	Sales/Net Fixed Assets	42.4	42.1	33.7	43.1	41.0	58.3
17.1	16.4	16.8		9.2	16.3	14.7	18.1	20.0	20.3
7.3	7.1	7.1		3.1	7.8	7.3	8.1	6.8	8.1
4.0	4.1	4.3	Sales/Total Assets	5.0	5.0	4.4	3.9	3.8	3.8
2.9	2.9	3.0		2.5	3.2	3.0	3.0	3.0	2.7
2.0	1.9	2.1		1.4	2.3	2.3	2.2	2.1	2.1
.8	.7	.7	% Depr., Dep., Amort./Sales	1.2	.8	.7	.7	.7	.4
(665) 1.7	(800) 1.6	(899) 1.7		(77) 2.6	(179) 1.9	(145) 1.7	(207) 1.6	(179) 1.4	(112) 1.0
3.7	3.5	3.6		8.5	3.9	3.8	3.3	3.3	2.6
2.3	2.0	2.2	% Officers', Directors' Owners' Comp/Sales	4.8	3.6	2.2	2.2	1.0	1.2
(383) 4.4	(465) 4.0	(548) 4.4		(49) 7.2	(154) 5.3	(101) 4.3	(130) 3.7	(79) 1.9	(35) 2.3
7.6	7.1	7.0		12.0	7.7	6.7	5.9	4.6	5.2
12376837M	18112652M	24332386M	Net Sales ($)	60554M	465904M	690082M	1690075M	3145115M	18280656M
4357122M	6010292M	7998529M	Total Assets ($)	35762M	164711M	283326M	665094M	1297231M	5552405M

© RMA 2007

M = $ thousand   MM = $ million
See Pages 11 through 21 for Explanation of Ratios and Data

MANUFACTURING

Current Data Sorted by Assets   Comparative Historical Data

	0-500M	500M-2MM	2-10MM	10-50MM	50-100MM	100-250MM	Type of Statement	4/1/02-3/31/03 ALL	4/1/03-3/31/04 ALL
		3	19	22	3	5	Unqualified	39	34
	1	1	10	3		1	Reviewed	14	12
	1	6	8	1			Compiled	9	31
	3	4	3				Tax Returns	1	5
	1	4	9	15	3	7	Other	27	31
		48 (4/1-9/30/06)		85 (10/1/06-3/31/07)					
NUMBER OF STATEMENTS	6	18	49	41	6	13		90	113
	%	%	%	%	%	%	ASSETS	%	%
Cash & Equivalents		5.1	4.6	10.1		5.7		9.7	6.9
Trade Receivables (net)		39.3	26.0	21.5		19.2		22.7	23.1
Inventory		24.0	27.0	19.1		21.2		20.2	20.3
All Other Current		2.9	3.2	3.0		3.5		4.1	4.4
Total Current		71.3	60.8	53.7		49.6		56.6	54.8
Fixed Assets (net)		18.6	30.7	35.7		35.1		35.5	34.5
Intangibles (net)		2.3	.9	2.2		9.7		1.3	2.5
All Other Non-Current		7.8	7.6	8.4		5.5		6.6	8.1
Total		100.0	100.0	100.0		100.0		100.0	100.0
							LIABILITIES		
Notes Payable-Short Term		11.5	14.8	8.9		11.6		11.0	7.9
Cur. Mat.-L.T.D.		2.6	3.4	3.4		2.4		2.6	4.5
Trade Payables		22.5	15.8	15.2		13.3		13.1	15.0
Income Taxes Payable		.1	.1	.3		.6		.4	.3
All Other Current		7.2	9.1	9.5		7.8		9.4	6.4
Total Current		43.9	43.2	37.3		35.6		36.6	34.1
Long-Term Debt		12.0	16.9	12.0		12.2		15.3	18.7
Deferred Taxes		.1	.2	.4		3.6		.6	.6
All Other Non-Current		2.0	4.8	1.7		3.2		3.1	5.2
Net Worth		42.0	34.9	48.6		45.4		44.5	41.4
Total Liabilities & Net Worth		100.0	100.0	100.0		100.0		100.0	100.0
							INCOME DATA		
Net Sales		100.0	100.0	100.0		100.0		100.0	100.0
Gross Profit		27.3	20.5	24.8		22.3		26.2	22.0
Operating Expenses		25.0	17.1	16.9		15.1		20.8	18.4
Operating Profit		2.3	3.4	7.8		7.2		5.4	3.6
All Other Expenses (net)		-1.6	.8	3.0		.4		.4	-.2
Profit Before Taxes		3.9	2.6	4.9		6.8		5.0	3.9
							RATIOS		
Current		2.8	2.0	2.2		2.2		2.4	2.5
		1.7	1.4	1.4		1.4		1.6	1.5
		1.0	1.1	1.0		1.0		1.2	1.1
Quick		2.0	1.1	1.3		1.1		1.4	1.4
		1.1	.6	.8		.6		.8 (112)	.8
		.6	.5	.5		.6		.6	.6
Sales/Receivables	25 14.8		16 23.3	20 18.6		18 20.8		20 18.0	20 18.7
	28 12.8		30 12.3	26 13.8		20 17.9		29 12.7	28 12.8
	50 7.3		40 9.1	38 9.7		40 9.2		40 9.0	39 9.3
Cost of Sales/Inventory	10 36.2		19 18.9	15 23.7		16 23.4		22 16.7	15 23.6
	26 14.1		38 9.7	34 10.7		37 9.9		36 10.3	29 12.6
	49 7.5		61 6.0	54 6.7		100 3.6		67 5.4	53 6.9
Cost of Sales/Payables	11 33.2		11 32.2	15 24.0		13 27.8		14 25.6	15 24.9
	22 16.3		21 17.4	25 14.7		28 12.9		25 14.3	21 17.6
	35 10.5		31 11.9	36 10.1		38 9.5		34 10.8	36 10.1
Sales/Working Capital		8.7	10.3	7.0		11.1		7.0	7.7
		13.1	18.5	17.0		16.4		12.9	16.0
		391.1	50.7	152.3		176.5		42.3	60.0
EBIT/Interest		19.5	8.7	21.4		11.9		15.8	14.3
	(15) 4.4		(47) 4.2	(38) 5.8		(12) 8.5		(82) 4.2	(103) 3.8
		2.5	1.8	2.3		4.3		1.7	1.3
Net Profit + Depr., Dep., Amort./Cur. Mat. L/T/D			8.1	98.3				8.7	14.6
		(14) 2.4		(12) 5.4				(17) 2.5	(25) 3.5
			1.2	3.2				1.9	.9
Fixed/Worth		.2	.5	.4		.8		.4	.4
		.3	.7	.7		1.0		.7	.8
		.9	1.9	1.3		1.6		1.9	1.7
Debt/Worth		.5	1.0	.5		1.1		.6	.6
		1.1	1.9	1.2		1.3		1.2	1.6
		4.8	4.5	2.3		6.5		3.1	3.1
% Profit Before Taxes/Tangible Net Worth		49.0	36.9	32.7		51.4		41.9	30.8
	(16) 28.5		(44) 16.7	(39) 20.3		32.8		(87) 19.5	(106) 20.5
		7.8	7.7	12.3		20.0		3.6	2.4
% Profit Before Taxes/Total Assets		12.4	14.5	16.3		15.0		18.2	15.5
		6.5	6.9	10.0		9.0		7.6	7.1
		3.6	2.9	3.1		4.2		1.4	.8
Sales/Net Fixed Assets		57.5	23.4	12.3		8.6		15.9	14.7
		28.8	11.9	6.6		5.3		8.0	8.3
		11.6	6.6	4.2		3.9		4.6	4.8
Sales/Total Assets		5.3	4.3	3.0		2.5		3.5	3.6
		4.1	3.4	2.2		2.1		2.5	2.6
		3.2	2.4	1.7		1.4		2.0	1.8
% Depr., Dep., Amort./Sales		.7	1.0	1.0				.9	1.0
	(15) 1.6		(45) 1.6	(40) 1.7				(84) 2.0	(103) 1.8
		1.8	2.6	2.9				3.1	3.1
% Officers', Directors' Owners' Comp/Sales			1.4					.7	1.3
		(15) 2.3						(26) 1.9	(28) 1.8
			3.3					3.4	3.7
Net Sales ($)	5171M	91204M	810041M	2163904M	969446M	6236726M		4367055M	4712778M
Total Assets ($)	2280M	21767M	243292M	908369M	422683M	2172603M		1908618M	2215346M

M = $ thousand   MM = $ million
See Pages 11 through 21 for Explanation of Ratios and Data

Comparative Historical Data — Current Data Sorted by Sales

4/1/04-3/31/05 ALL	4/1/05-3/31/06 ALL	4/1/06-3/31/07 ALL	Type of Statement	0-1MM	1-3MM	3-5MM	5-10MM	10-25MM	25MM & OVER
38	30	52	Unqualified	1			6	13	33
7	9	16	Reviewed		3	1	3	7	4
20	18	16	Compiled				7	3	1
6	7	10	Tax Returns	2		2	2	2	
23	36	39	Other		3		3	6	26
				48 (4/1-9/30/06)			85 (10/1/06-3/31/07)		
94	100	133	**NUMBER OF STATEMENTS**	3	6	8	21	31	64
%	%	%	**ASSETS**	%	%	%	%	%	%
9.4	9.5	6.6	Cash & Equivalents				5.6	4.9	8.4
20.2	23.0	25.3	Trade Receivables (net)				37.2	24.2	22.1
21.8	20.0	23.4	Inventory				24.8	23.4	21.2
3.7	3.5	2.9	All Other Current				4.9	2.6	2.8
55.1	56.1	58.2	Total Current				72.5	55.2	54.4
34.7	36.0	31.8	Fixed Assets (net)				23.7	34.9	33.6
4.2	2.2	2.5	Intangibles (net)				.3	1.0	3.9
6.0	5.6	7.5	All Other Non-Current				3.6	8.9	8.1
100.0	100.0	100.0	Total				100.0	100.0	100.0
			LIABILITIES						
8.3	9.8	13.0	Notes Payable-Short Term				13.3	12.7	10.2
3.5	4.0	3.1	Cur. Mat.-L.T.D.				3.6	3.7	2.9
15.7	16.4	15.9	Trade Payables				21.4	14.2	15.3
.2	.2	.2	Income Taxes Payable				.1	.1	.3
7.3	9.0	8.3	All Other Current				4.9	11.4	8.8
35.1	39.5	40.6	Total Current				43.4	42.2	37.6
20.3	19.5	15.5	Long-Term Debt				23.5	13.1	13.5
.7	.6	.6	Deferred Taxes				.1	.3	1.1
2.5	2.5	3.8	All Other Non-Current				1.0	4.0	2.4
41.3	37.9	39.5	Net Worth				32.1	40.4	45.4
100.0	100.0	100.0	Total Liabilties & Net Worth				100.0	100.0	100.0
			INCOME DATA						
100.0	100.0	100.0	Net Sales				100.0	100.0	100.0
25.4	23.2	23.8	Gross Profit				22.0	18.1	22.8
20.7	18.9	19.3	Operating Expenses				19.9	15.1	16.0
4.7	4.3	4.5	Operating Profit				2.2	3.0	6.9
1.8	1.2	1.1	All Other Expenses (net)				.0	.6	2.1
2.9	3.1	3.4	Profit Before Taxes				2.2	2.5	4.7
			RATIOS						
2.3 / 1.6 / 1.1	2.2 / 1.6 / 1.1	2.2 / 1.4 / 1.1	Current				2.5 / 2.0 / 1.2	1.9 / 1.4 / 1.1	2.0 / 1.4 / 1.1
1.2 / .8 / .5	1.4 / .8 / .5	1.3 / .7 / .5	Quick				1.8 / 1.0 / .6	1.1 / .6 / .5	1.3 / .7 / .5
17 21.2 / 25 14.5 / 35 10.3	17 21.2 / 26 14.0 / 38 9.7	19 19.7 / 29 12.6 / 41 8.8	Sales/Receivables				23 15.6 / 39 9.3 / 51 7.1	15 24.1 / 23 16.2 / 34 10.6	19 19.4 / 26 14.0 / 39 9.3
20 18.6 / 35 10.5 / 66 5.5	17 21.2 / 27 13.6 / 45 8.1	18 20.3 / 35 10.6 / 62 5.9	Cost of Sales/Inventory				14 25.8 / 28 13.3 / 66 5.5	13 27.6 / 30 12.3 / 46 7.9	17 21.3 / 36 10.0 / 54 6.7
16 22.3 / 24 15.5 / 36 10.2	14 25.2 / 22 16.9 / 32 11.4	13 27.8 / 23 15.8 / 36 10.3	Cost of Sales/Payables				16 23.5 / 22 16.8 / 41 9.0	8 45.8 / 20 18.1 / 28 13.0	15 25.0 / 24 15.2 / 36 10.2
7.7 / 14.3 / 45.6	8.5 / 17.2 / 65.1	9.5 / 17.0 / 109.2	Sales/Working Capital				6.2 / 11.6 / 23.4	14.0 / 23.1 / 122.9	10.2 / 16.5 / 63.8
12.2 / (81) 4.4 / 1.6	14.5 / (90) 5.2 / 1.9	10.8 / (123) 4.4 / 1.8	EBIT/Interest				7.7 / (20) 3.1 / 1.9	8.9 / (29) 4.4 / 1.8	12.7 / (60) 5.4 / 2.2
3.6 / (20) 2.5 / 1.3	7.8 / (23) 3.2 / 1.1	12.3 / (34) 3.5 / 1.5	Net Profit + Depr., Dep., Amort./Cur. Mat. L/T/D						97.5 / (21) 4.4 / 2.8
.5 / .9 / 2.2	.4 / .8 / 1.5	.5 / .8 / 1.8	Fixed/Worth				.2 / .7 / 1.8	.6 / .7 / 1.7	.5 / .8 / 1.3
.8 / 1.6 / 3.3	.6 / 1.5 / 3.0	.6 / 1.4 / 3.7	Debt/Worth				.9 / 1.9 / 8.8	.6 / 1.3 / 2.6	.6 / 1.3 / 2.4
32.0 / (87) 17.3 / 5.0	34.7 / (95) 19.6 / 7.2	35.0 / (119) 20.2 / 7.5	% Profit Before Taxes/Tangible Net Worth				37.8 / (18) 19.7 / 7.3	35.4 / (30) 15.2 / 6.4	36.6 / (61) 22.8 / 11.2
12.2 / 6.2 / 1.7	15.7 / 8.2 / 2.2	14.4 / 7.2 / 2.6	% Profit Before Taxes/Total Assets				12.4 / 6.1 / 3.0	15.3 / 7.3 / 2.4	15.3 / 9.1 / 2.7
17.0 / 8.4 / 4.6	21.3 / 8.9 / 3.8	25.7 / 9.7 / 5.2	Sales/Net Fixed Assets				40.9 / 22.6 / 7.2	16.8 / 11.2 / 6.8	14.0 / 6.7 / 4.3
3.5 / 2.5 / 1.8	3.8 / 2.7 / 1.9	3.8 / 2.8 / 1.9	Sales/Total Assets				4.4 / 3.3 / 2.4	4.3 / 3.4 / 2.6	3.5 / 2.3 / 1.8
1.1 / (81) 1.9 / 3.2	1.0 / (88) 1.9 / 3.5	1.1 / (119) 1.6 / 2.6	% Depr., Dep., Amort./Sales				.6 / (20) 1.6 / 2.6	1.1 / (28) 1.8 / 2.6	.9 / (58) 1.6 / 2.4
1.1 / (21) 2.0 / 3.6	1.4 / (25) 2.0 / 3.7	.6 / (32) 2.1 / 3.8	% Officers', Directors' Owners' Comp/Sales					1.1 / (10) 1.7 / 3.5	
4594759M	4926501M	10276492M	Net Sales ($)	1568M	8843M	33407M	153030M	551482M	9528162M
2316245M	2100235M	3770994M	Total Assets ($)	1072M	3488M	13014M	54652M	180791M	3517977M

M = $ thousand   MM = $ million
See Pages 11 through 21 for Explanation of Ratios and Data

Current Data Sorted by Assets							Comparative Historical Data	
	1	3	9	9	6	**Type of Statement** Unqualified	18	25
		1	2			Reviewed	1	2
	2	1				Compiled	4	10
	3					Tax Returns	2	2
		3	5			Other	13	15
	21 (4/1-9/30/06)		24 (10/1/06-3/31/07)				4/1/02-3/31/03 ALL	4/1/03-3/31/04 ALL
0-500M	500M-2MM	2-10MM	10-50MM	50-100MM	100-250MM			
	6	8	16	9	6	NUMBER OF STATEMENTS	38	54
%	%	%	%	%	%	**ASSETS**	%	%
DATA NOT AVAILABLE			6.0			Cash & Equivalents	4.7	3.8
			21.2			Trade Receivables (net)	19.9	18.5
			22.5			Inventory	19.2	20.0
			5.4			All Other Current	2.3	3.7
			55.0			Total Current	46.1	45.9
			41.3			Fixed Assets (net)	45.4	44.4
			.4			Intangibles (net)	3.5	3.3
			3.3			All Other Non-Current	5.0	6.3
			100.0			Total	100.0	100.0
						LIABILITIES		
			11.9			Notes Payable-Short Term	11.3	10.5
			6.3			Cur. Mat.-L.T.D.	2.8	3.5
			10.1			Trade Payables	11.1	11.8
			.4			Income Taxes Payable	.4	.2
			8.3			All Other Current	5.4	7.0
			37.0			Total Current	31.0	33.1
			20.7			Long-Term Debt	26.1	22.9
			1.9			Deferred Taxes	1.7	1.4
			.7			All Other Non-Current	3.2	5.0
			39.7			Net Worth	38.0	37.5
			100.0			Total Liabilties & Net Worth	100.0	100.0
						INCOME DATA		
			100.0			Net Sales	100.0	100.0
			20.6			Gross Profit	21.8	24.0
			17.4			Operating Expenses	17.7	20.8
			3.2			Operating Profit	4.1	3.2
			1.6			All Other Expenses (net)	.9	1.3
			1.6			Profit Before Taxes	3.2	1.8
						RATIOS		
			1.9				2.3	1.9
			1.8			Current	1.4	1.4
			1.4				1.1	1.1
			1.3				1.3	1.0
			.8			Quick	.7	.7
			.6				.5	.4
			31 11.8				25 14.5	25 14.7
			37 9.9			Sales/Receivables	34 10.8	34 10.7
			45 8.0				41 9.0	42 8.8
			18 19.8				16 23.1	27 13.6
			42 8.8			Cost of Sales/Inventory	43 8.4	45 8.2
			86 4.2				64 5.7	59 6.2
			13 28.6				16 23.3	14 26.1
			20 18.3			Cost of Sales/Payables	21 17.6	27 13.5
			34 10.6				29 12.6	46 8.0
			5.2				6.7	7.8
			7.8			Sales/Working Capital	14.1	16.9
			20.3				51.2	74.0
			5.1				6.1	5.9
			2.4			EBIT/Interest	(37) 2.4	(53) 2.1
			1.4				1.2	.6
							5.9	4.1
						Net Profit + Depr., Dep., Amort./Cur. Mat. L/T/D	(14) 3.2	(20) 2.0
							2.8	.4
			.6				.7	.8
			1.0			Fixed/Worth	1.3	1.4
			1.9				2.8	2.2
			.9				.9	.9
			1.1			Debt/Worth	1.7	1.8
			3.3				3.6	3.6
			14.9				30.6	19.8
			(15) 10.6			% Profit Before Taxes/Tangible Net Worth	(35) 13.6	(49) 10.6
			4.5				2.6	-6.3
			7.3				9.2	7.4
			4.4			% Profit Before Taxes/Total Assets	4.3	3.9
			1.2				1.0	-1.4
			10.6				6.7	7.0
			5.9			Sales/Net Fixed Assets	5.1	4.6
			2.3				2.5	2.6
			2.9				2.5	2.7
			1.9			Sales/Total Assets	2.0	2.0
			1.1				1.4	1.4
			1.9				2.2	1.6
			(15) 2.6			% Depr., Dep., Amort./Sales	(31) 2.8	(48) 2.4
			3.8				4.9	3.8
							1.6	1.7
						% Officers', Directors' Owners' Comp/Sales	(12) 3.3	(10) 2.9
							6.3	6.8
	18170M	111782M	751505M	907516M	1734809M	Net Sales ($)	3096560M	3542131M
	7688M	47964M	405901M	629561M	868340M	Total Assets ($)	1646673M	1969694M

M = $ thousand MM = $ million

See Pages 11 through 21 for Explanation of Ratios and Data

Comparative Historical Data				Current Data Sorted by Sales					
Type of Statement									
Unqualified	26	23	28			1		6	21
Reviewed	5	3	3						3
Compiled	5	4	3			2	1		
Tax Returns	1	1	3		2	1			
Other	10	14	8				1	3	4
	4/1/04-3/31/05 ALL	4/1/05-3/31/06 ALL	4/1/06-3/31/07 ALL	21 (4/1-9/30/06)			24 (10/1/06-3/31/07)		
				0-1MM	1-3MM	3-5MM	5-10MM	10-25MM	25MM & OVER
NUMBER OF STATEMENTS	47	45	45		2	4	2	9	28
ASSETS	%	%	%	%	%	%	%	%	%
Cash & Equivalents	5.2	5.4	5.1	DATA NOT AVAILABLE					3.4
Trade Receivables (net)	18.0	18.0	17.9						19.2
Inventory	19.8	23.0	23.5						23.7
All Other Current	3.4	3.4	4.3						5.8
Total Current	46.4	49.8	50.8						52.0
Fixed Assets (net)	45.2	40.2	39.8						39.8
Intangibles (net)	3.3	4.1	3.8						3.2
All Other Non-Current	5.1	5.9	5.6						4.9
Total	100.0	100.0	100.0						100.0
LIABILITIES									
Notes Payable-Short Term	8.2	10.7	12.3						11.9
Cur. Mat.-L.T.D.	3.5	2.8	3.9						4.8
Trade Payables	9.7	11.6	10.3						9.7
Income Taxes Payable	.3	.2	.3						.2
All Other Current	7.1	6.6	7.3						9.6
Total Current	28.7	31.9	34.1						36.2
Long-Term Debt	24.1	21.2	21.9						20.9
Deferred Taxes	2.1	1.4	1.7						2.6
All Other Non-Current	2.5	3.0	2.8						3.7
Net Worth	42.7	42.5	39.5						36.6
Total Liabilities & Net Worth	100.0	100.0	100.0						100.0
INCOME DATA									
Net Sales	100.0	100.0	100.0						100.0
Gross Profit	21.9	22.2	22.1						14.7
Operating Expenses	19.1	18.5	18.3						11.4
Operating Profit	2.9	3.8	3.8						3.3
All Other Expenses (net)	1.0	1.1	1.0						1.2
Profit Before Taxes	1.9	2.7	2.8						2.2
RATIOS									
Current	2.1	2.5	2.1						1.9
	1.7	1.7	1.8						1.5
	1.4	1.1	1.1						1.1
Quick	1.1	1.2	1.0						.9
	.8	.8	.7						.7
	.5	.5	.4						.4
Sales/Receivables	**23** 15.9	**22** 16.4	**21** 17.5						**30** 12.4
	31 11.9	**30** 12.1	**32** 11.3						**33** 11.1
	39 9.3	**39** 9.3	**41** 9.0						**43** 8.4
Cost of Sales/Inventory	**31** 11.7	**35** 10.5	**32** 11.5						**32** 11.5
	46 7.9	**46** 8.0	**57** 6.4						**49** 7.5
	57 6.4	**66** 5.5	**72** 5.1						**79** 4.6
Cost of Sales/Payables	**14** 26.6	**13** 27.5	**13** 28.4						**14** 26.7
	17 21.1	**21** 17.3	**21** 17.8						**19** 19.1
	30 12.4	**34** 10.9	**36** 10.1						**35** 10.3
Sales/Working Capital	7.0	6.7	6.0						6.4
	11.7	10.8	9.5						12.4
	25.6	36.5	34.2						30.5
EBIT/Interest	12.8	6.7	6.3						5.1
	(45) 4.0	(43) 3.0	(44) 3.0						3.0
	1.1	1.3	1.3						1.4
Net Profit + Depr., Dep., Amort./Cur. Mat. L/T/D	3.1	4.8	6.5						
	(21) 1.9	(17) 2.5	(12) 3.0						
	1.1	1.8	2.5						
Fixed/Worth	.6	.6	.6						.6
	1.2	1.0	1.2						1.2
	1.8	1.7	2.2						2.1
Debt/Worth	.7	.7	.9						1.0
	1.2	1.6	1.5						1.9
	2.9	3.1	4.1						3.8
% Profit Before Taxes/Tangible Net Worth	17.8	23.7	25.0						27.4
	(43) 12.8	(41) 12.9	(41) 13.7						(26) 14.3
	.9	4.2	5.9						6.8
% Profit Before Taxes/Total Assets	9.8	9.9	8.4						8.3
	3.4	3.8	4.9						5.8
	.2	1.2	1.5						1.3
Sales/Net Fixed Assets	8.8	9.8	10.2						8.1
	5.3	5.4	5.2						4.9
	2.3	3.1	2.6						2.5
Sales/Total Assets	2.8	2.8	2.7						2.7
	2.1	2.1	1.9						1.9
	1.3	1.5	1.4						1.3
% Depr., Dep., Amort./Sales	1.8	1.8	1.6						1.7
	(42) 3.0	(38) 2.8	(42) 2.8						(25) 2.6
	4.4	3.8	3.8						3.4
% Officers', Directors' Owners' Comp/Sales									
Net Sales ($)	**3795638M**	**3720055M**	**3523782M**		**2870M**	**15300M**	**18165M**	**141902M**	**3345545M**
Total Assets ($)	**1924239M**	**1892981M**	**1959454M**		**1615M**	**6073M**	**7164M**	**142607M**	**1801995M**

M = $ thousand MM = $ million

See Pages 11 through 21 for Explanation of Ratios and Data

Current Data Sorted by Assets   Comparative Historical Data

Type of Statement									
			2	9	3	1	Unqualified	28	25
	1	2	5	3	1		Reviewed	16	12
	2	4	6				Compiled	16	23
	1						Tax Returns	8	9
							Other	20	29
		30 (4/1-9/30/06)	11	37 (10/1/06-3/31/07) 11	2	1		4/1/02-3/31/03 ALL	4/1/03-3/31/04 ALL
	0-500M	500M-2MM	2-10MM	10-50MM	50-100MM	100-250MM			
	4	8	24	23	6	2	NUMBER OF STATEMENTS	88	98
	%	%	%	%	%	%		%	%

	0-500M	500M-2MM	2-10MM	10-50MM	50-100MM	100-250MM		ALL (88)	ALL (98)
ASSETS									
Cash & Equivalents			9.6	4.3				8.9	8.2
Trade Receivables (net)			15.3	20.2				15.5	14.7
Inventory			31.3	31.3				28.7	28.4
All Other Current			1.6	1.8				1.8	1.9
Total Current			57.8	57.6				55.0	53.2
Fixed Assets (net)			32.2	33.1				33.7	33.7
Intangibles (net)			3.1	5.4				3.1	5.0
All Other Non-Current			7.0	3.9				8.2	8.1
Total			100.0	100.0				100.0	100.0
LIABILITIES									
Notes Payable-Short Term			13.5	12.9				12.7	11.0
Cur. Mat.-L.T.D.			2.6	2.7				3.7	3.8
Trade Payables			12.9	13.8				11.5	10.0
Income Taxes Payable			.3	.7				.2	.4
All Other Current			5.9	7.9				7.7	9.1
Total Current			35.2	38.0				35.8	34.3
Long-Term Debt			17.6	8.1				16.8	14.8
Deferred Taxes			.9	1.7				.5	1.1
All Other Non-Current			7.7	6.7				8.7	8.9
Net Worth			38.5	45.5				38.3	41.0
Total Liabilities & Net Worth			100.0	100.0				100.0	100.0
INCOME DATA									
Net Sales			100.0	100.0				100.0	100.0
Gross Profit			37.1	22.2				34.3	37.7
Operating Expenses			34.1	17.0				31.1	32.8
Operating Profit			3.0	5.2				3.2	4.9
All Other Expenses (net)			.8	1.8				1.6	1.6
Profit Before Taxes			2.2	3.4				1.6	3.3
RATIOS									
Current			2.8	2.6				2.9	3.0
			2.0	1.4				1.5	1.6
			1.1	1.1				1.0	1.0
Quick			1.4	1.0				1.2	1.3
			.8	.6				.6 (97)	.6
			.3	.3				.3	.4
Sales/Receivables			11 34.8	17 21.7				13 28.2	12 29.7
			16 22.8	32 11.5				24 15.0	24 15.5
			41 9.0	48 7.5				40 9.2	38 9.7
Cost of Sales/Inventory			44 8.3	40 9.2				43 8.4	45 8.1
			75 4.9	68 5.4				76 4.8	71 5.2
			105 3.5	104 3.5				102 3.6	117 3.1
Cost of Sales/Payables			12 29.9	19 19.5				13 28.8	11 33.3
			25 14.5	27 13.7				23 15.8	24 15.5
			46 8.0	48 7.5				40 9.2	41 8.9
Sales/Working Capital			6.5	4.4				5.3	5.4
			10.5	13.0				14.1	12.2
			37.1	50.4				129.8	135.3
EBIT/Interest			12.1	10.1				9.0	8.5
			(22) 3.6	(20) 2.1				(79) 2.8	(89) 2.8
			1.0	1.3				1.1	1.1
Net Profit + Depr., Dep., Amort./Cur. Mat. L/T/D			11.7					9.5	3.9
			(10) 5.8					(28) 2.7	(30) 2.1
			2.4					1.4	1.2
Fixed/Worth			.4	.6				.3	.4
			.7	.9				1.0	.8
			1.9	2.6				2.4	2.0
Debt/Worth			.5	.4				.6	.6
			1.1	1.1				1.5	1.7
			2.5	6.8				4.5	4.6
% Profit Before Taxes/Tangible Net Worth			28.7	46.5				30.2	29.3
			(22) 22.9	(20) 15.5				(80) 11.1	(88) 9.6
			11.9	5.7				3.0	3.0
% Profit Before Taxes/Total Assets			13.9	13.3				11.2	11.0
			8.7	4.8				4.2	3.7
			.9	1.6				.7	.4
Sales/Net Fixed Assets			14.8	9.8				12.6	11.3
			9.1	5.9				6.4	6.0
			4.8	3.4				3.6	4.0
Sales/Total Assets			3.5	2.5				2.7	2.7
			2.4	2.2				2.0	2.0
			1.7	1.4				1.4	1.5
% Depr., Dep., Amort./Sales			1.4	1.7				1.6	1.7
			(21) 2.4	(20) 2.4				(80) 3.1	(83) 2.8
			3.4	3.2				4.3	4.1
% Officers', Directors' Owners' Comp/Sales								2.1	2.2
								(34) 4.9	(34) 5.6
								7.9	7.7
Net Sales ($)	6201M	28593M	232623M	1073902M	844640M	946874M		2527743M	3113814M
Total Assets ($)	1105M	9352M	106566M	559502M	452882M	362950M		1512379M	1766109M

© RMA 2007   M = $ thousand   MM = $ million
See Pages 11 through 21 for Explanation of Ratios and Data

Comparative Historical Data | | Current Data Sorted by Sales

			Type of Statement						
16	15	15	Unqualified				1	1	13
13	8	12	Reviewed				3	2	4
12	14	12	Compiled		1	2	3	2	
10	4	1	Tax Returns		4	3	3		
27	25	27	Other	1	2	1	5	5	14
4/1/04-	4/1/05-	4/1/06-			30 (4/1-9/30/06)		37 (10/1/06-3/31/07)		
3/31/05	3/31/06	3/31/07							
ALL	ALL	ALL		0-1MM	1-3MM	3-5MM	5-10MM	10-25MM	25MM & OVER
78	66	67	NUMBER OF STATEMENTS	1	7	6	12	10	31
%	%	%	ASSETS	%	%	%	%	%	%
7.6	8.3	8.3	Cash & Equivalents				10.4	5.8	3.9
16.1	16.4	16.1	Trade Receivables (net)				15.7	17.7	18.7
31.3	33.2	33.3	Inventory				32.5	33.0	35.1
2.4	2.2	2.2	All Other Current				2.0	1.6	2.2
57.4	60.1	59.8	Total Current				60.6	58.1	59.9
30.1	30.5	30.7	Fixed Assets (net)				32.0	36.3	31.2
6.2	5.2	4.4	Intangibles (net)				5.2	.7	5.1
6.4	4.2	5.0	All Other Non-Current				2.3	4.9	3.8
100.0	100.0	100.0	Total				100.0	100.0	100.0
			LIABILITIES						
14.6	18.8	13.3	Notes Payable-Short Term				8.9	10.5	11.5
3.2	3.1	2.9	Cur. Mat.-L.T.D.				3.7	2.9	2.8
13.4	12.8	12.7	Trade Payables				12.2	15.0	14.0
.5	.3	.5	Income Taxes Payable				.3	.4	.6
8.3	9.3	8.3	All Other Current				6.7	4.5	9.8
40.0	44.3	37.6	Total Current				31.7	33.2	38.7
17.4	19.0	14.9	Long-Term Debt				18.0	19.0	9.9
1.2	.6	1.0	Deferred Taxes				1.2	.7	1.4
10.4	3.5	7.3	All Other Non-Current				1.7	2.5	5.3
31.0	32.7	39.1	Net Worth				47.5	44.6	44.7
100.0	100.0	100.0	Total Liabilties & Net Worth				100.0	100.0	100.0
			INCOME DATA						
100.0	100.0	100.0	Net Sales				100.0	100.0	100.0
34.0	33.5	31.6	Gross Profit				36.3	34.8	22.2
30.9	29.9	27.3	Operating Expenses				30.2	31.2	17.6
3.0	3.5	4.3	Operating Profit				6.1	3.6	4.6
1.1	1.3	1.3	All Other Expenses (net)				.7	.9	1.6
1.9	2.2	3.0	Profit Before Taxes				5.4	2.8	3.0
			RATIOS						
2.8	3.0	2.9					2.9	2.9	2.8
1.5	1.8	1.7	Current				2.5	1.7	1.4
1.0	1.1	1.1					1.5	1.1	1.0
1.1	1.3	1.4					1.4	1.8	1.1
(77) .6	.7	.6	Quick				.9	.7	.6
.3	.3	.4					.5	.3	.3
8 44.3	12 29.5	10 34.9					10 36.5	11 32.8	16 22.7
20 18.3	21 17.5	23 15.7	Sales/Receivables				13 27.1	16 22.6	32 11.5
41 8.9	40 9.1	42 8.8					44 8.2	32 11.3	45 8.2
38 9.6	46 8.0	50 7.3					40 9.2	38 9.7	54 6.7
68 5.3	78 4.7	72 5.0	Cost of Sales/Inventory				77 4.7	71 5.1	72 5.1
104 3.5	110 3.3	111 3.3					102 3.6	95 3.9	112 3.3
14 26.8	13 27.9	13 27.7					12 29.9	10 35.1	18 20.6
25 14.8	25 14.7	21 17.3	Cost of Sales/Payables				22 16.4	26 13.9	27 13.7
44 8.3	39 9.3	44 8.4					43 8.5	51 7.2	48 7.5
5.7	5.1	6.0					6.2	7.7	4.4
15.3	11.7	10.8	Sales/Working Capital				9.0	10.9	10.9
UND	55.4	85.5					11.9	53.3	118.3
10.9	13.8	10.0					11.2	19.0	5.5
(69) 2.7	(62) 3.1	(62) 3.2	EBIT/Interest				(11) 5.2	3.6	(28) 2.1
.4	.1	1.3					2.5	1.8	1.3
6.6	11.0	10.3							9.3
(16) 2.5	(13) 2.7	(20) 5.0	Net Profit + Depr., Dep.,					(10)	1.7
1.2	1.7	1.3	Amort./Cur. Mat. L/T/D						.4
.4	.4	.4					.4	.4	.4
.9	.9	.8	Fixed/Worth				.6	.8	.9
5.5	2.4	1.6					2.3	1.7	1.4
.7	.6	.6					.6	.7	.6
2.0	1.3	1.7	Debt/Worth				.9	1.8	1.5
NM	8.4	4.9					4.1	2.5	5.7
32.4	37.5	37.6	% Profit Before Taxes/Tangible				58.4	28.7	33.5
(59) 14.9	(56) 13.9	(60) 18.2	Net Worth				(11) 23.0	25.9	(28) 12.0
.8	1.0	4.8					14.4	9.9	3.3
12.1	16.0	13.3	% Profit Before Taxes/Total				17.7	14.9	9.9
4.7	5.4	6.6	Assets				10.5	8.7	4.5
-1.8	-2.1	1.3					3.8	4.9	1.1
14.1	13.5	14.0					14.6	12.2	10.6
9.0	8.4	8.5	Sales/Net Fixed Assets				9.4	7.6	5.9
5.0	4.5	5.2					5.9	4.5	4.0
3.3	3.2	3.0					3.8	3.7	2.5
2.2	2.2	2.4	Sales/Total Assets				2.6	2.6	2.2
1.6	1.7	1.7					1.8	1.8	1.5
1.3	1.3	1.4					1.2		1.4
(63) 2.4	(53) 2.2	(58) 2.3	% Depr., Dep., Amort./Sales				(11) 2.0	(27)	2.3
3.2	3.3	3.3					3.2		3.1
2.7	2.1	1.8	% Officers', Directors'						
(25) 4.9	(21) 4.7	(17) 2.6	Owners' Comp/Sales						
7.0	7.2	6.4							
3808985M	3028375M	3132833M	Net Sales ($)	580M	13704M	25907M	93362M	133864M	2865416M
1915880M	1455126M	1492357M	Total Assets ($)	158M	4412M	19227M	40212M	53014M	1375334M

M = $ thousand   MM = $ million
See Pages 11 through 21 for Explanation of Ratios and Data

Current Data Sorted by Assets — Comparative Historical Data

0-500M	500M-2MM	2-10MM	10-50MM	50-100MM	100-250MM	Type of Statement	4/1/02-3/31/03 ALL	4/1/03-3/31/04 ALL
2		1	10	6	5	Unqualified	13	24
		4	5		1	Reviewed	9	10
	1	1	2			Compiled	1	2
1	3	3				Tax Returns	1	1
	1	2	7	2	3	Other	15	11
	24 (4/1-9/30/06)		36 (10/1/06-3/31/07)					
3	5	11	24	8	9	**NUMBER OF STATEMENTS**	39	48
%	%	%	%	%	%		%	%
						ASSETS		
		4.6	1.3			Cash & Equivalents	2.4	5.2
		26.6	17.9			Trade Receivables (net)	19.8	20.0
		29.4	36.6			Inventory	27.8	30.5
		3.1	1.6			All Other Current	4.0	3.3
		63.7	57.4			Total Current	54.0	59.0
		30.3	30.8			Fixed Assets (net)	38.4	34.2
		3.9	9.0			Intangibles (net)	2.8	1.4
		2.0	2.8			All Other Non-Current	4.8	5.3
		100.0	100.0			Total	100.0	100.0
						LIABILITIES		
		13.8	16.0			Notes Payable-Short Term	12.7	11.6
		3.6	2.2			Cur. Mat.-L.T.D.	3.0	3.2
		8.1	14.2			Trade Payables	18.4	13.3
		.0	.5			Income Taxes Payable	.4	.2
		21.4	6.4			All Other Current	13.8	17.1
		46.9	39.2			Total Current	48.3	45.4
		13.8	18.3			Long-Term Debt	17.5	19.0
		.0	.6			Deferred Taxes	1.2	1.0
		2.8	7.9			All Other Non-Current	4.7	5.8
		36.6	34.1			Net Worth	28.4	28.8
		100.0	100.0			Total Liabilities & Net Worth	100.0	100.0
						INCOME DATA		
		100.0	100.0			Net Sales	100.0	100.0
		19.8	19.1			Gross Profit	17.9	18.0
		17.4	13.4			Operating Expenses	14.7	13.8
		2.4	5.7			Operating Profit	3.2	4.2
		1.2	2.4			All Other Expenses (net)	1.8	1.4
		1.2	3.2			Profit Before Taxes	1.4	2.8
						RATIOS		
		1.8	1.7			Current	1.8	2.0
		1.3	1.5				1.2	1.4
		1.0	1.1				.9	1.1
		.9	.7			Quick	.7	.9
		.6	.4				.4	.5
		.4	.4				.3	.3
		23 16.0	31 12.0			Sales/Receivables	24 15.0	23 15.7
		25 14.6	41 8.9				35 10.4	31 11.7
		37 9.9	52 7.0				46 7.9	48 7.6
		12 31.6	62 5.9			Cost of Sales/Inventory	31 11.9	38 9.7
		66 5.6	119 3.1				72 5.1	82 4.4
		115 3.2	166 2.2				131 2.8	125 2.9
		2 186.9	27 13.7			Cost of Sales/Payables	17 21.5	13 28.5
		12 30.7	36 10.1				31 11.7	26 13.8
		23 16.2	56 6.5				56 6.5	42 8.8
		5.0	4.8			Sales/Working Capital	10.1	6.0
		44.5	10.0				24.1	11.7
		-999.8	46.0				-41.9	29.7
		7.2	4.9			EBIT/Interest	5.6	4.7
		(10) 2.5	(23) 2.1				(37) 2.8	(42) 2.5
		1.6	1.2				.4	1.0
						Net Profit + Depr., Dep., Amort./Cur. Mat. L/T/D	5.7	2.8
							(14) 2.4	(14) 1.6
							1.4	1.2
		.3	.5			Fixed/Worth	.8	.8
		1.0	1.2				1.3	1.2
		1.3	4.2				2.4	2.4
		1.0	1.2			Debt/Worth	1.5	1.0
		1.7	2.8				2.9	2.4
		9.2	9.0				8.2	6.6
		51.0	38.2			% Profit Before Taxes/Tangible Net Worth	45.3	42.6
		23.8	(20) 16.5				(34) 19.8	(45) 15.2
		2.1	5.1				.0	1.0
		19.2	10.1			% Profit Before Taxes/Total Assets	11.4	10.9
		4.5	3.3				2.5	4.2
		.5	1.2				-1.6	.2
		20.2	7.3			Sales/Net Fixed Assets	7.6	12.1
		9.7	4.9				4.1	5.3
		4.8	3.8				2.8	2.6
		3.9	1.7			Sales/Total Assets	2.4	2.4
		2.3	1.4				1.6	1.5
		2.0	1.2				.9	1.1
		1.0	1.4			% Depr., Dep., Amort./Sales	1.6	1.5
		1.4	(23) 2.7				(35) 3.3	(39) 2.9
		2.1	4.8				4.7	4.1
						% Officers', Directors' Owners' Comp/Sales		
3000M	16085M	200455M	989110M	835815M	1944945M	Net Sales ($)	1969905M	3493103M
635M	5336M	65444M	671023M	556837M	1638073M	Total Assets ($)	1285990M	2213412M

M = $ thousand   MM = $ million
See Pages 11 through 21 for Explanation of Ratios and Data

Comparative Historical Data | Current Data Sorted by Sales

Current data sorted by sales; middle-period columns: **24 (4/1-9/30/06)** and **36 (10/1/06-3/31/07)**

4/1/04-3/31/05 ALL	4/1/05-3/31/06 ALL	4/1/06-3/31/07 ALL	Type of Statement	0-1MM	1-3MM	3-5MM	5-10MM	10-25MM	25MM & OVER
17	20	24	Unqualified	2				2	20
10	7	10	Reviewed					4	6
2	4	4	Compiled					2	1
2	2	7	Tax Returns		1			1	
19	21	15	Other		4	1	2	3	11
50	54	60	NUMBER OF STATEMENTS	2	5	1	2	12	38
%	%	%	**ASSETS**	%	%	%	%	%	%
4.0	4.3	3.2	Cash & Equivalents					3.0	2.0
18.4	20.6	19.6	Trade Receivables (net)					19.8	19.4
33.0	33.9	34.7	Inventory					29.5	36.2
3.9	1.6	2.6	All Other Current					2.8	2.7
59.4	60.3	60.1	Total Current					55.1	60.4
31.5	29.5	31.8	Fixed Assets (net)					30.6	33.9
3.1	3.7	5.1	Intangibles (net)					10.9	3.2
6.0	6.6	3.0	All Other Non-Current					3.4	2.6
100.0	100.0	100.0	Total					100.0	100.0
			LIABILITIES						
16.4	14.7	14.8	Notes Payable-Short Term					17.6	16.5
2.6	3.1	3.5	Cur. Mat.-L.T.D.					4.4	2.2
13.0	15.1	13.3	Trade Payables					8.7	12.5
.4	.1	.3	Income Taxes Payable					.3	.3
9.5	10.0	11.4	All Other Current					8.0	13.0
41.8	42.9	43.3	Total Current					38.9	44.5
17.0	18.3	17.0	Long-Term Debt					17.6	16.8
.6	.5	.6	Deferred Taxes					.5	.7
5.7	4.7	6.0	All Other Non-Current					8.8	3.9
34.8	33.6	33.1	Net Worth					34.2	34.0
100.0	100.0	100.0	Total Liabilities & Net Worth					100.0	100.0
			INCOME DATA						
100.0	100.0	100.0	Net Sales					100.0	100.0
20.4	20.0	19.0	Gross Profit					20.6	17.0
16.4	15.4	14.7	Operating Expenses					14.5	11.7
3.9	4.6	4.2	Operating Profit					6.1	5.3
1.5	2.0	2.0	All Other Expenses (net)					3.0	1.5
2.4	2.6	2.2	Profit Before Taxes					3.1	3.8
			RATIOS						
1.9 / 1.4 / 1.1	1.9 / 1.5 / 1.0	1.8 / 1.4 / 1.1	Current					1.7 / 1.1 / 1.0	1.7 / 1.3 / 1.1
.7 / .5 / .3	.9 / .5 / .3	.8 / .5 / .3	Quick					1.3 / .5 / .3	.6 / .4 / .4
25 14.4 / 35 10.4 / 53 6.9	28 13.1 / 34 10.9 / 51 7.1	28 13.2 / 36 10.1 / 47 7.7	Sales/Receivables					25 14.4 / 39 9.4 / 57 6.4	30 12.1 / 38 9.6 / 47 7.7
50 7.3 / 97 3.8 / 168 2.2	43 8.4 / 95 3.8 / 176 2.1	54 6.7 / 100 3.7 / 153 2.4	Cost of Sales/Inventory					17 21.7 / 75 4.9 / 134 2.7	66 5.5 / 110 3.3 / 170 2.1
18 20.8 / 29 12.4 / 47 7.8	14 26.3 / 27 13.6 / 43 8.4	17 21.2 / 27 13.5 / 50 7.3	Cost of Sales/Payables					16 22.4 / 21 17.4 / 47 7.8	18 20.8 / 30 12.2 / 51 7.1
6.3 / 11.9 / 36.3	6.1 / 14.0 / 79.9	4.8 / 10.7 / 71.2	Sales/Working Capital					6.3 / 33.6 / NM	4.8 / 9.7 / 45.3
6.7 / (47) 2.5 / 1.4	5.4 / (50) 2.3 / .9	4.8 / (56) 2.4 / 1.2	EBIT/Interest					5.9 / 1.7 / 1.1	5.1 / (36) 3.2 / 1.5
4.9 / (14) 2.0 / 1.2	(13) 3.9	7.7 / 3.9 / 2.3	Net Profit + Depr., Dep., Amort./Cur. Mat. L/T/D						5.1 / (10) 3.9 / 2.9
.6 / .9 / 2.0	.6 / 1.0 / 2.4	.5 / 1.2 / 2.2	Fixed/Worth					.4 / 1.6 / 15.9	.7 / 1.2 / 1.9
1.1 / 2.1 / 4.1	1.2 / 2.7 / 5.3	1.1 / 2.4 / 7.0	Debt/Worth					1.1 / 5.0 / 40.0	1.2 / 2.3 / 4.3
33.5 / (47) 11.1 / 4.4	32.2 / (49) 16.7 / .9	40.1 / (53) 15.8 / 4.2	% Profit Before Taxes/Tangible Net Worth					46.9 / (10) 22.0 / 10.2	39.1 / (35) 15.8 / 4.1
7.7 / 3.5 / 1.2	8.9 / 4.2 / -.1	9.6 / 3.8 / .8	% Profit Before Taxes/Total Assets					14.0 / 2.8 / .6	9.5 / 4.8 / 1.2
9.5 / 4.7 / 2.4	13.0 / 5.8 / 3.0	10.2 / 4.9 / 3.3	Sales/Net Fixed Assets					11.0 / 5.6 / 3.8	8.0 / 4.6 / 2.9
2.2 / 1.4 / 1.1	2.9 / 1.6 / 1.0	2.2 / 1.5 / 1.2	Sales/Total Assets					2.3 / 1.7 / 1.0	1.9 / 1.4 / 1.2
1.1 / (45) 2.9 / 4.4	1.2 / (42) 2.9 / 5.3	1.4 / (56) 2.5 / 4.0	% Depr., Dep., Amort./Sales					1.5 / 2.0 / 5.0	1.4 / (35) 2.7 / 4.0
		(10) 1.7 / 3.3 / 9.8	% Officers', Directors' Owners' Comp/Sales						
3909637M	4476171M	3989410M	Net Sales ($)	424M	10265M	3372M	12921M	207268M	3755160M
2467314M	2653797M	2937348M	Total Assets ($)	292M	5465M	1545M	3854M	159847M	2766345M

M = $ thousand   MM = $ million
See Pages 11 through 21 for Explanation of Ratios and Data

Current Data Sorted by Assets   Comparative Historical Data

Type of Statement

0-500M	500M-2MM	2-10MM	10-50MM	50-100MM	100-250MM		4/1/02-3/31/03 ALL	4/1/03-3/31/04 ALL
		3	10	3		Unqualified	12	18
	1	5	4	1		Reviewed	16	14
3	1	1				Compiled	5	9
	6					Tax Returns		2
1	3	11	10	2	2	Other	15	19
	12 (4/1-9/30/06)		55 (10/1/06-3/31/07)					
4	11	20	24	6	2	NUMBER OF STATEMENTS	48	62
%	%	%	%	%	%	**ASSETS**	%	%
	10.2	6.6	5.6			Cash & Equivalents	7.0	8.6
	23.6	26.5	21.4			Trade Receivables (net)	17.3	18.6
	16.8	25.0	19.0			Inventory	18.1	19.2
	.7	1.6	3.4			All Other Current	1.2	2.4
	51.3	59.8	49.4			Total Current	43.6	48.8
	39.6	34.3	37.3			Fixed Assets (net)	40.6	36.8
	3.6	2.9	2.3			Intangibles (net)	10.4	4.8
	5.5	3.0	11.0			All Other Non-Current	5.4	9.5
	100.0	100.0	100.0			Total	100.0	100.0
						LIABILITIES		
	13.7	8.6	8.8			Notes Payable-Short Term	8.4	7.8
	4.7	4.2	3.4			Cur. Mat.-L.T.D.	5.5	4.9
	17.7	22.6	13.4			Trade Payables	13.7	15.9
	.0	.4	.1			Income Taxes Payable	.5	.5
	6.4	6.7	13.6			All Other Current	7.0	8.4
	42.5	42.6	39.3			Total Current	35.0	37.6
	27.5	10.9	13.2			Long-Term Debt	22.6	20.6
	.0	.4	1.6			Deferred Taxes	.7	.5
	1.7	12.1	4.2			All Other Non-Current	7.0	10.6
	28.3	34.1	41.7			Net Worth	34.8	30.8
	100.0	100.0	100.0			Total Liabilities & Net Worth	100.0	100.0
						INCOME DATA		
	100.0	100.0	100.0			Net Sales	100.0	100.0
	39.1	30.1	22.6			Gross Profit	29.4	34.8
	35.1	26.6	18.1			Operating Expenses	24.5	30.3
	4.0	3.5	4.5			Operating Profit	4.9	4.5
	1.7	1.0	1.2			All Other Expenses (net)	1.5	1.3
	2.3	2.5	3.4			Profit Before Taxes	3.3	3.1
						RATIOS		
	1.7	1.8	2.0			Current	1.8	2.0
	1.1	1.4	1.3				1.3	1.3
	.6	1.0	.9				.8	1.0
	1.2	1.2	1.1			Quick	1.1	1.3
	.7	.7	.7				.6	.7
	.2	.5	.4				.4	.5
	14 26.8	19 19.2	22 16.3			Sales/Receivables	16 22.4	20 18.4
	20 18.3	29 12.6	30 12.3				24 15.0	25 14.8
	40 9.1	33 10.9	34 10.7				32 11.5	33 10.9
	17 20.9	31 11.9	21 17.0			Cost of Sales/Inventory	26 14.3	26 13.8
	28 13.0	44 8.3	38 9.5				37 9.8	36 10.2
	40 9.2	58 6.3	64 5.7				50 7.2	59 6.1
	12 30.2	25 14.7	19 19.0			Cost of Sales/Payables	13 28.4	17 21.4
	22 16.7	36 10.0	25 14.8				28 13.1	29 12.7
	69 5.3	41 8.8	33 11.2				42 8.6	44 8.3
	21.5	11.6	9.7			Sales/Working Capital	11.7	8.6
	133.8	21.7	29.4				27.6	20.6
	-10.4	NM	-44.7				-43.6	-88.6
	5.8	12.5	12.5			EBIT/Interest	9.3	13.2
	4.3	(18) 5.7	(21) 5.3				(43) 3.8	(57) 4.1
	1.9	.9	2.1				1.1	1.0
						Net Profit + Depr., Dep., Amort./Cur. Mat. L/T/D	4.2	6.4
							(15) 2.0	(13) 2.8
							1.1	2.2
	.5	.4	.6			Fixed/Worth	.8	.5
	1.6	1.0	1.0				1.8	1.2
	3.8	1.5	1.7				NM	3.0
	1.5	.7	.8			Debt/Worth	.9	.9
	3.5	1.3	1.5				3.8	1.9
	5.9	2.0	2.7				NM	6.3
		50.1	38.3			% Profit Before Taxes/Tangible Net Worth	57.1	51.3
	(19) 23.0	(23) 23.1					(36) 36.2	(52) 21.7
	11.3	6.5					6.3	7.9
	16.3	15.7	12.7			% Profit Before Taxes/Total Assets	12.3	13.3
	8.6	9.8	7.9				7.0	7.6
	4.1	1.5	2.0				.6	.3
	47.9	24.4	12.8			Sales/Net Fixed Assets	11.6	17.3
	7.5	11.1	6.1				4.8	5.9
	2.9	4.2	4.0				3.2	3.5
	5.2	4.5	3.3			Sales/Total Assets	3.0	3.5
	2.8	3.2	2.4				2.3	2.4
	1.9	2.3	1.5				1.5	1.4
		1.0	1.3			% Depr., Dep., Amort./Sales	1.5	1.4
	(14)	2.1	(21) 1.6				(44) 2.6	(51) 2.4
		2.7	3.1				4.5	4.0
						% Officers', Directors' Owners' Comp/Sales		1.8
								(17) 2.9
								7.1
3040M	54530M	367938M	1675432M	909912M	231208M	Net Sales ($)	2112537M	1954420M
1472M	15330M	108702M	679920M	395621M	269362M	Total Assets ($)	1175898M	1018157M

M = $ thousand   MM = $ million
See Pages 11 through 21 for Explanation of Ratios and Data

Comparative Historical Data / Current Data Sorted by Sales

Label	4/1/04-3/31/05 ALL	4/1/05-3/31/06 ALL	4/1/06-3/31/07 ALL	0-1MM	1-3MM	3-5MM	5-10MM	10-25MM	25MM & OVER
		12 (4/1-9/30/06)					55 (10/1/06-3/31/07)		
Type of Statement									
Unqualified	24	13	16					4	12
Reviewed	13	14	11		2			2	6
Compiled	6	7	5		2		1	1	
Tax Returns	2	3	6	2	1		4		
Other	19	23	29	2		1	3	7	17
NUMBER OF STATEMENTS	64	60	67	4	5	1	8	14	35
ASSETS	%	%	%	%	%	%	%	%	%
Cash & Equivalents	5.7	9.8	5.7					6.7	4.9
Trade Receivables (net)	20.9	18.6	22.6					22.2	23.4
Inventory	17.4	17.8	20.3					24.4	20.6
All Other Current	2.0	1.4	2.2					2.1	2.8
Total Current	45.9	47.6	50.9					55.4	51.6
Fixed Assets (net)	39.9	38.2	36.7					38.1	30.9
Intangibles (net)	7.0	8.5	5.9					3.3	8.5
All Other Non-Current	7.2	5.7	6.5					3.2	9.0
Total	100.0	100.0	100.0					100.0	100.0
LIABILITIES									
Notes Payable-Short Term	8.1	10.5	11.0					6.3	10.5
Cur. Mat.-L.T.D.	5.9	4.9	4.0					4.8	3.4
Trade Payables	13.0	15.7	16.5					19.2	16.0
Income Taxes Payable	.3	.3	.2					.4	.2
All Other Current	10.8	6.9	9.3					5.9	11.9
Total Current	38.1	38.1	41.0					36.5	41.9
Long-Term Debt	18.5	21.2	18.5					11.1	14.9
Deferred Taxes	.9	.6	.7					.2	1.3
All Other Non-Current	5.1	7.1	7.9					3.5	9.3
Net Worth	37.3	32.9	31.9					48.6	32.6
Total Liabilties & Net Worth	100.0	100.0	100.0					100.0	100.0
INCOME DATA									
Net Sales	100.0	100.0	100.0					100.0	100.0
Gross Profit	30.4	31.3	28.2					32.3	21.9
Operating Expenses	26.3	27.4	24.1					28.6	17.1
Operating Profit	4.0	3.9	4.1					3.7	4.9
All Other Expenses (net)	1.0	1.9	1.5					.5	1.6
Profit Before Taxes	3.1	2.0	2.7					3.2	3.3
RATIOS									
Current	1.9	1.9	1.8					2.1	2.0
	1.2	1.2	1.2					1.3	1.3
	.8	1.0	.9					.9	.9
Quick	1.1	1.1	1.0					1.5	1.1
	.7	.8	.7					.7	.7
	.4	.5	.4					.4	.4
Sales/Receivables	20 18.0	20 18.6	20 18.0					21 17.5	23 16.0
	28 12.9	27 13.5	29 12.4					29 12.7	29 12.4
	37 9.9	35 10.6	35 10.4					38 9.5	34 10.7
Cost of Sales/Inventory	23 16.2	23 15.8	26 14.1					32 11.5	23 16.1
	34 10.7	36 10.3	38 9.7					45 8.1	38 9.7
	49 7.4	50 7.3	59 6.2					68 5.4	59 6.2
Cost of Sales/Payables	15 23.8	20 18.5	19 19.2					26 13.9	18 20.4
	24 15.3	30 12.2	28 13.1					36 10.0	25 14.5
	37 9.9	43 8.6	39 9.3					45 8.1	34 10.6
Sales/Working Capital	9.3	10.0	11.5					10.5	11.1
	25.4	29.6	30.3					21.7	26.9
	-50.5	-189.8	-43.9					-155.0	-67.2
EBIT/Interest	10.6	9.8	10.1					12.9	12.2
	(58) 3.9	(57) 3.9	(62) 4.8					(12) 5.8	(32) 5.2
	.9	.5	1.4					.6	2.1
Net Profit + Depr., Dep., Amort./Cur. Mat. L/T/D	3.6	4.9	5.5						6.6
	(23) 2.2	(21) 1.4	(21) 2.5						(16) 2.7
	.7	.7	1.9						1.8
Fixed/Worth	.6	.8	.6					.3	.6
	1.1	1.2	1.1					1.0	1.0
	2.8	3.2	2.4					1.6	1.9
Debt/Worth	.7	.9	1.0					.5	1.0
	1.9	1.9	1.9					1.2	1.6
	5.1	6.2	6.5					2.1	6.5
% Profit Before Taxes/Tangible Net Worth	47.4	35.2	46.9					42.6	39.8
	(56) 26.1	(48) 19.8	(56) 24.2					(13) 19.7	(30) 25.6
	3.9	5.7	11.7					5.6	13.2
% Profit Before Taxes/Total Assets	17.2	11.9	14.0					16.2	13.7
	8.4	5.4	8.5					9.7	8.0
	.1	-1.7	1.7					-.4	2.9
Sales/Net Fixed Assets	13.9	12.3	17.9					18.6	17.9
	5.7	6.0	7.3					7.2	7.7
	3.2	3.7	3.8					3.5	5.1
Sales/Total Assets	3.3	3.2	3.6					3.9	3.6
	2.3	2.3	2.5					2.7	2.5
	1.4	1.5	1.9					1.9	1.7
% Depr., Dep., Amort./Sales	1.2	1.5	1.2					1.0	1.2
	(56) 2.7	(50) 2.6	(54) 2.0					(10) 2.0	(29) 1.6
	3.9	4.2	3.0					3.0	2.5
% Officers', Directors' Owners' Comp/Sales	.6	2.3							
	(11) 2.9	(12) 3.5							
	3.7	7.7							
Net Sales ($)	3278239M	3032328M	3242060M	2792M	10937M	3372M	59916M	226001M	2939042M
Total Assets ($)	1498146M	1451355M	1470407M	1701M	5684M	1545M	17236M	102721M	1341520M

© RMA 2007

M = $ thousand   MM = $ million

See Pages 11 through 21 for Explanation of Ratios and Data

Current Data Sorted by Assets   Comparative Historical Data

0-500M	500M-2MM	2-10MM	10-50MM	50-100MM	100-250MM		4/1/02-3/31/03 ALL	4/1/03-3/31/04 ALL
						Type of Statement		
	1	3	14	7	4	Unqualified	28	27
	1	8	8			Reviewed	12	12
	1	2	1			Compiled	4	14
2	3	1				Tax Returns	1	1
1		9	8	5	6	Other	24	29
	37 (4/1-9/30/06)		48 (10/1/06-3/31/07)					
3	6	23	31	12	10	**NUMBER OF STATEMENTS**	69	83
%	%	%	%	%	%		%	%
						ASSETS		
		8.0	3.8	1.3	.9	Cash & Equivalents	3.7	4.4
		20.9	17.1	15.8	11.1	Trade Receivables (net)	16.7	15.9
		28.8	37.1	43.5	46.3	Inventory	34.8	34.8
		4.4	2.8	1.7	2.2	All Other Current	2.4	3.9
		62.0	60.8	62.4	60.4	Total Current	57.6	59.0
		28.9	29.8	31.6	30.5	Fixed Assets (net)	33.5	32.7
		4.7	2.5	1.6	5.7	Intangibles (net)	2.7	3.0
		4.5	7.0	4.5	3.3	All Other Non-Current	6.2	5.2
		100.0	100.0	100.0	100.0	Total	100.0	100.0
						LIABILITIES		
		9.2	14.1	16.1	23.4	Notes Payable-Short Term	11.4	11.9
		2.8	4.3	2.6	1.8	Cur. Mat.-L.T.D.	3.3	3.9
		23.0	18.2	14.4	4.9	Trade Payables	13.9	13.8
		.1	.2	.2	.2	Income Taxes Payable	.2	.2
		6.4	7.7	7.9	9.5	All Other Current	7.9	7.7
		41.4	44.4	41.2	39.7	Total Current	36.7	37.6
		15.1	11.1	15.9	21.9	Long-Term Debt	18.7	18.0
		.6	.4	.0	.5	Deferred Taxes	.8	.8
		6.6	3.6	6.9	8.7	All Other Non-Current	3.7	3.9
		36.4	40.6	36.0	29.2	Net Worth	40.2	39.7
		100.0	100.0	100.0	100.0	Total Liabilities & Net Worth	100.0	100.0
						INCOME DATA		
		100.0	100.0	100.0	100.0	Net Sales	100.0	100.0
		24.4	18.6	18.3	19.3	Gross Profit	21.8	22.0
		20.6	15.1	12.9	13.9	Operating Expenses	16.9	17.6
		3.8	3.4	5.3	5.4	Operating Profit	5.0	4.3
		.4	1.4	2.5	3.7	All Other Expenses (net)	1.6	1.0
		3.5	2.1	2.9	1.7	Profit Before Taxes	3.3	3.3
						RATIOS		
		2.2	2.2	1.8	2.1		2.6	2.7
		1.5	1.5	1.4	1.6	Current	1.6	1.7
		1.1	1.1	1.1	1.4		1.2	1.2
		1.2	.6	.6	.4		.9	1.0
		.6	.5	.4	.3	Quick	.5	.5
		.5	.3	.2	.2		.3	.3
		20 18.1	23 16.1	25 14.6	23 15.9		24 15.4	22 16.5
		25 14.6	30 12.1	35 10.5	28 13.1	Sales/Receivables	30 12.3	28 13.1
		36 10.2	34 10.8	42 8.7	38 9.5		40 9.2	35 10.5
		28 12.8	50 7.3	63 5.8	108 3.4		49 7.4	40 9.2
		46 7.9	75 4.8	122 3.0	142 2.6	Cost of Sales/Inventory	95 3.8	92 4.0
		105 3.5	136 2.7	172 2.1	224 1.6		137 2.7	135 2.7
		16 22.3	26 14.3	18 20.1	8 46.4		14 25.7	18 20.6
		32 11.3	38 9.6	28 12.9	13 28.1	Cost of Sales/Payables	27 13.3	27 13.5
		45 8.1	57 6.4	38 9.6	24 15.3		57 6.4	42 8.8
		6.4	5.2	5.6	5.1		5.1	4.8
		14.9	14.3	8.3	5.3	Sales/Working Capital	9.0	8.7
		63.6	68.1	39.8	6.9		21.7	24.5
		13.2	7.2	11.4	2.1		5.1	8.7
		(22) 5.3	(26) 1.6	3.3	1.8	EBIT/Interest	(63) 2.7	(76) 3.4
		1.8	-.1	1.1	.9		1.4	1.5
			5.9					5.3	4.8
			(16) 3.0			Net Profit + Depr., Dep., Amort./Cur. Mat. L/T/D	(29) 2.7	(35) 2.3
			1.1				1.0	1.0
		.5	.4	.4	.8		.5	.4
		1.0	.7	1.0	1.2	Fixed/Worth	.9	.9
		5.6	1.6	1.9	1.4		1.8	1.9
		.6	.7	.9	1.5		.8	.7
		2.2	1.4	1.8	2.0	Debt/Worth	1.6	1.8
		10.3	4.1	2.8	2.7		3.9	3.6
		41.3	26.5	29.7			24.5	30.9
		(19) 23.8	(28) 11.7	(11) 12.8		% Profit Before Taxes/Tangible Net Worth	(64) 16.1	(78) 17.1
		7.0	-1.4	2.6			10.3	5.6
		12.7	14.1	13.2	4.9		10.6	10.7
		7.9	2.1	4.1	2.3	% Profit Before Taxes/Total Assets	6.2	6.2
		1.5	-4.0	.0	-1.2		2.0	1.7
		27.2	12.8	11.1	5.9		9.8	11.0
		10.3	6.6	5.5	4.5	Sales/Net Fixed Assets	6.1	6.0
		4.1	4.8	3.7	3.1		3.6	3.7
		3.7	2.8	2.3	1.6		2.0	2.2
		2.5	2.0	1.8	1.6	Sales/Total Assets	1.7	1.7
		1.9	1.5	1.2	1.0		1.5	1.5
		1.0	1.3	2.2			1.6	1.5
		(21) 1.4	(29) 2.2	(11) 3.1		% Depr., Dep., Amort./Sales	(65) 2.4	(72) 2.3
		2.8	2.9	3.7			3.3	3.3
							1.2	1.3
						% Officers', Directors' Owners' Comp/Sales	(12) 2.8	(12) 2.0
							8.2	8.5
6098M	18586M	326473M	1563964M	1616941M	2413858M	Net Sales ($)	5705201M	6381700M
871M	7631M	118948M	731600M	864959M	1729759M	Total Assets ($)	3467093M	3839265M

M = $ thousand   MM = $ million
See Pages 11 through 21 for Explanation of Ratios and Data

Comparative Historical Data | | Current Data Sorted by Sales

			Type of Statement	0-1MM	1-3MM	3-5MM	5-10MM	10-25MM	25MM & OVER
32	27	29	Unqualified	1	1			2	25
15	15	17	Reviewed			1	2	8	6
5	6	4	Compiled			1		2	
3	4	6	Tax Returns	1	2	1	2		
24	24	29	Other	1	2	1	3	7	17
4/1/04-3/31/05 ALL	4/1/05-3/31/06 ALL	4/1/06-3/31/07 ALL		37 (4/1-9/30/06)			48 (10/1/06-3/31/07)		
79	76	85	**NUMBER OF STATEMENTS**	3	3	4	8	19	48
%	%	%	**ASSETS**	%	%	%	%	%	%
3.3	4.6	4.1	Cash & Equivalents					5.7	2.3
17.2	17.2	17.1	Trade Receivables (net)					19.7	16.9
37.0	36.2	35.9	Inventory					32.8	38.9
3.2	2.6	2.7	All Other Current					2.2	2.9
60.6	60.6	59.9	Total Current					60.5	61.1
29.9	32.6	30.6	Fixed Assets (net)					32.4	29.6
3.0	2.1	4.1	Intangibles (net)					1.1	3.7
6.4	4.7	5.3	All Other Non-Current					6.0	5.6
100.0	100.0	100.0	Total					100.0	100.0
			LIABILITIES						
15.1	14.8	14.7	Notes Payable-Short Term					11.1	16.3
3.0	2.5	3.0	Cur. Mat.-L.T.D.					2.2	3.6
14.8	17.7	16.4	Trade Payables					20.2	15.3
.2	.3	.1	Income Taxes Payable					.3	.1
7.5	6.2	7.7	All Other Current					3.8	8.7
40.6	41.6	42.0	Total Current					37.6	44.0
19.2	18.2	16.9	Long-Term Debt					11.8	14.2
.4	.7	.4	Deferred Taxes					.5	.3
6.0	4.7	6.7	All Other Non-Current					7.7	5.1
33.8	34.7	34.1	Net Worth					42.3	36.4
100.0	100.0	100.0	Total Liabilities & Net Worth					100.0	100.0
			INCOME DATA						
100.0	100.0	100.0	Net Sales					100.0	100.0
23.1	20.2	20.9	Gross Profit					19.0	19.1
18.0	17.6	17.2	Operating Expenses					14.9	15.2
5.0	2.6	3.7	Operating Profit					4.1	3.9
1.3	1.2	1.5	All Other Expenses (net)					1.2	1.8
3.7	1.5	2.2	Profit Before Taxes					2.9	2.1
			RATIOS						
2.2	2.1	2.2	Current					2.7	1.9
1.5	1.6	1.5						1.9	1.4
1.1	1.2	1.1						1.1	1.1
.8	.7	.7	Quick					1.2	.6
.5	.5	.5						.5	.4
.3	.3	.3						.4	.3
23 16.1	23 16.1	21 17.0	Sales/Receivables					22 16.4	23 16.0
30 12.3	30 12.1	27 13.4						30 12.1	31 11.9
37 9.9	37 10.0	37 9.9						38 9.7	37 9.9
46 7.9	47 7.7	44 8.3	Cost of Sales/Inventory					28 12.8	53 6.9
97 3.8	90 4.0	83 4.4						46 7.9	91 4.0
161 2.3	139 2.6	138 2.6						136 2.7	143 2.5
16 23.1	16 22.4	14 26.5	Cost of Sales/Payables					13 28.2	16 22.3
30 12.2	36 10.2	27 13.5						30 12.3	28 13.1
47 7.8	56 6.6	42 8.7						48 7.7	40 9.1
5.1	4.9	5.4	Sales/Working Capital					4.8	5.4
9.2	8.9	12.3						14.6	10.0
23.7	40.3	60.0						63.6	45.0
8.1	6.9	7.7	EBIT/Interest					12.5	7.6
(77) 2.8	(75) 2.5	(79) 2.1						(16) 2.8	(46) 2.0
1.5	1.0	.8						1.4	.8
5.6	6.5	8.3	Net Profit + Depr., Dep., Amort./Cur. Mat. L/T/D						10.1
(32) 2.2	(31) 2.7	(35) 3.3							(24) 3.6
1.5	1.3	1.4							1.8
.5	.7	.5	Fixed/Worth					.3	.5
1.0	1.0	1.0						.9	.9
1.8	1.8	2.0						2.7	1.3
1.1	1.1	.9	Debt/Worth					.5	1.0
2.2	2.0	2.0						.9	2.0
4.3	3.4	4.9						5.8	2.8
31.8	28.0	29.9	% Profit Before Taxes/Tangible Net Worth					29.3	28.9
(72) 17.5	(67) 14.8	(72) 12.7						(15) 12.8	(44) 12.3
2.9	6.1	2.6						7.0	1.9
10.5	9.1	12.7	% Profit Before Taxes/Total Assets					13.2	9.3
4.2	4.8	3.8						4.2	3.6
.9	.1	-1.5						1.3	-1.5
11.9	12.2	14.0	Sales/Net Fixed Assets					18.1	12.7
6.3	5.0	6.6						6.8	6.3
4.0	3.8	4.1						3.8	4.4
2.7	2.4	2.8	Sales/Total Assets					3.7	2.7
1.8	1.9	2.0						1.9	1.9
1.2	1.3	1.5						1.5	1.5
1.3	1.0	1.1	% Depr., Dep., Amort./Sales					1.0	1.2
(66) 2.3	(68) 2.4	(74) 2.2						(18) 1.6	(40) 2.2
3.3	4.0	3.3						3.1	3.3
1.2	1.2	.6	% Officers', Directors' Owners' Comp/Sales						
(17) 3.1	(13) 2.0	(17) 1.5							
7.3	6.0	3.9							
5998170M	6851121M	5945920M	Net Sales ($)	2118M	5037M	16275M	59752M	327085M	5535653M
3916512M	3845896M	3453768M	Total Assets ($)	2293M	4942M	13204M	22435M	168189M	3242705M

M = $ thousand   MM = $ million
See Pages 11 through 21 for Explanation of Ratios and Data

Current Data Sorted by Assets / Comparative Historical Data

0-500M	500M-2MM	2-10MM	10-50MM	50-100MM	100-250MM	Type of Statement		
1	2	3	3	2	2	Unqualified	15	13
	3	4	2			Reviewed	2	5
		1	1			Compiled	5	4
1		1				Tax Returns	1	1
1	1	4	4	2		Other	13	14
	16 (4/1-9/30/06)		22 (10/1/06-3/31/07)				4/1/02-3/31/03 ALL	4/1/03-3/31/04 ALL
2	7	13	10	4	2	NUMBER OF STATEMENTS	36	37
%	%	%	%	%	%		%	%

ASSETS

2-10MM	10-50MM		Hist ALL	Hist ALL
6.4	3.1	Cash & Equivalents	5.6	8.8
23.1	21.6	Trade Receivables (net)	17.2	21.7
36.1	37.1	Inventory	35.8	33.9
2.2	3.5	All Other Current	3.3	1.9
67.8	65.2	Total Current	61.8	66.3
25.3	24.0	Fixed Assets (net)	25.6	22.3
5.2	3.6	Intangibles (net)	5.7	5.7
1.7	7.2	All Other Non-Current	6.9	5.7
100.0	100.0	Total	100.0	100.0

LIABILITIES

2-10MM	10-50MM		Hist ALL	Hist ALL
10.2	17.0	Notes Payable-Short Term	16.7	17.2
3.9	2.4	Cur. Mat.-L.T.D.	4.7	1.6
25.2	16.0	Trade Payables	13.8	16.2
.4	1.0	Income Taxes Payable	.1	.3
9.9	3.4	All Other Current	6.6	7.5
49.6	39.8	Total Current	42.0	42.8
14.2	9.5	Long-Term Debt	15.9	12.8
.6	.6	Deferred Taxes	.8	.6
5.8	6.4	All Other Non-Current	11.0	7.6
29.8	43.7	Net Worth	30.2	36.2
100.0	100.0	Total Liabilities & Net Worth	100.0	100.0

INCOME DATA

2-10MM	10-50MM		Hist ALL	Hist ALL
100.0	100.0	Net Sales	100.0	100.0
40.9	23.4	Gross Profit	32.4	28.1
29.3	15.8	Operating Expenses	26.9	22.3
11.6	7.6	Operating Profit	5.6	5.8
4.9	.4	All Other Expenses (net)	2.0	1.7
6.7	7.2	Profit Before Taxes	3.6	4.2

RATIOS

2-10MM		10-50MM			Hist ALL		Hist ALL	
	2.1		2.3	Current		2.1		2.4
	1.9		1.7			1.6		1.6
	1.1		1.2			1.2		1.2
	1.8		1.1	Quick		.9		1.5
	.7		.7			.5		.7
	.4		.4			.3		.3
21	17.6	34	10.8	Sales/Receivables	27	13.5	31	11.9
36	10.0	38	9.6		37	9.8	37	9.9
52	7.0	59	6.2		50	7.3	44	8.3
26	14.1	61	6.0	Cost of Sales/Inventory	64	5.7	50	7.3
77	4.8	77	4.7		131	2.8	80	4.5
322	1.1	118	3.1		197	1.9	159	2.3
21	17.1	12	30.8	Cost of Sales/Payables	16	22.6	18	20.8
41	8.9	27	13.3		32	11.3	31	11.8
143	2.6	73	5.0		73	5.0	55	6.6
	5.5		6.1	Sales/Working Capital		4.8		5.3
	8.1		8.8			7.9		8.1
	NM		13.1			16.0		14.2
	10.0		19.5	EBIT/Interest		5.5		13.4
	5.2		3.1		(34)	2.0	(33)	3.0
	3.7		2.0			1.1		1.2
				Net Profit + Depr., Dep., Amort./Cur. Mat. L/T/D		9.7		7.6
					(15)	2.1	(16)	2.0
						.3		.6
	.5		.4	Fixed/Worth		.4		.3
	1.0		.7			.9		.7
	NM		1.3			4.1		1.3
	1.2		.6	Debt/Worth		1.1		.8
	1.7		2.3			3.0		2.4
	NM		3.6			7.4		4.5
	61.2		26.2	% Profit Before Taxes/Tangible Net Worth		56.3		41.9
(10)	21.3		18.1		(31)	14.8	(33)	13.8
	13.8		6.2			5.1		2.6
	20.2		17.9	% Profit Before Taxes/Total Assets		10.7		11.4
	7.2		4.7			2.5		4.4
	6.1		1.9			.5		-.2
	23.7		21.9	Sales/Net Fixed Assets		19.7		23.5
	12.2		8.4			5.9		7.7
	6.3		3.5			3.5		4.5
	3.1		2.4	Sales/Total Assets		2.3		3.2
	2.3		1.9			1.5		1.9
	1.5		1.3			1.1		1.2
	.7			% Depr., Dep., Amort./Sales		1.2		1.0
(11)	1.1				(33)	2.3	(33)	1.8
	2.0					3.2		2.7
				% Officers', Directors' Owners' Comp/Sales				

0-500M	500M-2MM	2-10MM	10-50MM	50-100MM	100-250MM		Hist	Hist
283M	22271M	147112M	522565M	481915M	499925M	Net Sales ($)	1851804M	1722903M
141M	9522M	65489M	277400M	289069M	326557M	Total Assets ($)	1400218M	1262660M

M = $ thousand　　MM = $ million
See Pages 11 through 21 for Explanation of Ratios and Data

Comparative Historical Data				Current Data Sorted by Sales					
			Type of Statement						
11	12	10	Unqualified				1	2	7
8	7	9	Reviewed	1	2		2	2	2
2	2	5	Compiled		3			1	1
3	1	3	Tax Returns	1	1		1		
14	9	11	Other				3	3	5
4/1/04-3/31/05 ALL	**4/1/05-3/31/06 ALL**	**4/1/06-3/31/07 ALL**		**16 (4/1-9/30/06)**			**22 (10/1/06-3/31/07)**		
				0-1MM	**1-3MM**	**3-5MM**	**5-10MM**	**10-25MM**	**25MM & OVER**
38	31	38	**NUMBER OF STATEMENTS**	2	6		7	8	15
%	%	%	**ASSETS**	%	%	%	%	%	%
7.3	6.5	5.8	Cash & Equivalents			**DATA NOT AVAILABLE**			5.9
19.6	18.0	20.2	Trade Receivables (net)						19.6
35.1	38.0	35.0	Inventory						35.6
3.5	2.2	2.3	All Other Current						3.9
65.5	64.8	63.3	Total Current						65.0
26.0	26.5	25.7	Fixed Assets (net)						24.4
3.7	1.8	4.2	Intangibles (net)						4.3
4.8	6.9	6.7	All Other Non-Current						6.3
100.0	100.0	100.0	Total						100.0
			LIABILITIES						
15.9	18.4	12.1	Notes Payable-Short Term						15.2
2.2	1.9	2.4	Cur. Mat.-L.T.D.						2.4
14.7	18.2	20.0	Trade Payables						17.4
.5	.2	.4	Income Taxes Payable						.7
8.2	4.8	7.2	All Other Current						4.9
41.4	43.5	42.0	Total Current						40.6
13.9	14.9	17.1	Long-Term Debt						20.3
.7	.5	.5	Deferred Taxes						.4
4.5	9.8	6.0	All Other Non-Current						9.9
39.5	31.3	34.4	Net Worth						28.8
100.0	100.0	100.0	Total Liabilities & Net Worth						100.0
			INCOME DATA						
100.0	100.0	100.0	Net Sales						100.0
33.3	27.7	32.1	Gross Profit						23.8
27.7	24.1	23.9	Operating Expenses						17.6
5.6	3.5	8.2	Operating Profit						6.2
2.1	3.2	2.6	All Other Expenses (net)						1.8
3.5	.4	5.6	Profit Before Taxes						4.4
			RATIOS						
2.4	2.5	2.1							2.0
1.5	1.5	1.8	Current						1.6
1.2	1.1	1.2							1.2
1.3	.8	1.1							.8
.7	.5	.6	Quick						.6
.3	.3	.4							.4
24 15.0	**31** 11.9	**23** 16.2							**33** 11.0
36 10.0	**36** 10.1	**37** 10.0	Sales/Receivables						**39** 9.3
43 8.4	**45** 8.2	**48** 7.6							**49** 7.4
60 6.0	**89** 4.1	**51** 7.1							**62** 5.9
79 4.6	**124** 3.0	**77** 4.7	Cost of Sales/Inventory						**78** 4.7
175 2.1	**169** 2.2	**119** 3.1							**113** 3.2
13 27.6	**19** 19.1	**18** 19.9							**17** 21.0
29 12.6	**51** 7.2	**31** 11.7	Cost of Sales/Payables						**30** 12.2
51 7.1	**100** 3.7	**80** 4.5							**83** 4.4
5.1	4.8	5.6							5.7
9.4	7.4	9.3	Sales/Working Capital						9.8
15.3	24.9	18.8							12.7
14.0	4.2	7.3							7.8
2.6	1.7	(37) 4.4	EBIT/Interest						2.4
1.0	-1.0	2.1							1.6
8.0	21.8	13.2							
(14) 2.5	(13) 3.5	(10) 3.2	Net Profit + Depr., Dep., Amort./Cur. Mat. L/T/D						
1.2	-1.2	1.4							
.4	.5	.5							.5
.7	.8	1.0	Fixed/Worth						1.1
1.2	12.6	1.9							2.6
.8	1.2	1.0							1.3
1.9	2.3	2.3	Debt/Worth						3.2
4.4	24.3	10.6							9.7
47.1	29.3	31.7							50.9
(35) 15.7	(24) 10.5	(34) 17.3	% Profit Before Taxes/Tangible Net Worth						(14) 18.1
2.0	.9	7.8							-3.2
14.8	6.2	15.0							15.0
3.3	1.6	6.3	% Profit Before Taxes/Total Assets						5.2
.1	-3.5	2.3							1.9
26.0	16.2	23.6							13.6
8.6	5.3	9.7	Sales/Net Fixed Assets						8.0
4.7	4.0	4.9							4.7
3.0	2.1	2.7							2.4
1.9	1.5	2.0	Sales/Total Assets						1.7
1.3	1.2	1.4							1.4
.9	1.0	.9							1.3
(34) 1.8	(30) 2.0	(35) 1.7	% Depr., Dep., Amort./Sales						(14) 1.9
3.2	3.5	2.5							2.8
			% Officers', Directors' Owners' Comp/Sales						
1673383M	1652625M	1674071M	Net Sales ($)	283M	12311M		49197M	114481M	1497799M
1148284M	1275277M	968178M	Total Assets ($)	141M	9075M		36089M	41431M	881442M

M = $ thousand MM = $ million

See Pages 11 through 21 for Explanation of Ratios and Data

Current Data Sorted by Assets   Comparative Historical Data

0-500M	500M-2MM	2-10MM	10-50MM	50-100MM	100-250MM	Type of Statement	4/1/02-3/31/03 ALL	4/1/03-3/31/04 ALL
3			13	5	5	Unqualified	31	29
1			3	1		Reviewed	11	12
	2	4				Compiled	5	3
	2	1				Tax Returns		3
	2	2				Other	9	18
		1						
14 (4/1-9/30/06)			50 (10/1/06-3/31/07)					
0-500M	**500M-2MM**	**2-10MM**	**10-50MM**	**50-100MM**	**100-250MM**	**NUMBER OF STATEMENTS**	**56**	**65**
4	6	8	23	15	8			
%	%	%	%	%	%	**ASSETS**	%	%
			5.4	8.3		Cash & Equivalents	7.3	7.6
			29.1	27.2		Trade Receivables (net)	28.1	25.0
			10.1	14.6		Inventory	10.8	12.1
			2.5	3.2		All Other Current	2.6	5.1
			47.2	53.3		Total Current	48.8	49.7
			46.7	38.7		Fixed Assets (net)	39.1	38.6
			1.0	1.2		Intangibles (net)	1.7	4.2
			5.2	6.9		All Other Non-Current	10.4	7.5
			100.0	100.0		Total	100.0	100.0
						LIABILITIES		
			7.1	10.6		Notes Payable-Short Term	5.2	9.8
			4.5	2.6		Cur. Mat.-L.T.D.	2.2	2.7
			21.8	20.3		Trade Payables	20.6	21.0
			.0	.9		Income Taxes Payable	.1	.1
			10.3	8.7		All Other Current	13.7	11.7
			43.8	43.1		Total Current	41.9	45.3
			19.0	19.2		Long-Term Debt	12.5	16.0
			.8	1.0		Deferred Taxes	.5	.5
			2.6	2.0		All Other Non-Current	2.5	3.9
			33.8	34.7		Net Worth	42.7	34.4
			100.0	100.0		Total Liabilities & Net Worth	100.0	100.0
						INCOME DATA		
			100.0	100.0		Net Sales	100.0	100.0
			23.5	18.3		Gross Profit	20.6	21.1
			21.7	15.7		Operating Expenses	17.6	18.9
			1.8	2.6		Operating Profit	3.1	2.2
			.5	.7		All Other Expenses (net)	.1	.7
			1.3	1.9		Profit Before Taxes	2.9	1.5
						RATIOS		
			1.3	1.6			1.6	1.6
			1.0	1.4		Current	1.2	1.2
			.8	1.1			1.0	1.0
			1.1	1.2			1.1	1.2
			.7	.9		Quick	.9	.8
			.5	.4			.6	.5
		24	15.2	24 15.1			21 17.2	23 16.1
		29	12.4	29 12.4		Sales/Receivables	25 14.8	27 13.4
		35	10.5	39 9.4			31 11.6	34 10.7
		10	35.1	7 51.6			6 63.0	8 44.1
		14	26.6	18 20.5		Cost of Sales/Inventory	12 30.4	15 23.9
		16	23.2	54 6.7			18 20.5	23 15.7
		22	17.0	18 19.8			17 21.7	20 18.7
		30	12.4	25 14.3		Cost of Sales/Payables	23 15.7	27 13.8
		33	11.2	41 9.0			30 12.3	34 10.8
			37.0	11.5			19.6	18.6
			314.5	19.4		Sales/Working Capital	48.3	46.1
			-41.8	113.3			-287.9	NM
			9.7	8.4			21.1	12.2
			(21) 3.1	(14) 2.7		EBIT/Interest	(52) 7.6	(59) 3.7
			1.3	1.4			3.0	.8
						Net Profit + Depr., Dep.,	10.8	6.8
						Amort./Cur. Mat. L/T/D	(17) 4.7	(22) 3.4
							3.0	1.6
			.7	.7			.6	.7
			1.4	1.0		Fixed/Worth	.9	1.1
			3.0	2.7			1.6	2.0
			1.1	.8			.7	.8
			2.2	1.3		Debt/Worth	1.3	1.8
			4.2	6.4			3.5	5.0
			34.1	34.8			34.4	31.4
			(21) 12.0	12.0		% Profit Before Taxes/Tangible Net Worth	(55) 18.7	(61) 12.2
			3.8	5.1			8.6	2.5
			10.0	10.7			14.1	12.1
			4.0	4.4		% Profit Before Taxes/Total Assets	8.4	4.2
			.7	1.5			2.5	.2
			9.9	10.3			18.5	13.8
			6.4	5.4		Sales/Net Fixed Assets	9.3	8.7
			5.1	3.6			5.8	5.2
			4.1	4.7			5.5	4.7
			3.3	2.5		Sales/Total Assets	3.5	3.1
			2.6	1.5			2.6	2.4
			1.6	.9			.7	.9
			(21) 2.3	1.6		% Depr., Dep., Amort./Sales	(52) 1.6	(60) 1.8
			3.3	3.1			2.4	2.6
						% Officers', Directors' Owners' Comp/Sales		
2014M	43286M	91768M	2487425M	3590323M	3319064M	Net Sales ($)	9017587M	10558643M
681M	7023M	32951M	705536M	1020365M	1334108M	Total Assets ($)	2071222M	2893392M

M = $ thousand   MM = $ million

See Pages 11 through 21 for Explanation of Ratios and Data

Comparative Historical Data   Current Data Sorted by Sales

Type of Statement	4/1/04-3/31/05 ALL	4/1/05-3/31/06 ALL	4/1/06-3/31/07 ALL	0-1MM	1-3MM	3-5MM	5-10MM	10-25MM	25MM & OVER
Unqualified	27	24	30	3	1		1	2	23
Reviewed	9	7	8		1		1	2	4
Compiled	1	6	4			1	2	1	
Tax Returns		3	3			1	1	1	
Other	17	22	19						19
					14 (4/1-9/30/06)		50 (10/1/06-3/31/07)		
NUMBER OF STATEMENTS	54	62	64	3	2	2	5	6	46
ASSETS	%	%	%	%	%	%	%	%	%
Cash & Equivalents	8.0	6.1	7.1						5.6
Trade Receivables (net)	27.4	25.5	26.2						27.3
Inventory	11.3	12.8	13.1						12.9
All Other Current	2.8	4.3	3.0						3.5
Total Current	49.6	48.7	49.4						49.3
Fixed Assets (net)	40.0	41.5	39.3						42.1
Intangibles (net)	2.7	2.6	3.0						1.9
All Other Non-Current	7.7	7.1	8.3						6.7
Total	100.0	100.0	100.0						100.0
LIABILITIES									
Notes Payable-Short Term	5.2	6.1	7.2						7.7
Cur. Mat.-L.T.D.	2.8	2.9	3.5						3.5
Trade Payables	20.4	21.3	20.8						21.7
Income Taxes Payable	.1	.2	.3						.4
All Other Current	9.5	10.8	10.2						9.5
Total Current	38.1	41.3	42.0						42.8
Long-Term Debt	14.6	14.4	18.1						17.6
Deferred Taxes	.6	.8	.7						.7
All Other Non-Current	7.1	5.7	3.9						4.1
Net Worth	39.7	37.8	35.3						34.7
Total Liabilties & Net Worth	100.0	100.0	100.0						100.0
INCOME DATA									
Net Sales	100.0	100.0	100.0						100.0
Gross Profit	17.6	19.6	22.3						20.7
Operating Expenses	16.0	17.7	19.4						18.2
Operating Profit	1.6	1.9	2.9						2.5
All Other Expenses (net)	.9	.7	1.0						.9
Profit Before Taxes	.7	1.2	1.9						1.6
RATIOS									
Current	1.7	1.8	1.6						1.4
	1.2	1.2	1.1						1.1
	1.0	1.0	.9						.9
Quick	1.4	1.2	1.1						1.1
	.9	.8	.7						.7
	.6	.4	.5						.5
Sales/Receivables	**23** 15.6	**18** 20.4	**22** 16.6						**24** 15.3
	26 14.0	**27** 13.6	**27** 13.5						**29** 12.6
	32 11.3	**33** 11.0	**34** 10.6						**37** 9.8
Cost of Sales/Inventory	**6** 56.3	**7** 52.3	**9** 39.1						**9** 40.0
	11 32.9	**13** 29.1	**14** 25.7						**14** 26.4
	23 15.7	**20** 18.4	**28** 13.2						**27** 13.3
Cost of Sales/Payables	**17** 21.6	**17** 21.4	**19** 19.4						**21** 17.8
	25 14.3	**25** 14.6	**26** 14.2						**26** 13.9
	32 11.4	**32** 11.4	**33** 11.1						**33** 10.9
Sales/Working Capital	16.8	13.6	19.4						19.3
	50.3	61.4	42.5						93.6
	205.4	-143.4	-148.2						-102.8
EBIT/Interest	22.5	8.4	9.2						9.2
	(48) 7.0	(54) 2.6	(55) 3.3						(41) 2.8
	1.5	.6	1.3						1.3
Net Profit + Depr., Dep., Amort./Cur. Mat. L/T/D	6.6	4.1	5.0						4.6
	(19) 3.6	(18) 1.9	(20) 2.0						(17) 2.1
	1.2	1.2	1.3						1.4
Fixed/Worth	.6	.6	.7						.7
	.9	1.1	1.2						1.2
	1.4	2.3	2.3						2.5
Debt/Worth	.8	.6	1.1						1.1
	1.4	1.6	1.8						2.1
	2.9	5.1	4.4						4.7
% Profit Before Taxes/Tangible Net Worth	25.9	26.9	36.3						35.9
	(52) 14.0	(57) 11.8	(59) 13.2						(44) 12.0
	3.7	-.8	4.1						4.2
% Profit Before Taxes/Total Assets	11.3	7.8	13.1						10.0
	5.2	3.2	4.4						4.0
	.2	-.7	1.6						1.0
Sales/Net Fixed Assets	21.2	22.9	13.7						10.4
	7.6	6.9	7.9						6.5
	4.8	4.8	5.0						4.8
Sales/Total Assets	5.1	5.4	4.5						3.8
	3.3	3.1	3.1						2.9
	2.3	2.3	2.2						2.2
% Depr., Dep., Amort./Sales	.6	.8	1.3						1.3
	(53) 1.7	(57) 2.1	(58) 1.8						(42) 1.9
	2.8	3.6	3.1						3.1
% Officers', Directors' Owners' Comp/Sales									
Net Sales ($)	9429136M	10473655M	9533880M	771M	2780M	7737M	38501M	87279M	9396812M
Total Assets ($)	2567690M	2951686M	3100664M	338M	3201M	1523M	10253M	25340M	3060009M

© RMA 2007

M = $ thousand   MM = $ million
See Pages 11 through 21 for Explanation of Ratios and Data

Current Data Sorted by Assets							Comparative Historical Data	

0-500M	500M-2MM	2-10MM	10-50MM	50-100MM	100-250MM	**Type of Statement**		
	1	8	14	2	4	Unqualified	21	27
	2	6	6		1	Reviewed	7	12
		5				Compiled	11	10
	1	2	1			Tax Returns	3	2
	5	5	8	4	5	Other	17	21
	20 (4/1-9/30/06)		**55 (10/1/06-3/31/07)**				4/1/02-3/31/03 ALL	4/1/03-3/31/04 ALL
	4	26	29	6	10	**NUMBER OF STATEMENTS**	59	72
%	%	%	%	%	%	**ASSETS**	%	%
D		7.8	5.7		7.3	Cash & Equivalents	7.0	5.9
A		23.5	21.1		18.1	Trade Receivables (net)	21.6	20.8
T		25.0	23.8		21.8	Inventory	25.4	25.6
A		2.4	1.4		2.1	All Other Current	2.1	2.0
		58.7	52.0		49.3	Total Current	56.0	54.3
N		36.1	40.3		38.8	Fixed Assets (net)	37.9	37.7
O		.6	3.2		8.7	Intangibles (net)	1.9	3.2
T		4.6	4.5		3.2	All Other Non-Current	4.1	4.8
		100.0	100.0		100.0	Total	100.0	100.0
A						**LIABILITIES**		
V		9.8	12.3		3.4	Notes Payable-Short Term	10.4	10.5
A		4.9	3.2		2.6	Cur. Mat.-L.T.D.	4.1	3.6
I		19.2	12.9		15.1	Trade Payables	14.9	16.4
L		.2	.1		.3	Income Taxes Payable	.1	.3
A		2.3	8.9		6.9	All Other Current	7.3	7.5
B		36.4	37.4		28.3	Total Current	36.8	38.3
L		19.0	20.9		30.8	Long-Term Debt	19.3	18.8
E		.9	.7		1.3	Deferred Taxes	.5	1.0
		3.2	2.2		2.6	All Other Non-Current	5.3	3.9
		40.5	38.8		37.1	Net Worth	38.1	38.0
		100.0	100.0		100.0	Total Liabilities & Net Worth	100.0	100.0
						INCOME DATA		
		100.0	100.0		100.0	Net Sales	100.0	100.0
		17.4	14.4		14.1	Gross Profit	16.4	18.9
		12.4	11.6		9.2	Operating Expenses	12.6	14.0
		5.0	2.8		4.9	Operating Profit	3.9	5.0
		.8	1.0		.9	All Other Expenses (net)	1.1	1.1
		4.2	1.8		4.0	Profit Before Taxes	2.7	3.9
						RATIOS		
		2.3	2.1		2.2		2.3	2.3
		1.7	1.5		1.8	Current	1.6	1.3
		1.1	1.0		1.6		1.1	1.0
		1.3	1.1		1.4		1.4	1.3
		.9	.7		1.0	Quick	.8	.6
		.5	.4		.7		.4	.3
		18 20.0	21 17.1		23 15.8		20 17.8	20 18.3
		30 12.3	28 12.9		25 14.6	Sales/Receivables	27 13.4	30 12.3
		39 9.5	34 10.7		33 11.1		33 11.2	38 9.6
		11 34.4	16 22.1		28 13.0		15 23.6	19 18.8
		33 11.1	28 13.0		35 10.5	Cost of Sales/Inventory	34 10.8	37 10.0
		59 6.2	72 5.1		50 7.3		70 5.2	72 5.1
		15 24.0	15 24.0		19 19.3		13 28.2	13 27.8
		23 15.6	24 15.4		24 15.0	Cost of Sales/Payables	20 17.8	26 14.2
		33 11.0	29 12.4		32 11.3		29 12.4	36 10.2
		8.8	8.8		8.7		8.3	7.9
		19.6	22.5		10.9	Sales/Working Capital	16.4	20.2
		109.1	NM		16.4		72.0	198.2
		10.4	4.3		43.9		8.7	14.7
		(23) 3.9	(28) 2.4		5.9	EBIT/Interest	(54) 3.6	(67) 3.5
		1.9	1.3		1.4		1.9	1.3
			4.0				8.4	6.8
			(13) 2.2			Net Profit + Depr., Dep., Amort./Cur. Mat. L/T/D	(18) 3.6	(23) 2.9
			1.6				2.5	1.2
		.5	.8		.6		.6	.6
		1.0	1.1		1.2	Fixed/Worth	1.1	1.0
		1.9	1.8		NM		1.4	2.6
		.7	1.0		.5		.7	.7
		1.5	1.5		2.2	Debt/Worth	1.7	1.7
		3.3	3.8		NM		3.5	5.2
		51.8	18.0				37.8	30.9
		(23) 12.7	(27) 13.7			% Profit Before Taxes/Tangible Net Worth	(55) 13.3	(64) 19.4
		3.6	4.3				3.3	5.9
		17.0	7.7		19.1		10.8	16.3
		8.9	3.8		7.0	% Profit Before Taxes/Total Assets	4.7	5.9
		2.3	1.0		2.2		2.0	.8
		20.0	11.8		10.2		12.2	12.4
		8.8	5.6		6.0	Sales/Net Fixed Assets	8.0	6.9
		4.2	3.3		4.7		4.2	3.8
		4.4	3.3		3.0		3.7	3.5
		3.3	2.5		2.6	Sales/Total Assets	2.6	2.5
		2.1	1.8		1.8		1.9	1.6
		1.1	1.3				1.3	1.2
		(24) 1.5	(28) 1.9			% Depr., Dep., Amort./Sales	(55) 2.0	(64) 2.0
		2.3	2.5				2.6	2.9
		.8					.5	1.4
		(13) 2.3				% Officers', Directors' Owners' Comp/Sales	(16) 1.1	(19) 2.3
		5.3					3.0	5.6
	18065M	492866M	2014436M	1305687M	4454761M	Net Sales ($)	4502938M	5983105M
	6045M	148831M	714095M	453325M	1743640M	Total Assets ($)	1812598M	2629482M

Note: Column 0-500M — DATA NOT AVAILABLE

M = $ thousand   MM = $ million
See Pages 11 through 21 for Explanation of Ratios and Data

Comparative Historical Data | Current Data Sorted by Sales

Type of Statement

4/1/04-3/31/05	4/1/05-3/31/06	4/1/06-3/31/07	Type of Statement	0-1MM	1-3MM	3-5MM	5-10MM	10-25MM	25MM & OVER
35	24	29	Unqualified			1	1	5	22
11	12	15	Reviewed			2	1	3	9
6	5	5	Compiled		1			3	1
3	2	4	Tax Returns				2		2
17	26	22	Other				1	6	15
ALL	ALL	ALL							

Header notes for current data: **20 (4/1-9/30/06)** and **55 (10/1/06-3/31/07)**.

Main Data

04-05 ALL	05-06 ALL	06-07 ALL		0-1MM	1-3MM	3-5MM	5-10MM	10-25MM	25MM & OVER
72	69	75	**NUMBER OF STATEMENTS**		1	3	5	17	49
%	%	%	**ASSETS**	%	%	%	%	%	%
5.6	5.3	6.6	Cash & Equivalents					8.0	6.6
21.8	22.0	21.5	Trade Receivables (net)					19.7	22.6
26.5	24.1	23.6	Inventory					20.5	21.9
2.5	1.8	1.8	All Other Current	DATA NOT AVAILABLE				2.4	1.7
56.4	53.2	53.6	Total Current					50.6	52.8
36.3	39.9	39.2	Fixed Assets (net)					43.3	39.1
2.7	1.8	2.9	Intangibles (net)					2.4	3.3
4.6	5.1	4.2	All Other Non-Current					3.7	4.8
100.0	100.0	100.0	Total					100.0	100.0
			LIABILITIES						
11.0	10.6	9.8	Notes Payable-Short Term					13.4	8.3
3.2	2.6	3.5	Cur. Mat.-L.T.D.					3.0	3.9
17.1	16.5	15.8	Trade Payables					13.9	16.4
.2	.1	.1	Income Taxes Payable					.3	.1
7.3	6.6	6.4	All Other Current						7.9
38.7	36.5	35.6	Total Current					34.1	36.6
16.3	19.7	21.3	Long-Term Debt					21.3	21.9
.9	.8	.8	Deferred Taxes					1.4	.7
10.7	4.2	3.0	All Other Non-Current					2.8	2.3
33.4	38.8	39.2	Net Worth					40.4	38.5
100.0	100.0	100.0	Total Liabilties & Net Worth					100.0	100.0
			INCOME DATA						
100.0	100.0	100.0	Net Sales					100.0	100.0
16.3	14.9	16.5	Gross Profit					16.3	16.1
13.0	11.5	12.7	Operating Expenses					12.3	12.6
3.3	3.4	3.8	Operating Profit					4.0	3.5
.6	.7	.9	All Other Expenses (net)					1.4	.6
2.6	2.7	2.9	Profit Before Taxes					2.6	2.8
			RATIOS						
2.3 / 1.4 / 1.1	2.1 / 1.6 / 1.0	2.2 / 1.6 / 1.1	Current					2.2 / 1.7 / 1.0	2.0 / 1.6 / 1.0
1.2 / .7 / .4	1.3 / .7 / .4	1.2 / .8 / .5	Quick					1.3 / .9 / .5	1.3 / .8 / .5
19 19.5 / 25 14.3 / 36 10.2	20 18.6 / 26 14.2 / 34 10.9	22 16.8 / 28 13.2 / 34 10.7	Sales/Receivables					19 19.3 / 33 11.1 / 40 9.1	22 16.5 / 27 13.7 / 32 11.6
18 20.4 / 30 12.3 / 71 5.1	16 22.7 / 29 12.6 / 54 6.7	17 21.3 / 31 11.7 / 58 6.3	Cost of Sales/Inventory					10 35.9 / 39 9.4 / 60 6.1	16 22.1 / 27 13.5 / 48 7.6
15 24.3 / 22 16.6 / 32 11.4	16 22.3 / 22 16.8 / 29 12.4	16 22.9 / 24 15.0 / 31 11.7	Cost of Sales/Payables					16 22.6 / 20 18.3 / 28 13.2	16 23.0 / 24 15.0 / 30 12.0
8.6 / 18.5 / 72.8	10.4 / 24.9 / 310.3	9.0 / 20.7 / 82.1	Sales/Working Capital					7.2 / 14.6 / 537.5	9.8 / 22.5 / 171.7
19.2 / (68) 4.4 / 1.3	10.1 / (63) 4.0 / 1.8	9.4 / (71) 3.2 / 1.3	EBIT/Interest					7.0 / (15) 2.3 / 1.2	13.3 / (48) 3.3 / 1.4
5.6 / (26) 2.5 / 1.8	9.4 / (19) 3.3 / 2.0	7.5 / (25) 2.2 / 1.6	Net Profit + Depr., Dep., Amort./Cur. Mat. L/T/D						9.8 / (18) 2.6 / 1.9
.6 / 1.2 / 2.3	.6 / 1.0 / 2.2	.7 / 1.1 / 2.2	Fixed/Worth					.7 / 1.1 / 1.9	.7 / 1.0 / 2.1
.7 / 2.4 / 6.4	1.0 / 1.8 / 3.7	.7 / 1.5 / 4.0	Debt/Worth					.7 / 1.6 / 3.4	.7 / 1.5 / 4.2
35.1 / (63) 20.9 / 7.3	35.7 / (67) 16.1 / 5.6	30.1 / (68) 13.7 / 4.4	% Profit Before Taxes/Tangible Net Worth					21.7 / (15) 12.7 / 3.6	31.3 / (44) 14.0 / 5.4
11.7 / 6.1 / 1.0	10.8 / 5.4 / 1.8	12.7 / 5.5 / 1.4	% Profit Before Taxes/Total Assets					14.7 / 4.6 / 1.4	11.9 / 5.7 / 1.3
12.0 / 8.2 / 4.9	15.5 / 7.9 / 4.2	13.6 / 7.0 / 4.0	Sales/Net Fixed Assets					12.3 / 4.3 / 3.3	14.0 / 7.5 / 5.2
3.6 / 2.6 / 1.9	3.9 / 3.1 / 1.9	3.8 / 2.7 / 2.1	Sales/Total Assets					3.5 / 2.3 / 1.8	4.2 / 3.1 / 2.2
1.2 / (69) 1.7 / 2.3	1.0 / (59) 1.5 / 2.1	1.3 / (67) 1.7 / 2.4	% Depr., Dep., Amort./Sales					1.6 / 1.9 / 3.1	1.2 / (43) 1.5 / 2.3
.6 / (18) 1.2 / 2.6	.6 / (18) 1.5 / 2.4	.8 / (22) 2.0 / 4.0	% Officers', Directors' Owners' Comp/Sales						.8 / (12) 2.0 / 5.3
7050082M	9030883M	8285815M	Net Sales ($)		1962M	10298M	38802M	281318M	7953435M
2510156M	3244404M	3065936M	Total Assets ($)		3210M	4594M	20405M	130725M	2907002M

Current Data Sorted by Assets   Comparative Historical Data

						Type of Statement		
			3	1	1	Unqualified	3	5
		3				Reviewed	5	1
		1				Compiled	2	4
		2				Tax Returns	7	
3	3	3	8		1	Other	5	9
1	2		26 (10/1/06-3/31/07)				4/1/02-	4/1/03-
	6 (4/1-9/30/06)						3/31/03	3/31/04
0-500M	500M-2MM	2-10MM	10-50MM	50-100MM	100-250MM		ALL	ALL
4	5	9	11	1	2	NUMBER OF STATEMENTS	22	19
%	%	%	%	%	%	**ASSETS**	%	%
			4.2			Cash & Equivalents	10.1	11.1
			12.0			Trade Receivables (net)	13.2	13.5
			18.2			Inventory	16.3	14.4
			3.1			All Other Current	1.8	3.2
			37.4			Total Current	41.4	42.2
			41.9			Fixed Assets (net)	49.4	40.9
			14.9			Intangibles (net)	4.3	9.6
			5.7			All Other Non-Current	4.9	7.4
			100.0			Total	100.0	100.0
						LIABILITIES		
			9.7			Notes Payable-Short Term	3.5	5.0
			7.8			Cur. Mat.-L.T.D.	8.6	5.5
			11.3			Trade Payables	11.8	11.5
			.0			Income Taxes Payable	.0	.1
			7.3			All Other Current	4.5	5.0
			36.1			Total Current	28.5	27.1
			21.3			Long-Term Debt	27.3	21.7
			2.7			Deferred Taxes	.1	1.2
			3.4			All Other Non-Current	3.5	4.0
			36.5			Net Worth	40.6	46.0
			100.0			Total Liabilties & Net Worth	100.0	100.0
						INCOME DATA		
			100.0			Net Sales	100.0	100.0
			19.9			Gross Profit	38.6	31.2
			18.4			Operating Expenses	32.4	25.6
			1.5			Operating Profit	6.2	5.6
			1.4			All Other Expenses (net)	1.3	1.0
			.1			Profit Before Taxes	4.9	4.6
						RATIOS		
			1.7				2.2	2.4
			1.2			Current	1.7	1.5
			.7				.7	.9
			.8				1.3	1.5
			.4			Quick	.8	.9
			.2				.3	.4
		13	27.9				3 141.8	13 28.0
		22	16.8			Sales/Receivables	17 21.6	17 20.9
		28	12.8				26 14.2	29 12.5
		18	20.7				13 27.2	18 20.3
		40	9.2			Cost of Sales/Inventory	31 11.9	26 14.1
		64	5.7				44 8.3	50 7.4
		16	23.3				3 121.5	11 32.8
		24	15.1			Cost of Sales/Payables	19 19.2	22 16.3
		41	8.8				25 14.7	37 9.9
			11.4				13.8	8.5
			92.7			Sales/Working Capital	24.0	17.5
			-15.8				-24.6	-38.2
			8.3				14.3	15.6
		(10)	3.8			EBIT/Interest	(20) 4.3	(17) 3.5
			-.1				1.0	1.1
						Net Profit + Depr., Dep., Amort./Cur. Mat. L/T/D		
			1.2				.6	.6
			1.7			Fixed/Worth	1.7	1.2
			5.1				4.5	3.3
			1.3				.8	.5
			3.3			Debt/Worth	2.5	1.1
			6.0				5.5	5.2
						% Profit Before Taxes/Tangible Net Worth	71.9	51.0
							(20) 36.2	(17) 13.7
							-.2	.8
			11.5			% Profit Before Taxes/Total Assets	30.3	19.2
			2.9				12.3	7.6
			-5.8				.1	.5
			11.5				11.6	7.3
			6.0			Sales/Net Fixed Assets	8.1	6.1
			2.6				3.7	3.6
			3.0				4.5	3.2
			1.8			Sales/Total Assets	3.3	2.2
			1.0				2.1	1.7
			2.1				1.9	2.6
			2.9			% Depr., Dep., Amort./Sales	(20) 2.6	(13) 3.2
			5.1				3.5	3.8
						% Officers', Directors' Owners' Comp/Sales		
1493M	16022M	98082M	515492M	92609M	691019M	Net Sales ($)	829771M	796206M
643M	4577M	40733M	260440M	60217M	319821M	Total Assets ($)	286143M	392117M

M = $ thousand   MM = $ million
See Pages 11 through 21 for Explanation of Ratios and Data

Comparative Historical Data — Current Data Sorted by Sales

4/1/04-3/31/05 ALL	4/1/05-3/31/06 ALL	4/1/06-3/31/07 ALL	Type of Statement	0-1MM	1-3MM	3-5MM	5-10MM	10-25MM	25MM & OVER
9	7	5	Unqualified					1	4
3		3	Reviewed					2	
3	4	1	Compiled				1	1	
1	1	8	Tax Returns	4	1	2	1	1	
5	13	15	Other	1	2	1	1	3	7
4/1/04-3/31/05 ALL	4/1/05-3/31/06 ALL	4/1/06-3/31/07 ALL			6 (4/1-9/30/06)			26 (10/1/06-3/31/07)	
21	25	32	NUMBER OF STATEMENTS	5	3	4	3	6	11
%	%	%	**ASSETS**	%	%	%	%	%	%
11.1	9.1	4.6	Cash & Equivalents						7.5
15.9	14.9	12.5	Trade Receivables (net)						14.3
21.4	21.7	17.2	Inventory						16.4
2.3	2.3	2.1	All Other Current						3.4
50.8	48.0	36.5	Total Current						41.6
39.4	40.6	46.3	Fixed Assets (net)						40.2
2.6	4.0	11.1	Intangibles (net)						12.6
7.3	7.4	6.1	All Other Non-Current						5.6
100.0	100.0	100.0	Total						100.0
			LIABILITIES						
6.1	12.1	10.1	Notes Payable-Short Term						9.4
3.4	3.8	5.5	Cur. Mat.-L.T.D.						7.6
14.3	14.3	13.0	Trade Payables						10.9
.0	.0	.0	Income Taxes Payable						.0
7.5	5.5	15.3	All Other Current						11.7
31.4	35.7	43.9	Total Current						39.6
18.4	26.3	28.3	Long-Term Debt						13.4
1.1	1.2	.9	Deferred Taxes						2.1
5.4	3.5	7.2	All Other Non-Current						8.2
43.8	33.3	19.7	Net Worth						36.7
100.0	100.0	100.0	Total Liabilties & Net Worth						100.0
			INCOME DATA						
100.0	100.0	100.0	Net Sales						100.0
31.3	30.6	34.0	Gross Profit						25.7
25.7	27.0	32.2	Operating Expenses						21.6
5.6	3.6	1.7	Operating Profit						4.1
.4	1.7	1.9	All Other Expenses (net)						1.3
5.2	1.9	-.2	Profit Before Taxes						2.7
			RATIOS						
2.8	1.7	1.8	Current						1.8
1.5	1.4	1.0							.9
1.1	1.0	.7							.7
2.3	1.2	.8	Quick						1.0
.8	(24) .6	.6							.6
.5	.4	.2							.2
10 35.4	13 27.9	8 44.8	Sales/Receivables					16 22.3	
19 18.9	19 19.6	19 19.0						22 16.8	
24 15.0	27 13.4	31 11.9						30 12.1	
20 17.9	23 16.1	14 25.5	Cost of Sales/Inventory					13 27.5	
46 7.9	45 8.0	33 11.2						26 14.1	
56 6.5	71 5.2	66 5.5						62 5.9	
11 31.9	19 19.5	17 21.6	Cost of Sales/Payables					16 23.3	
21 17.3	28 13.0	25 14.5						22 16.6	
29 12.8	42 8.6	41 8.9						35 10.4	
8.6	11.8	11.5	Sales/Working Capital						11.4
15.5	25.8	342.0							-71.0
82.6	NM	-15.9							-15.8
11.6	6.8	5.8	EBIT/Interest						6.9
(18) 4.7	(22) 1.3	(28) 1.5						(10) 2.3	
1.3	-.3	-.4							-.1
	3.6	6.5	Net Profit + Depr., Dep.,						
	(10) 1.8	(10) 2.9	Amort./Cur. Mat. L/T/D						
	.7	.4							
.5	.5	1.2	Fixed/Worth						.6
.9	1.8	3.5							1.9
1.6	6.5	-5.2							5.1
.5	.9	1.8	Debt/Worth						.8
1.1	3.2	4.5							3.9
2.7	8.8	-16.4							6.0
31.4	38.0	42.8	% Profit Before Taxes/Tangible						
(19) 8.0	(21) 11.4	(23) 7.9	Net Worth						
3.9	-2.2	-22.8							
16.3	16.6	8.3	% Profit Before Taxes/Total						14.3
5.1	1.9	1.9	Assets						6.8
1.3	-5.2	-6.2							-5.8
12.5	10.1	9.8	Sales/Net Fixed Assets						10.0
7.1	5.4	6.0							6.2
4.2	3.7	3.0							4.6
3.8	3.6	3.1	Sales/Total Assets						3.0
3.0	1.9	2.1							2.2
1.9	1.6	1.3							1.8
1.2	1.4	1.3	% Depr., Dep., Amort./Sales						1.4
(15) 2.5	(23) 2.4	(29) 3.1						(10) 2.9	
3.2	3.6	4.8							4.7
		2.4	% Officers', Directors'						
	(11) 3.3		Owners' Comp/Sales						
		4.4							
2193232M	1209368M	1414717M	Net Sales ($)	1737M	5747M	16400M	21520M	110898M	1258415M
767071M	594539M	686431M	Total Assets ($)	1171M	22219M	11972M	6289M	63136M	581644M

© RMA 2007

M = $ thousand   MM = $ million
See Pages 11 through 21 for Explanation of Ratios and Data

Current Data Sorted by Assets   Comparative Historical Data

Type of Statement

	0-500M	500M-2MM	2-10MM	10-50MM	50-100MM	100-250MM	Type of Statement	4/1/02-3/31/03 ALL	4/1/03-3/31/04 ALL
		27 (4/1-9/30/06)		77 (10/1/06-3/31/07)					
Unqualified			9	19	3	5	Unqualified	35	29
Reviewed		2	9	3	2		Reviewed	16	26
Compiled		4	5	4	1		Compiled	16	18
Tax Returns		1	1				Tax Returns	3	7
Other		6	8	16	2	4	Other	26	26
NUMBER OF STATEMENTS		13	32	42	8	9	NUMBER OF STATEMENTS	96	106

0-500M	500M-2MM	2-10MM	10-50MM	50-100MM	100-250MM		4/1/02-3/31/03	4/1/03-3/31/04
%	%	%	%	%	%	**ASSETS**	%	%
	3.1	8.9	7.7			Cash & Equivalents	8.2	9.4
D	28.7	25.3	23.7			Trade Receivables (net)	24.3	27.0
A	22.8	23.8	22.1			Inventory	21.7	19.6
T	2.0	2.2	2.4			All Other Current	4.4	2.6
A	56.6	60.2	55.9			Total Current	58.6	58.6
	36.7	28.2	33.8			Fixed Assets (net)	33.0	33.0
N	1.5	1.8	3.0			Intangibles (net)	2.3	1.7
O	5.1	9.8	7.3			All Other Non-Current	6.1	6.7
T	100.0	100.0	100.0			Total	100.0	100.0
A						**LIABILITIES**		
V	16.8	10.1	11.7			Notes Payable-Short Term	11.6	9.7
A	5.2	2.5	1.8			Cur. Mat.-L.T.D.	4.1	4.9
I	21.2	13.6	8.9			Trade Payables	11.9	12.8
L	.2	.1	.4			Income Taxes Payable	.2	.2
A	5.1	8.1	7.8			All Other Current	8.5	7.9
B	48.4	34.3	30.6			Total Current	36.4	35.5
L	19.7	15.8	16.4			Long-Term Debt	14.2	14.5
E	.1	.3	1.1			Deferred Taxes	.5	.5
	4.0	14.3	4.7			All Other Non-Current	5.9	6.6
	27.8	35.3	47.2			Net Worth	43.1	43.0
	100.0	100.0	100.0			Total Liabilities & Net Worth	100.0	100.0
						INCOME DATA		
	100.0	100.0	100.0			Net Sales	100.0	100.0
	26.1	15.8	15.8			Gross Profit	18.1	18.7
	23.5	14.1	11.6			Operating Expenses	14.6	15.8
	2.6	1.7	4.2			Operating Profit	3.6	2.9
	.8	.5	.1			All Other Expenses (net)	.2	.3
	1.8	1.1	4.1			Profit Before Taxes	3.4	2.6
						RATIOS		
	2.1	2.6	2.9			Current	2.8	2.9
	1.4	1.8	1.8				1.7	1.7
	1.0	1.1	1.3				1.3	1.2
	1.1	1.8	1.8			Quick	1.6	2.1
	.8	.8	1.0				.9	1.0
	.6	.6	.7				.6	.6
	18 20.8	13 27.8	14 25.6			Sales/Receivables	14 25.4	15 24.0
	21 17.4	18 20.0	20 18.6				19 19.0	21 17.5
	29 12.5	26 14.1	25 14.5				31 11.9	28 12.9
	11 33.6	13 27.4	11 34.5			Cost of Sales/Inventory	11 32.0	9 42.1
	21 17.5	21 17.2	22 16.8				22 16.5	21 17.3
	44 8.4	29 12.8	37 9.8				35 10.5	33 11.1
	9 39.8	6 59.7	5 71.2			Cost of Sales/Payables	6 64.4	6 57.9
	13 27.9	11 32.3	8 43.5				10 36.3	12 30.9
	32 11.4	17 22.1	15 24.0				17 21.0	18 19.9
	15.8	10.4	7.2			Sales/Working Capital	10.6	10.2
	21.9	21.6	17.7				19.2	21.8
	NM	121.7	43.0				45.8	67.4
	4.8	15.1	7.4			EBIT/Interest	14.3	14.1
	2.7	(28) 2.8	(34) 4.7				(88) 5.1	(96) 4.0
	.9	1.0	1.3				1.8	1.4
			6.5			Net Profit + Depr., Dep.,	7.5	7.1
		(10) 2.8				Amort./Cur. Mat. L/T/D	(30) 3.0	(32) 3.4
		1.9					1.0	1.2
	.2	.2	.4			Fixed/Worth	.4	.4
	1.3	.7	.8				.9	.8
	2.0	3.1	1.8				1.6	1.5
	1.6	.6	.7			Debt/Worth	.6	.6
	2.4	1.4	1.4				1.8	1.5
	5.3	6.5	2.6				3.8	3.6
	24.1	52.9	47.0			% Profit Before Taxes/Tangible	36.7	37.6
	(11) 19.1	(27) 23.6	20.2			Net Worth	(89) 16.8	(100) 18.5
	-7.5	1.6	5.1				6.5	6.1
	7.8	21.4	17.9			% Profit Before Taxes/Total	16.1	13.1
	4.2	4.7	9.1			Assets	8.3	6.2
	-.4	-.9	1.8				2.1	1.4
	49.1	94.1	24.9			Sales/Net Fixed Assets	27.3	33.0
	18.5	16.8	12.2				11.8	14.4
	3.4	8.0	5.4				6.4	6.0
	5.7	7.5	6.1			Sales/Total Assets	5.6	6.5
	4.9	4.6	3.7				3.9	3.9
	2.1	2.6	2.6				2.5	2.5
	.5	.3	.5			% Depr., Dep., Amort./Sales	.6	.5
	(11) 1.1	(26) 1.0	(39) 1.3				(85) 1.0	(95) .9
	2.0	1.9	2.1				1.9	2.2
			.6			% Officers', Directors'	1.1	.8
		(11) 1.4				Owners' Comp/Sales	(26) 2.4	(37) 2.3
		4.0					4.3	3.6
	80900M	895606M	3815739M	2326555M	3872137M	Net Sales ($)	9111829M	8899949M
	16617M	172084M	973375M	563044M	1692136M	Total Assets ($)	2414886M	2342329M

M = $ thousand   MM = $ million
See Pages 11 through 21 for Explanation of Ratios and Data

Comparative Historical Data

Current Data Sorted by Sales

	4/1/04-3/31/05 ALL	4/1/05-3/31/06 ALL	4/1/06-3/31/07 ALL	Type of Statement	0-1MM	1-3MM	3-5MM	5-10MM	10-25MM	25MM & OVER
	33	21	36	Unqualified				1	4	31
	19	16	16	Reviewed				2	3	10
	20	19	14	Compiled		1	1	4	2	6
	3	4	2	Tax Returns		1	1		1	
	23	27	36	Other		3	2	4	5	22
						27 (4/1-9/30/06)		77 (10/1/06-3/31/07)		
NUMBER OF STATEMENTS	98	87	104			5	4	11	15	69
	%	%	%	**ASSETS**	%	%	%	%	%	%
	6.1	8.2	7.3	Cash & Equivalents	D			11.8	9.5	6.5
	25.7	22.9	24.2	Trade Receivables (net)	A			19.8	24.8	25.6
	22.5	21.7	22.3	Inventory	T			23.2	21.3	23.2
	1.7	2.1	2.3	All Other Current	A			1.7	3.1	2.3
	56.1	54.9	56.1	Total Current				56.4	58.7	57.6
	34.3	35.0	33.3	Fixed Assets (net)	N			23.1	31.8	34.4
	1.7	1.8	3.1	Intangibles (net)	O			2.9	2.1	3.6
	7.9	8.3	7.6	All Other Non-Current	T			17.6	7.4	4.4
	100.0	100.0	100.0	Total				100.0	100.0	100.0
				LIABILITIES	A					
	12.8	14.1	11.9	Notes Payable-Short Term	V			11.6	5.1	13.3
	2.4	2.6	2.4	Cur. Mat.-L.T.D.	A			1.5	2.8	2.0
	13.4	11.2	12.1	Trade Payables	I			11.7	12.2	11.6
	.1	.2	.2	Income Taxes Payable	L			.0	.2	.3
	9.0	7.3	7.2	All Other Current	A			4.3	7.7	7.7
	37.7	35.3	34.0	Total Current	B			29.1	28.0	34.9
	16.6	17.7	17.2	Long-Term Debt	L			12.3	19.9	16.8
	.7	.7	.6	Deferred Taxes	E			.0	.4	.8
	4.5	4.6	8.1	All Other Non-Current				25.6	8.3	5.4
	40.5	41.7	40.1	Net Worth				33.0	43.3	42.0
	100.0	100.0	100.0	Total Liabilties & Net Worth				100.0	100.0	100.0
				INCOME DATA						
	100.0	100.0	100.0	Net Sales				100.0	100.0	100.0
	19.1	20.3	16.8	Gross Profit				20.8	18.6	13.7
	16.6	17.1	14.0	Operating Expenses				21.3	14.8	11.0
	2.5	3.2	2.7	Operating Profit				-.5	3.8	2.7
	.5	.4	.5	All Other Expenses (net)				.2	.5	.6
	2.0	2.8	2.3	Profit Before Taxes				-.6	3.3	2.2
				RATIOS						
	2.3	2.7	2.6	Current				4.0	5.2	2.4
	1.5	1.5	1.7					2.5	2.1	1.6
	1.1	1.1	1.2					1.1	1.4	1.2
	1.2	1.5	1.5	Quick				2.0	3.0	1.4
	.8	.8	.8					1.0	.8	.8
	.5	.5	.6					.6	.7	.6
	15 24.1	15 24.9	14 25.2	Sales/Receivables				17 21.3	12 31.7	15 25.1
	20 17.9	20 18.0	21 17.7					20 18.5	21 17.5	21 17.6
	30 12.1	27 13.8	27 13.4					28 13.0	29 12.6	26 14.0
	12 31.1	11 33.5	13 29.0	Cost of Sales/Inventory				19 19.7	12 29.2	11 32.0
	21 17.0	24 15.5	21 17.1					21 17.5	18 20.7	19 18.7
	37 9.8	44 8.3	37 9.8					44 8.4	29 12.7	31 11.6
	7 52.9	6 61.0	5 66.4	Cost of Sales/Payables				9 39.6	6 56.4	5 71.3
	13 29.0	12 31.0	11 32.8					13 29.1	11 34.0	10 36.7
	22 16.4	20 18.0	19 19.7					16 23.4	17 21.6	17 21.1
	14.8	10.4	10.6	Sales/Working Capital				4.0	8.2	12.1
	28.8	23.7	20.9					15.0	15.8	22.9
	159.8	96.2	57.5					104.6	31.6	58.5
	13.9	5.9	8.5	EBIT/Interest					14.7	7.8
	(91) 3.2	(78) 2.1	(91) 3.3						(14) 3.4	(60) 3.6
	1.1	.8	1.0						.9	1.1
	13.1	9.4	5.6	Net Profit + Depr., Dep., Amort./Cur. Mat. L/T/D						6.3
	(19) 3.6	(28) 2.9	(21) 2.7							(15) 2.8
	1.9	1.6	1.7							2.0
	.4	.4	.4	Fixed/Worth				.1	.3	.5
	.8	.8	.9					.3	.6	1.0
	2.0	2.1	2.3					1.3	3.1	2.1
	.7	.7	.8	Debt/Worth				.2	.5	.8
	1.9	1.7	1.6					1.2	1.4	1.5
	3.5	3.6	4.4					3.5	6.0	3.5
	33.1	28.5	42.3	% Profit Before Taxes/Tangible Net Worth					51.5	44.7
	(96) 18.2	(83) 10.2	(95) 16.7						(14) 14.1	(65) 22.1
	.8	1.9	1.6						-1.8	4.4
	12.5	12.5	14.6	% Profit Before Taxes/Total Assets				5.3	17.2	16.2
	5.0	3.0	6.1					3.9	4.4	8.7
	.1	.2	.5					.5	-1.1	1.0
	27.3	23.8	31.5	Sales/Net Fixed Assets				121.6	38.0	28.6
	12.4	11.3	12.8					18.5	14.0	12.7
	6.4	5.5	5.6					6.4	4.6	6.9
	6.6	5.4	6.0	Sales/Total Assets				5.1	6.5	6.7
	4.2	3.5	3.8					3.2	3.8	4.1
	2.4	2.3	2.4					1.9	1.8	2.8
	.5	.5	.5	% Depr., Dep., Amort./Sales				.3	.6	.5
	(87) 1.0	(82) 1.0	(89) 1.3					(10) 1.4	(13) 1.3	(59) 1.2
	2.1	2.2	2.0					2.1	3.3	1.9
	.7	.7	.5	% Officers', Directors' Owners' Comp/Sales						.2
	(28) 1.9	(31) 2.1	(29) 1.8						(14)	.5
	2.9	4.4	3.8							3.8
	9413161M	7864918M	10990937M	Net Sales ($)		10343M	16283M	84028M	257354M	10622929M
	2285971M	2432228M	3417256M	Total Assets ($)		7550M	21397M	36108M	81644M	3270557M

M = $ thousand   MM = $ million
See Pages 11 through 21 for Explanation of Ratios and Data

Current Data Sorted by Assets   Comparative Historical Data

Type of Statement	0-500M	500M-2MM	2-10MM	10-50MM	50-100MM	100-250MM	4/1/02-3/31/03 ALL	4/1/03-3/31/04 ALL
Unqualified		2	3	16	8	7	39	39
Reviewed		5	18	7			35	30
Compiled	1	9	17				21	38
Tax Returns	1	1	2				6	13
Other	2	2	21	21	3	5	30	47
	31 (4/1-9/30/06)		120 (10/1/06-3/31/07)					
NUMBER OF STATEMENTS	4	19	61	44	11	12	131	167

0-500M	500M-2MM	2-10MM	10-50MM	50-100MM	100-250MM		4/1/02-3/31/03 ALL	4/1/03-3/31/04 ALL
%	%	%	%	%	%	**ASSETS**	%	%
	11.0	7.6	7.2	4.5	4.8	Cash & Equivalents	8.1	7.1
	30.5	27.7	20.1	16.3	17.6	Trade Receivables (net)	24.2	25.6
	22.1	21.2	20.0	29.8	21.3	Inventory	20.4	20.1
	2.4	3.0	2.4	1.8	1.3	All Other Current	2.3	3.4
	66.0	59.5	49.7	52.4	45.0	Total Current	55.1	56.1
	24.4	31.0	41.7	40.0	39.3	Fixed Assets (net)	36.7	34.6
	6.2	3.6	2.6	3.2	6.4	Intangibles (net)	2.7	3.8
	3.4	5.9	6.1	4.3	9.2	All Other Non-Current	5.6	5.5
	100.0	100.0	100.0	100.0	100.0	Total	100.0	100.0
						LIABILITIES		
	7.8	12.4	9.5	11.9	9.2	Notes Payable-Short Term	11.0	11.0
	2.4	2.6	3.6	4.3	2.0	Cur. Mat.-L.T.D.	6.0	3.9
	16.3	17.8	11.0	5.9	8.8	Trade Payables	14.9	17.4
	.2	.2	.0	.0	.0	Income Taxes Payable	.2	.2
	6.7	7.4	9.4	12.6	8.3	All Other Current	7.7	8.1
	33.5	40.3	33.5	34.8	28.4	Total Current	39.7	40.4
	17.2	16.3	20.4	27.5	31.0	Long-Term Debt	20.4	16.2
	.9	.2	1.0	.9	.0	Deferred Taxes	.3	.3
	5.9	7.2	3.7	6.5	9.8	All Other Non-Current	6.2	5.7
	42.5	36.0	41.4	30.4	30.9	Net Worth	33.4	37.3
	100.0	100.0	100.0	100.0	100.0	Total Liabilties & Net Worth	100.0	100.0
						INCOME DATA		
	100.0	100.0	100.0	100.0	100.0	Net Sales	100.0	100.0
	20.2	21.5	18.4	14.3	18.0	Gross Profit	24.1	20.9
	17.7	17.0	13.8	11.0	15.3	Operating Expenses	19.0	17.3
	2.5	4.4	4.6	3.3	2.7	Operating Profit	5.2	3.6
	1.1	.4	.6	1.9	1.4	All Other Expenses (net)	1.1	.7
	1.4	4.0	4.0	1.4	1.2	Profit Before Taxes	4.1	2.9
						RATIOS		
	3.0	2.9	2.3	2.3	2.4		2.1	2.1
	1.9	1.4	1.3	1.5	1.3	Current	1.5	1.4
	1.4	1.0	1.1	1.0	1.1		1.1	1.1
	1.9	1.8	1.5	.8	.9		1.4	1.3
	1.1	.8	.7	.5	.8	Quick	.8	.8
	.8	.6	.5	.4	.4		.5	.5
	13 28.7	14 26.8	17 21.0	19 18.8	14 25.3		16 22.5	16 22.6
	22 16.7	21 17.7	22 16.4	25 14.5	20 17.9	Sales/Receivables	22 17.0	20 18.1
	28 13.0	26 13.8	27 13.4	26 13.9	23 15.8		28 13.0	28 13.1
	12 29.8	12 29.4	19 19.6	34 10.8	17 21.4		14 25.7	12 29.7
	16 22.8	18 20.3	27 13.7	52 7.0	28 13.1	Cost of Sales/Inventory	22 16.5	22 16.5
	20 18.2	32 11.5	42 8.6	60 6.1	58 6.3		38 9.6	38 9.7
	4 90.5	9 42.7	8 45.4	5 73.6	7 51.3		9 41.2	9 40.5
	12 31.0	16 22.9	12 31.1	9 41.1	16 22.5	Cost of Sales/Payables	15 23.9	17 21.7
	22 16.4	26 14.2	16 23.2	14 26.2	25 14.7		23 15.6	25 14.6
	11.0	10.4	9.3	8.5	11.8		10.2	12.6
	19.1	30.6	23.7	14.2	25.0	Sales/Working Capital	25.5	31.9
	43.4	NM	113.7	407.4	121.9		100.4	157.1
	9.4	8.0	11.8	4.5	16.2		10.2	14.0
	(18) 3.8	(58) 3.5	(41) 5.7	2.8	5.5	EBIT/Interest	(121) 5.5	(147) 4.5
	1.1	1.8	2.1	.2	.6		2.2	1.3
			5.0	27.5			Net Profit + Depr., Dep.,	9.4	6.9
		(15) 2.9	(12) 2.3				Amort./Cur. Mat. L/T/D	(40) 2.9	(40) 3.2
		1.0	1.2					1.4	1.5
	.3	.4	.6	.5	.7		.5	.4
	.6	.9	1.1	1.4	1.1	Fixed/Worth	1.0	.9
	1.2	2.2	1.6	2.4	21.1		2.0	2.3
	1.0	1.0	.7	.9	.8		.8	.9
	1.7	2.5	1.6	2.7	1.6	Debt/Worth	1.8	1.7
	4.6	5.6	3.6	4.0	31.8		4.4	5.0
	32.2	53.7	38.6	35.9	59.2	% Profit Before Taxes/Tangible	50.2	52.7
	(18) 17.6	(56) 19.3	(41) 24.1	(10) 15.6	(10) 23.7	Net Worth	(120) 27.2	(152) 24.2
	7.6	7.9	6.5	5.2	2.3		13.3	7.5
	11.7	13.5	19.7	12.9	18.5	% Profit Before Taxes/Total	18.0	17.3
	5.8	5.6	10.6	4.3	9.1	Assets	9.6	8.0
	.8	2.3	2.7	-1.9	-2.1		3.9	1.5
	58.3	48.5	16.7	10.9	13.4		19.7	26.5
	21.0	14.8	7.3	5.7	7.2	Sales/Net Fixed Assets	8.7	10.4
	15.5	6.3	3.8	3.4	4.4		5.5	5.2
	7.7	6.5	4.2	3.2	4.5		5.1	6.1
	5.8	4.2	2.8	2.3	2.6	Sales/Total Assets	3.5	3.4
	3.6	2.8	2.0	1.9	1.9		2.4	2.4
	.4	.6	.8	1.5			.9	.6
	.9	(56) 1.2	(40) 2.0	2.6		% Depr., Dep., Amort./Sales	(113) 1.6	(145) 1.4
	1.7	2.2	3.5	2.9			2.7	2.7
	.6	.9	.4				1.4	1.2
	(11) 2.1	(26) 1.8	(13) .8			% Officers', Directors' Owners' Comp/Sales	(41) 2.3	(50) 2.1
	7.6	4.3	1.9				4.4	4.8
11819M	170851M	1647934M	3227507M	1990967M	5811860M	Net Sales ($)	12284332M	14030134M
1759M	24756M	340222M	1003168M	755749M	1770889M	Total Assets ($)	3314075M	4309265M

M = $ thousand   MM = $ million
See Pages 11 through 21 for Explanation of Ratios and Data

Comparative Historical Data				**Current Data Sorted by Sales**					
36	30	36	Type of Statement				2	1	32
25	25	30	Unqualified	1			5	9	13
27	25	27	Reviewed			3	4	13	5
12	8	4	Compiled	1	3	1			
45	54	54	Tax Returns		2			2	
			Other		3		6	9	36
4/1/04-	4/1/05-	4/1/06-			31 (4/1-9/30/06)		120 (10/1/06-3/31/07)		
3/31/05	3/31/06	3/31/07		0-1MM	1-3MM	3-5MM	5-10MM	10-25MM	25MM & OVER
ALL	ALL	ALL							
145	142	151	NUMBER OF STATEMENTS	2	5	7	17	34	86
%	%	%	**ASSETS**	%	%	%	%	%	%
6.8	7.1	7.4	Cash & Equivalents				10.1	9.9	4.7
25.2	24.9	24.6	Trade Receivables (net)				20.0	30.1	23.6
22.1	20.6	21.5	Inventory				16.4	19.7	24.5
3.3	4.2	2.4	All Other Current				5.8	1.2	2.4
57.5	56.8	55.9	Total Current				52.3	60.8	55.2
34.4	33.5	34.7	Fixed Assets (net)				38.8	29.1	35.3
3.5	3.8	3.7	Intangibles (net)				4.5	2.9	3.8
4.6	5.9	5.6	All Other Non-Current				4.4	7.2	5.7
100.0	100.0	100.0	Total				100.0	100.0	100.0
			LIABILITIES						
10.7	9.8	11.0	Notes Payable-Short Term				6.1	11.9	11.8
2.9	4.0	2.9	Cur. Mat.-L.T.D.				1.3	3.1	2.9
16.6	14.7	13.8	Trade Payables				9.0	16.8	14.3
.2	.2	.1	Income Taxes Payable				.1	.2	.1
8.1	9.8	8.6	All Other Current				7.3	5.8	10.3
38.5	38.6	36.3	Total Current				23.9	37.9	39.5
15.6	18.0	19.6	Long-Term Debt				17.4	16.7	20.6
.3	.5	.5	Deferred Taxes				.1	.5	.6
4.8	5.8	6.0	All Other Non-Current				12.1	4.4	5.4
40.9	37.2	37.6	Net Worth				46.5	40.6	33.9
100.0	100.0	100.0	Total Liabilties & Net Worth				100.0	100.0	100.0
			INCOME DATA						
100.0	100.0	100.0	Net Sales				100.0	100.0	100.0
22.3	20.8	19.6	Gross Profit				31.8	19.8	15.4
18.9	17.4	15.7	Operating Expenses				24.3	17.7	12.2
3.4	3.4	4.0	Operating Profit				7.5	2.2	3.3
.5	.6	.8	All Other Expenses (net)				.9	.4	.7
2.9	2.8	3.2	Profit Before Taxes				6.6	1.7	2.6
			RATIOS						
2.5	2.5	2.6					5.1	3.0	1.9
1.5	1.5	1.5	Current				2.5	1.7	1.3
1.1	1.2	1.1					1.5	1.1	1.1
1.4	1.5	1.7					3.5	1.8	1.0
.8	.8	.8	Quick				1.7	1.1	.7
.5	.5	.5					.8	.6	.4
15 23.8	16 23.0	15 23.9					12 29.6	18 20.2	16 23.0
22 16.9	23 16.2	21 17.0	Sales/Receivables				22 17.0	22 16.5	21 17.5
29 12.7	30 12.3	27 13.6					30 12.0	28 13.1	26 13.8
11 31.9	14 25.9	14 26.1					14 26.1	12 29.2	15 24.2
24 15.3	24 15.1	24 15.4	Cost of Sales/Inventory				18 20.3	25 14.7	25 14.5
44 8.4	39 9.3	39 9.4					56 6.5	33 11.2	42 8.6
8 44.1	8 47.2	8 47.9					6 63.4	9 40.4	8 47.6
17 21.5	13 27.3	13 27.9	Cost of Sales/Payables				17 21.0	14 26.8	12 30.3
26 13.8	24 14.9	20 18.1					26 14.1	20 18.5	17 21.0
10.8	10.4	10.3					4.3	10.1	14.2
27.2	22.9	23.9	Sales/Working Capital				10.3	20.2	29.5
222.2	59.8	131.4					31.9	104.6	170.6
14.0	13.5	9.9					8.2	4.9	12.1
(125) 5.2	(126) 3.2	(144) 3.9	EBIT/Interest				4.5	(32) 2.8	(81) 4.9
1.2	1.4	1.6					1.4	1.3	2.0
8.3	6.9	8.6						3.5	9.5
(35) 3.1	(41) 3.1	(44) 2.8	Net Profit + Depr., Dep., Amort./Cur. Mat. L/T/D					(11) 1.4	(24) 3.3
1.1	1.7	1.1						.9	1.7
.5	.5	.5					.6	.3	.6
.8	.9	1.0	Fixed/Worth				.8	.6	1.1
1.7	2.2	2.0					1.3	1.3	2.4
.8	.9	.9					.7	.7	1.0
1.5	1.9	2.0	Debt/Worth				1.7	1.8	2.3
4.3	5.7	4.6					2.5	3.7	6.6
38.4	40.1	39.6					39.3	28.9	50.3
(138) 19.1	(126) 22.7	(138) 20.3	% Profit Before Taxes/Tangible Net Worth				14.6	(33) 15.7	(77) 28.7
1.6	6.3	7.1					4.1	4.4	9.1
16.2	14.2	14.5					14.3	9.0	16.2
7.0	5.7	7.0	% Profit Before Taxes/Total Assets				8.5	4.4	10.1
.6	.8	1.8					1.1	.8	3.1
30.0	31.7	28.6					18.8	58.7	23.1
11.5	10.3	11.3	Sales/Net Fixed Assets				10.0	20.9	11.1
5.7	5.7	5.1					2.2	5.3	5.1
6.0	5.1	6.1					4.6	6.3	5.7
3.6	3.3	3.6	Sales/Total Assets				1.9	4.0	3.4
2.4	2.4	2.2					1.3	2.9	2.4
.6	.7	.6					1.1	.4	.7
(132) 1.2	(131) 1.3	(137) 1.4	% Depr., Dep., Amort./Sales				(16) 2.2	(32) .7	(77) 1.4
2.2	2.3	2.8					3.8	2.2	2.5
1.1	.9	.7						.7	.4
(49) 3.2	(46) 1.5	(53) 1.4	% Officers', Directors' Owners' Comp/Sales				(20) 1.8	(23) .7	
6.0	4.6	4.2						4.4	1.4
9945156M	12395410M	12860938M	Net Sales ($)	870M	11093M	30359M	135508M	589150M	12093958M
3059745M	3685111M	3896543M	Total Assets ($)	1092M	7124M	7498M	83549M	178036M	3619244M

M = $ thousand   MM = $ million
See Pages 11 through 21 for Explanation of Ratios and Data

Current Data Sorted by Assets / Comparative Historical Data

Type of Statement	0-500M	500M-2MM	2-10MM	10-50MM	50-100MM	100-250MM	4/1/02-3/31/03 ALL	4/1/03-3/31/04 ALL
Unqualified		2	1	8	13	8	23	29
Reviewed		1	6	4	1	1	7	7
Compiled			1				1	8
Tax Returns				1			2	1
Other			4	5	9	4	16	7
	18 (4/1-9/30/06)		51 (10/1/06-3/31/07)					
NUMBER OF STATEMENTS		3	12	18	23	13	49	52
ASSETS	%	%	%	%	%	%	%	%
Cash & Equivalents	D		11.3	2.7	2.8	4.7	5.1	6.0
Trade Receivables (net)	A		22.1	15.7	13.9	13.7	18.5	16.3
Inventory	T		22.7	19.6	21.7	32.0	21.7	23.4
All Other Current	A		3.0	2.2	1.5	1.1	4.7	5.4
Total Current			59.1	40.2	39.9	51.5	50.0	51.1
Fixed Assets (net)			38.7	49.3	49.8	40.1	41.3	39.2
Intangibles (net)	N		.1	3.2	1.8	4.6	4.3	4.1
All Other Non-Current	O		2.1	7.3	8.5	3.8	4.4	5.6
Total	T		100.0	100.0	100.0	100.0	100.0	100.0
LIABILITIES								
Notes Payable-Short Term	A		11.8	8.1	6.0	9.4	7.7	7.8
Cur. Mat.-L.T.D.	V		8.2	4.8	3.5	2.8	4.0	4.5
Trade Payables	A		18.9	11.7	8.0	10.6	14.2	12.3
Income Taxes Payable	I		.1	.0	.2	.3	.2	.4
All Other Current	L		11.9	6.8	10.1	4.6	8.6	9.0
Total Current	A		50.9	31.4	27.8	27.7	34.6	33.9
Long-Term Debt	B		21.7	29.8	23.2	25.4	18.3	17.1
Deferred Taxes	L		.7	.6	1.7	2.1	1.2	1.5
All Other Non-Current	E		.0	1.1	3.3	4.2	2.9	3.6
Net Worth			26.7	37.1	44.0	40.7	43.1	43.9
Total Liabilties & Net Worth			100.0	100.0	100.0	100.0	100.0	100.0
INCOME DATA								
Net Sales			100.0	100.0	100.0	100.0	100.0	100.0
Gross Profit			27.0	25.6	15.4	16.1	17.2	16.4
Operating Expenses			25.2	22.0	13.6	16.8	14.6	13.2
Operating Profit			1.8	3.6	1.8	-.6	2.6	3.2
All Other Expenses (net)			1.0	.5	.7	.9	.4	.4
Profit Before Taxes			.8	3.1	1.1	-1.5	2.1	2.9
RATIOS								
Current			2.6	2.2	2.0	3.0	2.7	2.6
			1.2	1.4	1.4	2.0	1.5	1.5
			.9	.9	1.1	1.4	1.0	1.0
Quick			1.8	1.0	.9	.9	.9	1.2
			.8	.6	.6	.5	.6	.5
			.4	.4	.4	.4	.4	.4
Sales/Receivables			**11** 31.8	**17** 21.7	**19** 18.8	**18** 20.7	**15** 23.7	**15** 23.6
			22 16.8	**19** 19.0	**22** 16.8	**20** 18.1	**21** 17.1	**20** 18.3
			25 14.9	**26** 13.8	**31** 11.8	**24** 15.3	**30** 12.3	**26** 14.1
Cost of Sales/Inventory			**17** 21.8	**22** 16.7	**28** 13.2	**38** 9.7	**21** 17.1	**23** 15.9
			28 13.2	**31** 11.7	**41** 8.9	**47** 7.8	**37** 9.9	**35** 10.5
			42 8.7	**40** 9.0	**85** 4.3	**86** 4.2	**70** 5.2	**47** 7.7
Cost of Sales/Payables			**11** 32.0	**13** 27.5	**12** 31.5	**12** 29.5	**10** 37.4	**10** 35.0
			19 19.0	**20** 18.3	**15** 24.8	**18** 20.7	**16** 22.7	**15** 24.2
			24 14.9	**41** 9.0	**23** 15.6	**22** 16.5	**27** 13.4	**24** 15.0
Sales/Working Capital			8.1	10.4	9.3	6.1	8.9	8.3
			164.0	25.8	17.8	10.2	19.1	16.0
			-112.4	-189.4	131.8	26.9	NM	NM
EBIT/Interest			6.9	15.1	5.2	5.6	12.1	12.2
			2.0	1.8	(22) 1.5	(11) 2.5	(44) 4.8	(48) 4.4
			-.6	-2.1	.5	-5.3	1.5	1.7
Net Profit + Depr., Dep., Amort./Cur. Mat. L/T/D							7.0	4.3
							(14) 4.2	(19) 2.3
							1.2	1.3
Fixed/Worth			.5	.8	.9	.7	.7	.6
			1.3	1.3	1.2	1.2	1.1	1.0
			35.8	3.7	2.0	4.6	2.0	2.0
Debt/Worth			.6	1.1	.8	.6	.7	.6
			3.1	1.7	1.6	1.8	1.4	1.5
			38.8	4.1	3.3	15.7	4.9	2.8
% Profit Before Taxes/Tangible Net Worth			45.1	59.2	22.8	14.7	35.5	40.4
			(10) 21.6	(16) 5.4	7.1	5.8	(47) 15.5	(49) 15.9
			-1.9	-15.9	-3.1	-61.8	5.5	8.1
% Profit Before Taxes/Total Assets			10.5	20.2	15.0	7.3	12.4	12.0
			3.3	1.7	2.2	3.7	5.7	6.0
			-4.1	-9.0	-.9	-8.2	1.1	1.3
Sales/Net Fixed Assets			20.6	9.8	6.6	6.1	12.6	10.0
			12.2	6.6	4.9	4.6	6.4	6.3
			5.7	2.8	2.1	3.9	3.7	4.5
Sales/Total Assets			6.0	3.5	2.6	2.4	3.5	3.1
			3.9	2.6	2.0	2.0	2.3	2.6
			2.3	1.8	1.4	1.7	1.9	2.1
% Depr., Dep., Amort./Sales			.7	1.9	1.6		1.2	1.3
			(11) 1.3	(14) 2.5	(21) 3.0		(43) 2.3	(43) 2.0
			3.3	3.1	4.7		3.6	3.3
% Officers', Directors' Owners' Comp/Sales								
Net Sales ($)		18807M	255517M	1134799M	3406775M	4807873M	5170629M	7048256M
Total Assets ($)		4171M	57104M	473111M	1609007M	2031595M	2381990M	2820574M

M = $ thousand MM = $ million

See Pages 11 through 21 for Explanation of Ratios and Data

Comparative Historical Data | Current Data Sorted by Sales

Type of Statement	04-05	05-06	06-07	0-1MM	1-3MM	3-5MM	5-10MM	10-25MM	25MM & OVER
Unqualified	18	14	32		2		1	1	29
Reviewed	7	8	13			1		2	9
Compiled	5		1						1
Tax Returns	2	2	1						1
Other	18	22	22		1		1	2	18
	4/1/04-3/31/05 ALL	4/1/05-3/31/06 ALL	4/1/06-3/31/07 ALL	18 (4/1-9/30/06)		51 (10/1/06-3/31/07)			
NUMBER OF STATEMENTS	50	46	69	2	2	2	2	5	58
ASSETS	%	%	%	%	%	%	%	%	%
Cash & Equivalents	6.9	6.4	4.6						4.2
Trade Receivables (net)	21.4	19.0	16.5						15.7
Inventory	20.5	21.0	22.8						22.6
All Other Current	1.0	1.9	1.9						1.8
Total Current	49.8	48.4	45.8						44.3
Fixed Assets (net)	42.7	44.2	45.9						46.3
Intangibles (net)	3.2	2.2	2.3	DATA NOT AVAILABLE					2.8
All Other Non-Current	4.3	5.2	6.0						6.6
Total	100.0	100.0	100.0						100.0
LIABILITIES									
Notes Payable-Short Term	7.0	7.6	7.9						8.8
Cur. Mat.-L.T.D.	3.3	3.9	4.4						4.0
Trade Payables	17.7	13.6	11.5						11.3
Income Taxes Payable	.4	.1	.2						.2
All Other Current	6.8	9.4	10.0						8.7
Total Current	35.0	34.6	34.0						33.0
Long-Term Debt	16.1	19.6	25.1						24.5
Deferred Taxes	1.2	1.5	1.2						1.4
All Other Non-Current	5.8	3.1	2.3						2.6
Net Worth	41.9	41.2	37.4						38.5
Total Liabilties & Net Worth	100.0	100.0	100.0						100.0
INCOME DATA									
Net Sales	100.0	100.0	100.0						100.0
Gross Profit	19.3	20.5	20.1						19.2
Operating Expenses	14.2	15.9	18.2						17.0
Operating Profit	5.1	4.6	1.9						2.1
All Other Expenses (net)	.4	.6	.7						.7
Profit Before Taxes	4.6	3.9	1.2						1.5
RATIOS									
Current	2.4	2.2	2.4						2.1
	1.5	1.5	1.4						1.4
	1.1	1.0	1.0						1.0
Quick	1.3	1.2	1.0						1.0
	.8	.7	.6						.6
	.6	.4	.4						.4
Sales/Receivables	18 20.0	14 25.2	18 20.3						17 20.9
	21 17.5	20 17.8	20 17.9						20 18.0
	30 12.0	29 12.4	27 13.8						26 13.9
Cost of Sales/Inventory	17 21.2	21 17.1	23 16.1						23 15.8
	30 12.3	32 11.3	35 10.4						36 10.3
	43 8.4	46 8.0	67 5.5						65 5.6
Cost of Sales/Payables	14 26.7	14 26.7	12 31.5						12 31.5
	18 20.1	18 20.8	18 20.7						18 20.2
	23 15.8	22 16.7	24 15.5						23 15.6
Sales/Working Capital	10.3	9.9	8.7						9.6
	22.3	18.4	21.8						22.1
	66.0	379.3	-378.0						NM
EBIT/Interest	21.3	18.8	7.7						7.7
	(45) 10.4	(42) 7.5	(64) 1.7					(56)	1.9
	2.7	2.2	-.6						.0
Net Profit + Depr., Dep., Amort./Cur. Mat. L/T/D	8.1	6.3	2.9						2.1
	(14) 4.9	(14) 4.6	(23) 1.5					(20)	1.4
	2.8	2.7	.3						.3
Fixed/Worth	.7	.7	.8						.8
	1.1	1.0	1.2						1.3
	1.7	1.9	3.7						2.6
Debt/Worth	.7	.7	.8						.9
	1.3	1.2	1.7						1.7
	3.7	3.0	4.6						3.9
% Profit Before Taxes/Tangible Net Worth	40.8	41.3	33.9						34.2
	(47) 29.7	(44) 21.1	(64) 6.0					(55)	6.7
	10.2	9.6	-11.0						-11.4
% Profit Before Taxes/Total Assets	17.9	14.4	11.3						11.7
	9.6	9.2	2.2						3.6
	2.8	2.2	-3.3						-2.7
Sales/Net Fixed Assets	11.0	9.0	10.0						9.8
	6.7	5.8	5.5						5.3
	4.8	3.7	3.6						3.5
Sales/Total Assets	4.0	3.3	3.3						3.2
	2.9	2.5	2.3						2.3
	2.5	2.1	1.7						1.6
% Depr., Dep., Amort./Sales	1.1	1.4	1.5						1.4
	(42) 1.8	(40) 2.2	(56) 2.7					(47)	2.7
	2.9	3.1	3.6						3.6
% Officers', Directors' Owners' Comp/Sales	.5								
	(10) 2.8								
	3.7								
Net Sales ($)	6162916M	6614034M	9623771M		3748M	7807M	13150M	72025M	9527041M
Total Assets ($)	2289065M	2532002M	4174988M		126170M	7813M	6430M	16212M	4018363M

M = $ thousand   MM = $ million
See Pages 11 through 21 for Explanation of Ratios and Data

Current Data Sorted by Assets — Comparative Historical Data

Type of Statement

0-500M	500M-2MM	2-10MM	10-50MM	50-100MM	100-250MM	Type of Statement	4/1/02-3/31/03 ALL	4/1/03-3/31/04 ALL
		3	12	2	3	Unqualified	22	16
	1	3	3			Reviewed	11	11
	2	1				Compiled	2	5
	2	2	1			Tax Returns	7	7
1	5	10	7	2	7	Other	20	18
11 (4/1-9/30/06)			56 (10/1/06-3/31/07)				4/1/02-3/31/03	4/1/03-3/31/04
1	10	19	23	4	10	NUMBER OF STATEMENTS	62	57

Assets (%)

0-500M	500M-2MM	2-10MM	10-50MM	50-100MM	100-250MM	ASSETS	02-03 ALL	03-04 ALL
%	%	%	%	%	%		%	%
	4.7	6.7	5.5		9.2	Cash & Equivalents	5.1	7.4
	33.0	28.2	21.1		18.1	Trade Receivables (net)	22.9	27.2
	13.2	40.5	30.5		37.1	Inventory	29.5	27.9
	25.5	.5	1.2		4.8	All Other Current	2.6	3.8
	76.3	75.9	58.3		69.2	Total Current	60.1	66.4
	17.0	18.4	35.4		20.9	Fixed Assets (net)	30.5	25.1
	3.3	.3	.8		4.0	Intangibles (net)	3.2	2.4
	3.4	5.4	5.5		5.9	All Other Non-Current	6.2	6.1
	100.0	100.0	100.0		100.0	Total	100.0	100.0

Liabilities

0-500M	500M-2MM	2-10MM	10-50MM	50-100MM	100-250MM	LIABILITIES	02-03 ALL	03-04 ALL
	10.5	19.2	18.1		16.8	Notes Payable-Short Term	21.9	22.6
	1.8	4.4	3.8		1.2	Cur. Mat.-L.T.D.	4.7	3.2
	21.3	20.0	9.6		10.2	Trade Payables	16.4	17.3
	.9	.7	.3		.5	Income Taxes Payable	.0	.8
	5.2	4.0	9.1		9.4	All Other Current	7.7	7.3
	39.7	48.4	40.8		38.1	Total Current	50.8	51.3
	3.8	10.6	17.3		10.4	Long-Term Debt	17.4	12.1
	.3	.1	.2		.3	Deferred Taxes	.4	.3
	13.8	10.1	4.2		2.8	All Other Non-Current	5.7	3.9
	42.4	30.9	37.5		48.3	Net Worth	25.7	32.4
	100.0	100.0	100.0		100.0	Total Liabilities & Net Worth	100.0	100.0

Income Data

0-500M	500M-2MM	2-10MM	10-50MM	50-100MM	100-250MM	INCOME DATA	02-03 ALL	03-04 ALL
	100.0	100.0	100.0		100.0	Net Sales	100.0	100.0
	17.5	17.5	20.8		18.7	Gross Profit	18.1	16.9
	14.9	14.4	14.4		11.3	Operating Expenses	13.6	14.4
	2.6	3.1	6.4		7.4	Operating Profit	4.5	2.6
	.0	-.3	.7		1.0	All Other Expenses (net)	.9	.3
	2.6	3.4	5.7		6.4	Profit Before Taxes	3.5	2.3

Ratios

0-500M	500M-2MM	2-10MM	10-50MM	50-100MM	100-250MM	RATIOS	02-03 ALL	03-04 ALL
	7.1	2.7	1.6		2.8	Current	1.7	1.9
	1.8	1.3	1.4		2.1		1.3	1.4
	1.2	1.1	1.2		1.2		.9	1.1
	1.2	1.2	1.0		1.0	Quick	.8	1.1
	1.1	.8	.6		.7		.5	.6
	.6	.5	.5		.3		.4	.4
9 39.2	25 14.4	27 13.6		30 12.2		Sales/Receivables	22 16.3	19 19.2
17 21.2	36 10.2	36 10.1		37 10.0			27 13.4	31 11.9
36 10.1	49 7.4	45 8.0		42 8.8			37 9.8	39 9.3
2 241.0	42 8.7	30 12.0		47 7.8		Cost of Sales/Inventory	22 16.6	16 22.6
6 61.1	65 5.6	51 7.2		78 4.7			40 9.1	35 10.4
40 9.1	92 4.0	87 4.2		115 3.2			63 5.8	72 5.1
2 179.0	16 22.6	11 33.8		13 28.8		Cost of Sales/Payables	8 44.0	7 51.2
9 39.4	30 12.1	19 19.0		18 20.6			24 15.4	19 19.0
23 15.6	36 10.1	33 11.0		26 14.1			32 11.4	30 12.3
	3.7	5.5	8.9		4.5	Sales/Working Capital	12.0	8.7
	15.9	7.7	13.8		7.6		27.4	22.8
	162.3	30.6	28.0		16.9		-71.7	66.3
	18.6	5.3	5.5		26.0	EBIT/Interest	6.9	9.7
	4.8	3.5	3.1		3.4		(61) 2.5	(55) 2.7
	1.7	1.2	1.7		2.1		1.1	.5
						Net Profit + Depr., Dep., Amort./Cur. Mat. L/T/D	3.1	5.1
							(20) 1.7	(12) 2.6
							.6	1.6
	.3	.2	.7		.3	Fixed/Worth	.6	.4
	.5	.6	.8		.4		1.1	.7
	1.2	1.5	1.2		.8		2.4	2.2
	.6	.9	1.1		.6	Debt/Worth	1.3	1.2
	1.6	2.8	1.8		1.0		2.6	2.3
	9.6	4.7	2.9		3.5		6.0	8.6
	96.2	62.6	28.4		23.0	% Profit Before Taxes/Tangible Net Worth	40.4	60.7
	20.9	(16) 36.1	18.8		14.7		(56) 14.9	(50) 15.8
	2.4	3.6	8.9		9.4		.9	2.2
	14.8	16.6	13.4		13.0	% Profit Before Taxes/Total Assets	12.3	18.3
	6.7	6.7	6.0		6.0		4.4	4.4
	.9	.3	3.6		3.4		.4	-.4
	96.2	55.2	14.9		19.6	Sales/Net Fixed Assets	27.5	45.5
	41.0	29.8	7.3		10.2		10.8	16.0
	16.5	9.1	2.7		4.7		6.6	6.3
	12.0	3.5	3.2		2.4	Sales/Total Assets	4.4	4.6
	5.4	2.9	1.9		2.1		2.7	2.8
	2.2	2.1	1.3		1.5		2.1	1.9
		.4	.6		.3	% Depr., Dep., Amort./Sales	.8	.4
	(17) .8	(22) 2.0					(60) 1.4	(45) 1.1
	1.5	3.6					2.5	2.0
						% Officers', Directors' Owners' Comp/Sales	.8	.7
							(21) 1.3	(16) 2.0
							3.3	2.4
1807M	91914M	307455M	1178990M	325914M	3210662M	Net Sales ($)	2770420M	3148747M
451M	14156M	112417M	522764M	213866M	1625015M	Total Assets ($)	1319204M	1525527M

M = $ thousand   MM = $ million
See Pages 11 through 21 for Explanation of Ratios and Data

Comparative Historical Data / Current Data Sorted by Sales

4/1/04-3/31/05 ALL	4/1/05-3/31/06 ALL	4/1/06-3/31/07 ALL	Type of Statement	0-1MM	1-3MM	3-5MM	5-10MM	10-25MM	25MM & OVER
					11 (4/1-9/30/06)		56 (10/1/06-3/31/07)		
15	13	20	Unqualified					4	16
14	12	7	Reviewed				1	3	3
5	8	3	Compiled				1	2	
5	4	6	Tax Returns		3			2	1
17	25	31	Other		1	1	5	10	14
56	62	67	NUMBER OF STATEMENTS		4	1	7	21	34
%	%	%	ASSETS	%	%	%	%	%	%
5.6	6.6	6.3	Cash & Equivalents	DATA NOT AVAILABLE				9.1	5.3
25.3	26.1	24.2	Trade Receivables (net)					25.1	22.0
30.9	31.6	31.4	Inventory					27.6	36.4
3.4	4.5	5.3	All Other Current					4.0	2.6
65.3	68.8	67.1	Total Current					65.7	66.4
23.9	25.3	25.6	Fixed Assets (net)					26.1	26.3
3.1	1.7	2.1	Intangibles (net)					.7	3.0
7.8	4.2	5.1	All Other Non-Current					7.4	4.4
100.0	100.0	100.0	Total					100.0	100.0
			LIABILITIES						
23.4	20.6	16.6	Notes Payable-Short Term					11.4	19.7
4.3	4.2	3.1	Cur. Mat.-L.T.D.					4.8	2.6
16.7	18.3	14.7	Trade Payables					17.2	12.3
1.0	.3	.5	Income Taxes Payable					.8	.2
7.9	10.5	6.8	All Other Current					4.3	9.2
53.2	54.0	41.8	Total Current					38.6	44.0
13.5	10.7	12.3	Long-Term Debt					13.5	12.9
.4	.2	.2	Deferred Taxes					.2	.2
4.0	8.7	7.1	All Other Non-Current					7.4	2.4
28.9	26.4	38.6	Net Worth					40.3	40.5
100.0	100.0	100.0	Total Liabilties & Net Worth					100.0	100.0
			INCOME DATA						
100.0	100.0	100.0	Net Sales					100.0	100.0
19.9	19.3	20.1	Gross Profit					17.6	20.7
15.4	17.0	14.9	Operating Expenses					13.7	14.5
4.4	2.2	5.2	Operating Profit					4.0	6.2
.9	1.6	.3	All Other Expenses (net)					-1.1	.9
3.6	.6	4.8	Profit Before Taxes					5.1	5.3
			RATIOS						
1.8	1.7	2.3	Current					3.2	2.2
1.2	1.3	1.5						1.9	1.3
1.0	1.1	1.2						1.1	1.2
.9	.9	1.1	Quick					1.4	.8
.6	.6	.7						1.1	.6
.3	.4	.5						.6	.5
24 15.5	**19** 18.9	**25** 14.7	Sales/Receivables					**9** 39.4	**29** 12.5
31 11.6	**30** 12.2	**34** 10.7						**25** 14.4	**35** 10.4
39 9.4	**37** 9.7	**41** 8.8						**39** 9.4	**40** 9.1
27 13.3	**25** 14.3	**37** 10.0	Cost of Sales/Inventory					**3** 113.9	**44** 8.3
42 8.6	**49** 7.5	**55** 6.6						**44** 8.3	**72** 5.1
80 4.5	**80** 4.6	**87** 4.2						**70** 5.2	**129** 2.8
8 44.9	**10** 37.3	**12** 30.2	Cost of Sales/Payables					**6** 62.3	**13** 28.8
18 20.0	**22** 16.7	**21** 17.3						**16** 22.6	**20** 18.1
35 10.4	**44** 8.3	**33** 11.0						**30** 12.2	**34** 10.9
10.7	10.7	5.9	Sales/Working Capital					6.0	6.3
25.8	21.2	12.8						12.6	13.1
129.9	62.2	28.0						162.9	25.4
10.1	8.8	9.3	EBIT/Interest					6.0	11.4
(54) 3.3	(61) 3.1	3.3						3.5	3.2
1.0	1.0	1.7						1.1	2.0
9.4	7.5	16.3	Net Profit + Depr., Dep., Amort./Cur. Mat. L/T/D						16.3
(12) 3.7	(15) 2.0	(21) 9.4							(13) 9.4
1.8	-.3	2.9							3.0
.3	.3	.4	Fixed/Worth					.3	.4
.8	.8	.7						.7	.8
1.9	1.8	1.3						1.1	1.1
1.3	1.3	.9	Debt/Worth					.9	.9
2.6	2.5	1.7						1.0	1.8
6.5	6.7	3.6						3.1	3.2
50.1	50.1	42.9	% Profit Before Taxes/Tangible Net Worth					60.9	30.9
(49) 28.7	(53) 20.6	(63) 21.5						(20) 26.6	(33) 20.5
11.4	3.3	8.9						1.4	10.4
15.4	14.2	14.5	% Profit Before Taxes/Total Assets					17.2	13.1
6.6	4.4	6.6						6.7	6.3
.6	-.2	2.1						.1	3.4
36.8	36.9	41.9	Sales/Net Fixed Assets					54.5	20.6
15.7	12.9	11.9						18.2	10.6
7.8	6.4	4.4						7.5	4.2
3.6	4.5	3.4	Sales/Total Assets					4.4	3.2
2.8	3.2	2.3						2.9	2.1
1.9	1.9	1.6						2.0	1.6
.8	.4	.6	% Depr., Dep., Amort./Sales					.3	.8
(49) 1.1	(56) 1.2	(58) 1.1						(20) .9	(29) 1.2
2.5	1.9	2.2						2.3	2.4
.7	.9	.5	% Officers', Directors' Owners' Comp/Sales						
(17) 1.4	(18) 3.0	(16) 1.8							
3.1	5.8	4.6							
3324887M	3581061M	5116742M	Net Sales ($)		8652M	3724M	52207M	354618M	4697541M
1463510M	1579127M	2488669M	Total Assets ($)		4477M	6643M	31327M	151090M	2295132M

M = $ thousand MM = $ million

See Pages 11 through 21 for Explanation of Ratios and Data

	Current Data Sorted by Assets						Comparative Historical Data	
Type of Statement								
Unqualified			2			2	7	9
Reviewed		1	4	1			11	14
Compiled	10	26	31	4			41	83
Tax Returns	29	18	5			1	27	43
Other	21	16	12	5			15	30
		18 (4/1-9/30/06)		170 (10/1/06-3/31/07)			4/1/02-3/31/03	4/1/03-3/31/04
	0-500M	500M-2MM	2-10MM	10-50MM	50-100MM	100-250MM	ALL	ALL
NUMBER OF STATEMENTS	60	61	54	10		3	101	179
ASSETS	%	%	%	%	%	%	%	%
Cash & Equivalents	12.1	10.6	7.5	8.6	DATA NOT AVAILABLE		10.1	10.4
Trade Receivables (net)	6.0	4.0	7.3	1.3			4.8	3.2
Inventory	6.5	3.5	3.1	1.2			5.0	3.4
All Other Current	.3	3.6	2.1	1.8			2.2	2.4
Total Current	24.7	21.7	19.9	12.9			22.2	19.5
Fixed Assets (net)	46.5	46.9	45.9	49.4			53.0	53.8
Intangibles (net)	20.1	19.9	16.4	27.2			12.3	15.9
All Other Non-Current	8.6	11.4	17.7	10.5			12.5	10.8
Total	100.0	100.0	100.0	100.0			100.0	100.0
LIABILITIES								
Notes Payable-Short Term	3.9	1.3	2.4	7.0			6.3	4.1
Cur. Mat.-L.T.D.	3.8	5.8	7.8	5.9			6.3	6.9
Trade Payables	7.6	4.9	3.9	2.7			10.1	5.4
Income Taxes Payable	.1	.2	.1	.0			.2	.1
All Other Current	31.0	9.6	7.3	8.1			16.1	11.8
Total Current	46.4	21.8	21.5	23.7			39.0	28.3
Long-Term Debt	36.7	40.1	37.3	52.9			44.1	40.4
Deferred Taxes	.0	.0	.1	.0			.2	.0
All Other Non-Current	7.7	12.3	11.1	5.7			4.9	8.0
Net Worth	9.1	25.7	29.9	17.7			11.8	23.2
Total Liabilties & Net Worth	100.0	100.0	100.0	100.0			100.0	100.0
INCOME DATA								
Net Sales	100.0	100.0	100.0	100.0			100.0	100.0
Gross Profit	52.6	44.6	37.5	49.4			54.5	46.4
Operating Expenses	44.2	37.3	32.0	41.3			48.6	39.5
Operating Profit	8.4	7.3	5.5	8.1			5.9	6.9
All Other Expenses (net)	1.2	1.8	.8	2.0			2.4	1.1
Profit Before Taxes	7.2	5.5	4.7	6.0			3.5	5.8
RATIOS								
Current	2.1	2.2	1.3	1.1			1.4	1.5
	.6	1.0	.8	.5			.7	.7
	.2	.5	.3	.2			.2	.3
Quick	1.7	1.4	1.1				1.0	1.2
	.5	.8	.6				.5	(176) .4
	.1	.2	.2				.1	.2
Sales/Receivables	0 UND	0 UND	1 419.4	0 UND			0 UND	0 UND
	0 UND	1 633.0	2 149.7	0 UND			1 519.7	0 UND
	4 98.3	6 61.0	17 20.9	2 163.6			5 67.0	3 140.8
Cost of Sales/Inventory	3 129.3	2 165.8	2 158.1	2 185.6			2 172.4	2 175.8
	5 69.3	4 82.5	3 112.0	4 89.7			5 67.5	4 101.9
	14 25.6	10 35.0	7 53.6	6 58.0			19 19.7	10 37.7
Cost of Sales/Payables	0 UND	0 810.8	1 433.8	2 191.5			2 147.0	2 233.4
	3 121.6	4 86.8	7 53.6	7 49.1			10 35.3	7 50.7
	24 15.2	12 29.4	18 20.2	27 13.4			37 9.8	19 19.5
Sales/Working Capital	39.8	28.2	44.1	NM			39.9	31.2
	-57.2	-999.8	-55.6	-13.9			-75.8	-33.9
	-9.3	-24.2	-14.3	-11.0			-11.6	-14.0
EBIT/Interest	17.4	12.4	10.6	7.7			9.6	10.4
	(46) 6.3	(54) 4.6	(52) 5.6	4.8			(89) 2.9	(158) 5.2
	2.0	1.7	1.8	1.3			.8	2.0
Net Profit + Depr., Dep., Amort./Cur. Mat. L/T/D								
Fixed/Worth	.9	1.1	1.0	4.7			1.1	1.2
	5.4	4.0	2.7	-142.1			5.7	6.5
	-1.6	-1.7	-6.7	-.9			-2.1	-4.3
Debt/Worth	.9	1.0	1.4	5.8			1.1	1.4
	15.0	5.4	4.6	-255.5			7.4	6.8
	-2.9	-4.4	-10.6	-2.4			-4.8	-6.9
% Profit Before Taxes/Tangible Net Worth	264.1	116.1	97.5				89.0	133.3
	(32) 82.4	(34) 60.6	(37) 58.6				(58) 42.3	(113) 66.7
	36.6	21.9	19.5				7.4	26.6
% Profit Before Taxes/Total Assets	38.5	30.3	24.1	23.8			27.9	24.4
	19.5	15.1	12.9	14.0			7.7	13.4
	4.0	3.0	3.7	1.0			-1.6	3.9
Sales/Net Fixed Assets	13.7	10.3	6.9	7.3			13.3	6.9
	8.4	6.7	5.3	5.1			6.2	4.7
	5.0	3.2	3.3	2.2			4.0	3.2
Sales/Total Assets	5.4	3.7	2.9	2.3			5.2	3.4
	3.7	2.4	2.2	1.7			3.2	2.4
	2.4	1.4	1.5	1.3			2.1	1.7
% Depr., Dep., Amort./Sales	1.8	1.8	2.2	2.8			2.1	2.7
	(51) 2.7	(58) 3.5	(53) 3.3	4.0			(95) 3.4	(167) 3.7
	4.3	5.5	5.2	6.6			5.7	5.3
% Officers', Directors' Owners' Comp/Sales	2.2	.9	1.6				2.9	1.2
	(21) 4.3	(33) 2.8	(42) 2.6				(48) 7.1	(109) 3.1
	6.5	4.5	5.0				10.7	5.5
Net Sales ($)	64692M	173730M	562237M	295453M		906262M	2233230M	2632498M
Total Assets ($)	16619M	66193M	252513M	158243M		452517M	584439M	824334M

M = $ thousand MM = $ million

See Pages 11 through 21 for Explanation of Ratios and Data

Comparative Historical Data | Current Data Sorted by Sales

4/1/04-3/31/05 ALL	4/1/05-3/31/06 ALL	4/1/06-3/31/07 ALL	Type of Statement	0-1MM	1-3MM	3-5MM	5-10MM	10-25MM	25MM & OVER
5	4	4	Unqualified		1	1	1	2	2
18	5	6	Reviewed	6	17	14	16	14	2
61	57	71	Compiled	23	21	3	4	1	4
50	41	53	Tax Returns	17	13	5	10	6	1
28	43	54	Other						3
				18 (4/1-9/30/06)	170 (10/1/06-3/31/07)				
162	150	188	NUMBER OF STATEMENTS	46	52	23	31	24	12
%	%	%	ASSETS	%	%	%	%	%	%
10.0	10.7	9.9	Cash & Equivalents	8.5	11.6	13.6	8.8	7.6	8.5
4.6	4.8	5.5	Trade Receivables (net)	1.9	7.1	3.5	6.0	9.8	5.5
3.7	3.6	4.2	Inventory	4.0	5.6	1.9	4.1	3.8	4.0
1.8	2.9	2.0	All Other Current	.2	2.5	2.3	3.1	2.5	1.3
20.1	22.0	21.5	Total Current	14.7	26.8	21.3	22.0	23.8	19.4
47.6	47.3	46.6	Fixed Assets (net)	55.5	41.8	46.4	44.0	43.7	46.0
20.0	16.6	19.7	Intangibles (net)	21.8	21.7	14.1	18.8	14.8	26.6
12.3	14.0	12.2	All Other Non-Current	8.0	9.7	18.2	15.3	17.7	8.0
100.0	100.0	100.0	Total	100.0	100.0	100.0	100.0	100.0	100.0
			LIABILITIES						
3.2	2.7	2.8	Notes Payable-Short Term	2.5	3.7	.7	.8	3.9	6.3
6.7	8.0	5.7	Cur. Mat.-L.T.D.	3.0	5.3	6.9	7.3	8.5	5.0
7.0	5.5	5.3	Trade Payables	5.1	6.4	3.2	7.3	4.1	2.8
.1	.0	.1	Income Taxes Payable	.0	.1	.2	.2	.0	.0
12.9	14.6	15.7	All Other Current	35.0	10.8	11.8	6.3	8.6	9.3
30.0	30.8	29.6	Total Current	45.7	26.4	22.8	22.0	25.1	23.4
38.1	37.6	39.2	Long-Term Debt	45.7	37.0	38.5	36.0	35.5	40.8
.2	.1	.1	Deferred Taxes	.0	.0	.0	.0	.3	.1
11.6	11.9	10.5	All Other Non-Current	10.2	8.1	9.1	16.5	8.1	14.1
20.1	19.6	20.7	Net Worth	-1.5	28.5	29.6	25.6	30.9	21.5
100.0	100.0	100.0	Total Liabilities & Net Worth	100.0	100.0	100.0	100.0	100.0	100.0
			INCOME DATA						
100.0	100.0	100.0	Net Sales	100.0	100.0	100.0	100.0	100.0	100.0
44.7	46.3	45.3	Gross Profit	51.5	48.6	39.5	39.7	37.4	49.5
39.2	39.8	38.2	Operating Expenses	45.8	40.0	32.2	33.9	29.9	39.7
5.6	6.4	7.2	Operating Profit	5.6	8.6	7.3	5.8	7.5	9.8
.9	1.4	1.4	All Other Expenses (net)	2.6	1.0	.8	.9	.5	2.4
4.6	5.1	5.8	Profit Before Taxes	3.0	7.5	6.5	4.9	7.0	7.4
			RATIOS						
1.7	1.6	1.5	Current	2.5	3.2	1.3	1.4	1.4	1.7
.6	.9	.8		.5	1.1	.9	.8	.8	.7
.3	.3	.3		.1	.5	.5	.5	.3	.2
1.2	1.1	1.2	Quick	1.9	2.0	1.1	1.0	1.1	1.3
.4	.6 (187)	.6		.3	.8	.8	.6	.6 (11)	.5
.1	.2	.2		.1	.2	.3	.2	.3	.1
0 UND	0 UND	0 UND	Sales/Receivables	0 UND	0 UND	0 999.8	0 999.8	0 756.0	0 UND
0 887.2	1 419.4	1 373.1		0 UND	1 445.5	1 263.3	2 212.4	2 147.5	1 509.1
4 86.3	7 50.8	8 47.6		1 309.8	11 32.8	8 48.0	6 57.7	22 16.3	15 24.2
2 161.7	2 171.7	2 151.0	Cost of Sales/Inventory	4 96.5	3 134.2	1 265.7	2 165.5	2 151.2	2 166.9
4 98.8	4 90.7	4 89.3		6 61.8	4 88.4	3 124.5	3 113.7	3 105.9	6 65.1
10 36.0	12 30.9	10 37.2		15 24.4	12 31.3	5 79.9	7 53.0	6 60.6	22 16.4
3 120.8	2 220.0	0 822.0	Cost of Sales/Payables	0 UND	0 UND	0 UND	1 537.6	1 266.4	0 807.0
10 36.3	8 44.7	5 77.2		3 108.4	5 70.2	2 224.8	6 57.5	7 53.9	3 137.8
22 16.4	23 15.7	18 20.0		25 14.7	18 20.4	13 27.6	20 18.3	11 32.8	18 20.3
29.0	31.1	37.2	Sales/Working Capital	47.0	25.3	32.0	54.5	33.9	NM
-37.0	-96.3	-64.5		-17.7	619.3	-114.4	-61.8	-80.0	-43.0
-14.7	-14.4	-14.0		-5.7	-20.3	-24.7	-18.1	-12.9	-13.7
11.2	11.5	12.0	EBIT/Interest	7.5	16.6	18.2	12.2	11.4	10.1
(150) 4.2	(139) 4.0	(165) 4.9		(38) 2.6	(41) 5.3	(22) 8.2	(29) 5.5	(23) 6.5	6.6
1.4	1.5	1.7		.8	3.1	1.8	1.7	3.7	2.5
2.1	6.0		Net Profit + Depr., Dep., Amort./Cur. Mat. L/T/D						
(15) 1.7	(14) 2.9								
1.3	1.2								
1.4	1.3	1.1	Fixed/Worth	1.8	.8	1.0	1.4	.7	2.0
10.2	4.5	4.1		-22.0	2.0	1.9	3.5	2.1	6.0
-1.5	-1.8	-1.8		-1.5	-1.5	-2.6	-1.6	-5.9	-.6
1.6	1.4	1.3	Debt/Worth	2.4	.6	.9	2.0	1.2	1.6
17.7	8.6	7.8		-10.2	4.3	3.9	5.7	3.0	8.5
-3.1	-4.0	-3.4		-2.6	-3.1	-5.9	-8.3	-9.1	-2.1
153.6	128.9	149.7	% Profit Before Taxes/Tangible Net Worth	249.5	151.0	136.0	106.8	130.3	
(92) 68.6	(90) 53.7	(108) 62.0		(19) 48.0	(32) 63.3	(16) 62.5	(18) 68.7	(16) 54.1	
16.8	17.1	29.5		18.7	29.9	23.8	25.2	29.8	
22.5	25.9	29.9	% Profit Before Taxes/Total Assets	24.4	39.2	38.2	26.3	27.0	28.4
9.9	9.5	15.9		6.4	17.4	18.0	13.5	15.1	21.8
1.2	2.1	3.3		-1.8	5.4	4.3	2.2	9.0	6.8
9.7	8.9	9.7	Sales/Net Fixed Assets	7.4	13.7	13.0	9.4	8.0	7.3
5.6	5.8	6.4		4.6	8.4	6.4	5.4	5.8	6.5
3.7	2.9	3.5		1.4	5.7	2.7	4.6	3.4	4.9
4.0	3.3	3.8	Sales/Total Assets	3.5	4.8	4.0	3.5	3.0	3.0
2.4	2.3	2.6		2.1	3.1	2.8	2.5	2.4	2.6
1.7	1.4	1.6		1.0	2.3	1.6	1.7	1.7	1.8
2.4	2.6	2.1	% Depr., Dep., Amort./Sales	2.7	1.7	1.6	2.5	2.1	2.1
(148) 3.6	(137) 3.6	(173) 3.3		(42) 4.1	(46) 2.7	(22) 2.2	(29) 3.7	3.1	(10) 2.7
5.5	6.0	5.1		8.7	4.5	4.1	5.2	3.9	4.8
1.9	2.2	1.6	% Officers', Directors', Owners' Comp/Sales	.4	2.2	1.1	.8	1.7	
(94) 3.7	(102) 3.9	(104) 3.1		(10) 4.4	(31) 3.1	(16) 4.0	(22) 2.4	(17) 3.4	
7.5	6.7	5.1		8.2	4.5	6.8	4.8	4.8	
1933320M	1058011M	2002374M	Net Sales ($)	29446M	91996M	95785M	214371M	348048M	1222728M
963719M	665941M	946085M	Total Assets ($)	20786M	34117M	41390M	108394M	151227M	590171M

M = $ thousand   MM = $ million
See Pages 11 through 21 for Explanation of Ratios and Data

Current Data Sorted by Assets   Comparative Historical Data

0-500M	500M-2MM	2-10MM	10-50MM	50-100MM	100-250MM	Type of Statement	4/1/02-3/31/03 ALL	4/1/03-3/31/04 ALL
	3	4	18	10	5	Unqualified	38	23
	6	19	7	10		Reviewed	39	50
4	10	12	4	4		Compiled	29	33
8	9	5	1			Tax Returns	10	26
4	9	19	32	4	3	Other	34	53
	36 (4/1-9/30/06)		160 (10/1/06-3/31/07)					
16	37	59	62	14	8	NUMBER OF STATEMENTS	150	185
%	%	%	%	%	%	**ASSETS**	%	%
14.3	16.8	9.6	8.1	3.6		Cash & Equivalents	8.6	8.5
12.0	18.6	21.9	15.4	15.1		Trade Receivables (net)	18.8	17.3
7.9	12.2	11.0	9.0	7.9		Inventory	11.1	9.8
1.7	1.8	1.7	2.1	5.0		All Other Current	2.2	2.1
35.9	49.5	44.1	34.5	31.5		Total Current	40.7	37.7
51.2	40.4	47.4	53.4	59.0		Fixed Assets (net)	46.4	48.4
10.2	4.5	3.3	5.1	.4		Intangibles (net)	4.9	5.3
2.7	5.6	5.2	7.0	9.1		All Other Non-Current	7.9	8.6
100.0	100.0	100.0	100.0	100.0		Total	100.0	100.0
						LIABILITIES		
15.2	5.1	4.2	4.2	2.4		Notes Payable-Short Term	8.1	6.6
8.3	3.9	7.5	5.3	3.4		Cur. Mat.-L.T.D.	5.1	5.7
16.6	16.8	16.7	11.0	9.5		Trade Payables	14.9	13.7
.0	.0	.2	.4	.1		Income Taxes Payable	.2	.2
8.0	9.9	5.4	11.4	11.7		All Other Current	9.1	10.0
48.1	35.8	34.1	32.3	27.0		Total Current	37.4	36.3
22.7	25.5	26.6	27.1	24.2		Long-Term Debt	26.0	24.3
.0	.5	.4	.4	2.8		Deferred Taxes	.9	.8
54.8	7.6	6.8	5.2	5.6		All Other Non-Current	5.5	9.5
-25.5	30.7	32.1	35.0	40.4		Net Worth	30.1	29.1
100.0	100.0	100.0	100.0	100.0		Total Liabilities & Net Worth	100.0	100.0
						INCOME DATA		
100.0	100.0	100.0	100.0	100.0		Net Sales	100.0	100.0
44.2	37.8	32.7	28.6	39.2		Gross Profit	35.5	36.1
41.0	34.8	28.2	23.8	34.6		Operating Expenses	30.4	32.9
3.2	3.0	4.5	4.7	4.6		Operating Profit	5.2	3.2
1.1	1.3	1.4	1.3	1.0		All Other Expenses (net)	1.3	1.4
2.1	1.7	3.1	3.5	3.6		Profit Before Taxes	3.8	1.9
						RATIOS		
.9	3.7	1.9	1.8	1.7		Current	1.8	1.9
.7	1.5	1.5	1.1	1.0			1.1	1.2
.4	.8	.9	.8	.8			.7	.8
.8	2.6	1.5	1.2	.8		Quick	1.2	1.3
.6	1.1	.9	.8	.7			.8	.8
.2	.5	.6	.4	.5			.4	.4
0 UND	4 81.9	22 16.2	18 19.9	23 16.2		Sales/Receivables	18 20.1	17 21.0
0 UND	19 19.0	30 12.4	26 14.3	24 15.2			25 14.3	27 13.5
25 14.8	29 12.6	37 9.8	34 10.7	32 11.6			34 10.7	33 10.9
2 236.1	9 41.8	10 37.5	11 34.1	10 35.1		Cost of Sales/Inventory	10 37.3	9 40.4
6 61.7	21 17.7	20 18.5	20 17.9	15 24.8			18 20.3	18 20.4
21 17.3	27 13.3	32 11.4	31 11.9	21 17.5			31 11.6	31 11.8
1 506.0	12 30.9	21 17.2	14 25.3	21 17.0		Cost of Sales/Payables	17 21.5	15 24.7
20 18.0	27 13.6	30 12.2	26 13.9	25 14.6			25 14.3	29 12.5
54 6.8	39 9.3	46 7.9	41 8.9	36 10.0			38 9.5	44 8.3
-371.4	9.6	12.1	13.4	16.6		Sales/Working Capital	15.0	13.1
-27.7	19.6	22.6	41.1	-144.5			68.4	47.4
-14.2	-41.7	-85.2	-24.7	-53.0			-24.4	-22.0
9.0	6.1	10.9	10.6	14.8		EBIT/Interest	8.9	6.2
(14) 3.6	(32) 2.7	(55) 3.1	(59) 4.4	(13) 2.0			(138) 3.6	(172) 2.8
.1	.7	1.5	.5	.8			1.6	.2
		6.0	2.9			Net Profit + Depr., Dep., Amort./Cur. Mat. L/T/D	5.2	2.6
		(17) 3.0	(19) 2.1				(52) 2.4	(51) 1.8
		1.6	.8				1.5	1.1
1.7	.5	.6	.8	1.2		Fixed/Worth	.8	1.0
5.0	1.2	1.4	1.7	1.7			1.7	1.8
-1.7	9.0	4.9	3.0	2.7			4.5	4.6
1.7	.7	.9	.7	.8		Debt/Worth	.9	1.2
NM	1.7	2.2	1.9	1.7			2.7	2.5
-2.4	16.7	6.6	3.7	3.3			6.9	7.4
	51.6	52.9	44.6	26.8		% Profit Before Taxes/Tangible Net Worth	46.8	45.9
	(29) 13.9	(48) 21.9	(51) 24.7	(13) 12.8			(126) 20.5	(153) 16.4
	4.0	5.1	10.4	-2.7			7.3	1.9
37.3	16.0	15.0	15.4	12.8		% Profit Before Taxes/Total Assets	15.6	11.2
17.5	7.5	6.1	6.7	6.3			6.5	5.0
-2.9	1.1	.7	-2.5	-.5			1.4	-2.8
14.6	16.9	10.2	5.8	5.7		Sales/Net Fixed Assets	10.6	9.2
8.4	9.6	5.5	3.8	3.2			5.9	5.1
3.8	4.9	3.1	2.6	2.6			3.3	2.9
4.6	4.6	3.3	2.6	3.2		Sales/Total Assets	3.5	3.1
4.1	3.8	2.5	2.0	1.9			2.5	2.3
2.4	2.2	1.7	1.5	1.5			1.8	1.7
1.5	1.7	1.6	2.4	2.5		% Depr., Dep., Amort./Sales	2.0	2.2
(12) 2.6	(36) 2.2	(54) 2.8	(60) 3.0	3.3			(142) 3.0	(170) 3.4
3.6	3.5	4.2	5.2	5.1			4.6	5.1
	2.6	2.2	1.4			% Officers', Directors' Owners' Comp/Sales	1.8	2.1
	(17) 4.0	(26) 3.6	(12) 2.6				(60) 3.3	(64) 3.7
	9.4	5.8	4.2				6.3	6.0
19388M	158649M	797361M	2632442M	2160082M	1938153M	Net Sales ($)	6137464M	5657776M
5053M	42540M	304356M	1306696M	1002568M	1181649M	Total Assets ($)	2562443M	2881730M

© RMA 2007

M = $ thousand   MM = $ million

See Pages 11 through 21 for Explanation of Ratios and Data

Comparative Historical Data | Current Data Sorted by Sales

Hist ALL	Hist ALL	Hist ALL	Type of Statement	0-1MM	1-3MM	3-5MM	5-10MM	10-25MM	25MM & OVER
37	25	40	Unqualified		2		2	5	31
38	26	32	Reviewed		2	2	6	14	8
19	17	30	Compiled		7	5	9	2	5
23	18	23	Tax Returns	2	8	6	4		2
40	75	71	Other	3	6	6	4	21	31
4/1/04-3/31/05	4/1/05-3/31/06	4/1/06-3/31/07			36 (4/1-9/30/06)		160 (10/1/06-3/31/07)		
157	161	196	**NUMBER OF STATEMENTS**	8	25	19	25	42	77
%	%	%	**ASSETS**	%	%	%	%	%	%
9.0	9.8	10.2	Cash & Equivalents		11.6	14.7	13.0	9.5	6.6
19.8	18.5	17.6	Trade Receivables (net)		14.4	16.7	20.9	20.1	17.4
9.7	10.2	10.1	Inventory		8.4	11.0	15.2	8.5	10.2
2.0	2.8	2.1	All Other Current		3.0	.2	1.9	1.8	2.7
40.5	41.3	39.9	Total Current		37.4	42.7	51.0	39.9	36.9
47.5	45.8	49.2	Fixed Assets (net)		48.8	48.3	40.2	52.3	50.8
4.2	3.6	4.5	Intangibles (net)		8.7	3.8	3.6	3.1	3.8
7.8	9.3	6.3	All Other Non-Current		5.1	5.2	5.2	4.8	8.5
100.0	100.0	100.0	Total		100.0	100.0	100.0	100.0	100.0
			LIABILITIES						
5.5	5.8	5.1	Notes Payable-Short Term		9.8	2.5	4.9	3.5	4.3
5.0	4.8	5.7	Cur. Mat.-L.T.D.		10.8	2.7	3.2	8.3	4.2
14.8	14.3	14.1	Trade Payables		12.4	16.0	17.8	15.4	12.4
.3	.2	.2	Income Taxes Payable		.0	.0	.1	.1	.5
8.8	10.0	9.1	All Other Current		8.0	8.8	8.1	9.3	9.4
34.5	35.1	34.2	Total Current		41.1	30.0	34.1	36.6	30.8
24.3	26.4	26.1	Long-Term Debt		33.4	31.2	19.3	24.2	25.9
1.1	.8	.6	Deferred Taxes		.2	.0	.8	.3	1.0
7.2	7.3	10.2	All Other Non-Current		33.6	8.2	6.6	6.4	6.0
32.9	30.3	28.9	Net Worth		-8.2	30.5	39.1	32.6	36.3
100.0	100.0	100.0	Total Liabilities & Net Worth		100.0	100.0	100.0	100.0	100.0
			INCOME DATA						
100.0	100.0	100.0	Net Sales		100.0	100.0	100.0	100.0	100.0
35.3	36.4	33.2	Gross Profit		44.3	32.7	33.1	31.8	28.8
31.4	32.0	29.0	Operating Expenses		41.2	31.2	29.2	26.0	24.3
3.8	4.5	4.2	Operating Profit		3.1	1.5	3.9	5.8	4.5
1.1	.9	1.4	All Other Expenses (net)		3.0	.9	.6	1.3	1.2
2.8	3.6	2.9	Profit Before Taxes		.0	.6	3.3	4.5	3.3
			RATIOS						
2.1	1.9	1.9	Current		2.8	4.0	2.1	1.9	1.7
1.3	1.4	1.3			1.3	1.5	1.7	1.2	1.2
.9	.8	.8			.6	.6	1.1	.8	.8
1.6	1.3	1.3	Quick		2.0	2.6	1.5	1.5	1.1
.9	.9	.8			.7	1.1	1.0	.9	.8
.6	.5	.5			.4	.3	.8	.5	.5
18 19.9	16 22.3	18 20.5	Sales/Receivables		4 101.0	2 214.1	15 23.9	22 16.6	20 18.4
25 14.5	25 14.5	25 14.6			20 18.3	24 15.1	26 14.2	30 12.3	25 14.9
32 11.4	33 11.0	34 10.7			30 12.1	35 10.5	35 10.6	39 9.4	32 11.6
9 39.4	11 34.5	9 40.3	Cost of Sales/Inventory		5 80.7	9 42.2	6 56.6	10 38.2	11 34.3
17 21.0	17 21.0	19 19.7			14 25.8	21 17.3	20 18.2	19 19.0	17 21.1
27 13.4	27 13.3	28 13.1			29 12.6	27 13.3	32 11.4	25 14.5	29 12.4
17 22.0	16 22.5	16 22.4	Cost of Sales/Payables		15 23.8	5 68.6	19 19.7	16 22.3	17 21.2
26 14.2	28 13.0	27 13.5			28 13.1	21 17.7	29 12.5	32 11.3	25 13.5
40 9.2	41 9.0	43 8.5			47 7.8	57 6.4	43 8.5	47 7.8	34 10.6
12.2	12.1	13.0	Sales/Working Capital		10.4	8.5	12.8	11.0	14.3
32.6	25.8	32.1			32.6	17.8	18.4	54.5	37.9
-57.2	-36.1	-28.5			-14.8	-18.7	119.4	-42.3	-38.1
11.8	9.1	10.3	EBIT/Interest		7.3	8.1	9.5	12.1	11.5
(144) 2.8	(141) 3.8	(181) 3.1			(22) 1.7	(17) 2.6	(23) 3.2	(38) 3.1	(74) 4.3
.6	1.2	.8			.7	-4.0	1.7	1.2	1.0
4.1	5.4	4.6	Net Profit + Depr., Dep., Amort./Cur. Mat. L/T/D					6.5	4.8	3.9
(52) 2.2	(43) 2.9	(52) 2.7						(10) 2.9	(15) 2.6	(24) 2.7
.9	1.2	1.4						1.7	1.3	1.2
.8	.7	.8	Fixed/Worth		1.4	.5	.5	.7	.9
1.6	1.4	1.7			-27.3	1.4	1.1	2.0	1.6
4.7	3.9	4.9			-1.0	5.4	2.6	4.9	2.8
.8	.9	.9	Debt/Worth		1.9	.6	.8	.7	.9
2.3	2.1	2.0			-40.5	1.2	1.6	2.5	1.9
6.3	7.5	6.5			-3.1	4.9	5.6	5.7	3.2
41.9	44.8	48.4	% Profit Before Taxes/Tangible Net Worth		65.9	49.3	37.0	56.8	42.0
(130) 16.9	(133) 22.3	(157) 20.3			(11) 26.6	(17) 11.5	(22) 16.3	(34) 33.4	(67) 19.2
2.3	5.5	3.8			5.7	-11.9	3.5	14.4	1.1
14.5	17.2	15.4	% Profit Before Taxes/Total Assets		21.2	17.5	14.8	19.3	14.2
5.0	7.1	6.4			4.6	5.6	6.1	7.0	5.9
-1.2	.9	-.3			-2.4	-5.4	1.7	.5	-.1
10.7	10.9	9.3	Sales/Net Fixed Assets		11.2	14.5	17.4	7.6	6.4
5.7	5.4	5.1			7.1	9.0	8.3	3.9	4.2
3.2	3.2	2.9			3.6	2.5	6.2	2.8	2.8
3.8	3.4	3.4	Sales/Total Assets		4.2	4.4	4.4	3.0	2.9
2.7	2.4	2.3			2.6	2.6	3.6	2.2	2.2
1.8	1.8	1.7			1.5	1.5	2.4	1.5	1.7
1.7	1.5	2.0	% Depr., Dep., Amort./Sales		1.9	1.6	1.4	2.1	2.4
(146) 2.8	(149) 2.6	(179) 2.9			(23) 3.4	(18) 2.9	(24) 2.0	(40) 3.2	(69) 3.0
4.6	4.1	4.2			5.0	4.8	3.2	3.8	4.8
2.6	2.2	2.3	% Officers', Directors' Owners' Comp/Sales			2.6	4.0	1.2	1.0
(60) 4.4	(58) 4.1	(64) 3.9				(12) 3.7	(12) 5.8	(13) 1.7	(15) 3.4
6.1	7.6	6.2				15.1	7.5	2.9	4.4
5033343M	5890654M	7706075M	Net Sales ($)	4406M	48597M	74034M	184937M	693361M	6700740M
2434509M	2754881M	3842862M	Total Assets ($)	2682M	27014M	52974M	65860M	352188M	3342144M

M = $ thousand   MM = $ million
See Pages 11 through 21 for Explanation of Ratios and Data

Current Data Sorted by Assets

Comparative Historical Data

0-500M	500M-2MM	2-10MM	10-50MM	50-100MM	100-250MM	Type of Statement	4/1/02-3/31/03 ALL	4/1/03-3/31/04 ALL
		1	2		2	Unqualified	8	6
		2	4			Reviewed	4	6
	3	2	2	1		Compiled	5	5
	2					Tax Returns	5	2
1		1	4	2		Other	7	13
	4 (4/1-9/30/06)		23 (10/1/06-3/31/07)					
1	5	6	10	3	2	NUMBER OF STATEMENTS	29	32
%	%	%	%	%	%		%	%

ASSETS

0-500M	500M-2MM	2-10MM	10-50MM	50-100MM	100-250MM	ASSETS	4/1/02-3/31/03 ALL	4/1/03-3/31/04 ALL
			2.1			Cash & Equivalents	16.3	8.9
			18.2			Trade Receivables (net)	18.9	22.6
			12.8			Inventory	13.9	16.3
			2.6			All Other Current	.9	1.1
			35.8			Total Current	50.0	48.9
			53.5			Fixed Assets (net)	41.2	40.8
			6.0			Intangibles (net)	5.2	4.2
			4.8			All Other Non-Current	3.5	6.2
			100.0			Total	100.0	100.0

LIABILITIES

0-500M	500M-2MM	2-10MM	10-50MM	50-100MM	100-250MM	LIABILITIES	4/1/02-3/31/03 ALL	4/1/03-3/31/04 ALL
			6.9			Notes Payable-Short Term	6.7	9.3
			7.4			Cur. Mat.-L.T.D.	3.1	2.4
			11.2			Trade Payables	10.6	14.5
			.1			Income Taxes Payable	.4	.0
			8.0			All Other Current	7.9	7.4
			33.5			Total Current	28.7	33.5
			30.0			Long-Term Debt	21.0	12.7
			1.3			Deferred Taxes	.5	.4
			.9			All Other Non-Current	5.6	11.6
			34.2			Net Worth	44.1	41.8
			100.0			Total Liabilties & Net Worth	100.0	100.0

INCOME DATA

0-500M	500M-2MM	2-10MM	10-50MM	50-100MM	100-250MM	INCOME DATA	4/1/02-3/31/03 ALL	4/1/03-3/31/04 ALL
			100.0			Net Sales	100.0	100.0
			28.2			Gross Profit	40.0	32.3
			24.9			Operating Expenses	30.3	26.5
			3.3			Operating Profit	9.6	5.8
			1.5			All Other Expenses (net)	1.0	.4
			1.9			Profit Before Taxes	8.7	5.4

RATIOS

0-500M	500M-2MM	2-10MM	10-50MM	50-100MM	100-250MM	RATIOS	4/1/02-3/31/03 ALL	4/1/03-3/31/04 ALL
			1.8			Current	4.6	2.8
			1.1				1.7	1.4
			.7				1.0	1.1
			.9			Quick	2.8	1.9
			.6				1.1	.9
			.4				.6	.5
			27 13.7			Sales/Receivables	17 21.6	19 19.0
			33 10.9				28 13.1	29 12.8
			47 7.7				36 10.2	40 9.2
			21 17.6			Cost of Sales/Inventory	21 17.7	21 17.5
			33 11.1				35 10.5	36 10.1
			44 8.3				47 7.8	54 6.7
			21 17.2			Cost of Sales/Payables	10 37.4	14 26.6
			26 14.0				23 15.9	22 16.4
			54 6.7				38 9.5	41 8.9
			13.4			Sales/Working Capital	5.6	8.7
			317.1				10.7	22.3
			-16.5				NM	176.8
						EBIT/Interest	16.9	29.3
							(28) 7.6	(28) 7.7
							3.2	-.3
						Net Profit + Depr., Dep., Amort./Cur. Mat. L/T/D	19.6	
							(10) 4.5	
							1.8	
			1.1			Fixed/Worth	.6	.6
			1.7				.9	.9
			4.3				2.0	1.6
			1.2			Debt/Worth	.8	.4
			2.0				1.3	1.0
			6.6				3.4	2.5
						% Profit Before Taxes/Tangible Net Worth	76.9	43.0
							(27) 32.6	(29) 23.0
							18.6	4.3
			13.6			% Profit Before Taxes/Total Assets	22.8	24.9
			.8				15.8	8.3
			-1.1				6.2	-3.6
			4.4			Sales/Net Fixed Assets	13.1	12.2
			3.5				6.7	6.1
			2.4				3.7	3.5
			2.5			Sales/Total Assets	3.1	3.4
			1.9				2.6	2.1
			1.0				1.6	1.6
			2.1			% Depr., Dep., Amort./Sales	2.3	2.4
			2.8				(26) 3.1	(28) 3.0
			3.4				4.2	4.0
						% Officers', Directors' Owners' Comp/Sales	2.1	1.6
							(16) 4.3	(11) 2.9
							7.0	4.4
391M	19119M	73514M	305750M	465163M	569092M	Net Sales ($)	1083210M	1447545M
174M	4837M	34631M	168827M	201417M	347479M	Total Assets ($)	549656M	780786M

M = $ thousand   MM = $ million

Comparative Historical Data | Current Data Sorted by Sales

4/1/04-3/31/05 ALL	4/1/05-3/31/06 ALL	4/1/06-3/31/07 ALL	Type of Statement	0-1MM	1-3MM	3-5MM	5-10MM	10-25MM	25MM & OVER
9	8	5	Unqualified				1	1	3
5	1	6	Reviewed				2	1	3
4	5	6	Compiled			2	2		1
5	5	2	Tax Returns	1			1		
5	10	8	Other	1	1			1	6
					4 (4/1-9/30/06)			23 (10/1/06-3/31/07)	
28	24	27	NUMBER OF STATEMENTS	2	1	2	6	3	13
%	%	%	**ASSETS**	%	%	%	%	%	%
9.5	10.3	7.1	Cash & Equivalents						3.1
22.1	20.9	18.7	Trade Receivables (net)						19.3
13.1	13.4	14.2	Inventory						13.5
.6	.5	1.9	All Other Current						2.8
45.3	45.2	41.9	Total Current						38.8
38.2	34.0	38.9	Fixed Assets (net)						46.0
5.2	11.8	11.6	Intangibles (net)						11.1
11.3	9.0	7.5	All Other Non-Current						4.1
100.0	100.0	100.0	Total						100.0
			LIABILITIES						
8.3	14.2	13.2	Notes Payable-Short Term						10.2
3.6	4.2	4.3	Cur. Mat.-L.T.D.						5.5
15.5	12.4	12.7	Trade Payables						13.0
.4	.5	.1	Income Taxes Payable						.0
5.6	7.2	7.8	All Other Current						10.7
33.3	38.6	38.0	Total Current						39.4
20.5	17.2	24.8	Long-Term Debt						30.0
.7	.9	.6	Deferred Taxes						.4
6.0	2.5	5.5	All Other Non-Current						1.9
39.5	40.8	31.0	Net Worth						28.4
100.0	100.0	100.0	Total Liabilities & Net Worth						100.0
			INCOME DATA						
100.0	100.0	100.0	Net Sales						100.0
33.0	31.3	32.7	Gross Profit						23.5
27.8	25.7	27.8	Operating Expenses						20.9
5.2	5.6	5.0	Operating Profit						2.6
.4	.5	1.6	All Other Expenses (net)						1.8
4.8	5.1	3.4	Profit Before Taxes						.8
			RATIOS						
3.0	2.5	1.9	Current						1.6
1.3	1.1	1.3							1.2
.9	.9	.7							.7
2.2	1.7	1.2	Quick						.9
1.0	.8	.8							.7
.5	.5	.4							.4
24 15.2	24 15.0	22 16.7	Sales/Receivables						26 14.0
29 12.4	31 11.9	28 13.0							32 11.4
35 10.3	39 9.3	41 9.0							42 8.8
16 23.4	21 17.6	19 18.8	Cost of Sales/Inventory						21 17.7
33 11.0	29 12.4	36 10.2							36 10.2
44 8.2	51 7.1	51 7.2							41 8.8
15 23.9	15 23.9	22 16.9	Cost of Sales/Payables						20 18.6
33 11.0	22 16.6	28 12.9							28 12.9
48 7.6	42 8.6	43 8.5							38 9.6
7.5	10.8	8.8	Sales/Working Capital						14.5
25.7	33.8	22.9							25.2
NM	-40.2	-17.6							-18.1
18.2	10.4	6.2	EBIT/Interest						5.1
(25) 3.1	(21) 1.9	(23) 1.4						(12)	1.2
-.7	.7	.5							.6
			Net Profit + Depr., Dep., Amort./Cur. Mat. L/T/D						
.5	.4	.7	Fixed/Worth						1.2
1.1	.8	1.2							1.6
1.8	2.6	4.1							4.6
.7	.8	.8	Debt/Worth						1.4
1.5	1.5	2.3							1.8
3.8	5.8	327.3							6.8
36.7	36.0	49.8	% Profit Before Taxes/Tangible Net Worth						38.1
(25) 23.9	(19) 7.2	(21) 10.4						(11)	2.6
-4.5	-6.0	-2.1							-1.8
19.1	17.8	16.3	% Profit Before Taxes/Total Assets						9.7
5.5	6.8	2.8							.3
-1.9	-.2	-1.3							-1.5
11.1	22.9	12.2	Sales/Net Fixed Assets						6.5
4.9	5.9	5.6							5.5
3.5	3.7	3.4							3.1
2.9	3.4	3.0	Sales/Total Assets						2.8
1.9	2.2	2.1							2.2
1.6	1.4	1.5							1.6
2.0	1.1	1.6	% Depr., Dep., Amort./Sales						2.0
(26) 3.4	(20) 2.7	(24) 2.7						(12)	2.8
4.8	4.1	3.5							3.3
			% Officers', Directors' Owners' Comp/Sales						
817001M	1340467M	1433029M	Net Sales ($)	1295M	1800M	8989M	45418M	50962M	1324565M
414417M	654661M	757365M	Total Assets ($)	683M	890M	4547M	33909M	20767M	696569M

© RMA 2007

M = $ thousand MM = $ million
See Pages 11 through 21 for Explanation of Ratios and Data

Current Data Sorted by Assets / Comparative Historical Data

0-500M	500M-2MM	2-10MM	10-50MM	50-100MM	100-250MM	Type of Statement	4/1/02-3/31/03 ALL	4/1/03-3/31/04 ALL
1		3	4	3	1	Unqualified	14	14
		6	2			Reviewed	4	6
1	4	3				Compiled	3	6
1	3	1	1			Tax Returns	5	2
1	3	6	13	4		Other	11	18
	25 (4/1-9/30/06)		36 (10/1/06-3/31/07)					
4	10	19	20	7	1	NUMBER OF STATEMENTS	37	46
%	%	%	%	%	%	**ASSETS**	%	%
	10.0	3.5	4.8			Cash & Equivalents	6.3	6.0
	16.0	23.5	20.1			Trade Receivables (net)	20.3	18.5
	20.8	23.0	14.9			Inventory	12.4	13.4
	.7	.9	1.8			All Other Current	1.8	3.5
	47.5	50.9	41.5			Total Current	40.9	41.3
	31.5	38.3	39.5			Fixed Assets (net)	43.7	41.4
	7.9	1.2	12.7			Intangibles (net)	7.2	9.4
	13.1	9.6	6.2			All Other Non-Current	8.3	7.9
	100.0	100.0	100.0			Total	100.0	100.0
						LIABILITIES		
	3.2	8.6	7.6			Notes Payable-Short Term	7.2	10.8
	4.4	7.5	2.6			Cur. Mat.-L.T.D.	3.0	3.1
	18.0	13.9	14.0			Trade Payables	13.8	12.4
	.0	.6	.2			Income Taxes Payable	.2	.6
	6.4	8.8	13.3			All Other Current	10.9	9.7
	32.0	39.5	37.8			Total Current	35.1	36.6
	22.6	29.7	15.8			Long-Term Debt	20.2	16.6
	.0	1.2	.7			Deferred Taxes	1.2	1.0
	40.2	4.9	9.7			All Other Non-Current	2.8	4.5
	5.2	24.8	36.0			Net Worth	40.6	41.2
	100.0	100.0	100.0			Total Liabilities & Net Worth	100.0	100.0
						INCOME DATA		
	100.0	100.0	100.0			Net Sales	100.0	100.0
	34.6	26.6	25.3			Gross Profit	35.7	33.2
	33.3	24.1	22.1			Operating Expenses	31.2	30.4
	1.2	2.6	3.3			Operating Profit	4.4	2.9
	1.2	1.4	.8			All Other Expenses (net)	.9	.7
	.0	1.2	2.5			Profit Before Taxes	3.5	2.1
						RATIOS		
	4.6	2.6	1.6			Current	2.1	2.4
	1.2	1.1	1.2				1.2	1.1
	.9	.9	.8				.8	.8
	2.4	1.1	.9			Quick	1.6	1.5
	.6	.7	.6				.8	.6
	.4	.5	.5				.5	.4
	16 22.4	23 16.1	29 12.7			Sales/Receivables	24 15.2	22 16.4
	23 15.8	31 11.9	33 11.1				31 11.8	29 12.6
	33 11.2	40 9.1	39 9.3				36 10.1	35 10.5
	16 22.6	18 20.2	24 15.1			Cost of Sales/Inventory	16 23.3	19 19.2
	53 6.8	36 10.1	29 12.7				26 14.2	27 13.5
	83 4.4	76 4.8	41 8.9				35 10.5	38 9.6
	9 39.1	11 33.3	19 19.5			Cost of Sales/Payables	15 24.4	15 24.2
	28 12.9	22 17.0	29 12.8				22 16.5	25 14.7
	53 6.8	34 10.8	38 9.5				43 8.6	40 9.1
	6.4	7.1	14.4			Sales/Working Capital	10.4	8.3
	33.3	46.6	48.0				71.8	51.8
	-116.7	-43.2	-31.9				-30.0	-23.5
	10.3	4.3	6.6			EBIT/Interest	14.1	8.8
	1.3	(16) 2.0	2.7				(32) 4.5	(42) 3.6
	.1	1.2	.0				.1	-1.5
		3.7				Net Profit + Depr., Dep.,	5.5	6.0
		(10) 1.7				Amort./Cur. Mat. L/T/D	(10) 2.4	(16) 2.8
		.4					2.2	2.1
	.3	.7	.8			Fixed/Worth	.6	.6
	1.2	1.6	2.2				1.3	1.4
	-3.8	7.0	NM				3.5	4.8
	.5	1.2	.7			Debt/Worth	.4	.7
	2.4	3.0	3.7				1.2	1.6
	-9.5	13.3	NM				7.5	8.2
		41.7	78.3			% Profit Before Taxes/Tangible	60.8	35.3
		(16) 16.2	(15) 9.9			Net Worth	(31) 26.4	(38) 9.0
		1.4	-2.3				7.3	-3.5
	13.4	7.3	10.0			% Profit Before Taxes/Total	19.3	12.7
	2.2	3.2	4.0			Assets	7.5	3.4
	-2.7	-2.0	-3.6				.0	-5.9
	25.5	21.8	7.7			Sales/Net Fixed Assets	10.9	9.0
	6.4	6.5	5.3				6.1	6.0
	5.0	3.6	4.0				4.1	3.8
	3.1	3.8	2.6			Sales/Total Assets	3.3	2.9
	2.4	2.4	2.2				2.4	2.3
	1.7	2.2	1.6				1.9	1.8
		1.5	.8			% Depr., Dep., Amort./Sales	1.9	1.8
		(18) 2.3	(18) 2.3				(33) 3.1	(36) 2.6
		3.3	3.4				4.9	4.7
		1.4				% Officers', Directors'	.9	.9
		(10) 3.0				Owners' Comp/Sales	(11) 2.4	(10) 2.8
		4.4					11.3	6.0
2611M	23311M	260893M	1136570M	801305M	402586M	Net Sales ($)	2212966M	2831937M
725M	10237M	95846M	533010M	446731M	210174M	Total Assets ($)	1019740M	1321470M

M = $ thousand   MM = $ million
See Pages 11 through 21 for Explanation of Ratios and Data

Comparative Historical Data | | Current Data Sorted by Sales

13	10	12	Type of Statement						
6	8	8							
4	3	8							
4	3	6							
18	23	27							
4/1/04-3/31/05 ALL	**4/1/05-3/31/06 ALL**	**4/1/06-3/31/07 ALL**		**0-1MM**	**1-3MM**	**3-5MM**	**5-10MM**	**10-25MM**	**25MM & OVER**
					25 (4/1-9/30/06)			36 (10/1/06-3/31/07)	

H1	H2	H3		0-1MM	1-3MM	3-5MM	5-10MM	10-25MM	25MM & OVER
13	10	12	Unqualified	1				3	8
6	8	8	Reviewed		3		1		4
4	3	8	Compiled	1		1	1	5	
4	3	6	Tax Returns		4		1	1	
18	23	27	Other	1	2	2	3	3	16
45	47	61	**NUMBER OF STATEMENTS**	3	9	3	6	12	28
%	%	%	**ASSETS**	%	%	%	%	%	%
7.4	5.5	5.5	Cash & Equivalents					1.8	4.7
20.4	19.2	20.1	Trade Receivables (net)					22.0	21.3
14.6	18.2	19.8	Inventory					20.4	18.5
2.7	2.7	1.2	All Other Current					.9	1.7
45.1	45.7	46.6	Total Current					45.1	46.3
40.3	43.2	37.8	Fixed Assets (net)					41.0	38.2
7.8	5.4	7.3	Intangibles (net)					6.2	9.7
6.7	5.7	8.3	All Other Non-Current					7.7	5.8
100.0	100.0	100.0	Total					100.0	100.0
			LIABILITIES						
8.4	11.9	8.4	Notes Payable-Short Term					10.3	10.4
4.4	3.9	4.5	Cur. Mat.-L.T.D.					7.3	2.9
14.0	13.5	14.3	Trade Payables					13.7	14.0
.2	.3	.3	Income Taxes Payable					.8	.2
7.9	9.5	10.0	All Other Current					7.1	12.6
34.9	39.0	37.5	Total Current					39.2	40.1
22.3	22.5	24.8	Long-Term Debt					26.5	15.6
1.2	1.0	.9	Deferred Taxes					1.3	1.3
6.4	5.9	12.1	All Other Non-Current					7.0	7.5
35.1	31.6	24.6	Net Worth					25.9	35.4
100.0	100.0	100.0	Total Liabilities & Net Worth					100.0	100.0
			INCOME DATA						
100.0	100.0	100.0	Net Sales					100.0	100.0
29.9	31.1	28.8	Gross Profit					26.6	26.8
26.3	30.0	25.3	Operating Expenses					23.1	24.2
3.6	1.1	3.5	Operating Profit					3.6	2.6
.8	1.3	1.3	All Other Expenses (net)					1.7	1.1
2.7	-.2	2.2	Profit Before Taxes					1.9	1.5
			RATIOS						
2.8	1.7	2.1	Current					2.5	1.6
1.2	1.1	1.2						1.1	1.1
.8	.9	.9						.7	.8
1.8	.9	1.1	Quick					1.0	.8
.7	.6	.6						.6	.6
.5	.5	.5						.4	.5
25 14.8	25 14.4	23 15.9	Sales/Receivables					20 18.1	28 13.1
31 11.8	32 11.5	31 11.8						33 11.1	33 11.2
35 10.3	38 9.6	37 9.9						42 8.7	39 9.3
15 23.6	21 17.4	22 16.4	Cost of Sales/Inventory					12 29.5	25 14.7
27 13.4	33 11.2	35 10.3						27 13.6	32 11.3
46 8.0	50 7.3	56 6.5						66 5.5	43 8.4
17 21.8	15 24.9	17 21.9	Cost of Sales/Payables					7 49.6	19 19.3
28 12.9	25 14.5	27 13.6						24 15.5	28 13.2
43 8.5	46 8.0	38 9.7						39 9.3	36 10.1
7.5	9.3	10.2	Sales/Working Capital					7.8	14.3
33.9	41.9	44.0						165.0	70.0
-25.0	-52.2	-34.6						-12.9	-31.9
17.0	5.1	6.9	EBIT/Interest					3.8	6.5
(39) 3.4	(43) 1.7	(57) 2.2						(10) 2.0	(27) 2.2
.6	-.4	.5						1.0	.3
6.0	4.4	4.5	Net Profit + Depr., Dep., Amort./Cur. Mat. L/T/D						6.3
(16) 3.8	(16) 2.6	(24) 2.0							(14) 2.6
1.8	1.7	1.2							1.3
.6	.7	.7	Fixed/Worth					1.2	.7
1.9	1.3	1.6						5.4	1.5
4.0	7.1	NM						12.9	13.7
.8	.7	.8	Debt/Worth					3.5	.7
2.9	2.0	3.0						9.0	2.5
7.5	13.6	NM						20.2	20.3
40.3	26.3	47.4	% Profit Before Taxes/Tangible Net Worth					50.3	34.6
(39) 18.2	(38) 8.1	(46) 14.5						(10) 16.2	(22) 16.4
.1	-.9	-.2						-11.8	-1.1
12.3	6.8	10.3	% Profit Before Taxes/Total Assets					5.6	9.2
5.4	2.0	3.9						3.0	4.6
.1	-4.5	-1.9						-3.2	-1.5
10.0	8.8	11.2	Sales/Net Fixed Assets					8.1	11.2
6.0	5.2	6.1						6.4	5.3
3.5	3.7	3.8						3.2	3.7
3.1	3.0	3.1	Sales/Total Assets					3.6	2.6
2.2	2.0	2.3						2.3	2.2
1.5	1.5	1.7						1.6	1.6
1.7	1.7	1.2	% Depr., Dep., Amort./Sales					1.5	1.0
(40) 2.5	(41) 2.7	(52) 2.4						2.4	(24) 2.3
4.2	4.8	3.8						3.6	3.9
1.8	1.4	1.4	% Officers', Directors' Owners' Comp/Sales						
(13) 3.5	(15) 2.1	(21) 3.0							
9.0	8.6	6.0							
1804874M	2190354M	2627276M	Net Sales ($)	1368M	17362M	11922M	42220M	183086M	2371318M
972089M	1055089M	1296723M	Total Assets ($)	423M	8433M	4109M	17637M	81755M	1184366M

M = $ thousand   MM = $ million
See Pages 11 through 21 for Explanation of Ratios and Data

Current Data Sorted by Assets   Comparative Historical Data

			3	2	1	1	Type of Statement		
	1		6	4			Unqualified	9	9
			4				Reviewed	4	10
3	1						Compiled	9	4
2	2	11	8	2			Tax Returns	2	3
	9 (4/1-9/30/06)		42 (10/1/06-3/31/07)				Other	13	8
								4/1/02-3/31/03	4/1/03-3/31/04
0-500M	500M-2MM	2-10MM	10-50MM	50-100MM	100-250MM		ALL	ALL
5	4	24	14	3	1	NUMBER OF STATEMENTS	37	34
%	%	%	%	%	%	ASSETS	%	%
		4.6	4.5			Cash & Equivalents	8.2	7.0
		20.9	27.1			Trade Receivables (net)	20.0	19.5
		22.9	28.5			Inventory	23.4	22.9
		2.0	1.4			All Other Current	3.2	1.1
		50.5	61.5			Total Current	54.7	50.5
		34.3	32.7			Fixed Assets (net)	29.5	36.6
		8.5	2.0			Intangibles (net)	5.5	4.0
		6.8	3.8			All Other Non-Current	10.3	8.8
		100.0	100.0			Total	100.0	100.0
						LIABILITIES		
		10.4	14.2			Notes Payable-Short Term	8.7	9.9
		6.2	3.5			Cur. Mat.-L.T.D.	4.2	3.1
		15.7	16.7			Trade Payables	13.7	13.0
		.0	.1			Income Taxes Payable	.1	.3
		4.9	30.1			All Other Current	8.5	8.7
		37.2	64.5			Total Current	35.3	35.1
		20.4	16.1			Long-Term Debt	17.3	27.9
		1.3	.8			Deferred Taxes	.4	.5
		5.6	4.8			All Other Non-Current	9.6	7.6
		35.4	13.8			Net Worth	37.4	28.9
		100.0	100.0			Total Liabilties & Net Worth	100.0	100.0
						INCOME DATA		
		100.0	100.0			Net Sales	100.0	100.0
		45.5	36.2			Gross Profit	42.9	44.5
		42.7	28.9			Operating Expenses	38.4	39.7
		2.8	7.4			Operating Profit	4.5	4.8
		1.3	5.2			All Other Expenses (net)	1.1	1.1
		1.5	2.2			Profit Before Taxes	3.5	3.7
						RATIOS		
		1.7	2.2				3.0	2.5
		1.4	1.5			Current	1.3	1.4
		1.1	1.1				1.1	1.0
		1.0	1.2				1.9	1.3
		.7	.7			Quick	.8	.7
		.6	.4				.4	.5
		26 14.2	34 10.9				23 15.6	24 15.4
		31 11.8	37 9.8			Sales/Receivables	31 11.7	31 11.6
		40 9.2	47 7.8				39 9.4	40 9.1
		44 8.3	37 9.8				38 9.6	40 9.1
		65 5.6	66 5.6			Cost of Sales/Inventory	61 6.0	56 6.6
		82 4.5	86 4.2				95 3.9	96 3.8
		30 12.3	18 20.0				21 17.4	26 13.8
		49 7.5	34 10.7			Cost of Sales/Payables	38 9.6	34 10.7
		63 5.8	50 7.3				51 7.1	46 7.9
		10.3	7.0				5.5	7.0
		18.3	15.8			Sales/Working Capital	15.8	17.3
		69.1	86.2				64.0	NM
		4.5	8.0				9.6	11.1
		2.0	3.1			EBIT/Interest	(32) 3.6	(29) 3.2
		.8	1.5				1.2	.9
						Net Profit + Depr., Dep.,	10.1	10.7
						Amort./Cur. Mat. L/T/D	(12) 2.1	(12) 3.6
							1.8	2.6
		.6	.5				.3	.4
		1.3	1.0			Fixed/Worth	.9	1.0
		3.3	2.1				2.3	2.9
		1.2	1.1				.7	.7
		1.7	2.1			Debt/Worth	1.9	1.9
		4.1	3.0				4.3	7.0
		27.9	46.1				33.4	38.6
	(22)	12.0	(12) 19.4			% Profit Before Taxes/Tangible Net Worth	(33) 16.7	(30) 21.7
		-4.9	8.2				7.5	7.8
		9.4	15.3				13.7	14.4
		3.5	6.8			% Profit Before Taxes/Total Assets	5.9	8.6
		-.9	1.6				1.3	1.0
		24.0	14.2				15.3	13.8
		8.4	9.5			Sales/Net Fixed Assets	9.1	7.5
		3.5	5.6				4.7	3.8
		2.8	3.3				2.6	3.0
		2.4	2.6			Sales/Total Assets	2.5	2.2
		1.8	2.1				1.6	1.6
		1.8	1.1				1.7	1.6
	(21)	3.9	(12) 2.3			% Depr., Dep., Amort./Sales	(35) 2.6	(31) 3.3
		5.9	3.5				4.0	5.7
							1.6	2.1
						% Officers', Directors' Owners' Comp/Sales	(15) 5.9	(14) 4.2
							14.5	11.1
6106M	13965M	265833M	654103M	360705M	282383M	Net Sales ($)	1624406M	1265290M
1215M	5370M	118644M	245902M	179747M	109630M	Total Assets ($)	906314M	680878M

M = $ thousand   MM = $ million
See Pages 11 through 21 for Explanation of Ratios and Data

Comparative Historical Data | Current Data Sorted by Sales

Type of Statement	8 / 11 / 4 / 4 / 15	9 / 13 / 5 / 2 / 23	7 / 11 / 4 / 4 / 25	0-1MM	1-3MM	3-5MM	5-10MM	10-25MM	25MM & OVER
Unqualified							1	2	4
Reviewed							3	5	3
Compiled						1	1	1	2
Tax Returns									
Other				2	1	1	9	3	9
	4/1/04-3/31/05 ALL	4/1/05-3/31/06 ALL	4/1/06-3/31/07 ALL	9 (4/1-9/30/06)			42 (10/1/06-3/31/07)		
NUMBER OF STATEMENTS	42	52	51	3	4	2	14	12	16
ASSETS	%	%	%	%	%	%	%	%	%
Cash & Equivalents	5.5	3.7	6.1				3.4	5.5	4.9
Trade Receivables (net)	18.8	22.8	21.5				19.9	23.3	24.9
Inventory	23.3	25.2	23.9				21.4	29.1	27.9
All Other Current	1.3	2.2	1.7				2.7	1.1	1.8
Total Current	48.8	53.9	53.2				47.4	59.1	59.5
Fixed Assets (net)	36.3	31.9	32.9				43.2	26.6	31.1
Intangibles (net)	7.4	7.2	5.9				2.9	7.4	5.3
All Other Non-Current	7.4	7.0	8.0				6.5	6.9	4.2
Total	100.0	100.0	100.0				100.0	100.0	100.0
LIABILITIES									
Notes Payable-Short Term	11.6	13.8	15.4				6.9	16.7	11.4
Cur. Mat.-L.T.D.	4.9	3.6	5.1				7.7	3.9	3.4
Trade Payables	18.6	20.3	15.5				15.7	17.2	14.9
Income Taxes Payable	.3	.2	.2				.0	.0	.8
All Other Current	5.8	9.0	15.5				5.7	5.9	27.9
Total Current	41.3	47.0	51.7				36.0	43.6	58.4
Long-Term Debt	31.8	21.5	19.7				20.9	14.5	17.9
Deferred Taxes	1.4	.9	1.0				1.9	.8	1.0
All Other Non-Current	7.7	4.2	4.3				5.5	4.8	5.3
Net Worth	17.8	26.4	23.2				35.6	36.2	17.3
Total Liabilties & Net Worth	100.0	100.0	100.0				100.0	100.0	100.0
INCOME DATA									
Net Sales	100.0	100.0	100.0				100.0	100.0	100.0
Gross Profit	41.8	36.5	42.4				47.0	40.6	36.0
Operating Expenses	36.3	33.4	38.0				44.9	37.7	28.2
Operating Profit	5.4	3.1	4.4				2.2	2.9	7.8
All Other Expenses (net)	1.6	1.2	2.3				1.6	.6	4.6
Profit Before Taxes	3.8	1.9	2.1				.6	2.3	3.2
RATIOS									
Current	2.1	1.7	1.8				1.6	1.8	2.2
	1.4	1.2	1.3				1.3	1.3	1.6
	1.0	.9	1.0				1.1	1.0	1.1
Quick	1.1	.8	1.0				.9	1.0	1.2
	.6	.6	.6				.6	.6	.7
	.4	.4	.4				.5	.4	.4
Sales/Receivables	21 17.2	23 16.2	22 16.5				26 14.0	23 15.7	28 13.2
	32 11.4	36 10.2	31 11.6				31 11.8	35 10.4	34 10.6
	43 8.5	46 7.9	40 9.2				50 7.3	43 8.4	39 9.4
Cost of Sales/Inventory	40 9.1	39 9.4	35 10.3				57 6.4	37 9.8	34 10.7
	59 6.2	63 5.8	58 6.3				69 5.3	59 6.2	66 5.6
	91 4.0	80 4.6	82 4.5				83 4.4	81 4.5	87 4.2
Cost of Sales/Payables	27 13.8	35 10.6	18 20.1				34 10.7	18 20.8	18 20.7
	41 8.8	42 8.7	38 9.7				50 7.3	46 7.9	24 15.3
	61 6.0	63 5.8	59 6.2				67 5.5	64 5.7	39 9.3
Sales/Working Capital	9.0	9.3	10.3				10.3	8.2	7.8
	15.8	28.7	19.5				18.3	27.5	13.5
	-83.9	-49.3	183.4				43.6	158.5	47.5
EBIT/Interest	8.6	7.1	5.0				4.1	6.3	9.2
	(41) 3.5	(45) 3.1	2.8				1.6	2.6	3.7
	1.2	.9	.9				.6	1.0	2.6
Net Profit + Depr., Dep., Amort./Cur. Mat. L/T/D	5.2	5.8	6.8						
	(18) 2.0	(15) 2.2	(15) 1.9						
	1.7	1.1	1.4						
Fixed/Worth	.7	.6	.6				.9	.5	.6
	1.8	1.2	1.1				1.4	.9	.9
	UND	6.1	3.8				2.8	1.8	2.1
Debt/Worth	1.1	1.2	1.2				1.2	1.2	1.0
	2.6	3.0	2.1				2.4	1.7	2.0
	UND	8.2	5.4				3.9	4.1	4.6
% Profit Before Taxes/Tangible Net Worth	50.6	31.5	33.4				13.6	40.9	44.3
	(33) 25.1	(40) 13.3	(43) 13.5				3.9	(11) 11.3	(13) 26.6
	8.6	5.5	.9				-4.9	-.5	13.3
% Profit Before Taxes/Total Assets	12.8	9.0	12.8				5.1	11.2	16.3
	7.1	4.6	4.9				1.3	5.8	11.6
	1.2	-.3	-.2				-1.5	.0	4.6
Sales/Net Fixed Assets	11.2	14.0	16.9				10.9	44.3	15.8
	7.7	8.7	8.7				5.9	8.6	8.3
	3.8	5.8	5.0				2.6	7.0	6.0
Sales/Total Assets	3.0	3.3	3.1				2.6	3.0	3.2
	2.0	2.4	2.4				2.0	2.6	2.5
	1.6	1.8	1.8				1.6	1.9	2.1
% Depr., Dep., Amort./Sales	2.5	1.4	1.4				3.3	1.6	1.1
	(38) 3.5	(43) 2.7	(44) 2.8				(13) 5.2	(11) 2.4	(12) 2.3
	5.6	4.0	4.7				7.7	4.6	3.5
% Officers', Directors' Owners' Comp/Sales	2.4	.9	2.3						
	(18) 4.7	(19) 3.3	(16) 4.3						
	7.4	7.9	6.5						
Net Sales ($)	974738M	2783220M	1583095M	1759M	7507M	7533M	104676M	204052M	1257568M
Total Assets ($)	520011M	1226670M	660508M	688M	2435M	4970M	57123M	86297M	508995M

M = $ thousand   MM = $ million
See Pages 11 through 21 for Explanation of Ratios and Data

Current Data Sorted by Assets   Comparative Historical Data

0-500M	500M-2MM	2-10MM	10-50MM	50-100MM	100-250MM	Type of Statement	4/1/02-3/31/03 ALL	4/1/03-3/31/04 ALL
		2	2	1		Unqualified	6	9
	1	6	3			Reviewed	12	9
	2	3	1			Compiled	5	6
	1					Tax Returns	2	1
	1	4			1	Other	15	17
	7 (4/1-9/30/06)		24 (10/1/06-3/31/07)		1			
	5	15	9	1	1	NUMBER OF STATEMENTS	40	42
%	%	%	%	%	%		%	%
						ASSETS		
		5.4				Cash & Equivalents	8.8	8.0
		26.0				Trade Receivables (net)	19.7	19.0
		31.7				Inventory	27.5	25.0
		2.3				All Other Current	1.8	4.4
		65.3				Total Current	57.6	56.4
D		22.6				Fixed Assets (net)	27.6	32.6
A		9.4				Intangibles (net)	5.8	2.9
T		2.7				All Other Non-Current	8.9	8.0
A		100.0				Total	100.0	100.0
						LIABILITIES		
N		6.8				Notes Payable-Short Term	8.1	7.7
O		2.3				Cur. Mat.-L.T.D.	2.6	2.3
T		18.0				Trade Payables	11.8	12.3
		1.0				Income Taxes Payable	.7	.5
A		5.6				All Other Current	8.0	7.1
V		33.8				Total Current	31.2	30.0
A		9.0				Long-Term Debt	18.4	15.7
I		.3				Deferred Taxes	.3	.4
L		8.1				All Other Non-Current	4.0	6.4
A		48.9				Net Worth	46.1	47.4
B		100.0				Total Liabilties & Net Worth	100.0	100.0
L						**INCOME DATA**		
E		100.0				Net Sales	100.0	100.0
		34.1				Gross Profit	31.6	31.6
		24.1				Operating Expenses	27.2	26.1
		10.0				Operating Profit	4.4	5.5
		1.0				All Other Expenses (net)	1.4	1.2
		9.0				Profit Before Taxes	3.0	4.3
						RATIOS		
		3.0					3.0	3.1
		1.9				Current	2.1	1.8
		1.5					1.3	1.2
		1.4					1.7	1.7
		1.1				Quick	.9	.8
		.6					.6	.5
	16	22.3					20 18.4	23 15.6
	28	12.9				Sales/Receivables	32 11.3	35 10.5
	41	8.8					43 8.4	42 8.6
	42	8.7					39 9.4	47 7.8
	61	6.0				Cost of Sales/Inventory	54 6.7	57 6.4
	88	4.1					88 4.2	93 3.9
	26	14.1					16 22.8	21 17.4
	32	11.4				Cost of Sales/Payables	25 14.8	31 11.8
	46	8.0					38 9.7	38 9.5
		6.4					5.2	4.8
		11.2				Sales/Working Capital	9.8	9.6
		16.9					19.5	21.3
		213.6					6.7	8.6
	(14)	6.8				EBIT/Interest	(33) 3.7	(36) 4.1
		2.9					2.1	1.1
						Net Profit + Depr., Dep.,	8.8	4.4
						Amort./Cur. Mat. L/T/D	(11) 4.2	(13) 3.0
							1.9	1.6
		.1					.2	.3
		.5				Fixed/Worth	.7	.8
		1.4					1.5	1.3
		.5					.7	.4
		1.1				Debt/Worth	1.3	1.2
		3.8					2.5	2.4
		115.3				% Profit Before Taxes/Tangible	37.1	52.7
	(14)	51.7				Net Worth	(37) 18.6	(41) 26.4
		16.8					7.6	.0
		39.4				% Profit Before Taxes/Total	15.9	22.7
		16.6				Assets	7.0	8.8
		7.0					3.3	.0
		100.7					24.3	15.7
		21.4				Sales/Net Fixed Assets	9.1	6.6
		8.6					4.2	3.5
		3.6					2.9	2.8
		3.0				Sales/Total Assets	2.1	1.9
		2.0					1.4	1.5
		.6					1.3	1.4
	(12)	1.2				% Depr., Dep., Amort./Sales	(31) 2.0	(36) 2.6
		2.3					3.0	4.2
							1.8	1.3
						% Officers', Directors'	(11) 5.1	(11) 2.2
						Owners' Comp/Sales	7.7	5.7
	22957M	226819M	356222M	132571M	107692M	Net Sales ($)	1168251M	1384369M
	7798M	75446M	186673M	67257M	106863M	Total Assets ($)	738911M	874826M

© RMA 2007

M = $ thousand   MM = $ million
See Pages 11 through 21 for Explanation of Ratios and Data

Comparative Historical Data   Current Data Sorted by Sales

Type of Statement	4/1/04-3/31/05 ALL	4/1/05-3/31/06 ALL	4/1/06-3/31/07 ALL	0-1MM	1-3MM	3-5MM	5-10MM	10-25MM	25MM & OVER
							7 (4/1-9/30/06)		24 (10/1/06-3/31/07)
Unqualified	13	12	5				1		2 2
Reviewed	9	10	10		1	1	3	1	5
Compiled	1	7	6		1		4	1	
Tax Returns	2		1		1				
Other	10	15	9		1				
NUMBER OF STATEMENTS	35	44	31			3	10	7	11
	%	%	%	%	%	%	%	%	%
ASSETS									
Cash & Equivalents	11.2	8.9	6.7	DATA NOT AVAILABLE	DATA NOT AVAILABLE		3.5		5.9
Trade Receivables (net)	18.8	22.3	25.8				26.2		25.3
Inventory	22.7	27.3	27.2				27.5		22.7
All Other Current	3.3	3.1	2.5				1.0		3.3
Total Current	56.0	61.7	62.2				58.2		57.3
Fixed Assets (net)	29.9	25.3	26.8				21.2		32.9
Intangibles (net)	6.3	4.8	6.7				16.7		3.1
All Other Non-Current	7.9	8.3	4.3				4.0		6.7
Total	100.0	100.0	100.0				100.0		100.0
LIABILITIES									
Notes Payable-Short Term	7.5	10.6	8.5				5.0		5.1
Cur. Mat.-L.T.D.	4.3	2.5	2.4				3.0		2.5
Trade Payables	9.0	14.1	17.3				20.3		19.9
Income Taxes Payable	.6	.1	.9				.0		1.2
All Other Current	6.9	7.2	8.2				5.7		6.9
Total Current	28.3	34.6	37.3				33.9		35.6
Long-Term Debt	16.7	8.7	12.0				9.3		15.2
Deferred Taxes	.4	1.0	1.0				.5		1.0
All Other Non-Current	8.3	4.7	6.3				14.6		1.7
Net Worth	46.4	51.0	43.4				41.6		46.5
Total Liabilities & Net Worth	100.0	100.0	100.0				100.0		100.0
INCOME DATA									
Net Sales	100.0	100.0	100.0				100.0		100.0
Gross Profit	36.1	30.6	31.4				37.0		27.4
Operating Expenses	25.0	22.4	23.7				27.3		21.0
Operating Profit	11.1	8.2	7.7				9.6		6.4
All Other Expenses (net)	1.3	1.3	1.3				.8		1.3
Profit Before Taxes	9.8	6.9	6.4				8.8		5.1
RATIOS									
Current	3.5	3.3	2.7				2.9		2.7
	2.0	1.9	1.6				2.1		1.4
	1.1	1.1	1.2				1.3		1.1
Quick	2.4	2.1	1.4				1.6		1.3
	1.1	.7	.9				1.2		.7
	.5	.5	.6				.6		.6
Sales/Receivables	25 14.8	28 13.0	28 13.2				20 18.3		28 12.9
	29 12.5	37 9.9	37 10.0				36 10.3		42 8.6
	39 9.4	44 8.3	46 7.9				42 8.7		47 7.8
Cost of Sales/Inventory	37 9.8	41 8.9	37 9.8				33 10.9		30 12.0
	57 6.4	60 6.1	59 6.2				50 7.4		59 6.2
	85 4.3	91 4.0	83 4.4				91 4.0		89 4.1
Cost of Sales/Payables	12 30.2	18 20.0	26 14.2				24 15.2		32 11.4
	23 16.1	31 11.9	35 10.5				35 10.3		47 7.7
	33 11.2	44 8.4	48 7.6				48 7.7		52 7.0
Sales/Working Capital	5.4	4.0	6.4				7.5		5.2
	10.3	8.1	13.8				13.2		19.1
	39.9	31.7	23.3				17.1		45.7
EBIT/Interest	15.0	28.8	18.0				66.1		21.0
	(30) 4.5	(36) 5.9	(29) 5.0				5.0		3.7
	1.2	1.9	2.2				2.9		1.7
Net Profit + Depr., Dep., Amort./Cur. Mat. L/T/D	6.2	6.8	6.0						
	(12) 3.1	(17) 4.4	(14) 3.1						
	2.0	2.3	1.7						
Fixed/Worth	.4	.2	.2				.3		.3
	.7	.5	.8				.8		.8
	1.4	.9	1.4				2.2		1.3
Debt/Worth	.6	.4	.7				.6		.7
	1.3	.9	1.7				2.9		1.4
	3.5	2.6	3.0				10.7		2.0
% Profit Before Taxes/Tangible Net Worth	61.8	50.8	60.6						42.3
	(32) 28.6	(42) 18.5	(30) 36.4						20.8
	2.4	3.4	15.7						7.2
% Profit Before Taxes/Total Assets	30.6	19.0	22.3				30.1		20.7
	13.9	9.5	11.3				13.8		7.6
	2.9	2.2	4.4				4.8		2.3
Sales/Net Fixed Assets	20.2	20.7	22.6				160.2		11.3
	8.1	9.3	11.3				18.2		6.4
	4.2	5.1	5.4				7.7		5.3
Sales/Total Assets	3.2	3.0	3.4				3.7		3.3
	1.8	1.9	2.4				2.9		2.0
	1.4	1.4	1.7				1.9		1.7
% Depr., Dep., Amort./Sales	1.3	.6	1.0						1.3
	(31) 2.5	(39) 2.2	(28) 1.6						1.7
	3.3	3.3	2.4						2.3
% Officers', Directors' Owners' Comp/Sales									
Net Sales ($)	929196M	1364510M	846261M			11255M	80248M	117957M	636801M
Total Assets ($)	633820M	913026M	444037M			4057M	31960M	58145M	349875M

			Current Data Sorted by Assets			Type of Statement		**Comparative Historical Data**
	1		2	1	2	Unqualified	7	7
	1	3	3			Reviewed	8	4
	1	2	2			Compiled	5	9
2			1	1		Tax Returns	2	1
	4	3	20 (10/1/06-3/31/07)			Other	7	6
	11 (4/1-9/30/06)						4/1/02-3/31/03	4/1/03-3/31/04
0-500M	500M-2MM	2-10MM	10-50MM	50-100MM	100-250MM		ALL	ALL
2	7	8	11	1	2	NUMBER OF STATEMENTS	29	27
%	%	%	%	%	%	**ASSETS**	%	%
			4.3			Cash & Equivalents	6.2	9.5
			16.8			Trade Receivables (net)	21.1	17.9
			18.9			Inventory	24.1	22.5
			1.7			All Other Current	3.5	3.8
			41.7			Total Current	54.9	53.7
			49.8			Fixed Assets (net)	34.9	35.8
			7.3			Intangibles (net)	3.8	7.4
			1.1			All Other Non-Current	6.4	3.1
			100.0			Total	100.0	100.0
						LIABILITIES		
			11.6			Notes Payable-Short Term	9.4	7.7
			3.2			Cur. Mat.-L.T.D.	3.2	3.6
			11.3			Trade Payables	15.7	13.5
			.0			Income Taxes Payable	.0	.4
			5.6			All Other Current	16.3	6.8
			31.8			Total Current	44.6	32.0
			29.5			Long-Term Debt	15.6	17.2
			1.2			Deferred Taxes	.7	1.2
			3.5			All Other Non-Current	2.6	8.7
			34.0			Net Worth	36.4	40.9
			100.0			Total Liabilities & Net Worth	100.0	100.0
						INCOME DATA		
			100.0			Net Sales	100.0	100.0
			24.5			Gross Profit	32.6	29.6
			22.6			Operating Expenses	28.0	25.0
			1.9			Operating Profit	4.6	4.6
			2.1			All Other Expenses (net)	1.6	.9
			-.2			Profit Before Taxes	3.0	3.6
						RATIOS		
			2.5				1.8	2.9
			1.4			Current	1.2	1.6
			1.2				.9	1.0
			1.4				.9	1.4
			.8			Quick	.6	.9
			.4				.4	.5
		25	14.9				20 18.5	22 16.5
		31	12.0			Sales/Receivables	30 12.2	27 13.4
		42	8.7				37 9.8	34 10.8
		32	11.6				26 14.2	33 11.0
		40	9.0			Cost of Sales/Inventory	41 8.8	49 7.5
		70	5.2				77 4.7	64 5.7
		13	27.2				18 20.1	14 25.5
		33	11.0			Cost of Sales/Payables	27 13.5	26 13.9
		39	9.4				40 9.1	40 9.1
			7.1				9.4	5.2
			14.2			Sales/Working Capital	20.5	12.6
			28.5				-131.4	136.2
			3.1				7.1	8.8
			1.9			EBIT/Interest	(26) 4.3	(24) 4.3
			.7				1.3	1.9
			11.6			Net Profit + Depr., Dep.,	4.6	
			3.0			Amort./Cur. Mat. L/T/D	(12) 3.0	(12) 2.8
			1.4				1.4	1.1
			1.0				.5	.7
			1.5			Fixed/Worth	1.0	1.2
			4.5				3.4	2.9
			1.2				.7	.7
			2.8			Debt/Worth	1.9	2.1
			4.6				7.4	6.7
			21.9			% Profit Before Taxes/Tangible	44.8	37.2
		(10)	10.8			Net Worth	(26) 16.5	(24) 22.2
			-2.1				2.2	6.6
			6.0			% Profit Before Taxes/Total	11.0	12.3
			3.3			Assets	5.6	7.3
			-.7				1.7	2.9
			8.5				16.4	11.4
			5.1			Sales/Net Fixed Assets	6.8	6.0
			1.4				3.8	3.3
			3.0				3.5	3.3
			1.9			Sales/Total Assets	2.3	2.1
			1.0				2.0	1.7
			1.7				1.7	2.0
			2.7			% Depr., Dep., Amort./Sales	(28) 2.5	(25) 2.6
			3.3				3.2	3.7
						% Officers', Directors'	6.6	
						Owners' Comp/Sales	(11) 8.6	
							10.1	
1529M	21006M	65953M	568487M	120631M	569544M	Net Sales ($)	1019043M	774692M
298M	8396M	43876M	328122M	60011M	305439M	Total Assets ($)	589193M	426663M

© RMA 2007

M = $ thousand   MM = $ million
See Pages 11 through 21 for Explanation of Ratios and Data

Comparative Historical Data   ## Current Data Sorted by Sales

C1	C2	C3	Type of Statement	0-1MM	1-3MM	3-5MM	5-10MM	10-25MM	25MM & OVER
5	7	6	Unqualified	1					5
7	7	7	Reviewed			1	2	1	3
6	3	5	Compiled		2		2	1	1
1	2	3	Tax Returns				1	1	1
8	8	10	Other	1	1	3	2		2
4/1/04-3/31/05 ALL	4/1/05-3/31/06 ALL	4/1/06-3/31/07 ALL		11 (4/1-9/30/06)			20 (10/1/06-3/31/07)		
27	27	31	**NUMBER OF STATEMENTS**	2	4	3	6	4	12
%	%	%	**ASSETS**	%	%	%	%	%	%
10.8	6.8	3.8	Cash & Equivalents						3.9
18.1	20.2	18.3	Trade Receivables (net)						17.9
26.1	24.6	26.2	Inventory						21.5
1.5	1.5	1.6	All Other Current						1.9
56.5	53.2	49.9	Total Current						45.2
35.0	35.7	40.0	Fixed Assets (net)						45.0
3.6	3.9	7.0	Intangibles (net)						7.8
4.9	7.2	3.2	All Other Non-Current						2.0
100.0	100.0	100.0	Total						100.0
			LIABILITIES						
10.4	11.7	13.1	Notes Payable-Short Term						12.6
3.5	3.5	3.2	Cur. Mat.-L.T.D.						2.9
12.8	15.2	12.2	Trade Payables						11.0
.6	.3	.2	Income Taxes Payable						.1
7.1	7.3	7.6	All Other Current						8.4
34.4	38.0	36.4	Total Current						35.1
12.1	16.0	22.7	Long-Term Debt						20.1
.5	.7	1.3	Deferred Taxes						.8
3.3	6.2	8.6	All Other Non-Current						3.3
49.7	39.1	31.0	Net Worth						40.7
100.0	100.0	100.0	Total Liabilities & Net Worth						100.0
			INCOME DATA						
100.0	100.0	100.0	Net Sales						100.0
28.1	25.5	29.2	Gross Profit						23.5
23.2	21.8	24.8	Operating Expenses						20.6
5.0	3.7	4.4	Operating Profit						2.9
.7	1.0	2.1	All Other Expenses (net)						1.4
4.2	2.7	2.3	Profit Before Taxes						1.5
			RATIOS						
2.2	1.9	2.5	Current						2.1
1.7	1.5	1.4							1.3
1.3	1.2	1.1							1.1
1.2	1.0	1.3	Quick						1.2
.9	.7	.7							.8
.4	.5	.4							.4
19 18.8	19 18.8	25 14.9	Sales/Receivables						25 14.9
24 15.0	26 14.0	32 11.4							31 11.7
35 10.5	39 9.3	43 8.5							40 9.2
32 11.3	30 12.0	40 9.2	Cost of Sales/Inventory						30 12.2
46 7.9	47 7.8	65 5.7							40 9.0
68 5.3	78 4.7	98 3.7							69 5.3
14 25.6	15 24.2	13 27.2	Cost of Sales/Payables						13 27.7
18 19.8	27 13.3	27 13.5							27 13.5
45 8.2	37 10.0	39 9.4							34 10.8
5.7	10.1	7.1	Sales/Working Capital						9.3
11.7	14.1	16.4							15.9
24.3	38.5	56.6							49.6
10.2	14.7	6.2	EBIT/Interest						8.6
(23) 4.8	(26) 3.9	(29) 2.1						(11)	2.3
2.3	1.2	1.3							1.7
4.7	6.5	2.4	Net Profit + Depr., Dep., Amort./Cur. Mat. L/T/D						
(11) 2.5	(12) 2.9	(11) 1.9							
1.8	.9	.6							
.5	.6	1.0	Fixed/Worth						.7
.8	1.1	1.5							1.4
1.3	1.7	4.5							3.8
.7	1.0	1.2	Debt/Worth						.9
.9	1.9	2.0							1.8
2.3	3.1	8.2							3.7
25.9	31.5	26.2	% Profit Before Taxes/Tangible Net Worth						26.7
(25) 13.5	(25) 18.8	(25) 11.3						(11)	11.3
5.1	2.2	2.4							.3
11.6	15.2	9.2	% Profit Before Taxes/Total Assets						9.2
6.9	6.0	3.7							3.6
2.0	2.0	.7							.4
14.1	16.0	11.4	Sales/Net Fixed Assets						8.3
7.1	6.9	6.3							6.3
4.3	4.9	2.0							2.3
3.2	3.3	3.0	Sales/Total Assets						2.8
2.3	2.3	1.9							2.1
1.6	2.1	1.0							1.0
1.6	1.2	1.2	% Depr., Dep., Amort./Sales						1.7
(25) 2.3	(24) 2.2	(30) 2.3						(11)	2.7
3.2	3.4	4.2							3.5
			% Officers', Directors' Owners' Comp/Sales						
1022826M	1308831M	1347150M	Net Sales ($)	634M	8145M	10424M	43600M	59994M	1224353M
534865M	564477M	746142M	Total Assets ($)	676M	3726M	7143M	32270M	62676M	639651M

M = $ thousand   MM = $ million
See Pages 11 through 21 for Explanation of Ratios and Data

Current Data Sorted by Assets   Comparative Historical Data

	0-500M	500M-2MM	2-10MM	10-50MM	50-100MM	100-250MM		
Type of Statement							2 4/1/02- 3/31/03 ALL	3 4/1/03- 3/31/04 ALL
Unqualified			2	5	2		2	3
Reviewed		1	2	1			3	2
Compiled		2	3				2	1
Tax Returns	1		1				1	1
Other		2	5	7	2	1	5	7
	10 (4/1-9/30/06)			27 (10/1/06-3/31/07)				
NUMBER OF STATEMENTS	1	6	12	13	4	1	13	14
	%	%	%	%	%	%	%	%
ASSETS								
Cash & Equivalents			8.1	3.4			9.1	7.3
Trade Receivables (net)			23.8	19.7			18.5	20.8
Inventory			29.7	29.8			25.9	21.9
All Other Current			1.6	3.4			1.2	.5
Total Current			63.2	56.3			54.7	50.5
Fixed Assets (net)			26.7	31.3			39.9	40.3
Intangibles (net)			5.3	1.4			2.4	3.6
All Other Non-Current			4.7	11.0			2.9	5.6
Total			100.0	100.0			100.0	100.0
LIABILITIES								
Notes Payable-Short Term			10.7	7.0			20.8	7.9
Cur. Mat.-L.T.D.			1.7	2.1			5.9	4.6
Trade Payables			14.9	9.2			13.6	16.4
Income Taxes Payable			.3	.1			.2	.0
All Other Current			8.9	9.3			4.6	4.0
Total Current			36.4	27.6			45.1	32.9
Long-Term Debt			18.5	10.3			23.9	20.6
Deferred Taxes			.2	.5			.2	.0
All Other Non-Current			8.3	6.2			12.3	11.8
Net Worth			36.6	55.4			18.5	34.7
Total Liabilities & Net Worth			100.0	100.0			100.0	100.0
INCOME DATA								
Net Sales			100.0	100.0			100.0	100.0
Gross Profit			37.2	29.1			35.0	37.3
Operating Expenses			32.2	20.9			30.9	30.0
Operating Profit			5.0	8.2			4.1	7.3
All Other Expenses (net)			1.2	.2			2.0	1.1
Profit Before Taxes			3.8	8.0			2.1	6.2
RATIOS								
Current			3.3	3.5			2.6	2.2
			1.6	2.5			1.2	1.3
			1.2	1.3			.7	.6
Quick			1.9	1.6			1.2	1.4
			.7	.7			.5	.8
			.5	.6			.4	.4
Sales/Receivables			29 12.8	30 12.3			30 12.2	5 71.7
			40 9.2	40 9.2			39 9.4	37 9.9
			52 7.0	61 6.0			47 7.8	46 7.9
Cost of Sales/Inventory			48 7.6	47 7.7			37 10.0	30 12.2
			70 5.2	73 5.0			49 7.4	43 8.5
			106 3.4	131 2.8			112 3.3	58 6.3
Cost of Sales/Payables			26 14.0	19 19.7			21 17.2	31 11.9
			36 10.2	32 11.6			32 11.5	35 10.3
			51 7.2	50 7.3			58 6.3	56 6.5
Sales/Working Capital			5.3	3.2			6.9	7.1
			10.2	5.9			17.8	12.6
			26.7	10.1			-11.4	-14.6
EBIT/Interest			9.5	20.2			13.7	9.2
			(11) 3.4	(12) 5.4			1.9	(13) 6.2
			1.0	2.0			1.1	3.0
Net Profit + Depr., Dep., Amort./Cur. Mat. L/T/D								
Fixed/Worth			.3	.1			.9	.4
			.8	.6			1.7	1.1
			4.0	.9			4.4	1.9
Debt/Worth			.6	.4			1.9	1.0
			1.6	.5			5.3	1.9
			6.9	1.5			19.6	3.1
% Profit Before Taxes/Tangible Net Worth			45.1	37.6			31.6	49.4
			(10) 13.9	16.1			(11) 26.3	(13) 33.7
			3.4	7.4			7.4	20.6
% Profit Before Taxes/Total Assets			13.1	20.0			10.5	16.2
			4.1	8.4			3.1	10.7
			.2	2.4			.3	4.3
Sales/Net Fixed Assets			31.0	22.3			22.9	42.4
			12.1	5.7			4.4	6.8
			4.2	2.5			1.6	1.4
Sales/Total Assets			2.9	2.3			2.3	3.3
			2.3	1.6			1.7	2.1
			1.5	1.1			1.1	1.1
% Depr., Dep., Amort./Sales			.9	1.9			1.3	1.0
			1.5	(11) 2.6			(11) 2.8	(12) 2.7
			2.2	3.7			7.0	4.8
% Officers', Directors' Owners' Comp/Sales								
Net Sales ($)	1323M	25512M	117445M	506131M	357462M	106113M	113374M	158352M
Total Assets ($)	52M	5783M	59438M	339752M	291962M	100540M	71846M	122562M

M = $ thousand   MM = $ million
See Pages 11 through 21 for Explanation of Ratios and Data

Comparative Historical Data   Current Data Sorted by Sales

			Type of Statement						
4	7	9	Unqualified				1		6
3	2	4	Reviewed		1		2	2	1
1	2	5	Compiled		1		4		
	2	2	Tax Returns		1		1		
4	11	17	Other			2	2	6	7
				0-1MM	10 (4/1-9/30/06) 1-3MM	3-5MM	27 (10/1/06-3/31/07) 5-10MM	10-25MM	25MM & OVER
4/1/04-3/31/05 ALL	4/1/05-3/31/06 ALL	4/1/06-3/31/07 ALL							
12	22	37	NUMBER OF STATEMENTS		3	2	10	8	14
%	%	%	ASSETS	%	%	%	%	%	%
11.8	9.8	6.8	Cash & Equivalents				8.1		4.9
20.3	20.3	22.3	Trade Receivables (net)				27.3		19.4
25.3	24.6	28.7	Inventory				29.6		29.5
6.1	5.1	3.6	All Other Current	D A T A			1.3		4.5
63.5	59.7	61.4	Total Current				66.3		58.3
27.1	23.3	27.9	Fixed Assets (net)	N O T			28.4		28.2
1.0	5.9	2.9	Intangibles (net)				1.3		2.8
8.5	11.1	7.9	All Other Non-Current				4.0		10.7
100.0	100.0	100.0	Total	A V A I L A B L E			100.0		100.0
			LIABILITIES						
9.9	12.8	10.0	Notes Payable-Short Term				11.5		7.7
2.5	3.0	1.7	Cur. Mat.-L.T.D.				1.7		2.0
10.8	10.9	10.9	Trade Payables				15.9		8.7
.0	.1	.1	Income Taxes Payable				.3		.1
19.0	13.3	10.1	All Other Current				12.6		10.5
42.1	40.0	32.8	Total Current				42.0		29.0
12.9	8.4	20.1	Long-Term Debt				23.0		8.6
.2	.4	.3	Deferred Taxes				.2		.4
1.3	11.2	8.3	All Other Non-Current				7.6		6.1
43.5	40.0	38.5	Net Worth				27.2		55.9
100.0	100.0	100.0	Total Liabilities & Net Worth				100.0		100.0
			INCOME DATA						
100.0	100.0	100.0	Net Sales				100.0		100.0
35.6	32.6	32.6	Gross Profit				37.6		23.4
27.7	25.5	25.2	Operating Expenses				33.1		16.2
7.9	7.1	7.4	Operating Profit				4.6		7.2
1.0	.0	.6	All Other Expenses (net)				1.2		.0
6.9	7.1	6.8	Profit Before Taxes				3.4		7.2
			RATIOS						
2.8	2.2	3.3	Current				1.9		3.2
1.8	1.4	2.0					1.6		2.2
1.0	1.2	1.2					1.3		1.4
2.4	1.2	1.5	Quick				1.1		1.6
.8	.9	.7					.8		.8
.5	.4	.5					.6		.5
21 17.1	21 17.0	27 13.3	Sales/Receivables				27 13.5		28 13.2
36 10.2	37 9.9	39 9.4					33 11.0		39 9.3
52 7.0	50 7.3	50 7.3					46 8.0		61 6.0
39 9.3	39 9.3	47 7.8	Cost of Sales/Inventory				45 8.1		42 8.7
57 6.4	56 6.5	63 5.8					61 6.0		69 5.3
102 3.6	101 3.6	110 3.3					85 4.3		116 3.1
12 31.0	20 18.1	18 20.5	Cost of Sales/Payables				24 15.0		13 27.2
26 14.0	33 11.2	30 12.2					36 10.2		23 16.2
55 6.6	49 7.4	44 8.3					50 7.3		35 10.5
4.0	5.7	4.8	Sales/Working Capital				9.2		4.2
7.6	11.3	8.3					15.4		5.4
94.6	29.0	29.2					23.3		9.5
32.0	16.4	16.0	EBIT/Interest				16.3		21.5
(11) 9.4	(21) 9.5	(35) 5.1					4.0		(13) 5.1
4.4	3.9	1.1					1.1		.7
		8.8	Net Profit + Depr., Dep., Amort./Cur. Mat. L/T/D						
		(10) 4.9							
		1.9							
.2	.2	.1	Fixed/Worth				.3		.1
.9	.6	.6					.8		.5
1.6	1.8	1.2					2.2		.7
.8	.8	.5	Debt/Worth				1.1		.4
1.0	1.2	1.1					2.7		.6
2.9	5.7	3.8					5.2		1.6
66.7	42.5	61.1	% Profit Before Taxes/Tangible Net Worth						56.7
(11) 26.1	(19) 30.2	(33) 17.0							13.7
12.5	10.2	5.5							-.7
18.5	20.9	20.0	% Profit Before Taxes/Total Assets				13.4		24.9
10.9	8.7	7.4					3.0		7.4
4.4	4.7	.7					.3		-.4
19.3	24.5	33.1	Sales/Net Fixed Assets				45.8		31.7
8.2	10.9	12.3					12.1		12.0
3.0	3.9	3.2					3.3		2.7
2.3	2.4	2.9	Sales/Total Assets				4.2		2.3
2.0	1.9	1.8					2.8		1.6
1.4	1.3	1.4					1.5		1.3
1.6	.9	1.1	% Depr., Dep., Amort./Sales						1.1
(11) 2.8	1.9	(31) 2.1						(11)	2.6
4.4	3.0	3.4							3.7
		2.1	% Officers', Directors', Owners' Comp/Sales						
		(10) 2.5							
		7.9							
517828M	881821M	1113986M	Net Sales ($)		5808M	7816M	75955M	129121M	895286M
282327M	546708M	797527M	Total Assets ($)		1675M	2042M	30098M	126084M	637628M

M = $ thousand   MM = $ million
See Pages 11 through 21 for Explanation of Ratios and Data

Current Data Sorted by Assets | Comparative Historical Data

Type of Statement	0-500M	500M-2MM	2-10MM	10-50MM	50-100MM	100-250MM		4/1/02-3/31/03 ALL	4/1/03-3/31/04 ALL
Unqualified	4	1	11	28	8	3		38	47
Reviewed	1	5	25	9		1		22	36
Compiled	2	10	11	4				18	28
Tax Returns	6	5	3					8	20
Other	6	10	31	31	23	3		55	51
	54 (4/1-9/30/06)			160 (10/1/06-3/31/07)					
NUMBER OF STATEMENTS	19	31	81	64	13	6		141	182

ASSETS	%	%	%	%	%	%		%	%
Cash & Equivalents	16.9	9.8	7.4	5.7	4.3			8.0	6.9
Trade Receivables (net)	28.7	21.2	22.8	21.1	18.5			21.7	22.3
Inventory	20.9	21.0	25.8	26.3	22.0			21.9	24.2
All Other Current	1.4	2.0	1.4	2.7	1.8			2.4	3.1
Total Current	67.9	54.1	57.4	55.8	46.6			54.0	56.5
Fixed Assets (net)	21.5	28.9	33.0	34.0	37.1			34.7	32.3
Intangibles (net)	3.7	1.0	4.7	2.7	11.2			4.7	5.2
All Other Non-Current	6.9	16.1	4.8	7.5	5.0			6.6	5.9
Total	100.0	100.0	100.0	100.0	100.0			100.0	100.0

LIABILITIES									
Notes Payable-Short Term	13.5	12.1	11.4	11.3	13.4			9.8	10.3
Cur. Mat.-L.T.D.	15.2	5.7	3.1	3.2	4.6			4.3	4.0
Trade Payables	15.9	15.4	19.6	17.6	13.3			14.7	17.0
Income Taxes Payable	1.3	.0	.3	.3	.6			.5	.3
All Other Current	7.5	9.2	7.4	7.4	6.8			8.6	8.7
Total Current	53.4	42.5	41.9	39.9	38.6			37.9	40.4
Long-Term Debt	21.9	18.6	17.5	21.2	22.8			18.0	16.4
Deferred Taxes	.4	.3	.7	.4	1.0			.4	.6
All Other Non-Current	1.6	15.7	6.5	5.9	8.0			6.5	9.3
Net Worth	22.7	22.9	33.5	32.6	29.5			37.2	33.4
Total Liabilties & Net Worth	100.0	100.0	100.0	100.0	100.0			100.0	100.0

INCOME DATA									
Net Sales	100.0	100.0	100.0	100.0	100.0			100.0	100.0
Gross Profit	39.7	36.0	30.2	28.6	25.4			31.5	31.8
Operating Expenses	36.3	32.0	26.6	22.8	20.9			26.9	26.2
Operating Profit	3.5	3.9	3.6	5.8	4.5			4.6	5.6
All Other Expenses (net)	1.6	.8	1.2	1.6	1.0			1.2	1.6
Profit Before Taxes	1.9	3.1	2.4	4.1	3.6			3.4	4.1

RATIOS									
Current	5.0	3.3	2.4	1.9	1.4			2.2	2.1
	1.8	1.4	1.3	1.4	1.1			1.4	1.3
	.7	.9	1.0	1.1	.9			1.0	1.1
Quick	3.7	1.2	1.2	1.0	.7			1.2	1.1
	.6	.6	.7	.7	.5			.8	.7
	.5	.4	.4	.5	.5			.5	.5
Sales/Receivables	18 20.5	20 18.5	21 17.5	19 18.8	28 13.1			20 18.0	22 16.4
	20 18.0	25 14.6	29 12.4	30 12.2	30 12.3			30 12.3	30 12.3
	38 9.7	35 10.4	40 9.2	39 9.3	40 9.2			39 9.4	39 9.4
Cost of Sales/Inventory	5 75.8	10 35.2	23 15.9	23 16.2	27 13.6			20 18.5	18 20.0
	26 14.0	37 9.9	47 7.7	47 7.7	45 8.1			43 8.4	44 8.4
	93 3.9	63 5.8	84 4.4	77 4.7	94 3.9			79 4.6	82 4.5
Cost of Sales/Payables	1 505.0	4 83.4	23 15.8	21 17.6	19 19.3			13 28.2	17 20.9
	21 17.1	22 16.2	35 10.6	32 11.3	28 13.2			25 14.4	29 12.5
	40 9.1	36 10.1	50 7.3	49 7.5	49 7.4			39 9.5	47 7.8
Sales/Working Capital	7.3	7.4	7.4	9.6	9.2			6.9	7.4
	19.7	24.5	19.4	16.7	65.6			18.0	21.4
	-25.0	-57.6	NM	65.5	-96.4			218.2	136.9
EBIT/Interest	20.3	8.1	10.2	8.4	8.3			13.5	13.2
	(13) 3.6	(27) 1.6	(74) 2.5	(62) 3.3	(12) 4.3			(134) 3.3	(164) 4.3
	1.3	.1	1.1	2.2	2.7			1.4	1.6
Net Profit + Depr., Dep., Amort./Cur. Mat. L/T/D			16.3	6.7				7.1	11.4
			(24) 4.7	(30) 3.5				(45) 4.9	(64) 3.2
			.8	1.8				2.3	1.8
Fixed/Worth	.1	.3	.4	.4	1.3			.4	.5
	1.0	.8	1.1	1.2	1.9			.9	1.0
	-.9	3.2	3.6	2.6	NM			2.5	3.4
Debt/Worth	.3	.5	.9	1.1	1.8			1.0	.9
	1.7	2.8	2.0	2.6	3.5			1.9	2.1
	-5.5	134.2	9.5	4.8	NM			4.5	8.6
% Profit Before Taxes/Tangible Net Worth	134.5	44.4	42.8	38.6	56.3			45.6	53.8
	(14) 37.0	(24) 9.8	(69) 18.1	(58) 23.7	(10) 28.5			(125) 21.1	(148) 24.6
	-4.3	1.9	3.5	13.2	19.8			5.0	6.8
% Profit Before Taxes/Total Assets	49.6	26.1	13.7	14.4	11.9			15.4	16.5
	14.1	4.2	5.6	7.4	8.7			6.0	7.4
	-16.1	-.4	.5	4.1	5.1			1.5	1.9
Sales/Net Fixed Assets	97.9	29.8	21.9	14.7	7.4			20.6	20.5
	28.3	6.9	8.9	6.9	6.7			7.9	8.8
	11.1	5.3	4.3	4.1	3.6			3.7	4.9
Sales/Total Assets	9.9	4.1	3.9	3.0	2.8			3.8	3.6
	4.1	2.4	2.6	2.4	1.8			2.3	2.5
	2.3	1.8	1.5	1.9	1.5			1.6	1.7
% Depr., Dep., Amort./Sales	.6	1.5	1.0	1.0	1.5			1.2	1.2
	(10) 1.3	(25) 2.4	(73) 1.8	(59) 1.8	(12) 2.1			(121) 2.1	(150) 2.1
	2.7	3.8	3.1	3.2	3.0			4.3	3.4
% Officers', Directors' Owners' Comp/Sales		1.7	1.9					1.5	1.6
		(14) 2.5	(24) 3.5					(44) 3.8	(64) 3.3
		4.8	5.7					7.5	5.5
Net Sales ($)	23140M	117993M	1244327M	4167923M	1919930M	1928718M		6657276M	8440117M
Total Assets ($)	4224M	38440M	448595M	1585123M	893523M	888879M		2894652M	3792325M

M = $ thousand   MM = $ million
See Pages 11 through 21 for Explanation of Ratios and Data

Comparative Historical Data · **Current Data Sorted by Sales**

Hist 1	Hist 2	Hist 3	Type of Statement	0-1MM	1-3MM	3-5MM	5-10MM	10-25MM	25MM & OVER
51	55	55	Unqualified	2	3	1	1	9	39
32	43	41	Reviewed	1	2	2	5	19	12
19	30	27	Compiled	2	6	2	7	6	4
16	20	14	Tax Returns	3	5	3	1		
58	90	77	Other	6	7	6	12	12	34
4/1/04-3/31/05 ALL	4/1/05-3/31/06 ALL	4/1/06-3/31/07 ALL		54 (4/1-9/30/06)			160 (10/1/06-3/31/07)		
176	238	214	NUMBER OF STATEMENTS	14	23	14	27	47	89
%	%	%	**ASSETS**	%	%	%	%	%	%
6.6	7.1	8.0	Cash & Equivalents	17.2	7.7	13.5	9.4	6.9	6.0
20.1	22.2	22.2	Trade Receivables (net)	22.9	19.0	18.4	20.6	25.3	22.2
23.9	24.8	24.3	Inventory	14.4	20.3	19.6	24.6	28.2	25.5
3.5	1.9	1.9	All Other Current	2.5	2.4	1.7	.8	1.4	2.3
54.2	56.1	56.4	Total Current	57.0	49.4	53.2	55.4	61.7	56.1
33.3	32.0	32.1	Fixed Assets (net)	21.9	37.0	34.4	30.7	30.0	33.5
4.9	4.5	4.0	Intangibles (net)	4.3	1.6	3.0	7.6	3.3	4.1
7.6	7.4	7.5	All Other Non-Current	16.9	12.0	9.4	6.3	4.9	6.3
100.0	100.0	100.0	Total	100.0	100.0	100.0	100.0	100.0	100.0
			LIABILITIES						
10.6	11.4	11.5	Notes Payable-Short Term	14.6	13.0	5.3	11.6	11.7	11.4
4.0	4.1	4.7	Cur. Mat.-L.T.D.	9.9	10.5	1.8	3.6	4.5	3.2
17.2	18.5	17.5	Trade Payables	13.2	13.3	9.0	20.9	21.0	17.6
.2	.4	.4	Income Taxes Payable	.0	.0	1.8	.3	.4	.3
8.4	8.3	7.9	All Other Current	5.2	9.4	2.5	8.5	9.3	7.8
40.5	42.6	41.8	Total Current	43.0	46.2	20.3	44.7	46.9	40.4
21.0	18.1	19.4	Long-Term Debt	12.6	34.8	18.1	18.1	13.8	20.1
.5	.5	.5	Deferred Taxes	.6	.2	.4	.6	.8	.5
7.3	7.7	7.5	All Other Non-Current	6.1	15.2	11.1	3.6	6.9	6.7
30.6	31.1	30.7	Net Worth	37.8	3.7	50.1	32.9	31.7	32.3
100.0	100.0	100.0	Total Liabilities & Net Worth	100.0	100.0	100.0	100.0	100.0	100.0
			INCOME DATA						
100.0	100.0	100.0	Net Sales	100.0	100.0	100.0	100.0	100.0	100.0
30.0	29.6	31.0	Gross Profit	37.4	40.7	36.8	32.8	28.6	27.2
25.4	25.7	26.5	Operating Expenses	37.2	36.1	28.6	28.5	25.7	21.9
4.7	4.0	4.4	Operating Profit	.3	4.6	8.2	4.4	2.8	5.3
1.1	1.0	1.3	All Other Expenses (net)	1.9	1.4	.5	1.5	1.0	1.4
3.6	2.9	3.1	Profit Before Taxes	-1.7	3.2	7.6	2.9	1.8	3.9
			RATIOS						
2.1	2.2	2.2	Current	5.1	2.0	9.5	2.2	2.0	1.8
1.4	1.4	1.4		1.8	1.4	4.7	1.1	1.3	1.4
1.0	1.0	1.0		.7	.7	1.6	.9	.9	1.0
1.0	1.1	1.2	Quick	5.1	1.0	6.9	1.1	1.2	1.1
.6	.7	.6		1.0	.6	1.5	.6	.6	.6
.4	.4	.5		.4	.4	.7	.4	.4	.5
19 18.8	20 17.9	20 18.0	Sales/Receivables	19 19.5	19 19.2	12 31.1	18 20.2	23 16.2	21 17.1
27 13.4	30 12.3	29 12.6		26 14.1	30 12.4	23 15.7	27 13.5	29 12.5	30 12.3
40 9.2	40 9.2	38 9.5		39 9.2	46 7.9	34 10.6	40 9.0	36 10.0	38 9.5
19 18.9	18 19.9	21 17.5	Cost of Sales/Inventory	6 65.7	23 16.0	8 46.5	24 15.2	24 15.2	22 16.5
41 8.9	41 8.8	44 8.3		17 21.2	55 6.6	29 12.6	50 7.2	47 7.7	43 8.6
81 4.5	81 4.5	82 4.5		58 6.2	98 3.7	106 3.4	105 3.5	77 4.8	76 4.8
17 21.0	18 20.0	19 19.7	Cost of Sales/Payables	1 268.4	11 32.9	0 871.0	25 14.6	21 17.7	19 18.9
28 13.1	31 11.8	30 12.0		20 18.0	27 13.3	17 21.4	37 9.9	33 11.1	30 12.1
45 8.1	45 8.1	45 8.1		47 7.8	49 7.4	29 12.4	52 7.0	52 7.1	44 8.4
8.1	8.3	8.5	Sales/Working Capital	4.4	8.2	4.4	9.4	8.8	10.1
20.2	19.6	19.6		22.1	13.3	8.1	50.3	19.6	19.8
-109.7	-314.3	-175.0		-13.8	-22.2	27.3	-57.6	-81.3	135.3
9.7	9.3	8.7	EBIT/Interest		7.8	20.4	13.0	13.7	8.6
(165) 3.8	(218) 3.5	(194) 3.1		(20) 2.4	(12) 4.1	(25) 2.1	(46) 3.2	(83) 3.4	
1.0	1.1	1.3			.8	2.3	1.1	1.0	2.1
7.8	7.4	11.2	Net Profit + Depr., Dep., Amort./Cur. Mat. L/T/D					14.2	9.3
(50) 3.4	(80) 3.3	(68) 3.3						(18) 4.7	(41) 3.7
1.4	1.4	1.4						1.0	1.8
.5	.4	.4	Fixed/Worth	.2	.6	.3	.1	.3	.6
1.2	.9	1.2		1.3	1.3	.8	.9	1.1	1.2
3.4	2.3	3.3		-1.4	-.7	1.5	4.8	2.5	2.6
1.1	1.1	.9	Debt/Worth	.2	.9	.4	.8	.9	1.3
2.5	2.2	2.3		2.8	3.2	1.0	3.1	2.4	2.5
9.9	5.8	9.4		-12.0	-3.4	1.4	99.2	9.3	5.2
49.1	46.5	45.0	% Profit Before Taxes/Tangible Net Worth	78.4	44.9	91.7	42.4	44.6	44.8
(143) 22.4	(205) 20.9	(180) 21.9		(10) 10.4	(16) 25.7	(13) 24.8	(22) 12.6	(41) 18.1	(78) 26.3
8.7	4.8	8.0		-46.3	2.7	11.3	-9.9	2.5	14.1
13.3	14.7	16.1	% Profit Before Taxes/Total Assets	8.5	31.7	30.8	20.1	14.0	14.7
6.1	5.3	6.6		-.2	12.1	9.0	3.7	6.9	7.5
.3	.5	1.0		-30.5	.8	4.4	.3	.2	4.1
21.3	22.7	22.6	Sales/Net Fixed Assets	55.5	28.9	34.7	33.5	22.7	14.9
8.5	9.5	7.8		11.1	6.9	6.3	6.6	9.7	7.4
4.3	4.7	4.7		6.2	2.6	3.4	3.1	5.4	4.6
3.8	3.8	3.7	Sales/Total Assets	4.1	4.1	3.9	4.0	3.9	3.3
2.5	2.5	2.4		2.1	2.0	2.3	2.4	3.1	2.4
1.6	1.6	1.7		1.5	1.3	1.5	1.0	2.0	1.9
1.1	.9	1.0	% Depr., Dep., Amort./Sales		1.5		1.2	.8	1.0
(148) 2.0	(196) 1.8	(182) 1.9		(17) 3.1		(24) 2.5	(44) 1.5	(80) 1.8	
3.5	3.2	3.2			5.5		4.2	2.8	3.0
1.3	1.2	1.6	% Officers', Directors' Owners' Comp/Sales		2.1		2.5	1.3	.8
(64) 2.5	(00) 2.3	(57) 2.7		(11) 3.0		(11) 3.9	(13) 3.3	(13) 1.0	
4.7	5.3	5.6			4.1		5.7	8.6	2.3
8236576M	13116433M	9402031M	Net Sales ($)	7811M	46451M	55929M	202130M	761510M	8328200M
3518398M	5216492M	3858784M	Total Assets ($)	4096M	26492M	30815M	112430M	300309M	3384642M

© RMA 2007

M = $ thousand   MM = $ million
See Pages 11 through 21 for Explanation of Ratios and Data

Current Data Sorted by Assets   Comparative Historical Data

0-500M	500M-2MM	2-10MM	10-50MM	50-100MM	100-250MM	Type of Statement	4/1/02-3/31/03 ALL	4/1/03-3/31/04 ALL
1		4	21	7	7	Unqualified	45	39
	1	6	4			Reviewed	11	11
		1	1			Compiled	2	18
	1	2	2			Tax Returns	4	1
3	1	12	11	2	6	Other	39	27
	14 (4/1-9/30/06)		79 (10/1/06-3/31/07)					
4	3	25	39	9	13	NUMBER OF STATEMENTS	101	96
%	%	%	%	%	%	ASSETS	%	%
		5.9	9.2		2.1	Cash & Equivalents	6.7	7.8
		20.0	18.7		13.0	Trade Receivables (net)	18.5	19.1
		17.6	16.4		14.4	Inventory	14.6	17.8
		1.7	2.9		1.9	All Other Current	2.5	4.4
		45.2	47.3		31.4	Total Current	42.2	49.0
		42.7	31.3		32.6	Fixed Assets (net)	36.6	34.4
		4.2	10.4		24.0	Intangibles (net)	13.7	10.3
		8.0	11.0		11.9	All Other Non-Current	7.5	6.2
		100.0	100.0		100.0	Total	100.0	100.0
						LIABILITIES		
		12.1	7.9		6.2	Notes Payable-Short Term	8.0	11.7
		3.6	2.5		2.3	Cur. Mat.-L.T.D.	4.2	4.6
		22.0	15.2		11.6	Trade Payables	14.6	15.2
		.1	.1		.1	Income Taxes Payable	.3	.1
		7.4	9.3		9.4	All Other Current	8.6	7.7
		45.2	34.9		29.6	Total Current	35.6	39.3
		32.1	19.7		19.7	Long-Term Debt	21.2	18.2
		.0	1.2		2.7	Deferred Taxes	1.1	1.0
		6.8	4.6		3.2	All Other Non-Current	8.8	10.7
		15.9	39.5		44.9	Net Worth	33.3	30.8
		100.0	100.0		100.0	Total Liabilties & Net Worth	100.0	100.0
						INCOME DATA		
		100.0	100.0		100.0	Net Sales	100.0	100.0
		38.8	27.1		28.7	Gross Profit	34.0	31.3
		37.6	23.6		23.5	Operating Expenses	29.3	27.7
		1.2	3.5		5.2	Operating Profit	4.6	3.6
		1.8	.1		1.1	All Other Expenses (net)	1.1	.7
		-.6	3.4		4.1	Profit Before Taxes	3.5	2.9
						RATIOS		
		2.0	2.2		1.6		1.8	2.1
		1.1	1.4		1.2	Current	1.2	1.3
		.6	1.2		.8		.9	.9
		1.1	1.5		1.1		1.2	1.2
		.6	.8		.6	Quick	.7	.7
		.3	.5		.3		.4	.4
		24 15.4	19 19.0		25 14.6		18 19.9	21 17.5
		28 13.1	25 14.5		29 12.4	Sales/Receivables	27 13.5	29 12.6
		46 7.9	36 10.0		34 10.6		35 10.4	38 9.7
		19 19.5	17 22.0		17 20.9		19 19.3	22 16.4
		32 11.2	30 12.2		20 18.7	Cost of Sales/Inventory	27 13.6	29 12.5
		62 5.9	40 9.0		44 8.4		39 9.4	45 8.2
		25 14.5	15 24.4		12 31.4		17 21.4	18 20.3
		35 10.4	21 17.1		27 13.8	Cost of Sales/Payables	27 13.4	28 13.3
		121 3.0	48 7.7		44 8.2		44 8.4	44 8.2
		13.0	11.0		16.8		11.9	9.7
		52.1	18.6		60.2	Sales/Working Capital	34.8	30.0
		-8.6	117.5		-40.5		-72.7	-81.5
		6.6	14.1		8.3		14.5	10.0
		(23) 2.6	(36) 3.9		5.3	EBIT/Interest	(92) 3.3	(88) 2.5
		.0	1.1		1.6		1.0	1.1
			23.4			Net Profit + Depr., Dep.,	8.5	2.8
		(13) 5.0				Amort./Cur. Mat. L/T/D	(21) 2.2	(26) 1.4
			2.4				1.1	.7
		1.0	.5		.6		.6	.6
		3.1	1.0		1.5	Fixed/Worth	1.2	1.2
		-7.6	6.8		-1.7		6.1	13.9
		.6	.6		.7		.8	.7
		17.7	1.7		2.1	Debt/Worth	1.8	1.9
		-13.1	21.0		-4.3		10.2	24.9
		38.2	30.7			% Profit Before Taxes/Tangible	55.8	33.2
		(15) 18.4	(31) 14.8			Net Worth	(80) 22.3	(74) 16.9
		-11.7	3.0				5.5	3.3
		15.6	11.3		13.2	% Profit Before Taxes/Total	14.3	12.1
		7.7	6.2		6.4	Assets	6.1	3.7
		-3.5	.3		.7		.0	.3
		21.5	17.7		8.3		14.4	17.5
		5.8	9.4		7.2	Sales/Net Fixed Assets	6.6	7.0
		2.7	4.8		3.6		4.1	4.0
		3.7	3.2		2.5		3.4	3.3
		2.0	2.4		2.2	Sales/Total Assets	2.4	2.4
		1.5	1.7		1.5		1.5	1.5
		1.5	1.6				2.3	1.5
		(23) 3.7	(34) 2.9			% Depr., Dep., Amort./Sales	(80) 3.1	(76) 3.4
		10.9	4.2				4.5	4.8
						% Officers', Directors'	.9	1.0
						Owners' Comp/Sales	(17) 2.0	(20) 2.8
							6.0	6.3
3141M	11582M	300508M	2596324M	1143821M	4476357M	Net Sales ($)	8236077M	7049167M
711M	3352M	135055M	1067953M	609755M	2185154M	Total Assets ($)	4237811M	3178964M

M = $ thousand   MM = $ million
See Pages 11 through 21 for Explanation of Ratios and Data

Comparative Historical Data | Current Data Sorted by Sales

Type of Statement									
				Current Data Sorted by Sales					
Unqualified	38	37	40	1			1	3	35
Reviewed	7	12	11			1	1	6	3
Compiled	3	3	2				2		
Tax Returns	7	2	5		1		2	2	2
Other	29	28	35	3		1	5	8	16
	4/1/04-3/31/05 ALL	4/1/05-3/31/06 ALL	4/1/06-3/31/07 ALL	0-1MM	1-3MM	3-5MM	5-10MM	10-25MM	25MM & OVER
					14 (4/1-9/30/06)		79 (10/1/06-3/31/07)		
NUMBER OF STATEMENTS	84	82	93	4	3	3	10	17	56
ASSETS	%	%	%	%	%	%	%	%	%
Cash & Equivalents	6.9	9.5	6.8				14.3	5.4	6.2
Trade Receivables (net)	17.3	16.7	18.8				16.2	19.0	18.1
Inventory	15.2	17.7	16.3				11.9	20.4	15.7
All Other Current	2.8	3.1	2.3				1.3	2.7	2.7
Total Current	42.3	47.0	44.2				43.6	47.4	42.7
Fixed Assets (net)	36.9	34.5	35.1				37.3	32.6	34.1
Intangibles (net)	12.2	11.1	10.8				3.0	10.0	13.1
All Other Non-Current	8.7	7.4	9.9				16.0	9.9	10.1
Total	100.0	100.0	100.0				100.0	100.0	100.0
LIABILITIES									
Notes Payable-Short Term	6.8	5.1	7.9				5.8	14.4	6.6
Cur. Mat.-L.T.D.	5.3	4.6	2.6				2.0	2.9	2.6
Trade Payables	12.6	14.1	16.8				18.6	17.0	14.7
Income Taxes Payable	.3	.2	.1				.3	.0	.1
All Other Current	9.6	8.3	8.3				2.3	8.3	9.5
Total Current	34.5	32.4	35.7				29.0	42.7	33.5
Long-Term Debt	22.7	25.3	24.8				34.2	17.1	22.2
Deferred Taxes	1.3	1.1	.9				.0	.6	1.4
All Other Non-Current	7.3	6.5	5.8				5.6	5.4	5.5
Net Worth	34.1	34.7	32.8				31.2	34.2	37.5
Total Liabilities & Net Worth	100.0	100.0	100.0				100.0	100.0	100.0
INCOME DATA									
Net Sales	100.0	100.0	100.0				100.0	100.0	100.0
Gross Profit	36.2	31.7	32.5				41.0	39.7	27.2
Operating Expenses	33.1	27.3	29.6				36.8	37.3	23.0
Operating Profit	3.2	4.3	3.0				4.3	2.4	4.2
All Other Expenses (net)	.4	.7	1.0				-.1	.8	.5
Profit Before Taxes	2.7	3.6	2.0				4.3	1.6	3.7
RATIOS									
Current	2.3	2.3	2.2				8.6	2.3	2.0
	1.4	1.5	1.3				1.8	1.2	1.3
	.9	1.1	.9				.6	1.1	1.0
Quick	1.4	1.6	1.4				6.7	1.4	1.4
	.9	.8	.8				1.0	.8	.8
	.4	.5	.4				.3	.3	.5
Sales/Receivables	21 17.0	19 18.9	24 15.4				19 19.1	24 15.4	24 15.4
	29 12.5	30 12.3	28 13.2				29 12.5	26 13.9	27 13.8
	35 10.4	34 10.7	37 9.8				37 9.9	35 10.5	34 10.7
Cost of Sales/Inventory	20 18.4	19 19.3	18 20.0				21 17.0	15 23.8	18 19.8
	29 12.4	29 12.4	30 12.1				47 7.8	30 12.1	28 13.2
	42 8.6	50 7.3	48 7.6				63 5.8	77 4.8	38 9.6
Cost of Sales/Payables	15 23.7	14 25.3	16 23.2				25 14.6	18 20.7	15 24.7
	33 11.0	30 12.1	27 13.7				45 8.2	30 12.4	20 17.8
	45 8.1	46 8.0	49 7.4				173 2.1	58 6.3	42 8.7
Sales/Working Capital	10.0	7.6	11.1				3.5	11.7	11.8
	20.0	19.8	24.3				16.1	32.8	25.8
	-94.6	79.5	-104.4				-9.2	53.5	NM
EBIT/Interest	25.0	20.2	10.8					7.3	13.5
	(75) 2.9	(77) 3.2	(87) 3.1					3.1	(53) 5.0
	.7	1.4	.8					-.2	1.2
Net Profit + Depr., Dep., Amort./Cur. Mat. L/T/D	3.6	7.2	12.6						15.5
	(22) 2.2	(19) 4.0	(20) 4.6						(17) 5.0
	1.1	2.2	1.7						2.4
Fixed/Worth	.5	.5	.6				.0	.7	.6
	1.5	1.0	1.4				5.1	1.1	1.2
	7.4	10.2	-33.1				-342.3	9.8	11.3
Debt/Worth	.6	.6	.6				.1	.6	.6
	2.4	1.6	2.4				6.5	2.3	1.8
	12.8	12.0	-44.5				-430.7	61.9	30.8
% Profit Before Taxes/Tangible Net Worth	39.2	37.9	33.9					29.0	34.2
	(66) 23.8	(63) 20.6	(66) 19.1					(14) 14.4	(43) 20.7
	.4	6.7	2.9					-13.9	5.9
% Profit Before Taxes/Total Assets	14.6	12.8	13.7				13.8	14.6	14.9
	5.6	7.1	6.2				4.8	6.2	6.5
	-1.5	1.0	-.4				-2.7	-2.0	.8
Sales/Net Fixed Assets	12.7	14.0	14.8				23.5	25.0	11.3
	6.9	7.0	7.3				4.0	8.6	7.4
	4.2	3.9	4.0				2.5	4.6	4.5
Sales/Total Assets	3.3	3.2	3.2				2.5	3.7	3.1
	2.3	2.2	2.2				1.6	2.3	2.4
	1.6	1.5	1.5				1.0	1.5	1.8
% Depr., Dep., Amort./Sales	1.9	1.8	1.6					1.8	1.6
	(70) 3.3	(66) 3.0	(73) 3.0					2.8	(42) 2.7
	4.8	4.2	4.5					4.2	4.0
% Officers', Directors' Owners' Comp/Sales	1.2	.9	1.0						
	(10) 2.3	(10) 1.8	(12) 2.0						
	7.2	5.3	5.0						
Net Sales ($)	7277362M	7298572M	8531733M	1487M	6077M	11471M	70718M	284995M	8156985M
Total Assets ($)	3397354M	3371353M	4001980M	1124M	12440M	12663M	92539M	151118M	3732096M

M = $ thousand   MM = $ million
See Pages 11 through 21 for Explanation of Ratios and Data

Current Data Sorted by Assets   Comparative Historical Data

						Type of Statement	4/1/02-3/31/03	4/1/03-3/31/04
		2	2	2	3	Unqualified	6	9
	2	4	4			Reviewed	12	7
	2	3	1			Compiled	10	10
1	1					Tax Returns	7	7
2	3	7	7		1	Other	11	20
	7 (4/1-9/30/06)		40 (10/1/06-3/31/07)				ALL	ALL
0-500M	500M-2MM	2-10MM	10-50MM	50-100MM	100-250MM			
3	8	16	14	3	3	NUMBER OF STATEMENTS	46	53
%	%	%	%	%	%	**ASSETS**	%	%
		5.9	1.3			Cash & Equivalents	7.5	6.5
		16.6	18.5			Trade Receivables (net)	29.1	20.9
		13.0	18.8			Inventory	22.8	18.8
		1.8	1.5			All Other Current	2.1	1.9
		37.3	40.1			Total Current	61.5	48.0
		44.4	49.7			Fixed Assets (net)	27.3	36.8
		12.2	5.9			Intangibles (net)	4.1	9.5
		6.2	4.3			All Other Non-Current	7.2	5.7
		100.0	100.0			Total	100.0	100.0
						LIABILITIES		
		14.6	11.0			Notes Payable-Short Term	15.5	8.5
		6.4	3.1			Cur. Mat.-L.T.D.	3.1	5.1
		11.7	13.0			Trade Payables	20.8	12.7
		.2	.3			Income Taxes Payable	.2	.0
		13.3	5.0			All Other Current	6.0	10.8
		46.2	32.4			Total Current	45.6	37.0
		30.0	36.3			Long-Term Debt	20.0	29.6
		.0	.3			Deferred Taxes	.5	.4
		10.1	9.4			All Other Non-Current	2.5	7.8
		13.7	21.7			Net Worth	31.5	25.1
		100.0	100.0			Total Liabilities & Net Worth	100.0	100.0
						INCOME DATA		
		100.0	100.0			Net Sales	100.0	100.0
		44.9	25.1			Gross Profit	31.6	41.6
		39.8	21.6			Operating Expenses	28.3	38.6
		5.0	3.5			Operating Profit	3.3	3.0
		2.1	2.1			All Other Expenses (net)	1.1	1.1
		2.9	1.3			Profit Before Taxes	2.2	1.9
						RATIOS		
		1.7	1.9				2.2	2.4
		.9	1.2			Current	1.3	1.4
		.5	1.0				.9	.8
		1.0	.9				1.2	1.5
		.7	.6			Quick	.8 (52)	.7
		.3	.4				.4	.5
		21 17.5	28 13.0				20 18.0	20 18.6
		29 12.7	33 11.1			Sales/Receivables	32 11.3	27 13.5
		41 9.0	41 8.9				43 8.5	35 10.4
		15 24.8	34 10.7				14 26.8	25 14.6
		21 17.1	38 9.6			Cost of Sales/Inventory	30 12.0	44 8.3
		60 6.1	67 5.5				80 4.6	75 4.9
		23 15.6	18 20.0				15 24.2	14 25.6
		35 10.5	27 13.7			Cost of Sales/Payables	28 13.0	27 13.4
		45 8.2	44 8.3				60 6.1	41 9.0
		11.8	11.3				7.8	9.4
		-141.2	39.6			Sales/Working Capital	30.4	18.2
		-5.6	NM				-51.2	-24.9
		5.7	5.2				5.3	7.9
		(15) 1.6	1.6			EBIT/Interest	(39) 1.8	(48) 2.3
		1.0	1.0				-.4	.6
						Net Profit + Depr., Dep., Amort./Cur. Mat. L/T/D		
		1.1	1.1				.2	.5
		2.9	2.4			Fixed/Worth	.7	1.4
		-4.7	-5.5				2.8	7.7
		1.0	2.0				1.0	.9
		4.8	3.7			Debt/Worth	2.0	2.1
		-7.7	-9.4				6.3	21.4
			60.6				32.7	59.0
		(10) 21.5				% Profit Before Taxes/Tangible Net Worth	(40) 5.1	(41) 13.8
		8.7					-7.2	2.1
		14.9	13.5				11.0	12.9
		5.5	2.5			% Profit Before Taxes/Total Assets	1.5	4.3
		.3	-.4				-2.5	-2.3
		7.1	77.2				164.5	14.2
		3.5	3.0			Sales/Net Fixed Assets	12.2	6.7
		2.4	1.7				5.0	3.5
		2.6	2.5				4.1	3.5
		1.8	1.6			Sales/Total Assets	2.6	2.5
		1.3	1.0				1.7	1.4
		2.6	2.1				.3	1.4
		(13) 6.8	(13) 4.4			% Depr., Dep., Amort./Sales	(41) 1.7	(49) 4.7
		9.1	5.4				5.0	8.5
							1.4	2.3
						% Officers', Directors' Owners' Comp/Sales	(18) 2.7	(19) 5.0
							5.0	9.3
2674M	33180M	203645M	526462M	239067M	712075M	Net Sales ($)	1220282M	1084500M
1064M	8891M	95162M	310402M	217637M	460667M	Total Assets ($)	549141M	468054M

M = $ thousand   MM = $ million
See Pages 11 through 21 for Explanation of Ratios and Data

Comparative Historical Data / Current Data Sorted by Sales

	4/1/04-3/31/05 ALL	4/1/05-3/31/06 ALL	4/1/06-3/31/07 ALL	Type of Statement	0-1MM	1-3MM	3-5MM	5-10MM	10-25MM	25MM & OVER
	7	7	9	Unqualified				2	1	7
	18	7	10	Reviewed		2		3	3	2
	8	8	6	Compiled			1	2	2	1
	7	5	2	Tax Returns	2		1			
	20	12	20	Other	2		3	2	4	7
					7 (4/1-9/30/06)			40 (10/1/06-3/31/07)		
	60	39	47	**NUMBER OF STATEMENTS**	4	2	5	9	10	17
	%	%	%	**ASSETS**	%	%	%	%	%	%
	7.2	5.7	3.9	Cash & Equivalents					4.4	2.5
	22.8	22.8	17.6	Trade Receivables (net)					16.7	20.1
	23.6	21.7	15.8	Inventory					16.8	19.6
	3.7	2.4	2.8	All Other Current					1.6	2.2
	57.3	52.6	40.1	Total Current					39.6	44.4
	29.7	35.0	45.1	Fixed Assets (net)					53.1	37.1
	7.3	5.3	9.8	Intangibles (net)					1.5	13.9
	5.6	7.1	5.0	All Other Non-Current					5.8	4.6
	100.0	100.0	100.0	Total					100.0	100.0
				LIABILITIES						
	11.8	12.4	9.9	Notes Payable-Short Term					2.4	10.1
	5.7	4.6	6.5	Cur. Mat.-L.T.D.					3.9	3.5
	19.4	12.7	11.0	Trade Payables					10.6	13.5
	.1	.2	.2	Income Taxes Payable					.4	.1
	7.6	8.5	10.2	All Other Current					4.1	14.4
	44.6	38.4	37.8	Total Current					21.5	41.5
	21.7	16.8	33.8	Long-Term Debt					28.8	32.2
	.4	.3	.4	Deferred Taxes					.6	.7
	4.7	8.0	8.2	All Other Non-Current					6.3	10.4
	28.6	36.5	19.9	Net Worth					42.9	15.1
	100.0	100.0	100.0	Total Liabilities & Net Worth					100.0	100.0
				INCOME DATA						
	100.0	100.0	100.0	Net Sales					100.0	100.0
	36.3	39.1	39.0	Gross Profit					36.7	30.1
	33.6	34.8	33.8	Operating Expenses					28.7	25.3
	2.7	4.3	5.1	Operating Profit					8.0	4.8
	.9	1.2	2.5	All Other Expenses (net)					1.6	2.0
	1.8	3.1	2.6	Profit Before Taxes					6.3	2.8
				RATIOS						
	2.1	2.5	1.8	Current					2.5	1.7
	1.3	1.5	1.2						1.8	1.2
	.9	.8	.9						1.0	1.0
	.9	1.2	1.0	Quick					1.5	.9
	.7	.8	.7						1.0	.6
	.4	.5	.4						.7	.4
	21 17.8	19 18.8	21 17.7	Sales/Receivables					20 18.7	22 16.9
	28 12.9	32 11.5	32 11.5						28 13.1	33 11.0
	35 10.3	44 8.4	40 9.1						39 9.3	41 8.9
	19 19.7	14 26.7	16 22.2	Cost of Sales/Inventory					14 26.3	24 15.2
	41 8.9	34 10.6	32 11.5						36 10.3	39 9.4
	62 5.9	91 4.0	61 5.9						45 8.1	80 4.6
	19 19.6	13 28.1	14 26.4	Cost of Sales/Payables					13 29.1	18 20.3
	27 13.6	22 16.7	26 14.0						20 18.4	33 11.0
	44 8.3	37 9.8	43 8.5						38 9.6	43 8.6
	7.9	7.2	9.9	Sales/Working Capital					8.5	12.1
	19.8	16.8	32.0						14.5	32.0
	-78.7	-54.3	-26.0						NM	NM
	10.0	5.8	5.7	EBIT/Interest					17.7	6.2
	(54) 3.2	(36) 2.8	(43) 1.9						4.8	(16) 2.5
	.9	1.1	1.0						1.6	1.1
	2.3		2.7	Net Profit + Depr., Dep.,						
	(12) .7	(10) 1.2		Amort./Cur. Mat. L/T/D						
	.2		.3							
	.2	.2	1.1	Fixed/Worth					.2	1.0
	1.2	.8	2.7						1.4	2.4
	7.3	4.3	-3.3						2.6	-1.9
	1.0	.6	1.4	Debt/Worth					.7	1.8
	2.5	3.2	5.3						1.5	15.5
	12.9	7.6	-9.0						2.5	-4.4
	40.9	41.8	62.2	% Profit Before Taxes/Tangible					50.5	129.9
	(47) 23.8	(34) 25.9	(30) 25.1	Net Worth					25.1	(10) 30.5
	1.1	1.8	8.7						7.5	17.4
	13.9	13.5	13.5	% Profit Before Taxes/Total					17.2	13.7
	6.7	5.2	3.9	Assets					10.7	6.2
	-.4	.2	.2						2.4	.7
	54.3	50.1	10.1	Sales/Net Fixed Assets					53.9	16.7
	9.8	7.4	3.9						2.1	4.6
	4.2	2.8	2.2						1.2	3.0
	4.4	3.7	2.7	Sales/Total Assets					4.0	2.9
	2.7	2.2	1.9						1.5	2.3
	1.6	1.4	1.0						.9	1.0
	.5	1.2	1.9	% Depr., Dep., Amort./Sales						1.7
	(53) 2.7	(32) 4.8	(41) 4.8						(14)	3.8
	6.4	7.6	7.6							5.4
	.9	1.0	.6	% Officers', Directors'						
	(27) 2.0	(14) 2.7	(10) 2.2	Owners' Comp/Sales						
	5.4	4.8	3.6							
	2007580M	1097550M	1717103M	Net Sales ($)	2129M	3964M	19627M	69027M	172030M	1450326M
	813603M	623460M	1093823M	Total Assets ($)	2084M	1212M	11026M	47079M	160408M	872014M

Current Data Sorted by Assets | Comparative Historical Data

Type of Statement	0-500M	500M-2MM	2-10MM	10-50MM	50-100MM	100-250MM	4/1/02-3/31/03 ALL	4/1/03-3/31/04 ALL
Unqualified	1		2	5	3		9	12
Reviewed	1		3	2			7	8
Compiled	1	1	3	1			4	3
Tax Returns		1		1			1	4
Other	1	3	4	9	2	4	9	9
		5 (4/1-9/30/06)		42 (10/1/06-3/31/07)				
NUMBER OF STATEMENTS	4	5	13	16	5	4	30	36
ASSETS	%	%	%	%	%	%	%	%
Cash & Equivalents			3.5	4.1			11.2	8.9
Trade Receivables (net)			9.9	7.3			7.0	9.8
Inventory			17.0	10.7			10.0	15.7
All Other Current			3.8	3.3			1.1	1.4
Total Current			34.1	25.4			29.3	35.9
Fixed Assets (net)			46.8	62.7			58.9	52.0
Intangibles (net)			12.1	4.9			8.8	6.9
All Other Non-Current			6.9	6.9			2.9	5.3
Total			100.0	100.0			100.0	100.0
LIABILITIES								
Notes Payable-Short Term			6.6	1.8			2.4	4.4
Cur. Mat.-L.T.D.			4.7	3.0			4.1	3.9
Trade Payables			11.2	7.5			7.5	9.2
Income Taxes Payable			.0	.1			.5	.1
All Other Current			6.8	6.8			10.7	10.4
Total Current			29.2	19.1			25.2	28.0
Long-Term Debt			31.5	33.8			26.6	22.9
Deferred Taxes			2.1	1.7			.6	1.1
All Other Non-Current			.9	1.6			5.0	5.5
Net Worth			36.3	43.8			42.6	42.5
Total Liabilities & Net Worth			100.0	100.0			100.0	100.0
INCOME DATA								
Net Sales			100.0	100.0			100.0	100.0
Gross Profit			42.5	34.1			40.3	37.3
Operating Expenses			38.8	25.0			35.1	31.7
Operating Profit			3.7	9.1			5.1	5.6
All Other Expenses (net)			1.9	1.8			2.0	1.7
Profit Before Taxes			1.8	7.2			3.1	3.8
RATIOS								
Current			2.0	1.6			2.3	2.5
			1.1	1.0			1.5	1.3
			.9	.9			.6	1.0
Quick			.7	1.0			1.5	1.5
			.4	.6			.9	.6
			.3	.4			.3	.4
Sales/Receivables			5 77.4	3 112.9			5 76.1	10 36.3
			25 14.4	23 16.1			21 17.3	23 16.1
			36 10.1	35 10.3			28 12.9	30 12.4
Cost of Sales/Inventory			35 10.4	20 17.9			22 16.2	26 13.8
			63 5.8	38 9.5			39 9.2	42 8.6
			84 4.4	57 6.4			57 6.4	74 4.9
Cost of Sales/Payables			27 13.6	11 32.0			17 21.5	17 21.3
			38 9.6	29 12.8			28 13.1	29 12.6
			54 6.8	44 8.4			44 8.3	38 9.7
Sales/Working Capital			7.5	11.8			7.7	6.5
			65.7	-999.8			15.9	25.3
			-147.0	-114.8			-17.6	-177.7
EBIT/Interest			7.1	7.8			9.8	9.9
			1.9	(15) 4.4			(29) 2.2	2.9
			.4	3.2			.7	.7
Net Profit + Depr., Dep., Amort./Cur. Mat. L/T/D								3.1
								(13) 2.3
								.2
Fixed/Worth			1.0	1.2			1.2	.9
			1.6	1.8			1.8	1.3
			3.9	2.9			3.9	2.6
Debt/Worth			1.3	.8			.9	.7
			3.2	1.3			1.8	1.4
			5.7	3.0			4.5	5.3
% Profit Before Taxes/Tangible Net Worth			37.1	27.8			40.1	43.3
			(11) 11.9	(15) 14.8			(26) 8.6	(32) 19.5
			-12.8	8.0			.9	4.2
% Profit Before Taxes/Total Assets			7.8	13.3			13.6	14.8
			4.8	7.5			3.1	5.9
			-1.9	3.2			-.2	-.6
Sales/Net Fixed Assets			8.5	2.8			3.8	9.2
			3.9	1.8			1.6	2.4
			1.6	1.1			1.2	1.6
Sales/Total Assets			2.8	1.5			1.9	2.4
			1.5	1.2			1.1	1.5
			.8	.8			.9	1.0
% Depr., Dep., Amort./Sales			2.6	2.7			2.9	2.2
			(12) 4.1	(15) 4.7			(28) 6.0	(32) 3.7
			5.0	8.6			8.4	6.7
% Officers', Directors' Owners' Comp/Sales								
Net Sales ($)	2662M	14829M	137285M	524369M	483603M	631299M	853511M	1155588M
Total Assets ($)	1039M	4952M	71035M	403784M	329559M	636638M	663911M	825060M

M = $ thousand   MM = $ million
See Pages 11 through 21 for Explanation of Ratios and Data

Comparative Historical Data   Current Data Sorted by Sales

Hist 1	Hist 2	Hist 3	Type of Statement	0-1MM	1-3MM	3-5MM	5-10MM	10-25MM	25MM & OVER
14	9	11	Unqualified	1			1	2	7
9	4	6	Reviewed	1		1		4	
4	5	5	Compiled	1	1	1	2		
3	2	2	Tax Returns		2				
11	24	23	Other		3	3		6	11
4/1/04-3/31/05 ALL	4/1/05-3/31/06 ALL	4/1/06-3/31/07 ALL		5 (4/1-9/30/06)			42 (10/1/06-3/31/07)		
41	44	47	NUMBER OF STATEMENTS	3	6	5	3	12	18
%	%	%	ASSETS	%	%	%	%	%	%
9.2	10.2	7.8	Cash & Equivalents					5.8	7.7
10.1	11.5	8.3	Trade Receivables (net)					9.9	5.8
14.6	15.1	13.9	Inventory					11.5	10.3
1.5	3.2	5.6	All Other Current					.5	11.1
35.3	40.0	35.6	Total Current					27.7	34.9
50.9	48.7	50.0	Fixed Assets (net)					55.6	48.8
8.7	7.1	8.3	Intangibles (net)					4.6	10.3
5.0	4.3	6.1	All Other Non-Current					12.2	5.9
100.0	100.0	100.0	Total					100.0	100.0
			LIABILITIES						
3.3	3.8	4.4	Notes Payable-Short Term					1.2	1.7
5.1	3.6	3.2	Cur. Mat.-L.T.D.					4.8	1.9
9.3	10.7	10.9	Trade Payables					10.3	8.1
.4	.4	.1	Income Taxes Payable					.0	.2
7.3	8.4	9.5	All Other Current					5.4	13.7
25.4	27.0	28.0	Total Current					21.7	25.6
36.2	29.6	31.1	Long-Term Debt					34.1	26.3
1.3	1.5	1.7	Deferred Taxes					1.8	2.4
3.6	8.0	3.0	All Other Non-Current					2.5	1.0
33.5	33.8	36.3	Net Worth					39.9	44.8
100.0	100.0	100.0	Total Liabilities & Net Worth					100.0	100.0
			INCOME DATA						
100.0	100.0	100.0	Net Sales					100.0	100.0
36.9	34.9	41.0	Gross Profit					42.3	30.4
29.8	26.3	33.7	Operating Expenses					32.2	21.0
7.1	8.6	7.3	Operating Profit					10.1	9.4
1.1	.9	1.5	All Other Expenses (net)					2.2	1.6
6.0	7.7	5.8	Profit Before Taxes					7.9	7.8
			RATIOS						
2.4	2.4	2.0	Current					2.1	1.5
1.4	1.4	1.1						1.0	1.0
.8	1.0	.9						1.0	.9
1.3	1.3	1.0	Quick					1.2	.6
.7	.8	.6						.7	.5
.3	.5	.3						.4	.3
7 52.9	9 42.5	3 117.8	Sales/Receivables					8 44.1	2 163.3
22 16.4	22 16.3	22 16.6						26 13.8	21 17.6
30 12.3	36 10.0	35 10.5						37 9.8	34 10.6
22 16.9	25 14.9	29 12.4	Cost of Sales/Inventory					36 10.2	17 21.7
40 9.2	42 8.7	47 7.8						40 9.0	30 12.1
72 5.1	67 5.5	79 4.6						53 6.9	63 5.8
16 23.3	11 32.4	11 33.1	Cost of Sales/Payables					28 12.8	7 52.6
31 11.6	26 14.2	35 10.3						45 8.2	20 18.4
45 8.1	43 8.5	61 6.0						60 6.1	51 7.2
7.4	6.0	8.5	Sales/Working Capital					7.3	20.9
25.5	22.4	65.7						NM	584.1
-31.2	-999.8	-159.8						-200.4	-63.0
9.5	10.8	8.8	EBIT/Interest					7.2	37.4
3.8 (39)	4.2 (43)	3.8						4.1 (16)	5.0
.9	1.1	1.6						2.4	2.0
5.7	5.8	4.1	Net Profit + Depr., Dep., Amort./Cur. Mat. L/T/D						
(15) 2.8	(10) 3.0	(15) 3.1							
.0	1.8	2.0							
.9	.7	.7	Fixed/Worth					.8	1.1
1.6	2.0	1.6						1.7	1.6
NM	UND	3.3						3.2	3.1
.9	.6	.9	Debt/Worth					.8	.7
1.4	1.4	1.5						1.6	1.2
NM	UND	4.7						4.3	5.2
49.4	85.7	51.1	% Profit Before Taxes/Tangible Net Worth					52.1	33.0
(31) 24.2	(34) 33.0	(41) 18.0						(11) 14.8	(16) 18.9
8.2	8.8	7.3						9.4	7.0
17.4	21.1	14.7	% Profit Before Taxes/Total Assets					16.3	14.5
7.4	9.9	7.4						7.8	7.9
-.3	1.0	1.1						3.6	1.1
11.0	8.9	8.6	Sales/Net Fixed Assets					6.2	11.0
2.1	3.1	2.7						2.7	2.4
1.4	1.6	1.7						1.6	1.3
3.0	2.5	2.5	Sales/Total Assets					2.2	2.0
1.4	1.5	1.5						1.2	1.4
.8	.9	.9						1.0	.8
2.8	2.6	2.6	% Depr., Dep., Amort./Sales					3.0	1.5
(33) 5.8	(39) 3.7	(42) 4.0						(11) 4.1	(17) 3.5
8.2	6.5	5.2						8.8	4.9
		.6	% Officers', Directors' Owners' Comp/Sales						
	(11)	3.7							
		4.8							
1112026M	1856364M	1794047M	Net Sales ($)	1355M	11845M	18473M	23224M	189526M	1549624M
904939M	1522670M	1447007M	Total Assets ($)	622M	8042M	18424M	14279M	161018M	1244622M

M = $ thousand   MM = $ million
See Pages 11 through 21 for Explanation of Ratios and Data

Current Data Sorted by Assets   Comparative Historical Data

0-500M	500M-2MM	2-10MM	10-50MM	50-100MM	100-250MM	Type of Statement	4/1/02-3/31/03 ALL	4/1/03-3/31/04 ALL
1	1	4	9	7	5	Unqualified	21	29
		10	9	1	1	Reviewed	13	23
	2	3				Compiled	6	13
2	4	3	3			Tax Returns	5	16
6		18	11	6	2	Other	42	26
	28 (4/1-9/30/06)		89 (10/1/06-3/31/07)					
9	16	38	32	14	8	NUMBER OF STATEMENTS	87	107

0-500M %	500M-2MM %	2-10MM %	10-50MM %	50-100MM %	100-250MM %		4/1/02-3/31/03 ALL %	4/1/03-3/31/04 ALL %
						ASSETS		
	14.0	5.2	2.9	1.0		Cash & Equivalents	3.6	3.7
	7.9	8.8	7.8	9.7		Trade Receivables (net)	8.3	9.8
	52.4	45.4	36.3	31.3		Inventory	43.2	39.8
	.3	1.4	1.4	4.1		All Other Current	2.0	2.0
	74.7	60.8	48.4	46.0		Total Current	57.1	55.2
	21.0	32.4	46.8	41.6		Fixed Assets (net)	35.7	36.7
	1.3	2.7	1.0	4.1		Intangibles (net)	1.5	3.9
	3.0	4.1	3.8	8.3		All Other Non-Current	5.7	4.1
	100.0	100.0	100.0	100.0		Total	100.0	100.0
						LIABILITIES		
	4.2	13.6	8.3	10.0		Notes Payable-Short Term	13.4	13.8
	1.4	2.0	2.7	2.4		Cur. Mat.-L.T.D.	2.2	2.3
	10.0	7.1	5.5	7.8		Trade Payables	8.2	7.9
	.0	.3	.3	.1		Income Taxes Payable	.2	.2
	7.8	4.5	7.1	5.9		All Other Current	6.1	9.4
	23.3	27.6	23.8	26.2		Total Current	30.1	33.6
	11.0	20.3	24.8	20.6		Long-Term Debt	23.9	25.4
	.1	.4	.9	1.2		Deferred Taxes	.6	.4
	3.9	12.6	1.6	2.1		All Other Non-Current	6.2	4.5
	61.7	39.1	48.9	49.9		Net Worth	39.2	36.0
	100.0	100.0	100.0	100.0		Total Liabilities & Net Worth	100.0	100.0
						INCOME DATA		
	100.0	100.0	100.0	100.0		Net Sales	100.0	100.0
	54.8	52.0	48.1	42.1		Gross Profit	44.9	46.6
	45.9	37.8	31.2	27.4		Operating Expenses	36.7	36.9
	8.8	14.2	16.8	14.7		Operating Profit	8.2	9.7
	-.7	3.8	6.6	1.8		All Other Expenses (net)	4.2	3.8
	9.5	10.4	10.2	12.9		Profit Before Taxes	4.0	5.8
						RATIOS		
	12.9	7.0	3.4	2.8		Current	3.2	3.1
	3.9	2.9	2.1	1.7			2.0	1.8
	1.7	1.7	1.3	1.3			1.3	1.2
	4.6	1.5	.9	.6		Quick	.7	.8
	.9	.5	.4	.4			.4	.4
	.3	.2	.2	.2			.2	.2
	10 38.4	13 27.4	25 14.7	22 16.5		Sales/Receivables	27 13.3	18 20.7
	24 15.1	28 13.1	45 8.1	44 8.4			38 9.5	38 9.5
	42 8.7	47 7.8	57 6.4	58 6.3			54 6.7	63 5.8
	295 1.2	222 1.6	270 1.4	161 2.3		Cost of Sales/Inventory	230 1.6	185 2.0
	399 .9	404 .9	426 .9	346 1.1			443 .8	335 1.1
	705 .5	806 .5	733 .5	492 .7			761 .5	734 .5
	3 139.9	19 19.2	19 19.3	21 17.7		Cost of Sales/Payables	26 14.1	21 17.4
	21 17.0	43 8.4	49 7.5	40 9.1			51 7.1	46 7.9
	159 2.3	104 3.5	94 3.9	79 4.6			108 3.4	99 3.7
	1.3	1.3	1.8	2.3		Sales/Working Capital	1.3	1.5
	2.3	2.4	2.6	4.0			2.5	3.5
	3.6	4.0	6.5	5.9			6.1	11.7
	105.6	6.0	9.0	7.6		EBIT/Interest	6.8	6.1
	(12) 4.1	(33) 3.6	(28) 3.6	4.3			(81) 2.3	(97) 2.5
	.4	1.6	1.5	2.1			1.0	.7
		7.6		15.5		Net Profit + Depr., Dep., Amort./Cur. Mat. L/T/D	4.0	8.3
		(14) 5.2		(12) 4.4			(34) 2.7	(35) 2.2
		1.5		1.5			1.1	1.5
	.1	.3	.6	.5		Fixed/Worth	.4	.4
	.2	.7	.8	.7			.9	1.1
	.8	1.9	2.5	1.4			1.6	2.3
	.2	.5	.4	.9		Debt/Worth	.7	.8
	.5	1.7	1.2	1.0			1.3	1.8
	1.3	4.4	2.7	1.5			2.9	3.8
	30.9	35.5	30.1	23.3		% Profit Before Taxes/Tangible Net Worth	24.9	26.3
	(15) 14.1	(34) 23.1	(31) 19.7	15.5			(79) 10.5	(93) 12.3
	-5.2	12.5	5.5	6.6			.7	.8
	21.4	16.2	14.8	11.9		% Profit Before Taxes/Total Assets	8.9	9.5
	5.2	7.6	7.2	6.9			3.0	4.2
	-1.8	2.8	1.1	3.0			-1.0	-.7
	14.3	6.3	3.7	3.2		Sales/Net Fixed Assets	5.8	7.6
	6.6	3.3	1.4	1.8			2.2	2.2
	3.9	1.3	.5	1.1			1.1	1.0
	1.4	1.2	.8	1.0		Sales/Total Assets	.9	1.0
	1.0	.8	.6	.7			.6	.7
	.7	.5	.4	.4			.4	.4
	1.4	2.3	3.5	5.2		% Depr., Dep., Amort./Sales	2.5	2.2
	(11) 3.0	(34) 4.3	(31) 7.2	(13) 6.2			(76) 5.8	(97) 4.9
	4.4	6.3	10.7	9.8			10.1	9.1
						% Officers', Directors' Owners' Comp/Sales	2.5	4.5
							(12) 4.7	(18) 6.5
							6.5	11.5
5535M	25314M	180113M	642649M	832220M	1290284M	Net Sales ($)	1970630M	1881440M
2522M	22313M	187353M	957147M	1011404M	1353094M	Total Assets ($)	2818962M	2643448M

M = $ thousand   MM = $ million
See Pages 11 through 21 for Explanation of Ratios and Data

	Comparative Historical Data			Type of Statement	Current Data Sorted by Sales					
	25	22	27	Unqualified	1	1		3	8	14
	18	27	21	Reviewed	1	6	1	3	6	4
	6	8	5	Compiled	1	3	1			
	13	13	12	Tax Returns	3	5	7	2	2	
	29	40	52	Other	8	12		10	2	13
	4/1/04-3/31/05 ALL	4/1/05-3/31/06 ALL	4/1/06-3/31/07 ALL		0-1MM	28 (4/1-9/30/06) 1-3MM	3-5MM	5-10MM	89 (10/1/06-3/31/07) 10-25MM	25MM & OVER
	91	110	117	NUMBER OF STATEMENTS	14	27	9	18	18	31
	%	%	%	ASSETS	%	%	%	%	%	%
	4.0	6.4	5.0	Cash & Equivalents	5.7	9.6		4.1	2.1	2.4
	10.7	10.8	9.0	Trade Receivables (net)	11.4	6.0		7.9	8.8	10.7
	40.1	40.6	41.7	Inventory	43.9	50.0		42.5	31.1	39.9
	1.2	1.9	2.4	All Other Current	4.8	.7		1.4	1.0	4.1
	56.0	59.7	58.1	Total Current	65.9	66.2		55.8	43.1	57.0
	35.9	33.8	35.0	Fixed Assets (net)	30.7	27.9		38.5	51.2	32.4
	4.1	2.3	2.4	Intangibles (net)	2.8	2.0		1.9	.8	3.8
	4.0	4.2	4.5	All Other Non-Current	.6	3.8		3.8	4.9	6.8
	100.0	100.0	100.0	Total	100.0	100.0		100.0	100.0	100.0
				LIABILITIES						
	11.1	12.4	12.1	Notes Payable-Short Term	17.0	8.5		11.2	17.5	12.8
	2.4	2.0	2.4	Cur. Mat.-L.T.D.	3.2	1.5		1.8	3.9	2.3
	9.7	8.5	7.8	Trade Payables	8.5	9.4		5.3	6.9	8.1
	.3	.2	.2	Income Taxes Payable	.0	.0		.9	.2	.2
	7.3	7.4	7.1	All Other Current	14.9	6.0		6.2	5.3	7.0
	30.8	30.4	29.7	Total Current	43.7	25.6		25.5	33.8	30.4
	25.4	18.9	19.6	Long-Term Debt	19.7	18.3		23.0	26.3	15.3
	.7	.6	.6	Deferred Taxes	.4	.0		1.3	1.1	.8
	8.0	7.4	6.7	All Other Non-Current	4.9	9.9		1.5	3.6	4.4
	35.3	42.7	43.4	Net Worth	31.3	46.2		48.7	35.2	49.0
	100.0	100.0	100.0	Total Liabilties & Net Worth	100.0	100.0		100.0	100.0	100.0
				INCOME DATA						
	100.0	100.0	100.0	Net Sales	100.0	100.0		100.0	100.0	100.0
	47.5	47.0	48.6	Gross Profit	51.6	53.7		48.0	46.0	42.4
	38.8	33.3	35.7	Operating Expenses	53.4	42.4		32.4	33.0	25.5
	8.7	13.7	12.9	Operating Profit	-1.9	11.2		15.6	13.0	16.9
	3.6	3.9	3.6	All Other Expenses (net)	1.9	2.7		5.0	4.9	3.6
	5.1	9.8	9.3	Profit Before Taxes	-3.8	8.5		10.6	8.1	13.3
				RATIOS						
	3.8	3.8	4.1		5.5	6.7		5.3	2.5	4.0
	2.0	2.3	2.2	Current	2.2	2.5		2.4	1.6	1.8
	1.2	1.3	1.4		1.5	1.6		1.4	1.1	1.4
	1.1	1.1	.9		1.6	.8		1.6	.8	.9
	.5 (109)	.5	.4	Quick	.5	.5		.4	.3	.5
	.2	.3	.2		.0	.3		.2	.2	.3
	18 20.2	15 23.9	13 27.9		0 UND	6 56.7		20 18.6	33 11.2	23 15.9
	35 10.5	41 8.8	31 11.7	Sales/Receivables	9 42.5	22 16.3		36 10.0	51 7.2	39 9.4
	56 6.5	59 6.1	51 7.2		73 5.0	42 8.8		48 7.6	70 5.2	52 7.0
	175 2.1	212 1.7	218 1.7		168 2.2	316 1.2		280 1.3	181 2.0	158 2.3
	325 1.1	363 1.0	401 .9	Cost of Sales/Inventory	485 .8	410 .9		590 .6	384 1.0	313 1.2
	587 .6	601 .6	697 .5		839 .4	800 .5		686 .5	526 .7	470 .8
	17 21.9	22 16.7	15 24.3		0 UND	12 29.8		13 28.8	25 14.5	17 21.2
	47 7.7	52 7.1	45 8.1	Cost of Sales/Payables	38 9.6	50 7.2		37 9.7	52 7.1	42 8.6
	97 3.8	89 4.1	101 3.6		158 2.3	120 3.0		104 3.5	113 3.2	63 5.8
	1.7	1.7	1.7		.8	1.2		1.4	2.0	2.1
	3.3	2.7	2.8	Sales/Working Capital	3.4	2.1		2.4	3.5	3.7
	11.9	8.7	6.2		6.8	3.9		6.5	24.6	6.6
	8.3	10.0	7.3			10.6		5.2	4.4	13.0
	(87) 2.8	(101) 3.7	(101) 3.2	EBIT/Interest		(24) 2.6	(13)	3.9	2.1	(28) 5.7
	1.4	1.4	1.3			1.0		2.8	1.2	2.3
	3.5	7.2	9.5							23.1
	(27) 2.5	(34) 3.8	(40) 5.0	Net Profit + Depr., Dep., Amort./Cur. Mat. L/T/D					(16)	9.5
	1.1	1.7	1.7							4.7
	.5	.3	.3		.2	.2		.4	.7	.4
	1.1	.8	.8	Fixed/Worth	.8	.5		.8	1.1	.6
	2.3	1.9	1.7		-3.9	1.7		1.6	3.8	1.3
	.8	.5	.5		.6	.5		.3	.7	.5
	1.9	1.2	1.3	Debt/Worth	1.4	1.3		1.5	1.9	1.0
	4.3	3.4	2.8		-30.3	3.4		2.2	4.1	1.9
	37.3	33.0	30.5		9.4	25.9		30.9	31.5	30.7
	(77) 14.2	(101) 20.3	(106) 18.8	% Profit Before Taxes/Tangible Net Worth	(10) -3.2	(26) 14.5	(17)	22.9	(17) 11.8	(30) 19.1
	3.8	7.1	5.7		-18.0	2.0		19.3	.5	10.2
	11.1	13.7	12.7		1.4	13.2		16.8	10.7	15.8
	4.4	6.5	6.4	% Profit Before Taxes/Total Assets	-3.5	6.4		8.9	3.6	8.1
	1.1	1.1	1.1		-10.9	.7		6.0	.6	3.1
	7.1	8.9	6.1		6.2	14.3		4.1	3.3	6.8
	2.4	2.4	2.7	Sales/Net Fixed Assets	3.1	5.0		2.6	1.2	2.5
	1.3	1.3	1.3		1.4	1.5		.6	.5	1.5
	1.2	1.2	1.2		1.5	1.1		1.0	.9	1.3
	.7	.8	.8	Sales/Total Assets	.8	.9		.7	.6	.8
	.6	.5	.5		.5	.5		.4	.3	.5
	2.5	3.0	2.9		2.9	2.7		2.9	5.1	2.3
	(79) 4.6	(93) 4.5	(102) 5.2	% Depr., Dep., Amort./Sales	(10) 3.7	(22) 5.6		4.4	(17) 8.1	(29) 5.9
	8.0	6.9	7.9		5.2	8.3		6.4	12.6	7.4
	2.0	1.3	2.9							
	(20) 4.4	(20) 3.8	(20) 10.6	% Officers', Directors' Owners' Comp/Sales						
	11.5	7.4	16.7							
	2222915M	2246631M	2976115M	Net Sales ($)	7850M	53334M	33259M	117400M	271897M	2492375M
	2140751M	2533249M	3533833M	Total Assets ($)	11442M	80188M	34272M	226117M	511556M	2670258M

© RMA 2007   M = $ thousand   MM = $ million
See Pages 11 through 21 for Explanation of Ratios and Data

Current Data Sorted by Assets

Comparative Historical Data

0-500M	500M-2MM	2-10MM	10-50MM	50-100MM	100-250MM	Type of Statement	4/1/02-3/31/03 ALL	4/1/03-3/31/04 ALL
		1	8	3	2	Unqualified	9	15
	3	2	1			Reviewed	4	9
		1				Compiled	3	10
1	1	3	9	2	1	Tax Returns	2	1
						Other	10	11
	7 (4/1-9/30/06)		31 (10/1/06-3/31/07)					
1	4	7	18	5	3	**NUMBER OF STATEMENTS**	28	46
%	%	%	%	%	%	**ASSETS**	%	%
			6.4			Cash & Equivalents	8.0	5.4
			22.5			Trade Receivables (net)	20.6	16.7
			25.5			Inventory	20.1	26.0
			5.0			All Other Current	3.7	5.6
			59.5			Total Current	52.3	53.7
			28.6			Fixed Assets (net)	39.0	37.1
			5.7			Intangibles (net)	.2	.9
			6.2			All Other Non-Current	8.4	8.4
			100.0			Total	100.0	100.0
						LIABILITIES		
			7.7			Notes Payable-Short Term	9.2	8.1
			2.7			Cur. Mat.-L.T.D.	4.1	6.0
			10.5			Trade Payables	18.3	13.4
			.3			Income Taxes Payable	.5	.5
			8.3			All Other Current	4.1	3.1
			29.5			Total Current	36.2	31.1
			14.7			Long-Term Debt	16.8	16.6
			.5			Deferred Taxes	.9	1.4
			5.2			All Other Non-Current	4.4	7.8
			50.1			Net Worth	41.7	43.1
			100.0			Total Liabilities & Net Worth	100.0	100.0
						INCOME DATA		
			100.0			Net Sales	100.0	100.0
			19.5			Gross Profit	13.2	18.2
			13.4			Operating Expenses	11.9	16.5
			6.1			Operating Profit	1.4	1.6
			1.9			All Other Expenses (net)	.0	1.5
			4.1			Profit Before Taxes	1.4	.2
						RATIOS		
			4.1				2.4	3.0
			1.8			Current	1.4	1.6
			1.2				1.1	1.1
			1.6				1.3	1.4
			.8			Quick	.6	.6
			.6				.4	.3
		32	11.4				27 13.7	20 18.4
		42	8.6			Sales/Receivables	36 10.2	42 8.7
		54	6.7				49 7.4	54 6.7
		35	10.5				24 15.1	39 9.3
		60	6.1			Cost of Sales/Inventory	39 9.4	54 6.8
		101	3.6				65 5.7	79 4.6
		12	30.8				13 29.1	17 21.2
		22	16.8			Cost of Sales/Payables	25 14.5	27 13.3
		35	10.4				49 7.4	47 7.7
			4.0				6.7	4.2
			7.6			Sales/Working Capital	13.8	8.5
			17.2				29.8	124.1
			5.2				10.1	4.8
		(14)	2.3			EBIT/Interest	(27) 1.8	(41) 1.7
			1.2				-2.6	-.3
								1.4
						Net Profit + Depr., Dep., Amort./Cur. Mat. L/T/D	(13) 1.1
								-.1
			.2				.4	.3
			.6			Fixed/Worth	.8	.9
			1.3				1.4	2.0
			.3				.6	.5
			1.1			Debt/Worth	2.0	1.4
			3.8				2.9	2.3
			23.9				35.9	21.2
		(16)	8.0			% Profit Before Taxes/Tangible Net Worth	(26) 11.9	(41) 6.3
			4.0				-2.6	-3.5
			13.7				10.5	9.0
			4.0			% Profit Before Taxes/Total Assets	4.3	1.8
			1.1				-2.8	-4.2
			25.1				9.1	10.5
			6.3			Sales/Net Fixed Assets	4.0	4.6
			3.3				2.3	2.6
			2.9				2.2	2.3
			1.8			Sales/Total Assets	1.7	1.7
			1.2				1.2	1.2
			1.0				1.6	1.6
		(16)	2.2			% Depr., Dep., Amort./Sales	(26) 4.4	(35) 4.0
			5.9				6.9	7.2
								1.3
						% Officers', Directors' Owners' Comp/Sales	(13) 2.6
								3.9
536M	11061M	69317M	854465M	632759M	1107715M	Net Sales ($)	1156827M	1770160M
106M	4984M	33521M	456723M	316159M	574959M	Total Assets ($)	765033M	1077676M

M = $ thousand   MM = $ million
See Pages 11 through 21 for Explanation of Ratios and Data

Comparative Historical Data / Current Data Sorted by Sales

			Type of Statement						
17	16	14	Unqualified					3	11
11	4	6	Reviewed		2	2	1	1	
4	3	1	Compiled			1	1		
	1	2	Tax Returns	1					
12	17	15	Other						11
4/1/04-3/31/05 ALL	4/1/05-3/31/06 ALL	4/1/06-3/31/07 ALL		0-1MM	1-3MM [7 (4/1-9/30/06)]	3-5MM	5-10MM	10-25MM [31 (10/1/06-3/31/07)]	25MM & OVER
44	41	38	NUMBER OF STATEMENTS	1	2	3	2	7	23
%	%	%	ASSETS	%	%	%	%	%	%
4.7	4.2	5.9	Cash & Equivalents						4.7
18.4	22.6	20.7	Trade Receivables (net)						21.7
24.9	25.1	29.7	Inventory						24.0
1.7	2.5	4.2	All Other Current						5.8
49.7	54.5	60.5	Total Current						56.2
38.0	32.6	29.3	Fixed Assets (net)						30.8
3.4	2.5	3.3	Intangibles (net)						5.4
8.8	10.4	7.0	All Other Non-Current						7.5
100.0	100.0	100.0	Total						100.0
			LIABILITIES						
8.7	7.2	8.9	Notes Payable-Short Term						6.9
3.4	2.9	3.7	Cur. Mat.-L.T.D.						4.3
13.2	15.5	14.5	Trade Payables						10.2
.1	.3	.1	Income Taxes Payable						.2
4.1	7.6	5.8	All Other Current						7.4
29.6	33.5	33.0	Total Current						29.1
19.9	18.4	18.8	Long-Term Debt						14.3
1.1	1.1	.8	Deferred Taxes						.9
7.0	7.2	4.5	All Other Non-Current						5.6
42.4	39.8	42.9	Net Worth						50.1
100.0	100.0	100.0	Total Liabilities & Net Worth						100.0
			INCOME DATA						
100.0	100.0	100.0	Net Sales						100.0
18.0	13.8	17.8	Gross Profit						16.3
14.6	11.3	14.1	Operating Expenses						11.1
3.4	2.5	3.7	Operating Profit						5.3
.9	.9	1.2	All Other Expenses (net)						1.8
2.5	1.6	2.5	Profit Before Taxes						3.4
			RATIOS						
2.4	3.0	3.7							3.3
1.6	1.7	1.7	Current						1.8
1.2	1.0	1.1							1.1
1.3	1.5	1.3							1.2
.8	.8	.8	Quick						.8
.4	.6	.4							.5
19 19.6	26 14.0	21 17.3							27 13.7
36 10.0	42 8.7	39 9.3	Sales/Receivables						46 8.0
47 7.7	51 7.2	51 7.1							51 7.1
20 18.7	29 12.4	35 10.3							33 11.0
56 6.5	49 7.5	59 6.2	Cost of Sales/Inventory						44 8.3
86 4.2	75 4.9	86 4.2							68 5.4
10 35.0	17 21.1	14 25.9							13 28.1
21 17.2	30 12.1	22 16.8	Cost of Sales/Payables						19 18.7
46 8.0	44 8.4	45 8.0							32 11.5
5.4	4.4	4.3							4.5
9.8	7.7	7.8	Sales/Working Capital						7.7
28.3	357.6	25.0							21.2
8.6	7.8	3.9							3.8
(43) 2.3	(40) 2.6	(34) 2.0	EBIT/Interest					(20)	2.3
.9	.8	1.1							1.2
11.4	5.8	4.0							
(12) 5.7	(13) 3.9	(10) 2.4	Net Profit + Depr., Dep., Amort./Cur. Mat. L/T/D						
1.7	1.7	.9							
.4	.4	.3							.4
.9	.8	.6	Fixed/Worth						.8
1.7	1.9	1.4							1.3
.6	.7	.5							.4
1.4	1.5	1.5	Debt/Worth						1.0
2.2	5.4	4.5							3.5
22.9	23.3	14.9							22.8
(38) 11.9	(38) 10.2	(34) 5.3	% Profit Before Taxes/Tangible Net Worth					(21)	8.6
.3	.2	1.3							2.2
10.1	10.3	8.2							13.5
3.9	4.6	2.6	% Profit Before Taxes/Total Assets						3.4
-.2	-.6	.3							.6
10.2	12.5	25.1							17.8
5.2	5.9	7.9	Sales/Net Fixed Assets						7.0
2.6	3.2	3.5							3.4
2.6	2.5	2.7							2.7
1.8	1.8	2.0	Sales/Total Assets						1.9
1.4	1.3	1.6							1.4
1.6	1.3	.8							.8
(40) 3.6	(38) 2.8	(33) 2.2	% Depr., Dep., Amort./Sales					(20)	2.2
5.8	5.7	3.6							4.7
1.6		2.2							
(12) 3.3		(12) 3.3	% Officers', Directors' Owners' Comp/Sales						
3.6		5.7							
2106441M	2250800M	2675853M	Net Sales ($)	536M	3413M	10796M	12842M	117832M	2530434M
1179315M	1373135M	1386452M	Total Assets ($)	106M	1806M	6796M	4122M	68726M	1304896M

Current Data Sorted by Assets | Comparative Historical Data

0-500M	500M-2MM	2-10MM	10-50MM	50-100MM	100-250MM	Type of Statement	4/1/02-3/31/03 ALL	4/1/03-3/31/04 ALL
		4	11	2	3	Unqualified	35	22
1	3	10	4			Reviewed	17	23
		2	1			Compiled	11	27
1	1	2	3			Tax Returns	1	5
2		6	8	3	3	Other	19	25
	14 (4/1-9/30/06)		59 (10/1/06-3/31/07)					
4	7	24	27	5	6	NUMBER OF STATEMENTS	83	102
%	%	%	%	%	%	ASSETS	%	%
		4.9	4.5			Cash & Equivalents	6.7	6.2
		25.7	26.6			Trade Receivables (net)	26.8	25.8
		32.0	31.1			Inventory	26.3	25.4
		2.9	2.7			All Other Current	2.5	3.7
		65.4	64.8			Total Current	62.3	61.2
		29.0	24.4			Fixed Assets (net)	30.9	29.4
		2.4	5.4			Intangibles (net)	.6	3.3
		3.1	5.4			All Other Non-Current	6.2	6.1
		100.0	100.0			Total	100.0	100.0
						LIABILITIES		
		16.8	16.2			Notes Payable-Short Term	10.9	10.1
		3.6	1.9			Cur. Mat.-L.T.D.	3.4	2.9
		17.6	12.8			Trade Payables	16.4	16.4
		.7	.1			Income Taxes Payable	.1	.2
		8.8	5.2			All Other Current	6.2	10.9
		47.5	36.2			Total Current	36.9	40.6
		13.7	10.0			Long-Term Debt	13.9	13.0
		.1	.8			Deferred Taxes	1.1	.9
		5.5	12.5			All Other Non-Current	4.9	8.0
		33.2	40.5			Net Worth	43.2	37.5
		100.0	100.0			Total Liabilities & Net Worth	100.0	100.0
						INCOME DATA		
		100.0	100.0			Net Sales	100.0	100.0
		29.3	21.5			Gross Profit	23.5	28.5
		25.5	18.7			Operating Expenses	19.3	25.1
		3.8	2.8			Operating Profit	4.2	3.5
		1.1	1.1			All Other Expenses (net)	1.4	1.2
		2.6	1.7			Profit Before Taxes	2.8	2.3
						RATIOS		
		2.0	3.0			Current	2.5	2.8
		1.5	2.1				1.8	1.8
		1.1	1.3				1.2	1.2
		1.0	1.7			Quick	1.4	1.4
		.6	.8				.9	.9
		.4	.6				.6	.6
		19 19.6	41 9.0			Sales/Receivables	30 12.1	31 12.0
		37 9.9	57 6.4				44 8.2	45 8.1
		61 6.0	65 5.6				64 5.7	61 6.0
		40 9.1	57 6.4			Cost of Sales/Inventory	38 9.7	39 9.3
		69 5.3	90 4.0				63 5.8	67 5.4
		128 2.9	131 2.8				85 4.3	93 3.9
		18 20.3	19 19.7			Cost of Sales/Payables	16 23.3	16 23.0
		35 10.5	31 11.9				28 12.9	30 12.3
		55 6.7	51 7.1				51 7.2	52 7.0
		6.8	3.7			Sales/Working Capital	4.8	4.5
		11.5	6.2				7.7	7.2
		40.2	14.7				27.3	23.9
		5.5	8.4			EBIT/Interest	11.0	9.3
		(23) 3.0	(25) 2.7				(68) 3.2	(87) 4.4
		1.1	.3				1.0	.7
			12.4			Net Profit + Depr., Dep., Amort./Cur. Mat. L/T/D	2.8	6.0
		(10) 2.3					(23) 2.1	(24) 2.1
			1.1				1.3	.8
		.2	.3			Fixed/Worth	.2	.3
		.8	.7				.6	.6
		1.2	2.7				1.3	1.3
		1.1	.6			Debt/Worth	.5	.7
		2.0	1.2				1.3	1.4
		4.9	8.0				2.4	4.0
		48.0	29.2			% Profit Before Taxes/Tangible Net Worth	38.7	35.6
		14.5	(22) 7.7				(79) 14.9	(91) 16.2
		1.1	-8.4				.9	-.5
		11.9	12.1			% Profit Before Taxes/Total Assets	14.4	12.8
		3.8	4.1				5.8	5.4
		.5	-2.7				.0	-1.1
		32.3	10.7			Sales/Net Fixed Assets	27.7	19.0
		15.1	6.4				5.6	7.5
		3.9	4.7				3.6	3.6
		2.9	2.1			Sales/Total Assets	2.8	2.7
		2.3	1.8				1.9	2.0
		1.5	1.4				1.4	1.4
		.6	1.2			% Depr., Dep., Amort./Sales	1.3	.7
		(20) 1.7	(23) 1.8				(73) 2.8	(84) 2.1
		4.0	3.5				5.3	4.8
		2.5				% Officers', Directors' Owners' Comp/Sales	2.2	2.1
		(11) 4.5					(24) 4.0	(32) 3.8
		8.6					6.0	6.7
1037M	18097M	319730M	1142626M	651461M	2651203M	Net Sales ($)	3004143M	4560394M
274M	7212M	141291M	650369M	354673M	1095298M	Total Assets ($)	1720581M	2763246M

M = $ thousand   MM = $ million
See Pages 11 through 21 for Explanation of Ratios and Data

Comparative Historical Data | Current Data Sorted by Sales

				Type of Statement	0-1MM	1-3MM	3-5MM	5-10MM	10-25MM	25MM & OVER
	17		15	20	Unqualified				2	5	13
	18		17	18	Reviewed	1	1	2	4	7	3
	7		8	3	Compiled				2		1
	4		1	7	Tax Returns	1	1		2		3
	28		27	25	Other	2	3		2	5	13
	4/1/04-3/31/05 ALL		4/1/05-3/31/06 ALL	4/1/06-3/31/07 ALL			14 (4/1-9/30/06)			59 (10/1/06-3/31/07)	
	74		68	73	NUMBER OF STATEMENTS	4	5	2	12	17	33
	%		%	%	ASSETS	%	%	%	%	%	%
	6.6		4.1	5.9	Cash & Equivalents				5.7	4.2	6.5
	25.9		25.0	25.4	Trade Receivables (net)				18.6	29.5	24.9
	28.5		33.1	30.1	Inventory				29.1	34.0	29.2
	1.5		2.5	3.0	All Other Current				3.6	3.3	2.8
	62.5		64.7	64.4	Total Current				57.2	71.0	63.5
	27.7		26.3	26.2	Fixed Assets (net)				38.8	21.5	23.2
	3.7		4.0	2.9	Intangibles (net)				.5	2.7	4.8
	6.2		5.0	6.5	All Other Non-Current				3.5	4.8	8.5
	100.0		100.0	100.0	Total				100.0	100.0	100.0
					LIABILITIES						
	13.4		10.7	18.0	Notes Payable-Short Term				12.3	18.2	14.7
	2.5		3.6	3.5	Cur. Mat.-L.T.D.				1.9	3.7	3.6
	14.4		14.6	14.3	Trade Payables				11.6	19.5	12.6
	.2		.1	.3	Income Taxes Payable				.3	.1	.5
	4.7		7.9	7.2	All Other Current				4.9	9.6	7.3
	35.2		36.8	43.3	Total Current				30.9	51.2	38.7
	16.6		13.3	14.2	Long-Term Debt				18.6	11.7	11.3
	.7		.4	.4	Deferred Taxes				.7	.2	.4
	7.6		9.7	8.6	All Other Non-Current				2.8	14.9	8.2
	39.9		39.8	33.4	Net Worth				46.9	22.0	41.3
	100.0		100.0	100.0	Total Liabilities & Net Worth				100.0	100.0	100.0
					INCOME DATA						
	100.0		100.0	100.0	Net Sales				100.0	100.0	100.0
	25.0		23.5	23.9	Gross Profit				25.0	29.1	18.6
	21.5		21.2	21.8	Operating Expenses				23.1	25.0	17.2
	3.4		2.3	2.2	Operating Profit				1.9	4.2	1.4
	1.5		.9	1.4	All Other Expenses (net)				.9	.9	2.0
	2.0		1.4	.8	Profit Before Taxes				1.0	3.2	-.6
					RATIOS						
	2.6		3.2	2.3					2.5	2.2	2.3
	1.7		2.0	1.7	Current				2.0	1.6	1.7
	1.2		1.4	1.3					1.4	1.0	1.3
	1.3		1.5	1.3					1.3	1.3	1.2
	.8		.8	.8	Quick				.8	.7	.8
	.5		.5	.5					.4	.4	.6
30	12.0	33	10.9	31	11.8	Sales/Receivables	23 15.8	29 12.8	38 9.6		
46	7.9	41	8.8	45	8.1		37 9.7	53 6.9	46 7.9		
60	6.1	52	7.0	61	6.0		60 6.1	65 5.6	59 6.2		
43	8.4	45	8.1	41	8.9	Cost of Sales/Inventory	55 6.7	56 6.5	35 10.5		
62	5.8	71	5.2	66	5.5		62 5.9	91 4.0	66 5.5		
87	4.2	108	3.4	115	3.2		110 3.3	139 2.6	111 3.3		
19	19.7	17	20.9	17	21.0	Cost of Sales/Payables	17 21.4	28 13.1	15 24.4		
29	12.7	25	14.3	29	12.4		24 15.8	38 9.6	26 14.3		
50	7.4	40	9.2	42	8.8		55 6.7	64 5.7	41 9.0		
	5.6		4.6	5.6	Sales/Working Capital				4.9	6.3	5.3
	8.6		6.7	7.9					7.7	12.2	6.6
	23.6		16.4	19.7					10.3	NM	16.1
	7.9		9.0	6.0	EBIT/Interest				4.4	5.7	8.9
(68)	3.1	(60)	2.5	(65)	2.5		1.6	(16) 3.0	(31) 2.8		
	.3		-.4	.2					.8	1.2	-.4
	7.1		14.7	3.7	Net Profit + Depr., Dep., Amort./Cur. Mat. L/T/D						
(21)	1.4	(16)	3.1	(19)	1.8						
	.7		.9	1.4							
	.3		.2	.3	Fixed/Worth				.3	.2	.3
	.8		.6	.7					.8	.4	.6
	2.0		1.5	1.4					1.0	8.5	1.4
	.7		.6	.8	Debt/Worth				.4	1.7	.7
	1.6		1.8	1.5					1.2	3.0	1.2
	3.7		5.5	6.3					3.1	16.0	5.9
	30.1		27.1	29.4	% Profit Before Taxes/Tangible Net Worth				15.4	48.1	29.3
(65)	11.1	(59)	7.3	(64)	8.2		6.0	(15) 19.8	(28) 11.5		
	-8.0		-1.2	-5.4					-3.1	1.8	-19.1
	11.0		12.6	11.9	% Profit Before Taxes/Total Assets				6.1	12.8	11.9
	3.3		3.9	3.4					1.5	4.1	3.7
	-3.0		-.7	-2.8					-.6	.8	-5.5
	23.4		34.6	28.7	Sales/Net Fixed Assets				15.9	33.4	27.5
	8.9		10.8	9.4					4.6	11.4	8.4
	3.8		4.3	4.5					1.7	4.5	5.3
	2.5		2.7	2.7	Sales/Total Assets				2.6	2.9	2.4
	2.0		2.2	2.1					1.8	2.1	2.0
	1.4		1.6	1.4					.9	1.6	1.5
	1.0		.7	.8	% Depr., Dep., Amort./Sales				1.6	.8	.8
(59)	1.9	(51)	2.3	(58)	1.8		2.3	(13) 1.8	(26) 1.6		
	4.0		3.6	3.2					6.1	3.2	2.9
	1.9		1.4	1.9	% Officers', Directors' Owners' Comp/Sales						
(20)	3.5	(17)	2.6	(22)	3.2						
	7.5		6.0	7.8							
3371284M		3829870M		4784154M		Net Sales ($)	1037M	7956M	7742M	85401M	313332M	4368686M
1829566M		1925185M		2249117M		Total Assets ($)	274M	3923M	3589M	62235M	155420M	2023676M

M = $ thousand   MM = $ million
See Pages 11 through 21 for Explanation of Ratios and Data

Current Data Sorted by Assets   Comparative Historical Data

0-500M	500M-2MM	2-10MM	10-50MM	50-100MM	100-250MM	Type of Statement	4/1/02-3/31/03 ALL	4/1/03-3/31/04 ALL
		3	4			Unqualified	9	6
	1	1	1			Reviewed	13	9
2		5	1			Compiled	5	12
1	1	2	6		1	Tax Returns	1	1
						Other	9	16
	11 (4/1-9/30/06)		18 (10/1/06-3/31/07)					
3	2	11	12		1	**NUMBER OF STATEMENTS**	37	44
%	%	%	%	%	%	**ASSETS**	%	%
		8.6	8.3			Cash & Equivalents	8.5	4.3
		23.7	22.1			Trade Receivables (net)	21.8	21.7
		28.0	35.0			Inventory	31.7	25.2
		1.3	2.7			All Other Current	1.5	4.9
		61.7	68.1			Total Current	63.6	56.2
		22.4	19.1			Fixed Assets (net)	23.7	30.9
		2.9	4.9			Intangibles (net)	6.5	4.5
		13.1	7.9			All Other Non-Current	6.2	8.5
		100.0	100.0			Total	100.0	100.0
						LIABILITIES		
		15.1	11.5			Notes Payable-Short Term	9.6	10.0
		1.9	3.0			Cur. Mat.-L.T.D.	3.2	3.2
		14.5	12.4			Trade Payables	12.1	15.2
		1.5	.2			Income Taxes Payable	.3	.3
		8.1	9.8			All Other Current	11.4	12.7
		41.1	36.8			Total Current	36.7	41.4
		6.1	5.8			Long-Term Debt	11.3	13.2
		.1	.3			Deferred Taxes	.6	.7
		1.5	9.1			All Other Non-Current	4.9	3.9
		51.2	48.0			Net Worth	46.6	40.8
		100.0	100.0			Total Liabilities & Net Worth	100.0	100.0
						INCOME DATA		
		100.0	100.0			Net Sales	100.0	100.0
		22.2	27.6			Gross Profit	26.1	24.2
		21.5	22.4			Operating Expenses	22.2	21.0
		.7	5.1			Operating Profit	3.9	3.3
		.3	.4			All Other Expenses (net)	.8	1.1
		.3	4.7			Profit Before Taxes	3.1	2.2
						RATIOS		
		2.6	5.9				3.0	3.0
		1.6	1.6			Current	1.7	1.4
		.8	1.2				1.4	.9
		1.7	3.4				1.3	1.1
		.6	.8			Quick	.8	.6
		.4	.5				.6	.4
		26 14.3	37 10.0				33 11.1	33 11.1
		35 10.4	47 7.7			Sales/Receivables	41 8.8	40 9.2
		43 8.4	50 7.3				49 7.5	53 6.9
		38 9.6	55 6.7				53 6.9	40 9.1
		52 7.0	89 4.1			Cost of Sales/Inventory	72 5.1	65 5.6
		87 4.2	102 3.6				119 3.1	97 3.8
		21 17.7	16 23.2				14 26.7	20 18.6
		22 17.0	28 13.2			Cost of Sales/Payables	26 13.9	29 12.8
		36 10.1	42 8.7				36 10.1	42 8.6
		4.9	2.9				4.8	5.1
		8.6	8.0			Sales/Working Capital	7.5	15.9
		-29.8	24.4				16.2	-34.3
			25.9				10.4	9.9
		(10)	11.0			EBIT/Interest	(32) 4.4	(42) 4.0
			1.4				1.2	.1
							3.9	3.1
						Net Profit + Depr., Dep., Amort./Cur. Mat. L/T/D	(18) 2.7	(14) 2.0
							1.7	.1
		.2	.3				.2	.3
		.5	.5			Fixed/Worth	.5	.7
		.9	1.2				1.0	2.5
		.5	.2				.6	.6
		.9	1.4			Debt/Worth	1.2	1.8
		3.3	3.9				6.0	4.7
		7.4	31.3				36.9	43.2
		-8.3	(10) 10.2			% Profit Before Taxes/Tangible Net Worth	(33) 12.0	(39) 6.0
		-22.5	3.3				.9	-4.4
		4.6	22.2				13.7	9.3
		-1.9	5.6			% Profit Before Taxes/Total Assets	5.4	4.3
		-6.8	.9				.5	-4.6
		39.8	29.6				32.7	22.5
		13.5	9.9			Sales/Net Fixed Assets	8.3	6.6
		5.4	7.5				5.2	3.3
		3.1	2.2				2.3	2.0
		2.6	2.0			Sales/Total Assets	1.9	1.8
		1.7	1.7				1.5	1.4
		.8	.9				1.2	1.0
		(10) 2.6	2.3			% Depr., Dep., Amort./Sales	(34) 2.2	(36) 3.3
		5.1	2.7				4.1	5.0
							1.8	1.4
						% Officers', Directors' Owners' Comp/Sales	(16) 3.8	(16) 3.0
							8.5	6.0
1127M	8189M	134991M	488187M		169753M	Net Sales ($)	708851M	892657M
528M	2113M	57436M	256469M		106888M	Total Assets ($)	420451M	588256M

M = $ thousand   MM = $ million
See Pages 11 through 21 for Explanation of Ratios and Data

Comparative Historical Data | Current Data Sorted by Sales

Type of Statement	4/1/04-3/31/05 ALL	4/1/05-3/31/06 ALL	4/1/06-3/31/07 ALL		0-1MM	1-3MM	3-5MM	5-10MM	10-25MM	25MM & OVER
Unqualified	7	7	7					1	2	4
Reviewed	8	5	3				1		1	1
Compiled	6	7	8		1	1	4	1	1	1
Tax Returns	3	3								
Other	10	13	11		1	1	1	1	1	7
					11 (4/1-9/30/06)			18 (10/1/06-3/31/07)		
NUMBER OF STATEMENTS	34	35	29		2			6	5	13
	%	%	%		%	%	%	%	%	%
ASSETS										
Cash & Equivalents	6.6	11.0	7.7							5.7
Trade Receivables (net)	28.1	26.2	26.0							24.2
Inventory	29.9	28.2	29.7							34.3
All Other Current	1.2	1.5	1.6							1.6
Total Current	65.8	66.8	65.0							65.8
Fixed Assets (net)	25.3	20.0	21.0							21.7
Intangibles (net)	3.5	5.2	4.1							4.5
All Other Non-Current	5.4	8.0	10.0							7.9
Total	100.0	100.0	100.0							100.0
LIABILITIES										
Notes Payable-Short Term	14.1	17.7	12.9							11.2
Cur. Mat.-L.T.D.	2.4	3.1	2.4							2.8
Trade Payables	16.5	17.0	13.2							13.3
Income Taxes Payable	.4	.1	.6							.0
All Other Current	8.7	6.6	8.4							9.7
Total Current	41.9	44.5	37.5							37.0
Long-Term Debt	13.6	8.0	6.3							5.3
Deferred Taxes	.4	.2	.2							.4
All Other Non-Current	6.3	3.2	5.7							8.4
Net Worth	37.8	44.1	50.3							48.9
Total Liabilties & Net Worth	100.0	100.0	100.0							100.0
INCOME DATA										
Net Sales	100.0	100.0	100.0							100.0
Gross Profit	22.2	24.3	25.0							23.3
Operating Expenses	19.2	22.1	21.2							18.0
Operating Profit	3.1	2.2	3.8							5.2
All Other Expenses (net)	1.1	.9	.6							.5
Profit Before Taxes	2.0	1.4	3.2							4.7
RATIOS										
Current	2.9	3.0	3.9							5.3
	1.6	1.7	2.0							1.6
	1.0	1.1	1.1							1.2
Quick	1.5	1.7	2.0							2.2
	.8	.8	1.0							.9
	.4	.5	.5							.5
Sales/Receivables	35 10.5	34 10.6	29 12.5							37 10.0
	46 8.0	40 9.1	42 8.6							46 8.0
	64 5.7	46 8.0	50 7.3							50 7.3
Cost of Sales/Inventory	42 8.7	28 13.1	41 9.0							45 8.1
	76 4.8	61 6.0	68 5.3							82 4.4
	109 3.3	91 4.0	95 3.9							97 3.8
Cost of Sales/Payables	18 20.3	17 21.5	20 18.1							17 21.6
	35 10.3	23 16.0	24 15.1							28 13.3
	49 7.5	39 9.4	41 9.0							42 8.7
Sales/Working Capital	5.0	5.1	4.5							4.4
	8.4	8.5	8.6							7.5
	-93.5	63.5	42.4							23.4
EBIT/Interest	9.1	9.4	18.3							30.7
	(31) 1.8	(26) 2.9	(23) 2.8							(11) 11.1
	-.4	.6	.6							1.6
Net Profit + Depr., Dep., Amort./Cur. Mat. L/T/D	6.5		42.8							
	(12) 2.4		(10) 4.6							
	1.4		1.0							
Fixed/Worth	.2	.1	.1							.3
	.6	.5	.5							.5
	1.8	1.7	1.0							1.2
Debt/Worth	.7	.3	.3							.2
	2.1	1.4	.9							.8
	5.5	8.1	3.2							3.5
% Profit Before Taxes/Tangible Net Worth	29.4	37.5	28.4							28.4
	(30) 8.6	(31) 4.0	(27) 7.4							(11) 10.8
	-7.3	.0	-8.3							3.4
% Profit Before Taxes/Total Assets	11.6	8.7	15.4							22.0
	2.7	1.0	4.6							5.7
	-2.7	-.1	-2.7							.8
Sales/Net Fixed Assets	37.4	47.8	37.6							29.6
	8.8	8.4	10.0							9.7
	4.3	5.6	6.4							6.8
Sales/Total Assets	2.4	3.1	2.9							2.3
	1.9	1.9	2.1							2.0
	1.3	1.6	1.7							1.8
% Depr., Dep., Amort./Sales	.9	.6	.9							.9
	(30) 2.4	(29) 1.8	(26) 2.5							2.4
	4.1	4.0	3.8							2.7
% Officers', Directors' Owners' Comp/Sales	2.7	2.2								
	(13) 4.3	(13) 3.6								
	6.6	4.9								
Net Sales ($)	639585M	921915M	802247M		59M	1068M	8189M	44304M	78969M	669658M
Total Assets ($)	378407M	476576M	423434M		33M	495M	2113M	24103M	40916M	355774M

M = $ thousand   MM = $ million
See Pages 11 through 21 for Explanation of Ratios and Data

Current Data Sorted by Assets   Comparative Historical Data

Type of Statement

0-500M	500M-2MM	2-10MM	10-50MM	50-100MM	100-250MM	Type of Statement	4/1/02-3/31/03 ALL	4/1/03-3/31/04 ALL
		6	4	2	1	Unqualified	14	18
1	1	7	4			Reviewed	15	16
	5	5	1			Compiled	5	17
1	3	1				Tax Returns	9	8
1	5	5			3	Other	21	22
	13 (4/1-9/30/06)		44 (10/1/06-3/31/07)					
3	14	24	10	2	4	NUMBER OF STATEMENTS	64	81

0-500M	500M-2MM	2-10MM	10-50MM	50-100MM	100-250MM		4/1/02-3/31/03 ALL	4/1/03-3/31/04 ALL
%	%	%	%	%	%	**ASSETS**	%	%
	7.9	7.1	5.3			Cash & Equivalents	8.3	6.6
	30.7	26.9	24.0			Trade Receivables (net)	28.0	26.4
	25.1	33.0	34.9			Inventory	25.3	27.5
	.6	1.1	2.7			All Other Current	1.9	5.7
	64.3	68.2	66.9			Total Current	63.4	66.2
	22.8	22.6	26.5			Fixed Assets (net)	27.3	21.7
	6.6	1.3	.9			Intangibles (net)	3.8	5.4
	6.3	7.9	5.6			All Other Non-Current	5.5	6.6
	100.0	100.0	100.0			Total	100.0	100.0
						LIABILITIES		
	13.8	20.8	15.7			Notes Payable-Short Term	12.6	11.9
	1.9	1.9	3.3			Cur. Mat.-L.T.D.	4.4	7.0
	16.4	15.6	12.8			Trade Payables	17.6	18.1
	.2	.1	1.2			Income Taxes Payable	.2	.2
	8.7	8.4	13.8			All Other Current	7.3	8.7
	40.9	46.8	46.8			Total Current	42.0	45.7
	21.9	10.0	12.6			Long-Term Debt	17.5	11.7
	.0	.2	.0			Deferred Taxes	.3	.5
	11.7	4.0	3.1			All Other Non-Current	2.8	6.7
	25.5	39.0	37.5			Net Worth	37.4	35.4
	100.0	100.0	100.0			Total Liabilities & Net Worth	100.0	100.0
						INCOME DATA		
	100.0	100.0	100.0			Net Sales	100.0	100.0
	32.6	26.5	18.2			Gross Profit	30.4	29.9
	30.6	24.2	14.8			Operating Expenses	25.8	26.0
	2.0	2.3	3.4			Operating Profit	4.6	4.0
	1.2	1.0	1.2			All Other Expenses (net)	1.6	1.4
	.8	1.3	2.2			Profit Before Taxes	3.0	2.6
						RATIOS		
	3.0	3.1	2.1				2.5	2.6
	1.8	2.0	1.5			Current	1.6	1.4
	.9	1.3	1.0				1.0	1.0
	1.7	1.5	1.3				1.4	1.3
	1.1	1.0	.6			Quick	.9	.7
	.6	.5	.3				.5	.4
	29 12.5	29 12.5	24 15.1				24 15.0	23 16.0
	34 10.7	41 9.0	46 7.9			Sales/Receivables	40 9.2	39 9.3
	48 7.6	55 6.6	66 5.5				52 7.0	54 6.7
	25 14.8	30 12.1	18 20.6				4 104.1	11 32.4
	41 9.0	74 4.9	82 4.4			Cost of Sales/Inventory	42 8.6	52 7.1
	75 4.9	101 3.6	114 3.2				93 3.9	93 3.9
	17 21.7	20 18.4	4 90.1				14 26.2	16 22.9
	30 12.1	29 12.6	22 16.6			Cost of Sales/Payables	25 14.5	28 12.9
	37 9.9	48 7.6	39 9.4				47 7.7	56 6.5
	4.5	4.7	5.1				5.3	5.5
	12.9	6.3	12.1			Sales/Working Capital	12.7	11.4
	-67.6	15.0	NM				UND	-242.7
	7.3	11.4					9.8	12.3
	2.7	(23) 2.0				EBIT/Interest	(57) 3.1	(73) 3.0
	.7	-1.1					1.3	.5
							12.9	3.7
						Net Profit + Depr., Dep., Amort./Cur. Mat. L/T/D	(12) 3.7	(26) 1.7
							1.6	.6
	.3	.1	.3				.2	.2
	.8	.3	.6			Fixed/Worth	.5	.5
	-4.8	1.0	1.7				1.9	2.0
	.7	.6	1.0				.8	.8
	1.8	1.1	1.4			Debt/Worth	1.8	2.3
	-472.1	3.1	6.7				3.9	4.9
	49.3	53.4	33.2				35.6	25.9
	(10) 5.3	(23) 7.9	8.1			% Profit Before Taxes/Tangible Net Worth	(55) 11.7	(69) 8.3
	-.8	1.3	-19.7				4.0	1.0
	6.5	20.5	14.6				13.6	11.8
	2.3	3.3	2.4			% Profit Before Taxes/Total Assets	4.1	2.4
	-1.4	-3.7	-9.8				.5	-1.6
	142.1	43.6	22.0				40.6	54.6
	19.8	15.9	8.8			Sales/Net Fixed Assets	13.5	18.7
	6.9	4.9	5.3				6.7	7.3
	3.7	3.1	2.1				3.7	3.3
	2.5	2.0	1.8			Sales/Total Assets	2.7	2.3
	1.8	1.7	1.6				1.6	1.8
	.5	.7					.6	.5
	(11) 1.4	(22) 1.4				% Depr., Dep., Amort./Sales	(59) 1.5	(63) 1.4
	3.5	3.1					3.7	3.4
		2.3					2.5	2.1
		(13) 3.8				% Officers', Directors' Owners' Comp/Sales	(26) 3.8	(34) 3.9
		4.9					7.0	9.3
2603M	49507M	321631M	403178M	297229M	1424282M	Net Sales ($)	1535025M	2543021M
769M	17798M	140322M	214042M	138613M	619534M	Total Assets ($)	724483M	1173283M

© RMA 2007

M = $ thousand   MM = $ million
See Pages 11 through 21 for Explanation of Ratios and Data

Comparative Historical Data   Current Data Sorted by Sales

Type of Statement	4/1/04-3/31/05	4/1/05-3/31/06	4/1/06-3/31/07		0-1MM	1-3MM	3-5MM	5-10MM	10-25MM	25MM & OVER
Unqualified	20	11	13		1			2	6	5
Reviewed	19	12	13			2	2	1	7	2
Compiled	16	9	10			2	3	2	2	1
Tax Returns	7	10	5		1	2	2			
Other	11	15	16			1	2	2	3	6
	ALL	ALL	ALL			13 (4/1-9/30/06)			44 (10/1/06-3/31/07)	
NUMBER OF STATEMENTS	73	57	57		2	7	9	7	18	14
	%	%	%		%	%	%	%	%	%
ASSETS										
Cash & Equivalents	8.5	7.9	8.3						7.1	5.1
Trade Receivables (net)	25.6	27.4	27.1						21.6	29.9
Inventory	34.6	33.6	30.0						38.7	29.5
All Other Current	1.8	3.2	1.4						1.6	2.4
Total Current	70.4	72.2	66.9						68.9	67.0
Fixed Assets (net)	21.6	21.3	23.6						21.5	23.9
Intangibles (net)	2.4	1.4	3.0						.9	3.3
All Other Non-Current	5.6	5.1	6.4						8.7	5.8
Total	100.0	100.0	100.0						100.0	100.0
LIABILITIES										
Notes Payable-Short Term	16.4	19.1	16.1						20.9	6.6
Cur. Mat.-L.T.D.	3.4	4.0	2.1						1.5	3.2
Trade Payables	19.8	16.3	17.1						14.6	19.5
Income Taxes Payable	.3	.4	.4						.1	1.0
All Other Current	9.3	8.6	9.1						9.3	10.3
Total Current	49.2	48.4	44.8						46.3	40.7
Long-Term Debt	12.3	17.9	15.0						9.7	16.1
Deferred Taxes	.3	.4	.1						.3	.3
All Other Non-Current	6.3	7.5	5.4						2.7	4.1
Net Worth	31.9	25.9	34.7						41.0	38.8
Total Liabilities & Net Worth	100.0	100.0	100.0						100.0	100.0
INCOME DATA										
Net Sales	100.0	100.0	100.0						100.0	100.0
Gross Profit	29.7	28.4	28.8						21.6	25.9
Operating Expenses	26.1	25.5	25.9						18.7	21.5
Operating Profit	3.6	2.9	2.9						2.9	4.4
All Other Expenses (net)	1.1	1.4	1.4						.9	2.4
Profit Before Taxes	2.5	1.5	1.5						2.0	2.0
RATIOS										
Current	2.5	2.5	2.6						2.1	2.7
	1.6	1.6	1.7						1.5	2.0
	1.1	1.2	1.2						1.3	1.1
Quick	1.3	1.5	1.4						1.1	1.3
	.7	.8	1.0						.7	1.1
	.4	.4	.5						.4	.6
Sales/Receivables	28 12.9	28 13.1	29 12.5						22 16.2	38 9.7
	40 9.2	43 8.5	39 9.2						36 10.1	44 8.3
	52 7.0	56 6.5	56 6.6						51 7.2	74 5.0
Cost of Sales/Inventory	33 11.2	36 10.2	31 11.6						42 8.7	33 11.0
	63 5.8	64 5.7	67 5.5						77 4.8	51 7.2
	105 3.5	99 3.7	94 3.9						114 3.2	94 3.9
Cost of Sales/Payables	15 24.4	15 23.9	19 19.4						19 18.8	20 18.5
	28 13.0	27 13.3	31 11.9						27 13.6	37 9.9
	50 7.3	47 7.8	48 7.6						45 8.2	79 4.6
Sales/Working Capital	4.6	4.3	4.8						4.8	5.2
	10.9	8.7	9.0						9.7	8.2
	46.8	31.6	22.4						19.6	NM
EBIT/Interest	8.0	8.0	9.3						10.2	16.0
	(68) 3.5	(56) 2.1	(54) 2.1						(17) 2.5	(13) 1.9
	1.0	1.0	.1						-1.2	.4
Net Profit + Depr., Dep., Amort./Cur. Mat. L/T/D	7.3	7.6	3.6							
	(19) 2.7	(18) 3.3	(15) 1.8							
	1.0	.2	.0							
Fixed/Worth	.2	.1	.2						.3	.2
	.5	.5	.6						.4	.6
	1.6	2.4	1.4						.6	2.2
Debt/Worth	.9	1.0	.7						.9	.6
	1.7	2.1	1.6						1.5	1.8
	4.8	6.0	4.3						3.1	6.7
% Profit Before Taxes/Tangible Net Worth	41.8	29.7	45.3						47.3	39.8
	(63) 11.3	(46) 4.5	(50) 7.3						8.6	(13) 7.0
	1.2	-.4	-.9						-9.1	-2.7
% Profit Before Taxes/Total Assets	12.3	16.7	16.8						19.2	14.2
	3.7	1.7	2.8						3.2	1.4
	.1	-.1	-2.5						-3.3	-1.9
Sales/Net Fixed Assets	49.9	61.2	40.9						42.5	26.7
	20.7	20.5	12.9						13.1	8.1
	7.1	6.2	6.6						6.2	5.3
Sales/Total Assets	3.2	3.4	3.1						3.0	3.0
	2.4	2.3	2.0						2.0	1.9
	1.7	1.7	1.7						1.7	1.6
% Depr., Dep., Amort./Sales	.5	.4	.5						.4	.5
	(62) 1.3	(47) 1.1	(49) 1.4						(15) 1.4	(12) 1.7
	2.6	1.9	3.1						2.0	3.0
% Officers', Directors' Owners' Comp/Sales	2.7	2.2	1.9							
	(32) 5.2	(25) 3.3	(20) 3.8							
	8.6	6.3	5.8							
Net Sales ($)	1938573M	2214797M	2498430M		1022M	11827M	33429M	50088M	309184M	2092880M
Total Assets ($)	920490M	1131912M	1131078M		512M	5703M	18819M	17050M	148094M	940900M

M = $ thousand   MM = $ million
See Pages 11 through 21 for Explanation of Ratios and Data

Current Data Sorted by Assets   **Comparative Historical Data**

0-500M	500M-2MM	2-10MM	10-50MM	50-100MM	100-250MM	Type of Statement		
	1	1	5	1	2	Unqualified	7	8
	2	4	2			Reviewed	16	7
	1	3				Compiled	1	10
	1					Tax Returns	5	
	4	8	7	1		Other	9	12
	6 (4/1-9/30/06)		37 (10/1/06-3/31/07)				4/1/02-3/31/03 ALL	4/1/03-3/31/04 ALL
9	16	14	2	2		NUMBER OF STATEMENTS	38	37
%	%	%	%	%	%		%	%
						ASSETS		
		4.2	5.6			Cash & Equivalents	10.0	6.5
		23.6	27.1			Trade Receivables (net)	27.4	30.3
		33.6	28.4			Inventory	20.4	24.8
		1.0	2.1			All Other Current	1.7	2.1
		62.4	63.3			Total Current	59.4	63.6
		23.6	25.5			Fixed Assets (net)	26.5	24.8
		4.8	5.3			Intangibles (net)	5.5	3.4
		9.1	5.9			All Other Non-Current	8.6	8.2
		100.0	100.0			Total	100.0	100.0
						LIABILITIES		
		11.7	10.9			Notes Payable-Short Term	8.6	11.1
		4.2	2.2			Cur. Mat.-L.T.D.	3.3	4.9
		12.8	17.8			Trade Payables	16.0	16.8
		.1	.5			Income Taxes Payable	.2	.3
		8.0	7.8			All Other Current	7.4	9.0
		36.8	39.2			Total Current	35.5	42.0
		10.6	7.4			Long-Term Debt	18.9	17.5
		1.0	.8			Deferred Taxes	.5	.4
		6.8	13.6			All Other Non-Current	15.8	13.1
		44.8	39.1			Net Worth	29.4	27.0
		100.0	100.0			Total Liabilities & Net Worth	100.0	100.0
						INCOME DATA		
		100.0	100.0			Net Sales	100.0	100.0
		23.8	22.6			Gross Profit	27.6	26.4
		20.7	16.0			Operating Expenses	25.9	22.6
		3.1	6.6			Operating Profit	1.7	3.8
		1.6	.5			All Other Expenses (net)	1.3	.6
		1.5	6.1			Profit Before Taxes	.4	3.2
						RATIOS		
		3.1	2.3			Current	2.7	2.1
		1.5	1.7				1.5	1.5
		1.1	1.2				1.2	1.2
		1.5	1.3			Quick	2.0	1.3
		.7	.7				1.0	.8
		.5	.5				.6	.6
		36 10.1	39 9.4			Sales/Receivables	38 9.7	42 8.6
		40 9.2	48 7.6				49 7.5	51 7.2
		59 6.1	58 6.3				54 6.8	60 6.1
		48 7.5	45 8.2			Cost of Sales/Inventory	25 14.5	33 11.2
		72 5.1	55 6.7				45 8.1	52 7.0
		106 3.5	83 4.4				72 5.0	82 4.5
		12 30.4	26 14.3			Cost of Sales/Payables	19 19.4	18 19.9
		26 14.0	37 9.9				31 11.7	37 9.9
		42 8.7	46 7.9				47 7.7	46 7.9
		4.1	5.2			Sales/Working Capital	5.3	7.4
		8.2	10.3				11.6	12.0
		76.1	18.0				26.6	20.5
		13.1	27.0			EBIT/Interest	2.6	5.4
		2.5	(13) 8.2				(31) 1.5	(33) 2.3
		-.8	2.2				-1.4	1.1
						Net Profit + Depr., Dep., Amort./Cur. Mat. L/T/D	1.9	9.5
							(13) 1.2	(12) 1.3
							-.3	.4
		.1	.4			Fixed/Worth	.4	.4
		.4	.7				.8	.8
		2.3	1.4				1.9	2.1
		.4	.7			Debt/Worth	.5	.8
		1.8	1.5				2.0	2.1
		3.1	4.5				4.5	9.4
		41.3	56.8			% Profit Before Taxes/Tangible Net Worth	14.6	41.2
	(15) 7.8	(13) 24.2				(32) 3.1	(30) 15.5
		-11.4	6.2				-6.0	1.4
		9.8	21.9			% Profit Before Taxes/Total Assets	6.8	13.4
		3.1	6.5				1.5	4.2
		-6.5	1.4				-2.2	.3
		45.3	13.2			Sales/Net Fixed Assets	19.3	19.0
		9.7	5.9				9.3	9.5
		4.5	5.3				3.4	5.5
		2.6	2.3			Sales/Total Assets	2.9	2.5
		2.1	2.0				1.9	2.1
		1.4	1.5				1.2	1.6
		.3	1.2			% Depr., Dep., Amort./Sales	1.4	1.6
		2.0	(11) 2.5				(35) 2.3	(33) 2.5
		4.0	3.4				4.2	3.3
						% Officers', Directors' Owners' Comp/Sales	3.1	2.0
							(16) 4.7	(10) 3.1
							6.6	10.7
	29068M	174063M	699613M	203640M	719789M	Net Sales ($)	865802M	1038569M
	12542M	87682M	355094M	128286M	301293M	Total Assets ($)	482045M	515444M

M = $ thousand   MM = $ million
See Pages 11 through 21 for Explanation of Ratios and Data

Comparative Historical Data — **Current Data Sorted by Sales**

1	2	3	Type of Statement	0-1MM	1-3MM	3-5MM	5-10MM	10-25MM	25MM & OVER
12	9	10	Unqualified				1	1	7
13	14	8	Reviewed		1		2		2
5	3	4	Compiled	1		1	3	3	
1	3	1	Tax Returns				1		
9	15	20	Other	1	2	1	3	6	7
4/1/04-3/31/05 ALL	4/1/05-3/31/06 ALL	4/1/06-3/31/07 ALL			6 (4/1-9/30/06)			37 (10/1/06-3/31/07)	
40	44	43	**NUMBER OF STATEMENTS**	2	3	2	10	10	16
%	%	%	**ASSETS**	%	%	%	%	%	%
8.4	5.5	5.6	Cash & Equivalents				7.7	2.6	5.7
27.9	27.3	25.9	Trade Receivables (net)				25.9	23.7	28.6
29.1	29.2	30.5	Inventory				35.7	37.9	25.0
.9	1.5	1.3	All Other Current				.7	1.4	2.1
66.4	63.4	63.2	Total Current				70.0	65.6	61.4
23.6	28.0	26.7	Fixed Assets (net)				23.0	21.0	28.6
3.5	3.7	4.1	Intangibles (net)				4.5	3.2	4.8
6.5	4.9	6.0	All Other Non-Current				2.5	10.2	5.2
100.0	100.0	100.0	Total				100.0	100.0	100.0
			LIABILITIES						
15.8	11.9	10.9	Notes Payable-Short Term				12.3	14.2	9.7
5.9	2.5	3.1	Cur. Mat.-L.T.D.				2.5	5.1	2.0
17.2	20.1	13.7	Trade Payables				10.9	14.2	17.7
.2	.1	.2	Income Taxes Payable				.0	.1	.4
7.5	9.5	7.8	All Other Current				6.2	7.5	8.5
46.5	44.1	35.7	Total Current				31.9	41.1	38.3
9.2	14.5	9.7	Long-Term Debt				5.7	12.7	8.9
.4	.5	.7	Deferred Taxes				.5	1.1	.9
14.3	18.2	9.3	All Other Non-Current				6.2	9.0	13.1
29.6	22.8	44.5	Net Worth				55.7	36.1	38.8
100.0	100.0	100.0	Total Liabilties & Net Worth				100.0	100.0	100.0
			INCOME DATA						
100.0	100.0	100.0	Net Sales				100.0	100.0	100.0
28.8	21.9	27.4	Gross Profit				26.5	21.9	24.6
23.0	20.6	21.0	Operating Expenses				23.2	18.4	16.8
5.8	1.3	6.4	Operating Profit				3.2	3.5	7.8
1.0	.6	1.1	All Other Expenses (net)				.7	2.2	.5
4.8	.7	5.3	Profit Before Taxes				2.5	1.3	7.3
			RATIOS						
2.4	2.2	2.8	Current				4.2	3.0	2.3
1.5	1.5	1.7					2.2	1.6	1.7
1.2	1.1	1.2					1.5	.9	1.2
1.4	1.2	1.3	Quick				1.8	1.1	1.4
.9	.7	.8					1.1	.6	.9
.6	.4	.6					.7	.4	.7
35 10.4	35 10.4	37 9.9	Sales/Receivables				31 11.8	37 9.9	42 8.6
48 7.6	43 8.5	44 8.4					39 9.4	38 9.5	53 6.8
54 6.7	52 7.0	57 6.4					50 7.3	52 7.0	57 6.4
29 12.4	38 9.6	46 7.9	Cost of Sales/Inventory				47 7.8	52 7.0	40 9.1
65 5.7	61 6.0	70 5.2					86 4.2	72 5.1	51 7.1
90 4.1	85 4.3	102 3.6					96 3.8	109 3.4	78 4.7
22 16.4	25 14.7	16 22.5	Cost of Sales/Payables				12 30.8	20 18.2	21 17.6
36 10.1	37 9.8	32 11.6					16 22.2	31 11.8	37 9.9
45 8.2	51 7.1	40 9.1					34 10.7	41 8.9	48 7.6
5.8	5.9	5.0	Sales/Working Capital				4.6	4.0	5.4
9.3	13.2	8.0					6.4	9.0	11.0
25.4	65.2	20.7					11.9	-82.7	20.4
15.1	8.5	16.5	EBIT/Interest					10.5	26.7
(38) 6.3	(39) 2.6	(41) 3.8						1.9	(15) 14.1
2.2	-.1	1.4						-1.7	2.8
5.0	4.4	14.8	Net Profit + Depr., Dep., Amort./Cur. Mat. L/T/D						
(17) 3.7	(15) 2.4	(17) 3.7							
2.4	2.1	.8							
.3	.4	.2	Fixed/Worth				.1	.1	.5
.6	.7	.6					.3	.6	.8
.8	2.2	1.2					.8	15.4	1.8
.7	.8	.6	Debt/Worth				.4	.7	.7
1.3	1.6	1.5					.6	1.9	1.5
2.9	6.4	3.1					2.7	45.4	4.9
39.1	30.8	48.5	% Profit Before Taxes/Tangible Net Worth				43.8		67.7
(35) 20.6	(37) 18.0	(41) 18.3					10.0	(15) 25.8	
12.7	7.6	3.9					-2.0		7.3
15.6	11.8	18.7	% Profit Before Taxes/Total Assets				16.9	13.2	25.2
9.2	4.9	7.0					6.0	3.7	8.3
3.5	2.3	.7					-1.4	-8.8	2.6
22.0	18.0	26.4	Sales/Net Fixed Assets				123.4	51.4	12.8
11.0	7.8	6.3					12.9	8.5	5.9
4.8	4.6	4.5					4.1	5.1	4.6
2.9	3.1	2.7	Sales/Total Assets				3.1	2.7	2.4
2.3	2.1	2.0					2.4	2.1	2.0
1.5	1.7	1.4					1.5	1.4	1.5
1.2	1.2	1.0	% Depr., Dep., Amort./Sales						1.2
(36) 1.9	(38) 2.2	(39) 2.2							(14) 2.5
3.3	3.6	3.8							3.7
2.2	1.6	1.4	% Officers', Directors' Owners' Comp/Sales						
(15) 3.1	(12) 2.6	(12) 2.1							
8.2	3.7	6.2							
879248M	1079274M	1826173M	Net Sales ($)	1674M	6662M	6910M	69350M	157222M	1584355M
459641M	569228M	884897M	Total Assets ($)	2620M	5591M	2427M	35345M	82378M	756536M

© RMA 2007

M = $ thousand   MM = $ million
See Pages 11 through 21 for Explanation of Ratios and Data

Current Data Sorted by Assets   **Comparative Historical Data**

0-500M	500M-2MM	2-10MM	10-50MM	50-100MM	100-250MM	Type of Statement	4/1/02-3/31/03 ALL	4/1/03-3/31/04 ALL
1		5	7	2	1	Unqualified	15	15
		5	2			Reviewed	12	14
2	2	6				Compiled	7	21
3	1	2				Tax Returns	1	5
	2	7	5	2	2	Other	18	29
	15 (4/1-9/30/06)		42 (10/1/06-3/31/07)					
6	5	25	14	4	3	**NUMBER OF STATEMENTS**	53	84
%	%	%	%	%	%	**ASSETS**	%	%
		4.9	8.6			Cash & Equivalents	9.1	7.6
		37.1	23.8			Trade Receivables (net)	20.4	20.5
		33.5	29.2			Inventory	28.5	33.5
		1.6	5.1			All Other Current	5.0	5.5
		77.1	66.6			Total Current	63.0	67.1
		17.2	28.1			Fixed Assets (net)	26.4	24.7
		2.2	2.7			Intangibles (net)	3.4	1.9
		3.5	2.6			All Other Non-Current	7.2	6.3
		100.0	100.0			Total	100.0	100.0
						LIABILITIES		
		12.6	10.2			Notes Payable-Short Term	9.6	11.4
		2.9	3.6			Cur. Mat.-L.T.D.	2.9	3.5
		36.5	14.8			Trade Payables	17.8	19.7
		.9	.3			Income Taxes Payable	.2	.2
		24.3	6.7			All Other Current	12.6	11.5
		77.2	35.5			Total Current	43.2	46.2
		16.6	10.2			Long-Term Debt	16.7	14.0
		.5	.7			Deferred Taxes	.7	.5
		.5	.3			All Other Non-Current	4.3	4.8
		5.1	53.3			Net Worth	35.1	34.4
		100.0	100.0			Total Liabilties & Net Worth	100.0	100.0
						INCOME DATA		
		100.0	100.0			Net Sales	100.0	100.0
		26.2	25.9			Gross Profit	31.7	29.2
		22.4	18.9			Operating Expenses	25.7	25.9
		3.8	7.0			Operating Profit	6.0	3.3
		1.1	1.1			All Other Expenses (net)	1.4	.7
		2.7	5.9			Profit Before Taxes	4.6	2.6
						RATIOS		
		2.2	3.2			Current	2.4	2.4
		1.3	2.1				1.7	1.5
		1.0	1.3				1.0	1.1
		1.2	1.8			Quick	1.2	1.1
		.6	.9				.6	.6
		.3	.4				.5	.3
		20 18.5	32 11.5			Sales/Receivables	13 27.2	8 44.1
		42 8.8	37 9.8				34 10.9	28 13.2
		62 5.9	64 5.7				49 7.5	44 8.4
		21 17.1	50 7.3			Cost of Sales/Inventory	37 9.8	34 10.7
		66 5.5	80 4.6				61 6.0	72 5.1
		81 4.5	105 3.5				115 3.2	134 2.7
		27 13.4	25 14.6			Cost of Sales/Payables	24 15.0	25 14.5
		49 7.4	36 10.2				41 8.8	39 9.4
		67 5.5	55 6.6				64 5.7	59 6.1
		7.1	4.1			Sales/Working Capital	4.5	5.4
		14.0	6.8				9.8	10.6
		NM	11.0				136.1	59.8
		6.9	16.8			EBIT/Interest	10.5	7.7
		(24) 2.6	5.4				(44) 3.6	(76) 3.0
		.8	1.4				1.4	.8
						Net Profit + Depr., Dep., Amort./Cur. Mat. L/T/D	4.6	7.3
							(15) 2.3	(21) 1.9
							1.0	.8
		.2	.3			Fixed/Worth	.3	.3
		.5	.5				.8	.8
		NM	.9				1.4	1.6
		1.1	.4			Debt/Worth	.8	1.0
		2.8	.9				2.2	2.1
		NM	1.9				6.3	4.7
		72.7	46.6			% Profit Before Taxes/Tangible Net Worth	49.2	31.9
		(19) 20.0	12.4				(48) 27.7	(76) 13.2
		9.2	4.3				10.7	2.5
		18.8	26.1			% Profit Before Taxes/Total Assets	13.9	12.5
		5.4	6.1				8.0	4.4
		.2	1.5				1.7	.1
		64.7	17.1			Sales/Net Fixed Assets	19.0	29.7
		25.4	6.0				8.4	12.3
		11.2	4.3				4.9	4.4
		3.7	2.2			Sales/Total Assets	2.4	3.3
		2.9	1.9				2.1	2.0
		2.0	1.3				1.6	1.7
		.6	1.5			% Depr., Dep., Amort./Sales	1.3	.6
		(20) 1.0	2.3				(46) 2.7	(75) 1.7
		2.0	3.5				3.6	3.1
		.6				% Officers', Directors' Owners' Comp/Sales	2.1	1.3
		(10) 4.4					(13) 5.4	(23) 3.6
		7.5					11.8	6.6
7036M	16308M	399592M	615267M	528184M	666310M	Net Sales ($)	1875257M	2049345M
1533M	6683M	131042M	352551M	297938M	451886M	Total Assets ($)	1080627M	1205164M

M = $ thousand   MM = $ million

See Pages 11 through 21 for Explanation of Ratios and Data

Comparative Historical Data | Current Data Sorted by Sales

16	11	16	Type of Statement						
13	13	7	Unqualified	1			1	5	9
13	12	10	Reviewed			1		4	2
13	4	6	Compiled		3	1	1	5	
20	23	18	Tax Returns	1	3		1	1	
4/1/04-	4/1/05-	4/1/06-	Other	1	3	2	3	4	9
3/31/05	3/31/06	3/31/07							
ALL	ALL	ALL		0-1MM	15 (4/1-9/30/06) 1-3MM	3-5MM	42 (10/1/06-3/31/07) 5-10MM	10-25MM	25MM & OVER
75	63	57	NUMBER OF STATEMENTS	2	8	2	6	19	20
%	%	%	ASSETS	%	%	%	%	%	%
8.8	6.1	7.6	Cash & Equivalents					3.7	9.2
24.6	27.9	29.7	Trade Receivables (net)					35.1	27.0
30.8	34.5	31.6	Inventory					32.3	27.9
2.0	2.5	2.1	All Other Current					3.7	2.2
66.3	71.0	71.0	Total Current					74.7	66.4
27.1	23.6	22.6	Fixed Assets (net)					21.1	26.2
1.4	2.2	2.0	Intangibles (net)					.3	2.1
5.3	3.1	4.5	All Other Non-Current					3.9	5.2
100.0	100.0	100.0	Total					100.0	100.0
			LIABILITIES						
8.9	10.2	14.1	Notes Payable-Short Term					11.9	8.9
4.2	5.6	3.0	Cur. Mat.-L.T.D.					3.4	3.3
22.0	23.0	24.5	Trade Payables					37.0	14.8
.2	.1	.5	Income Taxes Payable					.0	.9
10.6	14.6	17.0	All Other Current					7.6	27.5
45.9	53.4	59.2	Total Current					59.9	55.4
15.8	15.5	17.9	Long-Term Debt					18.2	13.3
.6	.6	.4	Deferred Taxes					.7	.5
5.4	2.8	1.6	All Other Non-Current					.4	2.8
32.2	27.8	20.9	Net Worth					20.8	28.0
100.0	100.0	100.0	Total Liabilities & Net Worth					100.0	100.0
			INCOME DATA						
100.0	100.0	100.0	Net Sales					100.0	100.0
29.0	29.2	28.0	Gross Profit					24.0	25.1
24.9	25.2	23.6	Operating Expenses					20.8	18.0
4.1	4.0	4.4	Operating Profit					3.2	7.1
1.1	.8	1.4	All Other Expenses (net)					1.0	1.0
3.0	3.2	3.0	Profit Before Taxes					2.2	6.1
			RATIOS						
2.6	2.6	2.6						2.4	2.8
1.6	1.6	1.6	Current					1.5	2.1
1.1	1.0	1.0						1.2	1.3
1.5	1.4	1.3						1.3	1.7
.8	(62) .7	.7	Quick					.8	.9
.3	.4	.4						.3	.5
20 18.5	24 15.4	25 14.6						22 16.8	35 10.4
37 9.8	37 9.8	38 9.6	Sales/Receivables					38 9.6	41 9.0
51 7.1	55 6.7	58 6.3						58 6.2	60 6.1
24 15.3	36 10.3	25 14.9						23 16.1	33 11.0
69 5.3	72 5.0	74 5.0	Cost of Sales/Inventory					66 5.5	79 4.6
110 3.3	102 3.6	98 3.7						80 4.6	115 3.2
19 19.6	26 14.2	24 15.0						34 10.7	23 15.7
37 10.0	39 9.4	41 8.9	Cost of Sales/Payables					53 6.9	33 10.9
61 5.9	63 5.8	58 6.3						66 5.6	46 7.9
5.4	4.8	5.8						6.6	4.4
9.7	9.5	9.5	Sales/Working Capital					9.9	6.6
59.4	999.8	112.8						37.3	12.9
15.2	7.4	8.1						6.7	25.9
(68) 3.7	(60) 3.2	(53) 3.1	EBIT/Interest					2.7	(19) 6.2
1.4	1.6	.7						1.3	1.4
5.3	5.2	6.9	Net Profit + Depr., Dep.,						
(17) 3.2	(14) 1.5	(12) 2.4	Amort./Cur. Mat. L/T/D						
.7	.4	.6							
.3	.3	.2						.2	.3
.7	.7	.6	Fixed/Worth					.7	.6
1.8	2.1	2.1						1.1	1.4
.8	.9	.9						.8	.6
2.0	1.8	2.0	Debt/Worth					2.5	1.0
5.3	7.5	8.0						8.7	2.7
44.2	35.0	45.7	% Profit Before Taxes/Tangible					41.8	46.3
(66) 17.9	(54) 16.7	(47) 15.7	Net Worth					(16) 12.2	(19) 19.3
5.2	6.5	4.7						9.4	6.4
12.4	12.3	16.8	% Profit Before Taxes/Total					7.5	27.6
6.9	5.1	5.5	Assets					5.4	9.0
1.4	1.0	-1.0						1.7	1.8
29.1	34.4	27.7						33.1	16.3
9.0	13.6	12.9	Sales/Net Fixed Assets					18.6	6.4
5.7	6.5	5.4						9.2	4.7
3.8	3.2	3.4						3.7	2.4
2.2	2.5	2.2	Sales/Total Assets					2.8	1.9
1.6	1.8	1.6						2.0	1.4
.9	.7	.9						.7	1.4
(67) 2.0	(56) 1.6	(45) 1.8	% Depr., Dep., Amort./Sales					(17) 1.2	(16) 2.1
3.0	2.9	2.7						2.2	3.4
1.6	.8	1.6	% Officers', Directors'						
(27) 2.9	(21) 2.6	(16) 4.2	Owners' Comp/Sales						
7.0	9.0	7.2							
3572256M	1513391M	2232697M	Net Sales ($)	758M	14314M	7521M	43060M	335708M	1831336M
1494915M	738722M	1241633M	Total Assets ($)	435M	7097M	5093M	21236M	124361M	1083411M

© RMA 2007

M = $ thousand   MM = $ million

See Pages 11 through 21 for Explanation of Ratios and Data

		Current Data Sorted by Assets					Comparative Historical Data	
0-500M	500M-2MM	2-10MM	10-50MM	50-100MM	100-250MM	**Type of Statement**		
		4	3	1	2	Unqualified	20	20
	2	8	2			Reviewed	15	18
	3	2				Compiled	8	8
2	2	1				Tax Returns	3	6
	2	4	3	5	1	Other	15	18
		13 (4/1-9/30/06)	34 (10/1/06-3/31/07)				4/1/02-3/31/03	4/1/03-3/31/04
							ALL	ALL
2	9	19	8	6	3	**NUMBER OF STATEMENTS**	61	70
%	%	%	%	%	%	**ASSETS**	%	%
		7.9				Cash & Equivalents	9.0	5.9
		19.4				Trade Receivables (net)	28.1	26.6
		41.8				Inventory	35.5	37.1
		1.3				All Other Current	3.9	4.2
		70.3				Total Current	76.5	73.8
		18.7				Fixed Assets (net)	16.5	17.7
		1.4				Intangibles (net)	2.4	2.5
		9.6				All Other Non-Current	4.7	5.9
		100.0				Total	100.0	100.0
						LIABILITIES		
		13.0				Notes Payable-Short Term	12.1	14.8
		4.7				Cur. Mat.-L.T.D.	3.7	2.0
		22.9				Trade Payables	19.8	18.0
		.1				Income Taxes Payable	.1	.1
		11.3				All Other Current	9.9	11.6
		52.1				Total Current	45.7	46.5
		5.3				Long-Term Debt	10.8	8.5
		.1				Deferred Taxes	.2	.3
		2.8				All Other Non-Current	2.6	5.1
		39.7				Net Worth	40.8	39.6
		100.0				Total Liabilties & Net Worth	100.0	100.0
						INCOME DATA		
		100.0				Net Sales	100.0	100.0
		32.5				Gross Profit	29.8	29.5
		29.0				Operating Expenses	24.5	25.9
		3.5				Operating Profit	5.4	3.6
		.7				All Other Expenses (net)	.8	.7
		2.7				Profit Before Taxes	4.6	2.9
						RATIOS		
		2.3				Current	2.6	2.7
		1.3					1.8	1.6
		1.1					1.3	1.2
		1.1				Quick	1.5	1.4
		.5					.8	.8
		.4					.5	.4
		17 22.0				Sales/Receivables	25 14.7	26 14.3
		36 10.2					42 8.7	41 9.0
		51 7.1					59 6.2	53 6.9
		42 8.7				Cost of Sales/Inventory	41 8.8	49 7.5
		91 4.0					75 4.9	83 4.4
		171 2.1					113 3.2	113 3.2
		33 11.0				Cost of Sales/Payables	20 17.9	15 24.1
		47 7.8					31 11.9	32 11.4
		66 5.6					53 6.9	51 7.2
		4.8				Sales/Working Capital	4.3	4.9
		13.2					8.0	8.5
		43.4					15.6	18.7
		15.8				EBIT/Interest	8.1	12.4
		(16) 3.4					(51) 3.9	(64) 4.4
		1.7					2.0	1.4
						Net Profit + Depr., Dep., Amort./Cur. Mat. L/T/D	11.0	11.1
							(20) 4.0	(21) 2.3
							1.4	1.2
		.1				Fixed/Worth	.1	.1
		.4					.4	.4
		.9					.7	.8
		.7				Debt/Worth	.8	.7
		2.1					1.9	1.5
		4.2					3.3	3.3
		47.2				% Profit Before Taxes/Tangible Net Worth	48.4	41.8
		(17) 19.8					(58) 22.5	(63) 17.6
		4.5					6.5	4.5
		16.3				% Profit Before Taxes/Total Assets	14.1	13.6
		9.3					7.0	6.0
		1.5					2.3	.5
		87.6				Sales/Net Fixed Assets	41.1	44.6
		14.3					17.3	17.1
		8.0					9.4	8.9
		3.4				Sales/Total Assets	3.1	3.2
		2.0					2.3	2.4
		1.8					1.8	1.8
		.6				% Depr., Dep., Amort./Sales	.8	.8
		(17) 1.4					(52) 1.3	(56) 1.5
		2.7					1.7	2.4
						% Officers', Directors' Owners' Comp/Sales	2.4	2.2
							(21) 4.0	(30) 2.9
							8.9	5.6
3894M	38937M	217747M	342795M	800768M	884950M	Net Sales ($)	4509940M	3452805M
484M	12219M	86817M	168940M	472769M	527943M	Total Assets ($)	1215845M	1815821M

M = $ thousand   MM = $ million
See Pages 11 through 21 for Explanation of Ratios and Data

Comparative Historical Data   ## Current Data Sorted by Sales

Comparative Historical Data			Type of Statement	0-1MM	1-3MM	3-5MM	5-10MM	10-25MM	25MM & OVER
11	14	10	Unqualified		2		2	2	6
15	12	12	Reviewed	2	3		3	5	2
4	9	5	Compiled	1	1		2	1	
9	4	5	Tax Returns	3			2		
18	17	15	Other		1		3	3	8
4/1/04-3/31/05 ALL	4/1/05-3/31/06 ALL	4/1/06-3/31/07 ALL			13 (4/1-9/30/06)		34 (10/1/06-3/31/07)		
57	56	47	NUMBER OF STATEMENTS		6	2	12	11	16
%	%	%	ASSETS	%	%	%	%	%	%
8.6	9.0	7.7	Cash & Equivalents				11.4	5.9	4.4
27.2	28.6	21.1	Trade Receivables (net)	D			23.3	16.3	22.3
39.4	33.9	40.1	Inventory	A			38.9	41.3	43.1
2.2	1.6	2.7	All Other Current	T			3.0	1.1	3.5
77.4	73.1	71.7	Total Current	A			76.7	64.6	73.3
14.2	17.9	16.7	Fixed Assets (net)				13.5	22.3	11.7
3.7	2.5	5.6	Intangibles (net)	N			.0	7.4	10.3
4.6	6.5	6.0	All Other Non-Current	O			9.8	5.8	4.7
100.0	100.0	100.0	Total	T			100.0	100.0	100.0
			LIABILITIES	A					
14.0	13.4	12.6	Notes Payable-Short Term	V			9.6	14.8	13.2
2.2	3.3	2.8	Cur. Mat.-L.T.D.	A			5.0	3.7	1.5
19.5	17.9	20.2	Trade Payables	I			17.9	29.3	18.2
.1	.2	.2	Income Taxes Payable	L			.2	.2	.3
8.7	11.2	10.6	All Other Current	A			10.7	13.1	6.3
44.5	46.0	46.4	Total Current	B			43.4	61.0	39.4
9.8	10.6	8.1	Long-Term Debt	L			1.7	7.0	12.6
.6	.5	.7	Deferred Taxes	E			.1	.2	2.0
4.3	4.7	5.7	All Other Non-Current				7.0	1.6	6.7
40.7	38.2	39.1	Net Worth				47.9	30.2	39.2
100.0	100.0	100.0	Total Liabilties & Net Worth				100.0	100.0	100.0
			INCOME DATA						
100.0	100.0	100.0	Net Sales				100.0	100.0	100.0
33.8	31.2	32.7	Gross Profit				32.2	33.3	25.0
28.2	26.6	28.2	Operating Expenses				30.0	30.1	20.0
5.6	4.6	4.5	Operating Profit				2.2	3.2	4.9
.5	.7	1.1	All Other Expenses (net)				-.1	.4	2.8
5.1	3.9	3.4	Profit Before Taxes				2.3	2.9	2.2
			RATIOS						
2.9	2.8	2.4					2.6	1.4	2.9
2.0	1.7	1.5	Current				2.0	1.2	1.8
1.2	1.1	1.1					1.2	.8	1.4
1.5	1.7	1.1					1.2	.7	1.1
.8	.9	.6	Quick				1.0	.4	.7
.5	.5	.4					.5	.1	.4

Sales/Receivables

Hist1		Hist2		Hist3			Current					
33	11.2	20	18.7	19	19.0				25	14.4	5	67.3	33	11.1
45	8.2	41	8.9	36	10.2	Sales/Receivables			36	10.1	29	12.6	43	8.6
57	6.4	58	6.3	49	7.4				52	7.0	45	8.1	53	6.9
61	6.0	33	11.0	52	7.0				25	14.4	30	12.3	64	5.7
94	3.9	65	5.6	82	4.5	Cost of Sales/Inventory			66	5.6	64	5.7	101	3.6
125	2.9	102	3.6	136	2.7				153	2.4	136	2.7	137	2.7
18	20.3	16	23.5	24	15.2				19	19.5	38	9.7	30	12.1
30	12.0	31	11.7	41	8.9	Cost of Sales/Payables			40	9.1	48	7.6	39	9.5
46	8.0	45	8.2	52	7.0				56	6.5	51	7.1	54	6.7

Hist1	Hist2	Hist3	Ratio				Curr5-10	Curr10-25	Curr25+
3.7	5.1	4.6	Sales/Working Capital				4.5	13.2	3.7
6.4	8.9	8.1					7.0	16.3	6.0
21.2	35.8	36.7					19.7	-21.8	9.1
	17.9		11.4		13.8	EBIT/Interest		49.0		6.1
(46)	5.0	(49)	3.5	(39)	3.5		(10)	3.8	(14)	3.2
	2.2		1.7		.9			1.6		.9
	8.4		4.2		8.4	Net Profit + Depr., Dep., Amort./Cur. Mat. L/T/D				
(13)	2.0	(18)	1.4	(13)	2.6					
	1.3		.3		1.7					
.1	.1	.1	Fixed/Worth				.1	.4	.2
.3	.3	.4					.2	.7	.4
.5	.8	.9					.5	1.5	.9
.5	.5	.7	Debt/Worth				.3	2.1	.9
1.5	1.2	1.9					1.1	2.8	1.8
4.6	6.0	7.5					6.4	5.8	8.5
	55.8		49.7		56.9	% Profit Before Taxes/Tangible Net Worth		32.5		37.9
(51)	23.7	(50)	21.4	(40)	18.8			15.0	(13)	15.7
	9.1		7.6		4.8			-1.3		3.7
19.3	15.9	16.3	% Profit Before Taxes/Total Assets				12.1	17.9	10.5
7.5	7.3	6.6					6.2	9.3	4.7
2.9	2.1	1.5					-1.0	1.8	.0
62.1	76.3	50.5	Sales/Net Fixed Assets				88.1	42.0	36.7
25.3	30.9	18.8					49.2	12.9	22.9
9.2	8.0	8.9					12.3	7.5	7.9
2.8	3.6	3.1	Sales/Total Assets				3.5	4.3	2.3
2.2	2.8	2.1					2.1	2.3	1.7
1.7	1.9	1.7					1.7	2.0	1.4
	.6		.4		.7	% Depr., Dep., Amort./Sales		.5	.9	.8
(47)	1.4	(47)	1.0	(39)	1.4		(10)	.7	(10) 1.3	(12) 1.5
	2.1		1.7		2.4			1.9	2.5	2.5
	3.0		2.2		1.6	% Officers', Directors' Owners' Comp/Sales				
(20)	4.0	(17)	3.0	(12)	4.1					
	7.0		5.7		10.2					
1984312M	1779364M	2289091M	Net Sales ($)	14370M	7312M		89143M	174393M	2003873M
1202739M	783335M	1269172M	Total Assets ($)	7733M	2899M		40850M	64202M	1153488M

M = $ thousand   MM = $ million
See Pages 11 through 21 for Explanation of Ratios and Data

Current Data Sorted by Assets							Comparative Historical Data	
						Type of Statement		
		1	4	1		Unqualified	5	5
1	2	8	1			Reviewed	12	14
4	3	3				Compiled	11	17
4	4	1				Tax Returns	6	9
	8	3	5	1		Other	19	20
	11 (4/1-9/30/06)		43 (10/1/06-3/31/07)				**4/1/02-3/31/03**	**4/1/03-3/31/04**
0-500M	**500M-2MM**	**2-10MM**	**10-50MM**	**50-100MM**	**100-250MM**		**ALL**	**ALL**
9	17	16	10	2		**NUMBER OF STATEMENTS**	53	65
%	%	%	%	%	%	**ASSETS**	%	%
	9.1	6.8	5.0		DATA NOT AVAILABLE	Cash & Equivalents	6.9	5.4
	27.1	23.9	25.9			Trade Receivables (net)	25.5	25.5
	36.2	29.6	29.5			Inventory	32.3	31.8
	1.5	2.4	3.2			All Other Current	3.3	2.3
	74.0	62.7	63.7			Total Current	68.0	65.0
	17.6	22.7	30.9			Fixed Assets (net)	21.9	24.8
	5.3	.3	1.5			Intangibles (net)	3.7	2.5
	3.1	14.3	3.9			All Other Non-Current	6.3	7.6
	100.0	100.0	100.0			Total	100.0	100.0
						LIABILITIES		
	16.8	11.0	9.2			Notes Payable-Short Term	18.4	11.8
	4.5	2.4	2.3			Cur. Mat.-L.T.D.	4.2	3.9
	16.5	12.3	10.3			Trade Payables	14.3	14.5
	.1	.1	.0			Income Taxes Payable	.0	.4
	7.4	5.6	15.9			All Other Current	13.8	9.9
	45.2	31.4	37.7			Total Current	50.7	40.6
	15.1	12.2	13.9			Long-Term Debt	11.9	13.6
	.0	.4	.0			Deferred Taxes	.1	.2
	4.2	7.9	1.1			All Other Non-Current	4.1	6.0
	35.5	48.0	47.3			Net Worth	33.2	39.7
	100.0	100.0	100.0			Total Liabilties & Net Worth	100.0	100.0
						INCOME DATA		
	100.0	100.0	100.0			Net Sales	100.0	100.0
	30.8	33.1	28.3			Gross Profit	36.3	37.0
	26.9	28.0	21.6			Operating Expenses	33.3	33.9
	3.8	5.1	6.7			Operating Profit	3.0	3.0
	1.3	.0	.9			All Other Expenses (net)	.6	.0
	2.5	5.1	5.8			Profit Before Taxes	2.4	3.1
						RATIOS		
	3.7	4.2	3.1				2.6	2.6
	1.9	1.8	1.8			Current	1.7	1.8
	1.1	1.4	1.0				1.1	1.1
	1.9	1.4	1.3				1.2	1.3
	.8	.9	.8			Quick	.7	.8
	.5	.7	.6				.5	.5
	22 16.7	**33** 11.1	**32** 11.3				**22** 16.7	**22** 16.9
	37 9.9	**37** 9.9	**45** 8.1			Sales/Receivables	**36** 10.0	**33** 11.1
	46 7.9	**45** 8.1	**51** 7.2				**48** 7.6	**50** 7.2
	31 11.9	**54** 6.7	**44** 8.3				**45** 8.2	**51** 7.2
	82 4.4	**57** 6.4	**57** 6.3			Cost of Sales/Inventory	**70** 5.2	**77** 4.7
	136 2.7	**86** 4.3	**111** 3.3				**108** 3.4	**105** 3.5
	17 21.3	**17** 20.9	**12** 29.8				**16** 23.2	**16** 22.2
	29 12.5	**23** 15.9	**19** 19.1			Cost of Sales/Payables	**26** 13.8	**27** 13.3
	41 8.8	**46** 8.0	**32** 11.4				**47** 7.8	**49** 7.5
	4.4	4.2	4.5				6.3	5.7
	6.9	7.9	7.9			Sales/Working Capital	11.3	10.0
	NM	13.8	NM				146.8	40.0
	7.3	8.2	16.4				8.7	14.1
	(14) 2.0	(14) 3.4	6.7			EBIT/Interest	(51) 3.0	(60) 4.1
	.7	1.8	2.8				.6	1.4
							5.0	7.4
						Net Profit + Depr., Dep., Amort./Cur. Mat. L/T/D	(12) 2.2	(18) 3.1
							.1	1.7
	.1	.3	.3				.3	.3
	.3	.6	.5			Fixed/Worth	.6	.5
	.9	1.2	1.4				1.4	1.4
	.8	.5	.5				.7	.7
	1.6	1.1	1.0			Debt/Worth	1.5	1.3
	4.5	3.6	2.9				3.7	3.1
	43.5	73.0					26.2	41.4
	(15) 16.5	13.4				% Profit Before Taxes/Tangible Net Worth	(43) 12.2	(59) 13.3
	2.0	4.7					-3.6	2.6
	14.2	12.1	18.8				11.0	13.8
	4.1	6.5	11.8			% Profit Before Taxes/Total Assets	6.0	5.5
	.0	1.9	5.3				-1.0	.9
	165.9	28.4	18.5				25.3	27.7
	19.6	11.9	8.2			Sales/Net Fixed Assets	14.9	12.5
	9.7	6.2	4.2				7.9	7.5
	3.3	2.9	2.5				3.5	3.2
	2.6	2.3	2.1			Sales/Total Assets	2.4	2.6
	2.0	1.9	1.9				1.9	1.8
	.4	1.0	.8				1.0	1.0
	(12) 1.0	(15) 1.2	1.8			% Depr., Dep., Amort./Sales	(49) 1.7	(57) 1.5
	2.2	2.4	2.4				2.9	2.6
							3.8	3.2
						% Officers', Directors' Owners' Comp/Sales	(29) 7.2	(36) 6.4
							12.1	13.7
9679M	**54787M**	**171016M**	**452858M**	**230224M**		Net Sales ($)	**636220M**	**583310M**
2840M	**21097M**	**73682M**	**210070M**	**147151M**		Total Assets ($)	**348149M**	**275592M**

M = $ thousand MM = $ million

See Pages 11 through 21 for Explanation of Ratios and Data

Comparative Historical Data   Current Data Sorted by Sales

4/1/04-3/31/05 ALL	4/1/05-3/31/06 ALL	4/1/06-3/31/07 ALL	Type of Statement	0-1MM	1-3MM	3-5MM	5-10MM	10-25MM	25MM & OVER
4	6	6	Unqualified	1	1	1	3	5	5
17	11	12	Reviewed	1	6			3	1
12	15	10	Compiled	1	4	1	1		
8	7	9	Tax Returns	3		2	4		
15	12	17	Other		5				6
				0-1MM	**11 (4/1-9/30/06)**		**43 (10/1/06-3/31/07)**		**25MM & OVER**
56	51	54	**NUMBER OF STATEMENTS**	5	16	4	9	8	12
%	%	%	**ASSETS**	%	%	%	%	%	%
10.4	6.2	8.0	Cash & Equivalents		10.9				5.0
26.1	26.2	26.2	Trade Receivables (net)		26.5				26.3
31.5	33.5	31.8	Inventory		31.6				28.3
1.6	2.2	2.1	All Other Current		.5				3.0
69.6	68.2	68.1	Total Current		69.3				62.7
19.0	22.6	22.1	Fixed Assets (net)		21.9				29.9
5.0	3.5	2.5	Intangibles (net)		4.7				3.5
6.4	5.6	7.2	All Other Non-Current		4.1				3.9
100.0	100.0	100.0	Total		100.0				100.0
			LIABILITIES						
15.8	14.7	12.1	Notes Payable-Short Term		15.8				7.7
2.8	2.2	2.9	Cur. Mat.-L.T.D.		2.9				2.3
16.1	14.4	14.4	Trade Payables		14.5				11.1
.2	.1	.1	Income Taxes Payable		.1				.0
8.6	9.9	10.2	All Other Current		8.8				15.4
43.4	41.3	39.7	Total Current		42.1				36.5
18.0	16.5	13.6	Long-Term Debt		12.2				19.8
.1	.1	.1	Deferred Taxes		.0				.0
13.5	11.9	5.0	All Other Non-Current		4.0				.9
25.0	30.2	41.6	Net Worth		41.7				42.8
100.0	100.0	100.0	Total Liabilities & Net Worth		100.0				100.0
			INCOME DATA						
100.0	100.0	100.0	Net Sales		100.0				100.0
35.8	34.4	32.0	Gross Profit		35.3				29.4
31.9	29.1	27.6	Operating Expenses		32.2				21.6
3.9	5.3	4.4	Operating Profit		3.0				7.7
.8	.3	.7	All Other Expenses (net)		.9				1.0
3.1	5.0	3.7	Profit Before Taxes		2.2				6.8
			RATIOS						
3.0	3.0	3.5	Current		4.0				2.9
1.7	1.8	1.8			2.1				1.8
1.1	1.3	1.3			1.0				1.1
1.8	1.5	1.5	Quick		2.4				1.5
.9	.8	.8			1.0				.8
.4	.5	.6			.5				.6
22 16.6	23 15.9	27 13.3	Sales/Receivables		23 15.6				39 9.3
35 10.4	37 10.0	39 9.5			35 10.4				45 8.1
49 7.5	53 6.9	47 7.8			45 8.2				60 6.1
44 8.4	46 7.9	38 9.6	Cost of Sales/Inventory		33 11.1				49 7.4
70 5.2	71 5.1	58 6.3			69 5.3				63 5.8
113 3.2	120 3.0	124 2.9			133 2.7				102 3.6
15 25.1	14 26.7	17 22.1	Cost of Sales/Payables		15 23.8				13 27.2
32 11.3	27 13.4	25 14.9			26 13.8				22 16.5
45 8.1	53 6.9	38 9.5			54 6.8				34 10.8
5.0	5.2	4.7	Sales/Working Capital		4.3				4.3
10.5	9.4	8.7			7.2				7.0
56.9	20.7	19.4			NM				41.4
14.4	13.6	10.0	EBIT/Interest		16.4				12.4
(50) 4.8	(48) 4.1	(48) 3.5			(13) 1.7				7.6
1.4	1.6	1.4			-.3				3.4
7.3	7.9	5.3	Net Profit + Depr., Dep., Amort./Cur. Mat. L/T/D						
(12) 2.0	(13) 4.2	(12) 2.7							
.8	2.0	1.3							
.2	.2	.2	Fixed/Worth		.1				.3
.5	.6	.5			.4				.6
3.6	1.5	1.2			1.1				1.7
.7	.7	.5	Debt/Worth		.4				.5
1.4	1.5	1.4			1.1				1.4
11.4	3.9	3.7			3.5				3.0
30.4	55.4	41.3	% Profit Before Taxes/Tangible Net Worth		41.8				38.8
(43) 11.8	(43) 23.8	(49) 18.1			(14) 7.7				(10) 35.6
3.6	6.5	3.9			-7.3				14.0
15.7	22.4	16.2	% Profit Before Taxes/Total Assets		25.6				21.0
6.8	7.2	8.4			4.1				14.2
.4	2.2	1.3			-3.9				7.2
43.9	36.7	41.5	Sales/Net Fixed Assets		132.7				16.4
19.2	13.9	13.1			15.7				8.2
8.7	7.2	7.9			8.0				4.4
3.4	3.2	3.2	Sales/Total Assets		4.0				2.3
2.6	2.4	2.4			2.8				2.0
1.8	1.9	1.9			1.9				1.7
.6	.8	.8	% Depr., Dep., Amort./Sales		.5				.9
(50) 1.2	(43) 1.4	(46) 1.5			(14) 1.3				(11) 2.1
2.3	2.4	2.4			2.5				2.3
2.6	2.5	2.4	% Officers', Directors' Owners' Comp/Sales		2.5				
(27) 5.0	(26) 5.1	(24) 3.1			(10) 3.1				
9.8	8.5	8.0			6.2				
641235M	695393M	918564M	Net Sales ($)	3376M	35069M	15362M	63788M	117887M	683082M
299546M	316387M	454840M	Total Assets ($)	1522M	18891M	6161M	27941M	43104M	357221M

© RMA 2007

M = $ thousand   MM = $ million
See Pages 11 through 21 for Explanation of Ratios and Data

Current Data Sorted by Assets / Comparative Historical Data

Type of Statement

0-500M	500M-2MM	2-10MM	10-50MM	50-100MM	100-250MM	Type of Statement	4/1/02-3/31/03 ALL	4/1/03-3/31/04 ALL
	1	10	11		8	Unqualified	43	52
	4	16	4			Reviewed	38	39
4	9	18	2			Compiled	19	54
2	11	1				Tax Returns	12	13
1	9	18	13	2	2	Other	43	48
	36 (4/1-9/30/06)		111 (10/1/06-3/31/07)					
7	34	63	30	3	10	NUMBER OF STATEMENTS	155	206

Main Data

0-500M %	500M-2MM %	2-10MM %	10-50MM %	50-100MM %	100-250MM %		4/1/02-3/31/03 ALL %	4/1/03-3/31/04 ALL %
						ASSETS		
	8.5	6.5	8.2		4.5	Cash & Equivalents	7.4	8.0
	28.1	26.2	23.4		20.1	Trade Receivables (net)	23.7	24.6
	30.1	31.5	29.0		24.2	Inventory	32.5	28.2
	.9	1.6	1.7		3.9	All Other Current	4.6	4.5
	67.6	65.8	62.3		52.6	Total Current	68.2	65.2
	21.0	25.5	24.6		23.7	Fixed Assets (net)	20.6	23.7
	2.0	2.7	5.5		17.5	Intangibles (net)	4.4	5.2
	9.4	6.0	7.6		6.2	All Other Non-Current	6.8	6.0
	100.0	100.0	100.0		100.0	Total	100.0	100.0
						LIABILITIES		
	14.8	13.5	9.8		5.6	Notes Payable-Short Term	11.7	11.0
	3.7	5.5	2.4		3.1	Cur. Mat.-L.T.D.	4.0	3.9
	18.1	15.3	12.2		12.1	Trade Payables	15.3	14.8
	.4	.3	.5		.6	Income Taxes Payable	.3	.3
	13.3	10.4	10.0		9.2	All Other Current	12.9	12.6
	50.2	45.0	34.9		30.7	Total Current	44.2	42.6
	16.2	13.7	12.2		15.9	Long-Term Debt	14.8	18.0
	.5	.4	.4		2.2	Deferred Taxes	.4	.6
	3.1	7.5	4.1		3.4	All Other Non-Current	6.5	6.9
	30.0	33.4	48.4		47.9	Net Worth	34.2	32.0
	100.0	100.0	100.0		100.0	Total Liabilities & Net Worth	100.0	100.0
						INCOME DATA		
	100.0	100.0	100.0		100.0	Net Sales	100.0	100.0
	40.2	29.5	28.8		26.1	Gross Profit	28.1	31.1
	35.0	24.3	22.4		19.8	Operating Expenses	24.7	27.3
	5.3	5.2	6.3		6.3	Operating Profit	3.4	3.7
	1.1	1.4	1.0		1.4	All Other Expenses (net)	1.4	1.3
	4.2	3.7	5.3		4.9	Profit Before Taxes	2.0	2.5
						RATIOS		
	2.7	2.3	2.9		2.5		2.8	2.8
	1.5	1.6	1.9		1.7	Current	1.7	1.8
	1.0	1.1	1.3		1.3		1.1	1.2
	1.6	1.3	1.6		1.1		1.3	1.3
	.8	.7	1.1		.8	Quick	.8	.8
	.4	.5	.5		.6		.4	.5
	24 15.3	30 12.1	32 11.6		38 9.7		21 17.6	26 14.2
	34 10.8	42 8.6	46 8.0		47 7.8	Sales/Receivables	37 9.9	40 9.1
	47 7.8	53 6.9	57 6.4		63 5.8		53 6.9	58 6.3
	27 13.7	38 9.6	56 6.5		56 6.5		35 10.6	36 10.2
	60 6.1	69 5.3	77 4.7		80 4.5	Cost of Sales/Inventory	70 5.2	63 5.8
	111 3.3	111 3.3	113 3.2		91 4.0		108 3.4	104 3.5
	17 22.0	19 19.5	18 20.0		28 13.0		14 26.4	19 19.6
	28 13.3	28 13.0	29 12.4		33 11.0	Cost of Sales/Payables	27 13.5	30 12.0
	53 6.9	43 8.4	42 8.6		48 7.6		48 7.6	49 7.5
	7.0	5.5	3.9		4.8		4.5	4.5
	13.9	9.3	6.9		7.8	Sales/Working Capital	9.3	8.8
	-639.9	41.5	11.8		15.0		41.5	29.1
	8.2	7.3	14.9		8.2		6.8	8.1
	(32) 2.4	(59) 2.4	(25) 5.3		4.1	EBIT/Interest	(133) 2.7	(184) 2.6
	1.1	1.3	1.3		1.7		1.0	1.0
		8.9	19.5				5.9	5.5
	(18) 3.2	3.2	(11) 2.5			Net Profit + Depr., Dep., Amort./Cur. Mat. L/T/D	(37) 2.1	(53) 1.3
		1.6	.9				.8	.6
	.2	.3	.3		.4		.2	.2
	.6	.6	.6		.9	Fixed/Worth	.5	.7
	1.4	1.7	1.4		1.3		2.1	2.5
	.5	.7	.4		1.1		.8	.8
	1.9	1.8	1.1		1.9	Debt/Worth	2.0	2.1
	5.1	10.2	3.3		4.4		8.3	6.4
	52.5	40.3	38.9		62.8	% Profit Before Taxes/Tangible	41.3	37.5
	(30) 10.0	(52) 19.8	(27) 24.0		31.8	Net Worth	(131) 17.9	(173) 16.8
	1.8	3.1	6.3		7.9		2.0	.8
	18.4	15.6	15.2		13.2	% Profit Before Taxes/Total	13.1	13.3
	5.2	5.3	9.9		9.5	Assets	4.7	4.8
	.6	.6	.8		2.5		.2	.0
	50.9	28.5	16.7		19.0		45.0	42.0
	22.2	11.6	9.7		11.5	Sales/Net Fixed Assets	15.2	11.3
	8.7	5.0	5.9		5.0		6.8	5.3
	3.9	2.7	2.4		1.8		3.2	3.0
	3.0	2.1	2.0		1.7	Sales/Total Assets	2.2	2.1
	2.4	1.4	1.2		1.6		1.6	1.5
	.5	1.0	.9				.5	.8
	(27) 1.3	(57) 2.1	(28) 2.0			% Depr., Dep., Amort./Sales	(123) 1.5	(172) 1.9
	2.7	4.5	2.7				3.2	3.3
	2.2	3.1	1.1			% Officers', Directors'	2.5	2.6
	(18) 7.8	(20) 4.1	(10) 2.1			Owners' Comp/Sales	(44) 5.4	(74) 5.0
	13.2	6.2	4.2				9.2	8.9
8186M	128723M	670250M	1159445M	524174M	2924652M	Net Sales ($)	4929255M	6540195M
2083M	41894M	308617M	627521M	256443M	1793929M	Total Assets ($)	2722860M	3616699M

M = $ thousand   MM = $ million

See Pages 11 through 21 for Explanation of Ratios and Data

Comparative Historical Data | Current Data Sorted by Sales

4/1/04-3/31/05 ALL	4/1/05-3/31/06 ALL	4/1/06-3/31/07 ALL	Type of Statement	0-1MM	1-3MM	3-5MM	5-10MM	10-25MM	25MM & OVER
42	30	31	Unqualified		1	2	3	7	18
32	19	24	Reviewed		1	5	7	8	3
32	27	33	Compiled	1	7	11	7	5	2
11	11	14	Tax Returns	1	4	4	4	1	
48	67	45	Other	2	5	2	8	13	15
				36 (4/1-9/30/06)		111 (10/1/06-3/31/07)			
165	154	147	NUMBER OF STATEMENTS	4	18	24	29	34	38
%	%	%	**ASSETS**	%	%	%	%	%	%
7.8	6.6	7.1	Cash & Equivalents		6.6	9.7	6.2	6.9	7.3
25.2	25.1	25.6	Trade Receivables (net)		21.7	25.0	24.5	28.5	26.4
28.4	29.0	30.2	Inventory		31.5	24.6	33.8	32.6	29.5
2.9	2.2	2.4	All Other Current		1.3	1.8	1.2	1.1	2.7
64.2	62.9	65.2	Total Current		61.2	61.2	65.6	69.1	65.8
25.1	25.4	23.8	Fixed Assets (net)		23.5	32.1	22.5	23.3	19.8
4.2	6.7	4.0	Intangibles (net)		2.8	.4	2.4	2.5	9.0
6.5	5.1	7.0	All Other Non-Current		12.6	6.4	9.5	5.0	5.3
100.0	100.0	100.0	Total		100.0	100.0	100.0	100.0	100.0
			LIABILITIES						
13.4	13.6	14.2	Notes Payable-Short Term		25.1	9.7	17.1	12.4	7.8
3.6	3.6	4.2	Cur. Mat.-L.T.D.		2.1	8.0	7.6	1.9	2.4
15.3	16.3	15.5	Trade Payables		13.2	14.0	15.9	18.9	13.9
.6	.4	.4	Income Taxes Payable		.5	.2	.3	.2	.5
10.9	9.3	11.0	All Other Current		14.5	9.1	13.0	9.2	11.2
43.8	43.2	45.2	Total Current		55.3	41.1	54.0	42.6	35.9
16.2	17.4	17.6	Long-Term Debt		29.8	12.5	24.5	10.5	10.4
.5	.5	.5	Deferred Taxes		.8	.1	.4	.4	.9
8.7	9.7	9.7	All Other Non-Current		26.6	1.9	10.6	4.7	3.7
30.8	29.3	27.0	Net Worth		-12.5	44.4	10.5	41.8	49.1
100.0	100.0	100.0	Total Liabilities & Net Worth		100.0	100.0	100.0	100.0	100.0
			INCOME DATA						
100.0	100.0	100.0	Net Sales		100.0	100.0	100.0	100.0	100.0
30.8	32.6	32.0	Gross Profit		39.8	29.3	40.5	26.4	27.2
26.9	27.8	26.9	Operating Expenses		38.1	25.1	35.0	20.7	21.3
4.0	4.8	5.1	Operating Profit		1.7	4.2	5.5	5.6	5.9
1.2	1.7	1.2	All Other Expenses (net)		.0	.7	3.0	.9	1.0
2.8	3.0	3.9	Profit Before Taxes		1.7	3.5	2.5	4.7	5.0
			RATIOS						
2.5	2.5	2.6	Current		2.4	2.8	2.0	2.8	2.6
1.7	1.5	1.7			1.5	1.6	1.4	1.7	1.9
1.2	1.1	1.1			.7	1.0	.9	1.1	1.3
1.3	1.3	1.4	Quick		1.2	1.7	.8	1.4	1.4
.8	.8 (146)	.8			.7	.8	.5	.9	1.0
.5	.5	.5			.2	.5	.4	.6	.6
30 12.2	30 12.2	30 12.3	Sales/Receivables		18 20.2	31 11.6	27 13.7	33 11.2	36 10.0
39 9.2	41 8.9	41 9.0			26 13.9	39 9.5	38 9.7	46 7.9	47 7.8
54 6.8	60 6.0	53 6.9			37 9.8	51 7.1	48 7.7	53 6.9	59 6.2
29 12.6	37 10.0	38 9.5	Cost of Sales/Inventory		30 12.1	26 13.9	27 13.7	40 9.2	53 6.9
61 6.0	65 5.6	69 5.3			65 5.6	47 7.8	104 3.5	74 4.9	75 4.8
99 3.7	116 3.2	105 3.5			113 3.2	91 4.0	156 2.3	100 3.6	94 3.9
18 20.7	19 19.5	19 19.5	Cost of Sales/Payables		13 29.1	16 22.6	19 19.7	22 16.4	20 18.4
29 12.4	35 10.5	29 12.7			23 15.7	29 12.8	28 13.2	30 12.3	32 11.4
48 7.6	55 6.6	46 7.9			33 11.1	42 8.6	68 5.4	54 6.8	42 8.7
5.2	5.4	5.5	Sales/Working Capital		4.9	5.5	6.6	5.5	4.8
9.3	9.2	9.3			16.2	8.3	13.2	8.9	7.2
28.5	47.9	41.5			-9.8	NM	-84.0	34.9	11.6
8.5	9.2	7.5	EBIT/Interest		7.2	9.0	4.2	20.9	15.6
(145) 3.4	(139) 3.0	(136) 2.9			(23) 1.7	(28) 2.1	(29) 1.8	(34) 5.9	5.2
1.0	1.2	1.2			-.6	1.5	.4	1.2	2.0
4.9	9.7	10.0	Net Profit + Depr., Dep., Amort./Cur. Mat. L/T/D					5.1	19.5
(35) 3.0	(32) 2.6	(38) 2.4						(11) 3.4	(15) 3.9
1.4	1.4	1.1						2.1	1.0
.3	.3	.3	Fixed/Worth		.2	.3	.3	.2	.2
.7	.7	.6			.7	.6	1.4	.6	.5
2.2	1.8	1.6			NM	1.7	-1.3	1.5	1.1
.8	.9	.7	Debt/Worth		.7	.5	1.6	.6	.6
1.9	2.1	1.8			1.8	1.2	4.5	1.7	1.1
5.6	6.5	5.9			NM	3.8	-6.6	4.5	2.9
35.9	35.1	40.6	% Profit Before Taxes/Tangible Net Worth		33.6	31.4	41.4	40.0	48.4
(139) 15.8	(130) 16.7	(124) 18.5			(14) 9.0	(23) 10.4	(19) 10.3	(30) 25.5	(36) 27.8
1.6	5.5	3.7			-2.2	2.6	1.3	2.3	14.6
13.3	14.9	14.4	% Profit Before Taxes/Total Assets		10.1	8.2	12.4	19.7	14.8
5.6	5.9	6.6			3.3	4.2	2.4	7.2	10.1
.0	.6	.6			-5.8	.8	-1.8	.1	5.5
32.0	34.7	27.6	Sales/Net Fixed Assets		38.8	35.8	38.7	24.1	21.4
10.8	12.1	12.2			17.9	8.4	19.2	12.4	11.7
5.5	5.8	5.8			6.3	2.8	6.4	6.0	7.8
2.9	3.0	3.0	Sales/Total Assets		3.8	2.9	3.2	2.8	2.5
2.3	2.1	2.2			2.7	1.9	2.2	2.3	2.0
1.6	1.4	1.6			1.9	1.3	1.6	1.5	1.6
.8	.9	.9	% Depr., Dep., Amort./Sales		1.0	1.6	.7	1.0	.8
(137) 1.7	(129) 1.9	(128) 1.7			(16) 1.9	(20) 2.9	(26) 1.7	(31) 1.7	(32) 1.3
3.3	3.4	2.9			3.0	8.8	3.1	2.9	2.1
2.2	2.0	2.1	% Officers', Directors' Owners' Comp/Sales			1.7	3.7	1.9		
(58) 4.8	(47) 3.8	(52) 4.4				(11) 5.3	(13) 6.4	(10) 3.8	
8.9	7.9	8.6				8.3	13.7	4.4	
7195517M	5735449M	5415430M	Net Sales ($)	3173M	37596M	97331M	200957M	484409M	4591964M
3614981M	2914111M	3030487M	Total Assets ($)	1192M	16457M	57580M	114234M	236265M	2604759M

© RMA 2007

M = $ thousand   MM = $ million

See Pages 11 through 21 for Explanation of Ratios and Data

Current Data Sorted by Assets — Comparative Historical Data

Type of Statement	0-500M	500M-2MM	2-10MM	10-50MM	50-100MM	100-250MM	4/1/02-3/31/03 ALL	4/1/03-3/31/04 ALL
Unqualified			5	7	1	3	6	4
Reviewed		2	8	5			11	11
Compiled		4	1	1			6	13
Tax Returns	1	5	1				3	2
Other	1		2	5			5	7
	10 (4/1-9/30/06)			42 (10/1/06-3/31/07)				
	0-500M	500M-2MM	2-10MM	10-50MM	50-100MM	100-250MM		
NUMBER OF STATEMENTS	2	11	17	18	1	3	31	37
ASSETS	%	%	%	%	%	%	%	%
Cash & Equivalents		7.0	10.7	9.0			11.3	10.4
Trade Receivables (net)		29.6	26.5	30.8			25.4	23.9
Inventory		42.5	43.2	39.3			37.3	38.1
All Other Current		.3	3.6	2.8			5.6	6.2
Total Current		79.4	83.9	82.0			79.6	78.6
Fixed Assets (net)		13.0	9.6	6.4			14.2	14.6
Intangibles (net)		.6	2.8	4.8			1.5	1.4
All Other Non-Current		7.0	3.6	6.9			4.7	5.5
Total		100.0	100.0	100.0			100.0	100.0
LIABILITIES								
Notes Payable-Short Term		19.8	21.0	14.2			12.7	11.4
Cur. Mat.-L.T.D.		1.2	1.4	1.3			4.4	6.3
Trade Payables		16.8	15.5	11.7			13.4	17.7
Income Taxes Payable		.0	1.1	.1			.3	.4
All Other Current		4.1	7.4	8.0			11.4	8.5
Total Current		41.9	46.4	35.4			42.3	44.3
Long-Term Debt		5.0	9.3	1.1			10.4	10.3
Deferred Taxes		.0	.0	.0			.3	.2
All Other Non-Current		7.9	6.1	1.4			6.8	8.2
Net Worth		45.0	38.2	62.1			40.2	37.0
Total Liabilities & Net Worth		100.0	100.0	100.0			100.0	100.0
INCOME DATA								
Net Sales		100.0	100.0	100.0			100.0	100.0
Gross Profit		24.3	28.6	26.6			32.4	32.7
Operating Expenses		18.9	27.8	23.9			29.3	30.1
Operating Profit		5.5	.8	2.7			3.1	2.5
All Other Expenses (net)		1.3	.4	.5			.9	.8
Profit Before Taxes		4.2	.4	2.2			2.2	1.7
RATIOS								
Current		9.9	2.1	5.8			2.8	3.3
		2.0	1.8	3.3			2.0	1.7
		1.0	1.4	1.4			1.3	1.3
Quick		3.9	1.1	3.1			1.6	1.6
		.7	.6	1.5			.9	.8
		.3	.4	.6			.5	.4
Sales/Receivables	10 36.6	16 23.0	43 8.5				24 15.1	20 17.9
	25 14.4	38 9.6	57 6.4				43 8.6	41 8.9
	37 9.9	61 6.0	89 4.1				61 6.0	63 5.8
Cost of Sales/Inventory	13 27.6	48 7.6	94 3.9				49 7.5	61 5.9
	64 5.7	112 3.3	124 3.0				110 3.3	93 3.9
	106 3.4	196 1.9	135 2.7				148 2.5	174 2.1
Cost of Sales/Payables	4 90.8	18 20.7	24 15.3				13 27.4	17 22.0
	21 17.1	31 11.8	31 11.9				24 15.2	44 8.3
	47 7.8	37 9.8	48 7.6				39 9.5	89 4.1
Sales/Working Capital		5.1	4.2	2.2			3.3	3.2
		16.0	7.0	3.5			6.5	4.3
		-161.4	11.9	8.9			14.3	26.6
EBIT/Interest		26.0	3.2	8.7			10.0	8.9
	(10) 6.6	(16) 1.0	(15) 2.5				(28) 2.7	(35) 3.5
		1.1	-.5	1.5			1.5	-.6
Net Profit + Depr., Dep., Amort./Cur. Mat. L/T/D								
Fixed/Worth		.0	.0	.0			.0	.1
		.2	.2	.1			.2	.3
		.5	.8	.2			.7	.8
Debt/Worth		.1	.6	.2			.5	.5
		1.2	2.2	.3			1.3	1.5
		22.4	3.7	2.1			3.4	6.6
% Profit Before Taxes/Tangible Net Worth			17.1	22.9			24.9	33.9
		(16)	.2	6.9			(27) 11.9	(31) 10.8
			-16.7	-5.0			1.4	-.1
% Profit Before Taxes/Total Assets		34.6	7.6	9.0			13.0	10.8
		12.7	2.7	3.1			5.7	5.5
		1.8	-7.4	-3.5			.6	-4.3
Sales/Net Fixed Assets		202.6	207.7	56.6			106.3	86.4
		54.4	49.0	32.5			33.8	23.1
		23.3	10.7	19.6			8.3	8.1
Sales/Total Assets		4.8	2.9	2.0			3.1	3.4
		3.2	2.4	1.7			2.2	2.0
		2.8	1.5	1.3			1.3	1.1
% Depr., Dep., Amort./Sales			.2	.4			.3	.2
		(15)	.6	.8			(28) .7	(34) .7
			1.3	1.1			1.2	1.9
% Officers', Directors' Owners' Comp/Sales			2.1				2.9	1.3
		(10)	4.9				(18) 5.3	(17) 3.9
			7.6				7.5	6.7
Net Sales ($)	2402M	81952M	177718M	668139M	160143M	703729M	605487M	953864M
Total Assets ($)	818M	12337M	75424M	389981M	67070M	319707M	335253M	532686M

M = $ thousand   MM = $ million

See Pages 11 through 21 for Explanation of Ratios and Data

Comparative Historical Data   Current Data Sorted by Sales

13 / 9 / 10 / 8 / 7	16 / 14 / 10 / 1 / 6	16 / 15 / 5 / 7 / 9	Type of Statement	0-1MM	1-3MM	3-5MM	5-10MM	10-25MM	25MM & OVER
			Unqualified		1		1	6	9
			Reviewed	1	4		4	1	5
			Compiled		2	1		1	1
			Tax Returns	1	1	3	2	1	1
			Other		1	1		3	3
4/1/04-3/31/05 ALL	4/1/05-3/31/06 ALL	4/1/06-3/31/07 ALL			10 (4/1-9/30/06)			42 (10/1/06-3/31/07)	
47	47	52	**NUMBER OF STATEMENTS**	1	5	9	7	12	18
%	%	%	**ASSETS**	%	%	%	%	%	%
8.6	9.4	8.6	Cash & Equivalents					14.9	3.0
28.2	29.9	29.6	Trade Receivables (net)					28.0	31.9
37.7	40.1	40.2	Inventory					38.5	43.1
4.6	3.9	2.5	All Other Current					3.0	2.1
79.1	83.3	80.9	Total Current					84.4	80.1
12.1	7.9	10.6	Fixed Assets (net)					8.7	9.5
4.0	4.9	3.0	Intangibles (net)					.5	5.4
4.8	3.9	5.5	All Other Non-Current					6.4	5.0
100.0	100.0	100.0	Total					100.0	100.0
			LIABILITIES						
17.4	13.3	17.2	Notes Payable-Short Term					18.2	13.0
4.6	2.7	1.5	Cur. Mat.-L.T.D.					1.0	1.5
14.2	15.8	15.1	Trade Payables					13.6	16.9
.0	.6	.5	Income Taxes Payable					1.0	.5
6.4	8.9	8.2	All Other Current					6.2	9.4
42.7	41.3	42.5	Total Current					40.1	41.3
7.3	8.4	7.6	Long-Term Debt					3.2	4.1
.1	.3	.0	Deferred Taxes					.0	.1
7.2	6.6	5.4	All Other Non-Current					2.6	1.4
42.6	43.4	44.4	Net Worth					54.1	53.2
100.0	100.0	100.0	Total Liabilities & Net Worth					100.0	100.0
			INCOME DATA						
100.0	100.0	100.0	Net Sales					100.0	100.0
33.9	33.2	28.6	Gross Profit					24.1	27.4
30.9	28.6	25.8	Operating Expenses					23.3	24.2
3.1	4.6	2.8	Operating Profit					.8	3.2
.2	.8	.6	All Other Expenses (net)					.4	.8
2.9	3.8	2.2	Profit Before Taxes					.4	2.4
			RATIOS						
3.8	3.5	4.1	Current					6.8	4.4
1.8	2.0	1.8						1.7	1.8
1.4	1.4	1.3						1.4	1.3
1.4	1.6	2.2	Quick					4.1	1.9
.8	.9	.7						.9	.7
.5	.5	.5						.6	.5
23 16.0	24 15.1	26 14.0	Sales/Receivables					19 19.5	40 9.2
42 8.7	46 7.9	43 8.6						39 9.2	48 7.6
60 6.1	61 6.0	64 5.7						67 5.4	68 5.4
53 6.9	52 7.1	52 7.0	Cost of Sales/Inventory					62 5.9	68 5.4
93 3.9	94 3.9	107 3.4						98 3.7	108 3.4
149 2.4	169 2.2	136 2.7						134 2.7	130 2.8
18 20.8	21 17.7	21 17.8	Cost of Sales/Payables					22 16.3	22 16.3
29 12.5	30 12.3	30 12.0						26 13.9	32 11.4
48 7.6	50 7.3	47 7.7						46 7.9	54 6.8
3.6	4.0	3.5	Sales/Working Capital					1.8	3.4
6.4	6.1	7.6						7.5	7.3
12.2	9.0	16.0						14.3	20.3
9.8	17.2	6.8	EBIT/Interest						7.4
(40) 3.9	(38) 2.7	(47) 2.4							3.1
1.2	1.3	.7							1.0
			Net Profit + Depr., Dep., Amort./Cur. Mat. L/T/D						
.0	.0	.0	Fixed/Worth					.0	.1
.1	.1	.2						.1	.2
.5	.5	.5						.3	.5
.5	.6	.3	Debt/Worth					.2	.3
1.4	1.3	1.3						.9	1.1
2.6	3.0	3.7						2.8	3.1
25.6	31.1	29.2	% Profit Before Taxes/Tangible Net Worth					12.7	29.9
(42) 11.5	(41) 12.4	(48) 9.4						-2.5	9.4
3.8	4.6	-6.1						-15.5	2.2
9.5	15.5	12.1	% Profit Before Taxes/Total Assets					3.9	11.9
6.1	6.3	3.9						-.8	4.1
.9	1.7	-3.0						-6.7	.9
150.5	128.2	105.2	Sales/Net Fixed Assets					91.4	78.1
37.3	35.4	35.1						36.0	24.1
10.4	18.8	17.1						18.3	17.6
3.3	3.1	3.0	Sales/Total Assets					2.9	2.7
2.1	2.2	2.3						2.0	2.0
1.6	1.7	1.6						1.3	1.7
.2	.3	.3	% Depr., Dep., Amort./Sales					.3	.4
(40) .7	(39) .8	(45) .7						(11) .6	(17) .7
1.5	1.4	1.3						1.0	1.3
2.2	2.0	.7	% Officers', Directors' Owners' Comp/Sales						
(28) 4.1	(22) 2.9	(26) 2.3							
6.6	7.3	5.5							
1462036M	1750168M	1794083M	Net Sales ($)	892M	10516M	38881M	48446M	211026M	1484322M
726606M	843558M	865337M	Total Assets ($)	460M	6502M	17403M	28730M	117423M	694819M

© RMA 2007

M = $ thousand   MM = $ million
See Pages 11 through 21 for Explanation of Ratios and Data

Current Data Sorted by Assets / Comparative Historical Data

0-500M	500M-2MM	2-10MM	10-50MM	50-100MM	100-250MM	Type of Statement	4/1/02-3/31/03 ALL	4/1/03-3/31/04 ALL
			7	6	1	Unqualified	9	11
	1	5	2		1	Reviewed	9	10
	2	1				Compiled	3	5
	1					Tax Returns	1	
1		1	1		2	Other	5	4
1	2 (4/1-9/30/06)		30 (10/1/06-3/31/07)					
1	3	8	10	6	4	**NUMBER OF STATEMENTS**	27	30
%	%	%	%	%	%	**ASSETS**	%	%
			16.4			Cash & Equivalents	14.2	8.3
			39.3			Trade Receivables (net)	26.1	31.5
			28.2			Inventory	34.5	35.3
			3.1			All Other Current	2.4	5.5
			87.1			Total Current	77.2	80.6
			6.0			Fixed Assets (net)	13.5	8.7
			.6			Intangibles (net)	.2	3.3
			6.3			All Other Non-Current	9.0	7.4
			100.0			Total	100.0	100.0
						LIABILITIES		
			12.5			Notes Payable-Short Term	12.8	8.4
			2.6			Cur. Mat.-L.T.D.	1.9	.7
			21.3			Trade Payables	12.0	22.5
			.1			Income Taxes Payable	.5	.6
			6.8			All Other Current	12.2	13.6
			43.3			Total Current	39.4	45.7
			1.7			Long-Term Debt	8.8	1.4
			.0			Deferred Taxes	.2	.4
			3.2			All Other Non-Current	10.7	7.9
			51.8			Net Worth	40.9	44.6
			100.0			Total Liabilities & Net Worth	100.0	100.0
						INCOME DATA		
			100.0			Net Sales	100.0	100.0
			33.3			Gross Profit	29.5	33.0
			29.8			Operating Expenses	25.5	30.1
			3.5			Operating Profit	4.0	2.8
			.6			All Other Expenses (net)	1.2	.2
			2.9			Profit Before Taxes	2.8	2.7
						RATIOS		
			3.3			Current	3.8	3.7
			2.1				2.0	1.9
			1.4				1.3	1.3
			2.3			Quick	2.4	2.7
			1.5				1.1 (29)	.9
			.7				.6	.5
		34	10.7			Sales/Receivables	18 19.9	18 20.5
		45	8.0				35 10.4	31 11.9
		53	6.9				46 7.9	47 7.8
		22	16.3			Cost of Sales/Inventory	40 9.1	32 11.5
		39	9.4				52 7.0	44 8.2
		78	4.7				90 4.1	67 5.5
		26	14.3			Cost of Sales/Payables	9 39.3	16 22.9
		29	12.5				17 21.3	25 14.6
		44	8.2				25 14.9	37 9.9
			4.2			Sales/Working Capital	4.2	4.9
			9.7				7.7	13.1
			17.8				18.7	31.5
						EBIT/Interest	15.8	15.3
							6.8 (21)	7.8 (26)
							2.4	1.3
						Net Profit + Depr., Dep., Amort./Cur. Mat. L/T/D		
			.0			Fixed/Worth	.1	.1
			.1				.1	.1
			.1				.5	.5
			.5			Debt/Worth	.4	.5
			.8				1.1	1.4
			2.2				2.3	2.7
			39.5			% Profit Before Taxes/Tangible Net Worth	31.3	56.4
			13.0				18.2 (24)	20.1 (28)
			6.6				-5.9	3.7
			17.1			% Profit Before Taxes/Total Assets	19.5	18.6
			7.6				9.8	9.5
			3.6				-3.0	-.9
			331.2			Sales/Net Fixed Assets	126.5	346.6
			92.6				33.3	83.5
			37.4				11.4	39.1
			4.5			Sales/Total Assets	3.9	5.4
			3.1				3.1	3.8
			2.1				2.2	2.3
						% Depr., Dep., Amort./Sales	.2	.1
							.8 (21)	.3 (24)
							1.8	.9
						% Officers', Directors' Owners' Comp/Sales	1.5	2.1
							3.6 (13)	3.2 (11)
							5.5	6.9
15M	14659M	65189M	633249M	1073856M	1399940M	Net Sales ($)	1956292M	1850675M
11M	3543M	30320M	203868M	415398M	791114M	Total Assets ($)	933927M	577026M

M = $ thousand   MM = $ million
See Pages 11 through 21 for Explanation of Ratios and Data

Comparative Historical Data | Current Data Sorted by Sales

04-05 ALL	05-06 ALL	06-07 ALL	Type of Statement	0-1MM	1-3MM	3-5MM	5-10MM	10-25MM	25MM & OVER
11	15	14	Unqualified						14
12	4	9	Reviewed		1		4	1	3
5	1	1	Compiled		1	1			
1	2	3	Tax Returns	1			2		
3	7	5	Other						3
4/1/04-3/31/05 ALL	4/1/05-3/31/06 ALL	4/1/06-3/31/07 ALL		0-1MM	2 (4/1-9/30/06) 1-3MM	3-5MM	30 (10/1/06-3/31/07) 5-10MM	10-25MM	25MM & OVER
32	29	32	NUMBER OF STATEMENTS	1	1	3	6	1	20
%	%	%	ASSETS	%	%	%	%	%	%
14.1	6.5	13.6	Cash & Equivalents						11.9
28.7	20.5	28.3	Trade Receivables (net)						35.1
30.6	36.7	32.8	Inventory						29.8
8.9	8.0	7.3	All Other Current						4.1
82.3	79.6	82.0	Total Current						80.9
9.6	10.7	8.3	Fixed Assets (net)						8.8
.7	.4	4.0	Intangibles (net)						3.2
7.4	9.3	5.8	All Other Non-Current						7.1
100.0	100.0	100.0	Total						100.0
			LIABILITIES						
31.0	21.6	22.3	Notes Payable-Short Term						16.0
.4	4.5	5.2	Cur. Mat.-L.T.D.						3.1
14.8	14.5	14.6	Trade Payables						14.7
1.2	.5	.3	Income Taxes Payable						.5
8.2	8.7	9.3	All Other Current						8.4
55.6	49.7	51.6	Total Current						42.6
1.1	8.3	15.3	Long-Term Debt						11.8
.6	.7	.2	Deferred Taxes						.3
6.0	9.8	8.1	All Other Non-Current						8.8
36.8	31.5	24.6	Net Worth						36.5
100.0	100.0	100.0	Total Liabilities & Net Worth						100.0
			INCOME DATA						
100.0	100.0	100.0	Net Sales						100.0
32.5	34.1	34.6	Gross Profit						34.7
30.0	31.6	29.9	Operating Expenses						28.9
2.4	2.5	4.6	Operating Profit						5.9
1.1	.9	.8	All Other Expenses (net)						.7
1.3	1.7	3.8	Profit Before Taxes						5.1
			RATIOS						
4.8	3.3	3.6	Current						3.3
1.7	1.6	2.1							2.0
1.3	1.2	1.4							1.4
2.2	1.4	1.9	Quick						2.1
.9	(28) .8	.9							1.2
.5	.4	.5							.6
(5) 70.9	(18) 20.0	(23) 16.1	Sales/Receivables						(34) 10.6
(41) 8.8	(38) 9.7	(43) 8.5							(45) 8.1
(57) 6.4	(53) 6.9	(54) 6.8							(59) 6.2
(19) 19.4	(42) 8.6	(35) 10.3	Cost of Sales/Inventory						(35) 10.3
(46) 7.9	(60) 6.1	(66) 5.6							(51) 7.2
(102) 3.6	(113) 3.2	(113) 3.2							(94) 3.9
(11) 32.6	(13) 27.2	(19) 19.0	Cost of Sales/Payables						(21) 17.4
(22) 16.3	(25) 14.3	(25) 14.4							(26) 13.8
(42) 8.8	(42) 8.7	(37) 10.0							(35) 10.3
3.3	4.6	3.8	Sales/Working Capital						4.6
10.7	8.5	6.4							8.5
42.1	31.8	11.2							12.3
6.3	9.8	7.7	EBIT/Interest						10.6
(28) 2.7	(25) 2.0	(26) 3.2							(18) 5.8
.9	1.1	1.0							1.6
			Net Profit + Depr., Dep., Amort./Cur. Mat. L/T/D						
.0	.1	.0	Fixed/Worth						.0
.2	.2	.1							.1
.3	.9	1.4							NM
.4	.7	.5	Debt/Worth						.6
.9	2.1	1.0							1.1
2.7	5.1	4.7							NM
31.9	46.7	52.5	% Profit Before Taxes/Tangible Net Worth						58.3
(29) 13.5	(25) 10.5	(25) 14.9							(15) 25.8
1.9	1.7	7.6							8.0
17.6	13.3	20.9	% Profit Before Taxes/Total Assets						20.9
5.8	2.9	9.5							12.2
.7	.2	1.4							4.6
214.3	131.6	118.8	Sales/Net Fixed Assets						169.3
78.0	64.2	49.7							64.2
24.2	16.6	18.5							16.7
4.8	3.7	3.5	Sales/Total Assets						3.3
3.5	3.0	2.7							2.8
1.6	1.8	1.5							1.8
.2	.3	.3	% Depr., Dep., Amort./Sales						.3
(25) .4	(23) .4	(27) .4							(17) .4
1.1	1.1	1.0							1.1
1.6	.6	1.5	% Officers', Directors' Owners' Comp/Sales						
(16) 3.0	(12) 2.7	(14) 3.0							
8.6	3.8	5.7							
1570970M	2658383M	3186908M	Net Sales ($)	15M	2593M	11985M	39038M	15030M	3118247M
674623M	996030M	1444254M	Total Assets ($)	11M	500M	9511M	14322M	10267M	1409643M

M = $ thousand   MM = $ million
See Pages 11 through 21 for Explanation of Ratios and Data

Current Data Sorted by Assets   Comparative Historical Data

0-500M	500M-2MM	2-10MM	10-50MM	50-100MM	100-250MM		4/1/02-3/31/03 ALL	4/1/03-3/31/04 ALL
		2		2	6	Type of Statement	14	14
		4	2			Unqualified	5	2
			1			Reviewed	4	5
1	3	2				Compiled	1	2
1	1	2	1		1	Tax Returns	4	9
	11 (4/1-9/30/06)		18 (10/1/06-3/31/07)			Other		
2	4	10	4	2	7	**NUMBER OF STATEMENTS**	28	32
%	%	%	%	%	%		%	%
						ASSETS		
		3.6				Cash & Equivalents	6.9	11.1
		33.9				Trade Receivables (net)	25.0	25.0
		44.4				Inventory	45.6	40.3
		3.0				All Other Current	2.0	1.8
		84.9				Total Current	79.5	78.1
		10.0				Fixed Assets (net)	13.3	13.0
		.1				Intangibles (net)	.5	1.0
		5.0				All Other Non-Current	6.7	7.9
		100.0				Total	100.0	100.0
						LIABILITIES		
		11.9				Notes Payable-Short Term	15.2	16.2
		8.4				Cur. Mat.-L.T.D.	2.8	1.8
		21.4				Trade Payables	15.2	13.8
		.2				Income Taxes Payable	.6	.9
		10.5				All Other Current	10.9	13.4
		52.4				Total Current	44.7	46.1
		3.4				Long-Term Debt	18.1	11.4
		.3				Deferred Taxes	.3	.3
		2.5				All Other Non-Current	20.8	2.6
		41.4				Net Worth	16.0	39.6
		100.0				Total Liabilties & Net Worth	100.0	100.0
						INCOME DATA		
		100.0				Net Sales	100.0	100.0
		32.0				Gross Profit	28.8	33.0
		27.7				Operating Expenses	26.8	30.9
		4.4				Operating Profit	2.0	2.1
		-.2				All Other Expenses (net)	1.7	1.1
		4.5				Profit Before Taxes	.4	1.0
						RATIOS		
		2.2					2.7	2.7
		1.6				Current	1.9	1.8
		1.3					1.4	1.4
		1.5					1.4	1.7
		.8				Quick	.7	.7
		.4					.3	.3
		38 9.7					22 16.3	22 16.9
		44 8.4				Sales/Receivables	37 10.0	38 9.7
		66 5.6					62 5.9	55 6.7
		44 8.3					54 6.8	47 7.8
		105 3.5				Cost of Sales/Inventory	115 3.2	95 3.8
		126 2.9					160 2.3	155 2.4
		9 39.4					14 25.8	12 30.5
		39 9.2				Cost of Sales/Payables	35 10.5	29 12.4
		51 7.1					45 8.2	43 8.4
		5.7					5.0	3.3
		8.5				Sales/Working Capital	6.4	6.7
		15.6					9.6	15.1
		15.3					7.1	8.0
		2.1				EBIT/Interest	(25) 2.2	(28) 2.9
		1.4					1.3	1.5
						Net Profit + Depr., Dep., Amort./Cur. Mat. L/T/D		
		.1					.1	.1
		.2				Fixed/Worth	.3	.4
		.3					.6	.8
		1.0					.6	.7
		1.6				Debt/Worth	1.1	1.4
		2.6					3.2	2.7
		16.3				% Profit Before Taxes/Tangible	23.1	21.5
		8.1				Net Worth	(24) 6.2	(28) 7.4
		2.1					2.3	3.6
		9.6				% Profit Before Taxes/Total	11.5	9.8
		2.6				Assets	2.6	4.0
		1.0					.9	1.7
		215.8					63.3	92.2
		29.0				Sales/Net Fixed Assets	23.6	20.0
		17.2					11.7	10.7
		3.4					3.2	3.2
		2.7				Sales/Total Assets	2.1	2.4
		2.0					1.7	1.7
							.4	.4
						% Depr., Dep., Amort./Sales	(26) .8	(28) 1.2
							1.7	1.6
								2.3
						% Officers', Directors' Owners' Comp/Sales		(10) 3.9
								6.3
2033M	5939M	148465M	107218M	268891M	2350341M	Net Sales ($)	1736622M	2674120M
770M	2378M	50636M	60310M	188086M	1044528M	Total Assets ($)	824559M	1321560M

M = $ thousand   MM = $ million

See Pages 11 through 21 for Explanation of Ratios and Data

Comparative Historical Data / Current Data Sorted by Sales

	4/1/04-3/31/05 ALL	4/1/05-3/31/06 ALL	4/1/06-3/31/07 ALL	0-1MM	1-3MM	3-5MM	5-10MM	10-25MM	25MM & OVER
Type of Statement									
Unqualified	12	6	10						10
Reviewed	7	6	6		4				2
Compiled	2	1	1				1		
Tax Returns	5	5	6				3	3	
Other	4	7	6	2		1	1	1	1
				2	4	1	5	4	13
				11 (4/1-9/30/06)			18 (10/1/06-3/31/07)		
NUMBER OF STATEMENTS	30	25	29						
	%	%	%	%	%	%	%	%	%
ASSETS									
Cash & Equivalents	12.1	5.8	5.0						3.0
Trade Receivables (net)	26.4	23.4	32.3						39.3
Inventory	40.4	44.0	34.4						30.0
All Other Current	2.0	2.5	5.1						3.4
Total Current	80.9	75.7	76.8						75.7
Fixed Assets (net)	10.6	9.2	13.2						8.8
Intangibles (net)	2.6	6.2	3.0						6.6
All Other Non-Current	5.9	9.0	7.0						8.9
Total	100.0	100.0	100.0						100.0
LIABILITIES									
Notes Payable-Short Term	18.3	14.5	12.6						21.8
Cur. Mat.-L.T.D.	3.5	4.5	4.6						1.1
Trade Payables	18.2	15.9	17.2						14.7
Income Taxes Payable	.9	.4	.2						.3
All Other Current	7.0	5.3	8.1						8.2
Total Current	47.8	40.5	42.7						46.2
Long-Term Debt	27.5	22.5	12.7						10.6
Deferred Taxes	.1	.5	.4						.6
All Other Non-Current	1.8	3.3	2.1						1.2
Net Worth	22.8	33.2	42.1						41.4
Total Liabilities & Net Worth	100.0	100.0	100.0						100.0
INCOME DATA									
Net Sales	100.0	100.0	100.0						100.0
Gross Profit	38.2	36.0	37.8						32.2
Operating Expenses	33.3	30.8	30.7						27.0
Operating Profit	4.9	5.2	7.1						5.2
All Other Expenses (net)	.7	.9	1.7						1.2
Profit Before Taxes	4.2	4.3	5.4						4.0
RATIOS									
Current	3.3	3.2	2.8						2.6
	1.8	1.9	1.8						1.7
	1.3	1.4	1.3						1.2
Quick	1.8	1.2	1.6						1.4
	.8	.6	.8						1.2
	.5	.4	.5						.6
Sales/Receivables	(1) 363.4	(2) 156.3	(16) 22.3						(21) 17.1
	(39) 9.3	(38) 9.5	(53) 6.8						(63) 5.8
	(64) 5.7	(69) 5.3	(68) 5.3						(79) 4.6
Cost of Sales/Inventory	(46) 8.0	(60) 6.1	(43) 8.4						(43) 8.4
	(83) 4.4	(101) 3.6	(73) 5.0						(54) 6.7
	(165) 2.2	(124) 3.0	(124) 3.0						(95) 3.8
Cost of Sales/Payables	(10) 34.9	(17) 21.4	(16) 22.5						(14) 26.7
	(33) 11.2	(27) 13.3	(36) 10.1						(27) 13.5
	(78) 4.7	(47) 7.8	(55) 6.7						(37) 10.0
Sales/Working Capital	4.5	4.1	4.2						4.9
	6.7	6.5	7.1						7.9
	15.3	12.3	13.4						14.4
EBIT/Interest	9.6	9.7	6.1						6.3
	(28) 3.2	(24) 3.7	(26) 3.1						3.2
	.1	1.1	1.6						2.7
Net Profit + Depr., Dep., Amort./Cur. Mat. L/T/D			30.0						
			(12) 6.2						
			2.0						
Fixed/Worth	.1	.1	.1						.1
	.2	.3	.2						.2
	.7	.6	.3						.4
Debt/Worth	.8	.9	.8						.9
	1.5	1.1	1.4						1.4
	4.7	4.0	3.0						4.0
% Profit Before Taxes/Tangible Net Worth	36.1	40.8	30.6						35.1
	(27) 8.0	(23) 18.5	(27) 17.0						(12) 22.6
	-6.5	3.3	5.8						9.7
% Profit Before Taxes/Total Assets	15.3	19.4	12.8						12.4
	4.0	6.1	6.1						6.5
	-2.5	.3	2.3						4.5
Sales/Net Fixed Assets	64.3	151.8	67.0						64.9
	36.9	38.1	30.1						33.6
	19.7	17.4	15.8						17.4
Sales/Total Assets	3.1	3.0	3.2						3.3
	2.5	2.6	2.4						2.2
	1.8	1.6	1.8						1.6
% Depr., Dep., Amort./Sales	.4	.3	.3						.2
	(25) .7	(20) .9	(23) 1.0						(12) .8
	1.4	1.6	1.3						1.4
% Officers', Directors' Owners' Comp/Sales			1.6						
			(16) 3.0						
			7.2						
Net Sales ($)	1221410M	1461156M	2882887M	1014M	6958M	4873M	37810M	77812M	2754420M
Total Assets ($)	581620M	674493M	1346708M	977M	2171M	2434M	16993M	45205M	1278928M

© RMA 2007

M = $ thousand   MM = $ million

See Pages 11 through 21 for Explanation of Ratios and Data

Current Data Sorted by Assets | Comparative Historical Data

0-500M	500M-2MM	2-10MM	10-50MM	50-100MM	100-250MM	Type of Statement	4/1/02-3/31/03 ALL	4/1/03-3/31/04 ALL
		5	4	3	2	Unqualified	19	15
1	2	7	1			Reviewed	20	13
	1	1				Compiled	5	13
1	1					Tax Returns	4	2
1	1	4		3	1	Other	9	13
	8 (4/1-9/30/06)		31 (10/1/06-3/31/07)					
2	5	17	8	4	3	**NUMBER OF STATEMENTS**	57	56

0-500M %	500M-2MM %	2-10MM %	10-50MM %	50-100MM %	100-250MM %		%	%
						ASSETS		
		3.3				Cash & Equivalents	11.1	10.1
		30.6				Trade Receivables (net)	24.0	27.8
		38.1				Inventory	42.6	37.0
		4.5				All Other Current	2.5	2.3
		76.5				Total Current	80.2	77.2
		12.5				Fixed Assets (net)	13.5	11.6
		6.1				Intangibles (net)	1.1	6.0
		4.9				All Other Non-Current	5.2	5.1
		100.0				Total	100.0	100.0
						LIABILITIES		
		25.5				Notes Payable-Short Term	16.3	12.7
		2.7				Cur. Mat.-L.T.D.	4.2	2.2
		14.7				Trade Payables	11.5	17.7
		.1				Income Taxes Payable	.2	.1
		7.9				All Other Current	6.1	9.1
		50.8				Total Current	38.2	41.8
		8.2				Long-Term Debt	9.7	8.5
		.3				Deferred Taxes	.3	.2
		6.7				All Other Non-Current	8.2	9.8
		34.2				Net Worth	43.5	39.7
		100.0				Total Liabilities & Net Worth	100.0	100.0
						INCOME DATA		
		100.0				Net Sales	100.0	100.0
		34.2				Gross Profit	32.4	31.3
		32.3				Operating Expenses	30.4	27.7
		1.9				Operating Profit	2.0	3.6
		2.9				All Other Expenses (net)	.6	1.8
		-.9				Profit Before Taxes	1.3	1.8
						RATIOS		
		2.0					5.6	4.6
		1.6				Current	2.6	1.9
		1.2					1.3	1.2
		1.1					2.5	1.9
		.8				Quick	1.0	1.1
		.3					.5	.5
		29 12.7					25 14.4	30 12.1
		54 6.7				Sales/Receivables	43 8.6	46 7.9
		89 4.1					68 5.4	71 5.1
		74 4.9					79 4.6	51 7.1
		118 3.1				Cost of Sales/Inventory	129 2.8	86 4.3
		150 2.4					172 2.1	146 2.5
		16 22.7					13 29.0	16 23.5
		29 12.7				Cost of Sales/Payables	24 15.3	32 11.4
		59 6.2					42 8.6	58 6.3
		4.4					2.6	3.4
		7.6				Sales/Working Capital	4.6	6.4
		12.2					10.4	19.7
		2.6					7.1	13.5
		(16) 1.1				EBIT/Interest	(50) 2.7	(51) 2.5
		-.8					.8	1.5
							18.7	
						Net Profit + Depr., Dep., Amort./Cur. Mat. L/T/D	(22) 3.3	
							1.8	
		.1					.1	.1
		.3				Fixed/Worth	.2	.3
		.9					.5	1.1
		1.4					.4	.6
		1.9				Debt/Worth	1.1	2.2
		3.5					2.8	7.1
		37.7					33.4	71.2
		(15) 5.1				% Profit Before Taxes/Tangible Net Worth	(51) 7.2	(49) 14.4
		-11.8					-1.9	2.9
		10.2					10.1	12.4
		1.1				% Profit Before Taxes/Total Assets	3.1	5.9
		-5.2					-2.6	.8
		58.9					50.4	72.5
		23.3				Sales/Net Fixed Assets	20.9	24.5
		9.9					8.4	13.5
		2.5					2.5	2.9
		2.0				Sales/Total Assets	1.9	2.1
		1.5					1.5	1.5
		.5					.6	.4
		1.1				% Depr., Dep., Amort./Sales	(53) 1.4	(49) .9
		2.1					2.4	1.8
		1.4					2.2	2.2
		(10) 1.9				% Officers', Directors' Owners' Comp/Sales	(20) 3.7	(20) 3.5
		7.1					7.0	5.5
6050M	14127M	157346M	258380M	653000M	576489M	Net Sales ($)	1721038M	1571532M
457M	5414M	79430M	150719M	314923M	400422M	Total Assets ($)	1058466M	819441M

M = $ thousand   MM = $ million
See Pages 11 through 21 for Explanation of Ratios and Data

Comparative Historical Data | Current Data Sorted by Sales

				Type of Statement	0-1MM	1-3MM	3-5MM	5-10MM	10-25MM	25MM & OVER
	12	10	14	Unqualified				1	5	8
	10	12	11	Reviewed		1		1	3	1
	7	8	2	Compiled		1	5	1		
	6	2	2	Tax Returns	1	1	1			
	15	18	10	Other	1	2		2	2	3
	4/1/04-3/31/05	4/1/05-3/31/06	4/1/06-3/31/07			8 (4/1-9/30/06)		31 (10/1/06-3/31/07)		
	ALL	ALL	ALL							
	50	50	39	NUMBER OF STATEMENTS	2	4	3	8	10	12
	%	%	%	ASSETS	%	%	%	%	%	%
	7.4	7.2	4.1	Cash & Equivalents					2.5	5.1
	25.4	28.4	28.2	Trade Receivables (net)					26.0	28.5
	38.6	41.5	41.1	Inventory					48.9	41.8
	3.7	2.8	5.0	All Other Current					4.7	4.2
	75.1	79.9	78.4	Total Current					82.1	79.5
	14.9	11.5	10.4	Fixed Assets (net)					12.3	7.6
	2.9	3.0	3.7	Intangibles (net)					.2	3.3
	7.1	5.7	7.5	All Other Non-Current					5.3	9.6
	100.0	100.0	100.0	Total					100.0	100.0
				LIABILITIES						
	21.1	19.6	20.2	Notes Payable-Short Term					31.8	15.4
	3.2	1.5	2.0	Cur. Mat.-L.T.D.					1.9	2.1
	14.2	12.8	13.3	Trade Payables					14.8	12.6
	.2	.2	.4	Income Taxes Payable					.0	1.1
	8.8	5.3	9.0	All Other Current					9.0	10.0
	47.6	39.3	44.9	Total Current					57.5	41.3
	9.3	5.4	9.3	Long-Term Debt					5.3	12.8
	.2	.1	.2	Deferred Taxes					.1	.1
	9.4	14.8	16.3	All Other Non-Current					8.2	8.4
	33.5	40.4	29.3	Net Worth					28.9	37.4
	100.0	100.0	100.0	Total Liabilities & Net Worth					100.0	100.0
				INCOME DATA						
	100.0	100.0	100.0	Net Sales					100.0	100.0
	32.5	32.4	33.7	Gross Profit					31.7	32.6
	30.9	29.8	30.3	Operating Expenses					28.5	26.4
	1.5	2.6	3.4	Operating Profit					3.2	6.1
	.9	1.6	2.5	All Other Expenses (net)					2.5	2.3
	.6	1.0	.9	Profit Before Taxes					.6	3.8
				RATIOS						
	3.8	4.7	2.6						1.7	3.5
	1.6	2.3	1.9	Current					1.4	1.9
	1.0	1.7	1.3						1.2	1.6
	1.4	2.1	1.4						.8	2.1
	.7	1.0	.8	Quick					.4	.9
	.3	.4	.3						.2	.5

						Sales/Receivables								
9	38.9	33	11.1	29	12.7						24	15.2	43	8.5
44	8.3	49	7.4	49	7.4						35	10.5	60	6.1
59	6.2	66	5.5	69	5.3						81	4.5	68	5.4

						Cost of Sales/Inventory								
43	8.4	62	5.9	71	5.2						90	4.1	68	5.4
99	3.7	120	3.0	127	2.9						146	2.5	120	3.1
155	2.4	174	2.1	151	2.4						187	2.0	142	2.6

						Cost of Sales/Payables								
13	28.9	14	25.3	16	22.9						16	22.6	24	15.1
29	12.7	25	14.8	29	12.7						28	13.0	31	11.9
46	7.9	43	8.5	39	9.5						56	6.5	35	10.4

					Sales/Working Capital						
	3.5		2.7		3.9					4.4	3.5
	8.3		4.4		5.8					10.0	4.8
	NM		7.6		10.8					11.6	7.3

						EBIT/Interest								
	6.5		8.8		4.9								2.1	16.3
(46)	1.6	(43)	1.7	(37)	1.6								1.1	2.1
	-.2		1.0		.8								-.4	1.3

						Net Profit + Depr., Dep., Amort./Cur. Mat. L/T/D								
			7.0		3.2									
		(11)	2.1	(11)	1.5									
			1.0		.3									

					Fixed/Worth						
	.1		.1		.1					.0	.0
	.4		.2		.2					.2	.2
	3.2		.6		.7					1.2	.6

					Debt/Worth						
	.7		.4		1.1					1.4	.6
	2.0		1.3		1.9					2.4	1.2
	9.6		4.0		5.5					4.1	13.7

						% Profit Before Taxes/Tangible Net Worth								
	34.3		27.8		41.6									43.2
(41)	16.7	(43)	13.2	(33)	10.0							(11)		14.6
	-1.0		1.7		-.6									2.3

					% Profit Before Taxes/Total Assets						
	9.4		12.7		17.3					5.2	19.5
	1.8		4.1		2.7					.4	3.9
	-3.2		.1		-.3					-4.7	1.3

					Sales/Net Fixed Assets						
	87.8		73.7		77.0					167.6	146.6
	21.3		23.6		23.3					40.8	31.2
	10.1		12.3		12.3					12.8	13.6

					Sales/Total Assets						
	2.8		2.5		2.7					2.5	2.9
	2.1		1.9		1.9					2.0	1.7
	1.8		1.6		1.5					1.6	1.3

						% Depr., Dep., Amort./Sales								
	.4		.5		.4									.3
(43)	.9	(41)	1.3	(34)	1.1							(11)		1.4
	2.0		2.0		2.2									2.5

						% Officers', Directors' Owners' Comp/Sales								
	2.6		2.0		1.6									
(24)	4.6	(22)	4.1	(17)	3.0									
	7.5		6.6		7.6									

1502300M	1598556M	1665392M	Net Sales ($)	1365M	7579M	13059M	53716M	145789M	1443884M
796877M	913978M	951365M	Total Assets ($)	3923M	5611M	5687M	51964M	73230M	810950M

© RMA 2007

M = $ thousand   MM = $ million
See Pages 11 through 21 for Explanation of Ratios and Data

Current Data Sorted by Assets

Comparative Historical Data

0-500M	500M-2MM	2-10MM	10-50MM	50-100MM	100-250MM	Type of Statement	4/1/02-3/31/03 ALL	4/1/03-3/31/04 ALL
			1			Unqualified	13	9
	4	8	4	1		Reviewed	19	17
			2	1		Compiled	4	6
1	1		1			Tax Returns		1
1	1	3	4			Other	2	7
	5 (4/1-9/30/06)		27 (10/1/06-3/31/07)					
1	6	12	11	2		NUMBER OF STATEMENTS	38	40

0-500M %	500M-2MM %	2-10MM %	10-50MM %	50-100MM %	100-250MM %		%	%
						ASSETS		
		4.8	3.3			Cash & Equivalents	10.8	9.4
		36.3	38.7			Trade Receivables (net)	25.2	30.1
		30.6	36.2			Inventory	43.9	39.9
		4.4	1.8			All Other Current	4.2	4.9
		76.0	80.1			Total Current	84.2	84.4
		15.5	11.1			Fixed Assets (net)	7.1	8.4
		1.3	5.9			Intangibles (net)	2.9	1.5
		7.1	2.9			All Other Non-Current	5.6	5.7
		100.0	100.0			Total	100.0	100.0
						LIABILITIES		
		18.1	23.5			Notes Payable-Short Term	14.2	10.1
		.4	1.5			Cur. Mat.-L.T.D.	1.5	1.4
		27.2	17.7			Trade Payables	28.9	23.2
		.1	.4			Income Taxes Payable	.6	.3
		12.5	11.1			All Other Current	11.5	14.8
		58.3	54.2			Total Current	56.7	49.7
		3.8	3.8			Long-Term Debt	5.3	3.8
		.1	.4			Deferred Taxes	.2	.3
		4.7	5.5			All Other Non-Current	3.5	5.0
		33.0	36.1			Net Worth	34.0	41.1
		100.0	100.0			Total Liabilities & Net Worth	100.0	100.0
						INCOME DATA		
		100.0	100.0			Net Sales	100.0	100.0
		43.9	43.5			Gross Profit	31.8	33.0
		39.9	36.2			Operating Expenses	28.0	31.2
		3.9	7.3			Operating Profit	3.8	1.8
		.8	1.1			All Other Expenses (net)	.7	.4
		3.1	6.2			Profit Before Taxes	3.1	1.4
						RATIOS		
		1.7	1.7			Current	2.0	2.8
		1.4	1.5				1.5	1.7
		1.1	1.4				1.2	1.3
		.9	1.1			Quick	1.0	1.2
		.8	.8				.6	.7
		.5	.6				.2	.4
		25 14.7	28 13.0			Sales/Receivables	1 328.1	19 19.5
		41 8.9	47 7.8				25 14.8	36 10.2
		46 7.9	72 5.1				46 7.9	54 6.8
		38 9.7	45 8.2			Cost of Sales/Inventory	38 9.5	39 9.4
		49 7.5	68 5.4				56 6.5	57 6.4
		72 5.1	110 3.3				113 3.2	125 2.9
		17 21.7	26 14.2			Cost of Sales/Payables	25 14.7	19 19.1
		46 7.9	32 11.5				32 11.4	31 11.6
		99 3.7	53 6.8				46 7.9	52 7.0
		12.5	8.1			Sales/Working Capital	8.0	5.1
		22.0	11.7				14.0	11.2
		30.4	12.8				38.9	27.0
		8.4	21.7			EBIT/Interest	8.2	12.2
		(11) 3.3	5.0				(32) 4.2	(33) 4.0
		2.2	2.0				1.2	1.2
						Net Profit + Depr., Dep., Amort./Cur. Mat. L/T/D		
		.1	.1			Fixed/Worth	.0	.1
		.3	.2				.2	.2
		.9	1.1				.8	.4
		1.0	1.3			Debt/Worth	.8	.5
		3.9	1.9				1.9	1.4
		5.3	3.4				8.7	2.9
		41.8	77.5			% Profit Before Taxes/Tangible Net Worth	69.3	58.6
		26.5	(10) 31.1				(35) 27.1	(38) 17.3
		20.7	14.6				3.8	1.8
		14.2	36.2			% Profit Before Taxes/Total Assets	20.1	17.5
		7.3	11.3				11.3	6.7
		4.2	3.7				.6	.6
		192.2	113.2			Sales/Net Fixed Assets	367.7	227.3
		27.2	72.1				85.5	69.4
		23.5	20.7				28.3	21.7
		4.8	4.2			Sales/Total Assets	5.4	4.8
		4.1	2.9				4.0	3.3
		2.7	2.2				2.5	2.1
						% Depr., Dep., Amort./Sales	.2	.2
							(31) .3	(31) .5
							.9	1.4
						% Officers', Directors' Owners' Comp/Sales	2.2	2.2
							(14) 5.0	(18) 3.6
							9.0	7.3
113M	30172M	245763M	797880M	297234M		Net Sales ($)	1560678M	1425451M
58M	8676M	62234M	270094M	159647M		Total Assets ($)	554506M	503439M

Note: Columns 0-500M, 500M-2MM, 50-100MM, and 100-250MM are marked "DATA NOT AVAILABLE".

M = $ thousand   MM = $ million
See Pages 11 through 21 for Explanation of Ratios and Data

Comparative Historical Data / Current Data Sorted by Sales

Type of Statement	4/1/04-3/31/05 ALL	4/1/05-3/31/06 ALL	4/1/06-3/31/07 ALL	0-1MM	1-3MM	3-5MM	5-10MM	10-25MM	25MM & OVER
					5 (4/1-9/30/06)			27 (10/1/06-3/31/07)	
Unqualified	3	6	6					1	5
Reviewed	13	7	15		1	2	2	6	5
Compiled	1	1	1						1
Tax Returns	1	1	2				1		
Other	4	10	8	1			1	1	5
NUMBER OF STATEMENTS	22	25	32	1	1	2	4	8	16
	%	%	%	%	%	%	%	%	%
ASSETS									
Cash & Equivalents	7.6	4.4	5.8						5.6
Trade Receivables (net)	32.6	33.9	34.7						38.9
Inventory	43.8	32.4	34.6						33.8
All Other Current	3.8	3.0	3.0						1.5
Total Current	87.9	73.7	78.2						79.8
Fixed Assets (net)	6.0	11.4	12.5						10.4
Intangibles (net)	2.8	4.9	3.0						4.3
All Other Non-Current	3.4	10.0	6.3						5.4
Total	100.0	100.0	100.0						100.0
LIABILITIES									
Notes Payable-Short Term	17.2	22.4	18.3						26.3
Cur. Mat.-L.T.D.	2.9	2.0	.9						1.1
Trade Payables	25.9	23.0	27.1						15.9
Income Taxes Payable	.1	.3	.2						.3
All Other Current	10.3	10.1	15.1						10.6
Total Current	56.3	57.8	61.6						54.3
Long-Term Debt	2.4	3.9	4.3						3.9
Deferred Taxes	.3	.4	.2						.3
All Other Non-Current	1.5	1.9	4.2						5.2
Net Worth	39.5	35.9	29.8						36.4
Total Liabilties & Net Worth	100.0	100.0	100.0						100.0
INCOME DATA									
Net Sales	100.0	100.0	100.0						100.0
Gross Profit	32.4	37.8	41.3						41.5
Operating Expenses	30.2	35.4	38.3						34.4
Operating Profit	2.2	2.4	3.0						7.1
All Other Expenses (net)	.2	.1	.7						.8
Profit Before Taxes	2.0	2.3	2.3						6.3
RATIOS									
Current	2.3	1.5	1.8						1.7
	1.4	1.3	1.5						1.5
	1.2	1.1	1.2						1.3
Quick	.9	.8	1.1						1.1
	.6	.6	.8						.8
	.5	.5	.5						.7
Sales/Receivables	18 19.9	39 9.3	24 15.2						29 12.6
	43 8.4	54 6.7	42 8.8						46 7.9
	53 6.9	63 5.8	58 6.3						65 5.6
Cost of Sales/Inventory	49 7.4	51 7.2	44 8.2						45 8.2
	80 4.6	75 4.9	62 5.9						62 5.9
	135 2.7	129 2.8	111 3.3						102 3.6
Cost of Sales/Payables	20 18.2	26 14.2	24 15.0						21 17.2
	29 12.6	46 7.9	39 9.3						28 13.2
	60 6.1	88 4.1	82 4.4						38 9.5
Sales/Working Capital	5.8	9.4	8.7						8.3
	13.7	17.5	12.8						12.4
	21.1	183.7	27.3						18.3
EBIT/Interest	7.6	7.0	6.7						6.9
	(19) 3.1	2.7	(28) 4.2						(15) 4.7
	1.4	.3	2.0						2.0
Net Profit + Depr., Dep., Amort./Cur. Mat. L/T/D									
Fixed/Worth	.1	.1	.1						.1
	.2	.2	.2						.1
	.2	.8	1.1						1.0
Debt/Worth	.7	1.1	1.0						1.3
	2.2	2.2	2.2						2.2
	3.5	4.3	5.3						3.9
% Profit Before Taxes/Tangible Net Worth	35.2	44.8	43.1						69.9
	(21) 15.3	(24) 10.4	(28) 26.5						(15) 31.5
	4.1	-1.5	13.0						19.1
% Profit Before Taxes/Total Assets	13.4	14.2	14.5						23.8
	5.8	2.4	6.0						11.5
	.7	-1.8	3.2						3.9
Sales/Net Fixed Assets	140.2	119.0	163.5						154.1
	64.3	33.3	38.9						50.8
	28.4	15.5	21.3						20.4
Sales/Total Assets	4.6	3.6	4.4						4.4
	3.1	2.3	3.3						3.0
	2.3	1.5	2.4						2.3
% Depr., Dep., Amort./Sales	.2	.3	.2						.3
	(17) .4	(19) .6	(23) .7						(13) .7
	.5	1.4	1.1						.9
% Officers', Directors' Owners' Comp/Sales		2.2	1.5						
		(14) 3.3	(16) 2.8						
		7.5	6.3						
Net Sales ($)	827091M	931063M	1371162M	113M	1458M	6841M	27903M	130667M	1204180M
Total Assets ($)	369908M	385362M	500709M	58M	1497M	1933M	7625M	35442M	454154M

© RMA 2007

M = $ thousand   MM = $ million

See Pages 11 through 21 for Explanation of Ratios and Data

Current Data Sorted by Assets | Comparative Historical Data

	0-500M	500M-2MM	2-10MM	10-50MM	50-100MM	100-250MM	Type of Statement		4/1/02-3/31/03 ALL	4/1/03-3/31/04 ALL
							Unqualified		20	13
		5	4	3			Reviewed		39	23
		1	1				Compiled		4	5
		2					Tax Returns		1	2
	2	1		3	2	2	Other		5	9
		11 (4/1-9/30/06)		27 (10/1/06-3/31/07)						
							NUMBER OF STATEMENTS		69	52
	2	9	8	12	4	3				
	%	%	%	%	%	%			%	%
							ASSETS			
				10.8			Cash & Equivalents		7.4	7.4
				28.1			Trade Receivables (net)		30.2	30.6
				38.9			Inventory		42.1	41.1
				1.7			All Other Current		3.2	2.6
				79.6			Total Current		82.9	81.7
				10.0			Fixed Assets (net)		9.7	8.9
				4.6			Intangibles (net)		1.6	2.2
				5.8			All Other Non-Current		5.8	7.2
				100.0			Total		100.0	100.0
							LIABILITIES			
				15.4			Notes Payable-Short Term		12.4	12.7
				1.9			Cur. Mat.-L.T.D.		1.2	1.1
				8.2			Trade Payables		21.0	19.8
				.5			Income Taxes Payable		.4	.5
				12.2			All Other Current		11.8	14.0
				38.2			Total Current		46.8	48.0
				3.6			Long-Term Debt		5.4	2.5
				.5			Deferred Taxes		.1	.3
				1.1			All Other Non-Current		5.5	9.9
				56.6			Net Worth		42.2	39.3
				100.0			Total Liabilities & Net Worth		100.0	100.0
							INCOME DATA			
				100.0			Net Sales		100.0	100.0
				30.1			Gross Profit		29.9	29.6
				28.7			Operating Expenses		26.6	26.1
				1.4			Operating Profit		3.3	3.6
				1.0			All Other Expenses (net)		.4	1.4
				.4			Profit Before Taxes		2.9	2.2
							RATIOS			
				3.6					2.6	2.4
				1.8			Current		1.8	1.7
				1.7					1.4	1.4
				1.5					1.4	1.4
				1.0			Quick		.8	.8
				.7					.5	.4
			31	11.8				12	31.1	15	24.1
			44	8.4			Sales/Receivables	35	10.6	34	10.7
			60	6.1				59	6.2	63	5.8
			55	6.6				36	10.1	39	9.3
			67	5.5			Cost of Sales/Inventory	68	5.4	68	5.4
			188	1.9				112	3.2	105	3.5
			11	33.9				18	20.5	19	19.1
			20	18.7			Cost of Sales/Payables	31	11.9	29	12.6
			27	13.5				46	8.0	41	8.8
				4.2					4.7	5.2
				6.3			Sales/Working Capital		9.6	9.4
				9.8					17.6	15.2
				4.6					12.8	12.1
			(11)	2.6			EBIT/Interest	(64)	3.1	(48) 4.7
				1.8					1.6	1.1
									29.3	
							Net Profit + Depr., Dep., Amort./Cur. Mat. L/T/D	(16)	3.5	
									1.0	
				.1					.1	.1
				.1			Fixed/Worth		.2	.2
				.2					.5	.4
				.4					.8	.8
				1.2			Debt/Worth		1.4	1.7
				1.5					2.8	3.5
				25.2					35.3	41.1
				12.9			% Profit Before Taxes/Tangible Net Worth	(64)	14.7	(49) 24.8
				7.6					6.3	6.8
				8.9					16.0	16.0
				6.8			% Profit Before Taxes/Total Assets		6.5	7.9
				2.3					1.8	1.1
				116.4					131.3	81.4
				41.5			Sales/Net Fixed Assets		53.8	43.3
				15.8					18.7	19.8
				3.5					4.1	4.0
				2.5			Sales/Total Assets		2.8	2.8
				1.3					2.2	2.0
									.3	.2
							% Depr., Dep., Amort./Sales	(63)	.6	(42) .6
									1.1	1.3
									1.1	1.1
							% Officers', Directors' Owners' Comp/Sales	(27)	2.6	(20) 2.3
									4.5	3.9
	5204M	36899M	129218M	583515M	572613M	664084M	Net Sales ($)		3244161M	3298351M
	728M	11709M	43933M	226571M	255100M	586002M	Total Assets ($)		1286839M	1512271M

M = $ thousand   MM = $ million
See Pages 11 through 21 for Explanation of Ratios and Data

Comparative Historical Data | | Current Data Sorted by Sales

			Type of Statement						
11	6	12	Unqualified	1			1	3	8
18	9	12	Reviewed			1	5	3	2
5	3	2	Compiled		1			1	
4	5	2	Tax Returns						
5	12	10	Other		2 3	1		1	6
4/1/04-3/31/05 ALL	4/1/05-3/31/06 ALL	4/1/06-3/31/07 ALL		0-1MM	1-3MM 11 (4/1-9/30/06)	3-5MM	5-10MM	10-25MM 27 (10/1/06-3/31/07)	25MM & OVER 6
43	35	38	NUMBER OF STATEMENTS	1	5	2	6	8	16
%	%	%	ASSETS	%	%	%	%	%	%
10.1	13.1	9.5	Cash & Equivalents						9.7
31.2	25.9	29.4	Trade Receivables (net)						32.1
43.0	38.9	37.5	Inventory						34.6
1.1	1.3	2.9	All Other Current						2.9
85.4	79.2	79.2	Total Current						79.3
8.4	11.9	10.2	Fixed Assets (net)						6.1
.9	4.0	5.0	Intangibles (net)						7.2
5.4	4.9	5.5	All Other Non-Current						7.5
100.0	100.0	100.0	Total						100.0
			LIABILITIES						
15.2	13.1	15.6	Notes Payable-Short Term						18.4
5.5	2.2	3.6	Cur. Mat.-L.T.D.						3.0
16.9	14.3	12.3	Trade Payables						11.2
.1	.2	.3	Income Taxes Payable						.4
12.3	16.5	10.6	All Other Current						10.3
50.2	46.2	42.3	Total Current						43.3
3.7	7.9	10.5	Long-Term Debt						13.3
.0	.1	.3	Deferred Taxes						.1
5.6	5.6	6.6	All Other Non-Current						3.2
40.6	40.1	40.3	Net Worth						40.1
100.0	100.0	100.0	Total Liabilities & Net Worth						100.0
			INCOME DATA						
100.0	100.0	100.0	Net Sales						100.0
33.1	35.2	34.1	Gross Profit						28.7
30.1	30.7	30.6	Operating Expenses						22.3
3.1	4.5	3.4	Operating Profit						6.5
.9	.9	2.1	All Other Expenses (net)						1.9
2.1	3.5	1.4	Profit Before Taxes						4.6
			RATIOS						
2.9	2.7	2.7	Current						2.3
1.7	1.7	1.8							1.8
1.3	1.1	1.4							1.6
1.4	1.4	1.4	Quick						1.3
.9	.8	.9							1.1
.5	.4	.5							.6
18 20.2	12 31.7	24 15.5	Sales/Receivables						15 23.9
35 10.5	33 11.1	36 10.1							40 9.2
57 6.4	62 5.9	62 5.9							75 4.9
43 8.5	39 9.3	46 8.0	Cost of Sales/Inventory						47 7.8
94 3.9	76 4.8	76 4.8							64 5.7
133 2.7	110 3.3	123 3.0							98 3.7
15 24.5	12 29.2	14 26.1	Cost of Sales/Payables						12 29.4
28 13.2	25 14.8	23 15.8							17 21.6
39 9.2	40 9.1	36 10.0							38 9.7
5.6	4.7	4.5	Sales/Working Capital						5.3
8.0	9.7	7.1							7.1
15.1	30.4	12.7							12.7
29.1	13.5	7.0	EBIT/Interest						10.9
(40) 5.1	(32) 3.8	(36) 2.4							3.8
1.5	1.2	1.3							1.8
			Net Profit + Depr., Dep., Amort./Cur. Mat. L/T/D						
.1	.1	.1	Fixed/Worth						.1
.2	.2	.1							.1
.6	.9	.6							NM
.6	.6	.6	Debt/Worth						.6
1.4	1.4	1.5							1.4
4.3	4.8	5.7							NM
49.8	41.3	24.7	% Profit Before Taxes/Tangible Net Worth						27.7
(39) 22.1	(31) 16.4	(31) 13.3						(12)	24.2
9.5	-3.3	2.7							9.9
18.5	20.8	14.0	% Profit Before Taxes/Total Assets						14.8
7.6	9.1	5.7							8.7
.7	-.5	.6							3.5
129.7	179.2	121.0	Sales/Net Fixed Assets						184.0
43.3	47.4	54.8							90.0
19.2	20.0	18.6							51.7
3.9	4.0	3.6	Sales/Total Assets						3.7
2.7	3.0	2.6							2.8
2.1	2.0	1.8							1.9
.3	.2	.3	% Depr., Dep., Amort./Sales						.2
(38) .7	(29) .5	(30) .5						(12)	.3
1.3	1.3	1.4							.5
1.2	1.0	.8	% Officers', Directors' Owners' Comp/Sales						
(21) 3.0	(16) 2.7	(13) 1.6							
6.8	8.4	6.1							
1781531M	1748013M	1991533M	Net Sales ($)	976M	11607M	8053M	39663M	135299M	1795935M
590031M	904799M	1124043M	Total Assets ($)	1795M	3454M	2459M	29242M	73714M	1013379M

© RMA 2007

M = $ thousand   MM = $ million
See Pages 11 through 21 for Explanation of Ratios and Data

Current Data Sorted by Assets | Comparative Historical Data

Type of Statement	0-500M	500M-2MM	2-10MM	10-50MM	50-100MM	100-250MM		4/1/02-3/31/03 ALL	4/1/03-3/31/04 ALL
Unqualified		2	3	5	2	2		4	11
Reviewed		2	4	3				2	2
Compiled		3	4	1				4	10
Tax Returns		1	1						1
Other	1	3	1	5	1	1		10	7
		9 (4/1-9/30/06)		36 (10/1/06-3/31/07)					
NUMBER OF STATEMENTS	1	11	13	14	3	3		20	31
	%	%	%	%	%	%		%	%
ASSETS									
Cash & Equivalents		9.6	13.7	4.8				11.1	10.4
Trade Receivables (net)		31.7	14.0	27.0				23.9	28.7
Inventory		38.2	38.4	43.9				42.9	36.1
All Other Current		3.1	8.7	2.5				2.3	3.9
Total Current		82.6	74.9	78.1				80.2	79.1
Fixed Assets (net)		10.8	13.9	11.4				14.8	14.3
Intangibles (net)		.1	8.5	5.2				1.3	2.6
All Other Non-Current		6.5	2.8	5.2				3.7	4.0
Total		100.0	100.0	100.0				100.0	100.0
LIABILITIES									
Notes Payable-Short Term		20.0	16.7	20.2				23.4	17.4
Cur. Mat.-L.T.D.		2.7	.8	1.4				2.7	2.6
Trade Payables		23.0	14.7	13.1				16.6	17.8
Income Taxes Payable		.1	.2	.1				.5	.2
All Other Current		7.6	12.5	8.9				6.0	9.7
Total Current		53.3	44.9	43.6				49.2	47.6
Long-Term Debt		14.2	9.7	7.9				10.8	6.1
Deferred Taxes		.1	.4	.3				.0	.6
All Other Non-Current		1.3	1.9	.1				1.1	3.1
Net Worth		31.1	43.2	48.0				38.9	42.6
Total Liabilities & Net Worth		100.0	100.0	100.0				100.0	100.0
INCOME DATA									
Net Sales		100.0	100.0	100.0				100.0	100.0
Gross Profit		31.7	37.0	30.1				33.9	36.3
Operating Expenses		31.9	29.5	25.4				29.7	30.3
Operating Profit		-.1	7.6	4.8				4.2	6.0
All Other Expenses (net)		.3	1.2	1.3				1.1	.8
Profit Before Taxes		-.4	6.4	3.5				3.2	5.2
RATIOS									
Current		3.0	5.6	4.0				4.6	2.5
		1.9	1.7	1.5				1.6	1.6
		1.0	1.0	1.4				1.1	1.2
Quick		1.6	2.5	1.4				1.9	1.9
		1.1	.5	.7				.8	.9
		.3	.2	.5				.4	.4
Sales/Receivables		24 15.1	13 29.0	34 10.6				31 11.6	29 12.7
		38 9.6	24 15.3	53 6.9				41 8.9	46 7.9
		54 6.7	29 12.4	81 4.5				68 5.4	60 6.0
Cost of Sales/Inventory		29 12.7	42 8.6	93 3.9				68 5.4	41 9.0
		50 7.3	73 5.0	133 2.7				121 3.0	105 3.5
		166 2.2	186 2.0	204 1.8				197 1.9	145 2.5
Cost of Sales/Payables		16 22.9	6 58.7	24 15.1				16 23.2	22 16.9
		25 14.7	18 20.6	37 9.8				35 10.3	39 9.4
		77 4.7	47 7.8	51 7.2				59 6.2	53 6.9
Sales/Working Capital		5.7	4.7	2.3				2.6	3.8
		6.6	12.7	7.4				7.8	7.6
		58.1	298.4	9.7				27.0	21.7
EBIT/Interest		5.4	16.8	8.4				8.8	16.0
		2.6	(12) 7.0	4.1				(19) 3.8	(30) 6.4
		.3	2.0	1.0				.6	2.6
Net Profit + Depr., Dep., Amort./Cur. Mat. L/T/D									
Fixed/Worth		.1	.1	.1				.1	.1
		.2	.3	.2				.3	.3
		.7	1.8	.6				1.2	.6
Debt/Worth		.6	.5	.4				.3	.7
		1.3	.9	1.6				2.1	1.5
		20.9	15.0	3.0				5.8	3.6
% Profit Before Taxes/Tangible Net Worth		87.7	40.7	21.6				35.5	58.2
		(10) 28.1	(11) 31.2	(13) 1.9				(18) 22.2	(30) 30.0
		.1	6.0	-4.1				7.8	12.1
% Profit Before Taxes/Total Assets		11.4	26.4	9.4				13.9	22.2
		6.7	13.7	1.2				5.5	8.6
		-2.3	1.2	-.5				-.4	5.0
Sales/Net Fixed Assets		271.7	56.9	47.1				53.3	52.3
		41.4	28.6	20.8				24.7	21.9
		23.2	12.4	7.8				9.0	13.0
Sales/Total Assets		3.7	3.0	2.4				2.9	3.1
		3.5	2.2	1.8				1.7	2.3
		1.7	1.7	1.3				1.5	1.6
% Depr., Dep., Amort./Sales			.4	.4				.7	.7
		(11)	.5	(13) .7				(17) 1.8	(27) 1.5
			2.9	1.4				3.1	2.2
% Officers', Directors' Owners' Comp/Sales								2.0	3.1
								(10) 5.0	(10) 6.5
								12.7	14.8
Net Sales ($)	1290M	38962M	149515M	544378M	456603M	746132M		540028M	1454112M
Total Assets ($)	382M	13461M	64902M	329187M	254540M	520815M		346125M	868383M

M = $ thousand   MM = $ million

See Pages 11 through 21 for Explanation of Ratios and Data

Comparative Historical Data | Current Data Sorted by Sales

Type of Statement

	4/1/04-3/31/05 ALL	4/1/05-3/31/06 ALL	4/1/06-3/31/07 ALL	Type of Statement	0-1MM	1-3MM	3-5MM	5-10MM	10-25MM	25MM & OVER
	4	9	14	Unqualified		1	1	3	4	6
	4	4	9	Reviewed		1	2	2	2	4
	10	5	8	Compiled		2	2	1	1	1
	4	2	2	Tax Returns		1		1	1	
	6	9	12	Other		1	1		1	6
						9 (4/1-9/30/06)		36 (10/1/06-3/31/07)		
28	29	45		**NUMBER OF STATEMENTS**		6	6	7	9	17

Columns 0-1MM through 10-25MM for the ASSETS, LIABILITIES and INCOME DATA sections are marked: DATA NOT AVAILABLE.

ASSETS

4/1/04-3/31/05	4/1/05-3/31/06	4/1/06-3/31/07	ASSETS	25MM & OVER
%	%	%		%
15.7	10.1	10.1	Cash & Equivalents	7.9
23.4	22.8	23.7	Trade Receivables (net)	25.0
37.8	39.1	38.8	Inventory	41.3
1.8	2.0	4.5	All Other Current	2.8
78.8	73.9	77.1	Total Current	77.0
15.1	17.9	12.6	Fixed Assets (net)	11.2
.4	4.2	5.8	Intangibles (net)	9.6
5.7	3.9	4.4	All Other Non-Current	2.2
100.0	100.0	100.0	Total	100.0

LIABILITIES

4/1/04-3/31/05	4/1/05-3/31/06	4/1/06-3/31/07	LIABILITIES	25MM & OVER
11.7	17.3	16.3	Notes Payable-Short Term	14.0
3.6	4.0	1.6	Cur. Mat.-L.T.D.	1.8
18.8	19.5	15.4	Trade Payables	13.6
.3	.3	.1	Income Taxes Payable	.1
7.5	7.2	9.1	All Other Current	8.9
41.9	48.4	42.6	Total Current	38.4
8.9	23.7	11.1	Long-Term Debt	10.9
.2	.3	.3	Deferred Taxes	.4
8.5	6.7	2.3	All Other Non-Current	3.8
40.5	20.9	43.8	Net Worth	46.6
100.0	100.0	100.0	Total Liabilities & Net Worth	100.0

INCOME DATA

4/1/04-3/31/05	4/1/05-3/31/06	4/1/06-3/31/07	INCOME DATA	25MM & OVER
100.0	100.0	100.0	Net Sales	100.0
35.2	34.9	34.1	Gross Profit	33.1
31.0	31.5	28.9	Operating Expenses	27.0
4.2	3.3	5.2	Operating Profit	6.1
.2	1.5	1.2	All Other Expenses (net)	1.6
4.0	1.8	4.0	Profit Before Taxes	4.5

RATIOS

4/1/04-3/31/05	4/1/05-3/31/06	4/1/06-3/31/07	RATIOS	25MM & OVER
4.0	3.6	4.1	Current	5.6
1.9	1.5	1.8		1.7
1.5	1.1	1.3		1.4
2.0	1.6	1.8	Quick	1.7
.9	.7	.9		.9
.5	.4	.4		.6
18 20.1	20 18.2	24 14.9	Sales/Receivables	32 11.3
36 10.1	36 10.2	36 10.1		44 8.3
48 7.7	55 6.7	56 6.6		67 5.5
27 13.4	53 6.9	48 7.6	Cost of Sales/Inventory	75 4.9
89 4.1	85 4.3	124 2.9		130 2.8
133 2.8	179 2.0	178 2.0		147 2.5
21 17.6	22 16.3	17 22.1	Cost of Sales/Payables	23 15.9
34 10.8	41 8.8	31 11.8		36 10.2
67 5.5	68 5.4	48 7.7		45 8.2
4.5	3.5	3.3	Sales/Working Capital	2.8
7.5	10.6	6.5		6.5
13.3	39.1	17.9		9.8
22.3	6.1	9.3	EBIT/Interest	8.5
(24) 2.7	(28) 3.0	(44) 4.0		3.6
.7	.8	1.2		1.3
		17.1	Net Profit + Depr., Dep., Amort./Cur. Mat. L/T/D	
		(13) 3.4		
		.1		
.2	.2	.1	Fixed/Worth	.1
.3	.4	.2		.2
1.1	2.1	.8		.9
.4	.6	.5	Debt/Worth	.3
1.1	2.3	1.1		1.6
6.2	5.9	5.4		3.4
36.3	26.4	40.0	% Profit Before Taxes/Tangible Net Worth	22.4
(25) 18.0	(26) 7.7	(39) 14.3		(14) 5.9
-.3	.0	1.2		-1.1
22.8	7.5	17.3	% Profit Before Taxes/Total Assets	11.2
5.8	3.2	4.2		3.9
-1.3	-.3	.7		.6
38.7	34.0	50.5	Sales/Net Fixed Assets	49.8
20.4	16.8	23.2		22.8
11.1	7.0	9.7		10.3
3.5	2.9	2.9	Sales/Total Assets	2.5
2.5	2.2	2.1		1.8
1.6	1.5	1.5		1.6
.7	.6	.4	% Depr., Dep., Amort./Sales	.5
(26) 1.4	(28) 1.6	(39) .7		(15) .7
2.4	2.3	1.9		1.7
3.3	2.1	1.4	% Officers', Directors' Owners' Comp/Sales	
(13) 5.7	(11) 4.5	(15) 3.3		
11.6	10.4	5.4		

Net Sales / Total Assets

4/1/04-3/31/05	4/1/05-3/31/06	4/1/06-3/31/07		0-1MM	1-3MM	3-5MM	5-10MM	10-25MM	25MM & OVER
306459M	758602M	1936880M	Net Sales ($)		12530M	23834M	49466M	147843M	1703207M
146865M	467607M	1183287M	Total Assets ($)		24014M	7052M	22110M	85302M	1044809M

Current Data Sorted by Assets   Comparative Historical Data

	0-500M	500M-2MM	2-10MM	10-50MM	50-100MM	100-250MM	Type of Statement	4/1/02-3/31/03 ALL	4/1/03-3/31/04 ALL
		2	5	14	2	8	Unqualified	33	36
	2	2	19	6			Reviewed	28	41
	4	6	7	2			Compiled	21	26
	9	9	5				Tax Returns	12	17
	5	6	12	12	2	4	Other	34	41
		28 (4/1-9/30/06)		113 (10/1/06-3/31/07)					
NUMBER OF STATEMENTS	18	25	48	34	4	12		128	161
	%	%	%	%	%	%	**ASSETS**	%	%
	12.7	12.7	7.9	8.2		5.3	Cash & Equivalents	8.5	10.3
	26.5	31.5	31.4	29.9		19.8	Trade Receivables (net)	25.6	23.0
	33.6	29.2	34.2	36.9		31.6	Inventory	34.0	36.7
	.6	2.8	1.7	3.4		3.9	All Other Current	3.4	3.0
	73.4	76.1	75.3	78.4		60.7	Total Current	71.6	73.1
	16.5	16.9	16.1	8.9		15.0	Fixed Assets (net)	18.7	16.6
	6.6	3.4	2.1	6.0		17.7	Intangibles (net)	3.2	4.3
	3.5	3.6	6.5	6.7		6.6	All Other Non-Current	6.6	6.0
	100.0	100.0	100.0	100.0		100.0	Total	100.0	100.0
							LIABILITIES		
	10.8	19.2	19.2	14.7		5.8	Notes Payable-Short Term	13.1	14.2
	7.7	2.3	2.3	2.5		4.5	Cur. Mat.-L.T.D.	3.5	2.6
	15.8	16.0	15.8	17.4		10.9	Trade Payables	16.4	14.4
	.0	.0	.2	.4		2.0	Income Taxes Payable	.2	.5
	9.0	9.8	12.2	12.2		9.1	All Other Current	10.2	12.7
	43.3	47.4	49.6	47.3		32.3	Total Current	43.5	44.5
	28.6	14.7	9.8	6.3		16.1	Long-Term Debt	11.0	12.8
	.0	.0	.1	.0		2.1	Deferred Taxes	.5	.4
	22.8	5.7	5.8	3.5		12.0	All Other Non-Current	5.9	5.4
	5.2	32.2	34.6	42.9		37.5	Net Worth	39.1	36.8
	100.0	100.0	100.0	100.0		100.0	Total Liabilities & Net Worth	100.0	100.0
							INCOME DATA		
	100.0	100.0	100.0	100.0		100.0	Net Sales	100.0	100.0
	43.3	36.3	31.1	34.7		38.0	Gross Profit	34.4	34.2
	42.5	32.1	25.7	25.8		30.0	Operating Expenses	31.0	30.8
	.8	4.2	5.4	8.8		8.0	Operating Profit	3.4	3.3
	1.0	1.3	1.4	1.3		2.5	All Other Expenses (net)	.8	1.0
	-.2	2.9	4.1	7.6		5.5	Profit Before Taxes	2.6	2.4
							RATIOS		
	11.9	3.4	2.1	2.3		3.1	Current	3.1	3.1
	2.1	1.7	1.6	1.6		2.5		1.8	1.7
	.8	1.0	1.2	1.2		1.3		1.3	1.2
	3.7	2.1	1.3	1.1		1.4	Quick	1.4	1.4
	1.6	1.2	.8	.7		.9		.8	.7
	.5	.4	.4	.5		.5		.5	.4
	0 UND	23 16.0	31 11.7	35 10.3		35 10.5	Sales/Receivables	26 14.2	16 22.4
	31 11.9	36 10.2	41 9.0	48 7.6		46 8.0		39 9.4	36 10.1
	46 8.0	49 7.5	66 5.6	59 6.2		57 6.3		60 6.1	54 6.7
	0 UND	19 19.0	29 12.6	33 11.1		73 5.0	Cost of Sales/Inventory	31 11.6	44 8.3
	51 7.1	45 8.2	82 4.4	102 3.6		133 2.7		85 4.3	91 4.0
	102 3.6	130 2.8	153 2.4	188 1.9		147 2.5		148 2.5	156 2.3
	0 UND	12 29.9	16 23.5	16 22.9		23 15.7	Cost of Sales/Payables	19 18.7	16 22.6
	12 29.9	25 14.5	28 12.9	38 9.7		34 10.7		30 12.4	29 12.5
	54 6.8	49 7.4	46 7.9	52 7.0		63 5.8		46 7.9	50 7.3
	6.0	4.6	5.9	4.4		3.2	Sales/Working Capital	4.3	4.3
	17.1	16.9	9.2	7.9		5.7		7.8	7.8
	-82.6	NM	17.9	17.1		13.8		16.4	22.7
	7.4	8.9	9.0	12.1		7.0	EBIT/Interest	10.0	10.1
	(11) .7	(24) 2.5	(44) 3.1	(31) 5.2		5.0		(109) 4.0	(143) 3.6
	-3.1	1.0	1.2	2.3		.9		1.3	1.0
							Net Profit + Depr., Dep., Amort./Cur. Mat. L/T/D	8.9	4.6
								(28) 2.8	(27) 1.4
								1.2	.5
	.1	.1	.2	.1		.2	Fixed/Worth	.1	.1
	1.2	.4	.4	.2		1.0		.3	.3
	-1.3	2.4	1.3	.6		-.8		1.0	1.2
	.3	.6	.9	.7		.5	Debt/Worth	.6	.7
	2.3	1.9	2.2	1.9		2.9		1.2	1.6
	-8.7	13.2	4.6	3.9		-5.6		3.5	5.0
	95.9	54.3	47.6	65.8			% Profit Before Taxes/Tangible Net Worth	40.0	30.4
	(11) 42.9	(22) 13.5	(41) 22.5	(33) 40.5				(112) 15.4	(141) 13.1
	21.5	-6.7	4.4	15.3				3.5	1.7
	36.9	12.6	18.5	22.0		16.8	% Profit Before Taxes/Total Assets	12.6	13.6
	5.6	8.5	4.9	9.6		8.4		6.2	4.7
	-7.2	-.1	.9	4.4		.2		.7	.1
	140.3	99.2	39.7	96.1		21.7	Sales/Net Fixed Assets	41.4	62.6
	67.0	25.5	18.7	24.6		12.9		19.4	25.9
	16.7	9.4	9.8	14.4		6.5		8.2	8.7
	5.2	4.7	3.3	3.0		1.8	Sales/Total Assets	3.3	3.0
	4.0	2.8	2.6	2.3		1.6		2.2	2.3
	2.9	2.0	1.6	1.7		1.3		1.6	1.6
		.7	.7	.3		1.6	% Depr., Dep., Amort./Sales	.8	.6
		(19) 1.2	(43) 1.4	(30) .6		(11) 2.2		(111) 1.5	(127) 1.1
		1.6	2.0	1.4		2.7		2.6	1.9
	4.8	3.1	1.3				% Officers', Directors' Owners' Comp/Sales	3.4	2.3
	(10) 6.4	(14) 4.8	(19) 2.7					(44) 5.0	(49) 6.4
	12.0	9.5	5.2					9.4	9.6
	19277M	88381M	625929M	1835758M	796982M	2843980M	Net Sales ($)	5323777M	8102481M
	4892M	28964M	256455M	718795M	302000M	1793310M	Total Assets ($)	2926588M	4254696M

M = $ thousand   MM = $ million

Comparative Historical Data | Current Data Sorted by Sales

Type of Statement									
32	32	31	Unqualified	1	1		4	6	19
32	35	27	Reviewed		2		6	10	9
16	16	19	Compiled	2	5	2	4	4	2
14	18	23	Tax Returns	5	8	4	5		1
37	59	41	Other	3	3	4	4	10	17
4/1/04-3/31/05 ALL	4/1/05-3/31/06 ALL	4/1/06-3/31/07 ALL		0-1MM	1-3MM	3-5MM	5-10MM	10-25MM	25MM & OVER
				28 (4/1-9/30/06)		113 (10/1/06-3/31/07)			
131	160	141	NUMBER OF STATEMENTS	11	19	10	23	30	48

%	%	%	ASSETS	%	%	%	%	%	%
8.1	8.5	9.0	Cash & Equivalents	17.5	10.1	10.5	10.1	7.0	7.2
27.4	29.2	29.4	Trade Receivables (net)	19.6	30.6	25.6	35.7	25.7	31.1
36.5	33.7	34.1	Inventory	23.5	39.3	30.5	22.9	41.4	35.9
2.5	3.1	2.3	All Other Current	3.8	.1	.5	2.1	2.4	3.3
74.4	74.4	74.8	Total Current	64.4	80.2	67.0	70.7	76.6	77.5
16.4	13.7	14.5	Fixed Assets (net)	18.3	15.1	24.2	16.7	13.7	10.7
3.0	5.0	5.1	Intangibles (net)	13.2	2.2	1.5	4.4	2.5	7.3
6.1	6.8	5.6	All Other Non-Current	4.1	2.5	7.3	8.2	7.2	4.6
100.0	100.0	100.0	Total	100.0	100.0	100.0	100.0	100.0	100.0

			LIABILITIES						
15.8	17.6	16.4	Notes Payable-Short Term	21.0	16.2	15.6	12.4	21.1	14.7
1.6	2.9	3.2	Cur. Mat.-L.T.D.	8.6	3.2	3.8	2.9	2.2	2.5
15.6	14.8	15.8	Trade Payables	12.1	13.9	17.0	15.6	15.5	17.3
.2	.2	.3	Income Taxes Payable	.0	.0	.0	.2	.2	.8
9.4	12.4	11.1	All Other Current	8.0	8.5	7.7	12.9	11.7	12.2
42.5	47.9	46.7	Total Current	49.7	41.8	44.1	44.0	50.6	47.4
12.4	12.0	12.7	Long-Term Debt	32.2	20.3	22.1	13.5	6.7	6.5
.3	.1	.2	Deferred Taxes	.0	.0	.0	.0	.2	.5
5.8	7.0	8.2	All Other Non-Current	22.8	11.3	9.1	4.2	5.9	6.7
38.9	33.0	32.2	Net Worth	-4.8	26.6	24.7	38.3	36.5	38.8
100.0	100.0	100.0	Total Liabilties & Net Worth	100.0	100.0	100.0	100.0	100.0	100.0

			INCOME DATA						
100.0	100.0	100.0	Net Sales	100.0	100.0	100.0	100.0	100.0	100.0
35.4	36.1	34.8	Gross Profit	46.8	35.9	42.0	31.5	30.2	34.5
30.7	31.7	29.2	Operating Expenses	47.0	32.1	40.0	26.4	23.4	26.6
4.7	4.4	5.6	Operating Profit	-.2	3.8	2.0	5.0	6.9	7.9
.9	1.2	1.4	All Other Expenses (net)	1.5	1.5	1.5	1.4	1.5	1.3
3.8	3.2	4.2	Profit Before Taxes	-1.6	2.4	.6	3.6	5.4	6.5

			RATIOS						
3.2	2.4	2.6		3.8	6.4	3.5	2.5	2.0	2.5
1.9	1.7	1.6	Current	1.5	2.2	1.6	1.6	1.6	1.6
1.3	1.2	1.2		.6	1.5	1.0	1.1	1.3	1.2
1.5	1.5	1.5		2.5	3.6	2.4	2.0	1.0	1.2
.9	.8	.9	Quick	1.5	1.5	.8	.9	.6	.8
.5	.4	.5		.2	.5	.3	.6	.4	.5
22 16.4	29 12.6	29 12.7		0 UND	25 14.5	15 25.1	30 12.1	33 11.1	34 10.8
41 9.0	46 8.0	42 8.7	Sales/Receivables	32 11.5	44 8.2	25 14.6	41 9.0	41 8.9	45 8.1
60 6.1	60 6.0	54 6.8		46 7.9	60 6.1	43 8.6	59 6.2	55 6.7	58 6.2
41 9.0	34 10.8	25 14.7		0 UND	21 17.0	21 17.2	14 25.4	59 6.2	35 10.4
96 3.8	82 4.5	78 4.7	Cost of Sales/Inventory	47 7.8	78 4.7	68 5.4	37 9.8	106 3.4	91 4.0
153 2.4	141 2.6	142 2.6		185 2.0	135 2.7	125 2.9	101 3.6	178 2.1	138 2.7
17 21.3	16 22.8	15 24.5		0 UND	2 230.4	6 58.6	15 23.6	15 24.9	21 17.6
30 12.2	30 12.0	28 13.2	Cost of Sales/Payables	21 17.4	22 16.5	31 11.6	29 12.7	29 12.6	29 12.8
46 8.0	46 7.9	50 7.4		52 7.1	49 7.4	63 5.8	49 7.4	50 7.3	51 7.2
4.2	4.3	5.2		6.1	4.4	9.4	5.6	5.9	5.0
6.7	8.9	9.6	Sales/Working Capital	21.6	7.6	18.6	11.0	8.3	9.2
14.0	30.1	19.8		-6.7	19.7	-90.6	22.2	14.3	16.0
18.1	7.8	9.2			4.2	3.4	15.7	7.6	12.0
(119) 3.9	(142) 3.0	(126) 3.2	EBIT/Interest	(14) 1.9	1.0	(22) 2.4	(26) 2.9	(46) 6.5
1.3	1.1	1.2			1.0	.1	1.3	1.2	2.1
11.5	9.8	39.4							66.9
(28) 4.6	(24) 4.1	(25) 5.3	Net Profit + Depr., Dep., Amort./Cur. Mat. L/T/D					(13) 5.3
1.8	1.2	1.2							2.8
.1	.1	.1		.1	.1	.3	.1	.2	.1
.3	.4	.3	Fixed/Worth	2.1	.4	1.9	.3	.5	.2
.9	1.5	1.8		.0	2.8	NM	1.3	.9	.7
.6	.8	.8		.3	.5	1.5	1.3	.8	.8
1.3	2.3	2.0	Debt/Worth	2.4	2.2	11.5	1.8	2.0	1.9
3.5	6.8	7.8		-2.0	35.6	NM	3.6	5.6	5.7
42.0	41.2	53.5			53.0		51.4	46.3	96.0
(121) 15.5	(136) 18.5	(118) 25.6	% Profit Before Taxes/Tangible Net Worth	(15) 21.5		(22) 15.9	(24) 24.5	(43) 40.5
2.4	3.7	6.8			8.0		4.1	4.6	15.2
17.1	13.5	18.9		25.1	23.4	10.9	19.0	19.2	19.2
7.1	6.0	7.6	% Profit Before Taxes/Total Assets	2.2	7.2	.1	5.4	5.0	10.1
.8	.7	1.0		-11.0	-2.1	-4.9	1.0	1.0	4.6
59.4	59.1	57.9		80.4	152.5	47.8	87.8	31.1	63.0
19.5	25.8	22.8	Sales/Net Fixed Assets	21.5	25.5	18.3	26.0	17.9	24.8
10.5	11.4	10.5		9.3	8.0	7.7	9.3	12.4	12.8
3.3	3.2	3.6		4.4	4.2	6.1	4.0	2.6	3.3
2.2	2.2	2.6	Sales/Total Assets	2.6	3.6	2.6	3.0	1.9	2.5
1.7	1.6	1.6		1.4	2.0	1.9	1.9	1.6	1.7
.6	.5	.5			.7		.6	.8	.3
(105) 1.2	(128) 1.0	(115) 1.2	% Depr., Dep., Amort./Sales	(13) 1.4		(19) 1.7	(25) 1.3	(43) .8
1.9	1.9	1.9			1.9		2.0	2.1	1.9
2.2	2.2	2.4						1.1	1.4
(39) 3.7	(60) 4.7	(52) 4.3	% Officers', Directors' Owners' Comp/Sales				(10) 2.2	(12) 4.6
9.5	7.8	6.9						4.5	10.2
5766116M	5741050M	6210307M	Net Sales ($)	7711M	34766M	38054M	163543M	462748M	5503485M
2852632M	3046626M	3104416M	Total Assets ($)	3858M	15757M	14475M	88080M	241376M	2740870M

M = $ thousand   MM = $ million
See Pages 11 through 21 for Explanation of Ratios and Data

Current Data Sorted by Assets   Comparative Historical Data

						Type of Statement		
						Unqualified	13	13
						Reviewed	10	10
						Compiled	7	10
						Tax Returns	2	2
						Other	9	13
1	1	1	3				4/1/02-	4/1/03-
2	1	2	3				3/31/03	3/31/04
	2	3					ALL	ALL
	1							
3	3	10	3	2	2			
	8 (4/1-9/30/06)		32 (10/1/06-3/31/07)					
0-500M	500M-2MM	2-10MM	10-50MM	50-100MM	100-250MM			
3	8	16	9	2	2	NUMBER OF STATEMENTS	41	48
%	%	%	%	%	%	ASSETS	%	%
		6.7				Cash & Equivalents	7.9	8.1
		31.3				Trade Receivables (net)	25.8	29.7
		25.2				Inventory	25.5	26.9
		7.3				All Other Current	5.5	3.3
		70.6				Total Current	64.7	68.0
		19.8				Fixed Assets (net)	21.9	22.2
		7.9				Intangibles (net)	5.5	6.2
		1.7				All Other Non-Current	8.0	3.7
		100.0				Total	100.0	100.0
						LIABILITIES		
		11.5				Notes Payable-Short Term	16.2	15.6
		2.9				Cur. Mat.-L.T.D.	2.3	1.7
		16.7				Trade Payables	17.2	17.1
		.4				Income Taxes Payable	.3	.2
		9.9				All Other Current	10.3	12.6
		41.4				Total Current	46.3	47.2
		8.9				Long-Term Debt	13.5	11.5
		.3				Deferred Taxes	.1	.2
		5.5				All Other Non-Current	2.8	2.5
		43.8				Net Worth	37.4	38.6
		100.0				Total Liabilties & Net Worth	100.0	100.0
						INCOME DATA		
		100.0				Net Sales	100.0	100.0
		21.5				Gross Profit	27.8	25.6
		16.3				Operating Expenses	24.9	20.9
		5.1				Operating Profit	2.9	4.8
		1.8				All Other Expenses (net)	1.1	1.2
		3.3				Profit Before Taxes	1.9	3.6
						RATIOS		
		2.5					2.6	2.5
		1.7				Current	1.6	1.5
		1.1					1.0	1.0
		1.2					1.7	1.7
		.8				Quick	.7	.7
		.5					.4	.4
	22	16.6					28 13.3	35 10.5
	34	10.6				Sales/Receivables	38 9.7	43 8.4
	52	7.0					56 6.5	63 5.8
	15	24.8					20 17.9	23 16.1
	44	8.3				Cost of Sales/Inventory	44 8.3	43 8.5
	89	4.1					113 3.2	123 3.0
	10	38.3					13 27.3	15 24.1
	22	16.5				Cost of Sales/Payables	23 15.8	28 13.0
	36	10.2					40 9.2	46 8.0
		4.0					5.6	5.8
		11.1				Sales/Working Capital	11.4	11.5
		35.2					UND	818.3
		11.2					6.7	11.3
	(15)	2.6				EBIT/Interest	(35) 2.1	(45) 5.5
		1.2					.8	1.3
						Net Profit + Depr., Dep., Amort./Cur. Mat. L/T/D		
		.1					.2	.2
		.3				Fixed/Worth	.4	.6
		1.6					5.3	1.2
		.7					.6	.9
		1.5				Debt/Worth	1.5	1.6
		4.6					17.8	6.0
		31.2				% Profit Before Taxes/Tangible Net Worth	57.2	43.2
	(15)	12.7					(33) 16.5	(44) 26.2
		4.1					7.0	4.0
		15.8				% Profit Before Taxes/Total Assets	14.1	16.2
		3.4					6.0	6.6
		1.0					1.0	.5
		404.7					44.8	52.9
		13.9				Sales/Net Fixed Assets	13.7	18.3
		8.9					6.1	7.5
		4.4					3.4	3.2
		2.5				Sales/Total Assets	2.4	2.2
		1.3					1.5	1.4
		.2					.6	.8
	(14)	.8				% Depr., Dep., Amort./Sales	(35) 1.7	(40) 2.2
		2.6					2.7	3.7
						% Officers', Directors' Owners' Comp/Sales	1.9	3.2
							(12) 4.4	(14) 5.6
							10.0	9.7
583M	23699M	367560M	371534M	286064M	610856M	Net Sales ($)	2403259M	1936071M
322M	9151M	91703M	153436M	158567M	382430M	Total Assets ($)	1160535M	990165M

© RMA 2007

M = $ thousand   MM = $ million
See Pages 11 through 21 for Explanation of Ratios and Data

Comparative Historical Data | | | | | | Current Data Sorted by Sales

						Type of Statement						
	11		7		6	Unqualified	1	1			1	3
	15		17		8	Reviewed	2	1	2	1	2	2
	2		7		5	Compiled		1			2	
	4		2		1	Tax Returns	1					
	16		13		20	Other		1	4	2	5	8
	4/1/04-3/31/05		4/1/05-3/31/06		4/1/06-3/31/07			8 (4/1-9/30/06)			32 (10/1/06-3/31/07)	
	ALL		ALL		ALL		0-1MM	1-3MM	3-5MM	5-10MM	10-25MM	25MM & OVER
	48		46		40	NUMBER OF STATEMENTS	4	4	6	3	10	13
	%		%		%	ASSETS	%	%	%	%	%	%
	9.7		9.1		6.9	Cash & Equivalents					9.9	6.6
	24.9		28.0		28.0	Trade Receivables (net)					22.1	43.3
	29.6		29.6		31.7	Inventory					25.4	27.8
	2.9		2.8		4.4	All Other Current					9.1	1.8
	67.0		69.5		71.0	Total Current					66.5	79.5
	22.5		20.9		17.6	Fixed Assets (net)					16.5	8.5
	5.0		5.8		6.9	Intangibles (net)					15.4	5.5
	5.5		3.8		4.4	All Other Non-Current					1.6	6.5
	100.0		100.0		100.0	Total					100.0	100.0
						LIABILITIES						
	13.6		14.1		14.1	Notes Payable-Short Term					9.5	15.2
	3.1		2.5		2.5	Cur. Mat.-L.T.D.					2.5	3.0
	16.0		16.7		16.6	Trade Payables					17.5	22.5
	.3		.1		.2	Income Taxes Payable					.6	.3
	8.2		10.5		10.5	All Other Current					5.3	9.8
	41.3		43.9		44.0	Total Current					35.5	50.8
	10.2		12.5		12.3	Long-Term Debt					4.9	10.6
	.3		.2		.2	Deferred Taxes					.1	.3
	4.7		5.3		8.0	All Other Non-Current					8.7	9.8
	43.5		38.1		35.5	Net Worth					50.8	28.5
	100.0		100.0		100.0	Total Liabilities & Net Worth					100.0	100.0
						INCOME DATA						
	100.0		100.0		100.0	Net Sales					100.0	100.0
	30.6		26.4		25.4	Gross Profit					23.7	21.4
	26.2		21.8		20.3	Operating Expenses					17.1	16.5
	4.5		4.6		5.0	Operating Profit					6.5	4.9
	1.3		.9		1.6	All Other Expenses (net)					1.5	.9
	3.1		3.7		3.4	Profit Before Taxes					5.1	4.0
						RATIOS						
	2.9		3.0		2.3						4.3	2.1
	1.7		1.6		1.7	Current					1.9	1.7
	1.2		1.0		1.2						.9	1.2
	1.6		1.8		1.2						2.1	1.2
	.8		.9		.8	Quick					.5	1.1
	.5		.5		.4						.4	.7
28	12.9	24	15.2	25	14.8						21 17.6	33 11.0
44	8.3	43	8.5	38	9.6	Sales/Receivables					37 9.8	41 8.9
59	6.1	59	6.2	54	6.7						50 7.3	64 5.7
30	12.2	20	18.7	34	10.6						17 21.2	27 13.3
67	5.4	60	6.1	64	5.7	Cost of Sales/Inventory					50 7.3	58 6.3
113	3.2	124	3.0	106	3.4						91 4.0	70 5.2
19	19.2	10	37.5	12	30.5						12 29.5	19 19.3
31	11.9	24	14.9	28	13.1	Cost of Sales/Payables					34 10.8	38 9.5
46	8.0	46	7.9	50	7.3						49 7.4	55 6.6
	5.6		5.0		4.8						3.2	7.0
	9.4		14.3		9.6	Sales/Working Capital					11.4	12.5
	26.7		UND		30.8						-90.5	15.8
	11.5		14.0		11.2							10.8
(44)	4.0	(39)	2.9	(37)	2.9	EBIT/Interest						3.4
	1.3		1.2		1.1							1.7
	5.2				5.8	Net Profit + Depr., Dep.,						
(13)	2.2			(11)	1.8	Amort./Cur. Mat. L/T/D						
	.7				.7							
	.1		.1		.1						.1	.1
	.6		.7		.4	Fixed/Worth					.3	.2
	1.1		2.0		1.8						NM	1.2
	.8		.7		1.0						.4	1.6
	1.4		2.3		1.9	Debt/Worth					1.1	2.5
	5.0		13.9		7.2						NM	7.8
	43.3		64.8		60.5	% Profit Before Taxes/Tangible						67.4
(44)	14.7	(40)	15.0	(33)	16.4	Net Worth					(11) 34.0	
	4.3		-.1		3.4							4.1
	11.5		14.6		16.6	% Profit Before Taxes/Total					21.1	17.0
	6.2		4.7		7.3	Assets					10.1	10.7
	.6		.6		.1						2.4	2.1
	64.2		104.3		83.4						108.1	333.5
	14.4		14.1		14.0	Sales/Net Fixed Assets					14.0	28.3
	6.5		7.6		8.9						10.3	13.2
	3.3		3.6		3.2						3.5	4.8
	2.4		2.5		2.3	Sales/Total Assets					2.1	2.7
	1.5		1.5		1.3						1.3	1.9
	.7		.5		.5							.2
(44)	1.6	(40)	1.7	(36)	1.1	% Depr., Dep., Amort./Sales					(11) .9	
	3.1		3.3		2.7							1.2
	3.7		2.3		1.4	% Officers', Directors'						
(19)	5.7	(10)	5.2	(13)	2.9	Owners' Comp/Sales						
	7.0		9.2		6.1							
	1494878M		1961188M		1660296M	Net Sales ($)	1160M	10465M	23606M	26216M	143896M	1454953M
	720169M		995846M		795609M	Total Assets ($)	941M	4250M	15294M	24586M	67357M	683181M

© RMA 2007

M = $ thousand   MM = $ million
See Pages 11 through 21 for Explanation of Ratios and Data

Current Data Sorted by Assets | **Comparative Historical Data**

	0-500M	500M-2MM	2-10MM	10-50MM	50-100MM	100-250MM	Type of Statement	4/1/02-3/31/03 ALL	4/1/03-3/31/04 ALL
	1	9	6	35	12	10	Unqualified	69	69
			23	22		2	Reviewed	63	58
	2	14	21	6			Compiled	52	68
	8	9	7	2			Tax Returns	25	32
	1	9	22	40	11	7	Other	60	60
		70 (4/1-9/30/06)		209 (10/1/06-3/31/07)					
NUMBER OF STATEMENTS	12	41	79	105	23	19		269	287
	%	%	%	%	%	%	**ASSETS**	%	%
	7.2	4.7	3.1	2.8	5.9	6.2	Cash & Equivalents	5.1	6.0
	18.6	17.8	12.7	11.9	9.5	8.1	Trade Receivables (net)	10.3	11.5
	27.3	32.5	26.1	29.5	28.6	15.1	Inventory	26.2	26.0
	.3	3.3	3.8	3.3	8.0	4.0	All Other Current	4.8	4.8
	53.5	58.4	45.7	47.5	52.1	33.4	Total Current	46.3	48.2
	33.3	34.6	42.2	44.1	36.6	50.7	Fixed Assets (net)	44.3	43.0
	1.7	1.7	1.3	.7	3.7	.5	Intangibles (net)	1.0	1.2
	10.9	5.4	10.9	7.7	7.7	15.5	All Other Non-Current	8.4	7.6
	100.0	100.0	100.0	100.0	100.0	100.0	Total	100.0	100.0
							LIABILITIES		
	17.5	17.5	13.4	13.9	8.4	2.4	Notes Payable-Short Term	13.3	13.1
	8.3	5.6	4.4	6.4	4.0	5.7	Cur. Mat.-L.T.D.	7.0	6.2
	10.4	8.9	7.6	5.7	7.4	4.7	Trade Payables	6.0	6.3
	.0	.0	.3	.2	.1	.3	Income Taxes Payable	.1	.2
	24.0	5.2	8.5	7.1	6.3	3.6	All Other Current	4.8	5.4
	60.3	37.2	34.2	33.4	26.2	16.7	Total Current	31.2	31.3
	96.4	18.6	20.1	19.4	24.4	36.5	Long-Term Debt	25.1	26.1
	.0	.2	.5	.7	.9	1.4	Deferred Taxes	.6	.6
	21.9	6.3	4.0	6.3	3.5	2.4	All Other Non-Current	6.1	5.4
	-79.2	37.6	41.2	40.1	45.0	42.9	Net Worth	37.0	36.6
	100.0	100.0	100.0	100.0	100.0	100.0	Total Liabilties & Net Worth	100.0	100.0
							INCOME DATA		
	100.0	100.0	100.0	100.0	100.0	100.0	Net Sales	100.0	100.0
	33.8	25.3	21.1	13.9	10.9	13.7	Gross Profit	19.0	21.5
	28.5	24.8	18.7	11.2	10.0	9.6	Operating Expenses	17.0	17.8
	5.3	.5	2.5	2.7	.9	4.0	Operating Profit	1.9	3.7
	1.7	1.1	.9	1.4	1.0	.5	All Other Expenses (net)	1.2	1.0
	3.6	-.6	1.6	1.3	-.1	3.5	Profit Before Taxes	.8	2.7
							RATIOS		
	3.9	3.4	2.6	2.4	2.8	2.6	Current	2.5	2.9
	1.6	1.6	1.4	1.4	2.2	2.0		1.6	1.6
	.4	1.1	.9	1.1	1.4	1.0		1.1	1.1
	1.1	1.0	1.1	.8	.9	1.3	Quick	.9	1.1
	.7	.5	(78) .5	(104) .5	.5	.7		.4	.5
	.1	.3	.2	.3	.3	.4		.2	.2
	0 UND	8 45.7	10 38.1	14 26.5	15 24.7	18 20.7	Sales/Receivables	10 35.4	10 34.8
	14 26.7	16 22.3	17 21.2	19 19.1	20 18.3	22 16.5		17 21.9	17 21.2
	23 15.7	36 10.2	29 12.7	31 11.9	25 14.6	27 13.6		24 15.3	26 14.0
	0 UND	24 15.4	34 10.7	36 10.2	34 10.9	24 15.5	Cost of Sales/Inventory	27 13.6	31 11.9
	17 20.9	56 6.5	56 6.5	58 6.3	69 5.3	38 9.6		56 6.5	56 6.5
	28 12.9	105 3.5	98 3.7	97 3.8	99 3.7	77 4.7		91 4.0	95 3.8
	0 UND	3 117.7	4 86.4	6 57.6	10 37.4	9 39.2	Cost of Sales/Payables	5 80.6	6 65.4
	7 50.5	8 43.0	10 38.1	11 34.1	14 25.5	14 25.4		10 36.1	12 30.4
	18 20.1	13 28.7	18 20.5	18 20.6	22 16.5	19 19.4		20 17.9	18 20.2
	14.3	5.8	7.2	6.7	4.4	6.0	Sales/Working Capital	6.5	5.7
	515.4	11.5	14.8	13.4	6.8	9.6		13.0	11.4
	-16.4	532.9	-53.5	47.3	14.0	492.8		89.8	56.5
	2.5	4.8	4.6	6.5	2.4	3.5	EBIT/Interest	4.1	7.4
	(11) 1.8	(39) 1.4	(74) 1.8	(103) 2.2	1.0	(18) 2.2		(253) 1.7	(272) 2.6
	-1.0	-.2	.8	.2	-.4	.8		.1	1.1
			3.4	4.4			Net Profit + Depr., Dep., Amort./Cur. Mat. L/T/D	3.4	3.1
		(22) 2.4	(34) 2.3					(66) 1.6	(72) 2.0
			1.5	.2				.4	1.0
	2.3	.3	.5	.6	.4	.7	Fixed/Worth	.6	.5
	-.5	.8	1.0	1.1	.8	1.0		1.1	1.1
	-.2	1.5	2.1	2.0	1.4	1.9		2.7	2.3
	10.9	.8	.6	.6	.7	1.0	Debt/Worth	.7	.6
	-3.2	1.5	1.4	1.5	1.4	1.4		1.8	1.8
	-1.6	4.6	2.9	3.3	2.8	1.8		3.9	4.0
		16.3	21.0	25.4	11.0	15.6	% Profit Before Taxes/Tangible Net Worth	19.0	26.3
	(36) 7.0	(73) 10.1	(96) 11.8	(22) -2.0	10.7			(245) 7.1	(265) 10.5
	-7.6	.5	-2.3	-10.7	-.4			-4.4	1.4
	22.4	10.5	8.8	11.2	5.6	7.5	% Profit Before Taxes/Total Assets	7.1	10.3
	8.5	2.4	3.0	4.1	.0	3.3		1.9	3.8
	-14.2	-4.8	-.5	-2.7	-3.9	-.2		-2.1	.3
	137.5	22.3	8.1	6.7	7.2	5.6	Sales/Net Fixed Assets	8.2	9.2
	19.2	7.5	4.9	4.6	4.4	2.9		4.7	4.6
	7.6	5.4	2.8	2.6	2.6	1.3		2.9	2.8
	9.1	3.5	2.8	2.5	2.5	1.8	Sales/Total Assets	2.7	2.7
	6.1	2.4	2.0	1.9	1.4	1.2		1.8	1.8
	4.5	1.8	1.3	1.3	1.0	.9		1.2	1.2
	.2	1.3	1.8	2.1	1.9	2.5	% Depr., Dep., Amort./Sales	2.2	2.0
	(10) .9	(38) 2.2	(75) 3.3	(100) 3.2	(21) 2.4	(16) 2.9		(249) 3.7	(264) 3.8
	2.3	3.3	5.2	5.0	5.1	4.4		5.5	6.1
		2.0	1.3	.7			% Officers', Directors' Owners' Comp/Sales	1.1	1.3
		(23) 3.3	(28) 1.8	(16) 1.4				(86) 2.3	(90) 2.5
		5.7	2.9	2.4				3.7	4.7
	21666M	128152M	877533M	4152607M	2777706M	3483531M	Net Sales ($)	7727374M	8387657M
	2625M	46294M	423010M	2263353M	1641202M	2690841M	Total Assets ($)	4961739M	5294992M

M = $ thousand   MM = $ million
See Pages 11 through 21 for Explanation of Ratios and Data

Comparative Historical Data				Current Data Sorted by Sales					
			Type of Statement						
68	64	64	Unqualified	1			2	9	52
73	54	56	Reviewed		9	4	6	20	17
50	45	43	Compiled	1	8	12	9	8	5
26	28	26	Tax Returns	5	6	8	4	3	
56	87	90	Other	1	8	3	11	24	43
4/1/04-3/31/05 ALL	4/1/05-3/31/06 ALL	4/1/06-3/31/07 ALL		0-1MM	70 (4/1-9/30/06) 1-3MM	3-5MM	209 (10/1/06-3/31/07) 5-10MM	10-25MM	25MM & OVER
273	278	279	**NUMBER OF STATEMENTS**	8	31	27	32	64	117
%	%	%	**ASSETS**	%	%	%	%	%	%
5.5	4.9	3.8	Cash & Equivalents		4.3	3.9	5.3	2.5	4.0
12.2	12.6	12.8	Trade Receivables (net)		18.7	10.9	11.0	14.2	11.6
26.5	29.3	27.8	Inventory		28.0	25.7	28.6	28.9	28.0
4.1	3.5	3.8	All Other Current		3.3	6.4	1.7	2.7	4.7
48.2	50.2	48.3	Total Current		54.2	46.9	46.6	48.2	48.3
42.5	41.0	41.5	Fixed Assets (net)		35.9	40.2	40.8	40.7	43.2
.8	1.0	1.3	Intangibles (net)		1.7	.5	2.0	1.5	1.0
8.5	7.7	8.9	All Other Non-Current		8.2	12.3	10.6	9.6	7.4
100.0	100.0	100.0	Total		100.0	100.0	100.0	100.0	100.0
			LIABILITIES						
14.6	14.8	13.2	Notes Payable-Short Term		13.7	14.9	14.3	13.9	11.2
6.7	4.6	5.6	Cur. Mat.-L.T.D.		4.5	5.4	6.0	4.6	6.4
7.0	6.7	7.0	Trade Payables		9.8	7.6	9.4	5.7	6.4
.2	.2	.2	Income Taxes Payable		.1	.0	.1	.3	.2
5.9	6.8	7.6	All Other Current		7.8	9.5	7.5	7.0	6.5
34.5	33.1	33.6	Total Current		36.0	37.3	37.3	31.5	30.7
22.5	20.5	24.4	Long-Term Debt		43.9	17.9	20.1	19.0	21.5
.7	.6	.6	Deferred Taxes		.2	.1	.7	.6	.9
5.1	5.8	5.8	All Other Non-Current		11.6	6.3	1.7	5.7	5.3
37.3	39.9	35.5	Net Worth		8.2	38.3	40.2	43.1	41.7
100.0	100.0	100.0	Total Liabilities & Net Worth		100.0	100.0	100.0	100.0	100.0
			INCOME DATA						
100.0	100.0	100.0	Net Sales		100.0	100.0	100.0	100.0	100.0
23.8	21.3	18.2	Gross Profit		32.4	18.6	17.1	17.1	13.6
17.4	16.7	15.9	Operating Expenses		30.7	18.0	16.9	14.1	10.7
6.4	4.6	2.4	Operating Profit		1.7	.6	.2	3.0	2.9
1.0	.7	1.1	All Other Expenses (net)		1.6	1.5	1.7	.7	1.0
5.4	3.9	1.2	Profit Before Taxes		.2	-.9	-1.5	2.3	1.9
			RATIOS						
2.6	2.9	2.6	Current		3.6	2.8	2.6	2.2	2.6
1.6	1.6	1.5			1.7	1.4	1.2	1.5	1.7
1.1	1.1	1.0			.8	.8	.7	1.1	1.2
1.0	1.0	.9	Quick		1.6	.8	.9	.9	.9
.5	.5 (277)	.5			.5	.4	(30) .4	.5	.5
.3	.3	.3			.2	.3	.2	.3	.3
11 33.0	13 28.7	12 30.4	Sales/Receivables		6 56.7	4 81.5	11 34.4	12 30.0	14 25.6
17 22.1	18 20.0	18 20.0			16 22.9	15 24.0	20 18.0	21 17.2	19 19.1
26 14.1	26 14.1	28 12.9			35 10.4	18 20.6	29 12.5	32 11.5	26 13.8
30 12.3	34 10.9	30 12.3	Cost of Sales/Inventory		23 15.8	12 29.8	36 10.0	35 10.3	31 11.8
55 6.6	56 6.5	54 6.8			54 6.8	49 7.4	71 5.1	59 6.1	44 8.2
98 3.7	92 4.0	93 3.9			115 3.2	104 3.5	121 3.0	91 4.0	87 4.2
6 59.1	6 66.2	6 66.2	Cost of Sales/Payables		4 88.5	3 124.8	2 209.4	5 69.2	7 50.8
12 30.2	12 31.7	10 35.3			9 39.7	8 43.2	12 31.7	8 43.3	12 29.9
22 16.8	18 20.8	17 20.9			32 11.5	14 26.0	21 17.2	17 21.8	17 21.2
6.5	5.8	5.9	Sales/Working Capital		5.5	5.2	7.2	6.3	6.0
13.1	13.0	12.8			10.4	20.6	29.1	13.1	10.1
96.8	130.6	148.2			-33.3	-17.9	-15.3	62.9	25.5
12.9	8.6	4.9	EBIT/Interest		3.9	5.9	3.6	6.0	5.2
(259) 5.4	(264) 3.5	(268) 1.8			1.3	(24) 1.3	(28) 1.8	(63) 1.9	(115) 2.0
2.2	1.2	.4			-.2	-.1	-.5	.8	.3
3.8	4.2	4.1	Net Profit + Depr., Dep., Amort./Cur. Mat. L/T/D					3.3	5.3
(67) 2.4	(75) 2.4	(78) 2.3						(23) 2.6	(38) 2.8
1.3	1.2	.7						1.4	.6
.6	.5	.5	Fixed/Worth		.6	.3	.4	.5	.6
1.0	1.0	1.0			1.2	.8	1.2	.9	1.0
2.1	2.0	2.1			26.9	2.7	2.1	2.0	1.7
.7	.6	.7	Debt/Worth		.9	.8	.3	.6	.7
1.5	1.4	1.5			2.1	1.3	2.0	1.4	1.4
3.1	3.2	3.4			82.7	2.9	6.5	3.1	2.9
41.8	33.8	20.8	% Profit Before Taxes/Tangible Net Worth		15.8	16.3	31.0	23.5	22.5
(250) 24.2	(256) 16.2	(250) 10.2			(24) 7.0	(23) 6.2	(28) 11.2	(60) 10.3	(111) 10.5
9.6	3.9	-2.1			-2.2	-7.2	2.3	-1.6	-4.1
18.5	14.6	9.9	% Profit Before Taxes/Total Assets		9.3	8.8	10.9	9.4	11.2
8.1	6.2	3.0			1.7	.9	2.6	3.5	3.3
2.6	1.0	-1.8			-3.9	-8.1	-1.5	-.6	-1.7
9.2	9.6	8.2	Sales/Net Fixed Assets		19.3	13.1	7.6	7.9	7.6
5.3	5.5	5.4			5.9	6.1	4.8	5.2	4.7
3.0	3.0	2.9			3.2	2.6	2.5	3.0	2.8
2.7	2.8	2.6	Sales/Total Assets		4.1	2.9	2.7	2.7	2.5
2.0	1.9	2.0			1.9	2.0	1.6	2.0	2.0
1.4	1.3	1.3			1.4	1.4	1.1	1.3	1.2
2.0	1.5	1.8	% Depr., Dep., Amort./Sales		1.1	1.6	1.4	1.8	1.9
(253) 3.2	(257) 2.8	(260) 2.9			(30) 2.4	(23) 3.2	(29) 3.8	(61) 2.4	(110) 3.1
5.1	4.8	4.9			5.2	5.6	5.8	3.3	4.9
1.4	1.5	1.3	% Officers', Directors' Owners' Comp/Sales		2.6	2.1	1.1	.7	.9
(84) 2.2	(82) 2.4	(76) 2.3			(19) 3.3	(10) 3.6	(15) 1.4	(17) 1.6	(11) 1.5
4.4	4.6	3.9			5.6	6.5	2.3	2.3	4.4
9488755M	9813605M	11441195M	Net Sales ($)	5084M	70526M	102053M	227368M	1111512M	9924652M
6010379M	5706390M	7067325M	Total Assets ($)	1955M	39971M	64498M	191680M	677527M	6091694M

M = $ thousand   MM = $ million
See Pages 11 through 21 for Explanation of Ratios and Data

Current Data Sorted by Assets   **Comparative Historical Data**

						Type of Statement		
	1	4	9		1	Unqualified	13	17
		11	4			Reviewed	9	8
2	1					Compiled	7	8
		1				Tax Returns	2	1
		4	3		3	Other	16	9
	12 (4/1-9/30/06)		32 (10/1/06-3/31/07)				4/1/02-3/31/03	4/1/03-3/31/04
0-500M	500M-2MM	2-10MM	10-50MM	50-100MM	100-250MM		ALL	ALL
2	3	19	16		4	NUMBER OF STATEMENTS	47	43

0-500M %	500M-2MM %	2-10MM %	10-50MM %	50-100MM %	100-250MM %	ASSETS	ALL %	ALL %
		5.0	5.1			Cash & Equivalents	5.1	3.6
		20.6	19.9			Trade Receivables (net)	20.7	22.1
		35.9	43.4			Inventory	32.5	35.6
		2.4	1.1			All Other Current	1.8	2.2
		63.9	69.5			Total Current	60.1	63.6
		29.5	22.8			Fixed Assets (net)	30.0	27.9
		.6	1.9			Intangibles (net)	1.3	1.3
		6.0	5.8			All Other Non-Current	8.5	7.2
		100.0	100.0			Total	100.0	100.0

(DATA NOT AVAILABLE for 0-500M, 500M-2MM, 50-100MM, 100-250MM columns)

2-10MM	10-50MM	LIABILITIES	ALL	ALL
20.9	16.0	Notes Payable-Short Term	15.2	16.2
4.3	4.4	Cur. Mat.-L.T.D.	3.4	3.3
8.3	9.2	Trade Payables	9.3	11.6
.2	.2	Income Taxes Payable	.1	1.1
8.0	5.6	All Other Current	7.7	6.7
41.6	35.4	Total Current	35.7	38.9
7.8	16.4	Long-Term Debt	17.8	19.4
.7	.7	Deferred Taxes	.4	1.1
1.4	1.4	All Other Non-Current	1.5	4.2
48.5	46.2	Net Worth	44.6	36.4
100.0	100.0	Total Liabilities & Net Worth	100.0	100.0

2-10MM	10-50MM	INCOME DATA	ALL	ALL
100.0	100.0	Net Sales	100.0	100.0
19.9	11.7	Gross Profit	19.2	15.2
13.4	7.5	Operating Expenses	16.1	12.2
6.5	4.2	Operating Profit	3.2	2.9
.8	.7	All Other Expenses (net)	.5	.5
5.7	3.5	Profit Before Taxes	2.6	2.4

2-10MM	10-50MM	RATIOS	ALL	ALL
2.3	2.9	Current	3.0	2.7
1.6	1.8		1.7	1.8
1.0	1.4		1.3	1.2
1.1	.9	Quick	1.3	1.0
.5	.6		.8	.6
.4	.5		.4	.5
13 27.5	16 22.1	Sales/Receivables	12 30.8	19 19.6
19 19.4	21 17.6		21 17.0	26 13.9
31 11.9	35 10.4		30 12.0	34 10.6
24 15.2	49 7.5	Cost of Sales/Inventory	20 18.7	22 16.7
59 6.2	57 6.4		45 8.2	44 8.2
63 5.8	82 4.5		73 5.0	79 4.6
3 109.7	7 53.2	Cost of Sales/Payables	5 72.2	7 51.4
11 32.8	9 40.3		10 35.6	13 27.8
20 17.8	19 19.0		18 20.0	19 19.6
8.2	5.2	Sales/Working Capital	6.8	5.6
12.1	10.0		15.7	13.7
139.0	20.7		29.5	40.9
17.9	9.5	EBIT/Interest	11.1	9.2
5.7	5.0		(44) 5.3	(41) 3.7
1.9	1.7		2.0	1.1
		Net Profit + Depr., Dep., Amort./Cur. Mat. L/T/D	4.2	2.8
			(14) 2.4	(17) 1.9
			1.1	.7
.3	.3	Fixed/Worth	.4	.4
.5	.6		.7	.7
1.0	.9		1.1	1.4
.7	.8	Debt/Worth	.7	.9
1.4	1.3		1.1	1.9
1.8	2.9		2.2	3.8
71.1	46.0	% Profit Before Taxes/Tangible Net Worth	33.6	33.2
32.4	24.3		(44) 20.1	(39) 20.5
12.2	11.1		7.8	3.7
28.4	15.4	% Profit Before Taxes/Total Assets	14.2	16.6
11.0	11.1		6.8	6.6
4.5	3.2		1.9	.4
23.2	21.9	Sales/Net Fixed Assets	33.2	28.9
15.4	12.6		10.3	12.4
9.4	7.0		6.1	7.6
4.0	3.9	Sales/Total Assets	4.7	4.4
3.4	3.2		3.2	3.3
2.9	2.0		2.3	1.9
.7	.7	% Depr., Dep., Amort./Sales	.7	.7
1.2	(15) 1.0		(42) 1.2	(40) 1.1
2.4	1.3		2.5	1.7
		% Officers', Directors' Owners' Comp/Sales	.6	.5
			(17) 1.2	(17) 1.2
			2.7	2.4

0-500M	500M-2MM	2-10MM	10-50MM	100-250MM		ALL	ALL
7319M	47395M	439249M	1246732M	1280278M	Net Sales ($)	3054074M	2235006M
923M	3463M	112330M	404562M	758998M	Total Assets ($)	1071037M	791797M

M = $ thousand   MM = $ million
See Pages 11 through 21 for Explanation of Ratios and Data

Comparative Historical Data | **Current Data Sorted by Sales**

16	16	15	Type of Statement Unqualified						
9	10	15	Reviewed		1			2	12
5	3	3	Compiled		3			4	8
3	3	3	Tax Returns		1				1
12	13	11	Other	1	1			3	7
4/1/04-3/31/05 ALL	4/1/05-3/31/06 ALL	4/1/06-3/31/07 ALL		0-1MM	12 (4/1-9/30/06) 1-3MM	3-5MM	32 (10/1/06-3/31/07) 5-10MM	10-25MM	25MM & OVER
45	45	44	NUMBER OF STATEMENTS	1	1		5	9	28
%	%	%	ASSETS	%	%	%	%	%	%
6.5	4.6	6.0	Cash & Equivalents						5.1
23.7	22.2	18.7	Trade Receivables (net)						20.1
32.8	36.8	39.5	Inventory						43.0
2.3	2.4	2.1	All Other Current						1.1
65.3	66.1	66.4	Total Current	D					69.3
28.0	26.9	26.2	Fixed Assets (net)	A					22.6
.4	.9	1.0	Intangibles (net)	T					1.1
6.3	6.2	6.5	All Other Non-Current	A					7.1
100.0	100.0	100.0	Total						100.0
			LIABILITIES	N					
19.4	15.4	17.8	Notes Payable-Short Term	O					20.3
3.8	5.0	3.8	Cur. Mat.-L.T.D.	T					3.4
12.3	10.4	9.5	Trade Payables						8.9
.2	.2	.2	Income Taxes Payable	A					.2
7.4	6.6	7.2	All Other Current	V					5.8
43.1	37.7	38.6	Total Current	A					38.6
13.7	12.9	11.5	Long-Term Debt	I					13.7
.5	.7	.7	Deferred Taxes	L					.7
3.5	3.7	1.2	All Other Non-Current	A					.9
39.3	45.1	48.0	Net Worth	B					46.1
100.0	100.0	100.0	Total Liabilities & Net Worth	L					100.0
			INCOME DATA	E					
100.0	100.0	100.0	Net Sales						100.0
21.3	20.6	17.1	Gross Profit						12.3
15.2	15.3	11.1	Operating Expenses						8.0
6.2	5.3	6.0	Operating Profit						4.3
.3	1.0	1.4	All Other Expenses (net)						.7
5.9	4.3	4.6	Profit Before Taxes						3.6
			RATIOS						
2.5	2.7	2.6	Current						2.6
1.7	1.6	1.7							1.7
1.3	1.2	1.3							1.3
1.0	1.1	.9	Quick						.9
.7	.6	.6							.6
.4	.4	.4							.4
16 22.1	15 25.0	16 23.0	Sales/Receivables						16 22.1
26 14.2	23 16.0	20 17.8							20 17.8
35 10.5	37 9.9	33 10.9							31 11.7
21 17.5	25 14.9	31 11.9	Cost of Sales/Inventory						29 12.4
47 7.8	56 6.6	58 6.3							57 6.4
65 5.6	75 4.8	70 5.2							91 4.0
6 58.6	8 43.3	5 66.9	Cost of Sales/Payables						5 66.9
12 30.4	13 27.1	10 36.7							9 42.5
26 13.8	20 18.2	21 17.7							19 18.8
7.6	7.3	6.5	Sales/Working Capital						5.8
14.5	11.2	11.1							11.8
30.9	29.4	26.3							23.0
18.8	13.3	10.4	EBIT/Interest						10.8
(38) 8.6	(41) 6.1	(41) 4.8							4.7
2.7	2.2	2.0							1.8
7.6	5.1	11.7	Net Profit + Depr., Dep., Amort./Cur. Mat. L/T/D						7.9
(16) 3.2	(13) 2.6	(16) 2.8						(10)	3.3
1.7	1.0	1.3							.8
.3	.3	.4	Fixed/Worth						.4
.5	.5	.5							.5
1.4	.9	.9							.7
.7	.6	.7	Debt/Worth						.8
1.5	1.3	1.3							1.3
2.5	2.5	2.3							2.3
65.4	63.9	45.9	% Profit Before Taxes/Tangible Net Worth						45.4
(42) 40.7	(44) 29.1	24.1							24.1
13.1	15.2	12.1							10.3
23.4	19.4	19.0	% Profit Before Taxes/Total Assets						17.7
14.6	13.1	10.7							10.1
4.2	5.1	3.8							2.8
42.9	26.2	22.9	Sales/Net Fixed Assets						35.7
14.7	15.2	13.9							15.4
7.5	8.4	8.2							8.0
4.6	4.5	3.9	Sales/Total Assets						4.0
3.3	3.5	3.3							3.5
2.2	2.0	2.0							2.2
.6	.5	.7	% Depr., Dep., Amort./Sales						.6
(40) 1.1	(40) 1.1	(41) 1.2						(26)	1.0
2.3	2.0	2.2							1.3
1.0	.4		% Officers', Directors', Owners' Comp/Sales						
(13) 2.2	(13) 1.0								
4.3	1.5								
2194464M	2847190M	3020973M	Net Sales ($)	607M	2596M		32457M	156738M	2828575M
769950M	1038912M	1280276M	Total Assets ($)	450M	550M		10715M	57081M	1211480M

© RMA 2007

M = $ thousand   MM = $ million
See Pages 11 through 21 for Explanation of Ratios and Data

Current Data Sorted by Assets   Comparative Historical Data

	0-500M	500M-2MM	2-10MM	10-50MM	50-100MM	100-250MM	4/1/02-3/31/03 ALL	4/1/03-3/31/04 ALL
Type of Statement								
Unqualified			3	10	5		18	23
Reviewed		2	12	3			12	16
Compiled		3	3	1			7	11
Tax Returns	1	7	7	1		1	3	10
Other	2	3	14	12	3	2	24	19
		23 (4/1-9/30/06)		72 (10/1/06-3/31/07)				
NUMBER OF STATEMENTS	3	15	39	27	8	3	64	79
	%	%	%	%	%	%	%	%
ASSETS								
Cash & Equivalents		6.9	3.6	4.9			5.5	5.7
Trade Receivables (net)		28.9	21.2	19.7			18.0	19.7
Inventory		21.4	33.8	35.8			32.7	31.7
All Other Current		4.6	1.9	1.1			3.2	3.7
Total Current		61.7	60.6	61.5			59.4	60.8
Fixed Assets (net)		28.9	30.9	31.7			29.3	29.6
Intangibles (net)		.3	2.8	.8			3.7	3.1
All Other Non-Current		9.1	5.7	6.1			7.6	6.5
Total		100.0	100.0	100.0			100.0	100.0
LIABILITIES								
Notes Payable-Short Term		7.7	15.3	22.0			14.7	13.2
Cur. Mat.-L.T.D.		6.8	3.7	3.1			4.9	4.7
Trade Payables		14.1	13.4	8.0			12.2	9.8
Income Taxes Payable		.2	.2	.3			.2	.1
All Other Current		6.8	6.5	5.8			5.8	7.7
Total Current		35.6	39.2	39.2			37.9	35.6
Long-Term Debt		19.1	20.7	16.6			16.1	15.4
Deferred Taxes		.1	.6	.6			1.1	1.0
All Other Non-Current		11.1	3.7	2.1			2.5	5.0
Net Worth		34.1	35.9	41.4			42.4	43.1
Total Liabilties & Net Worth		100.0	100.0	100.0			100.0	100.0
INCOME DATA								
Net Sales		100.0	100.0	100.0			100.0	100.0
Gross Profit		24.2	24.9	18.4			18.9	20.1
Operating Expenses		23.9	18.9	13.7			16.5	17.8
Operating Profit		.3	6.0	4.7			2.4	2.3
All Other Expenses (net)		-.7	1.4	1.3			.8	.5
Profit Before Taxes		1.1	4.6	3.4			1.6	1.8
RATIOS								
Current		3.5	2.5	3.4			2.7	2.9
		1.5	1.4	1.4			1.6	1.9
		1.1	1.2	1.1			1.2	1.2
Quick		2.1	1.2	1.2			1.1	1.4
		.7	.6	.7			.6	.7
		.4	.3	.3			.4	.4
Sales/Receivables		23 15.7	23 16.1	23 16.0			17 21.0	18 19.7
		31 11.8	28 12.8	44 8.4			30 12.2	31 11.8
		61 6.0	47 7.7	50 7.3			50 7.3	48 7.6
Cost of Sales/Inventory		12 30.8	35 10.5	47 7.8			33 11.0	36 10.0
		33 10.9	69 5.3	95 3.8			68 5.4	87 4.2
		51 7.1	109 3.4	117 3.1			115 3.2	131 2.8
Cost of Sales/Payables		10 35.4	13 28.8	8 43.7			12 29.6	10 37.8
		21 17.4	21 17.8	17 22.0			18 19.9	17 20.9
		28 13.2	40 9.1	26 14.2			36 10.2	23 16.1
Sales/Working Capital		6.4	5.9	4.4			4.9	4.5
		11.8	13.9	8.8			11.7	9.7
		68.7	37.1	38.5			25.2	24.8
EBIT/Interest		10.3	6.4	11.7			4.5	6.0
		(14) 2.3	(36) 2.3	3.1			(61) 1.9	(77) 2.7
		-1.4	.3	1.0			1.1	.7
Net Profit + Depr., Dep., Amort./Cur. Mat. L/T/D				16.2			3.5	6.6
			(11) 4.6				(19) 1.9	(30) 1.8
				2.1			.9	.8
Fixed/Worth		.2	.4	.4			.4	.4
		.6	.7	.9			.7	.7
		5.2	2.3	1.3			1.4	1.2
Debt/Worth		.4	.9	.6			.7	.7
		3.4	2.1	1.5			1.4	1.5
		8.7	4.6	3.6			3.6	3.1
% Profit Before Taxes/Tangible Net Worth		49.9	48.3	32.3			14.2	20.9
		(13) 8.7	(34) 20.5	(26) 14.9			(59) 7.5	(73) 7.9
		-75.9	4.0	3.6			1.0	-.9
% Profit Before Taxes/Total Assets		18.4	18.1	9.9			5.7	7.9
		2.2	4.0	7.0			2.5	3.6
		-5.4	-1.7	.1			.0	-.5
Sales/Net Fixed Assets		89.2	24.9	12.4			15.5	16.2
		11.8	7.0	6.5			7.0	7.2
		3.5	3.8	4.0			3.9	3.8
Sales/Total Assets		3.7	2.7	2.3			2.6	2.5
		2.0	2.0	1.8			1.8	1.8
		1.7	1.6	1.2			1.4	1.3
% Depr., Dep., Amort./Sales		1.0	1.2	1.0			1.3	1.1
		(14) 2.1	(34) 2.1	(26) 1.9			(52) 2.6	(65) 2.6
		5.9	4.0	2.9			4.2	3.5
% Officers', Directors' Owners' Comp/Sales			1.3				1.3	1.5
			(17) 2.4				(11) 3.2	(14) 2.7
			3.2				5.1	7.2
Net Sales ($)	6730M	46050M	457704M	1025084M	864844M	887592M	2252865M	3584615M
Total Assets ($)	983M	17594M	187995M	538188M	518546M	418399M	1385344M	1937453M

M = $ thousand   MM = $ million
See Pages 11 through 21 for Explanation of Ratios and Data

Comparative Historical Data

Current Data Sorted by Sales

Type of Statement	04-05 ALL	05-06 ALL	06-07 ALL	0-1MM	1-3MM	3-5MM	5-10MM	10-25MM	25MM & OVER
Unqualified	16	20	18		1	5	6	5	13
Reviewed	16	19	17		2	1	1	3	2
Compiled	17	7	8	1	4	4	1	2	2
Tax Returns	7	11	16	1	4	2	7	11	12
Other	23	29	36						
Period	4/1/04-3/31/05	4/1/05-3/31/06	4/1/06-3/31/07	\[23 (4/1-9/30/06)\]			\[72 (10/1/06-3/31/07)\]		
NUMBER OF STATEMENTS	79	86	95	2	8	14	16	24	31

ASSETS	04-05 ALL	05-06 ALL	06-07 ALL	0-1MM	1-3MM	3-5MM	5-10MM	10-25MM	25MM & OVER
	%	%	%	%	%	%	%	%	%
Cash & Equivalents	6.4	5.6	5.0			5.4	4.4	4.9	4.6
Trade Receivables (net)	20.9	22.2	21.6			33.1	22.0	21.7	18.6
Inventory	33.1	31.2	31.0			22.2	31.7	34.3	35.1
All Other Current	2.9	3.5	2.1			1.4	2.6	1.1	1.3
Total Current	63.3	62.4	59.6			62.1	60.7	62.0	59.6
Fixed Assets (net)	28.3	29.3	30.4			33.1	30.3	27.4	28.4
Intangibles (net)	3.5	1.6	3.0			1.0	4.7	1.2	5.1
All Other Non-Current	4.9	6.7	7.0			3.8	4.3	9.4	7.0
Total	100.0	100.0	100.0			100.0	100.0	100.0	100.0

LIABILITIES	04-05 ALL	05-06 ALL	06-07 ALL	0-1MM	1-3MM	3-5MM	5-10MM	10-25MM	25MM & OVER
Notes Payable-Short Term	14.8	15.3	15.2			8.7	10.6	19.0	18.5
Cur. Mat.-L.T.D.	4.2	4.7	3.9			8.1	4.8	2.6	3.1
Trade Payables	14.7	10.7	11.0			14.6	9.9	12.3	8.1
Income Taxes Payable	.1	.2	.2			.1	.1	.1	.3
All Other Current	7.3	6.5	6.5			10.1	6.6	6.7	5.6
Total Current	41.1	37.4	36.7			41.7	32.2	40.8	35.6
Long-Term Debt	15.2	18.9	19.7			22.8	20.4	17.4	17.0
Deferred Taxes	.6	.6	.6			.4	.8	.3	1.0
All Other Non-Current	6.4	5.8	4.6			4.9	8.0	2.6	3.8
Net Worth	36.7	37.3	38.4			30.3	38.6	38.9	42.6
Total Liabilities & Net Worth	100.0	100.0	100.0			100.0	100.0	100.0	100.0

INCOME DATA	04-05 ALL	05-06 ALL	06-07 ALL	0-1MM	1-3MM	3-5MM	5-10MM	10-25MM	25MM & OVER
Net Sales	100.0	100.0	100.0			100.0	100.0	100.0	100.0
Gross Profit	21.9	21.7	22.3			28.2	22.9	22.7	16.7
Operating Expenses	18.7	18.0	17.5			22.3	16.6	17.9	11.8
Operating Profit	3.2	3.7	4.8			5.9	6.3	4.8	4.9
All Other Expenses (net)	1.0	.7	1.0			1.3	.7	1.2	1.2
Profit Before Taxes	2.2	3.0	3.7			4.6	5.6	3.6	3.7

RATIOS	04-05 ALL	05-06 ALL	06-07 ALL	0-1MM	1-3MM	3-5MM	5-10MM	10-25MM	25MM & OVER
Current	3.1	3.0	2.9			2.3	4.4	2.9	3.3
	1.6	1.8	1.5			1.4	1.5	1.5	1.5
	1.1	1.2	1.2			1.0	1.3	1.1	1.2
Quick	1.4	1.5	1.4			1.2	1.7	1.4	1.4
	.7	.8	.7			.7	.6	.7	.6
	.3	.4	.4			.5	.4	.4	.3
Sales/Receivables	24 · 15.5	21 · 17.5	23 · 16.2			24 · 14.9	24 · 15.5	20 · 17.9	17 · 21.2
	37 · 10.0	36 · 10.0	32 · 11.3			34 · 10.9	35 · 10.3	40 · 9.2	32 · 11.3
	47 · 7.8	54 · 6.7	48 · 7.6			62 · 5.9	49 · 7.4	49 · 7.5	46 · 7.9
Cost of Sales/Inventory	33 · 10.9	36 · 10.1	34 · 10.6			1 · 276.7	26 · 13.9	44 · 8.4	42 · 8.7
	79 · 4.6	55 · 6.6	63 · 5.8			40 · 9.2	96 · 3.8	74 · 5.0	71 · 5.1
	127 · 2.9	118 · 3.1	106 · 3.4			80 · 4.6	120 · 3.0	114 · 3.2	105 · 3.5
Cost of Sales/Payables	13 · 28.0	11 · 32.8	10 · 36.9			10 · 35.6	10 · 37.9	9 · 42.7	9 · 41.8
	22 · 16.4	18 · 20.1	18 · 20.0			22 · 16.9	18 · 20.6	17 · 21.1	17 · 22.0
	36 · 10.1	29 · 12.6	32 · 11.3			71 · 5.2	36 · 10.2	37 · 10.0	22 · 16.9
Sales/Working Capital	4.4	4.5	5.9			6.3	4.4	4.5	4.7
	8.4	8.7	11.4			17.6	9.7	11.2	10.5
	50.2	27.3	37.1			NM	17.1	115.2	32.1
EBIT/Interest	9.1	10.9	6.9			8.5	6.6	7.0	6.3
	(75) 4.1	(82) 4.0	(90) 3.1			(13) 1.6	(14) 3.1	(23) 2.3	4.2
	1.4	.9	.9			-.8	-.1	1.0	2.0
Net Profit + Depr., Dep., Amort./Cur. Mat. L/T/D	4.9	5.1	6.1						6.9
	(26) 1.7	(28) 2.5	(28) 3.1						(14) 3.2
	.8	.6	1.5						2.0
Fixed/Worth	.4	.3	.4			.3	.4	.3	.5
	.7	.7	.8			1.0	.7	.7	.8
	1.7	1.6	2.1			2.2	2.3	1.9	1.5
Debt/Worth	.9	.6	.7			1.4	.7	.8	.7
	1.9	1.3	2.0			2.3	1.7	2.1	1.4
	4.4	4.6	5.2			4.2	6.2	4.6	3.6
% Profit Before Taxes/Tangible Net Worth	40.1	41.7	37.5			108.7	53.9	28.1	32.3
	(68) 12.8	(78) 14.1	(84) 14.7			(12) 23.3	(14) 25.3	(23) 14.1	(27) 12.3
	4.4	3.4	1.2			-23.0	-5.8	1.4	7.4
% Profit Before Taxes/Total Assets	14.2	14.0	14.1			34.7	27.0	10.0	12.0
	5.3	6.1	6.1			5.8	8.9	4.3	7.0
	1.3	.5	.1			-9.4	-1.1	.2	2.9
Sales/Net Fixed Assets	20.3	18.8	20.5			58.2	12.2	25.9	13.5
	7.8	7.9	6.7			5.1	6.1	7.9	7.5
	4.5	4.1	3.8			3.3	4.1	3.8	4.7
Sales/Total Assets	2.8	3.2	2.7			4.7	2.7	2.7	2.6
	1.9	2.0	1.9			2.3	1.8	2.0	2.1
	1.5	1.3	1.5			1.5	1.3	1.6	1.4
% Depr., Dep., Amort./Sales	1.4	1.0	1.2			.2	1.2	1.5	1.0
	(69) 2.2	(73) 1.9	(87) 2.0			(11) 2.9	(13) 3.0	2.0	(30) 1.8
	3.7	3.7	3.6			4.7	3.8	3.2	2.8
% Officers', Directors' Owners' Comp/Sales	1.1	.6	1.4						1.0
	(21) 3.2	(18) 2.4	(28) 2.5					(13)	1.9
	4.9	4.3	3.8						2.8
Net Sales ($)	3833025M	3142989M	3288004M	1336M	15793M	53711M	112175M	400255M	2704734M
Total Assets ($)	1939813M	1793388M	1681705M	854M	10839M	25736M	62302M	229691M	1352283M

M = $ thousand   MM = $ million
See Pages 11 through 21 for Explanation of Ratios and Data

	Current Data Sorted by Assets						Comparative Historical Data	
Type of Statement								
Unqualified		2		5	1		11	9
Reviewed		1	18	2			23	19
Compiled	1	7	17	1			18	23
Tax Returns	2	5	5	1			5	8
Other	3	9	17	4	1		17	32
		17 (4/1-9/30/06)		85 (10/1/06-3/31/07)			4/1/02-3/31/03 ALL	4/1/03-3/31/04 ALL
	0-500M	500M-2MM	2-10MM	10-50MM	50-100MM	100-250MM		
NUMBER OF STATEMENTS	6	24	57	13	2		74	91
ASSETS	%	%	%	%	%	%	%	%
Cash & Equivalents		14.1	10.6	6.0		DATA NOT AVAILABLE	6.7	8.9
Trade Receivables (net)		29.1	21.7	26.8			27.0	28.3
Inventory		21.1	21.2	31.2			19.7	22.6
All Other Current		1.7	2.3	2.4			2.9	3.1
Total Current		66.0	55.9	66.4			56.3	62.9
Fixed Assets (net)		30.5	33.1	26.1			32.7	29.4
Intangibles (net)		1.8	2.8	.4			2.5	1.7
All Other Non-Current		1.7	8.3	7.1			8.5	6.1
Total		100.0	100.0	100.0			100.0	100.0
LIABILITIES								
Notes Payable-Short Term		14.4	9.9	13.2			13.8	9.8
Cur. Mat.-L.T.D.		3.1	4.8	5.6			4.5	3.9
Trade Payables		20.4	6.6	5.7			9.0	11.1
Income Taxes Payable		.1	.3	.1			.2	.3
All Other Current		9.1	9.7	10.4			11.1	10.8
Total Current		47.1	31.3	35.0			38.6	35.9
Long-Term Debt		14.6	17.8	16.8			22.7	16.4
Deferred Taxes		.1	.4	.6			.4	.4
All Other Non-Current		7.2	4.3	4.4			2.8	4.5
Net Worth		30.9	46.2	43.1			35.5	42.7
Total Liabilties & Net Worth		100.0	100.0	100.0			100.0	100.0
INCOME DATA								
Net Sales		100.0	100.0	100.0			100.0	100.0
Gross Profit		33.2	30.4	22.2			30.4	26.7
Operating Expenses		30.4	25.0	16.4			25.9	22.1
Operating Profit		2.7	5.4	5.8			4.5	4.5
All Other Expenses (net)		.3	.5	.8			.7	.6
Profit Before Taxes		2.4	5.0	5.0			3.8	4.0
RATIOS								
Current		3.5	4.0	4.2			2.5	3.3
		1.9	1.7	1.7			1.6	1.8
		1.2	1.3	1.4			1.1	1.3
Quick		1.9	2.3	2.1			1.6	1.8
		1.2	1.1	1.0			1.0	1.0
		.5	.6	.5			.6	.7
Sales/Receivables		20 18.3	17 21.8	22 16.7			23 16.1	24 15.1
		25 14.4	26 14.0	30 12.1			34 10.8	36 10.1
		44 8.2	36 10.2	51 7.1			45 8.1	46 8.0
Cost of Sales/Inventory		15 25.1	25 14.8	30 12.2			23 15.7	26 14.2
		42 8.7	35 10.6	52 7.1			33 11.0	36 10.2
		67 5.4	52 7.0	66 5.5			49 7.5	52 7.0
Cost of Sales/Payables		8 46.5	4 84.6	5 77.4			6 56.5	6 56.7
		22 16.9	9 42.4	8 43.6			15 24.7	15 24.5
		46 7.9	14 26.1	16 22.9			23 16.1	25 14.6
Sales/Working Capital		7.0	5.8	5.8			7.9	6.4
		10.6	11.0	8.3			16.0	11.4
		40.8	40.2	21.6			124.7	29.3
EBIT/Interest		16.9	12.1	10.5			9.1	12.2
		(22) 3.7	(54) 4.9	(11) 3.3			(69) 4.1	(81) 4.1
		.6	1.7	1.3			1.5	1.6
Net Profit + Depr., Dep., Amort./Cur. Mat. L/T/D			4.7				5.2	3.6
			(10) 2.5				(19) 3.4	(17) 2.0
			2.0				1.5	-.7
Fixed/Worth		.3	.4	.3			.5	.4
		.6	.7	.6			.8	.8
		5.6	1.6	1.1			2.3	1.3
Debt/Worth		.5	.5	.5			.7	.6
		1.4	1.3	1.0			1.9	1.4
		11.7	3.5	2.9			4.2	3.3
% Profit Before Taxes/Tangible Net Worth		73.9	52.0	43.8			53.7	55.4
		(19) 22.3	(53) 27.5	(12) 25.7			(65) 18.6	(87) 24.1
		7.9	11.2	2.2			6.1	5.5
% Profit Before Taxes/Total Assets		20.4	22.6	22.8			15.9	20.6
		5.1	9.6	6.7			6.7	7.3
		-.1	2.7	1.0			1.7	1.5
Sales/Net Fixed Assets		28.5	16.8	29.9			16.2	19.1
		9.9	10.4	10.8			9.1	11.0
		5.5	5.4	7.8			5.5	5.9
Sales/Total Assets		4.7	3.9	3.2			3.7	3.7
		3.0	2.5	2.5			2.6	2.7
		2.3	2.0	2.3			2.0	2.1
% Depr., Dep., Amort./Sales		1.3	1.0	.9			1.5	1.2
		(22) 2.4	(53) 2.0	(11) 1.6			(66) 2.1	(84) 1.9
		5.1	3.6	2.5			3.2	2.8
% Officers', Directors' Owners' Comp/Sales		1.4	1.3				1.7	1.7
		(10) 2.9	(18) 2.9				(23) 4.5	(34) 3.5
		6.3	5.7				7.4	6.4
Net Sales ($)	11881M	92991M	769697M	647218M	281206M		1967760M	1641506M
Total Assets ($)	2350M	28174M	257778M	222981M	129409M		974638M	573765M

M = $ thousand MM = $ million

See Pages 11 through 21 for Explanation of Ratios and Data

Comparative Historical Data   **Current Data Sorted by Sales**

			Type of Statement	0-1MM	1-3MM	3-5MM	5-10MM	10-25MM	25MM & OVER
17	11	8	Unqualified			2			6
18	21	21	Reviewed		1	2	16		2
15	21	26	Compiled	4	5	7	8		2
16	8	13	Tax Returns	4	2	3	3		1
27	23	34	Other	2	7	4	8	7	6
4/1/04-3/31/05 ALL	4/1/05-3/31/06 ALL	4/1/06-3/31/07 ALL			17 (4/1-9/30/06)		85 (10/1/06-3/31/07)		
93	84	102	**NUMBER OF STATEMENTS**	2	15	12	22	34	17
%	%	%	**ASSETS**	%	%	%	%	%	%
5.7	7.6	10.6	Cash & Equivalents		10.7	11.4	11.5	11.8	4.6
30.5	28.2	24.3	Trade Receivables (net)		25.0	24.7	19.6	24.8	28.9
22.3	22.8	23.0	Inventory		21.7	19.1	23.8	20.8	31.4
2.9	2.3	2.1	All Other Current		.9	1.1	3.0	2.4	2.3
61.5	61.0	60.0	Total Current		58.3	56.3	58.0	59.9	67.2
30.1	29.1	30.3	Fixed Assets (net)		32.1	36.4	31.1	30.3	21.7
3.7	4.8	3.5	Intangibles (net)		4.9	6.2	1.2	2.8	4.8
4.7	5.2	6.3	All Other Non-Current		4.7	1.1	9.7	7.0	6.3
100.0	100.0	100.0	Total		100.0	100.0	100.0	100.0	100.0
			LIABILITIES						
9.9	10.9	12.0	Notes Payable-Short Term		17.0	8.6	13.1	8.1	15.3
4.8	3.8	4.2	Cur. Mat.-L.T.D.		7.3	2.6	4.5	3.4	4.6
13.3	12.6	10.0	Trade Payables		12.3	22.5	6.7	7.6	8.4
.3	.1	.2	Income Taxes Payable		.0	.0	.1	.4	.2
8.5	11.3	9.5	All Other Current		7.4	6.7	9.5	10.7	11.1
36.7	38.8	36.0	Total Current		44.0	40.4	33.9	30.2	39.5
17.6	17.0	17.0	Long-Term Debt		19.9	19.9	20.9	12.6	17.7
.5	.5	.3	Deferred Taxes		.0	.3	.1	.5	.7
6.2	7.3	4.8	All Other Non-Current		1.2	5.1	9.3	3.8	4.8
38.9	36.4	41.8	Net Worth		34.9	34.3	35.7	52.9	37.4
100.0	100.0	100.0	Total Liabilties & Net Worth		100.0	100.0	100.0	100.0	100.0
			INCOME DATA						
100.0	100.0	100.0	Net Sales		100.0	100.0	100.0	100.0	100.0
26.2	26.8	30.3	Gross Profit		38.3	32.9	31.3	29.0	21.9
21.7	20.8	25.5	Operating Expenses		36.7	26.8	24.3	24.0	18.2
4.5	6.1	4.8	Operating Profit		1.6	6.0	6.9	4.9	3.8
.5	.6	.5	All Other Expenses (net)		.8	1.3	.8	-.3	1.0
4.0	5.5	4.3	Profit Before Taxes		.8	4.7	6.1	5.3	2.7
			RATIOS						
3.6	2.7	3.6	Current		5.9	4.5	3.1	4.9	3.1
2.0	1.6	1.7			1.4	2.7	1.9	1.9	1.5
1.1	1.1	1.2			.9	1.2	1.1	1.3	1.3
2.2	1.6	2.1	Quick		3.0	2.9	1.9	3.4	1.7
1.1	.9	1.1			.9	1.6	1.0	1.3	.7
.6	.5	.6			.4	.7	.5	.6	.5
27 13.6	22 16.9	19 19.7	Sales/Receivables		23 16.0	16 22.8	16 23.0	17 21.6	19 18.9
38 9.5	33 11.1	27 13.4			37 10.0	25 14.4	23 15.7	26 14.1	30 12.2
49 7.4	48 7.7	39 9.3			43 8.5	43 8.4	34 10.8	37 9.9	42 8.6
24 15.1	25 14.7	25 14.8	Cost of Sales/Inventory		23 15.9	26 14.3	26 14.3	19 19.2	30 12.2
34 10.7	35 10.4	38 9.6			53 6.9	38 9.7	35 10.3	32 11.4	47 7.7
53 6.9	51 7.2	58 6.3			78 4.7	58 6.3	56 6.6	54 6.8	57 6.4
8 43.7	7 50.3	5 78.7	Cost of Sales/Payables		9 40.7	2 180.0	4 90.3	5 72.5	5 72.9
15 24.1	13 27.7	9 38.9			21 17.1	3 112.5	11 34.3	8 43.3	9 41.4
26 14.2	30 12.2	20 18.3			47 7.8	24 15.2	14 25.6	14 26.8	18 20.8
6.3	7.0	6.1	Sales/Working Capital		6.5	6.1	6.4	5.8	6.5
11.5	13.0	10.6			11.7	8.5	11.3	11.4	13.3
54.5	63.1	39.7			-77.8	40.8	NM	30.6	35.7
15.6	15.7	11.9	EBIT/Interest		11.2	16.6	18.1	16.2	5.5
(85) 5.3	(79) 5.6	(95) 4.3		(14)	1.6	6.2	4.6	(31) 7.1	(15) 1.8
1.6	2.5	1.4			-3.1	1.7	1.7	3.9	.3
4.7	5.3	3.5	Net Profit + Depr., Dep., Amort./Cur. Mat. L/T/D						
(23) 2.1	(17) 3.1	(14) 2.3							
1.7	.9	1.8							
.4	.3	.4	Fixed/Worth		.3	.6	.4	.4	.3
.7	.7	.7			.8	.9	.6	.7	.7
2.9	2.4	1.5			-13.7	6.8	6.7	1.1	1.1
.5	.7	.5	Debt/Worth		.5	.5	.5	.5	.9
1.5	1.6	1.4			1.7	1.4	1.2	.9	2.0
7.2	7.8	3.6			-30.5	13.2	10.6	1.9	4.2
60.4	70.3	52.8	% Profit Before Taxes/Tangible Net Worth		49.9	84.4	66.5	51.4	38.8
(81) 28.7	(71) 35.9	(90) 27.4		(11)	21.7	(10) 41.9	(19) 29.1	(33) 30.6	(15) 14.0
13.9	14.1	9.8			-2.6	4.6	12.4	11.4	1.4
23.5	25.7	22.6	% Profit Before Taxes/Total Assets		19.7	40.8	27.6	22.9	10.0
9.8	12.4	8.3			3.7	7.2	11.5	12.2	2.9
1.9	3.9	2.1			-9.2	2.0	2.5	5.5	-1.0
21.3	23.4	25.1	Sales/Net Fixed Assets		40.1	10.1	27.6	17.8	41.3
9.0	10.6	11.4			11.3	7.1	7.0	12.6	16.5
6.2	6.7	5.6			2.7	5.2	5.3	5.9	10.3
3.5	3.6	3.9	Sales/Total Assets		3.7	3.6	3.8	4.0	4.6
2.5	2.9	2.8			2.7	2.8	2.4	2.8	3.2
2.2	2.3	2.1			1.5	2.0	2.1	2.3	2.4
1.1	.9	1.1	% Depr., Dep., Amort./Sales		1.4	1.7	1.1	1.0	.8
(86) 2.1	(76) 1.6	(91) 2.0		(11)	2.7	3.8	(20) 2.5	(33) 2.0	(14) 1.0
3.2	2.7	3.5			6.4	5.6	3.6	2.9	1.6
1.6	1.6	1.5	% Officers', Directors' Owners' Comp/Sales						
(32) 3.7	(29) 2.9	(33) 2.8							
6.1	5.1	5.9							
2199971M	1669779M	1802993M	Net Sales ($)	1834M	31598M	46505M	164128M	543649M	1015279M
1009949M	692949M	640692M	Total Assets ($)	1035M	15267M	16880M	65321M	187768M	354421M

Current Data Sorted by Assets

						Comparative Historical Data

		4	7	9	3	Type of Statement		
	9	28	7			Unqualified	29	36
	17	13	2			Reviewed	73	71
8	12	6				Compiled	47	59
10	20	28	20	4	1	Tax Returns	14	25
6						Other	56	57
	39 (4/1-9/30/06)		175 (10/1/06-3/31/07)				4/1/02-3/31/03	4/1/03-3/31/04
0-500M	500M-2MM	2-10MM	10-50MM	50-100MM	100-250MM		ALL	ALL
24	58	79	36	13	4	NUMBER OF STATEMENTS	219	248
%	%	%	%	%	%	ASSETS	%	%
8.8	5.7	6.1	5.7	5.0		Cash & Equivalents	7.5	7.3
25.3	35.2	29.1	20.7	18.6		Trade Receivables (net)	30.0	30.6
29.7	26.1	25.6	26.2	26.1		Inventory	23.2	22.8
2.3	1.1	3.2	3.7	3.5		All Other Current	3.1	3.5
66.1	68.1	63.9	56.2	53.2		Total Current	63.8	64.1
22.1	26.2	30.3	29.6	35.4		Fixed Assets (net)	27.4	28.8
3.7	1.1	2.5	7.3	9.3		Intangibles (net)	2.4	2.5
8.2	4.5	3.4	6.9	2.1		All Other Non-Current	6.4	4.5
100.0	100.0	100.0	100.0	100.0		Total	100.0	100.0
						LIABILITIES		
9.7	16.6	13.1	13.6	9.0		Notes Payable-Short Term	12.3	15.3
4.3	4.8	3.7	2.0	2.4		Cur. Mat.-L.T.D.	4.4	4.0
15.0	17.9	11.8	8.8	7.6		Trade Payables	13.6	14.3
.4	.0	.5	.1	.1		Income Taxes Payable	.4	.3
10.2	9.6	10.4	9.3	13.0		All Other Current	9.8	8.8
39.5	48.9	39.6	33.9	32.0		Total Current	40.5	42.6
16.3	20.8	18.6	17.7	11.4		Long-Term Debt	18.1	17.0
.0	.2	.5	.4	1.6		Deferred Taxes	.3	.3
32.7	9.7	5.3	6.3	8.3		All Other Non-Current	5.2	5.9
11.5	20.4	35.9	41.6	46.7		Net Worth	36.0	34.3
100.0	100.0	100.0	100.0	100.0		Total Liabilties & Net Worth	100.0	100.0
						INCOME DATA		
100.0	100.0	100.0	100.0	100.0		Net Sales	100.0	100.0
31.2	30.7	25.2	24.9	29.6		Gross Profit	29.3	27.2
27.5	28.1	19.7	20.7	24.1		Operating Expenses	25.6	24.6
3.7	2.6	5.6	4.2	5.5		Operating Profit	3.8	2.5
1.1	1.2	1.7	1.6	1.2		All Other Expenses (net)	.9	.8
2.6	1.4	3.9	2.5	4.3		Profit Before Taxes	2.9	1.7
						RATIOS		
3.2	2.3	2.6	2.8	2.2			2.7	2.6
1.5	1.5	1.5	1.6	1.8		Current	1.6	1.7
1.0	.9	1.2	1.3	1.1			1.1	1.1
1.8	1.5	1.7	1.3	1.0			1.6	1.5
.8	.9	.9	.9	.7		Quick	.9	.9
.1	.5	.5	.5	.5			.5	.5

1	259.6	25	14.6	26	14.1	21	17.0	16	22.4			Sales/Receivables	23	16.0	24	15.3
16	22.8	38	9.7	37	9.9	32	11.4	25	14.8				35	10.3	38	9.7
49	7.4	53	6.9	57	6.4	50	7.3	45	8.2				53	6.9	53	6.8
7	49.3	20	18.7	22	16.7	33	11.2	40	9.2			Cost of Sales/Inventory	17	21.0	15	24.3
27	13.7	40	9.2	46	8.0	65	5.6	60	6.1				39	9.4	41	9.0
50	7.3	62	5.9	74	4.9	81	4.5	79	4.6				68	5.4	66	5.5
4	102.6	13	27.2	9	39.5	9	40.0	9	40.8			Cost of Sales/Payables	12	31.6	11	32.4
13	27.5	22	16.3	17	21.2	13	29.2	17	20.9				20	18.0	19	18.8
27	13.4	44	8.4	32	11.5	28	12.8	25	14.3				36	10.2	34	10.9

7.8		8.5		5.9		5.6		7.5		
15.7		14.1		10.3		12.6		11.3		Sales/Working Capital
UND		-56.9		40.1		21.6		49.8		

	9.4		6.9		10.8		5.8		6.1		
(19)	2.6	(56)	3.8	(75)	3.3	(31)	2.7	(12)	3.0		EBIT/Interest
	-.6		1.2		1.0		.8		1.0		

			3.4		7.0			
		(10)	2.5	(19)	2.9			Net Profit + Depr., Dep., Amort./Cur. Mat. L/T/D
			.9		1.3			

.2	.3	.4	.5	.5		Fixed/Worth	
.5	1.2	.9	.9	.9			
17.3	NM	2.6	3.4	1.8			

.6	1.0	1.0	.5	.8		Debt/Worth	.7	.7
2.6	2.8	2.0	1.6	1.1			1.8	2.0
257.3	-25.9	6.2	7.3	2.8			5.4	5.3

	136.4		54.0		53.1		34.0		25.8			44.9	31.4
(19)	29.1	(43)	18.2	(69)	19.7	(32)	18.4	(12)	16.5	% Profit Before Taxes/Tangible Net Worth	(191)	17.3	(218) 14.3
	-3.8		7.7		4.2		2.6		.7			6.5	.0

20.7	12.0	17.4	14.8	11.3		14.4	12.2
14.5	6.0	6.0	6.5	7.1	% Profit Before Taxes/Total Assets	6.2	4.4
-5.5	.7	.3	.9	.6		1.6	-2.3

86.6	32.8	19.6	21.2	16.1		20.5	20.8
30.8	17.4	10.8	9.5	8.0	Sales/Net Fixed Assets	11.3	11.1
7.3	7.1	4.7	4.5	3.4		6.6	6.1

8.1	4.3	3.2	2.8	3.2		3.6	3.4
3.9	3.4	2.5	2.1	2.3	Sales/Total Assets	2.6	2.6
2.7	2.3	1.9	1.7	1.5		2.0	1.9

	.4		.9		.9		1.1	1.7		1.0	1.1
(16)	1.3	(51)	1.7	(77)	1.7	(35)	1.9	2.1	% Depr., Dep., Amort./Sales	(207) 1.8	(224) 1.9
	3.0		3.5		2.8		3.0	3.0		3.0	3.3

			2.1		1.2			2.0	1.7
		(32)	4.2	(30)	2.1		% Officers', Directors' Owners' Comp/Sales	(94) 4.7	(101) 4.0
			6.6		5.9			8.5	6.3

32383M	226502M	953294M	1691549M	2315790M	1279065M	Net Sales ($)	6887912M	5566939M
6818M	64838M	380190M	721994M	960198M	626327M	Total Assets ($)	2745665M	2572804M

M = $ thousand   MM = $ million
See Pages 11 through 21 for Explanation of Ratios and Data

Comparative Historical Data — Current Data Sorted by Sales

			Type of Statement	0-1MM	1-3MM	3-5MM	5-10MM	10-25MM	25MM & OVER
29	21	23	Unqualified				2	3	18
63	42	44	Reviewed		5	6	9	19	5
49	29	40	Compiled	3	14	4	11	6	2
17	25	28	Tax Returns	2	11	8	3	3	1
47	75	79	Other	4	11	8	16	21	19
4/1/04-3/31/05 ALL	4/1/05-3/31/06 ALL	4/1/06-3/31/07 ALL			39 (4/1-9/30/06)		175 (10/1/06-3/31/07)		
205	192	214	NUMBER OF STATEMENTS	9	41	26	41	52	45
%	%	%	**ASSETS**	%	%	%	%	%	%
6.5	7.0	6.2	Cash & Equivalents		7.6	7.7	6.6	4.6	5.9
31.8	31.6	28.1	Trade Receivables (net)		29.6	40.6	27.6	28.7	21.8
25.1	24.8	26.3	Inventory		24.7	24.5	30.9	23.6	28.2
2.8	2.3	2.7	All Other Current		2.2	.7	2.3	3.0	4.6
66.2	65.8	63.3	Total Current		64.1	73.5	67.4	60.0	60.5
27.7	27.1	28.5	Fixed Assets (net)		24.2	22.4	27.9	33.4	27.3
1.8	2.5	3.5	Intangibles (net)		4.1	.4	1.4	3.0	7.6
4.3	4.6	4.7	All Other Non-Current		7.6	3.7	3.4	3.6	4.6
100.0	100.0	100.0	Total		100.0	100.0	100.0	100.0	100.0
			LIABILITIES						
16.0	12.1	13.3	Notes Payable-Short Term		11.1	18.4	13.9	11.6	11.4
4.0	4.6	3.7	Cur. Mat.-L.T.D.		6.0	4.7	3.6	3.2	2.2
14.4	14.0	13.0	Trade Payables		16.4	21.4	10.3	13.2	9.1
.3	.2	.3	Income Taxes Payable		.7	.0	.0	.2	.5
10.0	10.0	10.3	All Other Current		12.2	6.4	8.1	12.4	11.6
44.6	40.9	40.5	Total Current		46.4	50.8	36.0	40.5	34.9
16.2	18.6	18.2	Long-Term Debt		17.8	24.7	17.8	19.6	12.2
.5	.4	.5	Deferred Taxes		.1	.4	.3	.6	.9
5.8	8.8	9.9	All Other Non-Current		22.4	6.8	11.5	3.2	6.6
32.9	31.2	30.9	Net Worth		13.3	17.3	34.5	36.1	45.4
100.0	100.0	100.0	Total Liabilities & Net Worth		100.0	100.0	100.0	100.0	100.0
			INCOME DATA						
100.0	100.0	100.0	Net Sales		100.0	100.0	100.0	100.0	100.0
27.1	29.4	27.6	Gross Profit		31.6	29.2	27.9	21.8	27.0
23.4	24.8	23.2	Operating Expenses		27.7	26.8	23.6	17.7	20.9
3.7	4.6	4.4	Operating Profit		3.9	2.4	4.3	4.1	6.1
.6	.9	1.4	All Other Expenses (net)		1.5	1.0	1.1	1.6	1.0
3.1	3.7	2.9	Profit Before Taxes		2.4	1.4	3.3	2.5	5.0
			RATIOS						
2.8	2.6	2.5			2.3	2.5	3.6	2.3	2.6
1.7	1.8	1.6	Current		1.4	1.9	2.0	1.5	1.8
1.1	1.3	1.1			.9	1.0	1.2	1.0	1.3
1.5	1.6	1.4			1.3	1.7	1.9	1.3	1.2
.9	1.0	.9	Quick		.8	1.0	.9	.9	.8
.6	.6	.5			.4	.7	.4	.5	.6
25 14.4	**23** 15.7	**22** 16.9			**18** 20.8	**33** 11.1	**18** 20.0	**23** 16.0	**20** 18.6
38 9.6	**36** 10.2	**35** 10.3	Sales/Receivables		**40** 9.1	**37** 9.8	**31** 11.7	**38** 9.6	**29** 12.7
57 6.4	**55** 6.7	**52** 7.0			**54** 6.8	**60** 6.0	**45** 8.2	**55** 6.6	**43** 8.5
22 16.6	**23** 16.2	**22** 16.7			**15** 25.1	**15** 24.4	**27** 13.6	**21** 17.5	**39** 9.4
44 8.3	**40** 9.2	**46** 8.0	Cost of Sales/Inventory		**40** 9.1	**39** 9.4	**46** 9.1	**40** 9.1	**61** 6.0
68 5.4	**67** 5.5	**73** 5.0			**78** 4.7	**61** 6.0	**75** 4.9	**71** 5.2	**77** 4.7
10 35.1	**9** 38.7	**9** 38.9			**15** 24.3	**16** 22.5	**7** 49.3	**10** 37.1	**9** 39.8
20 18.4	**18** 20.0	**18** 20.7	Cost of Sales/Payables		**26** 14.3	**26** 14.0	**16** 23.4	**18** 19.9	**16** 23.4
35 10.5	**32** 11.3	**32** 11.5			**44** 8.3	**48** 7.5	**22** 16.7	**32** 11.5	**23** 16.0
5.8	6.4	6.4			8.8	6.9	6.1	6.4	6.3
11.3	11.8	11.6	Sales/Working Capital		25.6	12.0	8.8	11.8	12.6
48.4	26.1	58.5			-50.4	NM	23.5	767.0	21.4
9.2	10.1	8.0			7.2	5.6	9.8	12.1	7.3
(186) 3.7	(176) 3.8	(197) 3.1	EBIT/Interest		(37) 2.9	2.0	(40) 2.7	(50) 3.8	(39) 3.2
1.4	1.3	1.1			.9	.5	.9	1.1	1.9
5.8	6.2	7.5	Net Profit + Depr., Dep.,				4.6	17.7	10.9
(47) 3.2	(36) 2.1	(43) 3.1	Amort./Cur. Mat. L/T/D				(10) 2.7	(11) 7.0	(11) 6.8
1.7	1.3	1.4					-.2	1.5	3.2
.3	.3	.3			.3	.2	.3	.5	.4
.8	.8	.9	Fixed/Worth		2.2	.9	.8	1.1	.8
2.0	2.1	3.5			NM	NM	1.8	3.6	1.3
.8	.9	.9			1.0	1.1	1.0	1.0	.6
2.1	2.0	2.0	Debt/Worth		4.4	2.5	1.9	2.0	1.3
5.2	6.9	7.7			-75.0	-11.5	4.8	7.1	3.0
42.4	51.9	52.2	% Profit Before Taxes/Tangible		66.8	19.8	50.3	65.0	51.7
(180) 20.4	(160) 20.6	(179) 19.8	Net Worth		(30) 28.2	(19) 13.2	(36) 23.3	(46) 19.2	(41) 22.6
5.1	7.5	5.4			9.0	.8	1.2	3.8	9.1
13.4	16.8	15.9	% Profit Before Taxes/Total		16.2	8.7	19.2	14.1	18.3
6.4	7.3	6.9	Assets		7.7	3.1	7.2	6.9	8.0
1.0	1.5	.7			.6	-3.3	-.2	1.2	4.8
22.8	27.6	26.2			51.7	76.0	26.1	18.5	19.8
11.6	14.0	10.9	Sales/Net Fixed Assets		11.8	23.0	16.1	8.6	10.9
6.4	6.7	5.4			6.1	7.1	4.9	4.0	6.8
3.5	3.9	3.7			4.3	4.0	4.2	3.5	3.2
2.8	2.9	2.7	Sales/Total Assets		3.2	3.3	2.6	2.6	2.5
2.0	2.1	2.0			2.0	2.4	2.1	1.7	1.9
1.1	.9	1.0			.9	.7	.9	.9	1.1
(190) 1.7	(165) 1.6	(194) 1.7	% Depr., Dep., Amort./Sales		(35) 1.8	(21) 1.7	(38) 1.6	(51) 2.0	(42) 1.6
2.8	2.4	3.0			3.5	2.6	2.4	3.3	2.4
1.7	2.0	1.2	% Officers', Directors',		2.3	2.6	1.4	.9	
(81) 3.3	(70) 4.2	(79) 2.8	Owners' Comp/Sales		(20) 5.1	(16) 3.9	(15) 2.1	(16) 2.0	
5.3	7.1	6.3			8.5	6.6	6.8	3.9	
6198238M	5617722M	6498583M	Net Sales ($)	4472M	77814M	104823M	291930M	835338M	5184206M
2636293M	2260399M	2760365M	Total Assets ($)	8964M	37626M	36005M	116112M	371003M	2190655M

M = $ thousand   MM = $ million
See Pages 11 through 21 for Explanation of Ratios and Data

Current Data Sorted by Assets   Comparative Historical Data

		4	8	1	1	Type of Statement		
	1	8	2			Unqualified	14	20
1	7	11	2			Reviewed	15	17
	7	2			1	Compiled	10	17
	3	6	9	1		Tax Returns	10	14
						Other	11	25
	14 (4/1-9/30/06)		61 (10/1/06-3/31/07)				4/1/02-3/31/03	4/1/03-3/31/04
0-500M	500M-2MM	2-10MM	10-50MM	50-100MM	100-250MM		ALL	ALL
1	18	31	21	2	2	NUMBER OF STATEMENTS	60	93
%	%	%	%	%	%	**ASSETS**	%	%
	6.3	4.3	6.1			Cash & Equivalents	5.1	6.8
	26.7	20.4	12.8			Trade Receivables (net)	16.4	15.6
	28.8	38.7	35.0			Inventory	33.3	31.7
	2.1	.7	1.3			All Other Current	1.2	2.5
	63.9	64.1	55.2			Total Current	55.9	56.7
	33.7	29.6	33.4			Fixed Assets (net)	37.6	34.6
	.1	2.2	2.7			Intangibles (net)	.9	1.9
	2.2	4.2	8.7			All Other Non-Current	5.6	6.8
	100.0	100.0	100.0			Total	100.0	100.0
						LIABILITIES		
	10.6	23.1	23.9			Notes Payable-Short Term	12.2	19.7
	5.7	3.3	2.7			Cur. Mat.-L.T.D.	7.4	4.0
	14.2	9.3	8.1			Trade Payables	10.3	12.6
	.0	.0	.0			Income Taxes Payable	.2	.1
	8.7	9.4	5.1			All Other Current	4.5	10.8
	39.2	45.1	39.7			Total Current	34.6	47.2
	22.8	15.8	13.3			Long-Term Debt	25.7	21.8
	.1	.0	.1			Deferred Taxes	.4	.2
	3.7	1.8	3.1			All Other Non-Current	.9	5.2
	34.2	37.3	43.8			Net Worth	38.4	25.7
	100.0	100.0	100.0			Total Liabilities & Net Worth	100.0	100.0
						INCOME DATA		
	100.0	100.0	100.0			Net Sales	100.0	100.0
	22.6	24.2	13.6			Gross Profit	20.7	22.2
	18.5	18.3	12.4			Operating Expenses	17.6	19.1
	4.2	5.9	1.2			Operating Profit	3.1	3.1
	1.0	2.5	.7			All Other Expenses (net)	1.0	.9
	3.2	3.4	.5			Profit Before Taxes	2.1	2.1
						RATIOS		
	2.4	2.7	2.4				2.7	3.1
	1.7	1.6	1.5			Current	1.7	1.5
	1.3	1.1	.9				1.1	1.0
	1.5	1.1	.9				1.2	1.3
	1.0	.6	.5			Quick	.6 (92)	.5
	.4	.3	.2				.3	.3
	8 45.0	14 25.2	11 32.5				16 22.6	13 27.4
	20 18.6	27 13.3	20 18.7			Sales/Receivables	23 15.7	24 15.1
	33 11.0	36 10.2	33 11.1				37 9.9	34 10.8
	9 38.7	43 8.5	38 9.7				35 10.5	36 10.1
	34 10.6	80 4.6	74 4.9			Cost of Sales/Inventory	62 5.9	73 5.0
	59 6.2	114 3.2	86 4.2				119 3.1	110 3.3
	4 95.7	5 75.2	6 61.7				7 50.4	7 51.7
	18 19.9	10 37.8	11 33.5			Cost of Sales/Payables	13 27.8	15 25.1
	38 9.5	21 17.6	24 15.2				28 13.2	31 11.7
	9.6	5.5	6.6				5.5	5.1
	24.1	14.6	12.7			Sales/Working Capital	8.1	10.9
	39.7	54.5	-23.9				212.3	226.9
	9.4	7.2	5.9				6.4	7.3
	4.6 (29)	2.8 (20)	1.9			EBIT/Interest	(58) 1.9	(87) 2.4
	2.1	1.2	.6				1.0	.8
							3.3	2.2
						Net Profit + Depr., Dep., Amort./Cur. Mat. L/T/D	(17) 1.4	(20) .9
							1.1	.4
	.3	.2	.4				.3	.4
	.9	.8	.9			Fixed/Worth	.9	1.1
	1.8	1.6	1.7				2.1	4.0
	.9	.8	.9				.5	1.2
	2.3	1.9	1.6			Debt/Worth	1.5	2.3
	3.3	3.7	4.1				4.7	7.3
	57.1	35.9	22.0				24.9	39.7
	(17) 37.0	(29) 17.8	6.3			% Profit Before Taxes/Tangible Net Worth	(52) 11.7	(81) 11.7
	11.0	4.9	-9.1				1.9	1.8
	22.8	13.2	6.1				10.4	12.7
	11.6	6.8	3.5			% Profit Before Taxes/Total Assets	3.4	3.4
	3.3	1.1	-3.0				.1	-.1
	29.2	86.0	12.9				12.4	13.6
	11.6	7.6	6.2			Sales/Net Fixed Assets	5.2	6.0
	5.8	4.1	3.8				3.4	4.1
	5.6	3.5	3.3				2.8	2.8
	3.2	2.1	2.1			Sales/Total Assets	2.0	2.1
	2.3	1.6	1.3				1.3	1.4
	1.0	.7	.9				1.8	1.5
	(16) 2.2	(26) 1.8	(19) 1.7			% Depr., Dep., Amort./Sales	(55) 3.4	(86) 2.6
	4.7	5.7	3.6				5.1	5.0
	2.1	1.2					1.0	1.1
	(11) 2.5	(15) 2.7				% Officers', Directors' Owners' Comp/Sales	(20) 1.7	(33) 3.0
	4.1	4.7					2.8	5.5
788M	87317M	412447M	1077241M	232118M	2145195M	Net Sales ($)	1396166M	1956022M
99M	21243M	166115M	496572M	137493M	367473M	Total Assets ($)	874446M	1191589M

© RMA 2007

M = $ thousand   MM = $ million
See Pages 11 through 21 for Explanation of Ratios and Data

Comparative Historical Data | | | Type of Statement | Current Data Sorted by Sales

			Type of Statement	0-1MM	1-3MM	3-5MM	5-10MM	10-25MM	25MM & OVER
25	15	14	Unqualified				1	3	9
21	14	11	Reviewed			2	4	2	3
10	6	21	Compiled	2		4	8	3	3
12	17	10	Tax Returns	1	1	1	4	2	1
16	23	19	Other		2	1	2	6	8
4/1/04-3/31/05 ALL	4/1/05-3/31/06 ALL	4/1/06-3/31/07 ALL		14 (4/1-9/30/06)			61 (10/1/06-3/31/07)		
84	75	75	**NUMBER OF STATEMENTS**	4	4	8	19	16	24
%	%	%	**ASSETS**	%	%	%	%	%	%
5.6	5.8	5.6	Cash & Equivalents				3.8	5.8	4.9
15.9	16.6	19.9	Trade Receivables (net)				22.1	23.3	15.7
34.9	31.3	34.2	Inventory				30.2	37.5	40.0
1.3	2.5	1.3	All Other Current				.7	1.1	1.2
57.8	56.3	61.0	Total Current				56.9	67.7	61.7
32.6	33.0	31.7	Fixed Assets (net)				36.5	25.8	27.0
1.4	2.3	1.7	Intangibles (net)				2.3	.7	2.9
8.3	8.4	5.7	All Other Non-Current				4.3	5.8	8.4
100.0	100.0	100.0	Total				100.0	100.0	100.0
			LIABILITIES						
17.7	17.7	20.7	Notes Payable-Short Term				18.7	22.0	27.9
3.8	4.9	3.6	Cur. Mat.-L.T.D.				5.7	1.6	2.8
9.4	10.2	10.6	Trade Payables				5.7	9.3	9.3
.0	.1	.0	Income Taxes Payable				.0	.0	.0
6.3	9.4	7.7	All Other Current				9.6	5.2	7.4
37.3	42.2	42.7	Total Current				39.8	38.2	47.5
21.9	22.0	16.7	Long-Term Debt				20.6	13.4	12.0
.3	.4	.1	Deferred Taxes				.0	.0	.1
7.2	6.2	2.5	All Other Non-Current				4.6	.4	2.8
33.3	29.2	38.0	Net Worth				34.9	48.0	37.6
100.0	100.0	100.0	Total Liabilties & Net Worth				100.0	100.0	100.0
			INCOME DATA						
100.0	100.0	100.0	Net Sales				100.0	100.0	100.0
22.6	23.0	20.6	Gross Profit				21.0	20.7	13.8
16.2	18.7	16.6	Operating Expenses				17.8	17.2	12.1
6.4	4.3	4.0	Operating Profit				3.2	3.5	1.7
1.2	1.9	1.6	All Other Expenses (net)				.8	-.1	1.7
5.2	2.4	2.4	Profit Before Taxes				2.4	3.6	.0
			RATIOS						
2.6	2.1	2.5	Current				2.4	3.6	1.9
1.5	1.3	1.5					1.8	2.0	1.4
1.1	1.0	1.1					1.0	1.2	.9
1.3	1.0	1.2	Quick				1.2	1.8	.7
.5	.5	.5					.9	.8	.4
.2	.3	.3					.2	.3	.2
14 25.2	13 27.6	12 30.2	Sales/Receivables				13 28.5	16 23.3	11 34.6
21 17.5	21 17.7	21 17.1					21 17.1	27 13.4	17 21.3
29 12.6	32 11.3	34 10.6					37 10.0	37 9.8	32 11.5
33 10.9	36 10.1	31 11.7	Cost of Sales/Inventory				18 20.3	41 8.9	36 10.2
64 5.7	53 6.9	55 6.7					56 6.5	74 4.9	58 6.3
107 3.4	96 3.8	90 4.0					116 3.2	112 3.3	81 4.5
7 48.8	7 55.7	5 68.7	Cost of Sales/Payables				2 184.9	5 79.4	6 56.2
12 30.7	12 30.5	12 31.7					6 63.7	13 28.5	11 32.8
21 17.7	28 13.2	26 14.0					12 31.7	22 16.8	20 18.2
6.0	7.5	6.0	Sales/Working Capital				5.7	4.1	9.4
12.1	18.9	17.1					18.1	11.2	14.6
70.1	-72.8	67.3					54.5	26.0	NM
9.4	6.0	6.6	EBIT/Interest				3.9	7.9	6.0
(79) 3.6	(72) 2.5	(71) 2.8					2.1	(14) 3.5	2.1
1.5	.6	1.2					1.2	1.6	.6
4.9	4.2		Net Profit + Depr., Dep., Amort./Cur. Mat. L/T/D						
(21) 2.0	(18) 2.4								
.3	1.7								
.3	.5	.3	Fixed/Worth				.6	.1	.3
.9	1.0	.8					1.1	.4	.7
2.2	2.2	1.7					3.3	1.0	1.7
1.0	1.1	.9	Debt/Worth				.7	.3	1.1
1.7	2.1	2.1					2.3	1.5	1.9
4.6	7.5	3.7					3.7	2.5	4.2
42.7	40.0	36.9	% Profit Before Taxes/Tangible Net Worth				24.9	38.0	30.1
(73) 24.9	(65) 26.2	(72) 16.6					(17) 13.8	18.4	9.8
9.1	5.1	3.2					5.2	3.1	-5.0
16.0	13.8	13.3	% Profit Before Taxes/Total Assets				11.2	16.9	7.4
6.4	3.2	5.4					3.6	7.1	3.9
2.0	.0	1.0					1.1	1.2	-1.6
14.5	14.4	24.5	Sales/Net Fixed Assets				22.6	123.6	27.5
7.9	7.5	8.0					6.2	9.5	9.0
4.9	4.5	4.3					3.3	3.9	5.5
3.0	3.3	3.8	Sales/Total Assets				3.2	4.1	4.4
2.2	2.3	2.3					2.0	2.3	2.7
1.8	1.6	1.6					1.6	1.6	1.7
1.1	1.6	.9	% Depr., Dep., Amort./Sales				.9	.7	.5
(76) 2.1	(64) 2.6	(63) 1.8					(18) 1.8	(13) 1.4	(19) 1.1
3.7	4.2	4.1					5.8	5.5	2.8
.9	.8	1.2	% Officers', Directors' Owners' Comp/Sales						
(24) 1.5	(21) 1.6	(29) 2.5							
3.5	4.2	4.3							
2309417M	2038987M	3955106M	Net Sales ($)	2461M	7862M	36442M	138240M	260455M	3509646M
1281741M	1099218M	1188995M	Total Assets ($)	6009M	3578M	15339M	82588M	135117M	946364M

M = $ thousand   MM = $ million
See Pages 11 through 21 for Explanation of Ratios and Data

Current Data Sorted by Assets							Comparative Historical Data	
			6	6	2	1	Type of Statement		
		7	13	4	2		Unqualified	4	6
		11	5	2			Reviewed	5	10
4		11	5	2			Compiled	11	12
6		4	6				Tax Returns	4	9
		6	12	8	1	1	Other	10	20
		23 (4/1-9/30/06)		84 (10/1/06-3/31/07)				4/1/02-3/31/03	4/1/03-3/31/04
0-500M		500M-2MM	2-10MM	10-50MM	50-100MM	100-250MM		ALL	ALL
10		28	42	20	5	2	NUMBER OF STATEMENTS	34	57
%		%	%	%	%	%	ASSETS	%	%
11.6		8.0	5.6	6.1			Cash & Equivalents	6.8	8.7
23.7		34.4	25.4	17.1			Trade Receivables (net)	23.1	27.4
25.5		21.6	27.7	30.8			Inventory	24.3	23.5
2.5		3.4	3.0	2.7			All Other Current	4.9	1.1
63.3		67.4	61.7	56.7			Total Current	59.1	60.7
29.7		27.4	31.8	27.0			Fixed Assets (net)	32.1	32.0
.0		2.3	1.2	7.4			Intangibles (net)	.7	1.0
6.9		2.9	5.3	8.9			All Other Non-Current	8.1	6.3
100.0		100.0	100.0	100.0			Total	100.0	100.0
							LIABILITIES		
20.7		14.1	13.1	9.4			Notes Payable-Short Term	10.7	12.9
15.3		3.8	4.5	3.1			Cur. Mat.-L.T.D.	4.6	4.3
18.9		14.8	11.1	5.8			Trade Payables	13.9	10.1
.0		.4	.4	.7			Income Taxes Payable	.2	.2
15.0		6.3	12.0	6.7			All Other Current	7.9	7.8
69.9		39.4	41.1	25.6			Total Current	37.3	35.4
18.2		20.9	23.4	20.1			Long-Term Debt	20.6	19.0
.0		.3	.2	.6			Deferred Taxes	.3	.2
7.9		8.7	5.4	4.2			All Other Non-Current	5.3	3.7
4.0		30.6	29.9	49.4			Net Worth	36.5	41.7
100.0		100.0	100.0	100.0			Total Liabilties & Net Worth	100.0	100.0
							INCOME DATA		
100.0		100.0	100.0	100.0			Net Sales	100.0	100.0
31.2		32.3	28.1	18.0			Gross Profit	24.5	30.0
28.3		29.3	20.9	12.3			Operating Expenses	20.4	24.3
2.8		3.0	7.1	5.7			Operating Profit	4.0	5.6
.6		.7	1.7	1.0			All Other Expenses (net)	.4	.8
2.3		2.3	5.4	4.7			Profit Before Taxes	3.6	4.9
							RATIOS		
5.2		3.0	2.3	3.9				3.3	4.2
.9		1.4	1.4	2.2			Current	1.6	1.7
.4		1.2	1.2	1.5				1.2	1.2
1.7		1.6	1.1	1.6				1.8	2.1
.4		1.0	.7	.9			Quick	.7	1.1
.1		.6	.5	.4				.5	.5
0 UND	23	15.8	17	21.1	19	19.3		17	21.8	20	18.2
9	38.8	36	10.2	30	12.3	25	14.7	Sales/Receivables	25	14.8	37	9.8
32	11.2	64	5.7	54	6.8	40	9.0		41	8.8	52	7.1
0 UND	7	53.6	22	16.4	39	9.4		17	21.8	19	19.0
22	16.6	35	10.5	47	7.7	66	5.5	Cost of Sales/Inventory	39	9.4	41	9.0
49	7.4	71	5.2	89	4.1	115	3.2		68	5.4	82	4.5
0 UND	12	29.8	10	35.6	6	57.2		8	46.6	8	45.2
9	42.9	24	15.3	22	16.7	11	34.4	Cost of Sales/Payables	18	19.9	16	23.1
45	8.2	48	7.5	31	11.7	15	24.7		34	10.9	28	12.9
15.0		6.3	7.9	3.5				7.0	5.4
NM		14.1	14.8	7.0			Sales/Working Capital	12.5	8.6
-5.9		27.3	23.6	21.8				37.8	34.0
		8.1	7.3	27.9				8.3	12.7
	(27)	3.3	(40) 2.3	(18) 2.8			EBIT/Interest	(28) 3.6	(50) 3.7
		.2	1.3	.9				1.1	1.1
			3.2						4.7
		(10) 2.0					Net Profit + Depr., Dep., Amort./Cur. Mat. L/T/D		(14) 1.5
		.5							.9
.2		.2	.7	.3				.5	.3
NM		.6	1.0	.8			Fixed/Worth	.8	.9
-2.3		2.3	2.4	2.7				2.3	1.8
1.6		1.0	.8	.3				.6	.6
NM		2.2	2.5	1.2			Debt/Worth	2.2	1.4
-8.2		9.9	6.7	6.0				7.3	3.6
		43.2	59.9	41.7				55.9	64.4
	(24)	16.3	(38) 20.7	(17) 18.2			% Profit Before Taxes/Tangible Net Worth	(30) 27.0	(52) 16.7
		-9.6	4.5	-2.1				1.1	5.3
24.0		15.3	14.3	26.8				20.9	19.3
5.1		5.9	6.5	10.0			% Profit Before Taxes/Total Assets	10.8	8.1
-19.9		-2.8	.9	.0				.2	1.4
291.2		41.1	14.1	16.1				20.8	18.4
19.6		17.1	8.6	8.2			Sales/Net Fixed Assets	7.6	8.5
11.8		4.2	5.3	4.7				4.6	4.8
11.2		3.6	3.3	3.0				4.2	3.1
4.1		2.8	2.5	2.0			Sales/Total Assets	2.7	2.3
2.2		1.8	1.8	1.3				1.8	1.7
		.8	1.5	1.3				1.6	1.3
	(26)	1.6	(37) 1.9	(17) 1.9			% Depr., Dep., Amort./Sales	(30) 2.8	(49) 2.6
		3.5	2.7	2.8				4.4	4.5
		2.6	1.6					1.3	1.7
	(13)	3.5	(22) 2.5				% Officers', Directors' Owners' Comp/Sales	(18) 3.1	(25) 3.5
		6.3	8.1					4.3	4.5
16919M		86588M	419043M	1046421M	539625M	708058M	Net Sales ($)	281565M	603785M
2694M		31879M	173848M	467151M	311471M	302858M	Total Assets ($)	123091M	295348M

© RMA 2007

M = $ thousand   MM = $ million
See Pages 11 through 21 for Explanation of Ratios and Data

Comparative Historical Data

Current Data Sorted by Sales

			Type of Statement	0-1MM	1-3MM	3-5MM	5-10MM	10-25MM	25MM & OVER
18	13	15	Unqualified		1			5	9
16	17	26	Reviewed		3	4	7	5	7
13	17	22	Compiled		7	5	3	3	1
11	16	16	Tax Returns	3	4	3	6		
21	22	28	Other	3	5	3	8	6	6
4/1/04-3/31/05 ALL	4/1/05-3/31/06 ALL	4/1/06-3/31/07 ALL			23 (4/1-9/30/06)		84 (10/1/06-3/31/07)		
79	85	107	NUMBER OF STATEMENTS	6	20	15	24	19	23
%	%	%	**ASSETS**	%	%	%	%	%	%
5.0	6.0	6.6	Cash & Equivalents	10.0	4.4	7.0	5.2	6.2	
30.0	28.5	25.3	Trade Receivables (net)	32.8	24.4	32.4	22.7	17.6	
25.7	25.6	26.1	Inventory	18.5	23.8	28.0	28.0	28.9	
2.7	1.8	2.8	All Other Current	4.4	1.7	3.4	2.5	2.4	
63.4	61.9	60.9	Total Current	65.7	54.3	70.9	58.3	55.1	
30.2	29.4	30.3	Fixed Assets (net)	28.3	38.2	25.9	32.2	27.3	
1.3	3.1	3.0	Intangibles (net)	.5	4.3	.5	4.6	6.4	
5.1	5.7	5.9	All Other Non-Current	5.5	3.3	2.7	4.9	11.1	
100.0	100.0	100.0	Total	100.0	100.0	100.0	100.0	100.0	
			LIABILITIES						
14.8	11.8	12.9	Notes Payable-Short Term	13.0	14.5	13.1	14.6	9.5	
5.7	7.2	5.2	Cur. Mat.-L.T.D.	8.6	5.0	4.0	5.6	3.5	
13.8	12.2	11.5	Trade Payables	12.3	15.7	11.3	11.8	7.3	
.2	.4	.4	Income Taxes Payable	.5	.0	.7	.2	.5	
9.0	10.7	9.5	All Other Current	3.1	6.5	19.3	8.2	7.7	
43.6	42.4	39.5	Total Current	37.4	41.7	48.5	40.5	28.6	
22.9	19.1	22.1	Long-Term Debt	19.2	37.6	16.5	19.9	20.1	
.2	.3	.3	Deferred Taxes	.2	.1	.4	.3	.4	
4.1	5.8	6.2	All Other Non-Current	6.4	10.4	6.9	3.4	3.9	
29.2	32.4	31.9	Net Worth	36.7	10.3	27.7	36.0	47.0	
100.0	100.0	100.0	Total Liabilties & Net Worth	100.0	100.0	100.0	100.0	100.0	
			INCOME DATA						
100.0	100.0	100.0	Net Sales	100.0	100.0	100.0	100.0	100.0	
26.6	29.0	27.5	Gross Profit	40.1	39.3	21.1	24.4	19.6	
22.8	25.5	22.3	Operating Expenses	30.2	37.1	17.3	19.1	13.7	
3.8	3.5	5.2	Operating Profit	10.0	2.3	3.8	5.3	5.9	
.6	1.1	1.3	All Other Expenses (net)	1.4	1.5	1.1	1.3	1.1	
3.2	2.5	4.0	Profit Before Taxes	8.6	.8	2.8	3.9	4.8	
			RATIOS						
2.2	2.8	2.5	Current	7.3	2.1	1.8	3.1	2.7	
1.5	1.4	1.4		2.1	1.3	1.4	1.3	2.1	
1.2	1.1	1.2		1.1	1.1	1.3	1.1	1.0	
1.4	1.4	1.1	Quick	4.4	1.0	1.1	1.6	1.1	
.8	.9	.9		1.1	.9	.8	.7	.9	
.4	.4	.4		.5	.3	.3	.3	.4	
21 17.5	22 16.7	17 21.1	Sales/Receivables	17 21.3	17 21.1	15 24.4	22 17.0	16 22.5	
37 10.0	35 10.5	29 12.7		46 8.0	29 12.7	30 12.2	32 11.5	23 16.1	
52 7.0	55 6.6	52 7.0		70 5.2	47 7.8	59 6.2	49 7.5	33 11.0	
14 26.6	23 15.8	24 15.2	Cost of Sales/Inventory	2 198.3	14 26.3	19 19.6	27 13.4	33 10.9	
38 9.5	50 7.3	40 9.1		26 14.2	45 8.2	32 11.3	69 5.3	61 6.0	
86 4.2	84 4.4	81 4.5		112 3.3	86 4.2	65 5.6	97 3.8	81 4.5	
11 33.5	9 39.1	8 43.8	Cost of Sales/Payables	6 60.4	20 18.4	9 42.9	8 46.3	6 58.5	
19 18.8	20 18.2	19 19.6		24 15.3	35 10.5	17 20.9	23 16.1	12 30.6	
37 9.9	36 10.2	32 11.3		49 7.5	44 8.3	26 13.9	32 20.0	18 20.0	
7.1	6.2	6.2	Sales/Working Capital	2.8	8.0	9.4	7.2	4.6	
14.8	14.5	14.4		7.8	17.6	14.3	17.5	8.7	
33.2	37.1	37.3		79.7	38.9	21.7	54.5	-656.9	
11.9	10.1	8.0	EBIT/Interest	58.7	2.7	6.1	9.9	25.3	
(75) 4.7	(78) 3.5	(100) 2.6		(16) 5.5	1.0	(23) 2.6	2.1	(21) 5.8	
1.5	.8	.9		-.1	-1.6	1.2	1.7	.8	
4.3	5.8	2.7	Net Profit + Depr., Dep., Amort./Cur. Mat. L/T/D						
(21) 1.6	(16) 2.2	(18) 1.6							
.9	1.6	.4							
.3	.4	.4	Fixed/Worth	.2	.4	.4	.6	.4	
1.0	.8	.9		.6	1.6	.9	1.0	.9	
3.0	4.4	2.8		6.5	-4.5	2.2	2.3	1.8	
1.0	.9	.8	Debt/Worth	.6	1.2	1.5	.8	.4	
2.5	1.7	2.4		1.8	3.4	2.7	3.2	1.3	
8.5	23.2	7.3		6.7	-8.7	5.9	5.9	6.1	
57.2	52.4	43.3	% Profit Before Taxes/Tangible Net Worth	74.5	44.7	47.1	73.5	40.7	
(66) 24.5	(68) 33.6	(90) 19.3		(16) 21.2	(10) 3.7	(23) 19.2	(17) 33.8	(20) 25.5	
5.7	11.3	1.0		3.6	-37.7	5.1	4.5	-2.6	
14.6	20.1	15.4	% Profit Before Taxes/Total Assets	26.2	6.8	11.2	19.7	26.9	
8.0	9.2	6.5		9.5	-.1	5.0	6.4	10.5	
1.9	-.6	-.3		-1.9	-7.3	.9	2.8	-.5	
22.3	19.5	18.9	Sales/Net Fixed Assets	35.2	42.7	23.7	14.2	16.3	
9.8	12.0	10.3		13.3	3.4	10.4	8.7	8.6	
5.2	5.6	4.3		4.2	2.9	6.9	3.6	5.0	
3.4	3.4	3.3	Sales/Total Assets	3.3	3.3	4.1	3.4	3.0	
2.6	2.5	2.4		2.0	2.4	3.1	2.2	2.1	
2.0	2.1	1.8		1.6	1.7	2.1	1.6	1.6	
1.1	1.2	1.2	% Depr., Dep., Amort./Sales	.8	1.2	.9	1.5	1.4	
(72) 2.2	(79) 2.1	(92) 1.8		(17) 1.4	2.0	(19) 1.7	2.0	(17) 2.1	
3.8	3.2	3.0		2.7	4.5	2.4	3.3	2.9	
1.5	2.1	1.6	% Officers', Directors' Owners' Comp/Sales		2.1		1.5		
(38) 3.2	(32) 3.1	(45) 2.8			(10) 3.9		(13) 3.4		
7.0	5.8	6.5			8.8		9.0		
1188745M	1539828M	2816654M	Net Sales ($)	4268M	40666M	55079M	184487M	294408M	2237746M
518009M	699388M	1289901M	Total Assets ($)	2251M	31512M	27816M	70852M	185222M	972248M

M = $ thousand   MM = $ million
See Pages 11 through 21 for Explanation of Ratios and Data

Current Data Sorted by Assets   **Comparative Historical Data**

Type of Statement	0-500M	500M-2MM	2-10MM	10-50MM	50-100MM	100-250MM		4/1/02-3/31/03 ALL	4/1/03-3/31/04 ALL
Unqualified		1		7		1		7	4
Reviewed	2	11	35	4	1	1		32	35
Compiled		21	23	1				39	39
Tax Returns	9	13	6			1		22	25
Other	2	24	28	5		5		35	52
	48 (4/1-9/30/06)			155 (10/1/06-3/31/07)					
NUMBER OF STATEMENTS	13	70	95	17	1	7		135	155

ASSETS	%	%	%	%	%	%		%	%
Cash & Equivalents	18.4	7.4	4.9	6.9				5.5	7.5
Trade Receivables (net)	27.6	32.5	31.0	24.5				27.1	28.8
Inventory	11.7	24.0	25.4	26.0				21.0	22.1
All Other Current	2.1	2.3	2.6	2.1				3.1	2.3
Total Current	59.9	66.2	63.9	59.5				56.7	60.8
Fixed Assets (net)	33.5	27.9	29.8	28.7				36.8	31.2
Intangibles (net)	.9	2.5	1.6	9.1				2.0	2.1
All Other Non-Current	5.7	3.4	4.7	2.7				4.5	5.9
Total	100.0	100.0	100.0	100.0				100.0	100.0

LIABILITIES									
Notes Payable-Short Term	10.8	10.7	14.5	8.5				14.0	16.6
Cur. Mat.-L.T.D.	4.4	4.1	5.1	3.8				5.1	4.7
Trade Payables	13.8	14.7	13.8	9.4				13.2	15.5
Income Taxes Payable	.0	.4	.1	.2				.1	.1
All Other Current	6.6	6.7	7.6	6.1				8.3	9.1
Total Current	35.6	36.6	41.2	27.9				40.8	46.1
Long-Term Debt	25.5	18.0	16.4	23.7				22.1	21.2
Deferred Taxes	.0	.2	.2	.0				.2	.3
All Other Non-Current	24.5	4.5	3.7	4.8				4.9	9.3
Net Worth	14.4	40.7	38.5	43.5				32.1	23.1
Total Liabilities & Net Worth	100.0	100.0	100.0	100.0				100.0	100.0

INCOME DATA									
Net Sales	100.0	100.0	100.0	100.0				100.0	100.0
Gross Profit	39.6	29.2	20.9	24.4				25.7	25.3
Operating Expenses	29.7	23.9	17.4	18.4				23.9	23.1
Operating Profit	9.9	5.3	3.5	6.0				1.8	2.2
All Other Expenses (net)	.7	.5	.6	1.1				.8	.8
Profit Before Taxes	9.2	4.8	2.9	4.9				1.0	1.4

RATIOS									
Current	4.1	3.6	2.2	2.7				2.4	2.2
	1.5	1.6	1.5	1.9				1.4	1.3
	.7	1.2	1.1	1.3				1.0	1.0
Quick	3.2	2.2	1.4	1.6				1.6	1.4
	.9	1.1	.8	1.0				.8	.7
	.5	.7	.6	.6				.4	.5
Sales/Receivables	0 UND	24 15.1	25 14.5	25 14.9				23 15.7	25 14.6
	37 9.7	33 11.0	33 11.2	30 12.1				34 10.8	34 10.7
	44 8.3	43 8.5	42 8.6	45 8.0				42 8.6	43 8.4
Cost of Sales/Inventory	0 UND	16 22.7	18 20.2	26 14.2				18 20.8	17 21.7
	16 22.3	30 12.1	37 9.8	36 10.0				32 11.5	32 11.4
	33 11.1	54 6.8	52 7.0	105 3.5				56 6.5	51 7.2
Cost of Sales/Payables	0 UND	12 31.4	10 37.8	11 33.4				9 42.8	10 38.0
	16 22.8	21 17.6	18 24.1	15 24.1				17 20.9	19 19.6
	37 9.9	28 13.1	27 13.6	23 15.6				29 12.6	34 10.7
Sales/Working Capital	8.2	6.4	8.6	6.4				7.5	8.4
	60.9	14.7	15.8	12.2				16.7	22.1
	-35.6	46.0	55.9	23.8				999.8	-127.4
EBIT/Interest	13.3	14.5	9.6	9.1				3.4	5.1
	(11) 5.4	(66) 4.3	(93) 3.3	(16) 3.4				(122) 1.7	(141) 2.1
	.1	2.1	1.7	2.4				-.3	-.1
Net Profit + Depr., Dep., Amort./Cur. Mat. L/T/D		7.0	2.4					2.6	2.9
		(10) 3.2	(25) 1.9					(24) 1.3	(28) 1.9
		1.9	1.2					.4	1.1
Fixed/Worth	.4	.3	.4	.5				.5	.5
	1.0	.6	.8	.8				1.3	1.2
	-30.7	2.0	1.4	2.0				3.9	3.5
Debt/Worth	.2	.5	1.0	1.0				1.0	1.1
	1.8	1.9	1.9	1.5				2.1	2.5
	-39.9	3.6	3.6	3.1				8.8	8.7
% Profit Before Taxes/Tangible Net Worth		77.9	41.2	42.9				34.1	35.7
		(62) 28.4	(92) 22.5	(15) 23.1				(114) 8.9	(125) 13.7
		8.7	10.9	11.4				-6.2	-3.9
% Profit Before Taxes/Total Assets	33.5	19.2	14.7	15.0				9.5	11.1
	19.0	9.1	8.1	10.7				2.4	4.1
	1.5	2.8	2.3	5.0				-3.8	-3.0
Sales/Net Fixed Assets	47.0	35.9	25.7	16.4				13.1	17.5
	12.0	14.9	12.2	11.7				7.7	10.0
	7.0	6.7	6.7	6.7				4.6	6.0
Sales/Total Assets	6.5	4.7	4.1	3.6				4.0	4.1
	3.5	3.3	3.2	2.5				2.8	3.0
	1.3	2.4	2.5	1.8				2.1	2.0
% Depr., Dep., Amort./Sales		.8	.9	1.7				1.6	1.2
		(65) 1.4	(92) 1.6	(15) 2.0				(125) 2.4	(146) 2.2
		2.8	3.0	2.5				3.8	3.8
% Officers', Directors' Owners' Comp/Sales		1.2	1.6					2.2	1.5
		(39) 2.9	(35) 2.3					(70) 3.6	(70) 2.9
		5.0	4.6					5.6	4.7
Net Sales ($)	18112M	314579M	1339489M	1037908M	86525M	2528463M		1192753M	1313923M
Total Assets ($)	4236M	88461M	412111M	391338M	63551M	1105110M		517280M	498760M

M = $ thousand   MM = $ million
See Pages 11 through 21 for Explanation of Ratios and Data

Comparative Historical Data / Current Data Sorted by Sales

Item	4/1/04-3/31/05 ALL	4/1/05-3/31/06 ALL	4/1/06-3/31/07 ALL	0-1MM	1-3MM	3-5MM	5-10MM	10-25MM	25MM & OVER
Type of Statement					48 (4/1-9/30/06)			155 (10/1-3/31/07)	
Unqualified	8	8	12	1	3	6	1	4	7
Reviewed	42	38	53	2	6	5	17	18	8
Compiled	43	29	45	2	9	6	13	17	2
Tax Returns	36	18	29	3	9	8	8	3	1
Other	39	55	64				16	13	15
NUMBER OF STATEMENTS	168	148	203	8	27	25	55	55	33
ASSETS (%)	%	%	%	%	%	%	%	%	%
Cash & Equivalents	4.7	6.1	6.7		6.5	11.2	6.3	4.0	4.1
Trade Receivables (net)	30.3	29.3	30.2		30.3	27.4	33.0	31.1	30.0
Inventory	22.7	23.3	23.7		17.9	26.0	25.3	25.7	23.9
All Other Current	2.2	1.8	2.7		1.9	.7	1.8	2.7	4.5
Total Current	59.8	60.5	63.3		56.7	65.3	66.4	63.5	62.6
Fixed Assets (net)	32.6	33.0	29.6		39.8	27.4	28.1	29.0	26.6
Intangibles (net)	2.1	1.4	2.7		.8	2.7	2.5	2.6	5.1
All Other Non-Current	5.4	5.2	4.3		2.8	4.6	3.0	4.8	5.7
Total	100.0	100.0	100.0		100.0	100.0	100.0	100.0	100.0
LIABILITIES									
Notes Payable-Short Term	16.1	13.0	12.4		6.7	10.7	15.3	13.0	14.6
Cur. Mat.-L.T.D.	5.7	4.7	4.5		5.6	3.0	5.8	3.9	4.4
Trade Payables	15.9	14.5	13.4		15.3	12.3	15.0	13.7	11.3
Income Taxes Payable	.1	.2	.2		.4	.1	.3	.1	.1
All Other Current	8.4	7.8	7.1		4.3	6.2	8.1	8.7	7.2
Total Current	46.1	40.3	37.6		32.3	32.3	44.5	39.4	37.5
Long-Term Debt	21.0	20.2	18.5		29.1	14.4	15.8	16.1	19.0
Deferred Taxes	.3	.3	.2		.0	.4	.0	.3	.1
All Other Non-Current	6.1	4.6	5.5		14.1	2.6	4.0	5.6	3.4
Net Worth	26.6	34.6	38.2		24.4	50.2	35.6	38.6	40.1
Total Liabilities & Net Worth	100.0	100.0	100.0		100.0	100.0	100.0	100.0	100.0
INCOME DATA									
Net Sales	100.0	100.0	100.0		100.0	100.0	100.0	100.0	100.0
Gross Profit	26.4	25.1	25.4		36.7	27.6	23.2	23.1	19.1
Operating Expenses	23.4	20.9	20.6		30.4	23.7	19.6	19.0	14.1
Operating Profit	2.9	4.2	4.8		6.3	3.8	3.7	4.1	4.9
All Other Expenses (net)	.8	.7	.7		1.2	.4	.7	.4	1.0
Profit Before Taxes	2.2	3.5	4.2		5.1	3.4	3.0	3.6	3.9
RATIOS									
Current	2.1	2.4	2.8		4.0	4.9	2.1	2.4	2.4
	1.3	1.4	1.6		1.6	2.0	1.5	1.5	1.7
	.9	1.1	1.2		1.1	1.3	1.1	1.2	1.1
Quick	1.4	1.3	1.5		2.7	3.1	1.3	1.4	1.4
	.8	.8	.9		1.2	1.5	.9	.9	.8
	.5	.5	.6		.8	.6	.6	.6	.6
Sales/Receivables	24 15.2	24 15.1	25 14.7		25 14.4	25 14.3	27 13.5	25 14.7	25 14.9
	35 10.5	32 11.4	33 11.1		39 9.3	33 11.1	34 10.8	30 12.0	30 12.1
	43 8.5	41 8.9	43 8.6		49 7.4	40 9.2	43 8.5	38 9.7	43 8.6
Cost of Sales/Inventory	18 20.4	17 21.3	16 22.3		16 22.3	19 19.3	18 20.6	12 30.6	16 22.4
	32 11.4	33 11.0	32 11.4		25 14.7	43 8.6	32 11.4	35 10.3	31 11.8
	54 6.8	52 7.1	54 6.7		68 5.4	62 5.9	50 7.3	49 7.4	69 5.3
Cost of Sales/Payables	10 36.1	9 41.1	10 37.2		9 38.5	14 26.7	9 39.1	9 39.1	10 36.8
	19 19.5	18 19.8	17 21.8		22 17.0	23 16.2	17 21.8	18 19.9	12 29.5
	33 11.0	31 11.6	28 13.2		40 9.1	28 12.9	31 11.9	23 15.8	18 20.7
Sales/Working Capital	9.8	8.9	7.8		5.1	6.0	9.6	8.9	7.4
	23.3	17.9	15.5		10.9	8.4	17.8	15.8	15.5
	-86.1	47.8	49.6		106.9	34.3	89.4	31.2	55.6
EBIT/Interest	8.1	9.2	9.8		13.3	20.9	9.1	14.1	9.5
	(157) 2.7	(142) 3.6	(193) 3.7		3.9	(24) 4.2	(53) 3.1	(53) 3.9	(31) 2.8
	1.0	1.7	2.1		.4	2.2	1.4	2.8	2.1
Net Profit + Depr., Dep., Amort./Cur. Mat. L/T/D	3.4	3.6	3.7				4.2	2.5	3.6
	(25) 1.9	(36) 2.4	(45) 2.3				(14) 2.2	(11) 2.2	(14) 2.3
	.9	1.5	1.5				1.1	1.7	1.6
Fixed/Worth	.5	.5	.4		.3	.2	.4	.5	.5
	1.2	1.0	.8		1.4	.7	.7	.8	.7
	4.1	2.0	1.5		7.9	.9	2.0	1.4	1.1
Debt/Worth	.9	.9	.8		.4	.5	.9	1.1	1.0
	2.4	2.0	1.8		2.0	1.0	2.3	1.9	1.8
	9.3	4.3	3.7		31.0	2.6	4.3	3.5	3.5
% Profit Before Taxes/Tangible Net Worth	42.9	48.3	46.4		82.4	51.5	41.4	59.0	31.8
	(138) 15.6	(137) 19.7	(183) 23.8		(21) 36.2	(24) 23.1	(50) 21.3	(52) 29.9	(30) 18.4
	2.6	7.2	9.2		15.2	6.9	4.7	14.5	11.3
% Profit Before Taxes/Total Assets	13.3	16.3	18.5		28.7	18.5	18.7	18.5	12.8
	3.7	7.2	8.9		9.4	6.6	5.7	9.8	6.7
	.0	2.0	2.9		-3.4	2.7	1.8	5.5	3.2
Sales/Net Fixed Assets	21.9	22.2	27.0		14.9	32.0	35.3	27.0	25.4
	10.6	10.9	12.3		9.8	15.1	13.9	13.7	11.7
	6.3	5.8	6.6		2.6	6.6	6.8	7.7	6.7
Sales/Total Assets	4.2	4.3	4.1		3.5	4.0	4.5	4.3	3.9
	3.0	3.2	3.2		2.5	3.2	3.5	3.4	2.6
	2.2	2.2	2.2		1.7	2.2	2.9	2.6	1.9
% Depr., Dep., Amort./Sales	1.3	1.1	.9		1.0	1.1	.9	.9	1.2
	(146) 2.2	(133) 2.0	(185) 1.7		(25) 2.4	(21) 2.5	(52) 2.0	(54) 1.5	(27) 2.0
	3.4	3.1	2.8		3.5	3.5	3.3	2.0	2.3
% Officers', Directors' Owners' Comp/Sales	1.3	1.0	1.6		1.9	1.0	1.5	1.9	
	(83) 2.2	(55) 2.2	(86) 2.6		(18) 4.4	(13) 2.9	(30) 2.3	(17) 2.6	
	3.9	4.3	4.9		5.8	5.1	3.9	5.1	
Net Sales ($)	1848319M	2886868M	5325076M	4131M	51649M	96950M	402372M	818395M	3951579M
Total Assets ($)	629199M	1187817M	2064807M	4911M	24437M	33561M	131667M	265191M	1605040M

M = $ thousand   MM = $ million
See Pages 11 through 21 for Explanation of Ratios and Data

Current Data Sorted by Assets   Comparative Historical Data

Type of Statement counts and dating: 7 (4/1‑9/30/06); 35 (10/1/06‑3/31/07)

0-500M	500M-2MM	2-10MM	10-50MM	50-100MM	100-250MM	Type of Statement	4/1/02-3/31/03 ALL	4/1/03-3/31/04 ALL
		2	5	3	1	Unqualified	11	11
	1	2	1			Reviewed	4	7
	4	2	1			Compiled	8	9
	1	2				Tax Returns	2	4
1	1	6	6		3	Other	16	10
1	7	14	13	3	4	**NUMBER OF STATEMENTS**	41	41

0-500M %	500M-2MM %	2-10MM %	10-50MM %	50-100MM %	100-250MM %		%	%
						ASSETS		
		12.1	26.0			Cash & Equivalents	10.6	11.3
		12.4	13.1			Trade Receivables (net)	15.0	13.8
		26.9	21.9			Inventory	25.3	27.3
		5.0	1.6			All Other Current	8.2	6.1
		56.3	62.7			Total Current	59.1	58.6
		34.6	28.7			Fixed Assets (net)	26.5	27.6
		.9	2.8			Intangibles (net)	5.4	5.7
		8.2	5.8			All Other Non-Current	8.9	8.1
		100.0	100.0			Total	100.0	100.0
						LIABILITIES		
		22.6	3.7			Notes Payable-Short Term	13.2	10.0
		.9	.5			Cur. Mat.-L.T.D.	3.3	1.4
		11.9	6.3			Trade Payables	8.6	9.5
		.0	.0			Income Taxes Payable	.1	.1
		16.7	18.2			All Other Current	14.3	18.6
		52.1	28.7			Total Current	39.6	39.7
		10.6	9.5			Long-Term Debt	10.3	12.4
		.1	1.8			Deferred Taxes	1.0	.8
		6.3	4.0			All Other Non-Current	4.2	9.1
		30.9	56.0			Net Worth	44.9	38.0
		100.0	100.0			Total Liabilities & Net Worth	100.0	100.0
						INCOME DATA		
		100.0	100.0			Net Sales	100.0	100.0
		30.3	21.9			Gross Profit	21.6	22.6
		22.9	14.6			Operating Expenses	19.3	19.9
		7.4	7.2			Operating Profit	2.3	2.7
		2.4	-.4			All Other Expenses (net)	.2	.8
		5.0	7.6			Profit Before Taxes	2.1	1.8
						RATIOS		
		1.9	3.7			Current	1.9	2.0
		1.2	1.9				1.5	1.4
		.5	1.3				1.0	1.1
		.8	2.4			Quick	1.1	1.0
		.3	1.0				.6	.6
		.1	.6				.3	.3
		0 UND	10 35.5			Sales/Receivables	13 27.8	9 39.3
		7 52.4	14 25.4				18 20.6	18 19.9
		21 17.3	27 13.6				25 14.9	23 15.9
		0 UND	13 28.6			Cost of Sales/Inventory	23 15.9	25 14.4
		31 11.7	44 8.2				32 11.5	38 9.5
		51 7.1	49 7.4				54 6.7	59 6.2
		0 UND	7 53.2			Cost of Sales/Payables	7 50.8	8 43.3
		8 43.5	10 35.5				12 29.3	12 29.4
		37 9.8	15 24.5				20 18.3	22 17.0
		9.8	4.7			Sales/Working Capital	7.6	8.5
		34.5	10.7				14.7	16.2
		-12.6	38.9				111.8	61.0
		17.4				EBIT/Interest	9.7	5.8
		(13) 5.5					(39) 2.5	(37) 1.8
		1.9					-1.6	-.3
						Net Profit + Depr., Dep., Amort./Cur. Mat. L/T/D		
		.3	.1			Fixed/Worth	.3	.2
		1.7	.6				.6	.6
		5.1	1.5				1.4	2.2
		1.0	.3			Debt/Worth	.7	.7
		2.4	.7				1.3	1.9
		21.8	2.2				2.7	5.5
		77.2	67.7			% Profit Before Taxes/Tangible Net Worth	31.5	41.2
		(12) 29.7	24.5				(38) 8.6	(38) 12.1
		8.2	-5.8				-13.0	-4.0
		22.2	36.3			% Profit Before Taxes/Total Assets	11.5	10.7
		4.4	21.5				4.1	3.0
		2.1	-2.9				-4.4	-3.2
		24.2	31.5			Sales/Net Fixed Assets	16.5	26.3
		13.0	12.3				10.0	12.5
		2.9	6.0				6.9	7.4
		4.0	3.5			Sales/Total Assets	3.6	4.0
		3.3	2.8				2.6	2.6
		1.2	2.1				1.5	1.5
		.4	.4			% Depr., Dep., Amort./Sales	.9	.8
		1.0	(11) 1.4				(35) 1.1	(37) 1.0
		6.2	2.0				1.6	2.1
						% Officers', Directors' Owners' Comp/Sales		
441M	28494M	238700M	750485M	563520M	895322M	Net Sales ($)	2644418M	1964454M
228M	8438M	75317M	319300M	258186M	711830M	Total Assets ($)	1410715M	1083342M

M = $ thousand   MM = $ million
See Pages 11 through 21 for Explanation of Ratios and Data

Comparative Historical Data — Current Data Sorted by Sales

Comparative Historical Data			Type of Statement	Current Data Sorted by Sales					
20	13	11	Unqualified				1		11
2	4	3	Reviewed			2	2		2
6	8	7	Compiled						2
2	3	4	Tax Returns	1		1			
13	20	17	Other	2	1		1	2	
4/1/04- 3/31/05 ALL	4/1/05- 3/31/06 ALL	4/1/06- 3/31/07 ALL		1	1 7 (4/1-9/30/06)	1	1 35 (10/1/06-3/31/07)	2	11
				0-1MM	1-3MM	3-5MM	5-10MM	10-25MM	25MM & OVER
43	48	42	NUMBER OF STATEMENTS	4	2	3	4	3	26
%	%	%		%	%	%	%	%	%
			ASSETS						
11.8	12.3	17.1	Cash & Equivalents						23.3
16.4	21.4	12.4	Trade Receivables (net)						12.0
30.9	27.6	25.6	Inventory						21.7
3.3	2.4	3.0	All Other Current						4.2
62.4	63.6	58.0	Total Current						61.1
24.8	27.0	29.9	Fixed Assets (net)						24.7
5.2	4.0	5.7	Intangibles (net)						8.7
7.6	5.3	6.4	All Other Non-Current						5.5
100.0	100.0	100.0	Total						100.0
			LIABILITIES						
14.3	17.0	17.6	Notes Payable-Short Term						5.1
1.2	1.3	1.2	Cur. Mat.-L.T.D.						.7
12.0	14.4	10.0	Trade Payables						7.2
.2	.1	.2	Income Taxes Payable						.3
14.6	16.3	17.6	All Other Current						20.6
42.3	49.0	46.5	Total Current						33.9
11.9	12.7	7.8	Long-Term Debt						7.6
.9	.6	1.0	Deferred Taxes						1.6
4.3	3.2	3.9	All Other Non-Current						4.4
40.7	34.5	40.7	Net Worth						52.5
100.0	100.0	100.0	Total Liabilties & Net Worth						100.0
			INCOME DATA						
100.0	100.0	100.0	Net Sales						100.0
19.7	25.3	26.2	Gross Profit						20.0
16.4	18.1	18.6	Operating Expenses						14.4
3.3	7.1	7.5	Operating Profit						5.6
.2	1.0	1.3	All Other Expenses (net)						-.2
3.1	6.2	6.2	Profit Before Taxes						5.8
			RATIOS						
2.1	2.2	2.1	Current						2.9
1.6	1.4	1.4							1.9
1.1	1.0	.7							1.3
1.1	1.3	1.2	Quick						2.3
.7	.7	.6							1.0
.3	.3	.2							.6
11 33.2	**12** 29.9	**4** 85.0	Sales/Receivables						**8** 43.0
16 22.5	**23** 15.7	**11** 33.7							**13** 27.9
27 13.6	**48** 7.6	**21** 17.2							**21** 17.1
26 14.1	**17** 22.0	**17** 21.2	Cost of Sales/Inventory						**19** 19.4
49 7.5	**39** 9.3	**34** 10.6							**35** 10.3
61 5.9	**64** 5.7	**49** 7.5							**48** 7.6
9 39.0	**5** 70.4	**7** 56.0	Cost of Sales/Payables						**7** 51.1
14 25.8	**15** 24.2	**10** 37.9							**9** 40.8
22 16.5	**32** 11.5	**15** 24.5							**13** 27.6
8.1	6.9	8.3	Sales/Working Capital						5.1
13.8	14.2	14.5							9.8
127.7	84.5	-36.4							38.9
5.7	11.3	25.8	EBIT/Interest						50.7
(33) 2.7	(38) 4.6	(34) 3.8						(19)	5.5
.3	2.5	-1.2							-1.2
			Net Profit + Depr., Dep., Amort./Cur. Mat. L/T/D						
.3	.2	.2	Fixed/Worth						.2
.6	.5	.6							.5
2.0	2.3	2.7							2.2
.7	.8	.6	Debt/Worth						.4
1.6	2.2	1.4							.8
4.6	7.4	5.5							3.1
31.1	69.7	69.5	% Profit Before Taxes/Tangible Net Worth						56.1
(39) 16.2	(45) 25.9	(36) 27.0						(23)	24.8
1.2	11.7	5.2							4.7
9.2	20.5	21.9	% Profit Before Taxes/Total Assets						22.4
4.7	9.7	8.2							12.1
.5	3.5	1.3							1.9
34.3	34.3	28.7	Sales/Net Fixed Assets						21.3
13.9	14.6	12.8							12.8
6.2	5.8	5.7							8.0
4.2	4.0	3.7	Sales/Total Assets						3.6
2.8	2.2	2.5							2.7
1.5	1.3	1.2							1.6
.6	.5	.4	% Depr., Dep., Amort./Sales						.5
(37) .9	(44) .9	(39) 1.0						(24)	1.0
1.8	1.7	2.0							1.4
	.7	.6	% Officers', Directors' Owners' Comp/Sales						
	(12) 1.3	(11) 1.7							
	3.3	3.5							
2153805M	2274109M	2476962M	Net Sales ($)	2435M	3934M	12570M	27619M	42841M	2387563M
1120907M	1253919M	1373299M	Total Assets ($)	4666M	3613M	5797M	16020M	10023M	1333180M

© RMA 2007

M = $ thousand   MM = $ million
See Pages 11 through 21 for Explanation of Ratios and Data

Current Data Sorted by Assets | Comparative Historical Data

							Type of Statement				
			6	10			Unqualified		12		20
1	1		14	4			Reviewed		18		25
1	4		4	1			Compiled		13		15
3	4		2				Tax Returns		6		7
	2		8	10	3		Other		18		25
	11 (4/1-9/30/06)			67 (10/1/06-3/31/07)					4/1/02-3/31/03		4/1/03-3/31/04
0-500M	500M-2MM		2-10MM	10-50MM	50-100MM	100-250MM			ALL		ALL
5	11		34	25	3		NUMBER OF STATEMENTS		67		92
%	%		%	%	%	%	ASSETS		%		%
	3.7		7.9	13.7			Cash & Equivalents		12.1		10.4
	17.4		19.5	16.8		D	Trade Receivables (net)		20.2		21.2
	46.5		24.8	24.0		A	Inventory		26.6		25.8
	1.2		3.3	3.8		T	All Other Current		1.6		2.6
	68.8		55.4	58.3		A	Total Current		60.5		59.9
	23.6		34.5	30.9			Fixed Assets (net)		28.8		30.2
	.1		4.0	3.5		N	Intangibles (net)		4.9		3.3
	7.5		6.1	7.2		O	All Other Non-Current		5.7		6.7
	100.0		100.0	100.0		T	Total		100.0		100.0
						A	LIABILITIES				
	21.2		9.3	9.0		V	Notes Payable-Short Term		13.2		12.8
	2.1		3.9	4.4		A	Cur. Mat.-L.T.D.		2.4		3.1
	8.8		9.7	10.1		I	Trade Payables		11.2		12.5
	.0		.2	.0		L	Income Taxes Payable		.2		.2
	17.4		17.8	20.5		A	All Other Current		16.5		15.3
	49.4		40.9	44.1		B	Total Current		43.4		43.8
	6.9		16.9	15.6		L	Long-Term Debt		15.1		16.8
	.0		.3	.5		E	Deferred Taxes		.1		.2
	3.3		5.0	6.7			All Other Non-Current		3.9		5.4
	40.4		36.9	33.2			Net Worth		37.5		33.8
	100.0		100.0	100.0			Total Liabilities & Net Worth		100.0		100.0
							INCOME DATA				
	100.0		100.0	100.0			Net Sales		100.0		100.0
	31.1		29.5	26.5			Gross Profit		30.4		28.9
	31.2		24.2	22.3			Operating Expenses		25.4		25.5
	-.2		5.4	4.2			Operating Profit		5.0		3.4
	1.0		.8	.1			All Other Expenses (net)		.7		.6
	-1.1		4.6	4.1			Profit Before Taxes		4.3		2.9
							RATIOS				
	4.4		2.0	2.7					2.5		2.2
	1.5		1.4	1.5			Current		1.6		1.4
	1.0		1.1	.9					1.1		.9
	3.0		1.1	1.3					1.8		1.2
	.3		.7	.7			Quick		.8		.8
	.1		.4	.2					.4		.4

	6	57.2	8	45.2	6	62.4			Sales/Receivables		9	40.4	9	39.4
	13	28.0	21	17.6	16	22.5					24	15.3	24	15.4
	23	16.2	37	10.0	31	11.9					37	9.8	47	7.7
	56	6.6	24	15.2	23	15.8			Cost of Sales/Inventory		27	13.6	26	14.1
	79	4.6	40	9.2	39	9.4					46	8.0	51	7.2
	120	3.0	77	4.8	68	5.3					67	5.5	69	5.3
	2	220.8	10	36.6	10	36.3			Cost of Sales/Payables		9	39.0	10	35.0
	9	42.9	13	27.2	16	23.2					16	22.6	21	17.3
	31	11.7	31	11.7	23	16.1					34	10.8	33	11.0

	7.4		8.4	7.6			Sales/Working Capital		6.3		7.9
	12.1		18.2	19.0					14.0		19.6
	58.6		43.6	-38.1					71.0		-69.5

		2.3		12.9		8.0			EBIT/Interest			20.5		11.9
		1.4	(32)	4.1	(24)	5.0				(62)	7.0	(85)	4.1
		-4.9		2.0		2.1					1.8		1.1

									Net Profit + Depr., Dep.,			20.4		16.3
									Amort./Cur. Mat. L/T/D	(21)	6.3	(21)	4.2
											2.4		1.2

	.2		.5	.4			Fixed/Worth		.4		.4
	.5		.9	1.1					.7		.9
	1.1		2.4	2.1					2.0		2.1
	.4		.9	1.0			Debt/Worth		.6		1.0
	1.7		1.9	2.4					1.7		2.2
	4.7		4.3	4.5					4.6		4.9

		12.3		64.5		42.7			% Profit Before Taxes/Tangible			62.6		52.2
	(10)	3.2	(30)	40.0	(22)	31.9			Net Worth	(58)	42.6	(83)	17.2
		-12.1		23.4		14.5					10.0		3.3

	4.5		20.7	14.6			% Profit Before Taxes/Total		24.4		16.6
	1.2		9.1	8.2			Assets		10.1		5.3
	-6.6		4.1	3.9					1.7		.6
	48.9		16.0	14.8			Sales/Net Fixed Assets		24.0		18.2
	17.8		8.6	10.6					10.6		9.8
	6.1		4.6	5.8					6.3		5.0
	3.6		3.2	3.5			Sales/Total Assets		3.6		3.5
	2.6		2.5	2.5					2.7		2.7
	2.2		2.0	1.9					1.8		1.8

		.4		1.2		1.0			% Depr., Dep., Amort./Sales			1.3		1.0
	(10)	1.8	(30)	1.9	(24)	1.8				(63)	1.9	(82)	1.6
		3.0		2.8		2.4					2.8		2.5

									% Officers', Directors'			1.3		1.2
									Owners' Comp/Sales	(20)	2.7	(22)	3.9
											5.6		7.6

6704M	33729M	444288M	1200719M	449212M			Net Sales ($)		1201951M	1363789M
1695M	11571M	176265M	441620M	233815M			Total Assets ($)		686549M	578996M

M = $ thousand   MM = $ million

See Pages 11 through 21 for Explanation of Ratios and Data

Comparative Historical Data | Current Data Sorted by Sales

			Type of Statement						
14	14	16	Unqualified				1	8	7
20	19	20	Reviewed		1		6	6	6
17	11	10	Compiled		1	1	2	3	
11	3	9	Tax Returns	1	1	3		1	
24	25	23	Other		7	1		1	
4/1/04-	4/1/05-	4/1/06-			1	1	6	1	14
3/31/05	3/31/06	3/31/07			11 (4/1-9/30/06)		67 (10/1/06-3/31/07)		
ALL	ALL	ALL		0-1MM	1-3MM	3-5MM	5-10MM	10-25MM	25MM & OVER
86	72	78	NUMBER OF STATEMENTS	1	10	6	15	19	27
%	%	%	ASSETS	%	%	%	%	%	%
11.8	12.5	9.0	Cash & Equivalents		5.2		8.9	7.9	12.2
23.0	17.8	18.4	Trade Receivables (net)		20.6		19.2	15.3	21.3
22.9	23.7	27.5	Inventory		30.5		23.3	25.3	24.0
4.2	5.0	3.5	All Other Current		7.1		.5	3.1	4.9
61.9	58.9	58.4	Total Current		63.4		51.9	51.7	62.4
28.0	29.9	30.8	Fixed Assets (net)		23.4		36.6	33.9	28.7
3.7	5.8	3.9	Intangibles (net)		.9		4.9	6.8	3.0
6.4	5.4	6.9	All Other Non-Current		12.4		6.6	7.6	6.0
100.0	100.0	100.0	Total		100.0		100.0	100.0	100.0
			LIABILITIES						
14.4	9.0	11.5	Notes Payable-Short Term		22.5		11.2	4.1	11.2
3.6	2.7	4.2	Cur. Mat.-L.T.D.		6.9		4.0	3.7	3.8
16.3	10.1	10.2	Trade Payables		14.2		8.1	9.6	10.8
.4	.5	.1	Income Taxes Payable		.0		.2	.2	.0
14.3	18.9	18.1	All Other Current		10.8		20.3	16.3	19.2
48.9	41.3	44.1	Total Current		54.5		43.7	34.0	45.1
12.6	17.2	16.5	Long-Term Debt		18.4		17.1	19.2	11.8
.2	.3	.3	Deferred Taxes		.0		.0	1.1	.0
4.6	4.1	5.1	All Other Non-Current		6.4		.9	6.7	6.7
33.7	37.1	34.0	Net Worth		20.8		38.3	39.1	36.4
100.0	100.0	100.0	Total Liabilities & Net Worth		100.0		100.0	100.0	100.0
			INCOME DATA						
100.0	100.0	100.0	Net Sales		100.0		100.0	100.0	100.0
27.7	27.5	28.8	Gross Profit		39.4		31.5	25.3	24.8
23.1	21.7	24.6	Operating Expenses		37.0		26.5	20.7	19.7
4.6	5.8	4.1	Operating Profit		2.4		5.0	4.6	5.1
.5	.8	.7	All Other Expenses (net)		2.5		-.5	.5	.7
4.1	5.0	3.4	Profit Before Taxes		-.1		5.5	4.2	4.4
			RATIOS						
2.0	2.2	2.0			1.6		2.0	2.2	2.6
1.3	1.5	1.4	Current		1.1		1.2	1.4	1.5
.9	1.1	1.0			1.0		.9	1.2	1.1
1.3	1.4	1.2			1.0		.9	1.4	1.4
.6 (71)	.7	.7	Quick		.4		.6	.7	.9
.4	.4	.3			.1		.4	.4	.2
13 28.5	6 61.9	7 53.1		4 95.3		8 43.5	5 79.5	9 41.0
28 13.0	17 20.9	18 19.8	Sales/Receivables	11 32.6		33 11.2	18 20.0	20 17.9
47 7.8	48 7.7	36 10.1		27 13.5		37 9.9	37 10.0	37 10.0
23 15.9	27 13.7	24 15.0		0 UND		26 13.9	22 16.4	23 15.8
40 9.0	46 7.9	43 8.4	Cost of Sales/Inventory	55 6.6		44 8.3	48 7.5	36 10.2
71 5.2	79 4.6	81 4.5		112 3.3		114 3.2	75 4.9	56 6.5
13 28.9	10 35.2	9 39.2		0 UND		11 33.8	10 37.6	10 36.6
21 17.3	20 18.6	15 24.6	Cost of Sales/Payables	16 22.9		22 17.0	13 27.1	15 24.7
48 7.5	31 11.9	30 12.3		60 6.0		42 8.7	30 12.1	21 17.4
9.0	6.7	8.2		20.6		7.9	8.3	7.8
20.1	17.7	20.4	Sales/Working Capital	37.6		39.7	15.6	19.0
-44.0	67.2	83.0		NM		-33.5	36.6	47.4
16.7	12.3	8.1		1.6		16.0	9.6	12.2
(80) 4.5	(69) 4.9	(75) 3.5	EBIT/Interest	.8	(14) 5.3	(18) 4.1	(26) 5.5
2.0	2.7	1.4		-5.0		3.0	1.4	2.2
8.9	9.3	8.3						
(20) 2.1	(19) 4.5	(20) 3.5	Net Profit + Depr., Dep., Amort./Cur. Mat. L/T/D					
.7	1.0	1.2						
.3	.5	.4		.3		.3	.5	.4
1.0	1.0	.9	Fixed/Worth	1.5		1.0	1.3	.8
2.4	2.6	2.4		-1.6		2.7	4.6	1.5
.9	.8	.8		.6		.8	1.0	.7
2.2	2.3	2.1	Debt/Worth	8.6		2.0	1.5	2.0
6.6	5.6	5.3		-7.6		3.6	5.4	3.8
49.0	63.3	53.4				60.1	48.6	55.0
(76) 30.1	(62) 30.3	(65) 32.4	% Profit Before Taxes/Tangible Net Worth		(14) 43.3	(16) 22.9	(24) 34.3
11.4	8.3	8.0				26.2	2.4	26.6
15.4	16.7	17.3		1.3		22.4	18.0	17.0
7.7	9.2	6.7	% Profit Before Taxes/Total Assets	-1.1		9.2	6.3	11.9
2.2	3.3	1.2		-7.6		6.0	1.3	5.1
24.6	14.7	17.8		69.7		17.0	15.7	16.5
9.2	8.8	9.5	Sales/Net Fixed Assets	16.9		6.3	9.1	10.6
5.4	4.5	5.1		5.4		2.7	4.7	6.9
3.1	2.9	3.5		4.2		3.0	3.0	3.6
2.5	2.3	2.6	Sales/Total Assets	2.5		2.3	2.4	2.9
2.0	1.8	2.0		1.9		1.5	1.5	2.3
.9	1.0	1.0				1.3	1.2	.9
(76) 1.6	(63) 1.6	(72) 1.8	% Depr., Dep., Amort./Sales		(12) 2.5	(18) 2.0	(26) 1.4
2.9	2.5	2.7				4.0	2.8	2.2
.8	1.2	2.0						
(27) 2.4	(12) 2.2	(22) 3.7	% Officers', Directors' Owners' Comp/Sales					
6.3	4.6	5.6						
1626337M	2196855M	2134652M	Net Sales ($)	645M	18301M	21768M	106636M	313202M	1674100M
671995M	1057350M	864966M	Total Assets ($)	373M	14867M	7419M	64381M	151674M	626252M

M = $ thousand   MM = $ million
See Pages 11 through 21 for Explanation of Ratios and Data

Current Data Sorted by Assets							Comparative Historical Data	
						Type of Statement		
1	2	6	13	3	3	Unqualified	31	32
1	3	31	11	2		Reviewed	42	51
5	14	11				Compiled	32	34
7	17	6	1			Tax Returns	19	32
6	21	21	13	4	2	Other	50	54
	43 (4/1-9/30/06)		161 (10/1/06-3/31/07)				4/1/02-3/31/03 ALL	4/1/03-3/31/04 ALL
0-500M	500M-2MM	2-10MM	10-50MM	50-100MM	100-250MM			
20	57	75	38	9	5	**NUMBER OF STATEMENTS**	174	203
%	%	%	%	%	%	**ASSETS**	%	%
12.4	6.2	7.6	3.3			Cash & Equivalents	6.8	6.5
27.3	28.9	23.3	20.5			Trade Receivables (net)	21.5	22.7
21.7	29.9	30.1	36.4			Inventory	26.2	27.9
1.5	.9	2.1	2.1			All Other Current	2.8	1.9
62.9	65.9	63.1	62.3			Total Current	57.3	59.1
29.5	26.4	27.2	26.9			Fixed Assets (net)	31.3	30.2
1.8	2.9	2.6	5.0			Intangibles (net)	4.0	4.3
5.6	4.9	7.2	5.8			All Other Non-Current	7.3	6.5
100.0	100.0	100.0	100.0			Total	100.0	100.0
						LIABILITIES		
22.4	12.4	15.2	13.2			Notes Payable-Short Term	14.1	13.9
5.4	5.7	4.2	3.2			Cur. Mat.-L.T.D.	4.7	4.3
14.3	12.8	13.3	10.6			Trade Payables	12.7	12.6
.5	.4	.1	.5			Income Taxes Payable	.4	.2
7.0	8.1	10.4	10.5			All Other Current	8.5	8.8
49.6	39.4	43.1	38.0			Total Current	40.4	39.7
25.7	19.9	16.2	16.6			Long-Term Debt	21.1	18.5
.2	.1	.3	.6			Deferred Taxes	.4	.3
16.0	9.3	3.9	4.0			All Other Non-Current	3.5	6.9
8.3	31.4	36.5	40.8			Net Worth	34.5	34.6
100.0	100.0	100.0	100.0			Total Liabilties & Net Worth	100.0	100.0
						INCOME DATA		
100.0	100.0	100.0	100.0			Net Sales	100.0	100.0
46.4	32.7	25.7	23.9			Gross Profit	27.4	28.2
38.9	27.0	20.8	17.5			Operating Expenses	22.9	24.3
7.5	5.7	4.8	6.4			Operating Profit	4.5	3.9
1.9	1.7	1.2	1.2			All Other Expenses (net)	1.3	1.1
5.7	4.1	3.6	5.3			Profit Before Taxes	3.2	2.8
						RATIOS		
3.6	3.3	2.3	2.2				2.3	2.4
1.7	1.7	1.6	1.6			Current	1.5	1.5
.7	1.1	1.1	1.2				1.1	1.1
2.2	2.1	1.5	.9				1.3	1.3
1.1	1.1	.7	.7			Quick	(172) .7	.7
.4	.3	.4	.4				.4	.4
11　33.5	18　20.7	21　17.8	24　15.5				18　20.7	20　18.2
33　10.9	30　12.1	31　11.8	34　10.6			Sales/Receivables	29　12.4	33　11.0
72　5.1	44　8.4	43　8.5	47　7.8				42　8.8	46　7.9
4　91.5	15　24.2	29　12.5	56　6.5				27　13.4	33　11.1
30　12.3	45　8.1	53　6.9	86　4.3			Cost of Sales/Inventory	52　7.0	56　6.5
142　2.6	91　4.0	108　3.4	114　3.2				84　4.4	86　4.2
8　47.4	5　75.0	9　42.1	14　26.2				9　41.1	10　37.6
30　12.2	20　18.7	23　16.1	21　17.4			Cost of Sales/Payables	18　20.1	20　18.1
42　8.6	38　9.5	40　9.1	33　11.2				36　10.2	38　9.7
5.8	6.0	6.6	5.6				7.2	6.2
14.3	11.9	10.8	9.3			Sales/Working Capital	13.1	12.4
-20.9	109.9	38.2	22.6				63.3	92.1
10.8	9.0	9.6	6.3				9.2	7.6
(16) 2.3	(54) 4.5	(68) 3.6	(35) 3.3			EBIT/Interest	(163) 3.1	(191) 2.7
1.2	.8	1.6	2.2				1.1	1.1
		2.9	4.1			Net Profit + Depr., Dep.,	3.8	3.7
	(18) 1.8	(15) 2.7				Amort./Cur. Mat. L/T/D	(44) 1.9	(48) 2.0
		1.3	1.4				1.0	1.0
.6	.3	.2	.4				.4	.4
1.8	.8	.7	.7			Fixed/Worth	1.1	.9
-.9	2.3	1.6	1.2				2.8	2.5
1.1	.7	.9	1.1				.9	.8
6.0	2.1	2.2	1.7			Debt/Worth	2.1	2.0
-5.3	7.4	3.7	3.1				7.7	5.6
178.6	85.0	44.0	41.6			% Profit Before Taxes/Tangible	50.4	38.8
(14) 71.7	(48) 33.7	(69) 22.4	(36) 25.6			Net Worth	(149) 20.6	(175) 14.8
34.7	5.0	9.0	9.5				5.5	2.6
22.9	21.9	18.0	13.7			% Profit Before Taxes/Total	16.7	12.4
8.3	8.8	6.6	7.7			Assets	6.3	4.7
2.4	-.8	2.1	4.0				.8	.1
37.6	36.0	36.2	14.6				19.9	23.8
14.5	15.0	11.1	9.8			Sales/Net Fixed Assets	7.9	8.1
4.3	6.4	4.6	5.4				4.7	4.3
5.7	3.7	3.2	2.6				3.5	3.3
2.8	2.9	2.2	2.1			Sales/Total Assets	2.4	2.3
1.5	2.0	1.8	1.6				1.6	1.6
.9	.9	.8	1.0				1.4	1.2
(14) 2.3	(46) 1.8	(65) 1.7	(36) 1.6			% Depr., Dep., Amort./Sales	(160) 2.4	(177) 2.3
3.7	3.2	3.1	2.8				4.0	3.9
		2.8	1.4				1.5	1.9
	(34) 4.1	(28) 2.4				% Officers', Directors', Owners' Comp/Sales	(61) 3.5	(77) 3.9
	8.1	4.8					6.7	7.0
16232M	197924M	1030309M	1565152M	1247617M	1604234M	Net Sales ($)	3404158M	4281048M
5206M	67927M	392092M	717077M	589326M	842400M	Total Assets ($)	1763696M	1862370M

© RMA 2007

M = $ thousand　　MM = $ million
See Pages 11 through 21 for Explanation of Ratios and Data

Comparative Historical Data   **Current Data Sorted by Sales**

			Type of Statement	0-1MM	1-3MM	3-5MM	5-10MM	10-25MM	25MM & OVER
34	34	28	Unqualified	1	2		3	7	15
45	52	48	Reviewed	1	2	1	6	28	10
29	37	30	Compiled	4	7	9	6	3	1
31	39	31	Tax Returns	5	11	8	4	3	
56	68	67	Other	5	7	15	13	11	16
4/1/04-3/31/05 ALL	4/1/05-3/31/06 ALL	4/1/06-3/31/07 ALL		43 (4/1-9/30/06)			161 (10/1/06-3/31/07)		
195	230	204	**NUMBER OF STATEMENTS**	16	29	33	32	52	42
%	%	%	**ASSETS**	%	%	%	%	%	%
6.8	6.7	6.6	Cash & Equivalents	10.9	7.4	9.9	2.4	6.6	5.2
25.2	23.7	24.5	Trade Receivables (net)	21.4	22.6	33.1	24.3	21.5	24.0
29.2	28.0	30.1	Inventory	23.0	31.8	23.9	30.8	32.6	32.8
1.9	2.7	1.9	All Other Current	.7	1.4	2.7	1.7	2.5	2.7
63.1	61.0	63.0	Total Current	55.9	63.2	67.8	59.2	63.2	64.7
26.7	28.6	27.8	Fixed Assets (net)	31.9	32.4	22.9	31.2	26.1	26.3
4.5	4.0	3.2	Intangibles (net)	2.3	.5	4.5	.8	4.7	4.6
5.7	6.4	5.9	All Other Non-Current	9.6	4.0	4.8	8.9	6.0	4.3
100.0	100.0	100.0	Total	100.0	100.0	100.0	100.0	100.0	100.0
			LIABILITIES						
16.0	16.1	14.4	Notes Payable-Short Term	26.5	11.0	11.4	17.1	12.8	14.3
4.8	3.8	4.4	Cur. Mat.-L.T.D.	3.2	7.2	3.7	5.9	4.2	2.8
13.5	12.7	12.5	Trade Payables	12.1	9.0	13.3	17.1	12.3	11.0
.2	.2	.3	Income Taxes Payable	.0	.6	.5	.1	.3	.2
8.4	6.8	9.2	All Other Current	4.3	14.3	8.8	7.3	7.8	10.9
42.7	39.6	40.8	Total Current	46.1	42.2	37.7	47.4	37.4	39.3
18.2	20.5	18.6	Long-Term Debt	27.8	22.7	19.7	18.7	16.6	13.8
.3	.4	.3	Deferred Taxes	.3	.1	.0	.5	.5	.2
6.3	4.5	6.5	All Other Non-Current	19.3	2.9	10.0	5.9	3.9	5.2
32.5	35.1	33.8	Net Worth	6.2	32.1	32.6	27.5	41.7	41.6
100.0	100.0	100.0	Total Liabilties & Net Worth	100.0	100.0	100.0	100.0	100.0	100.0
			INCOME DATA						
100.0	100.0	100.0	Net Sales	100.0	100.0	100.0	100.0	100.0	100.0
27.5	29.1	29.1	Gross Profit	44.4	40.1	33.7	23.8	24.3	22.0
22.8	24.4	23.5	Operating Expenses	36.0	35.1	27.6	20.5	18.4	15.9
4.8	4.6	5.6	Operating Profit	8.4	5.0	6.1	3.3	5.9	6.1
1.0	1.1	1.4	All Other Expenses (net)	2.7	1.3	2.1	1.3	1.0	.8
3.8	3.6	4.3	Profit Before Taxes	5.7	3.7	4.0	2.0	4.9	5.3
			RATIOS						
2.4	2.7	2.9	Current	3.2	3.4	3.8	2.1	3.5	2.5
1.5	1.5	1.6		1.3	1.9	2.0	1.3	1.7	1.6
1.1	1.1	1.1		.7	1.2	1.2	.9	1.3	1.3
1.3	1.4	1.6	Quick	2.0	2.9	2.7	.8	1.4	1.1
.7	.7	.8		.8	.9	1.6	.5	.8	.7
.4	.4	.4		.4	.2	.7	.3	.4	.5
22 16.6	20 17.8	19 19.4	Sales/Receivables	11 33.5	14 26.8	19 18.9	24 15.3	21 17.1	22 16.6
32 11.3	32 11.5	32 11.5		40 9.2	29 12.6	33 11.0	31 11.8	33 11.1	31 11.7
44 8.3	44 8.3	45 8.0		72 5.1	43 8.4	50 7.2	53 6.9	41 8.9	42 8.7
27 13.6	26 14.1	28 12.9	Cost of Sales/Inventory	2 155.9	20 18.1	12 31.0	29 12.6	35 10.3	38 9.6
51 7.1	55 6.6	56 6.5		39 9.4	62 5.8	37 9.8	52 7.0	75 4.8	65 5.6
103 3.5	97 3.5	105 3.5		158 2.3	151 2.4	61 6.0	107 3.4	114 3.2	88 4.2
10 36.3	10 36.2	10 36.7	Cost of Sales/Payables	12 29.9	3 139.4	4 94.3	14 25.7	12 30.4	11 32.0
20 18.0	20 18.3	22 16.7		30 12.2	18 20.7	16 22.1	26 13.9	22 16.7	19 18.7
37 9.9	34 10.6	38 9.7		42 8.6	34 10.9	42 8.7	46 8.0	40 9.2	30 12.3
5.8	6.8	5.9	Sales/Working Capital	5.4	4.0	6.9	7.5	5.7	6.2
11.5	12.7	10.1		33.0	8.8	9.5	16.7	9.6	9.7
51.0	38.0	36.4		-20.6	35.5	23.2	-68.5	16.8	22.0
10.1	8.7	7.7	EBIT/Interest	3.7	8.7	13.9	7.0	7.2	7.0
(179) 4.4	(216) 3.3	(185) 3.6		(15) 2.1	(25) 2.4	(31) 5.8	(27) 2.1	(48) 3.2	(39) 4.8
1.7	1.2	1.6		1.2	-.7	2.1	.3	1.8	2.4
5.7	4.0	4.0	Net Profit + Depr., Dep., Amort./Cur. Mat. L/T/D					3.7	6.8
(54) 2.4	(59) 1.9	(48) 2.6						(15) 2.4	(19) 3.7
1.4	1.2	1.4						1.5	2.3
.4	.3	.3	Fixed/Worth	.8	.4	.2	.5	.2	.3
.9	.8	.7		3.3	.7	.7	.9	.7	.6
1.9	2.4	1.6		-.7	1.8	2.0	6.9	1.4	1.2
.9	.7	.9	Debt/Worth	1.2	.9	.5	1.0	.9	1.0
2.2	2.2	2.0		8.0	1.5	2.2	2.3	2.2	1.6
5.4	5.4	4.4		-5.3	5.9	5.4	14.7	3.5	2.8
45.6	41.9	49.8	% Profit Before Taxes/Tangible Net Worth	150.0	66.4	85.9	59.6	40.2	43.1
(166) 21.4	(199) 23.6	(180) 27.8		(11) 51.0	(25) 24.6	(29) 37.1	(27) 14.6	(48) 25.3	(40) 24.0
6.6	3.6	10.7		31.4	1.2	15.0	2.8	9.8	17.2
14.5	16.9	17.1	% Profit Before Taxes/Total Assets	14.4	20.5	21.4	14.1	17.0	14.3
7.0	5.7	8.6		6.6	4.4	10.0	4.6	8.2	10.0
1.7	.5	2.3		1.4	-4.9	3.9	-1.9	3.2	5.1
24.7	25.1	26.0	Sales/Net Fixed Assets	36.0	18.5	42.0	24.3	32.1	23.2
9.5	9.4	10.9		5.7	8.5	21.7	8.2	9.9	11.0
5.3	4.6	5.0		2.7	3.2	7.7	4.4	4.6	5.8
3.5	3.6	3.3	Sales/Total Assets	3.4	3.0	3.8	3.1	2.9	3.4
2.5	2.3	2.4		1.9	2.0	3.1	2.2	2.1	2.4
1.7	1.6	1.7		1.3	1.5	2.6	1.8	1.7	1.8
.9	1.0	.9	% Depr., Dep., Amort./Sales	1.0	.9	.8	1.2	.6	.9
(173) 2.1	(208) 1.9	(174) 1.8		(11) 3.2	(23) 2.8	(25) 1.5	(28) 2.3	(48) 1.6	(39) 1.6
3.7	3.3	3.1		5.0	3.7	2.9	3.2	3.0	2.5
1.8	1.7	2.0	% Officers', Directors' Owners' Comp/Sales		3.9	2.6	2.3	1.7	
(70) 3.0	(87) 3.4	(75) 3.6			(17) 7.9	(17) 3.4	(13) 3.8	(19) 2.0	
5.5	5.8	6.6			11.8	5.1	8.9	3.5	
5400012M	6523388M	5661468M	Net Sales ($)	9227M	56472M	133076M	234745M	857031M	4370917M
2428848M	3244188M	2614028M	Total Assets ($)	5366M	34967M	45994M	112953M	421600M	1993148M

M = $ thousand   MM = $ million
See Pages 11 through 21 for Explanation of Ratios and Data

Current Data Sorted by Assets | Comparative Historical Data

0-500M	500M-2MM	2-10MM	10-50MM	50-100MM	100-250MM		4/1/02-3/31/03 ALL	4/1/03-3/31/04 ALL
						Type of Statement		
1		4	5	4	5	Unqualified	19	23
	2	5	4	1		Reviewed	14	11
1	3	2	2			Compiled	4	4
1	2	2				Tax Returns	3	3
	3	5	14	2	4	Other	25	22
	6 (4/1-9/30/06)			64 (10/1/06-3/31/07)				
3	10	18	23	7	9	NUMBER OF STATEMENTS	65	63
%	%	%	%	%	%	**ASSETS**	%	%
	10.7	6.3	3.1			Cash & Equivalents	5.2	4.1
	36.8	28.9	23.3			Trade Receivables (net)	24.1	22.9
	19.3	24.8	25.6			Inventory	18.2	17.8
	1.1	1.7	1.0			All Other Current	2.3	1.5
	67.9	61.6	53.1			Total Current	49.8	46.2
	28.3	30.6	36.6			Fixed Assets (net)	38.8	41.7
	.9	1.8	2.1			Intangibles (net)	4.4	4.8
	2.8	6.0	8.2			All Other Non-Current	7.0	7.2
	100.0	100.0	100.0			Total	100.0	100.0
						LIABILITIES		
	18.7	12.0	12.4			Notes Payable-Short Term	10.5	6.2
	5.3	6.1	4.1			Cur. Mat.-L.T.D.	4.2	3.2
	15.0	18.0	17.4			Trade Payables	15.0	14.8
	.0	.1	.2			Income Taxes Payable	.1	.1
	5.7	4.5	7.3			All Other Current	6.6	8.8
	44.6	40.6	41.4			Total Current	36.4	33.0
	18.6	16.2	19.7			Long-Term Debt	19.2	21.1
	.0	1.6	.6			Deferred Taxes	1.4	1.7
	3.5	3.1	4.8			All Other Non-Current	4.5	7.9
	33.3	38.5	33.4			Net Worth	38.6	36.2
	100.0	100.0	100.0			Total Liabilties & Net Worth	100.0	100.0
						INCOME DATA		
	100.0	100.0	100.0			Net Sales	100.0	100.0
	30.1	23.3	17.2			Gross Profit	24.6	25.9
	22.9	18.7	12.0			Operating Expenses	21.5	21.1
	7.3	4.6	5.2			Operating Profit	3.2	4.8
	1.6	.8	1.1			All Other Expenses (net)	1.5	1.3
	5.7	3.8	4.1			Profit Before Taxes	1.6	3.5
						RATIOS		
	3.3	2.0	2.5				2.2	2.0
	1.8	1.6	1.4			Current	1.4	1.5
	.8	1.1	.9				1.0	1.1
	2.4	1.4	1.2				1.4	1.2
	.9	.9	.8			Quick	1.0	.9
	.5	.6	.4				.5	.6
	37 9.9	27 13.4	31 11.8				34 10.7	32 11.3
	43 8.5	48 7.7	35 10.4			Sales/Receivables	44 8.3	38 9.5
	69 5.3	58 6.3	44 8.3				59 6.2	48 7.6
	12 30.0	14 25.3	28 12.8				29 12.6	18 20.8
	29 12.5	48 7.6	44 8.2			Cost of Sales/Inventory	48 7.7	38 9.7
	65 5.6	62 5.9	68 5.4				71 5.1	65 5.6
	15 24.8	17 20.9	17 20.9				21 17.4	24 15.4
	26 14.3	37 10.0	34 10.8			Cost of Sales/Payables	34 10.7	33 11.0
	41 8.9	59 6.2	41 8.8				54 6.8	44 8.3
	4.2	6.6	7.7				6.5	7.9
	11.1	12.9	20.6			Sales/Working Capital	12.8	16.3
	-25.4	288.9	-26.6				NM	78.6
		11.2	10.0				7.8	7.7
		(16) 3.8	3.8			EBIT/Interest	(60) 3.3	(57) 3.9
		.7	1.4				.8	1.6
							4.1	5.5
						Net Profit + Depr., Dep., Amort./Cur. Mat. L/T/D	(18) 2.6	(20) 3.2
							1.4	1.7
	.2	.3	.6				.4	.7
	.3	.7	1.6			Fixed/Worth	1.2	1.2
	10.5	1.9	2.4				2.7	3.9
	.5	1.1	1.0				.7	.9
	1.9	1.5	3.0			Debt/Worth	2.0	1.9
	20.2	3.2	4.5				5.9	5.3
		38.6	62.9				29.3	31.4
	(17) 23.5	(21) 36.4				% Profit Before Taxes/Tangible Net Worth	(54) 15.7	(54) 19.0
		1.5	9.1				1.2	3.9
	31.7	13.1	20.7				10.2	10.6
	22.7	4.4	7.6			% Profit Before Taxes/Total Assets	4.7	5.4
	1.3	-1.6	2.1				-.8	1.5
	31.4	25.5	9.9				15.3	9.4
	14.0	12.2	7.4			Sales/Net Fixed Assets	4.3	4.3
	3.1	1.7	5.2				2.3	2.1
	3.0	3.2	3.2				2.2	2.4
	2.4	2.2	2.3			Sales/Total Assets	1.6	1.8
	2.0	1.1	1.6				1.1	1.1
		.8	1.2				1.4	1.7
		1.5	(22) 2.2			% Depr., Dep., Amort./Sales	(50) 3.3	(50) 3.5
		5.0	2.9				5.6	5.1
							1.3	1.7
						% Officers', Directors' Owners' Comp/Sales	(18) 3.3	(17) 3.9
							5.9	5.3
2133M	35323M	249256M	1269661M	568595M	2262723M	Net Sales ($)	3337911M	3847893M
486M	13077M	101521M	515389M	442371M	1418516M	Total Assets ($)	2718305M	3011050M

© RMA 2007

M = $ thousand   MM = $ million
See Pages 11 through 21 for Explanation of Ratios and Data

Comparative Historical Data

Current Data Sorted by Sales

4/1/04-3/31/05 ALL	4/1/05-3/31/06 ALL	4/1/06-3/31/07 ALL	Type of Statement	0-1MM	1-3MM	3-5MM	5-10MM	10-25MM	25MM & OVER
21	24	19	Unqualified	1	2		1	1	14
9	9	12	Reviewed		1	1		5	5
3	4	6	Compiled	1	2		1	2	
5	3	5	Tax Returns		3	1			1
18	30	28	Other			5		6	17
					6 (4/1-9/30/06)			64 (10/1/06-3/31/07)	
56	70	70	NUMBER OF STATEMENTS	2	8	7	2	14	37
%	%	%	ASSETS	%	%	%	%	%	%
4.6	7.0	5.9	Cash & Equivalents					2.1	4.2
23.5	25.2	26.1	Trade Receivables (net)					34.2	21.0
21.1	22.1	21.6	Inventory					30.1	21.6
2.0	2.3	1.3	All Other Current					1.4	1.3
51.1	56.6	54.9	Total Current					67.8	48.2
42.1	36.0	36.9	Fixed Assets (net)					25.3	42.2
1.9	2.0	2.6	Intangibles (net)					2.3	3.2
4.9	5.4	5.6	All Other Non-Current					4.6	6.5
100.0	100.0	100.0	Total					100.0	100.0
			LIABILITIES						
10.4	10.9	11.0	Notes Payable-Short Term					14.9	9.5
3.6	2.9	4.9	Cur. Mat.-L.T.D.					2.1	3.5
14.7	17.5	15.9	Trade Payables					22.8	15.0
.0	.2	.1	Income Taxes Payable					.1	.2
8.8	8.4	5.8	All Other Current					4.4	6.9
37.6	40.0	37.7	Total Current					44.3	35.1
27.8	19.9	18.8	Long-Term Debt					11.5	20.4
.8	1.0	1.2	Deferred Taxes					1.0	1.3
2.5	3.9	4.6	All Other Non-Current					6.3	5.0
31.3	35.3	37.7	Net Worth					36.9	38.1
100.0	100.0	100.0	Total Liabilties & Net Worth					100.0	100.0
			INCOME DATA						
100.0	100.0	100.0	Net Sales					100.0	100.0
23.5	19.5	20.6	Gross Profit					15.3	17.2
20.2	15.8	15.3	Operating Expenses					11.5	12.2
3.3	3.7	5.3	Operating Profit					3.8	5.0
1.5	.9	1.0	All Other Expenses (net)					2.0	.9
1.9	2.8	4.3	Profit Before Taxes					1.7	4.1
			RATIOS						
2.2	1.9	2.3	Current					2.0	2.3
1.4	1.5	1.5						1.5	1.5
.9	1.0	.9						1.1	.9
1.1	1.2	1.3	Quick					1.1	1.3
.7	.8	.8						.8	.8
.4	.5	.5						.5	.5
29 12.6	31 11.8	31 11.7	Sales/Receivables					33 11.0	31 11.8
36 10.0	37 9.9	40 9.2						48 7.5	34 10.7
47 7.7	47 7.8	52 7.0						67 5.4	41 8.8
21 17.1	23 16.2	25 14.4	Cost of Sales/Inventory					44 8.3	27 13.4
42 8.7	41 8.9	44 8.3						59 6.2	43 8.4
62 5.8	59 6.2	65 5.6						70 5.2	60 6.1
18 19.9	21 17.4	20 18.6	Cost of Sales/Payables					22 16.4	19 19.2
32 11.6	30 12.0	33 11.1						40 9.1	32 11.4
46 8.0	42 8.7	43 8.5						64 5.7	41 9.0
6.9	7.8	7.0	Sales/Working Capital					5.2	7.8
14.7	15.1	12.1						12.2	12.8
-34.6	202.0	-76.9						48.2	-34.0
10.1	5.6	9.4	EBIT/Interest					5.9	10.0
(49) 3.4	(62) 3.0	(62) 3.6						(13) 2.7	(35) 3.7
.6	1.3	1.4						.4	1.4
3.6	5.7	3.8	Net Profit + Depr., Dep., Amort./Cur. Mat. L/T/D						
(15) 2.2	(24) 2.7	(16) 3.1							
1.6	1.3	1.7							
.6	.5	.4	Fixed/Worth					.3	.6
1.5	1.0	1.0						.7	1.2
2.9	2.0	2.5						2.0	2.8
1.0	1.0	.8	Debt/Worth					1.0	.7
2.1	1.9	1.6						1.4	1.7
4.8	4.3	4.5						7.1	4.4
28.7	44.7	47.5	% Profit Before Taxes/Tangible Net Worth					38.2	49.1
(48) 9.3	(63) 15.3	(62) 24.2						(12) 12.4	(32) 23.9
-.4	4.7	5.3						-4.7	6.2
9.0	11.2	16.9	% Profit Before Taxes/Total Assets					11.1	14.6
4.4	5.7	7.1						3.4	7.1
-.8	.9	1.7						-2.2	2.0
14.0	25.6	15.8	Sales/Net Fixed Assets					44.5	9.4
4.3	6.1	6.8						12.4	5.9
2.3	3.0	2.8						5.1	2.6
2.5	3.0	2.9	Sales/Total Assets					3.2	2.7
1.8	2.3	2.2						2.4	2.1
1.1	1.5	1.4						1.8	1.4
1.2	.6	1.1	% Depr., Dep., Amort./Sales					.3	1.5
(43) 3.6	(53) 1.8	(61) 2.3						(13) 1.1	(31) 2.3
6.0	4.4	4.2						2.3	3.8
.7	1.4	1.3	% Officers', Directors', Owners' Comp/Sales						
(14) 2.7	(14) 3.3	(15) 1.9							
4.5	5.2	3.8							
3958297M	6523031M	4387691M	Net Sales ($)	177M	18051M	30436M	12915M	223934M	4102178M
2693323M	3438327M	2491360M	Total Assets ($)	138M	15272M	17778M	10337M	138946M	2308889M

M = $ thousand   MM = $ million
See Pages 11 through 21 for Explanation of Ratios and Data

Current Data Sorted by Assets | Comparative Historical Data

Type of Statement	0-500M	500M-2MM	2-10MM	10-50MM	50-100MM	100-250MM		4/1/02-3/31/03 ALL	4/1/03-3/31/04 ALL
Unqualified			13	25	1	6		44	34
Reviewed	1	3	41	21	1			72	67
Compiled	1	8	12	3				34	55
Tax Returns	3	10	8	1				8	6
Other	1	5	29	21	3	1		74	62
		45 (4/1-9/30/06)		173 (10/1/06-3/31/07)					
NUMBER OF STATEMENTS	6	26	103	71	5	7		232	224
ASSETS	%	%	%	%	%	%		%	%
Cash & Equivalents		6.2	6.6	5.2				7.8	8.4
Trade Receivables (net)		41.1	29.9	24.5				25.8	26.7
Inventory		18.1	15.2	16.6				15.5	15.2
All Other Current		2.8	1.1	2.9				1.9	2.5
Total Current		68.2	52.8	49.1				51.0	52.8
Fixed Assets (net)		20.5	37.0	38.0				39.4	38.0
Intangibles (net)		3.4	2.5	5.5				2.4	2.2
All Other Non-Current		7.9	7.7	7.4				7.2	7.1
Total		100.0	100.0	100.0				100.0	100.0
LIABILITIES									
Notes Payable-Short Term		9.0	8.2	11.4				8.7	9.8
Cur. Mat.-L.T.D.		3.2	6.9	4.2				5.4	4.6
Trade Payables		27.1	16.1	14.2				14.9	14.6
Income Taxes Payable		.0	.1	.3				.1	.2
All Other Current		5.3	8.3	7.3				7.4	6.8
Total Current		44.7	39.7	37.3				36.5	36.0
Long-Term Debt		15.1	19.3	19.6				21.1	21.9
Deferred Taxes		.1	.7	1.0				1.0	.8
All Other Non-Current		13.3	6.4	5.8				5.9	4.8
Net Worth		26.8	33.9	36.3				35.6	36.5
Total Liabilities & Net Worth		100.0	100.0	100.0				100.0	100.0
INCOME DATA									
Net Sales		100.0	100.0	100.0				100.0	100.0
Gross Profit		31.3	26.7	23.4				25.6	26.3
Operating Expenses		28.3	22.4	19.0				22.7	23.8
Operating Profit		3.0	4.3	4.3				2.8	2.5
All Other Expenses (net)		.5	1.1	.7				.8	.8
Profit Before Taxes		2.5	3.2	3.6				2.0	1.7
RATIOS									
Current		2.6	2.1	2.0				2.5	2.6
		1.7	1.4	1.2				1.5	1.5
		1.3	1.0	1.0				1.0	1.0
Quick		1.7	1.4	1.3				1.6	1.7
		1.1	.9	.8				.9	.9
		.7	.6	.5				.6	.6
Sales/Receivables	37	9.8	31 11.8	32 11.4				30 12.3	31 11.6
	42	8.6	40 9.1	39 9.3				39 9.5	40 9.2
	55	6.6	47 7.7	47 7.7				47 7.8	47 7.7
Cost of Sales/Inventory	10	35.8	18 20.7	21 17.2				19 18.9	19 19.5
	22	16.9	25 14.4	31 11.8				28 13.1	28 13.0
	44	8.2	39 9.3	47 7.8				40 9.1	40 9.1
Cost of Sales/Payables	18	20.0	15 24.4	16 23.5				16 23.0	13 27.6
	34	10.8	26 14.2	24 15.2				25 14.4	24 15.3
	60	6.1	44 8.3	45 8.1				42 8.6	41 8.9
Sales/Working Capital		7.2	10.8	8.3				7.7	7.9
		13.4	20.1	23.0				15.7	16.0
		21.8	-134.0	-387.3				-173.6	-208.2
EBIT/Interest		7.9	8.3	6.5				6.1	6.6
	(22)	3.3	(98) 3.6	(70) 3.3				(223) 2.9	(208) 2.0
		1.3	1.7	1.9				1.2	.4
Net Profit + Depr., Dep., Amort./Cur. Mat. L/T/D			4.4	6.1				2.9	2.6
		(31)	1.9	(38) 2.7				(85) 2.0	(74) 1.4
			1.0	2.0				1.0	.6
Fixed/Worth		.3	.6	.7				.6	.5
		.8	1.1	1.3				1.2	1.2
		1.8	2.5	3.0				3.0	2.6
Debt/Worth		.6	.8	1.0				.7	.7
		1.9	2.1	2.4				1.9	1.9
		6.7	5.6	5.9				5.5	4.6
% Profit Before Taxes/Tangible Net Worth		39.5	38.1	40.1				29.8	27.6
	(22)	26.0	(93) 19.2	(64) 22.6				(204) 11.7	(197) 7.7
		10.9	8.2	10.8				1.9	-1.6
% Profit Before Taxes/Total Assets		14.8	12.3	10.1				10.3	8.4
		7.1	6.7	7.3				4.2	2.8
		.9	1.7	2.9				.2	-1.1
Sales/Net Fixed Assets		40.3	14.5	10.3				11.5	13.1
		17.8	8.0	5.2				6.0	5.9
		9.8	4.2	3.3				3.6	3.7
Sales/Total Assets		3.9	3.3	2.7				3.0	2.9
		3.2	2.6	2.2				2.3	2.3
		2.7	2.0	1.7				1.8	1.8
% Depr., Dep., Amort./Sales		1.0	1.5	1.8				1.9	1.8
	(23)	1.7	(97) 2.5	(69) 2.8				(217) 3.0	(206) 3.0
		2.6	3.7	4.4				4.2	4.5
% Officers', Directors' Owners' Comp/Sales		2.6	1.6	1.6				1.6	1.9
	(13)	4.1	(43) 3.4	(14) 2.0				(92) 3.2	(94) 3.3
		7.4	5.9	2.8				5.4	5.6
Net Sales ($)	4795M	108104M	1436207M	3265928M	570985M	1680974M		5955353M	5659081M
Total Assets ($)	1211M	33493M	540484M	1500659M	342636M	1007445M		3239665M	2882358M

© RMA 2007

M = $ thousand   MM = $ million
See Pages 11 through 21 for Explanation of Ratios and Data

Comparative Historical Data | **Current Data Sorted by Sales**

Hist 4/1/04-3/31/05 ALL	Hist 4/1/05-3/31/06 ALL	Hist 4/1/06-3/31/07 ALL	Type of Statement	0-1MM	1-3MM	3-5MM	5-10MM	10-25MM	25MM & OVER
36	51	45	Unqualified				3	8	34
70	64	67	Reviewed	1		1	12	32	21
43	23	24	Compiled	1	4	5	9	4	1
11	11	22	Tax Returns	2	2	4	9	4	1
68	78	60	Other	1	4	5	9	18	23
4/1/04-3/31/05 ALL	4/1/05-3/31/06 ALL	4/1/06-3/31/07 ALL		\<- 45 (4/1-9/30/06) ->			\<- 173 (10/1/06-3/31/07) ->		
228	227	218	NUMBER OF STATEMENTS	5	10	15	42	66	80
%	%	%	**ASSETS**	%	%	%	%	%	%
7.1	6.0	6.2	Cash & Equivalents		9.1	6.5	5.8	6.8	5.3
28.1	28.7	29.4	Trade Receivables (net)		39.2	31.0	29.1	28.6	27.9
16.3	16.5	15.8	Inventory		11.4	18.3	15.6	14.4	17.2
1.7	2.1	1.9	All Other Current		5.4	.7	2.7	1.6	1.6
53.2	53.2	53.2	Total Current		65.0	56.5	53.1	51.3	52.0
35.9	36.6	35.3	Fixed Assets (net)		17.9	30.7	38.6	36.3	36.7
3.5	4.0	4.0	Intangibles (net)		8.4	4.2	1.9	3.5	4.5
7.4	6.2	7.4	All Other Non-Current		8.7	8.6	6.5	8.9	6.8
100.0	100.0	100.0	Total		100.0	100.0	100.0	100.0	100.0
			LIABILITIES						
10.9	10.1	9.4	Notes Payable-Short Term		7.0	8.2	8.0	9.1	9.9
5.4	5.1	5.1	Cur. Mat.-L.T.D.		3.1	5.5	5.2	6.6	4.3
18.1	17.1	16.9	Trade Payables		15.0	25.9	17.0	15.0	16.2
.1	.2	.2	Income Taxes Payable		.0	.0	.1	.1	.3
6.3	7.5	7.8	All Other Current		10.0	5.6	6.8	7.7	7.8
40.8	40.1	39.4	Total Current		35.2	45.2	37.0	38.6	38.5
20.8	19.4	18.7	Long-Term Debt		17.0	19.3	23.3	17.8	17.7
1.0	1.1	.9	Deferred Taxes		.0	.2	.8	1.0	1.3
3.9	5.6	6.8	All Other Non-Current		11.8	19.3	3.4	8.0	4.6
33.5	33.8	34.2	Net Worth		36.1	16.0	35.5	34.7	38.0
100.0	100.0	100.0	Total Liabilities & Net Worth		100.0	100.0	100.0	100.0	100.0
			INCOME DATA						
100.0	100.0	100.0	Net Sales		100.0	100.0	100.0	100.0	100.0
25.5	25.6	26.0	Gross Profit		31.9	30.8	28.5	26.3	22.6
23.0	22.1	21.7	Operating Expenses		28.2	28.9	23.5	22.2	18.1
2.5	3.4	4.4	Operating Profit		3.7	1.9	5.0	4.1	4.5
.5	1.1	.8	All Other Expenses (net)		.1	1.3	1.5	.9	.3
1.9	2.3	3.6	Profit Before Taxes		3.6	.6	3.5	3.2	4.2
			RATIOS						
2.2	2.2	2.1	Current		2.8	2.1	2.0	2.2	2.0
1.3	1.4	1.4			1.8	1.5	1.5	1.4	1.3
.9	1.0	1.0			1.3	.7	1.1	1.0	1.0
1.4	1.5	1.4	Quick		2.7	1.6	1.4	1.4	1.3
.8	.9	.9			1.1	.8	1.1	1.0	.8
.6	.6	.6			.9	.5	.6	.6	.6
33 11.0	32 11.4	33 11.1	Sales/Receivables		39 9.4	30 12.3	30 12.2	32 11.3	33 11.2
40 9.2	40 9.2	40 9.1			50 7.3	40 9.1	41 8.8	39 9.3	40 9.2
48 7.7	46 7.9	48 7.7			67 5.5	49 7.4	52 7.0	45 8.1	47 7.7
20 18.2	19 18.9	18 20.3	Cost of Sales/Inventory		0 UND	16 23.3	20 17.9	16 22.6	21 17.5
30 12.3	30 12.0	29 12.6			18 20.0	27 13.6	31 11.9	23 15.7	30 12.3
45 8.0	44 8.3	41 8.9			30 12.3	64 5.7	47 7.8	43 8.4	40 9.0
17 20.9	17 21.5	16 23.2	Cost of Sales/Payables		11 33.1	27 13.5	20 18.0	14 26.5	16 22.3
30 12.1	27 13.3	27 13.6			19 19.4	35 10.4	26 14.0	23 15.6	24 15.3
49 7.5	43 8.5	46 8.0			49 7.5	59 6.2	47 7.8	45 8.1	45 8.2
8.5	8.6	9.5	Sales/Working Capital		5.9	8.4	8.8	8.3	10.3
21.9	17.6	18.8			10.4	19.4	15.1	19.9	20.8
-58.5	-239.7	991.1			19.3	-29.0	72.4	-155.7	150.2
8.1	9.6	7.4	EBIT/Interest				6.4	12.5	6.1	9.6
(211) 2.9	(216) 3.0	(206) 3.6				(12) 2.3	3.4	(61) 3.5	(79) 3.9
1.1	1.2	1.8				.2	1.4	1.7	2.4
2.4	2.9	4.9	Net Profit + Depr., Dep., Amort./Cur. Mat. L/T/D				3.5	4.8	7.5
(72) 1.5	(72) 1.6	(79) 2.4					(16) 1.7	(20) 2.2	(38) 2.9
.9	1.0	1.6					1.0	1.6	2.0
.5	.6	.6	Fixed/Worth		.2	.4	.6	.5	.7
1.3	1.2	1.1			.8	1.4	1.0	1.2	1.1
3.2	3.7	2.7			NM	2.3	2.6	2.7	2.6
.8	.8	.8	Debt/Worth		.8	.7	.7	.8	1.0
2.2	2.0	2.1			2.9	3.2	1.9	2.1	1.9
6.3	6.4	6.0			NM	7.1	6.8	5.6	5.2
33.0	36.6	37.7	% Profit Before Taxes/Tangible Net Worth			32.7	39.1	36.6	44.8
(194) 11.8	(190) 15.6	(193) 21.9				(13) 11.1	(37) 18.0	(59) 18.6	(74) 23.7
-2.4	3.5	9.6				-16.9	8.0	6.8	13.6
12.0	12.1	12.1	% Profit Before Taxes/Total Assets		13.1	7.4	14.7	11.3	12.7
4.1	5.0	6.9			8.2	3.0	4.5	6.9	7.8
.3	.5	2.4			4.3	-5.8	1.4	2.3	3.8
15.4	15.4	15.0	Sales/Net Fixed Assets		41.4	20.4	12.8	15.1	12.5
6.6	6.3	7.0			18.4	10.3	7.2	6.4	5.9
4.0	4.0	4.2			7.6	4.9	3.2	3.9	4.3
3.0	3.1	3.2	Sales/Total Assets		3.2	3.6	3.2	3.0	3.2
2.3	2.4	2.5			2.7	3.0	2.5	2.4	2.4
1.8	1.9	1.9			1.4	1.9	1.8	1.9	1.9
1.7	1.6	1.6	% Depr., Dep., Amort./Sales			1.4	1.7	1.4	1.8
(211) 2.7	(208) 2.5	(202) 2.6				(14) 2.0	(40) 3.3	(62) 2.5	(76) 2.6
3.8	3.8	3.8				4.3	4.2	3.4	3.5
1.7	1.8	1.8	% Officers', Directors', Owners' Comp/Sales				2.3	1.8	1.3
(86) 3.4	(78) 3.4	(74) 3.0					(10) 3.8	(20) 2.8	(10) 1.8
6.6	5.7	6.0					7.4	5.1	3.2
5584120M	7250281M	7066993M	Net Sales ($)	2568M	23527M	62397M	303946M	1077155M	5597400M
2576941M	3577212M	3425928M	Total Assets ($)	749M	11500M	26948M	160657M	524608M	2701466M

© RMA 2007

M = $ thousand   MM = $ million
See Pages 11 through 21 for Explanation of Ratios and Data

Current Data Sorted by Assets | **Comparative Historical Data**

Note: vertical marking "DATA NOT AVAILABLE" appears in the 100-250MM column area.

Type of Statement

Type of Statement	0-500M	500M-2MM	2-10MM	10-50MM	50-100MM	100-250MM	4/1/02-3/31/03 ALL	4/1/03-3/31/04 ALL
Unqualified			1	14			12	10
Reviewed		3	9	5			16	13
Compiled	1	2	1				2	13
Tax Returns		2	1				1	1
Other	1	3	3	7	4		12	13
	9 (4/1-9/30/06)			48 (10/1/06-3/31/07)				
NUMBER OF STATEMENTS	2	11	14	26	4		43	50

ASSETS (%)

	0-500M	500M-2MM	2-10MM	10-50MM	50-100MM	100-250MM	4/1/02-3/31/03 ALL	4/1/03-3/31/04 ALL
Cash & Equivalents		11.0	5.0	4.3			3.8	5.5
Trade Receivables (net)		38.0	24.1	18.1			20.3	20.4
Inventory		21.7	16.0	20.6			22.9	22.5
All Other Current		2.6	2.0	1.0			1.5	2.7
Total Current		73.2	47.1	44.0			48.4	51.0
Fixed Assets (net)		20.6	44.9	44.2			43.9	39.9
Intangibles (net)		3.2	2.0	6.0			1.3	3.2
All Other Non-Current		2.9	6.0	5.9			6.3	5.9
Total		100.0	100.0	100.0			100.0	100.0

LIABILITIES

	0-500M	500M-2MM	2-10MM	10-50MM	50-100MM	100-250MM	4/1/02-3/31/03 ALL	4/1/03-3/31/04 ALL
Notes Payable-Short Term		7.0	4.4	10.9			8.5	10.5
Cur. Mat.-L.T.D.		3.6	7.9	3.9			4.7	5.0
Trade Payables		20.1	11.8	12.4			12.5	12.9
Income Taxes Payable		.0	.0	.1			.2	.1
All Other Current		11.9	5.0	5.8			8.1	6.7
Total Current		42.6	29.1	33.0			34.0	35.1
Long-Term Debt		14.3	21.6	19.7			22.7	18.9
Deferred Taxes		.0	.0	1.3			2.0	1.4
All Other Non-Current		10.6	2.6	4.9			4.8	5.5
Net Worth		32.4	46.7	41.1			36.5	39.1
Total Liabilities & Net Worth		100.0	100.0	100.0			100.0	100.0

INCOME DATA

	0-500M	500M-2MM	2-10MM	10-50MM	50-100MM	100-250MM	4/1/02-3/31/03 ALL	4/1/03-3/31/04 ALL
Net Sales		100.0	100.0	100.0			100.0	100.0
Gross Profit		27.2	20.7	18.7			24.7	22.1
Operating Expenses		22.2	16.4	14.3			20.4	18.8
Operating Profit		5.0	4.3	4.4			4.3	3.3
All Other Expenses (net)		.7	.7	1.8			2.0	1.2
Profit Before Taxes		4.3	3.6	2.5			2.3	2.1

RATIOS

	0-500M	500M-2MM	2-10MM	10-50MM	50-100MM	100-250MM	4/1/02-3/31/03 ALL	4/1/03-3/31/04 ALL
Current		5.9	2.1	2.1			2.0	2.1
		1.8	1.5	1.3			1.3	1.3
		1.0	1.2	1.0			1.1	1.0
Quick		4.3	1.6	1.1			1.0	1.0
		1.2	1.1	.6			.7	.6
		.6	.7	.4			.5	.5
Sales/Receivables		49 7.5	31 11.7	30 12.2			29 12.5	28 12.9
		56 6.5	38 9.5	36 10.1			34 10.6	38 9.5
		60 6.0	43 8.6	44 8.3			47 7.8	48 7.7
Cost of Sales/Inventory		13 28.6	18 20.4	39 9.3			37 9.9	36 10.2
		44 8.2	29 12.5	55 6.6			56 6.5	53 6.9
		75 4.9	60 6.1	70 5.2			79 4.6	73 5.0
Cost of Sales/Payables		12 30.0	11 32.7	13 27.4			17 21.9	16 23.1
		25 14.7	20 18.1	23 15.9			28 12.8	25 14.5
		33 10.9	32 11.4	41 9.0			40 9.1	42 8.6
Sales/Working Capital		6.0	8.5	7.2			7.5	5.6
		7.0	14.3	15.9			18.4	14.4
		83.3	NM	111.2			30.8	-597.5
EBIT/Interest			8.0	5.9			4.9	5.9
			(12) 3.3	2.8			(42) 2.8	(47) 2.9
			1.2	.7			.8	1.2
Net Profit + Depr., Dep., Amort./Cur. Mat. L/T/D				3.6			2.2	2.4
				(13) 1.9			(15) 1.7	(15) 1.5
				.8			1.1	1.0
Fixed/Worth		.1	.6	.8			.8	.6
		.5	1.3	1.1			1.3	1.1
		2.5	2.1	2.0			2.2	2.2
Debt/Worth		.3	.8	.8			1.1	1.0
		5.3	1.1	1.5			1.9	1.7
		10.2	2.6	4.0			4.1	3.6
% Profit Before Taxes/Tangible Net Worth			52.6	22.8			21.2	25.8
			19.4	(24) 16.5			(42) 8.9	(46) 8.6
			4.1	5.4			-1.7	1.9
% Profit Before Taxes/Total Assets		18.2	14.6	8.9			7.5	8.8
		14.7	5.9	5.6			3.3	3.9
		.6	3.3	-.9			-.4	.4
Sales/Net Fixed Assets		27.3	8.9	5.7			7.6	7.7
		14.1	5.1	3.4			4.0	4.7
		7.3	3.5	2.9			2.6	2.8
Sales/Total Assets		2.9	3.0	2.1			2.5	2.4
		2.4	2.1	1.7			1.7	1.8
		2.3	1.8	1.4			1.4	1.3
% Depr., Dep., Amort./Sales			1.5	2.5			2.7	2.1
			(12) 2.4	(21) 4.3			(39) 3.7	(42) 3.1
			4.2	5.8			5.4	5.6
% Officers', Directors' Owners' Comp/Sales							1.2	2.0
							(10) 2.2	(17) 3.7
							7.2	6.3
Net Sales ($)	3951M	35799M	165511M	949511M	470656M		1346874M	1839062M
Total Assets ($)	800M	14425M	78723M	571975M	239156M		792457M	1000659M

© RMA 2007

M = $ thousand   MM = $ million
See Pages 11 through 21 for Explanation of Ratios and Data

Comparative Historical Data | Current Data Sorted by Sales

			Type of Statement	0-1MM	1-3MM	3-5MM	5-10MM	10-25MM	25MM & OVER
9	11	15	Unqualified					3	11
15	17	17	Reviewed		2	2	2	8	3
3	4	4	Compiled		2	1	1		
3	1	3	Tax Returns		1	2	1		
23	31	18	Other		1	3		5	9
4/1/04-3/31/05 ALL	4/1/05-3/31/06 ALL	4/1/06-3/31/07 ALL			9 (4/1-9/30/06)			48 (10/1/06-3/31/07)	
53	64	57	NUMBER OF STATEMENTS		6	8	4	16	23
%	%	%	ASSETS	%	%	%	%	%	%
3.9	5.0	5.8	Cash & Equivalents					3.0	3.9
21.5	23.3	24.9	Trade Receivables (net)					19.1	20.1
22.3	22.1	19.5	Inventory					15.9	22.4
1.7	2.2	1.9	All Other Current					1.8	2.3
49.3	52.6	52.2	Total Current					39.7	48.7
41.5	38.0	39.0	Fixed Assets (net)					44.5	44.5
1.5	4.1	3.9	Intangibles (net)					5.7	3.6
7.7	5.3	5.0	All Other Non-Current					10.0	3.3
100.0	100.0	100.0	Total					100.0	100.0
			LIABILITIES						
12.1	12.4	8.9	Notes Payable-Short Term					5.5	13.3
4.1	6.0	4.9	Cur. Mat.-L.T.D.					6.9	4.0
12.2	15.0	13.9	Trade Payables					11.8	11.7
.1	.2	.1	Income Taxes Payable					.0	.3
5.9	6.1	7.3	All Other Current					6.0	6.4
34.3	39.7	35.1	Total Current					30.3	35.6
22.1	21.3	18.6	Long-Term Debt					20.6	17.8
1.1	1.1	.7	Deferred Taxes					.3	1.5
2.3	3.1	5.3	All Other Non-Current					5.4	3.9
40.1	34.7	40.4	Net Worth					43.4	41.1
100.0	100.0	100.0	Total Liabilities & Net Worth					100.0	100.0
			INCOME DATA						
100.0	100.0	100.0	Net Sales					100.0	100.0
21.9	22.9	21.5	Gross Profit					17.7	18.9
18.0	19.1	17.2	Operating Expenses					14.5	14.3
3.9	3.8	4.4	Operating Profit					3.1	4.6
1.5	1.4	1.2	All Other Expenses (net)					1.4	1.4
2.4	2.3	3.2	Profit Before Taxes					1.7	3.3
			RATIOS						
1.9	2.1	2.3						2.2	2.0
1.4	1.3	1.5	Current					1.5	1.3
1.1	1.1	1.1						.9	1.1
1.1	1.2	1.4						1.1	1.0
.7	.7	.8	Quick					.8	.6
.5	.4	.5						.4	.5
30 12.2	30 12.2	33 11.1						25 14.6	32 11.2
37 9.9	41 9.0	39 9.3	Sales/Receivables					32 11.2	38 9.5
52 7.1	51 7.1	51 7.2						40 9.2	46 7.9
37 9.8	29 12.6	27 13.3						26 14.2	40 9.1
54 6.7	49 7.4	43 8.5	Cost of Sales/Inventory					36 10.1	56 6.5
76 4.8	75 4.9	65 5.6						63 5.7	67 5.4
18 20.0	15 24.1	13 28.2						10 37.8	16 23.4
29 12.7	27 13.4	23 16.0	Cost of Sales/Payables					18 19.9	22 16.4
38 9.6	47 7.8	35 10.5						29 12.6	38 9.6
9.0	8.5	7.2						9.5	7.5
13.9	17.6	12.7	Sales/Working Capital					16.9	14.6
57.8	407.3	73.9						-85.1	64.5
6.0	5.4	6.0						5.5	5.9
(50) 2.7	(60) 2.6	(52) 3.1	EBIT/Interest					(15) 2.0	3.5
1.4	.5	1.6						-2.0	2.0
4.7	3.3	3.7							3.9
(18) 2.3	(24) 1.6	(18) 1.9	Net Profit + Depr., Dep., Amort./Cur. Mat. L/T/D						(12) 1.8
1.4	1.0	1.5							1.5
.6	.5	.7						.7	.9
1.2	1.3	1.2	Fixed/Worth					1.1	1.2
2.1	2.3	2.0						2.5	1.6
.9	1.1	.9						.7	.9
1.7	2.0	1.5	Debt/Worth					1.3	1.5
3.2	3.8	5.0						3.9	2.7
27.8	37.3	33.9						36.0	22.8
(50) 10.1	(57) 13.3	(53) 18.6	% Profit Before Taxes/Tangible Net Worth					(15) 11.8	(22) 16.5
1.9	2.2	6.0						-1.8	9.4
9.8	13.0	12.3						10.2	9.6
3.6	4.6	6.0	% Profit Before Taxes/Total Assets					4.2	6.3
.6	-1.4	2.1						-1.4	3.2
8.3	9.7	9.4						6.6	5.1
4.0	5.7	4.9	Sales/Net Fixed Assets					3.9	3.9
3.0	3.3	3.2						3.2	3.0
2.1	2.6	2.4						2.3	2.1
1.8	2.0	2.1	Sales/Total Assets					2.0	2.0
1.4	1.5	1.5						1.4	1.5
2.7	1.8	2.1						1.4	2.6
(48) 4.2	(58) 3.0	(46) 3.6	% Depr., Dep., Amort./Sales					(11) 2.5	(20) 4.1
5.5	4.4	4.9						6.6	5.3
1.7	1.9	1.8							
(10) 3.0	(14) 2.3	(16) 2.5	% Officers', Directors' Owners' Comp/Sales						
5.0	4.2	3.4							
2043985M	2155007M	1625428M	Net Sales ($)		13575M	30271M	31030M	246914M	1303638M
1329226M	1196636M	905079M	Total Assets ($)		5709M	11619M	19116M	142569M	726066M

© RMA 2007

M = $ thousand   MM = $ million

See Pages 11 through 21 for Explanation of Ratios and Data

Current Data Sorted by Assets   Comparative Historical Data

0-500M	500M-2MM	2-10MM	10-50MM	50-100MM	100-250MM	Type of Statement	4/1/02-3/31/03 ALL	4/1/03-3/31/04 ALL
	1	6	11	1		Unqualified	14	17
	1	12	6			Reviewed	30	18
	1	1	1			Compiled	10	18
1	2					Tax Returns	2	2
		6	3	2	1	Other	11	14
	5 (4/1-9/30/06)		51 (10/1/06-3/31/07)					
0-500M	500M-2MM	2-10MM	10-50MM	50-100MM	100-250MM			
1	5	25	21	3	1	NUMBER OF STATEMENTS	67	69
%	%	%	%	%	%	**ASSETS**	%	%
		7.1	4.9			Cash & Equivalents	6.7	6.2
		26.2	23.3			Trade Receivables (net)	25.3	25.6
		20.9	17.1			Inventory	17.2	18.6
		1.2	1.2			All Other Current	1.6	2.1
		55.5	46.4			Total Current	50.9	52.5
		38.7	41.6			Fixed Assets (net)	40.0	39.2
		1.8	7.1			Intangibles (net)	4.2	2.5
		4.0	4.9			All Other Non-Current	4.9	5.8
		100.0	100.0			Total	100.0	100.0
						LIABILITIES		
		7.7	6.6			Notes Payable-Short Term	9.4	10.7
		13.0	4.4			Cur. Mat.-L.T.D.	6.5	4.2
		14.1	13.2			Trade Payables	12.3	13.9
		.0	.5			Income Taxes Payable	.1	.4
		8.9	4.2			All Other Current	6.0	5.6
		43.8	28.9			Total Current	34.3	34.9
		21.9	23.6			Long-Term Debt	23.7	22.6
		.8	1.3			Deferred Taxes	.8	1.0
		4.9	3.7			All Other Non-Current	5.6	4.8
		28.7	42.5			Net Worth	35.7	36.7
		100.0	100.0			Total Liabilities & Net Worth	100.0	100.0
						INCOME DATA		
		100.0	100.0			Net Sales	100.0	100.0
		24.1	22.4			Gross Profit	27.2	26.9
		18.6	17.0			Operating Expenses	23.8	24.3
		5.5	5.4			Operating Profit	3.4	2.6
		2.3	1.1			All Other Expenses (net)	1.2	.9
		3.2	4.3			Profit Before Taxes	2.2	1.7
						RATIOS		
		2.2	2.9				2.4	2.5
		1.2	1.5			Current	1.6	1.6
		1.0	1.2				1.1	1.1
		1.5	2.1				1.6	1.4
		.7	.9			Quick	1.0	.8
		.5	.6				.6	.6
		28 13.0	36 10.2				31 11.9	31 11.9
		37 10.0	38 9.5			Sales/Receivables	35 10.3	37 9.8
		46 7.9	49 7.5				44 8.3	51 7.2
		20 18.2	22 16.9				24 15.3	23 15.6
		37 9.8	33 11.2			Cost of Sales/Inventory	34 10.9	35 10.4
		57 6.4	61 6.0				53 6.9	66 5.6
		14 26.5	17 21.6				14 25.8	15 23.6
		20 17.9	32 11.3			Cost of Sales/Payables	25 14.7	29 12.8
		33 11.1	42 8.7				33 10.9	47 7.8
		8.3	5.3				7.3	6.1
		36.5	12.0			Sales/Working Capital	15.2	11.1
		-119.3	34.7				50.2	93.9
		4.2	7.2				4.6	5.7
		(23) 2.3	3.7			EBIT/Interest	(66) 2.5	(66) 2.4
		.1	2.3				.8	.9
						Net Profit + Depr., Dep.,	3.5	3.6
						Amort./Cur. Mat. L/T/D	(24) 2.5	(21) 2.5
							1.0	1.6
		.5	.7				.7	.7
		1.3	1.2			Fixed/Worth	1.1	1.2
		3.7	3.9				2.1	2.0
		1.0	.7				1.0	.8
		3.3	1.9			Debt/Worth	1.7	1.8
		7.4	6.2				4.4	3.4
		33.0	50.1			% Profit Before Taxes/Tangible	21.7	17.7
		(22) 13.1	(19) 20.8			Net Worth	(60) 9.8	(63) 9.6
		2.4	12.4				-2.0	-1.0
		6.4	13.6			% Profit Before Taxes/Total	10.0	7.6
		3.5	8.3			Assets	2.4	3.6
		-3.9	3.4				-1.0	-.1
		13.1	9.2				11.5	10.8
		6.3	4.5			Sales/Net Fixed Assets	5.0	4.7
		3.7	3.2				3.5	3.3
		3.0	2.4				2.7	2.9
		2.5	2.0			Sales/Total Assets	2.1	2.1
		1.8	1.4				1.6	1.5
		1.8	2.0				2.3	2.0
		(23) 3.0	(20) 2.8			% Depr., Dep., Amort./Sales	(64) 3.6	(66) 3.4
		4.6	4.9				5.3	4.5
		2.0				% Officers', Directors'	2.1	1.6
		(11) 2.7				Owners' Comp/Sales	(28) 4.6	(30) 3.9
		6.6					9.3	6.9
1355M	26271M	335785M	896582M	304534M	219854M	Net Sales ($)	1728201M	2102513M
405M	5230M	136437M	470922M	178515M	106407M	Total Assets ($)	871930M	1140277M

M = $ thousand   MM = $ million
See Pages 11 through 21 for Explanation of Ratios and Data

Comparative Historical Data   ## Current Data Sorted by Sales

					Type of Statement						
16		13		19	Unqualified	1		1	2	4	11
19		19		19	Reviewed				4	11	4
7		2		3	Compiled				1	1	1
4		2		3	Tax Returns		2	1			
25		21		12	Other	2		1	3	3	6
4/1/04-		4/1/05-		4/1/06-			5 (4/1-9/30/06)		51 (10/1/06-3/31/07)		
3/31/05		3/31/06		3/31/07		0-1MM	1-3MM	3-5MM	5-10MM	10-25MM	25MM & OVER
ALL		ALL		ALL							
71		57		56	NUMBER OF STATEMENTS	1	2	2	10	19	22
%		%		%	ASSETS	%	%	%	%	%	%
5.0		5.4		6.4	Cash & Equivalents				7.8	7.2	3.5
29.3		25.8		25.7	Trade Receivables (net)				27.9	25.8	24.4
19.8		18.1		18.4	Inventory				20.6	22.0	16.1
1.5		1.4		1.3	All Other Current				.7	1.5	1.5
55.5		50.8		51.8	Total Current				57.1	56.5	45.4
34.8		39.0		36.9	Fixed Assets (net)				35.5	31.2	44.1
3.4		4.1		4.9	Intangibles (net)				1.7	6.5	6.0
6.2		6.2		6.3	All Other Non-Current				5.7	5.7	4.4
100.0		100.0		100.0	Total				100.0	100.0	100.0
					LIABILITIES						
11.6		8.6		7.0	Notes Payable-Short Term				6.7	7.5	7.1
4.1		5.6		8.0	Cur. Mat.-L.T.D.				8.2	13.7	4.5
17.9		15.1		14.8	Trade Payables				13.3	14.1	13.2
.1		.3		.2	Income Taxes Payable				.0	.4	.2
6.4		5.8		6.8	All Other Current				10.6	7.6	5.4
40.2		35.3		36.9	Total Current				38.7	43.4	30.4
22.2		24.6		21.1	Long-Term Debt				17.2	19.1	23.0
1.0		.8		1.1	Deferred Taxes				1.3	.7	1.7
5.4		4.6		5.4	All Other Non-Current				11.0	2.8	4.9
31.1		34.7		35.5	Net Worth				31.8	34.0	40.0
100.0		100.0		100.0	Total Liabilties & Net Worth				100.0	100.0	100.0
					INCOME DATA						
100.0		100.0		100.0	Net Sales				100.0	100.0	100.0
24.5		24.4		23.4	Gross Profit				23.9	22.0	21.1
21.5		21.0		17.9	Operating Expenses				20.5	19.4	16.0
3.0		3.4		5.5	Operating Profit				3.4	2.6	5.1
.5		1.0		1.6	All Other Expenses (net)				.3	1.2	1.1
2.5		2.4		3.8	Profit Before Taxes				3.1	1.5	4.0
					RATIOS						
2.0		2.2		2.6					2.7	2.4	2.8
1.3		1.4		1.3	Current				1.1	1.5	1.3
1.0		1.0		1.0					.9	1.0	1.1
1.3		1.4		1.7					1.6	1.6	1.8
.8		.8		.8	Quick				.8	.7	.9
.6		.6		.5					.6	.5	.6
35	10.3	32	11.3	30	12.4				24	15.5	30	12.0	36	10.2
43	8.5	44	8.3	38	9.6	Sales/Receivables			33	11.0	38	9.7	41	9.0
54	6.7	49	7.4	48	7.6				55	6.6	47	7.7	49	7.5
25	14.4	20	18.0	19	18.9				18	19.9	23	15.7	20	18.0
38	9.6	34	10.7	32	11.5	Cost of Sales/Inventory			36	10.0	33	11.0	29	12.7
55	6.6	52	7.1	53	6.9				62	5.9	53	6.9	54	6.8
21	17.3	17	21.3	15	24.3				8	43.3	15	24.5	17	22.1
31	12.0	27	13.4	25	14.9	Cost of Sales/Payables			15	24.3	28	13.2	23	15.7
51	7.1	40	9.2	40	9.0				33	11.1	47	7.8	41	9.0
	7.1		7.2		6.9					16.9		7.6		6.2
	15.0		15.8		21.2	Sales/Working Capital				281.3		10.8		21.1
	332.5		696.1		NM					-124.1		399.5		33.5
	8.7		5.1		6.8					12.7		5.0		6.0
(63)	3.4	(54)	3.0	(53)	3.1	EBIT/Interest				3.0	(18)	2.7		3.6
	1.6		1.7		1.9					.1		.4		2.2
	4.4		2.9		4.6									5.3
(20)	2.4	(18)	1.5	(20)	1.7	Net Profit + Depr., Dep., Amort./Cur. Mat. L/T/D							(11)	2.1
	1.1		1.1		1.2									1.3
	.6		.8		.6					.5		.4		.8
	1.3		1.4		1.3	Fixed/Worth				1.1		1.3		1.3
	2.8		3.0		3.5					2.1		4.4		3.6
	1.1		1.2		.9					.9		.6		.8
	2.7		2.5		2.0	Debt/Worth				2.5		3.4		1.8
	5.5		5.4		6.3					5.4		8.4		6.0
	31.4		45.0		44.0							25.2		47.4
(63)	17.1	(51)	18.1	(49)	17.8	% Profit Before Taxes/Tangible Net Worth					(16)	12.5	(20)	23.6
	6.3		4.2		8.7							6.3		11.6
	10.6		11.3		13.1					23.8		8.0		13.5
	5.9		4.9		5.9	% Profit Before Taxes/Total Assets				4.5		3.5		7.6
	1.4		1.3		2.5					-3.9		-3.2		3.1
	12.4		10.6		13.1					25.6		14.4		6.4
	6.4		5.4		6.1	Sales/Net Fixed Assets				5.5		9.9		4.7
	3.7		3.6		3.8					3.6		5.2		3.2
	2.9		2.7		3.0					3.4		3.1		2.5
	2.2		2.1		2.4	Sales/Total Assets				2.3		2.7		2.1
	1.6		1.7		1.6					1.7		1.5		1.5
	1.9		2.1		1.8							1.8		2.1
(64)	3.2	(51)	3.3	(51)	2.9	% Depr., Dep., Amort./Sales					(18)	2.7		2.9
	4.2		4.8		4.3							3.8		4.4
	1.9		1.3		1.5									
(26)	3.5	(22)	2.7	(19)	2.5	% Officers', Directors' Owners' Comp/Sales								
	7.3		5.6		5.7									
2046448M		1798041M		1784381M	Net Sales ($)	742M	3323M	8406M	76307M	322016M	1373587M
949661M		918778M		897916M	Total Assets ($)	5091M	931M	2202M	34119M	146070M	709503M

M = $ thousand   MM = $ million
See Pages 11 through 21 for Explanation of Ratios and Data

Current Data Sorted by Assets

Comparative Historical Data

	0-500M	500M-2MM	2-10MM	10-50MM	50-100MM	100-250MM	Type of Statement	4/1/02-3/31/03 ALL	4/1/03-3/31/04 ALL
			4	16	2	2	Unqualified	23	19
	1	2	11	5			Reviewed	12	23
	1	3	6	3			Compiled	10	15
	1	5	2	1			Tax Returns	3	8
	2	7	10	13	2	3	Other	20	24
		21 (4/1-9/30/06)		80 (10/1/06-3/31/07)					
NUMBER OF STATEMENTS	4	17	33	38	4	5		68	89

ASSETS	500M-2MM %	2-10MM %	10-50MM %	4/1/02-3/31/03 %	4/1/03-3/31/04 %
Cash & Equivalents	7.8	6.1	4.1	5.8	6.8
Trade Receivables (net)	31.1	30.2	22.1	24.6	26.0
Inventory	31.2	25.9	22.4	21.0	22.7
All Other Current	.6	2.4	2.0	1.0	2.2
Total Current	70.9	64.6	50.6	52.4	57.7
Fixed Assets (net)	23.0	29.1	40.1	35.5	31.0
Intangibles (net)	.4	1.3	3.5	6.8	5.2
All Other Non-Current	5.8	4.9	5.8	5.3	6.1
Total	100.0	100.0	100.0	100.0	100.0
LIABILITIES					
Notes Payable-Short Term	13.9	12.9	10.2	8.7	10.4
Cur. Mat.-L.T.D.	3.2	3.3	3.7	5.3	4.8
Trade Payables	31.8	20.8	13.4	14.7	16.6
Income Taxes Payable	.3	.4	.3	.1	.1
All Other Current	11.8	6.5	6.0	7.6	10.6
Total Current	61.0	43.8	33.5	36.5	42.5
Long-Term Debt	18.1	14.3	18.0	21.6	19.4
Deferred Taxes	.0	.8	.6	.6	.4
All Other Non-Current	6.2	4.7	5.9	5.1	6.4
Net Worth	14.6	36.3	42.1	36.2	31.3
Total Liabilities & Net Worth	100.0	100.0	100.0	100.0	100.0
INCOME DATA					
Net Sales	100.0	100.0	100.0	100.0	100.0
Gross Profit	29.1	24.3	23.6	28.7	26.3
Operating Expenses	22.4	19.3	18.8	23.2	22.2
Operating Profit	6.7	5.0	4.8	5.5	4.0
All Other Expenses (net)	1.2	.8	1.0	2.1	.9
Profit Before Taxes	5.5	4.2	3.7	3.4	3.1

RATIOS	500M-2MM	2-10MM	10-50MM	4/1/02-3/31/03	4/1/03-3/31/04
	2.5	2.3	2.3	2.1	2.2
Current	1.6	1.5	1.6	1.4	1.4
	1.0	.9	1.2	1.1	1.0
	1.3	1.2	1.1	1.2	1.2
Quick	1.0	.8	.7	.8	.9
	.5	.5	.6	.6	.5
	30 12.1	32 11.5	33 11.2	30 12.3	30 12.2
Sales/Receivables	38 9.6	40 9.2	37 9.9	39 9.4	38 9.6
	48 7.6	48 7.7	46 7.9	48 7.6	47 7.8
	33 11.2	25 14.3	37 9.8	29 12.5	31 11.7
Cost of Sales/Inventory	56 6.5	40 9.1	50 7.4	50 7.2	48 7.6
	81 4.5	64 5.7	62 5.9	71 5.1	67 5.5
	20 18.4	20 18.2	18 20.2	16 22.4	16 22.5
Cost of Sales/Payables	38 9.7	34 10.8	30 12.0	30 12.1	33 10.9
	53 6.9	52 7.0	44 8.4	44 8.3	45 8.1
	6.1	6.7	6.2	8.8	7.4
Sales/Working Capital	9.8	11.2	9.6	14.3	14.8
	NM	-57.5	22.8	37.0	NM
	6.4	10.5	5.9	7.8	9.1
EBIT/Interest	(15) 3.4	(30) 5.0	(35) 3.1	(66) 3.6	(81) 3.4
	.9	1.9	1.5	1.2	1.1
Net Profit + Depr., Dep.,			8.0	5.6	2.9
Amort./Cur. Mat. L/T/D			(16) 3.9	(21) 1.9	(23) 1.7
			1.9	1.1	1.1
	.2	.3	.6	.5	.5
Fixed/Worth	.4	.7	.9	1.2	1.0
	1.6	2.6	2.3	2.6	4.0
	.9	.6	.6	1.1	1.0
Debt/Worth	2.0	1.9	1.4	2.1	2.8
	NM	6.4	3.9	5.3	8.6
% Profit Before Taxes/Tangible	80.5	46.9	41.3	49.1	41.7
Net Worth	(13) 25.5	(29) 26.4	(36) 19.5	(60) 18.9	(74) 21.3
	4.7	13.7	5.7	2.1	4.3
% Profit Before Taxes/Total	29.2	18.8	12.0	13.2	13.3
Assets	8.2	9.9	6.7	6.2	5.8
	.1	3.9	1.6	.4	.2
	65.5	19.0	7.2	11.0	13.9
Sales/Net Fixed Assets	12.2	11.0	5.2	6.9	7.7
	6.5	6.5	3.2	3.6	4.6
	3.6	3.5	2.7	2.9	3.2
Sales/Total Assets	2.6	2.7	2.0	2.1	2.2
	2.2	2.0	1.5	1.4	1.5
	.5	.9	1.9	1.3	1.2
% Depr., Dep., Amort./Sales	(13) 1.9	1.6	(35) 3.2	(61) 3.0	(81) 2.7
	3.6	3.3	4.0	5.1	4.0
% Officers', Directors'		3.0		1.6	2.0
Owners' Comp/Sales		(14) 6.0		(17) 4.1	(28) 3.7
		7.6		5.4	9.5

	0-500M	500M-2MM	2-10MM	10-50MM	50-100MM	100-250MM		4/1/02-3/31/03	4/1/03-3/31/04
Net Sales ($)	2645M	66498M	478070M	1769726M	578009M	1388585M		2578553M	3213099M
Total Assets ($)	762M	22976M	176805M	882002M	296175M	765459M		1582601M	1796995M

M = $ thousand   MM = $ million
See Pages 11 through 21 for Explanation of Ratios and Data

Comparative Historical Data | Current Data Sorted by Sales

	4/1/04-3/31/05 ALL	4/1/05-3/31/06 ALL	4/1/06-3/31/07 ALL		0-1MM	1-3MM	3-5MM	5-10MM	10-25MM	25MM & OVER
Type of Statement										
Unqualified	29	23	24		1			1	6	17
Reviewed	24	22	19					6	6	5
Compiled	9	11	13			3	1	6	6	3
Tax Returns	1	5	8			1	2	1	1	1
Other	27	37	37		3	2	2	5	11	14
					21 (4/1-9/30/06)			80 (10/1/06-3/31/07)		
NUMBER OF STATEMENTS	90	98	101		4	6	6	15	30	40
	%	%	%		%	%	%	%	%	%
ASSETS										
Cash & Equivalents	5.3	5.7	5.7					6.5	6.5	3.7
Trade Receivables (net)	27.3	29.9	26.0					35.2	25.4	23.3
Inventory	23.3	26.4	25.0					28.0	22.9	23.5
All Other Current	1.1	2.3	1.9					1.0	3.7	1.5
Total Current	57.0	64.3	58.6					70.7	58.4	52.0
Fixed Assets (net)	31.2	27.0	32.7					26.0	32.4	38.2
Intangibles (net)	5.6	4.2	3.7					.1	2.6	5.5
All Other Non-Current	6.3	4.4	5.1					3.2	6.6	4.3
Total	100.0	100.0	100.0					100.0	100.0	100.0
LIABILITIES										
Notes Payable-Short Term	12.9	14.7	11.5					14.9	9.7	11.0
Cur. Mat.-L.T.D.	4.1	4.5	3.4					3.2	3.9	3.4
Trade Payables	15.3	19.5	18.7					24.1	17.2	14.8
Income Taxes Payable	.4	.2	.3					.6	.2	.3
All Other Current	8.0	6.1	7.0					6.7	7.0	6.0
Total Current	40.6	45.1	41.0					49.5	38.0	35.6
Long-Term Debt	18.9	14.8	18.0					18.4	14.5	19.4
Deferred Taxes	.8	.8	.7					.0	1.1	.9
All Other Non-Current	5.2	6.1	6.3					.8	7.3	5.5
Net Worth	34.4	33.2	34.0					31.3	39.1	38.5
Total Liabilties & Net Worth	100.0	100.0	100.0					100.0	100.0	100.0
INCOME DATA										
Net Sales	100.0	100.0	100.0					100.0	100.0	100.0
Gross Profit	25.8	23.3	24.4					26.6	27.8	21.0
Operating Expenses	19.9	18.7	19.0					21.4	22.6	15.9
Operating Profit	6.0	4.6	5.4					5.2	5.2	5.1
All Other Expenses (net)	1.1	1.0	1.3					1.6	.7	1.4
Profit Before Taxes	4.9	3.6	4.1					3.6	4.5	3.7
RATIOS										
Current	2.4	2.4	2.4					2.1	2.5	2.1
	1.5	1.5	1.6					1.4	1.7	1.6
	1.0	1.0	1.1					1.0	.9	1.1
Quick	1.2	1.4	1.2					1.1	1.3	1.1
	(89) .8	.8	.8					.8	.7	.7
	.6	.5	.6					.6	.5	.6
Sales/Receivables	31 — 11.7	33 — 11.0	32 — 11.5					33 — 11.2	32 — 11.3	31 — 11.7
	40 — 9.0	40 — 9.2	38 — 9.5					46 — 7.9	38 — 9.7	37 — 9.9
	50 — 7.3	49 — 7.5	47 — 7.8					61 — 5.9	46 — 7.9	45 — 8.1
Cost of Sales/Inventory	29 — 12.5	31 — 11.9	33 — 11.2					29 — 12.8	26 — 14.1	37 — 9.9
	48 — 7.6	46 — 7.9	47 — 7.7					56 — 6.5	41 — 8.8	48 — 7.6
	69 — 5.3	65 — 5.6	66 — 5.5					81 — 4.5	79 — 4.6	57 — 6.5
Cost of Sales/Payables	16 — 22.3	20 — 18.5	18 — 19.9					29 — 12.4	20 — 18.3	18 — 20.4
	30 — 12.0	31 — 11.8	32 — 11.4					37 — 9.8	34 — 10.8	29 — 12.7
	43 — 8.4	49 — 7.5	47 — 7.8					64 — 5.7	42 — 8.7	43 — 8.4
Sales/Working Capital	6.8	6.2	6.5					6.5	6.5	7.1
	13.0	13.7	10.9					12.6	8.7	14.5
	82.3	122.6	70.3					-176.5	-35.5	45.7
EBIT/Interest	13.9	11.0	7.4					10.4	8.8	6.6
	(80) 4.4	(90) 4.3	(93) 3.4					3.4	(26) 4.8	(38) 3.3
	2.0	1.7	1.4					1.4	1.6	1.6
Net Profit + Depr., Dep., Amort./Cur. Mat. L/T/D	4.9	3.5	5.9							7.6
	(27) 2.5	(28) 2.6	(29) 3.4							(18) 3.5
	1.6	1.0	1.5							2.4
Fixed/Worth	.4	.3	.5					.2	.5	.7
	.9	.8	.8					.5	.7	1.2
	2.4	2.5	2.6					3.4	2.7	2.6
Debt/Worth	.8	.7	.8					1.2	.6	1.1
	2.1	1.9	2.0					2.4	1.3	1.8
	5.3	6.3	5.2					9.1	5.3	4.1
% Profit Before Taxes/Tangible Net Worth	48.1	42.0	47.1					81.9	46.0	41.3
	(79) 25.5	(82) 24.1	(87) 20.3					(14) 22.7	(26) 21.6	(36) 20.9
	10.1	11.2	7.5					5.4	8.7	13.5
% Profit Before Taxes/Total Assets	15.9	15.7	13.3					23.4	16.6	12.8
	7.8	7.1	7.9					9.7	7.8	7.9
	2.4	2.0	1.7					1.7	2.1	2.2
Sales/Net Fixed Assets	14.1	20.3	14.1					52.4	16.3	8.6
	7.5	10.2	7.4					12.2	9.3	6.2
	4.3	5.3	4.4					4.2	4.2	3.8
Sales/Total Assets	3.2	3.2	3.0					3.5	3.2	2.8
	2.1	2.4	2.3					2.4	2.5	2.1
	1.6	1.8	1.7					1.8	1.6	1.6
% Depr., Dep., Amort./Sales	1.2	1.0	1.5					.4	1.3	1.8
	(78) 2.4	(83) 1.9	(89) 2.3					.8	(29) 2.1	(36) 2.8
	3.5	3.2	3.6					3.2	4.0	3.6
% Officers', Directors', Owners' Comp/Sales	1.5	2.1	2.7							
	(20) 2.6	(23) 2.9	(27) 4.2							
	7.3	5.5	6.9							
Net Sales ($)	4138244M	4885389M	4283533M		2114M	13338M	22080M	116694M	504033M	3625274M
Total Assets ($)	2166391M	2389107M	2144179M		1508M	4655M	9091M	55246M	254990M	1818689M

M = $ thousand   MM = $ million
See Pages 11 through 21 for Explanation of Ratios and Data

Current Data Sorted by Assets   Comparative Historical Data

0-500M	500M-2MM	2-10MM	10-50MM	50-100MM	100-250MM	Type of Statement	4/1/02-3/31/03 ALL	4/1/03-3/31/04 ALL
1			12	1	5	Unqualified	16	18
1	3	14	6			Reviewed	31	31
1	4	3	1			Compiled	7	16
1	2	1				Tax Returns	2	9
1	5	10	10		2	Other	19	22
	15 (4/1-9/30/06)		69 (10/1/06-3/31/07)					
5	14	28	29	1	7	NUMBER OF STATEMENTS	75	96
%	%	%	%	%	%	**ASSETS**	%	%
	3.9	8.1	6.3			Cash & Equivalents	5.2	6.3
	34.9	29.0	25.3			Trade Receivables (net)	26.6	25.7
	25.3	24.8	28.5			Inventory	22.0	23.3
	3.1	1.0	2.4			All Other Current	1.5	2.0
	67.2	62.9	62.5			Total Current	55.3	57.3
	26.6	29.9	26.7			Fixed Assets (net)	33.9	31.2
	3.5	2.5	4.0			Intangibles (net)	4.5	5.0
	2.7	4.8	6.8			All Other Non-Current	6.3	6.6
	100.0	100.0	100.0			Total	100.0	100.0
						LIABILITIES		
	19.3	10.7	8.8			Notes Payable-Short Term	9.6	12.8
	6.6	3.2	2.2			Cur. Mat.-L.T.D.	6.1	4.3
	16.9	17.4	13.3			Trade Payables	15.5	14.3
	.0	.4	.5			Income Taxes Payable	.2	.1
	25.1	7.2	8.6			All Other Current	8.4	6.7
	67.9	38.9	33.4			Total Current	39.9	38.3
	14.4	19.0	9.7			Long-Term Debt	17.1	14.5
	.0	.4	1.1			Deferred Taxes	.9	.8
	16.9	6.8	7.4			All Other Non-Current	6.5	8.5
	.7	35.0	48.4			Net Worth	35.5	37.9
	100.0	100.0	100.0			Total Liabilities & Net Worth	100.0	100.0
						INCOME DATA		
	100.0	100.0	100.0			Net Sales	100.0	100.0
	32.3	28.5	23.1			Gross Profit	31.8	32.1
	35.9	24.7	17.1			Operating Expenses	28.1	28.1
	-3.7	3.8	6.0			Operating Profit	3.7	4.0
	1.9	1.0	1.4			All Other Expenses (net)	1.8	1.1
	-5.5	2.8	4.7			Profit Before Taxes	1.9	2.9
						RATIOS		
	1.6	2.9	2.8				2.1	2.7
	1.3	1.6	1.6			Current	1.5	1.6
	.9	1.1	1.3				1.1	1.1
	1.1	1.8	1.6				1.1	1.5
	.9	.9	.8			Quick	.8	.9
	.4	.6	.6				.6	.6
	30 12.0	33 11.0	33 11.1				37 9.7	33 11.0
	40 9.2	39 9.4	42 8.7			Sales/Receivables	43 8.4	43 8.4
	61 6.0	54 6.7	48 7.6				50 7.4	51 7.1
	23 16.1	23 16.1	37 9.9				27 13.3	31 11.9
	42 8.6	44 8.2	58 6.3			Cost of Sales/Inventory	43 8.5	49 7.4
	94 3.9	67 5.5	86 4.3				67 5.4	76 4.8
	12 31.6	20 18.5	12 30.8				21 17.1	15 24.4
	21 17.1	37 9.7	29 12.5			Cost of Sales/Payables	32 11.4	33 11.0
	50 7.3	49 7.5	48 7.6				45 8.2	44 8.2
	11.1	4.0	4.7				6.7	5.9
	22.5	10.9	9.3			Sales/Working Capital	17.4	12.2
	NM	37.9	16.0				95.3	107.8
	5.5	7.8	16.0				6.1	6.9
	(13) 1.3	(25) 3.0	(26) 3.4			EBIT/Interest	(69) 2.7	(87) 3.1
	-2.0	2.0	1.3				1.3	1.0
			7.1				3.6	3.0
		(12)	4.3			Net Profit + Depr., Dep., Amort./Cur. Mat. L/T/D	(27) 1.6	(32) 1.8
			2.0				1.1	.8
	.5	.3	.3				.5	.5
	.7	1.0	.5			Fixed/Worth	1.0	.9
	-2.1	2.3	1.2				2.4	2.2
	1.2	.9	.6				1.0	.7
	5.2	1.6	.9			Debt/Worth	2.0	1.8
	-4.1	5.1	2.4				5.0	4.8
		51.4	38.0				28.6	23.9
		(25) 17.0	(25) 14.4			% Profit Before Taxes/Tangible Net Worth	(66) 14.6	(83) 14.2
		3.2	5.2				2.2	2.2
	5.5	17.9	21.0				11.4	11.7
	.5	6.5	7.3			% Profit Before Taxes/Total Assets	4.2	3.4
	-19.5	2.0	1.6				.7	.2
	28.8	20.9	15.7				11.4	12.8
	14.9	9.6	8.4			Sales/Net Fixed Assets	7.0	7.6
	5.9	4.6	4.7				4.3	4.4
	4.0	3.1	2.8				2.8	2.8
	3.0	2.5	2.1			Sales/Total Assets	2.3	2.0
	1.7	1.8	1.6				1.7	1.6
	.8	1.3	1.5				2.0	1.6
	(12) 1.6	(26) 2.0	(28) 2.0			% Depr., Dep., Amort./Sales	(69) 3.1	(86) 2.8
	4.4	3.0	3.2				4.9	4.3
			1.9				2.4	3.9
		(11) 2.7				% Officers', Directors' Owners' Comp/Sales	(33) 4.4	(34) 6.3
		5.3					6.8	9.1
1625M	53990M	310259M	1403292M	118882M	1629217M	Net Sales ($)	2006729M	1646080M
601M	18260M	121104M	652422M	76500M	1085571M	Total Assets ($)	1182330M	1023308M

M = $ thousand   MM = $ million
See Pages 11 through 21 for Explanation of Ratios and Data

Comparative Historical Data | Current Data Sorted by Sales

Yr1	4/1/04-3/31/05 ALL	Yr2	4/1/05-3/31/06 ALL	Yr3	4/1/06-3/31/07 ALL	Type of Statement	0-1MM	15 (4/1-9/30/06) 1-3MM	3-5MM	69 (10/1/06-3/31/07) 5-10MM	10-25MM	25MM & OVER
	20		19		19	Unqualified					1	17
	27		17		24	Reviewed	1		4	5	8	5
	7		11		9	Compiled	1	1	2	4	1	
	6		7		4	Tax Returns	1	1	1	1		
	30		29		28	Other	1	3	3	2		11
	90		83		84	NUMBER OF STATEMENTS	5	6	10	12	18	33
	%		%		%	ASSETS	%	%	%	%	%	%
	6.7		5.2		6.0	Cash & Equivalents			4.3	9.0	7.6	5.3
	26.6		29.3		26.8	Trade Receivables (net)			32.1	27.7	31.5	24.8
	26.4		25.7		26.2	Inventory			29.4	29.7	17.2	29.1
	1.1		1.5		1.9	All Other Current			.2	.4	2.3	1.7
	60.8		61.7		60.9	Total Current			66.0	66.7	58.7	60.9
	29.7		28.6		29.4	Fixed Assets (net)			28.4	29.8	29.4	28.0
	3.3		3.4		4.5	Intangibles (net)			1.9	1.2	4.6	6.0
	6.2		6.4		5.2	All Other Non-Current			3.7	2.3	7.4	5.1
	100.0		100.0		100.0	Total			100.0	100.0	100.0	100.0
						LIABILITIES						
	10.9		14.1		12.2	Notes Payable-Short Term			11.7	9.6	12.2	8.9
	3.5		4.6		3.5	Cur. Mat.-L.T.D.			8.4	2.6	2.9	2.7
	15.1		16.0		14.9	Trade Payables			13.5	17.8	18.2	13.4
	.1		.2		.3	Income Taxes Payable			.0	.8	.3	.3
	7.0		7.2		10.6	All Other Current			10.9	6.1	7.8	8.8
	36.7		42.1		41.5	Total Current			44.5	37.0	41.4	34.0
	17.9		18.0		15.7	Long-Term Debt			17.9	9.5	19.4	13.2
	.7		.7		.6	Deferred Taxes			.4	.5	.3	1.1
	7.9		8.3		9.2	All Other Non-Current			15.2	8.5	4.2	9.1
	36.9		30.9		33.0	Net Worth			22.0	44.6	34.7	42.6
	100.0		100.0		100.0	Total Liabilties & Net Worth			100.0	100.0	100.0	100.0
						INCOME DATA						
	100.0		100.0		100.0	Net Sales			100.0	100.0	100.0	100.0
	29.1		28.1		28.2	Gross Profit			33.8	25.6	28.7	22.3
	24.6		23.0		24.5	Operating Expenses			32.7	21.9	22.0	16.5
	4.5		5.1		3.7	Operating Profit			1.2	3.8	6.8	5.8
	1.1		1.9		1.5	All Other Expenses (net)			1.4	.2	.6	1.5
	3.4		3.2		2.2	Profit Before Taxes			-.2	3.6	6.1	4.4
						RATIOS						
	2.7		2.5		2.4	Current			2.0	4.0	1.9	2.6
	1.7		1.4		1.5				1.4	1.9	1.4	1.6
	1.2		1.2		1.1				1.1	1.1	.9	1.2
	1.6		1.2		1.4	Quick			1.2	1.8	1.6	1.1
	.9		.8		.8				1.0	1.1	.8	.8
	.5		.6		.5				.5	.6	.6	.5
36	10.2	36	10.1	32	11.4	Sales/Receivables			34 10.6	31 11.9	34 10.8	34 10.8
43	8.6	43	8.6	40	9.2				44 8.4	33 10.9	40 9.1	42 8.7
53	6.8	54	6.7	49	7.5				48 7.7	41 8.9	53 6.9	49 7.5
30	12.1	29	12.6	30	12.1	Cost of Sales/Inventory			24 15.3	20 18.6	22 16.7	43 8.4
53	6.9	48	7.7	52	7.1				35 10.4	53 6.8	30 12.0	61 6.0
81	4.5	77	4.8	82	4.5				78 4.7	84 4.3	45 8.1	86 4.2
17	20.9	15	24.6	14	26.4	Cost of Sales/Payables			12 31.6	13 28.7	17 21.1	13 28.1
32	11.4	33	11.0	32	11.3				28 13.2	34 10.8	37 9.8	32 11.6
48	7.6	52	7.1	49	7.5				52 7.0	48 7.7	46 7.9	50 7.4
	5.1		7.0		5.8	Sales/Working Capital			9.2	3.4	9.0	5.3
	10.4		12.9		11.2				16.0	9.4	16.2	8.7
	27.5		38.6		38.3				39.3	35.6	-108.0	18.6
	8.7		6.1		7.4	EBIT/Interest			3.1	9.5	9.5	8.1
(79)	3.0	(76)	2.5	(74)	3.0				1.6	7.1	(16) 4.8	(29) 3.4
	1.1		1.4		1.3				.0	1.4	2.4	1.3
	3.5		3.2		5.3	Net Profit + Depr., Dep., Amort./Cur. Mat. L/T/D						8.4
(32)	2.4	(26)	2.6	(23)	2.6						(14)	3.0
	1.6		1.1		1.5							1.8
	.4		.3		.4	Fixed/Worth			.5	.3	.3	.4
	.8		.8		.8				.8	.6	1.0	.7
	1.8		5.1		3.5				NM	1.3	3.1	5.7
	.8		.8		.7	Debt/Worth			1.1	.6	.9	.7
	1.7		2.0		1.6				3.0	1.4	1.4	1.5
	4.6		30.2		10.4				NM	4.5	8.8	12.5
	31.0		41.2		45.1	% Profit Before Taxes/Tangible Net Worth				48.8	55.5	41.9
(78)	14.5	(66)	18.2	(69)	15.6					25.0	(15) 31.9	(27) 21.7
	1.3		6.9		5.4					1.1	13.4	6.0
	12.3		12.6		15.4	% Profit Before Taxes/Total Assets			3.7	20.4	24.3	15.8
	5.2		5.1		5.5				2.0	7.3	13.7	7.3
	.4		1.5		1.4				-3.7	.7	4.6	1.9
	15.7		20.5		17.8	Sales/Net Fixed Assets			33.3	19.8	19.2	15.7
	7.5		9.2		8.8				11.5	11.9	9.2	8.0
	4.3		4.7		4.8				5.0	4.4	5.2	4.6
	2.9		3.1		3.1	Sales/Total Assets			3.6	3.5	3.1	2.8
	2.0		2.4		2.3				2.6	2.4	2.5	2.1
	1.6		1.6		1.6				2.1	1.7	2.1	1.5
	1.7		.9		1.3	% Depr., Dep., Amort./Sales				.7	1.6	1.6
(81)	2.8	(73)	2.3	(75)	2.1					1.5	(17) 2.2	(31) 2.1
	3.6		3.6		3.3					2.3	2.9	3.4
	2.3		2.1		1.8	% Officers', Directors' Owners' Comp/Sales						
(32)	4.4	(27)	3.8	(23)	2.6							
	7.0		6.7		5.3							
	2777038M		3085352M		3517265M	Net Sales ($)	1625M	12957M	38418M	90958M	303148M	3070159M
	1536555M		1564882M		1954458M	Total Assets ($)	601M	8728M	15853M	38674M	133123M	1757479M

M = $ thousand   MM = $ million
See Pages 11 through 21 for Explanation of Ratios and Data

Current Data Sorted by Assets **Comparative Historical Data**

	0-500M	500M-2MM	2-10MM	10-50MM	50-100MM	100-250MM	Type of Statement		4/1/02-3/31/03 ALL	4/1/03-3/31/04 ALL
			2	8	1	1	Unqualified		15	21
			14	4			Reviewed		17	15
		3	2			1	Compiled		10	8
		3					Tax Returns		1	3
	1	1	8	9	3	1	Other		15	17
		16 (4/1-9/30/06)		46 (10/1/06-3/31/07)						
	1	7	26	21	4	3	NUMBER OF STATEMENTS		58	64
	%	%	%	%	%	%	ASSETS		%	%
			6.3	2.7			Cash & Equivalents		5.3	3.7
			25.9	31.4			Trade Receivables (net)		21.7	24.8
			31.0	20.9			Inventory		22.6	21.5
			1.0	2.1			All Other Current		1.2	2.0
			64.3	57.0			Total Current		50.8	52.0
			29.4	32.5			Fixed Assets (net)		38.7	39.2
			1.5	4.1			Intangibles (net)		3.4	3.0
			4.9	6.4			All Other Non-Current		7.1	5.7
			100.0	100.0			Total		100.0	100.0
							LIABILITIES			
			15.2	15.1			Notes Payable-Short Term		10.6	10.7
			3.8	4.5			Cur. Mat.-L.T.D.		5.9	5.3
			19.5	21.5			Trade Payables		16.7	18.4
			.5	.0			Income Taxes Payable		.5	.2
			7.7	5.2			All Other Current		6.9	8.2
			46.7	46.3			Total Current		40.6	42.7
			16.1	17.2			Long-Term Debt		18.5	20.4
			1.1	1.2			Deferred Taxes		1.5	1.4
			3.3	1.3			All Other Non-Current		12.0	12.1
			32.9	33.9			Net Worth		27.5	23.3
			100.0	100.0			Total Liabilties & Net Worth		100.0	100.0
							INCOME DATA			
			100.0	100.0			Net Sales		100.0	100.0
			23.5	19.0			Gross Profit		27.4	25.2
			20.7	14.3			Operating Expenses		23.7	21.6
			2.8	4.6			Operating Profit		3.7	3.7
			1.1	1.4			All Other Expenses (net)		1.8	1.7
			1.8	3.3			Profit Before Taxes		1.9	2.0
							RATIOS			
			2.2	2.0					1.8	1.9
			1.4	1.3			Current		1.2	1.2
			1.0	.9					.8	.9
			1.1	1.3					1.0	1.0
			.6	.7			Quick		.6	.6
			.5	.5					.4	.4
			30 12.0	36 10.3					29 12.5	34 10.6
			37 9.9	45 8.2			Sales/Receivables		41 8.9	43 8.5
			43 8.5	70 5.2					50 7.3	53 6.9
			33 11.1	34 10.8					37 9.9	41 9.0
			51 7.2	41 8.8			Cost of Sales/Inventory		53 6.9	52 7.0
			77 4.7	63 5.8					78 4.7	62 5.9
			22 16.9	27 13.4					27 13.7	29 12.6
			38 9.5	39 9.4			Cost of Sales/Payables		42 8.7	40 9.2
			44 8.3	51 7.1					60 6.0	52 7.0
			7.8	6.3					8.1	7.7
			15.5	18.4			Sales/Working Capital		20.5	27.2
			-362.1	-35.7					-30.6	-41.8
			8.3	9.2					4.6	5.1
			1.9	3.9			EBIT/Interest	(56)	2.3	(62) 2.3
			1.4	2.3					1.2	1.0
			6.9	5.7			Net Profit + Depr., Dep.,		4.3	4.0
		(13)	1.7	(10) 2.0			Amort./Cur. Mat. L/T/D	(25)	1.6	(26) 1.9
			1.2	1.6					1.3	1.2
			.4	.4					.7	.8
			.9	1.1			Fixed/Worth		1.4	1.5
			2.1	2.8					2.7	5.4
			1.5	1.4					1.1	1.4
			2.0	3.8			Debt/Worth		2.2	2.5
			4.2	8.3					6.1	10.4
			34.2	93.8			% Profit Before Taxes/Tangible		33.3	24.3
		(24)	7.6	(20) 28.7			Net Worth	(50)	11.7	(53) 12.2
			2.6	7.4					3.2	3.7
			9.0	13.4			% Profit Before Taxes/Total		8.9	7.4
			2.8	7.9			Assets		4.0	3.3
			1.0	3.7					.4	.0
			18.8	13.3					10.3	9.9
			7.6	7.8			Sales/Net Fixed Assets		5.0	4.6
			5.2	3.9					2.7	3.3
			3.2	2.6					2.5	2.6
			2.7	2.1			Sales/Total Assets		1.9	2.0
			2.0	1.6					1.5	1.6
			.6	1.2					2.5	2.4
		(23)	2.0	2.4			% Depr., Dep., Amort./Sales	(57)	3.6	(58) 3.6
			2.8	3.5					5.5	5.0
			1.8						1.9	1.7
		(11)	2.4				% Officers', Directors' Owners' Comp/Sales	(24)	3.3	(21) 2.4
			5.2						6.8	6.9
	713M	31635M	363547M	985471M	554061M	693257M	Net Sales ($)		1497456M	1629232M
	303M	8534M	141508M	455774M	264293M	457399M	Total Assets ($)		878849M	934743M

M = $ thousand   MM = $ million
See Pages 11 through 21 for Explanation of Ratios and Data

Comparative Historical Data   Current Data Sorted by Sales

	4/1/04-3/31/05 ALL	4/1/05-3/31/06 ALL	4/1/06-3/31/07 ALL	Type of Statement	0-1MM	1-3MM	3-5MM	5-10MM	10-25MM	25MM & OVER
	19	18	12	Unqualified				1	2	9
	11	18	18	Reviewed				2	11	5
	10	6	6	Compiled			3	1		2
	7	5	4	Tax Returns				1		
	17	27	22	Other	2	1		5	6	11
					16 (4/1-9/30/06)			46 (10/1/06-3/31/07)		
NUMBER OF STATEMENTS	64	74	62		2	1	3	10	19	27
	%	%	%	ASSETS	%	%	%	%	%	%
	5.4	6.4	5.6	Cash & Equivalents				4.4	6.1	3.3
	25.2	29.0	27.2	Trade Receivables (net)				30.3	25.2	29.5
	22.2	24.3	26.5	Inventory				39.0	26.0	23.0
	1.8	1.3	1.8	All Other Current				1.6	.5	2.1
	54.5	61.1	61.1	Total Current				75.2	57.8	57.9
	34.1	29.1	29.1	Fixed Assets (net)				17.7	35.0	31.2
	5.2	3.0	3.3	Intangibles (net)				2.8	2.1	4.5
	6.2	6.9	6.5	All Other Non-Current				4.2	5.1	6.5
	100.0	100.0	100.0	Total				100.0	100.0	100.0
				LIABILITIES						
	13.7	13.9	13.4	Notes Payable-Short Term				14.0	15.4	13.7
	4.8	4.9	3.7	Cur. Mat.-L.T.D.				1.9	4.8	4.0
	18.6	21.0	20.6	Trade Payables				25.8	17.0	21.6
	.3	.2	.3	Income Taxes Payable				.0	.6	.2
	6.4	8.2	6.6	All Other Current				9.2	6.6	6.2
	43.8	48.1	44.6	Total Current				50.9	44.2	45.8
	18.7	20.9	16.5	Long-Term Debt				12.5	19.8	16.4
	1.1	.7	1.1	Deferred Taxes				.3	1.3	1.5
	9.4	3.6	3.2	All Other Non-Current				.4	3.4	2.5
	26.9	26.7	34.6	Net Worth				35.9	31.2	33.8
	100.0	100.0	100.0	Total Liabilities & Net Worth				100.0	100.0	100.0
				INCOME DATA						
	100.0	100.0	100.0	Net Sales				100.0	100.0	100.0
	21.6	20.6	22.3	Gross Profit				26.2	23.1	18.2
	19.8	16.8	18.0	Operating Expenses				21.3	19.4	14.3
	1.8	3.8	4.3	Operating Profit				5.0	3.6	3.9
	.7	1.9	1.3	All Other Expenses (net)				1.4	1.4	1.3
	1.1	2.0	3.0	Profit Before Taxes				3.6	2.2	2.7
				RATIOS						
	2.3	1.7	2.5	Current				2.5	1.8	2.1
	1.1	1.2	1.4					1.5	1.3	1.4
	.9	.9	1.0					1.1	1.0	.9
	1.3	1.1	1.2	Quick				.9	1.1	1.2
	.6	.6	.7					.7	.6	.7
	.4	.4	.5					.4	.5	.5
	35 10.4	33 10.9	30 12.0	Sales/Receivables				32 11.3	31 11.8	34 10.7
	42 8.6	41 8.8	39 9.5					35 10.3	42 8.7	39 9.2
	51 7.2	50 7.4	47 7.7					40 9.1	48 7.6	51 7.2
	30 12.3	30 12.2	33 11.0	Cost of Sales/Inventory				39 9.4	34 10.8	36 10.3
	44 8.4	48 7.6	48 7.6					57 6.4	52 7.1	42 8.6
	70 5.2	71 5.2	70 5.2					116 3.1	80 4.6	64 5.7
	26 14.0	25 14.5	21 17.0	Cost of Sales/Payables				17 21.2	19 19.2	25 14.4
	37 9.8	38 9.7	39 9.4					40 9.2	30 12.4	39 9.4
	51 7.2	57 6.4	43 8.5					56 6.5	60 6.1	43 8.6
	6.6	8.2	7.1	Sales/Working Capital				7.3	8.3	7.1
	46.4	21.9	13.5					12.4	15.4	15.6
	-30.4	-39.2	-290.8					NM	-469.3	-42.5
	6.1	5.9	9.4	EBIT/Interest					4.1	8.3
	(59) 2.2	(67) 3.0	(61) 3.2						1.9	3.3
	-.8	1.4	1.5						1.4	1.4
	8.3	2.3	5.4	Net Profit + Depr., Dep., Amort./Cur. Mat. L/T/D					8.5	4.0
	(21) 1.9	(19) 1.8	(26) 1.9						(11) 2.9	(14) 1.9
	.9	1.2	1.3						1.3	1.6
	.6	.4	.4	Fixed/Worth				.0	.5	.7
	1.5	1.2	.9					.5	1.5	.9
	6.3	3.8	2.8					1.0	6.6	2.8
	1.0	1.4	1.3	Debt/Worth				1.2	1.3	1.4
	2.9	2.7	1.9					1.8	2.5	2.2
	16.4	10.3	4.8					4.2	11.4	4.7
	32.9	34.3	48.4	% Profit Before Taxes/Tangible Net Worth					34.2	48.9
	(55) 12.9	(63) 21.0	(55) 18.1						(18) 13.9	(24) 20.0
	-6.1	6.2	6.0						6.4	3.3
	7.9	10.0	12.5	% Profit Before Taxes/Total Assets				17.5	8.4	13.1
	3.3	5.3	5.5					8.7	2.9	5.6
	-3.4	1.2	1.3					2.3	1.4	.7
	10.2	18.3	16.9	Sales/Net Fixed Assets				UND	13.9	11.5
	5.7	7.9	7.8					20.1	5.9	7.8
	3.9	4.8	5.1					6.4	4.3	4.7
	2.6	2.8	3.1	Sales/Total Assets				3.7	2.9	3.0
	2.0	2.3	2.4					2.9	2.2	2.4
	1.5	1.6	1.8					1.9	1.7	1.8
	2.0	1.4	1.1	% Depr., Dep., Amort./Sales					1.0	1.2
	(53) 3.1	(66) 2.2	(56) 2.0						(18) 2.4	(25) 1.9
	5.1	3.3	3.2						3.8	3.3
	2.3	1.7	1.7	% Officers', Directors' Owners' Comp/Sales						
	(24) 4.1	(25) 2.5	(20) 2.4							
	5.0	4.5	5.0							
	2234433M	3000070M	2628684M	Net Sales ($)	1575M	2706M	12951M	75779M	288028M	2247645M
	1279280M	1542599M	1327811M	Total Assets ($)	803M	796M	4469M	31992M	141022M	1148729M

M = $ thousand   MM = $ million
See Pages 11 through 21 for Explanation of Ratios and Data

Current Data Sorted by Assets

Comparative Historical Data

	0-500M	500M-2MM	2-10MM	10-50MM	50-100MM	100-250MM	Type of Statement	11	10
		2	5 3 3	3 4		1	Unqualified	11	10
		2 1	3 1				Reviewed	9	10
		1	1				Compiled	2	2
		1 9 (4/1-9/30/06)	4	6 29 (10/1/06-3/31/07)	2		Tax Returns Other	8 4/1/02- 3/31/03 ALL	7 4/1/03- 3/31/04 ALL
	6	6	16	13	3		NUMBER OF STATEMENTS	30	29

0-500M	500M-2MM	2-10MM	10-50MM	50-100MM	100-250MM		ALL	ALL
%	%	%	%	%	%	**ASSETS**	%	%
		8.7	4.1			Cash & Equivalents	5.1	7.5
		31.7	25.9			Trade Receivables (net)	27.0	28.2
D		11.6	15.4	D		Inventory	18.2	16.3
A		1.7	1.0	A		All Other Current	1.7	1.0
T		53.7	46.4	T		Total Current	52.0	53.0
A		39.4	49.6	A		Fixed Assets (net)	41.2	38.2
		3.1	.5			Intangibles (net)	1.1	3.0
N		3.8	3.5	N		All Other Non-Current	5.6	5.8
O		100.0	100.0	O		Total	100.0	100.0
T				T		**LIABILITIES**		
		11.9	9.8			Notes Payable-Short Term	13.2	12.7
A		4.7	6.7	A		Cur. Mat.-L.T.D.	5.8	5.4
V		12.0	11.6	V		Trade Payables	11.2	11.3
A		.4	.2	A		Income Taxes Payable	.2	.1
I		6.0	8.6	I		All Other Current	6.5	6.2
L		35.0	36.9	L		Total Current	36.9	35.8
A		18.6	30.9	A		Long-Term Debt	22.0	20.0
B		1.0	.4	B		Deferred Taxes	.7	1.3
L		6.4	3.2	L		All Other Non-Current	9.5	5.6
E		39.0	28.6	E		Net Worth	30.8	37.3
		100.0	100.0			Total Liabilities & Net Worth	100.0	100.0
						INCOME DATA		
		100.0	100.0			Net Sales	100.0	100.0
		24.6	21.3			Gross Profit	24.8	27.3
		20.4	16.1			Operating Expenses	22.3	23.7
		4.1	5.2			Operating Profit	2.5	3.6
		.5	1.5			All Other Expenses (net)	1.6	.8
		3.6	3.7			Profit Before Taxes	.9	2.8
						RATIOS		
		3.0	1.8				2.2	2.1
		1.4	1.2			Current	1.4	1.4
		1.0	.9				1.1	1.1
		2.4	1.1				1.2	1.4
		1.0	.8			Quick	.8	.9
		.7	.6				.6	.7
	42	8.8	43	8.5			38	9.6	38	9.6
	50	7.3	48	7.6		Sales/Receivables	47	7.8	46	8.0
	58	6.3	50	7.3			59	6.2	55	6.6
	14	27.0	21	17.2			24	15.5	20	18.0
	19	19.7	34	10.8		Cost of Sales/Inventory	39	9.4	32	11.4
	34	10.8	45	8.1			58	6.3	69	5.3
	13	28.3	20	18.1			17	22.0	16	22.1
	20	18.2	26	13.8		Cost of Sales/Payables	21	17.8	22	16.4
	33	11.0	30	12.2			31	12.0	33	11.2
		6.6	10.7				7.0	6.3
		14.7	27.4			Sales/Working Capital	14.2	12.3
		NM	-34.4				56.0	61.3
		3.3	7.2				5.2	5.0
	(13)	2.3	3.1			EBIT/Interest	2.0	2.5
		1.2	1.1				.4	1.3
						Net Profit + Depr., Dep.,	3.0	2.8
						Amort./Cur. Mat. L/T/D	(11) 1.8 (14) 2.2	
							1.3	1.4
		.8	1.0				.9	.7
		1.1	2.4			Fixed/Worth	1.3	1.0
		1.9	11.1				2.5	2.0
		.8	1.1				1.2	1.0
		1.6	3.5			Debt/Worth	2.2	1.9
		5.5	21.7				4.7	4.1
		29.2	38.5			% Profit Before Taxes/Tangible	29.0	25.3
	(15)	19.0	(11) 17.4			Net Worth	(28) 10.1 (28) 8.4	
		2.7	7.0				-3.8	3.1
		10.9	12.3			% Profit Before Taxes/Total	11.1	10.1
		5.1	4.3			Assets	2.7	3.5
		.6	.6				-1.1	.9
		10.1	6.0				6.9	8.7
		6.8	3.7			Sales/Net Fixed Assets	4.7	5.2
		3.2	3.4				3.4	3.6
		2.9	2.3				2.4	2.7
		2.2	2.1			Sales/Total Assets	2.0	1.9
		1.8	1.9				1.7	1.4
		1.6	2.5				2.4	2.6
		2.9	3.3			% Depr., Dep., Amort./Sales	(28) 3.3	3.4
		3.6	4.4				5.1	4.6
						% Officers', Directors' Owners' Comp/Sales		
	26711M	206400M	582331M	386249M		Net Sales ($)	1010739M	1193326M
	8474M	93132M	279619M	225434M		Total Assets ($)	553508M	734488M

M = $ thousand   MM = $ million
See Pages 11 through 21 for Explanation of Ratios and Data

Comparative Historical Data				Current Data Sorted by Sales					
			Type of Statement						
15	13	9	Unqualified				1	4	4
11	7	9	Reviewed		1		2	3	3
1	2	5	Compiled			1	2	2	
1	2	2	Tax Returns			1	1		
9	12	13	Other		1		2	3	7
4/1/04-3/31/05 ALL	**4/1/05-3/31/06 ALL**	**4/1/06-3/31/07 ALL**			**9 (4/1-9/30/06)**		**29 (10/1/06-3/31/07)**		
				0-1MM	**1-3MM**	**3-5MM**	**5-10MM**	**10-25MM**	**25MM & OVER**
37	36	38	**NUMBER OF STATEMENTS**		2	2	8	12	14
%	%	%	**ASSETS**	%	%	%	%	%	%
5.2	4.3	6.0	Cash & Equivalents	**DATA NOT AVAILABLE**				6.7	2.6
29.5	34.2	30.2	Trade Receivables (net)					32.1	26.0
18.3	16.0	15.1	Inventory					13.9	15.4
.9	1.7	2.4	All Other Current					1.2	1.1
53.9	56.2	53.7	Total Current					54.0	45.1
41.3	38.5	39.9	Fixed Assets (net)					39.8	46.7
.6	1.7	1.6	Intangibles (net)					1.6	.9
4.1	3.6	4.8	All Other Non-Current					4.6	7.4
100.0	100.0	100.0	Total					100.0	100.0
			LIABILITIES						
11.5	15.8	11.2	Notes Payable-Short Term					16.7	8.3
5.7	5.3	5.2	Cur. Mat.-L.T.D.					4.3	5.9
12.6	16.2	13.4	Trade Payables					12.6	11.4
.1	.2	.2	Income Taxes Payable					.5	.2
7.4	9.1	7.9	All Other Current					6.3	8.6
37.3	46.7	37.9	Total Current					40.5	34.4
27.4	28.9	25.1	Long-Term Debt					20.0	26.3
.7	.5	.8	Deferred Taxes					.8	.6
6.1	4.9	4.4	All Other Non-Current					8.3	3.7
28.6	19.1	31.9	Net Worth					30.4	34.9
100.0	100.0	100.0	Total Liabilties & Net Worth					100.0	100.0
			INCOME DATA						
100.0	100.0	100.0	Net Sales					100.0	100.0
23.4	22.5	26.2	Gross Profit					25.6	22.7
20.9	18.9	21.2	Operating Expenses					21.6	17.2
2.6	3.5	5.0	Operating Profit					4.0	5.5
.7	1.0	.6	All Other Expenses (net)					.8	.7
1.9	2.5	4.3	Profit Before Taxes					3.2	4.8
			RATIOS						
2.0	1.5	2.8						3.2	2.1
1.3	1.2	1.3	Current					1.3	1.3
1.1	.9	1.0						.9	1.0
1.4	1.1	1.8						2.7	1.3
.8	.8	1.0	Quick					.8	.8
.6	.6	.6						.6	.7
39 9.4	**44** 8.3	**42** 8.8						**39** 9.3	**44** 8.4
47 7.8	**49** 7.5	**48** 7.5	Sales/Receivables					**50** 7.3	**48** 7.6
54 6.7	**56** 6.6	**52** 7.0						**58** 6.3	**52** 7.0
24 15.4	**16** 23.0	**17** 21.3						**14** 26.6	**22** 16.3
37 10.0	**27** 13.3	**29** 12.4	Cost of Sales/Inventory					**28** 13.0	**35** 10.5
48 7.6	**36** 10.1	**43** 8.5						**36** 10.2	**52** 7.0
18 20.0	**21** 17.8	**14** 26.6						**18** 20.6	**17** 21.9
23 16.1	**25** 14.8	**26** 14.2	Cost of Sales/Payables					**25** 14.8	**26** 13.9
33 10.9	**34** 10.7	**37** 10.0						**29** 12.8	**32** 11.3
7.5	12.6	6.4						6.6	7.6
16.7	30.1	19.5	Sales/Working Capital					19.5	24.8
51.4	NM	NM						-56.0	NM
6.0	4.9	7.4						4.2	8.2
2.4	(35) 2.8	(34) 2.8	EBIT/Interest					(10) 1.6	4.2
.8	1.0	1.1						1.0	1.0
3.6	3.0	4.0							
(17) 1.8	(12) 2.0	(10) 2.2	Net Profit + Depr., Dep., Amort./Cur. Mat. L/T/D						
.9	.8	1.2							
.9	1.0	.8						.8	.8
1.4	1.6	1.2	Fixed/Worth					1.3	1.4
2.5	5.6	3.8						8.2	3.8
1.2	1.4	.9						.8	1.1
2.2	3.3	1.9	Debt/Worth					4.9	1.4
5.0	8.9	7.1						11.4	5.7
27.4	26.0	32.2						30.4	38.2
(33) 14.2	(30) 13.6	(32) 16.2	% Profit Before Taxes/Tangible Net Worth					(10) 21.6	(13) 17.4
2.1	-.9	5.2						5.9	4.4
9.2	8.9	13.1						10.9	14.8
2.2	5.1	6.3	% Profit Before Taxes/Total Assets					5.0	6.1
-.7	.0	.7						.5	.0
7.7	13.3	9.1						9.7	6.1
5.1	6.4	5.1	Sales/Net Fixed Assets					6.2	4.2
3.4	3.8	3.5						3.8	3.5
2.8	3.0	2.7						3.0	2.3
2.0	2.4	2.1	Sales/Total Assets					2.3	2.1
1.6	1.8	1.8						2.0	1.9
2.5	1.5	2.2						2.2	2.5
(36) 3.2	(35) 2.6	(37) 2.9	% Depr., Dep., Amort./Sales					2.8	3.2
4.3	3.6	3.6						3.6	5.2
2.2	2.2	2.7							
(11) 3.1	(12) 2.9	(10) 6.4	% Officers', Directors' Owners' Comp/Sales						
5.4	5.1	7.3							
1163098M	1224564M	1201691M	Net Sales ($)		4330M	7364M	64991M	195962M	929044M
620831M	506769M	606659M	Total Assets ($)		3111M	2635M	31453M	87043M	482417M

M = $ thousand MM = $ million

See Pages 11 through 21 for Explanation of Ratios and Data

Current Data Sorted by Assets   Comparative Historical Data

0-500M	500M-2MM	2-10MM	10-50MM	50-100MM	100-250MM			Type of Statement	4/1/02-3/31/03 ALL	4/1/03-3/31/04 ALL
		1	6	2	4			Unqualified	12	15
		3						Reviewed	2	8
1	2	1	1					Compiled	3	5
								Tax Returns	2	2
			2	2	2			Other	8	10
		6 (4/1-9/30/06)	22 (10/1/06-3/31/07)							
1	3	5	9	4	6			NUMBER OF STATEMENTS	27	40
%	%	%	%	%	%			ASSETS	%	%
								Cash & Equivalents	7.1	6.8
								Trade Receivables (net)	23.6	22.2
								Inventory	25.9	24.8
								All Other Current	1.3	1.8
								Total Current	57.8	55.6
								Fixed Assets (net)	34.5	35.8
								Intangibles (net)	3.7	4.6
								All Other Non-Current	3.9	4.0
								Total	100.0	100.0
								LIABILITIES		
								Notes Payable-Short Term	5.7	5.8
								Cur. Mat.-L.T.D.	6.1	2.9
								Trade Payables	12.0	14.4
								Income Taxes Payable	.1	.2
								All Other Current	7.2	12.3
								Total Current	31.2	35.6
								Long-Term Debt	21.3	23.2
								Deferred Taxes	.8	.9
								All Other Non-Current	5.5	4.0
								Net Worth	41.3	36.3
								Total Liabilties & Net Worth	100.0	100.0
								INCOME DATA		
								Net Sales	100.0	100.0
								Gross Profit	33.8	29.1
								Operating Expenses	26.2	22.7
								Operating Profit	7.6	6.4
								All Other Expenses (net)	1.7	2.0
								Profit Before Taxes	5.9	4.4
								RATIOS		
									2.9	2.8
								Current	2.1	1.9
									1.4	1.1
									2.1	1.5
								Quick	1.1	.8
									.5	.4
						34	10.8	Sales/Receivables	29	12.4
						42	8.8		40	9.0
						51	7.2		50	7.2
						29	12.4	Cost of Sales/Inventory	35	10.3
						60	6.1		51	7.2
						94	3.9		89	4.1
						20	18.5	Cost of Sales/Payables	17	21.6
						33	11.2		33	11.2
						45	8.2		47	7.7
								Sales/Working Capital	5.3	6.0
									7.4	9.2
									22.2	57.4
								EBIT/Interest	26.9	19.6
						(23)	5.2		(38)	5.7
							.6			1.2
								Net Profit + Depr., Dep., Amort./Cur. Mat. L/T/D		3.0
									(13)	2.1
										1.2
								Fixed/Worth	.3	.5
									1.1	1.4
									1.7	3.4
								Debt/Worth	.7	.8
									1.3	1.8
									2.0	11.7
								% Profit Before Taxes/Tangible Net Worth	60.6	73.4
						(23)	40.3		(35)	27.6
							3.2			8.0
								% Profit Before Taxes/Total Assets	29.2	17.6
									7.4	9.4
									-.7	1.1
								Sales/Net Fixed Assets	17.3	11.4
									6.0	7.0
									3.1	3.2
								Sales/Total Assets	2.8	2.7
									1.9	1.9
									1.4	1.5
								% Depr., Dep., Amort./Sales	1.7	2.0
						(24)	2.9		(35)	3.0
							5.7			3.7
								% Officers', Directors' Owners' Comp/Sales		
281M	7370M	76880M	553304M	385118M	1581369M			Net Sales ($)	1605234M	3608372M
419M	2743M	22763M	237817M	221391M	1148378M			Total Assets ($)	1078313M	2024170M

M = $ thousand   MM = $ million
See Pages 11 through 21 for Explanation of Ratios and Data

Comparative Historical Data   ## Current Data Sorted by Sales

						Type of Statement	0-1MM	1-3MM	3-5MM	5-10MM	10-25MM	25MM & OVER
	9		13		13	Unqualified					1	12
	5		3		3	Reviewed					2	
	2		4		3	Compiled		2	1			
	2		1		2	Tax Returns	1		1	1		1
	8		3		7	Other						7
	4/1/04-3/31/05 ALL		4/1/05-3/31/06 ALL		4/1/06-3/31/07 ALL				6 (4/1-9/30/06)		22 (10/1/06-3/31/07)	
	26		24		28	NUMBER OF STATEMENTS	1	2	2	1	3	20
	%		%		%	ASSETS	%	%	%	%	%	%
	4.4		9.4		8.4	Cash & Equivalents						2.2
	23.6		24.6		23.1	Trade Receivables (net)			DATA NOT AVAILABLE			19.4
	27.4		21.1		20.6	Inventory						21.5
	4.3		2.7		1.6	All Other Current						1.9
	59.7		57.8		53.8	Total Current						45.0
	33.1		33.3		35.4	Fixed Assets (net)						44.8
	3.7		2.9		6.9	Intangibles (net)						6.9
	3.5		6.0		3.9	All Other Non-Current						3.4
	100.0		100.0		100.0	Total						100.0
						LIABILITIES						
	14.1		7.3		8.1	Notes Payable-Short Term						8.0
	4.0		2.4		2.2	Cur. Mat.-L.T.D.						2.8
	17.1		17.4		17.6	Trade Payables						17.2
	.0		.0		.2	Income Taxes Payable						.3
	5.7		10.5		6.9	All Other Current						5.0
	40.9		37.6		34.9	Total Current						33.3
	22.1		21.1		21.9	Long-Term Debt						29.6
	.8		.9		1.5	Deferred Taxes						1.9
	7.1		6.0		1.8	All Other Non-Current						2.3
	29.1		34.4		39.9	Net Worth						32.9
	100.0		100.0		100.0	Total Liabilties & Net Worth						100.0
						INCOME DATA						
	100.0		100.0		100.0	Net Sales						100.0
	30.0		23.5		22.2	Gross Profit						20.6
	21.6		15.6		14.4	Operating Expenses						13.2
	8.4		7.9		7.8	Operating Profit						7.4
	1.3		1.4		1.4	All Other Expenses (net)						1.9
	7.1		6.5		6.4	Profit Before Taxes						5.5
						RATIOS						
	2.6		2.2		2.4							2.3
	1.6		1.5		1.7	Current						1.5
	1.2		1.2		1.1							.9
	1.4		1.7		1.5							1.1
	.6		.7		.8	Quick						.6
	.4		.5		.5							.5
30	12.4	29	12.5	29	12.6						30	12.2
43	8.6	35	10.4	34	10.6	Sales/Receivables					36	10.2
49	7.4	44	8.4	45	8.1						44	8.2
44	8.3	34	10.8	26	13.9						36	10.1
61	5.9	47	7.8	49	7.5	Cost of Sales/Inventory					50	7.3
94	3.9	57	6.4	66	5.5						66	5.5
23	15.9	21	17.8	24	14.9						24	14.9
37	9.9	33	11.0	37	9.9	Cost of Sales/Payables					37	9.9
61	5.9	51	7.2	48	7.6						48	7.6
	5.7		8.3		6.8							7.4
	9.9		12.8		9.7	Sales/Working Capital						10.1
	30.7		34.2		64.3							-105.0
	17.3		13.8		9.7							6.8
(21)	4.4	(22)	3.5	(24)	4.6	EBIT/Interest					(19)	4.6
	2.8		.6		2.4							2.4
						Net Profit + Depr., Dep., Amort./Cur. Mat. L/T/D						
	.4		.2		.4							.9
	1.7		1.4		1.1	Fixed/Worth						1.4
	7.0		3.3		2.5							3.5
	1.0		.7		.9							1.6
	2.7		2.6		2.0	Debt/Worth						2.7
	14.9		4.8		3.6							4.0
	66.1		68.5		53.3							51.3
(21)	19.3	(19)	38.7	(24)	36.4	% Profit Before Taxes/Tangible Net Worth					(16)	40.5
	8.4		8.2		11.6							15.8
	20.2		22.3		17.3							15.8
	9.0		5.2		9.0	% Profit Before Taxes/Total Assets						9.0
	2.4		-2.0		4.0							3.9
	24.2		49.4		40.3							7.4
	5.7		6.5		4.5	Sales/Net Fixed Assets						4.2
	3.3		3.5		3.0							2.7
	2.7		2.9		2.7							2.3
	1.9		2.1		2.0	Sales/Total Assets						2.0
	1.4		1.7		1.5							1.5
	.8		.7		.5							1.8
(18)	2.4	(16)	2.5	(21)	2.1	% Depr., Dep., Amort./Sales					(15)	3.1
	5.0		3.5		3.7							3.8
						% Officers', Directors' Owners' Comp/Sales						
	1835615M		2226819M		2604322M	Net Sales ($)	281M	3473M	8885M		42472M	2549211M
	997163M		1218022M		1633511M	Total Assets ($)	419M	1292M	5369M		12387M	1614044M

M = $ thousand   MM = $ million
See Pages 11 through 21 for Explanation of Ratios and Data

Current Data Sorted by Assets   Comparative Historical Data

0-500M	500M-2MM	2-10MM	10-50MM	50-100MM	100-250MM	Type of Statement	4/1/02-3/31/03 ALL	4/1/03-3/31/04 ALL
		8	14	6	3	Unqualified	19	29
		19	4			Reviewed	17	25
	3	8	1			Compiled	19	18
2	2	1	1			Tax Returns	4	8
1	1	10	20	2	1	Other	26	36
		23 (4/1-9/30/06)		83 (10/1/06-3/31/07)				
3	6	46	39	8	4	**NUMBER OF STATEMENTS**	85	116
%	%	%	%	%	%	**ASSETS**	%	%
		5.1	2.8			Cash & Equivalents	8.9	6.9
		26.5	23.4			Trade Receivables (net)	27.6	25.4
		25.3	27.5			Inventory	22.2	24.0
		1.6	2.0			All Other Current	1.6	2.2
		58.5	55.8			Total Current	60.2	58.6
		31.9	35.3			Fixed Assets (net)	27.7	29.5
		2.0	3.4			Intangibles (net)	5.5	4.6
		7.6	5.6			All Other Non-Current	6.6	7.2
		100.0	100.0			Total	100.0	100.0
						LIABILITIES		
		11.1	14.7			Notes Payable-Short Term	13.9	9.8
		4.3	3.8			Cur. Mat.-L.T.D.	4.0	3.5
		18.0	14.0			Trade Payables	15.0	14.6
		.2	.2			Income Taxes Payable	.3	.3
		7.7	10.3			All Other Current	7.5	8.2
		41.3	43.1			Total Current	40.8	36.5
		15.4	19.6			Long-Term Debt	14.3	15.3
		.9	.1			Deferred Taxes	.4	.8
		5.8	3.4			All Other Non-Current	6.2	5.3
		36.5	33.7			Net Worth	38.3	42.1
		100.0	100.0			Total Liabilities & Net Worth	100.0	100.0
						INCOME DATA		
		100.0	100.0			Net Sales	100.0	100.0
		22.9	22.3			Gross Profit	25.8	25.8
		19.1	17.7			Operating Expenses	21.2	20.7
		3.7	4.6			Operating Profit	4.6	5.0
		1.1	1.5			All Other Expenses (net)	1.2	.7
		2.7	3.1			Profit Before Taxes	3.4	4.3
						RATIOS		
		2.2	1.7			Current	2.5	2.5
		1.3	1.2				1.6	1.7
		1.0	1.0				1.0	1.2
		1.3	.9			Quick	1.7	1.6
		.7	.6				1.0	.8
		.5	.4				.6	.6
		30 12.3	31 12.0			Sales/Receivables	33 11.1	29 12.4
		35 10.5	41 8.9				42 8.6	40 9.1
		46 7.9	51 7.2				51 7.1	50 7.3
		28 12.8	36 10.2			Cost of Sales/Inventory	26 14.1	31 11.9
		45 8.2	60 6.1				45 8.1	51 7.2
		68 5.4	79 4.6				66 5.5	79 4.6
		17 21.9	17 21.2			Cost of Sales/Payables	16 23.0	16 22.3
		27 13.5	28 13.2				27 13.4	29 12.5
		44 8.3	47 7.8				44 8.3	43 8.4
		6.4	7.5			Sales/Working Capital	4.8	5.4
		16.9	20.3				11.4	11.0
		-373.3	-345.6				215.2	30.3
		8.1	3.8			EBIT/Interest	6.7	10.3
		(44) 2.8	(35) 2.4				(78) 2.5	(107) 3.9
		2.1	1.1				.9	1.5
		3.2	2.6			Net Profit + Depr., Dep., Amort./Cur. Mat. L/T/D	5.3	4.5
		(17) 2.1	(12) 1.8				(22) 2.3	(28) 2.2
		1.0	.3				.4	1.4
		.5	.4			Fixed/Worth	.3	.3
		.8	1.0				.7	.8
		2.7	3.3				1.6	1.6
		.7	1.2			Debt/Worth	.8	.7
		1.7	2.5				1.7	1.8
		5.4	5.2				4.9	4.1
		32.7	34.2			% Profit Before Taxes/Tangible Net Worth	29.4	34.1
		(40) 14.8	(35) 20.2				(77) 13.1	(108) 16.3
		2.9	9.1				-1.0	3.0
		12.2	11.2			% Profit Before Taxes/Total Assets	11.3	14.1
		5.2	5.3				4.5	7.1
		1.5	.5				.2	1.1
		14.8	17.9			Sales/Net Fixed Assets	23.8	26.4
		9.9	7.8				8.1	8.0
		5.1	2.7				4.0	4.0
		3.3	2.6			Sales/Total Assets	3.3	2.9
		2.6	2.0				2.0	2.1
		1.9	1.3				1.4	1.5
		1.4	1.0			% Depr., Dep., Amort./Sales	1.3	1.3
		(44) 2.1	2.3				(68) 2.8	(102) 2.6
		3.5	5.0				4.5	4.2
		1.3	.8			% Officers', Directors' Owners' Comp/Sales	1.1	1.3
		(13) 2.2	(10) .9				(33) 3.0	(45) 3.1
		5.7	1.4				4.4	5.3
14316M	24023M	606562M	1995588M	1033702M	825882M	Net Sales ($)	2856781M	4059490M
818M	6556M	238089M	1037867M	484329M	440330M	Total Assets ($)	1529879M	2449116M

M = $ thousand   MM = $ million
See Pages 11 through 21 for Explanation of Ratios and Data

Comparative Historical Data				Current Data Sorted by Sales					
			Type of Statement						
18	21	31	Unqualified			1		8	22
20	21	23	Reviewed				9	9	5
19	12	12	Compiled		3		5	4	
8	7	5	Tax Returns		3			2	
30	41	35	Other		1		4	9	21
4/1/04-3/31/05 ALL	4/1/05-3/31/06 ALL	4/1/06-3/31/07 ALL		23 (4/1-9/30/06)			83 (10/1/06-3/31/07)		
				0-1MM	1-3MM	3-5MM	5-10MM	10-25MM	25MM & OVER
95	102	106	**NUMBER OF STATEMENTS**		7	1	18	32	48
%	%	%	**ASSETS**	%	%	%	%	%	%
8.1	6.8	4.7	Cash & Equivalents	DATA NOT AVAILABLE			5.7	6.7	2.6
27.3	27.4	25.4	Trade Receivables (net)				27.0	25.7	24.9
24.6	23.3	26.0	Inventory				21.3	24.7	27.7
2.1	1.3	1.7	All Other Current				2.1	1.5	1.9
62.1	58.8	57.8	Total Current				56.2	58.6	57.1
28.2	29.3	33.1	Fixed Assets (net)				34.5	33.3	32.7
4.2	4.1	3.2	Intangibles (net)				1.2	1.9	4.4
5.5	7.7	5.9	All Other Non-Current				8.2	6.2	5.7
100.0	100.0	100.0	Total				100.0	100.0	100.0
			LIABILITIES						
12.3	12.3	12.2	Notes Payable-Short Term				9.0	11.1	15.5
3.5	3.9	4.4	Cur. Mat.-L.T.D.				4.3	4.0	4.3
15.7	16.2	15.9	Trade Payables				18.1	16.3	15.2
.2	.2	.2	Income Taxes Payable				.5	.3	.1
8.4	7.6	8.8	All Other Current				7.0	5.7	11.5
40.2	40.2	41.5	Total Current				38.9	37.4	46.5
15.7	16.1	17.6	Long-Term Debt				15.8	17.7	18.6
.4	.4	.5	Deferred Taxes				1.8	.3	.3
5.2	5.2	6.7	All Other Non-Current				6.6	5.3	4.8
38.5	38.1	33.6	Net Worth				36.9	39.3	29.9
100.0	100.0	100.0	Total Liabilties & Net Worth				100.0	100.0	100.0
			INCOME DATA						
100.0	100.0	100.0	Net Sales				100.0	100.0	100.0
29.7	25.0	23.1	Gross Profit				21.7	22.5	21.4
23.1	20.6	19.0	Operating Expenses				18.7	18.4	16.7
6.6	4.4	4.2	Operating Profit				3.0	4.1	4.8
1.6	1.0	1.3	All Other Expenses (net)				.5	.9	1.5
5.0	3.5	2.9	Profit Before Taxes				2.5	3.2	3.3
			RATIOS						
2.7	2.2	2.1	Current				2.4	2.3	1.7
1.5	1.4	1.3					1.4	1.4	1.2
1.1	1.0	1.0					1.0	1.0	.9
1.5	1.3	1.1	Quick				1.5	1.3	.9
.8	.8	.7					.8	.8	.6
.5	.6	.5					.4	.5	.4
32 11.3	**33** 10.9	**30** 12.4	Sales/Receivables				**30** 12.0	**27** 13.3	**30** 12.2
41 8.8	**40** 9.0	**38** 9.6					**34** 10.8	**40** 9.1	**41** 9.0
50 7.3	**53** 6.9	**47** 7.7					**47** 7.7	**46** 7.9	**51** 7.2
29 12.4	**30** 12.3	**29** 12.7	Cost of Sales/Inventory				**27** 13.6	**26** 14.1	**34** 10.6
47 7.8	**45** 8.1	**48** 7.6					**47** 7.8	**44** 8.2	**54** 6.8
73 5.0	**75** 4.9	**77** 4.8					**67** 5.5	**67** 5.5	**86** 4.3
18 20.3	**20** 18.6	**17** 21.3	Cost of Sales/Payables				**16** 22.5	**15** 23.7	**19** 19.1
31 11.8	**33** 11.1	**28** 12.9					**32** 11.4	**27** 13.5	**28** 13.0
45 8.0	**44** 8.3	**43** 8.4					**48** 7.7	**44** 8.3	**40** 9.2
5.0	6.2	7.4	Sales/Working Capital				6.1	7.5	7.6
12.0	15.2	16.6					16.1	16.9	19.9
36.9	999.8	-418.6					186.7	NM	-72.9
10.5	7.6	6.0	EBIT/Interest				6.8	8.1	4.7
(85) 3.8	(93) 3.3	(100) 2.7					2.9	(30) 2.8	(44) 2.7
1.8	1.6	1.4					1.4	2.1	1.4
6.2	4.4	2.8	Net Profit + Depr., Dep., Amort./Cur. Mat. L/T/D						2.8
(22) 2.4	(25) 2.6	(35) 2.1							(18) 1.9
1.5	1.2	.8							.7
.3	.4	.4	Fixed/Worth				.5	.4	.5
.6	.8	.9					.9	.8	1.1
1.7	1.8	3.3					3.2	2.4	6.7
.7	.7	.7	Debt/Worth				.7	.7	1.2
1.8	1.9	1.9					1.5	1.8	2.7
3.5	4.9	5.5					5.4	4.0	9.2
39.8	36.5	33.4	% Profit Before Taxes/Tangible Net Worth				34.5	30.3	38.2
(84) 17.1	(93) 14.7	(91) 16.4					(16) 11.4	(30) 16.3	(39) 20.3
5.1	4.2	6.0					2.4	6.5	9.3
16.0	13.2	12.0	% Profit Before Taxes/Total Assets				9.1	14.5	12.3
5.8	3.8	5.3					5.0	5.6	6.3
1.5	1.4	1.4					1.0	3.8	1.5
29.1	21.5	15.1	Sales/Net Fixed Assets				10.5	15.3	15.1
8.5	8.0	9.4					6.6	11.3	9.4
4.7	4.6	4.2					3.2	4.4	4.2
3.0	3.1	3.3	Sales/Total Assets				3.1	3.6	3.2
2.2	2.2	2.2					2.0	2.6	2.1
1.6	1.6	1.6					1.4	1.9	1.4
1.3	.9	1.3	% Depr., Dep., Amort./Sales				2.0	1.3	1.0
(84) 2.0	(93) 2.0	(102) 2.1					2.6	(29) 2.3	(47) 1.8
3.9	3.4	3.6					4.6	4.6	3.1
1.5	1.2	.9	% Officers', Directors' Owners' Comp/Sales					.8	
(32) 3.2	(31) 3.0	(26) 1.5						(10) 1.3	
4.6	7.3	4.2						4.6	
2373153M	3596421M	4500073M	Net Sales ($)		14236M	4996M	145679M	492614M	3842548M
1335501M	1915372M	2207989M	Total Assets ($)		5885M	4848M	76880M	229354M	1891022M

M = $ thousand MM = $ million

See Pages 11 through 21 for Explanation of Ratios and Data

Current Data Sorted by Assets   Comparative Historical Data

0-500M	500M-2MM	2-10MM	10-50MM	50-100MM	100-250MM	Type of Statement	4/1/02-3/31/03 ALL	4/1/03-3/31/04 ALL
1	1	28	52	7	3	Unqualified	109	100
2	23	119	35			Reviewed	207	195
7	38	56	2			Compiled	144	187
29	37	19				Tax Returns	56	62
22	46	98	64	6	4	Other	180	210
	159 (4/1-9/30/06)		540 (10/1/06-3/31/07)					
61	145	320	153	13	7	NUMBER OF STATEMENTS	696	754
%	%	%	%	%	%	**ASSETS**	%	%
12.8	10.3	6.8	5.4	4.3		Cash & Equivalents	7.4	7.5
33.3	30.0	30.4	28.4	26.8		Trade Receivables (net)	27.8	27.9
7.0	10.1	10.6	10.8	8.7		Inventory	9.8	10.1
1.2	1.8	2.2	1.7	3.9		All Other Current	1.7	2.6
54.3	52.1	50.0	46.3	43.7		Total Current	46.8	48.1
33.8	37.9	42.6	43.7	34.9		Fixed Assets (net)	44.6	42.8
3.8	3.9	2.7	4.7	18.5		Intangibles (net)	3.2	3.6
8.1	6.1	4.8	5.2	2.9		All Other Non-Current	5.5	5.5
100.0	100.0	100.0	100.0	100.0		Total	100.0	100.0
						LIABILITIES		
19.2	9.7	7.8	7.7	9.0		Notes Payable-Short Term	7.7	8.9
6.3	7.5	7.9	6.7	3.7		Cur. Mat.-L.T.D.	8.2	7.1
18.2	17.8	15.2	12.9	13.2		Trade Payables	13.7	14.0
.0	.1	.1	.2	.5		Income Taxes Payable	.2	.2
9.1	6.9	7.7	9.0	13.3		All Other Current	8.4	10.2
52.8	42.0	38.7	36.4	39.6		Total Current	38.3	40.3
41.3	32.6	26.7	23.0	17.8		Long-Term Debt	30.8	27.1
.2	.4	.9	.8	3.7		Deferred Taxes	.7	.8
11.7	4.4	4.1	5.3	12.7		All Other Non-Current	4.3	5.8
-6.0	20.6	29.6	34.5	26.2		Net Worth	25.8	26.0
100.0	100.0	100.0	100.0	100.0		Total Liabilities & Net Worth	100.0	100.0
						INCOME DATA		
100.0	100.0	100.0	100.0	100.0		Net Sales	100.0	100.0
52.0	39.9	33.2	26.3	24.7		Gross Profit	34.6	34.0
48.7	36.6	29.0	20.8	19.0		Operating Expenses	32.0	31.1
3.3	3.3	4.2	5.4	5.7		Operating Profit	2.5	2.9
1.6	1.1	1.3	1.6	3.4		All Other Expenses (net)	1.8	1.4
1.7	2.1	2.9	3.8	2.4		Profit Before Taxes	.8	1.5
						RATIOS		
2.0	1.9	1.9	1.9	1.5			2.0	1.8
1.2	1.3	1.3	1.3	1.0		Current	1.3	1.2
.7	.9	1.0	1.0	.9			.9	.9
1.8	1.6	1.5	1.4	1.0			1.5	1.4
1.0	1.0	1.0	.9	.8		Quick	.9	.9
.5	.6	.7	.7	.6			.6	.6
17 21.8	30 12.1	40 9.2	45 8.1	45 8.1			37 9.9	36 10.2
34 10.8	39 9.3	49 7.5	54 6.8	55 6.6		Sales/Receivables	47 7.7	46 7.9
46 7.9	50 7.3	58 6.3	65 5.6	73 5.0			59 6.2	58 6.3
1 512.0	6 56.3	10 35.5	16 22.8	16 22.3			11 32.4	11 33.4
11 32.3	16 22.7	19 19.7	24 15.1	21 17.3		Cost of Sales/Inventory	21 17.5	21 17.4
25 14.4	30 12.0	34 10.8	37 9.9	34 10.8			34 10.7	36 10.2
9 41.5	18 20.5	19 18.9	22 16.6	23 15.5			18 20.1	19 19.0
28 13.0	29 12.6	32 11.5	30 12.3	32 11.4		Cost of Sales/Payables	31 11.9	30 12.2
48 7.7	53 6.9	51 7.1	45 8.2	52 7.1			47 7.7	47 7.8
13.7	9.7	9.0	8.2	13.3			8.5	9.9
58.9	28.9	20.5	20.3	-907.7		Sales/Working Capital	24.5	26.3
-19.8	-61.6	-188.9	-131.5	-22.3			-64.6	-45.8
5.5	5.4	5.3	6.4	5.4			3.7	4.3
(53) 1.4	(131) 2.5	(303) 2.4	(148) 3.1	3.3		EBIT/Interest	(665) 1.6	(714) 1.8
-.1	1.0	1.4	1.7	1.0			.3	.2
	2.8	2.8	4.8				2.6	2.5
	(28) 1.4	(108) 1.6	(59) 2.0			Net Profit + Depr., Dep., Amort./Cur. Mat. L/T/D	(233) 1.6	(231) 1.5
	.8	1.0	1.4				.9	.7
.8	.7	.8	.8	1.4			.9	.8
18.5	2.1	1.6	1.5	3.1		Fixed/Worth	1.9	1.8
-.5	-8.4	4.0	2.9	-.8			4.7	5.6
1.6	1.3	1.2	.9	2.1			1.3	1.3
50.0	3.7	2.9	2.3	6.0		Debt/Worth	2.9	2.8
-3.4	-24.3	7.5	4.3	-3.1			8.4	11.1
130.4	62.5	40.5	43.4				25.6	30.8
(32) 33.6	(100) 22.1	(280) 18.2	(138) 18.0			% Profit Before Taxes/Tangible Net Worth	(583) 7.8	(624) 10.9
1.8	5.1	6.1	8.7				-6.9	-5.1
26.5	13.5	11.7	12.0	9.1			7.5	8.6
7.8	5.8	4.3	5.6	8.0		% Profit Before Taxes/Total Assets	2.1	2.7
-4.5	.4	1.4	2.1	.0			-2.7	-2.6
35.5	15.9	8.4	6.2	6.8			7.9	9.0
15.2	7.4	5.0	4.2	4.6		Sales/Net Fixed Assets	4.5	4.9
7.5	4.3	3.2	3.1	3.0			3.0	3.1
5.6	3.6	2.6	2.2	1.9			2.6	2.8
3.8	2.7	2.1	1.9	1.7		Sales/Total Assets	2.0	2.0
3.2	2.0	1.6	1.4	1.2			1.5	1.5
1.0	2.6	2.8	3.1	2.8			3.5	2.9
(47) 1.9	(126) 4.4	(309) 4.3	(147) 4.5	3.9		% Depr., Dep., Amort./Sales	(661) 5.1	(698) 4.7
4.2	6.0	6.1	6.1	4.6			7.0	6.7
3.3	2.8	2.4	1.1				2.8	2.7
(37) 7.2	(76) 4.8	(147) 3.6	(33) 2.2			% Officers', Directors' Owners' Comp/Sales	(334) 4.7	(344) 4.5
11.1	9.2	5.8	5.1				7.6	8.6
78735M	474073M	3286175M	6119914M	1554501M	1157645M	Net Sales ($)	10468077M	11900788M
15604M	166550M	1529449M	3262408M	909722M	1030728M	Total Assets ($)	6234194M	7317599M

© RMA 2007

M = $ thousand   MM = $ million
See Pages 11 through 21 for Explanation of Ratios and Data

Comparative Historical Data / Current Data Sorted by Sales

			Type of Statement						
106	92	92	Unqualified	1		2	11	28	50
192	175	179	Reviewed	1	12	15	66	64	21
126	96	103	Compiled	4	28	14	28	28	1
78	96	85	Tax Returns	17	31	16	20	1	
202	252	240	Other	13	32	24	56	60	55
4/1/04-3/31/05 ALL	4/1/05-3/31/06 ALL	4/1/06-3/31/07 ALL			159 (4/1-9/30/06)		540 (10/1/06-3/31/07)		
				0-1MM	1-3MM	3-5MM	5-10MM	10-25MM	25MM & OVER
704	711	699	NUMBER OF STATEMENTS	36	103	71	181	181	127
%	%	%	ASSETS	%	%	%	%	%	%
8.1	7.4	7.7	Cash & Equivalents	11.9	11.6	8.8	6.8	6.9	5.1
30.0	30.2	29.9	Trade Receivables (net)	29.2	27.3	30.4	29.9	31.6	29.8
10.2	9.6	10.2	Inventory	6.1	8.9	8.8	9.9	11.6	11.5
1.6	1.8	1.9	All Other Current	.4	1.7	2.0	2.3	2.0	1.9
49.9	49.1	49.8	Total Current	47.7	49.5	50.1	48.9	52.1	48.3
41.1	41.3	40.9	Fixed Assets (net)	40.7	39.4	41.4	43.1	39.3	41.1
3.4	3.8	3.9	Intangibles (net)	5.1	3.8	4.4	2.7	3.4	5.7
5.6	5.9	5.4	All Other Non-Current	6.5	7.3	4.1	5.3	5.2	4.9
100.0	100.0	100.0	Total	100.0	100.0	100.0	100.0	100.0	100.0
			LIABILITIES						
8.6	9.3	9.2	Notes Payable-Short Term	22.1	9.8	7.0	8.2	9.0	8.0
7.5	7.3	7.3	Cur. Mat.-L.T.D.	6.9	9.4	6.0	7.8	6.7	6.4
14.5	15.3	15.4	Trade Payables	16.3	15.8	15.1	15.3	16.2	14.0
.3	.1	.1	Income Taxes Payable	.0	.0	.1	.1	.2	.2
7.9	7.9	8.1	All Other Current	8.4	7.1	7.1	7.1	8.0	10.6
38.8	40.0	40.0	Total Current	53.7	42.2	35.3	38.6	40.0	39.2
27.5	29.8	28.2	Long-Term Debt	46.5	39.7	33.2	25.1	23.7	22.1
.9	.8	.8	Deferred Taxes	.1	.4	.5	1.0	.8	.9
4.9	5.7	5.2	All Other Non-Current	15.4	5.1	4.3	3.7	4.7	5.8
27.9	23.7	25.7	Net Worth	-15.7	12.6	26.8	31.6	30.9	31.9
100.0	100.0	100.0	Total Liabilities & Net Worth	100.0	100.0	100.0	100.0	100.0	100.0
			INCOME DATA						
100.0	100.0	100.0	Net Sales	100.0	100.0	100.0	100.0	100.0	100.0
35.1	34.4	34.5	Gross Profit	56.4	43.0	38.2	35.1	29.8	25.1
31.3	30.6	30.3	Operating Expenses	53.5	39.7	34.2	31.2	25.3	19.5
3.8	3.7	4.2	Operating Profit	2.9	3.2	4.0	3.9	4.4	5.6
1.1	1.3	1.4	All Other Expenses (net)	2.2	1.6	1.2	1.1	1.2	1.7
2.7	2.4	2.8	Profit Before Taxes	.7	1.6	2.8	2.8	3.2	4.0
			RATIOS						
1.9	2.0	1.9	Current	2.1	1.9	2.2	1.8	1.9	1.7
1.3	1.2	1.3		1.3	1.2	1.3	1.3	1.3	1.3
1.0	.9	.9		.6	.8	1.0	1.0	1.0	.9
1.5	1.5	1.5	Quick	2.0	1.6	1.7	1.4	1.5	1.2
1.0	.9	1.0		1.0	.9	1.1	1.0	.9	.9
.7	.7	.7		.5	.6	.7	.7	.7	.7
38 9.5	36 10.1	37 9.7	Sales/Receivables	17 21.5	26 13.8	31 11.6	38 9.5	42 8.7	45 8.2
49 7.5	48 7.6	48 7.7		35 10.3	38 9.6	43 8.4	47 7.7	51 7.1	53 6.9
60 6.1	59 6.2	58 6.3		52 7.0	49 7.5	53 6.8	58 6.3	62 5.9	64 5.7
12 30.8	10 37.0	10 35.5	Cost of Sales/Inventory	0 UND	7 50.9	5 70.1	9 39.9	14 26.7	17 21.7
22 16.8	19 18.9	19 19.0		11 32.4	14 25.4	13 28.2	17 20.9	22 16.4	24 15.1
36 10.2	32 11.4	34 10.8		27 13.3	29 12.4	22 16.3	33 11.2	36 10.0	38 9.7
20 18.5	19 18.8	19 18.9	Cost of Sales/Payables	0 UND	17 21.7	17 21.4	19 19.2	20 18.1	22 16.3
31 11.7	31 11.6	31 11.9		37 10.0	29 12.6	27 13.4	32 11.5	31 11.9	30 12.3
50 7.3	49 7.4	49 7.4		63 5.8	52 7.0	49 7.5	51 7.1	51 7.2	43 8.6
8.7	9.1	9.5	Sales/Working Capital	13.4	9.7	8.7	9.2	8.4	10.8
21.2	23.6	24.1		57.4	47.3	26.5	22.5	18.4	26.4
-120.2	-58.7	-97.4		-15.5	-35.3	-237.9	-191.6	-445.6	-77.1
6.5	5.7	5.7	EBIT/Interest	4.7	5.9	5.9	7.1	5.0	6.8
(666) 2.4	(673) 2.5	(655) 2.6		(30) 1.0	(96) 2.1	(63) 3.4	(171) 2.5	(171) 2.4	(124) 3.4
.9	1.0	1.3		-1.1	.7	1.0	1.3	1.5	1.7
2.5	2.7	3.1	Net Profit + Depr., Dep., Amort./Cur. Mat. L/T/D		1.9	2.8	3.0	3.2	4.6
(227) 1.5	(223) 1.6	(209) 1.7			(22) 1.1	(13) 1.8	(52) 1.4	(73) 1.9	(49) 2.3
1.0	.8	1.0			.6	.7	.9	1.2	1.5
.8	.8	.8	Fixed/Worth	1.3	.9	.7	.8	.8	.8
1.7	1.8	1.7		-7.9	3.5	1.5	1.6	1.6	1.5
4.1	6.5	5.8		-.4	-3.1	102.2	3.9	3.0	3.2
1.2	1.3	1.2	Debt/Worth	1.8	1.7	1.3	1.1	1.2	1.1
2.7	2.9	3.0		-12.1	6.4	3.0	2.4	2.8	2.5
7.5	13.8	11.0		-2.4	-9.3	156.2	7.1	5.6	5.1
37.3	37.2	45.5	% Profit Before Taxes/Tangible Net Worth	75.4	64.0	52.1	40.5	43.8	43.9
(589) 15.9	(578) 15.7	(565) 19.2		(15) 25.0	(66) 15.7	(54) 27.6	(159) 18.4	(160) 16.7	(111) 26.3
2.2	2.5	6.6		.0	.4	5.8	5.8	7.2	9.7
11.4	10.8	12.3	% Profit Before Taxes/Total Assets	21.5	10.1	13.2	12.2	12.2	12.1
4.2	4.2	5.2		3.7	4.5	6.9	4.8	4.5	6.9
-.1	.0	1.2		-9.9	-2.0	.7	1.2	2.2	2.0
9.8	9.7	10.2	Sales/Net Fixed Assets	24.4	15.1	15.6	8.6	9.9	7.8
5.0	5.0	5.5		7.7	6.6	7.1	5.0	5.3	4.8
3.2	3.2	3.4		5.3	3.7	3.6	3.3	3.4	3.3
2.8	2.8	2.9	Sales/Total Assets	4.4	3.5	3.4	2.8	2.7	2.4
2.1	2.1	2.2		3.3	2.4	2.6	2.1	2.1	2.0
1.6	1.6	1.7		2.1	1.9	1.8	1.6	1.6	1.5
3.0	2.8	2.6	% Depr., Dep., Amort./Sales	1.0	2.6	2.7	2.8	2.5	3.1
(649) 4.5	(653) 4.4	(647) 4.2		(28) 2.7	(88) 4.9	(63) 4.1	(172) 4.5	(175) 3.8	(121) 4.2
6.3	6.1	5.9		5.8	7.1	5.7	6.2	5.3	5.7
2.6	2.6	2.3	% Officers', Directors', Owners' Comp/Sales	6.3	3.6	2.7	2.4	1.9	1.1
(340) 4.3	(318) 4.6	(294) 4.0		(19) 10.1	(52) 7.0	(39) 4.3	(97) 3.6	(60) 3.2	(27) 2.1
7.4	7.5	7.2		11.9	10.5	6.2	6.4	6.4	4.9
11003992M	13326449M	12671043M	Net Sales ($)	22363M	209914M	279850M	1306491M	2888931M	7963494M
6285317M	7189044M	6914461M	Total Assets ($)	7512M	94728M	122258M	647148M	1508661M	4534154M

M = $ thousand   MM = $ million
See Pages 11 through 21 for Explanation of Ratios and Data

Current Data Sorted by Assets | Comparative Historical Data

Type of Statement

	0-500M	500M-2MM	2-10MM	10-50MM	50-100MM	100-250MM		4/1/02-3/31/03 ALL	4/1/03-3/31/04 ALL
Unqualified			4	6		1		4	6
Reviewed	1	1	12	5				4	7
Compiled		9	6					3	7
Tax Returns	3	5	2					4	5
Other	4	4	14	9	3			4	6
NUMBER OF STATEMENTS	8	19	38	20	4	1		19	31

ASSETS

	500M-2MM %	2-10MM %	10-50MM %		ALL %	ALL %
Cash & Equivalents	5.9	7.6	7.8		6.1	9.5
Trade Receivables (net)	30.2	27.4	21.3		32.6	35.1
Inventory	13.3	12.9	16.4		10.8	9.9
All Other Current	1.6	1.7	1.9		1.4	.4
Total Current	51.0	49.7	47.5		50.9	55.0
Fixed Assets (net)	36.8	39.3	44.4		34.7	35.8
Intangibles (net)	6.7	6.6	4.2		8.8	2.2
All Other Non-Current	5.5	4.3	3.9		5.7	7.0
Total	100.0	100.0	100.0		100.0	100.0

LIABILITIES

	500M-2MM	2-10MM	10-50MM		ALL	ALL
Notes Payable-Short Term	8.5	12.3	8.2		7.8	7.1
Cur. Mat.-L.T.D.	7.0	7.1	3.4		8.0	10.7
Trade Payables	21.3	15.1	10.3		11.9	18.7
Income Taxes Payable	.1	.1	.0		.0	.0
All Other Current	5.1	9.2	8.0		7.8	7.0
Total Current	41.9	43.8	30.0		35.6	43.6
Long-Term Debt	34.0	23.9	16.6		22.8	20.6
Deferred Taxes	.1	.5	1.2		.5	.2
All Other Non-Current	5.9	3.7	.8		1.7	7.4
Net Worth	18.1	28.1	51.4		39.5	28.2
Total Liabilities & Net Worth	100.0	100.0	100.0		100.0	100.0

INCOME DATA

	500M-2MM	2-10MM	10-50MM		ALL	ALL
Net Sales	100.0	100.0	100.0		100.0	100.0
Gross Profit	42.7	34.9	27.8		40.3	38.6
Operating Expenses	39.6	30.7	20.9		37.2	35.7
Operating Profit	3.1	4.2	6.9		3.1	2.9
All Other Expenses (net)	.7	1.1	.8		1.3	1.4
Profit Before Taxes	2.4	3.0	6.1		1.9	1.4

RATIOS

	500M-2MM	2-10MM	10-50MM		ALL	ALL
Current	2.0	1.9	2.4		2.9	2.1
	1.1	1.3	1.4		1.4	1.5
	.8	.9	1.2		1.0	.9
Quick	1.5	1.3	1.2		2.4	2.0
	.9	1.1	1.0		1.1	1.2
	.5	.6	.6		.6	.7
Sales/Receivables	25 14.4	34 10.7	32 11.3		36 10.0	40 9.2
	35 10.5	42 8.6	41 8.9		41 8.9	48 7.6
	48 7.6	60 6.1	52 7.1		63 5.7	66 5.5
Cost of Sales/Inventory	8 47.3	13 27.9	27 13.6		15 24.0	7 49.3
	24 15.1	30 12.2	38 9.6		21 17.4	20 18.2
	42 8.8	43 8.4	59 6.2		36 10.3	38 9.7
Cost of Sales/Payables	26 14.2	16 22.6	19 19.4		9 39.8	17 21.1
	32 11.6	30 12.0	23 15.6		23 16.0	31 11.7
	51 7.2	53 6.8	35 10.4		44 8.3	48 7.6
Sales/Working Capital	9.9	9.4	7.0		7.0	8.7
	102.4	20.8	18.5		26.0	15.5
	-35.2	-123.6	32.0		999.8	-76.3
EBIT/Interest	7.0	5.9	8.3		5.4	4.1
	(17) 3.1	2.8	(19) 4.1		(17) 1.7	(29) 2.3
	1.3	.6	2.6		-.5	-.2
Net Profit + Depr., Dep., Amort./Cur. Mat. L/T/D		6.8				3.5
		(14) 1.7				(10) 2.3
		1.3				1.3
Fixed/Worth	.4	.8	.6		.5	.5
	2.1	1.7	1.0		1.1	1.4
	-2.0	6.8	1.5		-4.4	2.4
Debt/Worth	1.6	1.2	.6		.3	.8
	2.9	2.7	1.2		2.2	2.2
	-4.8	12.6	1.9		-14.9	4.1
% Profit Before Taxes/Tangible Net Worth	73.0	34.3	36.8		53.8	29.8
	(13) 24.1	(32) 15.5	24.3		(14) 11.5	(26) 15.1
	7.6	4.1	5.6		-.5	1.0
% Profit Before Taxes/Total Assets	15.9	10.2	14.4		12.0	9.5
	5.1	4.7	10.2		5.4	5.3
	.8	-1.3	2.7		-3.8	-1.1
Sales/Net Fixed Assets	17.3	10.9	6.6		12.2	14.4
	10.1	5.3	4.6		7.8	8.1
	5.4	3.3	3.3		5.5	3.5
Sales/Total Assets	3.8	2.8	2.4		3.2	3.3
	3.0	2.0	1.8		2.3	2.4
	2.0	1.6	1.5		1.6	1.6
% Depr., Dep., Amort./Sales	1.2	2.4	3.3		2.4	2.0
	(17) 2.6	(36) 4.5	(19) 4.0		4.4	(29) 3.9
	4.0	5.8	5.6		7.0	5.7
% Officers', Directors' Owners' Comp/Sales	2.8	1.0				2.1
	(12) 4.4	(17) 2.8				(15) 4.8
	8.1	6.1				9.8

	0-500M	500M-2MM	2-10MM	10-50MM	50-100MM	100-250MM		ALL	ALL
Net Sales ($)	9435M	65994M	395419M	810422M	566471M	233047M		215193M	926767M
Total Assets ($)	2181M	22927M	183500M	430234M	265640M	247065M		119330M	418004M

Comparative Historical Data   Current Data Sorted by Sales

				Type of Statement		19 (4/1-9/30/06)		71 (10/1/06-3/31/07)		
12	7	11		Unqualified		1		1	4	6
14	15	19		Reviewed		3			6	4
8	7	15		Compiled	1		5	4	2	
11	8	10		Tax Returns	1	4	3	2	1	
14	10	35		Other	1	7	2	1		12
4/1/04-3/31/05 ALL	4/1/05-3/31/06 ALL	4/1/06-3/31/07 ALL			0-1MM	1-3MM	3-5MM	5-10MM	10-25MM	25MM & OVER
59	47	90		**NUMBER OF STATEMENTS**	3	14	14	15	22	22
%	%	%		**ASSETS**	%	%	%	%	%	%
7.6	7.4	8.8		Cash & Equivalents		15.7	9.8	7.4	6.5	6.5
29.2	29.2	27.3		Trade Receivables (net)		28.2	23.9	32.4	29.6	24.0
11.2	12.8	13.0		Inventory		9.9	10.6	9.9	16.4	16.5
.9	1.1	1.8		All Other Current		1.7	.6	.8	2.4	2.6
48.9	50.5	50.8		Total Current		55.7	44.8	50.4	54.9	49.5
38.7	35.2	37.9		Fixed Assets (net)		29.7	41.7	38.5	37.9	39.6
4.0	7.3	6.6		Intangibles (net)		9.8	9.2	6.8	1.6	8.1
8.3	7.0	4.7		All Other Non-Current		4.9	4.4	4.3	5.6	2.8
100.0	100.0	100.0		Total		100.0	100.0	100.0	100.0	100.0
				LIABILITIES						
11.0	8.6	10.2		Notes Payable-Short Term		9.1	4.2	6.5	17.1	8.6
6.0	7.9	5.7		Cur. Mat.-L.T.D.		4.8	7.8	7.4	6.1	3.9
19.4	15.4	15.2		Trade Payables		14.5	12.3	17.0	19.4	11.7
.1	.1	.1		Income Taxes Payable		.1	.1	.1	.1	.1
6.0	9.1	8.3		All Other Current		9.8	4.2	10.9	7.7	9.1
42.5	41.0	39.5		Total Current		38.3	28.6	41.9	50.4	33.3
29.0	26.7	24.5		Long-Term Debt		27.1	26.7	34.4	18.4	17.6
.5	.8	.7		Deferred Taxes		.1	.4	.1	.9	1.6
6.6	5.5	5.1		All Other Non-Current		15.1	6.3	7.0	.9	1.6
21.4	26.0	30.2		Net Worth		19.4	38.0	16.7	29.4	46.0
100.0	100.0	100.0		Total Liabilities & Net Worth		100.0	100.0	100.0	100.0	100.0
				INCOME DATA						
100.0	100.0	100.0		Net Sales		100.0	100.0	100.0	100.0	100.0
37.7	34.4	35.8		Gross Profit		45.7	41.0	36.0	31.0	27.7
33.6	29.1	30.8		Operating Expenses		41.2	36.5	31.7	26.7	20.8
4.1	5.3	5.0		Operating Profit		4.5	4.6	4.3	4.2	6.9
1.0	1.9	1.3		All Other Expenses (net)		1.2	1.0	1.3	.9	1.4
3.0	3.4	3.7		Profit Before Taxes		3.3	3.6	3.0	3.3	5.5
				RATIOS						
2.0	2.1	2.0		Current		4.2	2.7	1.5	2.0	2.0
1.4	1.4	1.3				1.7	1.4	1.1	1.3	1.4
.9	1.0	1.0				.6	1.1	1.0	.9	1.1
1.5	1.4	1.5		Quick		3.7	1.6	1.3	1.3	1.3
1.1	1.0	1.0				1.5	1.2	1.0	.9	.9
.5	.6	.6				.4	.8	.8	.5	.7
31 11.8	39 9.3	32 11.3		Sales/Receivables		23 15.6	24 15.5	34 10.9	35 10.3	32 11.3
44 8.3	46 7.9	41 8.8				34 10.7	42 8.8	43 8.5	43 8.5	46 7.9
55 6.6	60 6.1	52 7.0				39 9.3	61 6.0	52 7.0	60 6.1	54 6.8
7 51.7	11 34.4	11 34.3		Cost of Sales/Inventory		1 344.5	10 37.5	11 33.9	21 17.1	25 14.8
22 16.6	26 14.2	29 12.6				9 42.4	19 19.0	24 15.1	33 11.0	38 9.6
35 10.5	47 7.7	46 8.0				30 12.3	42 8.6	53 6.9	42 8.8	52 7.0
17 21.0	20 18.2	19 19.3		Cost of Sales/Payables		11 33.0	19 19.3	20 17.9	16 22.6	19 18.7
31 11.8	30 12.3	30 12.3				28 13.0	31 11.7	29 12.5	35 10.3	27 13.6
53 6.8	47 7.7	45 8.1				40 9.1	43 8.6	51 7.2	56 6.5	37 9.8
10.5	9.1	9.2		Sales/Working Capital		8.3	7.5	9.9	9.9	7.1
19.6	12.7	20.1				17.1	21.2	55.2	20.4	18.5
-76.9	-88.3	458.8				-18.3	NM	-142.4	-58.3	41.7
4.8	5.2	7.3		EBIT/Interest		33.0	6.2	6.8	13.6	7.9
(57) 2.4	2.5	(86) 3.3			(12) 2.0	(13) 4.6	1.9	3.7	(21) 4.1	
.9	1.7	1.3				-1.2	1.3	.7	1.6	2.3
3.8	2.5	7.5		Net Profit + Depr., Dep.,					11.2	
(16) 2.3	(15) 1.6	(26) 2.1		Amort./Cur. Mat. L/T/D					(10) 2.1	
1.5	1.4	1.3							1.1	
.7	.7	.8		Fixed/Worth		.2	.5	.8	.8	.7
1.7	1.3	1.3				3.3	1.9	1.8	1.2	1.1
40.1	8.1	5.0				-1.2	8.4	-2.7	3.5	1.5
1.4	1.0	1.0		Debt/Worth		.6	.5	1.6	.6	.7
2.8	2.1	2.3				7.5	1.9	3.2	2.0	1.8
-93.3	12.4	10.9				-3.5	16.1	-5.2	6.2	2.6
51.0	42.4	42.4		% Profit Before Taxes/Tangible		75.4	24.1	51.3	41.1	
(44) 22.0	(38) 15.9	(74) 21.0		Net Worth		(13) 14.3	(11) 6.3	(19) 20.7	26.6	
-3.3	7.1	5.9				.9	-4.7	10.5	11.6	
12.1	9.6	13.3		% Profit Before Taxes/Total		18.1	17.2	8.4	11.3	14.2
5.0	4.0	6.7		Assets		4.6	6.1	2.5	6.9	9.6
-.3	2.2	1.1				-15.6	.6	-1.3	.5	3.0
13.8	14.4	14.6		Sales/Net Fixed Assets		55.4	11.2	16.3	13.2	8.8
6.5	7.5	6.7				14.6	5.3	4.4	7.1	5.0
3.6	3.8	3.4				6.7	2.6	3.3	4.2	3.3
3.0	2.7	3.0		Sales/Total Assets		5.4	2.9	3.3	3.3	2.4
2.1	2.2	2.2				3.1	1.8	2.1	2.5	2.0
1.8	1.7	1.7				2.0	1.4	1.7	1.6	1.7
2.3	2.3	2.3		% Depr., Dep., Amort./Sales		.6	3.0	1.9	2.3	2.9
(52) 4.3	(44) 3.7	(82) 3.5			(10) 1.6	(13) 4.2	4.7	(21) 3.1	(21) 3.4	
5.8	5.4	5.1				4.3	7.0	5.7	5.1	5.0
2.8	1.6	1.4		% Officers', Directors'						
(24) 4.4	(17) 4.5	(37) 3.1		Owners' Comp/Sales						
7.5	9.9	7.9								
1121560M	758866M	2080788M		Net Sales ($)	1981M	27035M	55142M	92690M	350988M	1552952M
590638M	404473M	1151547M		Total Assets ($)	1085M	10249M	33095M	51593M	167412M	888113M

Current Data Sorted by Assets   Comparative Historical Data

	0-500M	500M-2MM	2-10MM	10-50MM	50-100MM	100-250MM	Type of Statement	4/1/02-3/31/03 ALL	4/1/03-3/31/04 ALL
			3	5	1	1	Unqualified	6	4
	2	5	12	4			Reviewed	12	20
	4	4	9				Compiled	7	13
	3	6	1				Tax Returns	3	8
	4	9	10	6	1	1	Other	10	25
		17 (4/1-9/30/06)		74 (10/1/06-3/31/07)					
NUMBER OF STATEMENTS	13	24	35	15	2	2		38	70
	%	%	%	%	%	%	**ASSETS**	%	%
	10.1	5.4	8.5	8.2			Cash & Equivalents	9.9	8.6
	34.1	31.4	28.0	33.3			Trade Receivables (net)	28.1	26.8
	8.9	19.7	20.1	17.3			Inventory	11.3	15.3
	12.2	1.1	.9	3.9			All Other Current	1.2	1.6
	65.2	57.6	57.4	62.8			Total Current	50.6	52.3
	33.2	26.1	32.9	24.9			Fixed Assets (net)	39.8	37.8
	.7	6.1	4.2	9.4			Intangibles (net)	4.6	3.0
	.9	10.2	5.4	2.8			All Other Non-Current	5.1	6.9
	100.0	100.0	100.0	100.0			Total	100.0	100.0
							LIABILITIES		
	17.7	21.4	11.8	15.9			Notes Payable-Short Term	11.3	11.4
	3.6	4.7	4.5	5.2			Cur. Mat.-L.T.D.	6.9	5.3
	22.3	16.3	14.0	11.4			Trade Payables	14.3	15.1
	.0	.1	.1	.3			Income Taxes Payable	.3	.2
	35.0	7.4	8.9	9.0			All Other Current	7.0	7.4
	78.7	50.0	39.3	41.8			Total Current	39.7	39.4
	28.3	16.6	21.1	13.8			Long-Term Debt	24.9	24.6
	.0	.2	.2	.1			Deferred Taxes	.6	.8
	10.3	2.8	1.6	5.1			All Other Non-Current	4.2	4.1
	-17.3	30.5	37.8	39.1			Net Worth	30.7	31.2
	100.0	100.0	100.0	100.0			Total Liabilities & Net Worth	100.0	100.0
							INCOME DATA		
	100.0	100.0	100.0	100.0			Net Sales	100.0	100.0
	47.7	48.1	34.4	30.0			Gross Profit	41.0	38.9
	41.0	42.7	27.0	22.1			Operating Expenses	36.3	35.4
	6.7	5.3	7.4	7.9			Operating Profit	4.7	3.5
	1.3	1.7	.9	2.0			All Other Expenses (net)	2.3	1.0
	5.3	3.7	6.5	5.9			Profit Before Taxes	2.4	2.4
							RATIOS		
	2.4	2.4	2.1	2.4			Current	2.2	2.2
	1.0	1.4	1.4	1.6				1.4	1.4
	.5	.9	1.1	1.1				.9	.9
	1.1	1.6	1.6	1.8			Quick	1.6	1.7
	.6	.9	.8	1.0				1.0	.9
	.5	.6	.5	.7				.6	.6
	0 UND	31 11.9	34 10.8	50 7.3			Sales/Receivables	34 10.7	31 11.9
	27 13.4	41 9.0	48 7.7	61 6.0				45 8.1	41 8.9
	46 8.0	51 7.1	57 6.4	76 4.8				53 6.8	51 7.2
	0 UND	20 18.3	19 19.5	20 18.0			Cost of Sales/Inventory	12 30.4	12 31.2
	2 198.7	39 9.4	51 7.2	39 9.3				30 12.1	27 13.8
	28 13.0	69 5.3	68 5.4	74 5.0				48 7.6	53 6.9
	0 UND	27 13.4	18 20.6	17 22.0			Cost of Sales/Payables	24 15.0	18 20.8
	34 10.7	40 9.2	30 12.2	26 13.8				31 11.6	30 12.3
	49 7.5	69 5.3	48 7.5	31 11.9				53 6.9	47 7.8
	19.0	8.9	5.8	5.9			Sales/Working Capital	7.4	8.0
	813.0	18.8	11.9	9.9				22.2	16.9
	-8.0	NM	61.4	41.6				-25.7	-51.1
	10.4	7.6	19.3	8.7			EBIT/Interest	7.8	6.7
	(12) 3.8	(21) 2.0	(34) 4.8	4.9				(36) 2.4	(67) 1.9
	.7	.3	1.4	1.9				.1	.2
			3.3				Net Profit + Depr., Dep., Amort./Cur. Mat. L/T/D	14.0	5.9
		(11) 1.8						(18) 2.0	(18) 2.6
			1.2					.8	1.4
	.9	.4	.5	.4			Fixed/Worth	.7	.6
	UND	1.0	1.0	.7				1.4	1.1
	-.8	81.2	3.2	2.8				NM	7.4
	3.2	.9	1.0	.7			Debt/Worth	.9	.8
	UND	2.1	1.9	1.3				2.1	1.8
	-3.0	394.8	8.1	6.0				NM	17.2
		33.3	53.3	46.9			% Profit Before Taxes/Tangible Net Worth	32.1	36.7
		(19) 15.5	(31) 24.2	(13) 23.8				(29) 14.3	(56) 9.7
		-2.3	4.7	12.1				.7	-4.1
	36.1	10.9	18.6	19.0			% Profit Before Taxes/Total Assets	12.6	14.3
	5.4	5.1	8.5	8.0				4.2	3.2
	-.4	-4.9	2.8	2.6				-2.5	-3.1
	40.2	28.0	13.7	21.6			Sales/Net Fixed Assets	11.4	13.3
	17.3	12.6	6.4	9.4				4.6	7.0
	8.4	8.0	3.8	5.4				3.1	4.0
	8.1	3.8	2.9	2.5			Sales/Total Assets	3.0	3.1
	5.3	2.7	1.9	2.0				1.9	2.3
	2.9	1.9	1.6	1.6				1.5	1.8
		1.4	1.2	1.2			% Depr., Dep., Amort./Sales	2.3	1.8
		(17) 2.2	(31) 2.1	(14) 2.1				(36) 4.7	(66) 3.3
		4.7	4.1	3.4				6.3	5.4
	4.0	3.1	2.8				% Officers', Directors', Owners' Comp/Sales	3.2	4.9
	(10) 5.5	(11) 6.2	(13) 5.1					(18) 5.7	(32) 6.9
	13.2	12.5	8.9					8.5	12.9
	12912M	82405M	377014M	879176M	196846M	480044M	Net Sales ($)	368072M	1242423M
	2572M	29929M	179213M	266529M	120521M	382210M	Total Assets ($)	213121M	407521M

© RMA 2007

M = $ thousand MM = $ million
See Pages 11 through 21 for Explanation of Ratios and Data

Comparative Historical Data | Current Data Sorted by Sales

Comparative Historical Data			Type of Statement	Current Data Sorted by Sales					
			Unqualified	1	2	3	2	2	6
4	11	10	Reviewed				7	8	2
29	23	23	Compiled	2	3	3	6	2	1
13	16	17	Tax Returns	2	3	1	2	2	1
10	6	10	Other	5	5	7	2	6	5
21	22	31							
4/1/04-3/31/05 ALL	4/1/05-3/31/06 ALL	4/1/06-3/31/07 ALL		0-1MM	17 (4/1-9/30/06) 1-3MM	3-5MM	5-10MM	74 (10/1/06-3/31/07) 10-25MM	25MM & OVER
77	78	91	NUMBER OF STATEMENTS	10	13	14	19	20	15
%	%	%	**ASSETS**	%	%	%	%	%	%
10.1	9.2	7.5	Cash & Equivalents	7.2	9.6	2.7	12.0	5.2	7.8
29.1	29.5	30.2	Trade Receivables (net)	32.6	27.1	34.5	24.6	33.9	29.7
17.9	19.3	17.9	Inventory	5.5	18.4	22.2	20.0	18.3	18.4
2.3	1.9	3.1	All Other Current	15.8	.7	.5	.7	2.3	3.2
59.5	60.0	58.7	Total Current	61.1	55.8	59.9	57.2	59.8	59.1
30.8	31.2	29.9	Fixed Assets (net)	26.9	33.8	25.5	31.7	30.9	29.0
2.9	4.3	5.7	Intangibles (net)	.5	4.6	7.2	5.6	6.1	8.6
6.8	4.6	5.7	All Other Non-Current	11.5	5.7	7.4	5.6	3.2	3.4
100.0	100.0	100.0	Total	100.0	100.0	100.0	100.0	100.0	100.0
			LIABILITIES						
11.7	13.5	15.6	Notes Payable-Short Term	15.4	23.0	25.2	9.0	13.0	12.2
6.9	5.9	4.5	Cur. Mat.-L.T.D.	.9	5.5	4.3	6.1	4.6	4.2
15.8	16.8	15.0	Trade Payables	16.7	21.5	16.0	12.2	15.0	11.0
.1	.1	.2	Income Taxes Payable	.0	.2	.1	.0	.2	.4
10.5	10.2	12.5	All Other Current	42.9	4.7	5.9	9.2	11.5	10.4
44.9	46.5	47.8	Total Current	75.9	55.0	51.5	36.5	44.4	38.1
24.9	25.2	19.7	Long-Term Debt	20.1	27.4	17.6	16.0	21.3	17.1
.6	.5	.2	Deferred Taxes	.0	.2	.1	.1	.3	.6
6.1	7.3	4.0	All Other Non-Current	9.2	7.2	1.7	.5	2.8	6.2
23.5	20.6	28.3	Net Worth	-5.3	10.3	29.1	47.0	31.2	38.0
100.0	100.0	100.0	Total Liabilities & Net Worth	100.0	100.0	100.0	100.0	100.0	100.0
			INCOME DATA						
100.0	100.0	100.0	Net Sales	100.0	100.0	100.0	100.0	100.0	100.0
39.3	39.4	39.3	Gross Profit	53.7	43.4	45.2	37.7	31.7	33.1
34.4	34.6	32.4	Operating Expenses	40.0	40.6	41.5	30.9	25.5	23.0
4.9	4.8	6.9	Operating Profit	13.7	2.8	3.7	6.7	6.2	10.1
1.2	1.6	1.4	All Other Expenses (net)	1.6	2.0	1.6	.8	1.3	1.6
3.7	3.2	5.5	Profit Before Taxes	12.1	.8	2.1	5.9	4.9	8.5
			RATIOS						
2.3	2.5	2.1	Current	4.7	1.8	2.2	2.6	2.2	2.2
1.4	1.4	1.4		1.1	1.3	1.4	1.5	1.3	1.8
.9	1.1	1.0		.5	.7	1.0	1.2	.9	1.0
1.5	1.6	1.5	Quick	4.2	1.3	1.4	1.7	1.3	1.8
.9	.9	.8		.7	.6	.9	.9	.8	.8
.6	.6	.6		.5	.5	.5	.6	.5	.6
30 12.2	31 11.9	31 12.0	Sales/Receivables	0 UND	26 14.1	32 11.3	27 13.4	43 8.6	35 10.4
41 8.8	44 8.3	46 8.0		36 10.3	35 10.3	44 8.3	44 8.3	53 6.9	51 7.2
52 7.0	52 7.1	58 6.3		61 6.0	47 7.8	52 7.0	53 6.8	66 5.5	64 5.7
14 25.9	14 25.5	17 22.1	Cost of Sales/Inventory	0 UND	5 78.5	27 13.6	27 13.5	17 21.0	23 16.2
31 11.9	42 8.8	39 9.3		0 UND	24 15.3	53 6.9	48 7.5	36 10.0	48 7.6
63 5.8	90 4.0	68 5.4		48 7.6	66 5.5	79 4.6	68 5.4	59 6.2	74 5.0
19 19.5	19 18.8	17 22.0	Cost of Sales/Payables	0 UND	31 11.7	31 11.9	15 23.6	23 15.8	13 28.4
27 13.6	32 11.4	32 11.2		31 11.8	44 8.3	36 10.2	23 15.6	30 12.1	26 14.0
49 7.4	49 7.4	47 7.8		85 4.3	76 4.8	44 8.3	47 7.8	44 8.3	38 9.6
6.7	6.1	6.5	Sales/Working Capital	7.0	13.9	7.1	5.3	6.5	6.2
14.4	13.5	16.9		414.5	50.3	12.7	12.0	18.1	11.1
-85.7	46.9	999.8		-7.2	-16.9	NM	25.6	NM	112.8
7.9	10.5	10.0	EBIT/Interest		5.6	8.3	14.8	12.1	20.9
(70) 2.6	(75) 3.2	(86) 3.9			1.1	(12) 2.5	(18) 4.5	4.2	5.0
1.3	1.4	1.1			.1	.9	1.8	1.5	3.6
5.2	5.0	3.5	Net Profit + Depr., Dep., Amort./Cur. Mat. L/T/D						
(21) 2.0	(22) 2.4	(23) 1.8							
1.2	1.4	1.2							
.4	.6	.6	Fixed/Worth	.7	.7	.6	.5	.6	.4
1.0	1.3	1.0		UND	3.4	1.0	.8	1.8	.8
3.6	12.3	5.9		-1.0	-2.5	29.7	1.7	10.5	2.0
1.0	1.0	.9	Debt/Worth	1.4	1.3	.9	.5	1.0	.7
2.3	2.6	2.1		UND	7.1	2.3	1.6	3.6	1.3
8.1	21.9	15.0		-3.6	-5.6	142.0	2.1	33.1	5.4
52.9	45.5	53.2	% Profit Before Taxes/Tangible Net Worth			26.5	52.3	57.3	65.5
(68) 11.4	(62) 21.3	(73) 23.8			(12) 13.1	(18) 21.7	(16) 35.1	(13) 33.7	
1.3	10.4	3.6			-42.1	12.6	-3.9	12.1	
14.1	14.1	18.4	% Profit Before Taxes/Total Assets	37.4	18.0	10.3	18.4	22.5	40.8
4.8	6.6	8.0		5.5	.2	5.9	8.5	10.4	10.3
.7	.8	.2		-.2	-6.0	-1.9	4.2	2.7	5.9
23.6	19.3	18.7	Sales/Net Fixed Assets	70.4	17.7	30.5	12.7	20.8	18.9
9.9	9.7	8.9		18.7	9.5	10.7	8.6	9.5	7.8
5.7	5.1	5.0		4.4	5.1	7.3	4.8	4.3	4.9
3.3	3.1	3.2	Sales/Total Assets	6.0	6.2	3.4	3.3	2.9	2.6
2.5	2.5	2.3		2.9	2.3	2.7	1.9	2.1	2.0
1.9	1.7	1.7		1.8	1.7	2.0	1.4	1.7	1.6
1.4	1.5	1.3	% Depr., Dep., Amort./Sales		1.6	1.2	1.8	1.4	1.0
(69) 2.2	(72) 2.6	(73) 2.2			(12) 2.4	(10) 1.5	(16) 2.8	(18) 2.0	(13) 2.2
4.6	4.7	3.8			6.7	3.2	4.2	3.6	3.3
2.6	3.4	3.3	% Officers', Directors' Owners' Comp/Sales	4.9					
(38) 7.4	(33) 5.0	(36) 5.9		(10) 7.0					
12.3	11.0	10.1		15.2					
2048395M	1190912M	2028397M	Net Sales ($)	5580M	26266M	53505M	137311M	326111M	1479624M
505771M	678772M	980974M	Total Assets ($)	4119M	11982M	21629M	75873M	154869M	712502M

© RMA 2007

M = $ thousand   MM = $ million
See Pages 11 through 21 for Explanation of Ratios and Data

Current Data Sorted by Assets   Comparative Historical Data

						Type of Statement		
						Unqualified	15	16
	7		6			Reviewed	31	40
	8	2	4			Compiled	35	39
3	8	8				Tax Returns	11	15
7	15	2				Other	31	32
7	5	2	2	1			4/1/02-3/31/03	4/1/03-3/31/04
	16 (4/1-9/30/06)	11	74 (10/1/06-3/31/07)				ALL	ALL
0-500M	500M-2MM	2-10MM	10-50MM	50-100MM	100-250MM	NUMBER OF STATEMENTS	123	142
17	35	25	12	1				
%	%	%	%	%	%	ASSETS	%	%
12.5	8.0	4.5	6.7			Cash & Equivalents	6.9	6.9
23.8	27.6	29.3	26.3		D	Trade Receivables (net)	28.0	28.0
6.9	11.3	10.0	13.4		A	Inventory	9.4	8.9
.9	.6	2.0	.8		T	All Other Current	1.8	.9
44.1	47.5	45.8	47.3		A	Total Current	46.0	44.7
21.1	42.1	43.6	44.3			Fixed Assets (net)	43.5	43.6
18.6	4.0	1.2	3.1		N	Intangibles (net)	2.8	4.7
16.3	6.3	9.4	5.3		O	All Other Non-Current	7.6	7.0
100.0	100.0	100.0	100.0		T	Total	100.0	100.0
					A	LIABILITIES		
10.4	6.2	14.2	8.5		V	Notes Payable-Short Term	9.6	9.5
7.3	8.7	9.0	6.9		A	Cur. Mat.-L.T.D.	7.8	7.2
17.1	10.2	15.9	11.9		I	Trade Payables	16.1	14.2
.1	.0	.0	.1		L	Income Taxes Payable	.1	.2
8.6	6.0	8.8	6.8		A	All Other Current	6.8	6.9
43.5	31.1	47.9	34.2		B	Total Current	40.4	38.0
46.8	32.1	24.5	25.8		L	Long-Term Debt	31.7	33.5
.0	.3	.9	.7		E	Deferred Taxes	.9	.8
9.9	4.2	2.9	3.2			All Other Non-Current	5.1	5.7
-.2	32.3	23.9	36.2			Net Worth	22.0	22.0
100.0	100.0	100.0	100.0			Total Liabilities & Net Worth	100.0	100.0
						INCOME DATA		
100.0	100.0	100.0	100.0			Net Sales	100.0	100.0
						Gross Profit		
96.0	91.9	96.2	91.8			Operating Expenses	97.1	96.3
4.0	8.1	3.8	8.2			Operating Profit	2.9	3.7
1.1	1.9	1.4	.5			All Other Expenses (net)	1.7	2.1
2.9	6.1	2.4	7.7			Profit Before Taxes	1.3	1.6
						RATIOS		
1.5	2.5	1.3	1.8				1.8	2.0
.9	1.6	1.1	1.2			Current	1.2	1.1
.7	.9	.8	1.0				.8	.8
1.3	2.0	1.0	1.5				1.4	1.5
.7	1.2	.9	.8			Quick	.9	.9
.4	.6	.7	.6				.6	.6
12 29.7	27 13.6	43 8.5	41 8.9				34 10.7	33 10.9
23 16.1	37 9.8	48 7.6	49 7.5			Sales/Receivables	45 8.1	44 8.4
34 10.8	49 7.4	55 6.6	62 5.9				56 6.5	57 6.4
						Cost of Sales/Inventory		
						Cost of Sales/Payables		
37.5	7.5	20.7	10.1				10.8	9.7
-247.7	15.8	54.8	27.6			Sales/Working Capital	37.8	43.6
-24.3	-132.9	-24.8	NM				-23.8	-27.1
5.3	9.8	5.0	8.4				4.1	3.9
(14) 2.5	(31) 2.6	1.9	2.1			EBIT/Interest	(114) 1.5	(131) 1.5
.4	1.2	.7	1.0				.4	.0
							2.2	2.6
						Net Profit + Depr., Dep., Amort./Cur. Mat. L/T/D	(42) 1.5	(37) 1.3
							.8	.8
.3	.5	1.1	.8				.9	.9
-2.1	1.1	1.7	1.7			Fixed/Worth	1.7	1.9
-.4	2.8	3.0	3.2				208.0	9.8
29.7	.9	1.7	1.2				1.4	1.3
-6.2	1.4	3.0	2.5			Debt/Worth	3.1	3.1
-2.0	6.3	4.3	4.8				-98.4	27.6
	36.4	38.2	44.2				29.1	24.1
	(29) 16.4	(21) 20.1	(11) 33.6			% Profit Before Taxes/Tangible Net Worth	(92) 11.3	(113) 8.1
	.1	3.1	-.5				-3.3	-4.3
42.6	16.4	10.1	19.2				9.0	7.8
11.4	6.9	3.7	4.9			% Profit Before Taxes/Total Assets	1.9	1.9
-.9	.1	-.7	.2				-3.1	-4.3
52.2	13.0	9.6	5.7				8.2	9.7
22.0	5.9	4.3	4.1			Sales/Net Fixed Assets	4.8	5.1
11.7	3.5	3.6	3.5				2.8	2.7
6.8	3.4	2.6	2.4				2.9	2.9
3.8	2.5	2.1	2.1			Sales/Total Assets	2.1	2.1
3.1	1.9	1.7	1.6				1.5	1.5
1.6	2.3	3.2	3.2				2.9	3.0
(10) 3.8	(32) 4.2	4.0	3.9			% Depr., Dep., Amort./Sales	(116) 4.7	(129) 4.7
5.7	6.5	5.2	5.1				6.9	7.1
	2.5		2.7				2.7	2.6
	(22) 4.5	(12) 4.3				% Officers', Directors' Owners' Comp/Sales	(63) 5.2	(71) 5.4
	7.2	5.7					8.0	10.6
25341M	103400M	239237M	486468M	108568M		Net Sales ($)	1736154M	1826634M
4778M	40995M	114705M	268426M	62042M		Total Assets ($)	968276M	951034M

(Columns 50-100MM and 100-250MM marked "DATA NOT AVAILABLE")

M = $ thousand   MM = $ million
See Pages 11 through 21 for Explanation of Ratios and Data

Comparative Historical Data | | Current Data Sorted by Sales

			Type of Statement						
12	7	8	Unqualified		3	3	1	2	5
26	25	19	Reviewed		6	5	5	4	4
30	19	13	Compiled	1	11	5	1	6	
14	14	24	Tax Returns	5		5	3		
27	32	26	Other	2	6	5	5		2
4/1/04-3/31/05 ALL	4/1/05-3/31/06 ALL	4/1/06-3/31/07 ALL		0-1MM	16 (4/1-9/30/06) 1-3MM	3-5MM	74 (10/1/06-3/31/07) 5-10MM	10-25MM	25MM & OVER
109	97	90	NUMBER OF STATEMENTS	8	26	18	15	12	11
%	%	%	**ASSETS**	%	%	%	%	%	%
6.0	6.3	7.6	Cash & Equivalents		12.1	6.3	6.0	3.5	6.7
29.7	28.4	27.3	Trade Receivables (net)		22.0	31.1	33.7	31.1	27.8
9.4	9.8	10.4	Inventory		8.7	10.3	14.0	8.7	14.4
1.0	.9	1.1	All Other Current		.6	.7	3.3	.2	1.0
46.1	45.4	46.4	Total Current		43.4	48.5	57.0	43.4	49.9
43.9	39.9	38.9	Fixed Assets (net)		39.9	31.7	35.9	45.4	45.2
3.4	6.3	5.8	Intangibles (net)		10.9	2.9	1.3	2.4	1.1
6.7	8.4	8.9	All Other Non-Current		5.8	17.0	5.8	8.8	3.8
100.0	100.0	100.0	Total		100.0	100.0	100.0	100.0	100.0
			LIABILITIES						
9.9	11.1	9.4	Notes Payable-Short Term		5.6	9.6	19.7	3.9	8.4
7.6	8.0	8.2	Cur. Mat.-L.T.D.		9.1	11.4	5.8	6.6	6.2
14.5	14.3	13.4	Trade Payables		12.4	11.7	15.6	17.3	13.2
.0	.1	.0	Income Taxes Payable		.0	.0	.0	.0	.2
7.4	7.3	7.3	All Other Current		6.3	9.0	9.5	6.7	6.9
39.4	40.8	38.4	Total Current		33.5	41.6	50.5	34.6	34.9
30.2	30.3	32.1	Long-Term Debt		37.2	25.8	17.8	29.7	24.5
1.0	.5	.5	Deferred Taxes		.3	.2	1.3	.0	.7
4.6	3.7	4.7	All Other Non-Current		5.9	1.9	3.1	1.4	3.5
24.9	24.6	24.4	Net Worth		23.1	30.5	27.3	34.3	36.4
100.0	100.0	100.0	Total Liabilities & Net Worth		100.0	100.0	100.0	100.0	100.0
			INCOME DATA						
100.0	100.0	100.0	Net Sales		100.0	100.0	100.0	100.0	100.0
			Gross Profit						
95.6	93.2	93.9	Operating Expenses		94.1	94.3	97.4	93.5	92.2
4.4	6.8	6.1	Operating Profit		5.9	5.7	2.6	6.5	7.8
1.7	1.8	1.4	All Other Expenses (net)		1.1	1.2	.9	1.6	.0
2.7	5.0	4.7	Profit Before Taxes		4.8	4.5	1.7	4.9	7.7
			RATIOS						
1.7	1.8	2.0			2.3	2.4	1.4	1.8	2.0
1.2	1.1	1.2	Current		1.0	1.7	1.2	1.2	1.3
.8	.8	.8			.7	.8	1.0	.9	1.1
1.5	1.4	1.5			1.6	2.0	1.0	1.1	1.6
(108) .9	.8	.9	Quick		.8	1.3	.8	1.0	.9
.6	.6	.6			.6	.6	.6	.8	.6
33 11.2	33 11.0	27 13.5		21 17.5	26 14.1	42 8.7	43 8.4	41 8.9	
44 8.3	44 8.2	42 8.7	Sales/Receivables	30 12.0	37 9.9	46 7.9	53 6.8	48 7.6	
59 6.2	58 6.2	51 7.1		44 8.2	53 6.9	56 6.6	62 5.8	65 5.6	
			Cost of Sales/Inventory						
			Cost of Sales/Payables						
11.4	12.2	9.4			11.1	7.9	15.8	11.0	7.4
49.2	54.7	37.2	Sales/Working Capital		-946.2	13.2	33.0	46.4	27.2
-24.5	-22.1	-31.6			-20.9	-131.2	-165.0	NM	57.3
4.3	6.0	6.2			7.5	6.7	3.4	7.0	8.3
(103) 2.0	(91) 2.6	(83) 2.4	EBIT/Interest	(21)	2.9	2.2	1.9	5.0	1.9
-.3	1.3	1.0			1.1	1.2	1.0	2.5	.8
2.9	2.3	3.6	Net Profit + Depr., Dep.,						
(25) 1.2	(28) 1.8	(22) 1.6	Amort./Cur. Mat. L/T/D						
.8	1.0	1.0							
.8	.7	.7			.9	.3	.6	1.1	.7
1.8	2.0	1.7	Fixed/Worth		2.7	.8	1.4	1.4	1.6
4.6	8.5	NM			-1.3	4.1	2.5	2.0	3.0
1.5	1.2	1.2			1.1	.7	2.0	1.4	1.1
3.2	3.2	2.5	Debt/Worth		5.7	1.2	2.8	1.8	2.2
10.6	13.8	NM			-4.1	20.8	4.3	3.3	4.0
27.3	41.9	44.0	% Profit Before Taxes/Tangible		61.9	51.6	19.6	43.3	44.2
(92) 10.6	(75) 20.4	(68) 22.5	Net Worth	(16)	24.9	(15) 25.3	(13) 7.2	(11) 35.6	27.0
-10.9	6.2	1.0			-2.7	1.1	.5	23.3	-.5
8.6	11.9	15.7	% Profit Before Taxes/Total		18.4	35.9	4.4	14.3	20.6
3.0	5.6	5.0	Assets		10.1	4.7	2.4	10.1	6.8
-2.9	.6	.0			-.4	1.0	.0	4.2	-.3
10.2	10.9	13.3			22.6	21.9	15.5	6.0	5.8
5.1	5.4	6.1	Sales/Net Fixed Assets		5.2	9.8	9.3	4.1	4.1
3.3	3.2	3.8			3.4	5.5	3.8	3.5	3.7
3.0	2.9	3.4			3.5	4.0	3.5	2.4	2.5
2.2	2.2	2.4	Sales/Total Assets		2.6	2.7	2.7	2.2	2.1
1.6	1.5	1.8			1.5	1.9	1.9	1.8	1.7
3.3	2.7	2.8			1.7	2.7	2.4	2.8	3.5
(102) 4.6	(85) 4.1	(80) 4.0	% Depr., Dep., Amort./Sales	(20)	4.8	(15) 3.4	3.9	4.3	4.0
6.7	6.6	5.6			6.5	5.6	5.0	5.3	5.1
2.8	2.8	2.5	% Officers', Directors'		2.4	3.0			
(60) 5.4	(52) 5.5	(46) 4.5	Owners' Comp/Sales	(13)	4.5	(13) 4.5			
8.2	8.1	8.8			6.7	7.8			
1140479M	971343M	963014M	Net Sales ($)	4313M	48738M	67497M	111172M	171768M	559526M
631782M	559580M	490946M	Total Assets ($)	2485M	22614M	26131M	48925M	88444M	302347M

M = $ thousand   MM = $ million
See Pages 11 through 21 for Explanation of Ratios and Data

Current Data Sorted by Assets   Comparative Historical Data

						Type of Statement		
		1	2	2	1	Unqualified	7	9
	6	6	2			Reviewed	14	11
1	2	2				Compiled	6	13
4	3	1				Tax Returns	2	3
1	5	1	7		1	Other	23	14
	10 (4/1-9/30/06)		38 (10/1/06-3/31/07)				4/1/02-3/31/03 ALL	4/1/03-3/31/04 ALL
0-500M	500M-2MM	2-10MM	10-50MM	50-100MM	100-250MM			
6	16	11	11	2	2	NUMBER OF STATEMENTS	52	50
%	%	%	%	%	%	**ASSETS**	%	%
	8.1	5.5	9.0			Cash & Equivalents	7.5	9.0
	33.2	32.6	37.7			Trade Receivables (net)	34.4	35.9
	20.2	15.0	13.0			Inventory	16.9	14.4
	1.3	1.0	1.7			All Other Current	2.6	2.5
	62.8	54.1	61.4			Total Current	61.4	61.7
	23.0	35.1	22.6			Fixed Assets (net)	28.2	28.7
	7.1	6.2	7.8			Intangibles (net)	6.0	5.4
	7.1	4.6	8.3			All Other Non-Current	4.5	4.2
	100.0	100.0	100.0			Total	100.0	100.0
						LIABILITIES		
	8.0	5.3	13.3			Notes Payable-Short Term	9.4	10.4
	3.4	7.9	1.7			Cur. Mat.-L.T.D.	4.6	4.1
	17.2	19.0	24.0			Trade Payables	18.7	18.1
	.0	.0	.0			Income Taxes Payable	.4	.1
	11.1	6.4	10.8			All Other Current	9.6	9.4
	39.7	38.6	49.8			Total Current	42.7	42.1
	10.9	28.2	3.1			Long-Term Debt	15.1	15.3
	.3	1.2	.5			Deferred Taxes	.8	1.0
	4.5	3.2	6.0			All Other Non-Current	1.9	4.6
	44.7	28.7	40.5			Net Worth	39.4	37.1
	100.0	100.0	100.0			Total Liabilities & Net Worth	100.0	100.0
						INCOME DATA		
	100.0	100.0	100.0			Net Sales	100.0	100.0
	41.2	28.3	28.4			Gross Profit	31.4	29.9
	36.8	25.4	24.0			Operating Expenses	27.6	27.0
	4.3	2.9	4.5			Operating Profit	3.8	2.9
	1.3	.6	.3			All Other Expenses (net)	.8	.4
	3.0	2.3	4.2			Profit Before Taxes	3.0	2.6
						RATIOS		
	2.6	1.9	2.4			Current	2.2	2.2
	1.7	1.5	1.8				1.6	1.5
	1.2	1.0	.8				1.1	1.0
	1.6	1.3	2.2			Quick	1.5	1.5
	1.0	1.2	1.2				1.0	1.1
	.6	.7	.5				.7	.7
30	12.3 / 29 12.4	35 10.3				Sales/Receivables	33 11.1	32 11.3
40	9.0 / 49 7.4	49 7.4					39 9.4	40 9.1
65	5.6 / 56 6.5	81 4.5					48 7.6	54 6.8
12	30.3 / 11 33.2	15 24.2				Cost of Sales/Inventory	19 19.4	12 31.3
32	11.5 / 21 17.3	24 15.5					25 14.3	23 16.0
89	4.1 / 44 8.3	40 9.1					46 8.0	34 10.9
13	27.2 / 16 22.6	21 17.4				Cost of Sales/Payables	20 18.5	18 20.8
33	11.0 / 26 14.2	30 12.1					31 11.8	26 14.1
48	7.5 / 55 6.6	56 6.5					47 7.7	40 9.2
	5.7	11.0	7.2			Sales/Working Capital	8.5	8.7
	8.5	14.6	9.0				14.1	15.9
	57.8	103.2	-10.7				63.9	218.2
	10.9	5.7	35.3			EBIT/Interest	13.6	8.8
(12)	2.8	2.4	(10) 4.3				(45) 2.6	(46) 2.5
	.4	1.7	.5				.4	.5
						Net Profit + Depr., Dep., Amort./Cur. Mat. L/T/D	4.2	5.5
							(17) 1.4	(16) 1.8
							.9	1.0
	.2	.6	.3			Fixed/Worth	.3	.4
	.6	1.3	.6				.8	.7
	1.0	7.8	3.3				2.4	2.1
	.5	1.2	.5			Debt/Worth	.7	.8
	2.0	2.1	.9				1.3	1.6
	4.4	12.8	11.8				5.2	5.4
	36.8					% Profit Before Taxes/Tangible Net Worth	40.1	38.7
(15)	16.1						(46) 17.8	(44) 16.2
	-.5						-2.1	.1
	17.3	7.3	18.5			% Profit Before Taxes/Total Assets	18.9	12.6
	4.6	2.4	6.7				4.2	3.0
	-1.4	1.8	.5				-2.4	-.8
	49.1	14.6	17.2			Sales/Net Fixed Assets	24.5	26.1
	10.3	6.2	12.4				8.7	9.5
	5.9	4.9	6.7				4.9	5.7
	3.4	3.3	2.8			Sales/Total Assets	3.6	4.2
	2.5	2.6	2.6				2.6	3.1
	1.9	2.2	2.2				2.0	2.2
	.8	1.4				% Depr., Dep., Amort./Sales	1.4	1.2
(14)	2.6	2.8					(47) 2.8	(42) 2.5
	4.5	3.5					3.9	3.6
						% Officers', Directors' Owners' Comp/Sales	2.8	2.4
							(16) 5.1	(19) 4.4
							8.0	6.6
10942M	62212M	133937M	513573M	275835M	221988M	Net Sales ($)	1266550M	1116919M
2022M	22584M	51077M	220565M	138647M	287626M	Total Assets ($)	641993M	485294M

M = $ thousand   MM = $ million
See Pages 11 through 21 for Explanation of Ratios and Data

Comparative Historical Data　　　　　　　　　　　　Current Data Sorted by Sales

11 / 15 / 8 / 1 / 17	13 / 11 / 3 / — / 17	6 / 14 / 5 / 8 / 15	Type of Statement					
			Unqualified						
11	13	6	Reviewed		3	2	3	1	5
15	11	14	Compiled		1	1	2	4	2
8	3	5	Tax Returns	1	5	2	1	1	
1		8	Other		3	1		1	8
4/1/04-3/31/05 ALL	4/1/05-3/31/06 ALL	4/1/06-3/31/07 ALL		0-1MM	1-3MM 10 (4/1-9/30/06)	3-5MM	5-10MM 38 (10/1/06-3/31/07)	10-25MM	25MM & OVER
52	44	48	**NUMBER OF STATEMENTS**	1	12	6	6	8	15
%	%	%	**ASSETS**	%	%	%	%	%	%
6.3	7.4	7.5	Cash & Equivalents		7.4				8.1
35.4	35.6	34.3	Trade Receivables (net)		30.5				32.8
16.9	14.6	15.8	Inventory		20.2				11.3
2.4	3.2	1.1	All Other Current		.6				1.6
61.0	60.9	58.8	Total Current		58.7				53.8
30.3	27.2	25.1	Fixed Assets (net)		25.9				21.8
2.6	5.3	9.4	Intangibles (net)		8.5				17.2
6.2	6.7	6.7	All Other Non-Current		6.8				7.3
100.0	100.0	100.0	Total		100.0				100.0
			LIABILITIES						
11.4	10.2	11.9	Notes Payable-Short Term		17.6				10.1
5.3	3.9	4.1	Cur. Mat.-L.T.D.		4.0				2.8
19.1	19.7	18.8	Trade Payables		12.9				19.6
.2	.2	.2	Income Taxes Payable		.6				.0
10.1	10.6	10.3	All Other Current		11.9				10.6
46.0	44.7	45.3	Total Current		47.1				43.1
16.4	17.1	14.0	Long-Term Debt		10.9				9.7
.5	.5	.6	Deferred Taxes		.0				.8
2.6	3.7	4.0	All Other Non-Current		5.8				4.6
34.4	34.0	36.1	Net Worth		36.3				41.9
100.0	100.0	100.0	Total Liabilties & Net Worth		100.0				100.0
			INCOME DATA						
100.0	100.0	100.0	Net Sales		100.0				100.0
29.6	29.9	34.9	Gross Profit		47.5				31.5
28.0	25.7	30.7	Operating Expenses		41.4				26.0
1.6	4.2	4.2	Operating Profit		6.1				5.5
.2	.5	.7	All Other Expenses (net)		.2				1.2
1.4	3.6	3.5	Profit Before Taxes		6.0				4.2
			RATIOS						
2.0	2.1	2.2	Current		3.0				2.4
1.3	1.4	1.6			1.8				1.8
.9	1.0	1.0			.9				.8
1.4	1.5	1.6	Quick		1.7				2.0
.8	1.0	1.0			.8				1.2
.6	.5	.6			.6				.7
34 / 10.6	33 / 11.1	32 / 11.5	Sales/Receivables		22 / 16.8				35 / 10.3
43 / 8.6	45 / 8.1	42 / 8.8			32 / 11.4				49 / 7.4
58 / 6.3	60 / 6.0	56 / 6.6			63 / 5.8				68 / 5.4
14 / 25.3	12 / 30.8	12 / 30.8	Cost of Sales/Inventory		8 / 45.0				15 / 24.2
28 / 12.9	25 / 14.3	23 / 15.7			33 / 11.2				23 / 15.9
48 / 7.6	45 / 8.1	45 / 8.2			89 / 4.1				39 / 9.3
24 / 15.0	19 / 19.4	18 / 20.5	Cost of Sales/Payables		8 / 45.3				21 / 17.4
33 / 11.0	28 / 12.9	31 / 11.7			29 / 12.8				30 / 12.1
50 / 7.3	50 / 7.3	52 / 7.1			45 / 8.2				56 / 6.5
9.2	8.3	7.6	Sales/Working Capital		5.8				7.2
21.6	19.9	12.2			8.4				11.7
-76.1	-208.4	451.4			NM				-14.2
12.6	15.1	8.3	EBIT/Interest						20.4
(50) 2.7	(37) 4.3	(40) 3.2						(14)	4.3
.8	1.0	1.2							1.0
8.0	12.0	10.5	Net Profit + Depr., Dep., Amort./Cur. Mat. L/T/D						
(19) 2.0	(12) 3.8	(11) 4.0							
.9	.4	.5							
.3	.3	.3	Fixed/Worth		.2				.3
.9	1.1	.7			.8				.7
1.7	9.5	6.7			-1.8				-3.2
.9	.7	.6	Debt/Worth		.3				.6
1.9	2.1	2.1			2.0				.9
4.5	22.6	12.5			-5.6				-16.3
33.3	34.0	28.7	% Profit Before Taxes/Tangible Net Worth						29.3
(46) 15.3	(34) 22.3	(37) 13.6						(11)	23.1
.7	16.7	5.0							6.8
13.5	15.7	13.1	% Profit Before Taxes/Total Assets		38.9				13.4
4.0	6.1	6.0			15.8				6.7
-.1	1.2	.5			6.6				.5
25.8	23.4	27.1	Sales/Net Fixed Assets		39.5				18.8
9.1	10.9	11.6			10.2				12.4
5.6	6.8	6.3			4.7				6.7
3.6	3.3	3.4	Sales/Total Assets		5.7				2.7
2.5	2.7	2.6			2.9				2.2
2.0	2.0	2.0			1.8				1.5
1.4	1.6	1.5	% Depr., Dep., Amort./Sales		1.6				1.7
(46) 2.6	(33) 2.1	(40) 2.5		(10)	3.6			(12)	2.6
4.1	3.6	3.4			5.7				3.2
3.1		1.9	% Officers', Directors' Owners' Comp/Sales						
(17) 6.7	(14) 3.4	3.4							
8.3		7.5							
1117250M	1112757M	1218487M	Net Sales ($)	662M	25056M	22822M	42566M	115985M	1011396M
486520M	482610M	722521M	Total Assets ($)	148M	10890M	8206M	19705M	36734M	646838M

© RMA 2007

M = $ thousand　　MM = $ million
See Pages 11 through 21 for Explanation of Ratios and Data

Current Data Sorted by Assets   Comparative Historical Data

0-500M	500M-2MM	2-10MM	10-50MM	50-100MM	100-250MM	Type of Statement	4/1/02-3/31/03 ALL	4/1/03-3/31/04 ALL
		5	6		2	Unqualified	8	7
1	1	2	3			Reviewed	7	9
1	1	1				Compiled	2	2
1		1				Tax Returns		1
1	4	4	4			Other	7	10
	6 (4/1-9/30/06)		30 (10/1/06-3/31/07)					
3	6	12	13		2	NUMBER OF STATEMENTS	24	29
%	%	%	%	%	%	**ASSETS**	%	%
		10.5	5.7			Cash & Equivalents	3.4	8.2
		32.1	30.0			Trade Receivables (net)	27.8	34.0
		8.7	11.2			Inventory	13.5	13.1
		1.3	.5			All Other Current	4.0	2.5
		52.6	47.4			Total Current	48.8	57.7
		40.4	41.9			Fixed Assets (net)	40.0	31.9
		.3	2.7			Intangibles (net)	3.1	2.9
		6.7	8.1			All Other Non-Current	8.2	7.5
		100.0	100.0			Total	100.0	100.0
						LIABILITIES		
		6.3	5.1			Notes Payable-Short Term	9.4	11.7
		5.9	5.1			Cur. Mat.-L.T.D.	3.4	4.8
		16.5	11.0			Trade Payables	11.0	17.8
		.0	.0			Income Taxes Payable	.2	.0
		10.5	8.5			All Other Current	8.2	9.3
		39.3	29.7			Total Current	32.3	43.7
		21.3	13.7			Long-Term Debt	20.9	14.7
		.3	2.2			Deferred Taxes	1.3	.6
		5.8	3.5			All Other Non-Current	4.8	6.8
		33.2	50.9			Net Worth	40.7	34.1
		100.0	100.0			Total Liabilities & Net Worth	100.0	100.0
						INCOME DATA		
		100.0	100.0			Net Sales	100.0	100.0
		29.8	23.7			Gross Profit	28.7	34.0
		25.0	18.1			Operating Expenses	25.3	30.8
		4.8	5.6			Operating Profit	3.4	3.3
		.8	.7			All Other Expenses (net)	1.3	1.0
		4.0	4.8			Profit Before Taxes	2.1	2.2
						RATIOS		
		2.3	2.6			Current	2.6	2.7
		1.2	2.2				1.6	1.4
		1.0	1.3				1.0	.9
		1.7	2.2			Quick	1.9	2.0
		1.1	1.5				1.0	1.1
		.8	1.0				.6	.7
		38 9.5	51 7.1			Sales/Receivables	56 6.5	52 7.0
		52 7.1	66 5.5				60 6.1	61 6.0
		68 5.4	70 5.2				76 4.8	73 5.0
		9 40.4	17 21.1			Cost of Sales/Inventory	21 17.6	12 29.4
		20 18.7	26 14.1				30 12.2	24 15.0
		34 10.9	37 9.9				52 7.0	68 5.4
		18 19.7	20 18.4			Cost of Sales/Payables	18 20.0	21 17.5
		27 13.3	24 15.2				26 13.9	32 11.3
		55 6.6	38 9.6				54 6.8	77 4.7
		5.4	5.5			Sales/Working Capital	4.7	4.8
		25.5	7.4				10.1	12.1
		284.6	20.3				-383.9	-77.7
		4.2	8.2			EBIT/Interest	8.5	6.0
		(11) 2.7	(12) 4.8				(27) 2.4	2.1
		1.4	2.0				.1	1.1
						Net Profit + Depr., Dep., Amort./Cur. Mat. L/T/D	4.3	
							(10) 3.2	
							1.3	
		.8	.6			Fixed/Worth	.6	.4
		1.5	.7				1.1	.9
		4.4	1.1				1.8	2.6
		.8	.4			Debt/Worth	.6	1.1
		2.0	.7				1.3	2.2
		8.2	2.7				3.6	4.9
		58.5	34.5			% Profit Before Taxes/Tangible Net Worth	24.4	31.7
		13.9	(12) 12.1				(21) 6.1	(25) 9.1
		7.4	2.6				.0	.8
		11.1	18.7			% Profit Before Taxes/Total Assets	8.2	6.5
		5.8	7.2				2.4	2.3
		2.2	1.7				-2.3	.4
		28.3	5.6			Sales/Net Fixed Assets	6.7	41.5
		4.3	3.7				3.7	5.4
		2.5	2.7				2.5	3.7
		3.4	2.0			Sales/Total Assets	1.9	2.3
		2.3	1.6				1.6	1.9
		1.4	1.4				1.0	1.4
		1.9	2.8			% Depr., Dep., Amort./Sales	3.0	1.0
		(11) 4.0	(11) 5.0				(21) 4.5	(24) 3.4
		5.4	5.7				5.6	5.5
						% Officers', Directors', Owners' Comp/Sales		
2324M	18746M	168664M	579795M		487198M	Net Sales ($)	887837M	937751M
597M	8287M	70189M	345374M		383149M	Total Assets ($)	580166M	629317M

(Column 50-100MM: DATA NOT AVAILABLE)

M = $ thousand   MM = $ million
See Pages 11 through 21 for Explanation of Ratios and Data

Comparative Historical Data   Current Data Sorted by Sales

4/1/04-3/31/05 ALL	4/1/05-3/31/06 ALL	4/1/06-3/31/07 ALL	Type of Statement	0-1MM	1-3MM	3-5MM	5-10MM	10-25MM	25MM & OVER
6	11	8	Unqualified					4	8
9	9	10	Reviewed	1	1			1	4
2	2	2	Compiled			1			
4	2	3	Tax Returns		1	1	1		
11	7	13	Other	2	1	2	1	2	5
				6 (4/1-9/30/06)			30 (10/1/06-3/31/07)		
32	31	36	**NUMBER OF STATEMENTS**	3	3	4	2	7	17
%	%	%	**ASSETS**	%	%	%	%	%	%
7.6	9.5	8.5	Cash & Equivalents						4.5
29.0	28.7	29.5	Trade Receivables (net)						29.1
14.8	13.7	12.6	Inventory						11.3
3.2	1.3	1.1	All Other Current						.9
54.5	53.1	51.8	Total Current						45.9
34.4	35.8	38.1	Fixed Assets (net)						42.3
4.4	3.1	4.4	Intangibles (net)						4.0
6.7	8.0	5.7	All Other Non-Current						7.8
100.0	100.0	100.0	Total						100.0
			LIABILITIES						
8.2	7.7	7.4	Notes Payable-Short Term						4.6
2.6	4.0	4.1	Cur. Mat.-L.T.D.						5.9
13.8	13.5	14.0	Trade Payables						11.0
.1	.0	.2	Income Taxes Payable						.1
8.2	6.6	9.6	All Other Current						8.3
32.9	31.9	35.4	Total Current						30.0
18.1	31.9	18.0	Long-Term Debt						13.6
.7	2.0	1.1	Deferred Taxes						1.9
14.2	4.7	3.4	All Other Non-Current						3.5
34.1	29.6	42.2	Net Worth						51.0
100.0	100.0	100.0	Total Liabilties & Net Worth						100.0
			INCOME DATA						
100.0	100.0	100.0	Net Sales						100.0
32.4	30.2	29.8	Gross Profit						24.3
26.9	25.8	23.0	Operating Expenses						18.4
5.5	4.3	6.8	Operating Profit						5.9
2.2	1.1	.9	All Other Expenses (net)						.7
3.3	3.2	5.9	Profit Before Taxes						5.2
			RATIOS						
2.9	2.5	2.3	Current						2.5
1.8	1.9	1.7							2.1
1.3	1.2	1.2							1.2
2.1	2.0	1.8	Quick						1.9
1.3	1.5	1.2							1.3
.6	.8	.8							.8
42 8.8	47 7.8	40 9.1	Sales/Receivables						44 8.2
52 7.0	55 6.7	52 7.0							58 6.3
68 5.4	68 5.4	67 5.4							68 5.3
11 32.7	16 23.2	12 30.6	Cost of Sales/Inventory						16 22.6
30 12.2	26 14.2	26 13.8							26 14.1
56 6.5	48 7.6	42 8.8							40 9.1
20 18.3	21 17.6	19 18.8	Cost of Sales/Payables						20 18.6
29 12.4	25 14.5	25 14.4							24 15.2
46 7.9	57 6.4	47 7.7							31 11.7
4.9	6.2	5.7	Sales/Working Capital						5.7
7.2	8.3	9.9							7.5
25.0	21.0	44.7							38.9
12.6	5.7	8.5	EBIT/Interest						17.3
(28) 3.0	(29) 2.9	(31) 2.9						(16)	4.8
.1	1.4	1.4							2.0
	4.5		Net Profit + Depr., Dep.,						
	(10) 2.5		Amort./Cur. Mat. L/T/D						
	1.4								
.5	.6	.6	Fixed/Worth						.6
.9	.9	1.0							.8
3.0	2.0	3.8							1.1
.7	.6	.6	Debt/Worth						.4
1.7	1.0	1.3							.7
12.2	4.2	8.2							2.7
33.7	28.3	36.4	% Profit Before Taxes/Tangible						34.5
(27) 9.5	(27) 8.8	(33) 17.1	Net Worth						(16) 17.1
2.8	2.3	4.8							4.0
13.2	10.2	14.9	% Profit Before Taxes/Total						14.4
2.8	4.1	6.3	Assets						7.2
-.6	.5	2.1							2.5
13.3	7.5	11.6	Sales/Net Fixed Assets						6.5
6.4	4.8	3.9							3.7
3.2	3.3	3.0							3.0
2.6	2.2	2.7	Sales/Total Assets						2.3
1.9	1.7	1.7							1.6
1.4	1.4	1.4							1.4
1.9	3.0	2.2	% Depr., Dep., Amort./Sales						2.5
(27) 4.2	(26) 4.6	(29) 4.3						(13)	4.7
5.7	6.4	5.6							5.6
			% Officers', Directors' Owners' Comp/Sales						
1047510M	1165605M	1256727M	Net Sales ($)	1128M	5645M	15783M	15099M	96073M	1122999M
729269M	744119M	807596M	Total Assets ($)	1127M	2855M	9536M	3819M	44922M	745337M

© RMA 2007

M = $ thousand   MM = $ million
See Pages 11 through 21 for Explanation of Ratios and Data

Current Data Sorted by Assets   Comparative Historical Data

Type of Statement	0-500M	500M-2MM	2-10MM	10-50MM	50-100MM	100-250MM		ALL 4/1/02-3/31/03	ALL 4/1/03-3/31/04
Unqualified	2	1	20	21	9	6		49	61
Reviewed	2	15	54	17				83	74
Compiled	5	27	26	3	1			88	104
Tax Returns	24	26	11	1		1		49	45
Other	13	28	49	25	4	4		104	107
	94 (4/1-9/30/06)			301 (10/1/06-3/31/07)					
NUMBER OF STATEMENTS	46	97	160	67	14	11		373	391
ASSETS	%	%	%	%	%	%		%	%
Cash & Equivalents	10.9	11.4	8.4	8.6	4.1	3.7		8.5	8.8
Trade Receivables (net)	30.0	29.6	29.3	25.4	25.2	21.3		28.6	28.5
Inventory	7.5	11.9	12.3	14.1	10.5	9.2		11.4	11.7
All Other Current	1.3	2.8	1.6	1.4	1.6	2.4		1.9	2.4
Total Current	49.7	55.7	51.6	49.4	41.4	36.6		50.4	51.5
Fixed Assets (net)	35.2	32.5	39.3	39.1	38.0	39.6		40.1	37.9
Intangibles (net)	2.7	3.7	3.3	5.7	15.7	15.4		3.5	4.0
All Other Non-Current	12.5	8.0	5.8	5.8	4.9	8.4		6.0	6.5
Total	100.0	100.0	100.0	100.0	100.0	100.0		100.0	100.0
LIABILITIES									
Notes Payable-Short Term	17.3	9.5	8.9	7.6	2.8	12.4		7.9	9.4
Cur. Mat.-L.T.D.	10.6	6.6	6.0	5.9	5.2	4.7		7.7	7.8
Trade Payables	22.2	14.6	15.1	13.4	10.5	9.6		16.1	15.8
Income Taxes Payable	.2	.4	.1	.2	.3	.1		.3	.3
All Other Current	15.3	12.2	7.3	7.4	6.2	8.6		8.6	9.4
Total Current	65.5	43.2	37.4	34.5	25.1	35.4		40.6	42.6
Long-Term Debt	31.1	24.9	27.2	23.9	24.0	37.2		26.7	24.8
Deferred Taxes	.0	.4	.7	1.3	4.7	1.0		.6	.8
All Other Non-Current	5.7	4.4	4.3	4.0	2.2	33.7		3.3	5.8
Net Worth	-2.4	27.1	30.4	36.3	44.0	-7.3		28.8	26.0
Total Liabilities & Net Worth	100.0	100.0	100.0	100.0	100.0	100.0		100.0	100.0
INCOME DATA									
Net Sales	100.0	100.0	100.0	100.0	100.0	100.0		100.0	100.0
Gross Profit	51.4	43.5	34.2	30.2	25.6	30.1		36.6	35.7
Operating Expenses	47.9	40.0	28.6	23.7	17.6	22.8		32.9	32.0
Operating Profit	3.4	3.6	5.6	6.5	8.0	7.2		3.7	3.7
All Other Expenses (net)	2.9	1.1	1.6	1.2	2.0	2.9		1.5	1.3
Profit Before Taxes	.6	2.4	4.0	5.4	6.0	4.3		2.2	2.4
RATIOS									
Current	1.7	2.3	1.9	1.9	2.6	1.6		2.0	2.1
	.8	1.3	1.3	1.3	1.7	1.1		1.3	1.3
	.5	.8	1.0	1.1	1.2	.5		.9	.9
Quick	1.2	1.8	1.5	1.5	1.8	1.1		1.5	1.6
	.6	1.1	.9	.9	1.2	.8		.9 (390)	.9
	.3	.6	.7	.6	.9	.4		.6	.6
Sales/Receivables	13 27.7	29 12.7	36 10.3	38 9.6	47 7.8	33 11.0		35 10.5	34 10.8
	31 11.9	37 9.8	49 7.4	48 7.6	53 6.8	43 8.5		43 8.4	44 8.2
	38 9.6	50 7.3	59 6.1	62 5.9	67 5.4	56 6.6		56 6.5	55 6.6
Cost of Sales/Inventory	0 UND	4 94.6	11 32.8	19 18.8	16 23.3	15 23.8		11 33.4	12 31.2
	8 44.5	19 19.2	27 13.3	35 10.3	25 14.3	21 17.6		23 15.7	22 16.7
	29 12.5	41 8.8	41 8.9	58 6.3	41 8.9	31 12.0		40 9.0	41 8.9
Cost of Sales/Payables	15 23.9	16 22.9	18 20.3	21 17.2	23 15.7	21 17.5		20 18.6	19 18.9
	36 10.1	29 12.6	34 10.8	30 12.3	28 13.0	32 11.3		34 10.6	33 10.9
	65 5.6	56 6.5	52 7.0	51 7.1	41 8.9	37 9.8		51 7.1	50 7.3
Sales/Working Capital	23.9	8.3	8.0	6.9	6.0	16.0		8.7	7.1
	-38.6	19.0	17.7	15.7	11.9	64.4		21.3	20.4
	-9.5	-46.0	-413.0	60.5	29.4	-9.6		-49.9	-44.6
EBIT/Interest	4.9	8.0	6.3	6.0	10.7	15.8		5.1	7.0
	(39) 1.7	(89) 3.4	(146) 2.2	(63) 3.8	4.6	2.2		(351) 2.2	(362) 2.5
	.8	.4	1.0	1.9	3.2	1.2		.4	.9
Net Profit + Depr., Dep., Amort./Cur. Mat. L/T/D		2.7	3.0	2.7	4.4			2.3	2.7
		(19) 1.4	(41) 1.3	(30) 1.9	(10) 3.5			(98) 1.2	(90) 1.5
		.7	.9	1.3	1.7			.6	1.0
Fixed/Worth	.6	.5	.7	.7	.6	.9		.6	.6
	4.0	1.2	1.4	1.4	1.4	2.8		1.5	1.5
	-1.1	48.0	4.9	2.8	NM	-.3		4.5	6.9
Debt/Worth	1.0	1.1	1.0	1.1	.6	.8		1.0	1.0
	15.5	2.5	2.4	2.1	2.0	3.5		2.6	2.7
	-3.9	87.3	10.4	4.6	NM	-1.8		10.3	13.9
% Profit Before Taxes/Tangible Net Worth	91.9	66.7	56.3	46.5	47.1			40.8	41.0
	(26) 40.1	(74) 19.8	(138) 22.5	(60) 23.6	(11) 23.9			(310) 13.2	(309) 15.3
	-1.8	4.0	3.1	13.8	19.2			-.1	3.8
% Profit Before Taxes/Total Assets	28.3	16.7	14.6	12.1	13.7	12.0		11.7	11.3
	3.4	4.6	4.7	7.1	8.7	7.6		3.6	4.6
	-2.0	-1.7	.2	3.3	6.8	.9		-1.8	-.2
Sales/Net Fixed Assets	38.0	21.5	11.3	6.3	6.3	19.6		11.8	14.0
	17.0	10.3	5.7	4.5	4.7	4.9		5.6	6.1
	6.6	6.0	3.2	3.3	3.1	2.5		3.2	3.4
Sales/Total Assets	5.4	3.7	2.8	2.1	2.1	2.1		3.1	3.1
	4.0	2.9	2.2	1.7	1.7	1.6		2.2	2.2
	2.9	2.1	1.6	1.5	1.4	1.2		1.6	1.6
% Depr., Dep., Amort./Sales	1.3	1.3	2.0	2.5	2.8			2.6	2.2
	(32) 2.5	(84) 2.7	(150) 4.0	(65) 3.7	4.0			(346) 4.4	(352) 4.0
	3.7	5.5	5.8	5.2	5.0			6.4	6.1
% Officers', Directors' Owners' Comp/Sales	4.8	3.5	2.3	1.6				3.2	2.8
	(33) 8.0	(65) 6.1	(64) 3.6	(18) 2.3				(175) 5.2	(175) 4.6
	12.9	10.6	7.1	4.3				8.8	9.5
Net Sales ($)	51339M	315897M	1625666M	2482273M	1430665M	2635273M		6398156M	6331846M
Total Assets ($)	12869M	109278M	760488M	1349658M	865903M	1506396M		3495185M	3404971M

M = $ thousand   MM = $ million
See Pages 11 through 21 for Explanation of Ratios and Data

Comparative Historical Data | Current Data Sorted by Sales

			Type of Statement						
50	45	59	Unqualified	2	1	3	7	13	33
102	75	88	Reviewed	1	7	5	29	35	11
75	69	62	Compiled	5	18	13	16	8	2
41	55	63	Tax Returns	14	26	10	5	7	1
113	144	123	Other	10	24	15	22	26	26
4/1/04-3/31/05 ALL	4/1/05-3/31/06 ALL	4/1/06-3/31/07 ALL		94 (4/1-9/30/06)			301 (10/1/06-3/31/07)		
				0-1MM	1-3MM	3-5MM	5-10MM	10-25MM	25MM & OVER
381	388	395	NUMBER OF STATEMENTS	32	76	46	79	89	73
%	%	%	ASSETS	%	%	%	%	%	%
8.3	8.2	9.2	Cash & Equivalents	10.3	11.1	10.5	9.4	7.9	7.3
30.1	30.8	28.4	Trade Receivables (net)	24.7	27.2	27.1	30.6	31.6	26.0
12.6	11.6	11.8	Inventory	6.8	10.1	9.1	14.4	12.6	13.7
1.8	2.2	1.8	All Other Current	1.3	1.8	3.5	1.0	2.2	1.5
52.8	52.9	51.2	Total Current	43.1	50.1	50.2	55.4	54.3	48.5
37.9	36.5	37.1	Fixed Assets (net)	40.6	35.9	37.6	36.6	36.4	38.0
3.6	4.6	4.5	Intangibles (net)	6.7	3.5	4.1	2.1	4.0	8.1
5.7	6.0	7.1	All Other Non-Current	9.7	10.5	8.1	5.9	5.3	5.5
100.0	100.0	100.0	Total	100.0	100.0	100.0	100.0	100.0	100.0
			LIABILITIES						
11.2	10.5	9.7	Notes Payable-Short Term	9.8	10.9	12.1	9.7	9.2	7.4
6.3	6.3	6.6	Cur. Mat.-L.T.D.	12.2	5.9	7.4	6.7	5.6	5.5
15.9	16.7	15.2	Trade Payables	20.5	15.6	13.5	15.2	15.6	12.9
.3	.3	.2	Income Taxes Payable	.2	.4	.0	.1	.3	.2
7.5	8.8	9.5	All Other Current	16.5	10.6	11.2	7.6	7.9	8.0
41.1	42.6	41.1	Total Current	59.3	43.4	44.2	39.2	38.6	34.1
24.9	26.4	26.7	Long-Term Debt	40.8	30.1	23.6	26.3	22.6	24.4
.9	.7	.8	Deferred Taxes	.0	.1	.5	1.0	.8	1.8
6.6	8.0	5.2	All Other Non-Current	3.1	6.1	2.4	5.8	3.8	7.8
26.4	22.3	26.2	Net Worth	-3.2	20.4	29.3	27.7	34.2	31.9
100.0	100.0	100.0	Total Liabilities & Net Worth	100.0	100.0	100.0	100.0	100.0	100.0
			INCOME DATA						
100.0	100.0	100.0	Net Sales	100.0	100.0	100.0	100.0	100.0	100.0
34.2	35.4	37.4	Gross Profit	53.9	46.9	41.3	33.5	31.6	29.0
30.3	31.5	32.3	Operating Expenses	46.5	43.6	37.3	29.5	25.6	22.1
3.9	4.0	5.1	Operating Profit	7.3	3.3	4.0	4.0	6.1	6.9
1.4	1.3	1.6	All Other Expenses (net)	5.4	1.5	1.2	1.3	1.1	1.4
2.5	2.6	3.5	Profit Before Taxes	2.0	1.8	2.8	2.8	4.9	5.4
			RATIOS						
2.1	2.0	2.0	Current	2.0	2.1	2.2	1.9	1.9	2.3
1.3	1.3	1.3		.9	1.2	1.3	1.3	1.3	1.4
1.0	.9	.9		.5	.7	.9	1.1	1.0	1.1
1.6	1.5	1.6	Quick	1.5	1.7	1.8	1.5	1.4	1.6
1.0	.9	.9		.6	.9	.9	.9	.9	.9
.6	.6	.6		.2	.5	.6	.7	.7	.6
35 · 10.4	35 · 10.4	32 · 11.3	Sales/Receivables	13 · 27.1	26 · 13.9	34 · 10.9	33 · 11.1	39 · 9.4	39 · 9.4
45 · 8.1	46 · 7.9	44 · 8.3		32 · 11.3	35 · 10.5	43 · 8.5	44 · 8.3	52 · 7.1	48 · 7.6
57 · 6.4	59 · 6.2	57 · 6.4		50 · 7.2	49 · 7.5	51 · 7.1	57 · 6.4	63 · 5.8	59 · 6.2
11 · 31.9	9 · 41.1	9 · 38.9	Cost of Sales/Inventory	0 · UND	4 · 92.0	2 · 174.4	10 · 35.1	15 · 24.8	18 · 20.5
24 · 15.1	22 · 16.5	24 · 15.1		10 · 35.6	16 · 22.2	13 · 29.0	28 · 13.2	28 · 13.1	31 · 12.0
43 · 8.5	40 · 9.1	43 · 8.4		43 · 8.4	41 · 8.9	30 · 12.1	43 · 8.4	41 · 8.9	48 · 7.6
19 · 19.5	22 · 16.9	18 · 20.1	Cost of Sales/Payables	19 · 19.0	14 · 26.3	22 · 16.8	15 · 24.4	19 · 19.4	22 · 16.6
32 · 11.6	34 · 10.8	32 · 11.3		40 · 9.2	29 · 12.5	37 · 9.7	28 · 13.0	33 · 11.1	30 · 12.1
49 · 7.4	51 · 7.2	52 · 7.0		86 · 4.3	65 · 5.6	47 · 7.8	50 · 7.4	52 · 7.0	45 · 8.2
8.4	8.1	8.9	Sales/Working Capital	15.8	9.8	8.5	9.8	8.1	7.0
19.2	20.1	21.8		-66.4	33.4	37.7	16.8	18.6	13.7
-111.8	-75.4	-52.6		-8.0	-17.7	-65.8	126.5	154.9	74.5
7.3	7.3	7.0	EBIT/Interest	10.7	7.4	5.7	4.5	6.6	12.9
(356) 2.9	(364) 2.8	(362) 2.6		(23) 1.7	(69) 2.3	(45) 2.3	(72) 1.7	(82) 2.9	(71) 4.5
1.1	1.0	1.0		.1	.8	.7	.3	1.4	2.2
3.3	3.6	3.4	Net Profit + Depr., Dep., Amort./Cur. Mat. L/T/D		2.8	2.7	2.4	2.6	6.1
(111) 2.0	(93) 1.9	(106) 1.7		(12) 1.3	(12) 1.6	(21) 1.3	(27) 1.6	(34) 2.4	
1.0	1.2	1.1		.6	.9	.7	1.2	1.4	
.6	.7	.6	Fixed/Worth	.7	.5	.7	.6	.6	.7
1.4	1.6	1.5		NM	1.9	1.4	1.4	1.3	1.4
4.1	15.2	6.0		-.5	-8.4	5.8	5.1	2.4	2.9
1.0	1.1	1.0	Debt/Worth	.7	1.3	1.5	1.0	1.0	.8
2.5	2.8	2.6		NM	3.9	2.6	2.9	2.1	2.1
9.1	42.1	16.3		-3.3	-14.1	8.8	11.2	6.4	5.1
48.0	44.1	55.5	% Profit Before Taxes/Tangible Net Worth	288.7	68.8	62.2	48.7	63.3	46.4
(317) 20.5	(301) 21.9	(316) 22.5		(16) 34.5	(54) 17.2	(39) 25.4	(65) 11.6	(80) 22.5	(62) 27.0
4.8	7.3	5.1		5.3	-.8	9.7	-3.1	9.9	15.9
12.9	12.5	14.6	% Profit Before Taxes/Total Assets	30.6	16.0	13.1	13.0	14.8	13.7
5.2	5.6	5.9		3.6	4.1	4.8	2.9	6.5	9.8
.3	-.1	.0		-6.5	-1.9	-1.0	-2.3	1.6	4.6
12.4	12.8	15.2	Sales/Net Fixed Assets	35.4	20.8	12.8	15.2	12.2	7.0
6.6	6.7	6.4		8.4	11.0	6.3	7.6	5.7	4.9
3.6	3.9	3.7		2.5	4.0	3.6	4.0	3.3	3.6
3.2	3.1	3.1	Sales/Total Assets	5.3	3.9	3.0	3.1	2.8	2.3
2.3	2.3	2.2		2.9	3.0	2.5	2.4	2.1	1.9
1.7	1.7	1.7		1.0	1.8	1.7	1.9	1.6	1.6
2.4	2.1	1.9	% Depr., Dep., Amort./Sales	1.4	1.5	2.1	1.5	1.9	2.2
(345) 3.9	(352) 3.6	(352) 3.5		(21) 3.5	(63) 3.1	(44) 3.9	(70) 3.3	(85) 3.7	(69) 3.2
6.2	5.1	5.5		8.1	6.1	5.7	6.0	5.4	4.8
2.9	2.6	2.7	% Officers', Directors' Owners' Comp/Sales	6.0	4.8	2.9	2.1	2.1	1.5
(159) 4.6	(170) 4.4	(180) 5.1		(19) 8.6	(52) 7.2	(29) 5.3	(43) 3.4	(24) 3.5	(13) 2.7
7.2	7.6	8.6		14.6	11.2	8.8	4.9	7.5	4.4
6406692M	7310791M	8541113M	Net Sales ($)	21915M	148931M	184946M	590462M	1352276M	6242583M
3555284M	3668290M	4604592M	Total Assets ($)	15769M	69512M	92704M	268365M	710100M	3448142M

M = $ thousand   MM = $ million
See Pages 11 through 21 for Explanation of Ratios and Data

Current Data Sorted by Assets   Comparative Historical Data

0-500M	500M-2MM	2-10MM	10-50MM	50-100MM	100-250MM	Type of Statement	4/1/02-3/31/03 ALL	4/1/03-3/31/04 ALL
		1				Unqualified	3	5
	5	13	2			Reviewed	15	20
2	6	3	1			Compiled	15	14
1	3	1	1			Tax Returns	5	5
	2	4	2			Other	15	17
	10 (4/1-9/30/06)		37 (10/1/06-3/31/07)					
3	16	22	6			**NUMBER OF STATEMENTS**	53	61
%	%	%	%	%	%	**ASSETS**	%	%
	9.0	7.5				Cash & Equivalents	5.7	9.2
	23.4	23.0	D	D		Trade Receivables (net)	27.1	26.6
	7.7	17.9	A	A		Inventory	4.5	7.2
	1.8	1.3	T	T		All Other Current	.7	1.8
	42.0	49.7	A	A		Total Current	38.0	44.8
	46.5	39.6				Fixed Assets (net)	51.6	43.3
	4.9	4.4	N	N		Intangibles (net)	4.1	4.5
	6.7	6.4	O	O		All Other Non-Current	6.3	7.4
	100.0	100.0	T	T		Total	100.0	100.0
						LIABILITIES		
	9.8	6.4	A	A		Notes Payable-Short Term	9.2	10.1
	8.1	5.7	V	V		Cur. Mat.-L.T.D.	6.8	8.7
	8.2	10.2	A	A		Trade Payables	8.3	8.3
	.0	.6	I	I		Income Taxes Payable	.4	.4
	11.0	6.3	L	L		All Other Current	7.4	7.4
	37.1	29.1	A	A		Total Current	32.1	34.9
	32.8	22.3	B	B		Long-Term Debt	31.3	25.4
	.2	2.1	L	L		Deferred Taxes	1.9	.8
	10.1	13.0	E	E		All Other Non-Current	4.4	6.8
	19.7	33.4				Net Worth	30.2	32.0
	100.0	100.0				Total Liabilties & Net Worth	100.0	100.0
						INCOME DATA		
	100.0	100.0				Net Sales	100.0	100.0
	33.6	33.6				Gross Profit	37.8	35.1
	31.6	27.5				Operating Expenses	34.5	31.8
	2.0	6.0				Operating Profit	3.3	3.3
	1.9	1.7				All Other Expenses (net)	1.5	1.4
	.0	4.3				Profit Before Taxes	1.9	1.9
						RATIOS		
	2.1	3.4					2.0	2.4
	1.3	1.8				Current	1.3	1.4
	1.0	1.0					.8	.8
	2.1	2.2					1.7	1.9
	1.0	1.1				Quick	1.2	1.1
	.4	.7					.8	.7
26	14.0	39 9.3					38 9.6	36 10.0
45	8.1	43 8.4				Sales/Receivables	51 7.1	48 7.7
55	6.7	52 7.0					67 5.5	58 6.3
0	UND	6 64.5					0 UND	0 UND
5	76.0	27 13.4				Cost of Sales/Inventory	6 59.3	8 48.4
18	19.8	65 5.7					15 24.8	25 14.4
9	40.2	9 41.1					11 34.7	12 29.5
23	16.2	20 18.3				Cost of Sales/Payables	21 17.7	18 20.3
33	10.9	41 8.8					30 12.3	27 13.4
	10.9	6.1					9.3	6.6
	35.2	9.0				Sales/Working Capital	30.0	19.7
	NM	328.1					-29.5	-37.1
	4.5	6.1					4.4	4.1
	1.8	(21) 1.9				EBIT/Interest	(49) 2.0	(59) 1.6
	-.6	1.1					.6	.5
							11.4	2.1
						Net Profit + Depr., Dep., Amort./Cur. Mat. L/T/D	(11) 2.5	(20) 1.3
							.8	.9
	1.1	.7					1.0	.7
	2.1	1.0				Fixed/Worth	2.1	1.4
	NM	3.2					5.8	4.0
	1.8	.8					1.1	.9
	2.7	2.4				Debt/Worth	3.3	2.2
	NM	5.8					9.1	9.8
	62.1	31.5					43.6	17.5
(12)	16.7	(20) 16.6				% Profit Before Taxes/Tangible Net Worth	(46) 9.3	(51) 4.7
	-26.7	2.7					-4.2	-2.2
	15.2	14.5					12.0	6.6
	2.9	5.4				% Profit Before Taxes/Total Assets	3.2	1.5
	-11.9	.4					-1.7	-1.1
	9.4	11.7					6.7	8.2
	5.3	5.4				Sales/Net Fixed Assets	3.6	5.9
	3.3	2.6					2.1	2.8
	2.8	2.6					2.4	2.6
	2.2	2.0				Sales/Total Assets	1.8	1.9
	1.4	1.4					1.3	1.4
	2.7	1.7					3.8	3.3
	4.8	3.1				% Depr., Dep., Amort./Sales	(51) 5.8	(59) 5.4
	8.2	6.8					9.0	7.4
	4.9						3.1	3.5
	(10) 6.3					% Officers', Directors' Owners' Comp/Sales	(27) 4.4	(30) 6.3
	10.7						6.2	11.9
3997M	40623M	222600M	195584M			Net Sales ($)	387964M	459236M
894M	18457M	108674M	129323M			Total Assets ($)	223507M	261112M

M = $ thousand   MM = $ million
See Pages 11 through 21 for Explanation of Ratios and Data

Comparative Historical Data | | | | ## Current Data Sorted by Sales

			Type of Statement						
7	3	3	Unqualified		1	6	4	1	2
16	15	19	Reviewed		7	3		7	1
12	9	12	Compiled	1	3	2		1	
4	6	5	Tax Returns		2		2	4	
13	17	8	Other						
4/1/04-3/31/05 ALL	4/1/05-3/31/06 ALL	4/1/06-3/31/07 ALL		0-1MM	10 (4/1-9/30/06) 1-3MM	3-5MM	5-10MM	37 (10/1/06-3/31/07) 10-25MM	25MM & OVER
52	50	47	NUMBER OF STATEMENTS	1	13	11	6	13	3
%	%	%	ASSETS	%	%	%	%	%	%
8.2	7.5	7.2	Cash & Equivalents		5.3	12.2		6.0	
31.9	29.2	26.5	Trade Receivables (net)		31.5	20.9		20.8	
8.7	11.9	12.3	Inventory		8.8	6.6		23.6	
.5	1.6	1.3	All Other Current		.4	2.3		1.5	
49.3	50.2	47.2	Total Current		46.0	42.0		51.9	
40.2	36.3	41.0	Fixed Assets (net)		38.2	47.0		34.1	
4.4	7.2	5.4	Intangibles (net)		6.0	8.4		6.5	
6.2	6.3	6.4	All Other Non-Current		9.9	2.7		7.5	
100.0	100.0	100.0	Total		100.0	100.0		100.0	
			LIABILITIES						
12.2	11.2	8.5	Notes Payable-Short Term		16.1	3.1		4.6	
6.9	5.7	6.4	Cur. Mat.-L.T.D.		5.2	9.6		5.1	
9.1	10.4	9.3	Trade Payables		8.3	6.3		10.9	
.5	.4	.4	Income Taxes Payable		.4	.4		.6	
8.1	8.0	9.6	All Other Current		16.6	9.8		5.7	
36.8	35.7	34.2	Total Current		46.6	29.2		26.9	
24.7	19.5	26.6	Long-Term Debt		34.9	28.3		23.1	
.7	1.4	2.1	Deferred Taxes		3.8	.2		.4	
8.6	10.1	11.0	All Other Non-Current		6.9	14.7		13.0	
29.3	33.3	26.1	Net Worth		7.8	27.7		36.6	
100.0	100.0	100.0	Total Liabilties & Net Worth		100.0	100.0		100.0	
			INCOME DATA						
100.0	100.0	100.0	Net Sales		100.0	100.0		100.0	
35.0	36.1	34.1	Gross Profit		37.0	35.2		24.4	
30.2	31.7	30.0	Operating Expenses		39.1	26.9		19.7	
4.8	4.4	4.1	Operating Profit		-2.1	8.3		4.7	
1.4	1.4	1.8	All Other Expenses (net)		1.9	2.7		1.1	
3.5	3.0	2.3	Profit Before Taxes		-4.0	5.7		3.6	
			RATIOS						
2.3	2.2	2.5	Current		2.0	2.0		3.3	
1.3	1.3	1.4			1.1	1.2		2.0	
.9	1.0	1.0			.7	1.0		1.2	
1.8	1.7	2.1	Quick		2.0	2.0		1.9	
1.0	1.0	1.1			.7	1.0		1.2	
.7	.7	.7			.5	.7		.7	
43 8.5	35 10.5	39 9.4	Sales/Receivables		29 12.4	41 8.9		32 11.5	
51 7.2	51 7.2	46 7.9			43 8.4	50 7.4		46 7.9	
62 5.8	60 6.1	61 6.0			58 6.3	55 6.7		66 5.5	
0 UND	2 214.8	0 UND	Cost of Sales/Inventory		0 UND	2 207.8		24 15.1	
9 41.8	17 21.6	9 41.8			0 UND	5 72.8		31 11.9	
29 12.5	41 8.9	38 9.7			27 13.3	23 15.8		69 5.3	
11 32.8	13 27.4	11 33.0	Cost of Sales/Payables		9 40.2	8 43.9		13 29.1	
22 16.9	21 17.4	20 18.4			17 21.2	20 18.4		19 19.2	
32 11.5	36 10.2	35 10.5			33 11.1	34 10.8		39 9.4	
7.1	6.9	6.7	Sales/Working Capital		18.2	6.4		4.3	
22.7	13.6	19.5			45.9	22.5		8.8	
-100.1	-377.1	788.8			-18.7	999.8		45.3	
6.3	6.2	5.5	EBIT/Interest		3.2	8.1		5.8	
(51) 1.9	(47) 1.6	(46) 1.9			-.5	1.7		3.1	
1.0	.5	.8			-2.6	1.0		1.6	
2.5	3.4	4.4	Net Profit + Depr., Dep., Amort./Cur. Mat. L/T/D						
(16) 1.4	(16) 1.1	(11) 2.0							
1.0	.5	1.6							
.7	.6	.8	Fixed/Worth		1.6	1.0		.5	
1.3	1.2	1.7			2.8	1.8		.9	
3.7	4.4	4.5			-1.4	20.5		2.7	
.9	.8	1.3	Debt/Worth		2.2	1.7		.8	
2.3	2.3	2.4			4.9	2.2		2.2	
6.4	10.5	7.5			-6.4	65.9		5.6	
33.2	34.2	33.0	% Profit Before Taxes/Tangible Net Worth					44.5	
(44) 11.1	(40) 9.6	(38) 14.6						(12) 14.9	
1.6	.4	.6						7.7	
12.2	10.1	14.4	% Profit Before Taxes/Total Assets		12.7	16.3		13.8	
3.2	1.8	3.8			-10.8	4.5		4.7	
.2	-1.9	-.6			-23.7	.0		2.4	
9.1	13.5	11.0	Sales/Net Fixed Assets		15.2	7.6		21.1	
6.1	7.6	5.7			6.2	3.5		8.3	
3.5	3.4	2.8			3.5	1.6		2.6	
2.6	2.6	2.8	Sales/Total Assets		4.1	2.4		2.5	
2.1	2.0	2.2			2.3	2.0		1.8	
1.5	1.4	1.3			1.5	1.1		1.1	
3.1	2.2	1.9	% Depr., Dep., Amort./Sales		1.3	2.6		1.3	
(50) 4.2	(46) 3.9	(46) 3.5			2.8	6.7		(12) 2.4	
7.4	6.3	7.2			6.8	10.7		5.0	
2.3	2.8	2.8	% Officers', Directors' Owners' Comp/Sales						
(27) 5.0	(17) 5.9	(23) 5.5							
8.1	11.5	7.6							
429488M	528893M	462804M	Net Sales ($)	494M	24322M	45632M	40501M	200397M	151458M
219933M	301136M	257348M	Total Assets ($)	519M	11142M	32137M	18423M	141648M	53479M

M = $ thousand   MM = $ million
See Pages 11 through 21 for Explanation of Ratios and Data

Current Data Sorted by Assets   Comparative Historical Data

						Type of Statement		
		2	4			Unqualified	6	5
	1	6	2			Reviewed	10	15
	3	3				Compiled	11	15
1	1					Tax Returns	5	3
1	3	4				Other	16	18
	8 (4/1-9/30/06)		23 (10/1/06-3/31/07)				4/1/02-3/31/03	4/1/03-3/31/04
0-500M	500M-2MM	2-10MM	10-50MM	50-100MM	100-250MM		ALL	ALL
2	8	15	6			NUMBER OF STATEMENTS	48	56
%	%	%	%	%	%		%	%
		13.0		D	D	**ASSETS** Cash & Equivalents	10.5	13.0
		31.0		A	A	Trade Receivables (net)	29.5	31.4
		6.5		T	T	Inventory	9.2	9.7
		2.6		A	A	All Other Current	3.3	2.1
		53.1				Total Current	52.6	56.3
		38.1		N	N	Fixed Assets (net)	35.1	31.8
		5.4		O	O	Intangibles (net)	6.0	5.5
		3.4		T	T	All Other Non-Current	6.4	6.5
		100.0				Total	100.0	100.0
				A	A	**LIABILITIES**		
		7.3		V	V	Notes Payable-Short Term	7.5	7.2
		4.2		A	A	Cur. Mat.-L.T.D.	4.9	10.2
		7.0		I	I	Trade Payables	11.1	11.4
		.1		L	L	Income Taxes Payable	.1	.2
		9.8		A	A	All Other Current	7.7	8.7
		28.4		B	B	Total Current	31.3	37.7
		11.5		L	L	Long-Term Debt	24.0	16.5
		.4		E	E	Deferred Taxes	.6	.6
		2.4				All Other Non-Current	2.9	6.7
		57.3				Net Worth	41.3	38.6
		100.0				Total Liabilties & Net Worth	100.0	100.0
						INCOME DATA		
		100.0				Net Sales	100.0	100.0
		33.7				Gross Profit	39.6	40.1
		29.6				Operating Expenses	36.1	35.1
		4.1				Operating Profit	3.5	5.0
		.7				All Other Expenses (net)	1.2	.4
		3.4				Profit Before Taxes	2.2	4.6
						RATIOS		
		3.6					2.7	3.3
		2.0				Current	1.8	1.9
		1.0					1.1	1.0
		2.9					2.0	3.0
		1.7				Quick	1.4	1.5
		.7					.8	.8
	43	8.5					41 8.9	36 10.2
	56	6.5				Sales/Receivables	53 6.9	50 7.3
	83	4.4					64 5.7	66 5.5
	0	UND					10 34.8	10 36.7
	15	23.7				Cost of Sales/Inventory	19 19.0	17 21.2
	40	9.2					42 8.7	29 12.6
	10	36.9					16 22.9	14 27.0
	14	26.4				Cost of Sales/Payables	24 15.0	25 14.5
	41	9.0					43 8.4	36 10.2
		3.0					4.4	5.2
		8.8				Sales/Working Capital	11.1	10.4
		-292.9					63.3	168.6
		34.3					7.6	11.8
	(14)	4.4				EBIT/Interest	(44) 2.1	(50) 4.1
		.6					.6	1.6
						Net Profit + Depr., Dep.,	2.7	9.3
						Amort./Cur. Mat. L/T/D	(11) 2.0	(10) 1.9
							1.4	1.1
		.2					.5	.4
		.8				Fixed/Worth	1.1	.7
		2.0					2.1	1.7
		.3					.7	.5
		.7				Debt/Worth	2.0	1.4
		1.7					4.2	5.0
		39.4					42.0	46.1
		13.6				% Profit Before Taxes/Tangible Net Worth	(43) 19.2	(49) 19.7
		-5.1					-4.8	4.3
		17.1					13.0	19.1
		5.8				% Profit Before Taxes/Total Assets	3.3	7.2
		-1.9					-2.4	1.4
		10.5					10.2	19.5
		5.8				Sales/Net Fixed Assets	5.8	7.0
		2.8					3.9	4.1
		2.2					2.4	3.1
		1.7				Sales/Total Assets	2.0	2.0
		1.2					1.5	1.6
		2.8					2.7	2.3
		4.6				% Depr., Dep., Amort./Sales	(42) 4.1	(47) 4.4
		7.1					6.6	7.1
							3.6	3.9
						% Officers', Directors' Owners' Comp/Sales	(18) 6.2	(18) 7.4
							12.5	11.5
3632M	17317M	107012M	184822M			Net Sales ($)	656375M	812309M
902M	9069M	63160M	112871M			Total Assets ($)	466265M	540531M

© RMA 2007

M = $ thousand   MM = $ million

See Pages 11 through 21 for Explanation of Ratios and Data

Comparative Historical Data | Current Data Sorted by Sales

				Type of Statement	0-1MM	1-3MM	3-5MM	5-10MM	10-25MM	25MM & OVER
	8	7	6	Unqualified	1		3	2	3	3
	13	10	9	Reviewed		2		2	2	1
	14	8	6	Compiled		2	1		1	
	3	3	2	Tax Returns		4	3		1	
	17	20	8	Other						
	4/1/04- 3/31/05	4/1/05- 3/31/06	4/1/06- 3/31/07			8 (4/1-9/30/06)			23 (10/1/06-3/31/07)		
	ALL	ALL	ALL							
	55	48	31	NUMBER OF STATEMENTS	1	8	7	4	7	4
	%	%	%	**ASSETS**	%	%	%	%	%	%
	11.6	11.9	11.1	Cash & Equivalents						
	30.9	32.0	32.5	Trade Receivables (net)						
	10.9	10.1	9.2	Inventory						
	1.9	1.7	1.4	All Other Current						
	55.3	55.6	54.2	Total Current						
	32.7	33.3	38.0	Fixed Assets (net)						
	6.1	4.3	3.6	Intangibles (net)						
	6.0	6.8	4.3	All Other Non-Current						
	100.0	100.0	100.0	Total						
				LIABILITIES						
	9.1	7.5	6.5	Notes Payable-Short Term						
	15.1	5.1	5.7	Cur. Mat.-L.T.D.						
	14.2	12.9	9.9	Trade Payables						
	.2	.3	.1	Income Taxes Payable						
	9.9	10.7	7.9	All Other Current						
	48.4	36.5	30.2	Total Current						
	22.7	19.2	22.1	Long-Term Debt						
	.4	.4	.5	Deferred Taxes						
	8.2	7.0	2.1	All Other Non-Current						
	20.4	36.8	45.2	Net Worth						
	100.0	100.0	100.0	Total Liabilities & Net Worth						
				INCOME DATA						
	100.0	100.0	100.0	Net Sales						
	38.4	40.9	37.7	Gross Profit						
	33.8	34.2	32.7	Operating Expenses						
	4.6	6.6	5.0	Operating Profit						
	1.1	1.0	1.2	All Other Expenses (net)						
	3.5	5.7	3.8	Profit Before Taxes						
				RATIOS						
	2.4	2.8	3.6							
	1.5	1.7	1.8	Current						
	1.0	1.1	1.0							
	2.1	2.3	2.9							
	1.1	1.3	1.7	Quick						
	.5	.8	.8							
	35 10.4	39 9.3	43 8.5							
	52 7.0	51 7.1	59 6.2	Sales/Receivables						
	69 5.3	67 5.5	82 4.4							
	14 25.5	15 24.9	12 30.4							
	25 14.3	23 15.9	23 16.0	Cost of Sales/Inventory						
	46 8.0	43 8.6	40 9.2							
	10 37.9	16 22.5	10 35.6							
	28 13.3	35 10.4	23 15.8	Cost of Sales/Payables						
	63 5.8	52 7.0	44 8.4							
	5.4	5.4	3.6							
	17.2	10.6	9.1	Sales/Working Capital						
	-65.4	54.7	-292.9							
	8.0	13.3	16.9							
	(49) 3.6	(44) 4.4	(28) 3.6	EBIT/Interest						
	-.3	1.7	.4							
	4.9	3.5		Net Profit + Depr., Dep.,						
	(14) 2.3	(10) 2.0		Amort./Cur. Mat. L/T/D						
	1.0	1.1								
	.4	.3	.3							
	.9	.9	.9	Fixed/Worth						
	16.1	4.0	3.1							
	.7	.5	.3							
	2.3	1.9	1.1	Debt/Worth						
	37.1	8.7	5.1							
	48.7	48.3	40.2	% Profit Before Taxes/Tangible						
	(42) 18.7	(41) 25.7	(28) 19.3	Net Worth						
	1.2	8.3	-3.7							
	14.2	18.9	17.1	% Profit Before Taxes/Total						
	6.0	8.3	6.2	Assets						
	-.5	2.5	-1.9							
	13.7	12.3	10.5							
	7.4	6.0	5.5	Sales/Net Fixed Assets						
	4.6	4.3	3.1							
	3.3	2.7	2.2							
	2.1	2.0	1.8	Sales/Total Assets						
	1.4	1.5	1.2							
	2.9	2.6	2.9							
	(49) 3.9	(43) 3.7	(29) 4.6	% Depr., Dep., Amort./Sales						
	6.7	4.8	6.1							
	2.3	3.4	4.4	% Officers', Directors'						
	(20) 4.8	(24) 6.9	(14) 6.7	Owners' Comp/Sales						
	11.0	11.0	12.2							
	1455225M	1428342M	312783M	Net Sales ($)	855M	15762M	28289M	27388M	86315M	154174M
	932720M	961229M	186002M	Total Assets ($)	1359M	7646M	23710M	15196M	46491M	91600M

© RMA 2007

M = $ thousand   MM = $ million
See Pages 11 through 21 for Explanation of Ratios and Data

Current Data Sorted by Assets   Comparative Historical Data

Sub-period comparison: 9 (4/1-9/30/06)   35 (10/1/06-3/31/07)

0-500M	500M-2MM	2-10MM	10-50MM	50-100MM	100-250MM	Type of Statement	4/1/02-3/31/03 ALL	4/1/03-3/31/04 ALL
		3	1	3	3	Unqualified	15	26
	1	1	2			Reviewed	5	7
1	1	1	1		1	Compiled	1	4
	1					Tax Returns	3	4
	1	8	8	5	2	Other	15	16
1	3	13	12	9	6	**NUMBER OF STATEMENTS**	39	57
%	%	%	%	%	%	**ASSETS**	%	%
		10.0	8.3			Cash & Equivalents	10.9	12.4
		31.9	34.1			Trade Receivables (net)	21.3	20.7
		18.8	12.4			Inventory	15.9	14.0
		5.1	.5			All Other Current	6.5	1.9
		65.7	55.3			Total Current	54.6	49.1
		24.1	36.8			Fixed Assets (net)	34.3	36.7
		1.7	3.5			Intangibles (net)	3.0	3.7
		8.5	4.5			All Other Non-Current	8.2	10.5
		100.0	100.0			Total	100.0	100.0
						LIABILITIES		
		4.7	6.1			Notes Payable-Short Term	6.2	6.2
		3.4	4.5			Cur. Mat.-L.T.D.	3.0	3.4
		22.7	21.7			Trade Payables	20.6	18.2
		.4	.6			Income Taxes Payable	.3	.3
		10.9	10.4			All Other Current	9.8	6.5
		42.2	43.5			Total Current	39.9	34.6
		21.0	23.0			Long-Term Debt	9.4	13.5
		1.3	.1			Deferred Taxes	1.8	1.2
		5.1	2.7			All Other Non-Current	5.7	3.0
		30.5	30.8			Net Worth	43.2	47.7
		100.0	100.0			Total Liabilties & Net Worth	100.0	100.0
						INCOME DATA		
		100.0	100.0			Net Sales	100.0	100.0
		22.7	18.6			Gross Profit	20.3	21.5
		17.1	10.2			Operating Expenses	14.9	15.9
		5.5	8.5			Operating Profit	5.3	5.6
		.9	1.9			All Other Expenses (net)	.3	1.0
		4.6	6.5			Profit Before Taxes	5.1	4.6
						RATIOS		
		2.1	1.8				1.8	2.1
		1.5	1.4			Current	1.4	1.5
		1.1	1.0				1.0	1.1
		1.4	1.2				1.1	1.4
		1.1	1.1			Quick	.8	.9
		.5	.7				.5	.6
		13 28.0	16 22.4				17 21.1	18 20.2
		26 14.2	26 14.1			Sales/Receivables	28 13.1	25 14.8
		48 7.7	36 10.2				37 9.7	43 8.5
		4 100.1	4 95.9				10 36.3	10 37.4
		17 20.9	9 42.8			Cost of Sales/Inventory	21 17.6	20 18.1
		31 11.9	21 17.6				38 9.7	31 11.6
		12 30.9	8 44.1				19 19.5	15 24.2
		28 12.9	14 26.9			Cost of Sales/Payables	31 11.6	27 13.4
		31 11.7	41 8.9				45 8.1	44 8.3
		6.9	13.8				8.7	9.7
		14.7	41.4			Sales/Working Capital	22.8	16.5
		NM	NM				999.8	74.2
		17.7	32.8				31.7	16.1
		(11) 4.7	6.3			EBIT/Interest	(35) 7.4	(50) 5.6
		1.4	1.7				2.5	1.9
								6.7
						Net Profit + Depr., Dep., Amort./Cur. Mat. L/T/D		(14) 2.5
								.6
		.2	.3				.2	.4
		.6	1.1			Fixed/Worth	.8	.8
		8.7	NM				1.5	1.6
		.8	1.0				.8	.7
		1.8	1.7			Debt/Worth	1.6	1.2
		15.1	NM				2.6	2.2
		69.1					36.1	33.0
		(11) 40.4				% Profit Before Taxes/Tangible Net Worth	(37) 12.6	(53) 15.9
		3.5					6.0	2.4
		23.2	19.4				16.0	18.0
		20.7	10.1			% Profit Before Taxes/Total Assets	6.8	7.1
		1.5	1.8				1.7	.4
		51.1	88.7				29.0	18.5
		39.9	15.7			Sales/Net Fixed Assets	8.1	7.0
		8.2	3.5				3.9	3.4
		6.1	8.0				3.7	3.8
		3.1	4.3			Sales/Total Assets	2.4	2.3
		2.6	1.9				1.8	1.3
		.2	.6				.5	.8
		(10) .7	(11) .8			% Depr., Dep., Amort./Sales	(37) 1.7	(53) 1.4
		1.7	4.0				3.7	4.4
								.5
						% Officers', Directors' Owners' Comp/Sales		(10) 1.5
								2.8
469M	21473M	461714M	1718652M	2243987M	4951911M	Net Sales ($)	6786976M	8588491M
398M	4221M	84623M	305406M	688769M	1015240M	Total Assets ($)	2265149M	2923010M

M = $ thousand   MM = $ million
See Pages 11 through 21 for Explanation of Ratios and Data

Comparative Historical Data / Current Data Sorted by Sales

Type of Statement / NUMBER OF STATEMENTS

4/1/04-3/31/05 ALL	4/1/05-3/31/06 ALL	4/1/06-3/31/07 ALL	Type of Statement	0-1MM	1-3MM	3-5MM	5-10MM	10-25MM	25MM & Over
23	18	10	Unqualified	1			2	3	7
5	6	4	Reviewed					1	2
16	3	5	Compiled					1	3
1	1	1	Tax Returns			1	2	2	
14	20	24	Other						19
59	**48**	**44**	**NUMBER OF STATEMENTS**	**1**		**1**	**4**	**7**	**31**

Sub-periods (right side): 9 (4/1-9/30/06); 35 (10/1/06-3/31/07)

Note: For the ASSETS, LIABILITIES, INCOME DATA, and upper RATIOS sections, the current-data columns 0-1MM through 10-25MM are printed "DATA NOT AVAILABLE"; only the 25MM & Over column carries values.

4/1/04-3/31/05 ALL %	4/1/05-3/31/06 ALL %	4/1/06-3/31/07 ALL %		25MM & Over %
			ASSETS	
10.2	13.4	10.9	Cash & Equivalents	12.8
18.4	24.4	27.5	Trade Receivables (net)	28.1
17.6	13.9	15.4	Inventory	13.3
1.7	3.7	3.1	All Other Current	2.6
47.8	55.4	56.9	Total Current	56.8
40.6	34.0	35.5	Fixed Assets (net)	36.2
3.3	2.8	2.5	Intangibles (net)	2.6
8.3	7.8	5.1	All Other Non-Current	4.4
100.0	100.0	100.0	Total	100.0
			LIABILITIES	
3.1	2.5	4.0	Notes Payable-Short Term	2.9
2.5	2.6	3.6	Cur. Mat.-L.T.D.	3.9
21.5	23.1	20.6	Trade Payables	23.5
.3	.7	.4	Income Taxes Payable	.5
9.6	9.6	7.6	All Other Current	9.0
37.0	38.5	36.2	Total Current	39.6
23.9	17.6	18.8	Long-Term Debt	15.5
1.1	1.3	1.1	Deferred Taxes	.4
9.7	4.4	5.7	All Other Non-Current	5.2
28.4	38.2	38.3	Net Worth	39.2
100.0	100.0	100.0	Total Liabilities & Net Worth	100.0
			INCOME DATA	
100.0	100.0	100.0	Net Sales	100.0
14.5	20.5	19.4	Gross Profit	15.8
11.2	13.6	11.6	Operating Expenses	9.1
3.2	6.9	7.8	Operating Profit	6.8
.5	1.2	1.1	All Other Expenses (net)	.5
2.7	5.7	6.7	Profit Before Taxes	6.2
			RATIOS	
1.7	2.1	2.4	Current	2.2
1.3	1.4	1.6		1.5
.8	1.1	1.2		1.0
1.2	1.5	1.5	Quick	1.5
.8	1.0	1.1		1.1
.3	.7	.6		.7

Ratios with turnover counts:

4/1/04-3/31/05	4/1/05-3/31/06	4/1/06-3/31/07		25MM & Over
4 96.9	15 24.2	15 25.0	Sales/Receivables	15 24.1
19 18.9	19 19.2	22 16.5		22 16.7
31 11.8	37 9.9	30 12.0		26 14.0
10 35.1	6 56.2	5 69.5	Cost of Sales/Inventory	7 51.6
18 19.8	16 22.5	15 24.9		12 29.2
40 9.1	29 12.5	27 13.3		22 16.4
15 23.6	15 23.8	11 34.5	Cost of Sales/Payables	10 35.4
24 15.2	26 13.9	19 18.9		19 19.5
38 9.6	37 9.8	29 12.4		28 12.8
14.4	9.4	9.7	Sales/Working Capital	12.1
48.4	19.3	16.0		19.6
-41.8	198.5	62.2		-167.9
24.5	30.9	33.6	EBIT/Interest	38.1
(48) 4.4	(38) 7.9	(38) 7.1		(26) 7.5
2.0	3.3	2.2		2.0
33.4	87.2	80.7	Net Profit + Depr., Dep.,	
(12) 10.5	(15) 10.1	(11) 8.5	Amort./Cur. Mat. L/T/D	
2.2	3.2	1.1		
.4	.3	.4	Fixed/Worth	.4
1.0	.8	.9		.8
2.3	1.7	2.3		2.1
1.1	.7	.7	Debt/Worth	.7
1.7	1.3	1.6		1.5
11.3	3.0	3.4		2.6
44.5	64.7	71.2	% Profit Before Taxes/Tangible	70.7
(47) 26.3	(43) 32.6	(38) 40.7	Net Worth	(27) 32.8
8.3	14.8	14.1		12.6
15.7	24.6	24.8	% Profit Before Taxes/Total	25.6
5.0	14.5	14.0	Assets	12.9
.8	5.5	2.8		2.8
33.3	27.8	47.3	Sales/Net Fixed Assets	39.9
9.2	13.0	18.6		18.1
2.3	5.2	3.4		3.7
5.2	4.8	5.4	Sales/Total Assets	7.0
2.8	3.4	4.0		4.3
1.2	1.7	1.6		1.6
.7	.5	.5	% Depr., Dep., Amort./Sales	.5
(54) 1.3	(46) .9	(40) .8		(28) .7
3.1	2.8	3.2		3.8
			% Officers', Directors' Owners' Comp/Sales	

4/1/04-3/31/05	4/1/05-3/31/06	4/1/06-3/31/07		0-1MM	1-3MM	3-5MM	5-10MM	10-25MM	25MM & Over
12339749M	9057471M	9398206M	Net Sales ($)	469M	3007M		28660M	107710M	9258360M
3128495M	2680101M	2098657M	Total Assets ($)	398M	1398M		26048M	33858M	2036955M

M = $ thousand   MM = $ million
See Pages 11 through 21 for Explanation of Ratios and Data

Current Data Sorted by Assets   Comparative Historical Data

Type of Statement	0-500M	500M-2MM	2-10MM	10-50MM	50-100MM	100-250MM		4/1/02-3/31/03 ALL	4/1/03-3/31/04 ALL
Unqualified		2	10	11	3	5		21	22
Reviewed		3	5	6				23	17
Compiled	2	2	7	4				5	10
Tax Returns	3	3	1	1				3	7
Other	2	5	8	7		1		10	19
	14 (4/1-9/30/06)			77 (10/1/06-3/31/07)					
NUMBER OF STATEMENTS	7	15	31	29	4	5		62	75

	0-500M %	500M-2MM %	2-10MM %	10-50MM %	50-100MM %	100-250MM %		ALL %	ALL %
ASSETS									
Cash & Equivalents		17.7	14.1	11.7				11.7	11.8
Trade Receivables (net)		30.8	28.8	22.5				22.6	21.6
Inventory		6.8	8.7	13.6				8.8	8.4
All Other Current		3.3	4.4	7.6				5.2	5.9
Total Current		58.6	55.9	55.4				48.3	47.6
Fixed Assets (net)		34.7	34.1	36.1				39.7	42.4
Intangibles (net)		1.3	1.7	2.1				2.2	2.5
All Other Non-Current		5.3	8.3	6.3				9.8	7.5
Total		100.0	100.0	100.0				100.0	100.0
LIABILITIES									
Notes Payable-Short Term		3.4	5.5	6.7				9.4	7.1
Cur. Mat.-L.T.D.		4.4	5.2	4.1				6.1	5.2
Trade Payables		20.1	13.1	12.9				13.7	11.9
Income Taxes Payable		.4	.1	.1				.7	.5
All Other Current		5.6	7.8	9.0				5.7	8.5
Total Current		34.0	31.7	32.8				35.7	33.3
Long-Term Debt		20.3	14.8	16.7				14.8	25.2
Deferred Taxes		.0	.3	.1				1.4	1.5
All Other Non-Current		3.5	9.2	1.4				2.6	2.9
Net Worth		42.2	44.0	48.9				45.5	37.1
Total Liabilities & Net Worth		100.0	100.0	100.0				100.0	100.0
INCOME DATA									
Net Sales		100.0	100.0	100.0				100.0	100.0
Gross Profit		19.5	19.9	21.7				21.3	26.2
Operating Expenses		15.2	15.0	15.1				17.6	23.4
Operating Profit		4.3	4.9	6.6				3.6	2.8
All Other Expenses (net)		.4	1.0	1.0				.7	.9
Profit Before Taxes		3.9	3.9	5.6				2.9	1.9
RATIOS									
Current		3.1	3.7	3.2				2.1	2.5
		1.6	1.7	1.7				1.5	1.5
		1.1	1.0	1.2				.9	1.0
Quick		2.9	2.7	2.5				1.5	1.9
		1.4	(30) 1.6	1.0				1.0	1.1
		.9	.7	.6				.5	.6
Sales/Receivables		12 29.9	22 16.8	21 17.4				13 27.8	14 27.0
		27 13.5	36 10.0	37 9.8				36 10.2	44 8.2
		50 7.2	64 5.7	53 6.8				58 6.3	64 5.7
Cost of Sales/Inventory		0 UND	2 240.7	9 39.2				1 282.3	0 UND
		4 99.9	10 35.9	22 16.9				10 35.7	10 35.2
		21 17.2	29 12.7	36 10.2				30 12.2	31 11.7
Cost of Sales/Payables		9 40.8	6 58.3	14 25.8				11 32.1	11 33.8
		17 21.1	18 20.6	26 14.2				24 15.3	24 14.9
		40 9.2	37 10.0	43 8.6				52 7.0	41 9.0
Sales/Working Capital		6.8	4.2	5.5				7.5	5.7
		17.9	15.2	9.5				13.9	15.7
		72.8	163.2	33.9				-65.7	-208.8
EBIT/Interest		14.3	31.9	17.7				8.6	12.7
		(13) 3.9	(30) 4.7	(27) 4.9				(54) 4.5	(69) 3.7
		2.0	1.2	2.9				1.3	1.1
Net Profit + Depr., Dep., Amort./Cur. Mat. L/T/D								3.2	6.6
								(19) 1.5	(27) 2.0
								1.0	.9
Fixed/Worth		.3	.2	.4				.4	.5
		.7	1.0	.7				.9	.9
		2.3	2.4	1.4				1.6	2.9
Debt/Worth		.4	.2	.4				.5	.6
		1.9	1.2	1.2				1.2	1.3
		3.5	4.9	2.3				2.7	3.9
% Profit Before Taxes/Tangible Net Worth		64.3	51.3	41.8				31.1	30.0
		(14) 34.8	(27) 28.6	24.3				(59) 17.1	(70) 17.1
		9.2	12.8	11.1				4.9	3.4
% Profit Before Taxes/Total Assets		27.1	21.3	18.9				12.1	13.1
		9.0	11.0	10.3				5.8	6.2
		4.2	1.4	6.0				1.1	.5
Sales/Net Fixed Assets		18.1	19.4	8.6				10.0	9.9
		13.0	8.5	6.1				5.8	5.1
		5.3	3.3	3.6				2.9	2.8
Sales/Total Assets		6.1	3.4	2.6				2.8	2.9
		2.9	2.0	2.3				1.9	1.8
		2.2	1.6	1.8				1.3	1.3
% Depr., Dep., Amort./Sales		1.7	1.7	1.8				2.8	2.4
		(12) 2.6	(29) 2.7	(28) 3.2				(56) 3.7	(67) 3.5
		5.7	5.6	4.4				6.1	6.5
% Officers', Directors' Owners' Comp/Sales			.7					1.6	2.8
			(10) 1.7					(19) 2.8	(21) 5.3
			3.6					4.3	7.9
Net Sales ($)	7699M	59953M	525573M	1221752M	493945M	1282293M		1955895M	1768526M
Total Assets ($)	1777M	17020M	157510M	537065M	263509M	827194M		973660M	1090776M

M = $ thousand   MM = $ million
See Pages 11 through 21 for Explanation of Ratios and Data

Comparative Historical Data				Current Data Sorted by Sales					
			Type of Statement						
26	26	31	Unqualified	1	1	1	5	7	16
25	21	14	Reviewed		1		2	4	6
10	13	15	Compiled	3		1	2	4	4
7	2	8	Tax Returns	1	2	2	2	1	
18	22	23	Other	2	3	2	6	2	8
4/1/04-3/31/05 ALL	4/1/05-3/31/06 ALL	4/1/06-3/31/07 ALL			14 (4/1-9/30/06)		77 (10/1/06-3/31/07)		
				0-1MM	1-3MM	3-5MM	5-10MM	10-25MM	25MM & OVER
86	84	91	**NUMBER OF STATEMENTS**	7	7	8	17	18	34
%	%	%		%	%	%	%	%	%
			ASSETS						
14.2	10.2	12.8	Cash & Equivalents				11.0	11.9	13.2
22.8	24.4	26.9	Trade Receivables (net)				30.1	31.8	23.5
10.1	8.5	10.0	Inventory				9.3	9.4	11.7
4.5	5.5	4.8	All Other Current				2.9	2.3	6.9
51.6	48.8	54.6	Total Current				53.3	55.5	55.3
36.6	38.2	34.6	Fixed Assets (net)				35.6	36.4	33.8
1.6	4.1	3.0	Intangibles (net)				2.3	.6	4.8
10.2	8.9	7.8	All Other Non-Current				8.8	7.5	6.1
100.0	100.0	100.0	Total				100.0	100.0	100.0
			LIABILITIES						
9.2	5.5	5.3	Notes Payable-Short Term				6.5	8.4	3.6
5.2	4.4	4.7	Cur. Mat.-L.T.D.				6.7	5.0	3.3
13.9	15.2	15.3	Trade Payables				18.5	15.8	11.9
.5	.2	.2	Income Taxes Payable				.0	.0	.2
7.5	12.2	8.6	All Other Current				7.5	4.5	9.5
36.3	37.5	34.1	Total Current				39.2	33.7	28.5
21.4	20.7	16.2	Long-Term Debt				21.4	16.0	12.8
.8	.5	.5	Deferred Taxes				.2	.4	1.1
3.3	4.3	5.7	All Other Non-Current				5.7	7.0	2.0
38.2	36.9	43.5	Net Worth				33.5	42.8	55.7
100.0	100.0	100.0	Total Liabilities & Net Worth				100.0	100.0	100.0
			INCOME DATA						
100.0	100.0	100.0	Net Sales				100.0	100.0	100.0
24.7	20.4	20.5	Gross Profit				17.0	20.3	19.6
19.3	16.9	15.4	Operating Expenses				13.3	14.2	12.2
5.4	3.5	5.1	Operating Profit				3.7	6.1	7.4
.7	.8	.7	All Other Expenses (net)				2.1	.1	.6
4.7	2.7	4.4	Profit Before Taxes				1.7	6.0	6.8
			RATIOS						
2.8	2.6	3.1					3.1	3.2	3.2
1.5	1.3	1.7	Current				1.6	1.7	2.0
1.0	1.0	1.1					.9	.9	1.4
1.8	1.9	2.6					2.1	2.5	2.6
1.0	1.0 (90)	1.2	Quick				1.0	1.4	1.5
.7	.7	.7					.4	.6	.9
14 25.2	23 15.8	20 18.6					19 19.2	27 13.7	17 21.9
35 10.4	40 9.0	37 9.8	Sales/Receivables				38 9.7	41 9.0	41 8.8
58 6.2	59 6.2	54 6.8					67 5.5	53 6.9	54 6.8
2 166.3	0 999.8	2 166.9					0 UND	2 176.1	5 66.9
14 25.9	13 27.2	14 26.2	Cost of Sales/Inventory				13 27.8	13 28.2	15 24.4
32 11.5	25 14.6	33 11.1					30 12.3	32 11.5	35 10.4
10 37.7	14 26.2	11 33.1					11 34.1	18 20.0	13 28.1
28 13.0	26 13.9	23 16.1	Cost of Sales/Payables				37 10.0	31 11.8	22 16.4
46 7.9	44 8.2	41 9.0					63 5.8	46 8.0	34 10.8
5.5	6.6	5.9					3.8	5.9	6.6
13.9	20.4	13.5	Sales/Working Capital				15.2	19.1	9.6
133.6	572.6	97.4					-91.8	-69.2	17.9
20.5	9.0	17.8					12.7	36.6	27.0
(79) 5.1	(76) 3.4	(85) 4.9	EBIT/Interest				2.9	(17) 5.3	(31) 10.3
1.5	1.1	2.0					1.0	2.5	4.4
4.5	4.9	14.4							
(32) 3.2	(27) 2.1	(24) 3.2	Net Profit + Depr., Dep., Amort./Cur. Mat. L/T/D						
1.5	1.3	1.5							
.5	.5	.4					.6	.2	.4
.8	1.1	.9	Fixed/Worth				2.1	.9	.6
1.8	3.2	2.3					3.1	1.7	1.3
.7	.5	.4					1.0	.4	.3
1.3	2.0	1.3	Debt/Worth				3.4	1.2	1.0
3.3	5.1	3.8					20.0	3.1	1.8
41.2	34.0	51.3					99.5	50.6	52.2
(78) 22.4	(75) 14.3	(81) 28.3	% Profit Before Taxes/Tangible Net Worth			(15) 13.8		(17) 34.6	(33) 30.3
7.7	2.4	12.3					3.1	10.7	17.9
19.3	10.7	21.3					16.5	27.9	21.4
9.1	5.1	10.8	% Profit Before Taxes/Total Assets				4.7	11.7	13.8
1.3	.2	3.5					.1	4.5	8.8
11.1	12.3	14.7					17.3	20.2	10.2
6.3	6.1	6.4	Sales/Net Fixed Assets				5.6	6.2	6.3
4.1	3.8	3.6					2.0	3.5	4.2
3.0	2.9	3.1					3.1	3.5	2.9
2.4	2.3	2.2	Sales/Total Assets				1.9	2.0	2.3
1.5	1.7	1.8					1.0	1.7	1.8
2.0	1.5	1.9					1.9	1.8	1.8
(82) 3.2	(76) 2.7	(81) 2.8	% Depr., Dep., Amort./Sales			(16) 3.1		(17) 3.1	(32) 2.6
4.8	4.5	4.6					7.7	5.1	3.9
1.3	1.7	1.0						.9	
(31) 2.5	(26) 3.0	(27) 3.2	% Officers', Directors' Owners' Comp/Sales					(10) 1.7	
4.8	6.0	4.8						3.6	
2233839M	3097679M	3591215M	Net Sales ($)	4653M	12937M	31875M	120215M	274724M	3146811M
1224376M	1710990M	1804075M	Total Assets ($)	8509M	6717M	11149M	90587M	134510M	1552603M

© RMA 2007

M = $ thousand   MM = $ million
See Pages 11 through 21 for Explanation of Ratios and Data

Current Data Sorted by Assets   Comparative Historical Data

Type of Statement

	0-500M	500M-2MM	2-10MM	10-50MM	50-100MM	100-250MM		4/1/02-3/31/03 ALL	4/1/03-3/31/04 ALL
Unqualified		1	1	5	1	2		19	12
Reviewed		1	5	5				17	12
Compiled		1	2	1				7	7
Tax Returns		1	3		1			1	3
Other	3	4	9	3		1		11	14
		10 (4/1-9/30/06)		38 (10/1/06-3/31/07)					
NUMBER OF STATEMENTS	9	9	12	20	4	3		55	48

Note: For the 0-500M and 500M-2MM columns the center of the page is marked vertically "DATA NOT AVAILABLE."

	2-10MM %	10-50MM %		4/1/02-3/31/03 ALL %	4/1/03-3/31/04 ALL %
ASSETS					
Cash & Equivalents	5.2	9.0		7.9	6.6
Trade Receivables (net)	36.8	24.8		26.2	29.6
Inventory	29.9	29.0		24.4	22.9
All Other Current	2.3	2.9		1.9	2.3
Total Current	74.2	65.6		60.3	61.4
Fixed Assets (net)	16.7	25.0		27.5	30.8
Intangibles (net)	5.3	4.5		3.9	2.2
All Other Non-Current	3.7	4.9		8.3	5.5
Total	100.0	100.0		100.0	100.0
LIABILITIES					
Notes Payable-Short Term	12.9	10.5		9.4	9.3
Cur. Mat.-L.T.D.	2.7	2.5		3.2	4.0
Trade Payables	26.7	13.6		15.9	21.1
Income Taxes Payable	.1	.4		.4	.1
All Other Current	9.3	8.2		10.4	6.7
Total Current	51.7	35.1		39.3	41.2
Long-Term Debt	11.9	10.6		12.2	17.2
Deferred Taxes	.4	.6		1.0	.7
All Other Non-Current	1.0	11.3		4.8	10.8
Net Worth	35.0	42.4		42.7	30.1
Total Liabilties & Net Worth	100.0	100.0		100.0	100.0
INCOME DATA					
Net Sales	100.0	100.0		100.0	100.0
Gross Profit	31.0	33.7		34.3	36.7
Operating Expenses	26.1	26.6		28.3	33.6
Operating Profit	4.9	7.1		5.9	3.1
All Other Expenses (net)	2.5	.9		.7	.6
Profit Before Taxes	2.4	6.3		5.2	2.5

RATIOS

	2-10MM	10-50MM		4/1/02-3/31/03 ALL	4/1/03-3/31/04 ALL
Current	2.2	3.7		2.7	2.7
	1.2	2.2		1.5	1.5
	1.1	1.2		1.1	1.1
Quick	1.2	1.5		1.4	1.5
	.7	1.2		.9	.8
	.6	.5		.5	.5
Sales/Receivables	23 15.6	34 10.8		31 12.0	32 11.3
	50 7.4	44 8.2		45 8.1	45 8.0
	57 6.4	53 6.8		59 6.2	55 6.6
Cost of Sales/Inventory	24 14.9	46 7.9		34 10.7	32 11.2
	59 6.2	78 4.7		62 5.9	50 7.3
	93 3.9	100 3.6		73 5.0	75 4.9
Cost of Sales/Payables	22 16.8	19 19.2		23 16.2	24 15.1
	34 10.6	33 11.1		35 10.5	35 10.4
	51 7.2	42 8.6		53 6.9	56 6.5
Sales/Working Capital	8.3	3.9		6.1	6.2
	23.0	5.5		12.2	12.1
	53.2	20.7		62.7	73.3
EBIT/Interest	11.2	15.0		17.8	13.4
	(11) 5.4	(18) 4.0		(49) 6.8	(45) 4.0
	1.6	2.0		2.0	.1
Net Profit + Depr., Dep., Amort./Cur. Mat. L/T/D				8.1	6.0
				(17) 5.7	(14) 2.2
				1.3	1.0
Fixed/Worth	.1	.3		.3	.4
	.4	.4		.6	1.0
	2.1	1.1		1.7	2.0
Debt/Worth	.8	.8		.6	.9
	2.5	1.7		1.5	1.8
	12.3	2.8		3.9	6.3
% Profit Before Taxes/Tangible Net Worth	80.7	51.4		43.1	48.4
	(11) 13.4	(18) 22.9		(52) 19.8	(42) 16.2
	7.7	15.2		4.7	-1.2
% Profit Before Taxes/Total Assets	10.5	19.6		19.8	14.4
	4.5	9.7		9.1	5.3
	1.5	4.2		2.2	-1.3
Sales/Net Fixed Assets	84.5	16.6		18.4	17.6
	27.5	8.6		10.6	8.5
	9.2	6.0		4.5	4.8
Sales/Total Assets	4.0	3.2		3.1	3.4
	3.1	2.0		2.2	2.6
	1.9	1.4		1.5	1.8
% Depr., Dep., Amort./Sales	.2	.8		.9	.8
	(11) .7	(19) 1.9		(52) 1.9	(39) 1.8
	2.4	2.4		2.8	2.9
% Officers', Directors' Owners' Comp/Sales				2.0	2.6
				(17) 3.2	(13) 7.9
				4.9	12.9

	0-500M	500M-2MM	2-10MM	10-50MM	50-100MM	100-250MM		4/1/02-3/31/03 ALL	4/1/03-3/31/04 ALL
Net Sales ($)		29213M	223793M	1040850M	681692M	687382M		1609820M	1140462M
Total Assets ($)		9567M	62018M	467489M	316064M	386562M		929386M	536392M

M = $ thousand   MM = $ million
See Pages 11 through 21 for Explanation of Ratios and Data

Comparative Historical Data | Current Data Sorted by Sales

4/1/04-3/31/05 ALL	4/1/05-3/31/06 ALL	4/1/06-3/31/07 ALL	Type of Statement	0-1MM	1-3MM	3-5MM	5-10MM	10-25MM	25MM & OVER
13	13	10	Unqualified	1				1	8
18	13	11	Reviewed				2	4	5
5	3	4	Compiled			1	1	1	1
3	2	3	Tax Returns		3				
17	24	20	Other		1	1	4	2	12
				10 (4/1-9/30/06)			38 (10/1/06-3/31/07)		
56	55	48	NUMBER OF STATEMENTS	1	4	2	7	8	26
%	%	%	ASSETS	%	%	%	%	%	%
7.9	11.1	8.0	Cash & Equivalents						7.0
29.1	29.2	30.3	Trade Receivables (net)						27.7
24.3	24.1	28.3	Inventory						28.6
1.2	1.9	1.9	All Other Current						2.4
62.6	66.2	68.5	Total Current						65.7
26.6	23.5	21.2	Fixed Assets (net)						21.9
3.3	4.8	5.8	Intangibles (net)						7.7
7.5	5.6	4.4	All Other Non-Current						4.7
100.0	100.0	100.0	Total						100.0
			LIABILITIES						
12.8	9.2	8.9	Notes Payable-Short Term						8.9
3.5	3.4	3.5	Cur. Mat.-L.T.D.						3.4
17.4	19.2	19.7	Trade Payables						16.8
.2	.5	.4	Income Taxes Payable						.6
5.9	7.4	9.6	All Other Current						9.1
39.9	39.8	42.1	Total Current						38.8
14.1	13.5	12.7	Long-Term Debt						14.0
1.2	.9	.7	Deferred Taxes						1.0
8.7	8.3	7.2	All Other Non-Current						5.8
36.1	37.5	37.4	Net Worth						40.5
100.0	100.0	100.0	Total Liabilities & Net Worth						100.0
			INCOME DATA						
100.0	100.0	100.0	Net Sales						100.0
31.1	31.7	32.9	Gross Profit						31.3
26.0	26.6	27.6	Operating Expenses						23.9
5.1	5.0	5.3	Operating Profit						7.4
.8	.7	1.0	All Other Expenses (net)						.3
4.3	4.3	4.3	Profit Before Taxes						7.1
			RATIOS						
2.6	2.4	2.9	Current						2.7
1.6	1.6	1.9							2.0
1.1	1.2	1.1							1.1
1.5	1.4	1.4	Quick						1.4
.9	.9	1.0							1.1
.5	.5	.6							.5
34 10.7	34 10.7	36 10.2	Sales/Receivables						33 11.1
42 8.6	44 8.3	47 7.8							45 8.2
53 6.8	52 7.0	55 6.7							53 6.9
25 14.8	27 13.7	42 8.8	Cost of Sales/Inventory						44 8.4
54 6.7	48 7.6	66 5.6							66 5.5
85 4.3	78 4.7	93 3.9							79 4.6
19 19.6	26 13.9	21 17.3	Cost of Sales/Payables						21 17.6
29 12.5	32 11.5	37 9.9							27 13.4
49 7.4	46 7.9	47 7.8							40 9.2
4.9	5.5	4.2	Sales/Working Capital						4.7
11.5	10.5	9.4							8.1
35.6	44.9	53.2							118.9
20.0	8.1	13.2	EBIT/Interest						18.4
(54) 4.5	(49) 3.8	(43) 4.0							(24) 5.7
1.5	1.6	2.0							2.5
7.7	7.3	9.4	Net Profit + Depr., Dep., Amort./Cur. Mat. L/T/D						21.4
(17) 2.2	(15) 3.1	(18) 4.9							(11) 7.5
1.1	1.3	1.6							2.0
.4	.3	.3	Fixed/Worth						.3
.9	.6	.5							.6
1.8	1.9	1.9							1.5
.8	.8	.8	Debt/Worth						.8
2.5	2.1	1.7							1.7
4.6	5.6	4.3							4.0
51.1	52.7	51.4	% Profit Before Taxes/Tangible Net Worth						59.4
(51) 23.4	(50) 18.2	(42) 23.2							(23) 29.2
7.3	4.1	13.0							21.6
17.5	16.7	17.1	% Profit Before Taxes/Total Assets						20.4
6.7	5.4	7.1							10.1
1.8	2.3	2.6							4.7
23.0	25.1	32.1	Sales/Net Fixed Assets						17.9
10.1	12.7	14.7							8.8
5.0	7.1	6.4							6.3
3.3	3.5	3.4	Sales/Total Assets						3.3
2.4	2.2	2.2							2.1
1.7	1.6	1.6							1.5
.9	.7	.5	% Depr., Dep., Amort./Sales						1.0
(53) 1.6	(51) 1.7	(44) 1.3							(25) 1.7
2.7	2.4	2.4							2.3
1.6	1.6	1.6	% Officers', Directors' Owners' Comp/Sales						
(16) 3.1	(14) 2.8	(15) 3.9							
7.3	5.9	9.0							
2597041M	3024968M	2662930M	Net Sales ($)	271M	8534M	8067M	48731M	135092M	2462235M
1290606M	1402577M	1241700M	Total Assets ($)	604M	3376M	2575M	19003M	68969M	1147173M

© RMA 2007

M = $ thousand   MM = $ million
See Pages 11 through 21 for Explanation of Ratios and Data

Current Data Sorted by Assets   Comparative Historical Data

		2				Type of Statement		
	2	1	3	3		Unqualified	6	8
	1	2				Reviewed	4	2
	1	2				Compiled	2	12
1	1	6	4	1	1	Tax Returns	1	
	5 (4/1-9/30/06)		26 (10/1/06-3/31/07)			Other	6	8
							4/1/02-3/31/03	4/1/03-3/31/04
0-500M	500M-2MM	2-10MM	10-50MM	50-100MM	100-250MM		ALL	ALL
1	5	13	7	4	1	NUMBER OF STATEMENTS	19	30
%	%	%	%	%	%	ASSETS	%	%
		19.0				Cash & Equivalents	12.3	10.7
		33.0				Trade Receivables (net)	19.7	32.5
		21.3				Inventory	17.1	17.9
		3.8				All Other Current	3.2	2.2
		77.2				Total Current	52.3	63.4
		15.2				Fixed Assets (net)	33.6	27.6
		2.2				Intangibles (net)	2.3	3.0
		5.4				All Other Non-Current	11.8	6.1
		100.0				Total	100.0	100.0
						LIABILITIES		
		7.5				Notes Payable-Short Term	11.0	12.4
		1.7				Cur. Mat.-L.T.D.	4.4	4.9
		26.4				Trade Payables	12.5	21.2
		.2				Income Taxes Payable	.1	.2
		7.9				All Other Current	10.0	7.0
		43.8				Total Current	37.9	45.6
		21.3				Long-Term Debt	18.8	16.2
		.4				Deferred Taxes	.8	.6
		.2				All Other Non-Current	5.4	10.8
		34.3				Net Worth	37.2	26.9
		100.0				Total Liabilties & Net Worth	100.0	100.0
						INCOME DATA		
		100.0				Net Sales	100.0	100.0
		33.8				Gross Profit	21.4	27.2
		18.9				Operating Expenses	17.4	25.3
		14.9				Operating Profit	4.0	1.9
		1.5				All Other Expenses (net)	2.7	.6
		13.4				Profit Before Taxes	1.3	1.3
						RATIOS		
		4.6				Current	2.4	2.5
		1.9					1.3	1.7
		1.1					.8	1.0
		2.7				Quick	1.8	1.8
		1.5					.8	1.1
		.8					.3	.5
		29 12.7				Sales/Receivables	23 15.7	28 13.1
		42 8.7					40 9.2	46 7.9
		93 3.9					53 6.8	63 5.8
		2 213.3				Cost of Sales/Inventory	15 25.0	9 39.6
		33 11.1					46 7.9	34 10.6
		55 6.6					74 4.9	62 5.9
		0 UND				Cost of Sales/Payables	13 27.4	16 22.8
		26 13.9					38 9.7	41 8.9
		59 6.2					49 7.5	54 6.8
		1.4				Sales/Working Capital	5.9	6.7
		5.2					23.3	14.1
		195.4					-24.1	NM
						EBIT/Interest	6.5	12.4
							(13) 1.9	(23) 4.1
							.7	.9
						Net Profit + Depr., Dep., Amort./Cur. Mat. L/T/D		
		.1				Fixed/Worth	.2	.2
		.4					1.0	.9
		UND					3.1	2.8
		.7				Debt/Worth	.4	.8
		1.9					1.6	1.9
		UND					5.8	5.8
		81.3				% Profit Before Taxes/Tangible Net Worth	20.4	56.5
		(11) 37.8					(15) 11.6	(25) 14.2
		10.8					1.4	-3.3
		21.8				% Profit Before Taxes/Total Assets	14.5	13.2
		10.2					3.2	3.9
		2.0					-1.4	-2.9
		298.3				Sales/Net Fixed Assets	16.2	32.6
		22.1					6.7	11.6
		3.8					2.4	5.2
		4.0				Sales/Total Assets	2.8	3.3
		2.3					1.9	2.6
		.7					1.1	1.8
						% Depr., Dep., Amort./Sales	1.1	.8
							(16) 3.5	(25) 1.5
							6.4	4.1
						% Officers', Directors' Owners' Comp/Sales		
941M	19140M	169477M	734609M	897065M	421671M	Net Sales ($)	784244M	1268522M
169M	7393M	67069M	130422M	260366M	116725M	Total Assets ($)	619015M	723693M

© RMA 2007

M = $ thousand   MM = $ million
See Pages 11 through 21 for Explanation of Ratios and Data

Comparative Historical Data					Type of Statement	Current Data Sorted by Sales					
	7		6		8	Unqualified	1			1	1	7
	2		3		3	Reviewed			1	1	1	
	5		3		3	Compiled		1		1	1	
					3	Tax Returns		2			1	
	8		11		14	Other	1	1	1	2	5	4
	4/1/04-		4/1/05-		4/1/06-			5 (4/1-9/30/06)		26 (10/1/06-3/31/07)		
	3/31/05		3/31/06		3/31/07							
	ALL		ALL		ALL		0-1MM	1-3MM	3-5MM	5-10MM	10-25MM	25MM & OVER
	22		23		31	NUMBER OF STATEMENTS	2	4	2	4	8	11
	%		%		%	ASSETS	%	%	%	%	%	%
	8.5		6.8		12.8	Cash & Equivalents						7.4
	29.0		31.9		28.7	Trade Receivables (net)						30.3
	21.4		19.3		18.3	Inventory						14.7
	.7		4.5		4.3	All Other Current						7.4
	59.7		62.4		64.1	Total Current						59.8
	30.6		26.9		29.0	Fixed Assets (net)						33.6
	3.2		3.8		1.6	Intangibles (net)						.3
	6.5		6.9		5.2	All Other Non-Current						6.3
	100.0		100.0		100.0	Total						100.0
						LIABILITIES						
	9.4		5.5		9.7	Notes Payable-Short Term						11.5
	3.9		4.6		2.2	Cur. Mat.-L.T.D.						3.2
	19.6		15.8		20.6	Trade Payables						25.2
	.2		.9		.3	Income Taxes Payable						.6
	8.4		7.4		7.1	All Other Current						6.4
	41.5		34.2		39.9	Total Current						46.8
	13.7		18.4		20.3	Long-Term Debt						13.8
	1.8		1.5		.4	Deferred Taxes						.6
	10.3		7.4		2.6	All Other Non-Current						3.2
	32.8		38.5		36.9	Net Worth						35.7
	100.0		100.0		100.0	Total Liabilties & Net Worth						100.0
						INCOME DATA						
	100.0		100.0		100.0	Net Sales						100.0
	18.1		22.9		25.0	Gross Profit						11.9
	13.2		13.3		15.4	Operating Expenses						7.9
	4.9		9.6		9.6	Operating Profit						4.0
	.2		.6		.8	All Other Expenses (net)						.3
	4.8		8.9		8.8	Profit Before Taxes						3.7
						RATIOS						
	2.2		3.1		3.5							2.3
	1.4		1.9		1.6	Current						1.1
	.9		1.4		1.1							1.0
	1.7		1.9		2.7							1.1
	.8		1.1		1.0	Quick						.6
	.5		.8		.5							.4
28	13.0	26	14.0	22	16.4						9	40.0
40	9.2	43	8.4	35	10.4	Sales/Receivables					25	14.8
56	6.5	67	5.4	59	6.2						41	9.0
22	16.3	24	15.4	4	86.5						1	340.1
41	9.0	46	8.0	29	12.8	Cost of Sales/Inventory					20	18.5
62	5.9	69	5.3	53	6.9						31	11.7
15	25.1	12	29.8	7	54.0						11	32.8
30	12.0	25	14.4	21	17.0	Cost of Sales/Payables					17	21.9
63	5.8	49	7.4	39	9.3						32	11.4
	5.5		4.9		5.2							21.6
	20.1		7.6		15.4	Sales/Working Capital						53.1
	-111.4		27.0		343.2							353.9
	23.0		55.9		23.6							48.4
(19)	8.5	(22)	12.8	(26)	8.1	EBIT/Interest						5.9
	2.7		2.6		2.8							2.9
			40.3			Net Profit + Depr., Dep.,						
		(10)	7.4			Amort./Cur. Mat. L/T/D						
			2.3									
	.2		.3		.4							.4
	1.0		.8		.5	Fixed/Worth						.7
	1.9		1.5		2.4							2.3
	1.0		.8		1.0							1.0
	2.6		2.1		1.8	Debt/Worth						2.4
	4.1		5.7		5.7							5.4
	79.6		77.5		68.9	% Profit Before Taxes/Tangible						67.2
(20)	21.2	(22)	30.8	(28)	47.3	Net Worth						45.4
	8.1		13.6		19.4							21.0
	18.1		24.8		21.7	% Profit Before Taxes/Total						21.5
	6.9		12.1		10.5	Assets						14.3
	2.1		3.3		3.1							8.9
	40.5		31.1		25.1							75.4
	6.8		8.3		9.4	Sales/Net Fixed Assets						11.6
	3.1		4.2		4.3							5.1
	3.8		3.3		4.0							5.3
	2.2		2.2		2.8	Sales/Total Assets						3.6
	1.2		1.3		1.7							2.5
	.7		.6		.7							.5
(20)	1.1	(18)	1.7	(25)	1.2	% Depr., Dep., Amort./Sales					(10)	1.1
	3.7		3.7		2.9							1.8
						% Officers', Directors'						
						Owners' Comp/Sales						
	2106343M		2559386M		2242903M	Net Sales ($)	1462M	7941M	6611M	28758M	155584M	2042547M
	949706M		1079498M		582144M	Total Assets ($)	2794M	7886M	8780M	12826M	69084M	480774M

© RMA 2007

M = $ thousand   MM = $ million
See Pages 11 through 21 for Explanation of Ratios and Data

Current Data Sorted by Assets / Comparative Historical Data

Type of Statement	0-500M	500M-2MM	2-10MM	10-50MM	50-100MM	100-250MM	4/1/02-3/31/03 ALL	4/1/03-3/31/04 ALL
Unqualified			2	16	5	11	27	34
Reviewed	1	4	17	5			12	15
Compiled	1	4	3	1			4	17
Tax Returns	1	5	1				5	7
Other	3		9	11	2	6	27	20

Asset-size ranges: 18 (4/1-9/30/06), 90 (10/1/06-3/31/07)

	0-500M	500M-2MM	2-10MM	10-50MM	50-100MM	100-250MM		4/1/02-3/31/03 ALL	4/1/03-3/31/04 ALL
NUMBER OF STATEMENTS	6	13	32	33	7	17		75	93
	%	%	%	%	%	%	**ASSETS**	%	%
		9.2	6.9	7.3		3.8	Cash & Equivalents	8.5	5.9
		28.2	30.2	20.9		17.9	Trade Receivables (net)	23.5	26.7
		24.5	26.5	15.6		18.5	Inventory	18.5	21.6
		.4	1.5	4.4		3.0	All Other Current	2.2	3.2
		62.3	65.1	48.1		43.3	Total Current	52.8	57.4
		29.7	24.2	44.6		46.0	Fixed Assets (net)	35.1	30.9
		1.2	5.2	3.4		6.2	Intangibles (net)	5.9	2.9
		6.8	5.5	3.9		4.5	All Other Non-Current	6.2	8.8
		100.0	100.0	100.0		100.0	Total	100.0	100.0
							LIABILITIES		
		18.5	9.8	4.1		3.3	Notes Payable-Short Term	6.5	11.8
		5.4	2.8	3.5		4.2	Cur. Mat.-L.T.D.	4.5	4.5
		18.1	19.3	10.8		11.1	Trade Payables	15.7	18.9
		.3	.3	.4		.1	Income Taxes Payable	.2	.2
		6.6	7.7	11.9		8.1	All Other Current	10.2	12.4
		48.9	39.9	30.7		26.8	Total Current	37.2	47.7
		25.9	21.9	17.9		28.5	Long-Term Debt	18.7	14.3
		.0	.3	2.3		1.0	Deferred Taxes	.8	.8
		9.4	6.3	3.8		7.0	All Other Non-Current	5.3	8.2
		15.9	31.5	45.4		36.7	Net Worth	38.0	29.0
		100.0	100.0	100.0		100.0	Total Liabilities & Net Worth	100.0	100.0
							INCOME DATA		
		100.0	100.0	100.0		100.0	Net Sales	100.0	100.0
		35.6	30.8	34.8		24.5	Gross Profit	35.1	34.5
		38.2	23.4	24.4		13.9	Operating Expenses	28.8	30.2
		-2.6	7.4	10.4		10.6	Operating Profit	6.3	4.2
		4.1	2.3	1.2		3.3	All Other Expenses (net)	1.5	1.2
		-6.7	5.1	9.2		7.3	Profit Before Taxes	4.7	3.0
							RATIOS		
		1.7	2.7	2.9		2.3		2.2	2.0
		1.2	1.6	2.1		1.8	Current	1.5	1.3
		.9	1.2	1.2		1.4		1.0	.8
		1.2	1.6	1.5		1.5		1.4	1.1
		.7	1.0	1.1		.8	Quick	.9	.7
		.4	.7	.6		.6		.5	.5
		31 11.9	33 11.2	30 12.3		37 9.9		33 11.2	34 10.7
		41 8.9	40 9.2	38 9.5		48 7.6	Sales/Receivables	44 8.3	45 8.1
		49 7.5	54 6.7	61 6.0		56 6.5		54 6.8	56 6.5
		19 19.1	22 16.8	28 13.0		43 8.5		29 12.7	27 13.3
		52 7.1	42 8.7	47 7.7		60 6.1	Cost of Sales/Inventory	53 6.8	45 8.1
		71 5.2	69 5.3	75 4.9		114 3.2		93 3.9	85 4.3
		18 20.8	11 33.4	19 19.6		24 15.5		27 13.5	29 12.7
		26 14.0	29 12.4	33 11.1		35 10.4	Cost of Sales/Payables	43 8.6	38 9.5
		67 5.5	52 7.1	55 6.6		44 8.3		64 5.7	60 6.1
		11.1	6.0	4.3		5.6		6.0	6.8
		30.6	12.4	7.7		8.8	Sales/Working Capital	11.2	17.1
		-94.1	28.1	38.1		12.0		165.9	-24.6
		2.7	13.4	36.5		11.7		10.9	9.4
		(11) .6	5.8	(32) 6.9		2.4	EBIT/Interest	(72) 4.5	(85) 3.2
		-2.4	1.9	2.7		1.0		1.3	1.3
				7.4				5.8	3.1
				(17) 4.7			Net Profit + Depr., Dep., Amort./Cur. Mat. L/T/D	(30) 1.8	(27) 2.1
				1.8				.8	1.5
		.2	.2	.5		1.2		.5	.3
		3.2	.6	1.0		1.8	Fixed/Worth	.9	.8
		-3.3	4.1	2.7		3.1		2.5	3.0
		1.0	.8	.5		1.1		.7	.9
		6.3	1.6	1.0		2.6	Debt/Worth	1.5	2.2
		-6.2	18.4	3.1		6.3		3.9	6.9
			85.5	45.0		44.1		34.1	32.4
		(26)	29.0	(31) 25.7		(15) 15.2	% Profit Before Taxes/Tangible Net Worth	(65) 20.7	(82) 11.4
			10.8	15.1		.6		3.0	2.8
		6.7	20.7	23.6		15.2		14.1	10.2
		-1.8	11.0	11.8		4.8	% Profit Before Taxes/Total Assets	7.4	4.8
		-9.7	3.5	6.0		-.1		.5	.6
		103.4	55.4	6.1		4.5		11.2	27.6
		13.5	16.5	3.7		2.8	Sales/Net Fixed Assets	4.8	7.6
		4.9	6.3	2.4		1.6		2.7	3.2
		4.1	3.4	2.4		1.8		2.6	2.8
		2.6	2.6	1.5		1.2	Sales/Total Assets	1.6	1.9
		2.1	1.8	1.1		.9		1.1	1.3
		.7	.2	2.6				1.6	1.2
		(11) 1.4	(26) 1.2	(31) 3.9			% Depr., Dep., Amort./Sales	(67) 3.1	(80) 2.5
		5.9	3.2	5.6				4.8	4.5
								2.6	2.1
							% Officers', Directors' Owners' Comp/Sales	(18) 7.5	(25) 6.0
								19.2	14.2
	5301M	40871M	425831M	1152317M	774779M	4253396M	Net Sales ($)	2663219M	2889584M
	1471M	14456M	160482M	671770M	534888M	3159153M	Total Assets ($)	1906124M	1973033M

M = $ thousand   MM = $ million
See Pages 11 through 21 for Explanation of Ratios and Data

Comparative Historical Data   Current Data Sorted by Sales

Type of Statement

	4/1/04-3/31/05 ALL	4/1/05-3/31/06 ALL	4/1/06-3/31/07 ALL	0-1MM	1-3MM	3-5MM	5-10MM	10-25MM	25MM & OVER
Unqualified	33	24	34				1	5	28
Reviewed	21	19	27		3	3	7	11	3
Compiled	7	11	9	1	3	1	2	1	1
Tax Returns	8	5	7	1	4	1	1		1
Other	17	31	31	2	1	2	3		16
					18 (4/1-9/30/06)		90 (10/1/06-3/31/07)		
NUMBER OF STATEMENTS	86	90	108	4	11	7	14	24	48

ASSETS (%)

	Hist 1	Hist 2	Hist 3	0-1MM	1-3MM	3-5MM	5-10MM	10-25MM	25MM & OVER
Cash & Equivalents	5.6	7.3	7.0		10.8		5.9	5.0	6.8
Trade Receivables (net)	27.6	28.2	25.3		31.0		32.9	24.8	22.6
Inventory	18.9	19.8	21.0		20.9		30.0	22.0	18.6
All Other Current	1.3	2.3	2.7		1.2		1.2	2.4	3.8
Total Current	53.4	57.6	56.0		63.9		70.0	54.2	51.8
Fixed Assets (net)	36.9	32.0	35.0		31.0		19.2	36.3	39.5
Intangibles (net)	2.8	4.1	4.0		.3		8.0	3.5	4.2
All Other Non-Current	6.8	6.3	5.0		4.8		2.7	6.0	4.6
Total	100.0	100.0	100.0		100.0		100.0	100.0	100.0

LIABILITIES

	Hist 1	Hist 2	Hist 3	0-1MM	1-3MM	3-5MM	5-10MM	10-25MM	25MM & OVER
Notes Payable-Short Term	11.7	9.7	7.2		10.1		12.6	7.5	4.9
Cur. Mat.-L.T.D.	4.3	3.2	3.8		5.5		3.4	2.8	3.5
Trade Payables	17.0	16.5	15.1		18.0		18.2	14.9	13.1
Income Taxes Payable	.1	.1	.4		.1		.6	.3	.4
All Other Current	7.0	7.0	9.6		13.4		5.8	6.3	12.0
Total Current	40.1	36.6	36.0		47.1		40.6	31.8	33.8
Long-Term Debt	20.5	15.6	21.8		39.8		16.7	18.3	18.1
Deferred Taxes	1.3	1.0	1.0		.0		.1	1.6	1.3
All Other Non-Current	5.1	3.9	6.5		4.9		4.2	5.1	6.6
Net Worth	33.1	43.0	34.7		8.2		38.4	43.3	40.3
Total Liabilities & Net Worth	100.0	100.0	100.0		100.0		100.0	100.0	100.0

INCOME DATA

	Hist 1	Hist 2	Hist 3	0-1MM	1-3MM	3-5MM	5-10MM	10-25MM	25MM & OVER
Net Sales	100.0	100.0	100.0		100.0		100.0	100.0	100.0
Gross Profit	34.9	33.3	32.8		39.6		30.9	34.2	27.2
Operating Expenses	28.5	26.0	24.8		35.9		22.3	26.8	16.5
Operating Profit	6.4	7.4	8.0		3.8		8.6	7.4	10.7
All Other Expenses (net)	1.4	1.3	2.1		3.1		.6	1.1	2.1
Profit Before Taxes	5.1	6.0	5.9		.6		8.0	6.3	8.6

RATIOS

Ratio	Hist 1	Hist 2	Hist 3	0-1MM	1-3MM	3-5MM	5-10MM	10-25MM	25MM & OVER
Current	1.9	2.7	2.5		1.8		3.1	2.6	2.4
	1.4	1.7	1.7		1.3		1.7	2.0	1.8
	.9	1.1	1.2		1.0		1.3	1.2	1.3
Quick	1.1	1.6	1.5		1.5		1.7	1.5	1.5
	.8	1.0	.9		.8		1.3	1.1	.9
	.5	.7	.6		.6		.8	.6	.6
Sales/Receivables	34 10.8	36 10.1	32 11.4		35 10.4		27 13.7	34 10.7	29 12.4
	45 8.1	47 7.7	41 8.8		41 8.9		40 9.2	46 8.0	41 8.9
	62 5.9	61 6.0	57 6.4		47 7.7		83 4.4	61 6.0	56 6.5
Cost of Sales/Inventory	23 16.2	24 15.0	28 12.8		17 21.2		30 12.1	33 11.0	30 12.2
	42 8.7	45 8.0	52 7.1		31 11.9		59 6.2	66 5.5	46 7.9
	80 4.6	88 4.2	73 5.0		63 5.8		73 5.0	82 4.4	64 5.7
Cost of Sales/Payables	28 13.1	22 16.6	19 19.4		16 23.1		15 24.3	21 17.0	19 19.3
	42 8.6	39 9.3	33 11.0		23 15.6		23 15.9	41 9.0	35 10.4
	61 6.0	58 6.3	55 6.6		63 5.8		54 6.8	66 5.5	46 8.0
Sales/Working Capital	7.5	5.6	6.1		9.5		5.7	4.2	6.1
	13.4	9.4	10.2		13.3		10.2	8.3	9.0
	-62.0	62.3	31.5		-162.0		14.6	28.0	26.0
EBIT/Interest	12.8	20.6	15.8				24.1	7.8	36.1
	(80) 3.8	(80) 6.9	(104) 5.5				6.4	(47) 5.7	6.7
	1.5	2.1	1.7				3.9	3.7	2.2
Net Profit + Depr., Dep., Amort./Cur. Mat. L/T/D	3.4	5.2	7.7					5.3	11.7
	(29) 2.2	(22) 2.7	(31) 4.7					(10) 4.3	(18) 6.6
	1.2	1.4	2.2					2.3	1.9
Fixed/Worth	.5	.3	.4		.6		.1	.4	.5
	1.1	.8	1.0		3.6		.5	.9	1.2
	2.8	1.8	3.3		-.2		1.6	3.2	2.1
Debt/Worth	1.1	.6	.8		2.0		.8	.7	.8
	1.9	1.3	1.9		7.3		1.5	1.2	1.9
	4.1	3.6	6.5		-5.9		27.9	3.8	3.4
% Profit Before Taxes/Tangible Net Worth	39.9	44.2	55.3				90.9	37.6	64.4
	(76) 20.5	(82) 21.7	(92) 24.2				(12) 17.4	(22) 23.9	(44) 24.4
	7.6	8.6	10.3				9.9	11.2	11.5
% Profit Before Taxes/Total Assets	16.7	19.5	19.3		11.5		21.8	16.2	26.6
	6.7	9.2	9.5		3.2		10.1	9.9	10.1
	1.9	2.3	1.8		-4.8		6.3	3.5	3.0
Sales/Net Fixed Assets	17.7	22.2	16.8		33.2		214.6	19.2	8.3
	5.4	6.1	5.7		14.0		15.3	3.7	4.4
	2.3	3.1	2.9		5.3		5.6	2.4	2.2
Sales/Total Assets	3.3	3.2	2.8		4.0		3.1	2.6	2.5
	1.9	1.8	1.9		2.7		2.6	1.6	1.7
	1.1	1.2	1.3		2.3		1.7	1.1	1.2
% Depr., Dep., Amort./Sales	1.6	1.3	1.2		.8		.3	1.2	2.0
	(74) 3.5	(73) 3.0	(87) 2.8		(10) 1.5		(11) 2.4	(21) 3.2	(37) 3.1
	5.2	5.1	4.7		3.0		3.3	6.0	4.6
% Officers', Directors', Owners' Comp/Sales	1.7	1.7	1.5						
	(23) 4.4	(22) 2.7	(19) 2.7						
	10.0	5.8	6.5						
Net Sales ($)	3562200M	4242876M	6652495M	1255M	21130M	28217M	107522M	389645M	6104726M
Total Assets ($)	2571440M	3144846M	4542220M	1665M	12153M	20839M	56299M	259148M	4192116M

M = $ thousand   MM = $ million
See Pages 11 through 21 for Explanation of Ratios and Data

Current Data Sorted by Assets   Comparative Historical Data

0-500M	500M-2MM	2-10MM	10-50MM	50-100MM	100-250MM	Type of Statement	4/1/02-3/31/03 ALL	4/1/03-3/31/04 ALL
	1	2	21	22	8	Unqualified	26	28
1	2	10	6			Reviewed	9	15
	5	3	1			Compiled	8	6
1	1					Tax Returns	2	2
2	2	9	13	5	5	Other	23	30
	30 (4/1-9/30/06)		90 (10/1/06-3/31/07)					
4	11	24	41	27	13	NUMBER OF STATEMENTS	68	81
%	%	%	%	%	%	**ASSETS**	%	%
	7.7	12.7	5.5	14.1	7.9	Cash & Equivalents	7.7	6.5
	42.0	30.1	23.4	11.0	14.7	Trade Receivables (net)	23.4	21.7
	25.5	19.4	22.0	9.3	13.3	Inventory	19.6	17.0
	1.3	4.0	3.9	4.1	3.7	All Other Current	4.1	3.4
	76.5	66.2	54.8	38.4	39.6	Total Current	54.8	48.7
	17.0	30.5	33.6	53.3	37.1	Fixed Assets (net)	34.7	40.1
	1.0	.8	6.3	3.7	9.0	Intangibles (net)	3.5	5.1
	5.5	2.5	5.3	4.7	14.4	All Other Non-Current	7.1	6.1
	100.0	100.0	100.0	100.0	100.0	Total	100.0	100.0
						LIABILITIES		
	8.6	12.1	9.4	1.0	5.7	Notes Payable-Short Term	6.2	9.5
	5.6	3.0	2.6	3.1	2.2	Cur. Mat.-L.T.D.	3.2	4.8
	30.2	14.0	12.2	7.2	8.2	Trade Payables	12.3	14.0
	.1	.5	.7	.2	.3	Income Taxes Payable	.2	.3
	6.9	7.7	7.2	5.6	7.5	All Other Current	10.9	9.1
	51.4	37.3	32.2	17.0	24.0	Total Current	32.8	37.7
	22.5	18.5	16.5	15.9	20.6	Long-Term Debt	16.7	18.7
	.0	.5	1.2	.6	2.2	Deferred Taxes	1.2	.7
	24.4	3.3	5.0	.6	5.9	All Other Non-Current	4.8	9.0
	1.7	40.4	45.1	65.9	47.3	Net Worth	44.6	33.9
	100.0	100.0	100.0	100.0	100.0	Total Liabilties & Net Worth	100.0	100.0
						INCOME DATA		
	100.0	100.0	100.0	100.0	100.0	Net Sales	100.0	100.0
	34.6	36.0	27.2	40.0	33.4	Gross Profit	30.0	28.1
	31.4	30.0	16.9	9.3	16.8	Operating Expenses	23.3	21.9
	3.3	6.0	10.2	30.7	16.6	Operating Profit	6.7	6.2
	1.5	.0	.7	-.3	2.5	All Other Expenses (net)	.9	1.4
	1.8	6.0	9.6	31.0	14.1	Profit Before Taxes	5.8	4.8
						RATIOS		
	2.3	2.5	2.6	3.3	2.2		2.8	2.1
	1.2	1.8	1.8	2.9	1.8	Current	1.7	1.3
	1.0	1.2	1.2	1.8	1.1		1.3	.9
	1.6	1.6	1.5	2.2	1.6		1.3	1.2
	1.1	1.1	1.0	1.7	1.2	Quick	1.0	.7
	.6	.8	.6	1.1	.6		.6	.5
	37 9.9	32 11.4	37 10.0	19 19.3	31 11.9		36 10.0	23 15.6
	43 8.5	45 8.1	49 7.4	23 15.9	41 8.8	Sales/Receivables	47 7.8	42 8.8
	52 7.0	63 5.8	64 5.7	36 10.0	63 5.8		62 5.9	52 7.0
	41 8.8	20 18.0	29 12.4	19 19.2	37 9.8		22 16.8	18 20.8
	47 7.8	44 8.4	52 7.0	37 9.7	61 6.0	Cost of Sales/Inventory	51 7.2	35 10.5
	52 7.1	70 5.2	92 4.0	49 7.5	77 4.8		90 4.1	72 5.0
	35 10.5	18 20.1	17 21.0	15 24.1	15 23.9		19 19.0	19 19.5
	45 8.2	30 12.1	29 12.4	22 17.0	36 10.1	Cost of Sales/Payables	32 11.5	34 10.6
	72 5.1	50 7.2	51 7.2	40 9.0	72 5.0		51 7.2	57 6.4
	7.1	5.1	4.2	4.3	4.0		4.3	5.7
	27.4	8.3	7.3	6.0	6.7	Sales/Working Capital	8.8	20.2
	450.7	25.9	33.9	9.6	55.9		16.4	-53.7
	4.4	18.1	23.1	76.9	29.5		11.3	12.5
	1.8	4.4	(39) 8.5	27.1	8.6	EBIT/Interest	(61) 5.9	(74) 3.6
	.4	1.3	2.5	14.0	2.5		1.6	1.1
			20.3				13.6	10.6
		(19) 6.4				Net Profit + Depr., Dep., Amort./Cur. Mat. L/T/D	(20) 2.2	(21) 1.7
			2.6				.4	.4
	1.2	.3	.3	.7	.2		.2	.4
	-8.2	.7	.7	.8	1.3	Fixed/Worth	.6	1.2
	-.5	1.5	1.8	1.1	1.7		1.6	2.9
	3.8	.6	.6	.3	.5		.6	.7
	-74.6	1.6	1.9	.6	1.5	Debt/Worth	1.3	1.5
	-9.9	3.5	3.9	.7	2.3		2.9	5.1
		49.7	43.1	80.0	64.4		37.0	33.3
	(23) 32.1	(38) 31.2	62.1	(12) 18.5		% Profit Before Taxes/Tangible Net Worth	(64) 19.0	(69) 18.5
	4.2	16.9	44.4	13.4			4.8	1.6
	13.1	28.4	19.5	56.7	29.5		17.8	14.5
	7.6	8.4	11.0	40.7	9.9	% Profit Before Taxes/Total Assets	6.7	7.0
	-1.8	.8	5.0	20.7	4.7		2.0	.3
	81.9	20.5	16.1	3.2	15.8		23.4	11.6
	21.1	10.1	6.9	2.5	4.5	Sales/Net Fixed Assets	5.1	5.5
	14.0	4.1	2.8	2.1	1.4		2.3	1.7
	4.2	3.1	2.2	1.6	1.5		2.0	2.5
	3.8	2.5	1.6	1.3	.9	Sales/Total Assets	1.4	1.5
	3.2	1.3	1.2	1.1	.7		1.1	1.1
		.8	1.2	2.9	1.1		1.3	1.4
	(21) 1.8	(38) 2.1	(26) 3.4	(10) 2.4		% Depr., Dep., Amort./Sales	(58) 2.4	(67) 3.3
	3.0	4.0	4.7	4.4			5.0	5.9
		1.9					1.7	1.4
	(11) 2.8					% Officers', Directors' Owners' Comp/Sales	(16) 2.3	(12) 2.1
	4.5						7.5	9.6
4975M	55651M	319188M	1712454M	2821572M	2000880M	Net Sales ($)	2486877M	4242406M
1445M	16167M	139980M	1017567M	2111806M	1775921M	Total Assets ($)	1908228M	2743150M

M = $ thousand   MM = $ million
See Pages 11 through 21 for Explanation of Ratios and Data

Comparative Historical Data				Current Data Sorted by Sales					
27	34	54	**Type of Statement** Unqualified	1	1		6	5	47
19	19	19	Reviewed	1	1		6	6	5
3	5	9	Compiled	1	1		4	1	2
3	2	2	Tax Returns	1			1		
30	34	36	Other		2	2	3	8	20
4/1/04- 3/31/05 ALL	4/1/05- 3/31/06 ALL	4/1/06- 3/31/07 ALL		1	30 (4/1-9/30/06)		90 (10/1/06-3/31/07)		
				0-1MM	1-3MM	3-5MM	5-10MM	10-25MM	25MM & OVER
82	94	120	**NUMBER OF STATEMENTS**	1	6	5	14	20	74
%	%	%	**ASSETS**	%	%	%	%	%	%
6.6	6.8	9.9	Cash & Equivalents				9.7	5.7	9.1
23.2	24.8	23.0	Trade Receivables (net)				35.7	24.6	18.9
18.8	19.3	18.2	Inventory				19.5	25.1	15.6
2.7	3.8	3.7	All Other Current				1.8	5.4	3.4
51.3	54.7	54.8	Total Current				66.7	60.8	47.0
38.9	36.4	35.4	Fixed Assets (net)				23.7	35.3	41.2
3.3	3.2	4.3	Intangibles (net)				6.7	1.1	5.0
6.5	5.8	5.4	All Other Non-Current				2.9	2.9	6.7
100.0	100.0	100.0	Total				100.0	100.0	100.0
			LIABILITIES						
10.4	6.7	8.2	Notes Payable-Short Term				8.4	11.3	5.7
4.1	3.2	2.9	Cur. Mat.-L.T.D.				4.3	2.9	2.6
16.0	14.5	12.7	Trade Payables				22.1	11.7	10.7
.2	.2	.4	Income Taxes Payable				.7	.4	.4
7.0	8.3	7.5	All Other Current				3.2	7.4	7.0
37.7	32.9	31.7	Total Current				38.7	33.6	26.5
20.8	18.2	17.3	Long-Term Debt				18.0	18.6	16.7
1.1	.6	.9	Deferred Taxes				.1	1.4	1.0
7.6	5.5	6.1	All Other Non-Current				14.8	3.8	3.2
32.8	42.9	44.0	Net Worth				28.3	42.5	52.6
100.0	100.0	100.0	Total Liabilties & Net Worth				100.0	100.0	100.0
			INCOME DATA						
100.0	100.0	100.0	Net Sales				100.0	100.0	100.0
29.2	30.6	34.0	Gross Profit				43.3	31.1	31.9
22.9	21.8	20.5	Operating Expenses				35.6	23.9	13.6
6.3	8.8	13.4	Operating Profit				7.7	7.2	18.3
.8	.6	.6	All Other Expenses (net)				-.3	.6	.6
5.5	8.2	12.8	Profit Before Taxes				7.9	6.6	17.7
			RATIOS						
2.2	2.5	2.9	Current				2.5	2.5	3.0
1.5	1.7	1.9					1.9	1.7	2.0
1.1	1.3	1.2					1.1	1.4	1.3
1.3	1.6	1.8	Quick				1.6	1.3	1.8
.9	1.0	1.1					1.1	.8	1.2
.6	.7	.7					.8	.5	.8
29 12.5	26 13.9	24 15.1	Sales/Receivables				37 9.7	36 10.0	22 16.3
45 8.1	45 8.1	43 8.6					45 8.1	49 7.4	39 9.5
53 6.9	57 6.4	58 6.3					61 6.0	59 6.1	52 7.0
20 18.3	23 15.7	28 12.9	Cost of Sales/Inventory				16 22.5	26 14.2	30 12.0
44 8.3	47 7.8	46 7.9					46 8.0	64 5.7	43 8.5
75 4.9	75 4.9	68 5.4					77 4.7	95 3.8	63 5.8
20 18.7	19 19.5	17 21.1	Cost of Sales/Payables				28 13.0	17 21.5	16 22.9
37 9.9	30 12.0	30 12.1					45 8.2	29 12.5	27 13.3
56 6.5	52 7.0	47 7.8					73 5.0	53 6.9	44 8.3
6.6	5.0	4.6	Sales/Working Capital				5.7	4.2	4.4
13.4	9.3	8.0					8.9	6.9	7.6
81.5	22.0	26.5					NM	18.1	18.0
10.6	16.7	27.1	EBIT/Interest				19.1	22.0	34.8
(77) 4.3	(87) 6.4	(117) 8.9					7.8	3.6	(72) 14.6
1.4	2.2	2.3					1.2	1.6	4.0
6.8	14.6	17.2	Net Profit + Depr., Dep., Amort./Cur. Mat. L/T/D						19.0
(33) 2.1	(23) 3.7	(38) 4.7						(25) 7.1	
1.1	1.8	1.9							2.4
.6	.4	.4	Fixed/Worth				.3	.3	.5
1.4	1.0	.9					1.4	.8	.9
3.1	1.9	1.7					NM	2.1	1.4
.6	.5	.5	Debt/Worth				.7	.6	.5
1.9	1.2	1.5					4.2	1.6	.9
7.4	3.3	3.7					-64.1	3.7	2.1
47.1	46.7	63.7	% Profit Before Taxes/Tangible Net Worth				103.3	38.6	69.1
(69) 26.1	(85) 32.5	(107) 36.0			(10) 34.0			24.5	(71) 42.5
9.9	8.1	17.3					4.2	13.2	19.6
17.8	23.6	31.7	% Profit Before Taxes/Total Assets				21.7	25.5	36.7
7.4	9.6	12.9					12.3	5.8	17.5
1.9	1.9	4.8					.9	2.4	8.0
14.0	14.5	16.9	Sales/Net Fixed Assets				35.0	15.9	10.6
5.5	5.6	6.5					15.1	6.9	3.7
2.5	2.6	2.4					8.0	2.9	2.1
2.3	2.5	2.4	Sales/Total Assets				3.8	2.5	2.1
1.8	1.9	1.6					3.1	1.5	1.4
1.3	1.3	1.2					1.6	1.2	1.1
1.4	1.1	1.1	% Depr., Dep., Amort./Sales				.8	1.0	1.2
(75) 2.8	(83) 2.4	(106) 2.3			(10) 1.7			(19) 1.8	(69) 2.6
4.7	4.5	4.1					4.2	4.8	4.1
2.1	2.0	1.8	% Officers', Directors' Owners' Comp/Sales						
(19) 3.4	(19) 3.1	(25) 2.8							
8.1	7.6	4.5							
3943012M	4345231M	6914720M	Net Sales ($)	649M	9778M	21838M	104498M	314318M	6463639M
2657799M	3158857M	5062886M	Total Assets ($)	486M	5803M	21822M	52587M	192377M	4789811M

© RMA 2007   M = $ thousand   MM = $ million
See Pages 11 through 21 for Explanation of Ratios and Data

Current Data Sorted by Assets   **Comparative Historical Data**

Type of Statement	0-500M	500M-2MM	2-10MM	10-50MM	50-100MM	100-250MM		4/1/02-3/31/03 ALL	4/1/03-3/31/04 ALL
Unqualified			21	24	5	4		61	46
Reviewed	1	3	23	13				42	39
Compiled	2	10	8	1				21	43
Tax Returns	2	6	1	1				12	13
Other	1	18	35	25	6	8		61	64
		41 (4/1-9/30/06)		177 (10/1/06-3/31/07)					
NUMBER OF STATEMENTS	6	37	88	64	11	12		197	205
	%	%	%	%	%	%	**ASSETS**	%	%
Cash & Equivalents		13.8	5.8	4.0	3.6	4.4		5.5	5.9
Trade Receivables (net)		28.0	27.6	27.0	26.5	28.6		25.6	28.3
Inventory		26.8	22.8	23.9	17.9	20.4		22.3	21.4
All Other Current		.9	2.5	1.8	2.1	1.5		2.8	2.5
Total Current		69.5	58.7	56.6	50.0	54.9		56.2	57.9
Fixed Assets (net)		25.1	32.7	32.9	32.6	29.0		35.9	32.8
Intangibles (net)		1.0	4.6	6.0	11.6	11.6		3.3	4.2
All Other Non-Current		4.4	4.1	4.5	5.7	4.5		4.6	5.1
Total		100.0	100.0	100.0	100.0	100.0		100.0	100.0
							LIABILITIES		
Notes Payable-Short Term		13.6	11.0	13.4	8.8	8.0		9.9	12.7
Cur. Mat.-L.T.D.		3.3	3.6	3.9	3.1	1.6		6.3	4.7
Trade Payables		20.5	17.0	16.7	13.1	15.8		16.4	18.1
Income Taxes Payable		.2	.2	.2	.2	.2		.3	.2
All Other Current		7.6	8.5	7.8	4.6	8.2		9.9	12.1
Total Current		45.3	40.4	42.1	29.7	33.8		42.7	47.7
Long-Term Debt		21.6	18.9	19.0	16.6	26.7		21.6	18.3
Deferred Taxes		.2	.8	.9	.6	.3		1.0	1.2
All Other Non-Current		8.0	9.6	5.0	5.6	2.7		7.2	8.2
Net Worth		24.8	30.3	33.0	47.4	36.5		27.4	24.5
Total Liabilties & Net Worth		100.0	100.0	100.0	100.0	100.0		100.0	100.0
							INCOME DATA		
Net Sales		100.0	100.0	100.0	100.0	100.0		100.0	100.0
Gross Profit		32.5	25.9	19.8	21.9	19.1		26.8	27.0
Operating Expenses		28.8	19.3	13.6	12.0	14.5		22.1	21.6
Operating Profit		3.8	6.5	6.2	9.9	4.6		4.6	5.4
All Other Expenses (net)		1.2	1.7	1.8	2.0	1.7		1.5	1.6
Profit Before Taxes		2.6	4.9	4.4	7.9	2.8		3.1	3.8
							RATIOS		
Current		3.9	2.1	1.9	2.2	2.5		2.2	2.0
		2.0	1.5	1.4	2.0	1.9		1.4	1.4
		1.0	1.1	1.1	1.3	1.3		1.0	1.0
Quick		2.2	1.3	1.1	1.5	1.3		1.2	1.2
		1.2	.8	.7	1.1	1.1		.7	.7
		.3	.6	.5	.9	.8		.5	.5
Sales/Receivables		26 14.2	32 11.4	38 9.5	38 9.5	36 10.1		34 10.7	34 10.6
		40 9.1	41 8.8	47 7.7	51 7.2	48 7.6		45 8.1	46 7.9
		51 7.2	52 7.0	59 6.2	59 6.2	78 4.7		54 6.7	55 6.6
Cost of Sales/Inventory		21 17.6	25 14.9	34 10.7	28 13.1	34 10.6		33 11.1	31 11.9
		47 7.8	48 7.6	50 7.4	52 7.0	45 8.1		49 7.5	48 7.6
		76 4.8	71 5.1	78 4.7	59 6.2	64 5.7		65 5.6	68 5.4
Cost of Sales/Payables		15 24.1	18 20.4	23 15.9	24 15.2	25 14.9		21 17.0	24 15.4
		38 9.6	33 11.1	33 11.1	29 12.7	38 9.6		36 10.1	38 9.7
		60 6.1	44 8.4	48 7.7	43 8.5	48 7.6		48 7.6	51 7.1
Sales/Working Capital		5.6	6.6	7.3	6.2	6.0		6.6	7.3
		8.6	13.0	14.9	8.3	8.2		12.5	15.0
		NM	73.5	94.4	14.8	20.4		584.7	-140.2
EBIT/Interest		11.1	9.4	7.4	262.8	16.9		7.4	8.4
		(33) 2.7	(80) 3.8	(59) 3.3	(10) 5.1	(11) 2.4		(185) 3.0	(188) 3.1
		1.0	1.7	1.5	3.2	.8		.8	1.1
Net Profit + Depr., Dep., Amort./Cur. Mat. L/T/D			5.7	6.3				4.5	4.8
			(18) 3.1	(29) 3.5				(55) 2.1	(59) 2.1
			1.7	1.9				.8	1.1
Fixed/Worth		.2	.5	.5	.7	.6		.6	.5
		.7	1.2	1.3	.8	1.2		1.3	1.3
		6.1	3.6	3.9	1.1	3.2		3.1	3.2
Debt/Worth		.6	.9	1.0	.7	1.4		1.1	1.2
		2.5	2.6	2.3	1.4	2.2		2.2	2.5
		18.0	7.1	9.7	5.2	12.8		7.5	10.0
% Profit Before Taxes/Tangible Net Worth		45.1	45.7	48.6		79.2		41.7	50.6
		(31) 19.1	(75) 25.6	(55) 30.4		(11) 23.9		(171) 18.4	(174) 20.9
		.8	12.3	14.6		15.7		4.1	4.9
% Profit Before Taxes/Total Assets		21.4	17.4	14.4	21.4	14.0		12.8	16.8
		8.3	9.0	8.2	9.9	8.1		5.9	4.7
		.4	2.3	2.4	5.9	-.5		-.2	.6
Sales/Net Fixed Assets		37.5	15.9	12.6	8.2	9.4		12.7	16.2
		12.6	8.8	5.9	4.8	6.0		5.5	6.1
		7.6	4.3	3.4	3.6	3.0		3.3	3.8
Sales/Total Assets		3.7	2.9	2.6	2.2	2.8		2.8	2.8
		2.7	2.2	1.8	1.6	1.9		2.1	2.1
		1.9	1.7	1.4	1.1	.9		1.4	1.5
% Depr., Dep., Amort./Sales		.6	1.1	1.4	2.3			1.6	1.3
		(30) 1.8	(78) 2.1	(61) 2.2	(10) 3.1			(174) 3.2	(184) 3.0
		3.7	3.9	3.7	4.2			5.3	5.3
% Officers', Directors' Owners' Comp/Sales		2.2	1.3	.8				2.6	2.4
		(16) 5.1	(33) 2.6	(10) 1.2				(54) 4.6	(54) 5.1
		7.7	5.4	3.3				7.8	7.2
Net Sales ($)	7836M	115557M	1103450M	2960623M	1476536M	4831360M		9187583M	6849523M
Total Assets ($)	1701M	42192M	476852M	1483109M	754259M	2387357M		4808785M	3943602M

© RMA 2007

M = $ thousand   MM = $ million
See Pages 11 through 21 for Explanation of Ratios and Data

Comparative Historical Data

Current Data Sorted by Sales

			Type of Statement						
53	49	54	Unqualified				8	10	36
46	32	40	Reviewed	1	1	2	9	15	12
33	29	21	Compiled	1	6	5	5	3	1
19	12	10	Tax Returns		4	2	2	1	1
64	98	93	Other	4	10	11	14	25	29
4/1/04- 3/31/05 ALL	4/1/05- 3/31/06 ALL	4/1/06- 3/31/07 ALL			41 (4/1-9/30/06)		177 (10/1/06-3/31/07)		
				0-1MM	1-3MM	3-5MM	5-10MM	10-25MM	25MM & OVER
215	220	218	NUMBER OF STATEMENTS	6	21	20	38	54	79
%	%	%	ASSETS	%	%	%	%	%	%
6.2	5.9	6.5	Cash & Equivalents		11.6	11.5	5.6	6.4	3.8
27.9	30.1	27.2	Trade Receivables (net)		27.5	27.8	22.8	29.1	29.0
21.7	23.8	23.2	Inventory		25.0	23.0	25.8	21.8	23.6
2.2	2.4	2.5	All Other Current		3.9	1.4	3.0	2.6	1.5
57.9	62.2	59.5	Total Current		68.1	63.7	57.2	59.9	57.9
32.5	30.3	31.1	Fixed Assets (net)		27.4	30.7	35.8	28.5	31.1
4.1	3.3	5.0	Intangibles (net)		.8	1.4	4.2	6.3	6.7
5.4	4.2	4.4	All Other Non-Current		3.7	4.1	2.9	5.2	4.2
100.0	100.0	100.0	Total		100.0	100.0	100.0	100.0	100.0
			LIABILITIES						
11.8	12.6	11.6	Notes Payable-Short Term		13.2	14.6	10.4	11.0	12.2
4.8	3.9	3.5	Cur. Mat.-L.T.D.		4.6	2.2	4.9	2.9	3.4
18.4	18.3	17.2	Trade Payables		18.5	19.3	14.4	19.1	17.1
.3	.2	.2	Income Taxes Payable		.1	.1	.3	.3	.1
8.0	9.4	8.0	All Other Current		10.0	4.9	5.3	11.2	7.8
43.3	44.5	40.6	Total Current		46.4	41.1	35.3	44.6	40.7
18.8	16.7	19.6	Long-Term Debt		22.1	23.0	21.3	18.8	17.8
.8	.8	.7	Deferred Taxes		.2	.4	.9	.6	.8
5.7	9.4	7.2	All Other Non-Current		13.4	2.6	12.4	7.2	4.6
31.3	28.6	32.0	Net Worth		17.9	32.9	30.1	28.8	36.0
100.0	100.0	100.0	Total Liabilities & Net Worth		100.0	100.0	100.0	100.0	100.0
			INCOME DATA						
100.0	100.0	100.0	Net Sales		100.0	100.0	100.0	100.0	100.0
26.6	25.9	25.2	Gross Profit		36.9	29.9	24.3	23.6	19.9
22.0	21.1	19.2	Operating Expenses		34.7	23.3	20.1	17.6	13.5
4.6	4.8	6.0	Operating Profit		2.2	6.7	4.3	6.0	6.4
.9	1.4	1.6	All Other Expenses (net)		1.8	.7	1.8	1.4	1.6
3.6	3.4	4.4	Profit Before Taxes		.4	6.0	2.4	4.6	4.8
			RATIOS						
2.0	2.3	2.2			3.2	3.8	2.5	1.9	2.0
1.4	1.5	1.5	Current		1.8	2.0	1.7	1.4	1.5
1.0	1.1	1.1			1.0	1.5	1.1	1.0	1.1
1.2	1.4	1.4			1.7	2.2	1.6	1.3	1.2
.8	.8	.9	Quick		1.2	1.2	.9	.7	.9
.5	.6	.5			.3	.9	.5	.5	.6

34	10.9	38	9.7	33	10.9		29	12.7	26	13.9	27	13.3	36	10.0	37	9.8

Rows continuing (Sales/Receivables, etc.):

Hist ALL	Hist ALL	Hist ALL	Ratio	0-1MM	1-3MM	3-5MM	5-10MM	10-25MM	25MM & OVER
34 / 10.9	38 / 9.7	33 / 10.9	Sales/Receivables	29 / 12.7	26 / 13.9	27 / 13.3	36 / 10.0		37 / 9.8
47 / 7.7	48 / 7.6	44 / 8.3		45 / 8.1	36 / 10.2	37 / 9.8	46 / 8.0		47 / 7.8
56 / 6.5	57 / 6.4	54 / 6.7		62 / 5.9	48 / 7.6	49 / 7.4	59 / 6.2		56 / 6.5
28 / 13.1	30 / 12.3	27 / 13.7	Cost of Sales/Inventory	24 / 15.1	17 / 21.9	24 / 15.1	26 / 14.1		34 / 10.7
47 / 7.7	51 / 7.1	48 / 7.6		45 / 8.1	47 / 7.8	50 / 7.3	45 / 8.2		50 / 7.4
70 / 5.2	72 / 5.1	73 / 5.0		93 / 3.9	69 / 5.3	79 / 4.6	69 / 5.3		65 / 5.6
22 / 16.4	22 / 16.9	20 / 17.8	Cost of Sales/Payables	18 / 20.2	11 / 34.6	12 / 31.3	27 / 13.5		23 / 16.0
39 / 9.3	35 / 10.3	33 / 11.1		40 / 9.0	24 / 15.1	27 / 13.4	39 / 9.3		32 / 11.3
52 / 7.0	50 / 7.2	46 / 7.9		60 / 6.1	46 / 8.0	43 / 8.5	51 / 7.2		43 / 8.5

7.8	6.5	6.6	Sales/Working Capital		6.1	5.3	6.2	7.5	7.3
15.0	13.0	11.7			9.5	6.8	12.6	13.6	11.8
-999.8	74.1	57.0			-157.7	26.3	45.3	-102.1	43.6

Hist	Hist	Hist	Ratio	0-1MM	1-3MM	3-5MM	5-10MM	10-25MM	25MM & OVER
	11.9		8.5		10.5	EBIT/Interest		10.2		11.1		10.6		9.4		10.0
(201)	4.4	(198)	3.5	(197)	3.8		(20)	1.9	(18)	5.8		3.5	(47)	3.0	(72)	4.7
	1.7		1.1		1.5			-1.0		2.1		.1		1.6		1.8

	6.0		7.1		8.4	Net Profit + Depr., Dep., Amort./Cur. Mat. L/T/D								8.8		7.5
(62)	2.3	(65)	2.3	(57)	3.5								(12)	2.7	(34)	3.6
	1.2		1.2		1.9									1.4		2.2

.4	.4	.5	Fixed/Worth		.3	.3	.3	.5	.5
1.1	1.0	1.1			1.0	.9	1.2	1.4	1.0
2.9	2.2	3.5			5.6	3.2	3.9	4.6	2.2
1.0	1.0	.9	Debt/Worth		1.3	.6	1.0	.8	1.0
2.4	2.0	2.3			4.4	1.2	2.4	4.3	2.0
6.9	5.6	8.2			22.2	7.8	9.4	14.0	7.1

	41.1		48.8		48.6	% Profit Before Taxes/Tangible Net Worth		47.9		52.0		51.4		43.8		57.5
(190)	21.8	(188)	20.2	(187)	25.7		(18)	12.1	(17)	25.8	(33)	19.4	(44)	25.3	(70)	33.3
	7.8		2.5		11.7			-6.2		6.9		-4.4		17.0		18.1

13.9	15.5	16.1	% Profit Before Taxes/Total Assets		16.3	26.6	16.5	12.7	15.6
6.9	6.1	8.5			3.4	13.3	7.3	8.2	9.3
1.7	.0	2.1			-7.3	4.1	-2.5	2.4	2.6
17.5	18.3	16.2	Sales/Net Fixed Assets		32.7	23.3	16.4	16.5	13.9
6.6	7.5	7.6			11.8	11.3	6.5	9.3	6.5
4.0	4.3	4.0			6.7	4.1	2.5	4.5	3.7
3.0	2.8	2.9	Sales/Total Assets		3.2	4.2	2.9	2.8	3.0
2.1	2.2	2.1			2.4	2.6	2.1	2.2	2.1
1.5	1.6	1.6			1.6	1.7	1.6	1.6	1.5

	1.5		.9		1.0	% Depr., Dep., Amort./Sales		.6		1.5		1.1		1.0		.9
(195)	3.0	(193)	2.4	(193)	2.1		(19)	1.9	(16)	2.2	(36)	2.6	(47)	1.9	(71)	2.0
	4.9		3.8		3.7			4.4		3.8		5.1		3.1		3.4

	1.7		1.8		1.3	% Officers', Directors' Owners' Comp/Sales		1.2				1.4		1.2		.6
(70)	4.5	(56)	4.0	(65)	3.5		(10)	5.6			(17)	2.9	(19)	2.3	(10)	1.2
	7.1		7.3		5.9			12.9						5.9		5.1		4.3

7374122M	7663320M	10495362M	Net Sales ($)	3786M	43208M	80798M	275462M	910711M	9181397M
4342686M	3941088M	5145470M	Total Assets ($)	4161M	20444M	35091M	148349M	475838M	4461587M

M = $ thousand   MM = $ million
See Pages 11 through 21 for Explanation of Ratios and Data

Current Data Sorted by Assets   **Comparative Historical Data**

0-500M	500M-2MM	2-10MM	10-50MM	50-100MM	100-250MM	Type of Statement	4/1/02-3/31/03 ALL	4/1/03-3/31/04 ALL
	5	4	3	2	1	Unqualified	12	21
	2	3	1			Reviewed	11	6
	2	4				Compiled	2	6
1	3	2				Tax Returns	2	3
	7	6	3			Other	10	9
	17 (4/1-9/30/06)		32 (10/1/06-3/31/07)					
1	19	19	7	2	1	**NUMBER OF STATEMENTS**	37	45
%	%	%	%	%	%	**ASSETS**	%	%
	4.9	7.1				Cash & Equivalents	7.9	9.0
	21.9	24.5				Trade Receivables (net)	22.0	22.0
	34.5	24.1				Inventory	25.0	23.3
	2.1	.9				All Other Current	1.1	3.3
	63.4	56.7				Total Current	56.0	57.6
	30.2	30.3				Fixed Assets (net)	32.8	32.9
	3.2	3.6				Intangibles (net)	2.7	3.8
	3.2	9.4				All Other Non-Current	8.5	5.7
	100.0	100.0				Total	100.0	100.0
						LIABILITIES		
	12.7	12.6				Notes Payable-Short Term	12.1	10.2
	3.0	3.8				Cur. Mat.-L.T.D.	3.1	4.6
	26.3	16.3				Trade Payables	15.8	15.6
	.0	.3				Income Taxes Payable	.6	.5
	12.1	9.4				All Other Current	9.5	9.1
	54.1	42.3				Total Current	41.1	40.1
	18.1	20.3				Long-Term Debt	13.8	18.3
	.4	.9				Deferred Taxes	.8	.9
	7.0	4.9				All Other Non-Current	3.6	5.4
	20.4	31.5				Net Worth	40.6	35.4
	100.0	100.0				Total Liabilities & Net Worth	100.0	100.0
						INCOME DATA		
	100.0	100.0				Net Sales	100.0	100.0
	25.3	30.6				Gross Profit	32.3	27.9
	26.8	21.2				Operating Expenses	29.1	23.7
	-1.6	9.4				Operating Profit	3.2	4.2
	2.1	5.0				All Other Expenses (net)	.2	.9
	-3.7	4.4				Profit Before Taxes	3.0	3.3
						RATIOS		
	1.8	1.9					2.1	2.3
	1.4	1.5				Current	1.4	1.3
	.8	.9					1.0	1.1
	.7	1.6					1.3	1.3
	.5	.5				Quick	.7	.8
	.3	.4					.4	.5
(23) 15.8	(26) 14.1					Sales/Receivables	(21) 17.7	(26) 14.0
(33) 10.9	(34) 10.7						(36) 10.2	(38) 9.7
(47) 7.7	(49) 7.5						(60) 6.1	(57) 6.4
(43) 8.4	(26) 14.0					Cost of Sales/Inventory	(46) 8.0	(37) 9.8
(73) 5.0	(60) 6.1						(60) 6.1	(61) 6.0
(133) 2.7	(113) 3.2						(89) 4.1	(89) 4.1
(27) 13.4	(27) 13.5					Cost of Sales/Payables	(22) 16.3	(21) 17.3
(61) 6.0	(33) 11.2						(35) 10.5	(40) 9.1
(116) 3.2	(47) 7.7						(60) 6.0	(54) 6.8
	6.4	7.3				Sales/Working Capital	7.7	6.7
	18.5	16.7					19.2	14.4
	-19.8	-51.4					-84.1	47.1
	7.0	9.0				EBIT/Interest	5.6	6.3
	(18) 1.5	(16) 1.3					(36) 3.7	(44) 3.4
	-2.4	.9					1.1	.8
						Net Profit + Depr., Dep., Amort./Cur. Mat. L/T/D	6.5	10.6
							(13) 2.4	(16) 3.2
							1.0	2.2
	.5	.5				Fixed/Worth	.5	.5
	1.1	1.0					.8	.9
	7.7	5.7					1.5	1.7
	1.4	.9				Debt/Worth	.6	.8
	3.7	3.0					1.4	2.0
	24.9	9.7					2.6	4.1
	38.5	40.8				% Profit Before Taxes/Tangible Net Worth	31.1	27.7
	(15) 7.7	(15) 7.3					(35) 17.5	(42) 19.0
	1.2	.5					1.1	5.2
	8.3	9.8				% Profit Before Taxes/Total Assets	10.6	11.3
	2.5	1.2					6.5	5.4
	-10.5	-.3					.4	.0
	25.5	31.0				Sales/Net Fixed Assets	15.1	14.8
	15.2	8.3					7.0	5.8
	2.7	3.2					3.7	2.8
	3.4	3.7				Sales/Total Assets	2.8	2.5
	1.8	2.0					2.1	1.9
	1.2	1.3					1.5	1.3
	.5	1.1				% Depr., Dep., Amort./Sales	1.9	1.5
	(16) 1.3	(16) 1.9					(35) 2.6	(39) 2.5
	5.7	3.3					5.1	4.6
						% Officers', Directors', Owners' Comp/Sales	1.8	1.9
							(13) 3.9	(10) 5.0
							7.7	6.5
460M	54458M	201176M	382987M	317912M	550605M	Net Sales ($)	1223942M	1413326M
240M	23614M	88539M	189886M	106299M	123200M	Total Assets ($)	596216M	784428M

© RMA 2007   M = $ thousand   MM = $ million

See Pages 11 through 21 for Explanation of Ratios and Data

Comparative Historical Data

Current Data Sorted by Sales

Hist 1	Hist 2	Hist 3	Type of Statement	0-1MM	1-3MM	3-5MM	5-10MM	10-25MM	25MM & OVER
11	14	15	Unqualified	1	4	1	2	1	6
8	7	6	Reviewed		1		1	3	1
4	3	6	Compiled		3	1	1	1	
4	6	6	Tax Returns	1	3	1		1	
3	14	16	Other	2	2	2	3	4	3
4/1/04-3/31/05 ALL	4/1/05-3/31/06 ALL	4/1/06-3/31/07 ALL			17 (4/1-9/30/06)			32 (10/1/06-3/31/07)	
30	44	49	**NUMBER OF STATEMENTS**	4	13	6	6	10	10
%	%	%	**ASSETS**	%	%	%	%	%	%
10.3	5.4	6.2	Cash & Equivalents		3.9			5.7	6.0
21.5	25.2	23.9	Trade Receivables (net)		18.8			33.1	26.8
31.3	31.9	31.1	Inventory		25.8			33.3	36.8
1.4	1.3	1.7	All Other Current		2.8			1.1	2.1
64.5	63.8	62.9	Total Current		51.2			73.1	71.7
26.3	27.6	27.8	Fixed Assets (net)		35.5			20.5	19.4
1.7	2.9	3.8	Intangibles (net)		4.3			.3	5.8
7.5	5.7	5.5	All Other Non-Current		9.0			6.0	3.0
100.0	100.0	100.0	Total		100.0			100.0	100.0
			LIABILITIES						
17.1	13.4	16.0	Notes Payable-Short Term		11.1			19.8	25.5
4.2	3.8	3.1	Cur. Mat.-L.T.D.		4.1			3.3	2.3
13.8	23.7	22.1	Trade Payables		19.9			22.6	23.4
.3	.2	.2	Income Taxes Payable		.0			.1	.3
13.2	12.4	10.2	All Other Current		10.9			13.9	8.8
48.5	53.5	51.6	Total Current		46.1			59.7	60.3
11.9	17.3	17.5	Long-Term Debt		26.8			9.3	9.7
.7	.7	.7	Deferred Taxes		.6			.6	.7
2.5	4.1	5.5	All Other Non-Current		11.2			1.5	4.1
36.4	24.3	24.8	Net Worth		15.2			29.0	25.2
100.0	100.0	100.0	Total Liabilities & Net Worth		100.0			100.0	100.0
			INCOME DATA						
100.0	100.0	100.0	Net Sales		100.0			100.0	100.0
25.5	26.1	27.9	Gross Profit		23.1			21.9	23.7
21.5	21.4	24.2	Operating Expenses		22.3			17.7	21.4
4.1	4.7	3.7	Operating Profit		.8			4.2	2.4
.1	1.2	3.1	All Other Expenses (net)		2.1			.4	1.4
4.0	3.5	.6	Profit Before Taxes		-1.3			3.8	1.0
			RATIOS						
1.9	1.6	1.8			1.9			2.2	1.5
1.2	1.2	1.2	Current		1.4			1.4	1.2
1.0	1.0	.9			.8			.9	1.0
.9	.8	.8			.7			1.3	.7
.6	.6	.5	Quick		.4			.5	.5
.5	.4	.4			.3			.4	.4
15 24.6	21 17.5	26 14.2		22 16.5			25 14.8	29 12.4	
30 12.3	34 10.7	34 10.6	Sales/Receivables	34 10.7			33 11.1	42 8.6	
52 7.0	52 7.0	47 7.7		45 8.1			49 7.5	50 7.3	
36 10.3	41 8.9	42 8.8		43 8.5			24 15.1	47 7.7	
65 5.6	66 5.6	69 5.3	Cost of Sales/Inventory	69 5.3			35 10.4	67 5.5	
92 4.0	115 3.2	123 3.0		121 3.0			90 4.1	125 2.9	
11 33.7	27 13.4	27 13.5		31 11.7			16 22.5	26 13.9	
24 15.1	39 9.3	42 8.7	Cost of Sales/Payables	61 6.0			30 12.3	44 8.4	
45 8.1	56 6.5	76 4.8		100 3.7			40 9.0	58 6.2	
9.7	8.2	7.8		6.1			7.8	9.5	
18.2	21.4	18.5	Sales/Working Capital	12.9			18.6	27.1	
NM	142.2	-62.1		-27.6			-40.8	NM	
6.8	6.3	3.8			2.3				3.5
(28) 3.4	2.9	(45) 1.5	EBIT/Interest		(12) 1.5				1.6
1.5	1.5	.9			1.0				1.2
8.4	4.9	8.6	Net Profit + Depr., Dep.,						
(13) 2.7	(12) 2.5	(11) 2.9	Amort./Cur. Mat. L/T/D						
1.2	.7	1.0							
.5	.7	.6			.7			.4	.5
.9	1.0	1.0	Fixed/Worth		1.6			1.0	.8
1.2	1.3	5.8			-1.9			1.2	3.4
.9	1.2	1.3			1.3			.9	1.7
1.9	2.4	3.7	Debt/Worth		8.5			2.7	3.6
4.3	7.7	22.4			-6.9			5.9	10.5
28.5	29.3	36.4	% Profit Before Taxes/Tangible						
(29) 15.8	(36) 15.6	(39) 7.7	Net Worth						
4.6	7.8	.9							
10.1	10.3	8.4	% Profit Before Taxes/Total		4.1			16.1	3.3
6.4	4.2	2.5	Assets		2.5			3.2	2.3
1.5	1.6	-.2			.1			-1.1	1.3
20.2	19.8	25.9			20.3			58.6	19.5
10.0	9.2	9.9	Sales/Net Fixed Assets		3.3			17.8	13.2
4.2	5.7	3.2			2.6			8.2	7.1
3.4	3.2	3.4			1.8			4.5	3.1
2.4	2.4	1.9	Sales/Total Assets		1.5			3.2	2.4
1.5	1.6	1.4			1.2			2.2	1.8
1.0	.9	.7			.5				.6
(27) 2.1	(36) 1.5	(43) 1.7	% Depr., Dep., Amort./Sales		(11) 2.3				1.4
3.6	2.5	3.3			5.9				2.4
	1.7	3.4	% Officers', Directors'						
	(13) 3.7	(11) 5.3	Owners' Comp/Sales						
	7.5	10.2							
1300656M	2370489M	1507598M	Net Sales ($)	1956M	26823M	25584M	44274M	157457M	1251504M
467762M	970480M	531778M	Total Assets ($)	6898M	18543M	10554M	24359M	52039M	419385M

M = $ thousand   MM = $ million
See Pages 11 through 21 for Explanation of Ratios and Data

| Current Data Sorted by Assets | | | | | | | Comparative Historical Data | |

Type of Statement

0-500M	500M-2MM	2-10MM	10-50MM	50-100MM	100-250MM	Type of Statement	4/1/02-3/31/03	4/1/03-3/31/04
	1	1	3	1		Unqualified	3	7
	1	1	2			Reviewed	4	2
		1	1			Compiled	5	10
	2					Tax Returns		
		6	5		3	Other	8	6
	12 (4/1-9/30/06)	6	15 (10/1/06-3/31/07)		3		8 ALL	6 ALL
	4	9	10	1	3	NUMBER OF STATEMENTS	20	25

Financial Data

0-500M %	500M-2MM %	2-10MM %	10-50MM %	50-100MM %	100-250MM %		4/1/02-3/31/03 ALL %	4/1/03-3/31/04 ALL %
						ASSETS		
			7.8			Cash & Equivalents	5.3	8.8
			22.2			Trade Receivables (net)	20.0	21.4
			24.6			Inventory	28.8	25.4
			1.6			All Other Current	4.4	2.7
			56.1			Total Current	58.6	58.4
			34.0			Fixed Assets (net)	36.6	35.0
			1.7			Intangibles (net)	1.0	1.1
			8.2			All Other Non-Current	3.8	5.6
			100.0			Total	100.0	100.0
						LIABILITIES		
			11.1			Notes Payable-Short Term	11.1	12.7
			3.3			Cur. Mat.-L.T.D.	10.8	5.3
			20.4			Trade Payables	13.5	15.2
			.1			Income Taxes Payable	.2	.6
			12.1			All Other Current	6.8	6.6
			47.1			Total Current	42.3	40.5
			20.3			Long-Term Debt	10.1	16.4
			.9			Deferred Taxes	1.1	1.4
			2.2			All Other Non-Current	6.8	2.0
			29.6			Net Worth	39.7	39.7
			100.0			Total Liabilities & Net Worth	100.0	100.0
						INCOME DATA		
			100.0			Net Sales	100.0	100.0
			22.3			Gross Profit	33.0	31.1
			18.7			Operating Expenses	27.1	26.8
			3.6			Operating Profit	5.9	4.4
			.1			All Other Expenses (net)	1.4	.6
			3.5			Profit Before Taxes	4.4	3.8

(*Note: the 0-500M, 500M-2MM, 2-10MM, 50-100MM and 100-250MM current columns are marked* DATA NOT AVAILABLE.)

Ratios

10-50MM		4/1/02-3/31/03 ALL		4/1/03-3/31/04 ALL
1.6		2.4		2.6
1.2	Current	1.5		1.3
1.0		1.1		1.1
.9		.9		1.3
.6	Quick	.6		.6
.4		.3		.5
23 16.0		17 21.5	18	19.8
33 11.0	Sales/Receivables	34 10.8	38	9.6
47 7.7		57 6.4	47	7.8
36 10.3		40 9.1	40	9.0
67 5.4	Cost of Sales/Inventory	74 4.9	66	5.5
102 3.6		103 3.6	83	4.4
28 13.0		18 20.4	10	38.2
41 8.8	Cost of Sales/Payables	26 14.2	29	12.5
58 6.3		47 7.7	43	8.5
13.5		4.8		5.4
28.3	Sales/Working Capital	13.0		17.4
-234.6		35.5		52.7
		7.0		11.4
	EBIT/Interest	3.3	(23)	5.9
		1.5		.5
				7.6
	Net Profit + Depr., Dep., Amort./Cur. Mat. L/T/D		(10)	3.7
				1.8
.5		.4		.3
1.3	Fixed/Worth	.8		.6
2.7		2.3		1.4
1.7		.7		.6
2.7	Debt/Worth	1.3		1.5
4.8		4.2		4.7
34.7		35.6		37.8
22.4	% Profit Before Taxes/Tangible Net Worth	(19) 24.0	(22)	18.3
7.3		6.3		1.9
12.6		16.0		16.2
4.6	% Profit Before Taxes/Total Assets	5.1		7.3
1.9		1.1		-2.8
10.8		14.1		18.5
7.1	Sales/Net Fixed Assets	7.6		7.3
4.3		3.9		4.6
3.2		2.7		3.0
2.0	Sales/Total Assets	2.1		2.2
1.4		1.5		1.5
1.2		1.5		1.6
2.5	% Depr., Dep., Amort./Sales	(17) 2.2	(23)	2.5
4.0		4.1		4.9
	% Officers', Directors' Owners' Comp/Sales			

0-500M	500M-2MM	2-10MM	10-50MM	50-100MM	100-250MM		4/1/02-3/31/03	4/1/03-3/31/04
	12247M	90490M	439360M	76356M	1168403M	Net Sales ($)	936237M	530645M
	5157M	44790M	180158M	67180M	383863M	Total Assets ($)	430530M	273128M

M = $ thousand   MM = $ million
See Pages 11 through 21 for Explanation of Ratios and Data

Comparative Historical Data | Current Data Sorted by Sales

			Type of Statement	0-1MM	1-3MM	3-5MM	5-10MM	10-25MM	25MM & OVER
9	5	6	Unqualified		1		1	2	5
3	1	4	Reviewed				1		
7	1	1	Compiled			1			
	1	2	Tax Returns		2			3	
6	12	14	Other		3	2			6
4/1/04-3/31/05	4/1/05-3/31/06	4/1/06-3/31/07			12 (4/1-9/30/06)			15 (10/1/06-3/31/07)	
ALL	ALL	ALL							
25	20	27	**NUMBER OF STATEMENTS**		6	3	2	5	11
%	%	%	**ASSETS**	%	%	%	%	%	%
9.4	3.7	6.6	Cash & Equivalents	D					7.6
24.4	28.6	21.1	Trade Receivables (net)	A					28.0
28.6	24.7	25.0	Inventory	T					28.8
3.2	2.5	2.5	All Other Current	A					3.3
65.6	59.5	55.2	Total Current						67.6
28.1	33.8	37.8	Fixed Assets (net)	N					28.1
.4	.3	.7	Intangibles (net)	O					1.5
5.9	6.4	6.3	All Other Non-Current	T					2.7
100.0	100.0	100.0	Total						100.0
			LIABILITIES	A					
12.8	9.4	9.4	Notes Payable-Short Term	V					8.2
2.3	4.9	5.3	Cur. Mat.-L.T.D.	A					1.5
17.2	16.2	20.7	Trade Payables	I					35.6
.2	.0	.2	Income Taxes Payable	L					.1
9.1	10.3	12.0	All Other Current	A					9.1
41.6	40.8	47.6	Total Current	B					54.5
9.6	21.4	21.1	Long-Term Debt	L					15.7
1.7	1.3	.9	Deferred Taxes	E					.9
1.7	3.3	1.6	All Other Non-Current						.8
45.4	33.2	28.8	Net Worth						28.1
100.0	100.0	100.0	Total Liabilities & Net Worth						100.0
			INCOME DATA						
100.0	100.0	100.0	Net Sales						100.0
31.1	34.5	28.2	Gross Profit						18.3
24.3	31.5	25.0	Operating Expenses						13.6
6.7	3.0	3.1	Operating Profit						4.7
.8	2.4	1.7	All Other Expenses (net)						1.0
5.9	.6	1.4	Profit Before Taxes						3.7
			RATIOS						
2.4	2.3	1.6	Current						1.7
1.5	1.4	1.3							1.3
1.2	1.2	1.0							1.0
1.2	1.3	.8	Quick						1.0
.8	.9	.6							.6
.5	.5	.3							.3
19 19.7	28 13.1	18 20.6	Sales/Receivables						21 17.4
40 9.1	48 7.6	32 11.3							30 12.3
63 5.8	76 4.8	57 6.4							54 6.7
49 7.5	35 10.4	36 10.0	Cost of Sales/Inventory						35 10.4
82 4.5	76 4.8	72 5.1							48 7.5
105 3.5	102 3.6	111 3.3							85 4.3
22 16.9	24 15.1	24 15.2	Cost of Sales/Payables						31 11.8
32 11.3	34 10.7	38 9.6							45 8.1
54 6.8	66 5.5	62 5.9							71 5.2
5.1	5.2	11.6	Sales/Working Capital						12.7
11.0	13.0	16.2							16.2
19.2	21.1	-265.9							-265.9
9.3	9.0	3.8	EBIT/Interest						6.2
(22) 5.0	(18) 2.3	(26) 1.9						(10)	2.8
1.3	1.2	1.3							.6
			Net Profit + Depr., Dep., Amort./Cur. Mat. L/T/D						
.3	.3	.6	Fixed/Worth						.3
.6	.9	1.0							.9
.9	1.6	2.3							1.7
.6	.9	1.3	Debt/Worth						1.5
1.3	2.7	2.6							2.4
2.8	5.7	11.5							12.3
37.7	36.7	39.3	% Profit Before Taxes/Tangible Net Worth						64.8
23.1	(18) 14.1	(24) 17.3							20.2
1.4	1.7	3.0							.0
16.5	12.8	10.0	% Profit Before Taxes/Total Assets						13.6
7.2	4.1	3.6							5.8
.6	.4	.9							.0
18.0	11.8	12.7	Sales/Net Fixed Assets						58.4
9.5	6.6	4.9							7.6
3.5	3.0	2.5							4.2
2.6	2.8	3.2	Sales/Total Assets						3.9
1.8	1.8	1.7							3.2
1.4	1.4	1.2							1.7
1.4	1.8	1.5	% Depr., Dep., Amort./Sales						
(20) 2.2	(17) 2.9	(25) 2.6							
3.5	7.6	6.3							
			% Officers', Directors' Owners' Comp/Sales						
1494461M	1173683M	1786856M	Net Sales ($)		13169M	11236M	12947M	88508M	1660996M
639603M	465894M	681148M	Total Assets ($)		21495M	15277M	5189M	49343M	589844M

© RMA 2007

M = $ thousand   MM = $ million
See Pages 11 through 21 for Explanation of Ratios and Data

Current Data Sorted by Assets | Comparative Historical Data

0-500M	500M-2MM	2-10MM	10-50MM	50-100MM	100-250MM	Type of Statement	4/1/02-3/31/03 ALL	4/1/03-3/31/04 ALL
1	1	9	5	4	1	Unqualified	15	18
	1		3			Reviewed	5	5
	2		1			Compiled	4	8
1						Tax Returns		4
1		7		2		Other	7	6
	17 (4/1-9/30/06)		26 (10/1/06-3/31/07)					
3	3	19	11	6	1	NUMBER OF STATEMENTS	31	41
%	%	%	%	%	%	ASSETS	%	%
		11.0	7.6			Cash & Equivalents	5.4	9.8
		25.9	18.8			Trade Receivables (net)	23.1	24.8
		25.9	24.0			Inventory	32.1	25.3
		3.2	5.9			All Other Current	4.3	3.8
		66.1	56.2			Total Current	64.9	63.7
		25.4	15.7			Fixed Assets (net)	23.1	24.2
		3.2	19.3			Intangibles (net)	5.1	6.8
		5.3	8.7			All Other Non-Current	7.0	5.3
		100.0	100.0			Total	100.0	100.0
						LIABILITIES		
		15.7	3.1			Notes Payable-Short Term	13.3	8.8
		2.2	1.1			Cur. Mat.-L.T.D.	2.9	1.8
		11.4	9.8			Trade Payables	15.6	13.0
		.1	1.6			Income Taxes Payable	.4	.4
		8.7	14.4			All Other Current	9.4	8.9
		38.0	30.0			Total Current	41.6	33.0
		13.1	11.7			Long-Term Debt	11.4	15.7
		.3	1.4			Deferred Taxes	1.4	1.1
		2.5	9.7			All Other Non-Current	4.2	6.8
		46.1	47.1			Net Worth	41.4	43.4
		100.0	100.0			Total Liabilties & Net Worth	100.0	100.0
						INCOME DATA		
		100.0	100.0			Net Sales	100.0	100.0
		37.4	44.6			Gross Profit	29.8	36.1
		30.5	33.0			Operating Expenses	23.6	29.9
		6.9	11.6			Operating Profit	6.2	6.2
		1.5	1.0			All Other Expenses (net)	1.4	.8
		5.4	10.6			Profit Before Taxes	4.7	5.4
						RATIOS		
		3.0	2.7				2.1	3.6
		1.5	2.3			Current	1.6	2.2
		1.3	1.6				1.1	1.4
		1.6	1.3				1.1	1.8
		.9	.8			Quick	.8	1.0
		.6	.5				.4	.8
	36	10.3	37 9.7				31 11.7	28 13.0
	51	7.1	47 7.8			Sales/Receivables	37 9.8	38 9.6
	74	4.9	72 5.0				58 6.3	73 5.0
	55	6.6	89 4.1				48 7.7	39 9.3
	84	4.3	123 3.0			Cost of Sales/Inventory	95 3.9	81 4.5
	108	3.4	158 2.3				131 2.8	114 3.2
	17	22.0	25 14.8				23 15.6	10 37.9
	20	17.9	49 7.4			Cost of Sales/Payables	37 9.8	31 11.7
	64	5.7	96 3.8				61 6.0	51 7.1
		4.3	3.1				5.1	4.0
		8.2	4.4			Sales/Working Capital	6.9	5.6
		13.1	7.0				25.5	14.7
		11.4	77.3				6.9	17.9
		(17) 3.4	7.2			EBIT/Interest	(27) 3.2	(35) 5.0
		.9	3.3				1.8	2.0
						Net Profit + Depr., Dep.,	11.9	11.1
						Amort./Cur. Mat. L/T/D	(13) 3.3	(12) 4.0
							1.7	1.8
		.2	.4				.2	.2
		.7	.5			Fixed/Worth	.4	.4
		2.1	1.6				1.0	1.0
		.5	.5				.8	.5
		1.6	1.5			Debt/Worth	1.7	1.6
		4.0	44.3				3.4	3.7
		44.3	313.3			% Profit Before Taxes/Tangible	33.9	54.2
		16.1	(10) 35.9			Net Worth	(29) 17.1	(37) 19.4
		.0	24.3				5.2	9.8
		14.9	15.7			% Profit Before Taxes/Total	12.4	13.9
		7.7	11.2			Assets	6.1	7.9
		.0	6.7				2.3	3.3
		19.7	77.9				37.8	19.7
		8.3	10.3			Sales/Net Fixed Assets	11.1	10.9
		4.1	4.1				3.2	4.7
		2.4	1.7				2.5	3.0
		1.8	1.5			Sales/Total Assets	1.7	1.7
		1.3	.8				1.2	1.3
		1.0					1.1	.8
		1.5				% Depr., Dep., Amort./Sales	(26) 1.9	(37) 1.8
		2.6					4.0	3.3
						% Officers', Directors'		2.2
						Owners' Comp/Sales	(10)	3.5
								7.5
3451M	15638M	211881M	337096M	504936M	237679M	Net Sales ($)	1974867M	1324691M
1041M	3410M	106059M	226209M	397105M	108160M	Total Assets ($)	1204994M	961214M

© RMA 2007

M = $ thousand   MM = $ million
See Pages 11 through 21 for Explanation of Ratios and Data

Comparative Historical Data   Current Data Sorted by Sales

			Type of Statement	0-1MM	1-3MM	3-5MM	5-10MM	10-25MM	25MM & OVER
20	18	21	Unqualified	1	1	2	3	5	9
7	6	4	Reviewed				1	2	1
2	2	3	Compiled				3		
4	2	1	Tax Returns		1				
13	18	14	Other		3	2	3	3	3
4/1/04-3/31/05 ALL	4/1/05-3/31/06 ALL	4/1/06-3/31/07 ALL			17 (4/1-9/30/06)			26 (10/1/06-3/31/07)	
46	46	43	**NUMBER OF STATEMENTS**	1	5	4	10	10	13
%	%	%	**ASSETS**	%	%	%	%	%	%
9.9	9.8	9.6	Cash & Equivalents				13.0	13.3	5.5
22.7	22.6	24.5	Trade Receivables (net)				20.1	22.9	28.8
29.4	30.5	27.1	Inventory				23.7	23.5	34.1
3.4	3.9	4.4	All Other Current				2.6	5.7	1.2
65.4	66.8	65.6	Total Current				59.4	65.4	69.6
21.4	22.6	20.8	Fixed Assets (net)				20.5	20.5	19.7
4.7	5.0	8.1	Intangibles (net)				11.8	7.7	5.1
8.5	5.6	5.5	All Other Non-Current				8.3	6.4	5.6
100.0	100.0	100.0	Total				100.0	100.0	100.0
			LIABILITIES						
7.9	17.7	14.9	Notes Payable-Short Term				12.7	5.3	11.3
2.4	3.2	1.6	Cur. Mat.-L.T.D.				2.5	1.4	1.7
12.8	11.7	10.8	Trade Payables				13.5	7.9	12.4
.5	.4	.5	Income Taxes Payable				.5	.3	.8
11.5	11.9	12.1	All Other Current				6.0	15.6	16.4
35.2	44.8	39.9	Total Current				35.2	30.4	42.6
16.4	11.8	11.0	Long-Term Debt				13.0	15.2	4.9
1.2	1.2	.7	Deferred Taxes				.7	.4	1.4
5.6	3.8	5.1	All Other Non-Current				2.2	6.9	6.0
41.6	38.5	43.3	Net Worth				49.0	47.2	45.1
100.0	100.0	100.0	Total Liabilities & Net Worth				100.0	100.0	100.0
			INCOME DATA						
100.0	100.0	100.0	Net Sales				100.0	100.0	100.0
36.2	31.6	36.7	Gross Profit				38.3	47.0	27.2
30.1	25.3	29.1	Operating Expenses				27.9	38.7	20.5
6.1	6.2	7.6	Operating Profit				10.4	8.3	6.7
.9	1.7	1.4	All Other Expenses (net)				.4	1.0	2.0
5.1	4.6	6.2	Profit Before Taxes				9.9	7.3	4.7
			RATIOS						
3.2	3.0	2.7	Current				4.1	3.7	2.3
2.0	1.5	1.5					1.7	2.5	1.4
1.2	1.1	1.3					1.0	1.4	1.3
1.5	1.4	1.4	Quick				2.9	2.3	1.2
.9	.8	.8					1.1	1.0	.8
.5	.5	.5					.5	.5	.7
27 13.4	27 13.4	36 10.3	Sales/Receivables				22 16.2	35 10.5	44 8.3
35 10.5	50 7.4	51 7.1					46 7.9	42 8.7	62 5.9
60 6.1	66 5.5	70 5.2					78 4.7	70 5.2	67 5.4
58 6.3	54 6.8	56 6.5	Cost of Sales/Inventory				48 7.6	69 5.3	59 6.1
95 3.8	88 4.2	86 4.2					94 3.9	103 3.5	89 4.1
143 2.5	136 2.7	138 2.6					173 2.1	123 3.0	142 2.6
18 20.8	20 18.5	17 21.6	Cost of Sales/Payables				20 18.5	13 27.5	22 16.9
39 9.4	36 10.1	34 10.7					43 8.4	22 16.6	34 10.7
67 5.5	48 7.6	58 6.2					78 4.7	96 3.8	52 7.0
3.6	3.8	3.6	Sales/Working Capital				2.7	3.5	4.2
6.1	7.6	6.3					4.2	4.4	7.0
30.7	33.5	18.2					NM	10.4	13.6
12.3	15.7	13.2	EBIT/Interest				15.0		13.7
(41) 5.4	(39) 4.0	(40) 4.6					4.3		5.9
1.7	1.4	1.6					1.4		2.7
15.9	19.7	16.6	Net Profit + Depr., Dep., Amort./Cur. Mat. L/T/D						
(11) 3.6	(11) 2.7	(15) 6.0							
2.9	1.2	2.0							
.2	.2	.2	Fixed/Worth				.1	.1	.3
.5	.6	.7					.3	.9	.5
1.2	2.2	1.4					1.0	14.5	.7
.7	.7	.6	Debt/Worth				.5	.4	.7
1.7	2.0	2.0					2.0	1.2	1.4
3.5	6.3	4.0					2.9	60.4	3.5
40.3	43.9	43.6	% Profit Before Taxes/Tangible Net Worth				51.1		26.2
(42) 23.3	(39) 19.3	(42) 18.4					27.4		16.8
8.5	7.2	7.7					7.7		12.7
12.5	10.7	13.1	% Profit Before Taxes/Total Assets				17.1	28.7	10.5
6.1	6.4	7.7					7.5	10.4	7.0
1.8	2.5	2.0					1.6	1.9	2.8
26.6	25.4	27.3	Sales/Net Fixed Assets				55.9	-42.7	14.4
12.3	9.9	9.7					6.8	19.1	9.7
4.5	4.2	5.0					3.8	3.9	6.7
2.7	2.6	2.3	Sales/Total Assets				2.0	2.5	2.2
1.7	1.6	1.7					1.3	1.7	1.7
1.2	1.2	1.1					.8	1.3	1.3
1.0	1.3	1.1	% Depr., Dep., Amort./Sales						1.0
(36) 2.2	(35) 1.9	(36) 2.2							(12) 1.6
3.0	3.2	2.9							2.7
2.3			% Officers', Directors' Owners' Comp/Sales						
(12) 3.9									
8.3									
2888169M	3999517M	1310681M	Net Sales ($)	194M	11234M	17575M	76379M	176986M	1028313M
1802356M	1861134M	841984M	Total Assets ($)	262M	6286M	8578M	65386M	115915M	645557M

© RMA 2007

M = $ thousand   MM = $ million
See Pages 11 through 21 for Explanation of Ratios and Data

Current Data Sorted by Assets   Comparative Historical Data

0-500M	500M-2MM	2-10MM	10-50MM	50-100MM	100-250MM	Type of Statement	4/1/02-3/31/03 ALL	4/1/03-3/31/04 ALL
1		7	12	2	1	Unqualified	20	16
1	1	2	5			Reviewed	4	7
	2	5				Compiled	4	7
	3					Tax Returns	3	4
2	3	8	10	1	4	Other	27	21
	12 (4/1-9/30/06)		53 (10/1/06-3/31/07)					
4	9	22	22	3	5	**NUMBER OF STATEMENTS**	58	55
%	%	%	%	%	%	**ASSETS**	%	%
		15.4	8.9			Cash & Equivalents	7.8	9.2
		22.5	21.8			Trade Receivables (net)	23.2	20.3
		25.9	27.5			Inventory	27.7	27.8
		2.9	2.8			All Other Current	2.4	4.4
		66.8	60.9			Total Current	61.2	61.7
		24.7	28.6			Fixed Assets (net)	26.6	24.6
		4.4	6.3			Intangibles (net)	4.0	5.1
		4.2	4.2			All Other Non-Current	8.2	8.5
		100.0	100.0			Total	100.0	100.0
						LIABILITIES		
		7.8	13.1			Notes Payable-Short Term	7.8	7.1
		4.0	3.0			Cur. Mat.-L.T.D.	5.3	2.6
		12.8	12.5			Trade Payables	13.9	14.4
		1.5	.4			Income Taxes Payable	.6	.8
		10.0	9.4			All Other Current	13.0	12.7
		36.2	38.5			Total Current	40.7	37.6
		6.4	17.5			Long-Term Debt	10.7	7.5
		.9	.9			Deferred Taxes	.4	.8
		12.1	1.6			All Other Non-Current	5.5	10.8
		44.4	41.5			Net Worth	42.8	43.3
		100.0	100.0			Total Liabilities & Net Worth	100.0	100.0
						INCOME DATA		
		100.0	100.0			Net Sales	100.0	100.0
		46.1	42.0			Gross Profit	43.4	45.9
		40.6	36.1			Operating Expenses	37.1	38.8
		5.6	5.9			Operating Profit	6.3	7.1
		1.0	1.2			All Other Expenses (net)	1.8	1.0
		4.6	4.6			Profit Before Taxes	4.5	6.2
						RATIOS		
		2.8	1.9				2.1	2.6
		1.8	1.6			Current	1.5	1.7
		1.3	1.2				1.0	1.3
		1.8	1.2				1.3	1.4
		.9	.7			Quick	.7	.8
		.5	.5				.5	.4
		29 12.7	31 11.9				31 11.6	27 13.6
		39 9.3	44 8.3			Sales/Receivables	39 9.4	38 9.6
		55 6.7	62 5.9				60 6.1	56 6.5
		63 5.8	65 5.6				63 5.8	68 5.4
		91 4.0	90 4.1			Cost of Sales/Inventory	90 4.0	99 3.7
		140 2.6	147 2.5				144 2.5	158 2.3
		29 12.5	30 12.1				28 13.2	26 14.3
		42 8.7	39 9.3			Cost of Sales/Payables	41 9.0	43 8.5
		59 6.2	56 6.5				64 5.7	68 5.4
		3.9	4.9				5.6	4.4
		8.3	8.9			Sales/Working Capital	11.1	7.9
		13.1	16.5				100.7	17.8
		20.7	21.9				13.5	24.5
		(20) 2.2	3.2			EBIT/Interest	(51) 3.4	(47) 5.6
		.3	1.5				1.0	1.7
			17.5				3.9	13.9
		(10) 2.0	2.0			Net Profit + Depr., Dep., Amort./Cur. Mat. L/T/D	(20) 1.8	(22) 3.8
			1.2				.6	1.6
		.2	.4				.2	.3
		.5	.8			Fixed/Worth	.7	.5
		1.4	1.6				1.3	1.4
		.6	1.1				.8	.5
		1.2	1.6			Debt/Worth	1.4	1.1
		7.4	2.8				3.2	2.8
		51.2	45.6				44.4	42.3
		(21) 11.0	(20) 23.9			% Profit Before Taxes/Tangible Net Worth	(56) 22.7	(49) 21.0
		-2.4	2.8				.6	5.8
		17.3	28.7				16.4	18.4
		3.3	7.3			% Profit Before Taxes/Total Assets	6.4	6.6
		-1.0	2.6				.1	2.7
		49.6	16.8				22.5	16.9
		13.1	9.0			Sales/Net Fixed Assets	9.2	9.5
		3.4	2.3				4.5	5.2
		2.5	2.2				2.7	2.6
		2.0	1.8			Sales/Total Assets	2.0	1.8
		1.2	1.0				1.3	1.3
		.9	1.3				1.2	1.5
		(20) 2.1	2.0			% Depr., Dep., Amort./Sales	(48) 2.5	(46) 2.5
		4.3	3.7				4.4	3.5
							2.4	1.7
	(14)					% Officers', Directors' Owners' Comp/Sales	(14) 5.7	(18) 4.7
							15.4	12.9
5404M	27676M	240656M	1126614M	317844M	1357253M	Net Sales ($)	2451263M	2963094M
1686M	12894M	126463M	561450M	204621M	780465M	Total Assets ($)	1425039M	1963423M

M = $ thousand   MM = $ million
See Pages 11 through 21 for Explanation of Ratios and Data

Comparative Historical Data | Current Data Sorted by Sales

	4/1/04-3/31/05 ALL	4/1/05-3/31/06 ALL	4/1/06-3/31/07 ALL	Type of Statement	0-1MM	1-3MM	3-5MM	5-10MM	10-25MM	25MM & OVER
	23	27	23	Unqualified	1			2	6	13
	4	8	4	Reviewed		1	1	1	1	
	5	5	7	Compiled		1	2	3	1	
	6	7	3	Tax Returns		1				
	28	25	28	Other	5	2		3	6	12
					12 (4/1-9/30/06)			53 (10/1/06-3/31/07)		
	66	72	65	NUMBER OF STATEMENTS	1	8	8	9	14	25
	%	%	%	ASSETS	%	%	%	%	%	%
	9.9	10.8	12.9	Cash & Equivalents					6.8	12.9
	20.5	21.2	22.8	Trade Receivables (net)					24.5	17.4
	24.3	25.5	25.9	Inventory					27.3	26.7
	2.5	3.7	3.0	All Other Current					3.8	3.0
	57.2	61.2	64.6	Total Current					62.4	60.0
	25.8	25.5	25.0	Fixed Assets (net)					27.1	25.5
	10.9	7.7	6.9	Intangibles (net)					7.6	10.9
	6.0	5.6	3.5	All Other Non-Current					2.8	3.6
	100.0	100.0	100.0	Total					100.0	100.0
				LIABILITIES						
	8.4	9.1	8.9	Notes Payable-Short Term					10.5	9.6
	3.2	3.5	5.4	Cur. Mat.-L.T.D.					2.4	9.7
	11.7	14.4	14.7	Trade Payables					12.2	12.8
	.3	.5	.8	Income Taxes Payable					.6	.9
	11.7	14.0	10.5	All Other Current					11.7	11.3
	35.3	41.6	40.3	Total Current					37.4	44.4
	13.4	12.7	11.8	Long-Term Debt					11.7	12.7
	.5	.7	.9	Deferred Taxes					1.2	1.3
	8.7	9.0	8.0	All Other Non-Current					7.8	1.8
	42.1	36.1	39.1	Net Worth					42.0	39.8
	100.0	100.0	100.0	Total Liabilities & Net Worth					100.0	100.0
				INCOME DATA						
	100.0	100.0	100.0	Net Sales					100.0	100.0
	48.5	44.8	45.0	Gross Profit					45.4	45.0
	40.1	39.5	38.0	Operating Expenses					41.3	34.7
	8.4	5.3	6.9	Operating Profit					4.1	10.3
	.9	1.6	1.6	All Other Expenses (net)					1.7	1.2
	7.5	3.7	5.4	Profit Before Taxes					2.4	9.2
				RATIOS						
	2.6	2.3	2.7	Current					3.3	2.3
	1.7	1.6	1.6						1.5	1.7
	1.1	1.0	1.3						1.2	1.2
	1.3	1.2	1.3	Quick					1.7	1.2
	.8	.8	.8						.7	.7
	.5	.5	.5						.5	.5
	26 14.2	27 13.7	28 13.1	Sales/Receivables					31 11.8	12 29.9
	39 9.4	38 9.7	39 9.3						45 8.1	36 10.2
	53 6.9	56 6.5	58 6.3						61 6.0	56 6.5
	55 6.6	56 6.5	59 6.2	Cost of Sales/Inventory					75 4.9	58 6.3
	97 3.7	88 4.2	90 4.0						115 3.2	89 4.1
	138 2.7	134 2.7	143 2.5						150 2.4	142 2.6
	23 15.7	23 15.6	30 12.1	Cost of Sales/Payables					32 11.5	28 13.2
	39 9.4	38 9.5	42 8.7						39 9.3	41 8.9
	59 6.2	55 6.7	61 5.9						54 6.8	56 6.5
	5.1	5.0	4.6	Sales/Working Capital					4.4	5.4
	9.4	11.4	8.5						10.5	8.6
	36.3	62.8	16.2						15.9	20.3
	24.0	21.7	18.1	EBIT/Interest					3.2	38.3
(55)	5.8	(65) 6.9	(59) 2.8					(13) 2.1	(24) 6.0
	2.2	1.5	1.0						.7	1.8
	9.3	11.2	5.9	Net Profit + Depr., Dep., Amort./Cur. Mat. L/T/D						
(18)	4.8	(25) 3.1	(17) 2.4							
	2.6	1.3	1.4							
	.2	.3	.3	Fixed/Worth					.3	.4
	.5	.6	.7						1.0	.6
	1.8	2.4	1.5						2.0	1.7
	.6	.7	.7	Debt/Worth					.4	.9
	1.5	1.8	1.6						1.9	1.6
	4.3	6.5	6.5						9.2	3.2
	52.7	59.2	57.2	% Profit Before Taxes/Tangible Net Worth					35.1	65.3
(57)	26.2	(62) 24.6	(58) 25.2					(12) 14.8	(22) 34.9
	9.2	8.3	.3						-2.8	12.1
	24.1	19.1	19.2	% Profit Before Taxes/Total Assets					8.3	30.9
	11.9	7.7	7.7						4.9	15.9
	1.9	.8	.1						-.3	3.5
	22.2	20.2	21.6	Sales/Net Fixed Assets					21.9	18.0
	10.2	11.5	12.3						9.4	12.3
	4.8	5.7	3.6						2.3	5.4
	2.9	3.1	2.7	Sales/Total Assets					2.4	3.0
	1.8	1.9	2.0						1.6	2.0
	1.3	1.3	1.1						1.0	1.2
	1.3	1.0	1.2	% Depr., Dep., Amort./Sales					1.7	1.1
(53)	2.4	(58) 2.0	(58) 2.0					(12) 3.0	(23) 2.0
	3.7	3.8	3.5						4.8	3.0
	3.3	2.2	2.3	% Officers', Directors' Owners' Comp/Sales						
(11)	5.3	(12) 5.0	(15) 3.4							
	10.0	7.3	5.1							
	3562178M	3253069M	3075447M	Net Sales ($)	788M	14895M	32984M	64780M	209776M	2752224M
	2022537M	1929802M	1687579M	Total Assets ($)	338M	8153M	20666M	51692M	156682M	1450048M

© RMA 2007

M = $ thousand   MM = $ million
See Pages 11 through 21 for Explanation of Ratios and Data

Current Data Sorted by Assets   Comparative Historical Data

						Type of Statement		
	1	8	17	8	17	Unqualified	50	49
	10	10	4	1		Reviewed	16	21
	4	6	1			Compiled	11	41
	4	2	1			Tax Returns	6	5
1	5	19	21	10	9	Other	43	45
	24 (4/1-9/30/06)		125 (10/1/06-3/31/07)				4/1/02-3/31/03	4/1/03-3/31/04
0-500M	500M-2MM	2-10MM	10-50MM	50-100MM	100-250MM		ALL	ALL
1	14	45	44	19	26	NUMBER OF STATEMENTS	126	161
%	%	%	%	%	%	ASSETS	%	%
	6.2	11.4	8.2	14.5	17.2	Cash & Equivalents	13.8	14.5
	34.6	28.4	19.3	18.8	15.6	Trade Receivables (net)	25.3	25.6
	20.3	22.1	24.2	17.5	11.6	Inventory	18.9	21.2
	2.1	4.0	1.6	3.0	5.3	All Other Current	4.0	4.4
	63.3	65.9	53.3	53.8	49.7	Total Current	62.0	65.7
	17.9	21.7	29.7	24.4	21.8	Fixed Assets (net)	25.0	22.8
	4.0	3.5	8.4	14.5	20.7	Intangibles (net)	6.9	6.0
	14.8	8.8	8.6	7.3	7.7	All Other Non-Current	6.2	5.5
	100.0	100.0	100.0	100.0	100.0	Total	100.0	100.0
						LIABILITIES		
	19.4	9.8	8.3	3.3	4.4	Notes Payable-Short Term	6.5	6.0
	1.3	2.3	3.7	1.5	2.5	Cur. Mat.-L.T.D.	3.4	2.9
	29.0	15.5	12.7	7.4	5.9	Trade Payables	15.3	15.8
	.0	.6	.2	.3	.6	Income Taxes Payable	.7	.5
	25.3	10.4	9.8	11.3	12.2	All Other Current	10.5	10.9
	75.1	38.5	34.7	23.8	25.6	Total Current	36.4	36.2
	8.8	16.5	21.6	18.0	14.3	Long-Term Debt	16.1	14.2
	.6	.9	.7	1.2	.7	Deferred Taxes	.4	.6
	13.8	7.1	8.7	3.0	7.9	All Other Non-Current	6.4	5.2
	1.8	37.0	34.3	54.1	51.4	Net Worth	40.7	43.9
	100.0	100.0	100.0	100.0	100.0	Total Liabilties & Net Worth	100.0	100.0
						INCOME DATA		
	100.0	100.0	100.0	100.0	100.0	Net Sales	100.0	100.0
	55.8	46.8	37.9	47.0	54.1	Gross Profit	45.9	44.8
	57.2	39.0	32.6	42.3	40.5	Operating Expenses	35.1	37.6
	-1.4	7.7	5.4	4.7	13.6	Operating Profit	10.8	7.2
	.3	.9	1.5	1.1	1.8	All Other Expenses (net)	1.1	.5
	-1.7	6.8	3.9	3.7	11.7	Profit Before Taxes	9.6	6.7

RATIOS

	2.1		3.5		2.3		4.6		3.5	Current		3.0		3.5
	1.1		1.7		1.7		2.3		2.2			1.9		1.8
	.7		1.2		1.2		1.6		1.3			1.3		1.3
	1.2		2.0		1.1		2.7		2.2	Quick		2.2		2.0
	.6		.9		.8		1.4		1.4			1.0		1.1
	.5		.5		.5		.7		.6			.6		.6
23	15.6	29	12.5	33	11.1	43	8.5	46	7.9	Sales/Receivables	32	11.3	32	11.4
43	8.5	40	9.1	45	8.2	57	6.4	64	5.7		46	7.9	45	8.2
95	3.8	62	5.9	58	6.3	82	4.5	86	4.2		59	6.2	57	6.4
40	9.2	30	12.0	58	6.3	86	4.3	71	5.1	Cost of Sales/Inventory	33	11.1	50	7.2
68	5.4	89	4.1	102	3.6	116	3.1	97	3.7		77	4.7	82	4.4
94	3.9	130	2.8	143	2.6	165	2.2	129	2.8		129	2.8	125	2.9
41	8.9	21	17.0	22	16.4	18	20.0	29	12.5	Cost of Sales/Payables	25	14.5	27	13.5
81	4.5	36	10.2	45	8.2	33	11.0	51	7.1		40	9.2	44	8.3
210	1.7	84	4.4	67	5.5	64	5.7	97	3.8		62	5.8	70	5.2
	5.9		4.4		4.9		2.3		2.2	Sales/Working Capital		3.8		3.6
	531.1		6.3		8.4		4.3		3.4			7.5		7.6
	-7.5		23.8		25.0		7.5		17.5			16.3		19.2
	16.9		18.8		9.2		26.2		38.8	EBIT/Interest		27.8		26.9
(13)	2.9	(40)	6.5	(42)	4.3	(18)	4.0	(25)	19.5		(115)	7.5	(141)	8.7
	-4.2		1.8		.5		-3.0		3.1			2.8		2.4
			20.5		27.3					Net Profit + Depr., Dep., Amort./Cur. Mat. L/T/D		19.6		12.9
		(12)	5.0	(16)	3.7						(31)	3.5	(41)	2.7
			2.4		1.7							1.8		1.2
	.1		.3		.4		.2		.2	Fixed/Worth		.2		.2
	.7		.6		1.1		.7		.7			.7		.5
	-2.3		3.2		2.6		1.6		NM			1.4		1.3
	.9		.4		.8		.2		.4	Debt/Worth		.5		.6
	1.7		1.8		2.2		.7		.8			1.4		1.5
	-7.9		19.2		6.8		2.9		NM			4.7		3.1
			73.7		39.2		26.9		58.6	% Profit Before Taxes/Tangible Net Worth		68.7		56.6
		(36)	35.6	(35)	23.7	(16)	18.3	(20)	25.0		(110)	29.3	(142)	23.4
			13.7		9.4		-11.8		10.3			13.6		9.8
	17.2		23.8		11.8		10.9		22.3	% Profit Before Taxes/Total Assets		25.3		20.7
	5.0		9.9		7.6		6.6		7.8			13.0		9.8
	-8.6		1.9		-.4		-2.7		3.8			3.5		3.8
	68.0		23.2		18.3		12.9		9.6	Sales/Net Fixed Assets		30.7		27.6
	23.8		10.9		5.8		4.7		4.2			7.1		8.5
	4.0		5.6		3.3		2.4		2.2			3.8		3.9
	4.8		2.8		2.1		1.5		1.1	Sales/Total Assets		2.6		2.7
	2.2		2.1		1.5		1.1		.8			1.8		1.8
	1.4		1.2		1.1		.6		.5			1.1		1.1
	.4		.9		1.1		2.3		1.6	% Depr., Dep., Amort./Sales		1.2		1.1
	.5	(13)	.5	(40)	2.2	(42)	2.2	(18)	3.0	3.6	(96)	2.1	(137)	2.3
	1.4		3.2		4.6		5.5		6.5			3.7		3.7
			1.8							% Officers', Directors' Owners' Comp/Sales		1.4		2.2
		(15)	2.8								(30)	4.9	(46)	3.7
			6.7									14.1		8.9
1990M	61817M	547347M	1484753M	1497944M	3951226M	Net Sales ($)	5116983M	6827835M
484M	21250M	261684M	973566M	1366892M	4001440M	Total Assets ($)	4018632M	5491642M

M = $ thousand   MM = $ million
See Pages 11 through 21 for Explanation of Ratios and Data

Comparative Historical Data | Current Data Sorted by Sales

4/1/04-3/31/05 ALL	4/1/05-3/31/06 ALL	4/1/06-3/31/07 ALL	Type of Statement	0-1MM	1-3MM	3-5MM	5-10MM	10-25MM	25MM & OVER
43	44	51	Unqualified	1			2	15	33
23	20	15	Reviewed				6	6	3
18	12	11	Compiled		2	1	4	3	1
6	5	7	Tax Returns		1	1	1	1	1
52	61	65	Other		5	5	11	14	34
				24 (4/1-9/30/06)			125 (10/1/06-3/31/07)		
142	142	149	NUMBER OF STATEMENTS	1	6	7	24	39	72
%	%	%	**ASSETS**	%	%	%	%	%	%
11.9	12.4	11.3	Cash & Equivalents				8.0	12.7	12.4
24.3	21.8	22.8	Trade Receivables (net)				24.5	25.9	19.8
22.3	20.8	20.4	Inventory				23.3	21.1	19.5
2.9	3.1	3.2	All Other Current				4.9	2.4	3.2
61.5	58.1	57.7	Total Current				60.7	62.1	55.0
23.3	24.6	24.0	Fixed Assets (net)				26.3	25.6	23.2
8.5	9.1	9.4	Intangibles (net)				2.9	4.1	14.8
6.7	8.2	9.0	All Other Non-Current				10.1	8.2	7.0
100.0	100.0	100.0	Total				100.0	100.0	100.0
			LIABILITIES						
7.9	6.7	8.5	Notes Payable-Short Term				12.0	9.6	6.4
3.0	4.0	2.5	Cur. Mat.-L.T.D.				2.0	4.0	2.2
16.6	14.7	13.6	Trade Payables				18.6	15.0	10.1
.3	.3	.4	Income Taxes Payable				.9	.2	.4
9.6	11.3	12.0	All Other Current				15.1	11.5	11.6
37.5	37.0	37.0	Total Current				48.6	40.3	30.6
14.5	16.4	17.0	Long-Term Debt				12.4	20.4	16.4
.5	.6	.8	Deferred Taxes				.7	.6	1.0
7.7	7.4	7.8	All Other Non-Current				11.7	8.7	6.1
39.7	38.6	37.4	Net Worth				26.6	30.0	46.0
100.0	100.0	100.0	Total Liabilities & Net Worth				100.0	100.0	100.0
			INCOME DATA						
100.0	100.0	100.0	Net Sales				100.0	100.0	100.0
42.5	44.3	46.3	Gross Profit				52.9	39.5	46.0
36.3	37.6	39.5	Operating Expenses				49.1	33.6	37.5
6.2	6.7	6.8	Operating Profit				3.9	5.9	8.5
.8	.8	1.2	All Other Expenses (net)				.8	.3	1.8
5.4	5.9	5.6	Profit Before Taxes				3.0	5.5	6.8
			RATIOS						
2.5 / 1.8 / 1.3	2.7 / 1.8 / 1.1	2.8 / 1.8 / 1.2	Current				5.4 / 2.3 / 1.2	2.6 / 1.6 / 1.2	3.2 / 2.1 / 1.2
1.6 / (141) 1.0 / .6	1.6 / 1.0 / .5	1.7 / .9 / .6	Quick				2.0 / .9 / .6	1.4 / .9 / .6	1.8 / 1.1 / .6
32 11.4 / 44 8.2 / 62 5.9	34 10.7 / 46 7.9 / 58 6.3	33 11.1 / 47 7.7 / 71 5.1	Sales/Receivables				33 11.1 / 41 9.0 / 73 5.0	29 12.5 / 40 9.2 / 57 6.4	37 10.0 / 54 6.8 / 75 4.9
42 8.7 / 82 4.4 / 122 3.0	41 9.0 / 84 4.4 / 129 2.8	55 6.7 / 96 3.8 / 133 2.7	Cost of Sales/Inventory				38 9.6 / 108 3.4 / 153 2.4	34 10.7 / 89 4.1 / 130 2.8	71 5.2 / 101 3.6 / 141 2.6
27 13.4 / 43 8.4 / 77 4.8	24 15.5 / 42 8.6 / 81 4.5	25 14.9 / 43 8.4 / 82 4.5	Cost of Sales/Payables				14 26.6 / 40 9.1 / 155 2.4	26 13.9 / 39 9.4 / 70 5.3	20 18.2 / 41 9.0 / 71 5.1
4.2 / 6.7 / 20.2	4.0 / 7.3 / 34.9	3.7 / 6.3 / 29.9	Sales/Working Capital				3.7 / 5.2 / 26.5	5.5 / 8.4 / 25.3	2.9 / 5.6 / 22.5
15.9 / (126) 5.1 / 2.1	19.1 / (120) 6.1 / 1.1	21.2 / (139) 5.5 / 1.5	EBIT/Interest				31.0 / (21) 7.6 / 1.7	10.5 / (37) 4.6 / 1.8	27.7 / (68) 7.5 / 1.1
8.5 / (40) 2.9 / .9	8.2 / (44) 2.5 / .7	12.4 / (45) 3.9 / 1.7	Net Profit + Depr., Dep., Amort./Cur. Mat. L/T/D						10.9 / (27) 3.2 / 1.2
.3 / .7 / 1.7	.3 / .8 / 2.3	.3 / .7 / 2.9	Fixed/Worth				.3 / .6 / 2.3	.3 / 1.1 / 3.9	.3 / .7 / 2.1
.6 / 1.8 / 6.2	.7 / 1.6 / 6.6	.5 / 1.5 / 12.8	Debt/Worth				.4 / 1.0 / 5.0	.8 / 2.1 / 21.4	.4 / 1.4 / 7.5
53.0 / (119) 21.2 / 6.0	66.7 / (118) 25.3 / 4.6	53.8 / (117) 24.7 / 8.7	% Profit Before Taxes/Tangible Net Worth				66.3 / (20) 26.5 / 9.7	57.5 / (30) 28.9 / 14.3	43.0 / (57) 23.7 / 7.4
18.0 / 7.3 / 1.4	20.6 / 8.9 / -.3	17.3 / 7.8 / 1.3	% Profit Before Taxes/Total Assets				21.0 / 8.6 / -5.4	16.7 / 8.7 / 2.4	16.3 / 7.6 / 1.1
30.1 / 8.4 / 4.2	20.2 / 7.4 / 4.1	19.7 / 7.0 / 3.6	Sales/Net Fixed Assets				25.8 / 8.4 / 3.0	22.1 / 10.6 / 3.4	17.1 / 6.0 / 3.6
2.7 / 1.8 / 1.2	2.3 / 1.6 / 1.0	2.2 / 1.5 / .9	Sales/Total Assets				2.2 / 1.6 / 1.1	2.8 / 2.1 / 1.2	1.9 / 1.2 / .8
1.1 / (118) 2.3 / 3.8	1.1 / (118) 2.3 / 3.8	1.0 / (132) 2.3 / 4.4	% Depr., Dep., Amort./Sales				.6 / (21) 2.4 / 5.2	.8 / (37) 2.0 / 4.1	1.4 / (62) 2.3 / 4.4
2.2 / (38) 3.7 / 9.3	1.5 / (34) 3.3 / 10.4	2.3 / (31) 4.0 / 7.3	% Officers', Directors' Owners' Comp/Sales					1.6 / (14) 3.4 / 8.5	
5909388M	6667726M	7545077M	Net Sales ($)	965M	13023M	26379M	177718M	657777M	6669215M
4170239M	5246150M	6625316M	Total Assets ($)	1981M	7771M	21226M	134658M	456048M	6003632M

© RMA 2007

M = $ thousand   MM = $ million
See Pages 11 through 21 for Explanation of Ratios and Data

MANUFACTURING—Paint and Coating Manufacturing NAICS 325510 (SIC 2851, 2899)

Current Data Sorted by Assets | **Comparative Historical Data**

0-500M	500M-2MM	2-10MM	10-50MM	50-100MM	100-250MM	Type of Statement	4/1/02-3/31/03 ALL	4/1/03-3/31/04 ALL
		6	10	6	1	Unqualified	22	21
2	5	20	5	1		Reviewed	32	29
	5	10	2			Compiled	15	26
2	7	1	1			Tax Returns	6	8
2	7	11	11	2	1	Other	31	30
	24 (4/1-9/30/06)		94 (10/1/06-3/31/07)					
6	24	48	29	9	2	**NUMBER OF STATEMENTS**	106	114
%	%	%	%	%	%	**ASSETS**	%	%
	10.1	7.9	5.7			Cash & Equivalents	8.4	8.3
	33.8	25.6	24.8			Trade Receivables (net)	25.3	25.5
	27.1	26.7	26.3			Inventory	26.6	27.5
	1.5	3.1	2.9			All Other Current	2.1	3.7
	72.5	63.3	59.7			Total Current	62.4	64.9
	16.9	22.8	21.7			Fixed Assets (net)	25.8	23.0
	4.7	7.6	10.6			Intangibles (net)	4.2	4.5
	5.9	6.4	8.0			All Other Non-Current	7.6	7.6
	100.0	100.0	100.0			Total	100.0	100.0
						LIABILITIES		
	19.6	9.0	4.7			Notes Payable-Short Term	7.1	12.6
	2.1	3.7	3.6			Cur. Mat.-L.T.D.	6.4	3.1
	21.0	12.0	13.4			Trade Payables	14.8	16.2
	.2	.2	.5			Income Taxes Payable	.2	.1
	8.0	9.6	12.0			All Other Current	8.5	10.7
	50.9	34.5	34.1			Total Current	37.0	42.7
	12.5	11.0	16.9			Long-Term Debt	16.6	15.9
	.2	.2	.8			Deferred Taxes	.3	.3
	7.1	8.3	4.9			All Other Non-Current	3.6	6.0
	29.3	46.0	43.4			Net Worth	42.5	35.0
	100.0	100.0	100.0			Total Liabilities & Net Worth	100.0	100.0
						INCOME DATA		
	100.0	100.0	100.0			Net Sales	100.0	100.0
	33.9	33.8	31.5			Gross Profit	34.5	33.4
	29.3	26.5	26.4			Operating Expenses	30.9	30.4
	4.6	7.3	5.1			Operating Profit	3.6	3.0
	1.8	1.1	1.0			All Other Expenses (net)	.9	.7
	2.7	6.2	4.2			Profit Before Taxes	2.8	2.2
						RATIOS		
	2.9	3.5	3.0				3.2	3.1
	1.6	2.0	1.9			Current	1.9	1.8
	1.0	1.2	1.3				1.3	1.2
	2.0	2.2	1.6				1.6	1.7
	.9	.9	1.1			Quick	.9	.8
	.5	.6	.6				.6	.5
	31 11.7	32 11.4	32 11.3				34 10.8	33 11.0
	43 8.4	39 9.3	43 8.4			Sales/Receivables	42 8.7	45 8.2
	56 6.6	48 7.6	57 6.5				52 7.0	56 6.6
	11 33.9	45 8.2	54 6.8				51 7.2	53 6.9
	66 5.6	66 5.5	69 5.3			Cost of Sales/Inventory	70 5.2	70 5.2
	103 3.6	96 3.8	88 4.1				89 4.1	97 3.7
	23 16.1	15 23.9	21 17.1				21 17.0	24 15.5
	37 9.9	24 15.5	35 10.3			Cost of Sales/Payables	32 11.5	35 10.3
	47 7.7	43 8.4	47 7.7				48 7.6	53 6.8
	5.6	4.6	4.2				4.7	4.5
	9.4	8.8	7.4			Sales/Working Capital	7.7	7.4
	131.7	15.4	18.0				18.3	24.4
	10.3	18.8	17.4				9.9	9.2
	(22) 3.1	(45) 5.7	(28) 4.2			EBIT/Interest	(95) 3.9	(103) 2.1
	1.0	1.9	2.4				1.1	-.1
		12.7	17.6				7.5	8.6
		(12) 2.6	(13) 3.2			Net Profit + Depr., Dep., Amort./Cur. Mat. L/T/D	(27) 2.9	(28) 2.5
		1.0	.7				1.7	1.2
	.1	.2	.3				.3	.3
	.5	.6	.5			Fixed/Worth	.7	.5
	20.1	1.4	1.3				1.5	1.7
	.7	.5	.6				.5	.6
	2.3	1.4	1.6			Debt/Worth	1.3	1.8
	122.7	5.0	4.3				4.3	5.7
	65.8	52.2	35.5				29.0	25.0
	(19) 43.0	(42) 21.1	(27) 17.8			% Profit Before Taxes/Tangible Net Worth	(96) 11.4	(99) 6.7
	4.0	9.2	8.1				2.4	-2.7
	18.1	20.3	15.7				12.4	9.5
	3.8	9.8	6.7			% Profit Before Taxes/Total Assets	3.6	2.8
	1.0	2.6	3.3				.2	-2.9
	67.2	22.7	16.6				15.4	20.0
	22.9	10.7	12.4			Sales/Net Fixed Assets	9.3	10.9
	8.7	6.6	5.6				5.4	5.5
	3.5	3.0	2.6				2.6	2.9
	2.9	2.2	2.3			Sales/Total Assets	2.1	2.2
	2.3	1.5	1.6				1.6	1.6
	.6	.9	1.0				1.3	1.1
	(22) 1.4	(40) 1.4	(25) 1.9			% Depr., Dep., Amort./Sales	(88) 1.9	(100) 1.7
	3.2	2.1	2.4				3.4	2.8
	1.8	.6					2.2	1.4
	(15) 4.4	(10) 2.4				% Officers', Directors' Owners' Comp/Sales	(24) 3.8	(31) 4.5
	6.6	4.2					6.7	10.4
5568M	79828M	545318M	1482516M	1021429M	573648M	Net Sales ($)	3109220M	3012578M
1335M	28102M	244846M	723520M	566158M	294910M	Total Assets ($)	1624223M	1682079M

M = $ thousand   MM = $ million
See Pages 11 through 21 for Explanation of Ratios and Data

Comparative Historical Data | | | | **Current Data Sorted by Sales** | | | | |
|---|---|---|---|---|---|---|---|---|---|

Hist 1	Hist 2	Hist 3	Type of Statement	0-1MM	1-3MM	3-5MM	5-10MM	10-25MM	25MM & OVER
23	24	23	Unqualified				1	6	16
22	18	33	Reviewed	1	1	5	10	10	6
22	19	17	Compiled		2	3	5	4	3
14	10	11	Tax Returns	3	3	3	1	1	
33	37	34	Other	2	4	4	6	4	14
4/1/04-3/31/05 ALL	4/1/05-3/31/06 ALL	4/1/06-3/31/07 ALL		24 (4/1-9/30/06)			94 (10/1/06-3/31/07)		
114	108	118	NUMBER OF STATEMENTS	6	10	15	23	25	39
%	%	%	ASSETS	%	%	%	%	%	%
7.8	8.0	8.5	Cash & Equivalents		8.6	8.6	9.8	8.1	5.3
29.0	27.0	26.7	Trade Receivables (net)		31.7	30.6	26.5	28.0	25.5
26.2	25.7	26.1	Inventory		27.8	21.3	28.3	25.9	27.3
3.1	2.5	2.6	All Other Current		3.2	4.4	1.6	2.0	2.9
66.0	63.1	63.8	Total Current		71.2	64.9	66.2	64.0	60.9
22.4	24.0	21.5	Fixed Assets (net)		17.0	18.2	18.4	25.3	23.6
4.7	5.6	7.9	Intangibles (net)		6.5	11.2	7.7	5.0	7.6
6.9	7.3	6.8	All Other Non-Current		5.3	5.7	7.7	5.6	7.8
100.0	100.0	100.0	Total		100.0	100.0	100.0	100.0	100.0
			LIABILITIES						
12.9	10.3	9.4	Notes Payable-Short Term		23.6	15.3	9.0	7.2	5.7
3.6	3.1	3.7	Cur. Mat.-L.T.D.		2.5	2.5	2.6	4.9	3.8
17.5	16.4	14.4	Trade Payables		22.0	13.8	16.4	11.7	14.2
.2	.2	.3	Income Taxes Payable		.2	.4	.3	.2	.3
7.7	8.1	10.0	All Other Current		9.3	6.0	10.5	11.8	10.2
41.7	38.1	37.8	Total Current		57.6	38.0	38.7	35.9	34.2
15.1	14.6	18.4	Long-Term Debt		15.6	9.7	8.4	11.4	16.1
.3	.2	.4	Deferred Taxes		.0	.0	.3	.4	.8
11.3	7.7	6.8	All Other Non-Current		6.9	5.3	12.8	5.1	5.5
31.5	39.4	36.7	Net Worth		19.8	47.0	39.8	47.3	43.5
100.0	100.0	100.0	Total Liabilities & Net Worth		100.0	100.0	100.0	100.0	100.0
			INCOME DATA						
100.0	100.0	100.0	Net Sales		100.0	100.0	100.0	100.0	100.0
33.9	32.4	34.0	Gross Profit		33.6	33.7	33.2	33.0	31.6
29.9	28.2	28.3	Operating Expenses		30.1	28.0	26.4	25.4	26.7
4.0	4.3	5.6	Operating Profit		3.5	5.7	6.8	7.6	4.9
.5	1.0	1.4	All Other Expenses (net)		2.1	1.1	1.2	1.4	.7
3.5	3.3	4.2	Profit Before Taxes		1.4	4.6	5.6	6.2	4.3
			RATIOS						
2.7	2.7	3.2	Current		3.8	3.7	3.5	3.3	3.0
1.6	1.9	1.9			1.8	1.8	1.9	2.0	1.9
1.2	1.2	1.2			.6	1.3	1.1	1.4	1.4
1.6	1.6	1.8	Quick		2.0	2.2	2.4	1.8	1.6
.9	1.0	1.0			.8	1.0	.8	1.1	1.1
.6	.6	.7			.3	.5	.5	.7	.7
37 9.8	33 11.0	32 11.5	Sales/Receivables		35 10.4	22 16.9	31 11.7	34 10.6	33 11.0
47 7.7	46 7.9	41 8.8			43 8.4	44 8.2	43 8.5	39 9.3	45 8.2
56 6.5	57 6.4	53 6.9			54 6.8	66 5.5	53 6.9	45 8.0	55 6.6
42 8.6	44 8.3	40 9.0	Cost of Sales/Inventory		0 UND	14 26.8	37 9.7	44 8.2	56 6.5
67 5.5	71 5.1	67 5.4			57 6.4	73 5.0	69 5.3	65 5.6	69 5.3
90 4.1	93 3.9	94 3.9			113 3.2	102 3.6	111 3.3	73 5.0	87 4.2
25 14.5	25 14.9	20 18.4	Cost of Sales/Payables		16 22.5	21 17.6	22 16.8	13 27.5	22 16.3
41 8.8	38 9.7	31 11.7			34 10.8	27 13.6	30 12.0	26 14.2	35 10.3
54 6.8	53 6.9	45 8.1			49 7.5	45 8.0	47 7.8	43 8.5	46 7.9
6.0	5.1	4.7	Sales/Working Capital		5.3	4.2	4.5	5.5	4.3
9.2	8.0	8.8			13.1	9.1	10.2	8.8	7.3
27.5	18.1	23.2			-8.2	18.1	43.8	15.0	12.5
12.9	8.9	14.5	EBIT/Interest			14.1	16.8	24.1	14.5
(106) 4.4	(100) 3.5	(111) 5.5				(14) 5.8	(22) 4.5	(22) 5.8	5.6
1.1	1.0	1.8				1.4	1.4	2.4	2.5
11.9	4.2	16.8	Net Profit + Depr., Dep., Amort./Cur. Mat. L/T/D						22.2
(28) 2.9	(28) 2.2	(34) 4.2						(19) 5.5	
1.0	1.3	1.2							3.0
.3	.3	.3	Fixed/Worth		.1	.1	.2	.2	.3
.6	.7	.6			2.4	.5	.7	.6	.5
3.1	1.8	2.9			NM	4.0	6.0	1.3	.9
.6	.7	.6	Debt/Worth		.7	.4	.5	.6	.6
1.9	1.9	1.7			9.3	1.9	2.5	1.2	1.6
11.3	5.2	5.8			NM	5.5	24.0	2.2	3.3
37.6	37.8	52.3	% Profit Before Taxes/Tangible Net Worth			42.1	85.2	47.0	34.2
(96) 12.0	(98) 17.0	(101) 22.0			(12) 13.2	(19) 18.3	(23) 32.7	(38) 17.8	
1.2	5.8	11.1				2.0	12.0	11.2	11.1
13.1	12.8	16.6	% Profit Before Taxes/Total Assets		20.9	13.3	16.9	31.2	16.0
6.0	5.8	7.9			3.7	7.8	9.8	9.6	7.0
.2	.3	3.0			-3.2	1.2	2.4	4.8	3.3
24.0	19.4	23.9	Sales/Net Fixed Assets		61.3	70.8	29.8	22.7	15.6
10.4	9.7	11.5			19.0	14.2	11.6	9.3	10.0
6.0	5.2	6.6			6.8	7.8	9.4	6.5	5.8
2.9	2.8	3.0	Sales/Total Assets		3.7	3.2	3.3	3.1	2.5
2.2	2.2	2.3			2.7	2.3	2.2	2.4	2.3
1.6	1.6	1.6			1.9	1.3	1.6	1.8	1.7
1.0	1.3	1.0	% Depr., Dep., Amort./Sales			.5	.7	1.0	1.1
(97) 1.6	(96) 1.7	(101) 1.7			(12) 1.6	(20) 1.6	(21) 1.4	(34) 1.9	
2.6	2.5	2.6				2.9	2.6	1.9	2.6
1.1	1.1	1.1	% Officers', Directors' Owners' Comp/Sales						
(39) 4.0	(31) 2.6	(32) 3.1							
6.3	5.8	6.4							
2838559M	3835442M	3708307M	Net Sales ($)	3444M	20224M	54858M	161828M	391103M	3076850M
1457361M	2141925M	1858871M	Total Assets ($)	1560M	8358M	29053M	77456M	199630M	1542814M

M = $ thousand   MM = $ million
See Pages 11 through 21 for Explanation of Ratios and Data

Current Data Sorted by Assets   Comparative Historical Data

0-500M	500M-2MM	2-10MM	10-50MM	50-100MM	100-250MM	Type of Statement	4/1/02-3/31/03 ALL	4/1/03-3/31/04 ALL
		5	14	3	2	Unqualified	19	31
	4	11	4			Reviewed	20	19
	4	3	1			Compiled	8	16
	2	4				Tax Returns	5	6
	6	14	16	1	2	Other	22	26
0-500M	17 (4/1-9/30/06)		79 (10/1/06-3/31/07)					
	16	37	35	4	4	NUMBER OF STATEMENTS	74	98
%	%	%	%	%	%	**ASSETS**	%	%
	11.1	6.2	4.1			Cash & Equivalents	7.3	7.2
	30.0	32.8	26.1			Trade Receivables (net)	26.5	29.3
	26.0	27.2	23.1			Inventory	23.7	24.4
	2.3	2.0	2.2			All Other Current	3.0	3.4
	69.4	68.3	55.6			Total Current	60.5	64.4
	22.6	22.9	29.2			Fixed Assets (net)	22.2	23.7
	3.6	3.7	6.3			Intangibles (net)	8.3	3.7
	4.4	5.1	8.9			All Other Non-Current	9.1	8.3
	100.0	100.0	100.0			Total	100.0	100.0
						LIABILITIES		
	14.2	12.2	10.6			Notes Payable-Short Term	10.8	12.0
	1.6	3.2	3.5			Cur. Mat.-L.T.D.	4.4	3.3
	16.3	17.1	14.8			Trade Payables	16.4	18.5
	.1	.2	.2			Income Taxes Payable	.2	.5
	11.6	9.7	9.0			All Other Current	7.0	8.3
	43.7	42.5	38.1			Total Current	38.9	42.5
	10.7	12.7	16.3			Long-Term Debt	10.6	13.3
	.3	.6	.9			Deferred Taxes	.6	.9
	6.6	13.6	5.3			All Other Non-Current	5.3	4.1
	38.7	30.7	39.4			Net Worth	44.6	39.2
	100.0	100.0	100.0			Total Liabilties & Net Worth	100.0	100.0
						INCOME DATA		
	100.0	100.0	100.0			Net Sales	100.0	100.0
	39.0	30.1	29.0			Gross Profit	35.3	33.7
	36.3	25.2	23.9			Operating Expenses	29.4	29.6
	2.7	4.9	5.1			Operating Profit	5.9	4.0
	1.0	1.5	.9			All Other Expenses (net)	1.2	.7
	1.7	3.4	4.1			Profit Before Taxes	4.8	3.3
						RATIOS		
	3.3	3.2	2.1			Current	2.4	2.2
	2.0	1.6	1.5				1.5	1.5
	.9	1.1	1.1				1.2	1.2
	1.9	2.1	1.6			Quick	1.3	1.4
	.9	.9	.8				.7	.8
	.7	.5	.5				.5	.6
	22 16.9	33 10.9	38 9.6			Sales/Receivables	33 11.0	36 10.1
	37 9.7	42 8.7	46 8.0				40 9.0	48 7.6
	45 8.0	53 6.9	57 6.4				50 7.3	58 6.2
	23 15.8	35 10.4	39 9.3			Cost of Sales/Inventory	41 8.8	43 8.5
	44 8.3	49 7.5	48 7.6				57 6.4	62 5.9
	71 5.2	86 4.3	78 4.7				86 4.2	80 4.5
	14 25.3	20 18.1	25 14.5			Cost of Sales/Payables	24 15.5	25 14.8
	27 13.4	33 11.2	35 10.4				37 9.8	38 9.6
	55 6.6	51 7.1	47 7.8				54 6.8	60 6.1
	6.6	5.6	6.3			Sales/Working Capital	5.8	5.6
	10.4	9.9	12.6				11.2	9.5
	-63.2	45.9	42.0				31.1	31.0
	8.4	12.5	10.5			EBIT/Interest	6.4	10.5
	(13) 3.6	(33) 5.0	(33) 5.8				(66) 3.4	(86) 4.1
	.9	2.8	1.8				1.0	1.2
		11.8	17.1			Net Profit + Depr., Dep., Amort./Cur. Mat. L/T/D	3.7	6.4
		(12) 4.7	(19) 4.7				(27) 1.9	(35) 1.9
		1.3	1.4				1.0	1.1
	.1	.2	.4			Fixed/Worth	.2	.2
	.6	.7	.9				.6	.5
	3.3	2.1	1.9				1.3	1.4
	.8	.8	1.0			Debt/Worth	.7	.9
	1.5	1.7	1.6				1.7	1.6
	4.2	4.7	3.8				3.5	2.9
	63.6	53.0	46.6			% Profit Before Taxes/Tangible Net Worth	37.5	36.2
	(13) 19.7	(30) 26.4	(33) 29.3				(65) 15.4	(91) 13.8
	4.1	13.1	8.4				.5	2.6
	22.3	14.2	17.1			% Profit Before Taxes/Total Assets	14.8	14.1
	6.2	10.1	11.9				6.4	5.4
	-.5	3.4	2.9				.1	.5
	82.2	43.8	15.5			Sales/Net Fixed Assets	24.7	23.0
	15.1	13.7	8.3				10.3	10.3
	8.8	6.9	5.7				5.2	5.1
	4.0	3.4	2.6			Sales/Total Assets	2.7	2.8
	3.1	2.7	2.3				2.1	2.1
	2.4	1.8	1.8				1.5	1.6
	.7	.5	1.2			% Depr., Dep., Amort./Sales	1.1	.9
	(14) 1.1	(33) 1.3	(33) 1.8				(66) 2.2	(83) 1.9
	2.7	2.7	2.3				3.0	3.1
		1.9				% Officers', Directors' Owners' Comp/Sales	4.2	2.3
		(14) 3.3					(22) 7.2	(29) 4.1
		8.0					10.0	10.2
	63425M	460183M	1851523M	592806M	935201M	Net Sales ($)	2023294M	2527039M
	19122M	175108M	872011M	344647M	664386M	Total Assets ($)	1345912M	1439752M

M = $ thousand   MM = $ million
See Pages 11 through 21 for Explanation of Ratios and Data

Comparative Historical Data | Current Data Sorted by Sales

Type of Statement

Comparative Historical Data			Type of Statement	Current Data Sorted by Sales					
26	29	24	Unqualified		1	3	7	5	19
21	28	19	Reviewed	1	1	1	2	4	4
9	5	8	Compiled		1	1	3	1	2
7	4	6	Tax Returns						
23	35	39	Other	1	3	4	3	12	16
4/1/04-3/31/05 ALL	4/1/05-3/31/06 ALL	4/1/06-3/31/07 ALL		17 (4/1-9/30/06)			79 (10/1/06-3/31/07)		
				0-1MM	1-3MM	3-5MM	5-10MM	10-25MM	25MM & OVER
86	101	96	**NUMBER OF STATEMENTS**	2	6	9	15	23	41

%	%	%	**ASSETS**	%	%	%	%	%	%
7.4	7.4	6.2	Cash & Equivalents				8.4	4.3	4.7
28.6	28.7	29.1	Trade Receivables (net)				28.8	31.3	28.0
22.2	25.2	25.1	Inventory				30.3	26.1	24.0
2.1	2.2	2.4	All Other Current				4.3	2.3	2.7
60.3	63.6	62.9	Total Current				71.8	64.0	59.4
24.2	23.4	25.2	Fixed Assets (net)				20.3	24.2	26.7
5.9	6.8	5.4	Intangibles (net)				2.2	4.7	7.2
9.6	6.3	6.5	All Other Non-Current				5.8	7.0	6.8
100.0	100.0	100.0	Total				100.0	100.0	100.0

			LIABILITIES						
11.6	8.9	11.3	Notes Payable-Short Term				8.8	11.8	11.0
2.7	3.9	3.2	Cur. Mat.-L.T.D.				2.0	3.1	3.9
18.4	16.3	15.8	Trade Payables				19.0	16.6	15.1
.3	.3	.2	Income Taxes Payable				.6	.0	.3
8.6	8.2	11.2	All Other Current				9.1	9.0	13.0
41.6	37.5	41.8	Total Current				39.5	40.5	43.4
13.6	13.4	14.0	Long-Term Debt				14.7	12.1	15.3
1.2	1.0	.8	Deferred Taxes				.4	.9	1.1
5.8	6.0	8.9	All Other Non-Current				8.5	8.1	5.1
37.8	42.1	34.5	Net Worth				36.9	38.4	35.1
100.0	100.0	100.0	Total Liabilities & Net Worth				100.0	100.0	100.0

			INCOME DATA						
100.0	100.0	100.0	Net Sales				100.0	100.0	100.0
34.4	32.1	31.4	Gross Profit				33.8	28.5	30.0
28.0	27.4	26.8	Operating Expenses				30.3	23.1	24.3
6.4	4.7	4.6	Operating Profit				3.5	5.5	5.7
.9	1.0	1.5	All Other Expenses (net)				.5	1.8	1.6
5.5	3.7	3.2	Profit Before Taxes				3.0	3.7	4.1

			RATIOS						
2.7	2.7	2.6	Current				3.8	2.6	2.1
1.6	1.8	1.6					1.9	1.6	1.5
1.1	1.2	1.1					1.3	1.1	1.1
1.7	1.6	1.6	Quick				2.2	2.1	1.3
.9	.9	.9					.9	.9	.7
.6	.6	.6					.7	.5	.5
33 10.9	38 9.7	35 10.3	Sales/Receivables				19 19.6	35 10.3	38 9.7
44 8.3	44 8.3	42 8.6					36 10.1	43 8.5	47 7.8
55 6.6	55 6.6	55 6.7					50 7.3	50 7.3	61 6.0
38 9.5	40 9.1	39 9.5	Cost of Sales/Inventory				38 9.6	35 10.4	41 8.9
55 6.6	55 6.6	49 7.4					49 7.4	46 7.9	53 6.9
70 5.2	82 4.4	79 4.6					68 5.4	75 4.9	80 4.5
26 13.9	28 13.0	21 17.2	Cost of Sales/Payables				10 34.9	20 17.9	23 15.8
36 10.0	36 10.2	35 10.6					24 15.5	37 10.0	35 10.4
58 6.3	49 7.5	50 7.3					53 6.8	45 8.0	49 7.4
6.0	5.8	6.4	Sales/Working Capital				4.6	6.2	7.8
11.2	8.7	10.5					8.7	11.6	11.3
44.3	20.2	45.5					16.5	44.4	43.9
14.7	14.0	11.0	EBIT/Interest				12.1	16.7	15.5
(78) 6.2	(90) 4.8	(87) 4.9				(13)	5.7 (22)	4.3 (39)	5.7
1.6	1.3	2.0					4.4	2.5	1.8
8.6	5.1	13.9	Net Profit + Depr., Dep.,					9.6	9.7
(40) 2.8	(45) 2.5	(38) 4.6	Amort./Cur. Mat. L/T/D					(10) 3.2 (22)	4.6
1.8	1.1	1.3						-1.7	1.4
.3	.3	.3	Fixed/Worth				.2	.2	.4
.7	.6	.8					.4	.7	.9
2.1	1.3	2.1					1.4	2.1	1.9
.7	.7	.9	Debt/Worth				.8	.8	.9
1.7	1.6	1.7					1.7	1.6	2.3
5.3	3.2	4.5					2.4	4.3	4.9
55.4	40.3	46.6	% Profit Before Taxes/Tangible				47.0	53.5	46.5
(72) 20.9	(89) 18.4	(82) 26.8	Net Worth			(13)	19.7 (20)	26.9 (36)	29.1
7.8	3.5	9.1					9.8	4.1	9.5
16.5	15.5	16.9	% Profit Before Taxes/Total				15.4	21.9	17.0
8.1	6.5	9.7	Assets				8.7	10.1	12.1
2.9	1.0	2.1					4.1	5.4	3.4
24.2	23.7	19.4	Sales/Net Fixed Assets				75.0	40.0	15.9
10.5	10.3	11.3					14.7	13.6	8.5
6.0	5.9	6.0					6.4	7.5	5.8
3.1	2.8	3.1	Sales/Total Assets				4.1	3.5	2.7
2.2	2.2	2.4					2.6	2.9	2.3
1.7	1.7	1.8					1.8	1.9	1.8
.9	.9	.9	% Depr., Dep., Amort./Sales				.3	.6	1.2
(78) 1.9	(85) 1.7	(85) 1.6				(14)	2.0 (20)	1.2 (36)	1.7
2.7	2.5	2.6					3.1	2.2	2.0
2.8	2.9	1.9	% Officers', Directors'						
(27) 5.6	(24) 4.0	(25) 3.3	Owners' Comp/Sales						
9.3	10.6	7.5							
2833676M	3463685M	3903138M	Net Sales ($)	1374M	14118M	36493M	107624M	385322M	3358207M
1722278M	1893389M	2075274M	Total Assets ($)	3845M	9256M	16150M	43177M	207272M	1795574M

M = $ thousand   MM = $ million
See Pages 11 through 21 for Explanation of Ratios and Data

Current Data Sorted by Assets   Comparative Historical Data

Type of Statement

0-500M	500M-2MM	2-10MM	10-50MM	50-100MM	100-250MM	Type of Statement	4/1/02-3/31/03 ALL	4/1/03-3/31/04 ALL
1	1	4	5		1	Unqualified	14	13
	2	8	2			Reviewed	7	13
2	2	1	1			Compiled	6	13
1	3					Tax Returns	4	3
1	4	7	7	1	1	Other	11	10
5 (4/1-9/30/06)			50 (10/1/06-3/31/07)					
5	12	20	15	1	2	NUMBER OF STATEMENTS	42	52
%	%	%	%	%	%	**ASSETS**	%	%
	9.0	4.1	5.7			Cash & Equivalents	6.5	7.5
	22.8	32.5	23.2			Trade Receivables (net)	28.5	29.1
	30.1	34.6	27.9			Inventory	26.6	24.9
	1.7	2.0	1.4			All Other Current	4.0	3.2
	63.5	73.1	58.2			Total Current	65.7	64.7
	15.1	17.9	26.1			Fixed Assets (net)	26.1	22.9
	9.1	3.5	7.9			Intangibles (net)	3.2	4.9
	12.2	5.5	7.8			All Other Non-Current	4.9	7.4
	100.0	100.0	100.0			Total	100.0	100.0
						LIABILITIES		
	12.4	10.0	17.6			Notes Payable-Short Term	15.1	12.5
	2.0	4.6	2.7			Cur. Mat.-L.T.D.	4.0	5.3
	18.6	17.8	18.3			Trade Payables	18.4	19.9
	.0	.0	.4			Income Taxes Payable	.2	.3
	9.3	9.8	8.4			All Other Current	9.5	8.0
	42.4	42.2	47.4			Total Current	47.1	46.0
	19.9	11.6	16.0			Long-Term Debt	13.0	14.0
	.0	.0	.4			Deferred Taxes	.4	.1
	6.9	4.7	11.9			All Other Non-Current	5.4	2.9
	30.8	41.5	24.4			Net Worth	34.0	36.9
	100.0	100.0	100.0			Total Liabilities & Net Worth	100.0	100.0
						INCOME DATA		
	100.0	100.0	100.0			Net Sales	100.0	100.0
	40.3	41.6	32.8			Gross Profit	35.3	37.3
	36.9	34.1	27.8			Operating Expenses	30.9	32.9
	3.4	7.5	4.9			Operating Profit	4.3	4.3
	1.7	.2	2.5			All Other Expenses (net)	.8	1.2
	1.8	7.3	2.5			Profit Before Taxes	3.6	3.2
						RATIOS		
	2.9	2.5	1.8				2.4	2.0
	1.3	2.0	1.3			Current	1.6	1.5
	1.0	1.3	.8				1.1	1.1
	1.2	1.6	1.0				1.4	1.3
	.7	.9	.5			Quick	.8	.7
	.4	.7	.3				.5	.5
	18 20.3	30 12.2	34 10.8				31 11.8	33 11.0
	30 12.4	42 8.6	41 9.0			Sales/Receivables	40 9.1	45 8.1
	40 9.1	49 7.4	55 6.7				52 7.0	57 6.4
	40 9.1	54 6.8	52 7.0				38 9.6	40 9.2
	59 6.2	78 4.7	69 5.3			Cost of Sales/Inventory	60 6.1	55 6.7
	103 3.6	102 3.6	91 4.0				78 4.7	78 4.7
	16 22.1	27 13.5	29 12.6				23 15.8	30 12.1
	38 9.6	39 9.4	41 9.0			Cost of Sales/Payables	44 8.3	42 8.7
	74 4.9	57 6.4	74 4.9				63 5.8	71 5.2
	6.4	4.9	7.5				6.3	5.8
	26.9	8.8	13.4			Sales/Working Capital	11.3	12.0
	NM	18.2	-20.7				34.0	36.2
	18.2	56.3	8.5				11.4	16.2
	(10) 4.1	(19) 9.1	3.8			EBIT/Interest	(37) 4.4	(50) 3.6
	.3	2.5	.2				1.4	.7
						Net Profit + Depr., Dep.,	4.4	2.1
						Amort./Cur. Mat. L/T/D	(10) 1.8	(15) 1.4
							-.6	.8
	.1	.2	.5				.3	.3
	.5	.4	1.0			Fixed/Worth	.8	.6
	NM	1.0	-43.4				1.8	1.3
	.6	.7	1.2				.7	1.1
	1.4	1.5	2.7			Debt/Worth	1.9	1.9
	NM	6.4	-105.8				3.7	4.0
		84.2	55.5			% Profit Before Taxes/Tangible	35.5	48.8
		(19) 39.5	(11) 30.9			Net Worth	(37) 18.3	(47) 12.4
		11.4	3.3				1.7	-1.3
	17.9	37.3	17.3			% Profit Before Taxes/Total	14.1	20.3
	6.4	14.8	9.4			Assets	6.2	4.4
	-1.0	3.9	-6.0				.5	-1.0
	196.0	31.2	25.7				23.0	24.2
	42.5	21.4	10.7			Sales/Net Fixed Assets	9.7	10.2
	8.9	10.2	5.3				6.0	6.8
	3.8	3.2	2.6				3.0	3.0
	2.7	2.6	2.1			Sales/Total Assets	2.3	2.3
	2.0	2.2	1.5				1.8	1.6
		.9	1.3				1.4	1.0
		(18) 1.3	(14) 2.0			% Depr., Dep., Amort./Sales	(38) 2.0	(49) 2.0
		2.1	5.7				3.0	2.9
						% Officers', Directors'	2.6	2.2
						Owners' Comp/Sales	(13) 4.3	(15) 4.2
							11.8	7.7
3781M	45005M	250216M	695772M	34683M	483571M	Net Sales ($)	1398233M	1639564M
1947M	15760M	90008M	358439M	54169M	235321M	Total Assets ($)	705114M	903796M

M = $ thousand   MM = $ million
See Pages 11 through 21 for Explanation of Ratios and Data

Comparative Historical Data			Type of Statement	Current Data Sorted by Sales					
			Unqualified	1		2	1	2	6
16	9	12	Reviewed		1	1	4	3	3
10	7	12	Compiled	1	2	1	1		1
10	6	6	Tax Returns	1		1	1		
9	4	4	Other	1	1	1	6	6	6
22	17	21		5 (4/1-9/30/06)			50 (10/1/06-3/31/07)		
4/1/04-3/31/05 ALL	4/1/05-3/31/06 ALL	4/1/06-3/31/07 ALL		0-1MM	1-3MM	3-5MM	5-10MM	10-25MM	25MM & OVER
67	43	55	NUMBER OF STATEMENTS	4	5	6	13	11	16
%	%	%	ASSETS	%	%	%	%	%	%
7.0	4.2	6.4	Cash & Equivalents				3.4	6.0	3.3
26.7	28.4	25.9	Trade Receivables (net)				33.6	28.1	24.8
27.3	27.6	28.8	Inventory				33.1	30.8	30.1
2.6	1.6	2.3	All Other Current				1.5	2.9	.9
63.7	61.8	63.4	Total Current				71.6	67.9	59.0
24.1	22.2	22.8	Fixed Assets (net)				12.9	26.9	23.3
4.8	10.4	6.6	Intangibles (net)				7.9	2.3	10.3
7.4	5.6	7.1	All Other Non-Current				7.6	2.9	7.3
100.0	100.0	100.0	Total				100.0	100.0	100.0
			LIABILITIES						
13.5	14.4	12.4	Notes Payable-Short Term				9.2	11.0	19.4
3.4	3.9	3.7	Cur. Mat.-L.T.D.				3.3	5.5	2.7
20.4	17.7	17.5	Trade Payables				17.4	17.0	19.9
1.0	.3	.1	Income Taxes Payable				.0	.0	.4
8.2	9.6	8.8	All Other Current				13.2	10.5	6.3
46.5	45.9	42.5	Total Current				43.0	44.0	48.6
13.3	15.4	15.7	Long-Term Debt				15.2	14.6	12.2
.3	.8	.5	Deferred Taxes				.0	.2	.8
6.6	8.3	7.0	All Other Non-Current				3.8	13.8	5.8
33.4	29.5	34.3	Net Worth				38.0	27.4	32.6
100.0	100.0	100.0	Total Liabilities & Net Worth				100.0	100.0	100.0
			INCOME DATA						
100.0	100.0	100.0	Net Sales				100.0	100.0	100.0
36.1	32.4	37.5	Gross Profit				45.8	35.1	28.3
32.1	27.7	32.1	Operating Expenses				39.0	29.1	24.1
4.0	4.7	5.4	Operating Profit				6.8	6.0	4.1
1.1	1.3	1.4	All Other Expenses (net)				.1	2.2	1.6
2.9	3.4	4.0	Profit Before Taxes				6.6	3.8	2.6
			RATIOS						
1.9	2.3	2.3					2.6	2.1	1.7
1.3	1.2	1.5	Current				1.6	1.8	1.2
.9	1.1	1.0					1.2	1.3	.9
1.2	1.2	1.2					1.3	1.3	.9
.7	.7	.7	Quick				.7	.9	.5
.4	.5	.4					.6	.5	.3
27 13.5	32 11.5	28 12.9					36 10.1	28 12.9	34 10.9
41 8.9	42 8.8	39 9.4	Sales/Receivables				41 8.8	43 8.6	38 9.5
52 7.0	55 6.7	45 8.1					71 5.1	48 7.5	47 7.8
37 9.9	36 10.0	41 8.9					53 6.8	26 14.0	53 6.8
63 5.8	64 5.7	65 5.6	Cost of Sales/Inventory				84 4.3	54 6.8	67 5.5
93 3.9	87 4.2	96 3.8					112 3.3	103 3.5	88 4.2
26 14.3	22 16.6	28 13.1					28 13.2	33 10.9	28 13.0
39 9.4	36 10.3	40 9.0	Cost of Sales/Payables				49 7.5	37 9.8	40 9.0
70 5.2	58 6.2	61 6.0					72 5.1	47 7.7	59 6.2
9.1	8.1	5.9					4.6	5.7	9.3
17.2	22.3	12.2	Sales/Working Capital				10.3	10.6	24.9
-105.8	95.8	-219.6					30.3	20.5	-49.8
20.4	8.9	14.9					105.1	14.9	8.6
(60) 3.0	(39) 2.1	(51) 3.9	EBIT/Interest		(12) 4.2			3.9	3.1
.6	.0	1.0					.8	1.9	.6
21.4	4.9	8.5	Net Profit + Depr., Dep.,						
(14) 2.3	(10) 1.5	(13) 2.2	Amort./Cur. Mat. L/T/D						
.7	.9	.4							
.3	.3	.2					.2	.3	.4
.8	.9	.7	Fixed/Worth				.4	.5	.9
2.3	2.5	2.9					1.8	4.2	NM
.8	1.0	.8					.8	1.2	.9
1.8	2.2	1.6	Debt/Worth				1.7	1.6	2.7
5.7	7.4	13.2					11.0	42.8	NM
39.8	46.8	50.0	% Profit Before Taxes/Tangible				93.7		62.1
(55) 16.2	(34) 23.2	(45) 30.1	Net Worth		(12) 41.3			(12) 30.5	30.5
1.5	3.5	7.4					2.9		4.6
17.2	15.3	18.6	% Profit Before Taxes/Total				31.7	25.6	16.8
5.3	3.5	9.0	Assets				17.3	9.0	5.9
-1.0	-2.0	.4					1.2	2.4	-2.1
47.5	40.8	27.1					48.3	27.1	24.6
10.6	12.8	11.8	Sales/Net Fixed Assets				24.6	15.9	10.5
5.1	5.1	6.2					12.0	6.8	5.0
3.4	3.4	3.1					3.4	3.9	2.8
2.4	2.3	2.4	Sales/Total Assets				2.6	3.1	2.3
1.6	1.7	1.7					2.1	1.5	1.7
.7	1.2	.9						.6	.9
(56) 1.8	(34) 1.9	(46) 1.6	% Depr., Dep., Amort./Sales					1.6	(14) 1.5
4.1	4.4	2.5						2.2	3.5
1.6	1.4	3.1	% Officers', Directors'						
(22) 3.5	(13) 4.5	(17) 4.2	Owners' Comp/Sales						
6.4	6.1	6.5							
1777303M	1020370M	1513028M	Net Sales ($)	2679M	8871M	23987M	96974M	188396M	1192121M
873210M	676033M	755644M	Total Assets ($)	1504M	5144M	9989M	38695M	93359M	606953M

M = $ thousand   MM = $ million
See Pages 11 through 21 for Explanation of Ratios and Data

Current Data Sorted by Assets   Comparative Historical Data

0-500M	500M-2MM	2-10MM	10-50MM	50-100MM	100-250MM	Type of Statement	4/1/02-3/31/03 ALL	4/1/03-3/31/04 ALL
	1	5	6	2	1	Unqualified	15	16
	1	12	1			Reviewed	17	12
1	5	3	1			Compiled	8	10
5	3					Tax Returns	4	5
2	2	10	6		1	Other	29	29
	12 (4/1-9/30/06)		56 (10/1/06-3/31/07)					
8	12	30	14	3	1	NUMBER OF STATEMENTS	73	72
%	%	%	%	%	%	**ASSETS**	%	%
	5.7	8.2	6.5			Cash & Equivalents	7.0	7.4
	36.5	30.4	26.1			Trade Receivables (net)	27.7	30.5
	36.0	25.8	27.4			Inventory	23.7	25.3
	2.5	4.9	1.3			All Other Current	3.5	2.3
	80.8	69.3	61.3			Total Current	62.0	65.4
	11.2	18.5	23.5			Fixed Assets (net)	26.0	22.3
	1.5	6.6	8.0			Intangibles (net)	5.1	5.3
	6.6	5.6	7.2			All Other Non-Current	6.9	7.0
	100.0	100.0	100.0			Total	100.0	100.0
						LIABILITIES		
	15.5	14.8	10.5			Notes Payable-Short Term	9.7	12.5
	2.2	2.6	2.9			Cur. Mat.-L.T.D.	4.1	3.3
	23.2	17.9	14.5			Trade Payables	18.0	17.8
	.1	.1	.4			Income Taxes Payable	.5	.4
	5.1	8.3	10.7			All Other Current	12.1	9.5
	46.1	43.7	39.0			Total Current	44.4	43.5
	14.9	10.6	17.7			Long-Term Debt	16.2	12.5
	.0	.4	.8			Deferred Taxes	.3	.2
	7.8	5.3	9.9			All Other Non-Current	3.9	5.7
	31.1	40.1	32.6			Net Worth	35.2	38.1
	100.0	100.0	100.0			Total Liabilities & Net Worth	100.0	100.0
						INCOME DATA		
	100.0	100.0	100.0			Net Sales	100.0	100.0
	44.6	38.1	34.2			Gross Profit	38.9	38.3
	42.6	32.8	24.5			Operating Expenses	34.6	33.3
	2.1	5.3	9.7			Operating Profit	4.3	5.0
	.9	.9	1.3			All Other Expenses (net)	1.0	1.0
	1.2	4.4	8.4			Profit Before Taxes	3.2	4.0
						RATIOS		
	2.9	2.5	3.2			Current	2.2	2.3
	1.8	1.5	1.7				1.4	1.5
	1.3	1.1	1.0				1.1	1.2
	1.7	1.5	2.5			Quick	1.2	1.4
	1.0	.8	.7				.8	.9
	.5	.6	.6				.5	.6
	25 14.6	35 10.3	36 10.2			Sales/Receivables	32 11.4	38 9.7
	42 8.8	41 8.9	41 8.9				43 8.5	45 8.2
	51 7.1	51 7.1	50 7.3				53 6.9	54 6.8
	43 8.5	43 8.5	53 6.8			Cost of Sales/Inventory	43 8.5	39 9.4
	61 6.0	54 6.8	61 6.0				55 6.6	62 5.9
	118 3.1	104 3.5	82 4.5				79 4.6	88 4.1
	20 18.1	27 13.7	19 18.8			Cost of Sales/Payables	30 12.4	24 14.9
	39 9.3	40 9.0	26 14.1				43 8.6	39 9.3
	77 4.8	60 6.1	41 8.8				55 6.6	58 6.3
	6.7	4.9	5.4			Sales/Working Capital	7.1	6.8
	9.1	9.8	10.6				12.9	11.4
	23.2	23.4	NM				46.0	34.4
	45.0	14.0	9.2			EBIT/Interest	12.4	13.1
	(11) 3.0	(26) 4.6	(12) 4.8				(66) 4.6	(62) 5.4
	.9	2.3	1.5				1.5	1.5
		13.4				Net Profit + Depr., Dep., Amort./Cur. Mat. L/T/D	10.6	4.2
		(11) 3.2					(27) 2.5	(25) 2.1
		2.4					1.3	.6
	.2	.2	.5			Fixed/Worth	.4	.3
	.4	.5	1.0				.9	.8
	-.8	1.4	-1.4				1.8	1.9
	.5	.7	.5			Debt/Worth	.9	.7
	1.7	1.8	1.9				2.4	1.8
	-8.4	5.6	-8.7				5.7	6.1
		66.9				% Profit Before Taxes/Tangible Net Worth	47.0	39.0
		(27) 29.9					(68) 18.8	(64) 20.0
		12.1					3.0	6.9
	6.8	17.7	19.5			% Profit Before Taxes/Total Assets	12.4	14.2
	2.9	6.8	12.4				7.1	8.4
	-.5	4.4	3.4				1.3	1.0
	131.4	31.6	15.0			Sales/Net Fixed Assets	16.0	21.4
	34.6	14.7	10.0				10.3	13.8
	26.3	7.6	5.7				5.8	6.3
	5.2	2.8	2.8			Sales/Total Assets	2.8	2.9
	3.0	2.5	2.4				2.4	2.3
	2.6	1.8	1.7				1.6	1.8
	.3	.8	.8			% Depr., Dep., Amort./Sales	1.2	.8
	(11) .6	(26) 1.3	1.6				(65) 1.9	(62) 1.3
	2.8	2.0	2.5				2.6	1.9
		2.3				% Officers', Directors' Owners' Comp/Sales	3.2	2.1
	(12) 3.2						(24) 4.1	(23) 5.2
		5.3					9.9	12.3
7400M	53563M	363481M	872863M	443126M	284811M	Net Sales ($)	2201019M	1905876M
2284M	15415M	153852M	394657M	190096M	146014M	Total Assets ($)	1128267M	927275M

M = $ thousand   MM = $ million
See Pages 11 through 21 for Explanation of Ratios and Data

Comparative Historical Data | Current Data Sorted by Sales

Type of Statement

Type of Statement	4/1/04-3/31/05 ALL	4/1/05-3/31/06 ALL	4/1/06-3/31/07 ALL	0-1MM	1-3MM	3-5MM	5-10MM	10-25MM	25MM & OVER
Unqualified	19	17	15		1		2	4	8
Reviewed	18	19	14		1		5	7	1
Compiled	9	9	10	1	2	3	2	1	1
Tax Returns	3	3	8	1	2	3			
Other	20	22	21	2	2	1	7	4	7
				12 (4/1-9/30/06)			56 (10/1/06-3/31/07)		
NUMBER OF STATEMENTS	69	70	68	4	8	7	16	16	17

Main Data

	4/1/04-3/31/05 ALL %	4/1/05-3/31/06 ALL %	4/1/06-3/31/07 ALL %	0-1MM	1-3MM	3-5MM	5-10MM %	10-25MM %	25MM & OVER %
ASSETS									
Cash & Equivalents	6.7	7.6	7.0				11.7	4.8	7.2
Trade Receivables (net)	31.9	30.7	31.7				25.5	34.6	27.0
Inventory	26.2	25.7	27.2				29.6	26.4	27.7
All Other Current	1.9	2.4	3.5				7.9	1.2	2.0
Total Current	66.7	66.4	69.4				74.8	66.9	63.8
Fixed Assets (net)	20.3	21.4	18.4				14.1	24.5	21.5
Intangibles (net)	6.8	6.0	6.2				5.9	2.3	7.6
All Other Non-Current	6.1	6.1	6.0				5.3	6.3	7.0
Total	100.0	100.0	100.0				100.0	100.0	100.0
LIABILITIES									
Notes Payable-Short Term	12.4	14.3	13.3				11.9	17.1	10.3
Cur. Mat.-L.T.D.	3.2	2.8	3.0				1.7	3.3	3.0
Trade Payables	19.9	19.4	19.2				18.6	18.4	13.9
Income Taxes Payable	.1	.2	.2				.2	.1	.4
All Other Current	8.2	7.3	9.5				7.9	7.5	11.8
Total Current	43.9	44.0	45.2				40.3	46.4	39.3
Long-Term Debt	11.7	12.1	15.6				8.0	14.6	15.4
Deferred Taxes	.4	.2	.4				.3	.4	.7
All Other Non-Current	6.1	5.0	6.6				5.9	4.0	8.7
Net Worth	37.9	38.7	32.3				45.5	34.6	35.8
Total Liabilities & Net Worth	100.0	100.0	100.0				100.0	100.0	100.0
INCOME DATA									
Net Sales	100.0	100.0	100.0				100.0	100.0	100.0
Gross Profit	37.1	38.6	39.1				40.6	31.9	35.2
Operating Expenses	32.2	33.3	33.7				37.3	26.0	27.0
Operating Profit	4.8	5.3	5.4				3.3	5.8	8.2
All Other Expenses (net)	1.2	.7	1.1				.4	.8	1.0
Profit Before Taxes	3.6	4.6	4.3				2.9	5.0	7.3
RATIOS									
Current	2.2	2.6	2.8				2.6	2.1	3.1
	1.5	1.6	1.7				1.9	1.5	2.1
	1.1	1.1	1.1				1.3	1.1	1.2
Quick	1.2	1.6	1.5				1.5	1.3	1.9
	.8	.9	.9				.7	.8	.9
	.5	.5	.5				.6	.6	.5
Sales/Receivables	36 10.0	39 9.4	36 10.2				24 15.5	37 9.9	39 9.4
	45 8.1	44 8.2	41 8.9				36 10.3	43 8.6	43 8.5
	61 6.0	52 7.0	50 7.3				51 7.2	49 7.4	47 7.7
Cost of Sales/Inventory	43 8.5	39 9.4	45 8.2				42 8.6	40 9.1	53 6.9
	71 5.1	59 6.2	59 6.2				63 5.8	52 7.0	63 5.8
	96 3.8	87 4.2	94 3.9				106 3.4	69 5.3	79 4.6
Cost of Sales/Payables	29 12.5	28 13.2	23 15.6				21 17.7	25 14.8	19 19.4
	44 8.2	38 9.5	34 10.8				47 7.8	31 11.8	26 14.0
	66 5.6	53 6.9	59 6.2				70 5.2	51 7.2	41 8.9
Sales/Working Capital	6.6	6.1	5.6				4.9	6.0	5.0
	11.8	10.2	9.1				7.4	11.2	8.8
	30.8	47.6	24.4				20.0	41.2	44.1
EBIT/Interest	7.8	10.1	11.0				22.3	11.6	8.5
	(63) 3.0	(60) 3.4	(60) 3.6				(14) 4.2	(14) 3.9	(14) 4.7
	1.3	.4	1.7				2.2	2.3	1.5
Net Profit + Depr., Dep., Amort./Cur. Mat. L/T/D	4.6	4.8	11.4						
	(24) 1.8	(16) 2.7	(19) 3.0						
	1.2	1.4	2.0						
Fixed/Worth	.3	.2	.2				.1	.4	.4
	.7	.7	.6				.3	.7	.7
	1.4	1.9	NM				.8	1.8	-9.5
Debt/Worth	.8	.6	.7				.7	.7	.6
	2.2	2.1	1.8				1.5	1.5	1.6
	6.4	6.9	NM				3.6	5.9	-26.0
% Profit Before Taxes/Tangible Net Worth	28.4	50.5	54.0				47.1	59.8	30.5
	(61) 11.1	(61) 23.9	(51) 25.6				(15) 20.7	(14) 28.9	(12) 20.4
	1.0	4.5	7.6				8.1	7.5	6.2
% Profit Before Taxes/Total Assets	11.9	17.3	16.5				15.3	18.6	19.4
	5.1	6.4	6.0				6.0	6.0	10.2
	.6	.5	2.7				2.8	3.8	3.2
Sales/Net Fixed Assets	26.9	30.6	34.6				81.1	19.3	16.8
	14.3	15.5	14.7				27.3	11.6	9.7
	7.1	7.4	8.5				11.1	7.0	7.7
Sales/Total Assets	2.9	2.9	3.1				3.1	2.9	2.8
	2.3	2.3	2.6				2.5	2.6	2.4
	1.7	1.8	2.0				1.8	2.3	1.8
% Depr., Dep., Amort./Sales	.8	.8	.7				.4	1.0	.7
	(64) 1.3	(60) 1.3	(60) 1.5				(12) .8	1.3	1.3
	1.9	2.2	2.6				2.0	2.2	2.3
% Officers', Directors' Owners' Comp/Sales	2.3	1.8	2.3						
	(21) 5.2	(22) 3.8	(22) 4.2						
	9.2	6.2	6.4						
Net Sales ($)	1488721M	1812454M	2025244M	1842M	14023M	27499M	121501M	280006M	1580373M
Total Assets ($)	694834M	831976M	902318M	759M	10789M	8610M	52241M	114681M	715238M

© RMA 2007   M = $ thousand   MM = $ million
See Pages 11 through 21 for Explanation of Ratios and Data

Current Data Sorted by Assets   **Comparative Historical Data**

0-500M	500M-2MM	2-10MM	10-50MM	50-100MM	100-250MM	Type of Statement	4/1/02-3/31/03 ALL	4/1/03-3/31/04 ALL
		2	11	3	1	Unqualified	28	34
	1	8	7			Reviewed	12	15
	4	2		1		Compiled	11	21
		2				Tax Returns	5	1
2	3	16	12	3	2	Other	31	25
	8 (4/1-9/30/06)		72 (10/1/06-3/31/07)					
2	8	30	30	7	3	**NUMBER OF STATEMENTS**	87	96
%	%	%	%	%	%	**ASSETS**	%	%
		6.4	8.4			Cash & Equivalents	8.2	8.7
		27.5	25.1			Trade Receivables (net)	26.5	27.2
		31.4	31.3			Inventory	31.3	29.6
		1.4	3.7			All Other Current	2.3	3.3
		66.7	68.5			Total Current	68.3	68.7
		22.8	20.5			Fixed Assets (net)	20.2	18.5
		3.9	5.0			Intangibles (net)	6.8	7.6
		6.5	6.0			All Other Non-Current	4.7	5.1
		100.0	100.0			Total	100.0	100.0
						LIABILITIES		
		18.8	10.7			Notes Payable-Short Term	15.1	13.1
		.9	1.8			Cur. Mat.-L.T.D.	4.1	2.5
		23.0	17.9			Trade Payables	19.0	17.7
		.2	.2			Income Taxes Payable	.7	.6
		16.1	12.5			All Other Current	10.7	9.3
		59.0	43.1			Total Current	49.6	43.3
		6.2	10.0			Long-Term Debt	13.6	10.9
		.0	.2			Deferred Taxes	.3	.4
		9.4	4.5			All Other Non-Current	7.7	9.7
		25.4	42.2			Net Worth	28.7	35.6
		100.0	100.0			Total Liabilities & Net Worth	100.0	100.0
						INCOME DATA		
		100.0	100.0			Net Sales	100.0	100.0
		39.1	35.9			Gross Profit	39.4	40.2
		37.0	32.5			Operating Expenses	35.1	33.1
		2.1	3.4			Operating Profit	4.3	7.1
		1.7	1.0			All Other Expenses (net)	1.0	1.1
		.5	2.4			Profit Before Taxes	3.3	6.0
						RATIOS		
		1.8	2.5			Current	2.7	2.2
		1.3	1.7				1.5	1.6
		.9	1.3				1.1	1.2
		1.1	1.1			Quick	1.3	1.3
		.6	.8				.8	.8
		.3	.5				.5	.5
		25 14.8	34 10.8			Sales/Receivables	33 11.1	35 10.3
		34 10.7	50 7.2				46 7.9	45 8.2
		52 7.1	66 5.5				62 5.9	55 6.7
		33 11.2	61 5.9			Cost of Sales/Inventory	54 6.7	52 7.0
		78 4.7	88 4.2				82 4.4	84 4.3
		146 2.5	130 2.8				143 2.6	133 2.7
		23 15.9	31 11.6			Cost of Sales/Payables	24 15.0	28 13.0
		38 9.6	50 7.3				41 8.8	50 7.3
		81 4.5	70 5.2				74 5.0	69 5.3
		6.4	4.9			Sales/Working Capital	4.6	4.9
		26.9	6.9				10.7	8.9
		-19.3	13.1				25.2	21.4
		10.0	20.0			EBIT/Interest	9.2	19.7
		(28) 3.3	(27) 3.3				(80) 3.5	(85) 6.2
		-.3	.8				1.2	2.1
			8.3			Net Profit + Depr., Dep., Amort./Cur. Mat. L/T/D	10.1	10.5
			(11) 2.9				(33) 3.2	(27) 4.1
			1.5				.6	1.7
		.3	.2			Fixed/Worth	.2	.2
		.5	.4				.7	.6
		6.6	1.2				3.4	1.8
		1.5	.7			Debt/Worth	1.1	.8
		2.9	1.4				2.5	1.9
		12.6	5.3				15.2	6.2
		60.6	43.2			% Profit Before Taxes/Tangible Net Worth	45.9	63.4
		(25) 26.6	(27) 17.4				(70) 23.6	(84) 30.4
		-4.1	4.1				3.8	13.7
		17.5	15.7			% Profit Before Taxes/Total Assets	14.9	20.5
		7.5	6.9				7.2	10.2
		-7.8	.0				.6	2.9
		41.2	22.4			Sales/Net Fixed Assets	38.7	28.7
		14.7	11.5				11.2	14.2
		5.9	5.8				6.4	7.3
		3.4	2.6			Sales/Total Assets	2.8	2.8
		2.5	1.9				2.1	2.1
		1.6	1.4				1.5	1.5
		.4	.6			% Depr., Dep., Amort./Sales	1.2	1.0
		(25) 2.0	(28) 1.6				(71) 2.1	(78) 1.6
		4.1	2.6				2.9	3.0
		1.2				% Officers', Directors' Owners' Comp/Sales	1.9	1.8
		(16) 2.2					(26) 4.3	(20) 4.3
		5.0					9.5	8.4
832M	38375M	423175M	1315455M	650524M	702666M	Net Sales ($)	3851542M	3242981M
413M	11685M	155691M	672036M	474840M	408552M	Total Assets ($)	2264998M	1966404M

M = $ thousand   MM = $ million
See Pages 11 through 21 for Explanation of Ratios and Data

Comparative Historical Data | Current Data Sorted by Sales

Type of Statement				0-1MM	1-3MM	3-5MM	5-10MM	10-25MM	25MM & OVER
Unqualified	23	21	17				1	2	14
Reviewed	11	10	16			2		7	7
Compiled	6	10	7		2	2	1	1	1
Tax Returns	6	1	2		1		1		
Other	27	36	38	2	2	3	5	15	11
	4/1/04-3/31/05 ALL	4/1/05-3/31/06 ALL	4/1/06-3/31/07 ALL	\<— 8 (4/1-9/30/06) —\>			\<— 72 (10/1/06-3/31/07) —\>		
NUMBER OF STATEMENTS	73	78	80	2	5	7	8	25	33
ASSETS	%	%	%	%	%	%	%	%	%
Cash & Equivalents	6.6	9.3	8.7					7.6	7.0
Trade Receivables (net)	29.1	27.8	25.8					28.4	26.8
Inventory	35.0	32.3	30.2					33.0	31.5
All Other Current	2.5	1.8	2.5					2.1	3.3
Total Current	73.2	71.2	67.2					71.2	68.6
Fixed Assets (net)	15.4	17.6	21.3					18.0	19.5
Intangibles (net)	5.9	4.6	4.0					2.7	4.4
All Other Non-Current	5.4	6.6	7.5					8.2	7.5
Total	100.0	100.0	100.0					100.0	100.0
LIABILITIES									
Notes Payable-Short Term	19.1	13.1	12.7					16.8	9.6
Cur. Mat.-L.T.D.	3.1	2.7	2.4					.9	3.6
Trade Payables	22.8	21.2	19.1					21.0	19.4
Income Taxes Payable	.1	.4	.2					.3	.2
All Other Current	9.7	8.2	12.9					13.1	10.7
Total Current	54.8	45.7	47.3					52.2	43.5
Long-Term Debt	11.6	13.8	11.7					7.5	14.4
Deferred Taxes	.1	.5	.1					.0	.3
All Other Non-Current	4.2	7.6	6.0					2.3	5.0
Net Worth	29.3	32.4	34.9					38.0	36.9
Total Liabilities & Net Worth	100.0	100.0	100.0					100.0	100.0
INCOME DATA									
Net Sales	100.0	100.0	100.0					100.0	100.0
Gross Profit	40.7	38.7	39.4					34.5	37.2
Operating Expenses	34.1	30.7	34.8					33.3	29.7
Operating Profit	6.6	8.0	4.6					1.2	7.5
All Other Expenses (net)	1.2	1.1	1.5					.9	1.2
Profit Before Taxes	5.4	6.9	3.1					.2	6.3
RATIOS									
Current	2.3 1.5 1.2	2.6 1.7 1.2	2.4 1.5 1.1					2.4 1.5 1.0	2.3 1.5 1.3
Quick	1.2 .7 .5	1.4 .9 .5	1.2 .8 .4					1.1 .8 .4	1.2 .8 .5
Sales/Receivables	37 9.9 47 7.7 61 6.0	37 9.8 45 8.2 61 6.0	30 12.1 47 7.7 63 5.8					28 12.9 41 9.0 53 6.9	33 11.1 49 7.4 67 5.4
Cost of Sales/Inventory	59 6.2 93 3.9 149 2.4	50 7.3 85 4.3 151 2.4	53 6.9 83 4.4 136 2.7					45 8.1 84 4.3 133 2.7	61 5.9 94 3.9 140 2.6
Cost of Sales/Payables	22 16.5 51 7.2 76 4.8	28 13.3 44 8.3 73 5.0	26 13.8 45 8.0 75 4.9					20 18.3 39 9.3 74 4.9	33 11.0 49 7.5 66 5.6
Sales/Working Capital	4.9 8.7 23.4	4.0 7.6 20.8	5.0 8.1 33.5					5.5 11.6 NM	5.4 7.3 13.4
EBIT/Interest	16.2 (67) 5.7 1.7	19.0 (68) 5.0 1.8	14.0 (73) 3.2 .1					11.4 (23) 3.5 .4	18.1 (30) 4.6 1.0
Net Profit + Depr., Dep., Amort./Cur. Mat. L/T/D	7.7 (18) 1.6 .9	5.0 (19) 2.6 .8	8.2 (20) 2.9 1.0						8.3 (15) 3.0 1.2
Fixed/Worth	.2 .5 1.4	.1 .4 1.1	.2 .5 2.0					.2 .3 1.1	.2 .5 1.3
Debt/Worth	1.0 2.5 7.9	.7 1.6 4.2	.7 1.8 5.8					.6 1.7 5.7	.7 1.5 4.8
% Profit Before Taxes/Tangible Net Worth	74.2 (64) 35.1 10.4	56.1 (69) 27.9 9.8	54.8 (71) 21.6 -1.6					32.8 (24) 17.4 -5.3	52.5 (30) 26.3 4.2
% Profit Before Taxes/Total Assets	19.3 9.2 2.0	21.5 8.4 2.4	18.1 8.2 -2.0					14.8 7.8 -3.0	22.0 9.7 1.6
Sales/Net Fixed Assets	55.4 18.7 8.2	42.0 15.6 7.8	31.7 13.8 5.8					45.1 19.9 8.9	27.3 12.6 5.6
Sales/Total Assets	3.0 2.2 1.5	2.9 2.1 1.5	2.8 2.1 1.4					3.2 2.5 1.6	2.6 2.0 1.4
% Depr., Dep., Amort./Sales	.7 (64) 1.5 2.1	.7 (65) 1.4 2.4	.6 (67) 1.8 2.8					.4 (20) 1.8 2.8	.5 (31) 1.4 2.5
% Officers', Directors' Owners' Comp/Sales	2.2 (22) 4.0 8.2	1.8 (21) 2.8 9.0	1.6 (28) 2.5 5.1						
Net Sales ($)	2196536M	3226220M	3131027M	832M	12704M	26137M	60301M	439679M	2591374M
Total Assets ($)	1331110M	1618160M	1723217M	413M	11739M	27092M	22936M	210815M	1450222M

© RMA 2007

M = $ thousand   MM = $ million
See Pages 11 through 21 for Explanation of Ratios and Data

	Current Data Sorted by Assets						Comparative Historical Data	
Type of Statement								
Unqualified			1	5	1	1	5	2
Reviewed		1	3	2			6	9
Compiled		2	4				1	5
Tax Returns			1					
Other		5	4	4		1	5	5
		7 (4/1-9/30/06)		28 (10/1/06-3/31/07)			4/1/02-3/31/03	4/1/03-3/31/04
	0-500M	500M-2MM	2-10MM	10-50MM	50-100MM	100-250MM	ALL	ALL
NUMBER OF STATEMENTS		8	13	11	1	2	17	21
ASSETS	%	%	%	%	%	%	%	%
Cash & Equivalents	DATA NOT AVAILABLE		7.2	4.1			3.7	5.7
Trade Receivables (net)			26.9	28.6			27.5	31.1
Inventory			27.5	32.8			34.5	30.8
All Other Current			2.5	3.6			2.6	4.0
Total Current			64.1	69.1			68.3	71.6
Fixed Assets (net)			25.4	20.8			25.5	18.3
Intangibles (net)			9.1	7.3			3.8	3.4
All Other Non-Current			1.4	2.8			2.5	6.7
Total			100.0	100.0			100.0	100.0
LIABILITIES								
Notes Payable-Short Term			9.4	17.2			18.0	14.5
Cur. Mat.-L.T.D.			4.3	2.2			2.5	2.8
Trade Payables			20.7	12.4			21.9	22.2
Income Taxes Payable			.1	1.1			.7	.1
All Other Current			6.8	15.3			13.0	11.2
Total Current			41.2	48.2			56.1	50.7
Long-Term Debt			18.7	6.0			11.1	11.0
Deferred Taxes			.3	.6			.2	.3
All Other Non-Current			8.2	8.3			6.8	11.2
Net Worth			31.5	36.9			25.9	26.8
Total Liabilties & Net Worth			100.0	100.0			100.0	100.0
INCOME DATA								
Net Sales			100.0	100.0			100.0	100.0
Gross Profit			33.2	37.2			31.2	32.7
Operating Expenses			27.6	29.8			28.0	27.9
Operating Profit			5.5	7.4			3.3	4.7
All Other Expenses (net)			.0	1.0			.6	.9
Profit Before Taxes			5.5	6.4			2.6	3.9
RATIOS								
Current			2.2	2.3			1.6	2.9
			1.7	1.6			1.3	1.4
			1.1	.9			.9	1.1
Quick			1.0	1.0			.8	1.6
			.8	.6			.6	.8
			.6	.5			.4	.5
Sales/Receivables			34 10.6	41 8.9			25 14.5	35 10.3
			42 8.8	51 7.1			47 7.7	46 7.9
			48 7.7	54 6.7			53 6.9	51 7.1
Cost of Sales/Inventory			30 12.1	75 4.9			48 7.5	49 7.5
			63 5.8	98 3.7			77 4.7	63 5.7
			91 4.0	131 2.8			95 3.8	96 3.8
Cost of Sales/Payables			26 14.3	27 13.5			23 16.2	22 16.7
			39 9.5	34 10.7			39 9.4	35 10.4
			53 6.8	49 7.4			53 6.8	55 6.7
Sales/Working Capital			6.1	4.7			7.0	5.4
			12.5	8.4			15.4	10.5
			NM	-42.6			-35.4	124.1
EBIT/Interest			11.4	40.9			17.0	11.3
			6.9	(10) 13.3			(16) 4.6	(19) 3.7
			2.5	1.1			2.5	.8
Net Profit + Depr., Dep., Amort./Cur. Mat. L/T/D								
Fixed/Worth			.2	.4			.6	.4
			.7	.7			1.0	.9
			NM	-1.3			2.6	-4.8
Debt/Worth			1.5	.6			1.6	1.2
			2.6	1.6			1.9	2.8
			NM	-13.0			12.1	-24.9
% Profit Before Taxes/Tangible Net Worth			77.5				60.3	50.4
			(10) 41.9				(14) 27.2	(15) 21.9
			2.5				8.1	3.6
% Profit Before Taxes/Total Assets			18.5	21.1			18.1	18.7
			16.2	11.0			7.2	5.5
			.9	.4			3.5	.3
Sales/Net Fixed Assets			34.7	16.0			25.3	28.0
			18.8	9.3			9.0	12.4
			6.0	7.9			5.9	8.6
Sales/Total Assets			3.7	2.4			3.1	3.1
			2.7	2.0			2.4	2.4
			1.7	1.7			1.9	2.0
% Depr., Dep., Amort./Sales			.7	1.6			1.3	1.0
			(12) 1.1	(10) 2.0			1.8	(19) 1.6
			1.8	2.4			2.9	2.8
% Officers', Directors' Owners' Comp/Sales								
Net Sales ($)		25228M	157793M	432191M	77821M	614609M	388886M	383985M
Total Assets ($)		9819M	61893M	203316M	72974M	357278M	236981M	172994M

M = $ thousand MM = $ million

See Pages 11 through 21 for Explanation of Ratios and Data

Comparative Historical Data

Current Data Sorted by Sales

Type of Statement	H: 4/1/04-3/31/05 ALL	H: 4/1/05-3/31/06 ALL	H: 4/1/06-3/31/07 ALL		0-1MM	1-3MM	3-5MM	5-10MM	10-25MM	25MM & OVER
Unqualified	3	7	8					1	3	4
Reviewed	9	7	6			1	1	2	2	2
Compiled	3	2	6			1	1	2	2	1
Tax Returns	2									
Other	7	8	14		1	4	2	4	4	4
					0-1MM	**7 (4/1-9/30/06)** 1-3MM	3-5MM	**28 (10/1/06-3/31/07)** 5-10MM	10-25MM	25MM & OVER
NUMBER OF STATEMENTS	24	24	35			5	4	4	11	11
ASSETS	%	%	%		%	%	%	%	%	%
Cash & Equivalents	3.3	5.2	6.7	D					2.2	4.9
Trade Receivables (net)	32.2	28.0	27.9	A					28.3	31.6
Inventory	34.0	33.8	29.8	T					31.3	30.2
All Other Current	3.2	2.6	3.1	A					3.1	2.8
Total Current	72.6	69.7	67.5						64.9	69.4
Fixed Assets (net)	17.6	17.2	21.0	N					24.5	20.5
Intangibles (net)	4.3	5.0	9.0	O					9.3	6.8
All Other Non-Current	5.5	8.1	2.6	T					1.3	3.3
Total	100.0	100.0	100.0						100.0	100.0
LIABILITIES				A						
Notes Payable-Short Term	24.1	15.1	10.2	V					9.2	17.7
Cur. Mat.-L.T.D.	2.8	2.3	2.7	A					3.9	1.5
Trade Payables	22.0	23.1	16.9	I					18.0	16.0
Income Taxes Payable	.3	.3	.5	L					.7	.4
All Other Current	7.9	8.3	11.7	A					10.2	12.0
Total Current	57.1	49.1	42.0	B					41.9	47.7
Long-Term Debt	4.7	6.9	16.1	L					10.7	8.1
Deferred Taxes	.2	.3	.7	E					.5	.6
All Other Non-Current	10.2	7.5	6.4						9.2	7.6
Net Worth	27.8	36.1	34.7						37.7	36.0
Total Liabilities & Net Worth	100.0	100.0	100.0						100.0	100.0
INCOME DATA										
Net Sales	100.0	100.0	100.0						100.0	100.0
Gross Profit	30.5	31.0	35.8						38.5	28.2
Operating Expenses	28.6	26.8	29.9						29.6	25.3
Operating Profit	1.9	4.2	5.9						9.0	3.0
All Other Expenses (net)	.8	.7	.8						.6	1.2
Profit Before Taxes	1.1	3.6	5.1						8.3	1.8
RATIOS										
Current	2.0	1.9	2.3						2.3	2.0
	1.5	1.5	1.7						1.7	1.6
	1.0	1.2	1.1						1.0	1.1
Quick	1.0	.9	1.0						1.0	.9
	.7	.7	.8						.8	.7
	.5	.5	.6						.5	.6
Sales/Receivables	35 10.5	35 10.5	39 9.4						35 10.5	47 7.8
	43 8.4	46 8.0	47 7.8						42 8.8	51 7.1
	51 7.1	51 7.1	54 6.7						53 7.0	59 6.2
Cost of Sales/Inventory	49 7.5	56 6.5	49 7.5						48 7.6	55 6.7
	70 5.2	82 4.5	81 4.5						86 4.2	75 4.9
	89 4.1	114 3.2	114 3.2						131 2.8	98 3.7
Cost of Sales/Payables	24 15.4	24 15.1	27 13.4						22 16.8	30 12.4
	30 12.0	33 11.1	36 10.2						39 9.5	34 10.7
	60 6.1	70 5.2	51 7.2						53 6.9	43 8.4
Sales/Working Capital	7.5	7.7	5.5						5.8	6.8
	11.3	10.4	8.4						8.1	8.7
	145.4	55.9	35.0						-267.1	35.0
EBIT/Interest	16.1	16.1	13.8						27.3	12.6
	(23) 3.7	(21) 3.3	(31) 8.8						13.1	(10) 1.6
	2.1	1.0	1.4						6.9	.6
Net Profit + Depr., Dep., Amort./Cur. Mat. L/T/D			22.4							
			(13) 5.9							
			1.6							
Fixed/Worth	.3	.3	.4						.3	.4
	.6	.6	.7						.7	.6
	-12.5	1.1	5.7						5.7	-1.3
Debt/Worth	.9	1.0	1.0						.8	.9
	1.8	1.9	1.7						1.6	1.6
	-73.0	4.3	23.0						8.8	-13.0
% Profit Before Taxes/Tangible Net Worth	42.3	45.4	49.9							
	(17) 22.8	(22) 13.6	(27) 31.5							
	6.1	.3	3.0							
% Profit Before Taxes/Total Assets	13.7	15.4	20.2						21.1	7.0
	6.3	5.8	12.1						18.2	4.9
	.5	.4	.6						16.2	-1.3
Sales/Net Fixed Assets	29.4	26.9	24.7						18.8	16.0
	16.1	13.6	14.1						15.4	8.5
	11.7	8.1	7.9						7.8	7.9
Sales/Total Assets	3.5	2.8	3.0						3.0	2.4
	2.6	2.2	2.2						2.3	2.0
	1.9	1.9	1.6						1.7	1.8
% Depr., Dep., Amort./Sales	1.1	1.2	1.0						1.0	1.1
	(20) 1.5	(21) 1.6	(32) 1.6						1.5	(10) 1.9
	2.4	2.1	2.2						2.4	2.0
% Officers', Directors' Owners' Comp/Sales			1.1							
			(11) 3.0							
			8.5							
Net Sales ($)	405678M	1133205M	1307642M			7626M	14244M	31061M	190450M	1064261M
Total Assets ($)	185138M	596891M	705280M			8320M	5252M	12996M	88354M	590358M

M = $ thousand   MM = $ million
See Pages 11 through 21 for Explanation of Ratios and Data

Current Data Sorted by Assets   **Comparative Historical Data**

0-500M	500M-2MM	2-10MM	10-50MM	50-100MM	100-250MM	Type of Statement	4/1/02-3/31/03 ALL	4/1/03-3/31/04 ALL
		2	3			Unqualified	3	5
	1	2	1	1		Reviewed	3	3
		1	1			Compiled	3	5
						Tax Returns	1	1
1	2 (4/1-9/30/06)	5	22 (10/1/06-3/31/07)		4	Other	10	8
1	1	10	7	1	4	NUMBER OF STATEMENTS	20	22
%	%	%	%	%	%		%	%
		5.7				ASSETS Cash & Equivalents	5.2	5.9
		21.2				Trade Receivables (net)	28.4	21.7
		22.9				Inventory	21.3	27.7
		4.9				All Other Current	1.7	3.5
		54.7				Total Current	56.7	58.9
		38.6				Fixed Assets (net)	34.8	34.6
		1.1				Intangibles (net)	5.1	2.5
		5.6				All Other Non-Current	3.4	3.9
		100.0				Total	100.0	100.0
						LIABILITIES		
		12.0				Notes Payable-Short Term	13.3	12.4
		3.2				Cur. Mat.-L.T.D.	6.9	5.4
		16.9				Trade Payables	14.3	13.3
		.0				Income Taxes Payable	.0	.1
		3.6				All Other Current	6.9	5.7
		35.8				Total Current	41.3	36.9
		16.1				Long-Term Debt	20.7	23.0
		.3				Deferred Taxes	1.1	1.2
		4.9				All Other Non-Current	11.1	6.2
		42.9				Net Worth	25.8	32.8
		100.0				Total Liabilities & Net Worth	100.0	100.0
						INCOME DATA		
		100.0				Net Sales	100.0	100.0
		36.2				Gross Profit	31.9	35.2
		31.7				Operating Expenses	25.6	28.2
		4.5				Operating Profit	6.3	7.1
		1.9				All Other Expenses (net)	2.3	1.8
		2.7				Profit Before Taxes	4.0	5.3
						RATIOS		
		2.2					2.3	3.5
		1.7				Current	1.5	1.6
		1.3					.8	1.0
		1.6					1.7	2.2
		.9				Quick	.9	.7
		.4					.4	.4
		34 10.9					34 10.7	31 11.7
		39 9.3				Sales/Receivables	42 8.7	40 9.1
		43 8.5					59 6.2	49 7.4
		44 8.4					36 10.1	48 7.7
		52 7.0				Cost of Sales/Inventory	51 7.2	64 5.7
		74 4.9					67 5.4	119 3.1
		27 13.7					16 23.5	22 16.6
		39 9.3				Cost of Sales/Payables	33 11.1	40 9.2
		76 4.8					48 7.7	53 6.8
		6.2					6.4	4.7
		8.9				Sales/Working Capital	16.3	9.1
		17.8					NM	NM
		12.1					13.4	12.4
		2.9				EBIT/Interest	(21) 4.0	2.7
		-.1					1.4	2.0
						Net Profit + Depr., Dep., Amort./Cur. Mat. L/T/D		
		.4					.7	.6
		.8				Fixed/Worth	1.9	.9
		2.7					11.0	5.6
		.6					1.1	.7
		1.1				Debt/Worth	4.5	2.7
		5.2					20.8	12.6
		42.5					(17) 121.1	(20) 54.9
		25.6				% Profit Before Taxes/Tangible Net Worth	39.4	32.1
		-12.3					17.6	10.1
		22.1					20.7	15.4
		7.6				% Profit Before Taxes/Total Assets	5.9	10.0
		-3.4					2.0	3.3
		11.3					11.5	15.2
		5.9				Sales/Net Fixed Assets	7.0	5.6
		3.5					3.6	2.6
		2.4					3.1	3.0
		2.0				Sales/Total Assets	2.2	1.9
		1.7					1.5	1.3
							1.6	1.7
						% Depr., Dep., Amort./Sales	(19) 3.1	3.4
							4.9	4.6
							1.4	
						% Officers', Directors' Owners' Comp/Sales	(10) 3.8	
							12.8	
6M	4657M	93715M	389593M	180768M	1175544M	Net Sales ($)	605235M	628793M
1M	1452M	46491M	124651M	94546M	641330M	Total Assets ($)	360992M	361265M

Comparative Historical Data | Current Data Sorted by Sales

Type of Statement	5/4/2 → 10 4/1/04-3/31/05 ALL	5/3/5 → 16 4/1/05-3/31/06 ALL	5/4/3 → 12 4/1/06-3/31/07 ALL	0-1MM	1-3MM [2 (4/1-9/30/06)]	3-5MM	5-10MM [22 (10/1/06-3/31/07)]	10-25MM	25MM & OVER
Unqualified	5	5	5				1	1	3
Reviewed	4	3	4		1			1	1
Compiled	2	5	3			1	1		1
Tax Returns									
Other				1			1		1
NUMBER OF STATEMENTS	21	29	24	1	2	1	3	6	11

ASSETS

	%	%	%	%	%	%	%	%	%
Cash & Equivalents	3.5	4.1	3.4						1.4
Trade Receivables (net)	26.7	26.8	24.6						28.2
Inventory	26.9	25.9	25.9						24.3
All Other Current	1.3	1.9	2.7						1.3
Total Current	58.4	58.6	56.6						55.2
Fixed Assets (net)	27.6	31.8	35.1						32.9
Intangibles (net)	8.3	4.4	4.0						7.7
All Other Non-Current	5.7	5.2	4.3						4.2
Total	100.0	100.0	100.0						100.0

LIABILITIES

Notes Payable-Short Term	17.2	15.2	13.6						9.3
Cur. Mat.-L.T.D.	5.7	2.7	2.6						1.9
Trade Payables	14.6	15.7	17.0						18.7
Income Taxes Payable	.0	.1	.0						.0
All Other Current	10.0	6.6	5.5						7.0
Total Current	47.5	40.2	38.7						36.9
Long-Term Debt	11.2	12.7	18.2						21.8
Deferred Taxes	.7	.4	.2						.1
All Other Non-Current	15.6	4.1	6.0						2.8
Net Worth	25.0	42.7	36.9						38.4
Total Liabilities & Net Worth	100.0	100.0	100.0						100.0

INCOME DATA

Net Sales	100.0	100.0	100.0						100.0
Gross Profit	28.5	25.3	27.0						21.3
Operating Expenses	22.4	20.0	22.9						16.0
Operating Profit	6.1	5.3	4.1						5.3
All Other Expenses (net)	1.6	1.6	1.5						1.4
Profit Before Taxes	4.5	3.7	2.6						4.0

RATIOS

Current	1.5	2.1	2.2						2.5
	1.1	1.4	1.7						1.8
	1.0	1.1	1.2						1.1
Quick	.9	1.2	1.3						1.2
	.6	.7	1.0						1.0
	.4	.5	.5						.6
Sales/Receivables	39 9.4	33 11.0	36 10.1						37 9.9
	42 8.7	42 8.7	42 8.7						47 7.7
	56 6.6	49 7.5	48 7.6						54 6.7
Cost of Sales/Inventory	44 8.4	42 8.7	37 9.9						35 10.3
	70 5.2	55 6.6	52 7.0						56 6.6
	96 3.8	77 4.8	70 5.2						57 6.4
Cost of Sales/Payables	27 13.7	22 16.7	24 15.4						23 15.8
	38 9.5	29 12.5	31 11.7						37 10.0
	48 7.6	45 8.1	52 7.0						49 7.5
Sales/Working Capital	9.0	6.5	6.7						6.2
	32.3	14.4	10.3						8.9
	NM	34.9	35.8						37.4
EBIT/Interest	17.8	11.9	11.5						18.2
	(20) 5.7	(26) 2.3	(23) 3.9						5.9
	2.2	1.4	1.2						1.8
Net Profit + Depr., Dep., Amort./Cur. Mat. L/T/D									
Fixed/Worth	.5	.5	.7						.7
	1.0	.9	1.4						1.4
	5.1	1.5	2.8						1.6
Debt/Worth	1.0	.8	1.1						1.2
	2.5	1.4	2.5						2.3
	10.7	3.9	5.1						3.3
% Profit Before Taxes/Tangible Net Worth	56.7	41.4	43.3						36.0
	(17) 25.8	(28) 19.9	27.5						28.4
	8.5	6.1	3.2						9.5
% Profit Before Taxes/Total Assets	14.7	14.1	11.4						9.8
	10.5	5.3	7.3						8.2
	2.8	1.7	.3						4.2
Sales/Net Fixed Assets	14.4	16.6	12.5						20.2
	7.8	6.3	6.4						6.3
	5.4	4.8	3.7						3.6
Sales/Total Assets	2.9	2.8	3.3						3.4
	2.2	2.2	2.1						2.0
	1.7	1.7	1.7						1.6
% Depr., Dep., Amort./Sales	1.6	1.2	1.9						
	(19) 2.5	(27) 2.5	(20) 2.8						
	4.5	3.8	3.9						
% Officers', Directors' Owners' Comp/Sales									
Net Sales ($)	895059M	1556984M	1844283M	6M	3630M	4657M	18529M	96167M	1721294M
Total Assets ($)	428777M	785445M	908471M	1M	5878M	1452M	9272M	41733M	850135M

M = $ thousand   MM = $ million
See Pages 11 through 21 for Explanation of Ratios and Data

Current Data Sorted by Assets　　　　　Comparative Historical Data

						Type of Statement		
1			15	15	12	7	Unqualified	36	33
1	9		23	4	1		Reviewed	20	31
2	10		6	1			Compiled	11	32
6	10		6				Tax Returns	2	7
3	15		31	26	6	10	Other	33	51
	55 (4/1-9/30/06)			165 (10/1/06-3/31/07)				4/1/02-3/31/03	4/1/03-3/31/04
0-500M	500M-2MM	2-10MM	10-50MM	50-100MM	100-250MM		ALL	ALL
13	44	81	46	19	17	NUMBER OF STATEMENTS	102	154
%	%	%	%	%	%	ASSETS	%	%
6.6	9.7	9.4	4.9	7.0	7.2	Cash & Equivalents	10.3	6.8
39.1	34.7	27.4	27.6	23.3	20.2	Trade Receivables (net)	25.9	28.5
17.7	23.5	25.3	25.6	25.9	17.4	Inventory	23.1	23.8
2.8	1.8	2.4	3.4	5.7	2.2	All Other Current	2.9	3.6
66.2	69.7	64.5	61.6	61.8	47.0	Total Current	62.2	62.7
20.3	21.4	25.8	21.8	25.4	20.5	Fixed Assets (net)	28.0	26.5
8.3	2.3	6.0	9.3	9.9	20.3	Intangibles (net)	5.3	5.1
5.2	6.6	3.7	7.3	2.9	12.2	All Other Non-Current	4.5	5.7
100.0	100.0	100.0	100.0	100.0	100.0	Total	100.0	100.0
						LIABILITIES		
20.9	10.5	15.2	10.7	6.6	1.9	Notes Payable-Short Term	9.4	10.8
3.6	4.5	2.6	3.6	2.5	3.2	Cur. Mat.-L.T.D.	4.1	3.9
24.8	19.7	17.6	19.1	15.4	10.0	Trade Payables	18.5	18.9
.0	.3	.1	.4	.6	.2	Income Taxes Payable	.2	.4
16.0	9.6	11.1	7.6	9.3	10.9	All Other Current	9.8	9.8
65.3	44.6	46.7	41.4	34.4	26.1	Total Current	42.0	43.8
25.6	14.0	13.3	14.3	22.3	17.4	Long-Term Debt	15.5	12.3
.3	.0	.3	.9	1.1	3.3	Deferred Taxes	.5	.6
29.6	7.1	3.7	5.1	6.2	8.2	All Other Non-Current	6.0	5.9
-20.9	34.3	36.1	38.2	36.0	45.1	Net Worth	36.0	37.5
100.0	100.0	100.0	100.0	100.0	100.0	Total Liabilities & Net Worth	100.0	100.0
						INCOME DATA		
100.0	100.0	100.0	100.0	100.0	100.0	Net Sales	100.0	100.0
43.4	42.7	33.9	26.0	22.1	27.2	Gross Profit	34.2	34.9
41.8	36.1	30.1	19.0	13.5	22.0	Operating Expenses	28.3	30.6
1.6	6.6	3.8	6.9	8.6	5.2	Operating Profit	5.8	4.3
2.3	.8	.9	1.5	.7	2.1	All Other Expenses (net)	1.1	.8
-.7	5.7	2.9	5.4	7.9	3.1	Profit Before Taxes	4.8	3.5
						RATIOS		
3.1	3.0	1.9	2.5	2.5	2.3		2.7	2.3
1.1	1.6	1.4	1.6	1.8	1.9	Current	1.5	1.4
.7	1.1	1.0	1.2	1.3	1.5		1.1	1.1
2.8	2.0	1.3	1.4	1.2	1.4		1.3	1.2
.8	.9	.8	.8	1.0	1.0	Quick	.8	.8
.4	.6	.5	.6	.6	.5		.5	.5

30	12.2	31	11.9	38	9.7	34	10.8	23	16.0	45	8.0	Sales/Receivables	35	10.5	34	10.7
35	10.6	43	8.4	46	8.0	48	7.7	47	7.7	52	7.1		46	8.0	44	8.2
61	5.9	52	7.0	63	5.8	61	5.9	63	5.8	64	5.7		58	6.3	57	6.4
7	51.3	24	15.0	39	9.5	40	9.0	31	11.8	32	11.5	Cost of Sales/Inventory	32	11.3	35	10.4
35	10.4	50	7.3	61	6.0	61	6.0	56	6.6	66	5.5		56	6.5	59	6.2
58	6.3	72	5.0	109	3.3	97	3.7	107	3.4	100	3.6		90	4.1	87	4.2
18	20.3	19	19.2	26	14.2	25	14.6	23	15.8	23	15.8	Cost of Sales/Payables	22	16.4	23	15.6
37	9.8	33	11.2	41	8.9	40	9.1	34	10.7	34	10.7		39	9.3	38	9.6
61	6.0	63	5.8	70	5.2	56	6.5	49	7.5	50	7.4		59	6.2	66	5.5

6.7		6.3		5.7		5.0		3.4		3.2	Sales/Working Capital	4.3		5.7
106.2		12.9		14.0		9.4		6.3		7.3		9.5		13.1
-10.8		51.7		113.4		27.9		11.0		9.8		126.6		82.7

	18.1		14.4		7.2		12.9		12.7		12.4	EBIT/Interest		10.5		10.4
	3.6	(38)	4.4	(74)	3.8	(37)	4.4	(17)	5.5	(15)	4.6		(94)	3.5	(137)	5.3
	-.3		1.9		1.4		1.9		2.0		-.5			1.4		1.4

					7.4		8.9					Net Profit + Depr., Dep., Amort./Cur. Mat. L/T/D		9.6		5.6
		(23)			1.7	(20)	5.1						(36)	2.7	(47)	2.2
					1.0		1.8							.8		1.0

.6	.1	.2	.3	.5	.4	Fixed/Worth	.4	.3
41.0	.3	.6	.7	1.0	.8		.8	.7
-.1	3.1	2.3	4.3	3.4	2.2		2.2	1.9
1.6	.8	1.0	.9	1.1	.8	Debt/Worth	.7	.8
88.5	1.9	2.3	1.9	1.7	1.2		1.9	2.3
-2.4	10.6	6.2	17.6	20.7	11.7		6.9	5.9

			73.4		45.7		49.8		76.2		41.9	% Profit Before Taxes/Tangible Net Worth		49.7		47.3
		(36)	25.9	(73)	16.7	(37)	32.0	(15)	43.0	(14)	18.3		(89)	16.9	(139)	18.1
			4.3		5.9		14.0		16.2		-3.8			4.9		3.8
29.1		22.0		14.0		15.1		16.1		15.4	% Profit Before Taxes/Total Assets		16.2		14.0
5.5		8.2		4.0		7.6		9.8		6.8			7.1		6.0
-10.7		2.1		1.3		2.8		3.5		-2.0			1.2		1.4
92.1		76.2		40.9		19.5		14.4		11.7	Sales/Net Fixed Assets		20.4		28.3
14.7		24.0		11.1		10.5		6.1		7.2			7.7		8.9
12.1		7.0		4.7		5.1		5.4		5.1			4.8		4.5
6.3		3.8		2.9		2.5		2.0		1.6	Sales/Total Assets		2.6		2.9
3.3		3.0		2.1		2.1		1.7		1.2			1.9		1.9
1.9		2.1		1.4		1.3		1.2		.9			1.5		1.4

	.5		.5		.8		1.0		1.1		1.1	% Depr., Dep., Amort./Sales		1.0		.8
(10)	.6	(30)	1.5	(70)	1.7	(37)	1.8	(16)	2.1	(13)	2.4		(93)	2.3	(134)	2.0
	3.0		3.0		3.4		3.2		4.3		4.1			3.7		3.5

			3.0		1.1					% Officers', Directors' Owners' Comp/Sales		2.0		2.1
		(28)	4.3	(18)	2.2						(29)	3.7	(43)	5.5
			6.9		3.7							7.2		7.8

13303M	168132M	1453527M	2194717M	2382262M	3307138M	Net Sales ($)	4017244M	5224499M
3764M	55654M	392783M	1094527M	1346131M	2616396M	Total Assets ($)	2332718M	2884974M

M = $ thousand　　MM = $ million
See Pages 11 through 21 for Explanation of Ratios and Data

Comparative Historical Data / Current Data Sorted by Sales

			Type of Statement	0-1MM	1-3MM	3-5MM	5-10MM	10-25MM	25MM & OVER
39	42	50	Unqualified		3	1	2	12	32
36	24	38	Reviewed	1	5	4	9	14	5
18	18	19	Compiled	2	4	4	7	1	1
11	17	22	Tax Returns	4	4	10	3	1	
57	76	91	Other	2	11	15	10	17	36
4/1/04-3/31/05 ALL	4/1/05-3/31/06 ALL	4/1/06-3/31/07 ALL			55 (4/1-9/30/06)		165 (10/1/06-3/31/07)		
161	177	220	**NUMBER OF STATEMENTS**	9	27	34	31	45	74
%	%	%	**ASSETS**	%	%	%	%	%	%
7.7	8.3	8.0	Cash & Equivalents		14.2	8.0	5.7	8.7	6.3
28.8	31.3	28.7	Trade Receivables (net)		26.5	26.4	34.8	29.5	26.6
22.7	22.6	24.0	Inventory		20.7	24.3	27.6	25.1	23.6
3.3	1.9	2.8	All Other Current		.7	3.0	2.5	2.9	3.8
62.5	64.1	63.4	Total Current		62.1	61.6	70.6	66.1	60.3
26.8	23.2	23.3	Fixed Assets (net)		30.5	27.7	20.6	20.0	22.4
6.1	6.1	7.5	Intangibles (net)		3.7	5.4	3.2	9.5	10.0
4.7	6.6	5.7	All Other Non-Current		3.7	5.3	5.6	4.3	7.4
100.0	100.0	100.0	Total		100.0	100.0	100.0	100.0	100.0
			LIABILITIES						
11.3	9.8	11.9	Notes Payable-Short Term		17.9	10.7	15.4	13.0	7.9
3.5	2.7	3.3	Cur. Mat.-L.T.D.		3.4	3.4	3.8	2.3	3.4
19.1	21.3	18.0	Trade Payables		16.4	18.5	18.5	17.9	17.6
.3	.2	.3	Income Taxes Payable		.1	.4	.1	.1	.4
9.5	9.4	10.2	All Other Current		11.8	13.0	8.0	9.9	9.2
43.8	43.4	43.6	Total Current		49.6	45.9	45.8	43.1	38.5
14.0	14.2	15.5	Long-Term Debt		16.2	23.2	5.3	11.2	16.4
.6	.6	.7	Deferred Taxes		.2	.2	.1	.7	1.3
5.0	7.1	6.8	All Other Non-Current		10.1	1.7	5.8	4.2	5.4
36.7	34.7	33.5	Net Worth		23.8	29.0	42.9	40.7	38.3
100.0	100.0	100.0	Total Liabilities & Net Worth		100.0	100.0	100.0	100.0	100.0
			INCOME DATA						
100.0	100.0	100.0	Net Sales		100.0	100.0	100.0	100.0	100.0
33.1	32.8	33.0	Gross Profit		42.8	39.9	33.1	35.1	23.0
27.4	27.5	27.6	Operating Expenses		37.9	34.6	28.7	28.7	17.1
5.7	5.3	5.4	Operating Profit		4.9	5.3	4.4	6.4	5.9
.8	1.2	1.2	All Other Expenses (net)		1.0	1.6	.4	.8	1.3
4.8	4.0	4.2	Profit Before Taxes		3.9	3.7	3.9	5.6	4.6
			RATIOS						
2.2	2.3	2.4	Current		3.1	2.7	2.3	2.2	2.2
1.5	1.5	1.6			1.2	1.4	1.6	1.5	1.7
1.0	1.1	1.1			.7	.9	1.1	1.1	1.2
1.3	1.4	1.4	Quick		1.9	1.3	1.3	1.5	1.3
.8	.9	.9			.7	.8	.9	.8	.9
.5	.5	.6			.4	.4	.6	.6	.6
32 / 11.2	33 / 11.1	34 / 10.8	Sales/Receivables		34 / 10.6	29 / 12.4	32 / 11.4	37 / 9.9	35 / 10.3
47 / 7.8	46 / 7.9	46 / 8.0			50 / 7.3	44 / 8.2	46 / 7.9	42 / 8.7	48 / 7.7
57 / 6.5	57 / 6.4	60 / 6.1			65 / 5.6	52 / 7.0	63 / 5.8	51 / 7.2	60 / 6.1
35 / 10.3	26 / 14.2	32 / 11.4	Cost of Sales/Inventory		36 / 10.2	24 / 15.1	30 / 12.3	40 / 9.2	32 / 11.4
57 / 6.4	50 / 7.3	55 / 6.6			81 / 4.5	53 / 6.9	52 / 7.0	59 / 6.2	56 / 6.6
83 / 4.4	85 / 4.3	98 / 3.7			110 / 3.3	104 / 3.5	90 / 4.1	94 / 3.9	94 / 3.9
25 / 14.8	26 / 14.1	23 / 15.9	Cost of Sales/Payables		25 / 14.8	31 / 12.0	23 / 16.2	22 / 16.7	24 / 15.3
40 / 9.1	39 / 9.3	39 / 9.3			57 / 6.4	45 / 8.1	32 / 11.4	33 / 11.0	38 / 9.6
61 / 6.0	60 / 6.1	62 / 5.9			107 / 3.4	71 / 5.2	59 / 6.2	55 / 6.7	52 / 7.0
5.6	6.4	5.5	Sales/Working Capital		3.4	6.3	5.8	4.8	5.1
12.6	12.1	10.5			20.8	15.8	10.0	13.4	8.9
170.8	62.4	64.1			-12.5	-71.2	36.6	34.7	23.4
11.7	13.5	10.0	EBIT/Interest		12.2	7.2	10.6	10.7	11.4
(146) 4.6	(157) 4.3	(194) 3.9			(25) 3.4	(30) 2.1	(26) 6.0	(42) 3.9	(62) 4.6
1.8	1.6	1.6			.2	.5	2.4	2.4	1.7
5.7	9.3	8.4	Net Profit + Depr., Dep., Amort./Cur. Mat. L/T/D					8.9	9.1
(42) 3.0	(48) 2.5	(68) 3.5						(17) 5.3	(33) 3.4
1.6	1.2	1.1						1.0	1.2
.3	.3	.2	Fixed/Worth		.2	.2	.2	.2	.4
.8	.6	.7			2.0	1.3	.4	.6	.8
2.3	2.1	3.2			78.4	4.0	.6	1.6	2.2
.8	.9	.9	Debt/Worth		.8	.9	.8	1.1	1.0
2.1	2.4	2.5			7.7	3.3	1.2	2.0	1.7
6.5	7.6	10.1			-36.4	11.1	2.7	5.4	9.8
52.5	54.6	54.4	% Profit Before Taxes/Tangible Net Worth		30.5	60.6	52.3	53.8	52.9
(144) 24.7	(151) 27.7	(182) 26.9			(20) 10.6	(28) 26.7	(29) 27.1	(40) 32.8	(61) 28.4
8.1	10.0	6.4			-27.7	-6.0	6.4	11.3	9.7
16.6	17.0	15.6	% Profit Before Taxes/Total Assets		9.8	17.0	17.3	17.3	15.1
6.1	7.0	7.0			3.7	6.2	7.1	9.6	7.1
2.2	2.2	1.8			-3.9	-1.7	1.9	3.1	2.5
25.3	34.8	38.7	Sales/Net Fixed Assets		384.2	66.9	56.6	40.4	14.8
9.4	11.7	11.4			7.1	8.6	20.4	14.7	8.5
4.6	5.9	5.4			2.4	4.1	6.4	6.7	5.5
3.0	3.3	3.1	Sales/Total Assets		2.9	3.4	3.7	3.3	2.5
2.1	2.3	2.1			1.4	2.4	2.7	2.3	1.9
1.4	1.4	1.4			1.0	1.1	1.9	2.0	1.3
1.0	.8	.8	% Depr., Dep., Amort./Sales		1.4	.5	.8	.7	1.0
(143) 2.1	(143) 1.7	(176) 1.6			(15) 2.6	(28) 2.9	(25) 1.6	(41) 1.2	(59) 1.8
4.0	3.5	3.3			6.4	5.4	2.8	2.5	3.1
3.0	2.3	2.0	% Officers', Directors', Owners' Comp/Sales		2.1			1.8	
(47) 4.8	(48) 4.4	(55) 3.4			(21) 3.4			(11) 2.3	
7.0	8.4	6.4			6.4			2.7	
6669007M	7728618M	9519079M	Net Sales ($)	5178M	56524M	135285M	225233M	750060M	8346799M
3461022M	3991558M	5509255M	Total Assets ($)	2469M	53140M	83280M	101168M	390500M	4878698M

© RMA 2007

M = $ thousand   MM = $ million

See Pages 11 through 21 for Explanation of Ratios and Data

Current Data Sorted by Assets | Comparative Historical Data

							Type of Statement		
			6	20	4	1	Unqualified	16	22
	2		17	6			Reviewed	19	19
	6		5	2		1	Compiled	5	8
	2		2				Tax Returns	1	4
1	3		9	11	3	2	Other	30	24
	28 (4/1-9/30/06)			75 (10/1/06-3/31/07)				4/1/02-3/31/03	4/1/03-3/31/04
0-500M	500M-2MM		2-10MM	10-50MM	50-100MM	100-250MM		ALL	ALL
1	13		39	39	7	4	NUMBER OF STATEMENTS	71	77
%	%		%	%	%	%	ASSETS	%	%
	7.4		5.1	3.1			Cash & Equivalents	4.4	5.2
	37.5		30.8	26.6			Trade Receivables (net)	25.1	28.3
	26.8		29.5	28.5			Inventory	25.4	25.6
	.6		1.1	2.8			All Other Current	1.6	1.3
	72.3		66.6	61.0			Total Current	56.5	60.4
	19.3		23.6	34.7			Fixed Assets (net)	32.7	33.4
	.3		5.3	1.3			Intangibles (net)	3.5	1.8
	8.1		4.5	3.0			All Other Non-Current	7.2	4.4
	100.0		100.0	100.0			Total	100.0	100.0
							LIABILITIES		
	14.6		15.6	13.5			Notes Payable-Short Term	10.3	12.8
	4.1		3.1	3.6			Cur. Mat.-L.T.D.	4.0	3.3
	29.6		20.1	17.8			Trade Payables	17.7	17.4
	.6		.0	.3			Income Taxes Payable	.5	.6
	12.8		5.5	7.6			All Other Current	9.0	5.9
	61.6		44.4	42.7			Total Current	41.5	40.0
	15.1		12.4	19.3			Long-Term Debt	15.3	18.4
	.2		.5	.7			Deferred Taxes	.7	.5
	17.1		5.8	8.6			All Other Non-Current	8.9	7.8
	5.9		36.9	28.6			Net Worth	33.5	33.3
	100.0		100.0	100.0			Total Liabilties & Net Worth	100.0	100.0
							INCOME DATA		
	100.0		100.0	100.0			Net Sales	100.0	100.0
	27.6		22.5	21.9			Gross Profit	27.1	24.9
	26.1		17.7	15.9			Operating Expenses	22.7	21.1
	1.6		4.7	6.0			Operating Profit	4.3	3.8
	1.2		1.1	1.5			All Other Expenses (net)	.8	.9
	.3		3.6	4.6			Profit Before Taxes	3.5	3.0
							RATIOS		
	2.6		2.1	2.3				2.5	2.3
	1.1		1.7	1.6			Current	1.4	1.5
	.9		1.2	1.0				1.0	1.0
	1.9		1.2	1.1				1.4	1.4
	.8		.8	.7			Quick	.7	.8
	.5		.6	.4				.5	.5

							Sales/Receivables				
21	17.8	34	10.8	34	10.6			34	10.8	38	9.6
32	11.4	42	8.7	41	8.8		Sales/Receivables	43	8.5	46	7.9
48	7.5	54	6.8	49	7.4			50	7.2	56	6.6
17	21.3	37	9.8	42	8.7			40	9.2	36	10.1
35	10.3	51	7.2	52	7.0		Cost of Sales/Inventory	58	6.3	54	6.7
69	5.3	64	5.7	75	4.9			81	4.5	75	4.8
13	28.8	22	16.9	21	17.7			22	16.7	26	14.2
35	10.6	30	12.3	36	10.1		Cost of Sales/Payables	36	10.1	38	9.7
55	6.7	51	7.1	53	6.9			62	5.9	51	7.1

						Sales/Working Capital		
	8.1		6.9	5.9			6.2	5.8
	37.0		10.7	11.5		Sales/Working Capital	14.4	11.5
	-278.6		25.5	682.5			140.9	123.5

							EBIT/Interest				
	5.3		8.8		16.6				10.8		11.4
	1.6	(37)	2.8	(37)	4.1		EBIT/Interest	(67)	3.3	(74)	4.2
	-1.1		1.4		1.6				1.1		1.3

							Net Profit + Depr., Dep., Amort./Cur. Mat. L/T/D				
					4.3				8.3		5.6
			(13)			3.0		Net Profit + Depr., Dep., Amort./Cur. Mat. L/T/D	(27)	3.9	(19)	3.2
					1.5				1.6		2.1

						Fixed/Worth		
	.4		.4	.6			.3	.4
	1.6		.7	1.1		Fixed/Worth	1.0	.9
	-.7		1.3	2.7			3.1	2.4
	2.3		1.0	1.2			.8	.9
	5.3		2.0	3.1		Debt/Worth	2.0	1.8
	-4.1		3.6	7.1			4.4	5.9

							% Profit Before Taxes/Tangible Net Worth				
				54.9		60.7				46.2		36.8
			(34)	18.3	(36)	41.0		% Profit Before Taxes/Tangible Net Worth	(61)	16.7	(67)	15.3
				8.1		20.2				4.1		2.9

						% Profit Before Taxes/Total Assets		
	11.1		14.3	19.0			14.9	12.7
	3.6		6.1	10.4		% Profit Before Taxes/Total Assets	6.0	4.9
	-7.1		1.2	2.7			.3	.5
	68.4		26.7	10.9			20.4	18.1
	14.5		12.8	7.0		Sales/Net Fixed Assets	6.1	7.4
	11.7		7.8	4.4			3.1	3.4
	5.5		3.3	2.6			2.6	2.9
	3.0		2.8	2.1		Sales/Total Assets	1.9	2.2
	2.8		2.0	1.8			1.5	1.5

							% Depr., Dep., Amort./Sales				
				.9		1.8				1.1		1.2
			(36)	1.6	(34)	2.7		% Depr., Dep., Amort./Sales	(68)	2.5	(68)	2.8
				2.6		4.0				5.0		4.1

							% Officers', Directors' Owners' Comp/Sales				
				1.8						2.5		1.6
		(14)		2.7				% Officers', Directors' Owners' Comp/Sales	(19)	4.4	(18)	4.2
				5.5						6.2		8.2

374M	71716M		543026M	1871569M	877068M	1099869M	Net Sales ($)	2656157M	2624408M
479M	17456M		206455M	891488M	558631M	621586M	Total Assets ($)	1683095M	1526659M

M = $ thousand   MM = $ million
See Pages 11 through 21 for Explanation of Ratios and Data

Comparative Historical Data | Current Data Sorted by Sales

	4/1/04-3/31/05 ALL	4/1/05-3/31/06 ALL	4/1/06-3/31/07 ALL	Type of Statement	0-1MM	1-3MM	3-5MM	5-10MM	10-25MM	25MM & OVER
	21	29	31	Unqualified				4	2	25
	21	17	25	Reviewed				6	11	8
	8	6	14	Compiled				3	2	4
	4	6	4	Tax Returns				1	2	
	20	19	29	Other	1	1	3	3	8	13
		28 (4/1-9/30/06)						75 (10/1/06-3/31/07)		
NUMBER OF STATEMENTS	74	77	103		1	4	6	17	25	50
	%	%	%	**ASSETS**	%	%	%	%	%	%
	6.0	4.6	4.7	Cash & Equivalents				8.0	4.9	3.5
	30.6	31.4	29.1	Trade Receivables (net)				31.2	34.3	25.8
	26.4	26.7	28.0	Inventory				22.7	32.7	28.0
	1.3	1.2	1.8	All Other Current				1.3	1.8	2.3
	64.3	64.0	63.6	Total Current				63.2	73.7	59.6
	28.4	30.3	28.3	Fixed Assets (net)				26.1	19.6	33.7
	1.8	1.5	3.2	Intangibles (net)				7.3	2.0	2.3
	5.5	4.3	4.9	All Other Non-Current				3.4	4.7	4.4
	100.0	100.0	100.0	Total				100.0	100.0	100.0
				LIABILITIES						
	12.4	11.4	14.0	Notes Payable-Short Term				10.0	18.5	13.1
	3.0	5.2	3.6	Cur. Mat.-L.T.D.				4.2	2.7	3.7
	19.9	18.8	19.2	Trade Payables				21.2	22.3	16.8
	.5	.4	.3	Income Taxes Payable				.1	.0	.5
	7.4	7.0	8.1	All Other Current				5.5	6.8	8.2
	43.4	42.8	45.2	Total Current				41.0	50.2	42.2
	12.0	13.4	15.8	Long-Term Debt				18.2	9.0	17.8
	.6	.7	.6	Deferred Taxes				.6	.5	.8
	9.7	7.3	8.7	All Other Non-Current				9.1	7.8	7.7
	34.4	35.8	29.7	Net Worth				31.1	32.5	31.5
	100.0	100.0	100.0	Total Liabilities & Net Worth				100.0	100.0	100.0
				INCOME DATA						
	100.0	100.0	100.0	Net Sales				100.0	100.0	100.0
	25.2	22.7	22.8	Gross Profit				23.9	23.8	21.0
	20.2	17.9	18.4	Operating Expenses				19.5	19.5	15.3
	4.9	4.8	4.4	Operating Profit				4.4	4.3	5.7
	.9	1.0	1.2	All Other Expenses (net)				1.1	.9	1.1
	4.1	3.8	3.2	Profit Before Taxes				3.3	3.4	4.5
				RATIOS						
	2.5	2.3	2.3	Current				2.6	2.0	2.3
	1.5	1.6	1.6					1.7	1.6	1.5
	1.0	1.1	1.0					1.2	1.2	1.0
	1.5	1.2	1.2	Quick				1.2	1.3	1.1
	.8	.9	.8					1.1	.8	.7
	.5	.6	.5					.7	.5	.5
	38 9.6	38 9.7	34 10.7	Sales/Receivables				31 11.9	34 10.8	36 10.2
	50 7.3	49 7.5	42 8.6					43 8.4	38 9.5	43 8.5
	58 6.3	60 6.0	52 7.1					57 6.4	53 6.9	50 7.2
	43 8.4	39 9.3	37 9.7	Cost of Sales/Inventory				24 15.0	37 9.9	42 8.7
	56 6.5	55 6.7	51 7.1					46 7.9	48 7.7	55 6.6
	73 5.0	72 5.1	73 5.0					66 5.6	71 5.2	78 4.7
	28 13.1	22 16.7	21 17.7	Cost of Sales/Payables				20 18.1	22 16.5	20 17.9
	39 9.5	32 11.3	33 11.0					35 10.6	32 11.6	32 11.4
	53 6.9	52 7.0	51 7.1					51 7.2	51 7.1	52 7.0
	5.5	5.6	5.9	Sales/Working Capital				5.8	6.8	5.8
	10.3	9.8	11.5					9.5	12.5	13.3
	190.3	39.3	131.4					31.2	29.6	532.7
	15.4	10.7	10.1	EBIT/Interest				6.6	10.1	16.3
	(67) 5.0	(71) 4.1	(99) 3.6				(15)	4.5	(23) 2.7	4.3
	2.0	1.9	1.3					-.8	1.6	1.6
	8.0	4.2	5.0	Net Profit + Depr., Dep., Amort./Cur. Mat. L/T/D						3.7
	(19) 3.0	(23) 2.0	(31) 2.7						(24)	2.6
	1.8	1.4	1.5							1.5
	.3	.4	.5	Fixed/Worth				.5	.4	.6
	.8	.8	.9					1.1	.6	1.1
	1.9	1.7	2.3					2.1	.9	2.4
	.9	.9	1.1	Debt/Worth				1.3	1.0	1.0
	1.9	1.9	2.7					2.1	2.2	2.7
	4.1	4.1	5.6					4.9	3.9	6.0
	34.6	40.6	56.0	% Profit Before Taxes/Tangible Net Worth				65.6	42.3	56.9
	(66) 17.8	(69) 17.7	(88) 23.1				(14)	17.3	(22) 19.9	(46) 32.7
	6.3	7.1	8.0					2.7	8.1	13.6
	16.1	12.5	14.3	% Profit Before Taxes/Total Assets				25.1	13.4	15.9
	6.0	6.5	6.7					4.8	6.6	10.5
	1.6	1.8	1.1					-4.3	2.8	2.6
	23.0	16.2	15.6	Sales/Net Fixed Assets				30.0	33.2	11.0
	8.8	7.9	9.1					9.6	16.6	7.0
	4.2	4.1	5.2					6.0	8.8	4.4
	2.9	3.0	3.0	Sales/Total Assets				3.3	3.5	2.7
	2.1	2.2	2.5					2.5	2.8	2.1
	1.6	1.7	1.8					1.7	2.2	1.8
	1.0	1.0	1.2	% Depr., Dep., Amort./Sales				.6	.9	1.8
	(67) 2.3	(67) 2.3	(89) 2.1				(14)	1.9	(22) 1.4	(45) 2.7
	3.2	3.3	3.5					3.1	2.3	4.0
	2.0	1.3	1.4	% Officers', Directors' Owners' Comp/Sales						
	(23) 3.3	(20) 2.2	(24) 2.6							
	7.4	4.6	6.8							
	2139733M	3738625M	4463622M	Net Sales ($)	374M	10756M	24062M	123919M	417274M	3887237M
	1169652M	2024524M	2296095M	Total Assets ($)	479M	4589M	9067M	60586M	159165M	2062209M

M = $ thousand   MM = $ million
See Pages 11 through 21 for Explanation of Ratios and Data

Current Data Sorted by Assets   Comparative Historical Data

Type of Statement								
	2	1	9		2	Unqualified	8	14
1	5	7	3			Reviewed	10	15
1	4	12				Compiled	9	10
2	4	.1				Tax Returns	6	9
	6	14	6	2	3	Other	8	15
	14 (4/1-9/30/06)		71 (10/1/06-3/31/07)				4/1/02-3/31/03	4/1/03-3/31/04
0-500M	500M-2MM	2-10MM	10-50MM	50-100MM	100-250MM		ALL	ALL
4	21	35	18	2	5	NUMBER OF STATEMENTS	41	63
%	%	%	%	%	%		%	%
						ASSETS		
	9.6	9.2	7.2			Cash & Equivalents	8.2	7.3
	32.4	25.3	20.1			Trade Receivables (net)	24.1	22.2
	27.9	27.2	21.1			Inventory	18.1	20.6
	.6	1.9	.6			All Other Current	3.5	1.4
	70.4	63.6	49.0			Total Current	53.9	51.4
	25.2	29.8	39.0			Fixed Assets (net)	36.0	36.4
	.5	1.3	7.7			Intangibles (net)	3.0	4.2
	3.9	5.3	4.3			All Other Non-Current	7.1	8.0
	100.0	100.0	100.0			Total	100.0	100.0
						LIABILITIES		
	8.8	10.4	10.3			Notes Payable-Short Term	7.7	10.2
	5.1	6.3	6.1			Cur. Mat.-L.T.D.	5.4	5.4
	14.0	18.2	12.1			Trade Payables	13.5	12.8
	.0	.0	.0			Income Taxes Payable	.4	.1
	17.7	5.8	7.4			All Other Current	6.0	5.9
	45.6	40.7	36.0			Total Current	33.1	34.4
	20.8	18.4	17.3			Long-Term Debt	23.7	29.6
	.0	.3	.6			Deferred Taxes	.7	.5
	8.0	5.1	5.3			All Other Non-Current	2.8	3.0
	25.6	35.5	40.8			Net Worth	39.7	32.5
	100.0	100.0	100.0			Total Liabilties & Net Worth	100.0	100.0
						INCOME DATA		
	100.0	100.0	100.0			Net Sales	100.0	100.0
	34.2	26.1	20.7			Gross Profit	33.3	29.1
	27.3	21.8	15.4			Operating Expenses	29.6	25.0
	6.9	4.3	5.3			Operating Profit	3.7	4.1
	1.3	.9	1.7			All Other Expenses (net)	1.0	1.3
	5.5	3.4	3.6			Profit Before Taxes	2.7	2.8
						RATIOS		
	3.6	2.7	2.7			Current	3.7	2.6
	2.1	1.7	1.3				1.8	1.5
	1.1	.9	1.0				1.1	1.0
	2.3	1.7	1.7			Quick	2.2	1.5
	1.1	1.1	.7				.9	.8
	.7	.4	.4				.6	.5
	28 13.0	31 11.6	35 10.3			Sales/Receivables	31 11.7	29 12.4
	38 9.5	37 9.9	44 8.4				37 9.9	40 9.2
	64 5.7	56 6.5	53 6.9				58 6.3	50 7.3
	35 10.4	33 10.9	37 10.0			Cost of Sales/Inventory	21 17.4	33 11.2
	47 7.8	68 5.4	49 7.4				42 8.7	45 8.1
	107 3.4	91 4.0	66 5.5				70 5.2	69 5.3
	8 43.2	20 18.3	15 23.9			Cost of Sales/Payables	13 27.8	18 20.1
	21 17.5	30 12.0	26 13.8				30 12.1	27 13.3
	64 5.7	57 6.4	54 6.8				49 7.5	44 8.4
	4.9	4.7	6.0			Sales/Working Capital	5.2	5.3
	9.5	11.1	24.4				9.2	13.7
	NM	-75.1	-174.8				100.3	-356.8
	13.7	8.6	9.5			EBIT/Interest	9.8	7.0
(20)	6.2	(31) 2.1	(17) 2.8				(37) 2.9	(56) 2.5
	1.7	.5	1.6				.0	.6
						Net Profit + Depr., Dep., Amort./Cur. Mat. L/T/D		4.2
								(14) 2.4
								1.4
	.3	.3	.7			Fixed/Worth	.4	.4
	.8	1.0	1.9				.9	1.0
	NM	4.1	4.8				2.1	2.7
	.7	.7	.7			Debt/Worth	.4	.6
	2.3	2.0	2.3				1.1	1.5
	NM	9.9	9.2				4.4	8.8
	105.2	41.8	36.5			% Profit Before Taxes/Tangible Net Worth	24.9	27.5
(16)	29.2	(28) 13.6	(16) 22.5				(33) 10.9	(51) 9.2
	10.2	.0	5.7				.3	-5.8
	34.0	16.2	12.7			% Profit Before Taxes/Total Assets	12.0	9.7
	7.4	3.3	5.1				3.9	3.6
	2.6	-.6	1.5				-2.7	.0
	37.1	15.7	6.4			Sales/Net Fixed Assets	10.9	12.3
	17.7	7.6	5.1				6.7	6.5
	4.4	3.8	3.2				3.6	3.3
	3.8	3.1	2.2			Sales/Total Assets	2.7	2.8
	2.7	2.2	1.6				2.1	2.0
	1.8	1.6	1.3				1.4	1.4
	.5	1.3	2.7			% Depr., Dep., Amort./Sales	2.4	2.4
(16)	1.9	(32) 2.7	(17) 3.4				(37) 3.7	(58) 3.6
	4.2	4.2	4.8				6.1	6.1
	2.3	1.7				% Officers', Directors' Owners' Comp/Sales	3.0	2.7
(12)	5.5	(18) 2.8					(12) 4.3	(29) 4.7
	8.2	6.6					8.4	8.4
2936M	75949M	342827M	688354M	217610M	890318M	Net Sales ($)	661416M	1170000M
894M	27155M	152890M	375506M	165041M	747950M	Total Assets ($)	395657M	677452M

M = $ thousand   MM = $ million
See Pages 11 through 21 for Explanation of Ratios and Data

Comparative Historical Data | Current Data Sorted by Sales

Type of Statement

Hist 1	Hist 2	Hist 3		0-1MM	1-3MM	3-5MM	5-10MM	10-25MM	25MM & OVER
21	21	14	Unqualified						
35	24	16	Reviewed	1	1	5	2	3	8
15	13	17	Compiled	1	1	5	5	2	2
14	6	7	Tax Returns		4	5	3	5	
29	23	31	Other	2	1	3	1		10
4/1/04-3/31/05 ALL	4/1/05-3/31/06 ALL	4/1/06-3/31/07 ALL			14 (4/1-9/30/06)		71 (10/1/06-3/31/07)		
114	87	85	NUMBER OF STATEMENTS	3	11	14	19	18	20

Assets

%	%	%	ASSETS	%	%	%	%	%	%
6.0	6.2	8.3	Cash & Equivalents		12.3	13.1	6.4	7.6	5.9
27.1	26.0	25.4	Trade Receivables (net)		24.1	23.2	33.7	25.6	18.4
21.3	26.2	25.0	Inventory		27.5	30.1	27.1	22.1	21.7
1.1	1.0	1.5	All Other Current		.1	.2	.9	3.2	2.5
55.5	59.3	60.2	Total Current		64.0	66.7	68.1	58.5	48.6
34.7	30.0	31.3	Fixed Assets (net)		31.9	26.5	27.4	28.5	41.2
3.8	4.9	3.4	Intangibles (net)		.8	1.8	.5	7.2	5.6
6.0	5.8	5.1	All Other Non-Current		3.3	4.9	4.0	5.8	4.7
100.0	100.0	100.0	Total		100.0	100.0	100.0	100.0	100.0

Liabilities

			LIABILITIES						
12.9	10.8	9.3	Notes Payable-Short Term		3.8	3.9	18.4	6.5	10.0
5.1	5.7	5.3	Cur. Mat.-L.T.D.		4.3	4.0	7.0	9.2	2.7
17.2	17.1	15.3	Trade Payables		12.1	8.6	17.9	18.5	13.5
.1	.2	.0	Income Taxes Payable		.0	.0	.0	.0	.2
7.8	8.8	9.3	All Other Current		11.1	10.1	12.6	6.3	8.7
43.1	42.5	39.3	Total Current		31.3	26.5	55.9	40.5	35.0
20.2	17.1	19.3	Long-Term Debt		27.4	19.7	20.5	13.3	19.0
.5	.4	.8	Deferred Taxes		.0	.0	.3	.2	2.9
6.6	7.0	6.2	All Other Non-Current		3.3	9.7	7.9	2.8	7.5
29.6	33.0	34.5	Net Worth		38.0	44.1	15.4	43.1	35.5
100.0	100.0	100.0	Total Liabilities & Net Worth		100.0	100.0	100.0	100.0	100.0

Income Data

			INCOME DATA						
100.0	100.0	100.0	Net Sales		100.0	100.0	100.0	100.0	100.0
27.7	27.6	28.4	Gross Profit		33.4	34.6	27.6	24.0	24.9
23.6	22.8	23.0	Operating Expenses		25.8	30.5	22.0	18.6	20.2
4.1	4.8	5.4	Operating Profit		7.6	4.1	5.6	5.5	4.7
1.4	1.7	1.4	All Other Expenses (net)		1.7	.5	1.1	1.7	1.5
2.7	3.0	4.0	Profit Before Taxes		5.9	3.6	4.5	3.8	3.2

Ratios

			RATIOS						
2.1	2.1	3.1			4.4	9.1	2.0	2.3	2.5
1.4	1.4	1.6	Current		3.1	2.8	1.3	1.5	1.5
1.0	1.0	1.0			1.3	1.9	.9	1.0	1.0
1.3	1.1	1.7			2.7	4.2	1.3	1.2	1.4
.7	.7	1.0	Quick		1.1	2.1	.6	.9	.6
.5	.5	.4			.7	.9	.4	.5	.4
34 10.7	34 10.7	31 11.8			26 13.9	29 12.7	32 11.6	32 11.4	29 12.7
44 8.2	42 8.8	38 9.5	Sales/Receivables		42 8.8	37 9.9	38 9.5	44 8.2	38 9.7
54 6.8	55 6.7	53 7.0			69 5.3	56 6.5	49 7.5	59 6.1	44 8.3
30 12.3	34 10.7	35 10.5			36 10.0	63 5.8	30 12.3	26 14.1	35 10.4
46 7.9	58 6.3	59 6.2	Cost of Sales/Inventory		91 4.0	85 4.3	39 9.5	47 7.7	57 6.3
72 5.1	88 4.1	91 4.1			136 2.7	111 3.3	79 4.6	73 5.0	72 5.1
20 18.3	23 15.9	17 21.1			13 27.7	4 84.3	18 19.8	20 18.3	17 21.2
32 11.5	37 9.8	28 13.0	Cost of Sales/Payables		27 13.6	17 21.9	25 14.5	33 11.2	27 13.4
50 7.2	52 7.0	54 6.7			79 4.6	60 6.1	52 7.1	47 7.8	51 7.1
7.8	6.9	5.0			3.8	3.4	8.6	4.6	5.7
15.1	13.2	11.1	Sales/Working Capital		5.4	5.7	36.4	14.5	11.0
UND	-492.4	-237.6			18.3	10.5	-40.1	-186.3	87.3
14.0	9.8	10.5			11.2	32.3	7.1	14.2	9.4
(104) 3.0	(78) 3.1	(77) 2.9	EBIT/Interest		(10) 4.1	(11) 4.5	(18) 2.6	2.5	(19) 3.0
.8	.9	1.1			2.2	1.3	.9	1.0	.0
4.2	4.9	7.4	Net Profit + Depr., Dep.,						
(27) 2.6	(19) 1.5	(17) 3.8	Amort./Cur. Mat. L/T/D						
.9	1.3	1.3							
.5	.4	.4			.3	.2	.5	.2	.8
1.1	1.2	1.1	Fixed/Worth		.5	.7	1.1	.9	1.6
6.1	3.4	4.5			2.2	NM	-7.8	2.7	4.9
.6	.8	.8			.5	.3	1.7	.7	.9
2.1	2.4	2.3	Debt/Worth		.9	1.5	7.3	1.7	2.2
13.0	8.5	9.6			2.7	NM	-23.3	3.8	9.2
41.5	33.3	43.1			62.6	127.2	36.2	34.3	
(93) 17.0	(75) 16.4	(70) 20.6	% Profit Before Taxes/Tangible Net Worth		(11) 16.8	(14) 27.6	(16) 16.8	(17) 25.2	
.4	.0	4.5			-.1	5.1	1.3	2.6	
13.5	12.1	17.2			32.2	27.3	35.6	16.8	16.2
5.2	4.9	6.0	% Profit Before Taxes/Total Assets		9.3	4.9	9.8	4.0	6.2
-.4	-.3	.2			4.8	-1.0	.3	.1	-2.8
14.2	21.1	18.0			12.0	25.3	25.7	20.2	7.1
6.5	7.1	6.2	Sales/Net Fixed Assets		6.2	12.7	8.3	7.6	4.8
3.4	4.3	3.5			2.9	3.5	5.8	4.2	3.2
2.8	3.0	2.9			2.8	2.8	3.4	2.9	2.3
2.2	2.2	2.1	Sales/Total Assets		1.7	2.2	2.8	1.9	1.9
1.6	1.6	1.5			1.4	1.6	2.0	1.3	1.4
2.1	1.5	1.7			1.6	.8	1.2	2.8	
(102) 3.5	(74) 2.9	(72) 2.9	% Depr., Dep., Amort./Sales		(12) 2.6	(18) 2.5	(15) 1.7	(17) 3.9	
5.3	4.4	4.5			3.8	4.3	4.5	4.6	
2.4	2.1	2.1						2.1	
(44) 4.1	(28) 3.4	(33) 3.7	% Officers', Directors' Owners' Comp/Sales				(10) 3.3		
8.3	5.4	6.9					6.3		
2124734M	2730376M	2217994M	Net Sales ($)	1018M	23835M	56816M	139905M	267438M	1728982M
1214127M	1503971M	1469436M	Total Assets ($)	468M	13804M	33450M	56106M	148843M	1216765M

© RMA 2007

M = $ thousand   MM = $ million
See Pages 11 through 21 for Explanation of Ratios and Data

Current Data Sorted by Assets   Comparative Historical Data

0-500M	500M-2MM	2-10MM	10-50MM	50-100MM	100-250MM	Type of Statement	4/1/02-3/31/03 ALL	4/1/03-3/31/04 ALL
	1	6	14	1	6	Unqualified	28	33
	2	12	8			Reviewed	35	37
	15	6	1			Compiled	17	38
1	2	2				Tax Returns	4	5
3	4	12	13	2	6	Other	61	61
	30 (4/1-9/30/06)		87 (10/1/06-3/31/07)					
4	24	38	36	3	12	**NUMBER OF STATEMENTS**	145	174
%	%	%	%	%	%	**ASSETS**	%	%
	9.3	7.0	6.3		3.9	Cash & Equivalents	4.8	4.3
	28.5	23.3	25.1		24.3	Trade Receivables (net)	26.3	26.8
	27.1	25.8	23.1		21.5	Inventory	18.4	20.1
	2.0	.8	3.8		3.7	All Other Current	1.9	1.2
	66.9	56.9	58.3		53.4	Total Current	51.4	52.4
	26.5	36.8	31.6		28.2	Fixed Assets (net)	35.0	36.9
	2.0	1.9	4.7		12.2	Intangibles (net)	5.6	3.7
	4.5	4.4	5.4		6.2	All Other Non-Current	7.9	6.9
	100.0	100.0	100.0		100.0	Total	100.0	100.0
						LIABILITIES		
	7.5	11.6	6.7		13.2	Notes Payable-Short Term	12.4	13.2
	5.0	5.1	3.2		1.4	Cur. Mat.-L.T.D.	5.3	6.4
	17.5	13.1	14.2		13.0	Trade Payables	16.3	16.5
	.0	.3	.1		.4	Income Taxes Payable	.3	.1
	6.2	7.1	8.6		14.4	All Other Current	8.9	8.3
	36.3	37.3	32.8		42.3	Total Current	43.2	44.4
	12.8	17.0	14.0		16.8	Long-Term Debt	19.6	18.7
	1.3	.9	1.1		1.2	Deferred Taxes	1.1	.9
	3.0	7.0	5.1		2.4	All Other Non-Current	5.3	5.3
	46.7	37.8	47.0		37.2	Net Worth	30.9	30.7
	100.0	100.0	100.0		100.0	Total Liabilities & Net Worth	100.0	100.0
						INCOME DATA		
	100.0	100.0	100.0		100.0	Net Sales	100.0	100.0
	23.8	28.6	25.1		29.6	Gross Profit	26.0	27.1
	21.3	22.9	17.4		19.9	Operating Expenses	21.9	24.4
	2.5	5.7	7.7		9.8	Operating Profit	4.1	2.7
	.4	1.3	.4		1.0	All Other Expenses (net)	1.8	1.3
	2.1	4.4	7.3		8.7	Profit Before Taxes	2.4	1.4
						RATIOS		
	3.4	3.3	2.4		1.6		1.7	1.9
	2.1	1.4	1.9		1.2	Current	1.2	1.2
	1.2	1.0	1.3		1.0		.9	.9
	2.2	1.7	1.4		1.0		1.0	1.1
	.9	.7	.9		.6	Quick	.7	.7
	.6	.4	.6		.5		.5	.4
	26 14.0	26 14.1	31 11.7		36 10.2		36 10.2	36 10.2
	37 9.9	36 10.2	40 9.2		54 6.8	Sales/Receivables	48 7.7	47 7.8
	46 7.9	49 7.5	52 7.0		87 4.2		58 6.3	61 6.0
	20 18.0	36 10.1	37 9.9		47 7.7		27 13.7	30 12.2
	41 9.0	55 6.7	50 7.4		79 4.6	Cost of Sales/Inventory	48 7.6	45 8.1
	79 4.6	95 3.8	81 4.5		140 2.6		66 5.5	66 5.5
	14 26.6	12 29.6	14 25.6		25 14.7		26 14.0	22 16.7
	24 15.1	25 14.4	26 14.3		31 11.7	Cost of Sales/Payables	36 10.1	35 10.5
	37 9.9	44 8.2	47 7.8		54 6.7		53 6.9	56 6.5
	5.1	4.7	5.1		8.4		9.3	8.4
	7.4	11.5	7.9		12.4	Sales/Working Capital	18.3	22.9
	26.4	-193.9	22.8		NM		-42.3	-24.8
	11.4	10.7	22.3		8.9		8.7	9.0
	(19) 2.8	(36) 3.4	(35) 12.2		7.0	EBIT/Interest	(137) 2.3	(166) 2.0
	.2	1.1	3.9		2.5		.6	.4
		4.8	9.4			Net Profit + Depr., Dep.,	4.1	4.1
	(11) 2.2	(11) 4.7				Amort./Cur. Mat. L/T/D	(46) 2.5	(49) 1.9
	1.0	1.9					1.1	1.0
	.4	.4	.4		.4		.6	.6
	.5	1.0	.6		.9	Fixed/Worth	1.2	1.3
	1.0	1.9	1.2		1.6		4.6	3.5
	.4	.6	.7		.9		1.0	1.0
	1.2	1.8	.9		2.2	Debt/Worth	2.5	2.4
	2.7	5.9	2.1		4.3		13.8	10.2
	34.2	56.9	49.0		90.1	% Profit Before Taxes/Tangible	45.3	33.0
	(22) 7.4	(35) 18.1	(34) 28.7		(10) 40.2	Net Worth	(117) 18.9	(147) 11.6
	-2.7	3.9	15.0		8.3		.8	-1.0
	13.6	17.6	21.2		20.3	% Profit Before Taxes/Total	12.0	9.0
	4.6	8.0	15.2		11.2	Assets	4.2	2.9
	-2.5	.6	6.4		2.5		-.9	-1.5
	19.3	10.9	9.8		10.2		8.8	10.1
	11.2	5.9	6.7		5.8	Sales/Net Fixed Assets	5.6	5.9
	6.8	3.1	4.4		3.9		3.5	3.6
	3.6	2.7	2.5		2.1		2.4	2.5
	2.7	2.0	2.0		1.3	Sales/Total Assets	1.8	1.9
	2.3	1.6	1.5		1.1		1.3	1.4
	1.8	1.8	1.5				2.5	2.4
	(22) 2.8	(36) 3.1	(31) 2.2			% Depr., Dep., Amort./Sales	(127) 3.9	(158) 3.8
	4.3	5.0	4.6				5.0	5.4
	1.9	1.2				% Officers', Directors'	2.0	1.7
	(18) 4.6	(15) 3.3				Owners' Comp/Sales	(51) 3.5	(68) 3.3
	7.8	6.1					5.8	6.0
4713M	77771M	428010M	1678941M	338591M	3373057M	Net Sales ($)	4717603M	4655230M
1052M	27645M	196356M	822637M	185785M	2231670M	Total Assets ($)	2995444M	2773993M

M = $ thousand   MM = $ million

Comparative Historical Data | Current Data Sorted by Sales

			Type of Statement						
29	36	28	Unqualified		1		1	7	19
45	31	22	Reviewed			3	8	4	7
24	25	22	Compiled		6	9	5	1	1
2	4	5	Tax Returns		3		1	1	1
60	57	40	Other	1	4	5	3	9	18
4/1/04-3/31/05	4/1/05-3/31/06	4/1/06-3/31/07			30 (4/1-9/30/06)		87 (10/1/06-3/31/07)		
ALL	ALL	ALL		0-1MM	1-3MM	3-5MM	5-10MM	10-25MM	25MM & OVER
160	153	117	**NUMBER OF STATEMENTS**	1	14	17	18	22	45
%	%	%	**ASSETS**	%	%	%	%	%	%
4.9	4.7	7.6	Cash & Equivalents		12.3	6.3	9.0	6.2	5.8
27.0	28.9	25.1	Trade Receivables (net)		27.8	27.0	19.4	24.0	27.0
22.2	23.0	24.7	Inventory		23.1	31.1	26.2	22.8	23.0
1.6	2.2	2.3	All Other Current		3.8	.3	.7	1.0	3.9
55.7	58.9	59.7	Total Current		67.0	64.8	55.2	54.0	59.8
34.5	31.1	31.6	Fixed Assets (net)		26.5	26.9	39.8	38.2	28.5
3.0	2.3	3.8	Intangibles (net)		3.3	2.3	1.0	3.2	6.1
6.8	7.6	4.9	All Other Non-Current		3.2	6.0	3.9	4.6	5.6
100.0	100.0	100.0	Total		100.0	100.0	100.0	100.0	100.0
			LIABILITIES						
13.7	12.6	10.7	Notes Payable-Short Term		4.5	13.4	8.9	8.7	9.5
4.7	4.5	3.8	Cur. Mat.-L.T.D.		4.5	4.0	5.4	5.2	2.4
15.9	16.9	14.3	Trade Payables		18.0	14.3	10.6	15.3	14.4
.2	.4	.2	Income Taxes Payable		.0	.0	.3	.3	.2
7.9	7.4	8.1	All Other Current		5.4	8.3	6.1	8.3	9.8
42.4	41.7	37.1	Total Current		32.4	40.0	31.4	37.8	36.2
15.6	14.3	14.5	Long-Term Debt		9.6	14.3	15.7	20.4	13.1
1.0	1.0	1.0	Deferred Taxes		1.2	1.3	1.4	.7	1.0
6.1	6.7	6.0	All Other Non-Current		8.0	9.5	3.5	3.4	5.6
34.9	36.3	41.3	Net Worth		48.8	34.9	48.1	37.8	44.1
100.0	100.0	100.0	Total Liabilities & Net Worth		100.0	100.0	100.0	100.0	100.0
			INCOME DATA						
100.0	100.0	100.0	Net Sales		100.0	100.0	100.0	100.0	100.0
24.7	24.1	27.0	Gross Profit		29.0	26.2	33.1	23.6	25.6
21.3	19.5	21.1	Operating Expenses		26.7	23.7	26.0	18.5	17.2
3.4	4.6	5.9	Operating Profit		2.3	2.5	7.1	5.2	8.4
1.1	.9	.8	All Other Expenses (net)		.3	.8	1.6	1.0	.6
2.3	3.7	5.1	Profit Before Taxes		2.0	1.7	5.6	4.2	7.8
			RATIOS						
1.9	2.3	2.9			5.5	3.3	3.8	1.8	2.3
1.3	1.4	1.7	Current		2.4	1.5	2.6	1.4	1.8
.9	1.0	1.1			1.2	1.1	1.0	1.0	1.1
1.2	1.2	1.5			4.0	1.4	1.9	1.2	1.3
.7 (152)	.8	.9	Quick		1.3	.8	1.2	.7	.9
.5	.5	.5			.6	.5	.5	.4	.6
35 10.4	36 10.0	28 12.9		25 14.9	29 12.4	22 16.9	24 15.5	33 11.2	
45 8.0	49 7.5	38 9.7	Sales/Receivables	37 9.7	37 10.0	36 10.1	34 10.9	48 7.7	
57 6.4	64 5.7	52 7.0		52 7.0	48 7.5	44 8.3	48 7.6	56 6.5	
33 11.2	34 10.6	35 10.3		15 23.8	33 11.0	46 8.0	33 11.1	37 9.9	
49 7.5	49 7.5	50 7.3	Cost of Sales/Inventory	43 8.4	62 5.9	74 5.0	44 8.3	50 7.3	
79 4.6	73 5.0	83 4.4		80 4.6	110 3.3	115 3.2	71 5.2	80 4.6	
21 17.2	21 17.7	14 26.5		12 30.9	10 37.1	11 32.0	16 23.0	20 18.6	
34 10.6	36 10.2	25 14.4	Cost of Sales/Payables	26 14.0	16 22.5	27 13.6	28 13.0	26 14.2	
56 6.5	54 6.7	44 8.2		49 7.5	35 10.3	37 9.7	55 6.7	46 7.9	
7.3	5.9	5.3			4.1	5.4	3.7	5.8	6.0
16.9	12.0	9.3	Sales/Working Capital		6.6	9.3	6.3	11.5	10.4
-44.6	-143.6	46.1			36.1	33.9	-178.9	NM	27.9
7.1	13.1	14.0				14.7	14.3	13.1	21.2
(145) 3.2	(145) 3.5	(108) 5.8	EBIT/Interest			1.2	(16) 5.2	(43) 5.1	8.2
.7	1.2	1.8				-1.0	1.2	2.5	3.9
4.1	9.8	7.0							12.9
(48) 1.9	(52) 3.3	(37) 4.1	Net Profit + Depr., Dep., Amort./Cur. Mat. L/T/D					(16)	6.9
.9	1.4	1.5							2.6
.5	.5	.4			.1	.4	.4	.5	.4
1.1	.9	.7	Fixed/Worth		.5	.6	.8	1.0	.6
2.4	2.0	1.5			2.2	7.9	1.6	2.8	1.3
.8	.8	.7			.4	.8	.4	.8	.7
2.0	1.7	1.3	Debt/Worth		.8	1.3	.9	1.8	1.3
6.1	4.9	3.2			3.7	40.4	2.4	4.3	3.0
38.3	41.4	49.8			36.5	34.2	48.5	59.9	58.3
(138) 14.5	(134) 22.6	(107) 23.4	% Profit Before Taxes/Tangible Net Worth		(13) 7.6	(15) 4.0	(17) 11.1	(20) 19.1	(42) 33.7
2.4	5.2	5.7			3.1	-2.0	-2.3	12.7	12.7
10.6	17.6	20.1			7.5	17.1	17.7	14.1	21.6
4.4	5.6	9.5	% Profit Before Taxes/Total Assets		5.0	.8	8.2	9.5	16.6
-.7	.8	1.6			2.1	-4.8	-.8	2.7	4.9
11.2	12.2	12.9			25.1	14.8	10.0	10.6	10.4
6.6	6.9	7.2	Sales/Net Fixed Assets		12.9	10.6	4.3	5.3	6.7
3.6	4.2	4.4			5.9	6.3	3.1	3.4	4.7
2.6	2.5	2.9			3.2	3.5	2.2	2.8	2.7
1.9	1.9	2.1	Sales/Total Assets		2.6	2.5	1.7	2.2	2.0
1.5	1.5	1.6			1.7	1.7	1.6	1.4	1.4
2.0	1.5	1.7			1.8	1.5	2.3	1.7	1.2
(143) 3.5	(136) 2.8	(102) 2.8	% Depr., Dep., Amort./Sales		(12) 2.7	(15) 3.2	3.6	(21) 2.8	(36) 1.9
4.9	4.6	4.4			5.5	4.2	5.4	5.0	3.5
1.4	1.4	1.4				2.1	.6		
(66) 2.7	(54) 3.1	(42) 3.3	% Officers', Directors', Owners' Comp/Sales			(12) 4.7	(10) 3.1		
6.0	5.4	6.7				12.1	8.2		
5085896M	6358139M	5901083M	Net Sales ($)	338M	28450M	66658M	127738M	376403M	5301496M
2886413M	3281119M	3465145M	Total Assets ($)	14M	11565M	34939M	70291M	312624M	3035712M

M = $ thousand   MM = $ million
See Pages 11 through 21 for Explanation of Ratios and Data

Current Data Sorted by Assets

Comparative Historical Data

Period headers (left): 7 (4/1-9/30/06) · 34 (10/1/06-3/31/07)
Period headers (right): 11 — 4/1/02-3/31/03 ALL · 12 — 4/1/03-3/31/04 ALL

0-500M	500M-2MM	2-10MM	10-50MM	50-100MM	100-250MM		4/1/02-3/31/03 ALL	4/1/03-3/31/04 ALL
						Type of Statement		
		2	7	2	4	Unqualified	10	11
	4	2				Reviewed	4	5
1	1		1			Compiled	7	9
	1	1				Tax Returns	2	
1	2	4	6	2		Other	11	12
2	8	9	14	4	4	**NUMBER OF STATEMENTS**	34	37
%	%	%	%	%	%		%	%
						ASSETS		
			7.5			Cash & Equivalents	6.2	5.4
			21.4			Trade Receivables (net)	23.6	26.3
			20.6			Inventory	22.6	23.4
			1.3			All Other Current	.8	1.7
			50.8			Total Current	53.2	56.8
			39.3			Fixed Assets (net)	37.2	33.1
			2.0			Intangibles (net)	6.1	5.5
			7.9			All Other Non-Current	3.5	4.7
			100.0			Total	100.0	100.0
						LIABILITIES		
			10.4			Notes Payable-Short Term	13.6	15.1
			5.2			Cur. Mat.-L.T.D.	2.8	3.5
			16.1			Trade Payables	12.1	15.4
			.3			Income Taxes Payable	.0	.1
			8.7			All Other Current	7.4	9.5
			40.8			Total Current	36.0	43.6
			15.9			Long-Term Debt	17.8	19.1
			.7			Deferred Taxes	1.2	1.0
			6.0			All Other Non-Current	7.6	7.5
			36.7			Net Worth	37.4	28.7
			100.0			Total Liabilities & Net Worth	100.0	100.0
						INCOME DATA		
			100.0			Net Sales	100.0	100.0
			24.4			Gross Profit	27.4	28.2
			17.2			Operating Expenses	23.3	23.8
			7.2			Operating Profit	4.1	4.4
			1.8			All Other Expenses (net)	1.9	1.6
			5.4			Profit Before Taxes	2.2	2.7
						RATIOS		
			1.8				2.3	2.5
			1.2			Current	1.8	1.5
			1.0				1.2	1.0
			1.3				1.5	1.2
			.7			Quick	.9	.9
			.4				.7	.6
		33	11.2				34 10.8	40 9.2
		48	7.6			Sales/Receivables	41 9.0	46 8.0
		64	5.7				50 7.3	53 6.9
		34	10.8				38 9.7	41 8.9
		50	7.4			Cost of Sales/Inventory	48 7.6	54 6.8
		80	4.6				65 5.6	78 4.7
		25	14.5				21 17.5	29 12.7
		41	8.9			Cost of Sales/Payables	29 12.4	36 10.3
		51	7.1				42 8.8	59 6.2
			8.5				4.9	5.9
			22.9			Sales/Working Capital	9.1	12.6
			NM				26.4	255.9
			8.9				7.1	9.1
			(12) 3.1			EBIT/Interest	(29) 1.6	(34) 2.4
			.0				.4	.2
						Net Profit + Depr., Dep.,		2.8
						Amort./Cur. Mat. L/T/D		(15) 2.1
								1.5
			.8				.6	.5
			1.2			Fixed/Worth	.9	.9
			3.0				2.2	3.7
			.9				.6	.9
			1.7			Debt/Worth	1.7	2.3
			4.2				4.9	6.7
			70.6				27.9	38.0
			(12) 24.1			% Profit Before Taxes/Tangible Net Worth	(31) 16.1	(31) 13.4
			7.6				-6.4	-.9
			18.3				12.2	12.6
			7.2			% Profit Before Taxes/Total Assets	3.2	3.7
			-.3				-1.4	-1.5
			8.7				10.1	11.3
			7.0			Sales/Net Fixed Assets	4.9	5.6
			2.9				3.6	3.8
			2.4				2.4	2.6
			1.7			Sales/Total Assets	1.9	1.8
			1.4				1.6	1.4
			1.6				2.3	1.2
			(13) 2.3			% Depr., Dep., Amort./Sales	(31) 3.7	(31) 2.8
			5.1				5.6	5.1
							1.8	2.6
						% Officers', Directors' Owners' Comp/Sales	(11) 3.3	(17) 4.3
							4.5	6.0
1521M	35457M	124840M	589729M	449379M	1112473M	Net Sales ($)	1413727M	1145906M
709M	9677M	46497M	353127M	300272M	587368M	Total Assets ($)	936019M	840672M

© RMA 2007

M = $ thousand   MM = $ million
See Pages 11 through 21 for Explanation of Ratios and Data

Comparative Historical Data

Current Data Sorted by Sales

			Type of Statement						
15	8	15	Unqualified				3	12	
5	9	6	Reviewed	1	2	2	1	1	
8	6	3	Compiled	1	1			1	
4		2	Tax Returns		1		1		
12	15	15	Other	1	2		3	3	9
4/1/04-	4/1/05-	4/1/06-		0-1MM	7 (4/1-9/30/06)	3-5MM	34 (10/1/06-3/31/07)	10-25MM	25MM & OVER
3/31/05	3/31/06	3/31/07			1-3MM		5-10MM		
ALL	ALL	ALL							
44	38	41	NUMBER OF STATEMENTS	1	4	4	2	8	22
%	%	%	ASSETS	%	%	%	%	%	%
5.6	6.2	8.4	Cash & Equivalents						6.2
29.7	26.0	23.2	Trade Receivables (net)						21.7
20.8	23.9	21.3	Inventory						21.7
1.0	1.3	1.4	All Other Current						1.4
57.1	57.4	54.2	Total Current						50.9
30.6	34.1	34.9	Fixed Assets (net)						34.2
5.1	4.8	4.0	Intangibles (net)						5.6
7.2	3.8	6.9	All Other Non-Current						9.3
100.0	100.0	100.0	Total						100.0
			LIABILITIES						
11.4	9.6	6.7	Notes Payable-Short Term						8.1
4.2	3.6	4.5	Cur. Mat.-L.T.D.						4.5
15.8	16.4	18.3	Trade Payables						15.6
.1	.1	.3	Income Taxes Payable						.4
9.5	7.4	9.9	All Other Current						9.6
40.9	37.1	39.8	Total Current						38.2
16.7	17.5	17.0	Long-Term Debt						16.7
1.2	1.4	1.4	Deferred Taxes						2.1
6.3	10.6	6.8	All Other Non-Current						5.6
34.8	33.5	35.1	Net Worth						37.5
100.0	100.0	100.0	Total Liabilties & Net Worth						100.0
			INCOME DATA						
100.0	100.0	100.0	Net Sales						100.0
27.3	27.3	22.4	Gross Profit						22.2
21.5	23.4	19.0	Operating Expenses						16.2
5.8	3.8	3.4	Operating Profit						6.0
1.4	1.7	1.5	All Other Expenses (net)						1.8
4.4	2.1	1.9	Profit Before Taxes						4.2
			RATIOS						
2.5	2.6	2.2							1.9
1.5	1.5	1.3	Current						1.2
1.1	1.1	1.1							1.0
1.5	1.4	1.3							1.1
.9	.9	.9	Quick						.8
.6	.5	.4							.4
40 9.2	36 10.0	27 13.3						33	11.1
47 7.7	47 7.8	39 9.4	Sales/Receivables					42	8.7
54 6.7	53 6.8	50 7.3						53	6.9
30 12.2	39 9.4	34 10.8						37	9.8
49 7.5	58 6.3	41 8.9	Cost of Sales/Inventory					54	6.8
69 5.3	84 4.3	71 5.1						80	4.6
24 15.3	30 12.4	26 14.3						26	14.1
33 11.0	38 9.6	37 9.9	Cost of Sales/Payables					38	9.5
49 7.5	47 7.7	47 7.7						49	7.5
6.7	5.2	7.2							8.6
14.1	10.4	16.9	Sales/Working Capital						18.7
54.8	51.0	94.4							157.6
12.0	5.5	9.1							10.7
(41) 4.5	(37) 2.2	(38) 4.1	EBIT/Interest					(20)	3.4
1.8	1.0	1.4							1.2
6.3	4.5	4.1	Net Profit + Depr., Dep.,						4.1
(10) 2.2	(11) 2.2	(15) 2.4	Amort./Cur. Mat. L/T/D					(11)	2.4
1.2	.7	1.8							1.8
.5	.4	.5							.6
.9	1.1	1.0	Fixed/Worth						1.0
2.4	2.5	3.3							3.9
.7	.8	.8							.9
2.2	2.1	1.8	Debt/Worth						1.7
4.1	4.3	5.5							9.3
37.3	29.0	49.2	% Profit Before Taxes/Tangible						68.7
(38) 21.3	(32) 13.3	(34) 19.3	Net Worth					(18)	17.7
3.6	.6	5.2							8.5
11.9	9.7	13.3	% Profit Before Taxes/Total						12.5
7.2	4.5	5.5	Assets						5.9
3.0	.1	.6							1.6
15.6	10.7	13.0							8.4
6.1	5.1	6.7	Sales/Net Fixed Assets						6.6
4.4	3.5	3.5							3.4
2.7	2.3	3.0							2.4
2.0	1.8	2.0	Sales/Total Assets						1.8
1.6	1.5	1.5							1.4
2.0	1.6	1.6							1.9
(39) 3.1	(34) 3.4	(36) 2.8	% Depr., Dep., Amort./Sales					(20)	2.3
4.4	5.0	4.7							4.7
1.7	3.6	.9	% Officers', Directors'						
(13) 4.0	(11) 3.8	(12) 3.4	Owners' Comp/Sales						
5.2	5.8	5.0							
1879820M	1605222M	2313399M	Net Sales ($)	367M	6484M	15875M	14666M	105163M	2170844M
1113984M	958817M	1297650M	Total Assets ($)	414M	3340M	5222M	5633M	45953M	1237088M

M = $ thousand   MM = $ million
See Pages 11 through 21 for Explanation of Ratios and Data

Current Data Sorted by Assets   Comparative Historical Data

0-500M	500M-2MM	2-10MM	10-50MM	50-100MM	100-250MM	Type of Statement	4/1/02-3/31/03 ALL	4/1/03-3/31/04 ALL
	1	5	9	4	6	Unqualified	18	17
1	2	10	5		1	Reviewed	27	18
2	9					Compiled	9	13
1	8					Tax Returns	5	6
		1	16	1	1	Other	22	21
	17 (4/1-9/30/06)		78 (10/1/06-3/31/07)					
4	24	24	30	6	7	NUMBER OF STATEMENTS	81	75
%	%	%	%	%	%	ASSETS	%	%
	13.4	6.1	5.2			Cash & Equivalents	6.5	6.0
	27.7	31.9	27.0			Trade Receivables (net)	28.7	29.8
	21.9	20.9	21.0			Inventory	19.4	17.5
	1.6	2.3	1.7			All Other Current	1.9	2.8
	64.7	61.2	54.9			Total Current	56.4	56.0
	25.2	31.4	37.1			Fixed Assets (net)	35.4	36.2
	2.4	4.2	3.1			Intangibles (net)	2.7	1.5
	7.7	3.1	4.9			All Other Non-Current	5.5	6.2
	100.0	100.0	100.0			Total	100.0	100.0
						LIABILITIES		
	8.8	13.9	10.9			Notes Payable-Short Term	8.5	8.9
	6.5	2.8	3.5			Cur. Mat.-L.T.D.	4.6	4.1
	18.1	16.0	15.3			Trade Payables	17.1	18.8
	.0	.3	.1			Income Taxes Payable	.1	.2
	9.4	5.2	6.8			All Other Current	18.6	7.5
	42.8	38.2	36.5			Total Current	48.9	39.5
	25.6	16.6	23.1			Long-Term Debt	19.2	18.7
	.4	.3	.2			Deferred Taxes	.5	.8
	8.2	5.0	2.9			All Other Non-Current	3.4	3.4
	23.0	40.0	37.4			Net Worth	28.0	37.6
	100.0	100.0	100.0			Total Liabilities & Net Worth	100.0	100.0
						INCOME DATA		
	100.0	100.0	100.0			Net Sales	100.0	100.0
	25.9	29.2	23.5			Gross Profit	27.2	27.2
	24.2	21.4	18.3			Operating Expenses	23.9	23.3
	1.7	7.8	5.2			Operating Profit	3.2	3.9
	.6	.6	.8			All Other Expenses (net)	1.1	.8
	1.1	7.2	4.4			Profit Before Taxes	2.2	3.1
						RATIOS		
	2.5	3.2	2.6				2.2	2.4
	1.7	1.6	1.4			Current	1.4	1.4
	1.3	1.1	1.0				1.0	1.1
	1.6	2.0	1.3				1.6	1.4
	1.0	.9	.8			Quick	.8 (74)	.9
	.6	.7	.5				.6	.6
	18 20.4	43 8.5	30 12.3				31 11.7	36 10.2
	33 11.2	52 7.0	38 9.7			Sales/Receivables	44 8.3	44 8.3
	41 9.0	63 5.8	52 7.1				53 6.9	57 6.4
	14 25.5	34 10.6	27 13.6				26 14.1	21 17.5
	36 10.3	43 8.5	44 8.2			Cost of Sales/Inventory	39 9.4	33 10.9
	62 5.9	61 6.0	57 6.4				59 6.2	51 7.1
	9 40.0	20 18.0	18 19.9				21 17.5	24 15.2
	22 16.6	27 13.6	29 12.5			Cost of Sales/Payables	33 10.9	31 11.7
	43 8.4	48 7.7	42 8.7				47 7.8	45 8.0
	7.6	5.5	6.5				6.9	7.0
	13.2	10.3	19.3			Sales/Working Capital	13.9	14.2
	42.6	98.4	NM				99.5	57.2
	6.4	11.1	8.3				7.5	8.1
	(20) 2.5	5.9	(28) 3.9			EBIT/Interest	(74) 4.0	(66) 4.0
	.5	2.1	2.1				.9	1.4
							5.3	3.7
						Net Profit + Depr., Dep., Amort./Cur. Mat. L/T/D	(23) 2.1	(21) 1.9
							.9	1.1
	.3	.4	.5				.5	.5
	.7	1.0	.9			Fixed/Worth	1.0	1.0
	2.5	2.8	3.6				2.2	2.5
	.9	.7	1.0				.7	.7
	2.8	1.6	1.6			Debt/Worth	1.6	1.8
	8.8	12.0	4.3				5.2	4.6
	67.5	55.0	48.8				35.0	56.5
	(20) 20.5	(20) 30.8	(28) 28.8			% Profit Before Taxes/Tangible Net Worth	(70) 13.9	(67) 22.8
	5.9	14.2	7.9				5.6	6.1
	15.2	23.1	16.2				16.6	12.9
	4.9	12.7	7.8			% Profit Before Taxes/Total Assets	6.3	6.8
	-.7	3.5	3.6				-.2	.8
	33.0	12.3	10.9				14.8	15.0
	16.7	6.9	6.6			Sales/Net Fixed Assets	6.5	6.7
	8.1	5.0	3.8				4.1	3.5
	4.5	2.8	3.0				3.2	3.2
	3.2	2.3	2.2			Sales/Total Assets	2.4	2.4
	1.8	1.7	1.5				1.6	1.6
	.9	1.7	1.7				1.5	1.6
	(19) 1.6	(21) 2.7	(27) 2.9			% Depr., Dep., Amort./Sales	(74) 2.8	(68) 2.7
	4.0	3.7	4.0				4.5	4.3
	1.3						2.4	2.7
	(16) 4.6					% Officers', Directors' Owners' Comp/Sales	(28) 3.7	(26) 4.3
	7.4						6.2	8.1
4563M	115629M	238874M	1522443M	764583M	2202758M	Net Sales ($)	2596671M	2479185M
1182M	29542M	109261M	650378M	397605M	1206913M	Total Assets ($)	1419085M	1186512M

M = $ thousand   MM = $ million
See Pages 11 through 21 for Explanation of Ratios and Data

Comparative Historical Data / Current Data Sorted by Sales

4/1/04-3/31/05 ALL	4/1/05-3/31/06 ALL	4/1/06-3/31/07 ALL		0-1MM	1-3MM	3-5MM	5-10MM	10-25MM	25MM & OVER
			Type of Statement		17 (4/1-9/30/06)		78 (10/1/06-3/31/07)		
19	14	25	Unqualified		1		1	5	18
16	17	19	Reviewed		2	1	9	4	3
20	15	11	Compiled	2	5	2	1	1	1
5	6	6	Tax Returns	1	2			2	
20	23	34	Other		4		7	11	12
80	75	95	**NUMBER OF STATEMENTS**	3	14	4	18	23	33
%	%	%	**ASSETS**	%	%	%	%	%	%
6.0	7.6	8.1	Cash & Equivalents		11.4		5.6	8.4	5.9
30.4	29.0	28.2	Trade Receivables (net)		26.6		32.8	27.3	28.0
20.2	20.4	21.3	Inventory		19.9		20.2	20.4	21.2
1.8	1.5	1.8	All Other Current		1.7		2.8	1.2	2.0
58.5	58.4	59.4	Total Current		59.7		61.5	57.3	57.1
32.7	32.4	30.7	Fixed Assets (net)		23.7		31.4	37.2	30.1
3.3	3.9	4.1	Intangibles (net)		5.5		3.5	2.0	6.0
5.5	5.3	5.9	All Other Non-Current		11.2		3.7	3.6	6.8
100.0	100.0	100.0	Total		100.0		100.0	100.0	100.0
			LIABILITIES						
9.2	9.7	9.8	Notes Payable-Short Term		6.1		17.0	11.9	6.0
5.0	5.7	3.7	Cur. Mat.-L.T.D.		6.7		3.4	3.2	2.8
18.2	19.6	16.2	Trade Payables		17.2		17.0	17.5	14.2
.1	.2	.1	Income Taxes Payable		.1		.3	.0	.2
8.1	6.6	7.6	All Other Current		7.0		7.2	8.2	8.7
40.6	41.8	37.4	Total Current		37.0		45.0	40.9	31.9
18.6	17.9	21.0	Long-Term Debt		38.1		13.4	19.2	18.8
.7	.3	.5	Deferred Taxes		.7		.2	.2	.9
2.9	4.7	5.7	All Other Non-Current		8.0		2.8	4.5	3.8
37.2	35.2	35.4	Net Worth		16.2		38.6	35.2	44.6
100.0	100.0	100.0	Total Liabilties & Net Worth		100.0		100.0	100.0	100.0
			INCOME DATA						
100.0	100.0	100.0	Net Sales		100.0		100.0	100.0	100.0
28.6	27.9	25.3	Gross Profit		27.6		30.2	24.3	21.5
24.3	22.8	20.3	Operating Expenses		23.4		24.2	19.2	15.4
4.3	5.2	5.0	Operating Profit		4.2		6.0	5.1	6.0
1.0	.8	.8	All Other Expenses (net)		1.0		.8	.5	.7
3.4	4.4	4.2	Profit Before Taxes		3.2		5.2	4.6	5.3
			RATIOS						
2.4	2.0	2.6	Current		3.5		2.2	2.0	2.6
1.3	1.5	1.7			2.6		1.3	1.2	1.8
1.0	1.0	1.1			1.0		1.0	1.0	1.4
1.3	1.3	1.6	Quick		2.0		1.3	1.3	1.6
.8	.9	.9			1.4		.8	.9	1.0
.6	.6	.6			.4		.7	.5	.7
34 10.9	35 10.4	31 11.8	Sales/Receivables	29 12.7		38 9.5	27 13.8	32 11.3	
43 8.4	44 8.4	39 9.3		34 10.8		49 7.5	45 8.1	39 9.4	
59 6.1	54 6.7	55 6.6		40 9.1		64 5.7	55 6.6	51 7.1	
25 14.7	32 11.5	27 13.5	Cost of Sales/Inventory	23 15.8		26 13.9	27 13.6	27 13.6	
39 9.5	45 8.0	43 8.4		43 8.6		41 9.0	44 8.2	44 8.2	
60 6.1	57 6.1	61 6.0		63 5.8		56 6.5	62 5.9	55 6.7	
21 17.1	20 18.1	17 20.9	Cost of Sales/Payables	17 21.3		15 24.2	21 17.4	18 20.2	
35 10.3	36 10.1	27 13.8		33 11.1		24 15.3	32 11.3	25 14.4	
50 7.3	54 6.8	43 8.5		59 6.2		46 7.9	55 6.6	31 11.8	
6.7	7.6	6.8	Sales/Working Capital		5.7		6.8	9.7	6.2
21.1	13.2	12.5			7.8		24.0	46.0	9.5
99.6	-291.9	47.0			NM		UND	76.7	17.5
9.5	11.6	10.4	EBIT/Interest		6.1		10.6	7.8	16.3
(69) 4.8	(67) 4.1	(88) 4.1		(12) 2.6		4.1	(21) 3.2	(30) 6.9	
2.2	1.8	1.8			-1.7		1.8	1.8	3.4
3.2	5.0	6.2	Net Profit + Depr., Dep., Amort./Cur. Mat. L/T/D						10.2
(26) 2.5	(21) 2.9	(27) 3.7						(13) 5.2	
1.7	1.5	1.7							3.1
.4	.4	.4	Fixed/Worth		.3		.5	.4	.5
1.0	.9	.8			2.3		1.0	.7	.6
2.5	3.3	2.5			-39.8		1.4	5.2	1.6
.8	1.1	.8	Debt/Worth		.8		.7	.8	.7
1.8	2.1	1.8			4.1		1.8	2.5	1.3
7.0	5.7	6.8			-188.6		8.1	9.1	2.4
43.0	52.6	53.0	% Profit Before Taxes/Tangible Net Worth		66.7		54.9	78.1	46.9
(71) 26.2	(65) 23.1	(84) 27.3		(10) 16.8		(17) 31.5	(21) 28.0	(30) 26.5	
9.5	6.2	8.9			-42.3		10.9	5.6	12.5
16.0	15.1	17.5	% Profit Before Taxes/Total Assets		11.8		23.9	15.4	19.5
6.4	6.9	7.7			5.6		10.5	5.9	12.9
2.2	2.2	2.7			-7.6		2.7	3.0	5.2
14.8	16.1	15.0	Sales/Net Fixed Assets		30.4		18.0	22.3	11.9
7.0	7.3	8.2			10.5		7.8	6.3	8.3
4.5	4.0	5.1			6.1		4.8	3.8	5.6
3.0	3.3	3.2	Sales/Total Assets		3.3		3.4	3.0	3.1
2.4	2.2	2.4			2.4		2.4	2.3	2.4
1.6	1.6	1.7			1.8		1.8	1.5	1.6
1.6	1.7	1.5	% Depr., Dep., Amort./Sales				1.3	1.1	1.5
(70) 3.0	(67) 2.9	(80) 2.4			(16) 2.4		(21) 2.3	(29) 2.2	
3.9	4.8	3.8					3.4	4.1	3.7
2.3	1.6	1.0	% Officers', Directors' Owners' Comp/Sales						
(29) 3.5	(26) 3.8	(30) 3.3							
7.2	6.9	6.6							
1992494M	2342109M	4848850M	Net Sales ($)	2450M	26661M	16034M	137540M	367637M	4298528M
1113921M	1218339M	2394881M	Total Assets ($)	2081M	14363M	6078M	59404M	193074M	2119881M

© RMA 2007

M = $ thousand   MM = $ million
See Pages 11 through 21 for Explanation of Ratios and Data

Current Data Sorted by Assets | **Comparative Historical Data**

0-500M	500M-2MM 7 (4/1-9/30/06)	2-10MM	10-50MM 26 (10/1/06-3/31/07)	50-100MM	100-250MM	Type of Statement	9 4/1/02-3/31/03 ALL	8 4/1/03-3/31/04 ALL
		3	5	2	3	Unqualified	8	6
	1	2		1		Reviewed	2	5
						Compiled		5
						Tax Returns		
1	1	5	6	1	1	Other	9	8
1	2	11	11	4	4	NUMBER OF STATEMENTS	19	24
%	%	%	%	%	%	**ASSETS**	%	%
		8.1	1.5			Cash & Equivalents	3.4	5.1
		20.2	28.2			Trade Receivables (net)	15.1	16.5
		12.6	17.5			Inventory	15.9	13.5
		.7	4.8			All Other Current	2.0	2.6
		41.5	52.0			Total Current	36.4	37.7
		49.5	40.4			Fixed Assets (net)	55.5	53.5
		4.0	1.4			Intangibles (net)	4.0	5.7
		5.0	6.1			All Other Non-Current	4.2	3.1
		100.0	100.0			Total	100.0	100.0
						LIABILITIES		
		3.1	9.8			Notes Payable-Short Term	5.6	6.3
		8.8	3.6			Cur. Mat.-L.T.D.	6.0	7.1
		13.3	12.8			Trade Payables	11.4	10.8
		.1	.0			Income Taxes Payable	.7	.8
		5.8	24.0			All Other Current	6.6	11.6
		31.0	50.2			Total Current	30.2	36.5
		32.6	18.5			Long-Term Debt	29.5	23.7
		1.5	1.1			Deferred Taxes	.5	1.1
		9.0	7.8			All Other Non-Current	4.7	8.4
		25.9	22.4			Net Worth	35.0	30.3
		100.0	100.0			Total Liabilties & Net Worth	100.0	100.0
						INCOME DATA		
		100.0	100.0			Net Sales	100.0	100.0
		29.4	24.4			Gross Profit	30.9	20.8
		23.4	19.1			Operating Expenses	21.7	15.7
		6.0	5.2			Operating Profit	9.3	5.1
		2.1	2.5			All Other Expenses (net)	2.2	1.8
		3.9	2.7			Profit Before Taxes	7.1	3.3
						RATIOS		
		4.6	2.0			Current	1.6	2.4
		1.0	1.5				1.1	1.0
		.7	1.0				.7	.7
		2.6	1.2			Quick	.7	1.3
		.6	.8				.5	.6
		.3	.7				.4	.4
		28 13.2	44 8.3			Sales/Receivables	28 12.8	27 13.3
		35 10.6	50 7.3				39 9.4	34 10.7
		70 5.2	75 4.8				41 9.0	42 8.7
		17 21.7	29 12.7			Cost of Sales/Inventory	30 12.3	26 14.2
		35 10.3	50 7.3				44 8.2	34 10.6
		51 7.1	64 5.7				81 4.5	46 8.0
		19 19.7	22 16.8			Cost of Sales/Payables	30 12.2	19 19.7
		32 11.3	40 9.2				42 8.6	29 12.7
		73 5.0	53 6.9				55 6.7	41 8.9
		6.9	7.9			Sales/Working Capital	9.5	9.6
		-999.8	14.5				29.0	NM
		-13.1	91.7				-20.5	-20.3
		6.7	9.2			EBIT/Interest	6.8	7.1
		3.2	2.6				(18) 4.1	3.9
		.6	1.1				1.8	1.3
						Net Profit + Depr., Dep., Amort./Cur. Mat. L/T/D		
		.4	.8			Fixed/Worth	1.5	1.1
		2.9	1.8				2.1	2.0
		-8.3	2.5				2.5	2.9
		1.6	1.2			Debt/Worth	1.7	1.0
		3.0	2.7				2.1	1.9
		-14.7	3.9				3.1	3.8
			42.5			% Profit Before Taxes/Tangible Net Worth	59.7	39.3
			(10) 19.2				38.3	(20) 27.6
			2.5				12.8	16.2
		22.8	15.3			% Profit Before Taxes/Total Assets	18.8	12.6
		4.2	5.8				10.7	6.3
		-.8	.2				3.1	1.4
		11.6	10.7			Sales/Net Fixed Assets	3.5	6.1
		2.6	4.3				2.6	2.7
		1.4	2.3				1.9	1.9
		3.2	2.2			Sales/Total Assets	2.0	2.0
		1.3	2.1				1.5	1.5
		.9	1.3				1.1	1.1
		1.8				% Depr., Dep., Amort./Sales	3.5	1.2
		(10) 4.2					(14) 6.1	(18) 3.7
		10.0					7.8	7.5
						% Officers', Directors' Owners' Comp/Sales		
1851M	8216M	106619M	603221M	520338M	898379M	Net Sales ($)	1573589M	1550330M
401M	1757M	63794M	313824M	312398M	612537M	Total Assets ($)	1195280M	973329M

M = $ thousand   MM = $ million
See Pages 11 through 21 for Explanation of Ratios and Data

Comparative Historical Data

Current Data Sorted by Sales

	4/1/04-3/31/05 ALL	4/1/05-3/31/06 ALL	4/1/06-3/31/07 ALL	Type of Statement	0-1MM	1-3MM	3-5MM	5-10MM	10-25MM	25MM & OVER
	8	12	13	Unqualified	1			1	3	9
	3	4	4	Reviewed		1		1	2	1
		1	1	Compiled						
		2	2	Tax Returns		1				
	12	15	14	Other	3	1	3	1	2	6
	23	34	33	NUMBER OF STATEMENTS	4	3	3	3	7	16
	%	%	%	ASSETS	%	%	%	%	%	%
	7.9	3.9	8.8	Cash & Equivalents						7.0
	18.2	21.6	22.4	Trade Receivables (net)						22.8
	14.8	16.0	15.4	Inventory	DATA					14.3
	1.8	1.6	2.5	All Other Current						4.5
	42.7	43.0	49.1	Total Current	NOT					48.6
	49.1	47.3	42.2	Fixed Assets (net)						41.9
	4.1	5.0	4.0	Intangibles (net)	AVAILABLE					4.9
	4.1	4.8	4.7	All Other Non-Current						4.6
	100.0	100.0	100.0	Total						100.0
				LIABILITIES						
	2.6	6.6	6.7	Notes Payable-Short Term						6.8
	6.1	6.9	5.6	Cur. Mat.-L.T.D.						4.3
	8.9	16.0	13.2	Trade Payables						13.8
	.1	.1	.2	Income Taxes Payable						.3
	5.9	7.3	12.8	All Other Current						10.5
	23.6	36.9	38.6	Total Current						35.8
	21.7	31.5	25.6	Long-Term Debt						22.4
	1.0	.9	1.0	Deferred Taxes						1.1
	8.4	5.9	6.4	All Other Non-Current						6.9
	45.3	24.8	28.4	Net Worth						33.9
	100.0	100.0	100.0	Total Liabilities & Net Worth						100.0
				INCOME DATA						
	100.0	100.0	100.0	Net Sales						100.0
	24.8	26.5	28.3	Gross Profit						26.4
	17.1	20.3	20.8	Operating Expenses						17.0
	7.7	6.2	7.4	Operating Profit						9.4
	1.6	2.4	2.1	All Other Expenses (net)						1.9
	6.1	3.8	5.4	Profit Before Taxes						7.4
				RATIOS						
	2.9	1.7	2.1	Current						1.8
	1.8	1.3	1.3							1.4
	1.2	.8	.8							.9
	2.2	1.1	1.4	Quick						1.2
	1.0	.7	.8							.8
	.6	.5	.5							.5
	29 12.5	30 12.1	29 12.6	Sales/Receivables						33 11.2
	39 9.4	44 8.3	43 8.6							45 8.2
	52 7.0	49 7.4	66 5.6							49 7.5
	32 11.2	31 11.6	26 13.8	Cost of Sales/Inventory						27 13.7
	46 7.9	43 8.5	39 9.4							37 9.8
	68 5.4	61 6.0	55 6.6							51 7.1
	14 26.4	20 18.3	20 18.0	Cost of Sales/Payables						23 15.9
	22 16.3	36 10.3	33 10.9							41 8.9
	44 8.3	56 6.5	46 7.9							45 8.2
	6.4	9.3	7.5	Sales/Working Capital						8.1
	9.6	13.1	16.1							12.2
	17.7	-25.0	-27.5							NM
	12.3	8.3	10.6	EBIT/Interest						12.5
	3.6	4.0	(31) 3.5							5.6
	2.5	.9	1.2							1.9
		4.5	6.0	Net Profit + Depr., Dep., Amort./Cur. Mat. L/T/D						
	(13) 1.4		(16) 2.4							
	.9		1.5							
	.8	.9	.6	Fixed/Worth						.8
	1.3	1.7	1.8							1.4
	2.1	5.4	11.4							2.7
	.7	1.0	1.0	Debt/Worth						1.0
	1.5	1.6	2.5							2.5
	2.2	14.1	14.4							3.7
	30.8	32.1	42.2	% Profit Before Taxes/Tangible Net Worth						40.2
	(22) 17.9	(27) 25.9	(26) 31.5						(13) 31.7	
	8.9	8.3	8.3							11.0
	16.5	16.7	21.7	% Profit Before Taxes/Total Assets						24.9
	5.8	4.5	8.7							16.5
	3.3	-.6	.7							2.1
	4.3	6.1	11.1	Sales/Net Fixed Assets						6.2
	2.9	2.9	4.1							4.4
	1.9	1.7	1.9							3.4
	1.9	2.0	2.3	Sales/Total Assets						2.3
	1.5	1.5	1.8							2.1
	1.2	1.2	1.1							1.6
	3.6	2.7	2.5	% Depr., Dep., Amort./Sales						3.4
	(18) 6.4	(30) 5.9	(26) 4.6						(12) 4.8	
	8.5	7.9	5.4							5.4
		2.2		% Officers', Directors', Owners' Comp/Sales						
		(10) 4.8								
		7.4								
	1494920M	2245018M	2138624M	Net Sales ($)		8418M	11281M	18249M	116614M	1984062M
	1075823M	1482927M	1304711M	Total Assets ($)		16305M	9190M	19383M	68269M	1191564M

© RMA 2007

M = $ thousand   MM = $ million

See Pages 11 through 21 for Explanation of Ratios and Data

Current Data Sorted by Assets   Comparative Historical Data

Type of Statement	0-500M	500M-2MM	2-10MM	10-50MM	50-100MM	100-250MM		4/1/02-3/31/03 ALL		4/1/03-3/31/04 ALL
Unqualified	1	4	47	70	31	30		165		188
Reviewed	2	32	137	48	1			207		213
Compiled	7	42	50	5		1		114		137
Tax Returns	19	25	15	1				45		55
Other	9	37	133	75	30	16		307		266
		180 (4/1-9/30/06)			688 (10/1/06-3/31/07)					
NUMBER OF STATEMENTS	38	140	382	199	62	47		838		859
ASSETS	%	%	%	%	%	%		%		%
Cash & Equivalents	16.3	6.8	6.5	4.8	4.1	3.0		6.4		6.4
Trade Receivables (net)	31.2	28.7	28.1	24.8	24.2	20.3		24.7		26.2
Inventory	16.8	24.9	23.5	21.9	21.0	17.3		20.8		20.7
All Other Current	2.3	1.2	2.0	2.1	2.7	2.5		2.0		2.3
Total Current	66.6	61.7	60.1	53.6	52.0	43.1		53.9		55.6
Fixed Assets (net)	24.5	30.0	31.6	36.7	34.2	32.8		36.3		34.8
Intangibles (net)	2.4	2.9	2.7	5.0	8.0	18.5		4.2		4.1
All Other Non-Current	6.5	5.4	5.6	4.7	5.8	5.5		5.5		5.4
Total	100.0	100.0	100.0	100.0	100.0	100.0		100.0		100.0
LIABILITIES										
Notes Payable-Short Term	20.9	13.8	12.0	12.1	8.3	5.4		10.4		9.4
Cur. Mat.-L.T.D.	3.4	5.4	5.0	5.5	4.6	3.4		5.7		5.5
Trade Payables	16.5	20.6	16.4	14.4	15.7	13.7		14.6		14.8
Income Taxes Payable	.0	.2	.2	.2	.2	.6		.2		.2
All Other Current	13.3	11.9	8.6	7.9	10.8	7.8		8.7		9.5
Total Current	54.1	52.0	42.1	40.1	39.5	30.9		39.6		39.5
Long-Term Debt	26.9	19.7	17.7	19.6	20.5	37.7		19.8		18.6
Deferred Taxes	.0	.3	.4	1.0	1.4	2.7		.7		.7
All Other Non-Current	7.8	11.0	4.8	7.3	4.9	9.4		5.6		7.0
Net Worth	11.2	16.9	35.0	32.0	33.7	19.3		34.3		34.2
Total Liabilties & Net Worth	100.0	100.0	100.0	100.0	100.0	100.0		100.0		100.0
INCOME DATA										
Net Sales	100.0	100.0	100.0	100.0	100.0	100.0		100.0		100.0
Gross Profit	47.2	31.0	25.8	22.3	22.5	22.2		27.9		26.9
Operating Expenses	41.3	28.4	20.3	17.2	16.3	15.2		23.3		22.3
Operating Profit	5.9	2.6	5.5	5.2	6.3	6.9		4.6		4.6
All Other Expenses (net)	2.1	1.1	1.4	1.8	1.8	3.9		1.6		1.4
Profit Before Taxes	3.8	1.5	4.1	3.4	4.4	3.1		3.0		3.1
RATIOS										
Current	4.2	2.4	2.4	2.1	2.0	1.9		2.2		2.3
	1.2	1.3	1.5	1.3	1.4	1.5		1.4		1.5
	.9	.9	1.0	1.0	1.1	1.1		1.0		1.1
Quick	2.3	1.4	1.5	1.2	1.1	1.1		1.4		1.4
	1.0	(139) .7	.8	.7	.7	.9		(837) .8		.8
	.5	.5	.5	.5	.5	.6		.5		.5
Sales/Receivables	19 18.8	27 13.5	35 10.4	38 9.5	40 9.1	39 9.4		34 10.8		36 10.2
	33 11.1	38 9.6	44 8.2	45 8.1	48 7.6	45 8.1		45 8.1		47 7.8
	44 8.2	51 7.2	57 6.4	60 6.1	62 5.9	63 5.8		56 6.5		58 6.3
Cost of Sales/Inventory	0 UND	26 14.0	33 11.1	36 10.2	43 8.6	37 9.9		32 11.3		31 11.8
	20 17.8	44 8.4	48 7.6	51 7.2	56 6.5	54 6.7		49 7.5		49 7.5
	58 6.3	72 5.1	71 5.1	70 5.2	72 5.1	68 5.4		72 5.1		74 5.0
Cost of Sales/Payables	6 57.6	18 20.1	19 19.1	21 17.1	28 13.2	27 13.7		21 17.7		21 17.7
	25 14.8	35 10.3	32 11.3	32 11.4	37 9.8	33 11.0		34 10.8		33 11.2
	60 6.1	55 6.6	49 7.4	45 8.2	52 7.0	50 7.3		47 7.7		48 7.6
Sales/Working Capital	6.2	6.4	6.0	6.2	6.8	6.1		6.2		6.0
	32.7	20.2	12.2	16.5	12.0	10.0		13.2		11.9
	-26.1	-46.2	176.1	139.5	34.5	89.9		-324.6		86.1
EBIT/Interest	11.7	5.6	9.5	8.9	6.4	6.3		8.1		8.3
	(33) 3.4	(122) 1.9	(355) 3.1	(193) 3.3	(57) 3.5	(44) 2.1		(783) 2.9		(804) 3.1
	.5	.3	1.1	1.5	1.5	1.0		1.1		1.2
Net Profit + Depr., Dep., Amort./Cur. Mat. L/T/D		4.1	4.6	4.6	4.9	4.5		3.9		3.7
		(19) 2.5	(94) 2.0	(79) 2.5	(28) 2.5	(19) 2.3		(248) 2.1		(238) 1.9
		.5	1.6	1.4	1.5	1.0		1.1		1.1
Fixed/Worth	.1	.5	.4	.7	.7	1.0		.6		.6
	.8	1.5	1.0	1.3	1.1	2.1		1.1		1.2
	-1.6	-7.2	2.5	3.0	3.3	-1.6		2.8		2.9
Debt/Worth	.5	1.0	.7	1.0	1.2	1.4		.9		.9
	2.8	4.7	1.9	2.2	2.2	4.2		1.9		2.0
	-6.1	-22.2	5.9	5.3	11.0	-3.5		5.5		6.1
% Profit Before Taxes/Tangible Net Worth	84.4	60.1	44.3	35.3	42.5	26.3		40.3		38.0
	(24) 53.1	(98) 19.7	(332) 22.5	(173) 20.5	(55) 17.5	(28) 16.5		(722) 16.7		(744) 15.3
	8.4	1.4	5.2	6.7	4.1	.5		2.9		2.5
% Profit Before Taxes/Total Assets	37.1	13.7	15.8	12.5	11.2	9.7		12.7		11.8
	11.1	4.7	7.0	5.8	6.3	3.5		5.2		5.0
	-2.9	-3.2	.5	1.9	1.4	-.1		.2		.4
Sales/Net Fixed Assets	143.9	21.8	13.9	8.8	7.3	8.3		10.2		10.4
	18.5	9.8	7.3	4.9	5.4	4.7		5.6		5.7
	7.5	4.6	4.4	3.2	3.5	3.2		3.4		3.4
Sales/Total Assets	4.3	3.3	2.7	2.2	2.1	1.7		2.5		2.5
	3.3	2.5	2.2	1.8	1.7	1.5		1.9		1.9
	2.4	1.8	1.7	1.4	1.4	1.1		1.4		1.4
% Depr., Dep., Amort./Sales	1.8	1.4	1.5	2.0	1.8	2.3		2.4		2.3
	(23) 3.1	(119) 2.5	(352) 2.7	(186) 3.2	(56) 3.0	(30) 2.9		(769) 3.9		(755) 3.7
	4.2	4.3	4.4	4.6	4.5	4.7		5.6		5.3
% Officers', Directors' Owners' Comp/Sales	4.3	2.8	1.6	.9				2.0		1.8
	(23) 8.8	(72) 4.4	(127) 2.7	(38) 1.5				(262) 3.7		(247) 3.5
	12.7	7.0	4.9	3.9				6.8		6.3
Net Sales ($)	38367M	470961M	4404642M	7596953M	7686636M	10861614M		21309130M		23318369M
Total Assets ($)	10436M	172460M	1987906M	4069848M	4268459M	7314183M		13401841M		14714196M

M = $ thousand   MM = $ million

See Pages 11 through 21 for Explanation of Ratios and Data

Comparative Historical Data | | | | Current Data Sorted by Sales

Hist 1	Hist 2	Hist 3	Type of Statement	0-1MM	1-3MM	3-5MM	5-10MM	10-25MM	25MM & OVER
192	178	183	Unqualified	2	2	5	13	43	118
215	194	220	Reviewed	2	17	32	50	85	34
117	114	105	Compiled	4	22	20	39	17	3
47	44	60	Tax Returns	16	16	11	9	8	
266	340	300	Other	7	30	19	48	83	113
4/1/04-3/31/05 ALL	4/1/05-3/31/06 ALL	4/1/06-3/31/07 ALL		180 (4/1-9/30/06)			688 (10/1/06-3/31/07)		
837	870	868	NUMBER OF STATEMENTS	31	87	87	159	236	268
%	%	%	ASSETS	%	%	%	%	%	%
5.8	6.5	6.2	Cash & Equivalents	14.5	7.1	6.7	7.9	5.8	4.2
27.3	27.6	26.9	Trade Receivables (net)	26.3	27.0	26.6	26.9	28.3	25.6
21.1	21.9	22.6	Inventory	14.2	21.1	23.1	24.9	22.9	22.1
2.1	1.8	2.0	All Other Current	.7	2.6	1.4	1.8	1.7	2.6
56.3	57.8	57.6	Total Current	55.6	57.8	57.8	61.5	58.7	54.5
34.4	33.2	32.5	Fixed Assets (net)	33.7	33.6	31.8	29.0	33.0	33.8
3.9	3.5	4.5	Intangibles (net)	3.2	2.9	4.6	3.4	2.9	7.1
5.3	5.5	5.4	All Other Non-Current	7.5	5.7	5.8	6.1	5.4	4.6
100.0	100.0	100.0	Total	100.0	100.0	100.0	100.0	100.0	100.0
			LIABILITIES						
11.0	11.3	12.1	Notes Payable-Short Term	16.9	13.3	15.1	11.9	11.8	10.5
5.3	4.8	5.0	Cur. Mat.-L.T.D.	4.1	4.7	5.8	4.6	5.4	4.8
17.5	17.6	16.4	Trade Payables	15.7	16.4	17.2	17.0	16.4	16.0
.2	.2	.2	Income Taxes Payable	.0	.0	.3	.2	.2	.3
8.2	8.6	9.3	All Other Current	14.6	12.3	9.5	8.3	8.3	9.0
42.2	42.5	43.0	Total Current	51.4	46.7	47.9	42.0	42.0	40.6
18.7	19.6	20.1	Long-Term Debt	28.2	26.7	17.8	16.9	18.3	21.4
.8	.7	.7	Deferred Taxes	.6	.3	.5	.3	.5	1.3
6.6	7.6	6.8	All Other Non-Current	7.2	10.9	5.0	6.7	7.0	5.8
31.7	29.5	29.4	Net Worth	12.5	15.3	28.7	34.1	32.1	30.9
100.0	100.0	100.0	Total Liabilities & Net Worth	100.0	100.0	100.0	100.0	100.0	100.0
			INCOME DATA						
100.0	100.0	100.0	Net Sales	100.0	100.0	100.0	100.0	100.0	100.0
25.9	25.4	26.3	Gross Profit	50.5	33.2	28.6	27.2	24.8	21.5
21.3	20.9	21.3	Operating Expenses	44.6	30.1	25.3	22.0	19.1	15.8
4.6	4.5	5.1	Operating Profit	5.9	3.1	3.3	5.1	5.7	5.7
1.2	1.3	1.6	All Other Expenses (net)	2.9	1.7	.9	.9	1.8	1.9
3.4	3.2	3.5	Profit Before Taxes	3.0	1.4	2.4	4.2	3.8	3.8
			RATIOS						
2.1	2.1	2.2	Current	2.9	2.4	2.4	2.5	2.2	2.0
1.4	1.4	1.4		1.1	1.4	1.4	1.5	1.4	1.4
1.0	1.0	1.0		.8	.9	.9	1.0	1.0	1.1
1.2	1.3	1.3	Quick	1.8	1.5	1.4	1.5	1.3	1.1
(836) .8	.8	(867) .8		.8	.7	(86) .6	.8	.8	.7
.5	.5	.5		.5	.4	.5	.5	.5	.5
37 10.0	36 10.1	34 10.7	Sales/Receivables	19 18.7	30 12.2	33 11.2	32 11.5	35 10.4	38 9.7
47 7.7	48 7.7	44 8.3		32 11.2	41 8.9	44 8.3	42 8.7	44 8.2	45 8.1
59 6.2	61 6.0	57 6.4		50 7.4	57 6.4	60 6.1	52 7.0	57 6.4	60 6.1
31 11.9	32 11.3	32 11.3	Cost of Sales/Inventory	0 UND	25 14.5	36 10.1	35 10.4	31 11.8	35 10.6
47 7.7	48 7.6	49 7.4		35 10.3	45 8.1	55 6.6	50 7.3	46 7.9	52 7.1
70 5.2	71 5.2	70 5.2		97 3.8	84 4.4	80 4.6	70 5.2	70 5.2	67 5.4
23 16.1	21 17.0	20 18.2	Cost of Sales/Payables	8 43.1	15 24.1	20 18.7	19 19.6	20 18.3	24 15.3
36 10.1	37 9.8	33 11.2		31 11.6	36 10.2	34 10.8	30 12.0	34 10.6	32 11.3
54 6.8	54 6.8	50 7.3		72 5.1	61 6.0	52 7.0	51 7.2	46 7.9	48 7.6
6.8	6.4	6.2	Sales/Working Capital	5.6	5.7	5.8	5.7	6.4	6.7
13.9	13.5	13.6		55.3	16.5	14.4	13.1	13.3	12.5
-406.2	288.7	999.8		-21.4	-39.0	-40.3	143.1	125.1	78.6
8.8	9.3	8.1	EBIT/Interest	5.3	5.6	5.4	12.3	8.3	9.3
(770) 3.4	(811) 3.0	(804) 3.0		(26) 1.4	(75) 1.8	(78) 2.1	(147) 3.2	(222) 3.1	(256) 3.4
1.2	1.0	1.1		.3	-.1	.4	1.3	1.3	1.3
3.7	4.6	4.6	Net Profit + Depr., Dep., Amort./Cur. Mat. L/T/D		4.4	4.3	3.5	4.5	5.1
(270) 2.0	(258) 2.2	(241) 2.3		(10) 2.5	(22) 2.0	(36) 2.0	(60) 2.5	(110) 2.4
1.2	1.0	1.4			.6	1.3	1.4	1.5	1.4
.6	.5	.5	Fixed/Worth	.2	.5	.4	.3	.5	.7
1.3	1.2	1.1		3.0	1.6	1.5	.9	1.1	1.2
3.5	3.4	4.0		-1.3	-4.8	520.0	1.9	2.8	3.2
1.0	1.0	.9	Debt/Worth	.4	1.0	1.0	.7	.9	1.1
2.3	2.3	2.3		4.7	5.9	2.3	1.7	2.4	2.3
7.5	8.3	10.3		-6.7	-9.9	999.8	6.8	6.1	7.4
41.6	39.7	43.6	% Profit Before Taxes/Tangible Net Worth	72.4	58.5	47.9	44.6	43.2	39.3
(703) 19.6	(732) 16.4	(710) 21.1		(19) 33.3	(57) 17.8	(66) 21.4	(136) 22.1	(209) 20.9	(223) 20.7
4.8	3.1	5.2		-12.2	.9	1.8	6.1	5.3	6.5
12.8	13.5	13.7	% Profit Before Taxes/Total Assets	33.3	13.4	13.0	16.8	13.4	12.6
5.8	4.9	6.3		7.8	5.1	3.7	7.1	5.9	6.4
.5	-.1	.4		-3.2	-4.7	-2.7	1.4	.9	1.3
12.0	12.6	13.1	Sales/Net Fixed Assets	33.8	17.1	16.3	15.7	12.8	9.3
6.1	6.2	6.6		10.2	7.8	6.7	8.6	6.6	5.8
3.6	3.7	3.8		3.3	3.1	3.7	4.5	3.9	3.6
2.6	2.7	2.7	Sales/Total Assets	3.9	3.1	2.8	3.0	2.6	2.4
2.0	2.0	2.1		2.4	2.0	2.0	2.3	2.1	1.9
1.5	1.5	1.6		1.3	1.4	1.6	1.7	1.6	1.5
2.1	1.7	1.7	% Depr., Dep., Amort./Sales	1.8	1.9	1.6	1.4	1.5	1.9
(742) 3.3	(774) 2.9	(766) 2.8		(22) 4.0	(66) 3.5	(81) 2.8	(142) 2.7	(221) 2.8	(234) 2.8
5.0	4.6	4.4		7.2	6.6	4.3	4.0	4.5	4.3
1.7	1.8	1.7	% Officers', Directors' Owners' Comp/Sales	5.3	3.4	2.1	1.8	1.4	.8
(261) 3.3	(253) 3.1	(263) 3.3		(15) 9.8	(47) 5.0	(43) 3.3	(62) 3.5	(65) 2.4	(31) 1.4
5.6	6.1	5.9		16.3	7.4	7.7	5.0	4.4	4.0
24417904M	32867327M	31059173M	Net Sales ($)	19338M	180101M	346378M	1183211M	3772862M	25557283M
14439128M	17027451M	17823292M	Total Assets ($)	9385M	100508M	197525M	582397M	1964679M	14968798M

M = $ thousand   MM = $ million
See Pages 11 through 21 for Explanation of Ratios and Data

Current Data Sorted by Assets							Comparative Historical Data	
						Type of Statement		
		1	1			Unqualified	7	5
		4	3			Reviewed	10	10
	1	5		1		Compiled	17	24
2	5	3				Tax Returns	3	6
2	3	7	2			Other	8	7
	9 (4/1-9/30/06)		31 (10/1/06-3/31/07)				**4/1/02-3/31/03 ALL**	**4/1/03-3/31/04 ALL**
0-500M	**500M-2MM**	**2-10MM**	**10-50MM**	**50-100MM**	**100-250MM**			
4	9	20	6	1		**NUMBER OF STATEMENTS**	45	52
%	%	%	%	%	%	**ASSETS**	%	%
		6.8			DATA NOT AVAILABLE	Cash & Equivalents	5.2	6.6
		30.8				Trade Receivables (net)	23.9	24.9
		29.2				Inventory	29.1	33.7
		1.8				All Other Current	3.3	2.1
		68.5				Total Current	61.5	67.2
		26.4				Fixed Assets (net)	28.7	25.2
		1.5				Intangibles (net)	4.5	3.6
		3.5				All Other Non-Current	5.3	3.9
		100.0				Total	100.0	100.0
						LIABILITIES		
		7.0				Notes Payable-Short Term	8.7	8.6
		3.4				Cur. Mat.-L.T.D.	5.0	4.9
		25.0				Trade Payables	28.1	30.0
		.4				Income Taxes Payable	.0	.1
		11.2				All Other Current	12.7	8.1
		47.0				Total Current	54.6	51.7
		10.3				Long-Term Debt	18.4	20.5
		1.3				Deferred Taxes	.4	.3
		1.3				All Other Non-Current	1.8	4.9
		40.1				Net Worth	24.8	22.7
		100.0				Total Liabilties & Net Worth	100.0	100.0
						INCOME DATA		
		100.0				Net Sales	100.0	100.0
		32.9				Gross Profit	35.8	37.0
		28.8				Operating Expenses	33.2	34.4
		4.1				Operating Profit	2.6	2.6
		-.1				All Other Expenses (net)	.3	.1
		4.2				Profit Before Taxes	2.3	2.4
						RATIOS		
		1.9					1.5	1.9
		1.3				Current	1.1	1.4
		1.1					1.0	1.1
		1.2					.9	1.0
		.8				Quick	.5	.6
		.5					.3	.4
		27 13.5					**11** 32.8	**17** 20.9
		38 9.7				Sales/Receivables	**36** 10.0	**31** 11.7
		53 6.9					**46** 8.0	**45** 8.1
		29 12.7					**34** 10.9	**43** 8.6
		49 7.5				Cost of Sales/Inventory	**60** 6.1	**61** 6.0
		88 4.1					**88** 4.1	**94** 3.9
		28 13.2					**30** 12.3	**31** 11.8
		39 9.3				Cost of Sales/Payables	**50** 7.3	**61** 6.0
		59 6.1					**69** 5.3	**85** 4.3
		8.6					12.4	8.0
		15.0				Sales/Working Capital	42.8	20.9
		60.9					-88.0	111.5
		19.9					7.3	7.2
		6.0				EBIT/Interest	(43) 3.0	(48) 3.3
		2.7					1.5	1.7
							2.6	2.6
						Net Profit + Depr., Dep., Amort./Cur. Mat. L/T/D	(14) 1.7	(15) 2.1
							1.2	.6
		.4					.6	.4
		.8				Fixed/Worth	1.3	.8
		1.3					2.8	2.6
		.9					1.8	1.6
		1.7				Debt/Worth	3.9	3.4
		3.3					6.5	7.5
		49.2					61.4	39.8
		23.3				% Profit Before Taxes/Tangible Net Worth	(39) 18.6	(45) 20.2
		11.4					5.2	10.3
		20.6					10.3	10.0
		6.6				% Profit Before Taxes/Total Assets	3.9	4.7
		3.2					1.2	1.7
		25.3					20.3	29.2
		11.4				Sales/Net Fixed Assets	11.3	16.7
		6.2					6.3	7.8
		3.6					3.5	4.1
		2.9				Sales/Total Assets	2.7	2.8
		2.3					2.1	2.1
		1.3					1.4	1.2
		(19) 1.9				% Depr., Dep., Amort./Sales	(41) 2.1	(45) 2.0
		2.7					2.7	2.4
							.7	.8
						% Officers', Directors' Owners' Comp/Sales	(21) 2.3	(31) 2.3
							4.2	3.8
3238M	**34722M**	**301171M**	**411673M**	**140024M**		Net Sales ($)	**620107M**	**743837M**
775M	**11286M**	**101716M**	**170558M**	**59344M**		Total Assets ($)	**255758M**	**251903M**

M = $ thousand MM = $ million

See Pages 11 through 21 for Explanation of Ratios and Data

Comparative Historical Data

Current Data Sorted by Sales

			Type of Statement						
1	2	2	Unqualified						
7	7	7	Reviewed						
9	11	7	Compiled					3	1	1
8	8	10	Tax Returns		1		1	2	2
9	18	14	Other	1	3	1	1	4	1
4/1/04-3/31/05	4/1/05-3/31/06	4/1/06-3/31/07		1	3	1	3	1	1
ALL	ALL	ALL		1	2		3	4	3
				0-1MM	9 (4/1-9/30/06) 1-3MM	3-5MM	31 (10/1/06-3/31/07) 5-10MM	10-25MM	25MM & OVER
34	46	40	NUMBER OF STATEMENTS	2	6	2	10	12	8
%	%	%	ASSETS	%	%	%	%	%	%
3.6	4.7	8.4	Cash & Equivalents				7.1	6.4	
23.7	28.6	27.2	Trade Receivables (net)				26.6	38.8	
33.0	35.0	31.6	Inventory				29.8	26.5	
4.2	2.1	2.8	All Other Current				2.3	2.5	
64.5	70.4	69.9	Total Current				65.8	74.2	
25.2	20.9	24.3	Fixed Assets (net)				30.8	21.1	
5.4	4.1	2.4	Intangibles (net)				.4	1.6	
4.8	4.6	3.4	All Other Non-Current				3.0	3.0	
100.0	100.0	100.0	Total				100.0	100.0	
			LIABILITIES						
9.4	9.7	8.2	Notes Payable-Short Term				8.2	7.2	
3.7	5.9	2.9	Cur. Mat.-L.T.D.				2.9	3.4	
30.3	32.2	38.2	Trade Payables				25.0	31.3	
.1	.3	.4	Income Taxes Payable				.5	.2	
6.4	8.4	7.8	All Other Current				6.9	8.9	
49.9	56.5	57.5	Total Current				43.5	51.1	
28.2	19.0	11.8	Long-Term Debt				13.8	12.0	
.5	.4	.7	Deferred Taxes				2.4	.2	
2.5	3.9	5.3	All Other Non-Current				1.8	.2	
18.9	20.2	24.6	Net Worth				38.5	36.4	
100.0	100.0	100.0	Total Liabilties & Net Worth				100.0	100.0	
			INCOME DATA						
100.0	100.0	100.0	Net Sales				100.0	100.0	
38.5	32.7	32.3	Gross Profit				29.8	33.8	
37.8	30.5	29.2	Operating Expenses				25.6	29.2	
.7	2.2	3.1	Operating Profit				4.2	4.7	
.7	-.3	-.1	All Other Expenses (net)				.0	-.4	
.1	2.5	3.2	Profit Before Taxes				4.1	5.1	
			RATIOS						
1.8	1.7	1.8	Current				2.0	1.7	
1.2	1.2	1.4					1.5	1.3	
1.0	1.0	1.0					1.0	1.2	
.8	.9	1.0	Quick				1.4	1.3	
.5	.5	.7					.9	.9	
.3	.4	.4					.4	.5	
13 28.6	20 18.3	15 24.9	Sales/Receivables				15 24.7	32 11.5	
34 10.7	36 10.1	35 10.3					37 9.8	39 9.4	
49 7.4	49 7.4	49 7.4					49 7.4	65 5.6	
39 9.4	39 9.3	38 9.5	Cost of Sales/Inventory				28 13.3	29 12.8	
56 6.5	69 5.3	61 6.0					47 7.8	49 7.5	
81 4.5	96 3.8	80 4.6					72 5.0	87 4.2	
40 9.1	41 9.0	30 12.3	Cost of Sales/Payables				21 17.1	29 12.6	
60 6.1	58 6.3	54 6.8					41 9.0	49 7.5	
84 4.3	77 4.7	72 5.1					59 6.2	77 4.7	
8.9	10.1	8.6	Sales/Working Capital				8.6	6.5	
18.3	18.8	16.7					18.3	12.2	
NM	230.2	107.8					86.1	35.0	
5.8	7.4	14.3	EBIT/Interest					23.8	
2.2 (42)	3.7 (37)	4.6						6.0	
.5	1.3	2.3						2.9	
3.8	4.6	4.2	Net Profit + Depr., Dep., Amort./Cur. Mat. L/T/D						
1.8 (12)	1.7 (12)	2.8 (12)							
1.0	1.2	1.2							
.4	.4	.3	Fixed/Worth				.3	.4	
1.4	1.1	1.0					.8	.7	
NM	8.4	1.6					1.4	1.1	
1.8	1.6	1.1	Debt/Worth				.8	1.2	
3.8	4.5	2.8					1.5	2.0	
NM	81.3	4.9					3.2	4.1	
33.2	38.3	47.6	% Profit Before Taxes/Tangible Net Worth					54.3	
12.7 (26)	26.2 (36)	25.7 (35)						24.6	
-4.6	12.4	9.9						13.6	
7.4	9.7	12.5	% Profit Before Taxes/Total Assets				18.7	20.4	
2.2	4.4	5.3					6.6	6.5	
-2.6	.6	1.6					2.2	3.4	
30.0	30.0	31.0	Sales/Net Fixed Assets				15.1	41.0	
16.0	17.6	12.4					10.2	14.5	
6.8	7.6	6.3					5.8	6.1	
3.7	3.6	3.6	Sales/Total Assets				3.7	4.1	
2.6	2.6	2.9					2.9	3.0	
1.6	1.9	2.2					2.3	2.2	
.9	.9	1.1	% Depr., Dep., Amort./Sales				1.3	1.3	
1.8 (32)	1.7 (42)	2.1 (37)					2.6 (11)	1.9	
2.5	2.7	2.7					4.0	2.7	
1.3	1.0	.6	% Officers', Directors' Owners' Comp/Sales						
2.8 (18)	2.5 (19)	1.6 (17)							
5.6	3.9	3.4							
523633M	1172047M	890828M	Net Sales ($)	972M	9369M	8037M	73246M	206188M	593016M
187205M	529791M	343679M	Total Assets ($)	105M	4653M	2872M	26223M	103820M	206006M

© RMA 2007

M = $ thousand   MM = $ million
See Pages 11 through 21 for Explanation of Ratios and Data

Current Data Sorted by Assets | Comparative Historical Data

Type of Statement	0-500M	500M-2MM	2-10MM	10-50MM	50-100MM	100-250MM	4/1/02-3/31/03 ALL	4/1/03-3/31/04 ALL
Unqualified		1	6	3	1		9	11
Reviewed		1	6	3			3	6
Compiled		3	2	2			7	11
Tax Returns		2	1				1	1
Other		3	5	3	3	1	11	9
		13 (4/1-9/30/06)		33 (10/1/06-3/31/07)				
NUMBER OF STATEMENTS		10	20	11	4	1	31	38

ASSETS	0-500M	500M-2MM %	2-10MM %	10-50MM %	50-100MM %	100-250MM %	ALL %	ALL %
Cash & Equivalents		11.3	5.7	6.5			9.3	8.9
Trade Receivables (net)		23.1	29.4	21.4			24.0	24.5
Inventory		33.9	30.4	29.6			26.3	31.5
All Other Current		.8	1.0	4.0			1.0	3.8
Total Current		69.0	66.4	61.5			60.5	68.7
Fixed Assets (net)		24.1	22.0	21.6			28.9	22.2
Intangibles (net)		2.1	7.3	5.3			4.9	5.0
All Other Non-Current		4.9	4.2	11.6			5.7	4.1
Total		100.0	100.0	100.0			100.0	100.0

(DATA NOT AVAILABLE for 0-500M column)

LIABILITIES	0-500M	500M-2MM	2-10MM	10-50MM	50-100MM	100-250MM	ALL	ALL
Notes Payable-Short Term		5.2	12.3	4.0			5.7	9.4
Cur. Mat.-L.T.D.		4.9	3.5	2.0			3.9	3.2
Trade Payables		14.4	16.4	10.1			12.9	13.4
Income Taxes Payable		1.1	.3	.3			.4	.5
All Other Current		10.2	7.9	7.8			18.1	20.4
Total Current		35.8	40.5	24.2			41.0	46.9
Long-Term Debt		16.8	15.2	13.5			21.9	14.8
Deferred Taxes		.0	.4	.0			.3	.8
All Other Non-Current		13.1	4.9	.9			7.1	3.7
Net Worth		34.4	39.0	61.3			29.7	33.8
Total Liabilities & Net Worth		100.0	100.0	100.0			100.0	100.0

INCOME DATA	0-500M	500M-2MM	2-10MM	10-50MM	50-100MM	100-250MM	ALL	ALL
Net Sales		100.0	100.0	100.0			100.0	100.0
Gross Profit		37.5	29.9	33.9			32.8	30.3
Operating Expenses		30.5	22.5	26.2			26.6	24.8
Operating Profit		7.0	7.5	7.7			6.2	5.5
All Other Expenses (net)		.7	1.6	.0			1.9	.9
Profit Before Taxes		6.3	5.8	7.7			4.3	4.5

RATIOS	0-500M	500M-2MM	2-10MM	10-50MM	50-100MM	100-250MM	ALL	ALL
Current		3.4	2.4	3.9			5.1	3.3
		2.3	1.6	3.0			2.1	1.8
		1.2	1.0	2.4			1.2	1.3
Quick		1.7	1.2	2.4			2.5	1.7
		1.0	.9	1.1			1.4	.9
		.5	.6	1.0			.7	.5
Sales/Receivables	21	17.1	37 9.9	44 8.3			38 9.7	35 10.5
	34	10.9	48 7.7	49 7.5			46 7.9	43 8.6
	41	8.9	63 5.8	60 6.1			51 7.1	55 6.7
Cost of Sales/Inventory	44	8.3	42 8.7	71 5.1			36 10.1	51 7.1
	60	6.1	58 6.2	99 3.7			56 6.5	72 5.1
	105	3.5	99 3.7	127 2.9			85 4.3	112 3.3
Cost of Sales/Payables	15	24.8	23 15.7	24 15.5			16 22.1	18 19.8
	25	14.4	36 10.1	32 11.3			27 13.3	30 12.2
	49	7.5	48 7.6	47 7.7			44 8.3	43 8.4
Sales/Working Capital		4.8	5.3	3.2			3.6	3.8
		7.7	8.3	4.0			7.9	7.0
		78.5	NM	5.5			29.1	16.7
EBIT/Interest		32.7	10.2				(28) 9.1	(34) 22.3
		13.0	5.3				4.4	6.0
		1.7	1.4				2.3	.9
Net Profit + Depr., Dep., Amort./Cur. Mat. L/T/D								13.9
							(13)	1.5
								.8
Fixed/Worth		.2	.3	.1			.3	.3
		.4	.7	.4			.7	.5
		NM	5.5	.6			2.8	1.2
Debt/Worth		.8	.7	.3			.3	.4
		.9	2.2	.7			1.0	1.5
		NM	25.8	1.6			5.2	3.0
% Profit Before Taxes/Tangible Net Worth			62.7	27.2			43.2	50.6
		(17)	41.3	21.9			(25) 12.1	(35) 13.9
			-1.1	13.7			4.3	2.1
% Profit Before Taxes/Total Assets		31.0	18.1	17.1			17.4	13.3
		13.0	7.4	15.6			6.6	7.8
		4.1	.4	2.0			2.0	.1
Sales/Net Fixed Assets		24.0	40.4	24.0			17.0	31.3
		13.8	10.1	9.0			6.5	8.0
		10.0	6.0	3.6			4.1	5.3
Sales/Total Assets		3.1	2.7	1.8			2.7	2.7
		2.6	2.1	1.5			1.9	1.9
		2.0	1.6	1.3			1.3	1.4
% Depr., Dep., Amort./Sales		1.4	.6				1.1	1.2
		2.3	1.5				(30) 2.6	(33) 2.6
		2.9	3.0				5.1	4.2
% Officers', Directors', Owners' Comp/Sales								1.7
							(10)	2.8
								5.7
Net Sales ($)		28363M	244129M	366781M	725686M	295360M	717991M	892662M
Total Assets ($)		10608M	111303M	220928M	341204M	126773M	436229M	496997M

M = $ thousand   MM = $ million
See Pages 11 through 21 for Explanation of Ratios and Data

Comparative Historical Data — Current Data Sorted by Sales

Note: In the Current Data section, the columns 0-1MM, 1-3MM, 3-5MM, and 5-10MM are marked **"DATA NOT AVAILABLE"** (percentages and ratios suppressed); only the 10-25MM and 25MM & OVER columns show common-size and ratio data.

10 4/1/04-3/31/05 ALL	18 4/1/05-3/31/06 ALL	15 4/1/06-3/31/07 ALL	Type of Statement	0-1MM	1-3MM	3-5MM	5-10MM	10-25MM	25MM & OVER
10	10	11	Unqualified			1	2	3	5
8	11	10	Reviewed		2	2	3	3	2
5	6	7	Compiled		2	1		2	2
		3	Tax Returns		1		1	2	1
10	18	15	Other		1	1	3	3	3
				13 (4/1-9/30/06)				33 (10/1/06-3/31/07)	
33	45	46	**NUMBER OF STATEMENTS**		6	5	9	13	13
%	%	%	**ASSETS**	%	%	%	%	%	%
8.5	4.7	6.9	Cash & Equivalents					4.5	4.2
26.0	27.4	26.0	Trade Receivables (net)					26.3	29.4
28.4	31.8	31.0	Inventory					31.9	31.0
3.1	2.5	1.8	All Other Current					2.0	3.6
66.0	66.4	65.7	Total Current					64.7	68.1
21.5	21.2	22.5	Fixed Assets (net)					23.5	17.7
4.5	5.1	5.7	Intangibles (net)					4.7	6.5
8.0	7.3	6.0	All Other Non-Current					7.1	7.8
100.0	100.0	100.0	Total					100.0	100.0
			LIABILITIES						
8.7	10.3	8.4	Notes Payable-Short Term					8.9	11.9
2.3	3.1	3.2	Cur. Mat.-L.T.D.					2.3	1.6
13.6	14.9	14.1	Trade Payables					12.5	14.6
.4	.2	.5	Income Taxes Payable					.4	.4
8.9	8.7	9.1	All Other Current					10.1	8.7
33.9	37.2	35.3	Total Current					34.3	37.2
15.8	10.9	14.2	Long-Term Debt					20.1	4.5
.8	.4	.4	Deferred Taxes					.4	.8
4.7	4.7	6.4	All Other Non-Current					4.2	5.5
44.8	46.8	43.7	Net Worth					41.1	52.0
100.0	100.0	100.0	Total Liabilities & Net Worth					100.0	100.0
			INCOME DATA						
100.0	100.0	100.0	Net Sales					100.0	100.0
30.8	27.7	31.5	Gross Profit					32.6	26.6
26.3	22.1	24.6	Operating Expenses					24.7	21.5
4.5	5.6	6.9	Operating Profit					7.9	5.1
1.4	.8	.9	All Other Expenses (net)					.7	.3
3.0	4.8	6.1	Profit Before Taxes					7.3	4.8
			RATIOS						
3.0	2.8	3.0	Current					3.5	3.0
2.1	1.9	2.2						1.8	2.4
1.5	1.4	1.3						1.3	1.5
1.7	1.3	1.5	Quick					1.6	1.2
1.2	.9	1.0						1.0	1.0
.6	.5	.7						.7	.7
40 9.1	35 10.5	35 10.5	Sales/Receivables					41 8.8	41 9.0
49 7.5	49 7.4	45 8.0						52 7.0	49 7.5
62 5.9	55 6.6	60 6.1						66 5.5	56 6.5
54 6.7	40 9.1	46 8.0	Cost of Sales/Inventory					58 6.2	41 8.9
65 5.6	70 5.2	66 5.5						86 4.2	69 5.3
95 3.8	114 3.2	109 3.4						143 2.5	106 3.4
26 13.8	22 16.5	22 16.7	Cost of Sales/Payables					25 14.7	21 17.3
33 11.0	27 13.6	32 11.4						37 9.8	32 11.3
48 7.7	43 8.5	48 7.7						50 7.3	42 8.8
3.7	4.4	4.4	Sales/Working Capital					4.0	3.3
6.0	6.4	6.1						5.5	6.0
11.6	17.0	14.8						11.3	13.5
14.8	13.6	23.8	EBIT/Interest					25.8	16.3
(29) 5.2	(43) 7.3	(44) 7.9						(12) 6.8	(12) 9.8
1.9	3.0	1.9						1.4	2.2
	5.7	11.9	Net Profit + Depr., Dep., Amort./Cur. Mat. L/T/D						
	(12) 2.8	(17) 3.7							
	1.8	1.0							
.2	.2	.2	Fixed/Worth					.3	.2
.6	.5	.5						.7	.4
1.1	.7	1.2						1.2	.9
.6	.6	.7	Debt/Worth					.7	.6
1.2	1.1	1.0						2.4	.9
4.3	2.9	3.5						5.6	2.5
40.7	39.3	55.8	% Profit Before Taxes/Tangible Net Worth					62.7	31.6
(29) 18.5	(43) 18.2	(41) 22.6						27.2	(12) 19.1
3.2	8.9	3.0						7.6	2.8
13.0	13.7	17.9	% Profit Before Taxes/Total Assets					21.7	16.7
6.3	8.7	10.9						10.8	7.5
.8	4.5	1.7						1.2	1.6
16.4	19.3	22.7	Sales/Net Fixed Assets					21.4	31.5
8.0	9.8	10.3						8.4	10.0
5.2	6.5	5.9						3.5	7.8
2.2	2.8	2.6	Sales/Total Assets					2.4	2.6
1.7	2.1	2.0						1.5	2.0
1.4	1.5	1.5						1.4	1.7
1.5	1.1	.9	% Depr., Dep., Amort./Sales					.7	.4
(29) 2.5	(40) 1.9	(43) 1.8						(12) 2.0	(11) 1.8
3.9	3.5	2.9						3.4	2.7
1.5	1.1	2.4	% Officers', Directors' Owners' Comp/Sales						
(11) 3.2	(12) 3.9	(18) 3.9							
5.5	7.4	7.0							
423572M	1398964M	1660319M	Net Sales ($)		11043M	19665M	63382M	201802M	1364427M
293209M	729206M	810816M	Total Assets ($)		4693M	11865M	30026M	122118M	642114M

M = $ thousand   MM = $ million
See Pages 11 through 21 for Explanation of Ratios and Data

Current Data Sorted by Assets   Comparative Historical Data

0-500M	500M-2MM	2-10MM	10-50MM	50-100MM	100-250MM	Type of Statement	4/1/02-3/31/03 ALL	4/1/03-3/31/04 ALL
						Unqualified	3	3
						Reviewed	2	6
						Compiled	8	13
						Tax Returns	3	5
						Other	14	16
1 2	5 (4/1-9/30/06)	3 9 2 1 4	46 (10/1/06-3/31/07)	1				
3	14	19	11	4		NUMBER OF STATEMENTS	30	43

0-500M	500M-2MM	2-10MM	10-50MM	50-100MM	100-250MM		4/1/02-3/31/03 ALL	4/1/03-3/31/04 ALL
%	%	%	%	%	%	**ASSETS**	%	%
	3.3	8.0	5.8			Cash & Equivalents	8.2	4.9
	38.5	23.1	25.2			Trade Receivables (net)	34.2	31.9
	24.9	24.2	21.7		D	Inventory	19.0	19.6
	.4	4.7	2.7		A	All Other Current	3.0	1.4
	67.1	59.9	55.4		T	Total Current	64.3	57.8
	29.1	32.3	34.8		A	Fixed Assets (net)	30.3	34.6
	.3	3.7	3.1			Intangibles (net)	.5	4.1
	3.5	4.1	6.8		N	All Other Non-Current	5.0	3.5
	100.0	100.0	100.0		O	Total	100.0	100.0
					T	**LIABILITIES**		
	17.1	11.9	9.2			Notes Payable-Short Term	9.1	11.9
	1.6	4.1	4.0		A	Cur. Mat.-L.T.D.	6.5	6.6
	24.0	11.4	11.8		V	Trade Payables	17.5	19.3
	.0	.9	.2		A	Income Taxes Payable	.1	.7
	5.0	9.7	13.6		I	All Other Current	8.9	9.8
	47.7	38.0	38.9		L	Total Current	42.0	48.3
	15.4	15.2	15.6		A	Long-Term Debt	18.1	25.9
	.3	.8	.4		B	Deferred Taxes	.3	.7
	2.7	.3	24.0		L	All Other Non-Current	6.8	9.7
	34.0	45.6	21.1		E	Net Worth	32.8	15.5
	100.0	100.0	100.0			Total Liabilities & Net Worth	100.0	100.0
						INCOME DATA		
	100.0	100.0	100.0			Net Sales	100.0	100.0
	35.1	26.3	19.4			Gross Profit	32.3	28.6
	32.9	19.8	16.9			Operating Expenses	27.9	25.2
	2.2	6.5	2.5			Operating Profit	4.4	3.4
	.9	.4	2.2			All Other Expenses (net)	1.2	1.6
	1.3	6.1	.3			Profit Before Taxes	3.2	1.9
						RATIOS		
	5.7	2.2	3.0			Current	2.6	2.0
	1.2	1.6	2.1				1.6	1.2
	.9	1.1	1.2				1.0	.9
	2.7	1.4	2.0			Quick	1.5	1.3
	.7	.8	1.1				1.0	.8
	.5	.6	.4				.8	.4
	40 9.0	39 9.4	34 10.6			Sales/Receivables	36 10.3	39 9.3
	48 7.6	41 8.9	58 6.2				47 7.7	49 7.5
	55 6.7	49 7.4	62 5.8				65 5.6	57 6.5
	24 15.1	23 16.2	32 11.5			Cost of Sales/Inventory	26 14.0	25 14.8
	40 9.2	44 8.2	62 5.9				36 10.0	33 11.1
	63 5.8	108 3.4	97 3.8				49 7.5	66 5.6
	19 19.2	18 20.5	16 22.8			Cost of Sales/Payables	20 18.5	20 18.2
	36 10.0	22 16.3	30 12.3				37 9.9	40 9.2
	53 6.9	44 8.3	43 8.5				50 7.3	55 6.7
	7.0	4.8	5.0			Sales/Working Capital	6.0	7.9
	17.8	8.6	6.3				12.4	19.3
	-41.1	50.3	28.1				-810.1	-111.2
	25.2	9.5	8.2			EBIT/Interest	7.8	6.3
	7.6	(17) 3.2	(10) 1.3				(26) 2.4	(42) 2.8
	-.7	1.5	-1.2				.7	.8
						Net Profit + Depr., Dep., Amort./Cur. Mat. L/T/D		2.1
							(12) 1.5	
								.6
	.1	.3	.6			Fixed/Worth	.4	.5
	.8	.8	1.5				1.2	1.8
	NM	2.0	-2.0				2.4	-3.2
	.5	.6	.9			Debt/Worth	.7	1.5
	2.0	2.0	2.3				3.0	5.3
	NM	3.2	-5.8				5.9	-6.6
	76.1	44.6				% Profit Before Taxes/Tangible Net Worth	69.2	51.7
	(11) 20.1	19.7					(27) 14.5	(29) 20.0
	2.8	3.9					6.2	1.5
	29.8	11.9	13.9			% Profit Before Taxes/Total Assets	13.3	14.0
	10.8	6.6	1.7				5.9	7.3
	-5.5	2.5	-9.8				1.6	-.8
	43.8	10.7	11.1			Sales/Net Fixed Assets	22.4	12.9
	11.6	7.6	4.8				10.0	8.4
	7.6	4.1	3.5				3.7	4.8
	3.3	2.6	2.0			Sales/Total Assets	3.4	3.5
	3.0	1.9	1.6				2.7	2.4
	2.1	1.5	1.5				1.9	1.8
		2.0				% Depr., Dep., Amort./Sales	1.1	1.6
	(17)	2.8					(28) 2.5	(39) 2.9
		3.4					5.7	5.1
						% Officers', Directors' Owners' Comp/Sales	2.6	2.4
							(17) 5.2	(16) 4.3
							6.8	9.7
1367M	47685M	201947M	539088M	450648M		Net Sales ($)	353218M	650769M
345M	15134M	103862M	311203M	295721M		Total Assets ($)	210478M	441414M

M = $ thousand   MM = $ million
See Pages 11 through 21 for Explanation of Ratios and Data

Comparative Historical Data | Current Data Sorted by Sales

				Type of Statement						
6		6	12	Unqualified				1	2	9
6		3	12	Reviewed				1	9	1
6		9	4	Compiled	1	1	1	2		
2		3	5	Tax Returns	1	2		2		
4		17	18	Other	3	2	1	6	2	4
4/1/04-		4/1/05-	4/1/06-			5 (4/1-9/30/06)		46 (10/1/06-3/31/07)		
3/31/05		3/31/06	3/31/07		0-1MM	1-3MM	3-5MM	5-10MM	10-25MM	25MM & OVER
ALL		ALL	ALL							
24		38	51	NUMBER OF STATEMENTS	4	6	2	12	13	14
%		%	%	ASSETS	%	%	%	%	%	%
5.3		5.3	6.4	Cash & Equivalents				9.9	5.2	7.8
33.7		26.4	29.2	Trade Receivables (net)				29.8	26.0	24.5
20.1		22.3	22.6	Inventory				22.9	22.8	18.8
2.8		4.3	3.3	All Other Current				6.3	1.3	2.2
62.0		58.3	61.4	Total Current				68.9	55.3	53.3
30.0		31.7	31.0	Fixed Assets (net)				24.5	34.8	35.2
2.6		3.9	3.2	Intangibles (net)				1.3	5.4	5.2
5.4		6.2	4.4	All Other Non-Current				5.3	4.5	6.3
100.0		100.0	100.0	Total				100.0	100.0	100.0
				LIABILITIES						
11.8		11.7	12.4	Notes Payable-Short Term				12.1	14.5	7.1
4.5		6.6	3.0	Cur. Mat.-L.T.D.				2.8	4.0	3.2
16.4		18.9	15.3	Trade Payables				16.9	12.8	11.5
.4		1.1	.4	Income Taxes Payable				.1	1.1	.4
6.5		9.5	9.0	All Other Current				8.0	9.2	12.6
39.5		47.8	40.1	Total Current				40.0	41.7	34.7
21.6		21.1	15.9	Long-Term Debt				13.5	11.0	20.0
.3		.8	.9	Deferred Taxes				.9	.7	1.9
4.8		5.0	7.3	All Other Non-Current				.5	.4	20.9
33.8		25.2	35.8	Net Worth				45.2	46.3	22.5
100.0		100.0	100.0	Total Liabilities & Net Worth				100.0	100.0	100.0
				INCOME DATA						
100.0		100.0	100.0	Net Sales				100.0	100.0	100.0
32.0		30.5	27.0	Gross Profit				28.1	25.7	16.3
26.2		25.2	22.6	Operating Expenses				24.4	17.6	13.3
5.8		5.3	4.4	Operating Profit				3.7	8.1	3.0
1.4		1.2	1.2	All Other Expenses (net)				.8	.0	3.0
4.4		4.1	3.2	Profit Before Taxes				2.9	8.2	.0
				RATIOS						
2.0		2.2	3.0					5.6	2.0	3.2
1.7		1.3	1.6	Current				1.9	1.2	2.3
1.2		.9	1.1					1.3	1.0	1.1
1.4		1.4	2.0					3.4	1.2	2.3
1.0		.8	.8	Quick				.8	.6	1.5
.7		.4	.6					.6	.4	.6

42	8.6	30	12.2	39	9.3		29	12.8	37	9.9	44	8.3
55	6.7	40	9.1	46	7.9	Sales/Receivables	41	8.9	41	8.9	55	6.6
61	6.0	57	6.4	56	6.5		48	7.5	50	7.3	63	5.8
28	12.9	23	16.2	24	15.0		24	15.4	21	17.4	27	13.8
41	8.8	51	7.2	44	8.2	Cost of Sales/Inventory	50	7.4	38	9.7	48	7.6
62	5.9	87	4.2	82	4.5		100	3.6	96	3.8	68	5.3
21	17.7	24	15.4	18	20.8		10	37.3	18	20.0	15	23.7
38	9.5	39	9.3	25	14.7	Cost of Sales/Payables	20	18.1	25	14.8	24	15.5
46	7.9	53	6.9	48	7.6		47	7.8	43	8.4	44	8.4

	6.4		6.8		5.6		4.8	7.7	4.6
	11.7		14.9		8.6	Sales/Working Capital	6.7	28.1	6.2
	38.1		-43.2		60.8		19.0	NM	NM
	16.4		10.3		12.8		18.5	24.8	7.9
	6.1	(36)	4.9	(47)	3.4	EBIT/Interest	(10) 3.3	5.7 (13)	1.0
	2.8		1.2		.9		2.1	1.2	-.1
			3.6		7.9				
		(14)	2.1	(13)	3.0	Net Profit + Depr., Dep., Amort./Cur. Mat. L/T/D			
			1.3		.9				
	.4		.4		.3		.2	.6	.6
	1.1		1.0		.9	Fixed/Worth	.4	1.0	2.3
	3.3		3.7		2.5		1.7	1.9	-2.8
	1.0		1.1		.7		.3	.6	.8
	2.0		2.4		2.2	Debt/Worth	1.7	1.3	3.9
	6.1		6.7		5.0		2.5	3.4	-5.8
	67.4		70.1		44.6		30.6	45.3	
(22)	38.5	(32)	32.9	(43)	19.7	% Profit Before Taxes/Tangible Net Worth	(11) 18.5	19.7	
	8.4		5.9		2.8		3.9	6.7	
	19.8		16.6		13.9		13.3	24.5	10.7
	9.6		6.5		5.8	% Profit Before Taxes/Total Assets	7.0	10.4	.9
	2.4		.8		-.7		2.6	1.5	-6.3
	14.0		12.5		15.2		29.9	9.5	8.8
	9.3		7.8		8.0	Sales/Net Fixed Assets	10.3	5.9	4.5
	4.6		3.9		4.1		7.4	3.8	3.3
	3.2		3.2		2.9		3.3	2.8	2.0
	2.6		2.2		2.0	Sales/Total Assets	2.0	1.9	1.7
	1.6		1.7		1.6		1.8	1.5	1.3
	1.3		1.2		1.6			1.9	2.4
(22)	2.6	(33)	2.7	(37)	2.9	% Depr., Dep., Amort./Sales	(12)	2.8 (10)	3.6
	3.8		3.9		4.2				4.4	4.5
	4.1		3.5		3.5				
(10)	8.6	(17)	9.0	(16)	4.9	% Officers', Directors' Owners' Comp/Sales			
	11.2		13.1		10.0				

330937M		618186M	1240735M	Net Sales ($)	1861M	9856M	7630M	75493M	175656M	970239M
175551M		312293M	726265M	Total Assets ($)	1113M	4423M	2407M	33184M	90649M	594489M

M = $ thousand   MM = $ million
See Pages 11 through 21 for Explanation of Ratios and Data

Current Data Sorted by Assets

Comparative Historical Data

						Type of Statement		
							27	30
	5	6	10	4	1	Unqualified		
1	4	24	8			Reviewed	32	31
1	2	11	2			Compiled	13	22
	7	2	1			Tax Returns	6	8
		12	12	1	2	Other	37	31
	24 (4/1-9/30/06)		92 (10/1/06-3/31/07)				4/1/02-3/31/03	4/1/03-3/31/04
0-500M	500M-2MM	2-10MM	10-50MM	50-100MM	100-250MM		ALL	ALL
2	18	55	33	5	3	NUMBER OF STATEMENTS	115	122
%	%	%	%	%	%	ASSETS	%	%
	10.0	8.8	3.7			Cash & Equivalents	7.6	6.5
	31.1	30.0	22.5			Trade Receivables (net)	23.3	24.6
	21.4	23.3	20.5			Inventory	21.6	21.1
	.8	2.3	2.1			All Other Current	2.7	2.7
	63.2	64.4	48.9			Total Current	55.2	55.0
	23.5	28.3	29.9			Fixed Assets (net)	36.5	34.0
	2.4	2.3	8.6			Intangibles (net)	3.7	5.3
	10.9	5.0	12.7			All Other Non-Current	4.5	5.7
	100.0	100.0	100.0			Total	100.0	100.0
						LIABILITIES		
	14.1	11.4	8.9			Notes Payable-Short Term	9.4	10.1
	2.3	2.5	2.8			Cur. Mat.-L.T.D.	4.8	4.2
	20.8	15.7	12.4			Trade Payables	12.7	15.5
	.0	.1	.2			Income Taxes Payable	.3	.2
	14.2	8.8	9.0			All Other Current	9.9	10.3
	51.3	38.5	33.4			Total Current	37.0	40.3
	13.0	10.0	15.5			Long-Term Debt	18.2	17.4
	.0	.8	.9			Deferred Taxes	.9	.6
	5.5	3.4	7.1			All Other Non-Current	5.3	11.7
	30.2	47.4	43.1			Net Worth	38.6	30.0
	100.0	100.0	100.0			Total Liabilities & Net Worth	100.0	100.0
						INCOME DATA		
	100.0	100.0	100.0			Net Sales	100.0	100.0
	31.9	28.3	20.8			Gross Profit	29.5	28.1
	25.6	24.4	16.0			Operating Expenses	25.5	23.9
	6.4	3.9	4.8			Operating Profit	4.1	4.2
	3.8	.4	1.8			All Other Expenses (net)	1.2	1.4
	2.6	3.5	3.0			Profit Before Taxes	2.9	2.8
						RATIOS		
	2.8	3.1	2.6				3.1	2.7
	1.3	1.8	1.7			Current	1.7	1.5
	1.0	1.1	1.0				1.0	.9
	2.3	1.9	1.6				1.8	1.4
	.7	1.1	1.0			Quick	.9	.9
	.5	.6	.5				.5	.5
	28 13.0	33 11.0	38 9.5				33 10.9	34 10.7
	40 9.2	42 8.7	46 8.0			Sales/Receivables	43 8.4	43 8.4
	54 6.8	54 6.8	56 6.5				58 6.3	55 6.6
	28 12.8	25 14.5	29 12.6				32 11.5	26 13.8
	32 11.5	45 8.1	47 7.8			Cost of Sales/Inventory	56 6.5	45 8.1
	43 8.4	90 4.1	87 4.2				83 4.4	72 5.1
	16 23.2	16 23.3	20 18.4				18 19.8	17 21.8
	33 10.9	27 13.5	29 12.5			Cost of Sales/Payables	28 12.9	29 12.6
	47 7.8	41 8.9	43 8.6				40 9.0	42 8.7
	5.9	4.6	6.0				5.1	5.8
	23.2	9.7	9.5			Sales/Working Capital	9.8	13.8
	NM	28.4	NM				-211.8	-42.9
	13.4	10.9	21.0				8.1	8.8
	(16) 3.5	(47) 3.9	(32) 2.8			EBIT/Interest	(103) 2.9	(113) 2.5
	.1	1.3	.5				1.2	.0
		7.9					4.3	2.4
		(20) 2.1				Net Profit + Depr., Dep., Amort./Cur. Mat. L/T/D	(44) 2.2	(35) 1.2
		1.4					1.3	.8
	.2	.3	.4				.5	.4
	.8	.6	.9			Fixed/Worth	.9	1.0
	1.4	1.3	4.8				2.4	7.8
	1.1	.4	.4				.6	.7
	1.8	1.2	1.7			Debt/Worth	1.6	2.1
	5.0	3.4	7.9				5.9	13.6
	79.4	43.9	34.1				36.4	30.1
	(15) 47.3	(52) 12.8	(28) 11.3			% Profit Before Taxes/Tangible Net Worth	(99) 17.1	(97) 11.2
	6.7	3.8	-2.7				3.4	-1.1
	31.5	15.6	12.9				12.6	10.5
	11.2	4.4	3.5			% Profit Before Taxes/Total Assets	4.3	3.7
	-1.8	.9	-1.4				.2	-2.6
	31.0	20.0	15.6				11.1	14.9
	17.7	11.6	6.3			Sales/Net Fixed Assets	5.3	7.2
	7.4	4.1	4.0				3.0	3.5
	4.0	3.4	2.2				2.5	2.7
	2.9	2.1	1.8			Sales/Total Assets	1.8	2.0
	2.0	1.6	1.3				1.3	1.5
	.9	.8	1.6				1.8	1.6
	(15) 1.9	(53) 1.7	(29) 2.7			% Depr., Dep., Amort./Sales	(105) 3.4	(103) 2.8
	4.6	3.0	3.8				4.8	4.5
	2.5	1.7					1.9	2.6
	(11) 3.2	(21) 4.4				% Officers', Directors' Owners' Comp/Sales	(40) 4.8	(37) 5.4
	4.3	5.5					8.0	7.7
2879M	61741M	611452M	1083472M	518217M	624427M	Net Sales ($)	3098244M	3192372M
466M	20869M	260010M	612230M	305635M	388532M	Total Assets ($)	2087943M	1761633M

M = $ thousand   MM = $ million
See Pages 11 through 21 for Explanation of Ratios and Data

Comparative Historical Data

Current Data Sorted by Sales

			Type of Statement						
30	26	21	Unqualified		1		2	6	12
26	25	37	Reviewed		2	5	8	13	9
14	16	18	Compiled		2	6	8	1	1
2	6	6	Tax Returns		2	2		1	1
33	36	34	Other		6	4	4	9	11
4/1/04–	4/1/05–	4/1/06–			24 (4/1-9/30/06)		92 (10/1/06-3/31/07)		
3/31/05	3/31/06	3/31/07		0-1MM	1-3MM	3-5MM	5-10MM	10-25MM	25MM & OVER
ALL	ALL	ALL							
105	109	116	NUMBER OF STATEMENTS		13	17	22	30	34
%	%	%	ASSETS	%	%	%	%	%	%
6.6	7.4	7.1	Cash & Equivalents		12.3	8.1	9.9	4.9	4.8
27.2	27.9	27.9	Trade Receivables (net)	D	30.1	23.2	27.3	31.3	26.8
23.1	23.8	22.2	Inventory	A	13.9	20.1	24.9	23.9	23.1
2.5	1.4	2.0	All Other Current	T	1.6	2.2	2.5	2.0	1.8
59.4	60.5	59.2	Total Current	A	57.9	53.6	64.5	62.1	56.5
29.7	30.2	28.2	Fixed Assets (net)		31.4	32.2	26.1	25.6	28.6
3.7	2.9	4.4	Intangibles (net)	N	3.9	3.7	2.1	5.3	5.6
7.2	6.4	8.2	All Other Non-Current	O	6.7	10.5	7.3	7.0	9.4
100.0	100.0	100.0	Total	T	100.0	100.0	100.0	100.0	100.0
			LIABILITIES	A					
10.0	13.6	10.9	Notes Payable-Short Term	V	6.3	13.5	12.8	9.5	11.3
3.6	3.3	2.6	Cur. Mat.-L.T.D.	A	2.9	2.3	2.9	1.8	2.8
14.9	15.1	16.2	Trade Payables	I	26.4	11.3	12.2	18.6	15.3
.2	.2	.1	Income Taxes Payable	L	.0	.0	.1	.2	.1
10.1	10.0	9.9	All Other Current	A	15.2	12.5	7.1	9.5	8.6
38.7	42.3	39.6	Total Current	B	50.8	40.2	35.1	39.5	38.1
13.1	15.9	12.2	Long-Term Debt	L	24.6	10.1	11.5	7.8	12.7
.6	.9	.7	Deferred Taxes	E	.7	.9	.3	.8	.8
10.7	8.8	5.1	All Other Non-Current		3.1	3.7	7.5	5.6	4.5
36.9	32.1	42.4	Net Worth		20.7	45.1	45.6	46.3	43.9
100.0	100.0	100.0	Total Liabilities & Net Worth		100.0	100.0	100.0	100.0	100.0
			INCOME DATA						
100.0	100.0	100.0	Net Sales		100.0	100.0	100.0	100.0	100.0
28.3	27.1	26.4	Gross Profit		35.2	33.2	27.8	22.7	21.9
24.5	23.0	21.8	Operating Expenses		31.4	27.0	22.8	20.3	16.3
3.8	4.1	4.6	Operating Profit		3.8	6.2	5.0	2.4	5.6
.9	.7	1.4	All Other Expenses (net)		4.8	.7	.7	1.1	1.2
2.9	3.4	3.1	Profit Before Taxes		-1.0	5.4	4.3	1.3	4.4
			RATIOS						
2.6	2.5	2.7			2.9	2.2	3.1	3.0	2.5
1.6	1.6	1.7	Current		1.3	1.2	1.9	1.8	1.7
1.0	1.0	1.1			.7	1.0	1.1	1.2	1.1
1.6	1.7	1.6			2.4	1.5	2.0	1.9	1.4
.9	.9	1.0	Quick		.7	.6	1.1	1.2	.7
.6	.5	.6			.6	.5	.6	.6	.5

37	9.8	36	10.0	35	10.5			26	14.2	30	12.1	33	10.9	35	10.4	38	9.5
49	7.4	44	8.2	43	8.4	Sales/Receivables		50	7.2	37	9.9	43	8.4	44	8.3	45	8.0
60	6.1	55	6.6	53	6.9			61	5.9	46	7.9	53	6.8	55	6.6	54	6.8
33	11.0	28	13.3	28	13.1			2	233.3	30	12.1	29	12.4	26	14.2	29	12.4
46	7.9	44	8.3	44	8.2	Cost of Sales/Inventory		30	12.0	41	8.8	52	7.0	42	8.7	48	7.6
86	4.2	83	4.4	84	4.4			48	7.5	82	4.5	119	3.1	79	4.6	89	4.1
23	16.0	19	19.6	17	21.2			17	21.9	15	24.3	16	22.4	17	21.1	19	18.9
33	10.9	28	12.9	29	12.6	Cost of Sales/Payables		36	10.3	21	17.5	27	13.6	29	12.5	29	12.4
46	7.9	45	8.2	41	8.9			55	6.6	36	10.0	44	8.3	41	8.9	42	8.8

4.8	6.0	5.6			3.9	7.5	3.8	5.0	6.0
9.6	10.0	9.8	Sales/Working Capital		16.9	21.1	6.2	10.2	8.6
98.7	269.3	59.2			-23.4	NM	NM	30.1	46.5

	11.5		10.8		10.5				3.3		10.9		9.7		13.0		18.7
(92)	3.0	(95)	4.0	(104)	3.1	EBIT/Interest		(11)	.3	(15)	3.9	(19)	4.2	(27)	1.6	(32)	5.1
	1.3		.7		1.2				-3.9		1.1		2.0		-2.6		1.4
	6.3		6.1		8.3										9.2		8.1
(35)	4.0	(36)	3.3	(37)	2.5	Net Profit + Depr., Dep., Amort./Cur. Mat. L/T/D								(10)	1.7	(10)	2.9
	1.4		1.3		1.2										-1.7		1.4
	.4		.4		.3				.2		.3		.3		.3		.4
	.8		.9		.7	Fixed/Worth			1.6		.8		.5		.5		.7
	2.1		2.3		1.6				UND		1.4		1.1		1.3		1.6
	.6		.6		.4				1.1		.5		.4		.4		.4
	1.4		1.9		1.6	Debt/Worth			3.3		1.4		.8		1.4		1.8
	4.9		8.4		4.2				UND		3.2		5.1		5.4		3.1
	28.9		34.2		47.3	% Profit Before Taxes/Tangible Net Worth			79.1		75.5		63.8		24.4		42.7
(90)	13.0	(95)	13.4	(103)	15.0			(10)	13.9	(16)	17.6	(20)	17.1	(26)	5.8	(31)	18.2
	2.9		.9		3.8				-12.6		1.3		6.1		-10.4		4.7
	11.9		13.2		15.0	% Profit Before Taxes/Total Assets			9.3		22.2		17.1		13.7		15.0
	3.2		5.5		4.9				.9		14.7		6.7		2.4		5.3
	.9		.3		.4				-13.1		.8		2.5		-5.5		1.1
	13.7		26.6		21.5	Sales/Net Fixed Assets			27.8		24.6		22.2		25.1		14.9
	8.2		7.8		9.7				12.5		8.0		8.7		12.4		8.2
	4.2		3.5		4.4				3.0		3.6		4.7		4.7		4.6
	2.5		2.9		3.2				4.1		3.0		3.3		3.7		2.6
	1.9		2.0		2.0	Sales/Total Assets			2.0		1.9		1.9		2.1		2.0
	1.5		1.5		1.4				1.3		1.4		1.1		1.7		1.5
	1.5		1.1		1.0				1.6		.7		.9		.9		1.7
(95)	2.6	(98)	2.2	(106)	2.1	% Depr., Dep., Amort./Sales		(10)	4.2		1.8	(20)	1.5	(29)	1.7	(30)	2.5
	4.1		3.6		3.5				6.9		3.9		3.0		3.0		3.7
	2.0		2.0		1.6						2.3						
(31)	3.5	(39)	3.8	(37)	3.8	% Officers', Directors' Owners' Comp/Sales				(10)	3.1						
	7.8		6.9		5.5						4.2						

2931559M	2813936M	2902188M	Net Sales ($)		24761M	70365M	171129M	467704M	2168229M
1673024M	1498637M	1587742M	Total Assets ($)		16130M	40985M	112389M	229632M	1188606M

M = $ thousand   MM = $ million
See Pages 11 through 21 for Explanation of Ratios and Data

| Current Data Sorted by Assets | | | | | | | Comparative Historical Data | |

Type of Statement

0-500M	500M-2MM	2-10MM	10-50MM	50-100MM	100-250MM	Type of Statement	4/1/02-3/31/03 ALL	4/1/03-3/31/04 ALL
		7	8	2	2	Unqualified	14	11
	1	4	1			Reviewed	6	11
1		5				Compiled	2	9
	1					Tax Returns	1	2
2		1	4	1	2	Other	10	11
	10 (4/1-9/30/06)		34 (10/1/06-3/31/07)					
3	4	17	13	3	4	NUMBER OF STATEMENTS	33	44
%	%	%	%	%	%		%	%

ASSETS

2-10MM	10-50MM		4/1/02-3/31/03 ALL	4/1/03-3/31/04 ALL
8.2	8.6	Cash & Equivalents	7.3	8.5
21.0	12.6	Trade Receivables (net)	11.8	19.3
27.2	21.4	Inventory	21.3	19.4
1.1	5.2	All Other Current	1.6	3.5
57.4	47.7	Total Current	42.1	50.7
26.4	46.6	Fixed Assets (net)	49.2	40.9
11.4	1.0	Intangibles (net)	1.7	1.9
4.7	4.7	All Other Non-Current	7.0	6.6
100.0	100.0	Total	100.0	100.0

LIABILITIES

2-10MM	10-50MM		4/1/02-3/31/03 ALL	4/1/03-3/31/04 ALL
7.0	4.2	Notes Payable-Short Term	4.1	5.3
3.9	2.5	Cur. Mat.-L.T.D.	3.6	3.5
12.6	6.1	Trade Payables	5.4	7.8
.3	.5	Income Taxes Payable	.2	.3
6.3	5.2	All Other Current	7.3	6.8
30.1	18.6	Total Current	20.5	23.7
19.4	25.8	Long-Term Debt	30.2	24.9
1.6	2.4	Deferred Taxes	1.8	1.1
6.1	4.6	All Other Non-Current	1.8	1.7
42.8	48.6	Net Worth	45.7	48.6
100.0	100.0	Total Liabilties & Net Worth	100.0	100.0

INCOME DATA

2-10MM	10-50MM		4/1/02-3/31/03 ALL	4/1/03-3/31/04 ALL
100.0	100.0	Net Sales	100.0	100.0
31.4	29.1	Gross Profit	34.5	32.3
23.6	18.3	Operating Expenses	24.6	23.1
7.7	10.8	Operating Profit	9.9	9.2
1.8	1.3	All Other Expenses (net)	1.7	.9
5.9	9.5	Profit Before Taxes	8.2	8.3

RATIOS

2-10MM	10-50MM		4/1/02-3/31/03 ALL	4/1/03-3/31/04 ALL
4.1	3.9	Current	3.4	3.9
2.0	2.9		2.5	2.1
1.3	1.9		1.6	1.5
2.3	2.0	Quick	1.8	2.0
.7	1.4		1.1	1.1
.5	.6		.5	.6
30 12.0	31 11.8	Sales/Receivables	25 14.5	33 11.1
37 9.9	34 10.8		35 10.4	41 8.9
46 8.0	43 8.5		54 6.8	54 6.7
19 18.9	60 6.1	Cost of Sales/Inventory	51 7.1	40 9.1
57 6.4	78 4.7		91 4.0	64 5.7
104 3.5	112 3.3		160 2.3	115 3.2
16 23.5	15 24.5	Cost of Sales/Payables	16 23.3	19 19.7
30 12.3	23 15.7		25 14.8	26 13.9
46 8.0	27 13.4		35 10.3	36 10.2
4.0	3.8	Sales/Working Capital	3.0	3.5
5.9	4.7		4.2	5.2
18.4	6.8		9.2	10.7
12.0	28.2	EBIT/Interest	9.4	16.9
(15) 2.6	5.5		(31) 5.2	(41) 8.1
1.6	3.4		2.3	3.7
		Net Profit + Depr., Dep.,		4.7
		Amort./Cur. Mat. L/T/D	(13) 2.5	
				1.3
.3	.4	Fixed/Worth	.6	.4
.6	1.3		1.0	.9
3.1	2.0		1.9	1.6
.2	.5	Debt/Worth	.4	.5
1.6	1.1		1.5	1.1
NM	2.5		2.2	2.1
53.9	39.6	% Profit Before Taxes/Tangible Net Worth	27.8	43.0
(13) 33.6	23.7		(32) 17.0	(42) 18.3
7.9	16.1		7.3	9.0
24.4	13.6	% Profit Before Taxes/Total Assets	14.5	17.7
8.6	10.2		6.6	10.3
3.3	5.2		3.2	4.0
29.5	6.8	Sales/Net Fixed Assets	4.5	11.0
9.1	2.2		2.2	3.8
3.5	1.4		1.3	1.7
2.5	1.7	Sales/Total Assets	1.4	2.4
1.9	1.1		1.0	1.2
1.2	.8		.8	.8
1.2	2.5	% Depr., Dep., Amort./Sales	3.8	1.5
(15) 1.9	5.0		(31) 4.8	(37) 3.9
4.7	6.0		9.2	6.8
		% Officers', Directors' Owners' Comp/Sales		

0-500M	500M-2MM	2-10MM	10-50MM	50-100MM	100-250MM		4/1/02-3/31/03 ALL	4/1/03-3/31/04 ALL
6675M	16845M	160891M	379191M	162057M	606927M	Net Sales ($)	877196M	1156283M
1324M	5852M	85794M	312881M	219749M	564695M	Total Assets ($)	863241M	1006418M

M = $ thousand   MM = $ million
See Pages 11 through 21 for Explanation of Ratios and Data

Comparative Historical Data | | Current Data Sorted by Sales

						Type of Statement									
	16		16		19	Unqualified						4	7	8	
	10		10		6	Reviewed			2			2	2		
	1		5		6	Compiled		1				3	2		
	2		2		1	Tax Returns				1					
	18		16		12	Other		3		1		1	2	5	
	4/1/04-		4/1/05-		4/1/06-				10 (4/1-9/30/06)			34 (10/1/06-3/31/07)			
	3/31/05		3/31/06		3/31/07										
	ALL		ALL		ALL		0-1MM	1-3MM		3-5MM		5-10MM	10-25MM	25MM & OVER	
	47		49		44	NUMBER OF STATEMENTS		4		4		10	13	13	
	%		%		%	ASSETS	%	%		%		%	%	%	
	9.4		11.4		6.8	Cash & Equivalents						9.2	7.7	6.4	
	18.0		19.3		19.0	Trade Receivables (net)	D					18.6	21.3	11.1	
	22.7		21.7		24.4	Inventory	A					28.1	27.1	19.6	
	1.5		1.0		2.9	All Other Current	T					1.4	2.2	5.0	
	51.5		53.4		53.1	Total Current	A					57.2	58.2	42.1	
	37.4		38.1		35.1	Fixed Assets (net)						28.7	35.2	49.9	
	3.3		2.3		5.4	Intangibles (net)	N					7.9	2.9	2.5	
	7.8		6.2		6.4	All Other Non-Current	O					6.2	3.7	5.5	
	100.0		100.0		100.0	Total	T					100.0	100.0	100.0	
						LIABILITIES	A								
	4.9		10.9		7.1	Notes Payable-Short Term	V					4.2	6.1	3.0	
	6.2		2.7		2.6	Cur. Mat.-L.T.D.	A					3.9	3.6	1.9	
	8.8		11.6		10.7	Trade Payables	I					9.7	12.7	6.2	
	.1		.1		.3	Income Taxes Payable	L					.4	.2	.5	
	9.5		6.3		6.4	All Other Current	A					5.3	6.7	4.8	
	29.4		31.6		27.1	Total Current	B					23.3	29.3	16.5	
	25.2		21.2		23.4	Long-Term Debt	L					20.6	24.9	34.3	
	2.3		2.5		1.3	Deferred Taxes	E					2.7	1.2	1.2	
	6.2		7.3		5.3	All Other Non-Current						6.9	3.9	4.5	
	36.9		37.4		42.9	Net Worth						46.4	40.6	43.5	
	100.0		100.0		100.0	Total Liabilties & Net Worth						100.0	100.0	100.0	
						INCOME DATA									
	100.0		100.0		100.0	Net Sales						100.0	100.0	100.0	
	32.8		31.8		32.8	Gross Profit						34.5	24.4	34.3	
	24.4		22.5		23.9	Operating Expenses						23.9	17.1	21.2	
	8.4		9.3		8.9	Operating Profit						10.6	7.3	13.1	
	2.5		1.5		1.6	All Other Expenses (net)						2.3	1.1	1.9	
	5.9		7.8		7.3	Profit Before Taxes						8.3	6.2	11.2	
						RATIOS									
	3.3		3.5		3.9							4.9	4.1	3.8	
	2.1		2.2		2.1	Current						2.1	2.3	2.7	
	1.4		1.3		1.7							1.8	1.4	1.8	
	2.0		2.1		1.8							2.4	2.0	1.4	
	1.0		1.2		1.0	Quick						.7	1.5	1.1	
	.5		.6		.5							.6	.5	.8	
29	12.5	30	12.1	31	11.7						26	14.2	32	11.5	32	11.4
39	9.3	35	10.3	36	10.1	Sales/Receivables					35	10.5	37	9.9	36	10.2
52	7.0	47	7.8	45	8.1						44	8.4	43	8.5	44	8.4
41	9.0	34	10.7	42	8.7						20	18.2	53	6.9	53	6.9
81	4.5	76	4.8	76	4.8	Cost of Sales/Inventory					67	5.5	85	4.3	78	4.7
131	2.8	126	2.9	102	3.6						183	2.0	92	4.0	155	2.4
18	19.8	23	15.9	17	21.3						18	20.5	13	27.3	14	26.0
27	13.6	32	11.6	25	14.3	Cost of Sales/Payables					31	11.9	23	15.7	23	15.5
40	9.0	40	9.1	41	8.9						41	8.9	34	10.9	36	10.2
	3.5		3.5		4.0							3.8	4.1	3.2	
	4.6		5.2		6.1	Sales/Working Capital						4.8	7.2	5.4	
	9.9		15.2		11.8							9.8	14.3	6.9	
	13.1		16.4		15.8								11.4	32.7	
(45)	3.7	(47)	5.0	(40)	3.7	EBIT/Interest					(12)	3.9	(12)	5.2	
	1.8		1.8		2.1								2.1	3.5	
	11.9		12.4		8.1	Net Profit + Depr., Dep.,									
(13)	3.4	(11)	5.9	(15)	2.8	Amort./Cur. Mat. L/T/D									
	2.1		3.1		1.5										
	.4		.4		.3							.3	.3	.8	
	1.0		.9		.8	Fixed/Worth						.6	.7	1.6	
	3.0		2.0		2.4							2.9	1.9	3.3	
	.9		.8		.3							.3	.3	.6	
	1.7		1.6		1.4	Debt/Worth						1.2	1.1	1.9	
	4.3		4.5		5.8							6.3	6.8	5.1	
	43.3		36.1		47.1	% Profit Before Taxes/Tangible							33.7	51.6	
(40)	15.4	(46)	19.5	(39)	24.7	Net Worth						(11)	23.7	26.8	
	5.9		10.1		12.2								10.3	21.4	
	13.0		14.0		19.1	% Profit Before Taxes/Total						26.8	15.6	17.1	
	6.6		9.0		9.5	Assets						18.6	10.2	9.6	
	2.0		3.4		4.3							2.3	5.6	5.8	
	10.3		22.8		19.9							15.6	19.5	5.2	
	3.0		3.1		4.5	Sales/Net Fixed Assets						6.4	4.3	2.0	
	1.8		1.6		2.0							2.8	1.6	1.2	
	2.1		3.0		2.3							2.4	2.8	1.5	
	1.3		1.3		1.5	Sales/Total Assets						1.7	1.8	1.0	
	.8		.9		1.0							1.2	1.0	.7	
	2.5		1.4		1.2							.7	1.4	2.2	
(39)	5.3	(36)	4.8	(37)	2.8	% Depr., Dep., Amort./Sales						1.7	(11)	3.7	(11)	5.4
	8.1		6.7		5.5							4.8	5.9	5.8	
	1.8		3.0			% Officers', Directors'									
(15)	3.1	(11)	4.7			Owners' Comp/Sales									
	4.7		13.6												
	1278967M		2185623M		1332586M	Net Sales ($)		7927M	15239M		77287M	211795M	1020338M		
	1287623M		1544387M		1190295M	Total Assets ($)		6935M	7280M		49493M	153977M	972610M		

M = $ thousand   MM = $ million
See Pages 11 through 21 for Explanation of Ratios and Data

Current Data Sorted by Assets							Comparative Historical Data	
						Type of Statement		
		1	3	1	2	Unqualified	4	8
		2	2			Reviewed	5	3
	2	2				Compiled	5	8
	2					Tax Returns	1	3
	2	3	6		2	Other	6	2
	5 (4/1-9/30/06)		25 (10/1/06-3/31/07)				4/1/02-3/31/03 ALL	4/1/03-3/31/04 ALL
0-500M	500M-2MM	2-10MM	10-50MM	50-100MM	100-250MM			
	6	8	11	1	4	**NUMBER OF STATEMENTS**	21	24
%	%	%	%	%	%	**ASSETS**	%	%
			6.5			Cash & Equivalents	8.0	8.6
D			21.4			Trade Receivables (net)	28.9	20.3
A			20.2			Inventory	16.9	17.1
T			2.0			All Other Current	8.5	2.0
A			50.1			Total Current	62.4	48.0
N			30.6			Fixed Assets (net)	29.5	38.2
O			16.1			Intangibles (net)	4.3	5.0
T			3.2			All Other Non-Current	3.8	8.9
			100.0			Total	100.0	100.0
A						**LIABILITIES**		
V			7.3			Notes Payable-Short Term	7.0	3.7
A			4.3			Cur. Mat.-L.T.D.	5.2	10.7
I			13.0			Trade Payables	16.1	10.2
L			.0			Income Taxes Payable	.1	.1
A			7.4			All Other Current	11.4	11.6
B			32.0			Total Current	39.9	36.2
L			16.4			Long-Term Debt	16.4	24.2
E			1.0			Deferred Taxes	.2	.7
			5.1			All Other Non-Current	3.9	6.5
			45.5			Net Worth	39.5	32.4
			100.0			Total Liabilties & Net Worth	100.0	100.0
						INCOME DATA		
			100.0			Net Sales	100.0	100.0
			25.8			Gross Profit	29.9	31.1
			20.3			Operating Expenses	25.6	27.4
			5.5			Operating Profit	4.3	3.7
			.7			All Other Expenses (net)	-.2	.8
			4.8			Profit Before Taxes	4.4	2.9
						RATIOS		
			2.9				3.7	2.3
			1.5			Current	1.7	1.5
			1.0				1.1	.8
			2.0				1.4	1.4
			1.0			Quick	1.0	1.0
			.7				.8	.4
			29 12.8				**29** 12.7	**23** 16.1
			44 8.2			Sales/Receivables	**39** 9.4	**37** 10.0
			53 6.9				**44** 8.3	**48** 7.7
			27 13.7				**17** 21.3	**22** 16.4
			45 8.1			Cost of Sales/Inventory	**30** 12.2	**39** 9.3
			102 3.6				**45** 8.2	**55** 6.6
			14 26.8				**18** 20.3	**12** 31.6
			24 15.4			Cost of Sales/Payables	**28** 12.8	**23** 16.0
			50 7.3				**43** 8.5	**47** 7.7
			7.9				6.7	7.6
			16.9			Sales/Working Capital	12.3	15.8
			-139.6				NM	UND
			22.2				11.3	8.1
			4.2			EBIT/Interest	4.6	(20) 2.2
			1.8				2.0	1.2
						Net Profit + Depr., Dep., Amort./Cur. Mat. L/T/D		
			.6				.2	.8
			1.3			Fixed/Worth	1.5	1.2
			-1.1				4.7	NM
			.8				.5	.6
			1.6			Debt/Worth	1.8	2.2
			-5.6				7.5	NM
							27.8	35.7
						% Profit Before Taxes/Tangible Net Worth	(17) 23.0	(18) 16.0
							17.6	7.2
			14.3				15.3	20.6
			9.6			% Profit Before Taxes/Total Assets	10.1	5.3
			2.1				3.6	.8
			18.0				32.8	12.9
			8.4			Sales/Net Fixed Assets	9.6	7.5
			3.5				5.5	3.0
			2.3				3.4	3.1
			1.6			Sales/Total Assets	2.3	2.1
			1.4				1.8	1.3
							1.4	1.4
						% Depr., Dep., Amort./Sales	1.9	(23) 3.1
							4.5	4.9
						% Officers', Directors' Owners' Comp/Sales		
	25117M	82957M	499757M	120855M	1175786M	Net Sales ($)	512022M	969392M
	8379M	36552M	268698M	94469M	649597M	Total Assets ($)	259600M	541235M

M = $ thousand MM = $ million

See Pages 11 through 21 for Explanation of Ratios and Data

| **Comparative Historical Data** | | | | | **Current Data Sorted by Sales** | | | | | |

				Type of Statement							
5		2		7	Unqualified				1		6
4		3		4	Reviewed				1	2	1
4		2		4	Compiled			1	2	1	
2		2		2	Tax Returns	1					
5		5		13	Other	2	2		1		6
4/1/04-3/31/05 ALL		4/1/05-3/31/06 ALL		4/1/06-3/31/07 ALL		0-1MM	5 (4/1-9/30/06) 1-3MM	3-5MM	25 (10/1/06-3/31/07) 5-10MM	10-25MM	25MM & OVER
20		14		30	**NUMBER OF STATEMENTS**		2	4	5	6	13
%		%		%	**ASSETS**	%	%	%	%	%	%
6.4		6.9		13.3	Cash & Equivalents						5.7
27.0		38.0		24.9	Trade Receivables (net)						23.6
21.4		16.6		23.4	Inventory	D					21.0
1.0		2.1		1.6	All Other Current	A					2.4
55.8		63.5		63.2	Total Current	T					52.7
32.7		24.6		25.1	Fixed Assets (net)	A					31.0
2.5		7.3		8.1	Intangibles (net)						11.5
9.0		4.6		3.6	All Other Non-Current	N					4.8
100.0		100.0		100.0	Total	O					100.0
					LIABILITIES	T					
9.4		4.8		7.5	Notes Payable-Short Term	A					8.1
4.3		8.9		2.9	Cur. Mat.-L.T.D.	V					3.6
14.2		12.5		12.6	Trade Payables	A					13.5
.1		.0		.0	Income Taxes Payable	I					.0
10.3		12.7		12.6	All Other Current	L					11.0
38.3		38.9		35.7	Total Current	A					36.3
16.4		15.9		18.9	Long-Term Debt	B					19.8
.4		.0		.5	Deferred Taxes	L					.8
7.4		4.3		9.9	All Other Non-Current	E					9.4
37.5		41.0		35.1	Net Worth						33.7
100.0		100.0		100.0	Total Liabilties & Net Worth						100.0
					INCOME DATA						
100.0		100.0		100.0	Net Sales						100.0
29.5		30.7		31.5	Gross Profit						28.4
27.0		25.6		24.6	Operating Expenses						19.4
2.5		5.1		7.0	Operating Profit						9.0
.9		.7		.8	All Other Expenses (net)						1.2
1.5		4.4		6.1	Profit Before Taxes						7.8
					RATIOS						
2.3		2.7		3.3							2.7
1.6		1.6		1.8	Current						1.5
1.2		1.3		1.2							1.0
1.3		1.8		1.9							1.4
.9		1.2		1.1	Quick						1.0
.5		.6		.7							.6
25	14.5	34	10.9	28	12.9					36	10.2
34	10.6	40	9.0	46	7.9	Sales/Receivables				49	7.4
51	7.1	58	6.3	57	6.4					55	6.6
21	17.5	9	39.3	23	15.6					28	13.1
41	8.9	21	17.2	48	7.6	Cost of Sales/Inventory				45	8.2
70	5.2	50	7.4	107	3.4					76	4.8
16	23.3	7	53.1	13	27.2					14	25.8
29	12.4	19	19.2	32	11.6	Cost of Sales/Payables				35	10.6
41	9.0	44	8.2	42	8.7					46	8.0
8.1		7.4		3.7							7.0
13.3		13.4		9.5	Sales/Working Capital						16.9
41.9		25.5		31.4							-109.7
7.9		18.8		11.3							14.3
(18)	1.4		5.2	(28)	3.1	EBIT/Interest				(12)	3.1
-2.1		1.7		1.5							1.9
					Net Profit + Depr., Dep., Amort./Cur. Mat. L/T/D						
.5		.5		.5							.6
.8		.7		1.3	Fixed/Worth						1.3
2.1		2.0		22.6							NM
.8		.7		.8							.9
2.4		2.2		3.7	Debt/Worth						1.9
4.6		5.3		60.6							NM
30.2		51.5		55.2							103.0
(18)	16.5	(13)	27.2	(24)	27.0	% Profit Before Taxes/Tangible Net Worth				(10)	36.0
-2.9		12.2		14.4							24.4
11.7		19.3		13.5							13.4
3.8		7.0		7.8	% Profit Before Taxes/Total Assets						9.7
-3.5		1.6		1.2							5.1
22.6		24.4		23.1							19.1
11.5		11.6		10.8	Sales/Net Fixed Assets						5.3
3.6		8.6		4.4							3.3
3.4		3.8		2.9							2.4
2.6		3.0		1.9	Sales/Total Assets						1.9
1.7		2.2		1.5							1.3
1.6		1.6		1.0							1.2
(19)	2.8	(10)	2.4	(26)	2.3	% Depr., Dep., Amort./Sales				(11)	2.3
4.5		2.6		3.4							3.3
					% Officers', Directors' Owners' Comp/Sales						
954381M		708824M		1904472M	Net Sales ($)		4162M	15833M	39995M	109606M	1734876M
411872M		280392M		1057695M	Total Assets ($)		2603M	7358M	15403M	70749M	961582M

© RMA 2007

M = $ thousand   MM = $ million
See Pages 11 through 21 for Explanation of Ratios and Data

MANUFACTURING—Glass Product Manufacturing Made of Purchased Glass NAICS 327215 (SIC 3231)

Current Data Sorted by Assets

Comparative Historical Data

0-500M	500M-2MM	2-10MM	10-50MM	50-100MM	100-250MM	Type of Statement	4/1/02-3/31/03 ALL	4/1/03-3/31/04 ALL
		3	6	1		Unqualified	19	12
1	8	22	4			Reviewed	21	30
2	7	6				Compiled	17	19
4	8	5				Tax Returns	13	13
4	10	14	11		1	Other	35	34
	26 (4/1-9/30/06)		91 (10/1/06-3/31/07)					
11	33	50	21	1	1	NUMBER OF STATEMENTS	105	108
%	%	%	%	%	%	ASSETS	%	%
23.5	8.8	6.0	9.7			Cash & Equivalents	6.9	7.2
19.6	32.6	28.2	25.9			Trade Receivables (net)	26.0	26.9
20.1	22.9	25.3	21.9			Inventory	21.9	22.3
.3	4.0	4.8	3.4			All Other Current	2.7	2.7
63.5	68.4	64.2	60.8			Total Current	57.5	59.2
29.9	24.0	27.4	27.6			Fixed Assets (net)	32.4	30.9
.8	1.5	3.9	6.3			Intangibles (net)	4.6	4.1
5.8	6.1	4.5	5.2			All Other Non-Current	5.5	5.8
100.0	100.0	100.0	100.0			Total	100.0	100.0
						LIABILITIES		
28.5	10.2	8.8	12.3			Notes Payable-Short Term	10.6	10.7
3.3	5.0	3.9	2.7			Cur. Mat.-L.T.D.	4.7	4.8
9.3	17.5	14.8	13.2			Trade Payables	13.8	13.8
.0	.1	.1	.9			Income Taxes Payable	.3	.2
17.1	10.1	7.5	9.1			All Other Current	11.0	7.9
58.2	42.9	35.2	38.2			Total Current	40.4	37.4
26.0	13.2	20.0	12.6			Long-Term Debt	20.1	18.3
.0	.1	.3	1.3			Deferred Taxes	.6	.7
19.7	3.7	4.7	7.0			All Other Non-Current	5.0	5.2
-3.9	40.1	39.9	40.9			Net Worth	33.9	38.4
100.0	100.0	100.0	100.0			Total Liabilities & Net Worth	100.0	100.0
						INCOME DATA		
100.0	100.0	100.0	100.0			Net Sales	100.0	100.0
37.9	37.2	29.2	26.6			Gross Profit	32.1	31.2
34.8	33.1	24.2	20.7			Operating Expenses	28.2	29.0
3.1	4.1	4.9	5.9			Operating Profit	3.9	2.2
.8	1.0	1.2	.7			All Other Expenses (net)	1.4	1.0
2.3	3.1	3.7	5.2			Profit Before Taxes	2.6	1.2
						RATIOS		
4.7	3.5	2.9	2.4			Current	2.6	2.7
2.0	1.9	1.8	1.6				1.5	1.6
.5	1.1	1.2	1.1				1.0	1.0
3.2	2.1	1.8	1.5			Quick	1.4	1.7
1.0	.9	1.0	.9				.9	.8
.3	.7	.6	.7				.6	.5
0 UND	27 13.3	36 10.3	43 8.5			Sales/Receivables	30 12.1	32 11.6
32 11.4	41 8.9	43 8.4	49 7.5				43 8.6	40 9.2
52 7.0	55 6.7	60 6.1	59 6.2				54 6.8	52 7.1
0 UND	11 34.3	23 15.6	24 15.5			Cost of Sales/Inventory	27 13.7	28 13.0
37 9.9	41 8.9	38 9.7	55 6.6				50 7.3	48 7.6
67 5.4	108 3.4	90 4.0	75 4.9				81 4.5	86 4.2
0 UND	14 25.4	18 19.9	18 19.9			Cost of Sales/Payables	18 20.3	17 21.4
8 45.3	29 12.6	27 13.4	31 11.9				29 12.8	30 12.4
46 8.0	48 7.6	55 6.6	57 6.4				48 7.6	42 8.7
6.3	5.9	4.9	3.5			Sales/Working Capital	6.1	5.0
11.3	11.0	8.0	10.7				11.3	9.2
-30.6	44.5	33.5	25.8				UND	132.4
	20.5	15.9	8.8			EBIT/Interest	6.3	7.8
	(31) 3.2	(45) 2.5	(19) 3.9				(97) 2.8	(98) 2.4
	-1.2	1.1	3.0				1.1	.0
		5.9				Net Profit + Depr., Dep.,	3.6	3.9
		(15) 2.4				Amort./Cur. Mat. L/T/D	(25) 2.1	(28) 2.0
		1.7					1.0	.9
.3	.2	.2	.5			Fixed/Worth	.4	.5
-2.8	.6	.6	.6				1.0	1.0
-.4	2.9	1.6	1.7				2.9	2.2
1.2	.4	.5	.9			Debt/Worth	1.0	.8
-13.4	1.1	1.6	1.7				1.9	1.8
-3.4	6.1	5.3	4.6				8.2	4.8
	43.7	41.8	37.6			% Profit Before Taxes/Tangible	33.3	28.8
	(32) 23.1	(43) 19.2	(19) 16.8			Net Worth	(90) 14.6	(96) 12.8
	-3.5	2.4	9.0				2.2	-2.6
90.2	22.2	18.9	15.9			% Profit Before Taxes/Total	11.3	12.5
13.5	5.8	4.7	7.5			Assets	4.7	3.3
-8.5	-3.1	.4	4.8				.5	-1.8
51.0	31.3	26.6	14.7			Sales/Net Fixed Assets	14.4	15.2
21.4	13.4	9.4	6.7				8.0	8.5
6.1	8.0	5.1	4.5				4.1	4.1
5.8	4.1	2.9	2.2			Sales/Total Assets	2.7	3.1
3.9	2.8	2.1	1.8				2.2	2.1
2.2	1.9	1.7	1.4				1.6	1.6
	.8	1.1	1.4			% Depr., Dep., Amort./Sales	1.6	1.7
	(31) 1.7	(47) 2.1	(19) 2.2				(96) 2.8	(97) 2.9
	2.5	4.0	3.4				4.8	4.7
	2.0	2.7				% Officers', Directors'	3.3	1.3
	(14) 4.0	(16) 4.1				Owners' Comp/Sales	(43) 4.8	(46) 3.6
	7.5	10.3					7.4	7.9
11368M	108859M	523986M	909497M	99292M	328221M	Net Sales ($)	2045399M	2978163M
2647M	38302M	237168M	477329M	73522M	173961M	Total Assets ($)	1191460M	1625564M

M = $ thousand   MM = $ million
See Pages 11 through 21 for Explanation of Ratios and Data

Comparative Historical Data | Current Data Sorted by Sales

Hist 4/1/04-3/31/05 ALL	Hist 4/1/05-3/31/06 ALL	Hist 4/1/06-3/31/07 ALL		0-1MM	1-3MM	3-5MM	5-10MM	10-25MM	25MM & OVER
			Type of Statement		26 (4/1-9/30/06)		91 (10/1/06-3/31/07)		
9	14	10	Unqualified	1	3	6	2	3	5
26	30	35	Reviewed	2	4	3	12	10	3
16	10	15	Compiled	1	4	3	4	1	1
12	15	17	Tax Returns	1	7	4	3	1	1
29	43	40	Other	2	9	3	8	10	8
92	112	117	**NUMBER OF STATEMENTS**	6	23	16	29	25	18
%	%	%	**ASSETS**	%	%	%	%	%	%
7.2	6.7	9.3	Cash & Equivalents		18.1	6.4	5.4	10.1	6.3
28.4	29.4	28.1	Trade Receivables (net)		28.5	25.3	28.5	30.8	28.1
24.3	24.2	23.5	Inventory		20.5	27.6	19.8	27.6	22.3
2.4	2.9	3.8	All Other Current		1.7	4.5	7.1	3.1	2.9
62.2	63.2	64.7	Total Current		68.7	63.7	60.9	71.6	59.6
27.0	26.8	26.8	Fixed Assets (net)		24.1	23.7	30.8	21.8	28.8
4.4	4.0	3.4	Intangibles (net)		1.3	5.5	2.9	1.9	7.8
6.3	6.0	5.1	All Other Non-Current		5.9	7.0	5.4	4.7	3.7
100.0	100.0	100.0	Total		100.0	100.0	100.0	100.0	100.0
			LIABILITIES						
11.6	11.3	11.8	Notes Payable-Short Term		18.9	6.7	9.5	10.0	14.4
4.0	4.6	3.9	Cur. Mat.-L.T.D.		5.3	3.2	4.7	2.4	2.9
14.7	14.9	14.7	Trade Payables		10.6	18.4	14.9	17.1	13.9
.4	.6	.2	Income Taxes Payable		.0	.0	.2	.5	.5
10.5	8.3	9.3	All Other Current		8.6	9.8	7.4	8.2	9.5
41.2	39.7	40.0	Total Current		43.3	38.2	36.8	38.1	41.1
15.2	16.5	17.1	Long-Term Debt		13.4	13.0	19.9	16.5	13.1
.7	.6	.4	Deferred Taxes		.0	.1	.2	.6	1.4
6.0	7.9	6.3	All Other Non-Current		9.1	1.7	2.6	8.7	5.9
36.8	35.3	36.2	Net Worth		34.1	47.0	40.5	36.1	38.5
100.0	100.0	100.0	Total Liabilties & Net Worth		100.0	100.0	100.0	100.0	100.0
			INCOME DATA						
100.0	100.0	100.0	Net Sales		100.0	100.0	100.0	100.0	100.0
31.5	30.7	31.8	Gross Profit		40.8	34.6	27.8	28.8	26.9
28.6	27.5	27.0	Operating Expenses		34.9	31.6	23.9	22.4	20.4
2.9	3.2	4.9	Operating Profit		5.9	3.0	3.9	6.5	6.5
.6	1.0	1.0	All Other Expenses (net)		1.1	.9	1.1	1.1	.7
2.3	2.2	3.8	Profit Before Taxes		4.8	2.0	2.8	5.4	5.7
			RATIOS						
3.0	2.7	3.1			4.5	3.0	3.4	2.5	1.9
1.6	1.6	1.8	Current		1.9	2.3	1.4	2.1	1.4
1.2	1.2	1.1			1.2	1.3	1.0	1.5	1.1
1.7	1.5	1.8			2.7	1.8	1.7	1.8	1.2
.9	1.0	.9	Quick		1.4	.9	.9	1.1	.7
.6	.6	.6			.7	.5	.6	.7	.6
33 11.2	32 11.3	34 10.6			23 15.6	22 16.4	35 10.3	38 9.5	36 10.0
40 9.1	45 8.1	43 8.5	Sales/Receivables		41 8.9	40 9.1	44 8.2	43 8.5	47 7.7
52 7.1	59 6.2	57 6.4			54 6.7	63 5.8	59 6.2	57 6.4	58 6.3
26 14.3	24 15.4	18 19.9			5 68.6	14 26.7	18 20.4	20 18.0	33 11.1
43 8.5	43 8.5	47 7.7	Cost of Sales/Inventory		40 9.1	67 5.5	31 11.9	38 9.7	53 6.9
87 4.2	85 4.3	89 4.1			105 3.5	126 2.9	74 4.9	104 3.5	64 5.7
16 22.4	16 22.2	15 24.6			0 UND	21 17.4	14 25.9	20 18.0	19 19.7
27 13.5	29 12.6	28 13.1	Cost of Sales/Payables		23 15.7	26 13.8	22 16.2	34 10.8	30 12.1
48 7.7	43 8.5	49 7.5			40 9.2	58 6.3	43 8.5	61 6.0	41 9.0
5.1	5.0	4.6			6.3	3.5	4.7	3.6	6.0
10.8	9.5	8.8	Sales/Working Capital		11.3	7.1	13.5	6.8	16.5
34.5	25.0	31.2			27.1	16.0	605.8	14.4	33.6
9.4	6.5	15.0			17.6	21.0	9.8	19.5	17.0
(83) 3.9	(103) 2.8	(105) 3.6	EBIT/Interest		(21) 4.7	(13) 1.9	(26) 2.0	3.6	(16) 3.7
.6	1.1	1.1			.1	-4.6	1.1	1.2	2.5
3.5	4.6	10.0					8.5		
(19) 1.5	(34) 1.9	(27) 2.4	Net Profit + Depr., Dep., Amort./Cur. Mat. L/T/D				(12) 2.1		
.9	1.0	1.7					1.6		
.3	.3	.3			.2	.3	.2	.2	.4
.8	.8	.6	Fixed/Worth		.6	.4	.7	.6	1.1
1.9	2.5	2.9			3.9	.9	1.9	1.4	5.7
.6	.7	.6			.4	.4	.6	.7	1.1
1.7	1.8	1.6	Debt/Worth		1.4	.7	1.5	1.6	2.1
4.3	8.1	6.2			12.4	4.3	4.1	8.1	14.6
25.9	34.5	42.1			86.2	42.2	26.5	53.5	64.0
(75) 10.7	(93) 13.6	(101) 20.8	% Profit Before Taxes/Tangible Net Worth		(21) 29.1	(14) 19.9	(27) 10.2	(21) 31.3	(16) 28.7
.0	1.6	2.7			-5.2	-5.6	.6	7.6	11.2
11.4	11.9	20.0			37.1	20.9	13.2	19.6	19.9
4.5	4.8	6.5	% Profit Before Taxes/Total Assets		16.4	4.7	2.3	7.5	8.4
-1.9	.4	.3			-.8	-8.3	-.1	.8	4.8
18.1	19.7	23.9			42.3	22.3	19.3	47.5	14.6
10.3	9.6	10.2	Sales/Net Fixed Assets		22.6	11.5	9.6	10.2	7.1
5.3	4.7	5.3			6.9	8.4	5.0	4.9	4.8
3.1	3.0	3.1			4.0	3.7	2.9	3.5	2.6
2.3	2.1	2.2	Sales/Total Assets		2.8	2.2	2.0	2.1	2.0
1.8	1.7	1.7			1.7	1.5	1.7	1.5	1.7
1.1	1.2	1.1			.6	1.3	1.6	.7	1.3
(80) 2.3	(98) 2.3	(107) 2.1	% Depr., Dep., Amort./Sales		(19) 1.1	1.9	(28) 2.6	(22) 2.0	(17) 2.2
3.9	3.9	3.6			3.7	2.4	4.4	3.4	3.9
1.8	1.6	2.3					2.8		
(39) 3.5	(42) 2.8	(40) 3.9	% Officers', Directors' Owners' Comp/Sales				(10) 3.9		
7.0	5.7	9.6					7.1		
1733482M	2998917M	1981223M	Net Sales ($)	3135M	45881M	59439M	224109M	375393M	1273266M
931231M	1358873M	1002929M	Total Assets ($)	1354M	18299M	30486M	109475M	193033M	650282M

M = $ thousand   MM = $ million
See Pages 11 through 21 for Explanation of Ratios and Data

Current Data Sorted by Assets   Comparative Historical Data

0-500M	500M-2MM	2-10MM	10-50MM	50-100MM	100-250MM	Type of Statement		
		12	27	14	12	Unqualified	50	49
	5	26	20	2		Reviewed	54	46
	5	22	5		1	Compiled	38	57
4	13	20				Tax Returns	13	22
2	8	31	33	9	5	Other	51	61
	46 (4/1-9/30/06)		230 (10/1/06-3/31/07)				4/1/02-3/31/03 ALL	4/1/03-3/31/04 ALL
6	31	111	85	25	18	NUMBER OF STATEMENTS	206	235
%	%	%	%	%	%	ASSETS	%	%
	14.2	10.4	8.2	5.7	2.9	Cash & Equivalents	9.0	9.6
	25.9	27.1	23.2	17.2	19.4	Trade Receivables (net)	23.6	24.6
	9.0	5.2	7.8	8.3	8.5	Inventory	6.9	7.5
	5.8	2.2	2.3	4.1	2.8	All Other Current	2.5	3.0
	54.9	44.9	41.5	35.3	33.7	Total Current	42.0	44.6
	37.2	46.1	46.5	52.8	49.1	Fixed Assets (net)	48.8	46.6
	2.1	1.9	5.8	5.0	11.0	Intangibles (net)	2.1	2.2
	5.9	7.1	6.2	6.9	6.1	All Other Non-Current	7.1	6.5
	100.0	100.0	100.0	100.0	100.0	Total	100.0	100.0
						LIABILITIES		
	9.1	6.8	3.6	4.0	4.2	Notes Payable-Short Term	5.5	5.3
	4.8	4.8	6.0	6.1	4.0	Cur. Mat.-L.T.D.	6.0	5.6
	20.7	15.4	12.9	8.5	7.5	Trade Payables	13.8	13.2
	.1	.2	.2	.1	.4	Income Taxes Payable	.2	.2
	4.4	7.1	6.1	7.0	7.4	All Other Current	6.8	6.9
	39.1	34.3	28.8	25.6	23.5	Total Current	32.4	31.3
	27.7	22.5	20.0	24.4	28.7	Long-Term Debt	20.0	22.0
	.0	.8	1.4	3.2	1.6	Deferred Taxes	1.5	1.2
	2.5	2.6	3.9	4.1	2.6	All Other Non-Current	4.5	4.7
	30.7	39.8	45.9	42.6	43.6	Net Worth	41.7	40.9
	100.0	100.0	100.0	100.0	100.0	Total Liabilities & Net Worth	100.0	100.0
						INCOME DATA		
	100.0	100.0	100.0	100.0	100.0	Net Sales	100.0	100.0
	33.0	31.5	29.7	22.8	21.1	Gross Profit	29.0	28.9
	31.9	27.5	23.6	14.8	10.3	Operating Expenses	25.7	25.5
	1.2	4.0	6.1	8.0	10.7	Operating Profit	3.3	3.4
	.4	.1	.4	1.1	2.2	All Other Expenses (net)	.3	.5
	.7	3.9	5.8	6.9	8.6	Profit Before Taxes	2.9	2.8
						RATIOS		
	3.4	2.3	2.0	2.0	2.1		2.3	2.6
	1.9	1.4	1.4	1.4	1.6	Current	1.5	1.5
	.7	.9	1.1	1.0	1.3		.9	.9
	1.9	2.0	1.5	1.3	1.4		1.8	1.9
	1.7	1.2	1.0	.8	1.1	Quick	1.2	1.1
	.5	.8	.8	.6	.7		.6	.7
	21 17.7	32 11.4	36 10.2	33 11.2	41 8.9		31 11.6 / 31 11.7	
	33 10.9	43 8.6	45 8.1	43 8.6	45 8.1	Sales/Receivables	40 9.1 / 41 8.8	
	49 7.5	58 6.3	54 6.8	49 7.5	60 6.1		51 7.2 / 53 6.9	
	1 575.0	3 141.1	8 44.8	14 26.7	14 25.8		5 72.9 / 4 90.7	
	9 39.1	9 40.0	16 22.2	23 15.9	22 16.9	Cost of Sales/Inventory	13 27.1 / 11 32.6	
	33 11.1	18 20.6	38 9.7	44 8.3	48 7.7		31 11.9 / 28 13.0	
	15 24.3	21 17.2	23 15.7	17 21.2	17 21.3		19 19.2 / 18 20.0	
	29 12.5	33 11.2	31 11.7	23 15.8	23 15.9	Cost of Sales/Payables	27 13.3 / 28 13.0	
	58 6.3	46 8.0	45 8.1	35 10.6	33 11.2		43 8.5 / 40 9.0	
	5.7	7.5	7.7	8.1	7.9		7.5	6.8
	10.2	20.9	16.1	16.5	11.7	Sales/Working Capital	15.7	15.9
	-17.6	-83.4	84.3	NM	38.9		-68.5	-156.3
	6.1	11.8	12.5	11.6	15.0		7.6	8.5
	(28) 1.7	(101) 3.9	(82) 5.3	3.9	(16) 4.9	EBIT/Interest	(188) 3.6 / (214) 3.8	
	.1	1.5	2.1	2.2	2.1		1.4	.9
		6.8	6.0	3.4		Net Profit + Depr., Dep.,	3.4	3.3
		(31) 2.8	(31) 2.5	(15) 2.3		Amort./Cur. Mat. L/T/D	(63) 2.0 / (65) 2.0	
		1.1	1.3	1.2			1.3	1.3
	.4	.7	.7	1.2	.9		.6	.6
	1.4	1.1	1.2	1.3	1.8	Fixed/Worth	1.2	1.2
	6.7	2.3	2.0	2.1	5.5		2.4	2.3
	.6	.7	.7	.9	.6		.6	.6
	2.1	1.6	1.4	1.4	2.3	Debt/Worth	1.3	1.4
	38.0	3.9	2.6	3.3	9.3		3.1	3.3
	43.5	42.9	37.8	42.6	75.1	% Profit Before Taxes/Tangible	28.8	29.0
	(25) 23.3	(101) 16.7	(81) 19.0	(24) 21.0	(17) 26.8	Net Worth	(189) 13.0 / (209) 14.9	
	-6.0	6.8	7.2	10.9	15.1		2.7	3.2
	13.7	16.0	14.8	16.8	14.7	% Profit Before Taxes/Total	11.1	11.9
	3.5	6.5	8.1	7.6	7.1	Assets	4.9	5.4
	-2.4	1.3	2.7	3.4	5.8		.7	-.2
	14.7	7.3	5.6	4.8	4.3		6.7	7.4
	8.1	4.9	3.5	2.5	3.3	Sales/Net Fixed Assets	4.0	4.3
	4.3	3.1	2.7	1.8	1.9		2.5	2.8
	3.6	2.7	2.2	1.9	1.9		2.6	2.7
	2.4	2.2	1.8	1.3	1.4	Sales/Total Assets	1.9	2.0
	2.0	1.6	1.4	1.1	1.0		1.5	1.5
	4.0	3.2	3.1	3.5			3.5	3.1
	(25) 5.8	(105) 4.3	(77) 4.5	(23) 5.1		% Depr., Dep., Amort./Sales	(188) 5.3 / (213) 4.9	
	7.1	6.0	6.4	6.4			7.4	7.1
	2.2	1.4	1.1				1.5	1.3
	(15) 4.5	(46) 3.0	(23) 2.9			% Officers', Directors' Owners' Comp/Sales	(80) 2.5 / (79) 2.6	
	7.0	5.9	5.3				4.2	4.6
3531M	102669M	1246928M	3623777M	2682300M	4093744M	Net Sales ($)	6320909M	6465259M
1700M	36718M	550620M	2134639M	1773120M	2879075M	Total Assets ($)	4484821M	4230076M

M = $ thousand   MM = $ million
See Pages 11 through 21 for Explanation of Ratios and Data

Comparative Historical Data   Current Data Sorted by Sales

Key: M = $ thousand   MM = $ million. Current data period groupings: **46 (4/1-9/30/06)** and **230 (10/1/06-3/31/07)**.

4/1/04-3/31/05 ALL	4/1/05-3/31/06 ALL	4/1/06-3/31/07 ALL		0-1MM	1-3MM	3-5MM	5-10MM	10-25MM	25MM & OVER
			Type of Statement						
49	54	65	Unqualified				3	14	48
52	46	53	Reviewed	1	2	7	8	17	18
46	33	37	Compiled	4	7	3	6	10	7
21	16	35	Tax Returns	2	9	3	14	6	1
57	80	86	Other	7	7	7	11	17	44
225	229	276	**NUMBER OF STATEMENTS**	7	25	20	42	64	118
%	%	%	**ASSETS**	%	%	%	%	%	%
8.3	9.5	9.2	Cash & Equivalents		11.0	9.8	11.2	9.8	7.6
26.0	25.4	24.2	Trade Receivables (net)		18.5	22.8	28.3	27.9	22.6
6.6	6.9	7.4	Inventory		9.7	5.0	5.3	6.0	7.8
2.2	2.8	2.8	All Other Current		.4	10.0	2.5	1.9	2.7
43.1	44.6	43.6	Total Current		39.7	47.6	47.3	45.6	40.8
47.9	44.4	45.7	Fixed Assets (net)		51.0	45.8	41.3	44.9	47.3
2.6	3.3	4.0	Intangibles (net)		1.1	.9	3.3	3.5	5.8
6.4	7.7	6.7	All Other Non-Current		8.2	5.7	8.1	5.9	6.1
100.0	100.0	100.0	Total		100.0	100.0	100.0	100.0	100.0
			LIABILITIES						
4.3	5.5	5.6	Notes Payable-Short Term		9.7	7.8	7.9	6.4	3.1
5.9	5.9	5.3	Cur. Mat.-L.T.D.		5.4	4.4	4.2	5.4	5.7
14.7	13.7	14.2	Trade Payables		10.6	16.0	18.2	16.1	12.0
.2	.3	.2	Income Taxes Payable		.1	.0	.2	.4	.1
6.0	6.6	6.4	All Other Current		4.6	5.1	9.1	6.2	6.4
31.2	31.9	31.7	Total Current		30.4	33.4	39.7	34.5	27.3
22.4	21.9	23.2	Long-Term Debt		47.1	22.0	16.3	21.3	21.2
1.3	1.2	1.2	Deferred Taxes		.3	.1	.8	.9	1.8
4.0	3.2	3.2	All Other Non-Current		5.1	1.9	1.9	2.9	3.6
41.1	41.7	40.7	Net Worth		17.1	42.6	41.4	40.3	46.1
100.0	100.0	100.0	Total Liabilities & Net Worth		100.0	100.0	100.0	100.0	100.0
			INCOME DATA						
100.0	100.0	100.0	Net Sales		100.0	100.0	100.0	100.0	100.0
27.6	28.4	30.0	Gross Profit		40.7	33.2	30.2	29.1	27.2
23.7	23.9	25.1	Operating Expenses		38.0	30.9	27.1	24.2	19.8
3.9	4.5	4.9	Operating Profit		2.7	2.4	3.1	5.0	7.4
.4	.5	.5	All Other Expenses (net)		1.5	.2	-.1	.0	.7
3.5	3.9	4.4	Profit Before Taxes		1.2	2.1	3.1	5.0	6.7
			RATIOS						
2.3	2.4	2.2	Current		3.4	2.6	2.4	1.8	2.1
1.6	1.4	1.4			1.4	1.7	1.4	1.3	1.5
1.0	1.0	1.0			.6	1.0	.8	1.0	1.1
1.9	1.8	1.7	Quick		2.0	2.1	2.1	1.6	1.5
1.1	1.1	1.1			1.1	1.4	1.1	1.0	1.1
.7	.7	.7			.5	.4	.7	.7	.8
36 10.1	34 10.8	33 11.0	Sales/Receivables		21 17.3	24 15.0	30 12.1	33 11.0	35 10.5
43 8.4	44 8.4	43 8.5			34 10.7	36 10.1	44 8.3	44 8.3	43 8.4
57 6.4	56 6.5	54 6.7			57 6.4	58 6.3	60 6.1	52 7.0	53 6.9
5 74.3	5 72.6	6 63.8	Cost of Sales/Inventory		3 134.3	2 187.5	2 214.8	6 63.1	8 45.2
11 33.9	12 29.6	14 25.7			23 16.1	9 42.2	7 52.1	12 31.1	16 22.1
23 15.9	26 14.0	31 11.6			116 3.2	18 20.1	20 18.3	22 16.6	34 10.7
21 17.7	18 20.1	20 18.3	Cost of Sales/Payables		18 20.5	21 17.6	17 20.9	24 15.1	20 18.5
32 11.6	32 11.5	30 12.3			35 10.4	31 11.8	28 13.1	36 10.1	27 13.4
47 7.8	44 8.2	44 8.2			50 7.4	64 5.7	49 7.4	47 7.7	39 9.4
7.9	7.5	7.4	Sales/Working Capital		4.2	6.7	7.5	10.0	7.7
15.6	15.1	15.8			11.3	9.4	15.8	26.6	13.1
NM	UND	469.5			-12.1	NM	-37.9	NM	65.7
10.5	12.0	10.5	EBIT/Interest		2.6	10.9	10.2	13.6	12.9
(205) 4.5	(211) 4.5	(257) 3.9			(24) 1.6	(19) 4.8	(37) 3.9	(59) 3.8	(112) 5.7
1.8	1.5	1.6			.6	1.3	1.1	1.5	2.5
3.9	4.1	5.5	Net Profit + Depr., Dep., Amort./Cur. Mat. L/T/D				10.6	6.0	5.4
(69) 2.2	(78) 2.0	(82) 2.5					(10) 3.4	(19) 2.3	(48) 2.5
1.4	1.4	1.2					1.0	1.1	1.3
.7	.6	.7	Fixed/Worth		1.2	.6	.7	.7	.7
1.2	1.1	1.2			5.3	1.0	1.1	1.2	1.2
2.1	2.1	2.3			NM	2.7	1.9	2.1	2.1
.7	.7	.7	Debt/Worth		1.2	.5	.5	.8	.7
1.3	1.4	1.6			6.7	1.6	1.3	1.6	1.3
3.1	3.3	3.9			NM	4.5	4.8	3.3	2.9
32.3	35.9	41.2	% Profit Before Taxes/Tangible Net Worth		40.8	32.9	40.8	45.4	43.3
(203) 16.0	(213) 17.0	(252) 18.8			(19) 13.6	(19) 17.0	(35) 12.7	(60) 19.5	(114) 23.3
7.4	5.2	7.1			2.6	.6	4.6	5.5	11.8
12.6	14.1	14.9	% Profit Before Taxes/Total Assets		6.0	14.6	13.9	17.5	17.1
6.2	7.2	6.6			1.8	7.3	5.2	8.2	8.2
2.3	1.1	1.7			-1.6	-2.6	.4	1.4	4.0
6.9	7.7	6.9	Sales/Net Fixed Assets		5.7	8.8	8.3	7.2	5.8
4.3	4.6	4.4			3.1	4.5	5.2	4.7	3.8
2.6	3.0	2.8			1.6	2.5	3.7	3.4	2.6
2.7	2.5	2.5	Sales/Total Assets		2.3	2.6	3.1	2.7	2.2
2.0	2.0	2.0			1.7	2.0	2.3	2.2	1.8
1.5	1.5	1.4			1.0	1.4	1.8	1.6	1.3
3.1	2.7	3.1	% Depr., Dep., Amort./Sales		5.6	2.7	3.3	3.0	3.0
(210) 4.7	(203) 4.4	(245) 4.6			(23) 6.9	(15) 5.2	(40) 4.3	(57) 4.2	(103) 4.5
6.6	5.8	6.2			10.0	6.4	6.0	6.1	5.8
1.2	1.2	1.5	% Officers', Directors' Owners' Comp/Sales		2.2		1.1	1.3	1.0
(60) 2.3	(73) 2.8	(89) 3.2			(12) 4.5		(23) 2.5	(20) 3.4	(21) 1.8
4.1	6.0	5.8			5.5		5.7	6.3	5.0
7384450M	9368947M	11752949M	Net Sales ($)	4166M	53480M	81768M	315179M	978316M	10320040M
5104407M	5871456M	7375872M	Total Assets ($)	2776M	41643M	46820M	165746M	558221M	6560666M

M = $ thousand   MM = $ million
See Pages 11 through 21 for Explanation of Ratios and Data

Current Data Sorted by Assets / Comparative Historical Data

Type of Statement

Type of Statement	0-500M	500M-2MM	2-10MM	10-50MM	50-100MM	100-250MM	4/1/02-3/31/03 ALL	4/1/03-3/31/04 ALL
Unqualified		3	8	14	4	6	24	17
Reviewed		5	17	10			30	29
Compiled	1	3	8	1			11	14
Tax Returns		4	5				7	7
Other		5	19	16	2	5	26	43
		12 (4/1-9/30/06)		124 (10/1/06-3/31/07)				
NUMBER OF STATEMENTS	1	20	57	41	6	11	98	110

ASSETS (%)

	0-500M	500M-2MM	2-10MM	10-50MM	50-100MM	100-250MM	Hist 02-03	Hist 03-04
Cash & Equivalents		7.7	5.7	8.2		5.7	7.4	8.0
Trade Receivables (net)		22.4	20.1	16.4		13.5	19.9	19.4
Inventory		24.0	19.2	18.3		15.9	17.9	17.7
All Other Current		3.5	2.2	2.8		5.9	1.7	2.8
Total Current		57.6	47.1	45.6		41.0	46.9	47.9
Fixed Assets (net)		31.3	43.9	46.6		47.4	44.2	43.9
Intangibles (net)		2.8	1.6	3.2		5.8	2.3	1.9
All Other Non-Current		8.3	7.3	4.5		5.8	6.6	6.3
Total		100.0	100.0	100.0		100.0	100.0	100.0

LIABILITIES

	0-500M	500M-2MM	2-10MM	10-50MM	50-100MM	100-250MM	Hist 02-03	Hist 03-04
Notes Payable-Short Term		12.6	7.7	8.0		3.9	7.2	6.3
Cur. Mat.-L.T.D.		5.6	4.5	3.9		4.9	6.7	5.2
Trade Payables		13.5	11.6	8.6		6.9	11.1	11.6
Income Taxes Payable		.0	.1	.5		.2	.5	.2
All Other Current		9.5	6.9	7.5		6.0	5.8	7.9
Total Current		41.2	30.8	28.6		21.8	31.4	31.3
Long-Term Debt		27.8	22.5	22.0		21.4	24.1	25.0
Deferred Taxes		.1	.2	.7		1.2	1.0	1.0
All Other Non-Current		6.9	6.7	2.9		3.2	4.0	6.6
Net Worth		23.9	39.9	45.9		52.5	39.4	36.1
Total Liabilities & Net Worth		100.0	100.0	100.0		100.0	100.0	100.0

INCOME DATA

	0-500M	500M-2MM	2-10MM	10-50MM	50-100MM	100-250MM	Hist 02-03	Hist 03-04
Net Sales		100.0	100.0	100.0		100.0	100.0	100.0
Gross Profit		30.1	33.7	30.8		32.8	32.7	34.4
Operating Expenses		25.7	27.5	20.6		19.1	27.4	28.9
Operating Profit		4.4	6.2	10.3		13.7	5.4	5.5
All Other Expenses (net)		2.5	1.7	1.5		-.2	1.2	1.1
Profit Before Taxes		1.9	4.5	8.8		13.9	4.2	4.4

RATIOS

	0-500M	500M-2MM	2-10MM	10-50MM	50-100MM	100-250MM	Hist 02-03	Hist 03-04
Current		2.3	2.4	2.9		3.5	2.7	2.7
		1.4	1.6	1.8		1.8	1.6	1.6
		1.1	1.1	1.1		1.2	1.0	1.0
Quick		1.3	1.5	1.7		2.5	1.7	1.4
		.6	.8	1.0		.8	.8	.8
		.3	.3	.5		.6	.5	.5
Sales/Receivables		16 22.9	28 12.9	26 13.9		33 11.2	29 12.6	28 13.0
		35 10.5	39 9.3	34 10.7		36 10.2	39 9.3	39 9.4
		45 8.1	53 6.9	45 8.2		40 9.2	52 7.0	54 6.8
Cost of Sales/Inventory		16 22.8	31 11.8	41 9.0		51 7.1	28 13.1	31 11.6
		45 8.1	54 6.8	72 5.1		66 5.5	56 6.5	58 6.3
		91 4.0	98 3.7	102 3.6		75 4.9	89 4.1	92 4.0
Cost of Sales/Payables		11 33.0	18 20.5	21 17.2		22 16.7	17 21.3	18 20.0
		29 12.7	27 13.4	26 14.3		29 12.4	28 13.0	30 12.2
		44 8.2	52 7.1	34 10.8		32 11.4	43 8.6	46 7.9
Sales/Working Capital		8.9	6.5	5.3		3.6	5.7	5.3
		12.6	9.9	7.9		7.3	10.1	10.7
		61.0	85.0	36.5		22.9	-264.8	112.2
EBIT/Interest		20.3	13.2	19.9		18.7	9.2	8.3
		(19) 3.4	(52) 2.9	(40) 4.4		16.3	(93) 3.1	(96) 3.4
		.9	1.2	2.5		6.1	1.6	1.3
Net Profit + Depr., Dep., Amort./Cur. Mat. L/T/D			5.9	17.0			4.8	10.7
			(11) 2.0	(19) 4.6			(38) 2.3	(33) 2.6
			.1	2.6			1.4	1.3
Fixed/Worth		.4	.6	.6		.9	.6	.7
		.7	1.3	1.0		1.1	1.2	1.4
		2.6	3.2	2.2		1.7	2.2	3.1
Debt/Worth		.9	.5	.6		.4	.7	.8
		1.6	1.6	1.3		.9	1.6	1.8
		7.4	5.9	2.6		3.3	4.4	5.1
% Profit Before Taxes/Tangible Net Worth		64.3	38.5	33.3		50.1	32.8	45.6
		(17) 28.6	(50) 13.7	(40) 25.7		31.8	(89) 14.7	(96) 18.9
		3.1	7.5	12.8		25.3	4.3	5.5
% Profit Before Taxes/Total Assets		18.3	12.8	17.7		20.9	13.2	13.7
		6.1	5.4	9.6		17.0	5.6	6.2
		-1.5	1.2	4.6		12.1	1.7	.7
Sales/Net Fixed Assets		16.8	7.8	6.0		3.3	6.4	5.8
		7.5	3.7	3.1		2.9	3.8	3.8
		3.7	2.2	2.0		1.9	2.6	2.3
Sales/Total Assets		3.1	2.4	1.8		1.6	2.2	2.2
		2.2	1.7	1.5		1.4	1.7	1.7
		1.6	1.0	1.1		.9	1.3	1.2
% Depr., Dep., Amort./Sales		1.2	2.1	2.1			3.0	2.9
		(17) 2.9	(53) 3.6	(40) 4.1			(96) 4.2	(93) 4.7
		5.0	6.2	5.5			7.1	7.4
% Officers', Directors' Owners' Comp/Sales			2.0				1.7	2.0
			(17) 2.7				(33) 3.2	(30) 3.5
			4.2				6.2	5.9
Net Sales ($)	3753M	64776M	417450M	1464633M	531888M	2142993M	2500364M	3165747M
Total Assets ($)	488M	28171M	257154M	950713M	438884M	1592203M	1665301M	1987542M

M = $ thousand   MM = $ million
See Pages 11 through 21 for Explanation of Ratios and Data

Comparative Historical Data | Current Data Sorted by Sales

H: 4/1/04-3/31/05 ALL	H: 4/1/05-3/31/06 ALL	H: 4/1/06-3/31/07 ALL		0-1MM	1-3MM	3-5MM	5-10MM	10-25MM	25MM & OVER
			Type of Statement		12 (4/1-9/30/06)		124 (10/1/06-3/31/07)		
30	25	35	Unqualified		3	2	6	4	20
41	37	32	Reviewed		2	8	10	7	5
11	20	13	Compiled		2	1	8	2	8
4	6	9	Tax Returns		1	3	3	2	2
35	35	47	Other	2	5	5	5	8	18
121	123	136	**NUMBER OF STATEMENTS**	2	13	19	36	23	43
%	%	%	**ASSETS**	%	%	%	%	%	%
7.1	9.3	6.9	Cash & Equivalents		7.9	7.4	5.6	7.7	7.1
22.2	22.3	18.5	Trade Receivables (net)		14.3	22.2	20.4	16.3	18.1
20.5	18.2	19.3	Inventory		23.7	17.9	22.2	16.0	18.1
1.4	1.6	2.9	All Other Current		1.8	.7	4.2	3.1	3.2
51.2	51.3	47.6	Total Current		47.7	48.2	52.5	43.1	46.4
40.4	39.4	43.1	Fixed Assets (net)		45.2	40.2	38.6	47.9	44.4
2.5	2.6	2.9	Intangibles (net)		2.9	1.0	1.2	4.6	4.0
6.0	6.6	6.5	All Other Non-Current		4.2	10.7	7.8	4.3	5.3
100.0	100.0	100.0	Total		100.0	100.0	100.0	100.0	100.0
			LIABILITIES						
9.0	7.2	8.0	Notes Payable-Short Term		14.7	7.1	7.8	8.6	6.5
5.3	4.9	4.4	Cur. Mat.-L.T.D.		3.1	7.0	4.3	3.2	4.4
12.2	11.1	10.3	Trade Payables		10.0	11.1	13.2	9.4	8.5
.6	.4	.2	Income Taxes Payable		.0	.0	.1	.3	.5
6.7	6.9	7.3	All Other Current		12.3	7.4	6.6	6.2	7.2
33.8	30.5	30.2	Total Current		40.2	32.7	32.0	27.7	27.1
21.1	24.7	22.5	Long-Term Debt		37.9	29.2	17.3	20.8	18.9
.8	.6	.5	Deferred Taxes		.0	.3	.1	.7	1.0
4.0	3.8	5.3	All Other Non-Current		11.8	3.3	6.0	6.3	2.8
40.3	40.4	41.5	Net Worth		10.2	34.5	44.6	44.5	50.1
100.0	100.0	100.0	Total Liabilities & Net Worth		100.0	100.0	100.0	100.0	100.0
			INCOME DATA						
100.0	100.0	100.0	Net Sales		100.0	100.0	100.0	100.0	100.0
29.9	31.1	32.2	Gross Profit		31.0	31.0	32.2	33.2	30.3
23.2	23.7	24.1	Operating Expenses		26.2	28.7	26.6	23.0	19.6
6.7	7.4	8.1	Operating Profit		4.8	2.3	5.6	10.2	10.6
.7	1.4	1.5	All Other Expenses (net)		3.7	2.6	1.5	.8	.5
6.0	6.0	6.6	Profit Before Taxes		1.1	-.3	4.1	9.4	10.2
			RATIOS						
2.4	2.8	2.5			2.2	1.7	2.6	2.2	2.9
1.7	1.7	1.6	Current		1.4	1.4	1.9	1.9	1.8
1.1	1.2	1.1			.8	1.0	1.1	1.1	1.2
1.5	1.8	1.6			1.3	1.6	1.5	1.5	1.8
.9	1.1	.9	Quick		.4	.5	.9	1.0	1.0
.5	.5	.4			.2	.4	.3	.5	.7
29 12.6	27 13.4	27 13.4			20 18.5	29 12.8	20 17.9	26 14.2	32 11.5
39 9.4	39 9.4	37 9.9	Sales/Receivables		40 9.1	38 9.7	34 10.6	33 11.1	37 10.0
54 6.8	56 6.5	49 7.5			57 6.4	60 6.1	49 7.4	43 8.5	47 7.8
35 10.4	22 16.8	31 11.6			2 155.0	28 13.0	40 9.1	26 14.3	40 9.2
58 6.3	55 6.7	59 6.2	Cost of Sales/Inventory		75 4.9	46 8.0	59 6.2	54 6.8	66 5.5
91 4.0	92 4.0	97 3.8			191 1.9	98 3.7	98 3.7	87 4.2	82 4.5
23 15.9	18 20.8	20 18.6			14 25.5	20 18.3	15 25.1	21 17.8	20 17.9
33 11.0	27 13.5	27 13.5	Cost of Sales/Payables		43 8.5	39 9.3	24 15.1	26 14.2	26 13.8
45 8.0	45 8.2	43 8.5			100 3.6	55 6.6	37 9.9	43 8.5	33 11.0
6.1	5.1	5.9			5.2	6.5	6.7	5.1	5.8
8.8	7.8	10.4	Sales/Working Capital		11.7	12.7	8.7	10.7	7.9
38.7	28.8	40.0			-30.5	126.3	52.9	43.8	21.0
13.6	13.2	17.5			10.4	5.9	22.7	27.9	19.0
(111) 4.7	(111) 4.5	(128) 4.5	EBIT/Interest		1.2	(16) 1.8	(33) 4.1	(22) 9.2	9.1
1.9	1.6	1.6			-.4	-1.4	1.4	2.2	3.1
5.7	7.5	7.8							9.4
(40) 2.8	(42) 2.6	(37) 3.6	Net Profit + Depr., Dep., Amort./Cur. Mat. L/T/D					(19)	4.6
1.5	1.5	1.9							2.6
.6	.5	.6			.7	.5	.4	.7	.6
.9	.9	1.0	Fixed/Worth		1.2	.9	.7	1.5	1.0
2.0	2.2	2.3			NM	3.3	2.1	3.2	1.7
.7	.6	.6			1.1	.6	.4	.6	.5
1.3	1.4	1.4	Debt/Worth		2.7	1.6	1.6	1.7	1.0
3.3	3.9	3.2			NM	7.3	2.7	4.3	2.6
43.3	39.5	38.8			53.8	18.2	46.6	38.5	39.3
(109) 27.6	(111) 20.1	(124) 24.8	% Profit Before Taxes/Tangible Net Worth		(10) 14.7	(16) 11.1	(32) 16.5	(22) 25.7	(42) 27.9
8.6	8.7	10.2			-34.0	2.4	4.6	19.9	16.8
17.8	19.5	16.8			19.4	8.3	16.8	19.8	19.8
9.0	7.3	8.1	% Profit Before Taxes/Total Assets		1.1	3.1	6.9	9.6	13.2
2.7	2.0	3.0			-7.0	-4.2	1.4	6.0	6.0
8.6	8.3	7.2			8.4	6.9	13.8	6.5	5.2
4.2	4.6	3.6	Sales/Net Fixed Assets		2.2	4.0	5.5	3.6	3.2
2.8	2.4	2.2			1.5	2.1	2.7	2.2	2.5
2.3	2.3	2.2			2.2	2.2	3.1	2.2	1.8
1.7	1.6	1.6	Sales/Total Assets		1.2	1.5	2.0	1.5	1.5
1.3	1.2	1.1			.7	1.0	1.4	1.1	1.2
2.4	2.5	2.1			2.1	1.5	1.9	2.9	1.7
(109) 3.6	(111) 3.4	(122) 3.7	% Depr., Dep., Amort./Sales		(12) 3.4	(17) 4.7	(33) 3.2	(21) 4.3	(37) 3.3
6.3	5.6	5.7			12.6	5.6	5.7	5.5	5.6
1.8	1.8	2.1						2.1	
(35) 3.0	(38) 3.0	(28) 2.9	% Officers', Directors' Owners' Comp/Sales				(12)	3.2	
5.3	4.7	4.2						5.5	
3730008M	3744454M	4625493M	Net Sales ($)	1268M	24045M	71726M	262289M	355977M	3910188M
2320652M	2436910M	3267613M	Total Assets ($)	5261M	22206M	57888M	167742M	258941M	2755575M

M = $ thousand   MM = $ million
See Pages 11 through 21 for Explanation of Ratios and Data

	Current Data Sorted by Assets						Comparative Historical Data	
Type of Statement								
Unqualified				7		1	2	5
Reviewed		1	4	1				2
Compiled		1	4				2	1
Tax Returns			2				1	1
Other		2	5	3	3	1		3
		7 (4/1-9/30/06)		28 (10/1/06-3/31/07)			4/1/02-3/31/03	4/1/03-3/31/04
	0-500M	500M-2MM	2-10MM	10-50MM	50-100MM	100-250MM	ALL	ALL
NUMBER OF STATEMENTS		4	15	11	3	2	5	12
ASSETS	%	%	%	%	%	%	%	%
Cash & Equivalents	DATA NOT AVAILABLE		9.5	7.3				5.4
Trade Receivables (net)			26.1	27.4				26.9
Inventory			20.3	15.0				19.7
All Other Current			.8	3.9				.7
Total Current			56.8	53.6				52.7
Fixed Assets (net)			37.9	34.8				42.8
Intangibles (net)			3.9	6.7				1.6
All Other Non-Current			1.4	4.8				2.9
Total			100.0	100.0				100.0
LIABILITIES								
Notes Payable-Short Term			3.4	7.3				12.6
Cur. Mat.-L.T.D.			2.9	6.4				6.2
Trade Payables			11.6	11.9				12.3
Income Taxes Payable			.1	.6				.2
All Other Current			3.9	9.5				7.7
Total Current			21.9	35.8				39.0
Long-Term Debt			17.6	17.0				21.9
Deferred Taxes			1.0	.6				.3
All Other Non-Current			6.8	6.3				2.3
Net Worth			52.7	40.3				36.5
Total Liabilties & Net Worth			100.0	100.0				100.0
INCOME DATA								
Net Sales			100.0	100.0				100.0
Gross Profit			29.1	23.3				26.7
Operating Expenses			21.3	15.3				23.9
Operating Profit			7.8	7.9				2.9
All Other Expenses (net)			.8	1.1				1.3
Profit Before Taxes			7.0	6.9				1.6
RATIOS								
Current			4.8	2.8				2.1
			3.0	1.3				1.3
			2.6	1.1				1.2
Quick			2.7	1.5				1.2
			1.9	1.0				.8
			1.0	.6				.5
Sales/Receivables			**36** 10.1	**36** 10.2				**36** 10.3
			45 8.2	**56** 6.5				**52** 7.0
			66 5.5	**92** 4.0				**61** 5.9
Cost of Sales/Inventory			**27** 13.7	**17** 21.8				**32** 11.3
			36 10.0	**54** 6.8				**61** 6.0
			68 5.4	**71** 5.1				**86** 4.2
Cost of Sales/Payables			**17** 21.0	**17** 21.5				**15** 24.3
			23 15.8	**29** 12.8				**24** 15.4
			34 10.8	**42** 8.7				**45** 8.2
Sales/Working Capital			4.0	5.2				8.2
			5.0	14.7				11.5
			9.1	77.7				38.8
EBIT/Interest			51.7	10.1				4.8
			(14) 5.1	(10) 6.2				3.3
			2.1	2.0				1.6
Net Profit + Depr., Dep., Amort./Cur. Mat. L/T/D								
Fixed/Worth			.4	.4				.6
			.7	1.6				1.2
			1.6	2.3				3.6
Debt/Worth			.4	1.5				1.0
			.8	2.2				1.6
			2.4	5.5				5.0
% Profit Before Taxes/Tangible Net Worth			34.2	68.5				25.9
			(14) 28.8	(10) 24.8				14.8
			8.3	9.4				4.8
% Profit Before Taxes/Total Assets			20.5	20.5				7.5
			15.1	10.0				4.9
			4.0	2.9				1.7
Sales/Net Fixed Assets			7.8	15.1				8.6
			5.2	5.1				4.2
			3.3	2.0				2.6
Sales/Total Assets			2.4	2.2				1.9
			2.0	1.7				1.7
			1.6	1.2				1.3
% Depr., Dep., Amort./Sales			1.0	.5				1.9
			3.7	2.8				4.8
			4.8	5.0				7.4
% Officers', Directors' Owners' Comp/Sales			.9					
			(12) 3.4					
			6.8					
Net Sales ($)		16639M	118588M	436606M	284712M	531454M	54871M	223560M
Total Assets ($)		5072M	60564M	251145M	209021M	345496M	42999M	148049M

M = $ thousand MM = $ million

See Pages 11 through 21 for Explanation of Ratios and Data

Comparative Historical Data   Current Data Sorted by Sales

4/1/04-3/31/05 ALL	4/1/05-3/31/06 ALL	4/1/06-3/31/07 ALL	Type of Statement	0-1MM	1-3MM	3-5MM	5-10MM	10-25MM	25MM & OVER
5	6	8	Unqualified		1	1	2	2	6
3	3	6	Reviewed				3	1	1
	1	5	Compiled				1	2	
2	1	2	Tax Returns		1				
3	2	14	Other	1			5	2	6
				1	7 (4/1-9/30/06)		28 (10/1/06-3/31/07)		
13	13	35	NUMBER OF STATEMENTS		2		11	7	13
%	%	%	**ASSETS**	%	%	%	%	%	%
5.2	4.3	7.3	Cash & Equivalents				10.9		7.2
27.6	20.8	26.4	Trade Receivables (net)				30.3		24.5
20.6	14.5	17.2	Inventory				22.9		14.9
1.1	2.8	2.2	All Other Current				.5		3.8
54.4	42.3	53.1	Total Current		DATA		64.7		50.4
37.4	47.6	38.9	Fixed Assets (net)		NOT		28.3		40.8
2.4	3.5	4.8	Intangibles (net)		AVAILABLE		5.9		4.0
5.8	6.6	3.2	All Other Non-Current				1.0		4.8
100.0	100.0	100.0	Total				100.0		100.0
			LIABILITIES						
9.6	4.3	6.1	Notes Payable-Short Term				9.1		6.0
5.5	6.0	4.5	Cur. Mat.-L.T.D.				2.1		5.6
13.3	8.0	11.4	Trade Payables				14.2		11.2
.0	.0	.3	Income Taxes Payable				.1		.2
5.8	9.4	7.2	All Other Current				5.2		8.7
34.3	27.7	29.4	Total Current				30.7		31.7
28.5	23.4	18.3	Long-Term Debt				12.3		19.0
.7	1.8	.8	Deferred Taxes				.7		.7
4.4	3.2	7.3	All Other Non-Current				5.8		6.3
32.1	43.8	44.2	Net Worth				50.4		42.3
100.0	100.0	100.0	Total Liabilties & Net Worth				100.0		100.0
			INCOME DATA						
100.0	100.0	100.0	Net Sales				100.0		100.0
27.5	25.8	25.2	Gross Profit				31.6		24.3
22.8	20.5	17.5	Operating Expenses				23.3		14.8
4.7	5.3	7.7	Operating Profit				8.2		9.5
1.2	1.7	1.2	All Other Expenses (net)				1.2		1.1
3.5	3.5	6.5	Profit Before Taxes				7.1		8.4
			RATIOS						
2.8	2.6	3.1	Current				3.2		2.4
1.9	2.1	1.8					2.9		1.4
1.0	1.0	1.2					1.6		1.3
1.3	1.4	2.0	Quick				2.7		1.5
1.0	1.1	1.0					1.7		1.0
.7	.6	.8					.8		.5
36 10.3	20 18.6	36 10.2	Sales/Receivables				36 10.2		34 10.6
47 7.7	40 9.1	43 8.4					41 8.8		43 8.5
66 5.5	61 6.0	66 5.5					64 5.7		62 5.9
21 17.8	4 97.9	18 19.8	Cost of Sales/Inventory				26 14.1		14 25.3
64 5.7	41 8.9	36 10.0					35 10.3		43 8.4
101 3.6	70 5.2	68 5.4					68 5.4		71 5.2
21 17.1	11 34.2	17 21.5	Cost of Sales/Payables				15 24.2		18 20.3
31 11.9	21 17.8	23 15.8					26 13.8		25 14.3
52 7.0	32 11.3	34 10.7					34 10.7		42 8.6
4.5	5.6	4.8	Sales/Working Capital				4.0		5.9
8.5	9.6	9.1					7.2		10.5
125.0	NM	19.3					12.7		17.2
8.0	6.1	15.9	EBIT/Interest				61.2		15.4
2.6	(11) 5.1	(33) 5.0					15.4		(12) 7.5
.9	1.4	1.5					-.2		2.4
		6.4	Net Profit + Depr., Dep., Amort./Cur. Mat. L/T/D						
		(15) 4.2							
		1.4							
.4	.5	.5	Fixed/Worth				.3		.5
1.5	1.3	1.1					.5		1.1
3.4	4.2	2.2					1.6		2.4
.9	.5	.6	Debt/Worth				.4		.7
2.5	1.3	1.7					1.0		2.0
9.0	7.9	5.2					2.4		6.7
39.3	16.5	31.8	% Profit Before Taxes/Tangible Net Worth				39.9		96.0
(11) 16.0	(11) 7.0	(32) 24.4					(10) 31.1		(12) 25.1
-.8	-1.6	8.7					-11.5		18.7
13.0	11.6	20.0	% Profit Before Taxes/Total Assets				29.7		21.3
5.4	3.3	9.4					15.1		11.2
-.1	-.3	2.0					-3.5		6.7
10.0	7.9	9.5	Sales/Net Fixed Assets				27.2		8.0
5.6	4.5	5.1					7.8		4.1
2.6	2.1	2.8					3.4		2.2
2.0	2.5	2.3	Sales/Total Assets				2.8		2.2
1.8	1.9	1.9					2.1		1.7
1.4	1.1	1.4					1.6		1.3
1.9	2.9	1.3	% Depr., Dep., Amort./Sales				.9		.5
(12) 4.5	(12) 4.4	(32) 3.4					(10) 2.9		(11) 2.8
5.3	6.9	4.8					4.0		5.2
		.7	% Officers', Directors', Owners' Comp/Sales						
		(17) 2.6							
		5.1							
255746M	658416M	1387999M	Net Sales ($)	4318M	7834M		73436M	104641M	1197770M
177015M	365694M	871298M	Total Assets ($)	2002M	5053M		34165M	82606M	747472M

© RMA 2007

M = $ thousand   MM = $ million
See Pages 11 through 21 for Explanation of Ratios and Data

Current Data Sorted by Assets

Comparative Historical Data

Type of Statement

	0-500M	500M-2MM	2-10MM	10-50MM	50-100MM	100-250MM		4/1/02-3/31/03 ALL	4/1/03-3/31/04 ALL
Unqualified		2	7	12	9	5		32	37
Reviewed		6	22	9	1			49	40
Compiled		11	16	1	1			18	40
Tax Returns	8	14	3					11	14
Other	5	5	18	12		3		41	34
		22 (4/1-9/30/06)		148 (10/1/06-3/31/07)					
NUMBER OF STATEMENTS	13	38	66	34	11	8		151	165

0-500M	500M-2MM	2-10MM	10-50MM	50-100MM	100-250MM		4/1/02-3/31/03 ALL	4/1/03-3/31/04 ALL
%	%	%	%	%	%	**ASSETS**	%	%
12.1	9.3	8.5	9.1	2.4		Cash & Equivalents	7.2	8.1
15.6	27.4	28.8	28.8	27.8		Trade Receivables (net)	28.9	29.2
31.5	14.9	16.2	14.2	15.4		Inventory	13.3	14.5
.4	1.2	2.6	5.4	3.6		All Other Current	3.8	3.3
59.6	52.8	56.2	57.5	49.2		Total Current	53.2	55.2
33.8	30.4	35.9	32.4	39.5		Fixed Assets (net)	38.8	36.4
4.8	5.6	1.5	4.5	1.3		Intangibles (net)	2.0	1.8
1.8	11.2	6.4	5.7	10.0		All Other Non-Current	6.0	6.6
100.0	100.0	100.0	100.0	100.0		Total	100.0	100.0
						LIABILITIES		
2.3	8.0	5.7	7.1	4.2		Notes Payable-Short Term	7.3	6.7
3.7	6.0	4.5	3.4	3.0		Cur. Mat.-L.T.D.	4.8	4.6
8.9	14.6	13.0	12.4	9.2		Trade Payables	14.2	14.1
.0	.1	.3	.9	.0		Income Taxes Payable	.3	.3
7.7	5.7	7.9	11.3	8.8		All Other Current	9.5	8.0
22.6	34.5	31.4	35.1	25.2		Total Current	36.0	33.5
42.7	32.0	19.4	15.4	23.9		Long-Term Debt	22.4	19.6
.0	.5	.4	1.7	.8		Deferred Taxes	.3	.7
3.0	8.0	2.5	3.7	8.7		All Other Non-Current	3.8	4.3
31.7	25.0	46.3	44.1	41.4		Net Worth	37.4	41.9
100.0	100.0	100.0	100.0	100.0		Total Liabilities & Net Worth	100.0	100.0
						INCOME DATA		
100.0	100.0	100.0	100.0	100.0		Net Sales	100.0	100.0
44.1	41.6	32.9	27.4	27.1		Gross Profit	31.0	31.5
37.5	35.9	26.2	19.1	17.0		Operating Expenses	25.9	26.6
6.5	5.6	6.7	8.3	10.2		Operating Profit	5.2	4.9
.8	2.1	.8	.4	1.1		All Other Expenses (net)	.9	1.1
5.7	3.5	5.9	7.8	9.1		Profit Before Taxes	4.2	3.8
						RATIOS		
6.3	3.9	3.3	2.6	2.2			2.6	2.6
2.9	1.9	1.7	1.7	2.0		Current	1.7	1.7
1.7	1.1	1.1	1.2	1.5			1.1	1.2
3.5	3.0	2.0	1.7	1.7			1.7	1.8
1.1	1.2	1.2	1.2	1.1		Quick	1.1	1.2
.5	.6	.8	.7	.7			.6	.7
0 UND	33 11.2	38 9.7	40 9.2	46 8.0			33 11.0	39 9.3
13 28.8	42 8.7	48 7.6	57 6.4	61 6.0		Sales/Receivables	52 7.1	56 6.6
30 12.3	56 6.5	73 5.0	83 4.4	92 4.0			76 4.8	74 4.9
0 UND	8 43.3	12 29.2	13 27.5	41 8.9			12 29.9	15 25.1
68 5.4	33 11.0	36 10.1	31 11.7	58 6.3		Cost of Sales/Inventory	33 11.2	37 9.9
105 3.5	62 5.9	82 4.5	56 6.6	82 4.4			68 5.3	69 5.3
0 UND	19 19.3	16 22.5	15 24.6	25 14.5			17 20.9	19 19.5
10 35.6	33 11.2	30 12.2	34 10.8	29 12.8		Cost of Sales/Payables	29 12.4	32 11.3
34 10.8	54 6.7	46 7.9	50 7.3	33 11.2			49 7.5	50 7.3
4.9	5.3	4.4	5.0	4.6			5.3	5.3
10.4	10.3	10.8	8.5	6.3		Sales/Working Capital	9.5	8.1
73.8	NM	44.2	31.6	11.4			46.1	21.3
	7.5	10.2	15.9	17.1			10.0	13.1
	(36) 1.7	(59) 4.8	(30) 7.3	(10) 5.8		EBIT/Interest	(133) 3.5	(155) 4.2
	.9	1.8	3.4	3.4			1.4	1.0
		12.5	10.9				4.7	4.2
		(19) 2.3	(11) 5.8			Net Profit + Depr., Dep., Amort./Cur. Mat. L/T/D	(52) 2.5	(50) 1.8
		1.2	3.8				1.4	.8
.1	.4	.4	.4	.6			.5	.4
1.1	1.7	.8	.8	1.0		Fixed/Worth	.9	.9
-4.0	-33.0	1.6	2.0	1.8			1.8	2.1
.2	.9	.7	.9	.8			.6	.6
1.8	3.2	1.3	1.2	1.8		Debt/Worth	1.4	1.4
-3.8	-54.5	2.2	4.6	2.4			3.0	3.3
	49.1	49.5	72.4	49.3			38.8	37.1
	(27) 17.3	(64) 26.4	(32) 33.0	34.5		% Profit Before Taxes/Tangible Net Worth	(140) 20.2	(149) 17.5
	5.2	7.4	15.8	19.0			7.2	4.1
45.4	11.1	18.6	28.8	14.6			14.6	14.3
24.2	4.0	11.4	13.7	11.3		% Profit Before Taxes/Total Assets	7.3	5.8
13.0	-.2	2.2	5.8	6.6			1.5	.1
UND	16.4	11.2	11.1	6.0			8.5	11.0
19.5	7.0	5.3	5.7	4.6		Sales/Net Fixed Assets	4.9	5.4
7.3	4.2	3.6	4.0	2.2			3.0	3.2
6.9	2.9	2.5	2.3	1.9			2.4	2.4
3.5	2.0	1.9	1.8	1.4		Sales/Total Assets	1.9	1.9
2.5	1.5	1.4	1.3	1.0			1.4	1.3
	2.6	2.1	1.3				2.1	2.2
	(33) 4.6	(59) 3.1	(31) 2.4			% Depr., Dep., Amort./Sales	(139) 3.5	(148) 3.5
	7.2	4.6	3.7				5.4	5.4
3.1	2.1	1.5					1.6	2.0
(10) 4.0	(22) 4.0	(23) 2.6				% Officers', Directors', Owners' Comp/Sales	(56) 3.2	(60) 3.5
6.0	8.4	3.7					7.0	6.9
12765M	96500M	665783M	1424486M	1276321M	2302258M	Net Sales ($)	3074844M	4649120M
3095M	48004M	346820M	705848M	864013M	1374739M	Total Assets ($)	1817536M	2826868M

M = $ thousand   MM = $ million
See Pages 11 through 21 for Explanation of Ratios and Data

Comparative Historical Data | Current Data Sorted by Sales

4/1/04-3/31/05 ALL	4/1/05-3/31/06 ALL	4/1/06-3/31/07 ALL	Type of Statement	0-1MM	1-3MM	3-5MM	5-10MM	10-25MM	25MM & OVER
39	34	35	Unqualified		2		2	9	22
39	31	37	Reviewed		4	4	8	14	7
25	27	29	Compiled		10	7	4	7	1
13	11	25	Tax Returns	5	13	5	2		
42	68	44	Other	4	7	2	8	12	11
158	171	170	**NUMBER OF STATEMENTS**	9	36	18	24	42	41
%	%	%	**ASSETS**	%	%	%	%	%	%
6.8	8.7	8.6	Cash & Equivalents	8.9	9.0	8.7	6.7		8.2
29.0	30.3	27.3	Trade Receivables (net)	22.3	25.4	34.0	27.2		30.8
15.0	15.8	16.3	Inventory	17.2	21.8	14.7	14.9		13.7
3.0	2.5	2.9	All Other Current	1.1	.5	2.0	3.5		6.1
53.9	57.3	55.1	Total Current	49.5	56.8	59.4	52.3		58.8
36.9	32.9	34.2	Fixed Assets (net)	33.7	30.5	33.1	38.3		31.8
3.2	3.1	3.3	Intangibles (net)	5.5	4.8	2.3	2.2		2.6
6.1	6.7	7.4	All Other Non-Current	11.2	8.0	5.2	7.1		6.8
100.0	100.0	100.0	Total	100.0	100.0	100.0	100.0		100.0
			LIABILITIES						
8.9	6.5	5.9	Notes Payable-Short Term	8.1	4.3	5.4	6.5		5.0
5.0	4.6	4.3	Cur. Mat.-L.T.D.	5.2	7.1	3.0	5.6		2.4
13.8	15.2	12.4	Trade Payables	10.9	11.1	16.4	12.6		11.0
.4	.4	.3	Income Taxes Payable	.1	.0	.5	.3		.6
7.7	8.5	8.5	All Other Current	4.7	10.1	9.1	6.2		12.7
35.8	35.2	31.5	Total Current	29.1	32.5	34.5	31.1		31.8
21.1	20.2	23.6	Long-Term Debt	31.5	26.3	16.7	20.4		16.3
.7	.6	.7	Deferred Taxes	.5	.1	.4	1.6		.5
7.2	5.5	4.8	All Other Non-Current	8.5	3.6	1.0	3.1		6.4
35.1	38.4	39.5	Net Worth	30.4	37.5	47.5	43.7		45.1
100.0	100.0	100.0	Total Liabilities & Net Worth	100.0	100.0	100.0	100.0		100.0
			INCOME DATA						
100.0	100.0	100.0	Net Sales	100.0	100.0	100.0	100.0		100.0
30.2	32.3	33.7	Gross Profit	43.7	41.4	32.1	31.6		25.3
24.9	25.7	26.4	Operating Expenses	37.0	38.1	24.3	24.4		14.4
5.3	6.6	7.3	Operating Profit	6.8	3.3	7.8	7.2		10.9
1.0	.9	1.1	All Other Expenses (net)	2.4	-.1	.7	1.0		.4
4.3	5.7	6.2	Profit Before Taxes	4.3	3.5	7.1	6.2		10.4
			RATIOS						
2.5	2.8	3.3	Current	4.0	4.0	3.5	2.8		2.6
1.7	1.7	1.9		1.9	2.1	2.1	1.5		1.9
1.2	1.2	1.2		1.1	.9	1.1	1.1		1.4
1.6	1.9	2.0	Quick	3.5	2.7	1.9	1.7		1.8
(157) 1.1	1.2	1.1		1.1	1.2	1.5	1.0		1.2
.7	.8	.7		.6	.5	.8	.8		.8
39 9.3	35 10.5	34 10.8	Sales/Receivables	18 19.9	36 10.2	40 9.0	32 11.3	44 8.4	
56 6.5	49 7.5	46 7.9		39 9.4	45 8.2	54 6.7	46 7.9	63 5.8	
72 5.1	72 5.1	71 5.1		51 7.1	60 6.1	80 4.5	58 6.2	83 4.4	
15 24.2	12 29.8	11 32.2	Cost of Sales/Inventory	8 44.6	35 10.4	10 36.5	11 33.3	13 27.7	
39 9.5	32 11.4	38 9.7		44 8.4	58 6.3	28 12.8	34 10.9	30 12.3	
67 5.5	60 6.1	74 5.0		99 3.7	113 3.2	66 5.5	71 5.1	54 6.8	
20 18.5	17 20.9	17 21.9	Cost of Sales/Payables	11 32.7	18 20.7	24 15.2	15 24.9	17 21.1	
33 11.0	32 11.3	29 12.8		30 12.2	27 13.3	31 11.9	30 12.0	25 14.5	
50 7.3	50 7.3	46 7.9		49 7.4	52 7.0	54 6.8	47 7.8	41 8.9	
5.2	5.0	4.8	Sales/Working Capital	5.1	6.3	4.0	4.8		5.1
8.6	9.6	9.0		11.8	7.9	7.3	11.9		7.1
24.0	22.0	31.7		38.6	-54.4	65.7	47.3		12.4
10.4	14.8	10.6	EBIT/Interest	8.0	7.8	19.4	9.5		17.9
(145) 4.5	(157) 5.9	(150) 4.9		(33) 2.7	(15) 1.6	7.4	(37) 3.8	(36) 7.8	
1.5	2.4	1.7		.6	1.0	3.4	1.9		4.7
3.8	5.9	11.1	Net Profit + Depr., Dep., Amort./Cur. Mat. L/T/D					8.6	13.5
(48) 2.0	(53) 3.5	(41) 3.9						(13) 2.7	(15) 6.4
1.3	1.6	1.6						1.2	3.8
.5	.4	.4	Fixed/Worth	.4	.4	.3	.6		.4
1.0	.8	.9		1.4	1.1	.8	.9		.8
2.2	1.7	2.1		-17.8	3.1	1.5	1.5		1.5
.8	.8	.8	Debt/Worth	.6	.8	.6	.8		.7
1.6	1.4	1.5		2.7	2.4	1.2	1.3		1.3
3.7	3.7	4.0		-35.6	10.1	2.5	2.4		2.5
34.9	46.6	54.5	% Profit Before Taxes/Tangible Net Worth	69.1	40.5	52.5	39.7		75.8
(135) 15.5	(151) 25.6	(149) 28.3		(25) 24.4	(17) 16.5	34.3	(39) 20.0	(40) 37.9	
4.7	9.8	9.8		3.4	-5.6	13.5	8.6		20.5
13.7	20.1	21.8	% Profit Before Taxes/Total Assets	23.1	10.2	23.5	18.1		30.9
6.0	10.1	11.4		6.0	5.0	14.2	12.5		14.6
1.7	3.2	2.7		-.1	-.7	4.8	2.4		10.8
9.9	12.3	12.6	Sales/Net Fixed Assets	17.4	17.4	13.4	8.3		10.8
5.5	6.9	6.1		7.0	6.9	6.5	5.2		5.5
3.2	4.3	3.7		3.6	4.2	4.1	3.8		3.5
2.4	2.7	2.6	Sales/Total Assets	3.0	2.5	2.9	2.5		2.4
1.8	2.1	1.9		2.1	1.8	2.2	1.8		1.8
1.3	1.6	1.4		1.4	1.3	1.5	1.6		1.4
2.1	1.6	1.9	% Depr., Dep., Amort./Sales	2.2	2.6	1.3	2.1		1.4
(138) 3.4	(156) 2.7	(146) 3.1		(32) 4.5	(15) 4.7	(23) 3.6	(36) 3.1	(36) 2.5	
5.4	4.5	4.9		7.3	6.9	4.6	4.2		3.5
1.5	1.6	1.6	% Officers', Directors' Owners' Comp/Sales	2.4	1.6	1.3			
(60) 2.9	(65) 3.4	(62) 2.9		(22) 4.0	(11) 2.2	(10) 2.3			
5.4	6.5	5.3		6.2	10.6	3.2			
5853462M	4978457M	5778113M	Net Sales ($)	4788M	73343M	66644M	178882M	651650M	4802806M
3176797M	2675627M	3342519M	Total Assets ($)	6289M	42941M	43595M	101557M	361059M	2787078M

Current Data groupings: **22 (4/1-9/30/06)** and **148 (10/1/06-3/31/07)**

M = $ thousand   MM = $ million
See Pages 11 through 21 for Explanation of Ratios and Data

Current Data Sorted by Assets

Comparative Historical Data

						Type of Statement		
		6	2	1	1	Unqualified	8	11
4		10	2			Reviewed	16	15
2		4				Compiled	3	5
						Tax Returns	1	2
5		8	7	1	1	Other	7	9
	11 (4/1-9/30/06)		43 (10/1/06-3/31/07)				4/1/02-3/31/03	4/1/03-3/31/04
0-500M	500M-2MM	2-10MM	10-50MM	50-100MM	100-250MM		ALL	ALL
	11	28	11	2	2	NUMBER OF STATEMENTS	35	42
%	%	%	%	%	%	ASSETS	%	%
	4.4	5.6	9.6			Cash & Equivalents	5.9	7.0
	28.0	25.2	24.1			Trade Receivables (net)	24.7	28.5
	33.1	34.6	32.1			Inventory	24.7	27.2
	1.3	1.3	1.1			All Other Current	4.7	1.9
	66.8	66.7	66.8			Total Current	60.1	64.6
	27.2	26.4	27.9			Fixed Assets (net)	27.9	25.2
	.0	.8	2.5			Intangibles (net)	4.6	4.0
	5.9	6.1	2.8			All Other Non-Current	7.4	6.2
	100.0	100.0	100.0			Total	100.0	100.0
						LIABILITIES		
	15.9	13.4	10.5			Notes Payable-Short Term	11.2	12.9
	2.7	3.7	1.3			Cur. Mat.-L.T.D.	7.4	5.6
	27.4	15.7	12.4			Trade Payables	14.2	17.6
	.2	.4	.3			Income Taxes Payable	.3	.5
	7.9	6.4	7.3			All Other Current	6.0	7.2
	54.1	39.5	31.9			Total Current	39.1	43.7
	11.7	15.2	10.1			Long-Term Debt	15.6	10.5
	.1	.3	.3			Deferred Taxes	.4	.5
	6.0	4.0	2.6			All Other Non-Current	2.4	6.3
	28.0	41.1	55.1			Net Worth	42.4	39.0
	100.0	100.0	100.0			Total Liabilties & Net Worth	100.0	100.0
						INCOME DATA		
	100.0	100.0	100.0			Net Sales	100.0	100.0
	24.7	30.1	26.5			Gross Profit	30.5	28.8
	23.0	23.3	18.7			Operating Expenses	24.9	24.1
	1.7	6.8	7.8			Operating Profit	5.6	4.7
	1.1	1.6	.1			All Other Expenses (net)	1.6	.9
	.5	5.2	7.8			Profit Before Taxes	4.0	3.7
						RATIOS		
	1.9	2.4	4.2				2.9	3.2
	1.2	1.8	3.1			Current	1.6	1.5
	.8	1.1	1.5				1.0	1.1
	1.1	1.2	2.3				1.7	1.6
	.6	.7	1.5			Quick	.9	.9
	.5	.5	.5				.5	.5
34	10.8	35	10.5	32	11.3	Sales/Receivables	35	10.5	38	9.7
41	9.0	41	9.0	40	9.1		46	7.9	50	7.3
56	6.5	51	7.2	61	6.0		59	6.2	59	6.2
37	9.7	54	6.7	69	5.3	Cost of Sales/Inventory	39	9.4	49	7.4
67	5.4	67	5.4	82	4.4		68	5.3	70	5.2
115	3.2	83	4.4	99	3.7		84	4.4	92	4.0
31	11.8	18	20.8	14	26.0	Cost of Sales/Payables	15	24.0	20	18.6
43	8.4	32	11.3	26	13.9		27	13.6	36	10.2
58	6.3	50	7.3	41	8.9		46	8.0	53	6.9
	6.1	5.1	2.6			Sales/Working Capital	4.4	4.6
	34.1	8.2	5.6				7.8	10.2
	-31.3	39.9	7.3				148.9	42.0
	8.1	17.8	279.8			EBIT/Interest	10.1	13.4
	2.6	(26) 5.9	(10) 10.2				(41) 2.9	6.1
	1.2	1.6	3.7				1.3	1.5
						Net Profit + Depr., Dep., Amort./Cur. Mat. L/T/D	5.5	4.5
							(11) 2.2	(16) 1.3
							1.3	.4
	.3	.2	.2			Fixed/Worth	.4	.3
	1.0	.5	.6				.8	.6
	2.4	1.7	.8				2.0	1.8
	1.2	.7	.3			Debt/Worth	.6	.5
	2.1	1.5	.9				1.3	1.8
	9.1	4.0	1.7				5.0	8.2
	68.1	45.6	33.4			% Profit Before Taxes/Tangible Net Worth	32.3	35.5
	(10) 22.3	(25) 22.2	24.9				(33) 20.9	(38) 21.5
	5.5	10.8	12.2				1.7	4.7
	21.4	17.2	25.3			% Profit Before Taxes/Total Assets	10.6	14.1
	3.6	11.1	8.9				6.3	4.9
	.4	1.7	3.6				.8	1.0
	31.1	18.8	14.6			Sales/Net Fixed Assets	9.7	12.6
	14.1	9.5	8.1				6.8	7.5
	3.7	5.2	4.6				4.5	5.4
	3.2	2.9	2.2			Sales/Total Assets	2.3	2.3
	2.4	2.1	1.8				1.8	1.9
	1.7	1.8	1.5				1.4	1.4
		.9	1.5			% Depr., Dep., Amort./Sales	2.0	1.6
	(26)	1.7	2.2				(33) 2.9	(41) 2.4
		3.5	3.2				4.2	3.6
		1.2				% Officers', Directors' Owners' Comp/Sales	2.0	2.6
	(11)	2.6					(12) 3.6	(10) 4.6
		8.9					4.9	8.7
	35089M	315978M	485488M	175862M	438776M	Net Sales ($)	635832M	847687M
	14828M	137493M	270106M	116720M	303937M	Total Assets ($)	492525M	589385M

M = $ thousand   MM = $ million
See Pages 11 through 21 for Explanation of Ratios and Data

Comparative Historical Data   Current Data Sorted by Sales

Type of Statement	4/1/04-3/31/05 ALL	4/1/05-3/31/06 ALL	4/1/06-3/31/07 ALL	0-1MM	1-3MM	3-5MM	5-10MM	10-25MM	25MM & OVER
Unqualified	13	10	10				1	3	6
Reviewed	14	16	16		3	1	5	5	2
Compiled	9	8	6		2	2			2
Tax Returns	1		2						
Other	15	14	22		1	6	3	4	8
					11 (4/1-9/30/06)		43 (10/1/06-3/31/07)		
NUMBER OF STATEMENTS	52	50	54		6	9	9	14	16
ASSETS	%	%	%	%	%	%	%	%	%
Cash & Equivalents	7.5	9.6	7.0					5.3	11.8
Trade Receivables (net)	25.5	25.8	24.9					26.5	23.6
Inventory	25.7	29.9	32.3					41.4	29.2
All Other Current	2.6	2.0	1.4					1.4	1.4
Total Current	61.3	67.3	65.6					74.6	66.0
Fixed Assets (net)	28.9	25.5	27.1					23.2	25.5
Intangibles (net)	2.7	1.6	1.2					.1	2.5
All Other Non-Current	7.1	5.6	6.2					2.2	5.9
Total	100.0	100.0	100.0					100.0	100.0
LIABILITIES									
Notes Payable-Short Term	9.6	11.6	12.3					12.2	8.2
Cur. Mat.-L.T.D.	5.6	3.4	2.8					3.2	1.2
Trade Payables	13.8	15.0	17.1					17.2	13.5
Income Taxes Payable	1.1	1.0	.3					.1	.3
All Other Current	6.9	6.7	7.0					6.1	7.9
Total Current	37.0	37.6	39.6					38.7	31.1
Long-Term Debt	18.8	12.5	13.9					13.3	12.4
Deferred Taxes	.4	.3	.3					.2	.8
All Other Non-Current	4.4	6.3	4.6					1.7	4.7
Net Worth	39.5	43.2	41.6					46.1	51.0
Total Liabilities & Net Worth	100.0	100.0	100.0					100.0	100.0
INCOME DATA									
Net Sales	100.0	100.0	100.0					100.0	100.0
Gross Profit	30.9	31.1	28.1					28.9	25.4
Operating Expenses	23.6	24.5	21.9					20.8	18.2
Operating Profit	7.3	6.6	6.2					8.1	7.3
All Other Expenses (net)	.9	1.4	.8					.6	-.7
Profit Before Taxes	6.4	5.2	5.4					7.5	8.0
RATIOS									
Current	2.6	3.2	2.9					2.4	3.6
	1.9	1.7	1.8					2.2	2.5
	1.2	1.2	1.2					1.5	1.7
Quick	1.5	1.6	1.6					1.4	1.8
	.9	1.0	.9					.8	1.5
	.6	.5	.5					.5	1.0
Sales/Receivables	34 10.7	36 10.2	34 10.9					38 9.6	33 11.2
	47 7.7	45 8.1	41 9.0					43 8.4	39 9.3
	58 6.3	57 6.4	53 6.9					51 7.2	53 6.8
Cost of Sales/Inventory	48 7.6	47 7.7	55 6.6					58 6.3	47 7.7
	71 5.2	83 4.4	68 5.3					68 5.4	76 4.8
	105 3.5	126 2.9	91 4.0					110 3.3	96 3.8
Cost of Sales/Payables	18 19.9	13 28.0	18 19.7					27 13.7	16 23.4
	35 10.5	33 10.9	33 11.1					37 10.0	30 12.2
	48 7.6	49 7.5	50 7.2					50 7.3	44 8.3
Sales/Working Capital	4.7	3.8	5.0					4.2	4.2
	6.8	6.3	7.1					7.1	5.7
	20.7	20.6	36.2					9.6	7.1
EBIT/Interest	19.3	25.0	20.3					45.5	39.7
	(49) 7.0	(48) 6.1	(51) 5.9					(13) 9.3	(15) 11.1
	2.7	1.2	1.9					1.6	4.4
Net Profit + Depr., Dep., Amort./Cur. Mat. L/T/D	8.0	9.8	5.5						
	(15) 4.7	(13) 6.2	(15) 3.1						
	.8	2.0	1.2						
Fixed/Worth	.3	.2	.3					.2	.2
	.7	.6	.6					.4	.5
	2.1	1.1	1.4					1.2	.7
Debt/Worth	.6	.4	.5					.7	.3
	1.7	1.6	1.4					1.5	.9
	5.2	2.8	3.2					2.3	1.7
% Profit Before Taxes/Tangible Net Worth	63.9	39.8	39.2					51.6	38.7
	(48) 28.6	(47) 22.0	(49) 24.1					28.7	(15) 30.5
	13.2	5.8	10.7					9.8	14.8
% Profit Before Taxes/Total Assets	17.1	22.3	21.0					27.2	25.2
	9.2	7.6	11.1					11.6	13.4
	5.9	.9	2.8					2.5	4.9
Sales/Net Fixed Assets	12.1	15.1	17.7					39.1	14.2
	8.4	10.1	9.0					12.7	8.8
	3.7	4.0	4.7					5.8	4.8
Sales/Total Assets	2.6	2.6	2.8					3.1	2.5
	1.9	1.9	2.0					2.2	1.8
	1.4	1.5	1.7					1.8	1.5
% Depr., Dep., Amort./Sales	1.5	1.1	1.0					.7	1.2
	(46) 2.5	(45) 2.1	(50) 1.9					(13) 2.8	2.2
	4.0	3.8	3.2					3.6	2.9
% Officers', Directors' Owners' Comp/Sales	1.6	2.1	.9						
	(12) 3.6	(19) 3.3	(14) 2.6						
	6.6	7.4	9.1						
Net Sales ($)	1160084M	1358881M	1451193M		11571M	34303M	66507M	197600M	1141212M
Total Assets ($)	811738M	804461M	843084M		9455M	15191M	29375M	96479M	692584M

M = $ thousand   MM = $ million
See Pages 11 through 21 for Explanation of Ratios and Data

Current Data Sorted by Assets   Comparative Historical Data

0-500M	500M-2MM	2-10MM	10-50MM	50-100MM	100-250MM	Type of Statement	4/1/02-3/31/03 ALL	4/1/03-3/31/04 ALL
	2	5	3		1	Unqualified	10	17
1	2	12	3			Reviewed	12	14
2	11	13				Compiled	12	18
5	12	7			1	Tax Returns	16	21
6	13	19	4	2	3	Other	24	27
	13 (4/1-9/30/06)		114 (10/1/06-3/31/07)					
14	40	56	10	2	5	NUMBER OF STATEMENTS	74	97
%	%	%	%	%	%	ASSETS	%	%
9.2	7.6	7.2	2.4			Cash & Equivalents	5.4	10.3
22.0	27.6	28.4	20.0			Trade Receivables (net)	24.7	24.0
21.6	21.4	25.2	28.9			Inventory	22.2	22.4
4.7	5.0	2.3	1.4			All Other Current	3.1	5.5
57.6	61.6	63.2	52.6			Total Current	55.5	62.2
36.3	31.0	31.5	36.0			Fixed Assets (net)	36.3	32.1
1.1	.8	1.7	7.8			Intangibles (net)	2.0	2.1
4.9	6.7	3.7	3.6			All Other Non-Current	6.2	3.7
100.0	100.0	100.0	100.0			Total	100.0	100.0
						LIABILITIES		
15.2	9.4	9.8	13.2			Notes Payable-Short Term	8.4	11.0
4.9	3.3	3.5	3.7			Cur. Mat.-L.T.D.	4.8	4.2
27.9	16.8	14.2	10.8			Trade Payables	20.0	12.9
.2	.0	.4	.6			Income Taxes Payable	.1	.3
15.2	8.9	7.5	5.5			All Other Current	9.4	8.7
63.4	38.4	35.4	33.8			Total Current	42.8	37.2
66.0	26.7	18.5	19.8			Long-Term Debt	19.9	23.4
.6	.1	.3	.6			Deferred Taxes	.3	.5
22.1	9.2	6.7	2.3			All Other Non-Current	5.4	4.5
-52.1	25.5	39.1	43.5			Net Worth	31.6	34.4
100.0	100.0	100.0	100.0			Total Liabilities & Net Worth	100.0	100.0
						INCOME DATA		
100.0	100.0	100.0	100.0			Net Sales	100.0	100.0
42.5	40.5	34.5	29.9			Gross Profit	36.5	38.3
39.2	35.4	27.8	22.2			Operating Expenses	32.2	31.4
3.3	5.1	6.7	7.7			Operating Profit	4.3	6.9
1.3	1.9	.9	2.0			All Other Expenses (net)	1.2	1.1
1.9	3.2	5.8	5.7			Profit Before Taxes	3.0	5.9
						RATIOS		
1.4	2.3	3.0	2.7			Current	2.2	3.2
.9	1.7	1.8	1.5				1.6	2.0
.5	1.1	1.3	.9				1.0	1.4
1.2	1.8	1.8	.8			Quick	1.2	1.8
.4	1.1	.9	.6				.7	.9
.1	.3	.5	.4				.4	.6
0 UND	21 17.6	26 14.2	37 9.9			Sales/Receivables	23 16.1	21 17.5
11 34.2	39 9.3	38 9.7	48 7.7				35 10.5	35 10.3
32 11.5	54 6.7	54 6.8	63 5.8				45 8.1	55 6.7
0 UND	9 39.6	24 15.1	42 8.6			Cost of Sales/Inventory	17 21.8	26 13.8
28 12.8	34 10.8	62 5.8	92 4.0				44 8.2	49 7.5
58 6.3	74 4.9	121 3.0	207 1.8				95 3.8	87 4.2
22 16.9	6 59.4	15 24.1	19 19.1			Cost of Sales/Payables	14 25.6	14 26.8
48 7.7	30 12.2	30 12.0	33 11.2				27 13.8	24 15.0
78 4.7	47 7.8	55 6.7	60 6.0				52 7.0	39 9.4
22.7	7.6	5.5	3.0			Sales/Working Capital	7.0	4.8
-44.1	13.5	7.8	10.3				13.1	9.0
-8.4	32.8	24.6	-62.0				UND	16.5
8.7	7.6	16.1	7.0			EBIT/Interest	11.6	12.6
(13) 3.3	(33) 3.7	(53) 4.0	2.9				(70) 4.5	(86) 5.3
1.0	1.0	1.5	1.7				1.2	1.4
			4.9			Net Profit + Depr., Dep., Amort./Cur. Mat. L/T/D	5.8	5.4
		(14)	1.6				(17) 2.7	(23) 3.0
			1.2				1.0	1.1
.4	.5	.3	.7			Fixed/Worth	.5	.3
7.4	1.2	.8	1.0				.9	.9
-.7	8.0	2.0	3.0				3.1	2.2
1.9	1.1	.7	.6			Debt/Worth	.9	.7
NM	2.8	1.6	1.8				2.1	1.4
-2.2	24.7	3.7	5.6				7.1	4.1
	82.8	52.9	76.2			% Profit Before Taxes/Tangible Net Worth	68.7	51.4
	(33) 21.9	(49) 25.7	15.6				(61) 24.2	(84) 19.0
	6.3	8.9	5.7				7.9	10.0
22.4	19.9	23.9	16.0			% Profit Before Taxes/Total Assets	19.7	23.6
10.8	8.1	11.2	5.5				5.7	8.2
.3	1.2	2.4	2.6				.7	2.1
36.8	16.8	22.1	4.9			Sales/Net Fixed Assets	21.3	20.8
9.9	9.4	7.7	3.4				7.0	8.4
4.6	5.5	3.9	2.5				2.9	3.6
5.0	3.7	3.3	1.7			Sales/Total Assets	3.7	3.2
4.1	2.7	2.2	1.3				2.3	2.3
2.5	1.4	1.5	1.0				1.4	1.4
	.8	1.4	2.3			% Depr., Dep., Amort./Sales	1.9	1.4
	(30) 2.0	(52) 2.1	4.2				(64) 3.1	(85) 3.1
	3.4	3.9	4.9				6.8	5.0
	2.5	1.5				% Officers', Directors' Owners' Comp/Sales	2.0	2.5
	(26) 4.0	(28) 2.5					(43) 4.2	(53) 4.3
	6.0	4.2					6.9	7.6
12717M	113568M	623199M	264280M	137559M	1626222M	Net Sales ($)	1120953M	1068163M
3444M	41484M	266517M	190637M	156443M	554568M	Total Assets ($)	493389M	597199M

M = $ thousand   MM = $ million
See Pages 11 through 21 for Explanation of Ratios and Data

Comparative Historical Data — Current Data Sorted by Sales

4/1/04- 3/31/05 ALL	4/1/05- 3/31/06 ALL	4/1/06- 3/31/07 ALL	Type of Statement	0-1MM	1-3MM	3-5MM	5-10MM	10-25MM	25MM & OVER
12	11	11	Unqualified	1	1	2	1	4	4
20	15	18	Reviewed		1	1	6	6	3
27	29	26	Compiled	3	7	5	6	5	
19	29	25	Tax Returns	5	8	3	6	2	1
41	49	47	Other	5	10	3	13	10	6
				13 (4/1-9/30/06)		114 (10/1/06-3/31/07)			
119	133	127	NUMBER OF STATEMENTS	14	26	14	32	27	14

%	%	%	ASSETS	%	%	%	%	%	%
5.9	7.5	6.9	Cash & Equivalents	12.7	6.5	6.2	4.4	9.4	3.6
26.8	25.3	26.3	Trade Receivables (net)	15.9	24.1	32.1	26.4	32.4	22.7
25.2	21.4	23.4	Inventory	23.0	23.5	21.3	25.8	20.6	25.7
3.3	2.8	4.0	All Other Current	4.7	6.5	2.5	2.6	1.8	7.5
61.1	57.0	60.6	Total Current	56.2	60.6	62.1	59.1	64.2	59.6
31.3	34.0	32.4	Fixed Assets (net)	32.6	35.6	26.6	35.7	29.3	30.5
3.1	2.8	1.9	Intangibles (net)	1.2	.6	1.2	2.6	2.5	2.9
4.5	6.2	5.1	All Other Non-Current	9.9	3.2	10.0	2.5	3.9	7.0
100.0	100.0	100.0	Total	100.0	100.0	100.0	100.0	100.0	100.0

			LIABILITIES						
12.4	10.6	10.5	Notes Payable-Short Term	12.9	11.2	12.9	11.8	6.3	9.3
5.1	4.3	3.8	Cur. Mat.-L.T.D.	2.6	4.2	2.7	4.7	2.8	5.6
18.4	15.7	15.8	Trade Payables	21.4	17.4	18.3	14.9	14.4	8.9
.3	.2	.3	Income Taxes Payable	.0	.1	.0	.5	.4	.1
7.8	8.3	9.5	All Other Current	12.2	12.5	8.0	6.1	7.4	14.3
44.1	39.0	39.8	Total Current	49.1	45.4	41.9	38.1	31.4	38.2
19.9	25.2	26.8	Long-Term Debt	29.1	41.2	14.1	30.5	18.9	16.8
.3	.3	.3	Deferred Taxes	.6	.2	.2	.3	.3	.7
4.4	5.5	8.6	All Other Non-Current	18.5	9.9	11.8	11.2	1.0	2.0
31.4	30.0	24.5	Net Worth	2.7	3.3	32.0	19.9	48.4	42.3
100.0	100.0	100.0	Total Liabilities & Net Worth	100.0	100.0	100.0	100.0	100.0	100.0

			INCOME DATA						
100.0	100.0	100.0	Net Sales	100.0	100.0	100.0	100.0	100.0	100.0
34.7	37.2	36.9	Gross Profit	45.2	41.7	37.7	39.5	28.7	28.3
29.7	32.3	31.0	Operating Expenses	43.2	36.0	33.3	33.9	19.8	22.6
4.9	4.9	5.8	Operating Profit	2.0	5.7	4.4	5.6	8.9	5.7
1.0	1.1	1.4	All Other Expenses (net)	4.0	.8	.8	1.5	1.1	1.0
3.9	3.7	4.4	Profit Before Taxes	-2.0	4.9	3.6	4.1	7.9	4.8

			RATIOS						
2.2	2.6	2.5	Current	4.0	2.5	2.1	2.0	3.6	2.4
1.6	1.5	1.6		.9	1.7	1.5	1.6	2.1	1.4
1.1	1.0	1.1		.7	.8	1.1	1.2	1.4	1.1
1.3	1.4	1.7	Quick	3.1	1.8	1.5	1.3	2.3	1.0
.8	.8	.8		.4	.6	1.0	.8	1.2	.6
.5	.5	.4		.2	.2	.4	.4	.7	.5
25 14.6	22 16.4	22 16.4	Sales/Receivables	0 UND	10 35.6	22 16.4	26 14.3	25 14.3	27 13.4
37 9.9	37 10.0	38 9.5		11 32.1	33 11.1	41 8.9	38 9.7	46 7.9	44 8.2
55 6.7	46 7.9	55 6.6		59 6.2	50 7.3	62 5.8	55 6.6	61 5.9	61 6.0
23 15.8	18 20.2	15 24.1	Cost of Sales/Inventory	0 UND	7 51.8	11 32.1	20 18.4	11 34.2	27 13.5
52 7.0	32 11.5	54 6.8		30 12.2	55 6.7	38 9.6	79 4.6	32 11.5	63 5.8
97 3.8	88 4.2	114 3.2		104 3.5	79 4.6	121 3.0	146 2.5	67 5.4	175 2.1
17 21.4	15 23.6	16 23.4	Cost of Sales/Payables	22 16.9	9 42.9	5 69.4	19 19.3	9 40.6	10 35.0
34 10.6	28 13.1	31 11.9		46 8.0	30 12.2	36 10.2	34 10.6	30 12.1	20 18.4
57 6.4	51 7.2	55 6.7		95 3.9	50 7.3	68 5.3	55 6.7	54 6.8	29 12.8
7.0	6.3	6.9	Sales/Working Capital	10.9	6.0	7.5	7.0	5.0	7.2
12.0	14.5	12.0		-235.2	12.3	17.3	8.8	8.2	10.6
59.2	-165.0	57.7		-3.2	-15.4	46.0	33.3	25.5	NM
11.0	10.6	10.0	EBIT/Interest	9.8	7.9	10.5	4.5	22.3	11.4
(107) 3.9	(119) 3.5	(116) 3.7		(10) 3.2	(23) 2.2	(13) 4.1	(31) 2.5	(26) 9.9	(13) 5.5
1.7	1.5	1.4		-1.7	.6	3.4	1.3	2.7	1.3
6.7	2.4	5.8	Net Profit + Depr., Dep., Amort./Cur. Mat. L/T/D						
(23) 2.5	(27) 2.0	(30) 2.6							
1.4	1.1	1.5							
.4	.3	.5	Fixed/Worth	.2	.5	.3	.6	.2	.4
1.1	1.1	1.2		2.4	1.3	1.3	1.6	.8	.9
2.7	3.3	4.3		-1.7	NM	6.5	NM	2.0	1.7
1.0	.9	1.0	Debt/Worth	1.7	1.0	1.1	1.4	.6	.6
2.4	2.2	2.3		4.7	3.1	2.0	2.8	.9	1.2
7.4	5.9	11.8		-5.2	NM	14.0	NM	3.8	3.5
59.2	58.2	54.7	% Profit Before Taxes/Tangible Net Worth		83.2	74.2	37.4	65.9	21.6
(103) 22.6	(112) 29.9	(104) 20.5			(20) 29.2	(12) 20.9	(24) 13.3	50.9	(12) 14.1
5.7	9.0	7.3			3.3	11.4	4.2	19.5	5.2
20.2	20.9	20.5	% Profit Before Taxes/Total Assets	15.9	23.3	16.9	14.2	32.8	16.0
6.0	9.7	8.4		4.2	7.3	10.3	5.7	20.5	7.0
.9	1.1	1.9		-11.6	-1.7	4.5	1.2	5.7	1.6
18.6	21.8	18.6	Sales/Net Fixed Assets	27.5	11.5	47.2	13.8	22.4	22.8
10.0	8.5	8.0		7.9	9.0	11.0	6.1	10.6	3.8
4.4	3.4	3.8		3.7	4.9	5.3	3.3	3.8	2.7
3.5	3.8	3.5	Sales/Total Assets	4.3	3.6	4.1	3.2	3.6	3.4
2.3	2.5	2.4		2.4	2.6	2.7	2.0	2.7	1.5
1.6	1.6	1.4		.9	1.4	1.8	1.5	1.4	.9
1.2	1.4	1.3	% Depr., Dep., Amort./Sales		.8	.9	1.4	1.1	.8
(97) 2.2	(109) 2.4	(106) 2.3			(20) 2.6	(12) 1.8	(30) 2.9	(25) 1.7	(12) 4.3
3.8	4.1	4.4			4.5	3.7	4.8	2.6	4.9
2.2	2.6	1.8	% Officers', Directors' Owners' Comp/Sales		2.8	2.4	1.0	.6	
(58) 3.8	(56) 4.1	(63) 3.2			(17) 4.7	(10) 3.4	(15) 2.8	(13) 1.6	
5.7	5.8	5.8			6.0	5.9	4.7	3.1	
1373279M	1372683M	2777545M	Net Sales ($)	7564M	51571M	54170M	233642M	409717M	2020881M
645097M	874698M	1213093M	Total Assets ($)	5009M	23868M	22151M	127230M	195722M	839113M

Current Data Sorted by Assets   **Comparative Historical Data**

0-500M	500M-2MM	2-10MM	10-50MM	50-100MM	100-250MM	Type of Statement	4/1/02-3/31/03 ALL	4/1/03-3/31/04 ALL
		1	1	1	1	Unqualified	3	5
		8				Reviewed	11	15
2	1	2				Compiled	3	3
	1	2				Tax Returns	1	3
	5	8				Other	11	6
5 (4/1-9/30/06)			33 (10/1/06-3/31/07)					
2	7	21	6	1	1	**NUMBER OF STATEMENTS**	29	32
%	%	%	%	%	%	**ASSETS**	%	%
		8.1				Cash & Equivalents	9.3	10.0
		28.1				Trade Receivables (net)	25.8	23.1
		20.9				Inventory	17.8	13.8
		1.6				All Other Current	3.3	2.4
		58.6				Total Current	56.3	49.4
		34.9				Fixed Assets (net)	33.1	39.3
		1.0				Intangibles (net)	3.5	2.9
		5.5				All Other Non-Current	7.1	8.4
		100.0				Total	100.0	100.0
						LIABILITIES		
		8.7				Notes Payable-Short Term	8.9	5.8
		5.9				Cur. Mat.-L.T.D.	6.0	3.9
		13.9				Trade Payables	13.8	10.1
		.5				Income Taxes Payable	.1	.3
		7.4				All Other Current	8.0	6.8
		36.4				Total Current	36.9	26.9
		12.2				Long-Term Debt	12.5	19.2
		.7				Deferred Taxes	1.8	1.9
		4.6				All Other Non-Current	3.3	5.8
		46.1				Net Worth	45.5	46.1
		100.0				Total Liabilties & Net Worth	100.0	100.0
						INCOME DATA		
		100.0				Net Sales	100.0	100.0
		33.1				Gross Profit	36.8	34.1
		24.6				Operating Expenses	28.8	31.1
		8.6				Operating Profit	7.9	3.0
		1.1				All Other Expenses (net)	.6	.8
		7.5				Profit Before Taxes	7.3	2.1
						RATIOS		
		4.1				Current	2.7	3.0
		2.1					1.6	1.6
		1.1					1.2	1.2
		2.4				Quick	1.8	2.5
		1.3					1.1	1.1
		.6					.6	.7
	36	10.2				Sales/Receivables	30 12.2	36 10.0
	44	8.3					45 8.0	47 7.8
	57	6.4					71 5.2	73 5.0
	18	20.5				Cost of Sales/Inventory	26 14.2	17 21.9
	49	7.4					48 7.6	34 10.7
	82	4.5					78 4.7	79 4.6
	14	26.3				Cost of Sales/Payables	20 18.6	12 29.5
	24	15.3					33 11.0	33 11.2
	41	8.9					50 7.3	41 9.0
		4.2				Sales/Working Capital	5.0	5.0
		6.9					10.4	8.6
		270.6					41.2	29.8
		26.0				EBIT/Interest	12.2	8.9
	(17)	6.6					(28) 5.1	(28) 4.1
		1.8					2.8	1.1
						Net Profit + Depr., Dep., Amort./Cur. Mat. L/T/D		6.1
							(10)	3.2
								2.4
		.3				Fixed/Worth	.4	.5
		.8					.7	.9
		1.1					1.5	1.7
		.4				Debt/Worth	.6	.6
		.8					1.1	1.2
		2.1					3.5	3.0
		44.8				% Profit Before Taxes/Tangible Net Worth	36.7	34.5
	(19)	34.2					(26) 21.0	(30) 15.0
		12.2					8.2	-2.5
		26.0				% Profit Before Taxes/Total Assets	14.7	13.4
		12.2					8.4	3.9
		4.3					3.9	-2.8
		13.3				Sales/Net Fixed Assets	16.0	6.9
		6.1					6.1	4.8
		3.2					3.5	2.3
		2.7				Sales/Total Assets	3.0	2.1
		2.3					2.0	1.5
		1.4					1.2	1.2
		1.4				% Depr., Dep., Amort./Sales	1.2	2.3
	(15)	3.2					(26) 3.2	(30) 4.0
		4.5					5.5	6.1
						% Officers', Directors' Owners' Comp/Sales	2.0	2.7
							(10) 2.8	(12) 4.3
							8.9	9.0
2181M	26772M	229203M	199849M	141336M	108776M	Net Sales ($)	767456M	394483M
721M	9477M	105345M	124653M	56857M	122139M	Total Assets ($)	607594M	323775M

M = $ thousand   MM = $ million
See Pages 11 through 21 for Explanation of Ratios and Data

Comparative Historical Data   Current Data Sorted by Sales

Type of Statement

4/1/04-3/31/05 ALL	4/1/05-3/31/06 ALL	4/1/06-3/31/07 ALL	Type of Statement	0-1MM	1-3MM	3-5MM	5-10MM	10-25MM	25MM & OVER
6	4	4	Unqualified				3	5	4
11	9	8	Reviewed	1	1	1	1	1	
4	2	5	Compiled				1	1	
3	3	3	Tax Returns		1				2
1	11	18	Other		3	3	5	5	
					5 (4/1-9/30/06)		33 (10/1/06-3/31/07)		
24	29	38	NUMBER OF STATEMENTS	1	5	4	10	12	6

Financial Data

4/1/04-3/31/05 ALL %	4/1/05-3/31/06 ALL %	4/1/06-3/31/07 ALL %	Item	0-1MM %	1-3MM %	3-5MM %	5-10MM %	10-25MM %	25MM & OVER %
			ASSETS						
10.7	9.0	8.6	Cash & Equivalents				12.0	6.9	
26.7	31.9	26.1	Trade Receivables (net)				30.6	25.6	
16.8	20.2	18.8	Inventory				18.4	19.6	
.9	2.3	1.7	All Other Current				.9	.8	
55.1	63.4	55.1	Total Current				61.8	52.9	
34.4	31.1	33.0	Fixed Assets (net)				31.8	36.4	
3.6	.7	3.0	Intangibles (net)				1.2	2.2	
6.9	4.8	8.8	All Other Non-Current				5.1	8.5	
100.0	100.0	100.0	Total				100.0	100.0	
			LIABILITIES						
5.2	7.9	7.2	Notes Payable-Short Term				7.5	6.4	
5.8	2.9	5.8	Cur. Mat.-L.T.D.				3.1	10.4	
11.0	16.7	15.2	Trade Payables				17.4	14.4	
.5	.2	.3	Income Taxes Payable				1.0	.1	
5.8	9.6	7.1	All Other Current				6.6	10.6	
28.3	37.2	35.6	Total Current				35.5	41.7	
20.5	13.6	19.3	Long-Term Debt				9.9	12.2	
1.2	1.0	.6	Deferred Taxes				.0	1.2	
4.8	3.7	5.3	All Other Non-Current				2.8	4.9	
45.2	44.5	39.2	Net Worth				51.8	39.9	
100.0	100.0	100.0	Total Liabilities & Net Worth				100.0	100.0	
			INCOME DATA						
100.0	100.0	100.0	Net Sales				100.0	100.0	
36.7	33.1	33.8	Gross Profit				34.5	23.8	
27.1	25.8	25.9	Operating Expenses				27.5	15.9	
9.6	7.3	7.9	Operating Profit				7.0	7.9	
.9	.5	.6	All Other Expenses (net)				-.1	1.4	
8.7	6.8	7.3	Profit Before Taxes				7.1	6.5	

Ratios

4/1/04-3/31/05 ALL	4/1/05-3/31/06 ALL	4/1/06-3/31/07 ALL	Ratio	0-1MM	1-3MM	3-5MM	5-10MM	10-25MM	25MM & OVER
3.2	2.9	4.2	Current				5.2	3.2	
1.7	1.8	1.7					2.1	1.9	
1.3	1.1	1.0					1.1	.9	
2.3	1.8	2.1	Quick				2.9	1.9	
1.2	1.1	1.1					1.6	1.0	
.7	.7	.6					.7	.5	
32 11.4	34 10.9	35 10.5	Sales/Receivables				36 10.2	36 10.2	
42 8.7	45 8.2	43 8.5					47 7.8	45 8.1	
58 6.3	71 5.2	55 6.6					57 6.4	64 5.7	
16 23.0	15 24.4	20 18.0	Cost of Sales/Inventory				14 25.7	25 14.8	
35 10.5	47 7.7	42 8.6					58 6.3	47 7.7	
98 3.7	81 4.5	82 4.5					106 3.4	82 4.4	
18 20.0	21 17.1	15 24.0	Cost of Sales/Payables				13 28.6	17 21.0	
27 13.8	27 13.6	25 14.6					23 16.1	26 13.9	
43 8.5	50 7.2	45 8.1					42 8.6	41 8.9	
5.0	5.3	5.4	Sales/Working Capital				2.6	5.8	
12.2	9.5	10.0					10.9	7.5	
24.1	49.2	NM					NM	-26.5	
23.0	21.7	17.1	EBIT/Interest						
(23) 7.8	(26) 7.7	(32) 4.4							
3.0	2.2	1.7							
7.4			Net Profit + Depr., Dep.,						
(10) 3.6			Amort./Cur. Mat. L/T/D						
1.8									
.5	.3	.3	Fixed/Worth				.4	.3	
1.0	.5	.9					.7	.8	
1.6	1.6	2.1					1.0	6.9	
.6	.5	.5	Debt/Worth				.4	.5	
1.5	1.0	1.0					.7	.7	
3.5	2.6	4.9					2.1	12.0	
41.8	51.7	44.3	% Profit Before Taxes/Tangible					45.6	
(23) 25.4	(27) 33.4	(32) 27.9	Net Worth					(10) 29.6	
14.9	21.7	10.4						13.2	
20.7	20.9	25.5	% Profit Before Taxes/Total				26.7	24.6	
10.2	15.3	11.2	Assets				10.4	11.7	
6.4	4.6	3.0					1.8	3.8	
9.6	15.5	13.1	Sales/Net Fixed Assets				12.6	13.6	
6.5	10.0	6.1					6.5	5.3	
4.1	4.3	3.8					3.7	3.5	
2.7	2.8	2.7	Sales/Total Assets				2.9	2.6	
2.1	2.3	2.3					2.3	2.0	
1.5	1.6	1.5					1.2	1.3	
2.2	.5	1.4	% Depr., Dep., Amort./Sales						
(22) 3.2	(26) 1.7	(28) 3.3							
5.2	3.7	4.8							
2.8	3.5	.7	% Officers', Directors'						
(10) 5.2	(14) 4.8	(14) 5.5	Owners' Comp/Sales						
14.2	10.1	11.1							
692352M	574629M	708117M	Net Sales ($)	784M	9231M	14685M	72365M	168495M	442557M
416651M	241934M	419192M	Total Assets ($)	369M	7236M	5518M	37996M	106347M	261726M

M = $ thousand   MM = $ million
See Pages 11 through 21 for Explanation of Ratios and Data

Current Data Sorted by Assets   Comparative Historical Data

0-500M	500M-2MM	2-10MM	10-50MM	50-100MM	100-250MM	Type of Statement	4/1/02-3/31/03 ALL	4/1/03-3/31/04 ALL
		2	13	5	4	Unqualified	17	19
	2	13	6	1		Reviewed	14	24
2	4	9				Compiled	11	13
6	3	4	1			Tax Returns	4	12
1	7	12	13	4	3	Other	25	37
	31 (4/1-9/30/06)		84 (10/1/06-3/31/07)					
9	16	40	33	10	7	**NUMBER OF STATEMENTS**	71	105
%	%	%	%	%	%	**ASSETS**	%	%
	15.4	3.3	5.5	1.4		Cash & Equivalents	5.7	8.0
	38.1	34.6	24.5	22.3		Trade Receivables (net)	27.0	28.3
	14.0	25.6	28.4	38.4		Inventory	20.3	20.0
	3.9	3.4	1.5	3.7		All Other Current	3.8	2.4
	71.3	67.0	60.0	65.8		Total Current	56.8	58.7
	22.7	24.3	31.0	27.7		Fixed Assets (net)	32.5	29.4
	1.2	2.3	2.7	1.3		Intangibles (net)	2.6	3.4
	4.8	6.4	6.3	5.3		All Other Non-Current	8.0	8.6
	100.0	100.0	100.0	100.0		Total	100.0	100.0
						LIABILITIES		
	11.8	11.4	12.9	13.5		Notes Payable-Short Term	11.2	10.2
	3.4	3.9	3.5	1.7		Cur. Mat.-L.T.D.	4.0	2.6
	23.7	21.1	15.9	15.3		Trade Payables	15.6	17.7
	.0	.1	.2	.9		Income Taxes Payable	.3	.6
	6.3	10.3	7.9	6.3		All Other Current	8.8	11.3
	45.2	46.8	40.5	37.7		Total Current	39.9	42.4
	15.7	11.8	13.2	19.0		Long-Term Debt	16.5	15.2
	1.0	.1	1.5	.8		Deferred Taxes	.4	.7
	4.6	3.4	7.4	3.5		All Other Non-Current	6.1	9.5
	33.4	37.9	37.4	39.1		Net Worth	37.1	32.2
	100.0	100.0	100.0	100.0		Total Liabilities & Net Worth	100.0	100.0
						INCOME DATA		
	100.0	100.0	100.0	100.0		Net Sales	100.0	100.0
	33.3	23.1	17.5	17.4		Gross Profit	24.9	23.0
	26.5	18.4	11.2	6.9		Operating Expenses	20.3	21.3
	6.8	4.7	6.3	10.5		Operating Profit	4.7	1.7
	.4	1.3	1.1	1.5		All Other Expenses (net)	.8	.6
	6.4	3.4	5.2	8.9		Profit Before Taxes	3.8	1.1
						RATIOS		
	3.1	2.0	2.1	2.5		Current	2.4	2.5
	1.7	1.4	1.5	1.6			1.6	1.4
	1.1	1.0	1.0	1.4			1.0	1.0
	2.1	1.2	1.4	1.4		Quick	1.4	1.3
	1.3	.8	.6	.7			.9	.8
	.9	.6	.4	.4			.5	.6
	31 11.8	34 10.6	25 14.4	25 14.5		Sales/Receivables	37 9.9	34 10.6
	45 8.2	43 8.4	41 8.9	32 11.4			47 7.7	48 7.6
	64 5.7	56 6.5	57 6.4	61 6.0			57 6.5	63 5.8
	8 43.0	19 19.6	34 10.7	38 9.7		Cost of Sales/Inventory	16 23.5	15 23.7
	22 16.9	45 8.1	51 7.1	67 5.4			50 7.4	43 8.4
	43 8.4	70 5.2	95 3.9	91 4.0			92 4.0	80 4.5
	21 17.5	25 14.6	22 16.7	15 24.4		Cost of Sales/Payables	20 18.0	18 20.2
	48 7.6	34 10.8	28 12.8	28 13.1			33 11.2	35 10.3
	65 5.6	58 6.3	41 8.9	69 5.3			50 7.3	52 7.1
	5.8	7.5	7.0	5.6		Sales/Working Capital	4.5	4.9
	7.5	13.8	9.5	8.9			11.3	12.6
	78.7	95.8	-97.2	14.6			-154.9	-238.3
	23.2	14.6	21.9			EBIT/Interest	10.4	9.0
	(14) 8.3	(34) 5.4	(30) 4.5				(65) 3.6	(91) 2.9
	3.3	2.3	1.6				.7	-.6
		15.4	21.0			Net Profit + Depr., Dep., Amort./Cur. Mat. L/T/D		9.3
	(10)	4.8	(13) 3.5				(22) 4.5
		1.6	1.4					1.7
	.1	.3	.4	.3		Fixed/Worth	.4	.4
	.6	.6	.7	.6			.9	.8
	4.0	1.7	3.3	.9			2.1	2.6
	1.0	.9	.7	1.1		Debt/Worth	.6	.8
	3.1	1.7	1.7	1.8			2.2	2.4
	10.3	4.6	6.7	3.7			4.6	9.4
	75.5	59.0	41.9	73.5		% Profit Before Taxes/Tangible Net Worth	51.6	36.3
	(14) 33.8	(38) 29.3	(27) 24.1	43.7			(65) 24.3	(91) 6.9
	20.2	8.7	9.2	19.6			3.7	-5.0
	28.4	21.5	13.8	22.9		% Profit Before Taxes/Total Assets	16.4	8.1
	14.3	9.8	6.3	16.0			6.3	2.7
	5.3	3.5	2.1	8.2			-.6	-3.6
	36.5	22.1	16.2	26.6		Sales/Net Fixed Assets	14.4	18.5
	16.1	13.9	6.7	11.2			6.6	8.3
	9.4	8.0	4.5	4.2			3.0	3.6
	3.9	3.1	2.6	2.8		Sales/Total Assets	2.7	3.0
	3.3	2.8	2.1	2.5			1.9	2.1
	2.0	2.2	1.6	1.5			1.3	1.3
	1.4	.8	1.0	.6		% Depr., Dep., Amort./Sales	1.5	1.1
	(11) 1.5	(34) 1.5	(31) 1.8	1.3			(63) 2.9	(89) 2.5
	2.7	2.2	2.1	3.2			5.0	4.4
		1.5				% Officers', Directors' Owners' Comp/Sales	1.0	1.5
	(15)	2.3					(22) 1.9	(36) 2.4
		3.0					4.0	4.3
9492M	63089M	528484M	2060678M	1565843M	1902872M	Net Sales ($)	2363486M	3117697M
2095M	19335M	202478M	940269M	704036M	1292727M	Total Assets ($)	1576547M	1875985M

Comparative Historical Data | Current Data Sorted by Sales

Type of Statement

Historical			Statement Type	0-1MM	1-3MM	3-5MM	5-10MM	10-25MM	25MM & OVER
20	30	24	Unqualified				1	4	19
33	15	22	Reviewed				4	9	9
17	9	15	Compiled		2	2	5	5	1
11	11	14	Tax Returns		4	1	2	2	
35	48	40	Other		5	3	6	6	20
4/1/04-3/31/05 ALL	4/1/05-3/31/06 ALL	4/1/06-3/31/07 ALL		31 (4/1-9/30/06)			84 (10/1/06-3/31/07)		
116	113	115	NUMBER OF STATEMENTS	6	10	6	18	26	49

H: %	H: %	H: %		C: %	%	%	%	%	%
			ASSETS						
5.2	8.3	6.7	Cash & Equivalents		18.9		4.8	5.4	5.0
33.0	31.3	30.9	Trade Receivables (net)		38.4		35.1	31.6	24.9
24.9	21.8	25.1	Inventory		8.4		16.8	30.1	31.0
2.3	3.0	3.3	All Other Current		1.4		4.9	3.2	2.0
65.4	64.4	65.9	Total Current		67.1		61.6	70.3	62.9
26.1	28.9	25.6	Fixed Assets (net)		18.7		27.9	24.8	28.7
2.5	2.4	2.6	Intangibles (net)		6.8		.4	1.7	2.5
6.0	4.2	5.8	All Other Non-Current		7.4		10.1	3.2	5.9
100.0	100.0	100.0	Total		100.0		100.0	100.0	100.0
			LIABILITIES						
14.4	15.5	12.2	Notes Payable-Short Term		15.3		13.5	11.1	12.6
3.8	3.1	3.1	Cur. Mat.-L.T.D.		1.7		4.2	3.9	2.7
20.8	19.4	19.4	Trade Payables		24.6		21.9	22.4	15.6
.3	.3	.2	Income Taxes Payable		.0		.0	.1	.3
8.1	10.3	8.1	All Other Current		4.4		8.6	10.3	7.8
47.3	48.6	43.0	Total Current		46.0		48.2	47.8	38.9
13.8	18.4	17.4	Long-Term Debt		13.3		14.7	12.2	18.9
.7	.6	.9	Deferred Taxes		1.0		.1	.4	1.7
6.7	7.5	6.3	All Other Non-Current		3.3		1.2	5.1	7.1
31.6	24.9	32.4	Net Worth		36.3		35.9	34.5	33.4
100.0	100.0	100.0	Total Liabilities & Net Worth		100.0		100.0	100.0	100.0
			INCOME DATA						
100.0	100.0	100.0	Net Sales		100.0		100.0	100.0	100.0
24.3	23.6	23.5	Gross Profit		40.3		24.6	21.7	16.6
19.4	17.7	17.5	Operating Expenses		36.5		18.8	16.4	9.2
4.8	5.9	6.0	Operating Profit		3.8		5.8	5.4	7.4
.9	1.0	1.3	All Other Expenses (net)		.9		1.9	.8	1.4
3.9	4.8	4.7	Profit Before Taxes		2.9		3.9	4.6	6.0
			RATIOS						
2.1	2.4	2.3	Current		3.3		1.6	2.0	2.5
1.4	1.5	1.5			1.5		1.2	1.4	1.6
1.1	1.1	1.1			.9		.7	1.1	1.1
1.2	1.4	1.4	Quick		2.7		1.2	1.1	1.4
.7	.9	.9			1.3		.9	.8	.7
.6	.6	.5			.7		.5	.6	.4
34 10.6	31 11.7	30 12.3	Sales/Receivables		26 13.9		32 11.5	33 11.2	26 14.1
49 7.5	44 8.2	41 8.8			32 11.4		41 8.8	44 8.2	41 8.9
62 5.9	60 6.1	57 6.5			72 5.1		64 5.7	56 6.5	56 6.5
21 17.1	14 25.9	17 21.1	Cost of Sales/Inventory		11 34.6		0 UND	33 11.2	35 10.3
53 6.9	41 8.8	45 8.0			17 21.0		17 21.4	53 6.9	60 6.0
74 4.9	72 5.1	72 5.1			39 9.3		62 5.9	71 5.1	95 3.9
20 18.2	21 17.5	22 16.6	Cost of Sales/Payables		27 13.7		25 14.5	27 13.6	21 17.2
37 9.9	32 11.4	33 11.1			49 7.4		43 8.5	34 10.8	27 13.5
56 6.5	48 7.6	55 6.7			70 5.2		50 7.3	62 5.9	41 8.9
6.8	6.0	6.1	Sales/Working Capital		3.4		9.6	7.3	5.6
15.5	11.7	10.9			13.5		25.4	13.8	8.3
52.5	68.6	78.6			NM		-27.2	37.8	53.2
12.8	14.8	13.5	EBIT/Interest				9.3	17.4	9.6
(109) 5.0	(104) 5.5	(102) 4.7					(15) 3.5	(23) 6.1	(45) 4.3
1.8	2.2	1.7					2.4	2.9	1.7
15.5	17.6	13.4	Net Profit + Depr., Dep., Amort./Cur. Mat. L/T/D					21.9	6.8
(27) 3.9	(32) 4.4	(34) 4.8						(10) 5.5	(19) 3.5
1.7	2.6	1.5						1.5	1.5
.3	.4	.3	Fixed/Worth		.1		.3	.4	.4
.8	.9	.7			.6		.7	.8	.7
2.1	4.0	3.5			NM		2.3	1.4	4.0
1.0	.9	.9	Debt/Worth		.9		.8	1.1	.8
2.5	2.2	2.0			2.3		1.6	2.2	2.0
7.5	12.6	8.0			NM		7.3	3.9	8.6
65.6	66.3	59.4	% Profit Before Taxes/Tangible Net Worth				58.2	71.2	53.7
(101) 30.3	(95) 33.9	(98) 29.9					(17) 21.1	(24) 35.7	(40) 26.3
12.6	13.8	13.2					5.2	8.5	18.2
18.1	17.1	21.8	% Profit Before Taxes/Total Assets		30.3		20.3	21.9	20.9
8.9	8.3	9.8			22.3		8.9	9.7	8.9
1.5	2.6	2.6			-22.8		3.7	3.1	2.4
24.4	21.6	24.9	Sales/Net Fixed Assets		173.3		41.7	20.0	16.2
10.9	9.5	12.0			21.9		15.1	12.7	7.9
5.4	5.1	5.7			3.9		4.0	8.2	4.5
3.2	3.2	3.1	Sales/Total Assets		4.9		3.6	3.0	2.7
2.5	2.4	2.5			2.1		2.9	2.8	2.2
1.6	1.6	1.8			1.4		2.1	2.1	1.6
1.1	1.0	.9	% Depr., Dep., Amort./Sales				.3	.9	.9
(107) 2.2	(103) 1.7	(97) 1.6					(15) 1.4	(24) 1.5	(46) 1.7
3.3	2.7	2.3					2.2	2.2	2.3
1.2	1.0	1.2	% Officers', Directors', Owners' Comp/Sales						
(43) 3.3	(35) 3.5	(33) 2.9							
6.3	6.0	5.9							
4665948M	7058865M	6130458M	Net Sales ($)	2548M	20158M	21983M	127270M	406319M	5552180M
1962567M	3598872M	3160940M	Total Assets ($)	1077M	9695M	6921M	64720M	168583M	2909944M

M = $ thousand   MM = $ million
See Pages 11 through 21 for Explanation of Ratios and Data

Current Data Sorted by Assets   Comparative Historical Data

Type of Statement

0-500M	500M-2MM	2-10MM	10-50MM	50-100MM	100-250MM	Type of Statement	4/1/02-3/31/03 ALL	4/1/03-3/31/04 ALL
1	1	4	6	8	5	Unqualified	20	27
	2	9	6			Reviewed	13	29
	4	4	4			Compiled	9	19
3	5	4				Tax Returns	7	4
1	6	15	21	4	3	Other	24	25
	28 (4/1-9/30/06)		88 (10/1/06-3/31/07)					
5	18	36	37	12	8	NUMBER OF STATEMENTS	73	104

ASSETS

0-500M	500M-2MM	2-10MM	10-50MM	50-100MM	100-250MM		4/1/02-3/31/03 ALL	4/1/03-3/31/04 ALL
%	%	%	%	%	%	ASSETS	%	%
	6.0	11.4	5.0	3.3		Cash & Equivalents	6.2	5.2
	35.1	30.4	31.6	26.5		Trade Receivables (net)	30.4	31.5
	32.3	23.4	39.7	43.6		Inventory	26.1	25.2
	.4	4.0	1.7	1.8		All Other Current	1.8	2.5
	73.8	69.3	78.1	75.2		Total Current	64.4	64.4
	20.0	27.1	14.7	21.6		Fixed Assets (net)	28.7	28.9
	.7	1.8	3.3	1.0		Intangibles (net)	2.4	2.0
	5.5	1.8	4.0	2.2		All Other Non-Current	4.4	4.7
	100.0	100.0	100.0	100.0		Total	100.0	100.0

LIABILITIES

0-500M	500M-2MM	2-10MM	10-50MM	50-100MM	100-250MM		4/1/02-3/31/03 ALL	4/1/03-3/31/04 ALL
	11.2	7.4	14.7	10.0		Notes Payable-Short Term	14.1	16.2
	3.7	2.2	1.2	1.2		Cur. Mat.-L.T.D.	3.9	3.1
	22.4	22.4	17.9	15.4		Trade Payables	17.2	18.6
	.0	.6	.3	.7		Income Taxes Payable	.3	.2
	10.0	7.2	10.8	7.5		All Other Current	7.6	7.7
	47.3	39.8	45.0	34.8		Total Current	43.0	45.8
	12.8	15.7	8.3	22.3		Long-Term Debt	17.0	16.9
	.3	1.2	.6	.9		Deferred Taxes	.7	.8
	8.6	4.2	1.9	4.6		All Other Non-Current	6.2	8.4
	31.1	39.1	44.1	37.5		Net Worth	33.0	28.0
	100.0	100.0	100.0	100.0		Total Liabilities & Net Worth	100.0	100.0

INCOME DATA

0-500M	500M-2MM	2-10MM	10-50MM	50-100MM	100-250MM		4/1/02-3/31/03 ALL	4/1/03-3/31/04 ALL
	100.0	100.0	100.0	100.0		Net Sales	100.0	100.0
	27.7	22.5	20.9	14.5		Gross Profit	23.5	23.8
	22.1	17.4	11.9	7.8		Operating Expenses	20.7	20.6
	5.6	5.1	9.0	6.7		Operating Profit	2.8	3.2
	.7	.3	.6	.8		All Other Expenses (net)	.9	1.0
	4.9	4.9	8.4	5.9		Profit Before Taxes	1.9	2.2

RATIOS

0-500M	500M-2MM	2-10MM	10-50MM	50-100MM	100-250MM		4/1/02-3/31/03 ALL	4/1/03-3/31/04 ALL
	2.0	3.0	3.1	4.4		Current	2.3	2.5
	1.6	1.8	1.6	2.3			1.7	1.5
	1.2	1.1	1.3	1.5			1.1	1.0
	1.5	1.8	1.5	1.5		Quick	1.4	1.4
	.7	1.0	.8	.9			.8	.7
	.3	.7	.5	.6			.5	.5
	19 19.7	28 13.3	44 8.4	34 10.6		Sales/Receivables	36 10.1	38 9.5
	36 10.2	47 7.7	53 6.9	51 7.1			46 7.9	50 7.4
	48 7.7	54 6.8	62 5.9	59 6.2			60 6.1	69 5.3
	6 61.6	19 18.8	51 7.2	77 4.7		Cost of Sales/Inventory	32 11.5	30 12.3
	44 8.4	41 9.0	88 4.2	104 3.5			58 6.3	56 6.6
	104 3.5	74 5.0	120 3.0	117 3.1			91 4.0	89 4.1
	20 18.4	18 20.5	22 17.0	18 20.2		Cost of Sales/Payables	15 23.6	15 24.0
	36 10.2	37 10.0	32 11.5	34 10.7			32 11.2	33 10.9
	46 7.9	55 6.6	53 6.9	53 6.9			49 7.5	56 6.5
	6.2	4.2	3.6	3.4		Sales/Working Capital	5.1	4.6
	12.5	9.7	6.1	4.3			9.9	11.5
	44.1	41.3	13.5	6.2			67.6	-155.6
	49.2	8.4	26.9	18.6		EBIT/Interest	6.2	7.7
	(17) 7.7	(29) 6.5	(32) 10.8	(11) 4.6			(68) 2.0	(90) 2.4
	2.9	1.2	3.2	2.8			.3	.3
						Net Profit + Depr., Dep., Amort./Cur. Mat. L/T/D	6.4	4.9
							(15) 3.1	(28) 1.4
							1.3	.8
	.2	.2	.1	.4		Fixed/Worth	.4	.3
	.4	.9	.3	.6			1.1	1.1
	1.6	1.7	.7	1.1			3.4	3.7
	.8	.8	.5	.8		Debt/Worth	.9	1.0
	1.9	1.9	1.4	2.2			1.9	2.4
	7.4	4.3	3.1	5.5			9.7	8.6
	98.8	49.6	60.2	71.6		% Profit Before Taxes/Tangible Net Worth	38.9	40.8
	(17) 34.1	(33) 28.0	(35) 33.9	29.1			(62) 12.4	(88) 12.1
	11.8	10.8	27.2	9.8			-.4	-7.1
	25.2	16.8	25.2	20.3		% Profit Before Taxes/Total Assets	10.3	11.9
	8.8	7.8	14.7	5.8			3.8	3.3
	3.7	.7	6.9	4.3			-.5	-2.6
	46.6	24.0	73.3	16.4		Sales/Net Fixed Assets	19.2	19.8
	23.7	11.6	17.6	9.0			7.9	8.0
	7.0	5.4	8.9	4.3			4.2	4.0
	4.5	3.2	2.8	2.5		Sales/Total Assets	3.0	2.8
	3.4	2.5	2.0	1.9			2.2	2.0
	1.9	1.7	1.6	1.5			1.5	1.6
	.3	1.0	.4	.5		% Depr., Dep., Amort./Sales	1.1	1.1
	(15) 1.2	(32) 2.1	(35) .8	(11) 1.8			(70) 2.2	(90) 2.6
	2.1	3.4	1.7	3.1			4.2	4.0
	.5	1.1	1.5			% Officers', Directors' Owners' Comp/Sales	2.3	2.7
	(10) 3.6	(15) 1.6	(10) 4.0				(22) 6.6	(34) 5.1
	7.8	4.2	5.9				11.7	9.1
5910M	83388M	384300M	1748815M	1658720M	2901320M	Net Sales ($)	2789981M	3855320M
1593M	24972M	156618M	823954M	883808M	1330228M	Total Assets ($)	1694595M	2166942M

© RMA 2007

M = $ thousand   MM = $ million
See Pages 11 through 21 for Explanation of Ratios and Data

Comparative Historical Data | Current Data Sorted by Sales

	4/1/04-3/31/05 ALL	4/1/05-3/31/06 ALL	4/1/06-3/31/07 ALL	Type of Statement	0-1MM	1-3MM	3-5MM	5-10MM	10-25MM	25MM & OVER
	22	30	24	Unqualified		2		2	2	18
	17	16	17	Reviewed		2		4	9	2
	9	11	13	Compiled		1	1	5	3	3
	6	6	12	Tax Returns	1	5	2	2	2	
	25	36	50	Other		1	5	9	11	24
						28 (4/1-9/30/06)			88 (10/1/06-3/31/07)	
NUMBER OF STATEMENTS	79	99	116		1	11	8	22	27	47
	%	%	%	**ASSETS**	%	%	%	%	%	%
Cash & Equivalents	4.6	6.8	7.3			5.4		7.3	9.8	4.4
Trade Receivables (net)	31.3	31.6	31.4			23.9		32.8	32.7	30.3
Inventory	31.2	30.6	33.3			31.2		26.9	30.4	40.9
All Other Current	4.1	2.5	2.3			1.6		2.3	1.7	1.8
Total Current	71.2	71.5	74.3			62.1		69.3	74.6	77.3
Fixed Assets (net)	23.3	21.6	20.4			28.9		25.2	19.5	18.1
Intangibles (net)	1.2	1.7	1.9			5.9		.5	3.3	1.1
All Other Non-Current	4.3	5.2	3.4			3.2		5.1	2.6	3.4
Total	100.0	100.0	100.0			100.0		100.0	100.0	100.0
				LIABILITIES						
Notes Payable-Short Term	15.8	9.1	10.9			2.9		12.5	7.9	13.5
Cur. Mat.-L.T.D.	3.6	2.6	2.0			4.7		2.1	1.6	1.7
Trade Payables	17.5	18.6	19.8			18.7		21.2	24.6	17.2
Income Taxes Payable	.2	.5	.4			.0		.1	.9	.4
All Other Current	8.1	12.0	9.3			8.5		7.9	11.7	8.7
Total Current	45.3	42.8	42.3			34.9		43.7	46.7	41.5
Long-Term Debt	12.1	12.4	13.1			25.7		17.5	7.0	13.2
Deferred Taxes	.6	.9	.8			1.0		.8	.7	.9
All Other Non-Current	5.5	5.0	4.1			11.2		5.0	.6	3.6
Net Worth	36.5	38.9	39.7			27.2		33.0	44.9	40.9
Total Liabilities & Net Worth	100.0	100.0	100.0			100.0		100.0	100.0	100.0
				INCOME DATA						
Net Sales	100.0	100.0	100.0			100.0		100.0	100.0	100.0
Gross Profit	24.4	21.8	22.4			30.3		22.0	23.3	18.3
Operating Expenses	17.2	14.4	15.3			24.6		17.6	15.2	10.7
Operating Profit	7.1	7.4	7.1			5.7		4.4	8.1	7.7
All Other Expenses (net)	.7	.5	.5			1.5		.7	.1	.7
Profit Before Taxes	6.4	6.9	6.6			4.1		3.8	8.0	7.0
				RATIOS						
Current	2.4	3.1	2.9			3.5		2.3	3.1	3.2
	1.5	1.8	1.7			1.7		1.7	1.5	2.0
	1.2	1.2	1.3			1.4		1.2	1.1	1.4
Quick	1.2	1.8	1.6			1.5		1.7	1.5	1.4
	.8	.9	.9			1.1		.9	.8	.8
	.6	.6	.6			.3		.5	.6	.6
Sales/Receivables	38 9.6	37 9.9	32 11.3			14 25.9		25 14.8	28 13.1	40 9.0
	49 7.4	46 8.0	48 7.6			36 10.1		44 8.4	48 7.7	51 7.2
	65 5.6	57 6.4	56 6.5			61 6.0		53 6.9	55 6.6	59 6.2
Cost of Sales/Inventory	40 9.1	33 11.1	32 11.5			47 7.8		8 43.3	21 17.1	53 6.9
	71 5.2	59 6.2	66 5.6			87 4.2		40 9.2	45 8.0	92 4.0
	110 3.3	93 3.9	110 3.3			129 2.8		70 5.2	124 3.0	116 3.2
Cost of Sales/Payables	17 21.6	20 18.1	21 17.2			22 16.7		15 24.1	24 15.5	22 16.8
	32 11.2	32 11.4	35 10.4			30 12.0		27 13.4	33 8.6	33 11.0
	51 7.2	47 7.8	48 7.5			56 6.5		46 8.0	63 5.8	44 8.3
Sales/Working Capital	4.3	4.8	4.2			3.2		7.2	3.7	3.7
	7.9	8.8	7.7			8.5		11.6	11.1	5.5
	22.0	20.1	15.8			19.0		71.0	24.8	10.9
EBIT/Interest	17.1	22.5	22.8					10.1	47.8	22.8
	(69) 6.4	(82) 8.2	(100) 7.7					(21) 6.5	(21) 13.7	(44) 9.8
	3.6	3.3	2.6					.8	6.8	3.2
Net Profit + Depr., Dep., Amort./Cur. Mat. L/T/D	39.6	37.7	14.9							30.2
	(17) 5.3	(27) 6.0	(22) 7.0						(14)	9.8
	2.0	1.3	2.4							2.2
Fixed/Worth	.2	.2	.2			.3		.2	.1	.2
	.6	.5	.5			1.2		.8	.4	.4
	1.3	1.4	1.1			-4.0		1.8	.9	.8
Debt/Worth	.9	.8	.7			.9		.8	.5	.8
	1.8	1.5	1.6			2.0		1.5	1.9	1.4
	4.9	5.0	3.9			-359.0		6.6	3.2	3.3
% Profit Before Taxes/Tangible Net Worth	57.6	58.9	58.6					71.9	62.2	52.9
	(73) 29.2	(91) 38.0	(109) 33.4					(20) 26.6	40.9	(45) 32.9
	15.6	21.4	14.5					9.5	30.2	22.8
% Profit Before Taxes/Total Assets	18.6	25.8	22.3			16.2		20.2	23.3	22.9
	9.4	13.6	12.4			2.4		7.3	15.9	13.5
	5.8	5.2	4.4			.4		.0	8.2	4.9
Sales/Net Fixed Assets	35.0	29.7	42.7			50.0		46.6	50.1	42.1
	11.0	11.5	15.3			6.5		15.8	16.6	11.4
	4.8	5.4	6.6			5.6		8.6	8.8	7.2
Sales/Total Assets	2.7	3.1	3.0			2.9		3.9	3.7	2.7
	2.0	2.2	2.3			1.9		3.0	2.4	2.2
	1.5	1.7	1.7			1.2		2.4	1.6	1.7
% Depr., Dep., Amort./Sales	.9	.6	.5			.4		.5	.5	.4
	(67) 1.9	(86) 1.6	(104) 1.2			(10) 2.1		(20) 1.2	(24) 1.1	(44) 1.0
	3.4	2.9	2.4			4.4		2.9	2.2	1.9
% Officers', Directors', Owners' Comp/Sales	1.6	1.7	1.1						1.0	.4
	(22) 6.8	(29) 3.6	(37) 2.4						(10) 1.7	(11) 1.6
	9.8	6.3	5.7						2.4	5.5
Net Sales ($)	3498941M	6444414M	6782453M		148M	17643M	31448M	157995M	471829M	6103390M
Total Assets ($)	1859244M	2920536M	3221173M		41M	11693M	17532M	59369M	215176M	2917362M

M = $ thousand   MM = $ million
See Pages 11 through 21 for Explanation of Ratios and Data

Current Data Sorted by Assets | Comparative Historical Data

0-500M	500M-2MM	2-10MM	10-50MM	50-100MM	100-250MM	Type of Statement	4/1/02-3/31/03 ALL	4/1/03-3/31/04 ALL
		5	13	5	2	Unqualified	13	17
	3	10	4	1		Reviewed	21	16
1	2	10				Compiled	10	11
1	2	3				Tax Returns	3	6
	3	7	14	1	4	Other	14	23
	26 (4/1-9/30/06)		65 (10/1/06-3/31/07)					
2	10	35	31	7	6	**NUMBER OF STATEMENTS**	61	73
%	%	%	%	%	%	**ASSETS**	%	%
	14.3	6.1	4.5			Cash & Equivalents	5.9	5.3
	27.7	31.6	25.8			Trade Receivables (net)	24.7	25.0
	20.4	30.4	33.7			Inventory	29.5	28.1
	3.8	2.3	1.3			All Other Current	2.4	1.9
	66.2	70.3	65.3			Total Current	62.5	60.3
	19.4	22.8	28.5			Fixed Assets (net)	29.1	32.9
	7.3	2.3	1.9			Intangibles (net)	1.6	.8
	7.1	4.5	4.3			All Other Non-Current	6.7	6.0
	100.0	100.0	100.0			Total	100.0	100.0
						LIABILITIES		
	5.8	16.6	15.8			Notes Payable-Short Term	14.4	15.7
	3.7	3.5	3.3			Cur. Mat.-L.T.D.	4.3	3.7
	24.1	20.1	17.0			Trade Payables	15.9	16.0
	.0	.3	.3			Income Taxes Payable	.1	.2
	9.6	7.8	6.1			All Other Current	6.8	7.2
	43.2	48.3	42.5			Total Current	41.5	42.8
	19.6	10.3	19.0			Long-Term Debt	17.4	18.0
	.0	.0	.7			Deferred Taxes	.8	.7
	.1	3.9	7.7			All Other Non-Current	6.6	7.7
	37.1	37.5	30.0			Net Worth	33.7	30.8
	100.0	100.0	100.0			Total Liabilties & Net Worth	100.0	100.0
						INCOME DATA		
	100.0	100.0	100.0			Net Sales	100.0	100.0
	32.8	22.9	18.2			Gross Profit	21.9	22.3
	30.5	17.8	11.3			Operating Expenses	18.7	21.1
	2.3	5.0	6.9			Operating Profit	3.2	1.2
	.8	1.5	1.8			All Other Expenses (net)	1.2	1.1
	1.5	3.5	5.0			Profit Before Taxes	2.0	.1
						RATIOS		
	5.2	2.0	2.3				2.5	2.6
	1.8	1.5	1.4			Current	1.6	1.5
	.9	1.0	1.1				1.1	1.1
	2.8	1.2	1.2				1.2	1.3
	1.0	.8	.7			Quick	.8	.6
	.7	.5	.4				.4	.5
	21 17.0	32 11.6	37 9.8				36 10.2	37 9.9
	25 14.6	45 8.1	43 8.5			Sales/Receivables	46 7.9	46 7.9
	48 7.6	66 5.5	49 7.4				55 6.7	58 6.3
	0 UND	41 8.8	49 7.5				40 9.1	37 9.9
	33 11.1	57 6.4	68 5.4			Cost of Sales/Inventory	71 5.1	62 5.9
	97 3.8	82 4.4	96 3.8				102 3.6	98 3.7
	18 19.8	17 22.0	23 15.6				19 18.9	17 22.0
	25 14.5	36 10.3	33 11.1			Cost of Sales/Payables	33 11.2	35 10.5
	55 6.7	63 5.8	42 8.8				52 7.1	49 7.5
	3.9	5.7	6.7				4.9	5.6
	14.1	13.7	11.1			Sales/Working Capital	9.2	11.1
	-82.7	112.1	32.6				27.5	70.2
		11.5	6.8				8.8	4.9
		(31) 2.2	(28) 3.9			EBIT/Interest	(56) 2.2	(68) 2.3
		-.4	2.1				-.2	-.2
			8.4			Net Profit + Depr., Dep.,	7.3	5.4
		(18)	4.4			Amort./Cur. Mat. L/T/D	(17) 2.0	(25) 2.6
			1.9				.6	.4
	.2	.2	.4				.4	.5
	.6	.6	1.0			Fixed/Worth	.7	.9
	NM	3.0	2.0				2.0	2.1
	.1	.7	1.0				.7	.7
	1.6	1.8	3.1			Debt/Worth	1.7	2.0
	-3.3	7.0	5.7				5.5	4.2
		39.0	69.0			% Profit Before Taxes/Tangible	30.5	18.4
	(29)	21.3	(28) 32.4			Net Worth	(54) 7.3	(64) 6.6
		.4	19.0				-4.4	-2.3
	17.8	13.2	14.1			% Profit Before Taxes/Total	8.9	7.5
	5.2	4.3	9.0			Assets	3.3	2.4
	-1.4	-3.2	4.9				-2.2	-3.0
	28.9	25.5	16.4				13.7	14.6
	17.8	13.3	7.4			Sales/Net Fixed Assets	7.5	5.9
	11.6	7.1	4.8				3.8	3.0
	4.3	3.1	2.7				2.5	2.4
	2.5	2.4	2.2			Sales/Total Assets	1.9	1.9
	2.1	1.9	1.7				1.2	1.4
		.5	1.0				1.4	1.4
	(33)	1.5	1.7			% Depr., Dep., Amort./Sales	(57) 2.3	(70) 2.4
		3.5	2.3				4.0	4.4
		.8					1.1	1.6
	(12)	1.6				% Officers', Directors'	(18) 2.6	(19) 3.0
		4.3				Owners' Comp/Sales	4.3	5.4
8431M	32414M	507157M	1546078M	852347M	2073163M	Net Sales ($)	2442961M	3339373M
620M	10864M	200024M	702454M	452108M	964926M	Total Assets ($)	1624952M	1775113M

© RMA 2007

M = $ thousand   MM = $ million
See Pages 11 through 21 for Explanation of Ratios and Data

Comparative Historical Data | Current Data Sorted by Sales

			Type of Statement						
16	19	25	Unqualified			2	4	19	
20	19	18	Reviewed	2	2	2	7	5	
20	8	13	Compiled	4	1	1	7		
7	5	6	Tax Returns	1	1	2	2		
18	27	29	Other	1	1	3	6	18	
4/1/04-	4/1/05-	4/1/06-			26 (4/1-9/30/06)		65 (10/1/06-3/31/07)		
3/31/05	3/31/06	3/31/07							
ALL	ALL	ALL		0-1MM	1-3MM	3-5MM	5-10MM	10-25MM	25MM & OVER
81	78	91	NUMBER OF STATEMENTS	8	5	10	26	42	
%	%	%	ASSETS	%	%	%	%	%	%
5.7	8.6	7.4	Cash & Equivalents				12.9	8.3	3.9
28.4	29.0	27.7	Trade Receivables (net)				26.2	31.5	26.2
28.3	28.4	30.6	Inventory				28.7	29.2	34.5
2.3	2.6	2.0	All Other Current				3.2	2.1	1.5
64.8	68.5	67.7	Total Current				71.1	71.2	66.1
30.5	25.0	24.6	Fixed Assets (net)				21.8	22.7	27.6
.6	1.5	2.8	Intangibles (net)				2.4	1.5	1.9
4.2	5.0	4.8	All Other Non-Current				4.7	4.6	4.5
100.0	100.0	100.0	Total				100.0	100.0	100.0
			LIABILITIES						
22.5	18.6	13.8	Notes Payable-Short Term				11.9	16.9	13.7
3.6	2.6	3.4	Cur. Mat.-L.T.D.				6.1	2.7	3.1
18.0	16.0	18.9	Trade Payables				17.6	17.1	19.6
.2	.2	.2	Income Taxes Payable				.8	.2	.2
4.8	5.6	8.0	All Other Current				11.1	9.0	6.6
49.1	43.2	44.4	Total Current				47.5	45.9	43.2
16.8	14.6	15.6	Long-Term Debt				13.1	10.6	19.0
.9	.8	.3	Deferred Taxes				.1	.1	.6
7.0	7.3	6.0	All Other Non-Current				3.3	5.2	8.4
26.2	34.2	33.7	Net Worth				36.1	38.2	28.8
100.0	100.0	100.0	Total Liabilities & Net Worth				100.0	100.0	100.0
			INCOME DATA						
100.0	100.0	100.0	Net Sales				100.0	100.0	100.0
27.6	22.8	21.5	Gross Profit				26.6	22.1	16.4
22.9	17.0	16.0	Operating Expenses				23.8	18.3	9.0
4.8	5.8	5.6	Operating Profit				2.8	3.8	7.3
1.1	1.4	1.6	All Other Expenses (net)				.2	.8	2.1
3.6	4.4	3.9	Profit Before Taxes				2.6	2.9	5.2
			RATIOS						
2.3	2.7	2.3					2.1	3.1	2.2
1.5	1.9	1.6	Current				1.8	1.4	1.6
1.1	1.3	1.1					1.2	1.1	1.2
1.3	1.4	1.2					1.1	1.7	1.2
.9	.9	.8	Quick				.8	.7	.7
.5	.6	.5					.7	.5	.5

							Sales/Receivables						
37	10.0	33	11.0	32	11.6			21	17.3	32	11.5	35	10.6
47	7.7	42	8.6	42	8.6	Sales/Receivables		40	9.2	46	7.9	42	8.6
60	6.1	50	7.3	54	6.7			47	7.7	65	5.6	49	7.5
23	15.8	33	11.2	39	9.3			1	267.7	44	8.3	41	8.9
60	6.0	51	7.2	60	6.1	Cost of Sales/Inventory		60	6.1	59	6.1	68	5.4
100	3.6	80	4.6	89	4.1			95	3.8	82	4.4	90	4.0
21	17.0	16	23.5	21	17.6			0	UND	16	22.7	24	15.0
33	11.2	30	12.1	33	11.1	Cost of Sales/Payables		38	9.5	29	12.6	34	10.6
50	7.3	42	8.7	49	7.4			61	6.0	44	8.4	46	8.0

			Sales/Working Capital						
5.3	4.7	5.7					5.4	5.2	6.7
10.8	9.0	10.8	Sales/Working Capital				11.4	15.0	9.7
24.4	17.0	33.5					NM	54.9	30.8

						EBIT/Interest						
	16.2		17.2		9.0			9.9	17.9		7.3
(76)	4.6	(68)	4.6	(81)	3.5	EBIT/Interest		6.0	(22) 1.4	(38)	3.6
	1.3		1.5		1.0			1.9	-.8		2.3

						Net Profit + Depr., Dep., Amort./Cur. Mat. L/T/D					
	7.7		15.9		8.4					9.3
(20)	3.5	(23)	5.2	(34)	4.0	Net Profit + Depr., Dep., Amort./Cur. Mat. L/T/D			(22)	4.3
	1.7		1.9		1.7					1.9

			Fixed/Worth						
.4	.2	.3					.4	.2	.4
.7	.5	.6	Fixed/Worth				.6	.6	.9
2.5	1.6	2.0					NM	3.4	1.9

			Debt/Worth						
.8	.6	.9					1.0	.7	1.4
1.9	1.7	2.0	Debt/Worth				1.4	1.9	2.6
4.5	3.4	5.9					NM	10.6	5.8

						% Profit Before Taxes/Tangible Net Worth					
	48.0		49.8		50.3				41.4	69.0
(69)	21.3	(68)	22.4	(75)	22.8	% Profit Before Taxes/Tangible Net Worth		(21)	20.7 (36)	27.2
	6.0		5.7		7.2				-2.3	19.0

			% Profit Before Taxes/Total Assets						
16.2	19.4	14.1					14.8	13.2	14.9
6.2	9.4	8.3	% Profit Before Taxes/Total Assets				10.5	3.7	9.1
.5	1.4	.9					3.1	-4.3	5.3

			Sales/Net Fixed Assets						
19.3	32.7	24.1					212.2	25.3	21.0
8.6	12.8	12.4	Sales/Net Fixed Assets				21.5	11.6	8.9
4.6	5.9	5.6					7.1	6.6	4.7

			Sales/Total Assets						
2.8	3.3	2.9					4.0	3.1	2.7
2.2	2.4	2.3	Sales/Total Assets				2.5	2.4	2.3
1.6	1.7	1.8					2.0	1.8	1.9

						% Depr., Dep., Amort./Sales					
	1.0		.8		.9				.5	.9
(77)	1.9	(63)	1.6	(85)	1.6	% Depr., Dep., Amort./Sales			1.6 (40)	1.5
	3.5		3.1		2.9				2.7	2.3

						% Officers', Directors' Owners' Comp/Sales					
	.8		.7		.9					
(30)	2.5	(14)	2.9	(21)	2.1	% Officers', Directors' Owners' Comp/Sales				
	6.3		6.3		5.0					

4144025M	5092486M	5019590M	Net Sales ($)	18467M	20607M	68446M	442175M	4469895M	
2197579M	2204307M	2330996M	Total Assets ($)	8729M	13072M	26734M	201772M	2080689M	

M = $ thousand   MM = $ million
See Pages 11 through 21 for Explanation of Ratios and Data

MANUFACTURING—Steel Wire Drawing NAICS 331222 (SIC 3315)

Current Data Sorted by Assets | **Comparative Historical Data**

Type of Statement

	0-500M	500M-2MM	2-10MM	10-50MM	50-100MM	100-250MM		4/1/02-3/31/03 ALL	4/1/03-3/31/04 ALL
Unqualified			1	6	3	2		11	12
Reviewed		2	3	4				12	18
Compiled			4					5	4
Tax Returns								6	5
Other		2	3	7	1	1		18	19
		10 (4/1-9/30/06)		31 (10/1/06-3/31/07)					
NUMBER OF STATEMENTS		6	11	17	4	3		52	58

Data for the 0-500M and 500M-2MM asset columns is not available (percentages/ratios). Data shown is for the 2-10MM and 10-50MM columns.

2-10MM %	10-50MM %		4/1/02-3/31/03 ALL %	4/1/03-3/31/04 ALL %
		ASSETS		
5.6	5.3	Cash & Equivalents	5.9	6.3
29.7	22.5	Trade Receivables (net)	25.2	27.0
38.7	31.5	Inventory	33.2	28.2
1.8	.4	All Other Current	1.5	1.4
75.7	59.6	Total Current	65.8	62.9
16.5	36.2	Fixed Assets (net)	25.1	28.4
.8	1.0	Intangibles (net)	2.5	1.9
7.0	3.1	All Other Non-Current	6.6	6.7
100.0	100.0	Total	100.0	100.0
		LIABILITIES		
17.1	17.1	Notes Payable-Short Term	20.0	15.6
2.5	3.6	Cur. Mat.-L.T.D.	3.2	3.4
16.1	13.5	Trade Payables	16.8	17.2
.4	.0	Income Taxes Payable	.3	.2
5.1	4.4	All Other Current	5.5	7.6
41.3	38.5	Total Current	45.7	44.0
14.2	16.2	Long-Term Debt	10.9	11.0
.2	1.1	Deferred Taxes	.8	.6
1.7	2.7	All Other Non-Current	5.7	7.4
42.6	41.5	Net Worth	36.9	37.1
100.0	100.0	Total Liabilities & Net Worth	100.0	100.0
		INCOME DATA		
100.0	100.0	Net Sales	100.0	100.0
25.7	16.9	Gross Profit	21.9	17.3
20.5	12.6	Operating Expenses	19.9	16.2
5.2	4.3	Operating Profit	2.0	1.1
.4	1.3	All Other Expenses (net)	.4	.9
4.8	3.0	Profit Before Taxes	1.5	.1
		RATIOS		
4.1	3.9	Current	1.9	2.9
2.0	1.4		1.3	1.4
1.3	1.0		1.1	1.1
1.6	1.6	Quick	1.0	1.4
.8	.7		.6	.8
.4	.5		.4	.4
36 10.2	28 13.1	Sales/Receivables	35 10.4	38 9.7
42 8.7	43 8.5		46 7.9	45 8.1
47 7.7	55 6.7		55 6.6	55 6.7
53 6.9	37 9.9	Cost of Sales/Inventory	50 7.3	31 11.8
83 4.4	67 5.5		74 4.9	56 6.5
115 3.2	95 3.8		121 3.0	84 4.4
16 23.4	14 25.3	Cost of Sales/Payables	22 16.2	14 26.1
28 13.2	28 12.9		38 9.6	27 13.3
37 9.9	38 9.5		52 7.0	50 7.3
4.4	4.1	Sales/Working Capital	5.1	5.4
5.7	12.6		12.0	15.6
14.9	NM		62.3	72.8
28.6	18.0	EBIT/Interest	3.0	3.9
(10) 4.1	(15) 1.9		(45) 1.5	(52) 1.3
1.6	1.2		-1.7	-.9
		Net Profit + Depr., Dep., Amort./Cur. Mat. L/T/D	49.0	3.9
			(15) 2.6	(17) 1.6
			1.3	.7
.2	.4	Fixed/Worth	.2	.3
.3	.9		.7	.8
1.0	1.6		1.5	2.2
.4	.7	Debt/Worth	1.0	.9
2.0	1.9		1.9	1.9
3.3	3.9		3.6	6.7
67.8	19.8	% Profit Before Taxes/Tangible Net Worth	17.5	19.6
22.4	(16) 13.8		(47) 8.2	(52) 1.0
11.9	2.3		-5.3	-14.1
21.0	11.8	% Profit Before Taxes/Total Assets	5.3	5.8
13.9	3.2		2.0	.6
3.0	.7		-3.7	-3.5
41.1	12.0	Sales/Net Fixed Assets	25.1	23.6
24.5	7.2		8.9	8.4
7.8	3.0		4.5	4.6
3.2	2.6	Sales/Total Assets	2.3	2.6
2.4	2.1		2.0	2.2
1.9	1.3		1.3	1.6
.5	.8	% Depr., Dep., Amort./Sales	.7	1.2
(10) 1.3	(16) 2.1		(47) 2.0	(54) 2.4
2.2	5.8		4.0	4.1
		% Officers', Directors' Owners' Comp/Sales	2.1	1.7
			(18) 3.9	(19) 3.9
			8.1	7.3

500M-2MM	2-10MM	10-50MM	50-100MM	100-250MM		4/1/02-3/31/03 ALL	4/1/03-3/31/04 ALL
11800M	107711M	962977M	816577M	358873M	Net Sales ($)	1318766M	1619493M
5514M	46073M	448986M	287513M	370842M	Total Assets ($)	1088433M	829139M

M = $ thousand   MM = $ million
See Pages 11 through 21 for Explanation of Ratios and Data

Comparative Historical Data   **Current Data Sorted by Sales**

12	13	12	Type of Statement						
12	13	12	Unqualified				1	2	9
17	8	9	Reviewed	2			1	2	4
11	5	4	Compiled				3	1	
4	3	2	Tax Returns	2					
15	18	14	Other	2			1	3	8
4/1/04-3/31/05	4/1/05-3/31/06	4/1/06-3/31/07			10 (4/1-9/30/06)		31 (10/1-3/31/07)		
ALL	ALL	ALL		0-1MM	1-3MM	3-5MM	5-10MM	10-25MM	25MM & OVER
59	47	41	NUMBER OF STATEMENTS	6			6	8	21
%	%	%	**ASSETS**	%	%	%	%	%	%
6.1	5.5	4.6	Cash & Equivalents						3.6
30.7	28.0	25.2	Trade Receivables (net)	D	D		D	D	23.5
29.8	29.7	32.8	Inventory	A	A		A	A	33.6
.9	1.2	1.0	All Other Current	T	T		T	T	.7
67.6	64.4	63.6	Total Current	A	A		A	A	61.3
21.8	29.0	29.8	Fixed Assets (net)						34.0
4.2	3.2	1.6	Intangibles (net)	N	N		N	N	1.0
6.5	3.5	5.0	All Other Non-Current	O	O		O	O	3.7
100.0	100.0	100.0	Total	T	T		T	T	100.0
			LIABILITIES						
14.4	13.3	16.7	Notes Payable-Short Term	A	A		A	A	15.8
2.3	3.3	4.0	Cur. Mat.-L.T.D.	V	V		V	V	2.8
18.4	15.8	15.4	Trade Payables	A	A		A	A	15.6
.3	.2	.2	Income Taxes Payable	I	I		I	I	.1
5.8	8.8	5.9	All Other Current	L	L		L	L	6.3
41.2	41.3	42.2	Total Current	A	A		A	A	40.5
13.2	14.9	17.5	Long-Term Debt	B	B		B	B	15.6
.8	.8	.7	Deferred Taxes	L	L		L	L	1.2
6.9	4.8	2.8	All Other Non-Current	E	E		E	E	2.5
37.9	38.2	36.8	Net Worth						40.1
100.0	100.0	100.0	Total Liabilties & Net Worth						100.0
			INCOME DATA						
100.0	100.0	100.0	Net Sales						100.0
24.5	22.7	20.9	Gross Profit						14.1
19.7	18.3	16.4	Operating Expenses						10.2
4.8	4.4	4.6	Operating Profit						3.9
1.2	1.1	1.0	All Other Expenses (net)						.8
3.6	3.2	3.6	Profit Before Taxes						3.1
			RATIOS						
2.7	2.9	3.0							2.2
1.5	1.5	1.4	Current						1.4
1.1	1.1	1.0							1.1
1.7	1.7	1.4							1.1
.8	.8	.7	Quick						.7
.5	.5	.5							.5
34 10.7	35 10.4	31 11.6							31 11.9
49 7.5	45 8.1	42 8.7	Sales/Receivables						43 8.5
62 5.9	62 5.9	53 6.9							56 6.5
38 9.7	37 9.8	47 7.8							47 7.8
67 5.4	77 4.7	72 5.1	Cost of Sales/Inventory						64 5.7
93 3.9	97 3.8	98 3.7							91 4.0
14 25.4	15 24.9	20 18.6							20 18.6
31 11.6	34 10.8	29 12.8	Cost of Sales/Payables						32 11.6
51 7.2	48 7.6	44 8.4							44 8.4
5.7	4.9	5.3							6.2
10.1	10.7	10.3	Sales/Working Capital						11.1
22.9	34.7	235.8							35.4
11.5	9.0	11.4							16.4
(50) 5.1	(41) 3.6	(38) 2.2	EBIT/Interest					(20) 2.2	
2.0	1.1	1.3							1.4
6.6	10.6	5.8							6.6
(19) 3.4	(14) 3.8	(13) 2.5	Net Profit + Depr., Dep., Amort./Cur. Mat. L/T/D					(11) 2.9	
2.3	.5	1.6							1.6
.2	.3	.3							.6
.5	.8	1.0	Fixed/Worth						1.0
1.9	1.9	1.6							1.4
.8	.8	1.0							1.0
1.8	1.8	1.9	Debt/Worth						1.6
5.0	4.6	3.9							3.5
47.8	36.5	28.8							19.4
(52) 22.5	(41) 21.1	(38) 14.5	% Profit Before Taxes/Tangible Net Worth						13.3
12.1	2.5	6.3							5.5
14.3	13.7	14.1							11.3
7.3	6.4	3.3	% Profit Before Taxes/Total Assets						3.2
3.2	.7	1.1							1.2
33.4	21.0	20.1							14.9
11.5	7.8	8.5	Sales/Net Fixed Assets						8.3
6.5	4.0	4.5							3.2
2.8	2.8	2.9							2.7
2.2	2.0	2.2	Sales/Total Assets						2.1
1.6	1.3	1.6							1.5
.9	.5	1.0							.7
(48) 1.9	(44) 1.5	(38) 1.7	% Depr., Dep., Amort./Sales					(20) 1.5	
3.2	2.6	4.0							4.8
1.3	3.0	2.4							
(19) 4.0	(13) 3.6	(10) 4.3	% Officers', Directors' Owners' Comp/Sales						
8.9	10.5	5.9							
1632059M	1747439M	2257938M	Net Sales ($)		11800M		46686M	113097M	2086355M
702550M	740286M	1158928M	Total Assets ($)		5514M		18014M	73876M	1061524M

M = $ thousand   MM = $ million
See Pages 11 through 21 for Explanation of Ratios and Data

Current Data Sorted by Assets · Comparative Historical Data

Date ranges for current "Other" data: 4 (4/1-9/30/06) · 26 (10/1/06-3/31/07)

Type of Statement	0-500M	500M-2MM	2-10MM	10-50MM	50-100MM	100-250MM		6 / 4/1/02-3/31/03 / ALL	3 / 4/1/03-3/31/04 / ALL
Unqualified				5	2	1		1	1
Reviewed		2	2	2				4	4
Compiled			1					1	2
Tax Returns	1								1
Other	1		4	8	1			6	3
NUMBER OF STATEMENTS	2	2	7	15	3	1		12	11

0-500M	500M-2MM	2-10MM	10-50MM %	50-100MM	100-250MM		6 / 4/1/02-3/31/03 ALL %	3 / 4/1/03-3/31/04 ALL %
						ASSETS		
			3.9			Cash & Equivalents	3.6	5.2
			33.3			Trade Receivables (net)	31.7	38.4
			26.3			Inventory	18.2	17.4
			.7			All Other Current	6.8	.3
			64.1			Total Current	60.4	61.3
			30.2			Fixed Assets (net)	25.6	28.7
			.1			Intangibles (net)	7.5	2.6
			5.5			All Other Non-Current	6.5	7.4
			100.0			Total	100.0	100.0
						LIABILITIES		
			19.0			Notes Payable-Short Term	13.5	27.5
			8.0			Cur. Mat.-L.T.D.	2.2	2.0
			27.1			Trade Payables	14.2	22.8
			.2			Income Taxes Payable	.7	.0
			6.1			All Other Current	6.3	3.5
			60.3			Total Current	36.9	55.8
			15.7			Long-Term Debt	11.5	15.6
			.2			Deferred Taxes	.0	.2
			3.1			All Other Non-Current	4.6	2.8
			20.6			Net Worth	46.9	25.6
			100.0			Total Liabilities & Net Worth	100.0	100.0
						INCOME DATA		
			100.0			Net Sales	100.0	100.0
			16.0			Gross Profit	32.8	24.9
			11.3			Operating Expenses	28.4	22.0
			4.7			Operating Profit	4.4	2.9
			1.7			All Other Expenses (net)	.8	1.4
			2.9			Profit Before Taxes	3.6	1.6
						RATIOS		
			1.5			Current	4.9	3.4
			1.2				1.4	1.2
			.8				1.0	.7
			1.0			Quick	3.6	2.3
			.7				.7	.7
			.4				.5	.4
		26	14.3			Sales/Receivables	38 9.6	36 10.1
		39	9.5				45 8.1	51 7.2
		53	6.9				65 5.6	57 6.5
		16	22.5			Cost of Sales/Inventory	15 24.5	23 15.5
		37	9.8				31 11.8	29 12.5
		49	7.5				67 5.5	55 6.7
		31	11.9			Cost of Sales/Payables	13 27.6	22 16.4
		35	10.4				38 9.7	41 9.0
		47	7.7				45 8.2	55 6.7
			15.3			Sales/Working Capital	6.5	5.7
			40.0				16.6	27.7
			-25.9				119.1	-14.2
			5.7			EBIT/Interest	11.3	
		(14)	2.9				(11) 3.8	
			2.1				1.1	
						Net Profit + Depr., Dep., Amort./Cur. Mat. L/T/D		
			.6			Fixed/Worth	.2	.7
			1.6				.5	1.5
			2.9				3.7	-1.5
			2.1			Debt/Worth	.4	.6
			4.4				1.3	9.0
			11.3				16.4	-8.7
			53.2			% Profit Before Taxes/Tangible Net Worth	11.6	
		(14)	36.8				(11) 7.9	
			18.7				1.3	
			8.4			% Profit Before Taxes/Total Assets	11.5	15.6
			6.0				3.4	4.2
			3.7				.2	-10.0
			24.7			Sales/Net Fixed Assets	27.9	35.6
			9.7				8.2	8.8
			7.8				4.2	3.4
			4.1			Sales/Total Assets	3.5	3.7
			3.1				2.2	1.9
			1.8				1.2	1.4
			.6			% Depr., Dep., Amort./Sales	.6	.6
			1.4				(11) 2.2	2.7
			2.3				5.0	5.4
						% Officers', Directors' Owners' Comp/Sales		
3941M	7146M	75611M	1211836M	528720M	710054M	Net Sales ($)	342429M	155626M
923M	1657M	31037M	355757M	177542M	240355M	Total Assets ($)	157988M	69862M

M = $ thousand   MM = $ million
See Pages 11 through 21 for Explanation of Ratios and Data

Comparative Historical Data / Current Data Sorted by Sales

4/1/04-3/31/05 ALL	4/1/05-3/31/06 ALL	4/1/06-3/31/07 ALL		0-1MM	1-3MM	3-5MM	5-10MM	10-25MM	25MM & OVER
			Type of Statement						
4	4	8	Unqualified						8
4	6	4	Reviewed				1	1	2
3	1	1	Compiled				1		
		1	Tax Returns	1					
7	7	16	Other			3	2	5	6
					4 (4/1-9/30/06)		26 (10/1/06-3/31/07)		
18	18	30	**NUMBER OF STATEMENTS**	1		3	4	6	16
%	%	%	**ASSETS**	%	%	%	%	%	%
6.6	7.5	7.1	Cash & Equivalents		DATA NOT AVAILABLE				6.5
40.1	33.0	34.0	Trade Receivables (net)						37.2
21.8	28.4	25.2	Inventory						27.9
1.1	.5	1.1	All Other Current						1.6
69.7	69.4	67.3	Total Current						73.2
21.2	19.4	24.5	Fixed Assets (net)						23.0
.7	3.0	1.7	Intangibles (net)						.0
8.4	8.2	6.5	All Other Non-Current						3.8
100.0	100.0	100.0	Total						100.0
			LIABILITIES						
14.8	16.3	16.6	Notes Payable-Short Term						17.1
1.4	1.0	4.6	Cur. Mat.-L.T.D.						2.3
19.3	23.3	19.6	Trade Payables						25.3
.0	.2	.2	Income Taxes Payable						.4
11.8	11.8	7.7	All Other Current						7.2
47.3	52.5	48.7	Total Current						52.3
15.5	7.3	12.1	Long-Term Debt						14.6
.3	.4	.5	Deferred Taxes						.2
4.5	4.4	3.9	All Other Non-Current						4.2
32.4	35.4	34.7	Net Worth						28.7
100.0	100.0	100.0	Total Liabilties & Net Worth						100.0
			INCOME DATA						
100.0	100.0	100.0	Net Sales						100.0
20.6	19.9	21.4	Gross Profit						14.2
18.9	16.8	15.0	Operating Expenses						10.0
1.7	3.2	6.4	Operating Profit						4.2
.7	.9	1.1	All Other Expenses (net)						.8
1.0	2.3	5.3	Profit Before Taxes						3.4
			RATIOS						
4.3	2.9	2.8	Current						1.8
1.4	1.3	1.4							1.4
1.0	1.0	1.0							1.1
3.3	1.2	1.9	Quick						1.3
1.1	.8	.8							.8
.4	.5	.6							.6
38 9.7	**31** 11.6	**28** 13.1	Sales/Receivables						**30** 12.3
44 8.3	**44** 8.3	**37** 9.8							**40** 9.1
57 6.4	**52** 7.0	**54** 6.8							**58** 6.3
18 20.2	**24** 15.5	**16** 22.8	Cost of Sales/Inventory						**21** 17.7
35 10.5	**45** 8.2	**36** 10.0							**34** 10.6
68 5.4	**62** 5.9	**53** 6.9							**46** 7.9
9 41.1	**7** 55.3	**14** 25.5	Cost of Sales/Payables						**25** 14.6
35 10.3	**35** 10.5	**31** 11.6							**33** 11.1
45 8.1	**67** 5.4	**43** 8.5							**42** 8.6
4.7	8.5	7.1	Sales/Working Capital						7.7
15.5	16.2	16.4							20.4
NM	NM	-339.8							50.1
4.2	8.6	13.4	EBIT/Interest						11.2
(14) 1.6	(17) 3.9	(27) 4.0							3.6
.6	1.4	2.4							2.1
		8.1	Net Profit + Depr., Dep., Amort./Cur. Mat. L/T/D						
		(11) 4.4							
		1.4							
.2	.2	.3	Fixed/Worth						.4
.7	.7	.9							1.1
1.7	2.5	2.8							1.8
.4	.8	.7	Debt/Worth						1.4
2.3	3.1	3.2							3.6
14.2	10.3	7.3							7.4
27.5	44.3	57.1	% Profit Before Taxes/Tangible Net Worth						50.1
(17) 19.4	(15) 13.6	(29) 38.0							36.8
1.0	2.9	20.9							19.8
11.0	9.4	19.8	% Profit Before Taxes/Total Assets						15.8
1.6	3.2	9.6							6.7
-.3	1.4	5.5							3.9
51.8	58.6	29.3	Sales/Net Fixed Assets						27.7
14.3	12.6	15.4							15.0
5.4	6.5	8.8							9.1
3.9	3.5	4.3	Sales/Total Assets						4.1
2.8	2.7	3.0							3.2
1.5	2.0	1.8							2.8
.8	.5	.7	% Depr., Dep., Amort./Sales						.6
(15) 1.9	(16) 1.3	(26) 1.0							(15) .9
2.9	2.9	2.2							1.5
			% Officers', Directors' Owners' Comp/Sales						
477324M	736105M	2537308M	Net Sales ($)	817M		10270M	27133M	105967M	2393121M
194952M	232222M	807271M	Total Assets ($)	446M		2134M	15070M	50683M	738938M

M = $ thousand MM = $ million

See Pages 11 through 21 for Explanation of Ratios and Data

Current Data Sorted by Assets   Comparative Historical Data

	0-500M	500M-2MM	2-10MM	10-50MM	50-100MM	100-250MM	Type of Statement	4/1/02-3/31/03 ALL	4/1/03-3/31/04 ALL
			10	17	6	4	Unqualified	13	12
	1	5	12				Reviewed	7	13
1	1	4	1				Compiled	3	8
3	2	1	1				Tax Returns	3	6
1		6	10	3	1		Other	10	14
	11 (4/1-9/30/06)			79 (10/1/06-3/31/07)					
5	4	26	41	9	5		NUMBER OF STATEMENTS	36	53
%	%	%	%	%	%	**ASSETS**	%	%
		4.7	3.6			Cash & Equivalents	4.0	4.3
		28.6	28.9			Trade Receivables (net)	28.2	31.7
		32.9	22.8			Inventory	24.2	23.6
		1.2	3.4			All Other Current	2.1	1.8
		67.5	58.8			Total Current	58.5	61.4
		24.4	33.0			Fixed Assets (net)	34.2	32.7
		5.3	2.3			Intangibles (net)	3.2	2.2
		2.9	6.0			All Other Non-Current	4.2	3.6
		100.0	100.0			Total	100.0	100.0
						LIABILITIES		
		14.5	10.5			Notes Payable-Short Term	11.1	11.0
		2.1	3.4			Cur. Mat.-L.T.D.	4.2	5.1
		21.6	16.6			Trade Payables	16.3	18.3
		.5	.1			Income Taxes Payable	.1	.1
		7.6	10.5			All Other Current	8.8	9.5
		46.3	41.1			Total Current	40.3	44.0
		12.4	18.0			Long-Term Debt	15.5	17.9
		1.1	.8			Deferred Taxes	1.1	.7
		14.9	3.8			All Other Non-Current	15.0	10.7
		25.3	36.2			Net Worth	28.1	26.7
		100.0	100.0			Total Liabilties & Net Worth	100.0	100.0
						INCOME DATA		
		100.0	100.0			Net Sales	100.0	100.0
		22.6	16.3			Gross Profit	20.0	23.5
		15.3	11.5			Operating Expenses	16.0	20.2
		7.3	4.8			Operating Profit	3.9	3.4
		1.9	1.5			All Other Expenses (net)	1.5	1.0
		5.4	3.3			Profit Before Taxes	2.4	2.3
						RATIOS		
		1.9	2.1				2.9	2.3
		1.5	1.4			Current	1.4	1.3
		1.1	1.1				1.2	1.0
		1.0	1.0				1.3	1.3
		.7	.8			Quick	.9	.8
		.4	.6				.6	.5
		29 12.6	34 10.7				34 10.7	35 10.4
		40 9.1	48 7.6			Sales/Receivables	45 8.2	48 7.6
		50 7.3	55 6.7				61 6.0	63 5.8
		34 10.8	27 13.6				27 13.6	28 13.2
		55 6.7	44 8.3			Cost of Sales/Inventory	40 9.2	43 8.5
		92 4.0	59 6.2				78 4.7	72 5.1
		23 16.0	17 21.7				18 20.1	25 14.8
		32 11.6	29 12.4			Cost of Sales/Payables	30 12.2	34 10.9
		55 6.6	39 9.4				37 9.9	47 7.7
		7.0	6.7				5.1	7.4
		17.9	15.1			Sales/Working Capital	16.1	19.1
		52.3	44.9				42.2	-828.9
		10.3	13.3				8.5	8.3
		(24) 6.5	(39) 5.0			EBIT/Interest	(33) 3.4	(46) 3.4
		2.0	2.0				1.2	.7
			22.8				4.3	8.4
			(13) 5.8			Net Profit + Depr., Dep., Amort./Cur. Mat. L/T/D	(11) 2.8	(15) 2.2
			2.2				1.7	1.2
		.4	.5				.5	.6
		1.0	1.0			Fixed/Worth	1.0	1.5
		18.0	1.9				3.3	4.3
		.9	.9				.9	1.7
		2.6	1.9			Debt/Worth	2.1	3.1
		51.6	4.2				9.4	8.9
		104.8	37.2				53.9	52.9
		(21) 42.6	(36) 18.3			% Profit Before Taxes/Tangible Net Worth	(29) 11.3	(45) 19.2
		23.2	9.5				4.5	.1
		22.3	18.0				17.1	12.5
		11.0	6.4			% Profit Before Taxes/Total Assets	5.0	6.3
		4.6	1.7				.8	.4
		26.8	12.2				15.4	15.1
		16.4	6.2			Sales/Net Fixed Assets	7.0	8.2
		5.1	4.7				3.4	4.1
		3.8	2.8				3.0	2.8
		2.7	2.2			Sales/Total Assets	2.1	2.3
		1.6	1.8				1.5	1.8
		.7	1.1				1.7	1.2
		(23) 1.3	(37) 2.1			% Depr., Dep., Amort./Sales	(31) 2.5	(48) 2.3
		2.3	3.1				4.6	3.9
							1.0	1.6
						% Officers', Directors' Owners' Comp/Sales	(14) 1.9	(14) 2.6
							3.4	4.0
8007M	19113M	442010M	2203600M	1282031M	1459319M	Net Sales ($)	1190099M	1615423M
1739M	4830M	150079M	939011M	662228M	745669M	Total Assets ($)	631192M	826312M

M = $ thousand   MM = $ million
See Pages 11 through 21 for Explanation of Ratios and Data

Comparative Historical Data | Current Data Sorted by Sales

			Type of Statement	0-1MM	1-3MM	3-5MM	5-10MM	10-25MM	25MM & OVER
26	23	37	Unqualified				1	6	30
19	12	18	Reviewed			1	3	4	10
9	6	7	Compiled		2	2		1	2
1	3	7	Tax Returns		3	1		1	1
17	33	21	Other	1.	1	2	1	3	14
4/1/04-3/31/05 ALL	4/1/05-3/31/06 ALL	4/1/06-3/31/07 ALL		11 (4/1-9/30/06)			79 (10/1/06-3/31/07)		
72	77	90	**NUMBER OF STATEMENTS**	1	6	4	7	15	57
%	%	%	**ASSETS**	%	%	%	%	%	%
4.0	5.4	5.6	Cash & Equivalents					5.1	3.7
29.0	30.7	27.8	Trade Receivables (net)					28.5	29.2
25.1	25.4	26.2	Inventory					28.1	24.9
2.5	2.9	2.7	All Other Current					1.7	2.8
60.5	64.3	62.3	Total Current					63.4	60.5
30.2	30.1	29.2	Fixed Assets (net)					28.7	30.7
3.5	2.1	3.8	Intangibles (net)					2.3	4.1
5.8	3.4	4.7	All Other Non-Current					5.6	4.7
100.0	100.0	100.0	Total					100.0	100.0
			LIABILITIES						
14.2	12.5	10.5	Notes Payable-Short Term					11.9	9.8
3.9	4.1	3.0	Cur. Mat.-L.T.D.					2.1	3.2
19.0	19.8	18.5	Trade Payables					13.7	18.9
.2	.3	.2	Income Taxes Payable					.2	.3
7.7	10.0	8.5	All Other Current					7.8	8.8
45.1	46.7	40.8	Total Current					35.6	40.9
17.7	16.3	16.7	Long-Term Debt					14.3	15.2
.9	.7	1.1	Deferred Taxes					.4	1.2
5.9	4.1	9.7	All Other Non-Current					.4	9.4
30.4	32.2	31.9	Net Worth					49.3	33.3
100.0	100.0	100.0	Total Liabilities & Net Worth					100.0	100.0
			INCOME DATA						
100.0	100.0	100.0	Net Sales					100.0	100.0
22.0	20.6	19.8	Gross Profit					17.4	16.2
16.2	15.1	14.5	Operating Expenses					11.8	11.2
5.8	5.5	5.4	Operating Profit					5.6	5.0
1.1	1.1	1.4	All Other Expenses (net)					.7	1.3
4.7	4.4	3.9	Profit Before Taxes					4.9	3.7
			RATIOS						
1.7	2.1	2.1	Current					2.7	2.1
1.3	1.4	1.6						1.5	1.7
1.0	1.1	1.2						1.2	1.1
1.0	1.0	1.2	Quick					1.3	1.1
.7	.8	.8						1.0	.8
.5	.5	.6						.7	.6
32 11.4	35 10.4	29 12.7	Sales/Receivables					30 12.0	29 12.5
43 8.6	45 8.1	43 8.5						45 8.2	41 8.9
56 6.5	57 6.4	53 6.9						53 6.9	55 6.7
31 11.7	29 12.8	28 13.2	Cost of Sales/Inventory					46 7.9	27 13.4
50 7.4	50 7.3	49 7.5						58 6.3	44 8.3
76 4.8	72 5.1	68 5.4						66 5.5	57 6.4
24 15.2	22 16.7	21 17.5	Cost of Sales/Payables					15 23.6	21 17.2
34 10.7	33 11.2	30 12.1						29 12.4	30 12.4
47 7.7	46 8.0	43 8.4						32 11.4	41 9.0
8.5	6.7	6.8	Sales/Working Capital					5.9	7.2
16.3	17.1	12.4						10.5	12.4
76.9	72.5	26.8						20.9	41.7
11.1	9.9	12.8	EBIT/Interest					10.1	14.5
(66) 4.2	(71) 4.6	(85) 5.3						(13) 5.1	(54) 5.5
1.9	1.9	2.0						2.5	2.2
6.0	7.7	7.9	Net Profit + Depr., Dep., Amort./Cur. Mat. L/T/D						9.0
(23) 3.0	(24) 2.6	(28) 3.3							(22) 3.9
1.3	1.6	2.0							2.5
.4	.5	.5	Fixed/Worth					.3	.5
1.2	1.0	1.0						.7	1.1
2.7	2.0	2.2						1.8	1.9
1.5	1.3	.9	Debt/Worth					.2	.9
2.5	2.4	2.0						.9	1.9
8.7	6.1	7.8						3.2	5.0
64.0	65.4	51.8	% Profit Before Taxes/Tangible Net Worth					46.7	52.8
(63) 21.7	(73) 29.0	(76) 30.7						(14) 18.0	(50) 33.0
6.2	7.6	12.1						8.1	14.4
14.2	15.3	18.3	% Profit Before Taxes/Total Assets					22.4	18.0
7.3	8.0	8.1						8.3	8.5
1.8	2.1	3.4						2.1	4.4
16.9	18.8	17.9	Sales/Net Fixed Assets					25.4	14.9
7.4	7.2	8.3						8.3	8.2
4.6	4.5	4.7						4.5	4.8
3.0	3.0	3.3	Sales/Total Assets					3.1	3.3
2.1	2.3	2.3						2.1	2.5
1.6	1.8	1.7						1.6	1.9
1.0	1.2	1.0	% Depr., Dep., Amort./Sales					1.0	1.0
(66) 2.0	(66) 1.9	(78) 1.6						(14) 2.0	(51) 1.6
3.3	3.3	2.6						3.6	2.5
1.2	1.1	1.1	% Officers', Directors' Owners' Comp/Sales						
(24) 1.8	(19) 2.7	(19) 2.1							
3.4	3.9	3.1							
3121433M	3994374M	5414080M	Net Sales ($)	479M	10445M	15236M	53563M	276111M	5058246M
1547377M	1852256M	2503556M	Total Assets ($)	282M	6585M	7698M	30145M	137402M	2321444M

M = $ thousand   MM = $ million
See Pages 11 through 21 for Explanation of Ratios and Data

		Current Data Sorted by Assets					Comparative Historical Data	
		5	1	3	2	**Type of Statement**		
		8				Unqualified	10	6
	1	2	1			Reviewed	12	11
1		1	1			Compiled	5	3
		2	10		5	Tax Returns	1	1
						Other	11	13
	6 (4/1-9/30/06)		37 (10/1/06-3/31/07)				4/1/02-3/31/03	4/1/03-3/31/04
0-500M	500M-2MM	2-10MM	10-50MM	50-100MM	100-250MM		ALL	ALL
1	1	18	12	4	7	**NUMBER OF STATEMENTS**	39	34
%	%	%	%	%	%	**ASSETS**	%	%
		4.1	4.5			Cash & Equivalents	6.5	2.8
		29.2	43.1			Trade Receivables (net)	25.8	27.5
		34.4	23.2			Inventory	29.1	28.1
		.5	1.9			All Other Current	1.5	3.7
		68.1	72.7			Total Current	62.9	62.1
		28.4	22.7			Fixed Assets (net)	27.3	26.9
		.8	.7			Intangibles (net)	5.5	5.9
		2.6	3.9			All Other Non-Current	4.3	5.0
		100.0	100.0			Total	100.0	100.0
						LIABILITIES		
		15.5	13.6			Notes Payable-Short Term	12.1	12.6
		6.0	2.7			Cur. Mat.-L.T.D.	3.8	4.2
		23.2	27.0			Trade Payables	13.8	18.2
		.5	.0			Income Taxes Payable	.3	.2
		6.7	10.9			All Other Current	5.4	5.9
		51.9	54.2			Total Current	35.4	41.2
		16.2	13.4			Long-Term Debt	13.4	9.8
		.5	.1			Deferred Taxes	.9	1.1
		5.1	7.1			All Other Non-Current	4.6	8.5
		26.3	25.2			Net Worth	45.8	39.4
		100.0	100.0			Total Liabilties & Net Worth	100.0	100.0
						INCOME DATA		
		100.0	100.0			Net Sales	100.0	100.0
		23.4	15.9			Gross Profit	28.9	23.5
		18.7	11.4			Operating Expenses	24.3	19.6
		4.7	4.5			Operating Profit	4.6	3.9
		1.1	1.6			All Other Expenses (net)	1.9	1.0
		3.5	2.9			Profit Before Taxes	2.8	2.8
						RATIOS		
		1.7	1.7				3.0	2.4
		1.2	1.3			Current	2.0	1.4
		1.1	1.1				1.1	1.1
		.9	1.2				1.9	1.0
		.6	.9			Quick	.8	.7
		.4	.6				.6	.5
		29 12.4	35 10.5				37 9.7	41 8.9
		41 8.9	41 8.8			Sales/Receivables	42 8.6	45 8.1
		46 7.9	77 4.7				51 7.1	62 5.9
		41 8.8	9 41.0				52 7.0	46 8.0
		58 6.3	21 17.3			Cost of Sales/Inventory	74 4.9	65 5.6
		73 5.0	62 5.9				116 3.1	93 3.9
		24 14.9	28 12.8				20 18.5	29 12.5
		34 10.8	35 10.4			Cost of Sales/Payables	33 11.2	41 9.0
		52 7.1	39 9.4				43 8.5	57 6.4
		10.1	7.3				4.2	4.2
		16.4	20.1			Sales/Working Capital	8.0	12.4
		281.6	68.0				28.9	49.5
		9.4	66.0				5.5	12.3
		3.1	(10) 1.8			EBIT/Interest	(35) 2.1	2.9
		1.9	.1				.6	-.3
						Net Profit + Depr., Dep.,		12.1 3.7
						Amort./Cur. Mat. L/T/D	(13) 1.7 (14) 1.3	
							.4 .2	
		.4	.2				.3	.4
		1.5	.7			Fixed/Worth	.7	.8
		3.6	1.4				1.5	1.4
		1.8	1.5				.5	.9
		3.7	3.9			Debt/Worth	1.7	1.7
		7.8	11.9				3.1	4.4
		85.1	63.0			% Profit Before Taxes/Tangible	42.2	42.8
	(17) 28.5		(10) 24.3			Net Worth	(35) 12.2 (31) 15.4	
		7.8	-1.3				.4 -3.1	
		17.5	12.3				9.2	10.2
		8.4	3.9			% Profit Before Taxes/Total Assets	3.1	4.6
		1.9	-1.7				.0	-2.8
		24.5	52.2				17.9	14.1
		11.6	26.7			Sales/Net Fixed Assets	8.5	7.8
		6.6	14.8				3.6	4.9
		3.7	4.7				2.8	2.7
		3.0	2.9			Sales/Total Assets	2.0	2.0
		2.3	2.2				1.4	1.6
		.8					.8	1.3
		1.4				% Depr., Dep., Amort./Sales	(38) 2.2 (29) 2.5	
		2.7					3.7	3.6
						% Officers', Directors'	2.5	
						Owners' Comp/Sales	(10) 7.1	
							9.8	
1660M	3536M	267696M	1460718M	1013921M	2610464M	Net Sales ($)	1975633M	2512083M
381M	1987M	91411M	409350M	330431M	1155343M	Total Assets ($)	1209453M	1473122M

M = $ thousand   MM = $ million
See Pages 11 through 21 for Explanation of Ratios and Data

Comparative Historical Data				Current Data Sorted by Sales					
			Type of Statement						
8	10	11	Unqualified					4	7
10	5	8	Reviewed			1	1	6	
2	2	4	Compiled			1	1	1	1
1	1	3	Tax Returns		1			2	
11	15	17	Other				1	1	15
					6 (4/1-9/30/06)			37 (10/1/06-3/31/07)	
4/1/04-3/31/05 ALL	4/1/05-3/31/06 ALL	4/1/06-3/31/07 ALL		0-1MM	1-3MM	3-5MM	5-10MM	10-25MM	25MM & OVER
32	33	43	**NUMBER OF STATEMENTS**		1	2	3	14	23
%	%	%	**ASSETS**	%	%	%	%	%	%
4.2	6.1	4.4	Cash & Equivalents	DATA NOT AVAILABLE				4.6	4.9
28.4	28.5	33.9	Trade Receivables (net)					28.7	38.3
29.1	28.5	30.5	Inventory					31.1	28.8
2.3	2.3	1.5	All Other Current					.7	2.3
64.1	65.4	70.3	Total Current					65.0	74.2
27.6	26.1	23.4	Fixed Assets (net)					31.1	16.9
3.4	3.2	2.4	Intangibles (net)					.9	3.8
4.9	5.3	3.8	All Other Non-Current					3.0	5.0
100.0	100.0	100.0	Total					100.0	100.0
			LIABILITIES						
13.6	11.7	13.9	Notes Payable-Short Term					14.2	15.2
5.8	5.2	4.8	Cur. Mat.-L.T.D.					3.0	3.8
18.2	16.8	21.9	Trade Payables					21.8	21.9
.2	.3	.3	Income Taxes Payable					.6	.2
7.1	6.3	8.0	All Other Current					8.3	8.7
44.8	40.2	48.9	Total Current					47.9	49.8
10.8	10.2	13.9	Long-Term Debt					20.4	8.6
1.4	.8	.5	Deferred Taxes					.6	.6
5.3	7.0	5.6	All Other Non-Current					6.3	6.7
37.7	41.7	31.1	Net Worth					24.7	34.3
100.0	100.0	100.0	Total Liabilties & Net Worth					100.0	100.0
			INCOME DATA						
100.0	100.0	100.0	Net Sales					100.0	100.0
24.5	21.7	20.0	Gross Profit					22.1	14.6
21.1	16.8	14.5	Operating Expenses					18.6	9.0
3.4	4.9	5.5	Operating Profit					3.5	5.6
.5	1.1	1.3	All Other Expenses (net)					1.3	1.2
2.9	3.8	4.2	Profit Before Taxes					2.2	4.5
			RATIOS						
2.6	2.9	2.1						1.9	2.5
1.5	1.7	1.4	Current					1.2	1.5
1.1	1.2	1.1						1.0	1.1
1.1	1.6	1.0						1.1	1.1
.7	.8	.8	Quick					.7	.9
.6	.6	.5						.4	.6
41 8.9	**41** 8.9	**34** 10.7						**26** 14.2	**37** 9.8
47 7.8	**46** 7.9	**41** 8.9	Sales/Receivables					**41** 8.9	**41** 9.0
53 6.9	**52** 7.0	**50** 7.4						**49** 7.5	**54** 6.8
42 8.7	**33** 11.2	**28** 13.0						**27** 13.4	**14** 25.2
68 5.3	**75** 4.8	**53** 6.9	Cost of Sales/Inventory					**47** 7.8	**45** 8.1
91 4.0	**106** 3.5	**74** 5.0						**73** 5.0	**78** 4.7
25 14.4	**21** 17.5	**21** 17.3						**22** 16.5	**20** 18.7
38 9.6	**38** 9.7	**34** 10.7	Cost of Sales/Payables					**29** 12.7	**35** 10.5
50 7.3	**43** 8.4	**41** 8.9						**43** 8.5	**38** 9.7
4.7	4.2	6.3						9.8	4.2
9.9	7.8	12.3	Sales/Working Capital					16.4	12.3
39.5	23.3	57.5						NM	57.5
11.3	20.1	15.5						7.2	27.7
(30) 3.6	(32) 5.1	(41) 3.2	EBIT/Interest					2.5	(21) 3.9
1.1	1.6	1.7						1.5	1.7
13.9		6.0							
(13) 5.6		(14) 3.1	Net Profit + Depr., Dep., Amort./Cur. Mat. L/T/D						
1.7		1.8							
.4	.3	.2						.3	.2
.8	.6	.8	Fixed/Worth					1.5	.7
1.6	1.0	1.9						7.7	1.3
.7	.7	1.1						1.8	.6
1.9	1.3	3.5	Debt/Worth					3.8	3.5
4.0	4.0	9.2						12.7	9.2
37.9	31.3	73.3						61.7	63.3
(30) 21.5	(30) 18.8	(38) 30.9	% Profit Before Taxes/Tangible Net Worth					(12) 16.7	(20) 32.8
5.7	2.0	10.9						2.1	10.9
12.5	14.1	17.0						12.1	16.7
4.4	5.9	9.6	% Profit Before Taxes/Total Assets					4.5	10.9
1.1	.1	2.0						1.2	2.0
15.6	15.7	29.6						24.5	43.0
9.7	9.4	15.6	Sales/Net Fixed Assets					11.6	17.1
5.1	4.7	8.1						6.6	14.9
2.8	2.8	3.7						3.8	3.7
2.1	1.9	2.8	Sales/Total Assets					3.0	2.8
1.5	1.5	2.0						2.1	1.9
1.2	1.1	.7						.8	.5
(31) 2.9	(27) 2.4	(39) 1.3	% Depr., Dep., Amort./Sales					1.4	(20) 1.1
4.5	3.2	2.6						2.3	2.3
			% Officers', Directors' Owners' Comp/Sales						
2441568M	**3492996M**	**5357995M**	Net Sales ($)		**1660M**	**7169M**	**21632M**	**222595M**	**5104939M**
1255873M	**1731594M**	**1988903M**	Total Assets ($)		**381M**	**4284M**	**7321M**	**86985M**	**1889932M**

M = $ thousand MM = $ million

See Pages 11 through 21 for Explanation of Ratios and Data

Current Data Sorted by Assets | Comparative Historical Data

0-500M	500M-2MM	2-10MM	10-50MM	50-100MM	100-250MM	Type of Statement	4/1/02-3/31/03 ALL	4/1/03-3/31/04 ALL
			1			Unqualified	5	7
		1	6	1				
		3	6			Reviewed	4	7
		2	1			Compiled	3	5
1	2	1				Tax Returns	2	1
		5	4	2	1	Other	10	10
	13 (4/1-9/30/06)		25 (10/1/06-3/31/07)					
1	6	10	17	3	1	NUMBER OF STATEMENTS	24	30
%	%	%	%	%	%	ASSETS	%	%
		3.5	7.2			Cash & Equivalents	5.7	5.3
		23.7	30.0			Trade Receivables (net)	24.9	28.2
		25.2	41.4			Inventory	25.5	26.4
		1.1	2.6			All Other Current	.9	1.3
		53.6	81.3			Total Current	56.9	61.2
		37.1	15.0			Fixed Assets (net)	35.5	29.7
		7.4	1.4			Intangibles (net)	3.1	2.3
		1.9	2.3			All Other Non-Current	4.4	6.8
		100.0	100.0			Total	100.0	100.0
						LIABILITIES		
		16.1	18.0			Notes Payable-Short Term	13.4	16.0
		4.2	2.8			Cur. Mat.-L.T.D.	5.4	3.1
		14.8	19.3			Trade Payables	16.5	14.1
		.0	1.4			Income Taxes Payable	.0	1.0
		8.2	6.4			All Other Current	6.6	8.1
		43.3	47.8			Total Current	41.9	42.2
		18.4	8.3			Long-Term Debt	14.7	9.5
		.9	.2			Deferred Taxes	.2	.9
		8.6	3.1			All Other Non-Current	7.3	8.5
		28.8	40.5			Net Worth	35.9	38.9
		100.0	100.0			Total Liabilities & Net Worth	100.0	100.0
						INCOME DATA		
		100.0	100.0			Net Sales	100.0	100.0
		17.5	20.7			Gross Profit	21.6	24.5
		17.2	8.6			Operating Expenses	19.8	22.5
		.4	12.1			Operating Profit	1.8	2.0
		.6	.9			All Other Expenses (net)	1.0	.7
		-.2	11.2			Profit Before Taxes	.7	1.2
						RATIOS		
		2.6	2.3				3.1	2.6
		1.5	1.6			Current	1.3	1.6
		.7	1.4				.9	1.2
		1.4	1.2				1.6	1.3
		.6	.8			Quick	.7	.7
		.3	.4				.5	.5
		33 11.2	37 9.7				31 11.9	43 8.5
		38 9.5	51 7.1			Sales/Receivables	45 8.0	53 6.8
		57 6.4	63 5.8				53 6.8	66 5.6
		10 36.3	37 9.8				26 13.8	40 9.1
		58 6.3	91 4.0			Cost of Sales/Inventory	62 5.9	69 5.3
		98 3.7	125 2.9				81 4.5	107 3.4
		18 20.7	21 17.5				17 21.5	23 15.6
		36 10.1	31 11.8			Cost of Sales/Payables	23 15.5	34 10.7
		44 8.2	63 5.8				44 8.3	48 7.6
		4.6	3.5				5.2	4.3
		9.5	5.7			Sales/Working Capital	20.6	8.0
		-21.4	15.5				NM	23.2
			23.8				6.1	6.5
		(16)	6.7			EBIT/Interest	(22) 2.3	(25) 2.0
			4.1				1.4	.7
						Net Profit + Depr., Dep., Amort./Cur. Mat. L/T/D		4.0
							(11) 2.4	
								1.3
		.4	.1				.5	.2
		2.4	.3			Fixed/Worth	.8	.7
		-8.9	.5				2.2	1.2
		.9	.9				.6	.7
		3.7	1.5			Debt/Worth	2.0	1.5
		-16.9	2.4				5.0	4.6
			72.1				23.0	24.7
		(16)	36.8			% Profit Before Taxes/Tangible Net Worth	(21) 8.9	(28) 7.2
			24.0				-5.7	-1.6
		8.2	29.2				7.0	6.8
		1.4	14.5			% Profit Before Taxes/Total Assets	2.9	2.0
		-3.1	6.9				-1.4	-.9
		21.0	85.6				13.5	12.7
		5.0	25.6			Sales/Net Fixed Assets	6.8	6.6
		3.0	8.6				3.2	3.3
		2.6	3.0				3.4	2.7
		1.9	1.7			Sales/Total Assets	2.4	1.5
		1.1	1.5				1.1	1.2
		1.1	.2				1.3	1.2
		2.7	.8			% Depr., Dep., Amort./Sales	(21) 3.0	(26) 2.9
		5.5	1.7				4.6	4.0
						% Officers', Directors' Owners' Comp/Sales		
1799M	18746M	125693M	833478M	303617M	176238M	Net Sales ($)	708836M	1033247M
418M	6779M	57076M	391529M	207535M	112184M	Total Assets ($)	535169M	781337M

M = $ thousand   MM = $ million
See Pages 11 through 21 for Explanation of Ratios and Data

Comparative Historical Data						Current Data Sorted by Sales					

			Type of Statement		0-1MM	1-3MM	3-5MM	5-10MM	10-25MM	25MM & OVER
9	6	9	Unqualified			1			1	7
7	14	10	Reviewed			1		1	5	3
7	1	3	Compiled			1	1			1
1	3	4	Tax Returns			3		1		
8	10	12	Other				1	1		8
4/1/04-3/31/05 ALL	4/1/05-3/31/06 ALL	4/1/06-3/31/07 ALL				13 (4/1-9/30/06)			25 (10/1/06-3/31/07)	
32	34	38	**NUMBER OF STATEMENTS**			6	2	3	8	19
%	%	%	**ASSETS**		%	%	%	%	%	%
7.1	5.9	5.2	Cash & Equivalents							6.1
27.4	26.6	27.0	Trade Receivables (net)	D						29.0
28.1	32.6	32.3	Inventory	A						37.7
1.0	4.1	3.4	All Other Current	T						6.0
63.6	69.2	67.9	Total Current	A						78.7
28.3	24.0	26.1	Fixed Assets (net)							16.6
2.8	2.0	3.1	Intangibles (net)	N						1.8
5.2	4.9	2.9	All Other Non-Current	O						2.8
100.0	100.0	100.0	Total	T						100.0
			LIABILITIES	A						
13.5	15.8	16.1	Notes Payable-Short Term	V						20.7
5.4	2.9	2.9	Cur. Mat.-L.T.D.	A						3.0
16.9	17.9	16.5	Trade Payables	I						17.5
.2	.7	1.2	Income Taxes Payable	L						1.3
6.9	10.1	7.9	All Other Current	A						9.3
42.8	47.4	44.7	Total Current	B						51.8
13.6	10.4	13.9	Long-Term Debt	L						10.0
.6	.3	.4	Deferred Taxes	E						.3
10.1	7.5	5.5	All Other Non-Current							3.6
32.9	34.5	35.5	Net Worth							34.3
100.0	100.0	100.0	Total Liabilities & Net Worth							100.0
			INCOME DATA							
100.0	100.0	100.0	Net Sales							100.0
19.0	22.1	23.6	Gross Profit							20.6
14.0	15.9	16.0	Operating Expenses							9.1
5.0	6.2	7.5	Operating Profit							11.6
1.1	1.0	.8	All Other Expenses (net)							1.0
3.9	5.3	6.8	Profit Before Taxes							10.6
			RATIOS							
2.9	2.3	2.4								2.4
1.4	1.3	1.5	Current							1.5
1.1	1.1	1.1								1.2
1.3	.9	1.2								1.2
.7	.6	.7	Quick							.5
.5	.4	.4								.3
38 9.6	32 11.4	35 10.5								36 10.1
46 7.9	46 8.0	44 8.2	Sales/Receivables							44 8.2
57 6.4	59 6.2	60 6.1								59 6.2
31 11.9	37 9.8	29 12.7								36 10.1
57 6.4	76 4.8	80 4.6	Cost of Sales/Inventory							77 4.7
99 3.7	114 3.2	106 3.4								111 3.3
22 16.4	21 17.6	18 19.9								17 21.9
34 10.8	36 10.2	36 10.1	Cost of Sales/Payables							31 11.7
44 8.4	50 7.3	51 7.1								57 6.4
3.9	5.6	4.3								3.4
10.8	13.4	9.3	Sales/Working Capital							7.2
35.6	31.4	28.8								22.8
9.1	15.3	11.0								19.2
(30) 3.6	(32) 5.9	(36) 4.4	EBIT/Interest						(18)	8.3
1.5	.5	1.2								3.0
3.0	23.7	13.7								14.8
(14) 2.1	(12) 2.7	(11) 3.3	Net Profit + Depr., Dep., Amort./Cur. Mat. L/T/D						(10)	5.1
.4	-1.5	1.6								1.6
.4	.4	.2								.1
1.0	.6	.5	Fixed/Worth							.3
2.4	1.1	2.2								.9
1.0	.8	.9								.9
1.8	2.2	1.8	Debt/Worth							2.1
10.4	7.2	6.9								6.3
37.1	52.8	50.6	% Profit Before Taxes/Tangible Net Worth							79.1
(27) 18.8	(32) 30.0	(32) 27.4							(17)	38.0
10.6	.4	9.9								26.9
11.9	22.5	22.8	% Profit Before Taxes/Total Assets							29.7
5.2	8.3	7.9								17.0
2.1	-.6	1.4								5.2
20.2	18.5	33.7	Sales/Net Fixed Assets							82.6
7.3	9.9	8.7								25.6
3.8	5.0	4.5								7.1
2.8	2.6	2.8	Sales/Total Assets							3.4
1.6	2.0	1.9								1.9
1.3	1.5	1.4								1.3
.7	.7	.4	% Depr., Dep., Amort./Sales							.2
(30) 1.6	(32) 1.5	(37) 1.9								.8
3.5	3.0	3.4								2.0
1.8			% Officers', Directors' Owners' Comp/Sales							
(10) 2.2		(12) 3.8								
4.6		6.0								
1271524M	1746862M	1459571M	Net Sales ($)			13176M	7462M	21726M	128583M	1288624M
710688M	918000M	775521M	Total Assets ($)			6544M	6228M	15697M	70529M	676523M

M = $ thousand   MM = $ million
See Pages 11 through 21 for Explanation of Ratios and Data

Current Data Sorted by Assets | Comparative Historical Data

Current data periods: 14 (4/1-9/30/06) · 44 (10/1/06-3/31/07)

Type of Statement

0-500M	500M-2MM	2-10MM	10-50MM	50-100MM	100-250MM		4/1/02-3/31/03 ALL	4/1/03-3/31/04 ALL
		2	8	4	1	Unqualified	14	16
	3	1	5			Reviewed	8	11
	4	1	3		1	Compiled	5	5
	3					Tax Returns	1	2
2		3	10	6	1	Other	10	12
2	10	7	26	10	3	**NUMBER OF STATEMENTS**	38	46

0-500M %	500M-2MM %	2-10MM %	10-50MM %	50-100MM %	100-250MM %		%	%
						ASSETS		
	9.7		4.8	2.3		Cash & Equivalents	6.2	6.9
	27.8		35.2	21.6		Trade Receivables (net)	25.3	29.0
	35.6		32.3	45.8		Inventory	26.5	31.9
	3.3		1.4	5.0		All Other Current	2.6	1.8
	76.3		73.6	74.7		Total Current	60.7	69.6
	20.5		16.8	18.5		Fixed Assets (net)	27.8	22.5
	.1		3.0	3.2		Intangibles (net)	5.0	2.0
	3.0		6.5	3.6		All Other Non-Current	6.6	5.9
	100.0		100.0	100.0		Total	100.0	100.0
						LIABILITIES		
	15.0		21.5	13.8		Notes Payable-Short Term	11.4	19.6
	1.2		3.3	7.5		Cur. Mat.-L.T.D.	6.6	2.0
	26.3		25.2	16.8		Trade Payables	17.2	19.0
	.5		.9	.6		Income Taxes Payable	.5	.3
	21.7		7.4	7.8		All Other Current	10.6	8.5
	64.6		58.2	46.5		Total Current	46.3	49.4
	8.6		11.9	9.6		Long-Term Debt	10.6	8.4
	.3		.1	1.7		Deferred Taxes	.9	.8
	1.7		1.7	1.6		All Other Non-Current	4.9	6.6
	24.8		28.1	40.6		Net Worth	37.4	34.8
	100.0		100.0	100.0		Total Liabilities & Net Worth	100.0	100.0
						INCOME DATA		
	100.0		100.0	100.0		Net Sales	100.0	100.0
	23.6		14.2	16.0		Gross Profit	21.0	16.5
	20.1		9.0	8.2		Operating Expenses	18.1	14.4
	3.5		5.2	7.7		Operating Profit	2.8	2.2
	.5		1.6	.7		All Other Expenses (net)	.3	.6
	3.0		3.7	7.1		Profit Before Taxes	2.6	1.6
						RATIOS		
	2.5		2.0	2.8		Current	2.2	2.3
	1.6		1.2	1.8			1.4	1.4
	.7		.9	1.2			.9	1.0
	1.3		1.1	1.0		Quick	1.3	1.2
	.7		.7	.7			.7	.8
	.2		.4	.3			.4	.5
	1 307.6		20 18.6	19 18.7		Sales/Receivables	26 13.9	31 11.8
	31 11.8		44 8.2	36 10.3			42 8.7	42 8.8
	37 9.9		50 7.3	51 7.2			55 6.6	56 6.5
	8 45.2		23 15.7	61 5.9		Cost of Sales/Inventory	18 20.6	31 11.8
	36 10.2		37 9.9	76 4.8			46 7.9	47 7.7
	63 5.8		64 5.7	126 2.9			86 4.3	92 4.0
	1 380.9		13 28.0	18 20.0		Cost of Sales/Payables	19 19.7	19 19.4
	20 18.4		31 12.0	24 15.2			39 9.4	34 10.7
	41 8.8		47 7.7	49 7.5			50 7.3	45 8.1
	7.8		8.7	4.2		Sales/Working Capital	4.7	6.8
	22.0		26.1	7.5			17.9	15.1
	-35.0		-135.4	20.6			-50.0	UND
			19.6			EBIT/Interest	8.9	3.8
			(25) 5.2				(36) 2.1	(43) 1.8
			1.9				.6	.0
						Net Profit + Depr., Dep., Amort./Cur. Mat. L/T/D	5.1	3.4
							(10) 1.3	(16) 2.6
							.6	1.1
	.2		.2	.1		Fixed/Worth	.3	.3
	.5		.6	.4			1.0	.9
	NM		1.9	1.3			2.4	1.8
	.9		1.4	.6		Debt/Worth	.7	1.2
	1.3		3.5	1.8			1.7	2.8
	NM		12.7	6.3			6.8	7.9
			67.7			% Profit Before Taxes/Tangible Net Worth	25.1	20.2
			(23) 48.8				(35) 10.5	(45) 10.4
			15.3				-1.3	-4.6
	22.6		18.0	20.4		% Profit Before Taxes/Total Assets	9.2	7.9
	7.2		9.0	9.1			3.5	1.7
	4.8		3.1	6.6			-.8	-1.7
	107.5		58.5	38.8		Sales/Net Fixed Assets	25.7	24.3
	26.9		21.3	17.4			12.0	14.8
	12.3		11.4	6.4			4.4	6.4
	7.9		4.5	2.6		Sales/Total Assets	3.6	3.2
	3.7		3.6	2.3			2.1	2.7
	3.2		2.8	1.6			1.4	1.8
			.2			% Depr., Dep., Amort./Sales	.8	.6
			(25) .6				(34) 1.7	(43) 1.4
			1.3				3.4	2.6
						% Officers', Directors' Owners' Comp/Sales	2.0	.8
							(19) 2.9	(16) 1.6
							4.7	2.8
1558M	68427M	242461M	2429964M	1493928M	899414M	Net Sales ($)	2636779M	1748078M
664M	12465M	42324M	675239M	689655M	376625M	Total Assets ($)	972139M	804056M

M = $ thousand   MM = $ million
See Pages 11 through 21 for Explanation of Ratios and Data

Comparative Historical Data | Current Data Sorted by Sales

Type of Statement

Hist 1	Hist 2	Hist 3	Type of Statement	0-1MM	1-3MM	3-5MM	5-10MM	10-25MM	25MM & OVER
17	23	15	Unqualified				1	1	13
9	12	9	Reviewed			1	1	3	4
4	1	9	Compiled		1	1	1		5
1	1	3	Tax Returns		1	1	1		
17	26	22	Other	2		1		2	17
4/1/04-3/31/05 ALL	4/1/05-3/31/06 ALL	4/1/06-3/31/07 ALL			14 (4/1-9/30/06)		44 (10/1/06-3/31/07)		
48	63	58	NUMBER OF STATEMENTS	2	2	4	4	7	39

ASSETS

%	%	%	ASSETS	%	%	%	%	%	%
7.0	5.7	5.9	Cash & Equivalents						5.1
27.6	26.7	30.7	Trade Receivables (net)						31.6
31.0	34.9	34.4	Inventory						37.1
3.2	3.2	2.5	All Other Current						2.0
68.7	70.5	73.5	Total Current						75.9
22.8	22.0	18.9	Fixed Assets (net)						17.4
2.0	2.1	2.7	Intangibles (net)						1.6
6.6	5.4	4.8	All Other Non-Current						5.1
100.0	100.0	100.0	Total						100.0

LIABILITIES

Hist 1	Hist 2	Hist 3	LIABILITIES						25MM & OVER
14.9	18.4	17.3	Notes Payable-Short Term						19.2
3.0	2.8	3.5	Cur. Mat.-L.T.D.						3.4
20.0	22.4	23.2	Trade Payables						22.9
.6	.3	.8	Income Taxes Payable						.8
10.9	13.1	10.2	All Other Current						7.0
49.5	57.0	54.9	Total Current						53.2
12.6	11.3	13.6	Long-Term Debt						10.4
.7	1.0	.5	Deferred Taxes						.6
4.7	4.2	1.5	All Other Non-Current						1.7
32.6	26.4	29.4	Net Worth						34.2
100.0	100.0	100.0	Total Liabilities & Net Worth						100.0

INCOME DATA

Hist 1	Hist 2	Hist 3	INCOME DATA						25MM & OVER
100.0	100.0	100.0	Net Sales						100.0
18.9	16.4	16.6	Gross Profit						13.6
16.2	12.3	11.4	Operating Expenses						7.8
2.7	4.1	5.2	Operating Profit						5.8
.5	.8	1.1	All Other Expenses (net)						.7
2.2	3.3	4.1	Profit Before Taxes						5.1

RATIOS

Hist 1	Hist 2	Hist 3	RATIOS						25MM & OVER
2.2	2.2	2.1	Current						2.4
1.5	1.3	1.5							1.5
1.1	1.0	1.0							1.0
1.2	1.0	1.2	Quick						1.2
.8	.7	.8							.7
.4	.4	.3							.3
20 · 18.2	24 · 15.2	18 · 20.7	Sales/Receivables						18 · 19.8
40 · 9.0	35 · 10.4	37 · 9.9							40 · 9.2
54 · 6.7	49 · 7.4	48 · 7.5							48 · 7.6
27 · 13.5	24 · 15.2	23 · 15.7	Cost of Sales/Inventory						25 · 14.6
49 · 7.5	48 · 7.7	45 · 8.0							45 · 8.2
79 · 4.6	87 · 4.2	74 · 4.9							64 · 5.7
18 · 19.8	15 · 24.4	15 · 24.1	Cost of Sales/Payables						14 · 26.1
33 · 10.9	33 · 10.9	25 · 14.7							24 · 15.0
54 · 6.7	49 · 7.4	48 · 7.6							46 · 7.9
6.7	7.7	8.1	Sales/Working Capital						7.7
12.6	16.2	19.1							14.5
87.6	-237.1	-814.3							336.3
18.8	15.5	11.1	EBIT/Interest						16.9
(44) 5.2	(59) 3.7	(53) 6.3						(35)	6.5
1.8	1.4	1.9							2.3
8.4	13.0	12.7	Net Profit + Depr., Dep.,						16.3
(16) 2.8	(27) 2.7	(19) 3.8	Amort./Cur. Mat. L/T/D						(12) 2.9
2.0	1.3	1.4							1.4
.2	.4	.2	Fixed/Worth						.2
.7	.8	.5							.5
2.1	2.4	1.9							1.3
1.0	1.3	1.0	Debt/Worth						.7
2.8	3.0	2.1							2.1
5.5	6.9	8.8							5.4
44.7	49.8	68.2	% Profit Before Taxes/Tangible						75.6
(43) 22.7	(57) 29.3	(49) 36.7	Net Worth						(37) 42.3
10.6	6.1	15.0							19.5
15.6	17.2	23.1	% Profit Before Taxes/Total						26.8
5.3	6.4	9.0	Assets						12.5
1.1	1.1	3.4							6.3
35.0	37.0	71.7	Sales/Net Fixed Assets						70.9
14.4	14.9	24.0							26.2
6.0	6.9	9.9							10.9
3.7	3.7	4.5	Sales/Total Assets						4.5
2.6	2.5	3.4							3.5
1.5	1.7	2.3							2.3
.5	.4	.3	% Depr., Dep., Amort./Sales						.3
(40) 1.0	(59) .9	(51) 1.1						(35)	.7
2.1	2.3	1.9							1.6
.6	.5	.4	% Officers', Directors'						.3
(15) 1.6	(17) 1.4	(17) 1.3	Owners' Comp/Sales						(11) .9
5.7	4.1	4.4							1.3
2625784M	4951848M	5135752M	Net Sales ($)	1558M	4513M	16811M	28823M	125362M	4958685M
1049658M	1922003M	1796972M	Total Assets ($)	664M	1446M	8210M	22097M	49643M	1714912M

M = $ thousand   MM = $ million
See Pages 11 through 21 for Explanation of Ratios and Data

MANUFACTURING—Iron Foundries NAICS 331511 (SIC 3321, 3322)

Current Data Sorted by Assets   **Comparative Historical Data**

0-500M	500M-2MM	2-10MM	10-50MM	50-100MM	100-250MM		4/1/02-3/31/03 ALL	4/1/03-3/31/04 ALL
		5	13	2		Type of Statement		
	1	13	1			Unqualified	20	16
1	4	3	2			Reviewed	10	17
	2					Compiled	16	14
1	1					Tax Returns	1	1
						Other	25	30
1	8	17 (4/1-9/30/06) 6	53 (10/1/06-3/31/07) 8	3	5			
1	**8**	**27**	**24**	**5**	**5**	**NUMBER OF STATEMENTS**	**72**	**78**
%	%	%	%	%	%	**ASSETS**	%	%
		7.8	4.6			Cash & Equivalents	7.9	8.9
		27.6	28.4			Trade Receivables (net)	21.5	22.0
		18.1	19.2			Inventory	17.4	17.2
		1.5	4.1			All Other Current	2.0	2.6
		55.0	56.3			Total Current	48.8	50.7
		38.1	34.0			Fixed Assets (net)	41.4	40.1
		2.8	4.2			Intangibles (net)	1.5	3.2
		4.1	5.5			All Other Non-Current	8.4	6.1
		100.0	100.0			Total	100.0	100.0
						LIABILITIES		
		8.8	7.4			Notes Payable-Short Term	7.2	9.7
		4.7	2.7			Cur. Mat.-L.T.D.	5.8	5.1
		14.5	16.2			Trade Payables	12.9	12.4
		.0	1.1			Income Taxes Payable	.4	.3
		5.9	7.5			All Other Current	6.5	9.1
		34.0	34.9			Total Current	32.8	36.5
		14.9	18.4			Long-Term Debt	19.1	18.3
		1.9	1.6			Deferred Taxes	.9	1.2
		2.6	3.5			All Other Non-Current	5.4	5.2
		46.7	41.7			Net Worth	41.8	38.8
		100.0	100.0			Total Liabilties & Net Worth	100.0	100.0
						INCOME DATA		
		100.0	100.0			Net Sales	100.0	100.0
		22.0	19.5			Gross Profit	23.4	23.2
		15.7	11.5			Operating Expenses	21.6	19.9
		6.4	8.0			Operating Profit	1.8	3.2
		.8	1.5			All Other Expenses (net)	1.2	1.3
		5.6	6.6			Profit Before Taxes	.6	1.9
						RATIOS		
		2.3	2.7			Current	3.2	2.6
		1.7	1.5				1.6	1.5
		1.1	1.1				1.0	.9
		1.7	1.8			Quick	1.9	1.9
		1.0	1.0				.9	.8
		.6	.7				.5	.5
		42 8.8	43 8.4			Sales/Receivables	39 9.4	41 8.8
		48 7.6	51 7.2				49 7.4	47 7.8
		56 6.5	57 6.4				59 6.2	57 6.3
		19 19.0	26 14.0			Cost of Sales/Inventory	28 12.8	25 14.6
		30 12.1	40 9.2				38 9.7	38 9.6
		55 6.6	60 6.1				66 5.6	68 5.3
		17 21.5	21 17.4			Cost of Sales/Payables	18 20.5	18 20.8
		28 13.0	35 10.4				31 11.7	29 12.6
		35 10.3	41 9.0				43 8.6	43 8.5
		6.6	5.5			Sales/Working Capital	4.8	4.7
		13.4	10.8				10.5	12.4
		90.9	32.3				-360.4	-54.4
		21.0	14.6			EBIT/Interest	4.8	7.1
		(26) 3.7	4.5				(64) 1.2	(68) 2.3
		2.7	2.5				-1.3	.5
		6.1	5.2			Net Profit + Depr., Dep., Amort./Cur. Mat. L/T/D	3.0	3.8
		(15) 3.7	(13) 2.8				(20) 1.8	(30) 1.6
		1.7	1.7				1.0	1.0
		.6	.4			Fixed/Worth	.5	.5
		.9	.9				1.0	1.1
		1.4	1.7				2.9	3.0
		.5	.7			Debt/Worth	.7	.6
		1.1	1.6				1.3	1.4
		2.7	3.2				4.1	4.4
		46.0	52.4			% Profit Before Taxes/Tangible Net Worth	17.2	17.8
		(25) 25.2	(22) 23.5				(65) 5.7	(69) 8.7
		9.3	9.2				-9.8	-1.6
		20.0	22.9			% Profit Before Taxes/Total Assets	8.4	10.1
		9.1	8.4				.6	2.4
		4.0	3.9				-4.4	-1.3
		10.2	9.0			Sales/Net Fixed Assets	6.8	7.6
		6.2	6.8				3.8	4.0
		4.0	3.5				2.5	2.7
		2.8	2.3			Sales/Total Assets	2.0	2.1
		2.3	1.9				1.6	1.6
		1.7	1.4				1.2	1.2
		1.6	1.0			% Depr., Dep., Amort./Sales	2.8	2.2
		2.6	2.1				(65) 4.5	(73) 3.7
		3.7	3.8				7.4	6.3
						% Officers', Directors' Owners' Comp/Sales	1.6	1.3
							(18) 3.4	(23) 3.1
							6.0	7.8
637M	29315M	335956M	985706M	520676M	939749M	Net Sales ($)	1475869M	1863831M
242M	8590M	151144M	515575M	372435M	839156M	Total Assets ($)	1211984M	1473782M

M = $ thousand   MM = $ million
See Pages 11 through 21 for Explanation of Ratios and Data

Comparative Historical Data | Current Data Sorted by Sales

			Type of Statement						
23	20	20	Unqualified					4	16
19	14	15	Reviewed		1		6	5	1
14	10	10	Compiled	1	3	2	1	2	1
2	3	2	Tax Returns				2		
21	22	23	Other		1		3	4	15
4/1/04-	4/1/05-	4/1/06-			17 (4/1-9/30/06)		53 (10/1/06-3/31/07)		
3/31/05	3/31/06	3/31/07							
ALL	ALL	ALL		0-1MM	1-3MM	3-5MM	5-10MM	10-25MM	25MM & OVER
79	69	70	**NUMBER OF STATEMENTS**	1	5	4	12	15	33
%	%	%	**ASSETS**	%	%	%	%	%	%
7.4	6.9	8.2	Cash & Equivalents				7.4	8.3	7.3
28.0	29.1	26.4	Trade Receivables (net)				33.2	28.1	24.1
18.1	18.3	18.2	Inventory				14.0	23.0	16.3
1.6	1.4	2.3	All Other Current				1.8	.7	3.8
55.2	55.8	55.1	Total Current				56.4	60.0	51.5
34.8	34.4	35.7	Fixed Assets (net)				38.5	35.9	36.4
3.5	3.3	3.5	Intangibles (net)				1.0	.5	4.8
6.5	6.5	5.7	All Other Non-Current				4.1	3.7	7.3
100.0	100.0	100.0	Total				100.0	100.0	100.0
			LIABILITIES						
9.5	9.0	7.7	Notes Payable-Short Term				8.9	7.9	5.8
5.0	3.2	3.5	Cur. Mat.-L.T.D.				4.9	3.9	2.5
14.2	15.0	15.9	Trade Payables				21.2	14.8	13.7
.5	.2	.4	Income Taxes Payable				.0	1.4	.2
7.9	9.0	6.0	All Other Current				4.3	7.9	6.7
37.1	36.5	33.5	Total Current				39.4	35.8	28.9
16.1	16.2	17.3	Long-Term Debt				18.4	13.1	17.5
1.3	1.3	1.4	Deferred Taxes				1.0	2.3	1.6
8.4	5.4	3.4	All Other Non-Current				3.9	1.0	2.9
37.2	40.6	44.3	Net Worth				37.4	47.8	49.1
100.0	100.0	100.0	Total Liabilities & Net Worth				100.0	100.0	100.0
			INCOME DATA						
100.0	100.0	100.0	Net Sales				100.0	100.0	100.0
22.9	21.6	22.2	Gross Profit				22.6	23.8	19.9
17.4	15.1	15.7	Operating Expenses				16.9	15.7	11.5
5.5	6.5	6.5	Operating Profit				5.7	8.1	8.4
.9	1.0	1.0	All Other Expenses (net)				.9	1.4	1.4
4.6	5.4	5.5	Profit Before Taxes				4.7	6.7	7.0
			RATIOS						
2.2	2.5	2.5	Current				2.0	2.4	2.9
1.5	1.5	1.7					1.5	1.7	1.8
1.1	1.2	1.1					1.0	1.3	1.1
1.8	1.5	1.7	Quick				1.6	1.4	2.2
1.0	.9	1.1					1.1	1.0	1.1
.7	.7	.7					.7	.6	.7
40 9.1	39 9.4	39 9.4	Sales/Receivables				40 9.0	43 8.5	37 9.9
51 7.2	47 7.8	45 8.1					47 7.7	48 7.5	45 8.1
60 6.1	54 6.7	54 6.7					55 6.7	56 6.5	54 6.7
20 18.0	22 16.6	20 18.2	Cost of Sales/Inventory				15 23.7	25 14.8	25 14.5
33 11.0	30 12.0	33 11.0					20 17.9	41 8.9	34 10.7
60 6.0	51 7.2	62 5.9					32 11.6	77 4.7	63 5.8
18 20.5	20 18.2	19 18.7	Cost of Sales/Payables				30 12.1	20 18.5	18 20.1
31 11.8	28 13.1	31 11.9					33 11.2	28 13.0	33 11.0
42 8.7	38 9.7	39 9.2					46 8.0	38 9.5	39 9.3
5.6	7.4	5.4	Sales/Working Capital				8.8	5.4	5.1
11.8	13.2	10.8					16.6	13.0	8.5
82.0	38.4	40.7					NM	13.8	35.4
13.4	11.9	12.6	EBIT/Interest				11.0	21.0	18.7
(72) 4.9	(62) 5.5	(66) 4.0					6.4	(14) 6.1	(31) 3.9
1.9	2.4	2.7					2.9	3.1	2.8
4.9	7.3	6.8	Net Profit + Depr., Dep.,						11.0
(27) 2.3	(25) 3.0	(33) 3.8	Amort./Cur. Mat. L/T/D					(16)	3.8
1.3	2.0	1.7							1.8
.4	.5	.5	Fixed/Worth				.6	.6	.4
1.0	1.1	.9					.9	.9	.9
2.1	2.4	1.6					4.8	1.2	1.7
.8	.6	.6	Debt/Worth				.9	.6	.4
1.2	1.7	1.2					1.6	1.1	1.2
4.7	5.0	3.2					7.3	1.9	3.3
40.4	41.7	47.2	% Profit Before Taxes/Tangible				48.3	47.3	46.5
(68) 20.8	(63) 21.0	(63) 23.1	Net Worth			(11)	25.9	24.6	(31) 20.4
8.4	7.9	10.0					11.7	11.1	10.0
15.2	17.1	17.4	% Profit Before Taxes/Total				15.0	24.4	17.7
8.3	8.2	8.9	Assets				9.1	13.0	8.9
3.0	4.0	3.8					6.5	4.0	4.0
12.7	10.2	9.4	Sales/Net Fixed Assets				9.6	12.3	8.6
5.3	6.6	6.1					6.3	5.7	5.6
3.3	4.3	3.6					4.6	3.9	3.1
2.4	3.0	2.7	Sales/Total Assets				2.9	2.4	2.3
1.9	2.2	2.1					2.4	2.1	1.6
1.3	1.6	1.5					2.1	1.7	1.2
1.4	1.6	1.5	% Depr., Dep., Amort./Sales				1.8	1.5	1.0
(71) 3.0	(64) 2.4	(64) 2.4					3.5	2.3	(30) 2.4
4.7	3.5	4.1					4.1	3.6	4.6
1.2	.7	1.2	% Officers', Directors'						
(23) 2.3	(16) 1.8	(19) 2.0	Owners' Comp/Sales						
5.3	7.5	5.4							
2332418M	2376650M	2812039M	Net Sales ($)	637M	10238M	16271M	88676M	267602M	2428615M
1624059M	1257663M	1887142M	Total Assets ($)	242M	5842M	8896M	38615M	126181M	1707366M

© RMA 2007

M = $ thousand   MM = $ million

See Pages 11 through 21 for Explanation of Ratios and Data

MANUFACTURING—Steel Foundries (except Investment) NAICS 331513 (SIC 3325)

Current Data Sorted by Assets

Comparative Historical Data

Type of Statement

0-500M	500M-2MM	2-10MM	10-50MM	50-100MM	100-250MM		4/1/02-3/31/03 ALL	4/1/03-3/31/04 ALL
						Type of Statement		
		2	9	1	1	Unqualified	11	13
	2	11	4			Reviewed	14	16
4	2	3				Compiled	8	10
	2	3				Tax Returns	4	2
	3	9	6	1	7	Other	14	17
	18 (4/1-9/30/06)		52 (10/1/06-3/31/07)					
4	9	28	19	2	8	NUMBER OF STATEMENTS	51	58
%	%	%	%	%	%	ASSETS	%	%
		7.0	9.1			Cash & Equivalents	6.5	4.0
		37.8	32.2			Trade Receivables (net)	27.2	28.0
		21.9	22.3			Inventory	21.9	21.9
		5.2	4.1			All Other Current	2.2	2.4
		71.8	67.8			Total Current	57.8	56.3
		20.8	27.3			Fixed Assets (net)	33.4	33.8
		3.2	.7			Intangibles (net)	2.1	3.3
		4.3	4.2			All Other Non-Current	6.7	6.5
		100.0	100.0			Total	100.0	100.0
						LIABILITIES		
		9.7	7.6			Notes Payable-Short Term	13.2	12.7
		3.1	3.0			Cur. Mat.-L.T.D.	4.5	5.0
		22.8	16.9			Trade Payables	16.9	19.0
		.1	.4			Income Taxes Payable	.2	.1
		10.5	18.6			All Other Current	8.9	7.0
		46.2	46.5			Total Current	43.7	43.8
		12.2	11.1			Long-Term Debt	16.4	17.7
		.0	.1			Deferred Taxes	1.1	1.0
		5.9	4.7			All Other Non-Current	5.6	8.1
		35.6	37.5			Net Worth	33.2	29.4
		100.0	100.0			Total Liabilities & Net Worth	100.0	100.0
						INCOME DATA		
		100.0	100.0			Net Sales	100.0	100.0
		22.2	20.3			Gross Profit	24.6	21.9
		16.5	12.4			Operating Expenses	19.5	19.7
		5.7	7.9			Operating Profit	5.0	2.2
		.8	.7			All Other Expenses (net)	1.3	.9
		4.9	7.2			Profit Before Taxes	3.7	1.3
						RATIOS		
		2.1	1.7				2.2	1.7
		1.5	1.5			Current	1.3	1.2
		1.1	1.2				.8	1.0
		1.5	1.2				1.2	1.1
		1.0	.9			Quick	.8	.7
		.6	.7				.5	.5
		43 8.4	39 9.3				39 9.5	41 8.8
		48 7.6	54 6.8			Sales/Receivables	46 7.9	52 7.0
		60 6.1	58 6.3				58 6.3	61 6.0
		15 23.9	30 12.0				24 14.9	26 14.0
		36 10.1	48 7.7			Cost of Sales/Inventory	54 6.8	50 7.4
		60 6.1	60 6.0				99 3.7	81 4.5
		19 18.9	25 14.4				18 20.7	28 12.8
		31 11.8	34 10.7			Cost of Sales/Payables	33 10.9	45 8.1
		52 7.1	42 8.7				51 7.2	60 6.1
		6.5	7.3				6.5	7.1
		11.1	10.2			Sales/Working Capital	15.6	14.7
		37.6	17.2				-22.8	UND
		20.1	42.3				8.5	5.1
		(27) 4.3	(17) 8.9			EBIT/Interest	(44) 3.0	(52) 2.2
		1.7	2.2				.8	-.4
		9.2						5.2
		(10) 4.7				Net Profit + Depr., Dep., Amort./Cur. Mat. L/T/D	(16)	.9
		1.1						.3
		.2	.4				.5	.6
		.7	.6			Fixed/Worth	.9	1.2
		1.3	.9				2.8	2.9
		.9	.9				.7	1.4
		2.0	1.5			Debt/Worth	2.9	3.2
		3.6	5.3				6.0	7.3
		57.1	52.7				46.8	35.3
		(26) 39.5	(17) 32.5			% Profit Before Taxes/Tangible Net Worth	(47) 21.2	(54) 10.7
		7.9	18.1				-.9	-7.2
		19.0	23.1				14.2	9.0
		8.2	12.8			% Profit Before Taxes/Total Assets	4.4	2.4
		2.1	5.3				-.6	-3.2
		35.7	11.4				11.1	11.8
		14.8	8.7			Sales/Net Fixed Assets	6.1	6.0
		5.5	7.1				3.1	3.1
		3.3	2.8				2.7	2.6
		2.6	2.3			Sales/Total Assets	1.9	1.8
		1.9	1.6				1.2	1.4
		.8	1.1				1.2	1.3
		(25) 1.4	(18) 1.6			% Depr., Dep., Amort./Sales	(42) 2.4	(54) 2.8
		2.7	3.3				4.7	4.9
		1.3					2.1	1.8
		(11) 2.7				% Officers', Directors', Owners' Comp/Sales	(14) 3.3	(20) 3.8
		3.9					5.8	6.0
5380M	34132M	357205M	907417M	224745M	2489953M	Net Sales ($)	2155156M	2017924M
1203M	12211M	135286M	422682M	112207M	1315138M	Total Assets ($)	1269219M	1087512M

© RMA 2007

M = $ thousand   MM = $ million

See Pages 11 through 21 for Explanation of Ratios and Data

Comparative Historical Data　　　　　　　　　　　Current Data Sorted by Sales

			Type of Statement						
18	14	13	Unqualified					3	10
16	20	17	Reviewed		1	3	2	6	5
12	10	9	Compiled	3		2	4		
2	1	5	Tax Returns			1	3		
21	22	26	Other			4	2	5	15
4/1/04-3/31/05	4/1/05-3/31/06	4/1/06-3/31/07			18 (4/1-9/30/06)		52 (10/1/06-3/31/07)		
ALL	ALL	ALL		0-1MM	1-3MM	3-5MM	5-10MM	10-25MM	25MM & OVER
69	67	70	**NUMBER OF STATEMENTS**	3	1	10	11	15	30
%	%	%	**ASSETS**	%	%	%	%	%	%
5.3	5.2	7.3	Cash & Equivalents			8.6	7.4	5.8	7.6
30.7	32.3	34.1	Trade Receivables (net)			29.8	40.7	37.3	32.5
26.8	24.5	21.3	Inventory			24.6	19.7	17.0	24.8
2.0	3.6	3.4	All Other Current			.5	1.3	8.5	3.1
64.8	65.6	66.2	Total Current			63.5	69.1	68.6	68.1
28.4	28.2	27.3	Fixed Assets (net)			28.1	24.7	26.4	24.6
1.4	1.6	3.0	Intangibles (net)			5.9	.4	1.9	3.6
5.4	4.6	3.6	All Other Non-Current			2.5	5.7	3.1	3.8
100.0	100.0	100.0	Total			100.0	100.0	100.0	100.0
			LIABILITIES						
13.7	14.2	12.0	Notes Payable-Short Term			12.4	18.1	11.7	10.6
6.0	2.3	3.0	Cur. Mat.-L.T.D.			2.3	3.9	3.7	2.3
20.5	18.2	22.4	Trade Payables			36.4	21.2	21.8	19.4
.2	.2	.2	Income Taxes Payable			.2	.0	.1	.3
9.5	9.7	11.1	All Other Current			6.8	8.2	13.0	13.9
49.8	44.7	48.7	Total Current			58.2	51.4	50.3	46.4
13.9	12.0	14.6	Long-Term Debt			15.0	16.9	17.3	11.4
.7	.4	.4	Deferred Taxes			.2	.0	.0	.7
6.1	6.6	5.5	All Other Non-Current			4.3	9.0	3.5	5.5
29.5	36.4	30.8	Net Worth			22.2	22.6	28.8	36.0
100.0	100.0	100.0	Total Liabilties & Net Worth			100.0	100.0	100.0	100.0
			INCOME DATA						
100.0	100.0	100.0	Net Sales			100.0	100.0	100.0	100.0
23.8	22.6	23.7	Gross Profit			33.3	24.8	19.3	19.1
16.8	16.7	16.7	Operating Expenses			26.5	19.0	13.9	11.5
7.0	6.0	7.1	Operating Profit			6.8	5.8	5.4	7.6
2.1	1.0	1.0	All Other Expenses (net)			.6	1.3	1.1	.9
5.0	5.0	6.1	Profit Before Taxes			6.1	4.5	4.3	6.7
			RATIOS						
1.7	2.1	1.9	Current			3.8	2.5	1.8	1.8
1.3	1.5	1.5				1.4	1.4	1.4	1.5
1.1	1.1	1.1				.7	1.1	1.0	1.2
1.0	1.1	1.3	Quick			1.8	2.0	1.3	1.2
.7	.9	.9				.9	1.0	.9	.9
.5	.6	.6				.3	.6	.5	.7
39　9.5	37　9.8	41　9.0	Sales/Receivables			31　11.8	47　7.8	35　10.3	39　9.4
56　6.5	47　7.7	48　7.6				46　7.9	55　6.6	45　8.0	53　6.8
67　5.5	61　6.0	67　6.0				64　5.7	79　4.6	50　7.3	63　5.8
23　16.2	21　17.1	13　27.7	Cost of Sales/Inventory			8　44.2	14　26.5	1　326.3	29　12.6
53　6.9	47　7.7	36　10.3				28　13.2	35　10.3	25　14.4	48　7.7
81　4.5	62　5.9	56　6.5				81　4.5	62　5.9	45　8.1	72　5.1
30　12.1	25　14.7	24　15.2	Cost of Sales/Payables			16　23.5	16　23.0	18　19.8	28　13.0
41　8.8	34　10.8	36　10.2				33　10.9	24　15.0	28　12.9	39　9.4
57　6.4	43　8.4	49　7.5				49　7.5	65　5.6	53　6.9	45　8.2
6.6	6.1	6.6	Sales/Working Capital			6.4	4.9	6.8	6.3
13.0	11.0	12.7				18.3	9.5	19.0	11.0
48.4	45.8	50.5				-24.5	68.1	91.1	24.1
10.1	13.9	13.6	EBIT/Interest				15.4	20.1	14.9
(66)　4.5	(65)　5.2	(66)　6.0				(10)　3.0		4.3	(28)　8.6
1.8	2.0	2.3					1.3	2.5	3.0
4.8	5.7	18.1	Net Profit + Depr., Dep., Amort./Cur. Mat. L/T/D						48.1
(17)　2.3	(16)　3.6	(21)　5.7							(10)　6.5
1.1	2.0	2.7							4.3
.3	.3	.4	Fixed/Worth			.3	.2	.4	.5
.8	.7	.8				.8	.6	1.0	.7
2.2	1.2	1.7				3.3	2.5	1.7	2.1
1.3	1.1	1.0	Debt/Worth			1.0	.9	1.4	1.1
2.2	1.8	1.8				4.1	1.9	2.7	1.5
7.9	3.5	6.3				7.5	4.5	5.6	8.4
74.3	60.4	61.1	% Profit Before Taxes/Tangible Net Worth					56.7	87.4
(64)　24.5	(64)　24.6	(64)　39.1						(14)　39.5	(28)　32.9
3.6	7.0	11.9						11.1	18.4
16.8	19.7	20.7	% Profit Before Taxes/Total Assets			18.0	28.0	12.6	21.3
7.0	8.6	10.5				10.8	8.0	6.1	12.7
1.1	2.3	4.7				4.8	1.7	4.5	5.5
19.0	26.0	20.4	Sales/Net Fixed Assets			22.7	27.1	22.5	16.0
8.1	9.0	10.4				7.8	18.0	14.8	9.7
4.2	5.0	5.1				3.8	5.2	6.0	6.3
2.6	2.9	2.9	Sales/Total Assets			3.0	3.3	3.3	2.8
1.9	2.4	2.4				2.6	2.7	2.7	2.2
1.6	1.7	1.8				1.0	1.8	2.1	1.6
1.3	.9	.9	% Depr., Dep., Amort./Sales				.8	.9	.7
(56)　1.8	(55)　1.8	(63)　1.7					(10)　1.8	1.4	(26)　1.3
3.4	3.5	3.0					3.2	2.6	2.3
1.4	1.7	1.4	% Officers', Directors' Owners' Comp/Sales						
(20)　3.2	(18)　2.8	(18)　3.3							
4.6	5.6	4.0							
3310872M	3794054M	4018832M	Net Sales ($)	2367M	2078M	36106M	73291M	226767M	3678223M
1807657M	1878827M	1998727M	Total Assets ($)	1112M	1437M	21485M	29784M	91840M	1853069M

M = $ thousand　　MM = $ million
See Pages 11 through 21 for Explanation of Ratios and Data

Current Data Sorted by Assets | Comparative Historical Data

0-500M	500M-2MM	2-10MM	10-50MM	50-100MM	100-250MM	Type of Statement	4/1/02-3/31/03 ALL	4/1/03-3/31/04 ALL
		2	4	2	2	Unqualified	12	13
	1	9	7	1		Reviewed	16	22
		8	1	1		Compiled	10	14
	2	2				Tax Returns	3	5
1		5	9	2		Other	24	21
		12 (4/1-9/30/06)	47 (10/1/06-3/31/07)					
1	3	26	21	6	2	**NUMBER OF STATEMENTS**	65	75
%	%	%	%	%	%	**ASSETS**	%	%
		4.4	5.5			Cash & Equivalents	7.3	7.8
		32.9	30.0			Trade Receivables (net)	25.5	27.6
		20.1	21.5			Inventory	16.3	17.3
		.8	1.5			All Other Current	1.6	2.4
		58.1	58.5			Total Current	50.8	55.2
		35.3	31.2			Fixed Assets (net)	39.6	36.5
		2.1	2.8			Intangibles (net)	2.9	2.6
		4.5	7.5			All Other Non-Current	6.8	5.7
		100.0	100.0			Total	100.0	100.0
						LIABILITIES		
		8.7	9.6			Notes Payable-Short Term	8.8	10.1
		5.4	2.3			Cur. Mat.-L.T.D.	3.9	4.5
		18.3	13.9			Trade Payables	14.8	14.6
		.3	.0			Income Taxes Payable	.2	.2
		9.8	8.4			All Other Current	11.1	8.4
		42.5	34.2			Total Current	38.8	37.8
		22.3	12.0			Long-Term Debt	28.6	17.9
		.5	.5			Deferred Taxes	1.1	.7
		4.1	7.0			All Other Non-Current	4.8	5.5
		30.7	46.3			Net Worth	26.7	38.0
		100.0	100.0			Total Liabilties & Net Worth	100.0	100.0
						INCOME DATA		
		100.0	100.0			Net Sales	100.0	100.0
		21.4	16.0			Gross Profit	22.3	24.1
		18.2	10.0			Operating Expenses	19.1	20.7
		3.2	6.0			Operating Profit	3.2	3.4
		1.1	1.3			All Other Expenses (net)	.8	.8
		2.1	4.7			Profit Before Taxes	2.4	2.7
						RATIOS		
		2.0	2.4			Current	2.2	2.7
		1.3	1.5				1.3	1.5
		1.1	1.3				.9	1.0
		1.3	1.7			Quick	1.4	1.7
		.9	.8				.9	1.0
		.5	.7				.5	.6
		43 8.4	47 7.8			Sales/Receivables	38 9.5	42 8.7
		53 6.9	57 6.4				46 7.9	50 7.3
		76 4.8	63 5.8				60 6.1	60 6.0
		25 14.4	22 16.8			Cost of Sales/Inventory	22 16.9	24 15.4
		38 9.7	44 8.4				36 10.2	37 10.0
		72 5.0	69 5.3				58 6.3	59 6.2
		24 15.5	14 25.3			Cost of Sales/Payables	18 20.7	19 19.6
		35 10.4	31 12.0				29 12.7	32 11.3
		51 7.1	48 7.6				46 7.9	49 7.4
		5.4	5.6			Sales/Working Capital	7.1	5.6
		14.9	8.6				16.7	9.8
		NM	18.9				-28.8	102.4
		7.6	12.5			EBIT/Interest	7.5	8.9
		(24) 2.6	(18) 2.9				(61) 3.5	(70) 2.7
		.4	1.3				.8	.1
						Net Profit + Depr., Dep., Amort./Cur. Mat. L/T/D	9.8	3.3
							(23) 2.4	(26) 2.2
							.8	1.1
		.5	.3			Fixed/Worth	.5	.5
		1.2	.6				1.4	1.1
		3.3	1.5				3.2	2.4
		1.0	.5			Debt/Worth	.6	.6
		2.1	1.3				1.9	1.7
		7.3	3.1				5.3	4.7
		23.3	44.5			% Profit Before Taxes/Tangible Net Worth	32.1	30.1
		(22) 15.3	21.1				(56) 10.8	(68) 13.7
		5.4	.8				1.1	-.8
		9.5	19.4			% Profit Before Taxes/Total Assets	10.9	10.4
		4.6	9.7				4.3	4.6
		-2.7	.3				-.5	-2.5
		14.1	11.6			Sales/Net Fixed Assets	7.2	8.3
		6.1	8.5				4.9	5.1
		3.8	3.8				3.1	3.1
		2.6	2.3			Sales/Total Assets	2.2	2.3
		2.1	1.9				1.8	1.8
		1.5	1.7				1.5	1.5
		1.4	1.6			% Depr., Dep., Amort./Sales	2.1	2.0
		(25) 2.4	2.4				(59) 3.8	(69) 3.7
		4.1	5.0				5.5	5.2
		1.7				% Officers', Directors' Owners' Comp/Sales	1.6	1.1
		(17) 2.4					(23) 3.7	(30) 2.7
		4.2					6.3	6.8
1280M	13313M	252271M	919523M	725102M	480638M	Net Sales ($)	2055325M	2269031M
417M	4324M	115773M	481024M	414440M	324459M	Total Assets ($)	1215355M	1274956M

Comparative Historical Data | Current Data Sorted by Sales

4/1/04-3/31/05 ALL	4/1/05-3/31/06 ALL	4/1/06-3/31/07 ALL	Type of Statement	0-1MM	1-3MM	3-5MM	5-10MM	10-25MM	25MM & OVER
16	13	10	Unqualified				1	2	7
16	9	18	Reviewed		1		5	4	8
14	14	10	Compiled		2	2	3	2	2
4	6	5	Tax Returns	2	1		2		
15	20	16	Other	1			1	5	9
					12 (4/1-9/30/06)		47 (10/1/06-3/31/07)		
65	62	59	NUMBER OF STATEMENTS		4	4	12	13	26
%	%	%	ASSETS	%	%	%	%	%	%
5.9	6.2	5.4	Cash & Equivalents	D			1.5	5.3	7.4
29.1	29.1	31.5	Trade Receivables (net)	A			30.6	40.8	27.5
19.1	17.3	19.7	Inventory	T			24.3	23.4	17.1
1.4	1.9	1.2	All Other Current	A			.6	1.2	1.6
55.6	54.5	57.7	Total Current				56.9	70.6	53.7
36.3	34.4	33.9	Fixed Assets (net)	N			36.9	21.6	38.1
2.0	5.8	2.8	Intangibles (net)	O			.4	4.0	1.0
6.1	5.3	5.6	All Other Non-Current	T			5.8	3.8	7.3
100.0	100.0	100.0	Total				100.0	100.0	100.0
			LIABILITIES	A					
11.2	9.7	7.9	Notes Payable-Short Term	V			13.3	8.9	6.9
4.2	3.5	3.9	Cur. Mat.-L.T.D.	A			4.4	1.5	3.2
16.5	17.7	16.3	Trade Payables	I			15.4	23.2	13.8
.1	.1	.2	Income Taxes Payable	L			.4	.2	.1
7.8	9.4	9.7	All Other Current	A			6.4	14.3	10.7
39.8	40.4	37.9	Total Current	B			40.0	48.1	34.9
16.7	23.0	18.1	Long-Term Debt	L			19.9	13.0	13.9
.9	.6	.5	Deferred Taxes	E			.4	.0	.7
4.6	8.3	5.3	All Other Non-Current				4.7	6.3	6.8
38.0	27.7	38.2	Net Worth				35.0	32.6	43.8
100.0	100.0	100.0	Total Liabilities & Net Worth				100.0	100.0	100.0
			INCOME DATA						
100.0	100.0	100.0	Net Sales				100.0	100.0	100.0
23.9	21.7	19.5	Gross Profit				23.7	16.3	15.2
19.3	16.4	15.7	Operating Expenses				20.5	12.1	11.2
4.6	5.3	3.8	Operating Profit				3.3	4.1	4.0
.7	1.4	1.0	All Other Expenses (net)				1.1	.1	1.0
3.9	4.0	2.8	Profit Before Taxes				2.1	4.0	3.0
			RATIOS						
2.2	1.9	2.4	Current				2.5	1.9	2.4
1.3	1.4	1.5					1.4	1.4	1.5
1.0	1.0	1.2					.9	1.2	1.1
1.4	1.3	1.7	Quick				1.3	1.3	1.8
.8	.8	.9					.9	.8	.9
.6	.6	.6					.5	.8	.6
41 8.8	41 8.9	45 8.1	Sales/Receivables				31 11.8	43 8.5	47 7.8
53 6.8	53 6.9	57 6.4					53 6.8	59 6.1	57 6.4
66 5.6	63 5.8	66 5.6					65 5.6	76 4.8	63 5.8
23 16.1	20 18.4	24 15.5	Cost of Sales/Inventory				34 10.7	26 13.9	19 19.7
37 10.0	33 11.1	37 9.9					38 9.5	41 9.0	34 10.6
71 5.2	56 6.5	61 6.0					77 4.7	63 5.8	52 7.0
23 15.9	21 17.0	18 20.4	Cost of Sales/Payables				19 19.2	20 18.2	13 29.1
36 10.0	38 9.7	33 11.2					26 14.1	37 9.8	29 12.4
53 6.9	59 6.1	51 7.2					43 8.5	54 6.7	48 7.6
6.8	6.7	5.5	Sales/Working Capital				4.9	6.2	5.7
15.4	15.1	10.4					13.5	12.9	9.0
91.6	-115.7	30.4					-134.7	27.3	33.9
12.1	9.1	8.2	EBIT/Interest				16.0	6.8	14.0
(63) 3.8	(58) 3.2	(53) 3.0			(11) 2.5	(12) 3.1			(22) 3.6
2.2	1.4	.9					.3	1.6	.6
7.9	6.2	9.9	Net Profit + Depr., Dep., Amort./Cur. Mat. L/T/D						12.6
(20) 2.2	(25) 1.7	(20) 3.6							(10) 3.2
1.7	.5	.5							.7
.4	.5	.4	Fixed/Worth				.4	.2	.4
1.0	1.7	.9					.9	.9	.9
1.7	28.4	2.0					7.7	1.6	1.7
.8	.9	.8	Debt/Worth				.8	1.2	.5
1.7	3.4	1.4					1.5	2.6	1.1
4.7	51.7	3.8					16.4	4.0	3.0
36.1	56.0	35.2	% Profit Before Taxes/Tangible Net Worth				23.4	60.2	39.2
(60) 16.6	(48) 24.8	(53) 15.7			(10) 15.3	(12) 19.2			(25) 15.9
7.4	3.8	1.8					-.4	3.1	.4
12.9	14.6	12.5	% Profit Before Taxes/Total Assets				10.0	15.1	15.5
5.2	6.0	5.2					4.6	6.0	5.7
2.8	1.0	.0					-5.4	.7	-.9
9.8	9.6	13.1	Sales/Net Fixed Assets				13.1	49.3	9.2
5.2	5.8	7.3					6.6	13.1	4.8
3.6	3.5	3.4					3.6	5.8	3.1
2.4	2.6	2.4	Sales/Total Assets				2.7	2.8	2.3
1.9	1.8	2.0					2.0	2.3	1.8
1.5	1.4	1.7					1.7	2.0	1.6
2.0	1.5	1.4	% Depr., Dep., Amort./Sales				1.2	.4	1.9
(59) 3.3	(53) 2.7	(54) 2.4			(11) 3.8			1.5	(23) 3.3
5.3	4.2	4.3					5.3	2.5	5.3
1.0	1.6	1.4	% Officers', Directors' Owners' Comp/Sales						
(23) 1.8	(31) 2.8	(27) 1.9							
5.8	5.0	3.7							
2129972M	2090379M	2392127M	Net Sales ($)		7946M	14600M	85087M	225406M	2059088M
1086197M	1175249M	1340437M	Total Assets ($)		7130M	7112M	41368M	100317M	1184510M

M = $ thousand   MM = $ million
See Pages 11 through 21 for Explanation of Ratios and Data

Current Data Sorted by Assets							Comparative Historical Data	
						Type of Statement		
			2	1	1	Unqualified	8	5
		6				Reviewed	7	13
		2	1			Compiled	7	9
	6	2				Tax Returns	1	1
1	1		2	1		Other	3	8
1	9 (4/1-9/30/06)		19 (10/1/06-3/31/07)				4/1/02- 3/31/03 ALL	4/1/03- 3/31/04 ALL
0-500M	500M-2MM	2-10MM	10-50MM	50-100MM	100-250MM	**NUMBER OF STATEMENTS**	26	36
2	7	10	6	2	1			
%	%	%	%	%	%	**ASSETS**	%	%
		6.9				Cash & Equivalents	8.9	8.2
		29.9				Trade Receivables (net)	21.6	24.2
		23.5				Inventory	16.8	19.5
		1.9				All Other Current	2.6	2.7
		62.1				Total Current	49.9	54.7
		30.5				Fixed Assets (net)	38.4	34.6
		.4				Intangibles (net)	4.5	3.4
		7.0				All Other Non-Current	7.3	7.3
		100.0				Total	100.0	100.0
						LIABILITIES		
		12.6				Notes Payable-Short Term	5.1	7.2
		2.0				Cur. Mat.-L.T.D.	3.6	4.7
		19.3				Trade Payables	10.5	13.7
		.0				Income Taxes Payable	.3	.1
		6.2				All Other Current	7.7	9.4
		40.2				Total Current	27.2	35.2
		13.3				Long-Term Debt	15.8	16.6
		1.7				Deferred Taxes	.7	.4
		.6				All Other Non-Current	1.8	3.7
		44.3				Net Worth	54.5	44.1
		100.0				Total Liabilties & Net Worth	100.0	100.0
						INCOME DATA		
		100.0				Net Sales	100.0	100.0
		33.6				Gross Profit	23.1	21.8
		28.2				Operating Expenses	21.1	19.8
		5.4				Operating Profit	2.0	2.0
		-.2				All Other Expenses (net)	.3	.3
		5.6				Profit Before Taxes	1.7	1.7
						RATIOS		
		2.0				Current	2.7	2.2
		1.5					1.8	1.7
		1.1					1.4	1.4
		1.2				Quick	1.8	1.6
		.8					1.0	1.1
		.6					.8	.6
		37 9.8				Sales/Receivables	38 9.7	37 9.9
		46 7.9					48 7.6	45 8.1
		57 6.4					53 6.9	60 6.1
		30 12.0				Cost of Sales/Inventory	28 13.2	31 12.0
		51 7.2					43 8.6	37 9.9
		110 3.3					63 5.8	69 5.3
		20 18.1				Cost of Sales/Payables	15 24.3	15 24.3
		33 10.9					28 13.1	28 13.1
		95 3.8					37 10.0	46 7.9
		7.3				Sales/Working Capital	5.3	5.2
		11.7					8.2	9.7
		41.9					14.0	23.3
						EBIT/Interest	5.3	6.9
							(22) 2.7	(30) 3.0
							-1.7	-.7
						Net Profit + Depr., Dep., Amort./Cur. Mat. L/T/D		4.2
							(11) 2.2	
								1.1
		.3				Fixed/Worth	.5	.5
		.7					.8	.8
		1.6					1.2	2.2
		.7				Debt/Worth	.4	.5
		1.0					1.0	1.4
		3.3					2.0	3.2
		60.3				% Profit Before Taxes/Tangible Net Worth	21.1	25.0
		33.4					8.3	(32) 12.4
		9.3					-5.2	-5.1
		21.6				% Profit Before Taxes/Total Assets	10.7	11.2
		9.8					3.2	5.6
		3.8					-3.2	-3.8
		18.3				Sales/Net Fixed Assets	7.6	9.8
		7.4					5.3	6.7
		4.7					2.9	3.5
		2.5				Sales/Total Assets	2.6	2.4
		2.1					1.7	1.9
		1.7					1.2	1.5
						% Depr., Dep., Amort./Sales	3.2	2.3
							(23) 4.2	(31) 3.5
							7.8	4.4
						% Officers', Directors' Owners' Comp/Sales		2.3
							(16) 3.1	
								9.2
6559M	23717M	107989M	247661M	240175M	181197M	Net Sales ($)	1009419M	1155968M
359M	7630M	51665M	148256M	138381M	148639M	Total Assets ($)	610532M	601578M

© RMA 2007

M = $ thousand   MM = $ million
See Pages 11 through 21 for Explanation of Ratios and Data

Comparative Historical Data   **Current Data Sorted by Sales**

3	2	4	Type of Statement						
3	2	4	Unqualified						4
9	10	7	Reviewed				1	6	
7	7	9	Compiled		4	2	2	1	
	1	3	Tax Returns		1		1		
6	6	5	Other	1			1	1	3
4/1/04-3/31/05 ALL	4/1/05-3/31/06 ALL	4/1/06-3/31/07 ALL		0-1MM	9 (4/1-9/30/06) 1-3MM	3-5MM	5-10MM	19 (10/1/06-3/31/07) 10-25MM	25MM & OVER
25	26	28	**NUMBER OF STATEMENTS**	1	5	2	5	8	7
%	%	%	**ASSETS**	%	%	%	%	%	%
8.5	7.2	7.1	Cash & Equivalents						
27.7	28.5	29.6	Trade Receivables (net)						
16.6	22.1	23.7	Inventory						
2.1	1.3	1.8	All Other Current						
54.9	59.1	62.2	Total Current						
34.8	30.6	28.7	Fixed Assets (net)						
1.8	2.6	4.6	Intangibles (net)						
8.6	7.7	4.5	All Other Non-Current						
100.0	100.0	100.0	Total						
			LIABILITIES						
7.8	17.6	8.9	Notes Payable-Short Term						
2.0	2.7	2.3	Cur. Mat.-L.T.D.						
14.6	12.4	16.6	Trade Payables						
.0	.2	.1	Income Taxes Payable						
8.3	7.2	9.3	All Other Current						
32.7	40.1	37.2	Total Current						
15.5	11.8	17.9	Long-Term Debt						
.4	.8	.7	Deferred Taxes						
2.6	6.5	3.4	All Other Non-Current						
48.8	40.8	40.8	Net Worth						
100.0	100.0	100.0	Total Liabilties & Net Worth						
			INCOME DATA						
100.0	100.0	100.0	Net Sales						
20.3	21.3	24.9	Gross Profit						
19.4	18.1	20.6	Operating Expenses						
.9	3.2	4.2	Operating Profit						
-.5	.6	.2	All Other Expenses (net)						
1.4	2.6	4.0	Profit Before Taxes						
			RATIOS						
3.0	2.2	2.1							
1.8	1.6	1.7	Current						
1.3	1.2	1.2							
1.7	1.5	1.4							
1.1	1.0	.9	Quick						
.8	.6	.6							
42 8.6	41 8.8	38 9.6							
46 7.9	48 7.6	48 7.7	Sales/Receivables						
54 6.7	59 6.2	55 6.6							
23 16.0	27 13.6	24 15.2							
33 11.0	34 10.7	40 9.1	Cost of Sales/Inventory						
56 6.5	86 4.2	69 5.3							
13 29.0	10 36.5	16 22.6							
23 15.6	25 14.5	29 12.5	Cost of Sales/Payables						
44 8.2	43 8.6	46 7.9							
5.1	5.2	7.1							
9.4	11.1	11.4	Sales/Working Capital						
20.1	32.9	27.8							
12.3	10.1	16.0							
(22) 3.7	(22) 2.9	(25) 5.2	EBIT/Interest						
-1.7	.6	2.0							
	4.3								
(10) 2.5			Net Profit + Depr., Dep., Amort./Cur. Mat. L/T/D						
	-.3								
.3	.3	.3							
.7	.8	.8	Fixed/Worth						
.9	3.4	3.3							
.5	.5	.7							
.8	1.0	1.5	Debt/Worth						
1.8	4.6	3.9							
15.0	22.9	46.6							
(24) 5.2	(22) 10.4	(24) 19.4	% Profit Before Taxes/Tangible Net Worth						
-4.0	-6.7	4.2							
9.3	11.4	14.3							
3.7	3.9	6.6	% Profit Before Taxes/Total Assets						
-2.5	-2.2	2.3							
11.3	12.0	19.3							
6.3	6.5	7.3	Sales/Net Fixed Assets						
3.9	3.6	4.1							
2.4	2.2	3.3							
2.0	1.8	2.1	Sales/Total Assets						
1.4	1.4	1.6							
2.1	1.9	2.3							
(22) 3.9	(24) 3.4	(24) 3.7	% Depr., Dep., Amort./Sales						
4.5	5.5	5.2							
1.5	2.1	1.3							
(12) 2.1	(11) 2.9	(14) 3.1	% Officers', Directors' Owners' Comp/Sales						
3.6	4.5	6.9							
583619M	594204M	807298M	Net Sales ($)	614M	12180M	9070M	35736M	121894M	627804M
352663M	359565M	494930M	Total Assets ($)	278M	5976M	2205M	16529M	57713M	412229M

M = $ thousand   MM = $ million
See Pages 11 through 21 for Explanation of Ratios and Data

Current Data Sorted by Assets

Comparative Historical Data

						Type of Statement		
		2	2			Unqualified	6	12
1	1	2	4			Reviewed	8	14
2	2	2				Compiled	9	8
	1					Tax Returns		1
1	3	4	5			Other	10	10
	11 (4/1-9/30/06)		21 (10/1/06-3/31/07)				4/1/02-3/31/03	4/1/03-3/31/04
0-500M	500M-2MM	2-10MM	10-50MM	50-100MM	100-250MM		ALL	ALL
4	7	10	11			NUMBER OF STATEMENTS	33	45
%	%	%	%	%	%	ASSETS	%	%
		5.8	3.4	D	D	Cash & Equivalents	7.6	6.1
		26.7	29.8	A	A	Trade Receivables (net)	24.5	27.0
		12.7	24.0	T	T	Inventory	12.3	18.4
		.9	1.5	A	A	All Other Current	2.4	2.2
		46.1	58.7			Total Current	46.7	53.6
		48.1	32.9	N	N	Fixed Assets (net)	44.7	38.7
		.0	4.3	O	O	Intangibles (net)	3.2	2.2
		5.8	4.1	T	T	All Other Non-Current	5.3	5.5
		100.0	100.0			Total	100.0	100.0
				A	A	LIABILITIES		
		5.7	18.0	V	V	Notes Payable-Short Term	8.8	11.4
		3.5	2.0	A	A	Cur. Mat.-L.T.D.	4.2	4.4
		11.4	15.4	I	I	Trade Payables	11.6	13.8
		.0	.0	L	L	Income Taxes Payable	.1	.1
		8.0	7.8	A	A	All Other Current	7.1	6.5
		28.6	43.2	B	B	Total Current	31.7	36.1
		20.3	17.2	L	L	Long-Term Debt	23.1	19.0
		.3	.8	E	E	Deferred Taxes	.8	.5
		2.4	5.0			All Other Non-Current	5.1	6.6
		48.4	33.8			Net Worth	39.3	37.8
		100.0	100.0			Total Liabilties & Net Worth	100.0	100.0
						INCOME DATA		
		100.0	100.0			Net Sales	100.0	100.0
		24.7	19.9			Gross Profit	22.8	21.1
		17.0	17.0			Operating Expenses	21.7	17.2
		7.7	2.9			Operating Profit	1.1	3.9
		1.0	1.4			All Other Expenses (net)	1.7	1.0
		6.7	1.5			Profit Before Taxes	-.6	2.9
						RATIOS		
		3.5	1.7				2.6	2.7
		1.7	1.5			Current	1.6	1.5
		1.0	1.2				1.0	1.0
		3.2	1.1				1.9	1.7
		1.3	.9			Quick	1.0	.9
		.6	.5				.6	.6
	41	9.0	40	9.0			40	9.2	42	8.7
	49	7.4	51	7.2		Sales/Receivables	48	7.6	47	7.7
	58	6.3	71	5.2			60	6.1	59	6.2
	0	UND	36	10.0			19	19.2	23	15.7
	33	10.9	45	8.2		Cost of Sales/Inventory	28	13.2	34	10.7
	48	7.6	75	4.9			39	9.4	59	6.2
	5	72.0	26	14.1			17	21.9	14	26.3
	17	21.2	32	11.3		Cost of Sales/Payables	28	13.1	22	16.2
	51	7.2	52	7.1			36	10.0	42	8.7
		4.7	8.9				6.5	5.3
		15.2	11.7			Sales/Working Capital	14.2	11.9
		NM	20.3				458.3	-161.6
			5.1				3.2	3.5
			1.9			EBIT/Interest	(29) 1.1	(39) 2.1
			.8				-3.1	.2
						Net Profit + Depr., Dep.,		1.8
						Amort./Cur. Mat. L/T/D	(13)	1.3
								.5
		.6	.6				.6	.7
		.9	1.4			Fixed/Worth	1.5	1.2
		1.8	2.0				3.0	2.7
		.5	2.8				.7	.8
		1.1	3.4			Debt/Worth	2.1	2.1
		2.6	5.5				4.0	4.5
		56.0	21.5			% Profit Before Taxes/Tangible	24.9	34.5
		29.5	8.6			Net Worth	(29) .8	(40) 9.8
		11.6	-2.3				-9.1	.4
		17.9	6.0			% Profit Before Taxes/Total	9.1	10.9
		11.9	2.3			Assets	.2	3.3
		5.4	-.6				-6.3	-.5
		7.8	10.8				6.2	7.5
		4.7	5.7			Sales/Net Fixed Assets	4.3	5.2
		2.4	3.6				2.7	3.5
		2.5	2.6				2.3	2.4
		2.0	1.8			Sales/Total Assets	1.8	1.9
		1.5	1.5				1.3	1.5
			1.9				3.3	2.6
		(10)	3.2			% Depr., Dep., Amort./Sales	(31) 3.9	(43) 3.7
			5.0				5.8	5.0
						% Officers', Directors'	3.4	2.4
						Owners' Comp/Sales	(16) 5.8	(17) 3.3
							11.3	7.4
3448M	18460M	97131M	479238M			Net Sales ($)	473184M	815944M
1176M	9440M	49872M	210217M			Total Assets ($)	346348M	439522M

M = $ thousand   MM = $ million
See Pages 11 through 21 for Explanation of Ratios and Data

Comparative Historical Data

Current Data Sorted by Sales

					Type of Statement						
	6		5		4	Unqualified				2	2
	14		10		8	Reviewed		2		3	2
	12		6		6	Compiled	1	3		1	1	
	1		2		1	Tax Returns			1			
	15		12		13	Other	1	3	1	3	2	3
	4/1/04-3/31/05 ALL		4/1/05-3/31/06 ALL		4/1/06-3/31/07 ALL		0-1MM	11 (4/1-9/30/06) 1-3MM	3-5MM	21 (10/1/06-3/31/07) 5-10MM	10-25MM	25MM & OVER
	48		35		32	NUMBER OF STATEMENTS	2	8	2	5	8	7
	%		%		%	ASSETS	%	%	%	%	%	%
	5.3		3.8		6.0	Cash & Equivalents						
	29.5		31.0		30.5	Trade Receivables (net)						
	19.4		23.1		18.5	Inventory						
	2.1		2.1		.9	All Other Current						
	56.2		60.1		55.9	Total Current						
	38.9		32.0		38.7	Fixed Assets (net)						
	1.0		2.8		1.7	Intangibles (net)						
	3.8		5.0		3.7	All Other Non-Current						
	100.0		100.0		100.0	Total						
						LIABILITIES						
	8.2		11.4		10.7	Notes Payable-Short Term						
	4.1		4.6		4.5	Cur. Mat.-L.T.D.						
	16.6		15.6		14.5	Trade Payables						
	.1		.0		.0	Income Taxes Payable						
	7.4		8.9		7.7	All Other Current						
	36.3		40.6		37.3	Total Current						
	26.1		17.7		21.9	Long-Term Debt						
	.3		.6		.3	Deferred Taxes						
	14.4		21.0		4.4	All Other Non-Current						
	22.9		20.0		36.0	Net Worth						
	100.0		100.0		100.0	Total Liabilties & Net Worth						
						INCOME DATA						
	100.0		100.0		100.0	Net Sales						
	21.5		20.1		26.1	Gross Profit						
	17.2		17.3		20.4	Operating Expenses						
	4.4		2.8		5.7	Operating Profit						
	1.2		1.2		1.3	All Other Expenses (net)						
	3.2		1.6		4.4	Profit Before Taxes						
						RATIOS						
	2.8		2.2		2.6							
	1.6		1.4		1.5	Current						
	1.1		1.0		1.0							
	1.7		1.6		1.8							
	1.2		.8		.9	Quick						
	.6		.5		.6							
39	9.3	41	8.8	41	8.9							
51	7.2	48	7.6	49	7.5	Sales/Receivables						
62	5.9	59	6.2	60	6.1							
25	14.9	26	14.2	24	15.3							
36	10.2	41	8.8	40	9.2	Cost of Sales/Inventory						
58	6.3	63	6.5	56	6.5							
16	22.4	16	23.3	15	24.7							
33	11.2	29	12.5	28	13.0	Cost of Sales/Payables						
49	7.4	49	7.5	51	7.1							
	5.8		6.8		6.1							
	11.7		14.5		12.0	Sales/Working Capital						
	45.4		122.1		108.4							
	6.0		5.4		8.6							
(41)	3.4	(31)	1.3	(29)	2.9	EBIT/Interest						
	.9		-.7		1.2							
	1.8		1.6			Net Profit + Depr., Dep.,						
(10)	1.4	(11)	1.1			Amort./Cur. Mat. L/T/D						
	1.0		.0									
	.8		.6		.6							
	1.2		1.1		1.3	Fixed/Worth						
	3.6		3.1		2.0							
	1.1		.9		.9							
	2.2		2.4		2.5	Debt/Worth						
	6.7		8.6		4.8							
	44.8		24.6		47.9	% Profit Before Taxes/Tangible						
(41)	18.3	(30)	3.6	(30)	20.9	Net Worth						
	4.4		-14.7		4.5							
	13.2		10.2		17.3	% Profit Before Taxes/Total						
	4.9		1.0		5.4	Assets						
	-.1		-3.2		1.1							
	13.1		11.0		11.0							
	4.8		6.6		5.7	Sales/Net Fixed Assets						
	3.2		4.6		3.3							
	2.7		2.8		2.9							
	2.0		2.1		2.0	Sales/Total Assets						
	1.5		1.7		1.5							
	1.9		2.1		1.8							
(44)	3.5		2.8	(29)	2.8	% Depr., Dep., Amort./Sales						
	5.7		3.9		5.8							
	1.9		1.9		1.5							
(17)	4.1	(12)	3.9	(10)	2.8	% Officers', Directors'						
	8.5		10.2		8.7	Owners' Comp/Sales						
	927549M		692785M		598277M	Net Sales ($)	1200M	13245M	9584M	32117M	138029M	404102M
	444788M		336178M		270705M	Total Assets ($)	486M	10230M	3007M	17791M	77380M	161811M

© RMA 2007

M = $ thousand   MM = $ million
See Pages 11 through 21 for Explanation of Ratios and Data

Current Data Sorted by Assets

Comparative Historical Data

Type of Statement

						Type of Statement	4/1/02-3/31/03	4/1/03-3/31/04
		2	5			Unqualified	7	4
1		6	1			Reviewed	9	11
3		4				Compiled	10	12
3		1				Tax Returns	1	4
		5	4	1	1	Other	8	7
	10 (4/1-9/30/06)		27 (10/1/06-3/31/07)				ALL	ALL
0-500M	500M-2MM	2-10MM	10-50MM	50-100MM	100-250MM	NUMBER OF STATEMENTS	35	38
7		18	10	1	1			

0-500M %	500M-2MM %	2-10MM %	10-50MM %	50-100MM %	100-250MM %		Hist %	Hist %
						ASSETS		
		8.9	4.8			Cash & Equivalents	8.3	3.8
		32.0	33.8			Trade Receivables (net)	24.7	28.0
		22.5	29.9			Inventory	18.3	17.7
		.8	3.3			All Other Current	2.5	3.6
		64.2	71.7			Total Current	53.8	53.1
		31.2	23.2			Fixed Assets (net)	31.6	41.1
		.7	.6			Intangibles (net)	6.0	.9
		3.9	4.5			All Other Non-Current	8.6	4.9
		100.0	100.0			Total	100.0	100.0
						LIABILITIES		
		14.5	9.8			Notes Payable-Short Term	9.1	12.4
		3.3	2.0			Cur. Mat.-L.T.D.	4.8	6.8
		17.4	18.3			Trade Payables	13.1	14.6
		.1	.1			Income Taxes Payable	.3	.5
		10.6	11.3			All Other Current	9.5	7.2
		45.9	41.5			Total Current	36.9	41.5
		13.8	9.2			Long-Term Debt	20.5	19.7
		.5	1.0			Deferred Taxes	.4	.4
		4.6	4.6			All Other Non-Current	8.0	5.4
		35.3	43.7			Net Worth	34.2	33.0
		100.0	100.0			Total Liabilities & Net Worth	100.0	100.0
						INCOME DATA		
		100.0	100.0			Net Sales	100.0	100.0
		27.6	15.9			Gross Profit	26.2	24.4
		19.2	9.9			Operating Expenses	23.7	21.9
		8.5	6.0			Operating Profit	2.5	2.5
		.7	.8			All Other Expenses (net)	1.8	1.3
		7.7	5.2			Profit Before Taxes	.7	1.3
						RATIOS		
		1.9	2.7				2.5	2.2
		1.4	1.6			Current	1.7	1.5
		1.1	1.3				1.1	.9
		1.2	1.5				1.5	1.4
		.8	.8			Quick	1.0	.8
		.6	.6				.6	.5
		43 8.5	41 8.8				28 13.2	38 9.6
		55 6.6	63 5.8			Sales/Receivables	48 7.5	52 7.0
		75 4.9	72 5.1				59 6.2	69 5.3
		21 17.8	36 10.0				20 18.4	19 19.3
		50 7.4	47 7.8			Cost of Sales/Inventory	34 10.7	37 9.8
		67 5.4	129 2.8				61 6.0	68 5.4
		20 17.8	27 13.7				14 26.0	17 21.2
		38 9.6	34 10.9			Cost of Sales/Payables	24 15.4	35 10.4
		57 6.4	59 6.2				41 8.8	56 6.5
		4.7	5.0				7.3	6.2
		15.4	7.1			Sales/Working Capital	14.1	11.3
		50.0	13.2				38.1	-75.0
		11.7					7.5	5.4
		(16) 4.7				EBIT/Interest	(30) 1.8	(32) 1.6
		1.0					.1	-1.2
							3.1	
						Net Profit + Depr., Dep., Amort./Cur. Mat. L/T/D	(10) 1.3	
							-.6	
		.6	.2				.4	.6
		1.0	.6			Fixed/Worth	1.0	1.3
		2.3	1.1				6.3	2.4
		.9	.8				.5	.7
		2.2	1.6			Debt/Worth	1.8	1.8
		7.0	3.8				31.5	4.7
		65.1	49.2				25.9	25.5
		(17) 39.7	21.6			% Profit Before Taxes/Tangible Net Worth	(28) 16.7	(33) 13.0
		7.1	15.3				5.1	-2.7
		29.2	16.0				9.3	8.2
		8.3	11.9			% Profit Before Taxes/Total Assets	3.8	2.7
		1.5	3.5				.0	-3.8
		12.8	16.7				14.4	8.8
		5.6	9.5			Sales/Net Fixed Assets	8.0	4.4
		4.1	7.5				3.5	2.6
		2.5	2.5				2.7	2.5
		2.1	1.9			Sales/Total Assets	2.1	1.7
		1.4	1.6				1.4	1.4
		1.6					1.4	2.0
		(17) 3.8				% Depr., Dep., Amort./Sales	(31) 3.2	3.4
		4.7					4.1	5.1
							1.3	1.5
						% Officers', Directors' Owners' Comp/Sales	(10) 5.2	(16) 6.1
							7.8	9.0
28072M	180911M	412006M	71041M	67203M		Net Sales ($)	647485M	362669M
9691M	80463M	220624M	99818M	104216M		Total Assets ($)	453863M	232506M

(Left columns 0-500M and 500M-2MM marked "DATA NOT AVAILABLE")

© RMA 2007

M = $ thousand   MM = $ million
See Pages 11 through 21 for Explanation of Ratios and Data

Comparative Historical Data | Current Data Sorted by Sales

Note: For the current-data size categories 0-1MM, 1-3MM, 3-5MM, 5-10MM and 10-25MM the financial percentage/ratio detail is marked **DATA NOT AVAILABLE**; only the 25MM & OVER column carries full detail.

Type of Statement

4/1/04- 3/31/05 ALL	4/1/05- 3/31/06 ALL	4/1/06- 3/31/07 ALL	Type of Statement	0-1MM	1-3MM	3-5MM	5-10MM	10-25MM	25MM & OVER
3	7	7	Unqualified					2	5
10	10	8	Reviewed			4	1		2
5	5	7	Compiled		2	1	3	2	2
2	3	4	Tax Returns			2	2	1	
9	14	11	Other			1	3	1	3
					10 (4/1-9/30/06)		27 (10/1/06-3/31/07)		
29	39	37	NUMBER OF STATEMENTS		2	8	9	6	12

Data

4/1/04- 3/31/05 ALL	4/1/05- 3/31/06 ALL	4/1/06- 3/31/07 ALL		25MM & OVER
%	%	%	**ASSETS**	%
7.0	6.4	8.1	Cash & Equivalents	3.8
26.2	29.8	29.6	Trade Receivables (net)	31.4
22.1	23.3	23.7	Inventory	27.2
2.1	2.3	1.4	All Other Current	2.8
57.3	61.7	62.7	Total Current	65.1
37.2	29.5	30.5	Fixed Assets (net)	22.1
.4	4.5	3.5	Intangibles (net)	9.7
5.1	4.3	3.3	All Other Non-Current	3.1
100.0	100.0	100.0	Total	100.0
			LIABILITIES	
10.2	10.1	10.6	Notes Payable-Short Term	9.3
6.2	4.8	3.2	Cur. Mat.-L.T.D.	1.2
15.3	16.8	18.4	Trade Payables	19.1
.3	.5	.1	Income Taxes Payable	.1
8.7	10.7	9.0	All Other Current	8.0
40.7	42.8	41.3	Total Current	37.7
16.4	13.8	14.6	Long-Term Debt	11.3
.9	1.0	.7	Deferred Taxes	.9
3.1	5.5	4.4	All Other Non-Current	6.4
38.9	36.9	39.0	Net Worth	43.7
100.0	100.0	100.0	Total Liabilities & Net Worth	100.0
			INCOME DATA	
100.0	100.0	100.0	Net Sales	100.0
24.8	26.0	23.7	Gross Profit	17.4
18.2	18.9	15.7	Operating Expenses	10.5
6.7	7.1	8.0	Operating Profit	6.9
.9	.8	.9	All Other Expenses (net)	.8
5.7	6.3	7.1	Profit Before Taxes	6.1
			RATIOS	
2.1	2.2	2.0	Current	2.3
1.4	1.5	1.5		1.7
1.0	1.1	1.1		1.4
1.4	1.2	1.4	Quick	1.5
.8	.8	.8		.9
.6	.6	.6		.6
32 11.6	41 8.8	40 9.2	Sales/Receivables	44 8.3
46 8.0	53 6.9	53 6.9		59 6.2
61 6.0	70 5.2	64 5.7		65 5.6
24 15.2	30 12.3	25 14.6	Cost of Sales/Inventory	32 11.5
46 8.0	53 6.9	47 7.8		57 6.4
70 5.2	89 4.1	67 5.4		119 3.1
17 21.5	27 13.3	25 14.6	Cost of Sales/Payables	27 13.3
30 12.1	33 11.1	35 10.3		42 8.8
44 8.2	59 6.1	57 6.4		57 6.4
7.2	5.4	4.9	Sales/Working Capital	4.9
10.7	14.4	11.8		6.5
101.0	71.1	36.6		15.2
16.7	23.8	9.9	EBIT/Interest	11.3
(26) 6.7	(35) 5.0	(33) 5.3		5.4
2.4	1.8	2.1		2.8
3.8	8.2	6.9	Net Profit + Depr., Dep., Amort./Cur. Mat. L/T/D	
(10) 2.3	(14) 3.7	(10) 2.3		
1.5	2.1	1.9		
.6	.5	.4	Fixed/Worth	.3
1.1	1.0	1.0		.8
1.8	2.0	1.9		1.8
.7	1.0	1.0	Debt/Worth	1.0
1.7	1.8	2.3		2.3
3.8	7.1	5.2		4.2
58.9	68.8	57.8	% Profit Before Taxes/Tangible Net Worth	49.2
(27) 22.9	(34) 20.7	(34) 36.5		(10) 21.6
13.7	2.7	13.5		10.9
15.8	19.3	20.7	% Profit Before Taxes/Total Assets	15.4
9.8	7.6	9.4		10.2
3.6	1.2	3.4		3.3
13.0	13.7	14.2	Sales/Net Fixed Assets	13.7
5.3	7.7	7.2		9.1
3.4	4.9	3.9		4.3
2.7	2.7	2.6	Sales/Total Assets	2.6
2.0	2.0	2.0		1.8
1.5	1.5	1.5		1.5
1.8	1.4	1.6	% Depr., Dep., Amort./Sales	1.4
(27) 3.3	(36) 2.4	(34) 2.8		1.9
4.3	3.6	4.5		2.7
2.9	1.6	2.8	% Officers', Directors' Owners' Comp/Sales	
(12) 5.6	(13) 4.3	(10) 5.0		
9.0	6.5	6.6		

Net Sales and Total Assets ($)

4/1/04- 3/31/05	4/1/05- 3/31/06	4/1/06- 3/31/07		0-1MM	1-3MM	3-5MM	5-10MM	10-25MM	25MM & OVER
420480M	815610M	759233M	Net Sales ($)	3955M	31756M	66029M	86487M		571006M
250296M	436412M	514812M	Total Assets ($)	2052M	22705M	29213M	38452M		422390M

M = $ thousand   MM = $ million
See Pages 11 through 21 for Explanation of Ratios and Data

Current Data Sorted by Assets   Comparative Historical Data

0-500M	500M-2MM	2-10MM	10-50MM	50-100MM	100-250MM		4/1/02-3/31/03 ALL	4/1/03-3/31/04 ALL
						Type of Statement		
		2	14	5	5	Unqualified	23	17
4	11	9				Reviewed	20	21
5	5					Compiled	10	10
1 4	2	9	3	1		Tax Returns	8	5
1 3	9					Other	27	32
	28 (4/1-9/30/06)		67 (10/1/06-3/31/07)				4/1/02-3/31/03	4/1/03-3/31/04
2	16	29	33	9	6	**NUMBER OF STATEMENTS**	88	85
%	%	%	%	%	%	**ASSETS**	%	%
	12.2	4.6	5.3			Cash & Equivalents	5.9	6.2
	25.4	27.3	25.3			Trade Receivables (net)	22.6	24.8
	20.6	28.9	30.0			Inventory	23.3	23.1
	4.2	1.7	3.0			All Other Current	2.4	2.7
	62.5	62.5	63.6			Total Current	54.3	56.6
	27.9	31.6	29.3			Fixed Assets (net)	35.9	32.1
	2.2	2.4	4.5			Intangibles (net)	2.7	2.8
	7.5	3.4	2.6			All Other Non-Current	7.2	8.5
	100.0	100.0	100.0			Total	100.0	100.0
						LIABILITIES		
	6.6	14.1	7.1			Notes Payable-Short Term	13.6	14.8
	3.5	3.7	4.3			Cur. Mat.-L.T.D.	6.1	4.8
	15.2	19.0	14.5			Trade Payables	12.5	17.4
	.1	.2	.3			Income Taxes Payable	.1	.3
	8.3	9.8	13.0			All Other Current	7.5	7.6
	33.8	46.8	39.1			Total Current	39.9	44.9
	16.9	21.4	15.9			Long-Term Debt	20.7	13.8
	.1	.5	.2			Deferred Taxes	.8	.7
	4.8	2.5	6.3			All Other Non-Current	8.6	8.6
	44.4	28.8	38.5			Net Worth	30.0	32.0
	100.0	100.0	100.0			Total Liabilties & Net Worth	100.0	100.0
						INCOME DATA		
	100.0	100.0	100.0			Net Sales	100.0	100.0
	28.0	22.8	26.5			Gross Profit	23.8	26.7
	24.5	18.2	17.3			Operating Expenses	22.4	23.9
	3.5	4.6	9.1			Operating Profit	1.4	2.8
	-1.8	1.3	1.4			All Other Expenses (net)	1.2	.7
	5.3	3.3	7.8			Profit Before Taxes	.2	2.1
						RATIOS		
	4.2	2.0	2.4				2.1	2.5
	2.5	1.4	1.7			Current	1.4	1.5
	1.3	1.1	1.3				1.0	1.1
	2.6	1.1	1.3				1.2	1.3
	1.3	.7	1.0			Quick	.7	.8
	.9	.4	.4				.5	.5
	28 13.2	33 10.9	42 8.7				36 10.0	41 8.8
	40 9.2	43 8.5	49 7.5			Sales/Receivables	48 7.6	49 7.5
	53 6.8	60 6.0	59 6.2				60 6.1	59 6.2
	23 15.9	43 8.6	40 9.0				34 10.8	31 11.7
	39 9.4	62 5.8	82 4.4			Cost of Sales/Inventory	62 5.9	53 6.9
	59 6.2	87 4.2	147 2.5				105 3.5	94 3.9
	11 33.2	27 13.7	22 16.8				19 19.6	20 17.9
	21 17.1	33 10.9	33 11.2			Cost of Sales/Payables	32 11.3	32 11.4
	37 9.8	51 7.2	50 7.3				47 7.7	49 7.5
	3.8	7.7	5.0				5.7	4.7
	5.6	11.7	6.5			Sales/Working Capital	11.9	11.3
	22.8	47.8	18.9				786.4	59.6
	16.9	15.4	9.5				4.5	8.2
	(12) 5.7	3.2	(30) 4.5			EBIT/Interest	(80) 1.9	(78) 2.8
	2.7	1.7	1.7				.3	.4
			7.7				3.3	4.1
		(14) 3.4				Net Profit + Depr., Dep., Amort./Cur. Mat. L/T/D	(26) 2.0	(17) 2.4
			1.9				.6	1.6
	.2	.5	.4				.6	.3
	.6	1.1	.7			Fixed/Worth	1.2	.8
	1.5	2.5	2.1				3.6	2.1
	.3	1.1	.9				1.1	.8
	1.0	2.4	1.8			Debt/Worth	2.2	1.9
	2.8	5.7	3.9				8.6	5.1
	31.0	72.0	59.2				24.3	31.5
	(14) 19.6	(26) 30.5	(30) 23.7			% Profit Before Taxes/Tangible Net Worth	(69) 10.0	(75) 14.1
	9.6	8.0	8.9				-5.0	-1.9
	20.5	16.4	20.0				7.3	9.2
	9.3	8.5	10.1			% Profit Before Taxes/Total Assets	3.3	4.6
	4.3	1.9	1.5				-3.2	-.9
	24.0	14.8	13.1				9.5	13.3
	9.9	6.1	7.5			Sales/Net Fixed Assets	4.3	5.1
	4.5	4.2	3.7				2.9	3.2
	3.1	2.6	2.2				2.1	2.2
	2.4	2.3	1.8			Sales/Total Assets	1.7	1.7
	1.4	1.6	1.4				1.3	1.3
	.9	1.3	1.5				2.0	1.8
	(12) 2.6	2.4	(31) 2.5			% Depr., Dep., Amort./Sales	(82) 3.9	(80) 3.4
	3.7	3.6	4.1				6.0	5.6
			.9				2.5	1.9
		(11) 1.7				% Officers', Directors' Owners' Comp/Sales	(28) 6.2	(31) 4.1
		3.6					12.0	5.8
2833M	49579M	344799M	1165515M	1027891M	1015618M	Net Sales ($)	2157727M	2089133M
709M	21382M	150671M	663263M	617797M	768978M	Total Assets ($)	1637446M	1506072M

M = $ thousand   MM = $ million

See Pages 11 through 21 for Explanation of Ratios and Data

Comparative Historical Data · Current Data Sorted by Sales

4/1/04-3/31/05 ALL	4/1/05-3/31/06 ALL	4/1/06-3/31/07 ALL	Type of Statement	0-1MM	1-3MM	3-5MM	5-10MM	10-25MM	25MM & OVER
25	20	26	Unqualified		3	1	7	5	21
22	19	25	Reviewed		3	3	6	6	8
10	7	10	Compiled		3	3	1	1	1
4	4	8	Tax Returns		3		1	1	
38	38	26	Other				1	7	10
					28 (4/1-9/30/06)		67 (10/1/06-3/31/07)		
99	88	95	**NUMBER OF STATEMENTS**		12	7	16	20	40
%	%	%	**ASSETS**	%	%	%	%	%	%
5.7	6.9	7.3	Cash & Equivalents		12.7		3.6	4.1	8.2
26.0	25.8	24.7	Trade Receivables (net)		15.1		30.0	26.7	24.1
24.9	29.7	27.3	Inventory		18.9		25.4	35.3	28.8
1.3	2.1	2.4	All Other Current		4.5		2.6	3.4	1.2
57.9	64.4	61.7	Total Current		51.3		61.6	69.5	62.3
31.7	27.6	30.9	Fixed Assets (net)		35.8		32.4	24.1	31.1
3.5	2.8	3.3	Intangibles (net)		8.0		1.7	3.7	2.8
6.9	5.2	4.1	All Other Non-Current		5.0		4.3	2.6	3.8
100.0	100.0	100.0	Total		100.0		100.0	100.0	100.0
			LIABILITIES						
11.6	8.2	8.7	Notes Payable-Short Term		10.2		13.8	10.7	5.4
5.3	3.0	3.5	Cur. Mat.-L.T.D.		2.7		4.6	3.0	3.5
17.1	15.8	15.5	Trade Payables		12.4		21.0	14.7	15.5
.2	.2	.2	Income Taxes Payable		.0		.1	.3	.4
8.2	7.5	10.3	All Other Current		3.5		10.4	8.7	12.0
42.5	34.6	38.3	Total Current		28.8		50.0	37.4	36.8
15.4	16.9	20.8	Long-Term Debt		28.4		25.1	11.1	22.4
1.1	.9	.4	Deferred Taxes		.2		.1	.6	.6
6.3	7.5	4.8	All Other Non-Current		7.6		3.8	4.0	5.1
34.8	40.1	35.8	Net Worth		35.0		20.9	46.9	35.1
100.0	100.0	100.0	Total Liabilties & Net Worth		100.0		100.0	100.0	100.0
			INCOME DATA						
100.0	100.0	100.0	Net Sales		100.0		100.0	100.0	100.0
22.8	23.7	25.6	Gross Profit		35.6		21.9	25.7	23.6
18.3	17.0	18.7	Operating Expenses		31.7		20.5	16.0	14.9
4.5	6.7	6.9	Operating Profit		3.9		1.4	9.6	8.7
.8	.7	.8	All Other Expenses (net)		-1.3		1.4	.8	1.4
3.7	6.0	6.1	Profit Before Taxes		5.2		.0	8.9	7.3
			RATIOS						
2.2	3.2	2.5			3.9		1.9	2.3	2.7
1.5	1.8	1.7	Current		2.4		1.3	1.8	1.8
1.1	1.3	1.2			.8		1.1	1.4	1.2
1.3	1.6	1.4			2.3		1.2	1.4	1.3
.8	1.0	.9	Quick		1.5		.7	.9	1.0
.4	.6	.6			.5		.5	.5	.6
37 9.7	38 9.5	33 10.9			23 16.0		36 10.1	35 10.5	42 8.6
52 7.0	49 7.4	45 8.1	Sales/Receivables		32 11.3		52 7.1	42 8.6	48 7.6
63 5.8	61 6.0	57 6.4			42 8.6		63 5.8	56 6.5	59 6.2
42 8.7	41 8.9	29 12.4			8 43.2		40 9.0	51 7.2	25 14.5
58 6.3	69 5.3	60 6.1	Cost of Sales/Inventory		42 8.7		60 6.1	67 5.5	79 4.6
99 3.7	102 3.6	107 3.4			108 3.4		76 4.8	135 2.7	128 2.9
27 13.5	22 16.7	22 16.3			5 68.4		27 13.4	24 15.3	24 15.0
38 9.5	33 11.1	32 11.5	Cost of Sales/Payables		18 20.8		35 10.4	30 12.4	36 10.2
54 6.8	48 7.5	51 7.2			39 9.5		57 6.4	40 9.1	55 6.7
5.3	3.8	5.1			3.6		9.8	5.4	3.9
10.4	7.1	8.7	Sales/Working Capital		5.5		13.1	6.5	7.1
39.1	13.7	24.2			NM		56.3	10.5	19.5
9.6	9.3	11.7					3.3	46.5	13.8
(88) 3.2	(76) 4.9	(86) 4.1	EBIT/Interest				(15) 2.5	(19) 7.1	(37) 5.8
1.5	2.3	1.9					.6	3.3	1.4
8.1	6.5	11.1						8.3	14.7
(24) 2.2	(27) 2.6	(33) 3.1	Net Profit + Depr., Dep., Amort./Cur. Mat. L/T/D					(10) 5.1	(16) 4.6
.8	1.8	2.0						2.7	2.2
.5	.3	.4			.3		.9	.2	.4
.8	.7	.8	Fixed/Worth		1.0		1.7	.6	.7
2.4	1.3	2.2			-1.2		3.8	1.0	1.6
.9	.7	.8			.3		1.3	.8	.9
2.3	1.6	1.8	Debt/Worth		1.0		3.6	1.5	1.9
6.6	2.8	4.0			-3.6		12.5	2.3	3.8
45.8	37.4	46.9					52.4	71.9	50.4
(83) 17.9	(80) 23.9	(84) 25.1	% Profit Before Taxes/Tangible Net Worth				(14) 21.5	(19) 31.6	(36) 26.1
7.1	8.9	9.9					-.6	15.2	9.9
13.3	19.2	19.0			14.1		12.1	24.1	20.0
5.3	8.4	9.2	% Profit Before Taxes/Total Assets		5.0		4.1	12.4	9.9
2.0	3.1	2.5			1.3		-2.1	6.7	1.4
14.1	17.5	14.6			18.3		13.9	45.1	11.7
5.5	7.0	6.2	Sales/Net Fixed Assets		6.0		6.0	10.4	6.0
3.5	4.1	3.8			3.1		4.0	4.9	3.7
2.2	2.5	2.5			3.0		2.5	2.8	2.2
1.7	2.0	2.0	Sales/Total Assets		1.8		2.1	2.1	1.7
1.3	1.4	1.5			1.0		1.6	1.5	1.4
1.5	1.0	1.4					1.5	.9	1.5
(86) 3.3	(77) 2.4	(85) 2.7	% Depr., Dep., Amort./Sales				2.9	(19) 1.7	(36) 2.8
5.0	3.9	4.1					4.0	3.0	4.1
2.5	1.7	1.3							
(26) 5.0	(22) 3.3	(26) 3.0	% Officers', Directors' Owners' Comp/Sales						
8.2	6.4	7.3							
3136228M	3593946M	3606235M	Net Sales ($)		20866M	29283M	117243M	372727M	3066116M
2175892M	2097549M	2222800M	Total Assets ($)		14116M	14434M	58920M	184621M	1950709M

© RMA 2007

M = $ thousand   MM = $ million
See Pages 11 through 21 for Explanation of Ratios and Data

Current Data Sorted by Assets   Comparative Historical Data

Type of Statement	0-500M	500M-2MM	2-10MM	10-50MM	50-100MM	100-250MM		ALL 4/1/02-3/31/03	ALL 4/1/03-3/31/04
Unqualified			8	29	5	5		53	49
Reviewed		15	49	27				96	90
Compiled	3	23	24	4				64	74
Tax Returns	5	15	5	1				10	16
Other	6	16	48	26	3	4		84	76
		79 (4/1-9/30/06)		242 (10/1/06-3/31/07)					
NUMBER OF STATEMENTS	14	69	134	87	8	9		307	305
ASSETS	%	%	%	%	%	%		%	%
Cash & Equivalents	8.2	8.7	7.1	5.6				7.7	7.1
Trade Receivables (net)	22.3	30.3	27.0	26.5				25.4	26.3
Inventory	21.6	25.0	23.8	22.1				20.5	19.9
All Other Current	3.9	1.0	1.9	2.1				1.6	2.3
Total Current	56.0	65.0	59.8	56.3				55.2	55.7
Fixed Assets (net)	34.8	28.1	30.0	33.8				36.4	35.6
Intangibles (net)	2.9	2.2	3.5	5.4				2.9	2.4
All Other Non-Current	6.3	4.6	6.7	4.6				5.5	6.3
Total	100.0	100.0	100.0	100.0				100.0	100.0
LIABILITIES									
Notes Payable-Short Term	12.6	10.0	9.3	8.8				10.2	9.3
Cur. Mat.-L.T.D.	6.3	4.4	4.2	5.6				6.0	5.6
Trade Payables	10.9	15.5	15.2	14.2				13.3	13.5
Income Taxes Payable	.1	.6	.3	.1				.1	.1
All Other Current	11.1	8.3	7.5	9.2				8.9	8.6
Total Current	41.0	38.9	36.5	37.9				38.6	37.2
Long-Term Debt	30.7	17.0	15.7	17.9				18.8	16.8
Deferred Taxes	.3	.5	.6	.3				.6	.7
All Other Non-Current	18.3	5.4	5.5	7.1				5.7	6.1
Net Worth	9.7	38.3	41.7	36.8				36.3	39.2
Total Liabilties & Net Worth	100.0	100.0	100.0	100.0				100.0	100.0
INCOME DATA									
Net Sales	100.0	100.0	100.0	100.0				100.0	100.0
Gross Profit	44.1	30.6	25.0	19.4				25.0	25.4
Operating Expenses	40.6	26.5	19.7	14.0				23.0	22.4
Operating Profit	3.5	4.1	5.3	5.4				2.0	3.0
All Other Expenses (net)	1.6	.7	.5	1.2				1.4	1.0
Profit Before Taxes	1.8	3.4	4.7	4.2				.6	2.0
RATIOS									
Current	3.9	2.9	2.8	2.4				2.5	2.6
	1.3	1.7	1.7	1.5				1.4	1.5
	.8	1.0	1.2	1.1				1.0	1.0
Quick	2.2	1.9	1.7	1.4				1.6	1.5
	.7	1.0	.9	.9				.8	.9
	.4	.6	.6	.6				.5	.6
Sales/Receivables	19 18.9	30 12.0	36 10.3	38 9.5				36 10.0	39 9.4
	29 12.5	41 8.9	46 7.9	49 7.4				47 7.7	49 7.5
	44 8.3	54 6.8	55 6.6	59 6.1				57 6.4	59 6.2
Cost of Sales/Inventory	11 32.9	25 14.7	31 11.8	32 11.4				31 11.8	30 12.1
	39 9.4	49 7.5	50 7.2	46 8.0				46 7.9	46 7.9
	84 4.3	65 5.6	73 5.0	75 4.9				76 4.8	71 5.1
Cost of Sales/Payables	7 51.3	18 20.8	19 19.0	20 17.9				19 19.7	16 22.8
	20 17.8	21 17.3	32 11.4	31 11.6				30 12.1	31 11.8
	39 9.3	38 9.7	45 8.2	39 9.4				43 8.5	44 8.3
Sales/Working Capital	8.3	5.4	5.7	5.8				5.5	5.5
	31.3	12.1	9.4	10.6				11.6	10.3
	-26.0	130.6	29.2	28.5				-443.5	354.3
EBIT/Interest	7.0	7.2	11.4	9.5				5.3	7.2
	(11) 3.8	(61) 2.0	(127) 3.8	(82) 3.6				(287) 1.7	(277) 2.2
	-1.2	.7	1.9	1.3				.0	.1
Net Profit + Depr., Dep., Amort./Cur. Mat. L/T/D		4.4	5.2	5.4				3.1	2.7
		(17) 2.1	(33) 2.7	(28) 2.7				(94) 1.6	(81) 1.4
		1.5	1.2	1.0				.5	.4
Fixed/Worth	.6	.3	.5	.6				.5	.5
	3.1	.8	.8	1.1				1.0	1.0
	-1.2	3.0	1.7	2.8				2.9	2.4
Debt/Worth	1.1	.6	.6	.8				.7	.6
	9.1	1.4	1.7	1.8				2.2	1.7
	-4.2	8.8	3.8	7.2				5.6	4.5
% Profit Before Taxes/Tangible Net Worth		40.2	50.1	46.6				26.5	28.1
		(59) 16.9	(124) 22.5	(76) 19.9				(267) 8.4	(276) 8.8
		4.2	7.7	5.6				-5.8	-1.4
% Profit Before Taxes/Total Assets	29.3	14.4	16.7	16.2				9.2	10.1
	10.1	3.1	7.2	5.7				2.1	3.0
	-9.3	-.2	2.9	1.6				-2.6	-1.0
Sales/Net Fixed Assets	25.4	22.6	12.3	9.0				9.4	10.0
	10.3	13.5	7.2	5.8				5.3	5.5
	4.7	5.5	4.9	4.5				3.5	3.6
Sales/Total Assets	5.5	3.3	2.6	2.3				2.5	2.4
	2.7	2.6	2.1	2.0				1.9	1.9
	1.9	2.0	1.7	1.5				1.4	1.4
% Depr., Dep., Amort./Sales	.7	1.2	1.7	1.9				2.5	2.3
	(11) 1.5	(62) 2.5	(125) 2.6	(83) 2.7				(283) 3.7	(289) 3.7
	3.2	4.2	3.8	3.7				5.5	5.5
% Officers', Directors' Owners' Comp/Sales	4.8	3.0	1.6	1.0				2.1	2.0
	(10) 8.9	(36) 5.6	(58) 2.8	(17) 1.4				(137) 4.5	(138) 4.1
	13.0	10.1	6.2	6.9				7.8	6.9
Net Sales ($)	13971M	216186M	1379024M	3348969M	904325M	1769049M		5353564M	5317909M
Total Assets ($)	4242M	82138M	645854M	1750910M	554889M	1220512M		3372480M	3201289M

M = $ thousand   MM = $ million
See Pages 11 through 21 for Explanation of Ratios and Data

Comparative Historical Data   Current Data Sorted by Sales

	4/1/04-3/31/05 ALL	4/1/05-3/31/06 ALL	4/1/06-3/31/07 ALL	Type of Statement	0-1MM	1-3MM	3-5MM	5-10MM	10-25MM	25MM & OVER
	51	55	47	Unqualified				2	11	34
	99	97	91	Reviewed	1	8	11	24	30	17
	53	54	54	Compiled	2	10	15	14	11	2
	21	19	26	Tax Returns	5	11	1	7	1	1
	72	92	103	Other	5	13	12	20	28	25
						79 (4/1-9/30/06)		242 (10/1/06-3/31/07)		
	296	317	321	**NUMBER OF STATEMENTS**	13	42	39	67	81	79
	%	%	%	**ASSETS**	%	%	%	%	%	%
	6.2	6.1	6.9	Cash & Equivalents	5.4	7.7	8.6	9.0	6.6	4.4
	28.7	29.1	27.1	Trade Receivables (net)	16.8	24.9	29.9	28.7	26.9	27.3
	22.2	21.5	23.1	Inventory	17.0	24.4	23.8	24.3	23.4	21.7
	1.8	1.7	1.8	All Other Current	.7	3.6	2.4	2.4	.9	1.3
	58.9	58.4	58.9	Total Current	39.9	60.6	64.6	64.4	57.9	54.6
	31.8	32.4	31.1	Fixed Assets (net)	46.9	30.0	26.7	27.0	30.6	35.2
	3.3	3.8	4.1	Intangibles (net)	2.2	3.8	1.9	3.1	5.9	4.7
	6.0	5.3	5.9	All Other Non-Current	11.0	5.7	6.7	5.5	5.6	5.5
	100.0	100.0	100.0	Total	100.0	100.0	100.0	100.0	100.0	100.0
				LIABILITIES						
	10.7	10.0	9.4	Notes Payable-Short Term	14.0	8.4	10.4	9.5	8.9	8.9
	5.0	4.6	4.7	Cur. Mat.-L.T.D.	7.9	4.7	3.3	3.9	5.3	4.8
	15.5	16.3	14.7	Trade Payables	8.7	14.5	13.8	14.7	15.2	15.8
	.2	.1	.3	Income Taxes Payable	.0	.8	.3	.4	.1	.1
	8.3	7.7	8.3	All Other Current	13.4	7.6	10.7	8.1	7.1	8.0
	39.8	38.7	37.3	Total Current	44.0	36.0	38.6	36.5	36.5	37.7
	16.6	17.1	17.5	Long-Term Debt	42.8	17.0	14.9	15.8	16.1	17.8
	.7	.7	.5	Deferred Taxes	.3	.0	.7	.9	.5	.4
	7.7	7.5	7.1	All Other Non-Current	16.2	6.4	6.0	4.7	8.9	6.6
	35.2	35.9	37.6	Net Worth	-3.4	40.5	39.8	42.1	38.0	37.4
	100.0	100.0	100.0	Total Liabilities & Net Worth	100.0	100.0	100.0	100.0	100.0	100.0
				INCOME DATA						
	100.0	100.0	100.0	Net Sales	100.0	100.0	100.0	100.0	100.0	100.0
	25.1	24.1	25.0	Gross Profit	43.4	34.9	29.3	26.5	20.7	17.6
	21.0	19.2	20.0	Operating Expenses	42.0	29.6	25.3	21.2	15.7	12.3
	4.1	4.8	4.9	Operating Profit	1.4	5.4	3.9	5.4	5.0	5.4
	.9	1.0	.9	All Other Expenses (net)	3.7	.3	.2	.8	.7	1.3
	3.2	3.8	4.0	Profit Before Taxes	-2.3	5.0	3.7	4.5	4.3	4.0
				RATIOS						
	2.5	2.5	2.6	Current	1.5	3.2	2.5	3.1	2.2	2.3
	1.5	1.5	1.6		.8	1.6	1.8	1.8	1.6	1.4
	1.1	1.1	1.1		.3	1.0	1.3	1.2	1.1	1.1
	1.5	1.5	1.5	Quick	.7	2.0	1.7	2.0	1.4	1.4
	.9	.9	.9		.4	.8	1.0	1.1	.8	.9
	.6	.6	.6		.2	.5	.7	.7	.6	.6
	38 9.6	37 9.8	35 10.3	Sales/Receivables	10 36.8	27 13.3	41 9.0	36 10.3	36 10.1	39 9.5
	52 7.1	48 7.6	45 8.2		28 13.0	39 9.3	47 7.8	42 8.7	47 7.8	48 7.6
	63 5.8	58 6.3	56 6.5		45 8.0	53 6.9	54 6.7	57 6.4	55 6.6	58 6.3
	33 11.0	27 13.3	30 12.3	Cost of Sales/Inventory	10 37.4	23 16.0	26 13.8	31 11.8	36 10.1	30 12.2
	50 7.4	43 8.4	48 7.7		41 8.8	57 6.4	54 6.7	49 7.4	50 7.3	41 8.8
	72 5.1	65 5.6	71 5.2		78 4.7	92 4.0	65 5.6	74 5.0	68 5.4	65 5.6
	21 17.6	19 18.8	19 19.6	Cost of Sales/Payables	2 147.0	17 21.4	20 17.9	18 19.9	18 20.4	22 16.9
	34 10.8	32 11.4	30 12.3		16 23.1	29 12.7	29 12.7	29 12.5	31 11.6	33 11.1
	49 7.5	48 7.6	42 8.7		40 9.0	49 7.5	37 9.9	45 8.1	41 9.0	39 9.3
	5.6	6.1	5.8	Sales/Working Capital	10.9	4.7	5.5	4.9	6.3	6.0
	11.7	12.4	10.7		-29.1	14.8	8.2	8.7	10.6	12.9
	57.7	77.1	44.7		-4.9	NM	16.8	21.1	32.7	63.1
	12.0	9.3	9.0	EBIT/Interest	4.6	9.9	7.7	12.0	11.1	8.9
	(276) 4.2	(292) 3.1	(298) 3.3		(11) -.9	(35) 3.8	(36) 3.1	(62) 3.3	(79) 3.2	(75) 3.7
	1.0	1.3	1.4		-2.0	1.1	1.2	1.5	1.8	1.4
	4.5	4.5	4.4	Net Profit + Depr., Dep., Amort./Cur. Mat. L/T/D		4.9	3.5	6.8	5.4	4.3
	(76) 2.9	(111) 2.2	(88) 2.2			(10) 2.1	(11) 2.2	(13) 2.2	(23) 2.7	(30) 2.0
	1.4	1.3	1.2			1.0	1.8	1.2	.9	1.2
	.4	.5	.5	Fixed/Worth	1.3	.3	.3	.3	.5	.6
	.9	1.0	.9		-35.4	.9	.7	.7	.9	1.1
	2.8	2.7	2.7		-1.1	2.3	2.9	1.8	3.6	2.3
	.7	.8	.7	Debt/Worth	3.1	.6	.6	.6	.8	.8
	1.9	1.9	1.8		-36.5	1.4	1.2	1.7	2.0	1.8
	6.4	6.6	6.3		-3.5	4.3	7.4	4.2	6.2	6.4
	42.8	47.4	49.0	% Profit Before Taxes/Tangible Net Worth		65.5	40.2	49.4	60.1	45.4
	(250) 18.0	(272) 17.4	(280) 21.7			(38) 18.1	(35) 15.7	(62) 16.6	(69) 23.9	(70) 21.7
	2.2	3.7	5.5			5.5	5.5	4.0	8.7	5.4
	13.8	15.0	15.9	% Profit Before Taxes/Total Assets	16.4	16.5	15.4	18.8	14.3	15.3
	6.4	5.3	6.1		-3.8	6.4	4.8	5.8	6.7	6.4
	.0	.7	1.2		-12.4	.9	.2	1.3	2.7	1.6
	12.7	12.7	14.1	Sales/Net Fixed Assets	7.8	25.4	19.0	21.0	13.2	8.4
	6.9	7.1	7.0		5.3	10.8	11.7	8.2	7.3	5.7
	4.3	4.3	4.7		2.4	4.6	4.8	5.4	5.0	4.6
	2.6	2.7	2.7	Sales/Total Assets	2.4	2.9	2.8	2.9	2.6	2.4
	2.0	2.2	2.1		1.9	2.3	2.3	2.2	2.0	2.0
	1.5	1.7	1.7		1.0	1.7	1.8	1.7	1.7	1.6
	1.9	1.9	1.7	% Depr., Dep., Amort./Sales	.7	.7	1.5	1.6	1.9	1.9
	(267) 3.1	(295) 2.8	(295) 2.6		(11) 2.1	(35) 2.4	(38) 2.8	(61) 2.7	(75) 2.6	(75) 2.7
	4.7	3.9	3.8		10.8	4.7	4.8	4.1	3.6	3.7
	1.9	1.5	1.8	% Officers', Directors' Owners' Comp/Sales		3.4	2.0	2.1	1.2	.9
	(128) 3.8	(110) 3.2	(122) 3.9			(22) 5.7	(24) 4.1	(31) 3.9	(23) 2.1	(14) 1.3
	7.4	6.8	7.4			11.2	6.1	8.4	5.1	2.5
	6539378M	8069916M	7631524M	Net Sales ($)	8618M	87109M	156176M	479561M	1313674M	5586386M
	3752705M	4320740M	4258545M	Total Assets ($)	5697M	47283M	80361M	253415M	706069M	3165720M

© RMA 2007

M = $ thousand   MM = $ million
See Pages 11 through 21 for Explanation of Ratios and Data

Current Data Sorted by Assets   Comparative Historical Data

Type of Statement

	0-500M	500M-2MM	2-10MM	10-50MM	50-100MM	100-250MM		4/1/02-3/31/03 ALL	4/1/03-3/31/04 ALL
Unqualified		1	6	5	2	3		19	19
Reviewed		3	16	4	1			12	20
Compiled	1	8	6	1				9	9
Tax Returns	2	4	1	1				4	7
Other	4	7	11	9		1		12	19
	18 (4/1-9/30/06)			79 (10/1/06-3/31/07)					
NUMBER OF STATEMENTS	7	23	40	20	3	4		56	74

ASSETS

	0-500M	500M-2MM %	2-10MM %	10-50MM %	50-100MM	100-250MM		4/1/02-3/31/03 %	4/1/03-3/31/04 %
Cash & Equivalents		11.1	3.8	4.6				7.8	7.4
Trade Receivables (net)		27.8	21.8	24.2				24.9	25.3
Inventory		28.1	36.6	28.6				31.9	31.3
All Other Current		1.2	1.5	1.2				1.7	1.7
Total Current		68.3	63.8	58.6				66.3	65.7
Fixed Assets (net)		24.9	21.2	23.4				22.4	22.6
Intangibles (net)		.6	8.4	9.7				4.2	3.1
All Other Non-Current		6.2	6.7	8.3				7.1	8.7
Total		100.0	100.0	100.0				100.0	100.0

LIABILITIES

	0-500M	500M-2MM	2-10MM	10-50MM	50-100MM	100-250MM		4/1/02-3/31/03	4/1/03-3/31/04
Notes Payable-Short Term		5.5	14.1	10.1				8.7	15.7
Cur. Mat.-L.T.D.		3.1	4.3	2.8				4.0	3.5
Trade Payables		17.4	10.8	9.5				11.5	12.2
Income Taxes Payable		.1	.1	.6				.1	.2
All Other Current		5.8	9.9	5.5				10.4	9.1
Total Current		31.8	39.2	28.6				34.7	40.7
Long-Term Debt		22.2	18.3	16.2				17.1	14.7
Deferred Taxes		.4	.7	.3				.2	.3
All Other Non-Current		6.0	5.2	2.5				4.5	6.0
Net Worth		39.7	36.7	52.6				43.5	38.2
Total Liabilities & Net Worth		100.0	100.0	100.0				100.0	100.0

INCOME DATA

	0-500M	500M-2MM	2-10MM	10-50MM	50-100MM	100-250MM		4/1/02-3/31/03	4/1/03-3/31/04
Net Sales		100.0	100.0	100.0				100.0	100.0
Gross Profit		44.0	33.1	33.3				36.0	34.6
Operating Expenses		38.0	28.4	23.7				31.9	30.8
Operating Profit		6.0	4.7	9.6				4.1	3.8
All Other Expenses (net)		.8	1.7	2.0				1.1	1.0
Profit Before Taxes		5.2	3.0	7.6				3.0	2.8

RATIOS

	500M-2MM	2-10MM	10-50MM		4/1/02-3/31/03	4/1/03-3/31/04
Current	3.2	2.3	4.0		3.7	3.5
	1.9	1.6	2.0		2.3	2.1
	1.5	1.1	1.5		1.4	1.2
Quick	2.5	1.1	1.8		1.6	1.9
	1.4	.6	1.0		1.2	.9
	.7	.4	.7		.6	.5
Sales/Receivables	32 11.4	30 12.0	38 9.6		35 10.5	32 11.4
	46 7.9	38 9.7	54 6.7		45 8.1	46 8.0
	68 5.4	56 6.5	65 5.6		59 6.2	59 6.2
Cost of Sales/Inventory	26 14.2	59 6.2	68 5.3		52 7.1	56 6.6
	73 5.0	121 3.0	98 3.7		99 3.7	94 3.9
	133 2.7	181 2.0	116 3.2		139 2.6	128 2.9
Cost of Sales/Payables	25 14.8	16 23.5	16 22.7		15 24.4	15 24.6
	51 7.1	31 11.8	30 12.1		28 13.2	24 14.9
	75 4.9	54 6.8	36 10.1		47 7.8	38 9.6
Sales/Working Capital	3.5	3.6	4.3		3.4	3.5
	6.9	7.5	5.8		5.4	6.1
	13.3	190.1	7.6		13.6	16.2
EBIT/Interest	20.8	3.9	19.6		8.6	14.3
	(20) 2.9	2.2	(18) 5.0		(53) 4.2	(69) 4.2
	1.3	1.2	1.9		1.0	1.0
Net Profit + Depr., Dep., Amort./Cur. Mat. L/T/D		3.5			9.9	6.5
		(11) 1.4			(17) 2.4	(21) 2.2
		1.1			1.0	.4
Fixed/Worth	.2	.1	.3		.3	.3
	.6	.8	.5		.4	.6
	1.8	2.9	1.1		.9	1.4
Debt/Worth	.5	1.0	.5		.5	.5
	1.8	2.4	1.0		1.5	1.4
	8.2	13.7	1.7		4.6	5.2
% Profit Before Taxes/Tangible Net Worth	47.0	41.3	37.3		37.6	34.3
	(22) 7.4	(33) 11.9	(17) 21.0		(52) 12.8	(63) 12.1
	-2.3	3.0	7.8		1.8	1.5
% Profit Before Taxes/Total Assets	20.2	10.6	16.9		11.7	12.8
	4.8	3.1	9.9		6.9	5.9
	1.1	.8	3.6		.6	-2.0
Sales/Net Fixed Assets	30.6	21.6	14.8		21.1	21.9
	12.2	13.0	8.8		9.3	9.9
	5.1	4.7	4.8		5.1	4.7
Sales/Total Assets	2.8	2.3	2.1		2.5	2.6
	2.0	1.6	1.8		1.7	1.9
	1.5	1.3	1.2		1.4	1.5
% Depr., Dep., Amort./Sales	1.1	1.4	1.1		1.5	1.7
	(20) 3.6	(34) 2.1	(19) 1.9		(47) 2.6	(68) 2.9
	5.6	3.6	2.6		4.2	4.4
% Officers', Directors' Owners' Comp/Sales	3.4				3.4	2.9
	(13) 7.0				(19) 7.0	(26) 4.2
	9.0				9.4	8.9

	0-500M	500M-2MM	2-10MM	10-50MM	50-100MM	100-250MM		4/1/02-3/31/03	4/1/03-3/31/04
Net Sales ($)	9317M	66897M	368600M	680709M	360259M	1002731M		1944009M	1986201M
Total Assets ($)	1539M	27946M	198146M	400714M	198800M	710519M		1236281M	1104097M

M = $ thousand   MM = $ million
See Pages 11 through 21 for Explanation of Ratios and Data

Comparative Historical Data   Current Data Sorted by Sales

Type of Statement	4/1/04-3/31/05 ALL	4/1/05-3/31/06 ALL	4/1/06-3/31/07 ALL	0-1MM	1-3MM	3-5MM	5-10MM	10-25MM	25MM & OVER
Unqualified	17	20	17			1	1	8	7
Reviewed	23	18	24		3	3	11	4	3
Compiled	19	17	16	3	2	4	4	2	1
Tax Returns	6	6	8	1	4	1		2	
Other	20	19	32	2	7	5	5	2	8
					18 (4/1-9/30/06)		79 (10/1/06-3/31/07)		
NUMBER OF STATEMENTS	85	80	97	6	16	14	21	21	19
ASSETS	%	%	%	%	%	%	%	%	%
Cash & Equivalents	6.4	5.8	6.7		3.9	7.9	4.7	3.9	4.0
Trade Receivables (net)	25.6	23.9	24.5		28.2	20.8	20.3	27.3	25.7
Inventory	31.4	33.7	30.6		28.2	34.4	41.4	26.9	27.0
All Other Current	2.4	2.0	1.7		.6	3.8	1.2	1.2	3.0
Total Current	65.8	65.4	63.5		61.0	66.9	67.3	59.2	59.7
Fixed Assets (net)	23.3	23.1	22.2		24.7	24.1	22.9	21.9	20.1
Intangibles (net)	4.0	6.1	7.6		5.5	6.7	3.7	11.9	9.9
All Other Non-Current	6.8	5.4	6.7		8.8	2.2	6.2	6.9	10.4
Total	100.0	100.0	100.0		100.0	100.0	100.0	100.0	100.0
LIABILITIES									
Notes Payable-Short Term	14.2	12.9	12.4		10.9	11.9	12.1	10.4	11.7
Cur. Mat.-L.T.D.	3.8	2.9	3.3		4.1	3.0	4.4	3.9	1.4
Trade Payables	12.2	11.1	13.2		17.1	10.5	11.9	11.0	9.4
Income Taxes Payable	.1	.3	.2		.0	.1	.1	.1	.6
All Other Current	8.5	7.8	9.1		5.1	8.5	8.6	9.8	8.8
Total Current	38.8	35.0	38.1		37.2	33.9	37.0	35.2	31.8
Long-Term Debt	14.0	13.0	22.2		26.8	23.2	16.3	20.3	13.1
Deferred Taxes	.3	.3	.5		.0	.5	1.2	.3	.6
All Other Non-Current	5.1	7.2	4.8		6.4	4.4	3.9	6.4	3.8
Net Worth	41.9	44.5	34.4		29.7	38.1	41.6	37.9	50.8
Total Liabilties & Net Worth	100.0	100.0	100.0		100.0	100.0	100.0	100.0	100.0
INCOME DATA									
Net Sales	100.0	100.0	100.0		100.0	100.0	100.0	100.0	100.0
Gross Profit	35.6	35.6	36.1		39.8	39.8	33.4	35.6	28.2
Operating Expenses	30.6	30.2	29.4		31.3	33.8	30.6	26.8	19.7
Operating Profit	5.0	5.4	6.6		8.4	6.0	2.8	8.8	8.5
All Other Expenses (net)	1.1	1.0	1.6		1.2	1.5	.8	2.7	1.7
Profit Before Taxes	3.9	4.4	5.0		7.3	4.5	2.0	6.1	6.8
RATIOS									
Current	3.5	3.4	2.9		1.9	4.0	3.5	2.4	4.0
	1.9	1.9	1.8		1.4	2.1	2.1	1.8	1.9
	1.3	1.4	1.2		1.2	1.3	1.3	1.2	1.3
Quick	1.7	1.4	1.5		1.2	2.7	1.6	1.3	2.1
	.8	.8	.9		.9	.8	.6	.9	1.0
	.5	.6	.6		.6	.3	.4	.6	.6
Sales/Receivables	37 / 9.9	37 / 9.8	32 / 11.3		37 / 9.7	29 / 12.8	27 / 13.3	35 / 10.4	38 / 9.7
	47 / 7.7	45 / 8.1	43 / 8.5		46 / 7.9	40 / 9.2	33 / 11.0	55 / 6.7	46 / 8.0
	59 / 6.2	56 / 6.5	58 / 6.2		60 / 6.1	53 / 6.9	45 / 8.1	62 / 5.9	61 / 5.9
Cost of Sales/Inventory	58 / 6.3	68 / 5.4	53 / 6.9		48 / 7.6	50 / 7.3	67 / 5.5	54 / 6.8	53 / 6.9
	96 / 3.8	103 / 3.6	92 / 4.0		74 / 4.9	92 / 4.0	137 / 2.7	76 / 4.8	73 / 5.0
	157 / 2.3	139 / 2.6	138 / 2.6		149 / 2.5	176 / 2.1	191 / 1.9	127 / 2.9	100 / 3.6
Cost of Sales/Payables	18 / 19.8	16 / 22.4	16 / 22.7		26 / 14.1	17 / 21.0	15 / 24.2	15 / 23.8	14 / 26.5
	30 / 12.2	26 / 14.0	30 / 12.4		52 / 7.0	31 / 12.0	22 / 16.9	35 / 10.3	25 / 14.6
	45 / 8.1	47 / 7.8	53 / 6.8		73 / 5.0	55 / 6.7	53 / 6.9	46 / 7.9	34 / 10.8
Sales/Working Capital	3.6	3.9	4.0		5.1	3.4	3.4	4.9	4.2
	5.7	6.3	7.1		10.8	7.9	5.3	7.1	6.9
	13.8	10.8	16.9		35.5	10.6	15.6	17.7	18.8
EBIT/Interest	12.2	17.8	8.9		6.4	9.1	3.8	10.0	23.9
	(79) 3.8	(77) 3.2	(90) 2.9		(15) 2.9	(12) 2.3	1.7	3.2	(16) 4.1
	.9	1.5	1.3		1.4	.9	1.1	1.9	1.8
Net Profit + Depr., Dep., Amort./Cur. Mat. L/T/D	9.2	7.5	4.5						
	(26) 3.1	(23) 3.3	(27) 1.8						
	.7	2.1	1.1						
Fixed/Worth	.3	.2	.2		.4	.2	.1	.2	.3
	.6	.6	.7		1.2	1.1	.5	.6	.5
	1.3	1.4	2.5		2.8	2.4	2.7	2.5	.7
Debt/Worth	.4	.6	.7		1.2	.4	.6	1.0	.5
	1.3	1.4	1.8		3.2	2.3	1.8	2.0	1.1
	3.6	3.4	10.3		15.7	8.2	3.6	NM	6.6
% Profit Before Taxes/Tangible Net Worth	30.5	29.1	37.6		124.7	41.0	33.7	49.3	33.6
	(77) 15.1	(70) 15.0	(79) 15.6		(14) 26.4	(12) 10.8	(19) 4.9	(16) 21.2	(15) 21.6
	4.6	3.1	4.0		5.3	-4.1	2.9	10.5	5.6
% Profit Before Taxes/Total Assets	12.7	11.9	15.7		19.4	18.1	10.6	14.5	19.5
	6.0	5.7	5.8		5.3	6.4	2.0	9.6	10.9
	.1	1.4	1.7		2.0	.2	.3	2.9	3.6
Sales/Net Fixed Assets	16.8	21.4	28.1		29.0	24.9	18.9	23.9	31.9
	8.6	8.5	11.7		11.4	8.5	13.0	13.2	10.2
	5.1	5.0	4.8		3.8	4.8	4.9	4.1	6.1
Sales/Total Assets	2.3	2.2	2.5		2.7	2.3	2.3	2.6	2.2
	1.7	1.8	1.8		1.9	1.8	1.6	1.8	1.9
	1.2	1.4	1.4		1.4	1.4	1.3	1.2	1.5
% Depr., Dep., Amort./Sales	1.6	1.4	1.2		2.0	1.3	1.3	1.4	1.1
	(74) 2.9	(71) 2.6	(81) 2.2		(14) 4.3	(12) 3.0	(20) 1.8	(17) 1.9	(16) 2.0
	4.6	4.1	4.1		5.8	3.4	3.3	4.9	2.6
% Officers', Directors' Owners' Comp/Sales	2.5	2.7	2.4						
	(37) 5.2	(28) 5.8	(31) 4.6						
	7.8	7.0	7.7						
Net Sales ($)	1734231M	3053680M	2488513M	3299M	32846M	53269M	155678M	317321M	1926100M
Total Assets ($)	1194392M	1819600M	1537664M	1829M	21312M	31084M	92300M	207989M	1183150M

Current Data Sorted by Assets   Comparative Historical Data

Type of Statement

0-500M	500M-2MM	2-10MM	10-50MM	50-100MM	100-250MM	Type of Statement	4/1/02-3/31/03 ALL	4/1/03-3/31/04 ALL
	5	4	11	3	5	Unqualified	13	14
	6	10	2			Reviewed	18	21
		6	2			Compiled	4	10
1	4	5	1			Tax Returns	5	2
	2	8	13		4	Other	11	23
15 (4/1-9/30/06)			77 (10/1/06-3/31/07)					
1	17	33	29	3	9	NUMBER OF STATEMENTS	51	70

Main Data

0-500M	500M-2MM	2-10MM	10-50MM	50-100MM	100-250MM		4/1/02-3/31/03 ALL	4/1/03-3/31/04 ALL
%	%	%	%	%	%	**ASSETS**	%	%
	9.7	6.5	6.5			Cash & Equivalents	10.5	9.5
	29.0	36.0	29.1			Trade Receivables (net)	29.0	27.9
	26.9	25.3	27.9			Inventory	24.4	26.0
	2.2	4.4	4.9			All Other Current	3.9	3.7
	67.8	72.1	68.4			Total Current	67.8	67.2
	26.0	22.4	23.1			Fixed Assets (net)	26.6	26.3
	1.2	1.4	2.7			Intangibles (net)	1.0	1.7
	5.0	4.0	5.8			All Other Non-Current	4.7	4.9
	100.0	100.0	100.0			Total	100.0	100.0
						LIABILITIES		
	11.2	10.2	8.2			Notes Payable-Short Term	10.6	12.1
	3.8	3.2	1.8			Cur. Mat.-L.T.D.	2.9	3.7
	19.2	18.5	17.0			Trade Payables	16.3	15.1
	.1	.2	.3			Income Taxes Payable	.4	.2
	18.5	12.8	26.0			All Other Current	11.1	10.2
	52.9	44.8	53.1			Total Current	41.2	41.3
	11.7	15.2	10.0			Long-Term Debt	19.9	18.5
	.1	.2	.6			Deferred Taxes	.6	.9
	9.3	1.2	9.4			All Other Non-Current	4.7	5.5
	26.0	38.6	26.9			Net Worth	33.6	33.8
	100.0	100.0	100.0			Total Liabilities & Net Worth	100.0	100.0
						INCOME DATA		
	100.0	100.0	100.0			Net Sales	100.0	100.0
	29.2	26.2	26.1			Gross Profit	25.3	27.3
	23.5	20.9	19.9			Operating Expenses	22.9	22.9
	5.7	5.3	6.3			Operating Profit	2.3	4.4
	.7	.7	.8			All Other Expenses (net)	.4	.8
	5.0	4.6	5.4			Profit Before Taxes	1.9	3.6
						RATIOS		
	2.3	2.1	2.3				3.3	2.9
	1.1	1.7	1.5			Current	1.7	1.8
	1.0	1.2	1.2				1.3	1.2
	1.4	1.3	1.2				1.4	1.6
	.8	.9	.8			Quick	1.0	1.0
	.4	.6	.5				.6	.5
	16 23.5	33 11.1	33 11.0				27 13.5	29 12.4
	24 15.5	50 7.3	46 7.9			Sales/Receivables	38 9.6	45 8.0
	46 8.0	82 4.5	67 5.4				60 6.0	58 6.3
	6 59.3	20 18.5	32 11.4				29 12.4	30 12.2
	41 8.9	45 8.0	57 6.4			Cost of Sales/Inventory	43 8.5	52 7.0
	68 5.4	91 4.0	77 4.8				70 5.2	89 4.1
	17 21.7	21 17.6	18 19.9				13 27.7	16 22.3
	25 14.6	32 11.4	30 12.2			Cost of Sales/Payables	25 14.5	32 11.4
	36 10.2	53 6.9	44 8.3				42 8.8	52 7.0
	10.6	5.8	6.2				5.2	4.9
	52.1	9.8	10.7			Sales/Working Capital	10.0	8.8
	NM	19.3	24.3				20.1	23.9
	10.4	15.8	20.0				12.2	10.4
	(16) 3.8	(30) 7.5	(28) 6.5			EBIT/Interest	(48) 4.2	(68) 4.1
	3.2	1.9	3.9				1.2	1.5
		9.1	23.5				5.7	4.9
		(10) 3.4	(14) 8.4			Net Profit + Depr., Dep., Amort./Cur. Mat. L/T/D	(12) 2.0	(23) 2.8
		1.4	2.8				1.0	1.5
	.3	.3	.3				.3	.4
	.7	.5	.5			Fixed/Worth	.6	.7
	5.7	1.2	1.4				1.5	1.6
	1.0	.8	1.1				.6	1.1
	2.7	1.5	1.7			Debt/Worth	1.4	2.0
	19.2	3.0	2.5				3.0	4.2
	65.7	44.8	64.7				38.2	40.8
	(14) 31.9	(31) 24.4	(27) 35.6			% Profit Before Taxes/Tangible Net Worth	(47) 20.5	(63) 21.8
	10.3	10.8	14.9				2.3	5.9
	17.0	18.0	19.3				19.4	14.3
	10.0	8.2	12.3			% Profit Before Taxes/Total Assets	5.2	5.7
	4.1	2.8	6.0				.5	1.0
	45.8	24.8	26.3				21.3	15.2
	13.5	11.3	10.1			Sales/Net Fixed Assets	10.0	8.6
	7.8	6.4	6.5				5.9	5.5
	4.3	3.2	3.2				3.3	2.8
	3.4	2.3	2.4			Sales/Total Assets	2.4	2.1
	2.3	1.8	1.9				1.9	1.7
	.8	.8	.8				.9	1.2
	(16) 1.4	(32) 1.3	(28) 1.5			% Depr., Dep., Amort./Sales	(43) 1.8	(64) 1.9
	2.8	1.9	2.1				2.8	2.8
		2.2					2.5	1.4
		(14) 4.5				% Officers', Directors' Owners' Comp/Sales	(17) 4.7	(19) 4.3
		6.9					8.5	11.1
1123M	79225M	409844M	1941332M	480388M	2940213M	Net Sales ($)	3209776M	2645720M
315M	22454M	161537M	690108M	197779M	1450715M	Total Assets ($)	1434119M	1329456M

M = $ thousand   MM = $ million

See Pages 11 through 21 for Explanation of Ratios and Data

Comparative Historical Data | Current Data Sorted by Sales

Type of Statement	4/1/04-3/31/05 ALL	4/1/05-3/31/06 ALL	4/1/06-3/31/07 ALL		0-1MM	1-3MM	3-5MM	5-10MM	10-25MM	25MM & OVER
Unqualified	16	15	23					1	1	21
Reviewed	30	20	17			1		9	6	1
Compiled	12	10	14			1	5	4	3	1
Tax Returns	2	4	11		1	3		3	3	1
Other	26	24	27			1		5	5	16
						15 (4/1-9/30/06)		77 (10/1/06-3/31/07)		
NUMBER OF STATEMENTS	86	73	92		1	5	7	22	18	39
ASSETS	%	%	%		%	%	%	%	%	%
Cash & Equivalents	8.5	10.1	7.3					7.6	7.7	6.3
Trade Receivables (net)	28.5	32.5	30.9					34.3	33.9	28.9
Inventory	25.2	23.4	25.7					29.2	23.1	24.7
All Other Current	3.7	4.0	4.5					2.7	4.7	6.4
Total Current	66.0	70.0	68.4					73.8	69.3	66.3
Fixed Assets (net)	26.1	23.0	23.7					21.2	25.7	23.0
Intangibles (net)	2.6	2.1	3.0					1.5	1.8	5.2
All Other Non-Current	5.4	4.9	4.8					3.5	3.2	5.4
Total	100.0	100.0	100.0					100.0	100.0	100.0
LIABILITIES										
Notes Payable-Short Term	9.7	9.5	8.5					10.3	10.7	5.8
Cur. Mat.-L.T.D.	3.5	4.6	2.6					2.5	2.7	1.6
Trade Payables	16.7	20.9	17.8					22.1	13.2	17.8
Income Taxes Payable	.2	.4	.4					.1	.2	.9
All Other Current	15.6	16.1	18.6					13.6	13.4	24.8
Total Current	45.6	51.5	48.0					48.6	40.2	50.9
Long-Term Debt	14.9	12.7	13.3					9.9	16.8	10.5
Deferred Taxes	.5	.2	.4					.2	.3	.7
All Other Non-Current	4.2	7.4	5.5					5.6	2.0	7.8
Net Worth	34.8	28.2	32.9					35.8	40.7	30.2
Total Liabilities & Net Worth	100.0	100.0	100.0					100.0	100.0	100.0
INCOME DATA										
Net Sales	100.0	100.0	100.0					100.0	100.0	100.0
Gross Profit	27.2	26.6	27.0					26.8	24.1	26.0
Operating Expenses	22.6	22.3	20.4					22.1	17.6	19.2
Operating Profit	4.6	4.3	6.6					4.7	6.5	6.8
All Other Expenses (net)	.8	.8	.9					.1	.5	1.3
Profit Before Taxes	3.8	3.5	5.6					4.5	6.0	5.5
RATIOS										
Current	2.2 / 1.4 / 1.1	2.0 / 1.4 / 1.1	2.1 / 1.5 / 1.2					2.1 / 1.5 / 1.1	2.3 / 1.7 / 1.2	1.8 / 1.5 / 1.2
Quick	1.1 / .8 / .5	1.2 / .9 / .6	1.2 / .9 / .5					1.2 / .9 / .5	1.4 / 1.0 / .7	1.0 / .8 / .5
Sales/Receivables	23 15.8 / 38 9.5 / 64 5.7	33 11.2 / 44 8.4 / 64 5.7	27 13.6 / 43 8.5 / 66 5.5					23 15.7 / 49 7.4 / 82 4.5	27 13.5 / 40 9.0 / 70 5.3	33 11.1 / 43 8.6 / 60 6.1
Cost of Sales/Inventory	29 12.8 / 47 7.7 / 77 4.8	19 18.8 / 40 9.2 / 64 5.7	24 15.3 / 46 8.0 / 76 4.8					25 14.3 / 58 6.3 / 81 4.5	17 22.0 / 32 11.2 / 95 3.8	27 13.8 / 44 8.4 / 69 5.3
Cost of Sales/Payables	17 21.7 / 28 13.2 / 46 8.0	21 17.1 / 35 10.3 / 49 7.4	20 18.6 / 30 12.2 / 44 8.3					25 14.7 / 39 9.5 / 53 6.9	16 22.6 / 25 14.7 / 31 11.8	20 17.9 / 29 12.5 / 42 8.6
Sales/Working Capital	6.2 / 11.4 / 61.2	7.2 / 12.2 / 45.9	6.8 / 10.8 / 29.4					6.9 / 10.5 / 38.5	6.2 / 10.4 / 22.0	7.3 / 12.5 / 22.4
EBIT/Interest	18.6 / (85) 6.9 / 1.9	13.3 / (68) 5.3 / 2.3	16.1 / (85) 6.5 / 3.1					(19) 16.7 / 5.0 / 1.9	28.7 / 5.4 / 2.9	22.6 / (37) 7.2 / 3.6
Net Profit + Depr., Dep., Amort./Cur. Mat. L/T/D	6.9 / (36) 3.9 / 2.0	7.5 / (27) 3.1 / 1.7	17.6 / (32) 5.6 / 2.6							21.3 / (20) 8.4 / 2.9
Fixed/Worth	.4 / .8 / 2.6	.3 / .7 / 1.8	.3 / .7 / 1.5					.3 / .6 / 1.2	.3 / .5 / 1.3	.3 / .7 / 1.3
Debt/Worth	.7 / 2.0 / 9.1	1.2 / 2.4 / 5.4	1.0 / 1.7 / 3.1					.8 / 1.5 / 3.0	1.0 / 2.1 / 3.0	1.2 / 1.7 / 2.3
% Profit Before Taxes/Tangible Net Worth	41.8 / (73) 24.9 / 9.5	59.2 / (64) 27.8 / 12.4	54.6 / (83) 27.1 / 14.9					(20) 42.0 / 25.4 / 4.7	53.5 / 23.2 / 16.8	64.7 / (35) 27.5 / 19.2
% Profit Before Taxes/Total Assets	19.0 / 8.1 / 2.1	15.6 / 9.6 / 3.1	17.7 / 11.4 / 5.4					20.0 / 7.5 / 1.1	14.4 / 10.7 / 6.1	22.3 / 12.2 / 7.2
Sales/Net Fixed Assets	21.2 / 8.7 / 5.7	27.0 / 12.7 / 8.0	25.9 / 10.7 / 6.6					38.0 / 12.6 / 6.9	23.4 / 10.6 / 5.7	23.2 / 10.4 / 7.4
Sales/Total Assets	3.1 / 2.4 / 1.7	3.2 / 2.5 / 2.0	3.5 / 2.4 / 1.8					4.1 / 2.6 / 1.8	3.1 / 2.5 / 1.8	3.5 / 2.5 / 2.0
% Depr., Dep., Amort./Sales	1.1 / (77) 2.0 / 3.2	.7 / (65) 1.4 / 2.2	.8 / (86) 1.5 / 2.1					(17) .7 / 1.2 / 1.8	1.0 / 1.7 / 2.1	.8 / (36) 1.5 / 2.0
% Officers', Directors', Owners' Comp/Sales	2.4 / (25) 5.0 / 7.0	1.1 / (21) 3.0 / 7.3	2.3 / (24) 4.9 / 6.4							
Net Sales ($)	3991268M	4091816M	5852125M		968M	10902M	26127M	169327M	297350M	5347451M
Total Assets ($)	2026970M	1735141M	2522908M		797M	4995M	12483M	72816M	136620M	2295197M

© RMA 2007

M = $ thousand MM = $ million

See Pages 11 through 21 for Explanation of Ratios and Data

Current Data Sorted by Assets   Comparative Historical Data

Type of Statement

	0-500M	500M-2MM	2-10MM	10-50MM	50-100MM	100-250MM		4/1/02-3/31/03 ALL	4/1/03-3/31/04 ALL
Unqualified		6	17	44	4	12		78	80
Reviewed		25	99	32	1			141	146
Compiled	4	29	38	2				93	122
Tax Returns	15	24	10					28	42
Other	5	23	57	31	8	7		123	129
		87 (4/1-9/30/06)		406 (10/1/06-3/31/07)					
NUMBER OF STATEMENTS	24	107	221	109	13	19		463	519
	%	%	%	%	%	%		%	%
ASSETS									
Cash & Equivalents	15.9	8.6	7.2	8.8	6.7	3.4		9.8	8.4
Trade Receivables (net)	26.3	37.6	37.9	37.6	36.9	36.9		33.4	34.6
Inventory	12.4	18.5	18.4	19.7	26.6	20.3		15.9	16.4
All Other Current	.8	3.5	5.3	6.3	5.9	6.7		4.5	5.3
Total Current	55.4	68.1	68.8	72.4	76.1	67.4		63.6	64.7
Fixed Assets (net)	31.9	23.3	24.8	21.0	18.1	20.9		28.4	28.0
Intangibles (net)	1.1	1.8	1.5	2.2	.8	3.7		2.1	2.1
All Other Non-Current	11.5	6.8	4.9	4.4	5.0	8.1		5.9	5.2
Total	100.0	100.0	100.0	100.0	100.0	100.0		100.0	100.0
LIABILITIES									
Notes Payable-Short Term	22.0	10.0	10.2	11.6	10.2	12.8		11.4	11.9
Cur. Mat.-L.T.D.	8.6	4.3	3.1	2.2	1.2	2.5		4.1	3.8
Trade Payables	15.1	20.1	18.8	18.5	16.1	15.1		15.2	16.9
Income Taxes Payable	.0	.3	.6	.4	.9	.7		.5	.3
All Other Current	3.5	13.3	11.5	12.4	15.0	12.5		9.4	9.4
Total Current	49.2	48.0	44.2	45.1	43.4	43.6		40.5	42.3
Long-Term Debt	32.9	17.8	13.8	12.2	5.5	13.7		15.5	16.1
Deferred Taxes	.0	.2	.4	.4	1.2	1.1		.5	.4
All Other Non-Current	2.4	3.5	4.0	1.3	.9	1.9		4.2	5.8
Net Worth	15.5	30.5	37.6	41.1	49.0	39.6		39.3	35.3
Total Liabilities & Net Worth	100.0	100.0	100.0	100.0	100.0	100.0		100.0	100.0
INCOME DATA									
Net Sales	100.0	100.0	100.0	100.0	100.0	100.0		100.0	100.0
Gross Profit	44.2	32.7	24.4	19.9	16.4	22.4		27.6	26.5
Operating Expenses	38.2	28.6	18.3	13.7	8.8	15.3		24.7	25.1
Operating Profit	6.0	4.1	6.2	6.2	7.7	7.1		2.9	1.4
All Other Expenses (net)	.5	.4	.6	.6	-.1	.4		.9	.8
Profit Before Taxes	5.5	3.7	5.5	5.6	7.7	6.7		2.0	.6
RATIOS									
Current	3.6	2.4	2.2	2.2	2.3	2.5		2.6	2.4
	1.1	1.5	1.5	1.5	1.8	1.8		1.6	1.5
	.4	1.0	1.2	1.2	1.2	1.3		1.2	1.1
Quick	2.7	1.5	1.5	1.4	1.7	1.4		1.8	1.6
	1.0	1.0	1.0	1.0	1.0	1.1	(462)	1.1	1.0
	.2	.7	.7	.7	.6	.7		.7	.7
Sales/Receivables	0 UND	30 12.3	39 9.3	44 8.2	43 8.5	41 9.0		37 10.0	39 9.4
	20 17.8	47 7.8	54 6.7	62 5.9	54 6.8	62 5.9		51 7.1	55 6.7
	61 6.0	67 5.4	70 5.2	85 4.3	78 4.7	93 3.9		70 5.2	75 4.9
Cost of Sales/Inventory	0 UND	5 80.2	12 30.3	14 25.8	32 11.4	14 26.6		9 39.9	10 37.1
	0 UND	29 12.4	30 12.0	38 9.6	50 7.4	43 8.4		29 12.4	31 11.9
	34 10.6	67 5.5	58 6.3	66 5.5	95 3.8	87 4.2		61 6.0	61 6.0
Cost of Sales/Payables	0 UND	19 19.4	19 19.3	23 15.6	20 18.3	20 18.1		17 20.9	18 19.8
	5 75.6	34 10.8	32 11.4	33 11.0	30 12.1	41 8.9		31 11.9	32 11.3
	26 14.2	51 7.2	49 7.5	50 7.3	46 7.9	47 7.8		48 7.7	51 7.1
Sales/Working Capital	8.6	6.1	5.0	5.0	5.9	3.9		5.4	5.4
	62.7	13.3	10.1	9.4	7.2	6.6		9.9	10.4
	-37.8	141.4	29.7	17.4	20.4	14.8		28.8	38.4
EBIT/Interest	14.6	14.0	15.6	20.9	153.9	22.7		9.3	7.1
	(18) 3.1	(99) 5.1	(208) 5.3	(103) 6.1	(12) 20.9	(18) 9.0	(432) 2.7		(475) 1.9
	1.5	1.7	1.9	2.1	7.1	4.4		.5	-.7
Net Profit + Depr., Dep., Amort./Cur. Mat. L/T/D		5.0	8.6	9.3		24.9		3.7	4.2
	(14) 2.8	(62) 4.3	(35) 3.6		(12) 7.6		(137) 1.8		(135) 1.7
	1.4	1.9	2.4		3.0			.6	.9
Fixed/Worth	.5	.2	.3	.3	.2	.4		.3	.3
	1.7	.6	.6	.5	.3	.5		.7	.7
	UND	3.0	1.4	1.2	.7	.8		1.6	2.0
Debt/Worth	1.1	.9	.9	.7	.5	.7		.7	.8
	6.5	2.0	1.8	1.7	.9	1.4		1.7	1.9
	UND	8.7	3.6	3.8	3.1	2.6		4.0	4.8
% Profit Before Taxes/Tangible Net Worth	428.6	59.5	49.1	40.9	47.0	78.7		28.3	26.4
	(19) 125.1	(90) 25.2	(208) 31.2	(107) 25.9	33.5	(18) 31.8	(424) 10.1		(454) 7.8
	23.3	10.8	12.9	16.2	25.1	15.8		-.9	-6.3
% Profit Before Taxes/Total Assets	41.2	18.4	20.1	17.2	28.3	16.3		10.6	9.4
	13.4	9.8	10.9	8.9	17.8	12.3		3.4	2.4
	4.8	2.3	3.4	3.6	6.3	6.0		-1.1	-3.6
Sales/Net Fixed Assets	47.3	43.0	26.0	20.8	26.7	14.8		18.6	18.0
	23.3	16.1	13.0	11.4	13.1	9.5		8.5	9.3
	9.3	8.7	6.1	6.9	8.2	6.8		4.6	4.9
Sales/Total Assets	10.1	4.0	3.0	2.4	2.7	2.6		2.9	2.8
	4.9	2.8	2.4	2.1	2.1	1.9		2.1	2.1
	2.8	2.1	1.9	1.8	1.5	1.5		1.6	1.5
% Depr., Dep., Amort./Sales	.7	.5	.8	.8	.7	1.1		1.3	1.2
	(17) 1.6	(88) 1.4	(204) 1.3	(104) 1.3	(10) 1.2	(17) 1.5	(428) 2.2		(471) 2.3
	2.4	3.1	2.6	1.9	2.5	1.6		3.7	3.8
% Officers', Directors' Owners' Comp/Sales	3.0	2.5	1.4	1.3				2.3	2.5
	(17) 4.7	(57) 5.0	(83) 2.3	(20) 2.0			(195) 4.7		(208) 4.1
	7.6	7.7	4.5	3.5				8.3	7.5
Net Sales ($)	42582M	397627M	2793088M	4586158M	1848727M	6375186M		9062637M	9337410M
Total Assets ($)	6920M	129864M	1123129M	2188512M	843225M	3005088M		4944587M	5091264M

Comparative Historical Data   Current Data Sorted by Sales

93	93	83	Type of Statement						
163	158	157	Unqualified		5		3	20	55
67	57	73	Reviewed	1	7	21	39	58	31
50	47	49	Compiled	2	15	15	29	11	1
123	150	131	Tax Returns	3	19	11	7	9	
4/1/04-3/31/05	4/1/05-3/31/06	4/1/06-3/31/07	Other	7	8	8	31	35	42
ALL	ALL	ALL			87 (4/1-9/30/06)		406 (10/1/06-3/31/07)		
				0-1MM	1-3MM	3-5MM	5-10MM	10-25MM	25MM & OVER
496	505	493	NUMBER OF STATEMENTS	13	54	55	109	133	129
%	%	%	ASSETS	%	%	%	%	%	%
8.1	8.0	8.1	Cash & Equivalents	11.4	8.2	11.1	7.3	9.2	6.0
36.6	37.3	37.1	Trade Receivables (net)	34.4	32.0	31.0	35.6	41.2	39.3
19.3	18.3	18.7	Inventory	13.2	18.2	17.4	18.8	17.7	20.9
4.5	5.2	5.0	All Other Current	.3	3.1	4.3	3.8	6.3	6.3
68.5	68.8	68.9	Total Current	59.2	61.4	63.7	65.5	74.3	72.6
25.1	24.0	23.7	Fixed Assets (net)	37.7	26.9	26.0	26.9	20.3	20.6
1.2	1.3	1.8	Intangibles (net)	.1	2.0	1.8	2.3	1.3	1.9
5.2	6.0	5.6	All Other Non-Current	2.9	9.7	8.5	5.3	4.1	4.9
100.0	100.0	100.0	Total	100.0	100.0	100.0	100.0	100.0	100.0
			LIABILITIES						
13.4	11.5	11.1	Notes Payable-Short Term	14.3	10.8	10.0	11.4	9.5	12.9
3.7	3.6	3.4	Cur. Mat.-L.T.D.	6.8	7.0	3.6	3.4	2.4	2.4
19.1	18.5	18.6	Trade Payables	17.1	16.1	15.8	19.0	20.0	19.3
.4	.4	.5	Income Taxes Payable	.0	.3	.3	.3	.9	.5
9.5	11.2	11.8	All Other Current	3.7	12.2	11.6	10.4	12.9	12.6
46.0	45.1	45.4	Total Current	41.9	46.4	41.3	44.5	45.7	47.7
14.7	15.4	15.0	Long-Term Debt	41.8	22.6	18.1	14.6	11.5	11.8
.3	.4	.4	Deferred Taxes	.0	.2	.3	.2	.5	.5
4.2	4.2	3.1	All Other Non-Current	2.5	3.5	2.3	6.4	2.3	1.3
34.8	34.9	36.1	Net Worth	13.8	27.3	38.1	34.3	40.0	38.7
100.0	100.0	100.0	Total Liabilities & Net Worth	100.0	100.0	100.0	100.0	100.0	100.0
			INCOME DATA						
100.0	100.0	100.0	Net Sales	100.0	100.0	100.0	100.0	100.0	100.0
25.5	25.5	25.9	Gross Profit	51.9	34.0	32.5	26.4	23.3	19.3
22.2	20.4	20.1	Operating Expenses	42.7	30.5	27.7	21.1	16.5	13.0
3.3	5.0	5.8	Operating Profit	9.2	3.5	4.8	5.3	6.8	6.2
.7	.7	.6	All Other Expenses (net)	2.4	.3	.5	.5	.5	.6
2.6	4.4	5.2	Profit Before Taxes	6.8	3.2	4.3	4.7	6.3	5.7
			RATIOS						
2.2	2.2	2.3		3.5	3.2	3.1	2.1	2.4	2.1
1.5	1.5	1.5	Current	1.1	1.4	1.5	1.5	1.6	1.5
1.1	1.2	1.1		.8	.9	1.1	1.1	1.2	1.2
1.4	1.6	1.5		2.5	1.8	1.6	1.4	1.7	1.3
1.0	1.0	1.0	Quick	.9	1.0	.9	1.0	1.1	1.0
.6	.7	.7		.7	.4	.6	.7	.7	.7
40 9.0	38 9.7	37 9.9		21 17.1	29 12.4	29 12.5	35 10.4	42 8.6	43 8.4
56 6.6	53 6.8	55 6.7	Sales/Receivables	56 6.5	47 7.8	43 8.5	52 7.0	57 6.4	60 6.1
75 4.9	75 4.8	74 5.0		108 3.4	67 5.5	61 6.0	68 5.3	75 4.9	83 4.4
11 32.1	9 39.0	10 38.1		0 UND	1 318.5	4 87.2	11 31.8	12 31.5	16 22.2
35 10.6	31 11.7	32 11.4	Cost of Sales/Inventory	13 27.5	36 10.2	28 12.9	33 11.1	28 13.2	37 9.9
66 5.6	60 6.0	62 5.9		78 4.7	61 6.0	67 5.5	63 7.0	52 7.0	66 5.5
21 17.7	19 19.0	19 18.9		0 UND	10 35.3	14 26.0	19 19.4	20 18.3	23 15.9
35 10.4	33 11.2	33 11.2	Cost of Sales/Payables	27 13.4	27 13.4	28 12.8	33 11.1	34 10.8	33 11.0
54 6.7	50 7.2	49 7.5		85 4.3	46 7.9	45 8.2	50 7.3	50 7.4	45 8.1
6.2	6.0	5.8		5.7	5.6	5.7	7.3	5.4	5.7
10.2	10.5	10.2	Sales/Working Capital	39.9	13.0	11.8	11.9	9.4	9.5
36.8	29.5	31.1		-45.6	-48.4	35.6	42.6	21.5	23.6
12.5	14.8	17.1		10.8	13.4	12.6	11.8	30.0	21.7
(461) 4.0	(464) 5.5	(458) 5.7	EBIT/Interest	(10) 3.6	(50) 3.2	(49) 4.5	(105) 4.3	(120) 7.3	(124) 7.7
1.1	2.0	2.1		1.0	1.5	1.7	1.7	2.9	2.6
5.6	8.1	8.8			7.2		9.4	9.5	9.4
(137) 2.4	(140) 3.4	(128) 4.2	Net Profit + Depr., Dep., Amort./Cur. Mat. L/T/D		(11) 3.2		(20) 5.4	(45) 4.3	(45) 4.3
.9	1.7	2.0			1.5		1.6	2.4	2.4
.3	.3	.3		1.4	.2	.3	.3	.2	.3
.7	.6	.6	Fixed/Worth	4.5	.7	.6	.6	.5	.5
1.5	1.4	1.6		UND	5.0	2.2	2.2	.9	1.0
.9	.8	.9		1.4	1.0	.9	.9	.8	.8
2.0	1.8	1.8	Debt/Worth	10.4	2.5	1.8	2.0	1.6	1.7
4.5	4.5	4.4		UND	9.9	5.8	5.4	3.3	3.6
39.4	49.6	49.6		UND	69.9	48.5	56.0	48.6	45.1
(451) 15.3	(466) 25.9	(455) 30.2	% Profit Before Taxes/Tangible Net Worth	(10) 126.8	(44) 22.9	(50) 24.3	(99) 26.3	(126) 34.1	(126) 29.1
1.7	8.6	14.5		54.5	7.7	10.9	10.7	14.9	19.3
12.9	16.9	18.9		29.0	18.9	16.5	17.5	22.6	17.9
5.2	8.6	10.2	% Profit Before Taxes/Total Assets	12.4	7.6	7.6	10.2	11.6	9.9
.2	2.6	3.6		.0	1.6	2.2	2.9	4.3	4.7
22.0	25.4	27.2		21.7	43.8	39.1	24.4	29.5	23.9
11.0	13.2	14.0	Sales/Net Fixed Assets	7.8	14.9	14.0	10.8	15.2	12.2
6.2	6.5	6.9		2.5	7.1	6.3	5.7	8.4	7.3
2.9	3.0	3.1		3.5	3.8	3.4	3.2	3.1	2.7
2.3	2.3	2.4	Sales/Total Assets	1.7	2.8	2.4	2.4	2.4	2.2
1.7	1.8	1.9		1.4	1.9	1.8	1.9	2.0	1.9
1.0	.7	.8		1.1	.7	.8	.8	.8	.7
(454) 1.8	(449) 1.4	(440) 1.4	% Depr., Dep., Amort./Sales	(10) 2.0	(40) 1.9	(51) 1.5	(97) 1.6	(124) 1.2	(118) 1.2
3.1	2.6	2.5		7.5	3.4	3.5	3.2	2.1	1.7
2.0	1.7	1.7			3.0	2.3	1.7	1.2	1.2
(223) 3.5	(199) 3.3	(179) 3.1	% Officers', Directors' Owners' Comp/Sales		(34) 4.0	(27) 5.0	(47) 3.1	(40) 2.3	(21) 1.0
6.0	6.1	6.0			7.2	7.8	5.6	4.6	2.6
12095684M	14434389M	16043368M	Net Sales ($)	8291M	113155M	213541M	818419M	2179989M	12709973M
5842401M	6774892M	7296738M	Total Assets ($)	4613M	48350M	91718M	360404M	965819M	5825834M

M = $ thousand   MM = $ million
See Pages 11 through 21 for Explanation of Ratios and Data

Current Data Sorted by Assets   Comparative Historical Data

0-500M	500M-2MM	2-10MM	10-50MM	50-100MM	100-250MM	Type of Statement	4/1/02-3/31/03 ALL	4/1/03-3/31/04 ALL
1	3	12	11		2	Unqualified	25	27
	2	23	4	1		Reviewed	48	44
1	9	7			1	Compiled	25	26
2	5	2		1		Tax Returns	5	6
3	7	13	12	2	5	Other	37	37
	29 (4/1-9/30/06)		100 (10/1/06-3/31/07)					
7	26	57	27	4	8	NUMBER OF STATEMENTS	140	140
%	%	%	%	%	%	ASSETS	%	%
	10.2	9.3	9.5			Cash & Equivalents	8.0	10.0
	33.3	28.5	28.9			Trade Receivables (net)	26.9	28.5
	17.7	25.2	24.3			Inventory	19.4	19.5
	3.6	3.9	5.7			All Other Current	4.6	3.2
	64.8	66.8	68.4			Total Current	58.9	61.2
	27.0	25.3	25.1			Fixed Assets (net)	32.0	28.3
	1.8	2.0	2.1			Intangibles (net)	2.6	2.4
	6.4	5.9	4.5			All Other Non-Current	6.4	8.0
	100.0	100.0	100.0			Total	100.0	100.0
						LIABILITIES		
	13.5	8.6	7.4			Notes Payable-Short Term	13.6	12.3
	2.0	2.6	3.2			Cur. Mat.-L.T.D.	4.4	4.2
	14.6	14.7	13.6			Trade Payables	13.7	15.2
	.1	.5	.6			Income Taxes Payable	.3	.2
	12.2	17.3	25.4			All Other Current	11.4	10.0
	42.3	43.7	50.1			Total Current	43.4	42.0
	18.2	13.7	11.0			Long-Term Debt	16.5	15.0
	.2	.5	.2			Deferred Taxes	.4	.7
	5.7	5.3	13.6			All Other Non-Current	5.6	5.0
	33.6	36.9	25.2			Net Worth	34.1	37.3
	100.0	100.0	100.0			Total Liabilties & Net Worth	100.0	100.0
						INCOME DATA		
	100.0	100.0	100.0			Net Sales	100.0	100.0
	28.4	25.9	20.9			Gross Profit	26.7	26.0
	24.9	18.4	13.5			Operating Expenses	24.5	23.9
	3.5	7.5	7.4			Operating Profit	2.3	2.1
	-.1	.5	1.0			All Other Expenses (net)	1.2	1.0
	3.5	6.9	6.4			Profit Before Taxes	1.1	1.1
						RATIOS		
	2.4	2.9	2.1				2.4	2.8
	1.6	1.7	1.5			Current	1.4	1.6
	1.1	1.2	1.1				1.0	1.1
	1.9	1.6	1.3				1.4	2.0
	.8	.9	.7			Quick	.8	.9
	.6	.6	.5				.5	.6
	22 16.6	33 10.9	36 10.1				31 11.7	34 10.8
	41 9.0	48 7.7	47 7.8			Sales/Receivables	43 8.5	48 7.6
	63 5.8	61 5.9	70 5.2				61 5.9	64 5.7
	3 143.1	31 11.7	28 12.9				24 15.0	22 16.5
	38 9.5	64 5.7	57 6.4			Cost of Sales/Inventory	46 7.9	44 8.3
	62 5.9	95 3.9	88 4.2				72 5.0	74 4.9
	8 47.4	17 21.1	19 19.1				16 23.5	19 19.3
	30 12.3	30 12.0	32 11.5			Cost of Sales/Payables	27 13.6	30 12.2
	50 7.3	47 7.8	39 9.3				46 8.0	49 7.5
	6.2	4.7	6.3				5.6	4.1
	10.3	8.3	13.2			Sales/Working Capital	11.2	10.1
	74.0	23.1	24.5				283.1	91.5
	17.6	17.1	17.2				6.3	10.1
	(25) 5.2	(51) 5.2	(24) 9.3			EBIT/Interest	(131) 2.0	(127) 2.3
	1.9	1.7	2.2				.5	-.4
		4.6	14.0			Net Profit + Depr., Dep.,	3.8	4.3
	(15) 2.3	(10) 7.3				Amort./Cur. Mat. L/T/D	(33) 1.8	(41) 1.7
		1.7	1.3				.8	.4
	.2	.3	.4				.5	.4
	.5	.5	.9			Fixed/Worth	1.1	.8
	3.0	1.6	1.3				2.9	2.5
	.7	.6	1.0				.8	.6
	2.3	1.4	3.2			Debt/Worth	1.9	1.8
	5.1	3.5	5.4				8.1	5.6
	53.1	51.8	67.3			% Profit Before Taxes/Tangible	28.0	28.4
	(23) 24.8	(51) 25.2	(23) 39.8			Net Worth	(121) 10.1	(119) 11.3
	14.2	8.9	15.4				.3	-8.3
	17.5	22.2	21.2			% Profit Before Taxes/Total	8.3	11.5
	8.0	9.7	9.0			Assets	2.9	4.0
	3.5	2.4	3.6				-1.0	-5.2
	33.9	16.1	13.7				14.8	17.2
	16.2	10.2	7.8			Sales/Net Fixed Assets	7.4	7.8
	5.2	5.3	5.3				4.1	4.3
	3.7	2.5	2.4				2.6	2.6
	2.5	2.1	2.0			Sales/Total Assets	2.0	1.9
	1.9	1.6	1.4				1.5	1.4
	.7	.9	1.1				1.3	1.3
	(22) 1.5	(53) 1.6	(26) 1.5			% Depr., Dep., Amort./Sales	(134) 2.3	(126) 2.2
	3.2	2.7	1.9				3.8	3.7
	3.6	1.0				% Officers', Directors'	3.0	2.0
	(22) 5.9	(24) 3.5				Owners' Comp/Sales	(55) 5.1	(53) 4.6
	8.4	4.7					9.5	7.2
7755M	96396M	643173M	1075648M	423408M	3213478M	Net Sales ($)	2321631M	2804369M
2349M	34538M	305284M	550363M	238067M	1395385M	Total Assets ($)	1137665M	1670807M

© RMA 2007

M = $ thousand   MM = $ million
See Pages 11 through 21 for Explanation of Ratios and Data

Comparative Historical Data

Current Data Sorted by Sales

			Type of Statement						
27	28	29	Unqualified	1	1	2	4	8	13
53	31	30	Reviewed		1	1	11	14	3
19	19	18	Compiled		4	4	8	1	1
7	7	10	Tax Returns	1	4	1	3		1
42	39	42	Other	2	4	4	8	9	15
4/1/04-3/31/05 ALL	4/1/05-3/31/06 ALL	4/1/06-3/31/07 ALL		0-1MM	1-3MM (29 4/1-9/30/06)	3-5MM	5-10MM (100 10/1/06-3/31/07)	10-25MM	25MM & OVER
148	124	129	NUMBER OF STATEMENTS	4	14	12	34	32	33
%	%	%	**ASSETS**	%	%	%	%	%	%
7.6	8.4	9.5	Cash & Equivalents		9.1	16.4	9.0	11.9	6.1
29.5	30.5	29.4	Trade Receivables (net)		33.9	26.5	32.0	26.0	28.9
23.1	23.4	22.1	Inventory		18.6	15.1	23.3	27.4	19.8
4.3	4.5	4.5	All Other Current		5.9	.3	3.1	3.9	7.9
64.6	66.9	65.5	Total Current		67.6	58.3	67.3	69.2	62.6
26.4	24.0	25.4	Fixed Assets (net)		21.0	34.7	25.7	22.2	25.5
2.5	2.9	3.3	Intangibles (net)		6.7	.2	2.3	.9	6.8
6.6	6.3	5.8	All Other Non-Current		4.7	6.8	4.7	7.7	5.1
100.0	100.0	100.0	Total		100.0	100.0	100.0	100.0	100.0
			LIABILITIES						
11.8	8.5	9.1	Notes Payable-Short Term		14.6	7.6	10.6	7.8	6.9
3.5	3.9	2.4	Cur. Mat.-L.T.D.		1.3	4.0	2.4	2.1	2.7
16.5	15.9	14.9	Trade Payables		18.5	12.7	16.2	12.8	15.0
.5	.3	.4	Income Taxes Payable		.3	.0	.7	.4	.4
11.2	13.9	17.4	All Other Current		9.3	11.1	14.7	18.4	25.9
43.3	42.5	44.1	Total Current		43.9	35.4	44.7	41.5	50.8
15.3	13.7	14.4	Long-Term Debt		22.4	20.1	12.3	11.3	11.5
.4	.4	.5	Deferred Taxes		.1	.3	.4	.4	1.1
6.1	7.1	7.1	All Other Non-Current		4.4	5.2	5.5	2.7	14.6
34.9	36.3	33.9	Net Worth		29.2	39.0	37.1	44.1	22.0
100.0	100.0	100.0	Total Liabilities & Net Worth		100.0	100.0	100.0	100.0	100.0
			INCOME DATA						
100.0	100.0	100.0	Net Sales		100.0	100.0	100.0	100.0	100.0
24.9	23.9	25.7	Gross Profit		31.9	31.8	24.7	23.8	21.1
21.7	18.8	19.3	Operating Expenses		29.8	24.5	18.0	16.1	15.1
3.3	5.1	6.4	Operating Profit		2.1	7.3	6.7	7.8	6.0
.5	.7	.7	All Other Expenses (net)		.7	.1	.4	-.1	1.7
2.8	4.4	5.7	Profit Before Taxes		1.4	7.2	6.3	7.8	4.3
			RATIOS						
2.6	2.7	2.4	Current		3.8	2.5	2.6	2.5	2.0
1.6	1.7	1.6			2.2	1.9	1.6	1.6	1.4
1.1	1.2	1.2			1.0	1.3	1.1	1.2	1.1
1.6	1.6	1.5	Quick		2.4	2.4	1.9	1.4	1.2
.9	.9	.8			1.2	1.3	.9	.9	.7
.6	.6	.6			.7	.7	.6	.6	.4
38 9.7	34 10.7	33 11.1	Sales/Receivables		33 11.0	33 10.9	32 11.5	34 10.8	31 11.7
51 7.2	46 8.0	46 8.0			40 9.2	47 7.7	47 7.7	46 8.0	45 8.2
64 5.7	60 6.0	63 5.8			64 5.7	60 6.1	67 5.5	63 5.8	59 6.2
27 13.4	20 17.8	21 17.6	Cost of Sales/Inventory		12 31.4	2 200.7	28 13.1	32 11.6	22 16.5
54 6.8	47 7.8	47 7.7			40 9.2	39 9.5	48 7.6	67 5.5	39 9.4
85 4.3	77 4.7	81 4.5			70 5.2	71 5.2	74 4.9	110 3.3	69 5.3
20 18.5	18 20.4	17 21.5	Cost of Sales/Payables		8 47.3	18 20.5	13 27.6	18 20.7	19 19.6
30 12.0	29 12.4	32 11.3			37 9.9	34 10.6	37 10.0	31 11.8	27 13.4
49 7.5	43 8.5	46 8.0			50 7.2	58 6.2	53 6.9	37 9.7	42 8.8
4.4	4.5	5.3	Sales/Working Capital		3.7	5.8	4.7	4.8	6.8
9.2	8.0	9.9			10.3	9.3	11.5	7.5	13.2
47.5	24.2	24.5			NM	21.7	39.3	16.6	33.5
10.9	15.3	17.1	EBIT/Interest		7.2	17.7	20.5	22.6	16.5
(129) 3.7	(114) 6.5	(115) 5.2			(12) 2.2	(11) 5.2	(30) 6.5	(28) 7.7	(32) 5.0
1.1	1.8	1.7			.4	1.9	1.2	3.3	1.0
13.8	10.5	8.0	Net Profit + Depr., Dep., Amort./Cur. Mat. L/T/D					12.2	8.1
(43) 3.0	(35) 4.0	(32) 3.2						(10) 5.8	(11) 6.5
1.3	1.6	1.3						2.5	1.1
.4	.3	.3	Fixed/Worth		.2	.3	.2	.3	.5
.8	.7	.6			.4	.8	.5	.5	.9
1.7	1.5	1.9			-7.3	2.6	4.1	.9	3.3
.7	.8	.7	Debt/Worth		.7	.7	.6	.7	1.0
1.9	1.8	1.8			3.8	1.4	1.8	1.3	3.3
5.2	5.2	5.3			-24.7	5.1	7.2	2.8	17.9
43.2	51.7	55.7	% Profit Before Taxes/Tangible Net Worth		25.8	48.5	61.0	55.4	67.1
(131) 17.2	(114) 25.5	(112) 25.8			(10) 23.8	19.4	(29) 26.1	33.9	(26) 39.5
1.3	6.6	11.7			5.5	15.5	10.4	11.7	6.7
13.6	17.9	19.9	% Profit Before Taxes/Total Assets		12.0	15.7	22.0	24.3	16.2
5.2	6.9	9.0			4.8	8.8	12.3	9.4	9.0
.2	2.5	2.4			-.5	2.8	1.3	4.8	.2
18.6	19.0	20.2	Sales/Net Fixed Assets		31.5	16.6	22.3	15.7	20.6
8.2	10.5	9.9			20.3	6.5	10.8	9.8	10.2
4.8	5.6	5.3			7.6	3.1	5.4	6.1	5.6
2.7	2.7	2.7	Sales/Total Assets		3.0	3.4	2.8	2.3	3.1
1.9	2.2	2.2			2.4	2.3	2.3	2.0	2.2
1.5	1.8	1.6			1.9	1.6	1.6	1.7	1.5
1.3	.9	.9	% Depr., Dep., Amort./Sales		.8	.8	.8	1.1	.9
(136) 2.0	(115) 1.5	(115) 1.6			(12) 1.5	(10) 3.2	(30) 1.6	1.4	(29) 1.7
3.3	2.5	2.5			2.4	4.4	2.1	2.5	2.3
2.1	1.5	1.8	% Officers', Directors' Owners' Comp/Sales			4.5	3.1	1.2	.9
(49) 4.0	(43) 3.0	(50) 4.3				6.3	(10) 5.7	(17) 3.5	(11) 1.9
7.0	7.3	7.3				12.1	7.9	5.2	4.2
3487426M	4048991M	5459858M	Net Sales ($)	2668M	26491M	47402M	235916M	498260M	4649121M
1945703M	2014759M	2525986M	Total Assets ($)	1997M	12563M	30629M	126473M	278676M	2075648M

M = $ thousand   MM = $ million
See Pages 11 through 21 for Explanation of Ratios and Data

Current Data Sorted by Assets   Comparative Historical Data

0-500M	500M-2MM	2-10MM	10-50MM	50-100MM	100-250MM	Type of Statement	4/1/02-3/31/03 ALL	4/1/03-3/31/04 ALL
		8	11	1	4	Unqualified	28	23
	4	30	9			Reviewed	39	42
	4	4	2			Compiled	24	31
4	5	8				Tax Returns	3	9
1	8	17	24	5	4	Other	46	36
	29 (4/1-9/30/06)		124 (10/1/06-3/31/07)					
5	21	67	46	6	8	NUMBER OF STATEMENTS	140	141
%	%	%	%	%	%	**ASSETS**	%	%
	12.7	9.3	6.0			Cash & Equivalents	6.6	8.6
	37.9	36.1	27.4			Trade Receivables (net)	30.3	32.1
	23.9	24.3	22.2			Inventory	27.3	24.9
	4.5	2.8	3.5			All Other Current	3.4	2.9
	79.0	72.6	59.1			Total Current	67.6	68.5
	15.6	18.6	31.0			Fixed Assets (net)	23.4	22.8
	4.1	3.5	4.1			Intangibles (net)	3.6	2.4
	1.3	5.3	5.8			All Other Non-Current	5.3	6.3
	100.0	100.0	100.0			Total	100.0	100.0
						LIABILITIES		
	9.3	13.1	10.7			Notes Payable-Short Term	11.4	9.7
	1.2	2.7	2.7			Cur. Mat.-L.T.D.	3.7	3.6
	22.3	18.4	11.6			Trade Payables	16.9	17.1
	.1	.3	.1			Income Taxes Payable	.5	.2
	7.4	10.9	12.8			All Other Current	10.5	12.1
	40.2	45.4	38.0			Total Current	43.0	42.8
	11.2	11.5	17.9			Long-Term Debt	15.5	15.4
	.4	.2	.5			Deferred Taxes	.5	.5
	1.7	5.9	3.9			All Other Non-Current	6.7	5.6
	46.5	37.0	39.8			Net Worth	34.3	35.6
	100.0	100.0	100.0			Total Liabilities & Net Worth	100.0	100.0
						INCOME DATA		
	100.0	100.0	100.0			Net Sales	100.0	100.0
	35.8	28.1	26.5			Gross Profit	31.2	30.2
	32.5	24.3	21.5			Operating Expenses	26.9	25.9
	3.3	3.8	5.0			Operating Profit	4.3	4.3
	-.5	.7	.9			All Other Expenses (net)	1.2	.9
	3.8	3.1	4.0			Profit Before Taxes	3.1	3.4
						RATIOS		
	6.1	2.5	2.7			Current	2.7	2.7
	1.8	1.5	1.6				1.6	1.7
	1.2	1.2	1.2				1.1	1.2
	3.9	1.4	1.4			Quick	1.4	1.7
	1.1	1.0	.8				.9	.9
	.7	.7	.4				.6	.6
	22 16.3	30 12.4	27 13.6			Sales/Receivables	28 13.1	27 13.7
	50 7.4	45 8.0	34 10.7				41 8.9	41 8.8
	65 5.7	67 5.5	53 6.8				60 6.1	58 6.3
	17 22.1	23 16.0	34 10.7			Cost of Sales/Inventory	30 12.2	26 13.8
	44 8.2	48 7.6	48 7.6				54 6.8	45 8.1
	80 4.6	66 5.5	68 5.4				85 4.3	76 4.8
	14 25.3	18 20.5	15 24.5			Cost of Sales/Payables	15 24.1	14 25.6
	29 12.6	32 11.5	22 16.5				28 13.0	23 15.6
	59 6.2	49 7.4	34 10.8				43 8.5	41 8.9
	4.3	5.8	5.6			Sales/Working Capital	5.7	5.7
	8.5	11.5	9.0				10.4	9.5
	43.3	26.9	40.1				38.7	26.4
	11.9	8.2	12.7			EBIT/Interest	9.6	18.0
	(17) 1.9	(63) 3.6	(41) 4.5				(128) 3.0	(127) 3.7
	.8	1.3	1.8				1.3	1.8
		3.1	22.8			Net Profit + Depr., Dep.,	6.8	6.0
	(18) 2.0	(18) 3.4				Amort./Cur. Mat. L/T/D	(50) 2.5	(43) 3.1
	.2	1.2					1.2	.9
	.1	.2	.4			Fixed/Worth	.3	.3
	.3	.6	.8				.7	.5
	.9	1.4	1.7				1.6	1.3
	.2	.9	.8			Debt/Worth	.9	.7
	1.3	1.9	1.7				2.0	1.6
	7.2	5.5	3.2				5.4	3.9
	79.4	40.4	47.1			% Profit Before Taxes/Tangible	40.6	35.0
	(20) 18.6	(58) 23.3	(43) 22.6			Net Worth	(122) 17.6	(126) 15.7
	1.7	8.8	8.3				4.1	4.3
	18.1	12.8	18.2			% Profit Before Taxes/Total	16.0	16.1
	10.5	7.5	9.3			Assets	5.2	5.9
	.4	1.2	1.5				.8	1.3
	93.6	35.3	15.6			Sales/Net Fixed Assets	27.8	32.1
	46.5	17.3	7.0				13.4	14.2
	13.0	10.6	4.8				6.7	6.5
	3.8	3.3	2.8			Sales/Total Assets	3.4	3.3
	2.8	2.7	2.3				2.4	2.5
	2.5	2.1	1.6				1.9	1.9
	.7	.7	1.0			% Depr., Dep., Amort./Sales	1.0	1.1
	(13) 1.5	(64) 1.3	(41) 1.5				(128) 1.6	(122) 1.7
	2.2	2.2	2.7				2.5	2.6
	2.5	1.5				% Officers', Directors'	1.8	1.8
	(13) 4.0	(26) 2.7				Owners' Comp/Sales	(54) 3.6	(58) 3.8
	8.0	4.9						7.3
7257M	86468M	898808M	1905356M	1015383M	2108726M	Net Sales ($)	5580453M	3999891M
1309M	27490M	322307M	882858M	437622M	1055861M	Total Assets ($)	2922846M	1946817M

M = $ thousand   MM = $ million
See Pages 11 through 21 for Explanation of Ratios and Data

Comparative Historical Data / Current Data Sorted by Sales

	4/1/04-3/31/05 ALL	4/1/05-3/31/06 ALL	4/1/06-3/31/07 ALL	0-1MM	1-3MM	3-5MM	5-10MM	10-25MM	25MM & OVER
Type of Statement					29 (4/1-9/30/06)		124 (10/1/06-3/31/07)		
Unqualified	24	29	24				2	6	16
Reviewed	43	37	43			2	15	14	12
Compiled	21	15	10	3	2	3			2
Tax Returns	14	20	17		3	3	6	5	
Other	41	67	59	1	3	3	11	15	26
NUMBER OF STATEMENTS	143	168	153	4	8	11	34	40	56
ASSETS	%	%	%	%	%	%	%	%	%
Cash & Equivalents	7.3	8.0	8.3			26.1	8.6	7.8	4.4
Trade Receivables (net)	33.8	33.6	32.2			27.6	38.6	35.7	28.2
Inventory	26.4	25.0	23.4			23.8	23.5	22.7	23.3
All Other Current	2.4	2.0	3.3			4.6	4.2	4.1	2.7
Total Current	70.0	68.6	67.3			82.0	74.9	70.3	58.6
Fixed Assets (net)	21.6	22.7	24.3			13.8	15.6	20.7	32.6
Intangibles (net)	2.5	3.0	3.7			2.6	3.6	4.4	3.4
All Other Non-Current	5.9	5.7	4.7			1.6	5.9	4.6	5.4
Total	100.0	100.0	100.0			100.0	100.0	100.0	100.0
LIABILITIES									
Notes Payable-Short Term	11.1	11.0	14.2			7.5	11.0	12.0	13.5
Cur. Mat.-L.T.D.	3.5	3.1	2.6			2.3	1.5	3.5	2.6
Trade Payables	18.2	17.9	15.9			11.9	22.1	17.1	12.1
Income Taxes Payable	.3	.2	.2			.2	.4	.1	.2
All Other Current	11.3	11.8	10.7			5.2	10.4	13.5	11.7
Total Current	44.4	44.1	43.6			27.1	45.4	46.2	40.2
Long-Term Debt	14.4	14.5	15.5			19.0	10.2	13.2	16.1
Deferred Taxes	.5	.5	.4			.0	.2	.5	.7
All Other Non-Current	6.3	5.6	4.7			1.5	6.1	4.6	4.3
Net Worth	34.3	35.3	35.7			52.4	38.2	35.6	38.6
Total Liabilities & Net Worth	100.0	100.0	100.0			100.0	100.0	100.0	100.0
INCOME DATA									
Net Sales	100.0	100.0	100.0			100.0	100.0	100.0	100.0
Gross Profit	29.1	28.7	29.1			32.9	31.3	26.1	27.6
Operating Expenses	26.2	24.4	25.1			25.9	27.2	23.0	22.6
Operating Profit	3.0	4.4	4.0			7.0	4.1	3.1	5.0
All Other Expenses (net)	.6	.6	.7			-.3	.6	.8	.9
Profit Before Taxes	2.3	3.8	3.3			7.3	3.5	2.3	4.1
RATIOS									
Current	2.6	2.6	2.6			18.8	2.5	2.5	2.2
	1.7	1.6	1.6			2.7	1.5	1.5	1.5
	1.2	1.2	1.2			1.7	1.2	1.2	1.0
Quick	1.4	1.7	1.5			10.9	1.8	1.4	1.3
	1.0	1.0	.9			1.5	1.0	1.0	.8
	.6	.6	.6			.8	.6	.6	.5
Sales/Receivables	30 12.0	31 11.7	27 13.4			16 22.8	34 10.7	25 14.5	27 13.4
	46 7.9	44 8.2	42 8.7			33 11.1	54 6.8	45 8.2	35 10.5
	63 5.8	69 5.3	63 5.8			57 6.4	72 5.0	68 5.4	55 6.7
Cost of Sales/Inventory	33 11.1	32 11.3	29 12.4			34 10.8	23 16.2	22 16.5	32 11.4
	50 7.2	46 7.9	47 7.7			48 7.6	58 6.3	42 8.7	47 7.7
	80 4.6	72 5.1	68 5.4			79 4.6	83 4.4	59 6.2	68 5.4
Cost of Sales/Payables	18 20.3	17 21.9	16 23.5			10 38.0	24 15.5	15 24.0	16 22.2
	29 12.5	29 12.6	25 14.9			18 20.3	42 8.7	25 14.6	22 16.5
	44 8.2	45 8.0	44 8.3			31 11.7	56 6.5	39 9.4	33 11.0
Sales/Working Capital	5.6	5.9	5.7			2.8	5.1	5.8	6.2
	9.8	11.1	10.8			7.6	10.6	12.0	15.9
	27.1	23.4	34.9			10.8	27.8	47.7	87.3
EBIT/Interest	12.5	13.3	9.3				16.1	7.3	10.9
	(128) 3.4	(147) 4.2	(140) 3.5				(31) 4.1	(37) 2.6	(53) 3.5
	1.1	1.4	1.4				1.7	1.1	1.9
Net Profit + Depr., Dep., Amort./Cur. Mat. L/T/D	4.2	8.9	4.6					2.7	22.8
	(51) 2.1	(42) 3.7	(44) 2.5					(13) 1.3	(22) 3.5
	.8	1.7	.9					-.3	1.7
Fixed/Worth	.3	.3	.2			.0	.2	.3	.5
	.6	.7	.7			.3	.4	.6	.9
	1.6	2.2	1.6			.9	1.5	1.3	1.7
Debt/Worth	.8	.8	.8			.1	.7	.9	.9
	1.7	2.2	1.9			1.2	1.9	1.7	1.8
	5.7	6.7	5.4			2.0	6.9	5.2	3.5
% Profit Before Taxes/Tangible Net Worth	37.5	51.8	46.3			53.6	40.3	43.1	53.9
	(120) 15.5	(146) 21.6	(136) 22.0			(10) 22.2	(31) 28.9	(35) 21.7	(52) 21.6
	3.5	7.0	7.0			1.9	8.7	5.7	7.4
% Profit Before Taxes/Total Assets	14.2	14.8	15.8			21.8	17.3	11.7	16.8
	5.7	7.8	7.6			15.3	8.0	5.8	7.7
	.4	1.3	1.2			.7	2.2	.3	1.9
Sales/Net Fixed Assets	28.9	35.0	32.9			110.9	47.1	31.8	13.8
	13.1	12.9	13.2			46.3	16.9	19.3	7.4
	8.1	6.1	5.9			7.9	10.9	8.3	4.8
Sales/Total Assets	3.1	3.2	3.2			4.1	3.2	3.6	2.9
	2.5	2.5	2.6			2.6	2.7	2.7	2.5
	1.9	1.9	1.9			1.9	2.0	1.8	1.9
% Depr., Dep., Amort./Sales	1.0	.9	.8				.7	.7	1.0
	(128) 1.6	(139) 1.7	(134) 1.5				(36) 1.4	(50) 1.1	1.7
	2.4	2.5	2.4				2.2	2.1	2.4
% Officers', Directors' Owners' Comp/Sales	1.5	1.4	1.9				2.0	1.3	
	(56) 2.5	(65) 2.6	(51) 2.7				(15) 2.7	(11) 2.2	
	5.1	5.0	5.4				5.2	3.5	
Net Sales ($)	4010116M	5416703M	6021998M	2395M	18842M	46057M	243897M	689355M	5021452M
Total Assets ($)	1887181M	2495416M	2727447M	901M	7842M	21164M	99298M	290276M	2307966M

M = $ thousand   MM = $ million
See Pages 11 through 21 for Explanation of Ratios and Data

Current Data Sorted by Assets   Comparative Historical Data

	0-500M	500M-2MM	2-10MM	10-50MM	50-100MM	100-250MM		4/1/02-3/31/03 ALL	4/1/03-3/31/04 ALL
Type of Statement									
Unqualified	2	1	15	26	4	1		46	41
Reviewed	2	21	60	13				87	96
Compiled	7	28	29	3	1	1		73	77
Tax Returns	5	19	5	5				20	21
Other	3	20	46	19	2	2		75	86
		64 (4/1-9/30/06)		271 (10/1/06-3/31/07)					
NUMBER OF STATEMENTS	19	89	155	61	7	4		301	321
	%	%	%	%	%	%		%	%
ASSETS									
Cash & Equivalents	10.4	9.8	7.0	7.3				8.3	7.6
Trade Receivables (net)	33.5	35.9	32.0	26.0				28.2	32.1
Inventory	16.3	16.6	20.0	28.3				18.3	19.2
All Other Current	2.3	1.6	2.7	2.9				3.5	3.1
Total Current	62.6	63.9	61.7	64.5				58.4	62.0
Fixed Assets (net)	31.0	29.3	28.6	27.0				33.2	30.9
Intangibles (net)	3.2	1.8	2.9	4.7				3.1	2.6
All Other Non-Current	3.0	5.0	6.8	3.8				5.3	4.5
Total	100.0	100.0	100.0	100.0				100.0	100.0
LIABILITIES									
Notes Payable-Short Term	6.9	9.7	10.8	13.5				10.5	11.4
Cur. Mat.-L.T.D.	5.1	4.4	4.2	3.1				5.4	4.3
Trade Payables	20.6	15.5	14.4	12.6				13.3	15.9
Income Taxes Payable	.4	.2	.3	.1				.3	.3
All Other Current	27.5	14.7	8.3	9.3				8.9	9.5
Total Current	60.5	44.5	38.0	38.6				38.5	41.5
Long-Term Debt	30.8	16.0	18.0	13.7				19.6	18.3
Deferred Taxes	.7	.5	.5	.4				.4	.5
All Other Non-Current	22.1	3.8	3.8	3.9				4.7	6.4
Net Worth	-14.1	35.2	39.7	43.4				36.7	33.3
Total Liabilities & Net Worth	100.0	100.0	100.0	100.0				100.0	100.0
INCOME DATA									
Net Sales	100.0	100.0	100.0	100.0				100.0	100.0
Gross Profit	38.7	32.9	25.4	24.0				28.2	27.4
Operating Expenses	30.8	28.6	19.6	15.5				26.2	25.3
Operating Profit	7.9	4.3	5.9	8.5				1.9	2.1
All Other Expenses (net)	.7	.7	.9	.9				1.3	1.1
Profit Before Taxes	7.2	3.6	5.0	7.6				.7	1.0
RATIOS									
Current	1.8	2.8	2.4	3.1				2.5	2.6
	1.4	1.7	1.6	1.7				1.6	1.6
	.8	1.1	1.2	1.2				1.1	1.2
Quick	1.2	2.1	1.6	1.5				1.7	1.7
	.9	1.2	1.0	.9				.9 (320)	1.0
	.4	.7	.7	.5				.6	.6
Sales/Receivables	13 27.4	31 11.8	34 10.6	30 12.2				33 11.0	36 10.1
	26 14.3	44 8.4	44 8.3	44 8.3				46 7.9	50 7.3
	42 8.8	57 6.4	60 6.1	61 6.0				60 6.0	68 5.3
Cost of Sales/Inventory	0 UND	9 42.9	14 26.3	40 9.2				20 18.0	18 19.7
	15 25.0	23 15.9	36 10.1	55 6.6				41 8.8	41 8.9
	35 10.6	42 8.6	62 5.9	108 3.4				68 5.4	76 4.8
Cost of Sales/Payables	11 33.1	15 25.0	16 23.4	17 21.0				15 24.7	20 18.7
	25 14.5	24 15.0	27 13.8	29 12.6				26 13.8	29 12.5
	42 8.8	37 9.7	38 9.6	35 10.3				41 9.0	47 7.8
Sales/Working Capital	9.3	6.3	6.6	4.3				5.8	5.4
	29.9	11.1	11.4	8.8				10.6	10.1
	-29.8	51.5	21.1	20.4				59.5	30.2
EBIT/Interest	5.8	13.9	11.5	17.3				6.3	7.0
	(13) 2.0	(85) 4.2	(141) 4.9	(59) 5.5				(269) 1.8	(289) 2.2
	1.1	1.3	2.1	2.3				-1.0	-.9
Net Profit + Depr., Dep., Amort./Cur. Mat. L/T/D		3.3	6.3	21.3				3.6	6.1
	(17) 1.9	(44) 3.2	(25) 5.5					(80) 1.4	(94) 2.4
	1.0	1.6	1.8					.1	.8
Fixed/Worth	.4	.3	.3	.4				.4	.4
	57.5	.6	.7	.8				.9	.9
	-1.0	1.5	1.7	1.9				2.5	2.2
Debt/Worth	1.0	.7	.7	.6				.7	.7
	UND	1.6	1.8	1.6				1.9	1.8
	-3.7	4.2	4.2	3.9				5.6	5.3
% Profit Before Taxes/Tangible Net Worth	215.5	49.9	50.1	43.7				29.1	38.6
	(11) 159.7	(82) 26.4	(142) 26.7	(56) 27.0				(266) 7.4	(281) 11.4
	5.6	5.2	10.9	13.6				-11.6	-5.4
% Profit Before Taxes/Total Assets	36.2	21.0	21.5	17.4				11.9	11.2
	7.1	11.5	9.0	9.9				2.6	3.4
	1.6	.7	2.7	4.7				-5.2	-4.3
Sales/Net Fixed Assets	33.3	25.1	16.4	14.5				14.6	16.9
	13.4	11.4	9.9	8.5				6.7	7.5
	8.4	6.4	5.6	5.1				3.9	4.2
Sales/Total Assets	6.2	3.6	2.9	2.5				2.7	2.9
	4.3	2.8	2.4	2.1				2.1	2.2
	2.7	2.2	1.9	1.6				1.6	1.5
% Depr., Dep., Amort./Sales	.9	1.0	1.1	1.3				1.9	1.6
	(13) 2.3	(78) 2.7	(152) 2.1	(59) 2.0				(288) 3.2	(290) 2.9
	3.1	4.3	3.8	3.3				5.3	4.6
% Officers', Directors' Owners' Comp/Sales	5.7	2.8	2.0	1.2				2.3	2.1
	(11) 7.5	(51) 3.7	(78) 3.8	(11) 2.2				(143) 4.6	(129) 4.4
	12.4	7.7	7.2	3.5				7.5	6.9
Net Sales ($)	28316M	310924M	1667905M	2379430M	668339M	2001498M		3379011M	4809074M
Total Assets ($)	4979M	104149M	710297M	1202683M	479715M	725047M		1969078M	2423760M

M = $ thousand   MM = $ million
See Pages 11 through 21 for Explanation of Ratios and Data

Comparative Historical Data | Current Data Sorted by Sales

41 / 100 / 66 / 43 / 92	46 / 91 / 54 / 36 / 105	49 / 96 / 69 / 29 / 92	Type of Statement						
4/1/04-3/31/05 ALL	4/1/05-3/31/06 ALL	4/1/06-3/31/07 ALL							

Type of Statement

Hist 4/1/04-3/31/05	Hist 4/1/05-3/31/06	Hist 4/1/06-3/31/07	Type of Statement	0-1MM	1-3MM	3-5MM	5-10MM	10-25MM	25MM & OVER
41	46	49	Unqualified	2	1		9	11	26
100	91	96	Reviewed		10	13	25	36	12
66	54	69	Compiled	1	18	15	16	15	4
43	36	29	Tax Returns	4	8	8	8	1	
92	105	92	Other	3	11	13	22	25	18
					64 (4/1-9/30/06)		271 (10/1/06-3/31/07)		
342	332	335	NUMBER OF STATEMENTS	10	48	49	80	88	60
%	%	%	**ASSETS**	%	%	%	%	%	%
8.0	8.2	8.0	Cash & Equivalents	5.2	9.7	8.0	9.3	7.2	6.5
32.1	31.1	31.7	Trade Receivables (net)	41.5	30.5	31.7	32.8	33.1	27.4
20.0	20.8	20.6	Inventory	8.1	15.5	16.1	21.2	21.3	28.7
3.0	2.7	2.4	All Other Current	1.6	1.8	2.6	2.2	2.3	3.3
63.1	62.9	62.7	Total Current	56.4	57.6	58.3	65.5	63.9	65.9
29.5	29.5	28.7	Fixed Assets (net)	32.1	34.2	33.0	25.0	28.8	24.9
2.6	2.3	3.2	Intangibles (net)	7.2	2.6	2.9	1.7	3.6	4.7
4.8	5.3	5.4	All Other Non-Current	3.8	5.6	5.8	7.9	3.7	4.5
100.0	100.0	100.0	Total	100.0	100.0	100.0	100.0	100.0	100.0
			LIABILITIES						
12.1	11.0	10.6	Notes Payable-Short Term	5.0	10.9	9.6	10.4	10.7	12.5
5.4	5.2	4.1	Cur. Mat.-L.T.D.	3.4	5.0	5.3	3.8	4.1	2.6
15.7	15.5	14.6	Trade Payables	15.8	12.9	16.2	16.1	12.9	14.6
.2	.4	.3	Income Taxes Payable	.0	.1	.4	.2	.4	.1
8.9	10.1	11.3	All Other Current	13.9	8.0	8.5	18.1	9.0	10.2
42.3	42.2	40.8	Total Current	38.1	37.0	40.0	48.7	37.1	40.0
18.1	17.2	17.8	Long-Term Debt	53.3	17.5	23.0	14.9	15.6	14.9
.5	.5	.5	Deferred Taxes	.0	.8	.4	.3	.7	.5
5.8	5.9	4.9	All Other Non-Current	4.0	6.6	7.7	3.7	4.4	3.9
33.4	34.3	36.0	Net Worth	4.5	38.2	28.9	32.4	42.2	40.8
100.0	100.0	100.0	Total Liabilties & Net Worth	100.0	100.0	100.0	100.0	100.0	100.0
			INCOME DATA						
100.0	100.0	100.0	Net Sales	100.0	100.0	100.0	100.0	100.0	100.0
28.9	28.5	28.0	Gross Profit	35.7	37.3	32.4	25.6	24.4	24.1
24.0	23.5	21.9	Operating Expenses	30.5	32.6	26.2	20.5	17.6	16.7
4.9	5.0	6.1	Operating Profit	5.2	4.7	6.2	5.1	6.8	7.3
.9	.9	.9	All Other Expenses (net)	1.8	.9	1.1	.6	.8	.9
4.1	4.1	5.2	Profit Before Taxes	3.4	3.8	5.1	4.5	6.0	6.4
			RATIOS						
2.4 / 1.5 / 1.1	2.6 / 1.6 / 1.2	2.6 / 1.6 / 1.2	Current	3.8 / 1.6 / 1.0	2.7 / 1.6 / 1.1	2.8 / 1.5 / 1.0	2.4 / 1.6 / 1.1	2.7 / 1.7 / 1.3	2.7 / 1.6 / 1.2
1.6 / .9 / .6	1.6 / 1.0 / .6	1.7 / 1.0 / .7	Quick	3.3 / 1.3 / .7	1.7 / 1.1 / .7	1.8 / 1.1 / .6	1.7 / 1.0 / .7	1.8 / 1.1 / .7	1.4 / .8 / .5
35 10.5 / 49 7.5 / 63 5.8	31 11.7 / 44 8.2 / 59 6.2	31 11.7 / 43 8.4 / 57 6.4	Sales/Receivables	29 12.4 / 44 8.4 / 119 3.1	26 14.1 / 43 8.4 / 53 6.9	28 12.9 / 41 8.9 / 55 6.6	33 11.1 / 45 8.2 / 59 6.2	33 11.0 / 43 8.5 / 62 5.9	33 11.1 / 44 8.3 / 52 7.0
18 20.3 / 38 9.7 / 66 5.5	17 20.9 / 40 9.1 / 68 5.4	14 26.3 / 37 9.8 / 68 5.4	Cost of Sales/Inventory	0 UND / 15 24.2 / 37 9.8	11 32.9 / 23 15.9 / 39 9.4	8 45.6 / 22 16.3 / 48 7.6	14 25.7 / 39 9.4 / 61 5.9	16 23.0 / 39 9.3 / 63 5.8	40 9.2 / 61 5.9 / 108 3.4
18 19.8 / 33 11.2 / 46 7.9	18 19.9 / 29 12.7 / 42 8.7	16 22.4 / 26 13.8 / 37 9.9	Cost of Sales/Payables	19 19.2 / 34 10.8 / 53 6.9	14 25.8 / 24 15.5 / 35 10.6	19 19.2 / 27 13.3 / 41 8.8	17 22.0 / 28 12.9 / 39 9.5	12 29.7 / 21 17.4 / 35 10.5	21 17.2 / 29 12.4 / 38 9.7
6.2 / 11.0 / 64.5	6.1 / 10.5 / 30.5	6.3 / 11.1 / 29.2	Sales/Working Capital	3.1 / 21.3 / UND	6.4 / 13.7 / 103.8	6.6 / 12.7 / 147.1	6.6 / 10.6 / 51.3	6.3 / 10.1 / 19.3	5.3 / 9.2 / 19.4
10.2 / (309) 3.7 / 1.5	12.1 / (304) 4.0 / 1.7	12.8 / (308) 4.6 / 1.8	EBIT/Interest		7.4 / (44) 2.9 / .4	11.2 / (46) 3.6 / 1.3	12.3 / (75) 4.9 / 2.5	18.5 / (79) 5.4 / 2.1	16.3 / (57) 5.4 / 2.6
5.8 / (86) 2.5 / 1.3	8.4 / (83) 3.3 / 1.5	6.5 / (94) 3.0 / 1.6	Net Profit + Depr., Dep., Amort./Cur. Mat. L/T/D			2.4 / (12) 1.9 / .9	8.0 / (20) 4.1 / 2.4	4.4 / (28) 2.1 / 1.4	14.3 / (26) 5.0 / 2.3
.3 / .9 / 2.4	.3 / .8 / 2.3	.3 / .7 / 2.0	Fixed/Worth	.4 / UND / -.8	.3 / .9 / 2.9	.4 / .8 / 3.9	.3 / .6 / 1.3	.3 / .8 / 2.0	.4 / .7 / 1.4
.9 / 2.1 / 5.5	.8 / 1.8 / 5.2	.7 / 1.8 / 4.4	Debt/Worth	.9 / UND / -9.1	.5 / 1.6 / 5.2	.8 / 2.2 / 6.3	.8 / 1.8 / 4.3	.6 / 1.7 / 3.7	.7 / 1.7 / 3.9
55.5 / (301) 22.7 / 5.2	55.0 / (296) 25.9 / 8.0	50.4 / (299) 27.0 / 10.0	% Profit Before Taxes/Tangible Net Worth		56.4 / (41) 26.8 / .7	49.9 / (43) 28.0 / 7.5	47.6 / (72) 26.2 / 10.8	51.5 / (82) 28.7 / 13.1	53.1 / (54) 27.0 / 12.5
15.5 / 6.8 / 1.2	16.4 / 8.3 / 2.1	21.4 / 9.1 / 2.6	% Profit Before Taxes/Total Assets	31.8 / 5.7 / -1.5	19.4 / 5.1 / -1.9	25.1 / 9.6 / 1.5	19.5 / 9.6 / 3.1	22.5 / 10.6 / 3.8	17.9 / 9.7 / 4.4
18.0 / 8.6 / 5.0	21.6 / 9.4 / 5.2	18.6 / 10.0 / 5.8	Sales/Net Fixed Assets	13.3 / 9.6 / 4.1	19.7 / 9.0 / 4.5	23.4 / 7.6 / 4.2	19.0 / 11.8 / 7.3	18.8 / 9.5 / 5.5	16.3 / 9.7 / 6.3
3.0 / 2.3 / 1.7	3.1 / 2.4 / 1.8	3.1 / 2.5 / 1.9	Sales/Total Assets	4.6 / 2.0 / 1.3	3.1 / 2.7 / 2.1	3.4 / 2.6 / 1.8	3.1 / 2.6 / 2.1	3.0 / 2.5 / 1.9	2.8 / 2.2 / 1.7
1.3 / (308) 2.6 / 4.1	1.3 / (298) 2.4 / 3.8	1.2 / (313) 2.2 / 3.8	% Depr., Dep., Amort./Sales		.8 / (44) 2.6 / 5.9	1.1 / (44) 3.1 / 4.5	1.2 / (75) 2.1 / 3.6	1.3 / (86) 2.2 / 3.8	1.1 / (58) 1.8 / 2.4
2.4 / (143) 3.8 / 6.9	2.3 / (139) 4.2 / 7.6	2.2 / (152) 3.7 / 7.4	% Officers', Directors' Owners' Comp/Sales		3.4 / (29) 6.8 / 10.3	2.3 / (25) 3.6 / 5.7	2.0 / (43) 4.2 / 7.1	1.5 / (41) 2.8 / 6.6	
5459632M	6484462M	7056412M	Net Sales ($)	4853M	97027M	187506M	564752M	1343794M	4858480M
2900637M	2908281M	3226870M	Total Assets ($)	2180M	43469M	86206M	239594M	612993M	2242428M

Current Data Sorted by Assets   Comparative Historical Data

0-500M	500M-2MM	2-10MM	10-50MM	50-100MM	100-250MM	Type of Statement	4/1/02-3/31/03 ALL	4/1/03-3/31/04 ALL
	7	7	2		1	Unqualified	9	13
2	4	16	2		2	Reviewed	26	35
5	5	4	2			Compiled	10	17
2		4	1			Tax Returns	10	9
	8	12	2			Other	14	23
	9 (4/1-9/30/06)		79 (10/1/06-3/31/07)					
9	24	43	9		3	NUMBER OF STATEMENTS	69	97
%	%	%	%	%	%	**ASSETS**	%	%
	7.1	8.5				Cash & Equivalents	7.0	8.2
	47.7	43.0				Trade Receivables (net)	34.9	38.6
	23.5	15.6				Inventory	19.1	15.3
	1.8	8.4				All Other Current	5.4	6.1
	80.1	75.5				Total Current	66.4	68.2
	12.2	16.9		D		Fixed Assets (net)	25.4	22.7
	4.2	2.7		A		Intangibles (net)	3.0	2.7
	3.5	5.0		T		All Other Non-Current	5.2	6.5
	100.0	100.0		A		Total	100.0	100.0
				N		**LIABILITIES**		
	16.1	9.3		O		Notes Payable-Short Term	11.9	10.6
	1.3	2.4		T		Cur. Mat.-L.T.D.	4.5	2.9
	15.0	15.8				Trade Payables	15.8	19.2
	.9	.9		A		Income Taxes Payable	.9	.6
	14.7	19.5		V		All Other Current	10.6	11.0
	48.1	47.9		A		Total Current	43.7	44.3
	7.9	9.3		I		Long-Term Debt	16.6	13.3
	.3	.3		L		Deferred Taxes	.5	.6
	12.3	5.3		A		All Other Non-Current	5.0	4.8
	31.5	37.2		B		Net Worth	34.2	37.0
	100.0	100.0		L		Total Liabilities & Net Worth	100.0	100.0
				E		**INCOME DATA**		
	100.0	100.0				Net Sales	100.0	100.0
	32.8	30.7				Gross Profit	34.7	32.0
	28.5	23.4				Operating Expenses	31.8	29.2
	4.3	7.3				Operating Profit	2.9	2.9
	.7	.4				All Other Expenses (net)	.9	.9
	3.6	6.9				Profit Before Taxes	2.0	2.0
						RATIOS		
	2.7	2.4				Current	2.2	2.3
	1.6	1.5					1.6	1.6
	1.3	1.2					1.1	1.2
	1.6	1.5				Quick	1.5	1.8
	1.2	1.0					.9	1.1
	.9	.8					.6	.6
	34 10.7	46 7.9				Sales/Receivables	34 10.7	38 9.6
	66 5.5	64 5.7					53 6.8	53 6.9
	79 4.6	90 4.1					68 5.3	78 4.7
	0 768.4	5 77.8				Cost of Sales/Inventory	2 151.6	2 221.1
	41 8.9	21 17.6					33 11.0	25 14.4
	80 4.6	69 5.3					80 4.6	56 6.5
	14 26.6	21 17.5				Cost of Sales/Payables	14 26.0	20 18.2
	33 11.1	29 12.8					32 11.3	41 8.9
	39 9.4	48 7.6					48 7.6	60 6.1
	5.1	5.1				Sales/Working Capital	6.3	5.9
	8.5	7.1					9.5	9.6
	17.0	18.9					34.2	23.5
	12.6	14.6				EBIT/Interest	11.1	10.6
	(21) 5.0	(38) 6.1					(67) 2.5	(84) 2.7
	1.1	2.9					1.2	-.6
		6.2				Net Profit + Depr., Dep., Amort./Cur. Mat. L/T/D	5.3	5.5
		(13) 2.7					(21) 3.3	(19) 1.3
		1.3					1.4	-1.0
	.1	.2				Fixed/Worth	.3	.3
	.4	.4					.7	.5
	.6	1.1					2.1	1.6
	.7	.7				Debt/Worth	.8	.8
	2.4	1.7					1.9	1.8
	6.1	4.4					4.8	4.6
	70.1	73.3				% Profit Before Taxes/Tangible Net Worth	42.3	28.0
	(20) 31.9	(41) 35.9					(59) 10.5	(86) 14.6
	10.2	16.2					2.8	-3.2
	22.8	24.3				% Profit Before Taxes/Total Assets	11.3	13.8
	9.0	13.8					3.6	3.9
	.5	3.3					.6	-1.8
	45.6	34.2				Sales/Net Fixed Assets	29.3	24.6
	32.5	20.0					11.7	14.8
	17.0	8.9					4.9	7.4
	3.5	2.6				Sales/Total Assets	3.2	3.1
	2.7	2.3					2.3	2.5
	2.2	1.8					1.8	1.8
	.6	.7				% Depr., Dep., Amort./Sales	1.0	1.1
	(16) 1.1	(42) 1.1					(62) 2.0	(86) 2.2
	1.4	1.7					3.0	3.1
	3.7	2.0				% Officers', Directors' Owners' Comp/Sales	3.6	2.3
	(11) 6.4	(18) 2.6					(40) 5.8	(45) 4.8
	10.2	4.0					10.4	8.8
9438M	84938M	552569M	296634M		738260M	Net Sales ($)	1587389M	1524881M
2100M	29642M	248391M	154876M		403820M	Total Assets ($)	680188M	796216M

M = $ thousand   MM = $ million

See Pages 11 through 21 for Explanation of Ratios and Data

Comparative Historical Data | Current Data Sorted by Sales

Type of Statement

			Type of Statement	0-1MM	1-3MM	3-5MM	5-10MM	10-25MM	25MM & OVER
9	13	10	Unqualified		2	4	3	4	3
29	20	25	Reviewed				5	13	1
12	9	12	Compiled	3	3	4	2	2	1
17	12	15	Tax Returns		5	1	3	2	1
24	22	26	Other	1	4	6	5	7	3
4/1/04-3/31/05 ALL	4/1/05-3/31/06 ALL	4/1/06-3/31/07 ALL			9 (4/1-9/30/06)			79 (10/1/06-3/31/07)	
91	76	88	NUMBER OF STATEMENTS	4	14	15	18	28	9

Data (%)

04-05	05-06	06-07	Item	0-1MM	1-3MM	3-5MM	5-10MM	10-25MM	25MM&OVER
%	%	%	**ASSETS**	%	%	%	%	%	%
6.1	7.7	8.1	Cash & Equivalents		6.1	7.1	14.1	5.8	
37.1	34.6	40.6	Trade Receivables (net)		47.1	39.2	37.8	44.9	
21.3	21.4	19.0	Inventory		23.6	23.0	16.8	15.5	
4.2	3.2	4.9	All Other Current		.9	.7	7.3	9.3	
68.7	66.8	72.6	Total Current		77.6	70.0	76.0	75.5	
21.2	23.3	17.1	Fixed Assets (net)		11.1	18.5	12.4	17.3	
3.1	3.3	4.6	Intangibles (net)		4.1	8.0	4.5	1.9	
7.0	6.6	5.6	All Other Non-Current		7.1	3.5	7.1	5.2	
100.0	100.0	100.0	Total		100.0	100.0	100.0	100.0	
			LIABILITIES						
10.4	10.7	10.6	Notes Payable-Short Term		22.2	8.9	8.7	9.6	
5.9	3.6	2.7	Cur. Mat.-L.T.D.		1.2	1.6	1.4	3.9	
17.7	17.7	15.1	Trade Payables		14.8	15.6	12.4	16.6	
.5	.9	.8	Income Taxes Payable		.0	.1	2.7	.4	
14.1	12.2	16.4	All Other Current		11.9	11.3	21.3	20.1	
48.7	45.1	45.6	Total Current		50.2	37.6	46.5	50.6	
14.5	16.7	12.2	Long-Term Debt		15.3	10.1	7.1	7.9	
.5	.5	.3	Deferred Taxes		.1	.4	.6	.1	
6.5	7.8	8.7	All Other Non-Current		17.6	12.4	7.8	3.2	
29.8	29.8	33.2	Net Worth		16.8	39.6	38.1	38.1	
100.0	100.0	100.0	Total Liabilties & Net Worth		100.0	100.0	100.0	100.0	
			INCOME DATA						
100.0	100.0	100.0	Net Sales		100.0	100.0	100.0	100.0	
31.2	32.6	33.3	Gross Profit		37.5	31.7	31.9	29.4	
27.5	28.7	27.1	Operating Expenses		32.3	25.7	28.4	21.6	
3.7	3.9	6.2	Operating Profit		5.2	6.1	3.4	7.8	
.2	.7	.6	All Other Expenses (net)		1.0	1.4	-.3	.5	
3.5	3.2	5.6	Profit Before Taxes		4.2	4.6	3.8	7.3	
			RATIOS						
2.1	2.2	2.4	Current		3.1	2.8	2.4	2.1	
1.5	1.5	1.6			2.2	1.6	1.7	1.5	
1.2	1.2	1.2			1.2	1.4	1.2	1.2	
1.5	1.6	1.6	Quick		1.9	1.9	1.7	1.4	
.8	1.0	1.1			1.2	1.2	1.2	.9	
.7	.6	.8			.7	.7	.8	.8	
36 10.1	31 11.7	37 9.8	Sales/Receivables		33 11.2	36 10.3	45 8.1	46 7.9	
52 7.0	52 7.0	58 6.3			56 6.5	53 6.8	62 5.9	65 5.6	
72 5.0	74 5.0	81 4.5			72 5.0	76 4.8	80 4.6	100 3.7	
12 30.8	9 39.2	5 76.8	Cost of Sales/Inventory		0 UND	21 17.6	1 362.1	5 72.7	
42 8.7	47 7.8	37 9.9			35 10.3	51 7.2	48 7.6	23 15.9	
69 5.3	83 4.4	76 4.8			84 4.3	81 4.5	85 4.3	62 5.8	
19 18.9	21 17.0	19 19.4	Cost of Sales/Payables		8 46.8	31 11.7	17 21.9	20 17.9	
35 10.5	31 11.9	31 11.6			27 13.7	35 10.5	26 14.1	28 13.1	
51 7.2	47 7.7	48 7.6			41 8.8	48 7.6	48 7.6	49 7.4	
6.4	5.8	5.1	Sales/Working Capital		5.2	4.8	4.6	5.7	
10.5	10.7	8.3			9.1	8.1	6.5	9.3	
22.7	38.7	21.6			39.5	13.2	15.3	23.0	
12.2	13.2	11.8	EBIT/Interest		6.2	18.5	12.2	21.5	
(84) 5.3	(72) 5.9	(77) 5.3		(12)	2.5	(14) 5.0	(15) 4.8	(26) 8.8	
1.7	1.4	1.6			-1.6	.5	1.3	4.8	
11.0	22.1	7.8	Net Profit + Depr., Dep., Amort./Cur. Mat. L/T/D						
(24) 3.6	(22) 3.0	(20) 3.0							
1.8	1.2	1.6							
.3	.3	.2	Fixed/Worth		.1	.3	.1	.2	
.6	.7	.5			.2	.4	.3	.4	
1.3	1.5	1.4			1.7	26.0	.9	.8	
1.1	.9	.9	Debt/Worth		1.6	.6	.9	.7	
2.1	2.2	2.4			3.1	1.6	1.3	1.7	
3.9	6.0	5.4			NM	70.4	4.8	3.7	
46.7	51.4	78.0	% Profit Before Taxes/Tangible Net Worth		80.5	70.8	69.8	76.0	
(81) 24.3	(64) 22.8	(78) 36.1		(11) 58.3		(12) 21.6	(16) 37.6	(27) 40.9	
4.8	7.0	13.9			9.1	2.7	2.5	25.6	
14.1	18.3	23.7	% Profit Before Taxes/Total Assets		47.4	14.3	26.0	24.7	
6.6	8.5	11.4			5.0	11.5	11.5	14.1	
1.5	1.7	2.7			-1.6	-.5	2.2	10.2	
27.6	30.3	37.3	Sales/Net Fixed Assets		250.6	39.5	36.1	33.6	
14.8	12.8	19.3			51.0	20.5	17.9	23.6	
7.4	7.2	8.9			19.4	8.9	14.2	8.2	
3.3	3.2	3.0	Sales/Total Assets		4.6	3.4	2.6	2.8	
2.4	2.6	2.4			2.8	2.5	2.3	2.3	
2.0	1.9	2.0			2.1	2.2	1.3	1.9	
.8	.9	.7	% Depr., Dep., Amort./Sales		.7		.7	.6	
(78) 1.7	(67) 1.7	(72) 1.1			(11) 1.3		1.2	(27) 1.0	
2.6	2.5	1.8			2.1		2.2	1.5	
2.3	2.6	2.3	% Officers', Directors' Owners' Comp/Sales					2.0	
(47) 5.0	(33) 5.1	(38) 4.4					(13) 3.2		
8.8	9.4	7.2						4.1	

Net Sales / Total Assets ($)

04-05	05-06	06-07		0-1MM	1-3MM	3-5MM	5-10MM	10-25MM	25MM&OVER
2401663M	1729355M	1681839M	Net Sales ($)	1852M	25727M	58652M	129676M	443485M	1022447M
992225M	833633M	838829M	Total Assets ($)	623M	8573M	44243M	80209M	199213M	505968M

M = $ thousand   MM = $ million
See Pages 11 through 21 for Explanation of Ratios and Data

Current Data Sorted by Assets   Comparative Historical Data

Type of Statement	0-500M	500M-2MM	2-10MM	10-50MM	50-100MM	100-250MM	4/1/02-3/31/03 ALL	4/1/03-3/31/04 ALL
Unqualified			3	8	2		3	3
Reviewed	1	3	5	1			7	12
Compiled		2	1	1			4	3
Tax Returns	2	3	4				3	5
Other		7	4	4	1	2	4	8
		10 (4/1-9/30/06)		44 (10/1/06-3/31/07)				
NUMBER OF STATEMENTS	3	15	17	14	3	2	21	31
	%	%	%	%	%	%	%	%
ASSETS								
Cash & Equivalents		6.1	3.8	8.8			8.2	6.8
Trade Receivables (net)		42.0	24.4	23.6			24.8	28.1
Inventory		25.0	26.4	29.3			21.5	24.4
All Other Current		4.6	2.2	2.8			2.1	5.0
Total Current		77.7	56.8	64.5			56.7	64.2
Fixed Assets (net)		16.7	30.2	24.7			36.2	29.2
Intangibles (net)		1.7	7.4	8.0			3.9	3.1
All Other Non-Current		3.9	5.6	2.7			3.2	3.5
Total		100.0	100.0	100.0			100.0	100.0
LIABILITIES								
Notes Payable-Short Term		14.9	7.2	3.9			11.0	16.0
Cur. Mat.-L.T.D.		1.2	4.6	2.2			9.0	5.4
Trade Payables		21.6	16.7	14.4			12.6	13.1
Income Taxes Payable		.9	.2	1.4			.1	.5
All Other Current		8.5	9.5	7.8			6.9	5.2
Total Current		47.1	38.2	29.6			39.5	40.1
Long-Term Debt		12.0	26.1	13.0			19.5	17.5
Deferred Taxes		.0	.4	.6			.3	1.1
All Other Non-Current		3.3	5.4	4.6			5.4	1.6
Net Worth		37.6	29.9	52.1			35.3	39.6
Total Liabilties & Net Worth		100.0	100.0	100.0			100.0	100.0
INCOME DATA								
Net Sales		100.0	100.0	100.0			100.0	100.0
Gross Profit		29.4	30.4	24.5			35.2	37.2
Operating Expenses		24.3	25.1	15.3			32.4	31.5
Operating Profit		5.1	5.3	9.2			2.8	5.7
All Other Expenses (net)		.4	1.6	1.6			1.2	.9
Profit Before Taxes		4.7	3.7	7.6			1.6	4.7
RATIOS								
Current		2.7	3.0	3.0			2.6	2.8
		1.6	1.3	1.9			1.8	1.4
		1.2	.9	1.5			1.0	1.1
Quick		1.8	1.4	1.6			1.4	1.4
		1.1	.6	.9			1.0	.8
		.6	.5	.6			.4	.5
Sales/Receivables	42 8.6	33 11.1	37 10.0				39 9.4	32 11.3
	48 7.6	39 9.4	44 8.3				46 8.0	44 8.3
	58 6.3	52 7.0	54 6.7				62 5.9	52 7.0
Cost of Sales/Inventory	19 18.9	42 8.6	36 10.2				34 10.9	20 17.8
	40 9.2	69 5.3	56 6.5				55 6.6	43 8.4
	70 5.2	98 3.7	132 2.8				92 4.0	77 4.7
Cost of Sales/Payables	26 13.9	21 17.3	17 22.1				20 18.7	12 31.3
	32 11.5	30 12.2	30 12.1				28 12.8	30 12.2
	59 6.2	52 7.0	47 7.8				50 7.3	46 8.0
Sales/Working Capital		5.2	5.5	4.5			5.3	5.6
		9.7	13.6	8.9			9.8	12.0
		27.5	-68.8	13.4			NM	84.8
EBIT/Interest		41.3	6.1	14.9			8.4	9.6
		(14) 5.0	(16) 3.0	(13) 7.6			2.6	(29) 4.5
		2.5	1.1	3.7			.0	2.3
Net Profit + Depr., Dep., Amort./Cur. Mat. L/T/D								
Fixed/Worth		.2	.4	.2			.5	.3
		.3	1.6	.5			1.0	.7
		.8	NM	.9			3.2	2.0
Debt/Worth		.5	1.0	.6			.7	.8
		1.6	4.2	.9			3.0	1.9
		3.3	NM	1.7			8.5	3.4
% Profit Before Taxes/Tangible Net Worth		74.5	51.8	39.1			39.9	44.8
		(13) 27.2	(13) 21.9	(12) 24.7			(19) 13.4	(30) 24.4
		8.2	7.9	12.3			-4.1	12.0
% Profit Before Taxes/Total Assets		23.5	9.7	18.9			12.9	16.7
		7.7	6.3	10.0			7.0	8.5
		2.8	.8	4.6			-2.0	2.6
Sales/Net Fixed Assets		24.3	12.4	18.9			12.2	19.7
		21.2	6.7	7.7			7.0	9.9
		13.0	4.2	4.6			3.1	5.0
Sales/Total Assets		3.5	2.4	2.8			2.9	3.3
		3.1	2.0	2.1			1.7	2.4
		2.4	1.6	1.0			1.3	1.9
% Depr., Dep., Amort./Sales		.9	1.4	1.1			1.6	1.2
		(13) 1.3	(16) 2.9	(12) 1.6			(20) 3.9	(24) 1.6
		2.1	4.6	3.7			6.7	4.0
% Officers', Directors' Owners' Comp/Sales								2.5
							(16)	3.2
								7.1
Net Sales ($)	4578M	65102M	176304M	763693M	387809M	525931M	172643M	544195M
Total Assets ($)	951M	20723M	88170M	400776M	223338M	408368M	94110M	270375M

M = $ thousand   MM = $ million
See Pages 11 through 21 for Explanation of Ratios and Data

Comparative Historical Data | | | Type of Statement | | Current Data Sorted by Sales

						Type of Statement						
4		9		13		Unqualified				3	2	8
9		8		10		Reviewed		2	1	5	1	1
6		9		4		Compiled		1	1	1		1
4		4		9		Tax Returns		1	3	2	2	
12		8		18		Other	1	3		6	3	6
4/1/04-		4/1/05-		4/1/06-				10 (4/1-9/30/06)		44 (10/1/06-3/31/07)		
3/31/05		3/31/06		3/31/07			0-1MM	1-3MM	3-5MM	5-10MM	10-25MM	25MM & OVER
ALL		ALL		ALL								
35		38		54		NUMBER OF STATEMENTS	1	7	5	17	8	16
%		%		%		ASSETS	%	%	%	%	%	%
7.0		5.2		6.3		Cash & Equivalents				7.3		6.9
32.3		35.6		28.5		Trade Receivables (net)				26.6		24.4
27.4		22.6		25.8		Inventory				27.0		23.9
2.5		6.0		2.9		All Other Current				.8		3.2
69.3		69.3		63.6		Total Current				61.8		58.4
18.6		23.2		25.9		Fixed Assets (net)				25.9		31.6
7.6		4.3		6.6		Intangibles (net)				7.4		7.0
4.5		3.2		3.8		All Other Non-Current				5.0		3.1
100.0		100.0		100.0		Total				100.0		100.0
						LIABILITIES						
14.5		9.4		8.1		Notes Payable-Short Term				8.6		5.4
5.6		5.7		3.7		Cur. Mat.-L.T.D.				3.2		2.9
16.1		16.8		16.5		Trade Payables				13.5		14.9
.6		.3		.7		Income Taxes Payable				.4		1.3
8.9		13.3		12.1		All Other Current				9.7		11.2
45.6		45.5		41.1		Total Current				35.5		35.7
15.4		12.1		21.3		Long-Term Debt				26.1		13.6
.4		.8		.6		Deferred Taxes				.4		1.2
7.5		8.0		4.1		All Other Non-Current				5.5		4.3
31.0		33.7		32.9		Net Worth				32.5		45.2
100.0		100.0		100.0		Total Liabilties & Net Worth				100.0		100.0
						INCOME DATA						
100.0		100.0		100.0		Net Sales				100.0		100.0
30.3		26.9		28.1		Gross Profit				30.8		24.2
25.2		21.0		22.4		Operating Expenses				24.7		20.3
5.0		5.9		5.8		Operating Profit				6.1		3.9
1.2		1.2		1.3		All Other Expenses (net)				1.9		1.1
3.8		4.6		4.5		Profit Before Taxes				4.1		2.8
						RATIOS						
2.6		2.5		2.5						3.2		2.1
1.5		1.6		1.6		Current				1.3		1.6
1.0		1.0		1.1						1.1		1.4
1.3		1.5		1.4						1.4		1.4
.8		.8		.8		Quick				.7		.9
.6		.6		.5						.5		.6

35	10.6	38	9.5	34	10.7		Sales/Receivables				34	10.9	34	10.6
48	7.6	48	7.6	45	8.1						44	8.2	41	8.8
63	5.8	58	6.3	56	6.5						54	6.7	55	6.6
32	11.6	18	20.3	31	11.9		Cost of Sales/Inventory				29	12.5	40	9.2
54	6.8	35	10.4	55	6.7						55	6.6	55	6.7
91	4.0	59	6.2	83	4.4						98	3.7	65	5.6
21	17.4	20	17.9	18	19.8		Cost of Sales/Payables				15	24.2	17	21.2
34	10.8	31	12.0	30	12.1						28	13.2	36	10.0
38	9.7	43	8.6	47	7.8						39	9.2	49	7.5
	4.9		6.7		5.8		Sales/Working Capital					6.1		6.7
	11.0		13.8		10.1							10.3		9.4
	582.1		177.7		68.1							70.3		17.6
	14.8		21.8		10.7		EBIT/Interest					3.7		11.3
(32)	4.7	(37)	5.8	(50)	4.5					(16)		2.5		7.2
	1.5		2.4		2.4							.9		4.4
			10.2		7.9		Net Profit + Depr., Dep.,							
		(12)	4.1	(20)	2.0		Amort./Cur. Mat. L/T/D							
			1.2		1.1									
	.2		.3		.3		Fixed/Worth					.3		.5
	.8		.7		.6							1.0		.6
	2.9		2.4		4.2							-9.7		1.1
	.9		.9		.8		Debt/Worth					1.1		.8
	5.3		2.3		1.7							3.1		1.0
	9.7		7.8		9.0							-26.5		2.8
	46.1		45.9		48.1		% Profit Before Taxes/Tangible					33.4		40.7
(28)	25.0	(33)	27.7	(43)	25.5		Net Worth				(12)	12.2	(14)	26.4
	13.0		19.7		12.0							3.9		13.1
	15.7		18.8		17.7		% Profit Before Taxes/Total					10.1		15.4
	7.9		10.8		8.1		Assets					4.2		9.1
	2.7		3.1		3.0							.3		3.7
	45.9		23.7		22.8		Sales/Net Fixed Assets					17.9		16.2
	12.8		11.7		11.4							8.1		7.5
	8.8		7.4		4.8							5.1		4.4
	3.2		3.7		3.1		Sales/Total Assets					3.3		2.8
	2.5		2.9		2.4							2.0		2.1
	1.7		1.8		1.8							1.3		1.7
	.9		.9		1.1		% Depr., Dep., Amort./Sales					1.6		1.1
(28)	1.6	(33)	1.8	(47)	1.7						(15)	3.2	(15)	1.5
	2.7		3.2		3.3							4.8		4.2
	2.3		1.0		2.5		% Officers', Directors'							
(17)	3.7	(14)	3.5	(17)	4.9		Owners' Comp/Sales							
	6.5		5.8		7.9									

	702777M		1581649M		1923417M		Net Sales ($)	511M	15721M	20525M	118014M	131599M	1637047M
	328995M		577753M		1142326M		Total Assets ($)	145M	5452M	6840M	92223M	86703M	950963M

M = $ thousand   MM = $ million
See Pages 11 through 21 for Explanation of Ratios and Data

MANUFACTURING—Hardware Manufacturing NAICS 332510 (SIC 3429, 3499)

Current Data Sorted by Assets | Comparative Historical Data

Type of Statement	0-500M	500M-2MM	2-10MM	10-50MM	50-100MM	100-250MM	4/1/02-3/31/03 ALL	4/1/03-3/31/04 ALL
Unqualified			3	11	2	4	23	25
Reviewed		6	15	6			22	22
Compiled	3	6	8				9	25
Tax Returns	1	7	4				4	6
Other	1	5	10	6	2	1	24	12
		22 (4/1-9/30/06)		79 (10/1/06-3/31/07)				
NUMBER OF STATEMENTS	5	24	40	23	4	5	82	90

ASSETS	%	%	%	%	%	%	%	%
Cash & Equivalents		11.2	5.4	6.3			6.0	8.1
Trade Receivables (net)		24.1	28.3	17.2			21.3	23.2
Inventory		31.7	39.8	30.4			30.3	31.1
All Other Current		1.5	.9	1.5			2.3	2.2
Total Current		68.5	74.4	55.3			59.8	64.6
Fixed Assets (net)		22.4	20.1	20.4			28.1	24.2
Intangibles (net)		.5	2.0	12.5			5.3	5.9
All Other Non-Current		8.6	3.4	11.8			6.8	5.4
Total		100.0	100.0	100.0			100.0	100.0

LIABILITIES								
Notes Payable-Short Term		7.1	13.6	9.3			11.2	10.0
Cur. Mat.-L.T.D.		5.8	2.6	1.9			5.6	3.4
Trade Payables		15.7	15.5	10.9			11.2	13.3
Income Taxes Payable		.0	.3	.3			.3	.3
All Other Current		11.5	10.0	11.0			9.6	8.5
Total Current		40.1	41.9	33.4			37.9	35.5
Long-Term Debt		18.2	16.5	9.8			15.9	18.1
Deferred Taxes		.1	.7	1.0			.6	.7
All Other Non-Current		8.0	5.5	11.0			3.6	7.1
Net Worth		33.6	35.4	44.7			41.9	38.6
Total Liabilities & Net Worth		100.0	100.0	100.0			100.0	100.0

INCOME DATA								
Net Sales		100.0	100.0	100.0			100.0	100.0
Gross Profit		40.8	31.0	31.1			30.1	32.0
Operating Expenses		37.5	25.6	22.9			24.9	27.1
Operating Profit		3.3	5.4	8.2			5.2	4.9
All Other Expenses (net)		.1	.7	2.7			1.3	1.0
Profit Before Taxes		3.1	4.7	5.5			3.8	3.9

RATIOS

Ratio	500M-2MM	2-10MM	10-50MM	4/1/02-3/31/03 ALL	4/1/03-3/31/04 ALL
Current	2.8	3.2	3.3	2.8	4.0
	1.9	1.9	1.9	1.9	2.0
	1.2	1.3	1.0	1.3	1.3
Quick	1.4	1.4	1.6	1.3	1.8
	.9	.9	.7	.9	.9
	.4	.6	.5	.5	.6
Sales/Receivables	22 16.5	31 11.8	32 11.4	29 12.6	30 12.2
	36 10.1	42 8.7	40 9.0	38 9.6	42 8.7
	51 7.1	49 7.4	45 8.0	47 7.7	55 6.6
Cost of Sales/Inventory	31 11.8	43 8.4	62 5.9	46 8.0	55 6.7
	71 5.1	100 3.7	86 4.3	69 5.3	78 4.7
	180 2.0	153 2.4	145 2.5	109 3.3	117 3.1
Cost of Sales/Payables	12 31.2	19 19.4	15 24.2	13 27.9	13 27.6
	35 10.6	28 12.8	26 14.1	23 15.7	26 14.2
	64 5.7	49 7.4	38 9.6	35 10.4	39 9.4
Sales/Working Capital	3.9	4.4	3.2	4.7	3.8
	8.9	6.8	6.4	8.0	6.5
	23.6	13.7	243.7	16.0	14.8
EBIT/Interest	8.6	9.8	9.2	13.3	12.0
	(19) 3.6	(37) 3.6	(22) 4.7	(76) 3.3	(76) 3.3
	1.7	2.0	2.0	1.0	1.2
Net Profit + Depr., Dep., Amort./Cur. Mat. L/T/D		5.1	15.4	4.1	6.2
	(13) 3.4	(13) 2.4		(31) 2.4	(33) 2.3
	2.1	1.0		1.1	.9
Fixed/Worth	.2	.2	.3	.4	.2
	.6	.6	.7	.7	.6
	1.5	2.2	2.2	1.3	1.6
Debt/Worth	.9	.7	.6	.6	.4
	2.0	2.5	1.2	1.2	1.2
	5.3	7.8	10.0	4.2	4.6
% Profit Before Taxes/Tangible Net Worth	65.1	49.6	35.5	32.2	30.2
	(22) 21.9	(36) 28.2	(18) 16.9	(68) 16.3	(75) 13.5
	5.3	10.2	7.2	1.2	3.4
% Profit Before Taxes/Total Assets	17.8	17.3	14.5	16.2	11.8
	5.8	7.2	7.9	6.0	5.1
	1.9	2.2	.9	-.5	.4
Sales/Net Fixed Assets	44.8	55.1	15.6	17.2	19.0
	17.3	15.3	9.0	7.3	9.1
	9.2	5.7	5.0	4.4	4.6
Sales/Total Assets	3.1	2.7	2.1	2.6	2.5
	3.0	2.1	1.8	1.9	1.9
	1.5	1.7	1.1	1.5	1.3
% Depr., Dep., Amort./Sales	.4	.6	1.1	1.5	1.3
	(17) 2.1	(38) 1.9	(22) 1.8	(77) 3.0	(78) 2.2
	2.4	2.6	2.8	4.4	3.9
% Officers', Directors', Owners' Comp/Sales	2.8	1.5		2.4	2.6
	(15) 3.8	(13) 3.6		(28) 3.9	(34) 3.9
	6.0	5.5		6.1	7.2

	0-500M	500M-2MM	2-10MM	10-50MM	50-100MM	100-250MM	ALL	ALL
Net Sales ($)	5325M	73064M	436470M	865987M	406816M	1321655M	2285807M	2252171M
Total Assets ($)	1913M	27705M	194784M	499323M	272836M	872459M	1523779M	1615711M

M = $ thousand   MM = $ million
See Pages 11 through 21 for Explanation of Ratios and Data

Comparative Historical Data | Current Data Sorted by Sales

	4/1/04-3/31/05 ALL	4/1/05-3/31/06 ALL	4/1/06-3/31/07 ALL	Type of Statement	0-1MM	1-3MM	3-5MM	5-10MM	10-25MM	25MM & OVER
						22 (4/1-9/30/06)		79 (10/1/06-3/31/07)		
	26	22	20	Unqualified				4	3	13
	18	19	27	Reviewed		1	3	11	6	6
	21	15	17	Compiled	4	5		4	4	
	10	18	12	Tax Returns	2	3	4	2	1	
	24	42	25	Other		4	3	3	7	8
	99	116	101	NUMBER OF STATEMENTS	6	13	10	24	21	27
	%	%	%	ASSETS	%	%	%	%	%	%
	8.8	6.5	7.7	Cash & Equivalents		9.3	7.4	4.6	6.2	7.5
	24.9	22.6	23.3	Trade Receivables (net)		22.1	26.0	27.2	26.7	20.0
	28.6	32.4	33.4	Inventory		36.5	31.4	37.0	39.8	28.3
	2.8	2.1	1.4	All Other Current		1.1	2.4	1.4	.7	1.7
	65.1	63.7	65.8	Total Current		68.9	67.1	70.3	73.4	57.5
	26.5	25.3	22.8	Fixed Assets (net)		17.6	25.0	20.1	18.0	24.7
	3.3	4.6	4.4	Intangibles (net)		.7	3.3	7.0	3.4	6.0
	5.1	6.4	7.0	All Other Non-Current		12.7	4.7	2.7	5.2	11.8
	100.0	100.0	100.0	Total		100.0	100.0	100.0	100.0	100.0
				LIABILITIES						
	11.6	11.5	10.3	Notes Payable-Short Term		4.0	11.8	12.8	12.0	8.2
	6.7	2.5	3.0	Cur. Mat.-L.T.D.		7.1	4.0	2.6	2.5	2.0
	13.2	14.6	13.4	Trade Payables		15.0	12.6	14.6	16.8	10.9
	.2	.3	.2	Income Taxes Payable		.0	.3	.2	.3	.2
	9.5	8.3	10.4	All Other Current		14.0	15.2	6.7	11.6	11.0
	41.2	37.1	37.3	Total Current		40.1	43.9	36.8	43.2	32.3
	15.5	18.3	15.9	Long-Term Debt		16.0	19.4	18.1	13.0	10.0
	.6	.7	.6	Deferred Taxes		.0	.0	1.5	.3	.7
	8.3	8.8	8.0	All Other Non-Current		9.8	10.5	9.3	6.1	5.6
	34.4	35.1	38.2	Net Worth		34.1	26.2	34.2	37.4	51.4
	100.0	100.0	100.0	Total Liabilities & Net Worth		100.0	100.0	100.0	100.0	100.0
				INCOME DATA						
	100.0	100.0	100.0	Net Sales		100.0	100.0	100.0	100.0	100.0
	32.2	30.3	34.5	Gross Profit		40.8	39.4	34.7	28.7	29.4
	26.9	24.6	28.5	Operating Expenses		38.8	32.5	28.4	22.4	21.2
	5.3	5.7	6.1	Operating Profit		2.0	6.9	6.3	6.3	8.1
	1.4	1.4	1.1	All Other Expenses (net)		-1.5	.9	1.3	1.5	1.2
	3.9	4.3	5.0	Profit Before Taxes		3.5	6.0	5.1	4.8	6.9
				RATIOS						
	3.6	3.2	3.2	Current		2.7	2.7	3.2	3.2	4.1
	1.9	2.0	2.1			2.1	1.4	2.0	2.3	2.4
	1.2	1.3	1.3			1.3	.9	1.4	1.3	1.0
	2.2	1.6	1.5	Quick		1.4	1.4	1.5	1.3	1.6
	.9	.9	.9			.9	.9	.8	.9	1.1
	.5	.5	.5			.4	.3	.6	.6	.5
	31 11.7	32 11.4	28 13.0	Sales/Receivables		22 16.6	5 75.9	33 10.9	35 10.6	28 13.1
	45 8.2	40 9.1	39 9.3			34 10.8	25 14.6	40 9.2	45 8.2	38 9.5
	54 6.7	50 7.2	48 7.5			52 7.0	76 4.8	48 7.6	48 7.6	47 7.8
	40 9.1	49 7.4	47 7.7	Cost of Sales/Inventory		37 9.8	6 65.6	61 6.0	40 9.2	55 6.6
	74 5.0	80 4.6	86 4.3			81 4.5	29 12.5	94 3.9	99 3.7	76 4.8
	120 3.0	125 2.9	147 2.5			225 1.6	160 2.3	153 2.4	160 2.3	103 3.5
	20 18.5	18 20.5	15 24.3	Cost of Sales/Payables		11 33.8	0 UND	19 19.4	24 15.2	15 24.5
	32 11.5	29 12.5	28 13.2			19 19.7	30 12.2	30 12.3	31 11.9	22 16.5
	45 8.2	45 8.1	46 7.9			87 4.2	48 7.6	47 7.8	46 8.0	41 8.9
	3.6	4.6	3.9	Sales/Working Capital		3.5	5.8	5.2	3.1	4.0
	5.9	7.0	6.4			6.4	19.4	6.4	6.4	5.9
	24.4	19.6	18.6			19.0	-47.7	10.6	20.6	243.7
	16.2	11.0	13.6	EBIT/Interest		13.5		5.1	8.8	25.3
	(88) 3.2	(108) 3.7	(90) 4.7			(10) 4.3		(21) 3.6	(20) 3.9	(25) 6.7
	1.4	1.8	2.0			1.8		2.0	1.3	4.4
	6.6	6.0	7.7	Net Profit + Depr., Dep., Amort./Cur. Mat. L/T/D						17.5
	(29) 2.7	(31) 3.0	(30) 3.9						(14)	4.1
	1.2	1.4	1.6							1.5
	.3	.3	.3	Fixed/Worth		.2	.5	.3	.1	.3
	.6	.6	.6			.5	1.5	.7	.5	.5
	2.3	2.8	1.7			1.1	-2.0	4.5	2.1	.8
	.6	.7	.6	Debt/Worth		.7	1.5	1.1	.5	.3
	1.5	1.7	1.6			1.4	3.3	2.7	2.4	1.1
	5.8	8.5	5.6			8.7	-17.9	22.4	5.6	2.8
	39.2	45.1	47.4	% Profit Before Taxes/Tangible Net Worth		71.1		75.0	42.8	44.7
	(82) 17.0	(93) 24.0	(87) 23.1			(12) 15.0		(21) 26.4	(18) 28.9	(25) 23.1
	7.5	9.0	9.8			2.9		10.9	7.7	15.9
	13.4	14.4	17.2	% Profit Before Taxes/Total Assets		22.1	24.7	13.8	16.9	17.4
	5.8	8.6	7.9			5.2	16.4	7.8	10.7	10.2
	1.4	2.1	2.3			1.3	4.8	4.0	1.3	5.7
	20.0	20.4	25.7	Sales/Net Fixed Assets		21.2	52.0	40.3	54.8	13.6
	8.4	9.0	10.5			13.5	25.7	10.5	17.1	7.9
	5.2	5.0	5.3			9.9	6.2	5.6	6.1	5.0
	2.6	2.6	2.9	Sales/Total Assets		3.1	3.6	2.7	3.0	2.3
	2.0	2.0	1.9			2.0	3.0	2.1	1.9	1.8
	1.4	1.5	1.5			1.4	1.9	1.5	1.6	1.5
	1.3	1.1	.8	% Depr., Dep., Amort./Sales				.7	.6	1.1
	(89) 2.2	(99) 2.0	(91) 2.0					(23) 1.6	(19) 1.5	(26) 1.8
	3.8	3.4	2.7					3.3	2.6	3.2
	2.3	2.4	2.7	% Officers', Directors' Owners' Comp/Sales						
	(34) 4.7	(43) 4.3	(30) 3.7							
	7.0	6.4	6.1							
	2593886M	3883638M	3109317M	Net Sales ($)	3433M	26830M	40595M	170491M	318043M	2549925M
	1680532M	2404817M	1869020M	Total Assets ($)	3582M	13211M	16225M	101512M	171239M	1563251M

M = $ thousand   MM = $ million
See Pages 11 through 21 for Explanation of Ratios and Data

Current Data Sorted by Assets / Comparative Historical Data

0-500M	500M-2MM	2-10MM	10-50MM	50-100MM	100-250MM		4/1/02-3/31/03 ALL	4/1/03-3/31/04 ALL
						Type of Statement		
		3	6			Unqualified	2	3
	1	7	3			Reviewed	9	9
1	2	3				Compiled	9	7
2	2		1			Tax Returns	1	1
3	3	3	2	1		Other	8	12
3	8	16	12	1		**NUMBER OF STATEMENTS**	29	32
%	%	%	%	%	%	**ASSETS**	%	%
		9.5	4.3			Cash & Equivalents	8.0	5.1
		23.1	22.3			Trade Receivables (net)	23.7	23.7
		24.7	26.5			Inventory	23.5	22.7
		1.1	3.9			All Other Current	3.6	2.0
		58.4	57.0			Total Current	58.8	53.5
		33.7	32.0			Fixed Assets (net)	32.8	38.1
		1.6	3.8			Intangibles (net)	3.6	4.6
		6.3	7.2			All Other Non-Current	4.8	3.8
		100.0	100.0			Total	100.0	100.0
						LIABILITIES		
		9.7	7.6			Notes Payable-Short Term	11.6	13.6
		8.4	4.8			Cur. Mat.-L.T.D.	4.1	4.9
		10.3	8.0			Trade Payables	10.4	12.3
		.3	.1			Income Taxes Payable	.1	.1
		18.9	7.0			All Other Current	14.9	6.6
		47.6	27.6			Total Current	41.0	37.5
		15.5	16.2			Long-Term Debt	15.6	18.2
		.8	1.5			Deferred Taxes	.5	.8
		2.7	6.7			All Other Non-Current	8.9	5.2
		33.5	48.1			Net Worth	33.9	38.4
		100.0	100.0			Total Liabilities & Net Worth	100.0	100.0
						INCOME DATA		
		100.0	100.0			Net Sales	100.0	100.0
		24.7	29.6			Gross Profit	34.2	26.7
		19.9	25.5			Operating Expenses	27.2	22.7
		4.7	4.1			Operating Profit	6.9	4.1
		2.0	1.4			All Other Expenses (net)	1.4	1.0
		2.8	2.8			Profit Before Taxes	5.5	3.0
						RATIOS		
		2.6	3.0			Current	3.3	2.5
		1.9	2.1				1.7	1.7
		1.3	1.4				1.2	1.2
		1.7	1.5			Quick	1.4	1.6
		.8	.9				1.0	.8
		.6	.6				.6	.5
		38 9.6	43 8.5			Sales/Receivables	37 9.7 / 35 10.5	
		48 7.6	49 7.4				44 8.3 / 46 7.9	
		55 6.6	62 5.9				56 6.6 / 59 6.1	
		43 8.6	56 6.6			Cost of Sales/Inventory	45 8.1 / 38 9.6	
		65 5.6	75 4.9				64 5.7 / 50 7.3	
		86 4.2	99 3.7				100 3.6 / 91 4.0	
		15 24.2	16 23.5			Cost of Sales/Payables	12 30.5 / 18 19.9	
		27 13.7	22 16.3				25 14.5 / 29 12.4	
		37 9.9	28 13.2				44 8.3 / 40 9.2	
		4.3	4.5			Sales/Working Capital	5.2	5.5
		7.5	6.0				7.2	8.9
		15.1	12.6				22.8	34.5
		16.2	18.1			EBIT/Interest	8.0	8.6
		2.1	6.2				(28) 2.5	(30) 2.4
		1.2	.9				1.1	.7
						Net Profit + Depr., Dep., Amort./Cur. Mat. L/T/D		
		.4	.5			Fixed/Worth	.4	.4
		.7	.6				.8	.8
		2.5	1.2				1.6	2.2
		.6	.4			Debt/Worth	.5	.7
		.8	.7				1.0	1.1
		5.9	3.6				3.0	3.3
		30.7	31.2			% Profit Before Taxes/Tangible Net Worth	25.0	30.5
		(13) 11.1	(11) 13.2				(24) 5.4	(28) 7.3
		3.1	-.5				.2	.0
		10.8	18.5			% Profit Before Taxes/Total Assets	11.4	9.5
		5.0	5.1				3.4	4.1
		.5	-.3				.1	.0
		8.5	7.6			Sales/Net Fixed Assets	13.5	11.4
		4.9	5.0				7.3	5.2
		3.0	2.7				2.6	3.0
		2.3	2.0			Sales/Total Assets	2.5	2.3
		1.8	1.7				1.9	1.8
		1.4	1.3				1.3	1.5
		2.7				% Depr., Dep., Amort./Sales	2.3	2.2
		(15) 3.4					(27) 4.4	(28) 3.6
		6.0					5.2	5.7
						% Officers', Directors' Owners' Comp/Sales	3.0	2.7
							(16) 6.2	(13) 3.5
							12.7	8.1
3586M	22134M	183899M	410973M	101196M		Net Sales ($)	282075M	862891M
989M	7585M	97395M	247106M	58065M		Total Assets ($)	187592M	479661M

Current Data columns: **11 (4/1-9/30/06)** covers 0-500M, 500M-2MM, 2-10MM; **29 (10/1/06-3/31/07)** covers 10-50MM, 50-100MM, 100-250MM. DATA NOT AVAILABLE for 50-100MM and 100-250MM columns.

M = $ thousand   MM = $ million
See Pages 11 through 21 for Explanation of Ratios and Data

Comparative Historical Data — Current Data Sorted by Sales

4/1/04-3/31/05 ALL	4/1/05-3/31/06 ALL	4/1/06-3/31/07 ALL	Type of Statement	0-1MM	1-3MM	3-5MM	5-10MM	10-25MM	25MM & OVER
9	12	9	Unqualified			1		2	6
13	18	11	Reviewed		1	1	3	6	1
9	9	6	Compiled		3	1	2		
2	4	5	Tax Returns		3		1		1
7	9	9	Other		2		1	3	2
				11 (4/1-9/30/06)			**29 (10/1/06-3/31/07)**		
40	52	40	NUMBER OF STATEMENTS		9	3	7	11	10
%	%	%	**ASSETS**	%	%	%	%	%	%
7.6	6.1	6.5	Cash & Equivalents					11.4	5.2
25.9	27.4	25.3	Trade Receivables (net)					22.2	27.6
23.4	22.7	25.1	Inventory					22.5	30.1
1.3	1.2	1.9	All Other Current					2.2	4.6
58.2	57.4	58.8	Total Current					58.3	67.5
31.7	29.4	30.0	Fixed Assets (net)					36.2	26.0
3.4	4.1	4.1	Intangibles (net)					1.7	3.5
6.7	9.2	7.1	All Other Non-Current					3.7	3.0
100.0	100.0	100.0	Total					100.0	100.0
			LIABILITIES						
14.8	11.1	9.3	Notes Payable-Short Term					7.9	13.6
3.3	4.3	5.9	Cur. Mat.-L.T.D.					6.5	8.3
13.7	13.5	12.9	Trade Payables					9.3	10.6
.5	.1	.1	Income Taxes Payable					.4	.1
7.6	11.0	10.3	All Other Current					5.4	8.4
40.0	40.0	38.5	Total Current					29.4	41.1
15.9	15.3	15.1	Long-Term Debt					22.5	5.9
.9	1.0	.8	Deferred Taxes					1.5	1.5
3.6	5.6	5.2	All Other Non-Current					3.9	3.5
39.5	38.1	40.5	Net Worth					42.6	48.0
100.0	100.0	100.0	Total Liabilities & Net Worth					100.0	100.0
			INCOME DATA						
100.0	100.0	100.0	Net Sales					100.0	100.0
24.6	24.8	28.0	Gross Profit					29.9	24.1
20.3	19.7	23.4	Operating Expenses					26.4	19.7
4.3	5.1	4.6	Operating Profit					3.5	4.4
.7	1.3	1.3	All Other Expenses (net)					1.5	.9
3.6	3.9	3.3	Profit Before Taxes					2.0	3.6
			RATIOS						
2.3	2.8	2.5	Current					3.9	2.8
1.8	1.6	1.9						1.9	2.1
1.3	1.1	1.4						1.4	1.5
1.5	1.5	1.6	Quick					3.2	1.5
1.0	.9	.9						1.0	1.1
.6	.6	.6						.7	.5
41 8.9	43 8.5	36 10.1	Sales/Receivables					36 10.0	47 7.8
48 7.6	53 6.9	47 7.7						43 8.5	53 6.9
57 6.5	58 6.2	56 6.6						53 6.8	62 5.9
34 10.8	41 9.0	38 9.6	Cost of Sales/Inventory					42 8.7	48 7.6
49 7.4	52 7.1	63 5.8						65 5.6	70 5.2
79 4.6	75 4.9	88 4.1						79 4.6	98 3.7
13 27.2	19 19.5	15 24.2	Cost of Sales/Payables					13 27.2	18 20.0
29 12.7	28 12.9	24 15.4						20 18.6	25 14.8
44 8.4	43 8.5	38 9.6						54 6.8	28 12.9
5.1	4.7	5.3	Sales/Working Capital					4.5	4.3
8.9	8.9	7.5						6.6	5.6
16.6	35.1	14.2						14.1	13.4
13.3	12.3	16.1	EBIT/Interest					16.1	18.5
(35) 4.5	(49) 2.7	(39) 6.2						2.4	9.9
1.5	1.4	1.3						1.3	2.3
10.0	8.9	8.5	Net Profit + Depr., Dep., Amort./Cur. Mat. L/T/D						
(12) 3.0	(20) 1.7	(14) 5.8							
1.6	.9	1.4							
.5	.4	.4	Fixed/Worth					.3	.5
.8	.7	.7						.7	.6
1.7	2.1	2.6						2.8	1.1
.5	.6	.6	Debt/Worth					.6	.4
1.1	1.4	.9						.9	.7
5.0	5.0	6.4						7.3	3.4
38.0	32.2	36.2	% Profit Before Taxes/Tangible Net Worth					23.5	
(37) 19.6	(45) 14.7	(33) 18.4						(10) 10.7	
4.2	2.1	4.3						3.5	
15.2	13.0	16.2	% Profit Before Taxes/Total Assets					9.8	19.7
7.6	6.0	5.8						4.7	7.6
1.1	1.6	1.1						1.3	3.0
13.0	12.4	17.5	Sales/Net Fixed Assets					8.5	11.9
6.3	6.9	7.1						5.2	6.6
3.9	4.1	4.3						2.7	5.0
2.6	2.2	2.7	Sales/Total Assets					2.4	2.1
1.9	1.8	1.9						1.9	1.8
1.6	1.4	1.5						1.4	1.7
2.0	1.7	2.3	% Depr., Dep., Amort./Sales					1.9	
(35) 3.2	(48) 2.9	(34) 3.4						3.8	
5.5	4.2	5.3						6.8	
3.4	2.8	2.3	% Officers', Directors', Owners' Comp/Sales						
(14) 5.2	(17) 4.7	(15) 6.2							
8.7	9.1	10.7							
591462M	907014M	721788M	Net Sales ($)		16382M	11568M	54380M	165266M	474192M
346630M	525672M	411140M	Total Assets ($)		6286M	6103M	43090M	95905M	259756M

M = $ thousand   MM = $ million
See Pages 11 through 21 for Explanation of Ratios and Data

Current Data Sorted by Assets   Comparative Historical Data

0-500M	500M-2MM	2-10MM	10-50MM	50-100MM	100-250MM	Type of Statement	4/1/02-3/31/03 ALL	4/1/03-3/31/04 ALL
	1	10	32	3	5	Unqualified	37	41
	8	22	6			Reviewed	54	56
1	4	15	3		1	Compiled	25	39
3	7	3				Tax Returns	19	23
1	16	23	14	2	2	Other	70	61
	41 (4/1-9/30/06)		141 (10/1/06-3/31/07)					
5	36	73	55	5	8	NUMBER OF STATEMENTS	205	220
%	%	%	%	%	%	ASSETS	%	%
	11.7	7.0	3.8			Cash & Equivalents	6.9	7.8
	31.9	31.4	25.0			Trade Receivables (net)	25.1	26.7
	23.6	30.0	33.3			Inventory	25.0	25.6
	3.3	1.2	1.1			All Other Current	2.6	2.4
	70.5	69.5	63.3			Total Current	59.6	62.6
	20.8	23.5	26.5			Fixed Assets (net)	31.6	29.1
	2.2	2.7	4.8			Intangibles (net)	4.0	3.2
	6.6	4.3	5.4			All Other Non-Current	4.9	5.0
	100.0	100.0	100.0			Total	100.0	100.0
						LIABILITIES		
	9.4	11.1	13.8			Notes Payable-Short Term	10.8	12.8
	2.8	3.2	3.5			Cur. Mat.-L.T.D.	4.4	2.9
	21.1	16.0	15.8			Trade Payables	14.1	14.4
	.4	.3	.4			Income Taxes Payable	.3	.2
	12.4	8.9	7.0			All Other Current	8.3	9.0
	46.1	39.4	40.5			Total Current	37.9	39.3
	16.8	9.6	11.3			Long-Term Debt	18.0	14.5
	.1	.5	1.0			Deferred Taxes	.5	.6
	4.1	4.6	4.6			All Other Non-Current	4.3	6.1
	32.9	45.8	42.6			Net Worth	39.3	39.4
	100.0	100.0	100.0			Total Liabilties & Net Worth	100.0	100.0
						INCOME DATA		
	100.0	100.0	100.0			Net Sales	100.0	100.0
	35.3	27.0	22.3			Gross Profit	28.4	29.2
	28.0	20.8	15.8			Operating Expenses	24.6	25.4
	7.2	6.2	6.5			Operating Profit	3.9	3.8
	.3	.8	1.2			All Other Expenses (net)	1.6	1.4
	6.9	5.5	5.3			Profit Before Taxes	2.2	2.4
						RATIOS		
	3.3	2.9	2.3				2.7	2.8
	1.9	1.7	1.6			Current	1.6	1.7
	1.2	1.3	1.3				1.2	1.2
	2.2	1.9	1.2				1.6	1.7
	.9	.9	.7			Quick	.9	1.0
	.7	.7	.5				.5	.5
28 12.9	36 10.1	38 9.6					32 11.4	36 10.1
39 9.4	47 7.7	46 8.0				Sales/Receivables	43 8.4	47 7.8
53 6.9	67 5.5	52 7.1					55 6.6	57 6.4
10 38.1	43 8.4	54 6.8					35 10.4	32 11.3
26 14.0	62 5.9	73 5.0				Cost of Sales/Inventory	60 6.1	58 6.3
84 4.3	85 4.3	101 3.6					93 3.9	93 3.9
17 21.3	18 20.1	18 20.5					18 20.6	15 24.8
27 13.3	35 10.6	28 12.8				Cost of Sales/Payables	28 12.9	27 13.4
43 8.5	49 7.4	45 8.1					46 8.0	46 8.0
	5.3	4.8	5.3				4.7	5.0
	7.6	7.3	8.0			Sales/Working Capital	9.2	8.4
	30.6	16.7	21.6				27.8	28.3
	7.7	14.4	13.3				6.8	6.8
	(29) 3.5	(67) 4.5	(53) 3.6			EBIT/Interest	(183) 2.3	(199) 2.1
	1.5	2.0	2.1				1.0	.0
		3.2	11.0			Net Profit + Depr., Dep.,	3.6	3.5
	(23) 2.0	(26) 3.9				Amort./Cur. Mat. L/T/D	(66) 2.3	(61) 1.9
		1.7	1.4				1.0	.9
	.1	.2	.3				.4	.3
	.4	.5	.6			Fixed/Worth	.8	.7
	3.0	1.1	1.4				2.1	1.7
	.7	.5	.7				.6	.7
	1.1	1.2	1.6			Debt/Worth	1.7	1.5
	130.4	3.6	4.1				4.9	4.1
	62.2	46.4	46.1			% Profit Before Taxes/Tangible	28.5	36.5
	(28) 22.0	(70) 20.4	(52) 24.6			Net Worth	(182) 10.8	(200) 7.1
	6.8	8.2	10.3				.6	-2.2
	17.5	16.8	13.3			% Profit Before Taxes/Total	11.3	11.5
	8.0	8.3	7.9			Assets	4.1	2.9
	1.7	2.0	3.1				.1	-1.7
	90.6	31.2	17.4				20.4	22.3
	19.0	10.3	7.8			Sales/Net Fixed Assets	6.9	8.2
	5.6	5.0	4.2				3.7	4.1
	4.0	2.8	2.5				2.6	2.8
	2.6	2.1	2.0			Sales/Total Assets	1.9	2.1
	1.7	1.6	1.5				1.4	1.4
	1.4	.9	.9				1.3	1.2
	(24) 2.4	(68) 1.6	2.2			% Depr., Dep., Amort./Sales	(179) 2.9	(196) 2.3
	3.9	2.8	3.3				4.9	4.1
	4.7	1.9				% Officers', Directors'	2.5	2.1
	(14) 7.5	(29) 3.1				Owners' Comp/Sales	(82) 4.6	(89) 4.6
	10.3	6.1					9.1	7.5
9826M	124612M	800277M	2759058M	639709M	3992030M	Net Sales ($)	3940919M	4898699M
1208M	43056M	367121M	1270285M	372080M	1232612M	Total Assets ($)	2587274M	3156281M

M = $ thousand   MM = $ million
See Pages 11 through 21 for Explanation of Ratios and Data

Comparative Historical Data | Current Data Sorted by Sales

					Type of Statement						
41		35		51	Unqualified		1		4	13	33
53		34		36	Reviewed		4	3	11	12	6
30		29		24	Compiled		4	2	9	6	3
24		23		13	Tax Returns		7	2	2	1	
57		68		58	Other	1	11	9	11	11	16
4/1/04-3/31/05 ALL		4/1/05-3/31/06 ALL		4/1/06-3/31/07 ALL			41 (4/1-9/30/06)		141 (10/1/06-3/31/07)		
						0-1MM	1-3MM	3-5MM	5-10MM	10-25MM	25MM & OVER
205		189		182	NUMBER OF STATEMENTS	1	27	16	37	43	58
%		%		%	ASSETS	%	%	%	%	%	%
7.0		7.5		7.5	Cash & Equivalents		9.8	10.9	11.0	5.7	4.2
28.3		27.6		29.1	Trade Receivables (net)		29.3	28.1	32.9	28.6	26.9
25.9		29.6		29.2	Inventory		22.5	23.7	28.6	30.1	34.1
2.2		1.2		1.6	All Other Current		4.2	.8	1.7	.6	1.3
63.3		65.9		67.4	Total Current		65.7	63.4	74.3	65.0	66.4
29.0		25.8		24.0	Fixed Assets (net)		24.7	25.9	19.0	24.1	26.5
2.7		3.3		3.5	Intangibles (net)		2.1	7.8	1.9	4.7	3.2
5.0		5.0		5.0	All Other Non-Current		7.4	2.9	4.9	6.2	3.8
100.0		100.0		100.0	Total		100.0	100.0	100.0	100.0	100.0
					LIABILITIES						
10.6		12.8		11.8	Notes Payable-Short Term		6.4	5.7	12.6	12.5	14.5
4.0		3.5		3.2	Cur. Mat.-L.T.D.		4.3	2.3	2.8	3.9	2.8
16.3		16.6		17.2	Trade Payables		18.2	6.1	19.1	20.4	15.8
.3		.2		.4	Income Taxes Payable		.0	.3	.4	.4	.5
9.6		8.7		10.1	All Other Current		13.8	15.6	12.1	7.1	7.8
40.9		41.8		42.6	Total Current		42.7	29.9	47.1	44.4	41.5
18.0		18.7		14.4	Long-Term Debt		32.4	5.8	13.1	9.2	13.3
.5		.6		.6	Deferred Taxes		.2	.0	.4	.9	.7
7.7		6.5		4.6	All Other Non-Current		4.4	3.9	5.8	4.5	4.2
32.9		32.4		37.8	Net Worth		20.4	60.4	33.6	41.0	40.2
100.0		100.0		100.0	Total Liabilties & Net Worth		100.0	100.0	100.0	100.0	100.0
					INCOME DATA						
100.0		100.0		100.0	Net Sales		100.0	100.0	100.0	100.0	100.0
27.2		27.2		26.7	Gross Profit		37.4	31.2	27.9	27.5	19.0
23.0		22.1		20.3	Operating Expenses		29.5	20.4	23.4	20.5	13.8
4.2		5.1		6.4	Operating Profit		7.9	10.8	4.5	7.0	5.2
1.0		1.2		.9	All Other Expenses (net)		.5	.8	.8	1.2	1.0
3.2		3.9		5.5	Profit Before Taxes		7.4	10.0	3.7	5.7	4.2
					RATIOS						
2.5		2.7		2.4			3.5	4.5	2.2	2.5	2.2
1.6		1.6		1.7	Current		1.7	2.3	1.6	1.7	1.6
1.2		1.2		1.2			.9	1.1	1.2	1.3	1.2
1.5		1.4		1.4			2.3	3.3	1.3	1.4	1.2
.9		.9		.9	Quick		.8	1.7	.9	.8	.7
.6		.5		.6			.7	.9	.7	.6	.5

36	10.1	32	11.4	34	10.8		28	13.2	31	11.9	33	11.0	39	9.5	38	9.5
47	7.8	45	8.2	44	8.2	Sales/Receivables	40	9.0	41	8.9	48	7.5	44	8.3	44	8.2
57	6.4	57	6.4	58	6.3		60	6.1	69	5.3	66	5.5	54	6.8	55	6.7
31	11.9	32	11.5	35	10.6		4	87.1	12	30.1	37	9.7	48	7.6	40	9.2
57	6.4	62	5.9	62	5.8	Cost of Sales/Inventory	25	14.8	31	11.9	67	5.4	62	5.8	67	5.4
88	4.2	95	3.9	89	4.1		101	3.6	102	3.6	84	4.3	89	4.1	90	4.1
21	17.7	16	22.9	18	20.2		19	18.8	6	65.5	22	16.7	23	15.9	17	21.0
32	11.2	29	12.4	30	12.1	Cost of Sales/Payables	34	10.9	17	21.0	36	10.1	33	10.9	26	14.1
49	7.4	49	7.4	46	8.0		49	7.5	28	13.2	60	6.1	46	7.9	45	8.2

5.5		5.3		5.1			4.7	3.7	5.8	5.2	5.3
9.3		9.3		7.9	Sales/Working Capital		6.6	6.1	8.7	7.7	8.2
22.2		28.7		22.9			-104.3	32.1	20.4	17.1	23.2

9.2		9.1		11.0			5.8		36.6		9.4		11.5		13.0
(189)	4.2	(178)	3.9	(167)	3.7	EBIT/Interest	(22)	2.3	(14)	9.3	(35)	3.2	(38)	4.7	(57)	3.4
1.1		1.4		1.8			1.5		4.2		1.5		2.0		2.1

5.9		6.3		6.6							2.4		5.7		11.8
(55)	2.0	(45)	2.1	(60)	2.1	Net Profit + Depr., Dep., Amort./Cur. Mat. L/T/D			(11)	1.9	(17)	2.3	(26)	3.0
1.0		1.2		1.3							1.3		1.5		1.4

.3		.2		.3			.3	.0	.2	.2	.4
.8		.6		.5	Fixed/Worth		1.1	.6	.4	.5	.6
1.9		1.9		1.5			-1.2	1.2	5.0	1.1	1.4

.8		.7		.6			.9	.3	.8	.5	.8
1.7		1.7		1.3	Debt/Worth		1.1	.4	1.8	1.2	1.5
5.1		5.2		5.7			-20.9	3.1	16.7	3.8	4.5

46.3		45.6		46.6			61.2		102.0		45.4		47.0		46.1
(183)	19.7	(162)	17.5	(162)	20.6	% Profit Before Taxes/Tangible Net Worth	(20)	21.5	(15)	30.9	(32)	16.2	(38)	20.2	(56)	20.1
3.4		6.5		8.2			9.0		14.0		8.0		9.0		5.4

14.2		15.5		16.6			14.8	21.0	10.0	17.1	14.1
5.6		6.4		8.0	% Profit Before Taxes/Total Assets		8.9	14.9	5.2	8.3	7.0
.4		1.1		2.0			1.9	4.8	1.6	3.6	2.0

22.7		30.7		30.8			84.7	83.3	45.0	18.8	23.3
8.5		9.4		10.6	Sales/Net Fixed Assets		13.7	9.0	19.0	9.9	8.6
4.2		5.8		4.7			4.0	4.1	7.0	5.4	4.9

2.8		3.0		2.8			3.1	2.6	3.2	2.7	2.6
2.1		2.3		2.1	Sales/Total Assets		2.2	1.7	2.6	2.1	2.1
1.6		1.7		1.6			1.3	1.4	1.7	1.6	1.6

1.3		.7		.9			1.3		1.2		.8		1.1		.7
(180)	2.3	(167)	1.9	(162)	1.7	% Depr., Dep., Amort./Sales	(21)	2.6	(11)	2.5	(33)	1.4	(40)	1.7	(56)	1.6
4.1		2.9		3.2			4.4		2.9		2.4		2.9		3.3

2.3		1.7		2.1			5.0				3.2		1.6	
(77)	3.7	(72)	3.6	(55)	4.9	% Officers', Directors' Owners' Comp/Sales	(11)	7.5		(18)	5.2	(11)	2.3	
7.7		6.5		7.5			10.2				7.8		3.6	

6306781M		5647095M		8325512M	Net Sales ($)	300M	55218M	68374M	267371M	701582M	7232667M
3533535M		2668040M		3286362M	Total Assets ($)	67M	28202M	43083M	121198M	394227M	2699585M

M = $ thousand   MM = $ million
See Pages 11 through 21 for Explanation of Ratios and Data

Current Data Sorted by Assets   Comparative Historical Data

0-500M	500M-2MM	2-10MM	10-50MM	50-100MM	100-250MM	Type of Statement	4/1/02-3/31/03 ALL	4/1/03-3/31/04 ALL
		24	28	3	3	Unqualified	51	49
2	26	109	20		1	Reviewed	130	137
28	90	77	5		1	Compiled	167	193
65	95	35	1		1	Tax Returns	83	76
28	86	84	35	7	4	Other	154	158
|194 (4/1-9/30/06)|			|663 (10/1/06-3/31/07)|					
123	297	329	89	10	9	NUMBER OF STATEMENTS	585	613
%	%	%	%	%	%	**ASSETS**	%	%
11.5	9.3	8.1	6.6	.3		Cash & Equivalents	8.0	8.5
28.1	25.8	24.4	24.0	27.8		Trade Receivables (net)	23.3	25.6
10.6	15.3	21.6	23.2	26.6		Inventory	17.7	18.5
2.5	1.9	1.7	2.8	2.8		All Other Current	2.6	2.8
52.7	52.3	55.8	56.7	57.4		Total Current	51.5	55.4
37.3	39.1	35.7	32.1	28.6		Fixed Assets (net)	39.9	36.0
2.6	3.0	3.2	7.3	10.5		Intangibles (net)	3.0	2.4
7.5	5.6	5.3	3.9	3.5		All Other Non-Current	5.6	6.2
100.0	100.0	100.0	100.0	100.0		Total	100.0	100.0
						LIABILITIES		
14.6	7.9	8.7	9.3	23.6		Notes Payable-Short Term	10.9	10.9
7.3	7.4	5.7	5.8	4.9		Cur. Mat.-L.T.D.	7.5	6.7
13.4	11.5	12.0	13.1	17.2		Trade Payables	11.2	11.5
.1	.1	.5	.2	.0		Income Taxes Payable	.3	.2
8.0	6.9	7.4	8.9	7.3		All Other Current	7.8	8.9
43.3	33.8	34.2	37.3	53.1		Total Current	37.7	38.2
33.6	28.1	22.3	19.1	16.7		Long-Term Debt	25.6	23.2
.0	.3	.6	.7	.6		Deferred Taxes	.7	.6
8.8	5.7	4.9	6.1	7.3		All Other Non-Current	5.6	8.0
14.2	32.0	38.0	36.8	22.3		Net Worth	30.5	30.0
100.0	100.0	100.0	100.0	100.0		Total Liabilities & Net Worth	100.0	100.0
						INCOME DATA		
100.0	100.0	100.0	100.0	100.0		Net Sales	100.0	100.0
52.5	39.4	29.5	22.2	17.7		Gross Profit	33.2	34.0
46.3	32.3	21.7	15.0	13.9		Operating Expenses	30.9	31.1
6.2	7.1	7.8	7.2	3.9		Operating Profit	2.3	2.9
1.6	1.6	1.4	1.8	4.7		All Other Expenses (net)	2.0	1.7
4.6	5.4	6.4	5.4	-.8		Profit Before Taxes	.3	1.2
						RATIOS		
2.9	2.8	2.6	2.1	1.3		Current	2.6	2.9
1.5	1.6	1.7	1.5	1.1			1.4	1.6
.7	1.0	1.2	1.1	.8			1.0	1.0
2.4	2.0	1.7	1.2	.6		Quick	1.6	1.8
1.0	1.1	.9	.8	.6			.9	.9
.5	.6	.6	.5	.4			.5	.5
11 33.7	29 12.8	33 11.0	37 9.8	40 9.1		Sales/Receivables	31 11.8	36 10.0
28 13.0	42 8.6	47 7.8	48 7.5	52 7.0			45 8.1	49 7.4
46 7.9	53 6.9	58 6.3	63 5.8	76 4.8			58 6.3	61 6.0
0 UND	7 55.1	27 13.5	32 11.3	28 13.3		Cost of Sales/Inventory	14 26.7	15 24.6
3 110.5	25 14.6	48 7.6	57 6.4	54 6.7			40 9.1	39 9.2
32 11.5	58 6.2	84 4.3	102 3.6	92 4.0			79 4.6	83 4.4
1 317.0	12 30.2	14 25.2	21 17.7	28 13.2		Cost of Sales/Payables	14 26.9	15 24.5
18 20.4	22 16.2	25 14.5	33 11.2	41 8.9			26 14.2	27 13.3
49 7.5	41 8.8	40 9.1	44 8.3	48 7.6			42 8.7	43 8.4
8.8	6.2	5.0	4.5	11.7		Sales/Working Capital	5.8	4.9
24.5	14.0	9.8	9.2	50.5			12.9	10.1
-26.2	170.6	28.2	27.5	-19.3			391.1	104.2
11.8	9.3	10.2	9.4			EBIT/Interest	4.3	5.9
(106) 5.2	(276) 3.3	(313) 4.4	(81) 3.8				(548) 1.7	(559) 1.8
1.0	1.6	2.0	1.5				-.7	-.5
	4.2	4.8	3.2			Net Profit + Depr., Dep., Amort./Cur. Mat. L/T/D	2.9	2.4
	(55) 1.9	(93) 2.4	(22) 2.3				(156) 1.5	(129) 1.5
	1.0	1.2	1.4				.6	.6
.3	.5	.5	.4	.5		Fixed/Worth	.6	.4
1.3	1.3	1.0	1.0	1.6			1.2	1.1
19.0	4.6	2.3	2.1	NM			3.8	3.8
.9	.8	.8	1.0	2.0		Debt/Worth	.7	.7
3.7	2.0	1.7	1.9	4.3			2.0	2.1
UND	8.6	4.2	4.8	NM			7.1	8.4
119.6	58.5	54.5	45.3			% Profit Before Taxes/Tangible Net Worth	29.6	29.3
(93) 44.2	(242) 26.1	(300) 26.1	(79) 20.4				(493) 7.5	(499) 9.0
7.9	7.8	7.8	7.5				-8.3	-4.0
32.1	17.5	17.9	13.2	7.4		% Profit Before Taxes/Total Assets	9.4	10.4
13.8	7.5	8.4	7.5	2.4			2.5	2.9
.0	2.2	3.2	2.0	-2.4			-5.5	-4.1
33.5	11.8	11.4	9.7	19.1		Sales/Net Fixed Assets	10.8	10.9
10.6	6.3	5.7	4.5	6.2			4.9	5.7
4.7	3.7	3.3	3.3	3.2			2.8	3.2
4.9	2.9	2.4	2.1	2.2		Sales/Total Assets	2.5	2.5
3.4	2.2	1.9	1.6	1.9			1.8	1.8
2.1	1.6	1.4	1.2	1.5			1.3	1.3
1.6	2.4	2.1	2.1	2.3		% Depr., Dep., Amort./Sales	2.7	2.3
(90) 3.7	(259) 4.2	(309) 3.6	(85) 3.6	3.4			(558) 4.9	(550) 4.6
5.8	6.6	5.4	5.4	6.1			7.8	7.1
5.2	3.3	2.1	1.4			% Officers', Directors' Owners' Comp/Sales	2.9	3.0
(84) 8.3	(187) 5.5	(161) 3.5	(16) 1.8				(309) 6.0	(311) 5.2
14.2	8.5	6.7	4.0				10.2	8.8
129230M	832662M	2821721M	3028494M	1036156M	3158961M	Net Sales ($)	5838787M	7194882M
34916M	353421M	1464726M	1722479M	607451M	1420299M	Total Assets ($)	3277596M	3920997M

© RMA 2007

M = $ thousand   MM = $ million

See Pages 11 through 21 for Explanation of Ratios and Data

Comparative Historical Data | | | | **Current Data Sorted by Sales** | | | | | |

59	51	58	Type of Statement			6	9	25	18
			Unqualified						
164	141	157	Reviewed	2	17	28	50	49	11
186	167	201	Compiled	20	67	49	42	21	2
93	160	197	Tax Returns	40	85	36	24	9	3
194	278	244	Other	26	72	30	48	34	34
4/1/04-3/31/05 ALL	4/1/05-3/31/06 ALL	4/1/06-3/31/07 ALL		194 (4/1-9/30/06)		663 (10/1/06-3/31/07)			
				0-1MM	1-3MM	3-5MM	5-10MM	10-25MM	25MM & OVER
696	797	857	NUMBER OF STATEMENTS	88	241	149	173	138	68
%	%	%	ASSETS	%	%	%	%	%	%
8.0	8.7	8.8	Cash & Equivalents	11.1	9.3	9.5	7.9	7.8	7.4
25.8	26.9	25.3	Trade Receivables (net)	19.5	25.2	26.0	27.0	25.2	27.6
19.4	18.4	18.1	Inventory	10.2	13.7	17.2	21.6	24.3	24.9
2.2	1.7	2.0	All Other Current	1.4	2.4	1.2	1.7	2.8	2.6
55.4	55.7	54.3	Total Current	42.3	50.6	53.9	58.3	60.0	62.5
35.5	35.6	36.6	Fixed Assets (net)	46.3	39.5	37.4	34.7	30.6	29.3
2.7	2.8	3.5	Intangibles (net)	3.7	3.5	3.1	2.6	5.0	3.8
6.4	5.9	5.5	All Other Non-Current	7.6	6.4	5.7	4.5	4.3	4.4
100.0	100.0	100.0	Total	100.0	100.0	100.0	100.0	100.0	100.0
			LIABILITIES						
11.8	10.4	9.5	Notes Payable-Short Term	12.8	9.3	7.6	9.0	8.8	12.7
6.6	6.6	6.5	Cur. Mat.-L.T.D.	7.6	7.1	8.0	5.8	5.2	4.0
13.1	13.1	12.2	Trade Payables	9.2	12.0	10.5	12.5	13.3	16.9
.2	.3	.2	Income Taxes Payable	.0	.1	.2	.4	.5	.1
9.1	8.8	7.5	All Other Current	7.0	6.6	6.4	8.1	8.7	9.6
40.8	39.2	35.9	Total Current	36.6	35.2	32.8	35.8	36.6	43.2
23.4	24.8	25.6	Long-Term Debt	37.3	32.0	24.0	21.0	19.1	16.1
.5	.6	.4	Deferred Taxes	.1	.2	.6	.5	.7	.5
7.6	6.8	5.9	All Other Non-Current	9.9	5.5	5.2	6.1	4.7	5.2
27.7	28.7	32.2	Net Worth	16.1	27.1	37.4	36.5	38.9	35.0
100.0	100.0	100.0	Total Liabilities & Net Worth	100.0	100.0	100.0	100.0	100.0	100.0
			INCOME DATA						
100.0	100.0	100.0	Net Sales	100.0	100.0	100.0	100.0	100.0	100.0
33.2	34.4	35.4	Gross Profit	59.7	40.6	35.1	29.9	25.0	21.3
28.1	28.3	28.2	Operating Expenses	50.0	34.1	28.1	22.7	17.7	14.6
5.1	6.1	7.2	Operating Profit	9.7	6.5	6.9	7.2	7.3	6.7
1.3	1.4	1.6	All Other Expenses (net)	3.2	1.7	1.2	1.0	1.5	1.4
3.8	4.7	5.6	Profit Before Taxes	6.6	4.8	5.8	6.2	5.8	5.3
			RATIOS						
2.3	2.5	2.6	Current	3.0	2.8	2.8	2.6	2.3	2.0
1.4	1.5	1.6		1.5	1.6	1.8	1.7	1.6	1.4
1.0	1.0	1.1		.7	1.0	1.2	1.1	1.1	1.1
1.5	1.7	1.7	Quick	1.8	2.1	2.0	1.8	1.4	1.2
(695) .9	.9	1.0		.9	1.0	1.2	1.0	.8	.7
.5	.6	.6		.4	.5	.7	.6	.5	.5
33 11.0	31 11.8	29 12.6	Sales/Receivables	11 33.2	27 13.4	35 10.5	32 11.4	32 11.5	31 11.7
46 7.9	45 8.0	44 8.4		31 11.7	41 8.9	46 7.9	46 7.9	44 8.4	46 7.9
60 6.1	58 6.2	56 6.5		50 7.3	53 6.9	58 6.3	57 6.4	56 6.5	61 6.0
13 28.2	10 37.3	11 34.1	Cost of Sales/Inventory	0 UND	5 78.7	8 43.3	25 14.4	33 10.9	24 15.0
39 9.4	34 10.6	36 10.1		1 253.8	23 16.0	33 11.2	45 8.1	55 6.7	50 7.3
78 4.7	75 4.9	70 5.2		59 6.2	51 7.2	69 5.3	77 4.7	84 4.3	77 4.7
16 22.5	14 25.2	13 27.5	Cost of Sales/Payables	0 732.0	11 34.3	13 28.2	14 26.6	15 24.6	24 15.1
28 13.1	27 13.5	25 14.7		28 12.9	23 16.1	22 16.2	23 15.8	25 14.4	35 10.4
47 7.8	43 8.5	43 8.6		57 6.4	45 8.0	37 9.9	39 9.3	43 8.5	45 8.1
5.8	5.9	5.8	Sales/Working Capital	6.3	6.0	5.3	5.6	5.1	7.1
12.8	12.2	11.8		22.1	15.7	9.1	10.5	10.1	11.3
-678.2	114.7	68.6		-16.8	-164.8	27.3	37.7	32.1	40.4
8.7	9.0	9.9	EBIT/Interest	7.7	9.2	8.6	12.2	10.2	15.0
(637) 3.2	(745) 3.8	(793) 3.9		(72) 2.9	(227) 3.1	(140) 3.8	(160) 4.5	(128) 4.7	(66) 4.6
1.2	1.5	1.7		1.0	1.2	1.8	1.9	2.1	2.0
3.5	4.3	4.5	Net Profit + Depr., Dep., Amort./Cur. Mat. L/T/D		5.0	3.7	5.4	4.0	7.7
(166) 1.8	(154) 2.1	(181) 2.3		(28) 1.6	(44) 1.9	(44) 2.6	(44) 2.3	(13) 4.9	
1.1	1.2	1.2			.9	1.1	.9	1.5	1.8
.5	.5	.5	Fixed/Worth	.8	.5	.5	.4	.4	.4
1.2	1.2	1.1		2.6	1.3	1.1	1.0	.9	.9
3.4	4.4	3.1		16.9	10.9	2.5	2.2	2.0	1.8
.9	1.0	.9	Debt/Worth	1.4	.9	.8	.7	1.0	1.2
2.4	2.2	1.9		4.5	2.2	1.8	1.5	1.8	2.0
7.5	10.0	6.3		36.7	46.6	5.2	4.3	4.1	4.7
45.9	60.7	60.5	% Profit Before Taxes/Tangible Net Worth	101.6	69.0	49.6	55.3	60.7	65.4
(583) 20.5	(661) 25.5	(731) 27.6		(68) 34.6	(186) 23.8	(132) 27.9	(155) 26.4	(128) 27.5	(62) 33.9
4.8	7.1	7.8		4.0	6.3	7.1	9.7	9.6	10.8
14.2	16.8	18.7	% Profit Before Taxes/Total Assets	29.9	17.5	18.7	18.8	17.8	18.5
6.2	7.4	8.1		6.4	7.1	8.4	8.6	9.3	8.0
.7	1.5	2.5		-.6	.9	2.5	3.3	3.8	3.1
12.4	14.5	12.8	Sales/Net Fixed Assets	9.1	13.9	12.2	12.4	13.0	17.1
6.1	6.3	6.1		4.8	5.6	6.3	6.6	6.9	7.2
3.4	3.6	3.6		2.4	3.3	3.7	3.8	3.8	4.4
2.6	2.9	2.8	Sales/Total Assets	3.2	3.3	2.9	2.6	2.7	2.7
1.9	2.0	2.0		1.9	2.2	2.0	2.0	2.0	2.1
1.4	1.5	1.5		1.0	1.5	1.5	1.6	1.4	1.7
2.0	1.8	2.1	% Depr., Dep., Amort./Sales	2.6	2.2	2.7	2.2	1.8	1.0
(629) 4.1	(688) 3.6	(758) 3.8		(66) 5.6	(204) 4.2	(136) 4.3	(158) 3.6	(131) 3.2	(63) 2.6
6.5	6.0	5.9		10.1	6.7	6.1	5.0	5.0	4.0
2.5	2.9	2.7	% Officers', Directors' Owners' Comp/Sales	5.6	3.6	2.6	2.4	1.0	.6
(333) 4.9	(405) 5.3	(452) 4.9		(53) 8.9	(155) 5.8	(86) 5.0	(90) 3.8	(52) 2.6	(16) 1.4
8.6	8.4	8.7		17.2	9.5	7.1	4.8	4.8	3.1
8490362M	11155381M	11007224M	Net Sales ($)	54269M	456469M	586422M	1207103M	2114144M	6588817M
4682224M	5093686M	5603292M	Total Assets ($)	37962M	240936M	332949M	643376M	1290250M	3057819M

© RMA 2007   M = $ thousand   MM = $ million
See Pages 11 through 21 for Explanation of Ratios and Data

Current Data Sorted by Assets   Comparative Historical Data

	0-500M	500M-2MM	2-10MM	10-50MM	50-100MM	100-250MM	Type of Statement	4/1/02-3/31/03 ALL	4/1/03-3/31/04 ALL
			7	10		1	Unqualified	20	30
		8	46	12	1		Reviewed	59	68
	3	22	12	3			Compiled	39	40
	4	9	1				Tax Returns	7	12
	6	18	22	14		1	Other	45	38
		57 (4/1-9/30/06)		143 (10/1/06-3/31/07)					
NUMBER OF STATEMENTS	13	57	88	39	1	2		170	188
	%	%	%	%	%	%	**ASSETS**	%	%
	16.2	6.6	6.6	3.6			Cash & Equivalents	5.0	6.2
	33.5	28.9	22.7	21.8			Trade Receivables (net)	22.2	22.1
	8.1	21.5	25.6	21.8			Inventory	21.6	22.0
	.6	.6	1.6	1.2			All Other Current	1.6	1.0
	58.3	57.6	56.4	48.3			Total Current	50.3	51.2
	36.6	34.0	36.6	41.5			Fixed Assets (net)	40.3	39.5
	.7	2.6	2.5	3.9			Intangibles (net)	3.0	2.9
	4.4	5.8	4.5	6.2			All Other Non-Current	6.4	6.3
	100.0	100.0	100.0	100.0			Total	100.0	100.0
							LIABILITIES		
	14.0	8.0	10.5	10.1			Notes Payable-Short Term	9.8	11.5
	8.9	9.1	7.8	4.4			Cur. Mat.-L.T.D.	7.1	7.0
	8.3	14.1	13.6	11.7			Trade Payables	11.4	11.3
	.1	.1	.4	.2			Income Taxes Payable	.2	.1
	4.2	4.9	6.5	6.9			All Other Current	6.8	7.1
	35.4	36.2	38.7	33.4			Total Current	35.3	36.9
	35.7	21.2	20.4	21.5			Long-Term Debt	24.3	21.6
	.0	.5	.8	1.1			Deferred Taxes	.8	.9
	7.3	5.1	4.1	4.1			All Other Non-Current	4.2	7.3
	21.6	37.0	36.1	39.9			Net Worth	35.4	33.4
	100.0	100.0	100.0	100.0			Total Liabilities & Net Worth	100.0	100.0
							INCOME DATA		
	100.0	100.0	100.0	100.0			Net Sales	100.0	100.0
	43.7	32.6	24.0	21.5			Gross Profit	26.1	26.4
	40.6	27.5	18.9	15.5			Operating Expenses	25.0	24.6
	3.0	5.1	5.1	6.1			Operating Profit	1.1	1.7
	1.4	1.5	1.8	1.4			All Other Expenses (net)	2.2	1.5
	1.6	3.6	3.3	4.6			Profit Before Taxes	-1.1	.2
							RATIOS		
	3.4	2.7	1.9	2.1			Current	2.4	2.3
	1.5	1.4	1.5	1.4				1.4	1.5
	.8	1.0	1.2	1.0				1.0	1.0
	3.1	1.3	1.1	1.1			Quick	1.2	1.4
	.8	.9	.7	.7				.7	.8
	.7	.6	.5	.6				.5	.5
	16 22.9	35 10.6	33 11.0	42 8.7			Sales/Receivables	37 9.8	40 9.2
	36 10.1	42 8.7	43 8.5	55 6.7				43 8.4	48 7.6
	41 8.8	54 6.8	53 6.9	63 5.8				58 6.3	57 6.5
	0 UND	27 13.8	38 9.6	35 10.6			Cost of Sales/Inventory	29 12.6	32 11.5
	1 260.0	50 7.3	60 6.1	60 6.1				55 6.6	57 6.4
	23 16.1	66 5.5	86 4.3	87 4.2				89 4.1	92 4.0
	2 162.9	15 24.1	17 22.0	16 23.2			Cost of Sales/Payables	15 24.9	16 22.1
	10 37.4	25 14.6	27 13.4	31 11.7				26 14.1	30 12.3
	28 13.2	41 8.9	41 8.9	47 7.7				40 9.1	47 7.8
	9.0	6.0	5.9	5.7			Sales/Working Capital	5.9	5.8
	34.5	12.3	10.8	12.4				13.6	9.7
	-31.7	999.8	37.4	78.7				205.4	845.0
	9.0	4.8	5.2	10.7			EBIT/Interest	3.7	4.5
	(11) 2.3	(46) 1.9	(83) 3.0	(35) 2.6				(161) 1.4	(171) 1.4
	1.8	.9	1.5	1.7				-1.0	-.7
		4.2	3.7	5.1			Net Profit + Depr., Dep., Amort./Cur. Mat. L/T/D	2.4	2.7
		(12) 1.9	(35) 1.7	(14) 2.6				(58) 1.4	(55) 1.3
		1.2	1.2	.9				.7	.9
	.3	.4	.6	.5			Fixed/Worth	.6	.6
	1.3	.7	1.0	1.2				1.2	1.3
	-2.5	5.5	2.3	2.2				3.0	3.5
	.6	.6	.9	.7			Debt/Worth	.8	.8
	1.5	1.7	2.0	1.6				1.6	1.8
	-6.3	8.8	4.5	3.9				5.8	5.7
		36.2	33.4	29.4			% Profit Before Taxes/Tangible Net Worth	19.9	18.9
		(45) 13.7	(78) 16.2	(35) 19.2				(143) 5.4	(158) 5.9
		2.4	6.8	6.8				-8.8	-8.3
	21.2	11.6	12.0	14.3			% Profit Before Taxes/Total Assets	6.6	7.1
	7.0	4.4	5.4	5.5				1.5	1.3
	1.0	.4	2.0	1.8				-5.9	-4.5
	48.5	16.3	12.4	7.3			Sales/Net Fixed Assets	9.2	8.4
	16.3	7.6	5.2	3.7				3.7	4.1
	5.0	3.6	3.0	2.4				2.5	2.6
	7.8	3.0	2.4	1.8			Sales/Total Assets	2.2	2.0
	4.0	2.2	1.8	1.4				1.6	1.6
	2.5	1.5	1.4	1.2				1.2	1.2
		1.3	2.0	3.3			% Depr., Dep., Amort./Sales	2.9	3.1
		(52) 3.6	(85) 4.4	(36) 5.0				(159) 5.1	(179) 5.1
		6.7	5.7	7.1				7.6	8.3
		2.6	2.0	1.3			% Officers', Directors' Owners' Comp/Sales	2.8	2.5
		(36) 4.1	(35) 2.7	(10) 1.7				(91) 5.2	(94) 5.6
		9.3	4.7	2.6				8.7	9.3
	18420M	162438M	820587M	1183966M	102945M	422223M	Net Sales ($)	1378753M	1677630M
	3677M	69298M	432962M	784418M	75437M	243375M	Total Assets ($)	978671M	1148812M

M = $ thousand   MM = $ million
See Pages 11 through 21 for Explanation of Ratios and Data

Comparative Historical Data			Type of Statement	0-1MM	1-3MM	3-5MM	5-10MM	10-25MM	25MM & OVER
25	21	18	Unqualified			2	3	6	7
71	83	67	Reviewed		3	10	20	28	6
39	33	40	Compiled	3	15	9	7	5	1
19	16	14	Tax Returns	2	8	8	3	1	
44	45	61	Other	3	16	8	14	11	9
4/1/04-3/31/05 ALL	4/1/05-3/31/06 ALL	4/1/06-3/31/07 ALL		57 (4/1-9/30/06)		143 (10/1/06-3/31/07)			
198	198	200	NUMBER OF STATEMENTS	8	42	32	44	51	23
%	%	%	ASSETS	%	%	%	%	%	%
5.4	6.1	6.7	Cash & Equivalents		7.4	7.4	6.6	5.3	4.8
25.0	24.8	25.0	Trade Receivables (net)		25.8	26.1	24.9	25.2	23.4
23.4	22.3	22.5	Inventory		18.0	22.8	25.5	25.1	22.8
1.0	1.3	1.2	All Other Current		.6	1.9	1.4	1.1	1.7
54.8	54.5	55.4	Total Current		51.8	58.1	58.4	56.6	52.7
36.7	37.0	36.8	Fixed Assets (net)		37.4	37.1	34.1	36.0	39.6
4.0	3.3	2.7	Intangibles (net)		4.1	2.0	1.9	2.5	3.4
4.5	5.3	5.1	All Other Non-Current		6.6	2.8	5.6	4.9	4.2
100.0	100.0	100.0	Total		100.0	100.0	100.0	100.0	100.0
			LIABILITIES						
9.7	10.4	9.9	Notes Payable-Short Term		8.0	12.8	10.3	9.1	10.7
6.0	6.2	7.5	Cur. Mat.-L.T.D.		9.9	8.7	8.3	4.8	4.0
13.3	13.1	13.0	Trade Payables		10.8	12.2	15.4	14.3	12.9
.1	.1	.2	Income Taxes Payable		.0	.2	.2	.5	.1
7.1	6.8	6.3	All Other Current		5.6	4.5	6.5	6.7	10.4
36.1	36.5	37.0	Total Current		34.3	38.5	40.7	35.4	38.1
20.9	22.9	21.9	Long-Term Debt		29.1	16.7	19.8	17.6	22.0
.9	.7	.7	Deferred Taxes		.3	.7	.9	.9	1.0
8.1	6.8	4.5	All Other Non-Current		6.7	3.0	4.4	4.0	4.0
34.0	33.1	35.8	Net Worth		29.5	41.1	34.2	42.2	34.9
100.0	100.0	100.0	Total Liabilties & Net Worth		100.0	100.0	100.0	100.0	100.0
			INCOME DATA						
100.0	100.0	100.0	Net Sales		100.0	100.0	100.0	100.0	100.0
26.3	25.9	27.2	Gross Profit		36.6	26.6	22.8	23.6	19.4
22.0	21.3	22.0	Operating Expenses		31.3	21.5	18.9	17.2	15.4
4.3	4.6	5.2	Operating Profit		5.3	5.1	3.8	6.4	4.1
1.2	1.3	1.6	All Other Expenses (net)		2.2	1.5	1.7	1.2	.8
3.1	3.2	3.6	Profit Before Taxes		3.1	3.6	2.1	5.2	3.3
			RATIOS						
2.3	2.4	2.2			2.6	2.2	2.1	2.0	2.3
1.5	1.5	1.5	Current		1.3	1.5	1.5	1.5	1.3
1.1	1.1	1.0			.9	1.2	1.0	1.2	1.0
1.4	1.4	1.3			1.4	1.4	1.2	1.3	1.1
.8	.9	.8	Quick		.8	.9	.8	.8	.7
.5	.5	.5			.5	.5	.5	.6	.6
37 9.7	38 9.5	35 10.4		34 10.8	34 10.6	30 12.0	38 9.6	45 8.2	
50 7.2	47 7.7	43 8.4	Sales/Receivables	39 9.4	42 8.7	42 8.7	44 8.3	53 6.8	
60 6.1	59 6.2	56 6.5		53 6.9	56 6.5	53 6.9	59 6.2	61 6.0	
35 10.5	32 11.5	31 11.6		15 23.8	21 17.6	36 10.1	38 9.6	31 11.7	
57 6.4	54 6.8	55 6.7	Cost of Sales/Inventory	37 9.9	61 5.9	56 6.5	55 6.7	62 5.9	
94 3.9	83 4.4	80 4.5		65 5.6	83 4.4	83 4.4	81 4.5	80 4.5	
20 18.5	20 18.4	15 23.9		14 25.9	14 26.5	16 22.7	19 19.4	14 26.5	
31 11.7	30 12.2	27 13.7	Cost of Sales/Payables	25 14.9	24 15.0	28 13.0	31 11.6	38 9.7	
49 7.5	46 8.0	42 8.8		29 12.8	39 9.3	41 8.9	47 7.8	47 7.7	
5.7	5.8	5.9			6.9	5.8	5.8	6.2	4.8
10.0	10.1	11.7	Sales/Working Capital		18.7	10.3	10.8	10.9	13.8
44.8	66.3	557.2			-60.4	24.1	242.4	28.2	-84.0
7.6	6.5	6.1			4.6	4.9	4.4	10.6	8.7
(184) 2.6	(180) 2.4	(178) 2.7	EBIT/Interest	(36) 1.8	(28) 3.1	(41) 2.7	(48) 3.9	(20) 3.6	
.9	1.1	1.5			1.0	1.6	1.4	1.7	1.8
3.0	3.9	4.4					2.5	6.2	5.2
(63) 1.8	(63) 1.8	(65) 1.9	Net Profit + Depr., Dep., Amort./Cur. Mat. L/T/D			(18) 1.4	(17) 2.9	(11) 4.2	
1.3	.8	1.2					.6	1.7	1.8
.7	.5	.5			.5	.6	.4	.5	.5
1.2	1.2	1.1	Fixed/Worth		1.4	1.0	.9	1.0	1.2
3.0	4.0	2.6			-3.7	1.7	2.5	1.6	2.2
1.0	.8	.8			.8	.8	1.0	.9	.7
2.0	1.9	1.8	Debt/Worth		1.9	1.5	2.0	1.6	1.6
5.4	7.8	4.9			-12.9	2.6	5.2	3.5	3.9
33.1	30.1	33.2			32.4	37.0	27.7	35.5	25.7
(166) 14.7	(165) 13.5	(169) 16.4	% Profit Before Taxes/Tangible Net Worth	(29) 12.6	(30) 13.3	(38) 13.1	(48) 28.1	(19) 14.5	
1.8	1.7	5.6			2.3	4.0	6.3	7.7	4.3
12.3	10.2	12.5			11.1	15.0	9.4	18.8	12.5
4.6	4.4	5.4	% Profit Before Taxes/Total Assets		3.9	5.7	5.5	7.5	5.9
.0	.2	1.3			.5	1.4	2.9	2.1	.0
10.0	9.5	12.7			17.8	10.2	14.7	12.2	7.6
4.3	4.9	5.3	Sales/Net Fixed Assets		6.8	4.9	6.6	5.5	4.4
2.8	3.1	3.1			3.5	3.1	3.1	3.1	2.9
2.3	2.4	2.7			3.0	2.7	2.7	2.5	1.9
1.7	1.8	1.8	Sales/Total Assets		2.1	1.8	1.8	1.9	1.7
1.3	1.3	1.4			1.4	1.4	1.4	1.4	1.3
2.9	2.4	2.0			1.0	3.5	1.7	2.0	2.9
(181) 4.9	(191) 4.3	(183) 4.4	% Depr., Dep., Amort./Sales	(35) 3.9	(29) 5.2	(43) 3.8	(49) 4.1	(20) 4.5	
7.6	6.2	6.2			6.8	6.3	6.1	5.3	7.1
2.1	1.7	2.0			3.1	2.7	2.4	1.0	
(97) 3.8	(85) 3.3	(87) 3.5	% Officers', Directors' Owners' Comp/Sales	(25) 4.3	(20) 3.9	(17) 3.2	(17) 1.7		
7.7	6.4	6.4			8.9	8.7	8.1	2.6	
1904663M	2284671M	2710579M	Net Sales ($)	4645M	80667M	128923M	320951M	815195M	1360198M
1272672M	1440701M	1609167M	Total Assets ($)	3476M	42023M	72482M	179263M	460933M	850990M

© RMA 2007   M = $ thousand   MM = $ million
See Pages 11 through 21 for Explanation of Ratios and Data

Current Data Sorted by Assets   ## Comparative Historical Data

0-500M	500M-2MM	2-10MM	10-50MM	50-100MM	100-250MM		4/1/02-3/31/03 ALL	4/1/03-3/31/04 ALL
						Type of Statement		
		6	16	1	3	Unqualified	24	30
1	8	23	5			Reviewed	38	35
2	3	13	1			Compiled	18	26
2	3	3				Tax Returns	3	6
2	7	21	9	3	1	Other	28	31
	30 (4/1-9/30/06)		103 (10/1/06-3/31/07)					
7	21	66	31	4	4	**NUMBER OF STATEMENTS**	111	128
%	%	%	%	%	%	**ASSETS**	%	%
	9.0	4.3	6.0			Cash & Equivalents	7.1	4.8
	30.2	25.5	21.7			Trade Receivables (net)	22.6	24.4
	31.2	36.8	31.3			Inventory	29.1	29.8
	.4	1.8	2.7			All Other Current	1.8	2.2
	70.8	68.4	61.7			Total Current	60.5	61.1
	20.9	24.8	30.4			Fixed Assets (net)	30.2	30.1
	1.2	3.2	3.0			Intangibles (net)	4.3	4.0
	7.1	3.6	4.9			All Other Non-Current	5.0	4.8
	100.0	100.0	100.0			Total	100.0	100.0
						LIABILITIES		
	5.2	13.9	8.5			Notes Payable-Short Term	11.6	10.7
	10.8	4.2	3.6			Cur. Mat.-L.T.D.	5.1	4.2
	12.1	17.2	13.8			Trade Payables	12.2	12.9
	.4	.4	.3			Income Taxes Payable	.2	.2
	22.5	5.8	5.8			All Other Current	7.0	8.8
	50.9	41.5	32.0			Total Current	36.1	36.8
	14.0	17.5	13.1			Long-Term Debt	13.3	15.2
	.6	.4	.8			Deferred Taxes	.8	.7
	4.9	6.4	5.5			All Other Non-Current	5.0	5.0
	29.6	34.2	48.7			Net Worth	44.8	42.3
	100.0	100.0	100.0			Total Liabilities & Net Worth	100.0	100.0
						INCOME DATA		
	100.0	100.0	100.0			Net Sales	100.0	100.0
	38.8	26.4	24.4			Gross Profit	26.3	28.6
	34.9	20.9	17.2			Operating Expenses	23.1	24.8
	3.9	5.6	7.2			Operating Profit	3.2	3.8
	1.4	1.5	1.1			All Other Expenses (net)	1.2	1.3
	2.5	4.1	6.1			Profit Before Taxes	2.0	2.5
						RATIOS		
	2.9	2.7	3.5				3.0	2.9
	1.7	1.7	2.0			Current	1.7	1.7
	1.0	1.2	1.2				1.3	1.2
	1.9	1.0	1.6				1.4	1.5
	.8	.7	.7			Quick	.8	.8
	.6	.5	.5				.5	.5
30	12.3	38 9.7	37 9.8				37 9.8	39 9.5
37	9.8	44 8.2	47 7.7			Sales/Receivables	43 8.4	47 7.8
52	7.0	53 6.9	54 6.8				53 6.9	56 6.5
38	9.5	61 5.9	58 6.3				53 6.8	51 7.2
70	5.2	91 4.0	88 4.1			Cost of Sales/Inventory	77 4.7	75 4.9
121	3.0	112 3.3	138 2.7				114 3.2	115 3.2
15	25.0	20 18.5	19 19.6				17 21.1	19 19.5
22	16.7	35 10.3	36 10.0			Cost of Sales/Payables	29 12.8	33 11.2
40	9.0	54 6.8	56 6.6				46 8.0	44 8.2
	5.2	4.9	3.5				4.6	4.5
	7.7	7.2	5.5			Sales/Working Capital	7.5	7.9
	NM	17.2	25.3				18.8	21.4
	25.9	6.6	12.2				6.2	8.4
	(20) 3.0	(62) 2.7	(29) 5.5			EBIT/Interest	(96) 2.6	(117) 2.4
	1.4	1.5	2.2				.4	.4
		7.7	11.1			Net Profit + Depr., Dep.,	3.0	2.6
	(20) 3.1	(12) 1.8				Amort./Cur. Mat. L/T/D	(39) 2.0	(36) 1.3
	1.9	.9					1.1	.6
	.1	.3	.3				.4	.3
	.8	.7	.7			Fixed/Worth	.7	.7
	1.8	2.5	1.2				1.9	2.1
	.6	.8	.4				.4	.5
	1.5	2.2	1.1			Debt/Worth	1.3	1.3
	5.1	7.7	3.0				3.7	4.6
	25.9	52.1	25.8			% Profit Before Taxes/Tangible	23.5	26.7
	(17) 15.4	(60) 26.5	(29) 16.4			Net Worth	(99) 8.5	(115) 9.1
	6.5	6.1	11.0				-4.2	-3.2
	17.1	14.7	14.9			% Profit Before Taxes/Total	9.8	9.8
	5.1	6.1	7.3			Assets	3.2	3.4
	2.1	2.2	3.6				-3.1	-1.7
	51.9	18.3	9.5				11.1	15.0
	16.1	8.6	6.2			Sales/Net Fixed Assets	6.4	6.2
	7.6	5.2	4.1				4.1	3.6
	3.4	2.5	2.1				2.2	2.4
	2.7	2.0	1.8			Sales/Total Assets	1.7	1.8
	2.1	1.7	1.3				1.3	1.4
	1.0	1.2	2.1				2.0	1.4
	(18) 1.8	(59) 2.2	(30) 2.8			% Depr., Dep., Amort./Sales	(101) 3.6	(112) 2.8
	2.8	3.5	4.9				5.3	5.0
	3.8	2.2				% Officers', Directors'	2.5	1.6
	(13) 6.5	(27) 3.4				Owners' Comp/Sales	(32) 6.1	(47) 4.1
	14.1	8.0					8.2	6.6
6022M	69848M	649050M	1205429M	307148M	771832M	Net Sales ($)	2818190M	3407853M
2145M	25218M	317888M	706677M	259479M	453569M	Total Assets ($)	2141842M	2534176M

M = $ thousand   MM = $ million
See Pages 11 through 21 for Explanation of Ratios and Data

Comparative Historical Data / Current Data Sorted by Sales

4/1/04-3/31/05 ALL	4/1/05-3/31/06 ALL	4/1/06-3/31/07 ALL	Type of Statement	0-1MM	1-3MM	3-5MM	5-10MM	10-25MM	25MM & OVER
31	27	26	Unqualified				3	6	17
39	33	37	Reviewed	1	5	5	9	12	5
10	15	19	Compiled	2	1	6	6	3	1
8	9	8	Tax Returns	3	1	1	4		
34	54	43	Other		3	6	11	11	11
					30 (4/1-9/30/06)		103 (10/1/06-3/31/07)		
122	138	133	NUMBER OF STATEMENTS	6	10	18	33	32	34
%	%	%	**ASSETS**	%	%	%	%	%	%
4.4	5.2	5.5	Cash & Equivalents		6.3	8.9	4.3	3.9	4.9
27.5	26.9	25.3	Trade Receivables (net)		29.5	22.9	27.4	25.1	22.2
31.5	34.3	33.4	Inventory		37.2	27.1	34.0	41.2	29.8
1.5	1.7	1.7	All Other Current		.2	2.1	.6	2.8	2.2
64.8	68.2	65.8	Total Current		73.2	61.0	66.4	73.0	59.1
27.0	24.2	26.0	Fixed Assets (net)		18.5	27.8	27.1	22.8	29.7
3.7	1.7	3.0	Intangibles (net)		1.8	6.1	1.5	1.6	4.5
4.5	6.0	5.1	All Other Non-Current		6.6	5.1	5.1	2.6	6.7
100.0	100.0	100.0	Total		100.0	100.0	100.0	100.0	100.0
			LIABILITIES						
16.9	13.5	11.3	Notes Payable-Short Term		9.2	5.5	11.6	16.9	10.0
3.5	4.3	5.0	Cur. Mat.-L.T.D.		18.2	6.4	3.6	4.1	3.0
16.6	16.4	15.1	Trade Payables		14.0	11.7	19.7	14.4	13.6
.1	.2	.3	Income Taxes Payable		.5	.6	.1	.5	.3
6.7	8.0	8.5	All Other Current		4.1	24.9	5.5	6.6	5.8
43.8	42.5	40.2	Total Current		46.0	49.1	40.4	42.4	32.7
12.9	13.0	15.9	Long-Term Debt		16.4	25.2	15.7	14.9	12.8
.7	.6	.6	Deferred Taxes		1.0	.2	.4	.5	1.1
7.0	4.4	6.3	*All Other Non-Current		5.6	3.4	8.9	6.8	5.6
35.6	39.6	36.9	Net Worth		31.0	22.0	34.6	35.4	47.7
100.0	100.0	100.0	Total Liabilities & Net Worth		100.0	100.0	100.0	100.0	100.0
			INCOME DATA						
100.0	100.0	100.0	Net Sales		100.0	100.0	100.0	100.0	100.0
25.3	26.5	28.2	Gross Profit		35.2	33.3	25.1	28.0	23.3
21.1	21.4	22.8	Operating Expenses		32.0	29.2	20.1	21.1	17.4
4.2	5.1	5.5	Operating Profit		3.3	4.1	5.0	6.8	5.9
1.2	1.1	1.3	All Other Expenses (net)		.7	1.9	1.3	1.5	.9
3.0	4.0	4.2	Profit Before Taxes		2.5	2.2	3.7	5.3	5.1
			RATIOS						
2.2	2.4	3.0	Current		2.8	2.6	2.7	2.8	3.2
1.4	1.6	1.7			1.7	1.3	1.7	1.7	1.9
1.1	1.1	1.2			.9	.9	1.2	1.3	1.2
1.1	1.3	1.2	Quick		1.7	1.4	1.1	1.0	1.6
.8	.8	.8			.7	.8	.8	.7	.7
.5	.5	.5			.5	.4	.6	.5	.5
41 8.8	39 9.4	37 9.9	Sales/Receivables		30 12.2	25 14.8	39 9.3	39 9.3	39 9.3
50 7.2	46 7.9	44 8.2			38 9.5	34 10.6	47 7.8	47 7.8	45 8.0
59 6.2	54 6.7	53 6.9			51 7.2	44 8.4	55 6.6	54 6.8	53 6.8
55 6.6	50 7.3	56 6.6	Cost of Sales/Inventory		59 6.1	38 9.6	56 6.5	66 5.5	56 6.5
74 4.9	73 5.0	86 4.2			87 4.2	66 5.5	87 4.2	102 3.6	81 4.5
108 3.4	120 3.0	119 3.1			132 2.8	110 3.3	100 3.7	156 2.3	121 3.0
26 13.8	23 16.2	18 20.1	Cost of Sales/Payables		16 22.9	13 28.6	27 13.6	16 23.1	21 17.6
38 9.6	36 10.2	33 10.9			24 15.4	19 18.8	39 9.4	29 12.7	33 10.9
51 7.1	48 7.6	48 7.6			42 8.7	62 5.8	49 7.4	57 6.4	46 7.9
5.7	4.6	4.3	Sales/Working Capital		5.2	5.3	5.4	3.9	4.0
11.5	8.3	6.8			11.2	13.4	7.3	6.4	6.7
65.3	28.5	26.6			-40.6	-56.3	19.6	13.5	25.3
9.4	10.1	8.0	EBIT/Interest		5.3	7.6	5.8	8.5	11.1
(114) 3.6	(123) 3.7	(124) 3.0			2.0	(15) 2.1	(31) 2.5	3.5	(31) 4.6
.8	1.3	1.6			1.2	1.2	1.7	1.6	1.9
6.5	7.8	5.1	Net Profit + Depr., Dep., Amort./Cur. Mat. L/T/D				5.6	12.5	5.1
(33) 2.5	(46) 3.3	(44) 3.0					(10) 3.1	(11) 3.0	(15) 4.1
1.3	1.1	1.2					1.4	1.0	1.6
.3	.3	.3	Fixed/Worth		.1	.3	.3	.3	.4
.9	.6	.7			.5	1.7	.8	.6	.7
1.7	1.2	1.9			NM	-106.6	2.0	1.8	1.3
.8	.6	.6	Debt/Worth		.8	.8	.9	.6	.4
2.0	1.8	1.7			1.3	4.3	2.0	2.0	1.1
5.4	3.3	5.4			NM	-387.1	5.4	6.6	3.1
36.8	38.0	45.5	% Profit Before Taxes/Tangible Net Worth		46.4		45.2	52.3	26.5
(105) 16.4	(126) 18.5	(118) 18.8			(13) 21.4		(31) 16.1	(29) 32.5	(31) 16.0
1.8	4.8	6.6			4.3		7.4	11.4	8.5
12.8	16.2	15.0	% Profit Before Taxes/Total Assets		16.6	11.2	11.2	19.8	14.5
5.0	6.3	5.7			4.2	5.2	6.1	7.4	6.0
-.1	1.2	2.1			.4	1.6	1.6	2.6	3.0
18.7	22.4	16.1	Sales/Net Fixed Assets		130.2	26.5	17.0	18.4	9.4
7.3	10.0	8.4			15.6	11.9	7.8	11.6	6.4
4.8	5.6	4.7			9.1	4.7	5.2	5.0	4.3
2.4	2.7	2.5	Sales/Total Assets		3.6	3.2	2.6	2.4	2.2
1.9	2.1	2.0			2.5	2.2	2.1	2.0	1.8
1.5	1.6	1.6			1.8	1.8	1.7	1.6	1.3
1.4	1.1	1.3	% Depr., Dep., Amort./Sales			1.0	1.9	1.1	1.8
(110) 2.5	(127) 2.1	(121) 2.4				(16) 1.5	(29) 2.5	(29) 2.0	2.7
4.2	3.6	3.8				3.7	4.0	3.6	4.4
1.9	2.1	2.3	% Officers', Directors', Owners' Comp/Sales				2.0	2.4	
(37) 3.7	(47) 4.1	(49) 3.6					(13) 3.6	(12) 3.1	
5.1	8.7	8.4					8.7	10.0	
3052464M	3555313M	3009329M	Net Sales ($)	3827M	20612M	74107M	237592M	481163M	2192028M
1771686M	2028308M	1764976M	Total Assets ($)	1937M	8976M	35322M	118360M	270919M	1329462M

© RMA 2007

M = $ thousand   MM = $ million
See Pages 11 through 21 for Explanation of Ratios and Data

Current Data Sorted by Assets   Comparative Historical Data

0-500M	500M-2MM	2-10MM	10-50MM	50-100MM	100-250MM	Type of Statement	ALL	ALL
1		1	6			Unqualified	8	10
1	5	14	3			Reviewed	22	30
1	8	8				Compiled	16	21
1	5					Tax Returns	5	7
3	4	14	9	1		Other	16	23
	21 (4/1-9/30/06)		63 (10/1/06-3/31/07)				4/1/02-3/31/03	4/1/03-3/31/04
0-500M	500M-2MM	2-10MM	10-50MM	50-100MM	100-250MM		ALL	ALL
6	22	37	18	1		NUMBER OF STATEMENTS	67	91

0-500M %	500M-2MM %	2-10MM %	10-50MM %	50-100MM %	100-250MM %		%	%
						ASSETS		
	9.2	5.8	5.5			Cash & Equivalents	5.2	5.7
	32.3	30.3	19.7			Trade Receivables (net)	22.8	26.5
	3.3	10.2	7.3			Inventory	5.7	6.8
	3.3	1.3	.4			All Other Current	1.2	1.9
	48.1	47.5	32.9			Total Current	34.9	40.9
	40.9	40.7	54.9			Fixed Assets (net)	53.4	46.5
	4.0	4.5	7.2			Intangibles (net)	3.5	3.5
	7.0	7.3	5.0			All Other Non-Current	8.2	9.1
	100.0	100.0	100.0			Total	100.0	100.0
						LIABILITIES		
	7.9	8.5	4.6			Notes Payable-Short Term	8.7	8.9
	6.4	5.4	5.3			Cur. Mat.-L.T.D.	8.8	6.6
	10.4	11.2	8.5			Trade Payables	10.3	9.8
	.5	.6	.2			Income Taxes Payable	.1	.2
	16.5	11.9	6.2			All Other Current	5.8	8.0
	41.6	37.7	24.8			Total Current	33.8	33.5
	26.1	21.4	25.6			Long-Term Debt	26.6	22.8
	.4	.7	.6			Deferred Taxes	1.1	1.0
	12.5	7.9	4.3			All Other Non-Current	3.2	9.2
	19.4	32.2	44.8			Net Worth	35.3	33.5
	100.0	100.0	100.0			Total Liabilties & Net Worth	100.0	100.0
						INCOME DATA		
	100.0	100.0	100.0			Net Sales	100.0	100.0
	36.1	32.7	37.0			Gross Profit	34.8	37.6
	30.0	28.5	25.3			Operating Expenses	32.4	33.4
	6.1	4.2	11.7			Operating Profit	2.4	4.3
	2.4	1.2	2.0			All Other Expenses (net)	2.1	1.8
	3.8	3.0	9.8			Profit Before Taxes	.3	2.5
						RATIOS		
	3.8	2.2	2.1			Current	2.2	2.0
	1.6	1.3	1.2				1.0	1.3
	.9	.8	.9				.7	.9
	3.4	2.1	1.3			Quick	1.9	1.8
	1.4	.9	.9				.8	1.0
	.9	.6	.7				.5	.6
	40 9.0	49 7.5	46 8.0			Sales/Receivables	46 8.0	47 7.8
	51 7.2	55 6.6	50 7.2				55 6.7	53 6.9
	61 6.0	65 5.6	57 6.5				63 5.8	64 5.7
	0 UND	0 UND	0 UND			Cost of Sales/Inventory	0 UND	0 UND
	0 UND	6 56.2	15 24.1				1 281.1	4 87.3
	10 35.8	43 8.5	37 9.9				11 33.0	21 17.0
	15 24.0	13 27.8	15 23.9			Cost of Sales/Payables	15 24.1	15 23.8
	23 15.8	24 15.2	25 14.5				24 15.4	25 14.6
	30 12.0	36 10.2	36 10.2				52 7.0	46 7.9
	6.1	8.2	7.9			Sales/Working Capital	8.1	9.3
	10.6	12.8	34.9				264.7	23.6
	-59.1	-20.6	-78.1				-10.1	-29.0
	27.9	5.2	10.7			EBIT/Interest	2.8	5.2
	(20) 2.4	(33) 2.3	6.1				(58) 1.6	(88) 2.1
	.6	.5	2.1				.1	-.8
		3.6				Net Profit + Depr., Dep.,	2.6	5.3
		(10) 3.0				Amort./Cur. Mat. L/T/D	(24) 1.4	(26) 2.2
		1.5					.7	1.3
	.5	.7	1.0			Fixed/Worth	.9	.7
	2.0	1.5	1.8				2.0	1.3
	-5.0	12.3	1.9				4.5	3.6
	.6	.6	.8			Debt/Worth	.9	.7
	2.7	1.5	1.5				1.9	1.8
	-8.8	26.3	2.2				6.4	4.5
	71.5	42.9	45.5			% Profit Before Taxes/Tangible	23.8	25.1
	(15) 22.5	(30) 26.2	(17) 20.8			Net Worth	(57) 6.0	(75) 8.8
	9.4	7.0	12.6				-4.9	-6.4
	14.1	15.7	15.3			% Profit Before Taxes/Total	6.8	8.6
	8.3	6.2	9.5			Assets	2.4	2.7
	-4.9	.0	4.7				-4.3	-4.6
	10.9	14.8	3.8			Sales/Net Fixed Assets	5.6	7.1
	5.6	5.4	2.5				2.3	3.5
	3.3	2.6	1.4				1.4	1.9
	3.3	2.8	1.6			Sales/Total Assets	2.2	2.2
	2.3	2.1	1.2				1.4	1.5
	1.6	1.2	1.0				1.0	1.1
	2.8	1.8	3.9			% Depr., Dep., Amort./Sales	3.6	3.6
	(20) 4.2	3.9	5.6				(62) 6.6	(85) 5.9
	6.8	6.4	8.6				9.7	8.9
	3.8	3.4				% Officers', Directors'	2.8	3.3
	(14) 5.7	(18) 5.8				Owners' Comp/Sales	(28) 4.5	(43) 6.0
	8.7	7.7					8.1	9.2
7071M	76145M	358504M	545814M	12709M		Net Sales ($)	425808M	985871M
1804M	32507M	176250M	390020M	51524M		Total Assets ($)	329955M	698937M

Data not available for 0-500M, 50-100MM, and 100-250MM asset-size columns (DATA NOT AVAILABLE).

M = $ thousand   MM = $ million
See Pages 11 through 21 for Explanation of Ratios and Data

Comparative Historical Data / Current Data Sorted by Sales

4/1/04-3/31/05 ALL	4/1/05-3/31/06 ALL	4/1/06-3/31/07 ALL	Type of Statement	0-1MM	1-3MM	3-5MM	5-10MM	10-25MM	25MM & OVER
13	10	7	Unqualified				1	3	3
23	22	23	Reviewed		4	6	4	8	1
15	11	17	Compiled	1	5	5	4	2	
4	6	6	Tax Returns	1	2	2	1		
28	22	31	Other	2	4	4	6	11	5
				21 (4/1-9/30/06)			63 (10/1/06-3/31/07)		
83	71	84	**NUMBER OF STATEMENTS**	4	14	17	16	24	9
%	%	%	**ASSETS**	%	%	%	%	%	%
8.5	7.7	6.7	Cash & Equivalents		3.6	10.2	5.1	6.3	
25.9	25.7	28.7	Trade Receivables (net)		23.8	34.9	27.8	30.3	
7.0	6.3	7.9	Inventory		4.5	2.4	12.2	10.1	
1.2	1.0	1.7	All Other Current		.6	1.8	4.2	.7	
42.6	40.7	45.1	Total Current		32.4	49.4	49.3	47.4	
47.6	47.8	43.0	Fixed Assets (net)		54.7	40.1	35.2	43.0	
3.3	4.2	5.0	Intangibles (net)		6.8	5.2	3.4	4.1	
6.5	7.4	7.0	All Other Non-Current		6.1	5.2	12.2	5.5	
100.0	100.0	100.0	Total		100.0	100.0	100.0	100.0	
			LIABILITIES						
8.7	4.9	7.4	Notes Payable-Short Term		9.3	7.2	12.2	3.3	
6.5	5.9	6.3	Cur. Mat.-L.T.D.		9.2	4.2	7.4	4.4	
10.9	10.2	11.0	Trade Payables		8.9	8.5	10.1	12.8	
.2	.3	.5	Income Taxes Payable		.7	1.0	.0	.3	
6.4	11.7	14.4	All Other Current		3.1	21.4	14.7	10.7	
32.7	33.0	39.6	Total Current		31.3	42.3	44.4	31.6	
24.0	30.2	23.5	Long-Term Debt		28.0	25.1	19.0	26.5	
1.2	.9	.6	Deferred Taxes		.9	.4	.5	.8	
9.3	6.6	7.9	All Other Non-Current		6.2	12.7	14.7	3.8	
32.7	29.3	28.3	Net Worth		33.6	19.6	21.4	37.3	
100.0	100.0	100.0	Total Liabilties & Net Worth		100.0	100.0	100.0	100.0	
			INCOME DATA						
100.0	100.0	100.0	Net Sales		100.0	100.0	100.0	100.0	
36.1	36.6	36.2	Gross Profit		40.8	37.1	38.9	30.2	
28.6	28.8	29.6	Operating Expenses		33.7	30.9	33.2	23.5	
7.5	7.8	6.7	Operating Profit		7.1	6.3	5.7	6.7	
1.8	2.3	1.8	All Other Expenses (net)		4.0	1.4	.4	2.0	
5.7	5.5	4.8	Profit Before Taxes		3.1	4.9	5.2	4.7	
			RATIOS						
2.2	2.3	2.4	Current		2.2	4.0	2.1	2.3	
1.4	1.4	1.4			1.1	2.4	1.0	1.7	
.9	.8	.8			.7	.8	.8	1.1	
2.1	2.2	2.1	Quick		2.1	3.9	1.3	2.1	
1.1	1.1	1.0			.9	1.5	.8	1.2	
.6	.7	.6			.5	.8	.6	.7	
44 8.2	43 8.4	43 8.6	Sales/Receivables		42 8.8	42 8.8	49 7.5	47 7.8	
54 6.8	54 6.8	51 7.1			52 7.1	51 7.2	55 6.7	54 6.8	
66 5.6	62 5.9	60 6.1			60 6.0	65 6.0	69 5.3	60 6.1	
0 UND	0 UND	0 UND	Cost of Sales/Inventory		0 UND	0 UND	0 UND	0 UND	
5 72.3	5 76.8	6 60.7			6 59.9	0 UND	0 UND	11 32.3	
31 11.7	19 19.0	35 10.5			30 12.2	7 53.8	88 4.2	44 8.3	
17 21.2	14 25.2	16 23.5	Cost of Sales/Payables		19 19.1	15 24.6	12 29.3	10 36.3	
29 12.6	30 12.1	25 14.5			25 14.5	18 20.8	28 13.1	22 16.7	
48 7.7	47 7.8	35 10.3			47 7.8	28 13.0	41 8.9	35 10.4	
8.3	7.1	7.7	Sales/Working Capital		9.3	5.7	7.3	6.5	
12.4	14.2	16.4			NM	8.7	NM	10.5	
-29.6	-31.0	-29.5			-18.1	-27.6	-19.0	29.5	
9.5	8.6	9.1	EBIT/Interest		8.1	19.8	7.3	10.7	
(75) 4.3	(68) 3.3	(78) 2.6			(13) 2.1	(14) 2.4	2.5	(22) 3.2	
2.0	1.3	1.1			.2	1.2	1.0	1.4	
4.1	6.5	4.1	Net Profit + Depr., Dep., Amort./Cur. Mat. L/T/D						
(22) 2.2	(23) 2.5	(24) 2.6							
1.0	1.6	1.5							
.7	.8	.8	Fixed/Worth		1.0	.5	1.0	.4	
1.3	1.4	1.6			2.5	1.7	2.4	1.3	
2.8	4.2	5.7			-6.0	-1.3	18.1	2.0	
.7	.7	.7	Debt/Worth		.5	.5	1.5	.8	
2.0	1.7	1.8			3.1	1.7	8.2	1.3	
4.3	13.7	20.6			-9.4	-3.9	NM	3.6	
42.8	40.7	53.3	% Profit Before Taxes/Tangible Net Worth		66.0	67.4	86.2	40.3	
(73) 20.4	(58) 24.0	(66) 25.2			(10) 12.3	(12) 29.5	(12) 33.4	(20) 26.2	
5.0	2.7	10.3			-14.2	20.6	8.3	8.7	
13.2	16.7	14.8	% Profit Before Taxes/Total Assets		9.5	19.7	13.7	18.2	
7.0	6.0	7.2			4.3	11.7	5.6	8.9	
2.2	1.3	.8			-6.5	3.5	-.2	1.0	
7.0	8.4	11.3	Sales/Net Fixed Assets		3.9	10.3	18.2	13.8	
3.5	3.1	4.3			2.6	7.0	5.2	4.2	
1.8	1.7	2.6			1.4	3.9	2.6	1.9	
2.3	2.3	2.8	Sales/Total Assets		1.9	3.3	2.5	3.0	
1.5	1.7	1.9			1.5	2.3	1.9	2.1	
1.1	1.1	1.2			1.0	1.8	1.1	1.1	
2.7	2.7	2.3	% Depr., Dep., Amort./Sales		4.4	2.4	1.5	1.9	
(79) 5.0	(69) 4.8	(82) 4.3			(13) 6.8	3.1	(15) 4.6	3.4	
7.5	7.8	6.8			8.3	5.1	6.8	5.1	
3.5	3.0	3.9	% Officers', Directors' Owners' Comp/Sales				4.7		
(36) 6.4	(29) 5.1	(36) 6.1				(10) 6.1			
10.6	8.7	8.4					9.3		
995543M	744253M	1000243M	Net Sales ($)	2453M	33030M	67104M	111963M	372794M	412899M
718275M	560689M	652105M	Total Assets ($)	1016M	26907M	31453M	80579M	258400M	253750M

M = $ thousand   MM = $ million
See Pages 11 through 21 for Explanation of Ratios and Data

Current Data Sorted by Assets							Comparative Historical Data	

						Type of Statement		
	1	7	6	2	3	Unqualified	20	17
1	11	22	6			Reviewed	33	33
1	10	9				Compiled	21	23
7	5	1				Tax Returns	10	13
2	15	26	7	1	3	Other	43	44
	29 (4/1-9/30/06)		117 (10/1/06-3/31/07)				4/1/02-3/31/03	4/1/03-3/31/04
0-500M	500M-2MM	2-10MM	10-50MM	50-100MM	100-250MM		ALL	ALL
11	42	65	19	3	6	NUMBER OF STATEMENTS	127	130
%	%	%	%	%	%	ASSETS	%	%
18.0	6.6	6.3	5.3			Cash & Equivalents	6.9	7.4
31.8	31.0	28.4	28.4			Trade Receivables (net)	27.3	26.2
7.2	8.6	15.0	19.8			Inventory	12.3	11.4
.1	2.3	4.1	1.9			All Other Current	2.1	2.4
57.1	48.5	53.8	55.4			Total Current	48.6	47.5
30.0	41.6	34.7	34.8			Fixed Assets (net)	41.3	41.9
1.8	1.2	5.3	7.0			Intangibles (net)	3.7	1.8
11.0	8.7	6.2	2.8			All Other Non-Current	6.4	8.8
100.0	100.0	100.0	100.0			Total	100.0	100.0
						LIABILITIES		
14.5	11.1	10.8	10.4			Notes Payable-Short Term	11.6	11.8
4.0	6.2	4.9	2.7			Cur. Mat.-L.T.D.	5.8	6.1
14.8	13.0	12.8	16.3			Trade Payables	11.9	12.3
.0	.1	.3	.2			Income Taxes Payable	.1	.1
28.7	10.4	11.7	7.4			All Other Current	8.5	8.1
62.0	40.8	40.5	37.0			Total Current	38.0	38.3
39.9	16.5	14.2	16.3			Long-Term Debt	27.3	22.0
.0	.2	.8	.3			Deferred Taxes	.4	.5
29.0	8.8	3.8	5.6			All Other Non-Current	5.7	5.6
-30.9	33.7	40.7	40.7			Net Worth	28.8	33.7
100.0	100.0	100.0	100.0			Total Liabilities & Net Worth	100.0	100.0
						INCOME DATA		
100.0	100.0	100.0	100.0			Net Sales	100.0	100.0
63.4	31.7	27.8	22.7			Gross Profit	32.3	30.1
56.3	27.7	21.6	13.8			Operating Expenses	26.8	26.8
7.1	4.0	6.2	9.0			Operating Profit	5.5	3.3
3.9	1.1	1.2	1.0			All Other Expenses (net)	1.9	1.1
3.2	2.9	5.1	8.0			Profit Before Taxes	3.6	2.2
						RATIOS		
5.1	2.5	2.1	2.2				2.4	2.3
1.4	1.4	1.4	1.5			Current	1.3	1.3
.6	.9	.8	1.2				.8	.9
5.1	2.0	1.5	1.2				1.5	1.7
1.3	1.0	.8	1.0			Quick	.9	1.0
.5	.5	.6	.7				.6	.6
36 10.2	35 10.4	38 9.5	35 10.5				37 9.8	36 10.2
45 8.1	46 8.0	50 7.3	57 6.4			Sales/Receivables	48 7.7	48 7.6
54 6.7	54 6.8	62 5.9	64 5.7				61 6.0	60 6.1
0 UND	0 UND	13 27.9	21 17.7				12 31.1	8 47.8
13 28.0	12 30.8	23 15.7	45 8.1			Cost of Sales/Inventory	23 15.6	24 15.2
34 10.7	27 13.4	52 7.1	53 6.8				47 7.8	45 8.1
18 19.8	9 41.0	16 22.7	22 16.9				15 24.3	14 27.0
44 8.3	22 16.7	26 14.2	33 11.1			Cost of Sales/Payables	25 14.7	26 14.3
85 4.3	36 10.1	33 10.9	50 7.3				37 10.0	39 9.4
6.7	7.6	6.7	6.5				6.9	7.1
19.7	15.8	16.0	10.2			Sales/Working Capital	19.7	16.1
-6.1	-35.9	-31.2	30.9				-28.7	-43.4
	9.4	9.1	11.0				7.5	7.2
	(40) 3.2	(61) 3.9	(15) 5.2			EBIT/Interest	(120) 3.1	(116) 2.4
	-.8	1.9	2.4				.8	.3
		2.5				Net Profit + Depr., Dep.,	2.9	1.8
	(18) 1.8					Amort./Cur. Mat. L/T/D	(28) 1.5	(26) 1.3
		.8					.8	.4
.1	.5	.5	.6				.7	.6
1.8	.8	1.1	1.2			Fixed/Worth	1.6	1.1
-.7	3.7	2.8	2.6				9.7	4.6
.4	.4	.7	.9				.9	.7
4.5	1.6	1.8	2.0			Debt/Worth	2.2	2.0
-1.6	9.6	5.2	4.8				11.0	7.1
	61.8	60.5	68.2			% Profit Before Taxes/Tangible	44.9	29.0
	(36) 17.5	(59) 26.3	(17) 34.2			Net Worth	(104) 20.1	(108) 12.4
	-14.4	11.3	21.4				1.3	-.6
21.5	21.5	16.2	22.4			% Profit Before Taxes/Total	16.9	13.0
1.0	6.2	10.4	15.0			Assets	5.0	3.7
.0	-5.4	2.8	3.9				-.2	-1.5
125.0	13.8	12.5	15.3				11.8	10.3
12.7	5.4	6.2	5.4			Sales/Net Fixed Assets	5.0	5.2
5.6	3.4	4.1	3.5				2.6	2.6
4.3	3.2	2.6	2.9				2.5	2.8
3.1	2.3	2.2	1.8			Sales/Total Assets	1.8	2.1
1.8	1.7	1.6	1.4				1.2	1.2
	1.9	2.0	.9				2.0	1.9
	(39) 3.5	(58) 3.2	(16) 2.7			% Depr., Dep., Amort./Sales	(117) 3.5	(116) 3.7
	5.1	4.1	4.2				5.6	5.6
	3.4	2.6				% Officers', Directors'	2.4	2.7
	(19) 5.2	(19) 3.8				Owners' Comp/Sales	(46) 4.8	(44) 4.8
	8.5	8.2					8.6	9.6
9310M	129028M	575897M	1013327M	347069M	1706475M	Net Sales ($)	3738587M	3334180M
2951M	53124M	275657M	494932M	248239M	1088187M	Total Assets ($)	1605604M	1614957M

© RMA 2007

M = $ thousand   MM = $ million
See Pages 11 through 21 for Explanation of Ratios and Data

Comparative Historical Data | Current Data Sorted by Sales

			Type of Statement						
17	16	19	Unqualified		2	1	1	4	11
32	38	40	Reviewed	1	7	9	11	10	2
17	15	20	Compiled	1	5	7	5	2	
10	14	13	Tax Returns	4	6	2	1		
41	63	54	Other	2	10	7	13	13	9
4/1/04-3/31/05 ALL	4/1/05-3/31/06 ALL	4/1/06-3/31/07 ALL		0-1MM	29 (4/1-9/30/06) 1-3MM	3-5MM	117 (10/1/06-3/31/07) 5-10MM	10-25MM	25MM & OVER
117	146	146	**NUMBER OF STATEMENTS**	8	30	26	31	29	22
%	%	%	**ASSETS**	%	%	%	%	%	%
7.3	6.1	7.0	Cash & Equivalents		9.9	7.3	4.0	6.2	3.7
28.2	30.1	28.8	Trade Receivables (net)		22.9	32.9	35.3	25.8	26.3
12.5	12.3	13.7	Inventory		8.1	10.9	14.8	16.1	22.9
2.1	1.9	2.8	All Other Current		2.6	4.1	1.4	4.8	1.8
50.0	50.3	52.3	Total Current		43.5	55.2	55.5	52.9	54.7
39.7	38.6	36.5	Fixed Assets (net)		47.5	33.4	33.8	33.9	34.7
4.0	4.2	4.6	Intangibles (net)		1.8	2.9	3.5	8.8	7.1
6.4	7.0	6.7	All Other Non-Current		7.2	8.5	7.2	4.4	3.5
100.0	100.0	100.0	Total		100.0	100.0	100.0	100.0	100.0
			LIABILITIES						
11.0	10.5	10.6	Notes Payable-Short Term		9.1	11.0	13.2	9.0	9.1
4.1	5.4	4.7	Cur. Mat.-L.T.D.		7.4	4.9	4.9	4.0	2.3
11.7	13.9	13.5	Trade Payables		8.5	14.1	16.0	12.8	16.8
.3	.4	.2	Income Taxes Payable		.0	.2	.6	.1	.3
10.1	10.1	11.6	All Other Current		14.5	9.2	12.7	10.3	7.1
37.2	40.3	40.7	Total Current		39.5	39.4	47.4	36.2	35.6
26.6	19.8	18.4	Long-Term Debt		25.7	11.0	10.6	15.6	23.4
.4	.4	.5	Deferred Taxes		.2	.4	1.1	.3	.7
5.5	8.3	7.9	All Other Non-Current		12.0	7.4	4.6	1.8	9.2
30.3	31.2	32.4	Net Worth		22.6	41.8	36.3	46.1	31.0
100.0	100.0	100.0	Total Liabilities & Net Worth		100.0	100.0	100.0	100.0	100.0
			INCOME DATA						
100.0	100.0	100.0	Net Sales		100.0	100.0	100.0	100.0	100.0
32.5	29.9	30.5	Gross Profit		36.9	30.7	27.1	27.1	20.7
28.1	23.8	24.2	Operating Expenses		31.3	25.7	22.1	20.2	11.6
4.3	6.1	6.2	Operating Profit		5.6	5.0	5.0	6.9	9.0
1.2	1.3	1.4	All Other Expenses (net)		2.3	.5	1.4	.9	1.6
3.1	4.8	4.8	Profit Before Taxes		3.3	4.5	3.6	6.0	7.4
			RATIOS						
2.3	2.2	2.3			2.3	2.9	1.6	2.5	2.2
1.4	1.3	1.4	Current		1.4	1.7	1.1	1.5	1.5
1.0	.9	.9			.7	1.1	.9	.8	1.2
1.9	1.5	1.5			1.9	2.1	1.3	1.5	1.2
1.0	1.0	1.0	Quick		1.0	1.3	.7	.9	1.0
.6	.6	.6			.5	.8	.6	.6	.7
40 9.1	40 9.1	37 9.9			35 10.4	37 9.9	43 8.5	25 14.4	33 11.2
52 7.0	51 7.2	48 7.6	Sales/Receivables		42 8.8	48 7.6	51 7.1	45 8.2	56 6.5
63 5.8	63 5.8	61 6.0			49 7.5	56 6.5	65 5.6	60 6.1	65 5.6
7 53.0	6 57.9	10 35.9			0 UND	4 97.4	4 101.4	17 21.8	21 17.3
24 15.0	23 15.9	22 16.8	Cost of Sales/Inventory		11 33.0	22 16.9	24 15.4	28 13.1	46 7.9
49 7.5	53 6.9	48 7.6			28 13.0	35 10.4	61 6.0	45 8.0	69 5.3
15 23.9	19 19.4	15 23.8			9 42.5	8 43.2	19 19.0	18 20.6	23 16.0
27 13.8	28 13.1	26 13.9	Cost of Sales/Payables		19 19.6	21 17.5	28 12.8	26 13.9	34 10.6
49 7.5	42 8.7	40 9.1			33 11.0	41 8.8	36 10.1	35 10.4	57 6.4
6.5	6.7	6.6			6.0	6.1	8.2	6.6	5.7
14.6	17.4	15.1	Sales/Working Capital		15.5	10.9	84.1	14.7	10.8
NM	-48.9	-103.2			-21.1	49.5	-30.3	-36.5	28.3
8.2	9.6	9.7			7.7	10.8	7.0	10.0	11.8
(110) 3.1	(137) 4.6	(133) 3.8	EBIT/Interest	(29) -.9	(23) 1.8 4.8	1.2	(29) 2.8	(27) 4.7	(19) 5.1
.9	1.4	1.2			-.9	1.2	1.5	1.8	2.5
2.6	3.6	3.9					1.8		
(20) 1.9	(34) 1.6	(36) 2.1	Net Profit + Depr., Dep., Amort./Cur. Mat. L/T/D				(10) 1.0		
.6	.9	.8					.2		
.6	.6	.5			.6	.4	.5	.5	.6
1.2	1.2	1.1	Fixed/Worth		1.9	.7	1.1	1.2	1.3
3.6	3.2	3.3			11.6	3.1	2.4	3.1	NM
.9	.8	.6			.7	.3	.9	.5	1.2
2.2	1.9	1.9	Debt/Worth		3.8	1.1	2.6	1.8	2.3
6.9	7.6	8.8			17.0	8.1	4.3	4.2	NM
46.4	50.1	62.5			80.0	41.1	63.5	69.5	68.6
(98) 17.3	(121) 24.0	(123) 25.6	% Profit Before Taxes/Tangible Net Worth	(24)	19.1	(24) 20.7	(29) 24.6	(25) 23.6	(17) 45.0
.9	8.4	7.2			-14.4	1.1	10.0	10.3	23.4
14.3	16.0	17.1			18.5	17.8	13.7	20.3	17.1
5.2	8.5	9.5	% Profit Before Taxes/Total Assets		1.9	10.8	9.0	11.0	11.2
-2.0	2.0	.9			-6.6	-.1	2.1	3.1	5.7
10.7	10.6	13.7			8.8	15.4	12.3	16.6	15.9
4.7	5.9	6.3	Sales/Net Fixed Assets		3.9	7.5	8.0	6.5	6.2
2.5	2.8	3.5			2.5	4.4	3.7	4.5	2.8
2.5	2.7	2.9			2.6	2.8	2.9	3.0	3.0
1.8	2.0	2.2	Sales/Total Assets		1.8	2.2	2.5	2.1	1.8
1.4	1.4	1.5			1.3	1.8	1.6	1.6	1.2
2.0	1.9	1.8			1.7	1.7	2.2	1.9	.8
(102) 3.6	(125) 3.1	(124) 3.1	% Depr., Dep., Amort./Sales	(28)	3.8	(24) 2.8	(30) 3.2	(23) 3.4	(17) 2.2
5.6	5.7	4.5			6.7	4.5	4.1	3.8	4.1
3.1	2.2	3.1			5.1	3.1	1.1		
(44) 5.7	(44) 5.2	(47) 4.9	% Officers', Directors' Owners' Comp/Sales	(13)	6.9	(11) 3.6	(11) 3.4		
7.8	7.1	8.5			9.4	10.6	4.2		
2799535M	4034958M	3781106M	Net Sales ($)	3961M	60916M	108938M	223787M	428180M	2955324M
1596656M	2272383M	2163090M	Total Assets ($)	2257M	34887M	52273M	110352M	212119M	1751202M

Current Data Sorted by Assets   **Comparative Historical Data**

0-500M	500M-2MM	2-10MM	10-50MM	50-100MM	100-250MM	Type of Statement	4/1/02-3/31/03 ALL	4/1/03-3/31/04 ALL
	1	6	8			Unqualified	16	18
2	7	26	4	1		Reviewed	53	48
3	19	9	2			Compiled	35	45
7	11	5				Tax Returns	15	17
8	14	26	11		1	Other	48	54
0-500M	500M-2MM	2-10MM	10-50MM	50-100MM	100-250MM			
	37 (4/1-9/30/06)		134 (10/1/06-3/31/07)					
20	52	72	25	1	1	**NUMBER OF STATEMENTS**	167	182
%	%	%	%	%	%	**ASSETS**	%	%
13.9	7.7	8.3	4.8			Cash & Equivalents	8.8	8.2
30.0	33.4	28.1	25.5			Trade Receivables (net)	25.1	26.6
9.2	9.7	9.7	15.5			Inventory	8.1	8.5
.9	2.8	.8	.8			All Other Current	1.4	1.8
54.0	53.5	46.9	46.6			Total Current	43.4	45.1
35.8	37.9	44.9	40.1			Fixed Assets (net)	46.1	44.2
2.6	2.5	2.6	6.1			Intangibles (net)	2.2	3.7
7.7	6.0	5.7	7.2			All Other Non-Current	8.3	6.9
100.0	100.0	100.0	100.0			Total	100.0	100.0
						LIABILITIES		
10.7	8.9	9.2	15.5			Notes Payable-Short Term	12.2	13.4
6.9	5.6	4.9	4.5			Cur. Mat.-L.T.D.	6.2	4.8
15.6	15.6	12.5	15.2			Trade Payables	11.5	11.9
.0	.7	.3	.1			Income Taxes Payable	.1	.1
10.5	11.6	8.0	7.5			All Other Current	8.7	7.9
43.6	42.4	34.8	42.8			Total Current	38.6	38.0
26.7	25.8	21.9	20.7			Long-Term Debt	22.2	22.0
.0	.6	.6	.5			Deferred Taxes	.5	.6
18.8	10.7	6.3	6.7			All Other Non-Current	4.7	8.0
10.9	20.5	36.5	29.3			Net Worth	33.9	31.4
100.0	100.0	100.0	100.0			Total Liabilities & Net Worth	100.0	100.0
						INCOME DATA		
100.0	100.0	100.0	100.0			Net Sales	100.0	100.0
50.8	33.4	31.9	21.3			Gross Profit	32.6	33.9
45.2	28.2	26.0	16.4			Operating Expenses	29.3	30.5
5.6	5.2	5.9	5.0			Operating Profit	3.4	3.3
2.8	2.3	1.3	1.3			All Other Expenses (net)	2.1	1.7
2.9	2.8	4.6	3.7			Profit Before Taxes	1.3	1.6
						RATIOS		
2.3	2.8	2.7	1.5			Current	2.1	2.1
1.5	1.4	1.4	.9				1.3	1.3
.8	.9	.9	.8				.8	.9
2.2	2.2	2.2	1.1			Quick	1.6	1.7
1.0	1.1	1.1	.6				1.0	.9
.5	.7	.7	.5				.6	.6
17 21.9	35 10.3	43 8.5	43 8.4			Sales/Receivables	35 10.4	38 9.6
38 9.6	44 8.4	49 7.5	50 7.3				45 8.1	48 7.6
47 7.7	52 7.0	55 6.6	61 5.9				53 6.9	58 6.3
0 UND	1 549.4	7 52.4	7 48.9			Cost of Sales/Inventory	4 84.1	5 75.7
4 84.7	9 38.4	15 24.2	21 17.4				14 26.8	13 28.6
30 12.3	31 11.8	39 9.5	53 6.9				31 11.9	38 9.5
9 42.4	13 29.2	14 26.8	23 15.8			Cost of Sales/Payables	15 24.8	15 23.6
24 15.5	26 14.1	28 13.1	35 10.5				24 15.5	26 14.0
44 8.3	37 9.8	48 7.6	46 7.9				44 8.2	42 8.7
8.5	7.7	7.9	11.1			Sales/Working Capital	9.7	8.2
15.7	22.0	13.7	-38.8				22.4	21.9
-74.2	-102.1	-43.9	-16.6				-26.7	-43.5
13.7	11.5	9.3	4.8			EBIT/Interest	5.3	5.5
(16) 3.8	(46) 2.4	(68) 4.6	(24) 2.5				(158) 1.7	(173) 2.1
1.0	1.0	1.2	1.0				.0	-.3
		7.8	16.9			Net Profit + Depr., Dep., Amort./Cur. Mat. L/T/D	4.8	5.3
		(25) 2.8	(11) 3.5				(38) 1.9	(48) 1.9
		1.0	1.6				.6	1.2
.5	.6	.7	.9			Fixed/Worth	.7	.7
-18.2	1.4	1.1	1.6				1.4	1.6
-1.5	7.5	2.6	-5.6				3.0	3.3
.8	.5	.7	.9			Debt/Worth	.9	.8
-38.4	3.2	1.6	3.4				2.0	2.2
-5.0	31.7	4.7	-10.0				5.3	6.3
	48.6	51.3	43.0			% Profit Before Taxes/Tangible Net Worth	28.6	31.2
	(42) 18.7	(62) 25.1	(18) 20.1				(142) 9.2	(155) 7.8
	2.5	3.4	5.9				-3.6	-8.0
22.6	15.9	16.3	11.3			% Profit Before Taxes/Total Assets	10.0	9.5
13.3	5.5	9.2	4.5				2.5	2.7
-.5	.0	1.2	.4				-2.5	-3.4
20.6	12.6	10.8	7.6			Sales/Net Fixed Assets	8.5	9.1
11.7	8.4	4.4	4.4				4.3	4.2
4.0	4.5	2.7	3.1				2.5	2.7
4.4	3.6	2.7	2.2			Sales/Total Assets	2.8	2.6
3.3	2.8	2.0	1.7				2.0	1.9
2.1	1.7	1.4	1.4				1.3	1.2
1.0	1.3	1.8	2.1			% Depr., Dep., Amort./Sales	2.7	2.4
(18) 2.0	(49) 2.6	(71) 3.7	(23) 2.8				(154) 4.2	(172) 4.7
5.4	4.2	5.5	5.0				7.2	6.6
	4.8	2.3				% Officers', Directors' Owners' Comp/Sales	2.9	3.3
	(35) 6.3	(32) 4.2					(82) 5.4	(83) 5.6
	10.2	6.9					10.0	10.0
23628M	174592M	697067M	955963M	84638M	324331M	Net Sales ($)	1617666M	1634763M
7156M	63681M	325681M	497398M	52519M	197961M	Total Assets ($)	1041739M	1025803M

© RMA 2007

M = $ thousand   MM = $ million
See Pages 11 through 21 for Explanation of Ratios and Data

Comparative Historical Data | Current Data Sorted by Sales

4/1/04-3/31/05 ALL	4/1/05-3/31/06 ALL	4/1/06-3/31/07 ALL	Type of Statement	0-1MM	1-3MM	3-5MM	5-10MM	10-25MM	25MM & OVER
				37 (4/1-9/30/06)		134 (10/1/06-3/31/07)			
15	17	15	Unqualified			1	3	4	7
44	36	40	Reviewed	1	3	8	15	10	3
41	39	33	Compiled	4	12	9	5	3	
18	14	23	Tax Returns	4	11	5	2	1	
57	60	60	Other	3	10	10	10	20	7
175	166	171	**NUMBER OF STATEMENTS**	12	36	33	35	38	17
%	%	%	**ASSETS**	%	%	%	%	%	%
8.6	8.8	8.2	Cash & Equivalents	12.8	9.0	7.5	10.8	7.0	2.1
29.0	27.9	29.6	Trade Receivables (net)	19.5	27.8	31.3	31.0	31.1	31.1
10.2	11.4	10.5	Inventory	5.9	10.6	7.1	9.0	12.7	18.6
2.0	2.0	1.5	All Other Current	1.6	.8	3.5	1.0	.8	1.2
49.8	50.1	49.8	Total Current	39.9	48.2	49.4	51.7	51.6	53.1
40.7	38.8	40.9	Fixed Assets (net)	47.7	42.4	43.1	39.3	38.7	36.7
2.4	3.2	3.1	Intangibles (net)	7.8	.4	3.2	2.3	3.9	4.6
7.1	7.9	6.2	All Other Non-Current	4.6	8.9	4.2	6.7	5.7	5.6
100.0	100.0	100.0	Total	100.0	100.0	100.0	100.0	100.0	100.0
			LIABILITIES						
10.6	10.5	10.2	Notes Payable-Short Term	5.5	10.4	9.7	7.3	11.7	16.2
5.2	5.2	5.2	Cur. Mat.-L.T.D.	14.0	5.5	4.0	5.5	3.8	3.7
14.0	13.3	14.2	Trade Payables	9.0	14.7	11.4	15.3	14.7	18.8
.1	.1	.4	Income Taxes Payable	.0	.1	1.0	.2	.4	.3
10.1	9.2	9.3	All Other Current	8.2	11.4	9.2	6.6	10.8	8.3
40.0	38.4	39.3	Total Current	36.6	42.2	35.3	34.9	41.3	47.4
24.1	18.9	23.3	Long-Term Debt	38.5	30.5	24.6	17.5	18.0	19.1
.6	.6	.5	Deferred Taxes	.0	.0	1.4	.3	.5	.6
11.0	11.1	9.1	All Other Non-Current	17.2	16.3	4.3	10.3	4.3	5.8
24.3	31.0	27.8	Net Worth	7.6	11.1	34.5	37.0	35.8	27.1
100.0	100.0	100.0	Total Liabilties & Net Worth	100.0	100.0	100.0	100.0	100.0	100.0
			INCOME DATA						
100.0	100.0	100.0	Net Sales	100.0	100.0	100.0	100.0	100.0	100.0
32.5	32.5	33.0	Gross Profit	47.1	40.2	32.2	33.5	27.7	20.0
28.5	28.3	27.4	Operating Expenses	38.2	35.1	27.7	27.5	21.9	15.3
4.1	4.2	5.6	Operating Profit	8.9	5.1	4.5	6.1	5.8	4.7
1.6	1.1	1.8	All Other Expenses (net)	6.1	1.6	2.3	1.3	.8	1.0
2.4	3.1	3.8	Profit Before Taxes	2.9	3.4	2.2	4.8	4.9	3.6
			RATIOS						
2.5	2.1	2.6	Current	2.2	2.5	3.2	2.7	2.3	1.7
1.3	1.3	1.3		1.1	1.4	1.6	1.3	1.3	.9
.9	.9	.9		.7	.7	1.0	.9	.9	.8
1.9	1.7	2.0	Quick	2.2	2.0	2.8	2.1	2.0	1.2
1.0	1.0	1.0		.9	1.0	1.3	1.1	.9	.7
.5	.6	.6		.3	.4	.7	.7	.6	.5
36 10.0	40 9.2	37 9.8	Sales/Receivables	23 15.7	28 12.9	41 8.9	43 8.5	42 8.7	42 8.8
49 7.4	48 7.5	47 7.8		41 8.8	41 8.9	45 8.1	48 7.5	50 7.3	47 7.8
58 6.3	57 6.4	55 6.7		62 5.9	54 6.8	51 7.2	56 6.6	59 6.2	61 5.9
5 81.0	7 49.6	4 81.9	Cost of Sales/Inventory	0 UND	0 UND	1 348.4	3 118.4	7 49.2	8 44.2
14 25.3	17 21.7	14 25.5		8 45.8	14 26.5	10 35.1	17 21.2	17 22.0	37 9.8
32 11.4	41 8.9	39 9.3		30 12.0	44 8.3	25 14.7	39 9.3	44 8.2	59 6.2
16 23.5	16 22.2	13 27.1	Cost of Sales/Payables	0 UND	14 26.7	10 37.6	17 21.2	14 26.9	28 13.2
27 13.5	26 14.0	28 13.1		16 23.3	28 13.1	23 15.7	31 11.9	27 13.7	37 10.0
44 8.3	43 8.4	42 8.6		58 6.3	46 8.0	34 10.6	51 7.2	50 7.3	49 7.4
8.5	7.2	8.0	Sales/Working Capital	8.5	8.1	6.9	7.6	8.2	10.7
18.5	17.7	18.3		74.7	17.9	9.8	26.2	13.6	-38.8
-51.0	-50.1	-37.7		-23.2	-20.6	NM	-47.3	-33.6	-17.8
9.7	8.0	9.6	EBIT/Interest	6.8	8.0	8.3	9.6	15.1	9.4
(159) 4.0	(154) 3.3	(156) 3.7		(10) 2.5	(34) 2.6	(28) 3.6	(33) 3.6	(35) 7.0	(16) 3.9
.8	.8	1.0		1.0	-.3	.8	1.5	.8	1.4
4.7	4.8	8.7	Net Profit + Depr., Dep., Amort./Cur. Mat. L/T/D				5.9	8.3	34.7
(48) 2.4	(39) 2.1	(48) 2.9					(13) 1.7	(12) 2.9	(10) 8.1
1.4	1.2	1.1					1.1	.8	3.0
.6	.6	.6	Fixed/Worth	1.1	.7	.6	.7	.6	.6
1.2	1.1	1.3		-7.5	3.3	1.0	1.0	1.2	1.6
5.4	3.4	9.6		-1.2	-3.1	2.0	3.5	2.5	-5.5
.8	.8	.8	Debt/Worth	1.2	1.4	.3	.7	.7	1.0
2.1	1.8	2.0		-14.0	7.9	1.6	1.8	1.8	5.2
8.9	7.2	29.3		-2.8	-6.0	4.9	5.9	4.6	-10.0
48.2	45.1	49.6	% Profit Before Taxes/Tangible Net Worth		51.1	48.2	58.8	60.0	39.4
(145) 18.8	(141) 17.7	(133) 22.4			(23) 33.8	(31) 15.2	(30) 18.2	(32) 24.5	(12) 21.1
2.2	2.1	3.3			3.6	.0	3.4	4.6	9.0
16.3	16.4	16.1	% Profit Before Taxes/Total Assets	20.1	17.3	14.3	16.4	19.1	12.0
7.6	5.4	7.1		2.9	9.2	5.4	7.3	8.6	5.3
-1.4	-.3	.2		-.6	-2.8	-4.0	1.4	-.8	1.3
11.6	11.1	12.0	Sales/Net Fixed Assets	9.5	14.3	11.8	15.4	11.6	11.4
5.9	5.9	5.6		3.0	8.0	5.6	5.9	4.7	6.4
3.3	3.3	3.3		1.7	2.7	2.7	3.4	3.8	3.5
3.1	2.9	3.3	Sales/Total Assets	2.3	3.6	3.5	2.9	3.1	3.1
2.2	2.1	2.2		1.5	2.8	2.3	2.2	2.0	1.8
1.6	1.5	1.5		1.2	1.5	1.3	1.6	1.5	1.7
1.9	1.6	1.5	% Depr., Dep., Amort./Sales	4.2	1.4	1.3	1.4	1.8	3.1
(165) 3.5	(152) 3.0	(163) 3.0		(11) 5.3	(34) 2.7	(31) 3.5	(34) 3.5	(37) 2.4	(16) 2.7
5.7	5.0	4.8		6.7	4.5	6.0	4.6	4.1	3.2
3.4	3.7	3.3	% Officers', Directors', Owners' Comp/Sales		4.7	4.7	2.6	1.5	
(83) 5.9	(78) 5.7	(79) 5.3			(21) 8.2	(20) 6.7	(19) 5.2	(13) 3.0	
9.8	9.5	8.4			12.8	7.6	7.0	6.0	
2147368M	2478407M	2260219M	Net Sales ($)	7739M	71599M	131313M	253916M	585683M	1209969M
1162222M	1254450M	1144396M	Total Assets ($)	5395M	34068M	74048M	126389M	295681M	608815M

M = $ thousand   MM = $ million
See Pages 11 through 21 for Explanation of Ratios and Data

Current Data Sorted by Assets | Comparative Historical Data

Type of Statement

Type of Statement	0-500M	500M-2MM	2-10MM	10-50MM	50-100MM	100-250MM	4/1/02-3/31/03 ALL	4/1/03-3/31/04 ALL
Unqualified			3	9	4	1	12	12
Reviewed			9	1			11	14
Compiled		3	5				8	11
Tax Returns	1	6	2	1			9	8
Other	4	4	15	12	1	2	23	25

Current data periods: 15 (4/1-9/30/06) covering 500M-2MM, 2-10MM; 70 (10/1/06-3/31/07) covering 10-50MM, 50-100MM (a "2" appears under 0-500M on the period line).

	0-500M	500M-2MM	2-10MM	10-50MM	50-100MM	100-250MM		4/1/02-3/31/03 ALL	4/1/03-3/31/04 ALL
NUMBER OF STATEMENTS	7	13	34	23	5	3		63	70
ASSETS	%	%	%	%	%	%		%	%
Cash & Equivalents		7.9	6.1	4.6				6.2	8.0
Trade Receivables (net)		32.5	26.7	27.1				25.0	27.2
Inventory		17.4	33.7	38.0				31.3	26.5
All Other Current		4.3	1.8	1.4				1.5	1.9
Total Current		62.1	68.3	71.1				63.9	63.6
Fixed Assets (net)		33.2	20.1	17.5				26.6	26.9
Intangibles (net)		3.3	4.0	4.7				3.8	4.1
All Other Non-Current		1.4	7.6	6.7				5.7	5.3
Total		100.0	100.0	100.0				100.0	100.0
LIABILITIES									
Notes Payable-Short Term		3.0	16.3	13.1				14.3	10.4
Cur. Mat.-L.T.D.		10.9	3.7	1.4				7.1	4.6
Trade Payables		18.6	16.7	10.4				15.9	12.8
Income Taxes Payable		.0	.0	.5				.0	.1
All Other Current		5.0	7.4	15.9				8.5	10.1
Total Current		37.5	44.2	41.3				45.8	38.0
Long-Term Debt		24.5	11.4	11.6				16.9	14.9
Deferred Taxes		.2	.7	.2				.3	.6
All Other Non-Current		8.2	2.4	5.2				10.9	6.5
Net Worth		29.7	41.3	41.7				26.1	39.9
Total Liabilities & Net Worth		100.0	100.0	100.0				100.0	100.0
INCOME DATA									
Net Sales		100.0	100.0	100.0				100.0	100.0
Gross Profit		37.3	33.1	28.0				35.3	36.8
Operating Expenses		30.8	23.9	19.6				32.0	31.7
Operating Profit		6.6	9.2	8.3				3.2	5.1
All Other Expenses (net)		1.2	1.2	1.3				1.4	1.3
Profit Before Taxes		5.4	8.0	7.1				1.8	3.8
RATIOS									
Current		2.5	3.1	2.5				2.6	3.1
		1.8	1.4	1.9				1.6	1.9
		1.1	1.1	1.2				1.1	1.1
Quick		1.7	1.6	1.5				1.3	1.8
		1.3	.7	.7				.8	1.0
		.8	.5	.5				.5	.6
Sales/Receivables		29 12.4	44 8.3	41 8.9				32 11.3	40 9.1
		46 7.9	50 7.4	54 6.7				49 7.5	54 6.8
		54 6.7	56 6.5	64 5.7				58 6.2	63 5.8
Cost of Sales/Inventory		8 47.9	52 7.0	80 4.6				51 7.1	46 8.0
		26 14.0	102 3.6	113 3.2				75 4.9	83 4.4
		59 6.2	143 2.5	162 2.3				153 2.4	130 2.8
Cost of Sales/Payables		24 15.2	16 23.4	12 29.8				20 18.3	19 18.9
		37 9.9	33 11.1	25 14.6				30 12.0	31 11.7
		68 5.4	59 6.2	40 9.2				54 6.8	49 7.4
Sales/Working Capital		6.5	3.8	3.1				4.3	4.2
		12.7	8.7	5.7				9.6	6.1
		42.9	33.4	12.2				22.5	28.3
EBIT/Interest		12.4	9.3	13.5				3.9	10.9
		(12) 4.2	(32) 6.3	(21) 6.0				(58) 1.7	(62) 3.2
		2.9	2.9	2.4				-.8	1.0
Net Profit + Depr., Dep., Amort./Cur. Mat. L/T/D			5.4					3.6	5.1
			(10) 2.0					(17) .8	(14) 1.4
			1.1					.0	.8
Fixed/Worth		.7	.2	.2				.4	.2
		1.2	.4	.3				.9	.7
		NM	.9	.9				2.5	2.4
Debt/Worth		1.0	.9	.8				.7	.5
		2.4	2.1	1.3				2.2	1.7
		NM	3.9	4.0				17.6	5.2
% Profit Before Taxes/Tangible Net Worth		71.6	62.3	57.0				38.0	38.7
		(10) 28.1	(31) 31.0	(21) 23.1				(51) 9.2	(59) 16.1
		17.8	16.1	12.9				-7.5	2.2
% Profit Before Taxes/Total Assets		17.6	20.7	17.9				9.7	12.9
		8.6	14.0	11.6				1.8	5.8
		4.9	4.9	2.8				-5.5	.2
Sales/Net Fixed Assets		26.3	41.2	17.6				16.8	16.7
		13.2	12.9	11.0				8.3	8.2
		4.3	5.3	8.0				4.1	4.5
Sales/Total Assets		3.5	2.8	2.0				2.7	2.4
		2.3	1.9	1.7				1.9	1.9
		1.8	1.4	1.4				1.3	1.3
% Depr., Dep., Amort./Sales		1.6	1.3	.7				1.8	1.4
		(12) 2.2	(32) 2.4	(19) 2.0				(55) 2.7	(63) 2.8
		4.8	3.5	2.6				4.9	4.6
% Officers', Directors' Owners' Comp/Sales			1.5					2.5	4.3
		(18)	2.6					(22) 6.3	(28) 6.6
			3.7					9.1	10.3
Net Sales ($)	8521M	37062M	355319M	967701M	487257M	622711M		1107311M	1214180M
Total Assets ($)	1748M	15516M	185284M	548212M	380420M	395609M		805742M	840919M

M = $ thousand   MM = $ million
See Pages 11 through 21 for Explanation of Ratios and Data

Comparative Historical Data | Current Data Sorted by Sales

Type of Statement

4/1/04- 3/31/05 ALL	4/1/05- 3/31/06 ALL	4/1/06- 3/31/07 ALL	Type of Statement	0-1MM	1-3MM	3-5MM	5-10MM	10-25MM	25MM & OVER
16	12	17	Unqualified			2	3	5	12
9	16	10	Reviewed			3	3	3	2
11	22	9	Compiled		1	3	3	2	
7	25	13	Tax Returns		5	3	3	2	1
26	35	36	Other	2	5	2	8	6	13
ALL	ALL	ALL			15 (4/1-9/30/06)		70 (10/1/06-3/31/07)		
69	110	85	NUMBER OF STATEMENTS	4	11	9	16	17	28

Data

4/1/04- 3/31/05	4/1/05- 3/31/06	4/1/06- 3/31/07		0-1MM	1-3MM	3-5MM	5-10MM	10-25MM	25MM & OVER
%	%	%	**ASSETS**	%	%	%	%	%	%
5.3	9.8	7.8	Cash & Equivalents		6.0		7.5	6.1	5.7
28.7	27.3	28.0	Trade Receivables (net)		34.5		28.2	27.1	27.6
30.1	26.2	30.1	Inventory		14.5		30.3	38.8	36.4
1.9	2.5	2.0	All Other Current		1.4		.7	2.2	1.7
66.0	65.9	67.9	Total Current		56.4		66.8	74.2	71.4
24.4	25.6	22.8	Fixed Assets (net)		33.2		17.5	18.6	21.4
3.2	2.3	3.6	Intangibles (net)		6.2		7.1	1.4	2.4
6.4	6.2	5.7	All Other Non-Current		4.2		8.6	5.8	4.8
100.0	100.0	100.0	Total		100.0		100.0	100.0	100.0
			LIABILITIES						
15.4	10.9	11.2	Notes Payable-Short Term		7.0		18.2	14.3	9.7
3.9	3.6	4.1	Cur. Mat.-L.T.D.		8.8		1.6	2.6	2.5
12.4	14.9	14.2	Trade Payables		18.8		14.0	12.9	14.1
.4	.2	.2	Income Taxes Payable		.0		.0	.2	.4
14.4	10.5	9.7	All Other Current		6.0		7.0	12.2	14.3
46.5	40.2	39.5	Total Current		40.6		40.9	42.2	41.0
13.8	16.2	15.3	Long-Term Debt		23.0		11.9	8.8	15.1
.2	.2	.4	Deferred Taxes		.8		.2	.3	.3
9.8	6.5	4.3	All Other Non-Current		6.0		2.9	1.5	4.7
29.7	37.0	40.5	Net Worth		29.6		44.1	47.3	38.9
100.0	100.0	100.0	Total Liabilities & Net Worth		100.0		100.0	100.0	100.0
			INCOME DATA						
100.0	100.0	100.0	Net Sales		100.0		100.0	100.0	100.0
34.1	36.7	33.7	Gross Profit		39.0		32.2	31.2	30.3
28.0	29.3	24.9	Operating Expenses		32.0		22.4	23.1	19.9
6.0	7.4	8.8	Operating Profit		7.1		9.7	8.1	10.4
1.1	.8	1.1	All Other Expenses (net)		2.1		.9	.8	1.2
5.0	6.6	7.6	Profit Before Taxes		5.0		8.8	7.3	9.2
			RATIOS						
2.8	3.0	2.8	Current		2.4		2.9	4.6	2.5
1.7	1.8	1.9			1.5		1.7	1.6	2.0
1.0	1.3	1.2			1.1		1.2	1.2	1.3
1.5	1.6	1.6	Quick		1.6		2.0	1.9	1.2
.8	.9	.9			1.1		.6	.7	.8
.5	.6	.5			.8		.5	.5	.5
41 8.9	35 10.5	41 8.9	Sales/Receivables		36 10.2		50 7.3	43 8.5	41 8.8
54 6.8	46 7.9	49 7.5			52 7.0		57 6.4	48 7.6	49 7.4
64 5.7	59 6.2	61 6.0			61 6.0		67 5.5	55 6.7	63 5.8
44 8.2	36 10.3	42 8.8	Cost of Sales/Inventory		8 47.2		35 10.4	70 5.2	70 5.2
81 4.5	70 5.2	84 4.3			30 12.3		89 4.1	102 3.6	110 3.3
147 2.5	124 3.0	139 2.6			109 3.4		137 2.7	157 2.3	189 1.9
17 21.3	21 17.2	14 25.5	Cost of Sales/Payables		31 11.7		12 29.5	13 27.4	21 17.8
29 12.5	36 10.1	31 11.7			49 7.4		31 11.6	25 14.8	32 11.6
46 8.0	53 6.9	49 7.4			70 5.2		45 8.1	44 8.3	49 7.5
4.0	4.1	3.9	Sales/Working Capital		7.3		3.1	3.2	2.8
8.7	7.9	8.0			15.3		7.6	7.8	4.7
-161.0	25.7	24.7			76.5		14.2	28.0	12.3
16.9	27.1	10.0	EBIT/Interest		9.2		9.3	47.3	11.3
(63) 3.8	(97) 5.1	(77) 6.2		(10) 4.8			(15) 6.3	(16) 6.3	(25) 7.4
1.5	1.7	2.9			2.6		2.7	2.6	3.5
5.0	5.6	5.9	Net Profit + Depr., Dep., Amort./Cur. Mat. L/T/D						5.6
(20) 1.9	(21) 2.0	(26) 2.8						(12) 2.9	
1.2	1.7	1.4							1.6
.4	.3	.2	Fixed/Worth		1.1		.1	.2	.2
.9	.5	.5			1.3		.2	.4	.5
4.2	2.1	1.3			4.0		.5	.7	1.3
.5	.5	.8	Debt/Worth		1.2		.8	.3	.8
2.4	1.4	1.8			3.9		1.9	1.4	1.4
38.1	5.9	4.1			24.5		3.6	4.5	3.7
59.1	57.6	59.7	% Profit Before Taxes/Tangible Net Worth				69.5	40.1	73.9
(56) 27.0	(94) 28.2	(76) 27.6					(15) 35.9	(16) 26.1	(26) 28.8
8.4	8.8	17.5					11.9	19.0	18.4
19.8	24.2	20.1	% Profit Before Taxes/Total Assets		14.4		23.4	19.5	20.0
5.9	8.9	11.6			7.5		14.5	13.5	13.7
1.6	2.5	4.9			3.3		3.5	6.4	8.9
21.5	22.5	33.6	Sales/Net Fixed Assets		36.2		75.9	27.2	14.6
9.2	9.6	11.3			5.7		21.6	13.3	10.7
5.4	4.5	5.5			2.4		4.8	6.0	5.9
2.5	2.7	2.8	Sales/Total Assets		3.6		2.7	2.9	2.2
1.9	2.0	1.9			1.9		1.8	1.9	1.7
1.3	1.4	1.4			.9		1.0	1.5	1.4
1.5	1.1	1.1	% Depr., Dep., Amort./Sales				.4	1.3	.9
(64) 2.5	(97) 2.3	(73) 2.3			(14) 2.5		(16) 2.1	(24) 2.4	
4.2	4.0	3.4					3.4	3.1	3.5
2.1	1.7	1.7	% Officers', Directors', Owners' Comp/Sales						
(26) 3.9	(42) 3.5	(32) 3.2							
5.7	7.2	5.6							
2091642M	2003113M	2478571M	Net Sales ($)	2450M	20300M	33757M	121348M	250053M	2050663M
1206248M	1227879M	1526789M	Total Assets ($)	381M	14520M	14843M	81463M	135347M	1280235M

M = $ thousand   MM = $ million
See Pages 11 through 21 for Explanation of Ratios and Data

Current Data Sorted by Assets   Comparative Historical Data

0-500M	500M-2MM	2-10MM	10-50MM	50-100MM	100-250MM	Type of Statement	4/1/02-3/31/03 ALL	4/1/03-3/31/04 ALL
		4	3	1	1	Unqualified	14	14
		14	2			Reviewed	11	15
	3	1			1	Compiled	4	12
2	1	3				Tax Returns	2	2
2	2	8	8	3	4	Other	12	16
	18 (4/1-9/30/06)		43 (10/1/06-3/31/07)					
2	6	30	13	5	5	NUMBER OF STATEMENTS	43	59
%	%	%	%	%	%	ASSETS	%	%
		7.5	2.0			Cash & Equivalents	5.1	4.1
		26.6	22.2			Trade Receivables (net)	20.5	23.3
		34.4	35.2			Inventory	32.5	35.1
		4.5	5.3			All Other Current	2.8	2.8
		73.0	64.6			Total Current	60.9	65.4
		21.0	19.3			Fixed Assets (net)	29.5	24.5
		1.1	10.7			Intangibles (net)	3.5	3.8
		4.9	5.3			All Other Non-Current	6.2	6.4
		100.0	100.0			Total	100.0	100.0
						LIABILITIES		
		13.1	8.1			Notes Payable-Short Term	16.4	18.0
		3.1	3.4			Cur. Mat.-L.T.D.	5.6	4.4
		12.6	13.3			Trade Payables	13.3	13.8
		.1	.5			Income Taxes Payable	.0	.3
		10.1	7.3			All Other Current	9.0	8.7
		39.0	32.5			Total Current	44.3	45.2
		7.4	20.5			Long-Term Debt	17.8	11.9
		.3	.4			Deferred Taxes	.5	.4
		11.2	9.7			All Other Non-Current	5.4	6.1
		42.1	36.9			Net Worth	32.1	36.5
		100.0	100.0			Total Liabilities & Net Worth	100.0	100.0
						INCOME DATA		
		100.0	100.0			Net Sales	100.0	100.0
		32.6	25.4			Gross Profit	30.8	31.1
		28.0	16.8			Operating Expenses	26.9	27.5
		4.5	8.6			Operating Profit	3.8	3.7
		.8	1.3			All Other Expenses (net)	1.8	1.2
		3.7	7.3			Profit Before Taxes	2.1	2.4
						RATIOS		
		3.2	3.3				2.4	2.0
		1.8	1.9			Current	1.4	1.4
		1.3	1.3				1.0	1.1
		1.3	1.1				1.1	1.0
		.8	.8			Quick	.6	.5
		.6	.5				.3	.4
		37 9.9	42 8.7				32 11.3	37 9.9
		46 8.0	49 7.5			Sales/Receivables	46 7.9	47 7.8
		60 6.1	60 6.1				58 6.3	56 6.5
		36 10.3	47 7.8				54 6.8	48 7.6
		91 4.0	113 3.2			Cost of Sales/Inventory	101 3.6	96 3.8
		144 2.5	133 2.7				139 2.6	147 2.5
		16 22.8	26 14.3				20 18.6	24 14.9
		26 14.1	33 10.9			Cost of Sales/Payables	38 9.5	37 9.9
		51 7.2	52 7.0				54 6.7	56 6.5
		4.5	2.7				4.8	5.3
		5.6	5.5			Sales/Working Capital	11.3	11.0
		13.6	14.0				-75.5	26.7
		15.1	9.7				6.0	8.1
		(28) 3.9	(11) 4.6			EBIT/Interest	(40) 2.6	(55) 3.0
		1.5	2.5				.6	.6
		6.9				Net Profit + Depr., Dep.,	4.3	7.5
		(11) 3.6				Amort./Cur. Mat. L/T/D	(17) 2.4	(12) 3.4
		2.0					.9	.3
		.2	.3				.4	.3
		.5	.5			Fixed/Worth	.9	.7
		.9	1.0				2.4	1.4
		.6	.8				.9	.8
		1.3	1.6			Debt/Worth	1.6	1.6
		3.1	4.4				7.4	5.4
		31.4	61.0			% Profit Before Taxes/Tangible	21.9	24.4
		(29) 19.6	(12) 25.7			Net Worth	(37) 7.8	(48) 8.0
		6.3	13.9				-1.8	-.8
		10.8	14.6			% Profit Before Taxes/Total	6.7	8.5
		4.8	8.8			Assets	3.4	3.6
		2.3	4.7				-1.9	-1.5
		31.7	16.5				20.0	25.4
		11.7	14.6			Sales/Net Fixed Assets	6.2	9.6
		6.1	6.1				3.8	3.7
		2.4	2.3				2.4	2.4
		2.1	1.6			Sales/Total Assets	1.6	1.8
		1.6	1.4				1.0	1.3
		1.1	1.0				2.2	1.1
		(29) 2.1	1.9			% Depr., Dep., Amort./Sales	(37) 3.4	(46) 2.4
		2.9	3.7				5.8	4.6
		1.7				% Officers', Directors'	1.9	1.1
		(16) 4.1				Owners' Comp/Sales	(12) 3.8	(21) 4.3
		7.6					6.2	6.6
1226M	17127M	286558M	452444M	471621M	1003260M	Net Sales ($)	799962M	1387695M
454M	6883M	144181M	278474M	334860M	918751M	Total Assets ($)	511756M	1011960M

M = $ thousand   MM = $ million
See Pages 11 through 21 for Explanation of Ratios and Data

Comparative Historical Data				Current Data Sorted by Sales					
			Type of Statement						
12	11	9	Unqualified				1	5	3
17	13	16	Reviewed		2	2	8	4	2
11	8	5	Compiled		2	2			1
2	4	6	Tax Returns	2		2	1	1	
10	10	25	Other		3	1	1	7	13
4/1/04-3/31/05 ALL	4/1/05-3/31/06 ALL	4/1/06-3/31/07 ALL			18 (4/1-9/30/06)			43 (10/1/06-3/31/07)	
				0-1MM	1-3MM	3-5MM	5-10MM	10-25MM	25MM & OVER
52	46	61	**NUMBER OF STATEMENTS**	2	5	7	11	17	19
%	%	%	**ASSETS**	%	%	%	%	%	%
5.3	8.3	6.5	Cash & Equivalents				9.2	6.3	2.7
22.3	25.0	24.3	Trade Receivables (net)				25.7	28.1	21.1
33.1	33.2	32.1	Inventory				31.0	33.8	29.9
2.7	2.7	4.8	All Other Current				1.3	5.7	7.2
63.4	69.2	67.7	Total Current				67.3	74.0	60.9
25.3	21.0	23.7	Fixed Assets (net)				24.7	18.6	25.5
3.4	3.3	3.8	Intangibles (net)				.9	2.3	8.8
8.0	6.5	4.8	All Other Non-Current				7.1	5.2	4.8
100.0	100.0	100.0	Total				100.0	100.0	100.0
			LIABILITIES						
11.8	10.3	12.5	Notes Payable-Short Term				8.5	16.3	5.1
4.3	4.2	3.6	Cur. Mat.-L.T.D.				4.2	2.9	4.6
12.4	11.9	12.6	Trade Payables				9.7	14.4	12.9
.2	.5	.5	Income Taxes Payable				.3	.1	1.3
8.8	9.8	10.1	All Other Current				10.9	7.1	7.3
37.4	36.7	39.2	Total Current				33.7	40.8	31.2
15.2	18.6	15.1	Long-Term Debt				7.9	14.4	16.3
.6	.3	.4	Deferred Taxes				.4	.3	.6
2.7	5.7	9.0	All Other Non-Current				17.3	11.0	6.4
44.1	38.7	36.3	Net Worth				40.7	33.5	45.5
100.0	100.0	100.0	Total Liabilities & Net Worth				100.0	100.0	100.0
			INCOME DATA						
100.0	100.0	100.0	Net Sales				100.0	100.0	100.0
33.4	31.3	32.0	Gross Profit				31.0	25.3	25.4
29.8	24.9	25.7	Operating Expenses				29.2	17.8	16.9
3.6	6.4	6.3	Operating Profit				1.8	7.4	8.5
.9	1.1	1.2	All Other Expenses (net)				.9	1.7	1.7
2.7	5.3	5.1	Profit Before Taxes				.9	5.7	6.8
			RATIOS						
2.7	3.1	3.2					3.2	2.7	3.0
1.7	1.9	1.9	Current				2.4	1.8	2.0
1.3	1.4	1.3					1.1	1.3	1.3
1.1	1.4	1.2					2.1	1.1	1.1
.8	.8	.8	Quick				.8	.7	.9
.5	.6	.6					.6	.6	.5
35 10.6	34 10.8	38 9.5					36 10.0	42 8.7	43 8.6
48 7.6	46 8.0	48 7.6	Sales/Receivables				45 8.0	49 7.4	50 7.4
59 6.2	59 6.2	59 6.2					54 6.8	61 6.0	55 6.6
58 6.3	50 7.3	40 9.2					37 9.8	31 11.9	58 6.3
105 3.5	82 4.4	93 3.9	Cost of Sales/Inventory				95 3.8	89 4.1	86 4.2
163 2.2	145 2.5	142 2.6					167 2.2	138 2.6	140 2.6
18 20.3	19 18.8	19 19.6					10 36.6	20 18.1	30 12.2
31 11.8	29 12.6	33 11.2	Cost of Sales/Payables				23 15.6	29 12.8	33 10.9
50 7.3	39 9.4	51 7.2					41 9.0	51 7.2	51 7.1
3.8	3.2	3.7					3.9	4.1	2.9
6.7	6.2	5.5	Sales/Working Capital				5.7	5.2	5.4
16.2	13.7	14.0					29.9	14.0	14.0
12.4	12.3	9.7					8.9	7.7	12.6
(47) 3.7	(39) 5.1	(55) 4.5	EBIT/Interest				(10) 3.8	(16) 3.9	(16) 4.9
1.5	2.3	1.4					-1.3	1.5	1.5
3.6	10.5	6.9	Net Profit + Depr., Dep.,						8.5
(11) 2.0	(10) 5.1	(23) 3.8	Amort./Cur. Mat. L/T/D						(11) 3.8
.6	3.2	2.0							1.7
.2	.2	.2					.2	.2	.5
.5	.5	.6	Fixed/Worth				.6	.4	.6
1.2	1.1	1.1					1.6	.9	1.0
.7	.6	.8					.5	.8	1.0
1.5	1.3	1.4	Debt/Worth				1.1	1.8	1.4
2.3	4.3	3.1					3.2	3.6	2.6
32.7	57.8	38.2	% Profit Before Taxes/Tangible				30.7	36.3	54.3
(49) 12.9	(40) 22.9	(56) 21.3	Net Worth				(10) 14.1	(16) 20.8	(18) 22.9
3.1	10.3	10.1					5.3	12.0	12.2
12.2	14.7	14.4	% Profit Before Taxes/Total				9.3	15.2	14.9
3.9	8.1	8.1	Assets				4.9	7.6	10.4
.8	2.4	2.6					1.3	3.3	2.8
28.4	33.1	20.1					15.8	33.5	14.6
8.3	11.1	9.7	Sales/Net Fixed Assets				11.0	12.2	6.3
3.9	4.9	4.2					4.1	6.8	3.7
2.2	2.6	2.3					2.5	2.5	2.2
1.6	1.9	1.9	Sales/Total Assets				2.1	2.1	1.6
1.2	1.4	1.3					1.3	1.6	1.1
1.3	.7	1.3					1.6	.9	1.3
(44) 2.7	(41) 2.1	(59) 2.1	% Depr., Dep., Amort./Sales				2.1	2.1	(18) 2.2
4.7	3.3	3.3					2.9	3.0	3.6
3.4	3.2	1.7	% Officers', Directors'						
(21) 5.8	(10) 5.2	(23) 5.0	Owners' Comp/Sales						
10.6	15.4	8.2							
1411733M	1319142M	2232236M	Net Sales ($)	1226M	11042M	27562M	78442M	276186M	1837778M
1004635M	914500M	1683603M	Total Assets ($)	454M	7467M	14863M	43715M	172878M	1444226M

M = $ thousand   MM = $ million
See Pages 11 through 21 for Explanation of Ratios and Data

Current Data Sorted by Assets   Comparative Historical Data

Type of Statement

0-500M	500M-2MM	2-10MM	10-50MM	50-100MM	100-250MM		4/1/02-3/31/03 ALL	4/1/03-3/31/04 ALL
			7	4	1	Unqualified	3	10
	2	4	1			Reviewed	9	13
	1	2				Compiled	2	8
1						Tax Returns	1	3
		4				Other	8	7
	5 (4/1-9/30/06)		28 (10/1/06-3/31/07)					
1	3	10	9	7	3	**NUMBER OF STATEMENTS**	23	41
%	%	%	%	%	%	**ASSETS**	%	%
		14.3				Cash & Equivalents	6.7	5.3
		28.4				Trade Receivables (net)	30.5	28.1
		33.3				Inventory	33.4	35.0
		2.0				All Other Current	2.4	3.7
		78.0				Total Current	73.0	72.0
		14.9				Fixed Assets (net)	19.8	18.9
		.7				Intangibles (net)	2.9	2.7
		6.4				All Other Non-Current	4.3	6.3
		100.0				Total	100.0	100.0
						LIABILITIES		
		13.7				Notes Payable-Short Term	9.5	10.8
		2.3				Cur. Mat.-L.T.D.	3.4	2.4
		10.4				Trade Payables	13.6	14.8
		.3				Income Taxes Payable	.3	.4
		15.1				All Other Current	13.2	11.1
		41.7				Total Current	40.0	39.5
		8.4				Long-Term Debt	12.7	10.5
		.5				Deferred Taxes	.1	.6
		3.4				All Other Non-Current	5.0	9.3
		46.0				Net Worth	42.2	40.2
		100.0				Total Liabilities & Net Worth	100.0	100.0
						INCOME DATA		
		100.0				Net Sales	100.0	100.0
		43.3				Gross Profit	34.2	33.8
		33.3				Operating Expenses	29.6	30.6
		9.9				Operating Profit	4.7	3.3
		1.1				All Other Expenses (net)	.5	1.0
		8.8				Profit Before Taxes	4.2	2.2
						RATIOS		
		4.3					2.3	2.6
		2.6				Current	1.9	2.0
		1.5					1.4	1.4
		3.3					1.4	1.3
		1.1				Quick	.9	.9
		.4					.6	.6
		41 8.9					40 9.1	38 9.5
		44 8.2				Sales/Receivables	49 7.4	48 7.7
		60 6.1					66 5.6	62 5.9
		46 7.9					56 6.6	72 5.1
		128 2.8				Cost of Sales/Inventory	88 4.1	96 3.8
		187 2.0					139 2.6	131 2.8
		14 25.8					22 16.6	23 15.8
		35 10.5				Cost of Sales/Payables	30 12.4	30 12.4
		57 6.4					46 7.9	47 7.7
		3.8					5.0	4.1
		4.5				Sales/Working Capital	6.4	6.3
		13.2					9.3	11.3
							18.8	12.8
						EBIT/Interest	(22) 4.4	(39) 4.4
							2.4	-.2
								5.1
						Net Profit + Depr., Dep., Amort./Cur. Mat. L/T/D		(12) 2.8
								1.8
		.1					.2	.2
		.2				Fixed/Worth	.4	.4
		1.0					.9	1.3
		.3					.7	.7
		.8				Debt/Worth	1.1	1.2
		2.4					2.4	4.0
							37.7	39.2
						% Profit Before Taxes/Tangible Net Worth	(21) 21.6	(38) 9.5
							5.4	.4
		41.5					18.2	11.4
		10.6				% Profit Before Taxes/Total Assets	4.9	4.6
		-3.2					2.3	-.1
		48.0					26.1	29.9
		19.4				Sales/Net Fixed Assets	17.0	14.5
		9.5					8.0	6.6
		2.4					2.5	2.5
		2.0				Sales/Total Assets	2.1	2.2
		1.5					1.7	1.5
		.5					.7	.9
		.7				% Depr., Dep., Amort./Sales	(22) 1.8	(39) 1.7
		1.6					2.5	3.1
								1.9
						% Officers', Directors' Owners' Comp/Sales		(16) 5.7
								8.9
3115M	8937M	88550M	526746M	820667M	560374M	Net Sales ($)	1503110M	1299598M
428M	3417M	42168M	233976M	473783M	477779M	Total Assets ($)	715808M	745415M

© RMA 2007   M = $ thousand   MM = $ million

See Pages 11 through 21 for Explanation of Ratios and Data

Comparative Historical Data   ## Current Data Sorted by Sales

			Type of Statement						
7	10	12	Unqualified						12
3	3	7	Reviewed		3	3			1
5	5	3	Compiled	1	1	1	1		
3		1	Tax Returns		1				
13	13	10	Other		1			2	6
4/1/04-	4/1/05-	4/1/06-							
3/31/05	3/31/06	3/31/07			5 (4/1-9/30/06)		28 (10/1/06-3/31/07)		
ALL	ALL	ALL		0-1MM	1-3MM	3-5MM	5-10MM	10-25MM	25MM & OVER
31	31	33	NUMBER OF STATEMENTS		1	5	5	3	19
%	%	%	ASSETS	%	%	%	%	%	%
6.8	8.6	11.1	Cash & Equivalents	D					6.4
23.9	27.1	26.2	Trade Receivables (net)						26.5
37.0	35.8	34.5	Inventory	A					36.1
2.0	1.9	1.8	All Other Current	T					1.7
69.7	73.4	73.6	Total Current	A					70.7
17.2	16.2	15.3	Fixed Assets (net)						17.0
7.8	5.3	3.8	Intangibles (net)	N					6.0
5.3	5.1	7.4	All Other Non-Current	O					6.3
100.0	100.0	100.0	Total	T					100.0
			LIABILITIES	A					
11.1	14.1	11.0	Notes Payable-Short Term	V					9.5
2.2	2.6	3.5	Cur. Mat.-L.T.D.	A					4.8
12.0	15.6	10.8	Trade Payables	I					10.8
.1	.1	.8	Income Taxes Payable	L					1.3
9.9	13.7	13.0	All Other Current	A					13.6
35.2	46.1	39.1	Total Current	B					39.9
14.7	11.2	16.1	Long-Term Debt	L					21.9
.3	.4	.4	Deferred Taxes	E					.5
5.1	3.8	3.5	All Other Non-Current						4.0
44.6	38.4	40.9	Net Worth						33.7
100.0	100.0	100.0	Total Liabilities & Net Worth						100.0
			INCOME DATA						
100.0	100.0	100.0	Net Sales						100.0
33.0	31.2	37.8	Gross Profit						35.5
27.8	26.8	29.5	Operating Expenses						28.7
5.1	4.4	8.3	Operating Profit						6.8
.6	.3	1.0	All Other Expenses (net)						1.1
4.6	4.0	7.3	Profit Before Taxes						5.7
			RATIOS						
2.9	2.0	3.9							3.8
2.0	1.6	1.9	Current						1.5
1.4	1.4	1.4							1.3
2.0	1.3	2.1							1.5
.8	.8	1.0	Quick						.7
.6	.4	.5							.5

32	11.3	38	9.6	38	9.5	Sales/Receivables							39	9.4
42	8.8	44	8.2	45	8.1								50	7.3
62	5.9	54	6.8	58	6.3								58	6.3
63	5.8	56	6.5	74	4.9	Cost of Sales/Inventory							86	4.2
97	3.8	78	4.7	100	3.7								100	3.7
144	2.5	122	3.0	145	2.5								126	2.9
19	19.0	21	17.7	14	25.4	Cost of Sales/Payables							22	16.6
31	11.6	30	12.0	31	11.7								31	11.7
45	8.1	53	6.9	42	8.7								40	9.2

4.1	4.1	4.0	Sales/Working Capital					3.4
6.0	7.2	6.2						7.3
11.5	11.6	14.8						15.4
25.7	13.5	22.4	EBIT/Interest					9.4
(28) 6.6	(27) 3.7	(29) 3.9					(17)	4.0
1.8	1.6	1.7						1.9
3.7	10.5	11.9	Net Profit + Depr., Dep.,					
(11) 1.9	(14) 3.1	(11) 2.5	Amort./Cur. Mat. L/T/D					
1.0	1.3	2.3						
.2	.2	.2	Fixed/Worth					.3
.4	.4	.3						.5
1.4	1.8	1.1						9.5
.6	.6	.6	Debt/Worth					1.3
1.1	1.8	1.5						1.9
3.8	5.4	3.7						46.3
47.1	49.3	62.8	% Profit Before Taxes/Tangible					56.1
(27) 20.9	(26) 26.4	(30) 35.6	Net Worth				(17)	35.5
5.9	7.7	16.7						20.6
19.7	14.5	18.4	% Profit Before Taxes/Total					16.3
8.1	6.7	12.0	Assets					11.9
1.6	2.8	3.3						3.3
36.6	41.7	32.2	Sales/Net Fixed Assets					17.6
14.4	15.1	14.7						10.0
8.6	7.6	8.8						8.1
2.2	2.3	2.4	Sales/Total Assets					2.3
1.9	2.1	2.1						2.0
1.7	1.8	1.6						1.6
.6	.5	.6	% Depr., Dep., Amort./Sales					.9
(25) 1.8	(26) 1.3	(30) 1.0					(16)	1.2
2.9	2.2	1.6						1.7
			% Officers', Directors'					
			Owners' Comp/Sales					
1739555M	1997549M	2008389M	Net Sales ($)	1853M	17935M	34980M	45834M	1907787M
999461M	971712M	1231551M	Total Assets ($)	627M	8222M	20886M	16278M	1185538M

M = $ thousand   MM = $ million
See Pages 11 through 21 for Explanation of Ratios and Data

Current Data Sorted by Assets

Comparative Historical Data

0-500M	500M-2MM	2-10MM	10-50MM	50-100MM	100-250MM		4/1/02-3/31/03 ALL	4/1/03-3/31/04 ALL
						Type of Statement		
3	3	5	15	3	4	Unqualified	34	25
	4	5	5	4		Reviewed	20	22
2	2	6				Compiled	8	12
1	1	3				Tax Returns		2
1	6	9	14	1	3	Other	28	27
	24 (4/1-9/30/06)		71 (10/1/06-3/31/07)					
7	16	28	33	4	7	**NUMBER OF STATEMENTS**	90	88
%	%	%	%	%	%	**ASSETS**	%	%
	13.1	5.9	6.2			Cash & Equivalents	6.2	6.7
	26.6	27.8	26.9			Trade Receivables (net)	25.5	25.6
	18.1	40.3	32.0			Inventory	30.9	31.4
	5.8	1.1	1.6			All Other Current	2.0	2.4
	63.6	75.0	66.6			Total Current	64.5	66.1
	19.8	18.8	18.3			Fixed Assets (net)	24.0	21.7
	9.8	.5	6.9			Intangibles (net)	4.3	6.0
	6.8	5.7	8.2			All Other Non-Current	7.1	6.1
	100.0	100.0	100.0			Total	100.0	100.0
						LIABILITIES		
	9.6	13.5	10.9			Notes Payable-Short Term	14.2	12.3
	2.9	2.4	2.7			Cur. Mat.-L.T.D.	3.2	3.2
	20.9	18.4	12.9			Trade Payables	13.5	12.9
	.1	.4	.4			Income Taxes Payable	.2	.3
	12.1	9.3	9.3			All Other Current	7.6	9.7
	45.6	44.0	36.2			Total Current	38.6	38.3
	20.7	10.1	12.8			Long-Term Debt	11.5	10.1
	.1	.1	.3			Deferred Taxes	.5	.4
	3.2	2.2	4.7			All Other Non-Current	4.0	6.5
	30.4	43.5	46.0			Net Worth	45.4	44.7
	100.0	100.0	100.0			Total Liabilities & Net Worth	100.0	100.0
						INCOME DATA		
	100.0	100.0	100.0			Net Sales	100.0	100.0
	41.0	30.0	30.6			Gross Profit	31.1	32.3
	36.9	23.1	23.2			Operating Expenses	26.6	27.3
	4.1	6.9	7.4			Operating Profit	4.5	5.0
	1.1	1.1	.6			All Other Expenses (net)	.9	1.4
	3.0	5.9	6.8			Profit Before Taxes	3.6	3.6
						RATIOS		
	2.9	3.1	3.1			Current	3.2	3.3
	1.4	1.5	2.1				1.7	1.9
	.8	1.2	1.3				1.2	1.3
	2.1	1.4	1.9			Quick	1.4	1.8
	.8	.7	1.0				.8	1.0
	.4	.5	.6				.5	.5
	(12) 30.4	(34) 10.7	(40) 9.2			Sales/Receivables	(38) 9.6	(42) 8.7
	(34) 10.6	(46) 8.0	(50) 7.4				(49) 7.4	(52) 7.1
	(58) 6.3	(49) 7.4	(60) 6.1				(63) 5.8	(63) 5.8
	(12) 29.2	(56) 6.6	(62) 5.9			Cost of Sales/Inventory	(59) 6.2	(61) 6.0
	(30) 12.2	(108) 3.4	(87) 4.2				(88) 4.1	(92) 4.0
	(71) 5.1	(143) 2.6	(115) 3.2				(134) 2.7	(139) 2.6
	(17) 22.1	(15) 23.7	(22) 16.9			Cost of Sales/Payables	(20) 18.2	(20) 18.5
	(31) 11.6	(32) 11.4	(33) 11.1				(31) 11.9	(31) 11.8
	(61) 5.9	(62) 5.9	(43) 8.4				(47) 7.8	(47) 7.8
	5.3	4.1	4.1			Sales/Working Capital	3.5	3.7
	14.3	6.7	5.5				6.4	5.8
	-58.8	28.2	11.8				18.2	14.5
	12.9	19.0	31.5			EBIT/Interest	15.2	12.5
	(14) 2.7	(26) 6.6	(30) 6.8				(87) 3.0	(77) 3.8
	1.2	2.8	2.5				1.2	.9
			7.9			Net Profit + Depr., Dep., Amort./Cur. Mat. L/T/D	7.1	7.0
		(16) 4.6					(39) 1.8	(37) 3.2
			1.6				.8	.6
	.4	.2	.2			Fixed/Worth	.3	.2
	1.4	.3	.4				.5	.6
	-2.2	1.4	1.0				1.3	1.2
	.8	.3	.5			Debt/Worth	.5	.5
	5.8	1.8	1.4				1.4	1.3
	-9.2	4.7	3.5				3.5	3.3
	170.0	48.2	40.6			% Profit Before Taxes/Tangible Net Worth	28.7	30.2
	(11) 28.8	(27) 30.6	(30) 24.9				(80) 10.8	(77) 11.5
	3.1	7.2	9.5				1.7	4.1
	17.6	22.4	15.6			% Profit Before Taxes/Total Assets	11.0	11.0
	6.5	8.7	11.3				5.0	6.2
	.8	4.5	4.9				.3	.3
	58.3	40.7	17.1			Sales/Net Fixed Assets	18.9	23.4
	18.3	14.4	10.5				8.1	8.7
	6.3	7.2	8.0				4.7	5.1
	3.7	2.7	2.2			Sales/Total Assets	2.2	2.1
	2.6	2.2	1.9				1.6	1.7
	1.9	1.6	1.5				1.3	1.2
		.8	1.5			% Depr., Dep., Amort./Sales	1.2	1.2
		(29) 1.4	2.2				(83) 2.9	(77) 2.7
		3.2	3.0				4.0	4.7
						% Officers', Directors' Owners' Comp/Sales	1.6	1.7
							(33) 3.5	(22) 3.0
							7.6	6.1
5763M	63668M	346633M	1224027M	510035M	1504413M	Net Sales ($)	2600149M	2220917M
1242M	21998M	157254M	661938M	248813M	1042107M	Total Assets ($)	1726429M	1584391M

M = $ thousand   MM = $ million
See Pages 11 through 21 for Explanation of Ratios and Data

Comparative Historical Data — Current Data Sorted by Sales

			Type of Statement						
28	23	33	Unqualified	1	3	2	2	5	20
20	25	13	Reviewed		3		3	4	3
15	11	10	Compiled	2			4	3	1
5	5	5	Tax Returns	2	1		1	1	
30	31	34	Other	1	4	1	5	8	15
4/1/04-3/31/05 ALL	4/1/05-3/31/06 ALL	4/1/06-3/31/07 ALL		0-1MM	1-3MM	3-5MM	5-10MM	10-25MM	25MM & OVER
				24 (4/1-9/30/06)			71 (10/1/06-3/31/07)		
98	95	95	NUMBER OF STATEMENTS	6	8	6	15	21	39
%	%	%	ASSETS	%	%	%	%	%	%
7.4	7.4	7.8	Cash & Equivalents				8.6	4.1	7.7
26.3	28.4	26.9	Trade Receivables (net)				27.5	29.1	25.9
31.6	29.4	31.7	Inventory				33.1	36.6	33.3
2.1	2.6	2.3	All Other Current				3.6	2.1	1.8
67.4	67.7	68.6	Total Current				72.8	71.9	68.7
18.8	20.1	19.1	Fixed Assets (net)				22.5	16.6	18.4
6.9	5.7	5.3	Intangibles (net)				1.4	4.0	5.9
7.0	6.5	7.0	All Other Non-Current				3.4	7.5	7.0
100.0	100.0	100.0	Total				100.0	100.0	100.0
			LIABILITIES						
11.1	13.6	12.3	Notes Payable-Short Term				11.5	13.9	11.5
3.4	3.5	3.1	Cur. Mat.-L.T.D.				2.3	1.9	2.6
13.5	16.2	16.3	Trade Payables				21.4	16.2	11.8
.3	.5	.5	Income Taxes Payable				.0	.7	.7
10.6	9.1	9.5	All Other Current				9.2	8.8	8.2
38.8	42.8	41.7	Total Current				44.5	41.5	34.8
15.5	14.8	13.7	Long-Term Debt				16.2	4.2	14.9
.5	.4	.4	Deferred Taxes				.3	.2	.6
5.1	5.8	3.2	All Other Non-Current				4.4	1.1	4.5
40.1	36.1	40.9	Net Worth				34.6	53.0	45.2
100.0	100.0	100.0	Total Liabilities & Net Worth				100.0	100.0	100.0
			INCOME DATA						
100.0	100.0	100.0	Net Sales				100.0	100.0	100.0
32.5	29.9	32.1	Gross Profit				28.5	32.3	28.5
25.9	24.9	25.6	Operating Expenses				22.5	24.4	20.0
6.6	5.0	6.4	Operating Profit				6.0	7.9	8.4
1.1	.8	1.0	All Other Expenses (net)				.9	.5	.9
5.5	4.2	5.5	Profit Before Taxes				5.0	7.4	7.5
			RATIOS						
3.3	2.9	3.1					2.1	3.4	4.1
1.8	1.7	1.7	Current				1.6	1.7	2.3
1.2	1.2	1.2					1.3	1.2	1.3
1.9	1.6	1.8					1.3	2.3	2.5
.9	.9	.9	Quick				.8	.9	1.1
.6	.5	.5					.7	.5	.6
39 9.3	38 9.6	34 10.9					31 11.7	33 11.2	37 9.8
50 7.3	51 7.2	45 8.1	Sales/Receivables				46 7.9	47 7.8	47 7.8
63 5.8	68 5.4	58 6.3					49 7.4	64 5.7	58 6.3
56 6.6	44 8.3	45 8.0					42 8.8	59 6.2	61 6.0
91 4.0	81 4.5	81 4.5	Cost of Sales/Inventory				113 3.2	81 4.5	87 4.2
141 2.6	125 2.9	121 3.0					137 2.7	142 2.6	112 3.3
18 20.2	20 18.4	16 23.1					14 25.8	21 17.2	15 23.6
33 11.0	35 10.5	31 11.8	Cost of Sales/Payables				32 11.4	29 12.5	26 14.2
47 7.8	54 6.8	54 6.8					67 5.4	62 5.9	39 9.4
3.6	4.3	4.5					4.9	4.2	3.5
6.5	7.4	6.4	Sales/Working Capital				9.2	6.1	5.5
18.9	25.2	21.0					21.0	32.3	9.8
14.4	10.0	18.9					29.0	31.5	18.8
(81) 4.9	(88) 4.2	(84) 5.2	EBIT/Interest	(14) 4.8				(19) 13.6	(36) 6.3
2.2	1.8	2.0					2.6	3.9	1.9
7.3	7.4	11.9	Net Profit + Depr., Dep.,						7.9
(32) 4.5	(39) 3.7	(35) 4.3	Amort./Cur. Mat. L/T/D					(20)	5.3
1.8	1.8	1.8							1.6
.2	.3	.2					.2	.2	.2
.5	.5	.4	Fixed/Worth				1.6	.3	.4
1.3	1.5	1.4					4.1	.6	.9
.7	.9	.5					.5	.3	.5
1.8	2.0	1.9	Debt/Worth				3.5	1.0	1.6
5.1	5.6	5.5					15.8	2.9	2.9
42.0	47.4	46.8	% Profit Before Taxes/Tangible				46.8	47.7	50.9
(82) 20.8	(81) 21.2	(82) 27.6	Net Worth	(13) 31.4				(20) 19.5	(36) 32.0
9.1	8.6	7.6					23.1	8.0	10.1
15.0	16.4	17.4	% Profit Before Taxes/Total				20.7	19.5	18.4
7.5	5.7	7.9	Assets				7.8	13.3	13.0
2.1	3.2	3.6					5.0	5.5	4.1
23.8	28.5	26.7					54.0	24.5	20.4
11.0	10.8	11.3	Sales/Net Fixed Assets				9.8	13.0	10.4
6.0	7.2	7.5					4.4	8.8	7.6
2.5	2.4	2.6					3.0	2.8	2.3
1.7	1.9	2.1	Sales/Total Assets				2.1	2.1	1.9
1.4	1.4	1.5					1.5	1.5	1.6
1.2	.8	1.0					.7	1.1	1.0
(81) 2.5	(90) 2.0	(80) 1.9	% Depr., Dep., Amort./Sales	(13) 2.8				1.5	(34) 2.1
4.0	3.1	3.1					4.0	2.2	2.9
1.7	1.1	.9	% Officers', Directors'						
(28) 3.3	(24) 3.3	(23) 2.8	Owners' Comp/Sales						
6.8	8.2	9.4							
2751287M	3164711M	3654539M	Net Sales ($)	2370M	17551M	24185M	106574M	351409M	3152450M
1954563M	1882383M	2133352M	Total Assets ($)	1200M	9389M	8498M	55140M	188434M	1870691M

Current Data Sorted by Assets   **Comparative Historical Data**

0-500M	500M-2MM	2-10MM	10-50MM	50-100MM	100-250MM	Type of Statement	4/1/02-3/31/03 ALL	4/1/03-3/31/04 ALL
		2	5	1	2	Unqualified	6	3
		6	3			Reviewed	7	5
		5				Compiled	5	9
						Tax Returns		
1						Other	8	8
1	1	3	3	1	1			
7 (4/1-9/30/06)			27 (10/1/06-3/31/07)					
1	1	16	11	2	3	NUMBER OF STATEMENTS	26	25
%	%	%	%	%	%	ASSETS	%	%
		8.7	7.4			Cash & Equivalents	9.1	4.4
		25.2	23.7			Trade Receivables (net)	20.9	27.4
		28.0	34.0			Inventory	26.8	30.9
		3.1	3.3			All Other Current	1.8	3.5
		65.0	68.5			Total Current	58.5	66.3
		24.4	23.8			Fixed Assets (net)	28.8	24.2
		4.4	.4			Intangibles (net)	4.8	3.3
		6.2	7.3			All Other Non-Current	7.9	6.2
		100.0	100.0			Total	100.0	100.0
						LIABILITIES		
		10.3	12.0			Notes Payable-Short Term	7.5	11.7
		2.4	4.0			Cur. Mat.-L.T.D.	6.0	3.7
		11.0	11.0			Trade Payables	9.8	14.4
		.1	.1			Income Taxes Payable	.4	.3
		10.5	8.9			All Other Current	4.9	6.9
		34.3	36.1			Total Current	28.7	37.0
		8.9	10.3			Long-Term Debt	18.6	15.8
		.5	.3			Deferred Taxes	.5	.3
		10.4	4.1			All Other Non-Current	4.2	9.6
		45.8	49.2			Net Worth	48.0	37.4
		100.0	100.0			Total Liabilties & Net Worth	100.0	100.0
						INCOME DATA		
		100.0	100.0			Net Sales	100.0	100.0
		27.3	28.0			Gross Profit	27.0	32.3
		18.8	21.2			Operating Expenses	22.9	27.5
		8.4	6.8			Operating Profit	4.1	4.8
		1.3	3.6			All Other Expenses (net)	.9	.8
		7.1	3.2			Profit Before Taxes	3.2	4.0
						RATIOS		
		4.7	3.1			Current	4.2	3.5
		1.8	2.0				2.1	1.7
		1.4	1.1				1.2	1.1
		2.6	1.1			Quick	2.3	2.0
		.9	.9				1.1	.8
		.5	.7				.5	.4
		43 8.5	39 9.5			Sales/Receivables	42 8.8	33 10.9
		53 6.9	49 7.4				50 7.3	51 7.2
		63 5.8	62 5.8				59 6.1	61 6.0
		34 10.8	64 5.7			Cost of Sales/Inventory	59 6.2	50 7.3
		68 5.4	113 3.2				88 4.2	103 3.5
		132 2.8	138 2.7				131 2.8	170 2.2
		16 23.3	14 26.3			Cost of Sales/Payables	14 25.8	16 22.3
		23 15.6	33 10.9				28 12.9	36 10.2
		52 7.0	46 8.0				50 7.3	52 7.0
		2.7	3.2			Sales/Working Capital	2.6	2.6
		4.0	5.6				4.9	6.2
		15.8	21.1				11.4	246.6
		12.8	30.4			EBIT/Interest	8.0	5.7
		(15) 3.1	(10) 4.1				(22) 2.5	(20) 2.0
		1.5	1.6				.3	1.3
						Net Profit + Depr., Dep.,	7.4	
						Amort./Cur. Mat. L/T/D	(12) 2.4	
							.6	
		.1	.2			Fixed/Worth	.1	.1
		.6	.5				.6	.7
		1.6	.7				2.4	1.9
		.3	.3			Debt/Worth	.5	.5
		1.4	1.0				1.5	2.3
		7.1	2.6				3.8	3.3
		46.8	41.7			% Profit Before Taxes/Tangible Net Worth	23.0	32.7
		(13) 18.2	21.1				(25) 17.0	(22) 10.3
		-1.7	2.4				-7.4	1.2
		16.9	19.1			% Profit Before Taxes/Total Assets	11.5	9.8
		4.7	5.9				4.1	3.9
		-2.9	2.1				-2.0	.3
		20.6	13.9			Sales/Net Fixed Assets	11.6	32.4
		8.9	6.4				4.9	9.5
		3.4	4.4				2.7	3.4
		2.4	1.9			Sales/Total Assets	1.9	2.5
		1.7	1.6				1.5	1.8
		1.3	1.4				1.0	1.1
		1.7	1.5			% Depr., Dep., Amort./Sales	2.1	1.6
		(14) 2.6	2.2				(23) 3.4	(19) 3.6
		5.2	3.7				4.6	6.6
						% Officers', Directors' Owners' Comp/Sales		
3M	3810M	139205M	319672M	191047M	844150M	Net Sales ($)	878636M	547454M
8M	1202M	83535M	203190M	134829M	495533M	Total Assets ($)	840405M	497574M

Comparative Historical Data — Current Data Sorted by Sales

Type of Statement	4/1/04-3/31/05 ALL	4/1/05-3/31/06 ALL	4/1/06-3/31/07 ALL	0-1MM	1-3MM	3-5MM	5-10MM	10-25MM	25MM & OVER
Unqualified	8	4	10				1	5	4
Reviewed	8	5	9				5	1	3
Compiled	9	10	6		1	2	1	2	
Tax Returns	1		1						
Other	3	7	9	1	1	1		2	4
	4/1/04-3/31/05	4/1/05-3/31/06	4/1/06-3/31/07	\ 7 (4/1-9/30/06) \			27 (10/1/06-3/31/07)		
NUMBER OF STATEMENTS	29	27	34	1	2	3	7	10	11
ASSETS	%	%	%	%	%	%	%	%	%
Cash & Equivalents	6.3	8.9	7.0					6.6	5.0
Trade Receivables (net)	29.9	29.1	23.9					30.4	23.2
Inventory	32.7	30.7	31.0					24.4	37.7
All Other Current	1.1	2.2	3.2					5.1	3.5
Total Current	70.0	70.9	65.2					66.5	69.4
Fixed Assets (net)	19.6	18.9	22.7					28.2	17.3
Intangibles (net)	2.9	2.0	2.9					.0	2.6
All Other Non-Current	7.6	8.3	9.2					5.3	10.7
Total	100.0	100.0	100.0					100.0	100.0
LIABILITIES									
Notes Payable-Short Term	11.8	10.6	12.3					10.5	14.1
Cur. Mat.-L.T.D.	2.7	2.7	2.8					4.2	2.1
Trade Payables	16.8	16.4	11.4					14.1	12.3
Income Taxes Payable	.5	.5	.2					.1	.4
All Other Current	11.1	9.6	10.7					7.9	8.2
Total Current	42.9	39.7	37.4					36.7	37.0
Long-Term Debt	13.4	10.9	9.7					5.8	12.0
Deferred Taxes	.3	.4	.4					.3	.1
All Other Non-Current	11.1	10.0	6.9					14.6	5.3
Net Worth	32.3	38.9	45.6					42.6	45.6
Total Liabilties & Net Worth	100.0	100.0	100.0					100.0	100.0
INCOME DATA									
Net Sales	100.0	100.0	100.0					100.0	100.0
Gross Profit	28.3	30.7	27.5					27.9	25.4
Operating Expenses	22.8	22.5	19.8					19.8	18.4
Operating Profit	5.5	8.1	7.7					8.1	7.0
All Other Expenses (net)	1.9	.7	2.0					1.9	3.7
Profit Before Taxes	3.7	7.4	5.7					6.2	3.3
RATIOS									
Current	2.9	3.6	3.5					6.0	3.1
	1.9	2.4	1.8					1.9	1.8
	1.2	1.2	1.2					1.1	1.4
Quick	1.4	1.9	1.7					3.0	.9
	.8	.9	.8					1.1	.8
	.6	.5	.5					.5	.6
Sales/Receivables	34 10.7	34 10.6	41 8.8					51 7.1	45 8.1
	52 7.0	48 7.6	53 6.9					54 6.8	53 6.9
	70 5.2	56 6.5	62 5.9					63 5.8	58 6.3
Cost of Sales/Inventory	52 7.0	43 8.5	54 6.8					41 8.9	73 5.0
	84 4.4	72 5.1	96 3.8					72 5.1	128 2.9
	134 2.7	127 2.9	139 2.6					99 3.7	145 2.5
Cost of Sales/Payables	20 18.4	14 25.8	15 24.6					17 21.5	13 27.2
	34 10.8	35 10.5	33 11.0					31 11.9	37 9.9
	56 6.5	52 7.0	51 7.2					59 6.1	55 6.7
Sales/Working Capital	3.6	3.0	3.1					3.4	3.2
	4.9	5.2	5.5					8.7	5.5
	25.7	29.8	18.6					34.2	6.8
EBIT/Interest	14.2	22.5	18.7						18.7
	(27) 4.2	(22) 5.9	(31) 4.4						6.8
	2.0	2.2	2.1						2.4
Net Profit + Depr., Dep., Amort./Cur. Mat. L/T/D	9.0		8.9						
	(10) 2.9		(11) 4.9						
	1.1		1.1						
Fixed/Worth	.2	.1	.1					.3	.1
	.4	.4	.5					.7	.5
	1.7	1.5	.9					1.9	.7
Debt/Worth	.8	.6	.5					.4	.7
	2.5	.9	1.4					1.4	1.2
	6.3	5.4	2.9					6.1	2.0
% Profit Before Taxes/Tangible Net Worth	41.6	54.3	38.9						30.6
	(24) 19.5	(22) 21.6	(31) 21.1						25.1
	7.6	13.1	2.5						11.7
% Profit Before Taxes/Total Assets	12.7	21.0	15.3					28.0	14.7
	4.5	9.4	7.2					5.7	10.0
	1.7	3.6	2.1					-5.1	4.6
Sales/Net Fixed Assets	54.2	40.6	20.9					14.3	47.0
	12.7	11.2	7.0					6.5	10.2
	4.6	5.9	4.3					4.4	5.5
Sales/Total Assets	2.7	2.8	2.1					2.6	2.1
	1.8	1.9	1.7					1.8	1.6
	1.4	1.5	1.3					1.5	1.3
% Depr., Dep., Amort./Sales	1.1	1.1	1.4						.7
	(20) 2.1	(22) 2.0	(29) 2.3					(10) 1.8	
	5.3	3.9	3.8						2.3
% Officers', Directors' Owners' Comp/Sales									
Net Sales ($)	678736M	407133M	1497887M	3M	5153M	13594M	54171M	177538M	1247428M
Total Assets ($)	501536M	274204M	918297M	8M	9417M	7831M	36527M	100945M	763569M

M = $ thousand   MM = $ million
See Pages 11 through 21 for Explanation of Ratios and Data

Current Data Sorted by Assets | Comparative Historical Data

0-500M	500M-2MM	2-10MM	10-50MM	50-100MM	100-250MM	Type of Statement	16	19
		7	9	4	2	Unqualified	16	19
	3	13	7			Reviewed	22	23
2	10	7	2			Compiled	19	23
	3	2				Tax Returns	7	5
2	3	12	4	2	2	Other	22	26
	21 (4/1-9/30/06)		75 (10/1/06-3/31/07)				4/1/02-3/31/03 ALL	4/1/03-3/31/04 ALL
4	19	41	22	6	4	**NUMBER OF STATEMENTS**	86	96
%	%	%	%	%	%	**ASSETS**	%	%
	10.1	10.1	11.1			Cash & Equivalents	6.4	5.9
	40.7	33.2	34.9			Trade Receivables (net)	28.6	30.9
	22.8	25.0	25.5			Inventory	26.1	27.6
	4.4	2.8	4.1			All Other Current	3.1	2.8
	78.1	71.1	75.6			Total Current	64.1	67.2
	16.7	22.6	19.5			Fixed Assets (net)	29.5	25.1
	.2	2.5	1.4			Intangibles (net)	1.6	2.4
	5.0	3.8	3.5			All Other Non-Current	4.8	5.3
	100.0	100.0	100.0			Total	100.0	100.0
						LIABILITIES		
	14.9	11.2	13.8			Notes Payable-Short Term	10.5	15.1
	5.0	2.9	2.9			Cur. Mat.-L.T.D.	4.2	3.1
	20.5	15.4	14.8			Trade Payables	16.8	16.4
	.0	.4	.5			Income Taxes Payable	.3	.3
	6.7	7.6	12.7			All Other Current	9.0	9.6
	47.1	37.5	44.6			Total Current	40.8	44.4
	19.0	14.6	7.6			Long-Term Debt	15.9	14.1
	.1	.4	.6			Deferred Taxes	1.3	.6
	5.9	3.8	3.3			All Other Non-Current	4.3	5.4
	27.8	43.6	43.8			Net Worth	37.7	35.5
	100.0	100.0	100.0			Total Liabilities & Net Worth	100.0	100.0
						INCOME DATA		
	100.0	100.0	100.0			Net Sales	100.0	100.0
	31.0	27.3	24.9			Gross Profit	26.1	28.0
	28.7	19.1	13.1			Operating Expenses	23.1	26.2
	2.4	8.1	11.8			Operating Profit	3.0	1.8
	.5	.6	1.1			All Other Expenses (net)	1.1	1.3
	1.9	7.5	10.6			Profit Before Taxes	1.9	.5
						RATIOS		
	3.5	3.2	2.3			Current	2.3	2.5
	1.5	2.1	1.6				1.6	1.7
	1.2	1.5	1.3				1.3	1.1
	1.8	2.3	1.5			Quick	1.5	1.4
	1.0	1.2	.9				.8	.9
	.9	.6	.5				.5	.6
	32 11.6	34 10.6	50 7.3			Sales/Receivables	37 9.8	39 9.5
	49 7.4	48 7.6	59 6.1				47 7.7	52 7.0
	59 6.1	63 5.8	80 4.6				60 6.1	67 5.5
	15 24.3	21 17.8	27 13.5			Cost of Sales/Inventory	26 14.0	31 11.7
	37 10.0	46 7.9	68 5.4				55 6.6	67 5.5
	97 3.7	78 4.7	98 3.7				117 3.1	116 3.2
	14 25.5	12 30.2	17 20.9			Cost of Sales/Payables	17 21.0	17 21.1
	30 12.3	23 15.8	28 13.0				33 11.1	35 10.6
	40 9.2	56 6.5	50 7.3				51 7.1	51 7.1
	5.1	4.1	4.8			Sales/Working Capital	4.4	4.2
	8.6	5.9	8.1				9.2	8.7
	45.9	12.9	12.0				18.7	23.9
	12.7	26.1	22.9			EBIT/Interest	10.0	6.9
	(17) 5.2	(39) 6.8	(18) 7.5				(80) 2.3	(86) 1.8
	-.2	4.3	2.8				.0	.3
		8.5	34.9			Net Profit + Depr., Dep., Amort./Cur. Mat. L/T/D	7.3	5.6
		(11) 4.9	(11) 6.8				(35) 2.4	(26) 2.0
		3.1	2.2				1.3	.7
	.1	.2	.2			Fixed/Worth	.3	.3
	.3	.4	.4				.6	.6
	2.1	.7	.8				1.7	1.6
	.5	.5	.7			Debt/Worth	.8	.8
	1.7	1.1	2.0				1.6	1.4
	18.4	2.3	3.2				3.1	4.1
	42.1	54.3	68.8			% Profit Before Taxes/Tangible Net Worth	31.1	20.3
	(16) 7.7	(36) 31.0	45.5				(77) 11.3	(85) 7.7
	-5.6	14.5	25.3				-1.1	-2.6
	16.5	22.5	34.9			% Profit Before Taxes/Total Assets	12.2	11.5
	5.3	14.2	14.5				3.8	2.2
	-2.4	6.9	5.2				-1.9	-2.0
	115.4	26.2	22.6			Sales/Net Fixed Assets	21.2	26.2
	33.5	12.8	11.2				6.7	8.3
	11.4	6.8	7.5				3.7	4.1
	4.0	3.3	2.4			Sales/Total Assets	2.6	2.7
	3.2	2.3	1.9				1.9	1.9
	1.9	1.8	1.6				1.4	1.4
	.5	.9	.8			% Depr., Dep., Amort./Sales	1.0	1.1
	(15) 1.3	(36) 1.8	(21) 1.6				(83) 2.5	(87) 2.3
	3.2	3.2	2.3				4.3	3.5
	2.8	1.8				% Officers', Directors' Owners' Comp/Sales	2.4	2.1
	(12) 5.3	(13) 2.5					(34) 3.7	(35) 3.9
	7.2	7.7					7.6	10.5
7612M	78442M	444311M	1008070M	950225M	875596M	Net Sales ($)	2058050M	2185770M
1703M	21831M	183972M	513767M	465353M	570323M	Total Assets ($)	1123868M	1184238M

Comparative Historical Data | Current Data Sorted by Sales

			Type of Statement		21 (4/1-9/30/06)		75 (10/1/06-3/31/07)		
4/1/04-3/31/05 ALL	4/1/05-3/31/06 ALL	4/1/06-3/31/07 ALL		0-1MM	1-3MM	3-5MM	5-10MM	10-25MM	25MM & OVER
20	19	22	Unqualified			2	3	1	16
23	20	23	Reviewed		1	2	6	8	6
19	18	21	Compiled	1	5	5	4	6	
6	12	5	Tax Returns		2	1	1	1	
19	23	25	Other	1	3	1	6	5	9
87	92	96	**NUMBER OF STATEMENTS**	2	11	11	20	21	31
%	%	%	**ASSETS**	%	%	%	%	%	%
6.8	8.3	9.6	Cash & Equivalents		9.7	9.8	8.7	10.0	8.6
33.8	33.7	35.4	Trade Receivables (net)		36.1	37.0	34.8	38.5	34.0
25.5	25.5	25.1	Inventory		21.1	23.5	27.5	23.5	27.6
3.4	2.8	3.2	All Other Current		6.2	.3	3.3	4.6	2.4
69.4	70.3	73.3	Total Current		73.0	70.6	74.3	76.6	72.7
22.6	22.8	20.8	Fixed Assets (net)		20.1	25.9	19.5	17.6	20.9
2.6	1.7	1.9	Intangibles (net)		.2	1.1	4.2	.5	2.4
5.4	5.2	4.0	All Other Non-Current		6.7	2.3	2.0	5.3	4.1
100.0	100.0	100.0	Total		100.0	100.0	100.0	100.0	100.0
			LIABILITIES						
10.4	11.7	12.0	Notes Payable-Short Term		9.2	7.8	14.5	14.5	11.8
3.4	3.5	3.4	Cur. Mat.-L.T.D.		7.3	4.5	3.2	2.5	2.2
18.0	16.4	16.4	Trade Payables		15.3	21.0	19.3	15.7	14.7
.4	.6	.3	Income Taxes Payable		.0	.0	.3	.4	.6
7.4	8.9	8.5	All Other Current		6.1	10.0	4.8	9.3	11.1
39.6	41.1	40.6	Total Current		37.8	43.2	42.1	42.3	40.4
14.0	17.2	14.8	Long-Term Debt		26.8	9.8	14.5	5.5	16.8
.6	.6	.5	Deferred Taxes		.2	.5	.2	.3	.9
4.1	5.1	4.4	All Other Non-Current		6.4	1.8	4.4	5.0	2.6
41.6	35.9	39.7	Net Worth		28.7	44.6	38.8	46.9	39.2
100.0	100.0	100.0	Total Liabilities & Net Worth		100.0	100.0	100.0	100.0	100.0
			INCOME DATA						
100.0	100.0	100.0	Net Sales		100.0	100.0	100.0	100.0	100.0
28.7	29.0	28.0	Gross Profit		34.3	29.7	33.1	22.2	24.0
24.6	23.4	19.9	Operating Expenses		30.3	25.0	25.2	14.1	13.0
4.0	5.6	8.1	Operating Profit		4.0	4.7	7.9	8.1	10.9
.5	.9	.9	All Other Expenses (net)		.8	.4	.8	.3	.9
3.6	4.7	7.3	Profit Before Taxes		3.2	4.3	7.0	7.8	10.0
			RATIOS						
3.1	2.6	3.1			5.7	3.4	2.9	3.3	2.7
1.8	1.8	1.9	Current		2.8	2.2	1.9	1.8	1.8
1.3	1.3	1.3			1.1	1.3	1.2	1.3	1.3
1.8	1.6	1.9			2.6	1.7	2.2	2.3	1.4
1.0	1.0	1.1	Quick		1.8	1.3	.9	1.1	1.1
.7	.7	.7			.4	.7	.6	.6	.7
43 8.4	39 9.4	40 9.1			32 11.6	31 11.7	41 9.0	38 9.6	45 8.1
53 6.9	52 7.0	51 7.2	Sales/Receivables		49 7.4	49 7.5	48 7.6	51 7.2	59 6.2
66 5.6	66 5.5	65 5.6			55 6.6	78 4.7	54 6.7	65 5.6	78 4.7
31 11.6	27 13.6	21 17.7			17 21.4	21 17.5	18 20.2	7 53.9	29 12.5
54 6.8	50 7.3	58 6.3	Cost of Sales/Inventory		46 7.9	56 6.5	65 5.6	40 9.1	69 5.3
92 4.0	92 4.0	87 4.2			131 2.8	97 3.7	107 3.4	83 4.4	88 4.2
19 19.1	21 17.5	15 24.0			10 37.1	22 16.4	13 27.0	11 33.7	18 20.4
34 10.7	31 11.7	29 12.6	Cost of Sales/Payables		19 19.2	37 9.9	34 10.9	24 15.0	28 13.0
54 6.8	52 7.0	53 6.9			40 9.2	41 9.0	73 5.0	56 6.5	40 9.2
3.9	5.1	4.4			4.2	4.6	4.4	3.9	4.8
8.0	7.4	7.1	Sales/Working Capital		7.1	6.0	6.9	7.8	7.0
15.1	15.2	13.8			50.3	27.1	30.4	14.6	11.4
16.1	14.4	18.5					16.4	71.4	25.5
(79) 5.5	(86) 5.8	(87) 6.8	EBIT/Interest				(19) 5.9	4.8	(27) 9.4
1.4	2.1	2.9					4.6	2.3	4.6
4.4	7.4	17.7	Net Profit + Depr., Dep.,						34.4
(23) 3.3	(27) 3.9	(31) 5.2	Amort./Cur. Mat. L/T/D						(16) 12.3
1.7	1.9	2.2							5.5
.2	.3	.2			.1	.2	.3	.1	.2
.5	.5	.4	Fixed/Worth		.3	.5	.6	.4	.4
1.5	1.3	.9			-2.2	1.9	1.5	.7	.6
.6	.7	.5			.3	.4	.7	.4	.7
1.3	1.7	1.3	Debt/Worth		1.0	1.6	1.9	1.1	1.5
3.9	3.3	3.2			-3.3	2.7	3.2	2.0	3.2
38.8	51.2	60.3	% Profit Before Taxes/Tangible				62.8	51.7	70.1
(78) 14.1	(84) 23.4	(86) 32.0	Net Worth				(18) 42.4	(20) 28.2	(30) 42.5
1.5	5.9	14.6					22.6	9.0	25.2
13.8	20.2	23.1	% Profit Before Taxes/Total		37.2	10.2	26.3	31.4	26.1
7.0	8.0	13.7	Assets		14.7	7.4	15.4	13.2	16.3
.7	1.7	5.0			-6.1	2.1	8.7	3.5	8.0
32.3	26.3	32.3			88.1	40.3	23.9	38.7	30.1
12.9	12.1	14.1	Sales/Net Fixed Assets		33.5	11.6	16.9	17.9	10.9
5.4	6.0	7.9			10.5	2.5	9.5	7.4	6.5
2.9	3.0	3.3			3.9	3.6	3.3	3.6	2.8
2.2	2.2	2.2	Sales/Total Assets		2.4	2.6	2.4	2.2	1.9
1.5	1.7	1.7			1.7	1.3	1.9	1.7	1.6
.8	1.0	.8				1.0	1.1	.7	.8
(77) 2.2	(85) 1.7	(85) 1.6	% Depr., Dep., Amort./Sales			(10) 2.4	(16) 1.8	(19) 1.3	(30) 1.5
3.6	2.9	2.8				4.6	3.4	2.5	2.2
1.9	1.9	1.6	% Officers', Directors',						
(34) 3.1	(41) 2.5	(32) 2.9	Owners' Comp/Sales						
6.7	7.2	6.3							
1954019M	3580176M	3364256M	Net Sales ($)	1359M	20492M	45736M	143934M	327125M	2825610M
1084741M	1892572M	1756949M	Total Assets ($)	1102M	7850M	24362M	59908M	151604M	1512123M

M = $ thousand   MM = $ million
See Pages 11 through 21 for Explanation of Ratios and Data

Current Data Sorted by Assets | Comparative Historical Data

Type of Statement

Type of Statement	0-500M	500M-2MM	2-10MM	10-50MM	50-100MM	100-250MM		4/1/02-3/31/03 ALL	4/1/03-3/31/04 ALL
Unqualified		3	14	35	7	10		74	65
Reviewed	2	18	70	27	1			127	135
Compiled	13	26	39	7	1			99	128
Tax Returns	32	40	22	2	1	1		58	56
Other	6	44	80	51	9	2		149	161
		126 (4/1-9/30/06)		437 (10/1/06-3/31/07)					
NUMBER OF STATEMENTS	53	131	225	122	19	13		507	545

Main Data

0-500M	500M-2MM	2-10MM	10-50MM	50-100MM	100-250MM		4/1/02-3/31/03 ALL	4/1/03-3/31/04 ALL
%	%	%	%	%	%	**ASSETS**	%	%
14.4	8.7	7.9	5.8	5.2	11.0	Cash & Equivalents	9.1	8.6
28.8	30.1	26.2	27.0	25.9	18.5	Trade Receivables (net)	25.1	26.9
17.6	21.0	25.3	28.9	30.4	31.2	Inventory	21.2	21.8
1.5	2.4	2.7	4.3	4.6	6.2	All Other Current	2.8	2.6
62.2	62.2	62.2	66.1	66.0	67.0	Total Current	58.2	59.7
30.1	30.8	28.7	25.6	21.5	24.1	Fixed Assets (net)	34.0	31.4
.6	2.9	2.8	4.3	4.9	6.8	Intangibles (net)	3.2	3.5
7.1	4.1	6.4	4.0	7.6	2.1	All Other Non-Current	4.6	5.3
100.0	100.0	100.0	100.0	100.0	100.0	Total	100.0	100.0
						LIABILITIES		
23.8	10.8	8.5	10.0	17.1	8.3	Notes Payable-Short Term	10.4	12.2
15.6	5.4	4.1	3.2	3.5	7.5	Cur. Mat.-L.T.D.	5.4	4.9
19.3	18.2	13.6	13.7	14.8	15.7	Trade Payables	13.8	14.8
.0	.3	.4	.2	.2	.0	Income Taxes Payable	.3	.3
9.3	9.5	9.3	10.6	8.3	10.0	All Other Current	9.2	9.2
68.1	44.2	35.9	37.7	43.9	41.5	Total Current	39.1	41.3
21.4	19.7	17.2	15.1	21.5	14.6	Long-Term Debt	20.0	18.6
.0	.4	.5	.3	1.6	1.2	Deferred Taxes	.6	.6
16.8	6.5	5.3	5.7	3.1	16.9	All Other Non-Current	6.7	6.6
-6.2	29.2	41.1	41.2	29.9	25.8	Net Worth	33.7	32.8
100.0	100.0	100.0	100.0	100.0	100.0	Total Liabilities & Net Worth	100.0	100.0
						INCOME DATA		
100.0	100.0	100.0	100.0	100.0	100.0	Net Sales	100.0	100.0
49.9	33.1	28.8	23.9	18.1	23.6	Gross Profit	29.4	29.0
44.6	29.2	22.1	17.1	12.3	17.2	Operating Expenses	26.3	26.1
5.3	3.8	6.7	6.8	5.8	6.4	Operating Profit	3.1	3.0
1.9	.9	1.4	.9	1.0	2.3	All Other Expenses (net)	1.4	1.1
3.4	2.9	5.3	5.9	4.8	4.1	Profit Before Taxes	1.6	1.8
						RATIOS		
2.0	2.8	3.1	2.8	2.6	2.9		2.6	2.6
1.1	1.5	1.8	1.8	1.6	1.8	Current	1.6	1.6
.6	1.0	1.2	1.3	1.2	1.2		1.1	1.1
1.9	1.8	1.7	1.3	1.6	1.3		1.6	1.7
(52) .6	.9	1.0	.9	.7	.6	Quick	.9	.9
.3	.5	.6	.6	.4	.3		.5	.5
0 UND	26 13.8	31 11.8	36 10.3	33 11.0	22 16.7		32 11.6	32 11.5
27 13.3	37 9.8	43 8.4	48 7.6	44 8.2	43 8.4	Sales/Receivables	43 8.5	46 8.0
46 7.9	56 6.5	61 6.0	59 6.1	55 6.6	53 6.9		57 6.4	59 6.2
0 UND	6 56.8	28 13.2	38 9.6	52 7.0	58 6.3		23 15.9	23 16.1
14 26.2	40 9.2	55 6.7	63 5.8	60 6.1	71 5.2	Cost of Sales/Inventory	46 7.9	49 7.4
58 6.3	67 5.5	88 4.2	95 3.9	98 3.7	121 3.0		78 4.7	82 4.5
4 94.9	14 25.4	16 22.3	19 19.3	21 17.3	19 18.9		16 23.3	17 21.4
17 20.9	28 13.1	30 12.3	31 11.7	26 13.9	30 12.3	Cost of Sales/Payables	28 13.0	29 12.4
50 7.2	50 7.3	45 8.1	43 8.5	34 10.6	54 6.7		44 8.3	48 7.6
9.8	7.0	4.8	4.7	4.7	3.8		5.0	5.1
77.1	13.5	7.4	7.6	6.8	10.0	Sales/Working Capital	9.8	9.5
-12.1	-395.7	19.7	16.2	34.3	16.8		93.9	53.1
7.2	11.2	13.5	13.6	14.1	10.8		7.2	8.2
(45) 2.8	(118) 3.6	(205) 4.5	(115) 4.8	(18) 2.2	(12) 4.4	EBIT/Interest	(464) 2.6	(496) 2.4
1.4	1.1	1.9	2.2	.4	1.2		.1	.3
		9.6	7.1	5.3		Net Profit + Depr., Dep.,	5.1	4.2
	(22) 2.6	(58) 3.8	(45) 2.6			Amort./Cur. Mat. L/T/D	(119) 2.4	(126) 2.0
	1.3	1.5	1.7				1.1	.8
.0	.4	.2	.3	.3	.4		.4	.4
1.1	.9	.7	.6	.6	.6	Fixed/Worth	1.0	.9
-6.9	2.9	1.7	1.5	1.9	4.2		3.1	3.0
1.0	.8	.6	.8	.6	.9		.7	.7
10.0	2.0	1.6	1.5	3.1	1.3	Debt/Worth	1.8	1.9
-3.6	10.3	4.2	5.0	6.0	11.0		6.2	7.3
96.7	60.1	46.0	43.9	39.5	34.4	% Profit Before Taxes/Tangible	32.2	34.8
(33) 42.9	(107) 23.7	(209) 24.4	(114) 26.2	(18) 13.4	(11) 18.8	Net Worth	(430) 12.2	(463) 13.4
9.1	3.3	10.0	11.0	-37.5	8.8		-3.0	-1.8
32.4	18.9	18.1	17.1	22.7	17.2	% Profit Before Taxes/Total	12.6	11.9
9.1	5.9	8.7	9.4	4.9	4.5	Assets	4.2	3.6
1.6	.4	3.0	3.2	-2.2	1.2		-2.5	-1.9
447.0	27.3	17.4	17.3	37.0	23.2		13.4	16.3
21.3	10.1	8.7	8.5	8.8	6.7	Sales/Net Fixed Assets	6.7	7.4
6.1	5.1	4.6	5.2	5.6	5.8		3.4	3.9
5.8	3.6	2.5	2.5	2.7	2.1		2.6	2.7
3.6	2.7	2.0	2.0	1.8	1.8	Sales/Total Assets	1.9	2.0
2.4	1.8	1.5	1.5	1.2	1.4		1.5	1.5
1.4	1.5	1.0	1.0	.9		% Depr., Dep., Amort./Sales	1.7	1.4
(32) 2.8	(106) 2.7	(208) 1.9	(107) 1.9	(17) 2.3			(459) 3.2	(486) 3.0
5.0	4.5	4.3	3.1	2.6			5.7	5.3
4.8	2.3	2.1	.8			% Officers', Directors'	2.4	2.7
(35) 7.8	(80) 4.5	(97) 3.5	(23) 2.4			Owners' Comp/Sales	(211) 5.1	(226) 4.6
15.7	7.8	5.2	4.7				8.4	8.0
58181M	466962M	2264797M	5356173M	2695134M	4739113M	Net Sales ($)	8389389M	9663312M
14373M	165035M	1109569M	2541585M	1283465M	2303072M	Total Assets ($)	5277631M	5810475M

M = $ thousand   MM = $ million
See Pages 11 through 21 for Explanation of Ratios and Data

Comparative Historical Data

Current Data Sorted by Sales

4/1/04-3/31/05 ALL	4/1/05-3/31/06 ALL	4/1/06-3/31/07 ALL	Type of Statement	0-1MM	1-3MM	3-5MM	5-10MM	10-25MM	25MM & OVER
76	70	69	Unqualified		1	1	8	11	48
156	134	118	Reviewed	2	5	14	35	39	23
111	97	86	Compiled	5	22	19	18	15	7
82	69	98	Tax Returns	22	27	27	17	1	4
128	195	192	Other	7	19	22	53	41	50
				126 (4/1-9/30/06)			437 (10/1/06-3/31/07)		
553	565	563	NUMBER OF STATEMENTS	36	74	83	131	107	132
%	%	%	ASSETS	%	%	%	%	%	%
7.9	8.9	8.2	Cash & Equivalents	14.3	8.7	8.4	7.6	8.6	6.5
28.4	28.9	27.4	Trade Receivables (net)	20.0	29.3	26.6	28.5	26.8	28.0
23.9	23.8	24.7	Inventory	17.3	21.4	19.6	25.1	26.6	29.7
2.4	2.5	3.0	All Other Current	1.0	2.7	2.4	3.0	2.2	4.7
62.6	64.1	63.3	Total Current	52.6	62.1	57.0	64.3	64.3	69.0
29.0	27.1	28.3	Fixed Assets (net)	35.6	30.7	33.0	26.9	29.3	22.5
3.3	2.7	3.1	Intangibles (net)	3.6	3.0	2.6	2.9	2.2	4.1
5.2	6.1	5.3	All Other Non-Current	8.2	4.2	7.3	5.8	4.2	4.4
100.0	100.0	100.0	Total	100.0	100.0	100.0	100.0	100.0	100.0
			LIABILITIES						
12.7	12.0	11.1	Notes Payable-Short Term	18.9	13.5	12.2	8.2	9.2	11.3
4.4	3.9	5.3	Cur. Mat.-L.T.D.	20.5	7.8	4.2	3.6	4.1	3.2
15.8	15.4	15.3	Trade Payables	18.7	15.4	14.5	16.0	14.3	15.1
.3	.3	.3	Income Taxes Payable	.0	.2	.3	.5	.2	.2
8.2	10.2	9.6	All Other Current	7.3	9.2	8.7	10.0	10.1	10.3
41.4	41.8	41.7	Total Current	65.4	46.0	39.9	38.4	38.0	40.1
19.7	18.8	17.8	Long-Term Debt	27.1	21.4	20.9	17.6	14.9	13.9
.4	.5	.4	Deferred Taxes	.0	.3	.5	.5	.4	.6
7.1	5.6	6.9	All Other Non-Current	23.6	7.9	5.3	5.2	4.9	6.2
31.3	33.3	33.2	Net Worth	-16.1	24.4	33.5	38.3	41.8	39.1
100.0	100.0	100.0	Total Liabilties & Net Worth	100.0	100.0	100.0	100.0	100.0	100.0
			INCOME DATA						
100.0	100.0	100.0	Net Sales	100.0	100.0	100.0	100.0	100.0	100.0
29.9	30.4	30.2	Gross Profit	52.1	38.6	32.7	29.8	25.3	22.3
25.1	24.8	24.3	Operating Expenses	46.4	35.8	26.9	23.8	18.2	15.8
4.8	5.6	5.9	Operating Profit	5.7	2.8	5.8	6.0	7.1	6.5
1.2	.9	1.2	All Other Expenses (net)	3.6	1.1	1.6	1.2	.7	1.0
3.6	4.7	4.6	Profit Before Taxes	2.0	1.8	4.2	4.8	6.4	5.6
			RATIOS						
2.6	2.6	2.9	Current	2.8	2.7	2.6	3.1	2.8	2.9
1.6	1.6	1.7		1.0	1.5	1.5	1.8	1.7	1.8
1.1	1.2	1.1		.4	.9	1.0	1.2	1.2	1.3
1.5	1.6	1.6	Quick	2.0	1.8	1.9	1.6	1.7	1.5
.9	.9 (562)	.9		(35) .5	.8	.9	1.0	.9	.9
.6	.6	.5		.2	.4	.5	.6	.6	.5
32 11.4	31 11.8	28 13.0	Sales/Receivables	0 UND	26 14.0	26 14.3	31 11.7	28 13.2	30 12.0
46 7.9	44 8.2	42 8.6		30 12.2	38 9.7	42 8.8	43 8.4	43 8.4	46 8.0
60 6.1	59 6.2	58 6.3		57 6.4	52 7.0	58 6.3	63 5.8	59 6.2	56 6.5
26 14.1	20 18.3	22 16.4	Cost of Sales/Inventory	0 UND	8 48.4	8 44.9	25 14.3	32 11.2	39 9.3
52 7.0	50 7.3	51 7.2		36 10.1	36 10.0	39 9.3	54 6.8	52 7.0	61 6.0
87 4.2	82 4.4	83 4.4		87 4.2	85 4.7	77 4.7	83 4.4	79 4.6	90 4.0
19 19.3	17 21.8	16 23.3	Cost of Sales/Payables	7 52.9	13 27.5	13 28.8	16 23.0	19 19.5	19 19.2
31 11.8	30 12.2	29 12.8		24 15.5	28 13.2	28 13.1	29 12.8	32 11.5	28 13.1
47 7.8	44 8.4	46 7.9		94 3.9	50 7.3	52 7.0	44 8.3	45 8.1	40 9.2
5.3	5.4	5.4	Sales/Working Capital	7.8	6.1	6.6	5.0	4.5	5.0
9.5	9.8	9.2		UND	12.8	10.2	7.6	8.3	7.7
38.9	33.2	39.6		-6.3	-44.7	104.2	32.4	19.0	18.3
11.8	12.3	12.8	EBIT/Interest	9.5	7.4	6.4	12.8	15.5	14.8
(501) 4.0	(505) 4.4	(513) 4.2		(30) 3.3	(66) 2.5	(75) 3.3	(123) 5.1	(95) 5.3	(124) 5.0
1.3	1.6	1.6		.3	.5	1.4	2.1	2.4	2.0
6.9	6.4	7.2	Net Profit + Depr., Dep., Amort./Cur. Mat. L/T/D		11.4	5.6	6.5	8.4	7.6
(135) 2.7	(141) 2.6	(144) 3.1		(11)	5.3	(16) 1.7	(33) 2.1	(28) 3.4	(53) 3.5
1.5	1.3	1.5			1.3	.8	1.1	1.8	1.7
.4	.3	.3	Fixed/Worth	.2	.2	.4	.2	.3	.3
.8	.7	.7		5.6	.9	1.0	.7	.7	.6
2.7	1.9	2.3		-1.7	3.9	2.9	1.9	1.6	1.5
.8	.7	.7	Debt/Worth	1.3	.9	.8	.6	.7	.7
2.1	2.0	1.8		22.2	2.0	2.5	1.6	1.6	1.4
6.9	5.0	6.0		-3.9	NM	6.9	4.8	3.8	5.2
42.3	50.3	49.0	% Profit Before Taxes/Tangible Net Worth	195.1	53.7	44.2	48.9	55.6	43.3
(471) 20.5	(497) 23.2	(492) 24.7		(21) 43.8	(56) 19.1	(73) 17.4	(116) 26.2	(102) 28.4	(124) 26.9
5.2	6.2	8.2		4.2	1.2	3.5	8.7	10.9	11.0
14.4	18.9	18.9	% Profit Before Taxes/Total Assets	30.4	18.2	16.2	18.1	20.8	20.6
6.2	7.8	8.5		6.1	5.4	5.6	9.6	10.0	10.2
.9	1.8	2.0		-6.9	-2.0	1.3	2.5	4.1	2.9
18.2	24.0	21.9	Sales/Net Fixed Assets	27.5	38.9	17.9	25.2	18.1	21.9
8.5	10.2	9.2		6.4	10.7	9.4	9.6	7.6	11.3
4.7	5.5	5.1		2.7	4.4	4.7	5.4	4.7	6.3
2.8	3.0	3.1	Sales/Total Assets	3.5	3.9	3.3	3.0	2.6	3.0
2.1	2.2	2.2		1.9	2.3	2.4	2.1	2.0	2.1
1.6	1.7	1.6		1.3	1.5	1.5	1.6	1.6	1.7
1.4	1.0	1.0	% Depr., Dep., Amort./Sales	1.6	1.8	1.6	.9	1.0	.9
(482) 2.5	(498) 2.1	(479) 2.2		(25) 3.3	(55) 3.7	(68) 3.2	(120) 2.0	(95) 1.8	(116) 1.7
4.4	3.6	4.0		6.9	5.3	5.0	4.0	3.8	2.6
2.2	2.2	2.2	% Officers', Directors', Owners' Comp/Sales	4.9	3.1	2.7	2.1	1.7	1.1
(239) 4.0	(247) 4.4	(240) 4.0		(22) 8.2	(42) 5.8	(47) 4.5	(70) 3.3	(34) 2.6	(25) 2.7
7.7	7.9	6.9		13.1	9.3	6.3	5.0	7.3	4.9
9549691M	13591316M	15580360M	Net Sales ($)	19704M	140471M	332976M	936869M	1654137M	12496203M
5323381M	6137112M	7417099M	Total Assets ($)	15657M	69889M	171027M	510979M	881795M	5767752M

M = $ thousand   MM = $ million
See Pages 11 through 21 for Explanation of Ratios and Data

Current Data Sorted by Assets | Comparative Historical Data

0-500M	500M-2MM	2-10MM	10-50MM	50-100MM	100-250MM	Type of Statement	4/1/02-3/31/03 ALL	4/1/03-3/31/04 ALL
	1	13	16	1	3	Unqualified	33	38
1	3	16	10	2		Reviewed	24	31
2	9	11	2			Compiled	21	25
1	7	3				Tax Returns	9	20
1	4	16	16	5	4	Other	25	32
	46 (4/1-9/30/06)		101 (10/1/06-3/31/07)					
5	24	59	44	8	7	NUMBER OF STATEMENTS	112	146
%	%	%	%	%	%	ASSETS	%	%
	3.8	7.0	5.3			Cash & Equivalents	6.1	5.8
	10.4	18.7	19.3			Trade Receivables (net)	19.3	19.2
	61.3	47.1	44.4			Inventory	43.2	43.3
	4.2	1.7	2.8			All Other Current	1.8	2.4
	79.7	74.5	71.8			Total Current	70.4	70.7
	16.0	17.4	19.5			Fixed Assets (net)	20.8	20.3
	.8	2.6	4.4			Intangibles (net)	4.2	3.4
	3.5	5.5	4.2			All Other Non-Current	4.6	5.6
	100.0	100.0	100.0			Total	100.0	100.0
						LIABILITIES		
	20.3	15.2	19.3			Notes Payable-Short Term	19.0	15.7
	2.5	3.4	2.8			Cur. Mat.-L.T.D.	2.8	4.0
	7.4	11.5	9.7			Trade Payables	10.4	11.9
	.1	.2	.1			Income Taxes Payable	.2	.2
	9.2	11.4	10.0			All Other Current	11.0	10.1
	39.5	41.7	41.9			Total Current	43.4	41.8
	25.0	11.0	14.2			Long-Term Debt	14.0	14.6
	.0	.3	.5			Deferred Taxes	.3	.3
	9.1	5.6	3.8			All Other Non-Current	7.7	7.2
	26.4	41.4	39.6			Net Worth	34.6	36.0
	100.0	100.0	100.0			Total Liabilities & Net Worth	100.0	100.0
						INCOME DATA		
	100.0	100.0	100.0			Net Sales	100.0	100.0
	30.8	26.4	25.0			Gross Profit	27.2	26.5
	27.3	22.1	18.3			Operating Expenses	24.1	22.8
	3.5	4.3	6.7			Operating Profit	3.1	3.7
	1.6	1.3	2.1			All Other Expenses (net)	1.0	.9
	2.0	3.0	4.6			Profit Before Taxes	2.0	2.7
						RATIOS		
	5.1	2.6	2.5				2.9	2.9
	2.3	1.9	1.8			Current	1.7	1.7
	1.2	1.4	1.4				1.2	1.3
	1.2	1.1	.9				1.1	1.1
	.3	.7	.6			Quick	.6	.6
	.1	.3	.4				.3	.3
	6 58.3	19 19.0	25 14.8				18 19.8	18 20.3
	13 29.0	36 10.2	38 9.7			Sales/Receivables	35 10.3	36 10.1
	27 13.6	52 7.0	64 5.7				55 6.6	57 6.4
	119 3.1	70 5.2	82 4.4				73 5.0	68 5.4
	146 2.5	114 3.2	124 2.9			Cost of Sales/Inventory	105 3.5	113 3.2
	253 1.4	211 1.7	194 1.9				179 2.0	167 2.2
	4 95.8	14 25.7	14 26.0				13 28.7	13 28.6
	11 31.9	25 14.8	25 14.8			Cost of Sales/Payables	23 16.2	24 15.2
	29 12.6	39 9.3	47 7.8				42 8.8	49 7.5
	3.1	3.4	3.7				3.5	3.8
	5.4	6.2	5.2			Sales/Working Capital	6.9	6.5
	24.0	10.4	11.4				14.5	13.5
	3.9	5.1	8.5				6.2	6.8
	(23) 1.6	(53) 2.4	(42) 3.2			EBIT/Interest	(103) 2.1	(135) 3.3
	1.0	1.2	1.2				.8	1.2
			5.7				9.8	6.4
		(16)	2.9			Net Profit + Depr., Dep., Amort./Cur. Mat. L/T/D	(32) 3.6	(33) 3.0
			1.6				.9	.7
	.2	.1	.2				.3	.2
	.4	.3	.5			Fixed/Worth	.5	.5
	2.6	.9	.9				2.1	1.1
	.6	.7	.9				.6	.8
	4.0	1.7	1.4			Debt/Worth	1.7	1.8
	17.0	4.3	5.1				5.2	4.9
	25.2	31.3	32.6				25.0	27.8
	(20) 8.6	(58) 12.4	(42) 23.2			% Profit Before Taxes/Tangible Net Worth	(96) 8.3	(133) 12.4
	-.5	3.1	7.0				1.3	2.6
	5.1	11.2	13.7				7.9	8.9
	2.8	3.3	7.0			% Profit Before Taxes/Total Assets	2.1	4.5
	-.3	1.0	1.0				-.4	.6
	76.1	34.0	15.8				22.8	21.1
	20.6	15.2	8.2			Sales/Net Fixed Assets	9.3	10.6
	9.8	6.6	6.5				5.7	6.3
	2.6	2.4	1.9				2.2	2.4
	2.2	1.9	1.6			Sales/Total Assets	1.6	1.8
	1.5	1.3	1.3				1.3	1.3
	.7	.7	1.1				1.3	1.1
	(16) 1.2	(49) 1.4	(41) 1.7			% Depr., Dep., Amort./Sales	(99) 2.0	(125) 2.0
	2.4	2.1	2.6				3.3	3.1
	1.9	1.0					1.6	1.3
	(13) 3.0	(19) 2.3				% Officers', Directors' Owners' Comp/Sales	(37) 2.6	(51) 2.7
	6.0	8.7					5.2	5.1
6068M	58661M	544368M	1640248M	995021M	1494275M	Net Sales ($)	3241679M	4434951M
1820M	28199M	287755M	1040255M	564398M	1155871M	Total Assets ($)	2257617M	2900890M

M = $ thousand   MM = $ million
See Pages 11 through 21 for Explanation of Ratios and Data

Comparative Historical Data   Current Data Sorted by Sales

© RMA 2007

					Type of Statement						
	32		32	34	Unqualified		2	2	5	9	16
	30		21	32	Reviewed	1	3	1	6	13	8
	24		20	24	Compiled	1	8	4	8	1	2
	11		8	11	Tax Returns	3	6	1		1	
	29		51	46	Other		6	2	8		22
	4/1/04-3/31/05 ALL		4/1/05-3/31/06 ALL	4/1/06-3/31/07 ALL			46 (4/1-9/30/06)			101 (10/1/06-3/31/07)	
						0-1MM	1-3MM	3-5MM	5-10MM	10-25MM	25MM & OVER
	126		132	147	NUMBER OF STATEMENTS	5	25	10	27	32	48
	%		%	%	ASSETS	%	%	%	%	%	%
	7.5		5.7	6.0	Cash & Equivalents		3.7	4.5	5.9	7.6	5.1
	18.5		20.2	18.0	Trade Receivables (net)		12.0	8.8	17.1	22.2	21.4
	44.3		43.3	47.2	Inventory		51.6	59.0	51.6	47.2	40.7
	2.4		2.7	2.5	All Other Current		4.1	1.8	1.9	3.1	2.1
	72.7		72.0	73.7	Total Current		71.4	74.1	76.6	80.0	69.3
	19.0		20.2	18.1	Fixed Assets (net)		23.4	14.8	14.9	14.4	19.7
	3.2		4.0	3.8	Intangibles (net)		1.8	0	3.2	1.6	7.3
	5.1		3.9	4.4	All Other Non-Current		3.3	10.3	5.3	4.0	3.7
	100.0		100.0	100.0	Total		100.0	100.0	100.0	100.0	100.0
					LIABILITIES						
	13.4		16.3	16.9	Notes Payable-Short Term		19.5	26.0	13.6	19.5	15.4
	3.2		2.6	2.9	Cur. Mat.-L.T.D.		5.8	.8	1.2	2.8	3.2
	12.2		12.1	10.8	Trade Payables		8.2	8.6	13.1	9.8	12.4
	.4		.3	.2	Income Taxes Payable		.1	.0	.3	.1	.3
	11.6		11.7	10.2	All Other Current		6.6	13.2	12.4	11.1	10.3
	40.9		42.9	41.0	Total Current		40.2	48.7	40.5	43.3	41.6
	11.9		13.4	14.4	Long-Term Debt		17.2	22.9	11.4	10.8	13.0
	.2		.3	.3	Deferred Taxes		.0	.4	.4	.2	.6
	5.1		5.7	6.2	All Other Non-Current		10.6	2.6	5.9	5.4	4.4
	41.9		37.7	38.0	Net Worth		32.0	25.4	41.8	40.3	40.4
	100.0		100.0	100.0	Total Liabilties & Net Worth		100.0	100.0	100.0	100.0	100.0
					INCOME DATA						
	100.0		100.0	100.0	Net Sales		100.0	100.0	100.0	100.0	100.0
	25.3		25.3	26.6	Gross Profit		30.4	23.7	27.1	24.3	25.5
	20.5		20.2	21.8	Operating Expenses		28.2	18.7	22.2	20.1	18.7
	4.8		5.1	4.9	Operating Profit		2.2	5.0	4.9	4.2	6.8
	.9		1.0	1.4	All Other Expenses (net)		2.2	1.4	1.0	1.0	1.8
	3.9		4.1	3.4	Profit Before Taxes		.0	3.6	3.9	3.2	5.0
					RATIOS						
	3.2		2.9	2.8			4.9	2.8	2.7	2.5	2.6
	1.8		1.8	1.8	Current		1.5	1.7	1.8	1.9	1.7
	1.3		1.3	1.3			1.2	1.0	1.5	1.5	1.3
	1.2		1.2	1.1			1.1	.6	1.1	1.1	1.2
	.6		.6	.6	Quick		.5	.3	.5	.7	.7
	.4		.3	.3			.1	.2	.2	.4	.4
16	22.2	19	18.8	17	21.2	8	44.6	9	38.6	18	20.2	20	18.7	28	13.2

	Hist1		Hist2	Hist3	Ratio	0-1MM	1-3MM	3-5MM	5-10MM	10-25MM	25MM&Over
16	22.2	19	18.8	17 21.2	Sales/Receivables	8 44.6	9 38.6	18 20.2	20 18.7	28 13.2
33	11.1	38	9.6	34 10.6		20 18.4	20 18.5	35 10.3	42 8.7	38 9.5
59	6.2	58	6.3	56 6.5		37 9.9	32 11.3	52 7.0	61 6.0	75 4.9
71	5.1	74	4.9	82 4.5	Cost of Sales/Inventory	94 3.9	125 2.9	81 4.5	71 5.1	82 4.4
107	3.4	120	3.0	120 3.0		142 2.6	150 2.4	137 2.7	105 3.5	107 3.4
173	2.1	167	2.2	197 1.9		299 1.2	260 1.4	216 1.7	169 2.2	166 2.2
12	30.0	15	24.3	13 28.5	Cost of Sales/Payables	4 94.0	7 50.3	20 18.4	11 33.0	18 20.2
24	15.5	25	14.4	25 14.8		16 23.5	20 18.3	29 12.6	21 17.3	30 12.2
44	8.3	41	9.0	40 9.1		40 9.1	37 10.0	45 8.1	29 12.7	51 7.1
	3.4		3.4	3.6	Sales/Working Capital	3.3	4.3	3.2	3.5	3.9
	6.0		6.2	5.8		6.1	7.1	6.1	5.1	6.0
	10.3		14.4	12.1		24.4	NM	9.1	11.6	13.4
	11.1		8.9	5.9	EBIT/Interest	2.5		5.3	5.1	9.9
(112)	3.7	(120)	3.0	(138) 2.8		(24) 1.6	(25) 2.9	(29) 2.9	(46) 3.2
	1.8		1.2	1.3		.5		1.5	1.4	1.2
	7.5		6.5	4.3	Net Profit + Depr., Dep., Amort./Cur. Mat. L/T/D					4.7
(39)	3.9	(34)	2.7	(34) 2.6					(21) 2.9
	1.6		1.6	1.4						1.9
	.2		.2	.2	Fixed/Worth	.2	.1	.1	.1	.3
	.4		.6	.5		.5	.7	.3	.4	.6
	.9		1.5	1.0		3.1	-2.1	.8	.7	1.2
	.6		.7	.9	Debt/Worth	.9	.5	.9	1.0	.8
	1.5		1.9	1.7		3.9	2.2	1.7	1.9	1.4
	3.8		5.9	5.1		10.8	-16.1	3.5	4.1	6.4
	34.5		35.8	31.5	% Profit Before Taxes/Tangible Net Worth	20.2		31.9	31.0	35.3
(118)	15.0	(119)	17.3	(137) 15.2		(23) 6.1		15.5	12.6	(44) 23.8
	4.7		6.2	3.8		-6.5		5.3	4.3	7.2
	11.9		11.8	10.9	% Profit Before Taxes/Total Assets	4.7	18.0	10.6	10.2	13.9
	6.4		5.0	4.3		1.6	4.7	4.2	4.1	7.4
	1.8		.9	.9		-1.7	.1	1.2	2.1	1.0
	25.8		24.6	32.8	Sales/Net Fixed Assets	84.4	42.6	36.8	41.4	15.0
	11.3		11.4	11.4		12.3	19.0	16.8	17.9	8.4
	6.9		6.4	6.6		5.4	9.0	8.6	7.0	6.6
	2.4		2.3	2.3	Sales/Total Assets	2.6	2.4	2.4	2.4	2.2
	1.8		1.8	1.8		1.7	1.8	1.9	1.9	1.6
	1.4		1.3	1.3		1.1	.9	1.3	1.4	1.3
	.9		1.0	.9	% Depr., Dep., Amort./Sales	.7		.5	.7	1.2
(113)	1.5	(119)	1.5	(124) 1.5		(17) 1.3	(20) 1.4	(29) 1.5	(45) 1.6
	2.3		2.4	2.4		3.6		2.4	1.7	2.5
	1.3		1.0	1.0	% Officers', Directors' Owners' Comp/Sales				.8	
(36)	2.6	(31)	2.8	(43) 2.5				(11) 1.8	
	4.4		6.8	4.6					2.9	
	3127142M		4682180M	4738641M	Net Sales ($)	3994M	52200M	40647M	196304M	533866M	3911630M
	1945442M		2990433M	3078298M	Total Assets ($)	2724M	33344M	28462M	116296M	323778M	2573694M

M = $ thousand   MM = $ million
See Pages 11 through 21 for Explanation of Ratios and Data

Current Data Sorted by Assets   Comparative Historical Data

0-500M	500M-2MM	2-10MM	10-50MM	50-100MM	100-250MM		13	14
						Type of Statement		
		1	6	1		Unqualified	13	14
		5	3		1	Reviewed	3	2
	2	2				Compiled	5	4
	3	4				Tax Returns	7	7
1	3	4	3	2	3	Other	20	13
	10 (4/1-9/30/06)		34 (10/1/06-3/31/07)				4/1/02-3/31/03 ALL	4/1/03-3/31/04 ALL
1	8	16	12	3	4	**NUMBER OF STATEMENTS**	48	40
%	%	%	%	%	%	**ASSETS**	%	%
		11.2	3.8			Cash & Equivalents	5.5	6.9
		19.5	20.9			Trade Receivables (net)	20.2	20.6
		39.7	43.2			Inventory	42.5	38.6
		1.9	2.0			All Other Current	1.9	2.7
		72.3	70.0			Total Current	70.0	68.9
		17.7	19.3			Fixed Assets (net)	21.5	20.5
		4.2	4.7			Intangibles (net)	3.1	4.0
		5.8	6.0			All Other Non-Current	5.4	6.6
		100.0	100.0			Total	100.0	100.0
						LIABILITIES		
		17.8	14.9			Notes Payable-Short Term	16.7	15.9
		1.7	1.9			Cur. Mat.-L.T.D.	2.0	2.5
		21.0	12.6			Trade Payables	18.5	14.5
		1.2	.0			Income Taxes Payable	.4	.7
		10.0	12.5			All Other Current	10.4	7.5
		51.6	41.9			Total Current	48.0	41.1
		13.3	11.3			Long-Term Debt	16.2	7.8
		.2	.5			Deferred Taxes	.1	.3
		6.2	7.1			All Other Non-Current	5.0	6.0
		28.8	39.3			Net Worth	30.8	44.8
		100.0	100.0			Total Liabilities & Net Worth	100.0	100.0
						INCOME DATA		
		100.0	100.0			Net Sales	100.0	100.0
		34.3	19.4			Gross Profit	28.3	29.4
		27.7	15.9			Operating Expenses	25.5	25.5
		6.5	3.5			Operating Profit	2.8	3.9
		1.5	1.7			All Other Expenses (net)	1.3	1.2
		5.0	1.8			Profit Before Taxes	1.5	2.7
						RATIOS		
		2.6	2.4				2.9	2.9
		1.4	1.8			Current	1.6	1.7
		1.2	1.6				1.0	1.3
		1.1	1.1				1.3	1.3
		.6	.8			Quick	.5	.6
		.2	.3				.3	.4
		9 42.2	18 20.2				18 19.9	19 19.5
		29 12.4	39 9.4			Sales/Receivables	41 8.9	37 10.0
		63 5.8	52 7.1				58 6.2	65 5.6
		58 6.3	82 4.4				65 5.6	57 6.4
		99 3.7	110 3.3			Cost of Sales/Inventory	91 4.0	88 4.2
		134 2.7	123 3.0				165 2.2	155 2.4
		12 30.9	13 28.0				15 24.4	11 32.3
		36 10.3	22 16.5			Cost of Sales/Payables	28 13.1	29 12.6
		90 4.0	45 8.0				47 7.8	51 7.2
		6.5	4.2				3.9	3.8
		11.5	5.7			Sales/Working Capital	8.4	7.7
		19.7	9.1				97.7	22.6
		4.7	4.0				11.0	7.8
		(14) 1.3	2.3			EBIT/Interest	(46) 2.3	(37) 3.3
		.7	1.2				.3	.6
								6.1
						Net Profit + Depr., Dep., Amort./Cur. Mat. L/T/D		(13) 1.9
								1.7
		.2	.3				.3	.3
		.6	.5			Fixed/Worth	.5	.4
		NM	.7				1.3	.7
		.9	.7				.8	.5
		2.0	1.4			Debt/Worth	2.6	1.4
		NM	2.5				6.2	2.8
		65.1	20.2				37.3	24.2
		(12) 22.5	(11) 11.3			% Profit Before Taxes/Tangible Net Worth	(44) 17.6	(38) 9.2
		-7.5	.3				-3.3	.0
		22.0	7.1				9.1	8.8
		4.5	5.3			% Profit Before Taxes/Total Assets	4.3	3.4
		-.8	.4				-.8	-.4
		46.6	20.3				31.5	27.1
		16.1	11.5			Sales/Net Fixed Assets	8.6	9.8
		8.6	5.9				5.6	6.0
		3.1	2.4				2.9	2.5
		2.3	2.0			Sales/Total Assets	1.9	1.9
		1.9	1.3				1.4	1.4
		.9	1.3				1.4	1.2
		(13) 1.7	1.8			% Depr., Dep., Amort./Sales	(42) 2.1	(36) 2.0
		2.5	2.8				3.3	3.5
								1.3	1.9
						% Officers', Directors' Owners' Comp/Sales	(15) 3.2	(15) 3.4
							9.5	6.3
385M	18050M	202506M	565328M	506380M	897796M	Net Sales ($)	1852339M	2200348M
330M	9814M	71921M	318720M	216168M	589320M	Total Assets ($)	1047645M	1242683M

© RMA 2007

M = $ thousand   MM = $ million
See Pages 11 through 21 for Explanation of Ratios and Data

Comparative Historical Data | Current Data Sorted by Sales

4/1/04-3/31/05 ALL	4/1/05-3/31/06 ALL	4/1/06-3/31/07 ALL	Type of Statement	0-1MM	1-3MM	3-5MM	5-10MM	10-25MM	25MM & OVER
8	8	8	Unqualified			1	3	1	1
6	4	9	Reviewed					1	7
3	2	4	Compiled		1	2		1	5
7	4	7	Tax Returns		2	1	2		
19	22	16	Other	1	3	1	1	1	9
				10 (4/1-9/30/06)			34 (10/1/06-3/31/07)		
43	40	44	**NUMBER OF STATEMENTS**	1	6	5	6	4	22
%	%	%	**ASSETS**	%	%	%	%	%	%
6.3	8.8	8.2	Cash & Equivalents						6.4
21.9	19.7	18.9	Trade Receivables (net)						19.1
42.3	43.3	40.8	Inventory						39.6
3.3	3.1	3.2	All Other Current						4.5
73.7	74.9	71.1	Total Current						69.5
17.5	16.9	19.3	Fixed Assets (net)						21.0
4.4	4.3	5.0	Intangibles (net)						5.5
4.4	3.9	4.7	All Other Non-Current						4.1
100.0	100.0	100.0	Total						100.0
			LIABILITIES						
19.0	21.5	22.1	Notes Payable-Short Term						14.3
1.1	1.1	1.8	Cur. Mat.-L.T.D.						1.4
15.2	16.4	17.5	Trade Payables						14.8
.0	.5	.5	Income Taxes Payable						.1
7.6	10.0	9.6	All Other Current						13.5
42.9	49.4	51.5	Total Current						44.0
7.8	10.9	11.4	Long-Term Debt						9.5
.4	.6	.4	Deferred Taxes						.7
9.0	5.4	5.3	All Other Non-Current						5.6
40.0	33.8	31.4	Net Worth						40.3
100.0	100.0	100.0	Total Liabilities & Net Worth						100.0
			INCOME DATA						
100.0	100.0	100.0	Net Sales						100.0
28.3	28.7	28.3	Gross Profit						21.3
22.9	25.5	25.0	Operating Expenses						17.5
5.4	3.2	3.2	Operating Profit						3.9
1.2	2.1	1.6	All Other Expenses (net)						1.3
4.1	1.2	1.7	Profit Before Taxes						2.5
			RATIOS						
3.1	2.3	2.5							3.0
1.7	1.5	1.6	Current						1.7
1.3	1.1	1.2							1.3
1.4	1.0	1.1							1.1
.7	.6	.6	Quick						.5
.3	.3	.3							.3
23 15.9	13 28.5	17 21.3							17 21.0
41 8.8	35 10.5	36 10.1	Sales/Receivables						37 9.9
58 6.2	61 6.0	53 6.8							50 7.3
67 5.5	63 5.8	72 5.1							67 5.4
100 3.6	105 3.5	100 3.7	Cost of Sales/Inventory						99 3.7
148 2.5	158 2.3	134 2.7							117 3.1
15 24.0	13 28.9	16 23.3							16 23.3
32 11.4	33 11.2	32 11.4	Cost of Sales/Payables						25 14.8
45 8.2	60 6.1	60 6.1							45 8.0
3.5	4.2	4.4							4.0
7.2	8.9	8.2	Sales/Working Capital						8.0
11.2	21.7	18.4							15.0
13.5	5.4	4.7							6.9
(41) 4.2	(38) 2.9	(42) 1.4	EBIT/Interest						3.0
.9	1.1	.6							1.2
		22.0							
		(10) 1.7	Net Profit + Depr., Dep., Amort./Cur. Mat. L/T/D						
		.9							
.2	.1	.3							.3
.4	.4	.5	Fixed/Worth						.5
.8	1.0	1.1							.9
.6	.9	.7							.6
1.5	1.7	1.9	Debt/Worth						1.5
5.0	3.8	5.4							2.5
39.6	30.5	27.3							22.6
(37) 16.3	(34) 13.6	(35) 11.3	% Profit Before Taxes/Tangible Net Worth					(19)	14.5
6.6	6.5	-3.0							.3
20.6	8.2	11.9							11.0
4.7	4.1	3.2	% Profit Before Taxes/Total Assets						6.3
.2	-1.1	-1.0							.8
25.9	41.9	25.2							14.6
13.4	17.1	12.6	Sales/Net Fixed Assets						12.3
7.3	8.7	6.7							6.4
2.6	2.7	2.6							2.8
1.9	2.0	2.0	Sales/Total Assets						2.0
1.5	1.4	1.4							1.3
.7	.6	1.3							1.4
(39) 1.7	(33) 1.3	(39) 1.7	% Depr., Dep., Amort./Sales					(20)	1.6
2.9	2.3	2.7							2.7
1.3	1.2	1.5							
(12) 2.1	(10) 1.8	(10) 2.3	% Officers', Directors' Owners' Comp/Sales						
7.4	9.3	5.3							
2328873M	1724468M	2190445M	Net Sales ($)	385M	10098M	19582M	38946M	59166M	2062268M
1374323M	921061M	1206273M	Total Assets ($)	330M	7129M	9028M	20166M	23028M	1146592M

M = $ thousand   MM = $ million
See Pages 11 through 21 for Explanation of Ratios and Data

Current Data Sorted by Assets   Comparative Historical Data

Type of Statement	0-500M	500M-2MM	2-10MM	10-50MM	50-100MM	100-250MM		ALL 4/1/02-3/31/03	ALL 4/1/03-3/31/04
Unqualified			8	21	3	6		41	39
Reviewed	1	2	13	11				31	39
Compiled	2	5	5	1				19	22
Tax Returns		4	4	1				5	8
Other	1	7	8	15	5	2		40	44
		32 (4/1-9/30/06)		93 (10/1/06-3/31/07)					
NUMBER OF STATEMENTS	4	18	38	49	8	8		136	152

	0-500M %	500M-2MM %	2-10MM %	10-50MM %	50-100MM %	100-250MM %		ALL %	ALL %
ASSETS									
Cash & Equivalents		12.9	6.7	6.9				6.3	7.3
Trade Receivables (net)		27.5	22.3	24.6				25.3	27.1
Inventory		21.5	31.6	35.5				30.3	31.3
All Other Current		3.7	5.8	3.1				3.7	3.8
Total Current		65.7	66.4	70.1				65.7	69.5
Fixed Assets (net)		25.6	27.7	20.4				25.4	21.9
Intangibles (net)		4.1	1.2	4.5				3.6	2.9
All Other Non-Current		4.6	4.6	5.0				5.3	5.7
Total		100.0	100.0	100.0				100.0	100.0
LIABILITIES									
Notes Payable-Short Term		9.7	12.6	13.6				13.3	16.6
Cur. Mat.-L.T.D.		1.9	4.6	2.6				5.5	3.1
Trade Payables		19.8	13.6	14.1				13.1	12.9
Income Taxes Payable		.0	.5	.6				.3	.4
All Other Current		7.2	12.4	13.7				11.8	14.7
Total Current		38.6	43.7	44.5				44.0	47.8
Long-Term Debt		18.2	18.3	13.8				15.9	12.0
Deferred Taxes		.2	.3	.5				.5	.5
All Other Non-Current		6.1	4.7	5.9				4.5	5.7
Net Worth		36.9	33.1	35.2				35.0	34.0
Total Liabilties & Net Worth		100.0	100.0	100.0				100.0	100.0
INCOME DATA									
Net Sales		100.0	100.0	100.0				100.0	100.0
Gross Profit		33.8	25.6	26.7				27.3	28.9
Operating Expenses		28.6	18.4	19.4				24.1	25.4
Operating Profit		5.2	7.2	7.3				3.2	3.6
All Other Expenses (net)		.3	1.4	1.3				1.1	.8
Profit Before Taxes		4.9	5.9	6.0				2.1	2.7
RATIOS									
Current		2.6	2.1	2.3				2.6	2.6
		1.8	1.6	1.5				1.6	1.5
		1.3	1.2	1.2				1.1	1.1
Quick		2.1	1.0	1.0				1.4	1.4
		1.1	.6	.7				.7	.7
		.6	.5	.5				.4	.4
Sales/Receivables		17 21.0	26 14.0	37 9.9				34 10.7	33 11.1
		23 15.7	41 9.0	49 7.4				49 7.5	48 7.6
		43 8.5	56 6.5	68 5.4				71 5.2	70 5.2
Cost of Sales/Inventory		5 80.2	8 45.0	64 5.7				36 10.1	49 7.5
		45 8.1	88 4.2	95 3.8				87 4.2	79 4.6
		102 3.6	117 3.1	134 2.7				148 2.5	126 2.9
Cost of Sales/Payables		12 30.6	16 23.4	20 18.5				17 21.8	12 30.3
		25 14.8	27 13.4	32 11.3				30 12.2	26 14.3
		50 7.3	44 8.3	49 7.5				47 7.8	47 7.7
Sales/Working Capital		5.8	5.8	3.9				3.9	4.4
		12.3	8.9	7.4				7.7	8.0
		26.1	26.9	15.4				33.5	30.9
EBIT/Interest		23.9	13.1	10.4				6.3	9.3
		(15) 4.9	(37) 3.8	(46) 5.0				(130) 2.3	(140) 2.6
		2.2	1.4	2.5				.7	.9
Net Profit + Depr., Dep., Amort./Cur. Mat. L/T/D			4.1	5.4				3.7	4.9
			(10) 1.6	(19) 2.7				(35) 1.5	(48) 2.0
			-.5	1.6				.5	.8
Fixed/Worth		.1	.3	.3				.3	.3
		1.0	.6	.6				.8	.6
		12.8	1.4	1.6				2.6	1.5
Debt/Worth		.6	1.1	1.2				1.0	.9
		2.2	2.1	2.1				2.3	1.8
		30.0	3.9	7.2				7.3	4.9
% Profit Before Taxes/Tangible Net Worth		97.0	72.2	53.0				24.9	36.1
		(15) 29.1	(35) 25.4	(46) 25.0				(124) 11.8	(137) 10.8
		3.9	4.3	16.3				-1.4	.4
% Profit Before Taxes/Total Assets		21.4	20.2	13.0				9.2	11.7
		14.1	8.6	8.3				3.0	3.7
		2.4	1.0	6.0				-.7	-.1
Sales/Net Fixed Assets		118.4	28.6	18.3				20.6	23.0
		21.9	8.5	9.6				7.9	10.9
		6.1	5.3	5.8				4.1	5.7
Sales/Total Assets		4.0	2.6	2.2				2.6	2.7
		3.1	2.0	1.8				1.7	1.9
		2.2	1.7	1.3				1.2	1.3
% Depr., Dep., Amort./Sales		.4	.7	.9				1.4	1.0
		(13) 1.9	(33) 1.9	(45) 1.6				(118) 2.1	(140) 1.7
		3.2	2.9	2.3				3.4	3.0
% Officers', Directors' Owners' Comp/Sales		2.5						2.5	2.0
		(11) 4.2						(33) 4.8	(41) 3.6
		6.0						8.5	5.6
Net Sales ($)	4579M	71972M	393889M	2142421M	829459M	2044646M		3684849M	4020817M
Total Assets ($)	1488M	20868M	198404M	1193857M	548015M	1333903M		2457737M	2397041M

M = $ thousand   MM = $ million
See Pages 11 through 21 for Explanation of Ratios and Data

Comparative Historical Data | Current Data Sorted by Sales

					Type of Statement						
	36		41	38	Unqualified				3	14	21
	35		35	27	Reviewed	1	1	2	9	7	7
	13		12	13	Compiled	1	3	3	4	2	
	8		15	9	Tax Returns		3	1	3	1	1
	50		43	38	Other	1	3	3	5	6	20
	4/1/04-3/31/05		4/1/05-3/31/06	4/1/06-3/31/07			32 (4/1-9/30/06)		93 (10/1/06-3/31/07)		
	ALL		ALL	ALL		0-1MM	1-3MM	3-5MM	5-10MM	10-25MM	25MM & OVER
	142		146	125	NUMBER OF STATEMENTS	3	10	9	24	30	49
	%		%	%	ASSETS	%	%	%	%	%	%
	8.4		8.8	8.1	Cash & Equivalents		8.6		8.0	8.0	7.5
	25.5		23.9	23.9	Trade Receivables (net)		25.1		23.8	22.7	24.4
	32.2		31.5	32.3	Inventory		26.2		29.2	33.7	36.1
	3.7		3.0	4.0	All Other Current		3.6		3.3	5.5	3.4
	69.7		67.2	68.4	Total Current		63.5		64.4	69.9	71.4
	21.3		23.1	23.3	Fixed Assets (net)		24.1		28.4	22.6	18.5
	3.0		4.3	3.5	Intangibles (net)		7.3		1.3	4.1	4.4
	6.0		5.4	4.8	All Other Non-Current		5.0		5.9	3.5	5.7
	100.0		100.0	100.0	Total		100.0		100.0	100.0	100.0
					LIABILITIES						
	13.7		13.6	12.7	Notes Payable-Short Term		6.5		9.5	12.1	14.7
	3.0		3.5	2.8	Cur. Mat.-L.T.D.		2.6		4.2	3.8	1.8
	14.3		14.4	14.9	Trade Payables		15.5		15.6	11.7	15.6
	.6		1.3	.4	Income Taxes Payable		.0		.5	.5	.6
	11.9		11.1	12.4	All Other Current		8.9		12.0	11.8	14.7
	43.5		43.9	43.2	Total Current		33.5		41.9	40.0	47.3
	13.8		11.5	15.7	Long-Term Debt		22.7		19.4	14.2	12.2
	.6		.5	.4	Deferred Taxes		.4		.3	.7	.4
	6.4		5.5	5.5	All Other Non-Current		10.4		4.3	4.0	7.4
	35.6		38.6	35.1	Net Worth		33.0		34.1	41.1	32.7
	100.0		100.0	100.0	Total Liabilities & Net Worth		100.0		100.0	100.0	100.0
					INCOME DATA						
	100.0		100.0	100.0	Net Sales		100.0		100.0	100.0	100.0
	29.2		28.0	27.0	Gross Profit		41.4		26.2	25.4	24.5
	23.8		21.1	20.2	Operating Expenses		32.7		21.3	16.6	17.4
	5.5		6.9	6.8	Operating Profit		8.7		4.9	8.8	7.1
	.8		.9	1.0	All Other Expenses (net)		1.2		1.2	.9	1.1
	4.7		6.0	5.7	Profit Before Taxes		7.6		3.7	8.0	6.0
					RATIOS						
	2.6		2.2	2.2			3.9		2.1	2.3	1.9
	1.7		1.5	1.6	Current		1.8		1.8	1.7	1.4
	1.2		1.1	1.2			1.4		1.1	1.4	1.1
	1.4		1.2	1.2			1.5		1.3	1.3	.9
	.7		.7	.7	Quick		.9		.7	.7	.6
	.5		.5	.5			.6		.5	.5	.5
32	11.5	29	12.7	29	12.7	Sales/Receivables	15	24.5	33	11.2	23	15.7	37	9.9
44	8.4	42	8.8	42	8.6		35	10.5	45	8.2	40	9.1	46	8.0
62	5.9	54	6.7	61	6.0		64	5.7	58	6.3	67	5.5	62	5.9
39	9.4	37	9.9	42	8.6	Cost of Sales/Inventory	33	11.2	6	59.3	45	8.1	64	5.7
90	4.1	83	4.4	91	4.0		76	4.8	88	4.1	92	4.0	100	3.6
136	2.7	128	2.9	126	2.9		113	3.2	124	3.0	157	2.3	127	2.9
20	18.5	16	22.8	19	19.7	Cost of Sales/Payables	16	22.5	16	22.6	12	31.6	22	16.9
28	12.9	31	11.9	28	13.1		28	12.9	30	12.3	22	16.5	32	11.3
44	8.2	46	8.0	48	7.5		63	5.8	49	7.4	39	9.3	55	6.6
	3.9		5.0	4.9	Sales/Working Capital		4.0		4.7	3.9	5.0
	7.1		9.0	8.6			6.3		11.1	7.0	8.9
	23.1		31.4	18.7			14.1		35.7	10.3	30.2
	13.1		12.0	12.2	EBIT/Interest		8.0			13.2	10.9
(126)	5.3	(135)	5.1	(116)	4.9		2.1	(27)	8.5	(46)	4.9
	1.9		2.1	2.1			.4		4.0	2.2
	4.8		12.2	5.7	Net Profit + Depr., Dep., Amort./Cur. Mat. L/T/D				10.7
(47)	2.3	(45)	2.6	(34)	2.4					(14)	2.0
	1.0		1.9	1.5						1.6
	.3		.3	.3	Fixed/Worth		.2		.3	.3	.3
	.6		.5	.6			1.3		.8	.4	.6
	1.9		1.5	1.6			NM		1.6	1.1	1.7
	1.0		1.0	1.0	Debt/Worth		1.4		.8	.9	1.3
	2.0		1.9	2.1			2.1		2.0	1.7	2.4
	7.4		4.8	5.2			NM		3.2	3.6	8.4
	49.8		58.8	66.3	% Profit Before Taxes/Tangible Net Worth		31.1		82.1	58.7
(125)	19.3	(134)	21.4	(113)	25.4		(21)	11.0	30.3	(44)	29.7
	7.1		10.2	12.9			-4.1		16.5	18.8
	13.2		15.5	17.0	% Profit Before Taxes/Total Assets		26.3		11.0	19.1	15.4
	6.5		8.4	8.7			11.0		3.0	10.6	8.6
	1.7		2.8	3.1			-.1		-2.0	7.0	4.4
	31.5		27.9	22.2	Sales/Net Fixed Assets		118.4		15.8	33.9	18.3
	12.0		11.1	9.5			17.2		8.3	8.4	10.0
	5.3		5.9	6.0			3.0		6.2	3.9	6.8
	2.8		2.7	2.6	Sales/Total Assets		3.5		2.6	2.3	2.2
	2.0		2.0	1.9			2.2		1.9	1.9	1.8
	1.3		1.4	1.5			1.4		1.6	1.4	1.4
	.9		.7	.8	% Depr., Dep., Amort./Sales				1.4	.7	.8
(124)	1.7	(122)	1.5	(108)	1.7		(22)	2.1	(24)	1.8	(44)	1.6
	2.9		3.1	2.9					3.0	2.8	2.2
	1.9		1.6	2.4	% Officers', Directors' Owners' Comp/Sales						
(40)	3.5	(35)	3.5	(27)	3.6						
	5.4		6.6	5.0							
5996000M		6409252M	5486966M	Net Sales ($)	2223M	23026M	33996M	184367M	539552M	4703802M
3711894M		3497604M	3296535M	Total Assets ($)	998M	11992M	14800M	100995M	344237M	2823513M

M = $ thousand   MM = $ million
See Pages 11 through 21 for Explanation of Ratios and Data

Current Data Sorted by Assets · Comparative Historical Data

0-500M	500M-2MM	2-10MM	10-50MM	50-100MM	100-250MM	Type of Statement	4/1/02-3/31/03 ALL	4/1/03-3/31/04 ALL
		1	3	3	2	Unqualified	9	10
	3	9	6			Reviewed	7	10
1	1	6	1			Compiled	7	7
	5	8	3	2	1	Tax Returns	2	6
						Other	9	9
	9 (4/1-9/30/06)		46 (10/1/06-3/31/07)					
1	9	24	13	5	3	NUMBER OF STATEMENTS	34	42
%	%	%	%	%	%	ASSETS	%	%
		6.9	5.7			Cash & Equivalents	8.0	5.1
		28.3	22.3			Trade Receivables (net)	23.3	25.1
		31.5	41.5			Inventory	30.1	32.1
		5.9	2.3			All Other Current	1.8	1.5
		72.7	71.7			Total Current	63.2	63.8
		17.5	22.6			Fixed Assets (net)	25.3	24.4
		.2	2.1			Intangibles (net)	5.1	4.4
		9.6	3.5			All Other Non-Current	6.4	7.4
		100.0	100.0			Total	100.0	100.0
						LIABILITIES		
		10.1	14.7			Notes Payable-Short Term	8.9	11.1
		3.1	3.7			Cur. Mat.-L.T.D.	3.4	3.2
		17.1	14.7			Trade Payables	11.8	13.7
		.6	.0			Income Taxes Payable	.2	.1
		14.3	6.6			All Other Current	8.3	12.2
		45.3	39.7			Total Current	32.6	40.3
		11.2	9.6			Long-Term Debt	21.9	19.0
		.4	.4			Deferred Taxes	.3	.2
		3.6	1.3			All Other Non-Current	.9	4.7
		39.5	49.0			Net Worth	44.3	35.8
		100.0	100.0			Total Liabilities & Net Worth	100.0	100.0
						INCOME DATA		
		100.0	100.0			Net Sales	100.0	100.0
		29.5	27.1			Gross Profit	33.2	35.2
		22.2	16.6			Operating Expenses	30.3	31.5
		7.3	10.5			Operating Profit	2.9	3.7
		.6	.9			All Other Expenses (net)	.9	.7
		6.8	9.7			Profit Before Taxes	2.0	3.0
						RATIOS		
		2.5	2.7			Current	3.4	2.7
		1.6	2.1				2.0	1.6
		1.3	1.3				1.4	1.1
		1.2	1.1			Quick	1.6	1.2
		1.0	.8				1.0 (41)	.8
		.5	.5				.5	.5
		36　10.2	31　11.8			Sales/Receivables	38　9.6	37　9.9
		43　8.4	42　8.6				44　8.3	47　7.8
		59　6.2	61　6.0				56　6.6	63　5.8
		31　11.9	60　6.0			Cost of Sales/Inventory	38　9.6	36　10.1
		65　5.6	120　3.0				90　4.1	95　3.8
		141　2.6	151　2.4				182　2.0	176　2.1
		19　19.1	28　13.0			Cost of Sales/Payables	15　24.6	18　20.6
		38　9.7	34　10.8				36　10.0	32　11.3
		62　5.9	52　7.0				56　6.5	57　6.4
		4.3	2.9			Sales/Working Capital	3.7	3.7
		7.2	5.4				5.4	7.7
		18.9	16.1				14.2	20.9
		28.4	43.4			EBIT/Interest	11.3	12.1
		(23)　6.7	11.8				(32)　2.5	(41)　2.2
		3.0	4.0				1.2	.8
						Net Profit + Depr., Dep., Amort./Cur. Mat. L/T/D	5.3	9.3
							(14)　2.2	(15)　1.3
							1.5	.5
		.1	.3			Fixed/Worth	.3	.3
		.3	.3				.6	.7
		1.0	1.0				1.5	1.5
		.8	.5			Debt/Worth	.4	.7
		1.4	1.2				1.2	2.2
		3.4	2.1				7.0	4.9
		45.8	50.2			% Profit Before Taxes/Tangible Net Worth	25.7	25.1
		(22)　29.7	30.0				(31)　15.8	(37)　13.7
		10.8	22.7				4.7	1.8
		28.3	23.7			% Profit Before Taxes/Total Assets	9.2	9.6
		11.9	14.8				3.4	4.9
		2.9	9.7				.8	.1
		51.8	17.1			Sales/Net Fixed Assets	13.1	15.6
		18.9	8.6				6.4	8.1
		8.3	6.3				4.2	4.8
		2.6	2.3			Sales/Total Assets	2.1	2.4
		2.0	1.9				1.5	1.7
		1.7	1.7				1.2	1.1
		.6	.7			% Depr., Dep., Amort./Sales	1.4	1.8
		(22)　1.0	1.2				(30)　2.4	(39)　2.2
		2.1	3.1				3.6	3.6
		1.9				% Officers', Directors' Owners' Comp/Sales	.7	2.0
		(10)　3.6					(11)　4.0	(14)　4.2
		6.2					4.4	8.7
1013M	15624M	253228M	530991M	650651M	993828M	Net Sales ($)	925876M	1038698M
364M	10281M	113283M	288375M	359849M	528340M	Total Assets ($)	625599M	660332M

M = $ thousand　　MM = $ million
See Pages 11 through 21 for Explanation of Ratios and Data

Comparative Historical Data				Current Data Sorted by Sales					
			Type of Statement						
11	12	9	Unqualified					1	8
9	6	18	Reviewed		3	2	3	5	5
4	4	9	Compiled		2	1	4	1	1
3	1		Tax Returns						
14	20	19	Other		5		4	5	5
4/1/04-3/31/05 ALL	**4/1/05-3/31/06 ALL**	**4/1/06-3/31/07 ALL**			**9 (4/1-9/30/06)**		**46 (10/1/06-3/31/07)**		
				0-1MM	**1-3MM**	**3-5MM**	**5-10MM**	**10-25MM**	**25MM & OVER**
41	43	55	**NUMBER OF STATEMENTS**		10	3	11	12	19
%	%	%	**ASSETS**	%	%	%	%	%	%
9.4	8.4	6.7	Cash & Equivalents	D A T A N O T A V A I L A B L E	7.6		7.5	5.2	6.7
26.3	25.8	25.0	Trade Receivables (net)		24.0		27.2	31.1	20.8
32.1	30.5	35.4	Inventory		37.4		33.1	29.9	39.7
1.4	2.3	3.6	All Other Current		1.1		8.7	3.7	1.8
69.2	67.0	70.7	Total Current		70.2		76.5	69.8	69.0
23.1	23.1	19.8	Fixed Assets (net)		20.4		12.2	21.6	21.4
2.8	3.3	3.4	Intangibles (net)		6.4		.0	.5	6.1
4.9	6.7	6.1	All Other Non-Current		3.0		11.3	8.1	3.4
100.0	100.0	100.0	Total		100.0		100.0	100.0	100.0
			LIABILITIES						
10.6	7.2	10.7	Notes Payable-Short Term		11.5		15.5	8.8	10.0
4.3	4.7	2.8	Cur. Mat.-L.T.D.		2.1		2.9	3.3	2.9
20.2	19.2	17.0	Trade Payables		25.6		17.2	18.7	12.8
.3	.7	.3	Income Taxes Payable		.2		.8	.5	.0
7.3	13.1	13.4	All Other Current		17.8		13.0	13.8	10.9
42.6	45.0	44.2	Total Current		57.2		49.4	45.1	36.7
16.8	17.8	13.7	Long-Term Debt		20.7		7.5	14.8	13.2
.3	.4	.4	Deferred Taxes		.4		.9	.1	.4
5.1	4.2	7.4	All Other Non-Current		25.5		5.7	1.9	2.9
35.1	32.6	34.4	Net Worth		-3.9		36.6	38.1	46.8
100.0	100.0	100.0	Total Liabilties & Net Worth		100.0		100.0	100.0	100.0
			INCOME DATA						
100.0	100.0	100.0	Net Sales		100.0		100.0	100.0	100.0
31.9	30.2	30.7	Gross Profit		42.7		24.2	34.0	26.3
26.2	22.9	23.9	Operating Expenses		42.3		18.2	24.5	17.4
5.6	7.3	6.9	Operating Profit		.4		6.0	9.5	8.9
.8	1.1	.8	All Other Expenses (net)		1.4		1.0	.8	.5
4.9	6.1	6.0	Profit Before Taxes		-1.0		5.0	8.7	8.4
			RATIOS						
2.4	2.2	2.6			3.0		3.1	2.3	2.8
1.5	1.6	1.7	Current		1.3		1.8	1.5	1.8
1.1	1.0	1.2			.6		1.0	1.2	1.4
1.2	1.1	1.2			1.3		1.3	1.1	1.1
.8	.7	.8	Quick		.7		1.0	.9	.8
.6	.6	.5			.3		.3	.5	.6
38 9.7	**30** 12.3	**29** 12.7			**26** 14.1		**38** 9.5	**41** 9.0	**29** 12.7
45 8.1	**43** 8.5	**42** 8.6	Sales/Receivables		**45** 8.1		**46** 7.9	**46** 7.9	**37** 9.8
61 6.0	**58** 6.3	**61** 6.0			**63** 5.8		**69** 5.3	**61** 6.0	**58** 6.3
40 9.0	**30** 12.4	**46** 7.9			**24** 15.5		**25** 14.5	**37** 9.8	**51** 7.2
75 4.8	**66** 5.6	**90** 4.0	Cost of Sales/Inventory		**125** 2.9		**56** 6.5	**74** 5.0	**107** 3.4
123 3.0	**127** 2.9	**155** 2.4			**275** 1.3		**155** 2.4	**120** 3.0	**166** 2.2
28 13.2	**21** 17.4	**20** 18.3			**24** 15.4		**25** 14.6	**24** 15.3	**16** 23.2
43 8.4	**39** 9.3	**36** 10.2	Cost of Sales/Payables		**42** 8.7		**37** 9.9	**37** 9.9	**34** 10.8
62 5.9	**62** 5.9	**55** 6.6			**410** .9		**64** 5.7	**69** 5.3	**51** 7.2
4.3	5.2	3.9			4.4		3.3	4.5	2.9
9.5	7.7	6.4	Sales/Working Capital		NM		5.4	12.9	6.3
41.2	-295.2	19.0			-5.5		-436.7	18.9	14.7
12.5	21.8	30.4					37.8	28.3	40.7
(37) 3.9	(40) 6.8	(53) 6.9	EBIT/Interest				4.1	9.1	11.8
1.6	2.4	2.1					-1.9	3.3	4.6
5.0	8.9	25.0							
(16) 2.6	(15) 4.0	(13) 5.7	Net Profit + Depr., Dep., Amort./Cur. Mat. L/T/D						
1.4	1.3	3.8							
.3	.3	.2			.4		.1	.2	.3
.6	.5	.4	Fixed/Worth		-3.2		.1	.5	.4
1.7	1.1	2.1			-.1		1.4	1.0	.9
.9	1.0	.8			5.7		.6	.9	.6
2.5	1.8	1.5	Debt/Worth		-8.2		1.2	1.7	1.3
4.7	5.5	6.0			-3.5		4.1	2.9	4.2
39.1	69.6	49.8						68.3	63.1
(37) 20.9	(36) 27.2	(46) 28.3	% Profit Before Taxes/Tangible Net Worth					35.9	27.7
8.5	14.0	13.6						29.1	21.1
15.1	20.8	22.5			8.7		30.9	28.3	22.8
5.8	9.1	10.3	% Profit Before Taxes/Total Assets		1.2		5.0	16.5	12.8
1.5	3.7	2.3			-2.4		-10.2	9.2	6.9
21.0	25.8	37.7			173.7		62.3	40.6	16.2
10.8	10.5	10.8	Sales/Net Fixed Assets		17.2		37.7	14.0	8.3
5.9	6.7	7.0			6.1		8.5	5.1	6.7
3.0	2.8	2.4			2.8		2.5	3.2	2.3
2.0	2.2	1.9	Sales/Total Assets		1.7		2.0	2.1	2.0
1.5	1.5	1.6			1.2		1.5	1.8	1.4
1.1	.9	.7					.6	.4	.9
(39) 1.7	(37) 1.2	(49) 1.3	% Depr., Dep., Amort./Sales				(10) .8	(11) .8	(18) 1.4
2.9	2.1	2.6					1.8	3.1	2.9
.6		2.1							
(14) 2.5		(15) 3.9	% Officers', Directors' Owners' Comp/Sales						
3.9		7.6							
1238824M	**2826589M**	**2445335M**	Net Sales ($)		**16637M**	**14071M**	**85780M**	**200173M**	**2128674M**
711627M	**1465884M**	**1300492M**	Total Assets ($)		**10645M**	**7703M**	**45370M**	**86594M**	**1150180M**

M = $ thousand MM = $ million

See Pages 11 through 21 for Explanation of Ratios and Data

Current Data Sorted by Assets　　　　　　　　　　　　Comparative Historical Data

	0-500M	500M-2MM	2-10MM	10-50MM	50-100MM	100-250MM	Type of Statement	4/1/02-3/31/03 ALL	4/1/03-3/31/04 ALL
			2	7		4	Unqualified	16	18
		1	3	2			Reviewed	6	8
		2	12				Compiled	11	11
		1	3				Tax Returns	4	5
	1	6	16	10	5	3	Other	26	32
		16 (4/1-9/30/06)		62 (10/1/06-3/31/07)					
	1	10	36	19	5	7	NUMBER OF STATEMENTS	63	74
	%	%	%	%	%	%	ASSETS	%	%
		16.8	7.6	2.8			Cash & Equivalents	8.1	8.2
		31.5	33.0	23.3			Trade Receivables (net)	27.3	27.7
		22.0	24.8	28.3			Inventory	25.2	25.9
		.5	6.1	5.4			All Other Current	3.0	4.1
		70.8	71.6	59.8			Total Current	63.7	66.0
		27.2	24.0	29.9			Fixed Assets (net)	25.6	22.5
		.0	1.8	4.5			Intangibles (net)	6.5	5.6
		2.1	2.6	5.8			All Other Non-Current	4.2	5.9
		100.0	100.0	100.0			Total	100.0	100.0
							LIABILITIES		
		6.9	8.0	8.2			Notes Payable-Short Term	10.2	9.7
		2.1	3.8	1.9			Cur. Mat.-L.T.D.	4.4	3.3
		19.7	15.0	18.7			Trade Payables	11.8	12.1
		.0	.2	.6			Income Taxes Payable	.8	.3
		10.1	15.2	14.3			All Other Current	6.8	9.8
		38.8	42.2	43.7			Total Current	34.0	35.2
		13.2	15.2	19.8			Long-Term Debt	10.1	9.2
		.2	.3	1.2			Deferred Taxes	1.0	1.1
		13.1	3.3	6.5			All Other Non-Current	5.6	9.2
		34.8	39.1	28.9			Net Worth	49.3	45.3
		100.0	100.0	100.0			Total Liabilities & Net Worth	100.0	100.0
							INCOME DATA		
		100.0	100.0	100.0			Net Sales	100.0	100.0
		36.8	37.2	31.3			Gross Profit	34.8	34.7
		30.2	28.8	19.0			Operating Expenses	29.6	30.8
		6.6	8.5	12.3			Operating Profit	5.2	3.9
		1.9	.9	1.7			All Other Expenses (net)	2.0	1.1
		4.7	7.6	10.6			Profit Before Taxes	3.2	2.9
							RATIOS		
		4.5	2.4	1.7			Current	3.2	3.0
		1.7	1.7	1.3				1.9	1.8
		1.2	1.3	1.2				1.2	1.4
		3.6	1.6	.8			Quick	1.9	1.7
		1.4	1.0	.6				1.0	1.0
		.4	.6	.4				.6	.6
		25 14.3	44 8.3	32 11.3			Sales/Receivables	43 8.4	44 8.3
		59 6.2	56 6.6	40 9.2				57 6.4	58 6.3
		66 5.5	71 5.2	62 5.8				76 4.8	75 4.8
		0 UND	30 12.0	38 9.7			Cost of Sales/Inventory	23 16.2	24 14.9
		48 7.6	55 6.7	83 4.4				81 4.5	78 4.7
		171 2.1	138 2.7	157 2.3				123 3.0	146 2.5
		19 19.6	21 17.6	39 9.4			Cost of Sales/Payables	19 19.6	21 17.2
		51 7.2	37 9.8	67 5.5				37 9.9	35 10.6
		85 4.3	63 5.8	90 4.1				48 7.7	65 5.6
		5.5	4.3	8.1			Sales/Working Capital	3.6	3.2
		8.4	7.3	11.7				5.9	5.4
		16.4	13.7	19.0				13.5	12.6
			12.8	25.2			EBIT/Interest	8.8	10.7
			(35) 6.2	(18) 6.0				(60) 4.0	(68) 3.1
			3.4	3.3				.8	1.2
							Net Profit + Depr., Dep., Amort./Cur. Mat. L/T/D	6.8	4.0
								(16) 2.6	(27) 2.3
								1.5	1.0
		.2	.2	.4			Fixed/Worth	.2	.2
		.7	.8	1.3				.5	.5
		2.8	1.2	3.6				1.6	1.3
		.8	.9	1.7			Debt/Worth	.4	.6
		2.6	1.8	2.5				1.1	1.3
		6.8	3.2	6.4				2.8	4.1
			57.1	84.6			% Profit Before Taxes/Tangible Net Worth	25.6	26.4
			(35) 35.0	(17) 50.3				(58) 13.8	(69) 10.9
			19.8	30.0				2.0	2.9
		9.6	18.3	25.3			% Profit Before Taxes/Total Assets	12.9	10.5
		7.3	11.8	11.2				5.4	4.4
		.7	8.2	6.8				-.3	.9
		26.9	31.9	15.4			Sales/Net Fixed Assets	29.6	28.2
		7.6	8.9	7.3				6.7	8.0
		5.4	4.6	3.8				3.5	4.4
		3.0	2.5	2.8			Sales/Total Assets	2.4	2.3
		1.9	2.0	1.5				1.6	1.6
		1.4	1.5	.9				1.1	1.2
			.7	1.2			% Depr., Dep., Amort./Sales	1.4	1.7
			(31) 1.9	(16) 2.0				(53) 2.9	(63) 3.1
			3.1	4.7				4.4	4.7
			1.9				% Officers', Directors' Owners' Comp/Sales	2.7	3.6
			(10) 3.0					(19) 3.6	(20) 5.0
			4.9					8.9	10.7
	622M	36123M	313131M	714219M	355547M	1371467M	Net Sales ($)	2292622M	2212382M
	131M	16405M	157151M	447018M	294935M	1016190M	Total Assets ($)	1893606M	1832416M

M = $ thousand　　　MM = $ million
See Pages 11 through 21 for Explanation of Ratios and Data

Comparative Historical Data / Current Data Sorted by Sales

			Type of Statement	0-1MM	1-3MM	3-5MM	5-10MM	10-25MM	25MM & OVER
13	15	13	Unqualified					3	10
5	3	6	Reviewed		1		2	3	
14	8	14	Compiled		1	3	4	6	
9	7	4	Tax Returns				4		
29	32	41	Other	2	3	6	8	7	15
4/1/04-3/31/05 ALL	4/1/05-3/31/06 ALL	4/1/06-3/31/07 ALL			16 (4/1-9/30/06)			62 (10/1/06-3/31/07)	
70	65	78	NUMBER OF STATEMENTS	2	5	9	18	19	25
%	%	%	**ASSETS**	%	%	%	%	%	%
9.2	9.3	7.3	Cash & Equivalents				7.7	7.2	3.3
31.2	30.2	28.5	Trade Receivables (net)				34.7	33.7	24.0
22.4	25.0	25.3	Inventory				26.2	27.3	26.0
2.0	3.5	5.1	All Other Current				2.4	6.6	6.4
64.8	68.0	66.3	Total Current				71.0	74.9	59.7
25.4	21.8	26.0	Fixed Assets (net)				25.0	17.8	27.2
3.3	5.1	4.5	Intangibles (net)				.8	1.4	11.2
6.5	5.1	3.2	All Other Non-Current				3.2	5.8	1.9
100.0	100.0	100.0	Total				100.0	100.0	100.0
			LIABILITIES						
10.7	7.4	8.0	Notes Payable-Short Term				6.8	9.6	8.6
3.6	3.0	3.0	Cur. Mat.-L.T.D.				4.3	3.0	2.1
19.0	16.8	15.6	Trade Payables				13.2	20.3	14.6
.4	.6	.3	Income Taxes Payable				.5	.0	.6
8.2	12.6	13.4	All Other Current				17.6	16.4	11.4
41.8	40.4	40.3	Total Current				42.4	49.3	37.2
18.0	15.5	15.8	Long-Term Debt				14.4	12.0	15.8
.5	.5	.6	Deferred Taxes				.4	.3	1.3
5.0	6.3	5.4	All Other Non-Current				3.9	3.1	6.0
34.7	37.3	37.9	Net Worth				39.0	35.2	39.6
100.0	100.0	100.0	Total Liabilities & Net Worth				100.0	100.0	100.0
			INCOME DATA						
100.0	100.0	100.0	Net Sales				100.0	100.0	100.0
36.6	35.6	35.1	Gross Profit				33.2	32.9	30.0
31.8	26.7	24.9	Operating Expenses				27.2	25.7	15.7
4.7	8.9	10.3	Operating Profit				6.0	7.2	14.3
.4	1.1	1.3	All Other Expenses (net)				.5	.9	1.6
4.3	7.8	9.0	Profit Before Taxes				5.5	6.3	12.7
			RATIOS						
2.6	2.6	2.3	Current				2.1	1.8	2.3
1.6	1.8	1.6					1.8	1.3	1.7
1.2	1.3	1.3					1.5	1.2	1.2
1.8	1.4	1.6	Quick				1.8	1.5	1.4
1.0	1.0	.8					1.3	.8	.7
.6	.7	.5					.6	.5	.4
37 9.9	44 8.3	38 9.5	Sales/Receivables				49 7.5	42 8.7	33 11.1
52 7.0	61 5.9	56 6.5					58 6.3	60 6.1	55 6.7
79 4.6	81 4.5	71 5.2					65 5.6	64 5.7	76 4.8
22 16.6	32 11.2	30 12.1	Cost of Sales/Inventory				16 23.3	30 12.0	34 10.7
53 6.9	80 4.6	70 5.2					55 6.7	53 6.9	87 4.2
99 3.7	126 2.9	148 2.5					141 2.6	104 3.5	147 2.5
21 17.4	28 12.8	21 17.1	Cost of Sales/Payables				18 20.8	35 10.5	28 13.2
46 7.9	47 7.8	47 7.8					25 14.8	55 6.7	46 8.0
65 5.6	70 5.2	68 5.3					54 6.8	70 5.2	68 5.3
5.0	4.4	4.5	Sales/Working Capital				6.2	5.4	3.8
7.6	6.6	8.0					8.0	10.6	7.1
23.5	11.9	14.6					10.1	14.7	18.2
14.5	14.7	13.5	EBIT/Interest				9.1	17.6	32.6
(60) 3.6	(60) 6.7	(72) 6.3					6.8	5.2	(22) 6.9
.0	2.8	3.2					3.5	3.4	3.5
4.7	7.6	16.2	Net Profit + Depr., Dep., Amort./Cur. Mat. L/T/D						21.7
(20) 2.5	(25) 3.5	(22) 5.1							(11) 5.6
1.3	2.1	2.0							3.5
.2	.3	.3	Fixed/Worth				.2	.1	.4
.6	.6	.9					.8	.8	.8
2.0	1.2	1.6					1.1	1.3	4.8
.9	.9	1.0	Debt/Worth				.9	1.2	1.1
1.9	2.2	1.9					1.4	2.5	1.7
5.4	3.3	4.9					3.4	3.7	11.6
55.5	60.9	60.7	% Profit Before Taxes/Tangible Net Worth				51.4	50.3	80.4
(65) 16.9	(61) 29.3	(72) 38.9					25.0	(18) 37.1	(21) 50.1
-4.0	14.7	18.6					17.6	19.3	33.2
18.0	17.3	21.5	% Profit Before Taxes/Total Assets				14.1	18.7	28.4
6.4	10.5	11.1					9.8	10.5	20.5
-.7	5.4	6.8					7.0	6.8	7.7
26.4	26.4	19.8	Sales/Net Fixed Assets				33.3	50.0	13.9
9.4	9.7	7.7					12.0	11.7	7.5
4.0	5.0	4.5					4.2	5.6	4.0
2.8	2.6	2.5	Sales/Total Assets				3.2	2.5	2.4
2.1	1.8	1.7					2.1	2.0	1.5
1.4	1.3	1.3					1.6	1.6	.9
1.0	1.0	1.1	% Depr., Dep., Amort./Sales				.8	.7	1.3
(55) 2.4	(57) 1.7	(66) 2.1					(17) 1.7	(15) 1.6	(21) 2.0
4.2	3.6	3.0					2.5	3.0	2.8
2.3	2.1	1.7	% Officers', Directors', Owners' Comp/Sales						
(21) 7.2	(17) 4.3	(18) 2.4							
10.5	8.0	5.6							
2292371M	1935731M	2791109M	Net Sales ($)	1037M	11621M	36445M	131199M	261944M	2348863M
1316066M	1599644M	1931830M	Total Assets ($)	933M	10431M	24919M	68608M	166576M	1660363M

© RMA 2007

M = $ thousand   MM = $ million
See Pages 11 through 21 for Explanation of Ratios and Data

	Current Data Sorted by Assets						Comparative Historical Data	
						Type of Statement		
		3	6	2	2	Unqualified	8	8
1	1	9	1			Reviewed	5	6
	1	4				Compiled	4	3
2	1					Tax Returns	3	5
	5	4	1	1	1	Other	13	13
	10 (4/1-9/30/06)		35 (10/1/06-3/31/07)				4/1/02-3/31/03	4/1/03-3/31/04
0-500M	500M-2MM	2-10MM	10-50MM	50-100MM	100-250MM		ALL	ALL
3	8	20	8	3	3	**NUMBER OF STATEMENTS**	33	35
%	%	%	%	%	%	**ASSETS**	%	%
		6.8				Cash & Equivalents	7.7	7.5
		23.1				Trade Receivables (net)	25.5	29.2
		26.4				Inventory	24.0	19.3
		3.0				All Other Current	2.3	1.8
		59.3				Total Current	59.6	57.7
		30.3				Fixed Assets (net)	29.1	28.4
		6.2				Intangibles (net)	2.0	4.8
		4.2				All Other Non-Current	9.3	9.0
		100.0				Total	100.0	100.0
						LIABILITIES		
		12.7				Notes Payable-Short Term	16.3	22.0
		5.9				Cur. Mat.-L.T.D.	4.9	6.5
		15.3				Trade Payables	17.5	15.9
		.2				Income Taxes Payable	.5	.2
		11.8				All Other Current	15.1	13.7
		45.8				Total Current	54.3	58.4
		11.0				Long-Term Debt	15.0	19.3
		.3				Deferred Taxes	.3	.4
		6.7				All Other Non-Current	5.6	7.8
		36.2				Net Worth	24.8	14.1
		100.0				Total Liabilities & Net Worth	100.0	100.0
						INCOME DATA		
		100.0				Net Sales	100.0	100.0
		25.6				Gross Profit	26.4	30.8
		19.0				Operating Expenses	29.0	28.4
		6.5				Operating Profit	-2.6	2.4
		1.1				All Other Expenses (net)	1.3	1.1
		5.4				Profit Before Taxes	-4.0	1.3
						RATIOS		
		1.7					1.5	1.6
		1.3				Current	1.1	1.4
		.9					.8	.9
		.8					1.0	1.0
		.6				Quick	.6	.8
		.4					.3	.4
		32 / 11.2					23 / 15.5	38 / 9.7
		48 / 7.5				Sales/Receivables	46 / 7.9	48 / 7.7
		70 / 5.2					72 / 5.1	69 / 5.3
		27 / 13.3					32 / 11.3	23 / 16.2
		61 / 6.0				Cost of Sales/Inventory	59 / 6.2	52 / 7.0
		104 / 3.5					116 / 3.2	73 / 5.0
		22 / 16.3					25 / 14.7	20 / 18.6
		40 / 9.1				Cost of Sales/Payables	34 / 10.6	31 / 11.9
		54 / 6.7					63 / 5.8	51 / 7.1
		5.6					8.9	7.5
		13.8				Sales/Working Capital	30.7	14.1
		-65.5					-16.4	-61.5
		15.3					4.2	6.8
		(19) 5.5				EBIT/Interest	(28) 1.2	(33) 3.1
		1.9					-2.4	-2.8
								6.4
						Net Profit + Depr., Dep., Amort./Cur. Mat. L/T/D		(10) 1.1
								-.6
		.4					.5	.5
		1.2				Fixed/Worth	1.2	1.1
		2.5					NM	3.5
		.9					1.2	1.0
		2.6				Debt/Worth	3.9	3.7
		7.3					NM	9.1
		54.2					28.9	46.2
		(19) 34.8				% Profit Before Taxes/Tangible Net Worth	(25) 6.3	(27) 18.2
		18.3					-11.5	-9.4
		17.6					4.5	12.5
		10.0				% Profit Before Taxes/Total Assets	.0	5.3
		3.3					-12.6	-10.8
		16.8					18.6	21.7
		4.6				Sales/Net Fixed Assets	6.6	9.9
		3.4					3.3	4.1
		2.4					2.3	2.4
		1.7				Sales/Total Assets	1.8	1.9
		1.2					1.2	1.4
		1.8					1.2	1.7
		(19) 2.9				% Depr., Dep., Amort./Sales	(32) 3.9	(32) 3.0
		4.7					6.2	4.3
							3.9	2.9
						% Officers', Directors' Owners' Comp/Sales	(12) 6.0	(16) 5.0
							6.5	6.7
2543M	29531M	191654M	291451M	357382M	568318M	Net Sales ($)	296460M	316179M
904M	10651M	116350M	180296M	219646M	516655M	Total Assets ($)	155411M	184606M

M = $ thousand   MM = $ million
See Pages 11 through 21 for Explanation of Ratios and Data

Comparative Historical Data | Current Data Sorted by Sales

4/1/04-3/31/05 ALL	4/1/05-3/31/06 ALL	4/1/06-3/31/07 ALL	Type of Statement	0-1MM	1-3MM	3-5MM	5-10MM	10-25MM	25MM & OVER
3	5	13	Unqualified				1	3	9
9	9	12	Reviewed		3	5	3		1
1	3	5	Compiled				3	2	
2	2	3	Tax Returns					3	
8	10	12	Other	2	3		3	1	3
				10 (4/1-9/30/06)			35 (10/1/06-3/31/07)		
23	29	45	NUMBER OF STATEMENTS	2	6	5	10	9	13
%	%	%	**ASSETS**	%	%	%	%	%	%
8.6	5.8	7.9	Cash & Equivalents				11.8		4.1
25.3	27.0	22.2	Trade Receivables (net)				24.3		21.8
19.5	24.3	24.7	Inventory				20.7		21.1
2.8	1.4	3.1	All Other Current				8.3		3.3
56.1	58.4	57.9	Total Current				65.1		50.3
28.4	26.0	30.3	Fixed Assets (net)				22.9		36.3
4.4	5.0	6.2	Intangibles (net)				4.3		11.5
11.1	10.6	5.6	All Other Non-Current				7.8		2.0
100.0	100.0	100.0	Total				100.0		100.0
			LIABILITIES						
9.7	11.1	11.7	Notes Payable-Short Term				12.1		11.2
7.8	6.0	4.3	Cur. Mat.-L.T.D.				7.3		3.1
17.0	19.8	15.9	Trade Payables				20.6		11.8
.5	.3	.1	Income Taxes Payable				.1		.1
14.2	10.8	10.1	All Other Current				6.0		11.8
49.1	48.0	42.1	Total Current				46.1		38.0
24.3	14.7	13.6	Long-Term Debt				8.1		17.4
.4	.8	.5	Deferred Taxes				.1		1.0
4.9	4.0	6.0	All Other Non-Current				1.9		7.1
21.4	32.4	37.9	Net Worth				43.8		36.5
100.0	100.0	100.0	Total Liabilities & Net Worth				100.0		100.0
			INCOME DATA						
100.0	100.0	100.0	Net Sales				100.0		100.0
23.8	24.1	25.6	Gross Profit				27.0		21.5
20.6	20.1	19.1	Operating Expenses				17.7		15.3
3.2	4.0	6.5	Operating Profit				9.3		6.2
.8	1.2	1.3	All Other Expenses (net)				.8		1.9
2.4	2.8	5.2	Profit Before Taxes				8.4		4.4
			RATIOS						
1.5	1.5	2.1					2.7		1.9
1.2	1.3	1.2	Current				1.4		1.1
.9	1.0	1.0					.8		1.0
.9	1.1	.9					1.5		.9
.7	.7	.6	Quick				.6		.6
.4	.5	.4					.4		.5
30 12.3	36 10.1	30 12.2					20 18.3		40 9.1
46 7.9	57 6.4	46 8.0	Sales/Receivables				46 7.9		48 7.6
54 6.8	73 5.0	59 6.1					71 5.1		61 6.0
18 20.4	33 11.1	40 9.2					8 45.6		46 8.0
40 9.2	63 5.8	61 6.0	Cost of Sales/Inventory				45 8.2		63 5.8
63 5.8	97 3.7	89 4.1					112 3.3		69 5.3
25 14.6	31 11.7	22 16.4					22 16.6		25 14.4
38 9.7	46 7.9	34 10.7	Cost of Sales/Payables				36 10.3		29 12.7
51 7.1	63 5.8	46 7.9					81 4.5		41 9.0
10.0	8.4	5.5					4.6		8.7
24.0	17.7	20.6	Sales/Working Capital				7.9		37.2
-16.7	NM	-150.6					-21.9		NM
5.4	5.5	10.0							4.3
(22) 3.3	(26) 2.7	(39) 3.4	EBIT/Interest					(11)	1.7
-1.2	1.6	1.5							.4
	2.1	2.7							
	(11) 1.5	(11) 1.3	Net Profit + Depr., Dep., Amort./Cur. Mat. L/T/D						
	1.4	.4							
.6	.4	.4					.2		.9
1.1	1.0	1.2	Fixed/Worth				.5		1.9
8.4	3.0	2.4					1.3		2.9
1.7	1.4	.9					.6		1.9
3.7	3.5	2.3	Debt/Worth				1.7		2.7
12.5	7.2	6.4					5.1		7.5
47.1	41.0	52.2					60.1		38.9
(18) 19.6	(26) 12.7	(42) 23.7	% Profit Before Taxes/Tangible Net Worth				50.5	(12)	11.8
-21.4	5.2	4.0					25.0		-9.6
14.0	7.4	14.2					26.8		12.1
5.3	3.6	6.9	% Profit Before Taxes/Total Assets				12.6		4.5
-5.0	.6	2.3					7.4		-1.1
26.4	16.7	16.3					50.5		6.9
9.1	6.3	5.8	Sales/Net Fixed Assets				12.8		4.2
4.2	4.1	3.2					4.2		2.9
2.7	2.5	2.5					3.0		2.1
2.2	1.6	1.8	Sales/Total Assets				1.9		1.5
1.5	1.3	1.3					1.2		1.3
1.9	1.6	1.9							2.0
(19) 3.5	(28) 3.4	(38) 2.9	% Depr., Dep., Amort./Sales					(11)	3.2
4.1	4.3	4.7							5.3
	1.9	1.4							
	(11) 3.1	(13) 3.1	% Officers', Directors' Owners' Comp/Sales						
	6.6	8.7							
409311M	878715M	1440879M	Net Sales ($)	1406M	12633M	19064M	75556M	126752M	1205468M
225818M	559239M	1044502M	Total Assets ($)	462M	12659M	10512M	43770M	78433M	898666M

M = $ thousand   MM = $ million
See Pages 11 through 21 for Explanation of Ratios and Data

Current Data Sorted by Assets

Comparative Historical Data

						Type of Statement		
		1	3	2	2	Unqualified	8	10
	4	4	3		1	Reviewed	18	18
1	2	3				Compiled	8	4
	3	1				Tax Returns	2	2
	4	4				Other	16	14
	5 (4/1-9/30/06)		34 (10/1/06-3/31/07)				4/1/02-3/31/03	4/1/03-3/31/04
0-500M	500M-2MM	2-10MM	10-50MM	50-100MM	100-250MM	NUMBER OF STATEMENTS	ALL	ALL
1	13	13	7	2	3		52	48
%	%	%	%	%	%	ASSETS	%	%
	15.5	10.9				Cash & Equivalents	8.7	11.4
	29.4	33.0				Trade Receivables (net)	26.6	26.8
	24.6	33.8				Inventory	29.0	24.7
	1.7	.6				All Other Current	4.6	3.7
	71.2	78.3				Total Current	69.0	66.6
	19.3	15.3				Fixed Assets (net)	22.1	25.9
	7.0	.0				Intangibles (net)	2.6	1.8
	2.6	6.4				All Other Non-Current	6.4	5.6
	100.0	100.0				Total	100.0	100.0
						LIABILITIES		
	10.5	5.7				Notes Payable-Short Term	16.7	12.3
	3.9	2.0				Cur. Mat.-L.T.D.	3.4	3.1
	20.3	12.6				Trade Payables	16.0	12.2
	.3	.1				Income Taxes Payable	.1	.3
	24.9	19.7				All Other Current	17.9	16.5
	59.9	40.2				Total Current	54.0	44.4
	9.9	7.0				Long-Term Debt	11.4	13.6
	.1	.0				Deferred Taxes	.4	.5
	4.8	5.0				All Other Non-Current	10.3	6.0
	25.4	47.8				Net Worth	23.9	35.6
	100.0	100.0				Total Liabilities & Net Worth	100.0	100.0
						INCOME DATA		
	100.0	100.0				Net Sales	100.0	100.0
	30.2	29.1				Gross Profit	29.8	29.6
	27.7	21.5				Operating Expenses	26.8	26.4
	2.4	7.6				Operating Profit	3.0	3.3
	-.1	2.2				All Other Expenses (net)	1.0	.6
	2.5	5.5				Profit Before Taxes	2.0	2.6
						RATIOS		
	2.2	2.8				Current	2.1	2.4
	1.2	2.3					1.5	1.8
	.8	1.4					1.1	1.0
	1.0	1.7				Quick	1.0	1.2
	.8	1.5					.8	.9
	.6	.7					.5	.6
	24 15.0	35 10.3				Sales/Receivables	38 9.5	41 8.9
	39 9.3	53 6.9					49 7.4	51 7.2
	51 7.1	62 5.9					64 5.7	69 5.3
	19 19.3	46 8.0				Cost of Sales/Inventory	38 9.6	31 11.9
	32 11.3	63 5.8					76 4.8	62 5.9
	69 5.3	113 3.2					153 2.4	104 3.5
	14 26.6	11 32.7				Cost of Sales/Payables	21 17.0	13 27.4
	33 11.1	18 20.2					37 9.9	29 12.7
	53 6.9	34 10.6					52 7.0	43 8.4
	8.7	3.5				Sales/Working Capital	5.1	3.8
	27.5	8.4					8.6	8.2
	-27.3	13.3					34.0	80.9
	33.9	20.3				EBIT/Interest	5.3	6.9
	4.1	(10) 6.6					(48) 2.4	(44) 3.2
	1.8	3.4					-.8	.0
						Net Profit + Depr., Dep., Amort./Cur. Mat. L/T/D	4.3	3.8
							(16) 1.3	(15) 2.3
							-1.4	.3
	.3	.1				Fixed/Worth	.3	.3
	.5	.2					.7	.6
	NM	.5					10.3	3.4
	.8	.5				Debt/Worth	1.0	.6
	3.1	.9					2.2	1.5
	NM	2.2					70.8	6.8
	108.8	45.1				% Profit Before Taxes/Tangible Net Worth	43.6	24.2
	(10) 49.3	(12) 16.6					(43) 18.0	(42) 9.5
	8.7	7.0					-5.9	1.2
	29.0	19.0				% Profit Before Taxes/Total Assets	13.7	10.8
	8.3	8.3					3.2	3.0
	2.7	4.7					-4.2	-.8
	97.8	53.1				Sales/Net Fixed Assets	19.2	22.2
	20.1	15.9					10.4	9.1
	9.6	10.8					5.3	3.6
	4.3	3.9				Sales/Total Assets	2.6	2.2
	3.0	2.0					1.7	1.7
	2.1	1.6					1.2	1.1
	.4	.5				% Depr., Dep., Amort./Sales	1.4	1.5
	.9	(12) .7					(49) 2.1	(41) 2.1
	1.9	1.9					3.0	3.7
						% Officers', Directors' Owners' Comp/Sales	1.6	1.6
							(18) 3.1	(14) 3.1
							6.3	6.0
560M	55138M	153893M	236002M	205876M	554316M	Net Sales ($)	918974M	1085861M
309M	17711M	57732M	150862M	118774M	453269M	Total Assets ($)	683649M	844644M

© RMA 2007

M = $ thousand   MM = $ million
See Pages 11 through 21 for Explanation of Ratios and Data

Comparative Historical Data | Current Data Sorted by Sales

4/1/04-3/31/05 ALL	4/1/05-3/31/06 ALL	4/1/06-3/31/07 ALL	Type of Statement	0-1MM	1-3MM	3-5MM	5-10MM	10-25MM	25MM & OVER
8	4	8	Unqualified					1	7
12	8	12	Reviewed			4	3	3	2
9	4	6	Compiled	1	1	2	2	1	1
1	2	4	Tax Returns				1	1	
13	11	9	Other		3	1	1		1
				5 (4/1-9/30/06)			34 (10/1/06-3/31/07)		
43	29	39	NUMBER OF STATEMENTS	1	5	6	9	7	11
%	%	%	ASSETS	%	%	%	%	%	%
10.4	12.6	13.0	Cash & Equivalents						12.9
29.0	23.9	29.7	Trade Receivables (net)						26.1
28.5	32.5	29.3	Inventory						30.5
2.8	2.7	2.6	All Other Current						4.0
70.7	71.6	74.5	Total Current						73.5
22.4	18.2	17.7	Fixed Assets (net)						20.4
1.8	4.0	3.6	Intangibles (net)						3.4
5.0	6.1	4.1	All Other Non-Current						2.6
100.0	100.0	100.0	Total						100.0
			LIABILITIES						
11.7	13.4	7.7	Notes Payable-Short Term						4.5
2.1	1.5	2.8	Cur. Mat.-L.T.D.						1.4
14.0	15.7	17.2	Trade Payables						17.2
.3	.1	.3	Income Taxes Payable						.5
22.3	20.9	21.9	All Other Current						24.1
50.5	51.7	50.0	Total Current						47.6
12.6	5.9	7.4	Long-Term Debt						1.9
.4	.4	.1	Deferred Taxes						.2
10.6	5.7	4.5	All Other Non-Current						3.8
25.9	36.3	38.0	Net Worth						46.6
100.0	100.0	100.0	Total Liabilities & Net Worth						100.0
			INCOME DATA						
100.0	100.0	100.0	Net Sales						100.0
29.3	29.3	28.8	Gross Profit						24.1
26.3	25.5	23.8	Operating Expenses						19.0
3.1	3.8	5.0	Operating Profit						5.1
.9	.5	1.6	All Other Expenses (net)						.7
2.2	3.4	3.4	Profit Before Taxes						4.4
			RATIOS						
2.1	2.1	2.3	Current						2.2
1.4	1.4	1.6							1.6
1.2	1.1	1.1							1.1
1.2	.8	1.5	Quick						1.4
.7	.7	.8							.7
.6	.5	.6							.5
38 9.7	30 12.3	36 10.3	Sales/Receivables					38	9.5
48 7.6	47 7.8	48 7.6						56	6.5
63 5.8	58 6.3	58 6.2						58	6.2
38 9.7	47 7.8	32 11.3	Cost of Sales/Inventory					64	5.7
62 5.9	95 3.8	64 5.7						92	4.0
122 3.0	174 2.1	110 3.3						123	3.0
20 17.8	15 23.9	13 27.2	Cost of Sales/Payables					18	20.1
30 12.3	35 10.5	33 11.1						40	9.2
52 7.0	60 6.1	49 7.4						49	7.5
4.2	4.1	4.2	Sales/Working Capital						3.4
9.3	8.7	10.5							10.2
32.5	52.1	27.5							18.9
15.3	6.7	23.3	EBIT/Interest						
(35) 3.7	(24) 4.5	(33) 5.7							
.3	2.0	2.2							
			Net Profit + Depr., Dep., Amort./Cur. Mat. L/T/D						
.3	.2	.2	Fixed/Worth						.2
.7	.3	.4							.7
3.8	1.4	1.2							.9
.7	.7	.6	Debt/Worth						.6
2.0	1.7	1.6							1.6
10.6	3.6	4.1							2.3
39.5	39.3	55.1	% Profit Before Taxes/Tangible Net Worth						45.0
(36) 14.3	(26) 12.8	(35) 20.9							20.9
2.6	1.5	7.6							-.8
14.5	10.7	17.4	% Profit Before Taxes/Total Assets						12.0
4.5	6.1	8.3							8.7
-2.2	.5	3.9							-.6
29.0	42.5	44.6	Sales/Net Fixed Assets						11.0
10.7	15.3	12.6							8.8
5.0	5.9	7.8							5.7
2.7	2.5	3.0	Sales/Total Assets						2.1
1.9	1.8	2.1							1.6
1.3	1.2	1.6							1.3
.9	.8	.6	% Depr., Dep., Amort./Sales						.7
(42) 1.7	(27) 1.6	(38) 1.0							1.6
3.3	2.8	2.4							3.2
.9	1.9	1.7	% Officers', Directors' Owners' Comp/Sales						
(15) 2.6	(14) 2.6	(12) 2.4							
4.7	3.9	3.8							
712418M	613482M	1205785M	Net Sales ($)	560M	10718M	23865M	68956M	111663M	990023M
536366M	585056M	798657M	Total Assets ($)	309M	6186M	10116M	26750M	44994M	710302M

M = $ thousand   MM = $ million
See Pages 11 through 21 for Explanation of Ratios and Data

Current Data Sorted by Assets | Comparative Historical Data

							Type of Statement		
		1	3	2			Unqualified	12	11
		2	8	4			Reviewed	17	17
		6	3				Compiled	10	15
2		1	1				Tax Returns	4	3
		3	6	7	1	1	Other	12	15
		4 (4/1-9/30/06)		47 (10/1/06-3/31/07)				4/1/02-3/31/03	4/1/03-3/31/04
0-500M	500M-2MM	2-10MM	10-50MM	50-100MM	100-250MM			ALL	ALL
2	13	21	13	1	1		NUMBER OF STATEMENTS	55	61
%	%	%	%	%	%		ASSETS	%	%
	7.5	13.5	11.6				Cash & Equivalents	12.4	11.1
	28.1	26.3	22.2				Trade Receivables (net)	22.1	20.3
	36.9	27.7	22.0				Inventory	30.7	30.5
	1.2	1.2	3.9				All Other Current	4.8	5.7
	73.7	68.7	59.7				Total Current	70.0	67.6
	15.7	14.3	23.1				Fixed Assets (net)	21.0	22.6
	.3	13.3	5.4				Intangibles (net)	1.3	1.9
	10.3	3.8	11.7				All Other Non-Current	7.7	7.9
	100.0	100.0	100.0				Total	100.0	100.0
							LIABILITIES		
	11.6	13.8	4.0				Notes Payable-Short Term	10.5	14.3
	3.2	4.0	1.0				Cur. Mat.-L.T.D.	2.4	2.1
	16.4	12.5	11.6				Trade Payables	12.0	14.1
	.0	.1	.2				Income Taxes Payable	.2	.1
	22.5	16.4	10.7				All Other Current	15.3	12.8
	53.7	46.7	27.4				Total Current	40.5	43.4
	11.8	19.0	10.2				Long-Term Debt	7.6	9.3
	.3	.0	.4				Deferred Taxes	.4	.5
	5.6	1.2	1.8				All Other Non-Current	4.1	3.8
	28.6	33.2	60.2				Net Worth	47.4	42.9
	100.0	100.0	100.0				Total Liabilities & Net Worth	100.0	100.0
							INCOME DATA		
	100.0	100.0	100.0				Net Sales	100.0	100.0
	31.9	31.6	29.1				Gross Profit	30.7	30.5
	27.6	29.3	23.3				Operating Expenses	28.3	27.4
	4.3	2.3	5.8				Operating Profit	2.4	3.1
	1.8	1.6	.6				All Other Expenses (net)	.6	.4
	2.5	.7	5.3				Profit Before Taxes	1.8	2.7
							RATIOS		
	4.9	2.4	3.7					3.2	3.5
	1.5	1.5	2.3				Current	2.1	1.8
	1.2	.9	1.9					1.2	1.3
	1.7	1.2	1.9					1.5	1.6
	.6	.7	1.4				Quick	.9	.9
	.4	.5	.8					.6	.5

							Sales/Receivables				
23	16.2	33	11.0	48	7.7			28	12.9	29	12.8
53	6.9	48	7.7	50	7.3			43	8.5	42	8.7
63	5.8	66	5.5	75	4.8			55	6.6	51	7.1
18	20.7	38	9.6	37	9.9		Cost of Sales/Inventory	46	7.9	46	7.9
82	4.4	79	4.6	105	3.5			86	4.3	107	3.4
186	2.0	117	3.1	164	2.2			152	2.4	140	2.6
16	22.3	13	27.5	15	25.2		Cost of Sales/Payables	14	26.7	17	21.3
25	14.6	29	12.8	19	19.0			27	13.7	30	12.1
41	8.9	50	7.4	33	11.0			42	8.8	53	6.9

							Sales/Working Capital				
	3.9		4.6		2.5				2.8		3.0
	7.2		6.5		4.2				4.9		5.8
	28.8		-28.6		7.0				15.8		15.3
	4.1		5.4		5.8		EBIT/Interest		7.8		8.6
(11)	2.3	(16)	3.1	(11)	2.9			(47)	2.7	(54)	3.5
	-1.0		.6		-4.3				-.8		.1
							Net Profit + Depr., Dep., Amort./Cur. Mat. L/T/D		4.6		4.5
								(16)	1.7	(14)	1.7
									.2		-.2
	.1		.1		.2		Fixed/Worth		.2		.2
	.3		.3		.4				.4		.5
	.8		-1.3		.6				1.0		1.1
	1.0		1.2		.2		Debt/Worth		.4		.5
	2.3		1.7		.5				.9		1.1
	6.0		-10.8		3.4				2.5		3.2
	37.4		23.3		14.7		% Profit Before Taxes/Tangible Net Worth		26.7		24.9
(12)	5.1	(15)	8.7	(12)	4.8			(53)	9.0	(57)	10.6
	-34.5		1.1		-1.5				-3.7		-.1
	19.3		12.0		8.5		% Profit Before Taxes/Total Assets		10.1		9.9
	2.6		3.2		3.0				2.7		3.0
	-6.7		-.8		-.7				-2.4		-.6
	81.3		48.5		10.1		Sales/Net Fixed Assets		21.8		24.3
	27.9		16.6		5.2				9.6		10.7
	10.9		7.7		2.9				5.6		3.8
	3.4		2.1		1.5		Sales/Total Assets		2.6		2.5
	2.1		1.9		1.1				1.7		1.7
	1.4		1.2		.7				1.1		1.1
	.3		.7		1.4		% Depr., Dep., Amort./Sales		1.0		.6
	.8		1.2		3.7			(50)	2.0	(54)	1.9
	2.2		2.0		4.5				3.7		3.4
							% Officers', Directors' Owners' Comp/Sales		2.9		3.0
								(21)	4.4	(17)	4.0
									8.4		7.3

6139M	42860M	172981M	310271M	86624M	144058M		Net Sales ($)	503704M	997921M
602M	17969M	104846M	281680M	51468M	152915M		Total Assets ($)	373850M	817884M

M = $ thousand   MM = $ million
See Pages 11 through 21 for Explanation of Ratios and Data

Comparative Historical Data				Current Data Sorted by Sales					
			Type of Statement						
16	6	6	Unqualified			1	2	3	
11	9	14	Reviewed		2	1	5	5	1
6	9	9	Compiled		2	4	3		
6	1	4	Tax Returns		1	1	2		
8	18	18	Other		5		2	6	5
4/1/04-3/31/05 ALL	4/1/05-3/31/06 ALL	4/1/06-3/31/07 ALL		4 (4/1-9/30/06)			47 (10/1/06-3/31/07)		
				0-1MM	1-3MM	3-5MM	5-10MM	10-25MM	25MM & OVER
47	43	51	**NUMBER OF STATEMENTS**		10	7	14	14	6
%	%	%	**ASSETS**	%	%	%	%	%	%
7.6	9.9	11.5	Cash & Equivalents	D	7.0		19.8	9.6	
22.0	28.5	24.4	Trade Receivables (net)	A	19.5		22.8	19.4	
39.6	32.7	28.8	Inventory	T	35.9		24.0	29.7	
2.6	2.8	1.8	All Other Current	A	.9		.6	1.9	
71.7	73.9	66.6	Total Current		63.3		67.2	60.6	
18.4	13.8	17.2	Fixed Assets (net)	N	16.2		11.7	24.4	
2.6	4.7	7.6	Intangibles (net)	O	4.3		16.5	1.5	
7.3	7.5	8.6	All Other Non-Current	T	16.2		4.5	13.4	
100.0	100.0	100.0	Total		100.0		100.0	100.0	
			LIABILITIES	A					
11.2	13.2	10.1	Notes Payable-Short Term	V	11.2		5.8	11.3	
4.0	4.0	4.9	Cur. Mat.-L.T.D.	A	4.2		11.1	1.0	
13.5	16.7	13.7	Trade Payables	I	14.7		11.9	6.4	
.2	.2	.1	Income Taxes Payable	L	.0		.2	.1	
12.8	14.3	16.4	All Other Current	A	19.7		16.9	10.9	
41.7	48.4	45.1	Total Current	B	49.8		45.9	29.7	
11.7	11.0	14.1	Long-Term Debt	L	28.3		6.2	13.8	
.3	.3	.2	Deferred Taxes	E	.0		.0	.4	
3.7	3.4	2.8	All Other Non-Current		2.7		1.7	1.1	
42.5	36.9	37.8	Net Worth		19.3		46.2	55.0	
100.0	100.0	100.0	Total Liabilities & Net Worth		100.0		100.0	100.0	
			INCOME DATA						
100.0	100.0	100.0	Net Sales		100.0		100.0	100.0	
32.3	29.0	31.0	Gross Profit		36.0		31.6	28.8	
29.2	24.4	27.0	Operating Expenses		37.5		27.0	26.1	
3.1	4.7	3.9	Operating Profit		-1.5		4.6	2.7	
.4	.4	1.5	All Other Expenses (net)		2.6		1.7	.3	
2.7	4.3	2.4	Profit Before Taxes		-4.1		3.0	2.4	
			RATIOS						
2.8	2.5	2.7			2.6		1.9	3.3	
1.8	1.7	1.7	Current		1.2		1.5	2.3	
1.4	1.4	1.2			.8		.8	1.7	
1.3	1.4	1.4			.8		1.4	1.8	
.7	.8	.8	Quick		.6		.7	1.0	
.5	.5	.5			.4		.4	.6	
32 11.3	**37** 10.0	**36** 10.1			**25** 14.3		**18** 19.8	**43** 8.5	
40 9.1	**47** 7.7	**50** 7.3	Sales/Receivables		**54** 6.8		**37** 10.0	**49** 7.4	
60 6.1	**74** 4.9	**64** 5.7			**72** 5.0		**51** 7.2	**59** 6.2	
71 5.1	**40** 9.2	**29** 12.6			**20** 18.1		**8** 47.8	**65** 5.6	
122 3.0	**109** 3.4	**82** 4.4	Cost of Sales/Inventory		**104** 3.5		**46** 7.9	**103** 3.6	
157 2.3	**132** 2.8	**138** 2.6			**331** 1.1		**109** 3.3	**163** 2.2	
17 21.9	**19** 19.0	**15** 23.7			**24** 15.1		**9** 41.6	**16** 22.7	
32 11.5	**30** 12.2	**26** 14.1	Cost of Sales/Payables		**39** 9.3		**14** 26.1	**20** 18.4	
47 7.8	**60** 6.1	**53** 6.9			**112** 3.2		**48** 7.6	**28** 13.1	
3.6	3.8	3.7			3.3		5.3	3.2	
6.3	5.8	6.1	Sales/Working Capital		11.1		9.5	4.8	
12.9	25.3	25.2			-18.0		-52.7	6.8	
18.5	12.1	5.2					8.0	6.0	
(46) 3.5	(39) 4.2	(41) 2.9	EBIT/Interest				(10) 4.6	(13) 4.1	
1.3	1.6	-.4					2.6	-1.6	
	40.6		Net Profit + Depr., Dep.,						
	(12) 5.6		Amort./Cur. Mat. L/T/D						
	.5								
.2	.1	.1			.1		.1	.3	
.4	.3	.3	Fixed/Worth		.2		.2	.4	
.9	1.1	2.1			1.7		2.5	1.1	
.6	.6	.6			1.4		1.2	.2	
1.4	2.3	1.7	Debt/Worth		2.5		1.8	.7	
5.3	8.1	6.1			5.8		7.5	1.5	
34.3	62.3	22.6	% Profit Before Taxes/Tangible				32.3	15.6	
(45) 11.7	(38) 8.6	(42) 6.9	Net Worth				(12) 8.2	(12) 5.6	
4.4	3.3	-.4					2.1	.7	
12.4	14.2	13.9			16.7		14.5	7.3	
5.2	4.3	3.0	% Profit Before Taxes/Total Assets		.5		3.9	2.8	
.8	1.3	-.8			-15.4		1.4	-.3	
27.5	47.8	42.7			51.5		61.4	17.1	
12.3	19.0	14.5	Sales/Net Fixed Assets		24.7		43.3	6.0	
6.3	7.8	5.2			2.9		14.1	3.0	
2.2	2.4	2.1			2.2		2.8	2.0	
1.7	1.7	1.7	Sales/Total Assets		1.4		1.9	1.5	
1.3	1.1	1.1			.8		1.5	.7	
.8	.6	.6			.3		.4	1.3	
(40) 1.6	1.2	1.3	% Depr., Dep., Amort./Sales		.9		.9	1.7	
3.0	2.0	3.7			4.1		1.4	4.4	
	2.4	3.2	% Officers', Directors'						
	(13) 3.3	(19) 4.1	Owners' Comp/Sales						
	6.1	6.8							
915330M	**937279M**	**762933M**	Net Sales ($)		**21750M**	**27129M**	**100934M**	**226075M**	**387045M**
552066M	**651606M**	**609480M**	Total Assets ($)		**17918M**	**11368M**	**56907M**	**203554M**	**319733M**

M = $ thousand MM = $ million

See Pages 11 through 21 for Explanation of Ratios and Data

Current Data Sorted by Assets | Comparative Historical Data

0-500M	500M-2MM	2-10MM	10-50MM	50-100MM	100-250MM	Type of Statement	4/1/02-3/31/03 ALL	4/1/03-3/31/04 ALL
1		1	7		3	Unqualified	18	11
	5	9				Reviewed	18	10
1	3	3				Compiled	5	16
2	3	2				Tax Returns		4
1	4	3	4	4	2	Other	18	19
12 (4/1-9/30/06)			46 (10/1/06-3/31/07)					
5	**15**	**18**	**11**	**4**	**5**	**NUMBER OF STATEMENTS**	**59**	**60**
%	%	%	%	%	%	**ASSETS**	%	%
	8.0	8.7	5.9			Cash & Equivalents	8.4	9.3
	24.1	22.7	31.1			Trade Receivables (net)	22.0	27.1
	25.4	39.5	38.4			Inventory	31.8	26.3
	1.4	1.3	3.4			All Other Current	4.1	2.1
	58.8	72.2	78.8			Total Current	66.3	64.9
	32.6	21.4	11.9			Fixed Assets (net)	20.9	24.7
	2.5	2.1	3.0			Intangibles (net)	7.2	5.2
	6.1	4.2	6.3			All Other Non-Current	5.6	5.2
	100.0	100.0	100.0			Total	100.0	100.0
						LIABILITIES		
	13.7	12.0	7.6			Notes Payable-Short Term	7.9	15.8
	5.4	2.4	2.2			Cur. Mat.-L.T.D.	4.9	3.7
	17.4	18.3	19.3			Trade Payables	12.0	14.4
	.0	.3	.5			Income Taxes Payable	.4	.2
	28.7	15.1	24.2			All Other Current	17.6	15.0
	65.2	48.1	53.8			Total Current	42.7	49.1
	28.2	13.2	9.2			Long-Term Debt	12.3	15.0
	.0	.1	.3			Deferred Taxes	.4	.5
	6.3	9.6	8.1			All Other Non-Current	5.4	5.6
	.4	29.1	28.7			Net Worth	39.1	29.7
	100.0	100.0	100.0			Total Liabilities & Net Worth	100.0	100.0
						INCOME DATA		
	100.0	100.0	100.0			Net Sales	100.0	100.0
	39.3	32.3	30.9			Gross Profit	33.7	34.2
	33.5	27.3	25.5			Operating Expenses	31.1	31.6
	5.8	5.0	5.5			Operating Profit	2.6	2.6
	2.1	2.2	.6			All Other Expenses (net)	1.3	1.2
	3.7	2.8	4.8			Profit Before Taxes	1.3	1.5
						RATIOS		
	1.7	2.2	2.1				2.7	2.4
	1.2	1.6	1.5			Current	1.6	1.6
	.6	1.1	1.1				1.2	1.1
	1.0	.9	1.1				1.3	1.5
	.5	.7	.8			Quick	.8	.8
	.4	.4	.5				.4	.5
	25 14.4	39 9.4	38 9.7				33 11.0	34 10.7
	32 11.6	46 7.9	53 6.9			Sales/Receivables	45 8.1	43 8.4
	42 8.7	61 6.0	83 4.4				62 5.9	62 5.9
	18 19.9	68 5.4	67 5.5				56 6.5	21 17.6
	41 9.0	110 3.3	126 2.9			Cost of Sales/Inventory	82 4.5	75 4.9
	90 4.1	147 2.5	156 2.3				150 2.4	119 3.1
	18 20.5	23 15.8	26 13.8				20 18.5	22 16.5
	34 10.7	35 10.4	45 8.2			Cost of Sales/Payables	32 11.3	34 10.8
	79 4.6	66 5.5	72 5.1				46 7.9	45 8.1
	8.6	4.3	3.4				4.2	4.4
	38.0	7.5	6.5			Sales/Working Capital	7.1	8.9
	-7.8	27.7	21.1				17.9	33.5
	7.9	5.9	46.8				7.0	11.3
	5.6	(17) 2.5	10.4			EBIT/Interest	(54) 1.8	(52) 2.3
	.5	.8	1.8				-.2	-.4
							5.5	2.1
						Net Profit + Depr., Dep., Amort./Cur. Mat. L/T/D	(23) 1.2	(15) 1.0
							.2	.1
	1.7	.2	.2				.2	.2
	-10.3	.5	.3			Fixed/Worth	.6	.6
	-.5	1.2	1.9				1.4	2.4
	3.5	1.2	.7				.8	.8
	-15.2	3.2	5.7			Debt/Worth	1.9	1.9
	-5.3	10.0	122.5				3.7	7.6
		52.6					28.6	35.1
	(17)	12.1				% Profit Before Taxes/Tangible Net Worth	(52) 9.3	(52) 13.4
		4.3					-4.9	-2.6
	21.6	9.4	14.3				7.1	9.4
	9.2	3.1	9.0			% Profit Before Taxes/Total Assets	1.9	2.8
	-3.4	-.3	4.2				-3.2	-1.5
	37.2	33.7	101.1				31.9	30.7
	7.1	12.0	12.2			Sales/Net Fixed Assets	9.0	10.8
	4.7	6.5	8.3				4.9	4.0
	3.2	2.6	2.1				2.0	2.6
	2.5	1.6	1.9			Sales/Total Assets	1.6	1.6
	2.1	1.3	1.4				1.3	1.3
	.4	.5					1.1	1.1
	(13) 4.2	1.1				% Depr., Dep., Amort./Sales	(54) 2.7	(54) 2.9
	6.2	3.3					4.2	4.6
							3.9	2.7
						% Officers', Directors' Owners' Comp/Sales	(19) 7.5	(17) 4.4
							12.0	10.1
6403M	48276M	163929M	426607M	429868M	1126556M	Net Sales ($)	1914485M	2032417M
1930M	18384M	86908M	245425M	298991M	844721M	Total Assets ($)	1401816M	1348934M

M = $ thousand   MM = $ million
See Pages 11 through 21 for Explanation of Ratios and Data

Comparative Historical Data | Current Data Sorted by Sales

Current Data groupings: **12 (4/1-9/30/06)** covers 0-1MM, 1-3MM, 3-5MM; **46 (10/1/06-3/31/07)** covers 5-10MM, 10-25MM, 25MM & OVER.

4/1/04-3/31/05 ALL	4/1/05-3/31/06 ALL	4/1/06-3/31/07 ALL	Type of Statement	0-1MM	1-3MM	3-5MM	5-10MM	10-25MM	25MM & OVER
11	10	12	Unqualified		1			2	9
14	15	14	Reviewed		2	6	3	3	
5	4	7	Compiled		3	2	2		
3	2	7	Tax Returns	2	1		2	2	
22	20	18	Other	1	3	2	1	2	9
55	51	58	NUMBER OF STATEMENTS	3	10	10	8	9	18
%	%	%	**ASSETS**	%	%	%	%	%	%
9.8	8.0	7.7	Cash & Equivalents		4.7	13.0			5.1
23.6	25.5	25.4	Trade Receivables (net)		28.9	24.7			28.6
26.2	29.7	29.1	Inventory		20.5	29.8			28.4
3.0	2.8	2.0	All Other Current		1.5	1.1			2.5
62.6	66.0	64.2	Total Current		55.6	68.5			64.7
23.0	22.6	23.8	Fixed Assets (net)		30.4	25.0			13.2
7.7	5.7	5.9	Intangibles (net)		4.3	2.5			13.4
6.7	5.7	6.0	All Other Non-Current		9.8	3.9			8.7
100.0	100.0	100.0	Total		100.0	100.0			100.0
			LIABILITIES						
13.0	9.2	10.3	Notes Payable-Short Term		17.7	15.1			7.0
4.9	5.5	4.4	Cur. Mat.-L.T.D.		4.9	1.1			2.3
13.9	13.5	16.2	Trade Payables		14.8	16.4			15.3
.5	.3	.2	Income Taxes Payable		.1	.0			.2
14.0	17.1	21.2	All Other Current		27.1	28.8			21.6
46.2	45.5	52.3	Total Current		64.6	61.3			46.5
13.7	17.6	22.6	Long-Term Debt		36.8	11.9			16.9
1.2	.2	.3	Deferred Taxes		.0	.0			.7
3.2	6.8	7.1	All Other Non-Current		.4	3.3			7.7
35.7	29.9	17.8	Net Worth		-1.8	23.5			28.2
100.0	100.0	100.0	Total Liabilities & Net Worth		100.0	100.0			100.0
			INCOME DATA						
100.0	100.0	100.0	Net Sales		100.0	100.0			100.0
35.0	35.2	34.7	Gross Profit		39.1	37.7			28.1
31.4	30.9	29.1	Operating Expenses		35.1	34.8			23.4
3.6	4.3	5.6	Operating Profit		4.0	2.9			4.7
1.4	1.3	2.1	All Other Expenses (net)		2.8	1.8			2.1
2.2	3.1	3.5	Profit Before Taxes		1.1	1.1			2.6
			RATIOS						
2.0	2.3	1.9	Current		1.9	2.2			1.9
1.7	1.5	1.4			.8	1.3			1.5
1.1	1.1	.9			.5	.9			1.1
1.2	1.3	1.1	Quick		.9	1.3			1.2
.8	.7	.7			.6	.6			.8
.5	.5	.4			.2	.4			.5
37 9.8	30 12.1	30 12.0	Sales/Receivables		21 17.1	27 13.5			50 7.3
49 7.5	47 7.8	46 7.9			38 9.7	41 9.0			60 6.1
59 6.2	59 6.2	61 6.0			48 7.6	61 6.0			74 5.0
26 14.0	32 11.5	36 10.0	Cost of Sales/Inventory		0 UND	36 10.1			46 7.9
77 4.8	72 5.1	74 4.9			14 25.8	81 4.5			73 5.0
133 2.7	117 3.1	127 2.9			97 3.7	139 2.6			115 3.2
23 15.6	21 17.8	19 18.9	Cost of Sales/Payables		16 22.8	23 15.7			22 16.6
35 10.3	30 12.2	36 10.2			19 19.1	31 11.7			41 8.9
52 7.0	46 8.0	55 6.7			54 6.8	43 8.4			49 7.5
4.0	4.7	5.5	Sales/Working Capital		5.4	6.1			5.2
8.5	8.1	11.3			-44.9	20.7			7.3
62.6	35.1	-66.2			-4.9	-24.9			51.5
12.4	7.7	9.4	EBIT/Interest		4.7	10.2			11.4
(45) 3.7	(42) 3.7	(57) 3.1			1.7	4.8			3.7
.0	1.2	1.1			-.4	.0			1.3
2.4	7.5	14.8	Net Profit + Depr., Dep., Amort./Cur. Mat. L/T/D						
(14) .6	(12) 2.9	(12) 3.7							
-.6	.5	.4							
.2	.3	.3	Fixed/Worth		.4	.3			.2
.5	.7	1.1			NM	1.8			.5
2.0	2.2	-8.9			-.6	-1.4			-70.3
.9	1.1	1.7	Debt/Worth		3.2	.9			1.9
1.5	2.7	5.5			NM	3.1			5.8
4.2	55.1	-75.3			-2.4	-13.9			-181.4
36.3	45.3	61.4	% Profit Before Taxes/Tangible Net Worth						77.7
(49) 14.2	(41) 19.3	(42) 23.6						(13)	30.1
.7	6.0	3.7							8.4
10.5	10.2	14.5	% Profit Before Taxes/Total Assets		8.2	14.4			9.6
5.1	6.1	4.7			2.8	2.8			5.8
-1.7	1.2	.8			-15.8	-4.6			1.2
26.6	35.5	33.9	Sales/Net Fixed Assets		38.6	30.0			34.9
10.9	9.3	10.6			11.5	9.2			11.3
3.9	6.5	6.2			5.8	4.3			7.9
2.1	2.5	2.6	Sales/Total Assets		3.8	3.3			2.1
1.5	1.9	1.9			2.4	2.1			1.5
1.2	1.4	1.4			2.0	1.3			1.2
1.1	.7	.7	% Depr., Dep., Amort./Sales						.7
(48) 2.3	(47) 1.5	(51) 1.6						(14)	1.7
3.7	3.2	3.6							2.7
2.8	1.3	2.4	% Officers', Directors' Owners' Comp/Sales						
(12) 7.6	(13) 2.0	(18) 5.2							
9.2	7.6	7.4							
1888293M	2071534M	2201639M	Net Sales ($)	2203M	19708M	39764M	51114M	149309M	1939541M
1339002M	1271105M	1496359M	Total Assets ($)	1392M	9754M	21101M	27462M	75052M	1361598M

M = $ thousand   MM = $ million
See Pages 11 through 21 for Explanation of Ratios and Data

Current Data Sorted by Assets   Comparative Historical Data

0-500M	500M-2MM	2-10MM	10-50MM	50-100MM	100-250MM		4/1/02-3/31/03 ALL	4/1/03-3/31/04 ALL
						Type of Statement		
			1	9		Unqualified	21	11
	1	19	6			Reviewed	17	22
1	5	6				Compiled	12	14
2	2	1				Tax Returns	6	6
3	3	19		2	1	Other	17	23
22 (4/1-9/30/06)		69 (10/1/06-3/31/07)						
3	11	46	23	4	4	NUMBER OF STATEMENTS	73	76
%	%	%	%	%	%	**ASSETS**	%	%
	9.3	10.0	12.3			Cash & Equivalents	12.9	11.1
	33.2	25.2	20.8			Trade Receivables (net)	23.9	23.6
	31.7	34.6	27.1			Inventory	26.6	33.6
	5.2	2.9	1.4			All Other Current	3.5	3.2
	79.5	72.7	61.7			Total Current	66.8	71.4
	16.3	15.4	26.0			Fixed Assets (net)	20.3	18.0
	1.5	3.7	6.0			Intangibles (net)	5.9	5.3
	2.8	8.2	6.3			All Other Non-Current	7.0	5.3
	100.0	100.0	100.0			Total	100.0	100.0
						LIABILITIES		
	9.1	6.8	3.5			Notes Payable-Short Term	6.5	10.8
	7.3	2.2	2.4			Cur. Mat.-L.T.D.	3.5	3.1
	15.4	13.6	11.3			Trade Payables	10.5	12.2
	.1	.4	.4			Income Taxes Payable	.3	.2
	18.7	19.3	16.7			All Other Current	15.3	20.6
	50.6	42.3	34.2			Total Current	36.1	46.9
	12.0	11.2	14.0			Long-Term Debt	13.3	12.0
	.2	.2	.4			Deferred Taxes	.8	.4
	3.9	3.8	1.6			All Other Non-Current	5.8	9.5
	33.3	42.5	49.8			Net Worth	44.0	31.1
	100.0	100.0	100.0			Total Liabilities & Net Worth	100.0	100.0
						INCOME DATA		
	100.0	100.0	100.0			Net Sales	100.0	100.0
	44.6	33.4	38.4			Gross Profit	36.4	34.3
	39.9	27.9	30.9			Operating Expenses	30.5	30.0
	4.7	5.5	7.6			Operating Profit	6.0	4.2
	.8	.9	.4			All Other Expenses (net)	1.1	.7
	3.9	4.7	7.2			Profit Before Taxes	4.9	3.5
						RATIOS		
	3.2	2.7	3.3				3.0	2.2
	1.3	1.8	2.5			Current	1.8	1.4
	1.2	1.3	1.2				1.3	1.1
	1.6	1.5	1.9				1.7	1.1
	.6	.9	1.2			Quick	.9	.7
	.5	.5	.6				.6	.5
16 22.3	31 11.8	34 10.9					30 12.3	29 12.7
37 10.0	41 9.0	41 8.9				Sales/Receivables	41 8.9	42 8.8
90 4.0	52 7.0	56 6.5					54 6.8	55 6.7
10 36.5	47 7.8	80 4.6					43 8.4	60 6.1
81 4.5	93 3.9	94 3.9				Cost of Sales/Inventory	92 4.0	98 3.7
158 2.3	150 2.4	130 2.8					125 2.9	151 2.4
10 37.7	23 15.6	21 17.2					16 22.4	16 23.0
37 9.8	32 11.5	32 11.5				Cost of Sales/Payables	25 14.5	31 11.8
74 4.9	43 8.5	55 6.6					40 9.1	53 6.9
	4.7	4.5	3.5				3.8	4.7
	11.6	6.2	5.0			Sales/Working Capital	7.5	8.7
	28.3	15.0	17.7				17.5	24.1
	16.3	20.9	22.4				11.0	12.6
	(10) 4.1	(40) 5.4	(18) 7.3			EBIT/Interest	(62) 3.1	(67) 5.0
	1.0	2.4	4.3				1.2	1.9
		12.1	9.0			Net Profit + Depr., Dep.,	5.0	4.9
	(12) 5.6	(10) 7.5				Amort./Cur. Mat. L/T/D	(25) 1.5	(20) 1.7
		1.8	3.5				1.0	1.0
	.0	.1	.3				.2	.2
	.3	.3	.4			Fixed/Worth	.4	.5
	1.3	.8	1.3				1.5	1.3
	1.2	.7	.5				.5	1.3
	3.3	1.6	1.0			Debt/Worth	1.5	2.2
	4.7	3.1	2.5				3.8	5.2
	47.2	58.1	40.7			% Profit Before Taxes/Tangible	28.3	54.4
	(10) 28.2	(44) 19.0	(21) 30.7			Net Worth	(63) 11.6	(63) 16.1
	-1.2	8.2	15.3				-.7	5.3
	18.5	13.6	20.1			% Profit Before Taxes/Total	15.0	14.7
	7.9	6.5	12.4			Assets	5.6	5.1
	-.2	3.1	5.5				-.2	1.8
	99.6	34.0	12.0				20.6	34.4
	28.9	22.6	6.3			Sales/Net Fixed Assets	10.6	11.9
	6.9	8.9	3.7				6.9	7.6
	3.8	2.7	2.2				2.4	2.5
	2.7	2.2	1.7			Sales/Total Assets	1.8	1.9
	1.7	1.7	1.2				1.2	1.4
		.6	1.3				1.2	.9
	(39) .9	(20) 2.0				% Depr., Dep., Amort./Sales	(65) 2.1	(68) 1.8
		1.6	3.4				3.1	2.7
		2.2					3.5	3.0
	(14) 3.5					% Officers', Directors'	(22) 5.1	(21) 3.7
		10.1				Owners' Comp/Sales	9.6	6.0
1918M	32982M	490410M	975513M	370111M	979279M	Net Sales ($)	1784465M	1757707M
701M	12860M	226612M	529392M	261549M	696341M	Total Assets ($)	1436769M	1089398M

M = $ thousand   MM = $ million
See Pages 11 through 21 for Explanation of Ratios and Data

Comparative Historical Data | Current Data Sorted by Sales

20		17		15	Type of Statement					1		1		13
28		21		26	Unqualified		1		4		5		12		4
9		9		12	Reviewed		2		3		3		2		
5		11		5	Compiled	2	3		3		1				
23		26		33	Tax Returns	1	1		1		6		13		8
4/1/04-		4/1/05-		4/1/06-	Other										
3/31/05		3/31/06		3/31/07			22 (4/1-9/30/06)				69 (10/1/06-3/31/07)				
ALL		ALL		ALL		0-1MM	1-3MM		3-5MM		5-10MM		10-25MM		25MM & OVER
85		84		91	NUMBER OF STATEMENTS	3	7		12		16		28		25
%		%		%	ASSETS	%	%		%		%		%		%
9.4		11.1		10.4	Cash & Equivalents				2.5		10.5		14.7		8.8
28.1		26.3		24.5	Trade Receivables (net)				26.7		24.6		24.0		21.7
32.4		29.8		31.1	Inventory				37.6		34.5		30.8		26.3
2.9		2.8		2.8	All Other Current				3.1		1.4		3.9		2.0
72.8		70.0		68.8	Total Current				70.0		71.0		73.3		58.7
16.9		19.2		18.9	Fixed Assets (net)				15.8		14.1		19.0		23.3
4.9		4.4		5.8	Intangibles (net)				5.1		5.3		2.1		12.8
5.4		6.4		6.5	All Other Non-Current				9.1		9.6		5.6		5.1
100.0		100.0		100.0	Total				100.0		100.0		100.0		100.0
					LIABILITIES										
8.9		8.1		6.0	Notes Payable-Short Term				12.6		5.3		4.9		3.2
2.9		2.3		2.9	Cur. Mat.-L.T.D.				3.0		2.7		1.7		2.6
17.2		16.7		12.6	Trade Payables				14.0		14.6		12.6		11.9
.4		.4		.3	Income Taxes Payable				.6		.3		.2		.5
20.1		14.8		18.9	All Other Current				19.5		18.8		20.2		18.0
49.6		42.3		40.8	Total Current				49.6		41.7		39.6		36.1
13.2		15.1		13.4	Long-Term Debt				15.5		9.5		14.0		12.8
.3		.3		.3	Deferred Taxes				.3		.0		.2		.9
5.0		6.9		3.3	All Other Non-Current				.9		3.7		4.3		1.9
31.9		35.4		42.2	Net Worth				33.6		45.1		41.9		48.3
100.0		100.0		100.0	Total Liabilties & Net Worth				100.0		100.0		100.0		100.0
					INCOME DATA										
100.0		100.0		100.0	Net Sales				100.0		100.0		100.0		100.0
33.9		35.4		36.1	Gross Profit				37.6		33.4		33.3		35.7
29.8		30.5		29.7	Operating Expenses				31.8		27.9		27.8		26.7
4.1		4.9		6.5	Operating Profit				5.8		5.6		5.6		9.0
.6		1.3		.9	All Other Expenses (net)				1.2		1.0		.4		1.0
3.5		3.5		5.6	Profit Before Taxes				4.7		4.6		5.1		8.0
					RATIOS										
2.2		2.6		2.9					2.3		2.6		3.2		2.9
1.4		1.6		1.8	Current				1.3		2.0		2.1		1.9
1.1		1.3		1.2					1.1		1.2		1.4		1.2
1.1		1.4		1.5					.8		2.0		1.6		1.4
.7		.9		.9	Quick				.5		.9		1.1		.8
.5		.6		.5					.3		.3		.6		.6
34	10.9	30	12.3	32	11.5		18	19.7	26	13.9	33	11.0	33	10.9
41	8.9	37	9.8	41	8.9	Sales/Receivables	50	7.3	39	9.3	39	9.4	37	9.8
56	6.5	54	6.8	52	7.0		77	4.7	47	7.8	55	6.6	49	7.4
49	7.5	40	9.2	52	7.0		82	4.4	34	10.9	51	7.2	56	6.5
81	4.5	71	5.1	88	4.1	Cost of Sales/Inventory	122	3.0	93	3.9	90	4.0	87	4.2
131	2.8	129	2.8	145	2.5		173	2.1	146	2.5	129	2.5	121	3.0
23	15.8	19	19.7	21	17.2		26	14.0	28	13.0	21	17.5	23	15.6
38	9.7	35	10.5	31	11.6	Cost of Sales/Payables	39	9.3	33	11.0	27	13.8	32	11.5
60	6.1	57	6.4	43	8.4		45	8.1	45	8.2	37	9.8	48	7.7
	5.1		4.5		4.3			4.3		5.0		3.4		4.2
	11.2		8.3		6.4	Sales/Working Capital		12.9		6.6		5.7		8.3
	31.0		21.3		17.7			28.0		18.4		14.3		22.7
	18.5		17.3		20.8			16.1		21.5		25.9		25.0
(78)	4.8	(75)	5.9	(77)	5.1	EBIT/Interest	(14)	3.9	(22)	8.9	(21)	8.3		7.4
	1.3		1.1		2.4			1.5		2.5		2.7		4.3
	9.8		15.3		10.8										15.9
(30)	4.2	(31)	5.1	(27)	7.3	Net Profit + Depr., Dep., Amort./Cur. Mat. L/T/D					(11)			8.5
	1.5		1.7		2.3										3.7
	.2		.2		.2			.1		.1		.2		.3
	.5		.5		.4	Fixed/Worth		.3		.3		.3		.6
	1.3		1.1		1.1			2.9		.7		.9		1.8
	1.1		.8		.7			1.0		.6		.8		.5
	2.3		1.7		1.7	Debt/Worth		3.8		1.6		1.7		1.5
	6.4		5.2		4.0			7.7		3.0		2.8		5.2
	43.7		50.8		49.2	% Profit Before Taxes/Tangible Net Worth		102.1		58.1		41.9		48.2
(74)	14.3	(73)	21.4	(82)	21.9		(11)	34.7		18.4	(25)	19.7	(21)	35.8
	5.3		3.9		8.7			6.7		8.0		9.5		17.9
	12.3		20.5		18.3	% Profit Before Taxes/Total Assets		11.1		17.2		19.3		19.4
	4.9		6.9		8.4			6.2		7.6		8.2		13.3
	.4		.5		3.1			2.0		2.9		3.1		5.9
	31.6		34.0		30.4			48.0		43.0		29.9		19.5
	14.3		15.9		13.7	Sales/Net Fixed Assets		18.1		22.5		15.2		8.3
	8.1		7.8		6.3			6.7		12.0		5.4		5.6
	2.7		3.1		2.6			3.0		2.6		2.7		2.2
	2.0		2.2		1.9	Sales/Total Assets		1.7		2.2		2.1		1.7
	1.6		1.6		1.6			1.5		1.7		1.7		1.5
	.8		.8		.7					.7		.7		1.1
(71)	1.4	(75)	1.5	(75)	1.3	% Depr., Dep., Amort./Sales		(15)		.9	(22)	1.4	(22)	1.8
	2.1		2.5		2.0					2.0		2.1		3.2
	2.3		2.9		2.7	% Officers', Directors' Owners' Comp/Sales								
(29)	3.8	(21)	4.5	(24)	5.0								
	8.3		9.2		9.4									
2355836M		1861635M		2850213M	Net Sales ($)	1311M	15833M		47805M		114129M		443936M		2227199M
1433214M		1038829M		1727455M	Total Assets ($)	925M	9253M		27597M		57308M		241599M		1390773M

© RMA 2007

M = $ thousand   MM = $ million
See Pages 11 through 21 for Explanation of Ratios and Data

Current Data Sorted by Assets   Comparative Historical Data

0-500M	500M-2MM	2-10MM	10-50MM	50-100MM	100-250MM	Type of Statement		
	4	13	15	5	5	Unqualified	46	37
		27	7	2		Reviewed	23	29
1	18	19	1	1	1	Compiled	35	55
4	11	5		1		Tax Returns	11	12
3	12	21	20*	3	3	Other	53	49
	52 (4/1-9/30/06)		149 (10/1/06-3/31/07)				4/1/02-3/31/03 ALL	4/1/03-3/31/04 ALL
8	45	85	43	11	9	NUMBER OF STATEMENTS	168	182
%	%	%	%	%	%	**ASSETS**	%	%
	16.8	10.8	11.2	13.3		Cash & Equivalents	10.8	9.4
	29.0	27.3	23.6	21.7		Trade Receivables (net)	24.8	27.8
	24.9	29.0	29.9	18.7		Inventory	28.4	26.2
	5.2	2.4	5.1	6.4		All Other Current	4.4	3.7
	75.9	69.5	69.7	60.1		Total Current	68.3	67.1
	18.0	20.3	17.5	26.0		Fixed Assets (net)	21.8	23.3
	2.7	3.7	5.0	3.8		Intangibles (net)	2.5	3.8
	3.4	6.4	7.8	10.1		All Other Non-Current	7.4	5.7
	100.0	100.0	100.0	100.0		Total	100.0	100.0
						LIABILITIES		
	10.4	10.8	7.2	4.1		Notes Payable-Short Term	13.5	12.4
	2.4	3.8	2.0	3.5		Cur. Mat.-L.T.D.	3.2	4.1
	14.6	15.5	11.6	7.0		Trade Payables	12.3	14.6
	.1	.2	.4	.4		Income Taxes Payable	.2	.2
	18.6	13.9	15.4	24.1		All Other Current	14.6	17.6
	46.1	44.2	36.6	39.2		Total Current	43.9	49.0
	13.5	13.8	9.8	12.8		Long-Term Debt	11.7	14.5
	.2	.2	.6	.9		Deferred Taxes	.5	.6
	4.7	4.1	7.5	4.0		All Other Non-Current	3.9	6.4
	35.5	37.8	45.5	43.1		Net Worth	40.1	29.5
	100.0	100.0	100.0	100.0		Total Liabilities & Net Worth	100.0	100.0
						INCOME DATA		
	100.0	100.0	100.0	100.0		Net Sales	100.0	100.0
	37.8	32.7	29.0	34.8		Gross Profit	31.7	32.6
	31.7	25.8	20.5	27.4		Operating Expenses	29.6	29.9
	6.1	6.9	8.5	7.4		Operating Profit	2.0	2.7
	.7	.8	1.1	1.3		All Other Expenses (net)	1.0	.7
	5.4	6.1	7.5	6.1		Profit Before Taxes	1.0	2.0
						RATIOS		
	2.7	2.8	3.0	2.2		Current	2.6	2.6
	1.7	1.7	1.9	1.7			1.7	1.6
	1.1	1.1	1.4	1.0			1.2	1.1
	1.8	1.5	1.5	1.4		Quick	1.4	1.3
	1.0	.9	.9	.8			.8	.8
	.6	.5	.6	.5			.5	.5
	25 14.6	31 11.7	38 9.7	44 8.3		Sales/Receivables	34 10.8	38 9.6
	37 10.0	46 7.9	56 6.5	51 7.1			50 7.4	53 6.9
	51 7.1	59 6.2	69 5.3	81 4.5			71 5.1	69 5.3
	13 27.5	39 9.4	75 4.9	42 8.7		Cost of Sales/Inventory	45 8.1	37 9.8
	47 7.7	72 5.1	102 3.6	71 5.1			78 4.7	73 5.0
	106 3.4	123 3.0	134 2.7	129 2.8			137 2.7	123 3.0
	11 32.9	16 22.1	23 15.7	16 23.5		Cost of Sales/Payables	17 21.3	21 17.1
	27 13.7	35 10.5	38 9.7	20 18.6			32 11.4	37 9.8
	49 7.5	52 7.0	53 6.8	36 10.1			49 7.5	52 7.1
	5.7	4.6	3.0	2.4		Sales/Working Capital	3.5	3.8
	8.9	8.1	5.1	7.9			6.6	8.0
	41.9	519.5	7.6	-191.8			20.5	28.7
	34.7	13.5	48.5	139.2		EBIT/Interest	10.0	10.0
	(37) 7.2	(73) 4.0	(37) 6.0	6.0			(146) 2.7	(151) 2.5
	1.7	1.1	2.9	4.5			-.1	-.3
		7.7	24.4			Net Profit + Depr., Dep., Amort./Cur. Mat. L/T/D	5.4	2.7
		(24) 3.0	(11) 3.5				(47) 2.5	(50) 1.2
		1.4	1.8				.8	.5
	.1	.2	.2	.3		Fixed/Worth	.2	.3
	.4	.7	.4	.4			.5	.6
	1.2	1.7	1.2	.9			1.2	2.5
	1.0	.7	.6	.7		Debt/Worth	.5	.8
	1.8	1.9	1.5	1.2			1.5	1.8
	5.1	7.7	3.3	3.0			4.0	8.7
	71.7	58.2	45.8	52.9		% Profit Before Taxes/Tangible Net Worth	29.3	35.6
	(39) 23.5	(74) 28.9	(40) 29.0	27.4			(153) 8.0	(152) 13.8
	8.3	6.0	18.1	19.4			-5.7	.8
	22.3	22.5	19.8	17.4		% Profit Before Taxes/Total Assets	10.5	11.2
	12.7	9.6	12.6	15.4			3.1	3.9
	2.7	.7	6.0	5.6			-3.1	-1.8
	50.2	39.8	18.5	16.5		Sales/Net Fixed Assets	20.2	20.1
	17.5	14.0	8.5	6.1			9.4	9.8
	7.8	5.4	5.8	2.4			5.5	4.8
	3.5	2.7	1.8	1.7		Sales/Total Assets	2.2	2.3
	2.5	2.0	1.5	1.4			1.7	1.8
	1.9	1.5	1.2	.9			1.2	1.3
	.5	.5	.8	1.2		% Depr., Dep., Amort./Sales	1.4	1.1
	(36) 1.3	(78) 1.2	(39) 1.8	(10) 2.6			(152) 2.2	(164) 2.2
	3.0	2.6	2.7	5.9			4.1	4.0
	2.9	2.7				% Officers', Directors' Owners' Comp/Sales	2.9	2.5
	(26) 5.5	(28) 3.5					(52) 5.1	(54) 4.3
	11.6	6.0					8.9	8.2
5222M	154257M	850606M	1312484M	973775M	2428210M	Net Sales ($)	3269336M	3262391M
1781M	56701M	426714M	853130M	755754M	1529403M	Total Assets ($)	2522589M	2111858M

M = $ thousand   MM = $ million
See Pages 11 through 21 for Explanation of Ratios and Data

Comparative Historical Data | Current Data Sorted by Sales

4/1/04-3/31/05 ALL	4/1/05-3/31/06 ALL	4/1/06-3/31/07 ALL	Type of Statement	0-1MM	1-3MM	3-5MM	5-10MM	10-25MM	25MM & OVER
38	38	38	Unqualified				6	15	17
37	39	40	Reviewed		4	2	15	14	5
50	34	41	Compiled	1	11	8	11	6	4
9	24	20	Tax Returns	3	5	8	4		
62	85	62	Other	4	6	6	11	18	17
					52 (4/1-9/30/06)		149 (10/1/06-3/31/07)		
196	220	201	NUMBER OF STATEMENTS	8	26	24	47	53	43
%	%	%	ASSETS	%	%	%	%	%	%
10.4	9.6	12.4	Cash & Equivalents		16.4	12.8	11.4	10.9	11.3
26.8	27.5	27.0	Trade Receivables (net)		22.7	29.2	28.4	26.9	25.8
27.6	28.4	26.7	Inventory		29.3	25.5	26.7	28.5	25.7
3.8	3.7	3.7	All Other Current		3.0	4.8	3.8	2.6	5.6
68.7	69.2	69.8	Total Current		71.4	72.4	70.3	68.8	68.3
20.2	20.5	19.6	Fixed Assets (net)		22.8	19.8	20.5	16.9	19.0
4.3	3.9	4.4	Intangibles (net)		3.9	3.6	2.6	5.3	6.4
6.8	6.4	6.2	All Other Non-Current		2.0	4.3	6.6	9.0	6.3
100.0	100.0	100.0	Total		100.0	100.0	100.0	100.0	100.0
			LIABILITIES						
15.5	11.8	9.2	Notes Payable-Short Term		11.2	16.9	7.1	8.9	6.6
3.3	3.7	2.9	Cur. Mat.-L.T.D.		2.8	3.3	4.1	2.5	2.0
15.3	16.3	13.9	Trade Payables		12.3	13.8	15.1	14.5	14.5
.2	.3	.2	Income Taxes Payable		.1	.1	.3	.1	.5
14.5	15.1	16.9	All Other Current		13.4	16.9	13.8	16.0	16.1
48.8	47.3	43.2	Total Current		39.7	50.9	40.3	42.0	39.8
13.4	15.9	14.0	Long-Term Debt		16.4	12.7	14.7	11.6	9.5
.6	.5	.4	Deferred Taxes		.1	.0	.3	.2	1.0
4.7	5.3	5.7	All Other Non-Current		4.1	3.9	3.6	7.0	7.3
32.5	31.0	36.8	Net Worth		39.7	32.5	41.0	39.1	42.5
100.0	100.0	100.0	Total Liabilties & Net Worth		100.0	100.0	100.0	100.0	100.0
			INCOME DATA						
100.0	100.0	100.0	Net Sales		100.0	100.0	100.0	100.0	100.0
32.1	32.6	34.2	Gross Profit		38.1	38.3	34.2	30.6	28.6
27.9	27.2	26.9	Operating Expenses		31.7	30.2	27.8	22.9	21.6
4.2	5.4	7.3	Operating Profit		6.4	8.1	6.4	7.7	7.0
1.1	1.2	1.1	All Other Expenses (net)		1.2	1.2	.8	.9	1.4
3.1	4.2	6.2	Profit Before Taxes		5.2	6.9	5.6	6.8	5.6
			RATIOS						
2.6	2.4	2.8	Current		4.6	2.3	3.0	2.9	2.2
1.5	1.6	1.7			1.7	1.5	2.0	1.7	1.7
1.1	1.1	1.2			1.1	1.0	1.2	1.2	1.3
1.4	1.4	1.5	Quick		1.8	1.3	1.9	1.4	1.5
.8	(219) .8	.9			1.0	.8	1.0	.8	.9
.5	.5	.6			.5	.5	.6	.6	.6
31 11.7	32 11.4	34 10.7	Sales/Receivables	34 10.8	26 13.8	29 12.5	36 10.3	39 9.4	
47 7.7	46 7.9	47 7.8		41 8.9	44 8.4	45 8.0	50 7.3	55 6.7	
64 5.7	66 5.5	61 5.9		57 6.4	56 6.5	63 5.8	64 5.7	67 5.4	
30 12.2	30 12.3	34 10.7	Cost of Sales/Inventory	23 16.1	33 11.2	26 14.2	44 8.3	44 8.2	
74 4.9	73 5.0	75 4.9		93 3.9	47 7.7	53 6.8	80 4.6	77 4.8	
125 2.9	134 2.7	124 2.9		166 2.2	112 3.3	133 2.8	127 2.9	123 3.0	
18 20.1	20 18.1	16 22.4	Cost of Sales/Payables	12 29.9	12 29.3	17 21.7	22 16.7	19 19.0	
36 10.1	38 9.7	34 10.8		27 13.4	36 10.2	33 11.0	35 10.3	30 12.1	
64 5.7	59 6.1	53 6.9		56 6.5	55 6.7	51 7.1	51 7.2	53 6.9	
4.6	4.3	4.3	Sales/Working Capital		2.9	6.0	4.6	4.2	3.2
8.6	8.1	7.6			8.4	10.8	7.0	7.8	6.7
28.0	28.8	23.6			28.5	-431.6	28.4	20.0	13.8
12.2	14.2	20.1	EBIT/Interest		8.6	37.4	18.5	24.9	42.1
(168) 3.9	(195) 3.6	(169) 5.0		(22)	3.6	(21) 6.2	(40) 6.0	(45) 4.4	(37) 7.2
.6	1.1	1.7			1.4	.9	.8	2.4	3.4
5.4	5.6	8.2	Net Profit + Depr., Dep., Amort./Cur. Mat. L/T/D					11.1	8.7
(48) 2.1	(49) 2.7	(51) 3.4						(18) 4.7	(18) 3.6
.2	1.4	1.5						2.7	1.9
.2	.2	.2	Fixed/Worth		.1	.2	.2		.2
.5	.5	.5			.7	.6	.4	.5	.4
1.8	1.9	1.5			1.8	1.1	1.5	1.7	.9
.8	.8	.7	Debt/Worth		1.0	1.0	.6	.7	.7
2.2	2.0	1.8			1.8	2.1	1.1	2.2	1.4
5.5	6.0	5.8			4.9	5.9	5.4	7.6	3.4
53.2	55.4	57.4	% Profit Before Taxes/Tangible Net Worth		36.1	83.0	65.4	55.1	49.1
(169) 21.3	(187) 22.0	(175) 27.4		(23) 13.3	(20) 39.4	(42) 24.7	(48) 29.8	(39) 30.8	
2.7	5.8	9.6			3.5	5.3	2.3	16.9	21.2
17.0	16.6	19.8	% Profit Before Taxes/Total Assets		14.3	29.6	24.0	17.5	19.7
7.4	6.3	10.7			6.0	16.3	8.9	10.6	12.1
-.3	.4	2.0			1.7	-.3	-.1	2.2	5.4
36.4	40.9	30.3	Sales/Net Fixed Assets		19.2	51.7	35.9	57.6	18.0
15.2	13.0	13.1			10.0	16.2	15.5	14.2	10.8
5.6	5.8	6.2			4.8	6.3	6.0	6.4	5.6
2.7	2.7	2.7	Sales/Total Assets		2.4	3.4	3.1	2.5	1.9
2.0	1.9	1.8			1.9	2.1	2.2	1.8	1.7
1.4	1.4	1.4			1.4	1.6	1.5	1.2	1.2
.9	.9	.6	% Depr., Dep., Amort./Sales		.8	.4	.5	.6	.8
(170) 1.9	(185) 1.6	(173) 1.5		(23) 2.0	(21) 1.1	(41) 1.3	(46) 1.2	(39) 2.0	
3.3	3.1	2.9			4.5	3.0	2.9	2.0	3.2
2.6	2.1	2.6	% Officers', Directors' Owners' Comp/Sales		4.9	3.2	2.5		
(59) 5.1	(78) 4.8	(68) 4.5		(16) 7.0	(14) 5.0	(18) 3.5			
8.4	7.5	8.4			14.9	9.1	4.7		
9238955M	5592229M	5724554M	Net Sales ($)	4423M	55818M	95740M	350044M	849100M	4369429M
3476753M	3273377M	3623483M	Total Assets ($)	2439M	39439M	45272M	191999M	729441M	2614893M

M = $ thousand   MM = $ million
See Pages 11 through 21 for Explanation of Ratios and Data

Current Data Sorted by Assets | Comparative Historical Data

0-500M	500M-2MM	2-10MM	10-50MM	50-100MM	100-250MM	Type of Statement	4/1/02-3/31/03 ALL	4/1/03-3/31/04 ALL
	2	3	5	1	2	Unqualified	10	12
	1	10	2	1		Reviewed	8	12
1	3	5			1	Compiled	5	12
1	4					Tax Returns	1	2
2	4	8			1	Other	21	15
	10 (4/1-9/30/06)			47 (10/1/06-3/31/07)				
4	14	26	8	3	2	NUMBER OF STATEMENTS	45	53
%	%	%	%	%	%	**ASSETS**	%	%
	10.7	14.0				Cash & Equivalents	11.2	11.8
	30.8	22.1				Trade Receivables (net)	23.3	25.4
	21.0	27.1				Inventory	26.0	29.8
	2.6	3.7				All Other Current	4.8	2.5
	65.1	67.0				Total Current	65.3	69.5
	28.3	27.7				Fixed Assets (net)	23.9	22.1
	4.7	1.1				Intangibles (net)	3.8	2.6
	1.9	4.3				All Other Non-Current	6.9	5.9
	100.0	100.0				Total	100.0	100.0
						LIABILITIES		
	8.9	6.8				Notes Payable-Short Term	8.1	6.6
	6.3	4.0				Cur. Mat.-L.T.D.	3.2	4.0
	17.9	15.9				Trade Payables	10.4	12.9
	.0	.0				Income Taxes Payable	.1	.2
	8.7	12.2				All Other Current	9.3	11.4
	41.9	38.9				Total Current	31.3	35.2
	22.6	12.1				Long-Term Debt	13.1	14.4
	.1	1.2				Deferred Taxes	.3	.5
	6.7	3.9				All Other Non-Current	4.3	4.3
	28.7	43.9				Net Worth	51.0	45.7
	100.0	100.0				Total Liabilties & Net Worth	100.0	100.0
						INCOME DATA		
	100.0	100.0				Net Sales	100.0	100.0
	44.0	33.9				Gross Profit	40.5	41.7
	36.1	28.7				Operating Expenses	35.9	35.3
	7.9	5.1				Operating Profit	4.7	6.4
	1.0	1.1				All Other Expenses (net)	.8	1.9
	6.9	4.1				Profit Before Taxes	3.8	4.5
						RATIOS		
	2.5	2.9				Current	4.1	2.8
	1.4	1.7					2.1	2.2
	1.2	1.2					1.5	1.5
	1.4	1.6				Quick	2.5	1.6
	1.0	.9					1.0	1.1
	.6	.6					.6	.7
	28 12.9	33 10.9				Sales/Receivables	34 10.7	35 10.5
	37 9.8	40 9.1					46 7.9	47 7.8
	50 7.3	53 6.9					67 5.5	62 5.9
	15 24.4	34 10.9				Cost of Sales/Inventory	52 7.1	58 6.3
	32 11.5	87 4.2					103 3.5	97 3.7
	99 3.7	100 3.7					140 2.6	142 2.6
	18 20.2	20 17.8				Cost of Sales/Payables	17 21.8	18 20.1
	29 12.6	37 9.8					27 13.6	30 12.3
	52 7.0	47 7.8					53 6.9	58 6.2
	6.2	4.1				Sales/Working Capital	3.3	3.4
	10.9	5.9					4.9	5.2
	45.1	24.6					9.5	14.6
	9.4	7.0				EBIT/Interest	8.1	19.1
	(13) 4.8	(20) 3.2					(40) 3.1	(45) 4.3
	2.4	2.1					1.2	1.8
		2.9				Net Profit + Depr., Dep., Amort./Cur. Mat. L/T/D	6.5	21.1
		(10) 1.8					(11) 3.2	(14) 3.7
		1.5					.7	1.5
	.3	.2				Fixed/Worth	.2	.2
	.8	.9					.4	.4
	11.8	1.4					1.0	1.1
	1.1	.7				Debt/Worth	.4	.6
	2.1	1.3					1.0	1.0
	50.0	2.7					2.3	2.4
	133.9	47.6				% Profit Before Taxes/Tangible Net Worth	30.7	47.7
	(12) 53.2	17.3					(43) 14.9	(50) 19.7
	27.6	5.9					.5	7.3
	26.6	17.6				% Profit Before Taxes/Total Assets	14.0	17.9
	15.3	4.8					4.8	8.6
	4.9	2.8					.0	1.7
	40.4	29.8				Sales/Net Fixed Assets	18.4	27.2
	15.4	8.6					10.0	12.1
	6.5	3.3					5.1	6.5
	3.8	2.5				Sales/Total Assets	2.4	2.8
	2.9	1.8					1.7	1.8
	2.2	1.4					1.1	1.4
	1.7	1.1				% Depr., Dep., Amort./Sales	1.7	1.4
	(11) 3.7	(24) 2.9					(40) 2.7	(42) 3.1
	4.3	5.2					5.3	4.3
						% Officers', Directors' Owners' Comp/Sales	3.2	1.7
							(15) 5.1	(19) 4.4
							9.3	8.3
2496M	55333M	255042M	236350M	359027M	295104M	Net Sales ($)	1387863M	1317640M
1299M	18987M	129231M	160685M	213284M	307733M	Total Assets ($)	1162121M	957630M

M = $ thousand   MM = $ million
See Pages 11 through 21 for Explanation of Ratios and Data

Comparative Historical Data   Current Data Sorted by Sales

			Type of Statement						
11	11	13	Unqualified			2	1	4	6
7	6	13	Reviewed		2	1	2	7	1
6	6	11	Compiled			3	4	2	1
4	2	5	Tax Returns	1	1	1	2		
17	16	15	Other	1	2	1	2		1
4/1/04-	4/1/05-	4/1/06-		2		2			
3/31/05	3/31/06	3/31/07			10 (4/1-9/30/06)		47 (10/1/06-3/31/07)		
ALL	ALL	ALL		0-1MM	1-3MM	3-5MM	5-10MM	10-25MM	25MM & OVER
45	41	57	NUMBER OF STATEMENTS	4	5	9	15	15	9
%	%	%	ASSETS	%	%	%	%	%	%
10.1	12.1	11.3	Cash & Equivalents				10.5	10.4	
25.4	23.1	23.0	Trade Receivables (net)				22.9	22.7	
24.7	27.0	27.2	Inventory				24.5	29.5	
3.0	1.7	3.2	All Other Current				3.7	3.0	
63.3	63.9	64.7	Total Current				61.7	65.5	
23.0	25.6	26.8	Fixed Assets (net)				32.9	28.7	
8.4	6.2	3.9	Intangibles (net)				1.5	2.3	
5.4	4.2	4.6	All Other Non-Current				3.9	3.5	
100.0	100.0	100.0	Total				100.0	100.0	
			LIABILITIES						
6.7	5.1	14.6	Notes Payable-Short Term				10.9	7.3	
4.9	5.9	4.4	Cur. Mat.-L.T.D.				4.6	3.3	
13.2	15.2	15.2	Trade Payables				15.3	17.4	
.3	.3	.1	Income Taxes Payable				.0	.0	
11.4	10.1	9.9	All Other Current				8.0	9.0	
36.6	36.4	44.3	Total Current				38.8	36.9	
13.9	17.1	15.2	Long-Term Debt				21.2	12.3	
.6	.8	.6	Deferred Taxes				1.1	.6	
5.9	6.2	6.3	All Other Non-Current				8.4	9.5	
43.1	39.4	33.5	Net Worth				30.5	40.7	
100.0	100.0	100.0	Total Liabilties & Net Worth				100.0	100.0	
			INCOME DATA						
100.0	100.0	100.0	Net Sales				100.0	100.0	
41.3	36.6	39.0	Gross Profit				29.0	37.0	
35.2	32.1	33.0	Operating Expenses				27.8	29.6	
6.1	4.5	6.1	Operating Profit				1.3	7.4	
1.5	2.9	1.4	All Other Expenses (net)				.1	2.5	
4.7	1.7	4.6	Profit Before Taxes				1.2	4.8	
			RATIOS						
2.8	2.8	2.7					3.2	2.8	
1.9	1.8	1.6	Current				1.4	1.6	
1.3	1.4	1.2					1.0	1.4	
1.5	1.4	1.3					1.6	1.6	
1.0	1.1	.9	Quick				.9	.8	
.6	.6	.5					.5	.6	
33 11.0	33 11.0	33 10.9					34 10.8	31 11.8	
44 8.3	43 8.6	41 9.0	Sales/Receivables				40 9.1	42 8.8	
68 5.4	57 6.4	55 6.7					51 7.2	56 6.5	
34 10.7	38 9.6	33 11.0					19 19.6	57 6.4	
93 3.9	94 3.9	89 4.1	Cost of Sales/Inventory				88 4.2	87 4.2	
124 2.9	141 2.6	131 2.8					96 3.8	122 3.0	
19 19.4	21 17.6	20 18.5					22 16.6	18 19.8	
33 11.2	32 11.6	35 10.5	Cost of Sales/Payables				42 8.8	31 11.8	
52 7.0	51 7.1	50 7.4					49 7.5	49 7.4	
4.0	3.7	4.1					3.7	4.1	
7.8	5.8	7.8	Sales/Working Capital				14.9	7.6	
16.1	14.2	30.4					202.9	11.8	
13.0	10.4	8.2					3.6	17.1	
(39) 3.8	(35) 3.0	(48) 3.5	EBIT/Interest		(12) 2.6			(13) 3.3	
.7	.9	1.7					.8	1.9	
4.1	3.0	2.6	Net Profit + Depr., Dep.,						
(18) 2.7	(13) 2.2	(17) 1.8	Amort./Cur. Mat. L/T/D						
1.0	.8	1.3							
.2	.2	.2					.2	.1	
.5	.6	.7	Fixed/Worth				1.0	1.1	
2.7	2.1	1.5					8.8	1.5	
.6	.7	1.0					1.1	.7	
1.2	1.2	1.5	Debt/Worth				1.3	1.9	
5.2	4.9	3.8					29.4	3.6	
44.7	31.1	53.6	% Profit Before Taxes/Tangible				64.6	50.4	
(37) 25.2	(35) 14.2	(51) 26.9	Net Worth		(13) 14.2			(14) 20.9	
2.2	6.5	8.9					-.5	8.1	
17.9	13.6	16.1	% Profit Before Taxes/Total				8.9	20.3	
7.1	5.8	6.3	Assets				4.2	4.7	
-.1	-.6	2.7					-3.9	2.0	
26.8	26.1	27.3					19.9	41.7	
13.2	8.7	9.4	Sales/Net Fixed Assets				6.2	6.8	
4.9	3.6	4.2					3.2	3.4	
3.1	2.6	2.5					3.1	2.5	
1.8	1.8	2.0	Sales/Total Assets				1.8	2.0	
1.0	1.0	1.3					1.4	1.3	
1.5	1.1	1.6					1.5	.9	
(39) 2.9	(38) 1.9	(48) 3.4	% Depr., Dep., Amort./Sales		(14) 3.6			(14) 2.5	
5.2	4.0	5.2					6.3	5.1	
2.0		2.8	% Officers', Directors'						
(16) 4.3	(15) 5.8		Owners' Comp/Sales						
5.6		6.4							
1159721M	983745M	1203352M	Net Sales ($)	2496M	10662M	33261M	112517M	222965M	821451M
931677M	783431M	831219M	Total Assets ($)	1299M	5072M	15933M	61174M	122627M	625114M

© RMA 2007

M = $ thousand   MM = $ million
See Pages 11 through 21 for Explanation of Ratios and Data

Current Data Sorted by Assets   Comparative Historical Data

			4	1		Type of Statement		
		2	2			Unqualified	8	8
1						Reviewed	5	10
1		2				Compiled	3	1
1		2				Tax Returns	3	2
	1	3	3	3	1	Other	13	7
	5 (4/1-9/30/06)		20 (10/1/06-3/31/07)				4/1/02-3/31/03	4/1/03-3/31/04
0-500M	500M-2MM	2-10MM	10-50MM	50-100MM	100-250MM		ALL	ALL
3	1	7	9	4	1	NUMBER OF STATEMENTS	32	28
%	%	%	%	%	%	ASSETS	%	%
						Cash & Equivalents	8.2	7.7
						Trade Receivables (net)	22.6	22.5
						Inventory	24.1	31.1
						All Other Current	1.7	2.1
						Total Current	56.6	63.4
						Fixed Assets (net)	33.6	25.4
						Intangibles (net)	4.6	5.2
						All Other Non-Current	5.2	5.9
						Total	100.0	100.0
						LIABILITIES		
						Notes Payable-Short Term	12.6	10.1
						Cur. Mat.-L.T.D.	5.5	3.7
						Trade Payables	13.2	13.2
						Income Taxes Payable	.5	.7
						All Other Current	10.7	10.1
						Total Current	42.6	37.9
						Long-Term Debt	15.8	13.6
						Deferred Taxes	1.6	.5
						All Other Non-Current	1.9	4.2
						Net Worth	38.2	43.8
						Total Liabilities & Net Worth	100.0	100.0
						INCOME DATA		
						Net Sales	100.0	100.0
						Gross Profit	40.8	37.9
						Operating Expenses	37.6	33.7
						Operating Profit	3.2	4.2
						All Other Expenses (net)	1.6	.8
						Profit Before Taxes	1.6	3.3
						RATIOS		
						Current	2.0	3.0
							1.3	1.7
							.8	1.1
						Quick	1.0	1.3
							.6	.8
							.4	.5
						Sales/Receivables	28 12.8	24 14.9
							45 8.1	42 8.8
							59 6.1	58 6.3
						Cost of Sales/Inventory	34 10.7	44 8.2
							68 5.4	78 4.7
							111 3.3	137 2.7
						Cost of Sales/Payables	21 17.7	22 16.4
							38 9.5	27 13.7
							59 6.2	51 7.1
						Sales/Working Capital	7.3	4.3
							16.0	9.1
							-20.5	47.3
						EBIT/Interest	9.6	12.2
							(31) 3.1	(26) 5.4
							.8	2.0
						Net Profit + Depr., Dep., Amort./Cur. Mat. L/T/D	4.0	3.9
							(11) 1.8	(11) 1.5
							.4	.2
						Fixed/Worth	.5	.3
							.9	.6
							2.6	1.5
						Debt/Worth	.9	.9
							1.7	1.5
							5.5	4.4
						% Profit Before Taxes/Tangible Net Worth	32.0	38.9
							(30) 11.7	(27) 10.0
							.4	2.7
						% Profit Before Taxes/Total Assets	11.9	10.6
							3.1	4.2
							-.4	1.4
						Sales/Net Fixed Assets	19.4	23.4
							8.7	9.1
							2.9	3.5
						Sales/Total Assets	2.8	3.2
							1.9	2.0
							1.4	1.2
						% Depr., Dep., Amort./Sales	1.4	1.3
							(27) 3.6	(27) 2.6
							5.4	4.7
						% Officers', Directors' Owners' Comp/Sales		
2154M	799M	94560M	212818M	500337M	119598M	Net Sales ($)	905935M	866760M
649M	634M	41820M	120237M	263352M	238649M	Total Assets ($)	678305M	628776M

Comparative Historical Data   Current Data Sorted by Sales

			Type of Statement						
6	11	5	Unqualified				3		2
9	7	5	Reviewed		1		1		2
1	1	1	Compiled						
2	1	3	Tax Returns	1			1		
11	11	11	Other	1			5		5
4/1/04- 3/31/05 ALL	4/1/05- 3/31/06 ALL	4/1/06- 3/31/07 ALL		0-1MM	5 (4/1-9/30/06) 1-3MM	3-5MM	20 (10/1/06-3/31/07) 5-10MM	10-25MM	25MM & OVER
29	30	25	NUMBER OF STATEMENTS	3	1		2	10	9
%	%	%	ASSETS	%	%	%	%	%	%
7.5	9.0	11.1	Cash & Equivalents					15.6	
23.5	21.7	22.7	Trade Receivables (net)			D		18.9	
28.0	28.9	24.8	Inventory			A		26.0	
1.0	3.9	4.0	All Other Current			T		1.1	
60.0	63.5	62.5	Total Current			A		61.6	
29.3	24.4	21.7	Fixed Assets (net)					25.2	
4.7	5.6	8.4	Intangibles (net)			N		2.9	
6.0	6.6	7.3	All Other Non-Current			O		10.3	
100.0	100.0	100.0	Total			T		100.0	
			LIABILITIES			A			
13.0	9.7	12.5	Notes Payable-Short Term			V		2.8	
5.7	5.9	6.3	Cur. Mat.-L.T.D.			A		1.9	
13.1	11.9	17.5	Trade Payables			I		13.4	
.6	.5	.5	Income Taxes Payable			L		1.0	
12.8	9.1	6.5	All Other Current			A		4.8	
45.1	37.1	43.3	Total Current			B		23.8	
17.9	23.2	27.1	Long-Term Debt			L		17.9	
.5	.5	.5	Deferred Taxes			E		.9	
1.4	3.3	7.3	All Other Non-Current					9.0	
35.2	35.9	21.8	Net Worth					48.3	
100.0	100.0	100.0	Total Liabilities & Net Worth					100.0	
			INCOME DATA						
100.0	100.0	100.0	Net Sales					100.0	
36.6	37.6	36.1	Gross Profit					38.7	
30.7	30.4	32.1	Operating Expenses					33.6	
5.8	7.1	4.0	Operating Profit					5.2	
1.6	2.4	1.7	All Other Expenses (net)					1.0	
4.3	4.7	2.3	Profit Before Taxes					4.2	
			RATIOS						
3.0	2.9	3.7						5.1	
1.6	2.1	2.1	Current					3.1	
1.0	1.2	1.0						1.6	
1.6	1.8	2.1						2.9	
.7	.9	.8	Quick					1.5	
.4	.5	.5						.7	
31 11.7	31 11.8	30 12.2						36 10.2	
41 9.0	42 8.6	42 8.7	Sales/Receivables					45 8.1	
53 6.9	59 6.1	65 5.7						69 5.3	
39 9.3	46 8.0	43 8.5						49 7.5	
80 4.6	94 3.9	78 4.7	Cost of Sales/Inventory					92 4.0	
109 3.3	143 2.5	121 3.0						147 2.5	
17 21.1	20 18.6	18 19.9						30 12.3	
25 14.5	36 10.2	37 9.9	Cost of Sales/Payables					45 8.1	
45 8.1	45 8.0	57 6.4						68 5.4	
4.3	3.1	3.2						2.5	
8.4	6.6	8.0	Sales/Working Capital					3.9	
NM	28.6	NM						18.2	
12.0	8.2	7.9							
(27) 3.8	(28) 5.2	(24) 3.1	EBIT/Interest						
.7	1.7	1.4							
6.3	7.9		Net Profit + Depr., Dep., Amort./Cur. Mat. L/T/D						
(11) 4.0	(11) 1.9								
1.3	1.1								
.3	.3	.2						.1	
.8	.6	.7	Fixed/Worth					.7	
2.3	NM	NM						4.9	
.5	.5	.7						.4	
1.2	1.9	2.4	Debt/Worth					1.0	
6.0	NM	-27.7						9.6	
32.9	30.9	39.9							
(25) 11.9	(23) 18.1	(18) 15.3	% Profit Before Taxes/Tangible Net Worth						
.4	4.5	3.5							
15.3	15.7	13.4						10.9	
8.8	9.3	6.8	% Profit Before Taxes/Total Assets					6.9	
.1	2.2	.9						1.2	
21.2	20.2	40.7						41.9	
7.8	8.8	8.9	Sales/Net Fixed Assets					5.9	
3.9	3.9	4.1						3.5	
2.8	2.5	2.6						1.9	
2.0	1.8	1.9	Sales/Total Assets					1.7	
1.3	1.3	1.2						1.1	
1.4	1.3	.7							
(25) 2.3	(27) 3.2	(21) 1.6	% Depr., Dep., Amort./Sales						
5.1	4.7	5.0							
			% Officers', Directors' Owners' Comp/Sales						
996679M	1639850M	930266M	Net Sales ($)	1931M	1022M		14638M	158226M	754449M
637198M	1186831M	665341M	Total Assets ($)	911M	372M		7780M	107164M	549114M

M = $ thousand   MM = $ million
See Pages 11 through 21 for Explanation of Ratios and Data

Current Data Sorted by Assets   **Comparative Historical Data**

	0-500M	500M-2MM	2-10MM	10-50MM	50-100MM	100-250MM	Type of Statement	4/1/02-3/31/03 ALL	4/1/03-3/31/04 ALL
		2	9	11	6	5	Unqualified	43	32
		5	32	8	1		Reviewed	24	33
	5	18	20	2			Compiled	18	28
	9	10	3				Tax Returns	7	12
	3	11	18	22	4	4	Other	40	42
		37 (4/1-9/30/06)		171 (10/1/06-3/31/07)					
NUMBER OF STATEMENTS	17	46	82	43	11	9		132	147
	%	%	%	%	%	%	**ASSETS**	%	%
	13.1	8.4	8.3	6.6	2.7		Cash & Equivalents	6.4	8.0
	33.6	29.6	29.2	30.7	19.7		Trade Receivables (net)	27.6	28.3
	20.2	31.3	29.6	27.7	25.0		Inventory	29.4	27.8
	.3	1.3	4.3	3.4	1.5		All Other Current	2.9	3.2
	67.0	70.7	71.4	68.4	48.9		Total Current	66.2	67.4
	14.3	18.1	18.3	17.9	17.6		Fixed Assets (net)	22.0	20.9
	6.9	4.5	3.4	6.7	20.1		Intangibles (net)	5.5	5.1
	11.8	6.7	6.9	7.0	13.4		All Other Non-Current	6.2	6.7
	100.0	100.0	100.0	100.0	100.0		Total	100.0	100.0
							LIABILITIES		
	10.7	15.1	12.4	9.8	11.7		Notes Payable-Short Term	13.3	13.6
	10.0	4.9	3.0	2.3	3.6		Cur. Mat.-L.T.D.	7.3	4.1
	18.6	13.8	15.0	14.1	10.1		Trade Payables	13.4	15.5
	.3	.1	.4	.3	.7		Income Taxes Payable	.7	.1
	18.9	14.3	13.9	17.7	10.4		All Other Current	12.0	11.0
	58.5	48.3	44.7	44.2	36.4		Total Current	46.7	44.3
	12.2	21.1	10.0	10.1	23.2		Long-Term Debt	15.6	11.9
	.0	.3	.4	.2	3.3		Deferred Taxes	.2	.3
	19.0	5.3	4.5	2.4	4.0		All Other Non-Current	10.3	9.9
	10.3	25.0	40.4	43.1	33.0		Net Worth	27.2	33.5
	100.0	100.0	100.0	100.0	100.0		Total Liabilties & Net Worth	100.0	100.0
							INCOME DATA		
	100.0	100.0	100.0	100.0	100.0		Net Sales	100.0	100.0
	39.1	35.5	32.0	29.8	30.5		Gross Profit	35.0	33.9
	30.4	31.0	26.4	22.6	21.3		Operating Expenses	32.6	30.3
	8.7	4.4	5.7	7.3	9.2		Operating Profit	2.4	3.6
	1.9	1.7	.8	1.0	2.1		All Other Expenses (net)	1.5	.9
	6.8	2.7	4.9	6.3	7.1		Profit Before Taxes	.9	2.7
							RATIOS		
	3.6	2.6	2.4	2.3	2.0		Current	2.4	2.6
	1.3	1.5	1.7	1.6	1.2			1.7	1.6
	.9	1.0	1.3	1.2	1.0			1.2	1.1
	2.6	1.6	1.3	1.3	.8		Quick	1.4	1.3
	1.0	.7	.9	(42) .9	.5			.8	.9
	.5	.4	.5	.6	.3			.5	.5
	17 21.7	25 14.8	30 12.3	31 11.7	35 10.4		Sales/Receivables	34 10.8	32 11.6
	34 10.7	37 10.0	45 8.1	50 7.2	47 7.8			47 7.7	45 8.1
	40 9.1	57 6.4	65 5.6	70 5.2	56 6.6			64 5.7	61 6.0
	4 86.9	28 13.0	26 13.9	39 9.4	39 9.3		Cost of Sales/Inventory	46 7.9	36 10.2
	20 18.4	53 6.9	74 4.9	61 6.0	80 4.6			74 4.9	63 5.8
	68 5.4	94 3.9	127 2.9	91 4.0	156 2.3			116 3.1	108 3.4
	6 57.0	17 21.6	17 21.3	18 20.1	21 17.7		Cost of Sales/Payables	19 19.1	19 19.3
	26 13.9	24 15.2	30 12.0	32 11.4	28 12.8			34 10.7	33 11.0
	47 7.8	45 8.2	48 7.6	45 8.1	36 10.2			56 6.6	51 7.1
	5.2	5.8	4.6	5.4	5.0		Sales/Working Capital	4.5	4.9
	30.7	10.2	7.9	8.8	12.3			8.1	9.0
	-208.0	-106.6	14.8	16.8	-999.8			20.8	32.7
	26.3	7.4	16.9	20.2			EBIT/Interest	5.4	9.6
	(15) 7.0	(37) 2.8	(72) 5.3	(37) 6.8				(120) 2.4	(134) 3.1
	1.7	1.3	2.2	2.6				.5	1.0
			27.5	12.8			Net Profit + Depr., Dep., Amort./Cur. Mat. L/T/D	4.0	4.4
		(21) 2.2	(17) 6.3					(43) 1.8	(46) 1.9
			1.0	2.2				1.1	.6
	.2	.2	.2	.2	.7		Fixed/Worth	.3	.3
	.6	.5	.4	.4	1.1			.7	.6
	-1.4	NM	1.0	1.1	-.6			2.6	1.7
	1.3	.8	.7	.7	1.8		Debt/Worth	.9	.8
	3.8	2.1	1.5	1.4	5.3			2.1	1.9
	-10.3	-19.9	4.1	3.8	-5.1			9.2	7.3
	136.0	72.1	52.9	68.8			% Profit Before Taxes/Tangible Net Worth	30.4	38.4
	(11) 41.6	(34) 18.4	(77) 23.0	(40) 36.4				(115) 12.4	(129) 14.1
	12.5	3.3	5.7	18.4				-.6	2.0
	41.5	18.4	19.8	23.2	12.8		% Profit Before Taxes/Total Assets	8.8	12.0
	16.8	5.0	7.8	10.2	7.3			3.9	6.0
	4.7	.2	2.2	4.5	3.6			-1.4	.2
	97.4	83.0	32.3	24.3	28.4		Sales/Net Fixed Assets	28.8	33.6
	31.7	20.3	16.5	14.4	7.6			12.3	14.4
	14.0	7.5	6.2	7.0	5.5			5.5	6.9
	5.0	3.1	2.7	2.7	2.2		Sales/Total Assets	2.6	3.1
	3.8	2.6	2.1	2.0	1.5			2.0	2.2
	2.6	2.1	1.6	1.6	.7			1.5	1.6
	.3	.4	.7	.8			% Depr., Dep., Amort./Sales	1.0	.9
	(10) 1.0	(37) 1.2	(77) 1.3	(36) 1.7				(117) 1.8	(128) 1.8
	2.6	2.4	2.9	2.3				3.4	3.1
		4.6	2.4				% Officers', Directors' Owners' Comp/Sales	1.5	3.3
		(27) 5.6	(31) 3.9					(37) 3.1	(51) 5.2
		10.9	5.1					6.6	10.2
	21239M	136033M	840888M	2062477M	1041002M	2294522M	Net Sales ($)	4458459M	4714291M
	5160M	50789M	395204M	974624M	686959M	1388376M	Total Assets ($)	2714591M	2560812M

© RMA 2007

M = $ thousand   MM = $ million
See Pages 11 through 21 for Explanation of Ratios and Data

Comparative Historical Data / Current Data Sorted by Sales

				Type of Statement						
36		32	33	Unqualified		2	1	1	7	22
34		42	46	Reviewed		3	4	17	15	7
20		24	45	Compiled	5	9	14	11	6	
12		9	22	Tax Returns	3	12	3	1	3	
56		59	62	Other	4	5	7	8	13	25
4/1/04-3/31/05 ALL		4/1/05-3/31/06 ALL	4/1/06-3/31/07 ALL			37 (4/1-9/30/06)		171 (10/1/06-3/31/07)		
					0-1MM	1-3MM	3-5MM	5-10MM	10-25MM	25MM & OVER
158		166	208	NUMBER OF STATEMENTS	12	31	29	38	44	54
%		%	%	ASSETS	%	%	%	%	%	%
7.6		6.6	7.9	Cash & Equivalents	9.5	13.5	4.0	9.3	9.6	3.9
29.6		31.7	29.2	Trade Receivables (net)	21.7	33.3	27.8	27.2	31.2	29.0
27.1		27.4	28.2	Inventory	29.6	21.6	28.4	30.6	31.5	27.5
3.3		4.0	3.1	All Other Current	.1	.9	3.9	3.9	3.0	4.2
67.6		69.7	68.4	Total Current	60.8	69.3	64.1	70.9	75.3	64.6
20.6		18.5	18.1	Fixed Assets (net)	19.3	15.9	23.3	19.1	14.8	18.1
5.0		4.0	5.8	Intangibles (net)	13.9	3.4	6.5	2.6	3.5	9.3
6.7		7.7	7.7	All Other Non-Current	5.9	11.4	6.2	7.4	6.4	8.1
100.0		100.0	100.0	Total	100.0	100.0	100.0	100.0	100.0	100.0
				LIABILITIES						
16.0		12.5	11.9	Notes Payable-Short Term	8.1	17.0	13.1	10.1	12.7	9.6
3.6		2.7	3.9	Cur. Mat.-L.T.D.	11.8	4.0	6.7	2.4	2.5	2.6
16.4		16.0	14.4	Trade Payables	17.0	13.9	12.5	15.5	15.9	13.0
.3		.5	.3	Income Taxes Payable	.5	.0	.2	.5	.3	.4
11.3		13.2	15.0	All Other Current	12.0	18.1	11.6	13.3	14.8	17.0
47.5		44.7	45.4	Total Current	49.3	53.1	44.1	41.9	46.3	42.6
13.8		13.3	13.7	Long-Term Debt	29.4	14.1	20.8	10.3	8.9	12.6
.4		.3	.5	Deferred Taxes	.6	.2	.3	.4	.4	1.1
8.6		5.3	5.4	All Other Non-Current	24.1	7.5	6.5	3.9	1.8	3.7
29.7		36.3	34.9	Net Worth	-3.4	25.1	28.3	43.5	42.7	40.0
100.0		100.0	100.0	Total Liabilties & Net Worth	100.0	100.0	100.0	100.0	100.0	100.0
				INCOME DATA						
100.0		100.0	100.0	Net Sales	100.0	100.0	100.0	100.0	100.0	100.0
36.1		33.6	32.4	Gross Profit	42.8	39.4	28.3	32.7	31.2	29.1
31.8		29.1	26.2	Operating Expenses	34.6	33.2	26.0	27.4	24.1	21.4
4.3		4.5	6.2	Operating Profit	8.3	6.2	2.3	5.3	7.1	7.7
1.1		.9	1.2	All Other Expenses (net)	4.3	1.7	1.0	1.2	.3	1.1
3.2		3.6	5.0	Profit Before Taxes	4.0	4.5	1.2	4.2	6.8	6.6
				RATIOS						
2.3		2.3	2.4		2.8	3.2	2.5	2.9	2.1	2.3
1.5		1.5	1.7	Current	1.8	1.3	1.4	1.7	1.7	1.7
1.1		1.2	1.1		.8	.9	1.0	1.3	1.3	1.2
1.3		1.3	1.4		1.3	2.0	1.3	1.5	1.3	1.2
.9 (165)		.8 (207)	.8	Quick	.6	1.0	.7	.9	.8 (53)	.8
.5		.6	.5		.3	.6	.5	.5	.5	.5

35	10.6	34	10.7	29	12.5	Sales/Receivables	12	29.3	25	14.5	30	12.2	24 15.3 / 27 13.6 / 34 10.9
48	7.6	47	7.7	44	8.3		24	14.9	38	9.5	43	8.5	43 8.4 / 42 8.8 / 50 7.2
63	5.8	62	5.9	61	6.0		55	6.6	56	6.5	64	5.7	65 5.6 / 63 5.8 / 67 5.5
34	10.6	31	11.8	30	12.3	Cost of Sales/Inventory	0	UND	14	26.3	26	14.1	36 10.2 / 28 13.0 / 44 8.3
70	5.2	59	6.2	62	5.9		57	6.4	39	9.5	59	6.2	76 4.8 / 77 4.7 / 64 5.7
107	3.4	102	3.6	101	3.6		160	2.3	66	5.5	95	3.9	122 3.0 / 127 2.9 / 89 4.1
21	17.7	20	18.2	17	20.9	Cost of Sales/Payables	33	11.0	7	49.9	15	24.2	15 23.8 / 18 20.7 / 20 18.4
34	10.7	33	10.9	29	12.8		47	7.8	20	18.0	22	16.9	32 11.5 / 30 12.0 / 31 11.8
61	6.0	50	7.3	45	8.1		110	3.3	37	9.9	34	10.8	53 6.9 / 47 7.8 / 42 8.7

5.3		5.5	5.2	Sales/Working Capital	4.3	5.2	5.3	4.5	5.3	5.4
10.5		10.1	8.3		22.1	17.0	10.0	6.6	8.2	7.6
25.5		21.5	30.2		-33.6	-58.6	609.0	16.3	14.9	15.1
9.9		10.6	13.6	EBIT/Interest		15.8	5.9	9.0	23.1	11.8
4.2 (144)		3.8 (178)	4.7		(26) 3.8	(27) 2.8	(29) 2.7	(41) 7.0	(47) 6.4	
1.8		1.5	2.0		1.5	1.1	1.2	3.0.	2.7	
7.2		5.9	10.5	Net Profit + Depr., Dep., Amort./Cur. Mat. L/T/D				32.3		10.4
3.0 (50)		2.6 (42)	3.5 (57)			(10) 2.6		(26) 4.7		
1.3		1.1	1.2				1.1		1.9	
.2		.2	.2	Fixed/Worth	.4	.2	.2	.1	.2	.2
.6		.4	.5		NM	.4	.7	.4	.3	.5
2.2		1.3	1.5		-.3	6.4	NM	1.1	.7	1.1
1.0		.7	.8	Debt/Worth	2.4	.8	.8	.5	.8	.9
2.4		1.8	1.8		NM	2.3	1.8	1.7	1.4	1.8
7.3		4.2	5.3		-3.7	-17.2	NM	4.0	3.9	4.4
46.5		44.3	58.1	% Profit Before Taxes/Tangible Net Worth		92.9	18.9	55.6	67.6	58.6
21.1 (132)		21.1 (146)	25.5 (177)		(23) 22.4	(22) 8.9	(36) 16.2	(43) 37.5	(47) 33.1	
10.0		6.3	8.0		7.6	2.4	2.7	14.9	19.5	
13.8		14.5	20.4	% Profit Before Taxes/Total Assets	41.7	27.2	8.2	18.9	25.4	20.4
7.6		6.8	7.9		10.8	6.2	4.5	4.7	11.4	9.9
1.8		1.4	3.2		-.3	.6	1.1	.6	7.0	4.6
31.5		43.1	36.5	Sales/Net Fixed Assets	86.1	81.8	47.1	54.6	33.2	25.3
16.0		17.2	16.2		20.2	25.6	7.3	15.2	20.5	13.9
5.7		7.3	6.9		8.5	9.3	5.2	5.6	10.1	6.5
2.8		3.0	3.0	Sales/Total Assets	3.8	3.8	2.8	2.7	3.2	2.7
2.1		2.2	2.2		2.1	2.6	2.2	2.0	2.3	1.9
1.6		1.7	1.7		1.4	2.1	1.2	1.5	1.8	1.6
1.0		.7	.7	% Depr., Dep., Amort./Sales		.7	.8	.7	.6	.8
1.9 (139)		1.4 (146)	1.4 (176)		(23) 1.2	(26) 1.9	(33) 1.9	(42) 1.1	(44) 1.5	
3.1		3.0	2.7			3.1	4.4	3.9	1.8	2.7
1.9		2.0	2.6	% Officers', Directors' Owners' Comp/Sales		4.9	3.8	2.4	1.2	
3.9 (58)		4.1 (48)	4.4 (77)		(18) 7.6	(15) 5.3	(17) 3.9	(16) 2.9		
7.0		10.5	7.6			14.3	10.9	6.1	4.2	
4439603M		6734458M	6396161M	Net Sales ($)	7855M	59805M	117600M	283130M	663710M	5264061M
2325168M		2621788M	3501112M	Total Assets ($)	4835M	22374M	68214M	174788M	303495M	2927406M

Current Data Sorted by Assets   Comparative Historical Data

Type of Statement

0-500M	500M-2MM	2-10MM	10-50MM	50-100MM	100-250MM	Type of Statement	4/1/02-3/31/03 ALL	4/1/03-3/31/04 ALL
	2	4	6	4		Unqualified	10	10
		5	1			Reviewed	16	9
	3	5	1			Compiled	10	13
	1	2				Tax Returns	4	2
	2	5	10	2	2	Other	12	17
	8 (4/1-9/30/06)		47 (10/1/06-3/31/07)					
	8	21	18	6	2	NUMBER OF STATEMENTS	52	51

Data for 0-500M and 500M-2MM size categories: DATA NOT AVAILABLE (percentage and ratio columns shown only for 2-10MM and 10-50MM).

2-10MM %	10-50MM %		ASSETS	%	%
9.1	12.2		Cash & Equivalents	9.1	10.1
29.5	25.3		Trade Receivables (net)	28.1	32.2
24.0	19.9		Inventory	20.9	21.5
7.4	6.9		All Other Current	4.8	5.4
70.0	64.3		Total Current	62.8	69.1
16.9	24.7		Fixed Assets (net)	27.2	21.6
9.0	5.8		Intangibles (net)	3.7	3.6
4.1	5.3		All Other Non-Current	6.3	5.7
100.0	100.0		Total	100.0	100.0
			LIABILITIES		
9.1	7.6		Notes Payable-Short Term	11.2	10.3
2.9	2.0		Cur. Mat.-L.T.D.	4.3	2.9
14.5	10.5		Trade Payables	15.8	18.0
.3	.6		Income Taxes Payable	.2	.3
11.8	14.8		All Other Current	16.9	11.8
38.7	35.4		Total Current	48.3	43.3
12.0	11.8		Long-Term Debt	11.0	9.2
.3	.4		Deferred Taxes	.3	.3
12.6	2.8		All Other Non-Current	5.5	9.9
36.4	49.5		Net Worth	35.0	37.4
100.0	100.0		Total Liabilities & Net Worth	100.0	100.0
			INCOME DATA		
100.0	100.0		Net Sales	100.0	100.0
33.2	27.9		Gross Profit	33.5	31.9
24.0	17.7		Operating Expenses	29.1	27.9
9.2	10.2		Operating Profit	4.4	3.9
1.3	.4		All Other Expenses (net)	.8	.6
7.9	9.8		Profit Before Taxes	3.6	3.3

RATIOS

2-10MM	10-50MM	Ratio	ALL '02-'03	ALL '03-'04
2.5	3.0	Current	2.3	2.7
1.8	1.7		1.5	1.7
1.3	1.3		1.0	1.1
1.5	1.8	Quick	1.6	1.7
.9	1.0		.9	1.1
.7	.6		.5	.6
39 9.4	31 11.8	Sales/Receivables	37 10.0	40 9.1
50 7.3	48 7.6		49 7.4	52 7.0
70 5.3	66 5.6		63 5.8	67 5.5
37 10.0	41 9.0	Cost of Sales/Inventory	25 14.5	33 11.1
52 7.0	52 7.0		49 7.5	56 6.5
103 3.5	73 5.0		90 4.1	84 4.4
15 24.3	11 32.3	Cost of Sales/Payables	17 21.7	17 21.1
33 11.1	27 13.5		30 12.2	33 11.0
51 7.1	46 7.9		46 7.9	51 7.1
5.1	4.8	Sales/Working Capital	5.5	4.8
7.1	5.6		13.7	8.8
12.5	21.3		-151.1	39.5
51.3	14.7	EBIT/Interest	12.4	19.8
(19) 10.8	(12) 6.1		(45) 4.7	(45) 3.4
2.8	2.6		1.0	.6
		Net Profit + Depr., Dep., Amort./Cur. Mat. L/T/D	8.0	8.9
			(19) 4.6	(16) 2.1
			1.6	1.1
.2	.3	Fixed/Worth	.4	.3
.6	.6		.6	.7
NM	1.2		1.9	1.4
.8	.7	Debt/Worth	.6	.6
1.7	1.1		1.8	1.6
NM	2.3		8.1	5.7
67.4	62.0	% Profit Before Taxes/Tangible Net Worth	58.4	33.5
(16) 37.8	(17) 24.6		(44) 15.3	(44) 16.3
15.0	13.0		2.9	1.7
31.7	26.2	% Profit Before Taxes/Total Assets	13.8	15.2
11.6	11.2		7.8	4.4
3.8	5.3		.1	-.6
34.9	13.2	Sales/Net Fixed Assets	21.8	28.1
23.1	8.6		9.6	10.5
5.7	6.5		5.0	6.3
2.9	2.4	Sales/Total Assets	2.7	3.1
1.8	1.9		1.9	2.2
1.6	1.5		1.5	1.5
.6	1.3	% Depr., Dep., Amort./Sales	1.7	1.0
(19) 1.3	(15) 2.3		(47) 2.2	(44) 1.7
2.1	2.9		3.1	2.7
		% Officers', Directors' Owners' Comp/Sales	3.2	3.1
			(12) 5.7	(12) 6.0
			10.4	14.6

500M-2MM	2-10MM	10-50MM	50-100MM	100-250MM		ALL '02-'03	ALL '03-'04
26115M	226856M	877607M	763380M	641042M	Net Sales ($)	1288522M	1134938M
8934M	110953M	453840M	470326M	332890M	Total Assets ($)	644608M	654587M

M = $ thousand   MM = $ million
See Pages 11 through 21 for Explanation of Ratios and Data

Comparative Historical Data   Current Data Sorted by Sales

				Type of Statement	0-1MM	1-3MM	3-5MM	5-10MM	10-25MM	25MM & OVER
12		13	16	Unqualified			2	1	3	10
12		13	6	Reviewed				3	2	1
8		9	9	Compiled		2		4	2	1
4		4	3	Tax Returns	1					1
14		11	21	Other			2	4	5	11

4/1/04-3/31/05 ALL	4/1/05-3/31/06 ALL	4/1/06-3/31/07 ALL			8 (4/1-9/30/06)			47 (10/1/06-3/31/07)		
					0-1MM	1-3MM	3-5MM	5-10MM	10-25MM	25MM & OVER
50	50	55		NUMBER OF STATEMENTS	1	2	4	12	12	24
%	%	%		ASSETS	%	%	%	%	%	%
8.0	8.8	10.1		Cash & Equivalents				5.8	13.0	10.6
34.0	34.6	30.4		Trade Receivables (net)				29.7	25.7	30.8
19.1	20.5	21.1		Inventory				24.4	20.5	19.6
4.2	4.2	5.9		All Other Current				9.2	5.6	6.0
65.2	68.2	67.6		Total Current				69.1	64.8	67.0
22.0	22.2	20.8		Fixed Assets (net)				17.3	20.2	22.2
4.7	5.0	6.7		Intangibles (net)				10.3	9.4	4.8
8.0	4.6	4.9		All Other Non-Current				3.3	5.5	6.0
100.0	100.0	100.0		Total				100.0	100.0	100.0
				LIABILITIES						
11.6	11.5	7.5		Notes Payable-Short Term				10.6	8.0	6.2
3.3	2.5	2.0		Cur. Mat.-L.T.D.				3.5	2.3	1.6
15.9	16.0	14.7		Trade Payables				13.3	12.8	12.7
.4	.6	.5		Income Taxes Payable				.4	.2	.9
13.9	15.3	15.6		All Other Current				8.3	14.0	16.2
45.2	46.0	40.4		Total Current				36.1	37.3	37.7
11.4	15.2	12.4		Long-Term Debt				16.3	11.2	9.2
.7	.5	.4		Deferred Taxes				.2	.4	.6
4.9	7.1	8.2		All Other Non-Current				8.6	13.7	3.5
37.7	31.2	38.5		Net Worth				38.8	37.4	49.0
100.0	100.0	100.0		Total Liabilities & Net Worth				100.0	100.0	100.0
				INCOME DATA						
100.0	100.0	100.0		Net Sales				100.0	100.0	100.0
30.3	31.3	30.8		Gross Profit				39.1	31.1	26.9
24.6	26.1	22.1		Operating Expenses				28.9	21.1	18.2
5.6	5.2	8.7		Operating Profit				10.2	10.0	8.8
1.2	.5	.8		All Other Expenses (net)				1.7	.6	.5
4.4	4.7	7.9		Profit Before Taxes				8.4	9.4	8.3
				RATIOS						
2.3	2.7	2.5		Current				2.7	2.5	2.8
1.5	1.5	1.8						1.9	1.9	1.7
1.1	1.3	1.3						1.4	1.3	1.3
1.4	2.0	1.6		Quick				1.4	2.0	1.7
1.0	.9	1.0						.9	.9	1.0
.7	.7	.8						.7	.5	.8
44 8.3	49 7.5	40 9.2		Sales/Receivables			29 12.4	39 9.3	44 8.3	
58 6.3	60 6.1	54 6.8					45 8.1	50 7.4	64 5.7	
72 5.1	75 4.9	73 5.0					71 5.1	57 6.4	74 4.9	
24 15.1	26 14.1	34 10.6		Cost of Sales/Inventory			39 9.3	24 15.3	36 10.2	
46 7.9	50 7.3	52 7.0					51 7.2	57 6.4	52 7.0	
77 4.8	71 5.1	81 4.5					110 3.3	119 3.1	64 5.7	
22 16.7	24 15.4	21 17.8		Cost of Sales/Payables			12 31.2	23 15.8	21 17.6	
31 11.7	35 10.4	33 10.9					24 15.1	32 11.4	35 10.4	
49 7.5	50 7.3	49 7.4					52 7.0	44 8.3	47 7.8	
5.8	4.4	5.0		Sales/Working Capital				4.7	5.5	4.8
10.5	7.9	7.5						8.1	7.3	6.3
41.4	15.5	15.4						12.4	15.4	9.7
24.2	38.4	31.0		EBIT/Interest				27.7	30.0	41.2
(46) 4.1	(47) 9.2	(45) 8.8					(11) 14.9	(10) 5.9	(17) 12.7	
1.8	2.2	2.8						6.2	2.0	2.8
8.0	9.2	9.8		Net Profit + Depr., Dep.,						
(18) 4.6	(15) 4.8	(21) 3.7		Amort./Cur. Mat. L/T/D						
2.5	2.0	1.6								
.3	.3	.3		Fixed/Worth				.3	.3	.3
.6	.5	.5						.5	1.0	.5
1.6	2.5	1.2						.9	NM	.9
.8	.7	1.0		Debt/Worth				.6	1.0	.5
1.9	1.5	1.5						1.8	2.0	1.2
7.3	6.3	3.5						4.5	NM	1.9
55.4	47.0	58.0		% Profit Before Taxes/Tangible				131.6		56.6
(44) 21.3	(41) 17.5	(47) 34.4		Net Worth			(10) 50.5		(23) 26.2	
9.1	9.5	19.4						11.8		20.8
15.2	16.1	21.6		% Profit Before Taxes/Total				33.3	19.8	24.2
6.6	7.2	11.3		Assets				15.7	7.8	13.2
1.9	3.4	5.2						6.0	3.4	6.2
19.1	38.0	26.5		Sales/Net Fixed Assets				35.1	29.2	15.2
10.6	12.5	10.4						14.1	24.0	8.9
6.3	4.9	6.1						6.9	4.5	7.0
2.6	2.6	2.5		Sales/Total Assets				3.3	2.4	2.4
1.9	1.9	2.0						2.3	1.8	1.9
1.5	1.6	1.6						1.7	1.1	1.6
1.0	.7	.9		% Depr., Dep., Amort./Sales				.7	.3	1.2
(47) 1.9	(45) 1.4	(49) 1.5					(11) 1.5	(11) 1.4	(21) 1.8	
2.5	2.0	2.3						2.1	2.7	2.4
3.1	1.8			% Officers', Directors'						
(14) 3.8	(12) 5.5			Owners' Comp/Sales						
8.0	11.5									
1320623M	1642751M	2535000M		Net Sales ($)	953M	3084M	15463M	92410M	151170M	2271920M
800110M	978011M	1376943M		Total Assets ($)	1093M	1343M	5841M	46213M	96426M	1226027M

M = $ thousand   MM = $ million
See Pages 11 through 21 for Explanation of Ratios and Data

Current Data Sorted by Assets   Comparative Historical Data

						Type of Statement		
		9	14	4	3	Unqualified	22	27
	2	9	5			Reviewed	19	33
1	3	7	1			Compiled	10	18
1	3	1			1	Tax Returns	2	4
1	3	9	8	2	2	Other	18	21
	14 (4/1-9/30/06)		75 (10/1/06-3/31/07)				4/1/02-3/31/03	4/1/03-3/31/04
0-500M	500M-2MM	2-10MM	10-50MM	50-100MM	100-250MM		ALL	ALL
3	11	35	28	6	6	NUMBER OF STATEMENTS	71	103
%	%	%	%	%	%	ASSETS	%	%
	16.5	10.8	12.9			Cash & Equivalents	8.5	7.4
	40.5	25.5	28.7			Trade Receivables (net)	26.0	27.8
	31.3	35.5	29.0			Inventory	30.2	29.2
	.7	1.5	3.5			All Other Current	2.7	4.0
	89.0	73.3	74.0			Total Current	67.4	68.4
	7.2	19.6	16.5			Fixed Assets (net)	20.4	19.2
	2.9	1.8	4.1			Intangibles (net)	4.1	4.5
	.8	5.3	5.5			All Other Non-Current	8.2	7.9
	100.0	100.0	100.0			Total	100.0	100.0
						LIABILITIES		
	10.6	8.5	10.4			Notes Payable-Short Term	10.4	10.4
	1.9	3.1	2.2			Cur. Mat.-L.T.D.	3.2	4.2
	34.2	13.8	11.7			Trade Payables	13.0	14.7
	.0	.5	.4			Income Taxes Payable	.2	.2
	9.7	11.6	16.8			All Other Current	13.2	14.7
	56.4	37.5	41.5			Total Current	40.0	44.2
	5.7	12.3	6.4			Long-Term Debt	13.1	12.0
	.0	.5	.4			Deferred Taxes	.3	.4
	8.6	3.6	9.0			All Other Non-Current	6.4	7.3
	29.3	46.1	42.7			Net Worth	40.2	36.0
	100.0	100.0	100.0			Total Liabilities & Net Worth	100.0	100.0
						INCOME DATA		
	100.0	100.0	100.0			Net Sales	100.0	100.0
	32.6	30.2	30.0			Gross Profit	34.6	33.0
	31.5	22.8	25.2			Operating Expenses	30.6	29.0
	1.1	7.4	4.8			Operating Profit	4.1	4.0
	.8	1.0	1.0			All Other Expenses (net)	1.1	.7
	.3	6.4	3.8			Profit Before Taxes	3.0	3.3
						RATIOS		
	5.1	3.4	3.2				2.7	2.7
	2.1	2.1	1.9			Current	1.9	1.6
	.9	1.3	1.2				1.3	1.1
	4.4	1.9	1.6				1.4	1.4
	1.6	1.0	1.0			Quick	.8	.8
	.5	.5	.5				.6	.5
31	11.6 32	11.5 40	9.2				37 10.0	35 10.4
41	8.9 41	8.9 54	6.8			Sales/Receivables	51 7.1	50 7.2
50	7.3 58	6.3 70	5.2				61 6.0	64 5.7
22	16.2 35	10.4 48	7.6				47 7.8	47 7.8
51	7.1 78	4.7 90	4.0			Cost of Sales/Inventory	98 3.7	91 4.0
70	5.2 148	2.5 132	2.8				133 2.7	121 3.0
27	13.7 15	24.4 18	20.4				19 19.7	21 17.6
37	9.8 29	12.6 31	11.7			Cost of Sales/Payables	32 11.4	30 12.0
95	3.8 49	7.4 44	8.3				57 6.4	51 7.1
	4.0	3.7	4.3				4.1	4.6
	11.9	5.4	6.3			Sales/Working Capital	6.7	7.3
	-17.3	12.2	18.8				14.8	43.7
		12.7	15.9				7.0	12.5
	(26)	3.5 (25)	6.4			EBIT/Interest	(64) 2.8	(94) 4.9
		1.2	1.0				.6	1.2
			10.6			Net Profit + Depr., Dep.,	5.3	4.5
		(12)	3.0			Amort./Cur. Mat. L/T/D	(15) 3.3	(25) 1.7
			.9				1.5	1.0
	.1	.1	.2				.2	.2
	.1	.3	.5			Fixed/Worth	.6	.5
	-2.1	1.0	.9				1.7	1.4
	.2	.5	.8				.6	.7
	1.3	1.2	1.4			Debt/Worth	1.3	1.8
	-22.0	3.0	4.4				4.2	5.1
		58.6	48.4			% Profit Before Taxes/Tangible	34.8	41.5
	(33)	24.9 (26)	33.8			Net Worth	(61) 9.3	(91) 14.7
		5.8	7.4				.7	2.1
	44.7	21.9	23.5			% Profit Before Taxes/Total	12.1	12.5
	3.4	7.6	12.9			Assets	4.1	6.9
	-1.6	2.0	.8				-.7	.9
	179.3	36.4	35.3				24.3	28.6
	69.5	13.5	16.8			Sales/Net Fixed Assets	9.1	11.4
	28.5	5.1	7.5				5.7	5.5
	4.3	2.7	2.5				2.3	2.7
	3.5	1.9	2.1			Sales/Total Assets	1.7	2.0
	2.8	1.6	1.5				1.4	1.4
		.5	.7				1.3	1.1
	(29)	1.2 (25)	1.3			% Depr., Dep., Amort./Sales	(62) 2.0	(86) 1.8
		1.8	2.0				3.3	2.7
		1.7				% Officers', Directors'	2.6	2.1
	(13)	3.0				Owners' Comp/Sales	(20) 3.5	(33) 3.1
		10.8					8.0	4.9
2694M	45064M	385801M	1343034M	570406M	1269267M	Net Sales ($)	1653789M	2312796M
932M	12268M	176142M	694540M	404814M	893669M	Total Assets ($)	992436M	1440613M

M = $ thousand   MM = $ million
See Pages 11 through 21 for Explanation of Ratios and Data

Comparative Historical Data | | | | **Current Data Sorted by Sales** | | | | | |

Historical	Historical	Historical	Type of Statement	0-1MM	1-3MM	3-5MM	5-10MM	10-25MM	25MM & OVER
21	25	30	Unqualified			2	2	7	19
26	17	16	Reviewed			1	5	5	5
8	7	12	Compiled		2	2	7	1	
7	6	6	Tax Returns	2	1	1		1	1
18	28	25	Other	1	1	3	5	4	11
4/1/04-3/31/05 ALL	4/1/05-3/31/06 ALL	4/1/06-3/31/07 ALL		14 (4/1-9/30/06)			75 (10/1/06-3/31/07)		
80	83	89	**NUMBER OF STATEMENTS**	3	4	9	19	18	36
%	%	%	**ASSETS**	%	%	%	%	%	%
10.2	9.1	11.9	Cash & Equivalents				12.9	13.7	10.0
29.3	29.0	26.9	Trade Receivables (net)				29.7	26.4	25.4
28.3	32.2	31.1	Inventory				29.4	30.2	30.6
3.6	1.9	3.6	All Other Current				1.0	2.2	3.1
71.4	72.2	73.5	Total Current				73.0	72.5	69.1
19.1	19.2	16.2	Fixed Assets (net)				23.6	15.2	17.0
3.3	3.1	4.4	Intangibles (net)				.3	5.3	7.2
6.2	5.5	5.8	All Other Non-Current				3.1	7.1	6.7
100.0	100.0	100.0	Total				100.0	100.0	100.0
			LIABILITIES						
8.8	8.8	9.7	Notes Payable-Short Term				7.2	8.8	9.2
4.2	2.6	2.6	Cur. Mat.-L.T.D.				2.4	2.1	2.2
15.3	16.6	15.7	Trade Payables				18.2	12.0	12.6
.2	.3	.4	Income Taxes Payable				.0	1.0	.4
14.1	13.6	12.3	All Other Current				12.6	11.1	13.9
42.6	41.9	40.7	Total Current				40.3	34.9	38.4
12.4	14.0	11.0	Long-Term Debt				13.9	9.8	10.8
.3	.2	.4	Deferred Taxes				.8	.2	.6
5.8	6.9	8.0	All Other Non-Current				2.8	3.8	11.9
39.0	37.0	39.9	Net Worth				42.0	51.4	38.4
100.0	100.0	100.0	Total Liabilities & Net Worth				100.0	100.0	100.0
			INCOME DATA						
100.0	100.0	100.0	Net Sales				100.0	100.0	100.0
30.8	31.4	30.6	Gross Profit				29.0	31.3	29.5
26.4	25.3	25.3	Operating Expenses				23.5	20.7	23.6
4.4	6.1	5.3	Operating Profit				5.4	10.5	5.9
1.2	1.6	1.2	All Other Expenses (net)				.6	.8	1.4
3.2	4.5	4.2	Profit Before Taxes				4.9	9.7	4.5
			RATIOS						
2.9	3.1	3.2	Current				2.9	4.7	3.1
1.8	1.8	1.9					2.1	2.4	1.9
1.2	1.2	1.3					1.2	1.3	1.3
1.5	1.7	1.8	Quick				1.7	2.5	1.4
1.0	.9	.9					1.1	1.3	.8
.6	.6	.5					.6	.6	.5
32 11.4	35 10.5	36 10.1	Sales/Receivables				24 15.2	35 10.3	37 9.9
49 7.4	48 7.5	44 8.4					42 8.8	46 7.9	44 8.3
68 5.4	68 5.3	60 6.1					49 7.5	70 5.2	59 6.2
34 10.7	53 6.9	39 9.4	Cost of Sales/Inventory				28 12.8	30 12.3	51 7.1
68 5.4	79 4.6	77 4.7					65 5.6	88 4.1	83 4.4
106 3.5	116 3.2	130 2.8					104 3.5	139 2.6	119 3.1
14 25.2	21 17.2	18 20.3	Cost of Sales/Payables				17 20.9	14 25.3	21 17.1
31 11.9	34 10.7	33 10.9					32 11.2	22 16.8	32 11.5
50 7.3	59 6.2	49 7.4					47 7.8	50 7.2	44 8.2
4.7	4.0	4.1	Sales/Working Capital				5.4	3.7	4.7
8.2	7.0	6.4					8.9	5.1	6.4
23.2	20.9	15.2					21.1	12.7	16.6
14.2	10.9	13.0	EBIT/Interest				27.0	10.7	18.9
(72) 3.6	(71) 3.1	(73) 4.5			(15) 4.9	(11) 6.4	(33) 6.0
1.0	1.1	.8					2.0	2.4	.8
4.6	4.0	6.7	Net Profit + Depr., Dep., Amort./Cur. Mat. L/T/D						11.6
(28) 2.3	(27) 2.6	(27) 2.3						(16) 2.6
.7	1.2	.7							.6
.2	.2	.1	Fixed/Worth				.1	.1	.2
.6	.6	.3					.4	.3	.5
1.1	1.3	1.4					1.7	.9	1.6
.7	.6	.7	Debt/Worth				.7	.4	.8
1.6	1.6	1.5					1.3	.9	1.5
5.1	4.8	5.1					7.6	3.8	5.8
40.1	53.4	54.6	% Profit Before Taxes/Tangible Net Worth				67.0	60.9	51.4
(74) 13.5	(72) 20.3	(78) 29.3			(18) 26.1	(17) 31.4	(30) 31.4
1.9	4.8	5.6					4.5	15.9	-1.5
13.6	18.5	21.3	% Profit Before Taxes/Total Assets				20.7	28.1	22.4
5.4	6.7	7.6					7.6	14.2	9.8
.2	.5	1.0					2.2	3.8	-.4
44.6	28.6	46.7	Sales/Net Fixed Assets				69.5	39.9	35.3
13.8	13.3	17.2					15.9	14.1	14.1
6.1	6.0	6.2					4.6	10.0	6.0
2.9	2.8	2.8	Sales/Total Assets				3.2	2.3	2.5
2.2	2.1	2.1					2.4	1.9	2.1
1.6	1.5	1.5					1.7	1.6	1.4
1.1	.7	.6	% Depr., Dep., Amort./Sales				.4	.5	.7
(70) 1.6	(71) 1.4	(73) 1.2			(14) 1.2	(14) .9	(33) 1.3
2.9	2.3	1.9					2.0	1.7	2.2
1.9	1.3	1.8	% Officers', Directors' Owners' Comp/Sales						
(27) 3.6	(16) 2.8	(22) 6.7							
9.2	6.0	13.5							
2446082M	3314532M	3616266M	Net Sales ($)	2176M	7784M	35642M	133815M	296789M	3140060M
1382468M	1912582M	2182365M	Total Assets ($)	1112M	5620M	33396M	59336M	165815M	1917086M

M = $ thousand   MM = $ million
See Pages 11 through 21 for Explanation of Ratios and Data

Current Data Sorted by Assets   Comparative Historical Data

0-500M	500M-2MM	2-10MM	10-50MM	50-100MM	100-250MM	Type of Statement	4/1/02-3/31/03 ALL	4/1/03-3/31/04 ALL
		10	22	5	6	Unqualified	27	34
	2	15	4			Reviewed	15	14
1	6	7	1	1		Compiled	15	20
1	5	3				Tax Returns	4	11
1	7	10	9	2	3	Other	28	32
	15 (4/1-9/30/06)		106 (10/1/06-3/31/07)					
0-500M	500M-2MM	2-10MM	10-50MM	50-100MM	100-250MM		ALL	ALL
3	20	45	36	8	9	**NUMBER OF STATEMENTS**	89	111
%	%	%	%	%	%	**ASSETS**	%	%
	13.7	8.0	8.7			Cash & Equivalents	9.6	8.6
	34.4	37.1	27.7			Trade Receivables (net)	28.4	29.0
	28.6	25.8	26.5			Inventory	26.7	26.7
	2.4	3.7	2.8			All Other Current	3.1	5.4
	79.1	74.6	65.7			Total Current	67.8	69.6
	11.8	20.5	20.4			Fixed Assets (net)	20.7	19.8
	5.8	2.2	6.4			Intangibles (net)	4.9	4.4
	3.4	2.7	7.4			All Other Non-Current	6.6	6.2
	100.0	100.0	100.0			Total	100.0	100.0
						LIABILITIES		
	12.0	12.9	9.0			Notes Payable-Short Term	8.1	10.3
	1.5	2.5	2.3			Cur. Mat.-L.T.D.	2.9	3.3
	21.8	21.8	11.7			Trade Payables	15.8	17.9
	.9	.9	.3			Income Taxes Payable	.7	.4
	11.5	15.7	13.7			All Other Current	18.1	13.4
	47.6	53.7	37.0			Total Current	45.5	45.3
	19.2	12.1	10.3			Long-Term Debt	13.1	12.2
	.0	.4	.4			Deferred Taxes	.5	.7
	9.3	2.5	6.6			All Other Non-Current	7.7	7.5
	23.8	31.3	45.8			Net Worth	33.1	34.3
	100.0	100.0	100.0			Total Liabilities & Net Worth	100.0	100.0
						INCOME DATA		
	100.0	100.0	100.0			Net Sales	100.0	100.0
	33.0	26.2	29.0			Gross Profit	30.2	30.6
	29.1	21.1	22.3			Operating Expenses	25.8	25.4
	3.9	5.1	6.7			Operating Profit	4.4	5.2
	.3	.6	1.1			All Other Expenses (net)	.9	.8
	3.6	4.6	5.6			Profit Before Taxes	3.5	4.4
						RATIOS		
	2.4	2.2	3.1			Current	3.2	2.5
	1.8	1.5	1.8				1.8	1.6
	1.3	1.1	1.2				1.2	1.2
	1.7	1.3	1.9			Quick	1.8	1.5
	1.3	.9	.9				1.0	.9
	.7	.6	.5				.6	.5
	26 14.1	31 11.7	38 9.6			Sales/Receivables	31 11.8	30 12.1
	40 9.2	46 7.9	49 7.5				44 8.4	43 8.4
	44 8.2	62 5.9	62 5.9				59 6.2	55 6.7
	13 27.9	19 18.8	36 10.1			Cost of Sales/Inventory	42 8.7	25 14.5
	41 8.9	52 7.0	66 5.5				59 6.2	55 6.7
	77 4.7	66 5.5	114 3.2				92 3.9	99 3.7
	17 20.9	18 19.9	15 24.6			Cost of Sales/Payables	18 20.0	20 18.4
	32 11.3	33 11.0	29 12.5				29 12.5	32 11.5
	47 7.7	56 6.5	42 8.7				43 8.5	54 6.8
	6.5	7.1	3.8			Sales/Working Capital	4.4	4.4
	9.5	13.5	7.0				8.1	9.3
	24.1	49.1	19.8				20.6	26.5
	11.6	12.6	17.6			EBIT/Interest	12.4	13.3
	(17) 2.9	(41) 6.6	(31) 5.9				(73) 4.0	(97) 5.4
	1.3	2.8	1.8				1.5	1.8
		6.4	64.7			Net Profit + Depr., Dep., Amort./Cur. Mat. L/T/D	13.7	17.8
		(11) 2.5	(17) 9.1				(30) 3.5	(30) 5.4
		1.2	3.8				2.1	2.5
	.1	.2	.2			Fixed/Worth	.2	.3
	.4	.5	.4				.5	.6
	-.5	1.4	1.1				2.3	3.7
	.9	.9	.6			Debt/Worth	.7	.6
	2.2	2.1	1.4				1.8	2.0
	-6.7	5.6	3.6				5.7	9.8
	55.4	68.4	52.2			% Profit Before Taxes/Tangible Net Worth	52.5	51.7
	(13) 24.0	(40) 36.0	(33) 24.0				(74) 20.8	(90) 18.7
	17.5	16.6	14.5				3.4	6.6
	18.4	22.2	18.5			% Profit Before Taxes/Total Assets	17.3	14.8
	6.9	9.8	10.7				6.6	6.5
	2.0	3.1	3.8				1.1	2.1
	62.3	46.9	21.8			Sales/Net Fixed Assets	28.5	44.5
	39.9	18.8	12.2				12.3	15.5
	24.9	8.5	5.5				6.7	7.3
	4.1	3.6	2.7			Sales/Total Assets	2.9	3.3
	3.6	2.7	1.9				2.1	2.3
	3.0	2.1	1.4				1.7	1.5
	.4	.4	.7			% Depr., Dep., Amort./Sales	.8	.8
	(17) .7	(41) 1.1	(34) 1.4				(75) 1.5	(98) 1.6
	1.5	1.8	2.2				2.4	2.8
	2.1	.6				% Officers', Directors' Owners' Comp/Sales	2.2	2.4
	(10) 4.0	(12) 1.2					(22) 3.5	(34) 3.6
	4.6	2.0					7.3	7.7
4101M	86956M	594847M	1664200M	692678M	2240446M	Net Sales ($)	3537965M	3135489M
944M	24825M	205108M	832284M	540621M	1630360M	Total Assets ($)	1968623M	1549911M

M = $ thousand   MM = $ million
See Pages 11 through 21 for Explanation of Ratios and Data

Comparative Historical Data   Current Data Sorted by Sales

4/1/04-3/31/05 ALL	4/1/05-3/31/06 ALL	4/1/06-3/31/07 ALL	Type of Statement	0-1MM	1-3MM	3-5MM	5-10MM	10-25MM	25MM & OVER
34	31	43	Unqualified		1		3	11	28
29	22	21	Reviewed				4	14	3
6	11	16	Compiled		3	5	2	4	2
8	12	9	Tax Returns		3	2	4		
36	33	32	Other	2	1	1	12	4	12
					15 (4/1-9/30/06)			106 (10/1/06-3/31/07)	
113	109	121	NUMBER OF STATEMENTS	2	8	8	25	33	45
%	%	%	ASSETS	%	%	%	%	%	%
7.1	9.5	9.6	Cash & Equivalents				5.8	8.6	9.6
33.5	35.9	31.3	Trade Receivables (net)				37.9	34.5	26.4
24.8	22.6	25.6	Inventory				27.2	27.5	23.7
3.6	4.1	2.9	All Other Current				3.7	3.2	3.0
69.1	72.1	69.3	Total Current				74.5	73.7	62.7
18.2	17.8	19.0	Fixed Assets (net)				16.1	18.2	21.2
5.8	3.6	6.2	Intangibles (net)				6.5	3.8	8.5
7.0	6.4	5.5	All Other Non-Current				2.9	4.4	7.6
100.0	100.0	100.0	Total				100.0	100.0	100.0
			LIABILITIES						
10.3	11.9	10.7	Notes Payable-Short Term				13.5	11.0	7.6
3.7	3.6	2.2	Cur. Mat.-L.T.D.				3.0	2.4	1.9
17.3	20.5	17.2	Trade Payables				26.3	17.8	12.5
.4	.5	.6	Income Taxes Payable				.0	1.2	.4
14.5	14.6	13.4	All Other Current				15.1	14.7	13.1
46.2	51.0	44.2	Total Current				58.1	47.1	35.5
15.0	10.6	14.7	Long-Term Debt				21.6	8.2	13.0
.7	.6	.7	Deferred Taxes				.4	.7	1.2
5.4	5.0	6.0	All Other Non-Current				10.2	3.4	6.6
32.7	32.9	34.4	Net Worth				9.7	40.7	43.6
100.0	100.0	100.0	Total Liabilities & Net Worth				100.0	100.0	100.0
			INCOME DATA						
100.0	100.0	100.0	Net Sales				100.0	100.0	100.0
29.0	29.2	28.4	Gross Profit				29.6	27.4	26.7
24.1	24.0	22.8	Operating Expenses				27.2	21.7	19.7
4.9	5.2	5.6	Operating Profit				2.4	5.8	7.0
1.4	1.0	1.1	All Other Expenses (net)				.7	.4	1.9
3.6	4.2	4.4	Profit Before Taxes				1.7	5.3	5.1
			RATIOS						
2.2	2.3	2.4					2.0	2.5	2.8
1.5	1.5	1.6	Current				1.4	1.5	1.7
1.2	1.1	1.2					1.0	1.2	1.3
1.4	1.5	1.5					1.2	1.4	1.7
.9	1.0	1.0	Quick				.7	.9	1.0
.6	.6	.6					.5	.6	.6
37 9.7	36 10.0	34 10.9					38 9.7	36 10.2	34 10.7
49 7.5	49 7.4	45 8.1	Sales/Receivables				46 7.9	46 7.9	46 7.9
58 6.3	64 5.7	58 6.3					62 5.9	68 5.4	55 6.6
18 19.9	18 20.0	23 15.7					22 16.7	22 16.9	34 10.6
55 6.7	52 7.1	54 6.7	Cost of Sales/Inventory				54 6.7	56 6.6	60 6.1
90 4.1	73 5.0	91 4.0					92 4.0	100 3.7	92 4.0
19 19.3	21 17.5	17 21.1					32 11.5	16 22.9	15 25.1
31 11.9	35 10.5	31 11.9	Cost of Sales/Payables				43 8.6	26 13.9	28 13.0
46 8.0	53 6.8	46 7.9					79 4.6	48 7.7	38 9.7
5.6	6.2	5.4					6.8	4.3	4.6
10.3	10.9	9.5	Sales/Working Capital				17.0	9.5	8.6
25.1	30.8	26.9					NM	30.1	14.6
16.9	11.2	13.9					9.6	13.9	26.2
(98) 4.5	(94) 4.6	(107) 5.4	EBIT/Interest				3.9	(29) 5.7	(39) 6.6
1.7	1.8	1.8					1.1	2.8	1.9
6.9	12.0	11.7	Net Profit + Depr., Dep.,					9.2	31.2
(35) 2.3	(26) 3.7	(45) 4.6	Amort./Cur. Mat. L/T/D					(10) 2.9	(26) 8.1
.9	.8	1.4						.3.	2.0
.2	.2	.2					.2	.2	.2
.6	.5	.5	Fixed/Worth				1.3	.3	.5
1.8	1.5	1.8					-1.1	1.0	1.4
1.0	.8	.8					1.7	.8	.5
2.1	1.8	1.8	Debt/Worth				5.0	2.0	1.3
8.9	5.7	6.8					-4.4	3.9	3.5
47.7	47.7	60.5	% Profit Before Taxes/Tangible				63.8	67.0	45.7
(92) 18.9	(94) 20.9	(99) 31.5	Net Worth			(16) 35.6		(31) 39.0	(38) 29.1
8.3	8.4	16.0					23.7	15.8	12.7
13.1	15.7	19.5	% Profit Before Taxes/Total				18.0	21.8	18.8
6.0	7.2	9.1	Assets				6.0	9.0	11.2
1.5	2.8	2.9					-.6	3.2	3.9
42.6	46.6	41.6					52.4	46.9	23.0
17.7	17.5	15.2	Sales/Net Fixed Assets				33.1	18.8	9.6
7.0	8.9	7.1					10.0	9.1	5.6
3.3	3.3	3.4					3.6	3.6	2.7
2.4	2.5	2.4	Sales/Total Assets				2.9	2.3	2.0
1.7	1.8	1.6					2.3	1.6	1.4
.9	.6	.5					.2	.5	1.0
(94) 1.5	(90) 1.3	(112) 1.3	% Depr., Dep., Amort./Sales			(21) .7		(31) 1.0	(44) 1.5
2.9	1.8	2.2					1.5	2.2	2.3
1.6	1.5	.8	% Officers', Directors'				.9		
(28) 3.3	(31) 3.3	(31) 2.1	Owners' Comp/Sales				(12) 2.0		
6.9	6.2	4.5					4.8		
3743118M	4202040M	5283228M	Net Sales ($)	1288M	15611M	32784M	174937M	535775M	4522833M
2078722M	1946728M	3234142M	Total Assets ($)	1612M	6531M	11771M	144399M	260087M	2809742M

M = $ thousand   MM = $ million
See Pages 11 through 21 for Explanation of Ratios and Data

Current Data Sorted by Assets   Comparative Historical Data

Type of Statement

0-500M	500M-2MM	2-10MM	10-50MM	50-100MM	100-250MM		4/1/02-3/31/03 ALL	4/1/03-3/31/04 ALL
	1	4	9	1	1	Unqualified	3	4
1	8	34	8			Reviewed	15	10
2	13	10	1			Compiled	12	15
5	11	2				Tax Returns	3	11
4	18	20	11	1	1	Other	11	12
	42 (4/1-9/30/06)		124 (10/1/06-3/31/07)					
12	51	70	29	2	2	NUMBER OF STATEMENTS	44	52

0-500M %	500M-2MM %	2-10MM %	10-50MM %	50-100MM %	100-250MM %		%	%
						ASSETS		
18.2	10.6	6.3	3.8			Cash & Equivalents	5.3	6.9
31.8	29.9	27.2	26.2			Trade Receivables (net)	24.9	24.7
15.5	17.5	19.3	11.6			Inventory	11.6	11.1
1.7	1.2	4.3	7.6			All Other Current	3.8	2.0
67.2	59.2	57.2	49.2			Total Current	45.7	44.8
24.7	34.6	35.6	39.8			Fixed Assets (net)	47.2	45.9
2.1	2.3	2.6	4.5			Intangibles (net)	1.1	2.0
5.9	3.9	4.5	6.5			All Other Non-Current	6.0	7.3
100.0	100.0	100.0	100.0			Total	100.0	100.0
						LIABILITIES		
4.7	7.5	9.9	10.5			Notes Payable-Short Term	9.9	10.9
5.3	4.9	5.2	4.5			Cur. Mat.-L.T.D.	9.3	9.3
12.2	11.7	13.9	12.4			Trade Payables	7.1	9.1
.0	.5	.1	.0			Income Taxes Payable	.1	.1
17.5	11.8	11.3	10.6			All Other Current	7.8	6.7
39.7	36.5	40.4	38.1			Total Current	34.3	36.1
18.4	22.7	16.8	23.0			Long-Term Debt	20.7	26.3
.0	.2	1.2	1.3			Deferred Taxes	.7	1.5
16.4	4.0	5.6	5.1			All Other Non-Current	6.5	9.6
25.5	36.6	35.9	32.4			Net Worth	37.9	26.5
100.0	100.0	100.0	100.0			Total Liabilities & Net Worth	100.0	100.0
						INCOME DATA		
100.0	100.0	100.0	100.0			Net Sales	100.0	100.0
51.8	32.4	25.9	20.8			Gross Profit	26.9	34.1
45.2	28.6	20.7	14.7			Operating Expenses	26.9	32.5
6.6	3.8	5.2	6.2			Operating Profit	.0	1.6
1.0	.8	1.5	1.7			All Other Expenses (net)	1.9	2.3
5.6	3.0	3.7	4.4			Profit Before Taxes	-1.9	-.7
						RATIOS		
5.7	2.7	2.1	1.8			Current	1.8	2.1
2.4	1.5	1.5	1.3				1.3	1.3
1.2	1.1	1.1	1.0				1.0	.8
5.5	1.6	1.4	1.1			Quick	1.4	1.3
1.1	1.0	.8	.8				.9	.9
.8	.7	.6	.5				.6	.5
12 31.7	30 12.3	35 10.4	47 7.8			Sales/Receivables	34 10.8	37 9.8
37 9.8	42 8.6	49 7.4	60 6.0				53 6.8	48 7.7
52 7.0	55 6.6	64 5.7	77 4.7				71 5.2	58 6.3
6 62.9	17 21.6	18 20.2	16 22.6			Cost of Sales/Inventory	14 25.8	12 29.3
13 29.2	40 9.1	47 7.8	34 10.7				30 12.1	26 13.9
67 5.4	59 6.2	78 4.7	46 7.9				56 6.5	41 8.8
6 60.1	12 30.8	18 20.1	26 14.1			Cost of Sales/Payables	9 40.7	15 25.1
14 25.4	22 17.0	27 13.6	34 10.8				20 18.1	25 14.3
49 7.4	34 10.7	45 8.2	41 8.9				28 13.1	36 10.1
3.5	6.3	6.2	6.8			Sales/Working Capital	6.5	9.9
7.3	13.0	13.1	11.0				18.2	20.9
163.4	54.5	113.1	NM				471.3	-28.5
16.4	11.5	7.0	6.4			EBIT/Interest	3.1	2.9
7.7	(46) 3.1	(64) 2.3	(28) 2.6				(43) 1.1	(50) 1.5
-.5	.4	1.4	1.2				-.5	-.3
		3.9	2.2			Net Profit + Depr., Dep., Amort./Cur. Mat. L/T/D	1.9	1.7
	(20) 2.0	(13) 1.9					(16) 1.4	(13) 1.2
		1.4	1.1				.8	.7
.2	.4	.6	1.1			Fixed/Worth	.9	.9
.6	1.1	1.1	1.7				1.4	1.8
UND	2.2	2.3	2.6				1.9	5.7
1.0	.9	.8	1.3			Debt/Worth	.8	.9
1.3	2.2	1.8	3.7				1.8	2.8
UND	5.5	5.7	7.3				3.0	11.4
	42.1	38.8	41.6			% Profit Before Taxes/Tangible Net Worth	9.7	29.1
(47)	18.8	(63) 13.9	(28) 22.6				(41) 3.7	(45) 11.9
	-5.9	3.6	7.3				-19.7	-8.3
38.6	16.5	12.4	11.6			% Profit Before Taxes/Total Assets	4.9	8.3
21.9	6.9	3.7	4.9				1.2	1.6
-1.9	-2.6	1.6	1.3				-4.6	-4.4
42.0	17.2	10.0	5.6			Sales/Net Fixed Assets	5.2	8.4
17.0	7.9	5.1	3.8				3.5	3.8
7.2	3.8	3.3	2.6				2.6	2.8
3.7	3.1	2.4	1.9			Sales/Total Assets	2.0	2.2
3.0	2.5	1.8	1.4				1.6	1.8
2.1	1.8	1.4	1.2				1.2	1.5
	1.9	2.3	2.4			% Depr., Dep., Amort./Sales	4.4	3.9
(44)	3.9	(67) 3.7	(26) 4.3				(42) 6.7	(48) 5.5
	5.9	5.7	5.5				8.7	7.5
	3.0	1.5				% Officers', Directors', Owners' Comp/Sales	2.5	3.1
(37)	5.9	(34) 3.1					(25) 4.3	(35) 5.2
	8.4	4.9					7.9	6.9
12038M	152970M	561489M	824752M	209044M	413699M	Net Sales ($)	392543M	237918M
3541M	60927M	298328M	543317M	110643M	244060M	Total Assets ($)	256695M	148315M

M = $ thousand   MM = $ million
See Pages 11 through 21 for Explanation of Ratios and Data

Comparative Historical Data | Current Data Sorted by Sales

Type of Statement

			Type of Statement	0-1MM	1-3MM	3-5MM	5-10MM	10-25MM	25MM & OVER
11	21	16	Unqualified			1	2	5	8
45	44	51	Reviewed	1	4	8	19	16	3
32	25	26	Compiled	1	8	9	5	2	1
17	11	18	Tax Returns	3	10	3	2		
24	24	55	Other	4	14	5	14	11	7
4/1/04-3/31/05 ALL	4/1/05-3/31/06 ALL	4/1/06-3/31/07 ALL			42 (4/1-9/30/06)		124 (10/1/06-3/31/07)		
129	125	166	NUMBER OF STATEMENTS	9	36	26	42	34	19

Main Data

4/1/04-3/31/05 ALL	4/1/05-3/31/06 ALL	4/1/06-3/31/07 ALL		0-1MM	1-3MM	3-5MM	5-10MM	10-25MM	25MM & OVER
%	%	%	ASSETS	%	%	%	%	%	%
7.9	7.4	8.0	Cash & Equivalents		7.7	13.0	6.2	5.5	3.0
27.4	26.6	28.6	Trade Receivables (net)		28.8	30.1	26.8	31.3	27.8
16.0	17.8	17.0	Inventory		17.3	17.2	17.2	17.6	14.5
2.2	3.7	3.7	All Other Current		1.1	1.8	6.2	5.5	3.9
53.6	55.5	57.2	Total Current		54.9	62.1	56.4	59.8	49.3
38.0	34.3	35.2	Fixed Assets (net)		39.6	31.3	37.0	32.8	40.8
2.3	3.4	2.9	Intangibles (net)		2.4	2.0	1.9	1.3	7.2
6.1	6.8	4.7	All Other Non-Current		3.1	4.7	4.8	6.1	2.7
100.0	100.0	100.0	Total		100.0	100.0	100.0	100.0	100.0
			LIABILITIES						
12.0	11.0	9.2	Notes Payable-Short Term		7.9	6.9	9.8	11.2	10.5
7.1	5.3	4.9	Cur. Mat.-L.T.D.		5.9	5.1	5.6	4.1	4.5
11.6	11.3	12.7	Trade Payables		11.0	11.0	13.8	15.1	14.0
.2	.1	.2	Income Taxes Payable		.2	.6	.0	.1	.2
7.6	10.5	11.8	All Other Current		12.8	11.7	11.6	13.4	8.5
38.4	38.2	38.7	Total Current		37.8	35.4	40.8	43.9	37.7
21.3	18.2	19.6	Long-Term Debt		27.2	13.9	17.4	19.5	16.7
.9	.8	.8	Deferred Taxes		.2	.8	1.2	.9	1.5
7.7	7.1	5.9	All Other Non-Current		4.4	6.6	3.6	4.0	7.0
31.7	35.6	35.0	Net Worth		30.4	43.3	37.0	31.7	37.2
100.0	100.0	100.0	Total Liabilities & Net Worth		100.0	100.0	100.0	100.0	100.0
			INCOME DATA						
100.0	100.0	100.0	Net Sales		100.0	100.0	100.0	100.0	100.0
28.9	29.6	28.8	Gross Profit		37.1	29.3	26.8	18.2	22.0
26.0	24.5	23.7	Operating Expenses		31.3	25.1	22.3	12.7	15.1
2.8	5.1	5.1	Operating Profit		5.8	4.2	4.6	5.5	6.8
1.1	1.4	1.3	All Other Expenses (net)		1.6	1.2	1.1	1.3	1.1
1.8	3.7	3.9	Profit Before Taxes		4.2	3.0	3.5	4.3	5.7
			RATIOS						
2.3	2.4	2.2	Current		3.1	3.0	2.1	1.8	1.7
1.4	1.4	1.5			1.4	1.8	1.5	1.4	1.3
1.1	1.1	1.1			1.0	1.2	1.1	1.1	1.1
1.5	1.5	1.5	Quick		1.6	2.0	1.2	1.1	1.3
.9	.9	.9			.9	1.3	.8	.8	.9
.6	.6	.6			.5	.8	.6	.6	.5
37 9.8	38 9.5	35 10.5	Sales/Receivables		34 10.7	33 11.0	30 12.3	40 9.1	41 8.9
49 7.4	49 7.4	49 7.4			44 8.4	48 7.6	43 8.6	52 7.0	63 5.8
70 5.2	65 5.6	63 5.8			56 6.5	63 5.8	63 5.8	65 5.6	76 4.8
17 21.2	20 18.3	17 21.7	Cost of Sales/Inventory		11 32.7	17 21.3	17 21.6	15 24.1	25 14.8
39 9.3	39 9.5	39 9.3			35 10.4	39 9.4	41 8.9	36 10.1	37 9.8
60 6.1	67 5.4	66 5.6			73 5.0	67 5.4	72 5.1	57 6.4	49 7.5
14 25.3	14 25.8	15 24.6	Cost of Sales/Payables		10 35.4	12 29.2	16 23.3	21 17.0	20 17.8
26 13.8	27 13.7	25 14.3			22 16.8	24 15.0	26 13.9	28 13.1	34 10.7
40 9.1	45 8.1	40 9.2			40 9.1	36 10.2	42 8.7	38 9.5	42 8.7
6.1	5.6	6.3	Sales/Working Capital		5.1	4.9	7.0	7.0	6.7
12.4	10.9	11.9			22.0	8.9	13.3	12.9	10.0
76.4	48.6	72.9			212.5	37.5	76.6	60.6	164.0
5.7	5.8	8.4	EBIT/Interest		8.0	9.7	7.1	8.8	11.1
(124) 2.6	(114) 2.7	(154) 2.8			(34) 2.9	(24) 2.7	(39) 2.7	(31) 2.5	(18) 5.7
.7	1.1	1.3			.8	1.1	1.4	1.6	1.0
3.7	3.0	4.2	Net Profit + Depr., Dep.,				2.1		
(43) 2.1	(35) 2.1	(43) 2.0	Amort./Cur. Mat. L/T/D				(14) 1.6		
1.4	1.2	1.4					.9		
.6	.6	.6	Fixed/Worth		.5	.3	.6	.5	.9
1.1	1.1	1.2			1.6	1.0	.9	1.6	1.2
3.9	3.4	2.4			4.1	1.8	2.0	2.3	2.7
.8	.9	1.0	Debt/Worth		1.0	.8	.8	1.2	1.2
1.8	2.0	2.1			3.4	1.5	2.0	2.7	2.5
7.3	6.4	5.8			9.5	2.7	4.5	6.4	6.9
33.8	32.0	42.1	% Profit Before Taxes/Tangible		62.9	33.5	30.3	46.7	60.1
(109) 14.3	(106) 13.1	(151) 18.7	Net Worth		(34) 18.7	(24) 13.0	(39) 13.9	(31) 22.7	(18) 33.5
3.8	4.5	3.6			-11.0	4.3	1.9	9.0	10.4
11.4	13.7	14.1	% Profit Before Taxes/Total		13.8	11.6	12.8	13.2	16.5
4.3	5.4	4.7	Assets		3.8	4.3	3.7	4.3	9.6
-1.2	.4	.7			-3.7	-.6	1.2	2.5	.4
9.0	9.4	12.7	Sales/Net Fixed Assets		14.5	19.1	10.7	8.5	7.7
5.0	5.4	5.6			6.4	7.9	5.3	5.2	5.2
3.5	3.5	3.4			2.9	3.7	3.3	3.8	3.1
2.3	2.3	2.6	Sales/Total Assets		3.1	2.9	2.7	2.4	2.4
1.8	1.8	1.9			2.1	2.2	1.9	1.7	1.8
1.4	1.3	1.4			1.4	1.6	1.5	1.3	1.4
3.2	2.7	2.2	% Depr., Dep., Amort./Sales		2.2	1.7	2.4	2.4	2.1
(122) 4.5	(113) 4.0	(149) 3.7			(31) 5.2	(24) 4.0	(41) 3.6	(30) 3.5	(18) 3.5
6.5	5.5	5.4			8.0	5.1	5.1	5.0	4.9
2.4	2.3	2.4	% Officers', Directors'		2.9	3.5	1.6	.9	
(76) 5.0	(55) 4.5	(85) 4.5	Owners' Comp/Sales		(27) 7.0	(15) 5.9	(21) 3.2	(11) 2.9	
8.8	8.0	8.5			9.5	8.5	8.5		
1144656M	1415558M	2173992M	Net Sales ($)	5889M	69396M	101318M	279597M	509313M	1208479M
813076M	925070M	1260816M	Total Assets ($)	4187M	39472M	51229M	158375M	306991M	700562M

M = $ thousand   MM = $ million
See Pages 11 through 21 for Explanation of Ratios and Data

Current Data Sorted by Assets & Comparative Historical Data

0-500M	500M-2MM	2-10MM	10-50MM	50-100MM	100-250MM	Type of Statement	4/1/02-3/31/03 ALL	4/1/03-3/31/04 ALL
	7	7	7	5	5	Unqualified	21	29
6	18	43	11			Reviewed	63	61
6	14	25	2	1	1	Compiled	47	57
		7				Tax Returns	16	15
2	16	21	22	4	1	Other	44	46
	55 (4/1-9/30/06)		175 (10/1/06-3/31/07)				4/1/02-3/31/03	4/1/03-3/31/04
14	55	103	42	10	6	**NUMBER OF STATEMENTS**	191	208
%	%	%	%	%	%	**ASSETS**	%	%
17.0	10.0	9.3	7.5	15.1		Cash & Equivalents	7.1	7.2
40.8	27.6	24.9	20.5	23.5		Trade Receivables (net)	24.2	24.7
8.9	7.9	26.5	23.3	22.0		Inventory	20.7	22.7
.4	2.5	1.0	4.8	5.7		All Other Current	3.0	3.0
67.2	48.0	61.7	56.0	66.3		Total Current	55.0	57.5
28.8	44.3	31.9	31.6	26.5		Fixed Assets (net)	37.0	34.1
1.0	1.5	1.7	4.4	1.3		Intangibles (net)	1.5	1.8
3.0	6.3	4.6	7.9	5.9		All Other Non-Current	6.5	6.5
100.0	100.0	100.0	100.0	100.0		Total	100.0	100.0
						LIABILITIES		
4.3	9.3	8.8	6.7	9.0		Notes Payable-Short Term	11.9	13.7
5.5	6.6	5.6	4.0	1.5		Cur. Mat.-L.T.D.	6.2	6.1
18.5	10.4	12.3	11.7	7.4		Trade Payables	11.9	11.5
.0	.0	.1	.1	.1		Income Taxes Payable	.2	.2
2.4	5.3	11.5	15.0	16.2		All Other Current	9.6	12.6
30.7	31.7	38.3	37.5	34.3		Total Current	39.8	44.1
21.4	31.0	17.8	16.0	6.9		Long-Term Debt	21.1	17.0
.0	.5	.6	.5	1.1		Deferred Taxes	.4	.5
15.5	3.6	3.0	7.0	5.0		All Other Non-Current	4.1	6.8
32.5	33.1	40.2	39.0	52.8		Net Worth	34.6	31.7
100.0	100.0	100.0	100.0	100.0		Total Liabilities & Net Worth	100.0	100.0
						INCOME DATA		
100.0	100.0	100.0	100.0	100.0		Net Sales	100.0	100.0
44.7	41.2	29.8	26.5	36.8		Gross Profit	31.9	32.8
38.8	33.8	24.1	21.6	32.6		Operating Expenses	31.4	31.1
5.8	7.4	5.6	5.0	4.2		Operating Profit	.6	1.7
-.9	1.7	1.1	.8	.6		All Other Expenses (net)	1.6	1.4
6.7	5.7	4.5	4.2	3.6		Profit Before Taxes	-1.1	.3
						RATIOS		
7.3	2.7	2.8	2.2	5.3		Current	2.3	2.3
1.9	1.6	1.5	1.5	1.7			1.4	1.4
1.2	.9	1.1	1.2	1.4			1.0	1.0
5.2	2.7	1.7	1.0	4.2		Quick	1.2	1.3
1.5	1.2	.9	.8	1.0			.8	.8
1.0	.6	.6	.5	.6			.5	.5
33 11.2	29 12.5	40 9.2	40 9.2	32 11.6		Sales/Receivables	36 10.0	38 9.6
50 7.4	44 8.4	47 7.8	47 7.7	50 7.3			49 7.4	51 7.2
63 5.8	56 6.6	58 6.3	66 5.5	84 4.4			66 5.6	67 5.5
0 UND	0 UND	27 13.6	36 10.1	0 UND		Cost of Sales/Inventory	23 15.8	23 15.5
9 39.8	13 28.5	61 6.0	66 5.5	106 3.4			48 7.5	60 6.1
39 9.4	32 11.3	120 3.0	135 2.7	152 2.4			107 3.4	115 3.2
20 18.4	11 33.0	17 21.2	24 15.0	3 108.2		Cost of Sales/Payables	17 21.6	16 23.3
31 11.8	21 17.7	30 12.1	33 11.1	16 22.7			31 12.0	28 13.1
59 6.2	37 9.9	42 8.6	51 7.2	43 8.5			51 7.2	48 7.6
6.3	7.3	5.0	3.9	2.5		Sales/Working Capital	5.3	4.8
11.8	15.1	8.6	6.3	7.4			12.1	11.6
45.6	-69.2	38.8	19.4	13.0			-147.3	UND
74.2	10.2	8.6	9.1	128.8		EBIT/Interest	3.1	5.2
(12) 7.9	(49) 3.6	(96) 3.2	(40) 3.7	10.2			(170) 1.3	(192) 1.8
.4	1.9	1.3	1.1	-.6			-1.5	-1.0
		4.5	3.1			Net Profit + Depr., Dep.,	2.7	2.0
	(24) 2.5		(11) 1.8			Amort./Cur. Mat. L/T/D	(54) 1.4	(59) 1.1
		1.3	.7				.3	-.1
.2	.6	.3	.5	.2		Fixed/Worth	.5	.5
.4	1.0	.7	.7	.4			1.1	1.0
NM	3.3	1.7	1.8	1.0			2.4	2.6
.2	.9	.8	.9	.4		Debt/Worth	.7	.7
1.9	1.7	1.8	1.9	1.0			2.1	2.1
NM	5.5	3.4	2.8	2.1			5.2	5.4
96.5	59.4	40.0	40.3	34.5		% Profit Before Taxes/Tangible	22.3	24.0
(11) 42.9	(49) 27.7	(99) 19.6	(40) 17.4	13.8		Net Worth	(171) 2.5	(178) 6.6
4.9	12.4	4.5	2.2	-15.1			-16.1	-8.9
49.8	18.7	13.0	10.0	16.2		% Profit Before Taxes/Total	5.9	7.9
20.5	8.7	7.1	6.3	11.1		Assets	.7	1.4
-.3	3.4	1.2	.5	-4.5			-7.9	-5.4
62.3	10.4	15.2	9.6	27.5		Sales/Net Fixed Assets	10.4	11.8
15.1	6.1	6.8	5.8	7.3			4.7	5.0
6.1	2.9	3.3	3.2	4.8			2.8	3.0
4.4	2.8	2.3	2.0	2.8		Sales/Total Assets	2.1	2.2
3.2	2.2	1.8	1.4	1.4			1.6	1.6
2.3	1.6	1.4	1.0	1.1			1.2	1.2
1.1	1.9	1.3	1.3			% Depr., Dep., Amort./Sales	2.2	2.0
(13) 2.6	(51) 4.8	(99) 3.0	(40) 2.4				(178) 4.1	(191) 4.0
6.8	7.9	5.6	4.2				7.4	7.1
	3.4	1.7				% Officers', Directors'	3.1	3.4
	(39) 7.5	(36) 3.6				Owners' Comp/Sales	(85) 6.1	(95) 5.5
	11.3	6.1					10.6	9.5
16666M	137519M	833592M	1288107M	1795168M	1244456M	Net Sales ($)	2306298M	2488811M
4505M	60247M	464092M	865319M	657539M	954318M	Total Assets ($)	1637054M	1998244M

© RMA 2007

M = $ thousand   MM = $ million
See Pages 11 through 21 for Explanation of Ratios and Data

Comparative Historical Data | Current Data Sorted by Sales

			Type of Statement						
32	20	24	Unqualified			1	2	6	15
61	64	61	Reviewed		3	14	24	15	5
63	45	51	Compiled	5	15	14	12	3	2
17	27	28	Tax Returns	4	12	5	6		1
58	73	66	Other	4	12	8	10	15	17
4/1/04-3/31/05 ALL	4/1/05-3/31/06 ALL	4/1/06-3/31/07 ALL		0-1MM	55 (4/1-9/30/6) 1-3MM	3-5MM	175 (10/1/06-3/31/07) 5-10MM	10-25MM	25MM & OVER
231	229	230	NUMBER OF STATEMENTS	13	42	42	54	39	40
%	%	%	ASSETS	%	%	%	%	%	%
8.6	8.1	10.1	Cash & Equivalents	8.5	10.7	10.0	8.1	10.5	12.6
26.4	28.5	25.6	Trade Receivables (net)	25.2	28.6	26.6	24.4	23.9	24.9
21.7	21.9	20.1	Inventory	10.9	7.7	18.1	27.6	25.4	23.1
2.7	2.2	2.3	All Other Current	.7	3.0	.5	1.0	4.3	3.7
59.4	60.7	58.2	Total Current	45.3	50.0	55.2	61.1	64.0	64.3
32.0	30.7	34.2	Fixed Assets (net)	51.8	41.6	38.4	30.7	25.7	29.1
2.7	3.1	2.1	Intangibles (net)	1.2	1.6	1.0	3.3	2.8	2.0
5.8	5.5	5.5	All Other Non-Current	1.7	6.7	5.5	4.9	7.5	4.6
100.0	100.0	100.0	Total	100.0	100.0	100.0	100.0	100.0	100.0
			LIABILITIES						
11.0	10.1	8.1	Notes Payable-Short Term	10.8	9.5	5.8	9.0	8.3	6.6
5.9	5.1	5.3	Cur. Mat.-L.T.D.	5.7	8.1	6.2	4.5	4.7	2.9
12.6	13.2	11.8	Trade Payables	10.2	11.9	10.6	11.8	13.0	12.4
.2	.3	.1	Income Taxes Payable	.0	.0	.0	.2	.1	.0
10.3	11.0	10.5	All Other Current	3.3	6.2	6.4	13.4	10.8	17.6
39.9	39.7	35.8	Total Current	30.1	35.7	29.0	38.9	37.0	39.8
20.1	18.8	20.2	Long-Term Debt	44.5	27.5	20.9	19.6	14.6	10.2
.6	.5	.5	Deferred Taxes	.0	.3	.6	.9	.3	.6
4.5	5.1	4.7	All Other Non-Current	20.0	2.8	2.2	4.1	4.7	4.9
34.9	35.9	38.8	Net Worth	5.4	33.6	47.3	36.4	43.5	44.6
100.0	100.0	100.0	Total Liabilities & Net Worth	100.0	100.0	100.0	100.0	100.0	100.0
			INCOME DATA						
100.0	100.0	100.0	Net Sales	100.0	100.0	100.0	100.0	100.0	100.0
32.7	33.0	33.2	Gross Profit	43.1	39.7	38.4	29.7	28.3	27.3
28.7	27.8	27.1	Operating Expenses	39.2	33.3	31.3	23.6	22.8	21.5
4.0	5.2	6.1	Operating Profit	3.9	6.4	7.1	6.0	5.6	5.9
.8	.9	1.1	All Other Expenses (net)	2.0	.9	1.1	1.3	.6	1.0
3.2	4.4	5.0	Profit Before Taxes	2.0	5.5	6.1	4.7	4.9	4.9
			RATIOS						
2.7	2.6	2.8		3.0	4.1	3.0	2.5	3.0	2.3
1.5	1.6	1.6	Current	1.3	1.3	1.6	1.5	1.7	1.7
1.1	1.1	1.1		.8	.8	1.4	1.1	1.2	1.2
1.6	1.7	1.7		2.7	2.3	2.2	1.4	1.3	1.3
.9	1.0	1.0	Quick	1.0	1.2	1.3	.8	.8	.9
.6	.6	.6		.5	.5	.8	.6	.5	.6

							Sales/Receivables									
39	9.4	39	9.4	37	9.8	39	9.4	29	12.6	36	10.0	39	9.5	40	9.2	35	10.4
51	7.2	50	7.2	47	7.8	50	7.3	44	8.3	45	8.0	49	7.5	48	7.5	48	7.6
69	5.3	66	5.6	61	6.0	69	5.3	58	6.3	55	6.6	61	5.9	65	5.6	62	5.9

							Cost of Sales/Inventory									
19	19.0	18	19.9	15	25.1	0	UND	0	UND	7	55.8	34	10.8	31	11.8	28	12.8
54	6.7	44	8.3	42	8.7	32	11.4	6	62.8	31	11.8	61	6.0	75	4.9	66	5.6
104	3.5	107	3.4	97	3.8	71	5.1	26	14.2	98	3.7	111	3.3	145	2.5	121	3.0

							Cost of Sales/Payables									
16	23.0	21	17.6	16	22.3	17	21.5	10	35.5	16	23.5	16	22.6	22	16.9	17	21.5
32	11.4	30	12.0	29	12.6	29	12.6	23	16.2	29	12.5	28	12.9	34	10.8	28	12.8
48	7.6	49	7.5	42	8.6	40	9.2	42	8.6	45	8.1	40	9.0	51	7.2	43	8.6

			Sales/Working Capital						
4.5	4.8	4.9		7.5	6.3	5.5	5.2	3.6	4.8
9.3	8.9	9.2		21.4	19.1	10.7	10.1	5.2	8.6
34.1	35.1	37.8		-32.3	-22.9	19.8	46.9	19.8	19.4

							EBIT/Interest									
	9.1		10.8		10.2		4.2		13.3		9.0		8.4		8.6		15.2
(219)	3.3	(209)	4.3	(213)	3.6	(11)	1.1	(38)	3.8	(39)	3.3	(52)	3.0	(34)	3.8	(39)	5.0
	1.0		1.3		1.3		-1.8		1.1		1.9		1.3		2.4		.0

							Net Profit + Depr., Dep., Amort./Cur. Mat. L/T/D									
	2.9		4.0		4.6								3.3		4.8		17.6
(65)	1.8	(57)	2.3	(51)	2.2							(15)	2.2	(10)	1.5	(15)	4.1
	.7		1.0		1.3								1.3		.6		1.6

			Fixed/Worth						
.4	.3	.4		.9	.5	.5	.4	.2	.3
.9	.8	.7		4.8	1.2	.8	.8	.5	.6
2.2	2.4	2.0		-18.4	3.6	1.3	2.3	1.5	1.0

			Debt/Worth						
.8	.8	.8		.9	.8	.7	1.1	.7	.6
1.7	1.9	1.7		9.2	1.9	1.3	2.1	1.9	1.2
4.8	5.5	3.4		-38.1	6.7	2.2	4.6	2.9	2.1

							% Profit Before Taxes/Tangible Net Worth									
	38.1		40.9		43.3				69.8		44.9		44.4		39.0		43.2
(204)	13.6	(209)	19.7	(215)	21.3			(35)	34.8	(41)	21.2	(51)	19.7		19.6	(38)	20.3
	2.4		4.9		5.2				16.8		5.9		5.0		8.0		-4.1

			% Profit Before Taxes/Total Assets						
12.1	14.9	15.0		15.3	24.5	15.8	13.2	12.3	17.3
4.1	6.7	7.3		4.7	9.6	8.6	4.1	7.0	9.4
.2	1.4	1.2		-10.1	1.0	2.5	1.3	4.3	-2.1

			Sales/Net Fixed Assets						
12.1	17.1	14.8		6.9	16.4	11.0	15.4	19.3	14.9
6.0	6.9	6.7		3.5	5.6	6.1	6.8	7.1	7.3
3.3	3.9	3.4		1.1	2.5	2.5	3.4	3.8	4.8

			Sales/Total Assets						
2.4	2.5	2.5		2.5	2.8	2.5	2.6	2.0	2.4
1.7	1.8	1.9		1.8	2.1	1.8	1.8	1.5	1.9
1.2	1.4	1.3		.9	1.4	1.6	1.2	1.2	1.3

							% Depr., Dep., Amort./Sales									
	2.0		1.3		1.3		2.1		1.9		1.5		1.0		1.0		1.2
(208)	3.5	(210)	2.8	(217)	2.8	(12)	6.1	(38)	5.3		3.7	(50)	3.0	(38)	1.8	(37)	2.3
	6.6		5.2		5.8		8.5		8.3		6.1		6.1		3.7		3.7

							% Officers', Directors' Owners' Comp/Sales									
	2.6		2.7		2.6				3.8		3.7		1.5				
(105)	4.7	(91)	4.5	(92)	4.8			(25)	6.6	(22)	5.7	(23)	1.9				
	8.0		9.1		8.3				10.9		8.8		1.5				

3685649M	3565639M	5315508M	Net Sales ($)	8965M	76351M	172292M	40068M	602310M	4054972M
2482023M	2314661M	3006020M	Total Assets ($)	6684M	45179M	98796M	26602M	449220M	2140139M

M = $ thousand   MM = $ million
See Pages 11 through 21 for Explanation of Ratios and Data

Current Data Sorted by Assets   Comparative Historical Data

Type of Statement	0-500M	500M-2MM	2-10MM	10-50MM	50-100MM	100-250MM		4/1/02-3/31/03 ALL	4/1/03-3/31/04 ALL
Unqualified			8	4	2	2		15	11
Reviewed		5	16	3	1			29	32
Compiled	1	8	11	2				20	30
Tax Returns	2	6	2					7	15
Other	1	9	17	16	1			30	28
		28 (4/1-9/30/06)		89 (10/1/06-3/31/07)					
NUMBER OF STATEMENTS	4	28	54	25	4	2		101	116

	0-500M %	500M-2MM %	2-10MM %	10-50MM %	50-100MM %	100-250MM %		4/1/02-3/31/03 %	4/1/03-3/31/04 %
ASSETS									
Cash & Equivalents		11.5	8.3	4.4				7.6	9.1
Trade Receivables (net)		30.2	28.1	27.1				23.6	24.7
Inventory		17.1	28.3	22.1				22.9	21.2
All Other Current		1.3	4.0	8.1				3.1	4.5
Total Current		60.1	68.7	62.1				57.2	59.5
Fixed Assets (net)		32.7	23.1	21.1				31.2	29.9
Intangibles (net)		1.6	2.2	5.1				5.9	3.9
All Other Non-Current		5.5	6.0	10.1				5.8	6.8
Total		100.0	100.0	100.0				100.0	100.0
LIABILITIES									
Notes Payable-Short Term		11.4	11.9	12.8				13.2	12.3
Cur. Mat.-L.T.D.		5.4	2.7	4.0				7.2	7.5
Trade Payables		14.1	18.1	13.9				9.9	11.7
Income Taxes Payable		.3	.3	.1				.1	.2
All Other Current		9.8	12.9	21.1				12.3	13.1
Total Current		41.1	45.8	51.0				42.7	44.8
Long-Term Debt		17.7	12.4	18.1				22.2	17.6
Deferred Taxes		.1	.1	.3				.3	.4
All Other Non-Current		5.3	8.8	9.6				5.9	7.7
Net Worth		35.7	32.8	25.0				28.9	29.5
Total Liabilities & Net Worth		100.0	100.0	100.0				100.0	100.0
INCOME DATA									
Net Sales		100.0	100.0	100.0				100.0	100.0
Gross Profit		35.3	25.5	21.7				30.0	29.6
Operating Expenses		26.7	20.1	15.9				29.6	27.8
Operating Profit		8.6	5.4	5.8				.3	1.7
All Other Expenses (net)		2.4	.9	1.3				1.6	1.2
Profit Before Taxes		6.2	4.6	4.5				-1.3	.6

RATIOS

	0-500M	500M-2MM	2-10MM	10-50MM	50-100MM	100-250MM		4/1/02-3/31/03	4/1/03-3/31/04
Current		2.7	2.6	1.6				3.3	2.4
		1.9	1.6	1.3				1.4	1.6
		.9	1.2	1.0				1.0	.9
Quick		2.3	1.3	.7				1.7	1.6
		1.3	.8	.6				.8	.8
		.5	.6	.5				.5	.5
Sales/Receivables	24	15.4	37 9.9	45 8.1			38	9.6	35 10.5
	37	9.9	48 7.5	54 6.7			53	6.9	50 7.2
	58	6.3	59 6.2	71 5.2			64	5.7	72 5.0
Cost of Sales/Inventory	5	69.2	33 11.1	30 12.3			33	11.1	25 14.8
	22	16.4	70 5.2	52 7.0			67	5.5	61 6.0
	59	6.1	105 3.5	97 3.8			108	3.4	100 3.7
Cost of Sales/Payables	11	32.6	20 18.7	20 18.4			12	29.4	15 24.3
	22	16.5	32 11.3	31 11.9			25	14.6	28 13.2
	47	7.8	55 6.6	45 8.2			42	8.6	52 7.1
Sales/Working Capital		7.6	4.4	6.8				4.1	3.8
		11.0	9.1	13.9				9.4	9.6
		-127.9	32.0	NM				NM	-59.5
EBIT/Interest		14.3	12.2	7.7				5.6	5.7
	(25)	6.7	(48) 3.6	(24) 3.6			(92)	1.4	(102) 1.4
		2.3	1.3	1.4				-1.3	-.7
Net Profit + Depr., Dep., Amort./Cur. Mat. L/T/D			6.2	69.1				2.5	4.7
			(13) 1.7	(10) 2.9			(32)	1.4	(29) 1.6
			.8	.7				-.2	.3
Fixed/Worth		.2	.3	.4				.5	.4
		.6	.6	1.0				1.1	.8
		2.5	2.1	7.7				4.4	4.4
Debt/Worth		.6	.7	1.4				.7	.7
		1.3	1.9	3.9				2.5	2.0
		5.5	11.1	27.6				9.7	14.6
% Profit Before Taxes/Tangible Net Worth		76.9	6.0	76.9				25.1	21.5
	(24)	45.2	(44) 3.5	(21) 37.6			(80)	5.3	(92) 3.3
		11.9	1.5	11.3				-14.6	-6.8
% Profit Before Taxes/Total Assets		27.1	7.4	14.7				9.1	9.3
		11.2	7.2	5.9				.8	1.2
		2.8	1.5	2.1				-8.1	-5.2
Sales/Net Fixed Assets		41.8	28.4	23.7				11.1	14.6
		12.4	10.3	8.4				5.2	5.4
		3.7	5.0	5.1				3.2	3.5
Sales/Total Assets		3.8	2.6	2.1				2.1	2.1
		2.2	1.9	1.7				1.5	1.5
		1.8	1.5	1.3				1.1	1.1
% Depr., Dep., Amort./Sales		.8	1.2	1.4				2.3	1.6
	(23)	2.0	(49) 1.9	(20) 2.0			(91)	4.4	(104) 4.1
		5.3	3.2	3.9				6.7	6.8
% Officers', Directors' Owners' Comp/Sales		3.5	1.3					3.2	3.2
	(17)	6.8	(17) 2.5				(46)	5.6	(46) 5.9
		14.3	6.5					9.1	9.2
Net Sales ($)	2839M	83098M	551819M	932959M	345818M	490601M		1122927M	1130426M
Total Assets ($)	1169M	30358M	275321M	565777M	271917M	370298M		911569M	904310M

M = $ thousand   MM = $ million

See Pages 11 through 21 for Explanation of Ratios and Data

Comparative Historical Data				Current Data Sorted by Sales					
			Type of Statement						
10	17	16	Unqualified			1	3	6	6
28	21	25	Reviewed		3	3	8	9	2
28	23	22	Compiled	1	5	6	6	4	
10	9	10	Tax Returns	2	3	2	3		
36	40	44	Other	2	4	5	7	9	17
4/1/04-3/31/05 ALL	**4/1/05-3/31/06 ALL**	**4/1/06-3/31/07 ALL**		**28 (4/1-9/30/06)**			**89 (10/1/06-3/31/07)**		
				0-1MM	**1-3MM**	**3-5MM**	**5-10MM**	**10-25MM**	**25MM & OVER**
112	110	117	**NUMBER OF STATEMENTS**	5	15	17	27	28	25
%	%	%	**ASSETS**	%	%	%	%	%	%
8.5	9.5	8.9	Cash & Equivalents		11.3	10.5	10.8	9.5	4.9
25.7	26.4	28.3	Trade Receivables (net)		25.9	35.6	25.8	28.4	29.0
20.7	22.6	24.0	Inventory		14.5	18.7	29.2	28.8	25.1
3.7	4.5	4.0	All Other Current		2.0	4.2	4.0	4.0	5.7
58.6	63.0	65.2	Total Current		53.8	68.9	69.8	70.7	64.7
30.9	26.5	25.5	Fixed Assets (net)		36.9	23.9	20.7	22.7	20.7
3.9	4.5	2.9	Intangibles (net)		2.1	1.2	3.0	1.0	6.4
6.6	6.0	6.4	All Other Non-Current		7.2	6.0	6.5	5.5	8.2
100.0	100.0	100.0	Total		100.0	100.0	100.0	100.0	100.0
			LIABILITIES						
11.9	9.4	11.6	Notes Payable-Short Term		11.3	13.3	14.3	9.9	9.1
6.3	4.9	3.5	Cur. Mat.-L.T.D.		5.6	4.0	3.3	2.1	3.6
13.7	13.1	15.5	Trade Payables		10.1	15.8	17.5	19.2	13.0
.2	.2	.3	Income Taxes Payable		.4	.1	.4	.4	.1
10.9	13.3	13.9	All Other Current		10.9	12.8	13.7	8.6	24.9
43.0	40.9	44.7	Total Current		38.2	46.1	49.1	40.2	50.7
22.1	17.6	14.7	Long-Term Debt		24.3	15.2	9.9	9.4	15.0
.5	.4	.2	Deferred Taxes		.0	.4	.0	.1	.6
7.6	7.2	7.6	All Other Non-Current		6.7	7.7	7.6	6.9	8.3
26.8	33.9	32.7	Net Worth		30.7	30.7	33.4	43.4	25.5
100.0	100.0	100.0	Total Liabilties & Net Worth		100.0	100.0	100.0	100.0	100.0
			INCOME DATA						
100.0	100.0	100.0	Net Sales		100.0	100.0	100.0	100.0	100.0
29.4	30.1	28.3	Gross Profit		38.1	27.3	27.5	24.3	22.4
24.5	24.6	21.7	Operating Expenses		32.7	22.9	22.7	17.2	15.3
4.8	5.6	6.6	Operating Profit		5.5	4.4	4.9	7.1	7.2
1.2	1.1	1.3	All Other Expenses (net)		2.2	.6	1.1	.0	1.1
3.7	4.5	5.3	Profit Before Taxes		3.3	3.9	3.8	7.2	6.0
			RATIOS						
2.5	2.7	2.5			3.2	3.2	2.9	2.9	1.6
1.4	1.6	1.5	Current		1.6	1.8	1.9	1.9	1.3
1.1	1.0	1.1			.9	1.1	.8	1.3	1.0
1.6	1.6	1.5			3.1	1.9	1.3	1.8	1.0
.8	.8	.9	Quick		1.2	.9	.9	.9	.6
.5	.5	.5			.5	.6	.4	.6	.5
34 10.7	**35** 10.4	**36** 10.3			**29** 12.7	**38** 9.7	**28** 12.9	**36** 10.2	**43** 8.5
49 7.4	**49** 7.4	**48** 7.6	Sales/Receivables		**47** 7.8	**56** 6.6	**45** 8.2	**49** 7.5	**54** 6.7
70 5.2	**62** 5.9	**63** 5.8			**60** 6.1	**69** 5.3	**58** 6.3	**58** 6.3	**78** 4.7
24 15.5	**33** 11.2	**25** 14.8			**5** 77.9	**17** 21.4	**28** 12.9	**26** 13.9	**41** 8.8
52 7.0	**55** 6.6	**55** 6.6	Cost of Sales/Inventory		**28** 13.1	**43** 8.4	**73** 5.0	**55** 6.6	**79** 4.6
92 4.0	**94** 3.9	**96** 3.8			**74** 5.0	**66** 5.5	**118** 3.1	**108** 3.4	**102** 3.6
18 20.3	**18** 20.7	**17** 21.3			**13** 27.9	**18** 20.7	**16** 22.6	**20** 18.7	**18** 20.0
31 11.7	**31** 11.8	**29** 12.7	Cost of Sales/Payables		**19** 18.8	**34** 10.7	**28** 13.0	**31** 11.6	**27** 13.6
51 7.1	**47** 7.7	**47** 7.8			**70** 5.2	**47** 7.8	**55** 6.7	**58** 6.3	**41** 8.8
5.5	4.7	4.8			7.6	5.1	3.1	4.4	8.1
11.6	9.5	11.0	Sales/Working Capital		10.3	9.3	8.3	5.9	13.9
75.4	55.3	46.8			-10.5	33.9	-26.6	14.3	613.6
7.6	11.2	12.2			6.8	33.9	14.8	11.1	12.4
(103) 3.3	(95) 3.3	(103) 4.6	EBIT/Interest		(13) 4.2	(16) 3.5	(23) 3.5	(25) 6.1	(23) 4.0
1.1	1.5	1.4			2.2	-2.1	.6	2.4	1.2
3.4	3.9	8.9							16.4
(30) 1.8	(30) 2.5	(27) 1.9	Net Profit + Depr., Dep., Amort./Cur. Mat. L/T/D						(10) 3.6
.8	1.4	.8							.7
.4	.3	.3			.3	.3	.3	.2	.4
1.4	.7	.6	Fixed/Worth		1.2	.8	.6	.5	1.0
8.3	3.0	3.0			17.6	-5.5	3.2	1.0	11.1
1.0	.7	.7			.4	.5	.6	.7	1.5
3.1	1.7	1.9	Debt/Worth		2.3	1.1	1.2	1.4	4.4
16.4	10.9	11.2			18.0	-20.6	11.3	3.4	67.6
49.5	59.9	65.7			59.4	48.3	63.8	72.6	85.4
(91) 18.8	(90) 30.8	(98) 36.2	% Profit Before Taxes/Tangible Net Worth		(12) 21.0	(12) 33.3	(22) 32.0	(27) 36.2	(20) 53.8
1.5	7.5	11.3			-3.5	7.5	11.1	12.9	28.2
13.0	18.1	19.3			11.7	29.4	23.1	20.2	21.1
5.2	6.2	8.1	% Profit Before Taxes/Total Assets		8.9	10.0	6.0	12.5	9.5
.0	1.5	1.9			-4.9	-6.8	-.4	5.1	1.3
12.9	19.2	26.0			19.1	23.1	27.6	36.2	29.2
6.1	7.7	10.4	Sales/Net Fixed Assets		5.3	12.1	10.6	12.0	10.5
3.5	4.7	4.7			3.0	4.6	6.8	5.1	6.0
2.3	2.4	2.6			2.3	3.3	2.5	3.0	2.4
1.7	1.8	1.9	Sales/Total Assets		1.8	2.0	1.9	2.2	1.9
1.3	1.3	1.4			1.4	1.5	1.4	1.6	1.4
1.8	1.5	1.2			1.4	.8	1.2	.8	1.5
(97) 3.4	(92) 2.7	(102) 1.9	% Depr., Dep., Amort./Sales		(13) 2.7	(16) 1.8	(24) 1.8	(26) 1.7	(20) 2.2
5.7	5.0	3.7			10.4	4.5	3.1	3.0	3.5
2.8	3.2	1.4			8.6		1.3		
(51) 4.4	(43) 5.4	(41) 3.3	% Officers', Directors' Owners' Comp/Sales		(10) 14.5		(11) 3.2		
9.6	9.7	10.5			18.6		8.5		
1515654M	**1801825M**	**2407134M**	Net Sales ($)	**2795M**	**26667M**	**70405M**	**200954M**	**437983M**	**1668330M**
1168784M	**1217792M**	**1514840M**	Total Assets ($)	**2291M**	**15146M**	**36854M**	**114763M**	**248690M**	**1097096M**

M = $ thousand MM = $ million

See Pages 11 through 21 for Explanation of Ratios and Data

Current Data Sorted by Assets / Comparative Historical Data

0-500M	500M-2MM	2-10MM	10-50MM	50-100MM	100-250MM	Type of Statement	38 / 52 ALL	
	1	10	18	1	4	Unqualified	38	52
1	35	79	11			Reviewed	160	176
14	56	39	5	2		Compiled	172	161
13	13	7				Tax Returns	37	32
6	28	36	23	4	3	Other	145	129
102 (4/1-9/30/06)			307 (10/1/06-3/31/07)				4/1/02-3/31/03 ALL	4/1/03-3/31/04 ALL
34	133	171	57	7	7	NUMBER OF STATEMENTS	552	550
%	%	%	%	%	%	ASSETS	%	%
12.8	6.9	8.2	6.2			Cash & Equivalents	6.8	7.5
33.4	30.9	30.8	24.1			Trade Receivables (net)	27.4	29.0
11.0	15.4	18.6	19.5			Inventory	15.5	15.6
3.1	2.3	3.0	3.2			All Other Current	3.6	3.6
60.3	55.5	60.5	53.1			Total Current	53.3	55.6
31.8	34.7	32.2	33.2			Fixed Assets (net)	38.3	36.1
5.7	2.8	2.1	7.7			Intangibles (net)	2.4	2.0
2.3	7.0	5.2	6.0			All Other Non-Current	6.0	6.3
100.0	100.0	100.0	100.0			Total	100.0	100.0
						LIABILITIES		
16.3	13.7	11.7	9.3			Notes Payable-Short Term	14.5	13.4
15.6	6.0	5.1	5.4			Cur. Mat.-L.T.D.	7.6	5.9
15.0	11.5	11.5	9.6			Trade Payables	10.7	11.3
.3	.1	.2	.2			Income Taxes Payable	.2	.2
19.6	8.0	9.4	11.4			All Other Current	10.2	10.7
66.8	39.4	37.9	35.9			Total Current	43.2	41.5
24.9	21.7	14.5	19.0			Long-Term Debt	20.6	19.6
.1	.6	.5	1.1			Deferred Taxes	.6	.7
20.7	7.6	5.9	5.2			All Other Non-Current	6.4	6.4
-12.5	30.8	41.1	38.9			Net Worth	29.2	31.7
100.0	100.0	100.0	100.0			Total Liabilities & Net Worth	100.0	100.0
						INCOME DATA		
100.0	100.0	100.0	100.0			Net Sales	100.0	100.0
40.7	31.4	27.3	21.6			Gross Profit	28.3	29.9
36.9	27.4	21.5	15.8			Operating Expenses	26.9	26.7
3.8	4.0	5.8	5.8			Operating Profit	1.4	3.2
1.0	1.1	1.3	1.3			All Other Expenses (net)	1.9	1.2
2.8	2.9	4.5	4.5			Profit Before Taxes	-.5	1.9
						RATIOS		
3.0	2.6	2.9	2.1			Current	2.3	2.5
1.0	1.5	1.6	1.6				1.3	1.4
.6	.9	1.1	1.2				.9	.9
2.3	1.7	1.9	1.3			Quick	1.5	1.7
.8	.9	1.0	.9				.8	.9
.4	.6	.6	.5				.5	.6
19 19.3	35 10.4	40 9.0	45 8.1			Sales/Receivables	40 9.2	40 9.0
34 10.6	44 8.2	55 6.6	55 6.6				54 6.8	55 6.7
47 7.7	63 5.8	68 5.4	70 5.2				73 5.0	72 5.0
0 UND	9 42.0	21 17.5	30 12.0			Cost of Sales/Inventory	15 25.0	14 25.5
7 55.9	27 13.8	39 9.4	58 6.3				35 10.5	33 11.0
42 8.7	52 7.1	63 5.8	82 4.5				65 5.7	68 5.4
6 60.0	13 29.1	12 30.0	19 18.9			Cost of Sales/Payables	13 27.8	15 24.2
18 20.7	22 16.5	24 15.0	26 14.3				26 14.0	27 13.6
39 9.3	35 10.5	38 9.5	37 9.9				44 8.3	41 8.8
6.4	6.4	4.6	4.7			Sales/Working Capital	5.8	5.3
NM	14.2	9.2	7.8				14.9	12.0
-10.9	-69.1	39.0	23.0				-30.4	-43.4
15.0	6.9	8.6	6.6			EBIT/Interest	3.6	5.5
(28) 4.4	(116) 2.6	(161) 2.9	(55) 3.1				(523) 1.4	(516) 2.2
.9	.9	1.6	1.2				-1.1	.1
	2.1	4.1	4.4			Net Profit + Depr., Dep., Amort./Cur. Mat. L/T/D	2.5	2.3
	(28) 1.2	(46) 2.1	(24) 2.3				(165) 1.4	(146) 1.5
	.3	1.2	1.2				.3	.7
.4	.5	.4	.6			Fixed/Worth	.6	.5
NM	1.1	.8	1.0				1.2	1.2
-.8	3.6	1.9	2.1				3.8	3.0
.8	.8	.6	.8			Debt/Worth	.8	.8
-12.6	1.9	1.4	1.7				2.0	2.0
-3.0	14.0	4.2	4.8				8.6	6.2
54.1	45.6	39.1	28.8			% Profit Before Taxes/Tangible Net Worth	24.5	32.5
(15) 14.2	(105) 18.5	(157) 18.5	(50) 19.8				(464) 6.7	(469) 11.8
-3.5	.0	4.4	3.3				-13.3	-1.5
18.5	15.5	15.6	11.2			% Profit Before Taxes/Total Assets	7.2	10.1
6.0	6.0	5.4	5.6				1.7	3.1
-3.6	-.3	1.4	1.2				-7.0	-2.7
28.8	17.2	12.9	7.4			Sales/Net Fixed Assets	9.2	9.4
10.9	7.0	6.8	5.0				4.8	5.1
6.8	4.4	3.9	3.1				2.8	3.3
6.2	3.0	2.5	1.8			Sales/Total Assets	2.2	2.4
3.1	2.4	1.9	1.3				1.7	1.7
2.3	1.7	1.4	1.1				1.2	1.3
1.7	1.9	2.1	2.5			% Depr., Dep., Amort./Sales	3.3	2.9
(27) 3.6	(118) 3.8	(162) 3.2	(55) 4.4				(529) 5.0	(523) 4.7
6.5	5.8	5.3	6.1				7.6	7.0
3.6	2.8	2.3	1.2			% Officers', Directors' Owners' Comp/Sales	2.9	3.2
(19) 7.3	(88) 4.9	(84) 3.6	(12) 2.3				(319) 5.3	(291) 5.2
9.7	8.0	6.7	3.2				9.8	9.4
33890M	376882M	1379700M	1782834M	815720M	1171483M	Net Sales ($)	4687907M	5333364M
9888M	159555M	719099M	1247144M	398117M	1009291M	Total Assets ($)	3331962M	3692946M

© RMA 2007   M = $ thousand   MM = $ million
See Pages 11 through 21 for Explanation of Ratios and Data

Comparative Historical Data / Current Data Sorted by Sales

51	35	34	Type of Statement						
			Unqualified		1	1	4	13	16
160	148	126	Reviewed	1	24	22	50	26	3
130	104	116	Compiled	13	36	30	21	12	4
42	48	33	Tax Returns	9	13	4	6	1	
130	155	100	Other	8	21	11	24	11	25
4/1/04-3/31/05 ALL	4/1/05-3/31/06 ALL	4/1/06-3/31/07 ALL		0-1MM	102 (4/1-9/30/06) 1-3MM	3-5MM	307 (10/1/06-3/31/07) 5-10MM	10-25MM	25MM & OVER
513	490	409	NUMBER OF STATEMENTS	31	94	68	105	63	48
%	%	%	ASSETS	%	%	%	%	%	%
7.0	7.4	7.7	Cash & Equivalents	7.6	9.5	8.1	8.1	5.9	5.6
31.7	31.3	30.1	Trade Receivables (net)	25.6	30.3	30.8	33.1	27.9	28.0
15.6	16.6	16.9	Inventory	8.7	13.9	18.9	18.0	20.1	18.6
3.2	4.0	2.8	All Other Current	4.5	1.4	2.9	3.1	4.0	2.2
57.5	59.3	57.6	Total Current	46.5	55.1	60.7	62.3	58.0	54.4
34.9	33.4	33.2	Fixed Assets (net)	42.5	34.3	33.1	29.8	33.8	32.2
2.1	2.1	3.6	Intangibles (net)	4.2	4.1	1.3	2.6	3.0	8.1
5.5	5.2	5.6	All Other Non-Current	6.8	6.6	4.8	5.3	5.3	5.3
100.0	100.0	100.0	Total	100.0	100.0	100.0	100.0	100.0	100.0
			LIABILITIES						
14.3	12.8	12.7	Notes Payable-Short Term	18.4	12.5	13.6	11.6	10.2	13.8
5.2	5.9	6.2	Cur. Mat.-L.T.D.	15.3	6.4	6.2	4.6	5.5	5.0
12.1	12.8	11.5	Trade Payables	10.9	11.0	11.8	11.5	12.1	12.0
.2	.2	.2	Income Taxes Payable	.1	.2	.1	.3	.2	.2
10.6	10.8	10.1	All Other Current	8.0	11.6	9.1	8.8	11.2	11.0
42.4	42.4	40.7	Total Current	52.7	41.6	40.7	36.7	39.3	41.9
18.6	17.8	18.5	Long-Term Debt	30.4	22.4	14.9	13.7	17.7	19.5
.8	.5	.6	Deferred Taxes	.2	.5	.3	.7	.9	.8
6.2	8.6	7.5	All Other Non-Current	25.0	6.6	7.6	4.4	8.1	4.1
32.0	30.7	32.7	Net Worth	-8.2	28.9	36.4	44.5	34.1	33.6
100.0	100.0	100.0	Total Liabilties & Net Worth	100.0	100.0	100.0	100.0	100.0	100.0
			INCOME DATA						
100.0	100.0	100.0	Net Sales	100.0	100.0	100.0	100.0	100.0	100.0
29.0	27.5	28.8	Gross Profit	40.1	34.5	29.2	27.3	22.2	21.2
24.6	22.9	23.8	Operating Expenses	35.8	30.6	24.3	21.4	17.7	15.2
4.4	4.6	5.0	Operating Profit	4.4	4.0	5.0	6.0	4.5	6.0
1.2	1.3	1.3	All Other Expenses (net)	3.5	.6	1.0	1.1	1.4	1.6
3.2	3.3	3.7	Profit Before Taxes	.8	3.4	3.9	4.8	3.1	4.4
			RATIOS						
2.3	2.3	2.6	Current	3.1	2.8	2.0	3.1	1.9	2.1
1.4	1.5	1.5		.9	1.7	1.5	1.6	1.5	1.5
1.0	1.1	1.0		.5	.8	1.1	1.1	1.1	1.1
1.5	1.6	1.7	Quick	1.5	2.1	1.5	2.0	1.3	1.3
.9	1.0	.9		.7	1.2	.9	1.2	.8	.8
.6	.6	.6		.3	.6	.6	.7	.6	.6
41 8.8	42 8.7	37 9.9	Sales/Receivables	19 18.8	34 10.9	37 9.8	38 9.6	39 9.3	46 7.9
57 6.4	55 6.7	51 7.1		42 8.7	44 8.4	51 7.1	54 6.7	52 7.1	57 6.4
74 4.9	76 4.8	65 5.6		67 5.4	65 5.6	66 5.6	68 5.4	62 5.9	66 5.5
17 21.8	15 23.9	14 27.0	Cost of Sales/Inventory	0 UND	4 85.8	16 22.6	16 22.7	27 13.6	31 11.7
34 10.7	38 9.5	35 10.4		14 26.9	19 18.8	36 10.0	35 10.4	44 8.2	54 6.7
62 5.9	67 5.4	62 5.9		44 8.4	50 7.3	67 5.4	60 6.1	69 5.3	78 4.7
15 24.1	15 23.7	13 28.7	Cost of Sales/Payables	5 69.7	11 34.3	15 24.1	11 34.0	18 20.5	20 17.9
27 13.4	29 12.7	24 15.3		16 22.3	20 18.1	23 16.1	22 16.2	25 14.6	32 11.6
47 7.8	47 7.7	38 9.6		61 6.0	34 10.8	39 9.4	36 10.2	39 9.4	42 8.7
5.5	5.3	5.4	Sales/Working Capital	5.9	5.8	6.0	4.4	6.0	4.9
12.0	10.9	11.1		-64.0	12.3	9.6	9.3	12.3	11.8
-676.7	56.4	104.5		-2.5	-34.2	48.5	68.5	39.0	30.5
8.9	7.4	7.4	EBIT/Interest	4.6	9.3	5.8	12.0	7.3	6.7
(466) 3.1	(459) 3.2	(373) 2.9		(27) 1.8	(80) 3.0	(62) 2.5	(99) 3.7	(59) 1.9	(46) 3.7
1.2	1.3	1.3		-1.3	1.1	1.2	1.8	1.1	1.6
4.4	3.9	3.7	Net Profit + Depr., Dep., Amort./Cur. Mat. L/T/D		2.5	2.9	3.9	4.6	5.1
(139) 2.0	(129) 2.2	(107) 2.0			(17) 1.3	(18) 1.6	(28) 2.2	(22) 2.0	(19) 2.4
1.3	1.0	1.0			.4	.8	1.2	1.0	2.0
.5	.5	.4	Fixed/Worth	.4	.5	.4	.3	.5	.6
1.0	1.0	1.0		5.7	1.2	1.0	.7	1.1	1.0
2.9	2.8	2.9		-2.6	8.8	2.3	1.6	3.0	2.9
.8	.8	.7	Debt/Worth	.7	.7	.8	.5	.8	1.0
2.1	2.0	1.8		-12.5	1.6	1.9	1.4	1.7	2.1
5.8	6.4	7.2		-4.7	NM	4.7	3.1	5.1	.6.4
36.2	41.3	39.2	% Profit Before Taxes/Tangible Net Worth	19.1	38.3	47.7	43.3	34.2	32.4
(436) 15.6	(425) 16.7	(340) 17.4		(14) 9.7	(71) 15.5	(59) 17.4	(97) 21.9	(57) 13.9	(42) 21.7
2.9	3.8	3.0		-10.1	.0	5.3	7.2	1.7	9.2
12.1	12.2	14.7	% Profit Before Taxes/Total Assets	12.6	16.4	11.9	17.6	10.9	12.0
4.8	5.2	5.4		-.3	4.4	5.4	7.7	4.2	7.9
.4	.9	.6		-6.8	.0	1.4	1.9	.2	2.2
10.8	12.0	13.3	Sales/Net Fixed Assets	12.5	19.2	12.5	16.7	8.9	8.1
5.7	6.2	6.7		6.1	7.2	6.9	8.0	5.3	4.9
3.5	3.7	3.8		2.2	4.0	4.0	4.6	3.6	3.1
2.4	2.5	2.7	Sales/Total Assets	2.4	3.0	2.7	2.7	2.5	2.0
1.9	1.9	1.9		1.5	2.3	2.1	2.1	1.8	1.4
1.4	1.3	1.4		.8	1.5	1.6	1.6	1.3	1.1
2.4	2.0	2.0	% Depr., Dep., Amort./Sales	4.3	1.5	2.2	2.0	2.5	1.9
(471) 4.2	(460) 3.5	(370) 3.5		(25) 7.5	(84) 3.8	(62) 3.2	(99) 2.8	(58) 3.5	(42) 3.6
6.1	5.3	5.7		11.2	6.0	5.6	5.2	4.7	5.1
2.7	2.4	2.5	% Officers', Directors' Owners' Comp/Sales	3.8	2.9	2.8	2.2	1.8	
(261) 5.0	(262) 4.5	(206) 4.3		(14) 7.0	(70) 5.5	(40) 5.0	(47) 3.5	(29) 3.2	
8.3	8.9	7.4		16.0	8.2	7.6	5.1	5.0	
5851401M	6283093M	5560509M	Net Sales ($)	18424M	191400M	268708M	752523M	940099M	3389355M
3880660M	3998042M	3543094M	Total Assets ($)	16525M	98422M	138325M	393197M	581860M	2314765M

© RMA 2007

M = $ thousand   MM = $ million
See Pages 11 through 21 for Explanation of Ratios and Data

Current Data Sorted by Assets   **Comparative Historical Data**

0-500M	500M-2MM	2-10MM	10-50MM	50-100MM	100-250MM	Type of Statement	4/1/02-3/31/03 ALL	4/1/03-3/31/04 ALL
		4	11	4	3	Unqualified	14	20
	13	29	10			Reviewed	42	60
2	7	9	3			Compiled	36	40
1	10	6				Tax Returns	12	13
2	12	17	8	3	1	Other	51	40
	28 (4/1-9/30/06)		127 (10/1/06-3/31/07)				4/1/02-3/31/03	4/1/03-3/31/04
5	42	65	32	7	4	NUMBER OF STATEMENTS	155	173
%	%	%	%	%	%	**ASSETS**	%	%
	7.8	6.5	6.9			Cash & Equivalents	7.8	7.2
	31.8	27.4	19.0			Trade Receivables (net)	26.1	24.7
	22.6	31.2	33.6			Inventory	23.0	26.1
	.2	1.6	.9			All Other Current	2.4	2.6
	62.4	66.8	60.5			Total Current	59.2	60.5
	28.3	26.3	28.2			Fixed Assets (net)	31.6	29.5
	3.4	1.8	2.2			Intangibles (net)	4.2	3.5
	6.0	5.2	9.1			All Other Non-Current	5.0	6.5
	100.0	100.0	100.0			Total	100.0	100.0
						LIABILITIES		
	14.9	10.4	12.1			Notes Payable-Short Term	10.6	10.9
	5.0	4.8	4.1			Cur. Mat.-L.T.D.	6.5	6.4
	12.9	12.8	9.6			Trade Payables	10.4	11.5
	.4	.2	.1			Income Taxes Payable	.1	.2
	6.2	9.9	8.4			All Other Current	7.8	9.9
	39.5	38.2	34.3			Total Current	35.4	38.9
	19.3	14.2	13.0			Long-Term Debt	16.2	18.5
	.1	.4	.2			Deferred Taxes	.5	.6
	9.0	5.4	5.5			All Other Non-Current	6.1	9.1
	32.2	41.7	47.0			Net Worth	41.7	32.9
	100.0	100.0	100.0			Total Liabilities & Net Worth	100.0	100.0
						INCOME DATA		
	100.0	100.0	100.0			Net Sales	100.0	100.0
	38.1	32.0	33.9			Gross Profit	34.5	32.7
	34.4	26.3	26.2			Operating Expenses	32.5	31.1
	3.7	5.7	7.6			Operating Profit	1.9	1.6
	1.5	1.4	1.8			All Other Expenses (net)	1.5	1.6
	2.2	4.4	5.8			Profit Before Taxes	.4	.0
						RATIOS		
	2.7	3.3	2.6			Current	3.0	2.8
	1.8	1.9	1.8				1.7	1.7
	1.1	1.2	1.4				1.2	1.1
	1.6	1.7	1.3			Quick	1.8	1.6
	1.0	.9	.7				.9	.8
	.7	.6	.4				.6	.5
	38 9.7	41 8.9	36 10.2			Sales/Receivables	41 8.9	39 9.3
	44 8.3	47 7.7	44 8.3				49 7.4	50 7.2
	61 6.0	59 6.2	52 7.0				66 5.6	62 5.9
	21 17.7	42 8.8	65 5.6			Cost of Sales/Inventory	24 15.2	33 11.1
	48 7.6	77 4.7	93 3.9				64 5.7	80 4.5
	80 4.6	130 2.8	157 2.3				121 3.0	138 2.7
	15 25.1	15 24.1	20 18.5			Cost of Sales/Payables	15 23.8	18 20.1
	24 14.9	25 14.6	30 12.0				25 14.3	31 11.6
	40 9.2	47 7.8	40 9.1				42 8.7	44 8.2
	5.1	4.7	3.5			Sales/Working Capital	4.3	4.2
	8.9	7.2	6.2				7.7	7.6
	87.0	16.4	11.2				25.2	32.2
	7.3	7.0	15.6			EBIT/Interest	4.8	4.2
	(40) 1.8	(60) 3.2	(29) 3.8				(140) 1.6	(156) 1.7
	-.1	1.2	1.3				-.6	-.8
		4.3	2.6			Net Profit + Depr., Dep., Amort./Cur. Mat. L/T/D	2.3	2.7
		(26) 2.3	(13) 1.6				(44) 1.1	(54) 1.4
		1.6	.7				.1	.7
	.4	.3	.3			Fixed/Worth	.3	.4
	.8	.6	.6				.8	.8
	2.8	1.3	1.0				1.7	2.4
	.9	.6	.6			Debt/Worth	.6	.7
	2.0	1.5	1.2				1.4	1.6
	15.3	3.8	2.6				4.8	4.9
	34.9	37.8	21.0			% Profit Before Taxes/Tangible Net Worth	18.2	23.8
	(35) 13.7	(63) 18.7	(31) 14.9				(140) 4.9	(152) 4.3
	-7.6	1.4	3.2				-12.8	-8.4
	11.2	17.5	12.9			% Profit Before Taxes/Total Assets	6.8	8.3
	3.2	5.9	7.3				1.7	2.0
	-2.8	.5	1.2				-4.8	-4.6
	18.9	19.6	12.0			Sales/Net Fixed Assets	12.8	13.8
	8.5	8.0	5.1				5.9	6.1
	5.3	4.3	3.6				3.3	3.3
	3.2	2.5	2.0			Sales/Total Assets	2.3	2.3
	2.3	2.0	1.6				1.7	1.7
	1.8	1.6	1.1				1.1	1.2
	1.2	1.3	2.1			% Depr., Dep., Amort./Sales	2.0	2.1
	(39) 2.6	(62) 2.8	(30) 2.9				(138) 3.8	(151) 3.9
	5.8	4.0	4.2				6.3	5.7
	3.4	2.1				% Officers', Directors' Owners' Comp/Sales	3.6	4.1
	(34) 6.1	(27) 4.2					(70) 7.4	(80) 6.6
	11.9	6.3					10.5	11.4
5870M	126558M	621081M	1018487M	965736M	751586M	Net Sales ($)	3366155M	2008849M
1606M	49575M	298995M	682009M	551290M	618904M	Total Assets ($)	1695137M	1602178M

M = $ thousand   MM = $ million
See Pages 11 through 21 for Explanation of Ratios and Data

Comparative Historical Data   **Current Data Sorted by Sales**

	4/1/04-3/31/05 ALL	4/1/05-3/31/06 ALL	4/1/06-3/31/07 ALL	Type of Statement	0-1MM	1-3MM	3-5MM	5-10MM	10-25MM	25MM & OVER
	24	21	22	Unqualified				1	9	12
	51	53	52	Reviewed		5	12	15	15	5
	31	32	21	Compiled		8	3	6	2	2
	11	16	17	Tax Returns		7	3	4	3	
	41	51	43	Other	1	10	6	6	9	11
						28 (1/1-9/30/06)		127 (10/1/06-3/31/07)		
	158	173	155	NUMBER OF STATEMENTS	1	30	24	32	38	30
	%	%	%	**ASSETS**	%	%	%	%	%	%
	7.7	7.5	6.8	Cash & Equivalents		8.6	5.1	7.2	6.8	6.1
	27.4	28.8	26.3	Trade Receivables (net)		29.3	27.9	29.8	23.3	22.1
	23.9	24.6	28.8	Inventory		20.0	26.5	28.4	36.0	31.0
	2.2	1.9	1.6	All Other Current		.1	.8	1.7	1.3	4.3
	61.2	62.8	63.5	Total Current		58.1	60.3	67.1	67.4	63.4
	29.9	29.0	27.2	Fixed Assets (net)		30.7	30.3	25.9	24.3	26.3
	2.4	2.2	2.8	Intangibles (net)		4.2	3.5	1.8	2.1	2.8
	6.5	6.0	6.5	All Other Non-Current		7.0	6.0	5.1	6.2	7.5
	100.0	100.0	100.0	Total		100.0	100.0	100.0	100.0	100.0
				LIABILITIES						
	11.1	10.8	12.0	Notes Payable-Short Term		12.3	15.4	8.5	11.6	11.7
	5.6	5.5	5.0	Cur. Mat.-L.T.D.		6.7	5.7	4.8	5.4	2.4
	11.3	12.9	12.7	Trade Payables		14.6	11.2	12.3	14.2	11.0
	.1	.5	.2	Income Taxes Payable		.2	.6	.4	.1	.2
	7.9	8.1	8.8	All Other Current		7.1	5.8	7.9	9.2	13.6
	36.0	37.8	38.7	Total Current		40.7	38.7	33.9	40.5	38.9
	16.8	18.8	16.1	Long-Term Debt		24.8	13.5	14.7	15.0	11.9
	.8	.7	.4	Deferred Taxes		.1	.0	.5	.4	.8
	6.3	6.7	9.2	All Other Non-Current		21.4	7.2	6.6	4.7	7.5
	40.1	36.1	35.7	Net Worth		12.9	40.5	44.3	39.4	41.0
	100.0	100.0	100.0	Total Liabilities & Net Worth		100.0	100.0	100.0	100.0	100.0
				INCOME DATA						
	100.0	100.0	100.0	Net Sales		100.0	100.0	100.0	100.0	100.0
	33.6	33.9	33.3	Gross Profit		37.4	36.3	35.1	30.5	28.3
	29.4	28.7	27.7	Operating Expenses		34.3	33.2	28.1	23.8	21.7
	4.2	5.3	5.6	Operating Profit		3.1	3.1	6.9	6.7	6.7
	.7	1.3	1.5	All Other Expenses (net)		1.9	1.3	1.1	2.0	1.3
	3.5	4.0	4.0	Profit Before Taxes		1.2	1.8	5.8	4.8	5.3
				RATIOS						
	2.8	2.6	2.7	Current		2.4	2.8	3.4	2.3	2.4
	1.7	1.7	1.8			1.8	1.9	2.4	1.6	1.8
	1.3	1.2	1.2			1.0	1.0	1.3	1.2	1.3
	1.7	1.7	1.5	Quick		1.6	1.4	2.0	1.2	1.3
	.9	.9	.9			1.0	1.0	1.1	.7	.7
	.6	.6	.5			.6	.7	.7	.5	.5
	42 8.7	41 8.8	37 9.8	Sales/Receivables		37 9.9	38 9.7	42 8.6	37 9.8	36 10.2
	54 6.8	50 7.3	46 8.0			44 8.3	45 8.1	49 7.4	46 8.0	44 8.3
	65 5.7	63 5.8	58 6.3			67 5.5	59 6.1	59 6.2	55 6.6	56 6.5
	31 11.7	29 12.5	37 9.9	Cost of Sales/Inventory		12 31.0	32 11.3	32 11.4	57 6.3	54 6.8
	73 5.0	72 5.1	77 4.8			53 6.9	64 5.7	60 6.1	86 4.2	89 4.1
	124 3.0	119 3.1	129 2.8			80 4.6	127 2.9	136 2.7	153 2.4	113 3.2
	16 23.3	19 19.6	17 21.9	Cost of Sales/Payables		12 29.6	15 24.0	15 23.7	17 21.3	19 18.9
	28 13.0	30 12.3	28 13.3			29 12.7	30 12.1	23 15.6	29 12.6	29 12.7
	47 7.7	44 8.3	44 8.3			51 7.1	46 7.9	44 8.3	45 8.2	38 9.6
	4.1	4.9	4.7	Sales/Working Capital		5.1	5.1	3.9	3.6	4.6
	7.5	8.6	7.5			9.0	7.3	6.3	8.2	7.9
	18.1	19.9	17.0			101.6	171.7	16.4	14.9	12.6
	9.4	8.7	7.4	EBIT/Interest		5.0	3.7	11.1	5.8	9.4
	(148) 3.4	(162) 3.7	(142) 2.8			(27) 1.2	(23) 1.9	(29) 3.6	(35) 2.1	(28) 6.2
	1.4	1.5	1.0			-1.3	.7	2.1	1.3	1.6
	5.6	4.1	3.9	Net Profit + Depr., Dep., Amort./Cur. Mat. L/T/D				5.0	2.5	9.1
	(54) 2.2	(60) 2.2	(53) 2.1					(12) 3.4	(15) 1.6	(14) 2.0
	1.3	1.0	1.1					2.0	1.1	1.3
	.4	.4	.4	Fixed/Worth		.6	.3	.2	.3	.4
	.7	.7	.7			1.9	.7	.5	.6	.6
	1.4	1.9	1.7			-6.8	1.8	1.3	1.3	1.0
	.7	.8	.7	Debt/Worth		1.0	.6	.6	.9	.7
	1.4	1.9	1.7			4.6	1.1	1.5	1.9	1.6
	3.2	4.0	5.1			-620.1	10.3	3.1	5.2	2.7
	31.8	41.0	29.8	% Profit Before Taxes/Tangible Net Worth		38.3	15.0	45.7	28.1	27.6
	(144) 9.8	(158) 18.6	(140) 16.1			(22) 10.8	(20) 5.3	21.0	(36) 17.6	(29) 16.3
	2.5	4.7	1.3			-12.8	.8	6.2	7.4	1.3
	12.5	13.9	14.7	% Profit Before Taxes/Total Assets		14.4	9.2	20.1	13.7	15.5
	4.6	5.8	4.7			1.8	1.5	8.1	4.7	8.2
	.8	1.3	.2			-6.0	-.6	2.6	1.5	.5
	12.1	16.5	15.9	Sales/Net Fixed Assets		16.3	13.9	23.4	18.1	14.3
	5.6	6.9	7.1			7.0	6.4	9.8	7.9	5.6
	3.6	4.2	4.6			4.2	4.4	5.1	4.6	4.6
	2.3	2.4	2.5	Sales/Total Assets		3.2	2.6	2.5	2.4	2.2
	1.7	1.8	1.9			2.2	2.0	2.1	1.8	1.7
	1.3	1.4	1.5			1.5	1.5	1.7	1.4	1.4
	1.9	1.6	1.4	% Depr., Dep., Amort./Sales		1.5	1.5	1.0	1.4	1.5
	(145) 3.8	(161) 3.3	(141) 2.8			(26) 3.0	2.6	(31) 3.1	(36) 2.8	(24) 2.4
	5.6	5.2	4.2			7.5	4.1	4.0	4.1	3.7
	3.0	2.9	3.2	% Officers', Directors' Owners' Comp/Sales		4.1	3.4	2.3	2.1	
	(72) 5.1	(77) 5.1	(64) 4.6			(21) 6.4	(13) 4.6	(19) 4.2	(10) 3.2	
	9.3	7.8	8.1			10.9	12.7	6.3	5.5	
	2226746M	2505235M	3489318M	Net Sales ($)	6M	57186M	91267M	241732M	575706M	2523421M
	1606406M	1616227M	2202379M	Total Assets ($)	4M	28479M	48207M	124414M	358417M	1642858M

© RMA 2007

M = $ thousand   MM = $ million
See Pages 11 through 21 for Explanation of Ratios and Data

Current Data Sorted by Assets   Comparative Historical Data

	0-500M	500M-2MM	2-10MM	10-50MM	50-100MM	100-250MM	Type of Statement	4/1/02-3/31/03 ALL	4/1/03-3/31/04 ALL
			2	1	1	1	Unqualified	7	8
	1	5	17	1			Reviewed	16	16
	1	5	4				Compiled	13	15
	4	7	1				Tax Returns	3	10
	1	4	12	6	1	2	Other	11	23
		15 (4/1-9/30/06)		62 (10/1/06-3/31/07)					
	7	21	36	8	2	3	NUMBER OF STATEMENTS	50	72
	%	%	%	%	%	%	**ASSETS**	%	%
		8.6	10.5				Cash & Equivalents	12.5	9.2
		30.7	25.7				Trade Receivables (net)	26.7	30.3
		22.4	28.1				Inventory	20.1	22.0
		4.1	2.8				All Other Current	6.1	3.9
		65.9	67.0				Total Current	65.3	65.4
		27.4	21.4				Fixed Assets (net)	29.9	26.0
		2.0	7.5				Intangibles (net)	.8	1.9
		4.7	4.2				All Other Non-Current	4.0	6.8
		100.0	100.0				Total	100.0	100.0
							LIABILITIES		
		11.9	10.6				Notes Payable-Short Term	16.1	14.1
		6.2	4.6				Cur. Mat.-L.T.D.	4.3	3.2
		19.1	11.7				Trade Payables	11.1	14.4
		.1	.6				Income Taxes Payable	.2	.1
		7.6	15.6				All Other Current	14.3	15.2
		44.9	43.1				Total Current	46.0	47.0
		19.5	13.9				Long-Term Debt	18.6	18.4
		.3	.8				Deferred Taxes	.1	.3
		12.4	5.7				All Other Non-Current	7.1	8.4
		22.9	36.4				Net Worth	28.2	25.9
		100.0	100.0				Total Liabilities & Net Worth	100.0	100.0
							INCOME DATA		
		100.0	100.0				Net Sales	100.0	100.0
		31.0	29.3				Gross Profit	32.7	33.6
		27.3	22.8				Operating Expenses	30.9	30.0
		3.6	6.5				Operating Profit	1.8	3.6
		1.3	1.2				All Other Expenses (net)	2.2	1.5
		2.3	5.3				Profit Before Taxes	-.4	2.1
							RATIOS		
		2.8	2.8				Current	2.5	2.4
		1.4	1.5					1.6	1.5
		1.1	1.2					1.1	1.0
		1.8	1.5				Quick	1.5	1.6
		1.0	.8					1.0	.8
		.5	.5					.6	.5
		28 13.3	33 11.1				Sales/Receivables	36 10.1	42 8.7
		42 8.7	50 7.3					48 7.6	54 6.8
		53 6.9	77 4.8					70 5.2	70 5.2
		4 99.3	33 11.2				Cost of Sales/Inventory	9 42.2	22 16.4
		30 12.3	71 5.1					56 6.6	57 6.4
		94 3.9	124 2.9					100 3.6	106 3.4
		17 21.1	21 17.3				Cost of Sales/Payables	14 26.6	19 19.1
		39 9.3	32 11.4					23 15.7	33 11.1
		49 7.5	45 8.2					47 7.8	56 6.5
		4.6	3.9				Sales/Working Capital	3.9	4.2
		21.8	7.6					8.4	12.3
		64.2	20.3					41.9	-70.6
		6.5	17.3				EBIT/Interest	3.5	7.6
		(20) 1.6	(34) 3.5					(45) 1.0	(64) 1.7
		.1	2.2					-1.6	-.7
							Net Profit + Depr., Dep., Amort./Cur. Mat. L/T/D	7.6	2.8
								(13) 1.9 (13) 1.0	
								.1	-1.5
		.3	.2				Fixed/Worth	.6	.4
		3.6	.6					1.0	.9
		-4.2	4.9					2.9	11.5
		1.0	.7				Debt/Worth	.8	.9
		16.3	1.6					1.9	2.3
		-17.5	16.5					6.5	125.3
		52.8	39.0				% Profit Before Taxes/Tangible Net Worth	25.3	50.8
		(13) 20.4	(28) 20.3					(42) 3.2	(55) 13.9
		2.2	3.1					-9.6	-4.9
		16.0	15.3				% Profit Before Taxes/Total Assets	6.2	11.7
		2.8	8.8					.2	3.5
		-3.3	4.0					-4.3	-4.0
		30.8	29.3				Sales/Net Fixed Assets	20.5	20.0
		12.7	15.9					6.7	10.1
		7.9	3.9					2.8	4.2
		3.0	2.2				Sales/Total Assets	2.2	2.3
		2.7	1.6					1.6	1.7
		2.0	1.3					1.3	1.3
		1.3	.8				% Depr., Dep., Amort./Sales	1.3	.9
		(15) 3.9	(31) 1.9					(45) 3.5	(64) 2.8
		6.9	4.4					6.5	5.4
		3.1	2.3				% Officers', Directors' Owners' Comp/Sales	1.9	2.5
		(13) 6.0	(14) 3.2					(25) 4.0	(29) 5.4
		8.6	7.0					9.8	8.0
	8022M	58304M	327524M	318156M	258779M	627961M	Net Sales ($)	811700M	762349M
	1711M	22738M	180222M	178635M	160339M	526784M	Total Assets ($)	564662M	564156M

© RMA 2007

M = $ thousand   MM = $ million
See Pags 11 through 21 for Explanation of Ratios and Data

Comparative Historical Data / Current Data Sorted by Sales

			Type of Statement	2	5	3	9	6	3
12	9	5	Unqualified				1	1	3
18	20	24	Reviewed		5	3	9	6	1
15	9	10	Compiled	2	2	4	1	1	
4	8	12	Tax Returns	4	5	2	1		
17	21	26	Other	1	3	3	8	3	8
4/1/04-3/31/05 ALL	4/1/05-3/31/06 ALL	4/1/06-3/31/07 ALL			15 (4/1-9/30/06)		62 (10/1/06-3/31/07)		
				0-1MM	1-3MM	3-5MM	5-10MM	10-25MM	25MM & OVER
66	67	77	NUMBER OF STATEMENTS	7	15	12	20	11	12

'04-05 %	'05-06 %	'06-07 %		0-1MM %	1-3MM %	3-5MM %	5-10MM %	10-25MM %	25MM & OVER %
			ASSETS						
8.0	8.3	10.3	Cash & Equivalents		8.2	13.9	7.8	5.8	11.3
31.8	32.6	28.5	Trade Receivables (net)		32.5	30.1	22.2	33.3	24.4
23.0	23.1	24.8	Inventory		23.3	17.4	34.4	27.8	23.5
5.4	5.2	3.4	All Other Current		3.0	6.2	2.6	1.9	4.6
68.2	69.2	66.9	Total Current		67.0	67.7	67.0	68.7	63.8
24.1	23.6	23.0	Fixed Assets (net)		25.3	22.8	23.7	19.3	18.9
2.9	3.3	5.7	Intangibles (net)		3.7	5.3	3.0	10.7	10.4
4.7	4.0	4.4	All Other Non-Current		4.0	4.2	6.3	1.4	6.9
100.0	100.0	100.0	Total		100.0	100.0	100.0	100.0	100.0
			LIABILITIES						
14.2	12.4	10.6	Notes Payable-Short Term		11.3	10.8	12.0	11.7	5.4
3.4	4.1	5.1	Cur. Mat.-L.T.D.		8.0	3.9	4.7	3.3	2.7
14.2	15.3	14.0	Trade Payables		21.7	10.9	12.5	14.2	13.3
.1	.1	.4	Income Taxes Payable		.1	1.4	.0	.1	.6
14.4	14.3	12.5	All Other Current		9.1	10.1	12.3	17.9	19.5
46.3	46.2	42.5	Total Current		50.1	37.2	41.5	47.3	41.5
15.7	17.1	15.8	Long-Term Debt		19.9	10.6	16.2	11.7	16.1
.2	.4	.5	Deferred Taxes		.2	.8	.5	1.2	.5
10.7	9.2	6.9	All Other Non-Current		15.8	4.4	6.7	2.3	.5
27.2	27.1	34.3	Net Worth		14.0	47.0	35.1	37.5	41.4
100.0	100.0	100.0	Total Liabilties & Net Worth		100.0	100.0	100.0	100.0	100.0
			INCOME DATA						
100.0	100.0	100.0	Net Sales		100.0	100.0	100.0	100.0	100.0
31.8	32.7	30.9	Gross Profit		29.7	26.2	31.3	26.3	27.2
26.9	27.3	24.9	Operating Expenses		24.4	23.3	25.9	17.5	18.3
4.9	5.4	6.0	Operating Profit		5.3	2.9	5.4	8.8	9.0
1.0	1.1	1.4	All Other Expenses (net)		1.0	.5	1.7	1.5	1.6
4.0	4.3	4.6	Profit Before Taxes		4.2	2.4	3.8	7.3	7.4
			RATIOS						
2.5	2.5	2.7	Current		3.0	3.1	2.8	2.4	1.8
1.3	1.5	1.6			1.1	1.9	1.5	1.5	1.7
1.1	1.1	1.1			.9	1.4	1.1	.9	1.4
1.2	1.6	1.6	Quick		1.8	2.6	1.9	1.1	1.1
.8	.9	.9			1.0	1.4	.7	.8	.8
.5	.5	.5			.3	.6	.4	.7	.7
39 9.4	33 11.0	33 11.2	Sales/Receivables		22 16.7	34 10.8	27 13.3	50 7.4	36 10.1
54 6.7	54 6.7	46 7.9			40 9.1	48 7.7	37 9.8	57 6.4	52 7.1
76 4.8	74 4.9	62 5.8			58 6.3	85 4.3	58 6.3	96 3.8	69 5.3
19 19.5	23 16.0	18 20.1	Cost of Sales/Inventory		3 136.4	18 20.4	60 6.1	21 17.5	36 10.2
63 5.8	53 6.9	64 5.7			22 16.4	41 9.0	106 3.4	75 4.9	66 5.6
108 3.4	95 3.8	109 3.3			100 3.7	74 4.9	147 2.5	122 3.0	92 4.0
15 24.3	20 18.7	18 20.5	Cost of Sales/Payables		21 17.2	14 26.8	24 15.2	17 21.4	14 26.1
34 10.7	29 12.5	30 12.0			41 8.9	24 15.0	35 10.5	30 12.2	20 18.4
60 6.1	57 6.4	49 7.5			63 6.3	45 8.2	45 8.2	46 7.9	58 6.3
4.9	4.8	4.5	Sales/Working Capital		4.6	3.7	4.4	5.2	5.4
11.1	10.2	8.4			31.0	5.2	8.3	8.3	8.0
29.0	25.1	28.9			-26.5	13.8	24.8	-62.9	10.1
12.4	15.9	13.8	EBIT/Interest		6.4	5.1	49.3	16.1	26.9
(60) 3.0	(59) 3.3	(70) 3.3			(13) 2.2	1.6	(19) 3.5	8.0	(10) 4.4
1.1	1.5	.7			-.2	-4.1	2.2	2.5	1.2
8.5	4.6	3.2	Net Profit + Depr., Dep., Amort./Cur. Mat. L/T/D						
(16) 5.1	(16) 2.2	(19) 2.0							
1.3	1.0	.6							
.3	.2	.2	Fixed/Worth		.1	.2	.2	.4	.1
.6	.7	.6			-10.3	.5	.4	.6	.5
3.5	3.5	-8.2			-.9	3.0	4.1	-1.9	NM
1.0	1.1	.7	Debt/Worth		1.0	.5	.6	.6	.8
2.4	2.6	1.6			-26.9	1.2	1.6	1.6	1.1
11.2	10.4	-25.7			-9.5	12.8	7.7	-4.5	NM
35.8	59.4	50.3	% Profit Before Taxes/Tangible Net Worth			20.4	45.5		
(53) 18.4	(53) 21.8	(56) 21.7				(11) 6.1	(17) 25.8		
3.2	8.0	4.5				-14.7	8.2		
11.4	16.0	19.2	% Profit Before Taxes/Total Assets		25.3	7.2	20.7	15.5	21.9
5.7	5.8	8.2			12.5	1.8	8.8	9.1	11.0
.2	1.3	.1			-3.5	-5.2	3.1	4.9	1.1
31.0	32.8	34.2	Sales/Net Fixed Assets		41.3	18.4	30.0	26.6	55.2
10.7	12.3	12.9			18.2	10.4	18.4	10.1	11.3
4.2	4.5	4.4			9.0	5.5	3.9	6.6	5.1
2.5	2.7	2.7	Sales/Total Assets		3.2	2.6	2.3	2.2	2.4
1.9	1.9	1.9			2.7	1.6	1.8	1.8	1.8
1.3	1.4	1.4			2.1	1.2	1.3	1.4	1.3
1.1	1.0	1.0	% Depr., Dep., Amort./Sales			1.0	.9		1.0
(58) 2.6	(54) 2.2	(62) 2.2				2.3	(17) 1.8	(11) 1.6	
4.8	3.8	5.0				5.8	5.3		2.5
2.8	2.8	2.8	% Officers', Directors', Owners' Comp/Sales						
(25) 6.1	(26) 5.6	(33) 5.2							
8.1	8.1	8.5							
1128832M	1147601M	1598746M	Net Sales ($)	4430M	29770M	47985M	140230M	159106M	1217225M
877540M	687612M	1070429M	Total Assets ($)	3785M	12222M	30960M	91633M	86427M	845402M

© RMA 2007

M = $ thousand   MM = $ million
See Pages 11 through 21 for Explanation of Ratios and Data

Current Data Sorted by Assets   **Comparative Historical Data**

0-500M	500M-2MM	2-10MM	10-50MM	50-100MM	100-250MM	Type of Statement	4/1/02-3/31/03 ALL	4/1/03-3/31/04 ALL
		3	3		1	Unqualified	8	11
1		7	1			Reviewed	8	13
1		5				Compiled	7	4
			1			Tax Returns	2	
1		3	3			Other	12	7
		10 (4/1-9/30/06)	20 (10/1/06-3/31/07)					
3		18	8		1	**NUMBER OF STATEMENTS**	37	35
%	%	%	%	%	%	**ASSETS**	%	%
		5.7				Cash & Equivalents	10.1	10.0
		21.5				Trade Receivables (net)	24.7	20.5
		33.3				Inventory	23.0	26.4
		1.2				All Other Current	1.5	1.4
		61.6				Total Current	59.3	58.4
		26.1				Fixed Assets (net)	33.1	33.8
		2.2				Intangibles (net)	2.5	1.1
		10.1				All Other Non-Current	5.1	6.8
		100.0				Total	100.0	100.0
						LIABILITIES		
		8.5				Notes Payable-Short Term	9.7	7.9
		4.3				Cur. Mat.-L.T.D.	8.9	5.2
		10.1				Trade Payables	12.7	8.5
		.3				Income Taxes Payable	.1	.2
		9.9				All Other Current	7.4	7.4
		33.1				Total Current	38.8	29.2
		15.6				Long-Term Debt	14.0	12.2
		.1				Deferred Taxes	.5	.6
		5.3				All Other Non-Current	7.7	5.9
		45.9				Net Worth	39.0	52.0
		100.0				Total Liabilities & Net Worth	100.0	100.0
						INCOME DATA		
		100.0				Net Sales	100.0	100.0
		27.9				Gross Profit	29.8	23.9
		22.0				Operating Expenses	28.0	22.9
		5.9				Operating Profit	1.8	1.0
		1.0				All Other Expenses (net)	1.6	.4
		4.9				Profit Before Taxes	.1	.6
						RATIOS		
		2.2				Current	3.0	4.0
		1.7					1.7	2.6
		1.5					1.1	1.3
		1.3				Quick	2.3	2.8
		.8					1.1	1.0
		.5					.5	.5
		41 8.8				Sales/Receivables	39 9.3	47 7.8
		50 7.2					51 7.2	55 6.6
		55 6.6					63 5.8	65 5.6
		64 5.7				Cost of Sales/Inventory	35 10.3	43 8.5
		104 3.5					52 7.0	86 4.2
		124 2.9					94 3.9	130 2.8
		10 35.2				Cost of Sales/Payables	16 23.5	17 22.0
		30 12.1					25 14.3	32 11.4
		40 9.2					50 7.2	41 9.0
		4.6				Sales/Working Capital	3.5	2.9
		6.7					7.1	3.9
		9.2					97.3	17.7
		9.3				EBIT/Interest	4.3	4.7
		5.8					(34) 1.3	(30) 1.1
		2.1					-1.6	-2.4
						Net Profit + Depr., Dep., Amort./Cur. Mat. L/T/D		7.4
								(12) 1.2
								1.0
		.2				Fixed/Worth	.5	.4
		.6					.8	.6
		1.4					2.9	1.5
		.4				Debt/Worth	.5	.3
		1.5					1.7	.8
		2.7					6.7	3.0
		27.8				% Profit Before Taxes/Tangible Net Worth	12.2	13.9
		(16) 16.9					(32) 3.0	1.5
		1.1					-7.5	-7.4
		15.6				% Profit Before Taxes/Total Assets	4.4	5.7
		5.9					1.1	.3
		1.0					-5.1	-3.9
		13.7				Sales/Net Fixed Assets	11.2	7.1
		8.3					5.0	3.9
		3.6					2.9	2.7
		2.0				Sales/Total Assets	2.3	1.7
		1.6					1.7	1.3
		1.2					1.2	1.0
		2.1				% Depr., Dep., Amort./Sales	2.5	3.2
		3.5					(36) 4.7	5.4
		6.4					7.5	8.4
						% Officers', Directors' Owners' Comp/Sales	3.5	3.1
							(13) 6.0	(14) 5.3
							9.3	9.8
	6838M	157828M	264375M		243287M	Net Sales ($)	979007M	1009069M
	3904M	93563M	174337M		236172M	Total Assets ($)	934573M	847928M

Data marked "DATA NOT AVAILABLE" in the 0-500M and 10-50MM (second period) columns.

Comparative Historical Data | | | | Current Data Sorted by Sales

						Type of Statement							
	7		6		7	Unqualified						5	2
	11		7		9	Reviewed			4		2	1	2
	1		3		6	Compiled		2	2		2		
	1		1		1	Tax Returns							1
	11		11		7	Other		1	1		1	1	3
	4/1/04-3/31/05 ALL		4/1/05-3/31/06 ALL		4/1/06-3/31/07 ALL			10 (4/1-9/30/06)			20 (10/1/06-3/31/07)		
							0-1MM	1-3MM	3-5MM	5-10MM	10-25MM	25MM & OVER
	31		28		30	NUMBER OF STATEMENTS	3	7	5		7	8
	%		%		%	ASSETS	%	%	%	%	%	%
	9.1		3.9		5.3	Cash & Equivalents						
	23.5		28.4		22.0	Trade Receivables (net)						
	31.1		30.5		30.0	Inventory	D					
	1.0		2.7		1.0	All Other Current	A					
	64.6		65.4		58.4	Total Current	T					
	28.0		26.1		29.2	Fixed Assets (net)	A					
	1.2		2.9		4.8	Intangibles (net)						
	6.2		5.6		7.7	All Other Non-Current	N					
	100.0		100.0		100.0	Total	O					
						LIABILITIES	T					
	7.4		12.0		9.6	Notes Payable-Short Term						
	4.5		3.6		4.3	Cur. Mat.-L.T.D.	A					
	10.8		13.0		10.4	Trade Payables	V					
	.0		.2		.2	Income Taxes Payable	A					
	7.1		10.6		10.3	All Other Current	I					
	29.9		39.4		34.9	Total Current	L					
	10.4		11.3		17.8	Long-Term Debt	A					
	1.3		.1		.4	Deferred Taxes	B					
	3.3		9.3		5.9	All Other Non-Current	L					
	55.1		39.8		41.1	Net Worth	E					
	100.0		100.0		100.0	Total Liabilties & Net Worth						
						INCOME DATA						
	100.0		100.0		100.0	Net Sales						
	28.0		26.2		27.6	Gross Profit						
	22.7		21.6		20.2	Operating Expenses						
	5.4		4.6		7.4	Operating Profit						
	1.0		.3		1.2	All Other Expenses (net)						
	4.4		4.3		6.2	Profit Before Taxes						
						RATIOS						
	6.1		2.3		2.1							
	2.5		1.6		1.6	Current						
	1.4		1.3		1.3							
	3.5		1.1		1.2							
	1.2		.8		.8	Quick						
	.6		.6		.6							
42	8.8	42	8.7	42	8.6							
56	6.5	51	7.1	52	7.1	Sales/Receivables						
67	5.5	67	5.4	59	6.2							
59	6.2	59	6.1	68	5.4							
79	4.6	81	4.5	99	3.7	Cost of Sales/Inventory						
120	3.0	108	3.4	115	3.2							
16	23.2	19	19.6	12	29.5							
23	16.0	29	12.8	30	12.1	Cost of Sales/Payables						
42	8.7	37	9.7	42	8.6							
	2.9		5.2		5.0							
	4.6		7.4		7.8	Sales/Working Capital						
	10.4		18.5		14.9							
	16.2		8.9		8.8							
(27)	3.0	(26)	6.1		5.9	EBIT/Interest						
	.8		1.5		3.1							
					4.9	Net Profit + Depr., Dep.,						
				(10)	2.4	Amort./Cur. Mat. L/T/D						
					.9							
	.2		.2		.4							
	.5		.8		.9	Fixed/Worth						
	1.3		1.3		2.0							
	.2		.7		1.0							
	.8		1.7		2.0	Debt/Worth						
	2.1		3.2		3.6							
	25.5		37.9		50.8	% Profit Before Taxes/Tangible						
(30)	8.4	(26)	21.0	(26)	20.1	Net Worth						
	-1.1		2.0		3.7							
	12.3		13.9		15.6	% Profit Before Taxes/Total						
	5.9		6.7		9.7	Assets						
	-.3		.8		4.2							
	16.5		16.0		11.3							
	5.8		7.3		5.3	Sales/Net Fixed Assets						
	2.5		4.7		3.5							
	2.3		2.2		2.0							
	1.5		1.9		1.6	Sales/Total Assets						
	1.1		1.4		1.2							
	2.7		1.8		2.2							
(27)	4.8	(27)	3.0		3.7	% Depr., Dep., Amort./Sales						
	7.3		4.6		5.1							
	2.0				1.9	% Officers', Directors'						
(11)	3.7			(13)	5.7	Owners' Comp/Sales						
	10.1				8.0							
	742554M		719804M		672328M	Net Sales ($)		4783M	26307M	37691M	101497M	502050M
	591312M		474591M		507976M	Total Assets ($)		4205M	26472M	21742M	69161M	386396M

M = $ thousand   MM = $ million
See Pages 11 through 21 for Explanation of Ratios and Data

Current Data Sorted by Assets — Comparative Historical Data

0-500M	500M-2MM	2-10MM	10-50MM	50-100MM	100-250MM	Type of Statement	4/1/02-3/31/03 ALL	4/1/03-3/31/04 ALL
		5	6		1	Unqualified	11	7
	1	8	1			Reviewed	9	10
	1	3				Compiled	3	3
1	1	2	1			Tax Returns	1	2
1	2	7	5	1		Other	11	11
	8 (4/1-9/30/06)		38 (10/1/06-3/31/07)					
1	5	25	13	1	1	NUMBER OF STATEMENTS	35	33
%	%	%	%	%	%	ASSETS	%	%
		5.4	5.0			Cash & Equivalents	5.1	8.6
		25.7	24.7			Trade Receivables (net)	28.0	27.2
		35.2	27.5			Inventory	26.5	26.0
		1.8	6.3			All Other Current	3.0	1.5
		68.2	63.6			Total Current	62.6	63.4
		24.7	24.4			Fixed Assets (net)	28.1	26.8
		1.1	5.2			Intangibles (net)	3.9	4.3
		6.0	6.9			All Other Non-Current	5.4	5.4
		100.0	100.0			Total	100.0	100.0
						LIABILITIES		
		14.3	8.0			Notes Payable-Short Term	19.7	11.7
		4.2	3.3			Cur. Mat.-L.T.D.	3.8	3.7
		14.1	15.2			Trade Payables	11.5	14.3
		.2	.6			Income Taxes Payable	.7	.6
		8.0	11.6			All Other Current	11.7	8.6
		40.8	38.7			Total Current	47.3	38.9
		18.7	9.2			Long-Term Debt	26.0	16.6
		.4	.6			Deferred Taxes	.3	.4
		5.4	5.1			All Other Non-Current	6.0	4.3
		34.7	46.4			Net Worth	20.4	39.8
		100.0	100.0			Total Liabilties & Net Worth	100.0	100.0
						INCOME DATA		
		100.0	100.0			Net Sales	100.0	100.0
		33.0	29.4			Gross Profit	32.4	29.6
		26.7	20.1			Operating Expenses	27.3	27.2
		6.2	9.3			Operating Profit	5.2	2.4
		2.6	1.6			All Other Expenses (net)	1.6	1.3
		3.6	7.7			Profit Before Taxes	3.6	1.1
						RATIOS		
		3.2	2.8			Current	2.9	2.5
		1.8	1.4				1.8	1.9
		1.3	1.2				1.5	1.2
		1.4	1.5			Quick	1.4	1.5
		.9	.7				1.0	.9
		.5	.5				.8	.6
		35 10.4	43 8.6			Sales/Receivables	39 9.5	38 9.6
		50 7.3	52 7.0				51 7.1	53 6.9
		59 6.1	63 5.8				70 5.2	65 5.6
		36 10.2	44 8.3			Cost of Sales/Inventory	46 8.0	44 8.2
		102 3.6	73 5.0				85 4.3	73 5.0
		192 1.9	119 3.1				135 2.7	104 3.5
		21 17.2	14 25.6			Cost of Sales/Payables	12 30.4	20 17.8
		31 11.8	41 8.9				29 12.7	29 12.6
		61 6.0	66 5.5				53 6.9	43 8.4
		3.4	3.7			Sales/Working Capital	3.5	4.3
		7.7	9.1				6.3	7.2
		18.8	25.7				13.2	24.8
		16.0	21.8			EBIT/Interest	9.3	5.2
		(23) 3.5	(12) 8.6				(34) 3.8	(29) 1.3
		1.5	3.6				1.3	-3.1
						Net Profit + Depr., Dep., Amort./Cur. Mat. L/T/D		
		.2	.3			Fixed/Worth	.4	.5
		.4	.6				.8	.8
		1.3	1.1				1.2	2.4
		.7	.5			Debt/Worth	.8	.7
		1.5	1.2				1.5	1.2
		2.9	3.0				2.4	5.6
		26.8	47.2			% Profit Before Taxes/Tangible Net Worth	38.1	18.4
		(22) 16.7	(12) 24.4				(31) 14.3	(29) 1.0
		7.3	17.6				2.3	-10.2
		14.8	13.8			% Profit Before Taxes/Total Assets	12.9	8.8
		6.9	11.6				4.9	1.1
		1.9	5.7				1.2	-4.4
		29.6	15.2			Sales/Net Fixed Assets	15.3	14.5
		8.7	7.6				5.5	6.7
		4.0	4.0				3.6	4.2
		2.5	2.1			Sales/Total Assets	2.3	2.6
		1.9	1.8				1.7	1.9
		1.6	1.4				1.1	1.3
		1.1	1.1			% Depr., Dep., Amort./Sales	1.5	2.1
		(20) 2.5	2.1				(30) 2.9	(29) 3.1
		5.0	3.1				4.5	4.4
						% Officers', Directors' Owners' Comp/Sales		
3152M	18916M	243104M	548937M	127551M	243287M	Net Sales ($)	1018324M	839739M
431M	6045M	122009M	307346M	64898M	232978M	Total Assets ($)	825166M	647294M

© RMA 2007

M = $ thousand   MM = $ million
See Pages 11 through 21 for Explanation of Ratios and Data

Comparative Historical Data

Current Data Sorted by Sales

Type of Statement									
	6	6	12	Unqualified				3	3	6
	10	8	10	Reviewed		3		3	3	1
	5	4	4	Compiled		3		1		
	2	3	5	Tax Returns		3			1	1
	15	11	15	Other	1			5	4	5

Middle grouping: **8 (4/1-9/30/06)** covers 0-1MM, 1-3MM, 3-5MM; **38 (10/1/06-3/31/07)** covers 5-10MM, 10-25MM, 25MM & OVER.

	4/1/04-3/31/05 ALL	4/1/05-3/31/06 ALL	4/1/06-3/31/07 ALL	0-1MM	1-3MM	3-5MM	5-10MM	10-25MM	25MM & OVER
NUMBER OF STATEMENTS	38	32	46	1		9	12	11	13
ASSETS	%	%	%	%	%	%	%	%	%
Cash & Equivalents	7.3	5.2	5.8				7.4	3.4	5.7
Trade Receivables (net)	30.6	30.8	25.8				24.6	28.2	30.1
Inventory	26.7	32.6	30.9	DATA			33.8	34.2	24.9
All Other Current	2.0	1.7	3.5	NOT			4.2	2.0	5.4
Total Current	66.6	70.2	66.0	AVAILABLE			70.0	67.8	66.2
Fixed Assets (net)	25.2	22.7	25.4				25.3	22.0	24.7
Intangibles (net)	1.6	3.8	2.8				2.5	.4	5.1
All Other Non-Current	6.6	3.3	5.8				2.2	9.8	4.0
Total	100.0	100.0	100.0				100.0	100.0	100.0
LIABILITIES									
Notes Payable-Short Term	8.7	8.8	24.6				63.3	17.4	8.8
Cur. Mat.-L.T.D.	3.5	4.3	4.2				5.8	3.2	2.7
Trade Payables	14.9	14.8	14.2				13.1	17.2	15.0
Income Taxes Payable	.4	.5	.3				.7	.1	.2
All Other Current	11.9	11.3	9.5				10.0	5.3	14.7
Total Current	39.4	39.7	52.9				92.8	43.2	41.5
Long-Term Debt	11.3	9.9	19.8				19.6	12.6	6.0
Deferred Taxes	.7	1.0	.5				.8	.3	.4
All Other Non-Current	4.9	3.1	6.5				10.7	.2	5.9
Net Worth	43.8	46.3	20.3				-24.0	43.7	46.1
Total Liabilities & Net Worth	100.0	100.0	100.0				100.0	100.0	100.0
INCOME DATA									
Net Sales	100.0	100.0	100.0				100.0	100.0	100.0
Gross Profit	32.9	32.4	33.6				35.4	25.1	29.3
Operating Expenses	27.3	25.5	25.7				27.9	19.2	20.5
Operating Profit	5.6	6.9	7.9				7.5	5.9	8.9
All Other Expenses (net)	1.1	.8	2.2				3.6	1.6	1.7
Profit Before Taxes	4.5	6.1	5.7				3.9	4.3	7.2
RATIOS									
Current	2.9	3.1	2.9				3.1	3.6	2.3
	1.7	1.9	1.7				1.8	1.4	1.6
	1.3	1.2	1.2				1.2	1.1	1.3
Quick	1.4	1.6	1.3				1.3	1.7	1.5
	1.0	1.0	.9				.8	1.0	.8
	.7	.5	.5				.5	.4	.5
Sales/Receivables	38 9.6	37 9.9	40 9.2				33 11.0	46 7.9	43 8.6
	49 7.5	50 7.3	50 7.3				46 8.0	50 7.3	56 6.5
	61 5.9	63 5.8	61 6.0				69 5.3	53 6.9	69 5.3
Cost of Sales/Inventory	32 11.5	45 8.1	37 9.9				32 11.5	38 9.5	44 8.3
	76 4.8	78 4.7	79 4.6				125 2.9	85 4.3	72 5.1
	139 2.6	151 2.4	143 2.6				177 2.1	107 3.4	107 3.4
Cost of Sales/Payables	23 15.8	18 20.6	20 18.6				18 20.2	22 16.5	10 34.9
	33 11.1	27 13.3	31 11.8				28 13.3	33 11.1	29 12.5
	51 7.1	47 7.7	55 6.7				77 4.7	52 7.0	55 6.7
Sales/Working Capital	4.1	4.2	3.7				3.3	3.7	4.8
	9.6	7.0	8.2				6.9	14.2	9.1
	21.6	14.5	20.6				23.8	34.6	13.3
EBIT/Interest	22.1	22.7	16.6				12.5	16.6	27.7
	(31) 7.9	(30) 8.4	(43) 6.0				(10) 5.2	3.3	(12) 11.8
	4.6	2.8	2.6				1.4	1.4	5.9
Net Profit + Depr., Dep., Amort./Cur. Mat. L/T/D		4.3	7.4						
		(12) 2.1	(19) 3.0						
		1.2	1.9						
Fixed/Worth	.3	.3	.3				.4	.0	.4
	.6	.5	.6				.8	.3	.5
	1.1	1.2	1.5				NM	1.1	1.1
Debt/Worth	.6	.5	.6				.5	.4	.5
	1.3	1.3	1.7				2.0	1.0	1.2
	2.5	2.8	3.9				NM	3.5	2.8
% Profit Before Taxes/Tangible Net Worth	59.2	38.8	36.9					23.1	47.2
	(35) 16.2	(31) 24.7	(38) 20.8					(10) 16.3	(12) 26.9
	4.9	15.2	10.8					7.7	20.8
% Profit Before Taxes/Total Assets	17.0	20.3	18.2				23.8	12.2	16.7
	6.7	9.7	10.3				7.8	9.3	11.6
	2.1	4.0	4.9				1.6	1.1	7.3
Sales/Net Fixed Assets	15.5	26.2	21.5				16.4	64.2	15.2
	8.1	8.4	8.2				8.5	26.5	7.6
	5.0	5.1	4.4				4.4	3.5	5.3
Sales/Total Assets	3.0	3.2	2.4				2.5	3.0	2.3
	2.0	2.1	1.9				1.9	1.9	1.9
	1.4	1.6	1.5				1.3	1.6	1.5
% Depr., Dep., Amort./Sales	1.7	1.3	1.1						1.7
	(33) 2.9	(26) 2.2	(39) 2.4						2.4
	3.3	2.7	4.1						3.2
% Officers', Directors' Owners' Comp/Sales		2.0							
		(10) 2.8							
		7.0							
Net Sales ($)	1127958M	898779M	1184947M	785M		36940M	89556M	148754M	908912M
Total Assets ($)	652962M	434747M	733707M	616M		22017M	57262M	75068M	578744M

M = $ thousand   MM = $ million
See Pages 11 through 21 for Explanation of Ratios and Data

Current Data Sorted by Assets

Comparative Historical Data

0-500M	500M-2MM	2-10MM	10-50MM	50-100MM	100-250MM	Type of Statement	4/1/02-3/31/03 ALL	4/1/03-3/31/04 ALL
		4	14	1	2	Unqualified	30	19
		12	9			Reviewed	21	18
	6	4				Compiled	20	30
	4	3				Tax Returns	2	7
1	3	9	8	1	2	Other	39	34
	15 (4/1-9/30/06)		68 (10/1/06-3/31/07)					
1	13	32	31	2	4	NUMBER OF STATEMENTS	112	108
%	%	%	%	%	%	ASSETS	%	%
	9.4	5.6	5.7			Cash & Equivalents	8.4	7.5
	32.0	26.3	27.5			Trade Receivables (net)	28.2	28.7
	31.5	36.3	32.9			Inventory	30.0	31.4
	1.9	1.8	3.0			All Other Current	2.5	3.2
	74.9	70.0	69.1			Total Current	69.2	70.7
	15.4	18.5	22.0			Fixed Assets (net)	21.0	20.6
	2.1	6.8	3.3			Intangibles (net)	3.1	3.5
	7.6	4.8	5.6			All Other Non-Current	6.6	5.2
	100.0	100.0	100.0			Total	100.0	100.0
						LIABILITIES		
	8.5	8.6	7.5			Notes Payable-Short Term	11.1	13.5
	5.2	1.9	2.3			Cur. Mat.-L.T.D.	4.3	4.1
	19.9	16.6	9.9			Trade Payables	13.9	16.8
	.8	.4	.5			Income Taxes Payable	.2	.3
	5.5	8.8	12.4			All Other Current	10.8	8.5
	39.8	36.3	32.6			Total Current	40.2	43.2
	14.4	9.3	11.0			Long-Term Debt	10.6	10.2
	.1	.7	.6			Deferred Taxes	.4	.6
	7.4	7.4	5.0			All Other Non-Current	4.0	4.5
	38.4	46.4	50.8			Net Worth	44.7	41.6
	100.0	100.0	100.0			Total Liabilities & Net Worth	100.0	100.0
						INCOME DATA		
	100.0	100.0	100.0			Net Sales	100.0	100.0
	31.6	33.3	31.9			Gross Profit	32.5	32.2
	25.1	25.8	24.5			Operating Expenses	29.2	29.5
	6.5	7.5	7.4			Operating Profit	3.4	2.8
	1.5	1.0	.0			All Other Expenses (net)	1.2	.6
	5.0	6.5	7.4			Profit Before Taxes	2.1	2.2
						RATIOS		
	2.5	2.7	4.4			Current	3.6	3.2
	2.1	1.8	2.4				1.9	1.7
	1.5	1.4	1.5				1.2	1.2
	1.6	1.5	2.1			Quick	1.8	1.4
	.9	.8	1.0				1.0	.9
	.7	.6	.8				.6	.5
	24 15.5	33 11.1	44 8.3			Sales/Receivables	41 8.9	39 9.4
	46 8.0	42 8.7	55 6.7				51 7.2	49 7.4
	57 6.4	54 6.8	67 5.4				67 5.5	70 5.2
	32 11.6	61 6.0	78 4.7			Cost of Sales/Inventory	52 7.0	51 7.2
	58 6.3	78 4.7	99 3.7				85 4.3	80 4.5
	118 3.1	112 3.3	146 2.5				126 2.9	131 2.8
	20 18.2	22 16.7	19 19.6			Cost of Sales/Payables	19 18.8	21 17.3
	33 11.1	30 12.0	28 13.1				29 12.5	29 12.6
	57 6.4	58 6.3	41 9.0				52 7.0	49 7.5
	5.3	4.2	3.1			Sales/Working Capital	3.5	3.9
	9.3	7.8	5.1				6.3	7.4
	10.3	12.1	7.8				17.4	21.4
	23.9	14.8	39.1			EBIT/Interest	9.7	14.3
	2.5	(31) 6.3	(30) 9.1				(99) 3.0	(97) 3.2
	1.4	2.7	3.9				.4	.7
		9.1	20.2			Net Profit + Depr., Dep., Amort./Cur. Mat. L/T/D	4.7	4.2
		(15) 5.2	(10) 5.1				(31) 2.0	(32) 1.5
		1.0	1.7				.3	.8
	.1	.2	.2			Fixed/Worth	.2	.2
	.3	.3	.5				.4	.4
	1.7	1.0	.8				1.0	1.1
	.6	.6	.5			Debt/Worth	.5	.6
	1.5	1.5	1.1				1.2	1.4
	9.3	2.8	2.5				3.5	3.4
	59.0	49.9	40.9			% Profit Before Taxes/Tangible Net Worth	26.0	20.0
	30.1	(31) 29.7	(30) 23.8				(100) 10.0	(97) 9.9
	8.1	13.6	15.7				1.8	.8
	23.0	18.0	21.3			% Profit Before Taxes/Total Assets	9.7	9.2
	8.2	10.4	10.1				3.9	3.5
	1.1	7.7	6.2				-.7	-.6
	165.2	49.7	19.3			Sales/Net Fixed Assets	25.0	29.7
	23.7	17.9	8.7				10.8	10.3
	8.7	8.1	5.9				5.0	5.7
	3.6	2.9	2.3			Sales/Total Assets	2.4	2.5
	2.1	2.1	1.8				1.8	1.9
	1.8	1.5	1.4				1.3	1.4
	.4	.6	1.2			% Depr., Dep., Amort./Sales	1.1	1.0
	(10) 1.3	(29) .9	(29) 1.8				(99) 2.2	(92) 2.2
	2.1	2.0	2.1				3.3	3.9
		2.5				% Officers', Directors' Owners' Comp/Sales	2.0	3.1
		(14) 3.9					(29) 3.6	(36) 4.4
		5.7					9.2	10.6
1549M	39085M	364030M	1179361M	219075M	1188431M	Net Sales ($)	2069265M	1629986M
125M	14676M	178814M	658901M	134987M	608019M	Total Assets ($)	1368973M	1121651M

M = $ thousand   MM = $ million
See Pages 11 through 21 for Explanation of Ratios and Data

Comparative Historical Data | Current Data Sorted by Sales

4/1/04-3/31/05 ALL	4/1/05-3/31/06 ALL	4/1/06-3/31/07 ALL	Type of Statement	0-1MM	1-3MM	3-5MM	5-10MM	10-25MM	25MM & OVER
24	28	21	Unqualified		2			3	16
24	15	21	Reviewed				5	10	6
18	12	10	Compiled	4	1		3	2	
4	5	8	Tax Returns	3	2		2	1	
36	33	23	Other	1	2		4	7	9
					15 (4/1-9/30/06)			68 (10/1/06-3/31/07)	
106	93	83	**NUMBER OF STATEMENTS**	8	7		14	23	31
%	%	%	**ASSETS**	%	%	%	%	%	%
7.9	8.3	6.9	Cash & Equivalents	D			4.3	7.7	5.7
30.7	28.7	27.3	Trade Receivables (net)	A			29.9	26.2	28.9
31.1	33.4	33.8	Inventory	T			31.3	34.7	35.6
1.9	2.4	2.4	All Other Current	A			1.5	2.0	3.6
71.6	72.8	70.5	Total Current				67.0	70.7	73.9
20.3	19.0	19.4	Fixed Assets (net)	N			18.4	17.1	19.9
3.0	3.3	4.2	Intangibles (net)	O			9.8	4.6	2.6
5.2	4.9	5.9	All Other Non-Current	T			4.8	7.6	3.6
100.0	100.0	100.0	Total				100.0	100.0	100.0
			LIABILITIES	A					
12.5	13.7	7.5	Notes Payable-Short Term	V			8.5	6.4	6.8
2.6	2.3	2.4	Cur. Mat.-L.T.D.	A			2.3	1.2	2.1
14.9	15.3	14.3	Trade Payables	I			19.5	14.0	11.6
.3	.3	.5	Income Taxes Payable	L			1.2	.4	.5
10.6	11.8	12.0	All Other Current	A			7.3	8.1	20.2
40.9	43.5	36.8	Total Current	B			38.8	30.2	41.2
9.9	13.8	11.3	Long-Term Debt	L			10.1	7.7	10.0
.5	.6	.5	Deferred Taxes	E			.7	.3	.6
7.1	7.2	6.3	All Other Non-Current				4.5	7.6	4.4
41.6	34.9	45.1	Net Worth				46.0	54.2	43.8
100.0	100.0	100.0	Total Liabilties & Net Worth				100.0	100.0	100.0
			INCOME DATA						
100.0	100.0	100.0	Net Sales				100.0	100.0	100.0
31.6	32.9	32.3	Gross Profit				35.3	34.1	29.0
27.1	27.9	24.6	Operating Expenses				28.7	26.7	20.5
4.6	5.0	7.6	Operating Profit				6.6	7.4	8.5
.8	1.1	.6	All Other Expenses (net)				.8	-.1	.5
3.8	3.9	7.0	Profit Before Taxes				5.8	7.5	8.1
			RATIOS						
3.1	2.6	3.0	Current				2.2	4.9	3.0
1.9	1.8	2.1					1.7	2.6	2.2
1.3	1.2	1.5					1.4	1.4	1.5
1.5	1.4	1.6	Quick				1.6	2.1	1.4
.9	.8	.9					.8	1.3	.9
.6	.6	.7					.7	.7	.8
41 8.8	42 8.7	38 9.6	Sales/Receivables			32 11.4	39 9.3	44 8.3
55 6.6	53 6.9	47 7.7				38 9.7	52 7.1	52 7.0
70 5.2	65 5.6	61 6.0				53 6.9	65 5.6	62 5.9
58 6.3	61 6.0	58 6.3	Cost of Sales/Inventory			45 8.2	63 5.8	72 5.1
80 4.5	102 3.6	87 4.2				66 5.6	88 4.2	97 3.8
118 3.1	129 2.8	123 3.0				91 4.0	123 3.0	139 2.6
21 17.5	22 16.6	20 18.6	Cost of Sales/Payables			22 16.9	22 16.9	19 19.6
31 11.7	35 10.5	29 12.6				33 11.2	34 10.8	26 14.0
49 7.5	58 6.3	47 7.7				54 6.8	48 7.6	37 9.8
4.1	4.3	3.8	Sales/Working Capital				7.3	2.8	3.4
6.3	5.9	6.5					9.5	5.1	5.2
14.1	16.8	10.6					13.3	11.0	7.8
15.8	11.5	36.3	EBIT/Interest				12.3	35.7	57.1
(91) 4.8	(82) 4.9	(79) 7.1					7.9	(22) 8.0	(28) 13.1
1.4	1.3	2.7					2.7	4.0	3.3
8.5	8.3	9.1	Net Profit + Depr., Dep., Amort./Cur. Mat. L/T/D						
(26) 2.1	(28) 4.7	(27) 5.1							
.9	1.3	1.6							
.2	.2	.2	Fixed/Worth				.2	.1	.2
.5	.5	.3					.4	.2	.4
1.0	1.3	1.0					1.0	.5	.8
.6	.7	.6	Debt/Worth				.7	.5	.6
1.3	1.6	1.2					1.2	1.1	1.1
3.0	5.5	2.9					4.9	1.8	2.9
30.3	36.3	49.3	% Profit Before Taxes/Tangible Net Worth				52.3	41.9	49.2
(97) 13.9	(85) 19.4	(80) 27.8			(13)		29.7	27.3	(29) 26.3
5.1	9.2	15.6					13.5	12.6	20.6
13.3	16.2	21.6	% Profit Before Taxes/Total Assets				17.6	20.5	21.6
5.6	7.3	10.7					10.3	10.2	13.4
.7	1.4	6.2					6.6	7.8	6.8
35.8	32.8	39.0	Sales/Net Fixed Assets				48.2	55.8	19.8
10.9	11.3	12.3					15.5	18.5	8.8
5.6	6.1	6.3					8.7	7.0	6.0
2.5	2.3	2.5	Sales/Total Assets				3.2	2.5	2.3
1.9	1.9	2.0					2.7	2.0	2.0
1.5	1.5	1.5					1.7	1.3	1.5
1.0	.8	.7	% Depr., Dep., Amort./Sales				.6	.5	1.2
(94) 1.7	(82) 1.6	(72) 1.4			(12)		1.1	(21) .9	(27) 1.6
2.8	2.7	2.2					2.1	2.3	2.1
2.6	2.7	1.7	% Officers', Directors' Owners' Comp/Sales						
(34) 4.4	(32) 3.9	(27) 3.5							
5.8	7.0	6.5							
2123522M	2759021M	2991531M	Net Sales ($)	14285M	29458M		101993M	358096M	2487699M
1256314M	1562015M	1595522M	Total Assets ($)	6706M	15203M		51182M	213045M	1309386M

© RMA 2007

M = $ thousand   MM = $ million
See Pages 11 through 21 for Explanation of Ratios and Data

Current Data Sorted by Assets

Comparative Historical Data

						Type of Statement		
				4	2	Unqualified	5	4
1		5		2		Reviewed	7	7
	2					Compiled	4	8
						Tax Returns	1	1
1	2	4	4			Other	6	13
	6 (4/1-9/30/06)		21 (10/1/06-3/31/07)				4/1/02-3/31/03	4/1/03-3/31/04
0-500M	500M-2MM	2-10MM	10-50MM	50-100MM	100-250MM		ALL	ALL
2	4	9	10	2		NUMBER OF STATEMENTS	23	33
%	%	%	%	%	%	ASSETS	%	%
			2.3			Cash & Equivalents	7.7	5.6
			20.6		D	Trade Receivables (net)	34.3	27.8
			39.7		A	Inventory	30.8	31.5
			2.9		T	All Other Current	1.5	1.2
			65.5		A	Total Current	74.4	66.1
			23.3			Fixed Assets (net)	17.2	26.6
			4.9		N	Intangibles (net)	4.8	3.1
			6.4		O	All Other Non-Current	3.6	4.2
			100.0		T	Total	100.0	100.0
					A	LIABILITIES		
			11.6		V	Notes Payable-Short Term	11.1	16.0
			5.6		A	Cur. Mat.-L.T.D.	3.6	2.6
			9.7		I	Trade Payables	23.5	17.2
			.1		L	Income Taxes Payable	.1	.3
			14.1		A	All Other Current	12.4	9.0
			41.0		B	Total Current	50.6	45.0
			14.6		L	Long-Term Debt	13.6	14.7
			1.7		E	Deferred Taxes	.1	.2
			5.8			All Other Non-Current	13.1	8.0
			36.8			Net Worth	22.5	32.1
			100.0			Total Liabilties & Net Worth	100.0	100.0
						INCOME DATA		
			100.0			Net Sales	100.0	100.0
			28.2			Gross Profit	33.5	36.0
			20.3			Operating Expenses	30.1	32.5
			7.9			Operating Profit	3.4	3.5
			.4			All Other Expenses (net)	2.2	2.5
			7.5			Profit Before Taxes	1.2	.9
						RATIOS		
			1.8				1.9	2.5
			1.5			Current	1.4	1.7
			1.3				1.2	1.2
			.6				1.1	1.1
			.6			Quick	.8	.8
			.5				.6	.6
		38	9.6				42	8.8	43	8.6
		44	8.3			Sales/Receivables	53	6.9	53	6.9
		63	5.8				76	4.8	71	5.1
		93	3.9				31	11.7	56	6.6
		108	3.4			Cost of Sales/Inventory	100	3.7	92	4.0
		165	2.2				163	2.2	201	1.8
		19	19.5				24	15.2	21	17.7
		26	13.9			Cost of Sales/Payables	35	10.3	36	10.1
		47	7.8				105	3.5	73	5.0
			4.6				4.4	3.7
			6.8			Sales/Working Capital	13.1	6.3
			12.8				30.1	16.7
							12.9	9.7
						EBIT/Interest	(20) 3.8	(30) 2.4
							1.2	-.9
						Net Profit + Depr., Dep., Amort./Cur. Mat. L/T/D		
			.3				.1	.1
			.5			Fixed/Worth	.4	.7
			2.6				4.4	3.9
			1.0				1.1	.9
			2.6			Debt/Worth	2.2	2.0
			7.3				-34.6	5.4
			61.8				33.4	24.8
			39.8			% Profit Before Taxes/Tangible Net Worth	(17) 10.5	(27) 4.8
			14.9				1.6	-6.6
			15.0				12.9	8.0
			9.4			% Profit Before Taxes/Total Assets	4.4	2.2
			2.3				.7	-4.4
			18.9				54.6	41.8
			8.3			Sales/Net Fixed Assets	14.8	12.0
			5.4				9.6	4.0
			1.9				3.3	2.3
			1.8			Sales/Total Assets	1.9	1.5
			1.0				1.1	1.0
							.7	1.1
						% Depr., Dep., Amort./Sales	(20) 1.5	(25) 1.6
							3.7	3.7
							2.5	
						% Officers', Directors' Owners' Comp/Sales	(10) 4.5	
							7.6	
316M	8363M	99469M	356312M	88430M		Net Sales ($)	309898M	506968M
153M	4510M	46568M	256243M	130263M		Total Assets ($)	254450M	425253M

M = $ thousand   MM = $ million
See Pages 11 through 21 for Explanation of Ratios and Data

Comparative Historical Data | Current Data Sorted by Sales

			Type of Statement	0-1MM	1-3MM	3-5MM	5-10MM	10-25MM	25MM & OVER
2	8	6	Unqualified						6
9	9	8	Reviewed	1			1	4	2
1	2	2	Compiled		1	1			
1	2		Tax Returns		1				
11	9	11	Other	1	2	2	2		4
4/1/04-3/31/05 ALL	4/1/05-3/31/06 ALL	4/1/06-3/31/07 ALL			6 (4/1-9/30/06)		21 (10/1/06-3/31/07)		
24	30	27	NUMBER OF STATEMENTS	2	3	3	3	4	12
%	%	%	**ASSETS**	%	%	%	%	%	%
4.2	4.2	3.1	Cash & Equivalents						2.0
24.3	26.6	22.7	Trade Receivables (net)						21.6
38.0	36.1	34.0	Inventory						34.6
1.9	1.2	4.1	All Other Current						3.6
68.4	68.1	63.9	Total Current						61.8
18.7	23.7	22.9	Fixed Assets (net)						22.4
4.1	2.4	9.1	Intangibles (net)						10.2
8.8	5.8	4.2	All Other Non-Current						5.6
100.0	100.0	100.0	Total						100.0
			LIABILITIES						
18.0	13.2	14.5	Notes Payable-Short Term						15.0
1.9	5.1	4.6	Cur. Mat.-L.T.D.						5.0
12.7	14.9	12.7	Trade Payables						10.1
.2	.1	.2	Income Taxes Payable						.1
9.6	7.3	11.8	All Other Current						12.0
42.3	40.6	43.7	Total Current						42.2
11.6	15.6	15.5	Long-Term Debt						15.7
.4	.8	1.4	Deferred Taxes						2.8
10.3	10.8	13.0	All Other Non-Current						8.2
35.3	32.1	26.5	Net Worth						31.1
100.0	100.0	100.0	Total Liabilities & Net Worth						100.0
			INCOME DATA						
100.0	100.0	100.0	Net Sales						100.0
32.0	30.9	33.7	Gross Profit						29.3
27.5	26.1	23.7	Operating Expenses						20.0
4.5	4.8	10.0	Operating Profit						9.2
1.3	2.0	3.4	All Other Expenses (net)						1.7
3.2	2.8	6.6	Profit Before Taxes						7.5
			RATIOS						
2.5	2.6	1.8	Current						1.9
1.5	1.6	1.5							1.4
1.3	1.2	1.3							1.3
.9	1.2	.9	Quick						.7
.7	.8	.6							.6
.5	.5	.5							.5
35 10.4	44 8.3	37 9.9	Sales/Receivables					39 9.4	
57 6.5	52 7.0	46 7.9						44 8.3	
79 4.6	74 5.0	63 5.8						68 5.4	
85 4.3	80 4.6	72 5.0	Cost of Sales/Inventory					92 3.9	
104 3.5	108 3.4	93 3.9						108 3.4	
168 2.2	138 2.6	115 3.2						147 2.5	
21 17.3	33 11.0	23 16.0	Cost of Sales/Payables					23 15.9	
44 8.3	42 8.7	33 11.1						33 11.1	
64 5.7	67 5.4	49 7.5						48 7.6	
3.5	3.6	4.7	Sales/Working Capital						4.8
6.2	6.9	8.2							7.8
12.7	17.6	14.4							16.2
4.5	6.6	8.4	EBIT/Interest						7.1
(22) 1.4	(27) 2.8	(24) 3.7						(11) 3.5	
-1.0	.3	1.7							1.9
	7.1	7.7	Net Profit + Depr., Dep., Amort./Cur. Mat. L/T/D						7.7
	(11) 2.7	(13) 4.6							
	1.4	2.9							
.1	.3	.3	Fixed/Worth						.3
.5	1.0	1.4							1.6
1.9	3.0	7.5							3.2
.7	1.0	1.4	Debt/Worth						1.1
2.0	2.5	3.6							3.9
4.6	7.3	-44.9							10.6
24.3	33.3	92.8	% Profit Before Taxes/Tangible Net Worth						76.7
(22) 3.1	(27) 12.1	(20) 44.2						(11) 43.7	
-6.7	-4.8	15.9							19.0
9.0	11.1	18.3	% Profit Before Taxes/Total Assets						13.3
1.0	3.5	9.5							8.4
-2.9	-.9	2.7							3.6
47.8	21.7	21.9	Sales/Net Fixed Assets						21.0
11.3	10.1	9.5							10.7
4.9	3.9	5.8							4.9
1.9	2.2	2.3	Sales/Total Assets						2.0
1.5	1.7	1.9							1.8
1.2	1.0	1.0							.8
1.0	.8	.8	% Depr., Dep., Amort./Sales						.8
(18) 1.3	(27) 1.8	(24) 2.1						(10) 2.1	
3.0	3.1	3.1							3.2
			% Officers', Directors' Owners' Comp/Sales						
289981M	427514M	552890M	Net Sales ($)	316M	5216M	11700M	24739M	56263M	454656M
231131M	365883M	437737M	Total Assets ($)	153M	3113M	9948M	16336M	35254M	372933M

© RMA 2007

M = $ thousand   MM = $ million
See Pages 11 through 21 for Explanation of Ratios and Data

Current Data Sorted by Assets   Comparative Historical Data

0-500M	500M-2MM	2-10MM	10-50MM	50-100MM	100-250MM	Type of Statement	4/1/02-3/31/03 ALL	4/1/03-3/31/04 ALL
	1	5	10	1	4	Unqualified	21	19
1	4	23	12	1		Reviewed	35	44
1	9	9	1			Compiled	14	30
	4	2				Tax Returns	2	4
1	3	20	8	3	2	Other	31	26
	37 (4/1-9/30/06)		88 (10/1/06-3/31/07)					
3	21	59	31	5	6	NUMBER OF STATEMENTS	103	123
%	%	%	%	%	%	ASSETS	%	%
	6.4	7.1	16.5			Cash & Equivalents	9.0	10.5
	35.3	36.1	25.1			Trade Receivables (net)	31.8	31.4
	30.8	26.0	28.2			Inventory	22.6	24.9
	1.9	4.5	3.3			All Other Current	4.4	3.5
	74.3	73.6	73.0			Total Current	67.9	70.3
	17.9	16.2	18.3			Fixed Assets (net)	21.2	20.2
	.4	2.0	3.4			Intangibles (net)	4.5	2.5
	7.4	8.1	5.3			All Other Non-Current	6.4	6.9
	100.0	100.0	100.0			Total	100.0	100.0
						LIABILITIES		
	11.4	9.0	12.7			Notes Payable-Short Term	10.4	9.6
	2.1	2.1	2.2			Cur. Mat.-L.T.D.	3.9	3.5
	22.8	21.7	12.8			Trade Payables	15.6	14.4
	.6	.1	.5			Income Taxes Payable	.4	.3
	12.2	22.1	17.8			All Other Current	15.5	19.2
	49.0	55.0	46.0			Total Current	45.8	47.0
	12.8	10.9	13.5			Long-Term Debt	13.0	8.6
	.2	.4	.2			Deferred Taxes	.5	.7
	9.5	3.6	4.8			All Other Non-Current	8.0	6.5
	28.5	30.2	35.5			Net Worth	32.7	37.3
	100.0	100.0	100.0			Total Liabilties & Net Worth	100.0	100.0
						INCOME DATA		
	100.0	100.0	100.0			Net Sales	100.0	100.0
	32.5	30.6	29.3			Gross Profit	30.5	31.1
	30.4	26.5	21.8			Operating Expenses	27.9	27.9
	2.2	4.1	7.5			Operating Profit	2.6	3.2
	.7	1.3	.7			All Other Expenses (net)	1.1	.6
	1.4	2.8	6.7			Profit Before Taxes	1.4	2.6
						RATIOS		
	2.4	1.9	3.2			Current	2.3	2.4
	1.6	1.5	1.6				1.5	1.6
	1.1	1.0	1.2				1.1	1.1
	1.3	1.2	1.6			Quick	1.4	1.6
	.9	.8	.8				.8	.9
	.6	.5	.6				.6	.6
	37 10.0	41 9.0	42 8.7			Sales/Receivables	41 8.9	39 9.5
	45 8.1	51 7.2	55 6.6				52 7.0	52 7.1
	55 6.6	69 5.3	68 5.3				75 4.9	72 5.1
	34 10.6	29 12.8	48 7.7			Cost of Sales/Inventory	27 13.4	28 12.9
	57 6.4	56 6.5	87 4.2				58 6.3	51 7.2
	95 3.9	93 3.9	129 2.8				92 4.0	111 3.3
	23 15.8	29 12.8	26 14.0			Cost of Sales/Payables	21 17.2	18 20.3
	39 9.3	45 8.2	37 9.8				33 11.1	30 12.2
	55 6.7	58 6.3	54 6.8				54 6.8	44 8.3
	5.1	6.3	3.8			Sales/Working Capital	5.5	5.1
	9.7	11.6	5.5				8.8	9.4
	35.4	153.0	14.4				26.9	28.7
	7.8	19.6	34.0			EBIT/Interest	7.6	11.8
	(20) 3.6	(57) 3.2	(27) 5.1				(98) 2.8	(107) 3.6
	1.2	1.2	2.5				.9	.1
		8.3	10.7			Net Profit + Depr., Dep., Amort./Cur. Mat. L/T/D	4.2	3.6
	(16)	2.8	(13) 2.2				(42) 1.4	(38) 1.7
		.8	1.9				.5	.7
	.3	.2	.2			Fixed/Worth	.3	.3
	.6	.4	.4				.6	.6
	1.7	1.9	1.2				1.7	1.3
	.9	1.1	.7			Debt/Worth	.8	.6
	4.0	2.1	2.1				2.2	1.3
	7.8	7.5	5.9				7.5	5.7
	53.4	42.8	57.4			% Profit Before Taxes/Tangible Net Worth	27.3	31.4
	(19) 28.1	(51) 19.3	(28) 18.8				(89) 10.3	(104) 10.2
	3.4	4.2	4.7				.1	1.8
	11.6	15.5	15.7			% Profit Before Taxes/Total Assets	8.9	9.9
	6.5	4.5	10.3				3.9	4.1
	-.7	.1	2.3				-.1	-1.0
	49.5	51.3	17.2			Sales/Net Fixed Assets	21.8	28.2
	14.2	19.6	10.1				11.3	13.4
	6.6	8.3	5.5				5.9	5.8
	3.5	3.0	2.1			Sales/Total Assets	2.6	2.9
	2.5	2.2	1.7				2.0	2.1
	1.7	1.9	1.3				1.5	1.5
	1.2	.6	1.0			% Depr., Dep., Amort./Sales	1.1	1.0
	(18) 1.5	(54) .9	(29) 1.5				(100) 1.8	(110) 1.6
	2.0	1.8	2.2				2.7	3.1
	3.2	1.9				% Officers', Directors' Owners' Comp/Sales	2.2	2.1
	(10) 5.9	(17) 4.8					(29) 3.3	(34) 4.4
	10.5	10.5					7.8	7.9
3769M	74888M	618584M	1176961M	535441M	1205494M	Net Sales ($)	2141726M	2708009M
922M	27779M	262825M	689944M	336072M	837810M	Total Assets ($)	1363320M	1762421M

M = $ thousand   MM = $ million
See Pages 11 through 21 for Explanation of Ratios and Data

Comparative Historical Data | Current Data Sorted by Sales

Hist 1	Hist 2	Hist 3		0-1MM	1-3MM	3-5MM	5-10MM	10-25MM	25MM & OVER
			Type of Statement						
20	19	21	Unqualified				1	6	14
43	38	41	Reviewed	1		4	13	18	5
22	16	20	Compiled		5	4	7	3	1
5	9	6	Tax Returns		3	2		1	
26	34	37	Other	2	1	1	14	6	13
4/1/04-3/31/05 ALL	4/1/05-3/31/06 ALL	4/1/06-3/31/07 ALL		37 (4/1-9/30/06)			88 (10/1/06-3/31/07)		
116	116	125	**NUMBER OF STATEMENTS**	3	9	12	34	34	33
%	%	%	**ASSETS**	%	%	%	%	%	%
9.1	10.6	9.5	Cash & Equivalents			6.8	6.7	10.7	13.6
35.8	34.7	32.3	Trade Receivables (net)			34.3	33.7	35.0	28.9
22.8	24.4	26.8	Inventory			35.3	26.5	24.9	22.7
3.1	3.3	3.7	All Other Current			2.8	4.1	3.5	4.8
70.8	73.0	72.3	Total Current			79.2	71.1	74.1	70.0
20.0	17.5	17.7	Fixed Assets (net)			15.7	19.2	14.5	19.4
2.9	3.2	2.8	Intangibles (net)			1.1	1.2	3.2	5.6
6.3	6.2	7.3	All Other Non-Current			4.1	8.5	8.2	5.0
100.0	100.0	100.0	Total			100.0	100.0	100.0	100.0
			LIABILITIES						
13.3	11.1	9.9	Notes Payable-Short Term			15.1	11.1	7.0	9.6
2.9	1.8	2.1	Cur. Mat.-L.T.D.			2.2	1.8	2.3	2.2
19.2	17.9	19.6	Trade Payables			20.3	22.6	19.8	15.0
.4	.5	.3	Income Taxes Payable			1.0	.1	.1	.6
15.4	14.4	19.4	All Other Current			20.5	20.2	19.4	19.9
51.2	45.7	51.4	Total Current			59.1	55.8	48.7	47.4
9.5	9.6	12.3	Long-Term Debt			5.2	14.8	8.7	15.5
.4	.3	.3	Deferred Taxes			.1	.2	.6	.4
5.7	5.2	5.6	All Other Non-Current			15.4	3.2	2.8	7.2
33.2	39.2	30.3	Net Worth			20.2	26.0	39.2	29.5
100.0	100.0	100.0	Total Liabilities & Net Worth			100.0	100.0	100.0	100.0
			INCOME DATA						
100.0	100.0	100.0	Net Sales			100.0	100.0	100.0	100.0
28.9	30.9	29.9	Gross Profit			31.7	32.4	27.9	27.2
26.7	26.2	25.2	Operating Expenses			28.7	28.5	23.1	19.5
2.2	4.6	4.7	Operating Profit			3.0	3.9	4.8	7.7
1.0	.6	1.0	All Other Expenses (net)			1.5	1.9	.2	1.4
1.2	4.1	3.7	Profit Before Taxes			1.4	2.1	4.6	6.4
			RATIOS						
2.1	2.5	2.1	Current			1.9	1.9	2.1	2.1
1.4	1.6	1.5				1.4	1.3	1.5	1.6
1.1	1.3	1.1				1.1	.9	1.2	1.1
1.4	1.4	1.2	Quick			1.0	1.1	1.2	1.4
.9	1.0	.8				.8	.8	.9	.9
.6	.7	.6				.5	.5	.6	.7
43 8.5	43 8.6	40 9.1	Sales/Receivables			40 9.1	39 9.4	40 9.1	43 8.6
57 6.4	56 6.5	51 7.2				49 7.5	50 7.3	54 6.7	51 7.2
70 5.2	77 4.7	67 5.5				68 5.4	69 5.3	72 5.1	62 5.9
24 15.0	34 10.9	34 10.9	Cost of Sales/Inventory			36 10.2	38 9.7	24 15.3	19 18.9
53 6.9	60 6.1	58 6.3				74 5.0	55 6.7	58 6.3	62 5.9
99 3.7	96 3.8	112 3.3				171 2.1	96 3.8	107 3.4	123 3.0
26 14.2	24 15.2	26 13.8	Cost of Sales/Payables			29 12.7	29 12.5	23 15.6	26 13.8
38 9.6	37 9.8	40 9.1				40 9.2	47 7.7	40 9.1	36 10.2
55 6.7	59 6.1	56 6.5				49 7.5	57 6.4	53 6.8	55 6.7
5.1	4.3	5.2	Sales/Working Capital			6.7	6.4	5.1	5.0
10.8	7.8	9.5				13.6	13.7	11.1	7.6
40.5	18.0	48.8				56.0	-72.4	22.5	44.6
10.6	15.6	17.2	EBIT/Interest			6.7	8.2	35.8	17.8
(106) 3.8	(103) 6.3	(113) 4.0				(11) 4.0	2.4	(32) 8.2	(26) 6.5
-.6	2.0	1.6				2.3	-.5	2.5	3.4
3.4	13.8	9.3	Net Profit + Depr., Dep., Amort./Cur. Mat. L/T/D					8.9	27.4
(32) 1.5	(39) 4.0	(37) 2.8						(11) 4.2	(14) 4.9
-.1	1.8	1.7						1.9	1.9
.2	.2	.2	Fixed/Worth			.3	.2	.1	.3
.6	.5	.5				.9	.5	.3	.5
1.5	.8	1.4				2.3	2.5	.9	6.2
.8	.7	1.0	Debt/Worth			1.5	1.5	.9	.8
2.2	1.6	2.4				5.9	2.4	1.4	2.7
6.4	3.8	7.3				25.0	7.8	3.6	12.1
39.3	41.0	47.2	% Profit Before Taxes/Tangible Net Worth			83.1	40.3	46.3	57.1
(99) 13.3	(107) 19.6	(108) 22.1				(11) 51.2	(30) 12.9	(31) 25.0	(26) 22.4
-2.7	5.9	3.8				1.8	-.9	5.2	7.9
10.7	14.8	14.8	% Profit Before Taxes/Total Assets			7.3	10.1	19.0	15.6
4.7	6.8	6.8				6.9	3.6	6.8	11.0
-3.3	2.0	.9				-.2	-6.0	1.8	3.0
32.1	37.7	37.3	Sales/Net Fixed Assets			24.6	49.7	61.2	21.8
13.2	16.7	15.1				20.4	14.6	16.2	14.2
6.1	6.6	6.9				11.1	7.8	6.7	6.4
2.6	2.8	2.7	Sales/Total Assets			3.2	2.8	3.2	2.5
2.2	2.1	2.1				2.0	2.2	2.2	1.9
1.6	1.6	1.7				1.7	1.9	1.4	1.5
.9	.7	.7	% Depr., Dep., Amort./Sales			.6	.8	.6	.7
(109) 1.6	(98) 1.4	(114) 1.4				(10) 1.5	(31) 1.2	(33) 1.2	(30) 1.5
2.9	2.5	2.1				2.7	2.1	1.6	2.2
2.5	2.2	2.2	% Officers', Directors' Owners' Comp/Sales					2.1	1.7
(35) 4.3	(38) 3.2	(32) 4.5						(10) 7.8	(12) 3.6
8.0	4.8	8.0						14.0	6.7
2127139M	3225550M	3615137M	Net Sales ($)	2116M	17296M	48503M	252143M	527686M	2767393M
1344345M	2170228M	2155352M	Total Assets ($)	1434M	10625M	21755M	121479M	307040M	1693019M

© RMA 2007

M = $ thousand   MM = $ million
See Pages 11 through 21 for Explanation of Ratios and Data

Current Data Sorted by Assets							Comparative Historical Data	
						Type of Statement		
		3	3		1	Unqualified	7	3
	2	9	2		1	Reviewed	4	6
	3	6				Compiled	11	9
3	4					Tax Returns	2	4
2		3	5		1	Other	6	12
5 (4/1-9/30/06)		43 (10/1/06-3/31/07)					**4/1/02-3/31/03 ALL**	**4/1/03-3/31/04 ALL**
0-500M	**500M-2MM**	**2-10MM**	**10-50MM**	**50-100MM**	**100-250MM**			
5	9	21	10		3	**NUMBER OF STATEMENTS**	30	34
%	%	%	%	%	%	**ASSETS**	%	%
		7.6	6.0	DATA NOT AVAILABLE		Cash & Equivalents	5.7	7.0
		38.1	22.8			Trade Receivables (net)	32.5	30.8
		29.3	35.0			Inventory	29.5	28.7
		7.3	8.0			All Other Current	4.8	6.4
		82.4	71.8			Total Current	72.5	72.8
		10.4	22.5			Fixed Assets (net)	18.8	19.3
		1.9	3.5			Intangibles (net)	2.3	3.2
		5.4	2.2			All Other Non-Current	6.4	4.8
		100.0	100.0			Total	100.0	100.0
						LIABILITIES		
		10.4	11.2			Notes Payable-Short Term	9.7	13.2
		1.7	2.5			Cur. Mat.-L.T.D.	4.6	3.1
		16.8	16.9			Trade Payables	16.0	18.3
		1.1	.0			Income Taxes Payable	.5	.3
		17.0	11.2			All Other Current	10.8	14.7
		47.0	41.8			Total Current	41.5	49.6
		7.6	13.8			Long-Term Debt	10.6	10.8
		.2	.2			Deferred Taxes	.3	.3
		3.7	5.7			All Other Non-Current	5.1	3.3
		41.5	38.6			Net Worth	42.5	36.0
		100.0	100.0			Total Liabilties & Net Worth	100.0	100.0
						INCOME DATA		
		100.0	100.0			Net Sales	100.0	100.0
		28.2	29.4			Gross Profit	30.0	31.8
		20.2	15.2			Operating Expenses	26.3	28.5
		8.0	14.2			Operating Profit	3.7	3.3
		.7	3.6			All Other Expenses (net)	.3	.8
		7.3	10.6			Profit Before Taxes	3.4	2.5
						RATIOS		
		2.8	2.9				2.5	2.1
		1.7	1.8			Current	1.7	1.6
		1.3	1.1				1.3	1.3
		1.6	1.3				1.6	1.3
		.9	.7			Quick	1.0	.8
		.7	.3				.6	.6
		39 9.3	**38** 9.5				**40** 9.2	**34** 10.8
		55 6.6	**53** 6.9			Sales/Receivables	**52** 7.0	**48** 7.6
		69 5.3	**82** 4.4				**69** 5.3	**55** 6.6
		29 12.8	**55** 6.6				**39** 9.4	**28** 13.2
		66 5.5	**70** 5.2			Cost of Sales/Inventory	**71** 5.1	**66** 5.5
		108 3.4	**157** 2.3				**134** 2.7	**119** 3.1
		20 17.9	**29** 12.7				**20** 17.9	**16** 23.1
		30 12.4	**42** 8.7			Cost of Sales/Payables	**35** 10.6	**35** 10.5
		43 8.5	**84** 4.4				**61** 6.0	**50** 7.3
		5.1	2.8				5.2	5.1
		6.8	6.0			Sales/Working Capital	7.3	8.8
		13.4	NM				9.7	12.1
		59.5					14.6	11.7
		(18) 7.9				EBIT/Interest	(28) 4.5	(31) 3.2
		5.0					-.2	.3
							5.6	
						Net Profit + Depr., Dep., Amort./Cur. Mat. L/T/D	(12) 1.6	
							.0	
		.1	.1				.2	.2
		.2	.3			Fixed/Worth	.4	.5
		.5	3.9				1.0	1.4
		.6	.7				.6	.8
		2.0	1.9			Debt/Worth	1.3	1.6
		3.1	11.1				2.9	3.5
		59.3					36.7	41.6
		(20) 44.0				% Profit Before Taxes/Tangible Net Worth	(28) 14.4	(28) 7.2
		14.2					.7	-2.8
		24.5	20.7				14.9	14.0
		15.8	8.7			% Profit Before Taxes/Total Assets	5.5	4.9
		6.6	6.2				-.3	-1.4
		52.8	65.7				29.3	35.0
		40.5	16.1			Sales/Net Fixed Assets	12.1	17.4
		15.3	4.4				7.2	6.1
		3.2	2.3				2.7	3.2
		2.7	1.6			Sales/Total Assets	2.2	2.5
		2.0	1.0				1.3	1.3
		.7					1.3	1.2
		(18) .9				% Depr., Dep., Amort./Sales	(28) 1.8	(30) 1.6
		1.4					2.4	3.0
							2.4	1.9
						% Officers', Directors' Owners' Comp/Sales	(11) 4.2	(15) 3.7
							8.4	6.1
4789M	**23048M**	**286979M**	**319589M**		**845615M**	Net Sales ($)	**416214M**	**364948M**
1437M	**9317M**	**115110M**	**221296M**		**476488M**	Total Assets ($)	**226874M**	**226665M**

M = $ thousand MM = $ million

See Pages 11 through 21 for Explanation of Ratios and Data

Comparative Historical Data   Current Data Sorted by Sales

Hist 4/1/04-3/31/05 ALL	Hist 4/1/05-3/31/06 ALL	Hist 4/1/06-3/31/07 ALL	Type of Statement	0-1MM	1-3MM	3-5MM	5-10MM	10-25MM	25MM & OVER
5	7	7	Unqualified					4	3
6	7	14	Reviewed					8	2
10	6	9	Compiled		2	2	2	3	
3	2	7	Tax Returns	2	5	2	2		
7	8	11	Other	1	1		1	3	5
					5 (4/1-9/30/06)			43 (10/1/06-3/31/07)	
31	30	48	**NUMBER OF STATEMENTS**	3	8	4	5	18	10
%	%	%	**ASSETS**	%	%	%	%	%	%
4.3	9.2	8.3	Cash & Equivalents					7.7	6.1
34.4	35.0	32.8	Trade Receivables (net)					37.8	29.7
27.4	27.2	28.1	Inventory					24.8	39.1
7.7	6.7	6.6	All Other Current					11.8	2.4
73.9	78.0	75.8	Total Current					82.2	77.2
17.4	13.7	18.1	Fixed Assets (net)					11.5	17.5
4.4	3.5	2.2	Intangibles (net)					2.7	2.7
4.4	4.8	3.9	All Other Non-Current					3.5	2.5
100.0	100.0	100.0	Total					100.0	100.0
			LIABILITIES						
13.2	8.5	8.9	Notes Payable-Short Term					13.1	5.0
2.7	3.5	2.4	Cur. Mat.-L.T.D.					2.0	1.4
18.5	17.7	18.2	Trade Payables					16.9	19.2
.5	.8	.6	Income Taxes Payable					1.3	.3
11.6	15.1	16.0	All Other Current					16.5	14.4
46.4	45.7	46.1	Total Current					49.8	40.3
8.2	9.5	11.8	Long-Term Debt					9.2	7.2
.3	.2	.1	Deferred Taxes					.3	.0
5.2	6.0	5.0	All Other Non-Current					4.4	2.6
39.9	38.6	37.0	Net Worth					36.3	49.9
100.0	100.0	100.0	Total Liabilities & Net Worth					100.0	100.0
			INCOME DATA						
100.0	100.0	100.0	Net Sales					100.0	100.0
29.0	27.1	31.0	Gross Profit					28.5	23.7
26.0	22.6	22.6	Operating Expenses					20.3	15.0
3.0	4.5	8.4	Operating Profit					8.2	8.7
.4	.6	1.2	All Other Expenses (net)					1.3	.3
2.6	3.8	7.3	Profit Before Taxes					6.9	8.4
			RATIOS						
2.7	2.8	2.4	Current					2.4	2.9
1.6	1.8	1.7						1.7	2.0
1.1	1.3	1.2						1.2	1.4
1.3	1.8	1.3	Quick					1.8	1.3
.9	1.0	.9						.9	1.0
.5	.7	.6						.6	.7
47 7.8	46 7.9	38 9.7	Sales/Receivables					38 9.6	45 8.1
59 6.2	59 6.1	56 6.5						59 6.2	58 6.3
67 5.4	71 5.2	69 5.3						71 5.1	73 5.0
31 12.0	29 12.7	27 13.5	Cost of Sales/Inventory					26 14.2	52 7.0
54 6.8	68 5.4	61 6.0						53 6.9	76 4.8
107 3.4	97 3.8	87 4.2						79 4.6	157 2.3
25 14.6	22 16.3	24 15.3	Cost of Sales/Payables					23 15.8	31 11.7
34 10.7	34 10.8	34 10.9						30 12.3	38 9.6
53 6.8	53 6.8	50 7.4						46 7.9	52 7.0
4.8	4.3	4.1	Sales/Working Capital					5.6	3.6
7.5	7.2	6.8						7.9	5.6
47.7	18.2	19.7						16.1	7.6
9.2	23.6	22.0	EBIT/Interest					45.0	
(27) 2.3	(27) 6.9	(42) 5.7						(16) 6.9	
.5	1.8	3.2						4.7	
		37.4	Net Profit + Depr., Dep.,						
		(11) 24.8	Amort./Cur. Mat. L/T/D						
		3.8							
.2	.2	.1	Fixed/Worth					.1	.2
.3	.3	.3						.2	.3
2.1	1.0	1.3						.5	.6
.7	.6	.8	Debt/Worth					1.0	.6
1.6	1.9	2.0						2.1	.9
4.3	4.7	4.1						3.3	2.8
29.4	38.9	58.2	% Profit Before Taxes/Tangible					56.0	59.5
(28) 11.3	(29) 15.2	(43) 30.1	Net Worth					(16) 44.0	29.5
-3.9	4.7	11.6						16.4	17.9
11.2	12.5	20.0	% Profit Before Taxes/Total					23.9	20.7
3.2	5.1	11.1	Assets					13.7	14.1
-.9	1.0	4.6						8.3	6.2
51.9	48.6	50.7	Sales/Net Fixed Assets					65.9	36.7
24.5	18.7	22.6						41.6	16.1
6.4	9.0	10.7						14.3	6.1
2.9	2.9	3.0	Sales/Total Assets					3.1	2.3
2.2	2.3	2.4						2.6	1.7
1.4	1.6	1.7						1.9	1.5
.9	.6	.7	% Depr., Dep., Amort./Sales					.6	
(27) 1.4	1.1	(42) .9						(16) 1.0	
2.5	2.0	1.7						1.6	
1.8	1.8	2.2	% Officers', Directors'						
(15) 3.0	(14) 4.1	(22) 4.4	Owners' Comp/Sales						
6.7	7.5								
682916M	545370M	1480020M	Net Sales ($)	1696M	14650M	16353M	36891M	296276M	1114154M
397490M	297320M	823648M	Total Assets ($)	1169M	5421M	7278M	43948M	139088M	626744M

M = $ thousand   MM = $ million
See Pages 11 through 21 for Explanation of Ratios and Data

Current Data Sorted by Assets   **Comparative Historical Data**

0-500M	500M-2MM	2-10MM	10-50MM	50-100MM	100-250MM	Type of Statement	4/1/02-3/31/03 ALL	4/1/03-3/31/04 ALL
		2	11	3	1	Unqualified	22	16
		4	6			Reviewed	11	9
1	3	5	1			Compiled	4	5
2	2	4				Tax Returns	3	4
	3	5	8	2	1	Other	17	20
	12 (4/1-9/30/06)		52 (10/1/06-3/31/07)					
3	8	20	26	5	2	NUMBER OF STATEMENTS	57	54
%	%	%	%	%	%	**ASSETS**	%	%
		5.5	6.3			Cash & Equivalents	6.9	7.9
		28.8	18.7			Trade Receivables (net)	23.1	22.4
		31.8	32.4			Inventory	24.4	30.6
		7.3	1.7			All Other Current	1.6	3.6
		73.4	59.1			Total Current	56.0	64.5
		20.9	28.6			Fixed Assets (net)	29.1	26.6
		2.2	2.3			Intangibles (net)	6.0	3.5
		3.5	9.9			All Other Non-Current	9.0	5.4
		100.0	100.0			Total	100.0	100.0
						LIABILITIES		
		11.1	17.1			Notes Payable-Short Term	12.0	14.1
		2.8	7.0			Cur. Mat.-L.T.D.	3.4	5.1
		15.5	11.0			Trade Payables	15.1	13.7
		.3	.7			Income Taxes Payable	.3	.2
		12.4	12.5			All Other Current	9.2	9.7
		42.2	48.3			Total Current	40.0	42.8
		20.0	16.8			Long-Term Debt	28.6	23.1
		.2	.5			Deferred Taxes	.8	.5
		7.6	1.2			All Other Non-Current	5.4	7.4
		30.0	33.2			Net Worth	25.1	26.2
		100.0	100.0			Total Liabilities & Net Worth	100.0	100.0
						INCOME DATA		
		100.0	100.0			Net Sales	100.0	100.0
		24.6	25.2			Gross Profit	25.4	23.9
		20.4	19.1			Operating Expenses	22.7	20.6
		4.2	6.1			Operating Profit	2.7	3.3
		2.0	.7			All Other Expenses (net)	1.7	1.2
		2.2	5.4			Profit Before Taxes	1.0	2.1
						RATIOS		
		4.0	1.7			Current	2.5	2.6
		2.6	1.3				1.4	1.4
		1.2	.9				1.1	1.1
		1.6	.8			Quick	1.3	1.3
		1.0	.5				.8	.7
		.4	.3				.5	.4
		30 12.2	23 16.0			Sales/Receivables	33 11.0	18 20.0
		46 7.9	40 9.2				43 8.5	43 8.5
		64 5.7	46 8.0				55 6.7	51 7.1
		33 11.0	51 7.1			Cost of Sales/Inventory	30 12.0	29 12.7
		80 4.6	68 5.4				59 6.2	55 6.6
		134 2.7	130 2.8				101 3.6	89 4.1
		18 20.2	12 29.7			Cost of Sales/Payables	18 19.9	14 25.3
		27 13.7	27 13.4				27 13.3	22 16.4
		42 8.7	40 9.2				48 7.5	36 10.1
		3.3	8.7			Sales/Working Capital	4.5	5.5
		8.7	19.6				14.3	15.3
		19.9	-30.6				59.2	54.3
		10.3	6.2			EBIT/Interest	6.0	7.2
		3.1	(24) 2.5				(49) 1.4	(46) 2.0
		-.1	1.6				-1.3	-.4
			3.3			Net Profit + Depr., Dep., Amort./Cur. Mat. L/T/D	3.0	2.9
			(16) 2.3				(20) 1.4	(15) 1.6
			1.2				.1	.5
		.3	.4			Fixed/Worth	.4	.3
		.8	.9				1.0	.7
		2.0	4.3				3.8	3.3
		.7	1.1			Debt/Worth	.6	1.2
		1.9	1.9				2.4	2.6
		7.8	6.1				12.2	12.1
		50.8	41.2			% Profit Before Taxes/Tangible Net Worth	31.9	44.7
		(17) 29.0	(24) 25.6				(48) 9.4	(47) 17.2
		-.8	15.9				-7.2	-14.8
		20.0	13.2			% Profit Before Taxes/Total Assets	10.0	14.4
		5.6	6.9				1.3	3.6
		-2.2	2.1				-5.0	-5.4
		29.2	14.9			Sales/Net Fixed Assets	13.3	19.1
		16.0	7.6				6.6	9.8
		6.7	3.5				3.6	4.2
		3.8	2.6			Sales/Total Assets	2.2	2.9
		2.1	1.8				1.8	2.0
		1.5	1.3				1.3	1.5
		.6	.9			% Depr., Dep., Amort./Sales	1.4	.8
		(19) 1.4	1.8				(49) 2.8	(44) 2.1
		2.8	4.1				4.4	3.6
						% Officers', Directors' Owners' Comp/Sales		1.1
							(14)	3.1
								6.7
4359M	24955M	230604M	875141M	801616M	574924M	Net Sales ($)	1706237M	1068027M
1278M	10592M	93640M	431019M	347443M	243772M	Total Assets ($)	1080309M	575562M

M = $ thousand   MM = $ million
See Pages 11 through 21 for Explanation of Ratios and Data

Comparative Historical Data   Current Data Sorted by Sales

4/1/04-3/31/05 ALL	4/1/05-3/31/06 ALL	4/1/06-3/31/07 ALL	Type of Statement	0-1MM	1-3MM	3-5MM	5-10MM	10-25MM	25MM & OVER
18	11	17	Unqualified					5	12
7	8	10	Reviewed			1	2	6	1
4	8	10	Compiled		3	1	4	2	
6	8	8	Tax Returns	1	3	2		2	
18	22	19	Other	1	1	3		5	9
				12 (4/1-9/30/06)			52 (10/1/06-3/31/07)		
53	57	64	**NUMBER OF STATEMENTS**	2	7	7	6	20	22
%	%	%	**ASSETS**	%	%	%	%	%	%
4.4	6.3	5.6	Cash & Equivalents					4.6	4.6
25.7	25.0	22.8	Trade Receivables (net)					23.3	29.4
32.0	32.8	34.8	Inventory					33.1	33.2
1.8	1.6	4.3	All Other Current					3.5	1.5
63.9	65.8	67.5	Total Current					64.5	68.8
23.4	23.0	22.8	Fixed Assets (net)					25.0	20.0
5.3	3.8	3.1	Intangibles (net)					2.9	4.6
7.4	7.4	6.7	All Other Non-Current					7.6	6.6
100.0	100.0	100.0	Total					100.0	100.0
			LIABILITIES						
15.4	16.1	14.4	Notes Payable-Short Term					18.3	14.7
3.6	3.8	4.5	Cur. Mat.-L.T.D.					6.7	3.0
18.3	17.2	14.3	Trade Payables					12.1	16.6
.2	.3	.4	Income Taxes Payable					.2	.8
9.0	10.4	16.7	All Other Current					18.3	12.7
46.6	47.7	50.3	Total Current					55.6	47.9
15.9	15.2	17.3	Long-Term Debt					15.3	12.8
1.0	.6	.4	Deferred Taxes					.8	.4
6.1	5.2	4.4	All Other Non-Current					5.4	4.0
30.3	31.4	27.6	Net Worth					22.8	34.8
100.0	100.0	100.0	Total Liabilities & Net Worth					100.0	100.0
			INCOME DATA						
100.0	100.0	100.0	Net Sales					100.0	100.0
24.0	23.6	24.0	Gross Profit					25.9	23.0
20.3	18.9	18.8	Operating Expenses					23.8	14.6
3.6	4.7	5.2	Operating Profit					2.0	8.4
.9	1.6	1.2	All Other Expenses (net)					1.2	1.9
2.7	3.1	4.0	Profit Before Taxes					.8	6.5
			RATIOS						
1.7	1.7	2.3	Current					1.6	2.2
1.2	1.3	1.3						1.1	1.4
1.0	1.0	.9						.9	1.1
1.1	.8	1.2	Quick					1.0	1.2
.5	.6	.5						.4	.7
.3	.4	.4						.2	.5
15 23.7	25 14.8	24 15.5	Sales/Receivables					19 19.2	30 12.4
41 8.8	35 10.5	37 9.9						42 8.6	42 8.6
60 6.1	47 7.7	49 7.4						58 6.3	53 6.9
33 11.0	31 11.8	43 8.5	Cost of Sales/Inventory					44 8.3	40 9.2
65 5.7	61 6.0	70 5.2						99 3.7	57 6.4
112 3.3	81 4.5	127 2.9						141 2.6	87 4.2
22 16.7	17 21.7	15 23.8	Cost of Sales/Payables					18 20.4	13 27.2
37 10.0	27 13.4	27 13.6						27 13.6	29 12.4
61 6.0	39 9.3	40 9.0						45 8.0	40 9.1
7.3	8.3	6.5	Sales/Working Capital					9.1	6.9
18.7	16.8	15.3						21.8	15.2
153.6	787.2	-79.9						-22.0	40.4
14.1	9.4	7.0	EBIT/Interest					3.8	15.0
(52) 3.6	(54) 3.1	(59) 2.9						1.6	(20) 5.9
.3	1.3	1.4						.9	2.5
4.9	7.8	3.5	Net Profit + Depr., Dep.,					3.2	4.1
(19) 1.4	(15) 2.1	(26) 2.2	Amort./Cur. Mat. L/T/D					(13) 1.3	(10) 2.5
.5	1.7	1.2						.8	1.5
.3	.3	.3	Fixed/Worth					.6	.3
1.0	.7	.9						1.1	.5
2.1	3.5	4.2						10.3	1.0
1.2	1.2	1.1	Debt/Worth					1.5	1.0
2.8	2.5	2.7						4.4	2.0
9.3	9.4	13.4						23.3	5.2
50.6	50.7	46.7	% Profit Before Taxes/Tangible					28.5	60.6
(46) 15.4	(51) 23.5	(54) 27.5	Net Worth					(16) 18.2	(19) 38.6
3.5	11.3	14.8						.5	22.8
13.7	15.3	14.9	% Profit Before Taxes/Total					6.2	25.3
4.4	7.9	6.6	Assets					2.5	10.6
-1.2	1.4	1.7						-.7	6.1
27.2	45.3	29.2	Sales/Net Fixed Assets					23.4	37.4
12.6	14.1	13.7						7.7	15.2
7.1	6.4	6.1						4.2	8.4
3.2	3.7	2.9	Sales/Total Assets					2.2	3.3
2.3	2.5	2.1						1.7	2.5
1.5	1.6	1.5						1.3	1.9
.8	.6	.6	% Depr., Dep., Amort./Sales					.9	.6
(49) 1.3	(50) 1.1	(60) 1.4						2.0	(20) 1.0
2.6	2.4	3.1						3.9	1.9
1.8	2.1	1.5	% Officers', Directors'						
(16) 3.3	(18) 3.7	(21) 3.6	Owners' Comp/Sales						
5.0	5.1	5.3							
1940796M	1834468M	2511599M	Net Sales ($)	1507M	14244M	28092M	45741M	330350M	2091665M
974140M	895250M	1127744M	Total Assets ($)	2381M	8719M	15196M	25738M	206463M	869247M

M = $ thousand   MM = $ million
See Pages 11 through 21 for Explanation of Ratios and Data

Current Data Sorted by Assets | Comparative Historical Data

0-500M	500M-2MM	2-10MM	10-50MM	50-100MM	100-250MM	Type of Statement	4/1/02-3/31/03 ALL	4/1/03-3/31/04 ALL
		3	2			Unqualified	5	5
	2	7	4			Reviewed	10	15
	3	5				Compiled	5	10
2	1	2				Tax Returns	1	4
1	3	4	3	1	2	Other	7	7
	8 (4/1-9/30/06)		37 (10/1/06-3/31/07)					
3	9	21	9	1	2	NUMBER OF STATEMENTS	28	41
%	%	%	%	%	%	**ASSETS**	%	%
		12.1				Cash & Equivalents	9.0	7.9
		24.5				Trade Receivables (net)	30.8	28.4
		31.1				Inventory	27.1	24.2
		2.9				All Other Current	4.2	3.4
		70.6				Total Current	71.1	63.9
		17.8				Fixed Assets (net)	23.5	28.2
		2.1				Intangibles (net)	.9	2.2
		9.5				All Other Non-Current	4.5	5.8
		100.0				Total	100.0	100.0
						LIABILITIES		
		7.6				Notes Payable-Short Term	19.0	19.1
		1.8				Cur. Mat.-L.T.D.	2.2	4.2
		12.8				Trade Payables	18.9	14.0
		.0				Income Taxes Payable	.4	.4
		12.9				All Other Current	10.9	9.2
		35.2				Total Current	51.4	46.8
		11.6				Long-Term Debt	13.3	14.7
		.3				Deferred Taxes	.1	.1
		2.6				All Other Non-Current	4.5	7.1
		50.3				Net Worth	30.7	31.3
		100.0				Total Liabilties & Net Worth	100.0	100.0
						INCOME DATA		
		100.0				Net Sales	100.0	100.0
		34.5				Gross Profit	32.2	34.3
		28.7				Operating Expenses	28.3	31.5
		5.8				Operating Profit	3.9	2.9
		-.1				All Other Expenses (net)	1.6	1.3
		5.9				Profit Before Taxes	2.3	1.5
						RATIOS		
		3.5					2.9	2.4
		2.3				Current	1.5	1.4
		1.7					1.0	1.0
		1.7					1.3	1.8
		1.4				Quick	.9	.8
		.8					.5	.5
		39 9.3					38 9.6	38 9.5
		47 7.8				Sales/Receivables	49 7.5	53 6.9
		57 6.4					71 5.2	74 4.9
		51 7.1					39 9.3	22 16.8
		93 3.9				Cost of Sales/Inventory	77 4.8	58 6.3
		143 2.5					105 3.5	124 2.9
		22 16.6					15 24.3	13 27.3
		32 11.4				Cost of Sales/Payables	37 9.7	35 10.5
		55 6.7					71 5.1	52 7.1
		2.9					4.3	4.8
		4.7				Sales/Working Capital	8.4	9.2
		8.7					-67.8	NM
		18.4					6.7	5.5
		(18) 5.2				EBIT/Interest	(27) 1.8	(37) 3.2
		2.2					.1	.0
						Net Profit + Depr., Dep.,		4.1
						Amort./Cur. Mat. L/T/D		(10) 1.1
								-3.1
		.2					.3	.3
		.3				Fixed/Worth	.7	.8
		.7					NM	6.6
		.5					.7	.6
		.9				Debt/Worth	1.9	2.4
		2.0					NM	15.9
		40.0				% Profit Before Taxes/Tangible	45.9	44.1
		(19) 16.0				Net Worth	(21) 16.1	(34) 10.5
		8.7					4.9	-4.0
		19.0				% Profit Before Taxes/Total	10.7	10.0
		6.6				Assets	3.7	3.5
		1.9					-1.8	-2.8
		32.1					25.3	15.2
		12.5				Sales/Net Fixed Assets	7.8	7.2
		6.7					5.2	3.7
		2.2					2.6	2.6
		1.7				Sales/Total Assets	2.1	1.8
		1.4					1.4	1.3
		.7					1.3	1.0
		(19) 1.2				% Depr., Dep., Amort./Sales	1.7	(36) 1.8
		2.4					2.6	2.8
								4.8
						% Officers', Directors'		(16) 7.1
						Owners' Comp/Sales		10.0
4387M	29023M	209197M	295448M	93077M	279026M	Net Sales ($)	272404M	669945M
957M	8869M	117494M	173097M	64854M	243914M	Total Assets ($)	156529M	367215M

M = $ thousand   MM = $ million
See Pages 11 through 21 for Explanation of Ratios and Data

Comparative Historical Data / Current Data Sorted by Sales

			Type of Statement	0-1MM	1-3MM	3-5MM	5-10MM	10-25MM	25MM & OVER
10	2	5	Unqualified					3	2
13	11	13	Reviewed		1	1	5	4	2
5	6	8	Compiled		3	1	2	2	
4	5	5	Tax Returns		1	1	2		
19	26	14	Other	1	2	2	2	2	6
4/1/04-3/31/05 ALL	4/1/05-3/31/06 ALL	4/1/06-3/31/07 ALL			8 (4/1-9/30/06)		37 (10/1/06-3/31/07)		
51	50	45	NUMBER OF STATEMENTS	1	7	5	11	11	10
%	%	%	ASSETS	%	%	%	%	%	%
8.5	10.9	11.8	Cash & Equivalents				7.8	8.5	7.2
30.1	28.9	26.6	Trade Receivables (net)				25.6	29.3	29.4
22.8	25.7	26.7	Inventory				28.6	32.8	26.2
3.5	3.4	2.7	All Other Current				2.0	3.4	5.9
65.0	68.9	67.8	Total Current				63.9	73.8	68.6
25.4	23.1	21.3	Fixed Assets (net)				23.8	16.6	17.6
1.0	1.0	2.2	Intangibles (net)				1.1	.4	5.4
8.5	7.0	8.6	All Other Non-Current				11.2	9.2	8.3
100.0	100.0	100.0	Total				100.0	100.0	100.0
			LIABILITIES						
13.4	12.2	10.1	Notes Payable-Short Term				4.8	12.3	13.8
2.1	2.3	2.6	Cur. Mat.-L.T.D.				2.6	1.3	2.2
14.7	13.3	13.0	Trade Payables				13.6	16.4	10.5
.4	.3	.1	Income Taxes Payable				.0	.2	.2
12.1	14.2	13.2	All Other Current				13.4	19.0	7.7
42.7	42.3	39.0	Total Current				34.3	49.3	34.4
14.3	11.8	10.5	Long-Term Debt				15.3	7.6	6.0
.8	.4	.3	Deferred Taxes				.4	.2	.7
5.0	6.2	5.1	All Other Non-Current				3.5	3.7	11.8
37.2	39.3	45.1	Net Worth				46.5	39.3	47.1
100.0	100.0	100.0	Total Liabilities & Net Worth				100.0	100.0	100.0
			INCOME DATA						
100.0	100.0	100.0	Net Sales				100.0	100.0	100.0
32.2	31.5	35.6	Gross Profit				39.0	26.7	28.7
27.7	27.8	28.7	Operating Expenses				35.2	20.7	20.0
4.5	3.7	6.9	Operating Profit				3.8	6.0	8.7
.4	1.4	.6	All Other Expenses (net)				-.6	.8	1.7
4.1	2.3	6.3	Profit Before Taxes				4.4	5.2	7.0
			RATIOS						
2.7	3.0	2.7	Current				6.2	2.1	4.3
1.6	1.8	1.9					2.3	1.7	1.9
1.1	1.2	1.2					1.8	1.2	1.3
1.7	2.0	1.6	Quick				1.8	1.5	2.0
.9	.8	1.1					1.5	.8	.9
.6	.6	.7					.8	.4	.7
38 9.7	37 10.0	35 10.5	Sales/Receivables				38 9.5	40 9.2	39 9.4
52 7.0	49 7.4	47 7.8					46 8.0	55 6.6	66 5.5
69 5.3	69 5.3	62 5.9					56 6.5	64 5.7	92 3.9
22 16.8	14 26.7	30 12.2	Cost of Sales/Inventory				19 19.1	40 9.2	30 12.0
65 5.6	78 4.7	66 5.5					99 3.7	62 5.9	75 4.9
116 3.2	135 2.7	117 3.1					161 2.3	126 2.9	111 3.3
21 17.1	17 21.0	21 17.3	Cost of Sales/Payables				23 15.8	21 17.2	16 23.1
34 10.8	31 11.8	26 14.2					28 12.9	32 11.4	32 11.4
54 6.7	46 7.9	46 8.0					64 5.7	63 5.8	52 7.0
4.5	3.7	3.3	Sales/Working Capital				3.0	4.6	3.0
9.5	9.3	6.5					6.0	10.2	5.5
28.2	18.8	12.3					10.7	31.2	10.3
14.5	7.6	15.8	EBIT/Interest				18.4		
(43) 3.9	(45) 3.1	(34) 4.8					(10) 4.9		
1.5	.4	2.1					1.9		
5.0	10.1	6.1	Net Profit + Depr., Dep., Amort./Cur. Mat. L/T/D						
(13) 3.5	(13) 2.4	(10) 3.2							
1.7	1.4	2.0							
.2	.2	.1	Fixed/Worth				.2	.2	.1
.6	.6	.4					.6	.4	.5
1.6	1.1	.9					.9	.8	1.0
.6	.5	.6	Debt/Worth				.5	.6	.7
2.0	1.6	1.3					1.0	1.9	1.6
4.5	4.9	2.6					3.2	3.8	3.3
33.1	38.5	53.8	% Profit Before Taxes/Tangible Net Worth				52.8	53.5	47.6
(45) 12.9	(45) 17.5	(42) 30.2					(10) 23.6	(10) 30.2	28.5
4.7	1.8	10.1					1.0	11.0	13.2
17.1	13.7	20.8	% Profit Before Taxes/Total Assets				19.8	18.2	16.9
4.5	4.3	9.2					7.5	6.3	10.6
1.7	.4	3.6					.6	3.1	5.7
16.6	37.1	39.8	Sales/Net Fixed Assets				21.6	37.3	29.9
10.0	12.0	11.6					7.0	12.5	10.1
4.1	4.4	6.4					4.6	6.8	6.8
2.5	2.7	2.8	Sales/Total Assets				2.2	2.8	2.2
1.7	1.8	2.0					1.8	2.0	1.5
1.3	1.2	1.4					1.3	1.5	1.3
1.3	.9	.7	% Depr., Dep., Amort./Sales					.5	
(43) 2.7	(40) 1.5	(35) 1.4						(10) 1.2	
3.6	2.9	2.6						2.2	
2.4	1.3	1.7	% Officers', Directors' Owners' Comp/Sales						
(15) 3.7	(17) 3.4	(14) 3.5							
7.8	4.9	13.1							
1015855M	1234773M	910158M	Net Sales ($)	425M	14493M	19703M	75750M	175031M	624756M
773141M	681244M	609185M	Total Assets ($)	115M	5098M	10893M	48175M	99594M	445310M

M = $ thousand   MM = $ million
See Pages 11 through 21 for Explanation of Ratios and Data

Current Data Sorted by Assets							Comparative Historical Data	
						Type of Statement		
		8	15		1	Unqualified	17	11
	5	16	4			Reviewed	12	12
1	5	4	1			Compiled	14	14
2	2	2				Tax Returns	5	6
3	4	11	3		1	Other	11	26
	27 (4/1-9/30/06)		61 (10/1/06-3/31/07)				**4/1/02-3/31/03**	**4/1/03-3/31/04**
0-500M	**500M-2MM**	**2-10MM**	**10-50MM**	**50-100MM**	**100-250MM**		**ALL**	**ALL**
6	16	41	23		2	**NUMBER OF STATEMENTS**	59	69
%	%	%	%	%	%	**ASSETS**	%	%
	7.1	11.7	9.6	D		Cash & Equivalents	11.0	9.8
	34.1	25.2	24.6	A		Trade Receivables (net)	27.5	25.4
	29.1	35.9	35.1	T		Inventory	28.1	31.6
	5.7	1.9	3.6	A		All Other Current	3.4	3.1
	75.9	74.7	72.9			Total Current	70.0	70.0
	14.1	15.7	16.8	N		Fixed Assets (net)	18.0	18.1
	2.0	3.4	7.0	O		Intangibles (net)	5.5	6.2
	7.9	6.2	3.3	T		All Other Non-Current	6.4	5.7
	100.0	100.0	100.0			Total	100.0	100.0
				A		**LIABILITIES**		
	8.2	8.2	3.1	V		Notes Payable-Short Term	6.1	8.5
	1.5	2.8	2.0	A		Cur. Mat.-L.T.D.	3.1	1.7
	24.5	13.0	12.8	I		Trade Payables	17.2	15.8
	.1	.4	.4	L		Income Taxes Payable	.5	.5
	22.3	25.3	25.1	A		All Other Current	19.4	20.4
	56.5	49.7	43.5	B		Total Current	46.4	46.8
	12.1	10.2	7.0	L		Long-Term Debt	11.9	8.4
	.1	.1	.8	E		Deferred Taxes	.6	.5
	11.8	5.5	3.0			All Other Non-Current	4.7	6.5
	19.4	34.5	45.7			Net Worth	36.4	37.8
	100.0	100.0	100.0			Total Liabilties & Net Worth	100.0	100.0
						INCOME DATA		
	100.0	100.0	100.0			Net Sales	100.0	100.0
	36.5	31.6	28.6			Gross Profit	32.7	35.6
	35.1	27.5	23.5			Operating Expenses	29.1	30.9
	1.4	4.2	5.1			Operating Profit	3.6	4.7
	.5	.8	.1			All Other Expenses (net)	1.1	.9
	.9	3.3	5.0			Profit Before Taxes	2.5	3.7
						RATIOS		
	2.2	2.2	2.1				2.4	2.1
	1.6	1.5	1.7			Current	1.6	1.6
	1.1	1.2	1.4				1.2	1.2
	1.7	1.1	.9				1.3	1.1
	.8	.7	.8			Quick	1.0	.7
	.5	.5	.6				.5	.5
	35 10.6	**30** 12.2	**37** 9.9				**33** 11.1	**28** 13.2
	47 7.8	**40** 9.2	**46** 8.0			Sales/Receivables	**47** 7.8	**41** 8.9
	64 5.7	**48** 7.6	**63** 5.8				**59** 6.2	**53** 6.8
	24 15.0	**53** 6.9	**57** 6.4				**33** 11.1	**43** 8.4
	67 5.4	**87** 4.2	**94** 3.9			Cost of Sales/Inventory	**69** 5.3	**82** 4.5
	133 2.7	**134** 2.7	**135** 2.7				**146** 2.5	**144** 2.5
	25 14.6	**17** 22.0	**17** 21.1				**21** 17.7	**21** 17.4
	63 5.8	**28** 13.0	**28** 13.2			Cost of Sales/Payables	**36** 10.0	**30** 12.0
	90 4.0	**38** 9.6	**51** 7.1				**51** 7.2	**56** 6.5
	5.1	4.7	4.4				4.4	5.0
	8.9	10.5	6.5			Sales/Working Capital	7.9	7.7
	71.3	37.5	11.6				24.2	22.5
	6.3	14.4	85.3				13.9	18.1
	1.9	(34) 4.7	(17) 12.5			EBIT/Interest	(55) 3.4	(61) 5.3
	-.5	1.4	2.7				.2	1.6
		6.3	9.6				14.3	9.5
		(13) 2.1	(12) 4.0			Net Profit + Depr., Dep., Amort./Cur. Mat. L/T/D	(22) 3.1	(21) 2.6
		1.4	1.7				.8	1.1
	.2	.1	.3				.2	.3
	.8	.4	.4			Fixed/Worth	.4	.5
	-2.3	.9	.7				1.1	1.9
	1.2	.9	.7				.7	.9
	5.8	2.6	1.1			Debt/Worth	1.9	2.1
	-9.0	5.7	3.7				8.9	6.0
	27.3	51.0	31.7				66.6	48.9
	(11) 19.4	(36) 24.8	(22) 19.8			% Profit Before Taxes/Tangible Net Worth	(51) 12.4	(58) 18.4
	-5.7	3.7	6.0				1.4	3.1
	7.2	13.6	15.2				18.5	16.6
	2.5	8.2	6.4			% Profit Before Taxes/Total Assets	3.6	7.6
	-3.5	1.1	1.3				-1.3	1.0
	41.1	60.5	17.0				38.0	31.0
	25.5	25.7	10.7			Sales/Net Fixed Assets	12.4	14.1
	13.3	9.9	8.5				5.9	6.7
	2.7	2.9	2.1				2.5	2.6
	2.4	2.3	1.9			Sales/Total Assets	1.9	1.9
	1.8	1.5	1.4				1.4	1.5
	.6	.6	.9				.8	.8
	(15) 1.0	(38) .8	(20) 1.6			% Depr., Dep., Amort./Sales	(54) 1.5	(58) 1.6
	3.2	2.5	2.4				3.3	3.2
		2.1					2.1	1.9
		(12) 3.2				% Officers', Directors' Owners' Comp/Sales	(20) 3.9	(24) 3.5
		6.9					10.4	12.0
6665M	**46478M**	**534977M**	**856935M**		**712184M**	Net Sales ($)	**1043465M**	**1569537M**
1971M	**19062M**	**225950M**	**473797M**		**406276M**	Total Assets ($)	**686454M**	**991665M**

M = $ thousand **MM = $ million**

See Pages 11 through 21 for Explanation of Ratios and Data

Comparative Historical Data / Current Data Sorted by Sales

			Type of Statement						
15	20	24	Unqualified			2		10	12
21	25	25	Reviewed		1	6	8	6	4
8	12	11	Compiled		5	1	1	2	1
4	6	6	Tax Returns	1	4	1		1	
19	25	22	Other		5	2	3	8	4
4/1/04-3/31/05 ALL	4/1/05-3/31/06 ALL	4/1/06-3/31/07 ALL		0-1MM	27 (4/1-9/30/06) 1-3MM	3-5MM	61 (10/1/06-3/31/07) 5-10MM	10-25MM	25MM & OVER
67	88	88	**NUMBER OF STATEMENTS**	1	15	10	14	27	21
%	%	%	**ASSETS**	%	%	%	%	%	%
10.3	8.7	10.9	Cash & Equivalents		11.4	4.7	13.6	10.6	9.5
24.4	27.9	27.7	Trade Receivables (net)		33.9	27.1	19.6	29.4	27.2
29.9	32.6	32.7	Inventory		22.8	39.7	41.0	32.2	33.1
4.1	3.6	3.6	All Other Current		3.8	4.3	1.9	2.6	5.6
68.6	72.8	75.0	Total Current		71.9	75.8	76.1	74.9	75.4
15.7	13.7	15.0	Fixed Assets (net)		16.7	16.8	10.6	16.9	13.7
6.4	6.9	4.4	Intangibles (net)		3.0	1.8	4.4	4.1	7.3
9.2	6.5	5.6	All Other Non-Current		8.4	5.6	8.9	4.1	3.6
100.0	100.0	100.0	Total		100.0	100.0	100.0	100.0	100.0
			LIABILITIES						
9.0	8.7	6.6	Notes Payable-Short Term		8.4	11.3	4.7	7.1	4.0
1.9	2.2	2.1	Cur. Mat.-L.T.D.		.6	2.5	1.9	3.0	2.1
13.2	18.7	16.2	Trade Payables		27.1	19.9	10.0	15.5	12.4
.2	.3	.3	Income Taxes Payable		.1	.3	.5	.3	.4
21.6	25.5	28.2	All Other Current		38.0	14.7	30.4	23.8	31.3
45.9	55.4	53.4	Total Current		74.1	48.7	47.5	49.8	50.2
11.2	9.8	9.1	Long-Term Debt		14.2	11.0	8.1	8.3	6.8
.7	.6	.3	Deferred Taxes		.1	.0	.1	.3	.7
4.3	8.2	10.8	All Other Non-Current		39.9	6.2	3.7	6.9	2.7
38.0	26.0	26.3	Net Worth		-28.4	34.2	40.6	34.7	39.7
100.0	100.0	100.0	Total Liabilties & Net Worth		100.0	100.0	100.0	100.0	100.0
			INCOME DATA						
100.0	100.0	100.0	Net Sales		100.0	100.0	100.0	100.0	100.0
35.7	32.1	31.4	Gross Profit		37.5	35.6	29.3	33.3	24.3
30.8	28.4	27.7	Operating Expenses		36.6	33.3	25.1	27.6	20.9
4.9	3.7	3.7	Operating Profit		.9	2.4	4.1	5.7	3.4
.8	.8	.5	All Other Expenses (net)		.9	.3	.3	.9	-.1
4.1	2.9	3.2	Profit Before Taxes		.0	2.0	3.9	4.8	3.6
			RATIOS						
2.3	2.1	2.2			2.9	1.8	2.7	2.1	2.0
1.5	1.4	1.6	Current		1.2	1.5	1.6	1.7	1.5
1.2	1.0	1.2			.6	1.2	1.1	1.2	1.2
1.0	1.0	1.0			1.9	.8	1.2	1.1	.9
.8	.7	.7	Quick		.9	.6	.7	.7	.8
.5	.5	.5			.4	.4	.4	.5	.6
34 10.9	33 10.9	33 11.2		29 12.8	31 11.9	27 13.4	33 10.9	38 9.7
42 8.7	45 8.0	42 8.6	Sales/Receivables	43 8.5	43 8.5	33 11.0	43 8.5	42 8.6
56 6.5	60 6.1	54 6.7		62 5.9	53 6.9	50 7.3	50 7.3	61 6.0
50 7.3	49 7.5	43 8.5		12 30.1	83 4.4	72 5.1	33 11.0	49 7.5
92 4.0	77 4.7	84 4.4	Cost of Sales/Inventory	42 8.6	103 3.5	95 3.8	77 4.8	75 4.9
138 2.6	126 2.9	127 2.9		156 2.3	149 2.5	204 1.8	123 3.0	111 3.3
22 16.9	19 19.4	17 21.8		17 21.9	20 18.3	14 26.4	22 16.3	15 23.8
36 10.1	33 11.0	28 12.9	Cost of Sales/Payables	48 7.7	42 8.7	25 14.6	31 11.7	23 16.1
49 7.4	59 6.2	51 7.2		86 4.3	70 5.2	42 8.6	49 7.4	38 9.6
4.3	5.6	4.7			4.5	5.0	4.1	4.7	5.5
8.6	10.0	8.0	Sales/Working Capital		14.2	8.0	7.3	8.0	10.0
24.6	246.4	22.0			-5.2	36.4	NM	22.2	15.3
23.2	15.3	16.0			4.9		18.0	26.5	19.5
(60) 5.4	(74) 3.5	(72) 4.1	EBIT/Interest		(13) 1.5		(11) 4.8	(23) 6.6	(16) 13.2
1.2	1.6	1.4			-3.9		1.9	1.3	3.2
17.0	5.9	11.0	Net Profit + Depr., Dep.,					9.3	9.4
(22) 4.9	(29) 3.2	(30) 3.6	Amort./Cur. Mat. L/T/D				(12) 2.8	(11) 4.4
1.7	.9	1.7						1.6	1.7
.2	.2	.2			.4	.1	.1	.2	.3
.4	.5	.4	Fixed/Worth		4.0	.3	.3	.4	.4
1.1	1.9	1.3			-.8	NM	.8	1.4	.7
.8	.9	.9			1.9	.9	.8	.8	.9
1.9	3.0	2.5	Debt/Worth		-11.8	1.8	2.5	2.2	1.4
5.5	35.5	7.7			-2.9	NM	5.4	5.6	4.2
37.2	49.1	36.0	% Profit Before Taxes/Tangible		38.8	59.2	33.1
(60) 14.7	(72) 14.0	(72) 19.6	Net Worth			(13) 16.9	(24) 27.9	(19) 24.0
2.9	2.9	3.7					6.5	8.5	8.8
11.5	11.1	13.3	% Profit Before Taxes/Total		6.6	6.0	13.0	15.8	15.2
4.9	4.4	5.1	Assets		-.5	.9	7.5	10.5	5.5
1.3	.4	.7			-14.9	-2.2	2.3	1.3	2.5
43.4	49.0	39.6			96.5	46.0	47.7	44.9	33.0
19.9	23.0	20.6	Sales/Net Fixed Assets		23.6	27.3	25.3	19.0	12.4
7.2	9.2	10.3			8.1	11.3	15.8	8.0	9.3
2.2	2.7	2.7			3.8	2.8	3.0	2.7	2.6
1.8	2.1	2.1	Sales/Total Assets		2.6	2.0	1.6	2.3	1.9
1.3	1.6	1.6			1.8	1.4	1.3	1.9	1.4
.7	.7	.6			.5		.8	.6	.5
(60) 1.5	(76) 1.1	(79) 1.0	% Depr., Dep., Amort./Sales		(13) 1.0		(13) 1.0	(25) .8	(18) 1.2
2.5	2.1	2.5			2.9		2.1	2.2	2.1
1.8	1.2	2.1	% Officers', Directors'						
(18) 3.7	(19) 3.3	(21) 3.1	Owners' Comp/Sales						
7.2	6.6	4.3							
1610967M	2424256M	2157239M	Net Sales ($)	425M	24908M	38835M	110788M	463789M	1518494M
1161005M	1424434M	1127056M	Total Assets ($)	407M	12534M	19718M	64353M	205666M	824378M

M = $ thousand   MM = $ million
See Pages 11 through 21 for Explanation of Ratios and Data

Current Data Sorted by Assets   **Comparative Historical Data**

0-500M	500M-2MM	2-10MM	10-50MM	50-100MM	100-250MM	Type of Statement	4/1/02-3/31/03 ALL	4/1/03-3/31/04 ALL
		5	2			Unqualified	13	10
	3	10	2			Reviewed	12	11
	4	4				Compiled	7	3
	3				1	Tax Returns	3	2
1	2	3	4		1	Other	12	9
	11 (4/1-9/30/06)		34 (10/1/06-3/31/07)					
1	12	22	8		2	**NUMBER OF STATEMENTS**	47	35
%	%	%	%	%	%	**ASSETS**	%	%
	11.9	13.0				Cash & Equivalents	12.0	10.0
	37.9	34.0				Trade Receivables (net)	27.7	31.1
	31.6	16.4				Inventory	24.0	20.7
	3.5	6.9				All Other Current	4.0	5.2
	84.9	70.3				Total Current	67.8	66.9
	12.3	21.0				Fixed Assets (net)	21.3	20.4
	1.4	4.0				Intangibles (net)	3.8	6.6
	1.3	4.7				All Other Non-Current	7.1	6.0
	100.0	100.0				Total	100.0	100.0
						LIABILITIES		
	8.6	5.5				Notes Payable-Short Term	10.8	7.9
	3.9	3.4				Cur. Mat.-L.T.D.	6.2	4.0
	25.5	16.5				Trade Payables	15.6	15.6
	.0	.5				Income Taxes Payable	.4	.5
	23.7	29.3				All Other Current	14.5	12.7
	61.6	55.3				Total Current	47.4	40.7
	5.3	10.9				Long-Term Debt	14.8	14.8
	.0	.3				Deferred Taxes	.6	1.1
	2.8	1.8				All Other Non-Current	6.9	7.1
	30.3	31.8				Net Worth	30.3	36.2
	100.0	100.0				Total Liabilities & Net Worth	100.0	100.0
						INCOME DATA		
	100.0	100.0				Net Sales	100.0	100.0
	32.0	27.5				Gross Profit	30.5	30.7
	26.2	21.3				Operating Expenses	28.7	26.0
	5.8	6.2				Operating Profit	1.9	4.7
	.5	.5				All Other Expenses (net)	1.6	.7
	5.3	5.7				Profit Before Taxes	.3	4.1
						RATIOS		
	2.2	2.1				Current	2.2	2.2
	1.5	1.2					1.5	1.7
	1.0	1.0					1.1	1.4
	1.3	1.2				Quick	1.4	1.6
	.9	.9					.9	1.0
	.7	.6					.5	.6
	23 15.6	35 10.6				Sales/Receivables	37 9.9	36 10.1
	36 10.3	54 6.8					52 7.0	55 6.6
	48 7.7	67 5.5					69 5.3	63 5.8
	19 19.6	6 59.8				Cost of Sales/Inventory	25 14.5	22 16.4
	45 8.2	31 11.7					64 5.7	40 9.0
	87 4.2	82 4.4					95 3.8	87 4.2
	25 14.8	18 19.7				Cost of Sales/Payables	16 23.2	21 17.0
	33 11.0	32 11.3					31 11.7	29 12.6
	50 7.4	52 7.0					61 6.0	49 7.5
	6.5	6.5				Sales/Working Capital	5.5	5.1
	21.5	19.7					9.5	7.1
	221.2	-45.2					48.3	14.3
	14.1	14.7				EBIT/Interest	6.0	14.0
	(10) 6.3	(19) 8.7					(41) 1.9	(30) 4.5
	1.7	1.2					-.8	-.5
						Net Profit + Depr., Dep.,	2.8	4.0
						Amort./Cur. Mat. L/T/D	(19) 1.7	(10) 1.9
							.5	.0
	.1	.4				Fixed/Worth	.3	.3
	.4	.8					.8	.6
	2.0	1.4					3.2	1.2
	.6	1.1				Debt/Worth	1.0	.7
	2.4	2.9					2.6	1.7
	14.5	10.9					9.4	4.0
	62.3	76.9				% Profit Before Taxes/Tangible	60.8	61.3
	(10) 32.6	(20) 30.0				Net Worth	(41) 8.4	(30) 20.3
	2.0	10.6					-12.3	-1.3
	31.7	20.3				% Profit Before Taxes/Total	11.4	14.5
	8.2	3.5				Assets	3.0	6.5
	.2	1.5					-7.7	-7.3
	75.0	38.9				Sales/Net Fixed Assets	26.1	29.6
	52.8	16.1					12.8	13.7
	25.1	5.0					5.2	5.7
	4.9	3.2				Sales/Total Assets	3.0	3.0
	3.9	2.4					1.9	2.2
	3.0	1.5					1.3	1.3
	.1	.6				% Depr., Dep., Amort./Sales	1.5	.8
	(11) .4	(21) 1.6					(41) 2.2	(30) 2.1
	1.4	2.8					4.5	5.0
						% Officers', Directors'	3.3	
						Owners' Comp/Sales	(10) 5.0	
							6.7	
1945M	51864M	277665M	281897M		468912M	Net Sales ($)	559265M	395638M
234M	14855M	108760M	117395M		404054M	Total Assets ($)	386368M	234375M

M = $ thousand   MM = $ million
See Pages 11 through 21 for Explanation of Ratios and Data

Comparative Historical Data | **Current Data Sorted by Sales**

	4/1/04-3/31/05 ALL	4/1/05-3/31/06 ALL	4/1/06-3/31/07 ALL	0-1MM	1-3MM	3-5MM	5-10MM	10-25MM	25MM & OVER
Type of Statement									
Unqualified	13	13	7				4	2	1
Reviewed	10	10	15			2	7	5	1
Compiled	6	5	8			2	4	1	1
Tax Returns	2	2	4			2	1		1
Other	16	13	11		2	2		2	5
				11 (4/1-9/30/06)			34 (10/1/06-3/31/07)		
NUMBER OF STATEMENTS	47	43	45		2	8	16	10	9
ASSETS	%	%	%	%	%	%	%	%	%
Cash & Equivalents	9.6	8.3	13.2	DATA NOT AVAILABLE			16.3	13.6	
Trade Receivables (net)	33.9	32.0	35.7				32.1	37.8	
Inventory	20.0	18.1	20.8				21.3	13.6	
All Other Current	4.9	5.6	6.4				1.9	11.9	
Total Current	68.4	64.1	76.1				71.6	76.9	
Fixed Assets (net)	20.8	20.5	16.4				19.7	14.7	
Intangibles (net)	4.4	7.4	3.8				4.2	3.8	
All Other Non-Current	6.4	8.1	3.7				4.5	4.6	
Total	100.0	100.0	100.0				100.0	100.0	
LIABILITIES									
Notes Payable-Short Term	10.1	10.7	8.8				5.2	7.4	
Cur. Mat.-L.T.D.	3.9	3.5	3.0				5.0	2.0	
Trade Payables	19.8	17.8	20.1				20.2	16.6	
Income Taxes Payable	.1	.1	.4				.1	1.5	
All Other Current	16.7	16.0	27.4				19.6	36.0	
Total Current	50.6	48.1	59.7				50.0	63.5	
Long-Term Debt	13.4	12.3	7.8				12.0	6.7	
Deferred Taxes	.8	.4	.2				.1	.4	
All Other Non-Current	6.8	5.9	7.3				3.7	.7	
Net Worth	28.3	33.3	25.0				34.2	28.7	
Total Liabilities & Net Worth	100.0	100.0	100.0				100.0	100.0	
INCOME DATA									
Net Sales	100.0	100.0	100.0				100.0	100.0	
Gross Profit	31.5	30.7	29.5				32.3	26.9	
Operating Expenses	25.7	24.7	24.1				23.7	22.6	
Operating Profit	5.9	6.0	5.4				8.7	4.3	
All Other Expenses (net)	1.8	.8	1.0				.9	.3	
Profit Before Taxes	4.0	5.2	4.5				7.8	4.0	
RATIOS									
Current	2.0	2.3	2.1				2.7	1.6	
	1.5	1.5	1.3				1.7	1.1	
	1.0	1.0	1.0				1.0	1.0	
Quick	1.2	1.6	1.3				1.8	1.1	
	.9	1.0	.9				1.0	.8	
	.7	.6	.6				.8	.6	
Sales/Receivables	**39** 9.3	**48** 7.6	**31** 11.8				**36** 10.3	**39** 9.5	
	54 6.7	**62** 5.9	**49** 7.4				**46** 7.9	**52** 7.0	
	85 4.3	**85** 4.3	**60** 6.0				**64** 5.7	**75** 4.9	
Cost of Sales/Inventory	**20** 17.8	**17** 21.3	**10** 37.3				**7** 53.4	**7** 49.3	
	48 7.7	**47** 7.8	**34** 10.6				**44** 8.2	**27** 13.6	
	79 4.6	**82** 4.5	**81** 4.5				**92** 4.0	**56** 6.5	
Cost of Sales/Payables	**26** 13.8	**24** 15.1	**19** 19.0				**19** 18.7	**17** 22.0	
	38 9.6	**37** 9.9	**32** 11.5				**40** 9.2	**26** 14.2	
	61 6.0	**65** 5.6	**52** 7.0				**55** 6.6	**45** 8.1	
Sales/Working Capital	5.9	5.7	6.2				6.0	6.0	
	8.3	8.7	17.0				8.8	36.1	
	94.8	-69.0	-48.8				NM	NM	
EBIT/Interest	17.1	14.1	13.9				16.3		
	(42) 4.7	(38) 4.3	(39) 6.0				(14) 9.6		
	1.1	1.1	1.2				1.4		
Net Profit + Depr., Dep., Amort./Cur. Mat. L/T/D	6.3	5.9	9.1						
	(10) 3.2	(15) 1.9	(11) 2.1						
	.2	.6	1.0						
Fixed/Worth	.3	.3	.3				.2	.3	
	.6	.7	.6				.7	.7	
	9.5	20.7	1.6				26.4	1.2	
Debt/Worth	.9	.8	1.0				.6	1.4	
	2.0	1.9	2.5				2.0	4.2	
	48.1	81.4	12.6				76.1	10.0	
% Profit Before Taxes/Tangible Net Worth	62.5	74.8	53.9				71.8	41.3	
	(37) 20.1	(34) 24.9	(38) 30.0				(13) 41.9	30.0	
	6.4	8.3	8.2				12.2	13.1	
% Profit Before Taxes/Total Assets	16.6	13.6	18.4				29.0	17.4	
	5.5	7.3	3.9				6.3	7.0	
	.4	.8	.5				1.1	1.4	
Sales/Net Fixed Assets	29.0	22.4	74.9				68.9	57.4	
	12.2	11.8	27.4				26.6	19.1	
	6.2	4.2	10.5				4.6	14.0	
Sales/Total Assets	2.7	2.5	3.5				3.4	3.2	
	2.0	1.6	2.5				2.3	2.8	
	1.4	1.4	1.8				1.4	1.5	
% Depr., Dep., Amort./Sales	.9	.8	.4				.9	.4	
	(37) 1.5	(38) 1.7	(40) 1.0				(14) 2.1	.6	
	2.5	2.8	2.0				3.4	1.0	
% Officers', Directors' Owners' Comp/Sales	1.7	1.6	3.2						
	(10) 4.1	(14) 3.5	(11) 3.7						
	9.2	6.5	8.8						
Net Sales ($)	715573M	763145M	1082283M		4628M	31513M	107439M	166615M	772088M
Total Assets ($)	407271M	521483M	645298M		760M	12153M	56238M	76129M	500018M

M = $ thousand MM = $ million

See Pages 11 through 21 for Explanation of Ratios and Data

Current Data Sorted by Assets — **Comparative Historical Data**

Type of Statement	0-500M	500M-2MM	2-10MM	10-50MM	50-100MM	100-250MM		4/1/02-3/31/03 ALL	4/1/03-3/31/04 ALL
Unqualified	1		20	24	10	2		42	32
Reviewed		9	34	17				47	42
Compiled	4	15	16		1			24	29
Tax Returns	6	11	11	1				4	17
Other	4	18	25	15	2	2		42	50
		68 (4/1-9/30/06)		180 (10/1/06-3/31/07)					
NUMBER OF STATEMENTS	15	53	106	57	13	4		159	170
ASSETS	%	%	%	%	%	%		%	%
Cash & Equivalents	11.4	9.5	9.3	8.1	6.5			8.3	9.7
Trade Receivables (net)	35.7	31.4	28.7	25.6	25.2			26.8	29.1
Inventory	18.1	20.8	26.1	27.8	27.8			24.5	23.0
All Other Current	1.6	1.7	4.0	5.2	3.0			4.1	4.9
Total Current	66.7	63.4	68.1	66.7	62.4			63.7	66.8
Fixed Assets (net)	25.5	24.0	22.8	22.4	27.3			24.4	23.9
Intangibles (net)	5.5	5.4	3.9	4.9	5.2			5.2	3.5
All Other Non-Current	2.2	7.2	5.1	6.0	5.0			6.6	5.8
Total	100.0	100.0	100.0	100.0	100.0			100.0	100.0
LIABILITIES									
Notes Payable-Short Term	14.3	9.3	11.6	7.0	8.3			8.8	10.6
Cur. Mat.-L.T.D.	11.4	4.3	2.6	1.9	3.5			4.3	4.0
Trade Payables	22.1	16.1	16.0	12.3	12.1			11.4	15.0
Income Taxes Payable	.0	.3	.4	.7	.7			.3	.3
All Other Current	16.1	16.2	14.5	15.6	11.4			14.2	14.0
Total Current	63.9	46.1	45.0	37.6	36.1			39.1	43.9
Long-Term Debt	27.9	17.8	12.7	11.8	14.4			14.2	12.4
Deferred Taxes	.0	.2	.4	.6	1.0			.6	.5
All Other Non-Current	.3	4.7	7.4	4.3	11.0			4.6	7.3
Net Worth	7.9	31.2	34.5	45.8	37.6			41.5	36.0
Total Liabilities & Net Worth	100.0	100.0	100.0	100.0	100.0			100.0	100.0
INCOME DATA									
Net Sales	100.0	100.0	100.0	100.0	100.0			100.0	100.0
Gross Profit	39.5	38.6	32.9	27.5	25.3			31.4	32.2
Operating Expenses	32.6	32.5	26.4	20.2	14.9			27.6	29.6
Operating Profit	6.9	6.2	6.5	7.3	10.4			3.8	2.6
All Other Expenses (net)	.7	1.1	1.3	1.8	.7			1.2	1.0
Profit Before Taxes	6.1	5.1	5.2	5.4	9.6			2.7	1.6
RATIOS									
Current	1.9 / 1.0 / .7	2.1 / 1.4 / 1.0	2.8 / 1.5 / 1.1	2.6 / 1.7 / 1.3	3.1 / 2.3 / 1.3			2.6 / 1.7 / 1.2	2.4 / 1.6 / 1.1
Quick	1.1 / .8 / .5	1.4 / .9 / .6	1.5 / .8 / .6	1.6 / .9 / .6	1.5 / 1.0 / .6			1.6 / .8 / .5	1.5 / .9 / .5
Sales/Receivables	15 23.9 / 30 12.1 / 64 5.7	31 11.7 / 40 9.0 / 59 6.2	35 10.4 / 48 7.6 / 71 5.1	41 8.8 / 51 7.1 / 61 6.0	38 9.6 / 51 7.2 / 57 6.4			38 9.5 / 51 7.2 / 64 5.7	36 10.2 / 50 7.3 / 66 5.5
Cost of Sales/Inventory	0 UND / 10 36.4 / 62 5.8	14 26.6 / 44 8.4 / 77 4.8	29 12.5 / 62 5.9 / 107 3.4	46 7.9 / 73 5.0 / 109 3.3	40 9.2 / 80 4.5 / 116 3.1			35 10.5 / 74 5.0 / 112 3.3	24 15.5 / 57 6.4 / 97 3.8
Cost of Sales/Payables	7 50.2 / 32 11.3 / 38 9.6	18 20.7 / 28 13.2 / 45 8.1	22 16.8 / 34 10.7 / 50 7.3	23 15.6 / 34 10.7 / 44 8.3	23 15.6 / 29 12.7 / 43 8.6			19 18.8 / 28 13.1 / 43 8.5	20 18.5 / 33 11.2 / 51 7.2
Sales/Working Capital	15.8 / 88.1 / -23.1	6.4 / 15.5 / NM	4.7 / 9.3 / 36.5	4.3 / 6.8 / 13.8	3.9 / 6.0 / 11.7			4.2 / 8.8 / 27.5	4.5 / 7.4 / 44.6
EBIT/Interest	27.4 / (13) 6.8 / 2.5	10.7 / (45) 4.1 / 1.4	18.2 / (95) 6.5 / 1.5	21.4 / (49) 6.7 / 2.9	27.8 / 12.0 / 2.5			13.6 / (149) 3.9 / .5	13.9 / (152) 3.6 / .9
Net Profit + Depr., Dep., Amort./Cur. Mat. L/T/D		(27) 4.0	15.9 / 4.0 / 1.3	9.2 / (23) 4.3 / 1.6	16.3 / (10) 3.4 / 2.1			6.3 / (46) 2.4 / .4	6.8 / (52) 2.3 / .8
Fixed/Worth	.6 / 3.2 / -79.5	.3 / .7 / 9.7	.2 / .5 / 1.8	.2 / .5 / 1.3	.4 / .9 / 4.5			.3 / .6 / 1.4	.2 / .6 / 2.1
Debt/Worth	2.7 / 6.1 / -177.5	1.0 / 1.8 / 32.6	.6 / 1.8 / 6.4	.6 / 1.5 / 2.9	.7 / 2.2 / 16.5			.7 / 1.4 / 3.6	.7 / 1.6 / 5.2
% Profit Before Taxes/Tangible Net Worth	360.7 / (11) 105.5 / 23.2	86.3 / (41) 38.8 / 11.3	47.3 / (90) 26.0 / 10.5	47.4 / (53) 26.8 / 10.9	75.0 / (11) 31.6 / 16.1			26.8 / (142) 12.2 / .0	35.5 / (139) 16.0 / 2.2
% Profit Before Taxes/Total Assets	34.8 / 17.2 / 7.4	18.6 / 8.2 / 1.6	19.8 / 7.6 / 1.5	17.4 / 9.0 / 4.6	23.8 / 10.6 / 5.1			10.0 / 5.4 / -.6	12.4 / 5.4 / -.1
Sales/Net Fixed Assets	41.8 / 28.9 / 8.7	38.3 / 12.7 / 7.9	27.6 / 9.8 / 5.8	18.3 / 10.4 / 5.3	11.6 / 7.3 / 4.6			17.8 / 8.2 / 4.4	27.6 / 10.7 / 4.9
Sales/Total Assets	8.6 / 4.2 / 2.7	3.7 / 2.7 / 1.8	2.5 / 2.0 / 1.5	2.1 / 1.8 / 1.4	2.0 / 1.7 / 1.6			2.4 / 1.9 / 1.2	2.6 / 1.9 / 1.4
% Depr., Dep., Amort./Sales	.8 / (12) 1.8 / 3.3	1.0 / (46) 2.2 / 4.4	1.0 / (98) 2.0 / 3.4	1.2 / (55) 1.7 / 2.8	1.1 / (12) 1.8 / 3.1			1.4 / (141) 2.4 / 4.2	1.3 / (148) 2.1 / 4.2
% Officers', Directors' Owners' Comp/Sales		2.8 / (32) 5.9 / 9.4	2.1 / (39) 4.6 / 7.0					1.8 / (48) 3.6 / 6.5	2.5 / (52) 4.7 / 8.9
Net Sales ($)	20917M	175868M	1065475M	2026159M	1536360M	674055M		4421384M	3457764M
Total Assets ($)	4652M	63414M	518981M	1111785M	887768M	453946M		2872431M	2205449M

Comparative Historical Data / Current Data Sorted by Sales

Hist 1	Hist 2	Hist 3	Type of Statement	0-1MM	1-3MM	3-5MM	5-10MM	10-25MM	25MM & OVER
38	41	57	Unqualified	1			5	19	32
65	58	60	Reviewed		2	7	19	23	9
25	37	36	Compiled	4	10	9	11	1	1
15	19	29	Tax Returns	2	14	3	8	2	
63	63	66	Other	2	10	10	14	15	15
4/1/04-3/31/05 ALL	4/1/05-3/31/06 ALL	4/1/06-3/31/07 ALL		0-1MM	68 (4/1-9/30/06) 1-3MM	3-5MM	5-10MM	180 (10/1/06-3/31/07) 10-25MM	25MM & OVER
206	218	248	NUMBER OF STATEMENTS	9	36	29	57	60	57
%	%	%	**ASSETS**	%	%	%	%	%	%
7.5	8.7	8.9	Cash & Equivalents		11.7	10.0	10.5	8.4	5.9
30.2	30.3	28.9	Trade Receivables (net)		28.3	30.5	30.1	28.4	28.2
25.9	25.2	25.1	Inventory		18.1	25.6	23.4	29.1	28.5
4.2	4.4	3.6	All Other Current		3.3	1.3	3.5	4.5	4.4
67.8	68.6	66.5	Total Current		61.4	67.3	67.5	70.4	67.0
23.1	21.8	23.3	Fixed Assets (net)		25.4	22.1	23.5	18.5	24.2
3.6	4.2	4.6	Intangibles (net)		8.0	3.2	4.1	4.3	4.1
5.5	5.3	5.6	All Other Non-Current		5.1	7.4	4.9	6.8	4.8
100.0	100.0	100.0	Total		100.0	100.0	100.0	100.0	100.0
			LIABILITIES						
12.2	12.8	9.9	Notes Payable-Short Term		10.1	12.1	9.6	11.5	8.0
3.5	3.1	3.4	Cur. Mat.-L.T.D.		4.8	3.1	2.3	2.6	3.1
16.3	15.8	15.3	Trade Payables		17.8	15.2	15.1	16.9	13.7
.3	.3	.4	Income Taxes Payable		.3	.2	.0	.7	.8
16.3	13.9	15.1	All Other Current		11.0	13.5	17.2	17.0	13.5
48.5	45.8	44.2	Total Current		43.9	44.2	44.2	48.8	39.1
13.1	13.0	14.6	Long-Term Debt		20.7	13.4	11.3	11.8	13.1
.5	.5	.4	Deferred Taxes		.2	.2	.4	.4	.8
7.1	9.7	5.8	All Other Non-Current		5.8	2.2	8.8	6.2	5.0
30.7	31.0	34.9	Net Worth		29.3	40.0	35.3	32.8	42.0
100.0	100.0	100.0	Total Liabilities & Net Worth		100.0	100.0	100.0	100.0	100.0
			INCOME DATA						
100.0	100.0	100.0	Net Sales		100.0	100.0	100.0	100.0	100.0
31.7	32.2	32.8	Gross Profit		38.8	39.0	32.1	29.1	27.0
27.6	26.9	26.0	Operating Expenses		34.7	30.8	27.2	22.6	18.6
4.1	5.3	6.8	Operating Profit		4.1	8.3	5.0	6.5	8.4
.8	.9	1.3	All Other Expenses (net)		1.1	1.0	.5	1.7	1.4
3.3	4.5	5.5	Profit Before Taxes		3.0	7.2	4.5	4.7	7.0
			RATIOS						
2.3	2.5	2.5	Current		2.2	2.7	2.7	2.5	2.4
1.5	1.5	1.5			1.4	1.6	1.6	1.5	1.6
1.1	1.1	1.1			1.0	1.1	1.1	1.1	1.3
1.3	1.5	1.4	Quick		1.5	2.0	1.6	1.3	1.5
.8	.8	.9			.9	.9	.8	.8	.9
.5	.5	.6			.5	.6	.6	.5	.6
40 9.1	38 9.7	35 10.5	Sales/Receivables	27 13.5	36 10.0	31 11.9	38 9.7	40 9.1	
52 7.0	50 7.3	48 7.6		37 9.8	50 7.3	40 9.1	48 7.6	51 7.1	
68 5.3	64 5.7	62 5.9		53 6.9	73 5.0	62 5.9	67 5.5	61 6.0	
28 13.0	29 12.7	29 12.7	Cost of Sales/Inventory	8 47.1	28 13.1	27 13.3	35 10.3	43 8.6	
70 5.2	66 5.5	61 6.0		47 7.8	51 7.1	45 8.0	73 5.0	68 5.4	
108 3.4	100 3.7	100 3.6		88 4.2	138 2.6	94 3.9	116 3.2	94 3.9	
22 16.9	20 18.6	21 17.0	Cost of Sales/Payables	19 18.7	17 21.1	23 16.1	21 17.7	24 15.5	
32 11.5	32 11.6	32 11.3		33 11.0	28 13.2	33 11.2	35 10.3	34 10.8	
57 6.4	52 7.0	47 7.8		47 7.8	60 6.1	48 7.6	48 7.5	43 8.4	
5.6	4.7	4.8	Sales/Working Capital		5.9	4.3	5.9	4.5	4.5
10.2	9.6	9.5			16.2	9.0	9.5	8.8	7.7
43.1	44.8	29.1			NM	35.5	40.2	58.5	13.7
12.2	12.6	16.9	EBIT/Interest		12.6	15.7	19.3	16.6	19.3
(192) 4.8	(196) 5.2	(218) 6.1		(30) 3.3	(23) 5.0	(52) 7.0	(55) 5.0	(51) 7.7	
1.8	2.0	1.8			1.1	1.7	1.7	1.4	2.8
8.3	6.9	9.0	Net Profit + Depr., Dep.,				5.2	16.4	9.0
(55) 2.6	(57) 3.0	(68) 3.5	Amort./Cur. Mat. L/T/D			(12) 2.2	(19) 7.1	(30) 3.5	
.9	1.2	1.3					-.8	2.1	1.5
.3	.3	.3	Fixed/Worth		.4	.3	.2	.2	.3
.7	.6	.7			1.0	.6	.5	.5	.7
2.1	1.9	2.0			NM	1.5	3.1	1.7	1.3
1.0	.8	.8	Debt/Worth		.8	1.0	.9	.7	.7
2.1	2.2	1.8			2.3	1.6	2.1	1.7	1.6
6.6	7.7	6.0			-383.1	4.4	7.6	4.7	3.0
44.5	52.0	55.3	% Profit Before Taxes/Tangible Net Worth		98.8	84.2	56.3	44.4	47.6
(170) 19.5	(178) 25.0	(210) 27.0		(26) 19.2	(27) 38.8	(47) 30.8	(51) 23.2	(52) 30.7	
6.9	6.5	11.4			9.5	12.8	9.9	11.3	14.1
12.0	17.5	19.5	% Profit Before Taxes/Total Assets		15.5	24.5	21.7	14.5	20.2
6.2	7.7	8.8			7.8	14.2	7.7	7.6	10.3
1.2	1.7	2.9			1.2	3.4	1.2	2.0	4.6
31.1	27.8	25.5	Sales/Net Fixed Assets		32.7	36.9	32.6	30.3	17.0
11.2	12.0	10.4			12.5	10.1	11.6	12.3	8.6
5.2	6.1	5.9			5.7	5.8	5.9	6.9	5.3
2.7	2.8	2.8	Sales/Total Assets		4.0	3.0	3.0	2.6	2.3
2.0	2.1	2.0			2.4	2.1	2.2	1.9	1.9
1.4	1.5	1.5			1.5	1.4	1.7	1.5	1.5
.9	.9	1.0	% Depr., Dep., Amort./Sales		1.2	.9	1.0	1.0	1.0
(188) 1.9	(192) 1.7	(225) 1.9		(31) 2.4	(25) 1.8	(51) 2.0	(56) 1.6	(54) 1.7	
3.5	3.3	3.4			4.1	3.7	3.7	2.6	2.7
2.2	2.3	2.4	% Officers', Directors' Owners' Comp/Sales		4.4	2.3	2.2	1.6	
(74) 4.6	(76) 4.0	(85) 4.7		(21) 6.7	(15) 3.7	(24) 4.7	(15) 4.1		
7.0	6.9	8.3			9.4	7.0	8.0		
4208331M	4883498M	5498834M	Net Sales ($)	5994M	75184M	111136M	407539M	936467M	3962514M
2534586M	2714332M	3040546M	Total Assets ($)	4530M	34548M	59359M	208394M	507533M	2226182M

Current Data Sorted by Assets / Comparative Historical Data

Type of Statement

0-500M	500M-2MM	2-10MM	10-50MM	50-100MM	100-250MM		4/1/02-3/31/03 ALL	4/1/03-3/31/04 ALL
		2	6	2	3	Unqualified	11	14
	2	4	2			Reviewed	7	7
1	1	2	1			Compiled	6	5
2		3	1			Tax Returns	3	8
3		4	5	3	5	Other	33	25
	12 (4/1-9/30/06)		34 (10/1/06-3/31/07)					
1	8	13	11	5	8	**NUMBER OF STATEMENTS**	60	59
%	%	%	%	%	%		%	%
						ASSETS		
		1.8	22.1			Cash & Equivalents	13.2	17.0
		36.1	27.4			Trade Receivables (net)	26.7	32.2
		45.2	29.7			Inventory	26.1	24.9
		2.2	2.9			All Other Current	4.7	3.5
		85.3	82.2			Total Current	70.7	77.6
		6.8	10.5			Fixed Assets (net)	17.2	16.2
		2.5	3.5			Intangibles (net)	6.9	1.7
		5.5	3.8			All Other Non-Current	5.3	4.6
		100.0	100.0			Total	100.0	100.0
						LIABILITIES		
		15.0	14.2			Notes Payable-Short Term	12.1	9.3
		2.8	1.5			Cur. Mat.-L.T.D.	2.8	2.0
		20.4	14.0			Trade Payables	14.7	20.1
		.0	1.0			Income Taxes Payable	.6	.7
		10.2	11.3			All Other Current	10.2	11.4
		48.5	42.0			Total Current	40.5	43.5
		7.4	3.3			Long-Term Debt	12.5	8.4
		.0	.0			Deferred Taxes	.1	.0
		9.7	2.8			All Other Non-Current	6.0	7.5
		34.4	51.9			Net Worth	40.8	40.6
		100.0	100.0			Total Liabilities & Net Worth	100.0	100.0
						INCOME DATA		
		100.0	100.0			Net Sales	100.0	100.0
		25.2	27.5			Gross Profit	38.8	39.2
		23.1	26.0			Operating Expenses	35.9	33.9
		2.1	1.5			Operating Profit	2.9	5.3
		1.3	1.0			All Other Expenses (net)	1.0	.4
		.8	.5			Profit Before Taxes	1.9	4.9
						RATIOS		
		2.5	5.4				3.4	3.3
		1.7	2.3			Current	1.6	1.8
		1.3	1.1				1.2	1.3
		1.5	3.5				1.4	2.6
		.8	.8			Quick	.9	1.3
		.6	.6				.5	.7
		34 10.7	37 9.9				29 12.4	29 12.6
		44 8.3	45 8.1			Sales/Receivables	46 8.0	44 8.3
		71 5.1	58 6.3				69 5.3	57 6.4
		46 8.0	42 8.7				29 12.7	14 25.3
		79 4.6	68 5.3			Cost of Sales/Inventory	75 4.9	57 6.4
		159 2.3	123 3.0				108 3.4	92 4.0
		15 23.8	15 24.6				20 18.3	23 15.6
		30 12.3	32 11.2			Cost of Sales/Payables	37 9.8	41 8.9
		63 5.8	40 9.1				59 6.2	59 6.2
		4.9	3.0				4.2	4.1
		9.0	4.8			Sales/Working Capital	7.6	7.4
		14.3	24.5				25.0	18.8
		9.3					14.3	23.5
		(12) 5.6				EBIT/Interest	(51) 2.1	(48) 6.3
		.5					-2.5	1.8
						Net Profit + Depr., Dep., Amort./Cur. Mat. L/T/D		
		.0	.1				.1	.1
		.2	.2			Fixed/Worth	.5	.3
		.7	.7				1.5	.8
		.9	.2				.6	.5
		2.4	1.1			Debt/Worth	1.8	1.4
		5.4	3.8				5.6	3.7
		51.7	31.8				67.9	61.0
		(12) 22.1	21.6			% Profit Before Taxes/Tangible Net Worth	(54) 14.5	(51) 20.6
		5.2	7.2				-10.5	6.2
		17.1	7.4				12.7	21.1
		7.5	6.4			% Profit Before Taxes/Total Assets	3.7	8.7
		-1.2	4.2				-7.7	2.1
		160.2	54.5				60.9	82.0
		83.2	22.5			Sales/Net Fixed Assets	13.9	37.7
		29.0	10.1				4.9	11.5
		4.0	2.5				3.3	4.0
		2.8	2.3			Sales/Total Assets	1.9	2.5
		1.5	1.6				1.2	1.7
			.8				.6	.3
			(10) 1.1			% Depr., Dep., Amort./Sales	(42) 2.4	(50) 1.0
			2.1				4.0	2.0
							1.8	1.1
						% Officers', Directors' Owners' Comp/Sales	(13) 8.2	(23) 5.7
							11.5	14.7
630M	31978M	180393M	576360M	649706M	2083264M	Net Sales ($)	2265232M	1852936M
223M	7370M	66917M	282758M	385168M	1261297M	Total Assets ($)	1738511M	843948M

M = $ thousand   MM = $ million
See Pages 11 through 21 for Explanation of Ratios and Data

Comparative Historical Data | Current Data Sorted by Sales

14 11 3 6 28 4/1/04- 3/31/05 ALL	15 5 6 5 24 4/1/05- 3/31/06 ALL	13 6 4 3 20 4/1/06- 3/31/07 ALL	Type of Statement Unqualified Reviewed Compiled Tax Returns Other	0-1MM	1-3MM 12 (4/1-9/30/06)	3-5MM	5-10MM	10-25MM 3 3 2 1 4 34 (10/1/06-3/31/07)	25MM & OVER 10 12
62	55	46	**NUMBER OF STATEMENTS**	1	5	2	3	13	22
%	%	%	**ASSETS**	%	%	%	%	%	%
15.0	14.0	15.3	Cash & Equivalents					7.9	21.2
31.9	31.3	31.7	Trade Receivables (net)					35.6	27.3
27.2	28.1	27.6	Inventory					42.4	21.3
3.5	3.0	3.1	All Other Current					1.8	3.2
77.6	76.3	77.7	Total Current					87.6	73.0
13.6	14.5	11.2	Fixed Assets (net)					7.6	11.9
2.3	5.0	5.7	Intangibles (net)					1.4	10.2
6.5	4.1	5.4	All Other Non-Current					3.4	4.9
100.0	100.0	100.0	Total					100.0	100.0
			LIABILITIES						
13.7	14.6	12.2	Notes Payable-Short Term					12.6	9.5
1.4	1.2	2.4	Cur. Mat.-L.T.D.					2.5	2.1
16.7	18.8	16.8	Trade Payables					19.7	14.7
.4	1.3	.6	Income Taxes Payable					.0	1.2
10.3	10.0	11.1	All Other Current					8.2	13.5
42.4	45.9	43.2	Total Current					43.0	41.0
10.5	9.4	11.3	Long-Term Debt					6.9	17.0
.1	.2	.1	Deferred Taxes					.0	.2
6.5	15.6	9.8	All Other Non-Current					9.5	2.8
40.4	28.9	35.6	Net Worth					40.5	39.0
100.0	100.0	100.0	Total Liabilities & Net Worth					100.0	100.0
			INCOME DATA						
100.0	100.0	100.0	Net Sales					100.0	100.0
37.0	36.2	31.9	Gross Profit					22.0	30.7
32.8	32.4	27.2	Operating Expenses					20.5	25.6
4.1	3.8	4.7	Operating Profit					1.5	5.1
.4	1.0	1.0	All Other Expenses (net)					2.0	.2
3.7	2.8	3.7	Profit Before Taxes					-.4	5.0
			RATIOS						
3.9 2.0 1.2	2.9 1.6 1.2	2.8 1.7 1.3	Current					3.0 2.3 1.4	3.3 1.6 1.2
2.9 1.0 .7	1.5 .9 .6	1.9 1.0 .6	Quick					1.8 .9 .6	2.3 1.1 .6
30 12.4 45 8.1 57 6.4	30 12.2 42 8.6 60 6.0	32 11.5 49 7.4 63 5.8	Sales/Receivables					34 10.7 42 8.7 59 6.2	40 9.2 53 6.9 62 5.9
32 11.4 61 6.0 101 3.6	17 21.0 64 5.7 112 3.3	22 16.5 53 6.9 100 3.7	Cost of Sales/Inventory					43 8.5 73 5.0 123 3.0	41 8.9 58 6.3 89 4.1
16 22.2 34 10.6 56 6.5	22 16.7 40 9.2 54 6.8	16 22.3 36 10.2 61 6.0	Cost of Sales/Payables					15 24.3 27 13.3 50 7.3	23 15.6 36 10.2 64 5.7
3.1 6.8 20.2	4.0 8.2 21.6	3.6 7.7 19.0	Sales/Working Capital					4.5 7.4 13.3	3.0 6.9 25.5
30.4 (50) 5.7 1.1	19.8 (49) 4.7 1.3	11.5 (39) 4.4 1.4	EBIT/Interest					9.3 (11) 6.9 1.4	13.4 (18) 3.8 1.2
26.7 (13) 15.5 3.0		9.3 (11) 1.8 .9	Net Profit + Depr., Dep., Amort./Cur. Mat. L/T/D						
.1 .3 .6	.1 .3 1.2	.1 .2 .9	Fixed/Worth					.0 .2 .3	.1 .2 .8
.5 1.4 6.5	.6 1.8 5.3	.6 2.0 5.1	Debt/Worth					.6 2.0 4.6	.4 2.0 4.9
51.7 (55) 22.6 3.1	71.4 (49) 22.5 5.1	51.0 (41) 21.6 7.3	% Profit Before Taxes/Tangible Net Worth					51.7 (12) 22.1 7.6	31.0 (20) 18.0 6.7
20.4 11.1 .2	14.5 7.3 1.4	19.5 7.4 2.2	% Profit Before Taxes/Total Assets					17.1 7.5 1.6	9.3 6.6 1.9
70.3 32.7 10.5	65.9 32.4 9.7	114.8 42.8 9.9	Sales/Net Fixed Assets					160.2 73.3 11.8	56.1 24.6 8.9
3.8 2.4 1.6	3.4 2.4 1.6	3.1 2.4 1.6	Sales/Total Assets					4.0 2.8 2.0	2.5 1.7 1.3
.6 (51) 1.2 2.6	.5 (44) 1.1 2.6	.3 (31) .9 2.2	% Depr., Dep., Amort./Sales						.7 (16) 1.1 2.5
2.3 (22) 4.8 9.8	1.7 (15) 4.0 6.9		% Officers', Directors' Owners' Comp/Sales						
1680184M	2644447M	3522331M	Net Sales ($)	630M	10915M	6894M	20977M	217959M	3264956M
1093794M	1278641M	2003733M	Total Assets ($)	223M	6317M	1684M	6987M	93613M	1894909M

© RMA 2007   M = $ thousand   MM = $ million
See Pages 11 through 21 for Explanation of Ratios a... nd Data

Current Data Sorted by Assets | Comparative Historical Data

Current period samples: 18 (4/1–9/30/06) · 75 (10/1/06–3/31/07)

M = $ thousand   MM = $ million

	0-500M	500M-2MM	2-10MM	10-50MM	50-100MM	100MM & OVER		4/1/02-3/31/03 ALL	4/1/03-3/31/04 ALL
Type of Statement									
Unqualified		1	8	11	10	3		26	23
Reviewed		1	6					14	11
Compiled	2	2						2	15
Tax Returns	2	2	6	1				4	2
Other		5	10	11	5	7		27	22
NUMBER OF STATEMENTS	4	11	30	23	15	10		73	73
	%	%	%	%	%	%		%	%
ASSETS									
Cash & Equivalents		13.0	10.4	13.4	23.9	1.3		13.6	15.8
Trade Receivables (net)		27.8	36.4	27.1	25.9	.3		28.4	26.4
Inventory		24.5	27.0	22.9	24.1	3.7		23.2	21.2
All Other Current		1.5	1.6	3.9	4.5	4.4		3.8	2.8
Total Current		66.8	75.4	67.3	78.5	89.8		69.0	66.3
Fixed Assets (net)		13.0	11.7	15.4	7.7	7.1		14.7	19.1
Intangibles (net)		7.4	6.6	9.7	9.5	16.5		11.3	9.0
All Other Non-Current		12.8	6.3	7.6	4.3	6.6		5.0	5.7
Total		100.0	100.0	100.0	100.0	100.0		100.0	100.0
LIABILITIES									
Notes Payable-Short Term		6.1	9.9	8.7	4.2	3.4		6.5	11.5
Cur. Mat.-L.T.D.		4.8	1.9	3.1	.2	4.4		3.9	2.3
Trade Payables		19.0	18.1	15.2	15.7	11.4		16.3	13.1
Income Taxes Payable		.4	.2	.7	.5	.2		.3	.7
All Other Current		10.4	12.0	12.3	18.2	17.3		11.6	11.0
Total Current		40.7	42.1	40.0	38.9	36.7		38.6	38.5
Long-Term Debt		17.4	15.6	22.0	2.0	9.5		15.2	19.2
Deferred Taxes		.4	.4	.7	.4	.1		.7	.4
All Other Non-Current		6.8	8.0	5.1	15.0	18.0		6.8	5.2
Net Worth		34.8	33.8	32.2	43.7	35.7		38.7	36.7
Total Liabilties & Net Worth		100.0	100.0	100.0	100.0	100.0		100.0	100.0
INCOME DATA									
Net Sales		100.0	100.0	100.0	100.0	100.0		100.0	100.0
Gross Profit		50.6	40.8	34.5	34.0	33.4		36.6	41.6
Operating Expenses		42.7	34.4	31.8	37.4	36.7		35.1	38.2
Operating Profit		7.9	6.5	2.6	-3.5	-3.3		1.4	3.4
All Other Expenses (net)		.8	1.0	1.4	-.3	.9		1.5	1.5
Profit Before Taxes		7.1	5.4	1.2	-3.2	-4.1		-.1	1.9
RATIOS									
Current		3.1 / 1.5 / 1.0	3.2 / 1.7 / 1.2	2.9 / 1.6 / 1.1	4.8 / 2.7 / 1.2	4.8 / 2.1 / 1.4		3.4 / 1.6 / 1.2	3.0 / 2.0 / 1.3
Quick		2.0 / 1.2 / .6	2.0 / 1.0 / .7	1.3 / 1.0 / .5	3.2 / 1.8 / .6	4.0 / 1.2 / .9		2.3 / 1.0 / .7	2.1 / 1.1 / .6
Sales/Receivables		28 12.9 / 42 8.8 / 57 6.4	32 11.3 / 50 7.4 / 65 5.6	35 10.5 / 45 8.1 / 66 5.5	56 6.5 / 65 5.6 / 68 5.4	55 6.7 / 75 4.9 / 107 3.4		37 9.9 / 50 7.3 / 68 5.4	37 9.8 / 50 7.3 / 68 5.4
Cost of Sales/Inventory		14 25.7 / 99 3.7 / 140 2.6	43 8.5 / 70 5.2 / 91 4.0	31 11.8 / 71 5.2 / 124 2.9	39 9.3 / 78 4.7 / 87 4.2	29 12.4 / 64 5.7 / 89 4.1		20 18.0 / 68 5.4 / 112 3.3	29 12.4 / 68 5.4 / 102 3.6
Cost of Sales/Payables		39 9.4 / 66 5.6 / 108 3.4	25 14.6 / 43 8.5 / 58 6.3	24 15.2 / 36 10.0 / 61 6.0	22 16.9 / 38 9.7 / 67 5.5	31 11.8 / 40 9.2 / 75 4.9		26 13.8 / 41 8.9 / 60 6.1	23 15.6 / 41 8.8 / 60 6.0
Sales/Working Capital		4.7 / 13.0 / 238.0	3.7 / 7.5 / 27.6	4.6 / 6.2 / 23.0	1.9 / 3.8 / 19.0	.8 / 5.5 / NM		3.9 / 7.8 / 28.4	3.2 / 6.4 / 23.5
EBIT/Interest			(25) 8.5 / 4.0 / 1.6	(19) 14.6 / 2.4 / -.4				(64) 10.3 / 2.4 / -.7	(62) 22.9 / 2.2 / .3
Net Profit + Depr., Dep., Amort./Cur. Mat. L/T/D								(16) 11.7 / 1.8 / -2.9	(15) 4.5 / 2.5 / 1.8
Fixed/Worth		.0 / .4 / .8	.1 / .4 / 1.3	.1 / .3 / 1.8	.1 / .2 / 4.8	.1 / .2 / -.2		.1 / .4 / 1.1	.1 / .5 / 1.2
Debt/Worth		.5 / .9 / -6.2	.8 / 2.7 / 5.4	.5 / 1.8 / 8.2	.4 / 1.4 / 26.9	.7 / 1.4 / -2.6		.5 / 1.8 / 6.7	.5 / 1.2 / 4.0
% Profit Before Taxes/Tangible Net Worth			(28) 83.1 / 29.7 / 5.6	(19) 40.1 / 16.2 / -4.2	(13) 24.2 / 13.2 / -24.5			(62) 43.4 / 12.8 / -4.0	(63) 33.1 / 12.1 / -3.1
% Profit Before Taxes/Total Assets		18.4 / 13.4 / 1.3	17.3 / 8.3 / 2.2	13.8 / 4.1 / -4.3	13.5 / 3.9 / -11.0	9.7 / 6.1 / -13.8		15.1 / 4.6 / -3.3	15.5 / 3.4 / -2.6
Sales/Net Fixed Assets		124.8 / 34.2 / 9.2	79.3 / 37.8 / 14.2	30.9 / 21.8 / 7.8	45.6 / 21.9 / 9.5	58.0 / 20.3 / 9.3		42.5 / 15.8 / 8.5	28.9 / 14.5 / 6.3
Sales/Total Assets		3.1 / 2.2 / 1.2	3.4 / 2.6 / 1.5	2.6 / 1.8 / 1.2	2.2 / 2.0 / .9	1.9 / 1.6 / .5		2.8 / 1.8 / 1.1	2.5 / 1.6 / .9
% Depr., Dep., Amort./Sales			(21) .7 / 1.1 / 1.9	(19) 1.1 / 1.4 / 2.4				(56) 1.1 / 2.1 / 3.7	(59) 1.1 / 2.2 / 4.7
% Officers', Directors', Owners' Comp/Sales								(11) 2.7 / 6.5 / 10.4	
Net Sales ($)	2824M	32619M	423475M	965233M	2047777M	2478451M		3503991M	2363290M
Total Assets ($)	713M	14282M	127475M	571999M	1039708M	3410849M		2309632M	2212885M

© RMA 2007

M = $ thousand   MM = $ million
See Pages 11 through 21 for Explanation of Ratios and Data

Comparative Historical Data   **Current Data Sorted by Sales**

Type of Statement

Type of Statement	4/1/04-3/31/05 ALL	4/1/05-3/31/06 ALL	4/1/06-3/31/07 ALL	0-1MM	1-3MM	3-5MM	5-10MM	10-25MM	25MM & OVER
Unqualified	33	26	33		2		1	10	20
Reviewed	13	13	7		1	2	1	2	1
Compiled	6	2	4	2	1				
Tax Returns	3	6	11	2	1	3	1	4	
Other	20	36	38		4	1	4	9	21
				18 (4/1-9/30/06)			75 (10/1/06-3/31/07)		
NUMBER OF STATEMENTS	75	83	93	4	9	6	7	25	42

Main Data

	4/1/04-3/31/05 ALL	4/1/05-3/31/06 ALL	4/1/06-3/31/07 ALL	0-1MM	1-3MM	3-5MM	5-10MM	10-25MM	25MM & OVER
ASSETS	%	%	%	%	%	%	%	%	%
Cash & Equivalents	14.8	14.8	15.5					13.7	16.8
Trade Receivables (net)	28.1	28.5	29.3					31.8	32.0
Inventory	22.9	22.5	23.0					24.8	22.4
All Other Current	3.5	4.6	2.9					2.1	4.3
Total Current	69.4	70.4	70.7					72.4	75.5
Fixed Assets (net)	14.9	14.5	12.2					12.6	9.6
Intangibles (net)	9.4	8.5	9.6					6.8	9.1
All Other Non-Current	6.3	6.6	7.5					8.2	5.9
Total	100.0	100.0	100.0					100.0	100.0
LIABILITIES									
Notes Payable-Short Term	7.5	8.9	8.5					7.3	7.3
Cur. Mat.-L.T.D.	2.2	1.6	2.5					2.9	1.7
Trade Payables	15.6	15.1	16.0					17.9	15.8
Income Taxes Payable	.6	.7	.4					.1	.7
All Other Current	10.8	11.6	13.0					12.3	16.2
Total Current	36.7	37.9	40.4					40.5	41.8
Long-Term Debt	18.3	13.7	15.7					14.3	12.2
Deferred Taxes	.3	.3	.4					.2	.5
All Other Non-Current	3.9	7.7	9.3					11.1	11.2
Net Worth	40.9	40.4	34.2					33.9	34.4
Total Liabilties & Net Worth	100.0	100.0	100.0					100.0	100.0
INCOME DATA									
Net Sales	100.0	100.0	100.0					100.0	100.0
Gross Profit	40.1	38.6	39.5					43.1	29.8
Operating Expenses	34.0	33.5	36.6					38.2	30.3
Operating Profit	6.2	5.2	3.0					5.0	-.5
All Other Expenses (net)	1.0	.2	.9					1.3	.6
Profit Before Taxes	5.2	5.0	2.1					3.6	-1.1
RATIOS									
Current	3.5	4.2	3.2					3.4	3.1
	1.9	1.7	1.7					1.6	1.9
	1.2	1.3	1.2					1.2	1.3
Quick	2.1	2.7	2.3					2.8	2.3
	1.1	1.1	1.1					1.0	1.1
	.7	.7	.6					.6	.7
Sales/Receivables	39 9.5	38 9.7	34 10.6					33 11.0	41 8.9
	50 7.4	53 6.8	51 7.1					45 8.0	59 6.1
	62 5.9	67 5.4	68 5.4					70 5.2	70 5.2
Cost of Sales/Inventory	35 10.4	31 11.9	32 11.5					36 10.2	32 11.6
	61 6.0	70 5.2	73 5.0					67 5.4	66 5.5
	99 3.7	106 3.5	105 3.5					127 2.9	86 4.2
Cost of Sales/Payables	29 12.6	27 13.8	26 14.1					25 14.8	24 15.2
	42 8.6	38 9.7	41 8.8					44 8.3	36 10.1
	63 5.8	55 6.6	65 5.6					61 6.0	61 6.0
Sales/Working Capital	3.0	3.1	3.7					3.8	3.4
	5.9	6.4	6.9					7.3	5.8
	17.3	21.6	36.0					34.3	20.0
EBIT/Interest	21.7	26.6	13.6					11.7	22.2
	(60) 4.8	(68) 6.7	(73) 3.9					(21) 4.0	(30) 2.7
	1.4	1.7	.9					1.4	-.5
Net Profit + Depr., Dep., Amort./Cur. Mat. L/T/D	14.0	14.7	16.5						23.1
	(24) 4.2	(18) 4.8	(21) 3.1						(11) 3.4
	1.6	1.8	2.3						1.0
Fixed/Worth	.2	.1	.1					.1	.1
	.3	.3	.3					.4	.2
	.8	1.4	1.7					3.6	1.3
Debt/Worth	.5	.5	.6					1.0	.5
	1.2	1.5	1.8					3.3	1.5
	3.8	6.0	8.8					27.3	6.0
% Profit Before Taxes/Tangible Net Worth	43.0	47.3	51.3					108.9	38.6
	(65) 19.8	(70) 19.6	(78) 21.6					(22) 35.6	(35) 17.0
	7.0	6.2	4.5					9.9	-6.8
% Profit Before Taxes/Total Assets	14.4	16.2	13.9					21.0	11.7
	8.4	6.3	6.3					9.2	5.7
	2.4	1.1	-.8					1.7	-6.0
Sales/Net Fixed Assets	32.9	51.3	54.9					62.6	58.0
	17.6	20.0	24.4					28.7	22.6
	8.4	8.8	10.3					16.8	12.0
Sales/Total Assets	2.8	2.8	2.8					3.3	2.4
	1.9	1.9	2.0					2.2	1.9
	1.1	1.2	1.3					1.4	1.3
% Depr., Dep., Amort./Sales	1.1	.8	1.0					1.0	1.1
	(55) 1.7	(65) 1.7	(62) 1.6					(20) 1.2	(26) 1.6
	3.5	3.0	2.4					2.1	2.9
% Officers', Directors' Owners' Comp/Sales	1.6	1.9	.6						
	(10) 3.1	(13) 6.9	(12) 3.7						
	8.5	14.7	8.5						
Net Sales ($)	4011838M	4007153M	5719779M	2146M	17205M	22316M	48166M	406841M	5223105M
Total Assets ($)	2857003M	2680978M	3395226M	966M	13298M	12472M	21494M	326134M	3020862M

M = $ thousand   MM = $ million
See Pages 11 through 21 for Explanation of Ratios and Data

Current Data Sorted by Assets   **Comparative Historical Data**

0-500M	500M-2MM	2-10MM	10-50MM	50-100MM	100-250MM	Type of Statement	4/1/02-3/31/03 ALL	4/1/03-3/31/04 ALL
	1	2	1	1	4	Unqualified	9	16
	1	3				Reviewed	10	7
1	1	1				Compiled	3	6
2	1	3				Tax Returns		1
1	2	4	7	4		Other	18	18
	3 (4/1-9/30/06)		36 (10/1/06-3/31/07)			NUMBER OF STATEMENTS		
4	5	13	8	5	4		40	48
%	%	%	%	%	%	**ASSETS**	%	%
		13.8				Cash & Equivalents	14.6	14.9
		31.5				Trade Receivables (net)	25.8	23.5
		32.8				Inventory	25.1	22.6
		1.5				All Other Current	4.5	5.0
		79.7				Total Current	70.1	65.9
		7.2				Fixed Assets (net)	15.1	18.8
		3.7				Intangibles (net)	6.8	8.8
		9.4				All Other Non-Current	7.9	6.5
		100.0				Total	100.0	100.0
						LIABILITIES		
		14.1				Notes Payable-Short Term	12.0	13.7
		1.7				Cur. Mat.-L.T.D.	7.2	2.4
		23.1				Trade Payables	13.2	16.3
		1.9				Income Taxes Payable	.4	.9
		13.4				All Other Current	11.0	17.2
		54.2				Total Current	43.8	50.4
		5.5				Long-Term Debt	18.1	14.3
		.0				Deferred Taxes	.2	.5
		3.7				All Other Non-Current	6.0	10.0
		36.6				Net Worth	32.0	24.8
		100.0				Total Liabilities & Net Worth	100.0	100.0
						INCOME DATA		
		100.0				Net Sales	100.0	100.0
		42.1				Gross Profit	38.9	44.7
		37.7				Operating Expenses	36.5	39.6
		4.4				Operating Profit	2.4	5.1
		1.1				All Other Expenses (net)	2.2	1.7
		3.2				Profit Before Taxes	.2	3.4
						RATIOS		
		2.3					3.8	2.5
		1.2				Current	2.3	1.4
		1.0					1.2	.9
		1.4					2.4	1.2
		.7				Quick	1.2	.8
		.5					.6	.4
	37	9.9					25 14.6	26 13.9
	60	6.1				Sales/Receivables	44 8.4	40 9.1
	77	4.8					66 5.5	54 6.7
	36	10.1					43 8.6	38 9.5
	87	4.2				Cost of Sales/Inventory	85 4.3	63 5.8
	134	2.7					143 2.6	94 3.9
	25	14.5					18 19.9	27 13.3
	45	8.1				Cost of Sales/Payables	29 12.4	38 9.5
	110	3.3					56 6.5	60 6.1
		5.1					3.5	3.9
		7.9				Sales/Working Capital	5.4	13.5
		NM					18.1	-31.6
		31.0					13.1	19.3
	(11)	5.3				EBIT/Interest	(34) 2.3	(43) 4.3
		1.4					.1	.6
						Net Profit + Depr., Dep.,	263.1	72.3
						Amort./Cur. Mat. L/T/D	(10) 6.3	(14) 31.3
							.4	2.2
		.0					.2	.2
		.2				Fixed/Worth	.3	.6
		.5					1.2	NM
		.9					.5	.6
		1.7				Debt/Worth	1.7	2.5
		6.2					4.9	NM
		71.6				% Profit Before Taxes/Tangible	39.9	49.4
	(12)	25.0				Net Worth	(32) 14.5	(36) 16.6
		5.6					2.4	8.2
		26.2				% Profit Before Taxes/Total	12.7	13.2
		3.6				Assets	6.1	5.9
		.5					-5.4	-2.6
		133.9					38.2	59.2
		34.2				Sales/Net Fixed Assets	15.3	19.8
		22.7					9.0	5.1
		3.2					2.8	3.0
		2.2				Sales/Total Assets	2.0	1.8
		1.3					1.2	1.0
		.2					1.0	.8
	(10)	1.1				% Depr., Dep., Amort./Sales	(29) 1.7	(34) 2.1
		2.3					3.6	5.7
							3.8	
						% Officers', Directors'	(10) 7.4	
						Owners' Comp/Sales	11.4	
6688M	25569M	157519M	473570M	420655M	645220M	Net Sales ($)	2766984M	1728678M
1092M	7285M	72352M	225812M	383641M	592957M	Total Assets ($)	1309144M	1391883M

© RMA 2007

M = $ thousand   MM = $ million
See Pages 11 through 21 for Explanation of Ratios and Data

Comparative Historical Data

Current Data Sorted by Sales

					Type of Statement						
15		8		9	Unqualified		1			2	6
5		5		4	Reviewed		1		1	2	
2		2		2	Compiled		1			1	
3		3		6	Tax Returns		3		3		
14		17		18	Other	1	1	1	2	3	10
4/1/04-3/31/05 ALL		4/1/05-3/31/06 ALL		4/1/06-3/31/07 ALL			3 (4/1-9/30/06)			36 (10/1/06-3/31/07)	
						0-1MM	1-3MM	3-5MM	5-10MM	10-25MM	25MM & OVER
39		35		39	NUMBER OF STATEMENTS	1	6	2	6	8	16
%		%		%	ASSETS	%	%	%	%	%	%
14.0		14.1		17.2	Cash & Equivalents						19.0
27.2		27.3		26.8	Trade Receivables (net)						22.2
23.9		23.4		25.6	Inventory						23.9
4.5		3.0		3.8	All Other Current						4.3
69.5		67.9		73.4	Total Current						69.4
13.2		10.3		11.9	Fixed Assets (net)						10.1
8.4		11.3		7.2	Intangibles (net)						13.0
8.8		10.6		7.5	All Other Non-Current						7.4
100.0		100.0		100.0	Total						100.0
					LIABILITIES						
9.8		13.1		9.8	Notes Payable-Short Term						8.7
2.5		4.5		5.1	Cur. Mat.-L.T.D.						2.7
15.3		14.7		16.5	Trade Payables						11.7
.5		.3		.8	Income Taxes Payable						.4
17.3		10.3		14.2	All Other Current						8.7
45.5		42.9		46.3	Total Current						32.1
11.6		16.7		7.4	Long-Term Debt						5.5
.1		.1		.2	Deferred Taxes						.4
14.4		7.0		3.9	All Other Non-Current						4.3
28.4		33.3		42.2	Net Worth						57.6
100.0		100.0		100.0	Total Liabilties & Net Worth						100.0
					INCOME DATA						
100.0		100.0		100.0	Net Sales						100.0
39.7		40.2		39.3	Gross Profit						37.4
36.1		33.2		34.4	Operating Expenses						34.1
3.7		7.0		4.9	Operating Profit						3.3
.8		1.1		.4	All Other Expenses (net)						-.5
2.8		5.9		4.5	Profit Before Taxes						3.8
					RATIOS						
2.5		3.3		3.6							6.0
1.6		1.7		1.8	Current						2.4
1.1		.9		1.1							1.5
1.5		2.0		1.8							3.6
.9		1.2		1.0	Quick						1.5
.5		.5		.6							.9
33	11.1	35	10.3	31	11.9	Sales/Receivables				42	8.8
46	8.0	47	7.8	61	6.0					64	5.7
62	5.9	66	5.5	80	4.6					83	4.4
34	10.6	26	13.8	34	10.7	Cost of Sales/Inventory				62	5.9
67	5.4	82	4.5	83	4.4					96	3.8
118	3.1	117	3.1	112	3.3					128	2.8
22	16.9	29	12.7	21	17.4	Cost of Sales/Payables				18	19.8
30	12.3	41	9.0	33	11.2					35	10.4
58	6.3	62	5.9	64	5.7					60	6.1
4.6		2.5		3.0	Sales/Working Capital						1.8
11.3		10.1		6.2							3.4
54.4		-91.3		33.7							7.0
	42.0		25.5		27.2	EBIT/Interest					52.9
(35)	6.4	(27)	6.8	(32)	5.1					(13)	7.2
	-.5		.7		.7						2.3
					16.5	Net Profit + Depr., Dep., Amort./Cur. Mat. L/T/D					
			(10)		1.8						
					.3						
.2		.1		.1	Fixed/Worth						.1
.3		.3		.3							.2
2.4		3.7		1.1							.9
.5		.4		.4	Debt/Worth						.2
1.6		1.5		1.5							1.0
93.0		41.3		7.2							4.8
	65.9		43.8		64.2	% Profit Before Taxes/Tangible Net Worth					40.9
(30)	24.7	(29)	27.9	(32)	18.4					(14)	12.0
	5.1		5.7		5.6						3.7
15.4		19.3		16.4	% Profit Before Taxes/Total Assets						10.2
7.0		7.1		5.8							6.1
-1.9		-1.5		-.2							3.9
52.5		64.7		65.1	Sales/Net Fixed Assets						32.7
20.3		27.2		24.1							15.0
8.5		9.3		9.2							10.1
3.0		3.0		3.4	Sales/Total Assets						1.7
2.2		2.2		1.7							1.3
1.3		1.0		1.1							.9
	.9		.6		.5	% Depr., Dep., Amort./Sales					1.4
(29)	1.4	(26)	1.6	(33)	1.6					(14)	1.8
	3.7		2.6		2.6						2.6
					% Officers', Directors' Owners' Comp/Sales						
2533785M		1796310M		1729221M	Net Sales ($)	350M	13018M	7568M	48017M	132241M	1528027M
1562863M		1352792M		1283139M	Total Assets ($)	364M	6115M	7103M	17383M	68743M	1183431M

© RMA 2007

M = $ thousand   MM = $ million
See Pages 11 through 21 for Explanation of Ratios and Data

Current Data Sorted by Assets   Comparative Historical Data

Type of Statement	0-500M	500M-2MM	2-10MM	10-50MM	50-100MM	100-250MM	4/1/02-3/31/03 ALL	4/1/03-3/31/04 ALL
Unqualified	1	1	4	19	5	5	28	38
Reviewed	1		15	5			25	24
Compiled	1		6				12	12
Tax Returns	2	3	1				8	4
Other	1	4	19	11	3	5	32	26
		31 (4/1-9/30/06)		85 (10/1/06-3/31/07)				
NUMBER OF STATEMENTS	6	12	45	35	8	10	105	104
ASSETS	%	%	%	%	%	%	%	%
Cash & Equivalents		5.8	9.0	12.8		19.8	11.6	10.9
Trade Receivables (net)		33.0	33.3	26.6		12.7	25.3	26.6
Inventory		22.3	28.2	32.3		10.7	26.9	24.8
All Other Current		.6	3.4	3.6		3.5	3.6	4.0
Total Current		61.6	73.9	75.3		46.7	67.3	66.2
Fixed Assets (net)		31.8	18.1	16.2		22.2	21.0	21.3
Intangibles (net)		3.4	3.1	4.3		25.4	5.4	5.3
All Other Non-Current		3.2	4.9	4.3		5.7	6.3	7.2
Total		100.0	100.0	100.0		100.0	100.0	100.0
LIABILITIES								
Notes Payable-Short Term		10.6	9.7	7.0		1.2	14.9	9.8
Cur. Mat.-L.T.D.		3.5	5.4	2.3		1.1	3.1	3.8
Trade Payables		17.8	16.8	14.4		5.6	14.9	14.3
Income Taxes Payable		1.5	1.1	.1		.2	.1	.2
All Other Current		5.8	13.6	10.3		7.2	12.9	11.4
Total Current		39.1	46.7	34.1		15.3	45.9	39.6
Long-Term Debt		20.5	11.2	8.9		21.2	11.2	11.9
Deferred Taxes		1.7	.5	.1		1.7	.7	-1.4
All Other Non-Current		10.7	7.2	3.0		.4	3.0	6.6
Net Worth		27.9	34.4	53.9		61.4	39.3	40.5
Total Liabilties & Net Worth		100.0	100.0	100.0		100.0	100.0	100.0
INCOME DATA								
Net Sales		100.0	100.0	100.0		100.0	100.0	100.0
Gross Profit		46.4	38.4	31.1		45.3	39.2	34.2
Operating Expenses		40.6	33.6	22.5		38.0	35.4	31.1
Operating Profit		5.8	4.8	8.6		7.3	3.8	3.1
All Other Expenses (net)		.9	.8	.4		4.7	1.7	.8
Profit Before Taxes		4.9	4.0	8.2		2.6	2.2	2.3
RATIOS								
Current		3.2	3.0	4.4		5.0	3.4	3.1
		1.5	1.8	2.0		2.6	1.8	1.9
		1.1	1.2	1.5		1.7	1.1	1.2
Quick		2.2	1.6	2.7		3.7	2.1	1.7
		.9	.9	.9		1.9	1.0	1.0
		.6	.5	.7		.8	.5	.6
Sales/Receivables	26 13.8	35 10.3	40 9.2			31 11.7	32 11.3	32 11.3
	44 8.2	45 8.2	45 8.1			60 6.1	48 7.7	46 8.0
	47 7.8	66 5.6	60 6.1			76 4.8	62 5.8	58 6.3
Cost of Sales/Inventory	12 30.5	21 17.4	63 5.8			58 6.3	36 10.0	25 14.5
	43 8.4	64 5.7	96 3.8			90 4.1	77 4.7	59 6.2
	79 4.6	122 3.0	149 2.5			129 2.8	147 2.5	99 3.7
Cost of Sales/Payables	20 18.0	18 19.9	21 17.1			34 10.9	19 18.9	19 19.7
	34 10.8	43 8.6	28 12.9			46 7.9	36 10.0	29 12.8
	62 5.9	61 6.0	44 8.2			58 6.3	63 5.8	50 7.3
Sales/Working Capital		7.2	3.9	3.1		1.6	3.4	3.8
		12.7	7.0	5.2		2.9	6.5	7.5
		63.8	27.1	7.7		9.6	31.2	27.5
EBIT/Interest		27.6	13.0	81.8			11.6	14.4
		9.0	(42) 4.2	(28) 9.7			(85) 3.3	(86) 3.8
		1.2	1.5	2.7			-1.0	.5
Net Profit + Depr., Dep., Amort./Cur. Mat. L/T/D			13.9	9.8			3.6	9.0
		(14)	3.3	(11) 3.2			(33) 1.5	(35) 4.0
			1.0	1.1			-1.5	1.5
Fixed/Worth		.2	.1	.1		.1	.2	.1
		.4	.4	.3		.2	.4	.4
		4.2	4.5	.7		60.1	1.4	1.6
Debt/Worth		.9	.6	.3		.2	.5	.6
		1.3	2.0	1.1		.7	1.4	1.3
		6.3	15.7	2.1		67.0	4.3	4.8
% Profit Before Taxes/Tangible Net Worth		83.2	39.8	48.6			33.5	32.3
		(10) 63.8	(38) 19.6	(34) 18.8			(93) 11.6	(89) 15.5
		2.1	2.7	8.0			-11.9	1.2
% Profit Before Taxes/Total Assets		41.1	19.0	22.8		12.1	15.0	17.5
		11.9	6.4	12.3		3.2	4.6	4.8
		.2	.7	3.2		-5.1	-5.5	-1.7
Sales/Net Fixed Assets		50.1	41.1	43.2		30.8	25.6	34.6
		15.5	18.5	19.0		10.2	12.2	13.6
		4.8	10.6	6.7		3.0	5.4	6.4
Sales/Total Assets		3.5	3.1	2.2		1.0	2.5	2.7
		3.0	2.5	1.9		.8	1.9	2.0
		2.8	1.7	1.3		.5	1.3	1.6
% Depr., Dep., Amort./Sales		.5	.6	.5			1.1	.9
		(40) 1.5	(34) 1.4	1.3			(87) 2.2	(86) 2.0
		4.2	2.0	2.4			3.8	4.0
% Officers', Directors' Owners' Comp/Sales			3.0				2.5	2.7
			(14) 6.4				(31) 6.5	(26) 4.1
			11.7				11.8	8.5
Net Sales ($)	11823M	43764M	514643M	1540393M	809052M	1192970M	2951791M	4975899M
Total Assets ($)	1269M	13798M	211638M	802640M	525308M	1625087M	1646785M	2631130M

M = $ thousand   MM = $ million
See Pages 11 through 21 for Explanation of Ratios and Data

Comparative Historical Data | Current Data Sorted by Sales

Type of Statement

4/1/04-3/31/05	4/1/05-3/31/06	4/1/06-3/31/07	Type of Statement	0-1MM	1-3MM	3-5MM	5-10MM	10-25MM	25MM & OVER
28	32	35	Unqualified	1		2	7	25	5
21	16	21	Reviewed		1	7	6	5	
8	6	11	Compiled	1		3	3	2	1
9	5	6	Tax Returns	1		1	1	1	
23	30	43	Other	1		8	3	15	15
ALL	ALL	ALL		31 (4/1-9/30/06)		85 (10/1/06-3/31/07)			
89	89	116	NUMBER OF STATEMENTS	4	7	13	16	31	45

Main Data

4/1/04-3/31/05 %	4/1/05-3/31/06 %	4/1/06-3/31/07 %		0-1MM %	1-3MM %	3-5MM %	5-10MM %	10-25MM %	25MM & OVER %
			ASSETS						
10.4	12.5	11.2	Cash & Equivalents			11.8	9.0	9.2	13.5
29.7	26.5	27.9	Trade Receivables (net)			23.3	38.9	29.3	24.3
27.1	27.6	26.4	Inventory			14.5	25.7	30.6	26.0
3.8	3.4	3.4	All Other Current			1.8	2.9	3.9	3.7
71.1	70.0	68.9	Total Current			51.5	76.6	73.0	67.5
18.6	19.2	19.8	Fixed Assets (net)			32.1	18.4	21.0	15.8
3.8	4.5	6.0	Intangibles (net)			9.4	1.3	2.8	10.1
6.5	6.2	5.3	All Other Non-Current			7.0	3.8	3.3	6.6
100.0	100.0	100.0	Total			100.0	100.0	100.0	100.0
			LIABILITIES						
11.8	10.8	8.0	Notes Payable-Short Term			9.9	8.1	8.2	5.7
3.4	2.7	3.5	Cur. Mat.-L.T.D.			1.1	5.2	5.8	1.9
15.6	15.1	14.1	Trade Payables			13.8	20.0	14.1	12.8
.6	.4	.8	Income Taxes Payable			3.1	.8	.5	.7
13.1	11.3	11.2	All Other Current			12.2	10.4	11.8	9.8
44.6	40.2	37.6	Total Current			40.0	44.4	40.4	30.9
10.2	13.9	11.7	Long-Term Debt			13.8	8.3	16.9	7.9
.4	.9	.6	Deferred Taxes			.6	.9	.7	.7
4.6	6.4	5.6	All Other Non-Current			9.5	3.7	8.0	2.9
40.2	38.6	44.4	Net Worth			36.1	42.7	34.1	57.7
100.0	100.0	100.0	Total Liabilties & Net Worth			100.0	100.0	100.0	100.0
			INCOME DATA						
100.0	100.0	100.0	Net Sales			100.0	100.0	100.0	100.0
37.4	38.4	37.5	Gross Profit			56.0	35.7	34.5	33.6
30.0	32.5	30.8	Operating Expenses			52.7	30.4	26.8	25.9
7.4	5.9	6.7	Operating Profit			3.3	5.3	7.8	7.6
.9	1.1	1.1	All Other Expenses (net)			-.6	.5	2.8	.7
6.5	4.9	5.5	Profit Before Taxes			3.9	4.9	4.9	6.9
			RATIOS						
3.0	3.9	3.7	Current			2.7	3.7	3.9	4.4
1.5	2.1	1.9				1.5	2.2	2.0	2.0
1.1	1.2	1.3				.7	1.4	1.2	1.5
1.7	2.0	2.3	Quick			2.3	2.5	2.0	2.4
.8	1.0	1.0				.8	1.1	.8	1.1
.5	.5	.6				.4	.7	.6	.7
37 9.9	33 11.0	35 10.4	Sales/Receivables			21 17.6	40 9.2	34 10.6	36 10.0
52 7.0	48 7.6	45 8.0				43 8.4	55 6.6	41 8.9	55 6.7
65 5.6	63 5.8	62 5.9				61 6.0	80 4.5	52 7.0	67 5.5
40 9.0	47 7.8	34 10.6	Cost of Sales/Inventory			0 UND	0 UND	23 15.9	55 6.7
79 4.6	86 4.3	80 4.6				34 10.8	79 4.6	77 4.7	84 4.4
118 3.1	129 2.8	122 3.0				92 4.0	123 3.0	124 2.9	118 3.1
22 16.9	23 16.2	21 17.0	Cost of Sales/Payables			35 10.5	16 23.2	17 21.0	24 15.1
32 11.4	38 9.7	35 10.3				47 7.8	42 8.7	27 13.7	32 11.4
67 5.4	59 6.1	53 6.9				85 4.3	75 4.8	43 8.4	48 7.6
4.0	3.4	3.4	Sales/Working Capital			5.4	4.3	3.9	2.8
8.0	5.8	6.4				22.7	6.6	7.0	4.6
27.8	17.3	15.1				-10.0	12.5	18.8	10.4
26.8	15.3	20.6	EBIT/Interest			38.1	19.4	11.6	107.0
(70) 6.6	(65) 4.5	(100) 5.3		(11)		15.4	9.2	(27) 4.2	(37) 8.6
1.5	2.1	1.6				2.0	2.6	1.6	1.5
14.8	9.9	9.2	Net Profit + Depr., Dep., Amort./Cur. Mat. L/T/D						22.0
(30) 3.0	(30) 3.4	(32) 3.0						(14)	2.3
.8	1.4	.9							.7
.2	.1	.1	Fixed/Worth			.2	.3	.1	.1
.5	.4	.4				.9	.3	.5	.3
1.9	1.7	1.2				NM	.4	7.1	.6
.5	.5	.5	Debt/Worth			.8	.6	.6	.3
1.7	1.5	1.2				1.2	1.2	2.7	1.0
7.5	5.9	3.4				NM	2.9	25.7	1.9
44.7	49.5	47.0	% Profit Before Taxes/Tangible Net Worth			119.3	65.9	38.0	47.0
(76) 18.9	(81) 22.2	(104) 18.4		(10)		67.9	(15) 25.0	(26) 17.6	(43) 15.9
6.6	5.9	2.8				-13.3	13.5	2.7	2.7
17.9	17.0	20.3	% Profit Before Taxes/Total Assets			43.1	23.3	19.2	21.0
8.2	7.2	6.8				6.4	10.7	6.3	7.6
1.1	.5	1.1				-7.6	4.3	1.6	1.2
34.4	32.4	35.5	Sales/Net Fixed Assets			38.9	39.0	47.9	32.6
17.0	17.5	16.6				11.5	19.9	16.8	14.8
7.4	7.1	6.9				4.4	11.3	5.3	7.3
2.5	2.8	2.9	Sales/Total Assets			3.1	3.2	3.2	2.2
1.9	1.9	2.1				1.9	2.8	2.5	1.7
1.4	1.3	1.3				1.2	2.0	1.6	1.1
.7	.8	.7	% Depr., Dep., Amort./Sales			.7	.4	.6	.8
(74) 1.6	(73) 1.9	(104) 1.6		(12)		1.5	1.0	(27) 1.8	(39) 1.6
3.2	3.2	2.5				2.7	1.9	2.2	3.8
3.4	1.9	2.5	% Officers', Directors' Owners' Comp/Sales						
(24) 5.4	(20) 4.2	(26) 4.0							
9.0	7.5	9.0							
2882228M	3253213M	4112645M	Net Sales ($)	1170M	16013M	54081M	128819M	513615M	3398947M
1949809M	2610967M	3179740M	Total Assets ($)	611M	7381M	30726M	54696M	353359M	2732967M

M = $ thousand   MM = $ million
See Pages 11 through 21 for Explanation of Ratios and Data

Current Data Sorted by Assets

	0-500M	500M-2MM	2-10MM	10-50MM	50-100MM	100-25[0]MM
Unqualified		4	6	6	2	3
Reviewed		4	12	2		
Compiled	1	4	5	1		
Tax Returns	3	2	1			
Other	2	8	12	6		4
		18 (4/1-9/30/06)		68 (10/1/06-3/31/07)		
NUMBER OF STATEMENTS	6	18	36	14	5	7
	%	%	%	%	%	%

ASSETS

	500M-2MM	2-10MM	10-50MM
Cash & Equivalents	13.3	7.3	11.9
Trade Receivables (net)	39.9	33.0	30.8
Inventory	26.6	27.4	22.2
All Other Current	2.5	2.3	3.5
Total Current	82.3	69.9	68.4
Fixed Assets (net)	10.6	20.6	13.9
Intangibles (net)	2.5	3.8	12.7
All Other Non-Current	4.6	5.6	5.0
Total	100.0	100.0	100.0

LIABILITIES

	500M-2MM	2-10MM	10-50MM
Notes Payable-Short Term	13.5	11.2	4.7
Cur. Mat.-L.T.D.	4.8	3.9	2.2
Trade Payables	19.1	16.5	12.1
Income Taxes Payable	.1	.3	.0
All Other Current	9.3	11.1	14.8
Total Current	46.7	43.0	33.8
Long-Term Debt	4.8	9.5	25.7
Deferred Taxes	.0	.6	.8
All Other Non-Current	2.7	6.7	4.1
Net Worth	45.7	40.2	35.6
Total Liabilities & Net Worth	100.0	100.0	100.0

INCOME DATA

	500M-2MM	2-10MM	10-50MM
Net Sales	100.0	100.0	100.0
Gross Profit	41.4	39.0	37.6
Operating Expenses	38.5	31.6	29.4
Operating Profit	2.9	7.4	8.3
All Other Expenses (net)	.9	2.3	.5
Profit Before Taxes	2.0	5.2	7.7

RATIOS

	500M-2MM		2-10MM		10-50MM	
Current		2.5		2.7		3.8
		1.6		1.6		2.2
		1.3		1.1		1.4
Quick		2.4		1.4		1.8
		1.2		1.0		1.2
		.7		.5		.9
Sales/Receivables	33	11.2	34	10.9	43	8.5
	49	7.5	47	7.8	63	5.8
	66	5.6	61	5.9	74	4.9
Cost of Sales/Inventory	26	14.3	26	14.2	39	9.4
	54	6.8	57	6.4	69	5.3
	98	3.7	121	3.0	133	2.7
Cost of Sales/Payables	24	15.4	23	16.1	29	12.6
	31	11.7	31	11.8	35	10.3
	55	6.7	52	7.1	51	7.2
Sales/Working Capital		6.0		5.7		2.3
		9.0		10.3		5.9
		15.4		41.0		11.4
EBIT/Interest		16.8		23.6		19.0
	(15)	5.1	(34)	5.6	(11)	12.3
		-4.3		2.1		2.2
Net Profit + Depr., Dep., Amort./Cur. Mat. L/T/D				8.9		
			(14)	2.5		
				-1.8		
Fixed/Worth		.1		.2		.1
		.2		.5		.4
		.6		1.3		NM
Debt/Worth		.6		.8		.6
		1.6		1.9		1.0
		2.5		3.4		NM
% Profit Before Taxes/Tangible Net Worth		47.7		72.9		31.7
	(33)	28.2		29.0	(11)	29.2
		-39.2		7.4		19.6
% Profit Before Taxes/Total Assets		25.2		22.5		19.4
		12.6		10.7		9.9
		-13.4		2.8		4.1
Sales/Net Fixed Assets		66.7		31.6		38.7
		32.4		16.4		19.7
		16.0		7.4		6.7
Sales/Total Assets		3.8		3.0		2.7
		2.9		2.4		1.5
		2.2		2.0		.9
% Depr., Dep., Amort./Sales		.4		.9		.8
	(13)	.8	(33)	1.5	(12)	1.7
		1.8		2.8		3.5
% Officers', Directors' Owners' Comp/Sales				2.5		
			(16)	5.1		
				8.2		

	0-500M	500M-2MM	2-10MM	10-50MM	50-100MM	100-25MM
Net Sales ($)	7835M	67155M	454432M	674669M	605997M	1335252M
Total Assets ($)	1284M	21707M	166553M	410280M	365070M	1249281M

Comparative Historical Data

Type of Statement	4/1/02-3/31/03 ALL	4/1/03-3/31/04 ALL
Unqualified	28	29
Reviewed	13	17
Compiled	7	8
Tax Returns	4	6
Other	19	15
NUMBER OF STATEMENTS	71	75

ASSETS

	%	%
Cash & Equivalents	10.0	10.6
Trade Receivables (net)	31.2	30.2
Inventory	21.9	23.2
All Other Current	4.8	3.5
Total Current	67.9	67.5
Fixed Assets (net)	18.7	18.1
Intangibles (net)	6.2	8.2
All Other Non-Current	7.2	6.1
Total	100.0	100.0

LIABILITIES

Notes Payable-Short Term	12.2	10.7
Cur. Mat.-L.T.D.	3.5	2.5
Trade Payables	18.2	15.5
Income Taxes Payable	.5	.7
All Other Current	9.1	12.0
Total Current	43.4	41.4
Long-Term Debt	9.0	11.4
Deferred Taxes	1.0	1.0
All Other Non-Current	4.6	6.9
Net Worth	42.1	39.3
Total Liabilities & Net Worth	100.0	100.0

INCOME DATA

Net Sales	100.0	100.0
Gross Profit	38.3	40.2
Operating Expenses	37.0	36.2
Operating Profit	1.3	4.0
All Other Expenses (net)	1.4	1.8
Profit Before Taxes	-.1	2.2

RATIOS

	4/1/02-3/31/03 ALL		4/1/03-3/31/04 ALL	
Current		2.9		3.0
		1.8		1.7
		1.2		1.3
Quick		1.6		1.7
		1.0		1.0
		.6		.7
Sales/Receivables	35	10.5	39	9.3
	48	7.7	52	7.0
	60	6.0	63	5.8
Cost of Sales/Inventory	20	17.8	23	15.9
	59	6.2	71	5.1
	109	3.3	110	3.3
Cost of Sales/Payables	20	18.6	17	20.9
	37	10.0	39	9.3
	64	5.7	53	6.9
Sales/Working Capital		5.0		4.2
		8.0		6.7
		23.3		28.5
EBIT/Interest		10.7		17.5
	(60)	2.1	(61)	3.9
		-4.4		-.5
Net Profit + Depr., Dep., Amort./Cur. Mat. L/T/D		9.9		13.5
	(22)	2.6	(24)	1.9
		.2		1.0
Fixed/Worth		.2		.2
		.4		.5
		1.3		1.1
Debt/Worth		.5		.5
		1.5		1.5
		3.2		7.0
% Profit Before Taxes/Tangible Net Worth		39.7		43.3
	(62)	15.7	(60)	21.4
		-8.1		-.2
% Profit Before Taxes/Total Assets		14.5		16.4
		3.2		5.1
		-7.0		-3.3
Sales/Net Fixed Assets		32.4		37.7
		16.9		13.8
		7.9		6.5
Sales/Total Assets		3.5		3.0
		2.2		1.9
		1.2		1.2
% Depr., Dep., Amort./Sales		1.0		.8
	(56)	1.7	(55)	2.0
		3.6		3.5
% Officers', Directors' Owners' Comp/Sales		2.4		2.7
	(20)	6.8	(21)	7.1
		9.8		10.1
Net Sales ($)	2362951M		1672593M	
Total Assets ($)	1850816M		1287038M	

M = $ thousand　　MM = $ million

Comparative Historical Data / Current Data Sorted by Sales

			Type of Statement						
12	17	17	Unqualified	1	1	1	2	12
16	14	18	Reviewed	3	1	7	6	1
1	5	10	Compiled	2	2	5	1	
9	6	6	Tax Returns	2	2	2		
23	31	35	Other	2	5	3	6	8	11
4/1/04-3/31/05 ALL	4/1/05-3/31/06 ALL	4/1/06-3/31/07 ALL		0-1MM	1-3MM	3-5MM	5-10MM	10-25MM	25MM & OVER
					18 (4/1-9/30/06)		68 (10/1/06-3/31/07)		
61	73	86	NUMBER OF STATEMENTS	2	13	9	21	17	24
%	%	%	ASSETS	%	%	%	%	%	%
11.3	10.0	11.6	Cash & Equivalents		13.4		7.5	13.0	14.8
28.8	33.8	32.2	Trade Receivables (net)		28.8		32.5	36.7	28.7
27.5	23.5	25.7	Inventory		23.3		29.6	19.9	22.6
2.8	3.6	3.0	All Other Current		1.0		1.2	3.9	4.9
70.5	71.0	72.5	Total Current		66.5		70.8	73.5	71.1
14.5	15.5	16.1	Fixed Assets (net)		23.5		18.7	13.8	13.9
7.2	7.5	6.5	Intangibles (net)		3.4		5.0	7.5	10.6
7.9	6.1	4.8	All Other Non-Current		6.6		5.6	5.2	4.5
100.0	100.0	100.0	Total		100.0		100.0	100.0	100.0
			LIABILITIES						
10.9	11.7	8.9	Notes Payable-Short Term		13.3		12.4	5.6	3.4
3.3	2.8	3.1	Cur. Mat.-L.T.D.		1.1		3.7	2.0	1.3
15.9	16.3	15.9	Trade Payables		13.7		18.4	16.0	15.7
.6	.2	.2	Income Taxes Payable		.2		.0	.6	.3
9.4	11.6	12.2	All Other Current		9.8		7.3	13.3	19.1
40.1	42.6	40.3	Total Current		38.0		41.8	37.5	39.8
6.9	10.1	11.7	Long-Term Debt		16.1		8.3	7.0	19.7
.5	.4	.4	Deferred Taxes		.1		.9	.3	.5
7.7	5.2	5.3	All Other Non-Current		3.7		6.8	7.9	4.8
44.9	41.7	42.3	Net Worth		42.1		42.2	47.4	35.2
100.0	100.0	100.0	Total Liabilties & Net Worth		100.0		100.0	100.0	100.0
			INCOME DATA						
100.0	100.0	100.0	Net Sales		100.0		100.0	100.0	100.0
43.0	37.1	39.7	Gross Profit		44.9		41.3	38.4	34.7
37.7	31.7	33.4	Operating Expenses		43.8		34.1	25.1	31.4
5.3	5.4	6.3	Operating Profit		1.1		7.2	13.3	3.3
.9	.8	1.5	All Other Expenses (net)		3.3		2.0	.6	1.1
4.4	4.7	4.8	Profit Before Taxes		-2.2		5.2	12.8	2.2
			RATIOS						
3.0	2.7	3.1			4.7		2.9	3.6	3.0
1.8	1.8	1.8	Current		1.5		1.7	2.2	1.9
1.4	1.2	1.3			.7		1.1	1.3	1.3
1.9	1.6	1.7			3.4		1.3	1.9	1.6
(60) 1.0	1.1	1.1	Quick		1.2		1.0	1.4	1.1
.6	.7	.7			.4		.5	.9	.9
37 9.9	35 10.5	36 10.2		13 28.3		34 10.7	43 8.6	42 8.7
54 6.8	49 7.4	51 7.1	Sales/Receivables	44 8.2		41 8.8	54 6.8	58 6.3
69 5.3	69 5.3	64 5.7		62 5.9		55 6.6	94 3.9	70 5.2
33 11.2	24 15.4	32 11.2		10 38.1		41 9.0	7 55.9	40 9.2
75 4.9	60 6.1	61 5.9	Cost of Sales/Inventory	51 7.1		59 6.1	69 5.3	64 5.7
139 2.6	99 3.7	119 3.1		109 3.3		134 2.7	120 3.0	121 3.0
24 15.1	22 16.7	23 15.6		9 41.8		22 16.5	25 14.8	28 13.1
42 8.6	33 11.2	33 11.0	Cost of Sales/Payables	23 16.2		33 10.9	33 10.9	41 8.9
65 5.6	50 7.3	53 6.9		50 7.3		56 6.5	55 6.7	52 7.0
3.1	4.7	4.4			4.9		5.0	3.8	3.8
6.9	8.4	7.7	Sales/Working Capital		8.7		9.2	6.2	6.5
14.6	22.6	15.1			-17.6		44.4	14.2	11.6
15.0	13.8	19.0			6.0		16.2	89.8	15.1
(50) 4.8	(61) 5.6	(76) 6.0	EBIT/Interest	(11) 5.0		4.8	(14) 18.6	(22) 6.5
.5	1.6	1.6			-9.4		1.7	4.4	2.0
12.6	17.8	10.2							
(15) 2.3	(19) 7.0	(28) 3.5	Net Profit + Depr., Dep., Amort./Cur. Mat. L/T/D						
.3	1.3	.9							
.1	.2	.1			.1		.2	.1	.2
.4	.4	.4	Fixed/Worth		.3		.5	.4	.4
1.0	1.0	1.0			2.4		1.3	.9	1.0
.4	.7	.6			.3		.8	.5	.7
1.6	1.8	1.6	Debt/Worth		2.0		1.5	1.1	1.7
3.4	4.5	3.3			5.2		3.9	3.4	3.6
68.2	56.3	56.7			49.6		43.6	81.1	41.2
(52) 19.1	(64) 18.6	(77) 29.0	% Profit Before Taxes/Tangible Net Worth	(12) -.9	(19) 20.1	(15) 64.3	(20) 26.4
3.6	3.9	3.1			-151.2		7.4	31.5	6.7
16.9	18.1	22.6			28.8		19.9	43.4	15.3
7.8	8.5	11.8	% Profit Before Taxes/Total Assets		1.9		7.1	22.4	7.0
-.5	2.3	1.7			-24.7		1.8	14.9	2.9
43.9	54.5	45.8			67.2		35.2	44.6	37.4
17.1	20.3	18.8	Sales/Net Fixed Assets		16.3		16.3	21.4	15.8
10.2	9.1	8.8			8.4		8.9	6.9	8.7
2.8	3.2	3.1			3.5		3.2	3.0	2.5
1.9	2.6	2.4	Sales/Total Assets		2.8		2.5	2.4	1.5
1.0	1.6	1.5			1.7		2.1	1.7	1.0
.6	.5	.7			.6		.7	.7	1.0
(51) 1.0	(62) 1.2	(70) 1.5	% Depr., Dep., Amort./Sales	(11) 1.5	(20) 1.5	(15) 1.1	(19) 2.2
2.4	3.1	2.7			2.1		2.7	3.3	3.2
2.4	2.4	2.5					2.9		
(19) 5.0	(16) 5.4	(27) 4.6	% Officers', Directors' Owners' Comp/Sales		(14) 5.1		
9.6	8.6	8.4					10.3		
1283111M	2604869M	3145340M	Net Sales ($)	577M	25867M	36175M	143894M	298749M	2640078M
1084577M	1781542M	2214175M	Total Assets ($)	156M	18106M	12778M	63089M	188318M	1931728M

M = $ thousand   MM = $ million
See Pages 11 through 21 for Explanation of Ratios and Data

Current Data Sorted by Assets   Comparative Historical Data

Type of Statement	0-500M	500M-2MM	2-10MM	10-50MM	50-100MM	100-250MM	4/1/02-3/31/03 ALL	4/1/03-3/31/04 ALL
Unqualified			6	7	1	4	17	16
Reviewed			9	3			11	12
Compiled	1	2	3	1			5	9
Tax Returns	3	2	1				2	6
Other	1	12	14	8	4	7	21	19

Period split: 21 (4/1-9/30/06) · 67 (10/1/06-3/31/07)

	0-500M	500M-2MM	2-10MM	10-50MM	50-100MM	100-250MM		4/1/02-3/31/03 ALL	4/1/03-3/31/04 ALL
NUMBER OF STATEMENTS	5	16	33	18	5	11		56	62
	%	%	%	%	%	%	**ASSETS**	%	%
		16.7	5.3	14.0		14.7	Cash & Equivalents	9.4	11.9
		26.4	37.2	28.2		38.6	Trade Receivables (net)	26.8	29.5
		28.9	34.9	35.6		23.3	Inventory	34.0	32.2
		6.6	4.6	2.1		4.0	All Other Current	3.2	3.9
		78.6	82.0	79.9		80.6	Total Current	73.4	77.5
		13.4	13.4	11.0		12.3	Fixed Assets (net)	16.9	14.4
		2.9	1.8	4.1		4.9	Intangibles (net)	4.3	3.5
		5.1	2.8	4.9		2.3	All Other Non-Current	5.3	4.6
		100.0	100.0	100.0		100.0	Total	100.0	100.0
							LIABILITIES		
		11.2	12.9	10.3		10.3	Notes Payable-Short Term	14.4	14.8
		2.0	3.1	2.0		2.2	Cur. Mat.-L.T.D.	1.7	2.7
		16.5	16.9	14.1		25.6	Trade Payables	15.1	16.6
		.0	.6	.6		.9	Income Taxes Payable	.5	.4
		20.2	10.8	13.7		11.9	All Other Current	10.6	9.6
		49.8	44.4	40.7		51.1	Total Current	42.3	44.2
		12.3	8.0	5.5		7.6	Long-Term Debt	9.2	6.6
		.0	.2	.2		.5	Deferred Taxes	.3	.2
		2.7	5.5	3.3		4.2	All Other Non-Current	3.6	5.6
		35.2	41.8	50.3		36.6	Net Worth	44.5	43.4
		100.0	100.0	100.0		100.0	Total Liabilities & Net Worth	100.0	100.0
							INCOME DATA		
		100.0	100.0	100.0		100.0	Net Sales	100.0	100.0
		47.0	37.1	33.9		30.5	Gross Profit	34.7	38.1
		42.8	31.7	27.4		24.5	Operating Expenses	29.3	33.7
		4.2	5.4	6.5		6.1	Operating Profit	5.4	4.5
		1.5	.9	-.3		3.6	All Other Expenses (net)	.7	1.1
		2.7	4.5	6.7		2.5	Profit Before Taxes	4.7	3.4
							RATIOS		
		3.6	3.5	4.9		2.8		2.9	3.4
		1.5	1.7	2.0		2.2	Current	1.8	1.8
		1.1	1.4	1.3		1.0		1.2	1.2
		1.8	1.6	2.6		1.6		1.5	1.8
		.9	1.0	1.2		1.0	Quick	.9	.9
		.5	.7	.6		.7		.5	.6
		19 19.0	39 9.3	35 10.5		49 7.5		29 12.7	34 10.7
		37 9.8	58 6.3	48 7.7		61 6.0	Sales/Receivables	43 8.5	50 7.3
		64 5.7	71 5.1	59 6.2		96 3.8		60 6.0	71 5.2
		38 9.7	29 12.8	58 6.3		28 12.9		49 7.4	57 6.4
		86 4.3	81 4.5	106 3.4		93 3.9	Cost of Sales/Inventory	91 4.0	95 3.8
		154 2.4	155 2.4	169 2.2		164 2.2		122 3.0	139 2.6
		21 17.5	19 19.0	9 38.5		29 12.5		19 19.1	17 22.0
		27 13.3	34 10.7	28 13.0		57 6.4	Cost of Sales/Payables	32 11.3	35 10.4
		76 4.8	52 7.0	58 6.3		78 4.7		50 7.2	60 6.1
		3.7	4.4	2.7		3.4		4.4	3.2
		6.7	8.0	6.4		4.6	Sales/Working Capital	7.7	6.2
		122.9	12.1	13.8		130.9		19.0	18.9
		13.2	12.6	111.2				20.9	18.5
		(14) 5.4	(30) 4.7	(14) 7.8			EBIT/Interest	(48) 6.3	(55) 3.1
		.4	1.6	2.3				1.7	1.1
								7.6	5.8
							Net Profit + Depr., Dep., Amort./Cur. Mat. L/T/D	(14) 5.1	(12) 2.6
								2.1	.9
		.0	.1	.1		.1		.1	.1
		.4	.2	.2		.4	Fixed/Worth	.4	.3
		1.2	.5	.4		1.0		1.0	1.0
		1.0	.7	.3		.4		.6	.5
		1.7	1.4	1.8		3.5	Debt/Worth	1.4	1.2
		5.5	3.3	3.6		40.3		3.8	4.9
		51.0	49.0	41.1			% Profit Before Taxes/Tangible Net Worth	53.1	35.8
		(14) 28.4	(31) 32.6	26.4				(52) 21.3	(55) 18.1
		1.2	6.5	6.4				7.2	4.8
		16.5	22.0	25.8		10.9	% Profit Before Taxes/Total Assets	15.5	13.0
		8.9	9.1	6.9		4.1		8.2	5.5
		-.5	2.5	3.0		.4		2.1	.6
		289.6	64.0	77.2		94.6	Sales/Net Fixed Assets	39.8	41.2
		31.5	36.3	34.3		32.9		17.3	25.1
		8.3	12.7	18.8		6.2		7.0	9.7
		3.2	3.2	2.8		2.1	Sales/Total Assets	2.9	2.9
		2.3	2.2	2.3		1.7		2.1	2.1
		1.8	1.8	1.2		1.3		1.4	1.5
			.4	.6		.5	% Depr., Dep., Amort./Sales	.7	.7
			(25) .6	(14) 1.3		1.6		(49) 1.6	(53) 1.3
			1.2	2.3		3.2		2.9	2.8
			1.7				% Officers', Directors' Owners' Comp/Sales	2.0	2.7
			(12) 3.4					(15) 4.2	(19) 6.3
			6.1					7.7	8.8
	4468M	43624M	395295M	930199M	762693M	3580396M	Net Sales ($)	3369242M	2661576M
	1055M	17455M	157803M	441114M	364643M	1874546M	Total Assets ($)	1785046M	1637071M

© RMA 2007

M = $ thousand   MM = $ million
See Pages 11 through 21 for Explanation of Ratios and Data

Comparative Historical Data   Current Data Sorted by Sales

	4/1/04-3/31/05 ALL	4/1/05-3/31/06 ALL	4/1/06-3/31/07 ALL	Type of Statement	0-1MM	1-3MM	3-5MM	5-10MM	10-25MM	25MM & OVER
	20	19	18	Unqualified				3	3	12
	15	9	12	Reviewed		2	2	2	6	2
	3	4	6	Compiled		2	2	1	1	
	2	3	6	Tax Returns	3	2		1		
	19	30	46	Other	2	9		4	11	18
						21 (4/1-9/30/06)		67 (10/1/06-3/31/07)		
	59	65	88	NUMBER OF STATEMENTS	5	11	8	10	22	32
	%	%	%	ASSETS	%	%	%	%	%	%
	8.5	8.6	10.5	Cash & Equivalents		17.4		1.1	8.7	11.4
	33.3	30.7	32.2	Trade Receivables (net)		20.9		33.0	36.2	34.5
	35.3	36.6	33.0	Inventory		27.5		38.0	35.8	32.7
	2.2	3.3	4.0	All Other Current		8.9		8.6	2.7	2.9
	79.2	79.2	79.8	Total Current		74.7		80.7	83.4	81.5
	12.5	13.2	12.9	Fixed Assets (net)		15.1		12.1	11.0	11.0
	2.4	3.5	2.9	Intangibles (net)		4.0		3.5	1.2	4.8
	5.9	4.1	4.4	All Other Non-Current		6.2		3.7	4.4	2.8
	100.0	100.0	100.0	Total		100.0		100.0	100.0	100.0
				LIABILITIES						
	17.5	15.7	13.7	Notes Payable-Short Term		12.7		11.1	12.5	14.0
	2.7	2.9	2.6	Cur. Mat.-L.T.D.		4.0		6.0	1.5	2.0
	15.6	16.8	17.0	Trade Payables		12.0		20.3	15.0	19.2
	.4	.5	.5	Income Taxes Payable		.0		.7	.6	.7
	12.9	9.7	13.5	All Other Current		14.1		12.2	9.8	14.8
	49.2	45.5	47.2	Total Current		42.9		50.2	39.4	50.8
	6.1	10.8	8.3	Long-Term Debt		15.5		5.1	5.5	6.7
	.3	.4	.2	Deferred Taxes		.0		.0	.4	.3
	3.9	5.2	4.1	All Other Non-Current		2.1		9.7	3.4	4.3
	40.5	38.1	40.2	Net Worth		39.5		35.0	51.4	37.9
	100.0	100.0	100.0	Total Liabilities & Net Worth		100.0		100.0	100.0	100.0
				INCOME DATA						
	100.0	100.0	100.0	Net Sales		100.0		100.0	100.0	100.0
	37.5	39.2	37.9	Gross Profit		51.2		33.8	34.8	33.0
	33.1	33.9	32.3	Operating Expenses		44.6		31.0	29.2	26.9
	4.4	5.4	5.6	Operating Profit		6.6		2.8	5.6	6.1
	.6	.9	1.1	All Other Expenses (net)		1.8		1.7	-.2	1.7
	3.8	4.5	4.5	Profit Before Taxes		4.8		1.1	5.8	4.5
				RATIOS						
	2.7	2.9	3.4	Current		3.6		2.1	5.4	2.7
	1.5	1.9	1.7			1.6		1.7	1.7	1.6
	1.2	1.3	1.3			.9		1.2	1.5	1.2
	1.5	1.3	1.6	Quick		2.0		1.0	3.2	1.4
	.8	.9	1.0			1.0		.7	1.1	1.0
	.6	.7	.6			.5		.4	.8	.6
	40 9.2	38 9.7	34 10.7	Sales/Receivables		10 35.5		36 10.1	36 10.1	44 8.2
	53 6.9	47 7.7	47 7.8			27 13.4		51 7.1	46 8.0	57 6.4
	70 5.3	66 5.5	66 5.5			57 6.4		64 5.7	72 5.1	66 5.5
	58 6.3	72 5.1	45 8.1	Cost of Sales/Inventory		23 16.0		47 7.7	36 10.3	50 7.4
	100 3.6	105 3.5	92 4.0			92 4.0		75 4.9	91 4.0	97 3.8
	149 2.4	152 2.4	151 2.4			173 2.1		168 2.2	170 2.2	149 2.4
	16 22.9	27 13.8	20 18.0	Cost of Sales/Payables		21 17.6		30 12.3	14 26.1	27 13.5
	34 10.8	42 8.7	33 11.2			26 13.8		46 8.0	21 17.3	44 8.2
	55 6.6	58 6.2	58 6.3			69 5.3		81 4.5	40 9.1	66 5.5
	4.2	4.0	3.8	Sales/Working Capital		3.6		4.3	4.0	4.0
	7.9	5.7	7.9			6.7		7.9	8.1	7.5
	17.6	12.7	15.9			-64.9		19.7	9.9	17.6
	12.9	12.3	15.5	EBIT/Interest				7.5	76.0	12.8
	(53) 4.8	(55) 3.7	(75) 4.0					(18) 3.1	6.9 (26)	2.8
	1.5	1.3	1.6					1.6	1.3	2.2
	14.6	17.3	6.0	Net Profit + Depr., Dep., Amort./Cur. Mat. L/T/D						7.4
	(19) 5.9	(28) 4.1	(21) 2.6						(11)	2.6
	1.6	1.6	1.8							1.8
	.1	.1	.1	Fixed/Worth		.0		.1	.1	.1
	.3	.4	.2			.1		.3	.1	.2
	.6	.9	.6			1.0		NM	.3	.6
	.5	.6	.6	Debt/Worth		.4		1.0	.3	.7
	1.7	2.0	1.6			1.5		1.7	1.2	2.9
	4.1	5.3	3.8			4.3		NM	3.1	3.8
	44.4	28.5	48.7	% Profit Before Taxes/Tangible Net Worth					39.7	41.4
	(57) 17.0	(55) 16.0	(80) 26.9						24.2 (30)	24.6
	5.4	4.0	9.3						5.2	14.2
	15.0	14.2	18.4	% Profit Before Taxes/Total Assets		16.2		20.4	23.8	16.5
	7.3	5.3	8.1			13.2		3.6	8.1	6.3
	1.2	.8	2.4			-1.7		2.5	1.2	2.2
	53.3	65.9	77.8	Sales/Net Fixed Assets		319.8		55.3	75.2	81.9
	27.0	25.5	31.5			26.0		23.9	37.8	34.3
	12.5	13.3	13.7			7.6		12.9	16.2	16.8
	3.1	2.9	3.2	Sales/Total Assets		2.8		3.2	3.4	2.9
	2.1	2.1	2.2			1.9		2.1	2.5	2.0
	1.6	1.5	1.7			1.8		1.8	1.8	1.5
	.6	.6	.5	% Depr., Dep., Amort./Sales					.4	.6
	(52) 1.4	(55) 1.3	(64) 1.1					(16)	.7 (27)	1.3
	2.4	2.4	2.1						1.4	2.1
	2.0	1.3	2.0	% Officers', Directors' Owners' Comp/Sales						
	(14) 4.7	(16) 3.5	(24) 4.6							
	5.7	5.1	6.1							
	3119007M	3596638M	5716675M	Net Sales ($)	3904M	20776M	33044M	80758M	328666M	5249527M
	1675935M	1864546M	2856616M	Total Assets ($)	2016M	9640M	16390M	38157M	158280M	2632133M

M = $ thousand   MM = $ million
See Pages 11 through 21 for Explanation of Ratios and Data

Current Data Sorted by Assets   Comparative Historical Data

Type of Statement	0-500M	500M-2MM	2-10MM	10-50MM	50-100MM	100-250MM		4/1/02-3/31/03 ALL	4/1/03-3/31/04 ALL
Unqualified	1	2	5	13	5	3		26	22
Reviewed	2	11	12	5				34	31
Compiled	2	5	7					25	19
Tax Returns			4					5	8
Other		9	17	11	2	1		44	51
		33 (4/1-9/30/06)		84 (10/1/06-3/31/07)					
NUMBER OF STATEMENTS	5	27	45	29	7	4		134	131
	%	%	%	%	%	%		%	%
ASSETS									
Cash & Equivalents		8.0	8.5	6.7				8.5	8.8
Trade Receivables (net)		33.8	30.9	30.4				27.5	29.2
Inventory		19.5	23.9	31.7				23.6	23.0
All Other Current		.6	.9	2.4				1.1	1.5
Total Current		61.9	64.2	71.2				60.7	62.5
Fixed Assets (net)		29.9	22.5	15.5				31.7	29.3
Intangibles (net)		1.7	5.9	7.2				3.0	3.6
All Other Non-Current		6.5	7.4	6.0				4.7	4.6
Total		100.0	100.0	100.0				100.0	100.0
LIABILITIES									
Notes Payable-Short Term		12.3	10.2	14.0				12.1	9.5
Cur. Mat.-L.T.D.		8.8	4.0	3.4				6.6	5.0
Trade Payables		21.0	20.9	19.4				16.4	16.7
Income Taxes Payable		.1	.3	.1				.1	.1
All Other Current		8.6	6.8	8.5				8.1	13.8
Total Current		50.8	42.1	45.5				43.4	45.2
Long-Term Debt		12.8	17.7	12.7				15.4	14.5
Deferred Taxes		.0	.1	.5				.2	.3
All Other Non-Current		14.2	2.6	5.4				6.0	5.9
Net Worth		22.1	37.5	36.0				35.0	34.1
Total Liabilities & Net Worth		100.0	100.0	100.0				100.0	100.0
INCOME DATA									
Net Sales		100.0	100.0	100.0				100.0	100.0
Gross Profit		31.2	29.2	23.6				26.2	30.1
Operating Expenses		25.2	23.4	17.9				25.4	26.8
Operating Profit		6.1	5.8	5.6				.8	3.3
All Other Expenses (net)		1.1	1.0	2.2				1.2	1.2
Profit Before Taxes		5.0	4.8	3.4				-.4	2.1
RATIOS									
Current		2.3	2.2	2.2				2.1	2.3
		1.4	1.5	1.5				1.5	1.5
		1.0	1.2	1.1				1.0	1.1
Quick		1.9	1.6	1.2				1.5	1.6
		1.0	1.1	.8				.8	.8
		.5	.6	.6				.5	.5
Sales/Receivables		(33) 11.2	(39) 9.4	(42) 8.8				(38) 9.5	(40) 9.1
		(41) 8.9	(48) 7.6	(48) 7.6				(48) 7.7	(48) 7.6
		(54) 6.8	(57) 6.4	(59) 6.1				(57) 6.4	(59) 6.2
Cost of Sales/Inventory		(4) 81.4	(24) 15.5	(40) 9.1				(24) 15.3	(26) 14.1
		(29) 12.4	(44) 8.3	(63) 5.8				(45) 8.1	(49) 7.5
		(66) 5.5	(72) 5.1	(87) 4.2				(75) 4.9	(76) 4.8
Cost of Sales/Payables		(14) 26.6	(25) 14.8	(29) 12.7				(19) 19.1	(23) 15.9
		(33) 10.9	(41) 8.8	(38) 9.7				(34) 10.9	(38) 9.6
		(53) 6.8	(58) 6.3	(52) 7.0				(50) 7.3	(54) 6.8
Sales/Working Capital		9.6	6.1	5.6				6.2	6.5
		16.7	11.0	9.8				12.0	11.4
		-193.9	23.4	22.3				177.1	32.7
EBIT/Interest		10.4	12.6	16.7				8.0	9.3
		(25) 5.0	(41) 3.8	(26) 2.3				(123) 2.3	(118) 2.6
		3.1	1.2	1.0				-1.2	.0
Net Profit + Depr., Dep., Amort./Cur. Mat. L/T/D			7.6					4.2	4.2
			(13) 3.9					(42) 1.9	(35) 2.4
			1.3					.3	1.1
Fixed/Worth		.4	.3	.2				.5	.3
		.7	.5	.6				.8	.7
		2.3	1.1	1.6				2.8	2.3
Debt/Worth		1.0	.8	.9				.7	.7
		1.8	1.7	2.4				1.8	1.7
		6.2	5.7	6.6				8.4	5.0
% Profit Before Taxes/Tangible Net Worth		50.1	46.7	60.1				29.0	35.0
		(23) 22.7	(39) 25.2	(25) 26.4				(115) 12.0	(113) 11.6
		15.5	.9	1.4				-8.9	.6
% Profit Before Taxes/Total Assets		16.2	17.0	17.4				10.8	13.5
		9.3	9.6	7.1				3.0	4.1
		5.7	1.0	-1.0				-7.4	-2.5
Sales/Net Fixed Assets		33.6	21.4	31.3				15.9	19.3
		11.6	13.4	17.2				7.9	8.6
		5.8	6.1	9.1				4.0	4.0
Sales/Total Assets		4.0	2.8	2.7				2.8	2.9
		2.9	2.3	2.2				2.1	2.1
		2.2	1.8	1.8				1.5	1.6
% Depr., Dep., Amort./Sales		2.0	1.3	1.1				2.0	1.8
		(24) 3.1	(42) 2.4	(26) 1.9				(124) 3.3	(118) 3.1
		4.7	4.1	3.3				6.2	5.3
% Officers', Directors' Owners' Comp/Sales		.9	3.6					2.6	2.5
		(12) 3.7	(14) 5.9					(42) 4.8	(47) 3.8
		5.3	10.1					6.8	7.5
Net Sales ($)	5226M	107720M	506421M	1154870M	1125497M	994213M		2312011M	2480934M
Total Assets ($)	1943M	35039M	219553M	518504M	572433M	519492M		1356039M	1324110M

M = $ thousand   MM = $ million

See Pages 11 through 21 for Explanation of Ratios and Data

Comparative Historical Data

Current Data Sorted by Sales

			Type of Statement	0-1MM	1-3MM	3-5MM	5-10MM	10-25MM	25MM & OVER
23	14	26	Unqualified	1		1	1	7	17
17	17	20	Reviewed			2	7	7	3
17	19	20	Compiled	1	6	4	5	4	
13	8	11	Tax Returns	1	3	4	1	2	
43	47	40	Other	1	3	7	6	9	14
4/1/04-3/31/05 ALL	4/1/05-3/31/06 ALL	4/1/06-3/31/07 ALL			33 (4/1-9/30/06)		84 (10/1/06-3/31/07)		
113	105	117	NUMBER OF STATEMENTS	4	12	18	20	29	34
%	%	%	ASSETS	%	%	%	%	%	%
11.2	7.0	7.5	Cash & Equivalents		5.4	8.0	7.6	9.6	5.3
29.3	31.8	31.2	Trade Receivables (net)		30.6	25.6	37.9	31.1	31.2
22.6	24.2	26.0	Inventory		17.6	22.6	17.4	29.6	32.1
.8	1.5	1.3	All Other Current		.0	.5	.9	1.5	2.3
64.0	64.5	65.9	Total Current		53.6	56.7	63.8	71.9	70.9
25.7	25.3	22.2	Fixed Assets (net)		33.1	27.9	24.0	17.8	18.5
5.4	4.6	5.3	Intangibles (net)		6.3	3.1	4.9	5.7	5.8
5.0	5.6	6.6	All Other Non-Current		7.0	12.3	7.3	4.6	4.7
100.0	100.0	100.0	Total		100.0	100.0	100.0	100.0	100.0
			LIABILITIES						
8.9	11.9	11.1	Notes Payable-Short Term		9.3	13.9	6.6	10.6	14.4
4.1	4.4	4.9	Cur. Mat.-L.T.D.		8.4	10.7	3.2	2.9	3.6
16.7	19.6	20.8	Trade Payables		17.6	20.2	22.1	21.9	22.0
.3	.2	.2	Income Taxes Payable		.2	.0	.3	.3	.2
9.6	8.5	9.2	All Other Current		12.0	5.8	6.1	7.5	9.9
39.6	44.5	46.2	Total Current		47.5	50.7	38.3	43.2	50.1
20.5	14.1	15.3	Long-Term Debt		26.3	13.6	14.4	13.8	12.2
.3	.4	.2	Deferred Taxes		.0	.0	.1	.2	.5
7.0	5.8	6.8	All Other Non-Current		22.3	5.8	3.5	3.0	7.7
32.6	35.2	31.5	Net Worth		3.9	29.9	43.7	39.8	29.5
100.0	100.0	100.0	Total Liabilties & Net Worth		100.0	100.0	100.0	100.0	100.0
			INCOME DATA						
100.0	100.0	100.0	Net Sales		100.0	100.0	100.0	100.0	100.0
29.8	26.5	27.0	Gross Profit		38.6	34.2	30.7	22.3	19.4
26.0	23.1	21.5	Operating Expenses		28.1	29.1	27.2	17.0	14.4
3.8	3.3	5.5	Operating Profit		10.5	5.1	3.5	5.3	5.0
1.0	1.4	1.4	All Other Expenses (net)		2.3	.9	.6	.9	2.0
2.8	2.0	4.2	Profit Before Taxes		8.3	4.2	2.9	4.4	3.1
			RATIOS						
2.7	2.0	2.2	Current		1.9	2.6	2.2	2.6	2.0
1.7	1.5	1.5			1.3	1.3	1.7	1.6	1.5
1.3	1.1	1.1			.8	.7	1.4	1.2	1.1
2.0	1.4	1.5	Quick		1.4	1.8	1.9	1.5	1.1
1.1	.8	.9			.9	.7	1.3	1.0	.7
.6	.6	.6			.6	.5	.8	.6	.5
36 10.3	41 8.9	39 9.3	Sales/Receivables	35 10.3	34 10.9	34 10.6	39 9.4	43 8.4	
46 7.9	51 7.1	47 7.7		45 8.2	48 7.6	41 8.8	49 7.5	48 7.6	
59 6.2	60 6.1	57 6.4		55 6.7	56 6.5	52 7.1	62 5.9	58 6.3	
21 17.4	28 13.2	25 14.6	Cost of Sales/Inventory	14 25.2	2 190.7	4 84.5	30 12.4	39 9.5	
48 7.5	52 7.0	50 7.2		35 10.4	43 8.5	20 18.5	66 5.5	62 5.9	
84 4.3	79 4.6	79 4.6		82 4.5	82 4.5	56 6.5	81 4.5	80 4.6	
21 17.8	24 15.1	24 15.3	Cost of Sales/Payables	15 24.0	15 23.6	18 19.9	24 14.9	31 11.9	
35 10.6	36 10.1	38 9.7		30 12.3	44 8.3	32 11.3	45 8.2	38 9.6	
53 6.9	51 7.1	54 6.7		62 5.9	74 4.9	44 8.4	66 5.5	49 7.5	
5.3	6.6	5.9	Sales/Working Capital		6.8	5.1	8.5	5.2	7.0
8.4	10.7	12.6			34.8	18.4	15.3	10.1	11.1
20.7	30.6	35.8			NM	-12.5	20.7	19.0	25.5
7.7	6.7	11.9	EBIT/Interest		13.7	13.3	13.0	18.7	10.9
(95) 4.3	(97) 3.1	(107) 3.4		(11) 3.6	8.7	(18) 5.1	(25) 1.8	(32) 2.3	
1.3	1.0	1.1			1.5	1.3	1.4	1.1	.5
7.5	6.4	8.0	Net Profit + Depr., Dep., Amort./Cur. Mat. L/T/D						14.2
(26) 3.5	(26) 2.7	(32) 4.0						(12)	6.3
1.1	.7	1.6							2.1
.3	.4	.3	Fixed/Worth		.4	.4	.4	.3	.2
.7	.7	.6			1.1	.7	.6	.4	.7
1.7	1.6	1.6			4.6	2.3	.9	.9	3.7
.7	.9	.9	Debt/Worth		.8	1.1	.6	.7	1.0
1.7	1.9	2.2			2.2	2.2	1.5	1.8	2.5
4.7	5.4	6.4			NM	6.7	2.7	5.7	20.9
40.8	32.9	47.9	% Profit Before Taxes/Tangible Net Worth		78.9	51.0	45.3		52.6
(94) 16.1	(90) 11.3	(100) 21.6		(15)	24.0	(18) 20.5	(27) 18.0	(28)	25.4
4.0	3.1	1.4			4.9	10.1	.9		-.1
13.8	10.9	16.2	% Profit Before Taxes/Total Assets		21.1	11.4	15.5	17.1	16.0
5.3	5.0	8.1			14.5	8.2	9.9	4.8	5.7
1.2	.4	.2			2	1.3	3.2	-.3	-1.4
22.1	21.0	25.1	Sales/Net Fixed Assets		21.6	16.9	32.8	24.9	32.0
8.9	12.1	13.3			9.1	8.6	14.7	18.0	13.3
4.5	5.6	6.7			4.0	5.8	8.5	8.8	8.8
2.9	2.8	2.9	Sales/Total Assets		3.3	2.6	4.1	2.7	2.7
2.1	2.3	2.3			2.2	2.2	3.2	2.2	2.3
1.5	1.8	1.8			1.5	2.0	2.2	1.8	1.8
1.5	1.5	1.3	% Depr., Dep., Amort./Sales		1.6	2.5	1.3	1.3	1.1
(92) 2.6	(92) 2.6	(106) 2.3		(16) 3.1	3.6	(18) 2.2	(26) 2.0	(31) 1.8	
5.7	4.9	4.1			7.7	5.2	4.6	3.0	3.1
2.4	1.3	3.1	% Officers', Directors' Owners' Comp/Sales						
(40) 4.7	(30) 2.9	(32) 4.6							
6.8	5.4	8.5							
2274064M	3048053M	3893947M	Net Sales ($)	2751M	24654M	77990M	143851M	481122M	3163579M
1372393M	1451011M	1866964M	Total Assets ($)	1620M	13664M	38807M	50789M	246378M	1515706M

M = $ thousand   MM = $ million
See Pages 11 through 21 for Explanation of Ratios and Data

Current Data Sorted by Assets | Comparative Historical Data

Type of Statement	0-500M	500M-2MM	2-10MM	10-50MM	50-100MM	100-250MM		4/1/02-3/31/03 ALL	4/1/03-3/31/04 ALL
Unqualified		1	6	7	5	6		19	28
Reviewed		1	4	1				11	9
Compiled		1	1					3	3
Tax Returns		2						2	5
Other		4						21	31
		15 (4/1-9/30/06)		52 (10/1/06-3/31/07)					
NUMBER OF STATEMENTS		9	20	19	9	10		56	76

	0-500M	500M-2MM	2-10MM %	10-50MM %	50-100MM	100-250MM %		%	%
ASSETS									
Cash & Equivalents			11.4	20.5		30.8		15.3	14.6
Trade Receivables (net)			27.9	21.7		12.2		21.2	23.3
Inventory			28.0	20.8		15.1		26.6	24.8
All Other Current			1.4	2.8		5.6		2.8	3.5
Total Current	D		68.7	65.8		63.7		65.9	66.3
Fixed Assets (net)	A		24.2	24.3		21.0		23.9	22.9
Intangibles (net)	T		.2	4.5		7.4		5.0	5.4
All Other Non-Current	A		6.9	5.4		7.9		5.3	5.5
Total			100.0	100.0		100.0		100.0	100.0
LIABILITIES	N								
Notes Payable-Short Term	O		10.5	5.1		3.8		9.8	8.2
Cur. Mat.-L.T.D.	T		2.2	2.8		.2		3.5	2.5
Trade Payables			11.5	9.7		12.8		15.3	13.0
Income Taxes Payable	A		.5	.1		.2		.6	.5
All Other Current	V		10.7	13.2		10.9		10.8	14.5
Total Current	A		35.4	30.9		27.9		40.0	38.7
Long-Term Debt	I		8.8	18.2		2.8		14.3	9.8
Deferred Taxes	L		.4	.2		.2		.7	.4
All Other Non-Current	A		15.8	3.8		6.6		5.1	5.2
Net Worth	B		39.6	46.8		62.4		40.0	45.9
Total Liabilties & Net Worth	L E		100.0	100.0		100.0		100.0	100.0
INCOME DATA									
Net Sales			100.0	100.0		100.0		100.0	100.0
Gross Profit			29.9	35.5		33.3		28.5	32.2
Operating Expenses			23.8	35.4		33.0		30.0	30.6
Operating Profit			6.1	.2		.3		-1.4	1.6
All Other Expenses (net)			1.5	1.4		-1.3		2.0	.6
Profit Before Taxes			4.6	-1.2		1.5		-3.4	1.0

RATIOS

	2-10MM	10-50MM	100-250MM		4/1/02-3/31/03 ALL	4/1/03-3/31/04 ALL
Current	3.3	4.1	6.6		2.6	2.8
	2.3	2.4	2.6		1.9	1.9
	1.4	1.6	1.2		1.2	1.2
Quick	2.1	2.9	5.7		1.8	1.7
	1.1	1.7	2.1		.9	1.0
	.8	.5	.4		.6	.6
Sales/Receivables	32 · 11.5	37 · 9.8	22 · 16.6		37 · 9.7	40 · 9.1
	47 · 7.8	48 · 7.6	48 · 7.6		48 · 7.6	50 · 7.3
	66 · 5.5	66 · 5.5	64 · 5.7		64 · 5.7	63 · 5.8
Cost of Sales/Inventory	35 · 10.5	29 · 12.6	31 · 11.9		41 · 8.8	52 · 7.1
	55 · 6.6	71 · 5.2	72 · 5.1		76 · 4.8	79 · 4.6
	174 · 2.1	134 · 2.7	129 · 2.8		124 · 2.9	114 · 3.2
Cost of Sales/Payables	15 · 24.6	27 · 13.6	32 · 11.2		25 · 14.7	19 · 19.2
	26 · 14.2	33 · 11.1	46 · 8.0		38 · 9.7	37 · 9.9
	42 · 8.8	41 · 8.9	60 · 6.1		69 · 5.3	57 · 6.4
Sales/Working Capital	3.2	2.8	1.2		2.8	3.0
	5.0	3.6	2.7		5.4	5.2
	14.5	7.3	10.1		27.4	18.9
EBIT/Interest	36.7	24.9			10.2	6.3
	(19) 9.0	(15) 4.4			(45) 1.4	(64) 2.0
	2.0	-2.5			-2.1	-1.7
Net Profit + Depr., Dep., Amort./Cur. Mat. L/T/D					5.0	8.7
					(19) 1.7	(21) 3.0
					-1.1	1.4
Fixed/Worth	.3	.2	.1		.2	.2
	.4	.2	.4		.4	.4
	.8	1.1	.8		1.4	1.0
Debt/Worth	.3	.3	.2		.5	.5
	1.4	.7	.8		1.2	1.0
	3.6	1.4	1.6		6.8	4.0
% Profit Before Taxes/Tangible Net Worth	34.5	32.1	19.3		21.6	18.9
	(18) 13.5	(18) 9.5	4.0		(47) 2.3	(70) 3.3
	6.7	-23.6	-19.1		-12.9	-6.3
% Profit Before Taxes/Total Assets	15.5	16.8	9.1		7.7	7.7
	7.1	3.3	2.9		.6	1.2
	4.2	-11.8	-10.9		-11.9	-5.4
Sales/Net Fixed Assets	15.3	14.6	13.2		25.5	23.1
	7.8	9.0	4.7		9.6	8.2
	5.0	2.7	2.0		3.6	4.3
Sales/Total Assets	2.5	1.7	1.2		2.5	2.2
	1.8	1.3	.7		1.3	1.4
	1.2	1.0	.6		.8	1.0
% Depr., Dep., Amort./Sales	1.8	2.0			1.3	1.3
	(16) 2.5	(17) 4.3			(43) 2.9	(54) 2.9
	3.5	5.9			6.0	5.7
% Officers', Directors' Owners' Comp/Sales						2.0
					(16)	4.3
						8.5

	500M-2MM	2-10MM	10-50MM	50-100MM	100-250MM		4/1/02-3/31/03 ALL	4/1/03-3/31/04 ALL
Net Sales ($)	34058M	202338M	467412M	732247M	2397332M		2879958M	3875852M
Total Assets ($)	11100M	109250M	360126M	719026M	1604834M		2278426M	3094836M

M = $ thousand   MM = $ million
See Pages 11 through 21 for Explanation of Ratios and Data

Comparative Historical Data | | Current Data Sorted by Sales

4/1/04-3/31/05 ALL	4/1/05-3/31/06 ALL	4/1/06-3/31/07 ALL	Type of Statement	0-1MM	1-3MM	3-5MM	5-10MM	10-25MM	25MM & OVER
27	14	25	Unqualified	1			4	4	16
8	8	6	Reviewed				4	1	1
5	5	2	Compiled			1		1	
5	2	2	Tax Returns				1		
21	43	32	Other		2		6	10	11
					15 (4/1-9/30/06)			52 (10/1/06-3/31/07)	
66	72	67	**NUMBER OF STATEMENTS**	1	3	4	15	16	28
%	%	%	**ASSETS**	%	%	%	%	%	%
15.7	14.7	18.2	Cash & Equivalents				15.1	16.4	22.2
25.8	25.1	23.0	Trade Receivables (net)				23.9	26.4	18.1
26.0	27.1	23.7	Inventory				24.6	20.6	23.7
2.7	3.5	2.5	All Other Current				1.3	3.2	3.2
70.2	70.4	67.3	Total Current				64.9	66.6	67.2
18.3	17.2	23.1	Fixed Assets (net)				26.6	25.6	19.6
4.8	6.2	3.6	Intangibles (net)				.7	3.3	6.5
6.6	6.2	5.9	All Other Non-Current				7.8	4.6	6.7
100.0	100.0	100.0	Total				100.0	100.0	100.0
			LIABILITIES						
11.0	11.1	7.9	Notes Payable-Short Term				11.0	5.1	5.6
3.3	3.3	2.1	Cur. Mat.-L.T.D.				2.7	2.1	2.2
15.6	16.2	11.1	Trade Payables				9.6	9.8	12.4
.6	.6	.3	Income Taxes Payable				.0	.2	.5
9.6	15.0	11.5	All Other Current				11.7	10.9	10.7
40.0	46.2	32.9	Total Current				35.0	28.1	31.3
8.7	9.7	10.1	Long-Term Debt				8.8	7.2	14.4
.3	.4	.4	Deferred Taxes				.4	.1	.7
6.1	10.6	10.3	All Other Non-Current				5.9	4.8	7.5
44.8	33.1	46.3	Net Worth				49.8	59.9	46.1
100.0	100.0	100.0	Total Liabilties & Net Worth				100.0	100.0	100.0
			INCOME DATA						
100.0	100.0	100.0	Net Sales				100.0	100.0	100.0
33.9	33.4	33.8	Gross Profit				31.3	37.4	34.2
29.7	31.0	28.9	Operating Expenses				26.3	36.9	29.6
4.2	2.4	4.8	Operating Profit				5.0	.5	4.6
.8	1.1	1.1	All Other Expenses (net)				1.5	1.1	.9
3.4	1.3	3.7	Profit Before Taxes				3.5	-.5	3.7
			RATIOS						
3.4	2.9	4.1	Current				5.6	4.0	4.2
1.8	1.8	2.3					2.3	3.0	2.2
1.2	1.2	1.4					1.2	1.6	1.6
2.0	1.9	2.8	Quick				2.8	2.9	3.1
1.0	1.0	1.2					1.2	1.8	1.1
.6	.6	.7					.6	1.0	.6
37 10.0	41 8.9	36 10.1	Sales/Receivables				27 13.5	41 8.9	37 9.9
49 7.4	51 7.2	49 7.5					38 9.7	46 8.0	53 7.0
63 5.8	61 6.0	68 5.4					68 5.4	60 6.1	67 5.4
42 8.7	51 7.1	34 10.9	Cost of Sales/Inventory				29 12.7	31 11.6	40 9.0
75 4.8	85 4.3	76 4.8					43 8.6	68 5.4	81 4.5
115 3.2	143 2.5	137 2.7					178 2.0	131 2.8	188 1.9
24 15.1	27 13.4	20 18.3	Cost of Sales/Payables				16 23.3	17 21.8	27 13.3
38 9.6	38 9.5	32 11.2					26 13.8	28 13.1	38 9.5
61 6.0	56 6.5	47 7.8					42 8.7	34 10.8	56 6.5
2.5	3.1	2.6	Sales/Working Capital				3.6	2.8	1.7
6.8	7.2	3.9					4.9	4.0	3.6
29.0	22.6	9.9					16.6	6.9	8.4
16.0	8.8	17.7	EBIT/Interest				40.3	21.8	14.2
(58) 4.5	(61) 4.0	(53) 5.5					5.5	(12) 7.2	(20) 6.1
1.4	.7	.9					1.6	2.6	-.2
12.5	11.2	12.1	Net Profit + Depr., Dep.,						
(24) 3.0	(19) 4.9	(14) 7.0	Amort./Cur. Mat. L/T/D						
1.1	2.8	1.7							
.2	.2	.2	Fixed/Worth				.2	.2	.1
.4	.5	.4					.4	.3	.4
1.2	7.2	.9					.7	.9	.9
.5	.6	.3	Debt/Worth				.2	.3	.3
1.2	1.5	.8					1.1	.6	.8
4.2	51.9	1.9					1.9	1.6	2.3
43.0	30.4	32.7	% Profit Before Taxes/Tangible				22.2	38.7	32.7
(58) 10.4	(55) 11.9	(62) 14.8	Net Worth				(14) 12.5	20.4	(26) 8.3
1.1	1.0	-5.8					5.4	-16.0	-20.1
14.4	11.5	15.9	% Profit Before Taxes/Total				12.8	17.1	16.6
4.6	4.1	5.2	Assets				5.2	9.4	2.9
.2	-1.1	-3.6					4.0	-11.7	-7.8
29.3	26.0	18.3	Sales/Net Fixed Assets				9.4	15.4	21.8
12.8	13.8	8.3					6.6	9.7	9.1
5.9	6.1	3.0					4.7	2.9	2.9
2.5	2.4	2.1	Sales/Total Assets				2.4	2.1	1.7
1.7	1.5	1.3					1.4	1.4	1.1
1.1	1.1	.9					1.1	1.0	.7
1.0	1.3	1.8	% Depr., Dep., Amort./Sales				1.9	2.0	1.8
(54) 2.1	(60) 2.2	(53) 2.8					(12) 2.9	(13) 3.6	(21) 3.6
4.7	3.9	4.7					4.1	6.8	6.9
.8	2.6	2.2	% Officers', Directors'						
(16) 2.4	(15) 3.1	(12) 4.4	Owners' Comp/Sales						
5.7	9.0	9.0							
3385149M	4046445M	3833387M	Net Sales ($)	690M	6551M	15791M	109805M	273283M	3427267M
2134986M	2775103M	2804336M	Total Assets ($)	954M	3396M	8953M	76731M	210704M	2503598M

© RMA 2007

M = $ thousand   MM = $ million
See Pages 11 through 21 for Explanation of Ratios and Data

Current Data Sorted by Assets   Comparative Historical Data

0-500M	4 (4/1-9/30/06) 500M-2MM	2-10MM	26 (10/1/06-3/31/07) 10-50MM	50-100MM	100-250MM	Type of Statement	8 4/1/02-3/31/03 ALL	11 4/1/03-3/31/04 ALL
	3	4 5 1	2 1	1	1	Unqualified / Reviewed / Compiled / Tax Returns / Other	9 7 3	5 5 3 3
	3	15	9	2	1	NUMBER OF STATEMENTS	27	27
%	%	%	%	%	%	**ASSETS**	%	%
		9.6				Cash & Equivalents	3.4	5.2
		37.7				Trade Receivables (net)	25.9	30.0
D		22.2				Inventory	27.6	25.7
A		4.5				All Other Current	1.2	1.4
T		74.0				Total Current	58.0	62.4
A		19.7				Fixed Assets (net)	26.5	25.9
N		1.0				Intangibles (net)	9.4	3.6
O		5.3				All Other Non-Current	6.1	8.2
T		100.0				Total	100.0	100.0
A						**LIABILITIES**		
V		17.7				Notes Payable-Short Term	10.4	16.7
A		2.2				Cur. Mat.-L.T.D.	6.0	5.8
I		21.2				Trade Payables	13.2	13.0
L		.0				Income Taxes Payable	.4	.3
A		10.9				All Other Current	10.1	16.3
B		52.0				Total Current	40.1	52.2
L		15.3				Long-Term Debt	11.4	9.1
E		.8				Deferred Taxes	1.1	.6
		15.7				All Other Non-Current	12.8	10.8
		16.1				Net Worth	34.6	27.1
		100.0				Total Liabilities & Net Worth	100.0	100.0
						INCOME DATA		
		100.0				Net Sales	100.0	100.0
		31.3				Gross Profit	25.2	29.3
		24.2				Operating Expenses	22.7	27.6
		7.1				Operating Profit	2.5	1.7
		.4				All Other Expenses (net)	1.3	1.7
		6.6				Profit Before Taxes	1.2	.0
						RATIOS		
		2.8					1.9	2.0
		1.4				Current	1.6	1.4
		1.1					1.1	1.0
		1.9					1.0	1.1
		.9				Quick	.6	.7
		.7					.5	.4
	44	8.3					30 12.2	34 10.9
	50	7.3				Sales/Receivables	41 8.9	50 7.2
	61	5.9					49 7.4	57 6.4
	28	13.1					38 9.6	34 10.8
	55	6.7				Cost of Sales/Inventory	56 6.5	62 5.9
	85	4.3					85 4.3	119 3.1
	23	16.1					16 23.4	20 18.1
	41	8.9				Cost of Sales/Payables	24 15.0	33 11.1
	57	6.4					36 10.1	47 7.7
		5.5					6.2	5.8
		14.0				Sales/Working Capital	10.8	15.0
		69.2					75.5	UND
		26.6					3.4	10.2
	(13)	9.0				EBIT/Interest	(25) 1.6	(26) 2.3
		1.4					-1.4	-.8
						Net Profit + Depr., Dep., Amort./Cur. Mat. L/T/D		
		.2					.5	.4
		1.0				Fixed/Worth	.7	.7
		-.9					20.8	UND
		.8					.7	.8
		2.3				Debt/Worth	1.3	1.3
		-6.4					90.3	UND
		101.5				% Profit Before Taxes/Tangible	21.9	23.3
	(11)	41.0				Net Worth	(21) 7.1	(21) 10.5
		33.7					-11.9	1.6
		27.3				% Profit Before Taxes/Total	6.6	7.8
		18.1				Assets	3.2	1.1
		4.6					-5.9	-7.1
		34.6					14.1	14.1
		16.4				Sales/Net Fixed Assets	8.3	6.8
		9.2					6.0	4.7
		3.1					2.6	2.5
		2.6				Sales/Total Assets	2.1	1.8
		1.9					1.6	1.4
		.9					1.3	1.6
	(14)	1.8				% Depr., Dep., Amort./Sales	(24) 3.0	(21) 3.9
		3.2					4.9	5.0
						% Officers', Directors' Owners' Comp/Sales		
11636M	202838M	424613M	202900M	246570M		Net Sales ($)	829639M	714752M
3916M	78278M	239685M	103924M	148006M		Total Assets ($)	421505M	409320M

M = $ thousand   MM = $ million
See Pages 11 through 21 for Explanation of Ratios and Data

Comparative Historical Data | Current Data Sorted by Sales

Type of Statement counts and date ranges:

	4/1/04-3/31/05	4/1/05-3/31/06	4/1/06-3/31/07	Type of Statement	4 (4/1-9/30/06)		26 (10/1/06-3/31/07)			
					0-1MM	1-3MM	3-5MM	5-10MM	10-25MM	25MM & OVER
	8	7	8	Unqualified				1	4	3
	9	10	9	Reviewed			3	3	2	1
	3	2	1	Compiled					1	
	1			Tax Returns						
	16	12	12	Other				1	5	6
	ALL	ALL	ALL							
	37	31	30	NUMBER OF STATEMENTS	3	5	3	5	12	10

Note: columns 0-1MM and 1-3MM are marked "DATA NOT AVAILABLE."

Item	4/1/04-3/31/05	4/1/05-3/31/06	4/1/06-3/31/07	0-1MM	1-3MM	3-5MM	5-10MM	10-25MM	25MM & OVER
ASSETS	%	%	%	%	%	%	%	%	%
Cash & Equivalents	5.6	5.5	8.7					9.9	7.0
Trade Receivables (net)	31.2	32.4	32.5					31.8	33.8
Inventory	24.2	25.6	26.3					23.3	25.0
All Other Current	1.1	3.6	2.6					5.0	1.1
Total Current	62.1	67.1	70.2					70.0	67.0
Fixed Assets (net)	20.7	19.0	20.6					18.4	24.0
Intangibles (net)	6.5	5.9	4.4					6.8	5.0
All Other Non-Current	10.8	7.9	4.9					4.8	4.0
Total	100.0	100.0	100.0					100.0	100.0
LIABILITIES									
Notes Payable-Short Term	11.3	11.7	13.5					16.1	10.6
Cur. Mat.-L.T.D.	4.8	3.1	2.4					2.6	3.3
Trade Payables	16.2	19.6	18.9					21.4	21.0
Income Taxes Payable	.4	.5	.2					.0	.4
All Other Current	10.9	8.9	12.6					13.2	12.9
Total Current	43.7	43.8	47.5					53.3	48.1
Long-Term Debt	10.0	9.9	11.8					15.0	11.0
Deferred Taxes	.4	.3	.5					.8	.2
All Other Non-Current	8.5	5.7	9.9					21.5	.6
Net Worth	37.4	40.2	30.2					9.4	40.0
Total Liabilities & Net Worth	100.0	100.0	100.0					100.0	100.0
INCOME DATA									
Net Sales	100.0	100.0	100.0					100.0	100.0
Gross Profit	27.5	28.8	30.0					32.7	27.4
Operating Expenses	22.1	22.4	22.5					25.9	18.5
Operating Profit	5.3	6.3	7.6					6.8	8.8
All Other Expenses (net)	.5	.4	1.1					1.3	1.2
Profit Before Taxes	4.8	5.9	6.4					5.5	7.6
RATIOS									
Current	2.0	2.6	2.4					2.2	1.9
	1.5	1.4	1.5					1.6	1.3
	1.0	1.1	1.1					.9	1.1
Quick	1.4	1.5	1.7					1.6	1.2
	.8	.9	.9					.8	.9
	.6	.5	.6					.5	.6
Sales/Receivables	37 9.8	41 9.0	46 7.9					45 8.1	53 6.9
	49 7.4	53 6.9	53 6.8					51 7.1	60 6.0
	53 6.9	66 5.5	61 6.0					66 5.6	61 5.9
Cost of Sales/Inventory	33 11.1	33 10.9	31 11.6					29 12.7	31 11.9
	53 6.9	67 5.5	57 6.4					55 6.6	61 6.0
	79 4.6	93 3.9	102 3.6					139 2.6	90 4.1
Cost of Sales/Payables	21 17.7	30 12.4	23 15.8					26 14.0	30 12.1
	28 12.9	43 8.5	43 8.5					56 6.5	50 7.3
	45 8.1	58 6.3	59 6.2					66 5.6	66 5.5
Sales/Working Capital	6.2	4.8	5.0					4.7	7.0
	11.4	8.0	10.1					10.0	10.7
	547.4	56.3	28.7					NM	27.8
EBIT/Interest	16.9	16.8	21.4					17.5	24.4
	(36) 5.6	(28) 5.7	(27) 5.0					(11) 5.0	17.0
	2.0	1.6	1.3					.7	2.3
Net Profit + Depr., Dep., Amort./Cur. Mat. L/T/D	7.5								
	(12) 3.0								
	1.7								
Fixed/Worth	.3	.2	.3					.3	.4
	.5	.4	.7					2.0	.7
	1.5	1.1	NM					-.4	1.2
Debt/Worth	.8	.7	.8					.8	.9
	1.7	1.5	1.5					6.4	1.6
	5.4	4.2	NM					-4.3	4.8
% Profit Before Taxes/Tangible Net Worth	45.6	57.5	61.1						
	(33) 22.8	(28) 19.9	(23) 39.7						
	3.6	5.2	7.9						
% Profit Before Taxes/Total Assets	20.4	19.8	22.2					21.6	28.2
	6.7	9.6	14.3					17.9	16.8
	1.7	2.6	1.1					-2.1	2.9
Sales/Net Fixed Assets	32.3	18.6	29.3					34.9	19.0
	12.2	11.1	11.5					18.9	8.2
	6.4	8.0	5.0					4.3	4.5
Sales/Total Assets	3.2	2.7	2.9					3.1	2.7
	2.2	1.9	2.0					2.2	1.8
	1.5	1.6	1.6					1.4	1.4
% Depr., Dep., Amort./Sales	.9	1.2	.9					.7	
	(28) 2.6	(26) 1.9	(26) 1.7					(10) 2.0	
	3.4	3.2	3.2					3.9	
% Officers', Directors' Owners' Comp/Sales									
Net Sales ($)	1067066M	892136M	1088557M			11636M	32937M	184859M	859125M
Total Assets ($)	631023M	630519M	573809M			3916M	15424M	115571M	438898M

M = $ thousand   MM = $ million
See Pages 11 through 21 for Explanation of Ratios and Data

Current Data Sorted by Assets   Comparative Historical Data

Type of Statement								
		2	5			Unqualified	11	10
		4	3			Reviewed	4	8
	2	3	1			Compiled	4	8
	3	1				Tax Returns	2	3
1	2	5	5			Other	11	17
1	11 (4/1-9/30/06)		6	1	1		4/1/02-3/31/03	4/1/03-3/31/04
			30 (10/1/06-3/31/07)				ALL	ALL
0-500M	500M-2MM	2-10MM	10-50MM	50-100MM	100-250MM	NUMBER OF STATEMENTS	32	46
2	7	15	15	1	1			
%	%	%	%	%	%	ASSETS	%	%
		14.3	15.2			Cash & Equivalents	10.3	8.2
		22.5	24.3			Trade Receivables (net)	21.8	26.4
		23.5	26.6			Inventory	28.9	27.6
		2.7	2.9			All Other Current	2.8	3.1
		63.0	69.1			Total Current	63.9	65.3
		26.2	13.9			Fixed Assets (net)	28.3	21.9
		2.3	9.7			Intangibles (net)	4.0	9.1
		8.5	7.4			All Other Non-Current	3.9	3.8
		100.0	100.0			Total	100.0	100.0
						LIABILITIES		
		7.9	2.0			Notes Payable-Short Term	6.1	13.1
		5.9	1.1			Cur. Mat.-L.T.D.	4.7	4.4
		14.2	13.9			Trade Payables	9.6	12.7
		.0	.1			Income Taxes Payable	.4	.7
		7.9	8.5			All Other Current	14.1	9.2
		35.9	25.6			Total Current	34.8	40.2
		17.0	3.8			Long-Term Debt	13.5	14.2
		1.2	.8			Deferred Taxes	.5	.4
		11.0	11.2			All Other Non-Current	6.0	7.4
		34.9	58.5			Net Worth	45.2	37.7
		100.0	100.0			Total Liabilities & Net Worth	100.0	100.0
						INCOME DATA		
		100.0	100.0			Net Sales	100.0	100.0
		33.2	36.0			Gross Profit	35.2	33.3
		26.3	23.8			Operating Expenses	31.5	27.8
		6.9	12.1			Operating Profit	3.7	5.5
		.3	.6			All Other Expenses (net)	1.8	1.2
		6.6	11.6			Profit Before Taxes	1.9	4.3
						RATIOS		
		3.3	5.0				3.4	2.9
		1.6	3.5			Current	2.0	1.8
		1.2	1.9				1.6	1.2
		2.6	2.7				1.6	1.5
		.7	1.7			Quick	1.0	.8
		.5	1.0				.6	.5
		30 12.0	34 10.8				32 11.4	36 10.0
		36 10.2	46 7.9			Sales/Receivables	43 8.4	48 7.6
		43 8.4	59 6.2				58 6.3	63 5.8
		58 6.3	52 7.0				68 5.4	63 5.8
		63 5.8	90 4.1			Cost of Sales/Inventory	95 3.8	75 4.9
		76 4.8	127 2.9				119 3.1	106 3.4
		22 16.9	19 18.8				15 24.2	19 18.9
		33 11.2	30 12.4			Cost of Sales/Payables	27 13.4	31 12.0
		46 8.0	47 7.7				43 8.6	43 8.5
		3.6	2.4				4.2	4.1
		13.4	3.9			Sales/Working Capital	5.9	6.9
		27.8	5.3				10.4	20.0
		16.8	122.3				23.0	14.9
		(14) 5.2	(13) 9.7			EBIT/Interest	(28) 2.6	(42) 4.4
		1.9	3.4				-1.7	-1.3
							13.4	15.2
						Net Profit + Depr., Dep., Amort./Cur. Mat. L/T/D	(12) 2.6	(17) 3.5
							.4	1.7
		.2	.2				.3	.3
		.8	.3			Fixed/Worth	.6	.6
		1.9	.5				1.4	2.0
		.8	.3				.5	.9
		2.5	.8			Debt/Worth	1.3	1.6
		3.9	2.7				4.5	4.8
		65.2	70.2				39.4	44.1
		(12) 50.5	35.6			% Profit Before Taxes/Tangible Net Worth	(28) 17.7	(39) 16.2
		14.8	23.6				1.7	-12.4
		27.8	28.5				15.4	18.5
		15.8	21.6			% Profit Before Taxes/Total Assets	2.7	7.7
		2.3	9.7				-3.5	-2.1
		17.5	22.8				11.4	16.9
		11.4	13.2			Sales/Net Fixed Assets	6.1	9.7
		5.1	7.9				3.7	5.5
		2.6	2.4				2.5	2.3
		2.5	1.8			Sales/Total Assets	1.7	1.7
		1.7	1.4				1.3	1.3
		1.4	1.1				1.7	1.5
		(11) 2.1	(14) 1.4			% Depr., Dep., Amort./Sales	(26) 3.5	(40) 2.6
		3.2	3.6				5.3	4.0
								2.3
						% Officers', Directors' Owners' Comp/Sales		(11) 5.3
								6.9
1595M	32866M	186518M	608511M	79582M	274331M	Net Sales ($)	912468M	921081M
641M	10109M	83583M	359373M	99154M	145251M	Total Assets ($)	603061M	604699M

M = $ thousand   MM = $ million

See Pages 11 through 21 for Explanation of Ratios and Data

Comparative Historical Data / Current Data Sorted by Sales

	4/1/04-3/31/05 ALL	4/1/05-3/31/06 ALL	4/1/06-3/31/07 ALL		0-1MM	1-3MM	3-5MM	5-10MM	10-25MM	25MM & OVER
Type of Statement					11 (4/1-9/30/06)			30 (10/1/06-3/31/07)		
Unqualified	8	10	7						2	4
Reviewed	9	10	7			1		1	2	3
Compiled	5	2	6			1		1	2	2
Tax Returns	4	6	5			1	2	2		2
Other	12	16	16		1		2	5	5	2
NUMBER OF STATEMENTS	38	44	41		1	3	4	9	11	13
ASSETS	%	%	%		%	%	%	%	%	%
Cash & Equivalents	14.1	13.2	13.3						18.2	17.3
Trade Receivables (net)	20.7	25.4	25.1						23.8	23.2
Inventory	28.8	31.6	26.0						21.3	29.0
All Other Current	1.3	1.5	3.9						3.5	3.5
Total Current	64.9	71.7	68.3						66.8	72.9
Fixed Assets (net)	25.3	20.5	19.4						21.4	16.1
Intangibles (net)	4.0	3.3	5.6						.0	7.8
All Other Non-Current	5.8	4.5	6.6						11.8	3.2
Total	100.0	100.0	100.0						100.0	100.0
LIABILITIES										
Notes Payable-Short Term	14.6	7.6	7.7						2.9	3.1
Cur. Mat.-L.T.D.	4.7	2.9	4.0						3.3	1.9
Trade Payables	11.0	15.4	14.0						12.4	14.1
Income Taxes Payable	.4	.3	.1						.0	.1
All Other Current	9.6	9.9	9.5						6.7	9.2
Total Current	40.3	36.1	35.3						25.3	28.5
Long-Term Debt	16.7	15.2	15.6						14.5	4.3
Deferred Taxes	.6	.6	.8						1.8	.8
All Other Non-Current	4.9	9.3	12.0						17.9	3.4
Net Worth	37.5	38.8	36.3						40.5	62.9
Total Liabilties & Net Worth	100.0	100.0	100.0						100.0	100.0
INCOME DATA										
Net Sales	100.0	100.0	100.0						100.0	100.0
Gross Profit	35.8	34.7	37.5						32.5	38.0
Operating Expenses	30.4	28.8	29.3						22.2	26.1
Operating Profit	5.5	5.9	8.3						10.3	11.8
All Other Expenses (net)	1.4	.5	.6						.0	-.1
Profit Before Taxes	4.1	5.4	7.7						10.3	12.0
RATIOS										
Current	3.7	2.9	4.1						4.9	5.0
	1.9	2.0	2.6						2.7	3.5
	1.3	1.4	1.2						1.6	2.0
Quick	2.3	1.8	2.6						2.9	2.7
	1.1	1.0	1.1						2.5	1.7
	.5	.6	.6						.6	.9
Sales/Receivables	26 13.8	36 10.2	33 11.0						26 14.3	34 10.9
	39 9.3	44 8.3	41 8.9						38 9.5	40 9.2
	50 7.3	58 6.3	51 7.1						73 5.0	54 6.7
Cost of Sales/Inventory	54 6.7	55 6.6	52 7.0						26 14.3	59 6.2
	71 5.2	79 4.6	73 5.0						59 6.2	95 3.8
	109 3.4	110 3.3	96 3.8						81 4.5	113 3.2
Cost of Sales/Payables	16 23.2	19 19.1	22 16.8						22 16.9	22 16.9
	26 13.9	39 9.5	29 12.6						29 12.6	28 13.0
	42 8.7	55 6.6	46 7.9						40 9.0	40 9.2
Sales/Working Capital	4.1	4.2	3.3						3.3	2.4
	9.0	6.4	6.1						4.5	3.9
	17.7	11.2	22.0						13.4	9.6
EBIT/Interest	14.2	30.3	73.5							140.1
	(32) 4.9	(37) 7.4	(37) 7.0							(11) 75.5
	1.2	3.4	1.9							7.0
Net Profit + Depr., Dep., Amort./Cur. Mat. L/T/D										
Fixed/Worth	.2	.2	.2						.2	.1
	.5	.5	.4						.3	.3
	6.9	1.8	1.8						1.9	.5
Debt/Worth	.5	.6	.4						.8	.2
	1.1	1.4	1.2						1.3	.5
	15.8	8.0	5.1						2.9	2.0
% Profit Before Taxes/Tangible Net Worth	61.0	76.0	65.3						92.2	63.7
	(31) 35.5	(38) 31.1	(33) 43.2						(10) 43.0	39.2
	3.3	13.8	21.3						19.7	29.2
% Profit Before Taxes/Total Assets	23.1	18.1	30.5						27.8	30.5
	8.2	10.8	16.2						15.8	21.6
	.4	5.2	2.2						10.4	11.2
Sales/Net Fixed Assets	19.5	26.3	22.9						17.5	21.8
	11.0	13.1	13.2						13.1	16.0
	4.3	5.0	7.4						7.9	6.6
Sales/Total Assets	2.7	2.7	2.9						2.5	3.0
	2.0	2.1	2.1						2.1	1.9
	1.3	1.5	1.6						1.7	1.4
% Depr., Dep., Amort./Sales	1.2	1.5	1.2							1.1
	(30) 2.5	(38) 2.1	(31) 1.8							(11) 1.3
	4.7	3.4	3.2							4.1
% Officers', Directors' Owners' Comp/Sales	3.4	2.1	3.1							
	(12) 5.6	(15) 4.2	(14) 5.0							
	22.1	10.2	9.0							
Net Sales ($)	806272M	940879M	1183403M		140M	5387M	16946M	61393M	205152M	894385M
Total Assets ($)	398515M	567765M	698111M		161M	4290M	52898M	26471M	103047M	511244M

© RMA 2007

M = $ thousand   MM = $ million

See Pages 11 through 21 for Explanation of Ratios and Data

Current Data Sorted by Assets | Comparative Historical Data

0-500M	500M-2MM	2-10MM	10-50MM	50-100MM	100-250MM	Type of Statement	4/1/02-3/31/03 ALL	4/1/03-3/31/04 ALL
	2	18	18	4	3	Unqualified	49	53
	5	22	4			Reviewed	48	57
4	7	9	1			Compiled	30	33
2	9	3				Tax Returns	10	14
3	12	36	11	5	4	Other	77	64
	31 (4/1-9/30/06)		151 (10/1/06-3/31/07)					
9	35	88	34	9	7	NUMBER OF STATEMENTS	214	221
%	%	%	%	%	%	ASSETS	%	%
	8.4	6.4	6.9			Cash & Equivalents	10.3	9.7
	36.8	30.6	25.8			Trade Receivables (net)	26.9	30.4
	29.8	31.5	34.7			Inventory	28.5	28.9
	3.9	2.2	3.7			All Other Current	3.2	2.2
	78.9	70.8	71.1			Total Current	68.9	71.1
	14.6	21.2	18.6			Fixed Assets (net)	20.8	19.7
	1.4	2.5	5.7			Intangibles (net)	4.6	3.8
	5.2	5.6	4.7			All Other Non-Current	5.7	5.4
	100.0	100.0	100.0			Total	100.0	100.0
						LIABILITIES		
	10.9	13.0	11.5			Notes Payable-Short Term	11.4	11.2
	4.4	3.2	3.0			Cur. Mat.-L.T.D.	4.4	4.6
	20.4	19.0	13.1			Trade Payables	15.5	15.8
	.3	.2	.3			Income Taxes Payable	.4	.3
	14.2	9.1	9.2			All Other Current	12.1	13.0
	50.2	44.5	37.2			Total Current	43.7	44.9
	11.9	11.3	10.4			Long-Term Debt	12.6	11.5
	.1	.3	.4			Deferred Taxes	.4	.3
	3.2	3.6	4.9			All Other Non-Current	5.4	7.6
	34.6	40.3	47.0			Net Worth	37.8	35.5
	100.0	100.0	100.0			Total Liabilities & Net Worth	100.0	100.0
						INCOME DATA		
	100.0	100.0	100.0			Net Sales	100.0	100.0
	35.5	30.2	28.5			Gross Profit	31.2	31.9
	32.3	25.6	19.8			Operating Expenses	28.6	27.8
	3.2	4.7	8.8			Operating Profit	2.6	4.1
	.9	.7	.6			All Other Expenses (net)	1.7	1.0
	2.3	4.0	8.2			Profit Before Taxes	.9	3.1
						RATIOS		
	2.6	2.5	3.2			Current	3.0	3.0
	1.7	1.7	2.0				1.6	1.7
	1.2	1.2	1.4				1.2	1.2
	1.4	1.5	1.2			Quick	1.5	1.8
	.9	.8	.9				.8	.9
	.6	.6	.6				.5	.5
	31 11.7	39 9.4	43 8.5			Sales/Receivables	36 10.1	40 9.2
	50 7.3	48 7.6	55 6.7				50 7.4	52 7.0
	60 6.1	57 6.4	65 5.6				61 6.0	66 5.6
	31 11.9	46 8.0	86 4.2			Cost of Sales/Inventory	44 8.2	43 8.6
	64 5.7	72 5.1	106 3.4				81 4.5	82 4.5
	113 3.2	103 3.5	132 2.8				118 3.1	113 3.2
	17 21.7	23 16.2	23 15.6			Cost of Sales/Payables	19 19.1	22 16.2
	40 9.0	39 9.3	32 11.5				32 11.5	34 10.9
	60 6.1	55 6.7	54 6.8				54 6.7	53 6.9
	5.2	4.5	3.2			Sales/Working Capital	3.9	4.0
	13.7	8.0	5.7				7.9	7.3
	31.7	29.0	9.6				21.2	18.5
	12.7	15.0	21.3			EBIT/Interest	7.7	11.4
	(27) 4.8	(83) 4.7	(31) 6.6				(192) 2.8	(191) 3.7
	2.2	1.9	3.3				-.3	.9
		8.0	11.1			Net Profit + Depr., Dep., Amort./Cur. Mat. L/T/D	4.6	6.1
		(23) 3.9	(12) 3.3				(61) 1.5	(69) 2.1
		1.6	1.4				.4	.7
	.0	.2	.2			Fixed/Worth	.3	.2
	.1	.5	.3				.6	.5
	1.7	1.3	.8				1.5	1.1
	.8	.7	.7			Debt/Worth	.5	.7
	2.4	1.5	1.6				1.8	1.6
	9.7	4.7	2.3				5.2	4.0
	74.6	47.2	56.1			% Profit Before Taxes/Tangible Net Worth	28.3	45.7
	(31) 32.1	(81) 21.7	(32) 30.4				(186) 12.3	(194) 14.8
	5.5	4.2	15.1				-2.3	.8
	18.1	14.7	24.3			% Profit Before Taxes/Total Assets	11.5	13.6
	6.2	7.1	11.2				3.5	5.2
	.4	1.2	6.0				-3.3	-.3
	215.4	23.2	19.8			Sales/Net Fixed Assets	25.5	30.7
	63.6	14.1	10.7				10.2	11.5
	11.2	6.9	6.5				5.0	6.2
	3.6	2.8	2.1			Sales/Total Assets	2.5	2.5
	2.6	2.1	1.8				1.9	2.0
	1.9	1.7	1.3				1.3	1.5
	.2	.9	1.1			% Depr., Dep., Amort./Sales	1.4	1.0
	(24) 1.0	(74) 1.5	(32) 1.8				(178) 2.5	(189) 2.0
	2.8	2.3	2.6				4.5	3.3
	2.4	1.9				% Officers', Directors' Owners' Comp/Sales	3.1	3.3
	(17) 5.9	(25) 5.3					(61) 4.8	(61) 6.2
	9.6	9.3					11.3	9.2
8013M	130343M	988375M	1110427M	727497M	1355777M	Net Sales ($)	7214947M	5510992M
3167M	44057M	412582M	670780M	562037M	1258317M	Total Assets ($)	4137853M	3529886M

© RMA 2007

M = $ thousand   MM = $ million
See Pages 11 through 21 for Explanation of Ratios and Data

Comparative Historical Data | Current Data Sorted by Sales

	4/1/04-3/31/05 ALL	4/1/05-3/31/06 ALL	4/1/06-3/31/07 ALL	0-1MM	1-3MM	3-5MM	5-10MM	10-25MM	25MM & OVER
					31 (4/1-9/30/06)		151 (10/1/06-3/31/07)		
Type of Statement									
Unqualified	62	33	45			5	4	18	18
Reviewed	46	32	31		3	8	6	10	4
Compiled	32	29	21	5	2	4	4	6	
Tax Returns	21	12	14		9	3	2		
Other	48	78	71	4	4	4	20	22	16
NUMBER OF STATEMENTS	209	184	182	9	19	24	36	56	38
ASSETS	%	%	%	%	%	%	%	%	%
Cash & Equivalents	10.5	10.8	8.1		7.1	9.0	8.3	5.2	10.5
Trade Receivables (net)	29.1	30.5	30.3		29.2	30.7	33.1	31.6	26.7
Inventory	29.2	28.7	29.9		30.3	29.1	30.2	31.4	30.3
All Other Current	2.3	2.4	3.3		3.7	1.3	3.5	2.9	2.9
Total Current	71.1	72.4	71.6		70.3	70.1	75.1	71.1	70.3
Fixed Assets (net)	17.9	18.1	18.6		22.8	19.7	17.6	20.1	16.1
Intangibles (net)	4.1	4.0	4.5		1.2	5.7	1.6	2.9	10.6
All Other Non-Current	6.9	5.6	5.2		5.6	4.4	5.8	5.9	3.0
Total	100.0	100.0	100.0		100.0	100.0	100.0	100.0	100.0
LIABILITIES									
Notes Payable-Short Term	13.5	11.9	11.6		10.6	13.7	12.0	12.5	8.2
Cur. Mat.-L.T.D.	3.1	3.1	3.3		4.4	4.3	3.8	2.8	2.4
Trade Payables	15.0	14.7	17.0		14.1	16.9	20.5	20.3	12.0
Income Taxes Payable	.4	.4	.3		.1	.2	.3	.2	.6
All Other Current	9.8	9.5	10.3		15.0	10.7	8.7	9.7	10.5
Total Current	41.8	39.6	42.5		44.1	45.7	45.2	45.5	33.8
Long-Term Debt	11.1	10.5	11.7		16.7	14.2	11.2	8.9	11.8
Deferred Taxes	.4	.5	.3		.0	.2	.2	.4	.6
All Other Non-Current	8.2	6.8	4.6		6.3	4.7	4.5	3.5	5.8
Net Worth	38.6	42.5	40.9		32.8	35.2	38.8	41.7	48.0
Total Liabilities & Net Worth	100.0	100.0	100.0		100.0	100.0	100.0	100.0	100.0
INCOME DATA									
Net Sales	100.0	100.0	100.0		100.0	100.0	100.0	100.0	100.0
Gross Profit	33.5	32.5	32.7		35.9	35.4	36.3	26.0	32.4
Operating Expenses	28.2	27.0	26.9		31.1	32.5	31.0	21.2	21.7
Operating Profit	5.2	5.5	5.8		4.8	2.9	5.3	4.8	10.7
All Other Expenses (net)	.6	.9	.8		1.6	.7	.6	.6	.9
Profit Before Taxes	4.7	4.6	5.0		3.2	2.2	4.7	4.2	9.8
RATIOS									
Current	3.3	3.1	2.8		3.3	2.3	3.4	2.4	3.1
	2.0	1.8	1.8		1.9	1.7	1.7	1.6	2.1
	1.3	1.3	1.2		1.0	1.0	1.2	1.2	1.6
Quick	1.8	1.9	1.6		1.9	1.4	1.7	1.3	1.7
	1.1	1.0	.9		1.0	.9	.7	.8	.9
	.6	.7	.6		.3	.6	.6	.5	.7
Sales/Receivables	35 10.3	42 8.6	39 9.4		34 10.8	45 8.2	33 11.2	41 9.0	40 9.2
	48 7.6	52 7.1	50 7.3		43 8.6	51 7.2	46 7.9	49 7.5	53 6.9
	63 5.8	63 5.8	62 5.9		56 6.5	65 5.6	60 6.1	64 5.7	62 5.9
Cost of Sales/Inventory	42 8.7	42 8.7	45 8.1		38 9.6	38 9.6	36 10.1	45 8.0	71 5.1
	75 4.8	78 4.7	79 4.6		78 4.7	86 4.2	67 5.5	73 5.0	99 3.7
	107 3.4	111 3.3	114 3.2		130 2.8	135 2.7	106 3.4	110 3.3	119 3.1
Cost of Sales/Payables	18 20.2	22 16.6	21 17.4		16 23.3	18 20.6	20 18.5	27 13.5	24 15.3
	33 11.0	32 11.5	36 10.1		30 12.3	49 7.5	41 9.0	39 9.4	32 11.5
	49 7.4	45 8.1	55 6.6		50 7.2	64 5.7	58 6.3	57 6.4	40 9.2
Sales/Working Capital	4.1	3.8	4.3		4.3	4.2	4.3	5.2	3.3
	6.7	7.1	6.8		7.8	7.3	10.9	8.2	5.4
	14.1	13.3	18.4		171.8	NM	21.6	28.3	6.6
EBIT/Interest	20.5	18.5	16.9		13.9	5.8	9.0	16.8	27.9
	(185) 8.1	(163) 6.2	(161) 4.9		(17) 5.1	(19) 3.6	(31) 5.4	(52) 4.6	(35) 9.0
	2.4	1.7	2.0		2.6	1.3	2.0	2.1	3.7
Net Profit + Depr., Dep., Amort./Cur. Mat. L/T/D	8.5	7.2	7.9					8.0	9.7
	(58) 4.5	(53) 2.9	(46) 3.3					(19) 5.6	(14) 3.2
	1.8	1.7	1.6					2.4	1.9
Fixed/Worth	.2	.2	.2		.1	.1	.2	.2	.2
	.4	.4	.4		.3	.6	.4	.4	.4
	.8	.8	1.2		6.1	1.8	1.1	1.2	.8
Debt/Worth	.5	.6	.7		.6	.6	.7	.7	.6
	1.4	1.5	1.6		3.2	1.9	1.5	1.6	1.6
	3.5	3.3	4.8		22.2	19.9	4.8	2.7	2.6
% Profit Before Taxes/Tangible Net Worth	41.5	42.9	49.5		119.5	32.1	57.5	47.2	61.2
	(184) 21.6	(170) 19.0	(162) 26.1	(16)	34.5	(20) 14.3	(32) 27.9	(53) 23.2	(33) 32.4
	7.4	4.9	6.5		6.6	3.4	6.4	6.9	14.6
% Profit Before Taxes/Total Assets	16.7	15.6	16.7		14.8	10.5	20.9	15.3	27.2
	9.2	7.7	8.2		8.6	4.3	10.7	6.4	11.9
	2.8	1.9	1.5		1.5	.5	1.1	2.7	6.7
Sales/Net Fixed Assets	44.3	29.4	28.3		134.5	118.7	26.9	26.0	20.3
	15.0	13.3	14.8		15.4	21.4	14.4	14.8	12.0
	7.7	8.3	6.9		4.0	4.4	9.8	6.8	7.9
Sales/Total Assets	2.7	2.6	2.6		2.8	2.5	3.2	2.8	2.2
	2.1	2.1	2.0		2.0	2.0	2.5	2.1	1.8
	1.4	1.6	1.6		1.4	1.6	1.6	1.7	1.4
% Depr., Dep., Amort./Sales	1.0	.9	.9		.7	.4	.7	.8	1.0
	(171) 1.9	(146) 1.8	(148) 1.6	(13)	1.6	(19) 1.3	(28) 1.4	(49) 1.5	(35) 1.6
	3.0	2.9	2.6		3.7	1.8	2.6	2.5	2.6
% Officers', Directors' Owners' Comp/Sales	2.3	2.1	2.3		2.3	2.3			
	(56) 5.0	(52) 5.1	(51) 6.1		(12) 3.4	(13) 8.1			
	8.9	9.0	11.0		6.5	14.3			
Net Sales ($)	6056976M	5769763M	4320432M	6050M	38199M	99718M	265434M	890235M	3020796M
Total Assets ($)	4104474M	3621770M	2950940M	4261M	19269M	60705M	119759M	525315M	2221631M

M = $ thousand   MM = $ million
See Pages 11 through 21 for Explanation of Ratios and Data

Current Data Sorted by Assets

Comparative Historical Data

0-500M	500M-2MM	2-10MM	10-50MM	50-100MM	100-250MM	Type of Statement	4/1/02-3/31/03	4/1/03-3/31/04
1		4	9	2	6	Unqualified	15	13
		3	1			Reviewed	2	2
1	1	1				Compiled		1
		1				Tax Returns	4	5
	2	3	8	3	7	Other	13	18
	11 (4/1-9/30/06)		42 (10/1/06-3/31/07)				ALL	ALL
2	3	12	18	5	13	NUMBER OF STATEMENTS	34	39
%	%	%	%	%	%	ASSETS	%	%
		8.6	10.5		28.9	Cash & Equivalents	16.0	17.7
		27.4	18.2		18.6	Trade Receivables (net)	24.6	25.2
		32.2	24.6		13.7	Inventory	20.0	22.2
		3.3	2.9		4.2	All Other Current	5.1	4.9
		71.4	56.2		65.3	Total Current	65.6	70.0
		23.8	24.5		9.9	Fixed Assets (net)	18.0	16.9
		2.7	16.8		16.0	Intangibles (net)	9.1	7.9
		2.1	2.5		8.7	All Other Non-Current	7.2	5.2
		100.0	100.0		100.0	Total	100.0	100.0
						LIABILITIES		
		14.5	4.4		.1	Notes Payable-Short Term	8.8	10.9
		4.8	3.4		.5	Cur. Mat.-L.T.D.	2.8	1.1
		18.4	9.1		6.1	Trade Payables	11.0	9.6
		1.4	.1		.6	Income Taxes Payable	.3	.5
		8.3	8.0		13.4	All Other Current	13.3	13.2
		47.4	25.0		20.6	Total Current	36.2	35.3
		11.7	13.2		5.0	Long-Term Debt	9.2	8.8
		.2	.3		1.1	Deferred Taxes	.3	.4
		6.6	4.8		1.9	All Other Non-Current	5.8	4.6
		34.1	56.7		71.4	Net Worth	48.5	50.9
		100.0	100.0		100.0	Total Liabilities & Net Worth	100.0	100.0
						INCOME DATA		
		100.0	100.0		100.0	Net Sales	100.0	100.0
		45.5	45.2		55.4	Gross Profit	48.3	50.8
		39.8	43.0		42.0	Operating Expenses	44.5	43.1
		5.7	2.2		13.4	Operating Profit	3.9	7.8
		2.0	2.3		.2	All Other Expenses (net)	.1	1.0
		3.7	-.1		13.2	Profit Before Taxes	3.8	6.8
						RATIOS		
		3.8	3.7		5.8		4.3	4.7
		1.5	2.5		4.2	Current	2.6	2.7
		1.1	1.8		2.8		1.6	1.5
		1.6	1.7		5.0		2.5	3.2
		1.0	1.4		2.4	Quick	1.7	1.6
		.4	.8		1.7		.9	.8
		25 14.5	37 9.9		47 7.8		43 8.4	32 11.5
		46 7.9	45 8.1		59 6.2	Sales/Receivables	56 6.5	53 6.9
		75 4.9	62 5.9		84 4.3		77 4.7	76 4.8
		62 5.9	77 4.8		80 4.6		47 7.8	69 5.3
		98 3.7	125 2.9		107 3.4	Cost of Sales/Inventory	96 3.8	97 3.8
		135 2.7	169 2.2		155 2.4		143 2.6	143 2.6
		16 23.4	26 13.8		29 12.6		31 11.8	17 21.0
		44 8.2	40 9.0		50 7.4	Cost of Sales/Payables	41 8.9	36 10.2
		93 3.9	63 5.8		67 5.4		58 6.2	46 8.0
		3.8	2.7		1.4		2.2	2.3
		14.8	3.3		2.4	Sales/Working Capital	3.6	4.1
		33.2	6.7		3.7		11.3	9.2
		18.4	12.7				45.8	75.8
		2.7	(15) 2.3			EBIT/Interest	(30) 8.4	(29) 13.9
		.5	-2.6				-2.5	1.1
						Net Profit + Depr., Dep., Amort./Cur. Mat. L/T/D	74.4	41.6
							(12) 4.2	(15) 10.8
							1.2	2.0
		.2	.3		.1		.1	.2
		.5	.4		.2	Fixed/Worth	.3	.4
		6.9	.7		.4		.6	.6
		.5	.6		.2		.3	.3
		2.4	.7		.5	Debt/Worth	.6	.6
		27.5	1.3		1.9		1.4	2.1
		75.6	20.1		43.6	% Profit Before Taxes/Tangible Net Worth	28.9	63.2
		(11) 33.0	(16) 7.5		24.1		(28) 14.8	(36) 17.9
		-6.6	-19.2		12.7		-5.5	1.2
		24.4	7.9		19.3	% Profit Before Taxes/Total Assets	16.9	19.9
		9.7	4.1		7.6		8.1	11.7
		-2.3	-13.5		6.2		-3.6	.4
		30.6	14.9		19.9		16.1	19.3
		11.1	8.2		11.7	Sales/Net Fixed Assets	10.9	10.9
		5.4	3.7		7.9		6.3	6.5
		2.5	1.8		1.4		2.2	2.1
		2.1	1.4		.9	Sales/Total Assets	1.4	1.7
		1.3	.8		.7		.9	1.2
		.6	1.8		1.1		1.6	1.5
		(11) 2.1	(14) 2.8		(11) 2.0	% Depr., Dep., Amort./Sales	(26) 2.7	(31) 2.3
		5.0	5.6		4.2		3.8	3.9
						% Officers', Directors' Owners' Comp/Sales		
1432M	13227M	89232M	527703M	281785M	2182969M	Net Sales ($)	1175576M	1931541M
738M	4119M	47083M	385805M	374320M	2116883M	Total Assets ($)	995793M	1593282M

M = $ thousand   MM = $ million
See Pages 11 through 21 for Explanation of Ratios and Data

Comparative Historical Data | Current Data Sorted by Sales

	4/1/04-3/31/05 ALL	4/1/05-3/31/06 ALL	4/1/06-3/31/07 ALL	0-1MM	1-3MM	3-5MM	5-10MM	10-25MM	25MM & OVER
					11 (4/1-9/30/06)			42 (10/1/06-3/31/07)	
Type of Statement									
Unqualified	11	13	22	1		3	1	5	12
Reviewed	4	2	4			1		2	1
Compiled	4	5	3		1	1	1	1	
Tax Returns	7	5	1			1			
Other	19	25	23			1	5	2	15
NUMBER OF STATEMENTS	45	50	53	1	1	7	7	10	27
ASSETS	%	%	%	%	%	%	%	%	%
Cash & Equivalents	21.1	19.0	15.4					10.8	21.3
Trade Receivables (net)	24.8	25.3	20.9					17.6	19.3
Inventory	24.1	21.0	22.8					29.3	18.5
All Other Current	2.3	2.5	3.6					2.8	4.5
Total Current	72.2	67.9	62.7					60.5	63.6
Fixed Assets (net)	13.9	20.5	19.4					23.8	14.5
Intangibles (net)	7.5	7.9	13.2					13.5	15.0
All Other Non-Current	6.4	3.6	4.7					2.2	6.9
Total	100.0	100.0	100.0					100.0	100.0
LIABILITIES									
Notes Payable-Short Term	10.8	8.8	6.3					4.7	2.3
Cur. Mat.-L.T.D.	6.8	1.7	2.5					4.0	1.1
Trade Payables	14.5	12.2	10.2					11.1	8.0
Income Taxes Payable	.5	1.9	.5					1.7	.3
All Other Current	16.8	12.9	10.1					7.2	11.5
Total Current	49.5	37.4	29.6					28.7	23.2
Long-Term Debt	6.6	12.7	10.6					11.2	5.5
Deferred Taxes	.3	.7	.5					.5	.8
All Other Non-Current	12.0	8.3	3.7					7.3	1.6
Net Worth	31.6	40.8	55.6					52.4	68.9
Total Liabilties & Net Worth	100.0	100.0	100.0					100.0	100.0
INCOME DATA									
Net Sales	100.0	100.0	100.0					100.0	100.0
Gross Profit	48.1	50.9	49.1					44.9	51.6
Operating Expenses	40.2	45.0	42.4					39.4	45.0
Operating Profit	7.9	5.8	6.7					5.6	6.6
All Other Expenses (net)	.9	.5	1.6					3.2	.1
Profit Before Taxes	7.0	5.4	5.1					2.3	6.5
RATIOS									
Current	3.3	3.8	4.2					4.3	4.9
	2.6	2.0	2.7					3.5	2.7
	1.2	1.2	1.7					1.5	2.2
Quick	2.5	2.7	2.3					1.9	3.6
	1.3	1.2	1.5					1.5	1.8
	.5	.8	.8					.8	.8
Sales/Receivables	37 9.9	38 9.6	35 10.5					28 13.1	45 8.2
	50 7.4	54 6.8	50 7.3					41 8.8	56 6.5
	60 6.1	69 5.3	73 5.0					55 6.7	74 5.0
Cost of Sales/Inventory	59 6.2	36 10.1	77 4.8					88 4.1	79 4.6
	84 4.3	96 3.8	114 3.2					141 2.6	123 3.0
	131 2.8	144 2.5	158 2.3					170 2.1	168 2.2
Cost of Sales/Payables	21 17.8	30 12.1	27 13.4					18 20.4	35 10.5
	44 8.3	49 7.4	43 8.5					39 9.4	44 8.3
	65 5.7	65 5.6	72 5.1					64 5.7	59 6.1
Sales/Working Capital	2.9	2.5	2.2					2.6	1.5
	4.8	6.5	3.3					3.0	3.0
	27.9	23.7	8.9					11.6	4.3
EBIT/Interest	19.8	17.9	23.5						46.5
	(37) 8.2	(44) 9.7	(43) 4.0						(19) 8.8
	.6	1.5	.5						1.8
Net Profit + Depr., Dep., Amort./Cur. Mat. L/T/D	23.6	20.3	22.8						
	(11) 8.3	(11) 5.0	(14) 4.1						
	1.8	2.3	-.4						
Fixed/Worth	.1	.1	.2					.2	.1
	.3	.4	.4					.4	.3
	.9	.9	.6					NM	.4
Debt/Worth	.5	.6	.4					.2	.2
	1.1	1.0	.8					.8	.6
	8.2	4.6	2.8					NM	1.1
% Profit Before Taxes/Tangible Net Worth	84.4	42.1	34.4						27.5
	(39) 33.5	(42) 18.0	(50) 17.2						16.5
	2.8	3.9	2.3						6.0
% Profit Before Taxes/Total Assets	23.4	22.6	12.6					21.6	12.4
	10.1	7.8	7.1					5.7	7.4
	.9	.4	.3					-3.8	3.6
Sales/Net Fixed Assets	39.7	21.5	19.5					27.3	17.5
	16.5	12.3	9.3					9.3	9.6
	9.0	6.2	4.5					3.0	5.2
Sales/Total Assets	2.9	2.5	2.1					2.2	1.5
	1.7	1.7	1.3					1.5	1.0
	1.2	1.1	.8					.9	.7
% Depr., Dep., Amort./Sales	1.6	1.4	1.6						1.8
	(35) 2.2	(41) 2.3	(45) 2.9					(23)	2.9
	4.4	4.8	4.9						4.2
% Officers', Directors' Owners' Comp/Sales	1.9	1.9							
	(10) 2.7	(18) 5.3							
	5.2	8.7							
Net Sales ($)	1833963M	2419942M	3096348M	263M	1169M	28792M	53784M	165877M	2846463M
Total Assets ($)	1337607M	2052873M	2928948M	375M	363M	16290M	61785M	149199M	2700936M

M = $ thousand   MM = $ million
See Pages 11 through 21 for Explanation of Ratios and Data

Current Data Sorted by Assets | Comparative Historical Data

Type of Statement

0-500M	500M-2MM	2-10MM	10-50MM	50-100MM	100-250MM	Type of Statement	4/1/02-3/31/03 ALL	4/1/03-3/31/04 ALL
1		2	11	5	4	Unqualified	14	19
	2	7				Reviewed	9	8
	2	5				Compiled	5	8
						Tax Returns	2	1
		5	2	3	4	Other	22	9
	18 (4/1-9/30/06)		35 (10/1/06-3/31/07)					
1	4	19	13	8	8	NUMBER OF STATEMENTS	52	45

Financial Data

0-500M %	500M-2MM %	2-10MM %	10-50MM %	50-100MM %	100-250MM %		4/1/02-3/31/03 ALL %	4/1/03-3/31/04 ALL %
						ASSETS		
		11.7	21.3			Cash & Equivalents	13.2	13.0
		29.7	22.0			Trade Receivables (net)	30.2	28.6
		32.1	20.8			Inventory	23.1	25.6
		2.6	14.5			All Other Current	7.1	7.1
		76.2	78.6			Total Current	73.6	74.4
		15.1	14.6			Fixed Assets (net)	14.0	17.7
		5.4	.9			Intangibles (net)	6.4	2.2
		3.3	5.9			All Other Non-Current	6.0	5.7
		100.0	100.0			Total	100.0	100.0
						LIABILITIES		
		9.5	3.7			Notes Payable-Short Term	8.9	5.8
		3.8	1.6			Cur. Mat.-L.T.D.	1.9	2.4
		12.9	9.6			Trade Payables	11.9	13.0
		1.0	1.2			Income Taxes Payable	.4	.9
		9.5	12.7			All Other Current	13.0	14.2
		36.6	28.9			Total Current	36.0	36.3
		8.2	5.0			Long-Term Debt	5.6	10.8
		.6	1.5			Deferred Taxes	.6	.8
		8.4	11.6			All Other Non-Current	2.9	5.2
		46.2	53.0			Net Worth	55.0	46.8
		100.0	100.0			Total Liabilties & Net Worth	100.0	100.0
						INCOME DATA		
		100.0	100.0			Net Sales	100.0	100.0
		36.6	37.0			Gross Profit	37.3	41.3
		26.3	27.9			Operating Expenses	29.4	33.3
		10.2	9.1			Operating Profit	7.9	8.0
		.8	1.6			All Other Expenses (net)	.6	.7
		9.5	7.4			Profit Before Taxes	7.3	7.4
						RATIOS		
		4.2	5.5			Current	4.9	3.7
		2.7	3.1				2.4	2.1
		1.2	1.8				1.5	1.4
		2.0	3.4			Quick	3.1	2.0
		1.1	1.6				1.3	.9
		.7	.9				.7	.7
		43 8.5	34 10.6			Sales/Receivables	41 8.9	40 9.2
		50 7.3	47 7.8				65 5.6	50 7.3
		65 5.6	75 4.9				79 4.6	82 4.5
		45 8.1	10 36.7			Cost of Sales/Inventory	29 12.6	18 19.8
		95 3.8	95 3.9				94 3.9	89 4.1
		168 2.2	136 2.7				156 2.3	145 2.5
		19 18.9	18 20.1			Cost of Sales/Payables	19 19.1	27 13.4
		28 13.0	27 13.6				33 10.9	35 10.3
		47 7.8	54 6.7				56 6.5	54 6.8
		2.6	1.7			Sales/Working Capital	2.4	2.7
		4.7	2.5				4.9	5.5
		12.0	5.7				10.0	11.8
		36.1	119.5			EBIT/Interest	44.8	43.5
		(17) 4.7	(11) 26.0				(37) 6.7	(39) 7.7
		.8	1.9				1.3	1.5
						Net Profit + Depr., Dep., Amort./Cur. Mat. L/T/D	10.3	6.2
							(18) 4.2	(15) 3.2
							2.4	.4
		.1	.1			Fixed/Worth	.1	.1
		.3	.2				.2	.3
		.6	.3				.6	1.1
		.4	.3			Debt/Worth	.3	.5
		1.1	.6				1.0	1.0
		2.7	1.4				2.1	3.1
		58.9	51.1			% Profit Before Taxes/Tangible Net Worth	42.2	53.6
		(17) 27.6	(12) 17.6				(47) 21.5	(40) 19.4
		1.5	8.4				3.9	9.3
		37.0	18.8			% Profit Before Taxes/Total Assets	20.0	25.0
		9.0	12.4				9.6	8.9
		-.1	3.5				1.2	2.9
		40.6	19.6			Sales/Net Fixed Assets	29.3	29.0
		24.7	14.1				13.2	12.9
		6.3	6.3				5.4	5.9
		3.0	1.8			Sales/Total Assets	2.2	2.5
		1.7	1.4				1.5	1.7
		1.5	1.1				1.1	1.2
		.7	1.2			% Depr., Dep., Amort./Sales	1.1	1.0
		(17) 1.5	1.9				(43) 2.0	(41) 1.8
		2.9	2.5				3.3	3.1
						% Officers', Directors' Owners' Comp/Sales	2.3	
							(14) 4.3	
							6.6	
7M	10088M	197675M	405001M	748926M	1415531M	Net Sales ($)	2824709M	1086677M
4M	5367M	91518M	258201M	613885M	1208779M	Total Assets ($)	2113812M	812774M

M = $ thousand   MM = $ million
See Pages 11 through 21 for Explanation of Ratios and Data

Comparative Historical Data | | Current Data Sorted by Sales

19	20	22	Type of Statement						
19	20	22	Unqualified	1			2	4	16
11	14	8	Reviewed				4	2	2
4	9	7	Compiled		2	1		1	3
3	1		Tax Returns						
13	19	16	Other		1	2	2	7	3
4/1/04-3/31/05 ALL	4/1/05-3/31/06 ALL	4/1/06-3/31/07 ALL		0-1MM	1-3MM 18 (4/1-9/30/06)	3-5MM	5-10MM	10-25MM 35 (10/1/06-3/31/07)	25MM & OVER
50	63	53	NUMBER OF STATEMENTS	1	3	3	8	14	24
%	%	%	ASSETS	%	%	%	%	%	%
13.6	12.4	13.7	Cash & Equivalents					18.5	10.5
26.6	23.8	26.3	Trade Receivables (net)					29.8	27.2
23.6	25.9	25.4	Inventory					31.6	20.1
5.4	5.8	6.3	All Other Current					4.5	9.5
69.2	68.0	71.7	Total Current					84.4	67.3
17.5	18.7	15.2	Fixed Assets (net)					10.8	15.9
7.8	7.2	7.6	Intangibles (net)					.6	12.3
5.6	6.2	5.4	All Other Non-Current					4.2	4.4
100.0	100.0	100.0	Total					100.0	100.0
			LIABILITIES						
5.0	6.4	6.8	Notes Payable-Short Term					10.5	3.8
2.3	1.9	2.5	Cur. Mat.-L.T.D.					2.1	1.5
10.9	12.1	10.7	Trade Payables					15.4	10.4
.8	.7	.8	Income Taxes Payable					.1	1.0
14.0	10.5	10.4	All Other Current					11.0	12.8
33.0	31.7	31.1	Total Current					39.1	29.6
10.3	8.1	11.3	Long-Term Debt					2.3	13.0
.7	.7	.7	Deferred Taxes					.0	1.2
7.4	9.9	9.6	All Other Non-Current					3.7	9.8
48.6	49.6	47.2	Net Worth					54.9	46.4
100.0	100.0	100.0	Total Liabilities & Net Worth					100.0	100.0
			INCOME DATA						
100.0	100.0	100.0	Net Sales					100.0	100.0
36.8	36.8	36.3	Gross Profit					38.6	33.0
27.3	28.9	27.8	Operating Expenses					28.7	26.4
9.5	7.8	8.5	Operating Profit					9.8	6.6
.8	.5	1.1	All Other Expenses (net)					.8	1.4
8.7	7.4	7.4	Profit Before Taxes					9.1	5.3
			RATIOS						
3.4	4.0	4.0	Current					4.3	3.6
2.3	2.5	2.6						2.3	2.3
1.3	1.4	1.5						1.6	1.5
2.0	2.1	2.4	Quick					3.1	1.8
1.3	1.2	1.2						1.4	1.2
.7	.7	.8						.7	.8
38 9.7	32 11.5	43 8.4	Sales/Receivables					29 12.7	52 7.0
51 7.1	50 7.4	57 6.4						47 7.8	69 5.3
67 5.5	66 5.5	78 4.7						60 6.1	92 4.0
31 11.8	34 10.6	39 9.3	Cost of Sales/Inventory					33 11.1	39 9.4
83 4.4	101 3.6	95 3.8						85 4.3	90 4.1
136 2.7	150 2.4	150 2.4						138 2.6	131 2.8
20 18.4	19 19.7	19 18.9	Cost of Sales/Payables					19 19.6	26 14.0
30 12.0	31 11.7	34 10.7						33 10.9	36 10.0
44 8.3	52 7.1	51 7.2						51 7.2	53 6.8
2.9	2.8	2.4	Sales/Working Capital					2.4	2.4
4.9	4.8	3.8						5.5	3.8
15.1	11.4	8.2						10.6	6.1
29.2	26.0	31.8	EBIT/Interest					42.0	25.5
(42) 7.2	(51) 12.3	(47) 7.4						(11) 20.8	(23) 10.8
3.9	1.4	1.3						1.9	1.4
9.6	15.5	21.3	Net Profit + Depr., Dep., Amort./Cur. Mat. L/T/D						28.5
(22) 3.4	(18) 5.0	(23) 6.4							(15) 7.2
2.0	1.8	1.3							1.3
.1	.1	.1	Fixed/Worth					.1	.2
.4	.3	.3						.2	.3
1.1	.7	.9						.3	1.5
.4	.4	.4	Debt/Worth					.4	.6
1.1	.8	1.2						.9	1.3
4.1	2.9	2.8						2.1	3.2
47.3	57.9	51.3	% Profit Before Taxes/Tangible Net Worth					54.1	42.3
(42) 25.5	(58) 27.3	(47) 19.7						21.2	(21) 15.5
13.5	11.8	4.1						4.1	4.3
21.3	27.2	20.4	% Profit Before Taxes/Total Assets					37.2	13.4
10.4	9.5	8.6						16.8	6.8
4.1	2.8	.5						2.0	-.7
32.5	20.3	24.8	Sales/Net Fixed Assets					46.0	15.7
11.2	9.2	11.4						23.8	9.0
5.5	5.6	6.4						13.4	6.4
2.7	2.2	2.0	Sales/Total Assets					3.1	1.7
1.7	1.5	1.5						2.3	1.3
1.1	1.0	1.2						1.4	.9
1.3	1.3	1.1	% Depr., Dep., Amort./Sales					.7	1.6
(41) 2.4	(57) 2.0	(49) 2.0						(13) 1.5	(23) 2.6
3.1	3.2	3.1						2.2	3.1
1.8	2.0		% Officers', Directors' Owners' Comp/Sales						
(15) 3.7	(13) 4.6								
11.0	9.9								
1434814M	2697050M	2777228M	Net Sales ($)	7M	6947M	11914M	54906M	222600M	2480854M
1122558M	2332820M	2177754M	Total Assets ($)	4M	3403M	8619M	38312M	124268M	2003148M

Current Data Sorted by Assets | Comparative Historical Data

0-500M	500M-2MM	2-10MM	10-50MM	50-100MM	100-250MM	Type of Statement	4/1/02-3/31/03 ALL	4/1/03-3/31/04 ALL
	1	4	3	1	2	Unqualified	10	10
	5	4				Reviewed	6	6
3	2	1				Compiled	5	11
2	2	2				Tax Returns	4	3
1	2	4	1		1	Other	10	8
	8 (4/1-9/30/06)		31 (10/1/06-3/31/07)					
3	8	16	8	1	3	NUMBER OF STATEMENTS	35	38
%	%	%	%	%	%	**ASSETS**	%	%
		17.4				Cash & Equivalents	12.2	12.2
		33.2				Trade Receivables (net)	29.3	28.7
		27.2				Inventory	20.6	18.3
		.1				All Other Current	5.1	4.5
		78.0				Total Current	67.2	63.7
		14.9				Fixed Assets (net)	16.6	22.5
		3.1				Intangibles (net)	9.7	8.4
		4.1				All Other Non-Current	6.5	5.4
		100.0				Total	100.0	100.0
						LIABILITIES		
		10.6				Notes Payable-Short Term	5.4	8.3
		4.8				Cur. Mat.-L.T.D.	3.2	4.4
		20.3				Trade Payables	13.9	11.5
		.0				Income Taxes Payable	.1	.2
		9.2				All Other Current	12.4	11.1
		44.8				Total Current	35.1	35.5
		5.7				Long-Term Debt	13.6	10.3
		.1				Deferred Taxes	.5	1.0
		8.6				All Other Non-Current	2.0	6.4
		40.7				Net Worth	48.8	46.9
		100.0				Total Liabilties & Net Worth	100.0	100.0
						INCOME DATA		
		100.0				Net Sales	100.0	100.0
		37.0				Gross Profit	38.3	42.6
		27.0				Operating Expenses	33.2	36.4
		10.0				Operating Profit	5.1	6.2
		.8				All Other Expenses (net)	.3	.8
		9.2				Profit Before Taxes	4.8	5.4
						RATIOS		
		3.5				Current	3.1	3.2
		1.6					1.6	1.8
		1.2					1.4	1.4
		1.9				Quick	1.9	2.0
		1.0					1.3	1.2
		.8					.8	.8
		38 9.6				Sales/Receivables	40 9.1	41 9.0
		56 6.5					52 7.0	55 6.6
		81 4.5					67 5.4	72 5.0
		36 10.2				Cost of Sales/Inventory	34 10.7	24 15.2
		63 5.7					67 5.5	56 6.5
		136 2.7					106 3.4	91 4.0
		22 16.8				Cost of Sales/Payables	18 20.0	17 21.2
		31 11.7					24 15.2	27 13.3
		77 4.7					48 7.5	48 7.7
		4.0				Sales/Working Capital	3.7	3.9
		8.7					7.9	6.5
		17.3					17.2	12.4
		29.9				EBIT/Interest	12.9	20.6
		(14) 14.0					(31) 3.5	(32) 5.4
		4.6					-.7	-.7
						Net Profit + Depr., Dep., Amort./Cur. Mat. L/T/D		
		.1				Fixed/Worth	.2	.2
		.3					.3	.4
		1.1					.8	1.5
		.7				Debt/Worth	.5	.5
		2.1					1.5	1.1
		3.5					3.8	4.3
		83.4				% Profit Before Taxes/Tangible Net Worth	45.8	50.8
		57.8					(32) 9.6	(35) 20.0
		24.4					-3.2	4.5
		29.7				% Profit Before Taxes/Total Assets	16.8	15.7
		17.7					5.2	7.0
		6.2					-.1	-.9
		66.3				Sales/Net Fixed Assets	40.6	23.5
		21.0					17.4	8.9
		10.4					6.8	5.4
		2.5				Sales/Total Assets	2.3	2.2
		2.0					1.7	1.7
		1.6					1.5	1.5
		.6				% Depr., Dep., Amort./Sales	1.4	1.0
		(13) .9					(29) 2.2	(33) 2.3
		2.1					4.3	3.8
						% Officers', Directors' Owners' Comp/Sales	2.5	3.6
							(19) 5.7	(14) 7.2
							9.0	13.1
7673M	29907M	163232M	298514M	60871M	826484M	Net Sales ($)	602156M	963897M
776M	10272M	78874M	177140M	50659M	526454M	Total Assets ($)	383987M	629952M

M = $ thousand   MM = $ million
See Pages 11 through 21 for Explanation of Ratios and Data

Comparative Historical Data / Current Data Sorted by Sales

			Type of Statement	0-1MM	1-3MM	3-5MM	5-10MM	10-25MM	25MM & OVER
12	11	11	Unqualified		1		2	3	5
8	13	9	Reviewed				2	6	1
3	4	4	Compiled	2	1			1	
4	1	6	Tax Returns	3			3		
5	7	9	Other	1	1		3	2	2
4/1/04- 3/31/05 ALL	4/1/05- 3/31/06 ALL	4/1/06- 3/31/07 ALL		8 (4/1-9/30/06)			31 (10/1/06-3/31/07)		
32	36	39	NUMBER OF STATEMENTS	7	2		10	12	8
%	%	%	ASSETS	%	%	%	%	%	%
9.4	9.4	14.7	Cash & Equivalents				20.3	11.4	
36.5	35.5	35.2	Trade Receivables (net)	D			38.3	28.9	
17.9	23.2	24.6	Inventory	A			25.1	28.9	
2.3	4.9	2.8	All Other Current	T			.2	1.2	
66.1	73.0	77.2	Total Current	A			83.8	70.3	
22.6	16.9	15.0	Fixed Assets (net)				12.5	19.6	
7.3	4.5	3.6	Intangibles (net)	N			.4	3.5	
4.0	5.7	4.2	All Other Non-Current	O			3.3	6.5	
100.0	100.0	100.0	Total	T			100.0	100.0	
			LIABILITIES	A					
22.8	13.8	10.6	Notes Payable-Short Term	V			15.5	8.2	
3.9	4.1	2.8	Cur. Mat.-L.T.D.	A			3.9	3.9	
15.5	14.0	16.0	Trade Payables	I			17.1	13.0	
.5	.1	.2	Income Taxes Payable	L			.0	.0	
13.5	13.7	13.7	All Other Current	A			7.9	10.9	
56.2	45.7	43.2	Total Current	B			44.4	36.0	
13.9	13.3	11.2	Long-Term Debt	L			14.1	7.9	
.6	.8	.4	Deferred Taxes	E			.0	.9	
4.5	4.7	5.0	All Other Non-Current				9.2	8.4	
24.8	35.5	40.1	Net Worth				32.4	46.8	
100.0	100.0	100.0	Total Liabilities & Net Worth				100.0	100.0	
			INCOME DATA						
100.0	100.0	100.0	Net Sales				100.0	100.0	
36.4	31.9	36.1	Gross Profit				38.6	35.7	
29.8	27.4	29.5	Operating Expenses				31.1	26.9	
6.6	4.6	6.6	Operating Profit				7.6	8.8	
.8	.3	.7	All Other Expenses (net)				.6	1.1	
5.8	4.2	5.8	Profit Before Taxes				6.9	7.7	
			RATIOS						
2.3	2.2	3.4	Current				5.9	3.5	
1.4	1.4	1.7					1.6	1.8	
.9	1.2	1.3					1.3	1.3	
1.4	1.3	1.8	Quick				3.7	1.9	
1.0	.9	1.0					1.2	.9	
.6	.6	.8					.8	.7	
44 8.3	43 8.6	49 7.4	Sales/Receivables				33 11.1	40 9.0	
57 6.4	55 6.6	56 6.6					55 6.6	57 6.4	
65 5.6	69 5.3	65 5.6					70 5.2	61 6.0	
6 62.6	27 13.4	34 10.8	Cost of Sales/Inventory				0 UND	53 7.0	
50 7.3	55 6.6	64 5.7					43 8.5	68 5.3	
93 3.9	112 3.3	114 3.2					159 2.3	126 2.9	
18 20.0	21 17.1	19 19.6	Cost of Sales/Payables				14 25.3	22 16.8	
35 10.5	33 11.1	29 12.4					31 11.8	27 13.3	
57 6.4	52 7.1	54 6.8					58 6.3	45 8.1	
5.7	4.7	3.9	Sales/Working Capital				4.9	3.6	
10.8	8.6	7.5					9.0	7.6	
NM	18.1	16.9					68.8	15.3	
13.1	8.4	20.0	EBIT/Interest				39.2	54.5	
(30) 6.0	(32) 2.9	(34) 8.0					12.1	(10) 4.7	
2.4	1.7	1.5					4.3	1.3	
	2.9	5.9	Net Profit + Depr., Dep., Amort./Cur. Mat. L/T/D						
	(11) 1.9	(12) 2.9							
	1.0	1.4							
.3	.2	.2	Fixed/Worth				.2	.1	
1.1	.5	.3					.3	.4	
38.5	1.4	.7					1.7	1.1	
1.2	.9	.6	Debt/Worth				1.4	.5	
3.6	2.8	1.7					2.2	1.9	
60.6	5.1	3.7					5.5	3.4	
109.9	64.7	79.8	% Profit Before Taxes/Tangible Net Worth				292.9	63.8	
(26) 48.6	(33) 21.2	(37) 31.4					77.7	33.6	
15.6	3.4	8.3					10.3	6.9	
19.7	15.8	20.2	% Profit Before Taxes/Total Assets				36.6	21.2	
11.2	6.5	11.7					20.0	12.0	
2.4	1.6	1.6					12.4	1.5	
50.6	44.7	59.9	Sales/Net Fixed Assets				148.8	46.0	
11.4	19.4	21.6					27.9	15.1	
5.2	6.9	7.9					14.6	4.9	
2.8	2.4	3.5	Sales/Total Assets				4.2	2.4	
2.3	1.9	2.1					2.9	2.0	
1.4	1.3	1.6					1.7	1.5	
.6	.6	.5	% Depr., Dep., Amort./Sales					.8	
(27) 2.1	(34) 1.4	(34) 1.2						(11) 1.6	
2.9	2.5	3.0						4.4	
2.9	2.1	2.2	% Officers', Directors' Owners' Comp/Sales						
(13) 3.6	(13) 3.1	(13) 4.9							
8.6	8.3	7.3							
834319M	1046496M	1386681M	Net Sales ($)	15620M	6647M		70147M	190826M	1103441M
537868M	734548M	844175M	Total Assets ($)	7843M	2772M		27935M	104144M	701481M

© RMA 2007

M = $ thousand   MM = $ million
See Pages 11 through 21 for Explanation of Ratios and Data

Current Data Sorted by Assets · Comparative Historical Data

	1	8	12	3	2	Type of Statement		
1	6	28	6			Unqualified	41	34
2	8	9	1	3		Reviewed	29	42
3	3	2				Compiled	19	20
						Tax Returns	5	4
	9	19	14	6	8	Other	28	41
	37 (4/1-9/30/06)		114 (10/1/06-3/31/07)				4/1/02-3/31/03	4/1/03-3/31/04
0-500M	500M-2MM	2-10MM	10-50MM	50-100MM	100-250MM		ALL	ALL
6	27	66	33	9	10	NUMBER OF STATEMENTS	122	141
%	%	%	%	%	%	ASSETS	%	%
	9.2	8.8	9.9		12.3	Cash & Equivalents	10.4	10.7
	36.6	31.5	27.7		16.8	Trade Receivables (net)	31.7	31.1
	32.7	27.9	27.3		19.2	Inventory	25.7	25.4
	1.5	5.3	3.0		3.2	All Other Current	3.5	2.2
	79.9	73.5	67.9		51.6	Total Current	71.2	69.5
	12.9	15.2	19.8		10.1	Fixed Assets (net)	19.9	17.0
	1.1	4.3	5.1		34.6	Intangibles (net)	4.9	7.3
	6.1	7.0	7.2		3.7	All Other Non-Current	4.0	6.2
	100.0	100.0	100.0		100.0	Total	100.0	100.0
						LIABILITIES		
	14.2	11.6	8.5		2.0	Notes Payable-Short Term	10.7	12.2
	1.4	3.2	1.7		.7	Cur. Mat.-L.T.D.	2.9	2.7
	15.9	13.0	9.6		10.6	Trade Payables	14.7	13.6
	.7	.6	.7		.7	Income Taxes Payable	.5	.4
	19.6	14.5	14.7		9.1	All Other Current	12.2	12.5
	51.7	42.9	35.1		23.0	Total Current	41.0	41.4
	12.9	10.7	8.6		19.1	Long-Term Debt	15.7	11.7
	.4	.3	.4		.9	Deferred Taxes	.3	.4
	7.8	4.9	10.3		2.2	All Other Non-Current	5.9	6.3
	27.3	41.2	45.6		54.8	Net Worth	37.1	40.2
	100.0	100.0	100.0		100.0	Total Liabilities & Net Worth	100.0	100.0
						INCOME DATA		
	100.0	100.0	100.0		100.0	Net Sales	100.0	100.0
	42.7	42.0	39.3		38.1	Gross Profit	39.8	43.1
	38.0	36.1	30.9		27.4	Operating Expenses	36.3	36.3
	4.7	6.0	8.4		10.7	Operating Profit	3.5	6.7
	1.1	1.7	1.2		1.5	All Other Expenses (net)	1.1	1.5
	3.6	4.3	7.2		9.2	Profit Before Taxes	2.4	5.2
						RATIOS		
	3.5	2.7	3.2		2.5		3.2	3.1
	1.9	1.7	2.3		2.3	Current	2.0	1.9
	1.3	1.3	1.6		1.8		1.1	1.2
	2.0	1.4	1.8		1.4		1.9	1.8
	1.0	.9	1.3		1.2	Quick	1.0	1.1
	.6	.7	.8		1.0		.7	.7
40 9.1	42 8.8	46 8.0		52 7.1			42 8.7	45 8.2
49 7.5	49 7.4	53 6.9		60 6.0		Sales/Receivables	55 6.7	54 6.7
59 6.2	66 5.5	65 5.6		69 5.3			67 5.5	72 5.1
63 5.8	52 7.0	60 6.1		81 4.5			45 8.2	52 7.0
90 4.0	88 4.2	97 3.8		115 3.2		Cost of Sales/Inventory	94 3.9	92 4.0
140 2.6	142 2.6	131 2.8		142 2.6		133 2.7	147 2.5
23 16.1	22 16.5	21 17.8		37 9.8			20 18.3	18 19.9
35 10.5	37 9.9	29 12.7		49 7.5		Cost of Sales/Payables	31 11.8	36 10.1
51 7.1	58 6.3	42 8.8		69 5.3			52 7.0	58 6.3
	4.5	4.1	3.3		2.7		3.5	3.6
	7.4	6.9	4.9		4.2	Sales/Working Capital	6.0	6.5
	10.5	13.7	7.7		4.9		26.6	16.5
	6.3	17.8	23.9		37.2		13.4	16.8
	(24) 2.8	(60) 5.6	(28) 7.9		12.2	EBIT/Interest	(114) 2.8	(129) 4.5
	.6	1.4	1.8		4.5		.2	1.4
		13.2	20.0				12.3	12.2
	(17) 2.3	(12) 7.7			Net Profit + Depr., Dep.,	(46) 2.7	(39) 2.5
		.9	2.9			Amort./Cur. Mat. L/T/D	.5	.8
	.1	.1	.2		.2		.2	.2
	.5	.4	.5		.9	Fixed/Worth	.4	.4
	2.4	1.3	.8		NM		1.2	1.1
	.5	.7	.5		1.3		.5	.5
	2.5	1.5	1.0		3.5	Debt/Worth	1.4	1.4
	15.0	4.9	2.3		NM		4.8	5.3
	64.2	39.3	46.0				29.3	39.5
	(22) 22.4	(59) 20.5	(31) 27.8			% Profit Before Taxes/Tangible	(108) 9.2	(121) 16.7
	4.8	6.4	9.4			Net Worth	-2.6	3.9
	16.9	17.0	23.1		14.4		13.5	17.0
	4.0	6.8	9.4		9.6	% Profit Before Taxes/Total	3.5	6.9
	-1.8	1.2	4.1		5.0	Assets	-2.1	1.5
	94.2	42.9	21.1		26.6		30.6	36.6
	20.9	15.7	10.3		9.2	Sales/Net Fixed Assets	12.2	14.0
	10.9	7.9	4.5		5.1		5.6	7.1
	3.4	2.5	2.1		1.3		2.7	2.5
	2.6	1.9	1.6		1.0	Sales/Total Assets	1.9	1.8
	1.8	1.6	1.3		.7		1.4	1.4
	.7	.7	1.1				1.0	1.1
	(21) 1.7	(56) 1.6	(28) 1.7			% Depr., Dep., Amort./Sales	(107) 1.8	(119) 1.9
	2.8	2.9	2.6				3.0	2.8
	2.7	1.4					2.8	2.5
	(10) 4.4	(15) 6.5				% Officers', Directors'	(36) 5.6	(32) 5.3
	10.0	9.5				Owners' Comp/Sales	10.6	9.1
7089M	82837M	615198M	1141900M	891902M	1763151M	Net Sales ($)	2930395M	2452898M
1873M	32811M	317307M	634752M	645380M	1720427M	Total Assets ($)	1958985M	1966243M

© RMA 2007

M = $ thousand   MM = $ million
See Pages 11 through 21 for Explanation of Ratios and Data

Comparative Historical Data / Current Data Sorted by Sales

			Type of Statement						
27	22	26	Unqualified		1		2	10	13
33	33	41	Reviewed		3	8	18	7	5
17	17	20	Compiled		6	5	4	5	
7	6	8	Tax Returns	2	4	1	1		
43	52	56	Other		5	4	7	17	23
4/1/04-3/31/05 ALL	4/1/05-3/31/06 ALL	4/1/06-3/31/07 ALL			37 (4/1-9/30/06)		114 (10/1/06-3/31/07)		
				0-1MM	1-3MM	3-5MM	5-10MM	10-25MM	25MM & OVER
127	130	151	NUMBER OF STATEMENTS	2	19	18	32	39	41
%	%	%	ASSETS	%	%	%	%	%	%
9.2	9.5	9.1	Cash & Equivalents		5.7	8.5	10.8	9.2	9.6
33.8	31.0	30.1	Trade Receivables (net)		33.9	27.8	33.1	31.5	26.0
28.0	26.9	28.0	Inventory		32.8	30.7	30.5	25.9	24.0
2.6	3.4	4.3	All Other Current		3.2	2.3	3.4	5.8	5.0
73.7	70.9	71.5	Total Current		75.6	69.3	77.7	72.4	64.6
15.6	17.3	16.0	Fixed Assets (net)		17.6	17.2	11.8	18.0	16.1
5.6	4.5	6.0	Intangibles (net)		.3	6.0	2.8	4.8	12.4
5.2	7.3	6.6	All Other Non-Current		6.5	7.5	7.7	4.9	6.9
100.0	100.0	100.0	Total		100.0	100.0	100.0	100.0	100.0
			LIABILITIES						
14.4	11.8	10.5	Notes Payable-Short Term		18.3	8.5	13.1	9.4	6.7
2.1	2.6	2.8	Cur. Mat.-L.T.D.		6.1	3.7	1.7	3.4	1.2
15.5	13.7	12.5	Trade Payables		12.3	14.3	13.7	12.7	9.7
.4	.8	.6	Income Taxes Payable		.0	.2	.8	.9	.8
11.4	14.0	14.6	All Other Current		20.9	7.3	16.5	13.8	13.6
43.9	42.9	41.0	Total Current		57.7	34.1	45.8	40.1	32.1
10.0	10.1	11.6	Long-Term Debt		13.2	17.3	7.6	10.4	11.8
.4	.4	.5	Deferred Taxes		.0	.9	.1	.5	.8
9.2	7.5	6.3	All Other Non-Current		3.7	11.3	5.2	2.9	9.0
36.5	39.1	40.7	Net Worth		25.5	36.4	41.3	46.1	46.3
100.0	100.0	100.0	Total Liabilties & Net Worth		100.0	100.0	100.0	100.0	100.0
			INCOME DATA						
100.0	100.0	100.0	Net Sales		100.0	100.0	100.0	100.0	100.0
41.7	41.8	41.3	Gross Profit		44.4	40.1	44.7	41.0	37.7
35.1	34.9	34.3	Operating Expenses		41.6	36.1	37.7	34.0	27.4
6.6	6.8	7.0	Operating Profit		2.8	3.9	7.0	6.9	10.3
1.2	.9	1.4	All Other Expenses (net)		.9	.7	2.2	1.0	1.7
5.4	5.9	5.6	Profit Before Taxes		1.9	3.3	4.8	5.9	8.5
			RATIOS						
2.9	2.9	3.0			3.5	2.8	2.6	3.1	3.2
1.8	1.8	2.0	Current		1.9	1.9	1.8	1.9	2.3
1.3	1.3	1.4			1.0	1.5	1.3	1.3	1.8
1.6	1.8	1.7			2.0	1.5	1.5	1.6	1.7
1.1	1.1 (150)	1.1	Quick	(18)	1.0	1.0	.9	1.2	1.2
.7	.7	.7			.5	.6	.7	.7	.8
45 8.1	42 8.7	43 8.5			40 9.1	37 9.9	40 9.1	44 8.4	48 7.6
56 6.5	55 6.6	51 7.2	Sales/Receivables		54 6.8	43 8.5	47 7.8	53 6.9	55 6.6
69 5.3	67 5.5	63 5.8			79 4.6	50 7.2	70 5.3	62 5.8	67 5.4
57 6.4	54 6.7	57 6.4			43 8.5	63 5.8	65 5.6	48 7.6	61 6.0
91 4.0	88 4.2	91 4.0	Cost of Sales/Inventory		93 3.9	89 4.1	89 4.1	91 4.0	94 3.9
123 3.0	140 2.6	134 2.7			169 2.2	130 2.8	149 2.4	131 2.8	125 2.9
22 16.4	21 17.4	22 16.3			15 23.6	25 14.7	22 16.6	24 15.3	22 16.8
37 9.8	32 11.2	35 10.4	Cost of Sales/Payables		29 12.7	41 8.8	38 9.7	30 12.2	33 10.9
57 6.4	57 6.4	51 7.1			54 6.8	52 7.0	58 6.3	51 7.2	47 7.7
3.9	3.6	3.8			4.2	4.4	3.4	4.1	3.5
6.3	6.7	6.1	Sales/Working Capital		7.0	7.4	6.7	6.6	4.6
13.5	14.4	10.5			-101.3	8.6	12.2	13.6	7.0
16.5	17.2	18.0			11.5	6.6	16.7	18.7	29.3
(112) 6.0	(106) 3.9	(135) 5.4	EBIT/Interest	(17) 2.3	(16) 2.7	(29) 5.4	(36) 6.7	(35) 10.6	
1.5	1.9	1.5			-.1	1.6	1.2	2.3	3.1
9.4	12.0	18.0						9.1	24.2
(36) 2.8	(45) 4.1	(45) 6.0	Net Profit + Depr., Dep., Amort./Cur. Mat. L/T/D				(13) 4.0	(18) 7.7	
1.2	1.7	1.9						1.9	5.2
.1	.1	.2			.1	.2	.1	.2	.2
.4	.4	.4	Fixed/Worth		1.0	.5	.3	.4	.5
1.1	1.0	1.3			4.0	3.1	.7	1.0	1.2
.6	.6	.6			.4	1.1	.6	.6	.5
1.6	1.3	1.5	Debt/Worth		3.1	2.3	1.6	1.2	1.3
4.8	5.6	5.0			25.9	9.2	5.0	3.0	4.0
44.4	49.6	48.8			93.8	30.7	62.6	38.2	52.9
(108) 20.1	(116) 22.1	(133) 24.6	% Profit Before Taxes/Tangible Net Worth	(15) 9.7	(16) 14.1	(29) 21.6	(36) 24.0	(36) 32.9	
4.6	10.9	8.8			-4.4	6.8	6.8	8.3	14.5
19.3	16.7	18.3			43.3	14.3	19.9	18.3	18.9
5.7	7.9	9.0	% Profit Before Taxes/Total Assets		3.2	4.0	6.2	12.2	12.6
1.6	2.8	2.0			-12.2	1.7	.7	2.1	5.9
47.6	39.4	38.9			89.9	23.0	78.5	36.2	21.1
14.9	13.2	14.9	Sales/Net Fixed Assets		40.1	12.3	22.5	14.5	9.9
7.8	6.8	7.8			10.1	10.2	10.6	7.4	6.6
2.6	2.6	2.7			3.5	2.8	2.5	2.6	1.8
2.0	1.8	1.8	Sales/Total Assets		2.5	2.1	2.1	1.9	1.6
1.4	1.4	1.4			1.5	1.5	1.7	1.4	1.2
.8	1.0	.8			.4	1.0	.6	1.1	1.1
(108) 1.5	(105) 1.7	(129) 1.7	% Depr., Dep., Amort./Sales	(17) 1.7	(14) 2.7	(25) 1.1	(33) 1.9	(38) 1.8	
2.4	2.8	3.0			3.0	3.8	2.7	2.7	4.1
2.7	3.0	2.4					3.8		
(35) 5.5	(39) 5.7	(36) 5.6	% Officers', Directors' Owners' Comp/Sales			(10) 7.0			
11.6	12.6	9.6					9.8		
2960945M	2774067M	4502077M	Net Sales ($)	1900M	36214M	70133M	226536M	570706M	3596588M
2213410M	1881769M	3352550M	Total Assets ($)	593M	18868M	41196M	115034M	323232M	2853627M

M = $ thousand   MM = $ million
See Pages 11 through 21 for Explanation of Ratios and Data

Current Data Sorted by Assets   **Comparative Historical Data**

0-500M	500M-2MM	2-10MM	10-50MM	50-100MM	100-250MM	Type of Statement	4/1/02-3/31/03 ALL	4/1/03-3/31/04 ALL
		2	4	1	3	Unqualified	7	5
	2	4	2			Reviewed	10	13
3		3				Compiled	5	5
1	1	2				Tax Returns	1	
2	2	6	5		1	Other	10	10
	8 (4/1-9/30/06)		38 (10/1/06-3/31/07)					
6	5	17	11	3	4	NUMBER OF STATEMENTS	33	33
%	%	%	%	%	%	**ASSETS**	%	%
		6.3	9.1			Cash & Equivalents	11.0	12.1
		25.5	29.5			Trade Receivables (net)	22.9	24.6
		39.6	23.6			Inventory	31.9	31.1
		8.6	7.5			All Other Current	8.6	3.5
		80.1	69.7			Total Current	74.5	71.3
		14.0	22.6			Fixed Assets (net)	16.2	18.6
		2.4	4.0			Intangibles (net)	4.3	4.9
		3.5	3.7			All Other Non-Current	5.0	5.2
		100.0	100.0			Total	100.0	100.0
						LIABILITIES		
		15.2	5.5			Notes Payable-Short Term	12.2	13.2
		3.2	1.8			Cur. Mat.-L.T.D.	3.2	2.3
		17.0	10.2			Trade Payables	10.8	13.7
		.0	1.0			Income Taxes Payable	.3	.3
		6.0	16.6			All Other Current	11.8	14.2
		41.4	35.0			Total Current	38.3	43.7
		5.3	8.7			Long-Term Debt	7.8	8.0
		.2	.5			Deferred Taxes	.5	.7
		9.4	4.6			All Other Non-Current	5.6	9.5
		43.7	51.2			Net Worth	47.7	38.0
		100.0	100.0			Total Liabilties & Net Worth	100.0	100.0
						INCOME DATA		
		100.0	100.0			Net Sales	100.0	100.0
		38.6	37.8			Gross Profit	41.1	40.1
		31.8	25.8			Operating Expenses	37.8	35.0
		6.8	12.0			Operating Profit	3.3	5.1
		.9	.8			All Other Expenses (net)	1.0	.8
		5.9	11.2			Profit Before Taxes	2.4	4.2
						RATIOS		
		2.7	4.3				2.9	2.6
		2.2	1.9			Current	2.0	2.1
		1.4	1.5				1.3	1.5
		1.4	2.3				1.6	1.4
		.8	.9			Quick	.8	1.0
		.5	.6				.5	.6
		37 9.9	43 8.5				38 9.6	36 10.1
		49 7.4	50 7.3			Sales/Receivables	48 7.6	47 7.7
		67 5.5	76 4.8				60 6.1	59 6.2
		90 4.1	36 10.0				67 5.4	50 7.3
		134 2.7	75 4.9			Cost of Sales/Inventory	106 3.4	81 4.5
		158 2.3	99 3.7				156 2.3	136 2.7
		31 11.7	16 22.5				22 16.3	27 13.6
		53 6.9	33 10.9			Cost of Sales/Payables	36 10.1	46 8.0
		78 4.7	47 7.8				54 6.8	58 6.2
		3.9	3.8				3.3	3.5
		5.3	4.4			Sales/Working Capital	5.1	5.4
		6.6	10.6				8.5	9.5
		9.3	53.6				11.7	19.2
		(16) 3.4	18.9			EBIT/Interest	(31) 1.9	(29) 3.2
		1.3	7.6				-.1	1.1
						Net Profit + Depr., Dep.,	6.8	8.3
						Amort./Cur. Mat. L/T/D	(11) 1.9	(10) 4.2
							.8	2.4
		.1	.2				.2	.2
		.3	.4			Fixed/Worth	.3	.4
		.8	.8				.8	.9
		.6	.3				.5	.6
		1.4	.9			Debt/Worth	1.1	1.2
		2.7	2.2				3.0	1.9
		58.0	74.4				26.7	44.4
		(15) 12.3	(10) 43.5			% Profit Before Taxes/Tangible Net Worth	(31) 8.9	(29) 9.3
		3.1	17.3				-12.1	-2.6
		13.0	31.2				10.8	16.0
		4.0	24.5			% Profit Before Taxes/Total Assets	3.5	2.7
		.4	6.1				-1.8	-1.5
		40.4	17.8				32.7	33.7
		22.0	10.8			Sales/Net Fixed Assets	12.7	13.7
		10.2	7.7				6.7	6.9
		2.3	2.2				2.3	2.4
		2.0	1.7			Sales/Total Assets	1.7	2.0
		1.5	1.5				1.3	1.4
		.7	1.4				1.0	1.0
		(11) 1.1	1.7			% Depr., Dep., Amort./Sales	(30) 1.6	(25) 1.5
		2.4	3.0				2.6	2.6
							2.7	3.2
						% Officers', Directors' Owners' Comp/Sales	(11) 6.3	(12) 5.2
							9.2	9.9
4117M	25489M	156615M	430198M	300268M	1236501M	Net Sales ($)	670866M	758551M
1608M	7783M	83799M	235121M	188586M	535842M	Total Assets ($)	432741M	380055M

M = $ thousand   MM = $ million
See Pages 11 through 21 for Explanation of Ratios and Data

Comparative Historical Data / Current Data Sorted by Sales

						Type of Statement								
	10		7		10	Unqualified				1		1		8
	12		9		8	Reviewed			1	1		2	3	1
	7		5		6	Compiled		1	2			2	1	
	1		1		4	Tax Returns	1			1		2		
	16		17		18	Other	1	1		1		4	4	7
	4/1/04-3/31/05 ALL		4/1/05-3/31/06 ALL		4/1/06-3/31/07 ALL				8 (4/1-9/30/06)			38 (10/1/06-3/31/07)		
							0-1MM	1-3MM	3-5MM		5-10MM		10-25MM	25MM & OVER
	46		39		46	NUMBER OF STATEMENTS	3	4	4		11		8	16
	%		%		%	ASSETS	%	%	%		%		%	%
	9.4		10.3		9.4	Cash & Equivalents					1.7			11.4
	26.2		27.2		29.6	Trade Receivables (net)					27.4			29.5
	34.3		31.9		30.0	Inventory					38.3			23.9
	4.5		3.0		6.4	All Other Current					8.0			5.4
	74.4		72.4		75.4	Total Current					75.4			70.2
	15.6		14.7		18.1	Fixed Assets (net)					18.3			20.0
	2.7		6.0		2.5	Intangibles (net)					3.4			4.3
	7.3		6.9		4.0	All Other Non-Current					3.0			5.5
	100.0		100.0		100.0	Total					100.0			100.0
						LIABILITIES								
	12.2		8.4		10.4	Notes Payable-Short Term					16.1			6.6
	3.1		1.9		3.2	Cur. Mat.-L.T.D.					2.7			1.6
	14.7		12.2		15.3	Trade Payables					16.0			10.5
	.5		1.7		.6	Income Taxes Payable					.7			1.0
	11.4		12.8		8.9	All Other Current					6.1			14.6
	41.9		36.9		38.5	Total Current					41.6			34.2
	13.8		12.5		13.1	Long-Term Debt					5.0			7.5
	.4		.4		.3	Deferred Taxes					.2			.2
	4.8		8.3		6.4	All Other Non-Current					3.2			5.4
	39.0		41.8		41.6	Net Worth					49.9			52.6
	100.0		100.0		100.0	Total Liabilties & Net Worth					100.0			100.0
						INCOME DATA								
	100.0		100.0		100.0	Net Sales					100.0			100.0
	37.9		38.4		37.9	Gross Profit					33.3			38.7
	34.0		31.5		28.9	Operating Expenses					26.9			27.9
	3.9		6.8		9.0	Operating Profit					6.4			10.9
	.7		.8		.8	All Other Expenses (net)					.4			.2
	3.2		6.0		8.2	Profit Before Taxes					6.0			10.7
						RATIOS								
	3.3		3.4		3.3						2.6			4.4
	2.3		2.2		1.9	Current					1.9			1.8
	1.5		1.5		1.4						1.4			1.5
	1.8		1.8		1.6						1.4			3.1
	1.0		1.1		.9	Quick					.8			1.0
	.6		.6		.6						.6			.7
35	10.4	38	9.5	39	9.3				26	14.0			46	8.0
47	7.7	45	8.0	49	7.4	Sales/Receivables			49	7.5			51	7.2
62	5.9	60	6.0	65	5.6				74	4.9			68	5.4
50	7.4	54	6.8	43	8.4				71	5.2			66	5.5
101	3.6	92	4.0	93	3.9	Cost of Sales/Inventory			93	3.9			87	4.2
236	1.5	152	2.4	130	2.8				158	2.3			103	3.5
19	19.2	17	21.6	19	18.9				24	15.5			20	18.3
39	9.4	33	11.1	37	9.9	Cost of Sales/Payables			37	9.8			33	11.2
74	4.9	51	7.2	59	6.2				61	6.0			45	8.2
	3.3		4.0		3.9						4.5			3.6
	5.1		5.6		6.1	Sales/Working Capital					6.0			6.9
	8.6		8.6		9.9						6.8			10.2
	18.2		23.3		19.9						47.5			55.1
(39)	3.9	(33)	9.7	(42)	6.6	EBIT/Interest			(10)	4.6		(15)	19.1
	1.2		2.3		1.9						1.0			7.6
			27.0		10.5									
		(10)	2.6	(13)	5.6	Net Profit + Depr., Dep., Amort./Cur. Mat. L/T/D							
			1.4		2.9									
	.1		.1		.1						.1			.2
	.3		.3		.3	Fixed/Worth					.3			.4
	.7		.7		.9						.9			.7
	.5		.5		.5						.7			.2
	1.1		1.0		1.4	Debt/Worth					1.1			1.0
	2.3		2.6		2.6						1.5			2.3
	28.9		44.9		63.1						79.0			52.0
(40)	11.8	(34)	19.7	(41)	25.2	% Profit Before Taxes/Tangible Net Worth			(10)	10.7		(15)	35.6
	4.0		7.2		6.7						-.5			20.3
	14.0		15.6		27.4						37.0			28.9
	4.9		9.4		9.0	% Profit Before Taxes/Total Assets					2.5			16.8
	.5		2.4		2.5						-1.3			6.3
	31.0		32.2		25.9						38.9			15.1
	13.7		14.2		13.9	Sales/Net Fixed Assets					17.8			10.3
	8.5		7.4		7.9						7.1			5.8
	2.6		2.7		2.5						2.6			2.2
	2.1		2.1		2.1	Sales/Total Assets					2.2			1.7
	1.3		1.4		1.6						1.4			1.5
	.9		.7		1.0									1.6
(39)	1.7	(30)	1.4	(36)	1.9	% Depr., Dep., Amort./Sales							1.9
	2.4		2.2		2.9									2.8
	3.5		2.3											
(12)	8.1	(10)	5.8			% Officers', Directors' Owners' Comp/Sales							
	13.5		20.0											
	976121M		1124998M		2153188M	Net Sales ($)	419M	6376M	17251M		78137M		129593M	1921412M
	612300M		761772M		1052739M	Total Assets ($)	164M	2106M	8972M		38581M		73020M	929896M

M = $ thousand   MM = $ million
See Pages 11 through 21 for Explanation of Ratios and Data

Current Data Sorted by Assets / Comparative Historical Data

Type of Statement

	0-500M	500M-2MM	2-10MM	10-50MM	50-100MM	100-250MM	Type of Statement	4/1/02-3/31/03 ALL	4/1/03-3/31/04 ALL
		1	5	6	4	3	Unqualified	12	10
		3	6	1			Reviewed	8	8
	2	2	5				Compiled	5	8
	1	1					Tax Returns		2
		4	4	7	1	1	Other	10	12
		13 (4/1-9/30/06)		44 (10/1/06-3/31/07)					
	0-500M	500M-2MM	2-10MM	10-50MM	50-100MM	100-250MM		4/1/02-3/31/03 ALL	4/1/03-3/31/04 ALL
	3	11	20	14	5	4	NUMBER OF STATEMENTS	35	40

Data

0-500M	500M-2MM	2-10MM	10-50MM	50-100MM	100-250MM		4/1/02-3/31/03 ALL	4/1/03-3/31/04 ALL
%	%	%	%	%	%	**ASSETS**	%	%
	12.4	5.0	14.2			Cash & Equivalents	14.9	12.7
	26.3	29.2	25.8			Trade Receivables (net)	25.5	26.9
	32.1	33.7	20.9			Inventory	28.0	27.3
	2.0	.7	4.7			All Other Current	2.7	2.2
	72.9	68.6	65.5			Total Current	71.2	69.1
	15.0	13.8	19.3			Fixed Assets (net)	18.7	17.1
	4.0	8.2	6.9			Intangibles (net)	3.2	6.3
	8.1	9.4	8.3			All Other Non-Current	6.8	7.4
	100.0	100.0	100.0			Total	100.0	100.0
						LIABILITIES		
	15.2	10.4	2.1			Notes Payable-Short Term	7.9	9.3
	1.2	2.2	1.8			Cur. Mat.-L.T.D.	2.8	3.0
	12.0	10.9	8.9			Trade Payables	10.6	11.2
	.5	.2	1.1			Income Taxes Payable	.5	.3
	4.6	12.0	7.9			All Other Current	10.8	12.5
	33.5	35.8	21.7			Total Current	32.5	36.3
	8.0	6.8	14.3			Long-Term Debt	9.4	10.5
	.3	.7	.3			Deferred Taxes	.2	.1
	11.0	4.1	3.6			All Other Non-Current	5.0	10.3
	47.2	52.8	60.1			Net Worth	52.8	42.8
	100.0	100.0	100.0			Total Liabilities & Net Worth	100.0	100.0
						INCOME DATA		
	100.0	100.0	100.0			Net Sales	100.0	100.0
	47.6	43.1	42.7			Gross Profit	42.6	42.0
	41.8	36.9	34.6			Operating Expenses	41.0	40.1
	5.8	6.2	8.1			Operating Profit	1.6	1.9
	1.3	.0	1.0			All Other Expenses (net)	.8	1.3
	4.4	6.2	7.1			Profit Before Taxes	.8	.6
						RATIOS		
	4.8	2.7	7.2			Current	3.8	3.7
	2.1	1.9	3.3				2.5	2.3
	1.5	1.4	1.8				1.7	1.4
	2.7	1.8	4.1			Quick	2.1	2.0
	1.0	.8	1.8				1.4	1.2
	.5	.7	1.1				1.0	.8
	26 13.9	39 9.3	53 6.9			Sales/Receivables	38 9.7	48 7.6
	51 7.1	52 7.0	60 6.1				51 7.2	54 6.8
	76 4.8	69 5.3	81 4.5				69 5.3	71 5.2
	43 8.5	75 4.9	63 5.8			Cost of Sales/Inventory	74 4.9	72 5.1
	93 3.9	106 3.5	76 4.8				89 4.1	98 3.7
	132 2.8	155 2.4	117 3.1				147 2.5	147 2.5
	18 20.8	21 17.2	20 18.2			Cost of Sales/Payables	21 17.0	19 19.5
	37 9.9	24 14.9	37 9.7				33 11.2	33 11.2
	80 4.6	42 8.6	55 6.7				54 6.8	53 6.9
	2.2	4.5	1.7			Sales/Working Capital	2.7	3.1
	5.0	6.3	3.3				4.9	5.0
	10.7	10.0	5.3				7.2	9.6
		16.8	68.4			EBIT/Interest	17.5	13.5
		(18) 4.0	(11) 45.5				(29) 3.5	(36) 2.4
		.9	1.4				-1.1	.2
						Net Profit + Depr., Dep., Amort./Cur. Mat. L/T/D	6.8	12.8
							(15) 2.3	(17) 3.3
							.9	.6
	.1	.2	.1			Fixed/Worth	.2	.2
	.2	.3	.2				.3	.5
	1.1	.7	.8				.6	.9
	.2	.5	.2			Debt/Worth	.3	.5
	1.6	1.2	.7				.9	1.4
	3.6	2.9	1.6				1.4	6.0
	33.9	44.7	38.7			% Profit Before Taxes/Tangible Net Worth	23.5	24.9
	(10) 17.9	(19) 20.5	(13) 20.2				(32) 4.6	(33) 9.0
	4.4	-2.3	5.7				-5.5	-3.7
	11.7	24.8	21.8			% Profit Before Taxes/Total Assets	12.6	10.5
	7.4	8.1	9.0				2.5	3.3
	2.4	-.9	1.7				-4.1	-1.3
	38.4	47.9	17.3			Sales/Net Fixed Assets	24.1	25.0
	15.7	18.1	9.4				9.8	11.0
	7.1	10.6	5.7				5.7	6.6
	2.9	2.7	1.7			Sales/Total Assets	2.4	2.3
	1.9	2.2	1.3				1.7	1.7
	1.4	1.6	.9				1.1	1.1
		1.0	1.2			% Depr., Dep., Amort./Sales	1.3	1.1
		(18) 1.4	2.0				(30) 2.3	(37) 2.0
		2.8	2.8				3.8	3.2
						% Officers', Directors' Owners' Comp/Sales	3.5	3.3
							(12) 4.4	(12) 6.4
							9.6	11.7
5264M	24865M	178041M	432369M	489168M	524753M	Net Sales ($)	906546M	1006055M
1333M	11903M	90116M	312420M	377139M	589849M	Total Assets ($)	836395M	866969M

M = $ thousand   MM = $ million
See Pages 11 through 21 for Explanation of Ratios and Data

Comparative Historical Data

Current Data Sorted by Sales

				Type of Statement						
15		15	19	Unqualified		1		4	5	9
6		7	10	Reviewed		3	1	3	2	1
13		7	8	Compiled		2	2	2	2	
			3	Tax Returns		2				
				Other	1	1	3	3	4	5
16		21	17		1					
4/1/04-		4/1/05-	4/1/06-			13 (4/1-9/30/06)		44 (10/1/06-3/31/07)		
3/31/05		3/31/06	3/31/07							
ALL		ALL	ALL		0-1MM	1-3MM	3-5MM	5-10MM	10-25MM	25MM & OVER
50		50	57	**NUMBER OF STATEMENTS**	2	9	6	12	13	15
%		%	%	**ASSETS**	%	%	%	%	%	%
15.0		13.2	11.5	Cash & Equivalents				6.3	9.3	15.9
27.2		27.7	26.9	Trade Receivables (net)				30.6	23.8	23.5
29.5		30.3	26.5	Inventory				33.2	27.1	17.3
1.7		1.8	2.3	All Other Current				.9	3.2	3.4
73.4		73.1	67.2	Total Current				70.9	63.4	60.1
14.9		15.3	15.7	Fixed Assets (net)				11.8	18.2	18.8
4.6		4.3	8.7	Intangibles (net)				8.5	7.3	12.8
7.1		7.4	8.4	All Other Non-Current				8.8	11.1	8.3
100.0		100.0	100.0	Total				100.0	100.0	100.0
				LIABILITIES						
13.4		10.9	7.9	Notes Payable-Short Term				13.1	3.3	.5
2.3		2.9	2.2	Cur. Mat.-L.T.D.				1.9	1.7	2.2
11.1		10.5	10.6	Trade Payables				9.5	9.1	9.5
.4		.5	.6	Income Taxes Payable				.4	.5	1.0
16.3		9.5	9.6	All Other Current				10.1	7.6	12.6
43.6		34.3	30.8	Total Current				35.1	22.2	25.9
8.1		8.4	10.2	Long-Term Debt				6.0	12.6	11.5
.3		.3	.5	Deferred Taxes				.2	.7	.7
5.1		10.6	4.7	All Other Non-Current				5.7	2.9	2.7
42.8		46.4	53.8	Net Worth				53.0	61.5	59.2
100.0		100.0	100.0	Total Liabilities & Net Worth				100.0	100.0	100.0
				INCOME DATA						
100.0		100.0	100.0	Net Sales				100.0	100.0	100.0
45.1		43.8	45.5	Gross Profit				46.8	41.3	43.9
37.3		38.1	38.4	Operating Expenses				39.2	34.7	34.8
7.8		5.7	7.1	Operating Profit				7.7	6.5	9.1
1.1		1.0	.6	All Other Expenses (net)				-.2	1.1	.3
6.7		4.7	6.5	Profit Before Taxes				7.9	5.5	8.8
				RATIOS						
3.7		3.8	4.2					3.3	8.3	3.2
2.4		2.3	2.1	Current				2.0	4.2	2.1
1.6		1.6	1.6					1.6	1.7	1.8
2.3		2.3	2.7					2.3	4.2	2.0
1.5		1.2	1.1	Quick				1.1	1.5	1.4
.8		.8	.7					.6	.8	1.0

							Sales/Receivables									
38	9.6	43	8.6	43	8.5						41	8.8	37	9.8	51	7.2
55	6.7	52	7.0	58	6.3						57	6.4	53	6.9	63	5.8
70	5.2	66	5.5	71	5.1						70	5.2	68	5.4	75	4.9

							Cost of Sales/Inventory									
76	4.8	73	5.0	63	5.8						75	4.9	53	7.0	63	5.8
107	3.4	103	3.5	95	3.8						112	3.2	95	3.8	90	4.0
163	2.2	147	2.5	137	2.7						155	2.4	168	2.2	109	3.3

							Cost of Sales/Payables									
17	21.5	17	21.0	21	17.5						21	17.2	19	19.1	28	13.1
30	12.2	36	10.2	31	11.8						23	15.7	22	16.3	43	8.4
51	7.2	49	7.5	51	7.1						31	11.9	46	8.0	54	6.8

				Ratios (cont.)						
2.7		2.9	3.1					4.5	1.7	2.4
4.3		5.5	5.2	Sales/Working Capital				5.8	3.8	3.9
7.4		7.9	8.7					8.9	10.1	5.9

						EBIT/Interest					
	39.8		36.1		46.1				37.4		66.3
(42)	6.6	(43)	3.7	(46)	4.9			(11)	7.6	(12)	40.6
	2.6		1.5		1.4				2.7		3.7

						Net Profit + Depr., Dep., Amort./Cur. Mat. L/T/D					
	33.6		9.0		20.6						
(15)	6.6	(15)	2.7	(16)	3.9						
	.8		.8		1.0						

				Fixed/Worth						
.1		.1	.1					.1	.1	.2
.2		.3	.3					.3	.2	.4
.5		1.1	.9					.7	.8	.5

				Debt/Worth						
.3		.3	.3					.5	.1	.4
.6		.9	1.2					1.1	.9	.9
2.5		3.3	2.3					2.9	1.7	1.7

						% Profit Before Taxes/Tangible Net Worth					
	47.1		37.4		44.0				46.4	26.4	44.2
(47)	17.8	(44)	16.0	(53)	21.3			(11)	32.3	(12) 15.6	22.0
	4.5		5.1		4.3				-2.3	2.2	9.3

				% Profit Before Taxes/Total Assets						
17.1		18.8	21.0					24.8	23.7	18.2
8.5		8.7	7.4					14.9	6.6	8.6
3.4		1.1	1.9					-.2	.3	5.1

				Sales/Net Fixed Assets						
41.6		30.7	33.0					47.9	23.7	12.7
14.7		16.8	13.1					19.9	12.5	8.1
6.1		8.1	7.4					10.6	7.9	5.7

				Sales/Total Assets						
2.3		2.5	2.3					2.4	2.6	1.7
1.6		1.9	1.7					2.1	1.1	1.4
1.1		1.3	1.0					1.5	.9	.9

						% Depr., Dep., Amort./Sales					
	.9		.9		1.0				.9	1.0	2.1
(43)	1.8	(46)	1.7	(49)	2.0			(11)	1.3	(12) 1.5	(14) 2.4
	3.3		3.0		2.9				2.8	3.2	3.5

						% Officers', Directors' Owners' Comp/Sales					
	2.2		2.9		3.7						
(14)	7.3	(11)	5.1	(13)	7.4						
	12.0		11.2		11.0						

				Net Sales ($) / Total Assets ($)						
1597581M		1112437M	1654460M	Net Sales ($)	1363M	17277M	24012M	88035M	206459M	1317314M
1562173M		999828M	1382760M	Total Assets ($)	1056M	8459M	15109M	49821M	155197M	1153118M

© RMA 2007   M = $ thousand   MM = $ million
See Pages 11 through 21 for Explanation of Ratios and Data

Current Data Sorted by Assets

Comparative Historical Data

						Type of Statement		
	1	8	4	1	6	Unqualified	17	14
	3	5	2			Reviewed	9	17
	2	1				Compiled	5	9
3		2				Tax Returns	4	4
	1	8	5	3	3	Other	14	12
	15 (4/1-9/30/06)		43 (10/1/06-3/31/07)				4/1/02-3/31/03	4/1/03-3/31/04
0-500M	500M-2MM	2-10MM	10-50MM	50-100MM	100-250MM		ALL	ALL
3	7	24	11	4	9	NUMBER OF STATEMENTS	49	56
%	%	%	%	%	%	ASSETS	%	%
		12.4	9.1			Cash & Equivalents	9.1	10.0
		29.1	22.9			Trade Receivables (net)	26.8	27.2
		31.0	25.5			Inventory	31.3	25.9
		1.7	1.5			All Other Current	2.0	4.3
		74.1	59.0			Total Current	69.1	67.4
		10.8	13.5			Fixed Assets (net)	15.8	16.6
		7.7	18.7			Intangibles (net)	8.6	9.4
		7.4	8.8			All Other Non-Current	6.5	6.6
		100.0	100.0			Total	100.0	100.0
						LIABILITIES		
		6.6	4.3			Notes Payable-Short Term	11.1	10.2
		2.0	1.3			Cur. Mat.-L.T.D.	3.9	3.0
		10.7	11.8			Trade Payables	11.7	12.3
		.5	.5			Income Taxes Payable	.6	1.1
		14.2	16.3			All Other Current	13.8	12.8
		34.0	34.1			Total Current	41.1	39.3
		8.3	9.2			Long-Term Debt	14.6	9.4
		.4	.6			Deferred Taxes	.3	.4
		8.2	3.7			All Other Non-Current	4.8	6.7
		49.1	52.3			Net Worth	39.1	44.2
		100.0	100.0			Total Liabilties & Net Worth	100.0	100.0
						INCOME DATA		
		100.0	100.0			Net Sales	100.0	100.0
		47.8	47.0			Gross Profit	45.3	43.5
		39.7	41.2			Operating Expenses	43.1	38.4
		8.0	5.7			Operating Profit	2.3	5.2
		.6	.9			All Other Expenses (net)	1.5	.6
		7.4	4.8			Profit Before Taxes	.8	4.6
						RATIOS		
		4.5	3.1				2.9	3.5
		2.4	2.1			Current	1.6	1.6
		1.6	1.3				1.2	1.2
		2.3	2.0				1.4	1.5
		1.5	1.1			Quick	.9	.9
		.7	.6				.6	.6
	48	7.6	47	7.8			48	7.5	46	7.9
	61	6.0	57	6.4		Sales/Receivables	59	6.2	55	6.6
	71	5.1	78	4.7			72	5.1	71	5.1
	75	4.9	106	3.5			87	4.2	60	6.1
	116	3.2	123	3.0		Cost of Sales/Inventory	130	2.8	102	3.6
	172	2.1	137	2.7			192	1.9	162	2.3
	22	16.3	25	14.5			25	14.6	24	15.1
	31	11.7	45	8.1		Cost of Sales/Payables	46	7.9	38	9.5
	74	5.0	80	4.6			62	5.9	54	6.8
		2.5	3.4				3.1	3.2
		4.5	4.2			Sales/Working Capital	7.0	6.8
		9.8	13.1				13.5	20.3
		17.5					10.2	23.5
	(20)	8.7				EBIT/Interest	(46)	3.1	(49)	5.3
		3.1					.7	1.0
						Net Profit + Depr., Dep.,		6.7	8.2
						Amort./Cur. Mat. L/T/D	(13)	2.7	(24)	3.8
							.7	1.6
		.1	.1				.2	.2
		.2	.4			Fixed/Worth	.5	.5
		.4	7.4				NM	1.9
		.4	.3				.6	.4
		.9	1.3			Debt/Worth	2.1	1.7
		5.4	17.5				NM	9.1
		32.3				% Profit Before Taxes/Tangible	36.6	37.3
	(21)	26.7				Net Worth	(37)	17.9	(45)	15.9
		8.8					1.4	2.7
		18.8	25.2			% Profit Before Taxes/Total	9.4	11.7
		10.6	15.4			Assets	3.4	6.7
		4.3	2.5				-1.0	-.2
		39.1	70.5				27.6	37.2
		19.2	17.0			Sales/Net Fixed Assets	13.3	14.4
		12.9	7.4				5.8	6.5
		2.2	1.7				2.1	2.2
		1.7	1.5			Sales/Total Assets	1.7	1.7
		1.4	1.1				1.2	1.3
		1.0					1.6	1.3
	(19)	1.6				% Depr., Dep., Amort./Sales	(41)	2.3	(45)	1.9
		2.2					4.1	3.4
						% Officers', Directors'		4.0
						Owners' Comp/Sales	(10)	5.9
							12.8
4040M	26606M	214462M	352775M	254121M	1381152M	Net Sales ($)	1159129M	1339461M
1093M	9789M	118882M	247875M	222757M	1400832M	Total Assets ($)	1150079M	1136361M

© RMA 2007   M = $ thousand   MM = $ million

See Pages 11 through 21 for Explanation of Ratios and Data

Comparative Historical Data | **Current Data Sorted by Sales**

			Type of Statement	0-1MM	1-3MM	3-5MM	5-10MM	10-25MM	25MM & OVER
16	17	20	Unqualified		1		3	5	10
11	10	10	Reviewed		2	1	4	2	1
5	4	3	Compiled			2	1		
6	2	5	Tax Returns		1	1	1		
17	23	20	Other	1	2	1	6	4	8
4/1/04-3/31/05 ALL	4/1/05-3/31/06 ALL	4/1/06-3/31/07 ALL			15 (4/1-9/30/06)		43 (10/1/06-3/31/07)		
55	56	58	**NUMBER OF STATEMENTS**	1	6	6	15	11	19
%	%	%	**ASSETS**	%	%	%	%	%	%
8.9	9.3	11.8	Cash & Equivalents				11.9	9.0	14.7
27.9	26.6	26.6	Trade Receivables (net)				27.7	25.2	23.0
27.9	26.4	24.9	Inventory				35.0	30.8	15.7
3.9	2.9	1.7	All Other Current				1.6	1.8	2.6
68.7	65.1	65.0	Total Current				76.2	66.9	55.9
13.6	16.4	13.8	Fixed Assets (net)				12.4	6.6	16.5
11.2	10.2	11.8	Intangibles (net)				5.1	16.9	15.8
6.5	8.2	9.4	All Other Non-Current				6.3	9.7	11.7
100.0	100.0	100.0	Total				100.0	100.0	100.0
			LIABILITIES						
8.3	10.7	8.1	Notes Payable-Short Term				4.8	6.4	4.9
2.7	1.9	1.4	Cur. Mat.-L.T.D.				2.1	.9	1.2
13.1	12.0	11.8	Trade Payables				10.3	13.5	7.5
.6	.8	.6	Income Taxes Payable				.7	.7	.6
14.6	12.7	14.3	All Other Current				12.8	18.0	12.2
39.3	38.1	36.1	Total Current				30.6	39.5	26.4
8.1	10.4	9.4	Long-Term Debt				7.0	7.5	7.6
.6	.3	.8	Deferred Taxes				.6	.0	1.7
4.6	7.0	6.5	All Other Non-Current				3.7	14.3	5.3
47.5	44.1	47.2	Net Worth				58.0	38.7	59.0
100.0	100.0	100.0	Total Liabilities & Net Worth				100.0	100.0	100.0
			INCOME DATA						
100.0	100.0	100.0	Net Sales				100.0	100.0	100.0
43.8	46.0	45.6	Gross Profit				51.5	39.4	46.4
36.3	39.7	39.5	Operating Expenses				44.3	29.9	43.7
7.5	6.3	6.1	Operating Profit				7.1	9.4	2.7
.6	1.0	1.1	All Other Expenses (net)				.3	1.3	1.1
7.0	5.3	5.0	Profit Before Taxes				6.8	8.1	1.6
			RATIOS						
3.1	3.5	3.7	Current				5.5	2.9	3.6
1.6	2.0	2.2					2.6	1.4	2.2
1.2	1.5	1.4					1.7	1.3	1.7
2.0	1.8	2.1	Quick				2.4	1.6	2.3
1.0	1.0	1.2					1.3	.9	1.3
.6	.7	.7					.9	.5	1.1
46 7.9	45 8.1	46 8.0	Sales/Receivables				34 10.6	47 7.8	55 6.6
57 6.4	57 6.4	58 6.2					59 6.2	57 6.4	68 5.4
68 5.4	67 5.4	70 5.2					80 4.6	60 6.1	78 4.7
64 5.7	68 5.3	62 5.8	Cost of Sales/Inventory				84 4.3	65 5.6	61 6.0
109 3.3	105 3.5	102 3.6					145 2.5	107 3.4	104 3.5
159 2.3	145 2.5	146 2.5					228 1.6	151 2.4	125 2.9
23 15.6	27 13.7	22 16.2	Cost of Sales/Payables				22 16.3	19 19.7	23 15.9
43 8.4	43 8.6	44 8.4					26 13.9	30 12.1	46 7.9
59 6.2	58 6.3	62 5.9					82 4.5	47 7.7	53 6.9
3.5	2.9	3.0	Sales/Working Capital				2.5	4.1	2.9
6.7	5.8	4.8					4.4	9.9	4.1
20.3	9.6	10.4					8.6	13.1	5.7
33.4	20.0	33.4	EBIT/Interest				35.0		42.6
(50) 9.2	(47) 6.6	(50) 6.4					(13) 10.5	(16) 4.7	
4.2	2.4	2.1					3.9		-9.3
40.8	25.7	40.0	Net Profit + Depr., Dep.,						
(21) 10.0	(22) 9.6	(18) 5.1	Amort./Cur. Mat. L/T/D						
1.4	3.4	1.2							
.2	.2	.1	Fixed/Worth				.1	.1	.1
.4	.4	.3					.3	.3	.4
1.2	1.1	1.5					.4	-.2	.5
.4	.4	.4	Debt/Worth				.4	.4	.2
1.6	1.3	1.1					.8	2.7	.9
5.5	4.8	5.0					1.6	-5.4	1.5
53.7	42.1	36.2	% Profit Before Taxes/Tangible				33.7		28.5
(48) 27.3	(47) 29.5	(48) 22.5	Net Worth				28.3	(16) 6.5	
7.6	8.4	4.3					11.3		-20.7
19.0	16.2	17.0	% Profit Before Taxes/Total				20.4	16.6	12.1
9.4	8.6	8.9	Assets				12.4	8.5	5.3
3.3	2.6	2.4					7.2	3.7	-8.6
35.3	28.4	28.3	Sales/Net Fixed Assets				44.3	70.5	12.1
16.7	12.2	16.6					18.9	27.5	7.9
8.4	5.8	7.5					16.1	20.4	5.0
2.0	2.2	2.2	Sales/Total Assets				2.4	2.2	1.7
1.7	1.6	1.6					2.0	1.6	1.4
1.3	1.1	1.1					1.4	1.1	.7
.7	1.0	1.0	% Depr., Dep., Amort./Sales				.9		1.7
(43) 1.5	(47) 1.9	(44) 1.7					(12) 1.5	(15) 2.4	
3.6	4.0	2.7					2.3		3.3
		2.1	% Officers', Directors'						
	(12) 5.0		Owners' Comp/Sales						
		12.4							
1192098M	2343863M	2233156M	Net Sales ($)	586M	12573M	24799M	117598M	172510M	1905090M
910767M	2043841M	2001228M	Total Assets ($)	221M	6541M	13731M	64488M	113378M	1802869M

© RMA 2007   **M = $ thousand   MM = $ million**
See Pages 11 through 21 for Explanation of Ratios and Data

Current Data Sorted by Assets   Comparative Historical Data

0-500M	500M-2MM	2-10MM	10-50MM	50-100MM	100-250MM	Type of Statement	4/1/02-3/31/03 ALL	4/1/03-3/31/04 ALL
	2	5	11	5	4	Unqualified	23	19
1	4	16	5		1	Reviewed	15	17
	5	4	1	1		Compiled	12	8
	1					Tax Returns	2	4
1	2	23	12	2		Other	35	48
	15 (4/1-9/30/06)		90 (10/1/06-3/31/07)					
2	14	48	29	8	4	NUMBER OF STATEMENTS	87	96
%	%	%	%	%	%	**ASSETS**	%	%
	7.1	13.5	11.6			Cash & Equivalents	10.3	12.5
	32.7	29.8	31.6			Trade Receivables (net)	29.7	27.6
	36.0	27.1	22.7			Inventory	27.4	24.9
	1.2	4.6	4.0			All Other Current	4.4	3.9
	77.0	75.0	70.0			Total Current	71.8	68.9
	16.2	15.8	20.1			Fixed Assets (net)	16.0	19.1
	2.2	4.0	5.5			Intangibles (net)	7.7	6.4
	4.6	5.2	4.5			All Other Non-Current	4.5	5.6
	100.0	100.0	100.0			Total	100.0	100.0
						LIABILITIES		
	25.5	10.6	8.4			Notes Payable-Short Term	12.0	10.3
	3.0	3.6	2.3			Cur. Mat.-L.T.D.	4.1	3.2
	17.6	13.5	11.8			Trade Payables	12.5	12.5
	.1	.5	1.0			Income Taxes Payable	.4	.6
	16.0	13.8	15.1			All Other Current	14.9	15.5
	62.3	41.9	38.6			Total Current	43.8	42.1
	13.3	8.4	9.6			Long-Term Debt	10.7	10.0
	.3	.1	.4			Deferred Taxes	.2	.2
	4.2	6.1	1.6			All Other Non-Current	4.4	6.1
	19.9	43.5	49.7			Net Worth	40.9	41.6
	100.0	100.0	100.0			Total Liabilities & Net Worth	100.0	100.0
						INCOME DATA		
	100.0	100.0	100.0			Net Sales	100.0	100.0
	39.0	44.6	35.1			Gross Profit	40.9	43.9
	34.4	37.4	25.3			Operating Expenses	36.6	38.3
	4.5	7.3	9.8			Operating Profit	4.3	5.6
	.5	1.4	.6			All Other Expenses (net)	1.0	1.4
	4.0	5.9	9.2			Profit Before Taxes	3.4	4.2
						RATIOS		
	1.9	3.1	3.4				2.9	3.2
	1.3	1.8	2.0			Current	1.8	1.8
	.9	1.2	1.2				1.2	1.3
	1.0	2.1	2.1				1.7	1.8
	.6	1.1	1.1			Quick	1.0	1.0
	.4	.6	.7				.6	.6
	38 9.7	42 8.7	43 8.5				46 7.9	42 8.8
	45 8.1	59 6.2	72 5.0			Sales/Receivables	58 6.3	55 6.6
	59 6.1	72 5.1	98 3.7				68 5.3	68 5.4
	48 7.6	54 6.8	38 9.6				56 6.5	44 8.2
	95 3.8	108 3.4	103 3.5			Cost of Sales/Inventory	103 3.5	93 3.9
	154 2.4	148 2.5	140 2.6				148 2.5	156 2.3
	23 15.8	17 21.4	20 18.0				21 17.5	21 17.0
	45 8.1	32 11.4	39 9.5			Cost of Sales/Payables	35 10.3	36 10.1
	57 6.4	66 5.5	47 7.8				57 6.4	55 6.6
	5.1	3.3	2.9				3.2	3.2
	7.5	5.6	6.3			Sales/Working Capital	5.4	5.7
	-122.7	25.6	12.0				16.2	15.0
	5.3	18.8	14.6				7.4	11.7
	(13) 2.8	(43) 5.1	(24) 9.9			EBIT/Interest	(80) 2.8	(88) 4.5
	1.5	1.4	2.6				-.2	1.4
		6.9	28.0			Net Profit + Depr., Dep.,	6.9	5.8
		(10) 2.5	(10) 10.2			Amort./Cur. Mat. L/T/D	(30) 1.5	(28) 1.9
		1.5	5.4				.2	.5
	.2	.1	.2				.2	.2
	.6	.3	.4			Fixed/Worth	.4	.5
	-3.3	.7	.7				1.2	1.0
	1.6	.7	.5				.5	.6
	3.5	1.4	1.3			Debt/Worth	2.0	1.5
	-32.4	4.7	2.2				5.0	3.9
	40.7	40.7	51.8			% Profit Before Taxes/Tangible	39.6	37.5
	(10) 29.8	(43) 30.8	31.7			Net Worth	(75) 10.8	(81) 13.3
	2.5	8.4	13.0				-6.6	2.7
	14.2	20.4	21.1			% Profit Before Taxes/Total	10.2	14.2
	8.8	9.0	11.3			Assets	4.2	4.7
	1.3	2.1	5.9				-1.6	1.0
	53.4	57.8	17.3				27.1	22.7
	26.5	16.6	10.1			Sales/Net Fixed Assets	13.3	11.0
	11.9	7.3	5.8				6.5	6.0
	3.0	2.4	1.9				2.2	2.3
	2.5	1.7	1.4			Sales/Total Assets	1.8	1.7
	1.7	1.3	1.3				1.2	1.3
	.8	.8	.9				1.3	1.2
	(10) 1.7	(37) 1.6	(25) 1.6			% Depr., Dep., Amort./Sales	(72) 2.1	(81) 2.1
	3.1	2.3	3.8				3.3	3.3
						% Officers', Directors'	2.9	4.9
						Owners' Comp/Sales	(18) 6.2	(19) 8.6
							8.8	10.8
3128M	46121M	473855M	904388M	652043M	589733M	Net Sales ($)	1884905M	2082833M
726M	18825M	253698M	568114M	531033M	590128M	Total Assets ($)	1387395M	1435038M

© RMA 2007

M = $ thousand   MM = $ million
See Pages 11 through 21 for Explanation of Ratios and Data

Comparative Historical Data | | Current Data Sorted by Sales

30 14 7 5 34 4/1/04- 3/31/05 ALL	26 18 9 7 40 4/1/05- 3/31/06 ALL	27 26 11 1 40 4/1/06- 3/31/07 ALL	Type of Statement Unqualified Reviewed Compiled Tax Returns Other	1	2 4 4 15 (4/1-9/30/06) 0-1MM	2 4 4 4 1-3MM	2 5 1 1 4 90 (10/1/06-3/31/07) 3-5MM	2 5 1 1 11 5-10MM	10 12 4 13 10-25MM	13 3 8 25MM & OVER
90	100	105	NUMBER OF STATEMENTS	1	10	11	20	39	24
%	%	%	ASSETS	%	%	%	%	%	%
10.4	8.5	12.5	Cash & Equivalents		9.7	12.9	12.7	12.6	12.8
29.9	29.7	29.5	Trade Receivables (net)		21.5	32.1	32.6	29.5	29.7
22.6	27.3	26.1	Inventory		36.2	23.2	27.1	26.0	22.8
3.2	2.6	3.7	All Other Current		.0	3.3	4.0	4.1	4.4
66.1	68.2	71.7	Total Current		67.4	71.5	76.4	72.2	69.8
19.9	17.7	17.3	Fixed Assets (net)		18.3	13.6	15.9	17.7	17.7
7.5	7.4	5.9	Intangibles (net)		7.9	7.0	3.2	5.8	7.5
6.5	6.6	5.1	All Other Non-Current		6.4	7.9	4.5	4.3	5.1
100.0	100.0	100.0	Total		100.0	100.0	100.0	100.0	100.0
			LIABILITIES						
10.7	8.6	11.5	Notes Payable-Short Term		28.4	21.4	11.0	8.6	5.6
2.3	2.8	3.1	Cur. Mat.-L.T.D.		5.2	5.7	1.0	3.6	2.1
12.8	12.9	12.7	Trade Payables		18.4	15.9	11.2	13.9	8.5
.5	.7	.7	Income Taxes Payable		.0	.3	.6	.7	1.3
14.4	14.1	14.2	All Other Current		10.1	15.4	16.4	12.8	16.3
40.7	39.0	42.3	Total Current		62.1	58.7	40.2	39.7	33.7
12.0	13.9	9.3	Long-Term Debt		9.8	14.6	6.4	7.8	9.8
.4	.4	.4	Deferred Taxes		.1	.4	.1	.5	.6
8.6	8.2	4.0	All Other Non-Current		1.7	8.5	8.4	2.5	1.6
38.4	38.4	44.0	Net Worth		26.3	17.8	44.9	49.6	54.3
100.0	100.0	100.0	Total Liabilties & Net Worth		100.0	100.0	100.0	100.0	100.0
			INCOME DATA						
100.0	100.0	100.0	Net Sales		100.0	100.0	100.0	100.0	100.0
42.7	41.4	41.4	Gross Profit		43.6	43.4	45.7	40.7	37.2
35.2	33.7	33.8	Operating Expenses		40.8	37.6	41.1	29.9	29.7
7.5	7.7	7.6	Operating Profit		2.8	5.8	4.6	10.8	7.5
.7	1.5	1.0	All Other Expenses (net)		2.5	.6	1.8	.7	.4
6.7	6.1	6.6	Profit Before Taxes		.4	5.2	2.8	10.1	7.0
			RATIOS						
3.0	3.2	3.1			1.9	1.7	4.3	3.1	3.3
1.8	2.0	1.9	Current		1.3	1.1	2.1	1.8	2.5
1.1	1.3	1.2			.6	.9	1.2	1.2	1.5
1.8	2.0	2.1			1.1	.8	2.5	2.0	2.1
1.0	(99) 1.1	1.0	Quick		.5	.6	1.2	1.1	1.4
.6	.6	.6			.2	.5	.6	.7	.8
44 8.3	43 8.5	41 9.0			18 20.1	44 8.4	38 9.7	40 9.2	56 6.5
55 6.7	53 6.8	59 6.2	Sales/Receivables		39 9.4	53 6.9	63 5.8	58 6.3	72 5.1
70 5.2	69 5.3	81 4.5			61 6.0	79 4.6	77 4.7	82 4.4	90 4.0
42 8.6	45 8.0	48 7.6			23 15.9	0 UND	54 6.8	72 5.0	39 9.3
86 4.2	96 3.8	104 3.5	Cost of Sales/Inventory		110 3.3	94 3.9	112 3.3	104 3.5	93 3.9
131 2.8	136 2.7	148 2.5			172 2.1	149 2.5	149 2.4	141 2.6	156 2.3
22 16.4	19 19.0	19 18.8			10 36.5	23 15.5	21 17.3	17 21.5	20 18.0
37 9.9	32 11.4	38 9.7	Cost of Sales/Payables		46 8.0	52 7.1	34 10.7	34 10.8	37 9.9
53 6.9	51 7.1	59 6.2			75 4.9	116 3.1	53 6.9	70 5.2	45 8.1
3.5	3.5	3.1			4.9	7.4	3.0	3.3	2.2
7.5	5.9	5.6	Sales/Working Capital		27.5	33.6	5.3	5.6	4.2
44.8	13.5	24.1			-8.2	-19.4	11.9	18.4	7.5
19.9	23.3	14.9			5.0		34.9	19.1	17.1
(77) 6.9	(86) 6.4	(91) 5.1	EBIT/Interest		1.8		7.0	(31) 8.5	(20) 7.3
1.9	1.6	1.7			.4		1.3	3.1	2.1
10.5	14.1	12.3	Net Profit + Depr., Dep.,					7.7	67.1
(32) 4.3	(29) 3.8	(30) 3.5	Amort./Cur. Mat. L/T/D					(13) 5.1	(10) 13.4
1.2	1.0	1.7						1.8	1.6
.2	.2	.2			.1	.1	.2	.2	.2
.5	.5	.4	Fixed/Worth		.5	.5	.3	.4	.3
2.0	1.0	.9			-15.7	-1.6	.7	.8	.7
.6	.6	.5			1.3	2.5	.5	.5	.4
1.6	1.5	1.5	Debt/Worth		2.6	10.5	1.6	1.3	1.1
7.9	5.4	3.9			-21.4	-12.0	4.7	1.9	2.2
48.1	48.8	42.9	% Profit Before Taxes/Tangible				39.9	51.8	37.1
(74) 22.6	(89) 30.1	(95) 30.4	Net Worth			(18) 21.3		(37) 30.8	25.7
10.6	11.3	9.1					5.6	13.0	8.9
19.8	19.0	17.8	% Profit Before Taxes/Total		14.0	13.5	16.3	22.3	14.3
8.7	10.0	9.6	Assets		2.6	4.5	9.7	11.3	9.9
3.4	2.9	2.2			-2.4	.8	1.0	4.9	4.7
23.3	31.5	28.4			273.2	71.3	35.5	31.3	12.4
11.7	12.3	12.7	Sales/Net Fixed Assets		26.6	26.2	16.1	12.7	9.2
5.7	6.6	6.8			10.5	7.3	6.4	6.7	6.3
2.4	2.4	2.4			3.1	2.7	2.6	2.3	2.0
1.8	1.8	1.6	Sales/Total Assets		2.5	1.8	1.6	1.6	1.5
1.3	1.3	1.3			1.1	1.2	1.3	1.3	1.0
1.2	.9	.9					1.0	1.0	.9
(76) 2.1	(85) 2.0	(85) 1.7	% Depr., Dep., Amort./Sales			(14) 1.5		(35) 1.7	(21) 1.8
3.3	2.8	2.8					2.2	3.0	3.9
4.1	2.5	4.2							
(16) 7.5	(22) 5.8	(16) 6.2	% Officers', Directors' Owners' Comp/Sales						
13.9	9.0	9.4							
3377816M	2645779M	2669268M	Net Sales ($)	681M	22447M	41997M	146201M	620901M	1837041M
2457195M	1778784M	1962524M	Total Assets ($)	664M	14967M	24468M	86972M	423669M	1411784M

© RMA 2007

M = $ thousand   MM = $ million
See Pages 11 through 21 for Explanation of Ratios and Data

Current Data Sorted by Assets   Comparative Historical Data

Type of Statement	0-500M	500M-2MM	2-10MM	10-50MM	50-100MM	100-250MM		
Unqualified		1	2	5	2	2	13	10
Reviewed		2		1			8	9
Compiled	2	2	1	1			9	12
Tax Returns	2	2	1				2	3
Other	3		4	2	1	1	14	12
		7 (4/1-9/30/06)		27 (10/1/06-3/31/07)			4/1/02-3/31/03 ALL	4/1/03-3/31/04 ALL
NUMBER OF STATEMENTS	2	8	9	9	3	3	46	46

	0-500M %	500M-2MM %	2-10MM %	10-50MM %	50-100MM %	100-250MM %	%	%
ASSETS								
Cash & Equivalents							5.8	9.1
Trade Receivables (net)							27.8	26.8
Inventory							35.7	38.2
All Other Current							2.0	1.5
Total Current							71.3	75.5
Fixed Assets (net)							19.4	16.1
Intangibles (net)							3.1	2.4
All Other Non-Current							6.2	6.1
Total							100.0	100.0
LIABILITIES								
Notes Payable-Short Term							14.4	13.4
Cur. Mat.-L.T.D.							2.0	2.0
Trade Payables							17.4	16.1
Income Taxes Payable							1.4	1.2
All Other Current							11.1	11.5
Total Current							46.3	44.3
Long-Term Debt							13.0	9.1
Deferred Taxes							.2	.1
All Other Non-Current							5.6	9.0
Net Worth							34.9	37.5
Total Liabilties & Net Worth							100.0	100.0
INCOME DATA								
Net Sales							100.0	100.0
Gross Profit							33.3	38.6
Operating Expenses							28.4	33.0
Operating Profit							4.8	5.5
All Other Expenses (net)							1.2	.8
Profit Before Taxes							3.6	4.7
RATIOS								
Current							2.8	2.8
							1.5	2.0
							1.1	1.3
Quick							1.3	1.4
							.7	.9
							.5	.4
Sales/Receivables							28 13.0	30 12.1
							41 8.9	40 9.1
							56 6.5	58 6.3
Cost of Sales/Inventory							43 8.5	57 6.4
							71 5.1	107 3.4
							120 3.0	122 3.0
Cost of Sales/Payables							15 24.9	17 21.2
							28 13.3	27 13.4
							60 6.0	50 7.4
Sales/Working Capital							5.4	4.4
							9.8	6.5
							38.8	17.1
EBIT/Interest							16.4	33.0
							(43) 2.8	(41) 5.0
							1.2	1.5
Net Profit + Depr., Dep., Amort./Cur. Mat. L/T/D							17.0	15.9
							(13) 5.7	(12) 5.9
							1.8	1.3
Fixed/Worth							.2	.2
							.5	.3
							1.8	1.3
Debt/Worth							.8	.7
							2.4	1.3
							5.0	4.6
% Profit Before Taxes/Tangible Net Worth							51.3	49.0
							(41) 34.6	(39) 33.3
							10.6	9.1
% Profit Before Taxes/Total Assets							19.5	23.4
							7.5	8.7
							.8	1.9
Sales/Net Fixed Assets							53.7	40.0
							18.6	15.3
							7.0	10.0
Sales/Total Assets							3.3	2.9
							2.4	2.4
							1.7	1.9
% Depr., Dep., Amort./Sales							.7	.4
							(41) 1.5	(44) 1.2
							2.4	2.0
% Officers', Directors' Owners' Comp/Sales							1.4	1.4
							(18) 3.0	(15) 2.4
							5.0	3.8
Net Sales ($)	1819M	24284M	118532M	395493M	331350M	881201M	1346000M	1791217M
Total Assets ($)	548M	10084M	48361M	209455M	181436M	520477M	627230M	898503M

© RMA 2007

M = $ thousand   MM = $ million
See Pages 11 through 21 for Explanation of Ratios and Data

Comparative Historical Data | Current Data Sorted by Sales

			Type of Statement	0-1MM	1-3MM	3-5MM	5-10MM	10-25MM	25MM & OVER
11	11	12	Unqualified				2	1	9
11	7	3	Reviewed				2	1	
8	4	3	Compiled		1	1	1		
4	8	5	Tax Returns	2	1	1	1		
9	18	11	Other		3				5
4/1/04-3/31/05 ALL	4/1/05-3/31/06 ALL	4/1/06-3/31/07 ALL			7 (4/1-9/30/06)			27 (10/1/06-3/31/07)	
43	48	34	**NUMBER OF STATEMENTS**	2	5	2	8	2	15
%	%	%	**ASSETS**	%	%	%	%	%	%
6.9	7.5	8.2	Cash & Equivalents						2.4
27.8	24.9	27.3	Trade Receivables (net)						29.7
37.4	36.6	38.7	Inventory						38.9
1.7	1.4	1.9	All Other Current						2.5
73.8	70.4	76.0	Total Current						73.6
17.1	16.8	17.4	Fixed Assets (net)						20.1
5.4	7.7	2.3	Intangibles (net)						2.8
3.7	5.0	4.2	All Other Non-Current						3.6
100.0	100.0	100.0	Total						100.0
			LIABILITIES						
13.8	13.1	10.3	Notes Payable-Short Term						10.2
2.6	1.7	2.9	Cur. Mat.-L.T.D.						.8
14.8	14.8	18.1	Trade Payables						16.6
.4	.4	.7	Income Taxes Payable						.1
8.2	8.9	9.3	All Other Current						9.6
39.8	38.9	41.2	Total Current						37.3
17.6	14.3	14.8	Long-Term Debt						9.0
.2	.3	.3	Deferred Taxes						.2
7.9	12.6	9.3	All Other Non-Current						6.2
34.4	33.8	34.5	Net Worth						47.4
100.0	100.0	100.0	Total Liabilities & Net Worth						100.0
			INCOME DATA						
100.0	100.0	100.0	Net Sales						100.0
40.5	41.3	42.1	Gross Profit						36.4
34.2	34.6	35.3	Operating Expenses						30.4
6.3	6.6	6.8	Operating Profit						6.0
1.1	1.3	1.1	All Other Expenses (net)						1.0
5.2	5.3	5.6	Profit Before Taxes						5.0
			RATIOS						
3.1	2.8	2.9							4.1
2.0	2.2	2.0	Current						2.6
1.5	1.3	1.3							1.1
1.6	1.4	1.5							1.6
.9	.9	.8	Quick						.9
.5	.6	.5							.6
35 10.4	33 10.9	32 11.3							46 8.0
45 8.2	45 8.1	49 7.5	Sales/Receivables						51 7.1
62 5.9	61 6.0	66 5.6							69 5.3
76 4.8	79 4.6	60 6.1							60 6.1
105 3.5	114 3.2	137 2.7	Cost of Sales/Inventory						127 2.9
132 2.8	143 2.6	168 2.2							151 2.4
19 19.6	22 16.9	26 14.2							26 14.2
29 12.6	40 9.2	48 7.6	Cost of Sales/Payables						44 8.4
56 6.5	67 5.5	82 4.5							64 5.7
4.2	4.4	4.0							3.1
6.3	6.3	5.8	Sales/Working Capital						4.8
10.5	12.2	19.2							25.8
14.1	12.7	19.1							29.5
(40) 3.3	(43) 3.8	(30) 4.5	EBIT/Interest					(13)	9.2
1.6	1.8	1.5							2.0
	34.5		Net Profit + Depr., Dep.,						
	(12) 4.7		Amort./Cur. Mat. L/T/D						
	1.1								
.2	.3	.1							.2
.5	.5	.4	Fixed/Worth						.4
2.1	2.5	1.6							1.3
.8	.9	.7							.4
1.7	2.3	1.5	Debt/Worth						1.1
11.3	9.0	4.7							3.7
42.5	48.8	52.3	% Profit Before Taxes/Tangible						34.0
(34) 19.3	(40) 22.2	(30) 25.7	Net Worth					(14)	25.5
5.3	6.5	10.5							14.9
18.2	19.1	23.7	% Profit Before Taxes/Total						18.9
5.4	7.1	10.6	Assets						11.2
1.7	2.0	1.1							2.7
35.8	47.5	42.7							42.4
14.4	19.4	18.9	Sales/Net Fixed Assets						11.3
9.8	9.3	9.0							6.9
2.7	2.7	2.4							2.2
2.3	2.2	2.1	Sales/Total Assets						2.1
1.9	1.5	1.7							1.6
.8	.7	.6							.8
(39) 1.4	(44) 1.0	(27) 1.1	% Depr., Dep., Amort./Sales					(12)	1.5
2.1	1.8	2.8							2.7
1.6	1.3	1.4	% Officers', Directors'						
(12) 3.4	(19) 3.7	(12) 2.3	Owners' Comp/Sales						
6.8	6.4	4.5							
1451069M	1488753M	1752679M	Net Sales ($)	1819M	11157M	7259M	61958M	33332M	1637154M
805752M	895759M	970361M	Total Assets ($)	548M	5781M	2911M	41636M	11029M	908456M

© RMA 2007

M = $ thousand   MM = $ million
See Pages 11 through 21 for Explanation of Ratios and Data

Current Data Sorted by Assets   Comparative Historical Data

0-500M	500M-2MM	2-10MM	10-50MM	50-100MM	100-250MM	Type of Statement	4/1/02-3/31/03 ALL	4/1/03-3/31/04 ALL
		8	7	2	2	Unqualified	7	8
	2	8	2			Reviewed	17	14
	2	4				Compiled	6	7
	2	3	2			Tax Returns	3	2
1	5	12	6	1	2	Other	14	18
	13 (4/1-9/30/06)		58 (10/1/06-3/31/07)					
1	**11**	**35**	**17**	**3**	**4**	**NUMBER OF STATEMENTS**	**47**	**49**
%	%	%	%	%	%	**ASSETS**	%	%
	4.8	7.4	4.0			Cash & Equivalents	6.3	5.9
	39.2	33.2	33.2			Trade Receivables (net)	32.3	29.8
	30.3	29.4	27.6			Inventory	32.6	30.0
	.5	5.3	3.5			All Other Current	3.8	2.3
	74.8	75.3	68.4			Total Current	75.1	68.0
	17.7	16.2	15.1			Fixed Assets (net)	17.3	22.0
	3.1	2.4	12.6			Intangibles (net)	3.5	5.1
	4.4	6.1	4.0			All Other Non-Current	4.2	5.0
	100.0	100.0	100.0			Total	100.0	100.0
						LIABILITIES		
	12.2	11.0	16.4			Notes Payable-Short Term	16.4	14.7
	6.9	2.5	4.7			Cur. Mat.-L.T.D.	3.8	4.5
	15.9	21.0	17.6			Trade Payables	16.0	15.9
	.8	.4	.1			Income Taxes Payable	.5	.5
	12.3	12.6	11.6			All Other Current	12.0	9.5
	48.1	47.4	50.3			Total Current	48.7	45.2
	23.3	11.6	14.7			Long-Term Debt	10.7	14.9
	.1	.6	.5			Deferred Taxes	.3	.3
	7.9	3.5	3.2			All Other Non-Current	2.9	6.6
	20.6	36.9	31.2			Net Worth	37.5	33.0
	100.0	100.0	100.0			Total Liabilities & Net Worth	100.0	100.0
						INCOME DATA		
	100.0	100.0	100.0			Net Sales	100.0	100.0
	40.1	33.1	31.8			Gross Profit	34.0	36.3
	30.7	26.0	27.0			Operating Expenses	32.2	32.3
	9.5	7.1	4.8			Operating Profit	1.7	4.0
	2.0	.4	1.5			All Other Expenses (net)	1.2	1.1
	7.5	6.7	3.3			Profit Before Taxes	.5	2.8
						RATIOS		
	3.1	2.6	2.4			Current	2.2	2.2
	1.4	1.7	1.2				1.5	1.6
	.8	1.2	1.0				1.2	1.1
	1.6	1.7	1.1			Quick	1.3	1.3
	1.0	1.0	.7				.8	.8
	.6	.5	.5				.6	.6
	27 13.5	40 9.1	49 7.5			Sales/Receivables	33 11.2	40 9.1
	49 7.4	50 7.3	56 6.6				45 8.1	48 7.6
	60 6.1	62 5.8	63 5.8				63 5.8	59 6.2
	27 13.3	40 9.0	32 11.4			Cost of Sales/Inventory	32 11.3	43 8.4
	54 6.8	68 5.4	80 4.6				77 4.8	82 4.4
	108 3.4	105 3.5	100 3.7				110 3.3	118 3.1
	27 13.5	27 13.4	27 13.4			Cost of Sales/Payables	18 20.0	22 16.3
	41 9.0	38 9.5	39 9.4				33 11.0	41 8.8
	52 7.0	60 6.1	67 5.5				45 8.1	59 8.1
	5.8	5.3	6.2			Sales/Working Capital	5.2	4.7
	14.7	6.4	15.6				9.1	8.8
	-27.0	17.4	-610.4				21.3	105.5
	31.0	25.3	7.1			EBIT/Interest	8.9	10.0
	(10) 8.3	(34) 6.1	3.5				(42) 3.0	(47) 2.6
	2.7	2.5	.8				.3	-.3
		7.2				Net Profit + Depr., Dep.,	5.9	4.9
	(11)	3.7				Amort./Cur. Mat. L/T/D	(15) 1.2	(17) 1.4
		2.6					.1	-1.6
	.1	.2	.3			Fixed/Worth	.1	.2
	.2	.3	1.1				.5	.7
	2.0	1.0	-.9				1.2	8.5
	1.0	1.0	1.1			Debt/Worth	.6	.7
	2.7	1.4	3.4				1.9	2.0
	4.6	3.0	-7.3				5.0	21.2
		79.3	46.0			% Profit Before Taxes/Tangible	36.0	36.5
	(33)	27.4	(10) 37.1			Net Worth	(41) 9.8	(39) 15.4
		11.2	12.4				-3.4	2.4
	21.1	23.2	14.6			% Profit Before Taxes/Total	12.0	15.9
	11.7	9.8	5.1			Assets	3.1	3.8
	5.6	3.8	-.8				-1.8	-3.7
	106.1	41.5	28.3			Sales/Net Fixed Assets	67.2	39.2
	39.0	24.1	19.1				19.9	13.5
	9.6	10.6	8.2				9.8	4.9
	4.1	3.0	2.2			Sales/Total Assets	3.0	2.6
	2.8	2.4	2.2				2.5	2.0
	2.3	1.8	1.6				2.0	1.5
		.5	.8			% Depr., Dep., Amort./Sales	.5	1.0
	(31)	1.4	(15) 1.9				(42) 1.4	(37) 1.8
		2.3	2.2				2.8	3.7
		1.2				% Officers', Directors'	2.8	3.1
	(15)	3.3				Owners' Comp/Sales	(22) 4.6	(18) 5.1
							7.0	7.0
1554M	44672M	416201M	866392M	321484M	1228355M	Net Sales ($)	1051834M	1456692M
377M	13754M	173871M	433119M	234204M	803591M	Total Assets ($)	659739M	918624M

M = $ thousand   MM = $ million
See Pages 11 through 21 for Explanation of Ratios and Data

Comparative Historical Data / **Current Data Sorted by Sales**

4/1/04-3/31/05 ALL	4/1/05-3/31/06 ALL	4/1/06-3/31/07 ALL	Type of Statement	0-1MM	1-3MM	3-5MM	5-10MM	10-25MM	25MM & OVER
13	10	19	Unqualified				2	7	10
15	13	12	Reviewed		1	2	1	6	2
4	2	6	Compiled				5	1	
7	8	8	Tax Returns		2	1	2	1	2
15	18	26	Other		1	2	9	6	8
				13 (4/1-9/30/06)			58 (10/1/06-3/31/07)		
54	51	71	**NUMBER OF STATEMENTS**		4	5	19	21	22
%	%	%	**ASSETS**	%	%	%	%	%	%
5.2	7.6	5.8	Cash & Equivalents	DATA NOT AVAILABLE			8.4	5.8	4.5
31.8	33.3	32.8	Trade Receivables (net)				35.8	34.7	31.3
30.9	28.3	28.2	Inventory				28.5	26.0	26.2
2.2	4.9	3.8	All Other Current				4.7	5.0	3.3
70.1	74.2	70.6	Total Current				77.4	71.6	65.3
19.3	16.2	17.2	Fixed Assets (net)				13.2	19.0	16.7
6.9	4.4	6.7	Intangibles (net)				3.7	4.0	13.2
3.8	5.3	5.4	All Other Non-Current				5.7	5.5	4.8
100.0	100.0	100.0	Total				100.0	100.0	100.0
			LIABILITIES						
11.6	10.5	11.3	Notes Payable-Short Term				8.5	14.9	10.3
3.9	3.3	3.6	Cur. Mat.-L.T.D.				1.4	3.5	3.4
17.0	16.5	18.0	Trade Payables				20.9	19.3	15.7
.3	.6	.4	Income Taxes Payable				.6	.6	.3
12.8	11.5	12.4	All Other Current				10.9	16.1	12.4
45.7	42.3	45.8	Total Current				42.4	54.4	42.1
18.9	11.7	16.1	Long-Term Debt				14.1	10.5	17.4
.5	.4	.4	Deferred Taxes				.6	.8	.0
6.4	3.4	4.7	All Other Non-Current				5.5	1.5	2.8
28.5	42.1	33.0	Net Worth				37.4	32.8	37.7
100.0	100.0	100.0	Total Liabilties & Net Worth				100.0	100.0	100.0
			INCOME DATA						
100.0	100.0	100.0	Net Sales				100.0	100.0	100.0
35.5	38.4	34.6	Gross Profit				33.5	32.4	33.7
31.0	32.8	27.6	Operating Expenses				24.7	26.6	26.4
4.4	5.6	7.0	Operating Profit				8.8	5.8	7.3
1.3	.7	1.1	All Other Expenses (net)				.6	.4	1.9
3.1	4.8	5.9	Profit Before Taxes				8.1	5.4	5.4
			RATIOS						
2.4	2.6	2.6					2.7	1.8	2.6
1.7	1.7	1.6	Current				2.0	1.4	1.6
1.1	1.2	1.2					1.4	1.0	1.2
1.4	1.7	1.5					1.8	1.2	1.3
.9	1.0	1.0	Quick				1.0	.8	1.0
.5	.6	.5					.7	.5	.6
40 9.2	**41** 9.0	**40** 9.0					**43** 8.5	**46** 7.9	**44** 8.3
51 7.2	**50** 7.3	**52** 7.0	Sales/Receivables				**50** 7.3	**55** 6.7	**53** 6.9
64 5.7	**61** 6.0	**60** 6.1					**62** 5.8	**63** 5.8	**59** 6.2
45 8.2	**40** 9.1	**39** 9.2					**39** 9.2	**36** 10.1	**39** 9.3
80 4.6	**84** 4.3	**74** 4.9	Cost of Sales/Inventory				**67** 5.4	**62** 5.9	**79** 4.6
111 3.3	**105** 3.5	**107** 3.4					**122** 3.0	**87** 4.2	**108** 3.4
26 14.1	**20** 18.4	**25** 14.7					**31** 11.7	**23** 15.6	**22** 16.8
41 8.9	**39** 9.3	**38** 9.7	Cost of Sales/Payables				**45** 8.2	**38** 9.5	**31** 11.7
55 6.7	**60** 6.1	**56** 6.5					**56** 6.5	**64** 5.7	**42** 8.7
5.6	4.7	5.3					4.9	6.2	4.3
7.6	6.8	8.4	Sales/Working Capital				5.8	11.1	7.7
38.0	9.9	21.8					15.5	NM	22.8
12.2	24.6	19.2					46.5	18.4	22.2
(51) 4.0	(48) 5.6	(69) 4.6	EBIT/Interest				(18) 13.8	(20) 4.5	4.9
.8	1.8	2.1					2.6	2.6	.8
9.4	7.8	6.8							20.8
(20) 3.0	(15) 2.7	(24) 2.6	Net Profit + Depr., Dep., Amort./Cur. Mat. L/T/D						(10) 2.6
1.0	.1	.6							.2
.2	.2	.2					.1	.2	.2
.6	.3	.6	Fixed/Worth				.2	.8	.7
2.7	.9	1.5					1.0	1.2	-.9
1.0	.7	1.0					1.0	1.0	.7
2.8	1.5	2.4	Debt/Worth				1.9	2.3	2.6
11.5	2.9	5.1					3.1	5.6	-7.4
42.3	43.2	56.0					105.6	92.2	46.9
(44) 22.3	(45) 22.7	(57) 30.3	% Profit Before Taxes/Tangible Net Worth				(18) 28.9	(18) 32.1	(15) 32.2
.7	7.5	13.5					16.5	10.9	12.7
15.9	17.8	18.8					23.2	20.5	16.4
7.0	8.9	9.8	% Profit Before Taxes/Total Assets				11.7	6.5	11.0
-.6	1.1	3.4					5.9	3.7	-.8
40.1	37.7	39.0					83.2	34.1	22.1
14.1	20.5	19.5	Sales/Net Fixed Assets				30.5	14.6	18.9
7.8	10.4	8.9					10.6	8.6	6.4
3.0	2.9	2.9					3.3	3.1	2.6
2.1	2.2	2.2	Sales/Total Assets				2.4	2.3	2.2
1.7	1.6	1.7					1.8	1.7	1.4
.8	.7	.8					.5	1.1	.8
(47) 2.0	(42) 1.5	(59) 1.7	% Depr., Dep., Amort./Sales				(14) 1.1	(19) 1.9	(18) 1.7
2.7	2.7	2.3					2.1	3.4	2.4
2.1	2.0	1.2					1.1		
(21) 3.8	(17) 3.9	(25) 3.3	% Officers', Directors' Owners' Comp/Sales				(10) 2.7		
5.5	5.7	5.0					4.4		
1803959M	**2498479M**	**2878658M**	Net Sales ($)		**6885M**	**19161M**	**135094M**	**338645M**	**2378873M**
982596M	**1364811M**	**1658916M**	Total Assets ($)		**3320M**	**7211M**	**63236M**	**158116M**	**1427033M**

M = $ thousand MM = $ million

See Pages 11 through 21 for Explanation of Ratios and Data

	Current Data Sorted by Assets							Comparative Historical Data	
				2	1	3	**Type of Statement**		
	2	5	2				Unqualified	9	10
	4	4	2				Reviewed	7	11
1	1	1					Compiled	4	7
	1	7	11				Tax Returns	2	2
							Other	19	9
	9 (4/1-9/30/06)		36 (10/1/06-3/31/07)					4/1/02-3/31/03	4/1/03-3/31/04
0-500M	500M-2MM	2-10MM	10-50MM	50-100MM	100-250MM			ALL	ALL
1	8	17	15	1	3		**NUMBER OF STATEMENTS**	41	39
%	%	%	%	%	%		**ASSETS**	%	%
		8.4	4.8				Cash & Equivalents	5.6	11.2
		28.9	23.6				Trade Receivables (net)	20.7	21.2
		31.9	35.7				Inventory	31.3	28.8
		.8	4.5				All Other Current	2.2	2.1
		70.0	68.6				Total Current	59.8	63.4
		15.9	19.2				Fixed Assets (net)	21.5	19.0
		7.7	5.4				Intangibles (net)	9.6	7.9
		6.4	6.8				All Other Non-Current	9.1	9.7
		100.0	100.0				Total	100.0	100.0
							LIABILITIES		
		15.1	13.9				Notes Payable-Short Term	11.4	10.1
		2.3	2.3				Cur. Mat.-L.T.D.	3.2	3.4
		15.3	14.0				Trade Payables	12.4	11.7
		.4	.2				Income Taxes Payable	.7	1.0
		4.6	9.4				All Other Current	9.0	8.2
		37.7	39.9				Total Current	36.7	34.5
		14.0	11.1				Long-Term Debt	18.0	15.1
		.0	.2				Deferred Taxes	.2	.1
		2.1	14.4				All Other Non-Current	4.8	7.3
		46.2	34.4				Net Worth	40.3	43.1
		100.0	100.0				Total Liabilities & Net Worth	100.0	100.0
							INCOME DATA		
		100.0	100.0				Net Sales	100.0	100.0
		33.4	31.6				Gross Profit	35.1	37.0
		26.6	24.5				Operating Expenses	29.1	31.8
		6.8	7.0				Operating Profit	6.0	5.2
		1.6	1.8				All Other Expenses (net)	2.2	1.2
		5.1	5.3				Profit Before Taxes	3.8	4.0
							RATIOS		
		3.3	3.7					3.1	3.9
		2.3	2.4				Current	1.5	2.0
		1.3	1.1					1.0	1.3
		2.0	1.3					1.7	1.9
		1.0	.9				Quick	.7	.9
		.7	.4					.4	.5
	42	8.7	29	12.5			Sales/Receivables	24 15.0	27 13.7
	48	7.6	43	8.5				41 8.9	45 8.1
	58	6.3	57	6.4				57 6.4	53 6.9
	52	7.1	77	4.8			Cost of Sales/Inventory	48 7.6	57 6.4
	92	4.0	89	4.1				97 3.8	92 4.0
	128	2.8	116	3.1				138 2.6	138 2.6
	21	17.6	19	18.8			Cost of Sales/Payables	19 19.6	22 16.4
	36	10.2	36	10.2				30 12.3	32 11.5
	73	5.0	41	8.9				49 7.4	54 6.8
		3.0	3.7				Sales/Working Capital	3.8	3.7
		5.2	6.9					7.7	6.5
		16.7	29.6					508.6	15.2
		13.9	11.5					8.9	9.7
	(15)	3.5	(14)	5.4			EBIT/Interest	(39) 3.0	(33) 3.9
		2.3	2.6					.9	2.1
							Net Profit + Depr., Dep.,	3.9	
							Amort./Cur. Mat. L/T/D	(12) 2.5	
								.3	
		.1	.3					.2	.2
		.3	.7				Fixed/Worth	.5	.5
		3.0	1.3					1.7	1.3
		.4	.8					.7	.6
		1.2	1.9				Debt/Worth	1.6	1.7
		6.0	7.3					5.1	4.0
		40.3	76.6				% Profit Before Taxes/Tangible	38.5	40.3
	(15)	12.4	(14)	30.7			Net Worth	(36) 14.5	(36) 21.3
		5.4	8.1					2.6	4.2
		13.3	19.0				% Profit Before Taxes/Total	15.1	13.8
		7.8	10.3				Assets	5.5	5.6
		3.1	1.5					-.2	.2
		110.3	34.4					25.7	29.4
		19.1	13.8				Sales/Net Fixed Assets	10.2	12.0
		6.9	5.1					5.8	6.0
		2.4	2.6					2.3	2.3
		1.8	2.2				Sales/Total Assets	1.8	1.7
		1.3	1.5					1.3	1.4
		.6	.8					.9	1.1
	(13)	1.4	(14)	2.0			% Depr., Dep., Amort./Sales	(35) 1.6	(29) 2.1
		2.7	2.6					3.8	3.4
							% Officers', Directors'	1.2	3.8
							Owners' Comp/Sales	(15) 4.1	(15) 6.6
								6.6	8.2
1199M	20280M	174059M	696589M	82848M	809326M		Net Sales ($)	1548840M	1295381M
498M	8270M	95994M	334276M	53392M	554000M		Total Assets ($)	1181740M	832912M

© RMA 2007

M = $ thousand   MM = $ million

See Pages 11 through 21 for Explanation of Ratios and Data

Comparative Historical Data | | | Current Data Sorted by Sales

					Type of Statement						
	5		7		6		Unqualified						6
	14		12		9		Reviewed						2
	11		6		8		Compiled	1	2	1	3	
	1		6		3		Tax Returns	3	1	3	1	
	13		19		19		Other	2		1		
	4/1/04-		4/1/05-		4/1/06-				2	2	7	8
	3/31/05		3/31/06		3/31/07			9 (4/1-9/30/06)			36 (10/1/06-3/31/07)	
	ALL		ALL		ALL			0-1MM	1-3MM	3-5MM	5-10MM	10-25MM	25MM & OVER
	44		50		45		NUMBER OF STATEMENTS	6	5	7	11	16

	%		%		%	ASSETS	%	%	%	%	%	%
	7.1		11.6		9.6	Cash & Equivalents					8.8	6.5
	33.5		27.3		26.6	Trade Receivables (net)					27.7	25.8
	25.2		27.3		29.9	Inventory					29.0	35.5
	4.5		2.0		2.5	All Other Current					1.8	3.9
	70.2		68.2		68.5	Total Current					67.3	71.7
	16.9		20.7		17.0	Fixed Assets (net)					16.3	19.2
	6.4		4.5		6.3	Intangibles (net)					5.3	3.8
	6.5		6.7		8.2	All Other Non-Current					11.1	5.3
	100.0		100.0		100.0	Total					100.0	100.0
						LIABILITIES						
	11.7		10.7		13.6	Notes Payable-Short Term					9.6	12.8
	2.7		2.0		2.4	Cur. Mat.-L.T.D.					3.0	1.9
	14.1		13.5		15.8	Trade Payables					15.2	12.7
	.4		.3		.2	Income Taxes Payable					.6	.2
	10.0		8.3		9.9	All Other Current					3.5	9.9
	39.0		34.9		41.9	Total Current					31.9	37.6
	20.6		12.8		13.0	Long-Term Debt					14.5	8.2
	.1		.3		.1	Deferred Taxes					.4	.1
	2.7		6.1		6.8	All Other Non-Current					1.3	15.5
	37.6		45.9		38.1	Net Worth					52.0	38.6
	100.0		100.0		100.0	Total Liabilties & Net Worth					100.0	100.0
						INCOME DATA						
	100.0		100.0		100.0	Net Sales					100.0	100.0
	34.7		37.7		35.3	Gross Profit					31.9	32.3
	29.5		31.9		28.0	Operating Expenses					22.8	25.0
	5.2		5.8		7.3	Operating Profit					9.2	7.3
	2.7		.8		1.2	All Other Expenses (net)					1.4	1.4
	2.5		5.0		6.1	Profit Before Taxes					7.7	5.9
						RATIOS						
	2.9		3.4		3.3						4.2	3.7
	1.8		2.3		2.1	Current					3.1	2.5
	1.4		1.3		1.1						1.3	1.2
	1.6		2.1		1.6						2.9	1.5
	1.0		1.3		1.0	Quick					1.1	1.0
	.6		.6		.5						.6	.6
44	8.3	37	9.9	30	12.1					44	8.3	32	11.2
54	6.7	47	7.7	45	8.0	Sales/Receivables				49	7.4	50	7.3
64	5.7	60	6.0	58	6.3					60	6.1	65	5.6
36	10.2	54	6.7	51	7.1					42	8.7	79	4.6
68	5.3	77	4.7	81	4.5	Cost of Sales/Inventory				71	5.2	91	4.0
99	3.7	105	3.5	109	3.3					95	3.8	113	3.2
17	21.4	24	15.3	18	20.2					21	17.3	18	20.0
31	11.8	37	9.8	36	10.2	Cost of Sales/Payables				31	11.7	34	10.8
47	7.7	54	6.8	56	6.5					65	5.6	40	9.0
	4.2		4.2		3.5						3.2	3.5
	6.9		5.9		5.7	Sales/Working Capital					5.2	5.6
	12.2		9.2		46.3						16.9	25.1
	21.4		19.7		10.6						15.3	20.2
(40)	5.6	(44)	9.2	(39)	5.4	EBIT/Interest				(10)	7.1	(14)	6.5
	1.5		1.9		2.8						4.2	2.6
	34.6					Net Profit + Depr., Dep.,						
(12)	3.8					Amort./Cur. Mat. L/T/D						
	2.1											
	.2		.2		.2						.1	.2
	.4		.4		.4	Fixed/Worth					.3	.6
	1.2		1.2		2.4						.7	.9
	.7		.5		.6						.4	.6
	1.4		1.3		1.6	Debt/Worth					.8	1.3
	6.0		3.9		17.9						1.6	4.2
	35.2		55.4		52.7	% Profit Before Taxes/Tangible					85.7	49.3
(38)	25.7	(45)	22.0	(38)	24.3	Net Worth					26.8	(15)	29.9
	7.2		6.9		7.4						5.8	12.7
	14.9		20.2		20.0	% Profit Before Taxes/Total					18.3	21.1
	9.1		9.4		10.3	Assets					9.6	13.1
	1.1		2.5		4.0						4.2	2.4
	33.8		28.5		42.5						103.4	38.4
	13.1		12.1		19.1	Sales/Net Fixed Assets					7.9	13.8
	7.1		5.3		6.0						5.1	5.5
	3.0		2.5		2.5						2.5	2.5
	2.2		1.9		2.0	Sales/Total Assets					1.8	2.1
	1.4		1.5		1.5						1.5	1.6
	.7		.8		.8							.9
(38)	1.7	(44)	1.7	(39)	1.9	% Depr., Dep., Amort./Sales					(15)	1.9
	2.9		2.7		2.4							2.3
	4.2		4.0		3.7	% Officers', Directors'						
(12)	6.1	(17)	5.3	(13)	6.0	Owners' Comp/Sales						
	7.7		7.9		8.3							
	1354558M		1401303M		1784301M	Net Sales ($)	10234M	19110M	53068M	171800M	1530089M
	842232M		825738M		1046430M	Total Assets ($)	5080M	8351M	37188M	104663M	891148M

Current Data Sorted by Assets   **Comparative Historical Data**

0-500M	500M-2MM	2-10MM	10-50MM	50-100MM	100-250MM	Type of Statement	4/1/02-3/31/03 ALL	4/1/03-3/31/04 ALL
		6	8	3	1	Unqualified	19	16
		6	6			Reviewed	12	13
2	2					Compiled	9	8
2		1				Tax Returns	3	2
1	4	8	11	1	5	Other	21	16
	15 (4/1-9/30/06)		52 (10/1/06-3/31/07)					
5	6	21	25	4	6	**NUMBER OF STATEMENTS**	64	55
%	%	%	%	%	%	**ASSETS**	%	%
		9.4	4.5			Cash & Equivalents	9.8	7.8
		34.9	32.4			Trade Receivables (net)	27.3	28.2
		27.7	29.9			Inventory	29.4	23.2
		1.3	1.3			All Other Current	2.0	3.3
		73.4	68.2			Total Current	68.5	62.5
		19.9	17.3			Fixed Assets (net)	21.7	24.0
		2.1	7.8			Intangibles (net)	4.1	5.7
		4.7	6.7			All Other Non-Current	5.7	7.8
		100.0	100.0			Total	100.0	100.0
						LIABILITIES		
		10.4	12.0			Notes Payable-Short Term	10.1	13.1
		3.6	1.2			Cur. Mat.-L.T.D.	2.7	2.5
		21.1	16.0			Trade Payables	13.3	13.9
		.1	.6			Income Taxes Payable	.3	.3
		9.4	12.9			All Other Current	11.7	13.2
		44.6	42.8			Total Current	38.0	43.0
		8.9	13.7			Long-Term Debt	12.1	13.2
		.3	1.7			Deferred Taxes	.4	.5
		3.2	5.7			All Other Non-Current	3.6	6.7
		42.9	36.2			Net Worth	45.8	36.6
		100.0	100.0			Total Liabilties & Net Worth	100.0	100.0
						INCOME DATA		
		100.0	100.0			Net Sales	100.0	100.0
		25.6	29.0			Gross Profit	29.2	30.0
		20.2	23.2			Operating Expenses	25.6	25.7
		5.5	5.8			Operating Profit	3.6	4.2
		.8	2.0			All Other Expenses (net)	1.3	1.1
		4.7	3.8			Profit Before Taxes	2.3	3.1
						RATIOS		
		2.4	2.2				3.0	2.5
		1.7	1.5			Current	1.8	1.4
		1.2	1.1				1.4	1.1
		1.7	1.1				1.7	1.5
		1.0	.9			Quick	.9	.8
		.6	.6				.5	.5
		32 11.4	44 8.3				35 10.5	36 10.2
		51 7.2	56 6.5			Sales/Receivables	48 7.6	50 7.3
		62 5.9	70 5.2				58 6.3	62 5.9
		27 13.4	49 7.4				45 8.1	32 11.3
		58 6.3	89 4.1			Cost of Sales/Inventory	68 5.3	54 6.7
		76 4.8	143 2.6				98 3.7	73 5.0
		19 19.0	28 12.9				22 16.9	23 16.0
		40 9.2	40 9.2			Cost of Sales/Payables	31 11.8	32 11.5
		54 6.8	51 7.1				45 8.2	42 8.7
		5.9	4.1				4.6	6.9
		9.1	8.4			Sales/Working Capital	8.0	12.3
		29.7	31.1				13.4	30.2
		16.9	7.8				9.8	8.9
		(20) 4.0	3.7			EBIT/Interest	(54) 2.5	(49) 3.7
		1.8	1.4				.5	.9
			44.4				13.6	9.1
			(12) 20.7			Net Profit + Depr., Dep., Amort./Cur. Mat. L/T/D	(20) 3.8	(19) 3.4
			5.1				.5	1.7
		.2	.3				.2	.3
		.5	.7			Fixed/Worth	.4	.6
		1.0	1.2				1.4	2.5
		.6	1.0				.4	.7
		1.9	2.1			Debt/Worth	1.1	1.8
		3.2	6.0				3.4	8.2
		51.7	47.3				33.7	38.0
		31.7	(22) 29.2			% Profit Before Taxes/Tangible Net Worth	(55) 13.9	(46) 23.6
		6.2	9.8				-.2	3.1
		27.2	13.6				14.6	13.0
		9.2	10.1			% Profit Before Taxes/Total Assets	5.2	5.3
		2.2	1.4				-1.3	-.2
		28.4	25.1				19.4	23.5
		13.5	10.7			Sales/Net Fixed Assets	11.9	10.9
		8.5	7.6				5.9	6.3
		3.9	2.5				2.4	2.6
		2.8	1.8			Sales/Total Assets	2.0	2.2
		1.8	1.3				1.5	1.4
		.7	.7				1.0	1.0
		(20) 1.1	(21) 1.5			% Depr., Dep., Amort./Sales	(51) 1.7	(47) 1.6
		1.8	2.9				3.0	2.6
							3.1	2.8
						% Officers', Directors' Owners' Comp/Sales	(15) 5.6	(14) 7.1
							11.9	9.8
4541M	24367M	343809M	1159285M	453797M	988659M	Net Sales ($)	3671619M	3738437M
1655M	8538M	117004M	601054M	310287M	825366M	Total Assets ($)	2103864M	2126958M

M = $ thousand   MM = $ million
See Pages 11 through 21 for Explanation of Ratios and Data

Comparative Historical Data | Current Data Sorted by Sales

Type of Statement									
	15	15	18					8	10
Unqualified	13	10	12				2	7	3
Reviewed	3	6	4	2	1	1			
Compiled	1	3	3		2		1		
Tax Returns	24	26	30	1	1	1	1	6	16
Other	4/1/04-3/31/05	4/1/05-3/31/06	4/1/06-3/31/07	15 (4/1-9/30/06)			52 (10/1/06-3/31/07)		
	ALL	ALL	ALL	0-1MM	1-3MM	3-5MM	5-10MM	10-25MM	25MM & OVER
NUMBER OF STATEMENTS	56	60	67	3	4	2	8	21	29
ASSETS	%	%	%	%	%	%	%	%	%
Cash & Equivalents	5.7	6.6	6.9					5.5	6.4
Trade Receivables (net)	29.0	27.2	31.3					29.4	32.8
Inventory	32.2	27.2	27.6					27.2	24.4
All Other Current	1.5	1.9	1.3					1.9	1.1
Total Current	68.3	62.9	67.2					63.9	64.7
Fixed Assets (net)	21.8	21.9	18.9					21.9	15.4
Intangibles (net)	3.5	6.4	8.8					8.0	13.2
All Other Non-Current	6.4	8.8	5.2					6.2	6.7
Total	100.0	100.0	100.0					100.0	100.0
LIABILITIES									
Notes Payable-Short Term	12.7	10.9	9.9					12.6	7.4
Cur. Mat.-L.T.D.	2.2	2.0	2.4					2.9	1.1
Trade Payables	15.9	13.3	18.5					18.2	15.2
Income Taxes Payable	.2	.2	.3					.1	.6
All Other Current	11.6	11.9	10.6					8.0	12.3
Total Current	42.6	38.4	41.7					41.8	36.5
Long-Term Debt	13.6	14.2	14.6					11.8	17.3
Deferred Taxes	.3	.4	.9					1.5	.9
All Other Non-Current	7.3	6.8	5.0					4.4	5.0
Net Worth	36.2	40.1	37.8					40.4	40.3
Total Liabilities & Net Worth	100.0	100.0	100.0					100.0	100.0
INCOME DATA									
Net Sales	100.0	100.0	100.0					100.0	100.0
Gross Profit	27.2	31.6	29.0					29.5	24.5
Operating Expenses	23.9	24.9	22.5					25.4	17.5
Operating Profit	3.3	6.7	6.5					4.1	7.0
All Other Expenses (net)	1.2	1.0	1.9					1.1	1.7
Profit Before Taxes	2.2	5.7	4.6					3.0	5.2
RATIOS									
Current	2.3	2.2	2.4					2.1	2.5
	1.6	1.7	1.7					1.5	1.9
	1.2	1.3	1.1					1.1	1.4
Quick	1.3	1.3	1.5					1.3	1.4
	.8	.9	.9					.8	1.0
	.5	.6	.6					.5	.8
Sales/Receivables	39 9.4	41 8.9	38 9.7					35 10.4	44 8.3
	48 7.7	50 7.3	52 7.1					49 7.5	56 6.5
	60 6.1	62 5.9	68 5.4					57 6.4	70 5.2
Cost of Sales/Inventory	45 8.2	37 9.8	38 9.6					37 9.9	37 9.9
	75 4.9	67 5.4	69 5.3					69 5.3	60 6.0
	107 3.4	113 3.2	113 3.2					126 2.9	88 4.2
Cost of Sales/Payables	21 17.4	22 16.4	27 13.5					31 11.6	26 14.0
	31 11.6	33 11.2	40 9.2					43 8.6	37 9.8
	50 7.3	48 7.6	52 7.0					56 6.5	43 8.5
Sales/Working Capital	4.8	4.5	4.7					5.3	4.7
	8.9	8.1	8.4					15.0	8.4
	18.1	16.5	29.8					57.5	18.3
EBIT/Interest	9.4	15.4	9.7					7.3	16.1
	(54) 4.9	(57) 6.0	(66) 3.7					3.0	(28) 4.5
	1.0	2.0	1.9					.4	2.6
Net Profit + Depr., Dep., Amort./Cur. Mat. L/T/D	10.1	11.6	31.3						39.6
	(18) 4.0	(23) 4.1	(24) 10.1						(15) 15.2
	1.1	1.1	3.3						3.0
Fixed/Worth	.3	.2	.2					.3	.2
	.5	.5	.7					.8	.6
	1.1	1.3	1.6					1.3	1.5
Debt/Worth	.8	.7	.9					.9	.8
	1.8	1.5	2.6					1.9	3.4
	6.3	5.0	6.3					3.3	7.3
% Profit Before Taxes/Tangible Net Worth	38.1	51.7	57.6					46.0	63.4
	(49) 24.7	(51) 27.7	(59) 31.4					(19) 28.1	(24) 31.5
	6.5	10.8	7.8					4.2	21.3
% Profit Before Taxes/Total Assets	15.2	19.1	15.5					14.3	14.7
	6.4	8.7	8.6					4.8	10.1
	.2	2.3	2.2					-.7	4.2
Sales/Net Fixed Assets	27.7	31.2	29.8					21.4	29.0
	10.8	9.2	11.4					9.8	11.6
	5.6	6.2	8.0					5.6	8.6
Sales/Total Assets	2.8	2.7	2.9					3.0	2.7
	2.1	1.9	2.0					2.0	1.7
	1.4	1.4	1.4					1.3	1.4
% Depr., Dep., Amort./Sales	.9	.8	.7					1.1	.7
	(51) 1.6	(54) 1.2	(59) 1.4					(19) 2.0	(26) 1.4
	2.4	2.3	2.6					2.9	2.4
% Officers', Directors', Owners' Comp/Sales	1.7	3.1	1.7						
	(15) 2.8	(10) 6.1	(13) 4.0						
	8.7	8.3	6.3						
Net Sales ($)	2506396M	2806132M	2974458M	1182M	8368M	7162M	56886M	352467M	2548393M
Total Assets ($)	1412260M	1720294M	1863904M	953M	2818M	2918M	30175M	281571M	1545469M

© RMA 2007

M = $ thousand   MM = $ million
See Pages 11 through 21 for Explanation of Ratios and Data

Current Data Sorted by Assets   Comparative Historical Data

0-500M	500M-2MM	2-10MM	10-50MM	50-100MM	100-250MM	Type of Statement	4/1/02-3/31/03 ALL	4/1/03-3/31/04 ALL
		5	7	2	1	Unqualified	12	14
	1	5	8		1	Reviewed	10	8
	4	1				Compiled	5	4
1	1	3				Tax Returns	2	3
1	3	13	12	1	1	Other	18	13
	22 (4/1-9/30/06)		48 (10/1/06-3/31/07)					
1	9	27	27	4	2	**NUMBER OF STATEMENTS**	47	42
%	%	%	%	%	%	**ASSETS**	%	%
		7.5	9.8			Cash & Equivalents	8.2	8.7
		28.7	28.9			Trade Receivables (net)	26.6	31.9
		31.3	28.0			Inventory	27.0	24.5
		3.1	2.1			All Other Current	3.9	2.6
		70.6	68.8			Total Current	65.7	67.7
		19.0	24.4			Fixed Assets (net)	21.7	24.2
		6.4	2.8			Intangibles (net)	7.0	3.3
		4.0	4.0			All Other Non-Current	5.6	4.7
		100.0	100.0			Total	100.0	100.0
						LIABILITIES		
		11.4	14.3			Notes Payable-Short Term	9.6	12.2
		2.3	3.5			Cur. Mat.-L.T.D.	4.2	4.4
		15.2	12.5			Trade Payables	12.8	13.4
		.1	.4			Income Taxes Payable	.4	.0
		14.9	12.9			All Other Current	7.0	10.1
		44.0	43.6			Total Current	34.0	40.2
		12.5	16.7			Long-Term Debt	14.7	19.0
		.2	.5			Deferred Taxes	.6	.4
		4.8	6.6			All Other Non-Current	5.7	7.3
		38.4	32.6			Net Worth	45.1	33.2
		100.0	100.0			Total Liabilties & Net Worth	100.0	100.0
						INCOME DATA		
		100.0	100.0			Net Sales	100.0	100.0
		28.6	28.9			Gross Profit	28.0	27.1
		22.1	21.4			Operating Expenses	24.9	24.3
		6.6	7.5			Operating Profit	3.1	2.8
		1.9	.4			All Other Expenses (net)	1.9	1.9
		4.7	7.1			Profit Before Taxes	1.1	.9
						RATIOS		
		2.2	2.4			Current	3.5	2.7
		1.6	1.5				2.0	1.7
		1.2	1.1				1.4	1.3
		1.2	1.6			Quick	1.8	1.3
		.8	.8				.9	1.0
		.5	.6				.6	.6
		37 9.8	50 7.3			Sales/Receivables	40 9.0	44 8.4
		52 7.1	53 6.8				52 7.1	52 7.0
		57 6.4	62 5.9				62 5.9	68 5.4
		50 7.3	58 6.3			Cost of Sales/Inventory	38 9.5	39 9.3
		72 5.0	68 5.3				79 4.6	67 5.5
		133 2.7	104 3.5				124 2.9	99 3.7
		18 20.3	22 16.7			Cost of Sales/Payables	21 17.2	16 23.3
		39 9.5	28 13.2				30 12.2	26 14.2
		50 7.3	50 7.3				42 8.6	49 7.4
		4.4	5.0			Sales/Working Capital	3.2	4.0
		7.1	8.4				6.2	7.5
		32.1	24.2				12.4	14.1
		14.9	14.1			EBIT/Interest	7.6	8.0
		(25) 3.0	(24) 4.7				(44) 3.5	(41) 2.0
		1.7	.9				.6	-.5
			7.2			Net Profit + Depr., Dep., Amort./Cur. Mat. L/T/D	2.0	
			(10) 3.9				(15) 1.2	
			.5				.9	
		.3	.3			Fixed/Worth	.3	.3
		.5	.6				.6	.6
		1.0	2.0				1.4	3.3
		.9	1.0			Debt/Worth	.6	.6
		2.4	1.9				1.3	1.9
		5.2	5.4				5.7	9.0
		56.3	58.2			% Profit Before Taxes/Tangible Net Worth	23.4	23.6
		(23) 25.8	(25) 22.9				(42) 5.3	(35) 7.4
		18.1	2.6				-2.8	-3.7
		18.6	16.0			% Profit Before Taxes/Total Assets	8.1	10.1
		7.1	11.2				3.3	1.6
		3.0	.9				-1.6	-3.3
		29.3	15.2			Sales/Net Fixed Assets	18.2	31.1
		16.2	7.7				9.5	9.0
		6.8	4.8				4.2	3.8
		2.6	2.3			Sales/Total Assets	2.5	2.4
		1.9	1.9				1.7	1.9
		1.5	1.4				1.2	1.3
		.7	1.1			% Depr., Dep., Amort./Sales	1.6	.8
		(24) 1.7	(26) 2.2				(43) 2.6	(37) 1.9
		2.4	2.8				4.2	3.9
						% Officers', Directors' Owners' Comp/Sales	2.2	3.9
							(14) 5.3	(11) 5.6
							6.9	7.4
2465M	31980M	298987M	1011655M	571755M	1005169M	Net Sales ($)	1006134M	756217M
174M	11718M	142504M	536478M	273362M	387968M	Total Assets ($)	732385M	521832M

M = $ thousand   MM = $ million
See Pages 11 through 21 for Explanation of Ratios and Data

Comparative Historical Data / Current Data Sorted by Sales

			Type of Statement	0-1MM	1-3MM	3-5MM	5-10MM	10-25MM	25MM & OVER
16	15	15	Unqualified				2	5	8
14	14	15	Reviewed			1	4	7	3
5	9	5	Compiled	1	1	2		1	
4	3	5	Tax Returns		1	3		1	
14	26	30	Other			4	6	7	13
4/1/04-3/31/05 ALL	4/1/05-3/31/06 ALL	4/1/06-3/31/07 ALL				22 (4/1-9/30/06)		48 (10/1/06-3/31/07)	
53	67	70	NUMBER OF STATEMENTS	1	2	10	12	21	24
%	%	%	**ASSETS**	%	%	%	%	%	%
9.1	5.9	9.1	Cash & Equivalents			11.9	19.6	7.4	4.0
31.8	29.6	28.4	Trade Receivables (net)			23.2	23.3	31.0	31.5
27.9	31.1	29.8	Inventory			37.1	17.6	27.2	34.6
1.9	1.8	2.6	All Other Current			.4	2.2	3.7	2.2
70.7	68.4	69.8	Total Current			72.6	62.8	69.4	72.3
22.5	22.1	21.3	Fixed Assets (net)			16.7	24.8	23.1	20.6
3.2	4.8	4.4	Intangibles (net)			5.6	5.7	4.5	3.7
3.6	4.7	4.4	All Other Non-Current			5.1	6.7	3.0	3.3
100.0	100.0	100.0	Total			100.0	100.0	100.0	100.0
			LIABILITIES						
11.0	14.3	11.0	Notes Payable-Short Term			4.6	6.2	10.2	16.7
2.3	3.8	3.6	Cur. Mat.-L.T.D.			3.1	1.6	4.4	4.3
13.0	13.7	13.9	Trade Payables			17.2	8.6	16.1	14.4
.2	.4	.3	Income Taxes Payable			.2	.1	.3	.4
11.6	12.0	13.3	All Other Current			11.8	15.9	14.5	12.9
38.0	44.2	42.1	Total Current			36.9	32.3	45.4	48.9
14.6	14.5	14.5	Long-Term Debt			16.7	7.7	14.6	15.0
.4	.5	.5	Deferred Taxes			.0	.2	.6	.9
5.9	9.1	4.9	All Other Non-Current			7.8	4.1	2.0	7.4
41.0	31.7	37.9	Net Worth			38.6	55.7	37.4	27.8
100.0	100.0	100.0	Total Liabilities & Net Worth			100.0	100.0	100.0	100.0
			INCOME DATA						
100.0	100.0	100.0	Net Sales			100.0	100.0	100.0	100.0
28.9	27.6	30.3	Gross Profit			35.0	32.8	27.9	29.0
23.7	22.7	23.4	Operating Expenses			28.0	25.5	20.9	21.5
5.2	4.9	6.9	Operating Profit			7.0	7.3	6.9	7.6
.7	1.2	.7	All Other Expenses (net)			1.8	-.1	1.1	.9
4.5	3.7	6.1	Profit Before Taxes			5.3	7.3	5.8	6.7
			RATIOS						
3.1	2.4	2.7				3.8	4.7	2.1	2.3
2.0	1.4	1.7	Current			1.8	2.6	1.5	1.4
1.4	1.1	1.2				1.4	1.2	1.2	1.1
1.7	1.2	1.5				1.6	2.7	1.3	1.4
1.0	.8	.9	Quick			.8	1.3	.9	.6
.7	.5	.6				.5	.7	.5	.5
43 8.6	43 8.5	42 8.6				30 12.1	30 12.0	47 7.7	46 7.9
51 7.2	51 7.2	52 7.0	Sales/Receivables			45 8.1	54 6.8	52 7.1	52 7.0
65 5.6	62 5.9	61 6.0				54 6.8	61 6.0	64 5.7	62 5.9
43 8.6	53 6.9	54 6.8				44 8.4	15 23.8	50 7.3	61 5.9
75 4.9	68 5.4	72 5.1	Cost of Sales/Inventory			92 4.0	48 7.6	64 5.7	77 4.7
119 3.1	110 3.3	101 3.6				179 2.0	141 2.6	84 4.3	102 3.6
21 17.3	22 16.3	22 16.7				27 13.7	17 21.6	24 15.1	22 16.8
30 12.2	26 13.9	33 10.9	Cost of Sales/Payables			39 9.4	35 10.4	39 9.5	27 13.3
42 8.7	44 8.3	50 7.4				57 6.5	42 8.7	57 6.4	38 9.6
3.9	4.8	4.9				3.4	2.5	6.0	5.4
6.1	8.8	8.1	Sales/Working Capital			8.3	6.1	8.4	10.8
12.4	26.3	26.2				21.6	28.2	19.0	34.7
8.6	7.5	16.8					32.3	16.5	19.9
(47) 3.6	(62) 3.3	(62) 3.7	EBIT/Interest				(10) 6.3	(19) 3.5	(22) 4.7
1.2	1.1	1.6					1.1	1.5	1.6
13.3	4.8	5.9						5.2	19.5
(11) 2.8	(30) 2.0	(25) 3.2	Net Profit + Depr., Dep., Amort./Cur. Mat. L/T/D					(10) 2.9	(10) 4.9
1.7	1.1	.7						.5	2.4
.2	.3	.3				.3	.2	.4	.3
.6	.8	.5	Fixed/Worth			.4	.5	.5	.7
1.2	2.2	1.6				NM	.9	1.4	7.6
.6	.7	.8				.6	.3	1.4	.9
1.2	2.2	2.1	Debt/Worth			3.2	.6	2.3	2.2
3.4	7.7	5.1				NM	4.0	3.1	25.5
34.3	33.6	60.1	% Profit Before Taxes/Tangible Net Worth				24.5	59.2	66.4
(47) 12.6	(57) 20.4	(63) 25.8					(11) 19.5	(20) 26.5	(21) 28.3
2.0	3.7	13.1					17.3	3.7	15.3
16.0	13.7	17.9	% Profit Before Taxes/Total Assets			20.2	15.2	18.6	17.8
6.5	5.0	8.7				6.3	10.4	9.1	10.4
.8	.4	1.6				2.7	3.2	.8	1.3
22.7	21.3	29.4				56.6	25.5	20.8	23.0
10.5	9.8	12.4	Sales/Net Fixed Assets			23.3	9.6	7.8	10.7
5.0	5.0	5.8				9.1	3.2	4.3	6.8
2.5	2.5	2.6				3.4	2.0	2.6	2.6
1.8	2.0	2.0	Sales/Total Assets			2.4	1.7	1.9	2.1
1.3	1.5	1.5				1.3	1.2	1.3	1.9
1.2	.9	1.0					1.1	.9	1.1
(50) 2.3	(62) 2.0	(62) 1.7	% Depr., Dep., Amort./Sales				(11) 2.1	1.8	(22) 1.6
1.7	1.1	.7					3.0	2.5	2.8
3.3	2.0	1.7	% Officers', Directors' Owners' Comp/Sales						
(16) 5.8	(23) 5.1	(25) 3.3							
8.4	6.6	5.6							
1354056M	3342629M	2922011M	Net Sales ($)	319M	4664M	38647M	78695M	365656M	2434030M
800442M	1871084M	1352204M	Total Assets ($)	914M	1375M	18956M	62286M	209868M	1058805M

© RMA 2007

M = $ thousand   MM = $ million

See Pages 11 through 21 for Explanation of Ratios and Data

	Current Data Sorted by Assets						Type of Statement	Comparative Historical Data	
		1	1	3	1		Unqualified	12	9
	2	9	3				Reviewed	12	14
	1						Compiled	9	8
		1					Tax Returns	2	1
	2	6		2		2	Other	9	6
	5 (4/1-9/30/06)		29 (10/1/06-3/31/07)					4/1/02-3/31/03	4/1/03-3/31/04
0-500M	500M-2MM	2-10MM	10-50MM	50-100MM	100-250MM			ALL	ALL
	5	17	6	3	3		NUMBER OF STATEMENTS	44	38
%	%	%	%	%	%		ASSETS	%	%
		9.6					Cash & Equivalents	7.4	7.4
		37.0					Trade Receivables (net)	36.2	37.4
D		27.3					Inventory	21.7	25.0
A		1.9					All Other Current	4.7	3.9
T		75.8					Total Current	69.9	73.7
A		16.4					Fixed Assets (net)	22.7	18.1
		4.5					Intangibles (net)	2.8	4.0
N		3.3					All Other Non-Current	4.7	4.2
O		100.0					Total	100.0	100.0
T							LIABILITIES		
		11.3					Notes Payable-Short Term	11.2	13.3
A		3.0					Cur. Mat.-L.T.D.	2.8	2.9
V		18.0					Trade Payables	16.0	16.2
A		.7					Income Taxes Payable	.3	.2
I		10.0					All Other Current	10.3	9.1
L		43.0					Total Current	40.6	41.7
A		4.5					Long-Term Debt	10.4	8.9
B		.1					Deferred Taxes	.1	.3
L		3.1					All Other Non-Current	3.4	4.3
E		49.3					Net Worth	45.6	44.8
		100.0					Total Liabilities & Net Worth	100.0	100.0
							INCOME DATA		
		100.0					Net Sales	100.0	100.0
		30.8					Gross Profit	30.4	27.8
		25.0					Operating Expenses	26.7	24.4
		5.7					Operating Profit	3.7	3.5
		1.8					All Other Expenses (net)	.6	.7
		4.0					Profit Before Taxes	3.0	2.8
							RATIOS		
		4.5						3.1	3.3
		1.9					Current	1.8	1.9
		1.2						1.3	1.3
		2.2						1.6	2.0
		1.4					Quick	1.1	1.1
		.9						.7	.8
	42	8.7						44 8.4	44 8.3
	51	7.1					Sales/Receivables	54 6.8	52 7.0
	58	6.3						71 5.2	73 5.0
	32	11.3						22 16.5	28 13.1
	55	6.6					Cost of Sales/Inventory	47 7.7	46 7.9
	88	4.1						76 4.8	77 4.7
	14	26.6						21 17.1	16 23.2
	39	9.4					Cost of Sales/Payables	30 12.1	29 12.5
	52	7.1						41 9.0	48 7.7
		3.8						4.2	4.6
		8.8					Sales/Working Capital	7.3	6.4
		22.0						20.0	16.1
		116.5						17.5	25.1
		(14) 6.6					EBIT/Interest	(38) 4.5	(36) 5.8
		.8						1.1	1.4
							Net Profit + Depr., Dep.,	5.7	3.0
							Amort./Cur. Mat. L/T/D	(17) 2.3	(11) .8
								-.3	.0
		.1						.2	.1
		.3					Fixed/Worth	.4	.3
		.9						1.0	1.1
		.3						.6	.5
		1.3					Debt/Worth	1.1	1.6
		2.6						2.9	2.5
		42.3					% Profit Before Taxes/Tangible	38.1	33.3
		(15) 31.5					Net Worth	(42) 16.4	(35) 18.7
		11.3						3.2	6.1
		16.8					% Profit Before Taxes/Total	14.9	14.5
		12.6					Assets	8.3	6.1
		.6						.3	.6
		65.8						37.3	52.7
		33.0					Sales/Net Fixed Assets	14.1	17.1
		8.4						5.4	6.8
		3.0						3.0	3.1
		2.4					Sales/Total Assets	2.3	2.2
		2.1						1.6	1.8
		.4						1.0	.7
		(14) 1.7					% Depr., Dep., Amort./Sales	(40) 1.7	(35) 1.5
		2.5						3.1	2.5
							% Officers', Directors'	1.3	1.1
							Owners' Comp/Sales	(18) 6.0	(16) 4.6
								11.8	8.0
	20393M	188603M	256953M	293612M	610181M		Net Sales ($)	1233063M	974613M
	5678M	76273M	129450M	202379M	437443M		Total Assets ($)	695708M	609541M

M = $ thousand   MM = $ million
See Pages 11 through 21 for Explanation of Ratios and Data

© RMA 2007

Comparative Historical Data

Current Data Sorted by Sales

				Type of Statement									
15		10		6	Unqualified				1		1		5
12		7		14	Reviewed			1		8		4	1
5		5		1	Compiled		1						
3		3		1	Tax Returns			1					
16		19		12	Other		1	1		2		4	4
4/1/04-3/31/05 ALL		4/1/05-3/31/06 ALL		4/1/06-3/31/07 ALL			5 (4/1-9/30/06)			29 (10/1/06-3/31/07)			
						0-1MM	1-3MM	3-5MM	5-10MM	10-25MM		25MM & OVER	
51		44		34	**NUMBER OF STATEMENTS**		2	3	11	8		10	
%		%		%	**ASSETS**	%	%	%	%	%		%	
8.4		6.9		10.3	Cash & Equivalents				15.1			10.6	
33.3		37.5		32.4	Trade Receivables (net)	D			35.4			23.5	
26.1		27.3		27.4	Inventory	A			27.7			24.6	
2.6		3.6		3.8	All Other Current	T			1.5			8.2	
70.3		75.3		73.9	Total Current	A			79.7			66.9	
19.1		14.5		16.9	Fixed Assets (net)	N			14.7			19.9	
4.6		3.4		4.7	Intangibles (net)	O			4.2			8.1	
5.9		6.8		4.4	All Other Non-Current	T			1.4			5.1	
100.0		100.0		100.0	Total				100.0			100.0	
					LIABILITIES	A							
13.5		11.8		11.3	Notes Payable-Short Term	V			12.7			7.0	
2.6		1.7		3.1	Cur. Mat.-L.T.D.	A			2.9			3.8	
14.4		17.7		17.8	Trade Payables	I			22.5			13.0	
.5		.2		.4	Income Taxes Payable	L			.2			.1	
10.4		11.2		9.5	All Other Current	A			10.1			9.6	
41.4		42.7		42.0	Total Current	B			48.3			33.5	
11.1		7.0		4.7	Long-Term Debt	L			3.9			7.7	
.4		.1		.1	Deferred Taxes	E			.0			.3	
8.4		6.6		4.4	All Other Non-Current				2.7			5.5	
38.6		43.6		48.8	Net Worth				45.0			53.0	
100.0		100.0		100.0	Total Liabilities & Net Worth				100.0			100.0	
					INCOME DATA								
100.0		100.0		100.0	Net Sales				100.0			100.0	
28.1		27.8		29.0	Gross Profit				29.2			25.3	
22.7		22.4		23.3	Operating Expenses				25.4			19.1	
5.4		5.4		5.7	Operating Profit				3.7			6.3	
.6		.3		1.3	All Other Expenses (net)				1.2			.7	
4.7		5.1		4.4	Profit Before Taxes				2.6			5.6	
					RATIOS								
3.1		3.8		3.6					3.8			2.9	
1.6		1.8		1.8	Current				1.9			1.7	
1.2		1.3		1.3					1.0			1.4	
1.5		1.9		1.9					2.2			1.4	
1.0		1.2		1.1	Quick				1.4			1.0	
.7		.7		.7					.7			.6	
42	8.6	42	8.7	41	9.0				40	9.1		43	8.4
50	7.3	53	6.9	48	7.6	Sales/Receivables			45	8.0		51	7.2
63	5.8	68	5.4	56	6.5				55	6.6		61	6.0
39	9.3	37	9.9	35	10.5				34	10.6		59	6.2
61	5.9	60	6.1	66	5.5	Cost of Sales/Inventory			39	9.4		78	4.7
90	4.1	87	4.2	91	4.0				79	4.6		96	3.8
21	17.6	22	16.4	23	15.9				23	16.1		25	14.8
30	12.4	32	11.4	36	10.3	Cost of Sales/Payables			39	9.4		34	10.8
45	8.2	54	6.7	48	7.6				56	6.5		41	9.0
	4.4		3.5		4.1					4.2			4.0
	7.0		7.3		7.8	Sales/Working Capital				8.7			6.0
	19.8		13.0		20.6					512.5			8.6
	16.3		36.6		39.5					133.7			
(47)	6.2	(38)	10.7	(29)	7.0	EBIT/Interest				8.1			
	2.0		2.0		1.5					-.2			
	13.1				26.2	Net Profit + Depr., Dep.,							
(14)	2.8			(10)	4.3	Amort./Cur. Mat. L/T/D							
	.9				.2								
	.2		.1		.1					.1			.2
	.5		.3		.3	Fixed/Worth				.3			.4
	1.3		.7		.8					-1.5			.8
	.5		.4		.4					.3			.7
	1.6		1.1		1.2	Debt/Worth				1.1			1.3
	3.9		2.8		2.3					-31.0			1.8
	54.7		52.3		42.3	% Profit Before Taxes/Tangible							40.5
(46)	21.2	(38)	26.2	(31)	29.0	Net Worth							27.2
	5.2		6.6		11.3								8.1
	16.7		21.0		16.4	% Profit Before Taxes/Total				35.8			14.4
	7.4		10.2		11.9	Assets				14.6			11.9
	1.7		2.0		.9					-4.3			2.2
	29.9		48.8		58.6					80.5			25.8
	12.3		19.1		20.8	Sales/Net Fixed Assets				33.0			10.4
	6.5		9.5		7.0					12.6			3.7
	2.6		2.9		3.0					3.7			2.1
	2.2		2.3		2.3	Sales/Total Assets				2.9			1.5
	1.5		1.5		1.6					2.4			1.3
	.8		.3		.6					.5			
(43)	1.9	(36)	1.1	(28)	1.7	% Depr., Dep., Amort./Sales			(10)	1.2			
	2.8		2.2		2.4					2.0			
	2.7		1.8			% Officers', Directors'							
(20)	4.9	(17)	5.8			Owners' Comp/Sales							
	8.2		9.1										
1533867M		1385973M		1369742M	Net Sales ($)		4123M	12997M	84652M	153771M		1114199M	
1295509M		1069397M		851223M	Total Assets ($)		1718M	6996M	30974M	64128M		747407M	

Current Data Sorted by Assets   Comparative Historical Data

						Type of Statement		
	4	5	12	3	2	Unqualified	19	17
	6	8	4			Reviewed	16	23
2	3	4	2			Compiled	15	14
2	7	2				Tax Returns	4	7
		19	9	2	2	Other	26	23
	19 (4/1-9/30/06)		79 (10/1/06-3/31/07)				4/1/02-3/31/03	4/1/03-3/31/04
0-500M	500M-2MM	2-10MM	10-50MM	50-100MM	100-250MM		ALL	ALL
4	20	38	27	5	4	NUMBER OF STATEMENTS	80	84
%	%	%	%	%	%	**ASSETS**	%	%
	11.0	9.0	7.8			Cash & Equivalents	8.6	8.6
	38.1	31.6	27.7			Trade Receivables (net)	27.1	31.1
	20.6	36.5	31.1			Inventory	31.1	28.1
	5.8	1.4	1.6			All Other Current	2.3	3.4
	75.5	78.4	68.3			Total Current	69.2	71.2
	13.6	13.5	22.7			Fixed Assets (net)	18.5	17.1
	1.7	4.2	5.5			Intangibles (net)	6.7	5.0
	9.2	3.9	3.5			All Other Non-Current	5.6	6.7
	100.0	100.0	100.0			Total	100.0	100.0
						LIABILITIES		
	6.8	8.9	8.2			Notes Payable-Short Term	11.3	10.4
	1.4	2.6	2.8			Cur. Mat.-L.T.D.	2.6	3.3
	16.6	17.0	14.4			Trade Payables	13.0	13.9
	.1	.3	.3			Income Taxes Payable	.3	.1
	13.7	14.4	10.3			All Other Current	11.3	14.6
	38.5	43.2	36.0			Total Current	38.5	42.3
	8.5	12.6	12.3			Long-Term Debt	11.4	10.7
	.0	.2	.3			Deferred Taxes	.3	.4
	8.4	6.1	6.7			All Other Non-Current	8.9	7.6
	44.5	37.9	44.7			Net Worth	41.0	38.9
	100.0	100.0	100.0			Total Liabilities & Net Worth	100.0	100.0
						INCOME DATA		
	100.0	100.0	100.0			Net Sales	100.0	100.0
	40.2	36.9	28.5			Gross Profit	32.3	35.5
	31.4	29.4	22.5			Operating Expenses	28.4	32.0
	8.8	7.5	6.0			Operating Profit	3.9	3.5
	1.0	.6	.5			All Other Expenses (net)	1.3	.6
	7.8	6.8	5.5			Profit Before Taxes	2.6	2.9
						RATIOS		
	3.2	3.0	2.7				3.1	2.8
	1.9	1.9	1.9			Current	1.8	1.7
	1.4	1.4	1.5				1.3	1.1
	2.0	1.7	1.3				1.6	1.6
	1.0	1.0	.9			Quick	.9	.8
	.6	.6	.7				.6	.6
38 9.6	37 9.9	45 8.1					40 9.1	40 9.0
48 7.5	47 7.8	55 6.6				Sales/Receivables	51 7.2	50 7.3
67 5.5	62 5.9	68 5.4					63 5.8	63 5.8
4 87.5	54 6.7	51 7.2					44 8.2	45 8.0
36 10.0	95 3.8	96 3.8				Cost of Sales/Inventory	93 3.9	87 4.2
113 3.2	140 2.6	152 2.4					133 2.7	118 3.1
13 28.9	21 17.1	22 16.8					17 21.4	18 20.2
33 11.2	35 10.6	33 11.1				Cost of Sales/Payables	32 11.6	26 13.8
61 6.0	69 5.3	45 8.2					50 7.2	44 8.3
	3.5	3.9	3.6				3.9	4.5
	7.0	7.0	6.3			Sales/Working Capital	7.1	7.9
	13.8	13.1	9.1				13.9	23.7
	36.0	16.9	9.4				7.1	9.3
	(17) 5.7	(33) 5.5	(23) 3.3			EBIT/Interest	(72) 3.0	(74) 3.7
	2.2	3.0	1.1				-.1	1.0
		15.3	13.2			Net Profit + Depr., Dep.,	5.3	5.9
	(13) 3.7	(10) 2.9				Amort./Cur. Mat. L/T/D	(24) 1.7	(26) 2.5
	1.8	.9					.5	1.2
	.1	.2	.3				.2	.2
	.2	.4	.5			Fixed/Worth	.5	.5
	.9	1.1	1.1				1.0	1.4
	.4	.6	.8				.6	.5
	1.3	1.4	1.3			Debt/Worth	1.7	1.8
	2.6	6.8	2.6				3.3	5.3
	54.0	70.3	35.8			% Profit Before Taxes/Tangible	32.7	33.0
	(18) 23.7	(32) 37.5	(24) 14.9			Net Worth	(72) 13.1	(76) 9.7
	13.7	8.6	3.9				-7.2	.7
	25.4	25.3	15.4			% Profit Before Taxes/Total	12.6	12.7
	10.0	8.0	7.9			Assets	4.9	4.4
	4.8	4.4	1.3				-2.2	-.8
	63.1	34.1	20.6				24.2	27.0
	32.6	21.1	8.0			Sales/Net Fixed Assets	13.3	14.5
	13.6	10.4	5.1				5.7	7.1
	3.6	3.2	2.2				2.4	2.8
	2.3	2.2	1.8			Sales/Total Assets	1.9	2.1
	1.8	1.5	1.4				1.3	1.5
	.3	.6	1.2				1.2	1.0
	(14) 1.1	(35) 1.2	(23) 1.9			% Depr., Dep., Amort./Sales	(72) 2.3	(74) 1.8
	2.5	2.0	4.2				3.6	3.0
		2.1				% Officers', Directors'	2.6	1.2
	(11) 4.5					Owners' Comp/Sales	(26) 4.0	(33) 3.9
	6.6						8.3	8.6
3433M	69594M	425242M	1005705M	607067M	1310496M	Net Sales ($)	2134011M	2087681M
1393M	27763M	180349M	538835M	414129M	847950M	Total Assets ($)	1715695M	1247591M

© RMA 2007   M = $ thousand   MM = $ million

See Pages 11 through 21 for Explanation of Ratios and Data

Comparative Historical Data | Current Data Sorted by Sales

			Type of Statement						
14	15	22	Unqualified				2	5	15
20	16	16	Reviewed	1		2	6	5	2
11	15	12	Compiled		3	1	6	1	1
6	8	7	Tax Returns	2	2		2	1	
37	32	41	Other	2	5	5	9	9	12
4/1/04-3/31/05	4/1/05-3/31/06	4/1/06-3/31/07			19 (4/1-9/30/06)			79 (10/1/06-3/31/07)	
ALL	ALL	ALL		0-1MM	1-3MM	3-5MM	5-10MM	10-25MM	25MM & OVER
88	86	98	NUMBER OF STATEMENTS	5	10	8	25	20	30
%	%	%	ASSETS	%	%	%	%	%	%
10.7	9.7	8.9	Cash & Equivalents		11.2		9.3	10.4	6.4
30.6	32.2	30.9	Trade Receivables (net)		32.4		37.8	26.5	27.9
28.7	27.6	30.8	Inventory		23.0		33.6	35.7	29.3
2.5	2.6	2.8	All Other Current		6.7		1.0	1.0	3.1
72.5	72.1	73.4	Total Current		73.4		81.8	73.6	66.6
16.3	18.3	16.8	Fixed Assets (net)		16.1		10.7	19.0	22.4
4.3	3.2	4.2	Intangibles (net)		1.7		2.1	4.0	6.5
6.8	6.3	5.7	All Other Non-Current		8.8		5.4	3.3	4.5
100.0	100.0	100.0	Total		100.0		100.0	100.0	100.0
			LIABILITIES						
10.8	10.8	7.8	Notes Payable-Short Term		8.3		9.6	6.8	6.9
2.8	2.0	2.5	Cur. Mat.-L.T.D.		1.5		2.4	2.0	3.3
14.4	15.2	15.3	Trade Payables		16.3		19.1	13.5	15.6
.2	.3	.3	Income Taxes Payable		.0		.3	.3	.6
11.3	10.8	13.0	All Other Current		16.1		16.4	9.7	11.0
39.4	39.2	39.0	Total Current		42.2		47.9	32.3	37.5
9.8	9.7	12.2	Long-Term Debt		7.0		6.3	19.7	12.7
.2	.2	.2	Deferred Taxes		.0		.2	.3	.2
5.4	7.4	6.7	All Other Non-Current		8.8		7.5	2.4	8.9
45.1	43.4	42.0	Net Worth		42.0		38.2	45.3	40.7
100.0	100.0	100.0	Total Liabilities & Net Worth		100.0		100.0	100.0	100.0
			INCOME DATA						
100.0	100.0	100.0	Net Sales		100.0		100.0	100.0	100.0
36.1	37.5	34.5	Gross Profit		46.1		35.3	36.7	24.8
30.6	31.3	27.7	Operating Expenses		37.1		30.2	26.8	20.4
5.5	6.2	6.8	Operating Profit		9.0		5.1	9.9	4.3
.7	.6	.5	All Other Expenses (net)		.8		.5	.4	.1
4.8	5.6	6.3	Profit Before Taxes		8.2		4.7	9.4	4.2
			RATIOS						
3.3	3.5	2.9	Current		2.4		2.9	3.6	2.2
1.7	1.9	1.9			1.6		1.7	2.5	1.8
1.3	1.3	1.4			1.3		1.3	1.8	1.4
1.9	1.9	1.6	Quick		1.6		1.7	2.5	1.2
1.0	1.0	1.0			.8		.9	1.4	.9
.6	.7	.6			.6		.6	.6	.7
40 9.1	42 8.7	39 9.3	Sales/Receivables	27 13.3		40 9.1	38 9.7	42 8.6	
51 7.2	52 7.0	49 7.4		48 7.5		50 7.4	46 7.9	56 6.6	
66 5.5	65 5.6	65 5.6		80 4.6		64 5.7	57 6.4	68 5.4	
50 7.4	40 9.1	39 9.4	Cost of Sales/Inventory	0 UND		44 8.3	73 5.0	40 9.2	
83 4.4	88 4.1	88 4.2		42 8.6		93 3.9	98 3.7	64 5.7	
130 2.8	133 2.7	145 2.5		148 2.5		145 2.5	150 2.4	111 3.3	
19 19.1	17 21.5	20 18.6	Cost of Sales/Payables	0 UND		15 24.0	22 16.5	22 16.7	
33 11.0	35 10.3	33 11.1		58 6.3		36 10.0	29 12.5	33 11.1	
54 6.8	56 6.5	54 6.8		192 1.9		71 5.1	39 9.5	40 9.1	
4.3	3.7	3.6	Sales/Working Capital		3.4		4.0	2.9	5.1
7.2	6.8	6.7			6.2		7.9	5.8	7.5
11.8	15.4	13.1			18.4		20.1	8.0	14.1
14.5	17.1	16.6	EBIT/Interest				13.9	32.7	12.6
(73) 5.3	(76) 6.6	(85) 4.9			(20) 4.1		(16) 4.0	(28) 5.2	
1.5	1.4	1.9					2.2	1.6	.1
7.0	9.6	15.3	Net Profit + Depr., Dep., Amort./Cur. Mat. L/T/D						13.2
(23) 2.6	(25) 3.2	(32) 3.4						(13) 1.8	
.9	1.5	1.3							.0
.2	.2	.2	Fixed/Worth		.1		.1	.2	.3
.3	.4	.4			.2		.3	.4	.5
.9	1.0	1.0			NM		1.0	.9	1.5
.5	.5	.6	Debt/Worth		.3		.6	.3	.8
1.2	1.4	1.4			1.4		1.3	.9	1.5
3.1	3.2	3.6			NM		9.5	2.5	3.8
43.2	49.0	56.4	% Profit Before Taxes/Tangible Net Worth				63.0	72.0	65.0
(81) 18.3	(77) 21.8	(86) 21.2			(20) 22.6		(19) 25.4	(27) 21.2	
2.9	3.0	7.5					8.6	4.3	5.2
16.6	19.9	18.1	% Profit Before Taxes/Total Assets		17.7		23.6	30.3	16.0
5.6	8.4	7.9			10.6		5.5	8.8	8.1
.8	.8	2.6			1.8		3.3	2.6	-.4
32.4	33.6	34.1	Sales/Net Fixed Assets		57.6		61.7	22.9	19.4
14.5	13.0	15.1			30.1		30.5	12.4	9.3
7.7	6.9	7.8			5.6		13.8	6.7	4.9
2.7	2.7	2.7	Sales/Total Assets		3.8		3.1	2.9	2.5
2.0	2.0	2.0			1.9		2.5	1.8	2.0
1.4	1.6	1.5			1.0		1.8	1.4	1.5
1.0	.8	.8	% Depr., Dep., Amort./Sales				.5	1.2	1.1
(67) 1.8	(69) 1.6	(82) 1.6			(19) .7		(19) 1.7	(26) 1.8	
2.8	2.6	2.6					2.0	2.9	3.2
2.4	3.0	2.8	% Officers', Directors' Owners' Comp/Sales				1.8		
(24) 6.7	(27) 5.4	(24) 5.8			(10) 5.0				
10.1	10.3	10.0					7.9		
2774139M	3043225M	3421537M	Net Sales ($)	2937M	20102M	32262M	175181M	341825M	2849230M
1721312M	1687821M	2010419M	Total Assets ($)	2483M	14225M	19517M	80328M	191059M	1702807M

© RMA 2007

M = $ thousand   MM = $ million
See Pages 11 through 21 for Explanation of Ratios and Data

Current Data Sorted by Assets   Comparative Historical Data

Period headers — Current: **11 (4/1-9/30/06)** and **70 (10/1/06-3/31/07)**. Historical: **4/1/02-3/31/03 ALL** and **4/1/03-3/31/04 ALL**.

Type of Statement	0-500M	500M-2MM	2-10MM	10-50MM	50-100MM	100-250MM	4/1/02-3/31/03 ALL	4/1/03-3/31/04 ALL
Unqualified			5	7	3	4	12	12
Reviewed		3	6	5			19	14
Compiled	1	1	5	1			8	10
Tax Returns	2	3	2				3	5
Other		4	9	11	5	4	19	28
NUMBER OF STATEMENTS	3	11	27	24	8	8	61	69

ASSETS (%)

	0-500M	500M-2MM	2-10MM	10-50MM	50-100MM	100-250MM	4/1/02-3/31/03	4/1/03-3/31/04
Cash & Equivalents		2.8	4.6	7.6			7.3	5.5
Trade Receivables (net)		46.6	30.1	34.3			25.9	30.4
Inventory		29.3	38.0	27.5			28.7	28.9
All Other Current		.2	1.4	3.6			2.0	1.8
Total Current		78.9	74.1	73.0			63.9	66.7
Fixed Assets (net)		15.0	15.8	17.2			25.7	22.3
Intangibles (net)		3.8	5.6	3.4			5.2	3.8
All Other Non-Current		2.3	4.6	6.4			5.2	7.3
Total		100.0	100.0	100.0			100.0	100.0

LIABILITIES

	0-500M	500M-2MM	2-10MM	10-50MM	50-100MM	100-250MM	4/1/02-3/31/03	4/1/03-3/31/04
Notes Payable-Short Term		16.5	8.5	9.0			12.8	12.4
Cur. Mat.-L.T.D.		4.5	5.3	1.8			4.3	3.6
Trade Payables		28.5	16.0	21.8			13.3	16.7
Income Taxes Payable		.0	.2	.7			.3	.2
All Other Current		10.6	12.2	8.2			8.4	8.5
Total Current		60.0	42.0	41.5			39.0	41.5
Long-Term Debt		12.3	8.3	8.6			15.9	15.6
Deferred Taxes		.1	.2	.8			.4	.2
All Other Non-Current		.0	4.5	1.7			6.8	6.5
Net Worth		27.6	44.9	47.4			37.9	36.2
Total Liabilities & Net Worth		100.0	100.0	100.0			100.0	100.0

INCOME DATA

	0-500M	500M-2MM	2-10MM	10-50MM	50-100MM	100-250MM	4/1/02-3/31/03	4/1/03-3/31/04
Net Sales		100.0	100.0	100.0			100.0	100.0
Gross Profit		29.6	26.3	24.5			27.0	28.0
Operating Expenses		24.0	20.6	16.7			25.8	24.2
Operating Profit		5.7	5.7	7.8			1.2	3.8
All Other Expenses (net)		.9	.7	1.4			1.0	1.2
Profit Before Taxes		4.7	5.0	6.4			.2	2.6

RATIOS

	500M-2MM	2-10MM	10-50MM	4/1/02-3/31/03	4/1/03-3/31/04
Current	2.2	2.8	2.2	2.6	2.4
	1.5	1.9	1.7	1.6	1.6
	1.0	1.2	1.3	1.1	1.2
Quick	1.2	1.5	1.3	1.4	1.3
	.8	.8	1.0	.7	.9
	.6	.6	.7	.5	.6
Sales/Receivables	33 11.0	34 10.7	45 8.1	38 9.7	40 9.1
	46 8.0	44 8.3	53 6.9	45 8.1	48 7.6
	87 4.2	57 6.4	76 4.8	52 7.0	60 6.1
Cost of Sales/Inventory	5 76.5	56 6.5	40 9.2	46 7.9	51 7.2
	52 7.0	72 5.0	63 5.8	66 5.5	69 5.3
	82 4.4	96 3.8	93 3.9	98 3.7	97 3.7
Cost of Sales/Payables	20 18.5	22 16.2	24 14.9	21 17.8	25 14.9
	36 10.0	34 10.8	38 9.5	28 13.1	34 10.9
	86 4.2	41 8.9	57 6.4	40 9.1	43 8.5
Sales/Working Capital	6.4	4.5	4.5	4.7	5.3
	9.5	7.6	7.5	8.8	9.5
	-213.7	25.8	15.5	34.6	25.0
EBIT/Interest	11.5	8.8	19.2	7.3	10.2
	2.7	(23) 6.1	(19) 7.2	(55) 1.6	(65) 3.9
	-.2	2.0	4.3	-.7	.7
Net Profit + Depr., Dep., Amort./Cur. Mat. L/T/D				4.5	4.6
		(22) 1.7		(16) 2.5	
				.6	.9
Fixed/Worth	.2	.1	.2	.2	.2
	.5	.4	.3	.9	.6
	1.2	.7	.8	2.5	2.7
Debt/Worth	1.0	.5	.7	.8	.8
	5.7	1.3	1.2	2.0	2.0
	55.4	4.7	2.6	5.9	6.7
% Profit Before Taxes/Tangible Net Worth		49.8	65.9	24.1	46.5
	(24)	33.4	(23) 31.0	(54) 5.6	(60) 18.6
		12.6	12.6	-12.5	3.8
% Profit Before Taxes/Total Assets	20.8	21.7	25.8	11.0	14.7
	5.1	9.2	15.4	1.8	5.6
	-4.1	3.4	4.6	-4.7	-.7
Sales/Net Fixed Assets	119.0	55.3	29.6	21.2	28.6
	32.5	18.0	15.2	9.5	10.4
	11.3	7.9	8.6	5.1	5.7
Sales/Total Assets	3.9	2.8	3.0	2.8	2.8
	2.9	2.4	2.4	1.9	2.1
	2.3	2.0	1.5	1.3	1.6
% Depr., Dep., Amort./Sales		.9	.7	1.4	.9
	(20)	1.4	(19) .9	(57) 2.5	(64) 1.7
		1.9	1.8	4.3	3.2
% Officers', Directors' Owners' Comp/Sales				3.0	2.4
		(19) 6.8		(20) 4.6	
				8.9	7.2

	0-500M	500M-2MM	2-10MM	10-50MM	50-100MM	100-250MM	4/1/02-3/31/03	4/1/03-3/31/04
Net Sales ($)	5731M	41853M	345785M	1373354M	969990M	2284908M	1462498M	1619881M
Total Assets ($)	600M	13879M	141256M	580523M	529789M	1403116M	940265M	1017852M

Comparative Historical Data				Current Data Sorted by Sales					
			Type of Statement						
21	22	19	Unqualified			1		5	13
13	15	14	Reviewed			4	2	4	4
9	7	8	Compiled		1	1	3	3	
5	4	7	Tax Returns	1	2	1	2	1	
23	30	33	Other		2	4	2	7	18
					11 (4/1-9/30/06)			70 (10/1/06-3/31/07)	
4/1/04-3/31/05 ALL	4/1/05-3/31/06 ALL	4/1/06-3/31/07 ALL		0-1MM	1-3MM	3-5MM	5-10MM	10-25MM	25MM & OVER
71	78	81	**NUMBER OF STATEMENTS**	1	5	11	9	20	35
%	%	%	**ASSETS**	%	%	%	%	%	%
4.8	6.7	6.9	Cash & Equivalents			4.8		5.9	6.9
29.0	31.8	34.0	Trade Receivables (net)			42.4		27.4	33.2
30.4	29.5	29.5	Inventory			24.7		35.1	27.5
1.7	1.6	1.9	All Other Current			.2		4.3	1.7
65.9	69.5	72.3	Total Current			72.1		72.7	69.3
20.6	18.3	16.9	Fixed Assets (net)			15.9		16.3	19.6
4.3	5.7	6.0	Intangibles (net)			6.9		3.8	7.2
9.2	6.5	4.8	All Other Non-Current			5.1		7.2	3.9
100.0	100.0	100.0	Total			100.0		100.0	100.0
			LIABILITIES						
12.2	10.9	8.9	Notes Payable-Short Term			7.7		8.9	7.8
2.7	3.7	3.3	Cur. Mat.-L.T.D.			5.8		2.3	3.5
17.0	16.7	19.1	Trade Payables			24.0		17.6	17.4
.3	.4	.4	Income Taxes Payable			.2		.1	.9
10.0	7.6	10.7	All Other Current			7.9		10.3	9.5
42.2	39.3	42.4	Total Current			45.5		39.1	39.1
13.0	11.6	11.1	Long-Term Debt			8.4		8.6	14.1
.5	.5	.4	Deferred Taxes			.1		.2	.2
7.3	5.9	4.2	All Other Non-Current			.1		4.7	4.1
36.9	42.8	42.0	Net Worth			45.8		47.4	42.5
100.0	100.0	100.0	Total Liabilties & Net Worth			100.0		100.0	100.0
			INCOME DATA						
100.0	100.0	100.0	Net Sales			100.0		100.0	100.0
28.7	27.7	27.0	Gross Profit			27.1		28.2	24.9
23.5	22.3	20.3	Operating Expenses			22.1		20.8	16.8
5.2	5.4	6.7	Operating Profit			5.0		7.5	8.1
.7	.7	1.0	All Other Expenses (net)			1.9		.4	1.2
4.4	4.6	5.7	Profit Before Taxes			3.1		7.1	6.9
			RATIOS						
2.4	2.8	2.5				2.6		3.3	2.5
1.6	1.9	1.9	Current			1.5		1.8	2.0
1.2	1.3	1.3				1.2		1.3	1.3
1.2	1.5	1.4				1.4		1.5	1.3
.8	1.0	1.0	Quick			1.0		.8	1.1
.6	.7	.7				.7		.6	.7
42 8.7	**41** 8.9	**37** 9.9				**41** 9.0		**34** 10.7	**45** 8.1
47 7.7	**53** 7.0	**51** 7.2	Sales/Receivables			**55** 6.6		**47** 7.8	**52** 7.1
56 6.5	**67** 5.4	**68** 5.4				**87** 4.2		**62** 5.9	**62** 5.9
42 8.8	**43** 8.5	**45** 8.2				**27** 13.8		**54** 6.8	**41** 8.8
70 5.2	**65** 5.6	**67** 5.5	Cost of Sales/Inventory			**82** 4.4		**83** 4.4	**66** 5.5
106 3.4	**100** 3.6	**92** 4.0				**91** 4.0		**110** 3.3	**79** 4.6
23 16.0	**24** 14.9	**22** 16.4				**25** 14.6		**26** 14.0	**24** 15.2
32 11.5	**31** 11.8	**35** 10.5	Cost of Sales/Payables			**35** 10.6		**37** 9.8	**34** 10.9
45 8.1	**48** 7.6	**46** 8.0				**86** 4.2		**53** 6.9	**45** 8.2
5.2	5.0	4.4				4.3		4.0	4.4
8.5	7.8	7.5	Sales/Working Capital			6.8		7.2	7.5
26.4	18.9	24.1				56.4		21.6	12.0
13.9	12.4	15.5				12.8		8.6	19.1
(65) 5.3	(68) 5.3	(71) 5.9	EBIT/Interest			(10) 4.0		(15) 6.1	(32) 5.8
2.3	1.9	2.0				-.2		2.0	3.3
12.5	11.1	11.0							11.5
(23) 4.2	(24) 2.8	(21) 6.5	Net Profit + Depr., Dep., Amort./Cur. Mat. L/T/D						(15) 7.0
2.1	1.7	2.0							4.0
.2	.2	.2				.3		.1	.2
.5	.5	.5	Fixed/Worth			.4		.4	.5
2.0	.8	1.0				.7		.8	1.1
.8	.6	.6				.6		.3	.8
1.9	1.4	1.3	Debt/Worth			1.2		1.1	2.2
7.5	3.9	6.1				2.2		4.2	4.9
52.4	41.4	49.1				38.5		49.1	81.6
(60) 30.1	(68) 25.3	(69) 29.9	% Profit Before Taxes/Tangible Net Worth			(10) 13.1		(17) 39.0	(30) 30.4
11.6	5.1	12.4				-5.8		10.8	19.9
17.3	17.4	19.5				14.8		23.5	18.2
10.7	7.7	11.4	% Profit Before Taxes/Total Assets			9.2		12.8	13.0
3.2	1.3	3.4				-2.0		3.6	7.0
30.3	28.9	38.9				173.5		41.9	26.3
10.1	14.7	14.3	Sales/Net Fixed Assets			14.1		20.5	11.2
7.1	8.1	7.9				6.0		7.9	7.0
2.8	2.9	3.0				3.0		2.7	3.0
2.3	2.2	2.4	Sales/Total Assets			2.2		2.4	2.0
1.5	1.6	1.7				1.6		1.7	1.6
.8	.9	.7						.5	.8
(61) 1.7	(69) 1.5	(60) 1.4	% Depr., Dep., Amort./Sales					(19) 1.4	(27) 1.7
2.7	2.3	2.0						1.8	3.2
2.0	2.0	1.6							
(22) 3.4	(24) 5.1	(20) 3.8	% Officers', Directors' Owners' Comp/Sales						
7.5	7.8	6.4							
2669695M	**3827053M**	**5021621M**	Net Sales ($)	**700M**	**10979M**	**44111M**	**64365M**	**329632M**	**4571834M**
1544744M	**2054512M**	**2669163M**	Total Assets ($)	**164M**	**3788M**	**45306M**	**31755M**	**171842M**	**2416308M**

M = $ thousand MM = $ million

See Pages 11 through 21 for Explanation of Ratios and Data

Current Data Sorted by Assets   Comparative Historical Data

Type of Statement

	0-500M	500M-2MM	2-10MM	10-50MM	50-100MM	100-250MM	4/1/02-3/31/03 ALL	4/1/03-3/31/04 ALL
Unqualified		2	16	16	5	6	38	49
Reviewed		11	18	1			38	45
Compiled	1	9	9				19	40
Tax Returns	7	14	7				15	17
Other	2	19	26	20	6	5	56	61

Periods: 36 (4/1-9/30/06)   164 (10/1/06-3/31/07)

	0-500M	500M-2MM	2-10MM	10-50MM	50-100MM	100-250MM	4/1/02-3/31/03 ALL	4/1/03-3/31/04 ALL
NUMBER OF STATEMENTS	10	55	76	37	11	11	166	212
ASSETS	%	%	%	%	%	%	%	%
Cash & Equivalents	14.0	9.1	7.9	10.4	9.7	4.0	9.4	10.7
Trade Receivables (net)	45.8	32.5	34.4	22.6	25.8	33.5	29.7	29.2
Inventory	13.0	34.1	27.6	28.8	24.1	25.6	27.3	26.9
All Other Current	6.4	2.7	2.8	4.2	7.2	1.7	3.4	3.7
Total Current	79.2	78.5	72.7	65.9	66.9	64.8	69.7	70.4
Fixed Assets (net)	7.9	16.3	16.8	17.4	14.2	14.7	19.3	18.4
Intangibles (net)	6.1	1.5	3.4	7.6	15.0	13.6	5.4	5.4
All Other Non-Current	6.8	3.7	7.0	9.1	3.9	6.9	5.6	5.8
Total	100.0	100.0	100.0	100.0	100.0	100.0	100.0	100.0
LIABILITIES								
Notes Payable-Short Term	7.0	13.5	9.4	8.3	4.0	3.6	9.7	14.0
Cur. Mat.-L.T.D.	3.3	2.9	2.3	1.5	1.4	1.6	4.2	3.2
Trade Payables	20.5	17.7	16.6	13.1	15.4	15.9	15.2	15.2
Income Taxes Payable	.2	.2	.5	.5	.6	.6	.4	.4
All Other Current	11.7	8.2	11.8	13.9	11.0	10.2	11.4	11.6
Total Current	42.6	42.5	40.7	37.3	32.3	31.9	40.8	44.4
Long-Term Debt	20.3	8.5	9.6	9.4	14.8	21.8	13.5	11.7
Deferred Taxes	.0	.2	.2	.3	.0	1.0	.2	.3
All Other Non-Current	8.0	2.9	9.7	1.7	1.3	6.2	4.9	6.9
Net Worth	29.1	45.9	39.8	51.3	51.6	39.1	40.6	36.8
Total Liabilties & Net Worth	100.0	100.0	100.0	100.0	100.0	100.0	100.0	100.0
INCOME DATA								
Net Sales	100.0	100.0	100.0	100.0	100.0	100.0	100.0	100.0
Gross Profit	43.0	38.6	33.4	31.2	21.6	30.2	35.8	33.0
Operating Expenses	29.6	33.1	25.5	21.3	19.7	20.7	31.2	30.4
Operating Profit	13.4	5.4	7.9	10.0	1.9	9.6	4.7	2.6
All Other Expenses (net)	.7	.6	.7	.7	1.9	.8	1.3	1.2
Profit Before Taxes	12.6	4.9	7.2	9.3	.0	8.7	3.4	1.5

RATIOS

	0-500M	500M-2MM	2-10MM	10-50MM	50-100MM	100-250MM	4/1/02-3/31/03 ALL	4/1/03-3/31/04 ALL
Current	5.0	3.5	3.2	2.7	2.9	2.8	2.9	2.8
	2.2	1.9	1.9	1.9	2.3	1.9	1.8	1.7
	1.4	1.3	1.3	1.2	1.8	1.7	1.3	1.3
Quick	3.7	1.7	1.8	1.5	1.7	1.4	1.6	1.5
	1.9	1.0	1.0	1.0	1.2	1.1	1.0	.9
	.9	.7	.6	.5	.7	.9	.7	.6
Sales/Receivables	31 11.8	23 15.8	41 8.8	33 11.2	46 7.9	55 6.6	36 10.2	39 9.4
	64 5.7	42 8.7	52 7.0	43 8.4	57 6.4	66 5.5	49 7.5	49 7.5
	74 4.9	52 7.0	66 5.5	63 5.8	78 4.7	96 3.8	64 5.7	63 5.8
Cost of Sales/Inventory	0 UND	24 14.9	31 11.7	53 6.9	42 8.7	46 7.9	41 8.8	42 8.8
	6 56.4	75 4.9	68 5.3	100 3.6	69 5.3	81 4.5	81 4.5	68 5.4
	101 3.6	106 3.4	113 3.2	145 2.5	107 3.4	123 3.0	136 2.7	113 3.2
Cost of Sales/Payables	0 UND	18 20.9	19 18.8	22 16.3	32 11.6	15 24.6	19 19.6	19 19.6
	48 7.5	32 11.5	37 9.8	34 10.7	35 10.3	43 8.4	33 11.0	36 10.3
	89 4.1	46 8.0	53 6.9	48 7.6	43 8.6	53 6.8	52 7.1	57 6.4
Sales/Working Capital	5.6	5.1	4.1	3.1	3.3	3.4	4.1	4.0
	8.5	7.8	7.0	5.4	4.0	4.7	6.4	6.5
	NM	18.0	15.4	33.2	6.0	12.2	14.6	17.2
EBIT/Interest		19.9	18.6	31.2	12.7	14.8	11.3	8.5
		(53) 6.8	(66) 7.2	(32) 10.3	(10) 3.6	5.8	(151) 3.5	(190) 2.7
		2.7	2.8	3.1	-2.3	3.2	1.1	.2
Net Profit + Depr., Dep., Amort./Cur. Mat. L/T/D		6.3	15.8	87.8			6.5	3.7
		(11) 2.9	(19) 3.7	(13) 9.5			(48) 2.2	(56) 1.6
		1.8	2.0	2.3			1.2	.6
Fixed/Worth	.0	.1	.1	.2	.2	.3	.2	.2
	.2	.3	.3	.3	.3	.6	.4	.4
	NM	.7	.9	.6	.5	.8	1.3	1.4
Debt/Worth	.3	.5	.5	.6	.6	.8	.7	.7
	1.3	1.3	1.5	.7	1.4	2.8	1.6	1.6
	NM	2.9	4.2	2.0	3.5	4.8	4.1	5.0
% Profit Before Taxes/Tangible Net Worth		46.3	60.8	55.7	62.4		45.1	26.2
		(53) 20.6	(69) 34.4	(33) 25.7	15.7		(146) 17.2	(182) 8.2
		7.0	15.4	14.6	-9.4		2.9	-.6
% Profit Before Taxes/Total Assets	64.9	23.2	23.5	23.0	15.5	15.0	15.7	9.9
	30.7	8.4	12.0	11.3	7.2	11.8	5.6	2.6
	23.7	2.2	3.5	5.7	-7.4	7.3	.4	-1.3
Sales/Net Fixed Assets	UND	80.5	50.0	25.5	47.8	21.7	27.1	34.1
	125.4	35.2	16.7	11.4	12.2	11.8	12.9	14.0
	22.5	14.5	7.6	6.4	6.1	8.7	6.2	6.3
Sales/Total Assets	5.6	3.6	2.8	2.2	1.8	2.6	2.9	2.7
	2.8	3.0	2.3	1.6	1.5	1.7	1.9	2.0
	2.1	2.3	1.7	1.2	.8	1.3	1.4	1.4
% Depr., Dep., Amort./Sales		.6	.6	1.0		.9	1.3	1.0
		(48) 1.3	(63) 1.3	(32) 1.7		1.5	(141) 2.1	(180) 1.9
		2.0	2.6	2.6		1.7	3.3	3.3
% Officers', Directors' Owners' Comp/Sales		2.4	2.1				2.3	2.7
		(30) 5.2	(30) 3.6				(56) 4.8	(57) 4.8
		10.5	5.4				9.6	5.0
Net Sales ($)	10429M	211828M	808687M	1536358M	1184858M	3259949M	5163052M	5077280M
Total Assets ($)	3138M	68360M	358470M	880857M	819334M	1714148M	3039831M	3455707M

M = $ thousand   MM = $ million
See Pages 11 through 21 for Explanation of Ratios and Data

Comparative Historical Data / Current Data Sorted by Sales

		Comparative Historical Data		Type of Statement	0-1MM	1-3MM	3-5MM	5-10MM	10-25MM	25MM & OVER
	42	50	45	Unqualified		1	3	8	9	24
	42	30	30	Reviewed		1	7	15	6	1
	27	18	19	Compiled	1	3	6	6	3	
	26	14	28	Tax Returns	5	10	6	6	1	
	63	86	78	Other	2	7	10	12	22	25
	4/1/04-3/31/05 ALL	4/1/05-3/31/06 ALL	4/1/06-3/31/07 ALL		36 (4/1-9/30/06)		164 (10/1/06-3/31/07)			
NUMBER OF STATEMENTS	200	198	200		8	22	32	47	41	50
ASSETS	%	%	%		%	%	%	%	%	%
Cash & Equivalents	9.7	9.9	8.9			6.8	11.2	8.7	10.7	7.1
Trade Receivables (net)	31.1	30.7	31.7			33.3	30.4	35.8	31.6	29.3
Inventory	29.4	29.9	28.6			24.8	35.8	29.4	28.8	25.9
All Other Current	2.6	2.0	3.4			3.9	1.2	3.5	2.8	4.4
Total Current	72.8	72.5	72.6			68.9	78.7	77.3	73.8	66.6
Fixed Assets (net)	16.2	15.4	16.1			18.5	13.6	13.9	15.7	16.5
Intangibles (net)	6.0	6.3	5.0			3.6	2.4	3.0	3.7	10.4
All Other Non-Current	5.1	5.8	6.3			9.0	5.4	5.7	6.8	6.5
Total	100.0	100.0	100.0			100.0	100.0	100.0	100.0	100.0
LIABILITIES										
Notes Payable-Short Term	14.7	11.9	9.6			18.0	9.3	11.9	8.9	6.1
Cur. Mat.-L.T.D.	3.4	2.2	2.3			1.8	3.2	2.0	2.4	1.5
Trade Payables	16.6	17.1	16.3			11.2	15.6	16.4	20.1	16.3
Income Taxes Payable	.4	.4	.4			.2	.3	.2	.4	.8
All Other Current	11.5	11.4	11.1			10.3	12.1	11.8	11.2	11.4
Total Current	46.5	43.0	39.7			41.5	40.4	42.3	43.0	36.1
Long-Term Debt	11.5	10.9	10.8			17.3	9.7	8.3	7.7	13.2
Deferred Taxes	.3	.4	.3			.5	.1	.3	.1	.4
All Other Non-Current	5.6	5.6	5.6			6.6	6.8	7.8	6.8	2.2
Net Worth	36.1	40.1	43.7			34.2	42.9	41.2	42.4	48.1
Total Liabilties & Net Worth	100.0	100.0	100.0			100.0	100.0	100.0	100.0	100.0
INCOME DATA										
Net Sales	100.0	100.0	100.0			100.0	100.0	100.0	100.0	100.0
Gross Profit	35.1	34.1	34.1			42.5	42.8	31.9	33.1	26.4
Operating Expenses	29.3	28.6	26.4			35.2	35.1	25.9	25.2	17.7
Operating Profit	5.9	5.5	7.7			7.3	7.7	6.0	8.0	8.7
All Other Expenses (net)	1.1	1.3	.7			.6	.8	.4	.9	1.1
Profit Before Taxes	4.8	4.2	6.9			6.7	6.8	5.6	7.1	7.6
RATIOS										
Current	3.0	2.8	3.0			2.6	3.3	3.5	2.7	2.8
	1.8	1.7	1.9			1.9	2.0	1.7	1.9	1.9
	1.2	1.3	1.3			1.2	1.4	1.3	1.2	1.4
Quick	1.6	1.5	1.7			1.7	1.7	2.1	1.5	1.5
	1.0	.9	1.1			1.0	1.1	1.0	1.0	1.1
	.6	.6	.7			.7	.6	.7	.6	.7
Sales/Receivables	38 9.7	38 9.5	35 10.4		28 13.2	22 16.9	37 9.8	41 9.0	37 10.0	
	47 7.8	51 7.2	47 7.8		48 7.6	42 8.7	48 7.7	51 7.2	55 6.6	
	66 5.5	66 5.6	64 5.7		69 5.3	56 6.6	61 6.0	66 5.5	69 5.3	
Cost of Sales/Inventory	45 8.1	46 7.9	33 11.2		17 21.5	34 10.6	26 13.9	41 8.9	42 8.7	
	78 4.7	83 4.4	74 5.0		81 4.5	87 4.2	62 5.9	73 5.0	75 4.9	
	121 3.0	121 3.0	115 3.2		110 3.3	121 3.0	110 3.3	155 2.4	107 3.4	
Cost of Sales/Payables	20 18.0	21 17.2	19 19.0		9 41.6	18 20.6	18 20.8	24 15.0	23 15.6	
	34 10.6	37 9.9	34 10.7		22 16.8	33 11.2	31 11.6	39 9.3	35 10.3	
	57 6.4	55 6.6	50 7.3		51 7.2	47 7.8	42 8.7	62 5.9	48 7.6	
Sales/Working Capital	4.3	4.3	4.1			4.8	5.0	4.2	3.2	3.4
	7.4	7.0	6.9			7.1	7.6	7.2	6.3	5.9
	19.6	17.0	13.8			28.1	15.7	16.8	17.8	11.9
EBIT/Interest	19.1	16.4	19.4			27.4	22.6	21.0	16.5	17.3
	(177) 3.9	(169) 4.1	(177) 6.8		(19) 9.3	(31) 8.8	(39) 4.9	(38) 7.8	(45) 5.3	
	1.5	1.6	2.8			3.0	2.8	2.8	3.0	3.0
Net Profit + Depr., Dep., Amort./Cur. Mat. L/T/D	7.3	14.0	14.7					11.5	52.9	13.7
	(53) 2.7	(51) 3.5	(53) 3.9				(12) 3.5	(13) 10.2	(19) 4.8	
	.6	1.8	2.0					1.6	2.4	1.9
Fixed/Worth	.2	.1	.1			.2	.1	.1	.1	.2
	.3	.4	.3			.3	.2	.2	.3	.4
	1.2	1.0	.7			3.2	.6	.7	1.1	.6
Debt/Worth	.5	.6	.6			.4	.5	.5	.7	.6
	1.6	1.7	1.3			1.7	1.3	1.3	1.2	1.4
	5.6	5.4	3.3			10.3	3.2	2.9	4.8	3.5
% Profit Before Taxes/Tangible Net Worth	46.9	42.3	57.6			68.8	58.8	47.7	62.6	60.7
	(170) 20.1	(167) 19.5	(183) 30.5		(19) 44.2	(31) 33.3	(43) 22.1	(36) 34.9	(46) 37.5	
	3.9	5.8	11.0			10.8	5.3	11.7	10.9	14.8
% Profit Before Taxes/Total Assets	17.7	14.7	23.7			30.0	25.8	20.4	23.7	19.8
	6.1	7.9	11.1			10.0	15.9	9.2	13.2	10.8
	1.4	1.7	3.6			5.5	2.0	3.4	3.4	5.7
Sales/Net Fixed Assets	41.5	43.1	51.4			68.1	80.2	80.5	34.4	32.5
	17.3	18.1	18.8			16.6	42.2	22.6	16.5	13.1
	7.5	8.2	8.5			5.6	14.1	11.9	8.8	8.1
Sales/Total Assets	3.0	2.8	3.1			3.0	3.4	3.4	2.7	2.5
	2.2	2.0	2.3			2.3	2.7	2.7	2.1	1.7
	1.5	1.3	1.6			2.0	2.1	2.1	1.3	1.4
% Depr., Dep., Amort./Sales	.8	.7	.8			.9	.7	.6	.5	.8
	(161) 1.5	(162) 1.4	(167) 1.4		(17) 1.4	(28) 1.4	(38) 1.3	(35) 1.3	(44) 1.5	
	2.8	2.5	2.5			2.8	2.5	2.4	2.3	2.5
% Officers', Directors' Owners' Comp/Sales	2.4	2.3	2.2			3.7	2.6	1.4	2.0	
	(78) 3.7	(61) 4.6	(68) 4.5		(11) 8.4	(17) 5.2	(20) 3.5	(14) 3.5		
	8.3	7.6	7.9			12.7	8.4	4.6	5.7	
Net Sales ($)	5162953M	6343230M	7012109M		4448M	45305M	125582M	332702M	650852M	5853220M
Total Assets ($)	3284876M	4319960M	3844307M		4385M	22863M	51314M	148036M	371872M	3245837M

M = $ thousand   MM = $ million
See Pages 11 through 21 for Explanation of Ratios and Data

Current Data Sorted by Assets | Comparative Historical Data

0-500M	500M-2MM	2-10MM	10-50MM	50-100MM	100-250MM	Type of Statement	4/1/02-3/31/03 ALL	4/1/03-3/31/04 ALL
		1	6	1	6	Unqualified	14	13
	1	3	2			Reviewed	9	9
	3	4				Compiled	5	8
	2	1				Tax Returns	1	2
1	3	4	9	3		Other	15	11
	9 (4/1-9/30/06)			41 (10/1/06-3/31/07)				
0-500M	500M-2MM	2-10MM	10-50MM	50-100MM	100-250MM	NUMBER OF STATEMENTS	44	43
1	9	13	17	4	6			
%	%	%	%	%	%	**ASSETS**	%	%
		4.9	4.3			Cash & Equivalents	9.7	6.6
		21.2	26.7			Trade Receivables (net)	17.5	18.9
		44.0	14.0			Inventory	36.4	35.0
		1.2	2.1			All Other Current	3.7	2.6
		71.3	47.1			Total Current	67.4	63.1
		24.7	39.4			Fixed Assets (net)	21.9	23.5
		2.4	6.1			Intangibles (net)	4.0	5.3
		1.7	7.4			All Other Non-Current	6.8	8.1
		100.0	100.0			Total	100.0	100.0
						LIABILITIES		
		12.1	14.4			Notes Payable-Short Term	13.1	15.1
		2.0	2.6			Cur. Mat.-L.T.D.	4.9	3.5
		13.4	15.6			Trade Payables	14.7	16.3
		.1	.2			Income Taxes Payable	.6	.5
		16.6	7.6			All Other Current	16.8	14.3
		44.2	40.4			Total Current	50.1	49.6
		11.5	14.8			Long-Term Debt	36.1	15.5
		.5	1.5			Deferred Taxes	.5	.7
		10.4	9.3			All Other Non-Current	11.2	9.9
		33.4	34.0			Net Worth	2.1	24.3
		100.0	100.0			Total Liabilities & Net Worth	100.0	100.0
						INCOME DATA		
		100.0	100.0			Net Sales	100.0	100.0
		27.9	18.2			Gross Profit	21.9	24.2
		25.2	13.1			Operating Expenses	18.9	21.9
		2.7	5.1			Operating Profit	3.0	2.3
		2.0	.9			All Other Expenses (net)	.9	1.0
		.8	4.2			Profit Before Taxes	2.1	1.3
						RATIOS		
		2.2	2.2				2.0	1.7
		1.8	1.2			Current	1.3	1.2
		1.3	.6				1.0	1.0
		1.1	1.5				.9	.8
		.7	.7			Quick	.5	.5
		.3	.5				.3	.3
		19 19.1	44 8.2				8 45.5	9 40.9
		42 8.7	53 6.8			Sales/Receivables	28 12.8	31 11.8
		72 5.1	61 6.0				56 6.6	54 6.7
		67 5.5	4 89.1				40 9.1	31 11.6
		106 3.4	28 12.9			Cost of Sales/Inventory	59 6.2	68 5.4
		180 2.0	53 6.9				105 3.5	107 3.4
		13 27.7	27 13.7				10 35.8	11 32.2
		38 9.5	35 10.3			Cost of Sales/Payables	26 14.1	29 12.6
		73 5.0	55 6.6				54 6.8	48 7.7
		4.2	8.0				7.0	8.5
		5.6	26.7			Sales/Working Capital	17.3	16.5
		10.0	-12.7				-84.1	-194.0
		11.0	5.0				11.4	6.2
		(11) 3.1	(11) 3.6			EBIT/Interest	(37) 2.9	(35) 2.6
		-.6	2.3				.9	.4
						Net Profit + Depr., Dep.,	8.2	3.4
						Amort./Cur. Mat. L/T/D	(14) 2.3	(13) 1.3
							1.3	1.0
		.2	.7				.3	.4
		.8	1.6			Fixed/Worth	1.2	1.2
		NM	15.4				-3.1	4.9
		.6	.9				1.8	1.2
		1.3	3.3			Debt/Worth	4.7	3.8
		NM	31.9				-14.8	45.6
		26.4	49.9				39.3	40.8
		(10) 18.7	(14) 21.8			% Profit Before Taxes/Tangible Net Worth	(31) 23.7	(34) 11.4
		13.0	6.4				10.5	-3.9
		14.0	16.6				10.6	12.8
		8.9	7.1			% Profit Before Taxes/Total Assets	4.9	3.7
		-1.0	3.7				-.4	-.8
		22.8	15.3				34.5	39.1
		7.6	6.7			Sales/Net Fixed Assets	11.6	10.5
		3.5	2.1				5.8	4.3
		2.3	2.0				3.2	3.0
		1.8	1.7			Sales/Total Assets	2.3	2.1
		.9	1.4				1.5	1.3
		.7	2.0				.7	.6
		(15) 1.7	3.2			% Depr., Dep., Amort./Sales	(38) 1.6	(38) 2.2
		4.3	5.3				2.5	4.1
							.8	.4
						% Officers', Directors' Owners' Comp/Sales	(10) 1.4	(12) 2.5
							2.9	4.2
369M	44514M	135155M	852285M	762000M	1374313M	Net Sales ($)	2437935M	1977885M
392M	13847M	79129M	498787M	347828M	921092M	Total Assets ($)	1205527M	1209060M

M = $ thousand   MM = $ million
See Pages 11 through 21 for Explanation of Ratios and Data

Comparative Historical Data   Current Data Sorted by Sales

		Comparative Historical Data					Current Data Sorted by Sales		
Type of Statement	4/1/04-3/31/05 ALL	4/1/05-3/31/06 ALL	4/1/06-3/31/07 ALL	0-1MM	1-3MM	3-5MM	5-10MM	10-25MM	25MM & OVER
					9 (4/1-9/30/06)		41 (10/1/06-3/31/07)		
Unqualified	12	6	14				1	1	12
Reviewed	6	6	6				2	2	2
Compiled	6	6	7			1	5	1	
Tax Returns	1	4	3			1	1	1	
Other	16	20	20	1	3	2		2	12
NUMBER OF STATEMENTS	41	42	50	1	3	4	9	7	26
ASSETS	%	%	%	%	%	%	%	%	%
Cash & Equivalents	8.1	7.5	7.0						9.6
Trade Receivables (net)	18.5	21.0	23.3						25.7
Inventory	38.0	36.4	29.2						16.1
All Other Current	1.7	4.0	2.7						3.5
Total Current	66.3	68.9	62.2						54.9
Fixed Assets (net)	20.5	22.2	26.2						30.1
Intangibles (net)	7.9	4.1	4.7						7.5
All Other Non-Current	5.4	4.8	6.9						7.5
Total	100.0	100.0	100.0						100.0
LIABILITIES									
Notes Payable-Short Term	14.3	12.1	11.7						8.9
Cur. Mat.-L.T.D.	2.5	2.0	1.9						2.3
Trade Payables	16.4	19.0	14.9						14.5
Income Taxes Payable	.3	.9	.1						.2
All Other Current	13.9	16.9	16.3						13.7
Total Current	47.4	50.9	44.8						39.5
Long-Term Debt	14.6	15.7	14.7						16.2
Deferred Taxes	.9	.6	.8						1.0
All Other Non-Current	7.3	10.1	8.8						10.2
Net Worth	29.8	22.7	30.9						33.0
Total Liabilities & Net Worth	100.0	100.0	100.0						100.0
INCOME DATA									
Net Sales	100.0	100.0	100.0						100.0
Gross Profit	21.4	23.2	22.5						17.9
Operating Expenses	18.0	19.8	18.1						13.0
Operating Profit	3.4	3.5	4.3						4.9
All Other Expenses (net)	2.0	1.2	1.4						1.2
Profit Before Taxes	1.4	2.3	2.9						3.7
RATIOS									
Current	1.7	2.4	2.2						2.4
	1.3	1.5	1.6						1.5
	1.1	1.0	1.0						1.0
Quick	1.0	.9	1.2						1.6
	.5	.5	.7						.9
	.2	.3	.4						.6
Sales/Receivables	9 42.2	11 34.1	30 12.1						37 9.8
	28 13.0	36 10.2	44 8.2						51 7.1
	53 6.9	48 7.7	57 6.3						61 6.0
Cost of Sales/Inventory	34 10.8	29 12.5	24 15.0						15 24.9
	62 5.9	62 5.9	63 5.8						32 11.5
	119 3.1	109 3.3	111 3.3						68 5.3
Cost of Sales/Payables	11 33.4	14 26.1	26 14.1						26 14.0
	32 11.5	37 9.9	35 10.4						33 11.1
	54 6.8	52 7.0	57 6.4						57 6.4
Sales/Working Capital	8.1	5.6	4.5						5.0
	13.5	11.3	9.9						10.1
	116.3	-70.9	-41.6						NM
EBIT/Interest	5.8	16.8	12.7						5.1
	(29) 1.9	(37) 4.9	(40) 3.4						(19) 3.1
	-1.5	.8	.8						.7
Net Profit + Depr., Dep., Amort./Cur. Mat. L/T/D	5.2	8.5							
	(12) 1.2	(10) 5.0							
	-2.0	2.1							
Fixed/Worth	.3	.2	.3						.4
	1.0	1.5	1.5						1.6
	-6.3	-473.5	16.4						NM
Debt/Worth	.9	.8	.7						1.0
	2.6	5.5	3.3						3.3
	-34.0	-758.6	63.5						NM
% Profit Before Taxes/Tangible Net Worth	43.4	89.7	54.6						46.1
	(29) 14.7	(31) 23.7	(39) 19.3						(20) 17.0
	4.3	13.7	6.9						3.0
% Profit Before Taxes/Total Assets	9.0	14.6	17.0						16.5
	4.8	8.1	7.7						5.2
	-3.4	-1.0	.7						.3
Sales/Net Fixed Assets	27.3	31.7	21.8						18.1
	17.0	14.3	10.8						8.5
	6.6	6.1	4.1						2.9
Sales/Total Assets	3.4	3.2	2.4						2.1
	2.3	2.2	1.8						1.7
	1.6	1.7	1.2						1.2
% Depr., Dep., Amort./Sales	.6	.7	1.2						1.5
	(38) 1.1	(35) 1.4	(42) 2.2						(21) 2.7
	3.0	2.2	3.7						4.8
% Officers', Directors' Owners' Comp/Sales		1.2							
		(13) 2.6							
		4.6							
Net Sales ($)	2106203M	2568969M	3168636M	369M	5539M	14349M	69965M	106339M	2972075M
Total Assets ($)	1040912M	1277916M	1861075M	392M	5458M	6092M	39776M	55539M	1753818M

M = $ thousand   MM = $ million
See Pages 11 through 21 for Explanation of Ratios and Data

Current Data Sorted by Assets   Comparative Historical Data

0-500M	500M-2MM	2-10MM	10-50MM	50-100M	100-250MM	Type of Statement	4/1/02-3/31/03 ALL	4/1/03-3/31/04 ALL
1	2	7	9	9	5	Unqualified	44	49
	3	18	6	2	1	Reviewed	31	40
6	10	7	7	2		Compiled	15	24
2	5	2	2			Tax Returns	9	7
4	11	18	9	9	7	Other	41	60
34 (4/1-9/30/06)		130 (10/1/06-3/31/07)						
13	31	52	33	22	13	NUMBER OF STATEMENTS	140	180

%	%	%	%	%	%	ASSETS	%	%
14.3	4.5	6.7	3.9	3.7	6.5	Cash & Equivalents	5.1	6.1
16.4	21.7	24.0	21.8	18.1	26.2	Trade Receivables (net)	24.4	23.8
35.7	40.8	38.5	34.7	26.1	21.8	Inventory	27.3	28.4
.8	2.9	2.1	4.5	5.9	4.0	All Other Current	3.3	2.8
67.1	69.8	71.3	64.9	53.8	58.5	Total Current	60.1	61.1
22.3	14.7	23.7	26.6	27.7	26.5	Fixed Assets (net)	28.3	25.7
4.0	6.7	1.4	4.8	10.2	12.6	Intangibles (net)	5.0	6.2
6.5	8.7	3.6	3.7	8.3	2.4	All Other Non-Current	6.6	7.0
100.0	100.0	100.0	100.0	100.0	100.0	Total	100.0	100.0
						LIABILITIES		
14.5	20.7	17.4	14.0	15.4	5.5	Notes Payable-Short Term	16.5	11.8
3.1	5.9	3.0	3.2	2.1	1.5	Cur. Mat.-L.T.D.	5.5	4.5
33.2	20.5	17.8	18.9	14.4	17.3	Trade Payables	16.2	16.6
.3	.1	.2	.2	.5	.7	Income Taxes Payable	.2	.3
26.3	18.3	8.6	9.5	13.8	8.2	All Other Current	11.7	10.2
77.5	65.6	47.0	45.7	46.3	33.2	Total Current	50.0	43.3
16.9	11.8	13.1	13.7	16.2	15.1	Long-Term Debt	15.1	15.5
.1	.0	.4	.4	.9	2.1	Deferred Taxes	.7	.9
15.6	7.3	7.7	4.8	5.1	5.4	All Other Non-Current	6.3	6.7
-10.2	15.3	31.9	35.5	31.5	44.3	Net Worth	27.9	33.6
100.0	100.0	100.0	100.0	100.0	100.0	Total Liabilities & Net Worth	100.0	100.0
						INCOME DATA		
100.0	100.0	100.0	100.0	100.0	100.0	Net Sales	100.0	100.0
29.8	29.6	26.6	17.4	15.0	18.1	Gross Profit	24.7	24.0
31.0	28.3	22.5	13.0	10.4	11.4	Operating Expenses	22.0	20.4
-1.2	1.3	4.1	4.4	4.6	6.7	Operating Profit	2.8	3.6
.4	.9	1.2	1.1	1.0	1.8	All Other Expenses (net)	1.3	.9
-1.6	.4	2.9	3.2	3.6	4.9	Profit Before Taxes	1.4	2.7
						RATIOS		
1.4	2.0	2.3	2.1	2.5	2.7	Current	2.2	2.6
1.1	1.3	1.4	1.4	1.2	2.0		1.3	1.5
.6	.8	1.2	1.2	.9	1.4		.9	1.0
.8	.8	1.2	1.0	1.1	1.4	Quick	1.1	1.3
.4	.5	.6	.6	.6	1.2		.7	.7
.2	.2	.4	.4	.2	.8		.4	.4
5 71.7	11 32.4	23 15.6	22 16.9	22 16.6	41 8.9	Sales/Receivables	27 13.3	27 13.5
9 42.5	27 13.4	37 9.9	33 10.9	45 8.1	52 7.1		38 9.5	39 9.4
18 19.8	50 7.3	52 7.0	54 6.8	56 6.5	59 6.2		54 6.8	53 7.0
15 24.0	40 9.1	47 7.7	32 11.3	33 11.1	44 8.3	Cost of Sales/Inventory	30 12.1	29 12.4
29 12.5	64 5.7	77 4.8	54 6.8	48 7.6	56 6.5		54 6.7	52 7.0
64 5.7	119 3.1	115 3.2	103 3.6	99 3.7	67 5.5		88 4.2	86 4.3
2 190.8	14 25.8	20 18.4	19 19.1	19 19.4	22 16.5	Cost of Sales/Payables	19 19.1	17 21.5
15 24.5	28 13.0	35 10.5	30 12.3	32 11.4	45 8.0		32 11.6	30 12.1
40 9.0	63 5.8	48 7.6	48 7.5	44 8.3	55 6.6		44 8.3	46 7.9
24.9	6.4	6.5	5.5	5.6	4.6	Sales/Working Capital	6.3	5.9
117.0	15.6	11.8	12.7	24.6	6.0		16.2	12.7
-21.8	-19.4	25.4	30.2	-22.5	34.4		-34.3	-337.7
6.3	6.1	4.5	7.4	5.0	19.7	EBIT/Interest	6.9	8.3
(10) 2.4	(30) 2.7	(48) 3.1	(30) 2.6	(20) 2.1	5.0		(131) 3.0	(174) 3.4
-.9	-1.2	1.2	1.4	1.4	1.5		.5	1.1
		8.4	11.0			Net Profit + Depr., Dep., Amort./Cur. Mat. L/T/D	5.8	8.3
	(17) 2.6	(12) 5.6					(50) 2.6	(63) 3.2
		1.7	2.3				.8	.9
.1	.1	.3	.4	.7	.3	Fixed/Worth	.5	.4
1.0	.6	.7	.7	1.9	.7		.9	.8
-1.0	18.3	1.7	1.7	4.5	NM		3.7	3.1
2.0	1.4	1.1	1.2	2.2	.8	Debt/Worth	1.0	1.0
-13.8	3.7	2.6	2.8	4.9	1.1		2.3	2.4
-2.7	-46.4	4.0	4.4	19.9	NM		16.0	12.5
	42.6	43.0	33.2	31.5	42.2	% Profit Before Taxes/Tangible Net Worth	45.9	44.1
	(23) 17.7	(46) 24.6	(31) 11.7	(20) 22.4	(10) 29.2		(114) 15.0	(151) 15.9
	-52.5	11.5	3.5	5.2	7.4		1.2	3.4
21.7	18.3	12.8	11.2	10.5	18.6	% Profit Before Taxes/Total Assets	12.2	12.6
11.1	2.8	6.2	3.3	3.8	7.2		4.3	4.1
-7.5	-9.8	1.0	1.0	1.4	1.6		-1.4	.0
UND	98.6	33.5	23.7	12.6	14.9	Sales/Net Fixed Assets	18.6	22.7
42.5	26.4	15.6	10.1	6.5	9.1		8.4	9.3
5.6	16.0	5.6	4.9	4.1	5.1		4.4	5.0
8.0	4.4	3.1	3.1	2.1	2.4	Sales/Total Assets	2.9	3.0
5.3	2.7	2.3	2.3	1.8	1.7		2.0	2.1
3.1	1.8	1.7	1.4	1.2	1.2		1.5	1.5
	.3	.7	.8	.9	.7	% Depr., Dep., Amort./Sales	.9	1.1
	(23) .8	(50) 1.4	(29) 1.6	(21) 1.6	(11) 1.3		(122) 2.4	(149) 2.2
	2.3	2.5	4.4	4.2	3.6		4.4	3.8
	2.3	1.2				% Officers', Directors' Owners' Comp/Sales	1.6	1.4
	(16) 3.7	(16) 1.9					(39) 3.5	(51) 3.1
	9.2	4.4					5.2	4.9
21930M	123871M	621026M	1692426M	2683326M	3825366M	Net Sales ($)	6781114M	8332021M
3581M	40806M	245397M	711961M	1613186M	2145344M	Total Assets ($)	3949744M	4708671M

M = $ thousand   MM = $ million
See Pages 11 through 21 for Explanation of Ratios and Data

Comparative Historical Data			Type of Statement	Current Data Sorted by Sales					
47	46	33	Unqualified			2	2	6	23
37	31	27	Reviewed		4	7	11	5	
19	22	26	Compiled	2	8	5	5	4	2
12	9	9	Tax Returns	1	1	2	5		
64	61	69	Other	3	7	4	12	10	33
4/1/04-3/31/05 ALL	4/1/05-3/31/06 ALL	4/1/06-3/31/07 ALL		0-1MM	34 (4/1-9/30/06) 1-3MM	3-5MM	130 (10/1/06-3/31/07) 5-10MM	10-25MM	25MM & OVER
179	169	164	NUMBER OF STATEMENTS	6	18	15	31	31	63
%	%	%	ASSETS	%	%	%	%	%	%
5.1	5.4	5.9	Cash & Equivalents	9.6	6.1	6.9	4.9	5.0	
23.3	23.6	21.9	Trade Receivables (net)	18.7	21.4	23.7	23.5	22.2	
32.6	31.0	34.9	Inventory	36.9	39.7	42.8	36.3	30.0	
2.2	2.5	3.3	All Other Current	2.2	2.7	1.4	3.8	4.5	
63.2	62.5	66.0	Total Current	67.4	69.9	74.8	68.6	61.7	
25.5	25.4	23.2	Fixed Assets (net)	15.9	25.8	18.5	24.0	25.8	
4.9	4.5	5.4	Intangibles (net)	7.8	.8	1.9	3.4	7.5	
6.4	7.6	5.4	All Other Non-Current	8.8	3.5	4.8	4.0	5.1	
100.0	100.0	100.0	Total	100.0	100.0	100.0	100.0	100.0	
			LIABILITIES						
13.5	13.4	15.9	Notes Payable-Short Term	22.6	17.5	17.0	14.7	13.5	
4.0	4.2	3.4	Cur. Mat.-L.T.D.	5.7	4.6	4.2	2.7	2.2	
18.0	18.7	19.2	Trade Payables	33.3	16.4	16.6	19.3	17.8	
.3	.4	.3	Income Taxes Payable	.2	.1	.3	.2	.4	
11.4	11.7	12.7	All Other Current	7.6	10.3	11.5	10.7	10.9	
47.3	48.4	51.5	Total Current	69.5	48.9	49.5	47.6	44.9	
16.0	15.1	13.8	Long-Term Debt	16.8	16.6	12.8	12.4	13.5	
.6	.7	.5	Deferred Taxes	.1	.2	.3	.3	.9	
5.7	7.5	7.1	All Other Non-Current	9.1	8.3	5.7	7.2	4.8	
30.4	28.4	27.1	Net Worth	4.5	26.1	31.7	32.6	35.9	
100.0	100.0	100.0	Total Liabilities & Net Worth	100.0	100.0	100.0	100.0	100.0	
			INCOME DATA						
100.0	100.0	100.0	Net Sales	100.0	100.0	100.0	100.0	100.0	
22.9	22.2	23.3	Gross Profit	31.6	27.9	29.0	21.5	16.5	
19.0	17.3	19.9	Operating Expenses	30.5	26.2	24.7	17.0	11.9	
3.9	4.8	3.5	Operating Profit	1.1	1.8	4.3	4.6	4.6	
.9	1.1	1.1	All Other Expenses (net)	.4	1.4	1.0	1.1	1.2	
3.0	3.8	2.4	Profit Before Taxes	.7	.3	3.3	3.5	3.4	
			RATIOS						
2.4	2.2	2.2	Current	1.8	1.8	2.7	2.2	2.4	
1.5	1.4	1.4		1.1	1.5	1.4	1.5	1.5	
1.0	1.0	1.0		.6	1.2	1.2	1.0	1.0	
1.2	1.1	1.0	Quick	.9	.7	1.2	1.1	1.1	
.7	.6	.6		.5	.6	.6	.6	.6	
.4	.4	.4		.1	.3	.4	.3	.4	
28 13.1 / 23 15.7 / 18 19.8			Sales/Receivables	8 47.5	15 24.3	18 20.6	15 24.3	26 14.2	
37 10.0 / 38 9.6 / 35 10.4				22 16.7	32 11.3	33 11.0	33 11.1	43 8.5	
52 7.0 / 51 7.1 / 52 7.1				47 7.8	51 7.2	54 6.7	50 7.3	55 6.6	
35 10.6 / 30 12.2 / 34 10.8			Cost of Sales/Inventory	25 14.7	35 10.5	42 8.7	32 11.6	33 11.0	
60 6.1 / 56 6.5 / 60 6.1				61 6.0	109 3.3	64 5.7	55 6.6	54 6.8	
96 3.8 / 92 4.0 / 105 3.5				113 3.2	143 2.5	117 3.1	92 4.0	81 4.5	
16 23.1 / 16 23.4 / 17 22.0			Cost of Sales/Payables	15 24.4	13 28.0	14 26.0	21 17.5	21 17.3	
31 12.0 / 28 12.9 / 31 11.6				40 9.1	38 9.7	28 13.0	34 10.6	32 11.3	
46 7.9 / 48 7.6 / 48 7.6				76 4.8	63 5.8	39 9.5	42 8.7	47 7.7	
6.3	7.0	6.0	Sales/Working Capital	6.7	5.7	5.4	6.9	5.5	
12.9	12.4	12.9		184.8	10.3	9.6	11.8	12.7	
-999.8	294.3	207.1		-15.0	47.3	23.3	108.2	512.9	
9.2	9.6	6.1	EBIT/Interest	6.0	4.3	6.4	4.8	8.4	
(172) 3.6	(154) 3.6	(151) 2.7		(17) 1.5	2.3	(30) 3.2	(28) 3.2	(58) 2.6	
1.4	1.2	1.2		-2.7	-1.9	1.2	1.7	1.4	
7.3	6.3	9.3	Net Profit + Depr., Dep., Amort./Cur. Mat. L/T/D				8.7	12.4	
(50) 3.7	(47) 3.3	(47) 3.8				(12) 4.1	(23) 4.9		
1.5	1.4	1.8					1.8	1.7	
.4	.4	.3	Fixed/Worth	.0	.2	.2	.3	.4	
.9	.9	.8		.8	.6	.7	.9	.8	
2.6	2.7	2.5		-1.4	1.7	1.4	2.5	3.0	
.9	1.1	1.2	Debt/Worth	3.3	1.7	1.0	1.4	1.1	
2.4	2.6	2.9		NM	2.7	2.4	2.6	2.9	
8.6	6.9	11.8		-3.7	4.8	4.9	4.3	6.7	
43.3	45.7	42.2	% Profit Before Taxes/Tangible Net Worth		50.5	42.6	52.2	32.6	
(148) 21.8	(139) 23.1	(135) 19.4		(13) 19.4	(27) 18.8	(27) 38.4	(57) 18.7		
6.6	8.2	4.6			2.0	2.2	18.5	5.7	
12.3	15.5	13.2	% Profit Before Taxes/Total Assets	20.8	10.0	18.4	13.1	11.9	
5.5	5.7	5.0		7.2	6.2	4.6	6.4	4.6	
.9	1.1	.7		-10.3	-9.5	.6	1.2	1.4	
27.6	36.8	35.3	Sales/Net Fixed Assets	UND	48.0	58.3	34.3	17.2	
9.6	10.9	13.4		29.6	17.8	21.9	14.3	9.3	
5.6	6.1	5.6		10.2	3.8	7.2	5.0	5.1	
3.0	3.1	3.1	Sales/Total Assets	5.3	3.2	4.0	3.5	2.6	
2.2	2.3	2.2		2.0	1.9	2.5	2.6	2.1	
1.6	1.7	1.6		1.8	1.4	1.8	1.7	1.5	
.8	.8	.7	% Depr., Dep., Amort./Sales	.3	.7	.7	.7	.7	
(144) 1.8	(138) 1.6	(141) 1.4		(11) .7	(13) 2.6	(27) 1.4	(29) 1.4	(57) 1.4	
3.1	2.7	3.2		2.3	7.0	2.2	2.8	3.6	
1.5	1.5	1.4	% Officers', Directors' Owners' Comp/Sales	3.7		1.9			
(58) 2.6	(51) 3.1	(48) 2.9		(10) 4.8		(14) 2.6			
4.2	4.8	5.1		5.5		5.9			
8731249M	9834514M	8967945M	Net Sales ($)	1745M	35132M	59365M	219161M	478905M	8173637M
4612420M	4839850M	4760275M	Total Assets ($)	2050M	15170M	30884M	101115M	222483M	4388573M

M = $ thousand   MM = $ million
See Pages 11 through 21 for Explanation of Ratios and Data

Current Data Sorted by Assets / Comparative Historical Data

	0-500M	500M-2MM	2-10MM	10-50MM	50-100MM	100-250MM	Type of Statement	4/1/02-3/31/03 ALL	4/1/03-3/31/04 ALL
			2	11		1	Unqualified	19	16
	1	1	8	5			Reviewed	11	14
	1	5	12	2	2		Compiled	15	19
	2	6	2				Tax Returns	3	10
		7	11	12		1	Other	25	26
		17 (4/1-9/30/06)		75 (10/1/06-3/31/07)					
	4	19	35	30	2	2	NUMBER OF STATEMENTS	73	85
	%	%	%	%	%	%	**ASSETS**	%	%
		8.0	7.1	3.3			Cash & Equivalents	7.6	6.6
		26.1	16.6	20.5			Trade Receivables (net)	17.4	16.5
		40.4	47.5	42.6			Inventory	37.6	38.3
		.7	2.8	2.8			All Other Current	3.7	3.6
		75.2	74.0	69.2			Total Current	66.4	65.0
		20.7	20.2	20.8			Fixed Assets (net)	27.0	28.6
		1.0	2.7	6.5			Intangibles (net)	2.7	2.4
		3.1	3.1	3.6			All Other Non-Current	3.9	4.0
		100.0	100.0	100.0			Total	100.0	100.0
							LIABILITIES		
		18.1	13.0	16.3			Notes Payable-Short Term	14.0	15.3
		1.6	4.3	2.4			Cur. Mat.-L.T.D.	4.4	4.4
		22.2	17.8	12.1			Trade Payables	14.3	17.9
		.4	.1	.2			Income Taxes Payable	.1	.1
		11.3	13.5	12.3			All Other Current	9.0	7.9
		53.7	48.7	43.2			Total Current	41.8	45.7
		10.4	11.2	12.4			Long-Term Debt	19.5	18.6
		.1	.1	.7			Deferred Taxes	.5	.5
		3.8	4.7	4.7			All Other Non-Current	6.6	5.7
		32.0	35.3	39.0			Net Worth	31.6	29.5
		100.0	100.0	100.0			Total Liabilties & Net Worth	100.0	100.0
							INCOME DATA		
		100.0	100.0	100.0			Net Sales	100.0	100.0
		23.6	18.0	16.9			Gross Profit	22.4	21.8
		23.9	14.2	10.7			Operating Expenses	19.1	19.9
		-.3	3.9	6.3			Operating Profit	3.2	1.9
		.7	.3	.4			All Other Expenses (net)	1.5	.9
		-1.0	3.5	5.8			Profit Before Taxes	1.8	1.0
							RATIOS		
		2.3	2.6	1.9				2.5	2.4
		1.3	1.7	1.5			Current	1.6	1.4
		1.0	1.0	1.2				1.1	1.0
		1.1	.8	.8				1.1	.9
		.6	.5	.6			Quick	.6 (84)	.5
		.2	.3	.3				.4	.3
		9 42.1	8 46.2	16 23.0				14 26.2	10 36.0
		26 14.0	16 23.0	23 15.9			Sales/Receivables	23 15.6	22 16.9
		35 10.4	29 12.6	34 10.9				39 9.3	36 10.1
		21 17.4	44 8.2	43 8.4				43 8.5	38 9.6
		54 6.7	58 6.3	68 5.4			Cost of Sales/Inventory	65 5.6	63 5.8
		89 4.1	100 3.7	96 3.8				94 3.9	111 3.3
		10 37.6	10 37.4	9 41.0				12 29.9	14 26.9
		25 14.7	21 17.4	17 21.4			Cost of Sales/Payables	26 13.8	26 14.2
		49 7.4	31 11.9	26 14.0				42 8.6	46 7.9
		8.4	6.1	6.8				5.4	7.0
		19.9	10.3	13.3			Sales/Working Capital	12.1	16.5
		247.4	-174.9	38.0				30.5	-89.6
		4.8	13.4	15.4				5.5	6.2
		(16) 1.7	(30) 5.1	(29) 5.4			EBIT/Interest	(67) 2.3	(76) 2.1
		-2.8	1.2	2.9				-.1	.9
				18.8				13.2	6.7
				(10) 6.6			Net Profit + Depr., Dep., Amort./Cur. Mat. L/T/D	(20) 3.1	(19) 1.6
				1.6				1.3	.5
		.2	.3	.3				.3	.3
		1.0	.5	.5			Fixed/Worth	.8	.8
		2.4	1.7	1.5				1.8	3.8
		.7	.8	.6				.7	1.1
		2.9	1.9	1.7			Debt/Worth	2.3	2.2
		5.5	5.1	5.4				7.4	14.3
		52.6	66.6	68.5				37.4	35.9
		(15) 21.0	(34) 28.5	(26) 32.5			% Profit Before Taxes/Tangible Net Worth	(62) 7.9	(73) 10.2
		-17.7	4.7	15.4				-1.0	.4
		14.3	20.3	19.2				8.1	8.4
		2.7	6.3	12.7			% Profit Before Taxes/Total Assets	2.6	2.8
		-7.5	.6	7.4				-2.4	-1.2
		111.4	50.5	43.4				36.3	48.6
		22.0	21.7	23.7			Sales/Net Fixed Assets	10.6	8.9
		8.5	10.1	9.7				5.3	5.0
		6.1	4.8	4.3				3.5	3.4
		3.6	2.7	2.7			Sales/Total Assets	2.5	2.3
		2.6	2.0	2.1				1.6	1.7
		.5	.5	.5				.9	.8
		(18) .9	(32) .7	(26) .9			% Depr., Dep., Amort./Sales	(69) 1.6	(75) 1.7
		1.7	1.3	1.5				2.8	3.0
		1.3	1.2					.9	2.2
		(11) 5.5	(11) 2.2				% Officers', Directors' Owners' Comp/Sales	(17) 1.9	(23) 3.0
		6.1	2.9					3.9	5.6
	2792M	90540M	530459M	2006895M	295967M	478011M	Net Sales ($)	2274558M	1987891M
	623M	22381M	163760M	720500M	114954M	266944M	Total Assets ($)	1054498M	815219M

M = $ thousand   MM = $ million
See Pages 11 through 21 for Explanation of Ratios and Data

Comparative Historical Data | Current Data Sorted by Sales

Type of Statement	20 / 4/1/04-3/31/05 ALL	13 / 4/1/05-3/31/06 ALL	14 / 4/1/06-3/31/07 ALL	0-1MM	1-3MM	3-5MM	5-10MM	10-25MM	25MM & OVER
				17 (4/1-9/30/06)			**75 (10/1/06-3/31/07)**		
Unqualified	20	13	14				1	3	11
Reviewed	8	10	15	1			1	10	3
Compiled	17	22	22	1	4	4	7	4	6
Tax Returns	6	10	10	1		1	2	1	1
Other	24	20	31	1	2	1	10	4	14
NUMBER OF STATEMENTS	75	75	92	3	6	6	20	22	35
ASSETS	%	%	%	%	%	%	%	%	%
Cash & Equivalents	6.3	7.9	5.8				8.6	7.2	3.6
Trade Receivables (net)	19.7	20.7	19.0				23.0	17.1	19.6
Inventory	40.6	38.2	43.2				41.6	45.3	44.4
All Other Current	1.9	1.2	2.5				2.4	1.0	3.5
Total Current	68.6	68.1	70.5				75.6	70.6	71.1
Fixed Assets (net)	23.2	24.0	22.5				19.2	22.3	20.2
Intangibles (net)	4.7	3.8	3.6				3.1	1.7	5.8
All Other Non-Current	3.6	4.1	3.4				2.1	5.4	2.9
Total	100.0	100.0	100.0				100.0	100.0	100.0
LIABILITIES									
Notes Payable-Short Term	17.3	13.7	15.0				11.8	12.2	16.3
Cur. Mat.-L.T.D.	3.0	3.5	3.2				5.2	3.2	2.4
Trade Payables	17.1	20.0	15.9				19.2	15.1	13.4
Income Taxes Payable	.1	.2	.2				.1	.0	.1
All Other Current	10.5	10.5	14.7				15.3	9.7	12.2
Total Current	48.1	47.9	49.0				51.7	40.2	44.4
Long-Term Debt	19.3	14.8	12.5				10.5	13.9	10.8
Deferred Taxes	.3	.5	.3				.1	.9	.2
All Other Non-Current	7.9	4.8	4.3				6.7	4.9	3.9
Net Worth	24.4	31.9	33.8				31.0	40.0	40.8
Total Liabilities & Net Worth	100.0	100.0	100.0				100.0	100.0	100.0
INCOME DATA									
Net Sales	100.0	100.0	100.0				100.0	100.0	100.0
Gross Profit	21.0	19.0	19.1				21.9	19.0	16.0
Operating Expenses	17.6	14.8	15.5				18.2	14.3	10.2
Operating Profit	3.3	4.2	3.5				3.7	4.8	5.8
All Other Expenses (net)	.6	.4	.5				-.1	.5	.6
Profit Before Taxes	2.7	3.8	3.0				3.8	4.3	5.1

RATIOS

Ratio	4/1/04-3/31/05	4/1/05-3/31/06	4/1/06-3/31/07	0-1MM	1-3MM	3-5MM	5-10MM	10-25MM	25MM & OVER
Current	2.2	2.1	2.2				3.1	3.4	1.9
	1.5	1.4	1.4				1.6	1.7	1.5
	1.1	1.0	1.1				1.0	1.2	1.2
Quick	.9	1.0	.8				1.2	1.2	.7
	.5	.6	.5				.7	.5	.5
	.3	.3	.3				.4	.4	.3
Sales/Receivables	11 / 33.4	12 / 31.4	9 / 41.4				8 / 43.8	9 / 38.7	15 / 24.8
	25 / 14.6	24 / 15.4	20 / 18.5				25 / 14.6	25 / 14.6	17 / 20.9
	38 / 9.6	38 / 9.6	32 / 11.5				54 / 6.8	32 / 11.4	28 / 13.2
Cost of Sales/Inventory	44 / 8.4	34 / 10.6	37 / 9.8				40 / 9.1	46 / 7.9	34 / 10.6
	69 / 5.3	55 / 6.6	62 / 5.9				77 / 4.7	57 / 6.4	59 / 6.2
	95 / 3.8	84 / 4.3	95 / 3.8				102 / 3.6	115 / 3.2	95 / 3.8
Cost of Sales/Payables	13 / 27.3	11 / 32.5	9 / 40.8				11 / 32.9	7 / 54.5	9 / 40.9
	22 / 16.8	22 / 16.5	18 / 20.1				24 / 15.4	18 / 20.1	14 / 26.0
	40 / 9.2	39 / 9.3	35 / 10.4				33 / 10.9	40 / 9.0	23 / 16.1
Sales/Working Capital	6.6	7.8	6.9				4.9	5.8	8.2
	14.7	18.1	14.6				8.9	10.1	13.7
	42.1	-999.8	62.3				211.8	27.3	38.1
EBIT/Interest	11.3	15.7	14.1				21.9	8.2	17.5
	(70) 4.3	(71) 7.8	(82) 4.8				(16) 4.9	(19) 3.4	(34) 7.6
	2.2	2.5	1.3				.6	1.2	3.3
Net Profit + Depr., Dep., Amort./Cur. Mat. L/T/D	6.4	14.4	18.8						
	(15) 2.8	(14) 3.9	(18) 9.9						
	1.5	1.6	3.3						
Fixed/Worth	.3	.2	.3				.3	.2	.2
	.8	.7	.7				.7	.5	.5
	3.9	1.9	2.3				2.3	1.2	1.0
Debt/Worth	1.1	.9	.7				.6	.6	.6
	2.9	2.0	2.1				2.9	2.0	1.5
	18.0	9.9	6.0				66.2	3.6	4.9
% Profit Before Taxes/Tangible Net Worth	55.7	53.9	61.4				61.0	60.4	68.3
	(62) 23.2	(64) 33.4	(81) 29.9				(17) 38.5	20.1	(31) 33.0
	12.0	12.3	6.6				4.1	3.3	16.4
% Profit Before Taxes/Total Assets	15.4	22.8	19.0				16.5	18.6	21.8
	6.9	9.8	10.2				8.3	8.0	13.4
	1.6	3.3	.7				.6	.6	5.6
Sales/Net Fixed Assets	54.6	53.5	51.4				64.0	58.3	47.4
	13.1	24.6	20.2				23.2	20.2	26.4
	6.6	6.5	8.2				7.8	7.0	11.1
Sales/Total Assets	3.6	4.1	4.8				3.8	4.8	4.9
	2.6	3.3	3.2				2.6	3.0	3.3
	1.8	2.3	2.2				1.7	1.9	2.5
% Depr., Dep., Amort./Sales	.7	.5	.5				.5	.5	.5
	(63) 1.3	(63) .9	(82) .8				(19) .8	(20) .7	(30) .7
	2.2	2.0	1.6				2.6	1.3	1.1
% Officers', Directors', Owners' Comp/Sales	.7	.8	1.2						
	(16) 2.6	(19) 3.2	(26) 2.2						
	5.4	4.3	5.8						
Net Sales ($)	3415456M	3239164M	3404664M	1050M	12637M	23886M	136769M	372485M	2857837M
Total Assets ($)	1359969M	1201371M	1289162M	443M	4707M	6736M	55208M	181599M	1040469M

Current Data Sorted by Assets / Comparative Historical Data

	0-500M	500M-2MM	2-10MM	10-50MM	50-100MM	100-250MM		4/1/02-3/31/03 ALL	4/1/03-3/31/04 ALL
Type of Statement									
Unqualified		1	2	7	1	2		12	7
Reviewed			5	2	1			8	11
Compiled	1	4	5	1				6	8
Tax Returns		3	2					2	2
Other		3	3	6		1		18	15
		12 (4/1-9/30/06)		38 (10/1/06-3/31/07)				18	15
NUMBER OF STATEMENTS	1	11	17	16	2	3		46	43
	%	%	%	%	%	%		%	%
ASSETS									
Cash & Equivalents		18.0	5.7	7.4				9.9	9.7
Trade Receivables (net)		13.2	16.7	21.3				14.3	17.7
Inventory		39.2	45.2	46.3				42.5	43.5
All Other Current		1.0	1.5	2.2				1.8	1.9
Total Current		71.4	69.1	77.2				68.5	72.8
Fixed Assets (net)		13.2	23.2	12.5				21.1	19.7
Intangibles (net)		.4	2.5	7.5				3.5	3.6
All Other Non-Current		15.0	5.2	2.8				6.9	3.9
Total		100.0	100.0	100.0				100.0	100.0
LIABILITIES									
Notes Payable-Short Term		10.0	19.2	18.0				14.3	29.7
Cur. Mat.-L.T.D.		1.1	4.8	1.8				3.0	2.6
Trade Payables		20.0	13.8	20.3				17.5	15.8
Income Taxes Payable		.0	.0	.0				.1	.3
All Other Current		12.4	6.5	13.0				14.0	11.8
Total Current		43.6	44.4	53.1				49.0	60.2
Long-Term Debt		6.8	15.0	10.9				9.1	7.6
Deferred Taxes		.1	.3	.0				.2	.2
All Other Non-Current		4.1	8.2	6.9				4.5	5.5
Net Worth		45.4	32.1	29.1				37.1	26.5
Total Liabilties & Net Worth		100.0	100.0	100.0				100.0	100.0
INCOME DATA									
Net Sales		100.0	100.0	100.0				100.0	100.0
Gross Profit		21.3	19.6	12.4				21.3	20.0
Operating Expenses		16.7	16.4	12.7				17.9	17.4
Operating Profit		4.6	3.1	-.3				3.4	2.6
All Other Expenses (net)		.6	1.1	.9				.6	.3
Profit Before Taxes		4.0	2.1	-1.2				2.8	2.3
RATIOS									
Current		2.2	3.1	2.1				2.0	2.0
		2.1	1.5	1.5				1.4	1.4
		1.0	1.1	1.1				1.1	1.1
Quick		1.2	1.1	.9				1.0	1.2
		.8	.4	.5				.4	.6
		.1	.3	.3				.2	.2
Sales/Receivables	3	133.2	6 60.6	11 32.4				7 52.7	7 49.2
	4	89.6	15 24.9	18 20.2				15 24.8	16 23.4
	21	17.5	21 17.1	29 12.7				22 16.6	23 16.1
Cost of Sales/Inventory	17	21.9	31 11.7	37 10.0				33 11.0	33 11.2
	60	6.1	45 8.1	52 7.1				53 6.9	42 8.7
	117	3.1	58 6.3	70 5.2				114 3.2	99 3.7
Cost of Sales/Payables	4	101.9	9 40.6	9 42.4				8 46.3	7 53.5
	10	37.0	13 28.2	16 22.9				17 20.9	13 28.3
	42	8.7	20 17.9	42 8.7				36 10.2	28 13.1
Sales/Working Capital		5.7	9.7	7.4				7.2	9.0
		14.6	21.0	16.7				14.3	20.0
		UND	76.1	51.4				99.0	36.6
EBIT/Interest			6.2	6.3				9.7	20.0
			(14) 5.2	1.5				(43) 4.8	(40) 5.7
			1.3	-8.3				1.0	1.6
Net Profit + Depr., Dep., Amort./Cur. Mat. L/T/D								2.9	
								(10) 1.8	
								.5	
Fixed/Worth		.0	.2	.2				.1	.2
		.2	.7	.4				.4	.5
		.4	2.1	-2.2				1.5	1.1
Debt/Worth		.6	1.0	.8				.8	.8
		.8	2.2	3.1				1.7	1.9
		1.7	7.0	-18.0				4.9	6.8
% Profit Before Taxes/Tangible Net Worth		79.1	59.3	34.9				51.5	69.1
		(10) 41.4	(16) 31.5	(11) 6.0				(41) 20.4	(36) 32.1
		1.2	16.6	-44.7				4.6	10.3
% Profit Before Taxes/Total Assets		28.6	16.2	8.0				16.9	20.7
		15.3	9.7	2.1				8.0	9.9
		2.4	1.6	-20.1				.8	3.0
Sales/Net Fixed Assets		455.6	125.2	62.9				82.7	62.0
		45.4	21.7	33.8				22.5	21.7
		17.3	8.4	25.6				9.0	11.1
Sales/Total Assets		5.3	5.4	4.7				4.4	5.1
		3.3	4.7	3.4				2.8	3.6
		1.6	3.3	2.0				1.9	2.6
% Depr., Dep., Amort./Sales			.3	.4				.3	.4
			(14) .6	.6				(40) 1.1	(37) .6
			1.6	1.0				2.2	1.3
% Officers', Directors' Owners' Comp/Sales								1.0	.4
								(15) 1.8	(12) 1.0
								7.0	1.7
Net Sales ($)	2281M	52122M	331568M	1400317M	272282M	1973123M		2977942M	3695188M
Total Assets ($)	352M	12973M	73882M	376302M	109953M	561851M		1123845M	1107221M

© RMA 2007

M = $ thousand   MM = $ million
See Pages 11 through 21 for Explanation of Ratios and Data

Comparative Historical Data				Current Data Sorted by Sales					
			Type of Statement						
15	14	14	Unqualified				2		12
11	9	7	Reviewed				1	4	2
9	10	11	Compiled		4		1	3	3
5	2	5	Tax Returns		1	1	2	1	
11	11	13	Other			2	2	1	8
4/1/04-3/31/05 ALL	**4/1/05-3/31/06 ALL**	**4/1/06-3/31/07 ALL**			**12 (4/1-9/30/06)**		**38 (10/1/06-3/31/07)**		
				0-1MM	**1-3MM**	**3-5MM**	**5-10MM**	**10-25MM**	**25MM & OVER**
51	46	50	**NUMBER OF STATEMENTS**		5	3	8	9	25
%	%	%	**ASSETS**	%	%	%	%	%	%
9.3	7.3	9.6	Cash & Equivalents	**DATA NOT AVAILABLE**					6.5
22.5	21.8	16.9	Trade Receivables (net)						21.4
44.8	42.5	44.1	Inventory						47.2
1.8	1.4	1.9	All Other Current						2.6
78.4	73.0	72.4	Total Current						77.7
14.5	17.6	17.5	Fixed Assets (net)						13.2
2.6	5.1	3.5	Intangibles (net)						5.2
4.5	4.3	6.6	All Other Non-Current						3.9
100.0	100.0	100.0	Total						100.0
			LIABILITIES						
17.0	16.8	16.4	Notes Payable-Short Term						20.6
2.0	1.3	2.7	Cur. Mat.-L.T.D.						1.6
20.5	17.4	18.3	Trade Payables						19.2
.1	.1	.0	Income Taxes Payable						.0
12.6	12.1	10.9	All Other Current						13.7
52.2	47.7	48.3	Total Current						55.0
6.2	12.2	11.2	Long-Term Debt						8.7
.1	.1	.2	Deferred Taxes						.1
10.3	8.1	7.5	All Other Non-Current						5.3
31.2	31.9	32.8	Net Worth						31.0
100.0	100.0	100.0	Total Liabilities & Net Worth						100.0
			INCOME DATA						
100.0	100.0	100.0	Net Sales						100.0
18.5	18.7	17.9	Gross Profit						13.0
15.2	15.4	15.9	Operating Expenses						12.4
3.4	3.3	2.0	Operating Profit						.6
.9	.9	.8	All Other Expenses (net)						.7
2.5	2.4	1.2	Profit Before Taxes						-.1
			RATIOS						
2.2	2.1	2.2							2.1
1.5	1.5	1.6	Current						1.6
1.1	1.2	1.1							1.1
1.1	.9	.9							.8
.6	.6	.5	Quick						.5
.3	.4	.3							.3
8 46.0	**13** 28.0	**4** 87.5							**11** 32.0
17 22.0	**20** 18.6	**15** 24.2	Sales/Receivables						**18** 20.8
28 13.2	**29** 12.6	**21** 17.5							**23** 16.1
33 10.9	**35** 10.4	**31** 11.7							**34** 10.8
41 9.0	**45** 8.1	**48** 7.6	Cost of Sales/Inventory						**50** 7.3
69 5.3	**67** 5.5	**65** 5.6							**64** 5.7
8 47.0	**11** 33.0	**9** 41.5							**9** 40.8
18 20.1	**17** 21.1	**14** 26.1	Cost of Sales/Payables						**17** 21.5
30 12.0	**28** 12.9	**33** 11.1							**37** 10.0
8.0	8.6	9.0							9.2
17.0	16.9	19.3	Sales/Working Capital						14.2
73.4	37.8	69.9							50.9
14.5	17.9	6.6							7.1
(48) 5.8	(41) 4.3	(46) 2.6	EBIT/Interest						(23) 2.1
1.1	1.7	.2							-3.4
		13.3							
		(10) 1.0	Net Profit + Depr., Dep., Amort./Cur. Mat. L/T/D						
		-3.3							
.2	.2	.2							.2
.5	.7	.4	Fixed/Worth						.4
2.7	1.7	2.9							NM
.8	1.2	.8							.8
2.2	2.7	1.6	Debt/Worth						2.0
10.4	6.6	10.9							NM
76.2	58.0	46.5							35.4
(44) 22.9	(40) 40.0	(42) 29.1	% Profit Before Taxes/Tangible Net Worth						(19) 16.3
13.1	14.3	1.0							-5.1
18.0	18.3	16.0							12.9
6.9	9.7	7.6	% Profit Before Taxes/Total Assets						4.1
1.3	1.9	-1.1							-8.3
65.3	72.7	63.8							71.6
35.9	24.8	27.4	Sales/Net Fixed Assets						34.1
16.7	13.6	13.7							22.2
5.2	4.9	5.2							5.3
4.0	3.8	3.9	Sales/Total Assets						3.8
2.7	2.6	2.4							2.3
.2	.3	.3							.3
(47) .5	(39) .6	(42) .6	% Depr., Dep., Amort./Sales						(21) .5
1.1	1.1	1.0							.9
.5	1.0	.8							
(16) 2.0	(12) 2.1	(17) 1.6	% Officers', Directors' Owners' Comp/Sales						
4.1	3.0	2.4							
4564787M	**3089575M**	**4031693M**	Net Sales ($)		**8744M**	**12516M**	**60994M**	**162045M**	**3787394M**
1051833M	**825323M**	**1135313M**	Total Assets ($)		**3959M**	**6491M**	**15379M**	**37008M**	**1072476M**

M = $ thousand MM = $ million

See Pages 11 through 21 for Explanation of Ratios and Data

Current Data Sorted by Assets   Comparative Historical Data

	0-500M	500M-2MM	2-10MM	10-50MM	50-100MM	100-250MM		4/1/02-3/31/03 ALL	4/1/03-3/31/04 ALL
Type of Statement									
Unqualified			1	7		4		23	21
Reviewed		1	5	1				11	11
Compiled	1	3	3					14	10
Tax Returns	1	1	1					2	4
Other	1	1	8	10				12	15
		6 (4/1-9/30/06)		43 (10/1/06-3/31/07)					
NUMBER OF STATEMENTS	3	6	18	18		4		62	61
	%	%	%	%	%	%		%	%
ASSETS									
Cash & Equivalents			3.6	4.7				7.0	6.9
Trade Receivables (net)			27.4	29.3				29.9	28.5
Inventory			30.5	27.1				27.2	26.5
All Other Current			.6	2.6				2.4	3.2
Total Current			62.1	63.7				66.5	65.2
Fixed Assets (net)			25.5	21.1				25.5	24.3
Intangibles (net)			7.7	12.0				3.3	3.5
All Other Non-Current			4.7	3.3				4.7	7.0
Total			100.0	100.0				100.0	100.0
LIABILITIES									
Notes Payable-Short Term			10.9	10.9				14.7	13.4
Cur. Mat.-L.T.D.			4.0	2.7				4.8	3.0
Trade Payables			15.4	15.8				17.9	21.3
Income Taxes Payable			.3	.4				.5	.5
All Other Current			7.6	12.5				10.2	10.7
Total Current			38.3	42.4				48.0	48.9
Long-Term Debt			18.2	22.2				16.5	13.6
Deferred Taxes			.3	1.3				.2	.2
All Other Non-Current			5.9	8.6				4.6	6.0
Net Worth			37.3	25.5				30.8	31.3
Total Liabilities & Net Worth			100.0	100.0				100.0	100.0
INCOME DATA									
Net Sales			100.0	100.0				100.0	100.0
Gross Profit			24.9	28.6				28.6	30.7
Operating Expenses			21.8	22.1				26.2	26.6
Operating Profit			3.1	6.5				2.4	4.1
All Other Expenses (net)			.8	1.8				.5	.7
Profit Before Taxes			2.3	4.7				1.9	3.4
RATIOS									
Current			2.5	2.6				2.4	2.5
			1.6	1.6				1.3	1.5
			1.1	1.2				1.0	.9
Quick			1.2	1.6				1.3	1.4
			.9	.9				.9	.8
			.4	.4				.4	.5
Sales/Receivables			20 18.3	38 9.5				28 13.0	28 13.3
			31 11.8	49 7.4				38 9.5	37 9.9
			43 8.5	68 5.3				59 6.2	50 7.3
Cost of Sales/Inventory			26 14.0	31 11.8				20 18.3	25 14.3
			36 10.0	63 5.8				57 6.4	52 7.0
			53 6.9	129 2.8				102 3.6	92 4.0
Cost of Sales/Payables			10 37.9	20 18.2				18 20.6	18 20.0
			21 17.1	34 10.7				35 10.5	32 11.3
			44 8.3	47 7.8				51 7.2	55 6.6
Sales/Working Capital			9.5	5.5				6.3	7.3
			15.9	9.1				19.8	11.6
			57.8	22.2				215.1	-51.2
EBIT/Interest			14.2	19.1				10.3	20.5
			4.1	5.0				(58) 2.7	(58) 6.2
			.0	1.3				1.0	1.1
Net Profit + Depr., Dep., Amort./Cur. Mat. L/T/D								7.4	
								(18) 1.7	
								.6	
Fixed/Worth			.3	.4				.4	.4
			.7	.8				.9	.8
			9.2	NM				3.4	3.5
Debt/Worth			.5	.8				.9	.9
			1.8	2.7				1.7	1.7
			15.3	NM				21.1	15.4
% Profit Before Taxes/Tangible Net Worth			78.9	49.4				38.7	70.6
			(15) 18.8	(14) 30.6				(50) 15.0	(51) 26.3
			-6.3	14.9				3.1	5.5
% Profit Before Taxes/Total Assets			21.0	20.7				12.5	19.3
			6.7	10.9				3.3	10.2
			-2.9	1.9				.4	1.1
Sales/Net Fixed Assets			30.6	27.8				32.4	28.8
			15.9	13.5				14.1	13.4
			7.7	6.1				6.7	6.3
Sales/Total Assets			3.9	2.6				3.1	3.2
			3.1	2.1				2.2	2.2
			1.9	1.3				1.8	1.9
% Depr., Dep., Amort./Sales			.7	.8				1.0	1.0
			(17) 1.8	(15) 1.5				(55) 2.0	(54) 1.7
			3.1	2.6				3.0	2.8
% Officers', Directors' Owners' Comp/Sales								2.7	3.1
								(25) 4.0	(21) 5.4
								8.2	10.0
Net Sales ($)	1652M	24630M	303951M	913798M		1322298M		2279129M	2597199M
Total Assets ($)	465M	6734M	96572M	419791M		553992M		1006021M	1201629M

M = $ thousand   MM = $ million
See Pages 11 through 21 for Explanation of Ratios and Data

Comparative Historical Data

Current Data Sorted by Sales

			Type of Statement						
15	7	12	Unqualified					1	11
11	9	7	Reviewed		1		1	4	1
7	7	7	Compiled		2	1	2	1	1
3	1	3	Tax Returns	1		2			
21	23	20	Other	1		1		5	10
4/1/04-3/31/05 ALL	4/1/05-3/31/06 ALL	4/1/06-3/31/07 ALL		0-1MM	6 (4/1-9/30/06) 1-3MM	3-5MM	43 (10/1/06-3/31/07) 5-10MM	10-25MM	25MM & OVER
57	47	49	**NUMBER OF STATEMENTS**	2	3	4	6	11	23
%	%	%	**ASSETS**	%	%	%	%	%	%
6.6	7.2	5.9	Cash & Equivalents					6.6	3.5
30.9	28.4	28.6	Trade Receivables (net)					16.9	32.8
27.4	28.9	30.0	Inventory					24.2	29.2
2.5	3.2	1.7	All Other Current					.9	2.0
67.4	67.7	66.1	Total Current					48.6	67.5
22.6	24.7	22.2	Fixed Assets (net)					22.3	23.6
3.8	3.0	8.0	Intangibles (net)					23.2	5.0
6.2	4.5	3.8	All Other Non-Current					5.9	3.8
100.0	100.0	100.0	Total					100.0	100.0
			LIABILITIES						
12.2	10.8	11.0	Notes Payable-Short Term					10.1	9.5
2.0	2.0	2.9	Cur. Mat.-L.T.D.					2.6	2.5
17.5	16.4	17.9	Trade Payables					9.9	21.3
.9	.3	.3	Income Taxes Payable					.3	.3
10.8	8.4	9.4	All Other Current					7.3	12.6
43.3	38.0	41.4	Total Current					30.2	46.3
10.1	13.7	17.8	Long-Term Debt					18.2	20.1
.1	.4	.8	Deferred Taxes					.3	1.4
3.3	5.0	5.8	All Other Non-Current					13.8	4.8
43.2	42.9	34.1	Net Worth					37.6	27.4
100.0	100.0	100.0	Total Liabilties & Net Worth					100.0	100.0
			INCOME DATA						
100.0	100.0	100.0	Net Sales					100.0	100.0
30.2	27.0	27.6	Gross Profit					32.1	20.8
25.3	21.6	22.4	Operating Expenses					26.4	15.5
4.8	5.5	5.2	Operating Profit					5.7	5.2
1.2	.9	1.2	All Other Expenses (net)					1.3	1.8
3.7	4.6	3.9	Profit Before Taxes					4.4	3.5
			RATIOS						
3.2	3.8	2.7						4.1	2.5
1.7	1.9	1.6	Current					1.9	1.6
1.1	1.3	1.2						.8	1.2
1.7	1.9	1.5						2.1	1.3
1.0	1.0	.9	Quick					.7	.9
.5	.5	.5						.4	.4

33	11.1	30	12.0	27	13.7							21	17.3	34	10.7

								Ratio						
33	11.1	30	12.0	27	13.7	Sales/Receivables	21	17.3	34	10.7
46	8.0	41	8.9	41	8.9		28	13.1	45	8.1
57	6.4	56	6.6	54	6.7		43	8.5	58	6.3
20	18.2	33	11.1	27	13.4	Cost of Sales/Inventory	28	13.2	24	15.0
54	6.8	49	7.5	41	8.9		41	8.9	38	9.5
105	3.5	81	4.5	102	3.6		174	2.1	94	3.9
20	18.7	14	27.0	15	24.8	Cost of Sales/Payables	8	45.7	15	25.1
31	11.8	30	12.0	30	12.3		22	16.7	35	10.4
45	8.2	51	7.1	44	8.4		44	8.4	44	8.3
	4.9		4.4		6.1	Sales/Working Capital		5.2		7.7
	10.3		8.3		13.1			14.5		11.9
	45.5		19.4		26.2			-28.0		23.2
	27.1		18.4		14.0	EBIT/Interest		12.1		24.8
(51)	6.5	(44)	8.2	(48)	5.1			5.4		4.1
	-.3		2.5		1.1			.2		1.1
	11.6		12.6		8.6	Net Profit + Depr., Dep., Amort./Cur. Mat. L/T/D				
(13)	2.6	(14)	3.7	(11)	4.5					
	.8		1.8		1.9					
	.2		.2		.3	Fixed/Worth		.3		.4
	.5		.5		.7			.7		.9
	1.2		1.4		3.1			5.0		-3.5
	.6		.5		.6	Debt/Worth		.4		.8
	1.2		1.4		1.9			1.9		2.3
	4.1		3.1		9.3			9.0		-24.1
	54.3		41.9		55.7	% Profit Before Taxes/Tangible Net Worth		46.7		
(52)	17.6	(43)	21.3	(40)	29.0				(17)	27.8
	3.6		5.8		7.1					13.1
	16.8		18.2		22.4	% Profit Before Taxes/Total Assets		20.0		19.6
	8.5		10.1		9.7			6.3		10.1
	-.2		3.6		1.0			-2.2		.4
	29.0		29.6		29.4	Sales/Net Fixed Assets		36.6		28.3
	13.8		11.3		14.7			9.7		13.6
	6.0		5.0		8.4			5.3		6.2
	3.3		3.1		3.8	Sales/Total Assets		2.7		3.8
	2.4		2.4		2.5			1.8		2.5
	1.9		1.7		1.7			1.0		2.0
	.9		.7		.8	% Depr., Dep., Amort./Sales		.9		.8
(49)	1.7	(39)	1.6	(42)	1.6		(10)	2.0	(18)	1.1
	2.4		2.9		2.7			4.9		2.5
	3.2		3.5		2.4	% Officers', Directors' Owners' Comp/Sales				
(20)	4.5	(13)	6.3	(15)	3.9					
	6.7		11.5		5.9					

2109868M	2083668M	2566329M	Net Sales ($)	293M	6470M	16691M	45187M	179401M	2318287M
976529M	1057560M	1077554M	Total Assets ($)	131M	2066M	5576M	16054M	117239M	936488M

M = $ thousand   MM = $ million
See Pages 11 through 21 for Explanation of Ratios and Data

Current Data Sorted by Assets · Comparative Historical Data

0-500M	500M-2MM	2-10MM	10-50MM	50-100MM	100-250MM	Type of Statement	4/1/02-3/31/03 ALL	4/1/03-3/31/04 ALL
		2	14	1	6	Unqualified	25	31
	1	10	9	1		Reviewed	43	34
	3	9	3			Compiled	19	22
	1	1	1			Tax Returns	3	3
4	4	10	11	1	4	Other	49	63
	18 (4/1-9/30/06)		80 (10/1/06-3/31/07)					
4	9	32	38	5	10	**NUMBER OF STATEMENTS**	139	153
%	%	%	%	%	%	**ASSETS**	%	%
		5.8	4.6		1.6	Cash & Equivalents	6.5	6.3
		34.2	27.3		25.5	Trade Receivables (net)	26.9	28.2
		21.3	16.3		12.5	Inventory	15.2	15.3
		.9	3.1		3.2	All Other Current	2.7	2.8
		62.2	51.3		42.9	Total Current	51.4	52.6
		28.8	39.4		45.5	Fixed Assets (net)	40.2	38.6
		4.8	2.6		6.2	Intangibles (net)	1.9	3.0
		4.2	6.7		5.4	All Other Non-Current	6.5	5.9
		100.0	100.0		100.0	Total	100.0	100.0
						LIABILITIES		
		11.3	13.2		7.0	Notes Payable-Short Term	12.6	12.9
		4.1	4.1		3.3	Cur. Mat.-L.T.D.	5.5	5.3
		17.9	17.1		21.4	Trade Payables	14.2	16.4
		.0	.2		.0	Income Taxes Payable	.1	.2
		8.0	6.8		8.7	All Other Current	9.2	8.8
		41.3	41.4		40.4	Total Current	41.7	43.6
		13.4	15.3		20.2	Long-Term Debt	23.8	20.7
		.5	1.0		2.4	Deferred Taxes	.7	.9
		6.7	4.0		3.7	All Other Non-Current	5.6	7.1
		38.1	38.2		33.3	Net Worth	28.2	27.6
		100.0	100.0		100.0	Total Liabilities & Net Worth	100.0	100.0
						INCOME DATA		
		100.0	100.0		100.0	Net Sales	100.0	100.0
		22.6	13.6		11.0	Gross Profit	22.8	22.8
		19.2	11.2		5.7	Operating Expenses	19.7	19.6
		3.4	2.4		5.3	Operating Profit	3.2	3.1
		1.4	.6		1.6	All Other Expenses (net)	1.9	1.7
		2.0	1.8		3.6	Profit Before Taxes	1.3	1.4
						RATIOS		
		2.5	1.9		1.4	Current	1.9	2.1
		1.6	1.3		1.2		1.3	1.3
		1.1	.8		.7		.8	.9
		1.7	1.3		.9	Quick	1.1	1.4
		.9	.7		.7		.8	.8
		.6	.5		.5		.5	.5
		39 9.3	39 9.4		36 10.3	Sales/Receivables	38 9.6	41 9.0
		52 7.0	51 7.2		53 6.9		51 7.2	56 6.5
		72 5.1	63 5.8		62 5.9		62 5.8	68 5.4
		26 14.2	22 16.6		25 14.5	Cost of Sales/Inventory	23 16.2	23 16.1
		41 8.8	31 11.9		29 12.7		36 10.0	36 10.2
		60 6.1	50 7.2		32 11.5		52 7.0	57 6.4
		16 23.1	24 15.5		32 11.4	Cost of Sales/Payables	19 19.5	22 16.8
		34 10.8	31 11.7		46 7.9		32 11.3	34 10.8
		42 8.7	43 8.5		65 5.6		47 7.8	51 7.1
		5.9	8.2		12.1	Sales/Working Capital	7.5	6.2
		12.8	19.5		50.4		16.4	16.1
		46.6	-31.6		-19.5		-15.7	-23.2
		6.6	5.2		9.0	EBIT/Interest	4.6	5.9
		(31) 2.3	(37) 1.9		3.5		(127) 2.0	(138) 2.1
		.7	-.4		1.0		.6	.0
			5.4			Net Profit + Depr., Dep., Amort./Cur. Mat. L/T/D	3.9	4.6
			(15) 1.7				(38) 1.6	(55) 2.5
			1.0				1.0	1.2
		.4	.6		1.0	Fixed/Worth	.7	.6
		.9	1.5		1.8		1.5	1.5
		1.4	3.1		NM		3.5	4.8
		.8	.7		1.4	Debt/Worth	1.2	1.0
		1.6	1.9		2.2		2.7	2.6
		4.2	5.4		NM		6.4	7.4
		31.6	15.6			% Profit Before Taxes/Tangible Net Worth	32.9	33.8
		(28) 13.3	(36) 9.4				(117) 10.8	(125) 10.3
		-1.4	-14.1				1.1	-3.2
		9.8	7.8		17.2	% Profit Before Taxes/Total Assets	8.7	10.4
		5.8	2.5		2.6		2.7	3.2
		-1.3	-2.6		-.1		-1.4	-2.5
		14.7	7.4		6.5	Sales/Net Fixed Assets	8.1	8.3
		9.3	4.9		4.6		4.5	5.0
		5.0	3.5		2.4		2.9	3.1
		2.9	2.4		2.3	Sales/Total Assets	2.2	2.2
		2.1	2.0		1.7		1.8	1.7
		1.6	1.4		1.4		1.4	1.3
		1.7	2.5			% Depr., Dep., Amort./Sales	2.7	2.4
		(31) 2.8	3.9				(130) 3.9	(139) 3.8
		3.4	4.5				5.5	5.2
		1.8				% Officers', Directors' Owners' Comp/Sales	1.8	1.7
		(16) 3.1					(45) 5.9	(48) 4.3
		4.3					8.7	7.2
3285M	32431M	354969M	1790660M	531504M	2685190M	Net Sales ($)	4277342M	6162709M
901M	9591M	148198M	947594M	328045M	1484575M	Total Assets ($)	2717181M	3762789M

M = $ thousand   MM = $ million
See Pages 11 through 21 for Explanation of Ratios and Data

Comparative Historical Data | Current Data Sorted by Sales

	4/1/04-3/31/05 ALL	4/1/05-3/31/06 ALL	4/1/06-3/31/07 ALL	Type of Statement	0-1MM	1-3MM	3-5MM	5-10MM	10-25MM	25MM & OVER
	28	24	23	Unqualified				1	2	20
	35	27	21	Reviewed		1	2	3	9	6
	21	12	15	Compiled		3	2	3	4	3
	3	5	4	Tax Returns		1		1		2
	44	47	35	Other	2	5	2	3	9	14
					0-1MM	18 (4/1-9/30/06) 1-3MM	3-5MM	80 (10/1/06-3/31/07) 5-10MM	10-25MM	25MM & OVER
	131	115	98	**NUMBER OF STATEMENTS**	2	10	6	11	24	45
	%	%	%	**ASSETS**	%	%	%	%	%	%
	5.5	5.2	4.6	Cash & Equivalents		3.5		5.7	7.2	2.1
	29.7	29.0	29.6	Trade Receivables (net)		38.7		32.7	27.7	29.7
	18.2	18.3	16.9	Inventory		10.5		20.2	20.1	16.4
	2.6	2.4	1.9	All Other Current		.1		1.5	3.4	1.8
	56.1	54.8	53.0	Total Current		52.8		60.2	58.4	50.0
	35.8	35.5	37.9	Fixed Assets (net)		40.0		31.4	33.6	40.7
	3.6	4.4	3.8	Intangibles (net)		3.8		7.0	3.1	3.1
	4.5	5.3	5.2	All Other Non-Current		3.4		1.4	4.8	6.1
	100.0	100.0	100.0	Total		100.0		100.0	100.0	100.0
				LIABILITIES						
	12.3	11.6	13.5	Notes Payable-Short Term		17.1		17.2	8.0	12.7
	4.8	5.6	3.9	Cur. Mat.-L.T.D.		3.2		4.7	3.9	3.9
	17.8	19.6	17.9	Trade Payables		14.4		12.7	15.0	20.3
	.2	.1	.1	Income Taxes Payable		.2		.0	.0	.2
	9.2	8.3	7.5	All Other Current		8.5		9.7	5.8	7.5
	44.1	45.1	42.9	Total Current		43.5		44.3	32.8	44.5
	16.3	17.8	17.4	Long-Term Debt		29.5		16.6	16.9	15.8
	1.1	.9	1.7	Deferred Taxes		8.0		.7	.6	1.4
	7.7	5.5	6.7	All Other Non-Current		4.9		12.5	3.7	5.5
	30.8	30.7	31.3	Net Worth		14.1		25.9	46.1	32.8
	100.0	100.0	100.0	Total Liabilties & Net Worth		100.0		100.0	100.0	100.0
				INCOME DATA						
	100.0	100.0	100.0	Net Sales		100.0		100.0	100.0	100.0
	19.5	18.1	18.8	Gross Profit		29.5		20.7	16.9	12.8
	15.6	14.7	15.6	Operating Expenses		29.3		16.3	13.4	9.3
	3.9	3.4	3.2	Operating Profit		.2		4.5	3.5	3.5
	.5	1.0	1.3	All Other Expenses (net)		1.6		1.5	-.2	1.9
	3.4	2.4	2.0	Profit Before Taxes		-1.4		3.0	3.6	1.6
				RATIOS						
	2.1	1.8	2.0	Current		3.1		2.4	3.0	1.7
	1.3	1.3	1.3			.8		1.6	1.8	1.3
	.9	.9	.8			.7		.8	1.1	.8
	1.3	1.2	1.3	Quick		2.4		1.7	1.7	1.1
	.8 (114)	.8	.8			.7		.8	.9	.7
	.5	.5	.6			.4		.5	.6	.5
	42 8.6	40 9.2	36 10.2	Sales/Receivables		21 17.8		36 10.3	32 11.3	40 9.1
	56 6.6	53 6.9	50 7.2			44 8.4		57 6.5	49 7.5	51 7.1
	67 5.5	69 5.3	63 5.8			90 4.0		76 4.8	63 5.8	58 6.3
	21 17.6	25 14.8	22 16.7	Cost of Sales/Inventory		0 UND		28 12.9	23 15.9	24 15.4
	37 9.9	36 10.0	32 11.5			25 14.5		40 9.1	41 9.0	30 12.0
	60 6.0	54 6.8	51 7.1			64 5.7		56 6.5	55 6.7	43 8.5
	24 15.1	27 13.4	20 18.5	Cost of Sales/Payables		14 26.9		13 27.8	15 24.8	29 12.7
	34 10.6	38 9.5	32 11.3			23 15.9		34 10.7	31 11.6	36 10.0
	53 6.9	54 6.8	43 8.4			34 10.7		38 9.7	39 9.4	58 6.3
	6.3	6.1	8.2	Sales/Working Capital		6.4		6.5	4.1	9.1
	16.6	17.3	17.1			-35.7		13.5	10.4	20.6
	-29.5	-23.4	-27.7			-8.9		-22.0	46.6	-18.6
	7.6	6.5	5.7	EBIT/Interest				5.1	7.2	6.9
	(120) 3.2	(104) 2.2	(94) 2.3					1.8	(23) 3.2	2.3
	1.1	.6	.2					.7	1.0	.0
	4.5	5.4	4.8	Net Profit + Depr., Dep., Amort./Cur. Mat. L/T/D					7.4	
	(36) 1.9	(35) 2.0	(33) 2.0						(21) 3.2	
	1.1	.8	1.4						1.5	
	.6	.6	.7	Fixed/Worth		.9		.8	.4	.7
	1.3	1.3	1.2			1.9		1.2	.8	1.7
	3.3	2.9	3.3			-3.3		3.3	2.8	2.9
	1.0	1.0	.9	Debt/Worth		1.0		1.4	.4	1.1
	2.3	2.9	2.2			4.3		3.5	1.4	2.3
	7.8	5.8	5.5			-7.6		5.1	3.8	6.1
	38.0	27.5	32.3	% Profit Before Taxes/Tangible Net Worth					39.9	18.0
	(113) 14.1	(98) 14.5	(84) 11.6						(23) 13.3	(40) 8.2
	1.7	.6	-2.9						2.7	-14.1
	11.5	11.4	9.0	% Profit Before Taxes/Total Assets		14.9		10.0	9.0	8.0
	4.6	3.9	3.2			1.6		2.3	6.4	2.1
	.4	-.7	-1.7			-9.8		-1.5	.3	-2.8
	10.4	10.0	10.2	Sales/Net Fixed Assets		13.7		11.4	12.1	7.3
	6.0	6.0	5.8			9.1		6.1	6.1	5.1
	3.1	3.4	3.2			2.8		4.7	2.9	3.1
	2.4	2.4	2.7	Sales/Total Assets		4.1		3.1	2.9	2.4
	1.9	1.9	2.0			2.0		2.1	1.9	2.0
	1.5	1.5	1.5			1.4		1.5	1.5	1.6
	2.1	2.1	2.1	% Depr., Dep., Amort./Sales				1.8	1.7	2.3
	(115) 3.0	(97) 3.3	(90) 3.4					(10) 3.2	2.8	(41) 3.8
	5.0	4.8	4.5					4.2	4.0	4.5
	1.5	.9	1.8	% Officers', Directors' Owners' Comp/Sales					1.3	
	(42) 3.0	(27) 4.2	(27) 4.0						(10) 2.1	
	4.5	7.3	7.4						4.8	
	5972323M	6544754M	5398039M	Net Sales ($)	490M	20152M	24351M	80400M	399270M	4873376M
	3443985M	3756930M	2918904M	Total Assets ($)	348M	10530M	16444M	38796M	243014M	2609772M

© RMA 2007

M = $ thousand   MM = $ million
See Pages 11 through 21 for Explanation of Ratios and Data

Current Data Sorted by Assets | Comparative Historical Data

Type of Statement	0-500M	500M-2MM	2-10MM	10-50MM	50-100MM	100-250MM	4/1/02-3/31/03 ALL	4/1/03-3/31/04 ALL
Unqualified	2	1	15	42	16	26	94	105
Reviewed		4	38	21	1		78	88
Compiled	6	21	24	6			75	82
Tax Returns	7	10	10				18	23
Other	5	16	40	56	16	18	142	152
		76 (4/1-9/30/06)		325 (10/1/06-3/31/07)				
NUMBER OF STATEMENTS	20	52	127	125	33	44	407	450

ASSETS	%	%	%	%	%	%	%	%
Cash & Equivalents	10.8	5.3	5.6	5.1	3.9	5.3	7.3	6.6
Trade Receivables (net)	16.1	30.7	27.4	24.7	26.5	25.2	24.4	25.9
Inventory	29.3	27.7	32.0	26.3	17.8	16.9	24.5	23.7
All Other Current	7.1	1.7	1.7	2.9	2.8	4.1	2.3	2.8
Total Current	63.3	65.4	66.8	59.0	51.0	51.4	58.6	58.9
Fixed Assets (net)	31.2	26.9	25.6	30.1	37.4	35.3	31.7	32.6
Intangibles (net)	3.1	2.5	2.3	5.0	6.5	8.0	4.4	2.9
All Other Non-Current	2.4	5.2	5.3	5.8	5.1	5.3	5.4	5.5
Total	100.0	100.0	100.0	100.0	100.0	100.0	100.0	100.0

LIABILITIES								
Notes Payable-Short Term	15.4	11.0	16.0	12.8	9.0	7.8	12.8	12.1
Cur. Mat.-L.T.D.	3.9	4.1	4.0	4.2	5.2	3.0	4.7	4.9
Trade Payables	17.0	19.6	18.1	16.5	19.6	19.9	15.6	15.7
Income Taxes Payable	.1	.3	.4	.4	.2	.3	.2	.2
All Other Current	26.7	12.7	8.9	11.2	10.1	9.9	8.8	9.8
Total Current	63.1	47.7	47.4	45.1	44.1	40.8	42.1	42.7
Long-Term Debt	32.8	19.4	10.7	18.1	16.7	16.0	17.0	15.4
Deferred Taxes	.0	.3	.4	.7	.9	1.9	.6	.6
All Other Non-Current	10.1	4.7	5.8	3.9	3.1	11.0	6.0	7.7
Net Worth	-6.0	28.0	35.7	32.2	35.2	30.3	34.3	33.6
Total Liabilties & Net Worth	100.0	100.0	100.0	100.0	100.0	100.0	100.0	100.0

INCOME DATA								
Net Sales	100.0	100.0	100.0	100.0	100.0	100.0	100.0	100.0
Gross Profit	45.2	35.8	29.2	20.5	12.6	16.2	27.8	27.6
Operating Expenses	43.2	32.7	23.8	15.3	8.8	12.3	23.6	24.3
Operating Profit	2.0	3.1	5.4	5.2	3.8	3.9	4.1	3.3
All Other Expenses (net)	.7	.7	1.5	1.3	1.2	1.3	1.5	1.4
Profit Before Taxes	1.3	2.4	3.9	3.9	2.6	2.6	2.6	1.9

RATIOS								
Current	3.3	2.2	2.5	2.1	1.8	1.8	2.3	2.2
	1.6	1.3	1.4	1.3	1.2	1.2	1.4	1.4
	.8	1.1	1.0	1.0	.9	.9	1.0	1.0
Quick	1.1	1.2	1.2	1.1	1.1	.9	1.3	1.2
	.7	.8	(126) .7	.7	.8	.7	.7	.8
	.1	.5	.4	.5	.5	.6	.5	.5
Sales/Receivables	0 UND	31 11.8	30 12.1	37 9.9	36 10.1	37 9.8	30 12.2	33 10.9
	7 49.4	44 8.4	45 8.1	50 7.3	45 8.1	51 7.1	43 8.6	47 7.8
	29 12.5	60 6.1	61 6.0	58 6.3	53 6.9	61 6.0	57 6.4	60 6.1
Cost of Sales/Inventory	0 UND	26 14.0	41 8.8	32 11.3	21 17.2	16 23.0	26 14.3	25 14.5
	23 16.1	55 6.6	70 5.2	61 6.0	31 11.8	33 10.9	48 7.6	50 7.3
	63 5.7	104 3.5	108 3.4	84 4.3	49 7.5	66 5.5	97 3.8	90 4.1
Cost of Sales/Payables	0 UND	19 19.0	20 18.1	24 15.5	23 15.6	32 11.5	19 18.8	21 17.7
	12 30.9	37 9.9	36 10.0	37 10.0	34 10.8	41 8.9	32 11.5	32 11.3
	39 9.3	59 6.2	61 6.0	54 6.8	48 7.5	56 6.5	50 7.3	49 7.5
Sales/Working Capital	5.9	7.1	5.6	6.0	9.7	7.0	5.5	5.8
	27.1	15.2	13.2	13.1	27.1	19.2	11.9	12.8
	-47.6	86.2	-122.4	999.8	-26.6	-37.3	-838.7	-254.0
EBIT/Interest	5.8	7.0	10.6	8.5	6.4	8.6	7.4	9.9
	(17) 3.6	(39) 3.5	(116) 3.4	(119) 3.0	(30) 2.3	(39) 3.9	(368) 3.2	(415) 3.3
	-.6	.8	1.0	1.2	.2	1.0	1.1	.6
Net Profit + Depr., Dep., Amort./Cur. Mat. L/T/D			3.8	7.7	4.5	7.2	4.7	3.0
		(31) 1.7	(51) 2.8	(18) 2.8	(16) 3.0		(126) 2.1	(123) 1.8
		.6	1.3	1.0	.3		.8	1.0
Fixed/Worth	.2	.5	.3	-.5	.8	.7	.4	.4
	1.2	.9	.7	1.1	1.6	1.4	1.0	1.0
	-2.2	2.7	1.9	3.6	4.2	8.8	2.7	2.7
Debt/Worth	.8	1.0	.8	1.0	.9	1.2	.7	.8
	2.1	2.7	2.1	2.6	4.0	2.1	2.1	2.0
	-5.3	14.9	6.2	7.8	8.2	31.6	6.8	5.7
% Profit Before Taxes/Tangible Net Worth	40.8	46.6	47.2	47.5	37.6	33.0	38.1	36.5
	(13) 21.9	(43) 16.5	(110) 22.9	(106) 20.7	(28) 12.9	(35) 15.7	(355) 17.3	(399) 14.3
	10.7	6.6	5.0	6.4	.6	2.2	2.6	.1
% Profit Before Taxes/Total Assets	19.5	11.8	15.1	13.0	7.8	10.4	12.0	12.3
	11.5	5.2	7.3	5.7	2.2	6.5	5.4	4.8
	-1.4	-2.2	.4	.8	-1.3	.1	.3	-1.4
Sales/Net Fixed Assets	55.0	26.4	26.4	13.7	9.4	10.5	16.3	15.3
	18.3	10.0	11.0	6.9	5.8	5.8	7.2	7.0
	11.4	6.2	4.5	3.7	4.4	3.6	3.8	3.6
Sales/Total Assets	9.3	3.2	2.7	2.2	2.4	2.7	2.7	2.7
	4.7	2.5	2.2	1.8	2.0	1.9	1.9	1.9
	3.3	1.8	1.5	1.4	1.6	1.2	1.4	1.4
% Depr., Dep., Amort./Sales	1.1	1.0	1.1	1.4	1.3	.9	1.7	1.6
	(13) 2.5	(46) 2.3	(110) 1.9	(116) 2.4	(29) 3.0	(28) 3.2	(353) 2.9	(379) 3.2
	5.7	4.1	4.1	4.4	4.6	4.6	5.1	5.6
% Officers', Directors', Owners' Comp/Sales	5.0	4.1	1.6	.8			2.7	2.7
	(13) 7.0	(27) 5.7	(47) 3.2	(14) 1.6			(125) 5.0	(142) 4.3
	8.0	8.0	5.1	2.5			9.6	8.4
Net Sales ($)	33064M	169951M	1447123M	5121441M	4942571M	13913019M	20980771M	20574839M
Total Assets ($)	5821M	63906M	672234M	2793391M	2367886M	7039937M	10373785M	11328667M

M = $ thousand   MM = $ million

See Pages 11 through 21 for Explanation of Ratios and Data

Comparative Historical Data / Current Data Sorted by Sales

			Type of Statement	0-1MM	1-3MM	3-5MM	5-10MM	10-25MM	25MM & OVER
115	99	102	Unqualified	1	1	1	7	16	76
94	76	64	Reviewed		4	2	12	32	14
76	61	57	Compiled	3	14	12	14	11	3
25	26	27	Tax Returns	3	7	9	7	1	
156	181	151	Other	3	11	8	15	34	80
4/1/04-3/31/05 ALL	4/1/05-3/31/06 ALL	4/1/06-3/31/07 ALL			76 (4/1-9/30/06)		325 (10/1/06-3/31/07)		
466	443	401	NUMBER OF STATEMENTS	10	37	32	55	94	173
%	%	%	ASSETS	%	%	%	%	%	%
6.0	6.6	5.5	Cash & Equivalents	5.3	6.2	7.8	4.4	6.6	4.7
26.3	27.6	26.1	Trade Receivables (net)	16.2	23.3	25.5	30.0	25.8	26.4
26.5	26.0	26.7	Inventory	31.1	23.8	33.1	28.6	31.4	22.7
2.2	2.7	2.7	All Other Current	16.0	1.0	.8	2.0	1.8	3.4
61.0	62.9	61.0	Total Current	68.7	54.3	67.1	65.0	65.6	57.1
28.8	28.3	29.5	Fixed Assets (net)	28.2	37.7	26.5	25.0	26.3	31.6
3.9	3.2	4.2	Intangibles (net)	1.8	4.2	1.8	1.9	3.2	6.0
6.4	5.5	5.3	All Other Non-Current	1.3	3.8	4.6	8.1	4.9	5.3
100.0	100.0	100.0	Total	100.0	100.0	100.0	100.0	100.0	100.0
			LIABILITIES						
12.5	13.2	12.9	Notes Payable-Short Term	5.1	13.0	17.5	17.0	13.6	10.7
4.1	3.9	4.1	Cur. Mat.-L.T.D.	1.8	4.9	4.4	3.5	4.0	4.0
17.8	19.1	18.0	Trade Payables	12.1	16.5	16.8	18.5	17.2	19.2
.3	.4	.3	Income Taxes Payable	.0	.1	.9	.5	.1	.4
9.7	10.4	11.2	All Other Current	20.0	19.1	10.1	9.9	9.7	10.4
44.3	47.0	46.5	Total Current	39.0	53.6	49.7	49.4	45.0	44.8
15.3	15.7	16.3	Long-Term Debt	15.8	32.0	17.1	10.9	13.5	16.1
.8	.7	.7	Deferred Taxes	.0	.2	.4	.6	.5	1.0
6.7	6.1	5.6	All Other Non-Current	22.2	9.0	1.8	5.8	3.9	5.5
32.9	30.5	30.9	Net Worth	23.0	5.2	31.0	33.4	37.1	32.6
100.0	100.0	100.0	Total Liabilities & Net Worth	100.0	100.0	100.0	100.0	100.0	100.0
			INCOME DATA						
100.0	100.0	100.0	Net Sales	100.0	100.0	100.0	100.0	100.0	100.0
26.3	25.9	25.4	Gross Profit	44.5	39.7	34.3	31.5	25.4	17.5
22.1	21.9	20.8	Operating Expenses	41.1	39.0	29.0	26.4	19.0	13.4
4.2	3.9	4.6	Operating Profit	3.4	.8	5.3	5.0	6.4	4.1
1.1	1.1	1.2	All Other Expenses (net)	.3	1.1	1.2	1.6	1.3	1.2
3.1	2.8	3.3	Profit Before Taxes	3.1	-.3	4.1	3.4	5.1	3.0
			RATIOS						
2.2	2.1	2.1		3.4	2.7	2.0	2.6	2.5	1.8
1.4	1.4	1.3	Current	2.1	1.3	1.3	1.3	1.5	1.3
1.0	1.0	1.0		1.1	.9	1.1	.9	1.0	.9
1.1	1.1	1.1		1.1	1.3	1.2	1.2	1.4	1.0
(465) .8	(442) .8	(400) .7	Quick	.5	.8	.7	.7	(93) .7	.7
.5	.5	.5		.3	.4	.3	.4	.5	.5
33 11.1	33 10.9	32 11.5		0 UND	26 14.3	16 22.9	36 10.2	30 12.4	37 9.9
49 7.5	47 7.8	46 8.0	Sales/Receivables	26 13.9	42 8.7	39 9.4	49 7.4	42 8.6	48 7.6
61 6.0	61 6.0	59 6.2		59 6.2	56 6.5	63 5.8	64 5.7	57 6.4	59 6.2
27 13.5	25 14.3	28 13.2		0 UND	22 16.2	27 13.7	36 10.0	36 10.3	25 14.5
52 7.1	49 7.4	55 6.6	Cost of Sales/Inventory	79 4.6	55 6.7	66 5.5	67 5.5	66 5.5	43 8.5
102 3.6	90 4.0	93 3.9		300 1.2	111 3.3	132 2.8	101 3.6	103 3.5	74 4.9
22 16.4	22 16.6	22 16.3		0 UND	14 26.6	14 25.6	19 18.9	21 17.3	28 13.2
37 9.8	36 10.0	36 10.0	Cost of Sales/Payables	20 18.7	36 10.3	28 12.8	37 9.8	36 10.1	37 9.8
56 6.6	56 6.6	55 6.6		37 9.8	57 6.4	45 8.1	66 5.5	57 6.4	53 6.9
5.8	6.4	6.3		3.8	6.5	7.9	5.7	5.6	7.4
12.4	13.0	15.4	Sales/Working Capital	5.9	14.0	19.0	17.7	11.9	18.3
-999.8	999.8	-136.2		138.3	-39.2	81.6	-33.5	-105.1	-81.6
10.9	9.6	8.5			8.7	4.8	11.7	9.3	8.5
(415) 3.5	(397) 3.1	(360) 3.1	EBIT/Interest	(35) 3.0	(24) 2.7	(51) 3.5	(84) 3.5	(159) 2.8	
1.1	1.1	1.0			.0	.9	1.0	1.3	1.0
4.4	6.2	5.2					4.5	4.2	7.6
(137) 2.0	(132) 2.7	(126) 2.6	Net Profit + Depr., Dep., Amort./Cur. Mat. L/T/D			(15) 2.6	(29) 2.3	(70) 2.9	
1.1	1.1	1.0					.9	1.4	1.0
.4	.3	.4		.3	.6	.5	.3	.3	.5
.9	1.0	1.0	Fixed/Worth	.9	1.8	.8	.6	.7	1.2
2.8	2.7	3.0		-5.6	-2.5	1.9	1.9	2.4	3.3
.9	.9	.9		.8	.8	1.2	.7	.8	1.1
2.5	2.4	2.4	Debt/Worth	2.1	4.4	3.0	2.2	2.1	2.4
7.6	8.0	7.6		-9.9	-6.3	7.1	6.5	5.8	8.6
41.3	40.9	43.7			29.4	71.7	38.9	53.8	42.2
(400) 18.4	(376) 17.7	(335) 20.5	% Profit Before Taxes/Tangible Net Worth	(24) 14.9	(29) 19.4	(48) 17.8	(81) 24.7	(146) 19.6	
3.1	2.4	5.0			1.9	7.6	2.8	10.6	3.6
12.9	11.8	12.9		16.1	13.0	12.9	14.0	16.8	10.8
5.4	4.8	6.0	% Profit Before Taxes/Total Assets	7.1	3.1	4.9	6.6	8.8	5.2
.4	.3	.4		1.3	-8.3	1.3	.1	1.4	.4
20.1	21.3	18.4		38.7	17.3	27.8	26.7	23.4	12.9
8.3	8.8	8.2	Sales/Net Fixed Assets	16.7	7.6	9.6	9.3	9.0	7.0
4.0	4.5	4.4		6.3	3.5	5.8	4.8	4.4	4.0
2.5	2.8	2.7		4.7	3.9	3.2	2.6	2.7	2.5
1.9	2.1	2.1	Sales/Total Assets	2.3	2.2	2.4	2.1	2.1	2.0
1.4	1.5	1.5		1.4	1.6	1.6	1.4	1.5	1.5
1.4	1.1	1.2			1.2	1.0	1.2	1.1	1.2
(398) 2.7	(370) 2.3	(342) 2.4	% Depr., Dep., Amort./Sales		(32) 3.5	(27) 2.0	(49) 1.9	(81) 2.3	(145) 2.4
4.6	4.1	4.2			6.6	4.1	5.0	3.8	4.2
1.8	2.0	1.9			5.5	1.9	2.4	1.2	.8
(129) 3.4	(125) 3.8	(106) 4.0	% Officers', Directors' Owners' Comp/Sales		(20) 7.4	(21) 4.1	(22) 4.3	(29) 1.8	(10) 2.7
6.5	7.2	6.8			8.1	6.8	8.2	2.9	5.2
23427214M	25583082M	25627169M	Net Sales ($)	5771M	73109M	125317M	410779M	1528686M	23483507M
12571484M	13239514M	12943175M	Total Assets ($)	2831M	44572M	65613M	224265M	811204M	11794690M

© RMA 2007

M = $ thousand   MM = $ million

See Pages 11 through 21 for Explanation of Ratios and Data

Current Data Sorted by Assets   Comparative Historical Data

0-500M	500M-2MM	2-10MM	10-50MM	50-100MM	100-250MM	Type of Statement	4/1/02-3/31/03 ALL	4/1/03-3/31/04 ALL
1		1	12	1	2	Unqualified	15	17
	2	16	3			Reviewed	9	21
	1	4				Compiled	8	8
2	2	2	1			Tax Returns		1
1	5	13	13	3	4	Other	28	26
	18 (4/1-9/30/06)		71 (10/1/06-3/31/07)					
4	10	36	29	4	6	NUMBER OF STATEMENTS	60	73
%	%	%	%	%	%	**ASSETS**	%	%
	10.3	5.2	2.7			Cash & Equivalents	7.5	7.8
	25.1	23.6	19.1			Trade Receivables (net)	18.0	21.1
	22.7	43.8	38.9			Inventory	35.2	33.0
	8.3	1.7	1.9			All Other Current	1.7	4.1
	66.4	74.3	62.7			Total Current	62.3	65.9
	26.1	19.3	28.7			Fixed Assets (net)	27.8	25.8
	5.0	2.3	4.3			Intangibles (net)	6.5	3.9
	2.4	4.1	4.3			All Other Non-Current	3.4	4.5
	100.0	100.0	100.0			Total	100.0	100.0
						LIABILITIES		
	12.2	12.4	12.5			Notes Payable-Short Term	13.2	15.7
	4.0	3.7	2.8			Cur. Mat.-L.T.D.	6.3	4.0
	18.3	15.1	13.4			Trade Payables	13.5	12.3
	.0	.0	.0			Income Taxes Payable	.2	.9
	24.0	10.3	10.4			All Other Current	7.4	8.2
	58.5	41.5	39.2			Total Current	40.6	41.0
	8.7	14.4	20.1			Long-Term Debt	19.7	13.6
	.9	.3	.3			Deferred Taxes	.5	.4
	20.7	6.3	7.8			All Other Non-Current	4.5	6.1
	11.3	37.5	32.7			Net Worth	34.8	38.8
	100.0	100.0	100.0			Total Liabilties & Net Worth	100.0	100.0
						INCOME DATA		
	100.0	100.0	100.0			Net Sales	100.0	100.0
	40.4	31.7	25.3			Gross Profit	28.4	29.6
	29.6	24.1	17.8			Operating Expenses	23.1	23.6
	10.8	7.6	7.5			Operating Profit	5.3	6.0
	1.4	.8	1.3			All Other Expenses (net)	1.7	.9
	9.4	6.8	6.2			Profit Before Taxes	3.6	5.1
						RATIOS		
	1.9	2.5	2.0			Current	2.5	2.4
	1.4	1.9	1.5				1.5	1.6
	.8	1.4	1.2				1.1	1.1
	1.3	1.0	.8			Quick	.9	1.1
	.8	.7	.5				.6	.7
	.2	.4	.3				.4	.4
	2 214.9	22 16.7	36 10.1			Sales/Receivables	25 14.8	34 10.6
	28 13.2	41 8.8	52 7.1				43 8.5	47 7.8
	52 7.0	59 6.2	63 5.8				57 6.4	63 5.8
	0 UND	62 5.9	103 3.5			Cost of Sales/Inventory	79 4.6	70 5.2
	50 7.3	92 4.0	132 2.8				110 3.3	99 3.7
	114 3.2	191 1.9	187 1.9				151 2.4	151 2.4
	7 48.9	21 17.5	34 10.8			Cost of Sales/Payables	22 16.6	20 18.3
	26 13.8	33 10.9	43 8.5				40 9.2	33 10.9
	79 4.6	44 8.2	69 5.3				51 7.2	56 6.6
	6.7	3.7	3.7			Sales/Working Capital	3.8	3.4
	16.2	5.5	5.9				8.4	6.7
	-60.4	13.6	14.2				25.0	25.0
		12.1	4.8			EBIT/Interest	7.3	9.0
		(35) 4.8	(27) 2.4				(57) 2.7	(65) 2.2
		2.3	1.3				.9	.3
			7.1			Net Profit + Depr., Dep., Amort./Cur. Mat. L/T/D	6.2	5.7
			(16) 2.1				(25) 1.7	(23) 2.4
			1.2				.8	.7
	.2	.1	.6			Fixed/Worth	.4	.3
	.9	.4	1.1				.9	.6
	-1.3	1.4	2.1				3.0	1.5
	1.0	.9	1.5			Debt/Worth	1.0	.8
	2.0	1.8	2.3				2.2	1.6
	-5.0	5.3	4.0				10.3	4.5
		93.3	39.0			% Profit Before Taxes/Tangible Net Worth	32.2	41.0
		(34) 32.5	(26) 16.8				(50) 14.3	(66) 16.7
		14.3	3.5				-5.9	-.3
	47.3	20.7	7.9			% Profit Before Taxes/Total Assets	12.1	13.4
	18.3	11.2	4.2				5.7	5.3
	4.4	4.1	.8				-.7	-1.2
	28.1	32.3	8.8			Sales/Net Fixed Assets	13.3	11.4
	12.0	14.0	4.5				7.6	6.9
	7.4	6.9	3.5				3.6	3.5
	3.4	3.0	1.6			Sales/Total Assets	2.0	2.1
	2.8	2.0	1.3				1.4	1.5
	2.2	1.5	1.0				1.1	1.1
		1.6	2.4			% Depr., Dep., Amort./Sales	2.1	1.9
		(29) 2.5	(27) 3.0				(54) 3.4	(60) 3.3
		3.6	4.5				5.3	5.6
		1.7				% Officers', Directors' Owners' Comp/Sales	.9	1.1
		(14) 4.4					(18) 2.2	(16) 2.7
		11.3					5.7	6.7
5338M	31968M	396367M	854036M	296318M	1344469M	Net Sales ($)	1626394M	1919575M
1249M	11394M	190516M	640968M	253924M	824630M	Total Assets ($)	1249752M	1515183M

© RMA 2007

M = $ thousand   MM = $ million
See Pages 11 through 21 for Explanation of Ratios and Data

Comparative Historical Data / Current Data Sorted by Sales

4/1/04-3/31/05 ALL	4/1/05-3/31/06 ALL	4/1/06-3/31/07 ALL	Type of Statement	0-1MM	1-3MM	3-5MM	5-10MM	10-25MM	25MM & OVER
24	22	17	Unqualified	1			1	7	8
16	16	21	Reviewed		1	4	4	9	3
7	10	5	Compiled		1		3		1
2	4	7	Tax Returns		3	2	1	1	3
37	35	39	Other		3	2	7	10	17
			Statement period		18 (4/1-9/30/06)			71 (10/1/06-3/31/07)	
86	**87**	**89**	**NUMBER OF STATEMENTS**	1	8	8	16	27	29
%	%	%	**ASSETS**	%	%	%	%	%	%
7.5	6.5	5.3	Cash & Equivalents				5.5	5.3	3.9
20.5	20.3	20.7	Trade Receivables (net)				23.3	19.5	20.6
36.5	37.5	38.5	Inventory				39.6	41.7	37.8
1.9	1.6	2.5	All Other Current				1.2	2.2	1.5
66.4	66.0	67.0	Total Current				69.5	68.7	63.8
24.0	26.1	25.3	Fixed Assets (net)				23.6	22.5	29.5
3.8	2.3	3.6	Intangibles (net)				2.0	3.5	3.8
5.8	5.6	4.1	All Other Non-Current				4.9	5.2	2.9
100.0	100.0	100.0	Total				100.0	100.0	100.0
			LIABILITIES						
13.2	11.6	11.4	Notes Payable-Short Term				15.0	10.1	10.2
3.8	4.7	3.6	Cur. Mat.-L.T.D.				4.5	3.3	2.9
13.9	15.1	14.8	Trade Payables				9.6	17.3	12.8
.5	.3	.0	Income Taxes Payable				.0	.0	.1
9.3	12.8	12.4	All Other Current				8.0	11.5	11.0
40.6	44.4	42.3	Total Current				37.1	42.3	37.1
12.8	16.5	16.8	Long-Term Debt				15.3	13.5	22.8
.3	.3	.3	Deferred Taxes				.8	.2	.3
5.2	10.2	8.6	All Other Non-Current				8.1	3.8	8.0
41.1	28.5	32.0	Net Worth				38.7	40.2	31.9
100.0	100.0	100.0	Total Liabilities & Net Worth				100.0	100.0	100.0
			INCOME DATA						
100.0	100.0	100.0	Net Sales				100.0	100.0	100.0
27.6	27.3	29.6	Gross Profit				32.8	26.1	24.3
21.3	21.5	21.9	Operating Expenses				26.3	17.7	17.1
6.3	5.7	7.7	Operating Profit				6.4	8.4	7.2
.8	1.4	1.2	All Other Expenses (net)				1.8	.2	1.3
5.5	4.3	6.5	Profit Before Taxes				4.6	8.2	5.9
			RATIOS						
2.8	2.6	2.3	Current				2.3	2.5	2.7
1.7	1.5	1.6					1.8	1.5	1.7
1.2	1.1	1.2					1.5	1.2	1.3
1.3	1.2	1.0	Quick				1.2	.9	1.0
.6	.6	.6					.6	.5	.7
.4	.3	.3					.3	.4	.5
27 13.6	29 12.6	28 13.2	Sales/Receivables				27 13.3	23 15.6	36 10.2
47 7.7	41 8.9	46 8.0					44 8.3	40 9.2	51 7.1
66 5.6	61 5.9	59 6.2					57 6.5	56 6.5	60 6.1
71 5.1	60 6.1	68 5.4	Cost of Sales/Inventory				26 14.2	69 5.3	80 4.5
115 3.2	109 3.4	109 3.3					109 3.4	110 3.3	118 3.1
172 2.1	162 2.3	172 2.1					250 1.5	156 2.3	167 2.2
26 13.8	22 16.9	22 16.5	Cost of Sales/Payables				15 24.1	30 12.1	26 13.8
41 8.8	33 11.2	37 9.9					28 13.1	40 9.1	37 9.9
57 6.4	51 7.2	54 6.8					45 8.2	51 7.2	54 6.8
3.4	4.0	3.8	Sales/Working Capital				3.7	3.8	3.7
5.3	8.0	6.1					4.8	8.2	5.9
19.5	22.9	18.3					7.0	19.0	14.6
12.2	9.5	9.4	EBIT/Interest				7.7	17.5	7.6
(73) 4.2	(80) 3.8	(83) 3.6					3.6	(25) 3.8	(27) 3.5
1.2	1.5	1.8					1.7	1.8	1.9
6.3	3.9	8.4	Net Profit + Depr., Dep., Amort./Cur. Mat. L/T/D						8.4
(27) 2.2	(26) 2.6	(31) 2.5						(17)	2.6
1.1	1.1	1.3							1.7
.2	.2	.3	Fixed/Worth				.2	.2	.5
.6	.7	.8					.4	.6	1.2
1.1	2.1	2.1					2.4	1.1	5.7
.6	.9	1.1	Debt/Worth				1.1	.7	1.2
1.6	1.9	2.1					2.0	1.9	2.1
4.7	6.5	5.4					5.0	3.8	13.4
39.3	44.4	65.9	% Profit Before Taxes/Tangible Net Worth				73.1	81.9	49.3
(74) 12.9	(74) 23.3	(78) 24.7					22.5	(26) 30.8	(25) 23.7
5.1	12.2	7.7					6.1	6.8	13.8
12.8	15.5	17.4	% Profit Before Taxes/Total Assets				15.5	28.8	12.5
4.5	7.9	7.1					6.5	9.1	7.1
.7	2.3	2.9					3.2	2.3	2.9
16.8	17.6	18.2	Sales/Net Fixed Assets				32.1	16.3	10.4
7.3	7.9	8.8					11.6	7.7	6.3
3.8	3.7	3.9					6.6	3.8	3.3
2.0	2.6	2.5	Sales/Total Assets				2.9	2.7	1.8
1.5	1.5	1.7					2.0	1.8	1.3
1.0	1.2	1.3					1.1	1.3	1.2
1.5	1.6	1.8	% Depr., Dep., Amort./Sales				2.1	1.5	1.9
(74) 2.8	(69) 3.1	(76) 2.9				(13)	3.2	(22) 2.7	(27) 2.6
4.3	5.1	4.0					4.5	4.5	4.0
1.4	1.4	1.7	% Officers', Directors' Owners' Comp/Sales						
(18) 3.4	(20) 3.8	(23) 5.0							
5.6	9.8	7.1							
2963099M	2743771M	2928496M	Net Sales ($)	262M	14867M	31126M	111325M	438802M	2332114M
2386188M	2026868M	1922681M	Total Assets ($)	382M	4342M	18165M	78722M	274634M	1546436M

M = $ thousand   MM = $ million
See Pages 11 through 21 for Explanation of Ratios and Data

Current Data Sorted by Assets | Comparative Historical Data

Type of Statement

	0-500M	500M-2MM	2-10MM	10-50MM	50-100MM	100-250MM	Type of Statement	4/1/02-3/31/03 ALL	4/1/03-3/31/04 ALL
	1	1	5	14	2	1	Unqualified	23	33
		1	25	8			Reviewed	34	29
		3	10	2			Compiled	22	28
	2	3	6	1			Tax Returns	14	12
	1	8	30	19	2	5	Other	48	38
		32 (4/1-9/30/06)		118 (10/1/06-3/31/07)					
NUMBER OF STATEMENTS	4	16	76	44	4	6		141	140

ASSETS

	0-500M %	500M-2MM %	2-10MM %	10-50MM %	50-100MM %	100-250MM %	Item	ALL %	ALL %
		17.3	8.6	7.0			Cash & Equivalents	8.1	8.1
		28.8	25.4	20.2			Trade Receivables (net)	20.3	21.1
		25.5	36.9	37.3			Inventory	33.6	32.8
		.7	1.8	6.0			All Other Current	3.9	3.6
		72.3	72.5	70.4			Total Current	65.9	65.5
		19.2	22.2	20.7			Fixed Assets (net)	24.6	23.2
		3.6	1.8	3.3			Intangibles (net)	4.4	6.3
		4.9	3.4	5.6			All Other Non-Current	5.1	4.9
		100.0	100.0	100.0			Total	100.0	100.0

LIABILITIES

	0-500M	500M-2MM	2-10MM	10-50MM	50-100MM	100-250MM	Item	ALL	ALL
		8.9	10.9	8.3			Notes Payable-Short Term	11.3	8.9
		1.2	2.9	4.2			Cur. Mat.-L.T.D.	4.3	4.0
		11.2	13.7	13.4			Trade Payables	12.0	12.7
		.1	.5	.2			Income Taxes Payable	.2	.4
		19.1	9.5	8.3			All Other Current	8.1	8.4
		40.6	37.3	34.5			Total Current	35.9	34.3
		15.1	12.4	14.6			Long-Term Debt	17.3	19.1
		.2	.6	.3			Deferred Taxes	.5	.5
		7.0	4.7	2.6			All Other Non-Current	5.2	8.1
		37.1	45.0	48.0			Net Worth	41.2	38.0
		100.0	100.0	100.0			Total Liabilities & Net Worth	100.0	100.0

INCOME DATA

	0-500M	500M-2MM	2-10MM	10-50MM	50-100MM	100-250MM	Item	ALL	ALL
		100.0	100.0	100.0			Net Sales	100.0	100.0
		34.2	33.3	27.8			Gross Profit	31.5	31.8
		25.1	24.0	17.6			Operating Expenses	26.7	25.8
		9.1	9.2	10.2			Operating Profit	4.8	6.0
		2.0	1.7	1.1			All Other Expenses (net)	1.7	1.7
		7.1	7.5	9.1			Profit Before Taxes	3.1	4.4

RATIOS

	500M-2MM	2-10MM	10-50MM	Ratio	ALL	ALL
	4.9	3.1	3.9	Current	3.4	3.1
	2.0	2.0	2.2		1.9	1.9
	1.3	1.3	1.4		1.4	1.4
	3.3	1.5	1.6	Quick	1.6	1.4
	1.1	.9	.8		.7	.8
	.7	.5	.4		.5	.5
	35 10.3	35 10.5	37 9.9	Sales/Receivables	30 12.2	32 11.6
	56 6.5	47 7.8	48 7.6		42 8.7	44 8.3
	86 4.2	63 5.8	61 6.0		59 6.2	58 6.3
	13 28.3	73 5.0	63 5.8	Cost of Sales/Inventory	43 8.5	56 6.5
	57 6.4	109 3.4	125 2.9		102 3.6	100 3.7
	146 2.5	154 2.4	201 1.8		168 2.2	155 2.4
	12 31.5	20 18.3	21 17.1	Cost of Sales/Payables	16 22.7	18 19.8
	25 14.6	28 13.1	44 8.2		32 11.3	30 12.3
	39 9.5	47 7.8	62 5.9		50 7.3	45 8.1
	3.6	3.2	2.3	Sales/Working Capital	3.5	3.6
	7.6	5.4	4.5		5.6	5.2
	15.5	11.2	7.6		10.2	10.8
	10.6	12.6	14.6	EBIT/Interest	7.8	8.4
	(14) 4.9	(67) 4.5	(39) 6.2		(131) 3.5	(127) 4.4
	1.8	2.4	2.2		1.3	1.5
		8.4	7.4	Net Profit + Depr., Dep., Amort./Cur. Mat. L/T/D	6.2	5.4
	(16) 3.9		(17) 2.2		(48) 2.2	(49) 1.9
		1.5	1.4		1.1	.7
	.2	.2	.2	Fixed/Worth	.3	.3
	.8	.4	.4		.7	.6
	2.2	1.2	.9		1.5	1.8
	.6	.6	.5	Debt/Worth	.7	.8
	2.0	1.1	1.3		1.4	1.6
	9.4	3.2	2.9		4.2	5.5
	98.8	48.4	47.2	% Profit Before Taxes/Tangible Net Worth	32.5	38.5
	(14) 47.3	(70) 27.8	(40) 27.7		(131) 13.3	(121) 17.3
	7.8	10.2	10.0		3.4	5.8
	29.1	26.2	19.8	% Profit Before Taxes/Total Assets	12.2	12.8
	8.2	9.4	12.0		5.8	6.0
	3.9	3.7	5.2		.7	1.6
	36.1	22.8	20.2	Sales/Net Fixed Assets	21.5	20.8
	20.8	9.1	8.3		8.5	8.3
	5.7	5.0	3.8		3.5	4.1
	2.7	2.3	2.0	Sales/Total Assets	2.4	2.4
	2.1	1.8	1.6		1.5	1.6
	1.2	1.4	1.0		1.1	1.1
	.7	.9	1.1	% Depr., Dep., Amort./Sales	1.3	1.6
	(12) 1.2	(64) 2.5	(40) 1.8		(126) 2.9	(122) 2.7
	2.2	4.2	3.8		5.1	4.6
		1.1		% Officers', Directors' Owners' Comp/Sales	2.4	1.9
	(30) 2.7				(45) 4.0	(47) 3.9
		5.1			6.9	7.4

	0-500M	500M-2MM	2-10MM	10-50MM	50-100MM	100-250MM		ALL	ALL
	4381M	55122M	682773M	1456187M	375723M	1091616M	Net Sales ($)	3239654M	3458681M
	850M	22126M	360396M	964656M	260068M	890503M	Total Assets ($)	2388627M	2662666M

M = $ thousand   MM = $ million
See Pages 11 through 21 for Explanation of Ratios and Data

Comparative Historical Data   **Current Data Sorted by Sales**

4/1/04-3/31/05 ALL	4/1/05-3/31/06 ALL	4/1/06-3/31/07 ALL	Type of Statement	0-1MM	1-3MM	3-5MM	5-10MM	10-25MM	25MM & OVER
34	30	24	Unqualified	2		2	1	7	12
44	30	34	Reviewed			6	11	14	3
19	16	15	Compiled	1	3		8	1	2
15	18	12	Tax Returns	2	1		5	1	
48	68	65	Other		6	7	17	17	18
					32 (4/1-9/30/06)		118 (10/1/06-3/31/07)		
160	162	150	**NUMBER OF STATEMENTS**	5	10	16	42	42	35
%	%	%	**ASSETS**	%	%	%	%	%	%
8.3	7.4	8.9	Cash & Equivalents		11.2	10.7	9.7	7.6	7.4
20.9	21.2	23.6	Trade Receivables (net)		31.0	20.2	24.4	25.1	21.9
33.4	33.7	34.9	Inventory		34.9	31.5	37.3	39.1	32.6
3.4	3.7	3.6	All Other Current		.2	.6	2.1	4.0	4.9
66.0	66.0	71.0	Total Current		77.4	63.0	73.5	75.7	66.9
23.8	25.9	21.8	Fixed Assets (net)		18.8	30.5	23.0	18.0	21.0
4.4	3.8	2.9	Intangibles (net)		1.3	4.2	1.2	2.4	4.2
5.8	4.4	4.3	All Other Non-Current		2.6	2.3	2.3	3.9	7.9
100.0	100.0	100.0	Total		100.0	100.0	100.0	100.0	100.0
			LIABILITIES						
11.5	10.4	9.3	Notes Payable-Short Term		11.8	7.4	10.8	9.7	7.8
4.3	3.8	3.1	Cur. Mat.-L.T.D.		2.7	3.9	3.2	2.2	4.0
11.3	11.9	13.1	Trade Payables		17.0	9.4	12.8	15.2	12.7
.2	.2	.4	Income Taxes Payable		.0	.4	.3	.6	.3
8.4	8.0	9.9	All Other Current		29.4	12.6	7.3	7.9	9.6
35.8	34.3	35.7	Total Current		60.9	33.7	34.4	35.6	34.4
17.2	15.8	14.0	Long-Term Debt		10.8	23.1	12.2	10.1	15.7
.7	.5	.5	Deferred Taxes		.0	.9	.5	.5	.6
8.3	7.5	4.9	All Other Non-Current		25.3	2.2	5.7	3.0	1.8
38.0	41.7	44.9	Net Worth		3.0	40.0	47.3	50.8	47.4
100.0	100.0	100.0	Total Liabilties & Net Worth		100.0	100.0	100.0	100.0	100.0
			INCOME DATA						
100.0	100.0	100.0	Net Sales		100.0	100.0	100.0	100.0	100.0
32.5	31.1	31.9	Gross Profit		38.6	34.5	34.2	30.3	25.9
26.0	24.5	22.6	Operating Expenses		35.9	25.9	23.8	21.3	15.9
6.4	6.5	9.4	Operating Profit		2.6	8.6	10.3	9.0	10.0
1.3	1.4	1.6	All Other Expenses (net)		3.3	1.6	1.1	1.6	1.6
5.2	5.1	7.8	Profit Before Taxes		-.7	7.1	9.2	7.4	8.4
			RATIOS						
3.3	3.8	3.6	Current		2.2	4.5	3.8	3.9	3.6
2.0	2.0	2.1			1.6	2.0	2.2	2.1	2.2
1.4	1.4	1.4			.8	1.2	1.5	1.4	1.4
1.6	1.6	1.6	Quick		1.2	2.0	1.9	1.6	1.4
.8	.8	.9			.6	.9	1.0	.9	1.0
.5	.4	.5			.3	.6	.4	.5	.5
29 12.7	31 11.6	35 10.5	Sales/Receivables	29 12.8	27 13.4	40 9.1	34 10.8	33 11.1
45 8.0	43 8.6	48 7.6			47 7.8	45 8.1	48 7.7	49 7.5	48 7.6
58 6.3	57 6.4	63 5.8			60 6.1	52 7.0	63 5.8	60 6.1	64 5.7
61 6.0	60 6.1	56 6.5	Cost of Sales/Inventory		18 20.7	84 4.3	72 5.1	64 5.7	53 6.9
110 3.3	106 3.4	111 3.3			76 4.8	101 3.6	111 3.3	125 2.9	92 4.0
166 2.2	169 2.2	160 2.3			208 1.8	144 2.5	169 2.2	164 2.2	171 2.1
17 21.8	18 20.0	21 17.8	Cost of Sales/Payables		24 15.5	18 20.2	17 21.5	25 14.8	14 25.7
31 11.6	31 11.7	32 11.3			35 10.6	24 15.1	29 12.5	40 9.1	40 9.2
47 7.8	46 7.9	56 6.5			76 4.8	28 12.9	64 5.7	47 7.7	57 6.4
3.3	3.2	3.1	Sales/Working Capital		5.4	3.3	3.0	3.1	3.0
5.3	5.2	5.0			15.2	7.4	4.7	4.7	4.9
11.0	10.0	10.3			-20.8	14.2	8.3	9.5	8.5
9.3	12.9	11.9	EBIT/Interest			9.3	11.9	12.6	19.1
(143) 4.5	(146) 4.0	(130) 5.0			(14) 3.3	(38) 4.2	(35) 6.7	(31) 6.1
1.7	1.4	2.4				2.5	2.1	3.4	2.7
4.5	5.2	7.9	Net Profit + Depr., Dep., Amort./Cur. Mat. L/T/D					4.5	24.1
(44) 1.9	(46) 2.5	(38) 3.4					(15) 1.9	(14) 7.0
1.0	1.1	1.6						1.0	2.3
.2	.3	.2	Fixed/Worth		.5	.4	.1	.2	.2
.5	.6	.5			4.5	1.0	.5	.4	.4
1.5	1.2	1.1			-.3	2.2	1.2	.7	.8
.7	.6	.6	Debt/Worth		3.2	.9	.6	.4	.5
1.7	1.4	1.2			11.6	1.9	1.0	1.1	1.2
3.3	3.2	3.2			-5.4	4.1	2.9	2.1	2.9
41.7	44.9	47.7	% Profit Before Taxes/Tangible Net Worth			78.1	43.7	53.4	45.5
(148) 17.3	(148) 19.5	(136) 27.7			(14) 28.7	(40) 23.5	(40) 33.1	(32) 25.5
5.9	7.7	10.3				4.6	9.8	12.2	17.5
16.3	18.6	22.4	% Profit Before Taxes/Total Assets		22.6	25.9	29.7	26.5	19.2
6.5	7.6	9.9			3.7	8.1	7.9	12.9	12.3
2.0	1.3	4.7			-4.5	2.1	3.9	5.9	5.9
22.7	15.7	22.4	Sales/Net Fixed Assets		56.4	10.9	24.3	21.7	23.9
8.1	7.0	9.1			22.0	6.6	8.5	14.5	6.4
3.8	4.2	4.6			9.0	3.0	4.8	5.1	4.2
2.2	2.1	2.3	Sales/Total Assets		3.9	2.1	2.2	2.5	2.2
1.5	1.7	1.7			1.9	1.7	1.7	1.9	1.6
1.1	1.2	1.2			1.1	1.4	1.3	1.3	1.1
1.2	1.2	1.0	% Depr., Dep., Amort./Sales			.8	1.1	.8	1.1
(136) 2.8	(140) 2.6	(126) 2.1			(13) 2.1	(37) 2.9	(37) 1.9	(29) 1.8
4.8	4.4	3.9				4.3	4.4	2.8	3.5
2.2	1.7	1.2	% Officers', Directors' Owners' Comp/Sales				1.2	1.2	
(59) 4.0	(49) 3.6	(49) 3.0					(20) 3.9	(14) 2.2	
6.6	6.0	5.4					5.4	4.3	
4504396M	4269588M	3665802M	Net Sales ($)	2115M	23706M	62637M	300162M	701635M	2575547M
3141156M	3171748M	2498599M	Total Assets ($)	3604M	13322M	39399M	201533M	456178M	1784563M

© RMA 2007

M = $ thousand   MM = $ million
See Pages 11 through 21 for Explanation of Ratios and Data

Current Data Sorted by Assets   Comparative Historical Data

Current period splits: 9 (4/1-9/30/06)   29 (10/1/06-3/31/07)

0-500M	500M-2MM	2-10MM	10-50MM	50-100MM	100-250MM	Type of Statement	4/1/02-3/31/03 ALL	4/1/03-3/31/04 ALL
		2	1	2	2	Unqualified	20	16
	1	3	3			Reviewed	10	11
	1	2	1			Compiled	6	7
1	1					Tax Returns	1	
1	1	5	7	3	1	Other	15	18
2	4	12	12	5	3	NUMBER OF STATEMENTS	52	52
%	%	%	%	%	%		%	%
						ASSETS		
		6.1	6.5			Cash & Equivalents	8.3	10.0
		25.9	24.1			Trade Receivables (net)	22.2	23.4
		18.9	33.0			Inventory	25.2	23.2
		5.6	1.1			All Other Current	4.2	7.2
		56.5	64.8			Total Current	59.9	63.8
		27.7	20.0			Fixed Assets (net)	26.6	25.9
		10.0	8.6			Intangibles (net)	6.3	3.8
		5.7	6.6			All Other Non-Current	7.2	6.4
		100.0	100.0			Total	100.0	100.0
						LIABILITIES		
		9.1	11.9			Notes Payable-Short Term	9.9	10.8
		4.2	1.9			Cur. Mat.-L.T.D.	4.4	3.2
		15.9	14.5			Trade Payables	12.8	15.1
		.2	.0			Income Taxes Payable	.4	.3
		9.6	8.8			All Other Current	7.5	10.6
		39.0	37.1			Total Current	35.0	40.0
		17.4	12.7			Long-Term Debt	17.1	14.5
		.0	.0			Deferred Taxes	.6	.8
		3.8	1.6			All Other Non-Current	4.9	6.2
		39.9	48.6			Net Worth	42.4	38.6
		100.0	100.0			Total Liabilties & Net Worth	100.0	100.0
						INCOME DATA		
		100.0	100.0			Net Sales	100.0	100.0
		41.1	25.9			Gross Profit	31.8	31.4
		28.3	16.7			Operating Expenses	25.8	24.4
		12.8	9.1			Operating Profit	6.0	6.9
		.5	1.0			All Other Expenses (net)	2.8	2.0
		12.3	8.1			Profit Before Taxes	3.2	4.9
						RATIOS		
		3.0	2.6				2.7	2.7
		1.6	1.5			Current	1.7	1.8
		1.1	1.1				1.2	1.1
		1.6	1.2				1.5	1.5
		1.1	.6			Quick	.8	1.0
		.4	.5				.5	.5
		23 15.7	34 10.8				28 12.9	31 11.8
		31 11.7	47 7.7			Sales/Receivables	41 8.8	44 8.3
		64 5.7	96 3.8				58 6.3	57 6.4
		4 89.8	29 12.7				36 10.2	24 15.2
		30 12.0	101 3.6			Cost of Sales/Inventory	59 6.2	58 6.3
		76 4.8	164 2.2				99 3.7	106 3.5
		24 15.5	21 17.1				17 22.1	18 20.8
		40 9.2	34 10.8			Cost of Sales/Payables	37 9.8	36 10.2
		64 5.7	43 8.5				50 7.3	50 7.3
		5.2	3.7				4.7	4.5
		14.2	5.1			Sales/Working Capital	7.7	6.1
		50.8	NM				25.4	27.9
		37.3	35.4				7.5	14.9
		(10) 7.8	3.3			EBIT/Interest	(47) 2.6	(47) 3.6
		3.7	2.1				.3	.8
							4.0	3.9
						Net Profit + Depr., Dep., Amort./Cur. Mat. L/T/D	(24) 2.6	(15) 2.4
							1.3	.9
		.2	.2				.4	.3
		.9	.4			Fixed/Worth	.7	.6
		8.2	1.0				1.6	1.5
		.6	.6				.7	.7
		1.3	1.5			Debt/Worth	1.5	1.4
		28.7	6.6				3.5	3.9
		73.7	48.7				25.7	35.1
		(10) 49.5	20.8			% Profit Before Taxes/Tangible Net Worth	(47) 9.1	(45) 19.2
		31.7	8.3				-4.1	1.6
		34.6	20.8				8.3	13.7
		16.8	9.9			% Profit Before Taxes/Total Assets	4.1	6.8
		9.1	1.7				-1.9	-.4
		16.9	16.5				16.3	17.7
		10.0	8.8			Sales/Net Fixed Assets	6.9	7.8
		5.8	7.7				4.5	3.9
		3.0	2.1				2.2	2.5
		2.4	1.4			Sales/Total Assets	1.8	1.9
		1.4	1.0				1.3	1.3
		1.3	.7				1.5	1.5
		(11) 2.9	(11) 2.0			% Depr., Dep., Amort./Sales	(48) 2.7	(46) 2.5
		5.2	3.0				4.0	4.6
							1.8	
						% Officers', Directors', Owners' Comp/Sales	(10) 3.6	
							6.2	
1146M	13221M	143199M	448623M	562709M	674598M	Net Sales ($)	2880013M	2780317M
66M	4682M	59982M	282005M	307270M	402923M	Total Assets ($)	1560121M	1579372M

Comparative Historical Data — Current Data Sorted by Sales

			Type of Statement	0-1MM	1-3MM	3-5MM	5-10MM	10-25MM	25MM & OVER
9	9	7	Unqualified	1	1	1	1	2	5
2	4	7	Reviewed					2	1
3	7	4	Compiled				1	1	2
	2	2	Tax Returns	1	1				2
10	16	18	Other	2	2	2	3		9
4/1/04- 3/31/05 ALL	4/1/05- 3/31/06 ALL	4/1/06- 3/31/07 ALL			9 (4/1-9/30/06)			29 (10/1/06-3/31/07)	
24	38	38	NUMBER OF STATEMENTS	1	4	4	4	8	17
%	%	%	ASSETS	%	%	%	%	%	%
7.6	8.6	8.4	Cash & Equivalents						8.4
22.9	26.1	24.5	Trade Receivables (net)						23.1
31.1	26.4	27.0	Inventory						32.2
3.9	2.0	2.6	All Other Current						1.9
65.4	63.1	62.6	Total Current						65.6
22.7	25.0	22.7	Fixed Assets (net)						21.1
6.9	6.2	9.5	Intangibles (net)						10.2
5.0	5.7	5.1	All Other Non-Current						3.1
100.0	100.0	100.0	Total						100.0
			LIABILITIES						
17.0	10.5	8.7	Notes Payable-Short Term						8.1
2.6	3.4	2.6	Cur. Mat.-L.T.D.						1.7
18.6	14.8	14.4	Trade Payables						16.8
.5	.5	.2	Income Taxes Payable						.3
14.6	13.7	9.2	All Other Current						12.0
53.3	42.9	35.1	Total Current						38.9
16.7	15.2	21.3	Long-Term Debt						20.3
.8	.2	.4	Deferred Taxes						.6
6.3	3.9	3.1	All Other Non-Current						3.8
22.8	37.7	40.0	Net Worth						36.4
100.0	100.0	100.0	Total Liabilties & Net Worth						100.0
			INCOME DATA						
100.0	100.0	100.0	Net Sales						100.0
23.5	31.0	30.1	Gross Profit						21.9
20.6	23.0	20.5	Operating Expenses						13.6
2.9	8.1	9.6	Operating Profit						8.3
1.7	1.4	.8	All Other Expenses (net)						.8
1.2	6.6	8.8	Profit Before Taxes						7.5
			RATIOS						
2.1	2.4	2.9	Current						2.8
1.4	1.5	1.7							1.8
1.0	1.0	1.3							1.3
1.0	1.1	1.4	Quick						1.3
.6	.8	.7							.7
.3	.5	.5							.5
31　11.7	29　12.8	30　12.1	Sales/Receivables						34　10.8
46　8.0	42　8.7	42　8.7							43　8.6
57　6.4	54　6.7	65　5.6							49　7.5
47　7.7	37　10.0	27　13.3	Cost of Sales/Inventory						30　12.0
64　5.7	65　5.6	73　5.0							80　4.6
119　3.1	116　3.1	104　3.5							107　3.4
28　13.2	22　16.3	20　18.0	Cost of Sales/Payables						22　16.9
41　8.9	36　10.0	32　11.4							32　11.4
50　7.3	51　7.1	50　7.4							42　8.6
5.1	5.0	3.8	Sales/Working Capital						3.5
8.1	9.6	6.9							7.1
NM	NM	24.7							20.4
15.4	36.4	17.2	EBIT/Interest						25.6
(22)　2.4	(36)　4.5	(33)　6.1						(16)	7.0
-1.2	1.9	2.4							2.7
		10.3	Net Profit + Depr., Dep., Amort./Cur. Mat. L/T/D						
		(12)　5.0							
		2.2							
.4	.3	.3	Fixed/Worth						.3
.8	.7	.9							.8
-2.2	4.0	2.1							7.9
1.1	.6	.9	Debt/Worth						.9
2.1	1.8	1.7							1.6
-6.9	7.3	10.9							25.4
50.2	71.9	62.1	% Profit Before Taxes/Tangible Net Worth						52.9
(16)　20.6	(32)　33.6	(33)　36.5						(14)	24.9
8.0	9.5	15.7							14.1
16.7	29.3	21.6	% Profit Before Taxes/Total Assets						20.3
7.3	10.5	13.8							10.9
-11.4	2.6	3.6							4.1
19.9	29.1	17.8	Sales/Net Fixed Assets						17.6
8.9	8.4	9.6							10.3
5.3	5.2	6.3							6.1
2.8	3.0	2.5	Sales/Total Assets						2.4
2.0	2.0	2.0							2.1
1.3	1.3	1.1							1.3
1.6	.8	1.3	% Depr., Dep., Amort./Sales						1.0
(21)　2.0	(33)　1.7	(32)　2.1						(16)	1.7
2.9	2.9	3.2							2.8
			% Officers', Directors' Owners' Comp/Sales						
1910693M	2563966M	1843496M	Net Sales ($)	5M	6643M	17672M	27866M	135508M	1655802M
1005257M	1066868M	1056928M	Total Assets ($)	4M	7374M	11637M	11959M	107918M	918036M

© RMA 2007

M = $ thousand　　MM = $ million
See Pages 11 through 21 for Explanation of Ratios and Data

Current Data Sorted by Assets   Comparative Historical Data

						Type of Statement		
		4	12	4	5	Unqualified	17	20
		9	5	1		Reviewed	16	16
1	3	6	6			Compiled	8	11
	1	3				Tax Returns	1	2
		3	11	3	2	Other	18	18
	18 (4/1-9/30/06)		61 (10/1/06-3/31/07)				4/1/02-3/31/03	4/1/03-3/31/04
0-500M	500M-2MM	2-10MM	10-50MM	50-100MM	100-250MM		ALL	ALL
1	4	25	34	8	7	**NUMBER OF STATEMENTS**	60	67
%	%	%	%	%	%	**ASSETS**	%	%
		17.1	14.2			Cash & Equivalents	11.5	11.3
		21.9	17.7			Trade Receivables (net)	17.8	21.4
		15.7	14.6			Inventory	11.7	8.9
		8.9	14.0			All Other Current	12.4	9.4
		63.7	60.5			Total Current	53.4	50.9
		29.5	31.3			Fixed Assets (net)	36.9	34.6
		1.0	2.7			Intangibles (net)	2.6	4.7
		5.9	5.5			All Other Non-Current	7.2	9.7
		100.0	100.0			Total	100.0	100.0
						LIABILITIES		
		10.7	10.8			Notes Payable-Short Term	7.5	6.7
		2.6	5.4			Cur. Mat.-L.T.D.	3.6	3.0
		18.9	9.8			Trade Payables	12.8	12.6
		1.9	1.1			Income Taxes Payable	1.0	.5
		14.3	13.9			All Other Current	13.2	13.2
		48.4	41.1			Total Current	38.2	36.0
		10.6	14.7			Long-Term Debt	17.6	18.1
		1.0	.6			Deferred Taxes	1.5	1.2
		4.4	4.3			All Other Non-Current	3.7	4.8
		35.6	39.3			Net Worth	39.0	39.8
		100.0	100.0			Total Liabilities & Net Worth	100.0	100.0
						INCOME DATA		
		100.0	100.0			Net Sales	100.0	100.0
		30.7	29.1			Gross Profit	25.6	23.6
		27.1	21.7			Operating Expenses	21.1	19.8
		3.6	7.4			Operating Profit	4.5	3.9
		1.3	.2			All Other Expenses (net)	.7	1.1
		2.3	7.2			Profit Before Taxes	3.8	2.8
						RATIOS		
		2.3	2.2				1.9	2.3
		1.5	1.4			Current	1.4	1.4
		1.1	1.2				1.0	1.1
		1.5	1.3				1.3	1.7
		1.1	.8			Quick	.8	.9
		.5	.4				.4	.5
		20 18.2	12 29.3				10 37.6	23 16.0
		37 9.7	43 8.6			Sales/Receivables	30 12.2	42 8.6
		50 7.3	71 5.1				48 7.7	61 6.0
		1 354.9	0 UND				0 UND	0 UND
		15 24.8	5 67.0			Cost of Sales/Inventory	8 46.0	6 59.3
		62 5.9	66 5.6				30 12.4	37 9.8
		15 24.8	20 18.7				14 26.9	14 26.0
		23 16.0	31 11.6			Cost of Sales/Payables	21 17.1	22 16.6
		39 9.3	48 7.6				40 9.1	44 8.2
		5.2	5.5				8.0	6.8
		10.3	8.4			Sales/Working Capital	17.8	13.1
		89.4	18.3				NM	74.3
		8.6	21.4				7.7	8.4
		(21) 3.1	(30) 3.7			EBIT/Interest	(52) 3.5	(54) 3.6
		1.7	2.9				1.2	.7
		10.6	8.2				4.2	4.9
		(12) 4.0	(16) 3.8			Net Profit + Depr., Dep., Amort./Cur. Mat. L/T/D	(21) 1.9	(27) 1.7
		2.1	2.5				.9	.6
		.3	.4				.5	.5
		.8	.8			Fixed/Worth	1.0	1.0
		1.2	1.5				1.9	1.7
		.6	.9				.7	.7
		1.6	1.7			Debt/Worth	1.9	1.6
		4.0	3.3				3.2	3.3
		30.4	50.2				35.5	35.7
		(23) 18.3	(32) 25.2			% Profit Before Taxes/Tangible Net Worth	(53) 11.4	(60) 17.7
		6.0	13.1				3.5	3.2
		14.3	15.3				13.0	12.9
		5.2	6.4			% Profit Before Taxes/Total Assets	4.1	5.2
		.7	3.3				.3	-.9
		18.6	8.8				19.5	18.5
		9.2	4.4			Sales/Net Fixed Assets	6.0	6.5
		4.1	2.9				2.5	2.6
		3.5	2.0				3.1	2.8
		2.1	1.4			Sales/Total Assets	2.2	1.8
		1.3	.9				1.4	1.1
		1.1	1.0				1.4	.9
		1.6	(33) 2.4			% Depr., Dep., Amort./Sales	(50) 2.2	(59) 2.1
		3.2	3.0				3.4	4.3
		7.7					1.2	1.3
		(10) 10.3				% Officers', Directors' Owners' Comp/Sales	(18) 2.0	(13) 2.3
		13.9					5.0	5.7
1280M	16711M	259448M	1266958M	827258M	1692147M	Net Sales ($)	2177901M	2692442M
353M	5989M	114268M	829335M	535424M	1265218M	Total Assets ($)	1481224M	1850360M

© RMA 2007   M = $ thousand   MM = $ million
See Pages 11 through 21 for Explanation of Ratios and Data

Comparative Historical Data | Current Data Sorted by Sales

			Type of Statement	0-1MM	1-3MM	3-5MM	5-10MM	10-25MM	25MM & OVER
31	18	25	Unqualified			1	2	3	19
16	11	15	Reviewed			1	4	6	4
10	11	16	Compiled		3	2	4	4	3
3	1	4	Tax Returns			2	4		1
16	24	19	Other		1		3	5	10
4/1/04-3/31/05 ALL	4/1/05-3/31/06 ALL	4/1/06-3/31/07 ALL			18 (4/1-9/30/06)		61 (10/1/06-3/31/07)		
76	65	79	NUMBER OF STATEMENTS		4	6	14	18	37
%	%	%	ASSETS	%	%	%	%	%	%
10.0	11.8	13.9	Cash & Equivalents				17.8	14.1	13.5
16.2	17.7	19.6	Trade Receivables (net)				19.1	20.2	20.6
14.4	14.9	13.2	Inventory				15.7	16.1	8.1
10.4	10.9	12.0	All Other Current				8.4	12.4	14.7
51.1	55.2	58.7	Total Current				61.0	62.7	57.0
37.9	34.4	31.4	Fixed Assets (net)				31.1	28.9	31.9
2.6	1.8	2.7	Intangibles (net)				2.0	1.6	4.2
8.4	8.6	7.2	All Other Non-Current				5.9	6.8	7.0
100.0	100.0	100.0	Total				100.0	100.0	100.0
			LIABILITIES						
9.8	13.7	10.1	Notes Payable-Short Term				4.1	21.5	5.8
2.2	3.3	3.7	Cur. Mat.-L.T.D.				7.1	3.2	3.1
10.4	10.9	12.4	Trade Payables				10.8	10.1	12.5
.6	.4	1.1	Income Taxes Payable				2.3	.8	.9
12.7	14.8	17.6	All Other Current				12.0	14.6	19.6
35.8	43.1	45.0	Total Current				36.3	50.3	41.9
20.9	18.3	14.0	Long-Term Debt				15.7	10.0	14.0
.8	.7	.7	Deferred Taxes				.7	.4	.8
3.7	3.2	4.5	All Other Non-Current				4.0	5.7	4.3
38.8	34.8	35.8	Net Worth				43.3	33.6	39.0
100.0	100.0	100.0	Total Liabilities & Net Worth				100.0	100.0	100.0
			INCOME DATA						
100.0	100.0	100.0	Net Sales				100.0	100.0	100.0
25.4	26.9	28.6	Gross Profit				36.3	27.2	21.3
21.1	24.1	22.3	Operating Expenses				33.2	23.2	13.2
4.2	2.8	6.3	Operating Profit				3.2	4.0	8.0
.9	.6	.7	All Other Expenses (net)				-.7	-.3	.8
3.3	2.2	5.6	Profit Before Taxes				3.9	4.3	7.3
			RATIOS						
2.3	2.0	2.2					2.7	1.7	2.0
1.4	1.3	1.5	Current				1.9	1.3	1.5
1.1	1.1	1.0					1.2	1.0	1.1
1.4	1.3	1.3					1.7	1.2	1.3
.8	.6	.8	Quick				1.1	.8	.8
.4	.3	.4					.5	.3	.6
13 27.6	11 34.6	19 19.2					31 11.7	6 63.2	18 19.8
31 11.9	27 13.6	37 9.7	Sales/Receivables				44 8.3	39 9.3	37 9.8
48 7.7	50 7.3	57 6.4					51 7.1	61 5.9	68 5.4
1 339.9	1 249.3	1 433.8					4 96.1	0 UND	0 UND
12 31.1	7 55.8	5 66.7	Cost of Sales/Inventory				25 14.6	8 45.7	3 107.1
55 6.6	64 5.7	56 6.5					74 4.9	57 6.4	26 13.8
14 26.2	14 26.1	17 21.8					17 21.7	14 26.9	18 20.6
25 14.9	24 15.2	25 14.5	Cost of Sales/Payables				24 15.3	21 17.1	31 11.7
38 9.6	50 7.3	41 8.9					47 7.7	48 7.6	41 8.9
5.7	6.5	6.0					4.3	7.8	6.7
13.1	10.5	9.0	Sales/Working Capital				7.6	14.1	8.7
54.6	51.3	159.8					NM	NM	69.1
9.5	9.6	13.4					37.2	7.5	18.2
(67) 3.6	(57) 3.0	(68) 3.7	EBIT/Interest				(12) 2.4	(16) 3.1	(32) 6.3
1.0	.9	2.2					.8	2.2	3.1
9.3	5.6	9.3							7.7
(32) 4.0	(25) 2.6	(32) 4.0	Net Profit + Depr., Dep., Amort./Cur. Mat. L/T/D					(17)	4.0
1.6	1.3	2.4							2.5
.5	.4	.4					.3	.4	.6
1.0	.8	.8	Fixed/Worth				.9	.7	.8
2.0	1.9	1.8					2.4	1.5	1.7
.7	.8	.8					.6	.8	.9
1.9	2.0	1.7	Debt/Worth				1.2	2.1	1.5
4.5	3.9	4.5					4.8	3.8	4.5
37.3	38.8	39.6					23.7	34.2	50.2
(73) 17.5	(62) 13.3	(72) 24.8	% Profit Before Taxes/Tangible Net Worth				(12) 15.5	(17) 20.2	(36) 30.7
1.6	.4	10.0					1.6	9.8	15.3
11.9	9.8	15.1					14.1	11.6	15.9
4.9	4.8	6.7	% Profit Before Taxes/Total Assets				4.2	5.8	11.2
.0	-.3	2.5					-.1	2.9	3.7
11.0	11.9	12.1					11.1	18.0	8.7
4.4	5.9	5.7	Sales/Net Fixed Assets				5.0	8.0	5.9
2.6	3.1	3.1					2.2	2.9	3.5
2.5	2.5	2.6					2.4	3.5	2.0
1.6	1.7	1.6	Sales/Total Assets				1.8	1.8	1.6
1.1	1.2	1.2					.9	1.0	1.3
1.4	1.1	1.0					1.0	1.2	1.0
(70) 1.9	(60) 2.0	(77) 2.0	% Depr., Dep., Amort./Sales				(13) 2.0	2.0	1.9
4.3	3.3	3.1					4.5	3.1	2.7
1.3	2.6	1.7							
(19) 2.8	(18) 3.9	(20) 6.1	% Officers', Directors' Owners' Comp/Sales						
5.5	7.1	10.9							
2446730M	2358295M	4063802M	Net Sales ($)		9027M	27243M	108567M	301826M	3617139M
1783353M	1513053M	2750587M	Total Assets ($)		5330M	21137M	118773M	196332M	2409015M

M = $ thousand   MM = $ million
See Pages 11 through 21 for Explanation of Ratios and Data

Current Data Sorted by Assets   Comparative Historical Data

0-500M	500M-2MM	2-10MM	10-50MM	50-100MM	100-250MM		4/1/02-3/31/03 ALL	4/1/03-3/31/04 ALL
						Type of Statement		
	1	10	17	5		Unqualified	15	16
	1	9	5		1	Reviewed	13	13
	3	6				Compiled	16	17
	6					Tax Returns	9	6
1	3	7	16	4	2	Other	26	30
2	27 (4/1-9/30/06)		72 (10/1/06-3/31/07)					
3	14	32	38	9	3	**NUMBER OF STATEMENTS**	79	82
%	%	%	%	%	%	**ASSETS**	%	%
	8.1	9.2	12.5			Cash & Equivalents	11.3	9.6
	13.7	15.6	14.5			Trade Receivables (net)	12.3	13.5
	38.8	32.9	31.2			Inventory	32.9	33.7
	2.4	4.7	3.8			All Other Current	4.8	3.7
	63.0	62.4	61.9			Total Current	61.3	60.7
	30.5	28.0	28.8			Fixed Assets (net)	30.8	29.7
	3.1	3.4	4.9			Intangibles (net)	3.4	3.8
	3.4	6.1	4.4			All Other Non-Current	4.6	5.8
	100.0	100.0	100.0			Total	100.0	100.0
						LIABILITIES		
	18.6	11.5	9.5			Notes Payable-Short Term	9.7	13.7
	1.7	2.2	2.6			Cur. Mat.-L.T.D.	2.6	1.8
	15.4	18.2	12.9			Trade Payables	16.6	13.2
	.7	.1	.4			Income Taxes Payable	.6	.2
	12.8	14.2	16.7			All Other Current	14.9	13.1
	49.2	46.2	42.1			Total Current	44.4	42.0
	19.5	12.8	20.0			Long-Term Debt	15.2	12.8
	.0	.3	.2			Deferred Taxes	.3	.3
	17.5	6.3	3.3			All Other Non-Current	3.4	5.0
	13.9	34.4	34.5			Net Worth	36.7	39.9
	100.0	100.0	100.0			Total Liabilties & Net Worth	100.0	100.0
						INCOME DATA		
	100.0	100.0	100.0			Net Sales	100.0	100.0
	34.5	22.8	20.8			Gross Profit	25.0	25.3
	29.7	18.9	15.2			Operating Expenses	20.0	19.9
	4.8	3.9	5.6			Operating Profit	5.0	5.4
	2.9	.7	.9			All Other Expenses (net)	.7	.6
	1.9	3.2	4.7			Profit Before Taxes	4.3	4.8
						RATIOS		
	2.2	2.2	2.0				2.3	2.2
	1.8	1.4	1.4			Current	1.6	1.4
	1.1	1.1	1.2				1.1	1.1
	1.7	.9	1.1				1.2	1.1
	.6	.5	.7			Quick	.4	.5
	.1	.2	.3				.2	.3
	3 129.3	9 39.8	10 36.1				5 74.6	7 49.1
	14 26.6	17 20.9	19 18.9			Sales/Receivables	12 31.3	19 19.6
	34 10.6	40 9.1	35 10.5				22 16.3	30 12.2
	12 29.6	33 11.0	32 11.4				31 11.7	25 14.8
	55 6.6	49 7.4	57 6.4			Cost of Sales/Inventory	57 6.5	58 6.3
	192 1.9	87 4.2	101 3.6				83 4.4	110 3.3
	12 30.6	14 25.4	15 24.2				12 30.1	11 33.6
	22 16.6	27 13.3	23 15.6			Cost of Sales/Payables	24 14.9	19 19.3
	51 7.2	44 8.3	36 10.3				40 9.0	39 9.4
	7.1	7.2	6.4				6.1	6.9
	10.0	14.4	11.6			Sales/Working Capital	16.4	13.5
	35.3	48.9	39.2				85.1	54.7
	11.0	14.9	9.8				17.0	11.5
	3.0	4.2	(35) 4.7			EBIT/Interest	(70) 4.1	(73) 3.7
	.8	1.8	1.8				1.6	2.1
			8.4				9.1	7.5
		(10) 5.8				Net Profit + Depr., Dep., Amort./Cur. Mat. L/T/D	(23) 4.2	(25) 2.9
			2.5				1.0	1.7
	.6	.3	.4				.4	.4
	1.1	.8	1.2			Fixed/Worth	.8	.8
	NM	1.3	2.7				2.5	1.7
	1.1	1.0	1.2				.7	.7
	4.5	1.9	2.2			Debt/Worth	1.9	1.7
	NM	3.0	6.8				6.8	5.0
	65.7	61.5	58.4				47.5	47.8
(11) 26.6		(30) 16.9	(34) 24.4			% Profit Before Taxes/Tangible Net Worth	(71) 23.5	(77) 31.5
	5.8	6.9	12.3				6.6	9.7
	13.9	21.1	18.9				19.9	15.9
	7.4	7.8	6.1			% Profit Before Taxes/Total Assets	7.6	7.7
	-1.1	1.9	3.6				1.9	3.1
	20.4	24.5	13.9				19.2	23.5
	8.0	11.7	9.3			Sales/Net Fixed Assets	10.0	9.2
	4.9	5.7	4.8				6.2	5.3
	4.4	3.5	2.7				3.5	3.2
	2.1	2.8	2.2			Sales/Total Assets	2.7	2.4
	1.4	1.8	1.8				1.8	1.7
	.9	.7	.9				.8	.8
(13) 1.7		(31) 1.4	(37) 1.5			% Depr., Dep., Amort./Sales	(75) 1.5	(75) 1.5
	3.0	2.7	2.7				2.3	3.1
							.9	1.1
						% Officers', Directors' Owners' Comp/Sales	(25) 3.0	(30) 2.8
							7.0	6.1
6478M	54066M	476839M	2125386M	1375466M	465851M	Net Sales ($)	2401837M	3209516M
852M	18382M	168960M	940823M	677087M	483332M	Total Assets ($)	1078403M	1611811M

M = $ thousand   MM = $ million

See Pages 11 through 21 for Explanation of Ratios and Data

Comparative Historical Data   Current Data Sorted by Sales

Type of Statement

4/1/04-3/31/05	4/1/05-3/31/06	4/1/06-3/31/07	Type of Statement	0-1MM	1-3MM	3-5MM	5-10MM	10-25MM	25MM & OVER
21	25	33	Unqualified			1	2	9	21
15	16	16	Reviewed		2	1	1	5	7
8	11	9	Compiled		2		1	6	
15	10	7	Tax Returns	2	3	1	1		
29	33	34	Other	1	4		2	6	21
ALL	ALL	ALL			27 (4/1-9/30/06)			72 (10/1/06-3/31/07)	

4/1/04-3/31/05 ALL	4/1/05-3/31/06 ALL	4/1/06-3/31/07 ALL		0-1MM	1-3MM	3-5MM	5-10MM	10-25MM	25MM & OVER
88	95	99	**NUMBER OF STATEMENTS**	3	11	3	7	26	49
%	%	%	**ASSETS**	%	%	%	%	%	%
12.4	10.0	10.4	Cash & Equivalents		12.9			6.9	12.3
11.9	12.2	14.0	Trade Receivables (net)		9.3			15.7	13.1
35.4	33.0	32.1	Inventory		39.9			39.5	29.6
3.1	4.5	3.6	All Other Current		3.0			4.5	3.8
62.8	59.7	60.2	Total Current		65.1			66.6	58.8
27.8	29.0	28.7	Fixed Assets (net)		27.1			26.5	29.1
4.3	6.4	6.0	Intangibles (net)		4.3			2.9	6.7
5.1	5.0	5.1	All Other Non-Current		3.5			4.0	5.4
100.0	100.0	100.0	Total		100.0			100.0	100.0
			LIABILITIES						
11.7	10.7	10.2	Notes Payable-Short Term		20.2			14.1	7.2
1.6	2.5	2.2	Cur. Mat.-L.T.D.		1.3			2.5	2.3
14.5	15.1	15.7	Trade Payables		13.6			18.2	12.9
.3	.2	.3	Income Taxes Payable		.9			.1	.3
15.1	12.2	15.3	All Other Current		17.0			14.5	16.8
43.2	40.6	43.7	Total Current		52.9			49.3	39.6
14.0	19.7	17.5	Long-Term Debt		20.4			8.9	20.9
.4	.4	.3	Deferred Taxes		.0			.2	.5
4.9	11.2	7.6	All Other Non-Current		17.6			2.8	3.1
37.6	28.0	30.8	Net Worth		9.2			38.8	35.9
100.0	100.0	100.0	Total Liabilities & Net Worth		100.0			100.0	100.0
			INCOME DATA						
100.0	100.0	100.0	Net Sales		100.0			100.0	100.0
26.3	24.3	24.0	Gross Profit		35.3			20.9	20.8
21.6	19.2	19.1	Operating Expenses		35.6			16.2	14.2
4.7	5.1	4.9	Operating Profit		-.3			4.7	6.6
.8	1.3	1.1	All Other Expenses (net)		2.3			.6	.8
3.9	3.8	3.8	Profit Before Taxes		-2.6			4.1	5.8
			RATIOS						
2.2	3.0	2.1	Current		2.1			1.8	2.4
1.5	1.6	1.5			1.2			1.3	1.6
1.1	1.2	1.1			1.1			1.1	1.2
1.2	1.0	1.0	Quick		.9			.6	1.1
.6	.6	.6			.7			.4	.8
.2	.3	.3			.1			.2	.4
(3) 134.0	(6) 63.8	(9) 40.9	Sales/Receivables		(4) 84.4			(7) 50.9	(10) 37.2
(15) 24.5	(16) 22.2	(17) 20.9			(14) 26.9			(16) 23.3	(19) 19.5
(27) 13.5	(26) 14.2	(34) 10.7			(32) 11.3			(27) 13.4	(28) 13.1
(29) 12.4	(31) 11.7	(31) 11.6	Cost of Sales/Inventory		(36) 10.1			(36) 10.1	(31) 11.6
(61) 6.0	(49) 7.4	(54) 6.8			(93) 3.9			(57) 6.4	(54) 6.8
(111) 3.3	(97) 3.8	(94) 3.9			(200) 1.8			(88) 4.2	(98) 3.7
(12) 31.2	(11) 31.8	(14) 25.8	Cost of Sales/Payables		(9) 40.2			(15) 23.9	(14) 26.6
(22) 16.6	(23) 15.7	(23) 16.1			(37) 9.8			(24) 15.1	(21) 17.1
(36) 10.2	(35) 10.4	(37) 9.8			(51) 7.2			(41) 8.9	(27) 13.4
5.7	6.3	6.9	Sales/Working Capital		7.4			9.9	6.1
13.6	11.3	12.0			9.7			18.8	10.9
72.0	35.3	45.9			79.3			57.1	36.4
16.5	11.6	10.9	EBIT/Interest		7.2			14.6	10.9
(77) 5.5	(85) 2.8	(94) 4.4			1.0			(44) 5.4	6.3
1.6	1.6	1.8			-3.8			2.0	2.0
9.3	8.1	19.7	Net Profit + Depr., Dep., Amort./Cur. Mat. L/T/D						7.8
(12) 2.5	(24) 3.4	(20) 5.8							(12) 4.7
1.7	1.9	2.3							2.3
.3	.4	.4	Fixed/Worth		.3			.5	.4
.7	1.2	.9			1.1			.8	1.0
2.3	260.0	1.9			19.5			1.0	2.2
.7	1.0	1.0	Debt/Worth		1.1			1.0	.6
1.7	3.0	2.1			8.3			1.9	2.1
7.1	291.0	6.8			21.4			3.0	6.8
45.2	49.4	59.9	% Profit Before Taxes/Tangible Net Worth					68.7	43.0
(77) 25.0	(72) 27.8	(86) 21.1						(25) 21.9	(42) 23.5
7.2	7.1	10.4						7.7	12.8
19.5	16.4	18.3	% Profit Before Taxes/Total Assets		10.0			20.8	19.0
8.0	4.6	7.3			.1			8.8	8.6
2.0	1.7	2.8			-8.6			2.5	3.8
27.0	23.5	17.2	Sales/Net Fixed Assets		17.2			22.5	13.9
12.4	10.5	9.0			7.8			11.7	8.6
5.5	5.3	5.0			3.9			7.6	4.8
3.6	3.1	3.0	Sales/Total Assets		2.5			3.6	2.7
2.3	2.2	2.3			1.8			3.0	2.2
1.7	1.6	1.6			.7			2.6	1.6
.8	.6	.8	% Depr., Dep., Amort./Sales		1.0			.7	.9
(72) 1.5	(89) 1.3	(95) 1.5			2.0			(48) 1.4	1.4
2.4	2.5	2.6			3.5			2.3	2.5
1.5	1.1	.9	% Officers', Directors', Owners' Comp/Sales						
(34) 2.5	(30) 2.0	(22) 1.8							
4.3	4.1	3.8							
3780920M	4023962M	4504086M	Net Sales ($)	1582M	24084M	12439M	50955M	432923M	3982103M
1915161M	1910455M	2289436M	Total Assets ($)	2302M	20662M	9776M	25614M	160504M	2070578M

M = $ thousand   MM = $ million
See Pages 11 through 21 for Explanation of Ratios and Data

Current Data Sorted by Assets   Comparative Historical Data

0-500M	500M-2MM	2-10MM	10-50MM	50-100MM	100-250MM	Type of Statement	4/1/02-3/31/03 ALL	4/1/03-3/31/04 ALL
		1	2		1	Unqualified	3	7
		4	1			Reviewed	4	3
		6				Compiled	4	9
	4					Tax Returns	3	2
1	3	7	2	1	2	Other	13	12
	7 (4/1-9/30/06)		28 (10/1/06-3/31/07)					
1	7	18	5	1	3	**NUMBER OF STATEMENTS**	27	33
%	%	%	%	%	%	**ASSETS**	%	%
		8.1				Cash & Equivalents	7.7	7.7
		15.4				Trade Receivables (net)	19.7	16.9
		52.6				Inventory	43.4	50.4
		2.4				All Other Current	1.8	3.8
		78.4				Total Current	72.4	78.8
		15.6				Fixed Assets (net)	18.5	13.5
		1.4				Intangibles (net)	3.9	5.4
		4.6				All Other Non-Current	5.2	2.2
		100.0				Total	100.0	100.0
						LIABILITIES		
		18.3				Notes Payable-Short Term	21.2	21.8
		7.9				Cur. Mat.-L.T.D.	3.0	2.3
		16.1				Trade Payables	16.0	18.1
		.1				Income Taxes Payable	.3	.2
		8.6				All Other Current	15.7	15.6
		50.9				Total Current	56.2	58.0
		10.5				Long-Term Debt	17.3	11.6
		.1				Deferred Taxes	.1	.0
		8.0				All Other Non-Current	5.4	3.0
		30.5				Net Worth	21.1	27.4
		100.0				Total Liabilities & Net Worth	100.0	100.0
						INCOME DATA		
		100.0				Net Sales	100.0	100.0
		35.8				Gross Profit	33.2	28.6
		30.1				Operating Expenses	29.7	29.1
		5.7				Operating Profit	3.4	-.5
		1.7				All Other Expenses (net)	.4	.8
		4.0				Profit Before Taxes	3.0	-1.2
						RATIOS		
		3.0				Current	1.8	1.7
		1.9					1.4	1.4
		1.3					1.1	1.0
		1.1				Quick	.9	.7
		.5					.6	.5
		.2					.3	.1
		6 62.2				Sales/Receivables	7 50.5	3 108.1
		16 22.3					31 11.8	25 14.7
		37 10.0					42 8.8	44 8.2
		80 4.6				Cost of Sales/Inventory	57 6.4	66 5.5
		108 3.4					104 3.5	101 3.6
		147 2.5					145 2.5	142 2.6
		14 26.6				Cost of Sales/Payables	13 28.9	11 33.1
		29 12.7					26 13.8	20 18.3
		41 8.9					61 6.0	64 5.7
		5.4				Sales/Working Capital	7.1	5.8
		7.9					13.5	17.4
		14.9					28.9	73.2
		25.5				EBIT/Interest	15.2	8.6
		5.1					(25) 8.1	(29) 5.2
		1.4					1.7	-.3
						Net Profit + Depr., Dep., Amort./Cur. Mat. L/T/D		
		.1				Fixed/Worth	.2	.1
		.4					.7	.4
		2.1					3.0	-12.3
		.5				Debt/Worth	1.4	1.3
		1.8					3.0	3.5
		10.7					11.2	-43.4
		73.7				% Profit Before Taxes/Tangible Net Worth	62.7	50.4
		(15) 30.6					(21) 39.8	(24) 12.6
		9.5					23.0	-10.2
		23.6				% Profit Before Taxes/Total Assets	17.9	15.9
		12.4					10.9	2.3
		1.5					2.8	-7.5
		93.0				Sales/Net Fixed Assets	71.7	68.2
		38.0					16.4	27.3
		10.7					7.8	12.6
		3.5				Sales/Total Assets	3.4	3.8
		2.9					2.4	2.4
		2.0					1.7	1.6
		.5				% Depr., Dep., Amort./Sales	.5	.6
		(16) .9					(24) 1.0	(26) 1.4
		3.4					3.3	2.2
						% Officers', Directors' Owners' Comp/Sales		2.3
								(15) 4.0
								6.3
1202M	31832M	274190M	316076M	39182M	444871M	Net Sales ($)	1921387M	1356278M
362M	9293M	98895M	117416M	62107M	413714M	Total Assets ($)	846433M	684804M

M = $ thousand   MM = $ million
See Pages 11 through 21 for Explanation of Ratios and Data

Comparative Historical Data | Current Data Sorted by Sales

Note: For the current data columns, the categories 0-1MM, 1-3MM, 3-5MM and 5-10MM are marked "DATA NOT AVAILABLE" in the Assets, Liabilities and Income Data sections (too few statements to publish). Ratio, dollar and statement-count data for those columns are shown where printed.

	4/1/04-3/31/05 ALL	4/1/05-3/31/06 ALL	4/1/06-3/31/07 ALL	Type of Statement	0-1MM	1-3MM	3-5MM	5-10MM	10-25MM	25MM & OVER
	5	4	4	Unqualified				2	1	3
	3	5	5	Reviewed				1	2	1
	2	1	6	Compiled			3	1	5	
	6		4	Tax Returns		1	4	2		
	11	10	16	Other						
					7 (4/1-9/30/06)			28 (10/1/06-3/31/07)		
	27	20	35	**NUMBER OF STATEMENTS**		1	7	6	11	10
	%	%	%	**ASSETS**	%	%	%	%	%	%
	3.2	7.1	9.7	Cash & Equivalents					10.0	5.4
	17.5	20.9	16.5	Trade Receivables (net)					19.6	22.4
	52.9	42.3	45.9	Inventory					52.2	34.7
	1.1	1.6	1.8	All Other Current					3.5	1.7
	74.8	71.9	74.0	Total Current					85.3	64.2
	16.7	17.5	15.4	Fixed Assets (net)					10.6	16.7
	4.8	7.9	5.9	Intangibles (net)					1.1	16.8
	3.7	2.6	4.7	All Other Non-Current					3.0	2.3
	100.0	100.0	100.0	Total					100.0	100.0
				LIABILITIES						
	28.4	22.9	18.8	Notes Payable-Short Term					19.0	11.1
	2.4	2.6	6.2	Cur. Mat.-L.T.D.					10.2	3.5
	19.1	13.6	16.5	Trade Payables					22.7	9.3
	.3	.1	.1	Income Taxes Payable					.1	.1
	6.5	9.0	13.1	All Other Current					10.6	13.9
	56.6	48.2	54.6	Total Current					62.6	37.9
	15.6	14.1	13.5	Long-Term Debt					6.2	15.8
	.1	.1	.6	Deferred Taxes					.1	1.9
	3.2	9.5	12.5	All Other Non-Current					.6	15.4
	24.5	28.2	18.9	Net Worth					30.5	28.9
	100.0	100.0	100.0	Total Liabilities & Net Worth					100.0	100.0
				INCOME DATA						
	100.0	100.0	100.0	Net Sales					100.0	100.0
	33.7	33.8	33.5	Gross Profit					33.6	30.4
	30.3	26.1	28.0	Operating Expenses					29.0	22.8
	3.4	7.7	5.5	Operating Profit					4.6	7.7
	1.4	1.3	2.0	All Other Expenses (net)					1.0	3.1
	2.0	6.4	3.5	Profit Before Taxes					3.6	4.6
				RATIOS						
	2.1	2.2	2.6	Current					3.3	3.0
	1.4	1.6	1.6						1.4	1.7
	1.1	1.2	1.1						1.2	1.4
	.6	1.3	1.0	Quick					1.1	1.3
	.4	.6	.5						.5	.8
	.1	.3	.2						.2	.4
	9 41.6	9 41.0	8 45.7	Sales/Receivables					9 38.7	25 14.7
	31 11.8	29 12.7	23 15.8						26 14.3	41 8.9
	50 7.3	50 7.3	42 8.7						42 8.7	60 6.1
	81 4.5	46 8.0	61 6.0	Cost of Sales/Inventory					80 4.6	57 6.4
	118 3.1	112 3.3	98 3.7						98 3.7	76 4.8
	192 1.9	167 2.2	148 2.5						142 2.6	127 2.9
	12 30.8	10 36.1	15 24.0	Cost of Sales/Payables					16 23.2	8 43.4
	26 14.2	24 15.5	30 12.2						37 9.9	26 13.8
	72 5.1	41 8.8	51 7.1						108 3.4	32 11.4
	5.4	5.9	5.4	Sales/Working Capital					5.4	3.9
	9.1	10.3	8.3						7.5	8.6
	86.4	16.1	39.7						16.6	24.9
	7.8	9.3	9.7	EBIT/Interest					88.6	
	(26) 3.3	(18) 3.0	(33) 2.4						3.4	
	1.1	2.0	1.4						1.4	
			8.1	Net Profit + Depr., Dep., Amort./Cur. Mat. L/T/D						
			(10) 1.8							
			.6							
	.1	.3	.2	Fixed/Worth					.1	.4
	.4	.4	.5						.2	NM
	6.4	NM	-13.8						.4	-1.8
	1.5	1.1	.9	Debt/Worth					.5	.9
	2.2	3.4	4.0						2.9	NM
	12.8	NM	-185.6						4.3	-13.4
	44.3	89.9	74.0	% Profit Before Taxes/Tangible Net Worth					68.3	
	(21) 30.1	(15) 22.3	(25) 30.6						(10) 25.0	
	5.2	11.4	16.8						9.2	
	15.8	19.5	17.0	% Profit Before Taxes/Total Assets					22.9	12.0
	5.9	8.7	7.7						6.2	5.4
	2.0	2.9	1.9						1.9	2.7
	52.7	36.1	57.6	Sales/Net Fixed Assets					94.3	32.2
	26.4	17.3	27.2						44.8	16.3
	7.7	9.5	10.8						13.1	6.1
	3.2	3.7	3.6	Sales/Total Assets					3.4	3.6
	2.0	2.1	2.6						3.2	1.7
	1.7	1.4	1.7						2.3	1.0
	.6	.6	.5	% Depr., Dep., Amort./Sales					.2	
	(22) 1.2	(18) 1.2	(31) .9						.7	
	2.6	2.4	3.0						1.0	
			1.7	% Officers', Directors' Owners' Comp/Sales						
		(15) 3.6								
			6.5							
	1422895M	611284M	1107353M	Net Sales ($)		1202M	26949M	43780M	199957M	835465M
	760739M	386920M	701787M	Total Assets ($)		362M	11623M	20197M	77200M	592405M

M = $ thousand   MM = $ million
See Pages 11 through 21 for Explanation of Ratios and Data

Current Data Sorted by Assets   Comparative Historical Data

Type of Statement	0-500M	500M-2MM	2-10MM	10-50MM	50-100MM	100-250MM	4/1/02-3/31/03 ALL	4/1/03-3/31/04 ALL
Unqualified		2	2	4	2		12	8
Reviewed		1	5	2			7	12
Compiled		5	3	1			8	12
Tax Returns	3	6	1			1	5	9
Other	5	3	6	7	2		17	24
		10 (4/1-9/30/06)		51 (10/1/06-3/31/07)				
NUMBER OF STATEMENTS	8	17	17	14	4	1	49	65
	%	%	%	%	%	%	%	%
ASSETS								
Cash & Equivalents		8.0	5.2	5.1			9.1	9.4
Trade Receivables (net)		17.5	28.0	26.0			22.8	24.2
Inventory		47.2	39.5	36.2			34.5	29.0
All Other Current		1.4	3.1	2.2			3.3	2.6
Total Current		74.2	75.9	69.5			69.7	65.2
Fixed Assets (net)		12.6	16.9	22.2			19.3	24.8
Intangibles (net)		7.4	2.3	4.7			4.4	3.9
All Other Non-Current		5.9	4.9	3.7			6.6	6.1
Total		100.0	100.0	100.0			100.0	100.0
LIABILITIES								
Notes Payable-Short Term		20.6	21.9	15.9			15.3	16.2
Cur. Mat.-L.T.D.		6.3	3.7	2.2			4.9	4.8
Trade Payables		13.6	16.7	14.9			15.1	17.8
Income Taxes Payable		.0	.0	.0			.3	.2
All Other Current		8.9	7.7	12.9			11.4	9.1
Total Current		49.4	50.0	45.8			46.9	48.1
Long-Term Debt		15.3	8.3	11.1			17.8	21.8
Deferred Taxes		.1	.0	.3			.2	.2
All Other Non-Current		12.0	11.3	4.1			5.7	9.9
Net Worth		23.2	30.5	38.7			29.4	19.9
Total Liabilties & Net Worth		100.0	100.0	100.0			100.0	100.0
INCOME DATA								
Net Sales		100.0	100.0	100.0			100.0	100.0
Gross Profit		31.7	28.8	24.1			28.0	27.3
Operating Expenses		28.9	22.6	16.8			22.3	25.5
Operating Profit		2.8	6.3	7.3			5.6	1.8
All Other Expenses (net)		1.1	1.5	1.3			2.4	1.4
Profit Before Taxes		1.7	4.8	6.0			3.3	.4
RATIOS								
Current		2.7	1.9	2.6			2.9	2.1
		1.5	1.4	1.4			1.6	1.4
		.9	1.2	1.0			1.0	1.0
Quick		1.4	.9	1.7			1.0	1.1
		.4	.6	.7			.7	.7
		.3	.3	.4			.4	.4
Sales/Receivables		5 71.4	16 23.5	30 12.1			15 24.8	13 27.2
		21 17.1	38 9.6	40 9.1			31 11.8	30 12.4
		51 7.1	53 6.9	51 7.1			52 7.0	46 8.0
Cost of Sales/Inventory		47 7.7	33 11.0	55 6.6			31 11.9	20 18.1
		71 5.1	84 4.3	79 4.6			70 5.2	50 7.3
		123 3.0	148 2.5	99 3.7			123 3.0	100 3.6
Cost of Sales/Payables		4 93.2	16 22.8	14 26.0			17 21.8	17 21.3
		22 16.5	28 13.0	31 11.7			25 14.5	30 12.1
		62 5.9	49 7.5	42 8.7			40 9.1	42 8.8
Sales/Working Capital		6.9	6.2	4.7			5.5	7.2
		9.3	9.7	18.5			14.3	20.7
		-83.6	16.8	NM			529.2	-134.0
EBIT/Interest		16.6	9.9	10.7			10.2	5.5
		(15) 2.7	(16) 4.3	(13) 2.3			(46) 2.2	(58) 2.0
		-1.7	2.0	1.3			1.0	.8
Net Profit + Depr., Dep., Amort./Cur. Mat. L/T/D							8.2	8.1
							(11) 4.1	(18) .9
							.5	.0
Fixed/Worth		.1	.1	.2			.2	.5
		1.1	.5	.5			.7	1.0
		-1.2	1.3	3.9			2.6	-2.6
Debt/Worth		.9	1.4	.9			1.0	1.2
		5.1	2.2	1.7			2.6	4.3
		-7.3	4.0	8.3			10.0	-9.6
% Profit Before Taxes/Tangible Net Worth		62.4	71.5	62.2			71.9	46.3
		(12) 22.4	(16) 32.0	(12) 20.3			(40) 30.9	(44) 18.4
		16.1	8.8	5.7			3.9	5.8
% Profit Before Taxes/Total Assets		22.6	19.6	14.8			19.5	11.8
		4.1	11.9	7.0			6.8	4.2
		-5.6	2.5	1.4			.5	-1.4
Sales/Net Fixed Assets		103.2	52.1	43.1			42.5	30.2
		27.3	21.0	14.8			16.3	15.2
		16.0	11.1	5.2			9.9	6.5
Sales/Total Assets		3.5	3.5	2.8			3.5	4.2
		2.8	2.4	1.9			2.6	2.6
		1.8	1.9	1.5			1.8	2.1
% Depr., Dep., Amort./Sales		.3	.7	.8			.6	.7
		(12) .4	(16) 1.1	(11) 1.0			(43) 1.2	(56) 1.5
		2.5	1.7	2.1			3.0	3.3
% Officers', Directors' Owners' Comp/Sales							1.6	2.2
							(15) 3.7	(29) 5.6
							4.9	8.7
Net Sales ($)	10849M	53022M	226432M	653526M	678389M	488350M	1195012M	1516226M
Total Assets ($)	2257M	19015M	84444M	288883M	298939M	202782M	571390M	747176M

M = $ thousand   MM = $ million
See Pages 11 through 21 for Explanation of Ratios and Data

Comparative Historical Data / Current Data Sorted by Sales

	4/1/04-3/31/05 ALL	4/1/05-3/31/06 ALL	4/1/06-3/31/07 ALL	Type of Statement	0-1MM	1-3MM 10 (4/1-9/30/06)	3-5MM	5-10MM	10-25MM 51 (10/1/06-3/31/07)	25MM & OVER
	2	9	10	Unqualified		1	1	1		6
	4	7	8	Reviewed		1	1	3	1	3
	12	7	9	Compiled	1	5	3	2	1	1
	13	10	11	Tax Returns		5	3	2	2	
	29	23	23	Other	2		1	1	9	5
	60	**56**	**61**	**NUMBER OF STATEMENTS**	**3**	**12**	**9**	**9**	**13**	**15**
	%	%	%	**ASSETS**	%	%	%	%	%	%
	10.4	7.8	6.8	Cash & Equivalents		7.9			8.5	3.2
	26.2	20.4	23.2	Trade Receivables (net)		24.2			23.5	25.3
	32.4	42.1	41.2	Inventory		36.9			36.7	42.6
	3.1	2.2	2.7	All Other Current		.4			2.2	4.8
	72.0	72.6	73.9	Total Current		69.4			71.0	75.9
	20.4	18.5	17.9	Fixed Assets (net)		18.7			23.1	15.8
	4.7	4.4	3.9	Intangibles (net)		4.5			1.2	4.4
	2.9	4.4	4.3	All Other Non-Current		7.4			4.8	3.8
	100.0	100.0	100.0	Total		100.0			100.0	100.0
				LIABILITIES						
	16.5	15.1	19.3	Notes Payable-Short Term		9.1			16.0	23.4
	3.3	4.9	4.0	Cur. Mat.-L.T.D.		6.9			2.1	3.7
	17.3	14.8	15.9	Trade Payables		23.0			15.5	15.6
	.4	.3	.0	Income Taxes Payable		.0			.0	.0
	11.1	15.1	9.7	All Other Current		6.7			9.5	10.9
	48.6	50.2	48.8	Total Current		45.7			43.1	53.6
	14.0	14.6	12.4	Long-Term Debt		25.6			13.3	6.8
	.3	.1	.1	Deferred Taxes		.2			.1	.2
	10.8	13.9	13.8	All Other Non-Current		19.1			12.3	8.2
	26.3	21.2	24.9	Net Worth		9.5			31.1	31.3
	100.0	100.0	100.0	Total Liabilities & Net Worth		100.0			100.0	100.0
				INCOME DATA						
	100.0	100.0	100.0	Net Sales		100.0			100.0	100.0
	29.0	27.6	29.0	Gross Profit		40.5			28.4	17.8
	24.1	24.9	23.4	Operating Expenses		32.1			20.5	13.6
	4.9	2.7	5.6	Operating Profit		8.4			7.9	4.3
	1.7	.8	1.4	All Other Expenses (net)		2.1			1.2	1.4
	3.1	1.8	4.2	Profit Before Taxes		6.3			6.7	2.8
				RATIOS						
	2.3	2.2	2.4			2.7			2.4	2.3
	1.5	1.5	1.5	Current		1.6			1.6	1.2
	1.1	1.1	1.1			1.1			1.2	1.1
	1.3	1.0	1.3			1.4			1.7	1.0
	(59) .7	(55) .6	.6	Quick		.5			.6	.6
	.4	.4	.3			.4			.4	.3
	18 19.8	12 30.2	12 31.3		2 190.2				16 22.3	21 17.5
	35 10.5	33 11.2	30 12.2	Sales/Receivables	28 13.1				38 9.7	30 12.1
	49 7.4	42 8.6	48 7.6		53 6.9				45 8.2	48 7.6
	24 15.1	40 9.1	41 9.0		42 8.7				35 10.4	45 8.1
	60 6.1	90 4.1	72 5.0	Cost of Sales/Inventory	70 5.2				76 4.8	74 4.9
	113 3.2	160 2.3	123 3.0		115 3.2				150 2.4	100 3.6
	15 24.0	11 34.3	12 31.2		19 19.4				17 22.0	10 37.1
	32 11.5	22 16.8	30 12.2	Cost of Sales/Payables	33 10.9				30 12.2	19 19.7
	44 8.2	38 9.6	45 8.1		65 5.6				44 8.3	40 9.1
	5.4	5.5	6.7			8.1			5.1	6.7
	11.7	9.9	11.2	Sales/Working Capital		10.4			8.9	20.2
	39.9	26.7	38.6			112.3			23.7	39.9
	21.1	12.0	9.9			6.2			14.2	5.6
	(50) 3.8	(49) 3.0	(56) 3.4	EBIT/Interest	(11) 3.6				(12) 6.5	(14) 2.3
	1.3	1.4	1.7			2.0			1.9	1.1
	16.4			Net Profit + Depr., Dep.,						
	(13) 3.0			Amort./Cur. Mat. L/T/D						
	.6									
	.2	.2	.2			.6			.2	.2
	.5	.6	.7	Fixed/Worth		1.3			.9	.4
	2.4	3.7	3.5			-.9			2.5	1.4
	.6	.8	1.2			2.7			1.1	.9
	2.1	1.9	3.1	Debt/Worth		7.8			1.8	3.3
	19.6	28.7	16.7			-6.5			5.3	18.3
	52.6	48.2	70.0	% Profit Before Taxes/Tangible					66.7	61.2
	(48) 27.7	(46) 22.8	(51) 30.6	Net Worth					(12) 20.6	(13) 22.8
	13.6	10.4	15.7						8.8	5.2
	16.9	14.9	20.7	% Profit Before Taxes/Total		32.3			27.6	15.3
	6.5	5.5	8.2	Assets		11.5			6.3	5.0
	2.4	2.0	1.6			3.5			2.2	1.4
	43.4	47.0	58.9			39.0			41.2	57.3
	17.5	18.2	21.0	Sales/Net Fixed Assets		18.8			20.5	19.2
	7.2	7.6	9.6			8.5			6.5	9.4
	3.7	3.6	3.5			6.5			3.5	3.3
	2.5	2.5	2.4	Sales/Total Assets		2.9			2.1	2.4
	1.8	1.5	1.8			1.8			1.7	1.9
	.5	.6	.5						.6	.6
	(50) 1.2	(52) 1.1	(50) .9	% Depr., Dep., Amort./Sales					(11) .8	(13) 1.0
	2.4	1.8	1.8						2.0	1.6
	2.7	1.9	2.1	% Officers', Directors'						
	(21) 5.2	(12) 2.1	(20) 4.7	Owners' Comp/Sales						
	7.6	10.2	7.9							
	1306228M	1790733M	2110568M	Net Sales ($)	1968M	18948M	34991M	77688M	224138M	1752835M
	704071M	705293M	896320M	Total Assets ($)	1450M	7339M	10643M	37456M	107959M	731473M

© RMA 2007

M = $ thousand   MM = $ million
See Pages 11 through 21 for Explanation of Ratios and Data

Current Data Sorted by Assets | Comparative Historical Data

Type of Statement

	0-500M	500M-2MM	2-10MM	10-50MM	50-100MM	100-250MM		4/1/02-3/31/03 ALL	4/1/03-3/31/04 ALL
Unqualified			5	8		5		20	16
Reviewed	1	9	26	6				29	39
Compiled	3	21	10	3	3	1		49	60
Tax Returns	20	27	5	1	2	3		38	46
Other	7	27	32	9				46	59
	42 (4/1-9/30/06)			192 (10/1/06-3/31/07)					
NUMBER OF STATEMENTS	31	84	78	27	5	9		182	220

	%	%	%	%	%	%		%	%
ASSETS									
Cash & Equivalents	14.0	8.7	8.6	9.5				9.3	8.9
Trade Receivables (net)	20.1	31.5	31.7	22.8				24.4	28.7
Inventory	17.2	19.0	21.3	21.3				23.5	20.0
All Other Current	2.0	2.0	2.2	3.0				2.2	2.8
Total Current	53.3	61.2	63.8	56.5				59.5	60.4
Fixed Assets (net)	41.2	31.1	28.5	34.5				33.1	31.6
Intangibles (net)	1.4	2.7	2.0	6.0				2.0	2.2
All Other Non-Current	4.2	5.0	5.7	3.0				5.5	5.8
Total	100.0	100.0	100.0	100.0				100.0	100.0
LIABILITIES									
Notes Payable-Short Term	16.3	7.8	11.3	8.6				11.7	11.1
Cur. Mat.-L.T.D.	4.9	3.1	5.6	3.6				4.9	4.8
Trade Payables	16.1	14.7	13.1	10.3				15.1	14.9
Income Taxes Payable	.5	.2	.3	.2				.3	.3
All Other Current	12.6	21.3	11.5	11.3				12.4	12.7
Total Current	50.4	47.1	41.7	33.9				44.4	43.8
Long-Term Debt	31.6	24.8	16.2	14.4				19.1	21.0
Deferred Taxes	.0	.2	.5	.5				.2	.5
All Other Non-Current	4.1	6.6	5.4	13.4				4.3	7.4
Net Worth	13.9	21.3	36.2	37.7				31.9	27.3
Total Liabilities & Net Worth	100.0	100.0	100.0	100.0				100.0	100.0
INCOME DATA									
Net Sales	100.0	100.0	100.0	100.0				100.0	100.0
Gross Profit	45.9	33.1	31.0	29.4				35.1	35.2
Operating Expenses	42.4	28.7	27.1	25.0				30.6	31.4
Operating Profit	3.6	4.4	3.9	4.4				4.5	3.7
All Other Expenses (net)	.6	1.3	.8	1.5				.9	.9
Profit Before Taxes	3.0	3.1	3.1	2.9				3.6	2.8

RATIOS

	0-500M	500M-2MM	2-10MM	10-50MM	50-100MM	100-250MM		4/1/02-3/31/03 ALL	4/1/03-3/31/04 ALL
Current	3.2	3.3	2.8	2.3				2.3	2.3
	1.4	1.4	1.5	1.8				1.5	1.4
	.6	.9	1.1	1.3				1.0	1.0
Quick	2.0	2.1	1.7	1.4				1.6	1.3
	1.0	1.0	1.1	1.0				.8	.9
	.4	.4	.5	.7				.4	.5
Sales/Receivables	0 UND	23 15.8	24 15.0	21 17.3				12 29.4	18 19.9
	10 35.3	34 10.7	34 10.8	33 11.2				28 13.1	33 10.9
	41 8.9	50 7.3	58 6.3	55 6.7				44 8.2	47 7.7
Cost of Sales/Inventory	5 75.2	10 34.8	18 20.0	26 14.0				17 20.9	15 24.7
	13 27.3	27 13.3	36 10.2	41 8.9				30 12.0	31 11.7
	37 10.0	52 7.1	53 6.9	77 4.7				61 6.0	50 7.3
Cost of Sales/Payables	0 UND	10 34.9	9 40.3	7 49.0				11 34.1	13 27.7
	9 41.5	20 18.7	19 19.1	16 23.5				23 15.9	24 15.4
	38 9.7	37 9.9	39 9.4	28 13.0				38 9.7	40 9.1
Sales/Working Capital	11.0	6.3	7.0	6.3				8.1	8.9
	98.8	16.7	14.2	10.7				16.4	18.9
	-26.4	-49.0	160.3	20.1				-554.4	189.2
EBIT/Interest	13.0	19.4	17.6	15.8				12.2	10.6
	(23) 4.3	(71) 4.9	(74) 4.5	(25) 7.7				(164) 3.9	(197) 3.5
	1.0	1.5	1.6	2.1				1.5	.9
Net Profit + Depr., Dep., Amort./Cur. Mat. L/T/D		7.5	3.4					5.6	7.3
		(11) 2.8	(15) 2.4					(37) 2.5	(47) 3.6
		.7	1.2					1.2	1.4
Fixed/Worth	.5	.3	.3	.6				.3	.4
	2.4	1.1	.8	.8				1.0	1.2
	-1.7	9.8	2.5	1.5				3.2	4.9
Debt/Worth	.7	.6	.6	.7				.7	.9
	2.4	2.5	1.7	1.3				2.2	2.3
	-6.5	39.2	6.5	3.6				7.6	13.5
% Profit Before Taxes/Tangible Net Worth	223.0	72.3	52.8	46.7				51.1	53.0
	(19) 32.9	(64) 41.3	(67) 23.5	(25) 21.1				(157) 24.1	(177) 20.9
	8.0	10.5	8.2	-1.3				7.7	3.7
% Profit Before Taxes/Total Assets	32.8	24.7	22.2	22.5				20.8	15.7
	9.8	7.3	7.8	9.2				7.1	6.3
	.0	1.1	1.8	.2				1.7	-.3
Sales/Net Fixed Assets	59.0	31.3	17.7	12.2				26.1	23.9
	14.4	11.4	12.4	8.4				11.0	11.7
	7.1	5.8	7.9	4.8				5.5	5.9
Sales/Total Assets	8.5	4.0	3.7	3.0				4.0	4.1
	4.0	3.1	3.0	2.5				3.0	3.0
	2.9	2.1	2.3	2.1				2.2	2.2
% Depr., Dep., Amort./Sales	.7	.9	1.2	1.5				1.0	1.3
	(22) 2.1	(67) 1.8	(72) 1.9	(23) 1.8				(161) 1.8	(186) 2.3
	3.0	3.4	2.6	2.5				3.5	3.3
% Officers', Directors', Owners' Comp/Sales	4.4	2.2	1.5	.8				2.6	1.9
	(20) 7.8	(45) 3.7	(29) 2.5	(10) 1.8				(92) 5.1	(118) 4.1
	10.8	7.6	5.9	2.8				8.4	7.1
Net Sales ($)	47994M	290942M	1060856M	1524008M	748484M	4111093M		5548249M	5475480M
Total Assets ($)	8138M	93718M	347153M	640524M	339551M	1434296M		1677675M	1927569M

M = $ thousand   MM = $ million
See Pages 11 through 21 for Explanation of Ratios and Data

Comparative Historical Data | | | | Current Data Sorted by Sales

4/1/04-3/31/05 ALL	4/1/05-3/31/06 ALL	4/1/06-3/31/07 ALL	Type of Statement	0-1MM	1-3MM	3-5MM	5-10MM	10-25MM	25MM & OVER
21	22	21	Unqualified	5	3	7	14	3	18
44	32	42	Reviewed		9	8	9	10	8
66	45	37	Compiled	13	17	12	8	4	2
52	46	54	Tax Returns					2	2
65	55	80	Other	4	20	9	17	12	18
				42 (4/1-9/30/06)			192 (10/1/06-3/31/07)		
248	200	234	**NUMBER OF STATEMENTS**	22	49	36	48	31	48
%	%	%	**ASSETS**	%	%	%	%	%	%
8.3	9.2	9.2	Cash & Equivalents	11.0	7.5	10.7	8.5	10.0	9.0
28.9	27.1	28.5	Trade Receivables (net)	15.6	27.3	32.5	35.5	29.0	25.2
21.4	21.0	20.3	Inventory	15.1	17.2	21.6	18.2	22.9	25.3
2.3	2.4	2.1	All Other Current	2.4	2.7	1.2	2.3	1.5	2.4
60.9	59.6	60.1	Total Current	44.1	54.7	66.1	64.5	63.4	61.8
30.7	31.3	31.9	Fixed Assets (net)	44.6	36.7	27.2	29.2	27.4	30.4
2.7	3.2	3.2	Intangibles (net)	4.0	3.4	1.2	1.7	3.9	5.3
5.7	5.8	4.8	All Other Non-Current	7.3	5.2	5.5	4.6	5.4	2.6
100.0	100.0	100.0	Total	100.0	100.0	100.0	100.0	100.0	100.0
			LIABILITIES						
10.2	12.2	10.3	Notes Payable-Short Term	13.2	7.7	7.6	15.1	10.4	8.8
4.9	4.2	4.2	Cur. Mat.-L.T.D.	3.0	3.9	4.5	4.5	6.3	3.1
14.9	15.3	13.5	Trade Payables	8.9	16.9	13.0	14.8	13.6	11.1
.4	.2	.2	Income Taxes Payable	.7	.1	.2	.1	.4	.2
14.3	13.7	15.0	All Other Current	27.2	16.7	12.3	15.9	11.4	11.4
44.7	45.6	43.3	Total Current	53.1	45.4	37.6	50.4	42.1	34.7
20.0	19.1	21.0	Long-Term Debt	47.6	29.6	16.4	16.1	15.9	11.9
.3	.4	.4	Deferred Taxes	.0	.2	.8	.2	.1	.6
7.6	7.4	6.6	All Other Non-Current	2.9	5.8	7.1	7.3	6.2	8.4
27.3	27.5	28.7	Net Worth	-3.5	18.9	38.1	25.9	35.7	44.5
100.0	100.0	100.0	Total Liabilties & Net Worth	100.0	100.0	100.0	100.0	100.0	100.0
			INCOME DATA						
100.0	100.0	100.0	Net Sales	100.0	100.0	100.0	100.0	100.0	100.0
34.8	34.4	33.1	Gross Profit	42.6	38.2	33.7	30.0	33.4	26.3
30.9	30.4	28.9	Operating Expenses	42.1	33.8	28.5	26.0	28.4	21.6
3.9	4.0	4.2	Operating Profit	.5	4.4	5.2	4.0	5.0	4.6
.8	.8	1.1	All Other Expenses (net)	2.5	1.2	.2	1.0	1.5	1.0
3.1	3.2	3.1	Profit Before Taxes	-2.0	3.2	5.0	3.1	3.5	3.6
			RATIOS						
2.4	2.2	2.9		3.0	3.2	3.6	1.9	2.8	2.5
1.5	1.3	1.6	Current	.9	1.4	2.2	1.4	1.9	1.9
1.0	1.0	1.0		.5	.8	1.0	1.0	1.1	1.3
1.5	1.3	1.8		2.3	2.0	2.8	1.4	1.6	1.4
(247) .9	.8	1.0	Quick	.7	.9	1.4	1.0	1.0	.9
.5	.5	.5		.2	.4	.5	.5	.5	.7
16 23.1	16 23.1	19 18.9		0 UND	20 17.8	21 17.2	23 16.2	21 17.3	19 19.7
32 11.5	31 11.9	33 11.2	Sales/Receivables	16 22.4	32 11.5	40 9.1	38 9.6	30 12.2	31 11.7
49 7.4	47 7.8	51 7.1		56 6.5	49 7.4	52 7.0	54 6.7	52 7.0	42 8.6
12 30.1	12 29.2	14 26.8		2 163.3	8 46.6	12 31.4	12 30.9	21 17.5	29 12.7
32 11.6	32 11.3	32 11.3	Cost of Sales/Inventory	15 25.1	26 14.0	33 11.2	27 13.7	39 9.5	42 8.8
58 6.3	56 6.5	54 6.8		52 7.0	50 7.3	65 5.6	50 7.3	57 6.4	54 6.8
10 35.5	9 39.2	9 41.7		0 UND	9 39.6	10 38.3	9 39.6	8 48.3	8 46.3
23 15.6	21 17.4	18 20.0	Cost of Sales/Payables	8 47.1	20 18.6	18 19.7	20 18.0	21 17.5	14 25.9
41 8.9	38 9.5	37 10.0		42 8.7	46 7.9	35 10.4	36 10.0	38 9.7	27 13.7
9.0	8.6	7.0		11.0	5.9	5.4	9.5	7.1	7.1
16.4	19.8	14.5	Sales/Working Capital	UND	17.7	8.7	15.4	14.5	11.1
-135.2	-140.5	623.3		-4.9	-28.1	567.3	596.9	152.3	19.9
12.4	12.5	16.7		5.6	9.0	28.5	9.8	17.3	18.0
(210) 3.6	(180) 3.9	(207) 4.9	EBIT/Interest	(15) 1.9	(44) 4.4	(31) 11.3	(41) 3.1	4.3	(45) 8.6
1.0	1.2	1.6		-.5	1.1	2.0	1.2	1.7	2.3
4.7	8.1	11.9							16.6
(44) 3.1	(30) 3.1	(44) 3.1	Net Profit + Depr., Dep., Amort./Cur. Mat. L/T/D					(18)	8.1
1.1	1.1	1.2							2.5
.4	.4	.4		1.0	.4	.2	.5	.3	.5
1.0	1.1	1.0	Fixed/Worth	3.3	1.9	.7	1.0	.8	.7
5.2	6.9	4.1		-1.0	-39.6	2.9	6.5	3.4	1.1
.9	.8	.6		.6	.9	.5	1.1	.7	.6
2.5	2.3	1.9	Debt/Worth	7.3	3.3	1.6	2.4	1.8	1.2
14.6	15.7	12.6		-3.2	-9.7	10.6	11.3	31.8	3.0
64.7	58.6	60.8		71.5	72.7	65.5	44.2	52.9	52.6
(196) 27.5	(155) 30.3	(187) 28.3	% Profit Before Taxes/Tangible Net Worth	(12) 30.6	(35) 32.0	(31) 41.3	(38) 22.0	(26) 22.5	(45) 34.6
5.2	6.6	8.1		10.0	8.0	20.5	-.4	9.6	7.5
18.6	21.0	23.4		21.4	27.1	26.1	16.0	27.7	27.5
6.7	7.2	8.2	% Profit Before Taxes/Total Assets	5.1	8.3	9.7	4.8	8.3	13.0
.0	.8	1.6		-15.6	-2.0	3.3	-1.7	2.6	2.6
24.4	24.6	23.1		20.6	21.7	38.2	30.1	40.2	15.4
12.3	11.4	10.7	Sales/Net Fixed Assets	7.9	9.3	14.1	14.8	11.5	10.1
6.4	6.7	6.0		3.3	4.2	6.6	8.3	8.2	6.3
4.0	4.1	3.8		3.4	3.7	4.2	4.2	3.8	3.5
3.0	3.1	3.0	Sales/Total Assets	2.6	2.7	3.2	3.2	3.4	2.9
2.3	2.3	2.2		1.6	1.7	2.3	2.7	2.3	2.2
1.1	1.0	1.1		.6	1.4	1.2	1.1	.9	1.1
(211) 1.7	(167) 1.8	(196) 1.8	% Depr., Dep., Amort./Sales	(16) 2.2	(37) 2.4	(30) 1.8	(42) 1.7	(28) 2.0	(43) 1.6
2.8	2.5	2.9		4.6	4.4	2.9	2.6	2.5	2.5
1.8	2.1	2.1		5.2	2.4	2.6	1.4	1.1	1.2
(128) 3.8	(96) 3.5	(105) 3.7	% Officers', Directors' Owners' Comp/Sales	(16) 7.4	(22) 4.9	(23) 3.7	(21) 2.1	(10) 2.0	(13) 2.1
6.3	6.3	7.6		14.5	10.1	7.7	4.2	7.3	3.0
4321322M	6653993M	7783377M	Net Sales ($)	15419M	96103M	142814M	352095M	519945M	6657001M
1613075M	2091848M	2863380M	Total Assets ($)	8225M	40889M	50819M	117531M	211517M	2434399M

M = $ thousand   MM = $ million
See Pages 11 through 21 for Explanation of Ratios and Data

Current Data Sorted by Assets   Comparative Historical Data

Type of Statement

0-500M	500M-2MM	2-10MM	10-50MM	50-100MM	100-250MM	Type of Statement	4/1/02-3/31/03 ALL	4/1/03-3/31/04 ALL
		5	8		2	Unqualified	23	24
1	2	10	7	1		Reviewed	14	21
	9	4	1			Compiled	13	21
5	8	4				Tax Returns	1	7
1	4	7	8	4	5	Other	17	19
	17 (4/1-9/30/06)		79 (10/1/06-3/31/07)				4/1/02-3/31/03	4/1/03-3/31/04
7	23	30	24	5	7	NUMBER OF STATEMENTS	68	92

ASSETS (%)

0-500M	500M-2MM	2-10MM	10-50MM	50-100MM	100-250MM	ASSETS	4/1/02-3/31/03	4/1/03-3/31/04
	11.4	5.7	8.9			Cash & Equivalents	6.2	7.4
	18.4	26.7	22.1			Trade Receivables (net)	25.9	25.3
	42.4	37.5	35.1			Inventory	32.2	33.4
	1.6	4.6	2.5			All Other Current	3.8	2.3
	73.8	74.5	68.7			Total Current	68.0	68.4
	21.3	15.5	21.8			Fixed Assets (net)	22.5	20.2
	.1	.9	1.2			Intangibles (net)	2.1	3.2
	4.8	9.1	8.3			All Other Non-Current	7.3	8.1
	100.0	100.0	100.0			Total	100.0	100.0

LIABILITIES

0-500M	500M-2MM	2-10MM	10-50MM	50-100MM	100-250MM	LIABILITIES	4/1/02-3/31/03	4/1/03-3/31/04
	16.7	10.5	10.5			Notes Payable-Short Term	8.1	11.5
	1.2	1.6	1.3			Cur. Mat.-L.T.D.	2.4	1.8
	19.2	16.8	13.8			Trade Payables	15.1	16.4
	.2	.1	.4			Income Taxes Payable	.1	.3
	14.8	7.8	9.4			All Other Current	13.9	12.4
	52.2	36.8	35.4			Total Current	39.5	42.4
	13.6	9.6	12.6			Long-Term Debt	14.6	13.8
	.0	.5	.7			Deferred Taxes	.2	.4
	8.1	4.9	3.5			All Other Non-Current	2.7	5.2
	26.0	48.2	47.8			Net Worth	43.0	38.2
	100.0	100.0	100.0			Total Liabilities & Net Worth	100.0	100.0

INCOME DATA

0-500M	500M-2MM	2-10MM	10-50MM	50-100MM	100-250MM	INCOME DATA	4/1/02-3/31/03	4/1/03-3/31/04
	100.0	100.0	100.0			Net Sales	100.0	100.0
	35.9	26.6	23.9			Gross Profit	24.3	26.4
	29.8	24.0	21.3			Operating Expenses	19.9	24.2
	6.1	2.6	2.6			Operating Profit	4.3	2.1
	.9	.0	.3			All Other Expenses (net)	.4	.6
	5.2	2.6	2.3			Profit Before Taxes	3.9	1.5

RATIOS

0-500M	500M-2MM	2-10MM	10-50MM	50-100MM	100-250MM	RATIOS	4/1/02-3/31/03	4/1/03-3/31/04
	3.7	3.4	3.6			Current	3.3	2.8
	1.9	2.1	2.4				1.7	1.6
	1.0	1.5	1.3				1.2	1.2
	1.3	1.5	1.8			Quick	1.5	1.4
	.6	1.0	.8				.8	.7
	.2	.6	.5				.5	.5
	7 52.6	14 26.1	13 27.6			Sales/Receivables	15 24.0	21 17.8
	12 30.0	29 12.5	34 10.7				36 10.3	35 10.3
	33 10.9	40 9.1	49 7.5				47 7.7	46 7.9
	45 8.0	36 10.0	39 9.5			Cost of Sales/Inventory	33 11.2	36 10.1
	63 5.8	48 7.6	45 8.1				46 7.9	52 7.0
	112 3.3	64 5.7	92 4.0				74 4.9	88 4.1
	16 23.1	11 34.5	8 45.1			Cost of Sales/Payables	11 32.9	14 26.8
	25 14.4	20 18.7	17 21.7				19 19.4	21 17.1
	55 6.6	35 10.6	27 13.6				28 13.0	37 10.0
	4.4	5.9	5.1			Sales/Working Capital	5.2	5.8
	12.0	8.5	8.8				14.2	12.1
	787.5	20.3	12.9				31.3	29.6
	17.3	15.8	10.3			EBIT/Interest	20.4	15.3
	(19) 2.6	(27) 3.5	(20) 2.0				(62) 6.9	(83) 3.2
	1.1	1.6	.8				2.6	.1
						Net Profit + Depr., Dep.,	11.0	7.6
						Amort./Cur. Mat. L/T/D	(14) 3.5	(31) 2.9
							1.1	.5
	.2	.2	.2			Fixed/Worth	.2	.2
	.6	.3	.5				.6	.5
	3.1	.6	1.0				1.1	1.6
	.3	.5	.5			Debt/Worth	.4	.6
	2.8	1.0	1.2				1.4	1.8
	55.6	2.2	2.7				4.0	5.5
	132.6	33.9	17.6			% Profit Before Taxes/Tangible	50.9	34.5
	(18) 35.9	18.3	(23) 9.1			Net Worth	(62) 23.1	(80) 12.8
	19.3	3.1	.4				10.1	-1.0
	22.4	14.1	9.7			% Profit Before Taxes/Total	18.8	13.4
	10.4	8.5	4.9			Assets	8.9	4.1
	.3	1.6	.1				3.1	-1.8
	51.7	55.9	23.7			Sales/Net Fixed Assets	32.1	32.1
	27.8	21.5	13.7				14.2	15.7
	13.5	13.7	8.8				8.4	9.6
	4.3	5.1	3.8			Sales/Total Assets	4.0	3.6
	2.9	3.4	2.7				3.0	2.9
	1.9	2.5	2.2				2.1	1.9
	.3	.4	.8			% Depr., Dep., Amort./Sales	.5	.5
	(17) .5	(29) 1.0	(22) 1.0				(57) .9	(79) .9
	.9	1.5	1.2				1.3	1.6
	2.9	1.4				% Officers', Directors'	1.6	1.7
	(16) 3.8	(14) 2.7				Owners' Comp/Sales	(13) 2.5	(38) 3.0
	6.8	5.8					4.5	7.0
9362M	95699M	652190M	1492955M	815619M	1866665M	Net Sales ($)	5688298M	5091836M
1948M	28090M	172359M	495184M	403672M	947353M	Total Assets ($)	2041544M	2110743M

© RMA 2007

M = $ thousand   MM = $ million
See Pages 11 through 21 for Explanation of Ratios and Data

Comparative Historical Data   Current Data Sorted by Sales

4/1/04-3/31/05 ALL	4/1/05-3/31/06 ALL	4/1/06-3/31/07 ALL	Type of Statement	0-1MM	1-3MM	3-5MM	5-10MM	10-25MM	25MM & OVER
29	21	15	Unqualified				1	2	12
19	18	21	Reviewed		2		2	8	8
10	15	14	Compiled		3	1	3	6	1
6	7	17	Tax Returns	3	7	3		3	
18	28	29	Other	1	3	3		5	19
					17 (4/1-9/30/06)			79 (10/1/06-3/31/07)	
82	89	96	**NUMBER OF STATEMENTS**	4	15	7	6	24	40
%	%	%	**ASSETS**	%	%	%	%	%	%
4.7	6.0	7.8	Cash & Equivalents		12.4			5.4	8.2
23.9	26.8	23.7	Trade Receivables (net)		18.0			23.0	25.1
36.5	35.2	36.4	Inventory		45.0			39.9	33.0
2.6	2.9	2.8	All Other Current		1.7			4.3	2.9
67.7	70.9	70.6	Total Current		77.1			72.7	69.0
20.5	17.6	18.6	Fixed Assets (net)		15.4			16.2	21.0
3.2	4.1	2.3	Intangibles (net)		.2			.1	4.2
8.6	7.4	8.4	All Other Non-Current		7.2			11.0	5.8
100.0	100.0	100.0	Total		100.0			100.0	100.0
			LIABILITIES						
12.3	11.5	11.6	Notes Payable-Short Term		17.9			12.5	8.3
2.1	2.5	2.1	Cur. Mat.-L.T.D.		6.1			1.4	1.4
18.8	17.5	16.5	Trade Payables		21.8			14.6	14.9
.2	.2	.2	Income Taxes Payable		.0			.3	.3
10.6	10.4	10.5	All Other Current		19.2			7.8	9.7
44.0	41.9	41.0	Total Current		65.0			36.5	34.7
13.7	12.8	13.0	Long-Term Debt		12.3			10.6	13.2
.3	.3	.5	Deferred Taxes		.0			1.0	.6
3.1	5.5	5.9	All Other Non-Current		10.4			4.0	4.5
38.8	39.4	39.6	Net Worth		12.3			47.9	47.0
100.0	100.0	100.0	Total Liabilities & Net Worth		100.0			100.0	100.0
			INCOME DATA						
100.0	100.0	100.0	Net Sales		100.0			100.0	100.0
25.6	24.6	29.0	Gross Profit		39.7			27.6	23.1
23.8	21.4	25.1	Operating Expenses		35.0			24.8	19.6
1.8	3.2	3.8	Operating Profit		4.7			2.8	3.5
.5	.7	.5	All Other Expenses (net)		1.1			.5	.4
1.3	2.5	3.4	Profit Before Taxes		3.6			2.3	3.1
			RATIOS						
2.6	2.9	3.4			3.5			3.8	3.2
1.5	1.7	2.1	Current		1.6			2.1	2.5
1.2	1.2	1.2			.6			1.3	1.4
1.1	1.3	1.5			1.3			1.9	1.7
.7	.8	.9	Quick		.4			.9	1.0
.4	.5	.4			.1			.4	.6
13 28.0	19 19.4	12 29.8		4 90.8				10 35.2	15 25.1
31 11.9	31 11.6	29 12.4	Sales/Receivables	23 16.0				29 12.6	35 10.4
44 8.3	44 8.3	42 8.6		33 10.9				41 8.9	45 8.1
33 10.9	32 11.3	36 10.3		43 8.4				38 9.7	33 10.9
49 7.4	48 7.6	54 6.7	Cost of Sales/Inventory	94 3.9				50 7.3	45 8.1
87 4.2	75 4.9	91 4.0		115 3.2				108 3.4	75 4.8
13 28.1	14 26.4	12 30.9		15 24.1				7 52.4	12 30.0
25 14.5	21 17.5	20 17.9	Cost of Sales/Payables	25 14.4				16 22.6	18 19.8
38 9.7	38 9.7	35 10.4		67 5.5				33 11.1	30 12.0
6.6	6.2	5.3			4.4			5.0	5.3
15.3	11.9	9.8	Sales/Working Capital		12.1			8.5	8.2
41.3	28.7	27.5			-12.1			14.7	19.9
9.2	11.4	13.1			21.6			8.6	14.0
(75) 2.0	(81) 4.2	(84) 3.2	EBIT/Interest		(13) 2.0			(22) 2.9	(36) 3.7
.6	.9	1.3			.7			1.6	1.1
6.1	4.0	4.4							4.9
(27) 2.5	(20) 1.4	(20) 2.4	Net Profit + Depr., Dep., Amort./Cur. Mat. L/T/D						(12) 3.0
1.6	.7	.5							.6
.3	.2	.2			.1			.2	.2
.6	.5	.4	Fixed/Worth		.6			.3	.5
1.6	1.7	1.0			-1.1			.6	1.0
.7	.5	.5			.8			.5	.5
1.9	1.7	1.3	Debt/Worth		3.4			1.0	1.5
6.8	6.3	4.2			-3.0			2.0	3.1
30.9	42.8	37.4			141.2			27.6	35.9
(73) 9.3	(77) 18.1	(86) 19.8	% Profit Before Taxes/Tangible Net Worth		(11) 52.6			(23) 10.6	(37) 17.4
-1.3	.5	4.2			24.5			3.2	3.3
13.8	17.1	16.2			22.4			12.4	16.2
3.2	8.2	6.2	% Profit Before Taxes/Total Assets		5.5			6.9	5.7
-.9	.0	1.3			-1.8			1.8	.7
32.5	52.7	43.9			126.1			42.8	32.0
18.1	20.2	19.2	Sales/Net Fixed Assets		34.4			20.2	13.9
9.6	11.1	10.1			17.6			11.8	8.4
4.2	4.2	4.4			3.7			5.1	4.1
3.2	2.9	2.9	Sales/Total Assets		3.0			3.1	2.5
2.1	2.3	2.2			1.9			2.3	2.0
.5	.5	.4			.4			.6	.7
(70) .9	(74) .8	(81) 1.0	% Depr., Dep., Amort./Sales		(10) .5			(23) 1.0	(34) 1.1
1.4	1.5	1.4			.9			1.5	1.5
1.7	1.0	2.3			3.6			1.5	
(27) 2.1	(29) 2.3	(39) 3.9	% Officers', Directors' Owners' Comp/Sales		(10) 4.7			(12) 2.7	
4.8	3.0	6.8			9.3			5.4	
5084228M	4365919M	4932490M	Net Sales ($)	3202M	32056M	26687M	46245M	399015M	4425285M
2074018M	1821630M	2048606M	Total Assets ($)	1885M	12357M	9814M	13645M	146778M	1864127M

M = $ thousand   MM = $ million
See Pages 11 through 21 for Explanation of Ratios and Data

Current Data Sorted by Assets   Comparative Historical Data

Type of Statement

0-500M	500M-2MM	2-10MM	10-50MM	50-100MM	100-250MM	Type of Statement	4/1/02-3/31/03 ALL	4/1/03-3/31/04 ALL
		6	5	2	7	Unqualified	30	38
		11	8			Reviewed	31	33
5	16	5	1		1	Compiled	33	40
5	8		1			Tax Returns	15	19
4	7	15	7	4	4	Other	50	42
14	**31 (4/1-9/30/06)**	**38**	**21 94 (10/1/06-3/31/07)**	**6**	**12**	**NUMBER OF STATEMENTS**	**159**	**172**

0-500M %	500M-2MM %	2-10MM %	10-50MM %	50-100MM %	100-250MM %	ASSETS	%	%
11.9	6.4	7.5	5.8		5.2	Cash & Equivalents	7.0	6.5
23.8	19.2	23.6	25.3		18.7	Trade Receivables (net)	17.4	17.2
33.8	42.7	29.4	34.1		37.1	Inventory	39.6	38.9
1.6	2.7	5.2	4.8		2.9	All Other Current	2.3	2.5
71.0	71.0	65.6	70.0		63.8	Total Current	66.2	65.0
25.1	24.0	24.9	23.0		25.4	Fixed Assets (net)	26.4	26.4
.1	1.5	1.9	2.1		6.8	Intangibles (net)	2.4	2.1
3.8	3.5	7.6	4.9		4.0	All Other Non-Current	5.0	6.6
100.0	100.0	100.0	100.0		100.0	Total	100.0	100.0
						LIABILITIES		
33.1	11.4	16.7	8.5		14.4	Notes Payable-Short Term	12.0	12.0
4.1	3.2	2.6	1.2		1.1	Cur. Mat.-L.T.D.	3.3	4.4
13.3	14.4	16.2	13.4		11.6	Trade Payables	13.4	13.7
.0	.0	.5	.4		.4	Income Taxes Payable	.2	.2
37.4	15.5	11.9	11.5		30.6	All Other Current	11.9	13.9
87.9	44.5	47.8	34.9		58.0	Total Current	40.8	44.1
42.0	13.0	15.5	13.3		11.8	Long-Term Debt	17.2	16.8
.0	.1	.4	.4		.5	Deferred Taxes	.3	.3
1.6	7.7	3.1	6.0		5.0	All Other Non-Current	4.9	5.8
-31.6	34.6	33.2	45.3		24.7	Net Worth	36.8	33.1
100.0	100.0	100.0	100.0		100.0	Total Liabilities & Net Worth	100.0	100.0
						INCOME DATA		
100.0	100.0	100.0	100.0		100.0	Net Sales	100.0	100.0
37.4	32.2	28.1	21.8		24.0	Gross Profit	33.8	32.1
34.3	29.4	25.2	18.5		20.9	Operating Expenses	30.8	30.2
3.2	2.9	2.8	3.3		3.0	Operating Profit	3.0	1.9
1.7	1.2	.7	.5		2.0	All Other Expenses (net)	1.0	.8
1.4	1.6	2.2	2.8		1.0	Profit Before Taxes	2.0	1.1
						RATIOS		
3.2	3.0	1.8	3.7		3.2	Current	2.7	2.8
1.0	1.8	1.3	2.1		2.1		1.7	1.5
.5	1.0	1.0	1.4		.9		1.2	1.0
1.0	1.0	1.2	2.0		1.3	Quick	1.1	1.0
.7	.5	.6	.8		.8		.6 (171)	.5
.1	.3	.4	.5		.2		.3	.3
0 UND	4 85.2	19 19.5	28 12.9		20 18.4	Sales/Receivables	6 64.6	6 57.9
15 24.6	21 17.1	30 12.2	43 8.6		38 9.6		30 12.1	26 14.1
25 14.4	35 10.4	46 8.0	46 8.0		44 8.3		45 8.2	40 9.1
6 63.0	27 13.3	27 13.5	41 8.9		70 5.2	Cost of Sales/Inventory	42 8.6	44 8.2
42 8.8	78 4.7	51 7.2	69 5.3		86 4.3		85 4.3	81 4.5
83 4.4	138 2.6	78 4.7	93 3.9		100 3.6		135 2.7	124 2.9
1 292.8	11 33.1	15 24.6	10 36.1		10 35.1	Cost of Sales/Payables	15 24.3	12 29.4
7 53.1	24 15.0	26 14.3	21 17.4		15 23.6		24 14.9	23 15.6
28 13.0	36 10.0	42 8.6	33 11.1		26 14.1		42 8.7	45 8.1
8.5	6.8	7.1	3.8		4.3	Sales/Working Capital	4.9	5.0
NM	11.4	16.5	8.8		8.4		9.3	11.2
-8.1	-999.8	830.2	13.6		NM		25.6	184.0
17.0	6.8	7.6	25.1		19.7	EBIT/Interest	7.8	8.1
(13) 2.8	(28) 3.1	(37) 3.4	(20) 4.4		3.7		(144) 2.7	(156) 2.2
-1.3	1.0	.9	1.3		1.2		1.0	.0
			9.4			Net Profit + Depr., Dep., Amort./Cur. Mat. L/T/D	3.6	3.5
			(13) 5.1				(50) 2.5	(49) 1.9
			2.6				.9	.2
.3	.2	.3	.4		.3	Fixed/Worth	.3	.3
9.8	.5	.8	.6		.7		.6	.7
-.7	2.5	2.2	1.3		NM		1.8	3.0
1.5	1.1	1.2	.4		.6	Debt/Worth	.8	.7
25.5	1.7	2.5	1.4		1.0		1.7	1.9
-3.1	8.2	4.0	4.1		NM		5.2	7.0
	61.5	51.7	39.5			% Profit Before Taxes/Tangible Net Worth	29.5	31.0
	(28) 23.7	(34) 21.2	(20) 21.3				(139) 12.5	(146) 9.0
	-.4	7.0	3.3				.8	-1.9
34.2	16.5	14.1	15.5		10.7	% Profit Before Taxes/Total Assets	11.1	12.7
8.2	3.9	8.0	6.1		4.2		4.3	3.0
-21.5	-.2	-.3	1.3		1.1		.0	-1.4
87.5	27.9	26.5	38.6		13.2	Sales/Net Fixed Assets	27.9	25.6
27.9	17.7	13.3	10.0		7.7		11.1	12.0
16.0	8.7	7.0	5.3		6.0		5.5	5.8
8.3	3.7	3.1	3.6		2.3	Sales/Total Assets	3.4	3.3
4.0	2.9	2.4	2.4		2.2		2.3	2.3
2.1	2.4	2.0	1.6		1.7		1.7	1.8
	.7	.8	.7		1.2	% Depr., Dep., Amort./Sales	.8	.8
	(28) 1.1	(33) 1.4	(19) 1.4	(11)	1.7		(137) 1.6	(150) 1.7
	1.8	1.8	2.7		2.6		2.8	2.6
	2.8	1.1				% Officers', Directors' Owners' Comp/Sales	1.9	1.5
	(21) 3.6	(15) 2.2					(71) 3.5	(71) 2.8
	5.5	5.3					6.4	5.5
12662M	119101M	527560M	1285507M	1030221M	3797854M	Net Sales ($)	4800123M	6598606M
3405M	37934M	192210M	506686M	468780M	1719031M	Total Assets ($)	2468152M	2915642M

M = $ thousand   MM = $ million
See Pages 11 through 21 for Explanation of Ratios and Data

Comparative Historical Data   Current Data Sorted by Sales

4/1/04-3/31/05 ALL	4/1/05-3/31/06 ALL	4/1/06-3/31/07 ALL	Type of Statement	0-1MM	1-3MM	3-5MM	5-10MM	10-25MM	25MM & OVER
22	20	20	Unqualified				2	3	15
27	20	19	Reviewed			1	5	6	7
32	32	28	Compiled	4	6	6	8	3	1
20	16	14	Tax Returns	3	5	3	3		
42	46	41	Other	3	4	5	5	7	17
					28 (4/1-9/30/06)		94 (10/1/06-3/31/07)		
143	134	122	**NUMBER OF STATEMENTS**	10	15	15	23	19	40
%	%	%	**ASSETS**	%	%	%	%	%	%
7.4	7.1	6.9	Cash & Equivalents	9.0	10.6	5.7	10.0	3.1	5.5
17.3	19.9	22.1	Trade Receivables (net)	20.4	22.7	19.2	23.2	21.6	23.1
40.3	38.3	35.5	Inventory	32.2	47.3	37.5	30.4	28.7	37.2
3.3	2.4	3.7	All Other Current	1.1	2.6	1.4	3.3	8.0	3.8
68.2	67.6	68.2	Total Current	62.6	83.3	63.8	66.8	61.5	69.6
23.7	25.0	23.7	Fixed Assets (net)	31.8	14.3	28.4	24.3	30.6	19.7
2.3	2.0	2.9	Intangibles (net)	.8	.0	2.1	.8	3.2	5.9
5.7	5.4	5.3	All Other Non-Current	4.8	2.5	5.8	8.1	4.7	4.8
100.0	100.0	100.0	Total	100.0	100.0	100.0	100.0	100.0	100.0
			LIABILITIES						
13.5	16.3	14.9	Notes Payable-Short Term	24.6	22.7	13.7	12.5	16.8	10.6
4.4	2.9	2.5	Cur. Mat.-L.T.D.	3.4	3.3	2.2	4.1	2.0	1.5
13.1	15.3	14.0	Trade Payables	5.2	19.4	11.1	18.7	14.9	12.3
.2	.3	.2	Income Taxes Payable	.0	.1	.0	.4	.5	.3
14.7	14.1	17.2	All Other Current	33.3	21.0	16.4	13.4	10.0	17.8
45.7	48.9	49.0	Total Current	66.4	66.4	43.5	49.0	44.2	42.5
16.3	19.3	16.8	Long-Term Debt	32.4	24.1	12.8	19.9	16.1	10.2
.3	.3	.4	Deferred Taxes	.0	.1	.0	.1	1.0	.5
8.4	4.6	5.3	All Other Non-Current	.0	11.0	11.1	1.2	.7	6.9
29.2	26.9	28.5	Net Worth	1.1	-1.6	32.6	29.9	37.9	39.9
100.0	100.0	100.0	Total Liabilties & Net Worth	100.0	100.0	100.0	100.0	100.0	100.0
			INCOME DATA						
100.0	100.0	100.0	Net Sales	100.0	100.0	100.0	100.0	100.0	100.0
32.5	29.7	28.3	Gross Profit	35.7	39.4	32.2	26.0	28.4	22.0
30.7	27.9	25.3	Operating Expenses	33.1	35.7	29.9	23.8	24.6	19.0
1.7	1.8	3.0	Operating Profit	2.6	3.7	2.3	2.2	3.8	3.1
.9	1.1	1.1	All Other Expenses (net)	1.9	1.0	.3	1.2	.9	1.2
.8	.7	1.9	Profit Before Taxes	.7	2.7	2.0	1.0	3.0	1.9
			RATIOS						
2.7	2.5	3.0	Current	2.6	4.3	4.1	1.9	1.8	3.8
1.5	1.5	1.6		.9	1.8	1.4	1.2	1.5	2.2
1.1	1.1	1.1		.5	1.3	1.0	1.0	1.3	1.3
1.1	1.1	1.2	Quick	.9	1.5	2.2	1.1	.8	1.6
(141) .5	.6	.7		.5	.5	.5	.6	.6	.8
.2	.3	.4		.1	.1	.1	.4	.3	.5
8 47.8	10 38.1	16 22.9	Sales/Receivables	0 UND	0 UND	4 85.2	19 19.7	13 27.1	23 15.9
26 14.2	28 13.1	27 13.3		9 42.1	19 18.8	21 17.8	27 13.6	27 13.4	37 9.8
43 8.6	42 8.8	43 8.5		29 12.5	37 9.8	40 9.0	39 9.4	52 7.0	44 8.3
43 8.6	39 9.3	32 11.6	Cost of Sales/Inventory	0 UND	18 20.3	27 13.3	23 16.0	40 9.1	45 8.0
98 3.7	69 5.3	62 5.9		44 8.3	87 4.2	65 5.6	38 9.7	58 6.3	74 4.9
139 2.6	117 3.1	98 3.7		97 3.8	138 2.6	133 2.8	84 4.4	85 4.3	98 3.7
11 31.8	12 29.6	10 35.6	Cost of Sales/Payables	1 245.9	1 322.0	10 36.8	15 24.6	15 24.2	9 42.8
23 15.8	21 17.6	20 18.2		11 34.6	22 22.8	30 12.1	24 15.1	27 13.5	16 22.3
39 9.3	39 9.5	36 10.2		28 13.0	48 7.7	36 10.1	43 8.4	42 8.7	26 13.8
5.3	5.5	6.0	Sales/Working Capital	6.5	6.1	4.1	9.9	7.6	3.9
10.0	12.3	10.8		-23.5	8.2	12.5	17.7	13.6	8.9
72.3	62.8	233.2		-8.4	17.0	-355.4	-124.2	32.7	21.2
8.2	7.0	7.7	EBIT/Interest		14.0	5.9	7.7	5.9	12.2
(132) 2.2	(126) 2.8	(116) 3.4			(12) 4.3	1.4	3.3	3.4	(38) 3.7
.2	.2	1.0			1.3	-.5	.2	1.8	1.3
8.5	5.0	7.2	Net Profit + Depr., Dep., Amort./Cur. Mat. L/T/D						7.7
(36) 2.7	(36) 2.2	(32) 4.1						(18)	4.6
.9	.5	1.6							2.5
.3	.3	.3	Fixed/Worth	.3	.2	.3	.4	.4	.3
.6	.7	.6		9.8	.3	1.2	.9	.7	.6
2.6	2.4	2.6		-2.1	-40.0	4.0	3.7	1.3	1.7
.8	1.1	.9	Debt/Worth	2.9	.6	1.1	1.3	1.3	.3
2.3	2.2	1.8		25.5	1.7	1.8	2.7	1.6	1.3
7.7	8.1	7.2		-12.4	-186.3	45.7	6.9	3.0	5.2
32.5	39.2	45.3	% Profit Before Taxes/Tangible Net Worth		59.2	99.1	51.3	40.0	37.1
(121) 12.2	(115) 14.3	(104) 17.7		(11)	28.4	(13) 8.8	(20) 16.8	26.0	(34) 13.0
-1.4	-.2	2.8			16.3	-10.5	-7.3	8.5	4.2
11.2	12.3	15.6	% Profit Before Taxes/Total Assets	50.0	23.9	17.1	12.9	11.7	13.3
3.0	5.1	6.9		14.6	9.8	1.3	7.8	7.9	5.4
-2.4	-3.4	.0		-12.5	-.2	-3.4	-2.7	2.3	1.6
29.8	26.8	31.6	Sales/Net Fixed Assets	87.0	61.0	23.9	27.9	19.2	34.8
13.2	13.3	15.6		20.7	25.6	14.5	13.6	7.5	13.2
6.3	6.2	6.8		2.4	16.6	5.0	9.3	4.2	6.7
3.5	3.6	3.6	Sales/Total Assets	8.3	4.6	2.9	3.7	3.1	3.6
2.4	2.5	2.5		2.8	3.3	2.5	2.5	2.4	2.3
1.7	1.8	2.0		1.3	2.6	2.2	2.0	2.0	1.9
.7	.8	.8	% Depr., Dep., Amort./Sales		.7	.7	.7	.8	.8
(124) 1.5	(116) 1.4	(103) 1.4		(13)	1.0	(13) 1.1	(21) 1.4	(15) 1.7	(34) 1.3
2.8	2.3	2.5			1.5	3.1	3.5	2.6	2.5
2.3	1.7	1.7	% Officers', Directors' Owners' Comp/Sales		2.6		1.1		
(71) 3.0	(62) 3.0	(49) 3.1		(11)	3.4		(11) 2.9		
5.8	6.3	5.9			10.6		5.7		
4024195M	5113923M	6772905M	Net Sales ($)	5676M	29116M	56728M	168880M	336454M	6176051M
1983445M	2355843M	2928046M	Total Assets ($)	3067M	8847M	23432M	67313M	150299M	2675088M

Current Data Sorted by Assets | Comparative Historical Data

Type of Statement

	0-500M	500M-2MM	2-10MM	10-50MM	50-100MM	100-250MM		4/1/02-3/31/03 ALL	4/1/03-3/31/04 ALL
Unqualified	1		1	3				8	5
Reviewed		1	5	1				6	3
Compiled	1	4	3			1		3	5
Tax Returns		2						1	4
Other	1	4	2	4	2			8	10
		7 (4/1-9/30/06)		29 (10/1/06-3/31/07)					
NUMBER OF STATEMENTS	3	11	11	8	2	1		26	27

	0-500M %	500M-2MM %	2-10MM %	10-50MM %	50-100MM %	100-250MM %		%	%
ASSETS									
Cash & Equivalents		7.4	7.1					12.3	7.6
Trade Receivables (net)		13.0	31.7					22.9	23.0
Inventory		41.3	25.2					30.5	37.4
All Other Current		5.2	.3					3.1	3.0
Total Current		66.9	64.3					68.7	71.0
Fixed Assets (net)		26.3	29.1					18.6	20.5
Intangibles (net)		1.9	.8					5.0	5.2
All Other Non-Current		4.9	5.8					7.7	3.4
Total		100.0	100.0					100.0	100.0
LIABILITIES									
Notes Payable-Short Term		7.9	18.7					7.1	21.6
Cur. Mat.-L.T.D.		2.4	5.2					3.1	4.3
Trade Payables		18.7	19.7					14.4	16.3
Income Taxes Payable		.1	.1					.0	.2
All Other Current		22.1	13.6					17.0	9.7
Total Current		51.1	57.4					41.7	52.2
Long-Term Debt		20.6	9.7					7.0	12.7
Deferred Taxes		.0	.2					.1	.2
All Other Non-Current		20.0	5.2					6.1	14.3
Net Worth		8.3	27.5					45.1	20.6
Total Liabilties & Net Worth		100.0	100.0					100.0	100.0
INCOME DATA									
Net Sales		100.0	100.0					100.0	100.0
Gross Profit		39.2	26.7					34.0	34.8
Operating Expenses		32.6	18.5					29.2	30.9
Operating Profit		6.6	8.2					4.8	3.9
All Other Expenses (net)		-.1	1.4					.7	1.4
Profit Before Taxes		6.7	6.7					4.1	2.5
RATIOS									
Current		2.2	2.3					4.4	2.1
		1.3	1.2					1.5	1.3
		.9	.8					1.0	1.1
Quick		.7	.9					2.4	1.2
		.3	.7					1.0	.7
		.2	.6					.3	.2
Sales/Receivables		4 92.5	31 11.7					9 41.4	21 17.7
		10 35.0	39 9.4					38 9.7	36 10.1
		21 17.4	52 7.0					43 8.4	54 6.8
Cost of Sales/Inventory		57 6.4	20 18.0					42 8.7	42 8.7
		69 5.3	58 6.3					65 5.6	89 4.1
		142 2.6	123 3.0					108 3.4	159 2.3
Cost of Sales/Payables		13 29.0	19 19.5					15 24.6	20 18.0
		33 10.9	21 17.7					20 18.0	31 11.9
		67 5.4	53 6.9					47 7.7	61 6.0
Sales/Working Capital		6.5	5.1					3.5	6.6
		19.2	24.1					10.4	10.2
		-18.5	-19.1					-778.5	44.9
EBIT/Interest		74.9	11.2					19.4	10.6
		(10) 9.5	4.2					(20) 8.1	(25) 3.4
		1.3	1.5					1.3	1.0
Net Profit + Depr., Dep., Amort./Cur. Mat. L/T/D									
Fixed/Worth		.1	.7					.2	.3
		.5	.9					.5	.6
		5.5	-18.7					1.2	6.6
Debt/Worth		.7	1.1					.4	1.3
		2.1	3.8					1.7	3.6
		6.2	-35.5					5.0	28.2
% Profit Before Taxes/Tangible Net Worth								55.0	54.6
								(24) 11.2	(21) 16.9
								1.8	2.2
% Profit Before Taxes/Total Assets		32.4	22.8					18.3	12.7
		22.7	9.2					7.5	2.9
		2.4	2.9					.7	.5
Sales/Net Fixed Assets		49.6	20.9					45.4	49.4
		17.6	10.3					20.1	17.2
		6.1	5.4					6.9	5.7
Sales/Total Assets		3.8	3.0					3.9	3.2
		3.1	2.7					2.6	2.4
		1.5	1.5					1.7	1.6
% Depr., Dep., Amort./Sales		.5	.7					.9	.5
		(10) .9	(10) 1.5					(22) 1.5	(23) 1.3
		1.7	3.2					2.4	1.7
% Officers', Directors' Owners' Comp/Sales									.7
								(10) 3.0	
								6.2	
Net Sales ($)	1498M	41411M	148392M	541429M	359981M	161702M		1201170M	861292M
Total Assets ($)	693M	14105M	53146M	228511M	150893M	134042M		617935M	576796M

M = $ thousand   MM = $ million
See Pages 11 through 21 for Explanation of Ratios and Data

Comparative Historical Data

Current Data Sorted by Sales

			Type of Statement						
4	3	5	Unqualified	1			1	3	3
	5	7	Reviewed				3		1
7	5	9	Compiled	1	4		2	1	1
7	5	2	Tax Returns			2			
9	14	13	Other	1	1	1	3		7
4/1/04-3/31/05	4/1/05-3/31/06	4/1/06-3/31/07		0-1MM	1-3MM	3-5MM	5-10MM	10-25MM	25MM & OVER
ALL	ALL	ALL			7 (4/1-9/30/06)		29 (10/1/06-3/31/07)		
27	32	36	NUMBER OF STATEMENTS	3	9	3	9	4	12
%	%	%	**ASSETS**	%	%	%	%	%	%
7.4	6.8	7.2	Cash & Equivalents						6.3
30.8	26.3	22.3	Trade Receivables (net)						26.8
30.1	35.7	33.3	Inventory						30.9
1.9	3.3	2.0	All Other Current						1.0
70.1	72.1	64.7	Total Current						65.0
24.4	19.4	23.6	Fixed Assets (net)						18.0
1.6	3.7	3.4	Intangibles (net)						7.8
3.8	4.7	8.3	All Other Non-Current						9.3
100.0	100.0	100.0	Total						100.0
			LIABILITIES						
22.6	21.6	17.0	Notes Payable-Short Term						23.2
5.3	4.9	3.1	Cur. Mat.-L.T.D.						1.5
14.0	15.9	17.3	Trade Payables						18.8
.0	.1	.1	Income Taxes Payable						.1
14.2	17.5	15.5	All Other Current						9.3
56.1	60.1	52.9	Total Current						52.8
19.9	19.1	14.6	Long-Term Debt						14.5
.0	.0	.4	Deferred Taxes						1.1
5.4	7.8	11.2	All Other Non-Current						5.9
18.6	13.0	20.9	Net Worth						25.7
100.0	100.0	100.0	Total Liabilties & Net Worth						100.0
			INCOME DATA						
100.0	100.0	100.0	Net Sales						100.0
28.6	28.9	28.9	Gross Profit						18.6
25.0	25.5	23.6	Operating Expenses						16.2
3.6	3.4	5.3	Operating Profit						2.4
.6	1.6	1.4	All Other Expenses (net)						2.3
3.0	1.8	4.0	Profit Before Taxes						.1
			RATIOS						
1.7	2.1	2.3							2.4
1.2	1.1	1.3	Current						1.3
1.0	.9	.8							.8
.9	1.1	.9							1.3
.6	.5	.5	Quick						.6
.3	.3	.2							.3
15 24.3	18 20.8	11 34.5							23 16.2
40 9.1	40 9.1	28 13.0	Sales/Receivables						42 8.8
55 6.6	48 7.7	44 8.2							56 6.6
20 18.5	43 8.5	48 7.6							48 7.6
46 8.0	58 6.3	66 5.5	Cost of Sales/Inventory						58 6.3
92 4.0	114 3.2	122 3.0							81 4.5
8 46.6	13 29.1	17 21.3							21 17.4
20 17.9	25 14.5	31 11.8	Cost of Sales/Payables						35 10.5
35 10.5	44 8.4	48 7.6							48 7.6
10.4	7.8	6.7							6.1
19.6	36.9	18.4	Sales/Working Capital						15.4
-147.1	-36.7	-22.5							-17.1
13.9	14.1	10.7							
(25) 4.4	(30) 2.0	(32) 3.1	EBIT/Interest						
1.8	.0	.1							
			Net Profit + Depr., Dep., Amort./Cur. Mat. L/T/D						
.4	.4	.1							.2
1.0	1.2	.8	Fixed/Worth						1.1
5.4	-2.8	-11.3							-1.2
1.7	1.2	.8							.9
3.5	5.5	3.1	Debt/Worth						7.6
12.6	-36.3	-32.3							-4.8
87.6	68.3	65.1							
(23) 47.7	(21) 28.9	(26) 36.6	% Profit Before Taxes/Tangible Net Worth						
26.8	-1.3	11.3							
19.3	17.2	24.0							14.4
9.6	2.5	7.5	% Profit Before Taxes/Total Assets						3.5
2.4	-2.9	-2.4							-8.8
84.8	36.3	45.5							45.5
16.7	23.0	14.5	Sales/Net Fixed Assets						15.7
4.5	7.1	6.4							7.6
3.7	3.5	3.1							3.1
2.8	2.6	2.6	Sales/Total Assets						2.4
2.0	2.1	1.6							1.4
.7	.7	.8							1.0
(23) 1.1	(27) 1.0	(30) 1.3	% Depr., Dep., Amort./Sales						(10) 1.7
2.8	2.0	2.5							3.0
		1.7	% Officers', Directors' Owners' Comp/Sales						
	(10)	3.1							
		8.6							
720939M	1333800M	1254413M	Net Sales ($)	1498M	8899M	10741M	61027M	81230M	1091018M
255100M	578726M	581390M	Total Assets ($)	693M	6612M	3870M	24424M	23097M	522694M

M = $ thousand   MM = $ million
See Pages 11 through 21 for Explanation of Ratios and Data

Current Data Sorted by Assets | Comparative Historical Data

0-500M	500M-2MM	2-10MM	10-50MM	50-100MM	100-250MM			
						Type of Statement		
1	1	6	20	1	2	Unqualified	30	38
	7	18	6			Reviewed	36	39
2	10	8				Compiled	25	40
5	10	4				Tax Returns	12	18
1	9	18	23	1	4	Other	43	58
	26 (4/1-9/30/06)		131 (10/1/06-3/31/07)				4/1/02-3/31/03 ALL	4/1/03-3/31/04 ALL
9	37	54	49	2	6	**NUMBER OF STATEMENTS**	146	193
%	%	%	%	%	%	**ASSETS**	%	%
	10.0	6.2	4.1			Cash & Equivalents	7.1	7.9
	27.8	32.2	28.2			Trade Receivables (net)	29.2	28.7
	32.9	25.6	25.0			Inventory	24.2	25.2
	2.7	3.1	2.8			All Other Current	1.8	2.7
	73.4	67.0	60.1			Total Current	62.3	64.5
	18.3	22.2	26.5			Fixed Assets (net)	26.6	24.3
	1.1	4.0	7.1			Intangibles (net)	4.7	4.2
	7.2	6.7	6.3			All Other Non-Current	6.3	7.1
	100.0	100.0	100.0			Total	100.0	100.0
						LIABILITIES		
	16.8	14.0	14.5			Notes Payable-Short Term	10.7	12.6
	1.3	2.7	3.2			Cur. Mat.-L.T.D.	3.8	3.4
	18.4	13.5	13.5			Trade Payables	13.8	14.7
	.1	.2	.2			Income Taxes Payable	.3	.2
	14.9	10.7	11.9			All Other Current	9.9	10.9
	51.3	41.1	43.3			Total Current	38.6	41.8
	11.0	14.4	13.7			Long-Term Debt	18.5	14.4
	.4	.4	.4			Deferred Taxes	.4	.4
	4.4	4.4	4.2			All Other Non-Current	4.7	10.3
	32.8	39.7	38.5			Net Worth	37.8	33.1
	100.0	100.0	100.0			Total Liabilities & Net Worth	100.0	100.0
						INCOME DATA		
	100.0	100.0	100.0			Net Sales	100.0	100.0
	33.2	29.3	23.3			Gross Profit	31.1	31.7
	29.4	24.8	19.4			Operating Expenses	26.6	28.1
	3.8	4.5	3.8			Operating Profit	4.4	3.6
	.6	1.1	.9			All Other Expenses (net)	1.2	1.3
	3.2	3.4	3.0			Profit Before Taxes	3.3	2.3
						RATIOS		
	3.5	2.5	2.2			Current	2.5	2.8
	1.6	1.7	1.3				1.6	1.5
	1.1	1.2	1.0				1.2	1.1
	1.5	1.5	1.2			Quick	1.5	1.6
	.8	.9	.7				.9	.8
	.3	.5	.5				.6	.5
	11 32.2	28 13.0	33 11.1			Sales/Receivables	27 13.4	28 12.9
	31 11.6	45 8.2	46 7.9				39 9.3	39 9.4
	48 7.6	63 5.8	57 6.4				52 7.0	56 6.5
	22 16.3	33 11.0	33 10.9			Cost of Sales/Inventory	27 13.4	26 14.1
	54 6.8	50 7.3	48 7.6				50 7.3	50 7.3
	86 4.2	84 4.3	88 4.2				76 4.8	86 4.2
	12 30.1	17 21.0	18 20.0			Cost of Sales/Payables	16 23.2	14 25.2
	32 11.5	24 15.5	28 12.9				25 14.8	25 14.7
	48 7.6	36 10.3	39 9.3				38 9.6	44 8.4
	6.7	5.2	6.8			Sales/Working Capital	6.3	5.4
	11.1	10.5	12.4				11.2	11.0
	199.5	22.3	119.4				29.0	109.5
	13.3	7.9	6.2			EBIT/Interest	10.1	9.3
	(32) 3.7	(52) 3.8	2.9				(132) 3.3	(170) 3.0
	.9	.9	1.2				.8	.6
		4.4	9.1			Net Profit + Depr., Dep., Amort./Cur. Mat. L/T/D	3.8	9.3
		(13) 3.1	(19) 2.2				(30) 2.2	(42) 2.8
		.8	1.0				1.1	.7
	.1	.3	.5			Fixed/Worth	.3	.3
	.4	.5	.9				.8	.7
	1.5	1.6	1.7				1.8	2.2
	.5	.9	1.0			Debt/Worth	.8	.9
	1.8	1.7	2.1				1.9	1.9
	5.7	4.4	4.9				4.1	7.3
	61.8	40.1	33.8			% Profit Before Taxes/Tangible Net Worth	48.9	41.6
	(31) 28.0	(49) 18.4	(44) 18.7				(130) 18.4	(162) 16.9
	7.4	-1.3	2.8				2.8	-.1
	20.1	13.3	12.6			% Profit Before Taxes/Total Assets	15.5	15.4
	8.1	5.8	5.4				6.5	5.6
	.8	-1.0	.4				.7	-1.0
	67.6	29.1	22.3			Sales/Net Fixed Assets	31.5	31.0
	33.8	11.5	8.1				10.9	11.2
	9.5	7.1	5.6				5.6	5.6
	4.3	3.2	2.7			Sales/Total Assets	3.2	3.1
	3.3	2.5	2.0				2.4	2.4
	1.9	1.9	1.5				1.8	1.7
	.4	.6	.9			% Depr., Dep., Amort./Sales	1.1	.9
	(32) .8	(50) 1.3	(44) 1.8				(120) 1.9	(165) 2.0
	1.7	2.2	2.7				3.5	3.3
	2.6	1.4				% Officers', Directors', Owners' Comp/Sales	1.8	2.7
	(21) 3.8	(24) 2.8					(56) 4.3	(68) 5.5
	5.7	4.2					9.8	9.0
7176M	148447M	620767M	2094367M	280873M	1091125M	Net Sales ($)	3294535M	4172679M
1757M	44908M	249454M	988072M	142874M	815570M	Total Assets ($)	1622264M	2433545M

M = $ thousand   MM = $ million
See Pages 11 through 21 for Explanation of Ratios and Data

Comparative Historical Data / Current Data Sorted by Sales

			Type of Statement		26 (4/1-9/30/06)		131 (10/1/06-3/31/07)		
38	35	31	Unqualified	1		1	1	7	21
44	27	31	Reviewed		3	4	8	12	4
16	19	20	Compiled	3	4	5	6	2	
14	15	19	Tax Returns	3	6	4	4	2	
52	48	56	Other	1	5	3	11	12	24
4/1/04-3/31/05	4/1/05-3/31/06	4/1/06-3/31/07		0-1MM	1-3MM	3-5MM	5-10MM	10-25MM	25MM & OVER
ALL	ALL	ALL							
164	144	157	**NUMBER OF STATEMENTS**	8	18	17	30	35	49
%	%	%	**ASSETS**	%	%	%	%	%	%
6.8	6.2	7.1	Cash & Equivalents		6.7	9.7	8.9	6.4	4.0
28.5	30.4	29.1	Trade Receivables (net)		22.6	29.4	31.5	32.2	28.8
27.1	26.2	27.4	Inventory		32.6	29.4	27.2	25.0	26.0
2.4	3.3	2.7	All Other Current		1.0	2.3	5.7	1.4	2.8
64.8	66.0	66.2	Total Current		63.0	70.8	73.3	65.1	61.7
24.5	24.1	22.5	Fixed Assets (net)		17.7	22.5	20.9	21.5	25.9
3.9	5.1	4.2	Intangibles (net)		4.0	1.8	2.6	5.7	5.3
6.9	4.7	7.1	All Other Non-Current		15.3	4.8	3.2	7.7	7.1
100.0	100.0	100.0	Total		100.0	100.0	100.0	100.0	100.0
			LIABILITIES						
14.9	16.6	14.8	Notes Payable-Short Term		16.5	13.9	12.6	12.6	13.7
4.3	2.9	2.3	Cur. Mat.-L.T.D.		1.7	3.2	2.2	1.9	3.0
14.6	16.7	15.4	Trade Payables		20.3	16.3	17.6	13.4	14.2
.2	.2	.2	Income Taxes Payable		.0	.1	.0	.3	.3
11.9	12.0	12.2	All Other Current		19.6	12.7	10.4	11.2	11.5
45.9	48.4	44.8	Total Current		58.1	46.1	42.8	39.4	42.6
18.7	14.6	15.8	Long-Term Debt		24.3	22.1	13.1	9.9	16.4
.4	.4	.4	Deferred Taxes		.5	.1	.9	.0	.5
8.1	8.1	5.4	All Other Non-Current		3.2	5.5	4.1	4.1	5.4
26.9	28.5	33.6	Net Worth		14.0	26.2	39.1	46.6	35.1
100.0	100.0	100.0	Total Liabilities & Net Worth		100.0	100.0	100.0	100.0	100.0
			INCOME DATA						
100.0	100.0	100.0	Net Sales		100.0	100.0	100.0	100.0	100.0
29.3	29.2	28.9	Gross Profit		36.5	31.1	32.9	24.9	23.3
26.0	26.3	24.5	Operating Expenses		30.0	28.6	28.4	20.3	20.0
3.3	2.9	4.4	Operating Profit		6.6	2.5	4.5	4.6	3.3
1.5	1.5	1.3	All Other Expenses (net)		1.4	.5	1.1	.8	1.3
1.8	1.4	3.2	Profit Before Taxes		5.2	2.0	3.5	3.8	2.1
			RATIOS						
2.2	2.3	2.4	Current		2.1	3.1	2.7	2.7	2.2
1.4	1.5	1.6			1.4	1.6	1.9	1.6	1.5
1.0	1.1	1.1			.6	1.1	1.1	1.2	1.1
1.3	1.6	1.5	Quick		1.4	1.6	1.5	1.6	1.1
.8	.8	.8			.4	.8	1.0	.9	.8
.5	.5	.5			.2	.5	.5	.5	.5
28 13.0	27 13.3	29 12.4	Sales/Receivables		11 32.8	28 13.0	24 15.5	26 13.8	35 10.5
41 8.8	40 9.0	40 9.1			29 12.6	35 10.3	39 9.3	43 8.4	46 7.9
58 6.2	58 6.3	59 6.2			61 5.9	55 6.6	62 5.9	62 5.9	57 6.4
30 12.3	29 12.5	30 12.0	Cost of Sales/Inventory		24 15.3	34 10.6	34 10.8	23 16.0	34 10.6
53 6.9	47 7.8	51 7.2			63 5.8	58 6.3	53 6.9	49 7.4	51 7.2
85 4.3	77 4.8	87 4.2			174 2.1	79 4.6	84 4.3	87 4.2	88 4.2
13 28.1	15 23.8	16 22.7	Cost of Sales/Payables		21 17.1	12 29.8	13 29.0	16 22.5	18 20.0
25 14.3	28 13.2	27 13.7			39 9.4	23 15.8	32 11.6	23 16.0	27 13.7
48 7.7	43 8.5	41 9.0			62 5.8	43 8.6	47 7.8	33 11.1	40 9.0
6.9	6.2	6.0	Sales/Working Capital		6.7	5.3	5.9	5.8	6.3
16.0	13.1	11.1			11.7	11.0	9.0	10.7	11.5
135.3	49.7	41.5			-26.9	170.4	31.8	21.9	56.9
7.9	9.6	8.3	EBIT/Interest		13.1	4.3	13.3	13.2	6.2
(147) 3.1	(134) 3.5	(148) 3.1			(17) 4.3	(14) 1.8	(27) 4.1	4.2	2.9
.9	.9	1.1			1.4	-.2	1.1	.8	1.2
2.9	6.0	6.5	Net Profit + Depr., Dep., Amort./Cur. Mat. L/T/D						6.2	7.9
(32) 1.7	(31) 2.1	(40) 2.7						(13) 3.3	(20) 2.7
.4	1.0	1.0							1.8	.7
.3	.3	.3	Fixed/Worth		.1	.3	.2	.3	.5
.8	.7	.6			1.0	.6	.5	.5	.9
2.2	2.8	1.7			-.6	2.8	1.4	1.2	2.0
1.3	.8	.9	Debt/Worth		.9	1.0	.9	.6	1.0
2.6	1.9	1.8			1.9	2.2	1.8	1.6	2.1
8.9	9.6	6.1			-54.6	7.8	5.6	3.4	6.6
47.6	42.0	41.3	% Profit Before Taxes/Tangible Net Worth		55.7	39.1	63.2	41.1	28.7
(141) 16.7	(115) 18.1	(135) 20.9			(13) 28.0	(14) 12.1	(27) 27.5	(34) 15.9	(42) 19.0
3.2	6.3	2.9			6.4	.5	4.2	-2.2	7.7
11.4	12.3	15.4	% Profit Before Taxes/Total Assets		19.4	10.8	19.8	14.4	11.6
4.6	5.4	6.8			10.8	4.2	8.9	6.7	5.4
-.3	-.3	.4			1.7	-4.4	.5	-.7	.4
35.1	34.4	41.6	Sales/Net Fixed Assets		112.6	60.2	46.7	28.0	22.3
13.0	12.1	11.0			29.4	19.8	13.6	10.5	7.6
5.4	6.0	6.3			4.5	6.1	7.5	7.1	5.7
3.3	3.5	3.3	Sales/Total Assets		2.9	3.9	4.0	3.3	2.7
2.4	2.5	2.4			1.9	3.1	2.7	2.4	2.1
1.7	1.7	1.8			1.3	2.0	1.9	1.7	1.7
.7	.8	.6	% Depr., Dep., Amort./Sales		.4	.6	.4	.7	1.0
(141) 1.8	(121) 1.7	(138) 1.4			(15) .8	(15) 1.0	(28) 1.2	(31) 1.3	(44) 1.9
3.0	2.8	2.4			1.7	2.3	2.2	2.1	2.7
2.0	1.8	1.8	% Officers', Directors' Owners' Comp/Sales					1.6	1.2
(61) 4.4	(51) 4.3	(56) 3.2						(20) 3.1	(12) 2.9
6.9	7.7	5.1						6.3	3.9
4563967M	4723403M	4242755M	Net Sales ($)	5030M	36484M	69025M	218921M	583031M	3330264M
1912936M	1787974M	2242635M	Total Assets ($)	1857M	22049M	29797M	96458M	269485M	1822989M

M = $ thousand   MM = $ million
See Pages 11 through 21 for Explanation of Ratios and Data

Current Data Sorted by Assets / Comparative Historical Data

0-500M	500M-2MM	2-10MM	10-50MM	50-100MM	100-250MM	Type of Statement		
	1	2	4	1	1	Unqualified	12	10
	7	12	6	1		Reviewed	10	19
1	7	2	1			Compiled	9	14
1	2	2				Tax Returns	4	7
2	2	7	2			Other	16	15
	17 (4/1-9/30/06)		47 (10/1/06-3/31/07)				4/1/02-3/31/03 ALL	4/1/03-3/31/04 ALL
4	19	25	13	2	1	NUMBER OF STATEMENTS	51	65
%	%	%	%	%	%	ASSETS	%	%
	8.5	5.9	2.6			Cash & Equivalents	5.4	7.4
	36.6	34.8	30.7			Trade Receivables (net)	31.4	31.5
	14.2	25.9	24.3			Inventory	26.9	25.0
	4.3	5.1	8.1			All Other Current	3.0	3.1
	63.5	71.6	65.6			Total Current	66.7	66.9
	31.0	20.9	24.2			Fixed Assets (net)	25.3	24.9
	.5	2.8	.6			Intangibles (net)	2.2	2.0
	5.0	4.6	9.6			All Other Non-Current	5.8	6.2
	100.0	100.0	100.0			Total	100.0	100.0
						LIABILITIES		
	9.8	11.2	10.6			Notes Payable-Short Term	12.2	13.4
	5.1	4.4	1.3			Cur. Mat.-L.T.D.	5.0	3.2
	20.0	12.8	17.9			Trade Payables	17.7	16.4
	.4	.3	.2			Income Taxes Payable	.1	.3
	10.4	13.1	12.2			All Other Current	14.3	10.7
	45.6	41.7	42.1			Total Current	49.4	44.0
	21.6	20.1	6.6			Long-Term Debt	18.0	15.3
	.7	.6	1.8			Deferred Taxes	1.0	.7
	10.7	5.4	3.0			All Other Non-Current	2.2	5.9
	21.4	32.1	46.6			Net Worth	29.5	34.1
	100.0	100.0	100.0			Total Liabilities & Net Worth	100.0	100.0
						INCOME DATA		
	100.0	100.0	100.0			Net Sales	100.0	100.0
	35.3	25.2	23.6			Gross Profit	28.1	29.9
	31.8	21.6	18.1			Operating Expenses	27.3	27.8
	3.5	3.6	5.5			Operating Profit	.8	2.1
	1.8	1.1	.5			All Other Expenses (net)	.7	.6
	1.8	2.5	4.9			Profit Before Taxes	.0	1.5
						RATIOS		
	2.1	2.9	2.5			Current	2.0	2.2
	1.3	1.8	1.5				1.5	1.4
	1.0	1.2	1.1				1.0	1.2
	1.4	1.4	1.2			Quick	1.2	1.5
	.9	.9	.7				.7	.8
	.5	.7	.6				.5	.5
	28 13.2	32 11.3	34 10.7			Sales/Receivables	35 10.5	31 12.0
	41 8.9	45 8.1	43 8.5				45 8.1	41 9.0
	69 5.3	59 6.1	66 5.5				57 6.4	53 6.9
	3 123.7	19 18.9	36 10.2			Cost of Sales/Inventory	26 14.0	20 18.1
	15 25.1	40 9.2	53 6.8				58 6.3	47 7.7
	38 9.6	72 5.1	69 5.3				80 4.5	78 4.7
	17 21.9	10 37.6	20 18.3			Cost of Sales/Payables	18 20.6	13 28.0
	31 11.8	20 17.9	27 13.4				26 14.3	26 13.8
	43 8.5	30 12.3	43 8.5				43 8.6	41 8.8
	8.6	6.1	5.1			Sales/Working Capital	7.0	7.1
	17.9	8.9	10.9				14.7	13.5
	130.3	15.9	62.8				218.0	38.3
	9.5	7.3	16.2			EBIT/Interest	6.9	7.8
	(17) 3.2	(24) 3.7	9.4				(48) 1.7	(62) 2.3
	.9	2.1	1.5				-2.9	-.1
	8.6					Net Profit + Depr., Dep., Amort./Cur. Mat. L/T/D	8.5	4.0
	(10) 2.3						(15) 1.1	(17) 1.4
	.8						-1.1	.0
	.4	.3	.3			Fixed/Worth	.4	.3
	.8	.5	.6				.6	.6
	-2.0	1.5	.7				2.0	1.8
	1.0	.8	.6			Debt/Worth	1.0	1.0
	2.7	1.8	1.3				1.7	1.8
	-10.0	5.3	1.8				5.0	4.5
	53.7	33.8	40.4			% Profit Before Taxes/Tangible Net Worth	34.5	42.1
	(13) 13.1	(21) 24.7	18.4				(42) 10.5	(58) 13.0
	4.9	13.1	3.2				-13.1	-10.6
	26.1	15.1	15.0			% Profit Before Taxes/Total Assets	10.3	12.0
	7.0	10.1	10.3				2.4	3.3
	.3	3.7	1.0				-8.3	-3.7
	21.5	22.6	19.8			Sales/Net Fixed Assets	24.5	26.2
	12.8	15.3	8.1				11.6	13.3
	4.0	12.0	5.2				6.0	7.3
	4.2	3.6	2.6			Sales/Total Assets	3.1	3.3
	2.9	2.8	2.1				2.6	2.6
	2.0	2.2	1.7				2.0	1.9
	.9	.7	.8			% Depr., Dep., Amort./Sales	1.2	1.0
	(16) 2.4	(24) 1.4	(12) 1.5				(47) 2.3	(58) 2.1
	4.0	2.2	2.6				3.5	3.0
	4.0	1.7				% Officers', Directors' Owners' Comp/Sales	1.9	2.7
	(12) 5.9	(11) 2.3					(22) 4.8	(32) 5.3
	8.9	3.5					7.8	9.4
4843M	82396M	287472M	563021M	269316M	200191M	Net Sales ($)	988929M	746383M
1338M	24843M	105701M	258155M	149218M	106906M	Total Assets ($)	506743M	343192M

M = $ thousand   MM = $ million

See Pages 11 through 21 for Explanation of Ratios and Data

Comparative Historical Data   Current Data Sorted by Sales

Hist 1	Hist 2	Hist 3	Type of Statement	0-1MM	1-3MM	3-5MM	5-10MM	10-25MM	25MM & OVER
10	6	8	Unqualified		1			2	5
14	16	26	Reviewed		3	2	8	6	7
8	5	11	Compiled	1	3	1	3	3	
3	5	5	Tax Returns		3		2		
17	18	14	Other		2	2	3	5	2
4/1/04-3/31/05 ALL	4/1/05-3/31/06 ALL	4/1/06-3/31/07 ALL			17 (4/1-9/30/06)		47 (10/1/06-3/31/07)		
52	50	64	NUMBER OF STATEMENTS	1	12	5	16	16	14
%	%	%	**ASSETS**	%	%	%	%	%	%
4.8	9.8	5.9	Cash & Equivalents		9.7		9.0	4.8	2.1
35.0	28.5	33.0	Trade Receivables (net)		23.7		44.0	29.9	32.1
29.2	26.1	21.5	Inventory		17.3		14.5	33.4	22.3
4.8	2.9	5.6	All Other Current		3.5		8.7	4.7	5.7
73.7	67.2	66.0	Total Current		54.2		76.3	72.8	62.2
18.6	23.2	27.0	Fixed Assets (net)		42.4		17.4	20.2	28.2
2.0	3.2	1.5	Intangibles (net)		.7		.4	3.4	1.1
5.6	6.4	5.5	All Other Non-Current		2.7		6.0	3.5	8.5
100.0	100.0	100.0	Total		100.0		100.0	100.0	100.0
			LIABILITIES						
19.1	13.3	12.5	Notes Payable-Short Term		22.5		9.3	11.2	8.4
4.8	3.5	3.6	Cur. Mat.-L.T.D.		5.3		2.0	4.3	1.7
17.9	17.2	15.8	Trade Payables		13.0		22.3	11.1	17.6
.3	.7	.2	Income Taxes Payable		.1		.6	.2	.2
13.4	12.8	11.2	All Other Current		2.4		11.4	15.8	13.1
55.5	47.4	43.3	Total Current		43.3		45.5	42.6	40.9
15.3	15.1	17.1	Long-Term Debt		17.2		17.7	16.3	11.7
.9	1.0	.9	Deferred Taxes		.3		.7	1.4	1.0
11.3	4.8	6.1	All Other Non-Current		8.9		7.7	2.4	3.5
17.0	31.6	32.6	Net Worth		30.3		28.4	37.3	42.9
100.0	100.0	100.0	Total Liabilities & Net Worth		100.0		100.0	100.0	100.0
			INCOME DATA						
100.0	100.0	100.0	Net Sales		100.0		100.0	100.0	100.0
27.4	27.3	27.4	Gross Profit		32.2		23.5	26.6	25.2
27.0	25.1	24.2	Operating Expenses		31.2		20.8	22.5	19.2
.4	2.2	3.2	Operating Profit		1.0		2.7	4.1	5.9
1.1	1.0	1.1	All Other Expenses (net)		1.1		.7	.7	.8
-.7	1.2	2.1	Profit Before Taxes		-.1		2.0	3.4	5.2
			RATIOS						
2.2	1.9	2.3	Current		2.8		3.0	3.0	2.1
1.5	1.5	1.6			1.2		1.8	1.8	1.6
1.1	1.1	1.1			.9		1.2	1.3	1.2
1.3	1.0	1.3	Quick		1.7		1.7	1.1	1.3
.8	.7	.9			.7		1.1	.8	.9
.5	.5	.6			.3		.9	.6	.6
34 10.6	27 13.8	30 12.0	Sales/Receivables		14 25.8		35 10.5	25 14.6	40 9.1
48 7.6	35 10.3	42 8.8			37 10.0		42 8.8	33 11.0	47 7.8
61 6.0	53 6.9	61 6.0			54 6.7		73 5.0	50 7.2	65 5.6
24 15.5	21 17.4	15 23.8	Cost of Sales/Inventory		5 73.8		4 93.9	29 12.5	35 10.5
49 7.4	48 7.7	38 9.6			15 24.3		17 20.9	58 6.2	51 7.1
93 3.9	79 4.6	62 5.9			77 4.8		42 8.7	93 3.9	57 6.4
20 17.9	15 23.9	16 22.3	Cost of Sales/Payables		16 22.9		17 20.9	9 41.2	20 18.5
28 12.9	24 15.0	22 16.5			25 14.5		30 12.3	18 20.7	26 14.0
44 8.3	36 10.2	37 9.8			44 8.4		41 8.9	27 13.7	42 8.7
6.4	8.4	6.1	Sales/Working Capital		7.1		7.8	5.0	6.0
14.4	18.9	12.0			34.9		9.2	11.8	11.4
32.1	110.6	45.4			-119.0		22.6	23.4	42.5
9.2	6.3	9.7	EBIT/Interest		10.9		7.7	11.2	15.4
2.0	(45) 2.7	(59) 4.2			(10) 1.3		(13) 3.2	5.7	7.5
-.1	-.4	1.4			-1.1		2.0	2.8	3.6
4.2	4.1	7.6	Net Profit + Depr., Dep., Amort./Cur. Mat. L/T/D						
(20) 1.7	(15) 2.5	(27) 5.4							
1.0	.0	2.2							
.3	.3	.4	Fixed/Worth		.5		.3	.3	.3
.7	.6	.6			1.1		.5	.5	.6
2.8	1.5	1.8			NM		1.7	1.0	.9
1.3	1.2	.8	Debt/Worth		.5		.8	.5	.7
2.6	2.1	1.8			2.3		2.1	1.1	1.6
14.7	3.8	5.4			NM		5.8	3.2	2.1
35.4	34.8	37.9	% Profit Before Taxes/Tangible Net Worth				40.8	32.4	37.8
(42) 12.4	(45) 16.5	(53) 21.5					(13) 21.9	(13) 22.3	23.0
1.5	-.3	4.9					7.8	12.6	9.4
8.8	9.2	15.1	% Profit Before Taxes/Total Assets		7.9		24.0	14.9	15.6
2.8	4.6	8.1			-.5		8.0	11.1	9.0
-3.8	-2.1	1.3			-9.6		2.1	5.8	2.2
41.6	39.6	22.1	Sales/Net Fixed Assets		12.2		26.5	29.8	17.9
18.5	12.4	13.3			6.5		17.3	13.9	10.1
9.2	6.2	5.5			4.0		14.1	8.0	4.2
3.6	3.8	3.5	Sales/Total Assets		3.4		4.1	3.7	2.7
2.7	2.4	2.6			2.3		2.9	3.0	2.2
2.0	1.7	2.0			2.0		2.6	1.8	1.9
.8	.8	.9	% Depr., Dep., Amort./Sales		1.8		.6	.7	.9
(46) 1.6	(41) 2.0	(58) 1.7			(11) 2.5		(13) 1.2	1.3	(13) 1.7
2.7	3.3	2.7			4.0		1.9	2.5	2.7
2.3	1.6	2.0	% Officers', Directors' Owners' Comp/Sales						
(23) 4.2	(16) 3.3	(25) 4.0							
6.9	6.5	7.0							
852603M	1069946M	1407239M	Net Sales ($)	726M	23226M	18081M	118356M	253174M	993676M
352901M	475695M	646161M	Total Assets ($)	751M	10504M	9973M	37220M	105489M	482224M

© RMA 2007
M = $ thousand   MM = $ million
See Pages 11 through 21 for Explanation of Ratios and Data

Current Data Sorted by Assets   Comparative Historical Data

0-500M	500M-2MM	2-10MM	10-50MM	50-100MM	100-250MM	Type of Statement	4/1/02-3/31/03 ALL	4/1/03-3/31/04 ALL
		4	6	5	1	Unqualified	13	11
1	3	11	3			Reviewed	17	9
	2	1				Compiled	6	5
1	3	1				Tax Returns	1	1
2	5	7	9	1	3	Other	17	17
	16 (4/1-9/30/06)		53 (10/1/06-3/31/07)					
4	13	24	18	6	4	**NUMBER OF STATEMENTS**	54	43
%	%	%	%	%	%	**ASSETS**	%	%
	5.1	6.6	5.8			Cash & Equivalents	6.8	7.3
	36.7	30.6	26.6			Trade Receivables (net)	30.0	35.3
	21.9	30.0	18.5			Inventory	27.0	25.8
	8.6	2.7	1.8			All Other Current	3.6	2.7
	72.2	69.9	52.7			Total Current	67.4	71.1
	14.6	19.9	23.0			Fixed Assets (net)	22.6	17.9
	7.7	5.7	17.3			Intangibles (net)	5.0	5.1
	5.5	4.4	7.0			All Other Non-Current	5.1	5.9
	100.0	100.0	100.0			Total	100.0	100.0
						LIABILITIES		
	12.9	18.7	6.1			Notes Payable-Short Term	13.3	16.5
	4.2	3.1	5.1			Cur. Mat.-L.T.D.	3.3	3.1
	23.1	20.9	10.9			Trade Payables	13.8	19.8
	.0	.1	.3			Income Taxes Payable	.1	.2
	8.4	13.5	12.8			All Other Current	14.2	13.8
	48.6	56.3	35.3			Total Current	44.7	53.4
	15.2	11.8	18.5			Long-Term Debt	8.6	9.9
	.0	.3	1.1			Deferred Taxes	.5	.4
	10.3	8.9	4.9			All Other Non-Current	7.1	21.8
	25.9	22.7	40.2			Net Worth	39.1	14.5
	100.0	100.0	100.0			Total Liabilities & Net Worth	100.0	100.0
						INCOME DATA		
	100.0	100.0	100.0			Net Sales	100.0	100.0
	37.7	28.2	33.9			Gross Profit	29.7	29.4
	34.3	25.2	25.9			Operating Expenses	27.7	28.2
	3.4	3.0	8.0			Operating Profit	2.0	1.3
	.6	1.2	1.2			All Other Expenses (net)	.5	1.2
	2.8	1.8	6.8			Profit Before Taxes	1.5	.0
						RATIOS		
	2.5	1.6	2.1			Current	2.3	2.3
	1.8	1.3	1.4				1.7	1.5
	1.0	.9	1.1				1.2	1.1
	1.6	1.1	1.3			Quick	1.4	1.4
	.8	.6	1.1				.9	.9
	.6	.4	.6				.5	.6
	25 14.9	24 15.0	35 10.4			Sales/Receivables	31 11.9	36 10.1
	30 12.2	36 10.1	42 8.6				40 9.2	46 7.9
	42 8.7	50 7.3	56 6.5				48 7.6	57 6.4
	6 56.7	24 15.1	22 16.6			Cost of Sales/Inventory	24 15.2	25 14.6
	28 13.1	52 7.1	42 8.7				45 8.2	47 7.7
	58 6.3	73 5.0	88 4.1				74 5.0	68 5.4
	8 45.5	23 16.1	13 27.6			Cost of Sales/Payables	15 24.2	23 16.2
	30 12.1	35 10.3	25 14.4				22 16.8	40 9.1
	55 6.6	43 8.4	39 9.3				36 10.2	60 6.0
	6.2	9.0	7.9			Sales/Working Capital	7.1	7.5
	12.7	15.6	12.7				11.8	12.4
	NM	NM	NM				49.8	42.4
	9.4	7.5	15.9			EBIT/Interest	9.5	6.3
	(12) 5.8	(23) 2.8	(16) 5.6				(51) 3.3	(40) 2.8
	-.5	1.5	2.9				1.1	-1.5
			7.4			Net Profit + Depr., Dep., Amort./Cur. Mat. L/T/D	7.7	4.5
		(11) 2.9					(22) 3.1	(15) 2.9
			1.0				1.7	1.3
	.2	.3	.4			Fixed/Worth	.3	.3
	1.1	.8	1.0				.5	.8
	-3.3	NM	NM				1.2	3.4
	.8	1.3	1.0			Debt/Worth	.7	1.0
	2.5	2.7	2.4				1.4	2.6
	-74.2	NM	NM				3.5	14.6
		41.5	62.4			% Profit Before Taxes/Tangible Net Worth	32.4	38.8
	(18)	24.6	(14) 33.9				(49) 10.1	(34) 10.1
		4.7	10.7				2.4	-3.5
	32.8	10.7	21.4			% Profit Before Taxes/Total Assets	9.1	10.5
	13.5	5.0	12.3				4.5	3.3
	-4.4	.7	3.3				.7	-3.0
	88.6	38.0	34.2			Sales/Net Fixed Assets	35.7	58.7
	30.5	18.4	10.5				13.1	14.5
	15.5	10.2	4.8				5.8	8.5
	5.7	3.6	2.7			Sales/Total Assets	3.8	3.6
	4.2	2.8	1.9				2.6	2.5
	2.7	2.3	1.5				1.8	1.7
	.4	.5	1.1			% Depr., Dep., Amort./Sales	1.1	.8
	.6	(21) 1.0	(17) 1.7				(49) 2.4	(36) 1.8
	1.6	2.0	2.9				3.5	3.0
						% Officers', Directors' Owners' Comp/Sales	1.5	1.9
							(25) 3.4	(14) 4.5
							7.3	8.2
4703M	54231M	376854M	946590M	668653M	937258M	Net Sales ($)	1087681M	1158249M
1043M	13129M	130420M	422987M	368363M	625882M	Total Assets ($)	589378M	608883M

© RMA 2007

M = $ thousand   MM = $ million
See Pages 11 through 21 for Explanation of Ratios and Data

Comparative Historical Data   Current Data Sorted by Sales

Type of Statement

Type of Statement	04-05	05-06	06-07	0-1MM	1-3MM	3-5MM	5-10MM	10-25MM	25MM & OVER
Unqualified	13	18	16				2	2	12
Reviewed	11	19	18	1	1	1	5	8	2
Compiled	5	3	3			1	1	1	
Tax Returns	4	8	5		3	2			
Other	20	26	27	2	1	3	2	10	9
	4/1/04- 3/31/05 ALL	4/1/05- 3/31/06 ALL	4/1/06- 3/31/07 ALL		16 (4/1-9/30/06)			53 (10/1/06-3/31/07)	
NUMBER OF STATEMENTS	53	74	69	3	5	7	10	21	23

Data

	04-05 ALL %	05-06 ALL %	06-07 ALL %	0-1MM	1-3MM	3-5MM	5-10MM %	10-25MM %	25MM & OVER %
ASSETS									
Cash & Equivalents	2.8	7.5	6.4				10.9	2.8	6.5
Trade Receivables (net)	35.4	31.5	30.3				30.3	29.6	30.8
Inventory	22.9	21.7	24.6				25.1	27.8	19.6
All Other Current	2.5	3.3	3.4				4.0	2.8	2.3
Total Current	63.5	64.0	64.7				70.4	63.0	59.2
Fixed Assets (net)	23.0	22.4	19.3				20.4	20.9	18.7
Intangibles (net)	7.8	8.3	10.5				2.7	11.8	15.1
All Other Non-Current	5.7	5.3	5.5				6.5	4.3	7.0
Total	100.0	100.0	100.0				100.0	100.0	100.0
LIABILITIES									
Notes Payable-Short Term	16.0	11.8	12.4				20.9	17.3	8.3
Cur. Mat.-L.T.D.	2.6	4.2	4.5				3.6	2.8	4.7
Trade Payables	19.0	18.1	17.5				10.3	21.5	12.0
Income Taxes Payable	.3	.3	.2				.2	.1	.4
All Other Current	13.3	12.6	11.4				10.8	13.9	12.7
Total Current	51.2	47.0	45.9				45.9	55.6	38.0
Long-Term Debt	15.2	20.3	18.3				12.0	15.8	25.2
Deferred Taxes	.8	.5	.6				.6	.7	.9
All Other Non-Current	9.4	5.1	7.0				2.5	9.9	5.2
Net Worth	23.4	27.1	28.1				39.0	18.1	30.7
Total Liabilities & Net Worth	100.0	100.0	100.0				100.0	100.0	100.0
INCOME DATA									
Net Sales	100.0	100.0	100.0				100.0	100.0	100.0
Gross Profit	28.7	33.0	32.1				30.3	29.6	29.9
Operating Expenses	26.0	28.8	27.3				27.2	25.7	22.7
Operating Profit	2.7	4.2	4.8				3.1	3.8	7.1
All Other Expenses (net)	1.5	1.2	1.2				.7	1.4	1.9
Profit Before Taxes	1.2	2.9	3.6				2.4	2.4	5.2
RATIOS									
Current	1.5	2.2	2.2				2.6	1.4	2.2
	1.2	1.4	1.4				1.6	1.1	1.5
	1.0	1.1	1.1				1.3	.9	1.2
Quick	1.1	1.3	1.3				1.5	.9	1.4
	.7	.9	.8				1.0	.6	1.1
	.5	.5	.5				.5	.5	.7
Sales/Receivables	35 10.4	31 11.8	29 12.5				21 17.3	33 11.2	38 9.6
	48 7.7	43 8.5	42 8.7				32 11.3	44 8.2	46 7.9
	68 5.4	55 6.7	55 6.7				38 9.6	54 6.7	61 6.0
Cost of Sales/Inventory	25 14.4	24 14.9	23 16.0				16 23.0	24 15.1	24 14.9
	42 8.6	35 10.3	42 8.7				32 11.2	48 7.6	42 8.8
	60 6.1	68 5.4	83 4.4				121 3.0	77 4.8	83 4.4
Cost of Sales/Payables	20 18.0	19 19.1	14 25.3				8 43.5	23 16.0	13 27.1
	38 9.6	33 10.9	31 11.9				25 14.9	36 10.1	28 13.1
	46 8.0	49 7.5	47 7.8				32 11.5	52 7.0	44 8.3
Sales/Working Capital	10.1	7.9	7.5				4.4	12.6	7.3
	27.5	15.3	13.2				10.6	77.1	11.8
	106.0	93.1	95.7				NM	-56.3	24.6
EBIT/Interest	7.6	10.5	8.6				15.0	5.6	12.6
	(49) 2.9	(65) 3.6	(64) 3.5				6.3	(20) 2.5	(21) 3.2
	.2	1.4	1.4				1.5	.7	1.7
Net Profit + Depr., Dep., Amort./Cur. Mat. L/T/D	8.0	4.6	7.0						8.5
	(16) 2.1	(23) 2.9	(28) 2.6					(15)	2.8
	1.3	1.1	1.0						1.0
Fixed/Worth	.5	.4	.3				.3	.5	.3
	1.3	1.2	.9				.6	1.4	1.2
	-3.5	-4.3	-9.7				1.5	-1.0	-1.7
Debt/Worth	1.4	1.0	1.0				.7	2.1	.7
	3.3	3.6	2.5				1.4	5.2	4.4
	-17.0	-23.2	-32.8				4.9	-13.7	-7.9
% Profit Before Taxes/Tangible Net Worth	53.5	49.3	51.7					55.2	62.7
	(36) 22.0	(55) 29.0	(50) 23.9					(13) 23.8	(17) 25.5
	4.5	9.3	2.8					-2.1	6.3
% Profit Before Taxes/Total Assets	13.2	15.9	15.3				13.6	12.6	15.5
	4.1	5.3	6.6				3.9	5.6	5.8
	-4.1	1.9	1.1				.7	-1.0	2.1
Sales/Net Fixed Assets	32.2	44.7	39.4				30.6	32.0	43.9
	11.9	14.2	18.2				16.5	18.1	12.7
	4.7	5.8	7.6				8.5	7.4	7.2
Sales/Total Assets	3.6	3.8	3.7				4.4	3.5	3.4
	2.3	2.4	2.6				2.7	2.7	2.2
	1.6	1.9	1.7				1.5	1.7	1.7
% Depr., Dep., Amort./Sales	.9	.8	.5				.5	.5	1.1
	(49) 1.9	(66) 1.6	(63) 1.4				1.6	(18) 1.3	(21) 1.9
	3.0	2.8	2.4				1.9	2.7	3.2
% Officers', Directors' Owners' Comp/Sales	2.3	2.2	2.0						
	(16) 4.6	(21) 4.9	(17) 2.7						
	8.0	6.8	7.3						
Net Sales ($)	1341385M	3476244M	2988289M	1908M	10193M	27589M	78528M	386957M	2483114M
Total Assets ($)	813771M	1425370M	1561824M	1341M	3070M	8294M	37771M	166212M	1345136M

© RMA 2007

M = $ thousand   MM = $ million
See Pages 11 through 21 for Explanation of Ratios and Data

Current Data Sorted by Assets   Comparative Historical Data

0-500M	500M-2MM	2-10MM	10-50MM	50-100MM	100-250MM	Type of Statement	4/1/02-3/31/03 ALL	4/1/03-3/31/04 ALL
	1	8	10	2	1	Unqualified	24	18
	5	28	4			Reviewed	44	52
1	6	8	1			Compiled	37	38
1	8	3				Tax Returns	11	23
1	5	16	9	3	1	Other	56	64
	22 (4/1-9/30/06)		100 (10/1/06-3/31/07)					
3	25	63	24	5	2	NUMBER OF STATEMENTS	172	195
%	%	%	%	%	%	**ASSETS**	%	%
	10.9	7.3	6.4			Cash & Equivalents	7.9	7.7
	37.5	33.6	28.5			Trade Receivables (net)	30.6	30.0
	21.4	24.1	23.1			Inventory	22.2	22.3
	2.2	2.4	2.7			All Other Current	2.2	2.2
	72.1	67.4	60.7			Total Current	62.8	62.2
	21.7	26.0	27.0			Fixed Assets (net)	26.4	27.6
	2.3	3.5	8.0			Intangibles (net)	5.1	4.6
	3.9	3.2	4.3			All Other Non-Current	5.8	5.5
	100.0	100.0	100.0			Total	100.0	100.0
						LIABILITIES		
	19.0	12.5	13.5			Notes Payable-Short Term	11.3	12.3
	4.0	4.0	2.7			Cur. Mat.-L.T.D.	3.4	4.2
	18.3	15.2	10.8			Trade Payables	15.9	13.5
	.1	.2	1.0			Income Taxes Payable	.3	.3
	6.8	13.9	10.5			All Other Current	12.1	13.1
	48.2	45.7	38.5			Total Current	43.1	43.4
	16.1	19.2	18.5			Long-Term Debt	16.2	14.6
	.4	.3	.4			Deferred Taxes	.4	.4
	2.8	2.8	3.6			All Other Non-Current	7.0	9.0
	32.6	31.9	38.9			Net Worth	33.3	32.5
	100.0	100.0	100.0			Total Liabilties & Net Worth	100.0	100.0
						INCOME DATA		
	100.0	100.0	100.0			Net Sales	100.0	100.0
	33.5	28.3	28.5			Gross Profit	29.7	28.8
	28.8	23.3	21.8			Operating Expenses	26.8	25.7
	4.6	5.0	6.8			Operating Profit	2.9	3.1
	1.3	1.0	1.2			All Other Expenses (net)	1.0	.9
	3.3	4.0	5.6			Profit Before Taxes	1.9	2.2
						RATIOS		
	2.9	2.0	2.0				2.5	2.5
	1.4	1.4	1.5			Current	1.5	1.6
	.9	1.1	1.3				1.0	1.0
	1.6	1.3	1.3				1.6	1.6
	1.1	.8	.8			Quick	.9	.9
	.5	.6	.6				.5	.6
26	14.1	33 11.0	39 9.4				31 11.7	31 11.8
34	10.8	45 8.1	51 7.1			Sales/Receivables	45 8.2	44 8.4
60	6.1	61 6.0	62 5.9				60 6.1	59 6.2
4	87.7	24 14.9	23 15.8				26 14.0	25 14.8
21	17.7	43 8.6	60 6.1			Cost of Sales/Inventory	43 8.5	42 8.7
57	6.4	67 5.4	82 4.4				72 5.0	67 5.5
16	23.2	15 23.6	16 22.2				16 22.5	14 25.8
25	14.4	29 12.7	26 13.9			Cost of Sales/Payables	29 12.5	24 15.1
37	10.0	44 8.2	43 8.4				48 7.6	38 9.7
	6.0	7.7	5.8				6.4	5.7
	16.9	13.3	12.2			Sales/Working Capital	12.9	12.0
	NM	48.0	19.1				-553.9	284.7
	9.8	11.0	9.8				7.7	8.0
	(23) 6.6	(58) 3.1	3.4			EBIT/Interest	(155) 2.6	(176) 3.0
	1.5	1.4	2.4				.2	.7
		6.5	11.3			Net Profit + Depr., Dep.,	2.4	3.7
		(17) 1.7	(14) 4.6			Amort./Cur. Mat. L/T/D	(37) 1.1	(52) 2.1
		1.1	2.0				-.5	.7
	.2	.3	.5				.3	.4
	.8	.6	.9			Fixed/Worth	.9	.9
	2.3	1.9	2.0				2.6	3.6
	1.0	1.0	.8				.8	.7
	2.2	2.0	2.2			Debt/Worth	1.9	1.7
	11.9	3.5	4.3				7.5	16.2
	108.0	48.1	55.7			% Profit Before Taxes/Tangible	39.6	38.2
	(20) 26.0	(58) 15.4	(23) 31.1			Net Worth	(141) 12.5	(157) 12.7
	6.9	6.2	16.0				1.2	1.8
	26.7	17.1	19.5			% Profit Before Taxes/Total	12.9	12.4
	7.9	6.2	6.6			Assets	4.3	4.1
	.5	1.7	4.7				-2.0	-.7
	61.4	28.1	22.6				23.1	22.3
	20.7	11.5	8.4			Sales/Net Fixed Assets	11.4	10.0
	10.4	6.3	4.0				6.0	5.5
	4.0	3.3	2.6				3.1	3.2
	3.1	2.7	2.2			Sales/Total Assets	2.4	2.3
	2.7	1.8	1.8				1.8	1.8
	.5	1.0	1.0				1.0	1.1
	(20) 1.5	(57) 1.8	(21) 1.4			% Depr., Dep., Amort./Sales	(151) 1.9	(168) 1.8
	2.3	2.8	2.5				2.9	3.3
	2.9	2.0				% Officers', Directors'	2.7	2.1
	(16) 4.6	(26) 4.0				Owners' Comp/Sales	(65) 6.1	(71) 3.8
	7.6	5.8					9.7	7.5
5685M	97571M	819931M	1154508M	671469M	450501M	Net Sales ($)	5059905M	3865887M
1230M	29224M	311198M	542368M	356115M	272930M	Total Assets ($)	1978167M	2109915M

M = $ thousand   MM = $ million
See Pages 11 through 21 for Explanation of Ratios and Data

Comparative Historical Data   Current Data Sorted by Sales

			Type of Statement	0-1MM	1-3MM	3-5MM	5-10MM	10-25MM	25MM & OVER
26	31	22	Unqualified		1			2	19
50	35	38	Reviewed		4	4	6	21	3
34	23	16	Compiled		4	1	9	1	1
22	19	12	Tax Returns		5	2	4	1	1
49	48	34	Other		2	1	8	11	12
4/1/04-3/31/05 ALL	4/1/05-3/31/06 ALL	4/1/06-3/31/07 ALL			22 (4/1-9/30/06)		100 (10/1/06-3/31/07)		
181	156	122	**NUMBER OF STATEMENTS**		16	8	27	36	35
%	%	%	**ASSETS**	%	%	%	%	%	%
6.9	6.9	7.6	Cash & Equivalents		9.1		6.9	8.3	4.8
30.7	31.4	33.5	Trade Receivables (net)		35.5		34.5	34.3	32.5
24.8	23.7	23.1	Inventory		13.5		22.2	25.9	25.2
1.7	3.1	2.3	All Other Current		2.4		1.8	2.4	2.8
64.1	65.0	66.6	Total Current		60.5		65.4	70.8	65.3
26.9	25.1	25.4	Fixed Assets (net)		32.5		26.2	23.1	23.8
4.7	5.6	4.5	Intangibles (net)		1.7		4.4	3.9	7.1
4.3	4.3	3.5	All Other Non-Current		5.4		3.9	2.2	3.8
100.0	100.0	100.0	Total		100.0		100.0	100.0	100.0
			LIABILITIES						
13.7	13.2	13.8	Notes Payable-Short Term		17.7		16.3	12.1	11.7
3.9	2.9	3.7	Cur. Mat.-L.T.D.		5.0		3.3	4.8	2.2
16.3	17.1	15.1	Trade Payables		14.6		20.5	14.0	13.1
.2	.2	.3	Income Taxes Payable		.0		.1	.2	.8
11.3	12.7	11.6	All Other Current		7.5		8.2	15.1	14.1
45.4	46.1	44.5	Total Current		44.8		48.4	46.3	42.0
19.4	15.2	18.8	Long-Term Debt		25.1		15.1	22.6	16.5
.5	.4	.4	Deferred Taxes		.2		.8	.2	.4
7.7	8.1	3.2	All Other Non-Current		3.3		3.3	3.5	3.4
27.1	30.2	33.0	Net Worth		26.6		32.5	27.4	37.7
100.0	100.0	100.0	Total Liabilities & Net Worth		100.0		100.0	100.0	100.0
			INCOME DATA						
100.0	100.0	100.0	Net Sales		100.0		100.0	100.0	100.0
28.6	29.5	29.4	Gross Profit		35.9		26.2	30.8	26.0
25.0	25.2	24.3	Operating Expenses		30.5		22.7	23.4	20.8
3.6	4.3	5.1	Operating Profit		5.3		3.6	7.4	5.2
1.1	1.0	1.1	All Other Expenses (net)		1.6		1.7	.5	1.1
2.4	3.3	4.0	Profit Before Taxes		3.8		1.9	6.9	4.1
			RATIOS						
2.0	2.2	2.1	Current		2.7		1.9	2.1	2.0
1.5	1.5	1.4			1.4		1.3	1.5	1.4
1.1	1.1	1.1			.8		1.0	1.2	1.3
1.3	1.3	1.3	Quick		2.3		1.4	1.3	1.2
.8	.8	.8			.8		.8	.8	.8
.5	.5	.6			.5		.5	.6	.6
28 12.8	32 11.5	33 11.1	Sales/Receivables		27 13.6		32 11.5	33 11.0	38 9.5
45 8.2	44 8.2	45 8.1			35 10.5		40 9.0	48 7.7	49 7.5
61 6.0	63 5.8	62 5.9			63 5.8		60 6.1	64 5.7	62 5.9
24 15.2	22 16.7	21 17.1	Cost of Sales/Inventory		2 150.2		20 18.1	31 11.9	26 14.2
44 8.3	45 8.2	44 8.4			15 23.9		45 8.2	47 7.8	46 7.9
77 4.7	72 5.1	71 5.1			45 8.1		60 6.1	78 4.7	73 5.0
17 21.5	17 21.6	17 21.7	Cost of Sales/Payables		15 24.6		18 19.8	16 23.1	16 22.2
26 13.8	26 13.9	27 13.7			23 16.0		31 11.7	24 15.0	25 14.8
43 8.4	41 8.8	41 8.8			35 10.4		45 8.0	44 8.2	34 10.6
6.6	6.2	6.6	Sales/Working Capital		6.2		9.6	6.0	6.6
14.4	11.9	13.8			21.1		15.5	11.9	14.6
57.4	64.4	43.1			-24.0		-468.2	25.1	20.3
8.4	8.7	9.9	EBIT/Interest		8.9		6.4	16.0	8.6
(172) 3.4	(149) 3.2	(114) 3.5			(14) 2.5		(25) 2.2	(34) 4.3	(34) 3.7
.9	1.3	1.7			1.0		1.2	2.2	2.3
6.4	6.8	6.9	Net Profit + Depr., Dep., Amort./Cur. Mat. L/T/D					4.8	16.1
(41) 1.9	(32) 3.3	(43) 3.3						(11) 2.2	(21) 4.7
.7	1.6	1.1						1.1	1.2
.4	.3	.3	Fixed/Worth		.3		.4	.3	.4
.9	.9	.7			1.2		.9	.6	.7
4.1	2.7	1.8			4.4		2.5	1.7	1.3
1.1	.9	1.0	Debt/Worth		.7		1.3	1.0	1.0
2.2	2.0	2.1			2.3		2.7	2.0	2.2
12.2	7.1	4.5			NM		4.9	3.7	4.3
42.2	47.2	50.0	% Profit Before Taxes/Tangible Net Worth		108.0		26.5	71.5	50.2
(147) 14.6	(131) 22.9	(110) 18.1			(12) 17.2		(24) 13.0	(32) 27.6	(34) 25.3
.4	9.4	6.5			-.6		5.6	8.8	11.3
12.3	14.2	17.9	% Profit Before Taxes/Total Assets		28.2		7.7	28.5	13.3
4.2	5.2	6.3			4.2		4.1	15.4	6.2
-.5	.9	1.8			-.2		1.6	3.0	3.9
24.8	26.7	28.5	Sales/Net Fixed Assets		28.2		31.4	45.4	26.0
11.3	12.6	11.7			11.2		13.1	12.1	11.6
5.5	6.7	6.8			4.3		7.3	6.4	7.4
3.3	3.3	3.3	Sales/Total Assets		3.8		3.9	3.3	2.8
2.5	2.4	2.7			3.0		2.7	2.7	2.3
1.8	1.7	1.9			2.1		1.7	1.7	1.9
1.0	1.0	1.0	% Depr., Dep., Amort./Sales		1.1		.7	.9	.8
(164) 1.8	(134) 1.7	(106) 1.6			(11) 1.7		(25) 1.9	(33) 1.6	(30) 1.3
3.0	2.8	2.8			3.5		3.0	2.6	2.3
2.0	2.2	1.9	% Officers', Directors', Owners' Comp/Sales		2.9		1.7	1.7	
(70) 4.5	(53) 4.9	(48) 3.9			(10) 5.4		(12) 4.6	(14) 3.8	
6.3	8.1	6.4			7.8		5.6	4.9	
3263767M	3435135M	3199665M	Net Sales ($)		35964M	30682M	191640M	503953M	2437426M
1659623M	1844600M	1513065M	Total Assets ($)		14507M	18931M	79796M	225534M	1174297M

M = $ thousand   MM = $ million
See Pages 11 through 21 for Explanation of Ratios and Data

Current Data Sorted by Assets

Comparative Historical Data

0-500M	500M-2MM	2-10MM	10-50MM	50-100MM	100-250MM	Type of Statement	4/1/02-3/31/03 ALL	4/1/03-3/31/04 ALL
		5	6	1	1	Unqualified	9	12
		8				Reviewed	9	8
2	3	4				Compiled	6	16
		1				Tax Returns	5	5
2	3	5	2		1	Other	11	10
	6 (4/1-9/30/06)		38 (10/1/06-3/31/07)					
4	6	23	8	1	2	NUMBER OF STATEMENTS	40	51
%	%	%	%	%	%	**ASSETS**	%	%
		5.2				Cash & Equivalents	7.2	10.1
		33.0				Trade Receivables (net)	29.9	28.1
		21.9				Inventory	26.7	24.4
		4.2				All Other Current	2.8	3.6
		64.2				Total Current	66.6	66.3
		25.0				Fixed Assets (net)	24.6	22.6
		1.6				Intangibles (net)	3.7	5.0
		9.2				All Other Non-Current	5.1	6.1
		100.0				Total	100.0	100.0
						LIABILITIES		
		9.3				Notes Payable-Short Term	7.6	8.8
		2.7				Cur. Mat.-L.T.D.	3.5	3.2
		24.4				Trade Payables	20.6	20.7
		.3				Income Taxes Payable	.3	.1
		8.5				All Other Current	10.6	11.5
		45.2				Total Current	42.6	44.4
		7.8				Long-Term Debt	11.5	14.8
		1.2				Deferred Taxes	1.0	1.0
		10.4				All Other Non-Current	6.9	5.5
		35.3				Net Worth	38.0	34.3
		100.0				Total Liabilties & Net Worth	100.0	100.0
						INCOME DATA		
		100.0				Net Sales	100.0	100.0
		30.9				Gross Profit	32.9	30.6
		28.3				Operating Expenses	30.6	28.0
		2.6				Operating Profit	2.3	2.6
		.0				All Other Expenses (net)	.1	.4
		2.6				Profit Before Taxes	2.3	2.1
						RATIOS		
		2.0				Current	2.4	2.5
		1.5					1.6	1.5
		1.1					1.3	1.1
		1.1				Quick	1.2	1.4
		.8					.9	.9
		.6					.5	.5
	25	14.9				Sales/Receivables	26 14.3	24 14.9
	33	11.0					33 11.0	33 10.9
	49	7.5					40 9.1	43 8.5
	24	15.0				Cost of Sales/Inventory	25 14.7	24 15.1
	30	12.0					35 10.5	33 10.9
	38	9.6					65 5.6	51 7.1
	20	18.3				Cost of Sales/Payables	21 17.5	17 22.1
	34	10.8					32 11.3	28 13.1
	42	8.6					40 9.2	44 8.3
		8.4				Sales/Working Capital	9.1	8.3
		17.8					14.1	16.0
		75.9					28.0	37.6
		15.1				EBIT/Interest	12.5	10.2
	(22)	3.6					(35) 2.9	(47) 3.0
		-.9					.4	1.0
		10.1				Net Profit + Depr., Dep., Amort./Cur. Mat. L/T/D	5.6	7.9
	(11)	3.4					(14) 2.5	(21) 2.8
		-.1					.8	1.1
		.3				Fixed/Worth	.4	.3
		.7					.6	.7
		1.2					1.5	1.6
		1.0				Debt/Worth	.8	.9
		1.6					1.7	2.1
		3.9					3.5	3.6
		54.6				% Profit Before Taxes/Tangible Net Worth	39.0	36.3
	(21)	15.6					(36) 19.0	(45) 18.6
		-12.0					-1.3	9.0
		17.4				% Profit Before Taxes/Total Assets	18.3	10.4
		7.1					4.0	6.0
		-4.2					-1.3	.3
		32.5				Sales/Net Fixed Assets	24.5	28.4
		18.6					17.2	15.5
		13.3					8.8	9.1
		4.4				Sales/Total Assets	4.2	4.5
		3.6					3.2	3.2
		2.7					2.4	2.1
		.8				% Depr., Dep., Amort./Sales	.9	.8
		1.4					(31) 1.3	(49) 1.3
		1.8					2.2	2.4
						% Officers', Directors' Owners' Comp/Sales	.8	2.1
							(19) 5.2	(21) 3.7
							9.8	8.9
8196M	20190M	450158M	451499M	136714M	944598M	Net Sales ($)	2348527M	1498861M
1376M	6740M	130287M	194969M	62922M	392349M	Total Assets ($)	621198M	643153M

M = $ thousand   MM = $ million
See Pages 11 through 21 for Explanation of Ratios and Data

Comparative Historical Data / Current Data Sorted by Sales

				Type of Statement						
	7	8	13	Unqualified				1	5	7
	5	6	8	Reviewed					7	1
	16	14	9	Compiled				1	1	1
	6	3	1	Tax Returns	3	2	2	1	1	
	10	15	13	Other	2	3		1	2	5
	4/1/04-3/31/05	4/1/05-3/31/06	4/1/06-3/31/07		0-1MM	6 (4/1-9/30/06) 1-3MM	3-5MM	5-10MM	38 (10/1/06-3/31/07) 10-25MM	25MM & OVER
	ALL	ALL	ALL							
	44	46	44	NUMBER OF STATEMENTS		5	5	4	16	14
	%	%	%	ASSETS	%	%	%	%	%	%
	12.9	13.0	10.7	Cash & Equivalents					6.3	19.4
	27.5	27.7	25.8	Trade Receivables (net)	D				29.7	26.0
	23.7	26.0	22.3	Inventory	A				20.1	14.4
	3.1	1.9	2.7	All Other Current	T				4.4	2.8
	67.3	68.5	61.5	Total Current	A				60.5	62.5
	20.2	21.3	25.9	Fixed Assets (net)					29.3	25.4
	4.2	2.5	5.1	Intangibles (net)	N				1.9	3.3
	8.3	7.7	7.5	All Other Non-Current	O				8.2	8.7
	100.0	100.0	100.0	Total	T				100.0	100.0
				LIABILITIES	A					
	6.6	7.5	7.4	Notes Payable-Short Term	V				9.6	2.5
	3.2	3.3	3.6	Cur. Mat.-L.T.D.	A				6.1	2.3
	19.3	22.4	18.9	Trade Payables	I				26.4	16.4
	.2	.2	.2	Income Taxes Payable	L				.5	.0
	12.6	9.6	11.0	All Other Current	A				7.8	8.2
	42.0	43.0	41.0	Total Current	B				50.5	29.5
	9.5	10.6	12.6	Long-Term Debt	L				8.5	6.9
	.7	.5	.8	Deferred Taxes	E				1.2	1.0
	6.0	4.8	7.6	All Other Non-Current					11.1	6.3
	41.8	41.2	38.0	Net Worth					28.8	56.4
	100.0	100.0	100.0	Total Liabilties & Net Worth					100.0	100.0
				INCOME DATA						
	100.0	100.0	100.0	Net Sales					100.0	100.0
	34.8	34.2	34.1	Gross Profit					31.6	33.7
	30.4	29.8	30.3	Operating Expenses					29.9	29.5
	4.4	4.4	3.8	Operating Profit					1.7	4.2
	.1	.3	.2	All Other Expenses (net)					-.5	.1
	4.3	4.1	3.6	Profit Before Taxes					2.1	4.1
				RATIOS						
	3.2	2.8	2.7						1.6	3.9
	1.6	1.7	1.7	Current					1.2	2.3
	1.1	1.2	1.1						1.0	1.4
	1.8	1.5	1.7						1.0	2.8
	.8	.9	.9	Quick					.7	1.7
	.7	.6	.6						.5	.9

11	34.4	19	19.2	18	19.8	Sales/Receivables							19	18.8	23	16.1

11	34.4	19	19.2	18	19.8	Sales/Receivables	19	18.8	23	16.1
32	11.4	34	10.6	32	11.4		30	12.1	33	11.1
47	7.8	42	8.7	43	8.5		46	8.0	43	8.4
25	14.5	23	15.7	23	15.9	Cost of Sales/Inventory	24	14.9	17	21.8
34	10.9	35	10.6	33	10.9		30	12.1	25	14.7
54	6.8	57	6.4	44	8.4		35	10.5	40	9.0
16	22.6	16	22.3	16	23.0	Cost of Sales/Payables	21	17.5	14	25.3
28	13.0	31	12.0	25	14.9		26	14.1	30	12.2
41	9.0	42	8.7	38	9.6		45	8.0	38	9.6
	7.7		6.7		6.7	Sales/Working Capital		14.9		4.6
	13.9		11.5		13.3			53.7		10.6
	52.0		58.1		131.3			NM		21.7
	21.0		68.8		19.2	EBIT/Interest		15.4		100.3
(34)	7.9	(41)	7.5	(42)	6.1			3.2	(12)	7.9
	3.2		1.9		1.1			-1.4		2.9
	15.7		14.1		10.6	Net Profit + Depr., Dep., Amort./Cur. Mat. L/T/D				
(10)	3.9	(12)	3.7	(14)	3.8					
	1.3		.8		-.3					
	.2		.3		.4	Fixed/Worth		.6		.3
	.5		.5		.6			.8		.4
	1.7		1.1		1.2			2.1		.7
	.7		.7		.7	Debt/Worth		1.4		.3
	1.3		1.4		1.3			2.6		.7
	5.1		7.5		5.2			13.2		1.5
	47.2		61.8		41.9	% Profit Before Taxes/Tangible Net Worth		86.7		35.1
(38)	27.4	(43)	31.3	(36)	16.7		(13)	5.6	(13)	17.2
	13.4		6.2		2.2			-20.7		13.4
	23.9		28.1		21.4	% Profit Before Taxes/Total Assets		18.4		15.1
	12.4		11.6		9.9			2.3		10.1
	2.9		2.6		1.0			-7.0		6.1
	39.6		37.6		31.2	Sales/Net Fixed Assets		34.2		18.8
	19.3		18.3		17.0			17.4		13.5
	10.6		10.4		7.5			6.0		7.2
	4.3		4.4		4.4	Sales/Total Assets		4.6		4.2
	3.5		3.7		3.5			3.5		3.0
	2.5		2.5		2.3			2.7		2.1
	.5		.7		1.1	% Depr., Dep., Amort./Sales		.8		1.1
(41)	1.1	(39)	1.2	(40)	1.4			1.4	(13)	1.7
	1.5		1.5		1.8			2.0		2.0
	1.6		1.1		1.5	% Officers', Directors' Owners' Comp/Sales				
(19)	2.9	(18)	2.1	(14)	3.6					
	5.7		4.7		4.4					

1458889M		1771276M		2011355M	Net Sales ($)	8885M	18306M	29946M	286476M	1667742M
566748M		707936M		788643M	Total Assets ($)	2746M	7313M	14228M	87250M	677106M

M = $ thousand   MM = $ million
See Pages 11 through 21 for Explanation of Ratios and Data

Current Data Sorted by Assets / Comparative Historical Data

0-500M	500M-2MM	2-10MM	10-50MM	50-100MM	100-250MM		4/1/02-3/31/03 ALL	4/1/03-3/31/04 ALL
						Type of Statement		
		2	5		1	Unqualified	5	5
		5				Reviewed	9	7
4		4				Compiled	6	11
		2				Tax Returns	1	6
	1	5	1			Other	10	9
	5 (4/1-9/30/06)		25 (10/1/06-3/31/07)					
4	1	18	6		1	**NUMBER OF STATEMENTS**	31	38
%	%	%	%	%	%	**ASSETS**	%	%
		9.8		DATA NOT AVAILABLE		Cash & Equivalents	6.4	10.7
		30.4				Trade Receivables (net)	31.5	28.7
		39.8				Inventory	32.9	33.4
		2.5				All Other Current	2.0	2.4
		82.5				Total Current	72.8	75.2
		8.7				Fixed Assets (net)	19.1	16.1
		4.5				Intangibles (net)	3.0	4.3
		4.3				All Other Non-Current	5.1	4.4
		100.0				Total	100.0	100.0
						LIABILITIES		
		16.3				Notes Payable-Short Term	14.4	15.5
		3.7				Cur. Mat.-L.T.D.	3.5	4.0
		19.0				Trade Payables	21.2	24.3
		.1				Income Taxes Payable	.1	.1
		10.8				All Other Current	11.9	10.2
		49.8				Total Current	51.0	54.1
		7.7				Long-Term Debt	12.1	14.1
		.2				Deferred Taxes	.3	.2
		1.1				All Other Non-Current	6.3	10.6
		41.2				Net Worth	30.3	21.1
		100.0				Total Liabilties & Net Worth	100.0	100.0
						INCOME DATA		
		100.0				Net Sales	100.0	100.0
		27.7				Gross Profit	33.8	32.6
		23.6				Operating Expenses	29.9	28.9
		4.1				Operating Profit	3.9	3.7
		.7				All Other Expenses (net)	.8	.7
		3.4				Profit Before Taxes	3.1	3.0
						RATIOS		
		4.2					1.9	2.2
		1.8				Current	1.3	1.5
		1.0					1.1	1.1
		1.9					1.1	1.1
		.9				Quick	.8	.6
		.5					.5	.4
		25 14.8					**23** 15.8	**20** 18.6
		35 10.5				Sales/Receivables	**36** 10.2	**30** 12.2
		40 9.0					**47** 7.8	**42** 8.7
		41 9.0					**35** 10.3	**35** 10.4
		55 6.6				Cost of Sales/Inventory	**52** 7.0	**54** 6.7
		73 5.0					**84** 4.4	**87** 4.2
		21 17.6					**26** 14.1	**20** 18.3
		29 12.5				Cost of Sales/Payables	**36** 10.2	**33** 10.9
		41 9.0					**52** 7.1	**62** 5.8
		5.6					7.6	7.3
		10.0				Sales/Working Capital	20.9	17.3
		NM					56.7	110.4
		21.3					12.8	11.0
		(17) 8.0				EBIT/Interest	(28) 4.0	(32) 2.6
		2.8					1.7	.3
							2.6	
						Net Profit + Depr., Dep., Amort./Cur. Mat. L/T/D	(12) 1.7	
							.4	
		.1					.3	.3
		.2				Fixed/Worth	.6	.9
		NM					1.6	-2.3
		.3					1.4	1.3
		1.8				Debt/Worth	2.9	2.5
		NM					9.7	-11.6
		30.9					75.6	54.3
		(14) 17.4				% Profit Before Taxes/Tangible Net Worth	(28) 26.5	(25) 21.8
		9.2					6.1	3.9
		15.5					16.8	14.2
		9.5				% Profit Before Taxes/Total Assets	9.6	4.7
		4.5					1.1	-1.9
		66.6					48.7	52.8
		46.3				Sales/Net Fixed Assets	28.1	30.4
		28.3					8.5	10.2
		4.1					4.3	4.7
		2.9				Sales/Total Assets	3.2	3.3
		2.8					2.4	2.1
		.4					.7	.9
		(14) .7				% Depr., Dep., Amort./Sales	(27) 1.2	(33) 1.3
		2.2					3.2	2.9
		1.4					2.8	2.2
		(11) 4.1				% Officers', Directors' Owners' Comp/Sales	(18) 4.9	(19) 4.7
		7.2					7.8	6.2
7386M	**2237M**	**312540M**	**299299M**		**560346M**	Net Sales ($)	**705594M**	**640636M**
1198M	**1769M**	**101524M**	**144792M**		**244708M**	Total Assets ($)	**270216M**	**276014M**

M = $ thousand MM = $ million

See Pages 11 through 21 for Explanation of Ratios and Data

Comparative Historical Data | Current Data Sorted by Sales

Type of Statement	4/1/04-3/31/05 ALL	4/1/05-3/31/06 ALL	4/1/06-3/31/07 ALL	0-1MM	1-3MM	3-5MM	5-10MM	10-25MM	25MM & OVER
Unqualified	3	5	8					2	6
Reviewed	8	8	5					4	1
Compiled	4	4	8			1	2	2	
Tax Returns	2	3	2				2	2	
Other	8	11	7	1			2	4	
				5 (4/1-9/30/06)			25 (10/1/06-3/31/07)		
NUMBER OF STATEMENTS	25	31	30	1	3	1	4	14	7
	%	%	%	%	%	%	%	%	%
ASSETS									
Cash & Equivalents	6.9	8.6	9.4					10.0	
Trade Receivables (net)	33.1	34.6	28.1					28.7	
Inventory	32.2	27.9	34.7					38.9	
All Other Current	2.1	1.8	2.7					2.7	
Total Current	74.4	72.8	75.0					80.3	
Fixed Assets (net)	18.1	16.9	15.0					11.1	
Intangibles (net)	3.3	5.3	6.1					5.6	
All Other Non-Current	4.2	5.0	3.8					3.0	
Total	100.0	100.0	100.0					100.0	
LIABILITIES									
Notes Payable-Short Term	14.2	16.9	15.3					18.6	
Cur. Mat.-L.T.D.	2.9	2.4	2.8					4.4	
Trade Payables	23.9	24.4	16.0					18.5	
Income Taxes Payable	.0	.2	.3					.4	
All Other Current	15.5	16.0	12.3					9.2	
Total Current	56.5	59.9	46.7					51.0	
Long-Term Debt	16.0	14.3	12.9					6.9	
Deferred Taxes	.4	.2	.3					.2	
All Other Non-Current	4.2	5.6	14.3					1.4	
Net Worth	22.8	20.0	25.9					40.6	
Total Liabilities & Net Worth	100.0	100.0	100.0					100.0	
INCOME DATA									
Net Sales	100.0	100.0	100.0					100.0	
Gross Profit	30.2	32.0	33.1					28.9	
Operating Expenses	27.1	28.5	26.7					23.9	
Operating Profit	3.1	3.6	6.4					5.0	
All Other Expenses (net)	.7	.7	1.2					.8	
Profit Before Taxes	2.4	2.8	5.2					4.1	
RATIOS									
Current	2.2	1.7	4.1					5.6	
	1.4	1.3	1.8					1.7	
	1.1	.9	1.1					.9	
Quick	1.0	1.0	1.9					1.9	
	.7	.8	.9					.9	
	.5	.4	.6					.5	
Sales/Receivables	28 13.2	27 13.4	27 13.7					25 14.3	
	33 11.1	33 10.9	35 10.5					35 10.5	
	42 8.7	41 8.9	42 8.7					40 9.1	
Cost of Sales/Inventory	42 8.7	21 17.1	37 9.9					41 9.0	
	62 5.9	45 8.1	55 6.6					55 6.6	
	88 4.1	62 5.9	80 4.6					95 3.8	
Cost of Sales/Payables	18 20.8	18 20.0	14 25.2					16 22.4	
	26 14.3	29 12.6	27 13.4					33 11.0	
	49 7.4	50 7.3	39 9.3					45 8.1	
Sales/Working Capital	8.8	10.5	4.9					5.3	
	16.9	20.4	9.8					11.8	
	50.8	-34.0	66.0					-60.9	
EBIT/Interest	12.1	7.4	15.2					21.3	
	(24) 3.0	(27) 2.4	(25) 5.5					(13) 5.5	
	.8	.9	2.6					2.6	
Net Profit + Depr., Dep., Amort./Cur. Mat. L/T/D									
Fixed/Worth	.2	.2	.1					.1	
	.7	1.6	.4					.2	
	-3.5	-5.7	NM					-1.3	
Debt/Worth	1.0	1.3	.3					.2	
	2.6	5.4	2.0					2.0	
	-22.1	-48.6	NM					-8.2	
% Profit Before Taxes/Tangible Net Worth	30.8	98.8	36.3					36.7	
	(17) 13.8	(23) 22.0	(23) 17.7					(10) 13.7	
	5.3	7.1	9.9					9.2	
% Profit Before Taxes/Total Assets	10.8	18.8	18.0					15.8	
	4.1	3.4	11.0					9.5	
	-.7	.1	5.4					4.5	
Sales/Net Fixed Assets	43.5	50.7	57.2					66.6	
	23.5	27.3	31.4					31.9	
	9.4	12.5	15.2					16.3	
Sales/Total Assets	4.5	5.2	4.1					4.0	
	2.8	3.1	2.8					2.8	
	2.2	2.3	2.3					2.6	
% Depr., Dep., Amort./Sales	.8	.5	.4					.4	
	(22) 1.1	(28) .8	(22) .8					(11) 1.2	
	2.5	1.7	2.4					4.3	
% Officers', Directors' Owners' Comp/Sales	2.1	1.3	1.4						
	(13) 3.2	(16) 3.4	(11) 4.1						
	6.7	5.4	7.2						
Net Sales ($)	584430M	704287M	1181808M	637M	5788M	3198M	33561M	250706M	887918M
Total Assets ($)	241159M	285115M	493991M	119M	2629M	219M	18398M	93740M	378886M

© RMA 2007

M = $ thousand   MM = $ million

See Pages 11 through 21 for Explanation of Ratios and Data

Current Data Sorted by Assets   Comparative Historical Data

						Type of Statement				
		1	4	2		Unqualified		7		5
	4	2	3			Reviewed		7		8
1	2	1				Compiled		6		3
2		1				Tax Returns		3		1
	4	3				Other		6		9
	8 (4/1-9/30/06)		27 (10/1/06-3/31/07)					4/1/02-3/31/03		4/1/03-3/31/04
0-500M	500M-2MM	2-10MM	10-50MM	50-100MM	100-250MM			ALL		ALL
3	10	8	9	5		NUMBER OF STATEMENTS		29		26
%	%	%	%	%	%	ASSETS		%		%
	5.8					Cash & Equivalents		12.0		13.2
	34.3					Trade Receivables (net)		24.1		28.7
	32.5					Inventory		28.7		26.7
	.6					All Other Current		2.0		3.0
	73.1					Total Current		66.9		71.5
	21.6					Fixed Assets (net)		21.8		20.1
	1.5					Intangibles (net)		4.9		3.2
	3.8					All Other Non-Current		6.4		5.3
	100.0					Total		100.0		100.0
						LIABILITIES				
	9.7					Notes Payable-Short Term		9.8		7.2
	1.4					Cur. Mat.-L.T.D.		3.6		3.0
	17.2					Trade Payables		10.9		9.9
	.5					Income Taxes Payable		.0		.0
	12.2					All Other Current		12.8		13.3
	41.0					Total Current		37.1		33.4
	15.7					Long-Term Debt		11.7		11.8
	.2					Deferred Taxes		.2		.3
	4.8					All Other Non-Current		14.5		20.6
	38.3					Net Worth		36.4		33.9
	100.0					Total Liabilties & Net Worth		100.0		100.0
						INCOME DATA				
	100.0					Net Sales		100.0		100.0
	32.4					Gross Profit		39.4		41.1
	30.1					Operating Expenses		34.2		34.6
	2.3					Operating Profit		5.2		6.4
	.9					All Other Expenses (net)		2.0		1.3
	1.4					Profit Before Taxes		3.2		5.1
						RATIOS				
	3.2							3.3		3.9
	2.2					Current		1.7		2.6
	1.3							1.2		1.7
	2.2							2.5		2.7
	1.1					Quick		.9		1.5
	.4							.5		.7
39	9.3						33	11.1	40	9.2
54	6.8					Sales/Receivables	48	7.7	54	6.8
77	4.8						61	6.0	75	4.9
52	7.0						48	7.7	49	7.4
88	4.2					Cost of Sales/Inventory	84	4.3	73	5.0
169	2.2						120	3.0	134	2.7
13	27.8						15	24.5	21	17.5
28	13.1					Cost of Sales/Payables	26	14.2	32	11.3
73	5.0						66	5.5	51	7.2
	4.0							3.1		3.1
	5.5					Sales/Working Capital		6.9		4.3
	17.8							27.7		10.4
								9.1		25.2
						EBIT/Interest	(26)	1.8	(20)	6.7
								.7		1.0
						Net Profit + Depr., Dep., Amort./Cur. Mat. L/T/D				
	.1							.2		.2
	.6					Fixed/Worth		.4		.3
	NM							6.2		.8
	.3							.7		.3
	1.4					Debt/Worth		1.7		.7
	NM							11.2		2.3
								39.6		40.4
						% Profit Before Taxes/Tangible Net Worth	(25)	5.9	(23)	21.6
								-12.1		.8
	10.7							12.8		21.3
	2.4					% Profit Before Taxes/Total Assets		1.6		6.5
	1.1							-1.1		-1.1
	71.8							19.6		29.0
	15.0					Sales/Net Fixed Assets		12.9		11.9
	4.4							8.3		6.7
	2.9							2.5		2.4
	1.9					Sales/Total Assets		1.9		2.1
	1.3							1.5		1.2
	.9							.9		.9
	2.2					% Depr., Dep., Amort./Sales	(24)	1.5	(23)	1.9
	4.2							2.9		2.6
						% Officers', Directors' Owners' Comp/Sales				
1810M	25928M	84832M	362371M	336727M		Net Sales ($)		450081M		481210M
597M	12622M	36645M	205134M	315987M		Total Assets ($)		468453M		653902M

M = $ thousand   MM = $ million
See Pages 11 through 21 for Explanation of Ratios and Data

Comparative Historical Data | Current Data Sorted by Sales

			Type of Statement						
7	3	7	Unqualified					3	4
6	6	9	Reviewed		3	1		3	2
3	4	4	Compiled	1	1	2			
2	2	3	Tax Returns	1	1			1	
13	12	12	Other	1	1	1	2		5
4/1/04-3/31/05 ALL	4/1/05-3/31/06 ALL	4/1/06-3/31/07 ALL		8 (4/1-9/30/06)			27 (10/1/06-3/31/07)		
				0-1MM	1-3MM	3-5MM	5-10MM	10-25MM	25MM & OVER
31	27	35	NUMBER OF STATEMENTS	3	8	4	2	7	11
%	%	%	ASSETS	%	%	%	%	%	%
10.5	10.6	10.5	Cash & Equivalents						14.6
29.2	30.8	30.5	Trade Receivables (net)						22.9
24.8	23.6	27.6	Inventory						20.2
3.0	3.5	1.2	All Other Current						2.0
67.6	68.5	69.9	Total Current						59.8
19.6	18.5	18.6	Fixed Assets (net)						18.9
9.1	7.4	5.4	Intangibles (net)						14.0
3.8	5.5	6.1	All Other Non-Current						7.3
100.0	100.0	100.0	Total						100.0
			LIABILITIES						
6.5	6.4	11.0	Notes Payable-Short Term						9.0
2.6	2.6	1.1	Cur. Mat.-L.T.D.						1.0
12.7	14.8	15.4	Trade Payables						9.4
.1	.0	.2	Income Taxes Payable						.1
13.1	7.3	11.0	All Other Current						9.8
35.1	31.0	38.7	Total Current						29.3
15.3	11.5	13.7	Long-Term Debt						4.4
.6	.5	.4	Deferred Taxes						1.1
15.2	5.5	8.7	All Other Non-Current						8.4
33.9	51.4	38.5	Net Worth						56.8
100.0	100.0	100.0	Total Liabilities & Net Worth						100.0
			INCOME DATA						
100.0	100.0	100.0	Net Sales						100.0
43.7	39.5	38.5	Gross Profit						40.1
37.4	32.7	35.1	Operating Expenses						33.3
6.2	6.8	3.4	Operating Profit						6.8
1.6	.8	1.1	All Other Expenses (net)						1.6
4.6	6.0	2.3	Profit Before Taxes						5.2
			RATIOS						
3.7	3.9	3.3							4.3
2.2	2.2	2.1	Current						2.2
1.3	1.4	1.2							1.2
3.2	2.4	2.1							3.6
1.1	1.2	1.2	Quick						1.4
.5	.7	.5							.5
39 9.3	49 7.5	40 9.2						45	8.1
56 6.6	55 6.6	52 7.0	Sales/Receivables					52	7.0
76 4.8	69 5.3	76 4.8						75	4.9
56 6.5	48 7.7	50 7.3						61	6.0
72 5.1	84 4.3	85 4.3	Cost of Sales/Inventory					81	4.5
121 3.0	121 3.0	123 3.0						137	2.7
28 13.3	30 12.2	22 16.9						25	14.5
48 7.5	40 9.2	32 11.5	Cost of Sales/Payables					32	11.5
63 5.8	56 6.5	56 6.5						51	7.2
3.1	3.5	3.9							2.8
6.0	4.9	5.6	Sales/Working Capital						5.5
14.1	7.1	24.3							24.8
31.8	19.5	16.2							
(26) 6.1	(24) 3.8	(30) 1.7	EBIT/Interest						
1.2	1.2	.7							
		18.1							
	(11)	8.5	Net Profit + Depr., Dep., Amort./Cur. Mat. L/T/D						
		2.8							
.2	.1	.2							.2
.7	.3	.5	Fixed/Worth						.5
4.2	.7	2.8							1.1
.4	.6	.4							.3
1.6	1.0	1.9	Debt/Worth						1.0
21.0	3.2	6.2							2.4
51.6	37.3	23.5							
(25) 23.5	(25) 12.3	(29) 14.4	% Profit Before Taxes/Tangible Net Worth						
3.0	-6.6	1.2							
15.7	18.4	10.9							19.5
8.3	3.9	1.9	% Profit Before Taxes/Total Assets						5.4
.4	-1.1	-.7							.3
37.8	42.1	23.3							14.5
12.6	14.7	10.4	Sales/Net Fixed Assets						8.5
5.5	4.2	5.8							6.3
1.9	2.1	2.6							1.8
1.7	1.6	1.8	Sales/Total Assets						1.6
1.2	1.2	1.3							1.1
1.0	.9	.9							1.5
(25) 2.0	(24) 1.5	(33) 1.8	% Depr., Dep., Amort./Sales					(10)	1.9
3.3	3.2	3.0							2.4
			% Officers', Directors' Owners' Comp/Sales						
527586M	532637M	811668M	Net Sales ($)	1707M	17619M	16285M	16155M	122026M	637876M
403542M	467942M	570985M	Total Assets ($)	1245M	9399M	10460M	5138M	65780M	478963M

© RMA 2007
M = $ thousand   MM = $ million
See Pages 11 through 21 for Explanation of Ratios and Data

Current Data Sorted by Assets   Comparative Historical Data

Type of Statement

0-500M	500M-2MM	2-10MM	10-50MM	50-100MM	100-250MM		4/1/02-3/31/03 ALL	4/1/03-3/31/04 ALL
	2	7	23	11	8	Unqualified	51	51
	1	9	7		1	Reviewed	27	20
1	5	5	5		1	Compiled	20	17
	3	3	3			Tax Returns	3	8
3	11	27	24	9	6	Other	49	37
	35 (4/1-9/30/06)		131 (10/1/06-3/31/07)					
4	22	51	54	20	15	**NUMBER OF STATEMENTS**	150	133
%	%	%	%	%	%	**ASSETS**	%	%
	10.2	10.1	10.5	17.7	10.3	Cash & Equivalents	12.2	11.9
	27.3	24.3	22.4	14.2	16.4	Trade Receivables (net)	23.6	24.5
	25.1	28.9	22.5	14.4	16.7	Inventory	21.3	23.8
	.8	2.2	2.3	2.7	3.2	All Other Current	4.0	3.1
	63.5	65.5	57.8	49.0	46.6	Total Current	61.2	63.3
	25.0	22.1	18.7	21.1	19.0	Fixed Assets (net)	23.4	20.3
	6.3	6.9	17.1	24.6	30.0	Intangibles (net)	8.4	9.2
	5.3	5.5	6.4	5.3	4.4	All Other Non-Current	6.9	7.2
	100.0	100.0	100.0	100.0	100.0	Total	100.0	100.0
						LIABILITIES		
	10.1	6.0	4.1	5.2	1.2	Notes Payable-Short Term	6.9	7.3
	5.8	3.3	4.6	3.9	3.1	Cur. Mat.-L.T.D.	4.1	4.9
	12.6	12.7	10.2	5.3	5.4	Trade Payables	11.6	11.9
	.4	.3	.4	1.1	.7	Income Taxes Payable	.8	.7
	9.1	8.8	10.8	9.8	10.4	All Other Current	12.3	10.8
	38.1	31.1	30.1	25.3	20.9	Total Current	35.7	35.6
	15.4	13.0	13.1	14.1	16.2	Long-Term Debt	12.7	11.8
	.2	.2	.9	.7	1.4	Deferred Taxes	.6	.7
	5.6	8.1	4.5	2.7	5.7	All Other Non-Current	5.1	7.1
	40.7	47.5	51.4	57.2	55.8	Net Worth	45.9	44.6
	100.0	100.0	100.0	100.0	100.0	Total Liabilties & Net Worth	100.0	100.0
						INCOME DATA		
	100.0	100.0	100.0	100.0	100.0	Net Sales	100.0	100.0
	47.8	44.4	44.0	54.6	40.4	Gross Profit	44.2	46.4
	40.7	35.7	36.4	46.4	32.6	Operating Expenses	35.3	37.6
	7.1	8.7	7.6	8.2	7.8	Operating Profit	8.9	8.9
	.8	3.0	1.5	.7	3.2	All Other Expenses (net)	1.7	1.5
	6.3	5.7	6.1	7.5	4.5	Profit Before Taxes	7.2	7.4
						RATIOS		
	3.6	4.2	3.2	4.4	3.9		3.5	3.6
	1.8	2.1	2.0	1.6	2.8	Current	2.0	2.1
	1.1	1.3	1.3	1.3	1.7		1.2	1.3
	2.4	2.3	2.4	3.0	1.8		2.1	2.0
	(21) 1.1	1.1	1.1	.9	1.6	Quick	1.1	1.1
	.7	.7	.6	.6	.7		.6	.6
	34 10.7	**35** 10.5	**43** 8.6	**36** 10.1	**39** 9.4		**37** 9.8	**38** 9.6
	40 9.1	**46** 7.9	**58** 6.2	**46** 8.0	**52** 7.0	Sales/Receivables	**48** 7.6	**47** 7.7
	56 6.5	**56** 6.5	**63** 5.8	**63** 5.8	**69** 5.3		**62** 5.9	**59** 6.2
	43 8.5	**49** 7.5	**60** 6.0	**74** 4.9	**76** 4.8		**48** 7.7	**61** 6.0
	85 4.3	**98** 3.7	**89** 4.1	**129** 2.8	**105** 3.5	Cost of Sales/Inventory	**80** 4.6	**92** 4.0
	135 2.7	**161** 2.3	**142** 2.6	**157** 2.3	**127** 2.9		**122** 3.0	**134** 2.7
	14 26.6	**19** 19.6	**22** 16.8	**22** 16.3	**20** 18.6		**22** 16.9	**23** 16.0
	36 10.1	**40** 9.2	**33** 11.1	**36** 10.1	**33** 11.1	Cost of Sales/Payables	**31** 11.6	**34** 10.7
	73 5.0	**76** 4.8	**60** 6.0	**66** 5.6	**48** 7.6		**57** 6.4	**62** 5.9
	4.1	3.4	3.4	2.0	2.9		3.4	3.3
	6.4	4.8	5.5	7.0	4.3	Sales/Working Capital	6.1	6.1
	NM	15.5	17.6	14.8	7.0		16.9	17.9
	14.1	19.0	24.3	17.9	73.4		19.4	21.4
	(15) 3.2	(42) 5.3	(49) 5.3	(17) 6.8	(13) 3.9	EBIT/Interest	(130) 5.3	(119) 5.4
	1.7	2.2	1.9	.7	1.0		1.8	1.8
			9.6	19.0			15.3	16.4
		(14) 3.5		(25) 3.2		Net Profit + Depr., Dep., Amort./Cur. Mat. L/T/D	(56) 2.8	(49) 4.8
		2.0		.7			1.2	2.0
	.2	.2	.2	.3	.2		.2	.2
	.7	.5	.5	.8	.7	Fixed/Worth	.5	.5
	NM	1.2	2.1	5.0	-3.1		1.4	1.2
	.4	.3	.5	.4	.3		.4	.5
	3.3	1.2	1.2	1.2	1.1	Debt/Worth	1.3	1.5
	NM	4.1	4.9	10.5	-16.1		3.1	4.1
	108.8	46.7	48.3	85.4		% Profit Before Taxes/Tangible Net Worth	44.5	47.4
	(17) 27.0	(45) 31.1	(44) 20.9	(16) 29.7			(135) 22.7	(119) 24.6
	13.0	5.8	4.7	-2.7			7.3	10.0
	20.1	20.4	22.1	19.5	11.0	% Profit Before Taxes/Total Assets	17.1	17.6
	11.8	11.6	7.1	12.0	4.6		9.1	9.8
	5.6	2.5	2.3	-2.6	.0		2.0	3.1
	26.5	26.1	21.0	9.5	13.1		18.3	21.2
	16.7	11.2	9.1	5.9	7.5	Sales/Net Fixed Assets	7.4	8.7
	4.3	5.7	4.7	3.2	2.7		4.3	4.7
	3.4	2.5	1.9	1.5	1.6		2.2	2.4
	2.3	1.9	1.4	.8	1.0	Sales/Total Assets	1.6	1.7
	1.4	1.3	1.1	.6	.6		1.2	1.3
	1.3	1.2	1.4	3.1	1.9		1.6	1.5
	(18) 1.8	(42) 2.3	(47) 2.4	(19) 4.8	(10) 2.8	% Depr., Dep., Amort./Sales	(124) 2.7	(115) 2.7
	2.8	5.0	4.6	5.6	4.4		5.0	4.5
		3.2					2.6	3.0
		(16) 5.3				% Officers', Directors' Owners' Comp/Sales	(41) 4.9	(38) 5.5
		7.4					10.5	8.8
6120M	65051M	550869M	1776778M	1391043M	2770170M	Net Sales ($)	5087628M	4767366M
1686M	28149M	292421M	1284900M	1355580M	2502823M	Total Assets ($)	4240409M	3752560M

M = $ thousand   MM = $ million
See Pages 11 through 21 for Explanation of Ratios and Data

Comparative Historical Data			Type of Statement	Current Data Sorted by Sales					
48	34	51	Unqualified		1	1	5	11	33
23	14	17	Reviewed		1		7	6	3
8	7	12	Compiled	1	2	3	5		1
10	8	6	Tax Returns	1	2	1	5		
59	71	80	Other	1	9	6	10	20	34
4/1/04-3/31/05 ALL	4/1/05-3/31/06 ALL	4/1/06-3/31/07 ALL		0-1MM	35 (4/1-9/30/06) 1-3MM	3-5MM	131 (10/1/06-3/31/07) 5-10MM	10-25MM	25MM & OVER
148	134	166	**NUMBER OF STATEMENTS**	3	15	11	29	37	71
%	%	%	**ASSETS**	%	%	%	%	%	%
12.2	11.3	11.1	Cash & Equivalents		9.2	6.4	14.8	6.2	13.5
24.6	23.7	22.6	Trade Receivables (net)		26.5	25.2	22.5	22.0	21.5
23.5	23.6	23.2	Inventory		28.1	28.5	26.2	24.5	20.2
2.2	2.5	2.2	All Other Current		1.1	.3	2.2	1.4	3.0
62.5	61.2	59.0	Total Current		65.0	60.4	65.7	54.2	58.2
20.9	22.5	21.2	Fixed Assets (net)		25.4	29.1	18.4	22.7	18.7
11.7	9.0	14.2	Intangibles (net)		5.0	1.2	12.1	15.9	17.8
5.0	7.4	5.5	All Other Non-Current		4.6	9.3	3.8	7.2	5.2
100.0	100.0	100.0	Total		100.0	100.0	100.0	100.0	100.0
			LIABILITIES						
7.4	6.1	5.7	Notes Payable-Short Term		11.9	8.5	5.6	7.9	2.9
3.4	3.1	4.2	Cur. Mat.-L.T.D.		4.5	6.2	3.1	4.5	3.7
11.0	11.7	10.6	Trade Payables		12.2	11.9	13.8	11.2	8.4
.5	.4	.5	Income Taxes Payable		.1	.1	.4	.5	.7
11.5	10.5	9.6	All Other Current		6.3	10.9	7.5	10.0	11.1
33.9	31.8	30.5	Total Current		35.0	37.5	30.3	34.1	26.7
15.8	14.1	14.1	Long-Term Debt		14.7	17.1	15.4	16.4	11.4
.6	.5	.6	Deferred Taxes		.0	.0	.8	.4	.8
8.1	5.6	5.6	All Other Non-Current		2.0	23.9	3.7	3.8	4.3
41.6	47.9	49.3	Net Worth		48.3	21.5	49.8	45.3	56.8
100.0	100.0	100.0	Total Liabilities & Net Worth		100.0	100.0	100.0	100.0	100.0
			INCOME DATA						
100.0	100.0	100.0	Net Sales		100.0	100.0	100.0	100.0	100.0
44.7	47.4	45.9	Gross Profit		55.0	40.9	52.2	40.4	45.4
34.5	37.9	37.8	Operating Expenses		44.0	36.1	46.1	30.1	37.6
10.3	9.5	8.1	Operating Profit		11.0	4.7	6.1	10.3	7.8
1.1	1.2	1.9	All Other Expenses (net)		.8	1.4	3.2	2.8	1.2
9.1	8.3	6.2	Profit Before Taxes		10.2	3.4	2.9	7.5	6.7
			RATIOS						
3.7	3.7	3.9			4.7	3.3	4.1	2.8	4.3
1.8	2.1	2.1	Current		2.4	1.8	2.1	1.6	2.3
1.3	1.3	1.3			.8	.9	1.4	1.1	1.5
2.0	2.2	2.3			2.7	1.5	2.8	1.3	2.8
1.0	1.2	(165) 1.1	Quick		(14) 1.2	.9	1.2	.7	1.4
.7	.7	.7			.5	.5	.8	.6	.7
40 9.2	41 9.0	38 9.7		26 14.2	37 9.9	33 11.1	37 10.0	42 8.7	
48 7.7	49 7.4	49 7.4	Sales/Receivables	43 8.5	40 9.2	42 8.8	49 7.4	56 6.5	
60 6.1	58 6.3	62 5.9		60 6.0	52 7.0	60 6.1	61 6.0	63 5.8	
59 6.2	58 6.3	59 6.2		53 6.8	54 6.8	76 4.8	46 7.9	66 5.6	
80 4.5	100 3.7	95 3.8	Cost of Sales/Inventory	103 3.5	68 5.3	108 3.4	73 5.0	98 3.7	
114 3.2	123 3.0	141 2.6		296 1.2	161 2.3	155 2.3	135 2.7	134 2.7	
20 17.8	22 16.6	20 17.9		15 25.0	12 31.3	26 14.0	20 18.6	21 17.5	
35 10.0	36 10.0	35 10.3	Cost of Sales/Payables	36 10.2	28 13.0	50 7.2	32 11.3	32 11.3	
51 7.1	57 6.4	64 5.7		114 3.2	64 5.7	85 4.3	60 6.1	47 7.7	
4.0	3.6	3.4			2.3	3.6	3.3	4.1	3.2
6.7	7.1	5.7	Sales/Working Capital		5.8	6.6	4.8	10.1	4.6
18.5	12.2	16.4			-63.3	-59.4	13.4	60.0	12.5
18.4	24.1	16.2			12.0		12.3	14.2	55.2
(123) 5.0	(118) 7.0	(139) 4.9	EBIT/Interest		(10) 4.5		(25) 4.8	(32) 4.8	(60) 10.9
2.3	2.0	1.8			-.4		2.0	2.1	1.9
7.8	22.8	15.1					5.1	15.8	38.2
(43) 3.9	(49) 3.8	(57) 3.2	Net Profit + Depr., Dep., Amort./Cur. Mat. L/T/D				(12) 3.3	(12) 3.1	(32) 3.6
1.6	1.8	.8					.4	.9	1.0
.2	.2	.2			.2	.4	.2	.3	.2
.6	.6	.6	Fixed/Worth		.5	1.0	.4	.8	.5
2.9	1.4	2.6			3.3	2.8	1.5	3.5	1.0
.5	.4	.4			.2	1.0	.4	.7	.4
1.6	1.3	1.3	Debt/Worth		.6	1.9	1.4	1.9	.9
7.2	3.5	6.0			6.1	7.8	4.2	NM	3.5
61.2	52.8	48.8			81.9		56.7	68.5	43.4
(115) 27.6	(121) 25.3	(134) 26.4	% Profit Before Taxes/Tangible Net Worth		(12) 19.5		(25) 28.9	(28) 34.6	(59) 17.7
8.2	6.6	6.7			9.9		3.0	18.2	4.4
21.5	21.1	19.3			25.4	19.6	19.7	20.4	19.9
10.7	12.1	10.5	% Profit Before Taxes/Total Assets		11.2	8.0	10.5	11.6	10.5
3.4	2.1	2.3			6.0	-3.6	1.5	3.2	2.1
24.0	18.8	21.9			25.9	23.0	34.9	18.3	15.0
8.5	8.8	9.2	Sales/Net Fixed Assets		17.4	6.6	13.2	10.1	8.3
4.6	4.9	4.6			3.9	4.5	4.6	4.3	5.1
2.4	2.4	2.2			3.5	2.5	2.7	2.0	2.0
1.7	1.7	1.6	Sales/Total Assets		2.2	1.7	1.8	1.6	1.2
1.2	1.1	1.0			.9	1.4	1.0	1.2	.8
1.1	1.1	1.5			1.1		1.0	1.3	1.9
(125) 2.5	(113) 2.5	(138) 2.6	% Depr., Dep., Amort./Sales		(11) 1.7		(24) 2.4	(29) 2.7	(62) 3.0
4.5	4.0	4.8			2.5		7.3	5.3	4.7
2.0	2.4	2.9					3.6		
(32) 4.5	(37) 6.2	(34) 5.5	% Officers', Directors' Owners' Comp/Sales				(11) 5.3		
7.2	11.1	9.2					7.2		
5831627M	6708537M	6560031M	Net Sales ($)	1936M	29651M	42435M	208789M	599986M	5677234M
4367209M	5216848M	5465559M	Total Assets ($)	2287M	21196M	24844M	180392M	474284M	4762556M

M = $ thousand   MM = $ million
See Pages 11 through 21 for Explanation of Ratios and Data

MANUFACTURING—Surgical Appliance and Supplies Manufacturing NAICS 339113 (SIC 3842, 3851)

							Type of Statement		
		1	8	11	9	3	Unqualified	41	32
	1	4	13	3			Reviewed	18	25
	4	8	8	2			Compiled	14	21
	5	4	1				Tax Returns	4	14
	2	3	16	15	5	9	Other	37	43
		28 (4/1-9/30/06)		107 (10/1/06-3/31/07)				4/1/02- 3/31/03	4/1/03- 3/31/04
	0-500M	500M-2MM	2-10MM	10-50MM	50-100MM	100-250MM		ALL	ALL
	12	20	46	31	14	12	NUMBER OF STATEMENTS	114	135
	%	%	%	%	%	%	ASSETS	%	%
	8.1	9.3	7.3	8.3	11.6	5.9	Cash & Equivalents	6.5	7.8
	40.8	39.7	30.2	26.9	19.6	17.4	Trade Receivables (net)	28.5	25.6
	24.7	24.4	24.0	26.8	22.9	17.7	Inventory	23.0	26.8
	5.6	2.7	2.0	4.2	2.2	4.3	All Other Current	3.1	2.7
	79.3	76.0	63.4	66.3	56.3	45.3	Total Current	61.1	62.9
	16.9	14.8	25.0	18.0	23.0	20.0	Fixed Assets (net)	24.3	22.3
	1.3	2.9	5.0	8.0	16.6	30.2	Intangibles (net)	8.4	7.9
	2.6	6.3	6.7	7.7	4.1	4.5	All Other Non-Current	6.2	6.9
	100.0	100.0	100.0	100.0	100.0	100.0	Total	100.0	100.0
							LIABILITIES		
	19.5	5.0	12.3	8.4	8.1	1.0	Notes Payable-Short Term	9.3	10.8
	1.0	4.2	3.6	3.6	3.4	3.8	Cur. Mat.-L.T.D.	3.7	3.8
	14.0	19.0	12.7	13.3	7.9	7.4	Trade Payables	13.0	15.0
	.0	.0	.1	.2	.1	.2	Income Taxes Payable	.6	.7
	14.3	10.5	11.5	13.9	6.6	4.3	All Other Current	10.5	13.9
	48.8	38.7	40.2	39.6	26.1	16.6	Total Current	37.2	44.2
	7.0	11.8	17.7	12.4	17.9	21.9	Long-Term Debt	13.8	16.5
	.0	.0	.4	.3	.8	2.6	Deferred Taxes	.5	.4
	2.5	4.4	2.9	4.2	4.7	6.9	All Other Non-Current	5.5	7.0
	41.7	45.1	38.8	43.6	50.6	51.9	Net Worth	42.9	31.9
	100.0	100.0	100.0	100.0	100.0	100.0	Total Liabilties & Net Worth	100.0	100.0
							INCOME DATA		
	100.0	100.0	100.0	100.0	100.0	100.0	Net Sales	100.0	100.0
	47.7	43.1	38.5	37.9	42.3	42.0	Gross Profit	43.9	43.9
	44.3	37.5	33.6	30.7	35.8	33.1	Operating Expenses	37.9	38.2
	3.4	5.6	4.9	7.3	6.5	8.9	Operating Profit	6.0	5.8
	.6	.5	1.1	1.5	1.9	3.1	All Other Expenses (net)	1.0	1.1
	2.8	5.1	3.8	5.8	4.6	5.7	Profit Before Taxes	5.0	4.6
							RATIOS		
	7.8	3.8	2.9	2.5	4.3	4.8		3.3	2.7
	1.7	2.1	1.7	1.6	1.9	3.4	Current	1.9	1.6
	1.0	1.3	1.2	1.1	1.4	2.0		1.2	1.1
	1.5	2.5	1.9	1.4	3.0	2.5		1.9	1.5
	1.2	1.4	1.0	.8	1.1	1.6	Quick	1.0	.8
	.6	.9	.6	.5	.7	.9		.6	.5

															Sales/Receivables				
0	752.9	36	10.2	36	10.2	40	9.2	44	8.4	49	7.4					38	9.6	33	11.2
43	8.6	48	7.6	44	8.3	49	7.4	56	6.5	56	6.5		Sales/Receivables			47	7.7	45	8.0
76	4.8	63	5.8	66	5.6	56	6.5	68	5.3	67	5.5					59	6.2	60	6.1
0	UND	22	16.8	38	9.5	51	7.1	66	5.5	80	4.5					37	10.0	39	9.4
30	12.1	54	6.8	55	6.7	82	4.5	101	3.6	107	3.4		Cost of Sales/Inventory			67	5.5	73	5.0
80	4.5	106	3.4	92	4.0	135	2.7	139	2.6	143	2.5					108	3.4	116	3.2
0	UND	13	28.9	14	26.7	22	16.6	28	12.9	22	16.3					20	18.2	19	18.9
15	24.6	43	8.5	28	13.1	34	10.8	39	9.4	36	10.2		Cost of Sales/Payables			33	11.1	33	11.0
34	10.7	61	6.0	56	6.5	49	7.5	43	8.5	79	4.6					52	7.0	67	5.4

							Ratio		
	5.7	4.0	6.0	4.1	2.8	2.7		4.4	4.9
	10.7	8.6	10.2	7.7	5.3	3.6	Sales/Working Capital	9.0	10.2
	NM	21.8	22.8	34.7	14.0	4.9		22.9	44.1

															EBIT/Interest				
	19.9		22.6		10.2		35.3		12.7		9.1						17.7		19.2
(11)	1.0	(17)	6.3	(41)	2.6	(28)	4.1	(13)	3.6		5.5		EBIT/Interest		(100)	3.8	(119)	4.2
	-4.3		1.4		1.2		2.6		1.3		1.3						1.7		1.4

													Net Profit + Depr., Dep., Amort./Cur. Mat. L/T/D		
					7.0		17.8		5.7					8.0	11.8
		(13)	1.8	(15)	2.5	(10)	1.8				(42)	2.7	(42)	2.4
			.3		1.3		1.2						1.5	1.3

							Fixed/Worth		
	.0	.1	.3	.1	.3	.5		.3	.3
	.1	.3	.6	.6	.9	.7	Fixed/Worth	.7	.7
	.9	.6	1.6	1.1	NM	-17.4		1.5	2.1
	.8	.3	.7	.7	.4	.6		.6	.9
	1.4	1.2	2.0	1.2	2.4	1.8	Debt/Worth	1.5	1.9
	3.5	4.2	4.0	4.3	NM	-50.8		4.7	6.5

											% Profit Before Taxes/Tangible Net Worth		
	42.8	37.8	47.1	48.0	33.9				48.2		58.5
	6.4	(17)	8.1	(43)	19.4	(28)	26.1	(11)	16.2	% Profit Before Taxes/Tangible Net Worth	(99) 19.9	(111) 21.2
	-48.1	1.7	5.3	11.1	3.5				4.7		9.2

							% Profit Before Taxes/Total Assets		
	16.7	18.3	18.4	15.9	10.3	10.8		20.1	16.0
	4.9	8.4	8.0	8.0	7.4	7.0	% Profit Before Taxes/Total Assets	6.9	6.6
	-7.8	1.2	1.2	4.6	.8	.8		1.8	1.2
	448.1	32.2	31.1	26.1	9.4	9.2		20.7	25.0
	110.3	19.3	10.7	13.2	5.2	4.1	Sales/Net Fixed Assets	10.4	13.2
	13.4	16.3	4.7	7.0	4.7	2.7		4.9	6.2
	5.1	3.6	3.0	2.5	1.9	1.1		2.8	2.9
	3.7	2.9	2.2	2.0	1.3	.9	Sales/Total Assets	2.1	2.2
	3.1	1.7	1.7	1.5	.8	.6		1.4	1.6

											% Depr., Dep., Amort./Sales		
		.6		.8		.8	2.3			1.5	1.3
	(16)	1.4	(42)	1.9	(28)	1.6	3.1	% Depr., Dep., Amort./Sales	(95) 2.3	(110) 2.1
		2.4		3.4		2.6	4.4			3.6	3.6

											% Officers', Directors' Owners' Comp/Sales		
		4.2		3.9						4.2	3.8
	(12)	7.0	(21)	5.1				% Officers', Directors' Owners' Comp/Sales	(28) 5.6	(46) 5.5
		11.7		10.0						11.8	11.4

14948M	63706M	518309M	1560392M	1316489M	1935966M		Net Sales ($)	3874420M	3888843M
3619M	23920M	226263M	784516M	977235M	2032777M		Total Assets ($)	2543257M	2369452M

© RMA 2007

M = $ thousand   MM = $ million
See Pages 11 through 21 for Explanation of Ratios and Data

Comparative Historical Data / Current Data Sorted by Sales

4/1/04-3/31/05 ALL	4/1/05-3/31/06 ALL	4/1/06-3/31/07 ALL	Type of Statement	0-1MM	1-3MM	3-5MM	5-10MM	10-25MM	25MM & OVER
31	22	32	Unqualified		1		2	8	21
31	22	21	Reviewed	1	4	2	5	7	2
20	13	22	Compiled	2	5	3	8	2	2
7	14	10	Tax Returns		9	1			
47	40	50	Other		4	2	8	11	25
					28 (4/1-9/30/06)		107 (10/1/06-3/31/07)		
136	111	135	NUMBER OF STATEMENTS	3	23	8	23	28	50
%	%	%	**ASSETS**	%	%	%	%	%	%
8.8	9.0	8.2	Cash & Equivalents		7.4		7.4	6.4	9.9
26.5	28.9	29.5	Trade Receivables (net)		35.7		32.4	28.4	23.9
26.5	26.2	24.1	Inventory		24.5		21.9	27.6	23.8
2.0	2.5	3.1	All Other Current		4.5		2.7	1.6	3.9
63.7	66.5	65.0	Total Current		72.1		64.4	64.0	61.4
22.1	22.8	20.5	Fixed Assets (net)		16.1		24.8	21.1	19.9
7.9	4.6	8.5	Intangibles (net)		7.0		4.4	8.2	13.0
6.2	6.1	6.0	All Other Non-Current		4.8		6.3	6.7	5.7
100.0	100.0	100.0	Total		100.0		100.0	100.0	100.0
			LIABILITIES						
10.0	10.3	9.5	Notes Payable-Short Term		12.7		10.4	12.1	6.5
3.8	3.3	3.5	Cur. Mat.-L.T.D.		3.1		4.2	3.4	3.5
14.0	13.6	12.9	Trade Payables		12.5		15.2	11.0	11.3
.3	.2	.1	Income Taxes Payable		.0		.1	.2	.2
11.5	9.9	11.0	All Other Current		11.6		14.8	10.1	9.9
39.6	37.2	37.0	Total Current		39.9		44.6	36.7	31.5
14.2	18.0	15.0	Long-Term Debt		12.7		15.2	14.8	14.9
.4	.3	.5	Deferred Taxes		.0		.2	.6	.9
6.2	4.4	3.9	All Other Non-Current		4.4		2.9	3.7	4.2
39.5	40.2	43.5	Net Worth		43.0		37.0	44.1	48.5
100.0	100.0	100.0	Total Liabilities & Net Worth		100.0		100.0	100.0	100.0
			INCOME DATA						
100.0	100.0	100.0	Net Sales		100.0		100.0	100.0	100.0
44.6	43.4	40.6	Gross Profit		48.0		40.5	36.9	40.3
37.2	37.3	34.6	Operating Expenses		41.0		37.9	29.4	33.5
7.4	6.2	5.9	Operating Profit		7.0		2.6	7.6	6.8
.7	.9	1.3	All Other Expenses (net)		1.1		.7	2.2	1.2
6.7	5.3	4.6	Profit Before Taxes		5.9		2.0	5.4	5.6
			RATIOS						
3.1	3.1	3.2	Current		5.3		2.8	3.1	3.7
1.8	2.0	1.8			1.7		1.7	1.8	2.3
1.1	1.3	1.2			1.0		1.2	1.2	1.4
1.6	2.0	1.9	Quick		2.6		1.9	1.6	2.1
(135) .9	1.2	1.0			1.1		1.0	.9	1.1
.5	.6	.6			.6		.6	.6	.6
32 11.3	32 11.4	38 9.6	Sales/Receivables		32 11.3		39 9.4	33 11.0	41 8.8
47 7.8	46 8.0	49 7.4			53 6.9		48 7.7	41 8.9	52 7.0
59 6.2	59 6.2	64 5.7			83 4.4		70 5.2	49 7.4	62 5.8
41 8.9	36 10.1	39 9.4	Cost of Sales/Inventory		24 15.2		30 12.1	46 7.9	56 6.5
77 4.7	65 5.6	71 5.1			54 6.7		44 8.3	71 5.2	93 3.9
118 3.1	111 3.3	118 3.1			133 2.7		90 4.1	109 3.4	126 2.9
17 21.3	16 23.1	17 20.9	Cost of Sales/Payables		7 54.6		21 17.2	10 37.5	24 15.3
35 10.5	31 11.8	34 10.8			35 10.6		36 10.0	20 18.0	35 10.3
57 6.4	53 6.9	50 7.3			62 5.8		60 6.1	49 7.5	44 8.2
4.8	4.7	4.3	Sales/Working Capital		4.0		7.7	4.5	3.4
9.3	7.9	8.1			10.1		10.4	8.1	5.0
36.6	15.5	18.2			-92.3		21.9	24.6	14.0
26.6	19.5	12.5	EBIT/Interest		22.7		10.2	11.4	21.2
(120) 5.1	(99) 5.2	(122) 3.6		(20) 2.4		(20) 2.2	(26) 3.1	(46) 4.8	
1.8	1.7	1.3			.5		.6	1.7	2.4
6.2	11.3	7.2	Net Profit + Depr., Dep.,						15.4
(42) 2.6	(44) 2.7	(45) 2.2	Amort./Cur. Mat. L/T/D					(28) 3.2	
1.2	1.0	1.1							1.4
.3	.3	.2	Fixed/Worth		.0		.3	.3	.3
.7	.6	.6			.2		.6	.6	.6
1.9	1.2	1.6			6.4		1.9	1.4	1.6
.7	.6	.6	Debt/Worth		.3		.8	.5	.6
1.7	1.3	1.6			1.5		1.7	1.7	1.5
5.2	3.5	4.3			12.1		5.4	3.7	3.9
62.9	54.8	41.3	% Profit Before Taxes/Tangible		22.0		56.9	31.2	48.7
(114) 25.0	(97) 23.7	(119) 19.2	Net Worth	(20) 10.0		(22) 14.8	(25) 16.8	(43) 26.8	
8.6	6.5	4.1			-12.1		.9	5.3	10.7
19.0	21.3	14.7	% Profit Before Taxes/Total		17.8		21.7	16.4	13.4
7.7	9.0	8.0	Assets		6.6		4.4	8.7	8.7
1.1	1.7	1.2			.0		.2	1.6	2.8
24.0	27.0	26.1	Sales/Net Fixed Assets		129.5		30.3	28.1	14.1
10.4	10.6	11.9			21.3		13.8	13.7	8.5
6.0	5.7	5.6			13.0		4.7	5.6	5.0
2.8	3.3	3.0	Sales/Total Assets		3.6		2.9	3.2	2.1
2.1	2.1	2.0			2.7		2.3	2.1	1.7
1.5	1.6	1.4			1.5		1.8	1.6	1.1
1.2	.9	.9	% Depr., Dep., Amort./Sales		.4		1.4	.6	1.3
(111) 2.2	(97) 1.9	(112) 1.8		(15) 1.4		(21) 2.2	(26) 1.5	(40) 2.1	
3.8	3.2	3.1			3.1		4.6	3.4	3.1
2.4	2.8	3.9	% Officers', Directors'		4.0		4.3	3.9	
(35) 5.1	(44) 6.0	(43) 5.4	Owners' Comp/Sales	(14) 6.7		(10) 8.1	(11) 4.9		
7.3	11.0	10.1			12.6		10.4	5.5	
3971777M	3448390M	5409810M	Net Sales ($)	1941M	42191M	33280M	170133M	469697M	4692568M
2750431M	2259295M	4048330M	Total Assets ($)	683M	21591M	16627M	80716M	299280M	3629433M

M = $ thousand   MM = $ million
See Pages 11 through 21 for Explanation of Ratios and Data

Current Data Sorted by Assets   Comparative Historical Data

0-500M	500M-2MM	2-10MM	10-50MM	50-100MM	100-250MM		4/1/02-3/31/03 ALL	4/1/03-3/31/04 ALL
		2	3	1		Type of Statement — Unqualified	9	11
1	1	6	3			Reviewed	6	6
1						Compiled	3	4
2	3	2				Tax Returns	5	3
	2	3	3	1	2	Other	16	13
		4 (4/1-9/30/06)	32 (10/1/06-3/31/07)					
4	6	13	9	2	2	NUMBER OF STATEMENTS	39	37
%	%	%	%	%	%	ASSETS	%	%
		8.7				Cash & Equivalents	9.8	11.2
		28.0				Trade Receivables (net)	24.2	20.5
		18.3				Inventory	24.9	22.0
		4.2				All Other Current	2.0	4.7
		59.2				Total Current	60.9	58.5
		31.4				Fixed Assets (net)	25.5	26.3
		5.1				Intangibles (net)	8.6	10.9
		4.3				All Other Non-Current	5.0	4.4
		100.0				Total	100.0	100.0
						LIABILITIES		
		8.5				Notes Payable-Short Term	7.1	5.6
		4.8				Cur. Mat.-L.T.D.	2.9	4.5
		13.7				Trade Payables	11.7	8.9
		.1				Income Taxes Payable	.3	.3
		12.5				All Other Current	11.6	11.4
		39.5				Total Current	33.6	30.6
		19.0				Long-Term Debt	13.1	19.1
		.7				Deferred Taxes	.5	.9
		8.0				All Other Non-Current	6.2	6.8
		32.9				Net Worth	46.5	42.5
		100.0				Total Liabilties & Net Worth	100.0	100.0
						INCOME DATA		
		100.0				Net Sales	100.0	100.0
		43.9				Gross Profit	49.3	50.1
		37.2				Operating Expenses	41.3	42.7
		6.7				Operating Profit	8.0	7.4
		1.9				All Other Expenses (net)	.8	.8
		4.7				Profit Before Taxes	7.1	6.5
						RATIOS		
		2.5					3.0	3.0
		1.2				Current	1.7	2.1
		1.1					1.3	1.4
		1.4					1.7	1.5
		1.0				Quick	1.1	1.0
		.6					.7	.8
		33 11.1					32 11.5	34 10.8
		46 8.0				Sales/Receivables	44 8.3	45 8.0
		54 6.7					52 7.1	53 6.9
		19 19.4					44 8.2	53 6.9
		61 6.0				Cost of Sales/Inventory	83 4.4	90 4.1
		108 3.4					132 2.8	169 2.2
		27 13.7					18 19.8	22 16.3
		40 9.0				Cost of Sales/Payables	29 12.8	34 10.8
		50 7.3					53 6.8	43 8.5
		6.0					4.3	3.6
		17.2				Sales/Working Capital	8.6	6.1
		86.0					23.4	15.9
		20.4					16.6	13.6
		3.0				EBIT/Interest	(34) 6.0	(35) 5.3
		1.7					1.7	2.8
							10.9	5.5
						Net Profit + Depr., Dep., Amort./Cur. Mat. L/T/D	(12) 1.9	(15) 2.5
							.9	1.0
		.5					.3	.5
		1.0				Fixed/Worth	.6	.7
		2.6					1.3	1.6
		1.6					.7	.5
		2.7				Debt/Worth	1.6	1.3
		6.0					3.2	2.9
		41.5					61.9	33.5
	(12)	25.2				% Profit Before Taxes/Tangible Net Worth	(37) 22.8	(31) 22.0
		12.3					4.9	10.1
		16.4					21.6	18.9
		5.2				% Profit Before Taxes/Total Assets	10.2	9.9
		2.0					1.6	3.1
		23.4					16.8	11.3
		10.1				Sales/Net Fixed Assets	8.9	5.9
		3.9					4.9	3.8
		2.8					3.0	2.5
		2.3				Sales/Total Assets	2.1	1.6
		1.5					1.3	1.1
		1.3					1.3	1.6
		1.7				% Depr., Dep., Amort./Sales	(32) 2.1	(35) 2.3
		3.8					3.5	3.8
							2.0	3.9
						% Officers', Directors' Owners' Comp/Sales	(13) 4.2	(10) 5.6
							11.1	29.7
2483M	20604M	158954M	391244M	174390M	297159M	Net Sales ($)	1192985M	1391907M
1202M	7002M	73287M	170459M	137302M	308146M	Total Assets ($)	703756M	1001476M

M = $ thousand   MM = $ million
See Pages 11 through 21 for Explanation of Ratios and Data

Comparative Historical Data | Current Data Sorted by Sales

			Type of Statement	0-1MM	1-3MM	3-5MM	5-10MM	10-25MM	25MM & OVER
12	12	6	Unqualified					3	3
4	9	11	Reviewed	1	1		3	4	2
4	2	1	Compiled	1					
3	1	7	Tax Returns	2		3	2		
15	18	11	Other	1	1			4	5
4/1/04-3/31/05 ALL	4/1/05-3/31/06 ALL	4/1/06-3/31/07 ALL			4 (4/1-9/30/06)		32 (10/1/06-3/31/07)		
38	42	36	NUMBER OF STATEMENTS	5	2	3	5	11	10
%	%	%	ASSETS	%	%	%	%	%	%
9.1	9.4	10.6	Cash & Equivalents					10.3	13.5
25.8	24.8	25.1	Trade Receivables (net)					22.4	29.1
24.4	25.4	18.1	Inventory					18.3	17.1
2.6	3.9	2.6	All Other Current					5.0	3.4
61.9	63.5	56.5	Total Current					56.1	63.1
24.2	23.3	28.5	Fixed Assets (net)					31.1	20.3
7.6	6.9	8.7	Intangibles (net)					7.3	12.4
6.3	6.3	6.3	All Other Non-Current					5.5	4.3
100.0	100.0	100.0	Total					100.0	100.0
			LIABILITIES						
13.2	13.8	10.5	Notes Payable-Short Term					6.0	9.6
2.0	2.4	5.0	Cur. Mat.-L.T.D.					5.7	3.8
13.3	13.7	11.7	Trade Payables					13.0	11.8
.1	.1	.1	Income Taxes Payable					.1	.1
9.2	10.0	10.5	All Other Current					10.7	8.0
37.8	40.1	37.7	Total Current					35.5	33.4
14.1	11.8	19.4	Long-Term Debt					13.5	6.9
.9	.7	.6	Deferred Taxes					.5	1.0
9.5	6.8	6.2	All Other Non-Current					5.0	3.2
37.7	40.7	36.1	Net Worth					45.6	55.5
100.0	100.0	100.0	Total Liabilities & Net Worth					100.0	100.0
			INCOME DATA						
100.0	100.0	100.0	Net Sales					100.0	100.0
44.5	46.0	47.8	Gross Profit					37.4	50.2
36.6	37.5	42.2	Operating Expenses					34.4	44.2
7.9	8.5	5.7	Operating Profit					3.0	6.0
.5	1.2	1.2	All Other Expenses (net)					1.0	.7
7.3	7.3	4.4	Profit Before Taxes					2.0	5.3
			RATIOS						
3.4	4.0	2.8	Current					2.9	3.5
2.2	1.9	1.6						1.6	2.3
1.4	1.2	1.1						1.1	1.1
1.8	1.7	1.5	Quick					1.7	2.2
1.3	1.1	1.0						1.4	1.4
.7	.7	.7						.5	.9
34 10.8	29 12.5	33 11.2	Sales/Receivables					33 11.1	40 9.2
43 8.5	40 9.1	43 8.6						44 8.3	50 7.3
50 7.3	47 7.8	54 6.8						54 6.8	61 6.0
49 7.5	18 19.9	20 18.1	Cost of Sales/Inventory					16 22.3	28 13.0
74 5.0	77 4.7	59 6.2						64 5.7	63 5.8
111 3.3	124 2.9	112 3.3						83 4.4	127 2.9
19 19.2	20 18.3	24 15.2	Cost of Sales/Payables					24 15.2	25 14.8
29 12.6	29 12.7	36 10.1						31 11.8	30 12.0
44 8.2	50 7.2	54 6.7						55 6.6	46 7.9
4.4	4.3	5.0	Sales/Working Capital					5.0	4.1
8.0	8.8	11.5						9.0	5.6
13.2	23.9	80.9						73.5	28.1
17.1	16.1	26.6	EBIT/Interest					35.7	39.5
(35) 8.3	(37) 7.6	(34) 3.6						4.1	13.0
3.4	2.0	1.6						.8	1.9
19.6	8.7	3.6	Net Profit + Depr., Dep., Amort./Cur. Mat. L/T/D						
(13) 2.9	(18) 3.6	(15) 2.0							
2.0	2.0	.9							
.2	.3	.4	Fixed/Worth					.4	.3
.6	.5	1.0						.6	.5
1.2	1.1	2.2						2.0	1.1
.5	.4	.7	Debt/Worth					.6	.4
1.2	1.3	1.8						1.6	1.0
3.4	3.9	4.9						4.1	5.4
66.1	57.1	68.3	% Profit Before Taxes/Tangible Net Worth					42.5	49.8
(34) 36.9	(39) 29.0	(33) 25.5						24.9	23.8
18.1	12.0	10.6						-4.7	11.7
21.7	20.6	17.0	% Profit Before Taxes/Total Assets					15.1	16.7
10.8	11.3	8.1						8.6	9.0
5.7	4.2	1.9						-.9	3.1
24.7	23.1	17.9	Sales/Net Fixed Assets					13.4	28.1
8.7	11.6	8.2						4.6	10.8
4.5	6.3	3.6						3.5	3.2
2.9	3.4	2.7	Sales/Total Assets					2.6	2.9
2.3	2.3	1.9						1.8	1.9
1.5	1.5	1.3						1.3	1.3
1.0	1.3	1.3	% Depr., Dep., Amort./Sales					1.5	
(35) 2.0	(38) 1.8	(34) 1.8						3.7	
4.0	2.9	4.2						5.2	
2.9	3.7	3.0	% Officers', Directors' Owners' Comp/Sales						
(11) 4.2	(12) 5.2	(17) 5.3							
6.6	9.3	9.9							
1528159M	1965791M	1044834M	Net Sales ($)	3387M	3564M	14125M	34792M	163819M	825147M
891062M	961018M	697398M	Total Assets ($)	1938M	1995M	4878M	19107M	99930M	569550M

M = $ thousand   MM = $ million
See Pages 11 through 21 for Explanation of Ratios and Data

Current Data Sorted by Assets   Comparative Historical Data

0-500M	500M-2MM	2-10MM	10-50MM	50-100MM	100-250MM	Type of Statement	4/1/02-3/31/03 ALL	4/1/03-3/31/04 ALL
			2	2	4	Unqualified	7	4
	3	4				Reviewed	9	7
1	3	2				Compiled	5	12
1	1	1				Tax Returns	3	3
	1	4	1		1	Other	11	10
	9 (4/1-9/30/06)		25 (10/1/06-3/31/07)					
2	9	11	3	4	5	**NUMBER OF STATEMENTS**	35	36
%	%	%	%	%	%	**ASSETS**	%	%
		10.0				Cash & Equivalents	9.3	5.9
		26.2				Trade Receivables (net)	26.9	28.6
		22.0				Inventory	27.1	26.4
		2.1				All Other Current	2.6	2.1
		60.2				Total Current	65.9	63.0
		20.4				Fixed Assets (net)	20.2	29.0
		5.4				Intangibles (net)	9.1	3.0
		14.0				All Other Non-Current	4.7	5.0
		100.0				Total	100.0	100.0
						LIABILITIES		
		8.1				Notes Payable-Short Term	9.0	8.5
		1.9				Cur. Mat.-L.T.D.	4.8	5.8
		19.8				Trade Payables	14.2	25.3
		.3				Income Taxes Payable	.4	.4
		10.8				All Other Current	10.4	7.2
		40.9				Total Current	38.8	47.1
		10.2				Long-Term Debt	19.1	16.6
		.8				Deferred Taxes	.4	.4
		4.7				All Other Non-Current	6.7	10.4
		43.4				Net Worth	35.0	25.4
		100.0				Total Liabilities & Net Worth	100.0	100.0
						INCOME DATA		
		100.0				Net Sales	100.0	100.0
		47.7				Gross Profit	47.1	41.7
		43.9				Operating Expenses	40.8	37.5
		3.8				Operating Profit	6.2	4.2
		.6				All Other Expenses (net)	1.3	.9
		3.2				Profit Before Taxes	4.9	3.3
						RATIOS		
		2.0					2.5	2.1
		1.6				Current	1.8	1.5
		.9					1.2	1.2
		1.2					1.6	1.2
		.8				Quick	1.0	.9
		.7					.5	.5
		22 16.5					23 16.1	26 14.3
		43 8.5				Sales/Receivables	38 9.7	38 9.7
		48 7.7					47 7.8	50 7.3
		18 20.0					32 11.5	28 13.2
		55 6.7				Cost of Sales/Inventory	89 4.1	81 4.5
		136 2.7					132 2.8	129 2.8
		25 14.5					22 16.7	24 15.5
		47 7.7				Cost of Sales/Payables	31 11.8	39 9.4
		124 2.9					51 7.2	105 3.5
		8.1					7.5	6.7
		16.2				Sales/Working Capital	9.3	14.0
		-36.4					19.4	43.4
		14.2					13.9	10.0
		(10) 5.6				EBIT/Interest	(32) 6.0	(33) 3.7
		1.7					2.3	1.3
						Net Profit + Depr., Dep.,	6.9	7.1
						Amort./Cur. Mat. L/T/D	(13) 3.2	(12) 4.7
							1.2	1.2
		.2					.4	.5
		.4				Fixed/Worth	.6	.9
		1.1					1.9	3.1
		.6					1.0	1.1
		1.6				Debt/Worth	2.3	2.7
		4.2					13.1	8.4
		117.5				% Profit Before Taxes/Tangible	63.8	54.4
		(10) 14.1				Net Worth	(29) 34.2	(31) 23.6
		2.7					16.6	5.2
		17.3				% Profit Before Taxes/Total	23.2	16.1
		7.9				Assets	8.5	5.3
		1.4					4.2	1.1
		54.1					24.3	22.5
		15.7				Sales/Net Fixed Assets	14.0	10.9
		5.3					10.1	5.2
		2.8					3.5	4.2
		2.4				Sales/Total Assets	2.4	2.4
		1.7					1.8	1.6
		.3					1.6	1.6
		1.9				% Depr., Dep., Amort./Sales	(27) 2.0	(35) 2.3
		2.8					3.1	3.4
						% Officers', Directors'	3.9	3.9
						Owners' Comp/Sales	(19) 8.4	(13) 6.3
							16.5	10.0
1792M	37331M	137428M	43359M	524669M	759210M	Net Sales ($)	959250M	1168847M
552M	12258M	53607M	93414M	293789M	668710M	Total Assets ($)	544800M	726982M

Comparative Historical Data   Current Data Sorted by Sales

4/1/04-3/31/05 ALL	4/1/05-3/31/06 ALL	4/1/06-3/31/07 ALL	Type of Statement	0-1MM	1-3MM	3-5MM	5-10MM	10-25MM	25MM & OVER
6	8	9	Unqualified				2		7
7	7	7	Reviewed		1	1	5		
12	5	6	Compiled		2	1	1		
3	1	2	Tax Returns	1			1	1	
15	11	10	Other	1			3	2	4
				9 (4/1-9/30/06)			25 (10/1/06-3/31/07)		
43	32	34	NUMBER OF STATEMENTS	3	3	2	12	3	11
%	%	%	ASSETS	%	%	%	%	%	%
10.0	9.0	10.8	Cash & Equivalents				9.1		15.6
22.6	22.7	22.7	Trade Receivables (net)				22.6		22.2
23.2	23.2	21.3	Inventory				23.9		21.2
3.6	3.4	3.3	All Other Current				3.6		3.9
59.4	58.3	58.1	Total Current				59.2		62.9
22.0	27.0	20.1	Fixed Assets (net)				13.7		17.9
13.0	8.5	10.5	Intangibles (net)				12.2		13.9
5.5	6.2	11.3	All Other Non-Current				14.9		5.4
100.0	100.0	100.0	Total				100.0		100.0
			LIABILITIES						
7.1	10.7	8.7	Notes Payable-Short Term				8.4		5.4
3.5	7.0	3.6	Cur. Mat.-L.T.D.				3.2		4.1
14.9	17.2	15.7	Trade Payables				17.9		16.1
.4	.2	.2	Income Taxes Payable				.1		.2
11.3	10.3	8.8	All Other Current				11.4		7.5
37.2	45.6	37.0	Total Current				41.0		33.3
16.8	11.5	17.7	Long-Term Debt				12.9		17.2
.6	.8	.3	Deferred Taxes				.2		.2
4.0	10.4	11.5	All Other Non-Current				5.0		2.3
41.3	31.7	33.5	Net Worth				41.0		46.9
100.0	100.0	100.0	Total Liabilities & Net Worth				100.0		100.0
			INCOME DATA						
100.0	100.0	100.0	Net Sales				100.0		100.0
50.7	42.2	44.7	Gross Profit				51.7		40.6
44.1	35.6	37.9	Operating Expenses				43.4		30.7
6.6	6.6	6.8	Operating Profit				8.3		10.0
1.6	1.2	1.7	All Other Expenses (net)				1.5		2.8
5.0	5.4	5.2	Profit Before Taxes				6.8		7.2
			RATIOS						
2.8	2.7	2.2					1.9		3.3
1.7	1.4	1.6	Current				1.4		1.7
1.0	1.0	1.0					1.0		1.2
1.5	1.4	1.4					1.1		2.8
.8	.7	.8	Quick				.7		.8
.5	.4	.5					.3		.5
23 15.9	24 15.1	24 15.1					23 15.9		39 9.4
37 9.8	38 9.6	43 8.5	Sales/Receivables				45 8.1		44 8.3
51 7.1	46 7.9	57 6.4					58 6.3		62 5.9
31 11.9	26 13.8	27 13.6					20 18.7		38 9.6
76 4.8	68 5.4	75 4.8	Cost of Sales/Inventory				81 4.5		58 6.3
141 2.6	136 2.7	115 3.2					122 3.0		135 2.7
23 16.0	29 12.7	25 14.8					23 16.0		35 10.3
38 9.6	41 9.0	43 8.4	Cost of Sales/Payables				58 6.3		56 6.6
72 5.1	71 5.1	80 4.5					85 4.3		77 4.8
5.7	6.6	7.2					8.9		3.4
11.5	15.0	14.4	Sales/Working Capital				16.4		9.4
210.2	NM	NM					NM		15.0
17.3	11.3	10.1					10.1		22.2
(38) 7.9	(29) 3.8	(32) 4.0	EBIT/Interest				3.9	(10)	6.0
1.2	1.5	1.5					1.5		3.4
6.8	6.6	14.5							
(15) 4.5	(15) 6.3		Net Profit + Depr., Dep., Amort./Cur. Mat. L/T/D						
1.4	1.8								
.3	.4	.2					.1		.2
.6	1.1	.5	Fixed/Worth				.4		1.1
1.8	3.8	2.0					.7		2.9
.7	.8	.7					.8		.4
1.4	2.6	1.9	Debt/Worth				1.8		2.1
7.2	15.6	5.8					3.3		30.2
64.2	79.5	54.1					34.7		175.3
(38) 29.7	(27) 32.0	(29) 17.6	% Profit Before Taxes/Tangible Net Worth				(11) 10.6	(10)	44.6
3.9	11.1	5.2					2.9		10.6
17.7	12.6	12.4					11.3		12.4
8.6	8.6	6.2	% Profit Before Taxes/Total Assets				5.8		11.2
.8	.5	1.3					1.3		6.0
22.5	25.1	61.2					51.6		88.9
11.9	11.0	13.8	Sales/Net Fixed Assets				18.3		13.1
8.1	4.5	6.1					13.1		4.8
3.4	3.4	3.6					3.6		2.1
2.4	2.3	2.1	Sales/Total Assets				2.3		1.5
1.4	1.4	1.4					1.7		1.1
1.3	1.3	.7					.3		
(38) 2.1	(29) 2.6	(29) 2.1	% Depr., Dep., Amort./Sales				1.6		
3.2	3.9	2.9					2.4		
3.3	3.5								
(13) 6.6	(10) 5.0		% Officers', Directors' Owners' Comp/Sales						
15.6	11.1								
1146603M	1228250M	1503789M	Net Sales ($)	2123M	6797M	8181M	88961M	55345M	1342382M
932610M	782312M	1122330M	Total Assets ($)	2086M	6885M	2636M	98680M	18215M	993828M

M = $ thousand   MM = $ million
See Pages 11 through 21 for Explanation of Ratios and Data

Current Data Sorted by Assets   Comparative Historical Data

0-500M	500M-2MM	2-10MM	10-50MM	50-100MM	100-250MM	Type of Statement	4/1/02-3/31/03 ALL	4/1/03-3/31/04 ALL
		2		1		Unqualified	5	4
1	3	3	2			Reviewed	4	5
1	5	3				Compiled	12	10
5	9			1	1	Tax Returns	7	20
5	7	4		1	1	Other	7	8
12 (4/1-9/30/06)			42 (10/1/06-3/31/07)					
12	24	12	2	2	2	NUMBER OF STATEMENTS	35	47
%	%	%	%	%	%	ASSETS	%	%
12.8	14.4	15.1				Cash & Equivalents	13.4	18.8
21.0	27.8	25.7				Trade Receivables (net)	25.1	23.4
8.3	8.3	8.2				Inventory	5.4	5.0
7.9	2.7	7.6				All Other Current	1.7	4.4
50.0	53.2	56.6				Total Current	45.6	51.6
25.6	26.5	31.6				Fixed Assets (net)	34.6	35.7
13.2	11.0	4.9				Intangibles (net)	8.4	5.0
11.2	9.3	7.0				All Other Non-Current	11.4	7.7
100.0	100.0	100.0				Total	100.0	100.0
						LIABILITIES		
10.8	6.9	7.3				Notes Payable-Short Term	12.2	12.7
6.2	5.9	3.8				Cur. Mat.-L.T.D.	9.9	5.4
8.4	12.0	13.3				Trade Payables	8.8	8.9
.0	.0	.7				Income Taxes Payable	.2	.6
11.4	5.0	8.7				All Other Current	12.3	12.8
36.8	29.8	33.8				Total Current	43.4	40.4
24.7	25.2	18.8				Long-Term Debt	23.6	36.3
.2	.6	1.4				Deferred Taxes	.2	.4
10.2	4.0	4.5				All Other Non-Current	12.0	9.1
28.1	40.4	41.5				Net Worth	20.8	13.6
100.0	100.0	100.0				Total Liabilities & Net Worth	100.0	100.0
						INCOME DATA		
100.0	100.0	100.0				Net Sales	100.0	100.0
						Gross Profit		
85.6	96.2	94.5				Operating Expenses	90.4	93.8
14.4	3.8	5.5				Operating Profit	9.6	6.2
1.3	1.3	.1				All Other Expenses (net)	1.1	.5
13.1	2.4	5.4				Profit Before Taxes	8.5	5.7
						RATIOS		
4.1	3.7	2.4					2.9	3.0
1.8	2.0	1.6				Current	1.4	1.4
.9	1.4	1.3					.7	.8
2.9	3.2	2.3					2.4	2.6
1.4	1.7	1.2				Quick	1.1	1.1
.6	1.0	.7					.6	.6
0 UND	27 13.7	33 11.1					0 UND	0 UND
19 19.4	38 9.6	36 10.2				Sales/Receivables	31 11.9	35 10.4
39 9.3	44 8.3	40 9.0					39 9.5	40 9.2
						Cost of Sales/Inventory		
						Cost of Sales/Payables		
8.4	7.2	7.0					9.1	9.7
22.9	12.8	13.3				Sales/Working Capital	29.2	22.9
NM	23.8	24.0					-26.2	-48.9
28.9	11.9	24.2					14.2	14.8
(10) 2.5	(22) 4.5	(11) 3.9				EBIT/Interest	(29) 4.7	(36) 3.6
.1	1.4	2.1					.1	.1
						Net Profit + Depr., Dep., Amort./Cur. Mat. L/T/D	8.8	
							(11) 1.1	
							.5	
.4	.1	.3					.3	.3
1.1	.6	1.2				Fixed/Worth	1.0	1.0
NM	2.8	2.8					-6.0	-10.2
.3	.7	.6					.6	.7
2.3	1.5	2.2				Debt/Worth	2.5	2.0
NM	6.2	4.0					-17.1	-16.8
	50.1	85.1				% Profit Before Taxes/Tangible Net Worth	69.5	74.5
	(20) 30.4	26.0					(26) 20.9	(33) 8.9
	13.2	14.4					-2.4	-1.6
77.9	26.9	15.9				% Profit Before Taxes/Total Assets	32.7	37.7
12.4	9.4	10.1					14.5	4.1
-1.4	2.5	3.9					-2.7	-1.4
48.4	53.4	23.7				Sales/Net Fixed Assets	19.6	29.3
19.7	14.0	9.2					12.3	14.2
7.2	9.6	5.8					7.8	8.5
6.4	4.0	3.3				Sales/Total Assets	5.3	7.0
3.6	2.7	2.3					3.9	3.9
2.3	1.3	1.4					2.5	2.3
	2.0	1.4				% Depr., Dep., Amort./Sales	1.5	1.5
	(17) 2.8	(11) 1.8					(33) 2.0	(38) 2.3
	5.4	3.9					3.6	3.6
	3.9					% Officers', Directors' Owners' Comp/Sales	3.3	7.3
	(17) 7.1						(20) 7.6	(27) 12.6
	10.2						13.0	27.5
17572M	79311M	118225M	26098M	796577M	1070122M	Net Sales ($)	249153M	708512M
3942M	27018M	50289M	23526M	126974M	333105M	Total Assets ($)	120317M	195688M

M = $ thousand   MM = $ million
See Pages 11 through 21 for Explanation of Ratios and Data

Comparative Historical Data | Current Data Sorted by Sales

1	2	3	Type of Statement						
1	2		Unqualified				2		1
3	3	9	Reviewed		2		3	3	
12	7	9	Compiled	1	3	1	4		
11	21	16	Tax Returns	3	6	4	1		2
9	15	17	Other	2			2	1	2
4/1/04-	4/1/05-	4/1/06-							
3/31/05	3/31/06	3/31/07		12 (4/1-9/30/06)			42 (10/1/06-3/31/07)		
ALL	ALL	ALL		0-1MM	1-3MM	3-5MM	5-10MM	10-25MM	25MM & OVER
36	48	54	NUMBER OF STATEMENTS	6	19	8	12	4	5
%	%	%	ASSETS	%	%	%	%	%	%
14.9	13.1	13.1	Cash & Equivalents		16.2		13.3		
32.3	26.7	24.5	Trade Receivables (net)		22.4		32.3		
5.5	4.8	7.8	Inventory		4.7		10.4		
2.6	4.9	4.8	All Other Current		5.5		.9		
55.3	49.5	50.2	Total Current		48.7		56.8		
31.1	32.6	28.1	Fixed Assets (net)		25.7		33.3		
4.2	9.9	13.4	Intangibles (net)		14.7		2.9		
9.3	8.0	8.3	All Other Non-Current		10.9		7.0		
100.0	100.0	100.0	Total		100.0		100.0		
			LIABILITIES						
6.8	12.2	7.5	Notes Payable-Short Term		5.8		7.5		
5.2	3.9	6.5	Cur. Mat.-L.T.D.		6.9		6.2		
7.1	8.2	10.8	Trade Payables		9.5		12.5		
.1	.3	.2	Income Taxes Payable		.0		.0		
10.4	10.2	7.8	All Other Current		7.6		10.0		
29.6	34.7	32.8	Total Current		29.8		36.2		
24.0	25.6	24.2	Long-Term Debt		36.2		16.6		
.6	.7	.8	Deferred Taxes		.1		1.1		
7.0	5.2	5.5	All Other Non-Current		4.5		5.2		
38.9	33.8	36.8	Net Worth		29.5		40.9		
100.0	100.0	100.0	Total Liabilties & Net Worth		100.0		100.0		
			INCOME DATA						
100.0	100.0	100.0	Net Sales		100.0		100.0		
			Gross Profit						
95.1	94.3	92.9	Operating Expenses		92.9		96.3		
4.9	5.7	7.1	Operating Profit		7.1		3.7		
-.2	.7	1.4	All Other Expenses (net)		1.7		-.2		
5.1	5.0	5.7	Profit Before Taxes		5.4		3.9		
			RATIOS						
3.1	2.7	3.0			3.8		3.7		
1.8	1.7	1.6	Current		1.7		1.4		
1.3	.9	1.3			1.3		1.1		
2.6	2.4	2.5			3.1		3.1		
1.6	1.1	1.4	Quick		1.6		1.1		
1.0	.6	.8			.9		.8		
5 78.3	5 70.0	25 14.4			14 25.4		31 11.9		
36 10.1	33 11.2	36 10.2	Sales/Receivables		32 11.2		37 10.0		
42 8.7	40 9.1	42 8.8			40 9.0		42 8.8		
			Cost of Sales/Inventory						
			Cost of Sales/Payables						
9.2	10.5	7.8			5.7		8.2		
17.7	23.5	16.4	Sales/Working Capital		14.3		17.4		
79.0	-98.7	28.0			26.3		83.9		
15.1	12.1	12.6			10.7		38.6		
(22) 7.3	(40) 4.0	(49) 3.5	EBIT/Interest	(18) 3.2			(10) 3.6		
2.5	.5	1.4			1.2		2.1		
		2.7							
	(11) 1.8		Net Profit + Depr., Dep., Amort./Cur. Mat. L/T/D						
		1.6							
.2	.5	.4			.1		.4		
.6	1.1	1.0	Fixed/Worth		.8		1.2		
2.4	NM	5.0			2.9		2.8		
.5	.7	.8			.8		.5		
1.2	1.7	2.5	Debt/Worth		1.9		2.2		
3.9	NM	18.9			4.7		4.0		
85.2	62.3	82.5			106.7		52.9		
(28) 20.7	(36) 23.1	(43) 27.5	% Profit Before Taxes/Tangible Net Worth	(15) 34.2			(11) 19.2		
3.2	1.8	14.3			2.4		12.5		
24.6	31.8	28.7			30.7		23.9		
11.3	7.2	7.8	% Profit Before Taxes/Total Assets		6.9		6.0		
2.0	-.7	2.1			.8		3.6		
32.9	25.8	31.8			63.3		24.0		
16.1	14.4	12.3	Sales/Net Fixed Assets		15.0		9.2		
10.0	9.7	6.3			9.4		5.8		
5.2	5.0	4.0			3.6		4.7		
4.1	3.9	2.7	Sales/Total Assets		2.6		2.7		
3.2	2.8	1.3			1.4		1.8		
1.3	1.2	1.4			1.8				
(27) 2.1	(42) 2.1	(41) 2.5	% Depr., Dep., Amort./Sales	(13) 2.9					
3.5	2.9	3.9			5.7				
8.0	4.5	5.3			5.3				
(18) 11.8	(27) 11.6	(30) 7.1	% Officers', Directors' Owners' Comp/Sales	(11) 7.6					
25.7	16.7	12.5			12.8				
152664M	1372777M	2107905M	Net Sales ($)	3292M	34847M	30010M	94975M	52897M	1891884M
43480M	451518M	564854M	Total Assets ($)	2214M	15710M	9655M	38146M	34892M	464237M

© RMA 2007

M = $ thousand   MM = $ million

See Pages 11 through 21 for Explanation of Ratios and Data

Current Data Sorted by Assets   Comparative Historical Data

	0-500M	500M-2MM	2-10MM	10-50MM	50-100MM	100-250MM		4/1/02-3/31/03 ALL	4/1/03-3/31/04 ALL
Type of Statement									
Unqualified	1		7	17	5	2		15	28
Reviewed		6	28	17	1	1		53	54
Compiled	1	7	3	1				13	19
Tax Returns	3	7	5	1				6	7
Other		2	10	14	2	8		19	34
		29 (4/1-9/30/06)		120 (10/1/06-3/31/07)					
NUMBER OF STATEMENTS	5	22	53	50	8	11		106	142
	%	%	%	%	%	%		%	%
ASSETS									
Cash & Equivalents		10.5	5.8	3.6		6.0		7.7	6.1
Trade Receivables (net)		26.1	25.4	33.2		23.8		30.7	30.0
Inventory		45.2	48.2	50.8		54.8		44.6	46.1
All Other Current		1.4	1.1	1.2		.5		1.0	1.6
Total Current		83.3	80.4	88.9		85.1		84.0	83.7
Fixed Assets (net)		10.3	12.0	6.1		5.0		10.3	9.4
Intangibles (net)		3.0	3.6	.6		5.9		1.8	1.8
All Other Non-Current		3.4	3.9	4.4		4.0		3.9	5.1
Total		100.0	100.0	100.0		100.0		100.0	100.0
LIABILITIES									
Notes Payable-Short Term		14.5	25.2	35.2		39.8		18.2	22.4
Cur. Mat.-L.T.D.		4.6	2.0	.7		.8		1.6	1.3
Trade Payables		21.9	19.3	15.1		18.1		18.6	17.4
Income Taxes Payable		.0	.0	.1		1.7		.2	.4
All Other Current		7.8	5.8	6.3		7.2		9.4	9.8
Total Current		48.8	52.3	57.4		67.6		48.0	51.3
Long-Term Debt		11.2	7.9	3.6		6.0		5.5	5.5
Deferred Taxes		.0	.8	.3		.5		.0	.1
All Other Non-Current		8.9	2.2	2.9		2.5		2.3	4.4
Net Worth		31.1	36.7	35.9		23.4		44.2	38.7
Total Liabilities & Net Worth		100.0	100.0	100.0		100.0		100.0	100.0
INCOME DATA									
Net Sales		100.0	100.0	100.0		100.0		100.0	100.0
Gross Profit		30.9	30.6	21.4		19.3		32.3	28.7
Operating Expenses		27.2	25.6	16.5		14.2		28.5	25.0
Operating Profit		3.7	5.0	4.8		5.2		3.8	3.7
All Other Expenses (net)		1.6	1.3	1.7		1.9		.9	1.2
Profit Before Taxes		2.1	3.7	3.2		3.3		2.9	2.6
RATIOS									
Current		3.1	2.1	1.7		1.5		2.7	2.3
		1.5	1.5	1.4		1.3		1.7	1.6
		1.1	1.2	1.3		1.2		1.3	1.3
Quick		1.2	1.0	.8		.6		1.1	1.1
		.7	(52) .6	.6		.4		.8	.7
		.4	.3	.4		.3		.5	.5
Sales/Receivables		9 / 40.2	22 / 16.6	50 / 7.3		45 / 8.1		35 / 10.5	41 / 8.8
		34 / 10.9	42 / 8.6	72 / 5.1		73 / 5.1		59 / 6.2	68 / 5.3
		63 / 5.8	73 / 5.0	106 / 3.5		91 / 4.0		89 / 4.1	91 / 4.0
Cost of Sales/Inventory		38 / 9.7	61 / 6.0	99 / 3.7		114 / 3.2		69 / 5.3	75 / 4.9
		99 / 3.7	118 / 3.1	146 / 2.5		176 / 2.1		122 / 3.0	129 / 2.8
		176 / 2.1	250 / 1.5	247 / 1.5		311 / 1.2		215 / 1.7	225 / 1.6
Cost of Sales/Payables		13 / 28.8	17 / 21.3	9 / 40.4		11 / 32.5		18 / 19.8	19 / 19.4
		50 / 7.2	43 / 8.4	32 / 11.3		43 / 8.5		47 / 7.8	44 / 8.4
		80 / 4.6	81 / 4.5	82 / 4.5		99 / 3.7		83 / 4.4	82 / 4.5
Sales/Working Capital		2.5	4.1	3.5		3.9		3.6	3.4
		14.9	7.2	6.6		7.5		6.1	6.0
		69.6	16.2	9.2		9.3		9.9	10.4
EBIT/Interest		2.9	5.9	4.1		3.2		6.3	5.6
		(18) 1.6	(51) 2.9	(47) 1.8		2.2		(99) 2.0	(128) 2.6
		1.1	1.6	1.3		1.4		1.1	1.3
Net Profit + Depr., Dep., Amort./Cur. Mat. L/T/D			4.3					6.9	8.5
			(10) 2.1					(24) 2.1	(22) 2.0
			1.4					1.3	.7
Fixed/Worth		.1	.1	.0		.1		.1	.0
		.3	.2	.1		.1		.2	.2
		1.2	.7	.3		.6		.4	.4
Debt/Worth		1.2	1.1	1.3		2.5		.7	.8
		3.1	1.7	2.2		3.4		1.6	1.9
		14.8	4.5	3.9		12.0		3.2	3.6
% Profit Before Taxes/Tangible Net Worth		31.9	32.6	26.4				20.2	27.4
		(18) 13.6	(48) 12.2	10.0				(104) 8.7	(138) 9.8
		4.8	3.1	3.0				1.3	1.8
% Profit Before Taxes/Total Assets		7.4	9.6	6.6		4.3		7.8	8.1
		2.8	5.8	2.4		2.1		2.5	2.3
		.3	.8	.9		.4		.3	.5
Sales/Net Fixed Assets		130.0	83.9	244.6		142.2		83.8	147.0
		30.7	29.1	47.2		65.9		29.9	39.3
		18.9	8.7	17.7		9.2		13.0	15.1
Sales/Total Assets		3.2	2.8	2.0		1.6		2.5	2.3
		2.0	1.7	1.5		1.3		1.9	1.7
		1.7	1.3	1.1		.7		1.2	1.2
% Depr., Dep., Amort./Sales		.3	.3	.2				.3	.3
		(18) 1.1	(50) 1.0	(43) .5				(90) .8	(120) .7
		2.2	1.4	1.0				1.4	1.5
% Officers', Directors' Owners' Comp/Sales		2.4	1.9	1.2				1.9	2.0
		(16) 5.3	(29) 3.4	(25) 1.6				(59) 3.7	(77) 4.3
		9.3	5.3	2.6				7.6	7.9
Net Sales ($)	6398M	141235M	579977M	1710640M	920564M	2127544M		3428601M	4471002M
Total Assets ($)	1335M	27689M	264712M	1112792M	557760M	1695313M		1944476M	3082481M

M = $ thousand   MM = $ million
See Pages 11 through 21 for Explanation of Ratios and Data

Comparative Historical Data | Current Data Sorted by Sales

			Type of Statement	0-1MM	1-3MM	3-5MM	5-10MM	10-25MM	25MM & OVER
41	47	32	Unqualified	1			3	8	20
63	50	53	Reviewed		5	7	11	18	12
23	14	12	Compiled	2	5	2	1	2	
11	14	16	Tax Returns	1	5	3	3	2	2
56	50	36	Other		5	3	3	2	17
4/1/04-3/31/05 ALL	4/1/05-3/31/06 ALL	4/1/06-3/31/07 ALL		\<— 29 (4/1-9/30/06) —\>	\<——————— 120 (10/1/06-3/31/07) ———————\>				
194	175	149	NUMBER OF STATEMENTS	4	17	15	21	41	51
%	%	%	ASSETS	%	%	%	%	%	%
5.0	5.3	6.0	Cash & Equivalents		11.2	2.7	5.7	6.8	4.3
30.2	28.4	28.0	Trade Receivables (net)		16.0	27.4	30.4	29.8	30.7
47.5	48.5	48.7	Inventory		55.3	49.6	43.3	47.6	49.4
1.2	1.9	1.2	All Other Current		1.5	.7	.9	1.7	1.0
83.9	84.2	83.9	Total Current		84.0	80.4	80.3	86.0	85.5
9.3	10.2	9.4	Fixed Assets (net)		10.6	13.1	13.2	6.7	7.5
1.8	1.3	2.8	Intangibles (net)		2.3	2.0	3.3	2.6	3.3
5.0	4.3	3.9	All Other Non-Current		3.1	4.5	3.2	4.7	3.8
100.0	100.0	100.0	Total		100.0	100.0	100.0	100.0	100.0
			LIABILITIES						
28.9	28.8	27.5	Notes Payable-Short Term		18.3	27.8	18.4	27.7	35.4
2.2	2.0	1.9	Cur. Mat.-L.T.D.		2.9	4.1	1.8	1.3	1.4
18.0	17.2	17.9	Trade Payables		14.6	19.2	23.3	17.5	17.2
.4	.3	.3	Income Taxes Payable		.0	.2	.1	.0	.8
6.8	8.1	6.3	All Other Current		3.0	7.2	6.5	7.3	6.5
56.2	56.4	53.8	Total Current		38.8	58.5	50.1	53.8	61.2
6.4	6.2	7.0	Long-Term Debt		11.3	16.0	7.2	4.8	4.7
.8	.1	.4	Deferred Taxes		1.7	.1	.4	.1	.4
4.9	4.5	3.6	All Other Non-Current		2.5	3.3	5.2	2.3	3.9
31.8	32.7	35.2	Net Worth		45.7	22.1	37.1	39.0	29.8
100.0	100.0	100.0	Total Liabilities & Net Worth		100.0	100.0	100.0	100.0	100.0
			INCOME DATA						
100.0	100.0	100.0	Net Sales		100.0	100.0	100.0	100.0	100.0
26.6	26.3	27.0	Gross Profit		38.5	32.3	28.4	27.2	19.6
23.6	22.5	22.2	Operating Expenses		31.0	28.7	25.3	22.0	14.7
3.0	3.8	4.9	Operating Profit		7.4	3.5	3.0	5.2	4.9
1.5	1.6	1.6	All Other Expenses (net)		1.5	2.0	.9	1.7	1.6
1.5	2.2	3.3	Profit Before Taxes		5.9	1.5	2.2	3.5	3.3
			RATIOS						
2.0	2.1	2.1	Current	4.5	2.0	1.8	2.1	1.7	
1.5	1.4	1.4		2.6	1.4	1.7	1.5	1.3	
1.2	1.2	1.2		1.2	1.1	1.3	1.3	1.2	
.9	1.0	1.0	Quick	1.8	1.0	1.1	.8	.7	
.6	.6 (148)	.6		.6 (16)	.5	.8	.6	.5	
.4	.3	.4		.3	.3	.5	.4	.4	
39 9.5	33 11.0	29 12.6	Sales/Receivables	6 60.5	28 13.2	29 12.8	29 12.6	45 8.1	
62 5.9	56 6.5	55 6.6		33 11.1	49 7.4	50 7.3	59 6.2	62 5.9	
87 4.2	79 4.6	78 4.7		57 6.5	74 4.9	77 4.7	92 4.0	80 4.6	
79 4.6	74 4.9	74 4.9	Cost of Sales/Inventory	97 3.8	92 4.0	60 6.1	70 5.2	81 4.5	
143 2.6	157 2.3	137 2.7		172 2.1	177 2.1	81 4.5	129 2.8	137 2.7	
220 1.7	242 1.5	227 1.6		316 1.2	270 1.4	187 2.0	258 1.4	202 1.8	
16 22.2	13 28.4	12 29.6	Cost of Sales/Payables	3 105.8	6 63.1	34 10.7	13 28.2	9 40.4	
38 9.5	33 11.1	39 9.3		44 8.2	55 6.6	48 7.5	41 9.0	24 15.0	
84 4.4	78 4.7	81 4.5		82 4.5	93 3.9	81 4.5	70 5.2	82 4.4	
3.6	3.6	3.8	Sales/Working Capital	2.2	2.7	4.2	3.6	6.0	
6.4	6.6	7.2		3.4	16.2	7.3	6.3	7.8	
12.2	13.2	13.8		17.8	47.8	13.5	12.7	12.2	
6.1	4.5	4.5	EBIT/Interest	5.4	2.9	3.6	5.3	3.9	
(184) 2.3	(162) 2.3	(138) 2.0		(14) 3.2	2.0	(18) 1.7	(39) 2.6	(49) 2.0	
1.2	1.1	1.3		1.4	.6	1.4	1.2	1.4	
8.3	7.0	10.4	Net Profit + Depr., Dep., Amort./Cur. Mat. L/T/D					36.5	
(41) 3.2	(31) 2.4	(28) 3.4					(12) 6.0		
1.1	.2	1.5						2.8	
.0	.1	.1	Fixed/Worth	.0	.1	.0	.0	.1	
.2	.2	.2		.3	.2	.2	.1	.2	
.5	.6	.5		.6	-24.3	.9	.3	.5	
1.4	1.1	1.2	Debt/Worth	.4	1.4	1.1	1.1	1.7	
2.5	2.4	2.3		1.3	2.8	1.7	1.8	3.2	
4.3	4.8	4.7		5.3	-45.5	4.2	3.3	6.8	
27.9	23.5	31.3	% Profit Before Taxes/Tangible Net Worth	25.4	51.4	22.7	32.4	33.9	
(183) 10.6	(163) 9.9	(137) 11.4		(15) 11.4	(11) 8.7	6.3	(39) 13.0	(47) 13.0	
1.5	2.3	3.1		6.3	.5	.8	3.1	4.3	
7.2	6.8	7.9	% Profit Before Taxes/Total Assets	8.2	6.6	6.7	12.4	7.6	
3.1	3.0	3.2		4.3	1.9	2.2	4.0	3.3	
.3	.4	.7		2.0	-1.6	.3	.9	1.2	
108.0	84.0	122.7	Sales/Net Fixed Assets	43.7	102.9	88.1	160.6	142.2	
36.5	33.3	34.4		25.0	26.7	29.1	58.8	51.8	
15.9	12.8	12.3		8.2	8.6	10.6	15.8	13.9	
2.4	2.6	2.4	Sales/Total Assets	1.9	2.0	2.8	2.8	2.3	
1.7	1.5	1.6		1.6	1.6	1.9	1.6	1.6	
1.2	1.2	1.2		1.1	1.3	1.4	1.1	1.3	
.3	.3	.3	% Depr., Dep., Amort./Sales	.4	.3	.4	.2	.2	
(170) .7	(154) .7	(130) .8		(15) 1.3	(14) .8	(19) .9	(38) .8	(40) .5	
1.4	1.4	1.3		2.3	1.5	1.5	1.1	1.2	
1.4	1.0	1.3	% Officers', Directors' Owners' Comp/Sales	2.9	3.4	2.0	1.1	.5	
(106) 3.0	(90) 2.9	(79) 2.3		(11) 4.8	(11) 4.3	(14) 4.4	(23) 1.8	(18) 1.2	
5.2	5.7	5.5		7.7	12.3	7.5	2.9	1.6	
8632945M	6134520M	5486358M	Net Sales ($)	2136M	34576M	57207M	157027M	707940M	4527472M
4219702M	4329697M	3659601M	Total Assets ($)	1843M	32633M	37052M	90653M	505832M	2991588M

M = $ thousand   MM = $ million
See Pages 11 through 21 for Explanation of Ratios and Data

Current Data Sorted by Assets   Comparative Historical Data

0-500M	500M-2MM	2-10MM	10-50MM	50-100MM	100-250MM		4/1/02-3/31/03 ALL	4/1/03-3/31/04 ALL
						Type of Statement		
			3			Unqualified	5	2
	2	7				Reviewed	18	17
	2					Compiled	8	11
	2					Tax Returns	2	2
1	1	5				Other	9	4
1	7	12	3			**NUMBER OF STATEMENTS**	42	36
%	%	%	%	%	%	**ASSETS**	%	%
		11.7				Cash & Equivalents	8.2	8.0
		37.8				Trade Receivables (net)	36.8	36.1
		28.1				Inventory	21.7	21.1
		.8	D	D		All Other Current	.7	1.4
		78.5	A	A		Total Current	67.4	66.6
		10.2	T	T		Fixed Assets (net)	23.3	25.8
		5.3	A	A		Intangibles (net)	2.9	2.8
		6.1				All Other Non-Current	6.4	4.8
		100.0	N	N		Total	100.0	100.0
			O	O		**LIABILITIES**		
		12.3	T	T		Notes Payable-Short Term	16.6	16.3
		2.3				Cur. Mat.-L.T.D.	3.3	4.3
		24.2	A	A		Trade Payables	15.6	16.7
		.0	V	V		Income Taxes Payable	.2	.2
		8.3	A	A		All Other Current	10.3	13.2
		47.1	I	I		Total Current	46.0	50.5
		7.1	L	L		Long-Term Debt	14.9	12.9
		.0	A	A		Deferred Taxes	.5	.3
		3.7	B	B		All Other Non-Current	13.5	7.8
		42.1	L	L		Net Worth	24.8	28.5
		100.0	E	E		Total Liabilities & Net Worth	100.0	100.0
						INCOME DATA		
		100.0				Net Sales	100.0	100.0
		39.8				Gross Profit	35.4	35.0
		29.8				Operating Expenses	30.6	31.2
		9.9				Operating Profit	4.9	3.9
		.5				All Other Expenses (net)	2.5	.8
		9.4				Profit Before Taxes	2.4	3.0
						RATIOS		
		3.0					2.5	2.5
		1.9				Current	1.4	1.2
		1.2					1.0	.9
		1.6					1.4	1.4
		1.0				Quick	1.0	1.0
		.8					.6	.5
		26 14.1					38 9.7	36 10.3
		43 8.5				Sales/Receivables	49 7.5	43 8.4
		79 4.6					62 5.9	54 6.7
		19 19.0					10 35.0	12 31.2
		56 6.5				Cost of Sales/Inventory	43 8.5	31 11.6
		129 2.8					69 5.3	87 4.2
		23 16.2					17 21.6	20 18.2
		49 7.4				Cost of Sales/Payables	29 12.5	31 11.9
		64 5.7					41 9.0	48 7.7
		5.3					7.6	7.8
		8.7				Sales/Working Capital	10.8	22.2
		30.2					NM	-69.8
		29.9					9.0	15.7
		11.8				EBIT/Interest	(39) 3.1	(34) 3.9
		5.0					1.2	.5
							4.9	9.4
						Net Profit + Depr., Dep., Amort./Cur. Mat. L/T/D	(11) 2.5	(11) 7.1
							.8	1.7
		.1					.3	.2
		.2				Fixed/Worth	.8	.7
		.8					2.2	3.8
		.5					1.2	1.0
		1.6				Debt/Worth	2.3	2.6
		6.1					6.7	12.5
		133.5					51.1	45.2
	(10)	84.2				% Profit Before Taxes/Tangible Net Worth	(35) 17.7	(31) 26.6
		23.2					2.6	4.1
		33.0					22.8	16.1
		20.5				% Profit Before Taxes/Total Assets	5.7	5.2
		15.7					.6	-2.0
		72.1					37.7	41.9
		24.0				Sales/Net Fixed Assets	14.6	16.9
		19.4					7.5	6.2
		3.4					3.3	3.4
		2.8				Sales/Total Assets	2.8	2.6
		1.9					2.2	2.0
		.4					.7	.6
	(11)	.5				% Depr., Dep., Amort./Sales	(40) 1.5	(35) 1.8
		1.4					3.5	3.6
							3.5	2.8
						% Officers', Directors' Owners' Comp/Sales	(24) 6.2	(24) 5.8
							9.6	9.8
993M	24674M	156320M	194293M			Net Sales ($)	379084M	229232M
290M	10029M	57562M	93595M			Total Assets ($)	155099M	90881M

M = $ thousand   MM = $ million
See Pages 11 through 21 for Explanation of Ratios and Data

Comparative Historical Data   Current Data Sorted by Sales

4/1/04-3/31/05 ALL	4/1/05-3/31/06 ALL	4/1/06-3/31/07 ALL	Type of Statement	0-1MM	1-3MM	3-5MM	5-10MM	10-25MM	25MM & OVER
6	5	3	Unqualified						3
17	6	9	Reviewed		1	1	2	5	
7	5	2	Compiled		1	1			
1		2	Tax Returns		1	1			
7	6	7	Other	1		2	1	2	1
					3 (4/1-9/30/06)		20 (10/1/06-3/31/07)		
38	22	23	NUMBER OF STATEMENTS	1	3	5	3	7	4
%	%	%	ASSETS	%	%	%	%	%	%
8.7	9.4	11.1	Cash & Equivalents						
33.5	39.6	34.3	Trade Receivables (net)						
25.0	27.4	24.7	Inventory						
.4	.2	1.7	All Other Current						
67.6	76.6	71.7	Total Current						
21.8	15.7	16.1	Fixed Assets (net)						
3.6	3.0	7.3	Intangibles (net)						
7.0	4.7	4.9	All Other Non-Current						
100.0	100.0	100.0	Total						
			LIABILITIES						
16.7	18.7	12.7	Notes Payable-Short Term						
4.0	2.5	2.5	Cur. Mat.-L.T.D.						
16.1	19.2	18.4	Trade Payables						
.2	.1	.2	Income Taxes Payable						
7.8	9.3	7.0	All Other Current						
44.8	49.6	40.9	Total Current						
11.3	8.7	10.4	Long-Term Debt						
.5	.0	.0	Deferred Taxes						
9.0	3.8	3.0	All Other Non-Current						
34.4	37.9	45.7	Net Worth						
100.0	100.0	100.0	Total Liabilties & Net Worth						
			INCOME DATA						
100.0	100.0	100.0	Net Sales						
33.9	32.1	41.6	Gross Profit						
28.9	25.9	32.9	Operating Expenses						
5.0	6.2	8.7	Operating Profit						
1.1	1.0	.7	All Other Expenses (net)						
4.0	5.2	7.9	Profit Before Taxes						
			RATIOS						
2.7	2.7	3.5	Current						
1.5	1.6	2.2							
.9	1.1	1.2							
1.4	1.5	2.0	Quick						
1.0	1.0	1.0							
.7	.6	.8							
(35) 10.3	(32) 11.3	(24) 15.2	Sales/Receivables						
(47) 7.8	(53) 6.9	(47) 7.8							
(55) 6.6	(70) 5.2	(72) 5.1							
(18) 20.0	(19) 19.6	(18) 20.2	Cost of Sales/Inventory						
(57) 6.4	(39) 9.5	(57) 6.4							
(96) 3.8	(64) 5.7	(86) 4.3							
(14) 25.9	(19) 19.3	(12) 30.7	Cost of Sales/Payables						
(25) 14.8	(23) 15.6	(48) 7.6							
(53) 6.9	(48) 7.7	(56) 6.6							
6.0	5.2	5.1	Sales/Working Capital						
11.7	11.2	7.7							
-51.9	NM	32.0							
18.3	26.0	19.6	EBIT/Interest						
(33) 4.7	(19) 5.8	(22) 8.4							
1.3	2.1	3.8							
10.3			Net Profit + Depr., Dep., Amort./Cur. Mat. L/T/D						
(14) 2.4									
.5									
.2	.1	.1	Fixed/Worth						
.4	.2	.4							
1.9	1.1	.9							
.9	.8	.4	Debt/Worth						
1.9	1.4	1.6							
4.2	6.2	6.4							
62.7	96.6	87.1	% Profit Before Taxes/Tangible Net Worth						
(33) 23.4	(19) 23.9	(19) 33.9							
4.6	9.9	14.8							
21.4	20.7	32.7	% Profit Before Taxes/Total Assets						
6.7	9.4	17.8							
.3	5.6	7.6							
36.4	58.4	45.3	Sales/Net Fixed Assets						
17.7	28.3	23.0							
11.2	14.8	17.7							
3.5	3.8	3.4	Sales/Total Assets						
2.7	2.8	2.3							
2.1	2.2	1.9							
.8	.4	.5	% Depr., Dep., Amort./Sales						
(36) 1.5	(21) .8	(21) .6							
2.9	2.0	2.4							
2.5	2.2	2.4	% Officers', Directors' Owners' Comp/Sales						
(20) 5.9	(11) 5.7	(11) 4.1							
9.0	9.4	7.1							
485460M	349246M	376280M	Net Sales ($)	993M	7135M	21058M	23229M	100818M	223047M
244326M	121618M	161476M	Total Assets ($)	290M	4408M	8957M	8796M	37213M	101812M

© RMA 2007   M = $ thousand   MM = $ million
See Pages 11 through 21 for Explanation of Ratios and Data

Current Data Sorted by Assets   Comparative Historical Data

	0-500M	500M-2MM	2-10MM	10-50MM	50-100MM	100-250MM		4/1/02-3/31/03 ALL	4/1/03-3/31/04 ALL
Type of Statement									
Unqualified			16	16	8	5		41	45
Reviewed		5	18	8				31	38
Compiled	2	10	8	4				24	31
Tax Returns	8	5	5	1	1			8	16
Other	4	10	26	15	5	3		57	49
		56 (4/1-9/30/06)		127 (10/1/06-3/31/07)					
NUMBER OF STATEMENTS	14	30	73	44	14	8		161	179
ASSETS	%	%	%	%	%	%		%	%
Cash & Equivalents	7.0	7.6	4.9	5.4	4.4			6.5	6.5
Trade Receivables (net)	10.0	26.9	25.8	27.1	27.6			23.9	25.8
Inventory	47.5	42.1	42.2	37.0	27.8			37.9	38.8
All Other Current	.0	1.8	2.9	3.7	5.7			3.0	2.7
Total Current	64.5	78.4	75.8	73.1	65.4			71.3	73.8
Fixed Assets (net)	18.6	13.0	14.4	16.8	12.5			18.2	15.5
Intangibles (net)	7.8	1.9	4.5	5.4	7.4			5.8	5.1
All Other Non-Current	9.2	6.7	5.3	4.8	14.6			4.6	5.7
Total	100.0	100.0	100.0	100.0	100.0			100.0	100.0
LIABILITIES									
Notes Payable-Short Term	26.6	15.5	19.9	15.8	13.3			15.3	16.1
Cur. Mat.-L.T.D.	7.0	1.3	1.6	3.8	.7			3.6	3.2
Trade Payables	17.8	13.2	15.5	10.3	9.5			12.9	14.9
Income Taxes Payable	.0	.1	.4	.4	.1			.5	.2
All Other Current	15.2	8.0	9.3	8.4	10.8			9.5	10.9
Total Current	66.7	38.1	46.7	38.6	34.2			41.8	45.3
Long-Term Debt	9.7	11.8	8.4	10.4	9.8			13.3	12.7
Deferred Taxes	.0	.1	.3	.3	1.0			.2	.3
All Other Non-Current	5.6	15.4	4.7	7.1	5.1			7.2	5.3
Net Worth	18.0	34.5	39.9	43.6	49.9			37.4	36.4
Total Liabilities & Net Worth	100.0	100.0	100.0	100.0	100.0			100.0	100.0
INCOME DATA									
Net Sales	100.0	100.0	100.0	100.0	100.0			100.0	100.0
Gross Profit	46.4	37.0	33.5	33.9	33.2			35.8	35.1
Operating Expenses	38.1	33.3	29.1	28.1	29.0			31.2	30.1
Operating Profit	8.3	3.6	4.4	5.7	4.2			4.6	5.0
All Other Expenses (net)	1.3	1.5	1.2	1.7	-.1			1.4	1.1
Profit Before Taxes	7.0	2.1	3.2	4.0	4.2			3.2	3.9
RATIOS									
Current	2.8	3.6	2.7	4.1	2.4			3.1	2.5
	1.1	2.1	1.6	1.8	2.1			1.9	1.7
	.4	1.5	1.2	1.3	1.6			1.4	1.3
Quick	1.1	1.8	1.3	1.8	1.3			1.4	1.2
	.4	.8	.7	.9	1.1			.8	.7
	.1	.4	.4	.5	.8			.5	.4
Sales/Receivables	0 UND	22 17.0	26 14.2	37 9.9	55 6.6			26 14.0	26 14.3
	3 105.0	31 11.7	39 9.3	51 7.2	69 5.3			42 8.6	43 8.5
	20 18.1	43 8.5	57 6.4	76 4.8	80 4.6			63 5.8	65 5.6
Cost of Sales/Inventory	44 8.2	53 6.9	69 5.3	74 4.9	58 6.3			68 5.3	66 5.5
	75 4.9	98 3.7	97 3.8	110 3.3	79 4.6			103 3.5	97 3.8
	175 2.1	144 2.5	150 2.4	154 2.4	125 2.9			147 2.5	148 2.5
Cost of Sales/Payables	0 UND	10 35.6	19 18.8	19 19.6	26 14.3			18 20.8	15 24.5
	34 10.8	23 16.1	30 12.2	25 14.4	34 10.6			28 13.0	27 13.4
	57 6.5	34 10.6	51 7.1	42 8.7	39 9.3			42 8.8	50 7.3
Sales/Working Capital	8.9	3.7	4.5	3.4	3.4			3.9	4.8
	NM	6.8	7.9	5.5	5.2			6.5	7.7
	-13.7	12.3	17.7	10.3	6.8			13.4	17.0
EBIT/Interest	14.4	8.7	8.6	8.2	6.3			12.0	9.9
	(10) 5.6	(27) 3.5	(69) 3.2	(41) 2.5	(13) 2.4			(155) 4.2	(168) 3.4
	1.2	1.5	.9	1.0	1.0			1.3	1.5
Net Profit + Depr., Dep., Amort./Cur. Mat. L/T/D			8.3	4.9				13.5	8.5
		(19) 2.2	(17) 2.5					(52) 3.6	(41) 2.0
			.7	1.1				1.4	.9
Fixed/Worth	.1	.1	.1	.2	.1			.2	.2
	.8	.2	.3	.5	.4			.4	.4
	-2.5	.9	1.2	.9	.5			1.5	1.0
Debt/Worth	1.0	.4	.7	.8	.4			.7	.8
	2.0	1.1	1.9	1.6	1.1			1.7	1.7
	-4.8	6.0	4.6	3.4	5.9			6.8	5.0
% Profit Before Taxes/Tangible Net Worth		30.0	50.1	32.0	25.6			45.3	43.0
		(24) 13.8	(69) 13.9	(42) 13.6	(12) 13.3			(138) 21.1	(155) 18.8
		5.3	2.8	.2	.3			8.8	4.9
% Profit Before Taxes/Total Assets	43.0	17.1	18.8	13.1	10.8			13.8	14.6
	18.4	7.4	6.5	5.4	3.8			7.2	5.9
	.5	.6	.1	.2	-.1			1.7	1.3
Sales/Net Fixed Assets	81.1	79.2	73.9	29.7	29.9			34.2	44.9
	31.4	31.8	24.6	13.0	10.9			14.6	20.2
	8.1	20.4	9.6	6.9	7.5			6.4	8.9
Sales/Total Assets	5.7	3.2	3.1	2.3	1.8			2.7	2.8
	3.7	2.4	2.2	1.7	1.4			1.9	2.2
	1.8	2.1	1.7	1.4	1.2			1.4	1.5
% Depr., Dep., Amort./Sales		.4	.8	.7	1.6			.9	.8
		(25) .7	(61) 1.3	(39) 1.7	(12) 2.1			(140) 1.7	(153) 1.4
		1.3	1.9	2.8	2.8			2.8	2.5
% Officers', Directors' Owners' Comp/Sales		3.9	2.6					2.4	2.8
		(14) 6.6	(18) 4.5					(50) 3.8	(53) 5.2
		9.4	7.0					6.4	7.6
Net Sales ($)	14019M	103665M	918933M	1642989M	1367452M	1831269M		4644019M	3741566M
Total Assets ($)	4108M	37745M	381066M	869906M	948100M	1271738M		3046700M	2069605M

M = $ thousand   MM = $ million
See Pages 11 through 21 for Explanation of Ratios and Data

Comparative Historical Data   Current Data Sorted by Sales

Comparative Historical Data			Type of Statement	0-1MM	1-3MM	3-5MM	5-10MM	10-25MM	25MM & OVER
48	39	45	Unqualified		2	1	4	15	25
30	17	31	Reviewed			5	5	15	4
19	15	24	Compiled	1	10	4	1	6	2
19	15	20	Tax Returns	6	4	4	3	1	2
65	60	63	Other	1	8	4	9	23	18
4/1/04-3/31/05 ALL	4/1/05-3/31/06 ALL	4/1/06-3/31/07 ALL			56 (4/1-9/30/06)		127 (10/1/06-3/31/07)		
181	146	183	**NUMBER OF STATEMENTS**	8	24	18	22	60	51
%	%	%	**ASSETS**	%	%	%	%	%	%
5.8	6.6	5.6	Cash & Equivalents		7.5	6.1	7.4	4.4	5.2
25.8	26.5	25.1	Trade Receivables (net)		17.9	27.7	23.1	28.8	26.4
36.7	36.9	39.6	Inventory		45.6	45.8	37.6	41.0	33.1
3.0	2.6	2.9	All Other Current		2.4	2.2	3.9	2.7	3.6
71.2	72.6	73.1	Total Current		73.5	81.8	71.8	76.9	68.3
16.7	16.8	14.9	Fixed Assets (net)		15.8	12.4	19.2	12.7	15.8
5.6	5.7	5.7	Intangibles (net)		2.0	2.5	6.0	4.5	8.8
6.4	4.9	6.3	All Other Non-Current		8.6	3.3	3.0	5.9	7.1
100.0	100.0	100.0	Total		100.0	100.0	100.0	100.0	100.0
			LIABILITIES						
17.1	14.4	17.6	Notes Payable-Short Term		16.3	20.2	13.0	18.7	14.3
2.6	2.2	2.4	Cur. Mat.-L.T.D.		2.8	1.8	1.9	1.7	2.8
14.5	12.4	13.4	Trade Payables		12.1	17.0	14.0	15.6	10.7
.2	.3	.3	Income Taxes Payable		.1	.2	.4	.3	.4
9.3	11.1	9.4	All Other Current		9.4	10.5	7.6	9.2	9.8
43.7	40.4	43.1	Total Current		40.8	49.6	37.0	45.5	38.0
13.6	12.4	10.3	Long-Term Debt		12.9	8.6	12.3	6.3	13.0
.3	.4	.3	Deferred Taxes		.1	.2	.1	.3	.6
6.1	4.9	7.2	All Other Non-Current		13.9	9.6	2.0	6.4	6.4
36.3	41.8	39.1	Net Worth		32.4	32.0	48.6	41.4	42.0
100.0	100.0	100.0	Total Liabilties & Net Worth		100.0	100.0	100.0	100.0	100.0
			INCOME DATA						
100.0	100.0	100.0	Net Sales		100.0	100.0	100.0	100.0	100.0
36.7	36.5	35.1	Gross Profit		40.7	30.3	38.3	33.7	32.1
31.6	31.0	30.1	Operating Expenses		37.7	29.4	32.0	28.1	27.4
5.1	5.4	5.0	Operating Profit		2.9	.9	6.3	5.7	4.7
1.1	1.2	1.4	All Other Expenses (net)		.7	2.5	1.0	1.2	1.5
4.1	4.2	3.7	Profit Before Taxes		2.3	-1.6	5.3	4.4	3.2
			RATIOS						
2.8	3.8	2.9			3.6	3.2	3.3	2.8	2.8
1.8	2.0	1.9	Current		2.2	1.7	2.0	1.7	1.9
1.2	1.3	1.3			1.1	1.3	1.4	1.3	1.4
1.3	1.7	1.4			1.7	1.3	1.8	1.4	1.4
.8	.8	.8	Quick		.6	.6	.8	.7	.9
.4	.5	.4			.4	.4	.5	.5	.5
30 12.2	30 12.1	26 14.0		18 19.8	18 20.6	25 14.9	31 11.9	37 9.8	
45 8.2	45 8.1	41 8.9	Sales/Receivables	31 11.9	36 10.0	36 10.2	44 8.3	50 7.2	
66 5.5	67 5.5	62 5.9		43 8.5	69 5.3	63 5.8	65 5.6	74 5.0	
66 5.5	62 5.9	71 5.2		48 7.5	75 4.9	57 6.5	72 5.1	71 5.2	
101 3.6	91 4.0	97 3.7	Cost of Sales/Inventory	129 2.8	100 3.7	114 3.2	97 3.7	90 4.0	
160 2.3	157 2.3	148 2.5		233 1.6	140 2.6	183 2.0	132 2.8	118 3.1	
17 21.2	16 22.3	18 20.8		10 36.1	17 21.0	13 27.0	21 17.3	21 17.2	
32 11.3	26 14.3	29 12.5	Cost of Sales/Payables	23 15.7	29 12.8	29 12.6	34 10.9	30 12.2	
52 7.1	49 7.5	45 8.1		45 8.1	38 9.6	52 7.1	56 6.5	39 9.4	
4.1	3.5	4.0			2.8	4.9	3.4	4.2	4.2
7.4	6.2	6.9	Sales/Working Capital		5.9	7.8	6.0	8.0	5.6
15.6	15.7	14.6			UND	NM	11.5	15.1	12.8
10.4	11.7	8.5			9.1	7.8	12.5	9.9	7.5
(167) 4.1	(135) 4.4	(168) 3.1	EBIT/Interest	(21) 4.1	1.5	(20) 5.4	(56) 3.2	(48) 2.6	
1.3	1.3	1.0			1.4	.2	2.5	1.0	1.0
9.5	10.8	7.3						17.1	5.6
(43) 3.8	(42) 3.6	(46) 2.4	Net Profit + Depr., Dep., Amort./Cur. Mat. L/T/D				(16) 6.5	(19) 2.5	
1.3	1.5	1.0						1.1	1.2
.1	.2	.1			.1	.1	.1	.1	.3
.4	.4	.4	Fixed/Worth		.2	.4	.4	.3	.5
1.2	1.1	1.1			1.4	2.5	.8	.9	1.1
.8	.6	.7			.5	.7	.5	.7	.8
2.1	1.4	1.8	Debt/Worth		1.3	2.2	1.2	1.8	2.1
5.4	3.7	4.9			7.6	NM	3.5	4.6	4.0
40.7	40.4	40.2			29.4	27.0	58.3	47.3	31.3
(154) 16.8	(130) 18.2	(161) 14.2	% Profit Before Taxes/Tangible Net Worth	(21) 8.7	(14) 8.5	18.7	(56) 13.8	(44) 20.2	
3.8	3.6	2.4			3.2	-7.0	6.0	2.5	.1
13.1	16.2	16.8			19.1	13.9	17.5	20.6	11.4
6.0	6.2	6.6	% Profit Before Taxes/Total Assets		7.4	1.8	8.4	6.9	5.5
.6	1.2	.3			1.5	-6.9	3.2	.3	.0
46.5	34.5	52.3			63.8	77.8	59.1	73.1	31.3
18.4	17.5	21.0	Sales/Net Fixed Assets		27.9	26.8	13.6	25.2	11.2
7.8	8.3	8.8			9.4	14.7	5.1	11.5	8.0
2.7	2.9	2.9			3.0	3.2	3.1	3.1	2.4
1.9	2.0	2.1	Sales/Total Assets		2.1	2.4	2.1	2.2	1.8
1.4	1.5	1.5			1.4	2.1	1.4	1.7	1.4
.8	.8	.7			.5	.6	.8	.6	1.1
(150) 1.5	(121) 1.5	(150) 1.4	% Depr., Dep., Amort./Sales	(20) 1.1	(16) .9	(16) 1.7	(52) 1.2	(42) 1.9	
2.5	2.7	2.2			1.7	1.5	3.4	1.7	2.8
2.3	1.4	2.6			2.4			2.3	
(56) 4.5	(40) 3.6	(43) 4.2	% Officers', Directors' Owners' Comp/Sales	(12) 5.8			(10) 4.4		
7.0	6.7	7.1			9.7			8.9	
4940931M	5818616M	5878327M	Net Sales ($)	3999M	49990M	71235M	155532M	995337M	4602234M
2860489M	3347662M	3512663M	Total Assets ($)	1923M	28839M	31135M	86936M	489407M	2874423M

M = $ thousand   MM = $ million
See Pages 11 through 21 for Explanation of Ratios and Data

Current Data Sorted by Assets | Comparative Historical Data

						Type of Statement		
		3	10	4	2	Unqualified	15	10
	1	4	4			Reviewed	9	9
	1	1	1			Compiled	5	8
	1	1				Tax Returns	2	2
1	2	5	7			Other	21	26
	6 (4/1-9/30/06)		42 (10/1/06-3/31/07)				4/1/02-3/31/03	4/1/03-3/31/04
0-500M	500M-2MM	2-10MM	10-50MM	50-100MM	100-250MM		ALL	ALL
1	5	14	22	4	2	NUMBER OF STATEMENTS	52	55
%	%	%	%	%	%	ASSETS	%	%
		3.8	6.7			Cash & Equivalents	8.1	6.9
		32.4	33.1			Trade Receivables (net)	26.9	28.0
		33.4	31.6			Inventory	29.4	28.6
		.6	3.0			All Other Current	3.3	2.0
		70.2	74.4			Total Current	67.6	65.4
		11.4	12.0			Fixed Assets (net)	19.2	19.5
		13.3	8.6			Intangibles (net)	8.5	8.6
		5.2	4.9			All Other Non-Current	4.7	6.5
		100.0	100.0			Total	100.0	100.0
						LIABILITIES		
		18.0	24.4			Notes Payable-Short Term	20.8	12.8
		2.4	6.1			Cur. Mat.-L.T.D.	2.4	1.4
		19.7	16.5			Trade Payables	13.6	14.3
		.3	.1			Income Taxes Payable	.1	.2
		10.2	8.9			All Other Current	11.9	14.3
		50.6	55.9			Total Current	48.9	43.1
		4.5	13.3			Long-Term Debt	12.1	12.6
		.1	.5			Deferred Taxes	.5	.2
		10.6	3.2			All Other Non-Current	4.8	6.6
		34.1	27.1			Net Worth	33.8	37.5
		100.0	100.0			Total Liabilties & Net Worth	100.0	100.0
						INCOME DATA		
		100.0	100.0			Net Sales	100.0	100.0
		44.7	33.8			Gross Profit	38.6	36.4
		44.5	29.5			Operating Expenses	33.3	33.3
		.2	4.3			Operating Profit	5.3	3.1
		2.1	1.8			All Other Expenses (net)	1.2	1.0
		-1.9	2.6			Profit Before Taxes	4.1	2.2
						RATIOS		
		2.5	1.9				2.5	2.5
		1.4	1.3			Current	1.6	1.5
		.9	1.0				1.1	1.2
		1.4	1.0				1.5	1.4
		.7	.7			Quick	.7	.8
		.3	.4				.5	.5
		31 11.8	44 8.4				32 11.6	34 10.9
		63 5.8	61 6.0			Sales/Receivables	49 7.5	47 7.7
		103 3.5	85 4.3				67 5.4	90 4.1
		45 8.2	57 6.4				47 7.8	45 8.0
		108 3.4	108 3.4			Cost of Sales/Inventory	97 3.8	86 4.3
		198 1.8	139 2.6				136 2.7	132 2.8
		32 11.5	27 13.5				20 18.7	15 24.3
		71 5.2	49 7.5			Cost of Sales/Payables	37 9.9	31 11.6
		100 3.7	68 5.4				55 6.6	59 6.2
		4.2	6.5				5.3	4.5
		8.3	11.9			Sales/Working Capital	8.9	9.6
		-41.7	-136.4				29.2	29.6
		11.5	8.0				9.1	17.9
		2.3	(20) 2.2			EBIT/Interest	(47) 3.5	(49) 2.5
		-2.0	1.1				1.2	-.5
						Net Profit + Depr., Dep.,	6.1	
						Amort./Cur. Mat. L/T/D	(13) 1.7	
							-1.5	
		.2	.2				.2	.2
		.4	1.4			Fixed/Worth	.5	.5
		-5.7	-1.2				5.4	6.2
		.6	1.3				.8	.7
		3.1	6.3			Debt/Worth	1.7	1.5
		-13.7	-18.1				13.7	18.0
		57.8	73.5			% Profit Before Taxes/Tangible	49.1	39.1
		(10) 24.3	(13) 21.3			Net Worth	(42) 25.5	(42) 10.2
		-35.2	9.5				3.3	-3.2
		12.1	11.7			% Profit Before Taxes/Total	16.8	15.4
		3.4	4.3			Assets	7.4	2.0
		-14.9	-1.0				.9	-7.4
		51.0	40.0				31.1	31.3
		30.0	15.8			Sales/Net Fixed Assets	11.8	13.0
		7.0	10.9				6.4	5.9
		2.3	2.5				2.6	2.6
		1.6	1.7			Sales/Total Assets	1.9	1.8
		1.2	1.3				1.2	1.3
		.5	.9				1.3	.5
		(13) 2.6	(21) 1.6			% Depr., Dep., Amort./Sales	(41) 1.8	(43) 1.7
		3.8	3.9				3.8	3.5
						% Officers', Directors'	1.8	.8
						Owners' Comp/Sales	(16) 4.3	(18) 2.7
							10.6	8.0
13M	10260M	135986M	949241M	486530M	646153M	Net Sales ($)	1643236M	1767138M
10M	5007M	73477M	527557M	293507M	321043M	Total Assets ($)	1156975M	1131890M

Comparative Historical Data

Current Data Sorted by Sales

14	12	19	Type of Statement				1	3	15
8	5	9	Unqualified						
7	4	3	Reviewed		1	1	2	4	1
4	2	2	Compiled		1	1			1
25	24	15	Tax Returns		2				
			Other	1			1	3	6
4/1/04-	4/1/05-	4/1/06-							
3/31/05	3/31/06	3/31/07		1	6 (4/1-9/30/06)		42 (10/1/06-3/31/07)		
ALL	ALL	ALL		0-1MM	1-3MM	3-5MM	5-10MM	10-25MM	25MM & OVER
58	47	48	**NUMBER OF STATEMENTS**	1	8	2	4	10	23
%	%	%	**ASSETS**	%	%	%	%	%	%
6.7	6.0	5.2	Cash & Equivalents					10.6	3.2
27.3	31.1	32.4	Trade Receivables (net)					30.6	35.9
29.8	33.6	34.8	Inventory					29.5	33.9
4.2	3.1	1.9	All Other Current					.6	3.3
67.9	73.8	74.4	Total Current					71.2	76.3
14.8	13.5	12.0	Fixed Assets (net)					13.3	10.6
9.2	4.8	8.8	Intangibles (net)					10.2	7.5
8.1	8.0	4.9	All Other Non-Current					5.3	5.7
100.0	100.0	100.0	Total					100.0	100.0
			LIABILITIES						
21.3	19.5	26.5	Notes Payable-Short Term					16.5	21.3
1.5	2.5	5.0	Cur. Mat.-L.T.D.					3.3	4.6
14.7	14.8	17.4	Trade Payables					19.9	16.8
.8	.2	.1	Income Taxes Payable					.4	.1
8.9	9.8	9.4	All Other Current					11.2	8.3
47.1	46.8	58.5	Total Current					51.2	51.1
10.1	8.9	11.3	Long-Term Debt					8.2	13.7
.4	.3	.4	Deferred Taxes					1.2	.2
3.9	5.4	5.8	All Other Non-Current					2.1	4.0
38.5	38.5	24.1	Net Worth					37.2	31.0
100.0	100.0	100.0	Total Liabilties & Net Worth					100.0	100.0
			INCOME DATA						
100.0	100.0	100.0	Net Sales					100.0	100.0
39.5	37.9	36.5	Gross Profit					39.0	32.3
33.9	34.1	34.1	Operating Expenses					33.1	27.5
5.6	3.8	2.3	Operating Profit					5.8	4.9
1.4	1.7	2.2	All Other Expenses (net)					1.2	1.7
4.2	2.1	.1	Profit Before Taxes					4.7	3.1
			RATIOS						
2.6	2.5	2.1						2.2	3.0
1.6	1.7	1.5	Current					1.3	1.5
1.1	1.2	1.0						.9	1.0
1.6	1.3	1.2						1.6	1.2
.8	.8	.7	Quick					.7	.7
.4	.6	.4						.4	.5
32 11.5	41 8.9	39 9.3						30 12.2	46 8.0
58 6.3	63 5.8	65 5.6	Sales/Receivables					55 6.7	69 5.3
88 4.2	88 4.1	86 4.2						81 4.5	98 3.7
60 6.1	73 5.0	59 6.2						63 5.8	58 6.2
98 3.7	114 3.2	120 3.0	Cost of Sales/Inventory					124 2.9	104 3.5
143 2.6	161 2.3	151 2.4						150 2.4	138 2.6
21 17.6	19 18.9	23 16.0						26 14.1	22 16.4
37 9.8	36 10.1	46 8.0	Cost of Sales/Payables					60 6.1	46 8.0
70 5.2	81 4.5	82 4.4						113 3.2	67 5.5
4.1	3.8	4.7						4.5	3.8
7.4	7.0	9.2	Sales/Working Capital					11.1	8.7
28.8	15.8	-159.1						-40.1	54.0
26.4	9.4	7.4						12.2	9.9
(49) 3.7	(45) 2.2	(45) 2.3	EBIT/Interest					5.4	(21) 3.6
.9	.7	.0						1.9	1.2
	14.3	10.1	Net Profit + Depr., Dep.,						
	(14) 5.8	(11) 1.6	Amort./Cur. Mat. L/T/D						
	.4	.9							
.1	.1	.2						.1	.1
.4	.2	.5	Fixed/Worth					.6	.5
2.2	1.4	-5.9						-5.9	-35.4
.7	.6	1.0						.7	1.0
1.5	1.6	3.5	Debt/Worth					2.8	2.4
12.3	5.1	-22.9						-14.0	-504.4
76.9	30.1	48.4	% Profit Before Taxes/Tangible						63.5
(49) 29.9	(41) 11.8	(33) 21.3	Net Worth					(17) 21.3	
3.8	-8.5	7.4							16.3
23.4	10.8	10.8	% Profit Before Taxes/Total					10.9	14.9
9.3	4.0	4.1	Assets					7.4	6.7
.1	-5.0	-6.8						3.4	1.3
54.9	61.6	44.8						64.0	45.6
18.5	22.8	17.7	Sales/Net Fixed Assets					16.9	19.2
7.5	7.0	9.4						7.9	11.9
2.3	2.3	2.2						2.3	2.5
1.7	1.8	1.8	Sales/Total Assets					1.6	1.9
1.1	1.4	1.3						1.2	1.4
.9	.6	.8						.7	.7
(40) 1.8	(41) 1.9	(44) 1.7	% Depr., Dep., Amort./Sales					1.8	(22) 1.3
4.2	3.1	3.2						4.0	2.6
1.7	.7	.7	% Officers', Directors'						
(14) 3.6	(12) 2.1	(14) 1.6	Owners' Comp/Sales						
7.9	4.0	4.5							
4705109M	2039038M	2228183M	Net Sales ($)	13M	17648M	8446M	31340M	175698M	1995038M
1751386M	1173102M	1220601M	Total Assets ($)	10M	11484M	8378M	20229M	111291M	1069209M

© RMA 2007   M = $ thousand   MM = $ million
See Pages 11 through 21 for Explanation of Ratios and Data

						Type of Statement		
	1	11	14	2	1	Unqualified	33	27
	10	37	8			Reviewed	74	62
7	20	11	1			Compiled	36	42
11	14	1	1			Tax Returns	30	37
8	23	29	12	1	2	Other	58	64
	44 (4/1-9/30/06)		181 (10/1/06-3/31/07)				4/1/02-3/31/03	4/1/03-3/31/04
0-500M	500M-2MM	2-10MM	10-50MM	50-100MM	100-250MM		ALL	ALL
26	68	89	36	3	3	NUMBER OF STATEMENTS	231	232
%	%	%	%	%	%	ASSETS	%	%
13.8	7.1	7.6	6.5			Cash & Equivalents	6.6	8.8
33.1	35.8	36.7	36.5			Trade Receivables (net)	35.3	35.6
11.6	19.9	21.9	21.2			Inventory	18.5	17.6
4.7	1.0	2.9	5.6			All Other Current	3.0	3.2
63.2	63.7	69.1	69.8			Total Current	63.4	65.2
29.9	23.5	21.4	19.5			Fixed Assets (net)	26.4	24.3
2.6	4.3	5.1	5.1			Intangibles (net)	4.3	5.0
4.3	8.5	4.3	5.5			All Other Non-Current	6.0	5.5
100.0	100.0	100.0	100.0			Total	100.0	100.0
						LIABILITIES		
33.7	9.5	10.3	13.0			Notes Payable-Short Term	13.8	14.3
12.6	7.0	4.4	2.7			Cur. Mat.-L.T.D.	4.0	4.8
25.2	17.5	17.7	16.1			Trade Payables	16.9	16.4
.3	.2	.3	.6			Income Taxes Payable	.2	.5
9.3	13.9	16.5	12.4			All Other Current	12.0	13.3
81.0	48.1	49.3	44.7			Total Current	46.8	49.2
39.7	19.5	12.5	14.0			Long-Term Debt	17.4	18.1
.0	.5	.4	.4			Deferred Taxes	.4	.3
3.5	2.6	6.2	3.6			All Other Non-Current	4.7	5.7
-24.2	29.4	31.6	37.3			Net Worth	30.7	26.8
100.0	100.0	100.0	100.0			Total Liabilities & Net Worth	100.0	100.0
						INCOME DATA		
100.0	100.0	100.0	100.0			Net Sales	100.0	100.0
54.1	40.9	32.7	27.8			Gross Profit	37.1	36.8
53.0	37.7	27.9	23.2			Operating Expenses	34.8	34.4
1.2	3.1	4.8	4.6			Operating Profit	2.3	2.4
1.6	.7	1.0	.8			All Other Expenses (net)	.9	1.1
-.4	2.5	3.8	3.8			Profit Before Taxes	1.4	1.3
						RATIOS		
2.7	2.4	1.9	2.2				2.0	1.9
1.1	1.5	1.4	1.5			Current	1.3	1.3
.4	1.0	1.1	1.2				1.0	1.0
2.1	1.6	1.3	1.5				1.4	1.4
.8	1.0	.9	1.0			Quick (230)	.9	.9
.3	.6	.6	.6				.6	.6
8 44.1	30 12.1	38 9.6	46 7.9			Sales/Receivables	36 10.0	36 10.2
38 9.6	46 7.9	49 7.5	53 6.8				52 7.1	50 7.2
57 6.4	63 5.8	64 5.7	68 5.4				65 5.6	65 5.6
0 UND	18 20.1	23 15.9	15 24.9			Cost of Sales/Inventory	18 20.4	15 24.3
17 21.0	39 9.4	42 8.7	48 7.7				42 8.7	35 10.5
46 7.9	67 5.4	59 6.2	76 4.8				68 5.4	65 5.6
13 28.9	19 19.6	23 16.2	20 18.3			Cost of Sales/Payables	19 18.9	18 20.7
45 8.1	30 12.3	34 10.9	31 11.8				35 10.5	34 10.8
111 3.3	53 6.8	49 7.5	50 7.3				54 6.8	55 6.6
10.9	7.9	6.6	5.1			Sales/Working Capital	7.0	7.2
65.1	13.7	13.9	10.4				16.6	17.2
-7.7	300.9	41.0	22.2				289.1	-131.4
6.6	8.5	14.1	20.3			EBIT/Interest	6.7	7.9
(22) 1.6	(66) 3.3	(87) 4.0	(33) 3.1				(214) 2.3	(214) 2.2
-3.9	1.1	1.8	1.8				-.3	-.5
		5.4	3.1			Net Profit + Depr., Dep., Amort./Cur. Mat. L/T/D	6.4	3.3
	(27) 3.3	(11) 1.6					(74) 2.9	(54) 2.0
		1.3	1.1				1.0	.8
.5	.3	.3	.2			Fixed/Worth	.4	.3
2.1	.8	.7	.5				1.0	1.0
-1.1	4.4	1.8	1.2				4.0	4.4
2.0	1.1	1.1	1.1			Debt/Worth	1.0	1.3
NM	2.3	2.3	2.6				3.0	3.0
-2.6	13.3	6.7	3.7				10.4	19.5
159.2	47.6	58.5	43.8			% Profit Before Taxes/Tangible Net Worth	36.9	42.0
(13) 81.0	(53) 22.1	(79) 27.1	(33) 19.3				(192) 10.9	(185) 13.1
13.2	10.1	9.7	8.8				-2.1	-5.1
27.8	15.6	15.5	15.2			% Profit Before Taxes/Total Assets	10.5	11.4
3.4	7.1	8.5	5.6				3.2	2.8
-14.1	.3	2.8	1.9				-2.9	-3.8
51.9	26.6	29.1	44.3			Sales/Net Fixed Assets	23.4	26.3
14.7	13.2	15.7	13.8				12.0	13.0
7.3	8.3	8.1	6.3				6.1	7.2
5.1	3.5	3.1	2.7			Sales/Total Assets	3.3	3.3
3.2	2.7	2.5	2.2				2.4	2.5
2.5	2.3	2.1	1.7				1.7	1.9
1.4	1.2	.8	.7			% Depr., Dep., Amort./Sales	1.3	1.0
(19) 2.5	(59) 2.0	(85) 1.8	(33) 1.6				(210) 2.2	(190) 1.9
5.8	2.9	2.7	2.5				3.5	3.8
5.8	2.6	2.0				% Officers', Directors' Owners' Comp/Sales	2.8	3.1
(15) 7.8	(36) 4.4	(31) 3.4					(106) 5.4	(103) 5.1
9.9	7.5	5.6					8.4	8.8
23212M	228047M	1078599M	1527699M	284970M	865649M	Net Sales ($)	3857546M	3314701M
6341M	79552M	418880M	660408M	203455M	513247M	Total Assets ($)	1723297M	1589472M

© RMA 2007

M = $ thousand   MM = $ million
See Pages 11 through 21 for Explanation of Ratios and Data

Comparative Historical Data | Current Data Sorted by Sales

4/1/04-3/31/05 ALL	4/1/05-3/31/06 ALL	4/1/06-3/31/07 ALL	Type of Statement	0-1MM	1-3MM	3-5MM	5-10MM	10-25MM	25MM & OVER
31	22	29	Unqualified				6	7	16
51	53	55	Reviewed		3	5	13	27	7
36	43	39	Compiled	6	8	12	8	4	1
27	34	27	Tax Returns	3	15	6	2	1	
60	84	75	Other	9	9	17	10	15	15
				44 (4/1-9/30/06)			181 (10/1/06-3/31/07)		
205	236	225	**NUMBER OF STATEMENTS**	18	35	40	39	54	39
%	%	%	**ASSETS**	%	%	%	%	%	%
6.5	6.7	7.9	Cash & Equivalents	12.4	8.0	8.0	8.3	7.1	6.1
37.4	34.3	35.6	Trade Receivables (net)	31.4	33.4	31.5	39.7	38.6	35.5
18.6	18.7	19.9	Inventory	13.7	17.2	23.0	16.4	22.6	21.6
3.2	3.3	3.0	All Other Current	4.1	1.9	1.3	2.7	3.4	5.0
65.7	63.0	66.3	Total Current	61.6	60.4	63.8	67.1	71.8	68.2
25.4	25.7	22.9	Fixed Assets (net)	30.1	26.8	21.0	25.9	19.4	19.8
3.4	5.2	4.6	Intangibles (net)	3.0	4.9	7.7	2.4	5.1	3.3
5.5	6.2	6.2	All Other Non-Current	5.4	7.9	7.5	4.6	3.8	8.7
100.0	100.0	100.0	Total	100.0	100.0	100.0	100.0	100.0	100.0
			LIABILITIES						
14.8	13.9	13.2	Notes Payable-Short Term	29.7	17.1	7.8	11.3	12.7	10.4
5.1	5.1	5.8	Cur. Mat.-L.T.D.	15.4	6.1	7.9	4.9	3.7	2.6
17.2	16.1	18.1	Trade Payables	27.2	14.7	20.1	15.6	19.2	16.0
.3	.3	.3	Income Taxes Payable	.4	.1	.2	.6	.1	.6
14.9	14.6	14.2	All Other Current	10.0	8.4	16.9	15.6	16.5	13.9
52.2	50.1	51.6	Total Current	82.6	46.4	52.9	48.0	52.2	43.6
18.7	18.9	18.5	Long-Term Debt	35.8	31.0	16.7	13.1	12.8	14.3
.4	.4	.4	Deferred Taxes	.0	.7	.1	.6	.4	.4
5.2	7.3	4.4	All Other Non-Current	4.7	2.4	6.0	6.7	2.7	4.2
23.5	23.3	25.2	Net Worth	-23.1	19.5	24.3	31.6	31.9	37.5
100.0	100.0	100.0	Total Liabilties & Net Worth	100.0	100.0	100.0	100.0	100.0	100.0
			INCOME DATA						
100.0	100.0	100.0	Net Sales	100.0	100.0	100.0	100.0	100.0	100.0
36.3	37.5	36.9	Gross Profit	52.2	46.2	42.3	34.2	29.1	29.3
32.5	33.9	33.1	Operating Expenses	50.9	43.4	39.0	30.3	24.4	24.6
3.8	3.6	3.7	Operating Profit	1.3	2.8	3.3	3.9	4.7	4.7
.9	1.1	1.0	All Other Expenses (net)	1.6	.6	1.3	.9	.9	1.0
2.9	2.5	2.7	Profit Before Taxes	-.3	2.2	2.0	3.0	3.8	3.7
			RATIOS						
2.1	2.0	2.1		3.1	2.6	2.1	1.9	1.9	2.2
1.3	1.4	1.5	Current	1.1	1.6	1.3	1.6	1.3	1.6
1.0	1.0	1.1		.4	1.0	1.0	1.1	1.1	1.2
1.4	1.3	1.5		2.6	1.9	1.4	1.5	1.3	1.5
1.0	.9	.9	Quick	.8	1.1	.9	1.2	.9	.9
.6	.6	.6		.3	.6	.5	.8	.6	.6
38 9.5	35 10.3	35 10.3		11 32.4	26 13.8	29 12.6	44 8.4	38 9.6	42 8.8
50 7.3	50 7.3	49 7.4	Sales/Receivables	51 7.1	49 7.4	36 10.1	53 6.9	50 7.3	52 7.0
70 5.2	65 5.6	63 5.8		82 4.4	60 6.0	50 7.4	68 5.4	66 5.6	63 5.8
13 27.6	19 19.6	17 21.0		11 33.2	9 42.2	17 21.2	14 26.8	32 11.5	20 17.8
37 10.0	41 8.9	39 9.3	Cost of Sales/Inventory	27 13.6	38 9.6	40 9.1	32 11.3	44 8.2	52 7.0
68 5.4	68 5.4	65 5.6		101 3.6	60 6.1	70 5.2	43 8.5	61 6.0	70 5.2
20 18.6	20 17.9	20 18.1		14 26.1	17 21.4	19 18.9	18 19.9	24 15.3	20 18.1
33 11.1	34 10.9	33 11.1	Cost of Sales/Payables	91 4.0	29 12.7	35 10.4	26 14.0	38 9.7	29 12.4
54 6.7	50 7.3	54 6.8		152 2.4	50 7.2	62 5.9	46 8.0	48 7.7	50 7.3
6.8	6.9	7.1		4.7	7.4	8.5	5.9	6.9	5.6
15.7	16.2	13.7	Sales/Working Capital	NM	14.0	22.2	11.6	15.0	9.7
119.9	365.9	66.8		-5.2	494.3	-999.8	42.1	31.2	18.5
8.9	8.0	11.3		7.3	7.7	6.9	18.6	11.9	31.5
(185) 3.3	(213) 2.9	(213) 3.6	EBIT/Interest	(14) 1.0	(33) 2.8	3.5	(38) 3.4	(52) 3.9	(36) 4.7
1.5	1.0	1.3		-3.2	.5	1.3	1.1	2.0	2.3
4.0	4.8	4.4					4.7	7.2	6.1
(46) 1.5	(60) 1.7	(52) 2.8	Net Profit + Depr., Dep., Amort./Cur. Mat. L/T/D				(14) 2.7	(15) 3.3	(13) 2.5
1.0	.5	1.3					1.2	1.3	1.4
.4	.4	.3		.2	.4	.4	.3	.3	.2
1.0	1.1	.8	Fixed/Worth	1.4	1.2	.8	.9	.6	.5
3.3	3.9	2.5		-1.9	-2.5	NM	2.3	1.2	1.1
1.2	1.4	1.1		1.7	.6	1.1	1.2	1.2	1.0
2.7	3.2	2.6	Debt/Worth	NM	2.9	2.7	2.0	3.0	1.6
10.6	11.2	9.8		-2.7	-9.1	NM	6.0	6.6	3.5
56.4	47.7	54.4			67.9	39.4	48.1	54.7	72.7
(172) 22.0	(187) 23.5	(183) 24.8	% Profit Before Taxes/Tangible Net Worth		(23) 17.2	(30) 26.9	(37) 20.8	(48) 29.8	(36) 22.1
5.6	5.7	10.1			9.1	12.3	2.3	11.9	10.3
14.0	14.9	15.7		14.9	23.7	11.0	16.5	13.8	19.0
6.3	5.6	6.8	% Profit Before Taxes/Total Assets	1.6	5.5	8.1	5.3	7.9	7.4
1.2	.2	1.0		-12.8	-3.6	1.3	.3	2.8	3.4
21.6	22.7	30.2		52.9	27.9	28.6	19.8	35.0	45.6
12.7	12.0	14.8	Sales/Net Fixed Assets	13.0	11.5	15.8	9.9	18.3	15.9
6.9	6.5	8.0		4.1	7.4	11.0	7.7	10.0	6.2
3.4	3.3	3.3		3.1	3.6	3.6	3.0	3.3	3.0
2.5	2.5	2.6	Sales/Total Assets	2.4	2.5	2.7	2.5	2.7	2.3
1.9	1.9	2.0		1.6	1.9	2.4	2.1	2.1	1.8
1.1	1.1	1.0			.9	1.3	1.4	.7	.6
(172) 1.9	(205) 1.9	(200) 1.8	% Depr., Dep., Amort./Sales		(30) 2.4	(38) 2.0	(38) 2.2	(52) 1.6	(33) 1.4
3.4	3.1	2.8			4.7	3.0	2.9	1.9	2.5
2.4	2.1	2.4			3.7	2.2	2.1	1.6	
(84) 5.2	(92) 5.0	(89) 4.5	% Officers', Directors' Owners' Comp/Sales		(24) 5.1	(18) 3.9	(19) 4.9	(13) 3.0	
9.4	7.5	7.2			8.7	6.4	7.2	4.0	
4563527M	4215784M	4008176M	Net Sales ($)	10657M	66382M	154253M	273008M	832651M	2671225M
2318659M	2146975M	1881883M	Total Assets ($)	5497M	27816M	57228M	119970M	337731M	1333641M

© RMA 2007

M = $ thousand   MM = $ million

See Pages 11 through 21 for Explanation of Ratios and Data

Current Data Sorted by Assets   Comparative Historical Data

Type of Statement

	0-500M	500M-2MM	2-10MM	10-50MM	50-100MM	100-250MM		4/1/02-3/31/03 ALL	4/1/03-3/31/04 ALL
Unqualified			2	4	4	1		18	9
Reviewed		3	12	2				24	22
Compiled		3	8					13	17
Tax Returns		5	2					3	5
Other	3	4	5			4		21	22
	1	25 (4/1-9/30/06)		44 (10/1/06-3/31/07)					
NUMBER OF STATEMENTS	4	15	29	12	4	5		79	75

0-500M	500M-2MM	2-10MM	10-50MM	50-100MM	100-250MM		Hist ALL	Hist ALL
%	%	%	%	%	%	**ASSETS**	%	%
	8.8	8.5	9.0			Cash & Equivalents	8.4	6.9
	38.6	31.3	19.2			Trade Receivables (net)	28.0	27.9
	21.4	33.0	22.2			Inventory	24.5	26.0
	1.2	1.5	1.2			All Other Current	1.5	1.4
	70.1	74.2	51.6			Total Current	62.4	62.2
	22.8	20.2	30.3			Fixed Assets (net)	25.4	26.8
	.8	1.0	9.9			Intangibles (net)	5.5	5.1
	6.3	4.5	8.2			All Other Non-Current	6.7	6.0
	100.0	100.0	100.0			Total	100.0	100.0
						LIABILITIES		
	9.4	11.6	4.7			Notes Payable-Short Term	10.6	10.9
	1.6	1.9	2.7			Cur. Mat.-L.T.D.	3.6	3.0
	21.6	16.8	8.9			Trade Payables	13.4	13.4
	.2	.1	.4			Income Taxes Payable	.5	.4
	8.5	8.7	12.7			All Other Current	8.4	8.2
	41.4	39.2	29.3			Total Current	36.5	35.9
	16.7	13.6	15.7			Long-Term Debt	14.9	15.5
	.6	.8	.2			Deferred Taxes	.6	.7
	13.9	1.1	4.7			All Other Non-Current	5.0	5.2
	27.5	45.4	50.1			Net Worth	43.0	42.6
	100.0	100.0	100.0			Total Liabilities & Net Worth	100.0	100.0
						INCOME DATA		
	100.0	100.0	100.0			Net Sales	100.0	100.0
	40.8	27.4	30.1			Gross Profit	29.4	31.4
	36.8	22.6	21.7			Operating Expenses	26.5	29.1
	4.0	4.8	8.5			Operating Profit	2.9	2.3
	.3	.3	.7			All Other Expenses (net)	1.4	1.0
	3.7	4.5	7.8			Profit Before Taxes	1.5	1.2
						RATIOS		
	2.9	3.6	4.8				3.1	3.0
	1.9	2.2	2.2			Current	1.8	1.8
	1.4	1.4	1.2				1.1	1.2
	2.4	2.7	2.8				1.9	2.0
	1.3	.9	.8			Quick	1.0	.8
	.9	.7	.6				.7	.6
	38 9.7	37 9.9	28 12.8				38 9.5	33 10.9
	51 7.2	41 8.9	41 8.9			Sales/Receivables	47 7.8	42 8.7
	60 6.1	49 7.4	53 6.9				56 6.5	52 7.0
	4 84.9	40 9.1	28 13.1				32 11.4	31 11.9
	30 12.1	64 5.7	83 4.4			Cost of Sales/Inventory	57 6.4	59 6.2
	81 4.5	103 3.6	131 2.8				91 4.0	82 4.5
	23 15.7	20 18.1	15 24.0				17 22.0	15 24.9
	38 9.7	28 12.9	28 12.8			Cost of Sales/Payables	26 14.2	27 13.7
	77 4.7	38 9.6	36 10.1				46 8.0	41 8.9
	5.1	4.3	3.0				5.1	5.2
	9.6	6.8	6.0			Sales/Working Capital	8.3	8.5
	13.8	12.7	23.9				33.0	34.4
	16.9	15.6					9.7	9.2
	2.7	(25) 3.7				EBIT/Interest	(71) 2.4	(66) 2.9
	1.1	1.9					1.3	1.2
						Net Profit + Depr., Dep.,		3.9 3.3
						Amort./Cur. Mat. L/T/D	(31) 1.9	(22) 2.1
							1.0	1.4
	.2	.2	.3				.3	.3
	1.9	.4	.8			Fixed/Worth	.5	.6
	43.5	1.0	1.6				1.3	1.6
	.4	.4	.4				.5	.5
	6.7	1.4	1.2			Debt/Worth	1.4	1.6
	332.5	3.6	3.3				4.2	3.0
	69.1	31.7	42.6				36.2	28.2
	(12) 30.2	(28) 17.3	(11) 28.5			% Profit Before Taxes/Tangible Net Worth	(71) 10.2	(69) 9.9
	3.9	6.6	9.1				3.0	3.5
	17.1	14.4	16.5				10.4	10.3
	7.0	6.7	9.2			% Profit Before Taxes/Total Assets	4.0	3.7
	.2	3.5	7.2				.9	.7
	144.6	36.1	12.4				18.4	23.8
	15.5	16.4	6.0			Sales/Net Fixed Assets	9.5	11.1
	6.2	6.8	2.5				4.7	4.3
	3.7	3.1	2.1				3.0	3.1
	2.8	2.5	1.6			Sales/Total Assets	2.1	2.3
	1.9	1.7	1.0				1.6	1.5
	1.3	.6	.9				1.5	1.1
	(11) 1.7	(28) 1.2	(10) 3.9			% Depr., Dep., Amort./Sales	(71) 2.4	(69) 2.2
	3.8	1.9	5.6				4.3	4.2
	3.2	1.8					2.6	3.4
	(10) 6.3	(12) 4.2				% Officers', Directors' Owners' Comp/Sales	(26) 6.6	(22) 5.4
	11.3	5.8					10.4	9.0
3332M	44519M	350453M	341472M	430042M	705930M	Net Sales ($)	1564329M	807149M
1086M	16364M	146321M	221499M	273303M	760588M	Total Assets ($)	983407M	462118M

Comparative Historical Data   Current Data Sorted by Sales

			Type of Statement	0-1MM	1-3MM	3-5MM	5-10MM	10-25MM	25MM & OVER
14	15	11	Unqualified				2	1	8
22	23	17	Reviewed		2	2	5	7	1
17	16	11	Compiled		1	2	6	2	
6	8	10	Tax Returns	2	5		2	1	
25	24	20	Other	1	3	1	3	3	9
4/1/04-3/31/05 ALL	4/1/05-3/31/06 ALL	4/1/06-3/31/07 ALL			25 (4/1-9/30/06)			44 (10/1/06-3/31/07)	
84	86	69	**NUMBER OF STATEMENTS**	3	11	5	18	14	18
%	%	%	**ASSETS**	%	%	%	%	%	%
7.6	7.1	9.5	Cash & Equivalents		7.4		6.8	11.1	10.7
30.8	31.6	28.4	Trade Receivables (net)		31.7		30.0	28.1	22.3
26.7	28.8	25.4	Inventory		21.3		31.6	26.3	19.5
1.4	1.1	1.4	All Other Current		.7		1.5	1.9	1.4
66.4	68.6	64.6	Total Current		61.1		69.9	67.5	54.0
25.6	22.2	24.1	Fixed Assets (net)		30.5		20.5	22.0	27.7
2.6	4.1	4.8	Intangibles (net)		.9		.9	6.4	11.0
5.4	5.1	6.4	All Other Non-Current		7.5		8.8	4.1	7.3
100.0	100.0	100.0	Total		100.0		100.0	100.0	100.0
			LIABILITIES						
13.1	11.4	8.5	Notes Payable-Short Term		12.4		11.1	7.5	5.9
4.3	4.8	1.8	Cur. Mat.-L.T.D.		1.3		2.2	1.6	2.0
16.7	16.5	14.5	Trade Payables		16.6		19.1	13.7	10.7
.2	.4	.3	Income Taxes Payable		.3		.1	.1	.6
8.1	8.4	11.9	All Other Current		10.7		9.6	12.9	15.8
42.4	41.4	36.9	Total Current		41.3		42.1	35.8	35.1
11.4	16.8	15.1	Long-Term Debt		22.0		16.8	10.1	16.1
2.0	.5	.7	Deferred Taxes		.8		.7	.7	.9
3.2	4.2	6.0	All Other Non-Current		15.3		.9	1.0	9.6
41.1	37.2	41.4	Net Worth		20.5		39.5	52.4	38.2
100.0	100.0	100.0	Total Liabilties & Net Worth		100.0		100.0	100.0	100.0
			INCOME DATA						
100.0	100.0	100.0	Net Sales		100.0		100.0	100.0	100.0
31.0	31.3	34.4	Gross Profit		44.2		27.1	28.7	36.5
26.0	26.0	28.2	Operating Expenses		40.8		22.4	21.6	28.3
5.0	5.3	6.1	Operating Profit		3.4		4.7	7.1	8.2
.7	1.5	.9	All Other Expenses (net)		.3		.8	.2	1.9
4.3	3.8	5.3	Profit Before Taxes		3.1		3.9	6.9	6.3
			RATIOS						
2.9	2.6	3.4			2.9		2.7	3.9	3.7
1.8	1.8	1.9	Current		1.9		1.5	2.4	1.5
1.3	1.3	1.3			1.1		1.4	1.5	1.2
1.8	1.7	2.2			1.7		1.3	3.0	2.1
1.1	1.0	1.0	Quick		1.0		.8	1.0	1.1
.6	.6	.7			.7		.6	.7	.6
39 9.3	40 9.1	36 10.1			37 9.9		32 11.4	39 9.3	37 10.0
48 7.6	46 7.9	42 8.7	Sales/Receivables		46 7.9		40 9.1	47 7.8	42 8.7
56 6.5	57 6.4	53 6.8			60 6.1		49 7.5	51 7.1	66 5.5
35 10.4	35 10.5	34 10.9			4 84.9		40 9.0	33 11.1	38 9.6
56 6.5	59 6.2	60 6.0	Cost of Sales/Inventory		25 14.6		66 5.5	54 6.8	75 4.9
90 4.1	93 3.9	101 3.6			106 3.4		105 3.5	114 3.2	96 3.8
20 18.6	20 18.5	19 19.7			9 42.2		13 27.7	22 16.5	19 19.7
33 11.2	32 11.5	28 12.9	Cost of Sales/Payables		38 9.7		31 11.7	29 12.8	28 13.3
47 7.8	48 7.6	45 8.1			82 4.5		44 8.4	35 10.3	78 4.7
5.2	5.2	4.4			5.1		5.5	4.0	3.4
8.4	7.9	9.0	Sales/Working Capital		10.1		10.3	5.4	11.1
18.0	18.0	14.2			76.5		13.2	13.6	23.4
19.4	11.5	14.5			4.7		6.1	148.3	34.9
(75) 6.8	(80) 5.7	(60) 4.7	EBIT/Interest		2.7		(14) 2.2	(12) 11.3	(16) 6.1
2.4	2.5	1.9			1.1		.7	3.8	1.5
15.3	12.2	14.9							
(26) 2.9	(30) 2.3	(17) 3.5	Net Profit + Depr., Dep., Amort./Cur. Mat. L/T/D						
1.3	.8	1.5							
.2	.2	.2			.2		.3	.2	.4
.5	.5	.6	Fixed/Worth		2.2		.5	.5	.9
1.5	1.7	1.6			-18.5		1.1	1.1	2.0
.6	.7	.5			.8		.6	.4	.8
1.1	2.0	1.5	Debt/Worth		12.0		2.3	.9	1.8
3.7	11.1	6.5			-24.1		4.3	1.8	6.9
45.3	55.4	41.6					27.2	40.7	48.6
(76) 22.0	(74) 26.2	(61) 20.1	% Profit Before Taxes/Tangible Net Worth				(16) 11.6	(13) 20.1	(16) 30.9
6.9	9.7	8.7					4.5	14.2	14.3
20.3	14.9	15.2			11.4		10.5	21.2	14.3
8.2	8.4	8.9	% Profit Before Taxes/Total Assets		4.7		4.4	11.9	9.8
2.6	3.0	3.1			.2		1.3	7.3	3.3
29.6	34.9	32.8			33.1		67.8	20.4	12.7
9.8	13.0	9.7	Sales/Net Fixed Assets		7.8		19.2	12.2	6.8
5.9	6.4	4.6			3.4		5.8	6.2	2.9
3.1	3.0	3.0			3.6		3.5	2.9	2.4
2.1	2.4	2.3	Sales/Total Assets		2.8		2.4	2.2	1.6
1.7	1.7	1.5			1.9		1.6	1.5	1.0
1.1	.7	.8					.4	.9	1.2
(71) 2.1	(78) 1.6	(59) 1.5	% Depr., Dep., Amort./Sales				(17) 1.4	1.2	(15) 3.3
3.5	2.9	3.4					3.5	1.5	5.1
2.5	2.8	2.8							
(24) 5.6	(33) 5.3	(25) 5.1	% Officers', Directors' Owners' Comp/Sales						
8.1	7.8	9.7							
1496136M	1723555M	1875748M	Net Sales ($)	1966M	24026M	20280M	141449M	232342M	1455685M
769796M	1119011M	1419161M	Total Assets ($)	625M	9982M	8807M	80132M	126182M	1193433M

M = $ thousand   MM = $ million
See Pages 11 through 21 for Explanation of Ratios and Data

Current Data Sorted by Assets   Comparative Historical Data

Type of Statement

	0-500M	500M-2MM	2-10MM	10-50MM	50-100MM	100-250MM		4/1/02-3/31/03 ALL	4/1/03-3/31/04 ALL
Unqualified			1	5	2	3		11	4
Reviewed	1		4					5	8
Compiled		4	2					3	9
Tax Returns	1	2						3	2
Other	1	1	3	5		1		6	8
	9 (4/1-9/30/06)			26 (10/1/06-3/31/07)					
NUMBER OF STATEMENTS	2	7	10	10	2	4		28	31
	%	%	%	%	%	%		%	%

ASSETS

	2-10MM	10-50MM		4/1/02-3/31/03	4/1/03-3/31/04
Cash & Equivalents	8.1	3.3		7.4	8.8
Trade Receivables (net)	21.5	27.4		22.9	22.9
Inventory	43.3	45.2		36.4	36.9
All Other Current	.3	3.9		2.4	4.2
Total Current	73.1	79.8		69.0	72.8
Fixed Assets (net)	13.9	12.3		18.8	16.3
Intangibles (net)	1.3	5.0		1.9	5.2
All Other Non-Current	11.7	2.8		10.3	5.7
Total	100.0	100.0		100.0	100.0

LIABILITIES

	2-10MM	10-50MM		4/1/02-3/31/03	4/1/03-3/31/04
Notes Payable-Short Term	13.2	17.0		9.3	10.9
Cur. Mat.-L.T.D.	.4	.9		1.7	3.2
Trade Payables	7.8	8.0		12.4	8.9
Income Taxes Payable	.3	.1		.2	.4
All Other Current	11.0	9.2		16.1	10.3
Total Current	32.7	35.1		39.8	33.7
Long-Term Debt	3.4	5.9		12.3	13.6
Deferred Taxes	.5	.1		.6	.3
All Other Non-Current	.0	13.0		7.3	9.0
Net Worth	63.4	45.8		39.9	43.4
Total Liabilities & Net Worth	100.0	100.0		100.0	100.0

INCOME DATA

	2-10MM	10-50MM		4/1/02-3/31/03	4/1/03-3/31/04
Net Sales	100.0	100.0		100.0	100.0
Gross Profit	30.4	32.6		35.5	36.9
Operating Expenses	27.1	30.5		28.8	30.9
Operating Profit	3.3	2.1		6.7	6.0
All Other Expenses (net)	.0	3.0		1.1	1.3
Profit Before Taxes	3.3	-.9		5.6	4.7

RATIOS

	2-10MM	10-50MM		4/1/02-3/31/03	4/1/03-3/31/04
Current	4.2	4.4		3.6	4.5
	3.0	3.2		2.6	2.5
	1.6	1.4		1.2	1.6
Quick	1.3	1.4		1.8	2.3
	.9	.7		.9	1.1
	.8	.7		.5	.5
Sales/Receivables	24 15.0	34 10.6		27 13.4	31 11.8
	39 9.5	45 8.1		40 9.2	39 9.2
	59 6.2	99 3.7		54 6.7	60 6.1
Cost of Sales/Inventory	89 4.1	108 3.4		89 4.1	79 4.6
	146 2.5	183 2.0		130 2.8	142 2.6
	199 1.8	211 1.7		156 2.3	200 1.8
Cost of Sales/Payables	10 38.4	17 20.9		16 22.1	13 28.4
	13 28.6	27 13.7		24 15.0	19 19.2
	38 9.7	41 9.0		44 8.2	40 9.1
Sales/Working Capital	2.3	2.1		3.1	2.8
	3.9	3.0		4.6	4.4
	7.2	7.2		15.8	6.3
EBIT/Interest				12.4	10.9
				(21) 4.6	(26) 3.7
				1.6	1.4
Net Profit + Depr., Dep., Amort./Cur. Mat. L/T/D					10.8
					(14) 4.7
					1.5
Fixed/Worth	.1	.1		.2	.1
	.2	.2		.3	.4
	.5	NM		1.6	.9
Debt/Worth	.2	.3		.4	.5
	.3	.5		1.0	1.5
	1.8	NM		5.5	4.1
% Profit Before Taxes/Tangible Net Worth	18.4			33.7	47.4
	9.7			(26) 16.5	(26) 21.8
	-1.6			4.8	2.4
% Profit Before Taxes/Total Assets	10.0	20.0		16.8	15.9
	8.2	3.9		10.5	9.7
	-1.1	-10.7		2.6	1.5
Sales/Net Fixed Assets	48.2	42.4		23.9	52.4
	15.7	11.8		10.7	15.0
	8.9	9.7		5.4	6.3
Sales/Total Assets	2.1	2.0		2.2	2.2
	1.6	1.5		1.7	1.7
	1.3	1.2		1.5	1.2
% Depr., Dep., Amort./Sales	.8			1.1	.9
	1.5			(25) 2.0	(28) 1.7
	2.2			4.2	3.9
% Officers', Directors' Owners' Comp/Sales					

	0-500M	500M-2MM	2-10MM	10-50MM	50-100MM	100-250MM		4/1/02-3/31/03	4/1/03-3/31/04
Net Sales ($)	2616M	16240M	83269M	351130M	201260M	1185252M		1044715M	931567M
Total Assets ($)	914M	6752M	51990M	207555M	137913M	775192M		708892M	602255M

M = $ thousand   MM = $ million

See Pages 11 through 21 for Explanation of Ratios and Data

Comparative Historical Data | Current Data Sorted by Sales

Type of Statement

4/1/04-3/31/05 ALL	4/1/05-3/31/06 ALL	4/1/06-3/31/07 ALL	Type of Statement	0-1MM	1-3MM	3-5MM	5-10MM	10-25MM	25MM & OVER
3	8	11	Unqualified				1	2	8
7	7	5	Reviewed	1		1	2	1	
5	5	6	Compiled	1	1	2	2		
3	3	3	Tax Returns	1	1	1			
16	5	10	Other		2	1		3	4

Periods: 4/1/04-3/31/05 ALL; 4/1/05-3/31/06 ALL; 4/1/06-3/31/07 ALL. Current groupings: 9 (4/1-9/30/06); 26 (10/1/06-3/31/07).

34	28	35	**NUMBER OF STATEMENTS**	3	4	5	5	6	12
%	%	%	**ASSETS**	%	%	%	%	%	%
9.9	8.8	5.6	Cash & Equivalents						5.3
17.4	22.2	22.6	Trade Receivables (net)						24.3
37.0	36.5	36.4	Inventory						35.4
3.1	2.2	1.5	All Other Current						2.4
67.3	69.7	66.1	Total Current						67.4
19.1	20.4	21.6	Fixed Assets (net)						18.8
4.6	2.3	2.9	Intangibles (net)						3.7
9.0	7.6	9.4	All Other Non-Current						10.1
100.0	100.0	100.0	Total						100.0
			LIABILITIES						
11.8	8.5	11.7	Notes Payable-Short Term						12.1
1.9	2.0	2.0	Cur. Mat.-L.T.D.						3.7
11.6	10.0	12.5	Trade Payables						9.3
.1	.6	.3	Income Taxes Payable						.4
12.0	11.2	12.6	All Other Current						9.1
37.5	32.3	39.1	Total Current						34.6
16.7	11.5	22.0	Long-Term Debt						22.7
.4	.6	.2	Deferred Taxes						.2
7.5	7.8	7.9	All Other Non-Current						5.9
38.0	47.8	30.8	Net Worth						36.6
100.0	100.0	100.0	Total Liabilities & Net Worth						100.0
			INCOME DATA						
100.0	100.0	100.0	Net Sales						100.0
36.9	37.5	35.8	Gross Profit						36.6
30.9	31.4	31.2	Operating Expenses						26.4
5.9	6.1	4.7	Operating Profit						10.2
1.2	1.2	2.2	All Other Expenses (net)						2.2
4.7	4.9	2.5	Profit Before Taxes						8.0
			RATIOS						
3.8	4.6	3.4	Current						3.1
2.3	2.3	1.9							2.5
1.1	1.2	1.1							1.3
1.5	1.7	1.1	Quick						1.1
.8	1.0	.8							.9
.4	.6	.6							.7
17 21.6	27 13.7	25 14.5	Sales/Receivables						36 10.1
39 9.2	42 8.7	37 9.8							46 7.9
50 7.3	51 7.2	58 6.3							56 6.5
89 4.1	77 4.7	83 4.4	Cost of Sales/Inventory						86 4.3
148 2.5	109 3.3	132 2.8							121 3.0
172 2.1	185 2.0	185 2.0							146 2.5
19 19.6	16 22.9	14 26.2	Cost of Sales/Payables						17 22.1
30 12.0	21 17.3	32 11.3							30 12.3
59 6.2	43 8.4	52 7.1							48 7.6
3.4	2.7	3.0	Sales/Working Capital						3.4
5.3	5.1	5.1							4.9
35.8	12.5	20.9							14.2
11.5	37.3	12.0	EBIT/Interest						29.7
(30) 3.9	(25) 7.3	(32) 4.0						(11)	5.4
.6	1.1	.7							1.9
8.0	12.3	15.4	Net Profit + Depr., Dep.,						
(13) 4.2	(12) 7.5	(13) 5.7	Amort./Cur. Mat. L/T/D						
2.3	2.1	2.0							
.2	.2	.1	Fixed/Worth						.2
.4	.3	.4							.4
4.4	1.0	-16.0							NM
.4	.4	.4	Debt/Worth						.5
1.4	.9	2.2							1.9
10.2	3.0	-14.2							NM
42.3	35.7	34.8	% Profit Before Taxes/Tangible						
(28) 24.5	(25) 12.0	(25) 20.2	Net Worth						
6.6	4.3	2.3							
16.8	21.7	13.9	% Profit Before Taxes/Total						18.2
8.9	8.0	7.4	Assets						11.8
1.7	1.0	-.5							4.7
26.4	19.9	26.0	Sales/Net Fixed Assets						16.2
11.9	10.8	11.3							7.8
5.7	6.6	6.7							5.6
2.3	2.1	2.1	Sales/Total Assets						2.0
1.5	1.8	1.6							1.7
1.3	1.3	1.3							1.4
1.0	.9	1.0	% Depr., Dep., Amort./Sales						.9
(30) 1.6	(27) 1.7	(32) 1.7							1.6
3.0	3.1	2.6							2.8
		2.8	% Officers', Directors'						
		(10) 6.4	Owners' Comp/Sales						
		12.6							
1411449M	879657M	1839767M	Net Sales ($)	2766M	7353M	20465M	42942M	84509M	1681732M
1068470M	579049M	1180316M	Total Assets ($)	2278M	7194M	8649M	25476M	64419M	1072300M

Current Data Sorted by Assets							Comparative Historical Data	

Type of Statement

0-500M	500M-2MM	2-10MM	10-50MM	50-100MM	100-250MM			
	1	2	5	1		Unqualified	12	9
	6		1			Reviewed	6	8
	1	4				Compiled	1	7
		2				Tax Returns	1	
1	2	2	1	1	1	Other	10	11
	7 (4/1-9/30/06)		25 (10/1/06-3/31/07)				4/1/02-3/31/03 ALL	4/1/03-3/31/04 ALL
1	4	16	7	3	1	**NUMBER OF STATEMENTS**	30	35
%	%	%	%	%	%	**ASSETS**	%	%
		4.5				Cash & Equivalents	7.1	7.0
		24.3				Trade Receivables (net)	22.9	24.0
		38.7				Inventory	37.2	32.5
		.7				All Other Current	1.2	1.5
		68.2				Total Current	68.5	65.0
		23.8				Fixed Assets (net)	22.1	21.2
		1.9				Intangibles (net)	3.5	6.4
		6.1				All Other Non-Current	5.9	7.4
		100.0				Total	100.0	100.0
						LIABILITIES		
		9.5				Notes Payable-Short Term	8.1	12.8
		6.8				Cur. Mat.-L.T.D.	7.1	3.1
		12.5				Trade Payables	9.0	10.9
		.9				Income Taxes Payable	.5	.1
		7.9				All Other Current	7.6	8.1
		37.7				Total Current	32.4	35.0
		11.6				Long-Term Debt	14.8	11.2
		.6				Deferred Taxes	.8	.6
		3.3				All Other Non-Current	4.6	9.5
		46.9				Net Worth	47.4	43.7
		100.0				Total Liabilties & Net Worth	100.0	100.0
						INCOME DATA		
		100.0				Net Sales	100.0	100.0
		28.8				Gross Profit	32.5	29.8
		24.5				Operating Expenses	26.9	23.4
		4.3				Operating Profit	5.6	6.4
		-.2				All Other Expenses (net)	1.7	1.5
		4.5				Profit Before Taxes	3.9	4.9
						RATIOS		
		3.1				Current	3.7	3.9
		1.7					2.2	1.6
		1.2					1.5	1.3
		1.6				Quick	2.0	2.1
		.7					1.0	.7
		.5					.5	.5
		32 11.3				Sales/Receivables	33 11.1	35 10.3
		39 9.3					36 10.1	44 8.3
		46 8.0					44 8.2	49 7.4
		54 6.7				Cost of Sales/Inventory	70 5.2	67 5.5
		86 4.2					96 3.8	80 4.6
		111 3.3					122 3.0	97 3.7
		14 26.2				Cost of Sales/Payables	12 30.1	11 32.0
		23 16.0					21 17.8	24 15.2
		37 9.9					32 11.4	48 7.6
		4.7				Sales/Working Capital	4.4	4.6
		8.4					5.4	6.5
		27.6					10.7	17.3
		24.6				EBIT/Interest	5.8	7.3
		4.9					(26) 4.2	(30) 4.2
		1.2					1.5	1.8
						Net Profit + Depr., Dep., Amort./Cur. Mat. L/T/D	3.1	2.9
							(10) 2.4	(11) 2.0
							1.2	.7
		.2				Fixed/Worth	.2	.3
		.4					.5	.6
		1.2					1.0	1.1
		.5				Debt/Worth	.7	.6
		1.4					1.3	1.6
		2.8					2.1	2.5
		38.5				% Profit Before Taxes/Tangible Net Worth	28.4	31.4
		14.8					(29) 16.0	(31) 19.1
		2.9					7.9	8.5
		19.7				% Profit Before Taxes/Total Assets	15.7	16.0
		7.0					7.1	5.4
		.9					1.2	1.8
		35.3				Sales/Net Fixed Assets	21.8	17.9
		10.3					9.6	9.5
		5.1					5.7	6.1
		2.7				Sales/Total Assets	2.5	2.4
		2.0					2.1	2.0
		1.7					1.6	1.6
		.8				% Depr., Dep., Amort./Sales	1.4	1.3
		1.5					(23) 2.0	(27) 1.9
		3.1					4.4	3.1
						% Officers', Directors' Owners' Comp/Sales		
1139M	9911M	153152M	301954M	279027M	253745M	Net Sales ($)	786875M	682567M
388M	4295M	71870M	159618M	225961M	237561M	Total Assets ($)	434339M	385610M

M = $ thousand   MM = $ million
See Pages 11 through 21 for Explanation of Ratios and Data

Comparative Historical Data | Current Data Sorted by Sales

			Type of Statement	0-1MM	1-3MM	3-5MM	5-10MM	10-25MM	25MM & OVER
			Unqualified						
5	6	9	Reviewed		1		2		6
6	4	7	Compiled		2		2	4	1
4	4	5	Tax Returns	1			4		
1	1	3	Other	1	1		2		1
11	12	8		1	1		2	2	2
4/1/04-3/31/05 ALL	4/1/05-3/31/06 ALL	4/1/06-3/31/07 ALL		7 (4/1-9/30/06)			25 (10/1/06-3/31/07)		
27	27	32	**NUMBER OF STATEMENTS**	2	3		10	6	10
%	%	%	**ASSETS**	%	%	%	%	%	%
6.9	7.1	4.9	Cash & Equivalents				6.9		6.5
24.7	27.4	22.9	Trade Receivables (net)				24.7		22.4
36.4	32.8	34.6	Inventory				35.1		27.1
.9	1.5	1.5	All Other Current				.9		1.4
68.9	68.8	63.9	Total Current				67.5		57.3
22.2	20.5	23.8	Fixed Assets (net)				23.1		24.7
3.6	5.4	5.8	Intangibles (net)				1.9		13.7
5.3	5.3	6.5	All Other Non-Current				7.5		4.3
100.0	100.0	100.0	Total				100.0		100.0
			LIABILITIES						
6.8	12.3	11.3	Notes Payable-Short Term				5.9		7.8
2.9	2.6	5.2	Cur. Mat.-L.T.D.				8.9		4.5
13.0	11.8	16.0	Trade Payables				11.0		10.9
.1	.2	.5	Income Taxes Payable				1.2		.1
7.9	9.8	8.7	All Other Current				5.8		6.1
30.9	36.7	41.6	Total Current				32.8		29.3
15.4	13.4	16.5	Long-Term Debt				15.1		19.5
.7	.5	.5	Deferred Taxes				.1		.6
4.7	3.4	3.8	All Other Non-Current				4.2		5.5
48.4	46.0	37.5	Net Worth				47.9		45.1
100.0	100.0	100.0	Total Liabilities & Net Worth				100.0		100.0
			INCOME DATA						
100.0	100.0	100.0	Net Sales				100.0		100.0
30.8	32.5	32.4	Gross Profit				30.1		38.5
25.5	27.7	27.3	Operating Expenses				25.7		30.1
5.3	4.8	5.0	Operating Profit				4.4		8.5
1.1	1.2	.8	All Other Expenses (net)				-1.0		2.4
4.2	3.5	4.2	Profit Before Taxes				5.4		6.1
			RATIOS						
4.7	3.0	3.1					3.3		3.4
2.0	2.1	2.2	Current				2.4		2.3
1.7	1.4	1.2					1.4		1.3
1.9	1.6	1.4					1.6		1.6
1.1	.9	.9	Quick				1.1		1.0
.5	.6	.5					.5		.6
33 11.1	33 11.1	33 10.9					31 11.7		36 10.2
36 10.0	44 8.3	40 9.0	Sales/Receivables				37 9.9		50 7.3
48 7.7	55 6.6	50 7.3					47 7.7		54 6.7
58 6.2	55 6.6	57 6.4					57 6.4		72 5.0
78 4.7	78 4.7	86 4.2	Cost of Sales/Inventory				76 4.8		90 4.1
116 3.1	115 3.2	122 3.0					98 3.7		133 2.8
11 31.8	15 24.2	17 21.2					11 32.6		23 15.8
30 12.1	29 12.7	27 13.3	Cost of Sales/Payables				18 20.5		33 11.2
44 8.3	48 7.6	43 8.6					31 11.7		45 8.2
3.7	4.4	3.9					4.1		3.7
5.8	7.0	6.6	Sales/Working Capital				7.8		4.9
9.7	13.7	27.6					17.0		37.6
13.6	13.5	9.3					30.2		
(25) 2.6	(25) 4.1	(30) 2.7	EBIT/Interest				8.4		
1.5	.6	.8					1.1		
			Net Profit + Depr., Dep., Amort./Cur. Mat. L/T/D						
.2	.2	.2					.2		.3
.5	.3	.5	Fixed/Worth				.4		1.1
.8	1.4	2.1					.8		-2.2
.4	.5	.5					.5		.3
1.3	1.6	1.8	Debt/Worth				1.0		2.2
2.3	3.4	4.9					2.1		-6.4
31.1	27.1	30.2	% Profit Before Taxes/Tangible Net Worth						
(25) 12.4	(24) 14.5	(26) 16.6							
4.5	-8.6	2.5							
12.9	15.2	19.7	% Profit Before Taxes/Total Assets				20.2		20.6
4.1	5.3	5.4					11.2		7.4
1.6	-1.2	-.9					.4		.0
20.2	25.0	24.4	Sales/Net Fixed Assets				29.0		15.6
11.8	10.1	9.7					10.4		6.7
6.8	6.7	5.1					7.1		4.5
2.8	2.6	2.6	Sales/Total Assets				3.3		2.2
2.1	2.0	1.9					2.3		1.5
1.8	1.7	1.5					1.8		1.1
1.1	1.0	.9	% Depr., Dep., Amort./Sales				.8		
(21) 1.8	(25) 1.6	(26) 1.9					1.8		
3.2	3.3	3.2					3.4		
2.2			% Officers', Directors' Owners' Comp/Sales						
(10) 5.3									
8.6									
741561M	983547M	998928M	Net Sales ($)	1766M	5661M	4942M	77066M	97947M	811546M
445171M	622941M	699693M	Total Assets ($)	1224M	7165M	3116M	35201M	42252M	610735M

© RMA 2007

M = $ thousand   MM = $ million
See Pages 11 through 21 for Explanation of Ratios and Data

Current Data Sorted by Assets | Comparative Historical Data

Comparative dates: 102 (4/1-9/30/06) covers the 0-500M and 500M-2MM columns; 428 (10/1/06-3/31/07) covers the 2-10MM through 100-250MM columns.

Type of Statement	0-500M	500M-2MM	2-10MM	10-50MM	50-100MM	100-250MM	4/1/02-3/31/03 ALL	4/1/03-3/31/04 ALL
Unqualified		4	26	45	9	20	83	85
Reviewed	4	17	53	19	3		89	92
Compiled	4	36	23	4	1		65	121
Tax Returns	22	43	16	1	1		34	55
Other	12	36	74	42	9	6	142	171
NUMBER OF STATEMENTS	42	136	192	111	23	26	413	524
ASSETS	%	%	%	%	%	%	%	%
Cash & Equivalents	14.3	12.1	6.1	6.2	3.2	5.9	8.2	7.5
Trade Receivables (net)	25.3	30.5	27.0	25.4	24.4	22.1	24.7	26.4
Inventory	24.2	26.5	29.3	27.1	23.6	22.9	25.8	26.9
All Other Current	1.7	2.2	3.0	2.6	2.8	2.2	2.9	3.0
Total Current	65.5	71.4	65.4	61.4	54.1	53.2	61.6	63.7
Fixed Assets (net)	24.2	19.0	24.3	24.8	32.1	24.6	26.8	24.8
Intangibles (net)	6.0	3.2	4.7	8.7	6.6	15.7	5.6	5.6
All Other Non-Current	4.3	6.4	5.7	5.1	7.3	6.5	6.0	5.9
Total	100.0	100.0	100.0	100.0	100.0	100.0	100.0	100.0
LIABILITIES								
Notes Payable-Short Term	23.1	11.2	14.6	14.0	8.1	3.2	11.8	11.8
Cur. Mat.-L.T.D.	4.1	3.5	3.0	2.7	3.8	2.9	4.0	3.4
Trade Payables	22.2	16.5	16.0	14.3	14.0	10.0	14.4	15.2
Income Taxes Payable	.2	.2	.2	.3	.4	.4	.2	.3
All Other Current	14.8	10.6	8.9	11.5	9.2	12.8	10.7	11.6
Total Current	64.5	41.9	42.7	42.8	35.5	29.3	41.0	42.3
Long-Term Debt	24.6	14.2	14.0	14.9	22.4	25.5	18.5	16.1
Deferred Taxes	.0	.3	.5	.7	.7	1.8	.5	.5
All Other Non-Current	21.6	8.3	5.6	5.2	6.3	3.3	5.5	6.0
Net Worth	-10.7	35.3	37.3	36.3	35.1	40.0	34.5	35.0
Total Liabilities & Net Worth	100.0	100.0	100.0	100.0	100.0	100.0	100.0	100.0
INCOME DATA								
Net Sales	100.0	100.0	100.0	100.0	100.0	100.0	100.0	100.0
Gross Profit	44.0	37.8	32.0	28.4	29.2	34.8	35.5	34.5
Operating Expenses	42.2	32.1	27.2	22.8	22.8	25.8	30.5	30.0
Operating Profit	1.8	5.7	4.8	5.6	6.5	9.0	5.1	4.5
All Other Expenses (net)	1.6	1.0	1.4	1.7	1.9	3.9	1.4	1.1
Profit Before Taxes	.1	4.7	3.4	3.9	4.6	5.1	3.6	3.3
RATIOS								
Current	2.5	3.3	2.5	2.4	2.1	2.3	2.4	2.6
	1.3	1.8	1.5	1.5	1.6	2.0	1.5	1.6
	.7	1.2	1.1	1.1	1.2	1.8	1.1	1.1
Quick	1.6	2.1	1.3	1.1	1.2	1.3	1.3	1.4
	.6	1.1	.8	.8	.9	1.0	.8	.8
	.2	.6	.5	.5	.6	.7	.5	.5
Sales/Receivables	5 80.9	21 17.1	32 11.4	34 10.8	36 10.2	43 8.5	28 13.1	29 12.6
	22 16.3	35 10.3	47 7.7	48 7.5	53 6.9	56 6.6	41 8.9	42 8.6
	47 7.8	50 7.3	64 5.7	61 6.0	59 6.2	66 5.5	54 6.8	60 6.1
Cost of Sales/Inventory	6 62.6	17 21.4	44 8.2	44 8.4	37 9.9	57 6.5	35 10.5	36 10.1
	28 12.9	48 7.6	74 4.9	68 5.4	67 5.5	97 3.7	61 6.0	65 5.6
	91 4.0	107 3.4	119 3.1	103 3.6	95 3.8	140 2.6	102 3.6	103 3.5
Cost of Sales/Payables	7 53.4	13 27.7	19 18.9	22 16.3	22 16.4	27 13.4	17 21.9	18 20.2
	27 13.4	28 13.0	34 10.6	35 10.3	35 10.3	39 9.4	32 11.4	32 11.3
	62 5.9	52 7.1	58 6.3	51 7.2	52 7.1	51 7.1	49 7.5	53 6.9
Sales/Working Capital	6.7	4.8	5.0	5.3	5.8	3.9	5.6	5.1
	28.3	9.6	9.0	10.2	8.5	5.6	10.8	9.8
	-16.9	32.8	62.5	45.4	40.9	7.0	43.7	49.2
EBIT/Interest	13.6	12.0	8.4	10.1	13.6	11.3	8.2	11.0
	(37) 3.5	(115) 4.1	(177) 3.1	(103) 3.2	(22) 4.6	6.0	(370) 3.2	(470) 3.6
	.3	1.3	1.1	.9	1.8	2.4	1.2	1.1
Net Profit + Depr., Dep., Amort./Cur. Mat. L/T/D		5.7	8.3	8.6	8.9		4.6	7.4
		(13) 1.8	(37) 2.6	(47) 3.7	(13) 2.3		(101) 2.6	(119) 2.7
		1.0	1.0	1.6	.9		1.2	1.2
Fixed/Worth	.3	.1	.2	.4	.4	.4	.3	.3
	1.7	.4	.7	.8	1.0	.9	.8	.7
	-.6	1.3	2.4	1.8	2.4	5.2	2.8	2.3
Debt/Worth	1.0	.7	.7	.9	1.2	.8	.9	.8
	NM	1.8	2.0	2.2	2.7	2.1	2.2	2.0
	-2.9	9.3	6.9	6.5	6.6	16.2	6.4	6.1
% Profit Before Taxes/Tangible Net Worth	64.8	75.1	52.6	46.1	41.2	99.5	47.3	46.2
	(21) 44.2	(113) 26.3	(169) 19.7	(93) 21.6	(20) 23.9	(21) 28.9	(351) 20.7	(444) 20.9
	5.9	8.1	1.7	1.7	13.0	13.6	4.3	2.4
% Profit Before Taxes/Total Assets	31.5	21.3	15.3	14.3	15.6	15.1	14.5	15.0
	12.8	8.6	7.0	5.7	6.8	7.8	6.1	6.3
	-1.7	1.2	.2	-.2	2.5	3.8	.7	.3
Sales/Net Fixed Assets	87.6	56.0	25.5	16.5	19.1	9.5	24.7	26.1
	19.6	25.0	11.7	8.4	7.6	6.1	9.5	11.0
	10.7	8.7	4.8	5.5	3.7	4.2	4.6	4.9
Sales/Total Assets	5.6	4.0	2.6	2.5	2.2	1.6	2.9	3.0
	3.2	2.8	2.0	1.9	1.9	1.3	2.0	2.2
	2.4	1.9	1.4	1.4	1.5	1.1	1.4	1.5
% Depr., Dep., Amort./Sales	.6	.7	.8	1.1	1.2	1.6	1.2	1.0
	(29) 2.3	(106) 1.4	(175) 1.8	(100) 1.9	(19) 2.2	(18) 3.0	(365) 2.3	(434) 2.1
	4.0	2.9	3.2	2.9	3.2	4.5	4.4	3.6
% Officers', Directors' Owners' Comp/Sales	4.9	2.1	1.2				2.7	2.5
	(16) 6.8	(71) 4.4	(61) 2.9	(21) 2.6			(138) 4.4	(168) 4.7
	10.9	7.2	5.8	4.9			9.7	7.9
Net Sales ($)	48683M	450754M	2008113M	4419652M	3125922M	5792639M	9936618M	11791398M
Total Assets ($)	12303M	155094M	935624M	2358307M	1571465M	4246891M	6460579M	6922041M

M = $ thousand   MM = $ million
See Pages 11 through 21 for Explanation of Ratios and Data

Comparative Historical Data | | | | Current Data Sorted by Sales

Hist 1		Hist 2		Hist 3			0-1MM	1-3MM	3-5MM	5-10MM	10-25MM	25MM & OVER
						Type of Statement						
90		109		104		Unqualified	1	3	2	10	24	64
98		82		96		Reviewed	2	11	12	31	22	18
79		61		68		Compiled	5	16	19	13	11	4
68		70		83		Tax Returns	11	30	20	17	3	2
161		237		179		Other	12	30	20	30	41	46
4/1/04-3/31/05 ALL		4/1/05-3/31/06 ALL		4/1/06-3/31/07 ALL			102 (4/1-9/30/06)			428 (10/1/06-3/31/07)		
496		559		530		**NUMBER OF STATEMENTS**	31	90	73	101	101	134
%		%		%		**ASSETS**	%	%	%	%	%	%
8.2		7.9		8.2		Cash & Equivalents	12.0	11.2	12.3	8.0	5.1	5.4
27.0		27.8		27.1		Trade Receivables (net)	16.2	27.2	28.8	28.7	29.2	25.8
26.8		26.4		27.2		Inventory	25.7	27.4	25.6	27.1	29.2	26.7
3.3		3.3		2.6		All Other Current	1.9	2.7	1.6	2.5	3.7	2.3
65.3		65.3		65.0		Total Current	55.7	68.5	68.3	66.4	67.2	60.3
23.7		22.8		23.4		Fixed Assets (net)	27.0	23.0	21.7	23.8	20.9	25.3
4.9		5.2		5.9		Intangibles (net)	10.2	2.1	5.3	5.1	6.7	7.6
6.1		6.6		5.7		All Other Non-Current	7.1	6.4	4.7	4.7	5.2	6.8
100.0		100.0		100.0		Total	100.0	100.0	100.0	100.0	100.0	100.0
						LIABILITIES						
11.1		12.8		13.5		Notes Payable-Short Term	17.3	16.0	11.8	12.5	15.2	11.1
3.8		3.2		3.2		Cur. Mat.-L.T.D.	4.3	3.2	3.1	3.8	2.9	2.6
15.3		15.0		15.9		Trade Payables	10.4	17.5	16.1	14.7	18.5	14.8
.3		.2		.3		Income Taxes Payable	.3	.1	.1	.3	.4	.3
10.8		9.2		10.5		All Other Current	17.8	9.9	10.7	8.1	10.9	10.7
41.4		40.3		43.3		Total Current	50.2	46.7	41.9	39.5	47.9	39.5
18.1		17.0		16.0		Long-Term Debt	21.6	18.7	15.7	14.8	12.4	16.8
.5		.6		.5		Deferred Taxes	.1	.2	.4	.4	.6	.9
6.4		7.0		7.4		All Other Non-Current	14.8	13.8	7.4	5.7	3.4	5.6
33.7		35.1		32.8		Net Worth	13.3	20.6	34.6	39.6	35.7	37.3
100.0		100.0		100.0		Total Liabilities & Net Worth	100.0	100.0	100.0	100.0	100.0	100.0
						INCOME DATA						
100.0		100.0		100.0		Net Sales	100.0	100.0	100.0	100.0	100.0	100.0
35.2		34.0		33.7		Gross Profit	45.4	41.0	37.5	32.0	29.2	28.7
30.3		28.2		28.5		Operating Expenses	44.4	35.8	31.6	27.9	23.4	22.5
4.9		5.8		5.2		Operating Profit	1.0	5.2	5.9	4.1	5.8	6.2
1.1		1.1		1.5		All Other Expenses (net)	2.9	1.4	1.3	1.1	1.5	1.8
3.8		4.7		3.7		Profit Before Taxes	-1.9	3.8	4.7	3.0	4.3	4.5
						RATIOS						
2.8		2.8		2.6		Current	2.7	3.3	3.0	2.7	2.3	2.3
1.6		1.7		1.6			1.5	1.7	1.9	1.6	1.4	1.7
1.1		1.2		1.1			.8	1.0	1.2	1.2	1.0	1.2
1.5		1.5		1.4		Quick	2.1	1.7	2.0	1.7	1.1	1.2
.9	(558)	.9		.9			.7	.8	1.0	1.0	.7	.9
.5		.5		.5			.3	.4	.6	.6	.4	.6
29 12.8		30 12.3		29 12.8		Sales/Receivables	11 33.2	19 19.2	27 13.4	29 12.8	33 11.0	35 10.5
45 8.2		45 8.2		44 8.3			35 10.3	35 10.3	41 8.9	45 8.1	46 8.0	48 7.6
58 6.3		61 5.9		59 6.2			67 5.5	53 7.0	56 6.5	61 6.0	63 5.8	59 6.2
33 11.2		31 11.8		37 9.9		Cost of Sales/Inventory	10 37.0	10 36.8	21 17.8	37 9.8	41 8.9	44 8.3
64 5.7		62 5.9		65 5.6			114 3.2	65 5.6	61 6.0	59 6.2	72 5.1	68 5.4
114 3.2		104 3.5		109 3.3			363 1.0	114 3.2	120 3.1	94 3.9	115 3.2	99 3.7
18 20.7		17 21.5		18 20.0		Cost of Sales/Payables	14 26.7	9 42.7	14 25.2	15 24.8	19 19.0	24 15.2
32 11.3		31 11.9		33 11.2			36 10.0	32 11.4	29 12.8	29 12.5	37 9.8	36 10.1
54 6.7		53 6.9		53 6.9			96 3.8	55 6.6	57 6.4	45 8.1	57 6.4	51 7.2
4.9		4.6		5.0		Sales/Working Capital	2.1	4.6	5.1	5.2	5.9	5.4
9.5		9.0		9.3			6.4	10.7	9.2	9.0	10.9	9.2
34.4		30.2		42.9			-145.6	-724.9	30.2	20.2	NM	30.7
11.2		11.4		10.6		EBIT/Interest	5.4	12.6	14.0	7.1	7.2	13.5
4.2	(442)	4.4	(507)	3.6	(480)		1.2 (26)	4.5 (76)	3.7 (64)	3.6 (93)	3.0 (93)	4.4 (128)
1.3		1.8		1.1			-1.0	.9	.9	1.1	1.2	1.5
5.3		5.0		8.3		Net Profit + Depr., Dep., Amort./Cur. Mat. L/T/D				9.4	8.5	8.5
2.6	(113)	2.5	(120)	3.0	(121)				3.5 (20)	3.5 (28)	2.7 (59)
1.2		1.4		1.4						1.0	1.0	1.4
.2		.2		.3		Fixed/Worth	.3	.2	.2	.2	.3	.4
.7		.7		.7			1.7	.6	.7	.6	.8	.8
2.0		2.3		2.4			-1.6	5.8	2.4	2.6	1.7	2.0
.8		.8		.8		Debt/Worth	1.0	.7	.7	.6	1.1	.9
2.0		1.9		2.1			3.0	2.2	2.6	1.7	2.2	2.1
5.8		6.1		9.3			-3.7	127.7	20.7	6.9	5.7	6.4
49.5		49.5		57.0		% Profit Before Taxes/Tangible Net Worth	42.2	63.7	83.2	60.6	43.8	50.2
20.6	(430)	22.7	(475)	24.1	(437)		4.3 (17)	26.6 (69)	25.9 (61)	22.2 (88)	19.6 (85)	24.9 (117)
3.5		7.1		5.5			-1.3	8.6	5.2	5.0	4.1	8.4
15.6		16.3		17.5		% Profit Before Taxes/Total Assets	15.3	21.6	23.1	15.6	16.2	15.9
6.4		7.6		7.2			.6	8.7	8.1	7.0	5.8	7.3
.9		2.2		.4			-2.7	.4	.2	.7	.9	1.3
29.2		28.7		30.8		Sales/Net Fixed Assets	29.2	49.6	47.8	29.2	30.8	18.0
11.7		12.3		11.8			7.6	17.9	18.7	12.3	12.3	8.4
5.2		6.0		5.5			2.0	7.2	5.6	5.4	5.6	5.2
2.9		3.0		2.9		Sales/Total Assets	2.4	3.7	3.7	3.0	2.6	2.6
2.1		2.1		2.1			1.0	2.5	2.5	2.2	2.0	2.0
1.4		1.5		1.5			.5	1.6	1.7	1.5	1.5	1.5
1.0		.9		.9		% Depr., Dep., Amort./Sales	1.9	1.0	.7	1.0	.8	1.1
2.0	(423)	1.7	(457)	1.8	(447)		3.6 (21)	1.8 (69)	1.9 (62)	1.8 (88)	1.6 (90)	1.7 (117)
3.8		3.1		3.2			7.7	3.6	3.8	3.1	2.6	3.0
2.4		2.3		2.2		% Officers', Directors' Owners' Comp/Sales		2.9	2.6	2.1	1.5	1.0
4.5	(167)	4.1	(174)	3.8	(171)			5.0 (39)	4.6 (35)	3.3 (42)	2.4 (31)	2.5 (17)
7.7		7.3		7.2				10.9	6.8	6.8	3.5	6.6
11626603M		15605233M		15845763M		Net Sales ($)	16485M	176302M	296932M	740940M	1560479M	13054625M
6452657M		9383765M		9279684M		Total Assets ($)	19136M	104314M	146218M	399631M	884562M	7725823M

M = $ thousand   MM = $ million
See Pages 11 through 21 for Explanation of Ratios and Data

WHOLESALE TRADE

Current Data Sorted by Assets   Comparative Historical Data

0-500M	500M-2MM	2-10MM	10-50MM	50-100MM	100-250MM	Type of Statement		
	2	7	15	11	2	Unqualified	30	40
	8	24	21	3	2	Reviewed	74	55
5	26	24	5			Compiled	69	82
7	23	12	3	1		Tax Returns	29	50
7	15	62	39	7	7	Other	95	127
	44 (4/1-9/30/06)		294 (10/1/06-3/31/07)				4/1/02-3/31/03 ALL	4/1/03-3/31/04 ALL
19	74	129	83	22	11	**NUMBER OF STATEMENTS**	297	354
%	%	%	%	%	%	**ASSETS**	%	%
8.4	7.9	6.5	7.6	2.8	6.7	Cash & Equivalents	8.2	8.5
15.6	20.2	22.6	18.1	14.4	15.9	Trade Receivables (net)	16.4	16.4
46.1	48.9	46.2	48.3	53.3	39.5	Inventory	48.1	47.1
.1	3.2	3.0	2.8	3.7	2.6	All Other Current	4.9	3.4
70.3	80.2	78.4	76.7	74.2	64.6	Total Current	77.7	75.4
18.8	15.1	14.3	15.3	16.3	25.9	Fixed Assets (net)	14.7	16.8
1.1	1.2	3.1	3.0	1.7	5.8	Intangibles (net)	1.9	2.3
9.8	3.5	4.2	4.9	7.8	3.7	All Other Non-Current	5.8	5.4
100.0	100.0	100.0	100.0	100.0	100.0	Total	100.0	100.0
						LIABILITIES		
23.1	26.1	32.9	39.4	52.1	28.2	Notes Payable-Short Term	34.1	34.2
6.1	4.3	1.7	1.9	3.3	6.0	Cur. Mat.-L.T.D.	3.8	3.1
12.4	11.3	13.0	8.8	6.1	5.4	Trade Payables	11.2	11.7
.0	.1	.1	.3	.3	.3	Income Taxes Payable	.1	.1
21.6	12.7	7.8	11.6	7.0	13.6	All Other Current	11.4	10.4
63.2	54.5	55.6	61.9	68.8	53.6	Total Current	60.6	59.5
11.7	12.3	11.4	10.9	14.7	18.9	Long-Term Debt	10.4	11.2
.0	.0	.2	.3	1.0	1.0	Deferred Taxes	.5	.4
8.0	3.5	4.8	3.8	1.2	5.4	All Other Non-Current	2.6	4.4
17.2	29.7	27.9	23.1	14.3	21.2	Net Worth	26.0	24.5
100.0	100.0	100.0	100.0	100.0	100.0	Total Liabilities & Net Worth	100.0	100.0
						INCOME DATA		
100.0	100.0	100.0	100.0	100.0	100.0	Net Sales	100.0	100.0
27.3	24.4	25.1	19.9	15.5	27.5	Gross Profit	19.1	21.5
25.0	20.0	20.7	17.2	13.3	24.7	Operating Expenses	17.5	19.5
2.3	4.4	4.3	2.7	2.2	2.8	Operating Profit	1.7	2.0
.9	.7	.9	.4	.6	2.7	All Other Expenses (net)	.2	.2
1.4	3.7	3.4	2.3	1.6	.1	Profit Before Taxes	1.5	1.8
						RATIOS		
2.0	3.1	1.8	1.4	1.2	1.1		1.7	1.7
1.2	1.5	1.4	1.2	1.1	1.1	Current	1.2	1.2
.6	1.0	1.1	1.1	1.0	1.0		1.1	1.0
1.1	1.1	.9	.6	.3	.9		.6	.7
.3	.5	.4	.3	.2	.2	Quick	(294) .3	(353) .4
.1	.1	.3	.2	.1	.2		.2	.2
0 UND	0 829.1	8 48.3	7 50.0	9 40.2	11 34.4		4 94.1	5 77.7
5 69.3	9 40.1	17 21.7	17 21.7	16 23.5	17 21.5	Sales/Receivables	12 29.4	14 26.9
22 16.9	30 12.1	39 9.4	28 13.2	32 11.3	31 11.7		27 13.5	30 12.1
1 371.8	23 16.0	30 12.3	48 7.6	62 5.9	44 8.4		28 13.1	30 12.2
20 17.9	62 5.9	58 6.3	68 5.4	78 4.7	87 4.2	Cost of Sales/Inventory	54 6.8	59 6.2
83 4.4	103 3.5	86 4.3	99 3.7	147 2.5	117 3.1		96 3.8	96 3.8
0 UND	0 UND	4 95.9	5 78.7	5 66.4	5 75.9		3 122.3	3 116.9
0 999.8	4 87.9	9 39.4	10 37.6	8 45.4	11 32.8	Cost of Sales/Payables	8 44.9	9 39.5
22 16.6	26 13.8	36 10.1	17 21.1	14 25.4	52 7.1		20 18.1	24 15.4
10.5	6.8	7.6	11.2	27.1	31.5		11.1	10.6
101.4	18.4	16.1	30.0	38.4	36.2	Sales/Working Capital	26.1	23.9
-30.7	219.0	58.8	68.6	254.3	-999.8		112.8	158.2
6.0	5.9	6.3	5.1	3.1	2.6		5.5	7.4
(15) 1.2	(62) 2.7	(110) 2.2	(72) 2.0	(21) 2.5	(10) 2.1	EBIT/Interest	(261) 2.2	(311) 2.6
-3.0	1.2	1.2	1.3	1.0	1.5		1.2	1.3
		5.0	5.9			Net Profit + Depr., Dep.,	4.7	4.9
	(15) 1.7	(19) 1.3				Amort./Cur. Mat. L/T/D	(49) 1.8	(64) 1.3
		1.0	.9				.9	.7
.0	.0	.1	.2	.2	2.2		.1	.2
.5	.3	.3	.4	1.0	2.8	Fixed/Worth	.4	.5
9.9	1.1	1.3	1.8	2.5	-2.0		1.5	1.7
1.0	1.0	1.5	2.5	3.1	4.4		1.6	1.7
3.3	2.5	3.2	4.7	8.3	6.9	Debt/Worth	3.7	3.7
-11.3	15.3	10.9	9.5	18.0	-21.3		8.8	9.5
100.0	66.1	39.7	38.5	51.1		% Profit Before Taxes/Tangible	33.6	41.2
(14) 69.1	(63) 29.1	(110) 20.8	(79) 23.1	(19) 21.2		Net Worth	(265) 15.6	(319) 18.0
.3	5.6	4.7	11.9	12.1			4.1	4.5
40.2	15.5	11.7	8.4	7.1	5.1	% Profit Before Taxes/Total	8.3	10.4
4.5	5.6	4.9	3.9	3.6	3.5	Assets	3.7	3.6
-7.8	1.2	.9	1.3	.1	1.1		.5	.9
999.8	199.4	191.8	93.0	99.3	15.1		146.1	115.2
160.8	65.6	51.5	40.1	22.7	8.1	Sales/Net Fixed Assets	46.9	38.3
13.4	22.4	17.2	11.2	8.2	3.6		15.9	11.8
8.0	6.4	4.3	3.9	3.0	2.7		5.7	4.9
5.3	4.0	3.1	2.9	2.3	2.5	Sales/Total Assets	3.5	3.1
2.9	2.5	1.8	1.8	1.8	1.0		2.3	2.1
	.2	.2	.2	.3			.2	.3
	(52) .5	(106) .4	(75) .4	(21) .8		% Depr., Dep., Amort./Sales	(243) .5	(287) .6
	1.7	1.3	1.6	2.5			1.6	1.9
		.7	.4				.5	.7
	(34) 1.6	(58) 1.8	(28) .6			% Officers', Directors' Owners' Comp/Sales	(137) 1.1	(144) 1.6
	3.6	3.7	1.1				2.7	3.0
57131M	504357M	2361785M	8557715M	4095823M	3505970M	Net Sales ($)	9467805M	13877628M
5860M	89629M	678392M	1886690M	1580296M	1610004M	Total Assets ($)	3122431M	4503498M

M = $ thousand   MM = $ million
See Pages 11 through 21 for Explanation of Ratios and Data

Comparative Historical Data   Current Data Sorted by Sales

			Type of Statement						
48	40	37	Unqualified		3			3	31
60	54	58	Reviewed	1	3	1	12	14	27
68	50	60	Compiled	2	13	10	11	17	7
48	42	46	Tax Returns	4	11	4	9	9	9
120	116	137	Other	4	7	9	16	40	61
4/1/04-3/31/05 ALL	4/1/05-3/31/06 ALL	4/1/06-3/31/07 ALL		0-1MM	44 (4/1-9/30/06) 1-3MM	3-5MM	294 (10/1/06-3/31/07) 5-10MM	10-25MM	25MM & OVER
344	302	338	**NUMBER OF STATEMENTS**	11	37	24	48	83	135
%	%	%	**ASSETS**	%	%	%	%	%	%
7.3	8.6	7.0	Cash & Equivalents	9.8	5.6	8.4	6.4	8.1	6.3
18.8	18.9	19.8	Trade Receivables (net)	35.2	17.5	26.0	21.5	19.8	17.6
47.2	45.8	47.5	Inventory	15.9	49.1	44.0	47.4	48.6	49.8
3.1	2.4	2.9	All Other Current	.1	2.0	1.0	3.9	4.0	2.7
76.4	75.8	77.2	Total Current	60.9	74.1	79.4	79.1	80.5	76.3
16.5	17.1	15.5	Fixed Assets (net)	27.8	18.4	13.2	13.7	13.6	15.9
1.9	1.9	2.5	Intangibles (net)	.7	2.3	4.3	3.6	1.6	2.7
5.2	5.2	4.8	All Other Non-Current	10.7	5.3	3.1	3.5	4.4	5.1
100.0	100.0	100.0	Total	100.0	100.0	100.0	100.0	100.0	100.0
			LIABILITIES						
34.1	31.0	33.5	Notes Payable-Short Term	8.2	22.6	22.6	25.5	35.8	42.0
3.0	3.3	2.8	Cur. Mat.-L.T.D.	3.7	4.5	3.4	4.3	1.5	2.5
11.4	12.2	10.9	Trade Payables	19.1	9.5	16.5	13.7	11.3	8.3
.2	.1	.1	Income Taxes Payable	.0	.0	.1	.0	.0	.3
8.3	10.5	10.7	All Other Current	28.7	12.5	9.7	9.7	8.8	10.5
57.1	57.1	58.1	Total Current	59.7	49.2	52.3	53.2	57.5	63.6
11.4	12.4	12.0	Long-Term Debt	13.1	15.1	7.9	14.2	11.2	11.4
.4	.4	.3	Deferred Taxes	.0	.4	.1	.0	.1	.5
5.5	5.7	4.3	All Other Non-Current	8.5	4.9	6.4	7.5	2.4	3.4
25.7	24.5	25.4	Net Worth	18.7	30.3	33.4	25.0	28.8	21.3
100.0	100.0	100.0	Total Liabilities & Net Worth	100.0	100.0	100.0	100.0	100.0	100.0
			INCOME DATA						
100.0	100.0	100.0	Net Sales	100.0	100.0	100.0	100.0	100.0	100.0
22.1	23.2	23.2	Gross Profit	47.9	33.4	35.8	24.0	21.8	16.8
19.6	20.0	19.6	Operating Expenses	34.7	27.6	28.1	20.8	18.8	14.7
2.5	3.3	3.6	Operating Profit	13.2	5.8	7.8	3.3	3.0	2.1
.4	.8	.8	All Other Expenses (net)	1.5	2.3	.7	.7	.4	.6
2.1	2.5	2.9	Profit Before Taxes	11.6	3.5	7.1	2.6	2.6	1.5
			RATIOS						
1.8	1.8	1.7		1.7	3.0	2.5	2.6	1.8	1.3
1.3	1.3	1.2	Current	1.3	1.6	1.5	1.4	1.4	1.1
1.0	1.1	1.0		.6	1.1	1.0	1.0	1.1	1.0
.7	.9	.9		1.4	1.2	1.0	1.2	1.0	.5
.4 (301)	.4	.4	Quick	.9	.4	.7	.4	.4	.3
.2	.2	.2		.5	.1	.1	.2	.2	.2
6 61.1	6 64.3	6 60.6		5 69.3	0 UND	2 173.9	4 101.5	5 77.4	7 49.2
17 21.6	16 22.9	15 23.6	Sales/Receivables	35 10.6	20 18.7	30 12.3	14 26.8	15 24.0	14 25.4
36 10.1	34 10.7	33 11.0		292 1.3	43 8.6	67 5.4	39 9.4	33 11.0	24 15.4
34 10.8	30 12.3	33 11.0		0 UND	10 36.4	31 11.9	24 15.3	30 12.1	41 8.8
60 6.1	61 6.0	63 5.8	Cost of Sales/Inventory	8 48.1	89 4.1	69 5.3	54 6.8	59 6.2	62 5.8
93 3.9	94 3.9	95 3.8		140 2.6	170 2.1	119 3.1	73 5.0	86 4.2	89 4.1
3 119.0	3 107.5	3 128.0		0 UND	0 UND	2 239.7	2 186.8	3 127.2	4 93.7
10 36.6	10 38.2	8 44.0	Cost of Sales/Payables	4 101.0	16 22.3	27 13.5	9 42.2	7 53.0	8 45.9
26 14.0	30 12.3	24 15.4		305 1.2	49 7.5	51 7.2	34 10.8	27 13.4	14 26.8
10.4	9.0	8.8		3.5	4.0	4.1	7.5	8.6	18.6
21.1	24.8	23.2	Sales/Working Capital	4.8	10.5	10.8	16.9	15.8	36.2
109.2	77.7	99.4		-15.6	62.3	108.3	163.2	57.6	105.2
6.8	6.4	4.7			5.8	21.6	4.0	5.0	4.5
(308) 3.0	(275) 2.9	(290) 2.2	EBIT/Interest	(30) 2.4	(20) 3.4	(44) 1.9	(71) 2.5	(118) 2.0	
1.5	1.4	1.2			1.0	1.7	1.2	1.4	1.2
5.1	5.8	4.6							4.6
(58) 2.5	(54) 2.4	(53) 1.5	Net Profit + Depr., Dep., Amort./Cur. Mat. L/T/D					(33) 1.3	
1.0	.8	.9							.9
.2	.1	.1		.0	.1	.1	.1	.1	.2
.5	.5	.4	Fixed/Worth	.4	.4	.2	.6	.3	.6
1.7	1.8	1.6		1.2	1.5	4.9	1.4	1.1	2.3
1.5	1.7	1.5		.5	1.1	1.0	1.3	1.1	2.7
3.2	3.7	3.9	Debt/Worth	2.4	2.4	3.0	4.5	2.8	4.9
9.2	8.4	12.0		8.5	7.9	14.9	17.8	8.3	12.0
38.1	50.4	44.3			73.9	55.4	66.1	41.9	39.9
(302) 17.9	(267) 26.2	(292) 22.3	% Profit Before Taxes/Tangible Net Worth	(31) 29.1	(20) 25.2	(40) 16.4	(71) 20.9	(121) 22.5	
6.2	9.3	6.7			6.8	6.4	4.3	5.3	11.7
9.1	10.9	11.4		21.1	18.5	18.5	13.2	12.9	8.2
4.1	5.1	4.4	% Profit Before Taxes/Total Assets	4.5	6.7	8.1	3.7	5.2	3.7
1.3	1.3	.9		-3.3	-.5	1.7	1.0	1.1	.9
107.5	119.8	154.6		UND	174.4	76.7	134.3	268.3	114.3
33.8	41.4	46.2	Sales/Net Fixed Assets	16.7	26.4	35.8	54.2	57.3	41.5
12.0	11.5	12.8		3.1	7.8	14.7	22.5	18.0	11.2
4.6	4.5	4.4		2.7	3.9	3.6	6.1	4.7	4.3
3.1	3.0	3.1	Sales/Total Assets	1.2	2.1	2.9	3.6	3.4	3.1
2.2	2.1	1.9		.3	1.1	1.2	2.1	2.3	2.3
.3	.2	.2			.2	.3	.3	.1	.2
(285) .6	(240) .5	(268) .5	% Depr., Dep., Amort./Sales	(23) 1.1	(18) .5	(34) .7	(73) .3	(116) .4	
1.8	1.4	1.6			3.1	1.3	1.6	.9	1.6
.6	.6	.6			2.4	1.7	.6	.8	.3
(143) 1.3	(115) 1.3	(135) 1.2	% Officers', Directors' Owners' Comp/Sales	(11) 3.8	(15) 2.1	(22) 1.8	(39) 1.3	(46) .5	
3.2	3.5	2.7			10.3	5.2	5.5	2.2	1.1
14200217M	14794418M	19082781M	Net Sales ($)	5633M	73046M	92269M	360552M	1369592M	17181689M
5363800M	5691224M	5850871M	Total Assets ($)	6064M	48667M	58056M	139460M	466417M	5132207M

M = $ thousand   MM = $ million
See Pages 11 through 21 for Explanation of Ratios and Data

Current Data Sorted by Assets

Comparative Historical Data

Type of Statement							
Unqualified						59	57
Reviewed						125	112
Compiled						129	134
Tax Returns						68	54
Other						136	129

1	2	22	36	12	5		
3	14	69	31				
9	40	50	2				
10	36	19	2				
12	25	52	41	8	8		
	88 (4/1-9/30/06)		421 (10/1/06-3/31/07)		8	4/1/02-3/31/03	4/1/03-3/31/04
0-500M	500M-2MM	2-10MM	10-50MM	50-100MM	100-250MM	ALL	ALL

	0-500M	500M-2MM	2-10MM	10-50MM	50-100MM	100-250MM	ALL	ALL
NUMBER OF STATEMENTS	35	117	212	112	20	13	517	486
	%	%	%	%	%	%	%	%
ASSETS								
Cash & Equivalents	11.5	5.9	4.7	3.7	4.1	1.7	5.6	6.6
Trade Receivables (net)	24.9	24.7	25.3	23.6	23.6	22.5	23.4	23.7
Inventory	49.0	48.9	52.3	48.9	34.7	41.7	49.1	48.3
All Other Current	.4	1.7	1.5	2.7	1.9	1.4	2.0	1.6
Total Current	85.8	81.2	83.8	79.0	64.3	67.3	80.1	80.2
Fixed Assets (net)	8.3	11.2	9.9	12.8	18.4	15.7	12.1	11.9
Intangibles (net)	2.8	2.1	1.8	2.7	14.3	10.2	3.1	2.8
All Other Non-Current	3.0	5.5	4.5	5.4	3.1	6.9	4.7	5.1
Total	100.0	100.0	100.0	100.0	100.0	100.0	100.0	100.0
LIABILITIES								
Notes Payable-Short Term	22.6	14.9	17.8	20.4	21.2	8.8	16.3	15.3
Cur. Mat.-L.T.D.	2.5	2.9	2.1	1.6	1.8	1.6	2.7	3.0
Trade Payables	24.8	22.3	22.5	20.3	14.9	20.2	22.2	22.0
Income Taxes Payable	.0	.1	.2	.1	.4	.0	.2	.2
All Other Current	22.7	10.2	7.0	8.6	5.4	7.2	9.3	10.0
Total Current	72.6	50.4	49.6	50.9	43.7	37.8	50.7	50.4
Long-Term Debt	17.2	15.1	9.9	9.1	16.5	14.8	12.5	11.3
Deferred Taxes	.0	.0	.3	.3	.4	1.5	.1	.2
All Other Non-Current	15.0	6.7	4.7	4.2	2.8	6.9	4.9	5.2
Net Worth	-4.8	27.9	35.3	35.5	36.6	39.0	31.8	32.8
Total Liabilities & Net Worth	100.0	100.0	100.0	100.0	100.0	100.0	100.0	100.0
INCOME DATA								
Net Sales	100.0	100.0	100.0	100.0	100.0	100.0	100.0	100.0
Gross Profit	34.7	34.3	30.5	28.9	28.8	28.1	32.5	31.5
Operating Expenses	34.0	31.6	27.4	23.7	23.8	22.7	29.8	28.6
Operating Profit	.7	2.8	3.2	5.2	5.0	5.4	2.7	2.9
All Other Expenses (net)	.7	.8	.8	1.1	1.7	1.9	.6	.7
Profit Before Taxes	.0	1.9	2.4	4.2	3.3	3.5	2.1	2.2
RATIOS								
Current	2.9	2.9	2.3	2.4	2.7	3.3	2.5	2.5
	1.9	2.0	1.7	1.6	1.7	1.8	1.7	1.7
	.9	1.3	1.3	1.2	1.0	1.1	1.3	1.3
Quick	1.1	1.1	.9	.8	1.2	1.2	.9	1.0
	.7	.6	.6	.5	.6	.7	.6 (485)	.6
	.3	.4	.4	.4	.4	.5	.4	.4
Sales/Receivables	8 45.0	21 17.5	25 14.6	30 12.2	30 12.3	38 9.6	23 15.9	23 16.2
	20 17.9	31 11.6	35 10.5	39 9.4	42 8.7	53 6.8	33 11.1	32 11.3
	29 12.4	41 8.9	46 7.9	51 7.1	52 7.0	75 4.9	42 8.6	44 8.4
Cost of Sales/Inventory	28 13.2	56 6.5	78 4.7	80 4.6	45 8.1	105 3.5	65 5.6	64 5.7
	100 3.6	101 3.6	112 3.3	122 3.0	95 3.9	137 2.7	106 3.4	103 3.6
	174 2.1	143 2.5	170 2.1	179 2.0	142 2.0	196 1.9	165 2.2	161 2.3
Cost of Sales/Payables	12 30.4	24 15.0	24 15.4	19 19.2	23 15.7	39 9.4	24 15.2	24 15.0
	23 16.1	39 9.3	43 8.4	38 9.5	33 11.2	64 5.7	38 9.6	38 9.7
	60 6.1	61 6.0	71 5.2	67 5.5	48 7.6	79 4.6	65 5.6	63 5.8
Sales/Working Capital	4.0	4.1	4.6	4.2	4.8	3.4	4.7	4.5
	10.6	7.2	7.7	7.7	7.2	3.9	8.2	8.5
	-46.1	18.5	14.4	19.6	359.6	49.4	16.2	18.5
EBIT/Interest	5.8	7.9	6.1	7.0	2.9	8.5	6.7	8.6
	(30) 2.4	(103) 2.7	(196) 2.7	(104) 2.9	(19) 2.6	3.9	(478) 2.8	(449) 3.1
	.2	.7	1.3	1.7	1.7	2.1	1.2	1.3
Net Profit + Depr., Dep., Amort./Cur. Mat. L/T/D		4.1	5.0	10.2			4.6	5.6
	(17) 1.5	(65) 2.0	(37) 2.5				(146) 2.0	(128) 2.6
	.5	.9	1.1				1.0	1.2
Fixed/Worth	.0	.1	.1	.1	.3	.2	.1	.1
	.3	.2	.2	.3	1.6	.4	.3	.3
	-.2	.6	.5	.9	NM	1.2	.7	.8
Debt/Worth	1.0	.7	1.0	.9	1.4	.9	.9	.9
	5.3	1.8	2.0	2.5	3.7	2.0	2.0	2.1
	-2.9	6.6	4.0	5.3	NM	8.1	4.9	5.0
% Profit Before Taxes/Tangible Net Worth	64.4	42.3	34.3	41.8	27.4	49.5	29.9	35.6
	(20) 16.1	(102) 20.7	(201) 13.1	(104) 19.1	(15) 14.7	(12) 21.9	(457) 13.2	(441) 16.1
	4.9	2.2	2.5	7.7	8.1	5.8	2.8	3.4
% Profit Before Taxes/Total Assets	16.5	16.4	10.2	13.5	7.5	10.3	9.6	11.1
	5.1	5.5	3.7	5.2	5.3	5.4	3.9	4.3
	-2.7	-.4	.7	2.5	3.0	2.3	.5	.8
Sales/Net Fixed Assets	301.0	128.8	88.4	65.2	32.7	50.9	64.7	78.4
	90.9	48.5	38.4	32.4	14.6	17.4	34.2	36.2
	21.8	20.5	20.3	13.2	7.7	6.4	17.0	16.4
Sales/Total Assets	5.3	3.6	3.1	2.7	2.6	1.9	3.2	3.2
	3.3	2.7	2.4	2.1	1.9	1.4	2.4	2.5
	2.3	2.0	1.8	1.7	1.5	1.3	1.9	1.9
% Depr., Dep., Amort./Sales	.3	.4	.4	.4	.8	.7	.5	.5
	(23) .6	(91) .9	(190) .9	(104) .6	(17) 1.3	(12) 1.5	(454) 1.0	(409) .9
	1.4	1.4	1.3	1.1	3.0	3.3	1.5	1.5
% Officers', Directors' Owners' Comp/Sales	2.8	2.3	1.7	.6			2.0	1.6
	(15) 4.5	(58) 4.0	(92) 2.6	(26) 1.2			(217) 3.4	(204) 3.0
	8.5	7.6	4.7	3.1			6.1	5.5
Net Sales ($)	38541M	393208M	2781778M	4918760M	2870867M	3130640M	12106376M	11589002M
Total Assets ($)	9019M	132770M	1073329M	2235376M	1443260M	1874357M	5971613M	5069221M

© RMA 2007

M = $ thousand   MM = $ million
See Pages 11 through 21 for Explanation of Ratios and Data

Comparative Historical Data | Current Data Sorted by Sales

Hist 1	Hist 2	Hist 3	Type of Statement	0-1MM	1-3MM	3-5MM	5-10MM	10-25MM	25MM & OVER
71	73	78	Unqualified	1	2	3	7	18	47
120	107	117	Reviewed	1	9	8	26	44	29
119	100	101	Compiled	8	24	12	29	26	2
68	70	67	Tax Returns	6	24	15	11	11	
127	183	146	Other	9	19	14	17	36	51
4/1/04-3/31/05 ALL	4/1/05-3/31/06 ALL	4/1/06-3/31/07 ALL		88 (4/1-9/30/06)			421 (10/1/06-3/31/07)		
505	533	509	**NUMBER OF STATEMENTS**	25	78	52	90	135	129
%	%	%	**ASSETS**	%	%	%	%	%	%
5.8	6.1	5.1	Cash & Equivalents	9.4	6.9	3.9	6.1	4.7	3.4
24.3	24.8	24.6	Trade Receivables (net)	18.5	22.6	25.0	24.1	24.9	27.0
47.5	47.6	49.6	Inventory	45.9	53.1	51.0	49.2	52.0	45.3
1.6	1.5	1.8	All Other Current	.5	1.1	1.9	1.7	2.0	2.2
79.2	79.9	81.1	Total Current	74.3	83.7	81.8	81.2	83.6	77.9
12.2	12.2	11.2	Fixed Assets (net)	19.7	8.9	11.0	12.8	8.6	12.7
3.1	2.7	2.8	Intangibles (net)	1.3	2.5	2.6	1.5	1.8	5.5
5.6	5.2	4.8	All Other Non-Current	4.6	4.9	4.6	4.5	6.0	3.9
100.0	100.0	100.0	Total	100.0	100.0	100.0	100.0	100.0	100.0
			LIABILITIES						
16.4	16.0	17.9	Notes Payable-Short Term	27.0	15.0	22.5	14.5	16.7	19.8
2.3	2.2	2.2	Cur. Mat.-L.T.D.	2.8	2.5	3.1	2.9	1.6	1.6
22.3	20.8	21.8	Trade Payables	15.8	20.6	24.8	21.6	22.1	22.3
.2	.3	.2	Income Taxes Payable	.0	.0	.1	.2	.3	.1
8.4	8.3	9.1	All Other Current	28.0	9.1	8.8	7.3	6.9	9.0
49.6	47.5	51.1	Total Current	73.7	47.2	59.4	46.5	47.5	52.8
10.5	12.7	11.8	Long-Term Debt	26.5	15.3	13.2	13.6	7.5	9.4
.1	.2	.3	Deferred Taxes	.0	.1	.0	.4	.3	.4
5.5	6.0	5.8	All Other Non-Current	6.2	11.6	6.5	3.6	4.5	4.7
34.2	33.6	31.0	Net Worth	-6.4	25.8	20.9	35.8	40.2	32.6
100.0	100.0	100.0	Total Liabilities & Net Worth	100.0	100.0	100.0	100.0	100.0	100.0
			INCOME DATA						
100.0	100.0	100.0	Net Sales	100.0	100.0	100.0	100.0	100.0	100.0
31.3	31.5	31.2	Gross Profit	40.7	34.3	33.5	32.4	30.5	26.6
27.8	27.9	27.7	Operating Expenses	39.5	32.2	30.6	29.3	26.3	22.0
3.6	3.6	3.5	Operating Profit	1.2	2.0	2.9	3.1	4.2	4.5
.7	.6	.9	All Other Expenses (net)	2.6	.9	.4	.5	.8	1.1
2.9	3.0	2.6	Profit Before Taxes	-1.4	1.1	2.5	2.6	3.4	3.4
			RATIOS						
2.5	2.7	2.6	Current	2.6	3.0	2.6	2.6	2.5	2.2
1.6	1.7	1.7		1.3	2.3	1.7	1.8	1.7	1.5
1.2	1.3	1.3		.6	1.4	1.2	1.3	1.4	1.1
.9	1.0	1.0	Quick	.9	1.1	.8	1.0	1.0	.9
(504) .6	.6	.6		.4	.6	.5	.6	.6	.5
.4	.4	.4		.1	.4	.3	.4	.4	.4
23 16.0	23 15.6	24 15.0	Sales/Receivables	8 47.0	20 18.6	20 18.5	24 15.0	27 13.5	29 12.4
33 11.1	34 10.8	34 10.8		24 15.4	28 12.8	34 10.6	34 10.7	35 10.3	38 9.6
44 8.3	47 7.7	47 7.8		32 11.5	38 9.5	46 7.9	45 8.0	46 8.0	54 6.8
60 6.1	66 5.6	67 5.4	Cost of Sales/Inventory	57 6.4	67 5.4	65 5.6	73 5.0	80 4.5	55 6.7
101 3.6	103 3.6	111 3.3		157 2.3	123 3.0	114 3.2	111 3.3	114 3.2	96 3.8
150 2.4	157 2.3	167 2.2		205 1.8	207 1.8	168 2.2	167 2.2	174 2.1	144 2.5
25 14.8	21 17.0	23 16.2	Cost of Sales/Payables	10 35.5	23 15.6	24 15.4	26 14.1	23 15.6	21 17.8
41 8.9	39 9.4	40 9.1		33 11.2	41 8.9	42 8.6	43 8.4	43 8.6	37 10.0
62 5.9	63 5.8	66 5.5		65 5.6	65 5.6	68 5.4	70 5.2	69 5.3	62 5.9
5.2	4.6	4.3	Sales/Working Capital	3.0	3.5	3.9	4.1	4.6	5.4
8.7	8.1	7.6		16.8	5.1	8.0	7.9	7.3	9.4
21.4	15.8	18.1		-9.8	10.8	32.8	18.1	12.4	25.0
11.2	8.4	6.6	EBIT/Interest	3.5	7.9	5.3	7.1	7.3	6.4
(454) 3.8	(481) 3.5	(465) 2.8		(22) .8	(70) 2.2	(48) 2.5	(81) 2.6	(124) 3.0	(120) 2.9
1.5	1.6	1.3		-.3	.8	.9	1.2	1.3	2.0
7.5	8.0	6.6	Net Profit + Depr., Dep., Amort./Cur. Mat. L/T/D		2.2	4.5	4.5	8.0	9.9
(136) 3.0	(130) 3.1	(133) 2.0		(10) 1.0	(13) 1.4	(24) 2.4	(44) 1.9	(42) 3.0	
1.3	1.3	.9			.4	.4	.7	.9	1.9
.1	.1	.1	Fixed/Worth	.1	.1	.1	.1	.1	.1
.3	.3	.2		.4	.2	.3	.3	.2	.3
1.1	.8	.8		-.4	.7	1.2	.8	.4	1.2
1.0	.9	.9	Debt/Worth	1.1	.7	1.2	.9	.8	1.2
2.1	2.0	2.1		5.3	1.7	2.3	2.0	1.7	2.6
5.2	5.5	5.9		-3.4	9.0	6.9	4.1	3.2	6.3
37.2	39.5	36.7	% Profit Before Taxes/Tangible Net Worth	36.6	41.4	34.8	34.1	34.2	42.3
(446) 16.3	(474) 18.3	(454) 16.1		(16) 12.5	(64) 14.1	(44) 18.5	(85) 13.1	(130) 14.4	(115) 20.6
5.1	5.4	4.4		-3.1	1.4	4.0	2.8	3.3	11.1
11.8	12.8	12.0	% Profit Before Taxes/Total Assets	15.5	12.1	13.5	10.4	11.6	13.2
5.2	5.7	4.4		.8	3.5	4.6	4.0	4.2	5.9
1.2	1.5	.8		-5.3	-.7	-.5	.7	.9	2.8
84.6	71.3	86.5	Sales/Net Fixed Assets	132.4	125.8	100.0	74.6	90.6	69.0
39.2	34.4	37.0		26.9	45.2	41.8	28.8	42.5	34.1
17.5	17.1	17.8		8.4	19.9	19.1	12.9	27.2	13.6
3.2	3.2	3.1	Sales/Total Assets	3.2	3.2	3.5	3.3	3.1	2.9
2.5	2.5	2.4		1.9	2.4	2.6	2.3	2.5	2.4
1.9	1.8	1.8		1.0	1.8	1.8	1.8	1.9	1.9
.4	.4	.4	% Depr., Dep., Amort./Sales	.5	.4	.6	.5	.3	.4
(416) .9	(456) .8	(437) .8		(19) 1.4	(58) .9	(44) .9	(79) 1.0	(120) .8	(117) .7
1.6	1.4	1.3		3.1	1.4	1.5	1.4	1.2	1.2
2.0	1.5	1.7	% Officers', Directors' Owners' Comp/Sales	3.5	3.2	2.7	1.7	1.3	.6
(204) 3.4	(220) 2.8	(192) 2.9		(10) 8.4	(43) 3.4	(23) 3.7	(45) 2.7	(49) 2.3	(22) 1.3
6.8	6.1	5.7		11.4	7.1	8.4	5.6	3.8	2.8
12935148M	14222047M	14133794M	Net Sales ($)	13999M	158193M	202926M	650307M	2275763M	10832606M
5889335M	7320577M	6768111M	Total Assets ($)	9715M	79399M	87051M	304370M	1024244M	5263332M

M = $ thousand   MM = $ million
See Pages 11 through 21 for Explanation of Ratios and Data

Current Data Sorted by Assets   Comparative Historical Data

						Type of Statement		
		1	10	2	4	Unqualified	20	16
	7	17	14			Reviewed	34	43
1	8	17	9	1		Compiled	43	68
7	7	9			2	Tax Returns	22	13
5	9	18	18	2	5	Other	38	45
	36 (4/1-9/30/06)		137 (10/1/06-3/31/07)				4/1/02-3/31/03	4/1/03-3/31/04
0-500M	500M-2MM	2-10MM	10-50MM	50-100MM	100-250MM		ALL	ALL
13	31	62	51	5	11	NUMBER OF STATEMENTS	157	185
%	%	%	%	%	%	ASSETS	%	%
13.9	8.9	4.7	4.4		5.0	Cash & Equivalents	7.1	6.0
22.9	22.6	29.1	25.5		26.6	Trade Receivables (net)	27.1	27.9
29.6	39.6	42.8	39.6		35.1	Inventory	39.0	38.9
5.9	1.9	3.1	3.6		1.6	All Other Current	2.4	2.5
72.3	73.0	79.8	73.1		68.4	Total Current	75.7	75.3
26.1	21.4	14.9	20.8		22.4	Fixed Assets (net)	18.6	17.4
1.0	1.9	1.0	1.6		6.5	Intangibles (net)	1.8	2.0
.6	3.7	4.3	4.5		2.8	All Other Non-Current	3.9	5.3
100.0	100.0	100.0	100.0		100.0	Total	100.0	100.0
						LIABILITIES		
13.5	11.7	12.1	13.4		14.7	Notes Payable-Short Term	10.9	12.5
2.0	3.9	3.2	2.4		2.6	Cur. Mat.-L.T.D.	3.3	2.9
39.6	26.4	38.4	28.7		29.3	Trade Payables	31.0	33.0
.0	.2	.1	.2		.3	Income Taxes Payable	.2	.1
6.6	6.9	6.5	5.9		4.7	All Other Current	7.8	9.0
61.7	49.1	60.3	50.5		51.5	Total Current	53.1	57.5
24.9	11.6	8.5	9.2		15.2	Long-Term Debt	10.8	12.5
.0	.0	.2	.6		.3	Deferred Taxes	.2	.2
7.6	10.4	4.3	2.5		.7	All Other Non-Current	3.3	4.8
5.8	28.8	26.6	37.2		32.3	Net Worth	32.6	25.0
100.0	100.0	100.0	100.0		100.0	Total Liabilties & Net Worth	100.0	100.0
						INCOME DATA		
100.0	100.0	100.0	100.0		100.0	Net Sales	100.0	100.0
38.7	32.5	22.1	24.3		23.6	Gross Profit	28.1	28.5
41.0	31.0	20.5	21.5		19.9	Operating Expenses	26.0	26.7
-2.3	1.5	1.6	2.8		3.7	Operating Profit	2.1	1.8
.9	.9	-.3	.2		.7	All Other Expenses (net)	.1	.1
-3.2	.6	1.8	2.6		3.0	Profit Before Taxes	1.9	1.7
						RATIOS		
2.8	2.0	1.7	1.8		1.3		2.1	1.8
1.1	1.5	1.3	1.4		1.3	Current	1.4	1.3
.8	1.1	1.0	1.1		1.3		1.1	1.1
1.0	.9	.8	.7		.9		1.1	.8
.7	.7	.5	.5		.6	Quick	.6	.5
.2	.5	.3	.3		.4		.4	.4
8 45.4	14 25.7	28 12.8	21 17.6		25 14.4		20 18.1	20 18.3
15 24.9	22 16.6	36 10.1	31 11.8		36 10.1	Sales/Receivables	33 11.1	33 11.0
23 15.8	31 11.8	42 8.7	45 8.2		54 6.8		44 8.3	46 7.9
16 22.5	34 10.6	55 6.7	46 7.9		67 5.4		46 7.9	48 7.7
40 9.0	64 5.7	71 5.1	71 5.1		71 5.1	Cost of Sales/Inventory	67 5.4	68 5.4
56 6.5	75 4.9	86 4.3	100 3.6		101 3.6		89 4.1	93 3.9
21 17.8	15 24.2	39 9.3	28 13.3		35 10.4		27 13.5	32 11.3
39 9.3	37 9.9	61 6.0	46 7.9		53 6.9	Cost of Sales/Payables	52 7.0	55 6.7
70 5.2	57 6.4	77 4.7	71 5.2		67 5.5		76 4.8	81 4.5
9.2	8.5	9.0	7.7		9.5		7.5	8.1
53.5	14.0	18.2	14.1		15.1	Sales/Working Capital	14.3	16.5
-56.7	44.4	91.8	41.2		31.4		49.6	76.1
9.4	5.1	9.4	8.0		10.9		10.0	10.9
(10) 3.8	(29) 2.1	(58) 3.5	(47) 4.8		2.9	EBIT/Interest	(144) 3.8	(170) 4.4
-2.3	.5	1.2	2.3		1.8		1.7	1.7
		6.0	4.4			Net Profit + Depr., Dep.,	5.4	8.4
	(21) 1.8	1.8	(18) 2.5			Amort./Cur. Mat. L/T/D	(46) 2.2	(56) 2.8
		.7	1.2				1.0	1.4
.4	.1	.2	.2		.2		.2	.2
1.1	.4	.4	.5		.9	Fixed/Worth	.6	.5
NM	1.5	1.1	1.3		1.9		1.2	1.3
1.3	1.1	1.6	.9		2.3		1.0	1.3
4.1	2.2	3.6	2.2		2.6	Debt/Worth	2.3	2.5
NM	6.2	5.3	4.0		3.2		5.3	5.7
64.2	41.1	38.7	34.1		67.0	% Profit Before Taxes/Tangible	28.7	36.2
(10) 10.8	(26) 6.0	(58) 20.0	(50) 19.7		(10) 20.2	Net Worth	(142) 16.8	(167) 16.3
-26.2	.2	6.9	8.5		7.6		6.2	6.3
10.8	7.2	9.6	8.9		14.1	% Profit Before Taxes/Total	9.2	9.4
4.1	2.1	4.6	5.0		4.4	Assets	4.5	4.0
-19.0	-1.0	.5	2.5		1.9		1.3	1.2
47.1	59.1	68.9	34.3		40.9		44.2	47.2
18.5	29.5	30.9	18.7		16.5	Sales/Net Fixed Assets	23.2	25.6
14.3	10.8	13.7	8.0		5.7		11.3	12.4
5.6	4.2	3.8	3.3		2.8		3.7	3.6
4.3	3.4	3.2	2.9		2.2	Sales/Total Assets	3.1	3.0
3.6	2.7	2.5	2.4		2.2		2.4	2.3
.7	.5	.4	.6		.6		.6	.7
(10) 1.3	(28) 1.1	(58) .8	(46) 1.1		(10) 1.1	% Depr., Dep., Amort./Sales	(140) 1.1	(164) 1.1
2.0	2.1	1.4	1.7		1.7		1.7	1.9
		2.8	1.0		.7	% Officers', Directors'	1.2	1.2
	(18) 3.9	(22) 1.4	(12) .9			Owners' Comp/Sales	(63) 2.9	(75) 2.4
		5.3	2.1		2.7		5.9	4.6
16477M	131535M	961334M	3468678M	812706M	4214484M	Net Sales ($)	5131183M	5543145M
3568M	38573M	310994M	1209888M	368273M	1544075M	Total Assets ($)	1977439M	2207185M

M = $ thousand   MM = $ million
See Pages 11 through 21 for Explanation of Ratios and Data

Comparative Historical Data | Current Data Sorted by Sales

Period groupings (current): 36 (4/1–9/30/06) · 137 (10/1/06–3/31/07)

19 / 48 / 38 / 25 / 42 (hist.)			Type of Statement	0-1MM	1-3MM	3-5MM	5-10MM	10-25MM	25MM & OVER
4/1/04-3/31/05 ALL	4/1/05-3/31/06 ALL	4/1/06-3/31/07 ALL							
19	16	17	Unqualified				1		16
48	41	38	Reviewed		3	1	6	14	14
38	40	36	Compiled		3	3	11	6	13
25	18	25	Tax Returns	4	8	2	5	4	2
42	69	57	Other	2	5	4	4	16	26
172	184	173	**NUMBER OF STATEMENTS**	6	19	10	27	40	71
%	%	%	**ASSETS**	%	%	%	%	%	%
6.8	6.4	6.0	Cash & Equivalents		7.3	15.1	4.6	5.3	4.4
27.8	27.9	26.2	Trade Receivables (net)		17.7	22.0	27.3	29.9	26.9
38.2	41.3	39.8	Inventory		37.6	30.8	45.2	42.8	39.9
2.3	3.0	3.1	All Other Current		4.8	8.3	1.1	3.6	2.4
75.1	78.6	75.1	Total Current		67.4	76.2	78.1	81.7	73.7
17.5	15.7	19.2	Fixed Assets (net)		26.7	19.4	16.9	13.7	19.6
3.1	1.8	1.8	Intangibles (net)		2.2	1.7	.2	.9	2.7
4.3	3.8	3.8	All Other Non-Current		3.7	2.8	4.7	3.7	4.0
100.0	100.0	100.0	Total		100.0	100.0	100.0	100.0	100.0
			LIABILITIES						
13.8	12.3	12.9	Notes Payable-Short Term		13.1	8.1	12.4	14.2	13.7
2.1	2.4	3.0	Cur. Mat.-L.T.D.		2.7	3.9	4.1	3.2	2.4
35.0	34.3	32.7	Trade Payables		33.2	27.3	34.5	38.1	30.6
.2	.2	.2	Income Taxes Payable		.0	.5	.1	.2	.2
7.2	6.9	6.3	All Other Current		4.9	8.0	9.5	5.5	5.7
58.3	56.1	55.0	Total Current		53.9	47.9	60.6	61.2	52.6
9.0	9.0	10.9	Long-Term Debt		17.2	16.7	7.7	5.3	9.6
.3	.2	.3	Deferred Taxes		.0	.1	.2	.1	.5
4.3	2.5	4.9	All Other Non-Current		15.9	4.4	6.6	4.2	2.2
28.1	32.2	28.9	Net Worth		13.0	30.8	24.9	29.2	35.2
100.0	100.0	100.0	Total Liabilties & Net Worth		100.0	100.0	100.0	100.0	100.0
			INCOME DATA						
100.0	100.0	100.0	Net Sales		100.0	100.0	100.0	100.0	100.0
29.3	26.8	26.0	Gross Profit		35.9	29.3	22.6	24.8	23.5
27.5	23.8	24.1	Operating Expenses		35.9	29.1	21.9	22.0	20.7
1.8	3.0	1.9	Operating Profit		-.1	.2	.8	2.8	2.9
.1	.1	.3	All Other Expenses (net)		1.0	-.4	-.3	.2	.3
1.6	2.9	1.6	Profit Before Taxes		-1.1	.6	1.0	2.7	2.6
			RATIOS						
1.7 / 1.3 / 1.1	1.9 / 1.3 / 1.2	1.8 / 1.3 / 1.1	Current		1.8 / 1.4 / .8	4.1 / 1.6 / 1.1	1.7 / 1.2 / 1.0	1.7 / 1.3 / 1.0	1.7 / 1.3 / 1.1
.8 / (171) .6 / .4	.9 / (183) .6 / .4	.8 / .5 / .4	Quick		.8 / .5 / .2	1.9 / .9 / .6	.7 / .5 / .4	.8 / .5 / .3	.7 / .5 / .4
22 16.7 / 33 11.0 / 45 8.1	24 15.0 / 34 10.9 / 45 8.1	20 18.6 / 31 11.8 / 42 8.6	Sales/Receivables		6 57.0 / 15 24.0 / 29 12.6	16 22.7 / 30 12.3 / 47 7.7	22 16.7 / 30 12.2 / 40 9.0	27 13.6 / 37 9.9 / 44 8.3	24 15.0 / 33 10.9 / 45 8.2
47 7.7 / 66 5.5 / 84 4.4	54 6.8 / 70 5.2 / 93 3.9	46 7.9 / 68 5.4 / 87 4.2	Cost of Sales/Inventory		41 9.0 / 67 5.4 / 87 4.2	42 8.8 / 67 5.4 / 80 4.6	46 8.0 / 72 5.1 / 83 4.4	51 7.2 / 66 5.5 / 89 4.1	51 7.2 / 70 5.2 / 100 3.6
35 10.5 / 57 6.4 / 79 4.6	33 11.2 / 57 6.4 / 78 4.7	33 11.0 / 50 7.3 / 71 5.2	Cost of Sales/Payables		23 16.1 / 47 7.7 / 74 4.9	12 29.7 / 29 12.6 / 74 4.9	31 11.9 / 45 8.1 / 76 4.8	39 9.3 / 61 6.0 / 73 5.0	34 10.8 / 53 6.8 / 71 5.2
9.3 / 16.7 / 49.8	7.9 / 13.7 / 28.1	8.6 / 16.8 / 50.5	Sales/Working Capital		9.7 / 26.3 / -33.0	7.4 / 9.5 / 48.8	11.4 / 19.3 / 439.5	8.9 / 17.2 / 95.4	8.4 / 16.7 / 41.7
10.7 / (151) 4.0 / 1.9	16.4 / (172) 5.6 / 2.4	8.0 / (160) 3.4 / 1.6	EBIT/Interest		5.0 / (17) 2.2 / -.2		7.8 / 1.8 / .6	9.3 / (37) 4.0 / 1.4	8.3 / (66) 4.2 / 2.3
6.6 / (61) 2.5 / 1.9	8.6 / (51) 3.1 / 1.9	4.8 / (49) 2.3 / 1.3	Net Profit + Depr., Dep., Amort./Cur. Mat. L/T/D					10.3 / (13) 2.2 / .9	5.2 / (25) 2.7 / 1.6
.2 / .5 / 1.4	.2 / .4 / .9	.2 / .5 / 1.4	Fixed/Worth		.2 / .5 / UND	.1 / .5 / 1.3	.2 / .4 / 1.5	.2 / .4 / .9	.2 / .5 / 1.3
1.4 / 2.6 / 6.0	1.1 / 2.3 / 4.8	1.3 / 2.6 / 5.1	Debt/Worth		1.4 / 4.1 / -144.4	1.0 / 3.2 / 9.8	1.3 / 3.5 / 6.5	1.4 / 2.4 / 4.0	1.1 / 2.4 / 4.0
32.4 / (152) 15.7 / 7.9	39.6 / (176) 21.0 / 10.4	38.0 / (158) 19.0 / 4.4	% Profit Before Taxes/Tangible Net Worth		64.2 / (14) 5.4 / -4.9		39.5 / (25) 10.0 / -.2	39.3 / (37) 23.0 / 7.5	35.2 / (68) 22.0 / 9.1
8.8 / 4.2 / 1.4	12.1 / 6.0 / 2.8	9.1 / 4.5 / .8	% Profit Before Taxes/Total Assets		8.7 / 1.2 / -2.8	10.9 / 4.1 / 1.0	7.0 / 1.6 / -.8	12.6 / 5.2 / .7	9.7 / 5.3 / 3.1
50.5 / 25.5 / 11.1	58.0 / 26.0 / 12.8	54.8 / 24.8 / 10.8	Sales/Net Fixed Assets		68.8 / 22.3 / 8.2	134.0 / 18.3 / 7.6	55.2 / 37.3 / 12.7	70.9 / 30.7 / 14.2	41.0 / 21.8 / 8.0
3.8 / 2.8 / 2.3	3.7 / 3.0 / 2.3	3.8 / 3.1 / 2.4	Sales/Total Assets		5.0 / 3.4 / 2.3	3.6 / 2.8 / 2.2	4.2 / 3.6 / 2.7	3.9 / 3.3 / 2.7	3.3 / 2.9 / 2.2
.6 / (144) 1.1 / 1.7	.5 / (157) 1.0 / 1.6	.5 / (156) 1.0 / 1.6	% Depr., Dep., Amort./Sales		.7 / (17) 1.3 / 2.2		.4 / (26) .8 / 1.4	.4 / (37) .7 / 1.4	.5 / (64) 1.0 / 1.6
1.2 / (75) 2.3 / 5.1	.8 / (60) 1.8 / 3.0	.9 / (62) 2.0 / 4.5	% Officers', Directors' Owners' Comp/Sales		1.9 / (11) 4.1 / 5.2		1.4 / (13) 3.3 / 9.5	1.0 / (17) 1.3 / 2.0	.5 / (14) .7 / 2.0
6390529M	7747927M	9605214M	Net Sales ($)	4376M	37564M	37930M	205402M	699070M	8620872M
2547027M	3186374M	3475371M	Total Assets ($)	2634M	14251M	17333M	68229M	258503M	3114421M

M = $ thousand   MM = $ million
See Pages 11 through 21 for Explanation of Ratios and Data

Current Data Sorted by Assets							Comparative Historical Data	
						Type of Statement		
			4	1		Unqualified	1	5
	3	12	2			Reviewed	16	12
3	5	5				Compiled	11	10
6	12					Tax Returns	18	12
2	8	2	4	1		Other	16	13
16 (4/1-9/30/06)		54 (10/1/06-3/31/07)					4/1/02-3/31/03 ALL	4/1/03-3/31/04 ALL
0-500M	500M-2MM	2-10MM	10-50MM	50-100MM	100-250MM			
11	28	19	10	2		NUMBER OF STATEMENTS	62	52
%	%	%	%	%	%	**ASSETS**	%	%
7.4	5.6	9.9	2.7		DATA NOT AVAILABLE	Cash & Equivalents	4.9	7.2
10.6	13.9	23.3	27.4			Trade Receivables (net)	17.1	16.6
47.6	47.0	41.0	36.0			Inventory	41.4	46.5
.5	3.8	2.0	3.6			All Other Current	1.7	2.0
66.1	70.3	76.2	69.7			Total Current	65.0	72.3
28.1	20.3	14.2	11.4			Fixed Assets (net)	24.9	21.3
1.0	1.5	3.0	2.2			Intangibles (net)	4.1	2.5
4.9	7.8	6.6	16.7			All Other Non-Current	6.0	3.9
100.0	100.0	100.0	100.0			Total	100.0	100.0
						LIABILITIES		
12.4	7.6	11.1	18.8			Notes Payable-Short Term	17.4	16.3
.5	3.6	1.8	1.1			Cur. Mat.-L.T.D.	4.9	6.9
6.2	14.0	16.1	14.4			Trade Payables	10.4	10.6
.3	.0	.4	.2			Income Taxes Payable	.1	.0
31.4	10.5	5.6	7.0			All Other Current	12.4	14.0
50.8	35.8	35.0	41.6			Total Current	45.1	47.8
25.9	20.8	11.4	3.7			Long-Term Debt	14.6	18.4
.0	.1	.2	.3			Deferred Taxes	.2	.0
4.8	7.0	3.9	3.4			All Other Non-Current	4.7	3.1
18.5	36.2	49.6	51.0			Net Worth	35.4	30.7
100.0	100.0	100.0	100.0			Total Liabilities & Net Worth	100.0	100.0
						INCOME DATA		
100.0	100.0	100.0	100.0			Net Sales	100.0	100.0
45.7	42.2	29.0	32.7			Gross Profit	42.1	41.6
44.8	39.4	22.6	27.6			Operating Expenses	40.8	38.1
.9	2.8	6.4	5.1			Operating Profit	1.3	3.5
.4	.3	.6	.1			All Other Expenses (net)	.8	.4
.4	2.5	5.8	5.0			Profit Before Taxes	.5	3.0
						RATIOS		
8.1	4.0	4.0	1.8				2.6	2.9
3.0	2.3	2.2	1.6			Current	1.5	1.6
2.2	1.4	1.6	1.5				1.0	1.2
2.1	1.3	2.2	.9				1.0	.9
1.1	.6	.7	.5			Quick	(61) .5	(51) .6
.1	.1	.5	.3				.2	.2
0 UND	**10** 37.0	**10** 38.1	**10** 35.1				**7** 53.5	**3** 113.1
2 177.2	**22** 16.6	**28** 13.3	**43** 8.6			Sales/Receivables	**25** 14.8	**21** 17.4
24 15.5	**27** 13.6	**52** 7.0	**88** 4.2				**34** 10.8	**34** 10.7
36 10.2	**59** 6.2	**43** 8.6	**47** 7.8				**51** 7.2	**60** 6.1
102 3.6	**86** 4.2	**85** 4.3	**128** 2.9			Cost of Sales/Inventory	**108** 3.4	**103** 3.5
291 1.3	**153** 2.4	**122** 3.0	**164** 2.2				**148** 2.5	**197** 1.9
0 UND	**6** 63.7	**7** 52.4	**18** 20.1				**6** 59.9	**4** 93.9
4 91.3	**20** 18.0	**15** 24.9	**52** 7.0			Cost of Sales/Payables	**20** 18.5	**17** 21.2
17 21.1	**57** 6.4	**57** 6.4	**59** 6.2				**33** 11.2	**49** 7.4
5.0	4.1	3.4	4.6				5.7	5.3
9.5	7.7	6.5	7.7			Sales/Working Capital	12.7	8.2
38.3	21.0	17.1	12.3				-618.5	22.2
	6.2	13.1	8.1				6.3	7.3
	(25) 2.2	(15) 9.0	3.8			EBIT/Interest	(58) 3.4	(50) 4.3
	1.1	1.8	1.2				1.0	1.3
							3.0	
						Net Profit + Depr., Dep., Amort./Cur. Mat. L/T/D	(13) 1.7	
							.9	
.1	.2	.1	.1				.2	.2
.4	.4	.1	.2			Fixed/Worth	.6	.4
-1.6	2.2	.5	.4				1.9	1.2
.3	1.0	.5	.4				.8	1.0
.9	2.0	.9	1.6			Debt/Worth	1.6	1.9
-6.0	3.9	2.7	2.2				7.3	4.2
	23.6	50.0	30.3				25.3	48.2
	(25) 11.1	(18) 19.1	19.4			% Profit Before Taxes/Tangible Net Worth	(52) 12.2	(45) 17.0
	3.9	8.6	2.1				1.1	3.6
24.4	15.2	22.6	14.8				9.8	13.0
10.4	4.0	8.1	9.1			% Profit Before Taxes/Total Assets	3.7	5.2
-3.5	.8	2.6	.6				-1.3	1.0
52.3	42.2	191.4	85.0				36.0	46.8
17.1	24.2	37.8	19.4			Sales/Net Fixed Assets	14.8	18.5
8.9	9.7	11.7	7.6				5.8	9.1
4.8	3.7	3.7	2.2				3.5	3.9
3.3	3.0	2.7	1.9			Sales/Total Assets	2.5	2.5
1.5	1.7	1.6	1.2				1.7	1.7
	.8	.2					.8	.9
	(25) 1.1	(16) 1.0				% Depr., Dep., Amort./Sales	(56) 1.5	(42) 1.8
	1.9	1.8					3.2	3.5
	2.9						2.8	4.3
	(20) 4.5					% Officers', Directors' Owners' Comp/Sales	(30) 5.7	(23) 7.1
	8.2						10.2	10.2
12677M	112660M	264458M	310495M	482359M		Net Sales ($)	1313761M	1108505M
3295M	37402M	96534M	167854M	106530M		Total Assets ($)	660255M	491545M

M = $ thousand MM = $ million

See Pages 11 through 21 for Explanation of Ratios and Data

Comparative Historical Data | Current Data Sorted by Sales

2 8 14 13 11 4/1/04-3/31/05 ALL	7 12 12 18 17 4/1/05-3/31/06 ALL	5 17 13 18 17 4/1/06-3/31/07 ALL	Type of Statement	0-1MM	16 (4/1-9/30/06) 1-3MM	3-5MM	5-10MM	54 (10/1/06-3/31/07) 10-25MM	25MM & OVER
2	7	5	Unqualified			4	5	1	4
8	12	17	Reviewed		2	4	1	8	1
14	12	13	Compiled	3	8	4	4	2	
13	18	18	Tax Returns	3	4			3	
11	17	17	Other	1	1		2	2	3
48	66	70	**NUMBER OF STATEMENTS**	7	15	12	12	16	8
%	%	%	**ASSETS**	%	%	%	%	%	%
5.9	6.8	6.7	Cash & Equivalents		6.3	4.6	9.7	6.8	
18.2	18.2	18.2	Trade Receivables (net)		11.0	12.6	18.2	22.1	
44.5	43.9	43.9	Inventory		39.5	53.0	37.5	46.4	
1.9	2.6	2.8	All Other Current		.4	.7	8.2	2.8	
70.6	71.6	71.6	Total Current		57.2	70.9	73.6	78.0	
21.0	21.9	18.2	Fixed Assets (net)		32.8	16.4	20.2	9.4	
3.4	2.1	2.0	Intangibles (net)		3.2	.1	4.3	1.6	
5.0	4.5	8.2	All Other Non-Current		6.9	12.7	1.9	11.0	
100.0	100.0	100.0	Total		100.0	100.0	100.0	100.0	
			LIABILITIES						
14.1	12.8	11.6	Notes Payable-Short Term		7.7	9.2	11.2	12.0	
2.7	3.7	2.2	Cur. Mat.-L.T.D.		3.1	3.1	2.0	2.0	
12.5	11.6	13.8	Trade Payables		8.9	17.2	7.9	21.3	
.0	.2	.2	Income Taxes Payable		.1	.0	.1	.2	
8.4	9.6	11.9	All Other Current		9.7	5.0	8.9	6.3	
37.9	38.0	39.6	Total Current		29.6	34.5	30.2	41.8	
23.7	19.7	16.0	Long-Term Debt		34.9	22.5	9.8	6.4	
.0	.3	.1	Deferred Taxes		.0	.3	.2	.1	
5.1	5.7	5.1	All Other Non-Current		4.7	4.6	4.6	3.6	
33.3	36.4	39.2	Net Worth		30.9	38.1	55.2	48.1	
100.0	100.0	100.0	Total Liabilities & Net Worth		100.0	100.0	100.0	100.0	
			INCOME DATA						
100.0	100.0	100.0	Net Sales		100.0	100.0	100.0	100.0	
38.3	40.5	36.9	Gross Profit		49.5	32.9	36.5	33.9	
33.1	36.8	33.1	Operating Expenses		46.3	29.8	31.0	28.1	
5.2	3.7	3.8	Operating Profit		3.3	3.1	5.5	5.9	
1.1	1.0	.4	All Other Expenses (net)		-.3	.8	.4	.6	
4.1	2.7	3.4	Profit Before Taxes		3.5	2.3	5.1	5.3	
			RATIOS						
3.0	3.7	3.6	Current		6.7	3.7	12.0	2.2	
1.8	1.9	2.2			2.9	2.2	3.1	1.9	
1.3	1.4	1.5			1.1	1.7	1.4	1.5	
1.0	1.2	1.3	Quick		2.1	1.0	4.8	.8	
(47) .5	(65) .5	.7			.7	.5	1.2	.6	
.3	.3	.3			.1	.2	.6	.2	
7 50.2	10 34.9	8 47.4	Sales/Receivables	2 177.2	10 37.4	3 118.9	7 56.1		
21 17.0	26 14.3	23 16.1		13 28.8	15 24.8	20 18.4	37 10.0		
40 9.2	41 8.9	35 10.4		25 14.6	27 13.6	29 12.6	56 6.5		
60 6.0	58 6.3	46 7.9	Cost of Sales/Inventory	67 5.4	68 5.3	37 9.9	68 5.4		
97 3.8	95 3.8	88 4.1		102 3.6	94 3.9	68 5.3	88 4.2		
178 2.1	195 1.9	140 2.6		166 2.2	193 1.9	95 3.8	139 2.6		
7 51.1	7 51.5	5 75.7	Cost of Sales/Payables	0 UND	5 70.4	1 433.1	14 26.5		
20 18.4	17 20.9	17 20.9		17 21.1	32 11.3	11 32.7	52 7.0		
39 9.4	49 7.4	52 7.0		51 7.1	63 5.8	20 18.1	73 5.0		
4.4	3.7	4.1	Sales/Working Capital		5.0	3.5	3.7	4.8	
7.4	7.4	7.7			9.3	6.5	8.7	7.7	
15.0	18.3	17.4			56.8	14.3	16.8	17.2	
8.4	7.5	8.9	EBIT/Interest		7.6	6.9		11.3	
(45) 4.8	(59) 3.0	(60) 3.8			3.6	(11) 1.9		(13) 8.7	
1.3	1.2	1.5			1.3	1.2		3.1	
	6.3	3.2	Net Profit + Depr., Dep., Amort./Cur. Mat. L/T/D						
	(13) 2.8	(12) 1.7							
	1.3	1.0							
.2	.1	.1	Fixed/Worth		.2	.1	.2	.0	
.4	.3	.3			2.1	.3	.3	.1	
3.6	1.5	.9			4.2	.6	.9	.4	
1.1	.7	.5	Debt/Worth		.9	.7	.1	.5	
2.1	1.9	1.5			2.4	1.4	1.0	1.2	
6.3	3.5	3.0			16.8	4.2	2.0	2.5	
57.3	37.3	34.3	% Profit Before Taxes/Tangible Net Worth		60.8	34.3	17.3	44.7	
(41) 22.5	(59) 10.4	(63) 13.6		(12) 12.9	(11) 7.5	(11) 13.6	(15) 18.4		
4.0	1.7	4.5			10.8	-1.2	6.9	8.6	
16.9	11.7	19.2	% Profit Before Taxes/Total Assets		20.6	21.6	14.1	26.5	
3.9	4.4	7.0			7.4	3.2	5.3	11.8	
.5	.3	1.1			2.3	.0	1.9	3.5	
66.8	48.5	55.9	Sales/Net Fixed Assets		24.3	47.1	44.7	217.3	
20.0	17.4	24.3			12.6	28.3	23.8	48.0	
8.5	9.2	11.0			5.6	15.6	8.2	16.2	
3.6	3.3	3.8	Sales/Total Assets		3.5	3.7	4.4	3.7	
2.5	2.4	2.7			2.6	2.9	3.2	2.7	
1.7	1.5	1.7			1.7	1.6	2.1	1.5	
.6	.7	.6	% Depr., Dep., Amort./Sales		.9	.3	.7	.3	
(39) 1.6	(53) 1.4	(59) 1.0		(11) 2.0	1.0	(11) 1.5	(11) .9		
4.1	2.3	2.0			7.3	1.5	1.8	1.8	
3.5	2.7	2.3	% Officers', Directors' Owners' Comp/Sales				2.8		
(20) 5.8	(30) 5.2	(37) 4.3				(10) 3.9			
10.0	8.0	9.9				8.3			
438155M	1318431M	1182649M	Net Sales ($)	3682M	25531M	49541M	91840M	255639M	756416M
160423M	522663M	411615M	Total Assets ($)	2918M	12684M	22778M	35898M	121513M	215824M

© RMA 2007

M = $ thousand   MM = $ million

See Pages 11 through 21 for Explanation of Ratios and Data

Current Data Sorted by Assets   Comparative Historical Data

	0-500M	500M-2MM	2-10MM	10-50MM	50-100MM	100-250MM	Type of Statement	4/1/02-3/31/03 ALL	4/1/03-3/31/04 ALL
		1	18	21	4	1	Unqualified	35	45
	1	12	52	13	1		Reviewed	71	75
	5	15	18	2			Compiled	52	62
	9	14	3				Tax Returns	18	31
	7	23	31	27		1	Other	61	62
		45 (4/1-9/30/06)		234 (10/1/06-3/31/07)					
NUMBER OF STATEMENTS	22	65	122	63	5	2		237	275
	%	%	%	%	%	%	**ASSETS**	%	%
	13.3	8.3	7.5	6.1			Cash & Equivalents	9.7	8.2
	31.4	34.2	42.9	37.9			Trade Receivables (net)	38.2	36.9
	24.7	38.5	25.6	32.0			Inventory	29.9	30.2
	7.3	2.7	4.3	2.8			All Other Current	3.1	3.1
	76.8	83.6	80.3	78.8			Total Current	80.9	78.5
	19.2	10.1	11.8	10.5			Fixed Assets (net)	11.8	13.1
	1.4	.8	2.6	4.5			Intangibles (net)	1.4	1.8
	2.7	5.4	5.2	6.2			All Other Non-Current	6.0	6.6
	100.0	100.0	100.0	100.0			Total	100.0	100.0
							LIABILITIES		
	14.1	24.8	14.2	21.1			Notes Payable-Short Term	16.2	16.3
	1.4	1.8	1.7	1.4			Cur. Mat.-L.T.D.	2.3	2.1
	16.5	24.0	21.7	17.2			Trade Payables	20.6	21.2
	.0	.3	.2	.2			Income Taxes Payable	.2	.3
	16.0	15.3	18.4	17.0			All Other Current	15.4	17.0
	48.0	66.2	56.2	56.9			Total Current	54.7	56.9
	8.3	7.2	6.8	7.8			Long-Term Debt	7.4	8.0
	.0	.1	.1	.3			Deferred Taxes	.1	.1
	8.3	6.4	5.2	5.3			All Other Non-Current	5.0	4.5
	35.3	20.2	31.8	29.8			Net Worth	32.8	30.5
	100.0	100.0	100.0	100.0			Total Liabilities & Net Worth	100.0	100.0
							INCOME DATA		
	100.0	100.0	100.0	100.0			Net Sales	100.0	100.0
	33.2	30.5	27.8	28.2			Gross Profit	28.9	28.9
	30.4	28.2	25.0	23.7			Operating Expenses	27.6	27.0
	2.8	2.3	2.8	4.5			Operating Profit	1.3	1.9
	.5	1.0	.5	.4			All Other Expenses (net)	.3	.3
	2.4	1.3	2.3	4.2			Profit Before Taxes	1.0	1.6
							RATIOS		
	4.8	2.0	2.1	1.8				2.0	2.1
	1.5	1.3	1.4	1.4			Current	1.5	1.3
	.9	1.0	1.1	1.1				1.1	1.1
	2.9	1.1	1.2	1.2				1.3	1.2
	1.0	.6	1.0	.7			Quick	.9	.9
	.5	.4	.6	.5				.6	.5
	3 126.5	18 20.8	32 11.4	27 13.4				23 15.6	22 16.6
	19 19.3	34 10.8	45 8.2	44 8.4			Sales/Receivables	38 9.7	37 9.8
	50 7.3	45 8.1	54 6.7	64 5.7				56 6.5	51 7.1
	0 UND	19 19.0	9 41.1	21 17.6				11 31.9	12 31.1
	0 UND	53 6.9	26 13.9	54 6.8			Cost of Sales/Inventory	36 10.1	38 9.7
	81 4.5	143 2.5	78 4.7	93 3.9				86 4.2	88 4.1
	0 UND	16 22.6	16 22.7	15 23.7				13 27.9	16 23.1
	15 24.2	30 12.3	25 14.3	25 14.6			Cost of Sales/Payables	25 14.7	25 14.6
	26 13.9	48 7.5	42 8.6	38 9.5				43 8.5	44 8.3
	7.1	6.4	8.2	8.0				7.3	9.0
	30.5	19.7	15.8	14.2			Sales/Working Capital	15.0	17.9
	-105.5	NM	46.5	56.6				42.3	92.0
	8.8	5.1	10.0	10.1				8.0	11.1
	(17) 5.5	(60) 1.8	(116) 4.5	(56) 3.3			EBIT/Interest	(207) 2.3	(248) 3.1
	1.4	.8	1.6	1.7				.4	.6
			15.0	26.5				9.8	8.6
		(20) 3.5	(14) 5.6				Net Profit + Depr., Dep., Amort./Cur. Mat. L/T/D	(62) 2.8	(53) 2.5
			.8	1.1				.9	.1
	.0	.1	.1	.1				.1	.1
	.4	.3	.3	.5			Fixed/Worth	.3	.3
	3.4	NM	.9	1.4				1.2	1.0
	.3	1.1	1.1	1.2				1.0	1.1
	2.3	3.0	2.3	2.9			Debt/Worth	2.0	2.6
	NM	-42.4	6.3	11.7				5.7	6.4
	75.6	59.2	48.9	59.7				32.0	37.8
	(17) 37.1	(48) 23.2	(106) 27.5	(56) 34.0			% Profit Before Taxes/Tangible Net Worth	(210) 12.8	(248) 15.8
	14.0	8.9	7.3	7.8				.8	2.2
	26.6	16.6	14.7	17.8				10.7	11.4
	13.5	3.1	7.1	5.4			% Profit Before Taxes/Total Assets	3.2	3.9
	4.3	-.4	1.8	2.1				-1.3	-.6
	229.6	133.3	120.0	96.3				106.8	91.7
	56.9	53.9	59.0	47.3			Sales/Net Fixed Assets	45.6	41.9
	19.4	25.2	21.8	22.5				23.9	20.4
	6.6	4.4	4.8	3.6				4.5	4.6
	4.2	3.4	3.7	2.8			Sales/Total Assets	3.4	3.5
	2.8	2.3	2.6	2.3				2.6	2.6
	.3	.2	.3	.4				.3	.4
	(13) .4	(50) .4	(101) .6	(57) .6			% Depr., Dep., Amort./Sales	(209) .7	(223) .7
	1.4	.9	.9	.8				1.1	1.1
	2.0	2.2	1.3	.6				1.8	1.8
	(13) 5.6	(36) 3.7	(41) 2.1	(10) 1.2			% Officers', Directors' Owners' Comp/Sales	(110) 2.9	(107) 3.4
	8.7	5.8	4.5	2.9				5.6	5.6
	31923M	270304M	2137359M	4007003M	914314M	545175M	Net Sales ($)	6014937M	6550326M
	6607M	74769M	568917M	1384104M	354325M	229035M	Total Assets ($)	1775488M	1960598M

© RMA 2007

M = $ thousand   MM = $ million
See Pages 11 through 21 for Explanation of Ratios and Data

Comparative Historical Data | | | Type of Statement | Current Data Sorted by Sales

			Type of Statement						
46	34	45	Unqualified		1	1	3	7	33
79	68	79	Reviewed	1	4	6	12	32	24
36	31	40	Compiled	4	4	10	9	9	4
30	27	26	Tax Returns	2	12	4	6	2	
87	100	89	Other	5	13	9	11	21	30
4/1/04-3/31/05 ALL	4/1/05-3/31/06 ALL	4/1/06-3/31/07 ALL		0-1MM	1-3MM	3-5MM	5-10MM	10-25MM	25MM & OVER
				45 (4/1-9/30/06)			234 (10/1/06-3/31/07)		
278	260	279	NUMBER OF STATEMENTS	12	34	30	41	71	91
%	%	%	**ASSETS**	%	%	%	%	%	%
7.4	7.1	7.7	Cash & Equivalents	10.4	13.9	7.2	4.8	9.9	4.8
37.6	40.3	38.5	Trade Receivables (net)	22.4	26.2	33.7	38.2	43.1	43.4
31.7	30.8	30.1	Inventory	22.8	41.8	37.7	30.6	25.4	27.5
3.3	2.3	3.9	All Other Current	13.1	1.9	2.1	5.0	3.8	3.6
80.0	80.5	80.2	Total Current	68.7	83.9	80.7	78.6	82.2	79.2
11.3	11.5	11.9	Fixed Assets (net)	25.4	12.5	11.2	14.8	10.0	10.2
1.7	2.2	2.5	Intangibles (net)	3.3	.1	.6	1.5	2.7	4.1
7.0	5.8	5.5	All Other Non-Current	2.5	3.6	7.4	5.1	5.1	6.4
100.0	100.0	100.0	Total	100.0	100.0	100.0	100.0	100.0	100.0
			LIABILITIES						
17.0	17.4	18.5	Notes Payable-Short Term	25.5	17.4	22.5	16.7	13.9	21.0
1.9	2.0	1.7	Cur. Mat.-L.T.D.	2.0	.7	.9	3.8	1.6	1.3
20.7	19.7	20.6	Trade Payables	16.9	18.1	19.9	23.6	22.8	19.1
.3	.2	.2	Income Taxes Payable	.0	.5	.2	.2	.1	.2
17.2	16.4	17.1	All Other Current	19.2	17.4	12.2	17.5	16.0	18.9
57.1	55.7	58.0	Total Current	63.6	54.1	55.8	61.8	54.4	60.5
8.5	7.6	7.2	Long-Term Debt	12.5	8.4	6.0	7.7	6.0	7.0
.3	.1	.1	Deferred Taxes	.0	.0	.1	.1	.2	.2
5.1	5.8	5.7	All Other Non-Current	8.5	8.2	5.3	5.0	6.1	4.5
29.0	30.7	29.0	Net Worth	15.4	29.2	32.7	25.5	33.3	27.7
100.0	100.0	100.0	Total Liabilities & Net Worth	100.0	100.0	100.0	100.0	100.0	100.0
			INCOME DATA						
100.0	100.0	100.0	Net Sales	100.0	100.0	100.0	100.0	100.0	100.0
29.4	29.6	28.9	Gross Profit	31.0	35.1	30.1	29.1	28.9	25.8
26.8	26.6	25.8	Operating Expenses	33.1	32.9	27.3	25.5	24.8	22.7
2.6	3.0	3.1	Operating Profit	-2.2	2.2	2.8	3.6	4.1	3.2
.4	.3	.6	All Other Expenses (net)	.6	1.1	.6	.9	.3	.5
2.2	2.6	2.5	Profit Before Taxes	-2.7	1.1	2.2	2.6	3.7	2.7
			RATIOS						
2.2	2.2	2.1	Current	2.0	2.8	2.7	2.1	2.3	1.7
1.4	1.4	1.4		1.1	1.5	1.4	1.3	1.4	1.3
1.1	1.2	1.1		.8	1.1	1.0	1.0	1.1	1.1
1.2	1.3	1.2	Quick	1.1	1.8	1.1	1.0	1.3	1.1
(277) .9	.9	.8		.6	.6	.7	.8	1.0	.8
.5	.5	.5		.1	.3	.5	.5	.7	.5
24 15.3	27 13.4	24 15.2	Sales/Receivables	12 29.5	2 195.1	19 19.0	26 13.9	28 13.1	33 11.2
39 9.3	41 9.0	42 8.7		23 16.1	25 14.7	40 9.2	43 8.4	42 8.8	46 8.0
56 6.5	59 6.2	55 6.6		54 6.7	50 7.3	48 7.6	54 6.8	54 6.8	64 5.7
15 23.8	13 28.8	12 30.4	Cost of Sales/Inventory	0 UND	6 61.5	25 14.6	19 19.4	8 45.2	14 26.0
39 9.3	38 9.5	38 9.5		0 UND	81 4.5	76 4.8	49 7.5	25 14.8	31 11.9
94 3.9	93 3.9	94 3.9		85 4.3	202 2.4	153 2.4	67 3.3	67 5.5	77 4.7
15 24.3	14 26.2	15 23.8	Cost of Sales/Payables	9 38.9	8 45.5	14 25.7	17 21.0	16 22.4	15 24.5
26 13.8	25 14.5	26 14.3		23 16.0	28 13.2	25 14.6	27 13.4	27 13.7	21 17.0
42 8.7	40 9.2	42 8.8		59 6.2	44 8.2	38 9.7	48 7.6	45 8.1	36 10.2
7.4	6.8	7.9	Sales/Working Capital	3.6	5.9	5.4	7.8	7.9	10.0
14.9	15.0	15.4		UND	10.6	9.5	15.4	16.4	16.2
47.9	31.6	75.8		-18.8	65.7	-325.8	192.9	47.2	75.8
12.7	11.9	9.6	EBIT/Interest	6.3	8.1	5.0	11.6	9.9	11.0
(246) 4.0	(234) 4.0	(256) 3.4		(10) .7	(28) 1.8	(26) 1.7	(39) 4.5	(67) 4.5	(86) 3.8
1.3	1.4	1.3		-2.5	.8	.6	1.4	1.5	2.1
12.6	8.8	13.4	Net Profit + Depr., Dep., Amort./Cur. Mat. L/T/D					36.5	15.8
(54) 4.4	(41) 3.2	(43) 3.5					(13) 3.5		(22) 5.9
1.5	.9	1.1						.4	1.2
.1	.1	.1	Fixed/Worth	.0	.1	.1	.2	.1	.1
.3	.3	.3		2.1	.3	.2	.4	.3	.3
1.0	1.1	1.2		-2.4	NM	1.1	1.5	.8	1.4
.9	1.0	1.1	Debt/Worth	1.3	.6	.7	1.0	1.0	1.3
2.2	2.2	2.5		NM	1.6	2.5	2.7	2.3	2.9
6.4	7.7	11.1		-28.1	-30.8	12.3	9.8	6.2	10.3
46.6	53.0	53.2	% Profit Before Taxes/Tangible Net Worth		67.1	38.1	80.1	45.5	62.0
(244) 20.3	(226) 25.2	(234) 26.5			(25) 34.0	(26) 13.1	(34) 29.5	(62) 31.7	(81) 32.7
4.3	4.0	8.3			8.9	3.2	13.2	5.8	10.8
13.6	16.4	16.4	% Profit Before Taxes/Total Assets	11.1	24.0	15.3	16.9	16.6	15.7
5.5	6.3	6.2		-.9	6.3	2.9	8.5	7.0	6.2
.7	.9	1.0		-22.7	-.2	-.5	1.0	1.9	2.5
86.2	95.4	112.3	Sales/Net Fixed Assets	UND	229.6	183.5	80.7	120.2	104.1
41.7	48.8	52.7		30.4	38.5	57.2	35.0	68.4	55.0
20.7	21.2	21.5		5.3	13.1	17.7	20.3	26.4	23.3
4.2	4.5	4.4	Sales/Total Assets	3.6	4.1	4.3	4.2	5.0	4.4
3.3	3.4	3.3		1.9	2.8	2.9	3.4	3.7	3.4
2.5	2.4	2.4		1.5	2.1	1.9	2.3	2.7	2.5
.4	.3	.3	% Depr., Dep., Amort./Sales		.2	.1	.4	.3	.4
(224) .7	(215) .6	(228) .5			(24) .4	(21) .4	(34) .6	(60) .5	(81) .5
1.0	.9	.9			1.0	.8	1.0	1.0	.8
1.9	1.5	1.6	% Officers', Directors' Owners' Comp/Sales		2.3	2.0	2.1	1.2	.8
(108) 3.3	(100) 2.0	(101) 2.8			(19) 4.2	(18) 2.9	(20) 3.5	(25) 1.6	(16) 1.5
5.6	5.4	5.2			7.9	5.1	5.9	3.3	4.8
8607017M	6741256M	7906078M	Net Sales ($)	7939M	68156M	115031M	307997M	1108403M	6298552M
2768532M	2124201M	2617757M	Total Assets ($)	4627M	26070M	47921M	103372M	333845M	2101922M

Current Data Sorted by Assets   **Comparative Historical Data**

0-500M	500M-2MM	2-10MM	10-50MM	50-100MM	100-250MM	Type of Statement	4/1/02-3/31/03 ALL	4/1/03-3/31/04 ALL
1	3	19	27	5	5	Unqualified	41	52
2	7	36	25			Reviewed	67	73
2	18	21	3			Compiled	45	65
6	26	16	2			Tax Returns	24	34
4	16	38	56	5	5	Other	77	74
	50 (4/1-9/30/06)		298 (10/1/06-3/31/07)					
15	70	130	113	10	10	NUMBER OF STATEMENTS	254	298
%	%	%	%	%	%	**ASSETS**	%	%
18.2	11.1	8.3	4.5	6.4	11.2	Cash & Equivalents	6.4	7.3
23.8	29.2	34.7	31.9	22.5	24.9	Trade Receivables (net)	32.8	31.9
32.8	39.2	39.7	41.5	45.1	32.2	Inventory	39.8	39.0
1.8	2.0	2.3	2.6	1.7	1.5	All Other Current	2.6	2.9
76.7	81.6	85.0	80.5	75.8	69.8	Total Current	81.5	81.2
9.5	11.9	8.1	10.3	10.5	8.1	Fixed Assets (net)	11.5	11.6
.6	.9	1.5	3.1	8.8	20.6	Intangibles (net)	2.5	2.5
13.2	5.6	5.4	6.1	4.8	1.5	All Other Non-Current	4.5	4.7
100.0	100.0	100.0	100.0	100.0	100.0	Total	100.0	100.0
						LIABILITIES		
14.3	13.7	14.4	22.5	11.9	15.9	Notes Payable-Short Term	16.0	15.4
.2	2.3	2.0	1.5	2.2	3.0	Cur. Mat.-L.T.D.	3.6	2.2
11.2	19.5	22.4	18.8	18.3	10.7	Trade Payables	21.8	21.9
.0	.5	.2	.2	.2	.1	Income Taxes Payable	.3	.2
25.4	11.6	10.7	10.5	11.5	12.2	All Other Current	10.4	12.8
51.1	47.5	49.7	53.5	44.2	41.9	Total Current	52.0	52.6
19.4	9.6	6.1	4.9	6.9	15.3	Long-Term Debt	9.1	8.3
.0	.0	.1	.1	.7	.3	Deferred Taxes	.1	.1
9.7	9.0	6.0	5.7	9.0	5.6	All Other Non-Current	4.6	6.7
19.8	33.8	38.1	35.8	39.3	36.9	Net Worth	34.2	32.2
100.0	100.0	100.0	100.0	100.0	100.0	Total Liabilties & Net Worth	100.0	100.0
						INCOME DATA		
100.0	100.0	100.0	100.0	100.0	100.0	Net Sales	100.0	100.0
46.5	33.8	29.3	28.1	32.5	39.8	Gross Profit	31.4	32.6
38.0	29.9	26.5	22.7	25.5	32.1	Operating Expenses	28.3	29.1
8.5	3.9	2.8	5.4	7.1	7.7	Operating Profit	3.0	3.5
1.2	.8	1.0	1.2	4.2	4.7	All Other Expenses (net)	.5	.7
7.3	3.0	1.8	4.2	2.9	3.0	Profit Before Taxes	2.5	2.8
						RATIOS		
12.8	2.9	2.6	2.1	2.9	2.0	Current	2.4	2.3
1.8	1.9	1.7	1.5	1.8	1.8		1.6	1.6
.8	1.3	1.2	1.2	1.1	1.5		1.3	1.2
5.1	1.4	1.5	1.0	1.3	1.3	Quick	1.3	1.2
1.0	.9	.8	.7	.6	.8		.7	.7
.3	.5	.5	.5	.3	.5		.5	.5
4 82.5	23 16.1	33 11.1	30 12.0	31 11.6	30 12.1	Sales/Receivables	29 12.5 / 28 12.9	
26 14.1	35 10.5	43 8.5	40 9.1	36 10.1	53 6.9		38 9.6 / 40 9.2	
51 7.1	48 7.6	57 6.4	59 6.2	51 7.2	63 5.8		55 6.7 / 58 6.3	
0 UND	23 15.6	37 9.9	48 7.7	84 4.3	58 6.3	Cost of Sales/Inventory	38 9.6 / 43 8.5	
52 7.0	77 4.7	72 5.1	89 4.1	105 3.5	102 3.6		72 5.1 / 73 5.0	
131 2.8	160 2.3	124 2.9	122 3.0	174 2.1	164 2.2		123 3.0 / 126 2.9	
0 UND	17 22.0	16 22.7	14 26.6	20 18.2	17 22.1	Cost of Sales/Payables	18 20.5 / 20 18.6	
10 36.0	37 9.8	30 12.3	28 13.1	39 9.4	37 10.0		32 11.3 / 35 10.5	
28 13.2	55 6.6	58 6.3	47 7.7	87 4.2	48 7.6		55 6.7 / 59 6.2	
3.4	5.5	4.8	6.2	4.4	3.8	Sales/Working Capital	5.2	5.4
8.7	7.7	8.5	10.9	9.2	6.5		10.0	9.9
-49.5	17.4	17.3	24.5	NM	17.6		23.9	23.8
24.6	14.2	9.3	10.9		4.4	EBIT/Interest	11.9	10.7
(11) 4.8	(62) 2.7	(117) 3.2	(106) 3.6		3.1		(230) 3.6 / (269) 3.7	
-1.7	1.2	1.4	1.7		.2		1.5	1.4
		13.7	20.7			Net Profit + Depr., Dep., Amort./Cur. Mat. L/T/D	12.0	9.0
	(22) 8.2		(35) 3.8				(58) 4.5 / (62) 3.6	
		1.0	1.8				1.3	1.2
.0	.1	.1	.1	.1	.0	Fixed/Worth	.1	.1
.0	.2	.2	.2	.3	.5		.2	.2
3.9	1.0	.4	.8	.3	-.6		.7	.8
.4	.7	.8	1.0	.6	1.3	Debt/Worth	.9	1.2
1.5	1.6	1.9	2.3	1.2	2.1		2.1	2.3
-32.9	5.7	4.1	5.4	2.3	-4.6		4.0	4.9
119.9	34.4	36.9	51.6			% Profit Before Taxes/Tangible Net Worth	41.6	43.7
(11) 48.6	(63) 16.9	(122) 16.4	(100) 31.0				(233) 19.2 / (268) 19.2	
26.4	2.2	3.4	9.5				5.3	5.3
33.5	14.7	13.3	19.2	19.3	14.4	% Profit Before Taxes/Total Assets	12.8	13.5
20.5	5.5	4.5	6.9	7.3	3.1		5.4	4.7
-18.8	.9	.9	2.3	.8	-4.6		1.4	.7
UND	132.7	127.4	102.6	69.2	UND	Sales/Net Fixed Assets	94.4	90.2
85.3	33.9	49.9	57.8	20.3	23.4		48.0	43.2
16.0	21.7	28.2	21.6	14.2	13.4		20.0	19.0
4.4	3.9	3.6	3.6	2.8	3.3	Sales/Total Assets	3.9	3.7
3.4	2.8	2.8	2.6	2.2	1.5		3.0	2.9
2.3	1.9	2.0	1.9	1.3	1.2		2.1	2.0
	.2	.2	.3			% Depr., Dep., Amort./Sales	.4	.4
	(51) .8	(115) .5	(103) .5				(210) .7 / (246) .7	
	1.3	.9	.9				1.1	1.1
	2.3	1.4	.7			% Officers', Directors' Owners' Comp/Sales	1.5	2.0
	(46) 4.3	(62) 2.2	(40) 1.6				(117) 3.3 / (143) 3.6	
	6.5	4.1	2.6				7.5	6.2
17712M	280781M	1939141M	6595461M	1429545M	4229348M	Net Sales ($)	7510151M	8648537M
4939M	89578M	654193M	2378484M	688704M	1580440M	Total Assets ($)	2980970M	3625644M

© RMA 2007

M = $ thousand   MM = $ million
See Pages 11 through 21 for Explanation of Ratios and Data

Comparative Historical Data | Current Data Sorted by Sales

Hist 1	Hist 2	Hist 3	Type of Statement	0-1MM	1-3MM	3-5MM	5-10MM	10-25MM	25MM & OVER
53	55	60	Unqualified	1	1	2	4	14	38
74	60	70	Reviewed	1	2	7	9	22	29
39	37	44	Compiled	2	7	6	13	12	4
32	34	50	Tax Returns	4	14	10	14	6	2
78	103	124	Other	2	11	9	12	20	70
4/1/04-3/31/05 ALL	4/1/05-3/31/06 ALL	4/1/06-3/31/07 ALL		50 (4/1-9/30/06)			298 (10/1/06-3/31/07)		
276	289	348	NUMBER OF STATEMENTS	10	35	34	52	74	143
%	%	%	**ASSETS**	%	%	%	%	%	%
7.2	6.7	8.1	Cash & Equivalents	16.7	16.3	7.5	9.0	8.4	5.1
32.1	32.0	31.6	Trade Receivables (net)	15.6	22.9	28.0	33.0	34.1	33.9
39.7	39.4	39.8	Inventory	38.7	40.2	44.8	38.1	37.1	40.7
2.5	3.0	2.3	All Other Current	2.0	1.0	2.4	2.5	2.6	2.3
81.5	81.1	81.8	Total Current	73.0	80.4	82.8	82.6	82.2	82.0
11.1	10.2	9.7	Fixed Assets (net)	12.9	10.2	12.4	9.0	10.1	8.8
2.2	2.7	2.6	Intangibles (net)	.0	1.0	1.2	1.9	2.2	4.1
5.3	6.1	5.9	All Other Non-Current	14.1	8.5	3.6	6.6	5.5	5.1
100.0	100.0	100.0	Total	100.0	100.0	100.0	100.0	100.0	100.0
			LIABILITIES						
18.5	17.1	16.8	Notes Payable-Short Term	14.9	16.5	12.7	13.6	16.0	19.6
2.9	2.0	1.9	Cur. Mat.-L.T.D.	1.1	.5	4.4	1.5	1.7	1.8
22.1	20.9	19.7	Trade Payables	12.8	15.5	24.3	21.1	20.2	19.4
.2	.2	.2	Income Taxes Payable	.0	.0	1.0	.1	.2	.2
9.9	11.2	11.5	All Other Current	34.4	6.4	8.5	12.7	12.3	11.1
53.7	51.4	50.2	Total Current	63.2	38.9	50.9	49.0	50.3	52.2
8.9	10.7	7.3	Long-Term Debt	12.0	12.8	10.6	6.9	5.5	5.9
.2	.2	.1	Deferred Taxes	.0	.0	.0	.0	.2	.2
6.0	6.9	6.7	All Other Non-Current	5.4	9.1	12.7	7.0	5.2	5.5
31.2	30.8	35.7	Net Worth	19.4	39.2	25.7	37.0	38.7	36.3
100.0	100.0	100.0	Total Liabilities & Net Worth	100.0	100.0	100.0	100.0	100.0	100.0
			INCOME DATA						
100.0	100.0	100.0	Net Sales	100.0	100.0	100.0	100.0	100.0	100.0
31.3	31.2	31.0	Gross Profit	40.4	40.5	34.2	28.3	31.2	28.1
28.0	27.4	26.6	Operating Expenses	33.9	34.0	32.9	25.6	27.2	22.8
3.3	3.8	4.4	Operating Profit	6.5	6.5	1.3	2.6	3.9	5.3
.5	.8	1.3	All Other Expenses (net)	4.0	2.0	.6	.8	.5	1.6
2.8	3.0	3.1	Profit Before Taxes	2.5	4.5	.7	1.8	3.4	3.7
			RATIOS						
2.4	2.4	2.6	Current	2.3	4.2	3.3	2.4	2.6	2.1
1.5	1.6	1.7		1.5	2.3	1.7	1.8	1.7	1.6
1.2	1.2	1.2		.8	1.5	1.2	1.3	1.2	1.2
1.2	1.2	1.3	Quick	1.7	1.7	1.2	1.4	1.5	1.2
(275) .7	.7	.7		.5	.9	.7	.8	.7	.7
.5	.5	.5		.2	.3	.4	.5	.5	.5
28 13.1	29 12.7	28 12.9	Sales/Receivables	7 50.6	7 49.7	31 11.8	27 13.6	33 11.1	30 12.0
41 9.0	40 9.2	40 9.1		26 14.0	31 11.8	43 8.5	41 8.9	42 8.7	40 9.1
56 6.6	53 6.8	56 6.5		43 8.4	48 7.6	56 6.5	53 6.9	59 6.2	58 6.3
43 8.5	41 8.8	38 9.5	Cost of Sales/Inventory	0 UND	21 17.6	51 7.1	30 12.1	37 9.8	42 8.8
72 5.1	72 5.1	79 4.6		107 3.4	124 2.9	127 2.9	78 4.7	70 5.2	76 4.8
127 2.9	124 3.0	128 2.8		381 1.0	210 1.7	190 1.9	111 3.3	133 2.8	108 3.4
18 20.6	18 20.4	15 24.6	Cost of Sales/Payables	2 167.0	11 32.7	22 16.3	14 25.6	14 25.9	16 22.1
32 11.5	32 11.4	29 12.5		19 18.8	29 12.7	41 9.0	29 12.4	29 12.6	29 12.8
58 6.3	53 6.9	53 6.9		89 4.1	79 4.6	87 4.2	58 6.3	52 7.0	46 7.9
5.5	5.5	5.0	Sales/Working Capital	2.5	3.2	4.3	5.8	4.8	6.3
10.6	9.8	9.1		10.3	5.9	6.7	8.4	9.2	11.3
23.9	22.1	19.9		-20.7	8.7	17.0	17.1	17.0	22.9
13.0	10.5	10.1	EBIT/Interest		11.2	5.3	8.4	9.2	13.4
(249) 4.7	(262) 3.7	(314) 3.4			(29) 3.5	(31) 2.5	(49) 2.3	(64) 3.4	(134) 3.8
1.6	1.4	1.5			1.2	1.3	1.0	1.6	1.7
21.1	11.6	17.9	Net Profit + Depr., Dep., Amort./Cur. Mat. L/T/D					11.9	20.6
(72) 5.0	(61) 3.8	(70) 3.8						(17) 3.8	(41) 4.8
1.7	1.2	1.1						2.1	1.4
.1	.1	.1	Fixed/Worth	.0	.1	.0	.1	.1	.1
.2	.2	.2		.1	.2	.3	.2	.2	.2
.7	.5	.5		.7	1.4	1.1	.5	.5	.5
.9	.9	.8	Debt/Worth	1.1	.5	.7	.8	.7	1.0
2.1	2.3	1.9		1.7	.8	3.9	1.8	1.9	1.9
4.9	5.1	4.7		15.3	5.3	9.4	5.4	3.9	3.8
43.2	46.8	43.9	% Profit Before Taxes/Tangible Net Worth		38.7	34.1	35.4	43.6	50.4
(254) 21.5	(262) 21.8	(311) 18.7			(29) 22.0	(31) 14.1	(48) 13.1	(68) 16.9	(126) 31.0
5.3	5.5	5.9			6.2	2.5	.5	7.0	9.5
16.3	15.5	16.2	% Profit Before Taxes/Total Assets	21.9	18.8	10.5	9.6	14.1	20.2
6.2	5.3	5.8		3.8	7.4	3.3	3.4	5.9	7.3
1.3	1.1	1.2		-7.1	.8	.3	.0	2.0	2.3
107.1	106.2	112.8	Sales/Net Fixed Assets	UND	101.7	149.3	174.2	77.5	118.0
44.2	48.4	48.6		UND	42.4	27.6	49.5	41.2	58.6
20.3	21.9	23.1		15.0	22.3	11.7	27.3	22.8	24.3
3.8	3.8	3.8	Sales/Total Assets	3.5	3.4	3.6	3.6	3.7	4.0
2.9	2.8	2.8		1.3	2.4	2.2	3.0	2.8	3.0
2.1	2.0	1.9		.7	1.6	1.6	2.1	1.9	2.2
.3	.3	.3	% Depr., Dep., Amort./Sales		.2	.4	.2	.3	.3
(237) .6	(246) .6	(291) .6			(23) .5	(25) .9	(45) .5	(68) .6	(126) .5
1.1	1.0	1.0			1.6	1.4	1.0	1.0	.9
1.6	1.3	1.4	% Officers', Directors' Owners' Comp/Sales		2.3	2.0	1.8	1.2	.8
(123) 3.8	(122) 2.6	(156) 2.4			(20) 5.6	(21) 2.9	(32) 3.2	(35) 2.2	(45) 1.6
5.7	5.3	4.6			8.8	4.9	4.8	4.0	2.6
7807072M	10649498M	14491988M	Net Sales ($)	6312M	68607M	130539M	378168M	1153461M	12754901M
2910413M	3990779M	5396338M	Total Assets ($)	6858M	33675M	74218M	158569M	491988M	4631030M

M = $ thousand   MM = $ million
See Pages 11 through 21 for Explanation of Ratios and Data

Current Data Sorted by Assets   **Comparative Historical Data**

0-500M	500M-2MM	2-10MM	10-50MM	50-100MM	100-250MM	Type of Statement	4/1/02-3/31/03 ALL	4/1/03-3/31/04 ALL
	5	39	83	28	13	Unqualified	173	176
5	27	165	72	3	1	Reviewed	250	285
10	61	74	15			Compiled	150	232
15	38	34	5		1	Tax Returns	49	65
7	48	117	89	15	15	Other	212	201
	167 (4/1-9/30/06)		818 (10/1/06-3/31/07)					
37	179	429	264	46	30	**NUMBER OF STATEMENTS**	834	959
%	%	%	%	%	%	**ASSETS**	%	%
13.0	7.9	5.4	5.2	5.8	3.7	Cash & Equivalents	5.6	5.2
39.4	36.7	33.8	32.0	26.2	25.3	Trade Receivables (net)	34.3	36.4
17.1	33.3	36.8	34.0	34.1	27.1	Inventory	34.7	33.8
4.9	1.6	2.3	3.1	2.6	4.1	All Other Current	2.4	2.8
74.4	79.5	78.3	74.3	68.8	60.2	Total Current	77.1	78.2
13.9	12.9	15.0	17.8	20.9	21.8	Fixed Assets (net)	15.8	15.0
3.4	1.3	1.7	2.4	4.1	9.9	Intangibles (net)	1.4	1.6
8.3	6.3	5.1	5.5	6.3	8.0	All Other Non-Current	5.7	5.2
100.0	100.0	100.0	100.0	100.0	100.0	Total	100.0	100.0
						LIABILITIES		
26.2	18.7	20.2	21.1	16.7	15.4	Notes Payable-Short Term	21.3	21.5
1.4	3.1	2.5	2.1	2.1	1.7	Cur. Mat.-L.T.D.	2.8	2.6
14.3	17.5	13.9	12.2	11.8	11.4	Trade Payables	14.3	15.2
.3	.1	.3	.1	.1	.2	Income Taxes Payable	.2	.2
11.0	11.2	8.5	8.3	9.7	9.0	All Other Current	8.3	8.5
53.3	50.7	45.3	43.8	40.4	37.7	Total Current	46.9	48.0
11.4	8.2	8.6	9.7	13.8	14.3	Long-Term Debt	9.7	9.6
.0	.1	.2	.3	.6	.3	Deferred Taxes	.2	.2
6.4	5.1	5.3	2.3	2.6	5.0	All Other Non-Current	3.6	4.6
29.0	36.0	40.6	43.9	42.6	42.7	Net Worth	39.6	37.6
100.0	100.0	100.0	100.0	100.0	100.0	Total Liabilities & Net Worth	100.0	100.0
						INCOME DATA		
100.0	100.0	100.0	100.0	100.0	100.0	Net Sales	100.0	100.0
20.0	23.5	21.3	20.9	20.6	22.0	Gross Profit	21.0	20.2
18.0	21.1	18.6	17.4	16.4	17.9	Operating Expenses	18.7	18.2
2.0	2.4	2.6	3.4	4.2	4.1	Operating Profit	2.4	2.1
.7	.7	.5	.4	.3	1.2	All Other Expenses (net)	.5	.3
1.3	1.6	2.2	3.0	3.9	2.9	Profit Before Taxes	1.9	1.7
						RATIOS		
3.2	2.7	2.7	2.8	2.9	2.6		2.6	2.5
1.4	1.6	1.7	1.6	1.6	1.8	Current	1.6	1.6
.9	1.2	1.3	1.3	1.2	1.2		1.3	1.2
2.0	1.5	1.5	1.4	1.4	1.2		1.4	1.4
1.0	.9	.8	.8	.7	.8	Quick	.8	.8
.5	.5	.5	.5	.5	.6		.5	.6
13 28.6	20 18.2	22 16.5	25 14.4	17 21.0	23 16.0		23 16.1	25 14.8
22 16.5	29 12.7	32 11.3	34 10.8	30 12.0	31 11.8	Sales/Receivables	33 11.2	35 10.3
44 8.2	41 8.8	42 8.6	43 8.5	39 9.5	42 8.7		43 8.4	47 7.8
0 UND	16 23.4	29 12.5	32 11.5	39 9.5	33 11.0		27 13.5	27 13.6
4 103.0	42 8.7	46 8.0	45 8.2	49 7.5	48 7.6	Cost of Sales/Inventory	46 7.9	45 8.2
36 10.0	71 5.1	73 5.0	63 5.7	68 5.3	63 5.8		71 5.2	68 5.4
0 UND	9 41.5	8 44.9	9 39.7	9 41.6	10 35.7		8 44.8	9 41.6
9 39.3	17 21.8	15 24.3	14 26.4	14 26.0	18 20.7	Cost of Sales/Payables	14 25.9	16 22.8
30 12.2	29 12.6	24 15.3	21 17.4	22 16.9	24 15.3		25 14.4	26 14.3
5.9	6.5	6.9	6.5	7.2	5.8		6.7	6.8
34.0	13.5	10.8	12.1	12.8	10.8	Sales/Working Capital	12.6	12.2
-212.0	35.6	25.5	23.6	22.3	31.4		28.1	27.9
19.6	9.0	7.2	9.1	11.0	13.0		8.3	8.7
(29) 3.8	(164) 2.3	(410) 2.8	(251) 3.8	(45) 4.3	4.7	EBIT/Interest	(783) 3.1	(906) 3.4
1.3	.8	1.3	1.6	2.5	1.9		1.4	1.5
	4.8	8.9	13.3	12.3	3.4		8.2	6.5
	(31) 2.3	(101) 3.1	(106) 4.2	(20) 5.2	(11) 2.7	Net Profit + Depr., Dep., Amort./Cur. Mat. L/T/D	(231) 2.7	(267) 2.7
	1.0	1.2	1.9	2.5	.8		1.3	1.4
.0	.1	.1	.2	.3	.4		.1	.1
.2	.2	.3	.4	.5	.6	Fixed/Worth	.3	.3
2.0	.8	.7	.9	.9	3.1		.7	.7
.6	.8	.8	.7	.9	.6		.7	.8
1.7	1.7	1.6	1.6	1.8	1.4	Debt/Worth	1.7	1.8
79.9	5.3	3.5	2.9	2.6	16.9		3.3	4.0
121.9	42.1	35.5	33.9	46.3	35.6		30.4	30.1
(29) 42.3	(160) 12.8	(412) 15.9	(257) 19.2	(44) 20.7	(26) 21.9	% Profit Before Taxes/Tangible Net Worth	(783) 14.0	(904) 14.1
5.0	-.5	3.0	6.5	8.1	9.5		3.8	3.7
31.5	14.4	13.4	14.4	13.5	12.2		11.5	10.6
12.6	4.6	5.4	8.2	8.9	6.9	% Profit Before Taxes/Total Assets	4.9	4.5
1.4	-.7	1.1	1.9	3.7	1.0		1.0	1.0
UND	145.0	104.2	51.2	35.4	28.6		71.8	90.4
83.4	48.4	31.1	22.4	16.7	11.3	Sales/Net Fixed Assets	28.8	29.9
19.7	22.4	14.5	10.5	7.4	8.0		13.3	13.2
6.3	5.6	4.6	4.2	3.9	3.4		4.7	4.5
4.3	3.8	3.5	3.1	3.2	2.6	Sales/Total Assets	3.4	3.3
2.8	2.7	2.5	2.4	2.3	2.0		2.4	2.4
.3	.3	.4	.4	.4	.5		.4	.4
(24) .9	(137) .6	(387) .7	(252) .8	(45) .9	(26) .9	% Depr., Dep., Amort./Sales	(748) .8	(841) .7
1.8	1.4	1.2	1.2	1.5	1.2		1.1	1.4
1.9	1.6	1.2	.6				1.3	1.2
(11) 3.6	(91) 2.8	(185) 2.4	(62) 1.6			% Officers', Directors' Owners' Comp/Sales	(321) 2.3	(377) 2.3
5.1	3.7	2.6					4.1	4.1
65274M	1027350M	7954812M	20276461M	10369183M	15330303M	Net Sales ($)	33518828M	37478425M
11961M	221823M	2111293M	5816284M	3154271M	4630049M	Total Assets ($)	9925911M	10990805M

M = $ thousand   MM = $ million
See Pages 11 through 21 for Explanation of Ratios and Data

Comparative Historical Data | Current Data Sorted by Sales

			Type of Statement						
187	178	168	Unqualified			2	7	23	136
251	262	273	Reviewed	2	9	9	35	106	112
161	147	160	Compiled	4	23	21	36	49	27
80	62	93	Tax Returns	5	20	12	29	22	5
208	241	291	Other	4	17	21	45	66	138
4/1/04-3/31/05 ALL	4/1/05-3/31/06 ALL	4/1/06-3/31/07 ALL		0-1MM	167 (4/1-9/30/06) 1-3MM	3-5MM	818 (10/1/06-3/31/07) 5-10MM	10-25MM	25MM & OVER
887	890	985	**NUMBER OF STATEMENTS**	15	69	65	152	266	418
%	%	%	**ASSETS**	%	%	%	%	%	%
5.1	5.8	6.1	Cash & Equivalents	11.0	9.4	7.6	6.5	6.6	4.5
35.0	35.7	33.4	Trade Receivables (net)	24.9	30.3	30.5	35.3	33.2	34.2
35.0	34.3	34.3	Inventory	20.1	32.4	33.3	34.5	35.9	34.1
2.6	2.1	2.5	All Other Current	12.1	2.6	1.8	2.3	2.0	2.7
77.6	78.0	76.3	Total Current	68.1	74.8	73.1	78.5	77.7	75.6
15.1	14.7	15.8	Fixed Assets (net)	16.2	15.1	17.9	14.2	14.7	16.9
1.6	1.7	2.2	Intangibles (net)	2.6	2.8	2.1	1.5	2.1	2.5
5.7	5.7	5.7	All Other Non-Current	13.2	7.3	7.0	5.7	5.5	5.0
100.0	100.0	100.0	Total	100.0	100.0	100.0	100.0	100.0	100.0
			LIABILITIES						
21.1	21.1	20.1	Notes Payable-Short Term	25.8	22.2	17.7	17.5	20.0	20.8
2.5	2.1	2.4	Cur. Mat.-L.T.D.	8.0	2.8	2.1	3.1	2.1	2.2
15.5	15.4	13.9	Trade Payables	13.8	15.9	14.0	15.0	13.7	13.4
.2	.3	.2	Income Taxes Payable	.1	.3	.1	.2	.3	.2
8.7	9.8	9.1	All Other Current	8.8	12.4	10.9	8.8	8.2	9.0
48.1	48.7	45.7	Total Current	56.5	53.5	44.8	44.5	44.3	45.5
10.0	9.8	9.3	Long-Term Debt	9.5	12.4	11.4	9.8	8.1	9.1
.3	.2	.2	Deferred Taxes	.0	.0	.1	.1	.3	.3
3.9	4.3	4.3	All Other Non-Current	8.0	5.2	5.3	6.4	4.4	3.1
37.7	37.0	40.3	Net Worth	26.0	28.8	38.3	39.2	42.9	41.9
100.0	100.0	100.0	Total Liabilities & Net Worth	100.0	100.0	100.0	100.0	100.0	100.0
			INCOME DATA						
100.0	100.0	100.0	Net Sales	100.0	100.0	100.0	100.0	100.0	100.0
20.0	21.0	21.5	Gross Profit	29.4	26.0	25.4	23.1	21.0	19.6
17.1	17.8	18.6	Operating Expenses	23.9	23.9	23.8	20.5	18.4	16.2
2.9	3.2	2.9	Operating Profit	5.5	2.2	1.6	2.6	2.6	3.4
.3	.4	.5	All Other Expenses (net)	2.1	1.0	.5	.6	.5	.4
2.6	2.8	2.4	Profit Before Taxes	3.4	1.2	1.1	2.0	2.1	3.0
			RATIOS						
2.4	2.5	2.7	Current	1.5	2.5	3.9	2.6	3.1	2.5
1.6	1.6	1.6		1.3	1.5	1.6	1.8	1.7	1.6
1.2	1.2	1.2		.9	.9	1.2	1.3	1.3	1.3
1.3	1.4	1.5	Quick	1.0	1.3	1.6	1.6	1.6	1.4
.8	.9	.8		.9	.7	.9	.9	.9	.8
.5	.5	.5		.2	.3	.5	.5	.5	.6
23 15.8	23 15.8	23 16.2	Sales/Receivables	8 44.5	14 25.4	21 17.2	24 14.9	20 17.9	24 15.3
34 10.8	34 10.9	32 11.5		30 12.3	33 10.9	32 11.4	33 11.0	31 11.8	32 11.5
45 8.0	45 8.1	42 8.6		61 6.0	48 7.6	43 8.6	48 7.6	41 8.9	41 8.9
27 13.4	28 13.2	27 13.6	Cost of Sales/Inventory	0 UND	11 34.1	33 10.9	23 16.0	28 12.8	28 12.8
45 8.0	43 8.4	45 8.1		4 103.0	51 7.2	52 7.0	55 6.7	45 8.1	41 8.9
68 5.3	66 5.6	68 5.4		141 2.6	120 3.0	85 4.3	84 4.4	69 5.3	57 6.4
9 40.2	9 40.3	9 42.1	Cost of Sales/Payables	0 UND	7 49.6	10 37.4	10 37.0	8 47.8	9 41.1
16 22.9	16 22.4	15 24.5		21 17.5	19 19.6	17 21.8	18 20.5	14 26.3	14 26.7
26 13.8	27 13.8	24 15.4		36 10.0	44 8.4	29 12.5	29 12.4	23 15.7	21 17.4
7.1	7.4	6.8	Sales/Working Capital	4.9	5.2	5.7	6.2	6.7	7.6
13.1	13.0	11.8		5.7	10.2	11.2	9.6	10.9	13.8
27.3	26.5	28.9		-39.3	-41.4	30.8	25.6	27.9	26.3
12.2	10.0	8.6	EBIT/Interest		9.0	6.4	6.4	7.8	10.0
(834) 4.9	(829) 4.1	(929) 3.2			(63) 2.0	(61) 2.1	(142) 2.2	(249) 2.8	(406) 3.9
2.2	1.9	1.3			.4	.6	1.1	1.3	1.8
7.9	9.3	9.0	Net Profit + Depr., Dep., Amort./Cur. Mat. L/T/D			3.7	4.6	8.3	11.5
(260) 3.6	(234) 3.7	(272) 3.3				(13) 2.3	(24) 1.6	(71) 2.5	(155) 4.4
1.7	1.7	1.4				.7	.8	1.2	2.2
.1	.1	.1	Fixed/Worth	.0	.1	.1	.1	.1	.2
.3	.3	.3		.3	.3	.4	.3	.3	.4
.8	.7	.8		2.7	3.6	1.2	.8	.7	.8
.8	.9	.7	Debt/Worth	1.1	.7	.7	.8	.7	.8
1.8	1.7	1.6		9.1	2.6	1.9	1.6	1.5	1.7
3.7	3.7	3.5		13.3	79.9	7.4	3.4	3.1	3.1
40.6	43.4	37.7	% Profit Before Taxes/Tangible Net Worth	109.6	46.1	28.3	40.3	30.7	38.7
(839) 21.4	(831) 22.3	(928) 17.0		(13) 67.4	(53) 8.3	(60) 9.2	(140) 14.7	(258) 14.7	(404) 22.2
8.6	8.2	4.3		28.2	-6.1	-12.0	2.5	2.9	7.8
14.7	16.3	14.1	% Profit Before Taxes/Total Assets	23.5	14.4	13.7	12.7	13.0	14.7
7.0	7.5	6.0		9.4	3.3	3.3	3.7	5.8	8.4
2.6	2.4	1.3		5.5	-3.0	-2.4	.7	1.1	2.7
94.6	85.4	83.7	Sales/Net Fixed Assets	301.5	94.1	59.5	124.8	108.0	70.6
31.6	32.4	30.0		25.8	27.5	27.7	33.0	31.1	26.9
13.5	15.0	12.9		8.5	17.3	10.8	13.9	15.4	12.0
4.6	4.6	4.6	Sales/Total Assets	3.7	4.1	4.2	4.4	4.7	4.7
3.4	3.5	3.4		1.6	2.7	2.8	3.2	3.5	3.5
2.4	2.6	2.5		1.0	2.0	2.3	2.3	2.6	2.7
.3	.3	.4	% Depr., Dep., Amort./Sales	.8	.5	.6	.3	.3	.3
(754) .7	(785) .7	(871) .7		(10) 2.8	(50) .8	(53) .9	(129) .7	(236) .7	(393) .7
1.3	1.1	1.3		5.0	1.8	1.8	1.4	1.2	1.2
1.1	1.1	1.2	% Officers', Directors', Owners' Comp/Sales		1.9	2.6	1.6	1.1	.5
(337) 2.0	(320) 2.1	(352) 2.4			(31) 4.3	(31) 3.7	(85) 2.4	(111) 2.1	(93) 1.5
3.8	4.3	4.2			5.6	5.4	3.8	4.1	2.7
44340868M	47580276M	55023383M	Net Sales ($)	7792M	140203M	253973M	1110530M	4331903M	49178982M
12308659M	13435804M	15945681M	Total Assets ($)	7334M	57759M	94165M	382802M	1433542M	13970079M

© RMA 2007

M = $ thousand   MM = $ million
See Pages 11 through 21 for Explanation of Ratios and Data

Current Data Sorted by Assets / Comparative Historical Data

0-500M	500M-2MM	2-10MM	10-50MM	50-100MM	100-250MM	Type of Statement	39 / 4/1/02-3/31/03 ALL	37 / 4/1/03-3/31/04 ALL
	2	8	23	6	6	Unqualified	39	37
	7	53	18			Reviewed	73	73
4	24	33	3			Compiled	59	70
7	19	16	2			Tax Returns	25	35
9	25	41	28	6	1	Other	65	71
*56 (4/1-9/30/06)			*285 (10/1/06-3/31/07)					
20	77	151	74	12	7	**NUMBER OF STATEMENTS**	261	286
%	%	%	%	%	%	**ASSETS**	%	%
9.8	7.2	5.9	4.7	2.1		Cash & Equivalents	6.9	7.6
35.9	31.3	31.1	27.1	33.7		Trade Receivables (net)	29.4	30.1
25.5	33.8	36.0	34.1	25.9		Inventory	27.2	28.5
1.3	2.4	1.7	2.2	2.4		All Other Current	2.6	3.5
72.6	74.6	74.7	68.1	64.1		Total Current	66.1	69.7
19.9	17.7	18.8	23.5	26.5		Fixed Assets (net)	25.7	24.0
1.1	1.6	1.7	4.1	4.9		Intangibles (net)	2.2	1.8
6.5	6.1	4.8	4.3	4.4		All Other Non-Current	6.1	4.6
100.0	100.0	100.0	100.0	100.0		Total	100.0	100.0
						LIABILITIES		
13.3	11.5	14.1	14.1	12.9		Notes Payable-Short Term	13.9	11.6
3.0	3.6	2.4	3.3	3.3		Cur. Mat.-L.T.D.	4.4	3.6
16.1	24.1	22.4	19.3	18.1		Trade Payables	17.9	20.5
.2	.2	.3	.7	1.2		Income Taxes Payable	.3	.3
10.2	10.1	8.7	7.6	10.9		All Other Current	8.8	8.7
42.9	49.4	47.8	45.1	46.3		Total Current	45.3	44.6
18.0	13.1	9.1	17.1	15.5		Long-Term Debt	13.4	12.4
.0	.2	.3	.3	1.2		Deferred Taxes	.6	.4
18.0	3.2	3.8	5.0	3.8		All Other Non-Current	4.2	5.4
21.0	34.1	38.9	32.6	33.2		Net Worth	36.5	37.2
100.0	100.0	100.0	100.0	100.0		Total Liabilities & Net Worth	100.0	100.0
						INCOME DATA		
100.0	100.0	100.0	100.0	100.0		Net Sales	100.0	100.0
36.6	30.8	29.8	28.1	26.0		Gross Profit	30.0	31.2
30.7	26.0	25.6	23.4	18.6		Operating Expenses	26.3	27.5
5.8	4.8	4.2	4.7	7.4		Operating Profit	3.8	3.7
.9	.9	.1	1.0	.9		All Other Expenses (net)	.5	.5
4.9	3.9	4.1	3.7	6.5		Profit Before Taxes	3.2	3.2
						RATIOS		
3.3	2.3	2.3	2.3	2.0		Current	2.6	2.5
2.1	1.7	1.5	1.5	1.5			1.6	1.6
1.1	1.1	1.2	1.2	1.1			1.1	1.2
1.5	1.1	1.2	1.3	1.2		Quick	1.4	1.4
1.1	.8	.8	.7	.8			.8	.8
.7	.5	.5	.4	.6			.5	.6
13 27.2	19 19.5	29 12.7	32 11.5	35 10.3		Sales/Receivables	28 12.9	27 13.3
35 10.5	31 11.9	37 9.8	43 8.5	53 6.9			38 9.6	42 8.7
52 7.0	52 7.0	49 7.5	56 6.5	68 5.3			51 7.2	55 6.7
0 UND	23 16.2	40 9.1	39 9.4	22 16.3		Cost of Sales/Inventory	21 17.4	23 15.6
29 12.5	50 7.3	63 5.8	69 5.3	53 6.9			47 7.8	52 7.0
68 5.4	80 4.6	100 3.6	153 2.4	99 3.7			76 4.8	87 4.2
2 146.3	17 21.8	22 16.6	24 15.5	25 14.5		Cost of Sales/Payables	17 21.7	20 18.1
14 26.7	31 11.9	36 10.1	36 10.2	33 11.1			28 12.9	34 10.8
31 11.7	57 6.4	60 6.1	64 5.7	69 5.3			49 7.4	60 6.1
4.6	7.8	6.1	6.0	6.1		Sales/Working Capital	6.1	5.8
14.6	10.5	10.2	10.2	10.7			11.1	10.3
NM	98.2	22.6	26.3	43.7			32.6	27.2
24.6	17.2	14.4	8.6	10.5		EBIT/Interest	11.2	11.2
(17) 7.0	(69) 5.3	(135) 4.7	(70) 3.7	(11) 4.5			(242) 4.4	(263) 4.0
-1.3	2.3	1.7	1.0	3.6			1.6	1.6
		5.5	15.7			Net Profit + Depr., Dep., Amort./Cur. Mat. L/T/D	5.5	5.5
	(31) 2.9	(31) 4.1					(76) 2.9	(86) 2.0
		1.4	2.1				1.2	1.0
.1	.1	.2	.3	.5		Fixed/Worth	.2	.2
.7	.3	.4	.8	.7			.5	.6
1.5	1.0	.9	1.8	2.4			1.4	1.5
.7	.9	.8	1.2	1.4		Debt/Worth	.7	.8
4.0	1.8	2.0	2.6	2.6			1.8	2.1
11.5	5.6	3.7	5.7	6.7			5.2	4.7
136.9	82.5	47.6	44.9	139.3		% Profit Before Taxes/Tangible Net Worth	36.7	34.8
(17) 48.4	(71) 42.2	(144) 24.4	(68) 27.9	39.3			(243) 16.8	(268) 17.4
-20.0	10.6	6.5	6.5	30.6			5.2	5.1
87.5	24.9	17.3	15.8	15.3		% Profit Before Taxes/Total Assets	12.4	13.6
15.4	8.7	8.8	7.7	10.5			6.3	5.5
-10.5	2.5	1.8	.6	8.2			1.0	1.1
277.5	94.7	46.9	34.2	20.1		Sales/Net Fixed Assets	36.2	40.5
61.6	30.0	20.1	13.4	12.0			15.2	14.9
9.0	14.1	9.5	4.3	5.3			5.4	5.9
7.2	4.4	3.5	2.8	2.7		Sales/Total Assets	3.5	3.5
3.8	3.2	2.7	2.0	2.2			2.6	2.5
2.7	2.4	1.9	1.5	1.8			1.8	1.8
.3	.6	.6	.7	.5		% Depr., Dep., Amort./Sales	.9	.9
(12) .6	(56) 1.4	(134) 1.1	(66) 1.4	1.4			(237) 1.6	(241) 1.7
3.2	2.7	2.3	2.9	3.4			3.1	3.2
	1.9	1.9	1.2			% Officers', Directors' Owners' Comp/Sales	1.8	1.7
	(29) 3.2	(64) 2.6	(18) 1.5				(101) 3.3	(119) 3.0
	5.4	5.1	4.8				5.6	5.5
26193M	342202M	1930974M	3669324M	1845104M	2860805M	Net Sales ($)	4514090M	6530346M
5847M	97912M	703841M	1689524M	858499M	1185030M	Total Assets ($)	2246143M	3016236M

© RMA 2007

M = $ thousand   MM = $ million
See Pages 11 through 21 for Explanation of Ratios and Data

Comparative Historical Data   ## Current Data Sorted by Sales

4/1/04-3/31/05 ALL	4/1/05-3/31/06 ALL	4/1/06-3/31/07 ALL	Type of Statement	0-1MM	1-3MM	3-5MM	5-10MM	10-25MM	25MM & OVER
42	47	45	Unqualified				5	4	36
93	79	78	Reviewed		2	4	20	33	19
75	54	64	Compiled		15	13	14	17	5
29	35	44	Tax Returns	6	10	7	9	9	3
92	112	110	Other	2	16	19	20	20	33
					56 (4/1-9/30/06)		285 (10/1/06-3/31/07)		
331	327	341	NUMBER OF STATEMENTS	8	43	43	68	83	96
%	%	%	**ASSETS**	%	%	%	%	%	%
7.1	6.8	6.0	Cash & Equivalents		7.0	5.7	6.8	6.4	4.4
30.1	28.6	30.6	Trade Receivables (net)		23.7	33.5	30.0	33.0	31.0
30.9	31.8	33.7	Inventory		28.1	40.5	34.1	34.7	32.6
1.9	2.3	2.0	All Other Current		3.5	1.4	1.5	1.8	2.4
70.0	69.5	72.4	Total Current		62.2	81.0	72.4	75.9	70.4
22.4	21.8	20.0	Fixed Assets (net)		26.1	11.4	20.6	18.2	21.3
2.2	2.6	2.3	Intangibles (net)		3.2	1.1	2.2	1.0	3.8
5.4	6.1	5.3	All Other Non-Current		8.4	6.5	4.8	4.8	4.5
100.0	100.0	100.0	Total		100.0	100.0	100.0	100.0	100.0
			LIABILITIES						
13.2	12.9	13.4	Notes Payable-Short Term		11.6	11.3	14.5	14.2	14.3
2.9	2.9	3.0	Cur. Mat.-L.T.D.		5.1	3.1	2.3	2.8	2.5
20.5	23.6	21.4	Trade Payables		18.9	29.3	20.2	22.4	20.2
.2	.3	.4	Income Taxes Payable		.2	.2	.3	.2	.8
9.1	9.9	8.9	All Other Current		8.9	12.7	8.5	7.1	8.9
45.9	49.6	47.1	Total Current		44.7	56.5	45.7	46.7	46.6
12.9	13.1	12.7	Long-Term Debt		19.2	10.7	10.0	10.1	14.3
.4	.5	.3	Deferred Taxes		.1	.2	.5	.2	.5
4.7	4.3	4.7	All Other Non-Current		7.5	7.7	2.5	2.5	4.3
36.0	32.5	35.2	Net Worth		28.6	24.9	41.3	40.5	34.3
100.0	100.0	100.0	Total Liabilities & Net Worth		100.0	100.0	100.0	100.0	100.0
			INCOME DATA						
100.0	100.0	100.0	Net Sales		100.0	100.0	100.0	100.0	100.0
30.2	29.2	29.8	Gross Profit		38.0	32.9	28.8	26.8	27.9
25.6	24.6	25.0	Operating Expenses		32.3	27.9	25.3	22.2	22.5
4.6	4.6	4.8	Operating Profit		5.7	5.0	3.4	4.6	5.4
.3	.5	.6	All Other Expenses (net)		1.1	.3	-.1	.3	.7
4.3	4.1	4.2	Profit Before Taxes		4.6	4.6	3.5	4.2	4.7
			RATIOS						
2.2	2.1	2.3	Current		2.1	2.0	2.7	2.3	2.3
1.6	1.5	1.6			1.6	1.5	1.6	1.6	1.5
1.2	1.1	1.2			.9	1.2	1.2	1.2	1.2
1.3	1.2	1.2	Quick		1.1	1.1	1.4	1.2	1.3
.8	.7	.8			.6	.8	.8	.8	.7
.5	.5	.5			.3	.5	.5	.5	.5
31 11.7	28 13.1	27 13.3	Sales/Receivables		17 21.4	25 14.4	26 14.1	30 12.1	31 11.7
40 9.1	39 9.4	38 9.5			33 11.0	34 10.8	37 9.8	41 9.0	41 9.0
54 6.7	53 6.8	52 7.0			47 7.8	57 6.4	49 7.4	51 7.1	57 6.4
25 14.6	28 12.9	31 11.8	Cost of Sales/Inventory		11 34.3	45 8.1	35 10.5	30 12.2	35 10.3
57 6.4	58 6.3	55 6.7			42 8.8	75 4.9	52 7.1	55 6.7	56 6.5
94 3.9	101 3.6	100 3.7			86 4.2	135 2.7	100 3.7	92 3.9	96 3.8
20 18.3	21 17.2	20 18.0	Cost of Sales/Payables		15 24.9	27 13.4	16 22.3	20 18.5	24 15.3
35 10.3	35 10.3	33 11.0			37 10.0	49 7.5	30 12.1	31 11.9	33 11.0
62 5.9	64 5.7	60 6.1			84 4.4	106 3.4	55 6.7	54 6.8	58 6.3
5.9	6.5	6.5	Sales/Working Capital		7.6	6.5	6.3	7.0	6.1
10.1	11.4	10.3			20.7	10.8	10.0	9.9	11.1
23.7	33.0	31.7			-79.1	30.9	24.4	22.6	32.1
13.7	11.1	13.1	EBIT/Interest		19.4	15.6	9.8	15.0	12.0
(297) 5.4	(301) 4.7	(309) 4.7			(41) 4.9	(34) 3.9	(61) 4.2	(76) 5.7	(91) 4.4
1.9	2.1	1.8			1.2	1.6	1.0	2.3	1.9
6.5	9.7	8.9	Net Profit + Depr., Dep., Amort./Cur. Mat. L/T/D				6.1	15.9	10.3
(100) 2.7	(90) 4.3	(82) 4.1					(14) 2.1	(15) 4.1	(42) 4.4
1.5	2.0	2.0					1.3	1.6	3.2
.2	.2	.2	Fixed/Worth		.2	.0	.2	.2	.3
.5	.6	.5			.9	.4	.4	.4	.6
1.3	1.4	1.1			3.9	.8	.9	.9	1.3
.9	1.0	.9	Debt/Worth		1.0	1.2	.7	.7	1.2
1.9	2.0	2.1			2.8	3.0	1.6	1.7	2.6
3.9	5.1	4.7			8.5	11.4	3.5	3.4	4.2
45.6	56.1	59.5	% Profit Before Taxes/Tangible Net Worth		104.8	77.8	47.7	46.2	46.2
(301) 24.3	(289) 26.9	(319) 29.5			(38) 42.9	(37) 54.4	(66) 20.2	(81) 29.5	(90) 29.1
8.1	8.2	8.5			16.3	10.9	1.9	7.7	10.5
16.2	16.9	17.7	% Profit Before Taxes/Total Assets		25.1	20.1	17.6	17.4	16.6
7.0	8.2	9.3			10.3	8.7	6.0	10.7	10.0
2.2	2.4	2.2			.3	1.8	.5	2.6	2.9
44.1	43.5	53.3	Sales/Net Fixed Assets		56.9	208.6	41.6	49.7	38.2
16.0	17.4	19.8			15.1	38.3	19.6	22.2	18.5
6.7	6.9	8.4			6.6	9.7	9.7	10.1	6.7
3.3	3.5	3.5	Sales/Total Assets		3.5	3.6	3.7	3.9	3.3
2.5	2.6	2.7			2.7	2.5	2.7	2.9	2.6
1.7	1.8	1.9			1.6	1.9	2.0	2.0	1.7
.8	.7	.6	% Depr., Dep., Amort./Sales		.8	.1	.7	.6	.5
(279) 1.5	(270) 1.3	(284) 1.2			(33) 1.8	(25) .8	(64) 1.5	(73) .9	(84) 1.2
3.2	2.6	2.5			4.3	3.1	2.5	2.0	2.1
1.4	1.6	1.7	% Officers', Directors' Owners' Comp/Sales		2.9	2.1	2.2	1.2	1.1
(128) 3.1	(104) 3.1	(121) 2.9			(16) 4.2	(20) 3.1	(28) 4.1	(31) 2.1	(25) 2.0
5.8	5.4	5.7			7.4	5.0	6.6	4.3	5.2
7786414M	9807374M	10674602M	Net Sales ($)	4248M	87442M	177937M	486532M	1318722M	8599721M
3447364M	4602807M	4540653M	Total Assets ($)	2117M	53394M	74589M	199224M	523972M	3687357M

© RMA 2007

M = $ thousand   MM = $ million
See Pages 11 through 21 for Explanation of Ratios and Data

Current Data Sorted by Assets

Comparative Historical Data

						Type of Statement		
	1	6	14	7	1	Unqualified	20	24
	5	20	12	1		Reviewed	25	38
7	11	8	7			Compiled	32	38
2	4	5	1			Tax Returns	9	12
2	6	18	14		1	Other	35	55
	23 (4/1-9/30/06)		130 (10/1/06-3/31/07)				4/1/02-3/31/03	4/1/03-3/31/04
0-500M	500M-2MM	2-10MM	10-50MM	50-100MM	100-250MM		ALL	ALL
11	27	57	48	8	2	NUMBER OF STATEMENTS	121	167
%	%	%	%	%	%	ASSETS	%	%
11.2	11.5	6.0	4.4			Cash & Equivalents	6.6	5.9
30.2	33.2	42.2	39.7			Trade Receivables (net)	36.8	41.1
31.3	34.8	34.7	30.2			Inventory	29.6	28.9
2.0	2.6	2.5	2.5			All Other Current	3.3	2.5
74.8	82.1	85.4	76.8			Total Current	76.3	78.4
18.2	13.9	11.3	16.3			Fixed Assets (net)	15.6	13.5
.7	.6	1.0	2.1			Intangibles (net)	3.1	2.9
6.2	3.4	2.3	4.8			All Other Non-Current	5.0	5.2
100.0	100.0	100.0	100.0			Total	100.0	100.0
						LIABILITIES		
13.2	12.4	14.7	14.6			Notes Payable-Short Term	15.4	16.1
6.8	2.5	2.3	1.8			Cur. Mat.-L.T.D.	3.4	2.7
19.9	20.3	24.2	24.0			Trade Payables	25.4	29.1
.0	.3	.3	.1			Income Taxes Payable	.2	.3
11.5	6.5	10.6	8.9			All Other Current	7.1	7.2
51.5	42.0	52.0	49.4			Total Current	51.6	55.4
19.5	7.0	7.9	10.2			Long-Term Debt	8.7	8.5
.0	.2	.2	.1			Deferred Taxes	.2	.4
1.7	6.3	3.8	2.5			All Other Non-Current	2.3	4.2
27.3	44.5	36.1	37.9			Net Worth	37.2	31.5
100.0	100.0	100.0	100.0			Total Liabilties & Net Worth	100.0	100.0
						INCOME DATA		
100.0	100.0	100.0	100.0			Net Sales	100.0	100.0
32.7	27.7	22.4	25.8			Gross Profit	25.1	23.9
24.4	23.6	18.6	21.5			Operating Expenses	21.9	21.4
8.3	4.1	3.8	4.2			Operating Profit	3.2	2.6
-.5	.0	.5	.2			All Other Expenses (net)	.7	.2
8.7	4.1	3.3	4.1			Profit Before Taxes	2.5	2.4
						RATIOS		
8.6	3.9	2.0	2.2				2.2	2.0
1.9	1.8	1.7	1.5			Current	1.4	1.4
.6	1.4	1.4	1.1				1.1	1.1
3.3	1.9	1.4	1.3				1.2	1.2
.9	.9	.9	.9			Quick	.8	.8
.3	.6	.7	.6				.6	.6

											Sales/Receivables etc.				
0	UND	25	14.5	33	11.2	33	11.0				Sales/Receivables	33	11.2	32	11.3
36	10.1	34	10.7	44	8.3	45	8.1					45	8.0	44	8.3
41	8.9	53	6.9	60	6.1	61	6.0					57	6.4	56	6.5
0	UND	33	11.2	30	12.2	33	11.2				Cost of Sales/Inventory	28	13.0	27	13.4
63	5.8	61	6.0	49	7.5	48	7.6					46	7.9	43	8.5
93	3.9	89	4.1	68	5.4	68	5.4					70	5.2	63	5.8
0	UND	11	32.8	18	20.6	26	14.2				Cost of Sales/Payables	25	14.8	25	14.4
1	570.0	30	12.0	29	12.4	36	10.0					36	10.2	40	9.2
40	9.1	52	7.0	53	6.9	50	7.3					53	6.8	56	6.5

									Sales/Working Capital		
5.2		4.6		7.3		7.9			Sales/Working Capital	7.8	8.4
8.0		7.0		11.6		11.0				13.1	14.2
-17.5		18.0		15.6		44.5				35.9	49.6

										EBIT/Interest				
			15.7		16.3		15.8			EBIT/Interest		11.4		12.0
		(25)	5.7	(56)	4.7		5.5				(112)	4.7	(158)	4.6
			1.6		2.2		2.2					2.0		1.9

										Net Profit + Depr., Dep., Amort./Cur. Mat. L/T/D				
					8.7		15.5			Net Profit + Depr., Dep., Amort./Cur. Mat. L/T/D		11.2		12.1
				(17)	5.0	(16)	6.7				(39)	4.2	(40)	4.4
					3.1		1.9					2.1		1.8

									Fixed/Worth		
.0		.1		.1		.2			Fixed/Worth	.2	.2
.3		.2		.3		.4				.4	.4
2.3		.6		.6		1.0				1.2	1.2

									Debt/Worth		
.4		.5		1.0		.8			Debt/Worth	.7	1.1
1.1		1.3		2.1		1.7				2.0	2.5
-14.5		2.5		3.4		5.2				5.0	7.4

										% Profit Before Taxes/Tangible Net Worth				
			53.4		58.6		52.4			% Profit Before Taxes/Tangible Net Worth		40.1		48.3
		(26)	20.1	(56)	31.1	(46)	24.9				(110)	19.8	(146)	19.9
			2.3		8.9		12.0					7.0		7.2

									% Profit Before Taxes/Total Assets		
45.9		23.9		16.6		20.8			% Profit Before Taxes/Total Assets	12.1	11.7
30.8		8.8		9.7		8.8				6.7	6.1
3.0		.6		2.9		3.3				2.3	1.3

									Sales/Net Fixed Assets		
UND		113.9		100.4		45.0			Sales/Net Fixed Assets	54.0	76.3
23.4		39.4		39.2		25.4				24.7	33.6
12.7		13.9		19.8		16.6				13.0	16.5

									Sales/Total Assets		
4.0		3.9		4.0		3.7			Sales/Total Assets	3.8	3.8
3.3		3.1		3.3		3.1				2.9	3.2
3.1		2.2		2.8		2.5				2.4	2.6

										% Depr., Dep., Amort./Sales				
			.3		.4		.6			% Depr., Dep., Amort./Sales		.6		.5
		(25)	.5	(50)	.6	(47)	.8				(110)	.9	(149)	.8
			1.8		1.8		1.2					1.6		1.5

										% Officers', Directors' Owners' Comp/Sales				
			2.0		1.8		.9			% Officers', Directors' Owners' Comp/Sales		1.5		1.6
		(13)	2.6	(20)	3.1	(13)	1.9				(51)	3.3	(63)	3.1
			5.3		4.3		8.8					5.2		4.4

10082M	118646M	1010613M	3000198M	2003919M	1176502M	Net Sales ($)	3588154M	5180301M
2740M	37588M	287417M	985424M	580350M	340727M	Total Assets ($)	1327075M	1925093M

M = $ thousand   MM = $ million
See Pages 11 through 21 for Explanation of Ratios and Data

Comparative Historical Data   Current Data Sorted by Sales

			Type of Statement	0-1MM	1-3MM	3-5MM	5-10MM	10-25MM	25MM & OVER
22	23	29	Unqualified		1		2	4	24
36	35	38	Reviewed		1	3	2	14	18
33	26	33	Compiled	4	7	4	7	2	9
13	12	12	Tax Returns	1	1	1	4	3	2
54	47	41	Other	3	1	1	6	9	18
4/1/04-3/31/05 ALL	4/1/05-3/31/06 ALL	4/1/06-3/31/07 ALL		23 (4/1-9/30/06)			130 (10/1/06-3/31/07)		
158	143	153	**NUMBER OF STATEMENTS**	8	14	9	19	32	71
%	%	%	**ASSETS**	%	%	%	%	%	%
5.5	4.8	7.0	Cash & Equivalents		8.1		11.0	3.6	5.2
39.9	41.3	38.6	Trade Receivables (net)		33.0		40.5	40.7	40.9
33.3	33.0	32.7	Inventory		33.5		33.4	37.6	30.3
2.6	1.9	2.5	All Other Current		1.3		2.6	1.2	3.0
81.3	81.0	80.7	Total Current		76.0		87.4	83.1	79.4
12.2	12.5	14.0	Fixed Assets (net)		19.8		10.9	12.9	13.9
2.3	1.4	1.5	Intangibles (net)		1.1		.4	1.4	2.1
4.2	5.1	3.8	All Other Non-Current		3.1		1.3	2.6	4.5
100.0	100.0	100.0	Total		100.0		100.0	100.0	100.0
			LIABILITIES						
16.1	16.4	13.5	Notes Payable-Short Term		12.1		14.7	15.9	13.0
2.6	3.0	2.5	Cur. Mat.-L.T.D.		3.2		1.5	2.6	1.8
30.8	27.5	23.2	Trade Payables		23.3		22.6	24.9	24.7
.3	.1	.2	Income Taxes Payable		.0		.0	.1	.3
6.9	8.3	9.4	All Other Current		4.8		12.3	9.3	9.7
56.7	55.3	48.7	Total Current		43.3		51.1	52.8	49.4
9.4	8.5	10.2	Long-Term Debt		10.6		7.1	9.7	10.0
.2	.3	.1	Deferred Taxes		.0		.3	.2	.1
3.8	3.5	3.6	All Other Non-Current		5.7		3.9	1.4	3.4
29.9	32.3	37.3	Net Worth		40.3		37.6	36.0	37.1
100.0	100.0	100.0	Total Liabilties & Net Worth		100.0		100.0	100.0	100.0
			INCOME DATA						
100.0	100.0	100.0	Net Sales		100.0		100.0	100.0	100.0
24.1	24.7	25.2	Gross Profit		28.6		24.4	21.9	24.6
21.0	21.2	20.8	Operating Expenses		22.9		19.9	18.1	20.4
3.0	3.5	4.4	Operating Profit		5.7		4.5	3.8	4.2
.3	.4	.2	All Other Expenses (net)		-.4		.6	.6	.2
2.7	3.2	4.2	Profit Before Taxes		6.1		3.9	3.2	3.9
			RATIOS						
2.0	2.1	2.3	Current		4.0		2.5	2.0	2.2
1.4	1.5	1.7			1.8		1.7	1.5	1.6
1.1	1.1	1.3			1.1		1.4	1.3	1.3
1.1	1.2	1.4	Quick		1.8		1.5	1.2	1.4
.7	.8	.9			.8		.9	.8	.9
.6	.6	.6			.5		.7	.6	.7
33 11.1	34 10.8	30 12.3	Sales/Receivables		28 12.8		30 12.1	32 11.5	31 11.9
47 7.8	50 7.3	43 8.6			40 9.2		38 9.6	44 8.3	45 8.2
62 5.9	61 6.0	56 6.5			58 6.3		69 5.3	55 6.6	57 6.4
36 10.1	34 10.8	30 12.0	Cost of Sales/Inventory		0 UND		33 11.0	32 11.3	30 12.3
50 7.3	52 7.0	48 7.5			78 4.7		46 7.9	55 6.7	44 8.3
74 5.0	72 5.1	71 5.1			114 3.2		54 6.8	75 4.9	61 6.0
26 13.9	24 15.4	19 19.6	Cost of Sales/Payables		10 36.2		21 17.0	23 16.0	23 15.8
43 8.5	37 9.8	31 11.6			38 9.6		30 12.0	29 12.4	35 10.3
66 5.6	62 5.9	50 7.3			61 6.0		44 8.2	49 7.4	49 7.4
8.2	7.8	6.5	Sales/Working Capital		4.4		5.8	7.6	7.6
13.4	11.9	9.9			5.3		8.6	13.1	10.8
32.6	42.5	20.7			NM		18.0	23.5	23.0
13.8	15.5	16.0	EBIT/Interest		11.8		19.5	15.3	16.1
(148) 6.4	(136) 6.8	(146) 5.3		(12)	5.1	(18)	4.5	4.3	(70) 7.0
2.4	2.6	2.2			.1		2.6	1.5	2.9
9.6	8.8	10.8	Net Profit + Depr., Dep., Amort./Cur. Mat. L/T/D						15.5
(31) 4.5	(30) 4.3	(41) 4.4						(24)	4.7
2.6	1.7	1.9							2.2
.2	.2	.1	Fixed/Worth		.1		.0	.1	.2
.4	.3	.3			.3		.3	.3	.4
.9	.9	.7			1.0		.6	.6	.7
1.3	1.0	.9	Debt/Worth		.4		1.4	1.0	.9
2.6	2.3	1.8			1.5		2.1	2.0	1.8
6.4	7.4	3.8			7.7		2.9	3.9	5.0
62.2	55.8	56.2	% Profit Before Taxes/Tangible Net Worth		68.5		52.9	63.2	55.6
(146) 26.7	(131) 28.8	(145) 31.4		(12)	29.8	(18)	38.5	30.4	(68) 32.5
8.7	11.1	11.4			3.8		10.2	6.8	14.6
14.5	17.5	21.9	% Profit Before Taxes/Total Assets		28.2		19.3	16.7	21.7
7.5	9.6	10.4			9.5		10.6	7.8	10.6
2.5	2.3	3.0			-.3		3.1	2.3	4.8
67.4	72.5	75.7	Sales/Net Fixed Assets		59.4		221.9	96.0	49.2
37.9	33.4	31.8			20.5		67.9	39.3	28.5
19.0	17.7	17.6			10.4		12.3	19.1	17.9
3.7	3.7	3.9	Sales/Total Assets		4.0		4.1	4.0	3.9
3.1	3.1	3.2			2.8		3.1	3.3	3.4
2.5	2.3	2.6			1.7		2.6	2.8	2.8
.5	.4	.4	% Depr., Dep., Amort./Sales		.5		.2	.4	.5
(137) .7	(126) .7	(136) .7		(10)	1.1	(16)	.5	(28) .7	(69) .7
1.3	1.3	1.1			2.2		2.0	1.0	1.1
2.0	1.8	1.8	% Officers', Directors' Owners' Comp/Sales				1.4	1.8	.9
(54) 2.9	(47) 2.8	(51) 3.0					(10) 2.5	(10) 3.1	(19) 2.8
4.9	5.0	4.6					3.3	6.1	4.4
5823458M	5040804M	7319960M	Net Sales ($)	4195M	28417M	37269M	143504M	472949M	6633626M
2175750M	1687810M	2234246M	Total Assets ($)	1724M	13565M	13367M	47168M	148440M	2009982M

M = $ thousand   MM = $ million
See Pages 11 through 21 for Explanation of Ratios and Data

Current Data Sorted by Assets   Comparative Historical Data

0-500M	500M-2MM	2-10MM	10-50MM	50-100MM	100-250MM	Type of Statement	4/1/02-3/31/03 ALL	4/1/03-3/31/04 ALL
	3	4	25	4	5	Unqualified	36	33
1	15	47	19			Reviewed	83	94
1	18	26	4			Compiled	44	81
10	17	8				Tax Returns	20	30
11	22	35	22	2	2	Other	58	70
	49 (4/1-9/30/06)		252 (10/1/06-3/31/07)					
23	75	120	70	6	7	NUMBER OF STATEMENTS	241	308
%	%	%	%	%	%	ASSETS	%	%
12.6	9.0	6.9	4.6			Cash & Equivalents	6.7	7.0
30.5	35.3	38.9	35.1			Trade Receivables (net)	36.7	36.9
23.0	30.1	32.0	29.3			Inventory	30.3	30.5
6.2	1.5	2.9	4.5			All Other Current	2.1	2.9
72.3	75.9	80.7	73.6			Total Current	75.8	77.3
20.0	16.6	13.9	18.9			Fixed Assets (net)	17.2	15.3
.0	1.6	1.0	2.5			Intangibles (net)	1.8	2.3
7.9	5.9	4.4	5.0			All Other Non-Current	5.2	5.1
100.0	100.0	100.0	100.0			Total	100.0	100.0
						LIABILITIES		
24.6	12.0	15.9	16.7			Notes Payable-Short Term	14.3	15.9
2.9	2.3	3.1	2.5			Cur. Mat.-L.T.D.	2.6	2.5
15.8	21.0	20.4	17.8			Trade Payables	19.0	20.5
.0	.1	.3	.2			Income Taxes Payable	.3	.3
23.6	12.1	8.5	7.4			All Other Current	9.8	9.1
66.9	47.5	48.2	44.6			Total Current	46.0	48.2
15.8	16.3	9.9	12.0			Long-Term Debt	9.4	8.7
.0	.1	.3	.2			Deferred Taxes	.3	.3
20.8	4.2	3.4	2.5			All Other Non-Current	2.4	4.7
-3.3	31.9	38.3	40.8			Net Worth	41.8	38.2
100.0	100.0	100.0	100.0			Total Liabilities & Net Worth	100.0	100.0
						INCOME DATA		
100.0	100.0	100.0	100.0			Net Sales	100.0	100.0
39.3	30.1	26.8	23.6			Gross Profit	26.5	27.0
36.6	26.3	22.4	18.9			Operating Expenses	23.1	24.2
2.6	3.8	4.4	4.7			Operating Profit	3.3	2.9
1.5	.5	.4	.7			All Other Expenses (net)	.5	.2
1.1	3.3	4.0	4.0			Profit Before Taxes	2.9	2.7
						RATIOS		
2.9	2.9	2.4	2.4			Current	2.7	2.4
1.2	1.8	1.6	1.6				1.7	1.6
.7	1.2	1.3	1.3				1.2	1.2
1.8	1.5	1.6	1.6			Quick	1.5	1.4
.7	.9	.9	.8				.9	.9
.3	.7	.6	.6				.6	.6
18 19.9	23 15.8	31 11.9	29 12.6			Sales/Receivables	29 12.5	31 11.8
31 11.9	39 9.2	43 8.6	40 9.1				41 8.9	42 8.8
47 7.7	57 6.4	56 6.5	58 6.3				56 6.6	57 6.4
0 UND	26 13.9	28 13.1	31 11.7			Cost of Sales/Inventory	25 14.9	27 13.4
22 16.5	44 8.3	44 8.3	49 7.5				47 7.8	51 7.2
71 5.2	77 4.7	73 5.0	70 5.2				76 4.8	74 5.0
8 45.0	14 25.5	18 20.5	12 29.8			Cost of Sales/Payables	16 22.8	15 23.6
21 17.4	26 13.8	28 12.8	25 14.3				26 13.8	28 12.9
50 7.3	47 7.8	43 8.5	39 9.3				40 9.1	47 7.8
9.3	5.8	6.2	6.7			Sales/Working Capital	6.7	7.0
34.0	9.0	11.0	9.8				10.2	10.3
-27.9	32.2	22.8	21.5				24.6	28.2
8.0	10.2	14.6	13.4			EBIT/Interest	10.7	11.5
(19) 2.0	(70) 3.9	(111) 4.4	(67) 6.4				(225) 4.2	(273) 4.2
-1.6	1.6	2.4	2.3				1.9	2.0
		11.8	7.8			Net Profit + Depr., Dep., Amort./Cur. Mat. L/T/D	9.3	10.0
	(35) 2.8	(27) 3.8					(68) 4.1	(67) 2.7
		1.0	1.6				2.0	1.4
.4	.1	.1	.2			Fixed/Worth	.1	.1
1.2	.3	.2	.4				.3	.3
-.5	1.8	.6	1.0				.8	1.0
1.2	.9	.9	.7			Debt/Worth	.6	.7
4.0	2.3	1.9	1.5				1.3	1.9
-7.3	5.9	3.7	3.6				3.0	4.3
119.5	54.5	57.3	43.4			% Profit Before Taxes/Tangible Net Worth	34.7	38.0
(13) 35.8	(67) 31.0	(116) 27.3	(65) 27.8				(223) 19.3	(276) 17.9
17.1	5.2	11.9	14.0				5.1	5.9
28.8	17.1	16.7	16.9			% Profit Before Taxes/Total Assets	14.0	13.1
10.0	7.7	8.8	10.0				6.5	6.3
-4.5	1.7	3.4	4.5				1.6	1.9
51.0	87.3	71.1	36.8			Sales/Net Fixed Assets	51.3	61.9
28.5	41.0	32.2	19.5				27.3	29.2
10.8	11.5	14.9	10.6				12.4	13.8
5.9	4.2	3.8	3.5			Sales/Total Assets	3.9	3.9
4.2	3.2	3.2	2.9				3.0	3.1
2.7	2.5	2.6	2.0				2.4	2.3
.9	.4	.4	.5			% Depr., Dep., Amort./Sales	.5	.5
(14) 1.5	(60) .9	(105) .8	(64) .9				(215) .9	(267) .9
3.4	1.7	1.6	1.5				1.8	1.7
2.6	1.5	1.4	.3			% Officers', Directors' Owners' Comp/Sales	1.5	1.7
(10) 10.5	(32) 3.0	(43) 2.0	(11) 1.1				(91) 3.6	(129) 3.0
21.8	5.0	4.6					6.1	7.1
26826M	295007M	1864413M	4377934M	1306154M	2296613M	Net Sales ($)	6640747M	7411626M
6141M	87810M	558367M	1518893M	436124M	912552M	Total Assets ($)	2477175M	2488647M

© RMA 2007

M = $ thousand   MM = $ million
See Pages 11 through 21 for Explanation of Ratios and Data

Comparative Historical Data   Current Data Sorted by Sales

			Type of Statement						
38	38	41	Unqualified		1	2		8	30
96	81	82	Reviewed	1	5	6	15	32	23
49	53	49	Compiled	1	5	9	14	12	8
42	32	35	Tax Returns	5	13	6	6	3	2
61	89	94	Other	5	17	7	15	23	27
4/1/04-3/31/05 ALL	4/1/05-3/31/06 ALL	4/1/06-3/31/07 ALL		\<-- 49 (4/1-9/30/06) --\>			252 (10/1/06-3/31/07)		
				0-1MM	1-3MM	3-5MM	5-10MM	10-25MM	25MM & OVER
286	293	301	NUMBER OF STATEMENTS	12	41	30	50	78	90
%	%	%	**ASSETS**	%	%	%	%	%	%
6.9	8.0	7.3	Cash & Equivalents	11.1	8.5	10.7	7.6	7.0	5.2
37.8	36.3	36.3	Trade Receivables (net)	27.6	27.2	39.1	38.4	38.0	37.9
29.6	30.6	30.0	Inventory	28.7	28.4	29.1	28.1	32.1	30.6
2.5	1.9	3.1	All Other Current	1.8	6.5	1.2	2.7	1.6	3.9
76.8	76.8	76.7	Total Current	69.2	70.6	80.2	76.7	78.6	77.6
15.8	16.9	16.5	Fixed Assets (net)	18.4	24.3	13.4	13.8	15.8	15.7
2.2	2.1	1.7	Intangibles (net)	.0	.7	3.0	1.1	1.0	3.0
5.1	4.2	5.1	All Other Non-Current	12.8	4.4	3.3	8.4	4.6	3.6
100.0	100.0	100.0	Total	100.0	100.0	100.0	100.0	100.0	100.0
			LIABILITIES						
18.8	15.6	15.5	Notes Payable-Short Term	25.4	15.4	15.2	12.3	15.6	16.1
3.0	2.4	2.7	Cur. Mat.-L.T.D.	1.3	3.5	2.1	4.5	2.2	2.3
19.8	19.5	19.3	Trade Payables	13.7	16.8	20.0	20.8	19.9	19.6
.3	.3	.2	Income Taxes Payable	.0	.0	.2	.2	.3	.2
9.4	10.4	10.5	All Other Current	29.8	12.2	8.4	12.5	7.2	9.4
51.2	48.1	48.2	Total Current	70.2	47.9	45.8	50.2	45.2	47.7
10.2	11.4	12.7	Long-Term Debt	24.5	24.0	7.5	11.7	11.3	9.4
.3	.2	.2	Deferred Taxes	.0	.0	.3	.1	.4	.3
4.2	4.6	4.8	All Other Non-Current	38.0	4.4	4.7	4.5	2.7	2.6
34.1	35.6	34.1	Net Worth	-32.3	23.7	41.7	33.4	40.4	40.1
100.0	100.0	100.0	Total Liabilities & Net Worth	100.0	100.0	100.0	100.0	100.0	100.0
			INCOME DATA						
100.0	100.0	100.0	Net Sales	100.0	100.0	100.0	100.0	100.0	100.0
26.6	27.1	27.8	Gross Profit	41.6	35.1	31.8	27.4	25.7	23.6
22.3	23.0	23.6	Operating Expenses	42.0	30.7	26.7	22.8	21.5	19.2
4.3	4.1	4.3	Operating Profit	-.4	4.4	5.1	4.6	4.2	4.4
.3	.4	.6	All Other Expenses (net)	4.0	.1	.5	.9	.4	.5
4.0	3.7	3.6	Profit Before Taxes	-4.5	4.3	4.6	3.7	3.8	3.9
			RATIOS						
2.3	2.7	2.6	Current	2.6	2.7	2.9	2.6	2.5	2.4
1.5	1.6	1.6		1.2	1.9	2.0	1.5	1.7	1.6
1.2	1.2	1.2		.6	1.2	1.3	1.2	1.3	1.3
1.4	1.5	1.6	Quick	1.7	1.5	2.3	1.5	1.6	1.6
.9	.9	.9		.6	.8	1.0	.9	1.0	.9
.6	.6	.6		.3	.5	.6	.6	.7	.6
31 11.8	32 11.6	28 12.8	Sales/Receivables	27 13.5	20 18.1	33 10.9	26 14.1	29 12.6	29 12.6
43 8.4	43 8.4	42 8.8		55 6.7	34 10.6	46 7.9	43 8.6	42 8.6	40 9.2
59 6.2	55 6.6	56 6.5		87 4.2	46 7.9	69 5.3	56 6.5	58 6.3	56 6.6
27 13.7	28 13.2	26 14.0	Cost of Sales/Inventory	4 102.2	25 14.6	15 24.4	22 16.3	28 12.9	26 14.0
46 8.0	46 7.8	45 8.2		104 3.5	48 7.6	44 8.2	41 8.8	47 7.8	46 8.0
72 5.1	71 5.1	74 4.9		207 1.8	76 4.8	89 4.1	63 5.8	72 5.1	61 6.0
14 26.0	16 23.1	16 23.1	Cost of Sales/Payables	7 53.0	11 32.8	21 17.0	17 21.3	17 21.3	15 23.8
26 14.1	27 13.3	27 13.5		29 12.7	27 13.5	36 10.1	23 15.9	27 13.3	25 14.7
43 8.5	43 8.5	43 8.5		72 5.1	46 8.0	64 5.7	42 8.7	40 9.1	38 9.6
6.9	6.8	6.4	Sales/Working Capital	8.6	5.6	5.7	6.2	6.2	7.3
11.3	10.5	10.7		36.1	10.2	7.2	12.6	10.2	11.6
31.2	26.1	29.8		-6.1	46.9	21.9	37.7	19.3	24.0
13.7	11.3	11.0	EBIT/Interest	2.0	10.3	14.2	8.6	15.6	15.1
(264) 5.7	(266) 4.7	(279) 4.6		(11) .8	(36) 3.9	(27) 3.2	(48) 4.6	(71) 4.8	(86) 6.6
2.4	2.0	1.9		-1.9	.4	1.6	2.0	2.6	2.6
9.5	8.5	10.8	Net Profit + Depr., Dep., Amort./Cur. Mat. L/T/D					10.6	11.9
(64) 3.4	(64) 3.7	(77) 3.8					(27) 2.5	(35) 4.9	
1.4	2.1	1.5						1.0	1.9
.2	.1	.1	Fixed/Worth	.2	.2	.1	.1	.1	.2
.3	.3	.3		-49.5	.8	.2	.3	.3	.4
.9	.9	1.0		-.1	5.7	.7	.8	.6	.9
.9	.8	.8	Debt/Worth	3.6	1.3	.5	.9	.8	.8
2.0	1.9	2.0		-130.5	2.7	2.1	2.2	1.7	1.5
4.7	4.6	4.3		-2.1	11.9	3.6	4.8	3.5	3.5
55.3	44.8	53.3	% Profit Before Taxes/Tangible Net Worth		49.7	54.1	65.6	57.8	45.0
(264) 26.9	(268) 23.3	(273) 28.4		(33) 35.6	(28) 15.1	(46) 31.3	(76) 26.1	(85) 29.4	
12.0	8.6	12.2			17.8	5.0	10.8	12.4	15.5
16.8	16.1	17.2	% Profit Before Taxes/Total Assets	10.7	20.3	17.7	15.1	18.7	17.0
9.4	8.2	8.7		1.3	8.4	7.7	6.6	9.1	11.0
3.5	2.6	3.2		-15.8	-.9	1.6	3.2	4.0	4.4
60.4	73.0	65.8	Sales/Net Fixed Assets	78.3	48.4	64.1	124.5	68.5	53.2
28.5	29.4	28.4		30.7	21.2	41.2	37.5	29.2	27.4
13.8	12.9	12.5		9.6	8.0	14.3	13.1	13.9	12.7
3.7	3.8	3.9	Sales/Total Assets	3.8	4.0	4.2	4.1	3.8	4.0
3.0	3.1	3.1		1.8	2.7	2.6	3.3	3.2	3.3
2.4	2.4	2.4		1.2	2.2	1.8	2.5	2.6	2.7
.5	.5	.5	% Depr., Dep., Amort./Sales		.8	.4	.5	.4	.4
(235) .9	(241) .8	(252) .9		(29) 1.3	(27) 1.1	(40) .7	(68) .8	(81) .8	
1.6	1.5	1.6			2.2	1.6	2.1	1.7	1.2
1.9	1.7	1.4	% Officers', Directors' Owners' Comp/Sales		1.5	2.4	1.1	1.5	1.0
(106) 3.1	(95) 2.9	(97) 2.6		(16) 2.6	(12) 4.1	(20) 2.5	(24) 2.0	(20) 1.7	
5.8	5.1	5.0			5.0	8.0	3.9	5.1	4.0
8589558M	10008795M	10166947M	Net Sales ($)	6216M	81350M	116821M	334307M	1275253M	8353000M
2658344M	3375430M	3519887M	Total Assets ($)	2753M	32034M	50137M	124790M	455850M	2854323M

© RMA 2007

M = $ thousand   MM = $ million
See Pages 11 through 21 for Explanation of Ratios and Data

Current Data Sorted by Assets   Comparative Historical Data

						Type of Statement		
		3	2			Unqualified	8	7
	1	10	2			Reviewed	21	18
1	1	1				Compiled	7	10
1	3	4				Tax Returns	1	
1		2				Other	6	10
1	8 (4/1-9/30/06)	2 29 (10/1/06-3/31/07)	2	2	2		4/1/02-3/31/03	4/1/03-3/31/04
0-500M	500M-2MM	2-10MM	10-50MM	50-100MM	100-250MM		ALL	ALL
2	5	20	6	2	2	NUMBER OF STATEMENTS	43	45
%	%	%	%	%	%	ASSETS	%	%
		14.3				Cash & Equivalents	7.5	9.6
		33.2				Trade Receivables (net)	32.9	28.3
		30.7				Inventory	39.4	36.0
		2.4				All Other Current	1.7	1.9
		80.6				Total Current	81.6	75.9
		14.1				Fixed Assets (net)	10.9	14.8
		.7				Intangibles (net)	1.2	4.6
		4.6				All Other Non-Current	6.4	4.8
		100.0				Total	100.0	100.0
						LIABILITIES		
		9.0				Notes Payable-Short Term	18.9	14.7
		1.9				Cur. Mat.-L.T.D.	1.4	3.0
		28.4				Trade Payables	21.4	19.8
		.0				Income Taxes Payable	.8	.1
		10.1				All Other Current	10.8	13.5
		49.5				Total Current	53.3	51.0
		7.9				Long-Term Debt	6.7	11.1
		.0				Deferred Taxes	.1	.1
		8.9				All Other Non-Current	6.0	5.6
		33.7				Net Worth	33.8	32.2
		100.0				Total Liabilities & Net Worth	100.0	100.0
						INCOME DATA		
		100.0				Net Sales	100.0	100.0
		28.8				Gross Profit	30.2	31.1
		24.2				Operating Expenses	28.2	29.8
		4.6				Operating Profit	2.0	1.2
		.7				All Other Expenses (net)	.4	.6
		4.0				Profit Before Taxes	1.7	.6
						RATIOS		
		2.5				Current	2.0	2.1
		1.6					1.5	1.5
		1.2					1.2	1.2
		1.6				Quick	1.1	1.0
		1.0					.6	.7
		.7					.5	.5
		27 13.3				Sales/Receivables	27 13.4 23 16.1	
		36 10.1					36 10.1 37 9.7	
		42 8.6					63 5.8 54 6.7	
		31 11.9				Cost of Sales/Inventory	39 9.2 35 10.4	
		41 8.9					69 5.3 65 5.6	
		84 4.3					104 3.5 108 3.4	
		27 13.5				Cost of Sales/Payables	15 25.0 14 25.9	
		41 9.0					37 9.9 31 11.7	
		52 7.0					52 7.0 55 6.7	
		6.4				Sales/Working Capital	5.1	5.2
		11.2					9.8	9.7
		35.8					29.3	27.8
		33.4				EBIT/Interest	5.8	7.6
		(18) 4.4					(39) 1.9 (38) 2.2	
		1.2					.3	-.7
						Net Profit + Depr., Dep., Amort./Cur. Mat. L/T/D		
		.1				Fixed/Worth	.1	.1
		.3					.2	.5
		1.1					.8	1.3
		.6				Debt/Worth	.9	1.3
		1.6					2.2	3.2
		3.2					4.7	6.3
		61.7				% Profit Before Taxes/Tangible Net Worth	32.7	32.4
		(18) 11.3					(38) 10.9 (37) 5.8	
		2.0					.4	-4.8
		24.8				% Profit Before Taxes/Total Assets	8.3	6.4
		5.7					2.5	2.4
		.7					-1.5	-3.4
		207.6				Sales/Net Fixed Assets	162.6	112.7
		37.9					42.7	34.9
		13.5					18.2	11.3
		4.0				Sales/Total Assets	3.4	3.3
		3.5					2.8	2.8
		2.2					2.1	1.9
		.3				% Depr., Dep., Amort./Sales	.5	.6
		(18) .7					(31) .9 (39) .8	
		1.7					2.1	2.1
						% Officers', Directors' Owners' Comp/Sales	1.4	2.2
		(18)					(18) 4.1 (20) 3.1	
							7.5	8.0
1459M	30302M	364428M	257776M	254450M	522410M	Net Sales ($)	909694M	846712M
844M	8043M	111113M	85102M	122636M	254669M	Total Assets ($)	332852M	302451M

M = $ thousand   MM = $ million
See Pages 11 through 21 for Explanation of Ratios and Data

Comparative Historical Data   Current Data Sorted by Sales

4/1/04-3/31/05 ALL	4/1/05-3/31/06 ALL	4/1/06-3/31/07 ALL	Type of Statement	0-1MM	1-3MM	3-5MM	5-10MM	10-25MM	25MM & OVER
4	5	5	Unqualified					2	3
14	8	13	Reviewed					6	4
3	3	3	Compiled	1			1	3	1
3	2	7	Tax Returns	1			3	2	1
11	11	9	Other	1		1	1	2	5
				0-1MM	*8 (4/1-9/30/06)*			*29 (10/1/06-3/31/07)*	25MM & OVER
35	29	37	**NUMBER OF STATEMENTS**	2		2	8	12	13
%	%	%	**ASSETS**	%	%	%	%	%	%
14.0	13.8	10.6	Cash & Equivalents					13.6	9.4
30.0	38.4	35.5	Trade Receivables (net)		D			37.4	34.1
34.2	24.3	34.1	Inventory		A			30.8	28.7
3.0	3.4	3.4	All Other Current		T			3.6	6.1
81.1	80.0	83.6	Total Current		A			85.3	78.3
9.7	11.7	10.2	Fixed Assets (net)					9.9	9.1
1.9	4.4	3.1	Intangibles (net)		N			1.1	7.4
7.3	3.9	3.2	All Other Non-Current		O			3.7	5.2
100.0	100.0	100.0	Total		T			100.0	100.0
			LIABILITIES		A				
16.4	15.5	16.5	Notes Payable-Short Term		V			16.5	12.3
1.3	2.2	1.6	Cur. Mat.-L.T.D.		A			1.1	1.9
24.3	20.1	23.6	Trade Payables		I			30.6	19.0
.3	.1	.2	Income Taxes Payable		L			.2	.2
9.0	13.6	15.9	All Other Current		A			7.5	19.3
51.2	51.5	57.8	Total Current		B			56.0	52.7
5.1	6.0	6.5	Long-Term Debt		L			1.4	9.5
.0	.0	.0	Deferred Taxes		E			.0	.0
11.2	13.1	6.7	All Other Non-Current					1.1	15.5
32.6	29.4	29.0	Net Worth					41.5	22.4
100.0	100.0	100.0	Total Liabilties & Net Worth					100.0	100.0
			INCOME DATA						
100.0	100.0	100.0	Net Sales					100.0	100.0
31.4	29.8	30.7	Gross Profit					28.8	31.3
27.1	24.6	25.9	Operating Expenses					24.5	24.7
4.3	5.2	4.7	Operating Profit					4.3	6.6
.5	.7	.8	All Other Expenses (net)					.4	1.2
3.8	4.4	3.9	Profit Before Taxes					3.9	5.4
			RATIOS						
2.6	2.4	2.3	Current					2.7	1.7
1.6	1.5	1.5						1.4	1.5
1.2	1.1	1.2						1.1	1.2
1.4	1.8	1.1	Quick					2.0	1.0
.7	1.0	.8						.9	.8
.5	.5	.6						.5	.7
16 23.1	32 11.5	30 12.3	Sales/Receivables					29 12.4	28 13.0
34 10.8	45 8.0	42 8.6						42 8.8	38 9.7
54 6.7	66 5.6	49 7.5						73 5.0	51 7.2
38 9.5	0 UND	37 10.0	Cost of Sales/Inventory					14 27.0	38 9.7
54 6.8	38 9.5	58 6.3						69 5.3	41 9.0
80 4.6	93 3.9	110 3.3						110 3.3	64 5.7
18 20.0	16 23.3	23 15.6	Cost of Sales/Payables					30 12.1	5 73.3
37 9.9	32 11.3	37 10.0						45 8.1	27 13.6
53 6.9	50 7.4	54 6.8						53 6.9	39 9.4
5.6	6.5	6.7	Sales/Working Capital					6.1	7.1
11.8	11.9	10.5						15.9	12.5
27.5	47.0	34.9						46.0	19.9
21.4	20.2	10.8	EBIT/Interest					10.5	43.1
(28) 3.8	(22) 4.4	(35) 4.1						(11) 4.1	4.1
.9	1.5	1.2						.5	2.1
			Net Profit + Depr., Dep., Amort./Cur. Mat. L/T/D						
.1	.1	.1	Fixed/Worth					.1	.1
.2	.2	.3						.1	.3
.5	1.7	1.0						.7	.6
.8	.8	.8	Debt/Worth					.6	1.2
1.5	2.2	2.5						2.0	2.1
4.0	8.9	5.8						5.0	13.1
33.1	61.7	71.5	% Profit Before Taxes/Tangible Net Worth					78.5	58.4
(31) 12.6	(26) 25.6	(31) 30.3						(11) 15.6	(11) 52.7
3.6	5.3	3.6						-1.2	3.7
13.4	17.0	17.3	% Profit Before Taxes/Total Assets					19.3	21.8
5.2	7.4	7.1						5.0	13.9
1.5	1.8	.8						-.3	2.8
125.3	194.8	247.2	Sales/Net Fixed Assets					229.0	180.6
44.5	42.5	60.9						37.9	41.8
20.1	21.7	26.6						21.1	27.5
4.1	4.2	4.0	Sales/Total Assets					3.9	4.2
3.1	3.2	3.2						3.0	3.4
2.5	2.2	2.0						1.8	2.9
.3	.2	.3	% Depr., Dep., Amort./Sales					.2	
(30) .5	(21) .8	(27) .9						(11) .6	
1.9	2.6	1.5						1.5	
1.0		1.2	% Officers', Directors' Owners' Comp/Sales						
(12) 2.6	(15) 2.7								
7.2		6.2							
1664615M	1444252M	1430825M	Net Sales ($)	1459M		9827M	56092M	231581M	1131866M
529466M	507564M	582407M	Total Assets ($)	844M		4435M	16844M	89715M	470569M

© RMA 2007

M = $ thousand   MM = $ million
See Pages 11 through 21 for Explanation of Ratios and Data

Current Data Sorted by Assets   **Comparative Historical Data**

						Type of Statement		
1	8	8	16	2	1	Unqualified	22	13
	7	33	9			Reviewed	55	43
3	21	14	1			Compiled	39	54
2	13	8				Tax Returns	18	12
3	23	33	14		2	Other	43	37
	67 (4/1-9/30/06)		156 (10/1/06-3/31/07)				4/1/02-3/31/03	4/1/03-3/31/04
0-500M	500M-2MM	2-10MM	10-50MM	50-100MM	100-250MM		ALL	ALL
9	72	96	40	3	3	NUMBER OF STATEMENTS	177	159
%	%	%	%	%	%	ASSETS	%	%
	8.8	6.6	9.1			Cash & Equivalents	8.4	9.1
	32.2	33.7	30.4			Trade Receivables (net)	31.8	33.3
	34.6	33.6	22.7			Inventory	30.9	30.4
	3.0	3.8	4.3			All Other Current	2.8	3.3
	78.7	77.8	66.5			Total Current	74.0	76.1
	13.5	13.0	19.6			Fixed Assets (net)	16.4	14.5
	3.2	3.0	6.6			Intangibles (net)	2.9	3.4
	4.6	6.2	7.2			All Other Non-Current	6.7	6.1
	100.0	100.0	100.0			Total	100.0	100.0
						LIABILITIES		
	11.1	15.5	12.4			Notes Payable-Short Term	14.7	13.1
	2.5	3.9	2.9			Cur. Mat.-L.T.D.	4.2	3.9
	16.7	20.2	18.6			Trade Payables	19.1	19.5
	.4	.4	.2			Income Taxes Payable	.3	.5
	15.9	17.3	11.8			All Other Current	13.1	16.3
	46.6	57.3	46.0			Total Current	51.3	53.3
	13.9	10.2	10.3			Long-Term Debt	11.8	9.0
	.2	.3	.4			Deferred Taxes	.2	.2
	7.3	5.2	4.8			All Other Non-Current	5.1	7.9
	32.1	27.0	38.5			Net Worth	31.6	29.7
	100.0	100.0	100.0			Total Liabilities & Net Worth	100.0	100.0
						INCOME DATA		
	100.0	100.0	100.0			Net Sales	100.0	100.0
	40.8	36.2	37.5			Gross Profit	39.9	38.1
	38.8	33.0	32.4			Operating Expenses	37.2	35.5
	2.1	3.2	5.1			Operating Profit	2.7	2.7
	.0	.5	.6			All Other Expenses (net)	.6	.2
	2.1	2.7	4.5			Profit Before Taxes	2.2	2.5
						RATIOS		
	2.5	1.9	2.1				2.2	2.1
	1.8	1.4	1.3			Current	1.5	1.4
	1.2	1.2	1.0				1.1	1.1
	1.3	1.1	1.2				1.3	1.1
	.8	.7	.7			Quick	.8	.8
	.6	.4	.6				.5	.5
	22 16.7	27 13.5	34 10.8				25 14.4	29 12.5
	31 11.9	36 10.1	41 9.0			Sales/Receivables	33 11.0	37 9.9
	40 9.2	44 8.3	53 6.9				46 7.9	49 7.5
	39 9.4	38 9.5	42 8.8				25 14.6	34 10.8
	71 5.1	65 5.6	63 5.8			Cost of Sales/Inventory	64 5.7	67 5.4
	99 3.7	94 3.9	91 4.0				101 3.6	104 3.5
	12 30.9	15 24.7	17 21.1				19 19.4	14 25.4
	26 14.0	32 11.5	36 10.1			Cost of Sales/Payables	30 12.1	29 12.6
	44 8.3	52 7.1	58 6.2				50 7.3	55 6.7
	6.9	8.5	6.0				7.2	7.7
	10.5	15.4	17.3			Sales/Working Capital	14.7	13.6
	24.7	35.4	187.6				65.7	33.8
	10.8	12.1	7.3				9.6	9.7
	(57) 3.5	(84) 4.2	(35) 3.9			EBIT/Interest	(156) 3.2	(143) 3.3
	1.3	2.3	1.9				1.1	1.4
		3.1	10.7			Net Profit + Depr., Dep.,	4.9	3.3
		(27) 2.0	(12) 3.3			Amort./Cur. Mat. L/T/D	(47) 1.6	(37) 1.7
		1.0	1.2				1.0	1.0
	.1	.1	.2				.1	.2
	.4	.3	.5			Fixed/Worth	.3	.4
	1.4	1.1	1.9				1.5	1.3
	.8	1.1	1.3				.9	.9
	2.4	2.3	2.1			Debt/Worth	2.0	2.3
	8.5	6.4	7.0				6.4	5.9
	48.7	51.7	45.1			% Profit Before Taxes/Tangible	37.4	38.4
	(63) 21.6	(81) 25.2	(35) 22.9			Net Worth	(151) 16.8	(138) 15.1
	6.0	9.6	11.2				4.0	3.7
	16.0	14.7	11.1			% Profit Before Taxes/Total	12.7	10.3
	5.1	8.8	7.8			Assets	5.5	4.5
	.8	2.5	2.9				.7	.7
	89.8	92.4	55.1				71.3	69.3
	34.2	35.2	14.7			Sales/Net Fixed Assets	30.6	29.1
	20.6	18.2	6.9				13.5	12.7
	4.5	4.0	3.2				4.3	4.0
	3.4	3.1	2.1			Sales/Total Assets	3.1	3.0
	2.7	2.4	1.5				2.2	2.1
	.4	.4	.6				.6	.5
	(59) .9	(86) .9	(39) 1.2			% Depr., Dep., Amort./Sales	(147) 1.1	(138) 1.0
	2.0	1.9	3.8				2.3	2.3
	2.8	2.1				% Officers', Directors'	2.3	2.4
	(32) 4.6	(31) 3.7				Owners' Comp/Sales	(74) 3.7	(60) 4.1
	7.9	6.4					5.9	6.5
19246M	331825M	1476848M	1684030M	413953M	1358036M	Net Sales ($)	4393130M	4532127M
2864M	90279M	432759M	749823M	205976M	569175M	Total Assets ($)	1340931M	1116344M

© RMA 2007

M = $ thousand   MM = $ million

See Pages 11 through 21 for Explanation of Ratios and Data

Comparative Historical Data   Current Data Sorted by Sales

			Type of Statement						
23	22	36	Unqualified		3	3	3	12	15
49	41	49	Reviewed		1	4	11	22	11
43	46	39	Compiled	1	8	4	13	11	2
16	19	23	Tax Returns		7	6	6	3	1
40	98	76	Other	2	14	15	20	20
4/1/04-3/31/05	4/1/05-3/31/06	4/1/06-3/31/07			67 (4/1-9/30/06)		156 (10/1/06-3/31/07)		
ALL	ALL	ALL		0-1MM	1-3MM	3-5MM	5-10MM	10-25MM	25MM & OVER
171	226	223	NUMBER OF STATEMENTS	3	24	31	48	68	49
%	%	%	ASSETS	%	%	%	%	%	%
9.4	8.0	8.2	Cash & Equivalents		7.4	9.4	10.1	5.9	8.6
32.0	33.8	32.2	Trade Receivables (net)		32.3	27.8	32.0	32.4	36.2
29.9	30.7	31.4	Inventory		34.9	35.1	35.1	30.1	25.5
3.0	3.9	3.6	All Other Current		1.4	2.2	3.5	4.8	4.2
74.3	76.5	75.5	Total Current		76.1	74.5	80.7	73.2	74.5
14.6	13.1	14.3	Fixed Assets (net)		13.1	16.8	13.6	15.2	12.5
3.9	4.7	3.7	Intangibles (net)		3.8	2.9	1.6	4.5	4.7
7.1	5.8	6.5	All Other Non-Current		7.0	5.8	4.2	7.1	8.2
100.0	100.0	100.0	Total		100.0	100.0	100.0	100.0	100.0
			LIABILITIES						
13.7	14.4	13.6	Notes Payable-Short Term		10.8	10.5	13.4	13.8	17.0
4.2	3.1	3.1	Cur. Mat.-L.T.D.		3.1	3.5	2.2	4.6	1.9
18.6	22.8	19.0	Trade Payables		24.1	13.9	18.4	19.5	19.7
.5	.2	.4	Income Taxes Payable		.1	.7	.5	.4	.3
13.8	14.5	16.2	All Other Current		16.9	10.6	19.0	18.3	13.0
50.8	55.0	52.2	Total Current		54.9	39.1	53.5	56.6	51.9
11.8	11.2	11.6	Long-Term Debt		16.0	17.7	6.1	13.4	9.1
.3	.2	.3	Deferred Taxes		.0	.1	.6	.2	.3
8.7	9.3	6.3	All Other Non-Current		11.2	8.7	5.1	6.5	3.9
28.3	24.3	29.6	Net Worth		17.9	34.3	34.7	23.3	34.7
100.0	100.0	100.0	Total Liabilties & Net Worth		100.0	100.0	100.0	100.0	100.0
			INCOME DATA						
100.0	100.0	100.0	Net Sales		100.0	100.0	100.0	100.0	100.0
38.3	36.4	37.8	Gross Profit		45.1	40.7	36.5	39.8	30.7
35.7	33.6	34.6	Operating Expenses		43.4	36.7	34.7	36.1	26.6
2.6	2.8	3.2	Operating Profit		1.7	4.1	1.9	3.7	4.1
.0	.4	.3	All Other Expenses (net)		.7	.7	-.8	.6	.5
2.5	2.4	2.9	Profit Before Taxes		1.0	3.4	2.6	3.1	3.6
			RATIOS						
2.0	2.1	2.1			2.2	2.6	1.8	2.1	2.1
1.5	1.4	1.5	Current		1.6	2.1	1.5	1.3	1.3
1.1	1.1	1.1			1.1	1.6	1.2	1.0	1.1
1.2	1.2	1.1			1.1	1.5	1.2	1.1	1.2
.8	.8	.7	Quick		.8	.8	.7	.7	.7
.6	.5	.5			.5	.6	.6	.4	.6

27	13.4	27	13.7	25	14.7	Sales/Receivables	21	17.1	18	19.8	24	15.0	27	13.7	32	11.3
36	10.2	36	10.2	35	10.4		33	11.2	31	11.9	32	11.5	36	10.1	39	9.4
47	7.8	48	7.6	44	8.3		47	7.7	46	7.9	40	9.2	45	8.1	51	7.2

(Sales/Receivables expanded with 8 current columns: 0-1MM, 1-3MM, 3-5MM, 5-10MM, 10-25MM, 25MM & OVER)

Hist days						Ratio	0-1MM	1-3MM	3-5MM	5-10MM	10-25MM	25MM & OVER
35	10.5	30	12.0	37	10.0	Cost of Sales/Inventory	44 8.4	38 9.6	42 8.8	35 10.3	30 12.4
60	6.1	60	6.1	65	5.6		89 4.1	68 5.4	68 5.3	59 6.2	54 6.8
95	3.8	87	4.2	92	4.0		104 3.5	121 3.0	89 4.1	93 3.9	84 4.4
15	23.8	17	21.2	14	26.6	Cost of Sales/Payables	22 16.6	11 33.9	12 31.2	16 23.5	14 26.4
32	11.5	35	10.6	30	12.3		42 8.7	22 16.3	26 13.9	34 10.6	23 15.7
46	7.9	55	6.7	49	7.4		62 5.8	37 10.0	50 7.4	54 6.8	47 7.8

			Sales/Working Capital						
7.4	8.0	7.7			6.4	5.7	9.0	8.7	7.6
12.7	14.6	14.7			11.9	7.9	12.4	18.7	18.2
40.7	39.0	46.8			119.1	17.0	24.4	-194.2	36.5

						EBIT/Interest								
	10.8		11.4		10.9			4.2		6.8		17.3		11.5		8.6
(148)	4.5	(204)	3.4	(188)	3.9		(19)	1.4	(25)	4.0	(42)	6.4	(57)	3.7	(43)	5.2
	1.3		1.2		1.6			.6		1.5		2.3		2.0		2.2

						Net Profit + Depr., Dep., Amort./Cur. Mat. L/T/D								
	4.9		4.8		6.1							13.3		2.3		18.0
(43)	1.6	(51)	2.0	(50)	2.1				(10)	4.7	(24)	1.5	(10)	5.2
	.4		.6		.9							2.1		.8		1.1

			Fixed/Worth						
.1	.1	.1			.2	.1	.1	.1	.1
.4	.4	.3			.5	.4	.4	.3	.3
1.3	1.2	1.5			4.6	1.8	.8	24.5	.9

			Debt/Worth						
1.0	1.3	1.1			1.5	.6	1.1	1.5	1.2
2.1	2.8	2.3			4.5	2.3	2.0	2.8	2.1
8.8	10.7	8.0			23.9	5.1	5.0	34.7	6.9

						% Profit Before Taxes/Tangible Net Worth								
	43.9		51.7		51.5			48.7		47.7		49.9		53.5		51.2
(141)	15.6	(191)	22.8	(189)	23.8		(19)	16.4	(27)	19.7	(46)	21.3	(52)	25.0	(42)	29.2
	3.2		4.9		7.3			.3		6.1		7.6		10.1		11.9

			% Profit Before Taxes/Total Assets						
14.2	13.8	14.3			9.4	14.9	14.4	16.4	14.3
5.4	5.4	7.1			1.5	6.0	7.1	7.2	8.5
.7	.5	1.8			-1.5	1.6	2.8	2.2	2.9

			Sales/Net Fixed Assets						
66.7	89.5	82.6			67.8	90.0	105.8	77.5	147.2
30.9	36.8	33.0			28.5	26.7	33.7	32.2	39.8
14.5	17.0	15.2			20.8	13.0	17.4	17.8	13.8

			Sales/Total Assets						
4.3	4.4	4.3			4.5	4.4	4.4	4.0	4.3
3.0	3.0	3.1			3.0	2.9	3.3	3.1	3.0
2.1	2.3	2.3			2.1	2.5	2.8	2.3	1.9

						% Depr., Dep., Amort./Sales								
	.6		.6		.4			.6		.4		.4		.4		.3
(140)	1.1	(189)	1.0	(194)	1.0		(18)	1.2	(23)	1.3	(41)	1.0	(64)	.9	(46)	.9
	2.4		1.9		2.2			2.1		1.8		2.6		1.7		2.3

						% Officers', Directors' Owners' Comp/Sales								
	2.4		2.5		2.7			3.1		2.6		2.9		2.0		1.4
(65)	3.7	(77)	3.9	(73)	4.3		(12)	4.6	(16)	4.5	(18)	3.9	(15)	4.6	(11)	3.3
	5.8		6.4		6.1			8.0		5.0		6.3		8.3		5.5

2867339M	5058114M	5283938M	Net Sales ($)	2414M	53553M	122604M	340868M	1045224M	3719275M
1053815M	1724000M	2050876M	Total Assets ($)	1095M	18281M	43239M	108095M	428402M	1451764M

© RMA 2007

M = $ thousand   MM = $ million
See Pages 11 through 21 for Explanation of Ratios and Data

Current Data Sorted by Assets   Comparative Historical Data

0-500M	500M-2MM	2-10MM	10-50MM	50-100MM	100-250MM	Type of Statement	4/1/02-3/31/03 ALL	4/1/03-3/31/04 ALL
	2	12	24		7	Unqualified	58	53
1	6	29	8			Reviewed	53	52
3	12	9	2		1	Compiled	42	54
8	8	4	1			Tax Returns	29	20
6	31	38	18	7	7	Other	100	99
18	59	92	53	7	15	**NUMBER OF STATEMENTS**	282	278
%	%	%	%	%	%	**ASSETS**	%	%
22.0	10.3	14.0	10.1		6.8	Cash & Equivalents	13.7	13.8
37.3	45.8	46.4	45.6		35.8	Trade Receivables (net)	41.7	43.3
12.2	19.7	20.4	21.6		22.1	Inventory	19.1	19.4
3.7	2.8	3.6	4.1		2.8	All Other Current	2.7	2.7
75.3	78.6	84.4	81.5		67.4	Total Current	77.2	79.2
12.2	12.4	8.9	6.3		5.8	Fixed Assets (net)	12.0	10.2
4.5	2.7	1.9	9.5		15.9	Intangibles (net)	4.8	5.1
7.9	6.4	4.8	2.7		11.0	All Other Non-Current	6.0	5.6
100.0	100.0	100.0	100.0		100.0	Total	100.0	100.0
						LIABILITIES		
13.0	19.9	13.1	13.4		12.0	Notes Payable-Short Term	15.3	14.2
3.6	.9	1.7	1.0		6.3	Cur. Mat.-L.T.D.	2.7	2.0
26.7	24.7	28.1	28.3		25.3	Trade Payables	24.8	25.8
.0	.4	.6	.5		.2	Income Taxes Payable	.3	.3
22.2	14.0	12.1	11.5		9.0	All Other Current	13.7	16.7
65.5	59.8	55.6	54.7		52.8	Total Current	56.8	59.1
36.5	6.7	4.5	5.0		14.2	Long-Term Debt	6.2	3.8
.0	.1	.2	.4		.9	Deferred Taxes	.2	.2
1.9	11.8	5.3	5.8		3.9	All Other Non-Current	5.9	7.3
-3.9	21.7	34.4	34.2		28.1	Net Worth	30.9	29.7
100.0	100.0	100.0	100.0		100.0	Total Liabilties & Net Worth	100.0	100.0
						INCOME DATA		
100.0	100.0	100.0	100.0		100.0	Net Sales	100.0	100.0
41.3	39.7	34.4	23.2		20.1	Gross Profit	33.4	32.4
37.0	35.9	28.6	19.7		15.0	Operating Expenses	30.9	29.5
4.4	3.7	5.9	3.5		5.1	Operating Profit	2.5	2.9
.6	.0	.4	.5		5.5	All Other Expenses (net)	.3	.2
3.7	3.8	5.5	3.0		-.3	Profit Before Taxes	2.2	2.7
						RATIOS		
2.9	2.2	2.3	1.8		1.6	Current	2.1	1.9
1.0	1.3	1.5	1.4		1.2		1.4	1.3
.7	1.0	1.1	1.1		1.0		1.1	1.1
2.4	1.5	1.8	1.5		1.1	Quick	1.5	1.4
.8	.9	1.1	.9		.7		1.0	1.0
.5	.5	.8	.7		.5		.7	.7
5 76.2	24 15.2	30 12.3	40 9.2		30 12.2	Sales/Receivables	27 13.7	28 13.0
23 16.2	37 10.0	45 8.1	51 7.1		59 6.2		39 9.4	44 8.3
29 12.5	54 6.8	73 5.0	66 5.6		69 5.3		60 6.1	61 6.0
0 UND	4 83.8	2 207.4	6 62.6		4 87.9	Cost of Sales/Inventory	5 74.9	6 64.3
2 148.7	19 19.4	24 15.3	25 14.7		31 11.9		21 17.7	20 18.6
19 19.0	40 9.1	47 7.7	45 8.2		61 6.0		43 8.5	43 8.5
4 98.2	19 19.7	20 17.9	24 15.1		31 11.7	Cost of Sales/Payables	18 20.1	19 19.1
18 19.9	31 11.9	38 9.5	35 10.3		38 9.5		31 11.7	33 11.2
46 7.9	47 7.8	65 5.6	51 7.1		71 5.2		53 6.9	52 7.0
18.0	10.0	7.4	8.4		9.1	Sales/Working Capital	8.1	9.4
-677.2	22.5	14.3	15.3		17.0		19.5	21.3
-43.2	-255.1	48.9	31.1		-110.5		118.0	102.4
10.4	11.2	27.7	16.3		7.0	EBIT/Interest	13.6	16.1
(14) 2.7	(50) 3.3	(83) 8.8	(43) 4.2		(10) 2.1		(235) 3.5	(230) 3.8
1.4	.9	2.8	2.0		.9		1.0	1.1
		14.9	16.3			Net Profit + Depr., Dep., Amort./Cur. Mat. L/T/D	10.4	9.9
		(22) 3.5	(16) 6.4				(54) 3.9	(44) 2.9
		1.2	3.9				1.0	.7
.0	.1	.1	.1		.2	Fixed/Worth	.1	.1
2.0	.3	.2	.2		.8		.3	.3
-.8	7.9	.7	.7		-.1		1.3	.9
.2	1.4	1.0	1.3		1.5	Debt/Worth	.9	1.1
UND	2.4	2.3	2.6		13.8		2.4	2.3
-3.6	18.4	5.5	8.3		-4.8		8.4	11.2
57.5	89.0	68.7	59.7		48.8	% Profit Before Taxes/Tangible Net Worth	59.8	54.3
(10) 22.6	(45) 22.5	(82) 35.2	(45) 25.8		(10) 21.3		(244) 21.0	(233) 20.9
-68.8	4.3	12.7	11.6		-3.9		1.5	2.4
58.7	18.9	25.9	15.0		6.7	% Profit Before Taxes/Total Assets	14.8	14.9
8.6	7.1	12.9	7.5		2.5		5.6	4.5
-.2	-3.4	3.4	2.7		.0		-.2	.3
UND	229.5	199.4	258.6		103.9	Sales/Net Fixed Assets	150.2	170.3
127.1	77.1	83.1	92.1		63.5		51.7	51.8
41.6	23.6	36.6	29.6		21.6		20.4	26.5
9.8	5.2	5.0	4.3		4.0	Sales/Total Assets	5.3	5.2
6.9	4.0	3.6	3.3		2.1		3.8	3.6
4.9	3.0	2.7	2.1		1.5		2.4	2.5
	.2	.2	.2			% Depr., Dep., Amort./Sales	.3	.3
	(35) .6	(71) .4	(47) .4				(209) .7	(203) .6
	1.5	1.0	.8				1.6	1.4
4.8	2.8	1.1	.4			% Officers', Directors' Owners' Comp/Sales	2.0	1.7
(10) 7.5	(27) 5.4	(22) 1.6	(10) .7				(92) 4.0	(92) 3.5
12.3	8.2	4.0	3.3				7.4	7.0
26937M	298139M	1825197M	3597935M	1704704M	6317458M	Net Sales ($)	11349666M	10856361M
4069M	71033M	455684M	1208813M	531272M	2563104M	Total Assets ($)	3768482M	4016309M

M = $ thousand   MM = $ million
See Pages 11 through 21 for Explanation of Ratios and Data

Comparative Historical Data | Current Data Sorted by Sales

4/1/04-3/31/05 ALL	4/1/05-3/31/06 ALL	4/1/06-3/31/07 ALL	Type of Statement	0-1MM	1-3MM	3-5MM	5-10MM	10-25MM	25MM & OVER
43	47	51	Unqualified		1	2	4	6	38
43	33	44	Reviewed		2	1	11	15	15
33	18	27	Compiled	1	3	3	10	6	4
30	22	21	Tax Returns	3	6	3	4	3	2
86	104	101	Other	2	16	8	22	21	32
					43 (4/1-9/30/06)		201 (10/1/06-3/31/07)		
235	224	244	NUMBER OF STATEMENTS	6	28	17	51	51	91
%	%	%	**ASSETS**	%	%	%	%	%	%
12.0	13.0	12.1	Cash & Equivalents		10.3	7.2	14.8	13.2	9.5
42.5	43.7	44.4	Trade Receivables (net)		43.0	38.7	43.7	45.2	48.2
22.3	21.9	20.3	Inventory		17.3	23.0	18.3	22.4	21.5
2.6	3.3	3.6	All Other Current		3.5	3.1	4.2	4.2	2.9
79.5	82.0	80.4	Total Current		74.1	72.0	81.1	84.9	82.0
9.7	9.8	9.0	Fixed Assets (net)		15.9	11.3	10.7	7.2	5.8
4.8	3.3	5.1	Intangibles (net)		6.1	5.4	1.8	3.2	8.0
6.1	5.0	5.5	All Other Non-Current		3.9	11.2	6.4	4.7	4.2
100.0	100.0	100.0	Total		100.0	100.0	100.0	100.0	100.0
			LIABILITIES						
17.6	16.7	15.0	Notes Payable-Short Term		19.7	20.6	17.7	11.4	13.6
1.9	1.7	1.8	Cur. Mat.-L.T.D.		3.2	1.0	1.4	1.4	1.8
25.3	29.1	27.1	Trade Payables		26.7	22.0	24.0	27.9	30.6
.4	.7	.4	Income Taxes Payable		.0	1.1	.5	.6	.4
12.3	13.4	12.8	All Other Current		18.5	14.0	10.5	13.5	10.9
57.6	61.7	57.0	Total Current		68.1	58.8	54.1	54.8	57.4
6.8	6.8	8.4	Long-Term Debt		13.4	9.6	5.6	3.6	5.9
.2	.3	.2	Deferred Taxes		.0	.7	.2	.3	.3
7.9	6.0	6.6	All Other Non-Current		11.1	13.2	5.9	5.8	5.2
27.6	25.3	27.7	Net Worth		7.4	17.7	34.2	35.5	31.2
100.0	100.0	100.0	Total Liabilities & Net Worth		100.0	100.0	100.0	100.0	100.0
			INCOME DATA						
100.0	100.0	100.0	Net Sales		100.0	100.0	100.0	100.0	100.0
31.6	29.5	32.6	Gross Profit		46.9	41.3	37.7	34.4	21.4
27.9	25.7	28.0	Operating Expenses		43.6	35.8	33.8	27.9	17.8
3.7	3.8	4.6	Operating Profit		3.3	5.5	3.9	6.6	3.6
.2	.5	.7	All Other Expenses (net)		.2	1.6	-.3	.5	1.3
3.5	3.3	4.0	Profit Before Taxes		3.2	3.9	4.2	6.1	2.3
			RATIOS						
2.1	1.9	2.1	Current		2.6	2.0	2.5	2.8	1.7
1.4	1.4	1.4			1.0	1.2	1.5	1.5	1.4
1.1	1.1	1.0			.7	.9	1.1	1.1	1.1
1.5	1.3	1.5	Quick		1.7	1.1	1.8	1.9	1.4
1.0	1.0	.9			.7	.8	1.0	1.1	1.0
.7	.7	.6			.4	.4	.7	.8	.6
27 13.4	29 12.6	28 12.9	Sales/Receivables		20 18.5	20 18.0	30 12.1	26 14.1	35 10.6
41 9.0	45 8.2	42 8.6			28 13.2	32 11.5	38 9.7	47 7.8	50 7.3
60 6.1	63 5.8	64 5.7			46 7.9	61 6.0	66 6.5	73 5.0	67 5.4
5 67.0	6 56.6	3 144.9	Cost of Sales/Inventory		2 186.0	5 70.1	5 67.9	2 211.2	3 109.1
25 14.7	27 13.6	24 15.3			12 31.5	33 11.0	24 15.5	26 14.1	25 14.9
58 6.3	49 7.5	44 8.3			52 7.0	50 7.3	43 8.5	53 6.9	40 9.1
20 18.3	23 16.1	20 17.9	Cost of Sales/Payables		18 20.4	19 19.7	18 19.8	20 18.1	26 14.0
31 11.7	36 10.2	35 10.5			35 10.5	24 15.5	38 9.5	31 11.8	36 10.0
53 6.8	58 6.3	54 6.7			79 4.6	46 8.0	53 6.9	60 6.1	53 6.9
8.9	8.0	8.5	Sales/Working Capital		14.4	10.1	7.0	7.1	9.3
16.1	18.2	17.0			-665.7	28.1	13.4	14.6	16.5
66.7	72.0	138.0			-22.6	-144.4	88.2	37.8	45.2
17.7	15.9	18.6	EBIT/Interest		8.0	19.2	23.6	49.9	16.4
(200) 5.4	(190) 4.9	(206) 4.6			(23) 2.1	(16) 4.7	(46) 5.5	(44) 9.2	(74) 3.8
1.7	1.7	1.7			1.0	.6	1.3	2.5	2.0
22.5	14.9	13.0	Net Profit + Depr., Dep., Amort./Cur. Mat. L/T/D					43.6	13.7
(32) 8.1	(42) 4.9	(47) 4.5						(13) 8.3	(22) 5.4
2.4	1.5	1.4						1.5	1.4
.1	.1	.1	Fixed/Worth		.1	.1	.1	.0	.1
.2	.2	.2			2.0	.4	.3	.2	.2
1.2	.9	1.1			-.6	NM	.9	.6	.8
1.1	1.2	1.2	Debt/Worth		.7	1.8	.8	1.0	1.3
2.9	3.1	2.6			NM	5.5	2.3	2.3	3.1
11.3	9.3	13.8			-3.5	NM	5.0	6.3	9.0
60.1	64.1	63.4	% Profit Before Taxes/Tangible Net Worth		53.3	179.6	60.1	63.3	63.6
(195) 28.3	(189) 28.9	(198) 29.2			(14) 19.5	(13) 40.4	(45) 31.9	(43) 32.6	(78) 28.5
6.8	8.8	10.4			-12.4	10.0	5.0	11.0	11.6
16.2	15.7	19.4	% Profit Before Taxes/Total Assets		17.2	25.0	21.7	24.1	15.0
6.6	6.9	8.2			4.5	7.1	9.7	13.0	6.1
.8	1.5	1.9			-3.3	-2.2	.9	2.9	2.1
233.5	239.8	228.2	Sales/Net Fixed Assets		457.0	191.8	142.9	206.5	256.0
77.3	82.5	81.1			50.4	78.5	48.7	105.9	92.1
26.4	27.3	31.7			15.3	15.3	26.9	39.4	43.9
5.0	4.9	5.0	Sales/Total Assets		7.0	4.9	4.7	5.1	4.9
3.6	3.6	3.7			4.1	3.6	3.6	3.8	3.6
2.5	2.5	2.6			2.2	2.4	2.9	2.6	2.5
.2	.2	.2	% Depr., Dep., Amort./Sales		.5	.2	.4	.2	.1
(172) .5	(163) .4	(174) .4			(12) 1.2	(10) .5	(35) .7	(42) .4	(72) .3
1.1	1.1	1.2			1.8	1.7	1.3	.7	.7
1.2	1.5	1.2	% Officers', Directors' Owners' Comp/Sales		4.1		2.1	1.2	.4
(87) 3.5	(74) 2.7	(71) 3.4			(15) 6.1		(18) 4.9	(14) 1.6	(16) 2.7
6.9	5.4	6.8			12.1		7.2	2.8	2.4
11722369M	12728158M	13770370M	Net Sales ($)	3524M	53990M	69108M	374164M	834824M	12434760M
3659230M	4201914M	4833975M	Total Assets ($)	1264M	16648M	36297M	127900M	306193M	4345673M

M = $ thousand   MM = $ million
See Pages 11 through 21 for Explanation of Ratios and Data

Current Data Sorted by Assets   Comparative Historical Data

						Type of Statement		
						Unqualified	26	20
	1	10	11	3	4	Reviewed	63	58
1	12	26	8			Compiled	43	66
10	16	17	3			Tax Returns	17	24
4	19	5	1			Other	58	57
	15	34	15		4		4/1/02-	4/1/03-
	37 (4/1-9/30/06)		184 (10/1/06-3/31/07)				3/31/03	3/31/04
0-500M	500M-2MM	2-10MM	10-50MM	50-100MM	100-250MM		ALL	ALL
15	63	92	38	5	8	NUMBER OF STATEMENTS	207	225
%	%	%	%	%	%	**ASSETS**	%	%
18.3	10.4	7.5	4.4			Cash & Equivalents	7.1	8.7
33.8	38.9	36.3	28.2			Trade Receivables (net)	33.4	33.6
29.3	33.2	32.2	33.7			Inventory	35.7	34.1
1.4	2.0	3.6	4.7			All Other Current	2.7	2.8
82.7	84.6	79.6	71.0			Total Current	78.9	79.2
12.3	9.0	12.8	16.5			Fixed Assets (net)	11.8	12.0
.2	3.7	2.9	4.2			Intangibles (net)	3.4	3.5
4.7	2.8	4.7	8.2			All Other Non-Current	5.9	5.3
100.0	100.0	100.0	100.0			Total	100.0	100.0
						LIABILITIES		
12.3	12.2	17.6	16.8			Notes Payable-Short Term	14.8	14.0
7.1	1.9	2.9	2.2			Cur. Mat.-L.T.D.	2.9	2.8
23.8	25.8	21.6	14.4			Trade Payables	22.0	19.9
.3	.2	.2	.1			Income Taxes Payable	.1	.2
29.6	8.5	12.1	12.6			All Other Current	11.3	12.0
73.2	48.6	54.5	46.0			Total Current	51.2	48.8
10.4	11.8	6.9	8.8			Long-Term Debt	8.7	10.7
.0	.0	.2	.2			Deferred Taxes	.1	.2
3.2	5.3	3.3	4.0			All Other Non-Current	3.8	4.8
13.3	34.3	35.2	41.1			Net Worth	36.3	35.5
100.0	100.0	100.0	100.0			Total Liabilties & Net Worth	100.0	100.0
						INCOME DATA		
100.0	100.0	100.0	100.0			Net Sales	100.0	100.0
38.8	28.8	30.3	26.0			Gross Profit	29.9	33.1
32.0	25.6	26.5	19.1			Operating Expenses	27.3	29.7
6.8	3.1	3.9	6.8			Operating Profit	2.5	3.4
.5	-.5	.0	.2			All Other Expenses (net)	.5	.4
6.3	3.6	3.9	6.6			Profit Before Taxes	2.1	3.0
						RATIOS		
2.8	2.8	1.8	2.9				2.3	2.7
1.4	1.7	1.4	1.5			Current	1.5	1.7
1.0	1.1	1.2	1.2				1.2	1.2
2.8	1.7	1.0	1.3				1.2	1.4
1.0	1.1	.8	.7			Quick	.8 (224)	.9
.3	.7	.5	.5				.5	.6
3 135.4	21 17.6	29 12.7	37 9.8				28 13.0	24 15.3
22 16.9	37 9.9	41 9.0	44 8.3			Sales/Receivables	41 8.9	40 9.1
42 8.8	55 6.7	56 6.5	60 6.0				54 6.7	56 6.5
7 49.4	17 21.7	31 11.9	39 9.4				32 11.6	26 13.8
43 8.6	38 9.7	55 6.6	65 5.6			Cost of Sales/Inventory	63 5.8	64 5.7
53 6.9	80 4.6	93 3.9	99 3.7				106 3.5	101 3.6
0 UND	13 28.6	19 19.1	14 26.2				18 20.8	15 24.2
3 111.6	26 13.9	33 11.1	28 13.0			Cost of Sales/Payables	32 11.5	27 13.4
45 8.1	56 6.6	53 6.9	43 8.5				54 6.8	51 7.1
6.7	6.9	7.5	5.1				5.8	5.2
17.1	12.5	13.1	11.6			Sales/Working Capital	10.9	9.6
481.0	34.7	26.5	30.4				42.1	35.3
15.8	15.4	8.4	23.5				9.5	14.5
(11) 5.0	(53) 5.6	(82) 5.2	(37) 6.0			EBIT/Interest	(192) 3.4	(207) 5.3
2.5	1.6	2.0	2.8				1.0	1.9
		8.0				Net Profit + Depr., Dep.,	7.0	10.0
	(20) 3.5					Amort./Cur. Mat. L/T/D	(59) 1.9	(48) 2.9
		1.4					.4	1.2
.1	.1	.1	.1				.1	.1
.3	.2	.3	.2			Fixed/Worth	.3	.3
UND	1.0	.7	.7				.9	1.0
.5	.7	1.0	.7				.9	.7
2.3	2.8	2.2	2.1			Debt/Worth	2.0	2.1
-4.1	8.4	4.3	3.9				6.4	6.0
103.2	62.3	63.4	51.7			% Profit Before Taxes/Tangible	39.2	38.4
(11) 78.4	(54) 29.2	(86) 24.2	(37) 29.7			Net Worth	(188) 13.9	(197) 18.1
54.4	7.2	13.5	13.8				1.9	5.8
52.5	15.6	18.2	17.6			% Profit Before Taxes/Total	11.8	13.1
17.1	7.3	7.1	11.0			Assets	3.7	5.2
3.2	.7	3.1	5.0				.3	1.7
280.9	154.9	102.7	67.2				95.3	95.4
104.8	75.4	44.8	19.7			Sales/Net Fixed Assets	40.5	39.7
19.2	38.9	19.2	10.4				19.9	18.2
7.8	4.7	3.8	3.2				3.7	4.0
4.7	3.8	2.9	2.3			Sales/Total Assets	2.9	3.0
2.7	2.8	2.1	1.7				2.2	2.1
.1	.3	.3	.4				.5	.4
(11) .4	(45) .6	(81) .6	(33) 1.0			% Depr., Dep., Amort./Sales	(177) .8	(178) .8
.6	1.0	1.1	2.0				1.5	1.4
	2.2	1.9				% Officers', Directors'	2.0	2.0
	(31) 3.7	(30) 3.3				Owners' Comp/Sales	(84) 3.3	(91) 4.3
	6.5	5.0					5.3	7.8
20305M	322782M	1269892M	1849626M	515972M	2861785M	Net Sales ($)	4072011M	4326397M
4188M	78651M	422102M	703186M	347501M	1189919M	Total Assets ($)	1719271M	1835567M

© RMA 2007

M = $ thousand   MM = $ million
See Pages 11 through 21 for Explanation of Ratios and Data

Comparative Historical Data | Current Data Sorted by Sales

Hist A	Hist B	Hist C	Type of Statement	0-1MM	1-3MM	3-5MM	5-10MM	10-25MM	25MM & OVER
23	16	29	Unqualified		1		4	9	15
55	40	47	Reviewed		1	7	15	15	9
40	36	36	Compiled		4	7	17	7	1
28	25	35	Tax Returns	4	14	7	6	3	1
71	84	74	Other	3	8	3	17	20	23
4/1/04-3/31/05 ALL	4/1/05-3/31/06 ALL	4/1/06-3/31/07 ALL			37 (4/1-9/30/06)		184 (10/1/06-3/31/07)		
217	201	221	NUMBER OF STATEMENTS	7	28	24	59	54	49
%	%	%	ASSETS	%	%	%	%	%	%
8.4	8.5	8.5	Cash & Equivalents		11.5	11.1	8.4	7.2	5.4
33.0	33.1	34.9	Trade Receivables (net)		31.3	27.5	38.8	40.7	32.3
32.8	35.2	32.5	Inventory		32.6	36.0	28.4	31.8	34.0
3.1	3.0	3.3	All Other Current		2.3	1.1	4.1	3.1	4.5
77.3	79.9	79.1	Total Current		77.7	75.7	79.7	82.8	76.2
12.9	12.5	12.0	Fixed Assets (net)		15.5	12.8	13.4	9.7	10.6
3.0	2.8	4.1	Intangibles (net)		4.0	5.9	2.0	3.0	7.6
6.8	4.8	4.7	All Other Non-Current		2.8	5.5	4.9	4.5	5.7
100.0	100.0	100.0	Total		100.0	100.0	100.0	100.0	100.0
			LIABILITIES						
18.3	16.3	15.1	Notes Payable-Short Term		13.0	14.5	11.4	19.4	15.7
2.3	3.0	2.8	Cur. Mat.-L.T.D.		2.1	3.4	2.6	2.8	1.6
22.0	21.5	21.6	Trade Payables		27.4	15.7	23.7	25.0	17.4
.2	.2	.2	Income Taxes Payable		.2	.2	.3	.2	.1
14.7	10.9	12.2	All Other Current		8.2	10.1	10.4	11.6	12.5
57.4	51.9	51.9	Total Current		50.8	43.9	48.5	59.0	47.3
11.4	11.6	9.6	Long-Term Debt		16.0	12.7	8.1	6.0	9.6
.1	.2	.3	Deferred Taxes		.1	.3	.0	.1	.8
5.6	4.8	4.4	All Other Non-Current		2.5	10.9	1.7	4.5	5.8
25.4	31.5	33.8	Net Worth		30.6	32.2	41.7	30.3	36.5
100.0	100.0	100.0	Total Liabilities & Net Worth		100.0	100.0	100.0	100.0	100.0
			INCOME DATA						
100.0	100.0	100.0	Net Sales		100.0	100.0	100.0	100.0	100.0
29.8	30.4	29.3	Gross Profit		33.0	30.6	32.9	25.9	24.4
26.9	26.6	24.8	Operating Expenses		26.7	29.1	27.7	22.3	18.7
2.9	3.8	4.5	Operating Profit		6.3	1.5	5.2	3.7	5.7
.4	.6	.0	All Other Expenses (net)		-.9	-.3	-.4	.5	.7
2.6	3.2	4.5	Profit Before Taxes		7.2	1.8	5.6	3.2	4.9
			RATIOS						
2.3	2.3	2.2	Current		3.8	2.5	2.3	1.9	2.0
1.4	1.6	1.5			1.6	1.8	1.5	1.4	1.6
1.1	1.2	1.2			1.1	1.1	1.3	1.1	1.3
1.2	1.2	1.2	Quick		2.0	1.3	1.3	1.0	1.0
.8 (200)	.8	.8			.9	.9	.9	.9	.7
.5	.5	.6			.4	.5	.7	.7	.6
23 15.7	25 14.7	26 14.0	Sales/Receivables	11 33.0	16 22.1	29 12.5	27 13.5	34 10.8	
40 9.1	41 9.0	41 8.9		33 11.0	32 11.3	41 8.9	46 7.9	44 8.4	
57 6.4	58 6.2	56 6.5		53 6.9	46 7.9	57 6.4	60 6.1	55 6.6	
27 13.5	31 11.9	25 14.6	Cost of Sales/Inventory	16 23.0	33 10.9	21 17.7	22 16.6	31 11.6	
55 6.6	65 5.6	53 6.9		46 7.9	67 5.5	48 7.6	47 7.8	57 6.4	
96 3.8	103 3.5	86 4.2		114 3.2	106 3.5	81 4.5	81 4.5	76 4.8	
17 21.3	15 24.9	15 24.2	Cost of Sales/Payables	15 23.8	10 37.6	20 18.4	15 23.7	17 22.0	
31 11.9	33 10.9	31 11.8		41 8.8	22 16.7	39 9.3	32 11.3	29 12.8	
55 6.7	60 6.1	52 7.0		63 5.8	41 8.9	70 5.2	52 7.1	41 9.0	
6.2	5.6	6.9	Sales/Working Capital		4.9	6.2	7.1	7.8	5.8
12.6	11.1	12.2			12.8	9.8	9.8	15.2	10.5
38.9	23.6	29.5			33.4	83.6	19.6	49.8	21.2
15.9	10.3	12.2	EBIT/Interest		34.7	4.3	11.3	9.5	19.7
(201) 4.4	(175) 3.9	(196) 5.0			(22) 5.6	(18) 2.2	(51) 5.7	(52) 5.0	(48) 6.0
1.5	1.4	2.3			2.7	1.2	2.6	2.4	2.8
5.9	7.0	11.3	Net Profit + Depr., Dep., Amort./Cur. Mat. L/T/D				11.2	5.6	34.5
(49) 2.8	(31) 3.4	(42) 4.5					(11) 3.0	(10) 4.5	(14) 7.7
1.1	1.2	1.7					1.3	1.6	2.7
.1	.1	.1	Fixed/Worth		.1	.1	.1	.1	.1
.3	.3	.3			.3	.2	.3	.2	.3
.9	1.1	.8			5.0	9.7	.7	.5	.7
1.1	.9	1.0	Debt/Worth		.5	.7	.8	1.7	1.3
2.7	2.4	2.3			4.9	2.3	1.6	2.6	2.3
6.6	6.6	5.9			9.6	22.0	3.8	4.8	4.2
49.0	52.1	60.7	% Profit Before Taxes/Tangible Net Worth		82.1	34.8	55.4	67.3	53.2
(193) 20.0	(179) 25.1	(197) 29.2			(22) 57.1	(20) 7.2	(56) 27.4	(50) 24.3	(44) 31.8
7.1	6.9	11.8			18.0	1.6	11.8	14.8	15.6
12.9	14.5	17.5	% Profit Before Taxes/Total Assets		46.1	9.7	18.4	16.7	17.6
5.3	5.9	7.9			16.0	4.2	8.2	6.7	10.8
1.5	1.7	2.5			.9	.3	3.5	2.8	5.2
110.1	116.3	117.1	Sales/Net Fixed Assets		156.6	90.1	90.4	145.6	94.0
41.5	43.2	47.9			81.1	41.6	46.1	68.7	32.4
16.6	18.5	19.0			13.6	13.0	21.6	27.9	17.1
4.1	3.8	4.0	Sales/Total Assets		4.7	4.1	4.0	4.3	3.6
3.0	2.8	3.1			3.0	3.0	3.2	3.3	2.8
2.1	2.1	2.1			2.0	1.9	2.1	2.4	1.9
.4	.3	.3	% Depr., Dep., Amort./Sales		.3	.4	.5	.3	.3
(158) .8	(165) .6	(182) .6			(17) .4	(19) .7	(49) .8	(47) .5	(44) .7
1.3	1.4	1.1			1.3	1.6	1.1	1.1	1.3
1.7	2.0	2.0	% Officers', Directors' Owners' Comp/Sales		3.3		2.9	.9	
(84) 3.3	(75) 3.0	(77) 3.6			(14) 4.7		(29) 4.3	(15) 1.4	
7.0	6.1	5.3			9.6		5.5	2.3	
4881418M	4492834M	6840362M	Net Sales ($)	4377M	55508M	100388M	438968M	877936M	5363185M
1983598M	1842469M	2745547M	Total Assets ($)	1779M	35551M	44491M	182622M	304723M	2176381M

M = $ thousand   MM = $ million
See Pages 11 through 21 for Explanation of Ratios and Data

Current Data Sorted by Assets   **Comparative Historical Data**

						Type of Statement		
1		21	23	6	3	Unqualified	61	49
1	10	31	11			Reviewed	46	61
6	17	25	2			Compiled	51	79
12	22	10		1		Tax Returns	37	48
12	28	67	22	5	5	Other	87	102

							4/1/02-3/31/03	4/1/03-3/31/04
	52 (4/1-9/30/06)			291 (10/1/06-3/31/07)			ALL	ALL
0-500M	500M-2MM	2-10MM	10-50MM	50-100MM	100-250MM			
32	79	154	58	12	8	**NUMBER OF STATEMENTS**	282	339
%	%	%	%	%	%	**ASSETS**	%	%
14.9	9.2	7.0	6.3	6.6		Cash & Equivalents	8.9	9.4
35.1	36.2	38.4	30.8	25.2		Trade Receivables (net)	35.5	35.8
24.6	30.8	26.9	27.3	18.2		Inventory	27.7	27.7
2.4	1.0	2.5	2.0	2.2		All Other Current	2.5	2.7
76.9	77.2	74.7	66.5	52.1		Total Current	74.6	75.6
15.6	13.9	14.7	16.9	13.3		Fixed Assets (net)	15.2	14.1
3.2	3.2	5.3	9.3	31.3		Intangibles (net)	4.5	4.7
4.3	5.6	5.2	7.2	3.3		All Other Non-Current	5.7	5.5
100.0	100.0	100.0	100.0	100.0		Total	100.0	100.0
						LIABILITIES		
23.5	15.9	14.3	14.2	2.6		Notes Payable-Short Term	14.3	15.0
13.4	3.7	2.4	3.1	5.6		Cur. Mat.-L.T.D.	4.0	2.7
26.1	24.6	21.8	18.3	15.1		Trade Payables	23.0	21.9
.0	.4	.2	.6	.1		Income Taxes Payable	.4	.4
10.8	9.6	10.6	8.8	11.8		All Other Current	10.6	12.4
73.8	54.2	49.3	45.0	35.2		Total Current	52.3	52.3
10.9	14.8	9.7	10.3	25.2		Long-Term Debt	10.8	11.2
.0	.0	.2	.4	.6		Deferred Taxes	.1	.3
6.5	5.5	4.2	2.1	4.3		All Other Non-Current	5.4	5.3
8.8	25.5	36.5	42.2	34.7		Net Worth	31.3	30.9
100.0	100.0	100.0	100.0	100.0		Total Liabilities & Net Worth	100.0	100.0
						INCOME DATA		
100.0	100.0	100.0	100.0	100.0		Net Sales	100.0	100.0
52.4	45.5	38.3	39.9	39.9		Gross Profit	38.2	39.3
49.4	41.3	32.4	33.5	31.6		Operating Expenses	33.4	34.7
3.0	4.2	5.9	6.5	8.3		Operating Profit	4.8	4.7
1.3	1.0	1.1	.7	1.8		All Other Expenses (net)	.6	.7
1.7	3.2	4.7	5.7	6.5		Profit Before Taxes	4.2	4.0
						RATIOS		
2.0	2.2	2.6	2.4	1.9			2.4	2.3
1.3	1.4	1.5	1.4	1.4		Current	1.5	1.5
.7	1.0	1.2	1.1	1.2			1.1	1.1
1.8	1.2	1.6	1.3	1.2			1.5	1.5
.7	.8	.9	.8	.8		Quick	.9 (338)	.9
.4	.6	.6	.6	.6			.5	.6
6 63.3	30 12.2	36 10.2	38 9.7	34 10.8			33 11.1	32 11.4
30 12.3	41 9.0	47 7.7	49 7.4	57 6.4		Sales/Receivables	43 8.6	43 8.4
48 7.7	58 6.3	62 5.9	60 6.1	70 5.2			59 6.2	60 6.1
6 61.5	33 11.2	29 12.7	45 8.2	34 10.8			26 14.2	30 12.1
35 10.5	52 7.0	53 6.8	60 6.0	50 7.3		Cost of Sales/Inventory	55 6.6	52 7.0
75 4.8	117 3.1	103 3.5	101 3.6	110 3.3			85 4.3	93 3.9
9 38.9	23 15.6	22 16.6	25 14.6	22 16.3			22 16.6	21 17.2
27 13.7	44 8.3	41 8.9	37 9.7	34 10.6		Cost of Sales/Payables	38 9.5	37 9.7
68 5.3	80 4.5	63 5.8	58 6.3	47 7.8			65 5.6	65 5.6
10.2	7.2	6.1	6.1	6.3			6.2	6.6
37.1	14.5	13.2	13.1	16.3		Sales/Working Capital	12.8	11.8
-14.5	157.1	32.9	98.5	33.2			53.0	43.7
12.4	12.0	13.6	20.2	8.8			13.4	17.5
(25) 4.4	(73) 3.7	(138) 3.7	(55) 4.3	3.7		EBIT/Interest	(249) 4.0	(304) 4.9
.8	1.0	1.5	1.9	1.3			1.5	1.7
		6.1	31.5				6.2	6.2
		(25) 2.5	(20) 6.5			Net Profit + Depr., Dep., Amort./Cur. Mat. L/T/D	(70) 2.7	(61) 2.2
		1.0	2.2				1.0	1.3
.1	.1	.1	.1	.9			.1	.1
.4	.4	.3	.4	4.4		Fixed/Worth	.4	.5
-.5	5.9	1.3	.9	-1.1			1.2	1.4
1.4	1.2	.7	.7	2.4			1.0	1.0
6.1	2.7	2.1	2.2	10.0		Debt/Worth	2.4	2.8
-7.4	16.6	5.4	5.3	-10.9			7.1	9.1
98.3	81.6	60.6	55.9				53.4	64.6
(20) 66.9	(62) 20.6	(137) 22.2	(53) 22.8			% Profit Before Taxes/Tangible Net Worth	(247) 28.3	(292) 27.9
19.4	2.0	6.1	10.8				7.8	8.7
43.5	24.7	20.1	17.6	17.8			20.0	16.4
11.6	5.6	6.5	6.7	5.5		% Profit Before Taxes/Total Assets	6.8	7.6
-1.6	.0	1.6	2.7	1.2			1.4	1.9
713.1	90.6	108.6	108.4	49.7			94.6	109.0
53.1	37.0	32.8	21.4	19.2		Sales/Net Fixed Assets	33.4	34.4
23.7	13.7	12.4	8.1	4.6			11.0	11.6
8.1	3.8	3.8	3.3	3.3			3.9	4.1
3.9	3.0	3.0	2.5	1.5		Sales/Total Assets	3.0	2.9
2.4	2.1	1.8	1.3	.9			2.0	2.0
.3	.3	.3	.3				.4	.4
(18) .9	(58) .8	(125) .8	(53) .8			% Depr., Dep., Amort./Sales	(229) 1.1	(274) .9
1.9	1.7	2.7	2.5				2.2	2.1
3.9	3.4	1.6	1.0				2.4	2.4
(13) 6.2	(41) 5.5	(59) 3.1	(14) 2.0			% Officers', Directors' Owners' Comp/Sales	(113) 4.4	(126) 4.8
9.2	9.6	7.2	3.0				6.9	9.3
59029M	325548M	2133678M	3119048M	2185703M	2692642M	Net Sales ($)	7298734M	8207933M
8776M	95648M	713809M	1334837M	821484M	1115412M	Total Assets ($)	3289113M	3520025M

Comparative Historical Data | Current Data Sorted by Sales

Type of Statement										
Unqualified	61	52	56		1	2	4	10	9	30
Reviewed	62	51	53		1	4	3	16	16	13
Compiled	61	55	50		4	8	10	13	11	4
Tax Returns	55	44	45		6	10	9	12	6	2
Other	121	127	139		6	19	18	26	38	32
	4/1/04-3/31/05 ALL	4/1/05-3/31/06 ALL	4/1/06-3/31/07 ALL		52 (4/1-9/30/06)		291 (10/1/06-3/31/07)			
					0-1MM	1-3MM	3-5MM	5-10MM	10-25MM	25MM & OVER
NUMBER OF STATEMENTS	360	329	343		18	43	44	77	80	81
ASSETS	%	%	%		%	%	%	%	%	%
Cash & Equivalents	8.7	8.3	8.0		10.2	9.2	14.1	8.1	6.5	4.8
Trade Receivables (net)	34.7	35.0	35.6		33.7	32.1	38.1	32.4	38.0	37.3
Inventory	26.9	29.6	27.5		24.1	27.1	24.7	29.0	26.4	29.7
All Other Current	2.4	2.3	2.0		3.7	.9	2.1	1.5	2.7	2.0
Total Current	72.7	75.1	73.1		71.8	69.4	79.0	71.0	73.6	73.9
Fixed Assets (net)	14.9	13.7	14.8		14.9	18.8	11.8	16.8	16.0	11.3
Intangibles (net)	6.4	5.3	6.6		6.2	6.7	3.5	7.9	4.1	9.8
All Other Non-Current	5.9	5.8	5.4		7.1	5.2	5.8	4.3	6.4	5.0
Total	100.0	100.0	100.0		100.0	100.0	100.0	100.0	100.0	100.0
LIABILITIES										
Notes Payable-Short Term	14.5	17.1	15.4		24.5	17.1	12.5	12.9	14.6	17.3
Cur. Mat.-L.T.D.	3.0	2.5	3.9		9.2	9.4	3.9	3.1	2.4	2.3
Trade Payables	21.5	23.9	21.8		16.0	24.8	22.7	18.4	23.9	22.2
Income Taxes Payable	.3	.3	.3		.0	.6	.0	.1	.4	.5
All Other Current	10.8	10.5	10.1		9.3	8.3	15.4	8.9	10.7	8.8
Total Current	50.0	54.4	51.6		58.9	60.1	54.5	43.4	52.0	51.1
Long-Term Debt	13.8	10.1	11.8		16.6	22.0	10.0	12.0	8.1	9.9
Deferred Taxes	.3	.2	.2		.0	.0	.1	.3	.1	.4
All Other Non-Current	4.8	5.2	4.3		9.4	3.8	5.4	3.3	6.1	2.0
Net Worth	31.0	30.0	32.2		15.1	14.0	30.0	41.1	33.8	36.6
Total Liabilities & Net Worth	100.0	100.0	100.0		100.0	100.0	100.0	100.0	100.0	100.0
INCOME DATA										
Net Sales	100.0	100.0	100.0		100.0	100.0	100.0	100.0	100.0	100.0
Gross Profit	40.7	38.3	41.8		60.0	53.1	42.2	44.6	35.7	34.8
Operating Expenses	35.2	33.6	36.3		59.0	49.0	35.2	39.1	30.6	28.0
Operating Profit	5.4	4.6	5.5		1.0	4.1	7.0	5.5	5.1	6.8
All Other Expenses (net)	.8	.9	1.2		2.1	1.4	.8	1.5	.8	1.2
Profit Before Taxes	4.6	3.7	4.3		-1.1	2.7	6.2	4.0	4.3	5.6
RATIOS										
Current	2.3	2.1	2.3		3.0	2.3	2.3	2.8	1.9	2.1
	1.5	1.4	1.4		1.5	1.4	1.6	1.5	1.4	1.3
	1.1	1.1	1.1		.7	.8	1.3	1.2	1.1	1.1
Quick	1.5	1.3	1.4		2.0	1.2	1.6	1.5	1.5	1.2
	(359) .9	.8	.8		.6	.8	1.0	.9	.8	.8
	.6	.6	.6		.4	.5	.7	.7	.6	.6
Sales/Receivables	31 11.8	31 11.7	33 11.0		19 19.6	27 13.3	29 12.6	36 10.2	33 11.0	37 9.9
	45 8.1	41 8.9	46 8.0		47 7.8	41 9.0	42 8.8	49 7.4	41 9.0	48 7.6
	62 5.9	55 6.7	60 6.1		57 6.4	60 6.1	64 5.7	63 5.8	56 6.5	58 6.3
Cost of Sales/Inventory	31 11.9	31 11.8	31 11.9		0 UND	25 14.5	22 16.3	36 10.2	22 16.7	36 10.2
	53 6.9	53 6.9	54 6.7		72 5.1	56 6.5	49 7.5	73 5.0	44 8.3	52 7.0
	95 3.8	90 4.1	105 3.5		198 1.8	131 2.8	90 4.1	116 3.1	65 5.6	96 3.8
Cost of Sales/Payables	23 16.1	23 15.9	22 16.6		0 UND	24 15.1	19 19.4	24 15.4	20 18.3	26 13.8
	36 10.1	42 8.8	38 9.5		27 13.5	57 6.4	40 9.1	38 9.5	42 8.7	36 10.0
	67 5.4	65 5.6	63 5.8		90 4.0	102 3.6	79 4.6	68 5.4	60 6.1	51 7.1
Sales/Working Capital	6.4	7.3	6.4		5.8	4.4	6.9	5.3	8.8	7.0
	12.5	13.3	14.3		11.9	21.0	11.3	11.4	14.9	14.5
	39.2	43.0	49.1		-7.4	-32.4	28.3	23.8	41.0	45.6
EBIT/Interest	13.4	13.6	12.6		8.1	6.4	23.2	16.5	10.0	18.7
	(313) 4.9	(294) 4.3	(311) 3.8		(15) 2.8	(38) 3.3	(39) 5.6	(70) 3.6	(69) 4.0	(80) 4.1
	1.6	1.8	1.4		-1.1	-.1	1.1	1.3	1.7	2.1
Net Profit + Depr., Dep., Amort./Cur. Mat. L/T/D	6.2	9.3	8.4					9.7	8.1	21.2
	(70) 2.2	(73) 3.4	(62) 2.9					(11) 1.3	(13) 2.6	(26) 3.5
	1.3	1.6	1.3					1.0	.6	2.1
Fixed/Worth	.1	.1	.1		.2	.2	.1	.1	.1	.2
	.4	.4	.4		.4	1.0	.4	.4	.4	.4
	1.9	1.2	2.0		-.7	-.6	2.9	1.9	1.3	1.0
Debt/Worth	1.0	1.0	1.0		.8	1.4	1.0	.6	1.1	1.2
	2.6	2.6	2.6		10.9	6.2	2.2	2.0	2.4	2.9
	10.0	7.5	8.8		-5.0	-7.4	14.1	5.5	5.6	8.4
% Profit Before Taxes/Tangible Net Worth	56.8	61.8	65.3		82.5	88.8	91.8	59.9	54.7	70.4
	(302) 25.5	(283) 28.6	(284) 23.8		(11) 18.9	(28) 31.5	(36) 30.2	(68) 18.3	(71) 22.2	(70) 30.5
	9.8	10.1	6.7		-2.2	5.2	1.9	3.1	9.0	13.3
% Profit Before Taxes/Total Assets	17.1	18.2	21.2		32.1	24.8	29.2	17.6	20.5	20.3
	7.2	7.5	6.7		.0	7.5	6.9	6.2	6.3	7.1
	1.7	2.1	1.0		-13.0	-2.2	.6	.5	2.1	3.0
Sales/Net Fixed Assets	102.5	112.1	108.2		255.8	71.5	97.8	89.8	102.8	121.7
	36.4	37.9	32.6		19.1	25.9	36.3	26.6	41.9	42.5
	10.2	14.6	12.2		6.9	8.5	14.8	8.9	14.0	12.4
Sales/Total Assets	3.9	4.2	3.8		3.2	3.9	3.4	3.4	4.2	3.9
	2.7	3.2	2.9		2.5	2.2	2.8	2.5	3.3	2.9
	1.7	2.0	1.8		1.6	1.7	1.9	1.5	2.2	1.9
% Depr., Dep., Amort./Sales	.4	.3	.3		1.1	.3	.4	.3	.3	.3
	(291) .9	(268) .8	(268) .8		(11) 2.3	(31) 1.0	(29) .8	(62) 1.3	(66) .8	(69) .6
	2.3	1.8	2.3		6.2	2.0	1.7	3.0	2.8	1.3
% Officers', Directors' Owners' Comp/Sales	2.4	2.3	2.0		2.1	3.6	2.4	1.5	1.0	
	(128) 4.5	(120) 4.4	(129) 4.1		(14) 5.7	(21) 5.5	(37) 4.7	(31) 2.9	(18) 1.9	
	8.9	8.8	8.0		10.4	9.6	7.7	8.1	3.3	
Net Sales ($)	8969818M	10010653M	10515648M		11522M	81650M	169219M	567066M	1274157M	8412034M
Total Assets ($)	4197776M	3765305M	4089966M		5627M	38139M	73106M	306749M	547265M	3119080M

M = $ thousand   MM = $ million
See Pages 11 through 21 for Explanation of Ratios and Data

Current Data Sorted by Assets   Comparative Historical Data

0-500M	500M-2MM	2-10MM	10-50MM	50-100MM	100-250MM		ALL 4/1/02-3/31/03	ALL 4/1/03-3/31/04
						Type of Statement		
		4	3	2		Unqualified	4	6
	2	4	1			Reviewed	6	11
1	2	3				Compiled	5	3
1						Tax Returns	2	6
	3	1	2			Other	11	11
	6 (4/1-9/30/06)		23 (10/1/06-3/31/07)					
2	7	12	6		2	**NUMBER OF STATEMENTS**	28	37
%	%	%	%	%	%	**ASSETS**	%	%
		6.3				Cash & Equivalents	5.6	6.1
		32.0				Trade Receivables (net)	30.0	28.4
		42.5				Inventory	37.7	36.4
		.9				All Other Current	2.9	4.8
		81.7	DATA NOT AVAILABLE			Total Current	76.2	75.7
		7.0				Fixed Assets (net)	13.8	12.7
		2.8				Intangibles (net)	7.4	4.9
		8.5				All Other Non-Current	2.6	6.7
		100.0				Total	100.0	100.0
						LIABILITIES		
		8.7				Notes Payable-Short Term	17.1	20.3
		4.2				Cur. Mat.-L.T.D.	3.9	3.6
		28.4				Trade Payables	30.0	23.3
		.1				Income Taxes Payable	.2	.0
		4.7				All Other Current	9.5	9.1
		46.0				Total Current	60.7	56.4
		3.5				Long-Term Debt	17.2	14.4
		.0				Deferred Taxes	.1	.1
		2.6				All Other Non-Current	4.0	9.9
		47.9				Net Worth	18.1	19.3
		100.0				Total Liabilities & Net Worth	100.0	100.0
						INCOME DATA		
		100.0				Net Sales	100.0	100.0
		31.2				Gross Profit	42.5	42.7
		27.7				Operating Expenses	39.3	40.1
		3.5				Operating Profit	3.2	2.5
		.8				All Other Expenses (net)	1.5	.6
		2.7				Profit Before Taxes	1.7	1.9
						RATIOS		
		2.7					2.3	2.2
		1.6				Current	1.6	1.6
		1.2					1.1	1.3
		1.4					1.2	1.3
		1.0				Quick	.8	.7
		.6					.5	.4
		28 13.2					26 13.9	30 12.1
		34 10.7				Sales/Receivables	38 9.6	39 9.3
		50 7.3					49 7.5	51 7.1
		12 30.1					37 10.0	39 9.4
		80 4.6				Cost of Sales/Inventory	103 3.5	110 3.3
		207 1.8					193 1.9	182 2.0
		31 11.8					27 13.3	28 13.1
		34 10.7				Cost of Sales/Payables	54 6.8	51 7.2
		77 4.7					97 3.8	89 4.1
		5.2					5.5	5.3
		9.9				Sales/Working Capital	13.1	9.9
		40.9					35.9	18.2
		33.6					10.6	8.5
		4.4				EBIT/Interest	(26) 3.2	(33) 3.1
		.0					1.6	.3
							3.7	2.8
						Net Profit + Depr., Dep., Amort./Cur. Mat. L/T/D	(10) 1.5	(12) 1.7
							.5	.4
		.0					.2	.2
		.1				Fixed/Worth	.5	.4
		.4					-.5	1.8
		.5					.9	.9
		1.6				Debt/Worth	2.8	2.1
		1.9					-6.2	14.3
		44.3					54.4	46.8
	(11)	14.9				% Profit Before Taxes/Tangible Net Worth	(20) 24.1	(30) 12.6
		3.7					3.8	-10.8
		20.8					17.7	14.4
		7.6				% Profit Before Taxes/Total Assets	4.2	6.0
		-1.4					1.2	-2.3
		315.6					89.1	52.2
		88.2				Sales/Net Fixed Assets	27.3	24.3
		18.6					10.7	12.0
		3.9					3.9	3.4
		2.8				Sales/Total Assets	3.1	2.3
		2.2					1.8	1.6
							.4	.5
						% Depr., Dep., Amort./Sales	(24) .9	(31) 1.1
							2.3	2.1
							1.8	2.1
						% Officers', Directors' Owners' Comp/Sales	(13) 4.1	(15) 4.1
							6.9	4.7
1698M	35746M	203354M	296916M		557009M	Net Sales ($)	942463M	1431629M
348M	9513M	58861M	123520M		349165M	Total Assets ($)	644790M	781412M

M = $ thousand   MM = $ million
See Pages 11 through 21 for Explanation of Ratios and Data

Comparative Historical Data | Current Data Sorted by Sales

4/1/04-3/31/05 ALL	4/1/05-3/31/06 ALL	4/1/06-3/31/07 ALL		0-1MM	1-3MM	3-5MM	5-10MM	10-25MM	25MM & OVER
			Type of Statement						
5	8	9	Unqualified		1		1	1	6
5	5	7	Reviewed				3	2	2
4	4	6	Compiled	1		2	2		1
4	4	1	Tax Returns				1		
6	6	6	Other		2			2	2
	6 (4/1-9/30/06)	23 (10/1/06-3/31/07)							
24	23	29	**NUMBER OF STATEMENTS**	1	3	2	7	5	11
%	%	%	**ASSETS**	%	%	%	%	%	%
4.8	8.7	7.2	Cash & Equivalents						9.6
27.5	29.4	27.9	Trade Receivables (net)						33.4
39.0	40.3	39.7	Inventory						25.4
2.5	2.7	2.3	All Other Current						3.2
73.8	81.1	77.2	Total Current						71.6
15.7	10.5	11.0	Fixed Assets (net)						12.2
3.9	1.9	5.6	Intangibles (net)						10.1
6.6	6.4	6.3	All Other Non-Current						6.1
100.0	100.0	100.0	Total						100.0
			LIABILITIES						
12.2	14.7	11.2	Notes Payable-Short Term						6.1
13.9	2.1	2.5	Cur. Mat.-L.T.D.						2.1
24.0	21.1	26.0	Trade Payables						24.5
.0	.5	.1	Income Taxes Payable						.2
10.8	14.2	12.6	All Other Current						8.8
60.9	52.5	52.4	Total Current						41.9
12.4	14.6	8.0	Long-Term Debt						10.7
.1	.2	.0	Deferred Taxes						.1
7.8	5.2	2.0	All Other Non-Current						.8
18.8	27.5	37.6	Net Worth						46.5
100.0	100.0	100.0	Total Liabilties & Net Worth						100.0
			INCOME DATA						
100.0	100.0	100.0	Net Sales						100.0
40.3	40.4	37.4	Gross Profit						35.1
40.0	35.4	33.9	Operating Expenses						28.0
.3	5.0	3.5	Operating Profit						7.1
1.6	.9	.9	All Other Expenses (net)						.8
-1.3	4.2	2.6	Profit Before Taxes						6.3
			RATIOS						
2.3	2.0	2.1	Current						2.2
1.4	1.5	1.6							1.7
1.0	1.3	1.1							1.6
1.3	1.2	1.1	Quick						1.2
.6	.7	(28) .8							1.0
.3	.5	.5							.9
31 11.8	31 11.8	28 13.0	Sales/Receivables						34 10.9
40 9.1	37 9.9	35 10.5							35 10.3
50 7.3	52 7.0	44 8.4							47 7.8
58 6.3	63 5.8	44 8.3	Cost of Sales/Inventory						11 32.4
93 3.9	99 3.7	99 3.7							101 3.6
184 2.0	176 2.1	150 2.4							135 2.7
16 22.8	21 17.0	32 11.5	Cost of Sales/Payables						31 11.7
56 6.5	45 8.2	38 9.7							36 10.1
116 3.1	70 5.2	83 4.4							85 4.3
6.4	5.8	5.5	Sales/Working Capital						5.2
12.9	11.6	14.3							9.0
159.3	26.2	51.1							15.0
10.8	9.3	18.3	EBIT/Interest						37.3
(23) 2.0	(22) 3.7	(28) 4.0							12.0
-1.0	1.7	1.6							3.9
			Net Profit + Depr., Dep., Amort./Cur. Mat. L/T/D						
.2	.1	.1	Fixed/Worth						.1
.8	.2	.2							.5
NM	.7	.6							.6
1.0	1.1	.9	Debt/Worth						.7
2.1	1.9	1.7							1.1
NM	4.2	4.0							3.2
26.4	64.4	57.6	% Profit Before Taxes/Tangible Net Worth						75.4
(18) 13.3	(21) 23.7	(26) 31.5						(10)	36.3
-5.0	3.5	9.3							22.5
12.3	20.0	15.6	% Profit Before Taxes/Total Assets						19.5
2.7	7.5	10.8							14.0
-6.1	1.1	1.3							11.8
93.1	95.0	163.7	Sales/Net Fixed Assets						51.1
29.9	42.8	37.4							18.9
9.3	13.0	13.0							11.6
3.5	3.4	4.0	Sales/Total Assets						4.4
2.2	2.7	2.9							2.7
1.7	2.0	1.8							1.7
.6	.3	.3	% Depr., Dep., Amort./Sales						
(20) 1.0	(20) .8	(20) .7							
2.9	1.7	1.9							
2.9	1.4	2.1	% Officers', Directors' Owners' Comp/Sales						
(10) 5.5	(10) 4.0	(10) 4.1							
15.5	5.8	10.8							
283384M	366283M	1094723M	Net Sales ($)	175M	5441M	7442M	51325M	68938M	961402M
124311M	154130M	541407M	Total Assets ($)	55M	2258M	3436M	18561M	25129M	491968M

M = $ thousand   MM = $ million
See Pages 11 through 21 for Explanation of Ratios and Data

Current Data Sorted by Assets   Comparative Historical Data

						Type of Statement		
		4	5	2		Unqualified	15	14
1	4	17	4			Reviewed	36	28
1	8	7	1			Compiled	14	21
2	6	2				Tax Returns	13	12
2	4	8	7	2		Other	23	24
0-500M	15 (4/1-9/30/06) 500M-2MM	2-10MM	72 (10/1/06-3/31/07) 10-50MM	50-100MM	100-250MM		4/1/02-3/31/03 ALL	4/1/03-3/31/04 ALL
6	22	38	17	4		NUMBER OF STATEMENTS	101	99
%	%	%	%	%	%	ASSETS	%	%
	10.7	4.4	7.6			Cash & Equivalents	8.4	7.8
	36.8	39.1	23.1			Trade Receivables (net)	34.6	34.4
	29.8	34.0	29.5			Inventory	31.0	33.2
	2.0	4.5	3.4			All Other Current	3.0	2.6
	79.4	82.0	63.6			Total Current	76.9	78.1
	13.3	8.0	22.4			Fixed Assets (net)	11.5	12.6
	4.3	3.7	6.7			Intangibles (net)	5.7	4.7
	3.0	6.3	7.3			All Other Non-Current	5.8	4.7
	100.0	100.0	100.0			Total	100.0	100.0
						LIABILITIES		
	10.8	12.2	9.8			Notes Payable-Short Term	14.0	13.0
	1.8	3.3	6.5			Cur. Mat.-L.T.D.	3.7	2.7
	19.8	27.8	15.3			Trade Payables	22.5	22.5
	.2	.2	.0			Income Taxes Payable	.2	.2
	17.0	10.9	9.7			All Other Current	10.7	11.2
	49.5	54.3	41.3			Total Current	51.1	49.5
	11.1	6.5	13.8			Long-Term Debt	8.2	7.5
	.0	.1	.0			Deferred Taxes	.3	.2
	6.2	2.6	7.2			All Other Non-Current	4.0	7.2
	33.1	36.5	37.7			Net Worth	36.5	35.5
	100.0	100.0	100.0			Total Liabilities & Net Worth	100.0	100.0
						INCOME DATA		
	100.0	100.0	100.0			Net Sales	100.0	100.0
	38.7	32.5	36.8			Gross Profit	35.4	32.1
	33.1	28.6	30.5			Operating Expenses	31.6	28.8
	5.6	3.9	6.3			Operating Profit	3.7	3.4
	1.8	1.1	1.8			All Other Expenses (net)	.3	.9
	3.8	2.9	4.5			Profit Before Taxes	3.4	2.5
						RATIOS		
	2.3	2.3	2.6				2.5	2.3
	1.5	1.6	1.5			Current	1.6	1.5
	1.2	1.1	1.1				1.1	1.2
	1.6	1.2	1.1				1.4	1.2
	.9	(37) .9	.6			Quick	.8	.8
	.6	.6	.5				.6	.6
	23 15.9	35 10.4	36 10.1				31 11.9	31 11.8
	28 12.9	49 7.5	41 9.0			Sales/Receivables	42 8.8	41 8.9
	42 8.6	62 5.9	51 7.2				54 6.7	53 6.9
	26 14.0	37 10.0	41 8.9				28 13.0	30 12.0
	52 7.0	66 5.5	69 5.3			Cost of Sales/Inventory	60 6.1	64 5.7
	86 4.2	104 3.5	143 2.6				101 3.6	113 3.2
	16 23.1	25 14.8	25 14.6				19 19.1	23 15.6
	23 16.1	45 8.1	35 10.4			Cost of Sales/Payables	36 10.0	42 8.6
	34 10.9	76 4.8	62 5.9				65 5.7	61 6.0
	7.3	5.6	4.1				6.1	5.6
	14.8	8.4	10.1			Sales/Working Capital	11.9	11.2
	41.8	37.1	57.4				36.2	23.9
	19.2	7.1	18.2				16.8	11.4
	(21) 3.9	(36) 4.2	(16) 5.6			EBIT/Interest	(87) 5.0	(88) 4.8
	1.7	1.4	1.9				1.4	1.9
		44.2				Net Profit + Depr., Dep.,	7.6	6.0
		(11) 8.7				Amort./Cur. Mat. L/T/D	(18) 3.4	(19) 3.1
		1.8					1.3	1.7
	.1	.1	.3				.1	.1
	.2	.2	.6			Fixed/Worth	.3	.3
	1.3	.5	1.7				.8	1.0
	1.0	.8	1.0				.8	.9
	2.1	2.1	1.9			Debt/Worth	1.9	2.2
	6.7	7.4	7.1				6.6	5.2
	102.6	49.5	44.9			% Profit Before Taxes/Tangible	48.5	40.7
	(18) 48.0	(36) 12.7	(15) 28.5			Net Worth	(84) 22.4	(86) 17.8
	11.1	5.7	14.9				5.4	4.5
	29.7	9.5	17.6			% Profit Before Taxes/Total	15.8	11.2
	9.7	4.4	9.1			Assets	7.1	6.5
	1.4	1.0	2.6				1.2	1.5
	256.9	114.3	23.4				119.2	77.0
	78.5	59.9	10.7			Sales/Net Fixed Assets	35.9	32.8
	12.5	21.4	5.6				15.6	13.1
	5.0	3.3	2.4				3.6	3.8
	4.2	2.8	2.2			Sales/Total Assets	2.8	2.7
	3.1	2.1	1.5				2.2	2.1
	.2	.3	.9				.5	.5
	(18) .7	(34) .5	(15) 1.7			% Depr., Dep., Amort./Sales	(80) 1.0	(81) 1.1
	4.0						2.2	2.3
	2.9	1.9				% Officers', Directors'	1.8	2.2
	(11) 3.2	(19) 3.0				Owners' Comp/Sales	(44) 4.5	(48) 4.2
	7.8	4.4					7.5	7.9
8719M	100800M	499526M	757478M	275919M		Net Sales ($)	1761758M	1402368M
1444M	25873M	173892M	378720M	250727M		Total Assets ($)	665712M	620267M

M = $ thousand   MM = $ million
See Pages 11 through 21 for Explanation of Ratios and Data

Comparative Historical Data   Current Data Sorted by Sales

Type of Statement									
					15 (4/1-9/30/06)			72 (10/1/06-3/31/07)	
Unqualified	9	13	11					4	7
Reviewed	25	25	26	1	1	2	6	12	4
Compiled	13	11	17		4	1	7	4	1
Tax Returns	11	9	10		1	2	2	1	
Other	20	29	23	1	4	7	2	3	6
	4/1/04-3/31/05 ALL	4/1/05-3/31/06 ALL	4/1/06-3/31/07 ALL	0-1MM	1-3MM	3-5MM	5-10MM	10-25MM	25MM & OVER
NUMBER OF STATEMENTS	78	87	87	2	10	12	21	24	18

ASSETS

	%	%	%	%	%	%	%	%	%
Cash & Equivalents	6.9	6.6	7.1		10.9	14.3	4.4	6.6	4.4
Trade Receivables (net)	38.6	34.1	34.9		34.9	36.3	37.4	37.5	29.1
Inventory	29.5	33.6	31.2		24.8	30.1	27.2	35.7	29.1
All Other Current	3.0	2.0	3.2		1.2	2.7	6.3	2.1	3.1
Total Current	77.9	76.4	76.4		71.8	83.4	75.3	82.0	65.6
Fixed Assets (net)	12.4	13.2	13.3		20.4	10.8	9.5	11.3	19.4
Intangibles (net)	5.4	5.0	4.9		4.1	5.1	2.8	3.7	9.8
All Other Non-Current	4.3	5.5	5.4		3.7	.7	12.4	2.9	5.1
Total	100.0	100.0	100.0		100.0	100.0	100.0	100.0	100.0

LIABILITIES

Notes Payable-Short Term	16.1	12.2	11.6		5.2	9.9	10.2	13.5	9.7
Cur. Mat.-L.T.D.	3.0	2.8	3.2		2.8	1.3	1.6	4.4	5.1
Trade Payables	24.6	22.2	21.7		17.0	18.9	23.6	27.9	17.3
Income Taxes Payable	.3	.3	.1		.1	.3	.2	.1	.1
All Other Current	10.5	9.8	12.1		13.1	20.1	8.0	11.1	13.3
Total Current	54.5	47.3	48.8		38.1	50.5	43.5	57.0	45.5
Long-Term Debt	8.0	7.6	11.8		29.2	6.6	7.6	6.1	19.4
Deferred Taxes	.1	.1	.0		.0	.0	.0	.1	.0
All Other Non-Current	3.6	4.8	4.2		2.5	1.8	11.6	2.3	1.2
Net Worth	33.7	40.2	35.2		30.2	41.1	37.3	34.5	33.8
Total Liabilties & Net Worth	100.0	100.0	100.0		100.0	100.0	100.0	100.0	100.0

INCOME DATA

Net Sales	100.0	100.0	100.0		100.0	100.0	100.0	100.0	100.0
Gross Profit	33.7	33.7	35.3		43.8	35.2	33.6	32.3	35.4
Operating Expenses	30.9	29.5	30.3		41.3	27.1	29.1	27.9	30.9
Operating Profit	2.9	4.2	5.1		2.6	8.1	4.5	4.4	4.5
All Other Expenses (net)	.9	.8	1.5		1.0	1.3	2.4	.9	1.5
Profit Before Taxes	1.9	3.4	3.6		1.6	6.9	2.2	3.5	3.0

RATIOS

Ratio	H1	H2	H3	0-1MM	1-3MM	3-5MM	5-10MM	10-25MM	25MM & OVER
Current	2.3	2.5	2.6		3.4	2.0	2.8	2.6	2.0
	1.3	1.6	1.6		2.1	1.6	1.8	1.5	1.5
	1.0	1.2	1.2		1.2	1.3	1.3	1.0	1.1
Quick	1.3	1.3	1.2		2.7	1.3	1.3	1.4	1.2
	.8	.8	(86) .9		1.2	(20) 1.0	.9	.8	.7
	.6	.6	.6		.5	.7	.7	.6	.5
Sales/Receivables	34 10.6	33 11.2	28 13.1		19 19.5	22 16.2	31 11.9	32 11.5	37 9.8
	45 8.0	42 8.8	41 8.9		27 13.7	34 10.8	41 8.9	49 7.5	41 8.8
	55 6.7	52 7.1	53 6.9		44 8.3	53 6.9	48 7.6	58 6.7	54 6.7
Cost of Sales/Inventory	31 11.9	39 9.3	31 11.7		0 UND	18 20.2	8 45.2	40 9.1	32 11.5
	57 6.4	65 5.7	64 5.7		62 5.9	58 6.3	54 6.7	61 6.0	68 5.4
	103 3.6	120 3.0	103 3.5		93 3.9	96 3.8	101 3.6	101 3.6	164 2.2
Cost of Sales/Payables	22 16.4	24 15.4	21 17.1		7 51.5	15 24.5	20 18.0	24 14.9	26 14.1
	43 8.5	32 11.3	33 10.9		19 19.2	23 15.9	35 10.4	45 8.1	37 9.9
	62 5.8	54 6.7	58 6.3		35 10.3	34 10.9	66 5.5	62 5.9	61 5.9
Sales/Working Capital	6.4	5.4	5.6		8.0	6.0	4.7	7.7	5.0
	15.0	9.4	9.6		10.2	9.0	8.1	10.5	9.9
	142.2	24.9	35.3		NM	51.2	27.7	71.3	38.1
EBIT/Interest	12.0	10.1	11.1		8.8	106.5	13.0	7.4	9.9
	(70) 4.0	(78) 4.0	(82) 4.5		2.9	(11) 6.1	4.5	(21) 3.3	5.3
	1.9	2.1	1.6		1.4	2.6	1.2	1.9	1.5
Net Profit + Depr., Dep., Amort./Cur. Mat. L/T/D	5.1	6.4	27.5						
	(15) 1.9	(21) 3.1	(19) 7.8						
	1.2	1.8	2.0						
Fixed/Worth	.2	.1	.1		.2	.1	.1	.1	.1
	.4	.3	.3		.7	.2	.2	.3	.6
	5.6	.8	.9		NM	1.2	.5	.7	2.0
Debt/Worth	.8	.7	.9		.6	.8	.7	1.3	1.5
	2.5	1.9	2.1		2.2	2.0	1.7	2.7	2.2
	26.3	5.2	7.3		NM	5.7	5.4	9.2	7.8
% Profit Before Taxes/Tangible Net Worth	54.2	38.4	60.3			103.1	31.7	58.3	44.9
	(62) 14.8	(76) 18.3	(77) 26.5			(11) 79.3	(19) 11.6	(22) 18.3	(15) 27.5
	3.3	6.9	7.7			50.4	3.0	9.0	4.6
% Profit Before Taxes/Total Assets	10.5	11.9	16.6		11.7	53.8	16.1	8.7	16.8
	5.5	6.3	6.1		5.3	14.6	4.7	5.0	9.5
	1.4	1.6	1.6		.9	5.2	.6	1.9	1.5
Sales/Net Fixed Assets	91.5	91.3	137.2		198.3	262.6	232.1	87.1	72.6
	34.2	37.2	45.4		36.1	85.8	63.2	51.2	15.2
	12.3	10.6	12.3		4.6	15.6	13.3	18.0	6.0
Sales/Total Assets	3.7	3.6	3.9		5.2	5.9	4.2	3.3	2.8
	2.8	2.8	2.8		4.2	3.6	3.0	2.9	2.2
	2.1	2.0	2.0		2.0	2.0	1.9	2.1	1.4
% Depr., Dep., Amort./Sales	.5	.4	.3			.2	.2	.3	.5
	(65) .9	(71) .9	(74) .8			(10) .6	(18) .5	(22) .7	(15) 1.1
	2.5	2.2	2.1			1.3	2.1	1.5	4.0
% Officers', Directors' Owners' Comp/Sales	1.9	1.5	2.1				2.1		
	(38) 3.1	(37) 2.9	(36) 3.1				(12) 3.0		
	7.3	5.9	4.8				4.6		
Net Sales ($)	1694077M	2109094M	1642442M	147M	22062M	48377M	156220M	414810M	1000826M
Total Assets ($)	945095M	948474M	830656M	81M	7854M	15744M	66804M	157526M	582647M

M = $ thousand   MM = $ million
See Pages 11 through 21 for Explanation of Ratios and Data

Current Data Sorted by Assets							Comparative Historical Data	
2	2	19	67	27	23	**Type of Statement** Unqualified	119	96
2	7	96	66	4	2	Reviewed	165	169
4	33	50	16	1		Compiled	88	127
7	19	20	3			Tax Returns	25	30
10	32	74	61	11	19	Other	161	150
	134 (4/1-9/30/06)		543 (10/1/06-3/31/07)				4/1/02-3/31/03	4/1/03-3/31/04
0-500M	500M-2MM	2-10MM	10-50MM	50-100MM	100-250MM		ALL	ALL
25	93	259	213	43	44	**NUMBER OF STATEMENTS**	558	572
%	%	%	%	%	%	**ASSETS**	%	%
23.7	7.2	5.8	4.6	3.4	3.3	Cash & Equivalents	5.5	5.2
28.1	38.8	36.9	31.2	29.7	30.5	Trade Receivables (net)	31.7	33.9
16.1	34.6	39.6	44.8	47.2	43.1	Inventory	40.6	37.5
4.2	1.1	1.7	2.5	1.7	2.3	All Other Current	1.7	2.0
72.1	81.7	84.0	83.1	82.0	79.2	Total Current	79.5	78.6
15.8	12.8	11.3	11.7	11.1	12.4	Fixed Assets (net)	15.2	15.0
2.4	1.8	1.4	1.6	3.3	4.0	Intangibles (net)	1.7	1.6
9.7	3.6	3.4	3.5	3.6	4.4	All Other Non-Current	3.6	4.8
100.0	100.0	100.0	100.0	100.0	100.0	Total	100.0	100.0
						LIABILITIES		
17.5	18.3	19.6	22.6	23.0	13.7	Notes Payable-Short Term	21.3	21.3
1.1	2.0	1.5	1.4	2.6	1.0	Cur. Mat.-L.T.D.	2.9	2.2
25.4	28.2	23.4	20.2	17.2	18.6	Trade Payables	21.0	23.3
3.3	.2	.2	.5	.3	.3	Income Taxes Payable	.2	.1
12.2	6.4	7.4	7.5	6.9	11.9	All Other Current	6.3	7.0
59.4	55.1	52.1	52.1	49.9	45.4	Total Current	51.6	53.9
15.3	10.2	6.2	8.7	12.0	14.5	Long-Term Debt	9.1	8.9
.0	.2	.2	.4	.4	.6	Deferred Taxes	.3	.2
7.5	4.1	4.7	2.4	4.1	4.3	All Other Non-Current	4.0	5.9
17.7	30.5	36.9	36.4	33.5	35.1	Net Worth	35.0	31.0
100.0	100.0	100.0	100.0	100.0	100.0	Total Liabilities & Net Worth	100.0	100.0
						INCOME DATA		
100.0	100.0	100.0	100.0	100.0	100.0	Net Sales	100.0	100.0
28.3	24.7	20.7	17.7	15.9	14.3	Gross Profit	22.2	20.8
24.3	19.8	16.1	11.7	9.3	8.8	Operating Expenses	19.5	18.6
4.0	4.9	4.6	6.0	6.6	5.5	Operating Profit	2.7	2.2
.6	.8	.7	.7	.9	.8	All Other Expenses (net)	.9	.7
3.3	4.1	3.9	5.3	5.7	4.7	Profit Before Taxes	1.9	1.5
						RATIOS		
2.4	2.4	2.4	2.6	2.9	3.0		2.4	2.1
1.4	1.5	1.6	1.5	1.6	1.8	Current	1.5	1.4
.8	1.1	1.2	1.2	1.2	1.3		1.1	1.1
1.7	1.4	1.3	1.1	1.2	1.2		1.1	1.1
1.0	.8	.8	.7	.6	.8	Quick	.7	.7
.4	.5	.6	.5	.5	.5		.4	.5
0 UND	26 14.0	30 12.2	33 11.0	34 10.7	33 11.1		33 11.1	37 10.0
12 31.2	36 10.1	40 9.2	41 8.9	46 7.9	42 8.7	Sales/Receivables	43 8.5	44 8.2
44 8.2	49 7.5	53 6.9	48 7.6	52 7.1	52 7.0		53 6.9	55 6.6
0 UND	18 20.6	33 11.0	48 7.5	54 6.7	45 8.1		45 8.2	39 9.3
7 55.8	40 9.2	59 6.2	81 4.5	90 4.1	77 4.8	Cost of Sales/Inventory	76 4.8	69 5.3
27 13.6	85 4.3	93 3.9	111 3.3	132 2.8	94 3.9		115 3.2	103 3.5
0 UND	16 22.7	17 21.2	17 21.2	16 22.6	17 21.0		19 19.0	21 17.0
15 25.1	38 9.7	30 12.1	30 12.1	28 13.2	26 13.9	Cost of Sales/Payables	32 11.3	37 9.9
49 7.4	56 6.5	47 7.8	46 8.0	42 8.8	37 9.7		51 7.2	54 6.8
16.0	8.3	5.8	5.2	3.2	4.9		5.3	5.9
53.1	16.4	10.6	10.0	7.5	8.1	Sales/Working Capital	10.4	12.7
-43.5	46.1	21.5	21.4	18.9	16.3		29.2	35.5
24.7	12.3	13.2	13.3	12.8	11.8		6.4	6.5
(19) 4.1	(82) 6.0	(240) 4.8	(198) 5.1	4.9	(40) 5.8	EBIT/Interest	(527) 2.5	(525) 2.5
1.3	1.8	1.7	2.4	2.1	2.4		1.1	1.0
		10.1	27.6	19.3	32.8		6.0	4.8
	(51) 4.4	(62) 7.0	(14) 12.3	(21) 6.3		Net Profit + Depr., Dep., Amort./Cur. Mat. L/T/D	(134) 2.2	(113) 2.2
	1.9	2.8	6.1	1.6			.9	.8
.0	.0	.1	.1	.1	.2		.1	.1
.1	.2	.2	.2	.3	.4	Fixed/Worth	.3	.4
6.1	.9	.5	.8	.7	.7		1.1	1.0
1.1	1.0	.9	.9	1.4	1.1		1.0	1.2
3.1	2.8	2.0	2.3	2.4	2.6	Debt/Worth	2.2	2.6
NM	7.8	4.7	4.6	5.7	5.4		5.5	5.8
238.1	86.5	58.1	53.6	78.7	58.8		27.4	31.8
(19) 100.0	(84) 34.5	(248) 28.6	(203) 29.3	(38) 34.7	(40) 39.1	% Profit Before Taxes/Tangible Net Worth	(515) 12.3	(523) 12.0
.0	13.6	10.4	13.6	16.4	23.4		2.0	1.9
87.7	26.4	20.5	16.7	17.1	16.8		8.7	8.1
17.0	11.6	9.2	9.3	9.5	10.2	% Profit Before Taxes/Total Assets	3.4	3.1
-.6	2.3	2.1	3.2	3.2	5.6		.2	.1
UND	241.8	252.2	135.4	63.7	97.5		85.6	88.1
178.8	69.8	51.7	35.8	31.2	19.3	Sales/Net Fixed Assets	23.7	24.5
22.2	20.1	19.2	14.6	11.7	11.0		10.2	11.0
12.7	5.1	3.9	3.2	3.0	3.2		3.4	3.3
5.5	3.6	3.0	2.6	2.4	2.5	Sales/Total Assets	2.4	2.6
3.1	2.5	2.3	2.0	1.7	2.1		1.8	1.9
.3	.3	.2	.2	.3	.4		.4	.4
(12) .8	(59) .7	(208) .7	(193) .5	(37) .6	(40) .8	% Depr., Dep., Amort./Sales	(490) .9	(489) 1.0
2.4	1.5	1.2	1.0	.9	1.4		1.8	1.8
.8	1.6	1.2	.9				1.6	1.3
(12) 3.0	(52) 3.6	(111) 2.2	(52) 1.7			% Officers', Directors' Owners' Comp/Sales	(233) 3.0	(246) 2.6
	4.2	4.1	3.3				4.4	4.4
59499M	522060M	4487907M	14491732M	7003795M	19720252M	Net Sales ($)	19160328M	19353011M
6010M	123569M	1326830M	5024992M	2895152M	6745742M	Total Assets ($)	8476257M	8142997M

© RMA 2007

M = $ thousand   MM = $ million
See Pages 11 through 21 for Explanation of Ratios and Data

Comparative Historical Data | Current Data Sorted by Sales

			Type of Statement						
111	110	140	Unqualified	2			6	12	120
181	163	177	Reviewed		4	4	26	58	85
107	103	104	Compiled	3	9	14	34	22	22
36	41	49	Tax Returns	1	11	7	14	9	7
143	201	207	Other	7	12	14	33	40	101
4/1/04-3/31/05 ALL	4/1/05-3/31/06 ALL	4/1/06-3/31/07 ALL		134 (4/1-9/30/06)			543 (10/1/06-3/31/07)		
				0-1MM	1-3MM	3-5MM	5-10MM	10-25MM	25MM & OVER
578	618	677	NUMBER OF STATEMENTS	13	36	39	113	141	335
%	%	%	**ASSETS**	%	%	%	%	%	%
6.1	6.5	6.0	Cash & Equivalents	5.1	9.7	10.6	8.2	6.2	4.3
35.8	35.9	34.1	Trade Receivables (net)	33.3	29.2	31.6	35.8	35.8	33.8
39.1	36.6	40.4	Inventory	14.7	36.1	32.1	37.6	41.0	43.5
1.9	1.8	2.0	All Other Current	1.7	1.0	1.6	3.3	.7	2.3
82.9	80.8	82.5	Total Current	54.9	76.0	75.9	84.9	83.7	83.7
11.8	13.0	11.9	Fixed Assets (net)	30.3	15.6	16.5	10.4	11.9	10.7
1.1	2.0	1.8	Intangibles (net)	4.6	2.3	2.8	1.0	1.4	2.1
4.2	4.2	3.8	All Other Non-Current	10.3	6.0	4.8	3.8	3.0	3.5
100.0	100.0	100.0	Total	100.0	100.0	100.0	100.0	100.0	100.0
			LIABILITIES						
19.8	19.1	20.1	Notes Payable-Short Term	23.0	18.1	18.5	16.2	20.9	21.4
1.9	2.1	1.5	Cur. Mat.-L.T.D.	3.0	2.6	2.6	1.2	1.4	1.4
24.4	22.5	22.4	Trade Payables	14.6	28.4	26.2	23.9	21.2	21.7
.3	.4	.4	Income Taxes Payable	.0	2.3	.2	.2	.3	.3
7.3	6.9	7.7	All Other Current	8.7	6.6	7.1	7.9	7.6	7.8
53.7	51.0	52.2	Total Current	49.3	57.9	54.6	49.5	51.5	52.7
8.0	8.8	8.8	Long-Term Debt	14.4	12.0	12.3	8.8	5.4	9.2
.2	.3	.3	Deferred Taxes	.1	.1	.2	.2	.2	.3
5.0	5.4	3.9	All Other Non-Current	7.4	8.8	4.8	5.3	3.6	2.9
33.1	34.4	34.8	Net Worth	28.7	21.3	28.1	36.2	39.3	35.0
100.0	100.0	100.0	Total Liabilities & Net Worth	100.0	100.0	100.0	100.0	100.0	100.0
			INCOME DATA						
100.0	100.0	100.0	Net Sales	100.0	100.0	100.0	100.0	100.0	100.0
22.2	20.6	19.9	Gross Profit	40.7	28.7	25.5	22.5	22.4	15.5
16.6	15.2	14.6	Operating Expenses	36.1	24.0	20.5	17.9	16.5	10.2
5.6	5.3	5.3	Operating Profit	4.6	4.6	5.1	4.6	5.9	5.3
.5	.7	.7	All Other Expenses (net)	2.5	1.2	.9	.7	.7	.6
5.1	4.7	4.5	Profit Before Taxes	2.1	3.4	4.2	3.9	5.2	4.7
			RATIOS						
2.3	2.5	2.5		2.9	2.2	2.5	2.7	2.4	2.6
1.5	1.5	1.6	Current	1.7	1.2	1.5	1.7	1.5	1.6
1.2	1.2	1.2		.8	1.0	1.0	1.3	1.2	1.2
1.2	1.3	1.2		2.2	1.0	1.5	1.5	1.3	1.1
.8	.8	.8	Quick	1.1	.7	.7	.9	.8	.7
.5	.5	.5		.4	.4	.5	.5	.6	.5
32 11.3	33 11.2	30 12.0		13 28.4	22 16.9	29 12.5	29 12.7	31 11.6	31 11.7
44 8.4	41 9.0	40 9.2	Sales/Receivables	44 8.3	37 9.8	38 9.7	40 9.2	41 8.8	39 9.2
54 6.7	52 7.0	50 7.3		110 3.3	54 6.7	56 6.5	54 6.8	50 7.2	48 7.5
36 10.1	29 12.8	33 11.1		0 UND	18 20.8	18 19.9	31 11.7	35 10.4	39 9.3
67 5.4	56 6.5	65 5.6	Cost of Sales/Inventory	17 21.6	66 5.5	41 8.9	58 6.3	69 5.3	69 5.3
101 3.6	86 4.2	99 3.7		40 9.2	115 3.2	96 3.8	98 3.7	96 3.8	99 3.7
19 18.9	17 21.3	17 21.9		0 UND	16 22.6	25 14.7	16 22.7	18 20.8	17 22.0
34 10.8	29 12.8	29 12.4	Cost of Sales/Payables	31 11.9	45 8.1	44 8.3	31 11.6	30 12.3	27 13.5
53 6.8	46 8.0	47 7.8		88 4.2	71 5.2	63 5.8	54 6.8	47 7.8	42 8.8
5.9	6.3	5.8		3.5	9.4	4.6	5.2	6.5	5.7
10.8	11.1	11.0	Sales/Working Capital	25.9	16.8	11.4	9.6	11.4	10.6
23.1	26.7	24.7		-31.0	NM	170.2	22.6	20.7	24.0
21.3	14.6	13.0			10.5	28.0	13.0	13.5	12.9
(533) 8.6	(574) 6.3	(622) 5.1	EBIT/Interest		(32) 3.7	(35) 5.9	(102) 4.6	(132) 6.8	(312) 5.0
2.9	2.3	1.9			1.0	1.4	1.4	2.0	2.3
20.5	16.5	16.0	Net Profit + Depr., Dep.,			7.2	7.2	13.4	31.8
(119) 6.7	(137) 5.4	(157) 6.0	Amort./Cur. Mat. L/T/D			(20) 2.5	(33) 2.5	5.3	(96) 7.0
2.7	2.7	2.5					1.0	2.9	2.6
.1	.1	.1		.1	.1	.1	.0	.1	.1
.2	.3	.2	Fixed/Worth	1.0	.2	.3	.2	.2	.2
.7	.7	.7		NM	8.2	2.2	.6	.5	.7
1.0	1.0	1.0		.6	1.7	.7	.8	.9	1.0
2.4	2.2	2.3	Debt/Worth	2.6	5.2	2.3	2.0	2.0	2.4
4.9	4.9	5.2		NM	30.3	6.5	5.3	4.1	5.1
72.6	64.0	60.2	% Profit Before Taxes/Tangible	46.9	133.8	81.6	46.2	61.2	58.7
(541) 39.2	(575) 34.5	(632) 30.6	Net Worth	(10) 3.3	(31) 27.8	(34) 31.0	(104) 24.0	(139) 32.0	(314) 32.6
16.9	15.4	12.9		-4.3	4.9	5.9	9.5	13.4	16.1
22.3	21.0	18.9	% Profit Before Taxes/Total	15.9	23.4	22.2	21.8	21.6	17.4
10.6	10.6	9.6	Assets	.0	7.9	6.7	8.3	11.4	9.7
3.9	3.4	2.7		-3.9	.7	1.0	2.1	3.0	3.5
155.9	155.5	184.8		41.7	174.9	130.5	325.5	185.3	194.9
37.8	39.2	42.4	Sales/Net Fixed Assets	14.3	42.4	24.1	58.3	50.4	40.4
15.5	14.7	15.8		4.5	12.0	11.4	23.7	15.1	15.3
3.7	4.0	3.8		3.5	3.9	3.7	4.2	3.6	3.7
2.8	2.9	2.9	Sales/Total Assets	1.2	2.7	2.6	3.0	2.8	2.8
2.1	2.2	2.2		.5	1.7	1.8	2.2	2.3	2.2
.3	.3	.3			.3	.3	.4	.2	.2
(482) .7	(506) .7	(549) .6	% Depr., Dep., Amort./Sales		(23) .7	(28) 1.3	(80) .8	(118) .7	(291) .5
1.3	1.3	1.3			1.9	2.6	1.2	1.3	.9
1.2	1.1	1.2			3.2	1.3	1.5	1.4	.8
(229) 2.5	(243) 2.3	(236) 2.2	% Officers', Directors', Owners' Comp/Sales		(23) 4.3	(21) 2.3	(48) 2.7	(59) 2.3	(84) 1.7
4.9	4.1	4.2			6.5	5.9	4.4	4.1	3.0
29660649M	35344094M	46285245M	Net Sales ($)	6489M	77061M	153876M	839836M	2465522M	42742461M
11138345M	12118703M	16122295M	Total Assets ($)	8047M	33815M	85087M	314668M	902195M	14778483M

M = $ thousand   MM = $ million
See Pages 11 through 21 for Explanation of Ratios and Data

Current Data Sorted by Assets   Comparative Historical Data

Type of Statement	0-500M	500M-2MM	2-10MM	10-50MM	50-100MM	100-250MM	4/1/02-3/31/03	4/1/03-3/31/04
Unqualified			2	4	4		7	5
Reviewed			8	4			5	6
Compiled		2	8		1		5	8
Tax Returns		2	1				5	4
Other		3	4	4	3		11	16
		7 (4/1-9/30/06)		43 (10/1/06-3/31/07)			ALL	ALL
NUMBER OF STATEMENTS		7	23	12	8		33	39

Note: Data not available for the 0-500M, 500M-2MM, 50-100MM, and 100-250MM asset categories (marked "DATA NOT AVAILABLE").

	%	%	%	%	%	%	%	%
ASSETS								
Cash & Equivalents			6.6	4.6			15.2	8.0
Trade Receivables (net)			48.2	37.6			40.0	36.6
Inventory			18.7	30.7			16.8	20.0
All Other Current			1.4	3.5			3.0	7.7
Total Current			74.9	76.3			75.0	72.3
Fixed Assets (net)			16.9	12.6			16.3	16.2
Intangibles (net)			2.1	2.4			1.8	.9
All Other Non-Current			6.0	8.7			6.9	10.6
Total			100.0	100.0			100.0	100.0
LIABILITIES								
Notes Payable-Short Term			11.3	14.4			15.6	13.5
Cur. Mat.-L.T.D.			7.8	2.2			2.4	1.7
Trade Payables			31.4	21.6			30.5	25.2
Income Taxes Payable			.3	.0			.4	.1
All Other Current			11.8	5.6			4.3	11.0
Total Current			62.6	43.9			53.2	51.5
Long-Term Debt			8.9	7.0			9.9	12.6
Deferred Taxes			.0	.3			.3	.8
All Other Non-Current			4.2	10.9			4.6	4.6
Net Worth			24.3	37.9			32.1	30.5
Total Liabilities & Net Worth			100.0	100.0			100.0	100.0
INCOME DATA								
Net Sales			100.0	100.0			100.0	100.0
Gross Profit			14.8	12.3			12.0	19.1
Operating Expenses			11.3	6.8			10.2	15.5
Operating Profit			3.5	5.5			1.8	3.7
All Other Expenses (net)			.2	.6			.1	.5
Profit Before Taxes			3.3	4.9			1.7	3.2
RATIOS								
Current			1.5	3.6			2.2	2.2
			1.1	1.6			1.5	1.4
			1.0	1.1			1.0	1.0
Quick			1.2	1.8			1.7	1.2
			.9	1.0			1.0	.8
			.4	.4			.8	.6
Sales/Receivables		21	17.5	28 12.9			28 13.0	24 15.3
		32	11.6	42 8.7			42 8.6	34 10.7
		41	8.8	52 7.0			48 7.5	45 8.0
Cost of Sales/Inventory		0	UND	0 UND			0 UND	0 UND
		2	153.7	40 9.0			23 15.9	19 19.4
		65	5.6	85 4.3			45 8.1	67 5.5
Cost of Sales/Payables		11	32.8	10 37.8			16 22.4	14 25.4
		22	16.6	26 13.8			26 14.0	28 12.9
		42	8.8	55 6.7			54 6.7	51 7.2
Sales/Working Capital			31.4	4.7			6.2	7.0
			65.6	11.2			16.6	23.2
			-546.1	72.1			121.5	-999.8
EBIT/Interest			43.0	13.4			12.7	8.6
			5.0	(11) 4.2			(31) 4.4	(32) 3.6
			1.5	1.9			2.0	1.8
Net Profit + Depr., Dep., Amort./Cur. Mat. L/T/D								
Fixed/Worth			.1	.0			.0	.0
			.3	.2			.4	.4
			1.1	1.4			1.2	1.7
Debt/Worth			1.2	.7			.9	1.3
			3.9	1.6			1.9	3.3
			10.6	8.6			16.3	8.6
% Profit Before Taxes/Tangible Net Worth			53.3	51.8			34.7	47.2
			(20) 24.2	30.6			(28) 14.9	(36) 17.9
			13.9	10.8			5.4	7.7
% Profit Before Taxes/Total Assets			14.2	24.4			9.6	9.3
			7.0	11.7			3.5	4.1
			1.4	3.4			1.6	1.2
Sales/Net Fixed Assets			564.8	605.2			726.5	547.3
			67.9	106.7			60.1	38.0
			12.2	43.2			13.1	6.7
Sales/Total Assets			11.0	3.9			4.6	5.7
			4.5	3.2			3.1	2.3
			2.0	2.2			2.0	1.3
% Depr., Dep., Amort./Sales			.1	.1			.1	.0
			(19) .2	(10) .3			(26) .6	(28) .6
			1.5	1.4			3.0	1.6
% Officers', Directors' Owners' Comp/Sales							1.5	.5
							(12) 2.1	(14) 1.2
							3.8	2.8
Net Sales ($)		35967M	758677M	972704M	1505097M		1028991M	2095719M
Total Assets ($)		7626M	118487M	282163M	539394M		377306M	743046M

© RMA 2007

M = $ thousand   MM = $ million
See Pages 11 through 21 for Explanation of Ratios and Data

Comparative Historical Data   ## Current Data Sorted by Sales

						Type of Statement							
	6		10		10	Unqualified							10
	6		4		12	Reviewed			1		5		6
	10		11		11	Compiled		1	1	3	1		5
					3	Tax Returns		1		1			1
	14		17		14	Other			1		1		9
	4/1/04-		4/1/05-		4/1/06-			7 (4/1-9/30/06)			43 (10/1/06-3/31/07)		
	3/31/05		3/31/06		3/31/07		0-1MM	1-3MM	3-5MM	5-10MM	10-25MM	25MM & OVER
	ALL		ALL		ALL							
	36		42		50	NUMBER OF STATEMENTS		2	3	7	7	31
	%		%		%	ASSETS	%	%	%	%	%	%
	10.9		9.9		8.3	Cash & Equivalents						5.1
	32.4		33.3		40.7	Trade Receivables (net)	D					47.1
	17.5		19.9		22.1	Inventory	A					24.7
	1.9		1.9		1.9	All Other Current	T					2.4
	62.6		64.9		73.0	Total Current	A					79.3
	20.0		20.4		16.2	Fixed Assets (net)						10.8
	2.5		2.8		2.2	Intangibles (net)	N					1.9
	14.8		11.8		8.5	All Other Non-Current	O					7.9
	100.0		100.0		100.0	Total	T					100.0
						LIABILITIES	A					
	16.0		16.4		12.1	Notes Payable-Short Term	V					12.4
	5.2		3.6		5.1	Cur. Mat.-L.T.D.	A					4.9
	23.4		20.0		24.8	Trade Payables	I					26.6
	.2		.2		.2	Income Taxes Payable	L					.2
	7.7		9.9		10.9	All Other Current	A					9.4
	52.5		50.1		53.1	Total Current	B					53.6
	11.2		11.1		11.1	Long-Term Debt	L					9.5
	.2		.1		.1	Deferred Taxes	E					.2
	4.9		4.1		5.3	All Other Non-Current						5.7
	31.3		34.5		30.3	Net Worth						31.1
	100.0		100.0		100.0	Total Liabilities & Net Worth						100.0
						INCOME DATA						
	100.0		100.0		100.0	Net Sales						100.0
	19.3		12.1		18.0	Gross Profit						9.2
	13.9		10.8		13.7	Operating Expenses						5.9
	5.4		1.3		4.3	Operating Profit						3.3
	-1.0		-.3		.4	All Other Expenses (net)						.3
	6.4		1.7		3.9	Profit Before Taxes						3.0
						RATIOS						
	1.6		1.7		2.1							2.0
	1.2		1.3		1.2	Current						1.3
	.9		1.0		1.0							1.0
	1.1		1.3		1.3							1.3
	.7		.9		.9	Quick						1.0
	.5		.4		.5							.6
18	20.2	19	18.8	22	16.3						23	16.1
27	13.5	35	10.3	32	11.5	Sales/Receivables					30	12.3
41	8.9	48	7.6	45	8.1						50	7.2
0	UND	0	UND	0	UND						0	999.8
9	39.5	20	18.6	29	12.8	Cost of Sales/Inventory					30	12.2
50	7.3	57	6.4	61	6.0						56	6.6
11	32.3	14	25.9	10	37.5						11	32.8
25	14.4	22	16.7	22	16.5	Cost of Sales/Payables					22	16.6
35	10.4	29	12.6	40	9.1						32	11.3
	13.0		9.6		8.0							8.1
	40.9		18.4		45.8	Sales/Working Capital						31.4
	-54.9		-755.9		-536.0							277.8
	13.7		16.5		13.4							11.2
(33)	6.3	(39)	5.3	(47)	4.3	EBIT/Interest					(30)	4.3
	2.1		.8		1.7							1.7
					5.4	Net Profit + Depr., Dep.,						5.6
		(12)			3.0	Amort./Cur. Mat. L/T/D					(11)	3.7
					.9							1.6
	.0		.1		.1							.1
	.4		.5		.3	Fixed/Worth						.2
	1.1		1.7		1.7							.7
	1.4		1.0		1.0							1.3
	2.9		2.4		2.9	Debt/Worth						3.1
	8.3		5.0		11.0							10.0
	91.2		56.3		55.7	% Profit Before Taxes/Tangible						56.1
(35)	25.3	(39)	26.2	(45)	29.8	Net Worth						30.3
	9.8		12.2		14.6							13.2
	21.4		17.5		17.3	% Profit Before Taxes/Total						16.0
	6.4		9.5		7.2	Assets						5.9
	2.5		-.1		2.5							2.4
	475.1		231.7		336.9							687.3
	47.9		22.4		67.4	Sales/Net Fixed Assets						103.5
	6.8		5.6		11.8							39.8
	5.6		5.2		7.0							10.8
	3.7		3.1		3.7	Sales/Total Assets						3.9
	1.6		1.9		2.1							2.7
	.2		.1		.1							.1
(27)	.6	(35)	.7	(40)	.4	% Depr., Dep., Amort./Sales					(27)	.2
	2.7		3.2		1.7							1.4
					.6	% Officers', Directors'						
		(14)	1.7	(10)	1.4	Owners' Comp/Sales						
			1.0		3.0							
	1888184M		2693111M		3272445M	Net Sales ($)		4186M	13303M	56694M	106550M	3091712M
	737374M		1117648M		947670M	Total Assets ($)		2543M	5840M	25077M	36778M	877432M

M = $ thousand   MM = $ million

© RMA 2007

See Pages 11 through 21 for Explanation of Ratios and Data

Current Data Sorted by Assets　　　　Comparative Historical Data

	0-500M	500M-2MM	2-10MM	10-50MM	50-100MM	100-250MM	Type of Statement	4/1/02-3/31/03 ALL	4/1/03-3/31/04 ALL
	1		17	45	16	7	Unqualified	77	82
	3	23	88	35	4	1	Reviewed	155	142
	7	42	49	10		1	Compiled	99	137
	19	22	6	5			Tax Returns	38	27
	7	42	71	47	10	7	Other	113	130
	117 (4/1-9/30/06)			470 (10/1/06-3/31/07)					
	37	131	231	142	30	16	NUMBER OF STATEMENTS	482	518
	%	%	%	%	%	%	ASSETS	%	%
	16.5	7.8	6.4	5.1	4.5	6.1	Cash & Equivalents	6.5	5.4
	30.4	37.8	39.9	42.7	42.2	39.3	Trade Receivables (net)	38.2	38.3
	28.7	33.9	33.2	33.4	35.2	28.8	Inventory	34.4	35.2
	5.1	1.6	1.7	2.4	2.2	2.3	All Other Current	2.4	2.5
	80.7	81.1	81.2	83.6	84.0	76.4	Total Current	81.4	81.3
	12.1	9.3	10.9	10.1	11.1	12.0	Fixed Assets (net)	11.6	10.9
	3.4	4.0	3.0	1.7	3.1	5.2	Intangibles (net)	1.9	2.2
	3.8	5.7	4.9	4.5	1.8	6.3	All Other Non-Current	5.1	5.5
	100.0	100.0	100.0	100.0	100.0	100.0	Total	100.0	100.0
							LIABILITIES		
	23.4	16.1	15.9	15.1	11.8	7.6	Notes Payable-Short Term	16.9	16.5
	5.7	3.2	2.4	1.4	1.4	.8	Cur. Mat.-L.T.D.	2.5	2.1
	28.3	24.4	23.3	23.8	25.3	22.8	Trade Payables	24.1	23.8
	.0	.2	.3	.3	.2	.1	Income Taxes Payable	.2	.2
	10.7	11.5	9.7	8.6	10.1	6.5	All Other Current	8.5	9.4
	68.0	55.4	51.6	49.1	48.8	37.9	Total Current	52.1	52.0
	13.5	11.5	6.7	5.8	9.4	14.7	Long-Term Debt	7.9	8.2
	.0	.1	.2	.1	.1	.2	Deferred Taxes	.2	.3
	3.9	5.6	5.1	3.3	1.1	2.8	All Other Non-Current	4.2	4.6
	14.6	27.5	36.4	41.6	40.6	44.3	Net Worth	35.6	34.9
	100.0	100.0	100.0	100.0	100.0	100.0	Total Liabilties & Net Worth	100.0	100.0
							INCOME DATA		
	100.0	100.0	100.0	100.0	100.0	100.0	Net Sales	100.0	100.0
	44.1	32.3	27.2	23.9	21.4	25.0	Gross Profit	28.6	28.1
	38.8	28.7	22.7	18.4	15.8	17.1	Operating Expenses	26.8	25.9
	5.3	3.6	4.4	5.5	5.6	7.9	Operating Profit	1.8	2.1
	.8	.4	.5	.3	.3	.9	All Other Expenses (net)	.4	.4
	4.5	3.2	3.9	5.3	5.4	7.0	Profit Before Taxes	1.5	1.8
							RATIOS		
	2.2	2.4	2.3	2.3	2.7	2.4		2.4	2.2
	1.5	1.6	1.6	1.7	1.8	2.1	Current	1.6	1.6
	.9	1.1	1.2	1.3	1.3	1.6		1.2	1.2
	1.3	1.4	1.3	1.4	1.3	1.4		1.3	1.2
	.9	.8	1.0	.9	.9	1.2	Quick	.9 (517)	.9
	.4	.5	.6	.6	.7	.8		.6	.6
	5　77.1	31　11.6	39　9.3	43　8.5	45　8.2	43　8.5		38　9.5	38　9.6
	23　15.9	43　8.5	47　7.8	51　7.2	52　7.0	57　6.4	Sales/Receivables	47　7.8	47　7.7
	38　9.5	55　6.6	58　6.3	61　6.0	62　5.8	64　5.7		58　6.3	60　6.1
	5　72.5	25　14.5	33　10.9	38　9.6	37　10.0	38　9.6		38　9.7	39　9.3
	35　10.5	57　6.4	53　6.9	52　7.1	52　7.1	50　7.4	Cost of Sales/Inventory	57　6.4	58　6.3
	77　4.7	97　3.8	86　4.2	79　4.6	91　4.0	65　5.6		87　4.2	96　3.8
	22　16.9	23　15.5	23　15.7	26　14.1	30　12.2	33　11.0		24　15.0	26　14.0
	33　11.0	37　9.9	36　10.2	37　9.9	35　10.5	38　9.6	Cost of Sales/Payables	36　10.2	39　9.4
	58　6.3	54　6.8	50　7.4	48　7.6	50　7.3	49　7.5		52　7.0	53　6.9
	8.1	5.8	6.3	5.8	5.3	5.0		5.8	5.8
	19.9	10.0	9.6	9.3	8.6	6.8	Sales/Working Capital	9.8	9.8
	-69.2	53.1	23.9	16.2	15.6	11.2		20.3	19.2
	36.3	9.4	14.7	18.5	17.1	24.3		8.4	8.3
	(29)　7.4	(118)　3.2	(209)　4.5	(125)　7.7	(26)　9.0	12.3	EBIT/Interest	(436)　2.9	(473)　3.0
	1.7	1.4	1.9	3.9	5.2	4.4		1.1	1.4
		7.4	10.1	20.0			Net Profit + Depr., Dep.,	6.6	6.0
	(26)　2.4	(72)　3.4	(44)　8.3				Amort./Cur. Mat. L/T/D	(126)　2.5	(131)　2.0
	1.3	1.6	5.4					.9	.8
	.0	.1	.1	.1	.1	.1		.1	.1
	.3	.2	.2	.2	.2	.2	Fixed/Worth	.2	.3
	-2.5	2.2	.6	.4	.5	.7		.6	.6
	.8	1.0	.8	.9	1.1	.8		.9	1.0
	2.8	2.5	2.0	1.6	1.9	1.2	Debt/Worth	1.7	1.9
	-8.9	20.2	4.8	2.8	3.2	2.8		3.9	4.2
	111.6	60.0	48.8	52.5	52.7	69.4	% Profit Before Taxes/Tangible	27.0	24.6
	(25)　67.0	(104)　22.3	(213)　26.2	(140)　33.4	33.7	(15)　41.3	Net Worth	(437)　11.0	(470)　10.9
	31.1	9.7	9.8	20.5	25.8	20.4		2.1	2.1
	44.1	16.4	17.1	18.8	20.7	22.6	% Profit Before Taxes/Total	10.0	8.2
	14.5	6.1	7.6	11.9	13.0	14.1	Assets	3.4	3.1
	.2	1.6	2.7	6.5	9.2	8.6		.3	.5
	UND	198.2	89.5	103.7	104.1	66.1		77.7	77.9
	193.5	51.7	42.1	44.6	38.3	40.9	Sales/Net Fixed Assets	41.0	40.9
	39.4	25.9	21.6	18.4	14.9	20.5		17.8	19.7
	7.4	3.8	3.6	3.6	3.7	3.2		3.6	3.5
	4.1	3.1	2.9	2.9	3.1	2.9	Sales/Total Assets	2.9	2.8
	2.7	2.4	2.2	2.4	2.2	2.3		2.2	2.2
	.1	.3	.3	.3	.3	.3		.4	.4
	(20)　.5	(97)　.6	(204)　.6	(128)　.5	(29)　.4	(15)　.6	% Depr., Dep., Amort./Sales	(433)　.7	(439)　.7
	1.5	1.3	1.1	.7	.8	.7		1.1	1.3
	6.3	2.6	1.6	.9			% Officers', Directors'	1.6	1.6
	(19)　9.0	(60)　5.1	(96)　2.7	(35)　1.5			Owners' Comp/Sales	(200)　3.5	(210)　3.3
	17.5	7.5	5.0	3.1				6.5	6.0
	55713M	524217M	3464820M	9030190M	6137477M	6016965M	Net Sales ($)	13318029M	15885782M
	10217M	161685M	1164315M	3015048M	2045107M	2314670M	Total Assets ($)	4906663M	5952139M

© RMA 2007

M = $ thousand　　MM = $ million

See Pages 11 through 21 for Explanation of Ratios and Data

Comparative Historical Data

				Type of Statement						
88		89		88	Unqualified		2		3	16	67
157		136		154	Reviewed	2	8	13	25	59	47
91		93		109	Compiled	5	17	16	22	38	11
46		46		52	Tax Returns	8	17	14	4	4	5
107		164		184	Other	3	17	29	24	24	69

Current Data Sorted by Sales

4/1/04- 3/31/05 ALL		4/1/05- 3/31/06 ALL		4/1/06- 3/31/07 ALL		117 (4/1-9/30/06)			470 (10/1/06-3/31/07)		
						0-1MM	1-3MM	3-5MM	5-10MM	10-25MM	25MM & OVER
489		528		587	**NUMBER OF STATEMENTS**	18	61	72	78	159	199
%		%		%	**ASSETS**	%	%	%	%	%	%
6.4		6.1		7.0	Cash & Equivalents	13.0	9.0	9.3	8.1	6.3	5.1
39.6		40.0		39.6	Trade Receivables (net)	21.7	32.6	34.9	39.6	40.2	44.6
33.5		33.4		33.1	Inventory	37.1	30.6	36.3	28.8	34.6	32.9
2.3		2.1		2.1	All Other Current	9.2	1.3	2.1	1.7	1.5	2.4
81.8		81.6		81.7	Total Current	80.9	73.5	82.6	78.3	82.4	84.9
10.6		10.5		10.5	Fixed Assets (net)	12.0	13.4	9.6	12.7	10.0	9.3
2.6		3.0		3.0	Intangibles (net)	3.4	7.8	.8	4.1	2.8	2.0
5.0		4.9		4.8	All Other Non-Current	3.7	5.3	6.9	4.9	4.8	3.8
100.0		100.0		100.0	Total	100.0	100.0	100.0	100.0	100.0	100.0
					LIABILITIES						
15.5		15.1		15.8	Notes Payable-Short Term	20.3	16.9	16.5	18.9	15.6	13.7
2.3		2.2		2.4	Cur. Mat.-L.T.D.	6.9	3.2	3.5	3.5	2.2	1.2
24.6		24.1		24.1	Trade Payables	24.7	20.7	25.7	22.3	23.7	25.5
.2		.3		.3	Income Taxes Payable	.0	.0	.2	.3	.3	.3
9.5		9.8		9.8	All Other Current	8.2	14.8	9.5	7.9	9.4	9.5
52.0		51.5		52.4	Total Current	60.1	55.6	55.5	52.9	51.3	50.2
9.2		9.1		8.4	Long-Term Debt	7.9	18.0	10.5	9.9	5.6	6.3
.2		.1		.1	Deferred Taxes	.0	.1	.0	.1	.2	.1
4.5		4.9		4.4	All Other Non-Current	8.2	6.4	6.0	4.0	5.1	2.6
34.1		34.3		34.7	Net Worth	23.8	19.8	27.9	33.0	37.9	40.9
100.0		100.0		100.0	Total Liabilities & Net Worth	100.0	100.0	100.0	100.0	100.0	100.0
					INCOME DATA						
100.0		100.0		100.0	Net Sales	100.0	100.0	100.0	100.0	100.0	100.0
27.7		27.7		28.2	Gross Profit	48.1	36.8	31.9	30.3	27.1	22.6
24.6		23.8		23.5	Operating Expenses	42.5	33.1	28.5	26.0	22.2	17.1
3.1		3.9		4.7	Operating Profit	5.6	3.8	3.4	4.3	4.9	5.5
.4		.5		.5	All Other Expenses (net)	.9	.7	.5	.5	.6	.3
2.7		3.4		4.3	Profit Before Taxes	4.7	3.1	2.9	3.8	4.3	5.2
					RATIOS						
2.2		2.3		2.3		2.6	2.3	2.4	2.6	2.4	2.3
1.6		1.6		1.6	Current	1.6	1.6	1.5	1.6	1.6	1.8
1.2		1.2		1.2		.9	1.0	1.1	1.1	1.2	1.3
1.3		1.3		1.3		1.4	1.4	1.3	1.5	1.3	1.4
.9		.9		.9	Quick	.7	.9	.9	.9	1.0	1.0
.6		.7		.6		.2	.5	.5	.6	.6	.8

38	9.5	39	9.3	37	9.8		0	UND	30	12.3	30	12.1	38	9.6	39	9.4	43	8.5
48	7.6	49	7.4	48	7.6	Sales/Receivables	20	18.6	37	9.8	42	8.6	48	7.6	46	8.0	50	7.2
60	6.1	62	5.9	58	6.2		44	8.3	57	6.4	56	6.5	61	6.0	57	6.4	61	6.0
35	10.5	34	10.6	32	11.3		21	17.2	18	20.5	26	14.2	31	11.7	34	10.9	36	10.2
55	6.7	56	6.6	52	7.0	Cost of Sales/Inventory	69	5.3	58	6.3	66	5.5	49	7.5	55	6.7	47	7.8
83	4.4	85	4.3	85	4.3		196	1.9	122	3.0	98	3.7	84	4.3	91	4.0	66	5.5
27	13.4	27	13.6	24	14.9		27	13.6	18	20.2	24	15.4	21	17.2	23	15.8	27	13.4
38	9.7	40	9.2	36	10.1	Cost of Sales/Payables	45	8.0	35	10.3	40	9.1	35	10.5	36	10.2	36	10.1
52	7.0	52	7.0	49	7.4		84	4.4	55	6.6	55	6.6	48	7.6	51	7.1	47	7.8
	6.1		6.0		6.2			5.9		5.6		5.9		5.2		6.3		6.3
	10.2		10.5		9.7	Sales/Working Capital		9.7		9.0		10.2		10.0		10.2		9.4
	20.9		21.4		22.6			-36.5		131.0		80.8		37.5		24.2		16.2
	12.8		11.8		15.1			21.5		10.3		8.9		10.0		14.6		21.9
(443)	4.8	(473)	4.7	(523)	5.2	EBIT/Interest	(15)	3.0	(50)	3.0	(67)	3.2	(71)	3.0	(142)	4.8	(178)	9.5
	2.0		2.0		2.2			1.0		1.2		1.5		1.5		2.2		4.4
	11.3		12.6		14.5							5.0		6.5		10.7		27.8
(126)	3.5	(152)	4.7	(155)	5.4	Net Profit + Depr., Dep., Amort./Cur. Mat. L/T/D					(20)	2.0	(19)	2.7	(50)	3.5	(60)	9.2
	1.6		1.7		1.9							1.2		1.4		1.6		5.7
	.1		.1		.1			.0		.0		.1		.1		.1		.1
	.2		.2		.2	Fixed/Worth		.2		.4		.2		.3		.2		.2
	.6		.6		.6			4.4		NM		1.0		2.4		.5		.4
	1.0		1.0		.9			.6		1.1		.9		.7		.9		.9
	2.0		2.2		1.9	Debt/Worth		4.5		2.5		2.3		1.8		2.0		1.7
	4.3		4.6		5.1			NM		-8.2		14.6		9.0		4.5		2.9
	33.4		45.1		54.1			93.2		74.0		46.8		42.3		52.0		53.7
(446)	16.1	(484)	23.8	(527)	30.9	% Profit Before Taxes/Tangible Net Worth	(14)	35.6	(44)	35.4	(59)	19.6	(65)	18.8	(149)	30.4	(196)	35.0
	5.6		7.8		13.7			.0		9.7		7.4		5.4		11.5		22.6
	10.9		13.5		18.9			24.1		24.1		12.6		17.0		17.5		20.3
	5.1		7.3		9.5	% Profit Before Taxes/Total Assets		5.6		8.1		4.9		5.8		9.0		13.3
	1.6		2.2		3.4			.0		.8		1.6		1.5		3.0		7.3
	92.7		93.4		117.0			UND		152.6		155.6		160.6		91.8		99.9
	42.0		42.3		46.8	Sales/Net Fixed Assets		219.3		40.2		48.4		41.8		46.2		50.3
	20.7		21.7		21.1			10.3		11.5		26.3		15.7		24.2		21.9
	3.5		3.6		3.7			3.3		3.6		4.1		3.6		3.7		3.8
	3.0		2.9		3.0	Sales/Total Assets		2.8		2.7		3.0		2.9		3.0		3.2
	2.3		2.2		2.3			2.0		1.7		2.2		2.1		2.2		2.5
	.3		.3		.3			.1		.4		.3		.4		.3		.3
(416)	.6	(452)	.6	(493)	.5	% Depr., Dep., Amort./Sales	(11)	1.4	(42)	.8	(54)	.8	(62)	.7	(143)	.6	(181)	.4
	1.1		.9		1.0			3.1		1.7		1.2		1.5		1.0		.7
	1.7		1.7		1.7			6.2		3.2		3.1		2.3		1.2		1.0
(198)	3.3	(208)	3.3	(213)	3.2	% Officers', Directors' Owners' Comp/Sales	(10)	10.3	(27)	6.6	(33)	5.2	(34)	3.2	(67)	2.4	(42)	1.6
	6.3		6.4		6.2			22.5		10.0		8.0		5.0		4.6		2.8
15950341M		19739434M		25229382M	Net Sales ($)	10378M	116823M	283191M	554946M	2582182M	21681862M
5674184M		7230374M		8711042M	Total Assets ($)	4650M	49136M	100346M	218734M	950787M	7387389M

M = $ thousand   MM = $ million
See Pages 11 through 21 for Explanation of Ratios and Data

Current Data Sorted by Assets   Comparative Historical Data

0-500M	500M-2MM	2-10MM	10-50MM	50-100MM	100-250MM	Type of Statement	4/1/02-3/31/03 ALL	4/1/03-3/31/04 ALL
	1	4	13	8	1	Unqualified	33	37
	4	15	7	1		Reviewed	30	37
	8	12				Compiled	25	29
1	5	4	1			Tax Returns	8	9
1	3	25	14	5	2	Other	41	31
	25 (4/1-9/30/06)		110 (10/1/06-3/31/07)					
2	21	60	35	14	3	**NUMBER OF STATEMENTS**	137	143
%	%	%	%	%	%	**ASSETS**	%	%
	8.7	10.0	5.0	8.3		Cash & Equivalents	8.6	9.0
	33.3	36.5	35.0	29.8		Trade Receivables (net)	32.4	30.3
	43.5	39.4	40.3	39.3		Inventory	40.5	39.5
	2.3	1.9	1.7	2.0		All Other Current	1.8	2.1
	87.8	87.9	81.9	79.4		Total Current	83.3	81.0
	5.2	6.3	10.4	10.3		Fixed Assets (net)	10.2	11.1
	2.3	1.4	3.2	7.3		Intangibles (net)	2.6	1.6
	4.7	4.4	4.4	2.9		All Other Non-Current	3.9	6.4
	100.0	100.0	100.0	100.0		Total	100.0	100.0
						LIABILITIES		
	15.1	18.3	19.4	18.9		Notes Payable-Short Term	18.4	17.6
	1.3	2.3	1.0	1.7		Cur. Mat.-L.T.D.	2.9	1.7
	31.2	23.9	20.4	17.4		Trade Payables	22.9	21.9
	.2	.2	.1	.2		Income Taxes Payable	.1	.2
	4.6	12.9	11.0	13.7		All Other Current	11.6	10.7
	52.4	57.6	51.9	52.0		Total Current	55.8	52.1
	8.0	5.1	4.0	9.4		Long-Term Debt	4.0	7.1
	.0	.1	.1	.1		Deferred Taxes	.0	.1
	4.9	3.4	.9	4.4		All Other Non-Current	6.1	4.7
	34.7	33.9	43.2	34.1		Net Worth	34.0	36.1
	100.0	100.0	100.0	100.0		Total Liabilities & Net Worth	100.0	100.0
						INCOME DATA		
	100.0	100.0	100.0	100.0		Net Sales	100.0	100.0
	22.8	23.2	22.2	29.9		Gross Profit	24.4	25.8
	21.4	20.4	18.1	25.0		Operating Expenses	21.0	21.9
	1.4	2.8	4.2	4.9		Operating Profit	3.4	3.8
	.1	.3	.7	.6		All Other Expenses (net)	.4	.0
	1.3	2.5	3.4	4.2		Profit Before Taxes	3.0	3.8
						RATIOS		
	2.2	2.1	2.3	2.8		Current	2.4	2.3
	1.5	1.6	1.5	1.5			1.6	1.5
	1.3	1.2	1.2	1.1			1.2	1.2
	1.3	1.2	1.2	1.6		Quick	1.2	1.1
	.9	.8	.7	.6			.8	.8
	.4	.6	.5	.5			.5	.5
	30 12.3	29 12.5	27 13.7	29 12.7		Sales/Receivables	23 15.8	22 16.5
	36 10.2	38 9.7	34 10.6	43 8.4			36 10.2	34 10.7
	44 8.2	48 7.6	47 7.8	61 6.0			50 7.3	56 6.6
	37 9.8	39 9.4	38 9.7	49 7.4		Cost of Sales/Inventory	36 10.3	38 9.5
	51 7.2	62 5.9	61 6.0	75 4.9			62 5.9	64 5.7
	108 3.4	83 4.4	85 4.3	111 3.3			93 3.9	94 3.9
	19 19.1	21 17.7	17 21.1	12 30.0		Cost of Sales/Payables	15 24.8	19 19.0
	38 9.5	32 11.3	27 13.7	33 10.9			28 13.0	33 11.1
	58 6.3	49 7.4	38 9.7	45 8.1			47 7.8	50 7.3
	6.7	6.1	7.9	4.7		Sales/Working Capital	5.9	5.9
	10.1	8.9	11.9	12.1			10.8	11.5
	17.5	24.0	22.1	31.6			25.2	24.5
	5.2	9.2	23.3	14.8		EBIT/Interest	13.3	14.5
	(17) 1.8	(54) 3.0	(32) 4.9	4.3			(119) 4.3	(129) 4.6
	-.2	1.6	2.6	1.5			2.1	2.1
		20.8				Net Profit + Depr., Dep.,	7.9	14.9
		(10) 3.5				Amort./Cur. Mat. L/T/D	(20) 5.3	(30) 6.0
		.7					1.5	2.0
	.1	.0	.1	.2		Fixed/Worth	.1	.1
	.2	.1	.2	.4			.2	.2
	.3	.3	.4	1.1			.4	.5
	.9	1.0	.8	1.4		Debt/Worth	.6	.9
	2.8	2.1	1.4	4.0			1.5	2.0
	4.9	5.2	3.5	6.5			4.4	4.2
	54.6	48.4	58.5	49.1		% Profit Before Taxes/Tangible Net Worth	46.9	46.8
	(20) 10.9	(57) 15.1	(34) 31.0	(13) 29.4			(128) 21.9	(131) 19.3
	-7.4	8.2	12.9	12.9			6.2	5.9
	7.8	12.2	19.9	22.2		% Profit Before Taxes/Total Assets	16.6	15.4
	3.6	5.3	10.8	7.4			6.6	6.3
	-2.2	2.1	4.2	1.6			1.7	1.7
	374.2	220.7	87.9	53.2		Sales/Net Fixed Assets	204.5	162.5
	109.8	67.4	38.3	26.8			71.0	46.2
	46.3	38.4	24.2	17.2			24.1	18.9
	4.8	3.9	4.2	3.7		Sales/Total Assets	4.5	4.0
	3.3	3.0	3.2	2.6			3.3	3.1
	2.6	2.6	2.6	1.8			2.4	2.2
	.2	.2	.3	.3		% Depr., Dep., Amort./Sales	.2	.2
	(18) .3	(47) .3	(33) .5	(13) .5			(114) .4	(121) .5
	.6	.6	.8	1.2			1.0	.9
	2.9	1.2				% Officers', Directors' Owners' Comp/Sales	1.0	1.5
	(13) 5.0	(23) 1.9					(62) 1.9	(57) 2.5
	7.7	2.9					3.4	4.2
2732M	101314M	1032808M	2499514M	2949475M	1030410M	Net Sales ($)	5568675M	4973883M
620M	28612M	305488M	760749M	935740M	462553M	Total Assets ($)	1808552M	1668329M

© RMA 2007

M = $ thousand   MM = $ million
See Pages 11 through 21 for Explanation of Ratios and Data

Comparative Historical Data | Current Data Sorted by Sales

H1	H2	H3	Type of Statement	0-1MM	1-3MM	3-5MM	5-10MM	10-25MM	25MM & OVER
32	22	27	Unqualified			1		2	24
27	28	27	Reviewed		2	2	2	9	12
25	21	20	Compiled		1	4	6	6	3
12	11	11	Tax Returns	1	2	3	1	3	1
42	47	50	Other		2	1	13	10	24
4/1/04-3/31/05 ALL	4/1/05-3/31/06 ALL	4/1/06-3/31/07 ALL		\<25 (4/1-9/30/06)\>			\<110 (10/1/06-3/31/07)\>		
138	129	135	NUMBER OF STATEMENTS	1	7	11	22	30	64
%	%	%	**ASSETS**	%	%	%	%	%	%
9.4	9.1	8.2	Cash & Equivalents			3.4	10.8	10.1	6.5
30.3	33.2	34.7	Trade Receivables (net)			32.2	37.5	36.9	34.8
40.3	41.5	40.5	Inventory			54.9	34.7	40.8	39.8
2.4	1.8	1.9	All Other Current			1.1	5.3	.3	1.7
82.5	85.5	85.4	Total Current			91.6	88.3	88.1	82.8
10.5	8.5	7.7	Fixed Assets (net)			3.7	7.4	5.3	9.4
1.1	1.9	2.6	Intangibles (net)			4.2	.7	2.2	3.5
5.9	4.1	4.3	All Other Non-Current			.4	3.6	4.4	4.3
100.0	100.0	100.0	Total			100.0	100.0	100.0	100.0
			LIABILITIES						
16.7	16.4	17.9	Notes Payable-Short Term			23.5	13.3	21.8	17.8
1.5	1.7	1.7	Cur. Mat.-L.T.D.			5.1	.6	.7	1.9
23.4	24.3	24.4	Trade Payables			30.2	24.6	23.4	22.2
.2	.3	.2	Income Taxes Payable			.1	.6	.0	.1
10.2	9.8	10.9	All Other Current			5.2	7.6	14.2	12.5
52.1	52.5	55.0	Total Current			64.1	46.6	60.1	54.5
7.0	5.8	5.6	Long-Term Debt			2.4	8.9	3.2	5.0
.1	.1	.1	Deferred Taxes			.0	.0	.0	.1
4.5	3.1	2.9	All Other Non-Current			3.3	4.9	1.8	1.7
36.3	38.5	36.3	Net Worth			30.2	39.6	34.9	38.8
100.0	100.0	100.0	Total Liabilities & Net Worth			100.0	100.0	100.0	100.0
			INCOME DATA						
100.0	100.0	100.0	Net Sales			100.0	100.0	100.0	100.0
25.9	23.6	23.6	Gross Profit			23.7	25.5	21.2	23.3
21.9	20.0	20.6	Operating Expenses			21.3	23.1	18.7	19.6
3.9	3.7	3.0	Operating Profit			2.3	2.4	2.5	3.7
.3	.5	.4	All Other Expenses (net)			.6	.4	.4	.5
3.6	3.1	2.6	Profit Before Taxes			1.8	2.0	2.0	3.2
			RATIOS						
2.3	2.4	2.2				1.8	2.4	2.0	2.5
1.5	1.6	1.5	Current			1.4	1.8	1.4	1.6
1.2	1.2	1.2				1.2	1.5	1.1	1.2
1.2	1.2	1.2				.9	1.3	1.2	1.3
.7	.8	.7	Quick			.5	1.0	.8	.7
.5	.5	.5				.4	.7	.5	.5
22 17.0	26 13.9	28 12.8				30 12.4	33 11.1	30 12.3	26 13.9
31 11.7	36 10.3	37 9.9	Sales/Receivables			39 9.3	37 10.0	39 9.5	36 10.1
47 7.8	52 7.1	47 7.8				55 6.6	51 7.2	48 7.6	46 7.9
40 9.0	43 8.5	40 9.1				51 7.2	33 11.1	42 8.7	39 9.4
64 5.7	63 5.8	62 5.9	Cost of Sales/Inventory			101 3.6	62 5.9	64 5.7	57 6.4
90 4.1	103 3.5	91 4.0				154 2.4	89 4.1	80 4.6	84 4.4
18 20.6	18 20.6	19 18.8				36 10.0	21 17.7	19 19.1	18 20.4
30 12.3	32 11.2	32 11.5	Cost of Sales/Payables			48 7.6	31 11.7	31 11.9	29 12.4
47 7.7	52 7.1	48 7.6				68 5.4	60 6.1	47 7.8	41 8.9
6.5	5.9	6.5				5.0	4.3	7.1	7.7
11.1	10.3	10.6	Sales/Working Capital			9.4	6.8	12.8	11.7
24.9	21.6	22.1				18.8	13.3	72.3	22.9
17.9	15.8	10.7				2.9	6.5	10.8	19.9
(119) 4.9	(109) 5.8	(121) 3.4	EBIT/Interest		(10) 1.7	(17) 3.8	(27) 2.2	(61) 4.5
1.9	1.9	1.6				.7	1.2	1.7	2.3
38.2	14.8	9.7							15.9
(29) 5.0	(26) 4.2	(29) 4.3	Net Profit + Depr., Dep., Amort./Cur. Mat. L/T/D					(17) 4.8
1.8	1.8	1.1							1.4
.1	.0	.1				.1	.0	.1	.1
.2	.2	.2	Fixed/Worth			.2	.1	.1	.2
.6	.5	.4				.3	.5	.3	.4
.9	.8	.9				1.4	.9	.8	.9
2.0	1.9	2.0	Debt/Worth			2.8	1.6	2.4	1.7
5.0	4.5	4.7				4.2	4.0	6.6	4.3
57.8	52.9	53.6				33.3	39.9	48.4	55.9
(132) 20.6	(124) 22.2	(128) 18.3	% Profit Before Taxes/Tangible Net Worth		(10) 9.5	14.9	(28) 15.6	(61) 27.9
6.4	7.5	7.9				-.1	7.1	8.6	11.6
17.2	16.1	15.0				12.8	13.5	11.1	19.6
5.9	7.5	5.8	% Profit Before Taxes/Total Assets			2.9	5.7	4.0	7.7
1.5	2.4	2.0				1.5	1.5	2.1	3.0
133.5	168.5	171.8				422.6	216.6	255.6	106.9
44.5	59.3	60.3	Sales/Net Fixed Assets			108.0	87.6	72.2	40.7
24.0	26.2	29.7				36.9	33.1	43.0	23.8
4.1	4.0	4.0				3.3	3.9	3.8	4.3
3.3	3.0	3.1	Sales/Total Assets			2.5	3.0	3.2	3.2
2.5	2.3	2.5				2.0	2.3	2.7	2.6
.2	.2	.2					.2	.1	.3
(116) .5	(102) .4	(115) .4	% Depr., Dep., Amort./Sales			(18) .4	(24) .4	(58) .4
.9	.7	.8					1.2	.6	.8
1.2	1.4	1.4						1.4	1.2
(58) 2.4	(44) 2.2	(45) 2.2	% Officers', Directors' Owners' Comp/Sales				(11) 2.2	(12) 1.7
4.1	4.2	4.4						3.5	2.0
8067425M	5983439M	7616253M	Net Sales ($)	859M	12109M	44463M	172577M	491407M	6894838M
2187920M	2004744M	2493762M	Total Assets ($)	2332M	5301M	17405M	66528M	154379M	2247817M

M = $ thousand   MM = $ million
See Pages 11 through 21 for Explanation of Ratios and Data

Current Data Sorted by Assets   Comparative Historical Data

						Type of Statement		
1	3	18	33	11	6	Unqualified	73	67
2	15	56	17			Reviewed	103	99
1	21	29	4			Compiled	79	72
4	12	11	1			Tax Returns	20	44
4	17	48	31	11	6	Other	114	123
	79 (4/1-9/30/06)		283 (10/1/06-3/31/07)				4/1/02-3/31/03	4/1/03-3/31/04
0-500M	500M-2MM	2-10MM	10-50MM	50-100MM	100-250MM		ALL	ALL
12	68	162	86	22	12	NUMBER OF STATEMENTS	389	405
%	%	%	%	%	%	ASSETS	%	%
12.3	10.5	6.6	7.9	8.7	1.4	Cash & Equivalents	8.9	9.6
27.5	38.1	36.6	37.4	31.4	38.6	Trade Receivables (net)	36.2	36.2
35.4	29.5	38.5	34.0	29.7	28.1	Inventory	33.9	32.8
1.6	3.6	2.0	3.3	2.8	2.6	All Other Current	2.6	2.3
76.8	81.7	83.8	82.6	72.5	70.8	Total Current	81.6	80.9
8.4	10.2	8.9	8.4	7.9	6.5	Fixed Assets (net)	10.0	10.9
5.3	2.0	2.9	4.3	10.7	16.0	Intangibles (net)	3.1	2.5
9.5	6.2	4.5	4.7	9.0	6.7	All Other Non-Current	5.3	5.7
100.0	100.0	100.0	100.0	100.0	100.0	Total	100.0	100.0
						LIABILITIES		
15.9	15.1	15.3	12.3	17.7	10.6	Notes Payable-Short Term	15.2	16.0
13.0	2.2	1.1	1.2	1.0	4.2	Cur. Mat.-L.T.D.	2.5	2.3
18.1	24.8	23.7	26.2	17.6	21.0	Trade Payables	23.1	23.6
.0	.2	.3	.6	.6	.0	Income Taxes Payable	.3	.4
16.5	8.8	10.2	11.1	13.3	7.2	All Other Current	10.2	10.6
63.4	51.1	50.5	51.3	50.0	43.0	Total Current	51.3	52.9
8.9	10.4	7.0	6.8	7.2	19.4	Long-Term Debt	7.0	7.5
.0	.1	.2	.1	.3	.5	Deferred Taxes	.1	.2
1.5	3.1	5.2	2.8	1.9	1.7	All Other Non-Current	5.4	5.4
26.2	35.3	37.1	39.0	40.6	35.4	Net Worth	36.1	34.0
100.0	100.0	100.0	100.0	100.0	100.0	Total Liabilties & Net Worth	100.0	100.0
						INCOME DATA		
100.0	100.0	100.0	100.0	100.0	100.0	Net Sales	100.0	100.0
36.3	35.1	28.5	26.2	24.0	20.1	Gross Profit	29.5	31.3
33.6	31.6	24.8	22.0	18.8	17.6	Operating Expenses	27.5	29.0
2.7	3.5	3.7	4.1	5.3	2.4	Operating Profit	2.0	2.3
.9	.3	.6	.4	.9	1.0	All Other Expenses (net)	.4	.6
1.8	3.2	3.1	3.7	4.4	1.5	Profit Before Taxes	1.6	1.7
						RATIOS		
3.6	2.3	2.5	2.2	1.9	2.6		2.5	2.5
1.4	1.7	1.6	1.6	1.6	1.6	Current	1.7	1.6
.8	1.2	1.3	1.2	1.1	1.1		1.2	1.2
1.6	1.3	1.4	1.2	1.1	1.2		1.3	1.4
.9	.9	.9	.9	.9	1.0	Quick	.9	.9
.2	.6	.8	.6	.6	.5		.6	.6

14	26.4	23	15.8	34	10.8	39	9.3	41	8.9	55	6.6		32	11.4	33	11.0

Sales/Receivables, Cost of Sales/Inventory, Cost of Sales/Payables rows:

Col1	Col2	Col3	Col4	Col5	Col6	Col7	Col8	Col9	Col10	Col11	Col12	Ratio	H1n	H1	H2n	H2
14	26.4	23	15.8	34	10.8	39	9.3	41	8.9	55	6.6	Sales/Receivables	32	11.4	33	11.0
26	14.1	39	9.4	45	8.1	48	7.6	47	7.7	61	6.0		42	8.6	44	8.2
38	9.5	52	7.1	54	6.8	62	5.9	57	6.5	68	5.4		56	6.5	57	6.5
0	UND	18	20.5	37	9.9	32	11.3	40	9.0	42	8.7	Cost of Sales/Inventory	31	11.7	30	12.0
53	6.9	55	6.6	66	5.5	62	5.9	62	5.8	69	5.3		58	6.2	58	6.3
94	3.9	94	3.9	103	3.5	92	4.0	115	3.2	82	4.5		95	3.8	102	3.6
12	30.8	17	21.5	22	16.9	26	14.2	13	29.0	20	17.9	Cost of Sales/Payables	22	16.6	20	18.0
22	16.6	35	10.5	37	9.8	42	8.6	34	10.6	55	6.6		36	10.2	37	9.7
45	8.0	54	6.8	60	6.1	66	5.6	50	7.2	65	5.6		50	7.3	58	6.3

						Ratio		
6.4	6.7	5.6	5.3	4.6	4.8	Sales/Working Capital	5.4	5.6
22.3	12.1	9.4	9.1	11.1	7.4		9.4	10.6
-43.7	23.3	19.7	20.8	44.3	48.2		25.7	31.6

								Ratio				
	15.1		11.8		20.8		10.5		6.1	EBIT/Interest	8.0	10.7
(61)	4.2	(149)	3.7	(75)	6.7	(21)	4.3	(11)	1.3		(344) 2.5	(355) 2.8
	1.3		1.6		2.4		2.1		.5		.4	.9

						Ratio		
	7.7	13.3	13.0			Net Profit + Depr., Dep.,	8.2	8.5
(10) 3.0	(35) 3.0	(22) 8.5				Amort./Cur. Mat. L/T/D	(88) 2.6	(67) 2.4
	-.1	1.1	1.2				.7	.7

						Ratio		
.0	.0	.1	.1	.1	.2	Fixed/Worth	.1	.1
.3	.2	.2	.2	.3	.3		.2	.2
-.6	.7	.5	.4	.8	.6		.6	.8
.4	.9	.7	.8	.8	1.6	Debt/Worth	.8	.8
3.6	1.5	2.0	1.8	2.5	4.2		1.8	1.9
-8.8	5.5	4.5	4.3	7.4	7.6		4.9	6.2

								Ratio				
	66.2		41.6		51.2		51.4		36.3	% Profit Before Taxes/Tangible Net Worth	33.2	31.1
(60) 30.7	(151) 15.7	(78) 30.6	(20) 32.2	(10) 1.4							(357) 10.0	(358) 9.3
	4.7		6.6		11.8		12.1		-11.7		-1.7	.1

						Ratio		
24.6	27.6	14.2	17.8	13.7	9.5	% Profit Before Taxes/Total Assets	10.1	10.8
7.8	7.4	6.0	8.6	6.2	.6		3.0	3.0
-.4	1.0	1.4	2.7	2.9	-2.1		-1.2	-.7
UND	242.8	139.3	96.3	72.0	71.3	Sales/Net Fixed Assets	118.9	125.1
59.7	74.2	54.4	46.9	36.2	33.0		52.2	49.4
20.6	23.2	25.4	19.5	18.9	20.4		22.0	19.8
5.0	5.0	3.7	3.4	3.0	2.9	Sales/Total Assets	3.9	3.9
3.7	3.8	2.8	2.7	2.2	2.4		3.0	2.9
2.5	2.4	2.2	2.0	1.3	1.5		2.1	2.1

								Ratio				
	.2		.2		.3		.3		.2	% Depr., Dep., Amort./Sales	.4	.4
(49) .5	(144) .5	(77) .6	(20) .6	(11) .5							(317) .7	(318) .9
	1.1		1.0		1.2		1.2		2.8		1.3	1.5

								Ratio				
	2.8		1.5		.8					% Officers', Directors' Owners' Comp/Sales	2.3	2.0
(32) 4.6	(70) 2.7	(16) 1.5									(159) 3.7	(155) 4.0
	6.5		5.8		3.2						6.7	6.9

14691M	302569M	2320901M	5209644M	3434026M	3962543M	Net Sales ($)	11788056M	11739736M
3103M	80314M	812512M	1914660M	1452526M	1793685M	Total Assets ($)	4517429M	4526974M

M = $ thousand   MM = $ million
See Pages 11 through 21 for Explanation of Ratios and Data

Comparative Historical Data / Current Data Sorted by Sales

Type of Statement	4/1/04-3/31/05 ALL	4/1/05-3/31/06 ALL	4/1/06-3/31/07 ALL	0-1MM	1-3MM	3-5MM	5-10MM	10-25MM	25MM & OVER
Unqualified	70	67	72	1		1	6	13	51
Reviewed	97	102	90	2	3	5	22	39	19
Compiled	53	63	55	2	8	7	23	12	3
Tax Returns	30	42	28	2	6	6	4	8	2
Other	97	126	117	3	9	6	14	36	49

Current data periods: **79 (4/1-9/30/06)** covers 0-1MM, 1-3MM, 3-5MM; **283 (10/1/06-3/31/07)** covers 5-10MM, 10-25MM, 25MM & OVER.

	ALL	ALL	ALL	0-1MM	1-3MM	3-5MM	5-10MM	10-25MM	25MM & OVER
NUMBER OF STATEMENTS	347	400	362	10	26	25	69	108	124
ASSETS	%	%	%	%	%	%	%	%	%
Cash & Equivalents	9.0	7.6	7.8	8.0	11.5	9.5	7.9	7.7	6.7
Trade Receivables (net)	36.3	37.4	36.5	26.1	29.3	35.7	34.3	39.0	38.1
Inventory	33.7	34.9	34.7	44.9	28.1	36.3	31.1	38.5	33.7
All Other Current	2.5	2.5	2.7	1.9	4.6	1.2	3.8	2.0	2.7
Total Current	81.6	82.4	81.8	81.0	73.5	82.8	77.2	87.1	81.3
Fixed Assets (net)	9.2	9.7	8.8	9.1	11.2	9.6	12.8	7.2	7.4
Intangibles (net)	3.2	3.0	4.0	6.0	6.2	.2	3.2	2.2	6.2
All Other Non-Current	6.0	4.8	5.4	3.9	9.1	7.4	6.8	3.6	5.1
Total	100.0	100.0	100.0	100.0	100.0	100.0	100.0	100.0	100.0
LIABILITIES									
Notes Payable-Short Term	15.6	16.3	14.6	9.4	17.8	16.7	15.7	14.3	13.5
Cur. Mat.-L.T.D.	2.0	1.8	1.8	13.4	3.2	2.7	1.6	.9	1.3
Trade Payables	23.8	24.4	23.8	22.2	15.4	19.5	22.3	26.4	25.2
Income Taxes Payable	.4	.3	.3	.0	.0	.5	.2	.4	.4
All Other Current	10.8	10.1	10.4	19.3	3.8	10.0	11.0	10.3	11.0
Total Current	52.4	52.8	51.0	64.3	40.3	49.4	50.8	52.4	51.3
Long-Term Debt	7.8	8.0	8.1	9.4	13.3	16.7	9.7	4.4	7.5
Deferred Taxes	.2	.2	.2	.0	.0	.0	.3	.1	.2
All Other Non-Current	3.5	4.3	3.8	5.9	1.8	2.3	5.2	5.2	2.3
Net Worth	36.0	34.6	37.0	20.4	44.6	31.5	34.0	37.8	38.8
Total Liabilties & Net Worth	100.0	100.0	100.0	100.0	100.0	100.0	100.0	100.0	100.0
INCOME DATA									
Net Sales	100.0	100.0	100.0	100.0	100.0	100.0	100.0	100.0	100.0
Gross Profit	30.4	30.4	28.9	36.6	40.6	37.1	33.6	25.9	24.2
Operating Expenses	27.1	26.4	25.1	31.4	39.8	32.3	29.7	22.2	20.1
Operating Profit	3.3	4.0	3.8	5.2	.8	4.8	4.0	3.7	4.1
All Other Expenses (net)	.4	.5	.5	.6	.7	.7	.7	.4	.5
Profit Before Taxes	2.9	3.5	3.3	4.6	.2	4.0	3.2	3.3	3.6
RATIOS									
Current	2.4	2.2	2.3	2.9	4.0	2.3	2.1	2.5	2.2
	1.6	1.5	1.6	1.8	1.8	1.8	1.5	1.5	1.6
	1.2	1.2	1.2	.7	1.3	1.3	1.2	1.3	1.2
Quick	1.4	1.3	1.3	1.2	1.8	1.4	1.3	1.4	1.2
	.9	.8	.9	.8	1.2	1.0	.8	.9	.9
	.6	.6	.6	.2	.7	.6	.5	.6	.6
Sales/Receivables	(33) 11.0	(34) 10.8	(33) 11.0	(18) 20.7	(24) 15.1	(18) 20.0	(28) 13.0	(34) 10.6	(40) 9.1
	(45) 8.2	(45) 8.1	(45) 8.1	(35) 10.6	(40) 9.2	(40) 9.2	(44) 8.3	(45) 8.1	(50) 7.3
	(56) 6.6	(58) 6.3	(57) 6.4	(61) 6.0	(59) 6.1	(52) 7.0	(54) 6.7	(54) 6.8	(61) 6.0
Cost of Sales/Inventory	(34) 10.7	(34) 10.8	(35) 10.4	(56) 6.5	(39) 9.3	(24) 15.1	(28) 12.8	(32) 11.6	(37) 9.8
	(61) 6.0	(59) 6.2	(63) 5.8	(112) 3.3	(72) 5.0	(49) 7.5	(59) 6.2	(60) 6.1	(62) 5.9
	(91) 4.0	(97) 3.8	(98) 3.7	(172) 2.1	(110) 3.3	(108) 3.4	(100) 3.6	(102) 3.6	(88) 4.1
Cost of Sales/Payables	(22) 17.0	(24) 15.0	(21) 17.2	(17) 22.0	(15) 24.4	(20) 18.2	(17) 21.8	(23) 15.7	(23) 16.1
	(38) 9.6	(38) 9.5	(38) 9.7	(28) 13.0	(40) 9.1	(31) 11.8	(35) 10.3	(36) 10.2	(41) 8.8
	(56) 6.5	(56) 6.5	(59) 6.2	(134) 2.7	(74) 5.0	(44) 8.2	(60) 6.1	(60) 6.1	(59) 6.2
Sales/Working Capital	5.4	6.1	5.6	4.0	4.0	6.7	6.2	5.8	5.5
	10.2	11.1	10.1	6.5	8.3	11.5	11.6	9.5	10.1
	24.2	24.9	22.1	-8.1	18.6	18.5	28.1	21.7	22.1
EBIT/Interest	13.4	13.9	13.1		12.3	11.8	6.7	18.2	15.1
	(298) 4.9	(356) 4.7	(326) 4.2		(22) 2.2	4.0	(58) 3.3	(102) 5.1	(110) 5.6
	1.6	1.8	1.7		1.1	1.3	1.2	1.9	2.3
Net Profit + Depr., Dep., Amort./Cur. Mat. L/T/D	11.0	12.7	10.6				17.2	13.2	10.6
	(64) 4.2	(94) 3.8	(83) 3.5				(21) 3.4	(21) 6.4	(35) 6.1
	1.1	1.5	1.1				.9	1.1	1.3
Fixed/Worth	.1	.1	.1	.1	.0	.0	.1	.1	.1
	.2	.2	.2	.3	.2	.2	.3	.2	.2
	.6	.6	.6	-.8	.6	1.2	.8	.4	.4
Debt/Worth	.9	1.0	.8	1.0	.5	.9	.9	.6	.8
	1.9	2.1	2.0	3.1	1.0	1.5	2.2	2.0	2.0
	4.6	4.7	4.8	-5.3	5.1	4.8	5.1	4.2	4.8
% Profit Before Taxes/Tangible Net Worth	40.8	47.5	46.5		47.1	50.6	39.9	45.9	48.8
	(321) 17.9	(371) 20.8	(327) 20.8		(22) 6.1	(21) 23.6	(62) 14.0	(102) 17.7	(113) 30.5
	4.3	6.2	6.9		2.5	.0	4.7	7.6	11.3
% Profit Before Taxes/Total Assets	13.5	14.5	17.1	29.0	16.5	29.0	12.7	16.1	16.6
	5.2	6.9	6.9	10.4	2.4	11.4	4.7	6.6	8.0
	1.0	1.8	1.5	-2.6	.0	.6	-.1	1.9	2.8
Sales/Net Fixed Assets	125.2	134.2	133.1	107.5	237.7	520.6	123.6	158.8	98.3
	52.5	54.5	51.4	21.5	29.1	96.1	47.8	71.1	49.6
	21.8	22.3	22.0	16.1	15.9	17.7	14.9	32.7	22.5
Sales/Total Assets	3.7	3.8	3.8	3.7	3.2	5.2	4.2	3.9	3.5
	2.9	2.9	2.8	2.3	2.2	3.6	2.8	3.0	2.7
	2.2	2.2	2.2	1.8	1.9	2.4	2.0	2.4	2.1
% Depr., Dep., Amort./Sales	.4	.3	.3		.4	.3	.3	.2	.3
	(272) .7	(331) .6	(308) .5		(18) 1.1	(18) .6	(61) .8	(94) .4	(111) .5
	1.3	1.2	1.1		2.8	1.3	.8	1.1	1.1
% Officers', Directors' Owners' Comp/Sales	2.1	1.8	1.7		4.1	2.6	2.0	1.7	.8
	(122) 4.1	(143) 4.0	(127) 3.0		(13) 5.6	(13) 3.6	(33) 3.4	(42) 2.6	(22) 1.5
	7.1	7.3	6.2		12.4	6.2	6.2	5.4	3.4
Net Sales ($)	12894773M	19388059M	15244374M	6723M	55201M	97867M	498584M	1750538M	12835461M
Total Assets ($)	5426290M	6723973M	6056800M	3751M	26772M	30573M	216550M	631700M	5147454M

M = $ thousand   MM = $ million
See Pages 11 through 21 for Explanation of Ratios and Data

Current Data Sorted by Assets   Comparative Historical Data

0-500M	500M-2MM	2-10MM	10-50MM	50-100MM	100-250MM	Type of Statement	4/1/02-3/31/03 ALL	4/1/03-3/31/04 ALL
	1	7	17	3	2	Unqualified	45	39
1	10	46	17	1		Reviewed	74	69
2	18	25	2			Compiled	45	63
9	18	10				Tax Returns	22	27
4	14	31	19	3	1	Other	59	58
48 (4/1-9/30/06)		213 (10/1/06-3/31/07)						
16	61	119	55	7	3	NUMBER OF STATEMENTS	245	256
%	%	%	%	%	%	**ASSETS**	%	%
15.2	7.8	7.4	5.8			Cash & Equivalents	6.1	5.1
24.1	31.1	31.9	29.7			Trade Receivables (net)	29.0	31.3
44.8	42.5	42.2	42.9			Inventory	43.2	42.6
.3	1.1	1.1	1.7			All Other Current	2.4	2.3
84.5	82.5	82.6	80.1			Total Current	80.7	81.2
12.8	12.2	11.3	12.3			Fixed Assets (net)	12.4	11.7
.4	1.1	1.2	3.2			Intangibles (net)	2.3	2.0
2.3	4.2	4.9	4.4			All Other Non-Current	4.6	5.1
100.0	100.0	100.0	100.0			Total	100.0	100.0
						LIABILITIES		
13.7	14.5	15.4	16.4			Notes Payable-Short Term	16.2	17.6
1.1	2.3	1.7	1.1			Cur. Mat.-L.T.D.	3.2	2.1
23.0	24.3	17.9	19.1			Trade Payables	17.3	18.4
.1	.1	.4	.3			Income Taxes Payable	.2	.2
15.9	6.4	7.7	6.2			All Other Current	6.6	6.9
53.7	47.6	43.1	43.0			Total Current	43.4	45.1
11.0	14.4	10.2	8.2			Long-Term Debt	10.3	10.4
.0	.1	.3	.2			Deferred Taxes	.2	.1
5.0	3.6	3.9	1.7			All Other Non-Current	4.4	6.0
30.3	34.4	42.5	46.9			Net Worth	41.6	38.3
100.0	100.0	100.0	100.0			Total Liabilities & Net Worth	100.0	100.0
						INCOME DATA		
100.0	100.0	100.0	100.0			Net Sales	100.0	100.0
32.0	31.1	32.3	29.7			Gross Profit	32.9	32.2
29.5	27.1	27.8	24.0			Operating Expenses	29.6	29.2
2.5	4.0	4.5	5.7			Operating Profit	3.3	3.0
.7	.7	.5	.6			All Other Expenses (net)	.6	.5
1.8	3.4	4.0	5.0			Profit Before Taxes	2.7	2.5
						RATIOS		
3.1	3.1	3.4	3.6			Current	3.0	2.8
1.8	1.8	1.9	1.9				1.9	1.8
1.1	1.3	1.4	1.4				1.4	1.4
1.2	1.2	1.6	1.4			Quick	1.4	1.2
.8	.8	.9	.9				.8	.8
.4	.6	.6	.5				.5	.5
3 115.3	25 14.4	30 12.2	35 10.6			Sales/Receivables	31 11.7	32 11.6
23 15.7	35 10.5	36 10.1	42 8.6				40 9.1	43 8.4
37 9.9	42 8.6	49 7.5	53 6.9				50 7.4	54 6.7
12 30.1	41 9.0	52 7.0	59 6.2			Cost of Sales/Inventory	58 6.3	55 6.6
73 5.0	78 4.7	87 4.2	98 3.7				93 3.9	92 3.9
116 3.2	97 3.8	117 3.1	148 2.5				142 2.6	138 2.7
14 25.9	21 17.4	17 21.9	24 15.3			Cost of Sales/Payables	17 20.9	18 20.2
21 17.0	36 10.2	29 12.8	34 10.8				30 12.0	32 11.5
49 7.5	53 6.9	43 8.5	49 7.5				46 7.9	52 7.0
5.2	4.9	5.4	4.6			Sales/Working Capital	4.4	4.8
13.1	8.8	7.7	6.7				7.1	7.3
148.7	24.2	12.2	12.3				12.0	12.5
10.7	6.3	12.0	20.5			EBIT/Interest	8.0	8.7
(12) 4.2	(53) 2.7	(107) 4.4	(50) 5.7				(225) 3.3	(230) 2.7
1.7	1.5	1.8	2.5				1.5	1.2
		11.7	11.1			Net Profit + Depr., Dep., Amort./Cur. Mat. L/T/D	4.7	5.7
		(29) 4.2	(20) 5.4				(80) 1.3	(73) 2.3
		1.9	2.8				.6	.9
.1	.1	.1	.1			Fixed/Worth	.1	.1
.2	.2	.2	.2				.2	.3
1.6	1.1	.4	.5				.6	.6
.8	.8	.6	.5			Debt/Worth	.7	.7
1.4	2.0	1.3	1.5				1.4	1.8
7.3	7.9	2.6	3.2				3.2	4.0
58.3	42.3	34.7	40.6			% Profit Before Taxes/Tangible Net Worth	25.7	30.9
(13) 28.2	(55) 17.5	(111) 20.4	(54) 26.7				(227) 10.6	(238) 11.2
5.5	5.9	7.5	9.1				3.6	1.8
26.7	15.0	18.1	18.1			% Profit Before Taxes/Total Assets	10.2	9.2
10.5	4.5	8.1	8.7				4.5	3.9
3.0	1.9	2.5	3.3				1.0	.8
186.3	149.3	84.3	61.0			Sales/Net Fixed Assets	69.2	67.9
79.0	52.2	39.3	32.2				30.6	32.8
28.6	19.9	17.2	16.1				16.0	15.8
6.9	3.8	3.5	2.9			Sales/Total Assets	3.2	3.2
3.7	3.2	2.8	2.3				2.6	2.5
2.5	2.6	2.1	1.8				1.9	1.8
.3	.3	.4	.3			% Depr., Dep., Amort./Sales	.5	.4
(11) .5	(43) .8	(105) .7	(52) .6				(216) .9	(221) .8
.8	1.5	1.1	1.0				1.5	1.4
2.8	2.5	2.2	1.5			% Officers', Directors' Owners' Comp/Sales	1.7	2.0
(10) 7.0	(38) 3.4	(63) 3.7	(13) 2.9				(102) 3.9	(111) 3.8
13.0	6.8	7.5	5.9				8.1	7.2
22627M	269687M	1536533M	2444220M	975417M	1528673M	Net Sales ($)	5149064M	5259142M
4659M	80635M	544150M	1032172M	460429M	511580M	Total Assets ($)	2242163M	2278013M

M = $ thousand   MM = $ million
See Pages 11 through 21 for Explanation of Ratios and Data

Comparative Historical Data | Current Data Sorted by Sales

			Type of Statement						
36	35	30	Unqualified		1	1	6	22	
68	83	75	Reviewed	1	1	7	17	28	21
43	42	47	Compiled		4	11	16	14	2
24	18	37	Tax Returns	4	10	12	6	5	
56	67	72	Other	2	7	6	18	21	18
4/1/04-3/31/05 ALL	4/1/05-3/31/06 ALL	4/1/06-3/31/07 ALL			48 (4/1-9/30/06)		213 (10/1/06-3/31/07)		
				0-1MM	1-3MM	3-5MM	5-10MM	10-25MM	25MM & OVER
227	245	261	NUMBER OF STATEMENTS	7	22	37	58	74	63
%	%	%	ASSETS	%	%	%	%	%	%
5.6	6.1	7.6	Cash & Equivalents		11.0	9.4	9.6	4.0	7.1
30.8	30.8	30.5	Trade Receivables (net)		25.0	28.1	32.3	32.4	31.5
43.5	44.2	42.6	Inventory		35.0	46.2	39.2	45.0	41.4
1.2	1.1	1.2	All Other Current		.5	1.5	.8	1.4	1.6
81.0	82.2	81.9	Total Current		71.5	85.2	81.9	82.7	81.5
11.7	12.3	11.9	Fixed Assets (net)		23.1	8.4	13.1	10.4	11.5
2.2	1.4	1.8	Intangibles (net)		1.4	1.6	.7	2.1	2.9
5.1	4.1	4.4	All Other Non-Current		4.0	4.7	4.3	4.8	4.1
100.0	100.0	100.0	Total		100.0	100.0	100.0	100.0	100.0
			LIABILITIES						
18.1	16.6	15.1	Notes Payable-Short Term		12.8	14.5	12.4	19.3	14.6
2.8	2.5	1.9	Cur. Mat.-L.T.D.		2.1	2.1	1.9	1.5	2.2
19.5	19.6	19.9	Trade Payables		23.2	21.3	19.7	19.3	19.2
.3	.2	.3	Income Taxes Payable		.0	.2	.1	.5	.2
8.2	8.6	7.7	All Other Current		10.2	6.8	6.1	8.2	7.2
48.8	47.6	44.9	Total Current		48.4	45.0	40.2	48.8	43.5
11.2	10.5	10.9	Long-Term Debt		21.2	14.4	11.4	7.9	7.9
.2	.2	.2	Deferred Taxes		.3	.2	.1	.4	.1
6.3	5.2	3.4	All Other Non-Current		.6	5.2	3.7	3.7	1.3
33.5	36.5	40.7	Net Worth		29.6	35.2	44.6	39.2	47.2
100.0	100.0	100.0	Total Liabilties & Net Worth		100.0	100.0	100.0	100.0	100.0
			INCOME DATA						
100.0	100.0	100.0	Net Sales		100.0	100.0	100.0	100.0	100.0
31.6	30.4	31.2	Gross Profit		32.7	31.7	33.6	29.9	29.2
28.4	25.5	26.5	Operating Expenses		29.6	27.0	29.4	25.6	23.0
3.2	4.9	4.7	Operating Profit		3.1	4.8	4.2	4.3	6.2
.5	.6	.6	All Other Expenses (net)		.8	.8	.6	.6	.5
2.8	4.3	4.1	Profit Before Taxes		2.2	4.0	3.6	3.7	5.7
			RATIOS						
2.5	3.0	3.2			3.4	3.2	3.8	2.2	3.7
1.7	1.8	1.9	Current		1.7	1.9	2.2	1.7	1.9
1.3	1.3	1.4			1.0	1.5	1.4	1.4	1.3
1.2	1.2	1.4			1.1	1.5	1.8	1.1	1.6
.8	.8	.8	Quick		.7	.7	1.0	.7	.9
.5	.5	.5			.4	.5	.7	.5	.5
31 11.8	31 11.9	30 12.4			17 22.1	26 13.8	29 12.7	30 12.3	33 10.9
43 8.6	41 9.0	38 9.7	Sales/Receivables		31 11.8	36 10.2	39 9.2	37 10.0	41 9.0
51 7.1	51 7.1	48 7.7			38 9.7	43 8.5	49 7.4	48 7.6	50 7.4
55 6.7	58 6.3	48 7.6			26 13.9	44 8.3	47 7.7	52 7.0	51 7.2
90 4.1	91 4.0	86 4.3	Cost of Sales/Inventory		66 5.5	92 4.0	82 4.5	86 4.2	75 4.9
136 2.7	134 2.7	121 3.0			116 3.2	123 3.0	107 3.4	123 3.0	129 2.8
20 18.2	18 19.9	20 18.5			19 19.1	17 22.1	15 23.9	20 18.3	23 15.5
35 10.5	32 11.4	31 11.6	Cost of Sales/Payables		32 11.5	33 11.1	32 11.4	31 11.7	32 11.6
51 7.2	50 7.3	47 7.8			69 5.3	50 7.4	53 6.9	40 9.0	44 8.2
5.0	4.7	5.0			6.5	4.4	4.5	6.0	4.6
7.8	7.3	7.8	Sales/Working Capital		13.1	5.9	7.2	8.5	7.5
15.5	13.3	13.8			-95.9	12.9	13.5	12.4	14.6
11.5	12.6	11.4			5.8	7.5	10.2	10.1	21.1
(204) 4.1	(222) 4.7	(231) 4.2	EBIT/Interest		(18) 1.9	(34) 3.1	(50) 3.0	(67) 4.4	(57) 7.4
1.9	2.1	1.8			.6	1.7	1.7	1.8	2.7
11.3	7.4	10.2						11.9	12.0
(56) 3.4	(64) 3.7	(65) 4.3	Net Profit + Depr., Dep., Amort./Cur. Mat. L/T/D					(24) 4.2	(24) 6.6
1.3	2.0	2.0						1.9	3.7
.1	.1	.1			.1	.1	.1	.1	.1
.2	.3	.2	Fixed/Worth		.8	.2	.2	.2	.2
.6	.7	.6			2.8	.6	.5	.5	.5
.8	.9	.7			1.3	.7	.5	.9	.5
1.7	1.7	1.5	Debt/Worth		2.2	1.4	1.4	1.5	1.1
3.8	3.6	3.4			6.6	9.5	3.3	2.7	3.2
36.4	46.9	40.3			59.4	49.8	32.0	36.5	46.9
(200) 17.4	(229) 20.1	(242) 20.3	% Profit Before Taxes/Tangible Net Worth		(20) 7.9	(32) 11.2	(54) 16.1	(69) 20.6	(61) 28.6
5.2	7.7	7.1			-4.6	5.6	4.1	10.7	13.6
11.5	16.2	17.5			20.2	13.2	13.0	18.3	21.1
6.0	8.2	7.8	% Profit Before Taxes/Total Assets		4.4	4.5	6.2	8.1	12.8
1.7	2.3	2.7			-.5	2.2	1.7	3.1	4.6
72.5	78.7	86.7			101.2	130.0	114.9	94.5	56.4
34.0	37.4	38.9	Sales/Net Fixed Assets		31.4	60.7	32.6	48.2	32.2
17.2	16.4	18.7			7.0	22.0	15.0	21.2	20.0
3.4	3.3	3.6			5.0	3.7	3.5	3.9	3.2
2.6	2.6	2.8	Sales/Total Assets		2.9	2.8	3.0	2.9	2.6
2.0	2.0	2.1			1.8	2.0	1.9	2.3	2.1
.5	.4	.4			.3	.4	.4	.4	.3
(194) .8	(216) .6	(219) .7	% Depr., Dep., Amort./Sales		(18) 1.1	(27) .9	(48) .8	(65) .6	(57) .6
1.5	1.1	1.1			1.8	1.5	1.1	1.1	.9
2.2	2.1	2.2			3.1	2.1	2.1	2.1	1.0
(96) 4.4	(95) 3.6	(124) 3.5	% Officers', Directors' Owners' Comp/Sales		(14) 4.8	(24) 3.5	(33) 3.7	(35) 3.3	(13) 3.0
8.6	6.1	7.5			6.4	7.0	8.2	7.3	5.7
6752080M	6817850M	6777157M	Net Sales ($)	3696M	44927M	146260M	411042M	1175052M	4996180M
2685361M	2609698M	2633625M	Total Assets ($)	2322M	16862M	58226M	172928M	435901M	1947386M

© RMA 2007

M = $ thousand   MM = $ million
See Pages 11 through 21 for Explanation of Ratios and Data

Current Data Sorted by Assets | Comparative Historical Data

						Type of Statement		
1	2	12	22	8	2	Unqualified	62	57
12	12	72	30	1	1	Reviewed	137	126
7	30	45	7	1		Compiled	60	92
8	11	21	1			Tax Returns	22	37
1	12	44	32	6		Other	66	70
	62 (4/1-9/30/06)		326 (10/1/06-3/31/07)				4/1/02-3/31/03	4/1/03-3/31/04
0-500M	500M-2MM	2-10MM	10-50MM	50-100MM	100-250MM		ALL	ALL
17	67	194	92	15	3	NUMBER OF STATEMENTS	347	382

0-500M	500M-2MM	2-10MM	10-50MM	50-100MM	100-250MM		4/1/02-3/31/03 ALL	4/1/03-3/31/04 ALL
%	%	%	%	%	%	**ASSETS**	%	%
12.3	7.5	5.6	5.2	3.9		Cash & Equivalents	6.0	6.4
20.7	30.6	36.9	33.9	29.8		Trade Receivables (net)	32.9	33.8
37.3	42.6	39.9	41.7	37.1		Inventory	40.1	39.3
5.1	1.9	2.0	2.1	2.9		All Other Current	2.9	3.1
75.4	82.6	84.3	82.9	73.6		Total Current	81.9	82.5
8.0	10.5	8.7	11.2	15.6		Fixed Assets (net)	11.8	11.2
5.2	2.1	2.0	1.4	1.1		Intangibles (net)	1.5	1.6
11.3	4.8	5.0	4.5	9.7		All Other Non-Current	4.8	4.7
100.0	100.0	100.0	100.0	100.0		Total	100.0	100.0
						LIABILITIES		
16.3	15.7	16.2	18.6	17.1		Notes Payable-Short Term	17.2	17.1
5.0	3.6	2.5	1.3	3.4		Cur. Mat.-L.T.D.	2.9	1.9
14.8	18.6	21.5	18.9	17.4		Trade Payables	20.6	21.2
.0	.2	.3	.5	.2		Income Taxes Payable	.3	.4
10.0	6.9	9.1	7.8	6.8		All Other Current	11.1	9.9
46.1	45.2	49.5	47.1	44.8		Total Current	52.2	50.6
7.7	9.6	7.7	7.7	8.3		Long-Term Debt	7.8	6.7
.0	.4	.1	.1	.6		Deferred Taxes	.2	.2
3.2	4.6	3.2	2.8	6.0		All Other Non-Current	2.9	5.1
43.0	40.2	39.4	42.2	40.4		Net Worth	36.9	37.4
100.0	100.0	100.0	100.0	100.0		Total Liabilities & Net Worth	100.0	100.0
						INCOME DATA		
100.0	100.0	100.0	100.0	100.0		Net Sales	100.0	100.0
39.8	32.5	27.4	26.0	26.7		Gross Profit	28.5	28.6
34.1	29.8	23.8	21.2	22.9		Operating Expenses	26.5	26.5
5.7	2.7	3.6	4.7	3.8		Operating Profit	1.9	2.1
.7	.4	.1	.0	.3		All Other Expenses (net)	.1	.2
5.0	2.3	3.6	4.7	3.5		Profit Before Taxes	1.9	1.9
						RATIOS		
5.1	2.9	2.6	2.7	2.3			2.2	2.4
1.4	1.7	1.6	1.7	1.5	Current	1.5	1.6
.9	1.5	1.3	1.4	1.4		1.2	1.2
1.3	1.4	1.2	1.2	1.1			1.1	1.2
.7	.8	.9	.8	.8	Quick	.7	.8
.2	.5	.6	.6	.5		.5	.5
0 UND	23 15.7	36 10.1	37 9.9	32 11.5			34 10.8	34 10.8
16 22.5	34 10.6	44 8.3	43 8.5	40 9.1		Sales/Receivables	41 8.8	43 8.5
31 11.8	46 8.0	53 6.9	51 7.2	51 7.2		51 7.2	54 6.7
11 32.7	43 8.4	44 8.4	54 6.7	54 6.8			48 7.7	45 8.1
60 6.0	74 4.9	73 5.0	76 4.8	69 5.3		Cost of Sales/Inventory	73 5.0	76 4.8
107 3.4	105 3.5	103 3.5	101 3.6	82 4.5		108 3.4	108 3.4
0 UND	13 27.9	24 15.5	24 15.2	19 18.8			24 15.5	24 15.4
18 20.0	29 12.8	32 11.3	30 12.1	30 12.2		Cost of Sales/Payables	33 11.1	37 9.8
32 11.3	49 7.4	47 7.8	43 8.6	37 9.8		48 7.6	50 7.3
4.7	5.2	5.7	4.7	6.4			6.0	5.5
13.1	9.1	8.8	8.4	9.4	Sales/Working Capital	10.0	9.7
-145.3	15.3	15.9	14.0	13.2		19.6	18.7
12.9	12.4	11.2	13.9	10.4			9.3	9.8
(13) 4.6	(61) 3.7	(178) 4.2	(88) 6.7	(13) 5.2		EBIT/Interest	(321) 3.3	(346) 3.8
1.4	1.3	2.2	2.8	2.0		1.5	1.5
		5.2	36.9			Net Profit + Depr., Dep.,	8.6	8.1
		(47) 2.6	(36) 6.4			Amort./Cur. Mat. L/T/D	(125) 3.0	(121) 3.6
		1.1	2.5				1.1	1.6
.0	.1	.1	.1	.2			.1	.1
.2	.2	.2	.2	.4	Fixed/Worth	.3	.2
2.4	.4	.4	.4	.5		.6	.5
.2	.7	.8	.8	.9			.9	.8
2.2	1.7	1.7	1.6	1.5	Debt/Worth	1.9	1.8
11.9	2.7	3.5	2.9	2.2		3.8	3.7
83.8	35.0	42.6	43.2	36.8		% Profit Before Taxes/Tangible	26.1	27.4
(15) 36.6	(62) 14.8	(182) 22.4	30.6	32.6		Net Worth	(321) 11.6	(353) 13.9
8.3	5.7	8.6	15.5	8.4		4.1	3.5
41.1	12.4	15.5	20.6	16.2		% Profit Before Taxes/Total	9.5	9.7
11.0	5.5	7.5	9.7	10.1		Assets	4.1	4.6
3.2	1.7	2.7	5.0	3.3		1.0	1.0
292.3	115.1	90.6	60.1	32.7			67.5	65.0
77.4	50.1	45.5	32.3	19.9	Sales/Net Fixed Assets	33.9	34.1
32.4	24.3	25.5	16.5	13.3		18.3	19.4
5.7	4.3	3.7	3.2	3.2			3.4	3.3
3.9	3.0	3.0	2.7	2.9	Sales/Total Assets	2.8	2.8
3.3	2.5	2.2	2.3	2.3		2.2	2.3
	.4	.3	.4	.6			.4	.5
	(54) .6	(166) .6	(84) .5	(14) .9		% Depr., Dep., Amort./Sales	(305) .7	(333) .7
	1.1	.9	.7	1.5			1.2	1.1
4.1	2.4	1.3	.8			% Officers', Directors'	1.7	1.6
(13) 6.0	(32) 4.7	(90) 2.5	(30) 1.4			Owners' Comp/Sales	(158) 3.3	(156) 2.8
7.5	7.0	4.3	5.2				6.5	5.3
25576M	287983M	2980679M	5808954M	2915556M	1568492M	Net Sales ($)	8244861M	8629070M
5834M	89309M	1006277M	2069468M	1059334M	447362M	Total Assets ($)	3147672M	3384389M

© RMA 2007

M = $ thousand   MM = $ million

See Pages 11 through 21 for Explanation of Ratios and Data

Comparative Historical Data | Current Data Sorted by Sales

4/1/04-3/31/05 ALL	4/1/05-3/31/06 ALL	4/1/06-3/31/07 ALL	Type of Statement	0-1MM	1-3MM	3-5MM	5-10MM	10-25MM	25MM & OVER
54	47	47	Unqualified	1		2	3	4	37
134	118	116	Reviewed		2	6	17	51	40
69	75	89	Compiled	3	14	16	26	24	6
36	32	41	Tax Returns	3	8	5	10	12	3
81	113	95	Other		3	7	20	19	46

Period spans: **62 (4/1-9/30/06)** over 0-1MM & 1-3MM; **326 (10/1/06-3/31/07)** over 3-5MM through 25MM & OVER.

H: 4/1/04-3/31/05	H: 4/1/05-3/31/06	H: 4/1/06-3/31/07		0-1MM	1-3MM	3-5MM	5-10MM	10-25MM	25MM & OVER
374	385	388	**NUMBER OF STATEMENTS**	7	27	36	76	110	132
%	%	%	**ASSETS**	%	%	%	%	%	%
6.3	5.9	6.1	Cash & Equivalents		10.2	9.0	6.5	5.7	4.3
34.6	34.7	34.1	Trade Receivables (net)		21.1	24.2	34.7	37.6	36.8
39.0	39.5	40.5	Inventory		33.5	45.1	40.1	41.2	40.1
2.4	2.6	2.2	All Other Current		1.1	4.1	1.6	1.3	2.4
82.2	82.7	82.9	Total Current		65.9	82.5	82.9	85.9	83.5
10.3	10.3	9.8	Fixed Assets (net)		12.2	10.0	9.4	8.6	10.6
1.8	1.5	2.0	Intangibles (net)		6.7	2.9	2.6	.9	1.6
5.7	5.5	5.3	All Other Non-Current		15.2	4.6	5.1	4.6	4.3
100.0	100.0	100.0	Total		100.0	100.0	100.0	100.0	100.0
			LIABILITIES						
15.4	15.3	16.6	Notes Payable-Short Term		17.4	11.5	15.4	16.8	18.3
2.0	2.6	2.5	Cur. Mat.-L.T.D.		6.5	1.9	3.6	1.8	1.9
21.5	21.6	19.9	Trade Payables		13.2	19.4	19.8	22.0	20.3
.5	.4	.3	Income Taxes Payable		.4	.2	.1	.3	.4
9.6	9.5	8.4	All Other Current		9.2	6.4	8.1	9.9	7.8
49.0	49.5	47.8	Total Current		46.6	39.6	47.0	50.8	48.6
8.0	8.2	8.1	Long-Term Debt		15.9	6.4	9.3	7.0	7.3
.1	.1	.2	Deferred Taxes		.1	.0	.4	.1	.2
3.9	4.2	3.5	All Other Non-Current		3.8	3.4	3.3	3.9	2.8
38.9	38.0	40.5	Net Worth		33.5	50.7	40.0	38.2	41.0
100.0	100.0	100.0	Total Liabilities & Net Worth		100.0	100.0	100.0	100.0	100.0
			INCOME DATA						
100.0	100.0	100.0	Net Sales		100.0	100.0	100.0	100.0	100.0
28.7	29.0	28.4	Gross Profit		35.6	33.1	30.2	27.0	25.2
25.6	25.5	24.6	Operating Expenses		32.9	31.0	26.2	23.1	20.8
3.0	3.5	3.8	Operating Profit		2.7	2.1	3.9	3.8	4.3
.1	.2	.2	All Other Expenses (net)		.1	.0	.2	.1	.2
2.9	3.3	3.7	Profit Before Taxes		2.6	2.1	3.7	3.7	4.1
			RATIOS						
2.3	2.4	2.7	Current		2.3	4.5	2.8	2.4	2.3
1.7	1.7	1.7			1.5	2.1	1.7	1.6	1.6
1.3	1.3	1.4			.9	1.4	1.4	1.3	1.4
1.2	1.3	1.3	Quick		1.1	2.1	1.4	1.2	1.2
.8	.8	.8			.7	.8	.9	.8	.8
.6	.6	.6			.3	.4	.6	.6	.6
36 10.1	35 10.6	33 11.1	Sales/Receivables	11 33.6	18 19.7	35 10.4	36 10.1	37 10.0	
43 8.5	43 8.4	42 8.7		27 13.6	29 12.4	43 8.5	44 8.2	43 8.5	
52 7.1	53 6.9	51 7.1		45 8.1	43 8.6	53 6.8	52 7.0	50 7.2	
47 7.8	48 7.6	46 8.0	Cost of Sales/Inventory	25 14.4	53 6.8	41 8.9	45 8.1	48 7.7	
73 5.0	72 5.1	74 4.9		96 3.8	84 4.4	74 5.0	70 5.2	69 5.3	
98 3.7	100 3.7	102 3.6		122 3.0	152 2.4	118 3.1	104 3.5	90 4.1	
25 14.7	24 15.2	21 17.5	Cost of Sales/Payables	6 66.0	13 28.1	22 16.9	23 15.5	24 15.5	
37 10.0	35 10.3	31 11.9		22 16.8	25 14.7	33 11.0	33 11.2	30 12.1	
50 7.3	50 7.3	44 8.3		52 7.0	59 6.2	47 7.8	48 7.6	39 9.2	
5.6	5.6	5.3	Sales/Working Capital		5.3	3.8	4.9	5.9	6.0
9.5	9.2	8.8			11.7	6.7	8.9	8.8	9.5
16.1	15.6	15.2			-50.4	15.4	15.5	14.1	14.7
12.6	11.7	12.4	EBIT/Interest		8.5	16.3	11.5	10.9	13.5
(336) 5.3	(336) 4.4	(355) 4.8		(22) 3.0	(29) 4.5	(69) 3.6	(104) 4.1	(124) 6.4	
2.4	2.2	2.1			.7	1.6	1.5	2.3	2.9
13.6	14.3	7.8	Net Profit + Depr., Dep., Amort./Cur. Mat. L/T/D				3.3	7.4	13.7
(134) 4.0	(104) 4.6	(101) 3.2				(17) 2.1	(26) 3.1	(50) 4.7	
1.6	2.1	1.7					.8	1.3	2.2
.1	.1	.1	Fixed/Worth		.1	.1	.1	.1	.1
.2	.2	.2			.3	.2	.2	.2	.2
.5	.5	.4			3.3	.4	.4	.4	.4
.8	.8	.8	Debt/Worth		.6	.4	.8	.8	.9
1.7	1.7	1.6			1.8	1.0	1.4	1.9	1.6
3.2	3.7	3.4			14.3	2.2	3.7	4.3	2.9
34.0	37.1	42.8	% Profit Before Taxes/Tangible Net Worth		65.8	21.8	42.6	45.7	45.2
(351) 17.8	(362) 20.6	(368) 22.6		(22) 11.7	(33) 11.4	(72) 19.2	(105) 26.6	(130) 31.8	
6.3	7.2	8.8			2.9	6.2	5.8	9.6	15.7
12.3	14.1	16.8	% Profit Before Taxes/Total Assets		13.3	11.6	13.8	18.1	18.8
6.0	6.3	8.0			4.5	5.9	8.6	7.3	10.0
2.3	2.4	2.9			.2	2.0	2.0	2.4	5.0
75.2	82.1	83.6	Sales/Net Fixed Assets		133.4	106.2	98.3	102.6	71.2
37.5	39.2	40.6			30.3	43.6	43.1	49.3	34.1
20.9	21.7	22.1			17.5	20.9	23.7	23.3	20.0
3.4	3.4	3.7	Sales/Total Assets		4.1	3.4	3.6	3.8	3.5
2.9	2.8	2.9			3.4	2.7	2.9	2.9	2.9
2.2	2.3	2.3			1.6	2.1	2.0	2.4	2.4
.4	.4	.3	% Depr., Dep., Amort./Sales		.2	.3	.3	.3	.4
(320) .7	(323) .6	(330) .6		(21) .5	(27) .6	(63) .6	(96) .5	(119) .5	
1.1	.9	.9			1.3	.9	1.1	.8	.7
1.7	1.5	1.3	% Officers', Directors' Owners' Comp/Sales		3.3	2.7	1.9	1.1	.8
(146) 3.3	(168) 2.7	(165) 2.8		(17) 4.8	(16) 5.9	(47) 3.1	(47) 1.9	(35) 1.4	
5.9	5.7	6.1			6.5	6.5	6.3	3.5	3.6
9983103M	10861235M	13587240M	Net Sales ($)	5213M	54738M	142230M	552981M	1789545M	11042533M
3835663M	4052104M	4677584M	Total Assets ($)	1981M	23781M	58931M	221351M	651494M	3720046M

© RMA 2007

M = $ thousand   MM = $ million
See Pages 11 through 21 for Explanation of Ratios and Data

Current Data Sorted by Assets | Comparative Historical Data

Comparative Historical number of statements timing: 36 (4/1-9/30/06) for 500M–2MM through 2-10MM group; 207 (10/1/06-3/31/07) for 10-50MM through 100-250MM group.

0-500M	500M-2MM	2-10MM	10-50MM	50-100MM	100-250MM	Type of Statement	4/1/02-3/31/03 ALL	4/1/03-3/31/04 ALL
	1	6	23	7	1	Unqualified	51	50
	4	50	17		1	Reviewed	68	80
1	17	19	2			Compiled	40	63
8	11	12	1		1	Tax Returns	21	19
5	11	23	18	3	1	Other	54	65
14	44	110	61	10	4	**NUMBER OF STATEMENTS**	234	277
%	%	%	%	%	%	**ASSETS**	%	%
18.3	10.9	5.5	3.6	.7		Cash & Equivalents	6.1	5.9
30.8	45.9	41.5	35.5	33.8		Trade Receivables (net)	40.0	40.1
23.1	28.1	37.4	44.8	42.5		Inventory	33.7	33.7
1.2	1.4	1.8	2.5	2.0		All Other Current	2.9	2.8
73.3	86.3	86.2	86.4	79.0		Total Current	82.6	82.4
18.6	7.5	8.5	8.2	15.5		Fixed Assets (net)	10.8	10.6
1.6	.8	.7	2.4	1.3		Intangibles (net)	1.7	1.1
6.4	5.4	4.7	3.0	4.1		All Other Non-Current	4.8	5.8
100.0	100.0	100.0	100.0	100.0		Total	100.0	100.0
						LIABILITIES		
15.8	15.9	16.9	24.9	26.1		Notes Payable-Short Term	18.6	18.0
13.0	1.4	1.4	.8	1.5		Cur. Mat.-L.T.D.	2.7	1.8
17.8	30.7	26.3	15.2	12.1		Trade Payables	22.2	23.7
.0	.1	.3	.4	.2		Income Taxes Payable	.2	.2
24.4	6.8	10.5	10.4	9.2		All Other Current	10.5	12.7
71.0	54.8	55.4	51.7	49.0		Total Current	54.2	56.4
11.1	10.2	5.7	4.4	11.9		Long-Term Debt	9.3	7.4
.0	.0	.2	.2	.1		Deferred Taxes	.3	.2
36.1	2.3	3.3	4.6	2.4		All Other Non-Current	4.2	5.2
-18.2	32.6	35.5	39.1	36.6		Net Worth	32.1	30.8
100.0	100.0	100.0	100.0	100.0		Total Liabilties & Net Worth	100.0	100.0
						INCOME DATA		
100.0	100.0	100.0	100.0	100.0		Net Sales	100.0	100.0
36.0	30.1	26.9	24.4	23.9		Gross Profit	27.2	27.3
33.3	26.7	23.2	20.0	20.4		Operating Expenses	24.8	24.9
2.8	3.4	3.7	4.3	3.5		Operating Profit	2.3	2.4
.3	-.1	.2	.7	1.0		All Other Expenses (net)	.3	.2
2.5	3.5	3.5	3.7	2.5		Profit Before Taxes	2.0	2.2
						RATIOS		
2.4	2.2	2.1	2.6	2.1		Current	2.1	2.1
1.6	1.5	1.6	1.5	1.6			1.5	1.5
.8	1.2	1.2	1.3	1.3			1.2	1.2
1.9	1.4	1.1	1.3	.9		Quick	1.2	1.2
1.0	1.0	.9	.7	.7			.8	.8
.4	.7	.6	.5	.7			.6	.6
0 UND	36 10.3	33 10.9	34 10.9	41 8.9		Sales/Receivables	35 10.3	36 10.1
34 10.7	47 7.8	45 8.2	41 8.8	47 7.8			44 8.2	46 8.0
47 7.7	62 5.9	65 5.6	49 7.4	53 6.8			59 6.2	57 6.5
0 UND	5 72.0	26 14.0	50 7.4	60 6.1		Cost of Sales/Inventory	28 13.2	23 15.9
6 60.8	43 8.5	69 5.3	82 4.4	85 4.3			60 6.1	60 6.1
72 5.1	97 3.8	98 3.7	103 3.5	107 3.4			88 4.2	90 4.1
0 UND	30 12.0	23 16.2	10 37.7	16 22.2		Cost of Sales/Payables	19 18.8	22 16.9
22 16.6	48 7.6	36 10.1	21 17.3	19 19.7			34 10.8	34 10.6
41 9.0	58 6.3	63 5.8	37 9.9	27 13.3			51 7.2	52 7.0
7.0	6.0	6.4	5.7	6.8		Sales/Working Capital	6.7	6.3
23.7	11.5	10.3	9.5	7.7			10.7	10.2
-41.4	32.0	18.4	13.1	18.3			21.7	23.8
9.7	11.2	10.0	14.5	5.4		EBIT/Interest	7.7	10.2
(13) 2.1	(38) 4.2	(100) 3.5	(56) 4.1	3.2			(221) 3.1	(251) 3.9
-1.4	1.9	2.0	2.3	2.1			1.3	1.5
		7.3	36.6			Net Profit + Depr., Dep.,	8.9	11.5
	(29) 3.3	(22) 7.4				Amort./Cur. Mat. L/T/D	(72) 2.2	(76) 3.8
		1.4	1.9				.7	1.6
.0	.1	.1	.1	.2		Fixed/Worth	.1	.1
.6	.2	.2	.2	.3			.3	.3
-.3	.7	.5	.3	.6			.6	.6
1.1	.9	1.0	.9	1.3		Debt/Worth	1.0	.9
NM	2.2	2.3	2.0	2.2			2.0	2.2
-2.7	5.3	4.0	3.5	3.0			5.5	4.7
	62.0	39.2	40.3	28.8		% Profit Before Taxes/Tangible	30.3	32.4
	(40) 23.3	(107) 21.6	(58) 27.7	22.1		Net Worth	(213) 11.7	(250) 17.3
	5.9	9.9	13.2	11.8			2.8	4.8
34.6	17.2	15.6	13.6	9.2		% Profit Before Taxes/Total	9.8	11.7
8.2	6.8	6.9	9.3	6.6		Assets	3.7	5.4
-4.2	1.7	2.5	4.6	3.0			.6	1.2
UND	161.8	125.5	90.7	69.7		Sales/Net Fixed Assets	99.6	89.7
90.3	62.0	56.6	52.9	19.1			41.0	41.8
13.0	38.9	23.3	25.4	11.5			20.5	20.1
5.7	4.0	3.6	3.2	3.2		Sales/Total Assets	3.6	3.7
4.1	3.3	3.0	2.8	2.8			3.0	3.0
3.0	2.6	2.4	2.5	1.9			2.5	2.4
.2	.2	.3	.3	.3		% Depr., Dep., Amort./Sales	.4	.4
(10) .3	(33) .6	(97) .5	(59) .4	.7			(205) .7	(239) .7
1.2	1.3	.8	.7	.8			1.1	1.1
	2.6	1.5	1.2			% Officers', Directors'	2.0	1.6
	(28) 3.8	(47) 3.3	(12) 1.3			Owners' Comp/Sales	(95) 4.1	(103) 4.2
	5.9	7.0	2.5				7.4	7.2
16358M	199392M	1711145M	3560352M	1821368M	2163661M	Net Sales ($)	7508305M	8306197M
3586M	54278M	557000M	1255765M	672151M	663880M	Total Assets ($)	2562428M	2847397M

M = $ thousand   MM = $ million
See Pages 11 through 21 for Explanation of Ratios and Data

Comparative Historical Data | | | | | **Current Data Sorted by Sales**

Hist	Hist	Hist	Type of Statement	0-1MM	1-3MM	3-5MM	5-10MM	10-25MM	25MM & OVER
46	32	38	Unqualified		1	5	1	5	32
79	60	72	Reviewed		10	3	14	27	25
52	36	39	Compiled		10	3	12	11	3
22	35	33	Tax Returns	2	10	5	5	7	4
56	84	61	Other	4	3	4	13	11	26
4/1/04-3/31/05 ALL	4/1/05-3/31/06 ALL	4/1/06-3/31/07 ALL			36 (4/1-9/30/06)		207 (10/1/06-3/31/07)		
255	247	243	**NUMBER OF STATEMENTS**	6	24	17	45	61	90
%	%	%	**ASSETS**	%	%	%	%	%	%
5.9	7.3	6.6	Cash & Equivalents		15.2	3.8	8.7	6.4	3.3
39.2	41.3	39.7	Trade Receivables (net)		40.7	39.4	40.7	43.4	37.9
35.2	34.6	37.2	Inventory		19.3	45.2	34.5	36.0	42.3
2.1	2.1	1.9	All Other Current		2.1	1.0	1.3	1.8	2.4
82.3	85.3	85.3	Total Current		77.2	89.5	85.1	87.5	85.9
11.2	9.2	9.1	Fixed Assets (net)		14.2	6.1	7.4	7.8	9.2
1.7	1.3	1.2	Intangibles (net)		1.3	.6	.6	.8	1.9
4.7	4.2	4.4	All Other Non-Current		7.3	3.9	6.8	3.9	3.0
100.0	100.0	100.0	Total		100.0	100.0	100.0	100.0	100.0
			LIABILITIES						
18.4	19.3	19.0	Notes Payable-Short Term		20.7	16.3	13.7	17.6	23.2
1.7	1.5	2.0	Cur. Mat.-L.T.D.		1.4	1.2	1.5	1.4	1.2
22.0	23.9	23.3	Trade Payables		24.1	38.4	25.0	26.8	17.9
.2	.2	.3	Income Taxes Payable		.0	.3	.2	.3	.3
9.9	11.5	10.4	All Other Current		9.7	5.1	9.5	10.9	10.5
52.2	56.5	55.0	Total Current		56.0	61.2	49.9	57.2	53.2
10.0	7.1	6.8	Long-Term Debt		11.1	7.3	9.2	4.6	5.6
.3	.2	.1	Deferred Taxes		.0	.1	.1	.2	.2
4.6	5.0	5.3	All Other Non-Current		5.4	3.3	2.2	4.0	3.7
32.9	31.3	32.7	Net Worth		27.4	28.0	38.7	34.0	37.4
100.0	100.0	100.0	Total Liabilties & Net Worth		100.0	100.0	100.0	100.0	100.0
			INCOME DATA						
100.0	100.0	100.0	Net Sales		100.0	100.0	100.0	100.0	100.0
28.2	26.9	27.2	Gross Profit		32.6	27.4	28.3	27.0	24.4
25.2	23.6	23.4	Operating Expenses		28.7	24.8	24.2	23.4	20.3
3.0	3.3	3.8	Operating Profit		3.8	2.6	4.1	3.6	4.1
.3	.3	.3	All Other Expenses (net)		-.2	-.3	.4	.2	.6
2.7	3.0	3.5	Profit Before Taxes		4.0	2.9	3.7	3.4	3.6
			RATIOS						
2.3	2.1	2.1	Current		2.2	1.9	2.6	2.0	2.1
1.6	1.4	1.5			1.4	1.5	1.6	1.6	1.5
1.2	1.2	1.2			1.0	1.2	1.2	1.2	1.3
1.3	1.2	1.2	Quick		1.8	.9	1.4	1.3	1.1
.9	.8	.8			1.1	.7	.9	.9	.8
.6	.6	.5			.6	.5	.6	.6	.5
36 10.1	38 9.6	34 10.9	Sales/Receivables	33 11.0	37 9.9	31 11.7	32 11.3	35 10.5	
44 8.2	49 7.5	44 8.4		49 7.4	46 7.9	46 8.5	46 8.0	43 8.6	
57 6.4	62 5.9	58 6.3		65 5.7	59 6.2	60 6.1	67 5.5	52 7.0	
25 14.5	25 14.7	27 13.5	Cost of Sales/Inventory	0 UND	46 7.9	21 17.2	23 15.7	45 8.2	
65 5.6	64 5.7	70 5.2		20 18.3	94 3.9	64 5.7	66 5.5	76 4.8	
94 3.9	96 3.8	99 3.7		99 3.7	144 2.5	98 3.8	96 3.8	99 3.7	
21 17.0	22 16.8	17 21.6	Cost of Sales/Payables	18 20.3	47 7.7	26 14.3	20 18.0	13 27.9	
34 10.8	37 9.8	32 11.3		40 9.2	56 6.5	37 9.8	35 10.5	23 16.1	
48 7.6	51 7.1	54 6.7		58 6.3	72 5.1	62 5.9	60 6.1	36 10.1	
6.1	6.6	6.2	Sales/Working Capital		5.8	6.1	5.1	6.9	6.8
10.3	10.6	10.0			17.4	10.7	9.7	10.0	9.9
20.5	20.0	20.4			-228.5	34.4	23.5	17.2	16.3
12.4	11.5	10.0	EBIT/Interest		7.4	7.5	10.4	9.3	16.1
(236) 4.9	(227) 5.0	(221) 3.8			(23) 3.3	(15) 2.7	(40) 3.4	(55) 5.2	(83) 4.0
2.1	2.4	2.0			2.0	-.1	1.8	2.3	2.6
8.0	8.6	10.6	Net Profit + Depr., Dep., Amort./Cur. Mat. L/T/D					13.1	11.1
(67) 2.7	(61) 3.3	(60) 3.3					(16) 3.2	(31) 3.7	
1.5	1.7	1.7						1.2	1.8
.1	.1	.1	Fixed/Worth		.1	.1	.1	.1	.1
.2	.2	.2			.4	.2	.2	.2	.2
.7	.6	.5			1.7	3.5	.3	.5	.4
.9	1.2	1.0	Debt/Worth		.9	1.1	.8	1.0	1.2
2.0	2.4	2.2			2.8	2.5	1.6	2.2	2.1
4.4	4.8	4.3			8.8	39.3	3.6	4.4	3.4
35.0	45.7	41.2	% Profit Before Taxes/Tangible Net Worth		68.9	31.8	34.3	46.3	42.5
(231) 16.7	(226) 26.0	(226) 25.0		(21) 24.5	(14) 10.7	(44) 14.1	(58) 26.7	(87) 28.0	
5.7	12.5	10.0			8.9	-2.8	3.7	12.0	13.3
13.1	12.9	15.4	% Profit Before Taxes/Total Assets		24.2	20.4	13.8	17.4	14.7
6.3	7.7	7.4			7.4	4.1	6.7	8.0	9.1
1.8	3.1	2.6			1.7	-.7	1.7	2.9	4.6
103.4	111.1	124.6	Sales/Net Fixed Assets		226.0	127.7	94.6	190.0	88.2
45.8	55.5	56.1			40.2	63.2	64.3	77.3	44.6
22.1	25.7	24.8			12.4	27.5	38.0	19.0	23.3
3.8	3.8	3.6	Sales/Total Assets		4.0	3.8	3.8	3.6	3.6
2.9	2.9	3.0			3.1	2.8	3.0	3.1	2.9
2.4	2.5	2.5			2.4	2.0	2.4	2.5	2.5
.4	.3	.3	% Depr., Dep., Amort./Sales		.4	.1	.3	.2	.3
(212) .6	(216) .5	(213) .5		(19) 1.1	(14) .6	(39) .5	(51) .5	(87) .4	
1.1	.9	.9			2.1	1.2	.9	.7	.8
2.0	2.0	1.6	% Officers', Directors' Owners' Comp/Sales		3.1		1.8	1.5	1.2
(96) 3.7	(107) 3.5	(96) 3.3		(15) 4.5		(22) 3.7	(27) 3.3	(20) 1.6	
5.9	5.9	6.2			8.8		5.6	7.0	6.3
6451892M	11923856M	9472276M	Net Sales ($)	2771M	49387M	70731M	342285M	986958M	8020144M
2326045M	3223269M	3206660M	Total Assets ($)	710M	17528M	27394M	120538M	333750M	2706740M

© RMA 2007

M = $ thousand   MM = $ million

See Pages 11 through 21 for Explanation of Ratios and Data

| Current Data Sorted by Assets | | | | | | | Comparative Historical Data | |

Type of Statement

0-500M	500M-2MM	2-10MM	10-50MM	50-100MM	100-250MM	Type of Statement	4/1/02-3/31/03 ALL	4/1/03-3/31/04 ALL
	1	1	10	2		Unqualified	11	9
	6	8	2	2		Reviewed	11	17
1	9	3	3			Compiled	15	24
2						Tax Returns	6	1
1	6	8	3			Other	14	17
5 (4/1-9/30/06)			63 (10/1/06-3/31/07)					
4	22	20	18	4		NUMBER OF STATEMENTS	57	68

Data

0-500M	500M-2MM	2-10MM	10-50MM	50-100MM	100-250MM		4/1/02-3/31/03 ALL	4/1/03-3/31/04 ALL
%	%	%	%	%	%	**ASSETS**	%	%
	7.2	7.9	2.4			Cash & Equivalents	9.1	4.9
	36.9	24.8	23.8			Trade Receivables (net)	28.7	27.9
	32.4	44.4	54.9			Inventory	37.1	41.4
	2.2	2.1	1.2			All Other Current	1.5	2.2
	78.6	79.3	82.4			Total Current	76.5	76.5
	11.4	12.3	10.4			Fixed Assets (net)	13.7	15.4
	7.1	5.7	2.0			Intangibles (net)	3.2	3.4
	3.0	2.7	5.2			All Other Non-Current	6.7	4.7
	100.0	100.0	100.0			Total	100.0	100.0
						LIABILITIES		
	16.2	19.7	26.5			Notes Payable-Short Term	14.4	20.3
	1.6	2.0	1.1			Cur. Mat.-L.T.D.	2.0	1.7
	27.0	18.0	19.0			Trade Payables	20.0	19.1
	.2	.8	.1			Income Taxes Payable	.3	.3
	7.0	6.9	9.7			All Other Current	8.0	5.7
	52.0	47.5	56.6			Total Current	44.8	47.0
	13.4	10.2	8.6			Long-Term Debt	10.0	7.7
	.0	.2	.8			Deferred Taxes	.2	.3
	10.2	4.8	3.5			All Other Non-Current	5.9	6.2
	24.4	37.3	30.5			Net Worth	39.2	38.9
	100.0	100.0	100.0			Total Liabilities & Net Worth	100.0	100.0
						INCOME DATA		
	100.0	100.0	100.0			Net Sales	100.0	100.0
	31.3	28.0	22.4			Gross Profit	28.6	27.2
	28.2	22.7	18.1			Operating Expenses	26.2	24.9
	3.1	5.3	4.4			Operating Profit	2.4	2.3
	.9	1.3	1.1			All Other Expenses (net)	.1	.1
	2.2	3.9	3.3			Profit Before Taxes	2.2	2.2

(The columns 0-500M, 50-100MM, and 100-250MM are marked "DATA NOT AVAILABLE".)

Ratios

0-500M	500M-2MM	2-10MM	10-50MM	50-100MM	100-250MM		4/1/02-3/31/03	4/1/03-3/31/04
	2.2	2.5	2.1			Current	2.4	2.5
	1.7	1.8	1.4				1.7	1.5
	1.2	1.3	1.0				1.3	1.2
	1.5	1.0	.8			Quick	1.4	1.0
	.7	.6	.5				(56) .7	(67) .7
	.5	.4	.3				.6	.4
	25 14.4	25 14.8	24 14.9			Sales/Receivables	27 13.7	30 12.3
	34 10.6	32 11.3	35 10.5				34 10.8	38 9.7
	51 7.1	51 7.1	39 9.4				46 7.9	48 7.5
	16 23.5	59 6.2	68 5.4			Cost of Sales/Inventory	28 13.3	52 7.0
	41 9.0	77 4.7	115 3.2				66 5.5	75 4.9
	65 5.6	125 2.9	156 2.3				104 3.5	116 3.1
	21 17.4	22 16.5	19 18.8			Cost of Sales/Payables	18 20.0	21 17.7
	35 10.5	32 11.5	34 10.8				29 12.6	33 11.2
	65 5.6	53 6.9	44 8.3				44 8.2	53 6.9
	7.0	5.6	5.6			Sales/Working Capital	6.1	5.4
	14.8	7.9	11.1				9.2	10.8
	24.9	14.3	258.3				29.5	26.4
	19.4	4.2	9.2			EBIT/Interest	6.1	8.5
	2.8	(16) 2.2	3.4				(49) 2.9	(63) 3.6
	1.7	1.4	2.6				1.9	1.9
						Net Profit + Depr., Dep., Amort./Cur. Mat. L/T/D	6.2	8.2
							(13) 2.8	(18) 3.3
							.6	1.8
	.2	.1	.2			Fixed/Worth	.1	.1
	.2	.3	.4				.3	.3
	1.0	.7	.7				.9	.8
	1.1	.9	1.6			Debt/Worth	.6	.8
	2.5	2.5	2.6				1.5	2.3
	12.3	5.9	6.8				4.3	3.9
	47.5	45.0	45.6			% Profit Before Taxes/Tangible Net Worth	33.8	28.1
	(18) 17.8	(19) 24.5	(17) 27.6				(53) 12.7	(65) 14.7
	5.9	5.4	14.1				4.9	7.5
	12.3	14.9	13.4			% Profit Before Taxes/Total Assets	11.0	9.1
	4.7	4.5	9.5				4.3	4.5
	1.7	1.7	6.0				2.1	2.3
	97.8	93.6	59.3			Sales/Net Fixed Assets	92.1	80.4
	61.0	31.7	37.4				32.7	25.4
	27.2	8.3	14.9				14.7	9.8
	3.8	3.0	3.0			Sales/Total Assets	3.6	3.2
	3.4	2.5	2.4				2.8	2.5
	2.7	2.2	2.0				2.2	2.0
	.3	.3	.4			% Depr., Dep., Amort./Sales	.3	.5
	(15) .8	(19) .7	(17) .7				(53) 1.0	(61) .9
	1.2		1.1				2.0	1.6
	2.8					% Officers', Directors' Owners' Comp/Sales	1.7	1.6
	(16) 3.9						(25) 3.5	(28) 4.0
	7.9						5.9	4.7
4016M	100928M	225147M	967494M	561784M		Net Sales ($)	1026409M	1292654M
1053M	29223M	99893M	381430M	266697M		Total Assets ($)	394096M	583901M

Comparative Historical Data   Current Data Sorted by Sales

						Type of Statement						
	8		12		13	Unqualified				1	1	11
	20		18		13	Reviewed				5	5	3
	15		15		13	Compiled	1	1	2	5	1	3
	6		7		11	Tax Returns	1	2	4	4		
	14		22		18	Other		3	4	2	6	3
	4/1/04-		4/1/05-		4/1/06-			5 (4/1-9/30/06)		63 (10/1/06-3/31/07)		
	3/31/05		3/31/06		3/31/07							
	ALL		ALL		ALL		0-1MM	1-3MM	3-5MM	5-10MM	10-25MM	25MM & OVER
	63		74		68	NUMBER OF STATEMENTS	2	6	10	17	13	20
	%		%		%	ASSETS	%	%	%	%	%	%
	5.7		6.4		7.0	Cash & Equivalents			9.5	8.1	5.0	4.9
	30.2		29.7		28.6	Trade Receivables (net)			26.1	39.0	22.1	24.7
	42.9		36.4		41.0	Inventory			30.1	35.4	49.3	52.0
	2.0		3.7		1.9	All Other Current			.2	5.1	.6	1.3
	80.8		76.3		78.5	Total Current			65.8	87.6	76.9	82.9
	11.5		15.5		13.5	Fixed Assets (net)			11.6	7.5	15.1	11.8
	2.0		3.9		4.5	Intangibles (net)			19.0	3.2	2.0	1.8
	5.6		4.3		3.5	All Other Non-Current			3.6	1.7	5.9	3.4
	100.0		100.0		100.0	Total			100.0	100.0	100.0	100.0
						LIABILITIES						
	17.0		15.1		18.2	Notes Payable-Short Term			13.1	23.8	17.1	21.4
	2.0		3.8		2.2	Cur. Mat.-L.T.D.			1.7	1.1	2.7	.9
	21.2		19.8		20.3	Trade Payables			20.2	26.1	17.8	18.7
	.2		.3		.3	Income Taxes Payable			.2	.0	1.2	.1
	6.2		8.0		8.3	All Other Current			4.9	7.7	11.8	6.6
	46.7		46.9		49.4	Total Current			40.2	58.7	50.6	47.7
	8.8		12.6		10.1	Long-Term Debt			17.4	6.7	13.7	8.2
	.2		.2		.3	Deferred Taxes			.0	.2	.1	.8
	4.4		6.0		5.8	All Other Non-Current			1.4	2.4	4.7	3.9
	39.9		34.3		34.4	Net Worth			41.0	32.0	30.8	39.5
	100.0		100.0		100.0	Total Liabilties & Net Worth			100.0	100.0	100.0	100.0
						INCOME DATA						
	100.0		100.0		100.0	Net Sales			100.0	100.0	100.0	100.0
	26.6		26.9		29.0	Gross Profit			35.0	25.8	23.0	24.0
	23.9		21.8		23.6	Operating Expenses			29.2	21.3	19.1	18.5
	2.7		5.0		5.4	Operating Profit			5.8	4.5	3.9	5.5
	.4		.6		1.4	All Other Expenses (net)			1.0	1.1	1.3	.7
	2.3		4.5		4.0	Profit Before Taxes			4.8	3.3	2.6	4.8
						RATIOS						
	2.7		2.4		2.6				2.3	1.9	2.4	3.8
	1.6		1.7		1.7	Current			1.7	1.4	1.8	1.6
	1.3		1.2		1.2				1.1	1.2	1.1	1.3
	1.2		1.3		1.3				1.6	1.3	.9	.9
	.7		.7		.6	Quick			1.1	.7	.6	.6
	.5		.5		.4				.4	.4	.3	.4
32	11.6	30	12.2	25	14.8		28	12.9	26 14.3	24 15.1	25 14.7
37	10.0	37	9.8	34	10.7	Sales/Receivables	35	10.5	45 8.2	29 12.6	36 10.2
50	7.2	47	7.7	47	7.7		62	5.9	52 7.1	32 11.3	39 9.4
53	6.9	34	10.8	40	9.2		16	23.5	29 12.5	69 5.3	71 5.2
83	4.4	77	4.8	73	5.0	Cost of Sales/Inventory	39	9.5	49 7.4	85 4.3	107 3.4
125	2.9	115	3.2	125	2.9		102	3.6	72 5.1	168 2.2	141 2.6
25	14.8	20	18.7	20	18.0		25	14.3	18 20.6	20 18.4	17 21.3
38	9.6	34	10.6	32	11.3	Cost of Sales/Payables	39	9.4	31 11.7	32 11.2	32 11.3
51	7.1	49	7.5	51	7.1		73	5.0	55 6.6	47 7.7	44 8.3
	4.6		5.0		5.8				6.6	5.9	6.7	3.6
	8.4		8.2		9.8	Sales/Working Capital			8.0	13.6	11.3	7.1
	18.8		20.4		23.0				32.3	20.9	24.7	17.6
	9.4		11.4		9.2				32.4	12.1	4.3	14.6
(58)	4.4	(66)	4.8	(62)	3.1	EBIT/Interest	(15)	5.7	(15) 2.6	(11) 2.4	(19) 5.1
	2.4		2.5		1.8				1.4	1.4	1.1	2.9
	7.7		10.9		40.7	Net Profit + Depr., Dep.,						
(17)	2.7	(17)	2.9	(13)	8.3	Amort./Cur. Mat. L/T/D						
	1.5		1.7		1.8							
	.1		.1		.2				.1	.1	.2	.2
	.2		.3		.3	Fixed/Worth			.7	.2	.4	.4
	.5		1.2		.7				-.4	.6	1.0	.5
	.8		.7		1.0				.8	1.1	1.2	1.1
	2.0		2.6		2.2	Debt/Worth			2.2	2.8	4.4	1.9
	3.9		5.4		5.9				-3.1	7.8	8.7	3.1
	45.3		56.8		42.2	% Profit Before Taxes/Tangible			59.1	51.8	37.7
(61)	17.0	(66)	19.4	(62)	24.6	Net Worth		(16)	22.0	24.9	(19) 27.6
	4.0		10.2		9.3					9.5	2.7	19.2
	11.6		15.2		14.5	% Profit Before Taxes/Total			20.1	15.0	14.8	15.8
	5.2		6.8		7.6	Assets			6.8	3.6	5.7	11.2
	1.2		3.4		2.6				1.5	1.5	1.1	6.5
	89.7		76.0		75.5				384.1	92.4	76.9	52.5
	42.1		33.3		38.9	Sales/Net Fixed Assets			48.1	62.4	33.7	25.1
	16.1		12.7		12.3				7.9	32.3	7.0	12.3
	3.2		3.4		3.4				3.6	3.8	3.0	2.9
	2.6		2.6		2.7	Sales/Total Assets			2.8	3.5	2.4	2.4
	2.0		2.0		2.2				1.6	2.7	1.9	2.1
	.4		.4		.3				.3		.3	.4
(51)	.7	(62)	.8	(57)	.8	% Depr., Dep., Amort./Sales		(16)	.6	(12) .7	(19) .7
	1.4		1.3		1.1				.8	1.4	1.0
	2.3		2.3		2.6	% Officers', Directors'						
(27)	4.3	(28)	3.8	(27)	3.7	Owners' Comp/Sales						
	5.1		6.1		7.8							
	1193159M		1858647M		1859369M	Net Sales ($)	992M	11696M	35204M	120019M	190856M	1500602M
	517703M		831021M		778296M	Total Assets ($)	500M	4103M	22980M	39724M	85662M	625327M

© RMA 2007   M = $ thousand   MM = $ million
                              See Pages 11 through 21 for Explanation of Ratios and Data

Current Data Sorted by Assets   Comparative Historical Data

						Type of Statement		
1		17	53	19	25	Unqualified	94	90
8		61	36	3		Reviewed	66	81
3	10	27	8			Compiled	55	74
13	16	14	1			Tax Returns	21	31
4	11	35	39	11	15	Other	66	89
	60 (4/1-9/30/06)		370 (10/1/06-3/31/07)				4/1/02-3/31/03	4/1/03-3/31/04
0-500M	500M-2MM	2-10MM	10-50MM	50-100MM	100-250MM		ALL	ALL
21	45	154	137	33	40	NUMBER OF STATEMENTS	302	365
%	%	%	%	%	%	ASSETS	%	%
13.3	9.6	5.7	3.7	4.2	1.2	Cash & Equivalents	5.3	6.5
28.0	19.7	21.8	17.3	18.2	19.5	Trade Receivables (net)	18.4	18.9
31.9	42.8	44.4	49.6	49.7	47.8	Inventory	48.7	46.3
.6	4.9	1.0	1.6	3.0	1.3	All Other Current	1.7	2.3
73.8	77.1	72.9	72.2	75.2	69.9	Total Current	74.1	73.9
21.2	18.8	21.7	23.6	17.3	27.8	Fixed Assets (net)	20.0	20.2
.7	1.8	1.4	1.3	3.1	.3	Intangibles (net)	1.0	1.0
4.2	2.3	4.0	2.9	4.4	2.0	All Other Non-Current	4.8	4.9
100.0	100.0	100.0	100.0	100.0	100.0	Total	100.0	100.0
						LIABILITIES		
11.7	18.2	24.6	29.1	29.5	29.8	Notes Payable-Short Term	29.7	27.4
3.3	2.9	3.9	5.3	3.2	1.8	Cur. Mat.-L.T.D.	4.9	4.6
21.1	16.3	15.8	11.7	9.6	12.1	Trade Payables	12.6	14.2
.1	.3	.3	.3	.6	.3	Income Taxes Payable	.3	.3
5.6	7.6	7.5	9.1	10.5	8.9	All Other Current	6.4	7.5
41.8	45.2	52.1	55.6	53.3	52.9	Total Current	53.8	53.9
9.1	9.6	11.0	13.5	16.5	16.1	Long-Term Debt	11.3	12.2
.1	.0	.5	.4	1.3	.3	Deferred Taxes	.7	.7
34.5	9.2	3.4	2.8	1.9	1.5	All Other Non-Current	2.9	3.6
14.5	36.0	32.9	27.7	26.9	29.2	Net Worth	31.2	29.6
100.0	100.0	100.0	100.0	100.0	100.0	Total Liabilities & Net Worth	100.0	100.0
						INCOME DATA		
100.0	100.0	100.0	100.0	100.0	100.0	Net Sales	100.0	100.0
36.0	27.3	28.0	25.0	23.0	22.4	Gross Profit	25.7	26.7
26.6	21.8	22.6	19.4	16.2	16.0	Operating Expenses	23.1	23.3
9.4	5.5	5.4	5.6	6.8	6.4	Operating Profit	2.6	3.3
.7	1.4	1.1	1.4	1.6	.7	All Other Expenses (net)	1.0	.8
8.7	4.1	4.3	4.2	5.2	5.7	Profit Before Taxes	1.6	2.5
						RATIOS		
4.2	3.4	1.8	1.7	1.9	1.9		1.9	1.9
1.6	1.8	1.4	1.2	1.5	1.3	Current	1.4	1.4
1.1	1.3	1.1	1.1	1.2	1.1		1.1	1.1
2.0	1.6	.9	.6	.8	.5		.7	.8
.9	(44) .6	.5	.3	.4	.4	Quick	.4 (364)	.4
.5	.2	.2	.2	.3	.3		.3	.3

												Sales/Receivables				
5	72.6	0	UND	20	18.6	22	16.5	26	14.0	36	10.2		25	14.7	22	16.4
25	14.6	20	18.2	31	11.7	33	11.0	40	9.2	42	8.7		35	10.6	36	10.0
47	7.7	42	8.6	47	7.8	45	8.1	49	7.4	54	6.8		47	7.7	51	7.2
11	33.9	15	24.0	43	8.6	72	5.1	76	4.8	99	3.7	Cost of Sales/Inventory	66	5.5	63	5.8
43	8.5	66	5.5	100	3.7	135	2.7	141	2.6	137	2.7		131	2.8	116	3.1
89	4.1	126	2.9	181	2.0	207	1.8	233	1.6	188	1.9		218	1.7	192	1.9
0	UND	1	275.5	11	34.2	10	37.4	13	28.0	13	28.7	Cost of Sales/Payables	11	32.3	10	37.9
28	13.1	10	37.8	29	12.6	21	17.0	20	17.8	30	12.0		24	15.5	26	13.9
46	7.9	50	7.3	54	6.8	37	9.8	32	11.3	62	5.9		45	8.1	54	6.8

												Sales/Working Capital				
	5.8		4.2		6.1		6.2		4.4		4.8			4.7		4.9
	11.6		9.1		10.3		11.1		7.1		9.4			8.9		8.7
	89.3		28.2		30.2		32.6		13.1		40.0			22.4		29.1
	19.3		7.3		6.0		4.7		5.3		6.1	EBIT/Interest		4.0		4.8
(16)	6.6	(39)	2.1	(148)	2.7	(134)	2.6	(31)	2.6	(39)	4.5		(293)	1.9	(342)	2.1
	1.8		1.3		1.5		1.8		2.1		2.4			1.0		1.2
					9.5		6.9		9.4			Net Profit + Depr., Dep., Amort./Cur. Mat. L/T/D		4.7		5.1
				(46)	4.3	(49)	1.9	(11)	4.0				(91)	1.9	(99)	2.1
					1.2		.8		1.1					.7		.7
	.0		.1		.2		.2		.1		.4	Fixed/Worth		.2		.2
	.4		.4		.5		.5		.3		.9			.4		.4
	2.7		.9		1.5		1.5		1.2		1.3			1.2		1.3
	.8		.7		1.2		1.9		1.4		1.8	Debt/Worth		1.4		1.4
	2.7		2.1		2.5		3.6		3.0		2.7			2.5		2.7
	5.7		4.9		5.4		5.2		5.2		3.6			4.9		5.1
	166.5		39.9		43.3		38.1		35.8		34.5	% Profit Before Taxes/Tangible Net Worth		20.5		22.4
(18)	43.8	(39)	23.1	(150)	20.2	(134)	23.6	(31)	23.6		24.0		(289)	8.9	(341)	10.3
	7.9		7.2		8.0		12.0		8.3		18.0			1.3		2.6
	54.9		18.4		12.4		10.0		10.8		10.7	% Profit Before Taxes/Total Assets		5.9		6.4
	23.6		3.7		4.3		5.5		5.6		7.2			2.3		2.8
	3.3		1.5		2.0		2.5		2.7		4.1			.1		.6
	UND		146.6		52.8		43.7		44.2		15.6	Sales/Net Fixed Assets		44.2		40.0
	46.2		30.8		20.4		17.0		26.5		6.0			16.5		18.3
	9.3		11.9		6.6		3.7		9.4		3.3			5.8		5.8
	6.3		4.1		3.0		2.1		1.9		1.7	Sales/Total Assets		2.3		2.4
	4.1		2.7		2.3		1.7		1.6		1.5			1.6		1.7
	2.2		1.7		1.4		1.3		1.3		1.3			1.3		1.3
	.6		.4		.6		.6		.5		.7	% Depr., Dep., Amort./Sales		.7		.6
(13)	1.6	(37)	1.1	(137)	1.2	(113)	1.1	(24)	1.1	(17)	1.0		(233)	1.4	(294)	1.3
	2.7		3.3		2.8		6.8		3.7		1.3			3.8		3.8
	2.0		1.7		1.4		.6					% Officers', Directors' Owners' Comp/Sales		1.2		1.7
(13)	5.4	(19)	3.2	(60)	2.3	(25)	1.2						(108)	2.4	(120)	3.3
	8.2		7.5		2.8		2.3								5.1		5.8
23094M	185163M	1728864M	6138448M	3633694M	10943534M	Net Sales ($)	12809676M	13540286M
6264M	57451M	766528M	3563627M	2278363M	6980451M	Total Assets ($)	8543757M	9136908M

M = $ thousand   MM = $ million
See Pages 11 through 21 for Explanation of Ratios and Data

Comparative Historical Data				Current Data Sorted by Sales					
			Type of Statement						
111	100	115	Unqualified	1	3	3	20	88	
90	72	108	Reviewed	1	4	10	22	40	31
62	46	48	Compiled	2	10	6	14	12	4
25	29	44	Tax Returns	7	14	6	12	5	
93	109	115	Other	4	7	6	19	23	56
4/1/04-3/31/05 ALL	4/1/05-3/31/06 ALL	4/1/06-3/31/07 ALL		60 (4/1-9/30/06)			370 (10/1/06-3/31/07)		
				0-1MM	1-3MM	3-5MM	5-10MM	10-25MM	25MM & OVER
381	356	430	**NUMBER OF STATEMENTS**	15	35	31	70	100	179
%	%	%	**ASSETS**	%	%	%	%	%	%
5.6	6.1	5.3	Cash & Equivalents	15.6	9.5	7.2	4.8	6.2	3.0
21.5	20.1	20.0	Trade Receivables (net)	14.1	21.1	17.6	20.7	21.6	19.5
46.8	46.4	46.0	Inventory	30.0	36.5	44.0	46.1	45.2	50.0
2.1	1.6	1.8	All Other Current	2.8	5.6	1.1	.7	.9	1.9
76.0	74.2	73.1	Total Current	62.6	72.7	69.9	72.3	73.9	74.4
18.8	21.2	22.2	Fixed Assets (net)	32.9	19.9	26.6	22.3	21.4	21.4
.8	1.4	1.4	Intangibles (net)	.6	2.8	.5	1.5	1.3	1.3
4.4	3.2	3.3	All Other Non-Current	3.9	4.6	3.0	3.9	3.3	2.9
100.0	100.0	100.0	Total	100.0	100.0	100.0	100.0	100.0	100.0
			LIABILITIES						
26.7	27.2	25.6	Notes Payable-Short Term	7.8	20.6	20.1	23.1	24.6	30.5
4.2	3.7	4.0	Cur. Mat.-L.T.D.	5.3	1.7	5.5	5.4	3.9	3.5
15.4	15.9	14.0	Trade Payables	14.0	17.6	19.1	14.3	13.8	12.4
.4	.4	.3	Income Taxes Payable	.0	.1	.0	.2		.5
8.1	8.0	8.3	All Other Current	4.9	5.6	5.4	7.5	10.7	8.6
54.8	55.1	52.1	Total Current	32.1	45.6	50.1	50.5	53.4	55.4
12.2	12.6	12.5	Long-Term Debt	15.1	9.4	13.6	16.0	8.7	13.3
.7	.6	.5	Deferred Taxes	.0	.1	.5	.5	.4	.6
3.9	3.7	5.1	All Other Non-Current	40.6	12.8	6.0	2.9	3.7	2.0
28.4	28.0	29.9	Net Worth	12.2	32.1	29.9	30.0	33.8	28.7
100.0	100.0	100.0	Total Liabilties & Net Worth	100.0	100.0	100.0	100.0	100.0	100.0
			INCOME DATA						
100.0	100.0	100.0	Net Sales	100.0	100.0	100.0	100.0	100.0	100.0
24.7	25.1	26.5	Gross Profit	39.3	35.0	32.4	27.1	26.3	22.6
21.0	20.4	20.6	Operating Expenses	25.5	30.3	26.8	21.0	20.5	17.1
3.7	4.7	5.9	Operating Profit	13.8	4.7	5.6	6.0	5.8	5.5
.7	.7	1.2	All Other Expenses (net)	3.9	.4	.8	1.6	1.0	1.1
3.0	4.0	4.7	Profit Before Taxes	9.9	4.3	4.8	4.5	4.7	4.4
			RATIOS						
1.8	1.8	1.9		5.5	2.6	2.1	2.0	1.8	1.7
1.4	1.3	1.4	Current	1.8	1.6	1.4	1.4	1.4	1.3
1.1	1.1	1.1		1.4	1.1	1.0	1.0	1.1	1.1
.8	.8	.9		3.0	1.2	.8	.9	1.0	.6
(380) .5	.4	(429) .4	Quick	1.0	.5	(30) .6	.5	.5	.4
.3	.3	.2		.4	.2	.2	.2	.2	.2
23 15.8	20 18.0	20 18.0		0 UND	3 104.9	17 21.4	20 18.1	18 20.0	26 13.9
37 9.8	35 10.6	33 11.0	Sales/Receivables	17 21.9	31 11.6	28 13.2	31 11.9	30 12.0	36 10.1
51 7.2	47 7.8	47 7.8		51 7.1	48 7.6	42 8.8	48 7.6	46 7.9	46 7.9
59 6.2	52 7.1	50 7.2		0 UND	12 29.8	37 9.9	44 8.4	41 9.0	77 4.7
109 3.3	108 3.4	112 3.2	Cost of Sales/Inventory	72 5.1	75 4.9	81 4.5	96 3.8	108 3.4	131 2.8
179 2.0	178 2.1	187 2.0		124 2.9	228 1.6	191 1.9	167 2.2	168 2.2	197 1.8
11 32.3	12 31.3	10 38.2		3 134.6	5 67.0	9 42.9	10 38.3	9 38.6	11 33.5
25 14.6	25 14.5	23 15.9	Cost of Sales/Payables	27 13.8	20 17.9	35 10.5	30 12.0	21 17.8	21 17.0
52 7.0	58 6.3	48 7.7		37 9.9	61 6.0	74 4.9	54 6.7	42 8.7	43 8.5
5.6	6.3	5.7		4.0	2.8	5.7	6.1	6.2	5.8
10.0	10.7	10.2	Sales/Working Capital	6.2	7.2	9.3	11.7	10.3	10.2
25.3	29.3	28.9		22.6	105.1	61.4	132.6	33.4	20.9
6.6	7.2	6.0		11.5	12.9	5.8	4.9	8.8	5.6
(357) 3.3	(347) 3.5	(407) 2.8	EBIT/Interest	(10) 5.1	(32) 1.9	(28) 2.8	(68) 2.5	(96) 3.2	(173) 2.9
1.7	1.9	1.6		1.2	1.2	1.2	1.6	1.6	2.0
9.4	9.7	8.6	Net Profit + Depr., Dep.,				9.1	8.5	10.0
(108) 3.3	(95) 3.4	(114) 3.5	Amort./Cur. Mat. L/T/D			(14) 2.0	(35) 2.6	(54) 3.8	
1.4	1.9	1.0					.6	1.0	1.2
.1	.2	.2		.0	.0	.3	.1	.2	.2
.4	.5	.5	Fixed/Worth	.5	.4	.6	.6	.4	.5
1.2	1.5	1.4		2.1	1.4	2.4	2.0	1.3	1.2
1.6	1.5	1.4		.8	.8	1.2	1.1	1.2	1.7
2.8	3.0	3.0	Debt/Worth	1.6	3.6	3.7	3.6	2.3	3.1
5.1	5.2	5.0		4.0	7.9	6.4	6.4	4.4	4.7
30.6	40.8	41.0	% Profit Before Taxes/Tangible	119.2	40.9	55.6	43.5	48.0	36.3
(362) 18.0	(335) 22.9	(412) 23.2	Net Worth	(13) 19.8	(31) 17.8	(28) 15.8	(67) 25.1	(98) 20.9	(175) 23.9
7.8	10.4	10.5		4.4	4.4	4.3	10.5	10.6	12.6
8.4	10.9	11.5	% Profit Before Taxes/Total	56.6	26.2	13.7	15.0	12.4	10.2
4.5	5.8	5.6	Assets	7.7	2.3	3.7	5.0	6.5	5.9
1.7	2.3	2.4		1.4	.7	.8	2.4	2.3	2.9
53.3	49.6	46.5		UND	172.8	27.8	59.1	48.3	41.0
22.4	18.3	18.1	Sales/Net Fixed Assets	8.4	45.4	12.2	19.4	25.1	15.8
6.4	5.5	5.5		3.5	7.7	5.1	6.5	6.2	4.8
2.6	2.6	2.6		3.7	4.1	3.0	3.0	3.1	2.2
1.8	1.9	1.9	Sales/Total Assets	2.1	1.8	2.1	2.3	2.1	1.7
1.4	1.4	1.4		1.3	1.1	1.3	1.3	1.5	1.4
.6	.6	.6		.8	.5	.8	.6	.6	.5
(295) 1.2	(281) 1.1	(341) 1.1	% Depr., Dep., Amort./Sales	(11) 2.4	(25) 1.7	(28) 2.2	(59) 1.3	(90) 1.0	(128) .8
3.8	4.5	3.9		8.1	6.6	4.4	2.7	4.0	3.7
1.1	1.1	1.3			2.3	1.7	1.4	1.3	.5
(116) 2.7	(116) 2.6	(120) 2.2	% Officers', Directors' Owners' Comp/Sales		(10) 6.4	(10) 3.8	(30) 2.4	(34) 2.2	(22) 1.1
5.6	4.5	5.1			12.1	9.1	3.8	2.9	1.9
17133922M	18492330M	22652797M	Net Sales ($)	9694M	66884M	126908M	517490M	1733330M	20198491M
10055434M	11124845M	13652684M	Total Assets ($)	6058M	45247M	72636M	293074M	1035051M	12200618M

Current Data Sorted by Assets

Comparative Historical Data

						Type of Statement		
1		8	28	4	1	Unqualified	40	28
2	8	49	19	3		Reviewed	75	68
4	25	51	4			Compiled	95	103
7	18	26	3	1		Tax Returns	36	50
4	15	47	24	3	1	Other	106	84
	63 (4/1-9/30/06)		293 (10/1/06-3/31/07)				4/1/02-3/31/03 ALL	4/1/03-3/31/04 ALL
0-500M	500M-2MM	2-10MM	10-50MM	50-100MM	100-250MM			
18	66	181	78	11	2	NUMBER OF STATEMENTS	352	333
%	%	%	%	%	%	**ASSETS**	%	%
9.3	7.0	5.9	3.4	3.6		Cash & Equivalents	5.8	6.4
17.7	18.0	13.6	16.8	16.0		Trade Receivables (net)	14.3	14.7
49.5	54.7	64.0	56.0	46.5		Inventory	61.7	60.4
4.3	1.3	1.7	2.1	4.6		All Other Current	1.9	2.5
80.9	81.0	85.2	78.3	70.7		Total Current	83.8	84.0
12.8	12.8	9.2	14.6	11.1		Fixed Assets (net)	10.7	10.5
5.8	1.0	1.0	1.9	10.7		Intangibles (net)	1.0	1.0
.6	5.2	4.6	5.3	7.6		All Other Non-Current	4.6	4.4
100.0	100.0	100.0	100.0	100.0		Total	100.0	100.0
						LIABILITIES		
29.2	21.0	28.7	20.1	24.8		Notes Payable-Short Term	26.7	24.8
6.1	1.5	2.1	2.9	1.1		Cur. Mat.-L.T.D.	2.3	2.3
23.2	18.7	17.5	22.8	13.9		Trade Payables	20.1	19.7
.0	.2	.2	.1	.3		Income Taxes Payable	.3	.2
15.6	6.7	8.3	11.0	7.8		All Other Current	9.1	8.7
74.1	48.1	56.9	56.9	47.9		Total Current	58.4	55.8
20.1	13.2	5.8	8.1	13.6		Long-Term Debt	8.4	8.3
.0	.0	.2	.2	.1		Deferred Taxes	.2	.2
4.1	3.9	2.4	4.6	6.1		All Other Non-Current	3.3	3.7
1.8	34.7	34.7	30.2	32.3		Net Worth	29.6	32.0
100.0	100.0	100.0	100.0	100.0		Total Liabilities & Net Worth	100.0	100.0
						INCOME DATA		
100.0	100.0	100.0	100.0	100.0		Net Sales	100.0	100.0
24.8	23.8	21.4	19.8	22.4		Gross Profit	22.1	22.5
22.0	21.2	19.2	16.4	17.7		Operating Expenses	20.2	20.9
2.7	2.5	2.2	3.4	4.7		Operating Profit	1.9	1.7
2.3	.9	.4	.3	1.1		All Other Expenses (net)	.3	.0
.4	1.7	1.8	3.1	3.6		Profit Before Taxes	1.6	1.7
						RATIOS		
1.8	2.6	1.9	1.7	1.9			1.8	2.0
1.2	1.8	1.4	1.3	1.5		Current	1.4	1.4
.7	1.2	1.2	1.1	1.3			1.2	1.2
.6	1.0	.6	.7	.9			.6	.7
.2	.4	.3	.3	.4		Quick	(351) .3	.3
.1	.2	.1	.1	.2			.1	.1
3 · 134.8	6 · 59.8	7 · 54.4	8 · 46.1	19 · 19.1			7 · 49.7	6 · 60.8
7 · 54.7	17 · 21.0	16 · 23.1	23 · 16.0	26 · 14.0		Sales/Receivables	15 · 24.2	16 · 23.2
30 · 12.2	32 · 11.4	30 · 12.2	42 · 8.6	45 · 8.1			33 · 10.9	35 · 10.3
10 · 38.0	55 · 6.6	86 · 4.2	81 · 4.5	39 · 9.4			91 · 4.0	85 · 4.3
87 · 4.2	85 · 4.3	132 · 2.8	104 · 3.5	113 · 3.2		Cost of Sales/Inventory	130 · 2.8	127 · 2.9
133 · 2.7	173 · 2.1	191 · 1.9	142 · 2.6	165 · 2.2			184 · 2.0	176 · 2.1
0 · UND	3 · 135.4	8 · 43.7	13 · 28.1	9 · 39.7			9 · 40.9	8 · 43.1
16 · 23.1	19 · 19.3	24 · 15.2	32 · 11.2	29 · 12.6		Cost of Sales/Payables	24 · 15.0	26 · 14.0
38 · 9.7	47 · 7.8	52 · 7.0	73 · 5.0	42 · 8.7			63 · 5.8	65 · 5.6
6.6	4.8	5.4	6.3	6.5			5.7	5.4
53.1	7.7	9.3	13.6	9.8		Sales/Working Capital	9.6	9.3
-16.5	25.3	15.7	24.1	15.6			19.2	17.1
2.6	5.1	5.7	5.2	4.3			5.7	6.0
(15) 1.3	(63) 2.5	(177) 2.4	(77) 3.0	3.5		EBIT/Interest	(335) 2.2	(318) 2.8
-.4	1.0	1.3	1.7	1.7			1.1	1.3
		3.9	5.7			Net Profit + Depr., Dep.,	4.6	4.7
	(45) 2.4		(30) 2.9			Amort./Cur. Mat. L/T/D	(105) 2.1	(86) 2.2
		1.0	1.2				1.3	1.1
.0	.1	.1	.2	.3			.1	.1
18.0	.3	.3	.5	.5		Fixed/Worth	.3	.3
-.3	.8	.4	1.0	1.1			.7	.6
2.3	.8	1.0	1.5	1.1			1.3	1.3
-28.8	2.6	2.2	2.8	2.5		Debt/Worth	2.6	2.6
-3.2	6.3	4.3	5.5	8.9			5.4	4.8
	33.0	25.0	31.7			% Profit Before Taxes/Tangible	27.2	27.6
	(58) 15.2	(173) 11.2	(73) 21.7			Net Worth	(334) 11.0	(316) 11.3
	2.2	3.5	11.7				2.6	2.8
9.9	9.5	8.4	9.0	9.1			6.6	7.4
5.9	4.1	2.8	4.8	4.5		% Profit Before Taxes/Total Assets	2.7	3.2
-9.8	.2	.8	2.7	2.3			.3	.6
UND	124.3	68.1	44.2	35.2			66.2	69.7
49.2	42.7	36.7	20.4	17.4		Sales/Net Fixed Assets	32.6	35.3
19.5	20.1	17.7	12.8	11.3			15.7	15.8
4.8	3.9	3.0	2.8	2.1			2.9	3.0
3.0	2.8	2.3	2.3	1.8		Sales/Total Assets	2.2	2.3
1.7	2.0	1.8	1.8	1.4			1.7	1.7
.2	.3	.4	.4	.4			.5	.5
(10) 1.1	(53) .8	(159) .8	(74) .6	(10) .5		% Depr., Dep., Amort./Sales	(309) .8	(296) .8
3.0	1.4	1.2	1.1	1.1			1.3	1.3
2.1	1.8	1.0	.5			% Officers', Directors'	.9	1.0
(11) 3.7	(37) 3.0	(97) 1.5	(19) 1.6			Owners' Comp/Sales	(172) 1.7	(167) 2.2
7.6	5.8	3.4	3.6				3.6	3.9
27938M	260559M	2122627M	3709564M	1587096M	1018549M	Net Sales ($)	6345308M	6326221M
5277M	82941M	880355M	1646775M	698039M	295344M	Total Assets ($)	2872954M	2858546M

M = $ thousand   MM = $ million
See Pages 11 through 21 for Explanation of Ratios and Data

Comparative Historical Data   ## Current Data Sorted by Sales

			Type of Statement						
27	37	42	Unqualified	1			2	7	32
68	64	81	Reviewed	1	3	4	25	27	21
97	76	84	Compiled	5	14	13	16	31	5
47	34	55	Tax Returns	5	8	5	22	10	5
80	95	94	Other	4	6	10	21	26	27
4/1/04-3/31/05 ALL	4/1/05-3/31/06 ALL	4/1/06-3/31/07 ALL		0-1MM	63 (4/1-9/30/06) 1-3MM	3-5MM	5-10MM	293 (10/1/06-3/31/07) 10-25MM	25MM & OVER
319	306	356	NUMBER OF STATEMENTS	16	31	32	86	101	90
%	%	%	**ASSETS**	%	%	%	%	%	%
5.7	5.9	5.7	Cash & Equivalents	5.9	7.0	5.1	7.8	5.4	3.7
14.0	16.4	15.5	Trade Receivables (net)	15.5	13.7	18.8	12.6	16.2	16.7
62.7	59.7	59.3	Inventory	51.3	61.0	54.7	62.8	59.9	57.6
1.9	2.1	1.9	All Other Current	4.5	.7	1.5	2.0	1.6	2.4
84.3	84.0	82.3	Total Current	77.1	82.3	80.2	85.2	83.1	80.3
10.5	10.5	11.3	Fixed Assets (net)	15.5	10.5	13.8	9.7	11.0	11.7
.7	1.4	1.7	Intangibles (net)	6.2	.8	.4	.6	1.5	3.0
4.5	4.1	4.7	All Other Non-Current	1.2	6.4	5.6	4.5	4.4	5.0
100.0	100.0	100.0	Total	100.0	100.0	100.0	100.0	100.0	100.0
			LIABILITIES						
24.9	23.2	25.3	Notes Payable-Short Term	32.0	23.5	29.3	25.8	24.4	23.8
1.9	2.0	2.3	Cur. Mat.-L.T.D.	2.0	2.8	2.5	2.1	2.4	2.2
19.6	20.2	19.1	Trade Payables	9.7	15.5	13.1	22.5	17.1	23.2
.2	.2	.2	Income Taxes Payable	.0	.4	.0	.1	.3	.2
10.0	8.8	9.0	All Other Current	17.2	3.8	7.5	8.2	9.8	9.8
56.7	54.5	55.9	Total Current	60.9	46.0	52.4	58.7	54.0	59.1
8.4	9.9	8.6	Long-Term Debt	9.8	14.1	15.7	8.0	7.0	6.4
.3	.2	.1	Deferred Taxes	.0	.0	.0	.1	.3	.2
3.4	2.8	3.4	All Other Non-Current	1.7	9.0	3.4	1.9	2.0	4.6
31.2	32.7	31.9	Net Worth	27.6	30.9	28.5	31.3	36.7	29.6
100.0	100.0	100.0	Total Liabilties & Net Worth	100.0	100.0	100.0	100.0	100.0	100.0
			INCOME DATA						
100.0	100.0	100.0	Net Sales	100.0	100.0	100.0	100.0	100.0	100.0
21.3	22.5	21.7	Gross Profit	31.5	28.3	21.0	21.1	21.3	19.1
18.9	19.5	19.1	Operating Expenses	28.2	25.4	18.5	19.6	18.3	15.9
2.4	3.0	2.7	Operating Profit	3.3	2.9	2.4	1.5	3.0	3.3
.0	.3	.6	All Other Expenses (net)	2.8	1.3	1.0	.6	.0	.4
2.4	2.7	2.1	Profit Before Taxes	.4	1.7	1.4	.9	3.0	2.9
			RATIOS						
2.0	1.9	2.0	Current	2.2	2.7	1.9	1.9	2.3	1.7
1.4	1.5	1.4		1.4	2.1	1.6	1.5	1.4	1.3
1.2	1.2	1.2		.9	1.3	1.2	1.1	1.2	1.1
.6	.7	.7	Quick	.7	1.0	.8	.5	.8	.7
.3	.4	.3		.2	.3	.4	.2	.3	.3
.1	.1	.1		.1	.2	.2	.1	.1	.1
6 65.0	7 51.3	7 53.9	Sales/Receivables	0 UND	6 56.8	12 29.9	5 69.2	8 47.4	7 51.4
13 28.9	18 20.7	17 21.5		14 26.4	17 20.9	22 16.6	12 31.7	17 21.3	21 17.3
32 11.3	40 9.2	34 10.8		59 6.2	28 12.8	39 9.3	31 11.9	32 11.4	42 8.7
90 4.1	79 4.6	73 5.0	Cost of Sales/Inventory	86 4.2	68 5.4	70 5.2	79 4.6	74 5.0	68 5.3
124 2.9	122 3.0	114 3.2		173 2.1	103 3.5	120 3.1	126 2.9	123 3.0	98 3.7
172 2.1	177 2.1	177 2.1		443 .8	243 1.5	192 1.9	175 2.1	175 2.1	131 2.8
7 49.8	11 33.8	9 41.6	Cost of Sales/Payables	0 UND	2 159.3	10 37.6	9 38.9	9 41.2	10 35.3
24 15.3	32 11.3	25 14.3		6 59.5	19 19.2	22 16.6	32 11.3	19 19.0	34 10.8
57 6.4	59 6.2	52 7.0		23 15.7	39 9.3	46 8.0	57 6.4	48 7.5	68 5.4
5.7	5.3	5.7	Sales/Working Capital	2.0	4.6	5.0	5.6	5.6	7.5
9.3	8.4	9.8		8.2	6.8	6.9	9.6	10.4	13.9
18.5	15.1	20.0		-38.0	18.3	18.1	17.0	17.7	22.4
9.2	7.0	5.4	EBIT/Interest	2.4	6.9	3.1	4.9	6.0	8.0
(308) 3.8	(290) 3.2	(345) 2.5		(12) 1.4	1.7	2.1	(83) 2.1	(98) 2.6	(89) 3.5
1.7	1.6	1.3		-1.3	1.1	.9	.9	1.6	1.8
5.3	5.4	4.1	Net Profit + Depr., Dep., Amort./Cur. Mat. L/T/D				3.1	4.7	7.1
(92) 2.6	(87) 3.2	(89) 2.6				(22) 1.4	(24) 3.1	(33) 3.4	
1.2	1.1	1.0					-.1	1.5	1.4
.1	.1	.1	Fixed/Worth	.0	.0	.2	.1	.1	.2
.3	.3	.3		.1	.2	.4	.2	.3	.4
.5	.6	.7		26.5	5.6	.8	.6	.5	.8
1.3	1.3	1.1	Debt/Worth	.6	.7	1.5	1.1	.8	1.4
2.6	2.2	2.4		3.3	2.8	2.6	2.0	2.3	2.9
5.0	4.5	5.9		-8.8	12.3	6.6	6.4	3.9	5.5
31.1	30.4	28.4	% Profit Before Taxes/Tangible Net Worth	40.2	25.1	20.2	24.4	27.2	34.7
(301) 14.5	(291) 15.5	(323) 14.5		(11) 10.3	(25) 11.7	(29) 9.3	(78) 10.3	(98) 13.5	(82) 23.3
5.8	5.3	4.4		.2	2.3	-2.2	-.2	4.8	11.8
7.2	10.1	8.9	% Profit Before Taxes/Total Assets	8.1	9.5	6.7	8.0	9.8	9.6
3.8	4.0	4.0		3.2	2.8	2.4	2.7	3.9	5.8
1.3	1.5	1.0		-6.6	.4	-.7	-.2	1.6	2.7
70.7	70.8	70.6	Sales/Net Fixed Assets	UND	186.5	36.5	86.6	66.2	53.9
35.5	30.5	33.1		40.3	64.3	22.4	35.3	35.7	28.6
16.9	16.1	16.3		10.2	28.0	11.1	16.8	15.9	16.3
3.0	3.0	3.1	Sales/Total Assets	2.6	3.9	2.8	3.3	3.1	3.3
2.4	2.3	2.3		1.3	2.3	2.1	2.4	2.3	2.4
1.8	1.7	1.8		.8	1.4	1.5	1.8	1.8	1.9
.4	.4	.4	% Depr., Dep., Amort./Sales		.3	.5	.4	.4	.4
(274) .7	(265) .7	(308) .7			(23) .6	(28) 1.0	(74) .7	(91) .8	(84) .5
1.2	1.1	1.2			1.1	1.6	1.3	1.3	.8
.9	1.0	1.0	% Officers', Directors' Owners' Comp/Sales		2.3	1.3	1.1	1.0	.5
(160) 1.8	(138) 1.9	(166) 2.0			(17) 4.8	(19) 2.2	(49) 1.7	(49) 1.6	(24) .9
3.8	3.5	3.9			6.6	3.8	3.8	3.3	2.4
6746192M	6898449M	8726333M	Net Sales ($)	7971M	65535M	125627M	613944M	1520451M	6392805M
2937745M	3139655M	3608731M	Total Assets ($)	6961M	32498M	63268M	270871M	678646M	2556487M

M = $ thousand   MM = $ million
See Pages 11 through 21 for Explanation of Ratios and Data

WHOLESALE—Industrial Machinery and Equipment Merchant Wholesalers NAICS 423830 (SIC 5084, 5085)

		Current Data Sorted by Assets				Type of Statement	Comparative Historical Data	
2	4	58	105	24	15	Unqualified	214	201
6	53	209	70	4		Reviewed	378	341
11	91	128	8			Compiled	294	353
20	50	29	5			Tax Returns	81	109
12	67	136	98	19	17	Other	307	310
	276 (4/1-9/30/06)			965 (10/1/06-3/31/07)			4/1/02-3/31/03	4/1/03-3/31/04
0-500M	500M-2MM	2-10MM	10-50MM	50-100MM	100-250MM		ALL	ALL
51	265	560	286	47	32	**NUMBER OF STATEMENTS**	1274	1314
%	%	%	%	%	%	**ASSETS**	%	%
10.3	8.2	7.2	5.2	3.8	5.4	Cash & Equivalents	6.7	6.9
30.5	34.3	33.6	29.1	28.7	20.5	Trade Receivables (net)	33.0	32.9
31.3	36.6	35.3	36.4	35.3	40.9	Inventory	36.0	35.7
2.7	2.3	2.4	2.6	3.5	2.3	All Other Current	2.3	2.9
74.9	81.4	78.5	73.3	71.3	69.0	Total Current	77.9	78.5
17.8	10.9	13.3	19.5	19.1	17.4	Fixed Assets (net)	14.9	14.2
1.7	1.6	2.6	2.7	5.4	4.9	Intangibles (net)	1.9	1.8
5.7	6.1	5.6	4.5	4.2	8.6	All Other Non-Current	5.3	5.5
100.0	100.0	100.0	100.0	100.0	100.0	Total	100.0	100.0
						LIABILITIES		
31.4	15.5	15.2	18.0	10.3	15.6	Notes Payable-Short Term	17.9	17.8
2.7	2.6	2.9	3.8	3.5	1.3	Cur. Mat.-L.T.D.	3.6	3.4
23.7	24.0	19.9	16.4	17.5	15.2	Trade Payables	20.9	20.8
.6	.2	.3	.4	.7	.2	Income Taxes Payable	.2	.2
16.9	9.5	11.0	10.9	13.9	12.6	All Other Current	10.2	10.4
75.3	51.7	49.3	49.4	46.0	44.9	Total Current	52.8	52.5
15.2	11.3	8.8	11.8	15.5	13.4	Long-Term Debt	9.4	9.2
.1	.1	.4	.8	.6	1.1	Deferred Taxes	.2	.3
5.3	3.8	3.6	3.5	2.1	2.1	All Other Non-Current	3.6	4.0
4.2	33.1	37.9	34.5	35.8	38.5	Net Worth	34.0	33.9
100.0	100.0	100.0	100.0	100.0	100.0	Total Liabilities & Net Worth	100.0	100.0
						INCOME DATA		
100.0	100.0	100.0	100.0	100.0	100.0	Net Sales	100.0	100.0
34.7	32.5	29.3	28.3	26.9	31.1	Gross Profit	30.4	30.8
31.3	29.0	25.0	23.2	20.3	21.4	Operating Expenses	28.6	28.6
3.4	3.5	4.3	5.2	6.6	9.7	Operating Profit	1.8	2.1
.9	.4	.6	.9	1.0	1.0	All Other Expenses (net)	.7	.5
2.6	3.1	3.7	4.3	5.6	8.7	Profit Before Taxes	1.1	1.6
						RATIOS		
2.6	2.6	2.3	2.1	2.6	2.4		2.1	2.2
1.5	1.6	1.6	1.5	1.6	1.5	Current	1.5	1.5
.8	1.2	1.2	1.1	1.2	1.2		1.2	1.2
1.5	1.3	1.3	1.0	1.0	1.0		1.2	1.2
(50) .8	.8	.8	.7	.7	.5	Quick	.7	.8
.3	.5	.6	.5	.5	.3		.5	.5
4 102.3	25 14.6	32 11.4	35 10.3	41 8.8	35 10.5		33 11.0	34 10.7
33 11.1	38 9.6	42 8.7	45 8.2	51 7.1	40 9.1	Sales/Receivables	44 8.3	44 8.3
50 7.4	50 7.3	52 7.0	54 6.8	64 5.7	53 6.9		55 6.7	56 6.6
15 23.9	29 12.5	36 10.3	48 7.5	60 6.1	60 6.0		36 10.1	37 9.9
32 11.4	56 6.5	57 6.4	72 5.1	78 4.7	99 3.7	Cost of Sales/Inventory	67 5.4	66 5.6
73 5.0	99 3.7	104 3.5	119 3.1	119 3.1	178 2.0		110 3.3	112 3.3
3 116.9	19 19.0	19 19.5	21 17.7	20 18.3	23 16.0		21 17.7	20 18.3
22 16.3	32 11.3	32 11.3	31 11.8	35 10.3	39 9.4	Cost of Sales/Payables	34 10.8	34 10.8
69 5.3	55 6.7	50 7.4	45 8.1	56 6.5	54 6.7		54 6.8	55 6.6
8.0	6.2	5.9	6.3	4.3	4.1		5.7	5.6
19.7	10.0	10.4	10.2	8.3	7.1	Sales/Working Capital	10.6	10.6
-34.9	25.5	23.2	30.6	18.3	17.0		28.4	26.4
9.4	10.9	11.4	11.8	9.3	10.6		5.6	6.5
(37) 2.4	(237) 3.7	(506) 4.2	(271) 4.8	(46) 4.5	(28) 7.0	EBIT/Interest	(1163) 2.2	(1200) 2.6
.8	1.7	1.8	2.5	2.4	3.0		.7	1.0
	5.1	6.3	12.3	17.5	36.2		4.5	3.8
	(47) 2.1	(156) 2.9	(116) 3.9	(26) 4.8	(10) 5.6	Net Profit + Depr., Dep., Amort./Cur. Mat. L/T/D	(386) 1.7	(322) 1.5
	.8	1.6	1.8	1.3	4.7		.6	.6
.1	.1	.1	.2	.3	.1		.1	.1
.2	.3	.3	.5	.8	.5	Fixed/Worth	.4	.3
1.7	.8	.7	1.4	1.7	.9		1.0	1.0
.9	.9	.9	1.2	.8	1.2		.9	.9
1.9	2.0	2.0	2.1	2.7	2.3	Debt/Worth	2.0	2.1
-5.7	7.5	4.3	5.1	10.1	3.7		4.7	5.2
61.9	60.1	44.0	41.2	49.3	47.4	% Profit Before Taxes/Tangible Net Worth	23.6	29.3
(36) 18.8	(232) 22.5	(535) 21.6	(267) 24.5	(43) 26.0	(31) 29.0		(1166) 8.4	(1201) 9.6
2.1	6.7	7.8	13.2	18.0	15.9		.0	1.0
18.1	16.2	15.5	13.8	12.8	13.7	% Profit Before Taxes/Total Assets	7.3	8.5
4.9	6.1	6.5	7.6	6.8	9.3		2.6	3.0
-2.4	1.8	2.1	3.8	4.2	4.2		-.6	.1
212.4	121.3	88.9	48.7	32.1	57.3		64.9	67.0
35.3	48.1	38.2	19.4	17.1	17.7	Sales/Net Fixed Assets	29.3	28.5
14.0	19.4	14.3	7.0	5.9	4.5		11.7	12.5
6.0	4.1	3.6	2.9	2.6	2.3		3.5	3.4
3.9	3.3	2.8	2.3	1.9	1.6	Sales/Total Assets	2.6	2.6
2.7	2.4	2.0	1.7	1.6	1.2		1.8	1.8
.3	.3	.4	.5	.5	.5		.6	.5
(32) .8	(207) .7	(494) .7	(259) .9	(43) 1.0	(19) .8	% Depr., Dep., Amort./Sales	(1126) 1.0	(1124) 1.0
2.0	1.6	1.6	3.0	1.9	1.6		1.9	1.8
5.0	2.7	1.6	.8				2.2	2.1
(22) 8.0	(149) 4.7	(220) 3.3	(44) 1.8			% Officers', Directors' Owners' Comp/Sales	(522) 4.0	(520) 4.2
11.8	7.4	5.8	3.5				6.4	7.1
61822M	1033727M	7693698M	13655186M	7320469M	9239386M	Net Sales ($)	23734568M	25007693M
14230M	319549M	2681495M	5968426M	3580592M	5222637M	Total Assets ($)	11655315M	12303643M

© RMA 2007

M = $ thousand   MM = $ million
See Pages 11 through 21 for Explanation of Ratios and Data

Comparative Historical Data | Current Data Sorted by Sales

4/1/04-3/31/05 ALL	4/1/05-3/31/06 ALL	4/1/06-3/31/07 ALL	Type of Statement	0-1MM	1-3MM	3-5MM	5-10MM	10-25MM	25MM & OVER
201	188	208	Unqualified	1	3	4	15	47	138
338	302	342	Reviewed	5	19	41	69	120	88
263	216	238	Compiled	8	36	49	71	60	14
99	95	104	Tax Returns	3	38	23	21	13	6
295	348	349	Other	10	39	31	51	87	131
				276 (4/1-9/30/06)			965 (10/1/06-3/31/07)		
1196	1149	1241	**NUMBER OF STATEMENTS**	27	135	148	227	327	377
%	%	%	**ASSETS**	%	%	%	%	%	%
7.0	7.0	6.9	Cash & Equivalents	4.9	9.5	8.7	7.7	6.9	5.0
34.2	32.9	32.0	Trade Receivables (net)	30.5	28.1	30.7	33.1	33.4	32.3
35.2	34.6	35.8	Inventory	25.8	35.9	39.8	35.1	35.2	35.9
2.0	2.5	2.5	All Other Current	4.9	1.7	2.4	2.4	2.3	2.8
78.5	77.0	77.3	Total Current	66.1	75.2	81.5	78.3	77.9	76.0
14.2	15.0	14.7	Fixed Assets (net)	21.5	14.9	11.6	13.6	14.6	16.2
1.8	2.5	2.5	Intangibles (net)	3.0	2.9	1.8	2.1	2.4	3.0
5.5	5.6	5.5	All Other Non-Current	9.4	7.0	5.1	6.1	5.1	4.8
100.0	100.0	100.0	Total	100.0	100.0	100.0	100.0	100.0	100.0
			LIABILITIES						
16.9	16.4	16.4	Notes Payable-Short Term	25.7	19.5	13.2	15.7	15.5	17.0
3.2	3.2	3.0	Cur. Mat.-L.T.D.	2.5	3.5	3.1	2.9	2.8	3.1
21.5	21.0	19.9	Trade Payables	21.2	18.1	23.1	20.1	20.5	18.6
.3	.3	.3	Income Taxes Payable	.2	.3	.3	.2	.4	.4
10.0	10.6	11.0	All Other Current	29.3	7.5	8.6	11.6	10.8	11.8
52.0	51.5	50.7	Total Current	79.0	48.8	48.3	50.4	50.0	50.9
10.2	9.8	10.7	Long-Term Debt	24.3	14.3	12.4	8.8	8.1	11.1
.4	.3	.4	Deferred Taxes	.2	.2	.1	.3	.6	.5
4.2	3.9	3.6	All Other Non-Current	5.1	4.6	3.8	4.6	3.2	2.8
33.3	34.4	34.7	Net Worth	-8.6	32.1	35.4	35.9	38.1	34.6
100.0	100.0	100.0	Total Liabilities & Net Worth	100.0	100.0	100.0	100.0	100.0	100.0
			INCOME DATA						
100.0	100.0	100.0	Net Sales	100.0	100.0	100.0	100.0	100.0	100.0
30.0	30.2	30.0	Gross Profit	40.2	36.9	33.0	29.5	29.2	26.5
27.0	26.2	25.4	Operating Expenses	37.3	32.1	29.7	25.3	24.7	21.3
3.0	4.1	4.5	Operating Profit	3.0	4.9	3.3	4.2	4.5	5.2
.4	.5	.7	All Other Expenses (net)	2.5	.7	.4	.7	.5	.7
2.6	3.6	3.9	Profit Before Taxes	.5	4.2	2.9	3.5	4.0	4.5
			RATIOS						
2.2	2.1	2.3	Current	2.5	3.0	2.6	2.4	2.1	2.1
1.5	1.5	1.6		1.4	1.8	1.8	1.6	1.5	1.5
1.2	1.2	1.2		.5	1.2	1.3	1.2	1.2	1.2
1.2	1.1	1.2	Quick	1.2	1.6	1.3	1.3	1.2	1.0
(1195) .8	.8	(1240) .8		(26) .6	.9	.8	.8	.8	.8
.5	.5	.5		.3	.4	.5	.5	.6	.5
34 10.6	33 11.1	32 11.5	Sales/Receivables	33 11.1	23 15.7	24 15.0	31 11.7	33 11.1	34 10.6
44 8.3	43 8.4	42 8.6		50 7.4	37 9.8	40 9.2	42 8.7	42 8.7	44 8.3
56 6.5	55 6.6	53 6.9		103 3.5	55 6.6	51 7.2	52 7.1	52 7.0	53 6.9
36 10.1	36 10.1	37 10.0	Cost of Sales/Inventory	32 11.4	31 11.7	33 11.1	33 11.0	37 9.9	42 8.6
61 5.9	62 5.8	62 5.8		73 5.0	74 4.9	64 5.7	55 6.6	57 6.3	66 5.5
107 3.4	104 3.5	108 3.5		133 2.8	151 2.4	112 3.3	104 3.5	98 3.7	105 3.5
20 18.1	21 17.4	19 19.3	Cost of Sales/Payables	15 25.2	13 27.6	20 18.5	18 20.4	21 17.8	18 19.8
33 11.0	34 10.7	32 11.4		64 5.7	31 11.9	36 10.2	30 12.2	33 11.0	31 11.9
55 6.7	54 6.7	50 7.4		136 2.7	61 6.0	56 6.5	51 7.1	49 7.5	45 8.2
6.1	6.1	6.0	Sales/Working Capital	5.9	4.1	5.0	6.3	6.3	6.6
10.8	10.7	10.2		15.6	8.4	10.5	10.5	11.5	10.5
27.2	27.8	25.3		-4.4	20.8	24.8	24.4	24.6	27.8
10.2	12.1	11.0	EBIT/Interest	7.6	11.0	9.1	9.1	12.7	11.2
(1088) 3.8	(1051) 4.4	(1125) 4.3		(19) 1.3	(115) 3.7	(134) 3.0	(206) 3.7	(294) 4.4	(357) 5.5
1.7	2.0	1.9		-.4	1.5	1.4	1.8	1.8	2.7
5.8	6.5	7.6	Net Profit + Depr., Dep., Amort./Cur. Mat. L/T/D		4.1	4.3	6.6	7.1	16.3
(316) 2.1	(302) 2.8	(357) 3.2			(14) 2.0	(32) 2.1	(57) 1.9	(111) 3.2	(141) 4.8
1.0	1.3	1.5			.7	.8	1.4	1.7	1.8
.1	.1	.1	Fixed/Worth	.1	.1	.1	.1	.1	.2
.3	.3	.3		.4	.3	.2	.3	.3	.4
1.0	1.0	1.0		-2.2	1.1	.8	.7	.9	1.0
1.0	1.0	.9	Debt/Worth	1.0	.7	.8	.9	.9	1.2
2.2	2.1	2.0		9.0	1.6	1.9	2.1	1.9	2.3
5.1	4.9	4.9		-4.0	7.1	7.2	4.9	4.9	4.7
37.3	44.9	45.3	% Profit Before Taxes/Tangible Net Worth	23.8	62.6	39.0	46.3	40.6	45.5
(1093) 15.4	(1044) 20.3	(1144) 23.7		(17) 7.0	(115) 17.1	(132) 16.7	(209) 22.4	(312) 20.9	(359) 27.6
4.5	7.3	9.0		-15.2	4.1	4.9	7.2	9.3	15.5
11.1	13.1	15.0	% Profit Before Taxes/Total Assets	12.5	17.7	12.4	14.7	15.7	15.3
4.6	6.4	6.8		.0	6.1	4.9	6.4	6.6	8.3
1.4	2.2	2.3		-8.4	1.3	1.0	2.3	2.4	4.1
76.0	78.6	80.5	Sales/Net Fixed Assets	47.8	117.2	94.6	102.9	78.2	67.8
30.9	32.2	33.5		13.0	29.4	41.2	39.6	35.1	26.8
12.9	11.2	11.7		4.7	11.9	18.4	13.8	11.4	9.9
3.6	3.5	3.6	Sales/Total Assets	3.0	3.4	3.9	3.7	3.6	3.5
2.7	2.7	2.7		2.0	2.4	2.9	2.8	2.9	2.6
1.9	1.9	1.9		1.0	1.7	2.0	2.0	2.1	1.9
.5	.4	.4	% Depr., Dep., Amort./Sales	.7	.5	.4	.3	.4	.4
(982) .9	(991) .8	(1054) .8		(16) 2.0	(99) 1.1	(125) .7	(192) .7	(293) .7	(329) .8
1.9	1.8	1.8		5.9	2.1	1.5	1.6	1.8	1.6
2.0	2.1	1.9	% Officers', Directors' Owners' Comp/Sales		3.5	2.8	1.8	1.6	.7
(457) 4.0	(434) 3.9	(438) 3.8			(78) 5.7	(72) 4.6	(111) 3.6	(115) 3.3	(53) 1.7
7.2	6.9	6.4			9.5	7.3	6.0	5.1	3.1
26365280M	33202777M	39004288M	Net Sales ($)	13872M	271637M	593055M	1678912M	5185089M	31261723M
11675472M	14956344M	17786929M	Total Assets ($)	16099M	143108M	241107M	712155M	2186971M	14487489M

M = $ thousand   MM = $ million
See Pages 11 through 21 for Explanation of Ratios and Data

Current Data Sorted by Assets   Comparative Historical Data

Type of Statement	0-500M	500M-2MM	2-10MM	10-50MM	50-100MM	100-250MM		4/1/02-3/31/03 ALL	4/1/03-3/31/04 ALL
Unqualified		2	27	29	11	3		85	92
Reviewed	4	20	102	37	1			182	177
Compiled	8	40	65	1		1		130	157
Tax Returns	5	25	16	1		1		42	56
Other	8	33	60	47	9	4		167	165
		134 (4/1-9/30/06)		425 (10/1/06-3/31/07)					
NUMBER OF STATEMENTS	25	120	270	115	21	8		606	647
ASSETS	%	%	%	%	%	%		%	%
Cash & Equivalents	9.7	7.2	5.0	4.7	2.5			7.0	6.0
Trade Receivables (net)	45.9	35.6	34.3	32.0	28.8			31.9	33.4
Inventory	22.2	35.2	40.6	37.9	38.9			36.8	37.6
All Other Current	1.5	2.4	1.5	2.5	3.7			2.0	2.0
Total Current	79.3	80.4	81.4	77.1	73.8			77.6	79.0
Fixed Assets (net)	11.9	12.3	11.5	13.8	12.2			13.5	12.3
Intangibles (net)	2.4	3.0	2.4	4.0	9.6			4.2	3.5
All Other Non-Current	6.2	4.2	4.7	5.1	4.4			4.7	5.1
Total	100.0	100.0	100.0	100.0	100.0			100.0	100.0
LIABILITIES									
Notes Payable-Short Term	19.1	16.3	16.7	15.9	21.4			16.8	16.4
Cur. Mat.-L.T.D.	4.5	2.4	2.0	1.9	1.6			3.6	2.6
Trade Payables	24.2	24.4	22.4	18.7	15.2			19.6	21.8
Income Taxes Payable	.1	.1	.4	.2	.3			.2	.2
All Other Current	8.5	9.3	7.1	8.2	8.6			8.0	8.6
Total Current	56.3	52.5	48.5	44.9	47.2			48.2	49.7
Long-Term Debt	6.2	10.7	8.0	12.2	15.9			10.5	9.4
Deferred Taxes	.8	.1	.3	.2	.6			.2	.2
All Other Non-Current	17.8	3.7	3.6	2.8	3.8			4.0	4.5
Net Worth	18.9	33.0	39.6	39.7	32.5			37.1	36.2
Total Liabilities & Net Worth	100.0	100.0	100.0	100.0	100.0			100.0	100.0
INCOME DATA									
Net Sales	100.0	100.0	100.0	100.0	100.0			100.0	100.0
Gross Profit	36.7	32.1	28.9	29.3	27.8			30.5	30.3
Operating Expenses	32.3	27.9	24.3	22.7	20.8			28.3	27.5
Operating Profit	4.5	4.1	4.6	6.6	7.0			2.2	2.8
All Other Expenses (net)	1.1	.6	.7	.8	.8			.6	.6
Profit Before Taxes	3.3	3.6	3.9	5.8	6.2			1.7	2.2
RATIOS									
Current	4.0	2.6	2.5	2.7	2.6			2.7	2.5
	1.3	1.5	1.7	1.7	1.5			1.7	1.7
	.9	1.1	1.3	1.3	1.2			1.2	1.2
Quick	2.3	1.5	1.3	1.3	1.5			1.3	1.3
	1.0	.9	.8	.8	.6			.8	.8
	.7	.5	.5	.6	.5			.5	.6
Sales/Receivables	37 10.0	33 11.2	34 10.6	38 9.7	37 9.8			33 11.0	34 10.7
	47 7.8	40 9.0	41 8.9	44 8.3	43 8.6			41 9.0	43 8.6
	57 6.4	49 7.5	49 7.4	52 7.0	49 7.5			51 7.2	54 6.8
Cost of Sales/Inventory	12 30.1	32 11.3	42 8.7	47 7.8	57 6.5			42 8.7	44 8.4
	38 9.6	51 7.1	69 5.3	71 5.1	71 5.1			69 5.3	71 5.2
	73 5.0	95 3.8	103 3.5	103 3.5	108 3.4			110 3.3	114 3.2
Cost of Sales/Payables	22 16.8	22 16.8	23 16.1	23 15.7	22 16.9			20 18.2	23 16.0
	37 9.9	37 9.9	35 10.4	35 10.6	32 11.5			33 11.2	34 10.6
	58 6.3	55 6.6	49 7.5	46 7.9	42 8.7			48 7.6	52 7.1
Sales/Working Capital	5.8	6.7	5.6	5.0	6.1			5.2	5.4
	22.0	11.4	9.2	7.7	8.0			9.2	8.4
	UND	37.5	18.8	16.2	16.6			24.7	21.0
EBIT/Interest	7.7	9.2	11.5	14.4	11.6			6.7	8.0
	(19) 1.2	(111) 4.0	(251) 4.5	(112) 6.2	4.7			(550) 2.6	(592) 3.0
	.8	1.6	1.9	2.6	2.5			1.0	1.3
Net Profit + Depr., Dep., Amort./Cur. Mat. L/T/D		6.3	9.7	15.8	7.9			5.0	4.5
		(16) 2.1	(82) 3.1	(37) 4.8	(12) 5.6			(181) 1.7	(169) 1.8
		.7	1.1	2.3	3.8			.6	.9
Fixed/Worth	.1	.1	.1	.1	.2			.1	.1
	.4	.4	.2	.3	.7			.3	.3
	UND	1.1	.7	.7	1.1			1.0	.8
Debt/Worth	.9	.8	.7	.8	1.7			.8	.8
	5.3	2.0	1.7	1.6	3.8			1.7	1.8
	UND	7.3	3.7	4.4	6.1			5.1	5.0
% Profit Before Taxes/Tangible Net Worth	44.1	50.8	45.5	46.1	68.1			25.3	30.4
	(20) 22.1	(99) 26.1	(249) 23.3	(105) 31.0	(20) 49.9			(534) 10.4	(575) 11.9
	.6	6.9	7.5	15.3	22.7			1.9	2.6
% Profit Before Taxes/Total Assets	19.0	17.2	16.3	17.4	14.8			9.6	9.5
	1.0	7.5	7.4	10.9	8.3			3.5	3.9
	-1.0	1.9	2.1	5.6	5.1			.1	.6
Sales/Net Fixed Assets	324.5	143.5	102.8	67.2	37.4			71.0	79.4
	54.2	51.7	43.6	30.7	23.1			31.7	34.8
	24.0	22.3	18.6	11.0	13.4			14.4	16.2
Sales/Total Assets	4.2	4.0	3.7	3.2	3.1			3.5	3.4
	3.6	3.3	2.9	2.6	2.5			2.8	2.7
	2.4	2.2	2.2	1.8	1.7			2.0	2.0
% Depr., Dep., Amort./Sales	.4	.3	.4	.4	.3			.5	.5
	(14) .8	(94) .6	(239) .7	(103) .7	.8			(535) .9	(541) .9
	1.3	1.8	1.1	1.2				1.6	1.5
% Officers', Directors' Owners' Comp/Sales		3.1	1.6	.9				2.3	2.3
		(57) 5.3	(112) 2.5	(18) 2.6				(250) 3.8	(246) 4.0
		8.4	4.2	5.5				6.4	6.4
Net Sales ($)	29335M	527628M	3836565M	5945815M	3550537M	3044770M		12091072M	12143638M
Total Assets ($)	7790M	155158M	1308277M	2310591M	1524192M	1217363M		5488228M	5110697M

M = $ thousand   MM = $ million
See Pages 11 through 21 for Explanation of Ratios and Data

Comparative Historical Data | Current Data Sorted by Sales

Hist 1	Hist 2	Hist 3	Type of Statement	0-1MM	1-3MM	3-5MM	5-10MM	10-25MM	25MM & OVER
79	63	72	Unqualified	1		1	9	16	46
171	148	164	Reviewed	1	10	5	32	74	42
127	104	115	Compiled	1	19	16	34	36	9
42	41	47	Tax Returns	4	12	11	9	11	
148	177	161	Other	5	18	14	34	33	57
4/1/04-3/31/05 ALL	4/1/05-3/31/06 ALL	4/1/06-3/31/07 ALL		134 (4/1-9/30/06)			425 (10/1/06-3/31/07)		
567	533	559	NUMBER OF STATEMENTS	11	59	47	118	170	154
%	%	%	**ASSETS**	%	%	%	%	%	%
6.0	5.6	5.5	Cash & Equivalents	13.8	6.5	5.3	5.5	6.1	4.1
34.5	36.0	34.4	Trade Receivables (net)	35.5	32.7	32.6	34.6	34.3	35.5
36.5	36.7	37.9	Inventory	28.3	33.6	33.6	39.3	40.8	37.2
2.0	2.1	2.0	All Other Current	.3	3.3	2.2	1.6	1.4	2.5
79.0	80.4	79.8	Total Current	77.8	76.1	73.7	81.0	82.6	79.3
12.6	11.9	12.1	Fixed Assets (net)	12.9	12.8	19.5	11.0	10.5	12.1
2.8	3.0	3.4	Intangibles (net)	4.5	5.1	1.8	2.8	2.2	4.9
5.6	4.8	4.7	All Other Non-Current	4.4	6.0	5.1	5.2	4.6	3.7
100.0	100.0	100.0	Total	100.0	100.0	100.0	100.0	100.0	100.0
			LIABILITIES						
16.1	16.7	16.7	Notes Payable-Short Term	27.3	16.3	16.4	16.0	16.4	17.1
2.5	2.0	2.1	Cur. Mat.-L.T.D.	7.2	2.4	2.3	2.0	2.1	1.7
22.1	22.1	21.8	Trade Payables	15.3	20.9	22.6	21.9	23.6	20.4
.3	.4	.3	Income Taxes Payable	.0	.1	.1	.3	.4	.2
7.1	7.1	7.9	All Other Current	3.7	13.5	6.8	6.0	7.2	8.6
48.1	48.3	48.8	Total Current	53.5	53.2	48.3	46.2	49.7	48.0
9.8	8.6	9.8	Long-Term Debt	4.1	11.9	12.1	8.4	7.9	11.8
.3	.3	.3	Deferred Taxes	.0	.5	.3	.4	.2	.2
4.2	5.0	4.1	All Other Non-Current	22.9	7.1	3.3	3.7	3.4	3.0
37.6	37.8	37.0	Net Worth	19.5	27.3	36.0	41.3	38.7	36.9
100.0	100.0	100.0	Total Liabilities & Net Worth	100.0	100.0	100.0	100.0	100.0	100.0
			INCOME DATA						
100.0	100.0	100.0	Net Sales	100.0	100.0	100.0	100.0	100.0	100.0
29.9	30.1	29.9	Gross Profit	39.6	35.4	33.9	31.1	28.4	26.7
26.1	26.2	24.9	Operating Expenses	31.1	32.0	28.9	26.5	23.4	21.0
3.8	3.9	5.0	Operating Profit	8.6	3.4	5.0	4.6	4.9	5.7
.4	.6	.7	All Other Expenses (net)	2.3	.8	.9	.7	.5	.7
3.4	3.3	4.3	Profit Before Taxes	6.2	2.6	4.1	3.9	4.4	5.0
			RATIOS						
2.4	2.4	2.6	Current	9.8	2.9	2.6	2.7	2.5	2.6
1.7	1.7	1.7		1.1	1.4	1.6	1.7	1.6	1.7
1.3	1.3	1.2		.9	1.0	1.3	1.2	1.3	1.3
1.3	1.4	1.3	Quick	9.8	1.3	1.3	1.5	1.2	1.3
.8	.9	.8		.8	.8	1.0	.8	.8	.8
.6	.6	.5		.4	.4	.5	.5	.5	.6
35 10.3	36 10.2	35 10.4	Sales/Receivables	35 10.6	36 10.2	32 11.5	34 10.8	34 10.9	37 9.9
43 8.4	44 8.3	42 8.7		46 8.0	46 7.9	41 8.8	41 8.9	41 8.9	43 8.5
53 6.9	55 6.7	50 7.3		118 3.1	62 5.9	48 7.6	49 7.5	49 7.4	50 7.3
41 8.9	39 9.3	39 9.3	Cost of Sales/Inventory	61 6.0	33 11.1	31 11.8	42 8.6	41 8.9	43 8.5
62 5.9	62 5.9	64 5.7		86 4.3	69 5.3	45 8.1	66 5.5	66 5.5	61 5.9
104 3.5	100 3.6	101 3.6		114 3.2	122 3.0	105 3.5	104 3.5	101 3.6	92 4.0
23 16.1	23 15.7	23 16.2	Cost of Sales/Payables	16 22.6	22 16.5	25 14.5	22 16.6	23 16.1	22 16.5
35 10.4	36 10.1	35 10.4		34 10.7	40 9.1	42 8.6	36 10.2	34 10.7	33 11.1
51 7.1	51 7.2	49 7.4		70 5.2	72 5.1	52 7.0	50 7.3	50 7.4	43 8.4
5.5	5.7	5.9	Sales/Working Capital	2.7	4.4	7.0	5.5	6.2	6.4
9.1	9.4	9.5		26.2	10.8	11.2	8.1	9.7	9.3
20.9	18.9	22.1		-32.6	-69.0	25.0	21.8	17.4	18.1
11.0	11.0	11.9	EBIT/Interest		8.7	8.9	9.6	11.9	13.3
(515) 4.6	(480) 4.7	(521) 4.6			(52) 2.4	(45) 4.3	(107) 4.1	(160) 4.9	(150) 6.2
1.7	1.8	1.9			.9	2.2	1.7	1.9	2.6
8.0	9.7	10.7	Net Profit + Depr., Dep., Amort./Cur. Mat. L/T/D				4.8	12.8	14.5
(167) 2.8	(138) 4.2	(153) 4.1				(29) 2.9	(56) 3.8	(55) 5.9	
1.4	2.1	1.3					1.1	1.0	3.3
.1	.1	.1	Fixed/Worth	.0	.1	.1	.1	.1	.1
.3	.2	.3		.6	.4	.5	.2	.2	.3
.8	.7	.8		UND	-13.5	.9	.6	.6	.9
.8	.8	.8	Debt/Worth	.9	.7	1.0	.6	.7	.9
1.7	1.7	1.8		7.7	3.1	1.8	1.7	1.8	1.8
4.6	4.5	4.8		UND	-55.5	3.6	3.5	3.8	5.6
41.3	41.0	48.1	% Profit Before Taxes/Tangible Net Worth		39.0	49.5	39.3	46.9	57.7
(511) 16.4	(480) 18.8	(499) 26.1		(42) 16.1	(43) 25.3	(105) 20.0	(161) 24.3	(139) 35.1	
4.7	5.6	9.1		2.3	7.9	4.8	9.1	16.5	
13.0	14.0	16.3	% Profit Before Taxes/Total Assets	19.9	15.5	14.7	15.3	16.4	17.5
5.8	6.8	8.3		5.8	4.6	7.6	7.3	7.4	11.5
1.6	2.1	2.4		.0	-.9	2.6	1.4	2.3	5.5
89.1	97.4	102.8	Sales/Net Fixed Assets	UND	132.1	106.2	112.2	109.8	74.2
38.5	39.2	40.4		62.3	32.6	31.3	48.6	50.5	32.1
15.1	17.9	17.3		4.2	13.5	11.0	19.6	22.1	15.2
3.6	3.7	3.7	Sales/Total Assets	2.3	3.6	3.7	3.7	3.8	3.5
2.8	2.8	2.9		1.8	2.2	3.0	2.9	3.0	2.9
2.1	2.2	2.1		1.1	1.7	2.2	2.2	2.2	2.2
.4	.4	.4	% Depr., Dep., Amort./Sales		.4	.5	.3	.4	.3
(485) .8	(451) .7	(478) .7		(43) 1.1	(34) .7	(102) .7	(151) .6	(144) .6	
1.3	1.2	1.2		3.0	2.3	1.1	.9	1.2	
2.2	2.0	1.8	% Officers', Directors' Owners' Comp/Sales		3.6	3.2	2.1	1.5	.6
(225) 4.0	(211) 3.6	(198) 3.2		(22) 5.4	(22) 4.4	(58) 3.8	(68) 2.4	(26) 1.7	
6.5	6.3	5.6		7.5	9.5	7.6	3.5	4.0	
11233662M	14975858M	16934650M	Net Sales ($)	4903M	116791M	189052M	853769M	2697438M	13072697M
4426448M	5726917M	6523371M	Total Assets ($)	2970M	62312M	86797M	320462M	1020487M	5030343M

M = $ thousand   MM = $ million
See Pages 11 through 21 for Explanation of Ratios and Data

Current Data Sorted by Assets | Comparative Historical Data

Type of Statement	0-500M	500M-2MM	2-10MM	10-50MM	50-100MM	100-250MM		4/1/02-3/31/03 ALL	4/1/03-3/31/04 ALL
Unqualified		1	3	3		3		15	13
Reviewed	1	8	26	8				57	57
Compiled	4	18	13	4				34	42
Tax Returns	6	16	6					17	20
Other	3	9	14	8		2		38	36
	42 (4/1-9/30/06)			114 (10/1/06-3/31/07)					
NUMBER OF STATEMENTS	14	52	62	23		5		161	168

50-100MM column: DATA NOT AVAILABLE

	0-500M %	500M-2MM %	2-10MM %	10-50MM %	50-100MM	100-250MM		%	%
ASSETS									
Cash & Equivalents	10.6	6.8	7.3	5.6				5.7	5.4
Trade Receivables (net)	32.9	36.4	31.6	29.7				31.5	32.0
Inventory	32.8	36.3	33.0	36.9				35.8	34.8
All Other Current	1.1	3.4	3.0	6.2				3.3	2.4
Total Current	77.4	82.9	74.9	78.4				76.4	74.6
Fixed Assets (net)	15.1	11.1	14.7	11.3				13.8	14.8
Intangibles (net)	.4	1.8	4.5	6.1				4.8	4.2
All Other Non-Current	7.1	4.1	5.9	4.2				5.0	6.4
Total	100.0	100.0	100.0	100.0				100.0	100.0
LIABILITIES									
Notes Payable-Short Term	4.0	11.4	11.7	17.6				15.9	15.3
Cur. Mat.-L.T.D.	5.8	2.2	3.3	1.7				4.4	3.3
Trade Payables	20.8	25.0	19.7	17.2				23.4	21.2
Income Taxes Payable	.0	.2	.5	.2				.1	.1
All Other Current	24.4	8.1	10.2	14.2				9.5	10.6
Total Current	55.0	46.9	45.4	50.9				53.2	50.6
Long-Term Debt	5.4	8.2	14.1	8.7				12.7	11.2
Deferred Taxes	.1	.2	.2	.1				.2	.2
All Other Non-Current	6.3	11.4	4.0	8.8				4.6	5.1
Net Worth	33.1	33.4	36.2	31.5				29.3	32.9
Total Liabilities & Net Worth	100.0	100.0	100.0	100.0				100.0	100.0
INCOME DATA									
Net Sales	100.0	100.0	100.0	100.0				100.0	100.0
Gross Profit	34.5	33.7	30.6	32.3				32.4	31.6
Operating Expenses	32.0	31.1	26.8	28.9				30.1	28.9
Operating Profit	2.5	2.6	3.8	3.5				2.3	2.7
All Other Expenses (net)	-.5	-.1	.5	.6				.6	.7
Profit Before Taxes	3.0	2.7	3.3	2.9				1.7	2.0

RATIOS

	0-500M	500M-2MM	2-10MM	10-50MM	50-100MM	100-250MM		Hist 1	Hist 2
Current	3.6	2.7	2.3	2.0				2.0	2.1
	1.7	1.9	1.5	1.5				1.4	1.4
	.8	1.4	1.2	1.1				1.1	1.1
Quick	1.6	1.6	1.2	1.0				1.0	1.0
	.8	.9	.8	.5				.7	.7
	.5	.7	.6	.4				.5	.5
Sales/Receivables	23 16.1	26 14.3	31 11.9	19 19.7				26 14.1	23 16.2
	30 12.1	37 10.0	37 9.9	43 8.4				35 10.4	37 9.8
	42 8.7	46 7.9	46 7.9	53 6.9				47 7.8	49 7.5
Cost of Sales/Inventory	12 30.0	31 11.7	32 11.2	54 6.8				37 9.8	35 10.4
	43 8.5	52 7.0	53 6.8	77 4.7				58 6.3	55 6.6
	81 4.5	77 4.8	81 4.5	94 3.9				86 4.2	83 4.4
Cost of Sales/Payables	5 76.6	23 15.9	19 19.5	21 17.4				21 17.3	19 19.3
	26 14.2	35 10.5	34 10.8	29 12.8				34 10.8	32 11.6
	46 7.9	44 8.2	44 8.3	42 8.7				54 6.7	49 7.5
Sales/Working Capital	7.7	6.2	7.2	7.2				7.8	7.5
	15.7	10.6	12.4	14.9				13.9	15.3
	-11.7	21.0	23.5	42.6				40.5	62.4
EBIT/Interest		7.0	14.3	9.1				8.0	9.6
		(44) 3.9	(60) 3.6	2.9				(150) 3.0	(161) 3.8
		1.5	2.0	2.0				1.0	1.5
Net Profit + Depr., Dep., Amort./Cur. Mat. L/T/D		4.1	2.9	32.9				4.5	5.3
		(13) 2.1	(26) 1.9	(10) 7.9				(52) 1.7	(50) 2.6
		.9	.9	3.3				.6	1.2
Fixed/Worth	.0	.1	.1	.1				.2	.1
	.3	.4	.4	.7				.5	.4
	2.0	1.4	1.8	1.3				1.4	1.3
Debt/Worth	.7	.9	.9	1.4				1.1	1.0
	1.9	1.9	2.5	2.8				2.7	2.5
	10.0	6.0	5.9	15.9				7.9	5.9
% Profit Before Taxes/Tangible Net Worth	32.2	54.0	40.7	31.2				48.5	40.0
	(12) 12.1	(45) 20.7	(58) 20.4	(20) 22.1				(140) 17.9	(143) 18.4
	3.3	4.1	6.9	15.7				1.6	4.7
% Profit Before Taxes/Total Assets	12.9	13.5	14.0	12.0				13.3	12.8
	5.8	6.5	5.5	5.8				4.5	5.3
	.3	1.2	2.4	3.6				.3	1.2
Sales/Net Fixed Assets	UND	108.7	65.6	54.8				69.6	73.3
	76.8	42.1	34.5	25.9				30.4	31.0
	12.4	23.0	20.7	17.0				16.0	14.9
Sales/Total Assets	5.4	4.6	3.9	3.2				4.0	4.2
	4.0	3.7	2.9	2.8				3.1	3.2
	2.3	2.9	2.2	2.0				2.4	2.4
% Depr., Dep., Amort./Sales		.4	.5	.6				.6	.5
		(41) .8	(57) .7	(21) .8				(146) 1.0	(148) .9
		1.1	1.2	1.1				1.6	1.6
% Officers', Directors' Owners' Comp/Sales		2.4	1.8					1.8	1.9
		(33) 4.0	(31) 3.0					(77) 3.0	(84) 3.0
		6.2	6.3					5.6	5.5
Net Sales ($)	17981M	251462M	861763M	1354505M		3619155M		2602970M	2781291M
Total Assets ($)	4381M	66521M	286337M	497577M	847166M			1003723M	1005096M

M = $ thousand   MM = $ million
See Pages 11 through 21 for Explanation of Ratios and Data

Comparative Historical Data | Current Data Sorted by Sales

			Type of Statement						
9	14	10	Unqualified		1			4	5
38	40	43	Reviewed	1	1	7	10	15	9
27	24	39	Compiled	3	6	6	11	9	4
18	16	28	Tax Returns	2	8	4	9	5	
43	50	36	Other	2	1	7	5	9	12
4/1/04-3/31/05 ALL	4/1/05-3/31/06 ALL	4/1/06-3/31/07 ALL		0-1MM	42 (4/1-9/30/06) 1-3MM	3-5MM	114 (10/1/06-3/31/07) 5-10MM	10-25MM	25MM & OVER
135	144	156	**NUMBER OF STATEMENTS**	8	17	24	35	42	30
%	%	%	**ASSETS**	%	%	%	%	%	%
6.5	8.2	7.0	Cash & Equivalents		5.4	8.3	7.2	7.2	5.2
33.5	31.6	32.9	Trade Receivables (net)		34.9	34.0	32.6	34.1	31.3
33.5	34.8	34.6	Inventory		35.7	31.9	34.6	34.5	36.6
2.2	2.2	3.5	All Other Current		4.0	3.0	3.8	3.8	3.4
75.7	76.7	78.0	Total Current		80.1	77.2	78.2	79.7	76.5
13.7	13.3	13.0	Fixed Assets (net)		13.3	17.4	13.5	10.9	11.2
5.0	4.5	3.9	Intangibles (net)		3.0	1.1	2.2	4.2	8.8
5.6	5.5	5.1	All Other Non-Current		3.7	4.3	6.1	5.2	3.4
100.0	100.0	100.0	Total		100.0	100.0	100.0	100.0	100.0
			LIABILITIES						
14.9	13.7	11.6	Notes Payable-Short Term		8.8	9.1	13.3	11.1	15.8
2.5	2.7	2.9	Cur. Mat.-L.T.D.		4.2	2.9	2.2	3.7	1.5
22.4	22.9	21.4	Trade Payables		22.9	22.0	23.4	21.7	19.8
.2	.2	.3	Income Taxes Payable		.2	.2	.3	.6	.1
9.1	11.2	11.4	All Other Current		5.1	12.6	9.2	13.6	10.5
49.1	50.7	47.6	Total Current		41.3	46.9	48.4	50.6	47.7
11.3	9.8	10.9	Long-Term Debt		7.8	18.6	10.1	8.6	11.5
.2	.3	.2	Deferred Taxes		.1	.2	.3	.2	.2
7.0	6.7	7.3	All Other Non-Current		17.0	8.2	7.5	4.8	6.2
32.3	32.6	34.0	Net Worth		33.9	26.1	33.7	35.8	34.5
100.0	100.0	100.0	Total Liabilities & Net Worth		100.0	100.0	100.0	100.0	100.0
			INCOME DATA						
100.0	100.0	100.0	Net Sales		100.0	100.0	100.0	100.0	100.0
30.5	30.9	32.0	Gross Profit		33.4	37.0	31.1	28.6	30.2
26.9	28.6	28.7	Operating Expenses		30.5	33.9	28.9	25.2	26.0
3.6	2.3	3.3	Operating Profit		2.9	3.1	2.2	3.4	4.3
.5	.1	.2	All Other Expenses (net)		-.4	-.3	.1	.4	.6
3.1	2.2	3.1	Profit Before Taxes		3.3	3.5	2.0	3.0	3.6
			RATIOS						
2.2	2.4	2.5	Current		5.3	2.6	2.4	2.2	2.3
1.6	1.5	1.7			2.4	1.9	1.7	1.4	1.7
1.2	1.2	1.2			1.3	1.1	1.3	1.1	1.1
1.2	1.2	1.3	Quick		2.0	1.4	1.2	1.2	1.0
.7	.8	.8			.9	1.0	.8	.8	.7
.6	.5	.5			.7	.6	.6	.5	.5
25 14.8	25 14.8	26 14.2	Sales/Receivables		25 14.6	26 14.3	27 13.8	30 12.2	18 19.8
38 9.7	36 10.1	36 10.2			33 11.2	36 10.0	35 10.3	35 10.3	36 10.1
48 7.6	51 7.1	47 7.8			49 7.6	48 7.6	45 8.2	47 7.8	51 7.2
34 10.8	36 10.2	33 11.2	Cost of Sales/Inventory		29 12.6	22 16.8	31 11.7	32 11.5	38 9.7
51 7.2	57 6.4	54 6.8			68 5.4	51 7.2	48 7.5	56 6.6	57 6.4
77 4.7	87 4.2	84 4.3			87 4.2	81 4.5	80 4.5	76 4.8	93 3.9
20 18.4	20 18.3	21 17.1	Cost of Sales/Payables		12 30.6	26 14.1	24 15.2	19 19.5	22 16.7
31 11.6	34 10.7	33 11.2			38 9.6	34 10.7	37 9.9	33 10.9	27 13.3
45 8.1	57 6.5	44 8.3			50 7.3	56 6.5	42 8.7	42 8.6	41 8.9
7.9	6.9	6.7	Sales/Working Capital		4.1	6.2	7.5	7.8	7.5
12.8	11.0	11.2			8.3	10.4	13.2	12.8	11.5
29.4	27.6	23.5			19.5	26.6	23.2	26.2	29.0
9.2	8.2	8.0	EBIT/Interest		8.0	7.2	6.4	16.3	13.8
(119) 3.4	(129) 3.4	(138) 3.8			(12) 3.7	(19) 3.6	(34) 3.9	(40) 3.6	4.3
1.4	1.8	1.8			1.4	1.9	1.5	1.8	2.6
5.4	5.7	6.4	Net Profit + Depr., Dep., Amort./Cur. Mat. L/T/D				7.3	2.5	25.0
(36) 2.4	(36) 3.4	(54) 2.4					(14) 2.0	(16) 1.9	(15) 6.9
1.1	1.4	1.1					1.1	1.0	3.9
.2	.2	.1	Fixed/Worth		.1	.2	.2	.1	.1
.4	.4	.4			.3	.6	.4	.4	.4
1.9	1.3	1.7			1.8	6.1	1.7	1.4	1.5
1.0	.9	.9	Debt/Worth		.8	1.1	1.0	.9	1.2
2.3	2.4	2.5			2.6	2.5	2.0	2.4	2.7
7.9	7.0	6.0			6.7	26.0	5.6	8.7	8.4
44.0	41.7	38.5	% Profit Before Taxes/Tangible Net Worth		36.1	64.5	29.5	42.0	38.2
(113) 14.8	(124) 18.5	(139) 19.9			(16) 20.1	(19) 20.7	(32) 13.3	(39) 22.4	(26) 23.9
3.3	5.3	6.9			4.7	3.8	3.8	10.0	16.1
14.0	11.3	12.5	% Profit Before Taxes/Total Assets		12.6	13.7	10.6	12.7	13.1
4.8	4.8	5.8			6.3	6.6	5.5	5.1	6.9
1.0	1.5	2.3			1.0	1.2	1.5	2.4	3.7
71.9	69.5	73.1	Sales/Net Fixed Assets		103.0	106.7	73.0	116.5	61.9
33.3	34.9	35.8			48.3	25.5	35.1	39.4	38.4
18.5	16.4	19.9			24.0	12.4	22.4	25.7	18.6
4.3	4.1	4.2	Sales/Total Assets		4.9	4.2	4.3	4.3	3.8
3.4	3.1	3.2			3.3	3.1	3.8	3.4	3.1
2.4	2.2	2.4			2.4	2.3	2.6	2.4	2.6
.5	.4	.4	% Depr., Dep., Amort./Sales		.3	.3	.5	.4	.5
(113) .9	(118) .8	(131) .7			(14) .5	(20) .8	(31) .8	(36) .8	(27) .7
1.5	1.2	1.1			1.0	1.3	1.3	1.1	.9
2.1	2.7	1.8	% Officers', Directors' Owners' Comp/Sales		2.7	2.3	1.8	1.4	.7
(65) 3.1	(62) 4.6	(79) 3.2			(12) 5.4	(11) 4.4	(23) 3.2	(20) 2.5	(11) 1.8
6.1	7.0	5.7			6.3	7.0	4.9	4.9	3.9
2321011M	4036913M	6104866M	Net Sales ($)	3980M	33868M	94458M	246357M	634313M	5091890M
883610M	1741903M	1701982M	Total Assets ($)	2704M	15874M	36262M	77816M	221457M	1347869M

M = $ thousand   MM = $ million
See Pages 11 through 21 for Explanation of Ratios and Data

Current Data Sorted by Assets   Comparative Historical Data

Type of Statement	0-500M	500M-2MM	2-10MM	10-50MM	50-100MM	100-250MM		ALL 4/1/02-3/31/03	ALL 4/1/03-3/31/04
Unqualified		1	11	14	4	2		22	20
Reviewed	1	9	21	10				52	63
Compiled	6	10	13	3				37	46
Tax Returns	4	9	10	1				15	18
Other	1	13	28	19	5	2		47	44
		39 (4/1-9/30/06)		158 (10/1/06-3/31/07)				4/1/02-3/31/03	4/1/03-3/31/04
NUMBER OF STATEMENTS	12	42	83	47	9	4		173	191
ASSETS	%	%	%	%	%	%		%	%
Cash & Equivalents	21.6	13.6	8.6	6.7				8.0	8.4
Trade Receivables (net)	20.6	26.9	26.8	20.2				26.1	25.8
Inventory	31.4	42.5	41.3	44.8				43.8	42.4
All Other Current	8.0	3.9	1.1	6.6				2.6	2.0
Total Current	81.5	86.8	77.7	78.2				80.5	78.5
Fixed Assets (net)	13.7	9.4	13.7	14.2				12.2	13.4
Intangibles (net)	3.7	.2	2.1	1.6				1.9	1.8
All Other Non-Current	1.0	3.6	6.5	6.1				5.5	6.3
Total	100.0	100.0	100.0	100.0				100.0	100.0
LIABILITIES									
Notes Payable-Short Term	20.4	15.9	20.4	21.7				19.4	18.5
Cur. Mat.-L.T.D.	3.2	4.2	2.0	2.7				2.9	3.1
Trade Payables	14.8	26.6	18.0	15.6				21.2	19.4
Income Taxes Payable	.0	.4	.1	.5				.1	.2
All Other Current	21.3	8.1	7.3	9.9				9.1	10.3
Total Current	59.8	55.1	47.9	50.4				52.7	51.6
Long-Term Debt	10.6	10.6	7.4	11.9				8.4	8.5
Deferred Taxes	.0	.2	.2	.3				.5	.7
All Other Non-Current	11.4	4.3	4.9	3.1				4.1	4.6
Net Worth	18.2	29.9	39.6	34.3				34.3	34.7
Total Liabilties & Net Worth	100.0	100.0	100.0	100.0				100.0	100.0
INCOME DATA									
Net Sales	100.0	100.0	100.0	100.0				100.0	100.0
Gross Profit	45.5	27.9	28.7	24.6				28.8	29.6
Operating Expenses	37.2	25.6	22.9	18.4				26.1	26.6
Operating Profit	8.3	2.3	5.8	6.2				2.7	2.9
All Other Expenses (net)	.8	1.2	.8	.9				.4	.6
Profit Before Taxes	7.5	1.1	4.9	5.3				2.3	2.3
RATIOS									
Current	2.4	2.4	2.4	2.3				2.3	2.2
	1.7	1.8	1.6	1.4				1.5	1.5
	.9	1.3	1.2	1.2				1.2	1.2
Quick	1.1	1.5	1.3	.7				1.0	1.2
	.6	(41) .6	.8	.4				.6	.6
	.1	.4	.3	.2				.4	.4
Sales/Receivables	0 UND	11 33.3	17 21.4	12 30.4				21 17.5	21 17.1
	5 69.8	27 13.3	37 10.0	33 11.0				37 9.9	37 9.8
	19 19.7	42 8.6	59 6.1	56 6.5				49 7.5	56 6.5
Cost of Sales/Inventory	0 UND	10 35.5	34 10.6	48 7.6				49 7.5	42 8.7
	6 59.0	48 7.7	73 5.0	92 4.0				78 4.7	82 4.4
	123 3.0	132 2.8	127 2.9	192 1.9				136 2.7	146 2.5
Cost of Sales/Payables	3 111.5	6 57.6	16 23.2	15 24.5				19 19.3	17 21.4
	21 17.7	22 16.4	29 12.4	28 12.9				37 9.8	36 10.2
	42 8.6	49 7.4	53 6.9	46 8.0				56 6.5	61 5.9
Sales/Working Capital	5.1	5.7	4.5	3.6				5.5	5.0
	21.5	11.1	10.9	12.2				9.9	10.0
	NM	27.7	23.1	32.7				21.6	30.3
EBIT/Interest		10.3	15.4	9.6				10.3	6.6
		(33) 2.5	(69) 4.4	(46) 3.9				(159) 2.4	(176) 2.9
		1.0	1.7	2.0				.9	1.1
Net Profit + Depr., Dep., Amort./Cur. Mat. L/T/D			13.4	17.4				5.8	8.1
			(18) 1.8	(17) 3.5				(52) 1.9	(52) 2.5
			.6	1.4				.6	1.0
Fixed/Worth	.0	.0	.0	.1				.1	.1
	3.2	.1	.2	.3				.2	.2
	-.8	.8	.6	.8				.9	.8
Debt/Worth	.7	.7	.9	1.2				.9	1.0
	31.3	1.9	2.0	2.5				2.1	2.2
	-8.9	12.1	4.1	5.5				5.1	4.3
% Profit Before Taxes/Tangible Net Worth		44.8	62.3	47.0				31.1	31.9
		(35) 18.7	(81) 29.5	(46) 23.1				(158) 9.6	(180) 12.5
		3.1	11.3	11.0				1.4	2.4
% Profit Before Taxes/Total Assets	58.1	20.3	17.5	12.0				9.0	8.7
	11.8	4.0	7.8	6.7				3.7	3.7
	.0	.8	3.5	2.9				-.1	.3
Sales/Net Fixed Assets	999.8	262.0	148.4	71.5				82.6	100.5
	79.7	93.7	49.4	32.9				38.0	37.8
	31.7	30.0	15.4	12.4				18.5	15.4
Sales/Total Assets	11.5	6.3	3.5	2.9				3.5	3.5
	3.8	3.5	2.5	1.9				2.4	2.2
	3.0	2.0	1.7	1.4				1.7	1.5
% Depr., Dep., Amort./Sales		.1	.2	.4				.4	.4
		(29) .4	(64) .5	(43) .6				(152) .8	(149) .9
		.8	1.2	1.2				1.4	1.9
% Officers', Directors' Owners' Comp/Sales		1.9	1.8	.9				2.2	2.1
		(25) 4.1	(28) 4.3	(12) 1.6				(81) 3.6	(85) 3.5
		6.8	7.5	3.9				6.5	7.4
Net Sales ($)	14581M	268565M	1102754M	1714536M	1159861M	1088090M		3290884M	3128529M
Total Assets ($)	2832M	48743M	402079M	780911M	629555M	586567M		1621311M	1520257M

M = $ thousand   MM = $ million
See Pages 11 through 21 for Explanation of Ratios and Data

Comparative Historical Data / Current Data Sorted by Sales

4/1/04-3/31/05 ALL	4/1/05-3/31/06 ALL	4/1/06-3/31/07 ALL	Type of Statement	0-1MM	1-3MM	3-5MM	5-10MM	10-25MM	25MM & OVER
					39 (4/1-9/30/06)			158 (10/1/06-3/31/07)	
23	35	32	Unqualified				3	11	18
53	43	41	Reviewed	2	4	4	12	12	7
36	33	32	Compiled	3	7	5	7	8	2
31	16	24	Tax Returns	2	8	4	7	3	
42	61	68	Other	2	6	8	10	22	22
185	188	197	**NUMBER OF STATEMENTS**	7	25	21	39	56	49
%	%	%	**ASSETS**	%	%	%	%	%	%
7.7	8.4	9.8	Cash & Equivalents		13.6	13.2	11.1	7.5	9.2
24.6	26.0	24.6	Trade Receivables (net)		20.5	29.3	28.0	26.8	22.0
40.0	42.7	42.0	Inventory		36.7	36.4	42.6	42.8	43.7
2.6	3.1	3.8	All Other Current		1.6	5.4	2.3	3.1	5.1
74.9	80.1	80.3	Total Current		72.4	84.4	84.0	80.1	79.9
16.0	12.0	12.6	Fixed Assets (net)		22.2	9.7	9.2	10.5	13.0
2.6	1.5	1.7	Intangibles (net)		1.8	.3	.8	3.3	1.3
6.4	6.4	5.5	All Other Non-Current		3.7	5.6	5.9	6.1	5.8
100.0	100.0	100.0	Total		100.0	100.0	100.0	100.0	100.0
			LIABILITIES						
19.2	20.6	20.7	Notes Payable-Short Term		21.7	10.1	20.2	18.8	25.2
3.4	3.5	2.8	Cur. Mat.-L.T.D.		6.5	2.6	1.9	1.8	2.7
18.0	19.0	18.7	Trade Payables		18.9	18.8	22.5	17.2	18.5
.2	.2	.3	Income Taxes Payable		.0	.3	.1	.5	.3
10.8	10.2	9.0	All Other Current		14.4	4.7	6.6	10.0	8.6
51.7	53.5	51.5	Total Current		61.6	36.5	51.4	48.2	55.3
11.3	8.4	9.2	Long-Term Debt		13.9	7.7	11.1	6.4	8.3
.4	.3	.2	Deferred Taxes		.8	.0	.0	.1	.4
4.5	4.1	4.5	All Other Non-Current		9.4	2.3	2.8	5.1	3.2
32.0	33.7	34.5	Net Worth		14.3	53.4	34.7	40.2	32.8
100.0	100.0	100.0	Total Liabilities & Net Worth		100.0	100.0	100.0	100.0	100.0
			INCOME DATA						
100.0	100.0	100.0	Net Sales		100.0	100.0	100.0	100.0	100.0
28.1	28.3	28.0	Gross Profit		37.0	36.8	28.8	25.6	17.7
24.8	23.4	22.7	Operating Expenses		33.2	29.2	24.0	19.7	12.9
3.2	4.9	5.4	Operating Profit		3.9	7.6	4.8	5.9	4.8
.4	.9	.9	All Other Expenses (net)		1.0	1.1	.3	.7	.5
2.8	4.0	4.4	Profit Before Taxes		2.8	6.5	4.5	5.2	4.2
			RATIOS						
2.1	2.3	2.4			2.2	4.1	2.6	2.7	1.9
1.4	1.4	1.5	Current		1.4	2.2	1.7	1.7	1.3
1.1	1.1	1.2			1.0	1.6	1.2	1.2	1.2
1.0	1.0	1.2			1.2	3.3	1.4	1.2	.8
.6	.6	(196) .6	Quick		.6	1.2	(38) .7	.6	.4
.4	.3	.3			.2	.5	.4	.2	.3
17 22.0	15 23.8	12 29.4			5 70.0	23 15.7	21 17.4	12 30.2	12 30.7
35 10.4	38 9.7	31 11.8	Sales/Receivables		23 16.0	29 12.6	40 9.0	35 10.3	24 15.5
58 6.3	54 6.7	54 6.8			53 6.9	49 7.5	63 5.8	59 6.2	46 7.9
36 10.1	38 9.7	24 15.5			1 275.6	3 130.2	26 13.8	46 7.9	33 11.0
67 5.4	84 4.4	73 5.0	Cost of Sales/Inventory		99 3.7	48 7.6	70 5.2	79 4.6	60 6.1
137 2.7	173 2.1	151 2.4			149 2.4	193 1.9	214 1.7	170 2.1	106 3.4
16 23.5	17 21.5	13 28.7			4 85.8	14 25.6	21 17.4	15 25.0	8 44.2
30 12.2	31 11.6	25 14.3	Cost of Sales/Payables		15 24.6	43 8.5	33 11.1	24 15.0	21 17.7
60 6.1	55 6.6	50 7.4			61 6.0	56 6.5	49 7.4	52 7.0	43 8.4
5.2	5.1	4.4			6.5	2.7	3.4	4.3	8.2
11.7	11.8	11.2	Sales/Working Capital		17.4	5.6	10.6	8.9	17.5
63.3	37.1	32.5			588.2	11.3	35.1	22.3	44.4
9.0	8.8	10.8			4.7	15.7	12.1	12.5	11.3
(168) 3.4	(169) 4.0	(169) 3.7	EBIT/Interest		(22) 1.5	(14) 2.9	(34) 4.4	(49) 4.2	(46) 3.8
1.5	2.0	1.6			.7	1.1	2.3	1.7	2.1
7.0	8.8	9.8	Net Profit + Depr., Dep.,					21.0	5.1
(41) 2.5	(40) 2.3	(44) 2.0	Amort./Cur. Mat. L/T/D					(17) 4.0	(15) 2.0
1.3	1.3	1.3						1.3	1.3
.1	.1	.1			.0	.0	.0	.1	.1
.3	.2	.2	Fixed/Worth		1.2	.0	.1	.2	.3
1.3	.6	.7			NM	.3	.6	.6	.6
1.1	1.1	.8			1.2	.3	.6	.8	1.3
2.4	2.3	2.2	Debt/Worth		4.6	.8	2.4	1.6	2.8
6.8	4.9	5.5			-15.1	2.0	4.9	3.6	5.6
38.7	51.3	54.4	% Profit Before Taxes/Tangible		52.8	64.7	40.8	60.7	50.3
(164) 15.8	(179) 23.7	(183) 24.9	Net Worth		(18) 18.7	18.7	(36) 18.8	(55) 32.8	(48) 32.6
4.7	9.4	9.1			2.4	4.1	7.3	11.5	14.5
11.7	13.7	17.1	% Profit Before Taxes/Total		11.4	27.6	14.1	16.9	19.2
4.6	7.0	6.9	Assets		1.9	6.6	6.8	8.1	7.0
1.1	2.4	2.7			-.2	2.5	3.7	4.4	3.7
105.5	136.2	143.3			356.8	224.0	132.6	110.4	100.3
33.5	53.3	48.3	Sales/Net Fixed Assets		45.3	81.7	49.5	42.2	45.5
11.8	16.0	15.7			6.6	27.8	27.8	16.7	12.0
3.3	3.7	3.7			3.9	4.3	4.3	3.1	4.1
2.5	2.4	2.5	Sales/Total Assets		2.4	2.3	2.3	2.5	2.9
1.6	1.6	1.6			1.1	1.6	1.5	1.7	1.9
.4	.3	.3			.3	.2	.2	.2	.3
(143) .9	(139) .6	(154) .6	% Depr., Dep., Amort./Sales		(16) 1.8	(13) .6	(33) .7	(47) .5	(41) .5
2.0	1.3	1.2			3.4	1.7	.9	1.1	1.1
2.0	1.2	1.2	% Officers', Directors',		2.9				1.3	.7
(74) 3.5	(70) 3.3	(73) 4.1	Owners' Comp/Sales		(16) 6.8			(21) 4.3	(14) 2.4	(10) .9
6.4	5.9	6.8			14.5			6.1	4.6	1.8
3495752M	5443696M	5348387M	Net Sales ($)	3890M	48446M	82617M	284473M	905090M	4023871M
1523803M	2452113M	2450687M	Total Assets ($)	7818M	28638M	55169M	161294M	418027M	1779741M

© RMA 2007

M = $ thousand   MM = $ million
See Pages 11 through 21 for Explanation of Ratios and Data

Current Data Sorted by Assets   Comparative Historical Data

Type of Statement	0-500M	500M-2MM	2-10MM	10-50MM	50-100MM	100-250MM		4/1/02-3/31/03 ALL	4/1/03-3/31/04 ALL
Unqualified		1	13	20	5	5		49	39
Reviewed	1	10	40	20		1		59	64
Compiled	2	23	19	2	1			45	52
Tax Returns	15	24	11	1				29	39
Other	19	17	47	34	5	4		57	83
		64 (4/1-9/30/06)		275 (10/1/06-3/31/07)					
NUMBER OF STATEMENTS	37	75	130	77	11	9		239	277
ASSETS	%	%	%	%	%	%		%	%
Cash & Equivalents	10.9	8.4	6.9	5.6	2.2			6.2	7.4
Trade Receivables (net)	15.3	27.5	27.0	31.3	37.3			29.2	27.2
Inventory	47.1	45.3	47.0	43.0	32.9			44.1	44.4
All Other Current	2.8	1.6	1.8	3.4	5.3			2.5	3.7
Total Current	76.1	82.7	82.7	83.3	77.7			82.0	82.6
Fixed Assets (net)	15.0	8.8	8.5	9.0	5.3			10.2	10.5
Intangibles (net)	2.9	3.0	4.5	4.6	9.9			3.1	1.7
All Other Non-Current	6.0	5.4	4.3	3.1	7.2			4.7	5.2
Total	100.0	100.0	100.0	100.0	100.0			100.0	100.0
LIABILITIES									
Notes Payable-Short Term	18.9	15.8	16.6	23.3	8.8			19.3	19.5
Cur. Mat.-L.T.D.	2.6	2.5	1.6	2.3	1.2			3.3	1.9
Trade Payables	18.5	20.3	20.0	18.1	27.5			21.2	22.5
Income Taxes Payable	.2	.1	.3	.2	.5			.2	.3
All Other Current	15.2	8.4	8.2	13.3	12.7			8.2	8.4
Total Current	55.5	47.1	46.8	57.2	50.7			52.2	52.6
Long-Term Debt	10.4	17.0	6.0	5.4	17.5			8.7	8.9
Deferred Taxes	.0	.1	.2	.2	.3			.0	.1
All Other Non-Current	16.5	10.0	7.7	4.4	7.3			5.5	5.3
Net Worth	17.6	25.7	39.4	32.9	24.2			33.5	33.1
Total Liabilties & Net Worth	100.0	100.0	100.0	100.0	100.0			100.0	100.0
INCOME DATA									
Net Sales	100.0	100.0	100.0	100.0	100.0			100.0	100.0
Gross Profit	39.5	35.7	30.7	30.1	25.4			30.7	32.1
Operating Expenses	36.5	31.8	26.8	24.9	20.8			26.9	28.4
Operating Profit	3.0	3.9	3.8	5.2	4.6			3.8	3.7
All Other Expenses (net)	1.3	.7	1.0	1.3	2.9			.7	.3
Profit Before Taxes	1.7	3.2	2.9	3.9	1.8			3.1	3.3
RATIOS									
Current	3.7	3.4	3.1	2.0	2.6			2.6	2.7
	1.6	1.7	1.6	1.4	1.3			1.6	1.6
	.9	1.2	1.3	1.2	1.2			1.2	1.2
Quick	1.0	1.4	1.2	.9	1.2			1.2	1.1
	.5	.7	.7	.6	.7			.7	.6
	.2	.3	.4	.4	.5			.4	.4
Sales/Receivables	2 184.5	13 28.4	21 17.5	34 10.9	39 9.3			20 18.7	18 20.5
	10 36.2	31 11.8	36 10.2	53 6.9	67 5.4			35 10.5	34 10.8
	28 13.1	49 7.5	53 6.9	73 5.0	92 3.9			58 6.3	55 6.6
Cost of Sales/Inventory	34 10.8	50 7.2	61 6.0	75 4.9	68 5.4			49 7.4	52 7.1
	102 3.6	105 3.5	94 3.9	111 3.3	87 4.2			83 4.4	96 3.8
	168 2.2	164 2.2	145 2.5	158 2.3	115 3.2			142 2.6	150 2.4
Cost of Sales/Payables	10 37.2	13 27.2	15 24.4	16 23.1	25 14.5			12 29.6	14 26.5
	28 13.1	25 14.7	31 11.7	36 10.1	50 7.3			29 12.5	36 10.1
	49 7.5	57 6.4	55 6.6	59 6.2	81 4.5			55 6.7	63 5.8
Sales/Working Capital	5.2	3.8	4.8	4.4	5.9			4.6	4.6
	10.8	7.1	8.3	8.1	11.8			9.8	8.4
	UND	21.5	16.4	24.2	17.6			25.2	19.6
EBIT/Interest	9.0	6.9	7.9	8.3				9.3	10.4
	(27) 3.0	(69) 2.7	(121) 2.8	(72) 2.8				(220) 3.4	(245) 4.3
	.9	1.0	1.2	1.1				1.5	1.6
Net Profit + Depr., Dep., Amort./Cur. Mat. L/T/D		8.5	5.2	27.0				11.7	6.7
		(12) 1.6	(28) 2.7	(23) 6.3				(48) 2.7	(56) 3.4
		.4	.7	2.5				1.0	1.2
Fixed/Worth	.0	.1	.1	.1	.1			.1	.1
	.3	.2	.2	.3	.4			.3	.2
	-2.4	1.9	.4	.8	-2.3			.7	.7
Debt/Worth	.8	.6	.8	1.3	2.8			.9	.8
	3.0	2.4	1.9	2.9	5.9			2.2	2.2
	-14.7	33.6	4.4	9.0	-126.4			6.0	5.4
% Profit Before Taxes/Tangible Net Worth	51.1	38.6	32.9	44.5				46.5	44.6
	(25) 20.2	(58) 16.7	(117) 13.0	(69) 20.3				(213) 18.2	(244) 18.8
	2.3	4.7	3.7	2.8				5.0	4.2
% Profit Before Taxes/Total Assets	18.3	13.9	11.3	13.3	5.0			14.8	14.4
	5.9	5.9	3.2	5.6	2.5			6.1	6.7
	-1.8	.4	.8	.3	-.6			1.3	1.1
Sales/Net Fixed Assets	311.6	178.5	133.9	110.8	247.1			101.6	108.9
	45.2	53.5	54.2	43.5	49.1			41.9	44.7
	10.6	23.6	23.6	20.7	22.9			20.2	22.0
Sales/Total Assets	4.2	3.1	3.4	2.8	2.8			3.7	3.5
	3.1	2.5	2.6	1.9	2.2			2.7	2.5
	2.0	1.8	2.0	1.4	1.2			1.8	1.9
% Depr., Dep., Amort./Sales	.6	.3	.3	.3				.4	.4
	(17) 1.3	(52) .7	(104) .6	(68) .6				(204) .7	(223) .7
	2.1	1.3	1.0	1.0				1.2	1.3
% Officers', Directors' Owners' Comp/Sales	3.9	3.5	1.7	.6				2.2	1.9
	(14) 4.9	(53) 4.3	(55) 2.9	(18) 1.5				(105) 3.4	(131) 3.8
	13.3	7.2	5.4	2.9				6.4	6.6
Net Sales ($)	35437M	253725M	1581500M	3797419M	1660531M	2923635M		6009307M	7230294M
Total Assets ($)	11281M	86698M	580161M	1786810M	722235M	1281892M		2664158M	3231689M

M = $ thousand   MM = $ million
See Pages 11 through 21 for Explanation of Ratios and Data

Comparative Historical Data | Current Data Sorted by Sales

					Type of Statement						
	45		48		44	Unqualified		1	2	5	7	29
	64		68		71	Reviewed	1	2	9	18	22	19
	54		42		47	Compiled	4	13	8	9	10	3
	41		38		51	Tax Returns	9	20	8	8	5	1
	71		126		126	Other	14	21	9	20	25	37
	4/1/04-3/31/05 ALL		4/1/05-3/31/06 ALL		4/1/06-3/31/07 ALL			64 (4/1-9/30/06)			275 (10/1/06-3/31/07)	
							0-1MM	1-3MM	3-5MM	5-10MM	10-25MM	25MM & OVER
	275		322		339	NUMBER OF STATEMENTS	28	57	36	60	69	89
	%		%		%	ASSETS	%	%	%	%	%	%
	6.2		6.8		7.3	Cash & Equivalents	10.4	8.5	9.3	8.7	6.3	4.7
	26.9		27.6		27.0	Trade Receivables (net)	15.0	21.2	26.3	28.4	29.6	31.7
	45.4		42.6		44.8	Inventory	49.7	46.4	43.9	46.5	45.1	41.4
	3.2		2.8		2.4	All Other Current	.2	2.9	1.3	1.5	2.2	3.9
	81.6		79.8		81.5	Total Current	75.3	79.1	80.8	85.0	83.2	81.7
	10.8		10.2		9.5	Fixed Assets (net)	19.0	8.7	9.7	8.3	8.2	8.7
	2.8		4.7		4.2	Intangibles (net)	1.6	4.4	5.6	3.2	3.5	5.6
	4.8		5.2		4.8	All Other Non-Current	4.1	7.8	3.9	3.5	5.1	4.0
	100.0		100.0		100.0	Total	100.0	100.0	100.0	100.0	100.0	100.0
					LIABILITIES						
	19.8		18.2		17.8	Notes Payable-Short Term	26.2	13.5	16.0	12.3	22.9	18.3
	2.1		1.7		2.1	Cur. Mat.-L.T.D.	2.9	1.9	3.1	1.7	1.5	2.1
	19.5		21.5		19.7	Trade Payables	13.9	17.0	20.5	19.2	23.2	20.6
	.2		.3		.2	Income Taxes Payable	.1	.1	.3	.2	.2	.3
	9.8		10.1		10.5	All Other Current	10.9	10.6	6.3	8.7	8.9	14.2
	51.5		51.8		50.2	Total Current	54.0	43.2	46.3	42.2	56.8	55.5
	9.2		11.1		9.1	Long-Term Debt	20.0	11.0	9.8	13.3	2.8	6.3
	.1		.2		.2	Deferred Taxes	.0	.1	.1	.1	.3	.4
	7.4		10.3		8.4	All Other Non-Current	15.5	14.7	5.7	8.1	6.0	5.3
	31.8		26.7		32.0	Net Worth	10.3	31.0	38.1	36.3	34.1	32.6
	100.0		100.0		100.0	Total Liabilties & Net Worth	100.0	100.0	100.0	100.0	100.0	100.0
					INCOME DATA						
	100.0		100.0		100.0	Net Sales	100.0	100.0	100.0	100.0	100.0	100.0
	30.9		32.5		32.3	Gross Profit	41.5	37.1	33.6	34.2	30.5	25.9
	28.0		28.9		28.2	Operating Expenses	37.3	33.9	30.5	28.9	26.5	21.6
	2.9		3.6		4.1	Operating Profit	4.2	3.3	3.1	5.3	4.1	4.3
	.5		1.1		1.0	All Other Expenses (net)	2.0	1.4	.1	.5	1.0	1.3
	2.3		2.4		3.1	Profit Before Taxes	2.2	1.9	3.0	4.8	3.1	2.9
					RATIOS						
	2.5		2.5		2.9		3.0	4.8	4.8	3.7	1.9	2.1
	1.6		1.5		1.5	Current	1.6	2.1	1.7	2.0	1.4	1.4
	1.2		1.2		1.2		1.1	1.2	1.2	1.4	1.2	1.2
	1.1		1.1		1.2		1.0	1.4	1.6	1.8	.9	1.0
	.6		.6		.6	Quick	.5	.6	.8	.9	.5	.6
	.4		.4		.4		.1	.3	.3	.5	.4	.4

19	19.3	21	17.7	16	23.0		1	406.2	6	56.6	14	25.6	19	19.7	23	16.2	26	13.9
35	10.5	36	10.0	37	9.9	Sales/Receivables	17	22.0	28	13.2	35	10.4	30	12.0	43	8.5	45	8.2
55	6.6	62	5.9	60	6.1		54	6.8	57	6.4	60	6.1	45	8.1	58	6.3	70	5.2
55	6.6	62	5.9	63	5.8		99	3.7	53	6.9	53	6.9	62	5.9	62	5.9	65	5.7
105	3.5	97	3.8	101	3.6	Cost of Sales/Inventory	158	2.3	127	2.9	102	3.6	95	3.9	103	3.5	87	4.2
153	2.4	139	2.6	150	2.4		354	1.0	177	2.1	144	2.5	152	2.4	136	2.7	116	3.1
14	26.1	17	21.0	14	26.5		14	25.5	9	40.2	15	23.8	8	45.4	22	16.5	20	18.1
29	12.5	33	11.0	32	11.5	Cost of Sales/Payables	45	8.2	21	17.8	37	9.9	25	14.6	36	10.1	39	9.3
57	6.4	69	5.3	55	6.6		60	6.1	50	7.3	76	4.8	46	8.0	72	5.1	54	6.7
	4.7		4.9		4.3			3.4		3.4		3.8		3.9		6.6		6.0
	8.0		8.7		8.4	Sales/Working Capital		6.0		7.3		7.8		6.8		11.0		10.2
	18.1		21.1		20.8			23.8		28.7		16.5		12.0		20.9		23.7
	10.2		9.4		7.9			6.9		7.1		9.2		10.8		5.8		9.3
(249)	4.1	(300)	3.2	(307)	2.9	EBIT/Interest	(22)	2.1	(48)	2.9	(33)	2.3	(54)	3.5	(66)	2.0	(84)	3.4
	1.2		1.2		1.1			.8		.7		1.1		1.5		1.1		1.1
	12.4		11.5		11.4	Net Profit + Depr., Dep.,										10.0		13.3
(60)	4.7	(62)	5.2	(69)	3.2	Amort./Cur. Mat. L/T/D									(20)	2.6	(27)	4.6
	1.3		1.3		.7												.8		.9
	.1		.1		.1			.1		.0		.1		.0		.1		.1
	.2		.3		.2	Fixed/Worth		.8		.2		.3		.2		.2		.3
	.8		.9		.9			-.8		1.7		.9		.5		.5		.9
	.9		1.1		.8			1.1		.6		.4		.5		1.2		1.5
	2.2		2.6		2.2	Debt/Worth		5.9		2.0		2.2		1.3		2.5		2.8
	5.1		9.0		9.4			-13.2		NM		20.8		5.5		4.2		9.0
	40.9		40.6		38.2	% Profit Before Taxes/Tangible		57.3		37.6		34.2		45.9		34.8		42.0
(240)	19.8	(270)	16.4	(284)	15.3	Net Worth	(19)	13.3	(43)	13.9	(29)	15.4	(52)	19.9	(64)	12.9	(77)	19.3
	3.8		3.0		3.6			.0		2.4		7.3		7.3		1.4		5.9
	12.7		11.6		12.5			13.8		12.5		13.9		19.6		12.9		11.1
	4.9		4.2		4.6	% Profit Before Taxes/Total		2.4		5.0		4.2		6.7		3.0		4.6
	.3		.6		.5	Assets		-1.5		-1.7		.7		1.9		.5		.4
	109.0		136.3		130.1			79.0		273.0		106.6		227.2		95.5		116.4
	42.9		43.4		47.7	Sales/Net Fixed Assets		22.0		59.0		57.6		49.9		50.7		48.6
	17.6		18.4		21.3			7.1		22.0		13.5		23.4		24.8		25.2
	3.2		3.2		3.3			2.4		3.3		2.8		3.7		3.3		3.5
	2.4		2.4		2.4	Sales/Total Assets		1.5		2.5		2.2		2.7		2.6		2.5
	1.8		1.6		1.7			1.1		1.6		1.4		2.1		1.7		1.6
	.3		.3		.3			.7		.4		.4		.2		.3		.3
(224)	.6	(253)	.6	(255)	.7	% Depr., Dep., Amort./Sales	(17)	1.0	(33)	.9	(25)	.9	(43)	.7	(63)	.6	(74)	.5
	1.3		1.0		1.1			1.7		1.7		1.7		1.1		1.0		.9
	1.8		1.6		1.7			4.6		3.8		1.9		2.0		1.2		.3
(131)	3.4	(118)	3.0	(140)	3.8	% Officers', Directors' Owners' Comp/Sales	(10)	8.0	(33)	4.6	(26)	2.9	(32)	3.8	(25)	1.8	(14)	.7
	6.1		5.7		5.7			13.3		7.8		5.6		6.4		4.5		2.3
	7949915M		8825629M		10252247M	Net Sales ($)		16562M	109955M	138659M	462870M	1135170M	8389031M
	3602594M		3948651M		4469077M	Total Assets ($)		12254M	66080M	70855M	200293M	527110M	3592485M

© RMA 2007

M = $ thousand   MM = $ million
See Pages 11 through 21 for Explanation of Ratios and Data

WHOLESALE—Toy and Hobby Goods and Supplies Merchant Wholesalers NAICS 423920 (SIC 5092)

Current Data Sorted by Assets

Comparative Historical Data

Type of Statement

	0-500M	500M-2MM	2-10MM	10-50MM	50-100MM	100-250MM		4/1/02-3/31/03 ALL	4/1/03-3/31/04 ALL
Unqualified			2	12	4	2		28	21
Reviewed	1	3	14	6				31	21
Compiled	3	12	2					25	34
Tax Returns	6	9	7	1				17	27
Other	2	8	16	11	5			37	30
	26 (4/1-9/30/06)			100 (10/1/06-3/31/07)					
NUMBER OF STATEMENTS	12	32	41	30	9	2		138	133

0-500M	500M-2MM	2-10MM	10-50MM	50-100MM	100-250MM	Item	4/1/02-3/31/03 ALL	4/1/03-3/31/04 ALL
%	%	%	%	%	%	**ASSETS**	%	%
12.2	7.3	10.4	7.3			Cash & Equivalents	10.2	10.3
7.1	28.4	26.8	34.8			Trade Receivables (net)	26.7	25.8
49.6	38.0	41.4	35.8			Inventory	39.5	38.6
5.3	2.3	2.5	3.4			All Other Current	2.9	3.9
74.2	76.0	81.1	81.3			Total Current	79.4	78.6
17.8	11.2	9.9	13.6			Fixed Assets (net)	12.0	10.9
7.0	6.6	1.6	1.2			Intangibles (net)	3.4	4.2
1.1	6.2	7.4	3.9			All Other Non-Current	5.3	6.4
100.0	100.0	100.0	100.0			Total	100.0	100.0
						LIABILITIES		
40.1	20.2	17.2	24.8			Notes Payable-Short Term	14.8	15.0
3.0	2.4	1.0	2.0			Cur. Mat.-L.T.D.	2.7	1.8
25.5	18.9	20.2	16.7			Trade Payables	18.8	19.0
.0	.0	.4	.2			Income Taxes Payable	.2	.1
7.4	4.6	10.5	6.0			All Other Current	10.5	9.8
76.0	46.1	49.3	49.8			Total Current	47.1	45.7
17.4	13.1	4.1	12.9			Long-Term Debt	7.0	8.3
.3	.0	.1	.1			Deferred Taxes	.1	.1
6.0	9.1	7.3	3.4			All Other Non-Current	5.1	5.4
-.4	31.7	39.2	33.8			Net Worth	40.8	40.5
100.0	100.0	100.0	100.0			Total Liabilties & Net Worth	100.0	100.0
						INCOME DATA		
100.0	100.0	100.0	100.0			Net Sales	100.0	100.0
32.7	38.8	33.7	31.1			Gross Profit	36.4	37.5
35.0	34.6	29.4	25.8			Operating Expenses	31.3	32.4
-2.3	4.2	4.2	5.2			Operating Profit	5.0	5.1
2.4	1.5	.8	1.4			All Other Expenses (net)	.6	.7
-4.7	2.7	3.5	3.9			Profit Before Taxes	4.4	4.4
						RATIOS		
2.6	3.5	2.5	2.9			Current	3.1	3.3
1.0	1.8	1.6	1.7				1.7	1.8
.6	1.2	1.3	1.1				1.2	1.1
.8	1.9	1.3	1.6			Quick	1.6	1.5
.2	.8	.6	.9				.8 (132)	.8
.1	.3	.3	.5				.5	.5
0 UND	15 23.7	18 20.5	29 12.5			Sales/Receivables	23 15.9	20 18.6
4 87.4	29 12.5	36 10.1	58 6.3				39 9.2	37 9.8
16 22.7	76 4.8	49 7.5	75 4.9				56 6.5	51 7.1
30 12.0	67 5.4	34 10.8	46 8.0			Cost of Sales/Inventory	53 6.9	46 8.0
88 4.2	111 3.3	96 3.8	85 4.3				95 3.8	92 4.0
129 2.8	153 2.4	124 2.9	119 3.1				145 2.5	154 2.4
0 UND	9 40.1	20 18.5	13 27.3			Cost of Sales/Payables	13 28.0	16 23.2
27 13.4	26 13.9	32 11.5	37 9.9				30 12.0	34 10.6
48 7.6	59 6.1	55 6.6	49 7.5				60 6.1	55 6.7
8.9	3.8	6.4	4.3			Sales/Working Capital	4.0	4.3
NM	7.7	9.3	7.3				7.3	9.6
-5.5	24.7	20.7	25.4				20.5	30.8
	5.6	9.2	11.9			EBIT/Interest	17.1	23.5
	(28) 1.9	(35) 3.8	2.8				(126) 6.6	(122) 5.4
	.4	1.4	1.5				1.5	1.6
						Net Profit + Depr., Dep., Amort./Cur. Mat. L/T/D	11.6	15.8
							(30) 4.1	(21) 3.5
							2.6	2.7
.0	.0	.0	.1			Fixed/Worth	.1	.1
1.0	.2	.2	.3				.2	.2
-.2	1.4	.5	1.0				.6	.6
1.0	.8	.6	.8			Debt/Worth	.6	.7
50.5	1.7	1.7	2.7				1.5	1.4
-2.7	16.4	3.5	6.9				4.2	3.6
	34.4	72.4	55.9			% Profit Before Taxes/Tangible Net Worth	56.0	64.6
	(27) 19.4	(38) 14.3	(29) 17.3				(126) 25.1	(121) 28.3
	4.9	4.7	5.9				3.4	5.9
9.9	13.5	20.6	11.2			% Profit Before Taxes/Total Assets	18.2	21.9
-4.5	3.7	6.4	5.3				7.4	8.8
-23.1	-1.0	1.5	2.0				.7	1.3
UND	237.4	175.1	68.4			Sales/Net Fixed Assets	132.4	119.0
30.8	41.2	50.8	27.2				45.3	38.0
5.5	12.7	17.3	11.9				11.9	17.7
4.2	3.7	4.3	2.8			Sales/Total Assets	3.2	3.8
3.4	2.7	2.7	2.4				2.4	2.5
1.6	1.5	1.6	1.7				1.7	1.6
	.1	.2	.3			% Depr., Dep., Amort./Sales	.4	.3
	(25) .6	(32) .7	(29) .8				(116) .8	(97) .8
	1.3	1.2	1.5				1.8	1.7
	1.7	1.1				% Officers', Directors' Owners' Comp/Sales	2.2	1.8
	(19) 3.5	(17) 2.1					(64) 4.7	(57) 3.8
	5.8	8.6					9.6	9.4
13772M	102059M	491253M	1402766M	1406049M	459326M	Net Sales ($)	3583895M	4031151M
3588M	36203M	170853M	628421M	664884M	212385M	Total Assets ($)	1683325M	1598133M

M = $ thousand   MM = $ million
See Pages 11 through 21 for Explanation of Ratios and Data

Comparative Historical Data | | | Current Data Sorted by Sales

4/1/04-3/31/05 ALL	4/1/05-3/31/06 ALL	4/1/06-3/31/07 ALL	Type of Statement	0-1MM	1-3MM	3-5MM	5-10MM	10-25MM	25MM & OVER
24	28	20	Unqualified		2	1	2	2	16
16	22	24	Reviewed	1		1	4	9	7
19	18	17	Compiled	4	4	5	2	2	
21	20	23	Tax Returns	4	7	4	4	3	1
33	41	42	Other	1		1	7	8	16
					26 (4/1-9/30/06)			100 (10/1/06-3/31/07)	
113	129	126	**NUMBER OF STATEMENTS**	10	22	11	19	24	40
%	%	%	**ASSETS**	%	%	%	%	%	%
9.0	8.5	8.3	Cash & Equivalents	10.0	6.5	5.9	14.1	9.8	5.9
25.9	27.5	27.2	Trade Receivables (net)	24.1	18.8	24.2	27.0	29.5	32.3
39.7	40.3	40.3	Inventory	33.7	46.0	48.6	32.4	41.2	39.8
3.5	2.7	2.9	All Other Current	.6	4.8	2.5	2.5	2.5	3.4
78.2	79.1	78.7	Total Current	68.3	76.0	79.3	76.0	82.9	81.4
12.1	11.1	12.3	Fixed Assets (net)	21.1	13.2	9.4	12.3	8.7	12.6
3.8	3.3	3.8	Intangibles (net)	9.4	7.3	2.5	1.5	1.6	3.2
6.0	6.4	5.2	All Other Non-Current	1.2	3.5	8.8	10.2	6.8	2.8
100.0	100.0	100.0	Total	100.0	100.0	100.0	100.0	100.0	100.0
			LIABILITIES						
20.0	20.0	21.8	Notes Payable-Short Term	34.4	23.0	26.6	18.7	17.6	20.8
2.3	2.2	2.0	Cur. Mat.-L.T.D.	3.1	2.0	4.2	1.2	.3	2.5
19.9	18.8	19.0	Trade Payables	21.2	14.4	27.9	18.5	18.8	18.8
.1	.3	.2	Income Taxes Payable	.0	.0	.0	.2	.6	.1
8.9	7.5	7.4	All Other Current	4.0	7.6	4.5	5.9	11.7	6.9
51.1	48.9	50.4	Total Current	62.7	47.0	63.3	44.7	49.0	49.2
9.0	9.2	12.7	Long-Term Debt	18.4	14.7	12.5	4.5	6.7	17.6
.1	.5	.1	Deferred Taxes	.0	.1	.0	.1	.1	.1
6.1	6.4	8.1	All Other Non-Current	3.1	13.4	3.3	8.1	9.1	7.3
33.7	35.0	28.6	Net Worth	14.9	24.7	20.9	42.6	35.1	25.9
100.0	100.0	100.0	Total Liabilties & Net Worth	100.0	100.0	100.0	100.0	100.0	100.0
			INCOME DATA						
100.0	100.0	100.0	Net Sales	100.0	100.0	100.0	100.0	100.0	100.0
38.4	34.3	34.4	Gross Profit	42.6	36.2	39.3	37.3	31.8	30.4
35.6	31.2	30.3	Operating Expenses	40.6	35.6	35.6	31.3	26.7	25.0
2.8	3.0	4.2	Operating Profit	2.0	.6	3.7	6.0	5.1	5.4
.8	.9	1.4	All Other Expenses (net)	3.3	2.1	.6	.6	1.0	1.3
2.0	2.1	2.8	Profit Before Taxes	-1.3	-1.5	3.1	5.4	4.0	4.1
			RATIOS						
2.3	2.5	2.7		3.5	3.0	2.9	2.9	2.6	2.4
1.5	1.7	1.7	Current	1.4	2.0	1.7	1.6	1.7	1.7
1.2	1.2	1.2		.6	1.2	.5	1.3	1.3	1.2
1.1	1.4	1.4		2.4	1.2	1.3	1.6	1.3	1.2
.6	(128) .7	.7	Quick	.8	.4	.7	.6	.8	.7
.3	.4	.3		.1	.3	.3	.3	.4	.4
19 19.3	22 16.9	18 20.5		0 UND	2 164.6	6 63.8	22 16.3	17 22.0	26 13.9
32 11.2	38 9.6	33 11.2	Sales/Receivables	21 17.0	30 12.2	22 16.5	43 8.5	29 12.6	47 7.7
60 6.1	57 6.4	61 6.0		101 3.6	54 6.8	30 12.4	52 7.0	54 6.8	65 5.6
61 5.9	48 7.6	46 7.9		0 UND	83 4.4	57 6.4	20 18.6	33 11.2	49 7.4
100 3.6	98 3.7	96 3.8	Cost of Sales/Inventory	102 3.6	139 2.6	78 4.7	104 3.5	84 4.4	91 4.0
155 2.4	158 2.3	136 2.7		156 2.3	176 2.1	108 3.4	151 2.4	108 3.4	130 2.8
18 20.7	17 21.9	14 25.4		0 UND	1 508.2	17 21.8	20 18.5	12 30.7	20 17.9
37 9.9	32 11.4	32 11.5	Cost of Sales/Payables	27 13.4	25 14.5	36 10.1	36 10.1	28 16.1	37 9.9
66 5.5	56 6.5	54 6.7		94 3.9	57 6.4	60 6.1	76 4.8	50 7.2	49 7.5
4.7	4.9	4.6		3.0	2.9	5.0	6.2	5.7	4.2
9.6	8.5	8.5	Sales/Working Capital	53.3	8.4	8.5	9.3	8.6	7.2
23.6	20.9	23.2		-4.6	23.5	-16.3	22.1	21.3	19.8
8.7	7.1	9.1			2.1	11.2	7.6	10.1	11.3
(97) 2.4	(122) 3.3	(112) 2.8	EBIT/Interest	(21) .5	4.6	(14) 3.8	(22) 3.3	(39) 3.4	
.3	1.0	1.5			-2.8	2.4	1.8	1.8	1.6
13.4	21.7	14.0							12.9
(21) 4.4	(29) 4.7	(21) 3.8	Net Profit + Depr., Dep., Amort./Cur. Mat. L/T/D					(11) 4.2	
.0	.2	-.4							1.3
.1	.1	.0		.0	.0	.0	.0	.1	.1
.3	.2	.3	Fixed/Worth	1.0	.4	.2	.1	.1	.3
1.0	.8	1.2		-1.2	4.7	-.8	.6	.4	1.3
1.0	.8	.8		1.2	.9	.5	.6	.8	.8
1.6	1.7	2.0	Debt/Worth	2.6	1.7	2.2	1.6	1.9	2.9
7.0	5.1	8.5		-3.3	37.5	-6.1	3.4	6.8	7.1
42.4	47.2	52.9			21.0		72.7	72.4	65.7
(94) 13.3	(116) 11.7	(108) 14.8	% Profit Before Taxes/Tangible Net Worth		(18) 5.0		(17) 25.9	(22) 13.8	(36) 18.1
-1.9	1.0	4.9			-38.1		9.7	5.7	6.0
12.9	12.6	12.5		16.9	4.3	22.8	19.7	11.0	15.1
3.9	4.3	5.5	% Profit Before Taxes/Total Assets	.6	-.2	8.6	6.8	5.3	6.1
-1.8	.2	1.3		-19.5	-14.9	6.2	4.3	1.9	2.1
77.6	115.7	114.4		UND	194.3	534.0	157.8	284.1	77.8
31.4	40.5	39.9	Sales/Net Fixed Assets	11.7	30.2	45.5	43.8	71.1	27.0
14.4	14.5	13.4		3.2	7.2	26.1	14.0	26.8	12.9
3.2	3.5	3.6		3.3	2.9	4.4	3.2	4.4	3.2
2.4	2.4	2.6	Sales/Total Assets	1.6	2.0	3.6	2.0	3.5	2.5
1.6	1.7	1.6		.9	1.5	3.2	1.5	1.9	1.7
.5	.4	.3			.3		.1	.1	.4
(86) .9	(104) .9	(102) .7	% Depr., Dep., Amort./Sales		(16) .7		(15) .9	(21) .5	(36) .8
1.7	1.5	1.5			2.5		1.5	.9	1.7
2.3	2.0	1.4			2.4			.9	
(45) 5.0	(59) 3.7	(49) 3.2	% Officers', Directors' Owners' Comp/Sales		(12) 3.4			(11) 1.8	
9.6	6.9	5.9			5.1			3.6	
3298139M	4336015M	3875225M	Net Sales ($)	5366M	46691M	42419M	135842M	369614M	3275293M
1532157M	2109888M	1716334M	Total Assets ($)	3509M	24102M	12399M	65770M	141551M	1469003M

© RMA 2007

M = $ thousand   MM = $ million
See Pages 11 through 21 for Explanation of Ratios and Data

Current Data Sorted by Assets | Comparative Historical Data

Type of Statement	0-500M	500M-2MM	2-10MM	10-50MM	50-100MM	100-250MM		4/1/02-3/31/03 ALL	4/1/03-3/31/04 ALL
Unqualified		1	3	16	8	5		26	37
Reviewed		5	44	32	1	1		79	84
Compiled	5	16	31	4		1		71	86
Tax Returns	17	21	15	1				15	28
Other	7	16	55	34	6	3		70	72
	69 (4/1-9/30/06)			278 (10/1/06-3/31/07)					
NUMBER OF STATEMENTS	29	59	148	87	15	9		261	307

ASSETS	%	%	%	%	%	%		%	%
Cash & Equivalents	20.0	15.6	9.2	7.0	4.0			8.0	8.7
Trade Receivables (net)	14.4	23.9	30.6	39.2	32.5			25.5	28.4
Inventory	20.5	13.4	17.7	22.7	22.1			20.4	19.9
All Other Current	2.5	3.8	2.3	3.9	3.9			2.8	3.1
Total Current	57.4	56.7	59.8	72.7	62.5			56.6	60.0
Fixed Assets (net)	34.9	35.8	32.1	20.0	28.9			33.6	30.4
Intangibles (net)	.3	1.8	2.5	2.0	5.5			2.7	2.4
All Other Non-Current	7.4	5.7	5.5	5.3	3.1			7.1	7.2
Total	100.0	100.0	100.0	100.0	100.0			100.0	100.0

LIABILITIES									
Notes Payable-Short Term	11.2	9.6	9.3	13.6	8.6			13.9	13.5
Cur. Mat.-L.T.D.	7.4	4.1	4.3	2.5	4.9			5.0	4.6
Trade Payables	12.9	17.4	16.8	22.1	23.8			15.2	17.9
Income Taxes Payable	.0	.1	.5	.6	.1			.2	.2
All Other Current	13.5	8.3	8.1	7.7	6.8			8.0	8.1
Total Current	45.1	39.5	39.0	46.6	44.2			42.2	44.3
Long-Term Debt	25.7	28.8	16.8	8.4	21.1			16.0	14.8
Deferred Taxes	.0	.0	.4	.5	1.0			.4	.4
All Other Non-Current	4.1	4.6	4.2	2.4	4.9			7.9	7.5
Net Worth	25.1	27.1	39.6	42.1	28.7			33.5	33.1
Total Liabilties & Net Worth	100.0	100.0	100.0	100.0	100.0			100.0	100.0

INCOME DATA									
Net Sales	100.0	100.0	100.0	100.0	100.0			100.0	100.0
Gross Profit	43.3	35.6	25.7	16.6	13.8			26.9	26.8
Operating Expenses	35.6	29.0	19.0	10.5	8.9			23.3	22.7
Operating Profit	7.7	6.5	6.7	6.1	4.9			3.6	4.1
All Other Expenses (net)	-.2	.6	.7	.1	1.4			.8	.4
Profit Before Taxes	7.9	5.9	6.0	6.0	3.6			2.9	3.7

RATIOS	0-500M	500M-2MM	2-10MM	10-50MM	50-100MM	100-250MM		4/1/02-3/31/03	4/1/03-3/31/04
Current	4.2	3.3	2.7	2.6	1.9			2.1	2.1
	1.6	1.8	1.7	1.6	1.4			1.4	1.4
	.5	1.0	1.1	1.2	1.1			1.0	1.0
Quick	1.8	2.2	1.8	1.6	1.1			1.4	1.3
	.6	1.1	(147) 1.1	1.0	1.0			.8	.8
	.3	.5	.6	.7	.7			.5	.5
Sales/Receivables	0 UND	4 101.5	17 21.6	27 13.5	33 11.0		19	19.4	17 21.3
	0 887.5	23 16.0	30 12.1	35 10.6	35 10.3		32	11.5	36 10.2
	13 29.0	41 9.0	45 8.1	41 8.9	53 6.9		43	8.5	50 7.3
Cost of Sales/Inventory	0 UND	2 217.0	5 72.9	10 37.8	13 28.3		10	34.9	10 36.0
	15 25.1	9 39.9	15 23.8	23 15.7	28 12.9		24	15.0	25 14.4
	41 8.8	34 10.8	39 9.3	38 9.5	51 7.2		59	6.2	53 6.9
Cost of Sales/Payables	0 UND	3 116.5	10 37.4	13 29.1	22 16.8		9	41.6	11 32.9
	3 109.5	20 18.4	22 17.0	22 16.2	33 11.0		22	16.5	26 14.0
	33 10.9	43 8.5	34 10.8	31 11.8	55 6.6		35	10.3	44 8.3
Sales/Working Capital	14.0	9.0	8.6	8.2	5.2			8.7	8.6
	26.0	19.7	16.6	15.5	17.2			19.5	22.2
	-34.1	-234.5	70.2	48.5	52.2			-514.0	577.6
EBIT/Interest	17.3	23.9	29.9	37.9	7.1			6.5	11.3
	(23) 4.8	(51) 7.9	(142) 9.4	(79) 10.4	3.3		(239)	2.9	(284) 4.6
	1.0	1.0	3.1	4.2	2.4			1.3	1.7
Net Profit + Depr., Dep., Amort./Cur. Mat. L/T/D			11.4	20.4				3.9	4.7
			(30) 4.0	(24) 6.0			(55)	2.3	(67) 2.5
			1.6	2.8				1.3	1.8
Fixed/Worth	.2	.3	.3	.3	.8			.4	.4
	.7	1.1	.7	.4	1.6			.9	.9
	69.0	12.1	1.7	.8	7.5			2.9	2.2
Debt/Worth	.7	.7	.7	.7	1.1			.8	.9
	3.0	1.9	1.6	1.7	4.9			1.9	2.1
	140.9	15.7	3.2	3.6	26.1			7.2	5.4
% Profit Before Taxes/Tangible Net Worth	209.5	81.0	78.7	74.5	61.3			42.1	48.6
	(23) 105.3	(46) 52.8	(140) 44.9	(79) 51.3	(13) 31.2		(224)	14.6	(280) 21.7
	5.1	18.2	19.2	28.9	21.0			4.2	8.5
% Profit Before Taxes/Total Assets	88.9	42.2	35.3	27.8	10.5			12.1	15.4
	18.5	14.3	16.2	16.1	9.1			4.5	7.1
	.6	.1	4.8	8.9	3.5			1.0	2.0
Sales/Net Fixed Assets	117.1	50.4	30.0	63.9	19.2			21.2	24.5
	28.0	10.0	12.8	20.3	9.2			9.5	10.6
	10.6	5.1	6.2	12.1	5.4			4.9	5.6
Sales/Total Assets	10.3	5.6	4.8	5.4	3.4			4.1	4.3
	5.6	3.3	3.3	3.7	2.6			2.8	2.9
	3.1	2.3	2.3	2.9	1.9			2.0	2.0
% Depr., Dep., Amort./Sales	.9	.9	.8	.4	.9			1.1	1.0
	(20) 2.8	(49) 2.6	(133) 1.8	(79) 1.0	(14) 1.4		(236)	2.5	(275) 2.3
	4.5	5.9	3.4	1.6	2.1			4.3	4.0
% Officers', Directors' Owners' Comp/Sales	2.1	1.6	1.6	.4				1.6	1.2
	(17) 8.4	(31) 2.7	(67) 3.5	(29) .6			(116)	3.3	(146) 2.8
	16.5	5.5	5.6	1.6				5.6	5.8
Net Sales ($)	57994M	306365M	2898077M	8319791M	3104955M	3605448M		8714155M	10470261M
Total Assets ($)	8257M	74338M	757291M	2002058M	1084216M	1160431M		3566350M	3946381M

M = $ thousand   MM = $ million
See Pages 11 through 21 for Explanation of Ratios and Data

Comparative Historical Data | Current Data Sorted by Sales

			Type of Statement						
37	36	33	Unqualified		1			2	30
94	84	83	Reviewed		1	4	7	25	46
61	70	56	Compiled	3	6	6	9	19	13
38	28	54	Tax Returns	3	13	16	12	6	4
76	100	121	Other	8	7	6	19	28	53
4/1/04-3/31/05 ALL	4/1/05-3/31/06 ALL	4/1/06-3/31/07 ALL		0-1MM	1-3MM 69 (4/1-9/30/06)	3-5MM	5-10MM 278 (10/1/06-3/31/07)	10-25MM	25MM & OVER
306	318	347	**NUMBER OF STATEMENTS**	14	28	32	47	80	146
%	%	%	**ASSETS**	%	%	%	%	%	%
10.9	9.2	10.3	Cash & Equivalents	7.9	24.9	16.6	10.3	11.6	5.6
30.0	29.9	30.3	Trade Receivables (net)	18.0	11.9	16.7	25.5	30.6	39.3
21.2	18.4	19.3	Inventory	19.3	14.5	19.6	11.8	18.8	22.7
2.2	3.1	3.0	All Other Current	3.3	1.3	.4	5.3	2.7	3.2
64.3	60.6	62.8	Total Current	48.5	52.6	53.4	52.8	63.8	70.9
26.8	30.7	29.4	Fixed Assets (net)	42.8	40.6	38.8	36.2	29.7	21.7
1.9	1.7	2.2	Intangibles (net)	.2	2.0	2.1	4.4	1.7	2.0
7.0	7.0	5.5	All Other Non-Current	8.5	4.8	5.7	6.6	4.8	5.5
100.0	100.0	100.0	Total	100.0	100.0	100.0	100.0	100.0	100.0
			LIABILITIES						
10.8	10.3	11.0	Notes Payable-Short Term	4.5	8.3	11.8	10.4	7.9	13.8
3.4	4.2	4.0	Cur. Mat.-L.T.D.	6.8	4.9	4.7	5.3	3.9	3.1
19.8	19.0	18.2	Trade Payables	11.7	15.2	11.1	14.8	17.7	22.2
.3	.4	.4	Income Taxes Payable	.0	.0	.0	.3	.3	.7
8.4	8.0	8.4	All Other Current	11.2	10.1	6.5	15.8	5.8	7.3
42.7	41.9	42.0	Total Current	34.3	38.5	34.0	46.5	35.6	47.2
14.3	16.2	17.4	Long-Term Debt	29.8	40.5	25.9	22.5	13.4	10.5
.6	.4	.3	Deferred Taxes	.0	.0	.4	.2	.3	.5
5.3	4.8	3.8	All Other Non-Current	4.8	6.9	4.4	3.2	3.6	3.3
37.1	36.7	36.4	Net Worth	31.1	14.0	35.3	27.6	47.1	38.5
100.0	100.0	100.0	Total Liabilties & Net Worth	100.0	100.0	100.0	100.0	100.0	100.0
			INCOME DATA						
100.0	100.0	100.0	Net Sales	100.0	100.0	100.0	100.0	100.0	100.0
26.7	28.0	25.7	Gross Profit	59.8	40.2	33.3	32.5	26.2	15.5
20.2	21.6	19.2	Operating Expenses	47.9	33.4	26.1	25.9	19.3	10.0
6.5	6.4	6.5	Operating Profit	11.9	6.8	7.2	6.6	6.9	5.5
.4	.7	.5	All Other Expenses (net)	1.9	.6	.8	.5	.3	.3
6.2	5.7	6.0	Profit Before Taxes	10.0	6.2	6.3	6.1	6.6	5.2
			RATIOS						
2.6	2.3	2.7	Current	2.7	4.9	2.6	3.2	2.9	2.2
1.5	1.5	1.6		1.5	1.9	1.8	1.5	1.9	1.5
1.1	1.0	1.1		.5	.9	1.1	.6	1.2	1.1
1.8	1.5	1.7	Quick	1.4	4.7	2.0	2.1	2.0	1.5
.9	.9 (346)	1.0		.5	1.0	1.1	1.1 (46)	1.2	1.0
.6	.6	.6		.3	.3	.4	.5	.7	.7
17 21.9	17 21.4	16 22.2	Sales/Receivables	0 UND	0 UND	2 154.1	4 100.1	19 19.2	27 13.7
33 11.2	32 11.5	31 11.9		16 23.4	9 40.6	20 18.4	22 16.7	29 12.4	34 10.9
45 8.1	43 8.6	43 8.5		77 4.7	34 10.6	40 9.1	48 7.6	45 8.2	40 9.1
9 41.3	6 64.5	6 60.8	Cost of Sales/Inventory	0 UND	1 672.2	3 131.9	2 217.0	6 59.1	9 40.9
21 17.5	18 20.1	17 20.9		0 UND	16 23.0	17 21.0	9 42.1	15 24.7	22 16.9
43 8.5	40 9.2	40 9.1		277 1.3	44 8.2	40 9.0	22 16.7	47 7.8	38 9.6
12 31.6	11 32.9	8 44.2	Cost of Sales/Payables	0 UND	1 246.1	3 109.5	11 33.9	12 30.1	
25 14.9	22 16.4	21 17.2		38 9.6	31 11.8	16 22.3	13 27.1	24 15.1	21 17.6
41 9.0	37 9.9	35 10.4		89 4.1	58 6.3	26 14.1	33 11.2	38 9.5	31 11.8
8.0	9.6	8.9	Sales/Working Capital	7.9	10.1	6.0	9.9	7.6	9.4
16.9	19.7	17.5		19.8	29.8	14.9	22.5	12.7	17.6
101.7	450.0	70.8		-9.0	-53.4	104.2	-34.1	42.0	61.4
31.2	21.9	25.3	EBIT/Interest	16.5	25.7	21.7	16.3	50.5	18.4
(280) 9.5	(283) 8.5	(319) 8.2		(10) 2.4	(25) 2.0	(30) 5.2	(41) 6.5	(74) 10.8	(139) 8.2
4.0	2.7	2.9		.7	-1.1	1.2	3.2	4.3	3.8
11.3	7.9	11.1	Net Profit + Depr., Dep., Amort./Cur. Mat. L/T/D					22.8	11.7
(82) 4.0	(68) 3.0	(68) 3.8						(16) 3.1	(42) 4.1
2.2	1.4	1.7						1.5	1.9
.3	.3	.3	Fixed/Worth	.0	.5	.5	.4	.2	.2
.7	.8	.7		1.5	1.4	1.0	1.3	.6	.6
1.6	1.8	1.7		40.9	-9.2	6.0	7.0	1.3	1.3
.8	.7	.7	Debt/Worth	.5	.9	.4	.8	.6	.8
1.9	1.9	1.7		2.4	3.1	2.4	1.9	1.2	1.9
4.7	4.4	4.9		61.9	-15.5	15.6	11.1	2.2	4.9
74.1	69.5	80.1	% Profit Before Taxes/Tangible Net Worth	192.4	152.7	74.3	92.3	70.6	78.8
(280) 49.0	(291) 37.7	(317) 47.8		(12) 80.5	(20) 64.3	(26) 42.6	(40) 53.0	(77) 44.4	(142) 50.7
21.2	18.1	22.0		6.0	-5.6	10.7	24.0	16.3	28.4
31.7	28.4	33.5	% Profit Before Taxes/Total Assets	105.5	54.1	35.0	33.5	36.7	27.4
14.3	12.6	15.6		5.5	5.3	11.9	17.7	16.7	15.3
5.5	3.8	5.0		-.3	-4.4	.8	5.7	5.2	7.9
34.4	35.4	44.6	Sales/Net Fixed Assets	UND	30.6	41.3	27.6	26.4	54.7
15.2	13.4	14.9		5.2	8.4	9.0	10.6	13.3	20.0
8.3	6.6	7.1		1.6	3.2	3.8	6.4	6.5	11.1
4.9	4.8	5.3	Sales/Total Assets	3.4	5.5	3.7	5.3	4.8	5.6
3.6	3.5	3.5		2.1	2.8	2.9	3.4	3.5	3.9
2.5	2.4	2.5		1.2	1.7	1.5	2.4	2.4	3.0
.6	.7	.7	% Depr., Dep., Amort./Sales	2.4	1.6	.7	1.1	1.1	.4
(268) 1.4	(279) 1.8	(302) 1.5		(10) 8.3	(23) 4.0	(28) 2.6	(40) 2.7	(68) 1.8	(133) 1.0
2.8	3.1	3.0		26.5	7.4	6.1	4.1	3.0	1.7
1.2	1.3	.8	% Officers', Directors' Owners' Comp/Sales		1.6	2.7	1.5	1.8	.4
(147) 2.7	(137) 3.0	(148) 2.6			(14) 3.1	(17) 5.5	(26) 2.7	(36) 3.2	(49) .8
5.1	6.2	5.5			13.5	8.2	5.3	5.3	1.9
13662070M	14255796M	18292630M	Net Sales ($)	7475M	56050M	123808M	336677M	1247799M	16520821M
4107779M	4188645M	5086591M	Total Assets ($)	7042M	23092M	59534M	104656M	414712M	4477555M

© RMA 2007

M = $ thousand   MM = $ million
See Pages 11 through 21 for Explanation of Ratios and Data

Current Data Sorted by Assets | Comparative Historical Data

						Type of Statement		
1	3	7 26	6 33	4 1	6 1	Unqualified Reviewed	17 60	21 73
5	16 17	19 13	1 1			Compiled Tax Returns	29 20	41 26
6	8	19	25	5	1	Other	30	31
	57 (4/1-9/30/06)		167 (10/1/06-3/31/07)				4/1/02- 3/31/03	4/1/03- 3/31/04
0-500M	500M-2MM	2-10MM	10-50MM	50-100MM	100-250MM		ALL	ALL
12	44	84	66	10	8	NUMBER OF STATEMENTS	156	192
%	%	%	%	%	%	ASSETS	%	%
13.1	12.2	6.7	3.9	7.8		Cash & Equivalents	8.1	8.0
22.5	19.1	27.3	32.9	31.5		Trade Receivables (net)	32.0	29.4
33.2	54.7	49.5	53.0	51.1		Inventory	48.0	50.5
1.9	1.8	2.7	1.4	2.1		All Other Current	2.2	2.4
70.7	87.8	86.2	91.2	92.5		Total Current	90.3	90.4
17.1	8.4	7.0	4.5	2.5		Fixed Assets (net)	3.8	4.8
2.3	.1	2.6	1.4	4.4		Intangibles (net)	.8	1.1
9.9	3.7	4.2	3.0	.6		All Other Non-Current	5.1	3.7
100.0	100.0	100.0	100.0	100.0		Total	100.0	100.0
						LIABILITIES		
15.8	11.6	14.6	27.9	34.0		Notes Payable-Short Term	13.7	14.6
1.7	4.2	1.9	2.0	.6		Cur. Mat.-L.T.D.	1.2	.8
16.9	20.1	24.7	21.1	17.2		Trade Payables	28.5	24.8
.1	.9	.2	.1	.8		Income Taxes Payable	.3	.2
10.5	7.4	10.0	12.5	5.3		All Other Current	10.4	14.0
45.1	44.2	51.4	63.6	57.9		Total Current	54.1	54.4
14.8	7.7	5.0	5.1	2.7		Long-Term Debt	4.6	4.6
.0	.0	.0	.0	.2		Deferred Taxes	.1	.0
5.3	5.0	6.4	2.5	7.2		All Other Non-Current	5.1	4.6
34.8	43.2	37.2	28.8	31.9		Net Worth	36.2	36.4
100.0	100.0	100.0	100.0	100.0		Total Liabilties & Net Worth	100.0	100.0
						INCOME DATA		
100.0	100.0	100.0	100.0	100.0		Net Sales	100.0	100.0
52.5	34.2	29.2	21.9	24.4		Gross Profit	27.1	27.0
45.6	30.0	26.9	17.5	17.9		Operating Expenses	24.0	24.2
6.9	4.2	2.3	4.5	6.5		Operating Profit	3.1	2.8
.4	.8	.9	1.6	1.4		All Other Expenses (net)	.9	.7
6.5	3.4	1.3	2.9	5.1		Profit Before Taxes	2.3	2.1
						RATIOS		
6.2	4.1	2.4	1.7	2.4			2.4	2.6
2.4	2.4	1.7	1.4	1.4		Current	1.7	1.7
.7	1.4	1.3	1.2	1.3			1.3	1.3
5.2	2.0	1.1	.8	1.4			1.1	1.0
1.1	.6 (83)	.7	.5	.6		Quick	.8	.6
.1	.3	.3	.4	.3			.4	.4

3	137.4	4	89.2	14	25.7	45	8.2	17	21.5		Sales/Receivables	28	13.3	21	17.1
26	14.1	18	20.0	50	7.3	70	5.2	53	6.9			60	6.1	57	6.4
38	9.6	46	7.9	75	4.9	96	3.8	108	3.4			91	4.0	89	4.1

31	11.9	62	5.8	47	7.8	71	5.2	33	11.2		Cost of Sales/Inventory	66	5.5	67	5.5
112	3.2	110	3.3	125	2.9	149	2.4	193	1.9			121	3.0	135	2.7
205	1.8	333	1.1	289	1.3	268	1.4	305	1.2			193	1.9	240	1.5

14	26.3	12	30.8	13	28.8	9	39.9	17	21.5		Cost of Sales/Payables	35	10.4	27	13.4
50	7.4	38	9.7	45	8.0	58	6.3	38	9.7			62	5.9	57	6.4
75	4.9	85	4.3	111	3.3	102	3.6	84	4.3			104	3.5	104	3.5

0-500M	500M-2MM	2-10MM	10-50MM	50-100MM	100-250MM		ALL	ALL
4.9	2.2	2.9	4.2	3.3			3.5	3.0
9.2	4.2	6.3	6.7	5.2		Sales/Working Capital	5.9	6.2
NM	22.5	12.0	12.9	88.5			10.1	10.6
	9.1	6.8	4.2				7.6	7.7
	2.3 (31)	2.1 (77)	2.1 (62)			EBIT/Interest	2.6 (143)	2.5 (173)
	1.3	1.2	1.4				1.2	1.2
		11.4					11.6	31.0
		2.3 (10)				Net Profit + Depr., Dep., Amort./Cur. Mat. L/T/D	3.0 (17)	2.4 (16)
		-2.4					.3	.5
.0	.0	.0	.0	.0			.0	.0
.1	.1	.1	.1	.1		Fixed/Worth	.0	.1
NM	.4	.4	.4	NM			.1	.2
.6	.4	1.0	1.8	1.8			.8	.9
1.1	1.0	1.9	2.8	3.3		Debt/Worth	2.0	2.1
NM	5.6	3.5	4.8	NM			3.9	4.0
	59.4	22.4	26.8			% Profit Before Taxes/Tangible Net Worth	28.2	28.8
	7.3 (39)	8.2 (79)	11.0 (63)				9.5 (148)	7.8 (185)
	1.5	1.8	3.1				1.7	1.0
56.7	14.0	7.6	9.2	11.9		% Profit Before Taxes/Total Assets	8.2	8.1
13.7	3.7	3.5	2.3	7.8			2.6	2.6
-.7	.8	.5	.6	3.6			.3	.3
403.3	663.6	368.7	409.3	875.2		Sales/Net Fixed Assets	384.4	342.9
61.0	59.4	53.9	118.8	72.5			147.0	84.7
6.7	15.4	17.9	32.5	50.6			43.4	39.5
4.2	3.3	3.2	2.5	2.9		Sales/Total Assets	2.8	2.8
2.9	2.1	1.9	1.7	1.5			1.9	1.7
1.2	1.3	1.2	1.1	1.2			1.4	1.3
	.1	.1	.1			% Depr., Dep., Amort./Sales	.1	.1
	.5 (32)	.5 (67)	.2 (59)				.3 (121)	.4 (146)
	1.0	.9					.8	.7
	2.8	1.4	.7			% Officers', Directors' Owners' Comp/Sales	1.5	1.7
	5.7 (29)	2.8 (48)	1.2 (31)				3.4 (98)	3.3 (117)
	8.7	4.9	3.1				6.1	6.5
9341M	184078M	977835M	3202957M	4813600M	1361286M	Net Sales ($)	2335235M	8943155M
3240M	50697M	406536M	1411896M	729615M	967186M	Total Assets ($)	1285957M	2724792M

M = $ thousand   MM = $ million
See Pages 11 through 21 for Explanation of Ratios and Data

Comparative Historical Data   Current Data Sorted by Sales

	4/1/04-3/31/05 ALL	4/1/05-3/31/06 ALL	4/1/06-3/31/07 ALL	Type of Statement	0-1MM	1-3MM	3-5MM	5-10MM	10-25MM	25MM & OVER
	22	30	23	Unqualified				2	3	18
	67	73	64	Reviewed	1	2	8	13	16	24
	38	27	37	Compiled	1	13	1	12	9	1
	26	33	36	Tax Returns	8	9	4	5	9	1
	45	72	64	Other	7	5	5	12	14	21
						57 (4/1-9/30/06)			167 (10/1/06-3/31/07)	
	198	235	224	**NUMBER OF STATEMENTS**	17	29	18	44	51	65
	%	%	%	**ASSETS**	%	%	%	%	%	%
	7.4	6.6	7.5	Cash & Equivalents	13.4	9.4	5.8	8.4	6.9	5.5
	30.6	30.5	27.3	Trade Receivables (net)	11.1	19.2	23.9	26.8	31.2	33.2
	51.6	51.6	50.3	Inventory	49.2	56.2	54.6	48.3	50.1	48.3
	1.6	1.2	2.0	All Other Current	.4	1.9	2.0	4.0	1.2	1.9
	91.2	89.9	87.1	Total Current	74.1	86.7	86.3	87.5	89.3	89.0
	3.8	4.7	6.7	Fixed Assets (net)	16.1	9.5	4.6	6.2	5.9	4.7
	.9	1.3	2.0	Intangibles (net)	1.7	.3	4.0	2.8	.7	2.9
	4.1	4.2	4.1	All Other Non-Current	8.1	3.5	5.1	3.5	4.1	3.4
	100.0	100.0	100.0	Total	100.0	100.0	100.0	100.0	100.0	100.0
				LIABILITIES						
	21.3	19.7	19.3	Notes Payable-Short Term	12.7	17.9	12.8	14.1	21.6	25.1
	1.2	1.5	2.3	Cur. Mat.-L.T.D.	4.5	2.0	8.5	1.3	.8	1.9
	24.9	25.0	21.7	Trade Payables	12.3	23.9	16.4	21.4	26.3	21.2
	.1	.1	.3	Income Taxes Payable	.1	.7	.0	.9	.1	.2
	7.6	9.8	10.3	All Other Current	8.9	3.4	10.1	11.7	8.9	13.8
	55.0	56.1	53.8	Total Current	38.5	47.9	47.8	49.4	57.7	62.1
	5.2	5.6	6.0	Long-Term Debt	15.7	7.8	2.9	5.9	3.3	5.7
	.1	.0	.1	Deferred Taxes	.0	.1	.0	.0	.1	.1
	3.9	4.6	4.9	All Other Non-Current	9.1	3.8	4.6	5.1	5.9	3.5
	35.8	33.6	35.2	Net Worth	36.8	40.5	44.7	39.6	33.1	28.6
	100.0	100.0	100.0	Total Liabilities & Net Worth	100.0	100.0	100.0	100.0	100.0	100.0
				INCOME DATA						
	100.0	100.0	100.0	Net Sales	100.0	100.0	100.0	100.0	100.0	100.0
	26.8	26.8	28.9	Gross Profit	46.9	37.0	37.6	27.1	26.8	21.0
	22.8	22.7	25.1	Operating Expenses	43.1	32.1	34.5	24.8	23.0	16.4
	3.9	4.1	3.8	Operating Profit	3.9	4.9	3.1	2.3	3.8	4.6
	.8	1.3	1.1	All Other Expenses (net)	1.1	1.1	1.1	1.1	1.2	1.1
	3.1	2.8	2.7	Profit Before Taxes	2.7	3.8	2.0	1.1	2.7	3.5
				RATIOS						
	2.5	2.3	2.4	Current	10.0	2.9	3.2	2.8	2.2	1.6
	1.5	1.6	1.5		2.7	2.1	1.7	1.8	1.5	1.4
	1.3	1.3	1.2		1.1	1.5	1.3	1.3	1.2	1.2
	1.0	1.0	1.1	Quick	3.4	1.6	.9	1.2	1.1	1.0
	.7 (234)	.6 (223)	.6		.7	.4	.7 (43)	.6	.6	.6
	.4	.4	.3		.2	.2	.3	.2	.3	.4
	25 14.4	24 15.1	15 24.1	Sales/Receivables	0 UND	5 69.0	12 30.3	19 19.4	26 14.2	31 11.8
	64 5.7	59 6.2	48 7.6		10 35.5	29 12.5	46 8.0	50 7.3	55 6.6	57 6.4
	90 4.1	99 3.7	83 4.4		38 9.6	64 5.7	102 3.6	82 4.5	90 4.1	91 4.0
	74 4.9	83 4.4	60 6.1	Cost of Sales/Inventory	148 2.5	67 5.4	91 4.0	71 5.1	44 8.3	41 8.8
	141 2.6	154 2.4	129 2.8		267 1.4	183 2.0	230 1.6	120 3.0	101 3.6	120 3.1
	249 1.5	240 1.5	278 1.3		574 .6	410 .9	365 1.0	207 1.8	245 1.5	207 1.8
	23 15.8	21 17.8	12 29.6	Cost of Sales/Payables	1 323.1	36 10.0	8 43.8	10 35.3	20 18.2	8 44.6
	58 6.2	56 6.6	47 7.8		55 6.7	66 5.5	28 13.0	46 8.0	45 8.2	45 8.0
	103 3.5	106 3.5	99 3.7		111 3.3	97 3.8	171 2.1	120 3.0	96 3.8	81 4.5
	3.3	3.3	3.3	Sales/Working Capital	1.3	2.2	2.3	3.0	4.2	5.2
	5.5	5.1	6.2		3.0	4.0	3.4	5.1	7.3	7.7
	10.0	11.2	12.7		29.9	9.2	17.3	9.7	23.1	14.4
	10.2	7.8	6.3	EBIT/Interest	4.9	5.9	7.1	6.2	8.1	4.7
	(179) 3.3	(214) 2.4	(194) 2.2		(10) 1.6	(21) 1.7	(17) 2.5	(39) 2.0	(48) 2.4	(59) 2.6
	1.5	1.3	1.3		-.7	.4	1.3	1.1	1.3	1.7
	11.4	9.8	9.8	Net Profit + Depr., Dep., Amort./Cur. Mat. L/T/D						
	(25) 3.1	(28) 2.4	(25) 2.2							
	.4	1.0	.5							
	.0	.0	.0	Fixed/Worth	.0	.0	.0	.0	.0	.0
	.1	.1	.1		.2	.1	.1	.1	.1	.1
	.2	.2	.4		-2.5	.5	.2	.3	.4	.5
	.9	1.1	.9	Debt/Worth	.1	.6	.5	.8	1.2	2.0
	2.2	2.2	2.2		.9	1.2	1.5	1.4	2.2	3.1
	4.6	4.3	4.3		-5.7	3.5	3.9	3.4	4.1	5.6
	32.8	27.8	31.9	% Profit Before Taxes/Tangible Net Worth	46.0	42.5	27.1	33.6	28.1	32.4
	(190) 11.7	(219) 10.5	(205) 10.3		(12) 4.7	(26) 6.9	(17) 6.0	(42) 7.7	(48) 11.3	(60) 16.4
	3.3	3.2	2.6		-1.6	-.8	1.4	1.0	2.8	4.9
	9.3	8.7	10.1	% Profit Before Taxes/Total Assets	9.7	11.0	7.9	10.0	10.7	10.4
	3.4	2.8	3.3		3.1	1.6	3.5	2.3	3.6	4.0
	.9	.6	.7		-1.9	-.8	.7	.4	.6	1.1
	486.1	346.3	382.5	Sales/Net Fixed Assets	108.3	261.7	347.7	792.7	655.0	420.3
	99.8	94.0	65.4		8.3	39.9	66.5	64.6	99.0	114.4
	35.0	30.5	22.2		3.8	14.4	18.0	25.1	30.9	33.1
	2.5	2.5	2.8	Sales/Total Assets	2.0	2.3	2.7	2.7	4.4	2.9
	1.8	1.7	1.8		.9	1.8	1.3	1.8	2.0	1.8
	1.3	1.1	1.2		.7	1.3	1.0	1.1	1.4	1.3
	.1	.1	.1	% Depr., Dep., Amort./Sales	.7	.1	.1	.1	.1	.1
	(153) .4	(180) .3	(180) .4		(10) 1.2	(23) .5	(14) .3	(33) .4	(41) .5	(59) .2
	.9	.8	.9		1.9	.9	.8	.9	1.0	.7
	1.2	1.2	1.1	% Officers', Directors' Owners' Comp/Sales		3.4	3.0	1.4	.8	.5
	(124) 3.0	(119) 2.7	(121) 2.8			(17) 6.3	(13) 4.1	(23) 2.7	(31) 1.7	(31) 1.0
	6.7	5.6	5.5			10.3	6.5	5.4	4.6	2.5
	9031012M	6384255M	10549097M	Net Sales ($)	8975M	56627M	72093M	315546M	823269M	9272587M
	3676747M	3840004M	3569170M	Total Assets ($)	10118M	41261M	57293M	214259M	424452M	2821787M

M = $ thousand   MM = $ million
See Pages 11 through 21 for Explanation of Ratios and Data

Current Data Sorted by Assets | Comparative Historical Data

Type of Statement								
		1	12	27	6	3	59	55
Unqualified								
Reviewed	4	20	62	21			90	104
Compiled	8	48	49	8		1	93	139
Tax Returns	32	60	36	1			42	92
Other	16	51	73	38	8	1	92	110

93 (4/1-9/30/06)   493 (10/1/06-3/31/07)   Historical: 4/1/02-3/31/03 ALL, 4/1/03-3/31/04 ALL

	0-500M	500M-2MM	2-10MM	10-50MM	50-100MM	100-250MM	4/1/02-3/31/03 ALL	4/1/03-3/31/04 ALL
NUMBER OF STATEMENTS	60	180	232	95	14	5	376	500
ASSETS	%	%	%	%	%	%	%	%
Cash & Equivalents	17.9	8.7	6.8	5.4	3.3		9.3	9.3
Trade Receivables (net)	28.5	34.2	33.5	32.8	24.4		32.5	30.7
Inventory	28.4	32.4	38.6	40.7	35.8		34.9	34.8
All Other Current	4.1	2.4	2.5	2.9	2.3		2.4	2.5
Total Current	78.9	77.8	81.4	81.9	65.8		79.2	77.4
Fixed Assets (net)	15.4	13.3	10.7	10.6	15.7		13.0	13.1
Intangibles (net)	1.1	3.3	2.4	2.3	12.4		3.2	3.1
All Other Non-Current	4.6	5.6	5.6	5.3	6.2		4.6	6.4
Total	100.0	100.0	100.0	100.0	100.0		100.0	100.0
LIABILITIES								
Notes Payable-Short Term	27.3	16.1	16.1	17.5	15.6		18.1	15.6
Cur. Mat.-L.T.D.	3.7	3.3	2.6	2.2	4.1		2.7	3.5
Trade Payables	23.8	23.0	22.4	22.0	15.2		22.6	22.3
Income Taxes Payable	.2	.1	.3	.3	.1		.3	.3
All Other Current	16.0	8.8	9.4	9.9	9.4		10.1	9.2
Total Current	71.1	51.3	50.8	52.0	44.4		53.7	50.9
Long-Term Debt	20.0	12.1	7.8	9.1	13.9		7.8	10.2
Deferred Taxes	.0	.1	.2	.1	1.5		.1	.1
All Other Non-Current	11.2	6.0	4.7	5.7	8.5		4.8	5.4
Net Worth	-2.3	30.5	36.5	33.0	31.8		33.6	33.4
Total Liabilities & Net Worth	100.0	100.0	100.0	100.0	100.0		100.0	100.0
INCOME DATA								
Net Sales	100.0	100.0	100.0	100.0	100.0		100.0	100.0
Gross Profit	38.0	32.7	29.4	29.0	26.3		31.2	30.5
Operating Expenses	33.6	28.8	24.3	23.8	19.9		28.0	27.6
Operating Profit	4.4	3.9	5.1	5.2	6.3		3.2	2.9
All Other Expenses (net)	1.1	.6	.8	.8	1.9		.7	.3
Profit Before Taxes	3.2	3.3	4.3	4.4	4.5		2.5	2.5
RATIOS								
Current	4.7	2.5	2.6	2.1	2.2		2.3	2.5
	1.5	1.5	1.6	1.5	1.4		1.5	1.5
	.8	1.1	1.1	1.3	1.0		1.1	1.2
Quick	3.1	1.5	1.3	1.2	.9		1.3	1.4
	(59) 1.0	.8	.8	.7	.5		(499) .8	.8
	.3	.5	.5	.5	.4		.5	.5
Sales/Receivables	0 UND	23 16.1	26 14.0	34 10.8	33 11.0		27 13.4	23 15.6
	16 22.2	35 10.3	39 9.4	45 8.2	45 8.1		41 8.9	39 9.4
	43 8.5	49 7.5	54 6.8	61 5.9	73 5.0		56 6.5	52 7.0
Cost of Sales/Inventory	0 UND	14 25.3	35 10.5	49 7.5	44 8.3		34 10.9	29 12.5
	23 15.6	47 7.8	62 5.9	90 4.0	90 4.1		67 5.4	60 6.1
	95 3.9	105 3.5	109 3.3	135 2.7	132 2.8		109 3.4	104 3.5
Cost of Sales/Payables	0 UND	14 25.5	17 21.9	19 19.3	12 29.2		18 20.8	16 23.3
	23 16.2	30 12.1	33 11.1	34 10.7	27 13.7		33 10.9	31 11.9
	56 6.5	54 6.7	52 7.0	59 6.2	54 6.8		57 6.4	53 6.8
Sales/Working Capital	5.7	7.2	5.3	5.0	5.5		5.7	5.4
	24.3	12.6	10.4	8.9	11.1		11.7	11.6
	-27.2	48.2	41.9	19.3	NM		41.9	32.3
EBIT/Interest	6.5	12.6	11.3	13.5	11.3		8.9	12.6
	(45) 2.3	(162) 4.0	(213) 3.6	(87) 4.1	(13) 3.4		(336) 3.0	(436) 3.7
	.7	1.4	1.6	2.0	1.8		1.2	1.5
Net Profit + Depr., Dep., Amort./Cur. Mat. L/T/D		4.2	6.3	15.4			10.9	7.0
	(17) 1.2	(44) 2.2	(15) 8.7				(80) 2.4	(81) 2.1
	.3	1.0	3.1				.8	.9
Fixed/Worth	.0	.1	.1	.1	.0		.1	.1
	.4	.3	.2	.2	.7		.3	.3
	4.2	2.4	.7	.6	NM		1.0	1.0
Debt/Worth	.9	1.0	.8	1.1	1.0		.9	.8
	5.5	2.7	2.1	2.1	4.2		2.3	2.1
	-4.6	12.0	6.3	4.9	NM		5.7	5.5
% Profit Before Taxes/Tangible Net Worth	146.7	68.8	53.4	54.3	87.6		43.0	48.8
	(41) 51.9	(150) 32.9	(213) 26.8	(86) 35.5	(11) 39.0		(335) 14.0	(441) 20.2
	5.3	7.3	6.4	14.9	3.7		3.4	4.3
% Profit Before Taxes/Total Assets	30.2	18.5	15.5	18.5	24.8		12.4	13.6
	6.8	8.8	6.4	10.3	7.2		3.9	5.4
	-1.2	1.2	1.7	3.0	1.7		.7	1.1
Sales/Net Fixed Assets	746.0	172.5	139.2	118.5	57.1		100.8	103.6
	80.8	44.1	56.1	54.0	24.6		36.7	43.8
	16.9	16.5	25.1	21.5	10.9		15.4	17.5
Sales/Total Assets	5.6	4.6	3.8	3.1	3.4		3.8	3.9
	3.8	3.4	2.8	2.4	2.1		2.7	2.9
	2.7	2.2	2.0	1.6	1.0		2.1	2.0
% Depr., Dep., Amort./Sales	.6	.3	.3	.2	.5		.3	.4
	(33) 1.1	(132) .7	(183) .6	(78) .5	(12) 1.1		(320) .8	(398) .8
	2.7	1.6	1.1	1.0	2.0		1.6	1.6
% Officers', Directors' Owners' Comp/Sales	3.5	2.1	1.3	.6			2.1	1.8
	(33) 6.0	(93) 3.6	(114) 2.9	(22) 1.9			(191) 3.8	(235) 3.6
	8.8	6.5	5.5	4.7			6.9	6.8
Net Sales ($)	77181M	723497M	3173854M	4909680M	2249236M	1688825M	8031202M	8572306M
Total Assets ($)	16013M	203166M	1034597M	1800932M	928938M	698372M	3333586M	3850170M

© RMA 2007

M = $ thousand   MM = $ million
See Pages 11 through 21 for Explanation of Ratios and Data

Comparative Historical Data | Current Data Sorted by Sales

			Type of Statement						
37	43	49	Unqualified			1	5	7	36
102	92	107	Reviewed		7	11	28	39	22
109	106	114	Compiled	5	26	17	36	18	12
105	119	129	Tax Returns	19	43	18	33	14	2
137	168	187	Other	9	27	26	30	45	50
4/1/04-3/31/05 ALL	4/1/05-3/31/06 ALL	4/1/06-3/31/07 ALL		93 (4/1-9/30/06)			493 (10/1/06-3/31/07)		
				0-1MM	1-3MM	3-5MM	5-10MM	10-25MM	25MM & OVER
490	528	586	NUMBER OF STATEMENTS	33	103	73	132	123	122
%	%	%	ASSETS	%	%	%	%	%	%
8.6	8.8	8.3	Cash & Equivalents	19.2	10.3	6.8	9.6	6.0	5.4
32.8	32.7	32.9	Trade Receivables (net)	25.8	25.4	37.8	32.6	35.1	36.1
35.0	35.6	35.8	Inventory	30.1	35.3	30.2	36.2	38.4	38.0
2.1	2.1	2.7	All Other Current	.7	3.1	3.1	3.0	2.2	2.7
78.6	79.3	79.6	Total Current	75.8	74.2	77.9	81.4	81.8	82.3
11.8	11.7	12.2	Fixed Assets (net)	13.9	17.4	12.7	10.4	10.0	11.1
3.4	3.4	2.7	Intangibles (net)	3.5	3.2	3.1	2.2	2.5	2.8
6.1	5.6	5.4	All Other Non-Current	6.9	5.3	6.3	6.0	5.7	3.8
100.0	100.0	100.0	Total	100.0	100.0	100.0	100.0	100.0	100.0
			LIABILITIES						
16.3	16.2	17.4	Notes Payable-Short Term	31.4	18.7	13.2	15.8	16.0	18.2
2.9	2.4	2.9	Cur. Mat.-L.T.D.	3.5	4.4	3.0	2.5	2.2	2.8
22.8	25.4	22.4	Trade Payables	17.5	20.7	23.7	22.4	23.6	23.5
.2	.2	.2	Income Taxes Payable	.0	.2	.5	.2	.2	.3
9.8	10.3	9.9	All Other Current	16.5	8.9	10.4	9.1	10.3	9.3
51.9	54.5	52.9	Total Current	68.8	52.9	50.8	49.9	52.3	54.0
11.7	9.5	11.1	Long-Term Debt	29.7	14.7	12.3	7.7	7.3	9.7
.2	.1	.2	Deferred Taxes	.0	.0	.1	.2	.2	.3
5.2	5.5	6.0	All Other Non-Current	11.9	8.4	5.2	6.5	4.7	3.6
31.0	30.4	29.8	Net Worth	-10.4	24.0	31.7	35.7	35.5	32.3
100.0	100.0	100.0	Total Liabilties & Net Worth	100.0	100.0	100.0	100.0	100.0	100.0
			INCOME DATA						
100.0	100.0	100.0	Net Sales	100.0	100.0	100.0	100.0	100.0	100.0
30.5	31.0	31.2	Gross Profit	45.3	35.2	35.4	30.9	27.4	25.6
27.2	26.8	26.4	Operating Expenses	38.5	32.1	30.5	25.3	23.1	20.1
3.4	4.2	4.8	Operating Profit	6.9	3.1	4.8	5.6	4.3	5.4
.6	.7	.8	All Other Expenses (net)	2.8	.6	.7	.9	.5	.8
2.7	3.6	4.0	Profit Before Taxes	4.1	2.5	4.2	4.8	3.8	4.6
			RATIOS						
2.5	2.3	2.6		4.3	3.5	2.6	2.8	2.5	2.0
1.6	1.5	1.5	Current	1.5	1.5	1.5	1.6	1.6	1.5
1.2	1.1	1.1		.8	1.0	1.1	1.2	1.1	1.2
1.3	1.3	1.4		3.3	1.7	1.6	1.5	1.3	1.2
(489) .8	.8	(585) .8	Quick	(32) 1.0	.6	1.0	.8	.8	.7
.5	.5	.5		.3	.3	.5	.5	.5	.5
26 14.1	24 15.3	24 15.4		0 UND	15 23.9	24 15.5	22 16.9	32 11.5	30 12.2
40 9.2	40 9.1	37 9.8	Sales/Receivables	34 10.6	32 11.5	40 9.2	36 10.1	39 9.2	41 8.9
54 6.8	54 6.7	53 6.8		66 5.6	43 8.5	59 6.2	53 6.9	55 6.6	54 6.8
27 13.4	30 12.3	25 14.5		0 UND	20 18.3	13 28.1	27 13.3	31 11.6	36 10.3
58 6.3	59 6.2	58 6.3	Cost of Sales/Inventory	64 5.7	64 5.7	43 8.4	54 6.8	64 5.7	63 5.8
110 3.3	107 3.4	115 3.2		150 2.4	131 2.8	97 3.8	113 3.2	105 3.5	112 3.2
17 21.5	18 20.3	15 24.0		0 UND	9 38.9	15 24.5	17 21.8	16 22.1	17 22.0
33 11.0	37 9.9	31 11.8	Cost of Sales/Payables	25 14.5	31 11.7	33 11.1	29 12.6	33 11.0	31 11.8
55 6.7	59 6.2	54 6.8		64 5.7	59 6.2	72 5.0	52 7.0	51 7.2	50 7.3
5.7	5.9	5.7		3.9	5.6	6.7	5.3	5.6	6.6
10.9	12.0	10.5	Sales/Working Capital	9.7	11.8	10.1	10.6	10.5	10.3
31.3	45.8	46.2		-24.5	-451.0	36.1	33.7	48.6	23.6
12.9	13.5	11.3		4.5	8.8	12.8	15.5	9.5	12.2
(440) 4.0	(467) 4.4	(525) 3.8	EBIT/Interest	(26) 1.7	(90) 2.6	(64) 4.8	(122) 4.3	(108) 3.8	(115) 4.4
1.6	1.6	1.5		.4	1.1	1.8	1.4	1.7	2.3
5.8	7.9	7.4					2.9	6.7	12.7
(76) 2.1	(66) 2.3	(84) 2.2	Net Profit + Depr., Dep., Amort./Cur. Mat. L/T/D			(21) 1.5	(24) 3.3	(25) 4.9	
.6	.6	.9					.5	1.3	1.2
.1	.1	.1		.0	.0	.0	.0	.1	.1
.3	.2	.2	Fixed/Worth	.4	.5	.2	.2	.2	.2
.9	1.0	1.1		-.6	3.5	1.6	.5	.8	.7
.9	1.1	1.0		1.4	.9	1.1	.8	.8	1.2
2.3	2.4	2.4	Debt/Worth	23.3	4.2	2.7	2.1	2.0	2.1
6.5	8.8	8.2		-2.7	22.7	9.6	5.9	6.9	4.6
55.1	65.2	64.8		97.2	68.6	73.3	59.1	63.8	57.9
(430) 21.6	(456) 28.8	(505) 31.4	% Profit Before Taxes/Tangible Net Worth	(18) 54.9	(81) 25.2	(62) 37.1	(122) 30.0	(111) 26.8	(111) 35.4
5.2	7.8	8.1		-3.5	3.4	11.6	5.5	7.0	14.2
15.0	17.6	18.2		20.9	13.7	22.0	21.2	15.9	20.7
6.0	7.2	8.0	% Profit Before Taxes/Total Assets	1.6	6.0	9.8	7.3	5.5	9.5
1.1	1.7	1.5		-5.2	.5	1.5	1.1	2.1	3.7
140.8	170.6	153.4		UND	152.5	260.3	222.4	115.0	124.6
49.7	56.3	52.8	Sales/Net Fixed Assets	61.6	29.1	56.1	59.4	53.0	59.2
21.6	21.2	19.6		12.1	10.9	16.9	24.9	29.8	21.8
4.2	4.1	4.1		3.7	4.2	4.2	4.4	3.9	4.0
3.0	3.1	3.0	Sales/Total Assets	2.6	2.7	3.1	3.1	3.0	3.0
2.0	2.1	2.1		1.8	1.9	2.0	2.2	2.1	2.3
.3	.3	.3		1.0	.5	.3	.3	.2	.2
(376) .7	(395) .6	(443) .6	% Depr., Dep., Amort./Sales	(17) 1.8	(74) .9	(52) .6	(97) .6	(97) .5	(106) .5
1.4	1.2	1.3		4.7	2.5	1.5	1.2	1.0	1.0
1.9	1.7	1.6		3.0	3.2	1.8	1.7	1.2	.8
(229) 3.8	(262) 3.6	(264) 3.4	% Officers', Directors' Owners' Comp/Sales	(13) 6.3	(58) 5.4	(32) 3.4	(74) 3.4	(56) 2.3	(31) 1.7
7.3	7.1	6.3		11.2	8.0	7.0	5.7	4.9	5.5
10810106M	9564263M	12822273M	Net Sales ($)	19774M	205779M	281272M	966527M	1878891M	9470030M
4028691M	3775717M	4682018M	Total Assets ($)	10165M	83135M	116606M	372268M	748278M	3351566M

© RMA 2007

M = $ thousand   MM = $ million
See Pages 11 through 21 for Explanation of Ratios and Data

	Current Data Sorted by Assets						Comparative Historical Data	
Type of Statement								
Unqualified		2	3	13	3	7	22	27
Reviewed	1	1	15	4			20	35
Compiled	3	8	7	2			16	23
Tax Returns	5	2	4				7	16
Other	8	8	16	9	1	4	29	32
		27 (4/1-9/30/06)		99 (10/1/06-3/31/07)			4/1/02-3/31/03	4/1/03-3/31/04
	0-500M	500M-2MM	2-10MM	10-50MM	50-100MM	100-250MM	ALL	ALL
NUMBER OF STATEMENTS	17	21	45	28	4	11	94	133
ASSETS	%	%	%	%	%	%	%	%
Cash & Equivalents	8.6	7.8	4.0	1.7		3.5	7.4	7.6
Trade Receivables (net)	26.5	36.3	46.0	41.5		34.8	43.1	39.8
Inventory	7.5	37.6	24.3	29.7		25.0	25.1	24.3
All Other Current	5.9	3.2	1.4	1.6		3.4	3.1	3.5
Total Current	48.5	84.9	75.7	74.4		66.7	78.7	75.2
Fixed Assets (net)	19.3	8.3	16.9	13.8		15.5	13.0	16.1
Intangibles (net)	6.7	.1	1.8	2.2		6.1	4.2	3.2
All Other Non-Current	25.4	6.7	5.6	9.6		11.7	4.1	5.4
Total	100.0	100.0	100.0	100.0		100.0	100.0	100.0
LIABILITIES								
Notes Payable-Short Term	17.6	15.1	19.5	22.0		22.5	18.9	17.2
Cur. Mat.-L.T.D.	2.8	4.7	3.0	3.2		1.9	3.9	3.4
Trade Payables	20.2	33.1	22.6	24.8		28.5	25.2	22.9
Income Taxes Payable	.0	.0	.1	.2		.0	.1	.3
All Other Current	10.1	13.1	7.1	6.7		7.0	6.6	7.6
Total Current	50.7	66.0	52.3	56.9		60.0	54.7	51.3
Long-Term Debt	21.2	11.6	9.8	14.7		22.6	12.3	11.4
Deferred Taxes	.0	.0	.4	.1		.0	.1	.1
All Other Non-Current	8.1	4.4	2.4	5.3		5.6	8.6	6.6
Net Worth	20.0	18.0	35.1	23.1		11.8	24.3	30.5
Total Liabilities & Net Worth	100.0	100.0	100.0	100.0		100.0	100.0	100.0
INCOME DATA								
Net Sales	100.0	100.0	100.0	100.0		100.0	100.0	100.0
Gross Profit	38.6	27.8	21.2	15.9		22.4	24.5	25.3
Operating Expenses	34.9	27.4	18.6	14.1		18.6	21.7	23.0
Operating Profit	3.8	.4	2.7	1.8		3.8	2.8	2.3
All Other Expenses (net)	-.3	-.3	.6	.9		2.1	.7	.7
Profit Before Taxes	4.1	.6	2.1	.9		1.7	2.1	1.6
RATIOS								
Current	4.4	2.0	2.1	1.8		2.2	2.0	2.1
	.7	1.3	1.4	1.2		1.3	1.4	1.4
	.4	1.1	1.1	1.0		1.0	1.1	1.2
Quick	3.4	1.1	1.3	1.0		1.2	1.4	1.3
	.6	.6	.9	.7		.8	.9	(132) .9
	.3	.5	.7	.6		.1	.6	.6
Sales/Receivables	**8** 46.1	**26** 14.2	**34** 10.8	**36** 10.2		**2** 240.0	**34** 10.8	**32** 11.5
	17 21.5	**37** 9.9	**45** 8.1	**39** 9.3		**36** 10.1	**42** 8.7	**41** 8.9
	36 10.2	**43** 8.4	**56** 6.5	**49** 7.5		**50** 7.3	**53** 6.9	**50** 7.4
Cost of Sales/Inventory	**0** UND	**21** 17.4	**12** 30.2	**25** 14.7		**16** 22.2	**9** 39.6	**10** 36.7
	5 77.0	**44** 8.3	**32** 11.2	**38** 9.6		**26** 13.9	**29** 12.7	**32** 11.4
	9 42.5	**87** 4.2	**45** 8.1	**57** 6.4		**47** 7.7	**58** 6.3	**60** 6.1
Cost of Sales/Payables	**0** UND	**18** 19.9	**17** 21.7	**17** 21.2		**29** 12.8	**20** 18.6	**17** 21.4
	11 31.8	**33** 11.1	**24** 15.5	**28** 13.0		**33** 11.0	**32** 11.6	**27** 13.5
	53 6.9	**63** 5.8	**38** 9.5	**43** 8.4		**48** 7.7	**44** 8.2	**44** 8.2
Sales/Working Capital	9.2	5.9	9.1	11.0		8.1	8.2	8.6
	-98.9	25.4	18.9	22.4		23.4	18.0	15.7
	-8.8	70.3	65.0	NM		-403.5	63.8	41.9
EBIT/Interest	14.9	9.3	5.4	3.8		30.9	5.0	7.2
	(14) 4.0	(20) 3.4	(42) 2.2	(27) 2.3		2.0	(85) 2.4	(117) 2.4
	1.5	1.3	1.1	1.2		1.1	1.4	1.0
Net Profit + Depr., Dep., Amort./Cur. Mat. L/T/D							6.0	7.0
							(27) 1.8	(27) 1.8
							.5	.4
Fixed/Worth	.0	.0	.1	.1		.1	.1	.1
	.5	.5	.4	.2		.6	.4	.4
	NM	UND	.9	2.3		-.2	1.6	1.2
Debt/Worth	.4	1.2	1.2	1.9		.7	1.4	1.0
	2.1	4.3	2.2	3.6		3.4	3.6	2.6
	-3.7	UND	8.1	10.2		-5.9	16.9	10.0
% Profit Before Taxes/Tangible Net Worth	115.0	84.5	30.9	28.3			60.7	38.1
	(12) 60.1	(17) 35.8	(43) 16.1	(24) 17.0			(80) 12.7	(117) 10.4
	9.7	21.5	1.7	8.4			2.9	.7
% Profit Before Taxes/Total Assets	35.5	14.5	9.7	5.1		8.4	11.5	9.7
	13.3	5.5	3.4	3.6		2.8	3.0	2.8
	3.3	1.1	.4	.4		.5	.7	.1
Sales/Net Fixed Assets	UND	100.0	258.6	200.2		340.1	208.4	219.1
	46.9	71.2	46.8	56.5		102.3	48.9	40.7
	11.1	32.4	10.6	21.0		12.6	16.9	11.3
Sales/Total Assets	8.4	5.2	4.7	4.2		4.4	4.9	4.9
	4.2	3.5	3.9	3.3		3.6	3.7	3.5
	2.4	2.6	2.6	2.5		2.7	2.3	2.4
% Depr., Dep., Amort./Sales		.3	.1	.2			.2	.2
		(13) .5	(39) .4	(24) .4			(79) .5	(100) .6
		1.1	3.1	1.0			1.1	1.6
% Officers', Directors' Owners' Comp/Sales	2.8		.6				1.2	1.8
	(10) 4.8		(17) 2.3				(33) 2.9	(54) 2.8
	9.4		3.4				4.3	5.3
Net Sales ($)	**23586M**	**141104M**	**838617M**	**2444847M**	**954828M**	**6389862M**	**5845889M**	**7168953M**
Total Assets ($)	**4616M**	**30870M**	**214560M**	**632973M**	**320176M**	**1776551M**	**1733911M**	**1758740M**

M = $ thousand MM = $ million

See Pages 11 through 21 for Explanation of Ratios and Data

Comparative Historical Data / Current Data Sorted by Sales

			Type of Statement	0-1MM	1-3MM	3-5MM	5-10MM	10-25MM	25MM & OVER
23	23	28	Unqualified		1		1	3	23
26	22	21	Reviewed	1			1	8	11
21	16	20	Compiled	2		3	6	7	2
8	8	11	Tax Returns	3	3	2	2	1	
43	39	46	Other	5	7	2	5	11	16
4/1/04-3/31/05 ALL	4/1/05-3/31/06 ALL	4/1/06-3/31/07 ALL			27 (4/1-9/30/06)		99 (10/1/06-3/31/07)		
121	108	126	NUMBER OF STATEMENTS	11	11	7	15	30	52
%	%	%	**ASSETS**	%	%	%	%	%	%
5.1	4.8	4.6	Cash & Equivalents	10.0	3.4		4.7	2.4	3.0
42.3	43.0	39.6	Trade Receivables (net)	20.9	32.0		33.4	46.4	42.3
25.2	25.5	25.7	Inventory	9.9	15.8		26.6	32.1	27.7
2.5	1.8	2.7	All Other Current	8.6	5.8		.5	1.0	2.2
75.1	75.0	72.4	Total Current	49.5	57.0		65.3	81.9	75.2
13.8	13.8	14.6	Fixed Assets (net)	25.8	15.7		20.0	14.0	12.0
4.2	5.2	3.1	Intangibles (net)	9.4	3.1		2.4	.8	3.8
6.9	5.9	9.8	All Other Non-Current	15.4	24.2		12.3	3.3	9.1
100.0	100.0	100.0	Total	100.0	100.0		100.0	100.0	100.0
			LIABILITIES						
18.0	19.6	19.5	Notes Payable-Short Term	14.6	15.2		16.0	18.9	23.5
2.4	3.1	3.2	Cur. Mat.-L.T.D.	2.2	2.5		7.4	2.2	2.9
23.3	25.9	25.1	Trade Payables	17.7	25.8		15.6	30.3	26.2
.2	.1	.1	Income Taxes Payable	.1	.0		.3	.1	.1
11.6	9.3	8.3	All Other Current	11.1	8.1		11.0	10.3	6.4
55.6	58.1	56.1	Total Current	45.6	51.6		50.3	61.7	59.1
12.0	12.6	14.0	Long-Term Debt	29.4	17.3		17.6	10.1	12.0
.1	.4	.2	Deferred Taxes	.0	.0		.4	.3	.2
4.1	5.2	4.7	All Other Non-Current	2.3	13.6		.5	3.9	5.0
28.2	23.8	25.0	Net Worth	22.7	17.5		31.2	23.9	23.6
100.0	100.0	100.0	Total Liabilties & Net Worth	100.0	100.0		100.0	100.0	100.0
			INCOME DATA						
100.0	100.0	100.0	Net Sales	100.0	100.0		100.0	100.0	100.0
23.7	23.5	23.5	Gross Profit	48.9	27.1		34.2	18.8	16.5
20.3	20.9	21.2	Operating Expenses	45.9	27.6		32.7	16.7	14.2
3.3	2.7	2.3	Operating Profit	3.1	-.5		1.5	2.1	2.3
.6	.5	.5	All Other Expenses (net)	-2.0	.5		.8	.7	.9
2.8	2.1	1.8	Profit Before Taxes	5.1	-1.1		.7	1.4	1.4
			RATIOS						
2.1	1.9	2.0		5.5	3.2		2.2	1.7	1.9
1.5	1.3	1.3	Current	1.4	1.0		1.1	1.4	1.3
1.1	1.1	1.0		.5	.6		1.0	1.1	1.1
1.3	1.3	1.1		4.6	1.3		1.3	1.2	1.0
.9	.8	.7	Quick	.6	.6		.6	.8	.8
.6	.6	.6		.4	.5		.5	.7	.6
32 11.6	30 12.2	30 12.1		15 24.9	17 21.6		30 12.1	30 12.0	33 11.0
42 8.6	41 8.9	39 9.3	Sales/Receivables	26 14.1	34 10.7		43 8.6	40 9.2	39 9.3
51 7.1	49 7.4	49 7.5		59 6.1	44 8.3		48 7.6	58 6.3	49 7.5
12 30.5	12 29.5	13 28.4		0 UND	0 UND		16 22.2	19 19.3	22 16.8
28 12.9	29 12.8	32 11.4	Cost of Sales/Inventory	8 43.5	8 47.1		42 8.6	36 10.2	33 11.2
56 6.5	51 7.2	52 7.1		44 8.2	56 6.5		60 6.1	52 7.0	44 8.2
18 20.2	19 19.4	17 22.1		0 UND	8 46.0		11 33.0	20 18.0	17 21.1
27 13.7	28 13.0	26 13.9	Cost of Sales/Payables	13 29.1	23 16.1		21 17.6	30 12.3	28 12.9
39 9.4	40 9.0	44 8.2		122 3.0	57 6.4		51 7.2	42 8.6	40 9.2
8.9	9.1	9.2		4.2	4.9		8.1	10.4	10.3
17.7	20.9	23.2	Sales/Working Capital	14.0	-127.8		40.3	22.1	22.8
76.7	87.7	-999.8		-9.3	-8.2		-999.8	76.7	88.3
8.1	10.5	5.7			10.3		8.8	6.1	3.9
(105) 3.3	(103) 3.5	(118) 2.3	EBIT/Interest		(10) 1.2		(14) 1.8	(29) 2.8	(49) 2.2
1.4	1.5	1.1			-2.0		.2	1.2	1.2
5.2	10.5	3.5	Net Profit + Depr., Dep.,						
(23) 2.3	(19) 2.5	(20) 1.2	Amort./Cur. Mat. L/T/D						
.6	1.3	.4							
.1	.0	.1		.1	.0		.1	.1	.1
.3	.3	.4	Fixed/Worth	1.2	.6		.8	.4	.3
1.0	1.3	2.0		-.5	-1.0		21.2	1.1	1.1
1.2	1.3	1.3		.2	.4		.9	1.6	1.6
2.6	3.2	3.0	Debt/Worth	2.1	11.8		4.3	3.0	3.3
8.3	10.0	12.1		-2.0	-4.0		310.2	9.5	10.2
42.6	53.7	38.2	% Profit Before Taxes/Tangible				83.3	30.6	30.3
(105) 13.0	(93) 20.1	(106) 19.2	Net Worth				(13) 8.7	(28) 16.4	(43) 19.2
4.3	3.7	5.5					-6.2	4.6	10.4
10.4	13.1	11.3	% Profit Before Taxes/Total	17.4	20.2		7.2	10.9	7.3
3.6	4.3	3.9	Assets	6.5	3.1		2.0	3.6	3.7
.7	1.2	.6		.6	-8.7		-3.1	.7	.6
254.0	286.7	210.4		46.9	106.9		71.2	312.1	221.7
57.4	63.9	56.1	Sales/Net Fixed Assets	11.2	49.6		31.4	81.9	54.3
16.7	21.8	15.8		8.1	8.0		6.2	21.7	27.8
4.8	5.0	4.7		4.0	7.8		3.8	5.4	4.7
3.7	4.0	3.6	Sales/Total Assets	2.5	2.5		3.1	4.1	3.8
2.5	2.7	2.6		.6	1.1		2.6	3.1	3.0
.1	.2	.2					.5	.1	.1
(93) .5	(81) .4	(93) .4	% Depr., Dep., Amort./Sales				(11) 1.5	(24) .2	(42) .3
1.5	1.3	1.4					3.9	1.0	.7
1.3	.9	.8	% Officers', Directors'						.7
(40) 2.5	(38) 3.2	(40) 2.3	Owners' Comp/Sales					(11)	2.3
4.5	6.9	4.2							2.7
7903024M	8624322M	10792844M	Net Sales ($)	6206M	22911M	29415M	106072M	483944M	10144296M
2305467M	2133792M	2979746M	Total Assets ($)	3879M	11217M	9010M	35332M	134354M	2785954M

M = $ thousand   MM = $ million
See Pages 11 through 21 for Explanation of Ratios and Data

Current Data Sorted by Assets

Comparative Historical Data

								Type of Statement		
1			2	5			2	Unqualified	15	19
	9		27	4				Reviewed	46	36
3	11		12					Compiled	26	34
7	6		3					Tax Returns	16	19
4	9		10	11	2		4	Other	36	29
	21 (4/1-9/30/06)			111 (10/1/06-3/31/07)					4/1/02-3/31/03	4/1/03-3/31/04
0-500M	500M-2MM		2-10MM	10-50MM	50-100MM		100-250MM		ALL	ALL
15	35		54	20	2		6	NUMBER OF STATEMENTS	139	137
%	%		%	%	%		%	ASSETS	%	%
10.7	5.3		5.6	7.4				Cash & Equivalents	7.6	7.3
44.2	48.3		41.6	31.2				Trade Receivables (net)	40.5	39.7
19.4	25.3		30.6	32.0				Inventory	27.8	26.3
1.0	.7		1.9	3.5				All Other Current	1.7	2.1
75.3	79.6		79.7	74.1				Total Current	77.6	75.4
12.6	11.8		10.8	16.0				Fixed Assets (net)	14.4	14.3
4.6	5.2		3.4	6.7				Intangibles (net)	2.9	3.8
7.6	3.3		6.1	3.1				All Other Non-Current	5.1	6.6
100.0	100.0		100.0	100.0				Total	100.0	100.0
								LIABILITIES		
18.4	17.1		17.4	10.9				Notes Payable-Short Term	14.5	18.2
2.7	3.5		1.7	2.9				Cur. Mat.-L.T.D.	3.1	3.2
34.7	29.2		26.5	15.1				Trade Payables	25.6	23.6
.0	.8		.2	.1				Income Taxes Payable	.4	.1
13.3	8.9		8.1	14.2				All Other Current	10.3	11.4
69.1	59.5		53.9	43.2				Total Current	53.8	56.6
16.4	11.6		7.5	16.6				Long-Term Debt	10.4	9.4
.0	.2		.1	.9				Deferred Taxes	.1	.2
.8	4.1		4.4	18.7				All Other Non-Current	6.3	5.6
13.7	24.6		34.1	20.6				Net Worth	29.4	28.3
100.0	100.0		100.0	100.0				Total Liabilties & Net Worth	100.0	100.0
								INCOME DATA		
100.0	100.0		100.0	100.0				Net Sales	100.0	100.0
31.8	31.8		33.1	34.0				Gross Profit	31.0	33.0
27.0	29.6		29.5	28.5				Operating Expenses	28.7	30.9
4.7	2.3		3.5	5.4				Operating Profit	2.2	2.1
.8	.8		.7	1.9				All Other Expenses (net)	.4	.6
3.9	1.5		2.8	3.5				Profit Before Taxes	1.8	1.5
								RATIOS		
2.6	1.7		1.9	2.7					2.1	2.1
1.0	1.4		1.4	1.7				Current	1.6	1.4
.6	1.0		1.2	1.3					1.1	1.1
2.1	1.2		1.4	1.5					1.3	1.3
.8	.9		.9	.9				Quick	.9	.9
.5	.5		.6	.5					.6	.6

23	16.1	29	12.4	32	11.4	31	11.9					Sales/Receivables	30	12.0	30	12.1
28	12.8	38	9.5	41	9.0	39	9.3						39	9.3	39	9.4
35	10.5	57	6.4	51	7.2	50	7.3						50	7.3	48	7.6
1	348.0	10	36.3	19	19.1	36	10.1					Cost of Sales/Inventory	17	22.0	14	26.7
10	35.6	26	13.8	46	8.0	50	7.3						35	10.4	36	10.0
24	15.4	56	6.5	80	4.6	100	3.7						75	4.9	89	4.1
10	38.1	17	21.1	21	17.1	17	21.1					Cost of Sales/Payables	20	18.0	19	19.4
26	14.0	31	11.8	32	11.6	24	15.2						32	11.5	31	11.7
45	8.2	49	7.5	46	7.9	41	8.9						48	7.6	46	7.9
	14.4		11.4		7.5		6.3					Sales/Working Capital		7.4		7.3
	999.8		20.4		15.6		11.8							13.4		16.5
	-14.3		382.6		26.7		17.2							65.0		47.2
	9.2		7.4		5.8		6.0					EBIT/Interest		8.1		8.0
(10)	3.9	(30)	1.9	(49)	3.1	(18)	2.9						(126)	2.6	(130)	2.7
	.4		-.4		1.1		1.3							1.1		.9
					12.4							Net Profit + Depr., Dep.,		4.5		5.6
		(20)	3.4									Amort./Cur. Mat. L/T/D	(29)	1.9	(29)	2.2
			.7											1.0		.7
	.0		.1		.1		.1					Fixed/Worth		.1		.2
	1.6		.3		.4		.6							.4		.3
	-1.5		4.5		.6		1.1							1.8		1.5
	.6		1.6		1.2		1.5					Debt/Worth		1.0		.8
	23.5		2.4		2.6		2.1							2.4		2.0
	-7.9		13.7		4.7		3.0							10.9		9.3
			47.5		34.5		28.2					% Profit Before Taxes/Tangible		41.0		35.1
		(28)	22.8	(49)	20.7	(17)	17.8					Net Worth	(117)	13.9	(111)	13.1
			-3.1		4.9		5.8							1.1		.0
	46.9		12.5		10.5		12.4					% Profit Before Taxes/Total		11.4		11.3
	10.2		4.8		5.4		5.8					Assets		3.6		3.4
	-2.7		-2.5		.6		2.0							.2		-.9
	375.1		333.0		103.4		82.4					Sales/Net Fixed Assets		95.8		98.4
	68.3		104.6		49.0		16.0							40.9		40.4
	30.1		39.8		24.5		10.6							14.0		17.5
	7.9		5.6		4.7		3.9					Sales/Total Assets		4.7		5.1
	6.3		4.2		3.7		2.8							3.6		3.8
	3.8		3.1		2.7		1.9							2.5		2.2
			.2		.4		.7					% Depr., Dep., Amort./Sales		.4		.4
		(26)	.6	(45)	.6	(19)	.9						(119)	.7	(111)	.9
			1.4		1.3		1.9							1.5		1.7
	2.9		2.8		1.0							% Officers', Directors'		1.7		1.7
(10)	6.4	(20)	3.9	(25)	2.6							Owners' Comp/Sales	(57)	2.7	(66)	3.9
	9.1		7.1		6.0									4.7		7.9
28099M	197553M		849997M	1308852M	561826M		2768033M	Net Sales ($)	2738593M	3510132M
4300M	44828M		240361M	436687M	111419M		840346M	Total Assets ($)	980509M	1274490M

M = $ thousand   MM = $ million

See Pages 11 through 21 for Explanation of Ratios and Data

Comparative Historical Data | Current Data Sorted by Sales

4/1/04-3/31/05 ALL	4/1/05-3/31/06 ALL	4/1/06-3/31/07 ALL	Type of Statement	0-1MM	1-3MM	3-5MM	5-10MM	10-25MM	25MM & OVER
18	15	10	Unqualified	1			1	1	7
34	31	40	Reviewed			2	11	20	7
24	20	26	Compiled		5	4	5	9	3
7	15	16	Tax Returns	3	5	2	5	1	
36	48	40	Other	1	4	5	5	9	16
					21 (4/1-9/30/06)		111 (10/1/06-3/31/07)		
119	129	132	NUMBER OF STATEMENTS	5	14	13	27	40	33
%	%	%	**ASSETS**	%	%	%	%	%	%
6.3	7.3	6.2	Cash & Equivalents		3.7	13.7	5.7	6.8	4.4
39.7	37.2	42.2	Trade Receivables (net)		45.5	42.7	46.1	44.8	37.7
28.0	27.2	28.2	Inventory		24.4	21.9	28.2	29.1	31.3
2.8	2.5	2.0	All Other Current		.6	.6	1.3	1.3	4.5
76.7	74.3	78.5	Total Current		74.2	78.9	81.3	82.0	77.9
13.0	13.2	12.0	Fixed Assets (net)		10.3	11.5	10.0	9.1	14.0
4.0	6.9	4.7	Intangibles (net)		9.1	2.1	2.6	4.2	5.6
6.2	5.6	4.8	All Other Non-Current		6.4	7.6	6.1	4.6	2.5
100.0	100.0	100.0	Total		100.0	100.0	100.0	100.0	100.0
			LIABILITIES						
13.7	16.0	16.2	Notes Payable-Short Term		22.1	12.3	14.6	18.7	11.4
3.0	3.9	2.5	Cur. Mat.-L.T.D.		7.2	1.2	2.3	1.7	2.5
21.8	24.1	26.6	Trade Payables		38.9	26.1	28.4	27.8	21.7
.2	.1	.3	Income Taxes Payable		.0	.0	1.2	.2	.2
13.0	10.2	10.1	All Other Current		12.9	6.0	7.4	11.7	11.6
51.6	54.4	55.7	Total Current		81.1	45.7	53.9	60.1	47.4
13.0	12.1	11.2	Long-Term Debt		13.8	11.4	7.2	5.5	15.1
.2	.3	.3	Deferred Taxes		.4	.0	.1	.1	.7
5.2	7.5	6.1	All Other Non-Current		3.0	.8	4.2	5.3	13.1
29.9	25.7	26.6	Net Worth		1.7	42.1	34.6	29.0	23.6
100.0	100.0	100.0	Total Liabilties & Net Worth		100.0	100.0	100.0	100.0	100.0
			INCOME DATA						
100.0	100.0	100.0	Net Sales		100.0	100.0	100.0	100.0	100.0
34.1	32.7	31.6	Gross Profit		37.5	37.0	30.0	32.6	26.7
31.9	30.6	28.0	Operating Expenses		34.1	30.8	27.5	29.6	22.4
2.2	2.1	3.6	Operating Profit		3.4	6.2	2.5	3.0	4.4
.6	.8	.9	All Other Expenses (net)		1.4	.3	.3	.7	1.5
1.7	1.3	2.6	Profit Before Taxes		2.0	5.8	2.2	2.3	2.8
			RATIOS						
2.2	2.1	2.0	Current		1.3	2.7	2.0	1.7	2.6
1.6	1.5	1.4			.9	1.7	1.5	1.4	1.7
1.1	1.1	1.1			.8	1.2	1.3	1.2	1.2
1.4	1.3	1.3	Quick		.8	2.3	1.3	1.3	1.4
.9	.8	.9			.7	1.3	1.0	.8	.9
.7	.6	.6			.5	.6	.8	.6	.6
32 11.4	30 12.0	30 12.3	Sales/Receivables		34 10.9	14 26.6	32 11.5	31 11.7	32 11.6
41 8.9	40 9.2	38 9.6			37 10.0	31 11.9	38 9.7	44 8.4	38 9.7
50 7.3	53 6.8	51 7.2			51 7.1	54 6.7	48 7.6	53 6.9	50 7.2
16 23.5	16 23.5	15 24.9	Cost of Sales/Inventory		12 29.3	0 UND	11 32.4	18 20.1	28 13.1
38 9.6	38 9.5	33 11.2			24 15.2	11 32.4	29 12.7	35 10.3	45 8.0
90 4.1	100 3.7	76 4.8			76 4.8	93 3.9	62 5.9	68 5.3	88 4.1
20 17.9	22 17.0	19 19.3	Cost of Sales/Payables		33 11.2	12 31.3	23 15.5	19 19.1	17 20.9
31 11.9	33 11.1	30 12.1			47 7.8	26 14.0	31 11.8	30 12.3	26 14.2
42 8.7	51 7.2	46 8.0			89 4.1	52 7.1	43 8.5	45 8.1	45 8.2
7.1	7.5	8.9	Sales/Working Capital		32.3	8.1	7.9	13.6	6.4
12.8	17.0	16.9			-111.3	14.4	15.4	18.6	13.7
38.1	125.3	55.6			-17.2	54.4	23.9	30.6	36.7
7.7	4.9	6.2	EBIT/Interest		5.6	21.5	7.5	4.0	9.6
(106) 3.7	(115) 2.7	(115) 2.9			(12) 2.1	(11) 2.6	(23) 4.9	(35) 2.7	(31) 3.0
1.5	1.1	1.1			.5	1.6	1.1	.9	1.9
5.1	8.9	11.6	Net Profit + Depr., Dep., Amort./Cur. Mat. L/T/D					12.0	9.8
(27) 1.6	(35) 2.4	(34) 3.3						(15) 3.5	(14) 3.1
.8	.7	1.1						.3	1.1
.1	.1	.1	Fixed/Worth		1.0	.0	.0	.1	.2
.3	.4	.4			UND	.1	.2	.4	.6
1.0	2.1	1.5			-.2	2.8	.6	.6	1.2
1.1	1.1	1.4	Debt/Worth		16.5	.4	1.4	1.4	1.5
2.1	2.8	2.6			UND	2.0	2.1	3.0	2.5
7.3	11.1	7.2			-12.7	5.8	3.3	5.2	6.4
42.4	40.9	46.7	% Profit Before Taxes/Tangible Net Worth			53.8	47.5	32.2	47.0
(102) 16.6	(102) 12.3	(111) 21.5				(11) 32.4	(26) 21.0	(35) 20.0	(29) 22.5
4.2	3.8	6.0				18.2	2.2	2.5	10.0
11.2	9.7	12.8	% Profit Before Taxes/Total Assets		11.6	31.2	12.9	8.0	12.7
4.0	4.3	5.6			4.0	15.8	6.8	4.4	6.0
1.1	.8	.3			-2.3	3.3	.3	-.4	2.9
85.3	83.5	123.9	Sales/Net Fixed Assets		403.3	254.0	248.0	115.5	84.5
40.3	34.2	56.9			70.3	72.3	93.8	63.4	32.9
16.3	15.9	19.8			51.0	32.0	24.4	31.9	12.3
4.7	4.7	5.4	Sales/Total Assets		6.3	7.8	5.5	5.1	4.6
3.5	3.4	3.8			4.0	4.1	4.2	3.8	3.7
2.3	2.2	2.7			1.8	2.9	2.9	2.8	2.4
.4	.4	.4	% Depr., Dep., Amort./Sales				.2	.4	.6
(99) .8	(106) .8	(105) .7					(22) .6	(34) .6	(29) 1.0
1.4	1.4	1.3					1.5	1.0	1.8
1.7	1.5	1.4	% Officers', Directors' Owners' Comp/Sales			3.4	2.2	.8	
(58) 4.0	(59) 2.9	(59) 3.4				(10) 4.7	(17) 4.4	(17) 1.3	
6.6	6.3	6.7				7.9	7.4	3.2	
4035340M	4244765M	5714360M	Net Sales ($)	2677M	26899M	51264M	201412M	616234M	4815874M
1495261M	1527075M	1677941M	Total Assets ($)	1051M	9680M	14674M	58316M	180255M	1413965M

M = $ thousand   MM = $ million
See Pages 11 through 21 for Explanation of Ratios and Data

Current Data Sorted by Assets　　　　Comparative Historical Data

						Type of Statement		
		6	12	4	2	Unqualified	18	26
1	2	40	13	1	2	Reviewed	80	78
1	16	12	5	1		Compiled	54	59
3	9	4				Tax Returns	17	15
5	9	29	20	2	6	Other	50	49
	50 (4/1-9/30/06)		153 (10/1/06-3/31/07)				4/1/02-3/31/03 ALL	4/1/03-3/31/04 ALL
0-500M	500M-2MM	2-10MM	10-50MM	50-100MM	100-250MM	NUMBER OF STATEMENTS		
10	36	91	50	8	8		219	227
%	%	%	%	%	%	**ASSETS**	%	%
9.2	5.7	4.0	5.6			Cash & Equivalents	6.2	5.6
27.4	41.3	42.6	43.7			Trade Receivables (net)	40.8	39.3
37.3	32.9	30.1	28.1			Inventory	29.0	29.4
4.5	.6	2.4	2.7			All Other Current	2.7	2.4
78.4	80.5	79.0	80.1			Total Current	78.6	76.6
13.9	10.0	13.7	11.1			Fixed Assets (net)	13.8	15.3
3.0	2.8	2.6	3.3			Intangibles (net)	2.6	2.0
4.7	6.7	4.6	5.5			All Other Non-Current	5.0	6.1
100.0	100.0	100.0	100.0			Total	100.0	100.0
						LIABILITIES		
38.4	14.6	17.1	18.8			Notes Payable-Short Term	14.1	16.7
.5	2.0	2.7	1.3			Cur. Mat.-L.T.D.	2.9	2.7
21.7	37.8	26.6	25.8			Trade Payables	27.0	25.7
.4	.1	.5	.5			Income Taxes Payable	.2	.2
5.0	7.4	7.0	7.9			All Other Current	6.9	8.4
65.9	62.0	54.0	54.4			Total Current	51.0	53.7
11.4	7.7	8.8	9.7			Long-Term Debt	11.3	12.3
.0	.0	.1	.2			Deferred Taxes	.2	.2
2.8	9.0	3.6	2.8			All Other Non-Current	2.9	3.9
19.9	21.4	33.5	33.0			Net Worth	34.6	29.9
100.0	100.0	100.0	100.0			Total Liabilities & Net Worth	100.0	100.0
						INCOME DATA		
100.0	100.0	100.0	100.0			Net Sales	100.0	100.0
27.3	27.0	23.0	19.8			Gross Profit	23.3	24.9
24.6	24.1	19.9	17.2			Operating Expenses	21.7	22.8
2.7	2.9	3.1	2.6			Operating Profit	1.6	2.1
1.0	.7	.7	.3			All Other Expenses (net)	.3	.6
1.7	2.2	2.4	2.3			Profit Before Taxes	1.3	1.5
						RATIOS		
5.2	2.4	1.9	2.2			Current	2.3	2.2
1.1	1.2	1.4	1.4				1.6	1.5
.9	.9	1.2	1.1				1.1	1.1
1.6	1.5	1.2	1.4			Quick	1.4	1.2
.8	.8	.9	.9				.9	.8
.4	.5	.6	.7				.6	.6
0 UND	27 13.4	31 11.8	35 10.3			Sales/Receivables	30 12.3 / 29 12.5	
30 12.1	34 10.7	39 9.3	41 8.9				36 10.1 / 38 9.7	
38 9.6	41 8.8	51 7.1	47 7.8				45 8.1 / 46 8.0	
20 18.0	18 19.8	28 12.8	24 14.9			Cost of Sales/Inventory	22 16.4 / 24 15.2	
45 8.1	37 9.8	42 8.7	36 10.0				34 10.7 / 37 9.9	
97 3.8	56 6.5	56 6.5	47 7.8				52 7.0 / 56 6.6	
4 82.8	25 14.6	19 19.6	19 19.1			Cost of Sales/Payables	19 19.0 / 20 18.3	
16 23.5	39 9.4	30 12.2	28 13.1				27 13.4 / 27 13.4	
58 6.3	74 4.9	43 8.4	39 9.3				42 8.7 / 43 8.6	
4.4	9.8	8.1	8.9			Sales/Working Capital	8.5	9.1
57.0	24.5	14.2	16.6				14.1	15.5
-593.1	-39.4	31.0	51.9				36.3	57.6
	19.7	8.6	15.0			EBIT/Interest	10.4	8.6
	(32) 3.2	(88) 3.2	(48) 2.8				(198) 3.0 / (209) 3.2	
	1.2	1.3	1.6				1.4	1.3
		4.3	25.0			Net Profit + Depr., Dep., Amort./Cur. Mat. L/T/D	6.8	3.6
	(19) 2.2	(17) 3.3					(54) 2.2 / (61) 1.7	
	.7	2.1					1.0	.6
.1	.1	.1	.1			Fixed/Worth	.1	.1
.9	.4	.4	.3				.3	.3
NM	NM	.8	.9				1.1	1.0
.5	1.0	1.3	.8			Debt/Worth	.9	1.0
6.0	4.0	2.3	3.0				2.2	2.3
-23.2	NM	5.5	6.4				6.1	6.1
	110.1	38.0	32.7			% Profit Before Taxes/Tangible Net Worth	32.2	36.5
	(27) 26.9	(83) 17.6	(46) 21.1				(198) 11.3 / (204) 14.6	
	6.8	6.0	11.1				2.2	3.1
23.8	16.4	13.2	14.2			% Profit Before Taxes/Total Assets	8.3	9.3
3.4	4.0	5.8	4.8				3.5	4.3
-7.6	.8	1.2	1.8				.6	.7
480.8	222.6	160.8	119.4			Sales/Net Fixed Assets	140.4	117.5
73.5	77.8	50.5	56.8				54.6	48.4
19.7	47.3	15.7	25.5				17.9	14.2
6.8	6.1	4.6	4.5			Sales/Total Assets	4.9	4.9
3.7	4.3	3.7	3.8				3.9	3.8
2.7	3.4	2.8	3.2				3.0	3.0
	.1	.2	.2			% Depr., Dep., Amort./Sales	.3	.4
	(27) .4	(79) .5	(46) .4				(180) .7 / (198) .7	
	1.2	1.0	.7				1.3	1.3
	2.8	1.2	.6			% Officers', Directors' Owners' Comp/Sales	1.3	1.4
	(18) 4.1	(46) 2.2	(13) 1.2				(100) 2.3 / (103) 2.8	
	6.8	4.5	3.8				5.2	5.5
16786M	198379M	1628885M	4201724M	1915489M	4443096M	Net Sales ($)	6844926M	6172435M
3282M	43533M	433901M	1118968M	497590M	960029M	Total Assets ($)	1786517M	1754045M

M = $ thousand　　MM = $ million
See Pages 11 through 21 for Explanation of Ratios and Data

Comparative Historical Data / Current Data Sorted by Sales

			Type of Statement	0-1MM	1-3MM	3-5MM	5-10MM	10-25MM	25MM & OVER
23	35	24	Unqualified	1			1	3	20
70	73	57	Reviewed		5	5	12	20	24
32	32	35	Compiled		5		8	11	6
20	21	16	Tax Returns	1	5	1	6	3	
53	56	71	Other	3		4	11	12	37
4/1/04-3/31/05 ALL	4/1/05-3/31/06 ALL	4/1/06-3/31/07 ALL			50 (4/1-9/30/06)		153 (10/1/06-3/31/07)		
198	217	203	NUMBER OF STATEMENTS	5	14	10	38	49	87
%	%	%	ASSETS	%	%	%	%	%	%
5.0	4.5	4.9	Cash & Equivalents	4.1	4.7	5.3	3.9		5.2
42.1	42.3	41.8	Trade Receivables (net)	33.8	43.2	34.9	44.8		45.3
30.4	31.5	30.2	Inventory	29.1	38.7	35.8	29.6		26.9
2.1	1.9	2.4	All Other Current	.8	.3	2.1	2.4		2.7
79.6	80.2	79.3	Total Current	67.8	87.0	78.0	80.7		80.1
12.7	12.7	12.4	Fixed Assets (net)	18.7	7.4	13.1	13.4		10.9
1.8	2.4	3.0	Intangibles (net)	3.6	1.2	3.5	2.5		3.1
5.9	4.7	5.3	All Other Non-Current	9.9	4.4	5.3	3.4		5.9
100.0	100.0	100.0	Total	100.0	100.0	100.0	100.0		100.0
			LIABILITIES						
17.5	16.1	17.9	Notes Payable-Short Term	17.6	15.6	17.6	17.7		18.3
3.2	2.3	2.1	Cur. Mat.-L.T.D.	6.1	.9	1.8	2.6		1.4
28.3	27.5	28.3	Trade Payables	26.7	44.2	28.0	27.1		27.4
.2	.2	.4	Income Taxes Payable	.1	.2	.8	.4		.3
6.9	7.8	7.4	All Other Current	3.1	14.3	6.2	6.8		8.2
56.1	53.7	56.1	Total Current	53.6	75.2	54.4	54.6		55.6
10.7	11.3	9.5	Long-Term Debt	13.8	4.2	10.3	7.6		9.4
.2	.1	.1	Deferred Taxes	.0	.0	.1	.1		.2
4.0	4.3	4.3	All Other Non-Current	6.8	23.0	2.8	3.2		3.3
29.1	30.6	30.0	Net Worth	25.8	-2.3	32.5	34.5		31.6
100.0	100.0	100.0	Total Liabilties & Net Worth	100.0	100.0	100.0	100.0		100.0
			INCOME DATA						
100.0	100.0	100.0	Net Sales	100.0	100.0	100.0	100.0		100.0
23.2	23.2	22.7	Gross Profit	29.8	27.7	24.4	23.3		19.5
21.2	20.6	19.8	Operating Expenses	25.9	24.2	22.0	20.4		16.6
2.0	2.7	2.9	Operating Profit	3.9	3.5	2.4	2.9		2.9
.2	.4	.7	All Other Expenses (net)	1.4	1.2	.6	.5		.5
1.9	2.3	2.3	Profit Before Taxes	2.5	2.3	1.7	2.4		2.4
			RATIOS						
2.1	2.1	2.1		3.7	2.5	2.0	2.2		2.1
1.5	1.5	1.4	Current	1.1	1.2	1.5	1.5		1.4
1.1	1.2	1.1		.7	.9	1.2	1.2		1.1
1.2	1.3	1.2		2.0	1.5	1.1	1.3		1.4
.8	.9	.8	Quick	.6	.5	.8	1.0		.9
.6	.6	.6		.5	.4	.6	.6		.7
31 11.6	32 11.4	31 11.7		32 11.3	30 12.1	30 12.3	32 11.4		32 11.4
39 9.3	39 9.3	38 9.6	Sales/Receivables	37 9.9	35 10.4	37 10.0	38 9.7		40 9.2
51 7.2	49 7.5	46 7.9		51 7.2	45 8.0	44 8.3	47 7.8		47 7.8
27 13.7	27 13.8	25 14.8		22 16.6	20 18.6	32 11.4	25 14.6		22 16.9
39 9.3	42 8.6	40 9.1	Cost of Sales/Inventory	43 8.6	62 5.9	54 6.8	38 9.7		35 10.4
57 6.4	58 6.3	55 6.6		86 4.2	98 3.7	63 5.8	50 7.3		47 7.7
20 18.1	21 17.7	19 19.5		10 35.7	21 17.2	22 16.6	19 19.4		19 19.6
32 11.5	30 12.0	30 12.1	Cost of Sales/Payables	70 5.2	38 9.6	35 10.5	30 12.2		28 13.1
49 7.4	47 7.8	46 8.0		86 4.2	114 3.2	50 7.3	40 9.1		40 9.2
8.1	7.9	8.3		7.4	7.5	8.5	8.6		8.5
16.2	14.4	17.4	Sales/Working Capital	36.2	24.4	13.8	13.8		21.2
45.2	29.3	59.6		-13.6	-24.2	22.2	37.0		67.7
12.6	12.6	10.0		18.5		7.7	8.9		12.9
(187) 4.3	(207) 4.3	(190) 3.1	EBIT/Interest	(12) 2.3	(35) 2.8	(46) 3.2	(84) 3.3		
1.4	1.8	1.4		1.0		1.3	1.3		1.8
5.5	9.5	6.2						4.2	11.6
(55) 2.2	(53) 2.4	(45) 2.8	Net Profit + Depr., Dep., Amort./Cur. Mat. L/T/D					(11) 2.2	(26) 3.3
1.0	1.2	.8						.9	2.2
.1	.1	.1		.1	.0	.1	.1		.1
.3	.3	.4	Fixed/Worth	.9	47.7	.5	.3		.3
1.1	.9	1.2		-8.9	-.2	.9	.9		.9
1.1	1.1	1.2		.5	3.9	1.2	.7		1.4
2.6	2.4	2.8	Debt/Worth	6.0	134.7	2.3	2.3		3.1
6.8	6.1	8.5		-23.5	-4.3	8.7	4.8		6.6
43.8	41.7	48.0		144.1		48.4	34.7		47.7
(173) 17.2	(194) 19.6	(178) 21.1	% Profit Before Taxes/Tangible Net Worth	(10) 15.5	(35) 12.5	(42) 16.3	(82) 23.2		
4.3	7.9	7.1		-16.5		4.0	8.6		12.0
11.3	13.1	13.6		24.1	13.5	13.9	10.7		13.9
4.8	5.8	5.7	% Profit Before Taxes/Total Assets	.9	.1	3.5	5.8		6.0
.6	2.0	1.2		-6.7	-7.0	.6	1.3		2.0
141.4	127.2	147.6		103.1	603.7	169.7	214.5		117.9
50.0	57.0	58.8	Sales/Net Fixed Assets	30.5	71.6	48.2	51.7		66.9
17.0	19.8	18.6		8.3	62.7	14.7	18.8		28.8
4.6	4.5	4.7		4.3	4.9	4.3	5.0		4.6
3.7	3.7	3.7	Sales/Total Assets	3.1	3.5	3.5	4.0		3.9
2.8	2.9	2.9		1.7	2.4	2.4	3.1		3.3
.3	.2	.2				.3	.1		.2
(164) .5	(179) .5	(169) .5	% Depr., Dep., Amort./Sales		(29) .6	(42) .5	(79) .4		
1.1	1.0	.9				1.1	.8		.7
1.6	1.7	1.2				2.1	1.1		.7
(86) 2.8	(88) 2.7	(84) 2.7	% Officers', Directors' Owners' Comp/Sales		(22) 3.2	(30) 2.4	(22) 1.2		
4.3	4.4	4.8				5.2	5.1		3.3
6863084M	8976426M	12404359M	Net Sales ($)	3429M	28207M	39557M	279004M	744706M	11309456M
1970471M	2486859M	3057303M	Total Assets ($)	1279M	11446M	13647M	87138M	204418M	2739375M

M = $ thousand   MM = $ million
See Pages 11 through 21 for Explanation of Ratios and Data

Current Data Sorted by Assets   Comparative Historical Data

						Type of Statement		
		13	15	10	5	Unqualified	60	55
1	4	15	12	1		Reviewed	52	42
7	9	8	2	1		Compiled	37	51
5	11	8	1			Tax Returns	18	28
2	11	27	30	5	7	Other	66	67
	27 (4/1-9/30/06)		183 (10/1/06-3/31/07)				4/1/02-3/31/03	4/1/03-3/31/04
0-500M	500M-2MM	2-10MM	10-50MM	50-100MM	100-250MM		ALL	ALL
15	35	71	60	17	12	NUMBER OF STATEMENTS	233	243
%	%	%	%	%	%	ASSETS	%	%
17.8	11.9	13.0	7.0	1.8	6.2	Cash & Equivalents	9.4	9.1
30.9	34.4	37.3	34.8	31.7	39.6	Trade Receivables (net)	34.2	33.2
24.1	34.8	28.0	31.7	34.3	27.7	Inventory	31.4	32.5
1.4	5.0	2.7	3.5	5.6	2.3	All Other Current	3.9	4.1
74.1	86.2	80.9	77.1	73.4	75.9	Total Current	78.9	78.8
7.7	9.9	11.0	9.3	10.3	5.5	Fixed Assets (net)	10.3	10.6
5.3	2.5	4.3	9.6	7.1	15.2	Intangibles (net)	4.9	4.8
12.9	1.5	3.8	4.0	9.2	3.5	All Other Non-Current	5.9	5.8
100.0	100.0	100.0	100.0	100.0	100.0	Total	100.0	100.0
						LIABILITIES		
17.7	19.9	15.2	14.6	12.0	1.0	Notes Payable-Short Term	13.9	14.3
5.8	2.6	2.7	1.6	4.2	1.0	Cur. Mat.-L.T.D.	1.6	1.7
26.7	24.0	22.4	26.4	31.7	34.5	Trade Payables	27.3	26.5
.0	.0	.5	.2	.0	.2	Income Taxes Payable	.2	.5
11.3	7.7	8.3	11.1	8.8	8.2	All Other Current	12.5	12.2
61.4	54.3	49.2	54.1	56.7	44.9	Total Current	55.6	55.2
5.0	18.8	7.6	10.6	8.7	25.3	Long-Term Debt	9.3	9.4
.0	.0	.2	.2	.2	.2	Deferred Taxes	.4	.3
6.5	8.1	3.2	3.9	1.6	2.2	All Other Non-Current	3.2	5.6
27.1	18.8	39.9	31.2	32.8	27.4	Net Worth	31.5	29.5
100.0	100.0	100.0	100.0	100.0	100.0	Total Liabilities & Net Worth	100.0	100.0
						INCOME DATA		
100.0	100.0	100.0	100.0	100.0	100.0	Net Sales	100.0	100.0
51.3	32.2	32.4	32.3	27.9	15.8	Gross Profit	29.0	29.4
40.7	27.9	26.0	25.0	22.7	11.6	Operating Expenses	24.4	25.6
10.6	4.2	6.3	7.2	5.2	4.2	Operating Profit	4.6	3.8
-.6	.7	.5	.9	.3	1.1	All Other Expenses (net)	.6	.7
11.2	3.5	5.8	6.3	4.9	3.1	Profit Before Taxes	4.0	3.1
						RATIOS		
2.0	3.7	2.5	2.0	1.5	2.9	Current	2.0	2.1
1.3	1.9	1.7	1.4	1.4	1.7		1.4	1.5
.8	1.3	1.2	1.1	1.2	1.2		1.1	1.2
1.1	1.4	1.7	1.1	.8	1.8	Quick	1.2	1.3
.9	.8	1.0	.8	.6	1.0		.8 (242)	.8
.5	.6	.5	.6	.4	.6		.5	.5
1 485.0	14 26.1	30 12.2	33 10.9	25 14.7	30 12.2	Sales/Receivables	23 16.2	22 16.9
21 17.0	24 15.2	40 9.1	45 8.1	38 9.7	36 10.2		34 10.7	35 10.5
37 9.8	31 11.7	59 6.2	61 5.9	49 7.5	46 7.9		47 7.8	50 7.2
14 25.5	18 20.2	17 21.5	39 9.4	36 10.0	18 20.6	Cost of Sales/Inventory	22 16.6	22 16.8
60 6.1	37 9.7	44 8.2	58 6.3	48 7.6	23 15.8		44 8.3	46 7.9
97 3.8	69 5.3	85 4.3	112 3.3	72 5.1	66 5.6		80 4.6	91 4.0
1 580.7	11 34.5	15 24.7	28 12.8	23 15.7	21 17.6	Cost of Sales/Payables	21 17.5	18 19.8
30 12.1	25 14.4	31 11.7	43 8.5	40 9.2	41 8.8		34 10.7	35 10.4
61 6.0	36 10.0	56 6.5	71 5.2	56 6.5	56 6.5		54 6.8	57 6.4
7.0	7.9	5.5	6.4	10.5	7.2	Sales/Working Capital	8.3	8.0
27.2	13.5	11.1	14.1	17.7	14.5		16.8	13.7
-57.5	38.1	35.4	35.3	32.7	28.4		58.8	39.3
	25.9	19.6	14.5	41.5	10.7	EBIT/Interest	17.5	16.4
	(30) 2.7	(57) 5.1	(55) 5.0	4.8	(10) 4.2		(207) 5.9	(208) 4.7
	.8	1.8	2.9	2.5	2.6		2.0	2.0
			5.2			Net Profit + Depr., Dep., Amort./Cur. Mat. L/T/D	10.9	9.7
		(11) 3.6					(51) 3.7	(53) 3.4
		1.5					1.6	1.3
.0	.1	.0	.1	.1	.1	Fixed/Worth	.1	.1
.0	.2	.2	.2	.4	.2		.2	.3
1.0	-13.5	.8	.9	.7	NM		.9	1.0
1.0	.8	.7	1.7	2.0	1.8	Debt/Worth	1.2	1.2
4.0	3.0	1.7	2.9	2.8	5.5		2.7	2.7
38.8	-115.5	7.1	7.9	5.9	NM		8.0	9.8
200.4	101.6	65.7	80.1	141.0		% Profit Before Taxes/Tangible Net Worth	83.3	67.5
(13) 44.1	(26) 31.1	(66) 40.0	(52) 36.8	29.6			(202) 33.4	(211) 27.0
7.1	6.6	14.3	11.9	18.7			11.7	10.0
88.1	31.9	28.7	18.5	26.8	9.6	% Profit Before Taxes/Total Assets	21.6	18.7
7.1	8.3	11.3	8.8	6.5	7.7		7.3	6.6
.5	.3	2.8	4.4	3.7	3.5		2.2	2.0
UND	415.3	200.8	235.1	122.3	187.7	Sales/Net Fixed Assets	239.2	201.6
99.0	119.5	58.1	70.0	42.7	128.4		71.7	74.2
21.3	41.5	23.8	24.1	11.1	30.8		28.4	24.9
8.7	7.2	4.3	3.9	4.4	5.8	Sales/Total Assets	5.2	5.1
4.1	4.7	3.0	2.3	3.4	3.7		3.7	3.3
3.5	3.3	2.1	1.6	1.7	1.9		2.3	2.2
.0	.1	.0	.1	.4	.1	% Depr., Dep., Amort./Sales	.2	.2
	(23) .4	(53) .5	(53) .3	(16) .5	(11) .3		(189) .5	(191) .5
	.7	1.1	1.3	3.0	1.4		1.1	1.2
	1.6	1.1	.6			% Officers', Directors' Owners' Comp/Sales	1.4	1.0
	(19) 2.3	(28) 2.0	(12) 1.5				(88) 3.1	(89) 3.1
	4.6	5.2	6.1				6.8	6.0
26291M	210791M	1365617M	3779600M	4394272M	8016550M	Net Sales ($)	16011067M	19945843M
3969M	40421M	392948M	1362110M	1255413M	2122945M	Total Assets ($)	4402941M	5595421M

© RMA 2007

M = $ thousand   MM = $ million
See Pages 11 through 21 for Explanation of Ratios and Data

Comparative Historical Data   **Current Data Sorted by Sales**

4/1/04-3/31/05 ALL	4/1/05-3/31/06 ALL	4/1/06-3/31/07 ALL	Type of Statement	0-1MM	1-3MM	3-5MM	5-10MM	10-25MM	25MM & OVER
					27 (4/1-9/30/06)		183 (10/1/06-3/31/07)		
54	42	43	Unqualified				1	10	32
35	35	33	Reviewed			1	3	12	17
32	21	27	Compiled	4	4	3	6	7	3
21	23	25	Tax Returns	2	5	3	6	8	1
68	73	82	Other		6	5	14	14	43
210	194	210	**NUMBER OF STATEMENTS**	6	15	12	30	51	96
%	%	%	**ASSETS**	%	%	%	%	%	%
10.4	10.9	10.1	Cash & Equivalents		16.6	18.9	12.6	11.9	6.3
31.6	33.1	35.3	Trade Receivables (net)		27.5	32.1	31.1	37.8	37.1
34.1	32.0	30.4	Inventory		26.8	35.2	28.1	28.9	32.6
2.0	3.2	3.5	All Other Current		1.7	1.4	6.8	2.6	3.7
78.1	79.2	79.3	Total Current		72.6	87.6	78.7	81.1	79.6
11.2	9.7	9.7	Fixed Assets (net)		16.3	7.7	10.2	9.2	8.6
5.2	4.7	6.4	Intangibles (net)		5.2	3.0	7.1	5.8	7.3
5.4	6.5	4.5	All Other Non-Current		5.9	1.7	4.0	3.9	4.5
100.0	100.0	100.0	Total		100.0	100.0	100.0	100.0	100.0
			LIABILITIES						
13.5	15.0	14.9	Notes Payable-Short Term		7.7	12.2	17.9	13.4	14.9
2.7	1.9	2.6	Cur. Mat.-L.T.D.		5.4	4.7	3.1	2.4	1.9
25.7	25.0	25.6	Trade Payables		25.4	12.2	19.9	22.8	30.5
.4	.2	.3	Income Taxes Payable		.1	.0	.6	.4	.2
13.0	10.1	9.2	All Other Current		8.8	9.1	7.2	10.5	9.2
55.3	52.2	52.7	Total Current		47.3	38.2	48.7	49.5	56.6
11.4	11.1	11.2	Long-Term Debt		13.3	14.4	19.6	7.3	10.7
.3	.2	.1	Deferred Taxes		.0	.0	.0	.3	.2
5.4	8.7	4.3	All Other Non-Current		8.8	10.8	5.2	2.8	3.2
27.6	27.9	31.7	Net Worth		30.5	36.6	26.5	40.1	29.4
100.0	100.0	100.0	Total Liabilities & Net Worth		100.0	100.0	100.0	100.0	100.0
			INCOME DATA						
100.0	100.0	100.0	Net Sales		100.0	100.0	100.0	100.0	100.0
31.1	27.4	32.4	Gross Profit		48.8	32.7	37.4	33.1	25.7
26.1	22.3	26.0	Operating Expenses		39.6	30.1	27.7	28.0	20.3
5.0	5.1	6.3	Operating Profit		9.2	2.6	9.7	5.1	5.4
.6	.6	.6	All Other Expenses (net)		.8	.8	.8	.7	.6
4.4	4.6	5.7	Profit Before Taxes		8.4	1.8	8.9	4.4	4.9
			RATIOS						
2.0	2.2	2.4	Current		3.7	7.9	2.6	2.8	1.9
1.5	1.6	1.5			2.0	2.6	1.7	1.7	1.4
1.2	1.1	1.2			1.0	1.3	1.3	1.1	1.2
1.2	1.4	1.4	Quick		1.4	6.4	1.7	2.2	1.0
(209) .8	.8	.8			.8	1.3	.9	1.0	.7
.5	.5	.6			.6	.5	.6	.6	.5
19 19.0	21 17.1	26 14.1	Sales/Receivables		18 20.6	14 26.2	16 23.5	32 11.5	28 12.9
35 10.5	33 10.9	38 9.7			31 11.7	26 14.3	30 12.3	44 8.3	38 9.6
47 7.7	47 7.7	56 6.5			37 9.9	39 9.4	56 6.5	57 6.4	52 7.0
26 14.3	21 17.2	22 16.3	Cost of Sales/Inventory		21 17.1	9 38.5	24 14.9	16 23.5	24 15.5
48 7.5	44 8.2	49 7.4			67 5.5	51 7.1	38 9.5	53 6.9	48 7.6
89 4.1	84 4.3	91 4.0			88 4.1	100 3.6	71 5.1	121 3.0	86 4.2
19 19.5	15 24.6	18 20.0	Cost of Sales/Payables		17 21.3	5 76.4	17 21.7	14 26.3	23 15.8
33 11.0	30 12.3	36 10.0			32 11.6	14 27.0	33 11.2	33 11.1	40 9.2
55 6.6	52 7.1	58 6.3			74 5.0	34 10.8	43 8.5	58 6.3	58 6.2
7.3	7.4	6.4	Sales/Working Capital		6.2	4.0	5.6	5.4	8.8
15.2	13.6	14.1			12.2	10.5	12.3	8.7	17.6
41.4	40.2	35.5			553.5	21.9	26.7	45.8	34.6
19.4	13.7	17.6	EBIT/Interest		41.1		17.3	38.1	17.3
(178) 5.7	(161) 4.9	(177) 4.8			(13) 4.0		(23) 6.5	(42) 4.8	(88) 5.0
2.2	1.5	2.0			1.7		1.6	1.5	2.7
10.0	6.6	6.9	Net Profit + Depr., Dep., Amort./Cur. Mat. L/T/D						6.5
(45) 2.5	(35) 3.4	(30) 3.6							(20) 3.6
1.1	1.3	1.6							1.7
.1	.0	.1	Fixed/Worth		.0	.0	.0	.1	.1
.3	.2	.2			.3	.2	.2	.2	.2
1.0	.8	1.0			2.3	NM	1.2	.8	.7
1.1	1.0	1.0	Debt/Worth		1.0	.4	.7	.6	1.7
2.6	2.4	2.8			4.0	2.9	1.6	2.0	3.1
10.3	9.4	9.1			38.8	NM	15.3	9.1	6.4
79.1	63.3	83.8	% Profit Before Taxes/Tangible Net Worth		121.5		84.8	65.5	83.8
(180) 32.1	(163) 32.9	(183) 35.2			(13) 92.6		(24) 37.2	(47) 24.8	(87) 38.1
15.2	11.8	13.7			22.9		18.5	9.7	17.9
21.1	20.5	22.2	% Profit Before Taxes/Total Assets		50.0	11.4	33.5	21.6	21.9
8.8	9.3	8.9			9.3	1.5	14.7	8.1	8.9
3.2	1.6	3.2			3.4	-4.7	4.4	1.3	3.8
215.5	276.1	236.7	Sales/Net Fixed Assets		UND	409.8	186.6	170.4	254.6
68.7	80.2	69.0			53.0	94.3	79.1	56.5	70.0
21.6	30.2	26.7			20.4	40.3	32.7	23.9	32.5
5.0	5.0	4.8	Sales/Total Assets		5.7	6.9	4.9	4.1	4.8
3.5	3.3	3.4			3.7	5.0	3.7	2.9	3.5
2.4	2.3	2.0			2.8	2.0	1.8	2.1	2.1
.2	.1	.1	% Depr., Dep., Amort./Sales				.1	.2	.1
(159) .5	(150) .4	(164) .4					(20) .4	(42) .5	(83) .4
1.0	.9	1.1					.8	1.2	.9
1.6	1.4	1.3	% Officers', Directors' Owners' Comp/Sales				1.3	1.1	.5
(69) 2.6	(68) 2.8	(67) 2.2					(15) 2.5	(21) 2.1	(17) 1.5
7.2	4.2	5.4					4.3	5.0	3.9
18520430M	14532182M	17793121M	Net Sales ($)	1730M	27643M	48199M	213826M	835194M	16666529M
5248908M	4310856M	5177806M	Total Assets ($)	1180M	11418M	14631M	104472M	346805M	4699300M

© RMA 2007

M = $ thousand   MM = $ million
See Pages 11 through 21 for Explanation of Ratios and Data

Current Data Sorted by Assets   Comparative Historical Data

Type of Statement

0-500M	500M-2MM	2-10MM	10-50MM	50-100MM	100-250MM	Type of Statement	4/1/02-3/31/03 ALL	4/1/03-3/31/04 ALL
		11	10	2	2	Unqualified	20	23
	6	34	8			Reviewed	62	50
1	9	15	1			Compiled	20	46
4	10	4	2			Tax Returns	8	12
4	12	20	7	1	2	Other	32	31
32 (4/1-9/30/06)			133 (10/1/06-3/31/07)					
9	37	84	28	3	4	NUMBER OF STATEMENTS	142	162

Data

0-500M %	500M-2MM %	2-10MM %	10-50MM %	50-100MM %	100-250MM %		4/1/02-3/31/03 ALL %	4/1/03-3/31/04 ALL %
						ASSETS		
	14.5	7.1	4.1			Cash & Equivalents	9.6	8.6
	26.8	32.5	28.5			Trade Receivables (net)	31.9	33.2
	33.6	40.4	39.7			Inventory	37.8	36.8
	4.4	4.6	2.2			All Other Current	2.3	3.8
	79.2	84.7	74.5			Total Current	81.7	82.3
	10.1	7.8	14.3			Fixed Assets (net)	8.3	9.2
	3.7	2.6	1.3			Intangibles (net)	3.7	3.1
	7.0	5.0	9.9			All Other Non-Current	6.2	5.4
	100.0	100.0	100.0			Total	100.0	100.0
						LIABILITIES		
	11.5	19.9	16.3			Notes Payable-Short Term	13.0	15.9
	3.1	.9	2.2			Cur. Mat.-L.T.D.	1.8	1.5
	21.5	21.8	19.8			Trade Payables	22.5	23.2
	.3	.1	.3			Income Taxes Payable	.3	.2
	10.5	7.7	11.2			All Other Current	11.4	12.6
	47.0	50.5	49.7			Total Current	49.1	53.4
	5.4	5.4	6.1			Long-Term Debt	6.5	8.0
	.0	.0	.0			Deferred Taxes	.0	.0
	2.7	6.7	3.9			All Other Non-Current	5.0	4.0
	44.9	37.5	40.3			Net Worth	39.4	34.6
	100.0	100.0	100.0			Total Liabilities & Net Worth	100.0	100.0
						INCOME DATA		
	100.0	100.0	100.0			Net Sales	100.0	100.0
	32.0	29.8	25.4			Gross Profit	29.4	32.0
	26.8	26.0	22.9			Operating Expenses	26.6	29.1
	5.2	3.8	2.5			Operating Profit	2.9	3.0
	.6	.5	.4			All Other Expenses (net)	1.1	.8
	4.6	3.3	2.1			Profit Before Taxes	1.8	2.2
						RATIOS		
	2.9	2.9	2.3				2.3	2.3
	1.9	1.6	1.6			Current	1.7	1.6
	1.3	1.3	1.1				1.3	1.3
	1.7	1.2	1.2				1.4	1.2
	.9	.8	.6			Quick	.8	.8
	.5	.4	.4				.5	.5
	18 20.4	27 13.6	33 11.0				29 12.6	27 13.8
	32 11.3	49 7.5	44 8.3			Sales/Receivables	44 8.2	45 8.1
	60 6.1	69 5.3	55 6.6				59 6.1	64 5.7
	24 15.0	39 9.4	53 6.8				39 9.4	41 8.9
	68 5.4	96 3.8	70 5.2			Cost of Sales/Inventory	79 4.6	74 4.9
	93 3.9	174 2.1	123 3.0				120 3.0	113 3.2
	8 43.8	19 19.1	17 21.7				22 16.6	23 16.1
	29 12.8	42 8.8	30 12.0			Cost of Sales/Payables	43 8.6	35 10.4
	52 7.0	71 5.1	61 5.9				60 6.1	56 6.6
	4.2	4.2	5.5				4.7	4.5
	8.3	7.3	10.7			Sales/Working Capital	8.5	8.5
	25.0	14.9	40.2				14.8	17.4
	9.5	8.6	7.4				11.1	12.5
	(31) 2.8	(75) 3.2	(27) 2.7			EBIT/Interest	(121) 3.0	(139) 3.5
	1.0	1.6	1.0				1.3	1.5
		20.8					13.0	7.0
		(11) 4.7				Net Profit + Depr., Dep., Amort./Cur. Mat. L/T/D	(24) 3.3	(33) 3.6
		1.4					1.9	1.1
	.0	.0	.0				.0	.0
	.1	.1	.3			Fixed/Worth	.1	.1
	.5	.3	.8				.4	.6
	.4	.9	.9				.8	.9
	1.1	1.9	1.9			Debt/Worth	1.6	1.9
	3.6	3.8	3.7				3.2	3.9
	36.9	44.5	32.0				34.6	31.9
	(34) 11.7	(78) 16.0	12.8			% Profit Before Taxes/Tangible Net Worth	(130) 13.1	(148) 16.1
	4.5	6.2	.6				2.4	4.2
	14.9	13.5	13.7				12.2	10.7
	5.3	5.6	4.2			% Profit Before Taxes/Total Assets	4.9	4.4
	.4	.7	.0				.7	1.3
	238.2	327.9	170.4				192.9	177.4
	121.1	68.7	33.0			Sales/Net Fixed Assets	63.4	71.5
	38.2	25.5	10.5				25.5	22.6
	3.8	2.9	3.1				3.4	3.4
	2.6	2.4	2.5			Sales/Total Assets	2.5	2.7
	1.9	1.7	1.6				1.9	2.1
	.2	.2	.3				.2	.3
	(27) .4	(66) .4	(27) .5			% Depr., Dep., Amort./Sales	(108) .5	(130) .6
	.9	1.0	1.4				.9	1.0
	3.7	1.7					2.1	2.3
	(24) 5.2	(48) 2.9				% Officers', Directors' Owners' Comp/Sales	(70) 3.9	(80) 3.7
	7.8	4.8					8.3	8.0
12734M	137310M	1009485M	1431286M	411181M	1113959M	Net Sales ($)	4975807M	3096674M
2521M	44062M	415633M	532592M	213223M	660663M	Total Assets ($)	1803017M	1227163M

M = $ thousand   MM = $ million
See Pages 11 through 21 for Explanation of Ratios and Data

Comparative Historical Data				Current Data Sorted by Sales					
			Type of Statement						
31	28	25	Unqualified			2	2	6	15
49	49	48	Reviewed		2	5	11	24	6
33	28	26	Compiled	1	3	8	8	4	2
16	11	20	Tax Returns	3	6	5	3	1	2
44	36	46	Other	2	10	3	9	15	7
4/1/04-3/31/05	**4/1/05-3/31/06**	**4/1/06-3/31/07**		**32 (4/1-9/30/06)**		**133 (10/1/06-3/31/07)**			
ALL	**ALL**	**ALL**		**0-1MM**	**1-3MM**	**3-5MM**	**5-10MM**	**10-25MM**	**25MM & OVER**
173	152	165	**NUMBER OF STATEMENTS**	6	21	23	33	50	32
%	%	%	**ASSETS**	%	%	%	%	%	%
8.3	8.1	8.3	Cash & Equivalents		11.1	13.6	8.2	6.8	4.6
28.9	31.0	30.7	Trade Receivables (net)		33.9	27.1	26.7	33.5	34.6
41.3	38.1	37.2	Inventory		29.9	35.2	40.6	40.0	36.4
2.3	2.0	3.8	All Other Current		.9	3.3	6.6	5.0	1.6
80.7	79.3	80.0	Total Current		75.9	79.3	82.0	85.4	77.2
10.2	10.1	10.3	Fixed Assets (net)		13.8	7.2	12.3	6.2	10.4
2.9	3.1	3.1	Intangibles (net)		3.2	10.1	1.1	.8	3.4
6.2	7.5	6.6	All Other Non-Current		7.0	3.4	4.5	7.6	8.9
100.0	100.0	100.0	Total		100.0	100.0	100.0	100.0	100.0
			LIABILITIES						
15.5	16.9	16.7	Notes Payable-Short Term		12.0	16.1	15.6	21.1	16.3
2.3	2.4	1.9	Cur. Mat.-L.T.D.		5.1	2.5	.8	1.1	1.7
21.0	21.3	21.6	Trade Payables		17.7	25.6	25.0	18.7	22.4
.2	.1	.3	Income Taxes Payable		.4	.1	.4	.2	.2
8.9	7.7	8.7	All Other Current		9.1	12.7	5.5	7.4	11.3
47.9	48.4	49.2	Total Current		44.2	57.1	47.3	48.5	51.9
8.0	8.8	7.5	Long-Term Debt		6.1	9.0	6.5	2.9	7.2
.1	.1	.1	Deferred Taxes		.0	.0	.0	.0	.5
4.8	4.5	5.3	All Other Non-Current		3.2	3.0	4.9	7.0	5.2
39.3	38.2	37.9	Net Worth		46.4	31.0	41.3	41.5	35.2
100.0	100.0	100.0	Total Liabilties & Net Worth		100.0	100.0	100.0	100.0	100.0
			INCOME DATA						
100.0	100.0	100.0	Net Sales		100.0	100.0	100.0	100.0	100.0
33.0	30.9	30.4	Gross Profit		30.7	34.1	29.0	29.4	26.1
29.8	27.6	26.0	Operating Expenses		22.6	30.4	26.5	25.8	21.4
3.2	3.4	4.3	Operating Profit		8.2	3.6	2.5	3.6	4.7
.5	1.0	1.0	All Other Expenses (net)		2.6	.6	.3	.3	1.6
2.7	2.4	3.4	Profit Before Taxes		5.6	3.1	2.1	3.4	3.1
			RATIOS						
2.6	2.4	2.7			2.9	2.7	2.6	3.1	2.3
1.6	1.7	1.7	Current		1.9	1.5	1.7	1.8	1.3
1.3	1.2	1.2			1.3	1.1	1.3	1.3	1.1
1.2	1.2	1.3			1.7	1.1	1.2	1.4	1.2
.7	.8	.8	Quick		1.0	.6	.7	.9	.7
.4	.5	.5			.8	.4	.4	.5	.5
25 14.8	**27** 13.6	**22** 16.3			**20** 17.8	**18** 19.9	**21** 17.7	**26** 14.0	**34** 10.7
37 9.9	**43** 8.6	**42** 8.6	Sales/Receivables		**41** 9.0	**35** 10.5	**42** 8.7	**46** 8.0	**49** 7.5
57 6.4	**59** 6.2	**64** 5.7			**73** 5.0	**77** 4.7	**54** 6.8	**65** 5.6	**61** 6.0
49 7.4	**42** 8.7	**38** 9.6			**2** 225.0	**29** 12.7	**42** 8.7	**38** 9.6	**30** 12.1
86 4.2	**76** 4.8	**80** 4.5	Cost of Sales/Inventory		**59** 6.2	**87** 4.2	**95** 3.9	**90** 4.1	**65** 5.6
143 2.5	**150** 2.4	**144** 2.5			**85** 4.3	**178** 2.0	**161** 2.3	**145** 2.5	**125** 2.9
19 19.0	**20** 17.9	**15** 23.8			**7** 50.7	**28** 12.9	**21** 17.0	**16** 22.5	**17** 21.4
35 10.3	**39** 9.4	**37** 9.9	Cost of Sales/Payables		**32** 11.5	**40** 9.1	**44** 8.3	**33** 11.2	**40** 9.2
58 6.3	**61** 6.0	**64** 5.7			**59** 6.2	**105** 3.5	**75** 4.8	**50** 7.2	**56** 6.6
4.2	5.0	4.5			4.1	3.2	4.1	4.1	7.4
8.1	9.0	8.4	Sales/Working Capital		6.5	9.3	6.5	7.6	11.6
18.0	20.1	21.8			23.2	30.0	14.3	21.5	40.2
8.0	7.4	9.3			11.6	5.0	12.0	11.0	13.6
(143) 3.5	(134) 3.4	(147) 3.5	EBIT/Interest		(17) 4.6	(20) 3.2	(30) 2.4	(45) 4.1	(30) 5.3
1.4	1.6	1.2			1.2	1.8	.8	1.5	1.4
18.1	9.7	13.8							
(27) 3.4	(28) 4.2	(20) 4.4	Net Profit + Depr., Dep., Amort./Cur. Mat. L/T/D						
1.5	1.3	.6							
.0	.0	.0			.0	.0	.0	.0	.1
.2	.1	.1	Fixed/Worth		.1	.1	.1	.1	.3
.6	.5	.5			.7	.7	.4	.3	.8
.8	.9	.8			.4	.6	.8	.7	1.1
1.6	1.8	1.8	Debt/Worth		1.0	3.0	1.6	1.6	2.2
3.7	4.1	4.1			3.8	9.8	2.8	3.2	4.7
34.2	37.6	40.8			39.2	67.6	30.4	46.0	50.1
(159) 14.4	(142) 11.7	(150) 15.6	% Profit Before Taxes/Tangible Net Worth		(20) 10.9	(18) 13.8	(31) 9.2	(48) 18.1	(30) 28.9
2.3	3.0	4.9			3.9	6.9	.4	5.7	7.3
11.3	11.6	14.9			17.9	10.8	9.5	16.6	15.9
3.8	4.8	5.4	% Profit Before Taxes/Total Assets		5.4	4.4	4.2	7.3	6.8
.7	1.0	.9			1.3	2.4	-.1	1.5	.9
178.3	262.9	241.0			325.9	735.4	281.3	175.2	227.9
52.1	63.5	69.9	Sales/Net Fixed Assets		93.5	133.7	106.1	65.9	52.6
17.5	20.2	20.2			12.4	38.2	15.3	31.5	13.0
3.4	3.5	3.2			3.5	3.1	3.0	3.2	3.8
2.6	2.5	2.4	Sales/Total Assets		2.3	2.1	2.3	2.6	2.9
1.8	1.9	1.8			1.9	1.2	1.7	1.9	1.9
.3	.2	.2			.2	.1	.2	.2	.2
(120) .7	(123) .5	(130) .4	% Depr., Dep., Amort./Sales		(13) .5	(17) .3	(25) .5	(42) .4	(28) .5
1.3	1.3	1.2			1.3	.9	1.3	1.0	1.3
2.1	2.5	1.8			4.3	2.8	1.8	1.4	1.7
(95) 4.0	(81) 3.9	(89) 3.3	% Officers', Directors' Owners' Comp/Sales		(13) 5.1	(16) 4.7	(17) 3.8	(28) 2.6	(11) 1.9
7.9	5.8	5.2			7.8	7.0	4.6	3.9	3.3
3261095M	**4452092M**	**4115955M**	Net Sales ($)	**3957M**	**40454M**	**92584M**	**238769M**	**780456M**	**2959735M**
1412855M	**1801631M**	**1868694M**	Total Assets ($)	**2393M**	**19311M**	**54319M**	**124435M**	**335520M**	**1332716M**

M = $ thousand MM = $ million

See Pages 11 through 21 for Explanation of Ratios and Data

Current Data Sorted by Assets   Comparative Historical Data

0-500M	500M-2MM	2-10MM	10-50MM	50-100MM	100-250MM	Type of Statement	4/1/02-3/31/03 ALL	4/1/03-3/31/04 ALL
		1	16	2	4	Unqualified	46	43
	5	24	10			Reviewed	60	46
1	10	6		1		Compiled	24	24
2	7	2				Tax Returns	10	19
3	7	15	7		3	Other	27	31
	27 (4/1-9/30/06)		99 (10/1/06-3/31/07)					
6	29	48	33	3	7	NUMBER OF STATEMENTS	167	163
%	%	%	%	%	%	**ASSETS**	%	%
	8.7	5.0	5.1			Cash & Equivalents	8.9	10.7
	28.2	34.6	30.3			Trade Receivables (net)	33.3	31.5
	40.1	44.4	46.5			Inventory	40.9	40.9
	.7	2.7	2.4			All Other Current	1.9	1.6
	77.7	86.7	84.2			Total Current	85.0	84.7
	13.3	7.6	6.9			Fixed Assets (net)	8.2	9.4
	.6	3.1	3.2			Intangibles (net)	1.8	1.7
	8.4	2.6	5.6			All Other Non-Current	4.9	4.3
	100.0	100.0	100.0			Total	100.0	100.0
						LIABILITIES		
	19.4	26.3	18.0			Notes Payable-Short Term	18.2	15.6
	1.7	.6	.8			Cur. Mat.-L.T.D.	3.0	3.5
	21.7	15.9	17.5			Trade Payables	19.6	18.2
	.3	.3	.1			Income Taxes Payable	.3	.3
	4.4	6.4	6.4			All Other Current	10.6	11.9
	47.6	49.4	42.8			Total Current	51.6	49.5
	5.5	5.0	7.2			Long-Term Debt	7.7	9.0
	.1	.1	.1			Deferred Taxes	.1	.1
	7.7	6.7	2.6			All Other Non-Current	3.6	4.5
	39.1	38.8	47.4			Net Worth	37.0	36.9
	100.0	100.0	100.0			Total Liabilties & Net Worth	100.0	100.0
						INCOME DATA		
	100.0	100.0	100.0			Net Sales	100.0	100.0
	38.1	29.4	25.5			Gross Profit	28.6	30.3
	33.6	25.7	20.5			Operating Expenses	24.3	27.1
	4.5	3.7	5.0			Operating Profit	4.3	3.2
	.9	1.0	1.2			All Other Expenses (net)	1.0	.9
	3.6	2.8	3.8			Profit Before Taxes	3.2	2.3
						RATIOS		
	2.8	2.8	3.0				2.9	3.0
	1.8	1.7	2.1			Current	1.6	1.7
	1.1	1.3	1.5				1.3	1.5
	1.2	1.2	1.4				1.3	1.6
	.7	.8	.8			Quick	.8 (162)	.9
	.3	.5	.5				.5	.5
	5 74.5	35 10.3	34 10.7				25 14.4	26 13.9
	28 12.8	52 7.1	50 7.3			Sales/Receivables	42 8.6	43 8.5
	44 8.2	67 5.4	69 5.3				73 5.0	58 6.3
	22 16.4	51 7.1	82 4.5				40 9.1	42 8.6
	70 5.2	98 3.7	109 3.4			Cost of Sales/Inventory	80 4.6	93 3.9
	148 2.5	156 2.3	156 2.3				133 2.8	140 2.6
	6 64.1	16 22.4	18 20.2				17 21.5	14 26.8
	29 12.8	27 13.7	36 10.2			Cost of Sales/Payables	30 12.1	33 11.0
	52 7.1	46 8.0	59 6.2				51 7.2	51 7.2
	5.7	4.4	3.1				5.1	4.1
	6.7	8.1	5.0			Sales/Working Capital	7.4	7.2
	217.7	13.0	12.2				16.2	15.3
	15.7	7.7	18.3				8.0	12.6
	(22) 5.1	(45) 3.1	(31) 2.6			EBIT/Interest	(149) 4.4	(140) 4.3
	1.3	1.4	1.4				1.9	2.2
			20.1				17.3	18.5
		(10) 4.4				Net Profit + Depr., Dep., Amort./Cur. Mat. L/T/D	(36) 4.8	(38) 4.4
			2.2				1.3	1.8
	.0	.0	.0				.0	.0
	.2	.1	.1			Fixed/Worth	.1	.1
	.3	.4	.4				.4	.4
	.5	.9	.5				.8	.6
	2.0	1.7	1.2			Debt/Worth	1.9	1.6
	4.0	3.4	4.0				4.0	3.0
	44.6	36.6	34.8				39.7	36.8
	(28) 20.2	(44) 15.1	(31) 16.7			% Profit Before Taxes/Tangible Net Worth	(153) 25.4	(152) 16.8
	3.7	6.0	3.8				6.3	5.7
	16.0	11.5	14.9				13.9	12.2
	7.3	5.6	6.3			% Profit Before Taxes/Total Assets	7.7	6.4
	.8	1.9	1.3				2.4	1.6
	161.3	243.7	128.0				225.2	153.2
	39.4	71.9	75.0			Sales/Net Fixed Assets	61.8	63.0
	17.1	26.2	28.3				24.6	23.5
	4.0	2.8	2.5				3.3	3.7
	3.1	2.5	2.1			Sales/Total Assets	2.6	2.5
	2.2	1.9	1.5				1.9	1.8
	.3	.1	.3				.2	.3
	(21) .6	(41) .4	(29) .5			% Depr., Dep., Amort./Sales	(133) .5	(130) .6
	1.5	.7	.7				1.1	1.2
	3.4	1.2	1.1				1.4	1.8
	(16) 5.4	(25) 1.9	(13) 2.2			% Officers', Directors' Owners' Comp/Sales	(83) 2.8	(75) 3.3
	6.8	3.5	6.3				5.2	5.0
4441M	108026M	525043M	1751769M	475364M	1774690M	Net Sales ($)	6396311M	5946811M
1903M	32555M	212359M	812332M	251267M	1080179M	Total Assets ($)	2806483M	2883669M

© RMA 2007

M = $ thousand   MM = $ million
See Pages 11 through 21 for Explanation of Ratios and Data

Comparative Historical Data | | Current Data Sorted by Sales

Type of Statement

Type of Statement	4/1/04-3/31/05 ALL	4/1/05-3/31/06 ALL	4/1/06-3/31/07 ALL	0-1MM	1-3MM	3-5MM	5-10MM	10-25MM	25MM & OVER
Unqualified	22	27	23		1	4	17	4	19
Reviewed	39	33	39		7	2	5	8	9
Compiled	16	9	18	1	2	2	2	2	1
Tax Returns	9	12	11	2	2	2	4	1	
Other	29	44	35	2	1	2	6	9	9

Current Data date ranges: 27 (4/1-9/30/06); 99 (10/1/06-3/31/07)

Main Data

	4/1/04-3/31/05 ALL	4/1/05-3/31/06 ALL	4/1/06-3/31/07 ALL	0-1MM	1-3MM	3-5MM	5-10MM	10-25MM	25MM & OVER
NUMBER OF STATEMENTS	115	125	126	5	13	12	34	24	38
ASSETS	%	%	%	%	%	%	%	%	%
Cash & Equivalents	11.5	9.2	7.1		5.6	12.6	7.9	4.0	6.1
Trade Receivables (net)	30.7	32.0	31.3		14.7	32.9	33.1	33.2	34.2
Inventory	40.6	39.7	41.2		55.4	25.2	45.0	39.8	42.1
All Other Current	1.6	3.1	2.9		.0	1.1	3.2	2.7	4.2
Total Current	84.5	84.1	82.6		75.7	71.8	89.3	79.7	86.6
Fixed Assets (net)	8.0	8.9	10.1		18.9	13.4	6.5	9.9	6.7
Intangibles (net)	2.9	1.7	2.5		1.2	.1	2.1	6.3	2.1
All Other Non-Current	4.6	5.2	4.7		4.1	14.7	2.2	4.1	4.6
Total	100.0	100.0	100.0		100.0	100.0	100.0	100.0	100.0
LIABILITIES									
Notes Payable-Short Term	17.9	18.0	20.6		15.9	26.5	21.4	23.6	17.8
Cur. Mat.-L.T.D.	1.8	1.6	1.2		.5	3.7	.5	1.0	1.7
Trade Payables	19.9	19.0	17.3		20.4	15.5	18.6	17.0	17.6
Income Taxes Payable	.2	.3	.2		.5	.0	.3	.4	.1
All Other Current	7.2	12.3	7.2		2.4	4.9	5.3	7.3	7.4
Total Current	47.0	51.1	46.5		39.7	50.5	46.1	49.3	44.6
Long-Term Debt	7.2	9.3	5.8		7.7	6.0	5.1	6.1	6.3
Deferred Taxes	.1	.1	.1		.0	.1	.0	.3	.1
All Other Non-Current	6.1	6.3	7.0		4.8	8.5	7.3	7.3	2.5
Net Worth	39.6	33.1	40.6		47.8	34.8	41.4	37.0	46.6
Total Liabilities & Net Worth	100.0	100.0	100.0		100.0	100.0	100.0	100.0	100.0
INCOME DATA									
Net Sales	100.0	100.0	100.0		100.0	100.0	100.0	100.0	100.0
Gross Profit	30.2	31.0	32.4		41.2	38.2	26.8	31.9	28.8
Operating Expenses	25.7	27.0	28.2		35.6	35.9	22.5	28.4	23.2
Operating Profit	4.5	3.9	4.2		5.6	2.3	4.2	3.5	5.6
All Other Expenses (net)	.8	.9	.9		1.2	.6	.9	1.2	.5
Profit Before Taxes	3.7	3.0	3.3		4.4	1.7	3.3	2.3	5.1
RATIOS									
Current	3.3	3.3	2.9		2.7	3.4	3.4	2.4	2.9
	1.8	1.8	1.8		1.8	1.3	2.1	1.6	2.0
	1.4	1.3	1.2		1.2	.8	1.3	1.3	1.5
Quick	1.9	1.4	1.4		1.4	1.9	1.3	1.1	1.5
	1.0	.9	.8		.4	.7	1.0	.6	.8
	.5	.5	.4		.0	.5	.6	.4	.5
Sales/Receivables	31 11.7	31 11.7	29 12.6		0 UND	13 28.6	33 11.2	29 12.5	36 10.1
	46 7.9	49 7.4	47 7.8		17 21.4	43 8.5	46 8.0	53 6.8	52 7.0
	69 5.3	74 4.9	64 5.7		37 9.9	55 6.6	57 6.4	77 4.7	68 5.4
Cost of Sales/Inventory	53 6.9	55 6.6	48 7.6		63 5.8	15 24.0	51 7.2	53 6.9	52 7.0
	99 3.7	101 3.6	96 3.8		131 2.8	30 12.3	98 3.7	115 3.2	90 4.0
	153 2.4	146 2.5	150 2.4		307 1.2	122 3.0	151 2.4	157 2.3	142 2.6
Cost of Sales/Payables	17 21.0	20 18.3	16 23.0		0 UND	10 37.8	15 23.8	18 19.7	22 16.4
	34 10.8	33 11.2	31 11.8		19 18.7	32 11.2	22 16.2	36 10.1	31 11.7
	64 5.7	58 6.3	51 7.2		100 3.7	44 8.3	51 7.2	45 8.1	55 6.7
Sales/Working Capital	3.7	3.6	3.9		4.0	6.1	4.0	4.1	3.5
	5.8	7.1	6.6		6.5	16.3	5.2	10.3	5.7
	12.5	13.7	18.6		84.8	-26.9	12.8	18.0	12.1
EBIT/Interest	13.2	7.4	10.4		17.3	13.7	5.1	7.9	24.4
	(104) 4.6	(109) 3.7	(111) 3.1		(11) 5.5	(10) 8.9	(29) 2.9	(23) 3.3	(35) 4.2
	1.8	1.8	1.4		1.1	.8	1.5	1.0	1.6
Net Profit + Depr., Dep., Amort./Cur. Mat. L/T/D	9.9	15.7	16.0						15.3
	(25) 4.2	(23) 5.0	(25) 4.9						(15) 4.7
	2.2	2.9	2.6						2.0
Fixed/Worth	.0	.0	.0		.1	.0	.0	.1	.0
	.1	.1	.1		.3	.2	.1	.2	.1
	.3	.4	.4		.7	1.5	.3	.6	.4
Debt/Worth	.5	.6	.5		.7	.4	.5	.9	.5
	1.5	1.4	1.5		1.0	2.2	1.8	1.7	1.2
	4.3	5.2	4.2		2.3	8.1	4.3	5.8	4.5
% Profit Before Taxes/Tangible Net Worth	40.6	40.9	37.9		40.9	34.2	54.6	32.1	36.9
	(105) 18.5	(116) 17.9	(116) 15.8		13.7	(10) 8.9	(33) 18.2	(21) 15.8	(36) 17.1
	6.8	5.9	3.9		3.4	-1.4	4.3	3.7	6.3
% Profit Before Taxes/Total Assets	16.0	12.8	13.2		14.9	14.2	13.4	11.1	15.2
	7.8	6.2	6.3		7.3	3.9	6.1	6.4	7.0
	2.0	1.4	1.3		1.2	-2.2	2.2	.6	2.1
Sales/Net Fixed Assets	247.5	197.5	159.7		66.9	219.7	366.2	109.8	148.0
	70.2	68.1	56.2		20.9	98.9	98.4	34.2	82.5
	23.7	20.5	20.1		8.6	12.5	25.9	19.4	22.6
Sales/Total Assets	3.2	3.0	3.1		3.0	4.1	3.0	2.8	2.9
	2.1	2.2	2.4		2.2	3.3	2.6	2.4	2.2
	1.7	1.5	1.7		1.7	2.3	1.8	1.5	1.7
% Depr., Dep., Amort./Sales	.2	.2	.3		.5		.1	.4	.3
	(89) .6	(99) .5	(103) .5		(11) .8		(28) .4	(21) .7	(32) .5
	1.0	.9	.9		1.5		.6	1.0	1.0
% Officers', Directors' Owners' Comp/Sales	1.8	1.4	1.5					1.4	1.2
	(52) 4.1	(58) 2.9	(57) 3.2				(17) 2.9	(13) 2.9	1.6
	8.1	6.2	6.3					5.1	4.7
Net Sales ($)	3840250M	4297571M	4639333M	2640M	25324M	47911M	240922M	362130M	3960406M
Total Assets ($)	1911227M	2135062M	2390595M	1510M	11744M	19683M	118650M	184683M	2054325M

M = $ thousand   MM = $ million
See Pages 11 through 21 for Explanation of Ratios and Data

Current Data Sorted by Assets | | | | | | Comparative Historical Data

	0-500M	500M-2MM	2-10MM	10-50MM	50-100MM	100-250MM		4/1/02-3/31/03 ALL	4/1/03-3/31/04 ALL
Type of Statement									
Unqualified		1	7	14	3	4		43	40
Reviewed	3	9	22	8		2		47	61
Compiled	1	5	4					13	25
Tax Returns	7	10	4					10	14
Other	1	9	17	12	1	3		27	28
		34 (4/1-9/30/06)		113 (10/1/06-3/31/07)					
NUMBER OF STATEMENTS	12	34	54	34	4	9		140	168
	%	%	%	%	%	%		%	%
ASSETS									
Cash & Equivalents	21.0	17.2	11.3	9.2				10.9	10.1
Trade Receivables (net)	13.6	27.3	32.4	35.1				31.7	30.2
Inventory	37.4	34.9	38.0	36.7				38.2	39.1
All Other Current	10.3	5.5	1.7	4.2				3.0	3.2
Total Current	82.3	84.8	83.4	85.2				83.7	82.5
Fixed Assets (net)	13.2	5.4	7.0	5.6				6.8	7.9
Intangibles (net)	.1	.3	1.4	2.2				1.7	1.6
All Other Non-Current	4.4	9.4	8.2	7.1				7.8	7.9
Total	100.0	100.0	100.0	100.0				100.0	100.0
LIABILITIES									
Notes Payable-Short Term	18.7	16.9	19.7	16.8				16.6	14.4
Cur. Mat.-L.T.D.	2.3	2.0	.8	2.0				2.9	1.0
Trade Payables	18.5	23.7	17.2	21.4				19.1	19.2
Income Taxes Payable	.0	.2	.2	.5				.1	.3
All Other Current	12.3	6.2	8.5	7.3				10.9	11.7
Total Current	51.8	49.0	46.4	48.1				49.6	46.5
Long-Term Debt	7.1	2.7	4.4	3.8				4.7	3.8
Deferred Taxes	.0	.0	.1	.0				.1	.1
All Other Non-Current	3.9	3.6	2.2	3.9				5.5	4.6
Net Worth	37.2	44.7	47.0	44.1				40.1	45.0
Total Liabilities & Net Worth	100.0	100.0	100.0	100.0				100.0	100.0
INCOME DATA									
Net Sales	100.0	100.0	100.0	100.0				100.0	100.0
Gross Profit	44.8	35.3	33.7	29.0				30.6	32.7
Operating Expenses	39.2	31.6	29.8	22.4				27.1	28.6
Operating Profit	5.5	3.7	3.9	6.6				3.5	4.1
All Other Expenses (net)	1.5	.5	.2	.4				.6	.6
Profit Before Taxes	4.0	3.2	3.7	6.2				2.9	3.4
RATIOS									
Current	4.7	3.4	2.6	2.6				2.7	2.9
	1.9	1.7	1.8	1.7				1.7	1.8
	.9	1.2	1.4	1.3				1.3	1.3
Quick	1.0	2.3	1.4	1.5				1.4	1.7
	.4	1.0	.9	.9				.8	.9
	.0	.4	.6	.5				.5	.5
Sales/Receivables	0 UND	20 18.3	29 12.6	30 12.3				20 18.4	21 17.2
	0 UND	31 11.7	47 7.7	55 6.7				40 9.0	41 8.9
	18 20.0	55 6.6	63 5.8	81 4.5				62 5.9	59 6.1
Cost of Sales/Inventory	0 UND	34 10.8	50 7.4	41 8.9				42 8.6	44 8.4
	47 7.8	61 6.0	102 3.6	63 5.8				75 4.9	73 5.0
	231 1.6	108 3.4	156 2.3	106 3.4				125 2.9	125 2.9
Cost of Sales/Payables	2 165.8	6 58.1	12 29.2	17 21.3				12 29.8	14 26.3
	16 22.6	37 9.9	23 15.7	37 9.9				29 12.8	28 13.0
	49 7.5	73 5.0	51 7.2	58 6.3				54 6.8	45 8.2
Sales/Working Capital	4.9	4.1	4.4	3.8				4.7	4.4
	14.9	8.6	7.1	8.7				8.4	7.3
	UND	33.6	12.5	14.3				16.8	15.3
EBIT/Interest		7.1	11.9	15.8				10.8	12.1
		(28) 2.7	(45) 4.3	(32) 7.1				(127) 3.4	(149) 4.0
		.6	1.9	2.3				1.5	1.3
Net Profit + Depr., Dep., Amort./Cur. Mat. L/T/D								26.0	15.9
								(21) 2.4	(17) 4.3
								.2	1.5
Fixed/Worth	.0	.0	.0	.0				.0	.0
	.4	.1	.1	.1				.1	.1
	16.1	.2	.2	.2				.3	.3
Debt/Worth	.3	.4	.6	.6				.5	.6
	3.9	1.1	1.1	1.3				1.4	1.2
	172.1	5.6	2.2	2.5				3.7	3.2
% Profit Before Taxes/Tangible Net Worth	212.6	36.6	42.5	64.1				45.9	44.2
	(11) 67.7	(33) 11.7	(52) 17.6	(33) 38.3				(127) 17.7	(161) 15.1
	5.0	-3.6	6.7	10.1				3.4	3.4
% Profit Before Taxes/Total Assets	56.9	15.4	18.1	28.9				16.4	17.6
	7.5	5.4	6.6	12.1				6.8	6.0
	.3	-1.2	2.6	4.7				1.2	1.0
Sales/Net Fixed Assets	UND	395.6	301.3	271.9				237.0	208.6
	70.0	114.4	93.9	102.3				81.9	77.8
	25.5	51.1	20.6	37.5				33.1	31.6
Sales/Total Assets	6.9	3.9	3.0	3.2				3.5	3.6
	3.3	3.0	2.4	2.5				2.8	2.6
	1.3	1.9	1.8	1.8				1.9	1.9
% Depr., Dep., Amort./Sales		.1	.2	.1				.2	.2
		(24) .2	(38) .5	(29) .2				(113) .4	(131) .4
		.7	1.0	1.0				.8	.8
% Officers', Directors' Owners' Comp/Sales		1.7	1.5	.9				1.8	1.8
		(20) 2.9	(27) 3.4	(14) 1.6				(67) 2.7	(87) 3.6
		6.4	6.6	3.4				5.7	5.4
Net Sales ($)	8375M	131335M	657062M	2046739M	592480M	2353662M		4643589M	6778016M
Total Assets ($)	2579M	43149M	249815M	780872M	253652M	1350426M		1751217M	2668216M

© RMA 2007

M = $ thousand   MM = $ million
See Pages 11 through 21 for Explanation of Ratios and Data

Comparative Historical Data   Current Data Sorted by Sales

	4/1/04-3/31/05 ALL	4/1/05-3/31/06 ALL	4/1/06-3/31/07 ALL	Type of Statement	0-1MM	1-3MM	3-5MM	5-10MM	10-25MM	25MM & OVER
	25	42	29	Unqualified				4	3	22
	38	46	44	Reviewed	2	6	5	11	13	7
	21	15	10	Compiled	1	3	1	4	1	
	9	17	21	Tax Returns	5	7	4	3	2	
	40	48	43	Other	2	6	4	6	8	17
					34 (4/1-9/30/06)			**113 (10/1/06-3/31/07)**		
NUMBER OF STATEMENTS	133	168	147		10	22	14	28	27	46
	%	%	%	**ASSETS**	%	%	%	%	%	%
	10.6	11.3	13.0	Cash & Equivalents	23.4	11.6	18.8	10.6	15.6	9.6
	30.3	32.5	30.4	Trade Receivables (net)	13.4	23.4	31.0	31.9	32.5	35.1
	38.7	35.7	36.0	Inventory	31.5	41.3	31.2	41.1	32.9	34.8
	3.1	3.0	4.1	All Other Current	16.2	5.7	.4	1.6	2.1	4.6
	82.7	82.6	83.6	Total Current	84.4	82.1	81.3	85.2	83.1	84.0
	6.7	7.0	7.1	Fixed Assets (net)	10.5	11.2	3.2	7.8	4.0	7.0
	1.7	2.4	1.8	Intangibles (net)	.1	.2	2.0	.3	2.5	3.5
	8.9	8.0	7.5	All Other Non-Current	5.0	6.5	13.5	6.8	10.4	5.5
	100.0	100.0	100.0	Total	100.0	100.0	100.0	100.0	100.0	100.0
				LIABILITIES						
	18.5	19.3	18.5	Notes Payable-Short Term	22.4	16.2	20.5	18.8	19.0	17.5
	1.0	1.6	1.5	Cur. Mat.-L.T.D.	.2	3.4	.1	1.6	.7	1.8
	17.6	17.9	19.1	Trade Payables	19.8	19.3	20.1	20.5	14.7	20.4
	.3	.2	.3	Income Taxes Payable	.0	.0	.0	.6	.1	.5
	9.0	8.7	8.1	All Other Current	13.1	8.7	5.3	6.0	8.1	8.9
	46.3	47.6	47.5	Total Current	55.4	47.5	46.0	47.4	42.6	49.1
	6.1	6.5	4.8	Long-Term Debt	7.4	6.4	.3	2.8	5.7	5.6
	.1	.1	.1	Deferred Taxes	.0	.0	.0	.1	.0	.2
	4.7	3.3	4.8	All Other Non-Current	3.5	5.2	3.1	1.2	3.0	8.7
	42.8	42.5	42.8	Net Worth	33.7	40.8	50.5	48.4	48.7	36.5
	100.0	100.0	100.0	Total Liabilities & Net Worth	100.0	100.0	100.0	100.0	100.0	100.0
				INCOME DATA						
	100.0	100.0	100.0	Net Sales	100.0	100.0	100.0	100.0	100.0	100.0
	34.0	31.5	33.7	Gross Profit	43.7	36.2	33.2	37.7	29.8	30.2
	28.7	27.4	28.8	Operating Expenses	40.8	31.4	30.4	32.6	27.0	23.1
	5.2	4.1	4.9	Operating Profit	2.9	4.8	2.9	5.1	2.8	7.1
	.3	.7	.6	All Other Expenses (net)	1.6	1.1	.1	.0	.3	.9
	5.0	3.4	4.3	Profit Before Taxes	1.3	3.7	2.8	5.2	2.5	6.2
				RATIOS						
	3.0	2.9	2.8	Current	7.3	2.8	2.9	2.6	3.0	2.6
	1.8	1.7	1.8		1.2	1.9	1.8	1.7	2.0	1.7
	1.3	1.3	1.3		.9	1.2	1.4	1.3	1.5	1.3
	1.6	1.8	1.5	Quick	1.0	1.7	2.4	1.4	1.7	1.5
	.9	.9	.9		.4	.9	1.0	.9	1.1	1.0
	.5	.5	.5		.0	.2	.7	.5	.6	.5
	19 19.4	22 16.8	22 16.3	Sales/Receivables	0 UND	13 27.3	28 13.2	25 14.4	29 12.5	23 16.0
	40 9.2	45 8.1	43 8.4		0 UND	36 10.2	34 10.7	39 9.3	51 7.2	51 7.2
	63 5.8	68 5.3	63 5.8		23 16.2	79 4.6	51 7.1	61 5.9	60 6.1	72 5.1
	45 8.1	30 12.0	39 9.2	Cost of Sales/Inventory	0 UND	61 6.0	31 11.7	59 6.2	39 9.2	35 10.4
	79 4.6	67 5.5	75 4.9		53 6.9	137 2.7	52 7.0	92 4.0	70 5.2	66 5.6
	132 2.8	126 2.9	129 2.8		271 1.3	232 1.6	109 3.3	140 2.6	115 3.2	110 3.3
	13 28.3	11 34.3	14 25.8	Cost of Sales/Payables	3 105.3	18 20.6	0 UND	12 30.3	7 49.7	23 16.2
	28 13.3	23 15.8	28 13.1		22 16.7	54 6.8	10 35.8	21 17.2	20 18.2	33 11.0
	46 7.9	45 8.2	56 6.5		54 6.8	79 4.6	71 5.1	53 6.8	43 8.6	53 6.9
	3.8	4.1	3.8	Sales/Working Capital	1.3	2.5	4.0	5.0	4.6	3.9
	7.5	8.1	7.8		UND	7.0	7.5	8.2	6.9	8.5
	17.4	20.8	15.8		-43.3	22.4	13.3	17.3	12.3	15.3
	20.2	13.5	9.0	EBIT/Interest		6.7	4.1	20.9	6.4	12.6
	(112) 6.3	(149) 3.9	(125) 4.4			(18) 3.4	(11) 2.3	(25) 4.4	(22) 3.7	(43) 6.6
	2.0	1.4	1.9			.2	1.4	2.5	1.2	2.1
	14.4	13.3	27.0	Net Profit + Depr., Dep., Amort./Cur. Mat. L/T/D						83.8
	(17) 3.1	(27) 5.2	(22) 5.4						(13) 12.8	12.8
	1.4	1.3	2.8							2.9
	.0	.0	.0	Fixed/Worth	.0	.0	.0	.0	.0	.0
	.1	.1	.1		.7	.1	.0	.1	.1	.1
	.2	.3	.3		UND	.5	.1	.2	.1	.4
	.6	.6	.6	Debt/Worth	.2	.5	.5	.5	.5	.8
	1.2	1.4	1.3		5.4	1.1	1.1	1.2	1.0	1.9
	2.8	3.4	3.2		UND	7.1	1.9	2.5	2.2	3.9
	53.4	48.9	51.8	% Profit Before Taxes/Tangible Net Worth		43.0	19.6	52.1	38.2	67.4
	(126) 22.7	(156) 20.0	(139) 19.4		(20) 12.4	12.4	8.1	24.0	(26) 11.3	(42) 41.9
	7.8	3.6	5.8			-6.9	4.8	8.3	1.4	12.5
	21.7	18.0	18.2	% Profit Before Taxes/Total Assets	7.7	13.5	10.4	23.5	18.1	28.9
	8.7	6.0	8.0		2.4	5.4	3.9	10.7	5.2	12.8
	3.2	1.5	2.5		-.1	-3.6	1.7	4.1	.5	4.8
	262.3	300.1	286.4	Sales/Net Fixed Assets	UND	110.6	463.5	315.4	231.8	271.9
	90.1	93.1	91.7		UND	47.8	150.8	129.0	118.9	69.9
	30.7	33.4	29.3		31.3	23.4	58.8	17.9	46.1	22.0
	3.5	3.5	3.4	Sales/Total Assets	5.4	3.2	3.9	3.8	3.1	3.3
	2.6	2.6	2.5		2.5	1.8	2.5	2.8	2.8	2.5
	1.8	1.9	1.8		1.0	1.0	1.8	2.0	1.9	1.9
	.2	.2	.1	% Depr., Dep., Amort./Sales	.3	.1	.1	.1	.1	.1
	(96) .4	(131) .4	(109) .4		(16) .5	(10) .2	(20) .6	(20) .3	(39) .3	.3
	.8	.8	.9		.8	.7	1.2	.6	1.3	
	1.5	1.5	1.5	% Officers', Directors' Owners' Comp/Sales		2.5		1.1	.9	.7
	(69) 2.8	(78) 2.9	(68) 2.9			(11) 3.7		(14) 3.1	(16) 2.5	(16) 1.6
	5.3	6.6	6.2			6.7		6.9	6.2	3.8
	10272787M	8657488M	5789653M	Net Sales ($)	4605M	45245M	56941M	191821M	470354M	5020687M
	2960847M	3479553M	2680493M	Total Assets ($)	2255M	28751M	24540M	81904M	197953M	2345090M

M = $ thousand   MM = $ million
See Pages 11 through 21 for Explanation of Ratios and Data

WHOLESALE—Footwear Merchant Wholesalers NAICS 424340 (SIC 5139, 5199)

Current Data Sorted by Assets

Comparative Historical Data

						Type of Statement		
						Unqualified	21	16
		5	7	1		Reviewed	26	30
1	3	15	2			Compiled	8	14
	2	3				Tax Returns	5	6
3	2	3				Other	26	19
1	1	10	13	3	2		4/1/02-3/31/03	4/1/03-3/31/04
0-500M	**500M-2MM**	**2-10MM**	**10-50MM**	**50-100MM**	**100-250MM**		**ALL**	**ALL**
		14 (4/1-9/30/06)	63 (10/1/06-3/31/07)					
5	8	36	22	4	2	**NUMBER OF STATEMENTS**	86	85

0-500M	500M-2MM	2-10MM	10-50MM	50-100MM	100-250MM		ALL	ALL
%	%	%	%	%	%	**ASSETS**	%	%
		6.4	9.4			Cash & Equivalents	9.4	11.3
		39.0	35.1			Trade Receivables (net)	35.8	31.3
		43.9	37.9			Inventory	37.8	38.5
		2.0	3.8			All Other Current	2.6	2.8
		91.2	86.1			Total Current	85.6	83.8
		4.6	5.0			Fixed Assets (net)	7.2	6.0
		1.5	3.4			Intangibles (net)	2.2	4.1
		2.7	5.5			All Other Non-Current	5.0	6.1
		100.0	100.0			Total	100.0	100.0
						LIABILITIES		
		22.7	15.5			Notes Payable-Short Term	18.2	17.5
		.3	.3			Cur. Mat.-L.T.D.	1.4	.8
		25.1	16.5			Trade Payables	18.8	18.7
		.3	.1			Income Taxes Payable	.2	.1
		9.0	13.0			All Other Current	8.6	9.6
		57.4	45.3			Total Current	47.1	46.8
		2.0	3.4			Long-Term Debt	8.2	3.5
		.1	.3			Deferred Taxes	.2	.1
		7.6	4.5			All Other Non-Current	5.0	3.9
		33.0	46.5			Net Worth	39.5	45.8
		100.0	100.0			Total Liabilties & Net Worth	100.0	100.0
						INCOME DATA		
		100.0	100.0			Net Sales	100.0	100.0
		30.6	30.4			Gross Profit	32.6	34.4
		28.0	25.9			Operating Expenses	27.9	30.1
		2.6	4.5			Operating Profit	4.7	4.4
		.6	1.4			All Other Expenses (net)	1.3	.5
		2.0	3.0			Profit Before Taxes	3.4	3.8
						RATIOS		
		2.5	3.1				2.7	3.3
		1.7	2.0			Current	2.0	1.8
		1.3	1.4				1.4	1.3
		1.2	1.7				1.8	1.6
		.7	1.1			Quick	1.0	.9
		.6	.7				.7	.5
		38 9.5	41 8.9				41 8.9	34 10.7
		54 6.8	54 6.7			Sales/Receivables	56 6.5	48 7.6
		74 4.9	66 5.5				70 5.2	69 5.3
		61 6.0	46 8.0				47 7.7	49 7.5
		92 4.0	85 4.3			Cost of Sales/Inventory	84 4.4	87 4.2
		168 2.2	122 3.0				138 2.6	147 2.5
		14 26.8	9 39.6				18 20.3	14 26.8
		32 11.5	21 17.1			Cost of Sales/Payables	29 12.5	38 9.7
		83 4.4	52 7.0				56 6.5	61 6.0
		4.0	3.1				3.8	3.7
		6.1	5.0			Sales/Working Capital	5.1	5.7
		11.3	9.4				11.2	13.0
		4.8	5.5				9.2	12.7
		(31) 2.7	(20) 1.3			EBIT/Interest	(77) 3.5	(77) 3.5
		1.1	-1.2				1.5	1.1
							15.8	
						Net Profit + Depr., Dep., Amort./Cur. Mat. L/T/D	(12) 4.4	
							.3	
		.0	.0				.0	.0
		.1	.1			Fixed/Worth	.1	.1
		.2	.2				.3	.2
		.5	.4				.6	.5
		1.7	1.4			Debt/Worth	1.5	1.2
		4.2	3.3				2.9	2.9
		57.7	25.1				38.1	35.1
		(35) 15.7	(21) 6.5			% Profit Before Taxes/Tangible Net Worth	(80) 14.8	(80) 12.9
		3.8	-5.7				5.4	3.0
		14.2	16.9				13.2	15.5
		3.6	2.1			% Profit Before Taxes/Total Assets	5.2	4.7
		1.0	-1.8				1.3	.7
		389.4	137.8				175.9	236.7
		122.6	74.1			Sales/Net Fixed Assets	62.5	68.4
		57.1	36.7				23.9	22.0
		3.4	3.0				2.9	2.8
		2.5	2.2			Sales/Total Assets	2.3	2.2
		1.7	1.9				1.6	1.7
		.2	.2				.2	.2
		(27) .3	(18) .5			% Depr., Dep., Amort./Sales	(67) .5	(57) .7
		.7	.8				1.1	1.1
		2.2					2.5	1.8
		(17) 4.1				% Officers', Directors' Owners' Comp/Sales	(34) 3.6	(38) 3.1
		10.8					6.2	5.1
10812M	27435M	459429M	1401856M	529604M	191086M	Net Sales ($)	3251254M	3078885M
1557M	11994M	189147M	576009M	286437M	258225M	Total Assets ($)	1737943M	1720042M

M = $ thousand   MM = $ million
See Pages 11 through 21 for Explanation of Ratios and Data

Comparative Historical Data · **Current Data Sorted by Sales**

			Type of Statement						
9	9	13	Unqualified				2	2	9
30	24	21	Reviewed	2	2		6	10	1
7	11	5	Compiled	1	1	2	2	1	
11	4	8	Tax Returns		3	2	3		
17	32	30	Other	1		2	2	8	17
4/1/04-3/31/05 ALL	4/1/05-3/31/06 ALL	4/1/06-3/31/07 ALL			14 (4/1-9/30/06)			63 (10/1/06-3/31/07)	
				0-1MM	1-3MM	3-5MM	5-10MM	10-25MM	25MM & OVER
74	80	77	NUMBER OF STATEMENTS	1	6	7	15	21	27
%	%	%	ASSETS	%	%	%	%	%	%
10.5	8.1	11.1	Cash & Equivalents				7.1	6.0	11.1
31.8	33.6	33.4	Trade Receivables (net)				42.9	34.4	33.0
37.9	40.3	39.5	Inventory				40.1	47.4	33.4
2.1	3.3	2.8	All Other Current				.9	2.9	3.9
82.2	85.3	86.9	Total Current				91.0	90.7	81.4
7.4	7.1	5.4	Fixed Assets (net)				4.4	5.6	5.6
3.5	2.9	3.0	Intangibles (net)				.9	1.5	5.9
6.8	4.8	4.8	All Other Non-Current				3.7	2.3	7.1
100.0	100.0	100.0	Total				100.0	100.0	100.0
			LIABILITIES						
15.4	18.9	17.1	Notes Payable-Short Term				24.0	22.2	14.2
.8	1.0	.4	Cur. Mat.-L.T.D.				.5	.2	.3
23.2	19.8	21.2	Trade Payables				19.5	20.4	22.6
.1	.1	.2	Income Taxes Payable				.5	.1	.1
6.0	8.2	10.7	All Other Current				11.6	5.1	14.5
45.5	48.0	49.5	Total Current				56.1	48.1	51.7
4.7	3.1	3.3	Long-Term Debt				4.1	.5	4.6
.3	.0	.1	Deferred Taxes				.2	.0	.2
3.5	5.7	5.7	All Other Non-Current				7.2	4.1	8.1
45.9	43.1	41.3	Net Worth				32.4	47.2	35.4
100.0	100.0	100.0	Total Liabilities & Net Worth				100.0	100.0	100.0
			INCOME DATA						
100.0	100.0	100.0	Net Sales				100.0	100.0	100.0
35.2	32.9	31.9	Gross Profit				33.3	30.1	33.6
30.1	29.9	28.7	Operating Expenses				30.6	26.0	29.6
5.1	3.0	3.2	Operating Profit				2.8	4.1	3.9
.6	.7	.7	All Other Expenses (net)				.6	.3	1.1
4.5	2.3	2.4	Profit Before Taxes				2.2	3.7	2.8
			RATIOS						
3.2	3.1	3.0					2.1	2.8	4.4
1.6	1.8	1.9	Current				1.6	1.9	2.2
1.3	1.3	1.3					1.3	1.3	1.5
2.0	1.3	1.5					1.2	1.2	2.3
(73) .8	.9	.9	Quick				.9	.7	1.1
.6	.5	.6					.6	.5	.7
29 12.8	30 12.3	35 10.3					46 8.0	33 11.0	37 9.9
49 7.4	50 7.3	52 7.1	Sales/Receivables				69 5.3	50 7.3	54 6.7
76 4.8	72 5.1	72 5.1					93 3.9	63 5.8	67 5.5
52 7.1	47 7.7	56 6.5					54 6.8	67 5.4	40 9.1
95 3.8	101 3.6	88 4.1	Cost of Sales/Inventory				108 3.4	97 3.8	85 4.3
145 2.5	137 2.7	126 2.9					198 1.8	143 2.6	117 3.1
23 16.1	12 29.5	12 29.4					8 43.3	15 25.0	7 52.2
39 9.2	32 11.5	27 13.6	Cost of Sales/Payables				37 9.8	26 13.6	26 14.2
77 4.8	70 5.2	71 5.2					117 3.1	69 5.3	57 6.4
3.8	4.0	3.7					3.7	4.0	3.2
6.9	6.5	6.1	Sales/Working Capital				6.4	5.7	5.8
11.9	15.8	12.0					11.4	11.4	10.3
12.0	6.8	5.7					3.9	7.8	13.2
(63) 4.0	(65) 2.4	(64) 2.3	EBIT/Interest				(14) 2.3	(17) 2.7	(23) 1.6
1.7	1.0	.7					1.0	1.1	-1.5
			Net Profit + Depr., Dep., Amort./Cur. Mat. L/T/D						
.0	.0	.0					.0	.0	.0
.1	.1	.1	Fixed/Worth				.1	.1	.1
.3	.4	.2					.3	.2	.3
.5	.5	.4					1.2	.5	.4
1.5	1.6	1.4	Debt/Worth				2.0	1.4	1.2
3.2	4.5	4.1					8.1	2.8	4.6
52.2	42.0	32.8					30.2	61.2	29.5
(71) 19.3	(74) 14.9	(70) 12.3	% Profit Before Taxes/Tangible Net Worth				10.0	17.6	(23) 16.6
2.4	2.9	1.3					4.4	1.8	-2.3
17.0	12.1	14.5					11.6	18.2	17.9
6.6	4.5	4.2	% Profit Before Taxes/Total Assets				3.5	5.7	6.5
.8	.6	.2					.4	1.6	-1.6
277.3	244.0	265.5					741.1	214.7	132.2
72.9	69.7	86.9	Sales/Net Fixed Assets				86.9	117.8	71.6
18.0	26.4	34.8					56.4	39.2	37.6
2.9	3.1	3.2					3.3	3.4	3.0
2.2	2.3	2.3	Sales/Total Assets				2.1	2.3	2.4
1.7	1.8	1.8					1.6	1.9	1.8
.2	.2	.2					.2	.2	.2
(56) .7	(60) .5	(59) .5	% Depr., Dep., Amort./Sales				(12) .6	(16) .3	(22) .6
1.2	1.1	.8					.9	.7	.8
2.3	1.9	1.7							
(36) 4.2	(29) 3.3	(26) 3.9	% Officers', Directors' Owners' Comp/Sales						
6.3	5.7	12.7							
2642959M	2623434M	2620222M	Net Sales ($)	388M	13998M	23900M	113228M	336217M	2132491M
1323234M	1279688M	1323369M	Total Assets ($)	397M	4466M	23060M	57370M	137538M	1100538M

M = $ thousand   MM = $ million
See Pages 11 through 21 for Explanation of Ratios and Data

Current Data Sorted by Assets   Comparative Historical Data

Type of Statement

Type of Statement	0-500M	500M-2MM	2-10MM	10-50MM	50-100MM	100-250MM	4/1/02-3/31/03 ALL	4/1/03-3/31/04 ALL
Unqualified	1		14	36	11	19	91	75
Reviewed	1	6	58	23	1		82	82
Compiled	10	30	36	7			60	88
Tax Returns	15	17	21				28	43
Other	9	17	45	33	12	6	115	100
	121 (4/1-9/30/06)			307 (10/1/06-3/31/07)				
NUMBER OF STATEMENTS	36	70	174	99	24	25	376	388

ASSETS (%)

	0-500M	500M-2MM	2-10MM	10-50MM	50-100MM	100-250MM	ALL	ALL
Cash & Equivalents	15.9	9.5	7.5	5.3	5.6	4.0	7.6	7.0
Trade Receivables (net)	16.0	27.6	35.9	31.5	27.5	19.8	32.3	30.6
Inventory	33.2	30.4	31.2	30.8	25.6	29.8	30.5	30.6
All Other Current	1.7	1.4	2.7	3.0	6.4	2.8	2.5	2.7
Total Current	66.8	68.9	77.4	70.6	65.0	56.4	72.8	71.0
Fixed Assets (net)	18.5	18.6	16.4	21.7	21.7	31.7	18.2	19.9
Intangibles (net)	5.0	3.4	1.1	1.8	2.9	4.4	2.3	3.1
All Other Non-Current	9.7	9.2	5.2	5.9	10.4	7.5	6.7	6.0
Total	100.0	100.0	100.0	100.0	100.0	100.0	100.0	100.0

LIABILITIES

	0-500M	500M-2MM	2-10MM	10-50MM	50-100MM	100-250MM	ALL	ALL
Notes Payable-Short Term	10.3	10.0	16.1	16.7	12.9	6.7	15.5	14.9
Cur. Mat.-L.T.D.	3.7	4.4	2.2	2.6	2.8	3.5	3.0	2.9
Trade Payables	29.2	29.8	26.6	21.3	22.6	19.0	24.3	24.8
Income Taxes Payable	.6	.0	.2	.2	1.5	.5	.2	.3
All Other Current	14.2	7.7	8.8	8.1	8.7	9.2	9.4	9.0
Total Current	58.0	51.8	53.9	48.9	48.5	38.9	52.4	51.8
Long-Term Debt	35.3	15.3	9.3	11.9	15.1	18.2	11.1	11.5
Deferred Taxes	.0	.1	.1	.2	.4	.7	.3	.3
All Other Non-Current	10.4	8.0	4.1	3.9	2.7	9.6	4.4	5.5
Net Worth	-3.6	24.7	32.5	34.9	33.3	32.7	31.7	30.9
Total Liabilities & Net Worth	100.0	100.0	100.0	100.0	100.0	100.0	100.0	100.0

INCOME DATA

	0-500M	500M-2MM	2-10MM	10-50MM	50-100MM	100-250MM	ALL	ALL
Net Sales	100.0	100.0	100.0	100.0	100.0	100.0	100.0	100.0
Gross Profit	22.4	23.4	18.3	16.6	12.2	17.8	18.5	19.2
Operating Expenses	21.1	20.3	16.6	14.3	11.0	14.8	16.4	17.5
Operating Profit	1.3	3.2	1.7	2.3	1.2	3.1	2.1	1.8
All Other Expenses (net)	1.4	.1	.2	.4	.2	.8	.1	.3
Profit Before Taxes	-.2	3.1	1.6	1.9	1.0	2.2	2.0	1.5

RATIOS

	0-500M	500M-2MM	2-10MM	10-50MM	50-100MM	100-250MM	ALL	ALL
Current	2.8	2.1	2.0	2.0	1.7	1.8	2.0	2.0
	1.4	1.4	1.5	1.5	1.4	1.4	1.4	1.4
	.7	1.0	1.2	1.1	1.1	1.2	1.1	1.1
Quick	1.2	1.2	1.2	1.1	.9	.7	1.2	1.1
	.5	.6	.8	.7	.6	.6	(375) .8	.7
	.2	.4	.6	.5	.4	.5	.5	.5
Sales/Receivables	0 UND	3 104.9	17 21.2	15 24.0	7 54.6	8 43.6	13 27.7	13 28.5
	3 117.2	15 23.8	27 13.4	25 14.4	15 23.9	14 25.4	24 15.3	23 15.7
	19 19.3	27 13.6	40 9.2	37 10.0	22 16.2	26 14.0	32 11.4	34 10.9
Cost of Sales/Inventory	8 45.7	14 25.8	17 21.0	15 23.7	15 24.5	20 18.2	16 22.3	18 20.5
	20 18.5	22 16.4	28 13.0	27 13.5	19 19.2	29 12.5	25 14.6	28 13.1
	35 10.5	38 9.7	45 8.2	44 8.3	25 14.5	43 8.4	39 9.3	42 8.8
Cost of Sales/Payables	3 140.4	9 40.6	11 33.4	11 32.3	11 33.2	12 29.6	11 34.1	12 31.3
	11 34.7	19 19.0	21 17.6	18 19.8	15 24.9	18 20.1	19 19.1	19 19.5
	28 12.9	37 9.8	37 9.8	33 11.2	19 19.2	28 13.2	31 11.8	33 11.1
Sales/Working Capital	16.6	12.4	11.2	11.4	20.9	12.9	13.6	12.9
	49.6	36.9	21.9	21.3	35.0	36.4	25.5	24.2
	-53.0	-497.9	50.4	57.6	120.4	52.2	89.3	119.9
EBIT/Interest	6.6	9.7	12.2	7.2	6.6	6.0	11.0	9.1
	(27) 1.4	(61) 4.1	(161) 3.1	(86) 2.6	(22) 3.2	(23) 1.9	(345) 3.5	(346) 3.2
	-1.7	.5	1.5	1.5	1.7	1.5	1.7	1.6
Net Profit + Depr., Dep., Amort./Cur. Mat. L/T/D			4.8	8.8	3.2	9.8	7.6	5.4
		(40) 2.1	(37) 3.9	(12) 3.0	(10) 2.3		(123) 2.8	(115) 2.5
		.9	2.4	1.0	.8		1.1	1.3
Fixed/Worth	.1	.1	.1	.3	.3	.6	.2	.2
	.6	.5	.4	.6	.6	1.0	.5	.6
	-2.7	1.6	.9	1.4	1.2	2.6	1.2	1.5
Debt/Worth	.6	1.2	1.1	1.0	1.6	1.8	1.0	1.1
	4.8	2.2	2.4	2.7	2.1	2.2	2.5	2.5
	-7.6	10.2	5.4	4.6	4.3	4.9	5.3	5.7
% Profit Before Taxes/Tangible Net Worth	54.3	71.6	38.1	35.0	28.5	49.0	42.6	36.8
	(23) 21.1	(59) 27.2	(160) 17.4	(94) 18.0	16.1	(24) 13.8	(346) 16.9	(350) 15.7
	1.1	3.6	6.1	10.1	5.8	5.5	6.6	5.9
% Profit Before Taxes/Total Assets	12.4	19.9	12.0	11.7	7.0	7.3	11.0	9.9
	4.4	7.0	5.1	5.0	3.4	3.5	4.9	4.6
	-4.8	-.6	1.5	2.2	1.6	1.5	1.7	1.6
Sales/Net Fixed Assets	356.5	320.6	156.3	81.5	95.3	26.1	109.5	109.3
	57.5	62.4	47.3	35.4	24.6	14.7	38.6	36.5
	24.2	15.2	18.6	11.3	15.2	9.7	17.1	13.5
Sales/Total Assets	12.7	7.4	6.7	6.0	8.4	6.4	7.0	6.7
	6.7	5.7	4.7	4.6	5.0	4.3	5.0	4.8
	5.1	4.3	3.2	3.1	4.1	3.1	3.6	3.4
% Depr., Dep., Amort./Sales	.3	.2	.2	.2	.2	.6	.3	.3
	(22) .9	(50) .7	(150) .5	(91) .5	(22) .6	(18) .7	(334) .6	(332) .6
	2.1	1.5	1.0	1.0	.9	1.2	1.0	1.1
% Officers', Directors' Owners' Comp/Sales	.7	.8	.5	.4			.8	.9
	(18) 2.0	(47) 1.6	(86) 1.7	(21) .9			(147) 1.6	(150) 1.9
	5.8	4.8	2.7	2.7			3.5	3.5
Net Sales ($)	91496M	464355M	4488556M	11341803M	9930962M	16855578M	46405571M	37065431M
Total Assets ($)	9999M	74986M	850637M	2221235M	1668256M	3845923M	8110994M	7774508M

M = $ thousand   MM = $ million
See Pages 11 through 21 for Explanation of Ratios and Data

Comparative Historical Data   Current Data Sorted by Sales

Hist 1	Hist 2	Hist 3	Type of Statement	0-1MM	1-3MM	3-5MM	5-10MM	10-25MM	25MM & OVER
74	81	81	Unqualified	1			1	3	76
92	76	89	Reviewed		3	10	29		47
84	62	83	Compiled	2	8	13	12	27	21
47	35	53	Tax Returns	7	10	7	9	11	9
111	123	122	Other	2	8	10	13	31	58
4/1/04-3/31/05 ALL	4/1/05-3/31/06 ALL	4/1/06-3/31/07 ALL		121 (4/1-9/30/06)			307 (10/1/06-3/31/07)		
408	377	428	**NUMBER OF STATEMENTS**	12	26	33	45	101	211
%	%	%	**ASSETS**	%	%	%	%	%	%
7.4	6.7	7.7	Cash & Equivalents	27.1	11.5	6.9	8.3	8.1	6.0
28.7	31.0	30.5	Trade Receivables (net)	17.4	14.2	17.9	30.3	36.9	32.1
30.0	31.7	30.8	Inventory	19.7	33.9	36.1	29.4	29.9	30.8
3.3	2.7	2.7	All Other Current	2.3	1.5	2.4	1.9	2.6	3.1
69.4	72.0	71.6	Total Current	66.6	61.2	63.3	70.0	77.5	72.0
21.8	19.1	19.3	Fixed Assets (net)	17.1	27.8	19.4	20.4	15.5	20.0
2.9	2.4	2.3	Intangibles (net)	5.4	2.9	5.3	2.9	.6	2.2
6.0	6.5	6.8	All Other Non-Current	10.9	8.2	12.0	6.8	6.4	5.8
100.0	100.0	100.0	Total	100.0	100.0	100.0	100.0	100.0	100.0
			LIABILITIES						
14.9	16.9	14.0	Notes Payable-Short Term	3.5	11.9	8.0	12.9	15.6	15.3
2.7	2.3	2.9	Cur. Mat.-L.T.D.	6.5	2.8	6.1	2.8	2.7	2.3
22.2	24.1	25.5	Trade Payables	14.2	26.1	30.7	26.6	30.2	22.7
.2	.3	.3	Income Taxes Payable	.0	.9	.0	.1	.1	.4
9.0	8.4	8.9	All Other Current	9.2	11.7	10.7	11.0	8.1	8.2
48.9	51.9	51.6	Total Current	33.5	53.3	55.5	53.5	56.6	48.9
14.8	13.2	13.9	Long-Term Debt	53.6	21.2	30.2	10.0	9.0	11.4
.4	.3	.3	Deferred Taxes	.0	.0	.0	.3	.2	.4
6.2	5.1	5.4	All Other Non-Current	27.0	4.7	11.3	4.6	3.4	4.6
29.7	29.5	28.8	Net Worth	-13.7	20.7	3.0	31.6	30.8	34.7
100.0	100.0	100.0	Total Liabilities & Net Worth	100.0	100.0	100.0	100.0	100.0	100.0
			INCOME DATA						
100.0	100.0	100.0	Net Sales	100.0	100.0	100.0	100.0	100.0	100.0
18.9	18.9	18.7	Gross Profit	34.1	24.2	25.1	23.1	19.3	14.9
16.7	17.2	16.6	Operating Expenses	32.2	19.8	22.6	21.4	17.6	12.9
2.2	1.6	2.1	Operating Profit	2.0	4.4	2.5	1.8	1.7	2.0
.3	.2	.4	All Other Expenses (net)	2.6	.8	.1	.6	.0	.3
1.9	1.5	1.8	Profit Before Taxes	-.7	3.6	2.4	1.2	1.7	1.7
			RATIOS						
2.1	1.9	2.0	Current	16.3	3.2	2.0	2.4	1.8	1.9
1.4	1.4	1.4		1.9	1.4	1.3	1.4	1.4	1.4
1.1	1.1	1.1		1.2	.7	.8	1.0	1.2	1.2
1.2	1.0	1.1	Quick	14.4	1.2	.7	1.1	1.2	1.1
.7	.7	.7		1.1	.4	.5	.8	.8	.7
.5	.5	.5		.5	.2	.2	.5	.6	.5
8 46.1	11 33.6	12 31.3	Sales/Receivables	0 UND	1 629.4	0 827.3	6 58.6	19 18.9	12 29.6
21 17.4	22 16.4	22 16.7		11 33.9	19 19.4	10 38.4	24 15.0	28 12.9	20 17.9
32 11.3	33 11.0	34 10.6		30 18.6	27 13.3	20 18.6	43 8.4	40 9.1	29 12.4
16 23.5	16 23.2	15 25.0	Cost of Sales/Inventory	6 61.5	12 31.5	16 22.5	15 24.4	18 20.2	14 25.4
26 14.0	26 14.0	25 14.4		17 21.2	29 12.7	28 12.8	26 14.2	31 11.6	24 15.3
38 9.6	40 9.0	40 9.1		41 8.9	53 6.9	43 8.5	50 7.3	45 8.1	35 10.6
9 40.8	11 34.5	10 35.1	Cost of Sales/Payables	0 UND	2 197.5	9 40.4	10 37.1	12 30.4	11 33.4
16 22.2	18 20.5	18 19.8		11 33.1	15 24.7	19 18.9	22 16.4	23 15.8	16 23.4
28 13.2	32 11.4	35 10.5		51 7.2	48 7.6	40 9.2	56 6.5	39 9.4	28 13.2
12.4	13.3	12.3	Sales/Working Capital	9.9	7.4	13.3	10.8	11.2	13.8
25.6	28.3	26.6		18.4	30.6	81.6	29.6	21.6	27.8
122.2	74.1	87.6		49.5	-30.0	-38.3	-251.2	54.5	58.9
9.7	9.9	9.2	EBIT/Interest		3.9	10.9	7.9	10.1	9.5
(364) 3.1	(341) 3.0	(380) 3.0			(21) 1.2	(32) 3.5	(38) 2.9	(90) 2.8	(193) 3.2
1.5	1.5	1.5			-1.0	-.2	1.2	1.2	1.6
7.7	5.8	5.0	Net Profit + Depr., Dep., Amort./Cur. Mat. L/T/D				13.2	3.5	6.4
(106) 2.7	(112) 2.9	(108) 3.0					(11) .8	(25) 2.0	(71) 3.3
1.4	1.5	1.3					-.7	.5	1.8
.2	.2	.1	Fixed/Worth	.1	.3	.0	.1	.1	.2
.6	.5	.5		.3	.9	.8	.5	.4	.5
2.0	1.5	1.4		3.0	NM	-6.7	1.4	1.0	1.3
1.1	1.2	1.1	Debt/Worth	.1	.9	1.3	1.0	1.3	1.2
2.6	2.5	2.4		.8	3.5	6.8	2.4	2.6	2.2
7.3	5.5	5.4		NM	NM	-5.4	5.9	4.9	4.8
36.0	34.3	40.4	% Profit Before Taxes/Tangible Net Worth		88.7	84.5	58.6	33.5	39.4
(358) 17.5	(336) 15.2	(384) 18.2		(20) 25.6	(21) 37.8	(40) 11.8	(92) 16.4	(202) 18.6	
5.5	5.5	6.7			.7	5.6	4.6	3.4	9.2
11.0	10.8	11.9	% Profit Before Taxes/Total Assets	18.7	14.8	22.6	10.3	11.5	11.8
4.5	4.1	4.9		8.9	3.9	7.2	3.2	4.9	5.2
1.4	1.4	1.5		-2.6	-3.8	-4.4	.9	.7	2.1
90.1	127.8	128.9	Sales/Net Fixed Assets	204.9	102.7	299.4	124.3	151.8	104.9
32.3	41.9	42.8		61.2	24.7	67.5	54.1	42.6	42.3
14.0	14.7	14.3		8.0	9.0	16.4	12.1	17.4	14.7
6.9	7.2	6.9	Sales/Total Assets	7.5	5.6	9.1	6.7	6.0	7.4
4.9	5.1	5.1		6.1	4.5	5.6	4.6	4.5	5.4
3.4	3.5	3.5		2.4	3.1	4.3	2.6	3.2	3.7
.3	.3	.2	% Depr., Dep., Amort./Sales		.6	.3	.3	.2	.2
(339) .6	(315) .5	(353) .6		(20) 1.2	(19) .7	(35) .9	(85) .6	(185) .5	
1.2	1.0	1.1			2.1	2.5	1.7	1.0	.9
.9	.7	.4	% Officers', Directors' Owners' Comp/Sales		1.3	.2	.8	.8	.4
(149) 1.9	(135) 1.6	(174) 1.5		(13) 1.7	(22) 1.9	(28) 2.1	(50) 1.4	(56) 1.0	
3.6	3.0	2.9			2.9	4.1	3.7	2.7	1.9
37641804M	43993041M	43168750M	Net Sales ($)	7353M	52331M	137851M	336476M	1600893M	41033846M
8022980M	8484342M	8671036M	Total Assets ($)	2545M	22081M	29259M	91940M	414101M	8111110M

M = $ thousand   MM = $ million
See Pages 11 through 21 for Explanation of Ratios and Data

Current Data Sorted by Assets   Comparative Historical Data

0-500M	500M-2MM	2-10MM	10-50MM	50-100MM	100-250MM	Type of Statement	4/1/02-3/31/03 ALL	4/1/03-3/31/04 ALL
	1	5	13	5	3	Unqualified	27	21
1		16	9			Reviewed	24	33
1	3	4	3			Compiled	17	22
1	3	4	1			Tax Returns	6	9
2	5	15	22	4	3	Other	38	35
	40 (4/1-9/30/06)		84 (10/1/06-3/31/07)					
5	12	44	48	9	6	**NUMBER OF STATEMENTS**	112	120

0-500M %	500M-2MM %	2-10MM %	10-50MM %	50-100MM %	100-250MM %		%	%
						ASSETS		
	6.9	7.1	6.4			Cash & Equivalents	7.0	4.8
	44.8	33.0	32.4			Trade Receivables (net)	28.2	32.1
	27.3	31.2	33.8			Inventory	31.1	29.9
	2.1	2.3	2.4			All Other Current	4.0	3.6
	81.2	73.6	74.9			Total Current	70.3	70.4
	13.6	13.5	18.3			Fixed Assets (net)	20.1	20.4
	3.4	6.0	1.2			Intangibles (net)	1.5	3.5
	1.8	6.9	5.6			All Other Non-Current	8.2	5.6
	100.0	100.0	100.0			Total	100.0	100.0
						LIABILITIES		
	37.3	15.7	19.2			Notes Payable-Short Term	17.2	18.4
	2.7	1.8	2.1			Cur. Mat.-L.T.D.	2.7	3.0
	36.6	22.3	18.7			Trade Payables	23.4	23.7
	.5	.2	.3			Income Taxes Payable	.2	.2
	9.7	6.0	7.0			All Other Current	8.5	7.2
	86.8	46.0	47.3			Total Current	52.0	52.5
	8.0	10.3	13.0			Long-Term Debt	11.8	17.2
	.3	.4	.6			Deferred Taxes	.3	.2
	1.1	3.7	2.6			All Other Non-Current	4.1	6.2
	3.7	39.6	36.5			Net Worth	31.8	23.8
	100.0	100.0	100.0			Total Liabilties & Net Worth	100.0	100.0
						INCOME DATA		
	100.0	100.0	100.0			Net Sales	100.0	100.0
	27.7	19.0	16.1			Gross Profit	19.4	20.1
	24.1	16.4	13.4			Operating Expenses	16.4	18.0
	3.6	2.6	2.6			Operating Profit	3.0	2.1
	.4	.5	.3			All Other Expenses (net)	.2	.6
	3.2	2.1	2.4			Profit Before Taxes	2.8	1.5
						RATIOS		
	1.8	3.0	2.9			Current	2.0	1.9
	1.3	1.5	1.5				1.4	1.3
	1.0	1.2	1.1				1.1	1.0
	1.3	1.7	1.5			Quick	1.1	1.0
	.8	.9	.7				.7 (119)	.7
	.6	.4	.5				.5	.5
13	27.3	19 19.6	19 19.0			Sales/Receivables	15 23.6	17 21.3
19	19.0	24 15.1	26 14.1				23 15.7	26 14.0
31	11.7	36 10.1	38 9.6				34 10.6	34 10.8
9	38.8	21 17.4	23 16.0			Cost of Sales/Inventory	18 20.0	19 18.9
15	24.9	33 11.1	30 12.0				28 13.1	29 12.5
33	11.0	56 6.5	52 7.0				55 6.7	48 7.6
16	22.8	12 31.6	13 28.6			Cost of Sales/Payables	14 26.0	15 24.5
20	18.6	20 18.5	18 20.3				20 18.1	21 17.6
55	6.7	40 9.2	29 12.4				31 11.9	32 11.4
	15.5	8.1	8.6			Sales/Working Capital	11.4	12.2
	35.4	15.0	17.4				25.8	26.8
	779.6	34.7	68.2				60.7	134.5
	29.1	11.6	7.4			EBIT/Interest	8.3	6.8
	(10) 4.2	(40) 2.9	(44) 3.9				(95) 3.4	(108) 3.2
	1.8	1.5	1.2				1.5	1.4
		20.7	8.1			Net Profit + Depr., Dep., Amort./Cur. Mat. L/T/D	7.6	5.0
	(16)	4.1	(15) 2.6				(24) 2.0	(27) 2.3
		1.7	1.5				1.2	1.6
	.0	.1	.1			Fixed/Worth	.1	.2
	.2	.4	.4				.5	.6
	1.0	.7	1.1				1.2	2.4
	1.2	.5	.7			Debt/Worth	.9	1.2
	3.7	2.8	2.3				2.4	3.2
	11.3	7.3	4.0				5.7	10.3
	91.3	49.3	30.7			% Profit Before Taxes/Tangible Net Worth	48.9	35.9
	(10) 44.0	(39) 23.3	(45) 19.6				(104) 16.1	(105) 20.3
	9.0	8.4	3.4				6.8	6.5
	18.5	13.2	15.6			% Profit Before Taxes/Total Assets	10.5	10.5
	7.2	5.9	6.0				5.2	4.0
	3.1	2.0	.7				1.8	.9
	819.4	175.8	115.7			Sales/Net Fixed Assets	160.6	115.3
	95.1	54.4	38.1				31.5	40.1
	31.1	17.0	12.7				13.4	12.3
	8.8	5.1	6.3			Sales/Total Assets	6.1	6.2
	6.7	4.1	3.8				4.4	4.2
	4.1	2.5	2.9				2.7	2.6
		.2	.2			% Depr., Dep., Amort./Sales	.3	.3
	(38)	.6	(43) .5				(93) .6	(101) .7
		1.0	.8				1.4	1.4
		.7	.6			% Officers', Directors' Owners' Comp/Sales	.7	.8
	(19)	1.4	(11) 1.7				(35) 1.1	(50) 1.1
		2.5	3.8				1.6	3.4
2688M	98366M	1017785M	4300981M	2287225M	5844233M	Net Sales ($)	7518107M	7619135M
760M	15471M	250932M	967514M	546035M	1210922M	Total Assets ($)	2098292M	1736706M

M = $ thousand   MM = $ million
See Pages 11 through 21 for Explanation of Ratios and Data

Comparative Historical Data | Current Data Sorted by Sales

			Type of Statement						
32	27	27	Unqualified				2		25
21	20	26	Reviewed	1			2	12	11
18	10	11	Compiled	1			3	3	4
3	5	9	Tax Returns	1			2	5	1
33	48	51	Other	1	1	1	5	10	33
4/1/04-3/31/05 ALL	4/1/05-3/31/06 ALL	4/1/06-3/31/07 ALL			40 (4/1-9/30/06)			84 (10/1/06-3/31/07)	
				0-1MM	1-3MM	3-5MM	5-10MM	10-25MM	25MM & OVER
107	110	124	NUMBER OF STATEMENTS	4	1	1	14	30	74
%	%	%	ASSETS	%	%	%	%	%	%
6.8	6.3	6.4	Cash & Equivalents				13.3	6.2	5.2
31.8	33.5	32.6	Trade Receivables (net)				33.3	28.3	34.9
31.9	29.3	32.2	Inventory				24.4	32.8	34.2
3.1	2.0	2.5	All Other Current				2.5	1.4	2.6
73.5	71.1	73.7	Total Current				73.5	68.8	76.9
17.3	19.4	16.5	Fixed Assets (net)				16.0	17.7	15.9
2.7	2.7	4.0	Intangibles (net)				4.4	6.7	2.2
6.5	6.9	5.7	All Other Non-Current				6.1	6.8	4.9
100.0	100.0	100.0	Total				100.0	100.0	100.0
			LIABILITIES						
19.4	17.7	20.0	Notes Payable-Short Term				25.8	15.7	20.7
2.0	2.7	2.8	Cur. Mat.-L.T.D.				2.5	2.2	1.8
24.4	21.8	22.0	Trade Payables				20.5	22.9	22.4
.2	.2	.3	Income Taxes Payable				.6	.5	.1
7.8	7.7	7.4	All Other Current				11.8	4.7	7.4
53.9	50.2	52.4	Total Current				61.1	46.0	52.4
17.2	13.9	12.1	Long-Term Debt				8.0	13.7	11.3
.3	.3	.5	Deferred Taxes				.4	.3	.5
5.1	5.4	3.7	All Other Non-Current				2.8	2.7	3.3
23.4	30.3	31.3	Net Worth				27.6	37.2	32.5
100.0	100.0	100.0	Total Liabilties & Net Worth				100.0	100.0	100.0
			INCOME DATA						
100.0	100.0	100.0	Net Sales				100.0	100.0	100.0
18.5	20.9	19.4	Gross Profit				23.8	24.5	14.2
16.9	18.2	16.7	Operating Expenses				21.1	20.8	12.0
1.6	2.7	2.6	Operating Profit				2.8	3.7	2.3
.3	.5	.4	All Other Expenses (net)				.5	.8	.3
1.2	2.2	2.2	Profit Before Taxes				2.3	2.9	2.0
			RATIOS						
2.1	2.0	2.4					2.8	2.9	2.3
1.3	1.3	1.4	Current				1.7	1.5	1.3
1.1	1.1	1.1					1.3	1.1	1.1
1.1	1.4	1.5					1.5	1.6	1.4
.7	.7	.7	Quick				1.3	.8	.6
.4	.5	.5					.7	.4	.5
18 20.7	19 19.1	18 20.3					14 26.7	17 21.4	19 19.1
25 14.4	26 14.2	24 15.5	Sales/Receivables				21 17.7	23 16.1	26 14.3
36 10.0	40 9.2	36 10.0					33 11.1	33 11.0	38 9.6
19 18.7	16 23.3	18 20.8					10 37.0	21 17.0	18 20.5
31 11.7	28 12.8	30 12.3	Cost of Sales/Inventory				22 16.6	41 9.0	29 12.4
48 7.6	48 7.6	54 6.8					39 9.3	60 6.1	44 8.3
14 25.4	13 28.0	12 30.0					15 24.9	11 33.9	12 29.3
21 17.3	22 16.5	20 18.6	Cost of Sales/Payables				19 19.1	20 18.2	19 19.2
31 11.8	35 10.5	32 11.4					27 13.6	56 6.5	31 11.9
11.9	8.8	9.3					5.0	8.5	10.7
24.5	25.2	18.8	Sales/Working Capital				16.7	15.0	21.3
59.5	90.9	98.4					40.0	138.3	78.2
11.6	7.6	8.2					31.2	9.4	7.4
(93) 4.2	(100) 3.2	(113) 3.3	EBIT/Interest			(13)	4.4	(26) 2.6	(69) 3.3
1.8	1.5	1.4					1.9	1.1	1.4
16.3	9.2	10.4					28.5		8.9
(33) 4.3	(35) 3.8	(42) 5.4	Net Profit + Depr., Dep., Amort./Cur. Mat. L/T/D					(13) 1.8	(24) 6.2
1.3	1.1	1.7						.6	2.4
.1	.2	.1					.0	.1	.1
.5	.6	.5	Fixed/Worth				.3	.5	.5
1.2	1.4	1.1					.8	1.1	.9
1.1	1.0	.8					.7	.6	1.3
3.1	3.2	2.9	Debt/Worth				1.3	2.9	2.9
9.2	8.3	8.1					4.9	9.7	8.1
35.3	34.9	37.8					68.1	39.0	36.0
(92) 21.3	(97) 17.6	(109) 21.5	% Profit Before Taxes/Tangible Net Worth			(13)	11.6	(26) 18.8	(67) 25.5
11.4	7.8	7.0					6.9	7.6	7.0
11.0	9.6	14.3					17.1	13.4	14.7
5.4	4.8	5.6	% Profit Before Taxes/Total Assets				5.0	5.9	5.9
2.6	1.6	1.5					2.8	1.2	1.5
162.3	130.2	126.0					286.4	245.1	122.3
47.2	39.4	38.1	Sales/Net Fixed Assets				62.3	23.9	39.1
14.2	13.8	15.5					19.5	11.3	16.9
6.1	6.1	6.1					7.3	4.7	6.4
4.2	4.0	4.1	Sales/Total Assets				4.2	3.6	4.2
2.7	2.4	2.7					2.7	2.4	3.1
.2	.3	.2					.3	.5	.2
(91) .5	(91) .6	(104) .5	% Depr., Dep., Amort./Sales			(10)	.9	(23) .9	(67) .5
1.1	1.7	1.0					1.5	1.6	.7
.7	.7	.7						.5	.7
(31) 1.7	(34) 1.7	(41) 1.4	% Officers', Directors' Owners' Comp/Sales					(17) 1.0	(16) 1.4
4.0	2.9	2.7						2.2	2.6
8762294M	10650820M	13551278M	Net Sales ($)	1516M	1172M	3339M	103351M	485351M	12956549M
1991551M	2445646M	2991634M	Total Assets ($)	649M	111M	1941M	31809M	186140M	2770984M

© RMA 2007

M = $ thousand   MM = $ million
See Pages 11 through 21 for Explanation of Ratios and Data

Current Data Sorted by Assets   Comparative Historical Data

0-500M	500M-2MM	2-10MM	10-50MM	50-100MM	100-250MM	Type of Statement	4/1/02-3/31/03 ALL	4/1/03-3/31/04 ALL
		1	1	7	3	4 Unqualified	19	12
	1	13	4		4	Reviewed	19	19
1	5	11	4			Compiled	13	21
1	3	5	1			Tax Returns	10	9
	1	17	11		4	Other	21	11
	18 (4/1-9/30/06)		80 (10/1/06-3/31/07)				4/1/02-3/31/03	4/1/03-3/31/04
2	11	47	27	3	8	**NUMBER OF STATEMENTS**	82	72
%	%	%	%	%	%	**ASSETS**	%	%
	7.6	7.3	9.4			Cash & Equivalents	8.0	7.1
	46.0	38.3	34.7			Trade Receivables (net)	39.3	36.8
	17.3	22.7	22.1			Inventory	21.8	25.0
	1.4	2.7	2.2			All Other Current	1.2	2.2
	72.3	71.0	68.4			Total Current	70.3	71.2
	16.1	20.4	18.7			Fixed Assets (net)	21.3	20.4
	6.7	3.2	7.9			Intangibles (net)	2.2	2.3
	4.9	5.4	5.0			All Other Non-Current	6.2	6.1
	100.0	100.0	100.0			Total	100.0	100.0
						LIABILITIES		
	8.5	12.8	9.1			Notes Payable-Short Term	6.7	8.3
	.3	2.4	2.3			Cur. Mat.-L.T.D.	4.4	2.7
	31.0	34.1	35.1			Trade Payables	31.9	33.3
	.0	.1	.2			Income Taxes Payable	.2	.2
	4.6	8.4	7.9			All Other Current	13.3	11.0
	44.4	57.7	54.6			Total Current	56.4	55.4
	11.2	10.0	13.0			Long-Term Debt	13.2	15.4
	.0	.2	.3			Deferred Taxes	.1	.2
	11.0	3.1	1.3			All Other Non-Current	4.1	3.1
	33.4	29.0	30.7			Net Worth	26.2	25.8
	100.0	100.0	100.0			Total Liabilties & Net Worth	100.0	100.0
						INCOME DATA		
	100.0	100.0	100.0			Net Sales	100.0	100.0
	17.4	19.2	15.2			Gross Profit	18.6	19.3
	15.3	16.4	13.0			Operating Expenses	17.2	17.3
	2.1	2.8	2.2			Operating Profit	1.5	2.0
	.6	.4	.0			All Other Expenses (net)	.0	.1
	1.5	2.4	2.2			Profit Before Taxes	1.4	1.9
						RATIOS		
	2.5	1.7	1.6				1.6	1.9
	1.6	1.2	1.3			Current	1.2	1.3
	1.1	.9	1.0				1.0	1.0
	2.1	1.2	1.0				1.3	1.2
	1.1	.8	.8			Quick	.8	.7
	.8	.5	.6				.5	.5
	9 41.1	19 18.9	21 17.5				16 22.6	20 18.0
	37 9.8	25 14.3	25 14.7			Sales/Receivables	22 16.3	25 14.3
	42 8.8	35 10.4	36 10.2				34 10.7	33 11.1
	0 UND	7 48.9	10 37.7				6 59.1	10 37.3
	12 31.1	20 18.6	18 20.1			Cost of Sales/Inventory	17 21.5	20 18.0
	30 12.3	32 11.3	26 13.8				35 10.3	35 10.4
	18 20.1	18 20.5	20 18.0				14 25.9	22 16.7
	24 15.4	26 14.0	27 13.6			Cost of Sales/Payables	24 15.3	30 12.3
	42 8.6	42 8.6	35 10.3				39 9.5	40 9.1
	10.3	15.4	15.8				17.4	12.4
	14.9	31.7	28.4			Sales/Working Capital	42.9	29.5
	149.4	-102.9	-180.9				-877.5	430.7
	10.1		26.5				12.2	26.7
	(42) 3.8		(24) 9.5			EBIT/Interest	(67) 4.1	(63) 4.9
	2.1		1.8				1.7	1.7
	10.1					Net Profit + Depr., Dep.,	14.4	4.0
	(10) 3.2					Amort./Cur. Mat. L/T/D	(11) 1.8	(16) 2.0
	1.2						1.3	.5
	.0	.1	.1				.1	.1
	.2	.8	.6			Fixed/Worth	.7	.6
	1.3	2.5	4.4				1.5	2.0
	.7	1.2	1.3				1.3	1.2
	2.4	4.5	3.5			Debt/Worth	2.9	2.8
	6.1	8.7	7.2				6.1	6.1
	61.3	56.5	54.7			% Profit Before Taxes/Tangible	39.8	50.4
	(10) 22.5	(42) 32.3	(22) 21.6			Net Worth	(74) 21.0	(62) 17.2
	2.1	4.8	8.3				7.5	6.8
	19.6	14.5	19.5			% Profit Before Taxes/Total	12.3	12.7
	5.7	6.3	6.3			Assets	4.9	4.5
	.3	2.7	2.6				1.0	1.3
	662.1	211.5	923.6				327.9	279.5
	148.3	27.9	32.6			Sales/Net Fixed Assets	32.3	31.5
	17.7	11.4	13.3				12.9	10.2
	7.0	6.5	6.0				8.2	6.2
	6.1	4.8	4.5			Sales/Total Assets	5.2	4.7
	3.3	2.7	3.3				3.2	2.9
		.2	.6				.2	.2
		(40) 1.1	(22) .9			% Depr., Dep., Amort./Sales	(68) .9	(60) .9
		1.9	1.6				2.0	1.8
		1.1	.4				.6	.7
		(22) 1.9	(10) 1.3			% Officers', Directors'	(35) 1.9	(34) 1.7
		3.2	2.9			Owners' Comp/Sales	4.4	3.7
1722M	73450M	1274999M	2702862M	1330243M	4033610M	Net Sales ($)	7227127M	3861329M
247M	13683M	231536M	584304M	219992M	1311134M	Total Assets ($)	1273075M	917385M

M = $ thousand   MM = $ million
See Pages 11 through 21 for Explanation of Ratios and Data

Comparative Historical Data

Current Data Sorted by Sales

	14 20 10 10 20	15 20 12 7 25	16 18 21 10 33	Type of Statement	0-1MM	1-3MM	3-5MM	5-10MM	10-25MM	25MM & OVER
Unqualified	14	15	16			1		2	7	15
Reviewed	20	20	18			1	1	2	7	7
Compiled	10	12	21		1		1	8	4	7
Tax Returns	10	7	10			2	1		3	4
Other	20	25	33			2		1	7	23
	4/1/04-3/31/05 ALL	4/1/05-3/31/06 ALL	4/1/06-3/31/07 ALL			18 (4/1-9/30/06)		80 (10/1/06-3/31/07)		
NUMBER OF STATEMENTS	74	79	98		1	6	3	11	21	56
	%	%	%	**ASSETS**	%	%	%	%	%	%
Cash & Equivalents	11.2	7.5	9.1					3.6	10.4	8.3
Trade Receivables (net)	38.9	37.0	36.6					43.0	35.4	39.3
Inventory	21.6	23.6	21.5					24.8	23.4	20.1
All Other Current	2.1	2.7	2.6					4.8	.5	2.6
Total Current	73.8	70.9	69.8					76.2	69.7	70.3
Fixed Assets (net)	17.4	22.5	19.9					17.0	21.8	19.8
Intangibles (net)	1.5	2.6	4.8					1.2	1.3	5.0
All Other Non-Current	7.2	4.0	5.4					5.6	7.2	4.9
Total	100.0	100.0	100.0					100.0	100.0	100.0
				LIABILITIES						
Notes Payable-Short Term	9.5	9.7	11.3					14.3	9.6	11.3
Cur. Mat.-L.T.D.	1.9	2.5	2.1					2.5	2.5	1.9
Trade Payables	33.0	32.8	32.9					28.4	35.1	35.8
Income Taxes Payable	.3	.1	.1					.0	.1	.1
All Other Current	9.9	7.8	8.2					8.6	5.5	9.8
Total Current	54.7	53.0	54.7					53.8	52.8	59.0
Long-Term Debt	12.1	13.6	11.8					12.4	6.6	12.2
Deferred Taxes	.1	.2	.2					.2	.3	.3
All Other Non-Current	3.7	3.6	3.3					5.7	6.7	1.7
Net Worth	29.5	29.7	29.9					27.9	33.7	26.8
Total Liabilties & Net Worth	100.0	100.0	100.0					100.0	100.0	100.0
				INCOME DATA						
Net Sales	100.0	100.0	100.0					100.0	100.0	100.0
Gross Profit	16.7	18.4	17.9					18.9	18.3	15.0
Operating Expenses	14.2	15.2	15.5					16.3	15.5	13.2
Operating Profit	2.5	3.2	2.4					2.6	2.8	1.8
All Other Expenses (net)	-.2	.8	.3					-.5	.8	.1
Profit Before Taxes	2.7	2.4	2.1					3.1	2.0	1.7
				RATIOS						
Current	1.9	1.8	1.7					2.1	2.3	1.6
	1.4	1.3	1.3					1.4	1.4	1.2
	1.1	1.0	.9					1.1	.9	.9
Quick	1.4	1.2	1.2					1.6	1.7	1.0
	.9	.8	.8					.5	1.0	.8
	.6	.5	.5					.3	.5	.5
Sales/Receivables	18 20.5	20 18.6	19 18.8					22 16.7	20 18.6	19 18.8
	23 15.7	26 14.2	25 14.5					38 9.6	28 13.1	24 15.2
	35 10.3	33 11.2	37 9.8					45 8.0	37 9.7	32 11.5
Cost of Sales/Inventory	8 45.2	8 44.9	7 51.4					0 UND	10 35.1	6 62.2
	17 21.2	17 21.3	19 18.9					26 13.9	20 18.7	16 22.3
	31 11.9	35 10.4	32 11.4					78 4.7	26 14.1	30 12.2
Cost of Sales/Payables	18 20.6	19 19.5	18 20.6					17 21.3	19 19.6	18 20.8
	25 14.4	25 14.8	26 14.2					33 10.9	29 12.5	25 14.5
	34 10.6	42 8.8	41 8.9					42 8.6	55 6.7	37 9.8
Sales/Working Capital	14.3	11.8	14.7					10.3	10.2	20.3
	26.6	29.3	30.9					18.7	27.4	43.2
	91.2	-999.8	-104.6					67.9	-66.2	-69.4
EBIT/Interest	18.3	11.3	16.3						10.7	22.2
	(66) 6.7	(70) 3.1	(85) 3.8						(19) 3.3	(50) 4.2
	2.2	1.4	1.7						1.6	2.3
Net Profit + Depr., Dep., Amort./Cur. Mat. L/T/D	46.0	7.6	10.1							17.8
	(12) 9.2	(19) 2.2	(18) 2.2							(12) 5.3
	4.1	.5	1.2							2.0
Fixed/Worth	.1	.1	.1					.0	.1	.1
	.5	.8	.7					.3	.6	.7
	1.2	2.4	1.9					2.9	1.3	2.4
Debt/Worth	1.2	1.5	1.2					.8	.6	1.3
	2.2	2.8	3.6					4.5	4.8	3.6
	5.5	8.3	8.4					6.3	8.6	8.6
% Profit Before Taxes/Tangible Net Worth	45.6	39.9	49.8					49.3	124.4	45.4
	(66) 23.7	(72) 11.4	(86) 22.5				(10)	36.7	15.5	(47) 24.8
	12.3	3.4	6.9					21.3	4.1	11.6
% Profit Before Taxes/Total Assets	12.9	10.8	14.0					24.6	13.1	13.7
	6.5	3.5	5.9					10.4	6.3	6.2
	2.7	.7	2.0					3.1	.9	2.7
Sales/Net Fixed Assets	286.4	204.8	316.1					655.3	284.1	293.1
	45.6	31.5	31.6					51.0	67.6	29.7
	15.0	10.2	11.7					9.1	11.2	13.3
Sales/Total Assets	6.5	6.1	6.2					6.1	5.8	6.8
	5.1	4.9	4.9					3.2	4.9	5.0
	3.5	3.1	2.6					2.0	3.0	3.9
% Depr., Dep., Amort./Sales	.2	.3	.2					.1	.1	.2
	(62) .7	(64) .7	(77) .8				(10)	1.1	(18) 1.0	(45) .8
	1.4	1.5	1.6					2.4	2.1	1.4
% Officers', Directors' Owners' Comp/Sales	.7	.5	.6						1.4	.5
	(28) 1.6	(29) 1.4	(37) 2.0					(10)	2.3	(20) 1.3
	3.3	3.3	3.4						4.1	2.3
Net Sales ($)	6149421M	7493706M	9416886M		158M	13086M	12965M	92094M	335761M	8962822M
Total Assets ($)	1120212M	1579367M	2360896M		65M	7957M	3837M	28626M	98619M	2221792M

M = $ thousand   MM = $ million
See Pages 11 through 21 for Explanation of Ratios and Data

Current Data Sorted by Assets   Comparative Historical Data

Type of Statement	0-500M	500M-2MM	2-10MM	10-50MM	50-100MM	100-250MM		4/1/02-3/31/03 ALL	4/1/03-3/31/04 ALL
Unqualified			3	5	2	2		9	15
Reviewed	1	2	9	3				17	16
Compiled		2	3	1				14	14
Tax Returns	1	1	3	2					4
Other	1	3	2	6				11	14
	11 (4/1-9/30/06)		38 (10/1/06-3/31/07)						
NUMBER OF STATEMENTS	3	8	19	15	2	2		51	63
ASSETS	%	%	%	%	%	%		%	%
Cash & Equivalents			5.1	6.1				5.4	4.4
Trade Receivables (net)			44.2	42.9				43.8	41.8
Inventory			15.0	21.7				19.0	17.6
All Other Current			5.8	4.1				1.4	2.1
Total Current			70.2	74.7				69.5	66.0
Fixed Assets (net)			22.6	18.7				21.6	24.1
Intangibles (net)			1.2	1.8				1.6	1.8
All Other Non-Current			6.0	4.7				7.3	8.1
Total			100.0	100.0				100.0	100.0
LIABILITIES									
Notes Payable-Short Term			12.2	15.8				14.8	15.8
Cur. Mat.-L.T.D.			6.5	3.6				4.1	2.3
Trade Payables			25.0	19.5				30.0	27.1
Income Taxes Payable			.0	.0				.1	.3
All Other Current			7.5	8.1				8.6	12.9
Total Current			51.2	46.9				57.6	58.4
Long-Term Debt			7.9	7.7				11.5	10.8
Deferred Taxes			.1	.0				.5	.2
All Other Non-Current			1.8	1.9				4.7	4.8
Net Worth			39.0	43.4				25.6	25.8
Total Liabilities & Net Worth			100.0	100.0				100.0	100.0
INCOME DATA									
Net Sales			100.0	100.0				100.0	100.0
Gross Profit			12.8	17.5				11.8	16.8
Operating Expenses			11.2	14.5				11.0	14.7
Operating Profit			1.6	3.0				.8	2.1
All Other Expenses (net)			.2	.1				.4	.1
Profit Before Taxes			1.4	2.9				.4	2.0
RATIOS									
Current			2.1	4.2				1.7	1.5
			1.5	1.4				1.3	1.2
			1.1	1.1				1.0	.9
Quick			1.4	2.2				1.2	1.0
			1.1	1.0				.8	.7
			.9	.6				.6	.6
Sales/Receivables			16 22.6	16 22.8				16 22.6	19 19.7
			22 16.7	22 16.5				20 18.5	20 15.9
			25 14.7	29 12.4				25 14.8	29 12.6
Cost of Sales/Inventory			1 252.2	7 50.2				4 82.9	4 96.6
			8 44.6	13 28.6				9 42.8	10 37.7
			16 23.3	26 14.1				20 17.9	21 17.8
Cost of Sales/Payables			8 45.1	11 34.4				9 38.5	10 34.8
			14 25.2	14 25.7				18 20.2	18 20.5
			19 19.6	19 19.3				23 16.1	23 16.2
Sales/Working Capital			15.4	15.5				23.4	19.3
			36.5	26.9				45.2	60.4
			145.3	132.0				-304.0	-121.4
EBIT/Interest			6.5	24.8				9.0	11.2
			(18) 2.2	(14) 3.8				(46) 3.0	(56) 3.6
			1.2	.5				1.2	2.2
Net Profit + Depr., Dep., Amort./Cur. Mat. L/T/D								6.3	7.0
								(10) 1.5	(14) 2.2
								-1.0	1.4
Fixed/Worth			.1	.1				.1	.2
			.3	.2				.6	.8
			.7	1.6				2.2	1.8
Debt/Worth			.8	.3				1.6	1.4
			1.6	1.9				2.8	3.0
			3.1	5.4				7.4	6.9
% Profit Before Taxes/Tangible Net Worth			40.4	32.3				52.6	52.4
			(18) 6.3	(14) 20.6				(48) 20.5	(55) 27.9
			1.3	-5.0				2.1	5.3
% Profit Before Taxes/Total Assets			12.0	18.3				9.2	12.0
			3.8	8.8				4.3	5.9
			.5	-.3				.4	1.7
Sales/Net Fixed Assets			387.9	199.4				351.3	189.1
			57.3	55.2				48.7	40.9
			13.3	14.1				19.2	9.6
Sales/Total Assets			10.0	10.9				11.1	9.2
			7.8	7.0				8.1	6.6
			4.0	2.8				5.4	3.1
% Depr., Dep., Amort./Sales			.1	.2				.1	.3
			(17) .4	(13) .5				(42) .4	(47) .5
			1.9	1.7				.7	1.6
% Officers', Directors' Owners' Comp/Sales			.3					.3	.4
			(11) 1.4					(15) 1.5	(25) 1.2
			1.6					2.1	4.4
Net Sales ($)	8962M	97798M	659782M	1895845M	645222M	248230M		4229564M	5564678M
Total Assets ($)	1001M	10141M	90302M	325436M	159720M	435166M		1108107M	1685077M

M = $ thousand   MM = $ million
See Pages 11 through 21 for Explanation of Ratios and Data

Comparative Historical Data   Current Data Sorted by Sales

4/1/04-3/31/05 ALL	4/1/05-3/31/06 ALL	4/1/06-3/31/07 ALL	Type of Statement	0-1MM	1-3MM	3-5MM	5-10MM	10-25MM	25MM & OVER
18	16	12	Unqualified					2	10
8	11	15	Reviewed		2			5	8
9	5	6	Compiled					3	3
7	4	4	Tax Returns			1	1	1	1
9	14	12	Other			1	1	1	9
					11 (4/1-9/30/06)		38 (10/1/06-3/31/07)		
51	50	49	NUMBER OF STATEMENTS		2	2	2	12	31
%	%	%	ASSETS	%	%	%	%	%	%
7.9	4.1	6.4	Cash & Equivalents					2.5	5.4
38.1	34.8	43.6	Trade Receivables (net)					36.0	46.1
19.2	20.9	18.7	Inventory					22.5	17.8
3.6	3.5	4.7	All Other Current		DATA	NOT	AVAILABLE	5.5	5.2
68.8	63.4	73.4	Total Current					66.5	74.5
24.6	25.0	18.2	Fixed Assets (net)					25.2	17.5
1.5	2.5	2.5	Intangibles (net)					1.4	2.6
5.1	9.1	5.9	All Other Non-Current					6.9	5.5
100.0	100.0	100.0	Total					100.0	100.0
			LIABILITIES						
14.2	18.3	14.9	Notes Payable-Short Term					11.6	14.0
3.4	3.2	4.0	Cur. Mat.-L.T.D.					5.4	4.1
23.0	19.2	25.3	Trade Payables					16.5	23.7
.2	.2	.1	Income Taxes Payable					.1	.1
7.6	9.5	8.3	All Other Current					10.8	8.4
48.3	50.4	52.6	Total Current					44.3	50.4
13.6	16.2	8.5	Long-Term Debt					4.6	10.1
.0	.0	.0	Deferred Taxes					.1	.0
6.6	3.8	2.2	All Other Non-Current					1.2	2.7
31.4	29.5	36.7	Net Worth					49.8	36.7
100.0	100.0	100.0	Total Liabilities & Net Worth					100.0	100.0
			INCOME DATA						
100.0	100.0	100.0	Net Sales					100.0	100.0
14.7	16.5	16.9	Gross Profit					15.6	16.8
12.1	13.3	14.1	Operating Expenses					13.6	13.6
2.6	3.2	2.8	Operating Profit					2.0	3.2
-.1	.2	.3	All Other Expenses (net)					.1	.3
2.7	3.0	2.5	Profit Before Taxes					2.0	2.9
			RATIOS						
2.2	1.9	2.2						2.4	2.1
1.5	1.4	1.5	Current					1.7	1.6
1.1	1.0	1.1						1.1	1.1
1.5	1.3	1.5						1.4	1.6
1.0	.8	1.0	Quick					1.0	1.1
.6	.5	.6						.6	.6
16 22.4	19 19.4	16 22.9						15 24.4	17 21.0
20 17.9	24 15.0	22 16.7	Sales/Receivables					20 18.3	22 16.5
26 14.3	34 10.7	29 12.6						27 13.5	29 12.4
6 60.8	7 54.4	6 63.9						2 200.5	6 57.1
12 29.9	13 27.1	10 35.4	Cost of Sales/Inventory					14 25.8	10 35.4
23 15.7	40 9.1	24 15.4						21 17.3	24 15.2
8 47.5	7 55.0	8 45.7						2 156.8	10 37.4
14 26.5	15 24.2	15 24.8	Cost of Sales/Payables					14 25.2	10 24.8
22 16.6	27 13.7	25 14.9						17 22.0	21 17.8
12.8	11.5	16.4						14.2	15.5
32.8	34.1	31.6	Sales/Working Capital					25.2	31.6
160.9	999.8	93.2						249.5	73.7
11.7	11.9	7.3						21.1	7.8
(45) 3.7	(45) 4.5	(46) 2.4	EBIT/Interest					2.9	(28) 2.2
1.7	1.6	1.2						.2	1.2
7.3									
(12) 4.4			Net Profit + Depr., Dep., Amort./Cur. Mat. L/T/D						
2.0									
.2	.1	.0						.0	.1
.6	.5	.2	Fixed/Worth					.2	.3
1.8	1.4	1.3						.6	1.5
1.0	1.1	.8						.5	1.2
1.9	2.2	1.9	Debt/Worth					1.3	2.0
7.3	4.3	5.0						1.9	5.6
53.8	44.3	37.5						36.3	37.5
(45) 20.8	(41) 23.3	(45) 15.7	% Profit Before Taxes/Tangible Net Worth					5.1	(29) 15.7
4.9	6.3	1.9						-3.5	4.0
12.9	14.3	17.5						17.6	12.0
6.6	7.5	4.5	% Profit Before Taxes/Total Assets					2.6	4.5
1.1	1.4	.7						-1.7	.8
159.6	277.5	999.8						863.2	387.9
36.3	44.9	66.8	Sales/Net Fixed Assets					86.4	60.0
12.7	4.7	14.0						6.1	20.4
9.3	8.4	10.2						10.0	10.9
6.9	5.2	7.0	Sales/Total Assets					5.2	7.8
3.2	2.3	4.0						3.1	4.4
.2	.2	.1						.0	.1
(39) .5	(37) .8	(38) .4	% Depr., Dep., Amort./Sales					(10) 1.0	(25) .4
1.7	2.9	1.7						2.3	.9
.4	.4								.2
(19) 1.4	(14) 1.1	(18) 1.2	% Officers', Directors' Owners' Comp/Sales						(10) 1.0
3.5	5.9	3.2							4.7
4032465M	3747196M	3555839M	Net Sales ($)		5482M	7738M	13071M	181902M	3347646M
1195120M	1200966M	1021766M	Total Assets ($)		869M	904M	2545M	39080M	978368M

M = $ thousand   MM = $ million
See Pages 11 through 21 for Explanation of Ratios and Data

Current Data Sorted by Assets | | | Comparative Historical Data

0-500M	500M-2MM	2-10MM	10-50MM	50-100MM	100-250MM	Type of Statement	4/1/02-3/31/03 ALL	4/1/03-3/31/04 ALL
	1	9	3			Unqualified	15	17
	6	11	5			Reviewed	21	25
1	8	2				Compiled	21	26
5		8				Tax Returns	5	13
1	3		7	1		Other	21	17
	32 (4/1-9/30/06)		39 (10/1/06-3/31/07)					
7	18	30	15	1		**NUMBER OF STATEMENTS**	83	98
%	%	%	%	%	%	**ASSETS**	%	%
	9.7	6.9	2.0			Cash & Equivalents	6.9	7.1
	24.2	29.6	26.5			Trade Receivables (net)	24.3	25.1
	37.4	40.2	41.2			Inventory	33.9	34.2
	3.0	1.8	2.4			All Other Current	3.4	2.0
	74.3	78.5	72.2			Total Current	68.5	68.4
	14.3	15.4	23.6			Fixed Assets (net)	21.8	21.6
	4.4	2.0	.3			Intangibles (net)	2.7	3.1
	7.0	4.1	3.9			All Other Non-Current	7.1	7.0
	100.0	100.0	100.0			Total	100.0	100.0
						LIABILITIES		
	10.3	16.1	32.5			Notes Payable-Short Term	19.4	17.3
	2.8	1.8	2.3			Cur. Mat.-L.T.D.	2.6	4.2
	20.6	22.6	18.7			Trade Payables	15.6	17.5
	.0	.5	.0			Income Taxes Payable	.2	.2
	11.6	3.7	5.6			All Other Current	5.2	7.2
	45.4	44.6	59.1			Total Current	43.1	46.4
	13.5	10.2	7.7			Long-Term Debt	15.1	13.0
	.1	.2	.4			Deferred Taxes	.4	.3
	16.0	3.9	5.7			All Other Non-Current	3.6	4.2
	25.0	41.0	27.0			Net Worth	37.9	36.2
	100.0	100.0	100.0			Total Liabilties & Net Worth	100.0	100.0
						INCOME DATA		
	100.0	100.0	100.0			Net Sales	100.0	100.0
	25.3	22.7	19.1			Gross Profit	26.1	25.1
	25.8	19.7	16.9			Operating Expenses	23.5	23.3
	-.5	3.0	2.2			Operating Profit	2.6	1.8
	.6	.5	.9			All Other Expenses (net)	.4	.4
	-1.0	2.5	1.3			Profit Before Taxes	2.2	1.3
						RATIOS		
	3.8	3.1	1.4			Current	2.6	2.4
	1.6	1.6	1.2				1.5	1.5
	.9	1.3	1.0				1.1	1.1
	2.3	1.2	.6			Quick	1.3	1.1
	.8	.7	.5				.7	.7
	.4	.5	.3				.4	.4

Columns 50-100MM and 100-250MM: **DATA NOT AVAILABLE**

0-500M	500M-2MM	2-10MM	10-50MM		Ratio	4/1/02-3/31/03 ALL	4/1/03-3/31/04 ALL
	11	32.8	21	17.8	24	15.3	Sales/Receivables
	20	18.0	30	12.2	26	13.8	
	39	9.4	46	7.9	29	12.8	

Sales/Receivables:
	500M-2MM	2-10MM	10-50MM		4/1/02-3/31/03	4/1/03-3/31/04
	11 32.8	21 17.8	24 15.3		18 20.7	15 24.4
	20 18.0	30 12.2	26 13.8		25 14.4	25 14.9
	39 9.4	46 7.9	29 12.8		35 10.4	34 10.8

Cost of Sales/Inventory:
	500M-2MM	2-10MM	10-50MM		4/1/02-3/31/03	4/1/03-3/31/04
	21 17.4	29 12.8	33 10.9		27 13.6	25 14.7
	51 7.1	55 6.7	58 6.3		45 8.1	44 8.4
	80 4.6	91 4.0	82 4.5		82 4.4	76 4.8

Cost of Sales/Payables:
	500M-2MM	2-10MM	10-50MM		4/1/02-3/31/03	4/1/03-3/31/04
	10 35.7	13 28.0	11 31.8		10 37.4	11 34.5
	25 14.5	26 14.2	19 19.4		19 19.6	19 19.1
	40 9.1	45 8.0	33 11.1		34 10.7	34 10.8

Sales/Working Capital:
	500M-2MM	2-10MM	10-50MM		4/1/02-3/31/03	4/1/03-3/31/04
	7.2	6.4	15.7		8.1	9.3
	14.1	10.8	24.0		15.8	15.9
	-96.7	27.6	92.0		59.0	50.2

EBIT/Interest:
	500M-2MM	2-10MM	10-50MM		4/1/02-3/31/03	4/1/03-3/31/04
	25.7	4.2	3.8		6.8	7.6
	(27) 3.5	1.8	2.5		(78) 3.0	(91) 2.9
	-2.4	.3	1.7		1.6	1.4

Net Profit + Depr., Dep., Amort./Cur. Mat. L/T/D:
	500M-2MM	2-10MM	10-50MM		4/1/02-3/31/03	4/1/03-3/31/04
					8.2	6.2
					(31) 3.2	(23) 2.6
					1.9	.7

Fixed/Worth:
	500M-2MM	2-10MM	10-50MM		4/1/02-3/31/03	4/1/03-3/31/04
	.1	.2	.3		.2	.2
	.3	.4	.8		.6	.4
	-9.2	.7	1.0		1.2	1.0

Debt/Worth:
	500M-2MM	2-10MM	10-50MM		4/1/02-3/31/03	4/1/03-3/31/04
	.5	.6	1.5		.8	.7
	1.8	2.2	3.3		2.1	1.8
	-30.6	4.8	5.7		5.2	5.4

% Profit Before Taxes/Tangible Net Worth:
	500M-2MM	2-10MM	10-50MM		4/1/02-3/31/03	4/1/03-3/31/04
	54.5	35.6	34.8		39.3	29.3
	(13) 17.7	14.0	20.8		(78) 20.3	(89) 14.1
	3.1	-6.3	10.5		5.2	4.3

% Profit Before Taxes/Total Assets:
	500M-2MM	2-10MM	10-50MM		4/1/02-3/31/03	4/1/03-3/31/04
	21.2	10.9	8.2		11.3	9.3
	4.7	3.3	5.0		5.2	4.1
	-7.3	-2.4	2.1		2.6	.7

Sales/Net Fixed Assets:
	500M-2MM	2-10MM	10-50MM		4/1/02-3/31/03	4/1/03-3/31/04
	110.8	86.5	58.5		60.7	93.6
	42.9	30.2	17.6		25.8	28.1
	11.1	10.8	7.5		6.3	8.4

Sales/Total Assets:
	500M-2MM	2-10MM	10-50MM		4/1/02-3/31/03	4/1/03-3/31/04
	5.2	5.1	5.6		4.9	5.4
	3.3	3.4	3.5		3.3	3.6
	2.4	2.1	2.4		2.0	2.2

% Depr., Dep., Amort./Sales:
	500M-2MM	2-10MM	10-50MM		4/1/02-3/31/03	4/1/03-3/31/04
	.2	.2	.4		.4	.4
	(15) 1.0	(27) .7	.6		(73) 1.2	(80) .9
	2.5	1.9	2.1		2.4	2.3

% Officers', Directors' Owners' Comp/Sales:
	500M-2MM	2-10MM	10-50MM		4/1/02-3/31/03	4/1/03-3/31/04
	.9	.8			.7	1.0
	(10) 3.0	(15) 1.2			(34) 2.0	(44) 2.2
	5.8	3.8			3.1	4.5

0-500M	500M-2MM	2-10MM	10-50MM	50-100MM		4/1/02-3/31/03	4/1/03-3/31/04
14246M	81784M	432359M	997351M	188541M	Net Sales ($)	2835489M	3815719M
2001M	19551M	131352M	284905M	76919M	Total Assets ($)	1069297M	1220582M

M = $ thousand   MM = $ million
See Pages 11 through 21 for Explanation of Ratios and Data

Comparative Historical Data | Current Data Sorted by Sales

			Type of Statement	0-1MM	1-3MM	3-5MM	5-10MM	10-25MM	25MM & OVER
18	10	3	Unqualified						3
22	15	15	Reviewed				1	7	7
22	22	18	Compiled		5	2	4	7	
9	7	15	Tax Returns	2	6	3	2	2	
13	23	20	Other		1	2	4	6	7
4/1/04-3/31/05 ALL	4/1/05-3/31/06 ALL	4/1/06-3/31/07 ALL			32 (4/1-9/30/06)		39 (10/1/06-3/31/07)		
84	77	71	NUMBER OF STATEMENTS	2	12	7	11	22	17
%	%	%	**ASSETS**	%	%	%	%	%	%
6.2	7.5	8.0	Cash & Equivalents		14.7		9.2	6.6	2.6
27.0	27.6	25.3	Trade Receivables (net)		13.5		29.8	32.1	27.2
36.0	36.4	37.4	Inventory		37.7		37.0	38.1	41.6
2.0	1.5	2.1	All Other Current		1.3		2.6	3.0	1.2
71.2	72.9	72.8	Total Current		67.2		78.6	79.9	72.7
19.2	19.1	19.5	Fixed Assets (net)		18.5		13.0	15.3	23.3
3.0	2.9	2.8	Intangibles (net)		9.7		2.8	1.1	.5
6.7	5.0	4.8	All Other Non-Current		4.6		5.6	3.8	3.6
100.0	100.0	100.0	Total		100.0		100.0	100.0	100.0
			LIABILITIES						
17.4	24.1	18.7	Notes Payable-Short Term		10.6		13.3	16.6	30.8
2.7	3.1	2.1	Cur. Mat.-L.T.D.		2.3		1.7	2.4	2.2
18.0	17.3	19.4	Trade Payables		12.6		17.0	26.1	18.2
.2	.2	.2	Income Taxes Payable		.0		.6	.3	.0
10.1	5.8	10.1	All Other Current		9.2		7.9	4.2	8.1
48.5	50.5	50.4	Total Current		34.8		40.4	49.7	59.3
11.1	9.5	13.4	Long-Term Debt		29.1		9.2	11.6	6.9
.3	.4	.2	Deferred Taxes		.2		.1	.3	.4
3.6	4.5	7.0	All Other Non-Current		3.2		7.2	2.2	5.2
36.6	35.1	29.0	Net Worth		32.7		43.1	36.1	28.2
100.0	100.0	100.0	Total Liabilities & Net Worth		100.0		100.0	100.0	100.0
			INCOME DATA						
100.0	100.0	100.0	Net Sales		100.0		100.0	100.0	100.0
24.5	23.3	24.7	Gross Profit		32.1		22.8	23.5	19.3
22.3	21.2	22.6	Operating Expenses		29.2		20.8	19.9	16.8
2.2	2.1	2.1	Operating Profit		2.9		2.0	3.6	2.5
.5	.9	.6	All Other Expenses (net)		.4		.5	.6	.8
1.7	1.3	1.4	Profit Before Taxes		2.5		1.5	3.0	1.7
			RATIOS						
2.5	2.6	2.6	Current		9.7		4.7	2.6	1.5
1.5	1.3	1.4			2.3		1.6	1.5	1.2
1.1	1.1	1.1			.9		1.4	1.2	1.0
1.2	1.3	1.0	Quick		3.6		2.2	1.0	.6
.7	.6	.6			.9		1.0	.7	.5
.5	.4	.5			.5		.6	.4	.5
21 17.4	18 20.4	13 27.4	Sales/Receivables		3 135.0		19 19.4	17 20.9	22 16.7
28 12.9	29 12.8	26 14.0			19 19.3		33 10.9	27 13.5	26 13.8
36 10.1	39 9.5	37 9.8			26 14.0		45 8.2	39 9.3	30 12.2
29 12.7	27 13.4	25 14.3	Cost of Sales/Inventory		9 39.5		35 10.4	19 19.2	36 10.2
41 8.8	51 7.1	51 7.1			78 4.7		49 7.4	44 8.4	51 7.1
80 4.5	69 5.3	82 4.5			141 2.6		72 5.1	91 4.0	71 5.1
8 45.0	9 41.1	9 39.8	Cost of Sales/Payables		0 UND		7 49.4	14 26.2	12 30.2
23 16.1	20 18.5	22 16.3			14 25.8		23 15.6	28 13.1	19 19.4
38 9.7	33 11.0	35 10.4			47 7.8		45 8.1	47 7.7	31 11.7
7.7	8.0	8.6	Sales/Working Capital		3.9		6.4	9.4	15.7
15.4	13.6	16.8			14.4		11.3	15.9	36.9
70.0	56.1	72.2			NM		14.8	29.6	203.5
7.8	4.8	7.2	EBIT/Interest		32.8			7.2	4.1
(80) 3.2	(72) 2.1	(67) 2.5			(11) 6.3			2.8	2.5
1.3	1.1	.3			-2.3			1.1	1.5
11.7	3.3	9.8	Net Profit + Depr., Dep., Amort./Cur. Mat. L/T/D						
(26) 2.1	(24) 1.5	(16) 3.2							
1.3	.2	1.0							
.2	.1	.2	Fixed/Worth		.0		.2	.1	.3
.4	.5	.4			.4		.2	.4	.8
1.2	1.5	1.3			NM		.4	.9	1.2
.9	.8	.7	Debt/Worth		.3		.6	.9	1.7
2.1	2.3	2.4			.7		2.0	2.2	2.9
4.6	4.6	5.7			NM		4.9	4.5	5.6
32.0	28.7	49.8	% Profit Before Taxes/Tangible Net Worth				17.3	54.7	46.8
(80) 13.5	(74) 11.1	(64) 17.6					12.3	22.1	20.8
4.3	1.6	-.1					-8.1	1.4	8.2
9.4	7.2	10.1	% Profit Before Taxes/Total Assets		46.4		16.0	13.4	8.6
4.4	3.0	4.5			9.0		1.8	4.7	5.0
.6	.2	-2.4			-2.5		-3.3	.2	1.8
87.5	84.7	72.3	Sales/Net Fixed Assets		UND		99.4	88.7	45.5
28.4	27.5	26.5			43.8		46.9	37.5	17.6
9.7	9.9	10.9			11.7		10.3	18.7	9.3
5.3	4.7	5.3	Sales/Total Assets		4.5		5.3	6.1	5.1
3.5	3.5	3.4			3.0		3.0	3.7	3.5
2.1	2.1	2.4			2.4		1.9	2.5	2.6
.3	.4	.3	% Depr., Dep., Amort./Sales					.2	.4
(69) 1.0	(64) .8	(65) .9						.5	.7
1.7	1.6	2.1						1.3	2.3
1.0	1.0	.8	% Officers', Directors' Owners' Comp/Sales					.8	
(37) 1.9	(35) 1.9	(38) 2.1						(12) 1.1	
3.9	4.3	4.2						3.0	
3416457M	2998040M	1714281M	Net Sales ($)	1528M	24087M	29176M	78377M	357054M	1224059M
1263791M	904151M	514728M	Total Assets ($)	820M	8067M	9013M	25788M	108634M	362406M

© RMA 2007

M = $ thousand   MM = $ million
See Pages 11 through 21 for Explanation of Ratios and Data

Current Data Sorted by Assets   Comparative Historical Data

0-500M	500M-2MM	2-10MM	10-50MM	50-100MM	100-250MM	Type of Statement	ALL 4/1/02-3/31/03	ALL 4/1/03-3/31/04
		11	20	7	4	Unqualified	42	46
2	7	35	11			Reviewed	64	73
2	11	14	6		1	Compiled	46	54
7	11	8				Tax Returns	16	26
2	9	31	29	6	5	Other	61	56
	52 (4/1-9/30/06)		187 (10/1/06-3/31/07)					
13	38	99	66	13	10	NUMBER OF STATEMENTS	229	255
%	%	%	%	%	%	**ASSETS**	%	%
12.3	8.2	5.5	4.2	1.5	1.4	Cash & Equivalents	9.3	8.0
31.7	46.9	39.7	31.7	36.2	19.5	Trade Receivables (net)	36.1	36.0
17.7	22.8	34.0	41.0	48.3	51.8	Inventory	30.0	30.6
1.9	2.8	2.4	2.9	1.4	3.3	All Other Current	2.5	3.0
63.7	80.7	81.6	79.7	87.4	76.0	Total Current	77.9	77.6
18.8	11.0	13.2	15.1	9.2	11.7	Fixed Assets (net)	15.4	16.1
3.2	1.5	1.7	2.5	.1	5.1	Intangibles (net)	1.9	2.2
14.3	6.8	3.4	2.7	3.2	7.2	All Other Non-Current	4.8	4.1
100.0	100.0	100.0	100.0	100.0	100.0	Total	100.0	100.0
						LIABILITIES		
24.0	24.6	22.2	31.3	43.4	34.8	Notes Payable-Short Term	21.3	22.0
10.7	1.4	2.0	1.3	.6	.5	Cur. Mat.-L.T.D.	2.3	2.9
19.3	27.3	27.9	18.5	21.1	13.7	Trade Payables	25.1	25.0
.0	.1	.1	.2	.0	.4	Income Taxes Payable	.4	.1
36.6	6.1	7.3	5.6	3.0	8.2	All Other Current	6.7	7.5
90.6	59.6	59.4	56.9	68.1	57.8	Total Current	55.7	57.4
10.6	4.8	5.9	8.4	3.5	8.7	Long-Term Debt	8.7	8.7
.4	.4	.2	.2	.0	.8	Deferred Taxes	.2	.3
18.3	8.1	5.7	5.0	1.4	.2	All Other Non-Current	5.3	5.3
-19.8	27.1	28.8	29.4	27.0	32.4	Net Worth	30.1	28.3
100.0	100.0	100.0	100.0	100.0	100.0	Total Liabilities & Net Worth	100.0	100.0
						INCOME DATA		
100.0	100.0	100.0	100.0	100.0	100.0	Net Sales	100.0	100.0
17.9	16.5	13.8	13.5	12.4	14.6	Gross Profit	14.8	15.5
17.3	14.8	12.0	9.9	8.9	11.3	Operating Expenses	12.6	13.8
.6	1.8	1.8	3.6	3.5	3.3	Operating Profit	2.2	1.7
1.0	.8	.6	1.1	.9	.5	All Other Expenses (net)	.4	.4
-.4	1.0	1.2	2.4	2.6	2.8	Profit Before Taxes	1.7	1.2
						RATIOS		
1.7	1.9	1.7	1.7	1.4	2.2		2.0	1.9
.7	1.4	1.3	1.4	1.3	1.2	Current	1.4	1.3
.2	1.0	1.1	1.1	1.1	1.2		1.1	1.1
1.3	1.2	1.1	.8	.7	.7		1.3	1.1
.5	.9	.7	.6	.6	.3	Quick	.8	.7
.2	.6	.5	.4	.5	.2		.5	.5
0 UND	20 18.0	23 15.7	30 12.1	33 11.1	29 12.5		21 17.3	21 17.3
8 47.0	27 13.7	34 10.6	35 10.5	39 9.3	38 9.7	Sales/Receivables	28 13.0	29 12.7
21 17.4	39 9.3	44 8.3	43 8.5	47 7.8	47 7.8		39 9.4	37 9.9
0 UND	4 92.8	18 20.5	30 12.0	47 7.8	77 4.7		7 52.8	10 36.1
2 157.2	15 24.9	34 10.9	50 7.3	55 6.6	147 2.5	Cost of Sales/Inventory	27 13.6	27 13.4
21 17.0	34 10.7	57 6.4	82 4.4	91 4.0	172 2.1		54 6.8	56 6.5
0 UND	9 39.5	15 23.6	11 32.5	20 18.2	15 23.6		10 37.9	11 34.3
4 92.9	15 24.6	28 13.1	21 17.1	28 13.2	29 12.7	Cost of Sales/Payables	21 17.4	23 16.0
22 17.0	37 10.0	41 9.0	37 10.0	36 10.3	47 7.8		33 11.1	36 10.1
63.9	11.8	11.6	8.0	10.1	9.0		11.5	11.0
-30.1	39.1	24.6	13.5	15.8	12.0	Sales/Working Capital	25.4	25.1
-16.0	-196.7	50.3	28.7	39.7	20.8		73.9	95.1
7.4	6.9	5.2	4.6	4.1	5.1		8.0	7.0
.9	(34) 2.6	(95) 2.5	(63) 2.3	2.9	2.0	EBIT/Interest	(205) 2.9	(232) 2.9
-2.8	.6	1.1	1.4	1.1	1.2		1.3	1.2
		8.0	10.6			Net Profit + Depr., Dep.,	5.9	6.0
	(20)	5.1	(26) 3.9			Amort./Cur. Mat. L/T/D	(57) 2.1	(68) 2.2
		.8	1.5				1.2	.5
.4	.0	.1	.1	.0	.1		.1	.1
-3.1	.2	.3	.3	.1	.2	Fixed/Worth	.3	.4
-.4	1.1	1.0	.7	.5	.6		1.2	1.3
NM	1.1	1.5	1.5	1.5	1.3		1.2	1.4
-4.7	2.5	3.7	2.8	2.9	3.7	Debt/Worth	2.8	3.4
-2.3	11.3	6.1	6.9	10.7	5.7		6.9	7.3
	49.2	41.1	34.9	25.8	23.0	% Profit Before Taxes/Tangible	37.4	33.8
	(34) 20.6	(94) 16.0	(62) 21.0	17.6	15.1	Net Worth	(205) 17.3	(228) 15.1
	.5	2.7	6.9	5.3	6.1		5.1	4.3
26.1	15.7	8.7	9.5	6.6	7.8	% Profit Before Taxes/Total	10.2	8.2
-3.5	4.8	4.9	5.0	4.8	3.5	Assets	4.1	3.6
-16.5	-.7	.4	1.9	.4	.7		.9	.4
263.9	999.8	274.8	432.3	711.9	114.7		198.2	237.2
104.8	82.0	55.7	91.9	179.8	54.0	Sales/Net Fixed Assets	68.9	63.1
39.0	28.8	22.4	10.2	29.0	8.5		20.3	17.4
17.9	7.8	5.4	4.3	3.8	2.4		6.5	6.4
10.2	5.8	4.4	3.1	3.4	2.0	Sales/Total Assets	4.5	4.3
5.2	3.6	3.0	2.3	2.6	1.4		3.1	2.8
	.2	.1	.1	.0			.2	.1
	(27) .4	(85) .4	(58) .3	(12) .1		% Depr., Dep., Amort./Sales	(202) .4	(216) .4
	1.3	.9	.4				1.0	1.0
	1.0	.7	.5			% Officers', Directors'	.8	1.0
	(23) 2.7	(41) 1.4	(24) .9			Owners' Comp/Sales	(102) 1.7	(116) 1.8
	5.5	2.7	1.8				3.3	3.3
62290M	309592M	2176569M	4333220M	2741091M	3105671M	Net Sales ($)	6922029M	9754170M
3286M	48586M	493267M	1392142M	858727M	1633779M	Total Assets ($)	1934479M	2682957M

M = $ thousand   MM = $ million
See Pages 11 through 21 for Explanation of Ratios and Data

Comparative Historical Data | Current Data Sorted by Sales

4/1/04-3/31/05 ALL	4/1/05-3/31/06 ALL	4/1/06-3/31/07 ALL	Type of Statement	0-1MM	1-3MM	3-5MM	5-10MM	10-25MM	25MM & OVER
45	41	42	Unqualified		1			6	35
62	49	55	Reviewed		2		4	26	23
44	40	34	Compiled	1	2	4	10	7	10
34	31	26	Tax Returns	3	5	4	6	7	1
42	77	82	Other		2		10	22	48
					52 (4/1-9/30/06)		187 (10/1/06-3/31/07)		
227	238	239	NUMBER OF STATEMENTS	4	12	8	30	68	117
%	%	%	**ASSETS**	%	%	%	%	%	%
8.0	5.5	5.6	Cash & Equivalents		7.8		5.7	6.2	3.8
36.4	35.4	37.2	Trade Receivables (net)		30.5		37.4	42.6	35.9
30.1	34.9	34.8	Inventory		27.8		28.5	31.4	40.1
3.0	3.3	2.5	All Other Current		.9		2.2	2.8	2.8
77.6	79.1	80.0	Total Current		67.0		73.9	83.0	82.6
15.3	14.2	13.4	Fixed Assets (net)		21.8		19.6	11.6	11.9
2.3	1.9	2.1	Intangibles (net)		7.0		.8	1.7	2.3
4.9	4.7	4.5	All Other Non-Current		4.2		5.7	3.6	3.2
100.0	100.0	100.0	Total		100.0		100.0	100.0	100.0
			LIABILITIES						
23.9	25.4	26.9	Notes Payable-Short Term		24.8		16.5	23.3	31.9
2.1	1.7	2.1	Cur. Mat.-L.T.D.		3.8		1.7	2.5	1.0
24.6	22.9	23.8	Trade Payables		27.4		27.8	25.0	22.2
.1	.2	.1	Income Taxes Payable		.0		.2	.1	.2
7.0	5.5	8.0	All Other Current		7.0		8.9	7.2	5.4
57.7	55.7	60.8	Total Current		63.0		55.1	57.9	60.7
8.7	8.5	6.7	Long-Term Debt		13.6		11.6	4.5	6.2
.3	.3	.3	Deferred Taxes		1.1		.0	.4	.2
5.3	6.7	6.1	All Other Non-Current		14.7		7.4	6.1	4.1
28.0	28.9	26.1	Net Worth		7.6		25.9	31.1	28.9
100.0	100.0	100.0	Total Liabilities & Net Worth		100.0		100.0	100.0	100.0
			INCOME DATA						
100.0	100.0	100.0	Net Sales		100.0		100.0	100.0	100.0
14.2	14.4	14.3	Gross Profit		25.6		20.2	12.6	12.5
12.5	12.8	12.0	Operating Expenses		25.7		18.0	10.7	9.4
1.8	1.6	2.4	Operating Profit		-.1		2.1	1.8	3.1
.3	.5	.8	All Other Expenses (net)		1.8		1.0	.3	.9
1.5	1.1	1.6	Profit Before Taxes		-1.9		1.1	1.6	2.2
			RATIOS						
1.9	1.9	1.7	Current		1.5		1.9	1.9	1.7
1.3	1.4	1.3			1.2		1.2	1.3	1.3
1.1	1.1	1.1			.7		.9	1.1	1.1
1.1	1.1	1.0	Quick		.9		1.0	1.1	.9
.7	.7	.7			.5		.7	.8	.6
.5	.5	.5			.3		.6	.5	.5
20 18.5	22 16.9	24 15.3	Sales/Receivables		4 91.7		26 13.9	22 16.4	28 13.1
30 12.2	32 11.3	34 10.9			22 16.3		39 9.3	33 10.9	34 10.7
39 9.4	41 8.8	42 8.7			45 8.2		52 7.1	43 8.4	42 8.7
8 47.3	14 26.6	16 22.5	Cost of Sales/Inventory		8 46.5		15 24.5	10 35.1	26 13.9
26 14.2	36 10.3	38 9.6			21 17.0		35 10.6	28 13.1	45 8.1
49 7.5	70 5.2	68 5.4			92 4.0		66 5.5	56 6.5	79 4.6
7 53.4	9 41.0	11 32.7	Cost of Sales/Payables		8 44.6		14 25.8	8 46.8	13 28.1
20 18.1	21 17.1	24 15.3			29 12.4		33 10.9	21 17.0	24 15.2
33 11.1	31 11.9	37 9.8			61 6.0		54 6.8	35 10.4	36 10.3
10.9	9.8	10.5	Sales/Working Capital		13.5		9.6	11.3	10.3
28.9	18.7	21.9			77.5		22.7	26.6	17.0
126.0	63.4	81.3			-18.1		-98.7	53.1	42.2
6.9	7.3	5.0	EBIT/Interest		3.5		3.8	5.6	5.0
(211) 2.6	(222) 2.7	(228) 2.4			.3		(28) 1.5	(64) 2.7	(113) 2.6
1.4	1.4	1.1			-2.4		.4	1.1	1.4
9.2	8.9	11.9	Net Profit + Depr., Dep., Amort./Cur. Mat. L/T/D					4.0	13.7
(55) 4.0	(48) 3.7	(61) 4.3						(11) 3.3	(43) 6.1
1.3	1.4	1.5						1.4	1.9
.1	.0	.1	Fixed/Worth		.4		.1	.0	.1
.4	.2	.3			1.1		1.0	.2	.2
1.1	1.0	.9			-2.3		1.9	.8	.7
1.4	1.3	1.5	Debt/Worth		2.2		1.3	1.3	1.6
3.4	3.1	3.3			NM		5.1	3.3	2.8
8.0	6.7	8.0			-6.5		16.2	5.8	6.9
40.1	37.4	35.8	% Profit Before Taxes/Tangible Net Worth				27.0	45.5	35.5
(206) 19.4	(220) 18.2	(216) 18.1					(28) 10.2	(64) 18.0	(112) 20.6
4.5	4.5	4.0					-10.1	3.2	7.8
9.4	10.6	9.4	% Profit Before Taxes/Total Assets		6.3		9.0	9.6	9.5
3.7	3.9	4.7			-4.3		2.3	4.6	5.6
.8	.8	.7			-8.9		-2.1	.5	1.9
306.5	508.9	351.4	Sales/Net Fixed Assets		185.5		157.2	430.4	424.9
64.5	81.4	79.0			22.2		40.4	102.7	86.5
20.2	20.3	22.4			11.5		13.1	28.7	23.1
6.4	5.9	5.6	Sales/Total Assets		8.3		5.7	6.5	5.0
4.4	4.0	3.9			3.8		3.4	4.6	3.6
2.9	2.6	2.7			1.7		2.2	3.0	2.7
.2	.1	.1	% Depr., Dep., Amort./Sales				.2	.1	.1
(184) .5	(190) .4	(197) .4					(25) .4	(53) .4	(104) .3
1.0	1.0	.9					1.7	.9	.7
.9	.8	.7	% Officers', Directors' Owners' Comp/Sales				1.3	.7	.5
(107) 1.6	(100) 1.6	(97) 1.6					(13) 2.5	(33) 1.2	(37) 1.0
3.8	2.9	3.1					4.2	2.8	1.8
12180213M	11902660M	12728433M	Net Sales ($)	1883M	25952M	32245M	219993M	1073241M	11375119M
3165370M	3912246M	4429787M	Total Assets ($)	1151M	10481M	6269M	89226M	280341M	4042319M

M = $ thousand   MM = $ million
See Pages 11 through 21 for Explanation of Ratios and Data

Current Data Sorted by Assets   Comparative Historical Data

						Type of Statement		
		6	14	6	1	Unqualified	33	33
	8	42	6			Reviewed	56	51
3	11	21	3			Compiled	45	60
3	8	3				Tax Returns	17	22
3	8	26	18	3	2	Other	45	43
	42 (4/1-9/30/06)		153 (10/1/06-3/31/07)				4/1/02-3/31/03	4/1/03-3/31/04
0-500M	500M-2MM	2-10MM	10-50MM	50-100MM	100-250MM		ALL	ALL
9	35	98	41	9	3	NUMBER OF STATEMENTS	196	209
%	%	%	%	%	%	ASSETS	%	%
	9.8	6.9	8.0			Cash & Equivalents	7.3	8.0
	36.6	40.4	34.3			Trade Receivables (net)	39.3	39.5
	22.3	23.7	29.7			Inventory	25.6	23.8
	.8	2.2	2.0			All Other Current	1.9	1.9
	69.6	73.2	73.9			Total Current	74.2	73.2
	19.0	18.1	19.7			Fixed Assets (net)	17.6	18.8
	6.4	3.7	2.2			Intangibles (net)	2.3	2.5
	5.1	5.0	4.2			All Other Non-Current	5.9	5.5
	100.0	100.0	100.0			Total	100.0	100.0
						LIABILITIES		
	11.7	18.6	21.1			Notes Payable-Short Term	15.2	16.7
	2.3	2.4	3.3			Cur. Mat.-L.T.D.	3.6	2.4
	21.5	22.6	16.7			Trade Payables	24.4	22.5
	.0	.2	.3			Income Taxes Payable	.4	.1
	8.6	7.0	8.5			All Other Current	10.8	9.5
	44.1	50.8	49.9			Total Current	54.4	51.2
	13.0	14.0	6.7			Long-Term Debt	9.4	10.9
	.0	.1	.1			Deferred Taxes	.1	.1
	7.1	3.7	4.3			All Other Non-Current	4.5	4.2
	35.8	31.4	39.1			Net Worth	31.6	33.6
	100.0	100.0	100.0			Total Liabilties & Net Worth	100.0	100.0
						INCOME DATA		
	100.0	100.0	100.0			Net Sales	100.0	100.0
	14.4	15.7	13.9			Gross Profit	15.9	14.7
	12.8	14.2	11.6			Operating Expenses	14.5	13.6
	1.6	1.5	2.3			Operating Profit	1.4	1.1
	-.1	.3	.3			All Other Expenses (net)	.2	.3
	1.7	1.2	2.0			Profit Before Taxes	1.2	.8
						RATIOS		
	2.6	2.0	2.4				1.9	2.1
	1.5	1.4	1.3			Current	1.4	1.4
	1.2	1.1	1.1				1.1	1.1
	1.6	1.4	1.3				1.3	1.4
	1.0	.9	.9			Quick	.9	.9
	.6	.6	.5				.6	.7

	12	31.5	17	21.0	19	19.0	Sales/Receivables	15	23.8	15	23.6
	15	24.6	24	15.5	26	14.3		20	18.7	21	17.6
	21	17.3	32	11.5	34	10.8		27	13.6	29	12.8
	4	89.3	9	41.8	15	24.2	Cost of Sales/Inventory	9	40.5	8	44.9
	11	32.0	18	20.8	27	13.6		16	23.1	14	25.4
	19	19.1	29	12.6	57	6.4		28	13.1	25	14.8
	4	82.1	8	46.0	8	43.0	Cost of Sales/Payables	9	41.1	7	50.1
	12	31.0	13	28.0	13	27.4		15	25.0	13	28.9
	16	22.3	21	17.4	22	16.9		21	17.5	19	18.8

	20.6	15.1	9.9			Sales/Working Capital	18.0	17.5
	32.9	32.1	23.6				30.2	30.8
	87.3	94.0	69.4				88.5	106.1

		8.4		5.7		6.9	EBIT/Interest		11.5		9.6
	(30)	3.3	(84)	2.3	(37)	2.8		(174)	4.2	(190)	4.4
		1.3		1.4		2.0			1.7		1.8
				7.9		46.3	Net Profit + Depr., Dep., Amort./Cur. Mat. L/T/D		10.3		8.1
			(22)	4.0	(10)	7.6		(41)	4.4	(40)	2.3
				1.3		1.0			2.2		1.2

	.1	.1	.1			Fixed/Worth	.1	.1
	.4	.5	.5				.4	.4
	2.5	1.9	1.0				1.3	1.4
	.6	1.1	.8			Debt/Worth	1.0	1.0
	2.6	2.7	2.1				2.3	2.5
	14.3	10.0	4.1				5.8	5.4

		69.2		33.5		46.3	% Profit Before Taxes/Tangible Net Worth		41.8		41.1
	(30)	29.9	(83)	15.9		22.0		(174)	17.6	(192)	19.2
		2.8		3.3		8.7			6.8		5.1

	19.9	11.2	12.0			% Profit Before Taxes/Total Assets	12.6	10.9
	7.4	3.9	6.6				5.5	5.6
	.6	.6	2.9				1.6	1.7
	711.5	239.5	136.1			Sales/Net Fixed Assets	194.4	240.6
	73.5	57.6	29.5				59.9	62.3
	21.8	14.6	9.3				19.6	17.5
	12.4	8.2	6.5			Sales/Total Assets	9.4	8.8
	7.8	5.8	4.1				6.2	6.5
	4.6	4.1	3.0				4.3	4.3

		.1		.1		.2	% Depr., Dep., Amort./Sales		.2		.1
	(26)	.4	(88)	.4	(37)	.5		(166)	.6	(186)	.4
		1.1		.8		1.1			1.1		1.0
		.7		.5		.3	% Officers', Directors' Owners' Comp/Sales		.9		.6
	(21)	1.4	(43)	1.1	(13)	.7		(98)	1.5	(102)	1.3
		3.4		2.5		1.7			3.0		3.1

21085M	363405M	3075456M	4046421M	3551339M	2061855M	Net Sales ($)	13207090M	15440484M
2160M	44087M	462437M	865488M	648627M	464097M	Total Assets ($)	2138740M	2404669M

M = $ thousand   MM = $ million
See Pages 11 through 21 for Explanation of Ratios and Data

Comparative Historical Data   Current Data Sorted by Sales

4/1/04-3/31/05 ALL	4/1/05-3/31/06 ALL	4/1/06-3/31/07 ALL	Type of Statement	0-1MM	1-3MM	3-5MM	5-10MM	10-25MM	25MM & OVER
36	29	27	Unqualified					1	26
48	43	56	Reviewed				2	23	31
38	48	38	Compiled		1	6	10	11	10
20	12	14	Tax Returns		2	5	1	5	1
46	78	60	Other	2	2	2	6	16	32
				2	5	13 (4/1-9/30/06)=42		153 (10/1/06-3/31/07)	
188	210	195	NUMBER OF STATEMENTS	2	5	13	19	56	100
%	%	%	**ASSETS**	%	%	%	%	%	%
6.4	6.6	8.3	Cash & Equivalents			10.0	13.8	6.5	6.9
41.1	41.0	37.4	Trade Receivables (net)			18.3	25.5	39.6	41.9
24.4	26.3	24.8	Inventory			28.4	15.7	22.4	27.9
1.9	1.9	1.7	All Other Current			.3	1.1	1.4	2.4
73.8	75.7	72.4	Total Current			57.1	56.1	69.9	79.1
18.3	16.9	19.1	Fixed Assets (net)			23.4	32.8	20.0	15.6
3.1	2.9	3.6	Intangibles (net)			7.6	5.1	4.7	1.5
4.8	4.5	5.0	All Other Non-Current			11.9	5.9	5.4	3.8
100.0	100.0	100.0	Total			100.0	100.0	100.0	100.0
			LIABILITIES						
19.4	21.4	16.9	Notes Payable-Short Term			9.7	15.0	14.7	20.1
2.5	2.4	2.5	Cur. Mat.-L.T.D.			4.4	2.8	2.5	2.3
21.6	23.6	22.2	Trade Payables			28.7	11.1	22.4	23.7
.1	.1	.2	Income Taxes Payable			.0	.4	.1	.2
6.8	8.3	8.3	All Other Current			18.2	3.1	9.0	8.0
50.4	55.7	50.2	Total Current			61.0	32.5	48.7	54.3
11.8	8.8	12.2	Long-Term Debt			14.9	17.7	15.9	8.1
.1	.1	.1	Deferred Taxes			.0	.1	.1	.1
5.5	4.8	4.1	All Other Non-Current			5.9	7.5	4.2	3.5
32.2	30.5	33.4	Net Worth			18.2	42.2	31.0	34.0
100.0	100.0	100.0	Total Liabilities & Net Worth			100.0	100.0	100.0	100.0
			INCOME DATA						
100.0	100.0	100.0	Net Sales			100.0	100.0	100.0	100.0
15.3	14.7	15.1	Gross Profit			20.3	24.2	15.6	11.8
13.7	13.3	13.3	Operating Expenses			18.4	21.2	14.6	9.8
1.6	1.4	1.8	Operating Profit			1.9	3.0	1.0	1.9
.3	.2	.2	All Other Expenses (net)			.4	.3	.1	.2
1.3	1.2	1.6	Profit Before Taxes			1.5	2.7	1.0	1.7
			RATIOS						
2.1	1.8	2.2	Current			3.0	3.4	2.0	2.1
1.4	1.3	1.4				1.5	2.0	1.4	1.4
1.1	1.1	1.1				.5	1.1	1.0	1.2
1.5	1.2	1.4	Quick			2.0	2.6	1.3	1.2
.9	.8	.9				.5	1.3	1.0	.9
.6	.6	.6				.3	.5	.7	.6
16 22.5	17 21.9	15 23.7	Sales/Receivables			0 UND	17 20.9	15 24.5	17 21.8
22 16.5	23 15.8	22 16.8				15 24.0	24 15.2	22 16.8	23 16.2
28 13.0	32 11.3	31 11.8				21 17.4	35 10.5	30 12.2	31 11.7
8 45.4	10 37.7	8 48.5	Cost of Sales/Inventory			3 116.0	15 24.7	7 52.0	9 41.1
16 23.3	17 21.1	17 21.3				30 12.3	26 14.2	14 25.5	17 20.9
25 14.4	30 12.2	31 11.9				53 6.9	42 8.7	27 13.6	30 12.1
9 41.1	8 45.4	7 49.3	Cost of Sales/Payables			5 71.8	5 80.7	6 59.2	9 42.2
13 27.2	13 27.3	13 27.4				13 27.4	9 40.1	13 28.3	14 26.4
20 18.6	21 17.2	21 17.5				27 13.3	27 13.4	19 18.8	20 17.9
14.7	16.0	14.1	Sales/Working Capital			11.6	9.0	15.2	17.6
31.4	30.4	30.0				28.2	22.4	37.8	30.1
75.5	89.7	82.1				-52.4	63.0	846.7	65.2
10.4	6.8	6.2	EBIT/Interest				5.8	6.4	7.6
(176) 4.2	(197) 3.5	(164) 2.8					(17) 2.5	(49) 2.3	(87) 3.2
1.8	1.6	1.5					1.0	1.5	1.7
7.4	6.7	9.1	Net Profit + Depr., Dep., Amort./Cur. Mat. L/T/D					8.3	20.3
(35) 2.0	(38) 2.8	(39) 6.1						(13) 3.0	(22) 6.8
.8	1.1	1.4						1.3	2.3
.1	.1	.1	Fixed/Worth			.1	.2	.2	.1
.5	.4	.5				.5	.7	.7	.3
1.2	1.3	1.6				NM	2.7	3.3	1.0
1.1	1.4	1.0	Debt/Worth			.7	.3	1.1	1.1
2.5	3.0	2.5				3.2	1.7	2.7	2.4
5.9	6.4	6.2				NM	5.3	15.0	5.1
43.3	38.6	47.2	% Profit Before Taxes/Tangible Net Worth			83.8	28.4	56.7	40.2
(173) 21.1	(188) 17.4	(174) 22.0			(10) 45.0	(15) 18.6	(46) 15.2		(97) 24.6
7.0	5.6	6.0				1.0	.5	3.1	7.8
11.4	10.0	13.3	% Profit Before Taxes/Total Assets			31.9	15.0	13.5	12.3
5.6	5.0	6.0				2.3	5.5	3.6	6.7
1.7	1.2	1.2				-1.9	.1	.4	2.3
198.4	331.9	238.1	Sales/Net Fixed Assets			147.3	30.5	230.3	441.4
51.1	62.7	57.5				57.5	10.7	59.4	75.2
14.2	18.5	14.4				14.1	4.9	14.5	22.4
8.6	8.4	8.3	Sales/Total Assets			12.5	4.1	8.7	8.8
6.2	5.8	5.8				4.8	3.1	5.8	6.5
4.2	4.2	3.7				3.0	2.1	4.2	4.0
.2	.1	.1	% Depr., Dep., Amort./Sales			.2	.5	.2	.1
(170) .4	(179) .4	(167) .4			(11) .5	(18) .8	(45) .4		(89) .3
1.0	.9	.9				1.4	1.5	.9	.8
.8	.6	.5	% Officers', Directors' Owners' Comp/Sales				1.7	.5	.4
(95) 1.6	(86) 1.2	(82) 1.2					(10) 3.0	(26) .9	(35) .7
2.8	2.8	2.3					4.6	1.7	1.6
12305592M	14223508M	13119561M	Net Sales ($)	758M	10495M	49723M	144701M	901256M	12012628M
2147646M	2252020M	2486896M	Total Assets ($)	509M	2039M	11546M	53818M	159235M	2259749M

© RMA 2007   M = $ thousand   MM = $ million
See Pages 11 through 21 for Explanation of Ratios and Data

WHOLESALE—Fresh Fruit and Vegetable Merchant Wholesalers NAICS 424480 (SIC 5148)

Current Data Sorted by Assets | **Comparative Historical Data**

Type of Statement	0-500M	500M-2MM	2-10MM	10-50MM	50-100MM	100-250MM		4/1/02-3/31/03 ALL	4/1/03-3/31/04 ALL
			103 (4/1-9/30/06)		171 (10/1/06-3/31/07)				
Unqualified	1	2	12	19	5	2		40	42
Reviewed	1	8	38	25	2	1		64	60
Compiled	4	20	34	12				65	84
Tax Returns	5	10	8	1				28	23
Other	3	12	26	18	4	1		59	52
NUMBER OF STATEMENTS	14	52	118	75	11	4		256	261
ASSETS	%	%	%	%	%	%		%	%
Cash & Equivalents	4.6	10.7	9.9	8.0	3.1			10.2	11.5
Trade Receivables (net)	23.4	44.3	45.3	40.3	31.1			39.9	39.9
Inventory	9.7	10.5	9.3	9.6	5.5			9.9	10.6
All Other Current	3.9	1.3	4.8	3.2	5.8			5.2	5.6
Total Current	41.7	66.8	69.4	61.2	45.6			65.3	67.6
Fixed Assets (net)	36.4	22.8	21.3	27.9	35.0			23.7	21.7
Intangibles (net)	3.8	2.1	3.1	2.9	7.5			2.8	2.0
All Other Non-Current	18.1	8.3	6.3	8.0	12.0			8.2	8.8
Total	100.0	100.0	100.0	100.0	100.0			100.0	100.0
LIABILITIES									
Notes Payable-Short Term	20.0	8.6	10.9	7.2	10.7			8.6	9.6
Cur. Mat.-L.T.D.	13.3	2.1	1.9	2.0	3.2			2.6	2.6
Trade Payables	39.4	34.2	34.6	29.7	18.2			30.1	29.6
Income Taxes Payable	.0	.1	.1	.1	.0			.3	.2
All Other Current	25.8	7.7	10.0	8.0	7.8			9.5	10.9
Total Current	98.5	52.7	57.5	47.1	39.9			51.1	52.9
Long-Term Debt	36.7	9.6	8.2	15.8	21.2			11.4	10.6
Deferred Taxes	.0	.2	.8	.4	1.3			.3	.5
All Other Non-Current	4.5	5.9	2.7	3.9	1.3			2.7	4.1
Net Worth	-39.6	31.6	30.9	32.8	36.2			34.4	31.9
Total Liabilities & Net Worth	100.0	100.0	100.0	100.0	100.0			100.0	100.0
INCOME DATA									
Net Sales	100.0	100.0	100.0	100.0	100.0			100.0	100.0
Gross Profit	25.9	18.0	20.6	19.9	18.7			20.3	20.1
Operating Expenses	25.9	16.9	17.6	17.1	15.0			17.6	17.7
Operating Profit	.0	1.1	2.9	2.8	3.7			2.7	2.4
All Other Expenses (net)	.7	.2	.5	.9	.6			.2	.2
Profit Before Taxes	-.7	.9	2.4	1.9	3.1			2.4	2.2
RATIOS									
Current	.8	1.9	1.6	1.7	1.3			1.8	1.9
	.4	1.3	1.2	1.3	1.1			1.2	1.3
	.2	.9	1.0	1.1	.9			1.0	1.0
Quick	.6	1.6	1.3	1.4	1.0			1.4	1.3
	.3	1.1	1.0	1.0	.8			1.0	1.0
	.0	.6	.8	.7	.7			.7	.7
Sales/Receivables	0 UND	15 24.1	22 16.7	26 14.3	27 13.6			20 17.8	20 17.9
	3 114.0	23 15.6	29 12.6	31 11.6	31 11.7			27 13.4	26 13.8
	23 15.6	36 10.1	37 9.9	38 9.5	41 8.9			36 10.1	35 10.4
Cost of Sales/Inventory	0 UND	0 846.0	2 173.2	4 92.8	3 122.3			2 170.2	2 171.0
	0 UND	5 69.4	6 63.7	7 51.3	5 75.0			6 66.2	6 62.6
	7 50.8	12 31.4	11 32.4	16 22.3	13 28.6			13 27.1	15 24.5
Cost of Sales/Payables	0 UND	9 40.4	17 21.6	19 18.9	12 31.2			13 27.1	14 26.7
	5 76.7	23 15.8	25 14.4	27 13.7	21 17.6			23 15.6	23 16.0
	67 5.4	36 10.2	39 9.4	38 9.5	29 12.4			35 10.3	35 10.5
Sales/Working Capital	NM	23.3	17.6	14.8	32.8			18.1	15.5
	-16.0	60.9	55.1	34.4	108.8			46.1	40.2
	-7.6	-108.5	NM	201.2	-135.6			422.9	540.8
EBIT/Interest	6.8	11.2	14.8	14.5	7.0			14.1	17.7
	(12) -.2	(47) 2.9	(107) 3.4	(70) 5.6	4.6		(233) 4.4	(240) 4.4
	-4.2	1.1	1.2	2.3	2.5			1.5	1.6
Net Profit + Depr., Dep., Amort./Cur. Mat. L/T/D		8.7	9.6	9.7				10.7	6.0
		(12) 4.0	(29) 4.1	(23) 4.4			(63) 4.4	(71) 2.5
		2.6	1.6	2.5				1.5	1.4
Fixed/Worth	2.1	.2	.2	.4	.7			.2	.2
	UND	.5	.6	.9	1.0			.6	.6
	-.3	2.2	1.4	1.7	2.2			1.4	1.3
Debt/Worth	6.2	.9	1.5	1.2	1.5			1.0	1.0
	UND	2.3	2.6	2.2	2.3			2.3	2.4
	-1.8	8.9	4.8	5.2	3.4			4.7	6.3
% Profit Before Taxes/Tangible Net Worth		53.9	38.1	43.8	36.3			38.9	44.7
	(44) 13.1	(110) 14.2	(72) 23.6	(10) 20.2			(233) 17.2	(241) 18.7
		.7	3.4	11.6	5.1			5.6	5.8
% Profit Before Taxes/Total Assets	38.9	12.8	12.5	12.6	10.8			12.7	13.8
	-3.7	5.3	4.4	6.8	9.5			4.9	5.3
	-22.2	.2	.6	2.4	1.7			1.2	1.3
Sales/Net Fixed Assets	125.2	155.9	123.3	44.8	21.3			107.4	113.8
	22.0	44.3	35.4	15.9	9.4			33.7	36.6
	10.4	16.3	13.1	7.7	3.9			12.9	12.9
Sales/Total Assets	16.6	9.5	8.2	6.1	5.1			7.6	7.4
	9.3	7.4	5.8	4.2	3.4			5.4	5.6
	3.5	3.9	3.3	2.9	1.2			3.1	3.0
% Depr., Dep., Amort./Sales		.3	.2	.3	.6			.3	.2
		(46) .7	(111) .5	(67) .7	1.3		(220) .7	(228) .7
		1.3	1.4	1.3	2.8			1.6	1.6
% Officers', Directors' Owners' Comp/Sales		1.3	.9	.7				1.2	1.0
		(26) 1.8	(54) 1.6	(21) 1.5			(112) 1.8	(119) 1.6
		3.1	2.4	2.2				3.8	2.9
Net Sales ($)	47743M	519756M	3584317M	6963441M	2585288M	1938314M		16464379M	15963884M
Total Assets ($)	3425M	66558M	602461M	1644092M	776120M	679221M		2426680M	2996720M

© RMA 2007

M = $ thousand   MM = $ million

See Pages 11 through 21 for Explanation of Ratios and Data

Comparative Historical Data | Current Data Sorted by Sales

			Type of Statement						
44	44	41	Unqualified	1	1	2	3	8	26
63	51	75	Reviewed		2	3	2	20	48
62	49	70	Compiled	1	6	5	7	20	31
28	22	24	Tax Returns	1	4	3	6	6	4
61	78	64	Other	1	1	2	9	14	37
4/1/04- 3/31/05 ALL	4/1/05- 3/31/06 ALL	4/1/06- 3/31/07 ALL		0-1MM	103 (4/1-9/30/06) 1-3MM	3-5MM	5-10MM	171 (10/1/06-3/31/07) 10-25MM	25MM & OVER
258	244	274	NUMBER OF STATEMENTS	4	14	15	27	68	146
%	%	%	ASSETS	%	%	%	%	%	%
9.7	10.4	8.9	Cash & Equivalents	7.2	4.9	13.1	9.8	8.5
40.2	40.4	41.7	Trade Receivables (net)	23.8	37.1	33.2	42.1	45.4
10.2	10.2	9.6	Inventory	8.8	19.5	10.4	10.0	8.5
4.3	4.0	3.7	All Other Current	.2	3.0	1.9	5.2	3.9
64.5	65.0	63.9	Total Current	40.0	64.5	58.7	67.1	66.3
24.3	25.0	25.0	Fixed Assets (net)	39.1	30.4	32.0	23.3	22.2
3.3	2.6	3.1	Intangibles (net)	5.2	1.7	3.6	1.9	3.2
7.9	7.5	8.0	All Other Non-Current	15.7	3.4	5.7	7.7	8.3
100.0	100.0	100.0	Total	100.0	100.0	100.0	100.0	100.0
			LIABILITIES						
10.1	9.7	9.9	Notes Payable-Short Term	6.0	17.0	8.2	10.6	8.9
2.7	2.2	2.6	Cur. Mat.-L.T.D.	14.3	3.4	2.3	2.2	1.7
32.0	30.4	32.5	Trade Payables	31.9	21.4	28.8	32.8	33.6
.1	.2	.1	Income Taxes Payable	.0	.2	.0	.1	.1
9.6	10.7	9.7	All Other Current	15.1	17.1	5.1	8.9	10.0
54.6	53.2	54.8	Total Current	67.4	59.1	44.4	54.6	54.3
10.2	11.2	12.7	Long-Term Debt	35.8	20.3	15.6	8.1	11.0
.4	.5	.6	Deferred Taxes	.0	.2	.1	.4	.8
5.3	4.4	3.7	All Other Non-Current	3.4	1.6	4.4	4.6	3.1
29.6	30.7	28.3	Net Worth	-6.7	18.7	35.6	32.3	30.8
100.0	100.0	100.0	Total Liabilties & Net Worth	100.0	100.0	100.0	100.0	100.0
			INCOME DATA						
100.0	100.0	100.0	Net Sales	100.0	100.0	100.0	100.0	100.0
20.3	20.4	20.3	Gross Profit	29.6	30.8	28.8	19.9	17.0
18.1	17.0	17.5	Operating Expenses	29.3	27.6	25.5	17.0	14.2
2.1	3.3	2.8	Operating Profit	.3	3.2	3.3	2.8	2.9
.7	.5	.9	All Other Expenses (net)	1.4	.6	1.6	.3	1.1
1.5	2.8	1.9	Profit Before Taxes	-1.1	2.7	1.7	2.5	1.8
			RATIOS						
1.6	1.7	1.7		1.5	2.1	1.7	1.7	1.6
1.2	1.2	1.2	Current	.7	1.6	1.4	1.3	1.2
1.0	1.0	1.0		.4	.8	1.1	1.0	1.0
1.3	1.3	1.3		1.0	1.9	1.6	1.4	1.3
.9	1.0	.9	Quick	.6	.8	1.1	1.0	1.0
.6	.7	.7		.2	.6	.6	.6	.7
20 18.1	20 18.1	21 17.4		0 UND	19 19.1	19 18.8	17 21.1	25 14.8
28 13.0	29 12.4	28 12.9	Sales/Receivables	22 16.9	30 12.0	26 14.2	25 14.7	29 12.4
38 9.6	37 9.9	37 9.9		46 7.9	61 6.0	53 6.9	37 9.9	36 10.2
3 137.2	3 135.5	2 176.5		0 UND	0 999.8	3 118.9	2 162.9	2 171.3
6 59.0	6 59.1	6 60.0	Cost of Sales/Inventory	7 55.3	11 34.0	11 32.6	6 64.7	6 65.2
15 24.7	14 25.8	12 30.9		17 21.0	49 7.5	28 13.1	12 31.2	9 40.1
16 22.3	15 24.2	16 22.9		2 146.5	2 162.4	14 26.1	15 24.7	17 21.4
26 14.1	25 14.4	24 14.9	Cost of Sales/Payables	34 10.9	34 10.7	32 11.4	24 15.3	24 15.4
39 9.4	34 10.8	37 9.8		71 5.1	61 6.0	50 7.3	33 11.1	34 10.7
19.4	18.5	18.7		40.4	7.6	9.9	15.3	24.1
54.2	50.0	53.9	Sales/Working Capital	-54.5	14.6	29.2	43.2	56.8
-137.1	NM	-255.9		-7.6	-32.1	79.9	-432.4	714.9
16.0	13.9	12.3		1.9	15.1	11.0	13.2	16.2
(224) 4.9	(217) 4.5	(251) 3.8	EBIT/Interest	.5	(14) 1.9	(24) 2.8	(62) 3.5	(135) 5.1
1.4	2.0	1.3		-4.9	-.5	1.2	1.2	1.7
8.5	8.3	8.2					11.2	8.1
(76) 3.8	(68) 3.8	(72) 4.1	Net Profit + Depr., Dep., Amort./Cur. Mat. L/T/D				(18) 4.3	(41) 4.4
1.8	1.6	1.5					1.5	2.5
.3	.3	.3		.9	.2	.4	.2	.2
.8	.7	.7	Fixed/Worth	3.2	.6	.7	.8	.7
2.1	1.7	1.8		-1.2	3.5	2.4	1.6	1.5
1.2	1.2	1.2		2.1	.8	.7	1.1	1.5
2.9	2.4	2.4	Debt/Worth	7.7	3.2	2.2	2.2	2.4
7.0	5.0	5.3		-2.8	5.0	11.3	4.5	5.1
46.6	43.9	43.6			33.4	42.9	44.1	44.0
(229) 21.0	(221) 19.0	(247) 17.8	% Profit Before Taxes/Tangible Net Worth	(13) 11.2	(23) 10.2	(62) 17.7	(138) 22.7
3.5	6.7	4.8		-14.4	1.4	3.7	7.0
12.8	13.5	12.5		4.8	11.7	12.9	15.5	12.5
4.9	5.6	5.4	% Profit Before Taxes/Total Assets	-2.2	4.2	4.6	6.0	6.5
.6	1.4	.7		-22.2	-6.7	.2	.7	1.5
112.6	92.4	103.2		25.6	35.3	38.3	145.5	138.4
28.5	27.0	26.5	Sales/Net Fixed Assets	11.2	16.9	17.7	31.6	30.3
10.3	9.5	10.1		4.5	3.8	4.5	14.0	11.0
7.2	7.5	7.8		6.9	4.8	7.3	9.1	8.0
5.4	5.4	5.4	Sales/Total Assets	3.3	2.9	3.8	5.8	5.8
2.8	3.0	3.2		2.0	1.6	2.0	3.6	3.6
.3	.3	.3		.4	.7	.9	.3	.2
(212) .8	(216) .7	(247) .7	% Depr., Dep., Amort./Sales	1.5	(13) 1.2	(24) 1.4	(62) .8	(131) .5
1.7	1.4	1.4		4.3	2.4	3.1	1.3	1.0
.9	1.1	.9				1.5	.9	.7
(114) 1.6	(99) 1.7	(113) 1.7	% Officers', Directors' Owners' Comp/Sales	(13) 2.1	(29) 1.4	(57) 1.6
2.5	3.0	2.5				3.2	1.9	2.6
12840024M	13390948M	15638859M	Net Sales ($)	1489M	25088M	59370M	208559M	1090577M	14253776M
3397546M	3731487M	3771877M	Total Assets ($)	841M	9001M	25675M	74982M	266332M	3395046M

M = $ thousand   MM = $ million
See Pages 11 through 21 for Explanation of Ratios and Data

Current Data Sorted by Assets   Comparative Historical Data

						Type of Statement		
1	1	17	33	14	10	Unqualified	56	53
	7	46	18			Reviewed	79	67
7	25	22	4			Compiled	52	78
12	20	10	1			Tax Returns	30	35
5	13	40	40	11	6	Other	80	95
	97 (4/1-9/30/06)		266 (10/1/06-3/31/07)				4/1/02-3/31/03	4/1/03-3/31/04
0-500M	500M-2MM	2-10MM	10-50MM	50-100MM	100-250MM		ALL	ALL
25	66	135	96	25	16	NUMBER OF STATEMENTS	297	328
%	%	%	%	%	%	ASSETS	%	%
14.5	13.7	7.4	5.8	7.6	2.8	Cash & Equivalents	7.8	8.0
24.9	27.3	31.8	29.1	23.3	20.6	Trade Receivables (net)	29.0	27.5
30.6	24.4	30.9	33.1	28.8	21.7	Inventory	28.4	28.6
2.8	1.3	3.3	2.5	2.1	3.1	All Other Current	2.3	3.3
72.8	66.7	73.4	70.5	61.8	48.2	Total Current	67.5	67.5
20.4	22.6	17.5	19.1	23.9	23.5	Fixed Assets (net)	21.8	22.0
3.8	4.9	3.4	4.2	9.2	14.6	Intangibles (net)	4.9	3.8
3.0	5.8	5.7	6.1	5.1	13.8	All Other Non-Current	5.8	6.7
100.0	100.0	100.0	100.0	100.0	100.0	Total	100.0	100.0
						LIABILITIES		
22.9	12.4	18.0	18.5	14.1	17.5	Notes Payable-Short Term	13.5	13.2
1.9	5.6	2.1	2.1	1.7	3.5	Cur. Mat.-L.T.D.	4.9	2.8
17.1	27.1	25.8	18.8	17.3	14.3	Trade Payables	22.8	20.6
.0	.1	.1	.4	.5	.1	Income Taxes Payable	.2	.2
16.4	10.0	6.4	9.3	12.3	11.0	All Other Current	10.0	10.2
58.4	55.2	52.4	49.1	45.8	46.5	Total Current	51.3	47.0
28.3	16.4	11.5	10.2	15.7	20.6	Long-Term Debt	15.0	12.0
.0	.2	.5	.3	1.4	1.1	Deferred Taxes	.2	.3
6.3	5.0	4.9	3.9	3.9	3.3	All Other Non-Current	4.3	6.1
7.1	23.2	30.7	36.6	33.1	28.4	Net Worth	29.2	34.5
100.0	100.0	100.0	100.0	100.0	100.0	Total Liabilities & Net Worth	100.0	100.0
						INCOME DATA		
100.0	100.0	100.0	100.0	100.0	100.0	Net Sales	100.0	100.0
32.8	31.9	24.4	21.2	23.7	29.0	Gross Profit	28.0	27.3
29.7	28.5	21.7	17.1	19.7	26.4	Operating Expenses	24.4	24.6
3.1	3.5	2.7	4.1	4.0	2.5	Operating Profit	3.6	2.7
1.2	.5	.7	.7	1.2	1.0	All Other Expenses (net)	.7	.6
1.9	3.0	2.0	3.5	2.7	1.5	Profit Before Taxes	3.0	2.1
						RATIOS		
2.8	2.4	1.8	2.0	2.2	1.6		1.9	2.2
1.9	1.2	1.4	1.4	1.4	1.2	Current	1.3	1.4
.9	.9	1.1	1.1	1.1	.9		1.0	1.1
1.7	1.4	1.1	1.2	1.1	.9		1.2	1.2
.8	.8	.7	.7	.7	.5	Quick	.7	.7
.4	.3	.5	.4	.4	.4		.4	.5

													Sales/Receivables				
0	UND	15	24.9	20	18.3	21	17.3	17	21.7	21	17.6			21	17.5	19	19.3
18	20.3	24	15.0	29	12.6	31	11.6	26	13.9	32	11.6			30	12.3	28	13.1
37	10.0	35	10.4	39	9.4	41	8.8	35	10.5	44	8.2			40	9.2	39	9.5
10	38.3	11	34.7	18	20.8	23	15.6	22	16.6	10	37.6		Cost of Sales/Inventory	21	17.1	18	20.1
36	10.0	32	11.4	38	9.7	41	8.9	36	10.2	44	8.4			36	10.1	34	10.7
84	4.3	52	7.1	67	5.4	69	5.3	68	5.4	84	4.3			70	5.2	64	5.7
2	189.3	12	29.7	16	22.7	15	24.6	17	21.8	16	23.4		Cost of Sales/Payables	16	23.2	13	28.5
10	36.8	25	14.7	28	12.9	25	14.9	25	14.9	29	12.8			25	14.5	23	15.6
34	10.8	56	6.6	44	8.3	33	11.0	33	11.2	47	7.8			48	7.6	43	8.4

											Ratio		
6.8		11.6		10.4		7.9		8.8		11.3	Sales/Working Capital	10.1	8.8
21.3		33.0		21.8		20.9		20.4		33.3		24.7	20.4
-191.5		-97.2		68.9		51.0		83.1		-132.3		NM	73.5
	9.1		14.2		10.1		12.7		6.5	4.0	EBIT/Interest	11.1	10.9
(16)	3.6	(59)	3.3	(124)	2.9	(91)	3.4	(24)	3.7	2.3		(267) 3.8	(294) 3.8
	1.9		1.0		1.2		1.6		1.2	1.4		1.7	1.6
			7.2		7.0		18.9		12.3		Net Profit + Depr., Dep., Amort./Cur. Mat. L/T/D	7.2	7.5
		(11)	1.7	(31)	4.5	(34)	4.2	(13)	3.6			(81) 2.8	(77) 2.5
			.5		1.0		1.7		3.1			1.6	1.2
.1		.2		.1		.1		.3	.1	Fixed/Worth	.2	.1
.6		.8		.4		.6		1.0	1.3		.7	.6
-2.4		UND		1.5		1.1		2.0	NM		2.3	1.4
.9		1.0		1.1		.8		1.1	2.4	Debt/Worth	1.0	.8
2.1		3.3		2.3		2.5		3.5	4.3		2.8	2.2
-3.2		-79.9		5.0		6.4		14.9	NM		8.5	5.9
	51.2		93.7		42.8		46.9		44.0	22.2	% Profit Before Taxes/Tangible Net Worth	51.8	43.7
(15)	19.0	(48)	38.4	(119)	17.2	(89)	19.8	(22)	19.2	(12) 13.2		(250) 25.2	(299) 17.2
	12.8		11.2		5.6		7.8		7.6	-6.0		8.4	6.0
17.2		16.2		13.2		14.9		10.1	6.9	% Profit Before Taxes/Total Assets	13.8	12.1
10.9		7.6		4.6		6.7		6.2	3.6		5.8	5.0
3.5		-.1		.8		2.4		1.0	.7		1.6	1.2
202.8		146.3		153.8		122.8		74.5	159.2	Sales/Net Fixed Assets	81.5	95.5
27.9		30.8		40.7		29.1		9.9	12.6		23.8	24.7
14.8		12.6		11.5		10.8		5.0	7.2		8.4	9.5
8.2		7.0		5.6		4.6		3.7	3.8	Sales/Total Assets	4.8	4.9
4.1		4.3		3.7		3.0		3.1	2.2		3.2	3.2
2.7		2.4		2.5		2.4		2.0	1.1		2.1	2.3
.9		.4		.2		.2		.3		% Depr., Dep., Amort./Sales	.4	.3
(15)	1.2	(52)	.8	(119)	.6	(87)	.6	(21)	1.5			(267) 1.0	(284) 1.1
	3.0		2.9		1.7		1.4		2.5			2.2	2.5
2.0		1.7		1.1		.5				% Officers', Directors' Owners' Comp/Sales	1.3	.9
(13)	2.4	(33)	3.0	(53)	2.2	(25)	1.0					(121) 2.1	(124) 1.8
	5.4		5.0		4.4		2.2					4.9	4.1

29051M	394545M	2861107M	7124655M	6008044M	7774137M	Net Sales ($)	11973503M	16128443M
6192M	75625M	686659M	1995067M	1754971M	2666872M	Total Assets ($)	3314922M	4214197M

M = $ thousand   MM = $ million
See Pages 11 through 21 for Explanation of Ratios and Data

Comparative Historical Data | Current Data Sorted by Sales

Comparative Historical Data			Type of Statement	Current Data Sorted by Sales					
59	56	76	Unqualified	1	1	1	2	11	60
77	80	71	Reviewed	1	1	3	12	26	30
42	46	58	Compiled	4	11	6	14	16	7
35	29	43	Tax Returns	8	8	7	7	8	5
76	116	115	Other	3	7	8	8	26	63
4/1/04-3/31/05 ALL	4/1/05-3/31/06 ALL	4/1/06-3/31/07 ALL		97 (4/1-9/30/06)			266 (10/1/06-3/31/07)		
				0-1MM	1-3MM	3-5MM	5-10MM	10-25MM	25MM & OVER
289	327	363	NUMBER OF STATEMENTS	16	27	25	43	87	165
%	%	%	ASSETS	%	%	%	%	%	%
7.1	6.9	8.4	Cash & Equivalents	18.5	10.7	8.7	10.9	8.6	6.3
28.1	29.3	28.7	Trade Receivables (net)	23.3	19.4	30.9	24.0	31.4	30.3
29.3	29.5	29.7	Inventory	20.1	29.8	26.2	26.4	29.9	32.0
2.7	2.7	2.6	All Other Current	2.8	1.9	.4	4.0	2.6	2.6
67.2	68.4	69.5	Total Current	64.8	61.8	66.1	65.3	72.5	71.2
21.3	20.7	19.8	Fixed Assets (net)	27.3	27.9	19.3	24.8	17.0	17.9
4.2	4.9	4.8	Intangibles (net)	7.5	4.1	7.5	5.4	2.7	5.3
7.3	6.0	6.0	All Other Non-Current	.5	6.2	7.1	4.5	7.9	5.7
100.0	100.0	100.0	Total	100.0	100.0	100.0	100.0	100.0	100.0
			LIABILITIES						
14.6	14.9	17.1	Notes Payable-Short Term	10.9	25.0	21.6	14.3	15.3	17.5
3.1	2.6	2.7	Cur. Mat.-L.T.D.	1.4	3.6	3.1	4.4	3.2	2.0
23.3	22.4	22.5	Trade Payables	9.0	17.6	25.6	25.2	24.5	22.3
.2	.2	.2	Income Taxes Payable	.0	.1	.1	.1	.1	.4
7.9	8.7	9.1	All Other Current	23.1	10.1	7.1	7.7	6.6	9.6
49.1	48.8	51.7	Total Current	44.4	56.4	57.5	51.7	49.8	51.8
12.9	14.3	13.9	Long-Term Debt	34.1	24.0	16.7	14.9	10.5	11.4
.3	.4	.4	Deferred Taxes	.1	.0	.4	.5	.4	.5
6.5	5.9	4.6	All Other Non-Current	16.8	1.9	5.4	2.8	6.1	3.4
31.2	30.6	29.3	Net Worth	4.5	17.7	20.0	30.1	33.2	32.8
100.0	100.0	100.0	Total Liabilties & Net Worth	100.0	100.0	100.0	100.0	100.0	100.0
			INCOME DATA						
100.0	100.0	100.0	Net Sales	100.0	100.0	100.0	100.0	100.0	100.0
26.7	24.6	25.7	Gross Profit	39.6	37.1	35.8	28.6	23.5	21.3
23.5	22.0	22.3	Operating Expenses	35.6	33.3	34.0	25.1	20.9	17.6
3.2	2.6	3.3	Operating Profit	4.0	3.8	1.8	3.4	2.6	3.7
.3	.5	.7	All Other Expenses (net)	1.3	1.8	1.1	.4	.5	.6
2.9	2.2	2.6	Profit Before Taxes	2.7	2.1	.7	3.0	2.1	3.1
			RATIOS						
2.0	2.1	2.0	Current	3.0	2.7	2.4	1.8	2.2	1.8
1.4	1.3	1.4		1.9	1.5	1.2	1.4	1.4	1.3
1.1	1.1	1.1		1.0	.7	.8	.9	1.1	1.1
1.2	1.2	1.2	Quick	1.9	1.2	1.3	1.0	1.3	1.1
.7	.7	.7		1.0	.7	.7	.6	.8	.7
.5	.5	.4		.3	.3	.4	.4	.5	.4
20 18.3	19 19.6	18 20.2	Sales/Receivables	0 UND	13 27.9	21 17.6	16 22.6	19 19.3	19 18.9
27 13.4	27 13.3	28 12.9		19 19.1	27 13.5	31 11.9	24 15.2	29 12.6	28 13.2
38 9.7	38 9.6	39 9.5		53 6.9	38 9.7	41 9.0	37 10.0	43 8.6	36 10.1
19 18.8	20 18.6	18 19.8	Cost of Sales/Inventory	6 63.4	35 10.6	15 23.8	14 26.3	15 24.4	21 17.6
36 10.2	34 10.8	36 10.2		38 9.6	51 7.2	39 9.3	36 10.2	35 10.4	33 11.0
68 5.4	62 5.9	67 5.5		96 3.8	81 4.5	65 5.6	56 6.5	67 5.5	60 6.0
14 25.6	14 26.5	15 24.8	Cost of Sales/Payables	0 UND	8 44.6	16 22.7	18 20.7	17 21.2	15 24.9
26 13.9	25 14.4	26 14.2		7 53.4	28 13.0	32 11.3	29 14.7	29 12.4	24 15.1
43 8.6	41 9.0	38 9.5		38 9.6	43 8.5	59 6.1	54 6.8	41 9.0	33 11.0
10.2	10.4	9.9	Sales/Working Capital	3.3	9.5	9.3	8.9	10.0	11.0
21.5	19.7	22.0		8.1	29.0	32.2	24.4	18.5	23.3
123.5	72.5	101.8		NM	-11.8	-18.8	-146.6	94.8	63.1
12.8	9.6	10.2	EBIT/Interest	8.9	10.5	14.4	8.4	13.1	
(262) 3.8	(304) 3.3	(330) 3.1		(22) 2.0	1.4	(40) 5.6	(78) 2.5	(156) 3.7	
1.5	1.3	1.3		1.1	-2.9	1.4	1.2	1.6	
6.7	6.1	10.4	Net Profit + Depr., Dep., Amort./Cur. Mat. L/T/D					6.4	18.1
(81) 2.4	(94) 3.2	(96) 4.3						(21) 4.3	(59) 4.5
1.0	1.4	1.5						1.1	2.4
.2	.1	.1	Fixed/Worth	.0	.2	.1	.1	.1	.1
.5	.6	.5		1.4	.8	1.4	.6	.4	.5
1.7	2.0	1.9		-2.0	-9.1	-8.0	2.9	1.3	1.3
.9	1.1	1.1	Debt/Worth	1.1	.6	1.3	1.2	.9	1.2
2.3	2.7	2.7		NM	2.7	4.3	2.4	2.2	3.0
6.8	6.8	7.9		-2.9	-12.8	-8.6	5.6	5.3	6.8
46.5	47.3	47.0	% Profit Before Taxes/Tangible Net Worth		44.2	102.2	59.3	38.1	47.5
(249) 20.2	(281) 18.3	(305) 19.6			(19) 19.0	(15) 32.9	(38) 31.8	(77) 14.7	(148) 19.7
6.1	5.1	7.4			9.1	2.8	6.2	6.7	7.5
14.3	13.1	14.3	% Profit Before Taxes/Total Assets	15.8	13.5	28.4	18.4	12.2	13.9
6.0	5.3	6.3		5.0	6.9	1.4	9.2	4.3	6.6
1.1	1.0	1.4		-9.1	1.3	-3.7	2.0	.8	1.8
71.6	118.2	134.9	Sales/Net Fixed Assets	200.8	72.5	186.3	146.0	113.2	152.5
25.1	31.3	32.4		15.4	20.5	27.9	27.4	38.4	42.7
10.2	10.0	10.5		3.6	8.4	10.4	7.6	12.1	11.3
5.1	5.6	5.5	Sales/Total Assets	3.7	4.7	5.9	6.3	5.4	5.7
3.3	3.4	3.4		2.1	3.1	3.2	3.6	3.7	3.5
2.3	2.3	2.4		.9	1.9	2.3	1.9	2.5	2.4
.3	.3	.3	% Depr., Dep., Amort./Sales	1.1	1.1	.6	.3	.3	.2
(251) .9	(267) .7	(303) .7		(10) 2.6	(19) 2.4	(18) 1.1	(38) 1.1	(75) .7	(143) .5
2.2	1.9	2.0		5.1	5.2	3.1	3.3	1.5	1.3
.9	.9	.9	% Officers', Directors' Owners' Comp/Sales		2.0	2.7	1.7	.8	.5
(102) 2.0	(108) 1.9	(126) 2.3			(13) 3.6	(15) 3.2	(19) 2.9	(38) 1.4	(36) 1.0
5.3	4.6	4.0			6.1	4.8	5.1	3.3	2.9
11818390M	17114570M	24191539M	Net Sales ($)	8711M	48630M	102919M	321638M	1428022M	22281619M
3834990M	5249636M	7185386M	Total Assets ($)	6444M	19080M	38066M	120082M	457920M	6543794M

M = $ thousand   MM = $ million
See Pages 11 through 21 for Explanation of Ratios and Data

Current Data Sorted by Assets   Comparative Historical Data

0-500M	500M-2MM	2-10MM	10-50MM	50-100MM	100-250MM	Type of Statement	4/1/02-3/31/03 ALL	4/1/03-3/31/04 ALL
1	16	78	74	19	9	Unqualified	175	180
3	19	52	14		1	Reviewed	71	71
1	6	8	2	1		Compiled	19	23
2	4	3				Tax Returns	8	7
2	7	24	11	6	7	Other	38	34
	210 (4/1-9/30/06)			160 (10/1/06-3/31/07)				
9	52	165	101	26	17	NUMBER OF STATEMENTS	311	315
%	%	%	%	%	%	**ASSETS**	%	%
	12.2	7.1	4.9	4.7	4.1	Cash & Equivalents	8.2	9.0
	24.5	16.4	15.0	16.6	29.6	Trade Receivables (net)	18.8	16.4
	29.0	36.1	39.9	42.1	34.6	Inventory	31.7	30.4
	5.5	7.2	8.9	8.2	7.7	All Other Current	4.1	7.7
	71.2	66.8	68.6	71.5	76.0	Total Current	62.8	63.4
	21.2	26.6	25.0	22.2	19.2	Fixed Assets (net)	29.0	28.1
	1.1	.8	.5	.2	.8	Intangibles (net)	.5	.6
	6.4	5.8	5.9	6.1	4.0	All Other Non-Current	7.7	7.9
	100.0	100.0	100.0	100.0	100.0	Total	100.0	100.0
						LIABILITIES		
	17.2	17.7	24.1	27.7	26.1	Notes Payable-Short Term	17.0	17.0
	1.9	1.6	1.9	1.2	.7	Cur. Mat.-L.T.D.	2.4	2.0
	15.3	15.6	19.6	18.1	17.2	Trade Payables	15.0	17.4
	.2	.3	.3	.1	.6	Income Taxes Payable	.5	.3
	8.7	12.0	8.6	11.0	16.3	All Other Current	8.1	9.0
	43.2	47.2	54.6	58.0	60.9	Total Current	43.0	45.8
	6.2	9.6	11.2	12.2	12.1	Long-Term Debt	9.6	9.1
	.6	1.3	1.2	.8	.1	Deferred Taxes	1.0	1.1
	2.9	2.8	.7	3.0	1.0	All Other Non-Current	2.0	2.1
	47.0	39.0	32.3	26.0	25.8	Net Worth	44.4	41.9
	100.0	100.0	100.0	100.0	100.0	Total Liabilties & Net Worth	100.0	100.0
						INCOME DATA		
	100.0	100.0	100.0	100.0	100.0	Net Sales	100.0	100.0
	11.9	11.7	11.0	7.8	9.8	Gross Profit	13.7	10.6
	10.0	9.4	8.5	5.3	7.4	Operating Expenses	12.1	9.5
	1.9	2.2	2.6	2.5	2.3	Operating Profit	1.6	1.1
	.3	.6	.4	.4	.5	All Other Expenses (net)	.1	.1
	1.6	1.6	2.2	2.1	1.8	Profit Before Taxes	1.5	1.0
						RATIOS		
	3.0	1.8	1.4	1.5	1.5	Current	2.0	1.8
	1.5	1.3	1.2	1.2	1.3		1.4	1.3
	1.1	1.2	1.1	1.1	1.1		1.2	1.1
	1.4	.8	.6	.6	.9	Quick	1.0	1.0
	.8	.4	.3	.4	.6		.5	.5
	.4	.1	.1	.1	.2		.3	.2
	4 84.5	3 115.9	4 98.1	6 56.4	10 35.4	Sales/Receivables	7 49.5	2 188.3
	17 21.7	15 24.2	19 19.2	12 29.4	22 16.8		15 23.7	12 29.9
	35 10.6	29 12.7	34 10.8	28 12.9	42 8.8		33 11.1	28 12.9
	13 27.8	29 12.7	33 11.2	30 12.1	11 33.5	Cost of Sales/Inventory	21 17.4	13 27.6
	24 15.5	49 7.5	63 5.8	60 6.1	52 7.0		42 8.7	34 10.7
	63 5.8	91 4.0	95 3.8	97 3.8	114 3.2		75 4.9	71 5.2
	3 117.6	5 68.5	11 33.6	10 37.4	6 60.1	Cost of Sales/Payables	6 64.2	6 65.2
	8 44.0	13 27.1	23 16.2	14 26.0	13 28.1		14 25.4	15 25.0
	26 14.0	33 11.1	52 7.1	28 12.8	29 12.4		29 12.7	31 11.8
	7.3	9.5	13.0	18.8	14.3	Sales/Working Capital	9.1	11.5
	19.3	19.4	21.1	21.2	33.5		18.1	23.1
	51.6	40.6	38.5	60.7	68.9		41.2	46.5
	6.1	5.0	5.1	4.0	6.3	EBIT/Interest	6.7	6.0
	(45) 2.2	(160) 2.5	(98) 3.1	2.4	(16) 4.7		(291) 3.2	(302) 2.7
	1.3	1.4	1.8	2.0	2.1		1.5	1.2
	6.2	6.0	9.5	31.5		Net Profit + Depr., Dep., Amort./Cur. Mat. L/T/D	6.5	5.1
	(10) 3.2	(63) 3.1	(41) 5.1	(12) 9.7			(107) 3.5	(107) 2.7
	2.1	1.8	2.4	4.3			1.8	1.4
	.2	.3	.5	.4	.4	Fixed/Worth	.4	.4
	.5	.7	.8	.9	.8		.7	.7
	1.1	1.1	1.2	1.4	.9		1.0	1.0
	.4	.9	1.4	1.9	1.4	Debt/Worth	.7	.7
	1.1	1.6	2.1	3.0	3.8		1.4	1.4
	3.1	3.2	4.1	6.6	10.3		2.6	3.5
	34.2	18.3	23.9	26.5	68.4	% Profit Before Taxes/Tangible Net Worth	16.4	15.6
	(49) 11.6	(161) 9.5	(99) 13.3	13.2	19.4		(308) 8.8	(304) 7.2
	1.1	3.8	8.4	8.8	12.4		3.0	.8
	8.7	7.2	8.7	5.7	8.9	% Profit Before Taxes/Total Assets	7.1	5.7
	3.5	4.0	4.1	3.9	6.2		3.4	2.8
	.5	1.0	2.2	2.2	2.5		1.0	.4
	48.9	22.9	15.7	30.3	298.3	Sales/Net Fixed Assets	20.5	24.7
	17.6	10.8	9.7	11.1	19.6		10.2	11.3
	10.3	7.0	6.7	7.0	5.2		6.3	6.9
	5.5	3.9	3.3	3.9	7.7	Sales/Total Assets	4.0	4.6
	3.9	2.9	2.5	2.6	2.9		2.9	3.1
	2.6	2.0	1.8	2.0	1.6		2.0	2.1
	.4	.7	.9	.7	.0	% Depr., Dep., Amort./Sales	.9	.7
	(46) 1.0	(155) 1.3	(96) 1.3	(24) 1.0	.8		(295) 1.5	(304) 1.2
	1.4	1.8	1.7	1.5	1.6		2.0	1.8
	.4	.8	.1			% Officers', Directors' Owners' Comp/Sales	.4	.5
	(14) 1.5	(30) 1.2	(10) .8				(53) 1.3	(55) 1.2
	3.0	2.8	1.6				2.3	2.7
13481M	303471M	2634278M	5929516M	6618880M	14537298M	Net Sales ($)	11453395M	19166626M
3058M	66435M	820967M	2131339M	1783915M	2756419M	Total Assets ($)	3716276M	4703707M

M = $ thousand   MM = $ million
See Pages 11 through 21 for Explanation of Ratios and Data

Comparative Historical Data / Current Data Sorted by Sales

Historical columns: **4/1/04-3/31/05 ALL**, **4/1/05-3/31/06 ALL**, **4/1/06-3/31/07 ALL**
Current size columns grouped: **210 (4/1-9/30/06)** covering 0-1MM, 1-3MM, 3-5MM; **160 (10/1/06-3/31/07)** covering 5-10MM, 10-25MM, 25MM & OVER.

	4/1/04- 3/31/05 ALL	4/1/05- 3/31/06 ALL	4/1/06- 3/31/07 ALL	0-1MM	1-3MM	3-5MM	5-10MM	10-25MM	25MM & OVER
Type of Statement									
Unqualified	190	169	197	1	3	6	34	49	104
Reviewed	83	59	89	3	5	7	27	32	15
Compiled	17	11	18	1	3	2	2	7	3
Tax Returns	11	11	9	1	2	2	1	1	2
Other	41	44	57	1	3	7	7	14	25
NUMBER OF STATEMENTS	342	294	370	7	16	24	71	103	149
ASSETS	%	%	%	%	%	%	%	%	%
Cash & Equivalents	9.6	7.6	7.0		10.6	10.9	10.9	5.7	5.3
Trade Receivables (net)	15.7	18.1	17.6		22.2	18.7	16.1	15.2	19.7
Inventory	32.7	32.7	36.2		31.0	38.3	32.6	38.1	36.6
All Other Current	6.8	7.3	7.6		4.9	4.2	7.6	8.7	7.3
Total Current	64.8	65.9	68.5		68.7	72.1	67.2	67.7	68.9
Fixed Assets (net)	27.6	27.5	24.8		24.2	19.9	25.4	26.5	24.7
Intangibles (net)	.5	.4	.7		.1	.2	2.2	.4	.4
All Other Non-Current	7.1	6.2	6.0		6.9	7.9	5.2	5.5	6.0
Total	100.0	100.0	100.0		100.0	100.0	100.0	100.0	100.0
LIABILITIES									
Notes Payable-Short Term	17.2	17.6	20.5		13.1	19.9	19.4	20.3	22.1
Cur. Mat.-L.T.D.	1.8	1.6	1.7		1.8	2.2	1.6	1.6	1.7
Trade Payables	18.7	19.1	16.7		13.3	14.9	13.5	16.7	19.2
Income Taxes Payable	.4	.3	.3		.1	.0	.3	.3	.4
All Other Current	10.4	9.3	10.6		7.2	12.4	10.6	10.6	10.9
Total Current	48.5	47.9	49.8		35.5	49.5	45.4	49.5	54.3
Long-Term Debt	9.2	9.5	10.0		11.1	9.0	7.9	8.2	12.2
Deferred Taxes	1.1	1.4	1.1		.1	.3	1.3	1.4	1.0
All Other Non-Current	1.9	1.3	2.1		6.5	10.3	1.8	1.1	1.3
Net Worth	39.3	39.8	36.9		46.8	30.9	43.6	39.9	31.2
Total Liabilities & Net Worth	100.0	100.0	100.0		100.0	100.0	100.0	100.0	100.0
INCOME DATA									
Net Sales	100.0	100.0	100.0		100.0	100.0	100.0	100.0	100.0
Gross Profit	11.2	10.5	11.4		28.4	15.8	12.0	10.3	8.9
Operating Expenses	9.7	8.8	9.1		16.1	12.6	10.0	8.4	7.0
Operating Profit	1.5	1.8	2.4		12.3	3.2	2.0	1.9	1.9
All Other Expenses (net)	.2	.3	.5		4.0	.4	.4	.4	.2
Profit Before Taxes	1.3	1.5	1.9		8.3	2.8	1.7	1.5	1.7
RATIOS									
Current	1.7 / 1.3 / 1.1	1.7 / 1.3 / 1.1	1.7 / 1.3 / 1.1		2.3 / 1.9 / 1.3	2.8 / 1.3 / 1.1	1.9 / 1.4 / 1.2	1.6 / 1.3 / 1.1	1.5 / 1.2 / 1.1
Quick	.9 / .5 / .2	.8 / .5 (293) / .2	.8 / .4 / .2		1.3 / .8 / .3	1.4 / .5 / .3	1.0 / .5 / .2	.7 / .3 / .1	.7 / .4 / .2
Sales/Receivables	2 166.6 / 12 31.6 / 25 14.7	3 145.7 / 14 25.5 / 32 11.5	4 91.7 / 17 22.1 / 31 11.9		4 82.9 / 29 12.6 / 58 6.3	5 67.2 / 19 19.0 / 42 8.6	4 99.5 / 16 23.0 / 32 11.5	2 185.7 / 12 30.1 / 28 13.2	5 73.8 / 17 21.1 / 30 12.3
Cost of Sales/Inventory	14 25.6 / 39 9.5 / 66 5.6	19 19.2 / 39 9.3 / 69 5.3	24 15.0 / 49 7.4 / 90 4.0		18 20.2 / 53 6.9 / 120 3.0	28 12.9 / 73 5.0 / 124 3.0	20 18.4 / 44 8.4 / 96 3.8	32 11.4 / 50 7.4 / 91 4.0	24 15.1 / 48 7.6 / 78 4.7
Cost of Sales/Payables	7 54.5 / 15 24.0 / 32 11.4	8 46.6 / 17 21.7 / 35 10.5	6 58.7 / 15 24.9 / 37 10.0		2 164.6 / 14 26.9 / 51 7.2	3 115.7 / 14 26.8 / 51 7.1	5 81.1 / 12 30.3 / 36 10.1	6 60.5 / 15 24.3 / 35 10.4	8 43.3 / 15 24.0 / 37 9.9
Sales/Working Capital	12.4 / 24.6 / 53.3	11.1 / 21.8 / 41.3	10.5 / 20.3 / 41.3		3.4 / 6.4 / 15.0	7.5 / 13.3 / 36.1	8.4 / 13.7 / 26.0	11.0 / 20.0 / 40.5	15.6 / 28.4 / 47.0
EBIT/Interest	5.9 / 3.0 / 1.5 (326)	8.1 / 3.5 / 1.6 (279)	5.3 / 2.7 / 1.5 (351)		10.8 / 7.1 / 2.4	4.6 / 3.0 / 1.5 (21)	5.3 / 2.5 / 1.2 (67)	4.8 / 2.5 / 1.4 (100)	5.5 / 2.8 / 1.8 (143)
Net Profit + Depr., Dep., Amort./Cur. Mat. L/T/D	6.7 / 3.5 / 1.6 (116)	6.7 / 3.6 / 1.9 (104)	8.9 / 3.9 / 2.3 (131)				7.4 / 3.1 / 1.3 (23)	6.0 / 3.2 / 1.8 (46)	11.2 / 5.3 / 2.6 (58)
Fixed/Worth	.4 / .7 / 1.1	.4 / .7 / 1.0	.4 / .7 / 1.1		.2 / .5 / 1.0	.2 / .7 / 2.2	.3 / .6 / 1.0	.4 / .7 / 1.0	.4 / .9 / 1.3
Debt/Worth	.8 / 1.6 / 3.2	.8 / 1.6 / 3.5	1.0 / 1.8 / 4.0		.4 / 1.1 / 2.1	.5 / 3.1 / 6.0	.7 / 1.3 / 2.7	1.0 / 1.6 / 2.9	1.4 / 2.4 / 4.5
% Profit Before Taxes/Tangible Net Worth	17.6 / 8.9 / 2.5 (332)	18.1 / 9.4 / 3.5 (287)	21.4 / 11.7 / 4.8 (360)		100.0 / 25.0 / 8.2 (15)	45.3 / 16.8 / 6.4 (22)	18.8 / 8.2 / .9 (67)	14.7 / 10.0 / 4.2 (146)	26.3 / 13.6 / 8.4
% Profit Before Taxes/Total Assets	6.3 / 3.2 / .9	7.0 / 3.6 / 1.3	8.1 / 4.0 / 1.3		22.8 / 7.3 / 4.0	10.7 / 4.3 / 1.7	7.0 / 3.5 / .2	6.1 / 3.6 / 1.1	8.8 / 4.4 / 2.3
Sales/Net Fixed Assets	27.5 / 11.8 / 7.6	26.0 / 11.5 / 6.8	27.3 / 11.8 / 7.2		25.1 / 11.9 / 5.9	36.3 / 16.3 / 8.3	31.0 / 12.8 / 6.6	25.2 / 10.5 / 7.0	26.0 / 11.8 / 7.5
Sales/Total Assets	4.5 / 3.3 / 2.3	4.5 / 3.0 / 2.2	4.0 / 2.8 / 2.0		4.5 / 2.4 / 1.0	4.3 / 2.4 / 1.9	4.1 / 2.9 / 2.0	3.7 / 2.8 / 2.0	4.7 / 2.8 / 2.2
% Depr., Dep., Amort./Sales	.6 / 1.1 / 1.7 (323)	.7 / 1.3 / 1.7 (274)	.7 / 1.2 / 1.7 (344)		1.1 / 1.4 / 1.9 (14)	.4 / .9 / 1.6 (23)	.7 / 1.4 / 2.1 (66)	.8 / 1.3 / 1.8 (96)	.7 / 1.2 / 1.5 (141)
% Officers', Directors' Owners' Comp/Sales	.5 / 1.2 / 2.3 (51)	.7 / 1.3 / 3.4 (45)	.6 / 1.3 / 2.8 (59)				.3 / 1.0 / 3.0 (11)	.9 / 1.3 / 2.8 (23)	.2 / .8 / 1.6 (14)
Net Sales ($)	24490192M	23579690M	30036924M	3496M	38036M	98187M	527163M	1693875M	27676167M
Total Assets ($)	5294997M	5232804M	7562133M	3221M	21650M	43848M	235398M	674533M	6583483M

M = $ thousand   MM = $ million
See Pages 11 through 21 for Explanation of Ratios and Data

Current Data Sorted by Assets

Comparative Historical Data

	0-500M	500M-2MM	2-10MM	10-50MM	50-100MM	100-250MM		1 4/1/02-3/31/03 ALL	2 4/1/03-3/31/04 ALL
Type of Statement									
Unqualified			1	3	1			1	2
Reviewed			2					9	5
Compiled	1	2	3	1				4	9
Tax Returns	4	4						9	5
Other	1	6	7	1	1	1		5	7
		8 (4/1-9/30/06)		31 (10/1/06-3/31/07)			**NUMBER OF STATEMENTS**		
	6	12	13	5	2	1		28	28
	%	%	%	%	%	%		%	%
							ASSETS		
		12.6	2.7				Cash & Equivalents	18.3	6.6
		22.8	28.4				Trade Receivables (net)	22.5	24.9
		25.2	19.6				Inventory	24.8	26.8
		7.7	6.4				All Other Current	3.2	11.9
		68.2	57.2				Total Current	68.8	70.3
		25.7	30.2				Fixed Assets (net)	20.5	18.9
		.1	6.3				Intangibles (net)	1.7	2.7
		6.1	6.3				All Other Non-Current	9.0	8.1
		100.0	100.0				Total	100.0	100.0
							LIABILITIES		
		24.2	17.2				Notes Payable-Short Term	29.6	25.8
		1.1	2.1				Cur. Mat.-L.T.D.	3.9	1.6
		14.9	17.9				Trade Payables	8.5	8.0
		.3	.1				Income Taxes Payable	.0	.2
		10.4	16.3				All Other Current	8.1	16.7
		50.8	53.8				Total Current	50.0	52.4
		13.0	23.0				Long-Term Debt	12.5	10.2
		.0	.1				Deferred Taxes	.1	.1
		1.9	.5				All Other Non-Current	2.8	1.1
		34.3	22.6				Net Worth	34.5	36.2
		100.0	100.0				Total Liabilities & Net Worth	100.0	100.0
							INCOME DATA		
		100.0	100.0				Net Sales	100.0	100.0
		15.6	20.1				Gross Profit	16.3	26.4
		16.0	17.6				Operating Expenses	13.3	23.7
		-.4	2.4				Operating Profit	2.9	2.7
		-.8	2.3				All Other Expenses (net)	.1	.2
		.4	.1				Profit Before Taxes	2.9	2.5
							RATIOS		
		1.8	1.3					2.8	2.5
		1.2	1.0				Current	1.2	1.2
		.9	.8					.9	1.0
		1.0	.9					1.8	1.2
		.7	.5				Quick	.8 (27)	.6
		.5	.4					.4	.1
		3 114.8	8 43.0					3 132.1	0 884.6
		8 47.0	15 23.9				Sales/Receivables	8 44.2	13 29.1
		16 22.4	31 11.7					21 17.6	28 13.1
		2 174.0	2 194.8					1 494.7	3 137.5
		6 62.4	8 48.3				Cost of Sales/Inventory	11 33.4	9 38.6
		21 17.7	33 11.2					24 15.3	31 11.7
		0 888.3	2 192.1					1 590.1	0 UND
		4 88.9	10 37.3				Cost of Sales/Payables	2 154.2	2 149.3
		14 25.9	25 14.5					12 31.7	29 12.4
		33.3	166.2					15.2	11.1
		173.4	-955.1				Sales/Working Capital	102.9	77.4
		-317.2	-29.9					-385.6	-206.0
		12.3	8.0					6.1	4.9
		1.9	3.6				EBIT/Interest	(22) 2.1	(25) 1.9
		-.3	.7					.9	.6
							Net Profit + Depr., Dep., Amort./Cur. Mat. L/T/D		
		.1	.2					.2	.2
		1.1	1.5				Fixed/Worth	.7	.5
		4.1	5.6					1.4	1.2
		.6	2.4					.8	.9
		2.3	6.9				Debt/Worth	2.7	2.6
		16.8	14.8					7.9	5.4
		88.8	62.1				% Profit Before Taxes/Tangible Net Worth	53.1	35.4
		(11) 8.4	(11) 15.7					(25) 17.0	(26) 6.0
		-11.4	-21.9					2.4	-2.0
		21.3	12.5				% Profit Before Taxes/Total Assets	12.4	5.1
		2.5	6.6					5.0	2.7
		-3.5	-2.1					1.0	.1
		493.5	188.6					167.0	92.5
		48.0	27.5				Sales/Net Fixed Assets	68.0	38.0
		19.1	8.7					20.5	15.9
		23.9	13.3					28.5	8.3
		8.7	6.2				Sales/Total Assets	7.7	5.6
		4.7	1.8					4.0	2.3
		.1	.2					.2	.4
		(11) .4	(12) .7				% Depr., Dep., Amort./Sales	(25) .4	(25) .7
		.9	3.7					.8	2.1
							% Officers', Directors' Owners' Comp/Sales	.1	.4
								(11) .9	(12) 1.7
								2.2	3.8
	20062M	189930M	318386M	328444M	2163626M	500895M	Net Sales ($)	619901M	525627M
	1791M	13083M	52264M	104391M	146360M	104303M	Total Assets ($)	276406M	284026M

M = $ thousand   MM = $ million
See Pages 11 through 21 for Explanation of Ratios and Data

Comparative Historical Data | Current Data Sorted by Sales

			Type of Statement						
3	4	5	Unqualified					2	3
5	2	2	Reviewed					2	2
9	9	7	Compiled			1	1	4	1
8	7	8	Tax Returns			2		2	1
8	8	17	Other	3	2	1	3	3	8
4/1/04-3/31/05	4/1/05-3/31/06	4/1/06-3/31/07		2					
ALL	ALL	ALL		8 (4/1-9/30/06)		31 (10/1/06-3/31/07)			
				0-1MM	1-3MM	3-5MM	5-10MM	10-25MM	25MM & OVER
33	30	39	NUMBER OF STATEMENTS		5	4	4	11	15
%	%	%	ASSETS	%	%	%	%	%	%
8.9	4.3	9.9	Cash & Equivalents					8.7	8.4
16.8	26.3	25.8	Trade Receivables (net)					25.4	35.9
26.1	26.7	21.7	Inventory					23.5	21.9
8.6	7.6	6.6	All Other Current					5.1	5.3
60.5	64.9	64.1	Total Current					62.7	71.5
25.5	25.2	24.5	Fixed Assets (net)					27.0	19.8
3.9	3.1	2.2	Intangibles (net)					.1	.2
10.1	6.8	9.2	All Other Non-Current					10.3	8.6
100.0	100.0	100.0	Total					100.0	100.0
			LIABILITIES						
19.7	18.6	20.0	Notes Payable-Short Term					28.8	19.9
1.2	4.5	2.4	Cur. Mat.-L.T.D.					2.5	2.3
7.5	10.0	15.9	Trade Payables					20.4	15.0
.1	.1	.1	Income Taxes Payable					.1	.1
14.9	16.7	17.8	All Other Current					12.4	17.4
43.4	49.9	56.2	Total Current					64.3	54.7
16.9	12.1	20.4	Long-Term Debt					17.9	11.9
.1	.2	.1	Deferred Taxes					.0	.3
8.4	1.2	.9	All Other Non-Current					2.5	.2
31.2	36.7	22.3	Net Worth					15.4	32.9
100.0	100.0	100.0	Total Liabilities & Net Worth					100.0	100.0
			INCOME DATA						
100.0	100.0	100.0	Net Sales					100.0	100.0
29.2	23.7	18.8	Gross Profit					25.8	7.0
25.1	23.4	17.4	Operating Expenses					25.6	5.7
4.1	.3	1.4	Operating Profit					.3	1.3
2.1	-.6	.6	All Other Expenses (net)					.8	.4
2.0	.9	.9	Profit Before Taxes					-.5	1.0
			RATIOS						
3.4	1.6	1.8						1.1	1.8
1.3	1.3	1.1	Current					1.0	1.1
.9	1.0	.9						.8	1.0
1.6	1.0	1.1						.7	1.0
(30) .8	(29) .6	.8	Quick					.5	.8
.4	.4	.5						.3	.5
0 782.2	2 242.2	5 73.2						7 52.4	8 45.8
8 44.2	16 22.2	13 27.5	Sales/Receivables					15 23.9	14 25.5
21 17.5	26 14.3	24 15.2						26 14.2	29 12.6
2 167.7	3 108.6	2 194.8						5 67.0	2 209.0
14 26.2	17 21.4	6 57.9	Cost of Sales/Inventory					20 18.0	5 74.0
47 7.8	60 6.1	25 14.4						46 7.9	15 24.3
0 999.8	0 UND	0 974.6						0 974.6	1 372.9
5 80.8	4 83.7	4 81.5	Cost of Sales/Payables					14 25.8	2 158.8
24 15.1	24 15.2	14 25.8						40 9.0	8 43.2
12.5	16.1	26.7						152.4	26.7
124.2	84.8	178.7	Sales/Working Capital					-275.8	178.7
-508.8	392.0	-202.0						-117.7	-999.8
11.6	7.6	8.8						3.5	10.6
(31) 2.9	(28) 3.4	(37) 2.7	EBIT/Interest					1.0	3.6
1.3	.1	.6						-.3	1.4
			Net Profit + Depr., Dep., Amort./Cur. Mat. L/T/D						
.3	.5	.2						.7	.1
.7	.8	.7	Fixed/Worth					1.5	.2
2.5	1.7	1.9						4.9	1.0
.6	1.0	1.6						3.7	1.3
2.1	1.9	4.4	Debt/Worth					6.4	2.4
8.5	7.6	8.7						8.7	4.4
40.9	65.4	63.4						68.8	42.8
(28) 15.1	(27) 12.9	(35) 15.7	% Profit Before Taxes/Tangible Net Worth					(10) -.9	13.9
2.3	1.0	-4.2						-64.8	6.1
9.4	15.1	17.4						7.8	19.1
3.3	3.7	5.1	% Profit Before Taxes/Total Assets					-.2	4.2
.3	-2.6	-1.1						-4.3	1.1
73.8	73.2	285.9						70.7	530.9
34.4	24.5	39.1	Sales/Net Fixed Assets					33.2	91.2
8.2	8.2	13.3						5.1	16.8
14.0	11.1	14.9						13.1	17.7
5.3	4.3	8.1	Sales/Total Assets					7.4	11.4
2.3	2.4	3.0						2.2	4.7
.3	.5	.2						.3	.1
(29) .8	(27) .9	(35) .5	% Depr., Dep., Amort./Sales					.6	(13) .2
2.3	2.0	1.2						2.5	.6
.4	.6	.4							
(16) 1.8	(11) 1.0	(14) 1.2	% Officers', Directors' Owners' Comp/Sales						
5.3	1.6	1.9							
2024902M	2267467M	3521343M	Net Sales ($)	9312M	13439M	26907M	164822M	3306863M	
581135M	441786M	422192M	Total Assets ($)	5141M	2614M	7726M	57314M	349397M	

© RMA 2007

M = $ thousand   MM = $ million
See Pages 11 through 21 for Explanation of Ratios and Data

| Current Data Sorted by Assets | | | | | | | | Comparative Historical Data | |

Type of Statement

0-500M	500M-2MM	2-10MM	10-50MM	50-100MM	100-250MM	Type of Statement	4/1/02-3/31/03 ALL	4/1/03-3/31/04 ALL
	1	9	13	6	3	Unqualified	33	44
	1	18	6			Reviewed	22	25
1	4	6	1			Compiled	19	36
2	9	3				Tax Returns	12	10
	3	9	15	4	1	Other	19	21
	50 (4/1-9/30/06)		65 (10/1/06-3/31/07)					
3	18	45	35	10	4	**NUMBER OF STATEMENTS**	105	136

0-500M	500M-2MM	2-10MM	10-50MM	50-100MM	100-250MM		4/1/02-3/31/03 ALL	4/1/03-3/31/04 ALL
%	%	%	%	%	%	**ASSETS**	%	%
	10.5	7.4	6.2	6.6		Cash & Equivalents	9.0	9.9
	36.7	35.8	34.7	22.4		Trade Receivables (net)	29.9	28.5
	22.5	30.9	32.7	37.3		Inventory	32.3	30.8
	4.1	8.7	4.5	6.4		All Other Current	4.5	6.5
	73.8	82.7	78.1	72.9		Total Current	75.7	75.7
	15.0	12.9	16.6	18.6		Fixed Assets (net)	15.5	16.7
	2.5	.8	.6	3.5		Intangibles (net)	1.5	.9
	8.7	3.5	4.7	5.0		All Other Non-Current	7.4	6.7
	100.0	100.0	100.0	100.0		Total	100.0	100.0
						LIABILITIES		
	17.9	20.0	22.6	29.8		Notes Payable-Short Term	19.1	19.5
	2.6	1.2	1.2	.6		Cur. Mat.-L.T.D.	1.9	2.2
	26.9	22.1	20.4	12.6		Trade Payables	21.3	20.7
	.5	.0	.1	.1		Income Taxes Payable	.3	.3
	16.8	12.2	9.0	9.1		All Other Current	10.4	10.7
	64.7	55.5	53.4	52.2		Total Current	53.0	53.4
	11.4	7.5	8.4	6.6		Long-Term Debt	8.3	10.0
	.0	.4	.3	.0		Deferred Taxes	.1	.2
	3.6	2.4	3.9	4.2		All Other Non-Current	3.4	2.5
	20.4	34.2	34.0	36.9		Net Worth	35.2	33.9
	100.0	100.0	100.0	100.0		Total Liabilities & Net Worth	100.0	100.0
						INCOME DATA		
	100.0	100.0	100.0	100.0		Net Sales	100.0	100.0
	22.8	18.9	13.8	13.5		Gross Profit	17.5	18.4
	21.5	16.0	12.6	7.6		Operating Expenses	14.6	16.1
	1.3	3.0	1.3	5.9		Operating Profit	2.9	2.4
	-.7	1.4	.7	1.2		All Other Expenses (net)	.2	.1
	2.0	1.6	.6	4.7		Profit Before Taxes	2.7	2.2
						RATIOS		
	2.4	2.3	2.2	2.0			2.0	2.0
	1.2	1.4	1.3	1.3		Current	1.4	1.4
	.9	1.1	1.2	1.2			1.1	1.2
	1.5	1.3	1.0	.9			1.3	1.2
	.7	.6	.7	.6		Quick	.7	.7
	.4	.4	.5	.3			.3	.3
	13 28.3	19 19.1	27 13.5	16 22.4			19 19.5	19 18.9
	24 15.0	34 10.8	32 11.5	25 14.4		Sales/Receivables	32 11.2	30 12.0
	42 8.7	52 7.0	57 6.5	31 11.7			47 7.7	46 7.9
	1 254.1	5 71.7	17 21.7	15 23.6			15 23.8	11 31.9
	16 23.3	48 7.6	48 7.6	35 10.3		Cost of Sales/Inventory	43 8.5	36 10.0
	57 6.4	89 4.1	82 4.4	58 6.2			87 4.2	85 4.3
	1 280.5	10 35.3	10 37.4	4 101.9			8 47.5	9 40.3
	15 24.6	23 16.1	24 15.1	16 23.2		Cost of Sales/Payables	21 17.2	23 15.8
	38 9.7	53 6.9	38 9.6	23 16.2			45 8.1	52 7.0
	19.6	7.9	6.9	6.7			8.3	7.7
	67.6	16.7	17.1	16.7		Sales/Working Capital	15.7	16.3
	-755.6	47.5	31.9	33.1			42.5	34.1
	9.8	5.4	3.7	12.3			9.5	9.7
	(16) 4.5	(44) 2.1	(33) 2.2	4.2		EBIT/Interest	(92) 3.9	(125) 4.2
	1.2	1.2	1.1	1.9			1.5	1.4
							6.1	4.5
						Net Profit + Depr., Dep., Amort./Cur. Mat. L/T/D	(20) 2.6	(26) 2.6
							1.0	1.2
	.0	.0	.1	.2			.1	.1
	.4	.2	.2	.3		Fixed/Worth	.3	.3
	NM	.9	.9	.6			.9	.8
	1.0	.8	1.1	1.2			.9	.9
	4.6	2.4	2.5	2.3		Debt/Worth	2.3	2.3
	NM	6.4	5.1	4.4			5.8	4.3
	129.7	51.2	24.6	63.3			37.7	39.1
	(14) 29.4	(44) 12.9	(34) 12.3	33.2		% Profit Before Taxes/Tangible Net Worth	(99) 18.5	(130) 15.9
	1.9	2.1	3.1	8.8			7.4	2.9
	16.6	8.1	6.5	25.2			10.9	10.9
	4.1	3.1	4.0	9.0		% Profit Before Taxes/Total Assets	6.0	4.8
	-.4	.7	.3	2.5			1.1	.5
	470.7	849.1	253.0	79.4			230.9	153.6
	121.9	73.9	25.2	35.0		Sales/Net Fixed Assets	35.7	28.3
	19.1	9.4	12.3	10.2			12.2	8.8
	12.5	4.7	4.6	4.8			5.2	4.4
	4.8	3.4	3.2	3.5		Sales/Total Assets	3.0	2.9
	2.8	2.1	2.1	2.2			1.8	1.8
	.2	.1	.1				.1	.2
	(14) .4	(32) 1.0	(30) .6			% Depr., Dep., Amort./Sales	(92) .6	(114) .7
	2.2	2.5	1.3				1.4	2.1
		.7						.8	.8
	(11) 1.9					% Officers', Directors' Owners' Comp/Sales	(35) 1.0	(40) 1.7
	4.2							4.4
45348M	164996M	981257M	2876274M	3405410M	1628144M	Net Sales ($)	4717060M	7992666M
1121M	23100M	221996M	792730M	705462M	684843M	Total Assets ($)	1918402M	2352861M

M = $ thousand   MM = $ million
See Pages 11 through 21 for Explanation of Ratios and Data

Comparative Historical Data   Current Data Sorted by Sales

			Type of Statement						
30	28	32	Unqualified			1	5	4	22
22	23	25	Reviewed			3	3	8	11
17	10	11	Compiled	1		1	1	6	2
16	13	15	Tax Returns		4	1	4	2	4
25	31	32	Other		1	4	4	5	21
4/1/04-3/31/05 ALL	4/1/05-3/31/06 ALL	4/1/06-3/31/07 ALL		50 (4/1-9/30/06)			65 (10/1/06-3/31/07)		
				0-1MM	1-3MM	3-5MM	5-10MM	10-25MM	25MM & OVER
110	105	115	NUMBER OF STATEMENTS	1	5	10	14	25	60
%	%	%	ASSETS	%	%	%	%	%	%
8.9	8.8	7.3	Cash & Equivalents			7.0	8.2	9.5	7.8
29.6	33.1	33.7	Trade Receivables (net)			30.6	25.5	37.4	34.2
31.5	28.3	31.7	Inventory			27.2	32.8	25.5	34.9
4.0	4.2	6.1	All Other Current			5.2	5.6	8.0	6.0
74.0	74.4	78.8	Total Current			69.9	72.1	80.4	83.0
16.6	17.8	14.5	Fixed Assets (net)			25.5	19.3	11.9	11.8
.8	1.4	1.2	Intangibles (net)			.2	1.8	2.1	.9
8.6	6.5	5.6	All Other Non-Current			4.4	6.8	5.6	4.3
100.0	100.0	100.0	Total			100.0	100.0	100.0	100.0
			LIABILITIES						
19.5	17.9	21.5	Notes Payable-Short Term			17.4	21.1	18.7	24.6
2.9	1.4	1.3	Cur. Mat.-L.T.D.			5.6	.5	1.1	1.0
21.4	19.4	21.3	Trade Payables			27.9	16.5	21.6	22.0
.5	.3	.2	Income Taxes Payable			.0	.1	.4	.1
10.6	10.7	11.4	All Other Current			2.3	15.1	13.0	10.7
54.9	49.5	55.6	Total Current			53.2	53.3	54.8	58.3
8.5	10.1	7.9	Long-Term Debt			33.4	3.1	5.4	5.8
.3	.2	.2	Deferred Taxes			.0	.3	.3	.2
5.0	3.8	3.1	All Other Non-Current			2.1	1.2	3.6	3.1
31.3	36.3	33.1	Net Worth			11.4	42.2	35.9	32.5
100.0	100.0	100.0	Total Liabilties & Net Worth			100.0	100.0	100.0	100.0
			INCOME DATA						
100.0	100.0	100.0	Net Sales			100.0	100.0	100.0	100.0
19.7	18.4	17.3	Gross Profit			38.9	17.9	20.4	10.1
16.4	15.4	14.9	Operating Expenses			40.8	15.3	18.1	7.0
3.3	3.1	2.4	Operating Profit			-1.8	2.6	2.3	3.1
.1	.4	.8	All Other Expenses (net)			.8	.1	.9	1.2
3.2	2.6	1.7	Profit Before Taxes			-2.6	2.5	1.4	1.9
			RATIOS						
1.7	2.2	2.3	Current			2.8	1.9	2.5	1.9
1.3	1.4	1.3				2.3	1.3	1.4	1.3
1.1	1.1	1.1				.9	1.1	1.1	1.1
1.0	1.3	1.1	Quick			1.5	1.2	1.6	1.0
.7	.8 (114)	.6				.7	.5	1.0	.6
.4	.5	.4				.3	.4	.4	.5
22 16.5	19 19.5	19 19.3	Sales/Receivables			4 91.3	19 18.9	16 22.3	18 20.0
31 11.8	30 12.1	30 12.0				44 8.3	31 12.0	34 10.8	28 12.9
48 7.6	48 7.6	48 7.6				63 5.8	49 7.5	54 6.7	40 9.2
20 17.9	10 37.0	10 36.8	Cost of Sales/Inventory			9 42.7	0 UND	2 168.0	12 31.3
45 8.2	35 10.4	45 8.2				78 4.7	70 5.2	25 14.4	37 10.0
88 4.2	69 5.3	85 4.3				237 1.5	96 3.8	89 4.1	63 5.8
12 30.1	8 47.0	9 40.6	Cost of Sales/Payables			10 35.9	0 UND	6 64.5	8 44.8
22 16.2	19 19.0	20 18.0				36 10.1	27 13.6	23 16.1	16 22.3
47 7.7	39 9.4	38 9.6				131 2.8	38 9.6	53 6.9	32 11.5
7.6	7.6	8.1	Sales/Working Capital			3.1	7.3	7.9	12.0
19.0	17.1	20.0				5.0	17.4	20.9	21.1
47.9	37.5	54.5				-80.3	52.4	54.6	53.2
10.4	8.0	5.4	EBIT/Interest				5.8	7.9	4.9
(105) 3.9	(97) 4.1	(109) 2.4					2.3	(23) 1.8	(58) 2.5
1.5	1.6	1.2					1.5	1.0	1.4
8.2	15.3	8.5	Net Profit + Depr., Dep., Amort./Cur. Mat. L/T/D						20.0
(29) 3.9	(24) 5.5	(18) 4.7						(11)	4.8
2.1	3.0	2.8							3.4
.1	.1	.0	Fixed/Worth			.2	.1	.0	.0
.5	.3	.2				2.3	.4	.2	.2
.9	.9	.9				-1.4	1.1	.7	.7
1.3	1.3	1.1	Debt/Worth			1.0	.6	.8	1.1
2.3	2.2	2.5				5.5	1.8	2.3	2.5
5.3	4.0	5.2				-6.7	3.5	7.5	5.0
38.7	44.0	39.8	% Profit Before Taxes/Tangible Net Worth				55.9	56.2	33.0
(105) 20.5	(101) 21.7	(109) 14.4					7.9	(24) 16.9	(58) 16.1
5.9	5.5	2.9					2.4	.3	7.4
13.4	11.0	10.1	% Profit Before Taxes/Total Assets			7.2	4.9	12.8	10.1
5.1	5.8	4.0				-1.2	2.9	3.2	4.4
1.3	1.5	.8				-12.4	1.5	.1	2.0
81.7	129.1	379.7	Sales/Net Fixed Assets			56.0	140.2	537.7	999.8
25.9	29.1	46.0				12.1	13.0	110.4	81.4
9.7	10.1	11.1				2.7	5.8	15.2	16.6
4.5	4.6	5.0	Sales/Total Assets			3.5	4.0	4.7	5.7
3.1	3.1	3.4				1.8	2.5	3.8	3.5
2.0	2.0	2.3				.8	1.7	2.6	2.5
.4	.3	.1	% Depr., Dep., Amort./Sales				.2	.2	.1
(95) 1.1	(93) .7	(90) .5					(11) 1.9	(17) .6	(48) .3
2.1	1.8	1.0					3.0	1.9	1.0
.7	.5	.6	% Officers', Directors' Owners' Comp/Sales						.5
(35) 1.5	(32) 1.3	(29) 1.4						(13)	.7
3.3	2.7	3.5							1.9
6619137M	7943389M	9101429M	Net Sales ($)	934M	9357M	42612M	99365M	402346M	8546815M
2307967M	2371832M	2429252M	Total Assets ($)	143M	5294M	34762M	43515M	130328M	2215210M

© RMA 2007

M = $ thousand   MM = $ million
See Pages 11 through 21 for Explanation of Ratios and Data

Current Data Sorted by Assets / Comparative Historical Data

Type of Statement	0-500M	500M-2MM	2-10MM	10-50MM	50-100MM	100-250MM		4/1/02-3/31/03 ALL	4/1/03-3/31/04 ALL
Unqualified	1		5	7	3			18	16
Reviewed		3	33	10				30	28
Compiled	4	8	15	1				24	39
Tax Returns	1	11	4					6	11
Other	4	8	27	20		3		42	40
		28 (4/1-9/30/06)		140 (10/1/06-3/31/07)					
NUMBER OF STATEMENTS	10	30	84	38	3	3		120	134
	%	%	%	%	%	%		%	%
ASSETS									
Cash & Equivalents	19.9	9.4	5.9	4.9				5.4	6.2
Trade Receivables (net)	34.3	40.1	38.2	40.8				40.1	38.6
Inventory	21.9	26.4	31.0	34.9				29.9	28.2
All Other Current	1.9	.5	2.1	2.3				1.9	3.2
Total Current	78.1	76.4	77.2	82.9				77.4	76.1
Fixed Assets (net)	13.9	13.0	13.6	10.8				17.2	16.1
Intangibles (net)	5.8	1.3	2.6	1.9				1.7	2.5
All Other Non-Current	2.2	9.3	6.7	4.4				3.8	5.3
Total	100.0	100.0	100.0	100.0				100.0	100.0
LIABILITIES									
Notes Payable-Short Term	10.8	14.5	16.8	23.9				14.5	17.0
Cur. Mat.-L.T.D.	4.4	1.5	2.4	1.2				2.6	2.5
Trade Payables	24.5	26.0	24.8	22.3				27.5	26.5
Income Taxes Payable	.0	.2	.4	.2				.4	.1
All Other Current	13.6	11.9	6.5	8.3				10.9	7.8
Total Current	53.4	54.1	50.9	55.9				55.9	54.0
Long-Term Debt	18.8	7.2	6.1	6.6				9.8	7.9
Deferred Taxes	.0	.1	.2	.0				.2	.1
All Other Non-Current	.7	6.7	4.5	5.1				3.7	6.7
Net Worth	27.0	32.0	38.3	32.4				30.4	31.3
Total Liabilities & Net Worth	100.0	100.0	100.0	100.0				100.0	100.0
INCOME DATA									
Net Sales	100.0	100.0	100.0	100.0				100.0	100.0
Gross Profit	41.6	26.1	25.6	19.0				25.5	23.7
Operating Expenses	35.4	22.0	20.5	14.8				22.4	21.4
Operating Profit	6.2	4.1	5.1	4.2				3.0	2.2
All Other Expenses (net)	1.1	.5	.9	.6				.6	.7
Profit Before Taxes	5.1	3.6	4.2	3.7				2.5	1.6
RATIOS									
Current	2.4	2.4	2.2	1.9				2.0	2.0
	1.5	1.6	1.4	1.4				1.4	1.4
	1.1	1.0	1.2	1.2				1.1	1.1
Quick	2.1	1.5	1.1	1.0				1.1	1.3
	1.0	1.0	.8	.7				.8	.9
	.4	.5	.6	.6				.6	.6
Sales/Receivables	7 49.9	27 13.3	36 10.0	41 9.0				34 10.8	36 10.1
	23 15.7	36 10.1	44 8.3	50 7.4				43 8.5	46 8.0
	56 6.5	48 7.6	56 6.5	61 6.0				59 6.2	60 6.1
Cost of Sales/Inventory	0 UND	7 52.9	26 14.0	30 12.2				28 13.1	22 16.4
	2 217.7	31 11.8	50 7.3	55 6.6				46 7.9	50 7.3
	110 3.3	89 4.1	75 4.8	71 5.1				75 4.8	73 5.0
Cost of Sales/Payables	0 UND	12 30.3	24 15.5	18 20.7				25 14.5	23 15.9
	29 12.6	36 10.3	35 10.3	35 10.3				39 9.4	38 9.7
	64 5.7	49 7.4	47 7.7	47 7.8				58 6.3	56 6.5
Sales/Working Capital	7.8	7.4	7.0	6.3				7.4	7.7
	20.9	14.6	12.1	12.1				15.3	13.3
	99.9	NM	24.9	23.9				47.2	39.9
EBIT/Interest	35.7	21.6	17.8	8.6				9.0	11.5
	7.2	(26) 4.4	(77) 4.7	(36) 3.4				(105) 4.2	(122) 2.3
	-.4	1.8	2.5	1.5				1.2	.3
Net Profit + Depr., Dep., Amort./Cur. Mat. L/T/D			11.7					7.1	7.1
			(22) 6.1					(27) 3.2	(23) 1.8
			2.2					1.4	.0
Fixed/Worth	.0	.0	.1	.0				.1	.1
	.4	.2	.2	.2				.4	.4
	NM	.8	.7	.7				1.1	1.4
Debt/Worth	.9	.6	.9	1.3				1.2	1.0
	3.0	2.5	1.9	2.4				2.3	2.4
	NM	9.1	3.7	6.8				5.0	7.4
% Profit Before Taxes/Tangible Net Worth		63.3	48.2	42.5				46.9	40.1
		(25) 23.3	(79) 28.5	(35) 23.3				(108) 19.5	(116) 17.0
		16.7	9.1	14.8				3.6	-1.2
% Profit Before Taxes/Total Assets	52.7	21.4	19.8	12.4				12.7	13.1
	18.4	11.3	7.4	6.0				5.0	3.4
	-5.0	2.9	3.5	2.1				.4	-.9
Sales/Net Fixed Assets	323.3	493.8	157.1	415.2				130.4	160.3
	65.1	99.1	52.3	72.7				32.4	34.9
	30.8	15.8	11.6	17.3				9.7	9.4
Sales/Total Assets	5.1	5.1	3.7	3.5				3.9	3.6
	4.2	3.5	2.9	2.8				3.0	2.8
	2.7	3.2	2.3	2.3				2.3	2.2
% Depr., Dep., Amort./Sales		.2	.3	.2				.3	.2
		(23) .7	(74) .7	(32) .5				(101) 1.0	(117) .9
		1.3	1.3	1.0				2.2	2.6
% Officers', Directors' Owners' Comp/Sales		1.3	1.3	.5				1.6	1.4
		(19) 4.4	(40) 2.6	(13) 1.7				(59) 3.7	(59) 3.4
		7.2						5.7	5.5
Net Sales ($)	11507M	150101M	1327560M	2086637M	734467M	1617145M		4533156M	4946476M
Total Assets ($)	2934M	37329M	433838M	715066M	177124M	426484M		1499030M	1567468M

M = $ thousand   MM = $ million
See Pages 11 through 21 for Explanation of Ratios and Data

Comparative Historical Data | Current Data Sorted by Sales

4/1/04-3/31/05 ALL	4/1/05-3/31/06 ALL	4/1/06-3/31/07 ALL	Type of Statement	0-1MM	1-3MM	3-5MM	5-10MM	10-25MM	25MM & OVER
19	17	16	Unqualified	1			1	3	11
32	34	46	Reviewed			2	11	20	13
21	19	28	Compiled	1	5	2	10	7	3
13	14	16	Tax Returns		4	3	5	2	2
38	49	62	Other	3	5	4	5	17	28
					28 (4/1-9/30/06)		140 (10/1/06-3/31/07)		
123	133	168	NUMBER OF STATEMENTS	5	14	11	32	49	57
%	%	%	ASSETS	%	%	%	%	%	%
6.7	7.1	7.0	Cash & Equivalents		19.9	4.6	7.6	6.0	5.4
40.5	42.6	39.5	Trade Receivables (net)		35.9	34.4	37.8	41.4	42.8
28.2	28.1	30.5	Inventory		24.7	35.5	26.8	31.7	32.9
1.6	1.8	1.8	All Other Current		.5	.6	2.6	1.1	2.4
77.0	79.6	78.8	Total Current		81.0	74.9	74.8	80.3	83.5
16.3	12.6	12.5	Fixed Assets (net)		6.8	21.3	14.7	12.8	9.0
2.5	2.6	2.4	Intangibles (net)		3.5	.3	2.8	2.3	2.1
4.1	5.2	6.3	All Other Non-Current		8.7	3.5	7.8	4.7	5.5
100.0	100.0	100.0	Total		100.0	100.0	100.0	100.0	100.0
			LIABILITIES						
16.1	18.1	17.7	Notes Payable-Short Term		11.2	16.8	19.1	16.8	20.7
1.5	2.3	2.0	Cur. Mat.-L.T.D.		1.6	2.2	2.0	2.6	1.1
29.1	27.1	24.7	Trade Payables		25.0	18.6	25.2	23.9	26.7
.2	.4	.3	Income Taxes Payable		.2	.0	.2	.6	.1
7.6	10.0	8.2	All Other Current		18.9	4.4	7.4	7.8	7.3
54.4	58.0	52.9	Total Current		56.9	42.0	53.9	51.7	55.9
9.4	8.6	7.4	Long-Term Debt		8.8	5.3	7.2	5.5	6.4
.1	.3	.1	Deferred Taxes		.0	.1	.1	.2	.0
4.4	3.6	4.7	All Other Non-Current		.5	10.4	6.2	2.9	4.6
31.6	29.5	34.9	Net Worth		33.8	42.1	32.6	39.7	33.1
100.0	100.0	100.0	Total Liabilities & Net Worth		100.0	100.0	100.0	100.0	100.0
			INCOME DATA						
100.0	100.0	100.0	Net Sales		100.0	100.0	100.0	100.0	100.0
23.7	23.2	24.6	Gross Profit		31.6	30.4	27.2	24.1	17.9
20.1	19.4	19.9	Operating Expenses		26.4	25.4	22.7	19.1	13.9
3.6	3.8	4.7	Operating Profit		5.3	4.9	4.5	5.1	4.0
.6	.6	.7	All Other Expenses (net)		.5	.7	.8	1.1	.3
3.1	3.3	3.9	Profit Before Taxes		4.8	4.2	3.7	3.9	3.7
			RATIOS						
2.1	1.9	2.2	Current		2.6	2.6	2.2	2.2	2.0
1.4	1.3	1.4			1.5	2.2	1.3	1.5	1.5
1.1	1.1	1.2			1.1	1.2	1.2	1.2	1.2
1.3	1.2	1.2	Quick		1.8	1.5	1.2	1.3	1.1
.9	.8	.8			1.1	.8	.9	.8	.8
.6	.6	.6			.4	.6	.6	.6	.6
35 10.3	36 10.1	35 10.5	Sales/Receivables		20 17.9	35 10.5	34 10.8	39 9.4	40 9.1
44 8.3	48 7.6	45 8.2			27 13.4	41 8.9	45 8.1	45 8.2	46 7.9
59 6.2	61 6.0	55 6.6			39 9.4	53 6.9	57 6.4	56 6.5	53 6.8
25 14.9	18 20.3	22 16.7	Cost of Sales/Inventory		0 UND	22 16.4	18 19.8	26 13.8	24 15.4
44 8.2	45 8.2	48 7.5			13 29.0	114 3.2	45 8.2	51 7.2	43 8.6
67 5.4	71 5.1	74 4.9			77 4.7	124 2.9	71 5.1	87 4.2	67 5.4
26 14.2	23 15.7	22 16.9	Cost of Sales/Payables		17 21.5	12 29.3	19 19.3	23 16.0	24 15.2
39 9.3	42 8.7	35 10.4			35 10.5	23 15.9	37 9.9	35 10.5	34 10.7
57 6.3	55 6.6	48 7.6			51 7.1	47 7.8	47 7.8	52 7.1	47 7.8
7.8	7.9	7.4	Sales/Working Capital		7.8	6.4	7.5	6.8	8.0
14.2	15.8	12.2			21.0	8.1	14.1	11.8	12.2
41.7	53.5	27.6			99.9	15.2	43.6	23.5	29.4
14.2	16.0	17.2	EBIT/Interest		36.2	12.2	10.4	21.8	14.6
(115) 5.3	(119) 5.6	(155) 4.5			(12) 7.2	(10) 4.4	(30) 4.7	(45) 4.1	(53) 4.9
2.0	2.3	2.1			1.8	3.0	2.5	2.0	2.0
19.3	19.7	13.0	Net Profit + Depr., Dep., Amort./Cur. Mat. L/T/D					14.7	21.1
(23) 9.7	(21) 8.3	(36) 6.5						(15) 6.8	(11) 9.1
3.2	1.6	3.0						2.6	3.8
.1	.1	.1	Fixed/Worth		.0	.1	.1	.1	.0
.4	.2	.2			.2	.3	.3	.2	.1
1.0	1.0	.7			.6	1.2	.7	.7	.4
1.1	1.2	.9	Debt/Worth		.8	.6	.8	.9	1.0
2.9	2.7	2.0			2.3	1.9	2.4	1.7	2.4
7.7	7.1	5.6			8.7	5.7	6.4	3.8	6.6
63.7	67.6	47.0	% Profit Before Taxes/Tangible Net Worth		298.2	36.2	54.0	44.6	44.5
(115) 24.9	(120) 35.5	(153) 25.2			(13) 44.8	22.0	(27) 29.2	(46) 16.4	(53) 25.0
12.4	12.0	11.6			17.9	19.5	9.1	8.6	17.2
14.9	19.0	19.6	% Profit Before Taxes/Total Assets		26.5	15.0	17.3	22.0	20.7
6.2	7.5	8.4			16.5	12.3	9.0	7.3	8.1
2.1	3.5	3.1			5.3	4.2	3.7	2.4	3.2
140.5	256.1	296.2	Sales/Net Fixed Assets		475.7	226.9	182.2	155.3	418.9
33.8	71.9	64.9			99.1	14.6	33.2	63.3	124.5
10.6	15.7	15.2			30.8	12.1	11.8	10.8	26.2
3.9	4.0	3.9	Sales/Total Assets		4.8	3.3	3.7	3.7	3.9
3.0	3.0	3.1			3.9	2.7	3.2	2.9	3.2
2.3	2.4	2.4			3.1	2.0	2.3	2.4	2.6
.4	.2	.2	% Depr., Dep., Amort./Sales			.2	.4	.3	.1
(102) .8	(108) .6	(138) .6				(10) 1.0	(25) 1.0	(44) .6	(47) .4
1.6	1.1	1.1				2.5	1.9	1.2	.8
1.3	1.3	.9	% Officers', Directors', Owners' Comp/Sales				1.1	1.5	.5
(46) 2.3	(54) 2.4	(77) 2.7					(17) 2.7	(24) 2.8	(19) 1.7
5.2	4.8	6.2					6.3	4.1	2.1
5485608M	6449963M	5927417M	Net Sales ($)	3299M	26707M	45619M	231575M	758307M	4861910M
1955856M	2145217M	1792775M	Total Assets ($)	3893M	7237M	17982M	85821M	264959M	1412883M

© RMA 2007

M = $ thousand   MM = $ million
See Pages 11 through 21 for Explanation of Ratios and Data

Current Data Sorted by Assets | Comparative Historical Data

0-500M	500M-2MM	2-10MM	10-50MM	50-100MM	100-250MM	Type of Statement	4/1/02-3/31/03 ALL	4/1/03-3/31/04 ALL
1	2	13	33	11	8	Unqualified	59	65
	6	56	31			Reviewed	89	78
2	24	24	4			Compiled	43	67
12	9	9	1		2	Tax Returns	14	28
2	23	49	28	3	7	Other	87	88
	69 (4/1-9/30/06)		291 (10/1/06-3/31/07)					
17	64	151	97	14	17	NUMBER OF STATEMENTS	292	326
%	%	%	%	%	%	**ASSETS**	%	%
20.0	8.9	6.3	6.5	4.8	3.7	Cash & Equivalents	7.0	7.3
34.3	37.2	40.7	38.2	34.8	25.6	Trade Receivables (net)	37.3	37.7
24.1	22.3	31.1	29.5	18.4	15.1	Inventory	25.7	24.7
1.9	1.3	1.9	2.3	2.8	1.2	All Other Current	2.3	2.7
80.3	69.7	80.0	76.5	60.7	45.6	Total Current	72.4	72.4
11.9	16.8	12.9	17.7	22.4	30.3	Fixed Assets (net)	19.3	19.0
3.2	4.3	1.3	1.4	4.2	11.0	Intangibles (net)	2.6	2.5
4.6	9.2	5.8	4.4	12.7	13.0	All Other Non-Current	5.7	6.1
100.0	100.0	100.0	100.0	100.0	100.0	Total	100.0	100.0
						LIABILITIES		
14.3	12.4	18.3	18.1	9.7	9.1	Notes Payable-Short Term	14.2	15.3
.9	4.0	2.3	1.4	4.2	1.3	Cur. Mat.-L.T.D.	3.4	3.4
28.7	26.7	28.7	23.2	18.8	11.9	Trade Payables	26.7	25.8
.1	.3	.3	.3	.1	1.3	Income Taxes Payable	.3	.4
14.7	11.8	7.6	9.5	11.7	14.1	All Other Current	10.1	9.7
58.7	55.2	57.2	52.5	44.5	37.7	Total Current	54.6	54.6
2.8	12.1	8.4	8.4	17.4	21.6	Long-Term Debt	8.8	9.0
.0	.2	.2	.4	.9	2.4	Deferred Taxes	.2	.3
7.5	6.9	4.3	1.7	2.2	2.8	All Other Non-Current	3.7	5.4
31.0	25.6	29.9	37.0	35.1	35.5	Net Worth	32.8	30.7
100.0	100.0	100.0	100.0	100.0	100.0	Total Liabilities & Net Worth	100.0	100.0
						INCOME DATA		
100.0	100.0	100.0	100.0	100.0	100.0	Net Sales	100.0	100.0
36.2	32.7	23.6	19.8	23.0	28.5	Gross Profit	27.2	26.9
32.0	29.2	20.2	16.5	19.0	21.1	Operating Expenses	23.9	23.7
4.2	3.5	3.4	3.3	4.0	7.4	Operating Profit	3.4	3.2
.6	.8	.6	.0	.1	.9	All Other Expenses (net)	.6	.6
3.7	2.6	2.8	3.3	3.9	6.5	Profit Before Taxes	2.8	2.6
						RATIOS		
2.4	1.8	1.9	2.0	2.8	1.6	Current	1.9	1.9
1.5	1.2	1.4	1.4	1.2	1.4		1.3	1.3
1.2	1.0	1.1	1.1	1.1	.8		1.1	1.1
1.5	1.2	1.2	1.2	1.6	1.2	Quick	1.2	1.2
1.3	.8	.8	.8	.8	.8		.8	.8
.8	.6	.6	.6	.7	.4		.6	.6
10 37.3	32 11.4	35 10.6	37 9.9	39 9.4	27 13.3	Sales/Receivables	36 10.1	35 10.5
19 18.8	44 8.3	43 8.6	44 8.2	45 8.2	41 9.0		43 8.5	44 8.4
38 9.6	56 6.5	52 7.0	54 6.7	54 6.8	50 7.3		55 6.7	54 6.7
2 161.1	14 25.2	26 14.1	25 14.8	31 11.6	9 39.7	Cost of Sales/Inventory	23 15.7	22 16.8
19 19.4	41 8.9	45 8.1	44 8.3	47 7.8	24 15.4		42 8.8	42 8.7
47 7.8	60 6.1	69 5.3	58 6.2	53 6.8	55 6.6		71 5.2	66 5.5
15 24.7	22 16.5	24 15.2	24 15.0	11 32.9	11 32.6	Cost of Sales/Payables	26 13.9	24 15.1
25 14.4	45 8.1	38 9.6	32 11.4	32 11.3	34 10.8		43 8.5	40 9.0
39 9.3	68 5.4	56 6.5	46 7.9	45 8.0	44 8.3		57 6.4	60 6.1
10.2	8.5	8.2	7.0	5.5	11.5	Sales/Working Capital	8.4	8.8
20.2	23.1	14.9	13.8	28.6	17.6		16.5	18.1
89.8	-139.5	44.3	33.2	170.7	-61.1		70.5	68.1
27.2	7.4	8.8	9.8	18.5	9.9	EBIT/Interest	10.3	10.4
(12) 6.7	(57) 2.5	(138) 3.5	(91) 3.8	(13) 4.4	(16) 7.3		(252) 3.4	(293) 3.8
2.2	1.3	1.4	2.3	2.0	1.7		1.6	1.5
		8.4	8.4	3.5		Net Profit + Depr., Dep., Amort./Cur. Mat. L/T/D	6.9	6.3
	(37) 3.5	(34) 5.1	(10) 2.2				(74) 3.2	(90) 2.9
	1.2	2.1	1.4				1.4	1.3
.0	.1	.1	.1	.2	.3	Fixed/Worth	.1	.1
.2	.7	.2	.4	.5	.9		.4	.4
.9	2.7	1.3	.9	1.9	17.4		1.2	1.4
.7	1.3	1.1	1.0	1.0	1.3	Debt/Worth	1.0	1.1
1.7	3.9	2.4	2.2	2.7	2.9		2.3	2.7
6.5	21.2	7.4	4.4	6.5	21.4		5.5	7.0
85.9	83.2	59.8	40.6	57.2	66.5	% Profit Before Taxes/Tangible Net Worth	34.4	45.6
(15) 48.8	(54) 28.3	(135) 24.1	(96) 24.6	28.7	(14) 24.5		(267) 16.9	(288) 17.8
10.8	3.3	7.7	11.9	13.8	6.7		5.3	5.5
31.7	14.4	15.9	14.4	10.7	12.9	% Profit Before Taxes/Total Assets	11.0	12.3
17.3	5.4	7.0	6.4	6.9	8.4		4.7	5.0
.1	.4	1.8	3.6	4.4	1.6		1.0	1.2
UND	117.6	147.4	185.2	66.6	514.8	Sales/Net Fixed Assets	121.5	150.3
92.0	39.5	51.2	22.2	9.5	7.4		22.8	28.4
40.3	9.1	15.5	10.3	4.5	2.1		8.5	7.6
7.4	4.2	4.4	3.8	2.9	3.5	Sales/Total Assets	3.8	4.0
5.8	3.0	3.5	2.9	1.9	1.8		3.0	2.9
3.9	1.9	2.4	2.2	1.5	1.0		2.1	2.0
	.4	.2	.2	1.6	.7	% Depr., Dep., Amort./Sales	.4	.3
(51) .7	(131) .6	(86) .7	(12) 2.0	(13) 1.7			(254) 1.1	(277) 1.0
2.4	1.2	1.5	2.5	4.0			2.4	2.3
4.0	1.1	1.6	.6			% Officers', Directors' Owners' Comp/Sales	1.6	1.6
(15) 10.8	(28) 4.7	(59) 2.8	(21) 1.0				(108) 3.0	(120) 3.2
19.3	7.6	4.5	4.2				5.8	6.4
27617M	260982M	2528005M	6223696M	2507235M	6117659M	Net Sales ($)	9030310M	10899313M
4777M	80607M	734435M	2018163M	962651M	2797070M	Total Assets ($)	3629266M	3803343M

© RMA 2007

M = $ thousand   MM = $ million
See Pages 11 through 21 for Explanation of Ratios and Data

Comparative Historical Data / Current Data Sorted by Sales

			Type of Statement						
68	66	68	Unqualified	1	1		5	9	52
87	89	93	Reviewed		4	2	8	43	36
48	46	54	Compiled	2	8	12	8	18	6
30	21	33	Tax Returns	6	6	6	5	6	4
87	105	112	Other	1	12	7	16	29	47
4/1/04-3/31/05 ALL	4/1/05-3/31/06 ALL	4/1/06-3/31/07 ALL		69 (4/1-9/30/06)			291 (10/1/06-3/31/07)		
				0-1MM	1-3MM	3-5MM	5-10MM	10-25MM	25MM & OVER
320	327	360	NUMBER OF STATEMENTS	10	31	27	42	105	145
%	%	%	ASSETS	%	%	%	%	%	%
7.8	6.4	7.3	Cash & Equivalents	29.4	9.9	7.9	6.7	6.3	5.9
39.8	41.1	38.1	Trade Receivables (net)	22.2	31.0	39.5	37.5	39.5	39.8
25.3	27.1	27.5	Inventory	25.5	22.6	24.1	27.5	32.3	25.9
2.7	2.0	1.9	All Other Current	.1	1.6	1.6	2.7	1.7	2.1
75.5	76.5	74.9	Total Current	77.2	65.2	73.1	74.4	79.7	73.7
16.5	15.2	16.0	Fixed Assets (net)	12.9	19.8	17.3	16.7	12.9	17.3
2.5	3.0	2.5	Intangibles (net)	8.8	5.0	2.4	1.7	1.5	2.6
5.6	5.3	6.6	All Other Non-Current	1.1	10.0	7.2	7.1	5.9	6.5
100.0	100.0	100.0	Total	100.0	100.0	100.0	100.0	100.0	100.0
			LIABILITIES						
15.8	17.8	16.2	Notes Payable-Short Term	26.6	13.4	13.9	12.3	18.0	16.4
2.4	2.2	2.3	Cur. Mat.-L.T.D.	.2	3.5	4.4	4.6	1.7	1.6
26.9	27.3	25.7	Trade Payables	27.3	18.0	32.3	27.5	27.3	24.3
.2	.4	.3	Income Taxes Payable	.1	.1	.1	.4	.1	.6
9.0	9.6	9.7	All Other Current	27.6	7.4	10.5	9.3	7.6	10.4
54.3	57.3	54.2	Total Current	81.8	42.3	61.2	54.0	54.7	53.3
8.7	8.3	9.8	Long-Term Debt	.0	14.9	9.9	12.2	7.8	10.1
.3	.3	.4	Deferred Taxes	.0	.5	.0	.2	.1	.6
4.1	4.0	4.0	All Other Non-Current	.7	11.2	5.7	7.1	3.9	1.7
32.6	30.1	31.6	Net Worth	17.5	31.2	23.1	26.4	33.5	34.3
100.0	100.0	100.0	Total Liabilties & Net Worth	100.0	100.0	100.0	100.0	100.0	100.0
			INCOME DATA						
100.0	100.0	100.0	Net Sales	100.0	100.0	100.0	100.0	100.0	100.0
26.4	26.0	25.0	Gross Profit	39.8	37.0	32.8	27.7	23.6	20.1
22.9	22.2	21.4	Operating Expenses	36.9	32.9	29.9	24.7	19.7	16.5
3.5	3.7	3.6	Operating Profit	3.0	4.1	2.9	3.0	3.9	3.7
.5	.7	.5	All Other Expenses (net)	1.3	1.5	.8	.0	.6	.2
3.1	3.0	3.2	Profit Before Taxes	1.6	2.6	2.1	3.0	3.4	3.5
			RATIOS						
2.0	1.8	1.9		1.6	2.5	1.9	1.8	2.0	1.9
1.4	1.3	1.4	Current	1.2	1.5	1.2	1.4	1.5	1.4
1.1	1.1	1.1		.9	1.2	1.0	1.1	1.1	1.1
1.3	1.1	1.2		1.4	1.4	1.2	1.2	1.2	1.2
.8	.8	.8	Quick	1.1	1.1	.8	.8	.8	.8
.6	.6	.6		.1	.6	.6	.5	.6	.6
37 9.9	38 9.7	34 10.9		0 UND	30 12.3	28 13.0	32 11.3	34 10.7	37 10.0
47 7.8	47 7.8	43 8.6	Sales/Receivables	18 20.3	43 8.5	45 8.1	45 8.2	42 8.8	43 8.4
57 6.5	58 6.3	53 6.9		55 6.7	63 5.8	56 6.5	57 6.4	47 7.7	53 6.9
21 17.2	21 17.3	22 16.3		0 UND	3 142.0	18 20.3	23 15.9	28 13.2	20 17.9
43 8.6	42 8.8	43 8.4	Cost of Sales/Inventory	51 7.1	47 7.8	45 8.1	42 8.6	45 8.1	41 9.0
66 5.6	72 5.1	61 5.9		109 3.4	106 3.4	60 6.0	69 5.3	68 5.4	55 6.6
26 13.9	27 13.3	22 16.6		6 58.2	18 20.8	29 12.7	23 15.6	23 15.7	22 16.8
42 8.6	42 8.8	36 10.2	Cost of Sales/Payables	22 16.5	35 10.4	55 6.6	42 8.6	34 10.6	33 11.2
61 6.0	60 6.1	53 6.9		130 2.8	78 4.7	69 5.3	59 6.2	52 7.0	44 8.2
7.7	8.7	8.2		5.8	5.4	8.6	7.6	8.3	8.5
15.9	17.2	15.7	Sales/Working Capital	34.6	14.6	24.6	15.2	14.1	16.7
51.4	53.7	54.2		NM	131.4	-440.4	36.4	46.8	51.5
13.4	9.6	9.5			6.5	4.3	8.6	9.0	10.3
(283) 5.8	(292) 4.2	(327) 3.7	EBIT/Interest	(26) 2.1	(24) 2.0	(41) 3.2	(94) 3.7	(136) 4.3
2.1	1.7	1.8			1.3	1.1	2.1	1.4	2.2
8.4	7.6	8.2					9.3	7.1	8.9
(80) 3.8	(82) 2.6	(96) 4.0	Net Profit + Depr., Dep., Amort./Cur. Mat. L/T/D		(15) 4.4	(23) 3.2	(53) 5.1
1.5	1.2	1.7					1.0	1.2	2.2
.1	.1	.1		.0	.1	.2	.1	.1	.1
.3	.3	.3	Fixed/Worth	.1	.4	.8	.5	.2	.3
1.1	1.1	1.3		NM	10.1	2.1	2.7	1.1	.9
1.0	1.2	1.0		1.5	1.0	1.5	1.3	1.0	1.0
2.4	2.7	2.4	Debt/Worth	4.1	3.0	3.3	3.3	2.1	2.4
5.7	6.0	6.7		NM	37.5	30.2	10.4	5.4	5.5
48.9	50.6	50.8			77.6	51.4	49.6	64.6	43.1
(292) 22.4	(297) 23.1	(328) 26.4	% Profit Before Taxes/Tangible Net Worth	(25) 29.8	(24) 21.9	(34) 26.6	(99) 22.8	(138) 26.7
8.0	8.0	10.4			.1	1.3	10.2	7.9	13.0
14.1	13.9	15.0		34.3	22.0	14.3	11.7	17.3	13.5
6.8	6.0	6.7	% Profit Before Taxes/Total Assets	2.5	5.5	5.0	6.4	8.1	7.0
2.0	1.9	2.4		-20.5	.1	.2	3.0	1.7	3.5
182.4	174.6	150.4		UND	165.8	92.0	80.3	138.1	211.3
36.3	36.7	38.1	Sales/Net Fixed Assets	499.3	22.3	39.5	34.5	51.3	30.5
10.6	13.4	11.7		41.4	5.7	8.6	12.4	16.9	9.6
4.0	3.9	4.2		6.3	3.4	4.4	4.0	4.4	4.1
3.0	3.0	3.2	Sales/Total Assets	2.6	2.3	3.2	2.9	3.6	3.1
2.1	2.2	2.2		1.1	1.2	2.4	2.1	2.6	2.2
.3	.3	.3			.3	.3	.3	.2	.2
(264) .9	(275) .7	(302) .7	% Depr., Dep., Amort./Sales	(21) .9	(25) .8	(38) .7	(90) .6	(125) .7
2.0	1.6	1.7			3.1	2.7	2.2	1.1	1.8
1.5	1.2	1.4			2.7	1.1	1.5	1.3	.6
(114) 3.1	(109) 2.7	(123) 3.0	% Officers', Directors' Owners' Comp/Sales	(13) 10.2	(12) 2.7	(24) 3.6	(42) 2.4	(24) 1.9
6.1	6.3	5.8			14.3	9.6	5.7	4.2	4.3
10422088M	14804128M	17665194M	Net Sales ($)	6930M	59655M	104363M	314989M	1680106M	15499151M
4105335M	5032572M	6597703M	Total Assets ($)	3616M	35293M	35427M	126520M	531234M	5865613M

M = $ thousand   MM = $ million
See Pages 11 through 21 for Explanation of Ratios and Data

Current Data Sorted by Assets

Comparative Historical Data

	0-500M	500M-2MM	2-10MM	10-50MM	50-100MM	100-250MM	Type of Statement	4/1/02-3/31/03 ALL	4/1/03-3/31/04 ALL
		1	7	17	8	3	Unqualified	41	53
		3	57	28		2	Reviewed	94	96
	1	23	48	9	2		Compiled	88	103
	5	12	13				Tax Returns	13	13
	1	3	26	19	3	8	Other	66	57
		100 (4/1-9/30/06)			197 (10/1/06-3/31/07)				
NUMBER OF STATEMENTS	7	42	151	73	13	11		302	322

	0-500M	500M-2MM	2-10MM	10-50MM	50-100MM	100-250MM		4/1/02-3/31/03 ALL	4/1/03-3/31/04 ALL
%	%	%	%	%	%	%	**ASSETS**	%	%
		11.4	9.8	8.1	8.5	4.8	Cash & Equivalents	8.4	8.8
		33.6	37.7	32.3	22.7	35.6	Trade Receivables (net)	27.2	26.6
		15.3	14.3	12.2	13.1	22.6	Inventory	12.7	13.6
		5.4	3.2	2.7	1.9	1.8	All Other Current	3.9	4.9
		65.6	65.0	55.2	46.2	64.9	Total Current	52.2	53.9
		23.7	26.6	33.6	41.8	24.9	Fixed Assets (net)	37.8	35.6
		3.9	2.4	3.6	4.1	8.8	Intangibles (net)	2.4	3.4
		6.7	6.0	7.6	7.8	1.4	All Other Non-Current	7.6	7.1
		100.0	100.0	100.0	100.0	100.0	Total	100.0	100.0
							LIABILITIES		
		13.9	10.3	12.4	12.6	21.6	Notes Payable-Short Term	9.0	7.7
		3.8	3.3	3.7	3.4	1.7	Cur. Mat.-L.T.D.	4.5	4.0
		30.3	29.9	26.9	18.3	24.7	Trade Payables	22.6	21.9
		.2	.2	.1	.3	.2	Income Taxes Payable	.2	.2
		12.0	6.5	7.4	11.1	5.4	All Other Current	7.3	9.2
		60.2	50.2	50.6	45.6	53.6	Total Current	43.5	43.1
		17.9	15.0	16.7	21.9	21.9	Long-Term Debt	21.2	20.0
		.5	.9	1.1	.4	.9	Deferred Taxes	.6	.8
		3.5	3.3	3.2	1.4	3.3	All Other Non-Current	2.5	4.4
		17.9	30.6	28.4	30.7	20.3	Net Worth	32.2	31.6
		100.0	100.0	100.0	100.0	100.0	Total Liabilities & Net Worth	100.0	100.0
							INCOME DATA		
		100.0	100.0	100.0	100.0	100.0	Net Sales	100.0	100.0
		13.4	9.9	10.3	6.4	5.7	Gross Profit	13.1	13.4
		13.1	8.8	8.4	5.7	4.6	Operating Expenses	12.9	12.7
		.4	1.1	1.9	.7	1.1	Operating Profit	.2	.6
		.1	-.1	.0	-.1	.5	All Other Expenses (net)	-.2	-.3
		.3	1.1	1.9	.8	.6	Profit Before Taxes	.5	.9
							RATIOS		
		1.8	1.6	1.3	1.3	1.4		1.6	1.7
		1.2	1.3	1.1	1.0	1.3	Current	1.2	1.2
		1.0	1.1	.9	.7	1.1		1.0	1.0
		1.2	1.1	.9	.9	1.1		1.1	1.1
		.8	1.0	.8	.5	.9	Quick	.8	.8
		.5	.7	.6	.4	.5		.6	.6
		8 47.7	11 34.4	9 40.7	6 58.9	9 41.5		12 31.5	10 36.7
		15 24.1	17 21.7	15 24.5	9 42.5	16 22.9	Sales/Receivables	18 20.0	17 21.9
		24 15.1	28 13.2	23 15.6	15 23.6	22 16.6		27 13.4	28 13.0
		2 173.0	3 118.5	2 149.7	3 145.2	5 73.2		6 65.7	5 69.5
		6 63.9	7 52.5	6 60.3	7 52.6	10 38.4	Cost of Sales/Inventory	9 38.8	9 40.0
		11 34.4	12 30.3	10 36.6	9 38.5	16 23.2		16 23.1	16 22.7
		10 37.3	10 37.9	10 36.6	7 56.1	6 57.7		13 28.0	11 31.8
		14 26.6	14 26.2	13 27.3	12 31.4	8 43.1	Cost of Sales/Payables	18 20.7	16 22.7
		19 19.1	20 18.7	16 22.3	12 30.3	16 23.1		24 15.3	22 16.5
		24.7	29.6	42.4	92.2	33.8		22.5	22.0
		128.9	48.7	176.5	-424.3	68.3	Sales/Working Capital	73.3	59.4
		-232.2	227.4	-144.6	-56.7	141.5		-251.1	-296.9
		7.7	6.6	5.8	5.6	7.2		4.2	6.0
		(38) 2.8	(145) 2.7	(71) 2.9	2.2	5.0	EBIT/Interest	(285) 1.9	(308) 2.8
		.6	1.4	1.6	1.2	.8		.5	1.4
		7.5	3.6	3.4				3.5	4.2
		(15) 3.2	(62) 2.1	(34) 2.3			Net Profit + Depr., Dep., Amort./Cur. Mat. L/T/D	(107) 2.1	(116) 2.3
		1.4	1.1	1.3				1.0	1.2
		.4	.5	.6	.6	.6		.7	.6
		.8	.9	1.3	2.0	.9	Fixed/Worth	1.2	1.3
		1.9	1.5	2.5	3.9	11.8		2.4	2.7
		1.3	1.4	1.7	1.4	5.2		1.1	1.2
		2.9	2.6	3.1	3.8	8.1	Debt/Worth	2.4	2.5
		320.0	4.6	7.6	5.9	25.6		4.5	5.5
		36.4	31.7	37.3	22.1			18.7	23.8
		(33) 15.7	(142) 13.6	(69) 21.5	(12) 15.8		% Profit Before Taxes/Tangible Net Worth	(285) 6.2	(292) 10.6
		5.0	4.5	10.0	5.6			-2.8	3.5
		9.1	8.6	8.4	9.4	15.7		5.3	6.2
		4.1	3.9	5.1	3.6	7.2	% Profit Before Taxes/Total Assets	1.9	3.1
		-.4	1.3	1.7	.9	-1.3		-1.6	.8
		115.5	70.7	52.5	27.4	237.5		29.0	32.0
		52.3	33.3	24.8	14.6	169.0	Sales/Net Fixed Assets	12.8	15.1
		16.7	15.3	13.9	10.3	10.6		7.3	8.1
		13.1	10.9	10.4	9.5	14.2		6.5	7.3
		7.8	7.5	7.6	6.9	10.8	Sales/Total Assets	4.8	4.9
		4.9	4.9	5.1	5.2	4.2		3.5	3.5
		.2	.4	.3	.5	.1		.8	.7
		(38) .5	(142) .6	(72) .6	(11) .8	.1	% Depr., Dep., Amort./Sales	(288) 1.3	(302) 1.1
		.9	1.0	1.0	1.1	1.1		1.9	1.8
		.4	.2	.2				.4	.4
		(26) 1.0	(56) .5	(16) .3			% Officers', Directors' Owners' Comp/Sales	(114) .7	(109) .8
		1.9	1.0	.6				1.7	1.3
20274M	542549M	7542717M	13375278M	6643936M	15416772M		Net Sales ($)	17000300M	23448757M
2163M	51699M	846218M	1629557M	847218M	1625453M		Total Assets ($)	3854471M	4747891M

© RMA 2007

M = $ thousand   MM = $ million
See Pages 11 through 21 for Explanation of Ratios and Data

Comparative Historical Data — Current Data Sorted by Sales

4/1/04-3/31/05 ALL	4/1/05-3/31/06 ALL	4/1/06-3/31/07 ALL	Type of Statement	0-1MM	1-3MM	3-5MM	5-10MM	10-25MM	25MM & OVER
					100 (4/1-9/30/06)		197 (10/1/06-3/31/07)		
45	35	36	Unqualified			3	1	3	30
84	71	88	Reviewed			2	2	14	71
83	68	83	Compiled		3	3	10	21	46
18	19	30	Tax Returns	2	4	2	5	5	12
58	88	60	Other		3	1	3	6	48
288	281	297	**NUMBER OF STATEMENTS**	2	10	11	18	49	207
%	%	%	**ASSETS**	%	%	%	%	%	%
8.0	9.7	9.2	Cash & Equivalents		4.6	11.0	8.4	9.2	9.5
32.3	34.0	35.4	Trade Receivables (net)		32.1	15.0	34.4	33.2	37.2
14.3	13.5	14.3	Inventory		15.5	10.2	17.1	16.3	13.8
2.6	2.7	3.2	All Other Current		6.3	9.1	3.6	3.6	2.7
57.2	59.9	62.1	Total Current		58.5	45.3	63.6	62.2	63.3
32.9	29.9	28.3	Fixed Assets (net)		26.1	35.2	23.9	29.2	27.9
3.5	3.7	3.2	Intangibles (net)		1.0	10.6	5.2	2.3	2.9
6.5	6.5	6.4	All Other Non-Current		14.4	8.9	7.3	6.3	5.9
100.0	100.0	100.0	Total		100.0	100.0	100.0	100.0	100.0
			LIABILITIES						
9.9	11.3	12.0	Notes Payable-Short Term		14.7	9.6	9.2	13.3	11.7
3.7	3.4	3.4	Cur. Mat.-L.T.D.		3.7	4.3	3.1	4.4	3.1
25.8	26.8	28.8	Trade Payables		14.6	19.0	26.9	26.7	30.9
.2	.2	.2	Income Taxes Payable		.0	.3	.1	.2	.2
8.1	7.7	7.6	All Other Current		13.0	9.4	9.8	6.8	7.3
47.6	49.4	52.0	Total Current		46.1	42.6	49.0	51.4	53.2
18.1	17.6	16.5	Long-Term Debt		23.0	20.3	18.9	22.1	14.4
.8	.9	.9	Deferred Taxes		.0	2.4	.4	.8	.8
4.3	3.7	3.1	All Other Non-Current		4.0	6.6	7.3	3.3	2.5
29.1	28.3	27.6	Net Worth		26.9	28.1	24.3	22.3	29.1
100.0	100.0	100.0	Total Liabilities & Net Worth		100.0	100.0	100.0	100.0	100.0
			INCOME DATA						
100.0	100.0	100.0	Net Sales		100.0	100.0	100.0	100.0	100.0
12.5	11.0	10.7	Gross Profit		30.2	29.5	16.4	12.9	7.1
11.5	10.0	9.5	Operating Expenses		30.3	22.4	13.8	11.7	6.2
1.0	.9	1.2	Operating Profit		.0	7.1	2.6	1.2	.9
-.2	.0	.0	All Other Expenses (net)		1.4	-.3	.3	.2	-.1
1.2	.9	1.1	Profit Before Taxes		-1.4	7.4	2.2	1.0	1.0
			RATIOS						
1.6	1.6	1.6	Current		3.5	2.1	1.9	1.6	1.4
1.2	1.2	1.2			2.0	1.0	1.6	1.3	1.2
.9	1.0	1.0			1.1	.7	.9	1.0	1.0
1.2	1.2	1.1	Quick		2.8	.9	1.4	1.1	1.1
.8	.9	.9			1.2	.6	.8	.9	.9
.6	.6	.6			.2	.4	.6	.6	.6
12 30.0	11 34.4	9 38.4	Sales/Receivables		12 30.4	8 48.0	11 34.5	12 30.5	9 41.8
18 20.3	18 20.6	16 23.3			37 9.8	19 19.3	21 17.4	26 14.2	14 26.1
29 12.7	28 12.9	26 14.1			64 5.7	29 12.6	30 12.3	31 11.6	21 17.2
4 86.6	3 106.5	3 126.5	Cost of Sales/Inventory		0 UND	4 88.0	4 93.6	6 63.6	3 141.7
9 42.7	7 52.0	7 55.7			18 20.1	13 28.9	9 41.3	9 41.0	5 66.7
16 22.8	13 28.8	11 32.3			72 5.1	31 11.6	24 14.9	17 21.2	9 38.8
11 32.4	11 33.3	10 38.0	Cost of Sales/Payables		12 30.9	12 30.4	9 42.9	11 34.6	9 39.1
16 22.6	15 24.5	13 27.3			31 12.0	26 14.3	13 27.8	15 23.6	13 28.6
23 16.0	19 18.8	18 20.2			58 6.3	65 5.6	27 13.3	27 13.5	16 23.3
25.4	27.6	32.8	Sales/Working Capital		6.7	9.9	15.2	21.1	40.1
68.9	67.4	76.5			10.5	-245.3	31.0	41.0	106.0
-189.3	-374.0	-619.0			89.7	-15.1	-176.6	593.6	-696.6
5.1	5.7	6.5	EBIT/Interest		7.2		4.5	3.8	7.7
(273) 2.5	(268) 3.1	(282) 2.8			(10) 3.2		(16) 2.5	(48) 2.2	(198) 3.5
1.4	1.6	1.4			.6		1.7	1.0	1.6
3.4	4.5	3.9	Net Profit + Depr., Dep., Amort./Cur. Mat. L/T/D					3.2	4.2
(103) 2.1	(92) 2.1	(119) 2.3					(25) 1.6		(84) 2.4
1.2	1.0	1.3					1.0		1.4
.6	.5	.5	Fixed/Worth		.3	.6	.5	.4	.5
1.2	1.1	1.0			.5	1.6	1.2	.9	.9
2.6	2.3	2.0			UND	2.4	-5.2	2.0	1.9
1.5	1.6	1.5	Debt/Worth		.5	1.4	1.3	1.7	1.6
3.0	3.3	2.9			1.1	2.8	3.5	2.6	3.1
6.3	6.8	6.8			UND	-46.3	-21.1	4.8	6.4
24.7	36.7	35.1	% Profit Before Taxes/Tangible Net Worth				34.8	22.1	36.9
(261) 11.3	(254) 16.2	(269) 16.2					(12) 9.1	(44) 10.4	(195) 18.9
2.6	6.4	5.2					4.9	.2	5.6
6.1	8.4	8.7	% Profit Before Taxes/Total Assets		7.7	9.6	14.7	6.3	10.4
2.9	4.1	4.5			4.5	4.0	5.6	2.6	4.9
.8	1.5	1.1			-3.0	-1.5	2.2	.0	1.4
39.4	56.7	69.9	Sales/Net Fixed Assets		46.5	44.4	82.6	63.9	85.5
19.6	25.5	31.4			12.8	11.2	22.2	25.2	34.4
9.3	12.1	14.5			5.4	2.8	8.9	10.8	16.9
8.4	9.7	11.0	Sales/Total Assets		4.4	5.3	8.1	8.3	12.5
5.7	6.4	7.5			2.8	3.5	5.8	5.3	8.6
4.0	4.2	5.0			2.3	1.5	2.6	3.4	6.4
.5	.4	.3	% Depr., Dep., Amort./Sales				.2	.5	.3
(261) 1.0	(254) .7	(279) .6					.9	(47) .9	(196) .5
1.5	1.2	1.0					1.2	1.4	.8
.3	.3	.2	% Officers', Directors', Owners' Comp/Sales					.5	.2
(101) .7	(99) .6	(104) .5						(22) .8	(65) .3
2.0	1.6	1.2						1.8	.8
28159711M	36300976M	43541526M	Net Sales ($)	1259M	15571M	43200M	137137M	811070M	42533289M
4889465M	4808363M	5002308M	Total Assets ($)	1896M	11529M	29519M	35409M	195833M	4728122M

© RMA 2007

M = $ thousand   MM = $ million

See Pages 11 through 21 for Explanation of Ratios and Data

Current Data Sorted by Assets   Comparative Historical Data

	0-500M	500M-2MM	2-10MM	10-50MM	50-100MM	100-250MM	Type of Statement	4/1/02-3/31/03 ALL	4/1/03-3/31/04 ALL
		2	12	54	20	21	Unqualified	91	95
	2	5	91	79	8		Reviewed	168	174
	5	41	68	20	1		Compiled	128	162
	4	17	15	3			Tax Returns	29	45
	3	22	53	58	21	9	Other	165	117
	214 (4/1-9/30/06)			420 (10/1/06-3/31/07)					
	14	87	239	214	50	30	NUMBER OF STATEMENTS	581	593
	%	%	%	%	%	%	ASSETS	%	%
	13.4	10.1	10.3	8.2	6.9	6.5	Cash & Equivalents	9.1	8.9
	29.0	37.3	39.9	33.6	30.9	39.4	Trade Receivables (net)	30.6	30.8
	17.0	17.8	13.8	13.2	12.8	15.0	Inventory	13.1	12.4
	.7	2.4	3.8	3.8	3.4	4.0	All Other Current	3.4	4.2
	60.1	67.6	67.7	58.8	53.9	64.9	Total Current	56.2	56.4
	30.1	23.0	22.4	29.5	35.5	24.5	Fixed Assets (net)	32.4	33.0
	4.4	3.8	2.7	3.1	3.8	3.7	Intangibles (net)	3.3	2.6
	4.6	5.6	7.1	8.5	6.8	6.9	All Other Non-Current	8.1	8.0
	100.0	100.0	100.0	100.0	100.0	100.0	Total	100.0	100.0
							LIABILITIES		
	25.1	10.0	10.7	11.7	9.2	10.5	Notes Payable-Short Term	10.0	9.4
	3.7	3.6	2.9	3.4	2.4	1.2	Cur. Mat.-L.T.D.	4.0	3.7
	21.9	30.4	33.4	30.2	30.1	27.5	Trade Payables	24.3	24.5
	.0	.1	.3	.2	.3	.2	Income Taxes Payable	.2	.2
	8.2	10.3	7.3	6.8	6.6	10.4	All Other Current	8.2	7.8
	58.9	54.3	54.7	52.4	48.6	49.7	Total Current	46.8	45.6
	8.7	18.5	13.2	15.0	19.8	20.4	Long-Term Debt	18.6	19.8
	.4	.4	.5	.8	.8	1.0	Deferred Taxes	.7	.8
	10.2	8.4	3.8	2.5	2.2	3.0	All Other Non-Current	3.4	.3.7
	21.1	18.3	27.7	29.3	28.6	25.8	Net Worth	30.5	30.0
	100.0	100.0	100.0	100.0	100.0	100.0	Total Liabilities & Net Worth	100.0	100.0
							INCOME DATA		
	100.0	100.0	100.0	100.0	100.0	100.0	Net Sales	100.0	100.0
	20.1	16.8	10.1	9.0	7.0	7.7	Gross Profit	15.3	14.5
	18.0	15.3	9.0	7.9	5.6	5.3	Operating Expenses	14.2	13.3
	2.1	1.5	1.1	1.1	1.4	2.3	Operating Profit	1.1	1.2
	.7	.2	.1	-.1	-.1	.4	All Other Expenses (net)	.1	-.1
	1.4	1.3	1.0	1.2	1.5	1.9	Profit Before Taxes	1.0	1.3
							RATIOS		
	2.9	1.8	1.5	1.3	1.4	1.6		1.6	1.7
	1.5	1.3	1.2	1.1	1.1	1.3	Current	1.2	1.2
	.8	1.0	1.0	.9	.8	1.0		.9	.9
	2.6	1.3	1.2	1.0	1.0	1.3		1.1	1.2
	1.2	.9	.9	.8	.7	1.0	Quick	.8	.8
	.3	.6	.7	.6	.5	.7		.6	.6
0	UND	12 31.7	11 32.6	9 42.0	7 50.2	17 21.6		12 29.8	10 36.3
16	22.8	22 16.6	18 19.8	16 22.5	15 24.6	20 17.8	Sales/Receivables	22 16.5	20 18.7
24	14.9	37 9.7	30 12.1	27 13.7	26 14.2	33 11.2		35 10.4	32 11.3
0	UND	4 86.6	2 205.4	2 148.0	2 148.7	2 167.4		4 104.1	3 125.2
5	68.3	8 43.3	5 73.2	5 69.4	6 62.3	5 74.8	Cost of Sales/Inventory	9 41.5	8 47.2
17	21.0	21 17.1	14 26.6	12 29.5	13 27.8	14 26.4		19 19.5	17 22.0
0	UND	9 39.7	11 34.2	11 33.8	11 33.3	8 47.9		13 27.8	11 32.8
10	38.4	15 24.3	15 25.0	14 25.8	15 25.2	14 27.0	Cost of Sales/Payables	19 18.8	16 22.6
33	11.1	30 12.1	23 15.8	22 16.3	21 17.3	24 15.1		29 12.7	25 14.7
	19.9	18.4	24.1	36.8	56.0	20.4		20.2	19.2
	43.6	48.6	66.0	107.1	145.8	43.7	Sales/Working Capital	69.3	58.0
	-96.7	-368.9	-365.9	-197.6	-73.3	475.7		-114.2	-299.2
		3.7	6.9	8.2	7.3	6.3		4.9	7.5
		(74) 1.7	(223) 2.8	(212) 3.6	(49) 3.5	(29) 3.4	EBIT/Interest	(536) 2.1	(556) 3.1
		.7	1.6	2.1	1.8	2.1		1.1	1.6
		2.0	3.5	6.5	10.7			3.7	4.3
		(16) 1.2	(81) 2.0	(85) 2.9	(20) 5.0		Net Profit + Depr., Dep., Amort./Cur. Mat. L/T/D	(197) 1.8	(211) 2.2
		.8	1.2	1.4	2.6			1.0	1.3
	.1	.3	.3	.5	.7	.2		.5	.5
	.9	1.0	.8	1.2	1.4	.6	Fixed/Worth	1.2	1.1
	NM	-10.5	1.9	2.2	2.1	2.3		2.5	2.2
	.5	1.5	1.7	1.6	1.8	2.2		1.3	1.4
	2.0	4.4	3.1	3.3	3.2	3.6	Debt/Worth	2.7	2.5
	NM	-12.2	7.1	5.4	6.4	7.8		6.3	5.5
	67.2	30.2	38.7	36.6	51.7	62.6		25.9	31.0
(11)	14.8	(61) 11.7	(222) 20.0	(199) 21.6	(49) 24.6	(29) 41.6	% Profit Before Taxes/Tangible Net Worth	(533) 11.6	(551) 15.0
	3.4	.4	8.3	11.7	10.2	23.4		2.1	4.7
	13.7	8.1	9.4	9.5	11.5	12.4		6.3	8.3
	3.1	2.7	4.5	5.5	5.3	7.0	% Profit Before Taxes/Total Assets	2.9	3.8
	-.4	-.7	1.7	2.4	2.4	3.8		.3	1.3
	242.6	106.4	106.0	60.6	40.4	214.2		39.0	43.7
	37.0	41.6	42.2	26.9	17.2	47.7	Sales/Net Fixed Assets	15.3	17.6
	8.3	12.9	19.5	13.9	11.3	8.9		8.3	8.6
	10.9	9.7	11.1	9.9	9.1	9.4		6.7	7.3
	7.7	5.4	7.6	7.2	6.3	5.3	Sales/Total Assets	4.5	5.0
	3.2	3.1	4.7	4.7	4.7	4.0		3.1	3.4
		.4	.2	.3	.4	.1		.7	.5
		(72) .8	(218) .6	(201) .5	(47) .7	(22) .4	% Depr., Dep., Amort./Sales	(537) 1.2	(553) 1.1
		1.6	.9	.9	1.1	.9		1.9	1.8
		.6	.4	.1				.4	.5
		(40) 1.0	(103) .7	(50) .3			% Officers', Directors' Owners' Comp/Sales	(215) 1.0	(226) 1.0
		3.3	1.3	.6				2.2	2.1
	26976M	855735M	11462952M	35917981M	22989434M	29350755M	Net Sales ($)	38916855M	49397957M
	3901M	113256M	1315233M	4666356M	3438414M	4454553M	Total Assets ($)	8502091M	9152452M

M = $ thousand   MM = $ million
See Pages 11 through 21 for Explanation of Ratios and Data

Comparative Historical Data | Current Data Sorted by Sales

4/1/04-3/31/05 ALL	4/1/05-3/31/06 ALL	4/1/06-3/31/07 ALL	Type of Statement	0-1MM	1-3MM	3-5MM	5-10MM	10-25MM	25MM & OVER
97	101	109	Unqualified		1	1	1	2	104
175	154	185	Reviewed	1	2	2	6	26	148
115	107	135	Compiled	2	10	7	12	42	62
41	46	39	Tax Returns		5	6	2	15	11
117	170	166	Other	2	4	5	16	19	120
					214 (4/1-9/30/06)		420 (10/1/06-3/31/07)		
545	578	634	**NUMBER OF STATEMENTS**	5	22	21	37	104	445
%	%	%	**ASSETS**	%	%	%	%	%	%
9.1	9.0	9.2	Cash & Equivalents		9.0	14.2	7.2	8.6	9.2
35.4	36.3	36.4	Trade Receivables (net)		30.2	30.7	31.4	37.3	37.4
12.9	13.3	14.2	Inventory		12.5	19.0	23.0	17.5	12.6
3.5	3.2	3.5	All Other Current		3.1	.7	2.5	3.1	3.9
60.8	61.8	63.3	Total Current		54.7	64.5	64.1	66.5	63.1
28.7	27.3	26.2	Fixed Assets (net)		32.9	24.7	25.2	24.2	26.3
2.9	3.3	3.2	Intangibles (net)		7.5	5.7	4.8	2.1	3.0
7.5	7.6	7.3	All Other Non-Current		4.9	5.0	6.0	7.2	7.6
100.0	100.0	100.0	Total		100.0	100.0	100.0	100.0	100.0
			LIABILITIES						
11.2	11.6	11.1	Notes Payable-Short Term		17.5	10.9	13.5	11.1	10.7
3.6	3.2	3.1	Cur. Mat.-L.T.D.		3.1	3.1	3.7	3.5	2.9
28.0	29.8	31.1	Trade Payables		26.6	19.3	26.0	28.6	33.1
.2	.2	.3	Income Taxes Payable		.0	.2	.1	.1	.3
7.5	7.7	7.6	All Other Current		13.7	10.6	10.4	6.0	7.4
50.6	52.4	53.3	Total Current		60.9	44.2	53.7	49.3	54.5
17.3	16.7	15.3	Long-Term Debt		16.7	17.8	21.1	15.6	14.5
.6	.6	.7	Deferred Taxes		.3	.9	.6	.7	.7
3.6	3.9	4.0	All Other Non-Current		13.3	7.5	7.8	5.7	2.6
27.9	26.4	26.8	Net Worth		8.7	29.6	16.8	28.7	27.6
100.0	100.0	100.0	Total Liabilities & Net Worth		100.0	100.0	100.0	100.0	100.0
			INCOME DATA						
100.0	100.0	100.0	Net Sales		100.0	100.0	100.0	100.0	100.0
12.7	11.6	10.5	Gross Profit		27.0	23.8	22.8	12.4	7.3
11.8	10.4	9.2	Operating Expenses		23.1	22.0	20.2	11.4	6.3
.9	1.3	1.3	Operating Profit		4.0	1.9	2.6	1.0	1.0
-.1	.0	.1	All Other Expenses (net)		1.7	.4	.8	.0	-.1
1.0	1.3	1.2	Profit Before Taxes		2.3	1.5	1.9	1.1	1.1
			RATIOS						
1.5	1.5	1.5	Current		2.4	3.3	1.6	1.9	1.4
1.2	1.2	1.2			1.2	1.2	1.2	1.3	1.1
1.0	1.0	.9			.5	.9	1.0	1.0	.9
1.2	1.1	1.2	Quick		1.6	2.3	1.0	1.4	1.1
.9	.9	.9			.8	.9	.7	1.0	.9
.6	.6	.6			.3	.5	.5	.7	.6
11 31.9	10 35.3	10 36.3	Sales/Receivables		12 29.2	15 23.6	19 19.5	14 26.9	9 39.8
21 17.7	20 18.6	18 20.3			31 11.9	31 12.0	28 12.9	24 15.4	16 23.1
34 10.9	31 11.9	29 12.6			66 5.6	46 7.9	39 9.3	36 10.3	25 14.5
3 124.6	2 155.7	2 162.6	Cost of Sales/Inventory		8 46.1	4 98.9	8 47.3	4 86.7	2 188.1
8 48.5	6 57.0	6 61.6			15 24.7	14 25.9	16 23.1	8 45.6	5 77.7
15 24.7	13 27.6	14 26.0			43 8.6	29 12.5	45 8.1	31 11.9	9 38.6
11 33.0	11 32.8	10 34.9	Cost of Sales/Payables		1 285.8	8 46.6	12 29.8	11 34.2	10 34.9
16 22.5	15 23.6	14 25.5			26 14.3	25 14.7	25 14.3	15 24.2	14 26.9
26 14.3	24 15.5	23 15.6			78 4.7	50 7.3	40 9.0	33 11.0	19 18.9
24.9	28.0	26.8	Sales/Working Capital		6.6	12.6	17.6	17.6	36.7
65.8	82.6	82.6			32.3	55.9	37.0	34.8	107.5
-338.2	-439.2	-241.7			-6.3	-45.2	-271.0	349.6	-240.2
7.8	7.3	6.9	EBIT/Interest		7.1	3.0	5.2	4.3	7.5
(506) 3.0	(539) 3.3	(596) 3.1			(18) 1.2	(17) 1.6	(35) 3.1	(95) 2.1	(429) 3.5
1.5	1.7	1.6			-1.1	-.3	.4	1.4	2.0
4.1	4.3	5.1	Net Profit + Depr., Dep., Amort./Cur. Mat. L/T/D					3.4	5.8
(179) 2.3	(193) 2.3	(212) 2.4						(34) 1.7	(164) 2.7
1.3	1.4	1.3						1.0	1.5
.4	.4	.4	Fixed/Worth		.4	.1	.3	.3	.4
1.0	1.0	1.0			2.1	1.0	1.2	.6	1.1
2.2	2.4	2.4			-1.8	-15.5	NM	2.7	2.0
1.6	1.7	1.6	Debt/Worth		1.0	.6	1.3	1.6	1.9
2.8	3.4	3.3			6.6	3.9	5.0	2.6	3.4
5.5	6.5	7.1			-3.8	-7.4	-22.6	6.4	6.3
32.7	39.0	40.1	% Profit Before Taxes/Tangible Net Worth		65.6	61.6	63.4	25.6	42.2
(495) 15.1	(517) 19.4	(571) 20.3			(14) 17.2	(14) 3.6	(27) 19.5	(95) 13.9	(416) 23.0
4.3	7.8	8.9			-.1	-2.7	2.0	5.8	11.5
7.7	9.1	9.5	% Profit Before Taxes/Total Assets		12.8	9.9	14.3	7.3	9.7
3.6	4.5	4.8			2.0	2.6	3.3	3.3	5.2
1.1	1.6	1.8			-3.5	-1.7	-1.8	1.4	2.4
61.3	77.7	81.7	Sales/Net Fixed Assets		33.0	114.1	119.9	68.4	88.8
22.6	28.9	36.3			11.1	12.9	34.0	36.3	38.6
10.6	12.7	14.9			5.1	6.7	8.5	15.9	16.8
8.7	9.3	10.0	Sales/Total Assets		4.1	5.4	5.5	8.7	11.4
5.8	6.3	7.0			2.8	4.0	4.4	5.8	7.9
3.6	4.2	4.4			1.6	2.5	2.6	3.7	5.5
.4	.3	.3	% Depr., Dep., Amort./Sales		.9	.9	.7	.5	.3
(499) .9	(527) .6	(569) .6			(19) 1.3	(16) 1.6	(28) 1.0	(95) .8	(407) .5
1.5	1.2	1.0			3.1	3.5	2.9	1.3	.8
.3	.3	.3	% Officers', Directors' Owners' Comp/Sales		2.5		.8	.5	.2
(190) .8	(200) .6	(201) .6			(10) 4.0		(13) 1.8	(50) .7	(119) .4
1.4	1.3	1.3			7.1		4.0	1.4	.8
62022269M	76839726M	100603833M	Net Sales ($)	2677M	46694M	79268M	267722M	1771758M	98435714M
9039837M	11422166M	13991713M	Total Assets ($)	1919M	23063M	33806M	120139M	399258M	13413528M

M = $ thousand   MM = $ million
See Pages 11 through 21 for Explanation of Ratios and Data

WHOLESALE—Beer and Ale Merchant Wholesalers NAICS 424810 (SIC 5181)

Current Data Sorted by Assets							Comparative Historical Data	

						Type of Statement		
	5	24	58	18	9	Unqualified	104	96
1	10	57	41			Reviewed	115	106
1	17	41	7			Compiled	68	98
3	5	7	3			Tax Returns	19	22
1	6	48	76	10	5	Other	120	87
	52 (4/1-9/30/06)		401 (10/1/06-3/31/07)				4/1/02-3/31/03	4/1/03-3/31/04
0-500M	500M-2MM	2-10MM	10-50MM	50-100MM	100-250MM		ALL	ALL
6	43	177	185	28	14	NUMBER OF STATEMENTS	426	409
%	%	%	%	%	%	ASSETS	%	%
	14.4	14.3	10.6	8.1	8.5	Cash & Equivalents	10.9	12.3
	5.5	10.1	10.8	10.1	11.5	Trade Receivables (net)	10.1	9.2
	29.3	22.2	15.0	17.1	15.2	Inventory	21.6	20.9
	3.7	1.8	2.9	2.2	1.5	All Other Current	2.7	2.6
	53.0	48.3	39.3	37.5	36.6	Total Current	45.4	45.0
	24.3	23.2	23.2	19.8	23.0	Fixed Assets (net)	24.0	23.5
	12.6	19.3	29.9	34.5	34.1	Intangibles (net)	20.9	21.3
	10.1	9.1	7.6	8.2	6.3	All Other Non-Current	9.7	10.1
	100.0	100.0	100.0	100.0	100.0	Total	100.0	100.0
						LIABILITIES		
	15.5	7.5	4.6	1.8	12.2	Notes Payable-Short Term	7.9	6.4
	2.9	3.8	3.1	3.5	2.5	Cur. Mat.-L.T.D.	4.5	4.3
	14.4	11.3	9.6	10.6	14.3	Trade Payables	10.8	10.1
	.2	.3	.0	.1	.1	Income Taxes Payable	.2	.2
	14.5	7.8	6.1	6.9	5.3	All Other Current	9.0	7.7
	47.5	30.8	23.5	22.8	34.2	Total Current	32.4	28.8
	12.0	19.7	30.5	32.2	18.5	Long-Term Debt	25.2	23.3
	.1	.5	.4	.4	.1	Deferred Taxes	.3	.4
	2.9	3.4	2.4	4.5	3.6	All Other Non-Current	3.6	4.6
	37.5	45.7	43.2	40.1	43.6	Net Worth	38.5	42.9
	100.0	100.0	100.0	100.0	100.0	Total Liabilities & Net Worth	100.0	100.0
						INCOME DATA		
	100.0	100.0	100.0	100.0	100.0	Net Sales	100.0	100.0
	26.2	25.3	24.9	24.7	25.2	Gross Profit	25.0	25.9
	24.5	22.3	20.7	18.9	18.7	Operating Expenses	21.3	22.3
	1.7	3.0	4.2	5.7	6.6	Operating Profit	3.7	3.6
	.2	.2	.6	.6	.7	All Other Expenses (net)	.6	.4
	1.5	2.7	3.5	5.1	5.8	Profit Before Taxes	3.1	3.2
						RATIOS		
	2.2	2.6	2.4	2.3	1.9		2.2	2.6
	1.6	1.7	1.6	1.5	1.2	Current	1.4	1.6
	.8	1.0	1.1	1.0	.9		1.0	1.0
	1.1	1.4	1.4	1.4	.9		1.1	1.5
	.5	.7	.8	.6	.6	Quick	(425) .6	.7
	.2	.3	.4	.3	.3		.3	.3
0 UND	1 279.9	2 148.7	3 121.1	3 111.9			1 263.5	1 280.5
1 376.3	4 96.6	7 55.1	8 47.9	8 46.5		Sales/Receivables	4 96.1	3 106.9
3 122.3	16 22.5	21 17.1	21 17.1	26 14.0			18 19.8	17 21.3
12 29.4	13 27.3	12 30.8	19 19.1	17 21.0			14 25.9	14 26.2
23 16.1	22 16.3	22 16.5	25 14.8	26 14.0		Cost of Sales/Inventory	24 15.5	22 16.3
31 12.0	32 11.4	30 12.3	35 10.5	32 11.4			32 11.4	31 11.8
2 234.0	5 76.1	10 37.5	9 39.0	16 22.4			6 61.7	6 62.2
9 41.5	11 32.6	14 26.9	16 23.0	21 17.7		Cost of Sales/Payables	11 32.2	12 31.7
17 21.7	16 22.5	20 18.7	24 15.4	31 11.9			17 21.7	17 21.6
	19.8	13.1	12.0	12.7	11.1		14.1	12.9
	28.9	26.4	24.8	19.2	70.4	Sales/Working Capital	33.6	25.7
	-80.5	305.8	161.3	313.9	-93.0		-288.5	812.4
	7.2	14.3	10.1	14.5	12.2		10.9	15.8
	(38) 3.2	(155) 4.2	(172) 4.7	(27) 6.8	(13) 5.9	EBIT/Interest	(382) 4.3	(357) 6.0
	.4	1.8	2.3	3.6	3.1		2.1	2.5
		3.7	6.0				5.3	5.8
		(36) 2.2	(34) 2.7			Net Profit + Depr., Dep., Amort./Cur. Mat. L/T/D	(92) 2.4	(90) 2.9
		1.0	1.5				1.3	1.6
	.3	.4	.5	.9	.7		.4	.3
	.6	.7	1.7	9.2	NM	Fixed/Worth	1.1	.9
	3.3	8.4	-1.0	-.4	-1.3		-2.0	-3.3
	.6	.6	.9	1.0	1.0		.8	.6
	1.9	1.6	4.4	16.7	NM	Debt/Worth	2.7	2.0
	6.7	14.8	-3.8	-3.2	-5.0		-7.5	-10.2
	66.7	49.7	58.8	82.7			57.7	61.8
	(37) 20.0	(138) 23.8	(112) 31.9	(15) 34.6		% Profit Before Taxes/Tangible Net Worth	(286) 30.5	(291) 30.9
	-2.0	10.7	16.3	21.8			13.2	13.3
	24.2	18.0	15.2	15.8	19.5		17.7	18.0
	8.4	8.5	9.4	11.5	12.7	% Profit Before Taxes/Total Assets	9.3	10.6
	-1.6	2.8	4.5	9.4	6.5		3.5	4.2
	58.2	41.7	34.3	49.2	22.9		37.8	40.2
	32.4	24.6	16.1	17.4	12.8	Sales/Net Fixed Assets	20.5	20.6
	15.2	13.5	8.7	8.5	8.8		10.3	10.5
	8.9	5.5	3.8	3.2	3.2		5.4	5.1
	6.1	4.3	2.9	2.7	2.5	Sales/Total Assets	3.7	3.9
	4.5	3.1	2.3	2.1	2.4		2.8	2.6
	.6	.7	.8	.7	.7		.7	.8
	(37) 1.0	(163) 1.1	(172) 1.1	(26) 1.1	(12) 1.1	% Depr., Dep., Amort./Sales	(389) 1.2	(368) 1.2
	1.9	1.7	1.5	1.4	1.3		1.7	1.8
	1.6	1.2	.8				.9	1.1
	(25) 2.7	(85) 1.9	(48) 1.2			% Officers', Directors' Owners' Comp/Sales	(147) 1.8	(153) 1.9
	4.9	3.2	2.0				3.4	3.1
5053M	390304M	3815175M	12528929M	5753237M	4961534M	Net Sales ($)	23254343M	19066643M
1387M	57565M	894991M	4117846M	2011523M	1842109M	Total Assets ($)	6905645M	5799261M

M = $ thousand   MM = $ million
See Pages 11 through 21 for Explanation of Ratios and Data

Comparative Historical Data

Current Data Sorted by Sales

110	112	114	Type of Statement				3	18	93
98	102	109	Unqualified / Reviewed		1	2	9	42	55
69	50	66	Compiled	1		2	13	35	15
26	14	18	Tax Returns	3	1		3	8	3
102	134	146	Other	1	1	3	7	33	101
4/1/04-3/31/05 ALL	4/1/05-3/31/06 ALL	4/1/06-3/31/07 ALL		0-1MM	52 (4/1-9/30/06) 1-3MM	3-5MM	5-10MM	401 (10/1/06-3/31/07) 10-25MM	25MM & OVER
405	412	453	**NUMBER OF STATEMENTS**	5	3	7	35	136	267
%	%	%	**ASSETS**	%	%	%	%	%	%
12.4	12.2	12.1	Cash & Equivalents				9.3	16.4	10.6
9.9	9.4	10.1	Trade Receivables (net)				11.6	7.8	11.0
21.1	20.1	19.8	Inventory				26.7	19.4	18.3
2.2	2.5	2.5	All Other Current				3.3	2.4	2.3
45.5	44.2	44.5	Total Current				51.0	46.0	42.3
23.5	24.0	23.0	Fixed Assets (net)				23.9	24.0	22.7
21.3	22.5	24.2	Intangibles (net)				16.4	20.9	27.3
9.7	9.3	8.3	All Other Non-Current				8.7	9.1	7.7
100.0	100.0	100.0	Total				100.0	100.0	100.0
			LIABILITIES						
6.1	7.3	7.4	Notes Payable-Short Term				9.0	8.7	5.5
3.3	4.0	4.2	Cur. Mat.-L.T.D.				3.9	3.4	3.4
11.3	10.9	11.5	Trade Payables				16.6	9.6	10.6
.1	.1	.1	Income Taxes Payable				.0	.3	.1
7.6	7.8	7.6	All Other Current				10.3	6.1	7.7
28.4	30.1	30.0	Total Current				39.9	28.1	27.3
24.3	23.9	24.0	Long-Term Debt				18.1	23.3	25.5
.4	.4	.4	Deferred Taxes				.4	.4	.4
4.6	3.5	3.0	All Other Non-Current				2.2	3.6	2.7
42.3	42.0	42.7	Net Worth				39.5	44.6	44.1
100.0	100.0	100.0	Total Liabilites & Net Worth				100.0	100.0	100.0
			INCOME DATA						
100.0	100.0	100.0	Net Sales				100.0	100.0	100.0
25.8	25.2	25.1	Gross Profit				24.9	26.0	24.7
22.0	21.8	21.6	Operating Expenses				22.8	22.6	20.7
3.8	3.4	3.5	Operating Profit				2.1	3.4	4.0
.4	.3	.4	All Other Expenses (net)				.3	.5	.4
3.4	3.1	3.1	Profit Before Taxes				1.8	2.9	3.6
			RATIOS						
2.5	2.3	2.5	Current				2.2	2.9	2.4
1.6	1.5	1.6					1.6	1.7	1.6
1.1	1.0	1.0					1.0	1.1	1.0
1.4	1.4	1.3	Quick				.9	1.5	1.3
.7	.6	.7					.6	.9	.7
.3	.3	.3					.3	.4	.4
1 291.0	1 291.2	2 235.5	Sales/Receivables				1 724.5	1 366.7	2 152.6
4 93.8	4 100.4	5 79.2					3 108.5	3 133.1	6 64.6
19 19.4	18 20.2	18 19.8					20 18.5	14 25.9	20 17.9
16 23.0	13 27.9	13 28.0	Cost of Sales/Inventory				17 22.0	12 31.1	13 28.2
22 16.4	21 17.5	23 16.1					26 14.1	22 16.9	22 16.5
30 12.1	30 12.3	31 11.9					37 9.9	31 11.9	29 12.4
7 54.7	7 49.4	7 52.0	Cost of Sales/Payables				5 80.5	5 77.0	9 40.9
13 28.9	12 29.9	13 28.9					13 28.6	11 33.7	13 27.3
18 19.8	18 20.7	19 19.0					23 15.6	16 22.5	19 18.9
12.3	13.5	13.3	Sales/Working Capital				16.4	12.7	12.6
23.4	28.7	26.4					26.3	22.3	29.5
151.2	-419.6	999.8					-999.8	180.9	999.8
15.6	11.3	11.0	EBIT/Interest				5.3	12.4	12.2
(359) 5.5	(369) 4.7	(410) 4.6					(31) 2.4	(119) 3.8	(246) 5.3
2.8	2.3	2.0					.3	1.6	2.7
6.2	7.5	5.4	Net Profit + Depr., Dep., Amort./Cur. Mat. L/T/D					3.5	6.5
(88) 3.0	(89) 3.0	(84) 2.3						(21) 2.3	(54) 2.5
1.4	1.4	1.2						1.1	1.3
.3	.4	.4	Fixed/Worth				.3	.3	.5
1.0	1.3	1.1					.6	.7	1.4
-3.9	-2.6	-2.0					3.1	NM	-1.4
.7	.8	.7	Debt/Worth				.8	.5	.8
2.1	2.4	2.7					1.9	1.7	3.5
-9.5	-10.0	-9.0					6.7	NM	-5.4
55.8	51.6	57.6	% Profit Before Taxes/Tangible Net Worth				40.7	49.3	66.3
(286) 30.4	(283) 27.7	(312) 26.2					(28) 15.1	(102) 22.6	(172) 32.1
12.4	11.1	11.8					-.3	8.8	18.3
18.7	16.2	16.5	% Profit Before Taxes/Total Assets				10.8	16.5	17.6
10.1	9.4	9.3					4.3	8.4	10.8
4.1	4.2	3.9					-2.3	2.4	5.8
41.4	38.9	42.0	Sales/Net Fixed Assets				43.0	42.6	38.7
22.1	21.7	21.4					22.8	23.8	19.6
10.7	10.4	10.2					13.4	10.2	10.0
5.1	5.0	4.9	Sales/Total Assets				5.9	5.5	4.5
3.7	3.7	3.5					4.5	3.9	3.2
2.6	2.6	2.5					2.6	2.6	2.5
.8	.7	.7	% Depr., Dep., Amort./Sales				.7	.8	.7
(349) 1.2	(383) 1.0	(413) 1.1					(33) 1.4	(124) 1.2	(248) 1.1
1.7	1.5	1.6					2.2	1.7	1.4
1.2	.9	1.1	% Officers', Directors' Owners' Comp/Sales				1.3	1.5	.8
(141) 1.9	(148) 1.9	(160) 1.8					(21) 2.5	(60) 2.3	(72) 1.4
3.4	3.2	3.0					3.4	4.0	2.0
23253663M	23153407M	27454232M	Net Sales ($)	2859M	6143M	27115M	266097M	2312879M	24839139M
7571163M	7392936M	8925421M	Total Assets ($)	994M	2037M	9052M	74170M	727920M	8111248M

© RMA 2007

M = $ thousand   MM = $ million
See Pages 11 through 21 for Explanation of Ratios and Data

Current Data Sorted by Assets   Comparative Historical Data

	0-500M	500M-2MM	2-10MM	10-50MM	50-100MM	100-250MM	Type of Statement	4/1/02-3/31/03 ALL	4/1/03-3/31/04 ALL
	1		3	23	5	14	Unqualified	47	47
		3	9	9	1		Reviewed	30	22
		2	10	1	1		Compiled	21	41
	3	5	3				Tax Returns	10	13
	2	4	11	16	9	8	Other	45	28
		37 (4/1-9/30/06)		106 (10/1/06-3/31/07)					
NUMBER OF STATEMENTS	6	14	36	49	16	22		153	151
ASSETS	%	%	%	%	%	%		%	%
Cash & Equivalents		5.2	5.1	3.9	7.5	5.7		7.5	7.6
Trade Receivables (net)		18.0	21.8	23.5	22.1	23.9		23.1	25.5
Inventory		53.8	50.7	39.5	39.3	27.5		42.5	42.2
All Other Current		.7	3.1	3.6	2.3	2.5		2.8	4.0
Total Current		77.8	80.7	70.4	71.2	59.6		75.9	79.3
Fixed Assets (net)		11.7	10.4	11.0	10.4	9.5		10.1	8.8
Intangibles (net)		4.8	4.5	12.5	8.1	19.7		6.8	5.7
All Other Non-Current		5.6	4.3	6.0	10.3	11.2		7.2	6.2
Total		100.0	100.0	100.0	100.0	100.0		100.0	100.0
LIABILITIES									
Notes Payable-Short Term		16.0	15.2	14.3	12.3	8.6		12.2	13.1
Cur. Mat.-L.T.D.		6.3	.8	1.9	.8	1.7		2.3	1.6
Trade Payables		28.5	28.6	22.0	18.3	21.6		24.6	27.8
Income Taxes Payable		.0	.4	.3	.0	.1		.2	.2
All Other Current		10.7	11.1	15.1	10.3	7.4		11.6	11.8
Total Current		61.5	56.1	53.5	41.7	39.4		50.8	54.6
Long-Term Debt		6.7	5.0	10.2	18.8	25.0		10.8	8.6
Deferred Taxes		.1	.1	.2	.1	.4		.2	.2
All Other Non-Current		5.0	5.9	2.9	.9	3.5		3.9	5.8
Net Worth		26.8	32.9	33.2	38.5	31.8		34.3	30.8
Total Liabilties & Net Worth		100.0	100.0	100.0	100.0	100.0		100.0	100.0
INCOME DATA									
Net Sales		100.0	100.0	100.0	100.0	100.0		100.0	100.0
Gross Profit		28.8	25.0	24.1	25.2	27.1		25.6	24.8
Operating Expenses		25.9	21.4	20.9	18.7	22.3		21.8	21.7
Operating Profit		2.9	3.6	3.2	6.5	4.7		3.8	3.0
All Other Expenses (net)		1.0	.3	.5	-.1	1.2		.2	.1
Profit Before Taxes		1.9	3.3	2.7	6.6	3.5		3.6	2.9
RATIOS									
Current		1.7	1.9	1.6	2.9	2.1		2.3	2.2
		1.2	1.4	1.3	1.8	1.4		1.5	1.5
		1.0	1.1	1.1	1.2	1.2		1.1	1.1
Quick		.6	.6	.7	1.5	1.0		1.0	.9
		.4	.5	.5	.6	.7		.6	.6
		.1	.3	.3	.5	.5		.4	.4
Sales/Receivables		1 282.5	8 43.8	9 42.3	14 26.0	17 21.1		13 27.9	12 30.8
		7 53.2	26 13.9	30 12.1	35 10.4	39 9.3		31 11.9	32 11.3
		36 10.3	52 7.1	51 7.2	42 8.7	52 7.0		48 7.5	50 7.3
Cost of Sales/Inventory		39 9.3	51 7.2	40 9.1	55 6.7	34 10.6		41 8.8	44 8.3
		61 6.0	72 5.1	56 6.5	65 5.6	54 6.7		62 5.9	60 6.1
		112 3.3	109 3.4	82 4.4	73 5.0	87 4.2		94 3.9	83 4.4
Cost of Sales/Payables		7 55.8	22 16.8	21 17.0	28 13.0	26 14.1		18 19.8	22 16.9
		31 11.8	46 7.9	31 12.0	29 12.4	40 9.0		37 9.9	39 9.5
		56 6.5	69 5.3	45 8.1	44 8.4	59 6.1		55 6.6	59 6.2
Sales/Working Capital		12.8	6.5	11.5	3.8	6.3		6.7	6.5
		36.7	14.6	27.4	8.4	12.6		13.5	13.6
		NM	75.5	116.4	31.8	35.4		53.5	44.7
EBIT/Interest		19.0	11.8	14.3	62.3	6.4		14.4	14.1
		4.6	(32) 4.6	(47) 4.3	(14) 8.3	3.5		(136) 4.8	(131) 4.7
		1.3	1.7	1.4	5.7	1.4		2.2	2.0
Net Profit + Depr., Dep., Amort./Cur. Mat. L/T/D								11.1	10.8
								(31) 3.2	(33) 3.8
								1.7	1.9
Fixed/Worth		.0	.1	.1	.2	.1		.1	.1
		.5	.2	.4	.3	.3		.3	.2
		-1.3	.9	1.8	NM	NM		.9	.8
Debt/Worth		1.2	1.3	1.9	.5	1.8		1.0	1.3
		2.3	2.2	3.2	1.9	4.2		2.3	2.6
		-10.0	6.9	36.1	NM	-11.5		8.3	7.8
% Profit Before Taxes/Tangible Net Worth			45.9	71.4	34.7	23.5		59.1	41.4
			(31) 20.0	(40) 18.9	(12) 20.7	(15) 11.7		(129) 28.9	(129) 23.0
			4.6	4.4	16.6	4.9		14.5	8.6
% Profit Before Taxes/Total Assets		21.7	17.1	16.5	21.6	10.2		16.6	13.6
		6.9	5.6	6.5	12.1	5.1		6.7	5.9
		1.2	1.2	1.2	8.3	1.0		2.9	1.8
Sales/Net Fixed Assets		511.4	161.4	127.8	84.6	138.4		145.1	171.3
		60.1	96.0	51.6	45.7	43.4		48.2	68.5
		23.0	29.2	22.7	16.9	17.5		22.5	27.5
Sales/Total Assets		5.5	4.5	4.1	3.9	2.9		4.3	4.4
		3.9	3.2	2.7	3.1	2.4		2.9	3.0
		3.2	1.9	2.2	1.4	1.2		2.2	2.3
% Depr., Dep., Amort./Sales		.2	.3	.2	.3	.3		.3	.3
		(10) .4	(29) .4	(41) .6	(13) .8	(18) .4		(130) .6	(118) .5
		1.1	.7	.9	1.5	1.2		1.2	.9
% Officers', Directors' Owners' Comp/Sales			2.0					2.1	1.5
			(12) 4.1					(52) 3.1	(43) 3.0
			6.2					4.5	4.2
Net Sales ($)	3337M	75153M	618530M	3513429M	3326573M	7307641M		13860149M	12147541M
Total Assets ($)	1539M	17176M	181811M	1129544M	1134953M	3394206M		5053116M	4547167M

M = $ thousand   MM = $ million
See Pages 11 through 21 for Explanation of Ratios and Data

Comparative Historical Data

Current Data Sorted by Sales

			Type of Statement						
39	37	46	Unqualified	1		2	1	4	38
26	21	22	Reviewed				3	4	15
24	18	14	Compiled		1	2	2	5	4
8	14	11	Tax Returns		1	2	3	2	
47	57	50	Other	3	1	2	7	8	30
4/1/04-3/31/05 ALL	4/1/05-3/31/06 ALL	4/1/06-3/31/07 ALL		37 (4/1-9/30/06)			106 (10/1/06-3/31/07)		
				0-1MM	1-3MM	3-5MM	5-10MM	10-25MM	25MM & OVER
144	147	143	NUMBER OF STATEMENTS	6	3	8	16	23	87
%	%	%	**ASSETS**	%	%	%	%	%	%
5.9	7.9	5.5	Cash & Equivalents				6.4	6.7	4.7
22.2	24.6	22.0	Trade Receivables (net)				21.1	21.1	23.7
43.6	40.0	42.3	Inventory				52.5	46.4	38.2
3.3	2.9	2.7	All Other Current				.4	5.3	2.9
75.0	75.5	72.5	Total Current				80.5	79.5	69.5
9.8	8.9	11.0	Fixed Assets (net)				12.3	9.7	10.4
8.1	9.0	9.9	Intangibles (net)				4.1	2.3	14.0
7.1	6.6	6.6	All Other Non-Current				3.1	8.6	6.1
100.0	100.0	100.0	Total				100.0	100.0	100.0
			LIABILITIES						
14.4	13.6	14.3	Notes Payable-Short Term				18.5	11.4	13.1
1.8	2.2	1.8	Cur. Mat.-L.T.D.				3.8	1.7	1.5
23.9	25.6	23.7	Trade Payables				27.8	23.9	22.7
.2	.1	.2	Income Taxes Payable				.0	.7	.2
11.8	9.4	11.4	All Other Current				4.3	12.7	12.5
52.1	50.9	51.4	Total Current				54.5	50.3	50.0
11.5	10.5	12.2	Long-Term Debt				8.9	5.7	14.2
.3	.2	.2	Deferred Taxes				.0	.2	.2
5.8	5.2	4.4	All Other Non-Current				3.9	8.7	1.9
30.3	33.1	31.8	Net Worth				32.7	35.1	33.7
100.0	100.0	100.0	Total Liabilities & Net Worth				100.0	100.0	100.0
			INCOME DATA						
100.0	100.0	100.0	Net Sales				100.0	100.0	100.0
25.0	26.7	25.9	Gross Profit				25.7	25.9	24.3
22.6	22.8	22.2	Operating Expenses				22.1	21.8	20.4
2.4	4.0	3.7	Operating Profit				3.6	4.2	3.9
.2	.3	.6	All Other Expenses (net)				.5	.5	.5
2.2	3.7	3.1	Profit Before Taxes				3.1	3.7	3.4
			RATIOS						
2.4	2.3	1.9	Current				2.2	2.2	1.9
1.4	1.5	1.3					1.6	1.6	1.3
1.1	1.1	1.1					1.1	1.2	1.1
.8	1.0	.8	Quick				.7	.9	.8
.5	.6	.5					.6	.5	.6
.3	.4	.4					.3	.5	.4
8 44.7	10 35.0	8 44.1	Sales/Receivables			2 227.9	8 46.7	10 35.0	
28 12.9	32 11.3	30 12.2				36 10.0	30 12.1	30 12.1	
46 8.0	53 6.8	48 7.6				50 7.3	56 6.5	46 7.9	
46 7.9	41 8.9	44 8.3	Cost of Sales/Inventory			43 8.5	50 7.3	43 8.5	
64 5.7	61 6.0	62 5.9				83 4.4	79 4.6	56 6.6	
83 4.4	87 4.2	93 3.9				121 3.0	110 3.3	76 4.8	
20 17.8	22 16.6	23 16.2	Cost of Sales/Payables			29 12.6	15 25.1	24 15.2	
34 10.8	37 9.8	32 11.3				41 8.9	42 8.7	31 12.0	
52 7.0	58 6.3	53 6.8				72 5.1	65 5.7	45 8.1	
7.3	6.2	7.5	Sales/Working Capital				7.6	5.2	8.8
14.9	13.2	16.0					13.9	8.1	19.0
41.6	49.6	86.7					75.6	22.5	62.3
13.5	18.2	13.0	EBIT/Interest				6.9	18.5	13.5
(131) 5.2	(137) 5.0	(134) 4.5				(15) 3.0	(20) 8.4	(84) 4.5	
1.6	2.1	1.6					2.0	3.2	2.1
17.2	11.0	24.4	Net Profit + Depr., Dep., Amort./Cur. Mat. L/T/D						14.0
(30) 6.9	(25) 5.0	(22) 6.6						(15)	7.1
2.8	2.4	2.3							2.1
.1	.1	.1	Fixed/Worth				.0	.1	.1
.3	.3	.3					.3	.2	.3
2.2	1.0	1.8					.9	.6	2.0
1.0	1.1	1.4	Debt/Worth				1.3	1.1	1.6
2.4	2.5	2.6					2.0	1.5	3.1
30.6	13.8	56.6					7.9	5.6	119.3
42.3	53.5	46.4	% Profit Before Taxes/Tangible Net Worth				48.1	40.6	64.5
(112) 18.6	(118) 23.5	(110) 18.9				(15) 20.0	(19) 18.9	(67) 18.9	
6.5	6.9	5.7					9.1	4.6	6.7
12.0	14.7	16.4	% Profit Before Taxes/Total Assets				15.5	18.1	14.3
5.6	7.5	7.0					4.8	10.0	7.6
1.2	2.3	1.3					1.9	.9	2.8
127.0	159.4	151.9	Sales/Net Fixed Assets				428.6	256.0	120.6
55.1	62.6	52.9					159.9	87.9	50.7
26.3	31.3	22.8					19.3	24.5	23.1
4.4	4.1	4.1	Sales/Total Assets				3.6	4.5	4.1
3.1	3.0	2.9					2.9	2.8	2.9
2.3	2.1	2.0					1.8	1.8	2.4
.3	.3	.3	% Depr., Dep., Amort./Sales				.3	.3	.3
(113) .5	(117) .5	(114) .5				(11) .4	(18) .5	(74) .5	
.9	.9	.9					1.2	.8	.9
2.0	1.3	1.8	% Officers', Directors' Owners' Comp/Sales						1.4
(37) 3.7	(40) 2.4	(36) 3.4						(13)	2.7
9.2	5.5	7.7							7.7
14062489M	12507298M	14844663M	Net Sales ($)	3337M	5562M	33515M	111533M	408356M	14282360M
5075294M	5022957M	5859229M	Total Assets ($)	1539M	4044M	72731M	50242M	200186M	5530487M

M = $ thousand   MM = $ million
See Pages 11 through 21 for Explanation of Ratios and Data

Current Data Sorted by Assets   Comparative Historical Data

						Type of Statement		
2	32	266	253	32	23	Unqualified	609	598
2	15	46	14	1		Reviewed	93	77
4	13	27	4	1		Compiled	62	76
9	15	9	1			Tax Returns	20	22
5	21	50	32	8	2	Other	131	105
	405 (4/1-9/30/06)		482 (10/1/06-3/31/07)				4/1/02-3/31/03	4/1/03-3/31/04
0-500M	500M-2MM	2-10MM	10-50MM	50-100MM	100-250MM		ALL	ALL
22	96	398	304	42	25	NUMBER OF STATEMENTS	915	878
%	%	%	%	%	%	ASSETS	%	%
12.1	7.9	6.7	4.0	3.3	3.3	Cash & Equivalents	5.8	5.8
21.9	20.2	18.9	16.6	18.3	18.1	Trade Receivables (net)	20.8	16.7
35.5	31.4	30.3	31.0	28.7	33.5	Inventory	28.4	29.2
.6	3.8	7.1	11.4	14.8	11.7	All Other Current	3.4	7.9
70.1	63.3	63.0	63.1	65.1	66.6	Total Current	58.4	59.6
23.1	23.4	23.5	21.5	20.2	20.6	Fixed Assets (net)	25.5	25.1
1.1	1.1	.4	1.0	1.9	1.4	Intangibles (net)	.7	.4
5.7	12.2	13.2	14.4	12.9	11.5	All Other Non-Current	15.5	14.8
100.0	100.0	100.0	100.0	100.0	100.0	Total	100.0	100.0
						LIABILITIES		
20.6	11.5	15.2	22.1	22.2	24.3	Notes Payable-Short Term	15.3	15.7
4.3	1.6	1.6	1.8	1.5	2.1	Cur. Mat.-L.T.D.	2.0	2.1
20.7	15.8	16.9	18.6	18.8	16.1	Trade Payables	16.6	17.3
.2	.3	.3	.4	.3	.5	Income Taxes Payable	.3	.3
5.6	7.3	7.6	7.0	11.6	12.2	All Other Current	5.9	6.2
51.3	36.6	41.5	50.0	54.4	55.2	Total Current	40.0	41.5
15.1	10.5	6.1	8.7	11.2	12.1	Long-Term Debt	8.6	8.9
.0	.1	.3	.5	.5	.5	Deferred Taxes	.3	.3
16.8	2.3	1.2	1.4	1.4	2.9	All Other Non-Current	1.6	1.5
16.8	50.5	50.8	39.5	32.5	29.2	Net Worth	49.5	47.8
100.0	100.0	100.0	100.0	100.0	100.0	Total Liabilities & Net Worth	100.0	100.0
						INCOME DATA		
100.0	100.0	100.0	100.0	100.0	100.0	Net Sales	100.0	100.0
36.6	21.9	15.1	14.1	15.8	16.3	Gross Profit	19.5	16.5
32.7	20.6	13.9	12.0	10.5	12.7	Operating Expenses	18.5	15.3
3.8	1.3	1.2	2.1	5.3	3.6	Operating Profit	1.0	1.2
1.0	-.7	-.9	-.4	.6	.2	All Other Expenses (net)	-.7	-.6
2.8	2.0	2.1	2.4	4.7	3.4	Profit Before Taxes	1.7	1.8
						RATIOS		
2.6	3.6	2.0	1.4	1.3	1.3		1.9	1.8
1.7	1.9	1.5	1.2	1.2	1.2	Current	1.4	1.4
.8	1.3	1.2	1.1	1.1	1.1		1.2	1.2
1.3	1.6	.9	.6	.6	.6		1.0	.8
.6	.7	.6	.4	.3	.4	Quick	.7 (877)	.5
.3	.4	.4	.2	.2	.1		.4	.3

3	105.4	13	29.2	15	24.8	13	29.1	12	30.6	10	35.4	Sales/Receivables	19	18.8	12	30.1
12	30.4	21	17.1	25	14.7	23	15.9	20	18.3	29	12.5		29	12.5	22	16.6
41	8.9	34	10.7	35	10.4	37	9.8	33	11.1	50	7.3		43	8.5	35	10.4
6	64.8	27	13.6	33	11.1	38	9.7	33	10.9	44	8.2	Cost of Sales/Inventory	37	9.9	34	10.8
48	7.6	50	7.3	52	7.0	54	6.8	56	6.5	73	5.0		56	6.5	54	6.7
110	3.3	85	4.3	76	4.8	81	4.5	80	4.6	112	3.3		78	4.7	82	4.5
5	71.4	9	40.4	15	25.0	19	19.4	22	16.7	19	19.1	Cost of Sales/Payables	17	21.0	16	22.8
15	24.9	18	20.7	25	14.6	29	12.5	32	11.4	37	10.0		28	13.0	27	13.4
41	8.9	33	11.2	41	8.8	50	7.3	46	7.9	52	7.0		44	8.3	48	7.7

7.5	5.8	7.2	12.8	18.2	9.5	Sales/Working Capital	8.3	8.5
18.0	10.7	12.8	19.6	24.4	19.3		14.5	15.3
-18.6	25.2	24.8	28.3	32.4	34.4		28.0	27.2

	9.4		7.3		7.3		4.7		4.1	3.9	
(17)	2.1	(82)	3.3	(369)	3.4	(297)	2.9	(41)	3.0	(24) 3.0	EBIT/Interest
	-.5		1.4		1.7		1.9		2.1	2.3	

EBIT/Interest historical: 7.0 / (848) 3.3 / 1.6 ; 7.5 / (820) 3.6 / 1.7

			6.1		8.1		5.6	12.2	Net Profit + Depr., Dep., Amort./Cur. Mat. L/T/D
		(157)	4.1	(188)	4.9	(29)	4.3	(18) 5.7	
			2.5		3.0		3.5	2.0	

Net Profit + Depr. historical: 7.1 / (441) 3.9 / 2.3 ; 6.8 / (431) 4.1 / 2.4

.1	.2	.3	.4	.5	.5	Fixed/Worth	.3	.3
.2	.4	.4	.5	.6	.7		.5	.5
3.1	.7	.7	.7	.8	1.0		.8	.7
.7	.3	.5	1.0	1.5	1.7	Debt/Worth	.5	.6
2.5	.7	.9	1.6	2.2	2.1		1.0	1.1
NM	2.0	1.9	2.6	3.5	4.2		1.9	2.0

	41.0		19.8		15.4		18.8		22.3	28.7	% Profit Before Taxes/Tangible Net Worth
(17)	20.3	(92)	10.4	(394)	9.7	(299)	12.7	(41)	13.7	17.6	
	-3.6		2.3		4.7		7.0		8.5	13.5	

% Profit Before Taxes/Tangible Net Worth historical: 13.7 / (892) 7.2 / 2.6 ; 14.3 / (859) 7.8 / 2.6

18.9	10.0	8.4	7.1	6.6	7.2	% Profit Before Taxes/Total Assets	6.5	6.4
12.2	5.0	4.9	4.4	4.7	6.1		3.5	3.7
-5.2	.8	2.0	2.5	2.6	3.2		1.1	1.2
84.0	27.4	17.0	15.6	17.6	15.8	Sales/Net Fixed Assets	14.1	14.3
43.1	15.1	10.9	10.3	10.7	10.5		8.7	9.2
11.2	7.5	7.3	7.8	8.1	6.0		6.1	6.6
6.3	3.7	3.0	2.7	2.5	2.4	Sales/Total Assets	2.8	2.8
3.3	2.5	2.3	2.1	2.1	1.9		2.1	2.1
2.2	2.0	1.9	1.7	1.8	1.4		1.7	1.7

	.2		.7		1.0		1.1		1.1	.9	% Depr., Dep., Amort./Sales
(16)	1.0	(89)	1.3	(388)	1.4	(294)	1.5	(40)	1.4	1.4	
	5.9		2.4		2.0		1.9		1.8	1.8	

% Depr. historical: 1.3 / (895) 1.8 / 2.6 ; 1.3 / (855) 1.8 / 2.4

	.9		1.6		1.2		.8				% Officers', Directors' Owners' Comp/Sales
(11)	5.9	(26)	3.9	(40)	1.8	(12)	1.8				
	8.5		7.8		2.7		4.7				

% Officers' historical: 1.0 / (90) 2.0 / 4.7 ; 1.0 / (88) 2.0 / 4.7

31742M	393067M	5128044M	15790631M	8310629M	7900341M	Net Sales ($)	25548291M	25830804M
7224M	122262M	1998854M	6946038M	2815248M	3793798M	Total Assets ($)	11719920M	11382384M

Comparative Historical Data / Current Data Sorted by Sales

			Type of Statement						
636	649	608	Unqualified	1	17	28	98	184	280
83	63	78	Reviewed		8	10	19	28	13
58	56	49	Compiled	3	8	9	10	13	6
32	22	34	Tax Returns	5	9	7	7	5	1
116	124	118	Other	3	12	17	16	35	35
4/1/04-3/31/05 ALL	4/1/05-3/31/06 ALL	4/1/06-3/31/07 ALL		405 (4/1-9/30/06)			482 (10/1/06-3/31/07)		
				0-1MM	1-3MM	3-5MM	5-10MM	10-25MM	25MM & OVER
925	914	887	NUMBER OF STATEMENTS	12	54	71	150	265	335
%	%	%	ASSETS	%	%	%	%	%	%
5.9	5.8	5.8	Cash & Equivalents	14.0	8.2	8.5	7.4	5.8	3.8
16.9	17.5	18.3	Trade Receivables (net)	23.6	16.4	18.9	17.6	18.4	18.4
28.9	30.0	30.8	Inventory	33.8	32.9	29.3	31.9	30.3	30.5
8.3	8.2	8.6	All Other Current	.3	3.4	5.5	5.6	8.8	11.5
60.0	61.6	63.5	Total Current	71.7	60.9	62.1	62.6	63.3	64.4
24.4	23.2	22.5	Fixed Assets (net)	21.4	26.3	21.5	23.6	23.1	21.2
.5	.8	.8	Intangibles (net)	1.7	1.4	.4	.3	.5	1.1
15.1	14.4	13.2	All Other Non-Current	5.2	11.4	16.0	13.5	13.0	13.3
100.0	100.0	100.0	Total	100.0	100.0	100.0	100.0	100.0	100.0
			LIABILITIES						
15.2	17.2	17.9	Notes Payable-Short Term	22.7	12.4	14.5	14.1	16.2	22.3
1.7	2.0	1.8	Cur. Mat.-L.T.D.	3.2	2.8	1.6	1.5	1.7	1.7
18.0	17.6	17.5	Trade Payables	23.9	14.8	14.1	15.2	18.1	19.0
.3	.4	.4	Income Taxes Payable	.0	.3	.2	.4	.3	.5
6.7	6.8	7.6	All Other Current	6.9	6.7	7.6	6.7	7.8	8.1
42.0	44.0	45.1	Total Current	56.7	37.0	38.0	37.9	44.3	51.5
8.3	8.2	8.1	Long-Term Debt	21.4	16.0	5.1	5.7	6.8	9.2
.4	.3	.4	Deferred Taxes	.0	.1	.1	.3	.4	.5
1.5	1.7	1.8	All Other Non-Current	30.0	2.4	1.8	1.4	1.3	1.4
47.9	45.8	44.6	Net Worth	-8.2	44.5	55.0	54.7	47.3	37.5
100.0	100.0	100.0	Total Liabilities & Net Worth	100.0	100.0	100.0	100.0	100.0	100.0
			INCOME DATA						
100.0	100.0	100.0	Net Sales	100.0	100.0	100.0	100.0	100.0	100.0
16.1	15.5	16.1	Gross Profit	47.3	23.4	21.1	17.1	15.0	13.1
14.8	14.0	14.2	Operating Expenses	41.8	23.1	19.5	15.9	13.1	10.8
1.3	1.5	1.8	Operating Profit	5.4	.3	1.6	1.2	1.9	2.3
-.6	-.6	-.6	All Other Expenses (net)	1.9	-1.0	-1.2	-1.0	-.6	-.2
1.8	2.1	2.4	Profit Before Taxes	3.6	1.3	2.8	2.2	2.4	2.5
			RATIOS						
1.8	1.8	1.8	Current	2.0	3.5	2.9	2.6	1.9	1.4
1.4	1.3	1.3		1.2	1.8	1.6	1.7	1.4	1.2
1.2	1.2	1.2		.8	1.2	1.2	1.3	1.2	1.1
.8	.8	.8	Quick	1.3	1.5	1.4	1.1	.8	.6
.5	(913) .5	.5		.7	.6	.7	.6	.5	.4
.3	.3	.3		.2	.3	.4	.4	.3	.2
12 30.7	13 27.1	13 27.9	Sales/Receivables	0 UND	9 41.6	16 23.2	15 25.0	14 26.4	12 30.4
21 17.5	23 15.9	23 15.6		36 10.1	21 17.7	28 12.8	23 16.2	24 14.9	21 17.4
34 10.6	34 10.6	35 10.3		46 7.9	42 8.8	41 8.8	35 10.5	34 10.6	35 10.3
31 11.9	35 10.5	34 10.8	Cost of Sales/Inventory	3 123.6	41 9.0	33 11.2	37 9.8	33 11.2	34 10.8
51 7.2	52 7.0	53 6.9		97 3.8	69 5.3	61 6.0	59 6.2	52 7.0	49 7.5
74 4.9	77 4.8	81 4.5		152 3.5	95 3.8	103 3.5	87 4.2	77 4.8	73 5.0
15 24.0	17 21.6	15 23.7	Cost of Sales/Payables	0 UND	11 33.6	12 30.4	14 26.4	15 23.8	17 20.9
27 13.7	28 13.3	26 13.9		18 20.4	21 17.1	22 16.8	26 14.2	27 13.8	27 13.4
43 8.4	43 8.5	44 8.3		49 7.4	58 6.3	45 8.2	41 8.9	44 8.2	44 8.2
8.9	9.1	8.9	Sales/Working Capital	5.8	5.0	6.4	6.6	8.9	14.3
16.5	16.4	16.1		31.0	7.7	9.9	10.7	14.6	21.8
30.4	28.4	28.0		-18.3	35.9	22.3	21.6	24.1	31.7
7.6	6.7	5.7	EBIT/Interest	5.7	7.5	9.8	8.3	5.8	4.5
(868) 3.7	(861) 3.6	(830) 3.1		(10) 1.9	(48) 2.6	(58) 4.2	(137) 3.8	(246) 3.1	(331) 3.0
1.8	2.0	1.8		-1.6	1.0	2.2	1.4	1.8	1.9
6.5	7.7	7.0	Net Profit + Depr., Dep., Amort./Cur. Mat. L/T/D			13.2	5.7	6.7	7.9
(427) 4.1	(438) 4.3	(401) 4.5			(12) 3.1	(52) 4.2	(121) 4.4	(211) 4.9	
2.6	2.8	2.7				1.3	2.6	2.6	3.1
.3	.3	.3	Fixed/Worth	.1	.2	.2	.2	.3	.4
.5	.5	.5		.9	.4	.3	.4	.5	.6
.7	.7	.7		NM	1.6	.6	.7	.7	.8
.6	.6	.6	Debt/Worth	1.5	.4	.3	.4	.6	1.1
1.1	1.2	1.3		13.4	1.3	.6	.7	1.1	1.7
1.9	2.0	2.4		-5.5	3.0	1.7	1.7	2.0	2.8
14.7	16.8	18.2	% Profit Before Taxes/Tangible Net Worth		23.0	20.1	15.0	16.2	19.9
(901) 8.3	(891) 10.1	(868) 11.2			(50) 8.4	(70) 10.6	(149) 8.9	(263) 10.2	(328) 14.0
3.5	4.9	5.4			.6	4.7	3.2	5.0	8.2
6.7	7.3	8.2	% Profit Before Taxes/Total Assets	28.7	9.6	10.5	8.3	7.8	7.3
3.9	4.6	4.7		3.1	3.6	5.4	5.4	4.4	4.7
1.4	1.9	2.2		-7.2	-.1	2.4	1.1	2.2	2.7
15.7	16.3	17.8	Sales/Net Fixed Assets	78.1	27.5	24.1	17.8	16.2	16.8
10.2	10.3	11.0		41.2	12.2	13.1	10.9	10.5	11.0
7.2	7.4	7.5		14.4	4.7	6.4	6.8	7.4	8.3
3.1	2.9	3.0	Sales/Total Assets	3.2	2.8	2.5	2.9	3.0	3.0
2.3	2.3	2.2		2.7	2.1	2.0	2.2	2.3	2.3
1.8	1.8	1.8		2.1	1.5	1.6	1.8	1.8	1.9
1.1	1.1	1.0	% Depr., Dep., Amort./Sales		.7	.9	1.1	1.1	1.0
(890) 1.7	(887) 1.5	(852) 1.4			(50) 1.5	(66) 1.4	(146) 1.5	(255) 1.5	(327) 1.4
2.2	2.0	2.0			4.1	2.3	2.1	2.0	1.8
.7	1.1	1.1	% Officers', Directors' Owners' Comp/Sales		1.8	.9	1.1	1.0	.8
(95) 1.8	(89) 2.2	(91) 2.0			(19) 4.1	(12) 2.5	(17) 1.5	(22) 1.7	(16) 1.7
3.5	4.8	4.6			9.7	6.5	3.3	2.2	4.6
33086615M	35560087M	37554454M	Net Sales ($)	7466M	109825M	281565M	1108369M	4451903M	31595326M
12617367M	15014549M	15683424M	Total Assets ($)	3046M	60464M	145021M	508118M	2125879M	12840896M

M = $ thousand   MM = $ million
See Pages 11 through 21 for Explanation of Ratios and Data

Current Data Sorted by Assets   **Comparative Historical Data**

Date ranges: 9 (4/1-9/30/06) · 45 (10/1/06-3/31/07) · Historical columns 4/1/02-3/31/03 ALL and 4/1/03-3/31/04 ALL.

0-500M	500M-2MM	2-10MM	10-50MM	50-100MM	100-250MM		4/1/02-3/31/03 ALL	4/1/03-3/31/04 ALL
						Type of Statement		
		1	7	3	3	Unqualified	10	14
1	2	3	3			Reviewed	10	12
2	2	3	2			Compiled	4	13
1	3	1	1			Tax Returns	5	5
	4	3	1	1	1	Other	15	17
4	11	11	20	4	4	**NUMBER OF STATEMENTS**	44	61
%	%	%	%	%	%	**ASSETS**	%	%
	8.7	7.2	12.6			Cash & Equivalents	7.2	9.8
	19.6	35.6	25.1			Trade Receivables (net)	24.8	30.1
	51.3	34.0	28.6			Inventory	29.5	31.2
	2.7	2.0	6.2			All Other Current	5.3	7.4
	82.3	78.7	72.5			Total Current	66.8	78.5
	12.0	12.9	14.1			Fixed Assets (net)	14.8	15.8
	.6	1.1	2.8			Intangibles (net)	6.2	2.7
	5.1	7.3	10.6			All Other Non-Current	12.1	3.0
	100.0	100.0	100.0			Total	100.0	100.0
						LIABILITIES		
	7.5	12.4	8.8			Notes Payable-Short Term	8.4	8.2
	.9	1.0	.8			Cur. Mat.-L.T.D.	1.5	3.2
	17.8	23.9	31.1			Trade Payables	31.1	29.6
	.0	.1	.3			Income Taxes Payable	.8	.5
	11.6	4.0	5.0			All Other Current	16.5	11.8
	37.9	41.2	45.9			Total Current	58.3	53.3
	18.7	8.3	9.4			Long-Term Debt	17.2	8.0
	.0	.0	.2			Deferred Taxes	.3	.3
	12.7	4.5	3.1			All Other Non-Current	6.0	2.4
	30.6	46.0	41.3			Net Worth	18.1	36.0
	100.0	100.0	100.0			Total Liabilties & Net Worth	100.0	100.0
						INCOME DATA		
	100.0	100.0	100.0			Net Sales	100.0	100.0
	39.8	33.5	33.2			Gross Profit	38.0	38.4
	40.4	29.3	28.8			Operating Expenses	33.8	32.8
	-.5	4.2	4.4			Operating Profit	4.2	5.5
	.3	.1	.7			All Other Expenses (net)	1.3	.4
	-.8	4.1	3.6			Profit Before Taxes	2.9	5.2
						RATIOS		
	5.5	3.4	3.5			Current	2.3	2.5
	3.5	2.3	1.7				1.2	1.4
	1.0	1.4	1.0				.9	1.1
	1.9	2.2	1.5			Quick	.9	1.3
	.8	.9	.9				.6	.8
	.5	.7	.4				.4	.5
	7 55.4	16 22.2	22 16.3			Sales/Receivables	18 20.8	25 14.8
	24 15.1	44 8.3	31 12.0				40 9.0	44 8.4
	32 11.6	84 4.3	65 5.6				49 7.4	58 6.3
	31 11.6	13 28.4	27 13.3			Cost of Sales/Inventory	22 16.9	17 20.9
	42 8.6	68 5.4	62 5.9				72 5.1	58 6.3
	250 1.5	167 2.2	147 2.5				130 2.8	151 2.4
	17 21.0	22 16.9	26 14.0			Cost of Sales/Payables	28 12.9	19 19.7
	26 14.0	42 8.7	74 4.9				65 5.6	55 6.6
	40 9.1	90 4.0	101 3.6				91 4.0	100 3.6
	4.9	3.6	3.5			Sales/Working Capital	6.1	4.8
	8.2	6.8	7.4				19.1	11.6
	-172.1	10.7	NM				-34.4	37.4
	11.3		10.7			EBIT/Interest	6.9	21.3
	3.1		(12) 4.9				(42) 2.8	(52) 6.3
	-10.8		2.4				1.0	1.7
						Net Profit + Depr., Dep.,	4.7	7.3
						Amort./Cur. Mat. L/T/D	(13) 1.9	(18) 3.2
							.7	1.9
	.1	.1	.1			Fixed/Worth	.2	.1
	.4	.3	.2				.8	.3
	1.3	.4	1.3				-9.6	1.1
	.7	.3	.5			Debt/Worth	1.4	.9
	2.5	1.3	1.5				5.8	2.2
	11.5	2.7	4.9				-22.2	3.7
		24.7	35.4			% Profit Before Taxes/Tangible	34.3	82.3
	(10)	8.3	(19) 10.3			Net Worth	(30) 11.8	(55) 25.8
		4.7	2.1				7.2	6.7
	21.1	10.0	13.3			% Profit Before Taxes/Total	8.8	21.9
	7.8	5.4	4.6			Assets	3.9	7.0
	-12.2	1.8	1.4				.1	1.8
	68.5	51.3	88.0			Sales/Net Fixed Assets	46.3	66.9
	36.8	26.5	20.7				25.2	30.4
	22.0	9.5	10.8				11.2	12.4
	5.6	4.2	2.8			Sales/Total Assets	3.1	4.3
	5.2	2.2	2.0				2.2	2.3
	1.6	1.4	1.4				1.3	1.6
		.7	.4			% Depr., Dep., Amort./Sales	.6	.7
	(10)	1.1	(19) .8				(40) 1.1	(49) 1.2
		1.8	1.5				1.9	1.8
						% Officers', Directors'	1.8	3.5
						Owners' Comp/Sales	(19) 4.9	(15) 4.5
							10.5	9.6
5862M	49637M	219220M	864878M	403463M	1345401M	Net Sales ($)	2318839M	2431982M
1111M	12395M	64253M	442432M	276870M	770893M	Total Assets ($)	1349296M	1293115M

M = $ thousand   MM = $ million
See Pages 11 through 21 for Explanation of Ratios and Data

Comparative Historical Data / Current Data Sorted by Sales

			Type of Statement	0-1MM	1-3MM	3-5MM	5-10MM	10-25MM	25MM & OVER
10	12	14	Unqualified					1	13
10	7	9	Reviewed		2	1		2	4
5	6	6	Compiled		4			2	2
11	6	6	Tax Returns	1		2	1	1	1
17	15	16	Other	1	1	3	1	1	9
4/1/04-3/31/05 ALL	4/1/05-3/31/06 ALL	4/1/06-3/31/07 ALL			9 (4/1-9/30/06)			45 (10/1/06-3/31/07)	
53	46	54	**NUMBER OF STATEMENTS**	2	7	6	2	8	29
%	%	%	**ASSETS**	%	%	%	%	%	%
8.9	8.3	11.2	Cash & Equivalents						12.5
29.9	30.8	26.4	Trade Receivables (net)						25.4
30.0	29.4	33.1	Inventory						28.6
4.1	4.5	3.7	All Other Current						5.5
72.9	73.0	74.5	Total Current						72.0
15.3	16.1	15.0	Fixed Assets (net)						14.4
5.3	6.1	3.3	Intangibles (net)						5.4
6.5	4.8	7.2	All Other Non-Current						8.2
100.0	100.0	100.0	Total						100.0
			LIABILITIES						
10.4	16.0	9.1	Notes Payable-Short Term						10.0
3.0	2.5	.9	Cur. Mat.-L.T.D.						1.1
31.1	23.5	27.5	Trade Payables						29.9
.1	.3	.3	Income Taxes Payable						.5
8.9	8.5	9.1	All Other Current						7.5
53.5	50.8	47.0	Total Current						48.9
10.3	12.2	10.7	Long-Term Debt						9.2
.3	.3	.1	Deferred Taxes						.1
2.4	5.5	5.3	All Other Non-Current						3.4
33.5	31.1	36.9	Net Worth						38.3
100.0	100.0	100.0	Total Liabilities & Net Worth						100.0
			INCOME DATA						
100.0	100.0	100.0	Net Sales						100.0
36.8	36.0	35.4	Gross Profit						33.4
34.8	34.0	31.8	Operating Expenses						28.7
2.0	2.0	3.6	Operating Profit						4.7
.1	.5	.5	All Other Expenses (net)						.5
1.9	1.5	3.1	Profit Before Taxes						4.2
			RATIOS						
2.0	2.4	3.4							2.9
1.4	1.4	1.6	Current						1.4
1.0	1.0	1.0							1.0
1.1	1.3	1.4							1.4
.7	.8	.8	Quick						.8
.5	.4	.5							.5
23 / 15.9	19 / 19.6	16 / 23.4							17 / 21.2
44 / 8.3	35 / 10.5	34 / 10.8	Sales/Receivables						33 / 11.1
67 / 5.5	65 / 5.6	61 / 6.0							68 / 5.4
16 / 23.3	12 / 29.7	31 / 11.6							41 / 8.8
66 / 5.5	57 / 6.4	62 / 5.9	Cost of Sales/Inventory						61 / 6.0
126 / 2.9	121 / 3.0	156 / 2.3							132 / 2.8
31 / 11.6	13 / 27.5	23 / 15.8							35 / 10.5
62 / 5.9	45 / 8.2	58 / 6.3	Cost of Sales/Payables						74 / 5.0
91 / 4.0	79 / 4.6	97 / 3.8							123 / 3.0
4.7	5.8	4.0							4.1
11.0	17.7	10.0	Sales/Working Capital						13.6
128.9	167.8	NM							-992.1
17.6	10.3	14.2							24.3
(45) 3.5	(42) 4.0	(43) 5.4	EBIT/Interest						(23) 8.1
1.8	1.2	1.9							2.6
8.3	34.9	24.1	Net Profit + Depr., Dep.,						
(13) 2.1	(10) 7.4	(10) 5.0	Amort./Cur. Mat. L/T/D						
1.2	1.0	1.0							
.1	.2	.1							.1
.6	.4	.4	Fixed/Worth						.4
1.3	2.3	1.3							1.8
1.1	1.0	.6							.6
2.7	3.3	2.4	Debt/Worth						2.4
7.1	7.3	6.6							5.8
37.5	50.2	42.3	% Profit Before Taxes/Tangible						39.7
(47) 17.1	(38) 20.0	(49) 17.9	Net Worth						(27) 18.4
3.6	6.0	4.4							8.2
9.6	11.4	12.2	% Profit Before Taxes/Total						13.3
4.4	5.7	5.9	Assets						7.0
.7	1.1	1.6							2.3
48.6	58.8	51.5							44.0
27.7	42.2	23.5	Sales/Net Fixed Assets						18.0
10.6	14.2	11.0							8.9
3.4	5.2	4.6							3.0
2.3	2.2	2.2	Sales/Total Assets						2.1
1.5	1.7	1.4							1.4
.6	.5	.5							.5
(49) 1.2	(39) .9	(46) .9	% Depr., Dep., Amort./Sales						(26) 1.0
2.4	1.6	1.5							1.5
2.6	1.9	2.2	% Officers', Directors'						
(18) 5.7	(16) 5.6	(12) 4.2	Owners' Comp/Sales						
13.5	16.2	10.6							
1950974M	2070723M	2888461M	Net Sales ($)	1077M	14219M	23045M	12312M	121249M	2716559M
1203906M	930918M	1567954M	Total Assets ($)	967M	12177M	7967M	1694M	84268M	1460881M

M = $ thousand   MM = $ million
See Pages 11 through 21 for Explanation of Ratios and Data

Current Data Sorted by Assets / Comparative Historical Data

0-500M	500M-2MM	2-10MM	10-50MM	50-100MM	100-250MM	Type of Statement	4/1/02-3/31/03 ALL	4/1/03-3/31/04 ALL
	1	8	9	1		Unqualified	22	20
	2	20	4			Reviewed	32	34
6	14	20	1			Compiled	33	37
10	8	6	1			Tax Returns	14	22
7	6	9	11			Other	40	39
	47 (4/1-9/30/06)		97 (10/1/06-3/31/07)					
23	31	63	26	1		NUMBER OF STATEMENTS	141	152
%	%	%	%	%	%	ASSETS	%	%
15.8	12.0	8.9	2.5		D A T A	Cash & Equivalents	7.9	7.4
16.7	24.7	26.1	29.9			Trade Receivables (net)	25.4	26.1
22.0	34.6	28.8	25.9			Inventory	27.4	24.8
3.4	1.6	3.8	2.8			All Other Current	3.6	3.6
57.8	72.9	67.6	61.2			Total Current	64.3	61.8
30.5	18.1	21.9	28.6		N O T	Fixed Assets (net)	25.9	27.9
2.3	2.6	4.7	2.5			Intangibles (net)	2.7	2.4
9.4	6.4	5.9	7.8			All Other Non-Current	7.1	7.9
100.0	100.0	100.0	100.0			Total	100.0	100.0
					A V A I L A B L E	LIABILITIES		
34.8	21.1	18.2	16.2			Notes Payable-Short Term	11.3	14.3
10.2	2.2	1.9	4.1			Cur. Mat.-L.T.D.	4.4	4.0
16.6	20.5	17.5	19.1			Trade Payables	15.5	19.5
.2	.0	.5	1.0			Income Taxes Payable	.8	.7
12.9	6.8	8.5	11.6			All Other Current	9.3	8.0
74.7	50.6	46.6	51.9			Total Current	41.3	46.5
33.2	16.4	10.2	10.1			Long-Term Debt	15.9	15.8
.0	.3	.4	1.2			Deferred Taxes	.4	.3
16.9	8.8	3.2	7.1			All Other Non-Current	5.2	5.4
-24.8	23.8	39.6	29.7			Net Worth	37.2	32.0
100.0	100.0	100.0	100.0			Total Liabilties & Net Worth	100.0	100.0
						INCOME DATA		
100.0	100.0	100.0	100.0			Net Sales	100.0	100.0
37.9	35.1	33.4	32.9			Gross Profit	35.4	35.0
36.8	35.3	30.7	30.5			Operating Expenses	32.6	33.2
1.1	-.2	2.7	2.5			Operating Profit	2.8	1.8
2.1	.5	.6	-.2			All Other Expenses (net)	1.1	.5
-.9	-.7	2.1	2.6			Profit Before Taxes	1.7	1.3
						RATIOS		
2.2	3.3	2.3	1.8				2.7	2.4
.9	1.6	1.4	1.3			Current	1.5	1.5
.4	1.1	.9	1.1				1.0	.9
.9	1.8	1.1	1.0				1.5	1.3
(22) .6	.9	.7	.6			Quick	.8	.7
.2	.3	.4	.3				.4	.4
0 UND	**11** 34.6	**17** 21.3	**18** 20.7				**18** 19.9	**16** 22.8
12 31.5	**25** 14.7	**30** 12.0	**41** 8.9			Sales/Receivables	**30** 12.1	**29** 12.5
22 16.3	**36** 10.1	**42** 8.7	**57** 6.4				**46** 8.0	**43** 8.5
0 UND	**20** 18.2	**19** 18.9	**16** 23.1				**14** 27.0	**10** 36.8
12 30.3	**45** 8.1	**53** 6.9	**41** 8.8			Cost of Sales/Inventory	**44** 8.3	**36** 10.2
67 5.4	**162** 2.3	**111** 3.3	**167** 2.2				**119** 3.1	**100** 3.7
0 999.8	**13** 27.8	**9** 38.6	**18** 20.1				**12** 31.1	**14** 26.2
11 33.8	**29** 12.7	**31** 11.6	**29** 12.8			Cost of Sales/Payables	**24** 15.1	**28** 13.0
52 7.1	**52** 7.0	**53** 6.9	**55** 6.6				**40** 9.2	**51** 7.2
11.8	6.0	5.6	6.7				5.1	7.4
-444.8	9.8	16.7	15.2			Sales/Working Capital	14.9	20.4
-11.1	78.9	-87.8	69.8				NM	-58.4
15.5	17.3	9.2	3.7				6.6	6.5
(20) 1.3	(30) 1.6	(58) 2.5	2.7			EBIT/Interest	(126) 2.6	(144) 2.2
.0	-1.7	1.1	1.1				1.1	.2
		5.6	13.0				5.4	11.5
		(16) 4.1	(10) 4.8			Net Profit + Depr., Dep., Amort./Cur. Mat. L/T/D	(46) 2.9	(33) 1.8
		1.6	1.6				.8	.5
.8	.1	.1	.5				.2	.3
-10.7	.4	.5	.9			Fixed/Worth	.6	.8
-.8	9.8	1.7	1.6				2.2	3.1
4.0	1.4	.7	1.1				.8	1.0
-10.5	3.0	2.0	1.8			Debt/Worth	1.6	1.8
-3.1	14.8	4.6	3.8				5.1	7.6
311.5	63.9	31.1	28.2				31.3	39.1
(10) 87.1	(24) 22.4	(55) 12.2	(23) 8.6			% Profit Before Taxes/Tangible Net Worth	(122) 9.0	(131) 13.2
16.5	-2.2	4.3	3.9				1.6	.0
25.5	16.7	9.5	9.7				10.8	11.0
4.3	3.7	4.7	3.2			% Profit Before Taxes/Total Assets	3.8	3.8
-13.6	-6.5	.4	.1				.2	-1.3
45.3	60.0	47.7	50.0				37.7	32.5
20.0	26.9	20.8	9.0			Sales/Net Fixed Assets	18.0	13.9
11.2	10.8	6.9	3.8				4.9	5.9
7.8	4.7	3.8	3.4				3.9	4.5
5.4	3.3	2.6	2.6			Sales/Total Assets	2.7	2.8
2.3	2.3	1.9	1.4				1.6	2.0
.6	.4	.6	.5				.7	.7
(19) 1.2	(26) 1.1	(62) 1.0	1.3			% Depr., Dep., Amort./Sales	(126) 1.3	(134) 1.8
2.7	1.8	2.1	2.9				3.3	3.1
2.3	2.6	1.0					2.0	2.1
(11) 3.7	(20) 3.5	(30) 2.1				% Officers', Directors' Owners' Comp/Sales	(70) 4.4	(70) 4.1
6.9	6.0	7.0					6.8	7.7
42327M	121645M	846819M	1339377M	203725M		Net Sales ($)	3535376M	3306810M
6444M	34402M	281173M	622353M	99653M		Total Assets ($)	1981117M	1381783M

M = $ thousand MM = $ million

See Pages 11 through 21 for Explanation of Ratios and Data

Comparative Historical Data | | | Current Data Sorted by Sales

					Type of Statement						
20		12		19	Unqualified		1		1	7	10
30		22		26	Reviewed		2	2	7	12	3
33		34		41	Compiled	4	7	11	8	9	2
20		20		25	Tax Returns	5	5	6	6	2	1
40		30		33	Other	3	6	4	5	2	13
4/1/04- 3/31/05 ALL		4/1/05- 3/31/06 ALL		4/1/06- 3/31/07 ALL			47 (4/1-9/30/06)			97 (10/1/06-3/31/07)	
						0-1MM	1-3MM	3-5MM	5-10MM	10-25MM	25MM & OVER
143		118		144	NUMBER OF STATEMENTS	12	21	23	27	32	29
%		%		%	ASSETS	%	%	%	%	%	%
9.0		6.3		9.4	Cash & Equivalents	8.7	15.2	7.6	13.3	8.8	4.0
26.0		27.0		25.1	Trade Receivables (net)	14.1	15.9	21.3	26.3	30.0	32.7
25.4		27.4		28.6	Inventory	32.5	35.6	24.4	29.3	28.4	24.6
2.4		3.0		3.1	All Other Current	3.4	1.0	3.8	1.7	5.7	2.2
62.9		63.7		66.1	Total Current	58.8	67.8	57.1	70.7	72.9	63.6
25.6		25.5		23.5	Fixed Assets (net)	30.6	21.8	29.8	20.1	18.3	25.8
3.6		2.9		3.5	Intangibles (net)	.4	5.5	2.8	5.6	2.4	2.9
7.9		7.9		6.9	All Other Non-Current	10.2	5.0	10.3	3.7	6.4	7.7
100.0		100.0		100.0	Total	100.0	100.0	100.0	100.0	100.0	100.0
					LIABILITIES						
17.0		19.0		21.3	Notes Payable-Short Term	46.4	24.7	20.4	19.0	17.2	15.9
4.1		2.7		3.9	Cur. Mat.-L.T.D.	2.9	10.9	2.7	2.1	1.3	4.8
18.0		16.8		18.3	Trade Payables	20.0	12.1	20.0	14.7	19.7	22.6
.5		.3		.4	Income Taxes Payable	.2	.0	.3	.3	.7	.9
8.1		6.9		9.4	All Other Current	5.6	14.9	7.2	4.4	11.6	11.0
47.7		45.7		53.4	Total Current	75.1	62.5	50.6	40.5	50.5	55.2
16.9		16.9		15.1	Long-Term Debt	42.7	19.8	20.0	12.1	4.7	10.8
.4		.4		.5	Deferred Taxes	.0	.3	.0	.8	.7	.6
4.8		10.1		7.9	All Other Non-Current	5.4	17.0	11.2	2.8	3.9	9.1
30.2		26.9		23.1	Net Worth	-23.2	.4	18.3	43.9	40.2	24.3
100.0		100.0		100.0	Total Liabilities & Net Worth	100.0	100.0	100.0	100.0	100.0	100.0
					INCOME DATA						
100.0		100.0		100.0	Net Sales	100.0	100.0	100.0	100.0	100.0	100.0
36.2		36.2		34.4	Gross Profit	39.2	39.6	37.3	32.9	30.4	32.2
34.7		34.6		32.6	Operating Expenses	44.4	36.9	36.9	29.9	27.3	29.8
1.4		1.6		1.8	Operating Profit	-5.3	2.7	.4	3.1	3.1	2.4
.5		1.1		.7	All Other Expenses (net)	3.6	1.1	1.1	.5	.1	.0
1.0		.5		1.0	Profit Before Taxes	-8.8	1.7	-.7	2.6	3.0	2.4
					RATIOS						
2.0		2.4		2.1		1.7	4.7	1.9	4.0	2.1	1.8
1.4		1.4		1.4	Current	1.0	1.6	1.2	1.9	1.4	1.3
.9		1.0		.9		.4	.7	.8	1.0	1.1	1.0
1.1		1.2		1.1		.8	2.2	.9	2.0	1.1	1.1
.7 (117)		.7 (143)		.7	Quick	(11) .4	.5	.6	.9	.8	.7
.4		.4		.3		.1	.2	.3	.5	.4	.4
15	24.2	18	20.7	12	29.4	Sales/Receivables	1	462.5	0 UND	10	36.3	18	20.6	21	17.1	17	21.8
29	12.5	33	10.9	29	12.8		12	30.9	22	16.7	22	16.4	30	12.1	30	12.0	39	9.4
46	8.0	51	7.2	42	8.8		24	15.5	37	9.8	34	10.8	53	6.9	40	9.1	54	6.8
8	46.9	15	24.6	14	25.4	Cost of Sales/Inventory	0	UND	7	51.9	2	159.6	28	13.2	5	74.0	14	26.6
38	9.5	49	7.4	44	8.2		64	5.7	75	4.9	30	12.1	53	6.9	44	8.3	41	8.9
84	4.3	124	2.9	118	3.1		191	1.9	246	1.5	123	3.0	86	4.3	111	3.3	118	3.1
13	28.2	15	24.0	10	37.1	Cost of Sales/Payables	5	78.6	2	209.6	8	47.7	9	38.6	10	35.3	17	21.2
25	14.7	29	12.4	29	12.7		30	12.0	20	18.0	27	13.7	28	12.9	31	12.0	34	10.7
49	7.4	54	6.8	53	6.9		95	3.8	41	8.8	70	5.2	50	7.2	47	7.7	53	6.9
	7.8		5.6		6.4	Sales/Working Capital		7.7		3.9		7.8		4.2		5.6		10.7
	20.7		15.2		17.0			NM		9.1		36.7		10.6		16.3		17.4
	-221.9		NM		-62.7			-15.1		-56.2		-16.1		96.8		304.4		NM
	6.2		3.8		7.9	EBIT/Interest		2.1		16.7		6.5		18.0		15.0		4.1
(130)	2.3	(106)	1.5	(135)	2.2		(10)	.0	(19)	1.6	(22)	1.2	(25)	2.2	(31)	3.3	(28)	2.8
	.7		-.2		.3			-2.7		-1.2		-.5		.5		1.8		1.1
	9.3		7.4		5.7	Net Profit + Depr., Dep., Amort./Cur. Mat. L/T/D												5.8
(38)	4.4	(26)	2.7	(30)	3.8											(11)	4.6
	1.4		.0		1.5													.3
	.2		.2		.2	Fixed/Worth		.5		.1		.4		.1		.1		.6
	.7		.8		.9			NM		1.4		1.6		.8		.4		1.0
	2.6		6.3		3.6			-.7		-1.2		-7.0		1.5		1.0		2.5
	.9		1.1		1.0	Debt/Worth		3.9		.8		2.4		.4		.8		1.1
	2.0		2.7		2.6			-15.9		5.1		3.8		1.7		1.4		2.3
	5.9		14.9		13.6			-3.1		-5.8		-13.4		7.0		3.3		8.4
	37.2		19.9		41.1	% Profit Before Taxes/Tangible Net Worth				101.5		79.1		28.0		41.2		37.7
(123)	10.9	(92)	7.6	(112)	15.0				(13)	21.9	(17)	12.2	(24)	11.4	(29)	14.7	(24)	19.5
	1.8		.1		3.9					.3		-3.9		1.1		7.9		6.8
	11.5		5.7		13.1	% Profit Before Taxes/Total Assets		18.7		20.9		7.5		13.5		13.5		9.7
	2.9		1.8		3.6			-6.1		3.7		.4		5.2		5.0		3.6
	.0		-3.5		-2.6			-47.3		-4.7		-8.5		.1		2.5		.2
	40.0		34.3		47.1	Sales/Net Fixed Assets		36.2		55.9		41.1		50.4		48.8		88.9
	18.4		16.6		19.8			10.9		18.8		18.2		26.9		23.9		16.2
	5.9		5.0		7.8			5.8		10.4		5.6		6.7		11.8		5.3
	4.4		3.7		4.2	Sales/Total Assets		5.0		5.0		5.8		4.2		4.2		4.2
	2.9		2.6		3.0			2.6		3.0		2.5		2.8		3.1		3.0
	1.8		1.9		2.0			1.8		1.9		1.6		1.9		2.3		2.1
	.7		.7		.6	% Depr., Dep., Amort./Sales		.5		.3		.8		.6		.6		.4
(117)	1.6	(102)	1.3	(134)	1.2		(10)	2.4	(16)	1.2	(21)	1.4	(26)	1.1		1.0		1.2
	3.1		2.8		2.1			3.1		2.7		2.2		2.2		1.5		1.7
	1.9		2.1		1.8	% Officers', Directors' Owners' Comp/Sales				3.0		2.4		1.8		1.0		
(67)	4.3	(57)	4.4	(68)	2.9				(13)	5.3	(12)	4.7	(15)	2.7	(16)	1.9		
	6.9		6.8		6.3					7.4		9.8		6.0		2.4		
2423623M		2674683M		2553893M	Net Sales ($)	7467M	42223M	89037M	207123M	504699M	1703344M
1017982M		1259142M		1044025M	Total Assets ($)	3193M	20093M	37895M	92584M	207064M	683196M

M = $ thousand   MM = $ million
See Pages 11 through 21 for Explanation of Ratios and Data

Current Data Sorted by Assets   Comparative Historical Data

0-500M	500M-2MM	2-10MM	10-50MM	50-100MM	100-250MM	Type of Statement	4/1/02-3/31/03 ALL	4/1/03-3/31/04 ALL
		8	12	2	3	Unqualified	20	30
	1	25	16			Reviewed	37	30
1	3	13	2			Compiled	35	44
4	4	5			1	Tax Returns	5	10
1	3	14		1	1	Other	18	20
	27 (4/1-9/30/06)		102 (10/1/06-3/31/07)					
6	11	65	39	3	5	NUMBER OF STATEMENTS	115	134
%	%	%	%	%	%	**ASSETS**	%	%
	3.7	7.8	8.0			Cash & Equivalents	8.4	9.0
	38.8	33.9	36.9			Trade Receivables (net)	32.9	30.0
	34.8	39.1	31.5			Inventory	35.7	38.2
	.4	2.7	2.6			All Other Current	2.1	3.4
	77.7	83.5	79.1			Total Current	79.1	80.7
	9.7	9.9	12.0			Fixed Assets (net)	11.8	11.0
	3.1	1.1	1.5			Intangibles (net)	2.4	1.7
	9.5	5.6	7.4			All Other Non-Current	6.7	6.6
	100.0	100.0	100.0			Total	100.0	100.0
						LIABILITIES		
	31.1	23.2	30.3			Notes Payable-Short Term	23.8	21.2
	.9	1.9	1.0			Cur. Mat.-L.T.D.	2.0	2.5
	22.5	18.3	18.0			Trade Payables	16.2	17.5
	.0	.2	.0			Income Taxes Payable	.7	.3
	4.1	6.7	8.0			All Other Current	8.1	10.0
	58.6	50.1	57.4			Total Current	50.9	51.4
	7.3	9.0	7.6			Long-Term Debt	8.1	6.6
	.1	.2	.3			Deferred Taxes	.1	.1
	.1	4.8	3.6			All Other Non-Current	2.6	3.0
	33.9	35.9	31.1			Net Worth	38.2	38.8
	100.0	100.0	100.0			Total Liabilties & Net Worth	100.0	100.0
						INCOME DATA		
	100.0	100.0	100.0			Net Sales	100.0	100.0
	17.8	8.9	7.6			Gross Profit	10.1	10.3
	16.3	8.0	6.0			Operating Expenses	8.8	8.5
	1.5	.9	1.6			Operating Profit	1.3	1.8
	.0	.2	.2			All Other Expenses (net)	.3	.0
	1.6	.8	1.5			Profit Before Taxes	1.0	1.8
						RATIOS		
	2.5	2.6	1.7			Current	2.3	2.4
	1.3	1.7	1.4				1.5	1.5
	1.1	1.2	1.1				1.2	1.2
	1.5	1.4	1.0			Quick	1.2	1.1
	.6	.8	.8				.7	.8
	.4	.5	.6				.5	.5
	10 36.3	10 36.0	12 30.2			Sales/Receivables	10 35.0	8 46.4
	16 23.5	15 25.0	17 20.9				16 23.5	14 25.4
	24 15.1	21 17.1	25 14.5				22 16.4	21 17.4
	8 44.0	13 28.9	10 36.2			Cost of Sales/Inventory	10 35.6	11 33.3
	19 19.0	18 20.8	13 27.2				18 19.8	17 21.8
	58 6.3	37 9.9	24 15.2				26 14.0	26 14.1
	3 140.0	4 103.2	4 96.6			Cost of Sales/Payables	3 114.8	3 124.4
	9 42.9	7 54.0	6 60.0				7 55.8	7 56.1
	37 9.8	16 23.1	13 27.8				13 28.3	14 25.6
	7.5	14.5	13.0			Sales/Working Capital	16.9	18.0
	30.7	24.7	45.5				29.4	27.1
	148.6	56.7	176.0				89.9	73.4
	13.8	9.2	8.8			EBIT/Interest	8.2	9.7
	5.8	(63) 2.2	(37) 2.4				(104) 3.0	(118) 4.4
	1.5	1.0	1.1				1.6	2.0
		5.7	6.9			Net Profit + Depr., Dep., Amort./Cur. Mat. L/T/D	4.0	9.2
	(19)	2.5	(15) 3.0				(32) 2.1	(36) 3.9
		1.3	1.0				.9	1.7
	.0	.1	.2			Fixed/Worth	.1	.1
	.2	.2	.4				.3	.2
	.8	.7	1.5				.8	.6
	1.0	.8	1.3			Debt/Worth	.8	.7
	2.1	1.9	2.5				1.9	1.7
	9.7	6.3	7.9				4.2	4.0
	52.3	24.1	27.8			% Profit Before Taxes/Tangible Net Worth	27.1	30.3
	(10) 26.1	(60) 9.5	(36) 14.3				(108) 14.5	(128) 16.9
	-10.1	1.5	3.4				4.6	8.3
	20.1	6.9	9.9			% Profit Before Taxes/Total Assets	9.6	10.9
	10.6	2.5	3.4				4.3	6.3
	1.6	.1	.3				1.6	2.3
	371.1	441.3	221.5			Sales/Net Fixed Assets	221.2	231.9
	96.6	135.5	82.9				91.8	106.1
	23.6	56.0	45.4				39.1	44.4
	13.4	10.1	9.9			Sales/Total Assets	10.5	11.3
	5.1	7.7	8.0				8.1	8.3
	4.2	5.2	5.4				5.9	6.1
		.1	.1			% Depr., Dep., Amort./Sales	.2	.1
	(56)	.2	(36) .2				(101) .3	(117) .3
		.3	.4				.6	.4
		.2	.2			% Officers', Directors' Owners' Comp/Sales	.3	.4
	(27)	.5	(10) .4				(55) .6	(56) .6
		.9	1.6				1.5	1.2
29650M	96771M	2830166M	5912080M	1326585M	3025884M	Net Sales ($)	14527330M	15858677M
1676M	13424M	348846M	805157M	225614M	651454M	Total Assets ($)	2024399M	2381544M

© RMA 2007

M = $ thousand   MM = $ million
See Pages 11 through 21 for Explanation of Ratios and Data

Comparative Historical Data | Current Data Sorted by Sales

			Type of Statement						
26	34	25	Unqualified					1	24
45	38	42	Reviewed				1	9	32
30	16	19	Compiled			1	1	6	11
12	13	14	Tax Returns		3	2	4	3	2
20	25	29	Other	1			4	2	22
4/1/04- 3/31/05 ALL	4/1/05- 3/31/06 ALL	4/1/06- 3/31/07 ALL			27 (4/1-9/30/06)		102 (10/1/06-3/31/07)		
				0-1MM	1-3MM	3-5MM	5-10MM	10-25MM	25MM & OVER
133	126	129	NUMBER OF STATEMENTS	1	3	3	10	21	91
%	%	%	ASSETS	%	%	%	%	%	%
10.1	9.2	8.7	Cash & Equivalents				3.0	13.3	7.9
30.6	31.8	34.2	Trade Receivables (net)				30.2	34.3	35.2
35.5	34.1	35.8	Inventory				33.6	36.5	35.7
2.0	4.0	2.5	All Other Current				5.6	1.1	2.4
78.3	79.1	81.3	Total Current				72.4	85.2	81.2
12.6	10.8	10.5	Fixed Assets (net)				14.3	10.3	10.5
2.4	2.2	1.3	Intangibles (net)				.2	2.1	1.4
6.7	7.8	6.9	All Other Non-Current				13.2	2.4	6.9
100.0	100.0	100.0	Total				100.0	100.0	100.0
			LIABILITIES						
21.7	20.2	25.0	Notes Payable-Short Term				27.6	18.0	27.1
1.5	3.3	2.0	Cur. Mat.-L.T.D.				.7	1.2	2.4
15.7	17.8	19.2	Trade Payables				22.9	18.7	17.8
.3	.3	.1	Income Taxes Payable				.0	.1	.1
7.1	6.8	6.9	All Other Current				9.8	3.4	7.5
46.1	48.3	53.1	Total Current				61.1	41.3	54.9
8.9	12.3	9.1	Long-Term Debt				8.4	8.6	9.9
.2	.2	.2	Deferred Taxes				.1	.0	.3
4.7	3.4	4.1	All Other Non-Current				8.5	4.4	3.2
40.1	35.9	33.5	Net Worth				21.9	45.7	31.8
100.0	100.0	100.0	Total Liabilities & Net Worth				100.0	100.0	100.0
			INCOME DATA						
100.0	100.0	100.0	Net Sales				100.0	100.0	100.0
10.5	8.9	9.6	Gross Profit				19.6	11.9	7.3
8.5	7.5	8.2	Operating Expenses				16.4	10.5	6.2
2.0	1.5	1.4	Operating Profit				3.2	1.4	1.1
.1	.4	.1	All Other Expenses (net)				.2	.1	.1
2.0	1.1	1.3	Profit Before Taxes				2.9	1.4	1.0
			RATIOS						
2.7	2.5	2.5					2.2	3.1	2.3
1.5	1.5	1.4	Current				1.2	2.4	1.4
1.2	1.2	1.1					.9	1.7	1.1
1.4	1.3	1.4					1.2	1.8	1.2
.8	(125) .8	.8	Quick				.6	1.4	.7
.6	.6	.5					.0	.5	.6
10 37.9	10 38.3	11 34.7		1 648.8			9 40.2	11 33.1	
15 23.7	15 23.8	16 23.5	Sales/Receivables	22 17.0			14 26.1	16 22.9	
21 17.7	22 16.7	22 16.6		31 11.7			42 8.7	20 18.1	
11 33.7	10 35.4	11 33.9		10 36.6			9 39.9	11 33.6	
16 23.5	16 23.4	17 21.3	Cost of Sales/Inventory	43 8.4			21 17.1	16 23.2	
25 14.5	26 14.1	33 11.2		60 6.1			53 7.0	24 15.0	
3 120.8	4 100.0	4 98.4		5 69.1			3 145.5	4 97.8	
5 70.6	7 48.8	7 51.0	Cost of Sales/Payables	13 28.2			9 42.9	7 55.9	
12 30.7	13 27.4	16 23.3		35 10.5			28 12.8	13 27.8	
14.4	15.6	14.2					14.3	6.8	19.2
29.6	32.6	33.2	Sales/Working Capital				56.9	14.7	42.0
64.9	57.3	78.7					NM	18.7	93.7
10.0	9.9	9.7					15.0		6.2
(119) 3.5	(114) 2.8	(120) 2.2	EBIT/Interest				3.7	(86) 1.8	
1.6	1.3	1.1					1.5		1.0
15.3	8.3	5.8							6.3
(32) 3.8	(43) 3.3	(38) 2.7	Net Profit + Depr., Dep., Amort./Cur. Mat. L/T/D					(31) 2.8	
2.7	1.5	1.0							1.0
.1	.1	.1					.0	.0	.1
.3	.2	.3	Fixed/Worth				.3	.1	.3
.7	.7	.8					2.0	.4	1.0
.7	.8	.8					1.0	.5	1.1
1.7	1.8	2.2	Debt/Worth				5.0	1.4	2.5
4.2	4.5	6.9					12.8	2.4	7.0
28.3	25.4	30.4					31.1		22.1
(122) 14.3	(119) 11.1	(119) 12.0	% Profit Before Taxes/Tangible Net Worth			(20)	10.7	(83) 10.8	
6.2	5.2	4.1					4.1		2.9
9.2	6.8	9.8					22.1	9.0	7.7
4.4	4.2	4.3	% Profit Before Taxes/Total Assets				11.5	5.4	2.5
1.0	1.2	.4					.9	1.1	.1
236.8	356.3	332.2					UND	721.8	258.5
85.8	113.7	105.4	Sales/Net Fixed Assets				85.6	143.8	105.3
41.6	40.8	47.7					17.9	39.1	50.9
10.5	11.1	10.2					10.8	9.2	10.6
7.8	8.3	7.7	Sales/Total Assets				4.1	5.5	8.3
5.5	5.0	4.9					2.9	3.3	5.8
.1	.1	.1						.1	.1
(120) .3	(108) .2	(106) .2	% Depr., Dep., Amort./Sales			(16)		.2	(82) .2
.5	.4	.4						.5	.3
.3	.3	.3							.3
(53) .7	(47) .6	(48) .7	% Officers', Directors' Owners' Comp/Sales					(30) .5	
1.3	1.3	1.9							1.1
11444778M	16891458M	13221136M	Net Sales ($)	601M	7009M	10202M	76258M	375676M	12751390M
1968190M	2523983M	2046171M	Total Assets ($)	148M	899M	2667M	17665M	81085M	1943707M

M = $ thousand   MM = $ million
See Pages 11 through 21 for Explanation of Ratios and Data

Current Data Sorted by Assets   Comparative Historical Data

							Type of Statement		
	2	2	7				Unqualified	10	7
	2	10	5				Reviewed	20	16
	3	3	2				Compiled	16	20
1	7	6					Tax Returns	9	14
1	2	4	6				Other	15	10
	11 (4/1-9/30/06)		52 (10/1/06-3/31/07)					4/1/02-3/31/03	4/1/03-3/31/04
0-500M	500M-2MM	2-10MM	10-50MM	50-100MM	100-250MM		NUMBER OF STATEMENTS	ALL	ALL
2	16	25	20					70	67
%	%	%	%	%	%		ASSETS	%	%
	9.7	5.4	5.2				Cash & Equivalents	8.4	9.8
	28.4	31.3	31.7	D	D		Trade Receivables (net)	30.2	30.3
	40.1	36.1	36.5	A	A		Inventory	39.8	35.0
	1.5	1.1	5.4	T	T		All Other Current	1.5	4.0
	79.6	74.0	78.8	A	A		Total Current	79.9	79.1
	17.0	15.4	9.3				Fixed Assets (net)	11.9	12.4
	.8	3.5	6.2	N	N		Intangibles (net)	3.5	3.2
	2.6	7.1	5.8	O	O		All Other Non-Current	4.7	5.4
	100.0	100.0	100.0	T	T		Total	100.0	100.0
							LIABILITIES		
	10.3	15.2	13.0	A	A		Notes Payable-Short Term	11.9	11.8
	2.2	1.2	2.6	V	V		Cur. Mat.-L.T.D.	2.1	4.6
	24.0	30.3	21.8	A	A		Trade Payables	24.9	24.0
	.2	.4	.4	I	I		Income Taxes Payable	.4	.2
	4.3	6.1	11.6	L	L		All Other Current	7.7	10.6
	41.1	53.2	49.2	A	A		Total Current	47.0	51.2
	8.2	10.7	9.8	B	B		Long-Term Debt	9.5	8.4
	.0	.2	.4	L	L		Deferred Taxes	.2	.3
	3.1	2.9	4.8	E	E		All Other Non-Current	6.6	5.7
	47.7	33.0	35.9				Net Worth	36.6	34.5
	100.0	100.0	100.0				Total Liabilties & Net Worth	100.0	100.0
							INCOME DATA		
	100.0	100.0	100.0				Net Sales	100.0	100.0
	38.0	27.7	29.1				Gross Profit	33.3	32.8
	33.1	25.3	24.5				Operating Expenses	30.0	30.2
	5.0	2.4	4.5				Operating Profit	3.4	2.6
	.2	-1.1	.4				All Other Expenses (net)	.4	.0
	4.7	3.5	4.1				Profit Before Taxes	2.9	2.5
							RATIOS		
	3.3	2.3	2.4					3.1	2.3
	2.1	1.3	1.7				Current	1.7	1.6
	1.4	1.0	1.2					1.3	1.2
	2.0	1.3	1.1					1.5	1.3
	1.0	.6	.8				Quick	.8	.8
	.5	.4	.4					.5	.5
28	12.9	33	11.1	34	10.7			31	11.9	27	13.3
36	10.0	37	9.8	43	8.5		Sales/Receivables	40	9.1	36	10.1
45	8.1	51	7.2	45	8.1			50	7.4	47	7.8
44	8.3	42	8.8	49	7.4			50	7.3	39	9.3
84	4.3	77	4.8	67	5.4		Cost of Sales/Inventory	75	4.9	64	5.7
115	3.2	102	3.6	80	4.6			123	3.0	108	3.4
22	16.8	32	11.4	21	17.7			26	13.9	21	17.1
43	8.4	48	7.5	40	9.2		Cost of Sales/Payables	42	8.7	37	9.9
63	5.8	81	4.5	56	6.6			64	5.7	68	5.7
	5.6	8.0	6.1					5.5	6.5
	7.9	12.4	9.5				Sales/Working Capital	9.8	11.5
	13.3	533.7	16.6					15.9	23.8
	28.7	9.6	9.4					11.1	11.0
(15)	7.3	(22)	3.5		6.3		EBIT/Interest	(61)	3.6	(58)	3.6
	1.2	1.8	3.0					1.6	1.6
							Net Profit + Depr., Dep.,		15.2		15.7
							Amort./Cur. Mat. L/T/D	(20)	6.2	(19)	5.6
								3.5	1.2
	.1	.1	.1					.1	.1
	.3	.3	.2				Fixed/Worth	.3	.3
	.7	1.0	1.3					.9	1.0
	.6	1.1	.9					.6	.8
	.9	2.7	1.8				Debt/Worth	1.7	1.8
	2.7	6.9	33.2					5.9	6.5
	35.3	39.4	38.5				% Profit Before Taxes/Tangible	36.6	26.9
	18.9	(22)	26.1	(16)	23.4		Net Worth	(61)	18.5	(59)	14.5
	4.7	11.7	14.1					6.4	3.4
	19.7	11.9	14.9				% Profit Before Taxes/Total	13.4	9.9
	10.2	8.0	10.0				Assets	5.8	5.3
	1.1	2.1	6.1					1.9	1.0
	59.5	101.3	107.1					67.2	84.9
	24.5	33.3	65.3				Sales/Net Fixed Assets	32.7	38.4
	11.3	13.1	28.3					16.3	13.8
	3.8	3.8	3.4					3.6	3.6
	3.0	2.8	2.8				Sales/Total Assets	2.9	2.9
	2.1	1.8	2.4					2.0	2.3
	.6	.4	.4					.5	.5
(12)	1.0	(21)	.8	(17)	.6		% Depr., Dep., Amort./Sales	(62)	.9	(55)	.7
	1.8	1.5	.8					1.5	1.5
	1.8	1.7						1.5	1.4
(11)	3.4	(15)	3.0				% Officers', Directors'	(26)	3.6	(29)	3.0
	4.0	5.3					Owners' Comp/Sales	5.7	4.8
1867M	66368M	315959M	1448002M				Net Sales ($)	2530535M	1736261M
527M	22466M	114447M	528639M				Total Assets ($)	1341270M	738140M

M = $ thousand   MM = $ million
See Pages 11 through 21 for Explanation of Ratios and Data

Comparative Historical Data

Current Data Sorted by Sales

				Type of Statement						
7		2	11	Unqualified			2	1	1	7
14		12	17	Reviewed			5	7	5	5
10		8	8	Compiled			2	2	2	2
8		12	14	Tax Returns		5	3	4	1	1
19		17	13	Other	1	1	2	2	1	6
4/1/04-3/31/05 ALL		4/1/05-3/31/06 ALL	4/1/06-3/31/07 ALL		1	11 (4/1-9/30/06)		52 (10/1/06-3/31/07)		
					0-1MM	1-3MM	3-5MM	5-10MM	10-25MM	25MM & OVER
58		51	63	NUMBER OF STATEMENTS	1	6	9	14	12	21
%		%	%	ASSETS	%	%	%	%	%	%
7.3		5.5	6.4	Cash & Equivalents				6.5	1.7	5.6
28.5		32.2	31.8	Trade Receivables (net)				26.4	38.1	33.2
37.9		38.5	36.8	Inventory				43.2	38.7	35.6
4.1		2.0	2.5	All Other Current				1.0	1.0	5.1
77.7		78.3	77.5	Total Current				77.1	79.5	79.5
11.1		11.3	13.6	Fixed Assets (net)				12.1	11.1	8.9
4.2		4.8	3.6	Intangibles (net)				2.2	5.4	5.9
7.0		5.7	5.3	All Other Non-Current				8.6	4.0	5.7
100.0		100.0	100.0	Total				100.0	100.0	100.0
				LIABILITIES						
13.0		12.8	13.4	Notes Payable-Short Term				10.7	21.9	12.3
1.8		3.2	1.9	Cur. Mat.-L.T.D.				2.8	1.2	2.5
19.0		25.0	25.5	Trade Payables				30.7	36.1	23.5
.2		.3	.3	Income Taxes Payable				.4	.4	.4
11.9		10.2	7.8	All Other Current				4.6	5.6	11.1
46.0		51.5	48.9	Total Current				49.1	65.1	49.8
9.4		8.8	10.5	Long-Term Debt				7.9	8.3	9.3
.2		.2	.2	Deferred Taxes				.1	.3	.3
3.2		5.1	3.5	All Other Non-Current				2.1	2.0	4.5
41.3		34.5	36.9	Net Worth				40.8	24.3	36.0
100.0		100.0	100.0	Total Liabilities & Net Worth				100.0	100.0	100.0
				INCOME DATA						
100.0		100.0	100.0	Net Sales				100.0	100.0	100.0
33.6		31.2	30.6	Gross Profit				32.4	24.2	28.2
32.1		28.1	26.8	Operating Expenses				28.8	21.4	23.7
1.5		3.1	3.7	Operating Profit				3.6	2.8	4.5
.3		.2	-.2	All Other Expenses (net)				-.6	.3	.4
1.3		2.9	3.9	Profit Before Taxes				4.2	2.6	4.1
				RATIOS						
3.0		2.4	2.5					2.3	2.0	2.3
1.7		1.6	1.6	Current				1.5	1.3	1.7
1.2		1.2	1.2					1.2	1.0	1.2
1.4		1.2	1.3					1.0	1.3	1.2
.7		.7	.8	Quick				.6	.6	.8
.5		.5	.5					.4	.4	.5

29	12.7	27	13.6	31	11.7				24	15.2	28	13.0	35	10.5
39	9.2	37	9.8	39	9.3	Sales/Receivables			36	10.1	38	9.6	43	8.4
48	7.7	46	8.0	49	7.5				43	8.5	57	6.4	48	7.6
54	6.8	44	8.2	44	8.2				52	7.0	32	11.6	46	7.9
84	4.4	70	5.2	73	5.0	Cost of Sales/Inventory			98	3.7	58	6.3	65	5.6
130	2.8	91	4.0	101	3.6				113	3.2	86	4.2	80	4.6
20	18.4	22	16.4	25	14.9				36	10.1	31	11.7	22	17.0
40	9.1	38	9.6	44	8.4	Cost of Sales/Payables			57	6.4	46	8.0	42	8.7
59	6.2	60	6.1	64	5.7				91	4.0	68	5.4	57	6.4
	4.4		7.4		6.4					7.9		8.1		6.2
	8.1		9.9		9.9	Sales/Working Capital				10.6		23.1		9.9
	20.4		20.2		17.5					20.4		766.8		16.5
	10.6		14.7		10.3					29.1		14.7		9.4
(48)	4.2	(48)	5.3	(58)	5.7	EBIT/Interest		(13)		6.8		4.4	(20)	6.3
	1.4		2.2		1.9					1.2		1.9		3.0
	8.5		13.3		15.2	Net Profit + Depr., Dep.,								
(20)	2.5	(14)	7.4	(17)	5.9	Amort./Cur. Mat. L/T/D								
	-.2		1.7		2.0									
	.1		.1		.1					.1		.2		.1
	.2		.2		.3	Fixed/Worth				.3		.3		.2
	.8		.6		.9					.8		1.0		1.1
	.6		.7		.7					.7		1.8		.9
	1.4		1.8		1.8	Debt/Worth				2.1		4.5		1.8
	6.7		7.8		6.3					3.1		12.8		24.2
	38.0		37.7		38.7	% Profit Before Taxes/Tangible				37.9		49.4		36.8
(50)	15.5	(43)	21.0	(55)	22.8	Net Worth		(13)		19.3	(10)	25.6	(17)	23.6
	2.2		11.1		11.8					3.3		12.9		16.3
	12.0		13.1		14.5	% Profit Before Taxes/Total				18.0		11.2		14.6
	4.8		8.1		8.8	Assets				8.8		7.0		10.7
	.5		3.4		3.6					.5		2.2		6.3
	94.1		125.1		88.8					52.4		122.6		111.5
	33.3		48.2		36.6	Sales/Net Fixed Assets				31.6		50.0		66.0
	18.4		27.2		16.1					15.9		15.6		30.8
	3.2		4.0		3.6					3.5		4.1		3.6
	2.6		3.0		2.9	Sales/Total Assets				2.9		3.7		2.9
	1.6		2.5		2.2					2.4		2.7		2.4
	.5		.3		.4					.4		.4		.4
(47)	.8	(42)	.6	(51)	.7	% Depr., Dep., Amort./Sales		(13)		1.0	(10)	.4	(18)	.6
	1.3		1.0		1.3					1.5		1.1		.8
	2.0		2.0		1.8					1.6				
(25)	3.1	(21)	4.2	(29)	3.0	% Officers', Directors' Owners' Comp/Sales		(10)		2.8				
	5.6		7.0		3.9					5.6				

			Net Sales ($)						
2052753M	1730077M	1832196M	Net Sales ($)	585M	12250M	35436M	97251M	198094M	1488580M
1027426M	663509M	666079M	Total Assets ($)	131M	6272M	21284M	36667M	63176M	538549M

M = $ thousand   MM = $ million
See Pages 11 through 21 for Explanation of Ratios and Data

Current Data Sorted by Assets | Comparative Historical Data

						Type of Statement		
2	3	24	37	9	6	Unqualified	76	74
1	20	72	23	1		Reviewed	132	127
7	35	47	4			Compiled	94	174
33	73	32				Tax Returns	53	72
10	40	67	46	6	8	Other	128	151
	130 (4/1-9/30/06)		476 (10/1/06-3/31/07)				4/1/02-3/31/03	4/1/03-3/31/04
0-500M	500M-2MM	2-10MM	10-50MM	50-100MM	100-250MM		ALL	ALL
53	171	242	110	16	14	NUMBER OF STATEMENTS	483	598
%	%	%	%	%	%	ASSETS	%	%
15.6	9.5	8.3	6.1	14.8	8.7	Cash & Equivalents	9.2	8.5
25.3	35.0	34.3	31.7	25.1	29.4	Trade Receivables (net)	31.5	31.8
27.6	33.1	33.2	34.2	29.3	28.1	Inventory	35.2	34.0
3.3	1.5	2.8	3.0	6.9	3.6	All Other Current	2.5	3.1
71.7	79.1	78.7	75.0	76.1	69.8	Total Current	78.4	77.4
17.5	13.4	12.4	12.9	16.2	14.9	Fixed Assets (net)	12.6	14.3
4.4	2.4	3.7	4.2	3.8	12.3	Intangibles (net)	3.3	2.9
6.3	5.0	5.2	7.9	3.8	3.0	All Other Non-Current	5.8	5.4
100.0	100.0	100.0	100.0	100.0	100.0	Total	100.0	100.0
						LIABILITIES		
28.0	15.2	16.5	19.1	13.1	13.2	Notes Payable-Short Term	16.4	16.9
5.7	3.4	2.4	1.6	3.3	1.7	Cur. Mat.-L.T.D.	3.4	2.9
16.5	24.3	20.8	20.5	16.6	20.0	Trade Payables	21.4	20.4
.2	.1	.3	.2	.3	1.7	Income Taxes Payable	.3	.3
24.9	10.4	7.7	8.2	12.8	10.6	All Other Current	10.1	10.3
75.3	53.4	47.7	49.6	46.1	47.3	Total Current	51.6	50.8
27.5	10.0	8.9	9.6	9.3	15.6	Long-Term Debt	9.9	10.8
.0	.1	.1	.2	.6	.0	Deferred Taxes	.2	.3
11.4	7.2	4.6	6.3	4.0	8.3	All Other Non-Current	5.8	6.7
-14.2	29.3	38.8	34.4	39.9	28.8	Net Worth	32.5	31.5
100.0	100.0	100.0	100.0	100.0	100.0	Total Liabilties & Net Worth	100.0	100.0
						INCOME DATA		
100.0	100.0	100.0	100.0	100.0	100.0	Net Sales	100.0	100.0
44.1	32.0	31.8	29.4	30.7	27.1	Gross Profit	33.1	33.7
41.2	28.4	26.8	24.6	22.6	23.6	Operating Expenses	29.2	30.4
2.9	3.7	5.0	4.9	8.0	3.5	Operating Profit	3.9	3.3
1.9	.7	1.0	1.7	.7	2.7	All Other Expenses (net)	.8	.6
1.0	3.0	4.1	3.2	7.3	.8	Profit Before Taxes	3.1	2.7
						RATIOS		
3.2	2.6	2.7	2.1	2.2	2.2		2.6	2.4
1.3	1.5	1.7	1.5	1.7	1.7	Current	1.6	1.5
.5	1.1	1.2	1.2	1.2	1.1		1.2	1.1
2.0	1.4	1.5	1.2	1.3	1.1		1.3	1.2
.6	(170) .9	.8	.7	.8	1.0	Quick	(482) .8	.8
.2	.6	.6	.5	.4	.4		.5	.5

													Sales/Receivables				
5	66.6	21	17.4	27	13.4	32	11.4	7	50.2	20	18.4		Sales/Receivables	23	15.7	24	15.2
27	13.5	36	10.1	39	9.3	43	8.6	38	9.7	47	7.8			38	9.6	38	9.6
41	9.0	52	7.0	54	6.7	56	6.5	55	6.6	63	5.8			55	6.7	54	6.7
5	77.7	21	17.3	27	13.3	33	10.9	29	12.6	35	10.4		Cost of Sales/Inventory	33	10.9	28	13.0
52	7.1	46	7.9	55	6.7	70	5.2	82	4.5	70	5.2			65	5.6	60	6.1
123	3.0	90	4.1	107	3.4	111	3.3	112	3.1	87	4.2			118	3.1	113	3.2
0	UND	14	26.0	17	21.7	20	17.8	9	39.9	11	33.2		Cost of Sales/Payables	18	20.5	14	25.3
19	19.6	30	12.3	30	12.1	35	10.4	33	11.0	35	10.4			34	10.7	30	12.2
60	6.0	53	6.8	53	6.9	58	6.3	48	7.5	49	7.4			54	6.7	53	6.9

5.6	5.6	5.4	6.0	6.0	5.4	Sales/Working Capital	5.1	5.6
18.9	13.9	9.3	12.1	9.7	11.5		10.0	11.0
-11.9	79.3	26.9	25.1	15.8	42.0		32.6	40.2

	9.9		9.3		11.8		10.8		33.4		6.4		9.1		9.8
(41)	1.8	(148)	3.0	(219)	3.9	(104)	3.2	(14)	7.0	(13)	2.8	EBIT/Interest	(433)	3.6	(538)	3.6
	-.2		1.4		1.7		1.3		3.0		.2		1.5		1.3

					11.1		11.6				Net Profit + Depr., Dep., Amort./Cur. Mat. L/T/D		5.8		7.8
				(44)	3.0	(28)	3.0					(105)	2.4	(114)	2.8
					1.0		1.5						1.0		1.2

.0	.1	.1	.1	.1	.1	Fixed/Worth	.1	.1
.3	.2	.2	.3	.4	.8		.3	.3
-1.5	1.2	.8	1.1	1.0	-27.0		1.0	1.1
1.0	1.0	.8	1.0	.7	1.4	Debt/Worth	.8	.9
6.5	2.5	2.1	2.1	2.5	2.7		2.2	2.3
-2.1	8.9	4.7	5.7	4.2	-37.8		7.4	6.2

	91.1		61.5		53.9		40.0		61.2		42.6	% Profit Before Taxes/Tangible Net Worth		46.1		47.6
(33)	31.3	(141)	21.3	(220)	26.5	(98)	20.3	(15)	44.0	(10)	26.6		(423)	19.7	(522)	18.3
	.5		4.3		7.7		7.9		24.7		13.2			4.9		4.7

28.5	15.2	18.1	14.2	22.7	10.7	% Profit Before Taxes/Total Assets	13.3	13.5
6.7	6.4	7.8	6.1	12.9	6.8		6.1	4.9
-2.8	1.3	2.2	1.6	7.7	-4.8		.9	.7
UND	212.8	133.5	81.3	104.1	171.7	Sales/Net Fixed Assets	116.6	118.1
48.3	61.8	46.6	41.2	26.2	17.6		44.2	39.0
14.1	22.3	18.9	13.9	11.2	9.0		16.7	13.2
4.2	4.7	3.9	3.3	4.2	3.0	Sales/Total Assets	3.8	4.0
3.3	3.4	2.8	2.4	2.6	2.2		2.8	2.7
2.2	2.3	2.1	1.8	1.8	1.7		2.0	2.0

	.4		.3		.3		.3		.6		.3	% Depr., Dep., Amort./Sales		.4		.3
(27)	1.1	(129)	.5	(199)	.7	(99)	.8	(13)	1.4	(10)	1.8		(391)	.7	(479)	.7
	3.3		1.2		1.3		1.4		2.3		2.9			1.6		1.7

	3.5		2.0		1.3		.9					% Officers', Directors' Owners' Comp/Sales		2.0		2.1
(26)	5.6	(107)	4.0	(121)	2.6	(30)	2.1					(229)	3.3	(288)	4.0
	11.5		5.9		5.3		4.3							6.4		7.5

52382M	740647M	3465768M	6480312M	3179812M	5333891M	Net Sales ($)	15430283M	17271926M
14262M	194811M	1142461M	2328699M	1094082M	2242783M	Total Assets ($)	6132325M	6292023M

M = $ thousand   MM = $ million
See Pages 11 through 21 for Explanation of Ratios and Data

Comparative Historical Data | Current Data Sorted by Sales

H1	H2	H3	Type of Statement	0-1MM	1-3MM	3-5MM	5-10MM	10-25MM	25MM & OVER
68	61	81	Unqualified	1	2	3	4	18	53
112	105	117	Reviewed	2	8	8	24	47	28
102	70	93	Compiled	4	17	15	28	18	11
99	84	138	Tax Returns	25	38	24	30	18	3
141	200	177	Other	8	19	15	32	16	55
4/1/04-3/31/05 ALL	4/1/05-3/31/06 ALL	4/1/06-3/31/07 ALL		130 (4/1-9/30/06) →			476 (10/1/06-3/31/07) →		
522	520	606	NUMBER OF STATEMENTS	40	84	65	118	149	150

ASSETS (%)

H1	H2	H3	Item	0-1MM	1-3MM	3-5MM	5-10MM	10-25MM	25MM & OVER
9.3	8.9	9.1	Cash & Equivalents	12.1	10.4	10.3	9.5	8.2	7.4
30.5	32.9	32.9	Trade Receivables (net)	18.1	30.2	33.0	33.0	37.3	33.7
35.6	33.3	32.7	Inventory	27.6	33.0	32.4	33.7	33.7	32.1
2.7	2.8	2.7	All Other Current	4.2	1.6	.7	1.9	3.4	3.6
78.0	77.9	77.3	Total Current	61.9	75.2	76.4	78.2	82.5	76.9
13.4	13.1	13.4	Fixed Assets (net)	24.5	14.4	12.8	14.4	9.7	12.9
2.9	3.2	3.7	Intangibles (net)	5.9	3.1	5.3	2.9	2.7	4.4
5.6	5.9	5.7	All Other Non-Current	7.7	7.3	5.5	4.6	5.0	5.8
100.0	100.0	100.0	Total	100.0	100.0	100.0	100.0	100.0	100.0

LIABILITIES

H1	H2	H3	Item	0-1MM	1-3MM	3-5MM	5-10MM	10-25MM	25MM & OVER
17.6	17.6	17.4	Notes Payable-Short Term	29.0	15.4	16.0	16.7	16.7	17.5
3.0	2.4	2.8	Cur. Mat.-L.T.D.	7.8	3.4	3.3	2.6	2.2	1.7
21.7	22.5	21.2	Trade Payables	10.8	18.6	23.3	21.7	23.0	22.5
.2	.2	.2	Income Taxes Payable	.2	.2	.2	.1	.2	.4
9.8	9.0	10.3	All Other Current	27.4	11.3	11.3	7.4	7.9	9.3
52.2	51.7	52.0	Total Current	75.1	48.9	54.1	48.5	50.1	51.4
9.6	10.2	11.1	Long-Term Debt	33.3	13.7	12.9	8.2	7.5	8.8
.2	.1	.1	Deferred Taxes	.0	.0	.1	.1	.1	.2
6.0	7.6	6.3	All Other Non-Current	12.0	10.4	4.1	4.9	5.0	5.7
31.9	30.4	30.5	Net Worth	-20.4	26.9	28.7	38.3	37.3	33.9
100.0	100.0	100.0	Total Liabilities & Net Worth	100.0	100.0	100.0	100.0	100.0	100.0

INCOME DATA

H1	H2	H3	Item	0-1MM	1-3MM	3-5MM	5-10MM	10-25MM	25MM & OVER
100.0	100.0	100.0	Net Sales	100.0	100.0	100.0	100.0	100.0	100.0
32.1	31.7	32.4	Gross Profit	50.3	37.7	34.3	32.5	28.3	27.8
28.7	27.6	27.9	Operating Expenses	46.4	34.6	29.0	27.4	23.7	23.3
3.4	4.0	4.5	Operating Profit	3.9	3.1	5.3	5.1	4.6	4.5
.5	.7	1.1	All Other Expenses (net)	2.7	.7	1.8	.9	.6	1.4
3.0	3.3	3.3	Profit Before Taxes	1.2	2.4	3.6	4.1	3.9	3.1

RATIOS

H1	H2	H3	Item	0-1MM	1-3MM	3-5MM	5-10MM	10-25MM	25MM & OVER
2.4	2.4	2.5	Current	3.6	3.0	2.2	2.5	2.7	2.1
1.5	1.5	1.5		1.4	1.7	1.4	1.5	1.7	1.4
1.2	1.1	1.2		.5	1.1	1.1	1.2	1.2	1.2
1.2	1.3	1.4	Quick	2.1	1.5	1.2	1.4	1.5	1.1
.8 (519)	.8 (605)	.8		.6	.8	.9 (117)	.8	.8	.7
.5	.5	.5		.1	.5	.5	.6	.5	.5
23 16.0	24 15.2	24 15.1	Sales/Receivables	0 UND	21 17.4	21 17.4	24 15.0	30 12.3	27 13.5
36 10.1	38 9.6	38 9.7		24 15.2	38 9.7	37 9.8	37 9.8	41 8.9	39 9.3
53 6.9	55 6.6	54 6.8		41 8.9	58 6.3	56 6.6	53 6.9	55 6.7	52 7.0
29 12.5	25 14.4	26 13.9	Cost of Sales/Inventory	12 30.1	26 14.1	25 14.5	28 13.0	24 15.4	27 13.7
59 6.2	56 6.5	56 6.5		78 4.7	76 4.8	58 6.3	55 6.7	51 7.2	55 6.7
119 3.1	106 3.4	107 3.4		155 2.4	137 2.7	98 3.7	95 3.9	107 3.4	92 3.9
16 22.7	15 25.1	15 23.7	Cost of Sales/Payables	0 UND	13 27.9	14 25.6	15 23.8	18 20.6	18 20.4
31 11.6	31 11.8	31 11.7		15 25.1	32 11.4	39 9.3	31 11.6	30 12.0	32 11.3
50 7.3	54 6.7	53 6.9		52 7.1	65 5.6	60 6.0	53 6.9	50 7.3	47 7.8
5.3	5.3	5.5	Sales/Working Capital	3.8	4.5	5.6	5.8	5.2	7.2
11.4	11.7	11.6		11.6	8.3	11.6	12.5	9.1	14.2
34.9	39.4	32.5		-6.5	80.6	61.4	29.7	25.3	28.7
11.4	11.8	10.7	EBIT/Interest	5.7	7.3	8.0	12.9	10.9	12.3
(469) 3.9	(470) 3.9	(539) 3.4		(30) 1.2	(72) 2.2	(60) 3.2	(103) 4.3	(134) 3.5	(140) 4.3
1.4	1.5	1.4		-.3	.8	1.6	1.8	1.8	1.6
5.6	10.7	11.7	Net Profit + Depr., Dep., Amort./Cur. Mat. L/T/D				3.1	15.9	14.6
(87) 2.4	(95) 3.7	(94) 3.0				(17)	1.3 (29)	3.7 (39)	3.3
1.0	1.4	1.0					.6	1.2	2.1
.1	.1	.1	Fixed/Worth	.0	.0	.1	.1	.1	.1
.3	.2	.3		.8	.3	.2	.2	.3	.4
1.1	1.2	1.1		-1.4	8.0	1.6	.8	.8	1.1
.8	.9	.9	Debt/Worth	.7	.8	1.0	.9	.7	1.0
2.2	2.4	2.3		6.2	3.0	2.8	2.0	2.3	2.2
6.2	7.3	7.1		-1.9	UND	10.1	3.7	5.7	5.7
49.3	54.2	54.7	% Profit Before Taxes/Tangible Net Worth	82.7	56.9	48.0	62.9	54.5	51.2
(455) 19.5	(445) 20.3	(517) 23.0		(24) 17.9	(64) 11.6	(53) 21.5	(107) 25.6	(137) 27.2	(132) 27.5
3.9	6.1	7.2		.3	.2	8.6	7.3	8.8	10.8
15.3	14.4	16.1	% Profit Before Taxes/Total Assets	24.2	14.2	12.6	21.0	16.7	15.0
5.4	6.1	7.1		4.0	3.2	7.7	8.4	6.5	8.6
1.0	1.5	1.6		-3.4	-.5	2.1	2.6	2.2	2.6
114.0	128.9	151.7	Sales/Net Fixed Assets	351.8	167.4	238.8	157.6	153.0	110.0
41.5	47.8	48.1		25.4	42.2	55.7	46.6	60.6	47.6
15.3	15.8	16.9		7.9	13.2	20.9	18.9	22.1	14.5
4.1	4.1	4.0	Sales/Total Assets	3.5	3.5	4.0	4.7	4.3	4.1
2.8	2.9	2.8		2.2	2.6	3.0	3.1	2.9	3.0
2.0	1.9	2.0		1.2	1.8	2.1	2.1	2.1	2.2
.3	.3	.3	% Depr., Dep., Amort./Sales	.6	.3	.1	.3	.3	.3
(418) .7	(400) .7	(477) .7		(21) 1.8	(61) .7	(48) .6	(90) .7	(126) .6	(131) .8
1.6	1.5	1.4		4.4	2.2	1.2	1.3	1.2	1.5
1.7	1.7	1.6	% Officers', Directors' Owners' Comp/Sales	3.5	3.1	2.0	1.9	1.1	1.0
(236) 3.4	(228) 3.3	(285) 3.2		(15) 5.6	(47) 5.1	(41) 3.5	(67) 3.6	(71) 2.0	(44) 2.1
6.4	5.8	5.8		8.8	10.2	5.6	5.4	4.3	3.5
16597336M	17535170M	19252812M	Net Sales ($)	21468M	157676M	258545M	850858M	2351315M	15612950M
6695766M	6016377M	7017098M	Total Assets ($)	12702M	73160M	107571M	310662M	907934M	5605069M

M = $ thousand   MM = $ million
See Pages 11 through 21 for Explanation of Ratios and Data

Current Data Sorted by Assets   **Comparative Historical Data**

0-500M	500M-2MM	2-10MM	10-50MM	50-100MM	100-250MM		4/1/02-3/31/03 ALL	4/1/03-3/31/04 ALL
						Type of Statement		
	4	1	4			Unqualified		
	5	1	3			Reviewed		5
1	4	1				Compiled		1
	1	6	4			Tax Returns		3
						Other	1	2
	6 (4/1-9/30/06)		29 (10/1/06-3/31/07)					
1	14	9	11			**NUMBER OF STATEMENTS**	1	11
%	%	%	%	%	%	**ASSETS**	%	%
	17.8		9.5	D	D	Cash & Equivalents		11.3
	30.5		34.8	A	A	Trade Receivables (net)		48.0
	32.4		31.5	T	T	Inventory		29.9
	.7		1.1	A	A	All Other Current		.7
	81.5		76.8			Total Current		89.9
	12.4		11.2	N	N	Fixed Assets (net)		4.9
	3.6		9.5	O	O	Intangibles (net)		1.6
	2.5		2.4	T	T	All Other Non-Current		3.7
	100.0		100.0			Total		100.0
				A	A	**LIABILITIES**		
	12.3		16.8	V	V	Notes Payable-Short Term		20.9
	3.5		1.9	A	A	Cur. Mat.-L.T.D.		2.5
	23.8		20.8	I	I	Trade Payables		34.0
	.0		.6	L	L	Income Taxes Payable		.1
	6.8		7.4	A	A	All Other Current		4.4
	46.4		47.5	B	B	Total Current		61.9
	12.4		6.5	L	L	Long-Term Debt		11.4
	.0		.0	E	E	Deferred Taxes		.0
	7.9		2.8			All Other Non-Current		8.6
	33.3		43.2			Net Worth		18.1
	100.0		100.0			Total Liabilities & Net Worth		100.0
						INCOME DATA		
	100.0		100.0			Net Sales		100.0
	40.0		23.8			Gross Profit		33.3
	37.1		20.9			Operating Expenses		29.8
	2.9		2.8			Operating Profit		3.4
	.7		.2			All Other Expenses (net)		.1
	2.2		2.6			Profit Before Taxes		3.3
						RATIOS		
	2.4		2.8					2.4
	1.8		1.7			Current		2.0
	1.3		1.1					1.0
	1.7		1.3					1.8
	1.1		.9			Quick		1.0
	.7		.7					.7
	17 21.5		18 20.7				36 10.1	
	36 10.2		47 7.7			Sales/Receivables	51 7.1	
	55 6.6		54 6.8				75 4.9	
	23 15.6		25 14.9				30 12.1	
	57 6.4		44 8.2			Cost of Sales/Inventory	37 9.8	
	98 3.7		60 6.1				68 5.3	
	15 24.0		13 27.7				27 13.5	
	39 9.3		37 9.8			Cost of Sales/Payables	43 8.6	
	75 4.9		45 4.9				108 3.4	
	5.5		6.7					4.6
	9.4		15.2			Sales/Working Capital		7.2
	14.1		83.5					101.8
	3.8		11.6					7.2
	(12) 1.6		(10) 5.4			EBIT/Interest		4.3
	1.2		1.0					1.6
						Net Profit + Depr., Dep., Amort./Cur. Mat. L/T/D		
	.2		.1					.1
	.4		.3			Fixed/Worth		.3
	1.3		.7					-.2
	.7		1.0					.6
	2.0		1.9			Debt/Worth		4.4
	14.5		8.9					-5.1
	38.2		58.5			% Profit Before Taxes/Tangible Net Worth		
	(12) 8.3		(10) 24.5					
	2.4		11.7					
	11.4		17.7			% Profit Before Taxes/Total Assets		11.1
	2.7		11.7					4.2
	.7		.6					1.0
	72.3		135.5					236.5
	35.6		29.5			Sales/Net Fixed Assets		126.3
	22.2		14.2					23.3
	4.6		3.8					4.5
	3.4		3.3			Sales/Total Assets		3.3
	2.2		1.9					2.0
			.3					
			(10) .8			% Depr., Dep., Amort./Sales		
			1.8					
						% Officers', Directors' Owners' Comp/Sales		
15919M	48674M	155993M	870957M			Net Sales ($)	3546M	65000M
376M	14683M	39524M	256530M			Total Assets ($)	516M	20367M

M = $ thousand   MM = $ million
See Pages 11 through 21 for Explanation of Ratios and Data

Comparative Historical Data				Current Data Sorted by Sales					
			Type of Statement						
7	12	5	Unqualified					2	3
8	8	8	Reviewed			2	2	1	3
1	6	7	Compiled		4	1	1	1	
4	3	4	Tax Returns		1	2	1		
6	5	11	Other		1		1	4	5
4/1/04-3/31/05 ALL	**4/1/05-3/31/06 ALL**	**4/1/06-3/31/07 ALL**		**0-1MM**	**6 (4/1-9/30/06) 1-3MM**	**3-5MM**	**29 (10/1/06-3/31/07) 5-10MM**	**10-25MM**	**25MM & OVER**
26	34	35	**NUMBER OF STATEMENTS**		6	5	5	8	11
%	%	%	**ASSETS**	%	%	%	%	%	%
12.0	8.8	10.9	Cash & Equivalents	DATA NOT AVAILABLE					9.4
39.1	32.7	32.9	Trade Receivables (net)						35.6
31.1	28.3	34.3	Inventory						33.2
1.1	1.0	1.4	All Other Current						1.1
83.3	70.9	79.5	Total Current						79.2
7.8	18.2	13.3	Fixed Assets (net)						13.9
5.9	8.0	4.9	Intangibles (net)						4.4
3.0	2.9	2.3	All Other Non-Current						2.5
100.0	100.0	100.0	Total						100.0
			LIABILITIES						
16.3	17.1	13.9	Notes Payable-Short Term						16.5
1.9	2.5	3.4	Cur. Mat.-L.T.D.						1.6
25.3	17.7	23.3	Trade Payables						22.8
.1	.2	.2	Income Taxes Payable						.6
8.7	14.6	9.5	All Other Current						7.5
52.3	52.1	50.3	Total Current						48.9
9.9	11.7	11.0	Long-Term Debt						9.7
.1	.1	.0	Deferred Taxes						.0
5.0	1.6	4.7	All Other Non-Current						2.4
32.7	34.5	33.9	Net Worth						39.0
100.0	100.0	100.0	Total Liabilities & Net Worth						100.0
			INCOME DATA						
100.0	100.0	100.0	Net Sales						100.0
24.6	33.0	30.7	Gross Profit						21.6
24.6	30.3	28.0	Operating Expenses						18.3
.0	2.7	2.7	Operating Profit						3.3
.4	.7	.4	All Other Expenses (net)						.0
-.4	2.0	2.3	Profit Before Taxes						3.3
			RATIOS						
3.2	1.9	2.3							2.8
1.7	1.3	1.6	Current						1.7
1.1	1.0	1.2							1.2
1.8	1.2	1.3							1.3
.9	.8	.9	Quick						.9
.7	.5	.6							.7
32 11.5	**29** 12.6	**18** 20.7							**14** 25.3
49 7.5	**45** 8.1	**42** 8.7	Sales/Receivables						**44** 8.3
54 6.7	**59** 6.2	**54** 6.8							**50** 7.3
17 21.6	**13** 28.6	**18** 20.6							**25** 14.9
46 8.0	**46** 7.9	**50** 7.3	Cost of Sales/Inventory						**44** 8.2
79 4.6	**79** 4.6	**74** 5.0							**60** 6.1
14 26.5	**8** 48.3	**15** 24.1							**13** 27.7
31 12.0	**33** 11.0	**38** 9.7	Cost of Sales/Payables						**32** 11.3
50 7.3	**53** 6.8	**69** 5.3							**42** 8.7
6.1	8.4	6.7							6.7
10.5	15.9	12.7	Sales/Working Capital						15.2
39.7	NM	33.7							83.5
5.2	10.1	7.1							11.6
(22) 2.1	(32) 3.0	(31) 2.6	EBIT/Interest						(10) 5.4
-.7	.3	1.4							1.6
			Net Profit + Depr., Dep., Amort./Cur. Mat. L/T/D						
.1	.1	.2							.1
.2	.6	.3	Fixed/Worth						.3
1.1	3.8	1.2							.7
1.2	.9	1.0							1.0
3.3	2.5	2.2	Debt/Worth						1.9
10.5	7.4	11.1							5.9
21.1	37.0	51.5							58.5
(22) 7.9	(28) 21.3	(30) 15.2	% Profit Before Taxes/Tangible Net Worth						(10) 24.5
-19.9	6.3	4.0							15.2
8.7	10.7	17.6							17.7
1.9	4.5	4.0	% Profit Before Taxes/Total Assets						11.7
-3.4	-.7	.7							2.4
141.2	73.3	112.6							135.5
44.1	20.8	34.0	Sales/Net Fixed Assets						29.5
23.8	7.9	16.9							15.0
4.4	3.9	4.5							4.4
3.1	3.1	3.3	Sales/Total Assets						3.4
2.1	1.9	2.3							2.9
.3	.6	.4							.3
(21) .6	(30) 1.2	(27) .9	% Depr., Dep., Amort./Sales						(10) .8
1.5	2.4	1.4							1.3
	1.3	1.7							
	(10) 6.7	(12) 5.7	% Officers', Directors' Owners' Comp/Sales						
	14.1	8.0							
810474M	**1172424M**	**1091543M**	Net Sales ($)		**11399M**	**19371M**	**32368M**	**115601M**	**912804M**
274661M	**464211M**	**311113M**	Total Assets ($)		**4584M**	**5844M**	**10916M**	**71692M**	**218077M**

M = $ thousand MM = $ million

See Pages 11 through 21 for Explanation of Ratios and Data

Current Data Sorted by Assets

Comparative Historical Data

Type of Statement

	0-500M	500M-2MM	2-10MM	10-50MM	50-100MM	100-250MM		4/1/02-3/31/03 ALL	4/1/03-3/31/04 ALL
Unqualified			8	14	5	3			7
Reviewed		4	21	8					9
Compiled	5	8	9				1		6
Tax Returns	15	16	7				2		2
Other	4	20	26	10	4	3			7
	42 (4/1-9/30/06)			148 (10/1/06-3/31/07)					

Main Data

0-500M	500M-2MM	2-10MM	10-50MM	50-100MM	100-250MM		4/1/02-3/31/03 ALL	4/1/03-3/31/04 ALL
24	48	71	32	9	6	**NUMBER OF STATEMENTS**	3	31
%	%	%	%	%	%		%	%
						ASSETS		
14.7	15.2	7.6	5.9			Cash & Equivalents		8.2
36.4	37.4	36.9	38.4			Trade Receivables (net)		34.6
15.7	22.2	32.7	27.8			Inventory		27.0
1.5	3.1	3.6	2.9			All Other Current		2.5
68.3	77.9	80.8	75.0			Total Current		72.3
12.4	11.1	10.7	13.4			Fixed Assets (net)		17.0
6.8	3.2	3.0	5.9			Intangibles (net)		1.5
12.5	7.8	5.4	5.7			All Other Non-Current		9.2
100.0	100.0	100.0	100.0			Total		100.0
						LIABILITIES		
37.5	16.9	19.3	23.4			Notes Payable-Short Term		19.4
3.4	1.2	2.8	1.8			Cur. Mat.-L.T.D.		2.0
28.8	19.3	22.6	22.3			Trade Payables		24.3
.0	.2	.7	.1			Income Taxes Payable		.6
10.7	10.0	8.9	6.0			All Other Current		7.8
80.4	47.6	54.2	53.5			Total Current		54.1
14.5	9.3	8.1	13.6			Long-Term Debt		11.2
.0	.2	.1	.3			Deferred Taxes		.2
12.1	6.9	4.3	1.9			All Other Non-Current		6.5
-7.0	36.0	33.3	30.7			Net Worth		28.0
100.0	100.0	100.0	100.0			Total Liabilities & Net Worth		100.0
						INCOME DATA		
100.0	100.0	100.0	100.0			Net Sales		100.0
35.8	27.7	24.2	17.8			Gross Profit		28.6
31.3	23.2	19.9	14.3			Operating Expenses		26.7
4.5	4.5	4.4	3.5			Operating Profit		2.0
.6	.5	.4	.8			All Other Expenses (net)		.4
3.9	4.0	4.0	2.7			Profit Before Taxes		1.5
						RATIOS		
2.7	3.1	2.0	1.9					1.7
1.2	1.7	1.5	1.3			Current		1.4
.5	1.1	1.1	1.1					1.1
1.7	1.7	1.3	1.4					1.1
.8	1.1	.6	.8			Quick		.8
.3	.8	.5	.4					.4
2 192.2	13 28.3	20 18.3	24 15.2					22 16.9
25 14.9	29 12.7	35 10.5	42 8.7			Sales/Receivables		33 11.2
42 8.7	49 7.4	56 6.5	54 6.8					46 7.9
0 UND	0 UND	18 20.2	6 60.7					6 58.5
0 UND	23 15.9	38 9.7	29 12.5			Cost of Sales/Inventory		39 9.4
35 10.6	59 6.2	98 3.7	114 3.2					89 4.1
0 UND	8 47.6	10 36.7	9 39.0					20 18.4
16 23.2	17 21.3	33 11.0	23 15.7			Cost of Sales/Payables		31 11.9
94 3.9	39 9.3	55 6.7	41 9.0					54 6.8
10.9	6.7	6.0	8.5					8.1
56.5	15.2	14.5	19.8			Sales/Working Capital		21.0
-11.9	66.5	66.1	93.9					59.4
28.2	23.1	11.7	8.9					5.4
(19) 5.1	(40) 6.8	(60) 2.4	(29) 3.3			EBIT/Interest		(28) 2.0
2.1	2.3	1.1	1.8					1.5
		16.0				Net Profit + Depr., Dep.,		
		(17) 3.2				Amort./Cur. Mat. L/T/D		
		1.7						
.0	.0	.1	.1					.2
.3	.1	.2	.2			Fixed/Worth		.5
-.6	.5	.8	.8					2.3
1.5	.6	1.1	1.5					1.5
17.0	2.2	2.9	3.7			Debt/Worth		2.9
-3.1	9.6	6.4	6.3					7.8
92.7	100.6	49.9	62.8			% Profit Before Taxes/Tangible		31.4
(14) 56.8	(41) 30.8	(66) 22.3	(29) 21.7			Net Worth		(27) 15.3
4.5	7.3	3.2	10.9					6.3
37.5	27.3	15.7	12.1			% Profit Before Taxes/Total		9.4
23.2	8.0	5.4	6.6			Assets		2.9
4.8	2.8	1.1	2.2					1.4
UND	489.5	247.5	188.9					89.8
98.7	114.9	57.1	46.3			Sales/Net Fixed Assets		28.8
32.7	32.2	23.0	16.3					10.7
8.5	6.5	5.0	4.4					
5.3	3.6	3.3	2.9			Sales/Total Assets		3.2
3.9	2.0	2.0	2.0					2.3
.1	.2	.2	.2					.3
(11) .6	(26) .8	(57) .4	(25) .6			% Depr., Dep., Amort./Sales		(26) 1.0
1.2	1.6	.9	.2					2.6
4.6	2.4	.8				% Officers', Directors'		2.3
(10) 8.7	(26) 3.2	(31) 1.8				Owners' Comp/Sales		(13) 2.9
15.4	9.9	3.2						8.8
36729M	320605M	1372956M	2182211M	2404215M	5249992M	Net Sales ($)	11079M	658740M
5186M	53777M	350601M	671492M	648651M	1134696M	Total Assets ($)	4181M	239422M

M = $ thousand   MM = $ million
See Pages 11 through 21 for Explanation of Ratios and Data

Comparative Historical Data

Current Data Sorted by Sales

4/1/04-3/31/05 ALL	4/1/05-3/31/06 ALL	4/1/06-3/31/07 ALL	Type of Statement	0-1MM	1-3MM	3-5MM	5-10MM	10-25MM	25MM & OVER
19	40	30	Unqualified			1	2	4	23
21	38	33	Reviewed		2	1	8	10	12
18	32	22	Compiled		8	4	7	1	2
13	31	38	Tax Returns	5	15	3	10	3	2
23	47	67	Other	5	7	9	8	11	27
4/1/04-3/31/05 ALL	4/1/05-3/31/06 ALL	4/1/06-3/31/07 ALL		42 (4/1-9/30/06)			148 (10/1/06-3/31/07)		
94	188	190	NUMBER OF STATEMENTS	10	32	18	35	29	66

%	%	%	ASSETS	%	%	%	%	%	%
11.1	7.6	9.8	Cash & Equivalents	17.2	13.9	16.1	14.6	3.1	5.5
36.2	33.8	37.0	Trade Receivables (net)	26.3	36.7	22.8	40.0	42.2	38.7
28.3	32.5	26.9	Inventory	24.0	19.6	29.2	22.9	36.1	28.3
1.6	1.9	3.1	All Other Current	3.5	4.2	8.0	.6	1.6	3.1
77.2	75.7	76.8	Total Current	71.1	74.4	76.1	78.1	83.1	75.6
12.0	13.4	12.3	Fixed Assets (net)	11.6	11.0	12.6	9.9	9.7	15.2
4.1	4.2	3.9	Intangibles (net)	.0	5.7	4.7	5.7	.3	4.1
6.7	6.7	7.0	All Other Non-Current	17.4	8.9	6.6	6.2	6.9	5.1
100.0	100.0	100.0	Total	100.0	100.0	100.0	100.0	100.0	100.0

			LIABILITIES						
22.4	19.6	21.4	Notes Payable-Short Term	23.2	33.7	11.6	13.3	21.6	22.2
2.2	2.9	2.3	Cur. Mat.-L.T.D.	.2	3.6	1.4	.7	2.7	2.9
22.3	24.6	22.1	Trade Payables	19.5	25.0	12.8	21.4	27.8	21.6
.4	.2	.3	Income Taxes Payable	.0	.0	.4	.5	.8	.2
8.6	8.7	8.8	All Other Current	6.0	10.5	16.1	9.9	7.9	6.2
56.0	56.1	55.0	Total Current	48.8	72.8	42.4	45.7	60.7	53.1
9.7	12.3	11.0	Long-Term Debt	17.0	10.5	9.8	8.9	6.6	13.7
.4	.3	.2	Deferred Taxes	.0	.6	.0	.0		.3
5.5	6.0	5.7	All Other Non-Current	35.0	2.9	4.3	5.7	5.5	3.1
28.4	25.3	28.2	Net Worth	-.9	13.8	42.9	39.6	27.2	29.9
100.0	100.0	100.0	Total Liabilities & Net Worth	100.0	100.0	100.0	100.0	100.0	100.0

			INCOME DATA						
100.0	100.0	100.0	Net Sales	100.0	100.0	100.0	100.0	100.0	100.0
26.1	25.5	25.2	Gross Profit	44.1	34.6	34.6	26.0	21.3	16.4
22.8	22.1	21.0	Operating Expenses	36.1	30.1	27.3	21.4	18.3	13.6
3.3	3.4	4.1	Operating Profit	8.0	4.5	7.3	4.6	3.0	2.8
.5	.5	.5	All Other Expenses (net)	1.5	.9	.8	-.1	.3	.5
2.8	3.0	3.6	Profit Before Taxes	6.5	3.6	6.6	4.7	2.8	2.3

			RATIOS						
1.9	2.0	2.3	Current	7.0	3.3	2.8	2.8	1.8	2.0
1.3	1.4	1.4		1.7	1.2	2.0	1.7	1.4	1.3
1.1	1.1	1.1		.7	.8	1.2	1.3	1.1	1.1
1.2	1.2	1.5	Quick	4.9	1.7	1.4	2.2	1.1	1.5
.8	.7	.9		1.0	.8	.9	1.1	.6	.8
.5	.4	.5		.4	.3	.6	.6	.4	.5
21 17.7	22 16.5	19 19.3	Sales/Receivables	0 UND	12 31.0	13 27.4	19 19.4	22 16.4	19 19.0
33 11.2	35 10.5	34 10.7		32 11.4	32 11.5	34 10.8	36 10.1	31 11.8	34 10.6
50 7.3	49 7.4	49 7.5		47 7.8	48 7.5	51 7.1	73 5.0	49 7.4	46 7.9
6 64.6	19 18.8	4 86.1	Cost of Sales/Inventory	0 UND	0 UND	32 11.6	0 UND	21 17.5	7 52.6
33 10.9	49 7.4	29 12.7		20 18.5	6 64.3	52 7.1	28 12.9	33 11.0	28 13.2
83 4.4	97 3.8	77 4.8		217 1.7	66 5.5	93 3.9	96 3.8	92 4.0	77 4.8
9 38.7	14 25.9	8 44.6	Cost of Sales/Payables	0 UND	3 135.2	10 37.5	9 39.2	6 61.4	8 47.5
29 12.5	31 11.7	25 14.7		29 12.5	19 19.5	28 13.0	37 9.8	27 13.7	20 18.3
44 8.4	51 7.1	47 7.8		186 2.0	83 4.4	46 8.0	52 7.0	46 7.9	36 10.2
7.3	6.9	6.9	Sales/Working Capital	3.1	6.6	5.2	5.0	8.6	10.5
20.1	20.3	15.5		12.4	14.3	7.7	8.7	23.3	29.5
102.8	98.5	77.2		-12.8	-30.4	25.5	48.0	122.8	77.2
12.7	9.3	14.0	EBIT/Interest		23.1	37.0	20.1	12.2	7.9
(84) 3.8	(169) 3.5	(162) 3.7			(27) 4.1	(14) 7.2	(27) 11.9	(26) 3.2	(61) 2.7
1.1	1.5	1.7			1.8	2.6	1.7	.7	1.7
5.3	9.1	5.7	Net Profit + Depr., Dep., Amort./Cur. Mat. L/T/D						14.1
(23) 2.6	(44) 3.2	(36) 3.4							(18) 4.7
1.0	1.1	1.4							1.4
.1	.1	.1	Fixed/Worth	.0	.0	.1	.0	.0	.1
.3	.4	.2		1.4	.2	.1	.2	.2	.3
1.1	1.3	1.0		-.6	2.0	3.2	.4	.8	1.0
1.4	1.3	1.0	Debt/Worth	4.8	.8	.6	.6	1.3	1.5
3.5	2.6	2.8		NM	3.4	1.3	1.6	3.9	3.3
13.6	9.0	8.0		-8.6	20.9	8.1	10.2	6.2	6.6
53.6	53.6	61.3	% Profit Before Taxes/Tangible Net Worth		56.8	67.0	76.0	73.9	43.5
(80) 28.6	(158) 21.7	(163) 25.8			(25) 27.9	(16) 33.5	(29) 28.6	(28) 20.6	(60) 22.7
5.9	5.8	7.3			6.1	4.7	13.4	2.8	9.3
15.4	12.1	18.9	% Profit Before Taxes/Total Assets	67.0	25.5	26.0	26.4	15.5	10.6
5.8	4.9	6.7		16.7	7.4	7.8	15.7	5.8	5.8
.8	1.4	2.1		-1.9	2.9	2.4	4.5	.0	2.0
182.5	150.6	309.4	Sales/Net Fixed Assets	UND	999.8	85.0	328.3	773.4	228.2
47.4	44.9	57.1		67.7	105.2	31.2	87.5	94.7	50.3
17.3	15.1	23.1		21.2	29.3	25.2	27.9	14.3	19.1
5.7	5.0	5.6	Sales/Total Assets	5.0	5.7	3.9	5.9	5.5	6.2
3.1	3.1	3.5		1.8	3.6	2.2	3.5	4.0	3.7
2.3	1.9	2.0		1.2	1.9	1.2	2.3	2.6	2.3
.4	.3	.2	% Depr., Dep., Amort./Sales		.6	.5	.1	.1	.2
(70) .8	(149) .6	(131) .6			(19) .7	(11) .8	(27) .4	(21) .4	(52) .5
1.4	1.3	1.2			2.4	1.5	1.1	.7	1.2
1.4	1.2	1.0	% Officers', Directors' Owners' Comp/Sales		2.7		2.0	.7	.3
(32) 3.1	(69) 2.5	(75) 2.6			(17) 8.9		(19) 3.2	(13) 1.3	(15) 1.0
8.8	4.8	6.2			14.5		9.0	2.9	1.4
3298638M	9144804M	11566708M	Net Sales ($)	4839M	60492M	73272M	257299M	439976M	10730830M
1485431M	2987229M	2864403M	Total Assets ($)	2770M	25029M	51222M	93235M	125344M	2566803M

M = $ thousand   MM = $ million
See Pages 11 through 21 for Explanation of Ratios and Data

RETAIL TRADE

Current Data Sorted by Assets   ## Comparative Historical Data

Type of Statement

	0-500M	500M-2MM	2-10MM	10-50MM	50-100MM	100-250MM	Type of Statement	ALL 4/1/02-3/31/03	ALL 4/1/03-3/31/04
		2	46	89	23	9	Unqualified	172	150
		10	197	175	15	7	Reviewed	444	413
	1	24	71	41	3	2	Compiled	218	191
	6	31	183	55	2		Tax Returns	252	251
	11	102	1104	766	50	16	Other	1340	1646
		160 (4/1-9/30/06)		2,881 (10/1/06-3/31/07)					
NUMBER OF STATEMENTS	18	169	1601	1126	93	34		2426	2651

Assets (%)

Item	0-500M	500M-2MM	2-10MM	10-50MM	50-100MM	100-250MM	ALL '02-'03	ALL '03-'04
Cash & Equivalents	7.4	7.9	9.0	11.8	12.2	9.2	9.3	9.4
Trade Receivables (net)	9.8	6.2	6.9	7.4	10.6	8.1	8.1	7.8
Inventory	68.1	72.4	66.6	57.1	52.2	47.4	63.2	64.1
All Other Current	4.5	2.4	2.3	2.7	2.5	2.2	2.7	2.8
Total Current	89.8	88.8	84.8	79.0	77.4	66.8	83.3	84.2
Fixed Assets (net)	8.8	7.8	7.8	11.7	12.6	20.7	10.2	9.5
Intangibles (net)	.4	.9	2.1	2.8	2.3	4.2	1.5	1.6
All Other Non-Current	1.0	2.5	5.3	6.5	7.7	8.3	5.0	4.8
Total	100.0	100.0	100.0	100.0	100.0	100.0	100.0	100.0

Liabilities (%)

Item	0-500M	500M-2MM	2-10MM	10-50MM	50-100MM	100-250MM	ALL '02-'03	ALL '03-'04
Notes Payable-Short Term	40.9	50.2	54.4	50.4	50.4	36.8	52.3	51.9
Cur. Mat.-L.T.D.	3.7	1.9	1.7	1.5	1.7	2.6	2.3	1.8
Trade Payables	20.1	5.5	4.0	4.0	5.8	7.0	4.4	5.1
Income Taxes Payable	.0	.1	.1	.1	.2	.2	.1	.2
All Other Current	17.8	15.9	12.9	11.9	8.7	11.4	10.5	12.2
Total Current	82.5	73.6	73.1	67.9	66.8	57.9	69.6	71.1
Long-Term Debt	7.0	8.1	6.3	8.0	8.0	16.4	7.6	6.7
Deferred Taxes	.0	.0	.1	.2	.4	.4	.2	.1
All Other Non-Current	2.9	5.2	4.2	3.2	3.2	2.3	2.7	3.1
Net Worth	7.6	13.2	16.3	20.8	21.6	23.0	19.9	19.0
Total Liabilities & Net Worth	100.0	100.0	100.0	100.0	100.0	100.0	100.0	100.0

Income Data (%)

Item	0-500M	500M-2MM	2-10MM	10-50MM	50-100MM	100-250MM	ALL '02-'03	ALL '03-'04
Net Sales	100.0	100.0	100.0	100.0	100.0	100.0	100.0	100.0
Gross Profit	16.1	14.4	12.9	12.4	12.8	13.5	12.9	13.1
Operating Expenses	15.9	14.5	13.0	11.8	11.1	12.3	12.2	12.6
Operating Profit	.1	-.1	-.1	.6	1.7	1.2	.7	.4
All Other Expenses (net)	1.4	.4	-.3	-.5	.0	.1	-.5	-.6
Profit Before Taxes	-1.3	-.4	.2	1.1	1.7	1.1	1.2	1.0

Ratios

Ratio	0-500M	500M-2MM	2-10MM	10-50MM	50-100MM	100-250MM	ALL '02-'03	ALL '03-'04
Current	1.5	1.5	1.3	1.3	1.3	1.3	1.3	1.3
	1.0	1.2	1.1	1.1	1.1	1.1	1.2	1.2
	.9	1.0	1.0	1.0	1.0	1.0	1.1	1.0
Quick	.4	.3	.3	.4	.4	.4	.3	.3
	.2	(167) .1	(1597) .2	(1125) .2	.3	.3	(2416) .2	(2649) .2
	.0	.1	.1	.2	.2	.2	.1	.1
Sales/Receivables	0 UND	1 243.8	3 124.7	4 103.1	5 74.0	6 62.1	3 121.4	3 123.7
	2 228.4	3 109.0	5 70.6	6 59.1	9 40.5	10 37.3	6 64.4	6 63.5
	6 62.3	7 54.0	9 42.7	10 35.3	15 24.5	17 22.0	10 36.9	10 35.5
Cost of Sales/Inventory	29 12.5	60 6.1	57 6.4	52 7.1	51 7.1	53 6.9	51 7.2	56 6.5
	51 7.1	84 4.4	76 4.8	66 5.5	71 5.2	64 5.7	67 5.5	73 5.0
	147 2.5	113 3.2	99 3.7	85 4.3	89 4.1	76 4.0	86 4.3	91 4.0
Cost of Sales/Payables	0 UND	1 296.7	2 222.5	2 184.8	3 126.6	4 90.5	2 232.9	2 210.8
	0 UND	4 103.5	3 123.1	3 108.2	5 67.8	6 65.7	3 128.8	3 122.8
	15 24.2	9 41.1	5 72.7	6 65.2	8 46.3	12 30.6	5 71.9	5 70.6
Sales/Working Capital	14.5	11.7	18.3	19.3	18.3	22.0	18.4	17.4
	223.6	28.1	33.3	37.4	41.8	43.2	32.9	31.2
	-153.4	UND	121.3	127.9	292.7	703.2	97.6	101.7
EBIT/Interest		1.7	3.0	5.9	4.4	3.8	8.3	7.8
	(133) 1.0	(1202) 1.3	(850) 2.4	(81) 2.8	(32) 2.0		(1801) 3.0	(1861) 2.9
		-.1	.5	1.1	1.7	1.1	1.3	1.1
Net Profit + Depr., Dep., Amort./Cur. Mat. L/T/D		3.9	5.9	4.6	4.5		5.6	5.1
		(75) 1.5	(71) 2.9	(35) 3.5	(13) 1.5		(267) 2.0	(221) 2.0
		.3	1.1	1.3	.5		.8	.8
Fixed/Worth	.0	.1	.2	.2	.2	.5	.2	.2
	.3	.4	.4	.5	.6	.9	.4	.4
	UND	UND	1.7	1.5	1.4	3.6	1.3	1.2
Debt/Worth	3.7	2.5	2.9	2.7	2.6	2.5	2.6	2.8
	20.4	6.0	5.9	5.0	4.8	4.5	5.0	5.2
	-8.2	-43.8	17.9	11.3	8.9	14.4	11.5	11.0
% Profit Before Taxes/Tangible Net Worth	277.4	16.4	30.4	43.5	40.9	35.6	43.7	41.9
	(12) 3.6	(125) 6.2	(1316) 10.6	(1022) 21.9	(89) 25.2	(32) 11.5	(2213) 22.0	(2405) 19.8
	-34.8	-13.7	-4.9	6.4	12.1	2.0	6.1	4.9
% Profit Before Taxes/Total Assets	17.9	3.5	5.0	8.0	7.1	5.8	7.7	6.9
	.0	.0	1.1	3.7	3.9	2.4	3.7	3.0
	-7.7	-5.4	-2.0	.6	2.3	.2	.7	.4
Sales/Net Fixed Assets	UND	213.5	167.9	111.2	84.8	40.0	139.2	138.4
	967.7	89.4	79.7	54.6	38.8	19.9	69.2	66.3
	79.7	42.8	37.1	21.7	14.3	8.4	29.8	31.7
Sales/Total Assets	8.0	4.9	4.6	4.4	3.7	3.6	4.8	4.5
	6.1	3.8	3.7	3.5	3.1	3.0	4.0	3.7
	2.6	2.7	2.9	2.8	2.5	2.3	3.2	3.0
% Depr., Dep., Amort./Sales		.1	.1	.1	.2	.2	.1	.1
		(125) .2	(1348) .2	(1039) .2	(88) .4	(31) .4	(2165) .3	(2313) .3
		.5	.4	.4	.6	.6	.4	.4
% Officers', Directors' Owners' Comp/Sales		.6	.3	.2	.1	.2	.3	.3
		(91) 1.0	(984) .6	(654) .4	(51) .2	(10) .7	(1447) .6	(1642) .5
		1.8	1.0	.8	.6	2.0	1.2	1.1
Net Sales ($)	36672M	937716M	34893167M	78420443M	21649144M	14926860M	110677099M	120083741M
Total Assets ($)	3962M	232038M	9172900M	21439514M	6525719M	4693424M	29006137M	33325223M

© RMA 2007

M = $ thousand   MM = $ million
See Pages 11 through 21 for Explanation of Ratios and Data

Comparative Historical Data　　　　　　　　　　　　Current Data Sorted by Sales

			Type of Statement						
156	152	169	Unqualified	1	2	3	8	21	134
371	359	404	Reviewed		2	6	26	101	269
150	135	142	Compiled	1	9	13	17	37	65
265	206	277	Tax Returns	4	8	10	37	112	106
2307	2315	2049	Other	12	34	50	169	625	1159
4/1/04- 3/31/05 ALL	4/1/05- 3/31/06 ALL	4/1/06- 3/31/07 ALL		160 (4/1-9/30/06)			2,881 (10/1/06-3/31/07)		
3249	3167	3041	NUMBER OF STATEMENTS	0-1MM 18	1-3MM 55	3-5MM 82	5-10MM 257	10-25MM 896	25MM & OVER 1733
%	%	%	ASSETS	%	%	%	%	%	%
10.3	10.9	10.1	Cash & Equivalents	8.9	7.0	8.3	7.1	8.4	11.6
5.9	5.9	7.2	Trade Receivables (net)	7.7	6.5	6.3	7.3	6.5	7.6
64.8	62.9	62.8	Inventory	60.3	57.3	68.2	69.1	67.1	59.6
3.4	3.7	2.5	All Other Current	.6	4.4	3.6	1.8	2.1	2.6
84.4	83.4	82.5	Total Current	77.6	75.2	86.5	85.3	84.1	81.3
8.3	8.9	9.5	Fixed Assets (net)	14.4	18.7	8.9	8.7	7.7	10.3
3.3	3.7	2.3	Intangibles (net)	.2	.3	1.3	2.1	2.4	2.4
4.0	4.1	5.7	All Other Non-Current	7.8	5.8	3.4	3.9	5.8	6.0
100.0	100.0	100.0	Total	100.0	100.0	100.0	100.0	100.0	100.0
			LIABILITIES						
54.9	53.0	52.3	Notes Payable-Short Term	48.4	41.2	54.7	48.9	54.4	52.0
1.7	1.5	1.7	Cur. Mat.-L.T.D.	1.8	3.7	.9	1.4	1.6	1.7
4.0	4.2	4.3	Trade Payables	6.1	7.2	4.8	4.6	3.9	4.2
.1	.1	.1	Income Taxes Payable	.0	.1	.1	.0	.1	.1
12.5	13.8	12.6	All Other Current	13.7	14.1	14.7	15.5	12.8	11.9
73.3	72.6	70.9	Total Current	69.9	66.4	75.1	70.3	72.8	69.9
5.5	6.0	7.2	Long-Term Debt	11.1	14.0	6.5	8.1	7.1	6.8
.1	.1	.1	Deferred Taxes	.0	.4	.0	.0	.1	.2
3.1	3.4	3.8	All Other Non-Current	3.1	5.6	4.3	6.2	4.4	3.1
18.0	17.8	18.0	Net Worth	15.9	13.7	14.1	15.3	15.6	20.0
100.0	100.0	100.0	Total Liabilities & Net Worth	100.0	100.0	100.0	100.0	100.0	100.0
			INCOME DATA						
100.0	100.0	100.0	Net Sales	100.0	100.0	100.0	100.0	100.0	100.0
12.8	12.9	12.8	Gross Profit	18.8	30.0	15.3	14.3	12.7	11.9
12.5	12.6	12.6	Operating Expenses	16.8	27.1	15.9	14.6	13.1	11.4
.3	.2	.2	Operating Profit	2.0	2.9	-.6	-.3	-.4	.5
-.6	-.4	-.3	All Other Expenses (net)	4.0	3.3	.3	.0	-.4	-.5
.8	.6	.5	Profit Before Taxes	-2.0	-.4	-.9	-.3	.0	1.1
			RATIOS						
1.3	1.3	1.3	Current	1.6	1.5	1.4	1.4	1.3	1.3
1.1	1.1	1.1		1.1	1.1	1.1	1.2	1.1	1.1
1.0	1.0	1.0		1.0	.9	1.0	1.1	1.0	1.0
.3	.3	.3	Quick	.3	.4	.3	.3	.3	.4
(3241) .2	(3162) .2	(3034) .2		.1 (54)	.2 (81)	.1	.2 (893)	.2 (1731)	.2
.1	.1	.1		.1	.1	.1	.1	.1	.2
1 295.5	1 287.9	3 120.4	Sales/Receivables	0 UND	3 125.0	2 150.0	2 165.8	3 129.6	3 109.6
4 97.4	4 96.2	5 66.6		5 67.9	7 50.5	5 68.4	5 70.3	5 71.6	6 63.9
8 46.9	8 46.0	9 38.5		25 14.7	25 14.8	13 28.3	11 33.2	8 43.0	10 38.0
57 6.4	53 6.8	55 6.7	Cost of Sales/Inventory	49 7.4	48 7.6	68 5.4	75 4.8	64 5.7	49 7.4
75 4.9	71 5.1	71 5.1		147 2.5	123 3.0	113 3.2	97 3.7	83 4.4	62 5.9
95 3.8	92 4.0	94 3.9		385 .9	204 1.8	176 2.1	127 2.9	103 3.5	79 4.6
2 232.8	2 223.1	2 207.3	Cost of Sales/Payables	0 UND	1 473.0	2 174.2	1 260.5	2 219.7	2 193.5
3 127.7	3 119.6	3 113.5		0 UND	7 53.7	6 65.2	3 112.4	3 119.1	3 113.5
5 72.6	5 70.0	6 66.1		70 5.2	25 14.4	14 27.0	6 57.3	5 69.2	5 69.9
19.7	19.6	18.3	Sales/Working Capital	1.5	5.7	7.8	13.1	17.9	20.4
36.6	36.1	34.7		9.3	15.9	24.0	22.8	31.9	39.3
128.0	179.1	132.9		UND	-33.0	NM	55.3	122.2	140.8
6.1	4.4	4.0	EBIT/Interest		3.2	1.8	1.6	2.4	5.9
(2568) 2.3	(2661) 1.8	(2307) 1.7			(42) 1.0	(62) 1.0	(194) .6	(688) 1.2	(1312) 2.4
1.0	.8	.6			-.4	-1.1	-.6	.3	1.2
7.2	6.8	5.1	Net Profit + Depr., Dep., Amort./Cur. Mat. L/T/D				3.4	3.6	5.7
(199) 2.3	(191) 2.3	(199) 2.1					(10) 1.9	(42) 1.1	(141) 2.8
.9	.7	.8					-.1	.0	1.1
.2	.2	.2	Fixed/Worth	.0	.1	.1	.2	.2	.2
.4	.5	.5		.3	.4	.5	.5	.4	.5
1.3	1.8	1.7		20.8	18.9	-1.6	3.5	2.1	1.4
3.2	3.0	2.8	Debt/Worth	2.4	2.2	2.7	2.7	3.1	2.7
6.0	5.9	5.6		5.9	6.9	6.6	6.1	6.3	5.0
14.7	18.0	14.9		UND	-60.0	-28.2	56.0	23.4	11.5
43.6	42.8	36.3	% Profit Before Taxes/Tangible Net Worth	55.6	10.6	13.5	17.1	25.0	44.1
(2850) 19.0	(2678) 18.0	(2596) 15.3		(15) .0	(39) 2.6	(59) 6.3	(196) 2.1	(734) 7.4	(1553) 22.4
2.7	1.4	.4		-11.4	-26.8	-7.8	-16.5	-9.9	7.7
6.7	7.0	6.3	% Profit Before Taxes/Total Assets	.1	2.6	3.4	2.8	3.8	8.1
2.7	2.4	2.1		-.5	-.6	-.2	-.6	.6	3.6
.0	-.5	-1.0		-7.0	-5.4	-5.1	-4.2	-2.5	.6
160.0	156.2	144.5	Sales/Net Fixed Assets	UND	142.7	132.5	146.0	157.8	134.8
75.5	74.7	67.3		39.2	35.1	46.6	58.8	74.2	67.3
36.1	33.3	29.6		.8	6.0	21.7	29.3	35.3	27.8
4.5	4.6	4.5	Sales/Total Assets	3.3	2.8	3.9	3.9	4.2	4.8
3.6	3.7	3.6		1.0	1.8	2.4	3.0	3.3	3.9
2.9	2.9	2.8		.2	.5	1.8	2.2	2.7	3.1
.1	.1	.1	% Depr., Dep., Amort./Sales		.3	.1	.1	.1	.1
(2796) .2	(2737) .2	(2637) .2			(41) .6	(62) .3	(198) .3	(753) .3	(1579) .2
.4	.4	.4			2.7	.8	.6	.4	.4
.3	.3	.3	% Officers', Directors' Owners' Comp/Sales		.3	.4	.6	.4	.2
(2097) .5	(2074) .5	(1793) .5			(23) 1.6	(38) 1.4	(130) .9	(553) .6	(1046) .4
1.0	.9	1.0			4.9	2.3	1.5	1.4	.8
147948282M	155070896M	150864002M	Net Sales ($)	6249M	107362M	332913M	1975903M	15385413M	133056162M
41050841M	41872549M	42067557M	Total Assets ($)	26862M	131969M	185217M	827609M	5020106M	35875794M

© RMA 2007

M = $ thousand　　MM = $ million
See Pages 11 through 21 for Explanation of Ratios and Data

Current Data Sorted by Assets   Comparative Historical Data

Type of Statement

	0-500M	500M-2MM	2-10MM	10-50MM	50-100MM	100-250MM		4/1/02-3/31/03 ALL	4/1/03-3/31/04 ALL
Unqualified		2	7	5	2	1		18	11
Reviewed		14	21	7	1			45	27
Compiled	25	60	29	4		1		152	136
Tax Returns	92	118	42	2		2		177	200
Other	17	80	65	24	1	1		111	126
		70 (4/1-9/30/06)		553 (10/1/06-3/31/07)					
NUMBER OF STATEMENTS	134	274	164	42	4	5		503	500

ASSETS

	0-500M %	500M-2MM %	2-10MM %	10-50MM %	50-100MM %	100-250MM %		ALL %	ALL %
Cash & Equivalents	11.2	7.0	7.4	4.6				7.7	7.7
Trade Receivables (net)	9.1	12.2	16.2	30.1				11.2	10.3
Inventory	64.2	62.6	58.7	37.3				63.2	63.1
All Other Current	.6	1.5	3.1	5.9				2.5	2.3
Total Current	85.1	83.3	85.4	77.9				84.5	83.4
Fixed Assets (net)	11.2	11.6	9.8	12.4				10.6	10.8
Intangibles (net)	.7	1.2	.8	1.5				.8	.9
All Other Non-Current	3.0	3.9	4.1	8.1				4.1	4.8
Total	100.0	100.0	100.0	100.0				100.0	100.0

LIABILITIES

	0-500M	500M-2MM	2-10MM	10-50MM	50-100MM	100-250MM		ALL	ALL
Notes Payable-Short Term	34.5	38.3	41.8	44.6				40.7	39.0
Cur. Mat.-L.T.D.	5.7	3.0	2.1	1.6				3.2	3.0
Trade Payables	5.3	5.4	5.8	3.2				5.1	4.7
Income Taxes Payable	.1	.2	.1	.4				.1	.1
All Other Current	12.1	9.4	9.9	13.6				9.5	11.0
Total Current	57.7	56.2	59.7	63.4				58.7	57.8
Long-Term Debt	15.1	12.4	6.8	8.0				11.0	11.1
Deferred Taxes	.0	.3	.1	.1				.0	.0
All Other Non-Current	11.6	7.1	6.6	4.7				8.1	7.4
Net Worth	15.6	24.0	26.8	23.9				22.2	23.6
Total Liabilities & Net Worth	100.0	100.0	100.0	100.0				100.0	100.0

INCOME DATA

	0-500M	500M-2MM	2-10MM	10-50MM	50-100MM	100-250MM		ALL	ALL
Net Sales	100.0	100.0	100.0	100.0				100.0	100.0
Gross Profit	21.2	18.0	17.5	25.4				19.0	17.8
Operating Expenses	19.6	15.8	15.3	20.3				16.5	15.9
Operating Profit	1.6	2.2	2.2	5.1				2.5	1.8
All Other Expenses (net)	.5	.7	.4	1.4				.8	.5
Profit Before Taxes	1.0	1.4	1.7	3.7				1.7	1.3

RATIOS

	0-500M	500M-2MM	2-10MM	10-50MM	50-100MM	100-250MM		ALL	ALL
Current	5.2	2.3	1.9	1.3				2.3	2.4
	1.4	1.4	1.3	1.2				1.3	1.3
	1.0	1.1	1.1	1.0				1.1	1.1
Quick	1.2	.7	.6	1.2				.6	.6
	(133) .3	(272) .2	.2	.4				(494) .2	(492) .2
	.1	.1	.1	.1				.1	.1
Sales/Receivables	0 UND	0 UND	1 282.1	3 117.3				0 UND	0 UND
	1 527.4	3 143.5	5 72.7	13 27.2				2 210.0	2 211.3
	8 48.4	11 31.8	16 23.5	250 1.5				10 38.3	9 41.9
Cost of Sales/Inventory	34 10.8	40 9.2	46 7.9	38 9.5				38 9.7	40 9.1
	56 6.5	63 5.8	66 5.5	64 5.7				62 5.9	60 6.1
	92 4.0	94 3.9	95 3.8	90 4.1				91 4.0	89 4.1
Cost of Sales/Payables	0 UND	0 UND	1 255.2	3 136.3				0 UND	0 UND
	0 741.4	1 254.2	4 92.2	5 79.1				2 229.3	2 211.4
	3 122.0	6 65.7	9 40.9	11 33.2				6 62.3	6 63.5
Sales/Working Capital	7.2	8.2	8.2	4.7				8.2	9.4
	21.3	19.3	19.7	17.7				22.0	23.3
	UND	95.1	42.5	295.8				77.8	101.1
EBIT/Interest	4.1	3.6	4.0	5.9				4.9	5.4
	(108) 1.5	(246) 1.7	(139) 1.8	(40) 2.2				(448) 2.0	(425) 2.4
	.3	1.0	1.1	1.6				1.0	1.1
Net Profit + Depr., Dep., Amort./Cur. Mat. L/T/D			6.0					3.7	6.0
			(11) 2.2					(23) 2.1	(21) 1.9
			.3					.3	.5
Fixed/Worth	.0	.0	.1	.1				.0	.0
	.6	.3	.3	.3				.2	.3
	-201.5	2.7	.8	.9				1.2	1.9
Debt/Worth	1.1	1.3	1.5	2.2				1.4	1.4
	5.9	4.1	3.9	4.1				3.9	3.9
	-33.4	30.0	9.8	7.7				15.8	15.4
% Profit Before Taxes/Tangible Net Worth	84.3	56.4	46.0	49.9				51.1	54.2
	(96) 22.7	(226) 21.1	(156) 17.5	(41) 27.2				(421) 19.3	(410) 20.1
	.0	2.7	3.8	13.9				3.9	5.7
% Profit Before Taxes/Total Assets	17.7	9.9	10.3	9.6				12.8	12.2
	4.6	3.9	4.1	5.9				4.0	4.4
	-4.1	.2	.7	2.7				.1	.0
Sales/Net Fixed Assets	999.8	586.5	228.0	116.4				664.1	513.7
	192.0	96.2	71.7	35.7				109.1	103.2
	34.2	27.0	26.3	16.0				31.4	29.6
Sales/Total Assets	8.6	6.5	5.2	3.5				6.7	6.5
	5.2	4.4	3.9	2.1				4.4	4.4
	3.0	2.8	2.6	1.0				2.5	2.6
% Depr., Dep., Amort./Sales	.1	.1	.1	.2				.1	.1
	(83) .3	(188) .2	(132) .2	(34) .3				(341) .3	(334) .3
	.8	.6	.4	.6				.7	.6
% Officers', Directors' Owners' Comp/Sales	1.3	.9	.5	.2				.9	.8
	(65) 2.1	(162) 1.8	(100) 1.0	(14) .7				(286) 1.8	(271) 1.7
	4.0	3.0	1.7	3.8				3.7	2.9
Net Sales ($)	262972M	1439719M	2748339M	1975164M	213846M	2727450M		3975706M	5984214M
Total Assets ($)	39490M	291845M	684919M	815980M	274834M	803891M		1290717M	2047491M

M = $ thousand   MM = $ million
See Pages 11 through 21 for Explanation of Ratios and Data

Comparative Historical Data   Current Data Sorted by Sales

	4/1/04-3/31/05 ALL	4/1/05-3/31/06 ALL	4/1/06-3/31/07 ALL	Type of Statement	0-1MM	1-3MM	3-5MM	5-10MM	10-25MM	25MM & OVER
	15	14	17	Unqualified		1		4	3	9
	28	23	43	Reviewed		6	5	6	14	12
	136	134	119	Compiled	8	31	27	21	20	12
	240	214	256	Tax Returns	36	88	37	51	31	13
	151	181	188	Other	13	29	25	44	54	23
					70 (4/1-9/30/06)			553 (10/1/06-3/31/07)		
NUMBER OF STATEMENTS	570	566	623		57	155	94	126	122	69
	%	%	%	**ASSETS**	%	%	%	%	%	%
Cash & Equivalents	9.1	8.6	7.8		11.8	7.7	7.4	7.2	7.1	7.2
Trade Receivables (net)	11.3	12.7	13.9		18.2	13.2	12.2	13.6	15.3	12.7
Inventory	60.9	58.4	59.9		51.9	59.3	64.6	61.5	60.7	57.2
All Other Current	2.2	2.5	2.1		1.2	.7	1.0	2.3	3.3	5.3
Total Current	83.4	82.2	83.7		83.1	80.8	85.1	84.7	86.4	82.5
Fixed Assets (net)	10.2	11.4	11.1		13.8	13.9	9.0	10.7	8.8	10.6
Intangibles (net)	.9	1.2	1.0		.6	1.2	1.9	.5	1.2	.6
All Other Non-Current	5.5	5.3	4.1		2.5	4.0	4.0	4.2	3.6	6.3
Total	100.0	100.0	100.0		100.0	100.0	100.0	100.0	100.0	100.0
				LIABILITIES						
Notes Payable-Short Term	40.5	36.5	38.7		27.3	36.6	41.3	37.8	43.1	43.4
Cur. Mat.-L.T.D.	2.4	2.1	3.2		3.1	5.2	3.5	2.1	2.8	1.1
Trade Payables	5.0	5.3	5.3		1.4	4.5	4.3	8.3	5.7	5.5
Income Taxes Payable	.1	.1	.2		.0	.3	.2	.1	.1	.3
All Other Current	11.4	11.5	10.3		13.0	9.9	7.0	11.1	10.8	11.2
Total Current	59.4	55.5	57.7		44.9	56.5	56.3	59.5	62.5	61.5
Long-Term Debt	11.8	12.1	11.4		16.8	15.0	14.0	8.9	6.7	8.3
Deferred Taxes	.0	.0	.1		.0	.0	.7	.1	.1	.1
All Other Non-Current	7.5	7.2	8.3		6.7	10.9	7.7	7.4	6.5	9.6
Net Worth	21.3	25.1	22.4		31.6	17.6	21.3	24.1	24.2	20.5
Total Liabilties & Net Worth	100.0	100.0	100.0		100.0	100.0	100.0	100.0	100.0	100.0
				INCOME DATA						
Net Sales	100.0	100.0	100.0		100.0	100.0	100.0	100.0	100.0	100.0
Gross Profit	18.8	19.5	19.2		29.3	21.6	18.7	16.8	16.5	15.2
Operating Expenses	17.1	17.2	17.0		26.8	19.4	16.1	14.6	14.5	13.4
Operating Profit	1.8	2.3	2.2		2.5	2.2	2.5	2.2	2.0	1.7
All Other Expenses (net)	.3	.6	.7		1.2	.7	.9	.6	.8	-.2
Profit Before Taxes	1.4	1.7	1.5		1.3	1.5	1.6	1.6	1.2	1.9
				RATIOS						
Current	2.2	2.5	2.4		7.2	3.7	2.8	1.8	1.7	1.8
	1.4	1.4	1.3		2.1	1.3	1.4	1.3	1.3	1.2
	1.1	1.1	1.1		1.1	1.0	1.1	1.1	1.1	1.1
Quick	.7	.8	.8		2.3	1.0	.9	.6	.5	.5
	(562) .2	(563) .3	(620) .2		.7	(153) .3	(93) .2	.2	.2	.2
	.1	.1	.1		.1	.1	.1	.1	.1	.1
Sales/Receivables	0 UND	0 UND	0 UND		0 UND	0 UND	0 UND	0 999.8	1 651.0	0 755.2
	2 207.7	3 138.9	3 111.9		0 UND	3 139.3	2 164.9	4 92.2	4 83.8	4 86.1
	10 38.4	11 32.8	12 29.4		53 6.9	13 27.6	8 44.5	12 29.7	11 33.1	14 26.6
Cost of Sales/Inventory	39 9.3	40 9.2	40 9.2		46 8.0	48 7.6	49 7.5	39 9.3	33 11.1	36 10.2
	60 6.1	60 6.0	62 5.9		103 3.5	73 5.0	65 5.6	55 6.6	53 6.9	51 7.2
	87 4.2	90 4.0	93 3.9		189 1.9	108 3.4	84 4.4	89 4.1	74 4.9	77 4.7
Cost of Sales/Payables	0 UND	0 UND	0 UND		0 UND	0 UND	0 UND	1 635.9	1 388.1	2 176.4
	2 194.4	2 169.9	2 174.3		0 UND	1 329.3	1 251.1	3 142.5	3 115.7	4 82.5
	7 55.6	7 52.4	7 55.3		2 172.1	7 50.4	5 68.5	9 41.9	7 53.3	7 53.1
Sales/Working Capital	8.3	8.1	7.9		3.5	6.3	7.8	9.5	11.5	12.6
	21.5	19.3	18.9		7.2	17.8	15.8	18.5	29.6	28.1
	72.5	75.2	87.2		31.3	999.8	51.5	131.7	57.8	164.4
EBIT/Interest	5.6	4.6	3.8		3.2	3.3	3.6	3.4	4.7	6.6
	(476) 2.4	(489) 2.1	(542) 1.8		(43) 1.4	(140) 1.6	(86) 1.9	(108) 1.8	(105) 1.8	(60) 2.4
	.9	1.0	1.0		.3	.5	1.1	1.1	1.1	1.5
Net Profit + Depr., Dep., Amort./Cur. Mat. L/T/D	4.4	5.9	5.0							
	(21) 1.6	(20) 2.7	(24) 1.7							
	.3	1.0	.8							
Fixed/Worth	.0	.0	.0		.0	.0	.0	.1	.1	.1
	.2	.2	.3		.4	.6	.2	.3	.3	.3
	1.4	1.5	1.7		1.7	UND	16.8	1.6	.8	.8
Debt/Worth	1.3	1.2	1.4		1.0	1.2	1.3	1.4	1.8	1.6
	3.6	3.9	4.2		2.5	5.0	5.4	4.1	3.7	4.2
	17.1	16.2	18.2		15.1	-134.0	46.5	11.2	10.2	10.2
% Profit Before Taxes/Tangible Net Worth	55.9	55.6	56.6		63.8	59.9	66.9	52.3	44.7	57.1
	(472) 19.7	(471) 22.0	(525) 21.2		(50) 13.0	(114) 18.2	(75) 28.7	(109) 17.5	(112) 17.7	(65) 30.9
	3.8	4.9	3.7		-2.9	.0	6.8	3.0	4.4	16.0
% Profit Before Taxes/Total Assets	12.6	12.4	10.8		9.2	12.5	12.6	9.4	9.3	11.8
	4.5	4.4	4.2		3.4	3.5	4.6	4.0	4.1	6.4
	-.2	.2	.1		-4.5	-2.4	.8	.4	.7	2.1
Sales/Net Fixed Assets	578.9	426.7	461.7		839.0	580.0	524.6	206.3	627.1	279.6
	110.0	97.7	94.7		27.0	90.8	140.4	86.6	141.9	70.4
	32.4	29.2	26.1		6.0	16.2	50.3	28.1	34.0	29.7
Sales/Total Assets	6.1	6.1	6.3		3.6	5.6	6.1	6.9	6.9	6.7
	4.4	4.1	4.2		1.9	3.5	4.4	4.6	4.8	4.8
	2.7	2.5	2.5		1.2	2.2	3.1	2.7	3.4	2.8
% Depr., Dep., Amort./Sales	.1	.1	.1		.3	.2	.1	.1	.1	.1
	(360) .3	(383) .2	(440) .2		(33) 1.0	(98) .3	(66) .2	(99) .2	(88) .2	(56) .2
	.6	.6	.5		2.4	.8	.5	.4	.3	.3
% Officers', Directors' Owners' Comp/Sales	.8	.8	.8		3.2	1.8	1.1	.9	.5	.3
	(325) 1.6	(326) 1.6	(344) 1.5		(14) 5.7	(93) 2.6	(54) 1.6	(74) 1.4	(74) .8	(35) 1.3
	2.9	3.2	2.9		10.4	4.8	2.9	2.1	1.3	1.3
Net Sales ($)	7605276M	9235241M	9367490M		33096M	290811M	369931M	920913M	1896592M	5856147M
Total Assets ($)	2152229M	2652755M	2910959M		19472M	104419M	108298M	295275M	655317M	1728178M

© RMA 2007

M = $ thousand   MM = $ million
See Pages 11 through 21 for Explanation of Ratios and Data

RETAIL—Recreational Vehicle Dealers NAICS 441210 (SIC 5561)

	Current Data Sorted by Assets						Comparative Historical Data	
Type of Statement								
		1	1	4				
		4	23	17	1			
	3	26	56	3		1		
	13	27	33	4		1		
	4	34	62	18	5			
	52 (4/1-9/30/06)		289 (10/1/06-3/31/07)				4/1/02-3/31/03 ALL	4/1/03-3/31/04 ALL
Unqualified		1	1	4			4	10
Reviewed		4	23	17	1		38	49
Compiled	3	26	56	3		1	80	127
Tax Returns	13	27	33	4		1	43	94
Other	4	34	62	18	5		183	117
	0-500M	500M-2MM	2-10MM	10-50MM	50-100MM	100-250MM		
NUMBER OF STATEMENTS	20	92	175	46	6	2	348	397
ASSETS	%	%	%	%	%	%	%	%
Cash & Equivalents	8.5	9.3	6.5	5.1			7.3	7.5
Trade Receivables (net)	3.7	2.6	2.6	2.6			2.6	2.6
Inventory	66.3	72.4	79.2	77.8			77.4	77.3
All Other Current	.4	.4	.8	1.6			.6	.5
Total Current	78.9	84.7	89.1	87.1			87.9	87.8
Fixed Assets (net)	17.2	11.4	8.1	9.0			9.2	9.4
Intangibles (net)	2.3	2.3	1.6	1.7			1.8	1.7
All Other Non-Current	1.6	1.7	1.3	2.1			1.1	1.1
Total	100.0	100.0	100.0	100.0			100.0	100.0
LIABILITIES								
Notes Payable-Short Term	25.7	48.4	55.5	61.4			26.7	23.7
Cur. Mat.-L.T.D.	1.2	1.8	3.2	2.0			1.8	2.0
Trade Payables	8.5	6.7	6.2	5.5			32.4	33.6
Income Taxes Payable	.0	.0	.0	.5			.1	.1
All Other Current	14.2	5.1	7.6	7.9			8.4	9.1
Total Current	49.7	62.1	72.4	77.3			69.4	68.5
Long-Term Debt	11.2	9.1	4.7	5.3			5.8	6.5
Deferred Taxes	.0	.0	.0	.1			.0	.0
All Other Non-Current	11.8	3.3	3.1	1.7			2.3	2.6
Net Worth	27.4	25.4	19.8	15.6			22.5	22.3
Total Liabilities & Net Worth	100.0	100.0	100.0	100.0			100.0	100.0
INCOME DATA								
Net Sales	100.0	100.0	100.0	100.0			100.0	100.0
Gross Profit	34.3	22.3	19.3	18.3			20.0	19.3
Operating Expenses	31.2	20.3	16.6	16.1			17.3	16.5
Operating Profit	3.0	2.0	2.8	2.2			2.7	2.7
All Other Expenses (net)	1.6	1.7	1.6	1.1			.9	.8
Profit Before Taxes	1.4	.2	1.2	1.1			1.7	2.0
RATIOS								
Current	2.5	1.7	1.3	1.2			1.4	1.4
	1.5	1.3	1.2	1.1			1.2	1.2
	1.3	1.1	1.1	1.0			1.1	1.1
Quick	.6	.3	.2	.2			.2	.2
	.2	.1	.1	.1			.1 (395)	.1
	.1	.0	.0	.0			.0	.0
Sales/Receivables	0 UND	0 UND	1 726.7	1 620.6			0 999.8	0 999.8
	1 281.5	1 556.2	2 169.2	2 190.3			1 247.7	1 257.6
	7 55.4	3 120.6	5 80.7	4 90.6			4 85.7	4 98.8
Cost of Sales/Inventory	65 5.6	109 3.3	111 3.3	128 2.9			105 3.5	102 3.6
	187 1.9	146 2.5	152 2.4	151 2.4			137 2.7	129 2.8
	272 1.3	233 1.6	199 1.8	231 1.6			178 2.0	165 2.2
Cost of Sales/Payables	0 UND	0 UND	1 319.8	1 196.1			2 157.3	3 136.2
	1 337.3	3 115.3	3 121.4	4 83.8			23 15.7	31 11.8
	24 15.3	9 39.8	8 44.3	10 37.3			109 3.3	108 3.4
Sales/Working Capital	6.2	6.3	10.2	14.8			9.7	9.3
	9.1	12.1	18.3	24.4			17.7	18.6
	13.1	33.6	36.9	57.2			38.2	35.3
EBIT/Interest	3.2	2.1	2.3	2.9			3.2	4.2
	(16) 1.0	(84) 1.3	(168) 1.5	(41) 1.5			(328) 1.9	(381) 2.4
	-.2	.5	1.0	1.1			1.3	1.4
Net Profit + Depr., Dep., Amort./Cur. Mat. L/T/D				17.5			5.7	15.6
			(18) 6.0				(30) 3.2	(39) 5.5
				2.6			1.2	1.7
Fixed/Worth	.1	.1	.1	.1			.1	.1
	.5	.3	.3	.3			.3	.3
	NM	1.3	.8	1.5			.9	.9
Debt/Worth	1.0	1.7	3.0	3.6			2.4	2.3
	3.3	4.1	5.3	6.2			4.7	4.4
	NM	10.0	12.0	10.9			9.1	8.5
% Profit Before Taxes/Tangible Net Worth	39.0	23.3	32.7	31.4			44.1	51.7
	(15) 8.1	(80) 5.6	(162) 11.5	(42) 16.3			(326) 21.1	(374) 23.8
	-22.1	-7.7	2.7	1.6			7.4	8.5
% Profit Before Taxes/Total Assets	8.3	4.6	5.9	6.3			6.8	8.8
	1.2	1.3	2.4	1.8			3.6	4.4
	-6.5	-1.7	.1	.2			1.0	1.3
Sales/Net Fixed Assets	387.6	133.2	142.6	136.9			168.5	162.1
	21.5	48.5	64.3	38.0			61.4	63.2
	10.1	19.7	27.6	17.4			22.6	21.6
Sales/Total Assets	4.7	3.0	3.1	2.7			3.2	3.4
	2.0	2.3	2.4	2.2			2.6	2.6
	1.4	1.6	1.8	1.7			2.0	2.2
% Depr., Dep., Amort./Sales	.7	.3	.2	.1			.2	.2
	(15) 1.4	(73) .6	(139) .4	(38) .3			(261) .4	(297) .5
	2.1	.9	.7	.5			.9	.8
% Officers', Directors' Owners' Comp/Sales		1.9	.8	.5			.9	.9
		(51) 2.9	(107) 1.5	(21) .7			(214) 1.7	(230) 1.8
		4.6	2.5	1.7			3.1	2.9
Net Sales ($)	16813M	280064M	2066674M	1900237M	1054874M	3557731M	3908107M	8033582M
Total Assets ($)	5784M	119844M	819742M	807869M	401882M	413415M	1476923M	2726240M

© RMA 2007

M = $ thousand   MM = $ million
See Pages 11 through 21 for Explanation of Ratios and Data

Comparative Historical Data | Current Data Sorted by Sales

Date ranges (current data): **52 (4/1-9/30/06)** and **289 (10/1/06-3/31/07)**

4/1/04-3/31/05 ALL	4/1/05-3/31/06 ALL	4/1/06-3/31/07 ALL	Type of Statement	0-1MM	1-3MM	3-5MM	5-10MM	10-25MM	25MM & OVER
7	6	6	Unqualified		1			1	4
50	40	45	Reviewed	4	3	1	7	18	16
112	108	89	Compiled	9	13	17	24	22	9
82	60	78	Tax Returns		19	9	16	22	3
116	115	123	Other	5	22	22	27	30	17
367	329	341	**NUMBER OF STATEMENTS**	18	58	49	74	93	49
%	%	%	**ASSETS**	%	%	%	%	%	%
7.1	8.6	7.2	Cash & Equivalents	9.1	7.7	8.2	6.8	6.6	6.4
3.0	4.3	2.7	Trade Receivables (net)	5.2	2.2	2.3	1.8	3.0	3.7
76.2	73.5	76.2	Inventory	67.6	69.9	77.2	80.4	77.4	76.9
.6	1.2	.8	All Other Current	.1	.5	.9	.8	1.1	.9
87.0	87.6	86.9	Total Current	82.1	80.3	88.7	89.8	88.1	87.8
9.6	9.3	9.7	Fixed Assets (net)	14.8	14.5	8.7	8.3	8.3	7.6
2.2	2.0	1.9	Intangibles (net)	2.5	2.9	1.4	1.2	1.7	2.6
1.2	1.1	1.5	All Other Non-Current	.5	2.3	1.2	.7	1.9	2.0
100.0	100.0	100.0	Total	100.0	100.0	100.0	100.0	100.0	100.0
			LIABILITIES						
51.7	51.2	51.9	Notes Payable-Short Term	35.7	41.5	53.3	56.1	56.3	53.9
3.1	2.0	2.5	Cur. Mat.-L.T.D.	.4	2.9	.5	4.4	2.4	2.3
6.3	6.3	6.4	Trade Payables	8.2	6.0	6.0	7.7	5.7	6.0
.1	.1	.1	Income Taxes Payable	.0	.0	.0	.0	.2	.3
6.8	6.8	7.7	All Other Current	13.3	5.5	7.6	6.1	9.0	8.3
68.0	66.4	68.6	Total Current	57.7	56.0	67.4	74.3	73.5	70.8
7.0	6.1	6.4	Long-Term Debt	10.2	11.7	6.4	5.4	4.4	4.3
.0	.0	.0	Deferred Taxes	.0	.0	.0	.0	.0	.1
3.2	3.2	3.5	All Other Non-Current	7.9	5.5	3.9	2.3	2.8	2.1
21.7	24.2	21.5	Net Worth	24.3	26.8	22.3	18.0	19.3	22.7
100.0	100.0	100.0	Total Liabilities & Net Worth	100.0	100.0	100.0	100.0	100.0	100.0
			INCOME DATA						
100.0	100.0	100.0	Net Sales	100.0	100.0	100.0	100.0	100.0	100.0
20.4	20.1	20.8	Gross Profit	31.2	25.3	21.5	18.7	19.0	17.4
18.1	17.4	18.3	Operating Expenses	29.0	23.7	18.6	16.1	16.5	14.4
2.3	2.7	2.5	Operating Profit	2.2	1.6	2.9	2.6	2.6	3.0
.8	1.0	1.5	All Other Expenses (net)	1.7	2.0	1.7	1.9	1.1	1.1
1.5	1.7	.9	Profit Before Taxes	.5	-.5	1.2	.7	1.5	1.9
			RATIOS						
1.5	1.5	1.4	Current	2.2	1.9	1.7	1.3	1.3	1.3
1.2	1.2	1.2		1.4	1.3	1.2	1.2	1.1	1.1
1.1	1.1	1.1		1.2	1.1	1.1	1.1	1.1	1.1
.2	.3	.2	Quick	.3	.4	.3	.2	.2	.2
(365) .1	(328) .1	.1		.2	.1	.1	.1	.1	.1
.0	.1	.0		.1	.0	.0	.0	.0	.1
0 999.8	0 999.8	0 999.8	Sales/Receivables	0 UND	0 UND	0 924.5	0 999.8	1 456.9	1 372.0
1 259.3	2 237.9	2 211.6		2 182.6	0 754.8	1 302.2	2 202.3	2 165.7	2 172.1
4 85.3	5 66.5	5 85.1		5 66.6	3 108.9	6 65.3	4 92.5	4 93.3	6 64.3
107 3.4	101 3.6	110 3.3	Cost of Sales/Inventory	76 4.8	109 3.3	128 2.9	135 2.7	99 3.7	93 3.9
138 2.6	135 2.7	147 2.5		261 1.4	163 2.2	190 1.9	168 2.2	142 2.6	127 2.9
189 1.9	184 2.0	203 1.8		352 1.0	242 1.5	239 1.5	199 1.8	192 1.9	143 2.6
1 474.3	1 412.2	1 410.4	Cost of Sales/Payables	0 UND	0 UND	0 UND	1 306.7	1 246.2	1 275.8
3 126.7	3 123.5	3 114.9		1 337.3	3 143.8	3 104.3	3 111.9	3 112.2	4 96.2
9 42.3	7 50.5	9 41.3		31 11.9	11 33.7	9 38.4	8 45.5	9 42.5	8 48.4
9.2	8.3	8.5	Sales/Working Capital	4.6	6.1	6.1	10.1	13.9	11.8
18.1	16.6	17.0		7.5	9.4	13.6	17.1	22.0	24.5
36.4	37.9	36.9		11.1	32.3	25.6	35.5	43.4	62.7
4.1	3.3	2.4	EBIT/Interest	2.6	2.0	2.4	1.9	2.4	3.2
(344) 2.0	(308) 1.6	(317) 1.4		(14) .8	(52) 1.1	(47) 1.4	(72) 1.2	(85) 1.5	(47) 1.8
1.2	1.0	.9		-.5	.1	.9	.7	1.1	1.3
12.4	7.2	17.9	Net Profit + Depr., Dep., Amort./Cur. Mat. L/T/D						
(31) 5.2	(42) 3.5	(28) 6.0							
2.5	.9	2.9							
.1	.1	.1	Fixed/Worth	.0	.1	.1	.1	.1	.1
.3	.3	.3		.5	.4	.3	.3	.3	.3
1.0	.8	1.1		NM	2.3	.8	1.0	.9	1.0
2.5	2.4	2.5	Debt/Worth	1.2	1.4	2.2	2.7	3.1	3.0
4.6	4.3	5.2		3.8	4.1	5.4	5.4	5.7	6.1
11.7	9.7	11.5		NM	30.3	13.0	18.7	10.2	10.8
39.4	37.4	30.9	% Profit Before Taxes/Tangible Net Worth	23.1	19.5	28.4	26.8	30.6	56.5
(333) 16.6	(303) 14.0	(307) 11.0		(14) .3	(49) .8	(43) 10.9	(68) 9.2	(86) 11.8	(47) 25.5
4.5	2.5	.0		-24.6	-24.5	-2.1	-5.1	3.6	11.7
7.1	7.0	5.7	% Profit Before Taxes/Total Assets	6.6	4.1	6.1	4.1	5.8	9.0
2.8	2.5	2.1		-1.2	.3	2.5	1.6	2.2	4.3
.7	.3	-.4		-6.2	-6.0	-.6	-1.6	.5	1.5
127.7	155.6	142.4	Sales/Net Fixed Assets	UND	87.3	121.2	190.0	122.7	215.7
54.2	57.5	52.8		20.0	32.3	52.8	61.1	62.5	84.5
21.8	21.2	20.6		6.9	14.9	19.1	23.9	29.2	20.6
3.2	3.2	3.0	Sales/Total Assets	2.4	2.7	2.8	3.2	3.2	3.7
2.5	2.6	2.3		1.6	2.0	2.0	2.2	2.6	2.8
1.9	1.8	1.7		1.3	1.5	1.6	1.8	2.0	2.4
.2	.2	.2	% Depr., Dep., Amort./Sales	1.1	.3	.2	.2	.2	.1
(287) .4	(270) .3	(269) .4		(12) 1.5	(46) .7	(40) .4	(53) .3	(78) .4	(40) .3
.9	.8	.8		2.6	1.4	.8	.7	.7	.4
.9	.9	.9	% Officers', Directors' Owners' Comp/Sales		2.1	1.5	1.1	.8	.3
(212) 1.6	(196) 1.7	(190) 1.9			(36) 3.9	(23) 2.1	(43) 1.7	(57) 1.5	(25) .6
2.8	2.9	3.3			5.1	2.9	2.7	2.7	.8
6102998M	7464842M	8876393M	Net Sales ($)	10797M	120182M	201645M	532164M	1462116M	6549489M
2320631M	2614240M	2568536M	Total Assets ($)	6220M	64928M	103121M	255648M	624435M	1514184M

© RMA 2007

M = $ thousand   MM = $ million

See Pages 11 through 21 for Explanation of Ratios and Data

Current Data Sorted by Assets   Comparative Historical Data

0-500M	500M-2MM	2-10MM	10-50MM	50-100MM	100-250MM	Type of Statement	4/1/02-3/31/03 ALL	4/1/03-3/31/04 ALL
	2	4	5	1	1	Unqualified	5	6
	4	30	11			Reviewed	24	40
4	14	50	10			Compiled	58	92
1	25	40	2			Tax Returns	47	58
2	19	101	21			Other	78	77
	32 (4/1-9/30/06)		315 (10/1/06-3/31/07)					
7	64	225	49	1	1	NUMBER OF STATEMENTS	212	273
%	%	%	%	%	%	**ASSETS**	%	%
	5.5	6.7	5.7			Cash & Equivalents	8.7	9.3
	2.9	3.5	4.9			Trade Receivables (net)	4.3	3.7
	76.1	68.5	48.2			Inventory	66.4	66.6
	.9	1.4	1.4			All Other Current	1.8	1.4
	85.4	80.1	60.3			Total Current	81.2	81.1
	11.2	11.8	24.3			Fixed Assets (net)	12.6	12.6
	2.7	5.6	12.0			Intangibles (net)	2.9	3.6
	.7	2.5	3.5			All Other Non-Current	3.3	2.7
	100.0	100.0	100.0			Total	100.0	100.0
						LIABILITIES		
	39.9	34.2	28.0			Notes Payable-Short Term	32.9	31.9
	3.2	3.6	2.9			Cur. Mat.-L.T.D.	3.6	2.9
	10.3	12.1	8.0			Trade Payables	12.2	11.5
	.0	.1	.4			Income Taxes Payable	.3	.1
	9.2	9.6	7.7			All Other Current	9.5	10.2
	62.7	59.6	47.0			Total Current	58.5	56.5
	12.3	10.0	16.5			Long-Term Debt	9.6	8.1
	.0	.0	.1			Deferred Taxes	.0	.1
	8.1	4.0	2.8			All Other Non-Current	3.3	4.3
	16.9	26.4	33.7			Net Worth	28.6	31.0
	100.0	100.0	100.0			Total Liabilties & Net Worth	100.0	100.0
						INCOME DATA		
	100.0	100.0	100.0			Net Sales	100.0	100.0
	21.9	21.7	25.4			Gross Profit	22.1	22.2
	20.0	19.4	20.3			Operating Expenses	18.7	19.4
	1.9	2.3	5.1			Operating Profit	3.3	2.8
	1.4	.4	.0			All Other Expenses (net)	.0	-.2
	.5	1.9	5.1			Profit Before Taxes	3.4	2.9
						RATIOS		
	1.6	1.6	1.6			Current	1.8	1.9
	1.3	1.3	1.2				1.3	1.4
	1.1	1.1	1.1				1.1	1.1
	.2	.3	.3			Quick	.4	.4
	.1 (223)	.1	.2				.2 (272)	.2
	.0	.1	.1				.1	.1
	0 UND	2 223.5	3 111.3			Sales/Receivables	1 316.6	1 377.2
	1 289.0	4 98.9	5 76.2				4 103.9	3 113.1
	5 69.4	6 57.1	10 36.5				7 54.3	6 59.7
	106 3.4	100 3.6	94 3.9			Cost of Sales/Inventory	77 4.7	83 4.4
	155 2.4	129 2.8	116 3.1				112 3.3	107 3.4
	205 1.8	168 2.2	150 2.4				156 2.3	149 2.4
	2 232.6	5 67.9	6 60.4			Cost of Sales/Payables	5 80.5	5 76.0
	4 81.9	10 37.8	12 31.2				11 34.1	10 34.8
	14 25.9	23 15.9	23 16.1				23 15.9	23 16.0
	9.0	8.0	10.0			Sales/Working Capital	8.4	8.1
	12.8	14.1	16.2				14.3	13.1
	26.8	25.5	77.1				35.5	28.2
	2.8	6.3	7.4			EBIT/Interest	11.4	10.5
	(58) 1.2	(212) 2.2	(44) 4.2				(193) 4.3	(244) 4.0
	.5	.9	1.9				1.6	1.7
		3.6				Net Profit + Depr., Dep.,	13.8	10.5
		(10) 1.9				Amort./Cur. Mat. L/T/D	(25) 5.6	(36) 3.7
		.4					2.0	.7
	.1	.2	.5			Fixed/Worth	.1	.1
	.4	.4	1.1				.4	.4
	4.9	2.9	2.7				1.2	1.1
	2.5	1.8	1.7			Debt/Worth	1.4	1.2
	4.4	4.2	4.1				3.0	2.9
	24.1	22.3	7.1				7.8	7.1
	46.6	47.7	76.3			% Profit Before Taxes/Tangible	49.3	56.4
	(53) 17.5	(186) 21.6	(43) 24.2			Net Worth	(185) 26.9	(240) 31.3
	-.9	1.5	10.5				12.0	11.6
	7.3	10.8	12.8			% Profit Before Taxes/Total	18.4	16.8
	1.6	4.4	7.5			Assets	6.8	6.8
	-2.2	-.4	3.4				2.0	2.5
	109.7	85.4	22.2			Sales/Net Fixed Assets	75.3	70.7
	50.2	31.4	13.4				37.3	33.3
	15.9	14.3	4.0				15.6	16.8
	3.2	3.1	2.5			Sales/Total Assets	3.6	3.7
	2.3	2.5	1.8				2.6	2.8
	1.8	1.9	1.5				2.0	2.0
	.3	.4	.5			% Depr., Dep., Amort./Sales	.4	.4
	(45) .5	(176) .8	(46) .8				(179) .6	(226) .7
	.9	1.2	1.7				1.0	1.2
	1.1	.8	.8			% Officers', Directors'	1.2	1.0
	(31) 1.8	(124) 1.4	(19) 1.4			Owners' Comp/Sales	(128) 2.0	(155) 1.8
	3.6	2.8	3.5				4.0	3.7
13934M	223495M	2610864M	1824532M	105821M	214505M	Net Sales ($)	2632649M	3333995M
1679M	80831M	1071655M	932648M	67258M	116935M	Total Assets ($)	985582M	1219524M

Comparative Historical Data | Current Data Sorted by Sales

9 / 47 / 107 / 53 / 92	2 / 44 / 90 / 58 / 98	13 / 45 / 78 / 68 / 143	Type of Statement	0-1MM	1-3MM	3-5MM	5-10MM	10-25MM	25MM & OVER
			Unqualified		1		2	3	7
			Reviewed		2	2	8	23	10
			Compiled	2	6	11	21	30	8
			Tax Returns	1	12	10	23	22	
			Other	3	11	14	42	58	15
4/1/04-3/31/05 ALL	4/1/05-3/31/06 ALL	4/1/06-3/31/07 ALL			32 (4/1-9/30/06)		315 (10/1/06-3/31/07)		
308	292	347	NUMBER OF STATEMENTS	6	32	37	96	136	40
%	%	%	**ASSETS**	%	%	%	%	%	%
8.0	8.7	6.4	Cash & Equivalents		5.5	5.1	6.3	7.7	4.9
3.4	3.9	3.5	Trade Receivables (net)		2.9	2.1	3.1	4.0	5.3
67.0	66.9	66.6	Inventory		74.2	76.4	69.7	64.9	52.1
1.6	1.0	1.3	All Other Current		1.2	.3	1.1	1.6	1.8
80.1	80.6	77.8	Total Current		83.8	84.0	80.2	78.2	64.1
11.4	12.1	13.8	Fixed Assets (net)		11.7	11.9	12.4	12.2	22.6
5.1	4.9	6.1	Intangibles (net)		3.6	3.0	5.8	6.2	10.4
3.4	2.4	2.3	All Other Non-Current		.8	1.1	1.6	3.3	3.0
100.0	100.0	100.0	Total		100.0	100.0	100.0	100.0	100.0
			LIABILITIES						
33.3	34.7	34.2	Notes Payable-Short Term		41.6	40.8	37.6	29.5	30.0
3.2	2.4	3.4	Cur. Mat.-L.T.D.		1.1	4.4	3.9	3.3	3.5
13.0	12.7	11.1	Trade Payables		11.3	13.3	8.3	13.0	9.7
.1	.2	.1	Income Taxes Payable		.0	.0	.1	.2	.1
9.3	8.2	9.3	All Other Current		8.9	11.7	8.3	10.0	7.1
58.8	58.2	58.0	Total Current		62.9	70.2	58.2	56.0	50.5
8.9	10.5	11.8	Long-Term Debt		14.6	12.7	13.0	8.0	14.9
.1	.0	.1	Deferred Taxes		.0	.0	.0	.1	.1
4.3	4.4	4.8	All Other Non-Current		16.9	3.9	3.5	3.5	3.3
28.0	26.8	25.3	Net Worth		5.6	13.1	25.3	32.4	31.0
100.0	100.0	100.0	Total Liabilities & Net Worth		100.0	100.0	100.0	100.0	100.0
			INCOME DATA						
100.0	100.0	100.0	Net Sales		100.0	100.0	100.0	100.0	100.0
22.2	23.0	22.2	Gross Profit		22.3	19.3	19.8	23.3	24.9
19.4	19.8	19.6	Operating Expenses		20.8	18.5	18.0	19.8	21.2
2.8	3.2	2.6	Operating Profit		1.5	.8	1.8	3.5	3.8
.0	.5	.6	All Other Expenses (net)		1.5	1.4	.4	.2	.0
2.8	2.7	2.1	Profit Before Taxes		.0	-.6	1.4	3.3	3.8
			RATIOS						
1.7	1.7	1.6	Current		1.4	1.4	1.6	1.9	1.5
1.3	1.3	1.3			1.2	1.2	1.3	1.3	1.2
1.1	1.1	1.1			1.1	1.0	1.1	1.1	1.1
.3	.4	.3	Quick		.2	.1	.2	.3	.2
(307) .2	.2	(345) .1			.1	(36) .1	.1	(135) .2	.2
.1	.1	.1			.0	.0	.1	.1	.1
1 335.5	1 386.0	1 289.0	Sales/Receivables		0 UND	0 UND	1 623.2	2 171.7	3 112.3
3 110.6	3 116.3	4 99.1			2 190.6	3 140.2	3 137.0	5 75.0	5 76.4
6 60.3	7 54.4	6 56.4			7 54.1	4 82.9	6 66.0	7 53.6	7 49.1
90 4.0	88 4.1	99 3.7	Cost of Sales/Inventory		137 2.7	145 2.5	112 3.3	92 4.0	86 4.2
116 3.1	117 3.1	130 2.8			185 2.0	168 2.2	142 2.6	112 3.3	105 3.5
158 2.3	154 2.4	170 2.1			249 1.5	217 1.7	171 2.1	146 2.5	130 2.8
4 81.4	5 80.4	4 85.4	Cost of Sales/Payables		2 232.6	3 139.5	3 117.1	6 60.4	6 62.7
10 35.9	11 34.3	9 40.6			6 59.6	9 42.6	8 47.4	10 34.9	11 32.6
22 16.9	24 15.5	21 17.2			16 23.0	35 10.5	16 23.0	24 15.2	23 16.0
8.1	8.3	8.7	Sales/Working Capital		7.9	8.8	8.1	8.0	13.0
13.2	14.1	14.5			12.9	14.3	12.1	14.7	18.5
30.3	33.5	29.5			20.9	44.5	23.0	26.3	84.1
9.2	7.0	5.2	EBIT/Interest		2.2	2.1	4.1	10.0	6.9
(292) 3.6	(275) 2.6	(321) 2.1			(29) 1.0	1.2	(88) 1.8	(124) 3.5	(39) 3.6
1.4	1.2	1.0			.5	.4	.7	1.3	1.8
15.7	7.6	4.7	Net Profit + Depr., Dep., Amort./Cur. Mat. L/T/D						55.3
(36) 5.1	(32) 3.0	(24) 2.5						(10) 3.9	
2.6	.2	.8							1.2
.1	.2	.2	Fixed/Worth		.1	.2	.2	.1	.5
.4	.5	.5			1.1	.5	.5	.4	.9
1.4	1.6	3.5			7.0	-7.6	3.8	1.4	2.6
1.5	1.4	1.8	Debt/Worth		4.2	2.3	1.7	1.5	1.8
3.3	3.6	4.2			12.4	9.7	5.1	2.3	4.5
10.5	13.0	22.9			NM	-29.6	37.8	8.1	6.7
52.2	57.0	49.4	% Profit Before Taxes/Tangible Net Worth		53.3	43.2	56.9	47.6	53.6
(263) 24.5	(241) 22.7	(286) 21.6			(24) 21.4	(25) 12.2	(77) 22.0	(121) 23.0	(35) 24.0
7.6	7.4	3.5			-8.1	-.9	-2.3	7.1	10.5
13.2	12.6	10.7	% Profit Before Taxes/Total Assets		6.2	4.4	9.4	14.1	12.2
5.8	4.9	4.5			.4	1.0	3.2	6.4	6.0
1.6	1.0	-.1			-2.2	-3.4	-1.3	1.5	1.7
84.5	81.5	81.5	Sales/Net Fixed Assets		94.9	80.0	98.7	91.8	27.7
40.3	35.4	29.3			37.1	39.7	30.3	32.1	13.8
16.8	15.8	13.5			15.1	10.6	13.7	14.6	6.5
3.3	3.4	3.1	Sales/Total Assets		2.5	2.5	2.9	3.3	3.1
2.6	2.6	2.3			1.9	2.1	2.3	2.7	2.3
2.0	2.0	1.8			1.6	1.6	1.7	2.1	1.7
.3	.3	.4	% Depr., Dep., Amort./Sales		.3	.3	.4	.4	.5
(250) .6	(244) .6	(275) .7			(24) .6	(27) .4	(70) .8	(110) .7	(39) .7
1.0	1.0	1.2			1.1	.9	1.3	1.2	1.3
1.0	.9	.9	% Officers', Directors' Owners' Comp/Sales		1.0	1.6	.9	.7	.6
(177) 1.6	(155) 1.6	(176) 1.4			(16) 1.8	(17) 2.1	(54) 1.4	(70) 1.2	(18) 1.0
2.9	3.2	2.8			4.2	3.3	3.1	2.6	2.5
3855304M	4211764M	4993151M	Net Sales ($)	2612M	64134M	139487M	731048M	2066067M	1989803M
1562534M	1615763M	2271006M	Total Assets ($)	3394M	33228M	78833M	356839M	850915M	947797M

M = $ thousand   MM = $ million
See Pages 11 through 21 for Explanation of Ratios and Data

Current Data Sorted by Assets   Comparative Historical Data

0-500M	500M-2MM	2-10MM	10-50MM	50-100MM	100-250MM		4/1/02-3/31/03 ALL	4/1/03-3/31/04 ALL
						Type of Statement	5	8
		1				Unqualified	5	8
	4	20	2			Reviewed	27	37
6	25	37	16	1		Compiled	85	94
8	25	25	9		1	Tax Returns	46	64
2	31	39	9		2	Other	80	75
16	85	122	38	2	2	**NUMBER OF STATEMENTS**	243	278
43 (4/1-9/30/06)		222 (10/1/06-3/31/07)						
%	%	%	%	%	%	**ASSETS**	%	%
11.2	7.2	5.1	8.9			Cash & Equivalents	7.5	8.0
8.7	2.2	3.2	4.2			Trade Receivables (net)	3.9	3.8
54.1	76.8	76.0	65.5			Inventory	71.4	70.6
2.6	.5	1.9	1.8			All Other Current	1.0	1.2
76.5	86.7	86.2	80.4			Total Current	83.9	83.6
18.3	9.5	9.8	14.8			Fixed Assets (net)	12.8	12.7
2.4	1.4	2.0	1.4			Intangibles (net)	1.4	1.8
2.7	2.4	2.0	3.4			All Other Non-Current	1.9	1.9
100.0	100.0	100.0	100.0			Total	100.0	100.0
						LIABILITIES		
15.2	43.8	51.1	47.1			Notes Payable-Short Term	37.6	34.2
.3	2.6	2.0	4.3			Cur. Mat.-L.T.D.	2.2	3.3
12.4	6.2	6.2	6.7			Trade Payables	13.4	15.4
.2	.1	.1	.1			Income Taxes Payable	.1	.1
14.4	7.7	11.0	11.0			All Other Current	11.3	10.4
42.4	60.4	70.5	69.3			Total Current	64.6	63.5
20.9	11.9	10.2	11.5			Long-Term Debt	11.3	11.4
.1	.0	.2	.0			Deferred Taxes	.0	.0
24.2	3.0	2.9	1.5			All Other Non-Current	5.3	5.9
12.3	24.7	16.3	17.6			Net Worth	18.7	19.2
100.0	100.0	100.0	100.0			Total Liabilities & Net Worth	100.0	100.0
						INCOME DATA		
100.0	100.0	100.0	100.0			Net Sales	100.0	100.0
35.3	25.4	22.2	19.3			Gross Profit	23.7	22.9
31.3	21.9	19.6	15.5			Operating Expenses	21.3	20.4
4.0	3.5	2.6	3.8			Operating Profit	2.4	2.4
2.0	1.9	1.6	2.0			All Other Expenses (net)	1.0	.8
2.0	1.6	1.0	1.8			Profit Before Taxes	1.4	1.6
						RATIOS		
5.5	2.0	1.3	1.2				1.6	1.6
1.7	1.3	1.2	1.1			Current	1.2	1.2
1.3	1.1	1.1	1.0				1.1	1.1
1.1	.3	.2	.3				.3	.3
.6	(84) .1	.1	.1			Quick	.1	.1
.2	.0	.0	.0				.1	.1
0 UND	0 999.8	1 266.1	2 160.2				0 939.0	1 656.5
2 147.1	1 260.8	4 86.0	5 76.8			Sales/Receivables	3 121.2	4 103.9
9 41.0	6 63.8	8 46.5	14 26.8				8 44.9	8 46.5
32 11.4	125 2.9	151 2.4	150 2.4				120 3.0	112 3.3
67 5.5	193 1.9	210 1.7	205 1.8			Cost of Sales/Inventory	169 2.2	166 2.2
141 2.6	246 1.5	274 1.3	273 1.3				230 1.6	219 1.7
0 UND	0 UND	1 243.6	2 158.4				1 285.1	2 222.8
3 111.0	2 203.3	5 80.6	7 55.4			Cost of Sales/Payables	6 60.6	6 58.2
16 23.2	9 38.4	11 33.7	15 24.3				23 15.9	37 9.8
7.8	5.6	7.5	10.0				6.9	7.1
14.0	9.4	13.6	20.9			Sales/Working Capital	13.8	14.1
70.8	34.4	45.9	NM				45.3	42.1
4.8	2.8	2.7	3.2				3.9	4.3
(15) 3.6	(80) 1.4	(118) 1.3	(37) 1.6			EBIT/Interest	(231) 1.7	(267) 2.1
1.0	.9	.9	1.1				1.1	1.1
		3.9					4.4	6.6
		(17) 1.7				Net Profit + Depr., Dep., Amort./Cur. Mat. L/T/D	(39) 2.7	(29) 3.5
		1.1					.1	1.2
.1	.1	.2	.2				.2	.2
2.1	.3	.4	.6			Fixed/Worth	.5	.5
NM	1.1	2.0	2.3				1.8	1.8
2.0	1.5	3.2	2.9				2.3	2.2
18.7	4.5	7.5	7.0			Debt/Worth	4.8	5.3
-20.8	25.6	31.4	11.5				15.1	18.2
91.2	39.3	34.8	37.7				41.3	46.3
(11) 36.7	(72) 12.4	(103) 16.3	(35) 21.7			% Profit Before Taxes/Tangible Net Worth	(205) 14.9	(238) 19.3
-4.2	.9	.6	4.1				4.8	4.9
18.7	6.8	6.3	6.7				6.1	7.4
7.4	2.1	1.6	2.4			% Profit Before Taxes/Total Assets	2.6	3.2
-.7	-.2	-.8	.4				.4	.4
153.2	114.8	95.5	68.6				77.1	97.7
35.4	37.7	41.8	19.8			Sales/Net Fixed Assets	33.9	31.7
14.6	17.1	13.1	5.8				13.5	13.0
6.8	2.5	2.3	2.0				2.8	2.8
4.6	1.9	1.7	1.4			Sales/Total Assets	2.0	2.0
2.3	1.5	1.3	1.2				1.6	1.6
.3	.4	.3	.4				.4	.4
(11) .7	(64) .7	(104) .5	(37) .6			% Depr., Dep., Amort./Sales	(199) .7	(223) .7
2.1	1.2	1.0	1.0				1.4	1.4
	1.5	.9	.6				1.2	1.3
	(47) 2.5	(78) 1.6	(14) .9			% Officers', Directors' Owners' Comp/Sales	(127) 2.2	(152) 2.2
	4.3	2.4	1.6				4.3	4.2
26148M	224637M	1048237M	1246071M	501161M	3070682M	Net Sales ($)	2608261M	2635722M
4493M	103522M	565298M	760108M	105241M	438606M	Total Assets ($)	1169738M	1301147M

M = $ thousand   MM = $ million
See Pages 11 through 21 for Explanation of Ratios and Data

Comparative Historical Data			Type of Statement	Current Data Sorted by Sales					
			Unqualified				1		2
			Reviewed		2	4	8	16	11
10	.7	3	Unqualified						
37	39	41	Reviewed						
78	63	77	Compiled	3	13	22	25	12	2
61	55	61	Tax Returns	6	21	10	12	9	3
71	104	83	Other	4	26	11	19	16	7
4/1/04-3/31/05 ALL	4/1/05-3/31/06 ALL	4/1/06-3/31/07 ALL		43 (4/1-9/30/06)			222 (10/1/06-3/31/07)		
				0-1MM	1-3MM	3-5MM	5-10MM	10-25MM	25MM & OVER
257	268	265	NUMBER OF STATEMENTS	13	63	47	64	53	25
%	%	%	ASSETS	%	%	%	%	%	%
7.5	6.2	6.9	Cash & Equivalents	8.7	7.8	5.4	5.6	5.0	14.4
3.8	3.9	3.3	Trade Receivables (net)	5.1	3.2	2.8	2.7	3.4	4.9
70.7	72.9	73.0	Inventory	61.5	70.7	76.0	78.9	76.0	57.6
1.1	1.5	1.5	All Other Current	.2	.9	.9	2.3	1.6	2.6
83.0	84.5	84.7	Total Current	75.6	82.6	85.1	89.5	86.0	79.5
12.9	12.2	11.2	Fixed Assets (net)	19.6	12.3	10.6	7.3	10.8	15.9
1.4	1.8	1.7	Intangibles (net)	3.8	2.0	1.5	1.6	1.5	1.3
2.7	1.5	2.3	All Other Non-Current	1.0	3.1	2.8	1.6	1.7	3.3
100.0	100.0	100.0	Total	100.0	100.0	100.0	100.0	100.0	100.0
			LIABILITIES						
46.0	48.1	45.9	Notes Payable-Short Term	29.6	36.3	49.8	47.8	57.4	41.3
3.3	1.7	2.5	Cur. Mat.-L.T.D.	1.1	2.5	2.7	2.3	3.1	2.0
7.4	7.5	6.6	Trade Payables	7.7	6.4	5.0	8.6	5.7	6.5
.1	.1	.1	Income Taxes Payable	.2	.1	.1	.2	.1	.5
7.7	10.3	10.1	All Other Current	9.7	8.7	8.9	13.5	8.2	11.0
64.5	67.8	65.2	Total Current	48.4	54.1	66.4	72.5	74.5	61.3
10.7	11.6	11.7	Long-Term Debt	17.0	19.0	8.6	9.9	6.3	12.0
.2	.3	.1	Deferred Taxes	.0	.0	.0	.2	.1	.1
4.4	3.1	4.0	All Other Non-Current	15.0	1.7	9.4	4.1	1.5	2.2
20.2	17.2	19.0	Net Worth	19.8	25.2	15.5	14.3	17.7	24.5
100.0	100.0	100.0	Total Liabilities & Net Worth	100.0	100.0	100.0	100.0	100.0	100.0
			INCOME DATA						
100.0	100.0	100.0	Net Sales	100.0	100.0	100.0	100.0	100.0	100.0
25.1	23.9	23.6	Gross Profit	38.0	28.0	24.4	20.4	21.0	17.6
22.0	20.6	20.5	Operating Expenses	37.1	24.0	21.2	17.6	18.1	13.9
3.1	3.2	3.2	Operating Profit	.8	3.9	3.2	2.8	2.9	3.7
1.0	1.4	1.8	All Other Expenses (net)	2.7	2.0	2.1	1.6	1.5	1.1
2.1	1.8	1.4	Profit Before Taxes	-1.8	1.9	1.1	1.2	1.5	2.6
			RATIOS						
1.6	1.4	1.6	Current	4.9	2.1	1.5	1.4	1.3	1.8
1.2	1.2	1.2		1.5	1.6	1.2	1.2	1.1	1.2
1.1	1.0	1.1		1.0	1.2	1.0	1.1	1.0	1.0
.3	.2	.3	Quick	1.1	.5	.2	.2	.2	.8
(254) .1	.1	(264) .1		.2	(62) .1	.1	.1	.1	.2
.1	.0	.0		.0	.0	.0	.0	.0	.1
0 779.7	1 581.1	1 394.9	Sales/Receivables	0 UND	0 999.8	1 530.7	1 255.5	1 246.3	2 219.2
3 113.0	3 112.5	3 109.8		1 498.0	2 197.4	2 162.1	4 93.7	4 94.7	4 86.5
8 43.6	8 44.9	8 47.7		12 30.9	6 62.6	8 46.8	7 52.4	10 38.1	9 42.8
121 3.0	133 2.7	132 2.8	Cost of Sales/Inventory	137 2.7	127 2.9	140 2.6	144 2.5	136 2.7	43 8.5
182 2.0	185 2.0	196 1.9		259 1.4	194 1.9	198 1.8	203 1.8	208 1.8	127 2.9
255 1.4	241 1.5	259 1.4		441 .8	261 1.4	256 1.4	277 1.3	266 1.4	179 2.0
1 416.1	1 300.4	1 411.8	Cost of Sales/Payables	0 UND	0 UND	1 318.3	2 230.5	2 229.8	1 310.1
4 92.4	5 79.3	4 99.8		2 174.0	2 182.2	3 106.6	5 75.2	4 85.8	5 75.6
11 33.0	15 24.7	11 32.1		58 6.3	12 31.0	9 41.5	9 39.4	12 31.3	19 19.5
7.1	7.5	6.7	Sales/Working Capital	3.0	4.4	7.4	7.2	10.2	9.2
13.1	16.2	13.1		4.6	8.8	13.2	15.0	18.0	21.4
35.5	58.9	49.3		NM	28.4	63.2	50.6	52.3	311.8
4.5	3.4	3.0	EBIT/Interest	4.5	2.8	2.5	2.7	2.7	4.6
(245) 2.0	(256) 1.6	(253) 1.5		(12) .9	(57) 1.5	1.2	(62) 1.4	(52) 1.4	(23) 3.2
1.2	1.1	1.0		.2	.9	1.0	.7	1.1	1.5
7.0	5.5	5.1	Net Profit + Depr., Dep., Amort./Cur. Mat. L/T/D					4.7	
(34) 3.9	(42) 2.4	(30) 1.8						(11) 1.9	
1.8	1.3	.7						1.2	
.2	.2	.2	Fixed/Worth	.0	.1	.1	.1	.2	.2
.4	.6	.4		.8	.4	.5	.4	.4	.6
1.4	3.2	2.1		-3.5	4.2	2.0	4.8	1.6	2.2
2.3	2.9	2.6	Debt/Worth	1.8	1.6	2.6	3.6	3.2	1.6
5.3	7.3	6.3		12.0	3.6	5.5	8.5	6.7	5.0
13.9	21.4	28.8		-11.1	18.0	30.3	78.7	14.6	9.4
44.7	44.7	38.8	% Profit Before Taxes/Tangible Net Worth		45.4	35.9	48.5	33.4	39.4
(229) 17.0	(222) 17.5	(224) 19.5			(54) 13.1	(40) 15.1	(51) 23.9	(48) 9.3	(23) 31.9
5.1	4.9	1.1			.3	1.1	.4	1.4	18.7
7.2	6.7	7.1	% Profit Before Taxes/Total Assets	7.4	9.2	6.2	6.6	5.4	9.8
3.3	2.1	2.0		-1.0	2.9	1.1	2.4	.9	6.7
.5	.2	-.2		-3.9	-.3	.0	-1.1	.2	2.1
90.5	88.4	94.0	Sales/Net Fixed Assets	280.0	64.3	96.3	155.7	79.1	53.3
33.5	36.0	35.8		13.6	30.1	43.2	53.3	42.0	29.3
11.9	11.2	12.9		5.5	14.9	11.1	20.1	13.0	10.0
2.7	2.5	2.5	Sales/Total Assets	2.7	2.3	2.2	2.4	2.7	3.5
1.9	1.9	1.8		1.3	1.8	2.0	1.8	1.7	2.1
1.5	1.5	1.4		1.0	1.5	1.3	1.4	1.3	1.6
.4	.4	.3	% Depr., Dep., Amort./Sales		.5	.4	.2	.3	.4
(202) .7	(208) .7	(219) .6			(47) .8	(43) .6	(48) .4	(48) .4	(24) .4
1.3	1.2	1.0			1.4	1.0	.9	.9	.9
1.3	1.0	1.0	% Officers', Directors' Owners' Comp/Sales		1.6	1.1	1.1	.7	
(126) 2.0	(138) 1.8	(148) 1.8			(31) 2.7	(35) 1.7	(41) 1.6	(25) 1.3	
3.9	3.9	3.5			4.2	4.2	2.4	2.3	
2376729M	4519886M	6116936M	Net Sales ($)	7872M	124156M	181236M	445873M	801976M	4555823M
1298903M	2000518M	1977268M	Total Assets ($)	8126M	70189M	108054M	257132M	492612M	1041155M

© RMA 2007   M = $ thousand   MM = $ million
See Pages 11 through 21 for Explanation of Ratios and Data

Current Data Sorted by Assets   Comparative Historical Data

0-500M	500M-2MM	2-10MM	10-50MM	50-100MM	100-250MM		4/1/02-3/31/03 ALL	4/1/03-3/31/04 ALL
						Type of Statement		
	3	10	19	8	2	Unqualified	17	34
3	3	27	17		3	Reviewed	31	48
5	19	30	5			Compiled	39	54
13	26	24	4			Tax Returns	39	44
7	19	42	26	7	2	Other	74	75
	43 (4/1-9/30/06)		278 (10/1/06-3/31/07)					
25	70	133	71	15	7	**NUMBER OF STATEMENTS**	200	255
%	%	%	%	%	%	**ASSETS**	%	%
18.3	11.9	6.9	8.0	5.8		Cash & Equivalents	8.2	8.5
9.6	9.3	10.7	13.0	11.7		Trade Receivables (net)	12.0	11.0
44.2	54.6	58.8	51.5	59.0		Inventory	54.4	51.1
1.4	1.5	2.6	3.0	5.2		All Other Current	2.4	3.2
73.6	77.4	78.9	75.5	81.7		Total Current	77.0	73.9
21.6	16.6	15.9	16.1	11.4		Fixed Assets (net)	16.4	18.6
2.5	1.2	.7	1.1	.6		Intangibles (net)	1.3	1.6
2.4	4.8	4.5	7.3	6.3		All Other Non-Current	5.3	5.9
100.0	100.0	100.0	100.0	100.0		Total	100.0	100.0
						LIABILITIES		
37.6	37.7	37.7	39.6	49.7		Notes Payable-Short Term	35.5	36.9
3.8	1.7	4.2	3.6	4.7		Cur. Mat.-L.T.D.	3.5	5.0
10.1	8.2	11.2	7.7	7.3		Trade Payables	10.5	8.8
.1	.1	.1	.2	.3		Income Taxes Payable	.2	.2
15.6	8.9	8.7	11.8	5.6		All Other Current	8.5	8.9
67.3	56.6	62.0	62.8	67.5		Total Current	58.2	59.8
18.5	18.3	11.7	11.3	7.5		Long-Term Debt	13.4	14.0
.0	.0	.2	.4	.8		Deferred Taxes	.3	.3
5.8	2.7	2.6	2.6	1.6		All Other Non-Current	4.2	5.6
8.4	22.5	23.5	22.9	22.6		Net Worth	23.9	20.3
100.0	100.0	100.0	100.0	100.0		Total Liabilities & Net Worth	100.0	100.0
						INCOME DATA		
100.0	100.0	100.0	100.0	100.0		Net Sales	100.0	100.0
31.7	24.3	20.3	17.5	14.5		Gross Profit	22.2	21.6
30.3	20.6	17.4	15.5	11.3		Operating Expenses	20.4	20.0
1.4	3.7	2.9	2.0	3.2		Operating Profit	1.8	1.6
1.7	1.5	.4	.3	.3		All Other Expenses (net)	1.0	.6
-.3	2.2	2.5	1.7	2.9		Profit Before Taxes	.9	1.0
						RATIOS		
2.2	2.3	1.5	1.4	1.4			1.7	1.6
1.1	1.2	1.3	1.2	1.2		Current	1.2	1.2
.7	.9	1.1	1.0	1.1			1.0	1.0
1.1	.8	.5	.5	.4			.6	.6
.5	.3	.2	.3	.2		Quick	(197) .3 / (253) .3	
.0	.1	.1	.2	.1			.1	.1
0 UND	0 UND	5 76.6	7 55.0	6 57.3			3 131.2	3 119.1
2 218.7	5 78.6	10 36.3	12 30.9	14 25.3		Sales/Receivables	9 42.5	9 40.5
13 27.1	17 21.2	18 20.3	20 18.5	23 16.2			20 18.0	20 18.3
6 63.7	33 10.9	51 7.1	53 6.9	68 5.4			46 7.9	46 8.0
61 6.0	89 4.1	94 3.9	72 5.1	98 3.7		Cost of Sales/Inventory	71 5.1	71 5.2
119 3.1	130 2.8	151 2.4	119 3.1	121 3.0			113 3.2	108 3.4
0 UND	1 388.2	2 152.3	4 97.7	7 54.3			2 189.5	2 171.6
1 372.7	8 46.1	9 42.2	8 45.3	8 48.2		Cost of Sales/Payables	8 47.7	8 48.6
20 18.4	18 20.6	24 15.3	17 21.8	11 34.2			21 17.2	20 18.7
12.6	5.5	8.9	14.3	8.9			10.6	11.2
59.6	22.7	16.7	26.0	30.4		Sales/Working Capital	24.0	31.8
-49.8	-75.9	63.3	157.1	37.8			181.0	125.2
5.6	3.5	5.9	4.7	5.0			4.5	4.8
(20) 1.4	(63) 2.0	(124) 2.2	(66) 2.4	3.3		EBIT/Interest	(161) 2.0	(211) 2.2
.2	1.0	1.2	1.5	2.2			1.2	1.2
		4.8	10.0			Net Profit + Depr., Dep.,	2.6	2.1
	(21) 2.4	(14) 2.6				Amort./Cur. Mat. L/T/D	(28) 1.6	(32) 1.1
	1.2	1.1					.9	.6
.1	.0	.2	.2	.3			.1	.2
4.0	.4	.5	.6	.5		Fixed/Worth	.5	.6
-1.8	2.5	1.1	1.5	.7			2.1	2.2
1.7	.9	1.9	2.6	2.1			1.9	2.3
65.8	5.6	3.8	4.9	4.9		Debt/Worth	4.2	5.2
-7.2	26.6	9.2	7.3	9.5			9.2	12.9
189.1	53.6	47.3	41.0	47.8		% Profit Before Taxes/Tangible	39.9	45.5
(15) 25.0	(57) 24.2	(121) 21.8	(69) 25.0	31.4		Net Worth	(181) 13.9	(230) 18.1
.0	4.6	6.1	11.6	20.0			3.2	4.5
18.1	12.3	10.1	7.5	7.8		% Profit Before Taxes/Total	8.2	7.5
.0	5.4	4.7	4.3	5.3		Assets	2.3	3.3
-5.3	-.3	1.0	2.0	3.9			.3	.5
435.6	341.8	89.6	91.7	52.3			132.7	122.3
57.1	50.8	36.6	26.8	39.0		Sales/Net Fixed Assets	40.5	33.0
9.2	11.0	12.8	11.8	18.9			10.8	9.4
9.3	4.0	3.6	4.0	2.9			4.5	4.1
3.7	3.0	2.8	2.9	2.6		Sales/Total Assets	3.2	2.9
2.3	1.7	1.8	2.1	2.3			2.2	2.0
.3	.3	.2	.2	.3			.3	.2
(16) 1.6	(52) .7	(119) .6	(62) .5	.4		% Depr., Dep., Amort./Sales	(164) .6	(205) .6
6.3	2.2	1.5	1.7	.8			1.8	1.8
	1.3	.7	.3				.6	.6
	(38) 2.6	(51) 1.0	(22) .4			% Officers', Directors'	(121) 1.4	(126) 1.5
	6.0	2.1	.8			Owners' Comp/Sales	3.6	4.0
43783M	291542M	1979510M	4681870M	3078811M	2485424M	Net Sales ($)	4549794M	10875377M
5758M	84126M	693462M	1529962M	1092856M	1105344M	Total Assets ($)	1776504M	2851376M

Comparative Historical Data | Current Data Sorted by Sales

31	31	42	Type of Statement		1	1		7	33
43	36	50	Unqualified			5	5	16	22
50	48	59	Reviewed	5	10	8	13	18	5
53	52	67	Compiled	12	12	12	10	15	6
68	100	103	Tax Returns	2	11	12	14	25	39
4/1/04- 3/31/05 ALL	4/1/05- 3/31/06 ALL	4/1/06- 3/31/07 ALL	Other	0-1MM	43 (4/1-9/30/06) 1-3MM	3-5MM	278 (10/1/06-3/31/07) 5-10MM	10-25MM	25MM & OVER
245	267	321	**NUMBER OF STATEMENTS**	19	34	38	44	81	105
%	%	%	**ASSETS**	%	%	%	%	%	%
9.3	8.3	9.0	Cash & Equivalents	10.3	16.6	7.6	9.8	7.7	7.6
13.5	13.6	10.9	Trade Receivables (net)	10.9	11.8	8.9	8.6	10.9	12.5
49.5	52.5	55.0	Inventory	46.6	42.0	58.1	61.4	57.1	55.2
3.3	2.6	2.4	All Other Current	.0	1.7	.5	1.8	2.7	3.8
75.6	77.0	77.4	Total Current	67.9	72.1	75.0	81.5	78.4	79.1
17.3	16.6	16.3	Fixed Assets (net)	29.2	22.1	16.9	12.9	15.5	14.0
1.3	1.4	1.1	Intangibles (net)	.3	3.9	.3	1.3	.3	1.1
5.8	5.0	5.2	All Other Non-Current	2.6	1.9	7.8	4.2	5.8	5.8
100.0	100.0	100.0	Total	100.0	100.0	100.0	100.0	100.0	100.0
			LIABILITIES						
33.2	32.6	38.8	Notes Payable-Short Term	30.9	27.9	34.6	34.6	41.7	44.6
3.9	3.6	3.5	Cur. Mat.-L.T.D.	8.0	.7	3.7	6.1	1.8	3.8
11.6	13.1	9.6	Trade Payables	6.5	10.4	9.2	12.5	10.7	8.0
.2	.1	.1	Income Taxes Payable	.0	.2	.1	.1	.1	.1
11.0	9.4	9.8	All Other Current	17.6	4.2	11.2	7.4	9.4	10.8
59.9	58.7	61.8	Total Current	63.1	43.5	58.8	60.8	63.7	67.4
12.8	11.8	13.5	Long-Term Debt	34.2	24.8	13.4	10.6	11.5	8.8
.3	.4	.2	Deferred Taxes	.0	.0	.0	.1	.3	.4
3.1	4.6	2.9	All Other Non-Current	7.7	2.3	4.6	3.3	1.3	2.6
23.9	24.5	21.7	Net Worth	-5.0	29.4	23.2	25.2	23.2	20.8
100.0	100.0	100.0	Total Liabilities & Net Worth	100.0	100.0	100.0	100.0	100.0	100.0
			INCOME DATA						
100.0	100.0	100.0	Net Sales	100.0	100.0	100.0	100.0	100.0	100.0
20.1	20.9	21.0	Gross Profit	39.4	33.4	22.6	22.1	18.4	14.7
17.8	17.7	18.2	Operating Expenses	37.8	27.8	19.4	19.1	15.8	12.7
2.3	3.2	2.8	Operating Profit	1.6	5.6	3.2	3.0	2.6	2.0
.5	.7	.7	All Other Expenses (net)	3.1	1.8	1.1	.7	.1	.3
1.8	2.5	2.1	Profit Before Taxes	-1.5	3.8	2.1	2.3	2.5	1.7
			RATIOS						
1.8	1.7	1.6	Current	2.1	3.9	2.4	2.0	1.4	1.3
1.2	1.3	1.2		1.0	1.7	1.2	1.4	1.2	1.2
1.0	1.1	1.0		.5	1.0	1.0	1.1	1.1	1.0
.7	.6	.5	Quick	.8	1.4	.7	.5	.5	.4
.3	(266) .3	.3		.3	.5	.2	.1	.3	.3
.1	.2	.1		.0	.1	.1	.1	.1	.2
4 96.7	4 98.1	4 97.9	Sales/Receivables	0 UND	1 709.2	1 326.1	1 457.1	5 73.5	6 64.3
10 34.9	12 31.3	10 38.0		6 64.4	8 48.4	7 53.3	5 76.6	10 35.3	12 31.1
23 15.9	24 15.3	19 18.9		36 10.0	27 13.5	17 21.6	13 28.8	18 20.4	20 17.9
42 8.8	47 7.7	49 7.5	Cost of Sales/Inventory	26 13.8	27 13.7	41 8.9	60 6.0	49 7.4	52 7.0
65 5.6	77 4.7	87 4.2		91 4.0	104 3.5	97 3.8	104 3.5	89 4.1	69 5.3
114 3.2	114 3.2	133 2.7		274 1.3	160 2.3	142 2.6	187 2.0	134 2.7	104 3.5
2 150.3	4 100.2	2 164.8	Cost of Sales/Payables	0 UND	0 UND	2 220.5	3 131.5	2 165.6	3 113.1
9 40.5	10 38.3	8 45.3		6 58.3	13 27.8	9 40.4	9 40.8	5 49.7	8 48.2
21 17.3	24 15.3	19 19.2		28 13.2	36 10.2	18 19.9	32 11.3	19 19.1	13 27.4
9.4	8.9	10.0	Sales/Working Capital	3.5	3.7	7.7	7.0	9.8	15.3
24.4	19.3	22.5		UND	11.5	28.8	12.7	19.6	32.2
109.3	72.7	151.2		-5.4	NM	-490.7	47.4	63.1	156.5
6.4	6.1	4.7	EBIT/Interest	2.1	4.8	3.1	4.7	6.0	5.0
(211) 2.6	(248) 2.9	(295) 2.2		(14) 1.0	(30) 2.2	(36) 1.6	(40) 2.1	(76) 2.5	(99) 2.6
1.3	1.6	1.3		.0	1.0	.9	1.2	1.5	1.6
6.1	5.7	6.1	Net Profit + Depr., Dep., Amort./Cur. Mat. L/T/D					5.2	8.2
(36) 2.3	(42) 2.2	(49) 2.4						(13) 2.4	(24) 3.8
1.2	1.2	1.1						1.2	1.4
.2	.1	.2	Fixed/Worth	.7	.0	.1	.1	.2	.3
.5	.4	.5		-8.4	.5	.6	.3	.5	.6
1.9	1.6	1.7		-.5	3.6	2.7	1.2	.9	1.3
1.8	1.6	1.8	Debt/Worth	6.5	1.0	.8	1.3	1.8	2.9
4.4	3.6	4.8		-11.5	4.7	7.5	4.5	3.3	4.9
10.7	9.3	10.7		-7.1	14.7	46.2	9.9	7.4	9.3
40.1	48.8	48.0	% Profit Before Taxes/Tangible Net Worth		59.4	43.2	55.5	46.2	47.3
(214) 19.3	(241) 24.0	(284) 25.0		(28) 34.3	(32) 21.1	(41) 20.6	(74) 25.5	(101) 27.3	
7.4	10.5	8.5			7.2	-.2	4.5	9.2	11.8
7.9	11.0	9.1	% Profit Before Taxes/Total Assets	1.1	15.6	9.8	11.2	11.6	7.9
3.7	5.1	4.6		-.3	5.7	2.9	5.0	4.9	4.6
.9	1.6	.9		-6.1	.1	-.8	.8	1.6	1.9
111.8	128.0	111.9	Sales/Net Fixed Assets	148.0	146.6	158.5	246.9	86.4	96.1
40.0	44.2	35.6		10.1	21.0	33.9	61.8	35.5	38.2
13.3	12.3	12.1		1.4	7.3	10.3	15.5	13.6	14.8
4.4	4.2	3.8	Sales/Total Assets	2.6	3.3	4.0	3.7	4.0	4.2
3.1	2.9	2.8		1.3	2.2	3.0	2.6	2.9	3.0
2.1	2.0	1.9		.8	1.5	1.8	1.6	2.0	2.3
.3	.3	.2	% Depr., Dep., Amort./Sales	.3	.4	.4	.2	.2	.2
(190) .6	(201) .6	(269) .6		(14) 6.1	(25) 1.8	(29) .9	(37) .6	(72) .6	(92) .4
1.5	1.6	1.8		13.0	4.6	2.3	1.6	1.2	1.0
.8	.6	.5	% Officers', Directors' Owners' Comp/Sales		1.7	1.5	.8	.5	.2
(116) 1.5	(98) 1.4	(125) 1.3		(19) 4.4	(18) 2.1	(15) 1.3	(32) .9	(34) .4	
3.0	2.8	2.7			5.8	4.3	2.0	1.9	.8
7582651M	9741178M	12560940M	Net Sales ($)	9404M	69148M	147732M	317450M	1267426M	10749780M
2744825M	3537518M	4511508M	Total Assets ($)	8493M	38168M	67752M	137002M	495334M	3764759M

M = $ thousand   MM = $ million
See Pages 11 through 21 for Explanation of Ratios and Data

Current Data Sorted by Assets | Comparative Historical Data

Type of Statement

0-500M	500M-2MM	2-10MM	10-50MM	50-100MM	100-250MM	Type of Statement	4/1/02-3/31/03 ALL	4/1/03-3/31/04 ALL
	1	4	9	3	6	Unqualified	29	21
2	18	25	14		1	Reviewed	68	79
24	34	31	5		1	Compiled	100	105
46	50	16	2			Tax Returns	51	90
22	33	20	17	1	2	Other	86	95
69 (4/1-9/30/06)			317 (10/1/06-3/31/07)					
94	136	96	47	4	9	NUMBER OF STATEMENTS	334	390

ASSETS

%	%	%	%	%	%	ASSETS	%	%
9.3	7.4	5.0	4.7			Cash & Equivalents	6.1	7.2
15.5	17.4	18.1	17.3			Trade Receivables (net)	18.9	18.3
43.4	46.3	55.2	44.2			Inventory	45.8	46.0
3.7	2.0	1.5	2.8			All Other Current	2.2	1.7
71.9	73.1	79.9	68.9			Total Current	72.9	73.2
18.6	19.0	14.5	17.8			Fixed Assets (net)	18.4	18.0
4.4	3.4	1.7	4.1			Intangibles (net)	2.8	2.9
5.1	4.5	3.9	9.3			All Other Non-Current	5.9	5.8
100.0	100.0	100.0	100.0			Total	100.0	100.0

LIABILITIES

						LIABILITIES		
14.6	10.9	13.8	13.5			Notes Payable-Short Term	11.1	10.7
8.1	3.1	3.8	3.9			Cur. Mat.-L.T.D.	3.4	3.1
23.9	19.3	20.4	18.2			Trade Payables	24.3	22.8
.1	.1	.1	.1			Income Taxes Payable	.2	.2
11.4	6.5	6.8	7.6			All Other Current	7.2	7.4
58.1	39.9	44.9	43.4			Total Current	46.2	44.1
35.4	19.5	11.9	15.8			Long-Term Debt	18.7	17.6
.0	.1	.1	.4			Deferred Taxes	.1	.2
7.1	4.6	4.7	3.9			All Other Non-Current	5.7	5.8
-.7	35.9	38.4	36.5			Net Worth	29.2	32.2
100.0	100.0	100.0	100.0			Total Liabilities & Net Worth	100.0	100.0

INCOME DATA

						INCOME DATA		
100.0	100.0	100.0	100.0			Net Sales	100.0	100.0
41.7	36.4	34.4	37.6			Gross Profit	35.9	35.8
38.3	33.1	31.2	32.1			Operating Expenses	33.2	33.0
3.4	3.2	3.3	5.5			Operating Profit	2.6	2.8
1.1	.6	.3	.3			All Other Expenses (net)	.5	.3
2.3	2.6	2.9	5.2			Profit Before Taxes	2.1	2.5

RATIOS

0-500M	500M-2MM	2-10MM	10-50MM	50-100MM	100-250MM	RATIOS	Hist 1	Hist 2
3.6	3.5	2.5	2.6				2.5	2.8
1.6	2.0	1.7	1.5			Current	1.6	1.7
.8	1.3	1.4	1.2				1.1	1.2
1.0	1.1	.7	.8				.9	.9
.4	.6	.5	.5			Quick	.5	.6
.2	.3	.3	.3				.3	.3
0 UND	9 40.5	16 22.5	14 25.8				12 31.1	12 30.3
8 45.6	23 15.8	27 13.7	25 14.8			Sales/Receivables	25 14.4	25 14.6
19 19.0	34 10.8	37 9.8	41 9.0				35 10.3	35 10.5
31 11.7	55 6.6	76 4.8	80 4.6				55 6.6	55 6.6
59 6.2	96 3.8	111 3.3	110 3.3			Cost of Sales/Inventory	94 3.9	95 3.8
123 3.0	140 2.6	215 1.7	186 2.0				146 2.5	147 2.5
0 UND	17 21.6	26 14.0	33 11.1				27 13.7	25 14.4
25 14.6	35 10.4	43 8.5	53 6.9			Cost of Sales/Payables	43 8.5	43 8.5
41 8.9	58 6.3	60 6.0	70 5.3				63 5.8	62 5.9
7.5	4.5	4.3	4.2				5.4	5.0
16.9	7.7	7.7	8.7			Sales/Working Capital	10.8	9.5
-42.5	22.2	15.9	30.0				35.7	34.2
10.1	6.3	7.2	11.9				6.1	8.0
(74) 2.0	(121) 2.5	(92) 2.3	(44) 3.6			EBIT/Interest	(303) 3.2	(359) 3.2
.2	1.3	1.5	1.7				1.2	1.3
	6.9	9.3	7.4				3.9	3.8
	(19) 2.4	(21) 2.4	(11) 2.3			Net Profit + Depr., Dep., Amort./Cur. Mat. L/T/D	(84) 2.0	(85) 2.1
	1.4	1.4	.8				.8	1.0
.1	.1	.2	.2				.2	.2
.7	.4	.3	.4			Fixed/Worth	.5	.4
-2.0	1.5	.7	1.1				1.4	1.3
1.0	.8	1.0	1.0				1.1	1.0
2.9	1.9	1.7	2.2			Debt/Worth	2.1	2.1
-6.0	5.7	3.7	4.0				6.0	5.6
76.5	38.6	32.6	29.7				34.5	34.4
(60) 25.6	(121) 14.0	(93) 11.6	(43) 20.0			% Profit Before Taxes/Tangible Net Worth	(289) 14.6	(348) 14.4
3.3	3.3	3.7	11.6				2.8	4.0
29.1	10.8	10.0	11.2				10.4	10.2
8.7	4.3	3.3	6.4			% Profit Before Taxes/Total Assets	4.5	4.9
-1.8	.9	1.4	2.4				.4	.9
131.3	65.0	47.7	29.9				51.0	60.9
36.3	27.1	26.4	16.8			Sales/Net Fixed Assets	21.3	22.4
16.4	11.1	12.8	8.1				11.5	11.5
6.0	3.5	3.4	2.8				3.7	3.7
4.2	2.8	2.3	2.2			Sales/Total Assets	2.7	2.7
2.7	1.8	1.8	1.5				2.1	2.0
.4	.5	.6	.8				.7	.7
(62) .9	(110) 1.1	(83) 1.0	(41) 1.2			% Depr., Dep., Amort./Sales	(300) 1.3	(335) 1.1
1.9	1.9	1.4	1.9				1.9	2.0
3.3	2.2	1.2	1.0				2.0	1.6
(52) 4.8	(78) 3.2	(43) 2.2	(11) 1.8			% Officers', Directors' Owners' Comp/Sales	(171) 3.3	(211) 3.2
7.5	4.9	3.1	3.0				6.3	5.7
116870M	470270M	1129364M	2084415M	389171M	4593305M	Net Sales ($)	5902652M	6003226M
25701M	160659M	431325M	973984M	260730M	1343525M	Total Assets ($)	2551923M	2861223M

© RMA 2007

M = $ thousand   MM = $ million
See Pages 11 through 21 for Explanation of Ratios and Data

Comparative Historical Data | Current Data Sorted by Sales

4/1/04-3/31/05 ALL	4/1/05-3/31/06 ALL	4/1/06-3/31/07 ALL	Type of Statement	0-1MM	1-3MM	3-5MM	5-10MM	10-25MM	25MM & OVER
23	24	23	Unqualified			1	1	2	19
65	42	59	Reviewed	2	8	7	8	21	13
88	84	95	Compiled	12	26	18	21	11	7
61	101	114	Tax Returns	29	40	21	15	8	1
65	125	95	Other	14	25	16	14	13	13
				69 (4/1-9/30/06)		317 (10/1/06-3/31/07)			
302	376	386	NUMBER OF STATEMENTS	57	99	63	59	55	53
%	%	%	ASSETS	%	%	%	%	%	%
7.8	7.8	6.8	Cash & Equivalents	6.8	9.2	7.6	6.6	4.7	4.0
19.2	17.8	17.0	Trade Receivables (net)	9.0	17.1	19.5	18.9	20.2	17.1
48.7	46.4	47.3	Inventory	44.1	43.3	53.5	49.9	49.3	46.0
1.5	1.9	2.5	All Other Current	4.8	2.2	1.7	1.1	2.6	2.6
77.3	73.8	73.6	Total Current	64.6	71.8	82.3	76.5	76.8	69.8
15.7	18.5	17.6	Fixed Assets (net)	22.7	20.3	12.2	17.8	14.4	16.6
2.2	2.8	3.4	Intangibles (net)	5.6	4.3	1.4	1.6	2.4	5.1
4.9	4.9	5.4	All Other Non-Current	7.1	3.6	4.1	4.1	6.4	8.6
100.0	100.0	100.0	Total	100.0	100.0	100.0	100.0	100.0	100.0
			LIABILITIES						
10.4	11.7	12.8	Notes Payable-Short Term	18.5	9.9	11.6	12.5	12.7	13.7
3.9	4.0	4.5	Cur. Mat.-L.T.D.	7.8	5.2	2.5	3.5	5.6	4.5
22.6	23.4	20.7	Trade Payables	17.7	19.7	22.6	22.9	19.4	22.4
.3	.2	.2	Income Taxes Payable	.1	.1	.0	.2	.1	.5
6.7	9.8	7.9	All Other Current	13.7	6.9	6.9	6.2	7.4	7.5
44.0	49.2	46.1	Total Current	57.7	41.8	43.6	45.2	45.2	46.6
16.4	20.1	21.0	Long-Term Debt	55.0	19.6	11.9	15.5	12.8	12.4
.1	.1	.1	Deferred Taxes	.0	.0	.1	.1	.0	.4
6.0	5.7	5.2	All Other Non-Current	5.8	7.5	2.4	4.9	4.4	4.7
33.5	24.9	27.6	Net Worth	-18.5	31.1	42.0	34.3	37.5	35.9
100.0	100.0	100.0	Total Liabilties & Net Worth	100.0	100.0	100.0	100.0	100.0	100.0
			INCOME DATA						
100.0	100.0	100.0	Net Sales	100.0	100.0	100.0	100.0	100.0	100.0
36.2	37.1	37.4	Gross Profit	44.9	39.2	35.0	35.0	32.9	36.3
33.1	34.3	33.8	Operating Expenses	40.4	35.7	31.6	31.5	29.8	32.4
3.1	2.8	3.6	Operating Profit	4.5	3.5	3.4	3.5	3.1	4.0
.3	.5	.6	All Other Expenses (net)	2.1	.5	.1	.6	.1	.5
2.8	2.3	3.0	Profit Before Taxes	2.3	3.0	3.3	2.9	3.0	3.5
			RATIOS						
3.1	2.8	3.0	Current	4.2	3.6	3.3	2.8	2.2	2.3
1.9	1.7	1.7		1.5	2.1	1.9	1.7	1.7	1.4
1.3	1.2	1.2		.7	1.3	1.5	1.3	1.3	1.1
1.0	.9	.9	Quick	.7	1.2	1.0	.8	.8	.8
(301) .6	(375) .5	.5		.2	.6	.6	.5	.5	.4
.4	.3	.3		.1	.3	.4	.3	.4	.3
12 29.5	10 38.3	8 48.0	Sales/Receivables	0 UND	7 55.7	15 24.1	10 36.6	12 29.5	12 31.5
24 15.0	21 17.1	22 16.9		6 56.4	21 17.5	26 13.8	22 16.5	26 14.0	23 16.1
34 10.6	33 11.2	33 11.0		19 19.3	32 11.4	36 10.1	33 11.1	41 8.9	37 9.8
56 6.5	46 7.9	55 6.7	Cost of Sales/Inventory	45 8.2	42 8.6	62 5.9	50 7.2	64 5.7	69 5.3
92 4.0	84 4.4	95 3.8		88 4.1	78 4.7	109 3.3	89 4.1	92 4.0	99 3.7
148 2.5	132 2.8	161 2.3		195 1.9	141 2.6	158 2.3	166 2.2	158 2.3	165 2.2
27 13.5	21 17.5	19 19.7	Cost of Sales/Payables	0 UND	11 32.2	24 15.3	22 16.8	20 18.6	33 10.9
45 8.2	40 9.1	36 10.0		21 17.1	31 11.8	36 10.1	41 8.8	37 9.9	56 6.5
60 6.1	63 5.8	60 6.1		42 8.7	59 6.2	58 6.3	59 6.1	56 6.5	67 5.4
4.5	5.4	4.9	Sales/Working Capital	3.9	4.5	4.4	5.3	5.3	6.0
8.2	11.1	9.5		16.8	8.5	7.3	9.7	9.3	11.1
22.2	40.1	33.3		-28.2	34.9	16.5	35.9	22.6	43.0
10.8	9.7	7.4	EBIT/Interest	6.0	6.2	9.5	7.5	11.1	11.2
(271) 3.7	(320) 3.3	(343) 2.6		(44) 2.3	(85) 2.1	(58) 3.9	(53) 2.3	(54) 3.0	(49) 3.7
1.7	1.3	1.3		.1	.8	1.7	1.3	1.6	1.7
4.1	9.1	7.2	Net Profit + Depr., Dep., Amort./Cur. Mat. L/T/D				5.4	13.1	9.3
(80) 2.3	(64) 3.4	(61) 2.3					(10) 2.3	(14) 2.7	(18) 2.2
1.1	1.4	1.3					.8	1.7	1.3
.1	.2	.1	Fixed/Worth	.1	.1	.1	.1	.2	.2
.3	.4	.4		1.8	.3	.2	.6	.3	.4
1.1	1.9	1.5		-.9	6.6	.6	1.5	.7	1.4
.8	.9	.9	Debt/Worth	.9	.9	.8	1.1	.9	1.1
1.7	2.3	2.0		33.0	1.9	1.6	2.2	1.5	2.5
4.9	11.8	6.9		-3.7	10.3	3.1	8.2	4.0	5.6
32.1	43.6	41.2	% Profit Before Taxes/Tangible Net Worth	68.5	43.4	32.8	45.7	24.8	41.7
(267) 15.2	(312) 18.8	(327) 16.0		(30) 33.6	(81) 13.6	(61) 14.0	(55) 12.2	(53) 17.3	(47) 19.2
4.3	5.6	4.6		4.3	1.5	2.6	4.6	5.0	11.6
10.9	13.9	14.0	% Profit Before Taxes/Total Assets	19.7	15.4	13.9	12.7	10.7	13.6
5.3	5.3	4.8		5.2	4.3	5.5	3.6	4.5	6.4
1.3	.8	1.0		-3.9	-.2	1.3	1.5	1.7	2.8
58.7	58.8	62.3	Sales/Net Fixed Assets	90.6	61.2	86.2	56.6	57.5	36.3
26.0	26.0	25.8		24.0	24.6	32.1	25.2	34.6	18.5
13.2	12.7	11.8		8.3	10.2	14.1	12.2	12.1	11.9
3.6	4.0	3.9	Sales/Total Assets	5.0	4.3	3.5	3.9	3.7	3.2
2.8	2.9	2.8		2.8	2.8	2.8	3.1	2.6	2.4
2.1	2.1	1.9		1.8	1.7	1.9	2.0	1.9	1.7
.7	.6	.5	% Depr., Dep., Amort./Sales	.4	.6	.4	.7	.5	.8
(255) 1.2	(320) 1.2	(306) 1.1		(40) .8	(74) 1.2	(53) 1.0	(45) 1.2	(49) .9	(45) 1.1
1.7	1.8	1.7		2.3	1.9	1.6	1.5	1.5	1.7
2.0	1.9	2.0	% Officers', Directors' Owners' Comp/Sales	3.9	2.7	2.0	1.4	.9	1.1
(163) 3.9	(182) 3.9	(187) 3.2		(29) 4.9	(55) 3.8	(38) 3.0	(29) 2.2	(25) 1.6	(11) 2.4
7.2	7.2	5.4		8.8	7.2	4.5	3.7	3.0	9.5
4960335M	8226328M	8783395M	Net Sales ($)	37895M	179621M	244029M	395513M	899032M	7027305M
2256828M	2641113M	3195924M	Total Assets ($)	18812M	86612M	97506M	151908M	424615M	2416471M

M = $ thousand   MM = $ million
See Pages 11 through 21 for Explanation of Ratios and Data

Current Data Sorted by Assets   Comparative Historical Data

0-500M	500M-2MM	2-10MM	10-50MM	50-100MM	100-250MM		4/1/02-3/31/03 ALL	4/1/03-3/31/04 ALL
	26 (4/1-9/30/06)		114 (10/1/06-3/31/07)			**Type of Statement**		
		1	6	2	4	Unqualified	6	7
	3	18	8			Reviewed	5	11
7	11	18	6		1	Compiled	26	31
11	19	6				Tax Returns	16	23
3	5	6	6		2	Other	15	21
21	38	49	22	4	6	**NUMBER OF STATEMENTS**	68	93
%	%	%	%	%	%	**ASSETS**	%	%
7.0	9.9	5.6	3.6			Cash & Equivalents	7.9	9.1
19.2	20.9	21.5	18.9			Trade Receivables (net)	20.8	20.1
39.0	37.4	42.8	39.6			Inventory	41.2	38.9
4.1	1.9	1.0	4.9			All Other Current	1.5	2.0
69.4	70.1	70.9	67.1			Total Current	71.5	70.1
22.8	19.6	22.0	24.2			Fixed Assets (net)	21.3	21.0
.6	2.9	1.4	3.0			Intangibles (net)	1.3	2.3
7.2	7.4	5.7	5.7			All Other Non-Current	5.9	6.7
100.0	100.0	100.0	100.0			Total	100.0	100.0
						LIABILITIES		
15.5	10.7	8.6	12.1			Notes Payable-Short Term	10.0	10.0
3.9	3.6	2.4	2.3			Cur. Mat.-L.T.D.	3.9	4.4
31.6	26.1	34.5	31.5			Trade Payables	30.6	25.4
.0	.3	.3	.1			Income Taxes Payable	.3	.2
7.0	6.5	6.3	7.5			All Other Current	8.7	7.1
57.9	47.2	52.1	53.6			Total Current	53.4	47.2
25.0	16.1	8.9	13.1			Long-Term Debt	17.9	20.9
.0	.3	.2	.1			Deferred Taxes	.0	.2
16.0	3.8	1.8	4.1			All Other Non-Current	10.5	5.6
1.1	32.7	37.0	29.1			Net Worth	18.1	26.2
100.0	100.0	100.0	100.0			Total Liabilities & Net Worth	100.0	100.0
						INCOME DATA		
100.0	100.0	100.0	100.0			Net Sales	100.0	100.0
43.3	36.2	31.9	33.1			Gross Profit	36.5	35.8
42.1	33.6	29.3	29.0			Operating Expenses	35.2	34.1
1.2	2.6	2.6	4.1			Operating Profit	1.3	1.6
-.2	.5	-.3	.4			All Other Expenses (net)	.3	.2
1.4	2.1	2.8	3.7			Profit Before Taxes	1.0	1.4
						RATIOS		
5.9	2.9	1.8	1.6			Current	2.6	2.4
1.3	1.4	1.4	1.2				1.5	1.6
.7	.9	1.0	1.1				1.1	1.2
1.8	1.6	.7	.6			Quick	1.0	1.1
.5	.6	.4	.4				.6	.5
.2	.3	.3	.3				.3	.4
9 38.5	7 53.6	15 23.8	9 38.6			Sales/Receivables	9 40.6	11 34.1
14 26.8	21 17.6	22 16.8	30 12.1				20 18.1	23 16.2
29 12.7	40 9.1	33 11.0	49 7.4				32 11.3	32 11.3
38 9.7	40 9.1	50 7.2	64 5.7			Cost of Sales/Inventory	30 12.0	38 9.5
61 6.0	59 6.2	73 5.0	87 4.2				65 5.7	67 5.5
84 4.3	95 3.8	98 3.7	104 3.5				110 3.3	100 3.7
16 22.8	30 12.2	40 9.1	44 8.3			Cost of Sales/Payables	23 15.5	23 15.9
34 10.7	40 9.2	55 6.6	59 6.2				44 8.4	41 8.9
91 4.0	53 6.9	75 4.9	84 4.4				67 5.5	64 5.7
5.5	6.4	9.5	8.2			Sales/Working Capital	6.3	7.0
30.8	15.6	20.3	13.8				14.1	13.4
-23.2	-78.7	NM	54.5				93.5	48.0
6.6	5.7	8.2	6.7			EBIT/Interest	11.8	6.5
(18) 2.2	(33) 2.5	(47) 4.7	(21) 3.8				(62) 2.9	(81) 2.5
-.6	1.7	1.7	2.9				.7	1.4
		2.6	9.7			Net Profit + Depr., Dep., Amort./Cur. Mat. L/T/D	7.2	4.6
	(15) 1.0	(10) 3.9					(17) 2.3	(25) 2.2
		.9	2.6				1.7	1.8
.2	.2	.2	.5			Fixed/Worth	.2	.2
16.7	.5	.5	1.0				.5	.6
-.7	1.8	1.1	2.0				1.7	1.4
.9	.6	1.0	1.6			Debt/Worth	1.0	1.0
-147.0	2.8	1.9	3.4				2.6	2.3
-2.7	6.6	4.2	6.2				6.9	5.1
68.8	43.2	31.5	53.3			% Profit Before Taxes/Tangible Net Worth	26.6	25.5
(11) 16.1	(33) 16.5	(46) 16.2	(21) 25.3				(58) 11.5	(80) 11.1
1.3	4.1	4.0	8.3				1.2	3.5
15.2	12.2	12.5	9.1			% Profit Before Taxes/Total Assets	9.1	10.4
7.1	4.8	4.6	5.9				2.4	3.3
-8.5	1.7	1.3	3.3				-1.1	.9
86.1	59.9	38.8	18.3			Sales/Net Fixed Assets	54.6	38.8
30.7	28.4	18.0	12.5				25.8	20.2
7.5	10.9	11.3	5.9				12.5	11.0
5.3	3.9	3.8	3.4			Sales/Total Assets	5.2	4.3
3.6	3.1	3.2	2.4				3.4	3.1
2.6	2.4	2.6	1.8				2.6	2.2
.4	.5	.6	1.1			% Depr., Dep., Amort./Sales	.7	.8
(17) .9	(34) 1.1	(46) 1.3	1.5				(61) 1.3	(84) 1.5
3.9	1.8	1.7	1.8				2.2	2.3
4.2	1.8	.7				% Officers', Directors' Owners' Comp/Sales	1.1	1.3
(15) 5.0	(26) 3.0	(26) 1.8					(39) 2.7	(63) 3.1
7.9	5.3	4.4					4.9	6.0
22187M	140717M	792990M	1148702M	742192M	2469642M	Net Sales ($)	1344816M	2988548M
6175M	41558M	250930M	464169M	256046M	711747M	Total Assets ($)	498784M	1010949M

M = $ thousand   MM = $ million
See Pages 11 through 21 for Explanation of Ratios and Data

Comparative Historical Data					Current Data Sorted by Sales					

				Type of Statement						
11	11	13		Unqualified					1	12
8	11	29		Reviewed		1	1	4	15	8
46	43	37		Compiled	3	9	3	9	10	3
32	15	36		Tax Returns	8	10	9	4	5	
18	35	25		Other	2	5	2	1		12
4/1/04- 3/31/05 ALL	4/1/05- 3/31/06 ALL	4/1/06- 3/31/07 ALL			26 (4/1-9/30/06)			114 (10/1/06-3/31/07)		
					0-1MM	1-3MM	3-5MM	5-10MM	10-25MM	25MM & OVER
115	115	140		NUMBER OF STATEMENTS	13	25	15	18	34	35
%	%	%		ASSETS	%	%	%	%	%	%
9.3	7.9	6.4		Cash & Equivalents	7.1	7.1	10.5	6.5	6.0	4.3
19.6	18.9	20.5		Trade Receivables (net)	20.0	17.4	19.0	25.0	19.5	22.4
36.4	38.2	40.5		Inventory	38.8	34.7	48.2	39.7	39.1	43.8
2.2	2.8	2.4		All Other Current	5.7	2.3	.9	1.0	3.4	1.5
67.5	67.9	69.9		Total Current	71.6	61.6	78.5	72.2	68.1	72.0
22.9	24.2	21.8		Fixed Assets (net)	24.7	24.3	15.1	20.3	24.5	20.0
3.1	2.5	1.9		Intangibles (net)	.4	3.4	3.1	.3	1.4	2.3
6.5	5.4	6.4		All Other Non-Current	3.3	10.7	3.3	7.2	6.1	5.7
100.0	100.0	100.0		Total	100.0	100.0	100.0	100.0	100.0	100.0
				LIABILITIES						
10.0	13.0	10.9		Notes Payable-Short Term	9.0	13.7	16.2	10.3	8.6	9.9
3.6	3.0	2.9		Cur. Mat.-L.T.D.	2.7	4.2	4.7	2.6	2.0	2.1
32.3	31.9	30.9		Trade Payables	27.0	25.6	29.2	26.3	34.9	35.3
.3	.3	.2		Income Taxes Payable	.0	.1	.8	.2	.2	.2
7.3	10.8	7.3		All Other Current	6.3	7.7	3.3	10.0	4.9	9.8
53.4	59.0	52.1		Total Current	45.0	51.4	54.1	49.3	50.7	57.3
19.0	19.5	15.1		Long-Term Debt	18.5	29.3	11.4	11.4	9.2	12.9
.1	.1	.2		Deferred Taxes	.0	.0	.1	.4	.2	.2
3.7	4.5	5.0		All Other Non-Current	22.9	3.2	5.9	1.9	2.0	3.6
23.8	16.8	27.6		Net Worth	13.6	16.2	28.5	37.0	37.8	26.0
100.0	100.0	100.0		Total Liabilties & Net Worth	100.0	100.0	100.0	100.0	100.0	100.0
				INCOME DATA						
100.0	100.0	100.0		Net Sales	100.0	100.0	100.0	100.0	100.0	100.0
35.6	37.0	34.4		Gross Profit	43.1	38.9	39.6	29.2	33.2	29.8
34.0	35.2	31.7		Operating Expenses	40.4	36.6	36.7	26.7	30.2	26.7
1.6	1.8	2.8		Operating Profit	2.7	2.2	2.9	2.5	3.0	3.1
.1	.4	.1		All Other Expenses (net)	-.4	1.2	.0	-.4	-.1	.0
1.5	1.4	2.7		Profit Before Taxes	3.2	1.0	2.9	2.9	3.1	3.0
				RATIOS						
1.9	1.8	2.0			8.8	2.5	2.4	2.1	1.6	1.6
1.3	1.2	1.4		Current	3.7	1.2	1.4	1.5	1.3	1.2
1.0	.9	1.0			.8	.7	1.2	1.1	1.1	1.0
.9	.8	.8			3.9	1.0	1.5	1.0	.7	.7
.5	.4	.5		Quick	.7	.5	.5	.5	.5	.5
.3	.3	.3			.2	.2	.3	.4	.3	.3

9	40.7	9	41.8	11	33.7	Sales/Receivables	6	59.4	7	49.4	6	57.2	12	30.4	14	25.6	12	31.3
19	19.1	19	19.6	22	16.9		21	17.7	14	26.6	23	15.9	29	12.6	21	17.3	26	13.9
33	11.2	32	11.2	36	10.0		42	8.7	28	13.2	39	9.4	44	8.3	35	10.4	39	9.4
45	8.1	48	7.7	50	7.3	Cost of Sales/Inventory	44	8.3	36	10.2	43	8.5	41	8.8	51	7.1	55	6.6
64	5.7	64	5.7	70	5.2		66	5.5	56	6.6	65	5.6	70	5.2	75	4.9	76	4.8
92	4.0	90	4.0	98	3.7		130	2.8	88	4.2	124	2.9	95	3.8	98	3.7	98	3.7
29	12.5	33	11.0	33	11.0	Cost of Sales/Payables	2	237.3	28	13.2	33	11.0	33	10.9	39	9.4	38	9.6
51	7.2	58	6.3	49	7.4		23	16.2	35	10.5	44	8.4	47	7.8	56	6.6	56	6.5
81	4.5	77	4.7	74	4.9		113	3.2	67	5.5	65	5.6	70	5.2	84	4.3	72	5.0
	8.4		9.4		7.5	Sales/Working Capital		3.5		8.0		4.5		6.8		9.3		12.4
	20.8		28.0		16.6			6.6		33.4		11.6		15.8		19.8		20.3
	-285.5		-45.3		-582.0			-22.4		-25.2		43.4		NM		56.0		999.8
	7.8		7.7		7.8	EBIT/Interest		7.3		3.3		4.9		7.4		8.0		11.5
(99)	3.3	(111)	3.5	(129)	3.5		(11)	5.1	(22)	1.7	(13)	2.8	(17)	4.3	(33)	3.4	(33)	5.2
	1.3		1.3		1.8			.3		.1		1.4		1.9		1.9		3.2
	10.1		5.8		5.5	Net Profit + Depr., Dep., Amort./Cur. Mat. L/T/D												7.8
(27)	3.5	(34)	3.3	(40)	2.6											(18)	5.2
	1.6		1.4		1.0												3.3
	.3		.4		.3	Fixed/Worth		.1		.2		.3		.1		.3		.4
	.8		1.1		.7			16.7		1.3		.4		.5		.7		.8
	2.8		6.2		1.8			-.7		-5.1		1.1		.9		1.1		1.8
	1.0		1.5		1.0	Debt/Worth		.2		1.2		1.4		.8		.9		1.3
	2.8		3.6		2.8			147.0		4.4		3.0		1.7		2.4		3.2
	12.5		26.4		7.6			-4.9		-36.4		4.5		3.9		4.2		9.4
	36.4		45.5		38.7	% Profit Before Taxes/Tangible Net Worth				56.2		43.7		39.5		25.0		67.7
(95)	14.5	(91)	19.8	(120)	21.1				(18)	14.2	(13)	20.5	(17)	16.5	(32)	18.8	(33)	28.4
	3.2		6.9		6.8					.9		6.2		9.9		4.1		8.3
	9.9		10.1		12.6	% Profit Before Taxes/Total Assets		15.2		8.4		16.8		13.5		12.0		10.5
	4.4		4.8		5.3			12.6		2.5		5.9		6.5		4.7		6.8
	.3		1.1		1.7			1.9		-4.1		1.6		2.3		1.4		3.4
	41.9		36.4		47.8	Sales/Net Fixed Assets		139.3		74.6		51.7		70.8		37.8		32.4
	19.9		19.3		17.9			17.8		26.7		34.8		18.0		15.5		16.3
	9.3		9.0		9.0			6.1		8.2		13.2		12.1		8.0		10.6
	4.2		4.4		3.8	Sales/Total Assets		4.4		3.8		5.9		3.6		4.1		3.9
	3.2		3.3		3.1			2.7		3.1		3.1		3.0		3.1		3.2
	2.5		2.5		2.4			2.0		2.2		2.4		2.6		2.4		2.4
	.8		.7		.6	% Depr., Dep., Amort./Sales		.3		.5		.6		.6		.6		.8
(94)	1.3	(108)	1.4	(128)	1.3		(10)	1.2	(22)	1.2	(14)	1.1	(15)	1.4	(33)	1.1	(34)	1.4
	2.3		1.9		1.8			3.7		2.2		2.2		1.9		1.9		1.6
	1.0		1.3		1.3	% Officers', Directors' Owners' Comp/Sales				2.9		1.8		1.1		.7		
(67)	2.2	(44)	2.8	(76)	3.0				(17)	4.7	(12)	2.7	(10)	2.9	(20)	1.7		
	5.7		4.7		5.7					6.4		4.2		7.6		5.2		

3281733M	5403026M	5316430M		Net Sales ($)	9734M	48323M	60138M	120018M	561510M	4516707M
1149740M	1758442M	1730625M		Total Assets ($)	3697M	19304M	27703M	42510M	240751M	1396660M

© RMA 2007

M = $ thousand   MM = $ million
See Pages 11 through 21 for Explanation of Ratios and Data

Current Data Sorted by Assets   Comparative Historical Data

						Type of Statement		
1		9	23	8	11	Unqualified	64	46
3	22	47	24		1	Reviewed	101	109
22	79	61	6			Compiled	134	198
45	70	31	2		1	Tax Returns	88	154
26	53	82	47	5	12	Other	132	142
	146 (4/1-9/30/06)		545 (10/1/06-3/31/07)				4/1/02-3/31/03	4/1/03-3/31/04
0-500M	500M-2MM	2-10MM	10-50MM	50-100MM	100-250MM		ALL	ALL
97	224	230	102	13	25	NUMBER OF STATEMENTS	519	649
%	%	%	%	%	%	ASSETS	%	%
12.3	8.0	8.5	8.7	6.5	10.0	Cash & Equivalents	9.7	9.0
7.0	11.2	15.2	15.2	13.0	15.4	Trade Receivables (net)	14.1	12.4
54.5	55.9	46.4	40.7	36.9	26.7	Inventory	48.0	50.4
3.2	2.4	2.3	2.3	2.2	3.2	All Other Current	2.1	2.2
77.0	77.5	72.3	66.9	58.6	55.4	Total Current	73.9	74.0
15.4	16.8	20.7	23.2	30.0	28.2	Fixed Assets (net)	18.5	18.4
3.0	1.2	1.5	3.2	2.4	11.5	Intangibles (net)	2.0	1.8
4.5	4.5	5.5	6.7	8.9	5.0	All Other Non-Current	5.6	5.8
100.0	100.0	100.0	100.0	100.0	100.0	Total	100.0	100.0
						LIABILITIES		
13.3	12.9	10.9	11.4	12.8	8.8	Notes Payable-Short Term	9.8	10.4
5.3	1.9	2.3	3.1	1.5	1.5	Cur. Mat.-L.T.D.	2.7	2.3
20.6	19.1	21.0	15.7	12.1	13.4	Trade Payables	18.0	19.1
.1	.1	.2	.2	.1	.6	Income Taxes Payable	.3	.3
20.1	18.3	16.7	19.1	16.0	13.0	All Other Current	16.8	18.4
59.4	52.3	51.0	49.5	42.6	37.4	Total Current	47.6	50.5
15.6	14.7	12.7	14.3	18.9	18.3	Long-Term Debt	13.8	13.6
.0	.0	.1	.1	.1	.2	Deferred Taxes	.1	.1
5.4	6.9	4.5	4.8	.3	4.0	All Other Non-Current	5.5	4.8
19.6	26.0	31.7	31.4	38.1	40.1	Net Worth	33.0	31.0
100.0	100.0	100.0	100.0	100.0	100.0	Total Liabilties & Net Worth	100.0	100.0
						INCOME DATA		
100.0	100.0	100.0	100.0	100.0	100.0	Net Sales	100.0	100.0
42.3	41.5	41.2	41.7	44.9	44.0	Gross Profit	41.1	41.0
39.6	39.8	39.6	38.8	41.9	40.8	Operating Expenses	38.3	38.9
2.7	1.7	1.6	2.9	3.0	3.2	Operating Profit	2.8	2.1
.9	.8	.0	.6	-1.2	.2	All Other Expenses (net)	.4	.5
1.7	.8	1.6	2.3	4.2	3.0	Profit Before Taxes	2.4	1.6
						RATIOS		
2.8	2.7	2.2	2.1	2.1	1.8		2.5	2.3
1.4	1.6	1.4	1.3	1.3	1.4	Current	1.6	1.6
.9	1.1	1.0	1.0	1.0	1.1		1.1	1.1
.7	.7	.8	.9	.8	.9		.9	.9
(95) .3	(222) .3	(228) .3	.4	(12) .4	.4	Quick	.4	(643) .3
.1	.1	.1	.1	.1	.2		.1	.1
0 UND	0 UND	1 405.2	2 178.8	1 495.1	1 255.4		0 826.4	0 815.5
0 999.8	4 96.9	5 72.0	5 79.1	3 106.4	6 59.6	Sales/Receivables	5 73.4	5 71.0
12 30.4	18 20.2	34 10.6	39 9.3	15 24.9	90 4.1		25 14.5	22 16.9
51 7.2	82 4.4	66 5.5	64 5.7	93 3.9	68 5.4		65 5.6	67 5.4
88 4.2	122 3.0	118 3.1	107 3.4	104 3.5	78 4.7	Cost of Sales/Inventory	111 3.3	110 3.3
153 2.4	180 2.0	162 2.3	142 2.6	159 2.3	108 3.4		158 2.3	168 2.2
0 UND	18 19.8	23 16.0	21 17.3	22 16.6	28 13.3		19 18.8	18 19.9
21 17.3	34 10.7	36 10.0	35 10.4	37 9.9	46 8.0	Cost of Sales/Payables	32 11.3	34 10.7
43 8.4	53 6.9	59 6.2	51 7.2	51 7.2	60 6.1		53 6.9	53 6.9
7.4	5.4	5.9	6.5	8.5	6.2		5.7	6.1
16.5	11.0	14.6	20.4	14.8	19.3	Sales/Working Capital	11.5	12.5
-50.8	41.2	109.6	459.5	156.7	46.0		40.7	45.9
8.4	5.4	8.1	7.4	5.5	8.6		10.4	9.3
(72) 2.9	(182) 1.6	(210) 2.7	(89) 2.3	(11) 1.9	(22) 3.5	EBIT/Interest	(454) 3.3	(556) 3.0
-.1	.2	.7	1.2	1.5	1.5		1.3	.9
	2.1	9.0	9.1		17.0		9.0	7.7
	(22) .9	(44) 2.3	(28) 3.6		(10) 3.3	Net Profit + Depr., Dep., Amort./Cur. Mat. L/T/D	(108) 3.1	(107) 2.4
	-.1	.2	1.0		1.5		1.1	.8
.1	.1	.2	.2	.5	.6		.1	.2
.5	.5	.5	.9	.9	.8	Fixed/Worth	.4	.5
UND	4.3	1.8	2.1	1.6	1.8		1.5	1.5
1.0	1.0	.9	1.3	.9	1.2		.9	.9
3.5	2.5	2.4	2.4	2.2	1.8	Debt/Worth	2.1	2.1
UND	19.3	5.8	5.5	4.5	2.6		5.4	6.5
103.6	34.0	38.2	33.6	39.2	19.7		36.9	32.3
(73) 34.7	(177) 10.3	(206) 11.5	(91) 15.2	16.2	(20) 12.7	% Profit Before Taxes/Tangible Net Worth	(462) 15.1	(559) 13.1
1.1	-.5	.6	3.8	8.1	6.3		4.5	1.5
25.1	9.9	9.2	13.3	10.3	10.2		12.1	11.2
5.2	2.4	3.5	4.0	5.4	5.7	% Profit Before Taxes/Total Assets	4.9	3.7
-5.0	-2.9	-.9	.9	1.8	2.2		1.0	-.3
247.7	71.7	44.5	41.8	10.5	11.8		53.7	52.0
51.5	26.4	19.3	18.3	9.1	6.4	Sales/Net Fixed Assets	25.3	23.4
21.3	11.1	8.9	7.7	7.0	3.9		9.5	10.5
6.4	3.7	3.8	3.6	3.2	2.8		3.9	4.1
3.8	2.8	2.7	2.7	2.1	1.7	Sales/Total Assets	2.8	2.8
2.4	2.0	1.8	1.7	1.4	1.1		1.9	1.9
.4	.4	.5	.6	1.4	1.3		.6	.5
(61) .6	(175) .6	(199) .8	(88) 1.0	(22) 1.9	1.5	% Depr., Dep., Amort./Sales	(430) .9	(560) .9
1.1	1.1	1.2	1.3	2.4	2.0		1.5	1.5
2.8	1.9	1.3	.6				1.7	1.8
(50) 5.6	(128) 3.7	(105) 2.7	(32) 1.3			% Officers', Directors' Owners' Comp/Sales	(267) 3.6	(333) 3.5
9.3	6.0	4.6	2.9				6.2	6.0
125086M	776573M	3036809M	5996796M	2053099M	8252752M	Net Sales ($)	13686982M	13964407M
29146M	258558M	1035694M	2229532M	986146M	4124469M	Total Assets ($)	5623144M	5469454M

© RMA 2007

M = $ thousand   MM = $ million
See Pages 11 through 21 for Explanation of Ratios and Data

Comparative Historical Data / Current Data Sorted by Sales

4/1/04-3/31/05 ALL	4/1/05-3/31/06 ALL	4/1/06-3/31/07 ALL	Type of Statement	0-1MM	1-3MM	3-5MM	5-10MM	10-25MM	25MM & OVER
51	46	52	Unqualified	1	9	1	2	6	42
102	80	97	Reviewed	2		7	19	35	25
133	127	168	Compiled	9	55	37	37	23	7
154	117	149	Tax Returns	21	60	28	28	9	3
162	203	225	Other	23	39	24	24	45	70
				146 (4/1-9/30/06)			545 (10/1/06-3/31/07)		
602	573	691	**NUMBER OF STATEMENTS**	56	163	97	110	118	147
%	%	%	**ASSETS**	%	%	%	%	%	%
8.3	9.0	8.9	Cash & Equivalents	8.5	9.4	10.0	8.7	7.7	8.9
11.9	12.4	12.7	Trade Receivables (net)	9.6	10.2	9.7	13.1	15.9	15.8
50.9	48.9	48.9	Inventory	49.8	52.8	52.7	53.0	48.7	38.7
1.9	2.3	2.5	All Other Current	2.1	3.5	2.4	1.4	2.1	2.9
73.0	72.6	73.0	Total Current	70.0	75.9	74.7	76.1	74.5	66.2
18.8	18.9	19.5	Fixed Assets (net)	21.1	18.9	18.0	15.2	19.5	23.8
2.4	2.1	2.2	Intangibles (net)	3.4	1.8	.8	1.9	1.3	4.3
5.8	6.4	5.2	All Other Non-Current	5.4	3.5	6.6	6.7	4.6	5.7
100.0	100.0	100.0	Total	100.0	100.0	100.0	100.0	100.0	100.0
			LIABILITIES						
11.9	12.0	11.9	Notes Payable-Short Term	15.1	13.0	13.2	9.2	11.3	11.3
3.0	2.4	2.6	Cur. Mat.-L.T.D.	3.7	4.2	1.2	2.2	2.2	2.2
18.6	19.4	19.1	Trade Payables	16.5	18.2	18.3	20.1	22.1	18.6
.2	.3	.2	Income Taxes Payable	.1	.0	.1	.2	.1	.3
19.1	18.8	17.9	All Other Current	15.1	13.9	20.1	18.8	19.6	20.0
52.8	52.9	51.7	Total Current	50.5	49.2	52.8	50.5	55.3	52.4
14.9	14.2	14.3	Long-Term Debt	19.1	20.6	10.7	11.4	9.9	13.6
.1	.1	.1	Deferred Taxes	.0	.0	.1	.0	.1	.1
4.7	6.3	5.4	All Other Non-Current	5.9	6.5	6.1	6.9	3.2	4.0
27.5	26.5	28.5	Net Worth	24.3	23.6	30.4	31.2	31.5	29.9
100.0	100.0	100.0	Total Liabilities & Net Worth	100.0	100.0	100.0	100.0	100.0	100.0
			INCOME DATA						
100.0	100.0	100.0	Net Sales	100.0	100.0	100.0	100.0	100.0	100.0
41.3	42.3	41.7	Gross Profit	44.7	42.7	42.5	39.7	40.6	41.2
39.0	40.1	39.6	Operating Expenses	42.7	40.9	40.5	38.1	39.2	37.9
2.3	2.2	2.1	Operating Profit	2.0	1.8	2.0	1.6	1.4	3.2
.4	.7	.5	All Other Expenses (net)	1.8	.9	.2	.0	.1	.4
1.9	1.4	1.6	Profit Before Taxes	.2	1.0	1.8	1.6	1.3	2.8
			RATIOS						
2.3	2.2	2.4	Current	3.1	3.2	2.6	2.7	1.9	1.7
1.4	1.4	1.4		1.7	1.6	1.6	1.5	1.3	1.3
1.1	1.0	1.1		.9	1.1	1.1	1.1	1.0	1.0
.8	.8	.8	Quick	.8	.9	.9	.8	.8	.8
(597) .3	(571) .3	(684) .3		(55) .3	(161) .3	(94) .3	.3	.2	(146) .4
.1	.1	.1		.1	.1	.1	.1	.1	.1
0 999.8	0 999.8	0 999.8	Sales/Receivables	0 UND	0 UND	0 UND	0 758.5	1 364.7	1 371.5
4 83.0	4 86.8	4 86.2		8 46.8	3 124.6	3 106.4	5 70.1	5 74.2	5 80.5
18 20.3	18 20.8	23 15.9		20 17.9	18 20.2	12 29.3	27 13.4	33 10.9	32 11.6
68 5.4	66 5.5	67 5.4	Cost of Sales/Inventory	71 5.2	89 4.1	69 5.3	69 5.3	56 6.5	55 6.7
114 3.2	106 3.4	111 3.3		151 2.4	131 2.8	113 3.2	106 3.4	111 3.3	90 4.0
161 2.3	152 2.4	160 2.3		261 2.0	188 1.9	187 2.0	154 2.4	148 2.5	124 3.0
19 19.7	20 18.2	19 19.0	Cost of Sales/Payables	0 UND	15 24.5	19 19.3	20 18.7	23 16.0	22 16.3
32 11.4	36 10.2	34 10.7		24 15.4	34 10.6	33 11.0	35 10.6	36 10.2	34 10.7
53 7.0	56 6.5	54 6.7		75 4.9	62 5.9	51 7.2	54 6.7	55 6.6	51 7.2
6.4	6.6	6.1	Sales/Working Capital	4.2	4.2	6.0	5.7	8.4	8.5
15.4	14.7	13.8		8.3	9.6	12.7	11.5	21.3	25.8
112.7	209.3	95.2		-47.1	34.2	86.8	41.1	NM	228.7
11.0	7.7	7.2	EBIT/Interest	4.1	5.2	7.4	8.2	7.3	10.7
(514) 3.4	(497) 2.5	(586) 2.3		(42) 1.3	(138) 1.8	(80) 2.3	(91) 2.4	(106) 2.4	(129) 3.4
1.0	.5	.7		-2.5	.1	.6	.7	.6	1.4
6.6	6.5	9.1	Net Profit + Depr., Dep., Amort./Cur. Mat. L/T/D			1.3	5.0	9.9	14.2
(101) 2.6	(93) 2.5	(106) 1.9			(12) .9	(19) 1.2	(23) 4.1		(42) 3.7
.9	.5	.5			-.6	-1.4	.6		1.4
.2	.2	.2	Fixed/Worth	.1	.1	.2	.2	.2	.4
.6	.6	.6		.6	.6	.5	.4	.6	.9
2.8	2.7	2.6		UND	10.3	2.2	1.3	1.8	2.0
1.0	1.0	1.0	Debt/Worth	.8	1.0	.9	.7	1.0	1.4
2.5	2.7	2.5		3.8	2.7	2.2	1.8	2.6	2.5
11.8	12.3	9.8		-11.7	23.7	7.7	7.2	5.0	7.4
42.4	48.4	37.9	% Profit Before Taxes/Tangible Net Worth	72.6	43.3	34.5	21.4	32.2	48.8
(492) 17.2	(477) 15.0	(580) 12.5		(39) 7.5	(130) 12.3	(83) 9.7	(91) 10.0	(109) 11.7	(128) 18.5
3.0	.3	.6		-2.9	.2	-.1	.1	-.5	6.3
13.1	11.4	11.9	% Profit Before Taxes/Total Assets	11.1	12.4	12.1	8.2	10.2	13.8
4.5	4.0	3.5		1.0	2.6	3.3	3.5	3.4	6.5
.1	-1.0	-1.0		-8.2	-3.2	-1.8	-1.1	-1.3	1.6
53.1	60.1	59.6	Sales/Net Fixed Assets	134.5	90.2	52.6	73.8	66.0	37.4
24.2	23.2	22.7		30.8	22.5	25.1	28.7	22.5	14.2
10.2	10.2	9.7		5.9	9.4	10.5	14.9	10.5	7.4
4.0	4.1	3.9	Sales/Total Assets	3.6	3.5	4.1	3.9	4.1	3.8
2.9	2.9	2.8		2.1	2.5	2.8	2.8	3.1	2.9
2.0	2.0	1.9		1.2	1.7	2.1	2.0	2.1	1.8
.5	.4	.4	% Depr., Dep., Amort./Sales	.6	.4	.4	.3	.4	.6
(480) .9	(471) .8	(558) .8		(31) .9	(122) .8	(78) .6	(93) .7	(108) .7	(126) 1.1
1.5	1.3	1.3		2.3	1.3	1.0	1.0	1.0	1.7
1.6	1.7	1.4	% Officers', Directors' Owners' Comp/Sales	5.3	2.6	2.1	1.0	1.3	.5
(282) 3.3	(294) 3.2	(317) 3.2		(23) 8.9	(91) 4.3	(61) 3.8	(60) 2.3	(49) 2.5	(33) 1.0
5.5	5.6	6.0		11.1	6.7	6.4	4.5	3.7	2.6
14243279M	18232096M	20241115M	Net Sales ($)	31553M	326742M	382419M	776316M	1952851M	16771234M
5657152M	7495661M	8663545M	Total Assets ($)	18933M	167749M	153273M	319932M	750578M	7253080M

M = $ thousand   MM = $ million
See Pages 11 through 21 for Explanation of Ratios and Data

Current Data Sorted by Assets   Comparative Historical Data

						Type of Statement		
	1	8	7	1		Unqualified	11	15
	14	33	1	1		Reviewed	46	48
12	51	25	3			Compiled	83	107
37	38	17				Tax Returns	77	99
12	38	46	10	2	1	Other	66	81
	71 (4/1-9/30/06)			287 (10/1/06-3/31/07)			4/1/02-3/31/03	4/1/03-3/31/04
0-500M	500M-2MM	2-10MM	10-50MM	50-100MM	100-250MM		ALL	ALL
61	142	129	21	4	1	NUMBER OF STATEMENTS	283	350
%	%	%	%	%	%	ASSETS	%	%
12.3	9.2	7.1	2.7			Cash & Equivalents	9.9	9.4
24.0	35.6	31.0	28.4			Trade Receivables (net)	26.2	27.6
31.8	29.1	34.2	41.1			Inventory	34.5	34.7
2.9	2.2	3.3	2.3			All Other Current	2.6	2.8
71.0	76.1	75.6	74.6			Total Current	73.1	74.4
16.0	16.1	15.7	22.0			Fixed Assets (net)	16.9	16.7
1.2	2.4	3.3	.6			Intangibles (net)	3.3	2.5
11.7	5.4	5.5	2.8			All Other Non-Current	6.6	6.3
100.0	100.0	100.0	100.0			Total	100.0	100.0
						LIABILITIES		
17.4	10.5	15.1	20.9			Notes Payable-Short Term	11.9	13.1
7.4	1.8	1.8	1.5			Cur. Mat.-L.T.D.	3.8	3.7
27.3	18.3	18.0	19.6			Trade Payables	21.4	22.4
.1	.3	.1	.3			Income Taxes Payable	.4	.2
16.0	15.1	16.3	14.1			All Other Current	12.9	16.7
68.1	46.1	51.3	56.4			Total Current	50.5	56.2
13.1	11.8	10.3	14.8			Long-Term Debt	12.8	10.8
.0	.1	.1	.0			Deferred Taxes	.1	.0
6.5	4.4	4.3	2.4			All Other Non-Current	4.8	5.5
12.3	37.6	34.0	26.4			Net Worth	31.9	27.5
100.0	100.0	100.0	100.0			Total Liabilities & Net Worth	100.0	100.0
						INCOME DATA		
100.0	100.0	100.0	100.0			Net Sales	100.0	100.0
36.3	33.2	33.3	32.9			Gross Profit	35.5	35.5
34.3	30.0	29.9	29.4			Operating Expenses	33.3	33.1
2.0	3.2	3.4	3.5			Operating Profit	2.1	2.4
.6	.1	.5	1.6			All Other Expenses (net)	.3	.2
1.4	3.1	2.9	1.9			Profit Before Taxes	1.9	2.3
						RATIOS		
2.5	3.0	2.1	1.5			Current	2.4	2.3
1.5	1.7	1.4	1.2			Current	1.5	1.4
.6	1.2	1.1	1.1				1.1	1.1
1.2	1.9	1.1	.7			Quick	1.4	1.3
.5	1.0	.7	.6			Quick	(282) .8	.7
.2	.5	.4	.3				.4	.3
7 51.9	17 21.9	14 26.4	13 28.5			Sales/Receivables	10 35.5	10 37.4
13 28.3	28 13.1	31 12.0	30 12.0			Sales/Receivables	22 16.3	25 14.5
26 14.0	47 7.7	48 7.5	64 5.7				39 9.4	39 9.3
13 29.0	15 24.6	24 15.5	40 9.1			Cost of Sales/Inventory	23 16.1	20 18.6
28 13.3	34 10.7	52 7.0	72 5.0			Cost of Sales/Inventory	45 8.1	42 8.8
59 6.2	56 6.5	98 3.7	145 2.5				83 4.4	76 4.8
9 42.9	12 31.6	16 23.4	23 15.8			Cost of Sales/Payables	14 25.9	13 27.4
25 14.4	23 15.8	24 15.2	35 10.4			Cost of Sales/Payables	24 15.2	25 14.8
44 8.4	35 10.5	40 9.1	52 7.0				40 9.1	41 8.9
10.2	6.8	7.6	8.3			Sales/Working Capital	8.0	8.8
27.0	11.7	14.0	19.1			Sales/Working Capital	14.7	18.5
-15.1	44.5	62.4	94.5				66.7	127.1
10.5	16.5	15.9	7.7			EBIT/Interest	11.1	10.7
(47) 3.7	(128) 5.0	(122) 4.4	(18) 2.1			EBIT/Interest	(248) 3.7	(292) 3.4
-.5	1.7	1.3	1.2				1.4	1.1
	3.3	5.1				Net Profit + Depr., Dep.,	5.9	6.9
	(18) 2.5	(22) 2.4				Amort./Cur. Mat. L/T/D	(58) 2.0	(63) 2.3
	.6	1.1					1.1	.7
.1	.1	.1	.2			Fixed/Worth	.2	.2
.6	.3	.3	.4			Fixed/Worth	.4	.4
-78.7	1.1	1.4	2.0				1.5	1.6
1.2	.8	1.0	1.7			Debt/Worth	.9	.9
2.9	1.4	2.2	4.0			Debt/Worth	2.2	2.4
-12.7	4.1	5.7	6.8				6.8	8.5
95.5	54.3	59.3	70.6			% Profit Before Taxes/Tangible	48.0	56.2
(44) 29.3	(129) 22.5	(120) 25.9	17.6			Net Worth	(244) 18.7	(294) 20.8
12.0	8.1	4.7	-.7				5.8	2.5
22.9	19.3	17.1	14.1			% Profit Before Taxes/Total	16.3	16.7
10.4	8.1	5.7	4.2			Assets	6.0	5.7
1.6	2.0	1.6	.1				1.1	.7
246.1	89.6	86.4	61.2			Sales/Net Fixed Assets	62.0	66.5
39.5	38.1	39.5	27.7			Sales/Net Fixed Assets	32.2	35.3
17.4	20.0	16.9	6.3				17.0	18.1
6.9	5.0	4.6	3.9			Sales/Total Assets	5.1	5.5
6.0	3.9	3.3	3.0			Sales/Total Assets	3.8	3.9
3.6	3.1	2.5	1.7				2.6	2.9
.3	.4	.3	.5			% Depr., Dep., Amort./Sales	.5	.4
(42) .8	(115) .6	(110) .7	.7			% Depr., Dep., Amort./Sales	(246) .8	(293) .8
1.6	1.1	1.1	1.3				1.4	1.3
3.7	2.0	1.1				% Officers', Directors'	2.4	2.2
(41) 5.3	(101) 3.6	(72) 1.9				Owners' Comp/Sales	(177) 4.1	(217) 3.9
8.3	5.8	3.6					7.1	6.3
84451M	649454M	1966863M	1021914M	987488M	723020M	Net Sales ($)	3123689M	4792539M
15711M	162419M	556086M	373047M	285382M	136020M	Total Assets ($)	966821M	1275570M

© RMA 2007

M = $ thousand   MM = $ million
See Pages 11 through 21 for Explanation of Ratios and Data

Comparative Historical Data

Current Data Sorted by Sales

Comparative Historical Data			Type of Statement	Current Data Sorted by Sales					
			Unqualified		1		1	6	9
17	11	17	Reviewed		2	6	11	24	6
41	47	49	Compiled	6	25	23	20	12	5
80	83	91	Tax Returns	16	30	18	18	9	1
111	93	92	Other	2	21	18	23	26	19
83	115	109			71 (4/1-9/30/06)		287 (10/1/06-3/31/07)		
4/1/04-3/31/05 ALL	4/1/05-3/31/06 ALL	4/1/06-3/31/07 ALL		0-1MM	1-3MM	3-5MM	5-10MM	10-25MM	25MM & OVER
332	349	358	NUMBER OF STATEMENTS	24	79	65	73	77	40
%	%	%	ASSETS	%	%	%	%	%	%
8.7	7.5	8.5	Cash & Equivalents	12.4	10.3	9.2	6.8	7.5	6.6
26.8	29.0	31.1	Trade Receivables (net)	21.7	23.4	32.0	38.8	34.7	29.9
36.9	36.2	32.2	Inventory	38.1	33.0	29.3	31.3	31.2	35.6
2.5	2.4	2.8	All Other Current	1.5	2.3	1.8	3.0	4.0	3.3
74.9	75.1	74.6	Total Current	73.6	69.0	72.3	79.9	77.3	75.3
16.5	15.6	16.4	Fixed Assets (net)	18.0	19.6	19.1	12.3	15.4	14.6
3.1	3.0	2.6	Intangibles (net)	.2	2.9	2.7	2.0	1.8	5.4
5.5	6.3	6.4	All Other Non-Current	8.0	8.5	5.9	5.9	5.5	4.6
100.0	100.0	100.0	Total	100.0	100.0	100.0	100.0	100.0	100.0
			LIABILITIES						
11.7	12.0	13.9	Notes Payable-Short Term	18.2	11.7	14.2	13.6	12.7	17.5
2.8	1.9	2.8	Cur. Mat.-L.T.D.	10.8	4.0	1.1	1.7	1.9	1.7
22.0	21.3	19.8	Trade Payables	32.2	18.1	18.2	19.5	18.7	20.8
.2	.4	.2	Income Taxes Payable	.1	.1	.3	.3	.2	.2
14.7	15.7	15.7	All Other Current	9.7	13.8	14.8	19.1	16.2	17.7
51.4	51.2	52.3	Total Current	70.9	47.7	48.7	54.2	49.8	57.8
13.3	12.9	12.0	Long-Term Debt	22.1	15.8	12.4	8.3	9.6	8.9
.1	.1	.1	Deferred Taxes	.0	.1	.0	.1	.0	.1
4.0	4.5	4.6	All Other Non-Current	4.3	5.9	3.3	4.6	5.2	3.4
31.3	31.4	31.0	Net Worth	2.8	30.5	35.6	32.7	35.4	29.8
100.0	100.0	100.0	Total Liabilities & Net Worth	100.0	100.0	100.0	100.0	100.0	100.0
			INCOME DATA						
100.0	100.0	100.0	Net Sales	100.0	100.0	100.0	100.0	100.0	100.0
34.9	35.3	33.9	Gross Profit	41.1	36.8	32.6	32.7	30.3	34.5
32.2	32.5	30.7	Operating Expenses	39.3	33.8	29.1	29.9	26.8	31.0
2.7	2.8	3.1	Operating Profit	1.9	3.0	3.5	2.8	3.5	3.5
.2	.2	.4	All Other Expenses (net)	1.8	.4	.3	.3	.4	.0
2.5	2.6	2.7	Profit Before Taxes	.1	2.6	3.2	2.5	3.2	3.5
			RATIOS						
2.5	2.4	2.4	Current	4.3	3.3	2.7	2.1	2.3	1.8
1.5	1.5	1.5		1.9	1.7	1.4	1.5	1.4	1.3
1.1	1.1	1.1		.5	1.0	1.1	1.2	1.1	1.0
1.3	1.3	1.4	Quick	2.2	1.5	1.8	1.4	1.4	1.0
(331) .7	(348) .7	.7		.5	.7	.8	.9	.8	.6
.3	.4	.4		.2	.3	.4	.4	.5	.4
6 56.3	11 33.9	12 30.8	Sales/Receivables	4 84.9	8 45.6	15 23.9	19 18.8	16 23.3	10 38.4
22 16.4	25 14.5	26 13.9		12 30.3	20 17.9	27 13.5	32 11.4	32 11.5	27 13.6
39 9.4	42 8.6	43 8.5		27 13.7	34 10.6	42 8.7	54 6.7	43 8.6	41 8.9
24 15.5	24 15.4	20 18.5	Cost of Sales/Inventory	12 29.4	16 23.4	16 23.0	19 18.9	19 19.4	23 15.6
49 7.4	50 7.3	38 9.5		48 7.7	42 8.7	37 9.7	38 9.6	37 9.8	49 7.5
91 4.0	89 4.1	77 4.8		157 2.3	80 4.5	74 4.9	69 5.3	69 5.3	81 4.5
15 24.8	16 22.9	13 27.9	Cost of Sales/Payables	11 33.3	9 38.6	12 30.1	15 23.7	16 23.5	13 28.6
25 14.7	29 12.8	24 15.0		34 10.9	27 13.5	25 14.8	22 16.3	24 15.4	24 15.1
42 8.7	47 7.8	40 9.2		69 5.3	43 8.4	40 9.2	33 11.0	38 9.6	46 7.9
7.8	7.2	7.7	Sales/Working Capital	5.1	6.8	7.6	8.1	8.7	12.1
14.7	15.8	14.3		15.1	11.3	18.3	12.7	14.9	17.3
69.5	81.0	71.5		-13.2	430.2	51.7	45.7	56.3	129.8
17.2	13.7	14.9	EBIT/Interest	3.5	23.4	9.6	14.2	30.5	19.4
(282) 5.1	(303) 4.0	(320) 4.2		(20) 1.0	(64) 4.7	(61) 4.6	(66) 3.4	(72) 7.1	(37) 5.3
1.6	1.4	1.4		-4.8	1.7	1.3	1.2	1.7	1.8
5.2	7.3	5.0	Net Profit + Depr., Dep., Amort./Cur. Mat. L/T/D				5.2	5.1	32.0
(41) 2.6	(43) 2.8	(49) 2.9				(15) 2.5	(11) 2.9	(10) 3.6	
1.0	1.4	1.0					1.1	.1	1.3
.1	.1	.1	Fixed/Worth	.2	.1	.1	.1	.1	.2
.3	.4	.4		1.6	.4	.4	.3	.3	.3
1.6	1.5	1.6		-.5	2.6	1.5	.9	1.1	1.5
.7	.8	.9	Debt/Worth	1.2	.8	.9	1.0	.9	1.3
1.9	2.2	2.1		4.3	1.8	1.9	1.6	2.2	3.1
7.1	8.3	6.1		-5.7	12.0	5.7	4.4	5.5	6.2
56.0	53.1	59.9	% Profit Before Taxes/Tangible Net Worth	93.3	47.0	61.3	48.3	74.8	75.3
(282) 21.2	(299) 21.1	(318) 25.2		(14) 15.2	(66) 24.2	(60) 25.3	(67) 17.8	(75) 30.3	(36) 41.9
5.9	3.3	7.2		-4.3	10.4	8.6	3.8	7.8	7.6
17.8	16.2	19.2	% Profit Before Taxes/Total Assets	13.4	17.4	17.0	18.8	22.4	25.0
6.9	5.9	7.7		3.1	8.2	7.6	5.2	9.1	12.1
1.0	1.0	1.8		-12.6	2.7	1.7	.9	2.3	2.5
73.5	78.9	89.6	Sales/Net Fixed Assets	82.3	153.1	86.4	94.1	95.0	74.6
40.5	34.8	37.4		27.1	33.3	28.7	46.1	46.7	34.5
18.5	17.2	17.3		13.3	13.2	11.1	22.0	21.3	17.7
5.2	4.6	5.1	Sales/Total Assets	6.4	5.9	4.9	5.0	5.0	5.0
3.8	3.6	3.8		5.3	3.5	3.6	3.8	3.9	4.0
2.7	2.7	2.8		1.8	2.5	2.8	3.0	2.9	3.0
.4	.4	.3	% Depr., Dep., Amort./Sales	.5	.3	.4	.3	.3	.3
(273) .7	(288) .6	(293) .7		(21) .9	(54) .7	(51) .6	(61) .6	(68) .7	(38) .6
1.2	1.1	1.2		1.8	1.7	1.1	1.2	.9	1.0
2.2	2.0	1.7	% Officers', Directors' Owners' Comp/Sales	3.8	3.1	1.9	1.4	1.0	.6
(207) 3.5	(216) 3.6	(221) 3.3		(16) 6.0	(52) 4.8	(45) 3.3	(48) 2.5	(47) 1.8	(13) 1.5
6.4	6.7	5.9		9.2	7.6	5.3	5.8	3.4	2.6
3870191M	5309673M	5433190M	Net Sales ($)	15925M	152874M	258103M	512904M	1197941M	3295443M
1181879M	1374048M	1528665M	Total Assets ($)	7700M	58855M	92384M	150570M	375925M	843231M

© RMA 2007

M = $ thousand   MM = $ million

See Pages 11 through 21 for Explanation of Ratios and Data

Current Data Sorted by Assets   Comparative Historical Data

						Type of Statement		
1		2	4	2		Unqualified	20	15
1	3	9	2			Reviewed	9	19
5	14	11				Compiled	34	57
23	30	6			1	Tax Returns	27	51
12	18	11	5	3	3	Other	31	34
	29 (4/1-9/30/06)		137 (10/1/06-3/31/07)				4/1/02-3/31/03	4/1/03-3/31/04
0-500M	500M-2MM	2-10MM	10-50MM	50-100MM	100-250MM		ALL	ALL
42	65	39	11	5	4	**NUMBER OF STATEMENTS**	121	176
%	%	%	%	%	%	**ASSETS**	%	%
18.0	6.6	7.5	12.8			Cash & Equivalents	10.9	10.5
12.8	11.4	14.1	10.8			Trade Receivables (net)	11.1	11.8
43.9	56.3	49.3	37.2			Inventory	51.1	51.1
3.0	2.6	1.3	2.6			All Other Current	2.3	2.2
77.8	76.8	72.2	63.3			Total Current	75.4	75.5
19.2	12.8	18.7	26.1			Fixed Assets (net)	17.6	16.3
1.4	4.8	3.0	1.7			Intangibles (net)	3.2	3.3
1.6	5.5	6.2	8.9			All Other Non-Current	3.9	4.9
100.0	100.0	100.0	100.0			Total	100.0	100.0
						LIABILITIES		
12.8	10.7	18.7	13.7			Notes Payable-Short Term	10.3	9.8
6.2	4.3	2.4	2.0			Cur. Mat.-L.T.D.	3.7	2.4
14.9	21.0	19.0	17.0			Trade Payables	20.3	18.7
.0	.2	.2	.9			Income Taxes Payable	.2	.3
14.2	12.0	15.9	18.6			All Other Current	13.9	16.8
48.1	48.2	56.2	52.2			Total Current	48.5	48.0
19.6	20.9	13.2	8.3			Long-Term Debt	13.4	15.8
.0	.0	.0	.0			Deferred Taxes	.3	.2
9.7	6.0	4.6	3.4			All Other Non-Current	6.7	6.7
22.6	24.9	26.0	36.2			Net Worth	31.1	29.4
100.0	100.0	100.0	100.0			Total Liabilities & Net Worth	100.0	100.0
						INCOME DATA		
100.0	100.0	100.0	100.0			Net Sales	100.0	100.0
48.7	41.3	44.7	44.8			Gross Profit	44.5	43.9
45.3	38.4	41.1	42.5			Operating Expenses	40.4	40.1
3.4	2.9	3.6	2.3			Operating Profit	4.1	3.8
1.2	1.1	1.5	.6			All Other Expenses (net)	.9	.7
2.3	1.8	2.1	1.7			Profit Before Taxes	3.3	3.1
						RATIOS		
3.0	2.4	1.9	2.5			Current	2.6	2.6
1.9	1.6	1.3	1.4				1.7	1.8
1.2	1.2	1.0	.9				1.1	1.1
1.1	.8	.6	1.3			Quick	.9	.9
.6	.3	(38) .4	.3				(117) .4	(175) .5
.2	.1	.2	.1				.2	.1
0 UND	0 UND	0 778.9	0 UND			Sales/Receivables	0 UND	
4 85.8	10 35.3	8 45.9	12 30.7				3 116.9	5 76.3
26 14.3	27 13.6	37 9.9	18 19.9				25 14.9	26 13.8
35 10.5	75 4.9	76 4.8	65 5.6			Cost of Sales/Inventory	65 5.6	62 5.8
109 3.4	130 2.8	132 2.8	89 4.1				117 3.1	117 3.1
164 2.2	204 1.8	216 1.7	92 4.0				169 2.2	173 2.1
3 112.4	16 22.2	36 10.2	23 15.8			Cost of Sales/Payables	16 22.8	15 24.3
23 15.6	44 8.3	45 8.2	34 10.8				38 9.7	34 10.7
57 6.4	73 5.0	67 5.4	42 8.8				62 5.8	59 6.2
5.2	4.4	5.6	10.5			Sales/Working Capital	6.0	5.4
8.5	9.8	14.8	14.5				11.6	10.3
32.3	46.5	66.9	-85.6				33.4	45.8
11.0	8.7	6.7	19.3			EBIT/Interest	15.9	18.1
(33) 2.8	(61) 3.0	(37) 2.2	(10) 2.0				(98) 3.8	(144) 4.5
-.7	.9	.9	-.1				1.3	1.6
						Net Profit + Depr., Dep., Amort./Cur. Mat. L/T/D	12.6	9.9
							(26) 5.1	(22) 3.7
							1.7	2.3
.1	.1	.2	.2			Fixed/Worth	.1	.1
.6	.4	.5	.5				.5	.4
-1.4	15.7	3.0	3.1				1.4	1.8
.5	1.3	1.5	.7			Debt/Worth	.7	.9
3.0	2.6	2.8	1.3				1.8	2.0
-16.1	58.5	8.0	10.4				6.0	7.4
102.7	40.3	52.8				% Profit Before Taxes/Tangible Net Worth	38.3	44.6
(31) 34.9	(50) 15.2	(34) 13.7					(99) 20.9	(144) 20.6
5.5	5.1	2.8					5.6	5.2
25.0	12.4	13.7	20.2			% Profit Before Taxes/Total Assets	15.6	15.3
6.5	4.4	4.4	5.4				6.7	6.8
-5.7	-.4	.3	-1.5				1.4	.9
159.9	80.1	43.8	29.3			Sales/Net Fixed Assets	63.2	71.6
26.3	30.7	19.9	15.0				24.0	27.8
11.3	16.6	9.8	9.8				11.0	12.4
4.4	3.6	3.6	4.2			Sales/Total Assets	4.2	4.1
3.2	2.6	2.7	3.0				3.0	2.9
2.4	1.8	1.6	1.8				2.1	2.0
.6	.3	.4	.4			% Depr., Dep., Amort./Sales	.5	.5
(26) 1.4	(48) .6	(33) 1.2	(10) .9				(99) .9	(146) .9
1.8	1.5	1.7	1.1				1.5	1.7
3.2	2.6	1.9				% Officers', Directors' Owners' Comp/Sales	2.3	3.1
(24) 5.6	(44) 3.6	(20) 3.4					(64) 4.1	(90) 5.3
9.8	6.5	10.2					9.1	9.0
34087M	201051M	403996M	655683M	718905M	1601139M	Net Sales ($)	3773673M	3204599M
10883M	72947M	155435M	218275M	351543M	598941M	Total Assets ($)	1754528M	1338139M

M = $ thousand   MM = $ million
See Pages 11 through 21 for Explanation of Ratios and Data

Comparative Historical Data | Current Data Sorted by Sales

			Type of Statement						
9	11	9	Unqualified	1			1		7
15	15	15	Reviewed		2	1	3	7	2
46	33	30	Compiled	4	9	7	7	3	
54	57	60	Tax Returns	17	23	11	7	1	1
44	49	52	Other	10	15	7	4	6	10
4/1/04-3/31/05	4/1/05-3/31/06	4/1/06-3/31/07		29 (4/1-9/30/06)			137 (10/1/06-3/31/07)		
ALL	ALL	ALL		0-1MM	1-3MM	3-5MM	5-10MM	10-25MM	25MM & OVER
168	165	166	**NUMBER OF STATEMENTS**	32	49	26	22	17	20
%	%	%	**ASSETS**	%	%	%	%	%	%
8.7	10.8	10.2	Cash & Equivalents	15.4	10.5	5.9	8.3	11.1	8.2
17.0	11.9	12.1	Trade Receivables (net)	9.8	13.7	13.1	9.5	15.4	10.5
45.4	47.3	49.9	Inventory	42.7	52.6	55.6	56.7	44.8	44.4
2.2	1.5	2.6	All Other Current	3.6	2.1	2.4	2.3	1.0	4.3
73.3	71.5	74.8	Total Current	71.4	79.0	77.0	76.7	72.3	67.3
18.1	18.4	16.9	Fixed Assets (net)	23.2	12.6	12.3	18.5	16.7	22.0
2.8	3.5	3.4	Intangibles (net)	4.4	3.6	5.2	.4	1.7	3.8
5.7	6.7	4.8	All Other Non-Current	1.0	4.9	5.6	4.3	9.3	6.8
100.0	100.0	100.0	Total	100.0	100.0	100.0	100.0	100.0	100.0
			LIABILITIES						
12.4	11.9	13.4	Notes Payable-Short Term	15.6	10.4	9.6	17.3	16.5	15.6
2.9	3.6	4.0	Cur. Mat.-L.T.D.	5.6	3.2	6.5	5.2	.8	1.4
18.0	15.6	18.5	Trade Payables	14.5	15.4	24.5	24.8	19.8	17.0
.3	.2	.2	Income Taxes Payable	.0	.0	.0	.9	.3	.5
14.6	13.0	14.0	All Other Current	10.0	15.3	11.5	11.4	21.9	16.8
48.2	44.3	50.2	Total Current	45.7	44.3	52.1	59.6	59.2	51.3
14.1	18.1	17.2	Long-Term Debt	25.7	24.1	9.5	15.6	6.0	7.6
.1	.1	.0	Deferred Taxes	.0	.0	.0	.0	.0	.0
4.3	7.8	6.4	All Other Non-Current	13.6	3.3	7.6	3.2	5.9	4.3
33.3	29.7	26.3	Net Worth	14.9	28.2	30.8	21.7	28.8	36.8
100.0	100.0	100.0	Total Liabilties & Net Worth	100.0	100.0	100.0	100.0	100.0	100.0
			INCOME DATA						
100.0	100.0	100.0	Net Sales	100.0	100.0	100.0	100.0	100.0	100.0
43.0	44.9	44.7	Gross Profit	50.2	43.3	40.9	44.3	42.7	46.7
40.1	41.4	41.5	Operating Expenses	48.0	39.4	36.7	42.8	39.5	43.0
2.9	3.5	3.2	Operating Profit	2.2	4.0	4.2	1.5	3.2	3.7
.5	1.2	1.1	All Other Expenses (net)	2.0	1.2	1.1	.6	.5	.7
2.4	2.3	2.1	Profit Before Taxes	.1	2.8	3.2	.8	2.7	3.0
			RATIOS						
2.4	2.8	2.4		3.6	2.7	2.0	1.7	2.0	2.3
1.7	1.9	1.6	Current	1.9	1.9	1.6	1.5	1.3	1.4
1.1	1.1	1.1		1.2	1.3	1.1	1.0	1.0	1.1
1.0	1.0	.7		1.0	1.0	.7	.6	.6	.5
.5 (162)	.5 (165)	.4	Quick	.6	.3	.3 (21)	.3	.4	.4
.2	.2	.2		.2	.2	.1	.1	.2	.1
1 282.6	0 UND	0 UND		0 UND	0 UND	0 UND	0 999.8	1 603.8	0 UND
18 19.8	8 48.3	8 45.4	Sales/Receivables	3 138.0	10 35.2	14 25.9	6 57.0	8 45.9	7 50.5
33 11.0	25 14.8	27 13.6		23 15.8	29 12.5	34 10.8	20 18.2	36 10.0	28 13.2
55 6.7	67 5.4	68 5.4		37 10.0	71 5.1	89 4.1	75 4.9	58 6.2	68 5.4
103 3.6	117 3.1	117 3.1	Cost of Sales/Inventory	129 2.8	141 2.6	123 3.0	121 3.0	91 4.0	90 4.0
179 2.0	189 1.9	192 1.9		194 1.9	258 1.4	158 2.3	223 1.6	125 2.9	157 2.3
15 23.6	12 29.3	17 21.2		2 235.0	16 23.5	8 45.9	34 10.7	18 20.6	21 17.4
35 10.5	30 12.1	41 8.8	Cost of Sales/Payables	32 11.4	40 9.2	45 8.1	48 7.5	39 9.5	38 9.7
65 5.6	56 6.5	64 5.7		65 5.6	72 5.1	75 4.8	79 4.6	49 7.5	58 6.3
5.3	4.6	5.0		4.9	4.2	4.3	5.6	8.7	5.4
11.1	9.7	10.3	Sales/Working Capital	8.1	6.8	10.0	17.2	19.8	14.0
56.0	36.0	56.0		20.0	14.6	81.4	NM	NM	131.7
15.4	11.6	10.0		7.3	13.7	19.9	7.1	13.3	13.6
(145) 3.1	(141) 2.8	(150) 2.9	EBIT/Interest	(27) 1.3	(43) 3.1	(23) 3.1	1.7	(15) 4.2	6.9
.9	.7	.9		-1.8	1.0	1.3	-.7	1.8	1.1
5.5	9.0	12.5	Net Profit + Depr., Dep.,						
(27) 3.0	(20) 2.5	(14) 3.3	Amort./Cur. Mat. L/T/D						
1.5	1.3	.9							
.1	.1	.1		.2	.1	.1	.3	.2	.1
.4	.4	.4	Fixed/Worth	1.2	.3	.4	.7	.4	.5
1.6	2.8	4.5		-1.1	29.0	.8	3.0	2.9	1.5
.8	.9	1.1		.5	1.0	1.3	1.6	1.1	.7
1.9	2.1	2.4	Debt/Worth	12.6	2.1	2.8	3.2	2.1	1.6
5.9	16.1	20.4		-3.7	49.9	5.3	8.6	12.2	5.3
44.3	49.3	59.2	% Profit Before Taxes/Tangible	80.5	58.4	61.9	35.2	64.4	66.1
(143) 16.1	(132) 16.2	(133) 18.5	Net Worth	(20) 24.2	(39) 19.2	(23) 15.9	(19) 7.4	(14) 19.6	(18) 14.5
1.5	2.8	3.7		2.0	5.0	5.7	-25.6	8.4	2.1
13.1	16.1	14.7	% Profit Before Taxes/Total	16.2	13.8	15.4	12.8	18.7	19.4
4.6	3.9	4.9	Assets	4.0	4.4	6.6	1.4	5.7	6.6
-1.0	-1.4	-.1		-14.9	.2	1.8	-5.0	3.6	.4
58.5	69.7	62.6		46.7	146.3	62.0	39.8	112.1	29.0
27.8	29.1	24.4	Sales/Net Fixed Assets	17.3	34.3	32.8	21.8	29.3	15.2
9.9	10.5	12.0		8.6	13.6	18.4	10.2	11.6	10.2
3.8	3.9	3.7		3.7	3.4	3.6	3.9	4.6	3.9
2.6	2.7	2.7	Sales/Total Assets	2.5	2.1	3.0	3.1	3.3	2.6
1.8	1.8	1.9		1.9	1.6	2.2	2.1	2.6	1.8
.6	.4	.4		1.0	.4	.3	.3	.6	.4
(137) 1.0	(128) 1.0	(123) 1.0	% Depr., Dep., Amort./Sales	(23) 1.5	(30) .9	(20) .6	(20) .7	(14) 1.2	(16) .9
1.7	1.7	1.6		1.8	1.9	1.3	1.7	1.9	1.4
2.0	3.3	2.6	% Officers', Directors'	5.0	2.8	1.5	2.6		
(100) 4.3	(89) 4.7	(92) 4.1	Owners' Comp/Sales	(16) 7.5	(32) 4.7	(19) 2.9	(12) 4.4		
7.1	9.3	8.0		10.2	7.5	4.6	13.2		
2965342M	3664031M	3614861M	Net Sales ($)	18640M	90598M	102063M	156101M	269802M	2977657M
1112794M	1323335M	1408024M	Total Assets ($)	8283M	47385M	42621M	57503M	85984M	1166248M

M = $ thousand   MM = $ million
See Pages 11 through 21 for Explanation of Ratios and Data

Current Data Sorted by Assets | Comparative Historical Data

						Type of Statement		
1		3	2	2		Unqualified	8	13
	2	9	2			Reviewed	15	10
4	14	9	2			Compiled	34	41
17	9	9				Tax Returns	22	21
4	11	18	5			Other	34	28
	31 (4/1-9/30/06)		92 (10/1/06-3/31/07)				4/1/02-3/31/03	4/1/03-3/31/04
0-500M	500M-2MM	2-10MM	10-50MM	50-100MM	100-250MM		ALL	ALL
26	36	48	11	2		NUMBER OF STATEMENTS	113	113
%	%	%	%	%	%	ASSETS	%	%
19.4	8.1	8.9	8.8			Cash & Equivalents	11.0	11.6
17.9	15.1	14.6	12.8			Trade Receivables (net)	15.4	14.4
41.3	50.2	50.7	42.2			Inventory	46.5	44.0
.4	2.2	4.4	5.4			All Other Current	2.6	3.0
79.0	75.7	78.6	69.2			Total Current	75.5	73.1
17.2	16.9	13.0	23.7			Fixed Assets (net)	16.4	18.6
.2	3.2	1.9	.6			Intangibles (net)	2.4	2.5
3.6	4.3	6.6	6.5			All Other Non-Current	5.7	5.8
100.0	100.0	100.0	100.0			Total	100.0	100.0
						LIABILITIES		
13.0	15.7	6.1	21.7			Notes Payable-Short Term	14.1	13.5
3.4	4.3	1.6	.9			Cur. Mat.-L.T.D.	3.7	2.0
18.8	24.1	23.4	18.6			Trade Payables	25.6	22.4
.0	.2	.1	.1			Income Taxes Payable	.5	.2
15.4	14.4	18.5	27.1			All Other Current	12.1	12.9
50.6	58.7	49.6	68.4			Total Current	55.9	51.1
17.0	14.0	8.4	11.9			Long-Term Debt	11.8	12.1
.0	.0	.1	.3			Deferred Taxes	.1	.1
13.4	7.9	5.9	3.4			All Other Non-Current	4.4	4.1
19.1	19.3	36.0	16.0			Net Worth	27.8	32.7
100.0	100.0	100.0	100.0			Total Liabilities & Net Worth	100.0	100.0
						INCOME DATA		
100.0	100.0	100.0	100.0			Net Sales	100.0	100.0
39.6	35.3	31.1	30.0			Gross Profit	33.0	35.7
36.7	33.1	27.2	29.1			Operating Expenses	30.6	33.7
3.0	2.2	4.0	.9			Operating Profit	2.4	2.0
.6	1.1	-.4	-.5			All Other Expenses (net)	.2	.1
2.4	1.1	4.3	1.4			Profit Before Taxes	2.2	2.0
						RATIOS		
2.8	2.0	2.4	1.3				1.9	2.0
1.6	1.5	1.6	1.2			Current	1.4	1.4
1.1	1.0	1.1	.8				1.1	1.1
1.3	.8	.7	.4				.8	.9
.8	.3	.4	.3			Quick	.4	.5
.2	.2	.3	.2				.2	.3

											Sales/Receivables				
3	127.1	5	70.6	6	61.9	6	63.3					4	87.0	4	90.5
10	36.9	11	32.4	13	29.1	14	26.5					11	33.4	12	31.7
30	12.1	19	19.0	26	14.3	18	20.1					23	16.0	25	14.3
36	10.1	50	7.4	52	7.0	50	7.3				Cost of Sales/Inventory	41	8.9	48	7.7
52	7.0	86	4.3	82	4.5	74	4.9					66	5.5	75	4.9
97	3.8	170	2.1	117	3.1	80	4.6					108	3.4	112	3.3
8	45.6	21	17.2	15	23.9	18	19.7				Cost of Sales/Payables	14	25.6	20	17.9
24	14.9	34	10.6	37	9.8	33	11.1					32	11.5	36	10.1
47	7.8	65	5.6	57	6.4	44	8.3					55	6.6	56	6.5

									Sales/Working Capital		
8.4		7.6		6.3		20.3				8.2	7.7
15.1		15.3		11.9		26.4				20.2	14.6
43.5		-285.0		57.3		-23.3				61.6	36.5
	22.5		9.1		22.2				EBIT/Interest	15.0	12.7
(16)	3.3	(31)	3.4	(43)	5.4					(99) 5.1	(104) 4.3
	.6		.9		2.0					1.8	.7
									Net Profit + Depr., Dep., Amort./Cur. Mat. L/T/D	4.1	5.8
										(24) 2.0	(24) 3.0
										1.1	.7
.3		.1		.1		.4			Fixed/Worth	.2	.2
.6		1.0		.3		1.2				.5	.4
-8.0		-7.3		.9		1.8				1.0	1.3
.6		2.2		.8		2.4			Debt/Worth	1.3	1.1
4.9		7.9		2.0		3.7				2.6	2.4
-71.1		-48.2		7.6		9.9				6.0	5.4
	77.4		79.9		41.8		41.3		% Profit Before Taxes/Tangible Net Worth	45.8	42.3
(19)	50.0	(25)	27.4	(43)	20.9	(10)	33.1			(99) 23.9	(104) 17.7
	8.1		4.0		9.0		6.9			8.9	2.5
15.7		13.2		16.8		11.7			% Profit Before Taxes/Total Assets	12.0	12.1
9.6		4.3		5.9		7.3				5.5	4.7
1.6		-.3		4.0		.5				2.3	-.3
156.9		145.8		100.1		46.5			Sales/Net Fixed Assets	66.3	52.9
36.4		38.5		51.2		36.0				33.2	33.3
15.7		9.6		20.0		10.5				13.2	12.8
5.8		4.6		4.1		4.3			Sales/Total Assets	4.7	4.2
4.1		3.4		3.0		3.3				3.6	3.3
3.0		1.9		2.5		2.2				2.6	2.2
	.8		.4		.3		.5		% Depr., Dep., Amort./Sales	.5	.6
(16)	1.4	(27)	1.1	(42)	.6		.6			(98) .8	(91) 1.0
	2.5		1.8		1.2		1.0			1.3	1.9
	2.2		1.2		1.0				% Officers', Directors' Owners' Comp/Sales	2.1	2.2
(16)	4.4	(23)	3.5	(20)	1.8					(60) 3.3	(62) 5.1
	9.1		5.2		2.6					6.0	8.0
31873M	129626M	797076M	675839M	474278M		Net Sales ($)	3877474M	7706028M
7423M	37674M	240175M	238107M	153318M		Total Assets ($)	1293632M	1830548M

© RMA 2007

M = $ thousand   MM = $ million

See Pages 11 through 21 for Explanation of Ratios and Data

(Note: columns 50-100MM and 100-250MM marked "DATA NOT AVAILABLE")

Comparative Historical Data				Current Data Sorted by Sales					
6	8	8	**Type of Statement** Unqualified	1			4	2	5
12	12	13	Reviewed		1	6	2	2	6
46	33	29	Compiled	3	7		5	6	2
29	26	35	Tax Returns	9	11	3	9	2	1
27	36	38	Other	4	8	4	4	8	8
4/1/04-3/31/05 ALL	4/1/05-3/31/06 ALL	4/1/06-3/31/07 ALL		31 (4/1-9/30/06)			92 (10/1/06-3/31/07)		
				0-1MM	1-3MM	3-5MM	5-10MM	10-25MM	25MM & OVER
120	115	123	**NUMBER OF STATEMENTS**	17	27	13	24	20	22
%	%	%	**ASSETS**	%	%	%	%	%	%
9.3	10.4	10.8	Cash & Equivalents	17.6	11.4	10.2	6.9	9.7	10.2
14.8	19.4	15.8	Trade Receivables (net)	6.9	18.8	16.6	15.9	15.6	18.5
50.5	43.8	47.7	Inventory	46.1	41.4	43.8	57.6	52.1	43.9
2.5	3.1	2.9	All Other Current	1.3	1.8	4.1	4.2	2.1	4.3
77.1	76.7	77.2	Total Current	71.9	73.5	74.7	84.6	79.5	77.0
16.7	16.0	15.9	Fixed Assets (net)	22.7	15.8	18.9	8.9	13.6	18.5
2.2	2.9	1.8	Intangibles (net)	1.1	3.3	1.3	.9	3.0	.5
3.9	4.3	5.2	All Other Non-Current	4.2	7.4	5.1	5.6	3.8	4.1
100.0	100.0	100.0	Total	100.0	100.0	100.0	100.0	100.0	100.0
			LIABILITIES						
14.7	11.5	12.3	Notes Payable-Short Term	15.4	18.9	7.1	4.7	9.3	16.2
2.9	3.1	2.7	Cur. Mat.-L.T.D.	3.3	2.1	5.1	4.6	1.2	.7
23.1	24.7	22.1	Trade Payables	10.5	20.0	25.0	25.9	30.9	19.6
.2	.1	.1	Income Taxes Payable	.0	.2	.2	.0	.1	.1
16.3	16.6	17.2	All Other Current	15.6	11.1	9.2	27.3	15.2	21.6
57.2	56.0	54.4	Total Current	44.8	52.3	46.6	62.5	56.7	58.2
16.3	14.2	12.1	Long-Term Debt	25.2	11.5	15.3	6.9	9.8	8.3
.1	.1	.1	Deferred Taxes	.0	.0	.0	.0	.2	.2
4.2	5.7	7.8	All Other Non-Current	23.5	3.5	10.6	7.3	4.5	2.7
22.2	24.0	25.6	Net Worth	6.5	32.7	27.4	23.2	28.8	30.7
100.0	100.0	100.0	Total Liabilties & Net Worth	100.0	100.0	100.0	100.0	100.0	100.0
			INCOME DATA						
100.0	100.0	100.0	Net Sales	100.0	100.0	100.0	100.0	100.0	100.0
34.5	34.0	34.3	Gross Profit	47.8	34.1	40.0	26.8	29.6	33.2
32.5	31.2	31.3	Operating Expenses	45.4	29.1	38.5	25.6	26.9	29.1
2.0	2.9	3.0	Operating Profit	2.4	4.9	1.5	1.2	2.8	4.1
.3	.5	.3	All Other Expenses (net)	1.8	.2	.6	-.6	.3	-.1
1.7	2.3	2.7	Profit Before Taxes	.6	4.7	.9	1.8	2.4	4.2
			RATIOS						
2.1	2.2	2.3		4.4	2.0	2.3	2.2	2.0	2.3
1.4	1.3	1.5	Current	2.4	1.8	1.5	1.3	1.5	1.2
1.1	1.1	1.1		1.1	1.0	1.1	1.0	1.1	1.1
.7	.9	.9		1.3	1.2	1.2	.6	.5	1.2
.4	.5	.4	Quick	.3	.7	.5	.3	.4	.4
.2	.3	.2		.1	.3	.2	.2	.3	.2
5 76.4	6 64.5	5 69.6		0 UND	3 116.7	9 39.1	4 83.6	7 50.4	7 52.8
12 29.7	17 21.6	12 30.4	Sales/Receivables	8 44.5	11 32.3	11 32.5	11 34.0	13 28.2	14 26.1
24 15.0	30 12.3	23 15.7		23 15.7	30 12.2	23 16.1	26 14.1	25 14.6	19 18.9
53 6.9	48 7.6	49 7.5		65 5.6	38 9.5	31 11.7	59 6.2	51 7.2	51 7.2
88 4.1	82 4.4	75 4.9	Cost of Sales/Inventory	140 2.6	50 7.3	60 6.1	95 3.9	83 4.4	65 5.7
142 2.6	112 3.2	118 3.1		295 1.2	94 3.9	95 3.8	134 2.7	117 3.1	81 4.5
15 24.2	23 16.2	16 22.2		6 57.2	16 22.6	11 34.0	21 17.1	24 14.9	16 22.7
36 10.1	41 8.8	33 11.1	Cost of Sales/Payables	26 13.8	31 11.7	34 10.7	37 9.8	50 7.3	30 12.0
60 6.1	65 5.6	57 6.4		67 5.5	43 8.5	69 5.3	54 6.8	60 6.1	46 8.0
6.9	6.7	7.5		4.7	8.1	7.5	6.2	8.1	8.8
15.0	14.1	15.1	Sales/Working Capital	8.7	13.4	15.5	15.8	13.0	22.7
92.0	129.7	84.3		23.8	-325.5	329.2	-111.1	78.1	60.5
8.3	11.3	9.7		4.3	18.4	6.4	7.9	14.8	27.7
(106) 2.4	(106) 3.3	(100) 3.5	EBIT/Interest	(11) 1.6	(20) 5.8	(11) 3.1	(21) 2.7	(19) 5.7	(18) 3.7
.6	1.4	1.2		-.8	1.4	.5	1.6	2.0	2.0
7.3	9.4	25.1							
(17) 1.8	(14) 4.2	(13) 4.8	Net Profit + Depr., Dep., Amort./Cur. Mat. L/T/D						
.5	1.0	2.1							
.2	.2	.2		.2	.3	.1	.0	.2	.2
.6	.5	.5	Fixed/Worth	39.7	.5	.5	.1	.5	.4
1.8	2.6	4.0		-.6	1.3	5.3	NM	1.3	1.3
1.3	1.4	1.4		.5	.9	1.4	1.6	1.6	1.1
3.3	3.6	3.1	Debt/Worth	108.7	2.9	2.4	5.2	3.0	2.5
8.6	15.5	16.0		-9.5	11.3	21.5	NM	8.4	4.3
42.1	49.1	55.8			74.7	52.4	42.3	40.0	60.3
(100) 18.4	(91) 24.9	(99) 22.2	% Profit Before Taxes/Tangible Net Worth		(21) 35.3	(12) 13.6	(18) 18.8	(18) 20.6	(21) 34.5
.2	10.5	8.1			4.6	1.7	11.0	9.9	14.1
12.6	12.2	14.7		14.6	20.9	11.6	7.8	14.0	17.9
3.7	6.3	5.5	% Profit Before Taxes/Total Assets	6.8	6.9	4.3	4.1	5.0	9.5
-.4	.8	1.0		-7.3	2.1	-.7	2.8	1.0	2.4
60.2	73.9	102.7		84.5	74.1	110.8	334.2	88.3	82.9
26.9	38.4	38.0	Sales/Net Fixed Assets	17.3	34.7	42.4	104.2	32.7	38.2
11.3	15.7	14.1		4.1	14.1	10.7	39.2	17.9	13.2
4.1	4.2	4.5		3.6	4.8	5.2	3.9	4.4	4.6
3.0	3.1	3.4	Sales/Total Assets	2.0	3.5	4.3	3.3	3.2	3.7
2.1	2.1	2.4		1.2	2.0	2.8	2.5	2.6	2.9
.6	.4	.4		1.2	.8	.4	.2	.2	.4
(98) 1.1	(98) .8	(98) .8	% Depr., Dep., Amort./Sales	(14) 2.2	(16) 1.4	(10) 1.1	(18) .4	(18) .6	.6
1.5	1.3	1.6		5.2	1.7	2.2	1.3	1.0	1.0
1.8	1.5	1.3			2.2		.9		
(55) 3.3	(56) 2.5	(60) 2.7	% Officers', Directors' Owners' Comp/Sales		(15) 4.1		(15) 1.3		
6.2	6.4	6.1			6.9		6.1		
3331718M	2031450M	2108692M	Net Sales ($)	10920M	51657M	48896M	185560M	331941M	1479718M
805111M	854460M	676697M	Total Assets ($)	6694M	30706M	13416M	58897M	104098M	462886M

Current Data Sorted by Assets   Comparative Historical Data

						Type of Statement		
2		2	12	2		Unqualified	12	13
	2	9	3			Reviewed	22	18
4	12	3	1		1	Compiled	28	25
13	12	5	1	1	1	Tax Returns	26	22
5	18	19	9	2		Other	22	36
	25 (4/1-9/30/06)		112 (10/1/06-3/31/07)				4/1/02-3/31/03	4/1/03-3/31/04
0-500M	500M-2MM	2-10MM	10-50MM	50-100MM	100-250MM		ALL	ALL
24	44	38	25	5	1	**NUMBER OF STATEMENTS**	110	114
%	%	%	%	%	%	**ASSETS**	%	%
12.5	10.0	15.5	10.1			Cash & Equivalents	10.1	10.4
20.1	23.9	28.7	22.6			Trade Receivables (net)	17.3	17.0
37.0	38.4	31.6	41.8			Inventory	40.2	42.0
4.4	1.6	6.0	2.6			All Other Current	2.9	3.1
74.0	74.0	81.9	77.1			Total Current	70.4	72.4
18.1	18.1	11.6	14.7			Fixed Assets (net)	21.3	18.5
.2	1.6	2.3	2.6			Intangibles (net)	2.8	3.0
7.7	6.3	4.2	5.6			All Other Non-Current	5.4	6.2
100.0	100.0	100.0	100.0			Total	100.0	100.0
						LIABILITIES		
13.0	11.3	8.7	16.4			Notes Payable-Short Term	14.1	13.7
1.0	1.9	1.3	2.8			Cur. Mat.-L.T.D.	4.7	2.9
18.0	26.0	31.7	26.8			Trade Payables	21.4	21.0
.5	.2	.1	.3			Income Taxes Payable	.4	.2
26.9	14.5	13.8	13.4			All Other Current	10.2	11.8
59.3	53.9	55.7	59.6			Total Current	50.9	49.5
21.2	12.5	4.3	4.0			Long-Term Debt	15.2	16.0
.1	.2	.1	.1			Deferred Taxes	.2	.1
6.9	7.3	3.6	10.0			All Other Non-Current	4.0	5.8
12.5	26.2	36.3	26.2			Net Worth	29.8	28.5
100.0	100.0	100.0	100.0			Total Liabilities & Net Worth	100.0	100.0
						INCOME DATA		
100.0	100.0	100.0	100.0			Net Sales	100.0	100.0
40.7	39.4	36.0	30.7			Gross Profit	36.2	35.9
34.9	37.4	32.1	26.5			Operating Expenses	34.0	33.5
5.8	2.1	3.9	4.2			Operating Profit	2.2	2.4
1.1	.5	-.1	.5			All Other Expenses (net)	.4	.6
4.7	1.5	4.0	3.7			Profit Before Taxes	1.8	1.7
						RATIOS		
2.3	1.9	2.2	1.8				2.1	2.3
1.7	1.4	1.4	1.3			Current	1.4	1.5
1.0	1.0	1.1	1.0				1.1	1.1
1.4	1.0	1.3	1.1				1.0	.9
(23) .6	.7	.8	.5			Quick	(109) .5	.5
.4	.3	.4	.2				.2	.2
0 UND	13 27.5	9 40.4	6 57.5				4 97.6	3 109.7
10 35.2	21 17.4	24 15.2	15 23.8			Sales/Receivables	15 25.0	13 28.1
30 12.3	32 11.3	43 8.5	38 9.7				35 10.4	31 11.7
17 21.2	26 14.0	19 18.8	27 13.5				34 10.6	43 8.4
27 13.7	57 6.4	40 9.1	77 4.8			Cost of Sales/Inventory	63 5.8	73 5.0
72 5.1	115 3.2	91 4.0	88 4.1				113 3.2	125 2.9
3 135.3	25 14.5	23 15.9	15 23.6				17 20.9	13 28.6
17 22.0	42 8.7	49 7.4	33 11.0			Cost of Sales/Payables	32 11.5	33 11.1
33 10.9	56 6.5	81 4.5	73 5.0				50 7.4	52 7.0
12.0	9.6	6.7	10.0				9.6	6.5
22.7	14.6	13.7	21.1			Sales/Working Capital	17.4	16.3
677.9	121.6	74.9	-566.5				113.7	54.2
12.9	6.2	44.7	34.2				11.7	13.5
(18) 3.9	(39) 2.0	(29) 11.9	(22) 3.5			EBIT/Interest	(94) 2.8	(96) 2.4
2.1	-1.4	2.4	1.4				.8	1.0
							8.4	8.3
						Net Profit + Depr., Dep., Amort./Cur. Mat. L/T/D	(26) 2.9	(21) 1.1
							1.2	.2
.2	.2	.1	.3				.2	.2
.6	.7	.3	.6			Fixed/Worth	.6	.5
3.8	1.6	.7	1.6				2.0	2.2
1.3	1.3	.8	1.0				1.1	1.0
3.0	2.8	2.5	4.4			Debt/Worth	2.1	2.8
9.7	8.4	6.9	18.1				5.9	9.5
130.6	55.4	78.3	86.8				51.1	45.7
(20) 48.2	(37) 12.8	(33) 25.2	(21) 41.7			% Profit Before Taxes/Tangible Net Worth	(95) 20.4	(94) 12.1
27.5	-18.1	7.7	10.2				1.0	1.8
24.1	12.2	23.8	25.8				15.7	17.2
15.6	3.7	8.9	7.1			% Profit Before Taxes/Total Assets	4.7	3.5
8.3	-7.0	2.2	1.7				-.7	-.1
168.2	87.9	71.9	65.5				51.0	52.7
28.3	34.1	43.2	33.1			Sales/Net Fixed Assets	21.4	21.8
19.7	12.3	22.7	14.1				10.4	11.3
8.1	4.6	4.8	3.9				4.8	3.8
5.1	3.6	3.6	3.4			Sales/Total Assets	3.3	2.9
4.2	2.6	2.7	2.9				2.4	2.3
.3	.4	.2	.5				.6	.5
(19) .6	(33) .8	(32) .6	(23) .7			% Depr., Dep., Amort./Sales	(92) 1.0	(85) 1.0
1.1	2.2	1.2	1.3				2.0	1.7
3.4	1.6	1.1					2.2	3.1
(15) 7.3	(27) 2.9	(13) 2.4				% Officers', Directors' Owners' Comp/Sales	(58) 4.4	(46) 5.4
9.0	5.6	5.5					10.4	13.2
40445M	199071M	797290M	1981074M	1314452M	422468M	Net Sales ($)	3303419M	3856514M
6715M	49026M	188582M	552172M	336621M	135411M	Total Assets ($)	915993M	1111974M

© RMA 2007

M = $ thousand   MM = $ million
See Pages 11 through 21 for Explanation of Ratios and Data

Comparative Historical Data   Current Data Sorted by Sales

Type of Statement	4/1/04-3/31/05 ALL	4/1/05-3/31/06 ALL	4/1/06-3/31/07 ALL	0-1MM	1-3MM	3-5MM	5-10MM	10-25MM	25MM & OVER
Unqualified	10	15	18		1		1	1	15
Reviewed	19	16	14		1		2	5	6
Compiled	23	12	22	1	6	3	7	1	4
Tax Returns	27	31	30	7	9	6	5	3	
Other	36	42	53	2	13	6	7	7	18
				\<25 (4/1-9/30/06)\>			\<112 (10/1/06-3/31/07)\>		
NUMBER OF STATEMENTS	115	116	137	10	30	15	22	17	43
ASSETS	%	%	%	%	%	%	%	%	%
Cash & Equivalents	11.3	11.7	12.3	11.4	10.4	10.5	12.2	20.3	11.2
Trade Receivables (net)	21.5	20.3	24.8	15.1	26.0	18.2	22.7	27.6	28.6
Inventory	39.2	40.2	36.4	39.1	31.0	44.2	44.0	29.1	35.7
All Other Current	3.6	2.1	3.5	2.8	6.7	2.8	1.6	2.6	3.0
Total Current	75.6	74.2	77.0	68.4	74.2	75.8	80.5	79.6	78.5
Fixed Assets (net)	15.2	17.4	15.7	23.4	18.6	13.1	13.6	15.2	14.2
Intangibles (net)	2.7	2.3	1.7	.1	1.5	1.1	1.6	1.2	2.6
All Other Non-Current	6.4	6.1	5.6	8.0	5.7	10.1	4.3	4.0	4.7
Total	100.0	100.0	100.0	100.0	100.0	100.0	100.0	100.0	100.0
LIABILITIES									
Notes Payable-Short Term	13.4	13.8	12.0	14.7	13.3	9.6	9.4	6.2	15.0
Cur. Mat.-L.T.D.	3.6	4.3	1.7	.4	2.3	1.6	1.0	1.7	2.0
Trade Payables	27.2	25.9	26.5	10.7	21.2	26.2	28.9	41.0	26.9
Income Taxes Payable	.2	.1	.2	.0	.4	.1	.3	.5	.1
All Other Current	11.8	11.5	16.0	25.0	20.9	19.1	11.3	12.2	13.4
Total Current	56.2	55.7	56.5	50.8	58.1	56.7	50.8	61.5	57.4
Long-Term Debt	10.8	10.4	9.8	17.3	20.6	11.2	5.5	7.2	3.3
Deferred Taxes	.2	.1	.1	.0	.3	.0	.0	.2	.1
All Other Non-Current	5.0	7.7	6.5	17.2	7.1	.8	6.4	4.2	6.5
Net Worth	27.7	26.0	27.1	14.6	13.9	31.3	37.2	26.9	32.7
Total Liabilities & Net Worth	100.0	100.0	100.0	100.0	100.0	100.0	100.0	100.0	100.0
INCOME DATA									
Net Sales	100.0	100.0	100.0	100.0	100.0	100.0	100.0	100.0	100.0
Gross Profit	36.9	35.8	36.9	48.6	40.7	39.3	32.0	36.2	33.5
Operating Expenses	34.5	32.8	33.2	43.9	37.0	35.9	30.1	31.7	29.2
Operating Profit	2.4	2.9	3.8	4.6	3.7	3.4	1.9	4.5	4.4
All Other Expenses (net)	.4	.6	.4	2.3	.7	.0	.0	.0	.3
Profit Before Taxes	2.0	2.3	3.3	2.3	3.0	3.3	2.0	4.5	4.1
RATIOS									
Current	2.0	2.3	2.0	3.1	1.9	1.9	3.5	1.7	2.2
	1.4	1.5	1.4	1.8	1.4	1.2	1.5	1.2	1.4
	1.0	1.1	1.1	.9	1.1	1.0	1.1	1.0	1.0
Quick	1.1	1.2	1.2	1.4	.9	1.0	1.7	1.3	1.3
	.6	.6	(136) .7	.6	.7	.5	(21) .8	.8	.7
	.2	.3	.3	.1	.3	.3	.4	.3	.2
Sales/Receivables	6 57.8	5 81.1	6 56.2	0 UND	8 43.6	4 92.1	4 88.6	2 172.2	8 43.7
	18 20.1	20 18.6	18 20.2	16 22.9	19 18.9	16 22.2	17 21.5	25 14.9	19 19.1
	38 9.7	37 9.8	35 10.6	33 11.1	43 8.6	28 13.1	31 11.8	43 8.5	35 10.4
Cost of Sales/Inventory	32 11.3	32 11.4	21 17.0	32 11.5	20 17.8	27 13.5	18 20.1	12 30.9	23 16.1
	66 5.5	70 5.2	47 7.8	67 5.4	37 9.9	83 4.4	50 7.3	29 12.4	48 7.7
	110 3.3	122 3.0	90 4.0	117 3.1	104 3.5	116 3.2	99 3.7	80 4.6	79 4.6
Cost of Sales/Payables	24 15.2	21 17.1	18 20.1	0 UND	18 19.8	36 10.1	23 15.8	24 15.5	16 22.8
	43 8.5	39 9.3	38 9.7	20 17.9	38 9.7	51 7.1	38 9.5	42 8.7	33 11.0
	71 5.1	70 5.2	65 5.6	40 9.0	53 6.9	57 6.4	65 5.6	77 4.7	74 4.9
Sales/Working Capital	9.1	6.7	8.3	4.2	10.2	10.5	6.9	9.8	8.4
	17.8	14.7	17.4	9.3	17.0	22.3	12.4	17.3	21.4
	-999.8	85.7	122.3	NM	UND	113.8	59.9	-272.7	-999.8
EBIT/Interest	14.7	8.2	16.5		12.3	20.0	17.3	33.1	66.0
	(100) 3.1	(98) 3.1	(111) 3.7		(27) 3.1	(12) 4.1	(18) 2.4	(14) 5.0	(33) 7.6
	.7	.9	1.4		.3	-1.2	.9	1.3	2.2
Net Profit + Depr., Dep., Amort./Cur. Mat. L/T/D	6.7	5.4	14.3						
	(17) 2.8	(19) 2.2	(16) 4.9						
	.7	.6	1.3						
Fixed/Worth	.2	.2	.2	.4	.4	.1	.1	.1	.2
	.4	.4	.5	.9	.9	.3	.3	.4	.4
	2.6	2.7	1.5	NM	3.6	21.3	.5	NM	1.2
Debt/Worth	.9	.9	1.0	2.0	1.4	1.2	.7	1.4	.8
	2.7	2.3	2.7	3.6	3.1	2.4	2.4	3.0	2.5
	8.8	12.0	8.9	NM	7.9	100.6	5.1	NM	11.8
% Profit Before Taxes/Tangible Net Worth	51.0	40.4	75.8		129.8	58.1	36.0	96.7	84.3
	(97) 20.0	(94) 18.3	(117) 30.2		(25) 32.6	(12) 34.0	(21) 12.0	(13) 24.5	(38) 38.1
	-.2	1.7	6.8		-10.3	6.7	2.5	6.9	16.7
% Profit Before Taxes/Total Assets	17.6	14.7	22.1	28.7	20.1	18.4	13.4	28.1	26.9
	4.3	5.1	8.5	8.3	12.0	10.7	4.0	6.2	14.7
	-.6	.4	1.4	-.7	-1.2	1.2	.6	.7	2.8
Sales/Net Fixed Assets	83.4	-77.4	70.6	32.9	57.1	68.4	163.8	93.2	73.8
	27.9	24.3	32.4	15.9	24.8	36.5	58.2	43.0	33.1
	13.9	13.0	15.6	7.6	12.1	15.8	27.4	19.5	17.0
Sales/Total Assets	4.6	4.2	5.0	4.5	5.2	4.4	5.6	5.4	4.6
	3.2	3.2	3.7	3.3	3.9	3.8	3.7	3.7	3.6
	2.4	2.3	2.8	2.0	2.1	3.0	2.7	2.9	3.1
% Depr., Dep., Amort./Sales	.6	.4	.4		.6	.3	.1	.4	.4
	(92) 1.0	(97) .8	(112) .7		(22) .8	(11) .8	(20) .6	(14) .6	(38) .6
	1.8	1.5	1.3		1.6	1.6	1.6	1.1	
% Officers', Directors' Owners' Comp/Sales	1.4	1.9	1.6		3.2	.8	1.3		.9
	(47) 3.5	(57) 4.2	(62) 3.4		(17) 5.5	(10) 2.9	(13) 2.5		(11) 1.7
	8.4	6.9	7.2		7.4	5.5	5.6		7.0
Net Sales ($)	3010061M	3491071M	4754800M	6708M	58542M	57161M	158156M	266644M	4207589M
Total Assets ($)	843187M	1076065M	1268527M	3027M	26811M	16484M	41589M	76163M	1104453M

M = $ thousand   MM = $ million
See Pages 11 through 21 for Explanation of Ratios and Data

Current Data Sorted by Assets   Comparative Historical Data

						Type of Statement		
	2	2	1	2	4	Unqualified	16	14
4	4	10			1	Reviewed	19	15
11	6	6		1	1	Compiled	25	33
6	13	8		1		Tax Returns	22	29
	14	13	2	1		Other	31	44
	20 (4/1-9/30/06)		91 (10/1/06-3/31/07)				4/1/02-3/31/03 ALL	4/1/03-3/31/04 ALL
0-500M	500M-2MM	2-10MM	10-50MM	50-100MM	100-250MM	NUMBER OF STATEMENTS		
21	39	39	3	4	5		113	135
%	%	%	%	%	%	ASSETS	%	%
11.1	10.5	10.7				Cash & Equivalents	13.4	12.7
25.6	35.6	44.4				Trade Receivables (net)	37.8	38.6
24.2	23.0	18.2				Inventory	20.8	19.9
.2	3.3	1.8				All Other Current	2.5	3.5
61.0	72.4	75.1				Total Current	74.5	74.7
18.2	9.9	15.3				Fixed Assets (net)	15.5	15.5
12.0	10.4	5.3				Intangibles (net)	3.4	2.5
8.5	7.3	4.3				All Other Non-Current	6.6	7.3
100.0	100.0	100.0				Total	100.0	100.0
						LIABILITIES		
34.6	14.9	10.4				Notes Payable-Short Term	12.9	16.8
2.5	3.4	1.5				Cur. Mat.-L.T.D.	3.5	2.2
22.6	27.6	25.4				Trade Payables	27.2	23.9
.7	.1	.1				Income Taxes Payable	.1	.4
17.5	14.0	23.7				All Other Current	14.4	14.6
77.9	60.1	61.1				Total Current	58.0	57.8
29.7	10.9	12.8				Long-Term Debt	13.4	10.1
.1	.1	.2				Deferred Taxes	.1	.2
17.8	5.7	8.8				All Other Non-Current	6.5	7.7
-25.6	23.2	17.1				Net Worth	22.0	24.2
100.0	100.0	100.0				Total Liabilities & Net Worth	100.0	100.0
						INCOME DATA		
100.0	100.0	100.0				Net Sales	100.0	100.0
49.3	32.6	37.7				Gross Profit	34.8	38.4
46.7	29.7	31.6				Operating Expenses	34.5	34.9
2.6	2.9	6.1				Operating Profit	.3	3.5
.8	.7	1.4				All Other Expenses (net)	.3	.8
1.8	2.2	4.8				Profit Before Taxes	.0	2.7
						RATIOS		
1.5	2.1	2.2					2.1	2.0
1.1	1.2	1.4				Current	1.3	1.3
.5	.8	1.1					.9	1.0
1.1	1.3	1.5					1.5	1.3
.7	.8	1.0				Quick	.9	1.0
.2	.6	.6					.6	.6
9 39.8	15 24.3	30 12.1					17 21.0	23 16.1
19 19.5	29 12.7	48 7.6				Sales/Receivables	30 12.1	36 10.2
54 6.8	49 7.5	72 5.1					46 7.9	55 6.6
10 37.9	8 43.4	1 383.2					5 74.0	5 78.8
38 9.5	25 14.4	20 18.0				Cost of Sales/Inventory	17 21.1	21 17.6
91 4.0	42 8.8	50 7.3					43 8.5	52 7.0
15 23.9	23 15.5	24 15.4					16 22.5	17 21.8
30 12.1	29 12.6	39 9.4				Cost of Sales/Payables	28 13.0	30 12.4
76 4.8	49 7.4	88 4.2					47 7.7	59 6.2
20.9	9.7	7.2					10.0	8.5
51.2	35.6	18.7				Sales/Working Capital	25.5	20.3
-10.7	-41.4	81.4					-135.0	184.7
7.0	8.0	18.8					6.6	12.0
(20) 2.0	(32) 2.7	(32) 5.2				EBIT/Interest	(101) 2.0	(117) 3.1
-.8	.5	1.8					-.5	.5
							2.9	7.7
						Net Profit + Depr., Dep., Amort./Cur. Mat. L/T/D	(16) .4	(13) 2.0
							-.6	.7
1.2	.1	.2					.1	.1
-7.5	.6	.7				Fixed/Worth	.5	.4
-.3	-.6	16.9					8.2	1.5
4.7	1.5	1.0					1.1	1.1
-81.0	5.3	3.6				Debt/Worth	2.6	2.6
-2.0	-11.3	285.6					48.1	9.6
112.8	71.1	80.2					37.7	58.6
(10) 47.4	(26) 36.4	(30) 34.4				% Profit Before Taxes/Tangible Net Worth	(88) 7.7	(111) 20.3
-55.6	4.9	11.1					-.6	2.1
24.9	17.2	18.3					9.5	17.1
5.1	5.3	7.7				% Profit Before Taxes/Total Assets	2.4	6.2
-7.5	.1	3.1					-3.4	.1
90.3	304.1	99.5					85.2	153.4
27.8	41.6	35.1				Sales/Net Fixed Assets	36.3	35.1
11.4	23.2	14.0					21.0	15.2
6.3	6.8	4.4					6.0	5.0
3.3	4.1	3.4				Sales/Total Assets	4.5	3.8
2.3	2.5	2.3					2.8	2.5
.5	.2	.3					.5	.3
(14) 1.3	(30) .6	(36) .7				% Depr., Dep., Amort./Sales	(94) 1.0	(95) 1.0
2.9	1.2	1.4					1.7	2.1
3.0	1.4	1.5					2.5	2.8
(13) 6.7	(24) 3.4	(16) 2.8				% Officers', Directors' Owners' Comp/Sales	(50) 4.9	(55) 5.6
12.6	6.6	5.4					8.9	9.2
16493M	223939M	673710M	412562M	1205855M	4596718M	Net Sales ($)	1525249M	1680193M
4037M	48589M	194156M	86794M	320598M	902909M	Total Assets ($)	466649M	612290M

M = $ thousand   MM = $ million
See Pages 11 through 21 for Explanation of Ratios and Data

Comparative Historical Data | Current Data Sorted by Sales

4/1/04-3/31/05 ALL	4/1/05-3/31/06 ALL	4/1/06-3/31/07 ALL	Type of Statement	0-1MM	1-3MM	3-5MM	5-10MM	10-25MM	25MM & OVER
14	15	11	Unqualified				2	1	8
22	14	14	Reviewed		1	2	3	4	4
25	13	17	Compiled	4	1	4	4	6	1
29	27	33	Tax Returns	9	8	4	3	7	2
43	44	36	Other	5	6	3	11	5	6
				20 (4/1-9/30/06)			**91 (10/1/06-3/31/07)**		
133	113	111	**NUMBER OF STATEMENTS**	18	16	10	23	23	21
%	%	%	**ASSETS**	%	%	%	%	%	%
11.5	14.6	10.3	Cash & Equivalents	6.1	17.4	4.2	14.9	8.9	7.9
36.9	37.9	37.3	Trade Receivables (net)	21.5	33.3	40.5	30.4	54.2	41.5
21.7	18.7	21.6	Inventory	23.1	18.3	17.7	24.8	17.0	26.3
3.8	2.4	2.1	All Other Current	.2	2.7	3.3	1.8	2.5	2.6
73.9	73.6	71.4	Total Current	51.0	71.8	65.7	71.9	82.7	78.3
13.8	15.3	13.2	Fixed Assets (net)	25.5	7.2	16.6	12.1	11.0	9.3
4.7	5.6	9.2	Intangibles (net)	14.0	13.3	13.2	9.7	1.1	8.4
7.6	5.5	6.1	All Other Non-Current	9.3	7.8	4.5	6.3	5.1	3.9
100.0	100.0	100.0	Total	100.0	100.0	100.0	100.0	100.0	100.0
			LIABILITIES						
16.0	17.8	16.7	Notes Payable-Short Term	34.8	14.5	23.2	11.1	11.9	10.9
6.4	2.6	2.3	Cur. Mat.-L.T.D.	3.1	6.4	2.0	1.1	1.6	.8
27.8	31.8	26.6	Trade Payables	20.7	15.3	37.3	23.6	33.9	30.7
.8	.7	.3	Income Taxes Payable	.8	.0	.3	.1	.1	.7
11.7	17.2	18.1	All Other Current	17.8	14.9	17.1	29.6	14.5	12.6
62.7	70.1	64.0	Total Current	77.3	51.0	79.9	65.5	61.9	55.7
12.0	12.2	14.3	Long-Term Debt	31.7	21.0	13.0	15.9	5.1	3.4
.2	.4	.2	Deferred Taxes	.1	.0	.3	.3	.1	.5
6.0	7.2	8.5	All Other Non-Current	6.6	26.5	7.7	3.9	5.7	4.8
19.1	10.1	12.9	Net Worth	-15.8	1.5	-1.0	14.4	27.1	35.6
100.0	100.0	100.0	Total Liabilities & Net Worth	100.0	100.0	100.0	100.0	100.0	100.0
			INCOME DATA						
100.0	100.0	100.0	Net Sales	100.0	100.0	100.0	100.0	100.0	100.0
38.1	37.7	36.6	Gross Profit	56.1	45.5	28.0	40.6	25.0	25.6
33.7	35.2	32.7	Operating Expenses	52.8	39.6	27.2	36.1	20.4	22.5
4.5	2.6	3.9	Operating Profit	3.3	6.0	.7	4.5	4.6	3.0
1.0	1.3	1.0	All Other Expenses (net)	1.4	1.5	1.2	.8	.7	.4
3.4	1.3	3.0	Profit Before Taxes	1.8	4.5	-.5	3.7	3.9	2.6
			RATIOS						
1.8	1.8	1.8	Current	1.6	1.8	1.2	2.9	1.3	1.7
1.3	1.2	1.2		1.0	1.5	.9	1.1	1.3	1.4
1.0	.9	.9		.4	.9	.6	.6	1.1	1.0
1.2	1.3	1.4	Quick	1.1	1.4	1.0	2.1	1.4	1.3
.8	.9	.8		.6	1.0	.6	.8	1.1	.8
.5	.4	.5		.2	.7	.3	.4	.8	.5
21 17.6	13 27.3	15 24.0	Sales/Receivables	10 37.1	18 20.5	24 15.3	12 31.6	27 13.6	10 36.3
34 10.6	31 11.9	38 9.7		17 21.3	41 8.9	37 10.0	35 10.5	39 9.3	38 9.6
54 6.8	59 6.2	60 6.1		53 6.9	99 3.7	65 5.6	66 5.6	61 6.0	65 5.6
9 38.9	1 397.8	6 63.1	Cost of Sales/Inventory	10 36.6	4 82.1	8 46.8	9 39.5	0 UND	1 244.0
27 13.3	16 22.6	26 14.0		50 7.3	35 10.5	26 14.1	26 14.0	14 26.0	27 13.4
55 6.7	35 10.5	53 6.9		93 3.9	83 4.4	44 8.3	42 8.8	26 13.8	43 8.5
20 18.4	16 22.5	23 15.5	Cost of Sales/Payables	20 18.3	4 92.9	24 15.1	24 15.1	23 15.5	25 14.8
37 10.0	31 11.7	36 10.2		36 10.3	42 8.7	56 6.5	36 10.2	32 11.6	34 10.6
62 5.9	59 6.2	52 7.0		86 4.2	56 6.5	71 5.1	94 3.9	44 8.3	42 8.7
9.9	12.3	11.6	Sales/Working Capital	20.7	7.0	31.8	8.4	10.3	12.2
21.1	35.4	32.3		-252.0	17.5	NM	48.1	24.7	18.7
-624.0	-47.6	-42.7		-9.2	NM	-12.9	-12.1	81.4	117.2
10.5	14.2	9.2	EBIT/Interest	5.8	10.1		8.3	31.0	19.8
(112) 3.5	(90) 3.5	(95) 3.5		(17) 1.5	(15) 2.8		(16) 4.2	(19) 7.7	(19) 5.6
1.0	1.0	1.0		-1.0	.6		1.1	1.3	1.6
2.9	7.2	8.4	Net Profit + Depr., Dep., Amort./Cur. Mat. L/T/D						
(20) 1.5	(15) 3.4	(15) 4.7							
.1	1.7	2.1							
.1	.2	.1	Fixed/Worth	1.4	.1	.8	.1	.1	.1
.5	.6	.8		NM	NM	NM	.6	.3	.2
2.4	UND	-1.2		-.3	-.2	-.3	-10.4	.8	1.2
1.4	1.7	1.6	Debt/Worth	5.6	1.8	3.2	.6	1.0	1.1
3.0	4.1	4.9		NM	NM	NM	4.9	3.9	2.2
23.5	-72.6	-10.1		-2.0	-3.2	-2.9	-18.4	8.0	11.1
80.7	70.0	73.8	% Profit Before Taxes/Tangible Net Worth				69.7	82.3	53.8
(104) 24.7	(83) 27.9	(76) 34.8					(16) 30.9	(19) 57.1	(19) 31.5
5.1	4.2	9.7					11.1	10.0	7.7
16.4	20.4	18.3	% Profit Before Taxes/Total Assets	20.2	20.4	9.1	21.0	34.2	13.1
5.2	5.5	7.0		4.2	7.4	3.2	8.0	9.2	7.9
.4	.1	.5		-7.3	-1.6	-12.6	1.1	.6	1.3
121.3	181.5	123.7	Sales/Net Fixed Assets	44.1	180.3	52.8	190.1	253.5	138.3
44.3	41.0	41.1		17.8	35.6	20.6	39.7	80.2	56.8
18.3	16.2	17.3		8.6	17.5	16.8	23.2	28.8	22.6
5.0	6.4	5.3	Sales/Total Assets	4.8	3.9	5.0	5.2	6.6	5.7
3.7	3.9	3.6		2.6	2.1	3.8	3.5	4.4	4.5
2.5	2.6	2.3		2.0	1.6	2.4	2.3	3.4	3.4
.4	.3	.3	% Depr., Dep., Amort./Sales	.8	.5		.3	.1	.3
(95) .9	(78) .8	(88) .7		(14) 1.4	(11) .8		(20) .6	(18) .3	(17) .5
1.8	1.5	1.3		4.1	1.2		1.2	.9	.8
1.6	2.6	1.6	% Officers', Directors' Owners' Comp/Sales	5.3	1.8		1.2	2.1	
(55) 3.9	(48) 5.0	(57) 3.6		(11) 11.4	(13) 5.2		(10) 2.4	(11) 2.7	
7.6	9.4	7.3		13.0	8.6		5.7	3.6	
2672702M	3304183M	7129277M	Net Sales ($)	9615M	31579M	40051M	163728M	335718M	6548586M
837616M	809377M	1557083M	Total Assets ($)	5124M	13813M	12147M	59148M	82220M	1384631M

© RMA 2007

M = $ thousand   MM = $ million

See Pages 11 through 21 for Explanation of Ratios and Data

Current Data Sorted by Assets   Comparative Historical Data

Type of Statement								
						Unqualified	85	82
						Reviewed	211	199
						Compiled	183	220
						Tax Returns	77	90
						Other	159	142
1	2	21	29	8	5			
	18	75	40	4				
5	41	65	11	1			4/1/02-	4/1/03-
10	34	18	2				3/31/03	3/31/04
7	28	46	31	11	4		ALL	ALL
67 (4/1-9/30/06)		450 (10/1/06-3/31/07)						
0-500M	500M-2MM	2-10MM	10-50MM	50-100MM	100-250MM			
23	123	225	113	24	9	**NUMBER OF STATEMENTS**	715	733
%	%	%	%	%	%	**ASSETS**	%	%
20.5	7.3	6.1	6.3	5.6		Cash & Equivalents	5.9	6.0
23.8	28.4	30.0	26.8	26.2		Trade Receivables (net)	30.1	30.4
29.5	37.3	34.5	29.0	27.6		Inventory	34.4	33.1
2.5	2.1	2.0	2.4	5.3		All Other Current	2.2	3.1
76.4	75.1	72.6	64.5	64.7		Total Current	72.5	72.6
17.9	15.6	18.5	24.9	26.0		Fixed Assets (net)	19.4	19.6
2.6	2.6	1.9	3.6	3.3		Intangibles (net)	1.6	1.8
3.0	6.8	7.0	7.0	6.0		All Other Non-Current	6.4	6.0
100.0	100.0	100.0	100.0	100.0		Total	100.0	100.0
						LIABILITIES		
25.2	14.8	15.1	13.5	9.6		Notes Payable-Short Term	16.1	16.3
3.3	3.3	2.4	2.0	3.0		Cur. Mat.-L.T.D.	3.7	3.1
20.7	18.6	14.8	11.6	12.4		Trade Payables	15.8	16.1
.0	.0	.1	.2	.2		Income Taxes Payable	.2	.3
21.9	8.0	7.5	8.0	8.4		All Other Current	7.9	8.0
71.1	44.8	40.0	35.3	33.6		Total Current	43.8	43.8
36.0	16.6	12.4	13.9	16.0		Long-Term Debt	12.4	13.4
.0	.1	.2	.4	.9		Deferred Taxes	.2	.2
19.4	3.2	3.9	3.2	3.0		All Other Non-Current	3.9	4.5
-26.6	35.3	43.5	47.2	46.6		Net Worth	39.7	38.1
100.0	100.0	100.0	100.0	100.0		Total Liabilities & Net Worth	100.0	100.0
						INCOME DATA		
100.0	100.0	100.0	100.0	100.0		Net Sales	100.0	100.0
31.6	29.0	25.8	28.0	29.0		Gross Profit	26.9	26.7
32.5	26.8	23.0	23.6	24.2		Operating Expenses	25.0	24.4
-.9	2.2	2.8	4.5	4.7		Operating Profit	1.9	2.2
1.4	.4	.0	.5	.3		All Other Expenses (net)	.2	.1
-2.3	1.8	2.8	4.0	4.4		Profit Before Taxes	1.7	2.1
						RATIOS		
3.3	3.3	3.1	3.4	3.3			2.8	2.7
1.4	1.7	1.9	1.8	2.0		Current	1.7	1.7
.9	1.2	1.3	1.3	1.3			1.3	1.3
1.5	1.3	1.5	1.8	1.6			1.4	1.4
.8	.8	.9	.9	.9		Quick	.8 (728)	.8
.3	.6	.6	.6	.4			.6	.6
3 117.0	**20** 17.8	**27** 13.3	**27** 13.7	**31** 11.9			**25** 14.5	**27** 13.5
17 20.9	**29** 12.5	**34** 10.7	**35** 10.3	**35** 10.4		Sales/Receivables	**35** 10.3	**38** 9.6
31 11.8	**43** 8.6	**48** 7.7	**46** 8.0	**44** 8.3			**46** 7.9	**49** 7.4
0 UND	**30** 12.0	**35** 10.4	**35** 10.3	**36** 10.2			**37** 9.8	**38** 9.7
29 12.5	**63** 5.8	**55** 6.6	**51** 7.1	**49** 7.4		Cost of Sales/Inventory	**55** 6.6	**55** 6.7
107 3.4	**94** 3.9	**82** 4.4	**68** 5.4	**77** 4.8			**80** 4.6	**77** 4.7
6 62.0	**14** 26.2	**14** 25.7	**14** 26.8	**14** 26.1			**15** 24.5	**15** 23.8
24 15.3	**23** 15.7	**21** 17.6	**19** 19.6	**21** 17.2		Cost of Sales/Payables	**22** 16.7	**24** 15.3
37 9.7	**43** 8.4	**33** 10.9	**25** 14.7	**33** 11.0			**34** 10.6	**36** 10.1
6.1	5.5	5.7	5.8	6.3			6.1	5.9
23.2	9.8	9.0	10.3	10.5		Sales/Working Capital	10.2	9.7
-13.9	31.0	16.5	22.0	15.8			21.1	20.0
6.2	6.5	9.6	10.9	22.5			7.5	8.7
(18) 2.0	(114) 2.3	(215) 2.8	(109) 3.8	11.0		EBIT/Interest	(671) 3.0	(676) 3.5
-2.1	.9	1.5	1.8	1.7			1.2	1.5
	1.7	6.5	15.4	54.9			6.2	4.5
	(24) .7	(69) 3.3	(36) 6.8	(12) 5.8		Net Profit + Depr., Dep., Amort./Cur. Mat. L/T/D	(211) 2.5	(197) 2.0
	.1	1.5	3.1	1.5			1.1	.9
.2	.1	.2	.3	.3			.2	.2
-5.7	.4	.4	.6	.7		Fixed/Worth	.4	.4
-.4	1.2	.7	1.1	1.3			1.0	1.0
2.0	.8	.6	.6	.5			.7	.8
-22.8	1.9	1.3	1.3	1.8		Debt/Worth	1.6	1.7
-2.0	4.8	3.0	3.1	2.3			3.2	3.5
144.1	38.0	32.7	36.4	45.1			26.2	28.8
(10) 54.9	(104) 7.8	(214) 12.9	(111) 20.9	25.7		% Profit Before Taxes/Tangible Net Worth	(657) 11.7	(672) 15.1
31.6	-.7	4.2	6.1	6.0			2.9	3.6
19.6	13.3	13.1	16.3	19.2			9.7	11.1
6.5	2.6	4.7	8.7	12.6		% Profit Before Taxes/Total Assets	4.2	4.9
-11.2	-.4	1.5	2.5	2.5			.7	.9
394.7	58.5	37.4	22.4	22.7			35.7	37.4
20.2	24.8	18.9	11.0	10.8		Sales/Net Fixed Assets	18.5	18.7
10.4	13.9	10.7	7.2	6.4			10.6	10.0
7.6	3.9	3.6	3.3	3.1			3.6	3.6
4.6	3.1	2.9	2.7	2.7		Sales/Total Assets	2.9	2.8
2.7	2.4	2.2	2.0	2.0			2.2	2.2
.5	.5	.6	.8	.8			.8	.8
(17) .8	(103) 1.0	(208) 1.0	(109) 1.2	(22) 1.1		% Depr., Dep., Amort./Sales	(649) 1.1	(658) 1.2
2.1	1.6	1.5	1.7	1.6			1.7	1.8
1.3	1.9	1.0	.5				1.4	1.5
(11) 4.5	(67) 3.1	(101) 1.9	(34) 1.1			% Officers', Directors' Owners' Comp/Sales	(363) 2.6	(352) 2.5
10.3	4.8	4.0	2.1				5.2	4.7
30935M	490784M	3697869M	6967295M	4330465M	2779135M	Net Sales ($)	18228380M	16176286M
6619M	147620M	1081935M	2504502M	1700660M	1338801M	Total Assets ($)	6348597M	6394768M

M = $ thousand   MM = $ million
See Pages 11 through 21 for Explanation of Ratios and Data

Comparative Historical Data | Current Data Sorted by Sales

			Type of Statement						
70	64	66	Unqualified	1		2	1	15	47
189	150	137	Reviewed		7	8	27	42	53
133	123	123	Compiled	4	16	23	32	35	13
70	50	64	Tax Returns	5	19	11	18	8	3
121	160	127	Other	5	14	18	16	29	45
4/1/04-3/31/05	4/1/05-3/31/06	4/1/06-3/31/07		67 (4/1-9/30/06)			450 (10/1/06-3/31/07)		
ALL	ALL	ALL		0-1MM	1-3MM	3-5MM	5-10MM	10-25MM	25MM & OVER
583	547	517	**NUMBER OF STATEMENTS**	15	56	62	94	129	161
%	%	%	**ASSETS**	%	%	%	%	%	%
5.5	6.3	7.0	Cash & Equivalents	17.2	8.6	8.3	5.8	7.0	5.7
31.2	29.9	28.4	Trade Receivables (net)	16.6	23.7	26.1	28.5	32.4	28.7
35.5	34.5	33.3	Inventory	31.3	35.0	36.5	37.0	32.2	30.5
2.1	2.3	2.3	All Other Current	1.8	2.1	2.4	1.2	2.5	2.9
74.3	73.0	71.0	Total Current	66.9	69.3	73.2	72.4	74.0	67.8
17.8	18.9	19.7	Fixed Assets (net)	25.2	18.0	18.3	18.3	17.9	22.6
1.6	1.8	2.7	Intangibles (net)	.4	5.4	1.7	1.9	1.5	3.7
6.4	6.3	6.7	All Other Non-Current	7.5	7.3	6.8	7.5	6.5	6.0
100.0	100.0	100.0	Total	100.0	100.0	100.0	100.0	100.0	100.0
			LIABILITIES						
15.0	14.0	14.7	Notes Payable-Short Term	13.1	16.8	16.7	15.0	14.9	13.1
2.6	2.7	2.7	Cur. Mat.-L.T.D.	3.7	2.6	4.8	2.1	2.3	2.5
17.5	16.0	15.1	Trade Payables	9.2	16.3	19.0	15.2	16.3	12.6
.2	.2	.1	Income Taxes Payable	.0	.1	.0	.1	.2	.1
8.4	8.3	8.4	All Other Current	30.5	6.8	7.5	6.0	8.0	9.1
43.8	41.3	41.1	Total Current	56.5	42.6	48.0	38.5	41.6	37.5
14.3	12.7	15.2	Long-Term Debt	30.9	30.1	15.7	12.5	11.0	13.2
.3	.3	.2	Deferred Taxes	.0	.0	.0	.2	.3	.4
4.7	4.5	4.2	All Other Non-Current	18.3	5.7	4.7	4.6	3.3	2.6
36.9	41.3	39.3	Net Worth	-5.7	21.7	31.7	44.1	43.7	46.3
100.0	100.0	100.0	Total Liabilties & Net Worth	100.0	100.0	100.0	100.0	100.0	100.0
			INCOME DATA						
100.0	100.0	100.0	Net Sales	100.0	100.0	100.0	100.0	100.0	100.0
27.0	26.6	27.5	Gross Profit	43.0	30.4	28.2	27.0	25.3	26.7
24.2	23.3	24.5	Operating Expenses	45.0	27.6	25.0	24.7	22.5	22.7
2.8	3.3	3.0	Operating Profit	-2.0	2.8	3.2	2.3	2.9	4.0
.0	.1	.3	All Other Expenses (net)	1.3	.9	.3	.4	-.1	.3
2.7	3.2	2.7	Profit Before Taxes	-3.4	2.0	2.8	1.9	2.9	3.7
			RATIOS						
2.6	2.8	3.2	Current	6.9	4.7	2.7	3.2	3.0	3.0
1.8	1.8	1.8		1.6	2.1	1.5	2.1	1.8	1.9
1.3	1.4	1.3		.7	1.2	1.1	1.4	1.3	1.3
1.3	1.4	1.5	Quick	1.5	1.4	1.2	1.4	1.5	1.6
(580) .9	.9	.9		.8	.9	.7	.9	.9	.9
.6	.6	.6		.4	.5	.5	.6	.6	.6
27 13.7	26 14.1	25 14.8	Sales/Receivables	7 54.3	15 24.0	21 17.2	24 15.4	28 13.3	28 13.3
37 9.8	36 10.1	33 11.0		19 19.5	27 13.5	31 11.7	31 11.8	35 10.5	35 10.5
49 7.5	47 7.7	46 8.0		46 8.0	46 7.9	44 8.3	46 8.0	47 7.7	44 8.2
38 9.5	38 9.7	34 10.7	Cost of Sales/Inventory	29 12.8	31 11.9	30 12.4	44 8.4	30 12.2	34 10.7
56 6.5	55 6.6	54 6.8		114 3.2	70 5.2	70 5.2	63 5.8	49 7.5	49 7.5
83 4.4	81 4.5	81 4.5		196 1.9	119 3.1	95 3.7	71 5.1		66 5.6
17 22.0	15 24.2	14 26.3	Cost of Sales/Payables	0 UND	11 32.6	16 23.1	15 23.9	14 26.4	14 26.6
24 15.0	22 16.9	21 17.6		25 14.7	22 16.7	24 14.9	24 15.3	20 18.2	19 19.6
38 9.5	32 11.2	33 11.0		54 6.8	41 8.9	47 7.8	34 10.6	32 11.5	25 14.3
6.2	6.2	5.7	Sales/Working Capital	3.1	4.1	5.7	5.3	6.4	6.6
9.5	9.6	9.8		15.4	9.0	11.5	8.1	10.1	10.3
18.1	16.4	20.3		-9.7	33.7	42.2	14.0	22.0	16.6
11.2	10.6	9.4	EBIT/Interest	8.2	5.7	7.6	5.9	9.0	13.4
(550) 4.8	(502) 4.3	(489) 3.0		(11) .4	(50) 2.2	(60) 2.5	(88) 2.2	(123) 2.8	(157) 4.3
2.0	2.0	1.4		-4.6	.9	.9	1.1	1.6	1.8
6.7	6.7	7.2	Net Profit + Depr., Dep., Amort./Cur. Mat. L/T/D			2.7	6.7	6.5	17.1
(173) 3.0	(159) 3.3	(147) 3.3			(13) .9	(29) 4.0	(37) 2.6	(60) 4.4	
1.4	1.4	1.2				.1	1.5	1.2	2.6
.2	.2	.2	Fixed/Worth	.2	.1	.2	.2	.2	.3
.4	.4	.4		2.7	.5	.5	.4	.4	.5
.9	.9	1.0		-1.1	-9.3	2.2	.6	.7	1.0
.8	.7	.7	Debt/Worth	1.8	.8	.6	.6	.7	.6
1.6	1.4	1.5		12.6	2.1	2.1	1.2	1.6	1.3
3.2	3.3	3.5		-4.0	-24.3	9.9	2.7	3.0	2.6
36.1	35.5	36.4	% Profit Before Taxes/Tangible Net Worth		40.7	38.4	26.9	37.5	38.0
(537) 18.3	(509) 19.1	(471) 15.1			(39) 10.3	(49) 8.0	(91) 9.3	(126) 15.3	(157) 22.3
7.5	7.8	3.8			.3	-1.4	1.4	5.1	8.2
13.1	15.5	14.3	% Profit Before Taxes/Total Assets	5.2	12.6	13.2	9.0	14.6	16.6
6.4	7.2	5.0		-.6	3.5	4.3	2.9	5.0	8.8
2.3	2.6	1.2		-24.7	-.4	-.3	.5	1.9	2.6
40.6	42.4	36.9	Sales/Net Fixed Assets	12.9	57.6	45.3	40.2	49.1	25.2
21.4	18.5	18.0		8.4	21.4	20.5	18.6	21.2	14.6
10.8	9.8	9.3		3.9	8.9	10.7	11.1	11.6	9.0
3.7	3.6	3.7	Sales/Total Assets	3.2	3.8	3.7	3.6	3.9	3.6
2.9	2.9	2.9		1.7	2.7	2.8	2.9	3.0	2.9
2.3	2.3	2.2		1.3	1.8	2.1	2.0	2.4	2.4
.7	.6	.6	% Depr., Dep., Amort./Sales	1.0	.6	.6	.5	.6	.8
(515) 1.0	(485) 1.0	(466) 1.0		(11) 1.9	(46) 1.3	(55) 1.0	(82) 1.0	(120) .9	(152) 1.1
1.6	1.5	1.6		7.4	1.9	1.6	1.7	1.4	1.5
1.3	1.4	1.1	% Officers', Directors' Owners' Comp/Sales		2.4	1.8	1.3	1.0	.4
(277) 2.6	(240) 2.6	(218) 2.2			(26) 3.9	(33) 2.8	(54) 2.2	(51) 2.7	(49) 1.1
4.2	4.3	4.1			5.3	4.0	4.4	4.0	1.8
13698556M	16576687M	18296483M	Net Sales ($)	8331M	119578M	234431M	658685M	2042394M	15233064M
5160062M	5767767M	6780137M	Total Assets ($)	8550M	66931M	97028M	271602M	710923M	5625103M

M = $ thousand   MM = $ million
See Pages 11 through 21 for Explanation of Ratios and Data

Current Data Sorted by Assets   Comparative Historical Data

0-500M	500M-2MM	2-10MM	10-50MM	50-100MM	100-250MM	Type of Statement	4/1/02-3/31/03 ALL	4/1/03-3/31/04 ALL
	1	1				Unqualified	2	5
	5	7		1		Reviewed	21	25
4	3	4				Compiled	27	24
7	9	5				Tax Returns	11	26
1		1	1	1		Other	19	17
	12 (4/1-9/30/06)		38 (10/1/06-3/31/07)					
12	18	17	1	2		NUMBER OF STATEMENTS	80	97
%	%	%	%	%	%	**ASSETS**	%	%
10.9	5.6	6.2				Cash & Equivalents	9.6	10.9
18.1	31.0	22.2				Trade Receivables (net)	22.0	21.7
57.8	34.0	36.7				Inventory	38.0	37.2
.2	.8	.9				All Other Current	2.2	2.5
87.0	71.4	66.0				Total Current	71.8	72.3
9.3	14.9	14.9				Fixed Assets (net)	12.5	12.4
2.8	1.7	3.0				Intangibles (net)	1.8	1.3
.9	12.0	16.2				All Other Non-Current	13.9	14.0
100.0	100.0	100.0				Total	100.0	100.0
						LIABILITIES		
6.8	17.3	12.6				Notes Payable-Short Term	9.7	9.8
5.3	2.5	3.7				Cur. Mat.-L.T.D.	2.5	2.4
24.9	22.0	16.8				Trade Payables	24.0	23.6
.0	.7	.2				Income Taxes Payable	.6	.4
21.2	6.4	12.5				All Other Current	8.9	6.3
58.2	48.8	45.8				Total Current	45.7	42.6
19.8	14.7	14.3				Long-Term Debt	7.8	12.1
.0	.5	.3				Deferred Taxes	.0	.1
9.1	6.2	12.4				All Other Non-Current	15.8	16.6
12.8	29.9	27.3				Net Worth	30.6	28.6
100.0	100.0	100.0				Total Liabilities & Net Worth	100.0	100.0
						INCOME DATA		
100.0	100.0	100.0				Net Sales	100.0	100.0
41.9	35.0	31.4				Gross Profit	34.8	34.3
40.9	33.2	30.8				Operating Expenses	33.7	33.7
1.0	1.8	.6				Operating Profit	1.1	.6
1.2	.3	.2				All Other Expenses (net)	.2	.2
-.2	1.5	.4				Profit Before Taxes	.9	.4
						RATIOS		
2.9	2.5	2.1					2.7	3.1
1.6	1.5	1.6				Current	1.6	1.8
1.0	1.0	1.1					1.2	1.2
1.0	1.4	1.1					1.2	1.7
.6	.6	.6				Quick	.6	.6
.3	.5	.3					.3	.3
14 25.6	18 19.9	20 17.9					16 23.1	15 25.2
25 14.8	40 9.1	33 10.9				Sales/Receivables	25 14.4	24 14.9
47 7.8	53 6.8	44 8.3					40 9.1	39 9.4
78 4.7	47 7.8	43 8.4					49 7.4	45 8.1
128 2.9	64 5.7	83 4.4				Cost of Sales/Inventory	81 4.5	78 4.7
231 1.6	79 4.6	146 2.5					134 2.7	129 2.8
15 23.8	16 22.8	17 21.7					19 19.7	19 19.1
31 11.7	41 8.8	35 10.4				Cost of Sales/Payables	43 8.5	42 8.8
49 7.5	59 6.2	91 4.0					83 4.4	79 4.6
5.6	7.3	6.3					5.8	5.3
8.6	10.5	13.9				Sales/Working Capital	8.4	8.3
UND	NM	25.1					26.5	21.1
15.0	6.4	6.1					7.2	10.3
(11) 1.9	2.3	2.3				EBIT/Interest	(68) 2.6	(77) 1.8
-1.9	.2	1.0					-1.7	-1.4
							2.6	4.3
						Net Profit + Depr., Dep., Amort./Cur. Mat. L/T/D	(26) .9	(29) .4
							-2.1	-4.6
.1	.2	.2					.1	.1
NM	.6	.7				Fixed/Worth	.3	.3
-.6	1.1	NM					.9	1.3
1.0	1.3	1.1					.7	.8
NM	2.5	4.0				Debt/Worth	2.3	3.0
-8.5	7.4	NM					11.8	9.8
	28.3	34.7					29.9	33.4
	(16) 11.7	(13) 18.9				% Profit Before Taxes/Tangible Net Worth	(68) 8.3	(82) 5.9
	-25.1	5.3					-9.7	-4.9
8.7	13.3	7.0					9.2	9.5
1.3	3.9	2.2				% Profit Before Taxes/Total Assets	3.0	1.9
-6.8	-2.4	-.3					-4.2	-4.1
92.7	136.5	64.1					88.4	61.9
23.8	25.3	28.9				Sales/Net Fixed Assets	31.4	32.8
14.5	12.7	13.5					14.7	14.6
3.5	3.5	3.3					3.6	3.8
2.6	3.0	2.5				Sales/Total Assets	2.7	3.0
1.5	2.5	1.2					1.7	1.8
	.7	.4					.6	.6
	(13) .9	(14) .9				% Depr., Dep., Amort./Sales	(64) 1.0	(84) 1.0
	1.4	1.5					1.6	1.6
							4.1	2.7
						% Officers', Directors' Owners' Comp/Sales	(44) 5.4	(61) 5.2
							7.2	8.8
10159M	73818M	165168M	44110M	74762M		Net Sales ($)	531518M	774643M
3295M	23634M	70098M	23398M	110199M		Total Assets ($)	328263M	450890M

© RMA 2007

M = $ thousand   MM = $ million

See Pages 11 through 21 for Explanation of Ratios and Data

Comparative Historical Data — Current Data Sorted by Sales

Type of Statement

4/1/04-3/31/05	4/1/05-3/31/06	4/1/06-3/31/07	Type of Statement	0-1MM	1-3MM	3-5MM	5-10MM	10-25MM	25MM & OVER
4	6	2	Unqualified				1		1
9	19	13	Reviewed		1	3	6	2	1
18	10	11	Compiled	4	2	2	1	2	
22	17	21	Tax Returns	4	7	5	4	1	
6	11	3	Other	1		1			1
4/1/04-3/31/05 ALL	4/1/05-3/31/06 ALL	4/1/06-3/31/07 ALL		12 (4/1-9/30/06)			38 (10/1/06-3/31/07)		

Financial Data

4/1/04-3/31/05 ALL	4/1/05-3/31/06 ALL	4/1/06-3/31/07 ALL		0-1MM	1-3MM	3-5MM	5-10MM	10-25MM	25MM & OVER
59	63	50	NUMBER OF STATEMENTS	9	10	10	12	6	3
%	%	%	**ASSETS**	%	%	%	%	%	%
7.1	7.4	7.1	Cash & Equivalents		10.2	5.4	3.2		
30.1	26.0	24.1	Trade Receivables (net)		17.8	33.9	23.3		
34.6	31.2	41.3	Inventory		42.2	29.8	45.5		
2.6	2.8	.8	All Other Current		.6	1.0	.2		
74.4	67.4	73.2	Total Current		70.7	70.0	72.2		
17.4	16.1	13.6	Fixed Assets (net)		11.0	20.0	9.1		
3.3	2.9	2.3	Intangibles (net)		2.9	.3	3.6		
4.9	13.6	10.9	All Other Non-Current		15.4	9.7	15.1		
100.0	100.0	100.0	Total		100.0	100.0	100.0		
			LIABILITIES						
13.4	8.5	12.1	Notes Payable-Short Term		14.3	15.8	15.4		
2.5	1.5	3.4	Cur. Mat.-L.T.D.		1.5	3.3	4.1		
23.1	21.2	19.9	Trade Payables		31.7	19.9	15.3		
.9	.5	.3	Income Taxes Payable		.2	1.0	.0		
9.3	11.6	11.9	All Other Current		13.1	6.9	6.5		
49.2	43.5	47.6	Total Current		60.8	47.0	41.3		
20.0	23.9	14.9	Long-Term Debt		12.8	16.4	15.2		
.1	.1	.3	Deferred Taxes		.0	.9	.1		
4.5	15.6	9.0	All Other Non-Current		7.9	3.4	17.8		
26.2	16.9	28.2	Net Worth		18.5	32.3	25.6		
100.0	100.0	100.0	Total Liabilities & Net Worth		100.0	100.0	100.0		
			INCOME DATA						
100.0	100.0	100.0	Net Sales		100.0	100.0	100.0		
35.3	34.1	35.7	Gross Profit		33.5	36.3	32.8		
33.6	32.2	34.5	Operating Expenses		32.9	35.6	32.0		
1.7	2.0	1.2	Operating Profit		.6	.7	.8		
.0	.5	.4	All Other Expenses (net)		1.0	-.3	-.1		
1.7	1.5	.8	Profit Before Taxes		-.5	.9	.9		
			RATIOS						
2.5	2.7	2.5	Current		2.6	2.5	2.7		
1.6	1.6	1.7			1.1	1.7	1.8		
1.2	1.1	1.1			.8	1.2	1.1		
1.3	1.4	1.4	Quick		1.1	1.4	1.5		
.8	.8	.6			.5	.8	.5		
.5	.4	.4			.2	.5	.3		
19 18.9	15 23.6	20 17.9	Sales/Receivables		12 29.2	31 11.9	19 19.4		
30 12.3	30 12.0	34 10.8			25 14.7	53 6.9	33 11.1		
43 8.4	42 8.8	50 7.3			32 11.5	60 6.0	40 9.1		
26 14.0	25 14.4	58 6.3	Cost of Sales/Inventory		52 7.0	30 12.0	63 5.8		
48 7.6	56 6.5	80 4.6			67 5.5	73 5.0	76 4.8		
96 3.8	108 3.4	130 2.8			138 2.6	108 3.4	123 3.0		
20 18.5	21 17.4	17 21.6	Cost of Sales/Payables		33 11.0	21 17.2	15 24.2		
33 11.0	31 11.9	37 9.7			50 7.3	50 7.3	18 20.7		
50 7.3	71 5.1	63 5.8			90 4.1	79 4.6	60 6.1		
7.0	6.7	6.0	Sales/Working Capital		6.1	7.2	5.8		
13.1	12.1	9.3			NM	9.3	8.1		
28.4	32.9	28.7			-22.0	20.0	64.6		
8.7	8.8	8.9	EBIT/Interest			6.8	4.3		
(55) 3.5	(57) 2.6	(48) 2.3				2.1	1.8		
1.2	.9	.6				-1.2	.6		
5.7	13.7	7.2	Net Profit + Depr., Dep., Amort./Cur. Mat. L/T/D						
(10) 3.3	(18) 1.4	(10) 1.6							
2.3	-.4	-.6							
.2	.2	.2	Fixed/Worth		.1	.2	.0		
.4	.5	.6			.6	.6	.4		
2.0	3.7	NM			.0	1.5	-50.6		
1.4	1.0	.9	Debt/Worth		1.3	1.0	1.0		
2.5	3.1	2.6			4.9	2.6	4.7		
8.2	62.6	NM			-5.9	5.9	-307.3		
56.7	47.7	27.5	% Profit Before Taxes/Tangible Net Worth			25.8			
(53) 16.3	(48) 10.9	(38) 10.3				8.1			
3.9	2.6	1.2				-3.9			
10.6	13.1	7.4	% Profit Before Taxes/Total Assets		10.5	7.3	6.4		
3.7	2.7	2.8			1.0	2.8	1.3		
.3	.0	-1.9			-6.5	-2.9	-1.4		
53.4	65.9	63.4	Sales/Net Fixed Assets		245.4	58.6	159.0		
26.4	23.2	24.8			81.5	16.7	34.8		
12.5	13.1	12.3			20.7	9.6	23.7		
4.5	4.1	3.3	Sales/Total Assets		3.5	3.0	3.6		
3.4	3.0	2.7			2.7	2.8	2.8		
2.1	1.8	1.8			1.5	2.2	2.1		
.6	.5	.7	% Depr., Dep., Amort./Sales						
(47) 1.1	(50) 1.0	(37) 1.0							
1.8	1.7	1.5							
1.9	1.8	2.4	% Officers', Directors' Owners' Comp/Sales						
(31) 3.4	(33) 3.6	(27) 3.6							
7.0	6.4	8.0							
720662M	847564M	368017M	Net Sales ($)	4690M	18577M	41009M	89204M	95665M	118872M
372542M	463265M	230624M	Total Assets ($)	2289M	9967M	20673M	39140M	24958M	133597M

© RMA 2007   M = $ thousand   MM = $ million
See Pages 11 through 21 for Explanation of Ratios and Data

Current Data Sorted by Assets | Comparative Historical Data

0-500M	500M-2MM	2-10MM	10-50MM	50-100MM	100-250MM	Type of Statement	4/1/02-3/31/03 ALL	4/1/03-3/31/04 ALL
1	4	2	2		2	Unqualified	17	17
11	14	30	5			Reviewed	54	52
19	61	21	1		1	Compiled	110	109
6	47	9	1		1	Tax Returns	52	78
	46	27	13	2		Other	76	89
	62 (4/1-9/30/06)		264 (10/1/06-3/31/07)					
37	172	89	22	2	4	NUMBER OF STATEMENTS	309	345
%	%	%	%	%	%	ASSETS	%	%
5.9	6.8	5.1	4.3			Cash & Equivalents	6.0	6.4
8.5	12.2	14.3	17.2			Trade Receivables (net)	13.8	13.6
59.8	52.6	49.9	45.8			Inventory	50.5	50.1
2.3	2.1	2.0	1.1			All Other Current	1.8	1.9
76.5	73.8	71.4	68.4			Total Current	72.2	71.9
11.1	15.0	18.7	20.5			Fixed Assets (net)	17.0	16.7
3.5	1.7	2.1	.8			Intangibles (net)	1.7	1.5
8.9	9.5	7.8	10.3			All Other Non-Current	9.2	9.8
100.0	100.0	100.0	100.0			Total	100.0	100.0
						LIABILITIES		
19.1	7.5	10.2	10.5			Notes Payable-Short Term	11.3	9.4
4.1	2.9	4.0	1.0			Cur. Mat.-L.T.D.	3.5	2.9
12.9	13.6	13.3	15.7			Trade Payables	15.5	15.3
.1	.2	.1	.4			Income Taxes Payable	.2	.2
8.0	7.1	6.0	7.6			All Other Current	7.0	7.3
44.3	31.3	33.6	35.2			Total Current	37.4	34.9
26.4	23.3	15.2	11.5			Long-Term Debt	19.0	20.6
.0	.1	.2	.4			Deferred Taxes	.1	.1
7.5	9.2	5.6	2.9			All Other Non-Current	5.0	5.1
21.8	36.2	45.5	49.9			Net Worth	38.5	39.2
100.0	100.0	100.0	100.0			Total Liabilities & Net Worth	100.0	100.0
						INCOME DATA		
100.0	100.0	100.0	100.0			Net Sales	100.0	100.0
37.0	37.3	36.3	34.4			Gross Profit	35.7	36.1
37.1	34.5	33.2	32.1			Operating Expenses	33.1	33.9
-.1	2.8	3.1	2.3			Operating Profit	2.5	2.3
1.1	.1	.2	.3			All Other Expenses (net)	.2	-.1
-1.2	2.7	2.9	1.9			Profit Before Taxes	2.3	2.3
						RATIOS		
3.6	4.4	3.3	3.6				3.7	3.7
2.6	2.7	2.4	2.2			Current	2.2	2.4
1.6	1.8	1.6	1.5				1.5	1.5
.7	1.4	1.1	1.0				1.1	1.1
.3	.5	.5	.5			Quick (308)	.5	.6
.1	.3	.3	.2				.2	.3
4 90.6	8 45.6	8 48.2	7 54.9				7 49.8	6 56.5
10 36.5	13 28.5	15 24.6	18 20.1			Sales/Receivables	14 26.5	14 26.3
16 23.5	22 16.3	33 11.2	46 7.9				29 12.4	28 13.2
115 3.2	98 3.7	84 4.3	83 4.4				85 4.3	80 4.6
152 2.4	135 2.7	130 2.8	124 2.9			Cost of Sales/Inventory	120 3.0	120 3.0
192 1.9	190 1.9	187 1.9	154 2.4				171 2.1	174 2.1
11 32.7	17 21.7	14 26.0	22 16.5				17 21.3	18 20.6
23 15.6	25 14.6	28 12.9	33 11.0			Cost of Sales/Payables	30 12.3	28 13.2
51 7.1	40 9.1	41 9.0	54 6.8				50 7.4	44 8.3
4.2	3.7	4.1	4.6				4.2	4.0
7.1	5.4	5.3	6.2			Sales/Working Capital	7.0	6.2
68.0	8.7	11.4	14.6				12.3	12.1
3.1	7.8	7.2	16.5				8.1	7.8
(35) 1.8	(156) 3.3	(86) 3.3	(21) 5.5			EBIT/Interest (269)	2.8 (314)	3.1
.4	1.4	1.2	1.3				1.1	1.2
	2.2	6.0				Net Profit + Depr., Dep.,	5.5	5.2
	(26) 1.2	(25) 1.9				Amort./Cur. Mat. L/T/D (73)	2.4 (74)	1.9
	.8	.3					.5	1.1
.1	.1	.2	.1				.2	.1
.3	.3	.4	.4			Fixed/Worth	.4	.4
-.7	1.2	.7	.9				1.0	.9
.7	.7	.5	.5				.7	.6
2.5	1.7	1.4	.8			Debt/Worth	1.5	1.5
-5.9	5.8	2.6	1.8				3.7	4.1
17.8	39.7	26.3	20.1				29.2	29.6
(24) 12.1	(149) 15.1	(86) 9.1	11.0			% Profit Before Taxes/Tangible Net Worth (277)	11.9 (315)	12.3
1.5	5.7	1.7	4.4				2.2	3.0
9.1	11.9	11.4	8.4				11.5	10.4
3.0	5.7	4.3	4.7			% Profit Before Taxes/Total Assets	4.7	4.5
-2.8	1.6	.8	1.8				.2	.6
82.0	59.4	39.5	36.7				41.1	42.9
27.9	23.3	16.6	14.2			Sales/Net Fixed Assets	19.6	21.5
13.0	11.5	8.3	7.8				9.2	10.9
3.1	2.9	2.8	2.8				3.1	3.0
2.6	2.4	2.3	2.4			Sales/Total Assets	2.4	2.4
1.8	1.6	1.8	1.6				1.8	1.8
.6	.6	.7	.9				.7	.7
(28) 1.1	(137) 1.3	(82) 1.3	1.0			% Depr., Dep., Amort./Sales (266)	1.2 (291)	1.2
2.6	2.3	1.7	1.7				2.0	2.0
3.0	2.2	1.3					2.3	2.1
(27) 4.3	(103) 3.5	(55) 2.5				% Officers', Directors' Owners' Comp/Sales (168)	4.0 (201)	3.4
6.2	5.7	4.3					7.0	5.7
34372M	468770M	941948M	1228558M	217944M	2078034M	Net Sales ($)	3762671M	4042329M
12798M	191258M	398409M	531366M	102550M	740764M	Total Assets ($)	1607310M	1667038M

M = $ thousand   MM = $ million
See Pages 11 through 21 for Explanation of Ratios and Data

Comparative Historical Data　　　　　　　　Current Data Sorted by Sales

4/1/04-3/31/05 ALL	4/1/05-3/31/06 ALL	4/1/06-3/31/07 ALL	Type of Statement	0-1MM	1-3MM	3-5MM	5-10MM	10-25MM	25MM & OVER
21	12	10	Unqualified	1	4	8	13	2	4
51	51	50	Reviewed	1	10	8	13	13	5
94	81	94	Compiled	6	44	21	15	7	1
60	77	77	Tax Returns	17	33	15	7	3	2
81	86	95	Other	11	24	21	12	13	14
				62 (4/1-9/30/06)			264 (10/1/06-3/31/07)		
307	307	326	NUMBER OF STATEMENTS	35	115	65	47	38	26
%	%	%	**ASSETS**	%	%	%	%	%	%
6.1	6.1	6.0	Cash & Equivalents	4.6	6.5	5.6	6.7	7.0	4.7
14.6	14.6	12.6	Trade Receivables (net)	7.4	9.9	14.0	15.2	17.6	16.7
50.0	51.3	52.2	Inventory	59.2	53.7	52.6	47.9	49.4	47.4
1.4	2.4	2.0	All Other Current	.9	2.7	1.8	2.3	1.1	1.9
72.2	74.4	72.9	Total Current	72.1	72.7	74.0	72.1	75.2	70.8
16.6	14.3	16.1	Fixed Assets (net)	14.9	16.4	14.0	15.7	16.4	22.6
2.3	2.6	2.0	Intangibles (net)	4.8	1.8	1.1	2.7	1.3	1.3
8.9	8.7	8.9	All Other Non-Current	8.2	9.1	10.9	9.6	7.2	5.4
100.0	100.0	100.0	Total	100.0	100.0	100.0	100.0	100.0	100.0
			LIABILITIES						
10.4	11.7	9.9	Notes Payable-Short Term	15.7	9.4	7.2	9.9	9.6	11.2
3.5	3.3	3.2	Cur. Mat.-L.T.D.	3.7	2.7	4.7	3.6	2.5	1.0
14.7	15.2	13.7	Trade Payables	14.7	11.2	14.4	15.1	14.6	17.4
.2	.2	.2	Income Taxes Payable	.0	.2	.2	.2	.1	.3
6.9	7.3	6.9	All Other Current	5.1	6.9	6.1	7.6	9.1	7.4
35.7	37.7	33.8	Total Current	39.2	30.3	32.7	36.4	35.9	37.4
21.3	19.5	20.3	Long-Term Debt	35.5	24.6	18.5	11.7	13.9	9.9
.2	.2	.1	Deferred Taxes	.0	.0	.1	.1	.2	.4
4.9	7.4	7.6	All Other Non-Current	11.4	8.3	10.1	4.8	2.6	5.3
37.9	35.3	38.2	Net Worth	13.8	36.7	38.6	47.0	47.4	47.0
100.0	100.0	100.0	Total Liabilities & Net Worth	100.0	100.0	100.0	100.0	100.0	100.0
			INCOME DATA						
100.0	100.0	100.0	Net Sales	100.0	100.0	100.0	100.0	100.0	100.0
35.6	36.0	36.7	Gross Profit	38.3	37.9	37.3	35.5	33.9	34.4
32.6	34.1	34.2	Operating Expenses	38.9	35.1	34.4	32.9	30.2	31.7
3.0	2.0	2.5	Operating Profit	-.6	2.8	2.8	2.6	3.6	2.7
.2	-.1	.2	All Other Expenses (net)	1.2	.3	.1	-.2	.0	.2
2.7	2.1	2.3	Profit Before Taxes	-1.8	2.5	2.7	2.8	3.6	2.5
			RATIOS						
3.5	3.5	3.9	Current	4.3	4.6	4.1	3.2	3.6	2.9
2.3	2.1	2.5		2.3	3.0	2.6	2.1	2.4	1.7
1.5	1.5	1.6		1.6	1.7	1.8	1.6	1.4	1.3
1.1	1.0	1.1	Quick	.6	1.4	1.4	1.0	1.3	1.2
.6	.5	.5		.3	.5	.5	.6	.7	.4
.3	.2	.2		.1	.2	.2	.3	.3	.2
6　58.1	7　55.3	7　50.5	Sales/Receivables	5　69.3	8　48.6	8　45.7	9　42.5	8　46.5	7　55.6
15　24.0	14　26.3	13　28.6		11　34.2	13　28.6	12　30.7	17　21.5	19　19.5	14　26.9
31　11.6	31　11.8	25　14.6		16　22.7	20　17.9	26　14.3	24　15.0	37　10.0	45　8.1
76　4.8	79　4.6	92　4.0	Cost of Sales/Inventory	154　2.4	115　3.2	94　3.9	75　4.9	59　6.2	77　4.8
116　3.1	121　3.0	136　2.7		209　1.7	152　2.4	125　2.9	98　3.7	108　3.4	97　3.8
161　2.3	178　2.0	187　2.0		323　1.1	191　1.9	168　2.2	167　2.2	180　2.0	147　2.5
18　20.7	17　21.6	15　24.5	Cost of Sales/Payables	11　31.8	13　27.2	17　21.1	19　19.0	15　24.9	21　17.6
28　13.0	27　13.3	27　13.7		28　13.2	25　14.7	27　13.5	27　13.4	24　15.3	33　11.0
42　8.8	45　8.1	43　8.6		56　6.6	38　9.7	47　7.8	39　9.3	39　9.4	54　6.8
4.4	4.1	3.9	Sales/Working Capital	2.7	3.6	4.1	4.2	4.8	5.1
6.8	6.6	5.5		4.4	5.0	6.2	6.8	6.1	8.7
12.6	12.1	9.7		10.5	7.1	10.1	12.2	11.6	19.1
9.1	8.5	7.2	EBIT/Interest	3.0	5.5	9.3	8.2	10.5	17.5
(285)　3.7	(282)　3.1	(304)　3.0		(33)　1.5	(104)　2.6	(62)　4.8	(45)　3.4	(34)　4.7	4.5
1.4	1.3	1.3		-.4	1.2	1.3	1.3	1.6	1.0
5.1	3.8	2.9	Net Profit + Depr., Dep., Amort./Cur. Mat. L/T/D		2.0	2.8	3.4	10.0	
(63)　2.0	(56)　1.6	(63)　1.5			(14)　1.3	(14)　1.5	(14)　2.0	(10)　1.7	
.7	.6	.8			.8	.5	.7	.8	
.1	.1	.1	Fixed/Worth	.1	.1	.1	.1	.1	.2
.4	.4	.3		1.4	.3	.3	.4	.3	.5
1.1	.9	1.0		-1.1	1.3	.8	.7	.7	.9
.7	.8	.7	Debt/Worth	1.8	.7	.7	.5	.4	.6
1.7	1.7	1.5		4.4	1.5	1.4	1.6	1.2	1.1
4.6	4.5	3.8		-5.9	4.9	3.8	2.9	2.3	1.8
30.2	29.7	32.3	% Profit Before Taxes/Tangible Net Worth	22.3	33.9	41.3	30.5	36.9	30.5
(274)　13.6	(269)　13.5	(287)　12.3		(21)　6.8	(98)　13.7	(59)　13.1	(36)　10.0	12.3	11.9
4.2	3.7	4.3		-2.2	5.6	4.5	2.5	4.7	3.5
11.2	10.5	11.1	% Profit Before Taxes/Total Assets	6.3	11.9	12.3	11.0	13.6	13.3
5.2	5.3	4.8		2.4	4.8	5.2	4.7	7.1	6.4
1.0	.7	1.0		-5.2	.9	1.2	1.4	3.1	.5
49.9	59.6	52.0	Sales/Net Fixed Assets	40.5	59.4	60.1	46.1	57.0	37.9
21.1	22.9	20.3		13.9	21.1	23.7	18.5	20.2	14.2
9.8	10.7	9.8		8.4	9.0	12.5	9.8	10.2	7.8
3.2	3.1	2.8	Sales/Total Assets	2.3	2.7	3.1	3.2	3.3	3.0
2.5	2.5	2.4		1.6	2.2	2.5	2.5	2.5	2.6
1.9	1.9	1.7		1.2	1.6	2.0	2.0	2.3	1.9
.7	.5	.7	% Depr., Dep., Amort./Sales	.6	.6	.7	.5	.7	.8
(249)　1.2	(262)　1.0	(274)　1.2		(26)　2.0	(94)　1.3	(53)　1.3	(43)　1.1	(33)　1.0	(25)　1.0
2.0	1.9	2.0		3.4	2.7	1.7	2.0	1.9	1.9
1.7	2.0	1.8	% Officers', Directors' Owners' Comp/Sales	3.0	2.2	2.1	1.3	1.3	
(164)　3.5	(187)　3.4	(193)　3.2		(23)　4.5	(69)　3.7	(44)　3.2	(31)　3.0	(19)　1.8	
6.2	5.7	5.3		8.2	5.7	5.1	4.8	2.2	
5346164M	5361226M	4969626M	Net Sales ($)	24032M	215140M	247741M	336160M	620293M	3526260M
2015818M	1926895M	1977145M	Total Assets ($)	16500M	109029M	106265M	157126M	251225M	1337000M

Current Data Sorted by Assets | Comparative Historical Data

Type of Statement

Type of Statement	0-500M	500M-2MM	2-10MM	10-50MM	50-100MM	100-250MM	4/1/02-3/31/03 ALL	4/1/03-3/31/04 ALL
Unqualified			12	15	4	3	29	27
Reviewed	2	24	48	23	2		76	74
Compiled	9	39	33	9			61	78
Tax Returns	41	57	26	3		1	26	59
Other	14	32	52	19	3	1	37	67
	55 (4/1-9/30/06)		417 (10/1/06-3/31/07)					
NUMBER OF STATEMENTS	66	152	171	69	9	5	229	305

Main Data

	0-500M %	500M-2MM %	2-10MM %	10-50MM %	50-100MM %	100-250MM %	4/1/02-3/31/03 ALL %	4/1/03-3/31/04 ALL %
ASSETS								
Cash & Equivalents	11.8	7.9	5.1	6.1			6.7	6.8
Trade Receivables (net)	24.6	30.3	34.0	27.7			32.1	32.9
Inventory	33.6	34.8	32.3	30.1			31.8	32.1
All Other Current	3.5	2.2	2.0	3.2			3.1	1.9
Total Current	73.6	75.2	73.4	67.1			73.6	73.6
Fixed Assets (net)	16.7	16.9	17.7	22.6			17.3	18.4
Intangibles (net)	3.4	1.8	3.1	3.3			1.7	2.0
All Other Non-Current	6.3	6.1	5.8	7.0			7.3	6.0
Total	100.0	100.0	100.0	100.0			100.0	100.0
LIABILITIES								
Notes Payable-Short Term	13.0	13.9	14.0	13.5			16.7	15.9
Cur. Mat.-L.T.D.	5.8	3.5	2.9	2.9			3.7	3.6
Trade Payables	21.8	18.9	17.6	13.6			19.7	19.9
Income Taxes Payable	.1	.1	.6	.3			.2	.2
All Other Current	20.6	9.2	9.0	9.2			7.5	7.3
Total Current	61.3	45.6	44.1	39.4			47.7	46.9
Long-Term Debt	24.0	14.5	13.1	11.6			13.4	12.5
Deferred Taxes	.0	.1	.3	.4			.3	.3
All Other Non-Current	18.0	7.6	5.6	5.3			5.8	4.1
Net Worth	-3.3	32.2	36.9	43.3			32.8	36.3
Total Liabilities & Net Worth	100.0	100.0	100.0	100.0			100.0	100.0
INCOME DATA								
Net Sales	100.0	100.0	100.0	100.0			100.0	100.0
Gross Profit	35.8	31.1	28.0	28.3			29.3	29.5
Operating Expenses	32.8	28.4	25.1	23.5			27.5	27.9
Operating Profit	3.0	2.7	2.8	4.8			1.8	1.7
All Other Expenses (net)	.8	.7	.3	-.1			.4	.2
Profit Before Taxes	2.2	2.0	2.6	4.9			1.4	1.5
RATIOS								
Current	2.7	3.0	2.4	2.2			2.3	2.4
	1.5	1.8	1.7	1.8			1.6	1.6
	.8	1.3	1.3	1.2			1.2	1.2
Quick	1.5	1.6	1.2	1.4			1.3	1.3
	.7	.9	.8	.8			(228) .8	.8
	.3	.5	.6	.6			.5	.6
Sales/Receivables	4 89.7	19 19.2	28 12.9	27 13.4			28 13.1	29 12.8
	16 23.0	32 11.6	38 9.5	38 9.6			39 9.3	40 9.2
	32 11.4	42 8.7	50 7.3	50 7.2			54 6.8	55 6.7
Cost of Sales/Inventory	8 46.4	22 16.6	28 13.2	31 11.9			33 11.2	34 10.8
	40 9.1	55 6.6	56 6.6	61 6.0			51 7.1	56 6.5
	76 4.8	92 4.0	81 4.5	83 4.4			88 4.1	83 4.4
Cost of Sales/Payables	5 67.8	11 33.5	17 21.7	14 25.4			19 19.6	18 20.6
	22 16.9	24 15.2	25 14.7	21 17.1			33 11.0	30 12.3
	43 8.6	40 9.1	40 9.2	42 8.6			46 8.0	49 7.5
Sales/Working Capital	6.9	6.5	6.8	6.3			6.1	6.1
	24.7	10.1	10.3	10.6			11.2	11.3
	-64.3	27.5	19.8	21.1			28.5	29.2
EBIT/Interest	9.8	7.5	7.1	11.5			5.7	7.6
	(50) 2.4	(135) 2.7	(157) 3.1	(64) 5.0			(212) 2.3	(277) 3.1
	.3	.8	1.5	2.4			.9	1.3
Net Profit + Depr., Dep., Amort./Cur. Mat. L/T/D		8.5	7.4	14.6			3.5	6.4
		(22) 2.6	(39) 3.0	(23) 3.3			(65) 1.8	(82) 2.5
		.8	1.0	.9			.6	1.1
Fixed/Worth	.1	.2	.2	.2			.2	.2
	.8	.4	.4	.6			.4	.4
	-.7	1.6	1.0	1.1			1.0	1.1
Debt/Worth	1.0	.7	.9	.8			.9	.8
	8.0	2.4	1.8	1.5			1.9	2.0
	-5.3	10.1	4.3	3.1			4.9	4.8
% Profit Before Taxes/Tangible Net Worth	93.7	64.2	44.4	43.1			29.5	30.0
	(39) 24.1	(130) 19.1	(157) 16.6	(67) 23.4			(207) 11.2	(282) 11.7
	-2.6	4.5	5.3	9.3			1.5	2.0
% Profit Before Taxes/Total Assets	23.4	14.5	12.3	16.5			8.4	8.6
	6.3	5.5	5.7	8.4			2.8	3.7
	-3.1	.0	1.5	3.4			-.2	.4
Sales/Net Fixed Assets	179.1	68.7	47.5	33.8			49.1	55.9
	54.0	29.2	23.8	11.2			25.2	22.7
	21.9	12.8	11.1	6.8			11.1	11.0
Sales/Total Assets	6.2	4.1	4.0	3.2			3.8	3.7
	4.7	3.3	2.9	2.5			2.8	2.9
	3.3	2.5	2.2	2.0			2.0	2.0
% Depr., Dep., Amort./Sales	.4	.4	.5	.6			.6	.6
	(50) .8	(127) 1.0	(149) .9	(66) 1.1			(203) 1.1	(267) 1.1
	2.1	1.5	1.4	1.6			1.9	2.1
% Officers', Directors' Owners' Comp/Sales	3.4	2.0	1.1	1.0			1.8	1.6
	(33) 5.3	(84) 3.3	(74) 2.1	(16) 2.0			(122) 3.7	(170) 3.2
	8.2	5.3	3.5	4.8			7.3	5.9
Net Sales ($)	95680M	566193M	2413307M	3424579M	1120036M	2496956M	4412425M	6489973M
Total Assets ($)	17979M	166118M	789690M	1387190M	640813M	859776M	1992379M	2450443M

© RMA 2007

M = $ thousand   MM = $ million
See Pages 11 through 21 for Explanation of Ratios and Data

Comparative Historical Data | Current Data Sorted by Sales

© RMA 2007

				Type of Statement						
28		35	34	Unqualified		1	1	1	10	21
58		85	99	Reviewed	1	7	15	27	23	26
57		75	90	Compiled	3	23	19	12	24	9
64		68	128	Tax Returns	19	55	14	19	15	6
80		93	121	Other	5	23	13	26	27	27
4/1/04-3/31/05 ALL		4/1/05-3/31/06 ALL	4/1/06-3/31/07 ALL		55 (4/1-9/30/06)			417 (10/1/06-3/31/07)		
					0-1MM	1-3MM	3-5MM	5-10MM	10-25MM	25MM & OVER
287		356	472	NUMBER OF STATEMENTS	28	109	62	85	99	89
%		%	%	ASSETS	%	%	%	%	%	%
7.8		7.2	7.2	Cash & Equivalents	8.5	10.4	8.4	5.4	5.4	5.7
32.0		32.9	30.2	Trade Receivables (net)	17.5	24.8	31.4	35.4	34.7	29.8
33.5		32.5	32.8	Inventory	43.9	32.3	34.0	31.8	31.3	31.6
2.5		2.1	2.4	All Other Current	5.0	2.7	1.8	1.6	1.5	3.4
75.8		74.7	72.6	Total Current	74.9	70.3	75.6	74.3	73.0	70.5
16.9		18.3	18.4	Fixed Assets (net)	15.5	20.8	15.0	17.8	17.2	20.4
1.4		1.4	2.8	Intangibles (net)	4.4	2.5	1.3	3.9	2.6	2.8
5.9		5.6	6.3	All Other Non-Current	5.2	6.4	8.1	4.1	7.2	6.4
100.0		100.0	100.0	Total	100.0	100.0	100.0	100.0	100.0	100.0
				LIABILITIES						
14.8		14.1	13.7	Notes Payable-Short Term	8.6	13.8	12.6	16.4	12.6	14.6
3.4		2.4	3.6	Cur. Mat.-L.T.D.	3.0	5.7	2.8	3.3	2.8	2.6
19.6		20.8	17.8	Trade Payables	20.2	18.8	18.1	19.0	17.3	15.2
.4		.3	.3	Income Taxes Payable	.1	.1	.5	.1	.6	.3
7.9		8.7	10.7	All Other Current	29.3	11.8	7.7	8.1	9.3	9.3
46.1		46.3	46.0	Total Current	61.2	50.3	41.6	47.0	42.6	42.0
13.0		13.1	15.3	Long-Term Debt	28.1	20.1	12.9	14.8	11.2	12.4
.2		.2	.2	Deferred Taxes	.0	.1	.1	.3	.3	.3
5.2		6.3	7.8	All Other Non-Current	26.1	10.3	5.4	5.4	6.1	4.8
35.6		34.1	30.6	Net Worth	-15.4	19.3	39.9	32.6	39.9	40.5
100.0		100.0	100.0	Total Liabilities & Net Worth	100.0	100.0	100.0	100.0	100.0	100.0
				INCOME DATA						
100.0		100.0	100.0	Net Sales	100.0	100.0	100.0	100.0	100.0	100.0
29.2		28.7	30.1	Gross Profit	41.1	34.3	30.2	29.0	26.9	26.1
26.0		25.6	27.0	Operating Expenses	40.0	31.5	27.8	25.4	23.8	21.8
3.3		3.2	3.1	Operating Profit	1.2	2.8	2.4	3.6	3.1	4.3
.1		.3	.4	All Other Expenses (net)	1.1	.8	.1	.6	.0	.2
3.2		2.9	2.7	Profit Before Taxes	.1	1.9	2.3	3.0	3.1	4.1
				RATIOS						
2.6		2.4	2.5		4.8	2.6	3.1	2.4	2.4	2.4
1.7		1.7	1.7	Current	1.9	1.7	1.9	1.6	1.7	1.7
1.2		1.2	1.2		.9	1.1	1.4	1.2	1.3	1.2
1.5		1.3	1.4		2.3	1.4	1.7	1.3	1.3	1.3
.9	(355)	.9	.8	Quick	.5	.8	.9	.8	.8	.8
.5		.5	.5		.5	.4	.6	.5	.7	.6
25	14.5	24	15.1	22	16.7	Sales/Receivables	6	56.8	13	28.0	25	14.3	24	15.0	28	13.1	26	13.9

Sales/Receivables
						Sales/Receivables												
25	14.5	24	15.1	22	16.7		6	56.8	13	28.0	25	14.3	24	15.0	28	13.1	26	13.9
37	9.9	36	10.2	34	10.9		17	21.1	26	14.3	34	10.6	38	9.6	37	10.0	38	9.6
50	7.3	48	7.6	47	7.7		37	10.0	38	9.5	48	7.6	59	6.2	47	7.8	49	7.5

Cost of Sales/Inventory
34	10.6	28	13.2	27	13.7	Cost of Sales/Inventory	40	9.1	15	24.2	18	20.1	26	14.0	27	13.4	30	12.2
52	7.0	47	7.8	54	6.7		62	5.9	59	6.1	62	5.9	46	7.9	49	7.5	57	6.4
82	4.5	80	4.6	85	4.3		173	2.1	92	4.0	91	4.0	78	4.7	72	5.1	77	4.7

Cost of Sales/Payables
15	23.6	17	22.1	14	26.1	Cost of Sales/Payables	16	22.3	7	54.2	14	26.6	15	24.9	15	24.1	13	27.0
26	13.8	27	13.4	24	15.5		25	14.5	25	14.4	24	15.5	28	13.0	21	17.1	21	17.4
47	7.8	43	8.4	40	9.1		73	5.0	44	8.4	43	8.5	46	7.9	34	10.8	34	10.9

6.0		6.8	6.6	Sales/Working Capital	4.8	6.6	5.6	7.0	7.2	7.0
11.1		11.3	10.8		8.5	14.0	8.2	10.8	10.8	11.5
25.4		29.9	29.6		UND	142.5	18.8	46.0	19.8	21.1

EBIT/Interest
	11.6		11.0		8.1	EBIT/Interest		5.9		6.5		9.0		7.4		7.9		12.0
(256)	4.2	(322)	4.0	(418)	3.3		(21)	.8	(93)	2.4	(54)	3.4	(77)	2.8	(91)	3.6	(82)	5.0
	1.8		1.6		1.2			-3.4		.1		.4		1.4		1.8		2.4

Net Profit + Depr., Dep., Amort./Cur. Mat. L/T/D
	7.3		6.0		9.2	Net Profit + Depr., Dep., Amort./Cur. Mat. L/T/D						4.8		10.2		4.5		14.6
(56)	3.9	(84)	3.1	(91)	3.0				(13)	2.0	(18)	4.9	(24)	3.1	(31)	3.4
	1.1		1.4		.9							-.6		1.1		.9		1.7

Fixed/Worth
.1		.2	.2	Fixed/Worth	.0	.2	.1	.2	.2	.2
.4		.5	.5		.5	.8	.3	.6	.4	.5
1.1		1.1	1.5		NM	-6.3	.9	2.0	.7	1.0

Debt/Worth
.8		.9	.8	Debt/Worth	.6	1.0	.7	1.0	.9	.8
1.8		1.9	2.0		6.2	3.4	1.5	2.6	1.7	1.7
4.4		4.0	6.0		-4.8	-16.6	3.5	8.9	3.4	3.4

% Profit Before Taxes/Tangible Net Worth
	39.2		43.8		49.7	% Profit Before Taxes/Tangible Net Worth		25.2		88.5		43.5		54.6		44.8		47.0
(259)	20.4	(317)	22.3	(406)	19.1		(18)	-1.6	(78)	23.5	(58)	13.2	(72)	15.3	(94)	16.8	(86)	27.6
	7.9		7.1		6.5			-12.5		5.9		.7		9.1		5.2		12.6

% Profit Before Taxes/Total Assets
15.4		15.8	14.8	% Profit Before Taxes/Total Assets	14.3	17.0	13.5	12.4	15.0	18.8
6.5		6.7	6.4		-.1	5.5	5.9	4.5	7.3	8.6
2.3		1.1	.9		-8.2	-4.5	.1	1.5	2.0	3.4

Sales/Net Fixed Assets
58.6		54.4	57.5	Sales/Net Fixed Assets	151.6	62.7	71.7	71.1	47.5	37.6
25.5		24.6	25.6		37.0	27.4	29.8	26.6	27.2	18.1
11.4		11.9	10.7		11.1	12.0	13.9	10.9	12.0	7.6

Sales/Total Assets
3.9		4.3	4.1	Sales/Total Assets	4.1	4.6	3.9	4.4	4.0	3.7
3.0		3.3	3.1		3.0	3.4	3.0	3.1	3.3	2.8
2.2		2.4	2.3		1.7	2.4	2.2	2.3	2.4	2.1

% Depr., Dep., Amort./Sales
	.6		.5		.5	% Depr., Dep., Amort./Sales		.5		.5		.4		.4		.5		.6
(242)	1.0	(304)	1.0	(405)	1.0		(20)	1.4	(91)	1.1	(50)	.9	(75)	.9	(85)	.9	(84)	1.0
	1.9		1.5		1.5			3.0		2.4		1.7		1.5		1.4		1.4

% Officers', Directors' Owners' Comp/Sales
	1.6		1.4		1.5	% Officers', Directors' Owners' Comp/Sales		3.2		2.9		2.0		1.0		1.0		1.0
(132)	3.0	(183)	2.8	(210)	3.1		(11)	6.7	(62)	4.4	(32)	3.4	(35)	2.4	(44)	1.7	(26)	1.8
	6.4		5.5		5.2			12.1		5.9		5.7		4.7		3.0		3.3

7635115M		8239317M	10116751M	Net Sales ($)	15617M	219575M	247741M	626812M	1558244M	7448762M
2788633M		3150716M	3861566M	Total Assets ($)	18090M	77032M	89318M	247972M	540046M	2889108M

M = $ thousand   MM = $ million
See Pages 11 through 21 for Explanation of Ratios and Data

Current Data Sorted by Assets   Comparative Historical Data

Type of Statement

	0-500M	500M-2MM	2-10MM	10-50MM	50-100MM	100-250MM	Type of Statement	4/1/02-3/31/03 ALL	4/1/03-3/31/04 ALL
Unqualified		1	1				Unqualified	1	5
Reviewed	1	11	12	2			Reviewed	2	6
Compiled	4	9	11				Compiled	12	17
Tax Returns	6	10	2	3			Tax Returns	8	11
Other	4		12	1			Other	2	6
	13 (4/1-9/30/06)			77 (10/1/06-3/31/07)					
	0-500M	500M-2MM	2-10MM	10-50MM	50-100MM	100-250MM	NUMBER OF STATEMENTS	25	45
	15	31	38	6					
	%	%	%	%	%	%	**ASSETS**	%	%
	7.7	8.1	4.5		D	D	Cash & Equivalents	6.5	7.9
	5.9	16.1	11.8		A	A	Trade Receivables (net)	12.8	11.1
	59.2	56.1	62.3		T	T	Inventory	50.7	50.6
	1.4	1.7	2.0		A	A	All Other Current	.6	1.2
	74.3	82.1	80.6				Total Current	70.6	70.8
	22.1	15.0	14.1		N	N	Fixed Assets (net)	24.9	22.9
	.1	.8	2.1		O	O	Intangibles (net)	.1	1.3
	3.5	2.1	3.2		T	T	All Other Non-Current	4.3	4.9
	100.0	100.0	100.0				Total	100.0	100.0
					A	A	**LIABILITIES**		
	27.3	17.9	26.6		V	V	Notes Payable-Short Term	17.2	21.5
	3.7	4.4	1.9		A	A	Cur. Mat.-L.T.D.	2.7	2.2
	22.8	27.6	20.6		I	I	Trade Payables	16.2	15.0
	.0	.1	.6		L	L	Income Taxes Payable	.0	.1
	14.0	7.7	7.5		A	A	All Other Current	12.3	7.7
	67.8	57.7	57.2		B	B	Total Current	48.4	46.5
	22.8	11.6	11.7		L	L	Long-Term Debt	22.3	20.0
	.0	.2	.1		E	E	Deferred Taxes	.0	.4
	14.4	2.5	3.6				All Other Non-Current	.1	5.6
	-5.0	28.0	27.5				Net Worth	29.2	27.5
	100.0	100.0	100.0				Total Liabilities & Net Worth	100.0	100.0
							INCOME DATA		
	100.0	100.0	100.0				Net Sales	100.0	100.0
	34.3	30.5	23.6				Gross Profit	33.2	28.9
	35.8	27.8	21.3				Operating Expenses	31.1	26.7
	-1.5	2.6	2.3				Operating Profit	2.0	2.2
	1.2	1.2	.3				All Other Expenses (net)	1.7	.8
	-2.8	1.4	2.0				Profit Before Taxes	.4	1.4
							RATIOS		
	1.8	1.8	1.9					2.9	2.2
	1.1	1.4	1.5				Current	1.6	1.5
	.6	1.0	1.2					1.1	1.2
	.5	.8	.4					1.1	1.1
	.2	.3	.2				Quick	.3 (44)	.3
	.1	.1	.1					.1	.2
	0 UND	3 126.2	5 70.3					2 227.8	4 82.3
	4 91.1	7 52.1	13 28.9				Sales/Receivables	13 28.8	12 31.3
	16 22.4	22 16.9	30 12.1					25 14.8	25 14.4
	50 7.3	55 6.6	93 3.9					52 7.0	67 5.4
	101 3.6	101 3.6	128 2.9				Cost of Sales/Inventory	102 3.6	113 3.2
	190 1.9	327 1.1	164 2.2					177 2.1	148 2.5
	0 UND	8 46.0	10 36.4					3 141.7	9 39.0
	14 26.1	41 8.9	27 13.4				Cost of Sales/Payables	22 16.8	22 16.9
	65 5.6	87 4.2	69 5.3					63 5.8	48 7.6
	8.9	4.6	6.0					6.7	5.5
	72.2	14.0	9.7				Sales/Working Capital	12.2	11.0
	-19.9	-516.0	26.1					54.1	27.9
	2.1	5.4	4.4					3.5	5.9
	(14) 1.3	(30) 1.3	(37) 2.5				EBIT/Interest	(24) 1.4	(44) 2.3
	-2.7	.4	1.6					.5	1.1
							Net Profit + Depr., Dep., Amort./Cur. Mat. L/T/D		
	.3	.1	.1					.2	.2
	16.0	.4	.3				Fixed/Worth	.5	.5
	-1.1	1.6	1.3					2.7	2.7
	2.1	1.3	1.6					.9	1.0
	44.8	2.7	2.6				Debt/Worth	2.4	2.7
	-11.6	8.5	8.8					10.2	12.6
		24.7	31.1					17.7	33.8
		(29) 9.8	(34) 19.2				% Profit Before Taxes/Tangible Net Worth	(22) 5.6	(38) 10.9
		-6.0	6.8					-5.3	2.3
	5.2	7.6	8.8					7.3	7.1
	.7	1.2	3.9				% Profit Before Taxes/Total Assets	.8	3.2
	-17.8	-3.1	1.6					-1.9	.4
	75.1	55.5	96.7					49.4	51.1
	33.7	22.8	33.5				Sales/Net Fixed Assets	18.6	16.8
	8.8	13.2	12.3					6.3	5.4
	4.9	3.7	3.1					3.4	2.9
	3.4	2.7	2.3				Sales/Total Assets	2.5	2.5
	1.5	1.5	1.8					1.8	1.8
	.7	.6	.4					.8	.7
	(10) 2.0	(19) 1.4	(32) 1.1				% Depr., Dep., Amort./Sales	(21) 1.3	(36) 1.3
	4.5	1.8	1.6					2.8	2.9
	1.7	2.1	.9					1.8	1.6
	(10) 2.9	(18) 2.5	(18) 1.1				% Officers', Directors' Owners' Comp/Sales	(12) 4.0	(23) 3.5
	7.7	6.4	1.9					7.9	6.6
	16580M	96171M	414183M	240113M			Net Sales ($)	109976M	309638M
	4352M	34095M	169078M	112080M			Total Assets ($)	44047M	136258M

(Columns 50-100MM and 100-250MM display "DATA NOT AVAILABLE".)

M = $ thousand   MM = $ million
See Pages 11 through 21 for Explanation of Ratios and Data

Comparative Historical Data   Current Data Sorted by Sales

			Type of Statement					
1	1	1	Unqualified				1	
6	13	16	Reviewed	2	1	2	6	1	3
16	24	26	Compiled	6	5	7	5	4	1
14	12	20	Tax Returns	5	8	1	2	6	3
11	13	27	Other		5	5	5	6	2
4/1/04-3/31/05	4/1/05-3/31/06	4/1/06-3/31/07		13 (4/1-9/30/06)			77 (10/1/06-3/31/07)		
ALL	ALL	ALL		0-1MM	1-3MM	3-5MM	5-10MM	10-25MM	25MM & OVER

4/1/04-3/31/05	4/1/05-3/31/06	4/1/06-3/31/07		0-1MM	1-3MM	3-5MM	5-10MM	10-25MM	25MM & OVER
48	63	90	**NUMBER OF STATEMENTS**	13	19	15	17	17	9
%	%	%	**ASSETS**	%	%	%	%	%	%
9.6	5.5	6.2	Cash & Equivalents	6.1	7.4	7.6	3.8	7.6	
12.3	13.3	12.7	Trade Receivables (net)	5.9	15.8	12.5	10.8	14.7	
51.0	60.8	59.4	Inventory	61.5	60.2	56.8	63.1	55.9	
1.2	1.7	1.8	All Other Current	.1	.5	2.7	.5	4.6	
74.1	81.2	80.1	Total Current	73.6	83.9	79.6	78.2	82.8	
19.8	12.7	15.3	Fixed Assets (net)	20.9	14.7	18.0	13.9	13.9	
.8	1.8	1.8	Intangibles (net)	1.4	.1	.6	3.9	.0	
5.4	4.2	2.8	All Other Non-Current	4.1	1.4	1.8	4.0	3.3	
100.0	100.0	100.0	Total	100.0	100.0	100.0	100.0	100.0	
			LIABILITIES						
25.6	17.2	23.0	Notes Payable-Short Term	18.2	27.5	24.5	32.5	16.6	
2.5	5.3	3.0	Cur. Mat.-L.T.D.	3.8	2.6	5.7	2.1	2.0	
14.3	21.5	24.0	Trade Payables	19.4	27.6	20.5	19.4	27.7	
.1	.1	.3	Income Taxes Payable	.0	.1	.1	.3	1.2	
12.1	9.6	8.3	All Other Current	15.9	6.2	12.2	5.6	6.2	
54.7	53.7	58.6	Total Current	57.3	64.0	62.9	60.0	53.7	
16.3	13.9	13.3	Long-Term Debt	26.9	13.6	7.3	9.8	14.3	
.4	.4	.2	Deferred Taxes	.0	.1	.2	.4	.1	
6.2	5.8	5.4	All Other Non-Current	7.1	7.6	2.7	2.0	6.1	
22.4	26.2	22.5	Net Worth	8.7	14.7	26.9	27.9	25.8	
100.0	100.0	100.0	Total Liabilties & Net Worth	100.0	100.0	100.0	100.0	100.0	
			INCOME DATA						
100.0	100.0	100.0	Net Sales	100.0	100.0	100.0	100.0	100.0	
27.4	24.6	27.7	Gross Profit	37.3	29.4	27.7	22.7	24.5	
25.9	22.3	25.8	Operating Expenses	36.6	26.7	26.7	21.5	21.8	
1.5	2.3	1.8	Operating Profit	.7	2.7	1.0	1.2	2.6	
.6	.2	.8	All Other Expenses (net)	2.7	1.0	.7	.5	-.1	
1.0	2.1	1.0	Profit Before Taxes	-2.0	1.7	.3	.7	2.8	
			RATIOS						
2.2	2.0	1.8		4.2	1.8	1.6	1.6	2.2	
1.4	1.4	1.4	Current	1.7	1.3	1.2	1.3	1.8	
1.1	1.2	1.1		.8	1.0	1.0	1.1	1.2	
1.0	.7	.5		.7	.6	.8	.6	.6	
.4	.3	.3	Quick	.1	.3	.3	.1	.4	
.1	.2	.1		.0	.1	.1	.1	.2	
4 90.5	5 72.5	3 106.7		0 UND	2 219.3	4 101.9	4 91.1	7 54.0	
13 28.2	11 32.0	11 33.9	Sales/Receivables	4 95.1	7 51.2	12 30.4	12 30.2	14 26.3	
22 16.5	26 14.2	24 15.5		9 40.0	22 16.9	30 12.1	23 15.7	33 11.2	
47 7.8	87 4.2	76 4.8		112 3.3	66 5.5	38 9.5	88 4.2	60 6.1	
81 4.5	117 3.1	120 3.0	Cost of Sales/Inventory	342 1.1	96 3.8	124 2.9	134 2.7	100 3.6	
137 2.7	176 2.1	178 2.1		407 .9	157 2.3	211 1.7	217 1.7	140 2.6	
7 49.1	6 61.2	9 39.7		0 UND	8 46.0	8 47.8	8 43.2	11 32.1	
20 18.1	23 16.1	34 10.6	Cost of Sales/Payables	14 26.1	39 9.3	29 12.8	27 13.6	40 9.2	
32 11.3	67 5.5	76 4.8		154 2.4	81 4.5	65 5.6	52 7.0	96 3.8	
8.1	5.6	6.2		2.5	8.9	9.3	6.4	6.2	
15.2	11.4	10.6	Sales/Working Capital	4.5	18.9	19.0	12.1	7.9	
51.3	20.6	193.7		-14.9	-98.9	-516.0	28.6	23.9	
5.2	5.4	4.7		2.3	4.9	4.1	3.5	12.7	
(45) 3.0	(61) 3.1	(87) 1.9	EBIT/Interest	(12) .0	1.4	(14) 1.2	2.1	(16) 2.9	
1.1	1.7	.9		-2.3	1.0	-.1	.9	1.9	
	9.2	8.0							
(14) 4.9	(15) 3.5		Net Profit + Depr., Dep., Amort./Cur. Mat. L/T/D						
1.6	1.5								
.1	.1	.1		.2	.2	.1	.1	.1	
.6	.4	.3	Fixed/Worth	1.2	.3	.8	.3	.3	
2.1	1.6	2.0		-1.2	6.3	3.6	1.4	1.0	
1.4	1.6	1.6		1.1	2.1	1.1	1.7	1.6	
3.0	3.5	3.1	Debt/Worth	5.9	3.9	3.4	2.1	2.7	
10.3	11.1	14.7		-8.7	52.3	30.4	12.8	8.4	
40.6	38.4	28.0			58.4	22.7	27.4	54.6	
(42) 15.2	(59) 19.1	(77) 14.6	% Profit Before Taxes/Tangible Net Worth		(16) 12.2	(14) 10.5	(15) 10.2	(16) 21.8	
2.6	10.3	1.4			2.1	-21.4	.0	10.1	
7.8	10.0	7.5		6.2	5.4	7.0	5.4	14.9	
4.4	3.8	2.9	% Profit Before Taxes/Total Assets	-3.4	3.1	.9	3.3	4.7	
.4	1.6	-.4		-13.8	.1	-3.1	-.4	2.2	
84.8	72.6	71.7		43.8	81.9	55.5	127.8	77.1	
21.1	40.2	30.0	Sales/Net Fixed Assets	7.7	23.0	29.3	34.6	32.7	
10.1	13.1	12.7		3.5	17.1	12.5	12.1	13.6	
4.2	3.1	3.4		1.6	4.2	3.2	2.9	3.5	
2.9	2.4	2.5	Sales/Total Assets	1.4	3.0	2.6	2.3	2.6	
2.3	1.8	1.6		1.1	2.3	1.6	1.7	2.2	
.7	.4	.5			.5	.6	.5	.4	
(41) 1.1	(54) .8	(67) 1.2	% Depr., Dep., Amort./Sales		(13) 1.1	(10) 1.2	(13) 1.0	(15) 1.3	
2.7	1.8	1.8			1.6	2.0	1.6	1.8	
1.1	.9	1.1			1.8		.9		
(31) 2.4	(35) 2.5	(46) 2.1	% Officers', Directors' Owners' Comp/Sales		(12) 2.3		(11) .9		
6.0	4.9	3.5			5.0		1.9		
379043M	674004M	767047M	Net Sales ($)	8149M	35077M	59030M	119759M	220889M	324143M
132953M	272317M	319605M	Total Assets ($)	6862M	12311M	25982M	57067M	81423M	135960M

M = $ thousand   MM = $ million
See Pages 11 through 21 for Explanation of Ratios and Data

Current Data Sorted by Assets							Comparative Historical Data	
		3	4	1	1	**Type of Statement**		
						Unqualified	23	20
	9	24	8			Reviewed	42	51
17	43	19				Compiled	86	86
17	28	5		1	1	Tax Returns	54	54
15	18	19	10		1	Other	52	56
	41 (4/1-9/30/06)		203 (10/1/06-3/31/07)				4/1/02-3/31/03	4/1/03-3/31/04
0-500M	500M-2MM	2-10MM	10-50MM	50-100MM	100-250MM		ALL	ALL
49	98	70	22	2	3	**NUMBER OF STATEMENTS**	257	267
%	%	%	%	%	%	**ASSETS**	%	%
10.5	8.0	6.0	3.1			Cash & Equivalents	8.7	8.9
8.1	14.3	13.8	9.7			Trade Receivables (net)	13.9	13.5
34.2	35.7	32.4	44.6			Inventory	33.8	37.9
1.9	2.3	2.7	6.5			All Other Current	2.8	2.1
54.7	60.3	54.9	63.9			Total Current	59.2	62.4
32.9	32.0	34.9	21.0			Fixed Assets (net)	33.4	30.2
5.7	1.8	.9	4.2			Intangibles (net)	2.1	1.3
6.7	5.8	9.3	10.9			All Other Non-Current	5.3	6.1
100.0	100.0	100.0	100.0			Total	100.0	100.0
						LIABILITIES		
19.0	13.4	11.2	13.1			Notes Payable-Short Term	14.0	14.2
8.2	5.3	3.4	3.0			Cur. Mat.-L.T.D.	5.3	4.9
15.6	16.4	13.5	14.4			Trade Payables	14.1	14.9
.2	.1	.3	.5			Income Taxes Payable	.4	.5
17.0	6.7	12.1	21.1			All Other Current	7.2	9.4
60.0	41.8	40.5	52.0			Total Current	41.0	44.0
34.3	24.0	15.2	14.9			Long-Term Debt	21.5	21.6
.1	.1	.7	1.6			Deferred Taxes	.4	.5
17.2	4.9	6.5	1.7			All Other Non-Current	6.8	3.6
-11.6	29.1	37.1	29.8			Net Worth	30.3	30.3
100.0	100.0	100.0	100.0			Total Liabilties & Net Worth	100.0	100.0
						INCOME DATA		
100.0	100.0	100.0	100.0			Net Sales	100.0	100.0
40.1	37.0	37.6	37.0			Gross Profit	39.3	37.6
38.2	34.2	33.4	35.1			Operating Expenses	36.7	35.1
2.0	2.8	4.2	1.9			Operating Profit	2.6	2.5
1.4	1.1	.6	1.0			All Other Expenses (net)	.8	.8
.6	1.7	3.5	.9			Profit Before Taxes	1.9	1.8
						RATIOS		
1.9	2.2	2.3	1.7				2.8	2.7
.9	1.6	1.3	1.1			Current	1.6	1.6
.4	1.0	.8	.9				1.1	1.1
.9	1.1	.9	.4				1.4	1.2
.2	.4	.5	.1			Quick	(254) .6	.5
.1	.2	.2	.1				.2	.2
0 UND	2 179.9	5 80.8	2 180.8				3 138.8	3 130.0
3 131.0	10 36.6	16 22.9	10 38.2			Sales/Receivables	9 39.5	12 30.8
9 40.5	25 14.5	35 10.5	18 20.7				29 12.7	26 13.8
0 UND	29 12.4	44 8.4	60 6.1				28 13.1	36 10.3
50 7.4	74 4.9	70 5.2	176 2.1			Cost of Sales/Inventory	68 5.4	71 5.1
97 3.8	126 2.9	108 3.4	293 1.2				125 2.9	121 3.0
0 UND	10 36.1	15 24.5	25 14.5				9 40.4	10 34.8
9 41.8	24 15.3	28 13.1	43 8.4			Cost of Sales/Payables	23 15.9	22 16.9
40 9.2	48 7.5	47 7.8	57 6.4				42 8.6	48 7.7
13.4	7.3	7.0	6.0				7.0	6.4
-61.9	14.1	15.0	37.2			Sales/Working Capital	13.9	12.7
-11.9	-351.3	-23.6	-18.6				96.2	58.9
4.3	4.4	8.8	7.5				6.7	5.7
(46) 2.1	(92) 1.7	2.8	(20) 3.7			EBIT/Interest	(241) 2.6	(246) 2.3
-.3	.7	1.6	-.6				.8	.9
		3.3	5.8			Net Profit + Depr., Dep.,	5.0	4.5
	(25) 2.3	(10) 1.2				Amort./Cur. Mat. L/T/D	(54) 2.2	(56) 2.1
		1.4	-1.4				1.0	1.0
.5	.4	.4	.3				.4	.3
2.3	1.0	.9	.6			Fixed/Worth	.9	.8
-1.2	3.5	1.6	NM				4.3	2.3
1.0	.9	.8	1.4				.8	.8
6.8	2.7	1.9	2.7			Debt/Worth	1.8	1.9
-3.3	9.8	4.0	NM				8.7	6.8
64.6	38.1	24.6	43.5			% Profit Before Taxes/Tangible	35.5	37.3
(32) 25.7	(82) 10.0	(64) 13.8	(17) 22.4			Net Worth	(217) 12.6	(230) 14.0
-2.6	-.6	5.4	1.7				2.2	2.7
15.9	9.8	10.2	10.9			% Profit Before Taxes/Total	10.8	11.3
7.0	2.4	4.5	4.1			Assets	4.3	4.0
-4.9	-1.4	1.3	-5.1				-.7	.0
45.2	27.9	14.0	15.7				22.3	26.0
18.3	11.6	8.9	8.7			Sales/Net Fixed Assets	10.6	12.2
7.0	5.0	4.3	4.9				4.7	5.1
6.5	4.0	3.1	2.4				4.4	3.7
4.4	3.0	2.5	1.7			Sales/Total Assets	2.7	2.6
2.8	2.0	1.6	.9				1.7	1.9
.7	.8	1.1	.9				1.2	1.0
(38) 1.5	(90) 1.5	(67) 1.8	(18) 1.2			% Depr., Dep., Amort./Sales	(233) 2.0	(238) 1.9
2.4	2.9	3.3	1.9				3.3	3.5
1.9	2.2	1.5				% Officers', Directors'	2.5	1.9
(30) 4.7	(60) 3.9	(30) 2.3				Owners' Comp/Sales	(133) 4.3	(118) 3.9
6.9	6.4	4.1					6.4	6.0
72406M	314824M	732235M	870856M	638433M	1587362M	Net Sales ($)	5991720M	3424385M
15668M	102068M	293996M	464269M	123443M	588337M	Total Assets ($)	1298190M	1226801M

M = $ thousand   MM = $ million
See Pages 11 through 21 for Explanation of Ratios and Data

Comparative Historical Data   Current Data Sorted by Sales

4/1/04- 3/31/05 ALL	4/1/05- 3/31/06 ALL	4/1/06- 3/31/07 ALL	Type of Statement	0-1MM	1-3MM	3-5MM	5-10MM	10-25MM	25MM & OVER
15	10	9	Unqualified				1	3	5
48	47	41	Reviewed	2	4	4	10	16	5
79	65	79	Compiled	8	32	16	18	5	
52	50	52	Tax Returns	9	24	11	5	1	2
49	65	63	Other	7	17	9	15	7	8
				41 (4/1-9/30/06)			203 (10/1/06-3/31/07)		
243	237	244	**NUMBER OF STATEMENTS**	26	77	40	49	32	20
%	%	%	**ASSETS**	%	%	%	%	%	%
6.6	7.7	7.4	Cash & Equivalents	9.0	7.1	10.3	8.7	3.9	3.5
14.1	13.0	12.7	Trade Receivables (net)	2.5	11.1	13.5	14.4	22.4	10.3
37.1	38.0	35.0	Inventory	34.2	38.7	30.3	32.8	33.3	39.5
1.6	1.6	2.8	All Other Current	3.9	2.6	1.9	1.9	3.0	5.4
59.4	60.3	57.9	Total Current	49.7	59.6	56.0	57.8	62.6	58.7
32.5	29.4	31.8	Fixed Assets (net)	38.4	32.5	32.5	32.6	27.6	23.4
2.1	2.1	2.9	Intangibles (net)	7.3	2.8	1.2	.7	1.4	8.6
6.0	8.2	7.4	All Other Non-Current	4.7	5.1	10.2	8.9	8.4	9.3
100.0	100.0	100.0	Total	100.0	100.0	100.0	100.0	100.0	100.0
			LIABILITIES						
15.5	15.1	13.9	Notes Payable-Short Term	14.4	16.3	13.1	11.0	12.3	15.0
5.2	5.2	5.1	Cur. Mat.-L.T.D.	8.4	6.7	4.7	3.4	2.4	3.0
15.0	16.6	16.8	Trade Payables	13.0	16.8	13.1	12.6	17.9	37.5
.5	.3	.2	Income Taxes Payable	.0	.2	.0	.2	.6	.4
10.5	10.5	11.6	All Other Current	11.1	9.0	11.6	13.6	14.1	13.8
46.7	47.7	47.6	Total Current	46.8	49.1	42.4	40.9	47.4	69.7
22.0	19.4	22.9	Long-Term Debt	31.9	27.9	25.9	16.3	12.6	18.5
.5	.5	.4	Deferred Taxes	.0	.1	.3	1.5	.2	.4
5.7	9.7	7.8	All Other Non-Current	10.9	11.6	6.0	4.2	4.9	5.9
25.2	22.7	21.3	Net Worth	10.3	11.3	25.3	37.2	35.0	5.5
100.0	100.0	100.0	Total Liabilities & Net Worth	100.0	100.0	100.0	100.0	100.0	100.0
			INCOME DATA						
100.0	100.0	100.0	Net Sales	100.0	100.0	100.0	100.0	100.0	100.0
36.5	37.0	37.6	Gross Profit	42.6	38.3	41.0	35.4	31.9	36.5
34.2	34.8	34.8	Operating Expenses	39.8	36.1	36.8	32.8	28.8	33.3
2.2	2.2	2.9	Operating Profit	2.7	2.3	4.3	2.6	3.1	3.1
.6	.8	1.0	All Other Expenses (net)	2.8	1.2	1.1	.0	.4	1.8
1.7	1.4	1.8	Profit Before Taxes	-.1	1.1	3.2	2.6	2.7	1.4
			RATIOS						
2.1	2.2	2.2		3.2	2.2	2.3	2.4	2.3	1.4
1.4	1.3	1.3	Current	.9	1.4	1.4	1.5	1.3	1.1
1.0	1.0	.8		.6	.7	.9	.9	.8	.9
1.0	.9	.9		.3	.9	1.3	1.3	1.0	.3
(242) .4	.4	.3	Quick	.1	.2	.5	.5	.6	.1
.1	.2	.1		.0	.1	.2	.2	.2	.1
3 113.4	3 134.7	2 180.2		0 UND	1 435.2	3 130.7	5 74.5	4 99.4	3 119.6
11 34.7	10 37.2	9 40.3	Sales/Receivables	1 430.5	8 47.4	11 33.0	14 26.3	22 16.4	6 57.6
32 11.4	26 14.1	24 15.4		11 32.0	19 18.9	29 12.6	25 14.7	50 7.3	15 24.2
29 12.5	37 9.9	33 11.0		42 8.6	43 8.5	12 30.0	37 9.9	31 11.9	44 8.4
78 4.7	71 5.2	70 5.2	Cost of Sales/Inventory	111 3.3	78 4.7	45 8.1	65 5.6	63 5.8	65 5.6
140 2.6	117 3.1	118 3.1		241 1.5	127 2.9	92 4.0	107 3.4	86 4.3	167 2.2
7 50.2	11 34.6	9 42.3		0 UND	10 36.0	5 77.5	7 49.6	13 29.0	30 12.2
25 14.7	26 13.8	28 13.3	Cost of Sales/Payables	30 12.2	22 16.6	26 14.3	28 13.2	23 15.6	40 9.1
53 6.9	49 7.5	47 7.8		69 5.3	48 7.7	43 8.4	39 9.3	49 7.4	54 6.7
6.9	7.4	8.2		9.8	7.4	10.4	8.9	7.2	12.7
16.2	18.3	20.4	Sales/Working Capital	NM	13.4	17.8	17.3	22.7	67.3
-121.3	-201.8	-31.8		-9.8	-31.7	NM	-232.5	-153.9	-55.8
7.4	6.9	5.6		6.5	3.5	5.8	10.0	7.9	6.4
(232) 2.7	(224) 2.9	(233) 2.1	EBIT/Interest	(25) .9	(74) 1.5	(36) 2.4	(47) 2.3	3.1	(19) 3.7
.6	.8	.8		-1.1	.2	1.2	1.2	1.7	-.1
4.5	3.8	3.4					2.9		
(51) 2.0	(43) 2.4	(46) 2.3	Net Profit + Depr., Dep., Amort./Cur. Mat. L/T/D				(20) 2.4		
1.1	1.0	1.2					1.3		
.4	.3	.4		.5	.5	.4	.3	.3	.4
1.0	.9	1.0	Fixed/Worth	3.1	1.2	.9	.9	.8	.6
4.6	3.4	3.9		NM	UND	3.6	1.8	1.4	NM
1.0	1.1	.9		.7	1.0	.8	.7	.8	1.5
2.3	2.4	2.6	Debt/Worth	5.6	3.2	2.8	1.8	2.2	2.5
12.5	9.5	9.8		-19.3	UND	8.9	4.2	4.3	NM
33.6	37.3	36.8		52.0	32.5	47.1	23.1	35.4	29.5
(195) 14.4	(193) 13.6	(198) 14.2	% Profit Before Taxes/Tangible Net Worth	(19) 8.9	(58) 5.9	(33) 18.5	(45) 11.3	(28) 14.0	(15) 22.4
2.6	1.0	.9		-4.1	-2.7	7.5	1.1	5.3	12.0
9.8	11.6	11.6		10.6	11.8	16.7	10.2	10.3	11.6
3.5	4.4	3.6	% Profit Before Taxes/Total Assets	.3	1.3	5.9	3.7	5.1	6.1
-.7	-1.2	-.3		-7.9	-2.1	2.0	.2	1.9	-2.2
21.8	28.4	25.4		18.8	28.7	40.9	17.7	31.7	22.2
10.9	12.1	10.8	Sales/Net Fixed Assets	5.4	12.2	11.8	8.5	12.0	14.9
4.6	5.5	4.9		3.3	5.1	4.6	4.9	8.4	9.5
3.8	4.1	4.0		2.9	4.2	4.4	3.8	3.8	3.8
2.5	2.8	2.8	Sales/Total Assets	2.1	3.0	3.2	2.7	3.0	2.3
1.6	1.9	1.9		1.0	2.0	2.0	1.7	2.2	1.7
1.0	.9	.9		.8	.9	.6	1.2	1.0	.8
(218) 2.0	(204) 1.6	(216) 1.5	% Depr., Dep., Amort./Sales	(19) 2.4	(71) 1.5	(34) 1.4	(44) 2.0	(31) 1.1	(17) 1.1
3.5	3.2	2.6		5.0	2.8	2.8	3.2	1.9	1.7
2.0	1.9	1.7			2.1	2.2	1.8	.5	
(116) 3.5	(130) 3.4	(129) 3.7	% Officers', Directors' Owners' Comp/Sales	(54) 4.5	(24) 3.0	(22) 4.1	(16) 1.8		
5.9	6.0	6.2			6.8	5.1	6.2	3.4	
4547125M	2443870M	4216116M	Net Sales ($)	18813M	151609M	152495M	331827M	506490M	3054882M
1223698M	984696M	1587781M	Total Assets ($)	20403M	56331M	57669M	213219M	205706M	1034453M

M = $ thousand   MM = $ million
See Pages 11 through 21 for Explanation of Ratios and Data

Current Data Sorted by Assets   Comparative Historical Data

Type of Statement	0-500M	500M-2MM	2-10MM	10-50MM	50-100MM	100-250MM		4/1/02-3/31/03 ALL	4/1/03-3/31/04 ALL
Unqualified	1	3	11	29	16	22		103	86
Reviewed		16	52	24	3			108	114
Compiled	23	65	56	12	3			182	223
Tax Returns	53	95	36	5	2	1		158	209
Other	16	53	75	42	16	21		207	224
		150 (4/1-9/30/06)			601 (10/1/06-3/31/07)				
NUMBER OF STATEMENTS	93	232	230	112	40	44		758	856
ASSETS	%	%	%	%	%	%		%	%
Cash & Equivalents	13.9	11.6	14.8	11.4	8.1	8.5		12.4	13.0
Trade Receivables (net)	4.1	3.6	4.6	5.1	5.7	6.6		4.9	4.6
Inventory	42.4	34.8	26.3	25.5	19.9	24.0		28.6	29.0
All Other Current	2.5	2.8	2.2	2.4	4.0	2.8		3.0	3.0
Total Current	62.9	52.9	47.9	44.4	37.6	41.8		48.9	49.6
Fixed Assets (net)	26.7	33.6	34.8	42.1	50.4	46.2		38.6	37.1
Intangibles (net)	4.9	5.2	6.2	5.2	4.0	3.6		3.8	4.1
All Other Non-Current	5.7	8.4	11.1	8.4	8.0	8.4		8.6	9.2
Total	100.0	100.0	100.0	100.0	100.0	100.0		100.0	100.0
LIABILITIES									
Notes Payable-Short Term	10.9	3.9	4.0	3.7	2.6	2.9		4.1	4.2
Cur. Mat.-L.T.D.	4.0	3.3	4.3	5.4	3.8	4.0		4.7	4.5
Trade Payables	13.3	20.3	17.8	19.6	16.2	16.9		19.2	17.8
Income Taxes Payable	.1	.2	.1	.2	.2	.2		.3	.2
All Other Current	12.7	12.8	9.5	9.3	11.6	11.6		11.3	11.5
Total Current	41.0	40.4	35.7	38.3	34.4	35.5		39.6	38.2
Long-Term Debt	31.4	27.6	24.5	23.1	25.3	23.8		29.0	28.3
Deferred Taxes	.0	.1	.2	.5	.6	.6		.3	.3
All Other Non-Current	11.0	8.5	6.4	3.6	5.0	7.7		6.8	7.5
Net Worth	16.6	23.5	33.2	34.5	34.7	32.3		24.4	25.7
Total Liabilities & Net Worth	100.0	100.0	100.0	100.0	100.0	100.0		100.0	100.0
INCOME DATA									
Net Sales	100.0	100.0	100.0	100.0	100.0	100.0		100.0	100.0
Gross Profit	23.3	24.5	26.6	25.1	24.9	26.0		24.9	24.0
Operating Expenses	22.6	23.5	25.2	23.8	22.8	23.8		23.6	23.0
Operating Profit	.7	1.0	1.4	1.3	2.1	2.2		1.3	1.0
All Other Expenses (net)	-.4	-.5	-.3	.0	.3	.3		-.1	-.2
Profit Before Taxes	1.1	1.5	1.7	1.3	1.8	1.9		1.4	1.3
RATIOS									
Current	5.2	2.8	2.3	1.6	1.5	1.5		2.2	2.3
	2.2	1.6	1.5	1.2	1.1	1.2		1.3	1.4
	1.1	1.0	1.0	.9	.8	.9		.9	.9
Quick	1.7	.9	1.0	.7	.6	.6		.8	.9
	(92) .6	.4	(229) .5	.4	.2	.4		(746) .4	(846) .4
	.1	.1	.2	.2	.2	.3		.2	.2
Sales/Receivables	0 UND	0 UND	0 755.0	1 310.7	2 182.3	2 160.9		0 999.8	0 999.8
	0 999.8	1 425.5	2 218.0	3 130.5	3 126.2	5 78.3		2 237.9	1 284.9
	2 170.4	2 177.6	3 113.0	5 75.7	4 81.6	7 55.2		4 90.8	4 102.2
Cost of Sales/Inventory	12 30.1	18 20.7	17 21.7	17 21.3	15 25.2	18 20.2		16 23.2	15 24.5
	25 14.8	25 14.4	24 15.2	23 15.8	20 18.6	25 14.6		23 16.0	23 15.7
	40 9.1	35 10.5	32 11.4	31 11.9	26 14.1	32 11.4		32 11.3	32 11.4
Cost of Sales/Payables	0 UND	5 68.8	10 36.3	12 29.5	11 34.2	15 24.7		8 45.4	7 52.4
	4 89.8	12 30.9	14 25.3	18 20.6	17 21.8	19 19.1		14 25.7	14 27.0
	11 32.6	19 18.8	22 16.8	24 15.0	26 14.3	23 15.8		21 17.0	21 17.5
Sales/Working Capital	12.6	17.3	16.6	27.1	32.0	24.2		19.7	19.7
	32.3	36.7	39.0	66.7	255.5	81.0		55.5	47.6
	193.1	781.3	-842.3	-99.0	-80.4	-104.2		-98.7	-168.2
EBIT/Interest	7.2	9.3	7.6	10.5	13.2	7.3		6.6	7.8
	(56) 1.8	(195) 3.5	(209) 3.4	(107) 3.5	(38) 4.7	(42) 3.9		(662) 2.9	(720) 2.9
	-.7	1.0	1.3	1.4	2.9	1.6		1.2	1.1
Net Profit + Depr., Dep., Amort./Cur. Mat. L/T/D		4.9	7.1	6.7	8.3	7.3		4.6	4.6
		(27) 2.1	(33) 2.7	(42) 2.4	(16) 3.6	(10) 4.8		(164) 2.1	(165) 2.1
		1.2	1.4	.8	1.8	2.1		1.3	1.0
Fixed/Worth	.2	.4	.4	.8	.9	1.0		.6	.5
	1.4	1.6	1.2	1.5	1.7	1.7		1.6	1.4
	-.7	-9.3	3.5	4.1	2.8	4.9		7.2	9.0
Debt/Worth	.6	1.0	1.0	1.0	.9	1.4		1.1	1.1
	2.4	3.0	2.2	2.6	2.0	2.1		2.8	2.7
	-4.4	-24.6	7.0	7.3	3.7	5.7		16.9	23.0
% Profit Before Taxes/Tangible Net Worth	47.4	72.9	40.2	36.4	41.9	32.0		50.2	50.0
	(57) 28.6	(168) 29.1	(190) 19.5	(99) 18.7	(36) 17.7	(38) 22.6		(606) 21.5	(685) 20.0
	4.0	6.6	6.0	8.5	8.0	12.8		6.7	5.1
% Profit Before Taxes/Total Assets	21.6	18.0	15.4	11.5	11.2	11.0		12.9	13.0
	6.4	6.1	6.7	6.4	6.9	6.3		5.7	5.5
	-3.7	.0	1.2	1.2	3.3	2.9		.9	.2
Sales/Net Fixed Assets	151.7	49.5	35.4	20.5	14.9	12.9		34.5	40.9
	55.7	23.7	16.7	11.8	9.8	9.1		14.7	16.8
	13.2	11.4	8.0	7.7	6.4	6.9		7.6	7.4
Sales/Total Assets	11.9	8.8	7.1	5.9	6.0	5.2		7.3	7.5
	8.3	6.2	4.9	5.0	4.7	4.5		5.2	5.1
	4.1	4.5	3.3	3.8	3.6	3.4		3.5	3.5
% Depr., Dep., Amort./Sales	.3	.5	.7	.9	1.0	.8		.8	.7
	(73) .6	(210) .8	(213) 1.1	(107) 1.3	(34) 1.5	(19) 1.5		(678) 1.2	(753) 1.2
	1.8	1.4	1.8	1.8	2.0	1.8		1.8	1.9
% Officers', Directors' Owners' Comp/Sales	1.1	.8	.6	.3				.6	.6
	(49) 2.1	(119) 1.3	(84) 1.2	(27) .6				(283) 1.4	(347) 1.3
	4.3	2.4	2.2	1.1				2.6	2.6
Net Sales ($)	241171M	1796676M	5526619M	15558465M	14736986M	29165263M		51828206M	55884406M
Total Assets ($)	27765M	267602M	1053757M	2874661M	2819919M	6896221M		12471756M	12111223M

M = $ thousand   MM = $ million
See Pages 11 through 21 for Explanation of Ratios and Data

Comparative Historical Data | Current Data Sorted by Sales

04-05	05-06	06-07	Type of Statement	0-1MM	1-3MM	3-5MM	5-10MM	10-25MM	25MM & OVER
77	74	82	Unqualified		2	2	3	7	70
80	104	95	Reviewed		2	5	12	23	53
209	135	159	Compiled	2	9	21	43	50	34
235	188	192	Tax Returns	13	41	38	41	39	20
210	222	223	Other	7	11	21	36	44	104
4/1/04-3/31/05 ALL	4/1/05-3/31/06 ALL	4/1/06-3/31/07 ALL		150 (4/1-9/30/06)			601 (10/1/06-3/31/07)		
811	723	751	**NUMBER OF STATEMENTS**	22	65	85	135	163	281
%	%	%	**ASSETS**	%	%	%	%	%	%
13.5	13.0	12.5	Cash & Equivalents	10.6	11.6	9.2	12.8	16.2	11.4
4.7	4.8	4.5	Trade Receivables (net)	3.2	2.6	3.8	4.5	3.5	5.8
29.4	29.5	30.3	Inventory	28.3	32.9	36.4	31.7	30.8	27.1
2.5	2.0	2.6	All Other Current	1.0	3.7	2.6	2.4	2.3	2.7
50.0	49.3	49.8	Total Current	43.0	50.8	52.0	51.6	52.9	46.9
36.7	36.7	36.0	Fixed Assets (net)	42.9	37.5	33.2	34.2	30.7	39.9
4.3	4.7	5.3	Intangibles (net)	7.1	4.8	6.1	5.4	4.2	4.2
9.0	9.3	8.8	All Other Non-Current	7.1	6.9	8.7	8.8	9.8	8.9
100.0	100.0	100.0	Total	100.0	100.0	100.0	100.0	100.0	100.0
			LIABILITIES						
4.1	3.9	4.6	Notes Payable-Short Term	19.7	4.1	8.6	3.1	3.8	3.6
4.0	3.8	4.1	Cur. Mat.-L.T.D.	7.1	2.4	2.5	3.4	4.3	4.8
17.6	19.0	18.1	Trade Payables	4.8	8.5	14.6	20.7	20.1	20.1
.2	.1	.2	Income Taxes Payable	.1	.1	.1	.1	.2	.2
11.5	10.8	11.1	All Other Current	8.4	5.4	14.7	14.9	9.7	10.6
37.3	37.7	38.1	Total Current	40.0	20.5	40.6	42.2	38.1	39.4
27.8	26.2	26.1	Long-Term Debt	30.2	41.2	37.6	25.3	22.3	21.4
.3	.4	.2	Deferred Taxes	.0	.1	.0	.1	.2	.4
6.4	8.6	7.2	All Other Non-Current	17.4	7.5	6.5	8.4	9.7	4.4
28.2	27.1	28.4	Net Worth	12.4	30.7	15.2	24.0	29.7	34.4
100.0	100.0	100.0	Total Liabilties & Net Worth	100.0	100.0	100.0	100.0	100.0	100.0
			INCOME DATA						
100.0	100.0	100.0	Net Sales	100.0	100.0	100.0	100.0	100.0	100.0
24.4	25.7	25.2	Gross Profit	29.1	25.1	23.6	25.4	26.0	24.8
23.3	24.1	23.9	Operating Expenses	31.1	22.3	22.9	24.2	24.8	23.4
1.2	1.5	1.3	Operating Profit	-1.9	2.7	.7	1.2	1.2	1.4
-.3	-.2	-.3	All Other Expenses (net)	-.1	-.2	-.3	-.3	-.6	-.1
1.5	1.7	1.5	Profit Before Taxes	-1.8	2.9	1.0	1.5	1.8	1.5
			RATIOS						
2.4	2.3	2.4	Current	6.1	11.0	3.3	2.7	2.2	1.7
1.4	1.5	1.4		1.9	3.0	1.6	1.6	1.5	1.2
.9	.9	1.0		.7	1.5	1.0	.9	1.0	.9
1.0	.9	.9	Quick	2.9	2.8	.8	1.0	1.0	.7
(807) .5	(715) .5	(749) .4		.6	(64) .8	.4	(134) .4	.5	.4
.2	.2	.2		.1	.2	.1	.2	.2	.2
0 999.8	0 999.8	0 999.8	Sales/Receivables	0 UND	0 UND	0 UND	0 999.8	0 905.2	1 316.1
1 285.2	1 296.5	1 243.4		0 UND	0 UND	1 541.3	1 356.5	1 294.4	3 134.6
3 112.1	3 110.0	3 107.3		1 506.3	2 181.3	2 147.0	3 122.5	2 151.8	5 75.7
15 23.6	16 23.3	17 22.1	Cost of Sales/Inventory	16 23.1	19 19.0	18 20.2	17 21.5	16 23.3	16 22.2
23 15.7	23 15.9	24 15.2		46 7.9	27 13.5	30 12.0	25 14.8	22 16.8	23 15.9
32 11.5	31 11.8	33 11.1		129 2.8	45 8.1	40 9.2	35 10.5	31 11.8	30 12.2
7 52.9	8 45.8	7 49.1	Cost of Sales/Payables	0 UND	0 UND	4 99.2	6 58.4	8 45.1	12 29.2
13 28.0	14 25.7	14 26.0		0 UND	4 89.8	10 37.2	12 30.6	13 27.5	17 21.3
20 18.3	21 17.0	21 17.2		18 20.4	16 22.7	17 21.3	20 18.4	20 17.8	23 15.8
17.7	18.0	17.8	Sales/Working Capital	7.0	11.5	15.6	17.3	17.9	27.0
43.1	40.1	42.9		14.2	17.4	39.3	35.7	41.9	68.7
-469.4	-207.8	-478.2		-15.8	62.5	607.0	-195.0	437.4	-120.2
9.8	9.1	8.6	EBIT/Interest	3.2	8.0	4.5	10.6	10.0	9.7
(667) 3.1	(611) 3.4	(647) 3.5		(16) 1.4	(46) 2.1	(63) 2.0	(111) 3.2	(143) 3.5	(268) 4.4
1.0	1.0	1.3		-5.8	1.2	.2	.9	1.1	1.7
4.5	4.9	6.8	Net Profit + Depr., Dep., Amort./Cur. Mat. L/T/D				4.3	6.6	7.3
(139) 2.1	(130) 2.3	(131) 2.6					(17) 1.9	(24) 3.1	(83) 2.9
1.3	1.4	1.2					.8	2.0	1.6
.5	.5	.5	Fixed/Worth	1.1	.3	.4	.4	.4	.7
1.3	1.5	1.4		3.5	1.8	3.8	1.4	1.2	1.3
8.3	7.8	7.2		-.7	-7.2	-1.9	7.2	7.3	3.1
.9	1.0	1.0	Debt/Worth	.9	.8	1.1	.7	.9	1.0
2.8	2.5	2.4		3.9	2.3	6.0	2.9	2.0	2.2
23.8	16.8	15.7		-4.2	-13.0	-4.8	12.2	15.1	5.3
50.4	52.8	48.4	% Profit Before Taxes/Tangible Net Worth	29.3	74.4	63.7	60.9	64.7	37.8
(646) 20.1	(577) 23.7	(588) 21.7		(13) 3.7	(45) 30.7	(49) 30.3	(105) 19.5	(126) 21.2	(250) 21.1
6.6	5.6	7.0		1.4	9.4	5.5	6.1	6.3	8.9
14.3	15.6	15.2	% Profit Before Taxes/Total Assets	8.0	25.0	14.3	16.4	19.6	13.3
5.5	6.2	6.4		1.5	9.1	4.7	5.3	6.9	7.1
.3	.5	.9		-6.5	2.5	-4.2	-.4	.4	2.0
43.0	39.7	40.1	Sales/Net Fixed Assets	15.8	74.6	73.2	53.5	45.6	26.5
16.9	16.6	16.7		5.0	18.3	19.0	19.3	25.6	13.7
8.3	8.1	8.5		1.4	6.0	7.4	9.4	11.5	8.7
7.5	7.8	7.6	Sales/Total Assets	3.4	7.9	8.6	8.2	8.9	6.8
5.3	5.4	5.3		1.7	4.2	5.2	6.0	6.1	5.3
3.6	3.7	3.7		1.0	2.8	3.3	3.6	3.9	4.1
.7	.6	.6	% Depr., Dep., Amort./Sales	1.1	.5	.4	.5	.4	.8
(690) 1.2	(638) 1.0	(656) 1.0		(17) 2.0	(54) 1.2	(72) .9	(121) .8	(149) .9	(243) 1.2
1.9	1.6	1.6		5.5	2.2	1.9	1.6	1.4	1.6
.8	.8	.7	% Officers', Directors' Owners' Comp/Sales		1.3	1.0	.8	.5	.5
(306) 1.4	(279) 1.4	(282) 1.3			(33) 2.2	(43) 1.4	(62) 1.5	(76) .9	(59) .8
2.7	2.4	2.6			3.1	2.4	2.6	1.7	1.6
48044464M	54414670M	67025180M	Net Sales ($)	12740M	121937M	338840M	1003847M	2592143M	62955673M
10839977M	11957628M	13939925M	Total Assets ($)	13591M	35148M	83632M	218506M	527914M	13061134M

M = $ thousand   MM = $ million
See Pages 11 through 21 for Explanation of Ratios and Data

Current Data Sorted by Assets   Comparative Historical Data

Type of Statement

Type of Statement	0-500M	500M-2MM	2-10MM	10-50MM	50-100MM	100-250MM	4/1/02-3/31/03 ALL	4/1/03-3/31/04 ALL
Unqualified	1			9	6	4	2	7
Reviewed			4	6			3	6
Compiled	7	13	5	1			9	14
Tax Returns	60	42	5	1		1	16	39
Other	14	12	9	8		2	6	10
	21 (4/1-9/30/06)			195 (10/1/06-3/31/07)				

Data

	0-500M	500M-2MM	2-10MM	10-50MM	50-100MM	100-250MM	4/1/02-3/31/03 ALL	4/1/03-3/31/04 ALL
NUMBER OF STATEMENTS	82	67	23	24	13	7	36	76
ASSETS	%	%	%	%	%	%	%	%
Cash & Equivalents	13.7	12.8	9.0	10.5	10.5		13.3	11.8
Trade Receivables (net)	2.4	4.0	9.8	10.7	3.5		4.4	4.8
Inventory	44.3	20.9	20.0	10.9	17.5		24.3	29.2
All Other Current	1.2	2.3	1.3	2.3	1.8		2.5	2.6
Total Current	61.7	39.9	40.1	34.5	33.3		44.6	48.4
Fixed Assets (net)	23.2	47.9	50.6	55.2	56.7		46.5	38.6
Intangibles (net)	11.5	7.4	1.7	6.3	.6		3.4	6.9
All Other Non-Current	3.7	4.8	7.6	3.9	9.4		5.5	6.1
Total	100.0	100.0	100.0	100.0	100.0		100.0	100.0
LIABILITIES								
Notes Payable-Short Term	3.0	3.4	6.5	2.3	3.2		10.9	2.8
Cur. Mat.-L.T.D.	2.0	4.5	3.7	5.5	2.2		4.3	2.3
Trade Payables	10.1	12.3	17.9	17.1	12.9		10.4	12.8
Income Taxes Payable	.0	.0	.3	.2	.0		.2	.4
All Other Current	19.2	11.8	4.2	9.3	14.0		8.4	9.1
Total Current	34.3	32.1	32.6	34.3	32.4		34.2	27.4
Long-Term Debt	23.0	39.5	36.1	39.0	22.5		33.8	35.9
Deferred Taxes	.0	.0	.0	1.3	.4		.2	.2
All Other Non-Current	14.7	8.6	11.3	2.9	2.2		6.0	7.3
Net Worth	28.1	19.8	20.0	22.4	42.5		25.7	29.1
Total Liabilties & Net Worth	100.0	100.0	100.0	100.0	100.0		100.0	100.0
INCOME DATA								
Net Sales	100.0	100.0	100.0	100.0	100.0		100.0	100.0
Gross Profit	23.4	16.8	18.3	15.0	16.7		23.0	19.8
Operating Expenses	21.9	14.0	14.7	14.0	16.2		21.0	18.8
Operating Profit	1.5	2.8	3.6	1.0	.5		2.0	1.0
All Other Expenses (net)	-.3	.8	.8	.3	-.8		1.0	-.7
Profit Before Taxes	1.7	1.9	2.8	.7	1.3		1.0	1.8
RATIOS								
Current	7.0	3.9	2.0	1.4	1.4		1.8	4.0
	2.2	1.6	1.3	1.0	1.0		1.4	1.7
	1.0	.8	.6	.7	.7		.8	1.2
Quick	1.6	2.1	1.2	.9	.9		1.1	1.2
	.5	(65) .6	(22) .4	.5	.5		(35) .6	(73) .6
	.1	.1	.2	.4	.3		.2	.3
Sales/Receivables	0 UND	0 UND	1 505.2	2 184.1	0 UND		0 UND	0 UND
	0 UND	0 UND	2 163.8	4 89.2	2 160.6		1 442.0	2 240.6
	1 521.7	2 149.5	4 87.6	7 51.1	5 70.4		5 66.9	4 81.4
Cost of Sales/Inventory	12 30.3	8 44.8	7 50.8	6 58.1	9 42.9		11 33.6	12 31.4
	24 15.3	12 29.3	11 34.4	10 36.8	12 31.2		16 23.3	20 18.6
	51 7.1	27 13.3	27 13.6	12 31.1	19 19.4		36 10.1	31 11.7
Cost of Sales/Payables	0 UND	0 UND	2 194.1	9 40.7	7 51.3		0 UND	1 377.5
	0 UND	2 182.4	11 31.8	14 25.9	11 31.8		8 45.6	10 37.4
	6 63.4	14 25.4	17 21.9	18 20.0	21 17.2		16 22.2	15 23.8
Sales/Working Capital	12.2	15.6	23.8	37.0	61.9		20.2	18.4
	44.3	54.6	72.7	726.1	999.8		45.3	32.5
	-391.1	-88.7	-36.5	-67.6	-110.3		NM	95.4
EBIT/Interest	14.0	3.9	5.7	5.0	11.7		4.8	7.0
	(43) 4.3	(58) 2.2	(18) 2.3	(21) 1.6	(11) 3.5		(29) 2.5	(63) 2.8
	-.2	.5	1.2	.8	2.3		.4	1.0
Net Profit + Depr., Dep., Amort./Cur. Mat. L/T/D								
Fixed/Worth	.1	.5	.9	1.5	.9		.7	.7
	.8	5.5	4.2	3.2	2.0		2.3	1.6
	NM	-5.5	29.3	58.7	3.1		UND	-15.7
Debt/Worth	* .9	1.0	2.1	2.4	.7		1.2	.9
	2.6	11.4	6.3	4.5	2.2		3.5	2.1
	-15.6	-8.9	31.7	74.4	3.6		UND	-30.1
% Profit Before Taxes/Tangible Net Worth	84.2	63.3	70.3	76.9	22.9		32.3	39.8
	(58) 41.8	(43) 28.6	(18) 45.0	(19) 32.8	19.4		(28) 8.9	(54) 17.1
	6.2	11.9	8.5	7.7	6.3		-2.0	2.3
% Profit Before Taxes/Total Assets	25.3	13.5	13.6	14.5	7.9		9.5	12.6
	10.4	5.5	3.8	2.5	4.4		2.1	6.0
	-2.1	-1.8	.3	.6	2.7		-2.1	-.8
Sales/Net Fixed Assets	281.8	67.7	33.4	17.4	11.8		35.3	59.2
	63.0	9.8	12.5	8.3	7.3		12.2	15.7
	15.5	3.8	2.2	6.1	5.6		4.7	5.6
Sales/Total Assets	14.0	9.0	9.3	7.1	5.9		5.8	8.6
	7.4	4.6	4.1	4.8	5.0		4.0	5.1
	3.8	2.5	1.8	3.6	2.9		2.8	3.2
% Depr., Dep., Amort./Sales	.4	.6	.6	.9	.8		.7	.7
	(57) .8	(57) 1.2	(20) 1.1	(23) 1.2	(11) 1.1		(35) 1.3	(66) 1.4
	1.8	1.9	2.0	1.4	1.6		2.4	2.6
% Officers', Directors' Owners' Comp/Sales	1.0	.7					.6	.9
	(43) 2.9	(29) 1.3					(19) 2.0	(40) 2.2
	4.7	2.8					4.6	4.0
Net Sales ($)	149439M	378084M	599491M	2960582M	5291020M	15148313M	621739M	823084M
Total Assets ($)	17051M	63974M	104731M	586268M	971570M	1107840M	150665M	176185M

M = $ thousand   MM = $ million
See Pages 11 through 21 for Explanation of Ratios and Data

Comparative Historical Data   Current Data Sorted by Sales

			Type of Statement						
7	9	20	Unqualified				1		19
10	11	10	Reviewed				1	2	7
9	27	26	Compiled	5	2	1	9	5	4
66	83	109	Tax Returns	30	39	17	16	3	4
22	34	51	Other	6	12	7	4	4	18
4/1/04-	4/1/05-	4/1/06-		21 (4/1-9/30/06)			195 (10/1/06-3/31/07)		
3/31/05	3/31/06	3/31/07							
ALL	ALL	ALL		0-1MM	1-3MM	3-5MM	5-10MM	10-25MM	25MM & OVER
114	164	216	**NUMBER OF STATEMENTS**	41	53	25	31	14	52
%	%	%	**ASSETS**	%	%	%	%	%	%
10.0	10.5	12.1	Cash & Equivalents	13.7	9.8	12.1	16.2	17.9	9.3
3.8	3.5	4.8	Trade Receivables (net)	.4	1.6	6.9	5.5	8.5	9.1
26.8	31.9	28.2	Inventory	36.3	36.8	21.2	25.5	32.0	17.2
2.0	2.0	1.8	All Other Current	.1	2.1	2.2	2.3	1.7	2.4
42.6	47.9	47.0	Total Current	50.4	50.3	42.4	49.4	60.1	38.0
41.4	35.7	40.6	Fixed Assets (net)	30.7	40.3	42.8	35.3	26.7	54.8
10.0	10.0	7.6	Intangibles (net)	16.0	6.7	8.8	5.5	8.8	2.3
5.9	6.4	4.8	All Other Non-Current	3.0	2.7	6.0	9.8	4.4	4.9
100.0	100.0	100.0	Total	100.0	100.0	100.0	100.0	100.0	100.0
			LIABILITIES						
6.5	4.8	3.3	Notes Payable-Short Term	3.9	4.1	1.8	2.3	2.4	3.8
3.4	2.9	3.4	Cur. Mat.-L.T.D.	3.6	3.1	3.4	3.3	1.4	4.1
13.0	14.1	12.9	Trade Payables	5.7	5.0	15.0	15.8	28.1	19.8
.2	.1	.1	Income Taxes Payable	.0	.0	.0	.0	.2	.2
12.5	10.0	13.7	All Other Current	12.0	15.7	7.5	18.5	22.6	10.7
35.6	31.8	33.4	Total Current	25.2	27.8	27.6	39.9	54.8	38.6
33.4	36.5	31.9	Long-Term Debt	21.0	38.7	50.1	27.3	19.1	31.0
.2	.2	.2	Deferred Taxes	.0	.0	.0	.0	.0	.7
10.2	10.8	10.0	All Other Non-Current	20.6	10.4	13.5	6.1	5.0	3.2
20.6	20.6	24.6	Net Worth	33.2	23.1	8.8	26.7	21.1	26.6
100.0	100.0	100.0	Total Liabilties & Net Worth	100.0	100.0	100.0	100.0	100.0	100.0
			INCOME DATA						
100.0	100.0	100.0	Net Sales	.100.0	100.0	100.0	100.0	100.0	100.0
20.6	22.0	19.2	Gross Profit	30.8	20.0	13.7	13.8	20.9	14.5
18.7	19.9	17.2	Operating Expenses	26.9	16.7	13.7	13.2	19.5	13.4
2.0	2.1	2.0	Operating Profit	3.9	3.3	.0	.6	1.4	1.0
.6	-.2	.2	All Other Expenses (net)	.2	1.3	.3	-.8	.1	-.3
1.4	2.3	1.8	Profit Before Taxes	3.7	2.0	-.3	1.4	1.3	1.3
			RATIOS						
4.1	5.1	3.3		27.9	5.1	4.2	4.9	1.4	1.4
1.4	1.8	1.4	Current	2.4	2.0	1.8	2.0	1.3	1.0
.7	1.0	.8		1.0	.9	.7	.7	.9	.6
1.1	1.3	1.4		5.1	1.3	1.8	2.5	.8	.8
(112) .4	(162) .5	(213) .5	Quick	.5	(51) .4	.8	.6	.6	(51) .5
.1	.2	.2		.1	.1	.1	.1	.2	.3
0 UND	0 UND	0 UND		0 UND	0 UND	0 UND	0 UND	0 UND	2 237.0
0 905.3	0 UND	0 999.8	Sales/Receivables	0 UND	0 UND	1 561.1	1 505.2	0 762.3	4 94.8
4 99.3	2 217.6	3 127.4		0 UND	1 433.7	3 116.7	3 123.6	5 79.8	6 66.3
11 32.3	9 42.0	9 41.9		29 12.6	11 33.0	6 59.7	7 50.4	11 33.0	7 53.4
17 21.8	18 20.7	13 27.3	Cost of Sales/Inventory	50 7.3	15 24.2	8 44.6	10 36.4	14 25.7	10 36.7
34 10.9	40 9.2	31 11.8		69 5.3	32 11.3	12 30.2	19 19.7	27 13.5	13 27.5
0 UND	0 UND	0 UND		0 UND	0 UND	0 UND	0 UND	5 70.3	10 37.2
5 69.9	4 97.0	4 87.0	Cost of Sales/Payables	0 UND	0 UND	5 72.0	5 80.4	15 25.1	13 28.1
16 23.1	14 26.0	14 26.2		3 144.4	4 100.1	14 25.4	14 25.3	18 20.1	18 20.8
18.9	12.9	20.8		6.6	17.0	27.0	25.4	31.8	49.7
59.7	37.0	65.3	Sales/Working Capital	13.0	46.7	64.8	57.9	73.9	999.8
-54.8	999.8	-100.3		-273.1	-312.7	-105.0	-38.1	NM	-50.4
6.3	6.0	6.0		10.6	7.2	2.1	13.0	20.9	5.8
(86) 1.8	(119) 2.9	(158) 2.4	EBIT/Interest	(20) 3.0	(37) 2.6	(20) .5	(23) 2.3	(12) 3.8	(46) 2.8
.4	1.2	.7		.1	1.1	-1.5	.6	.6	1.5
	5.1	3.0	Net Profit + Depr., Dep.,						2.9
	(13) 1.6	(17) 2.1	Amort./Cur. Mat. L/T/D					(12) 2.1	2.1
	1.4	1.0							1.0
.7	.4	.4		.2	.2	.3	.2	.5	1.3
2.6	3.0	2.5	Fixed/Worth	1.4	2.6	-58.7	1.8	1.5	2.7
-6.2	-10.5	-179.0		-15.7	24.9	-2.2	-27.8	NM	5.0
1.2	1.1	1.3		1.0	1.2	1.6	.5	1.5	1.7
4.3	5.8	4.1	Debt/Worth	3.9	5.7	-63.3	2.3	14.3	3.5
-9.1	-10.3	-65.1		-30.4	-12.2	-3.6	-41.7	NM	7.5
50.6	76.3	67.4	% Profit Before Taxes/Tangible	75.8	94.5	148.6	48.3	64.7	65.5
(77) 10.1	(108) 38.1	(157) 28.8	Net Worth	(30) 37.7	(38) 39.1	(11) 37.0	(21) 28.6	(11) 37.1	(46) 20.9
-.2	14.6	8.0		9.3	10.0	1.8	6.3	8.3	6.9
11.3	18.8	17.3	% Profit Before Taxes/Total	23.8	19.3	6.6	17.5	20.4	13.7
2.4	7.1	5.5	Assets	9.7	8.5	1.3	5.8	3.8	4.5
-2.3	1.1	.2		.5	.8	-12.1	-1.3	-1.4	2.1
44.7	121.6	90.2		84.5	200.0	128.0	161.8	208.6	21.6
13.4	17.9	17.0	Sales/Net Fixed Assets	17.6	17.5	14.7	33.8	37.1	9.2
6.4	6.0	5.3		4.8	4.2	3.6	8.5	17.6	6.5
9.3	10.6	9.4		5.6	11.6	13.8	12.7	11.9	8.2
5.4	4.7	5.4	Sales/Total Assets	3.2	5.4	4.8	8.5	7.4	5.4
2.7	2.7	3.1		1.9	2.9	2.2	4.5	4.4	4.1
.8	.4	.6		.5	.7	.6	.3	.2	.7
(94) 1.3	(121) 1.0	(170) 1.1	% Depr., Dep., Amort./Sales	(32) 1.4	(40) 1.2	(19) 1.5	(25) .8	(11) .8	(43) 1.1
2.2	1.7	1.7		2.6	2.2	2.1	1.4	.9	1.3
.7	.8	.9	% Officers', Directors'	1.8	.9		.6		
(52) 1.7	(69) 2.2	(80) 1.7	Owners' Comp/Sales	(24) 4.5	(25) 1.6		(11) 1.2		
3.7	4.6	3.6		8.3	3.5		2.6		
3710576M	9480645M	24526929M	Net Sales ($)	26597M	104644M	97214M	227848M	215633M	23854993M
708396M	1359663M	2851434M	Total Assets ($)	15590M	22432M	30493M	40754M	74732M	2667433M

M = $ thousand   MM = $ million
See Pages 11 through 21 for Explanation of Ratios and Data

Current Data Sorted by Assets							Comparative Historical Data	
		1	3			Type of Statement Unqualified	5	3
1		3	2			Reviewed	7	10
1	7	2				Compiled	13	20
5	7	1				Tax Returns	7	26
	2	2	1	1		Other	12	10
	14 (4/1-9/30/06)		25 (10/1/06-3/31/07)				4/1/02-3/31/03	4/1/03-3/31/04
0-500M	500M-2MM	2-10MM	10-50MM	50-100MM	100-250MM		ALL	ALL
7	16	9	6	1		NUMBER OF STATEMENTS	44	69
%	%	%	%	%	%	ASSETS	%	%
	13.6				DATA NOT AVAILABLE	Cash & Equivalents	10.8	13.4
	12.8					Trade Receivables (net)	11.7	15.6
	19.7					Inventory	22.8	21.8
	.4					All Other Current	3.1	1.6
	46.5					Total Current	48.4	52.4
	39.2					Fixed Assets (net)	33.6	34.8
	3.5					Intangibles (net)	4.3	3.4
	10.8					All Other Non-Current	13.6	9.4
	100.0					Total	100.0	100.0
						LIABILITIES		
	6.6					Notes Payable-Short Term	8.7	8.1
	1.5					Cur. Mat.-L.T.D.	6.4	2.0
	18.6					Trade Payables	17.6	19.1
	.1					Income Taxes Payable	.5	.2
	6.3					All Other Current	8.9	9.1
	33.1					Total Current	42.1	38.4
	33.0					Long-Term Debt	30.3	22.9
	.0					Deferred Taxes	.1	.1
	1.5					All Other Non-Current	8.4	11.1
	32.4					Net Worth	19.0	27.5
	100.0					Total Liabilties & Net Worth	100.0	100.0
						INCOME DATA		
	100.0					Net Sales	100.0	100.0
	28.0					Gross Profit	32.3	29.7
	25.6					Operating Expenses	31.0	27.4
	2.3					Operating Profit	1.2	2.3
	.9					All Other Expenses (net)	-.1	-.3
	1.5					Profit Before Taxes	1.4	2.7
						RATIOS		
	3.6						2.9	2.4
	1.6					Current	1.2	1.6
	.9						.7	.9
	2.9						1.5	1.7
	(15) 1.2					Quick	(42) .6	(68) .8
	.2						.3	.4
	0 UND						0 UND	0 UND
	4 83.6					Sales/Receivables	1 253.7	3 124.0
	11 33.6						18 20.6	19 19.3
	4 90.3						10 35.1	7 54.3
	13 27.8					Cost of Sales/Inventory	22 16.3	13 27.6
	22 16.4						39 9.4	39 9.3
	0 UND						7 56.1	2 187.0
	10 36.2					Cost of Sales/Payables	15 23.6	11 31.8
	24 15.4						24 15.4	23 15.6
	10.7						18.2	11.0
	30.0					Sales/Working Capital	124.9	40.5
	-180.1						-34.1	-276.7
	14.5						14.5	11.7
	(14) 3.3					EBIT/Interest	(39) 4.1	(50) 3.1
	1.0						1.3	.8
						Net Profit + Depr., Dep., Amort./Cur. Mat. L/T/D		
	.5						.2	.2
	1.4					Fixed/Worth	1.6	.9
	2.6						-10.0	4.7
	.9						.7	.7
	2.2					Debt/Worth	2.8	1.7
	10.3						-21.0	8.7
	47.9						48.1	54.4
	(14) 16.1					% Profit Before Taxes/Tangible Net Worth	(32) 24.4	(55) 21.2
	7.6						9.4	4.3
	13.7						13.1	22.5
	5.0					% Profit Before Taxes/Total Assets	7.4	7.6
	.5						.8	1.4
	25.7						43.4	43.2
	10.5					Sales/Net Fixed Assets	18.1	19.6
	4.6						8.5	8.9
	7.4						6.6	8.2
	3.7					Sales/Total Assets	4.4	5.3
	2.4						3.2	3.0
	.6						.7	.6
	(15) 1.6					% Depr., Dep., Amort./Sales	(36) 1.8	(58) 1.3
	3.5						3.5	2.6
	.7						1.2	1.2
	(11) 1.1					% Officers', Directors' Owners' Comp/Sales	(22) 2.8	(36) 2.5
	2.3						5.5	4.4
12934M	110104M	185705M	631368M	97628M		Net Sales ($)	668565M	604548M
1776M	19216M	45795M	172023M	72851M		Total Assets ($)	145917M	118385M

M = $ thousand MM = $ million

See Pages 11 through 21 for Explanation of Ratios and Data

Comparative Historical Data   ## Current Data Sorted by Sales

			Type of Statement						
			Unqualified						
8	3	4	Reviewed					1	3
15	10	10	Compiled		1	2	2	2	2
12	8	13	Tax Returns	1	3	2	3		1
11	11	6	Other	1	7	1	1	3	3
4/1/04-3/31/05 ALL	4/1/05-3/31/06 ALL	4/1/06-3/31/07 ALL		0-1MM	14 (4/1-9/30/06) 1-3MM	3-5MM	5-10MM	25 (10/1/06-3/31/07) 10-25MM	25MM & OVER
46	35	39	**NUMBER OF STATEMENTS**	2	11	5	6	6	9
%	%	%	**ASSETS**	%	%	%	%	%	%
8.7	10.2	13.4	Cash & Equivalents		11.3				
20.0	20.7	17.9	Trade Receivables (net)		12.1				
20.4	21.6	23.8	Inventory		15.9				
1.4	3.5	1.8	All Other Current		3.2				
50.5	56.0	56.9	Total Current		42.4				
36.4	31.9	26.2	Fixed Assets (net)		41.6				
3.1	3.9	9.2	Intangibles (net)		11.7				
10.0	8.3	7.7	All Other Non-Current		4.3				
100.0	100.0	100.0	Total		100.0				
			LIABILITIES						
8.1	11.5	9.9	Notes Payable-Short Term		6.7				
4.5	1.7	1.8	Cur. Mat.-L.T.D.		4.5				
20.0	23.7	18.1	Trade Payables		8.8				
.0	.0	.0	Income Taxes Payable		.0				
9.3	9.5	8.7	All Other Current		7.1				
42.0	46.4	38.6	Total Current		27.1				
25.5	29.9	22.8	Long-Term Debt		53.2				
.1	.1	.1	Deferred Taxes		.0				
13.0	7.5	2.5	All Other Non-Current		3.0				
19.4	16.1	35.9	Net Worth		16.7				
100.0	100.0	100.0	Total Liabilties & Net Worth		100.0				
			INCOME DATA						
100.0	100.0	100.0	Net Sales		100.0				
27.3	31.5	32.2	Gross Profit		40.4				
26.1	28.7	28.9	Operating Expenses		34.5				
1.2	2.8	3.3	Operating Profit		5.9				
.1	.8	.7	All Other Expenses (net)		2.5				
1.1	2.0	2.6	Profit Before Taxes		3.4				
			RATIOS						
2.1	2.0	3.4			4.2				
1.3	1.2	1.6	Current		2.0				
.8	.8	1.0			1.1				
1.2	1.3	2.1			3.0				
.7	.7	(38) .8	Quick		1.0				
.3	.2	.3			.2				
1 454.5	1 269.1	0 999.8			0 UND				
8 47.9	7 55.5	8 44.0	Sales/Receivables		9 41.8				
23 15.6	26 14.3	25 14.5			18 20.4				
8 47.4	12 31.4	11 32.2			5 69.6				
16 22.6	19 18.7	23 15.7	Cost of Sales/Inventory		14 25.7				
35 10.5	33 11.0	61 6.0			26 13.9				
6 58.6	10 36.8	8 47.4			0 UND				
14 26.5	14 26.3	18 19.8	Cost of Sales/Payables		13 28.0				
24 15.1	32 11.5	31 11.6			26 13.8				
19.0	17.0	9.3			6.5				
47.9	61.8	33.0	Sales/Working Capital		10.8				
-162.0	-33.8	-424.8			125.3				
12.0	11.0	11.8			6.2				
(39) 3.8	(31) 4.2	(34) 3.5	EBIT/Interest		1.2				
1.6	1.2	1.1			.5				
			Net Profit + Depr., Dep., Amort./Cur. Mat. L/T/D						
.2	.3	.2			1.4				
1.8	2.6	1.1	Fixed/Worth		-5.6				
280.1	-5.1	3.2			-.4				
1.3	1.6	.8			.8				
3.7	4.4	2.2	Debt/Worth		-7.8				
NM	-38.0	21.7			-3.9				
38.9	37.6	32.5	% Profit Before Taxes/Tangible Net Worth						
(35) 9.0	(25) 16.4	(31) 18.1							
.3	2.5	8.7							
16.0	12.3	13.8	% Profit Before Taxes/Total Assets		9.6				
4.1	5.5	6.3			.7				
.4	.6	.6			-3.8				
85.5	200.3	141.0			53.7				
15.2	19.5	15.2	Sales/Net Fixed Assets		9.0				
7.0	7.2	7.9			2.8				
7.7	7.4	6.8			5.8				
5.4	4.9	3.5	Sales/Total Assets		2.7				
2.6	2.7	2.2			1.5				
.4	.2	.4	% Depr., Dep., Amort./Sales						
(35) 1.2	(31) 1.2	(30) 1.0							
2.2	2.4	3.0							
1.1	1.2	1.1	% Officers', Directors' Owners' Comp/Sales						
(23) 1.9	(16) 3.2	(19) 2.0							
4.5	7.3	5.6							
1623012M	931213M	1037739M	Net Sales ($)	1237M	19650M	20764M	40638M	94587M	860863M
198285M	174136M	311661M	Total Assets ($)	112M	11308M	7381M	7165M	32964M	252731M

M = $ thousand   MM = $ million
See Pages 11 through 21 for Explanation of Ratios and Data

Current Data Sorted by Assets   Comparative Historical Data

0-500M	500M-2MM	2-10MM	10-50MM	50-100MM	100-250MM	Type of Statement	4/1/02-3/31/03 ALL	4/1/03-3/31/04 ALL
						Unqualified		
2		2	1			Reviewed	6	7
5	3	5				Compiled	10	8
1	2	2				Tax Returns	8	6
		1	1			Other	2	2
	5 (4/1-9/30/06)		20 (10/1/06-3/31/07)					
8	5	10	2			NUMBER OF STATEMENTS	26	26
%	%	%	%	%	%	**ASSETS**	%	%
		13.5				Cash & Equivalents	17.0	13.5
		29.0				Trade Receivables (net)	11.0	12.1
		15.1				Inventory	19.7	24.3
		5.3				All Other Current	1.9	5.4
		62.9	DATA		DATA	Total Current	49.6	55.2
		22.1	NOT		NOT	Fixed Assets (net)	41.6	36.7
		.1	AVAILABLE		AVAILABLE	Intangibles (net)	3.3	2.6
		14.9				All Other Non-Current	5.6	5.5
		100.0				Total	100.0	100.0
						LIABILITIES		
		10.1				Notes Payable-Short Term	6.4	7.8
		.5				Cur. Mat.-L.T.D.	3.4	5.1
		45.5				Trade Payables	21.6	24.3
		1.5				Income Taxes Payable	.1	.2
		21.8				All Other Current	10.8	8.0
		79.3				Total Current	42.3	45.4
		.1				Long-Term Debt	24.2	16.0
		.0				Deferred Taxes	.3	.4
		1.9				All Other Non-Current	5.8	13.9
		18.6				Net Worth	27.4	24.4
		100.0				Total Liabilities & Net Worth	100.0	100.0
						INCOME DATA		
		100.0				Net Sales	100.0	100.0
		23.0				Gross Profit	33.9	31.4
		21.8				Operating Expenses	29.6	28.9
		1.3				Operating Profit	4.3	2.5
		.1				All Other Expenses (net)	.5	.7
		1.2				Profit Before Taxes	3.8	1.8
						RATIOS		
		1.2					2.3	2.0
		.9				Current	1.2	1.6
		.3					.7	.8
		1.0					1.3	1.0
		.7				Quick	.6	.5
		.1					.2	.1
		0 UND					0 UND	0 UND
		4 92.5				Sales/Receivables	1 546.5	1 540.0
		33 11.1					15 24.8	20 18.2
		5 70.3					3 113.9	9 38.5
		7 49.4				Cost of Sales/Inventory	11 32.1	18 20.7
		11 32.2					21 17.2	45 8.2
		7 53.5					4 93.6	5 66.9
		32 11.5				Cost of Sales/Payables	9 41.1	19 19.6
		40 9.1					27 13.4	40 9.0
		103.3					34.3	15.9
		-90.8				Sales/Working Capital	126.4	44.1
		-22.2					-37.2	-48.5
							12.5	11.4
						EBIT/Interest	(18) 4.1	(21) 5.3
							.6	.5
						Net Profit + Depr., Dep., Amort./Cur. Mat. L/T/D		
		.3					.5	.5
		1.0				Fixed/Worth	1.9	1.1
		NM					NM	5.4
		1.5					.6	.7
		4.7				Debt/Worth	2.7	2.0
		NM					NM	8.9
							123.5	80.4
						% Profit Before Taxes/Tangible Net Worth	(20) 34.9	(22) 31.3
							5.0	6.1
		20.4					37.2	19.5
		2.1				% Profit Before Taxes/Total Assets	12.6	8.0
		-1.7					-.4	-1.5
		136.4					36.4	51.5
		51.2				Sales/Net Fixed Assets	21.6	18.5
		20.3					10.5	6.4
		10.2					10.9	9.4
		7.7				Sales/Total Assets	7.4	5.5
		5.9					4.2	2.8
		.2					.8	.7
		.4				% Depr., Dep., Amort./Sales	(22) 1.0	(24) 1.4
		.8					1.6	2.3
							1.4	1.4
						% Officers', Directors' Owners' Comp/Sales	(16) 3.2	(11) 2.5
							7.8	5.4
24122M	36247M	294224M	119267M			Net Sales ($)	496352M	861702M
1915M	6255M	32949M	32364M			Total Assets ($)	68140M	319351M

M = $ thousand   MM = $ million
See Pages 11 through 21 for Explanation of Ratios and Data

Comparative Historical Data   ## Current Data Sorted by Sales

Type of Statement	4/1/04-3/31/05 ALL	4/1/05-3/31/06 ALL	4/1/06-3/31/07 ALL		0-1MM	1-3MM	3-5MM	5-10MM	10-25MM	25MM & OVER
Unqualified	1	2	1						1	1
Reviewed	2	3	2					1	4	1
Compiled	8	7	7				1	2	1	1
Tax Returns	6	12	10		3	1	2	2		2
Other	4	6	5			1		1		
					5 (4/1-9/30/06)			20 (10/1/06-3/31/07)		
NUMBER OF STATEMENTS	21	30	25		3	2	3	6	6	5
	%	%	%		%	%	%	%	%	%
ASSETS										
Cash & Equivalents	17.8	12.9	17.0							
Trade Receivables (net)	14.7	18.4	19.2							
Inventory	19.5	19.6	20.7							
All Other Current	3.9	3.3	2.3							
Total Current	55.8	54.3	59.3							
Fixed Assets (net)	35.2	32.2	25.2							
Intangibles (net)	4.5	8.3	3.0							
All Other Non-Current	4.4	5.2	12.5							
Total	100.0	100.0	100.0							
LIABILITIES										
Notes Payable-Short Term	4.4	12.0	9.4							
Cur. Mat.-L.T.D.	3.3	1.4	.3							
Trade Payables	30.9	29.1	30.5							
Income Taxes Payable	.2	.4	.6							
All Other Current	14.6	12.6	21.6							
Total Current	53.4	55.5	62.4							
Long-Term Debt	18.6	10.4	11.0							
Deferred Taxes	.4	.4	.0							
All Other Non-Current	16.2	10.4	3.6							
Net Worth	11.4	23.4	23.0							
Total Liabilities & Net Worth	100.0	100.0	100.0							
INCOME DATA										
Net Sales	100.0	100.0	100.0							
Gross Profit	29.2	26.7	26.2							
Operating Expenses	28.4	24.6	24.9							
Operating Profit	.8	2.1	1.3							
All Other Expenses (net)	.4	.2	-.6							
Profit Before Taxes	.4	2.0	2.0							
RATIOS										
Current	2.3	1.8	1.7							
	1.1	1.1	1.1							
	.9	.7	.7							
Quick	1.5	1.3	1.1							
	.8	(27) .9	.7							
	.1	.0	.1							
Sales/Receivables	0 UND	0 UND	0 UND							
	0 933.4	1 354.7	2 187.0							
	13 29.0	21 17.0	24 14.9							
Cost of Sales/Inventory	5 77.7	5 69.1	4 82.2							
	10 35.1	10 37.6	8 46.8							
	21 17.7	22 16.3	19 18.9							
Cost of Sales/Payables	12 30.5	7 51.7	0 UND							
	23 16.0	19 19.4	13 28.4							
	32 11.3	35 10.4	36 10.3							
Sales/Working Capital	32.6	26.7	43.0							
	169.0	544.3	114.8							
	-89.8	-49.8	-40.5							
EBIT/Interest	18.4	13.6	22.5							
	(17) 2.6	(22) 3.0	(17) 4.4							
	-1.9	-.7	-1.7							
Net Profit + Depr., Dep., Amort./Cur. Mat. L/T/D										
Fixed/Worth	.8	.5	.3							
	1.7	1.5	1.1							
	NM	-2.7	UND							
Debt/Worth	1.4	1.1	1.3							
	5.7	2.8	4.4							
	NM	-8.1	UND							
% Profit Before Taxes/Tangible Net Worth	342.1	87.6	109.7							
	(16) 19.8	(21) 30.7	(19) 34.9							
	5.3	1.4	6.7							
% Profit Before Taxes/Total Assets	25.2	25.8	23.2							
	4.4	7.7	11.9							
	-7.1	-1.6	-2.2							
Sales/Net Fixed Assets	51.0	67.0	117.1							
	31.6	31.9	33.1							
	8.4	9.5	15.0							
Sales/Total Assets	10.5	8.8	9.2							
	6.6	6.3	7.0							
	4.3	4.4	5.0							
% Depr., Dep., Amort./Sales	.4	.2	.3							
	(19) .8	(27) .6	(22) .5							
	1.6	1.3	1.2							
% Officers', Directors' Owners' Comp/Sales		.7	1.0							
	(16)	1.1	(10) 2.5							
		2.6	5.8							
Net Sales ($)	272561M	1009945M	473860M		1651M	4441M	13691M	50001M	124606M	279470M
Total Assets ($)	40640M	225199M	73483M		398M	531M	1477M	8523M	15281M	47273M

M = $ thousand   MM = $ million
See Pages 11 through 21 for Explanation of Ratios and Data

RETAIL—Confectionery and Nut Stores NAICS 445292 (SIC 5145, 5441)

	Current Data Sorted by Assets							Comparative Historical Data	

					2		2	**Type of Statement**		
				1				Unqualified	3	4
	3	1		1				Reviewed	4	3
	8	5				2		Compiled	4	6
		4		1	2		1	Tax Returns	16	9
		3 (4/1-9/30/06)			28 (10/1/06-3/31/07)			Other	9	8
									4/1/02-3/31/03	4/1/03-3/31/04
	0-500M	500M-2MM	2-10MM	10-50MM	50-100MM	100-250MM			ALL	ALL
	11	10	3	4	2	1		NUMBER OF STATEMENTS	36	30
	%	%	%	%	%	%		**ASSETS**	%	%
	37.9	13.8						Cash & Equivalents	11.1	12.4
	3.8	6.8						Trade Receivables (net)	9.0	9.0
	14.1	10.8						Inventory	26.6	22.9
	1.0	1.1						All Other Current	1.5	3.0
	56.9	32.5						Total Current	48.3	47.4
	23.9	55.5						Fixed Assets (net)	34.9	38.6
	9.9	6.0						Intangibles (net)	9.3	7.0
	9.1	6.0						All Other Non-Current	7.5	7.1
	100.0	100.0						Total	100.0	100.0
								LIABILITIES		
	14.1	6.0						Notes Payable-Short Term	9.0	8.5
	4.7	6.4						Cur. Mat.-L.T.D.	3.8	4.9
	14.2	2.8						Trade Payables	13.9	15.2
	.2	.0						Income Taxes Payable	.1	.1
	11.9	11.2						All Other Current	6.1	9.9
	45.1	26.3						Total Current	32.8	38.7
	43.8	27.2						Long-Term Debt	29.6	22.6
	.0	.0						Deferred Taxes	.3	.6
	.0	.0						All Other Non-Current	10.5	6.2
	11.1	46.4						Net Worth	26.9	32.1
	100.0	100.0						Total Liabilties & Net Worth	100.0	100.0
								INCOME DATA		
	100.0	100.0						Net Sales	100.0	100.0
	57.8	49.2						Gross Profit	53.2	47.8
	46.5	38.2						Operating Expenses	49.9	45.4
	11.4	11.0						Operating Profit	3.4	2.4
	1.2	1.7						All Other Expenses (net)	1.2	1.0
	10.1	9.3						Profit Before Taxes	2.2	1.5
								RATIOS		
	9.6	3.6							2.7	2.0
	.9	2.1						Current	1.6	1.1
	.8	.9							.8	.9
	9.0	2.3							1.2	.9
	.7	1.3						Quick	.5 (29)	.7
	.3	.2							.3	.1
	0 UND	0 UND							0 UND	0 UND
	0 UND	0 UND						Sales/Receivables	2 195.2	1 366.0
	1 512.0	12 31.5							20 18.6	18 20.7
	2 182.0	0 UND							18 20.3	21 17.3
	10 37.0	14 25.7						Cost of Sales/Inventory	43 8.4	50 7.3
	37 9.8	50 7.2							121 3.0	94 3.9
	0 UND	0 UND							11 32.5	9 42.0
	0 UND	8 44.2						Cost of Sales/Payables	23 15.9	17 21.3
	44 8.4	13 27.8							54 6.8	68 5.3
	14.0	4.8							8.5	15.6
	-999.8	23.3						Sales/Working Capital	22.4	61.6
	-56.2	NM							-58.7	-45.6
									10.8	13.5
								EBIT/Interest	(32) 2.5	(26) 1.4
									.6	-.9
								Net Profit + Depr., Dep., Amort./Cur. Mat. L/T/D		
	.0	.6							.4	.4
	.9	1.1						Fixed/Worth	1.3	1.6
	-.1	NM							4.0	9.7
	.2	.6							1.0	.8
	32.8	1.2						Debt/Worth	3.6	2.3
	-3.2	NM							UND	26.9
									40.6	44.4
								% Profit Before Taxes/Tangible Net Worth	(27) 20.1	(24) 10.0
									9.6	.0
	96.0	37.6							11.6	18.5
	27.4	10.7						% Profit Before Taxes/Total Assets	2.9	3.0
	2.7	.8							-2.3	-4.4
	360.5	10.4							32.7	21.0
	56.9	4.2						Sales/Net Fixed Assets	6.8	6.9
	4.9	2.0							4.2	3.7
	6.8	2.6							4.5	5.0
	3.5	1.9						Sales/Total Assets	2.5	2.6
	2.2	1.2							2.0	1.8
									.9	.6
								% Depr., Dep., Amort./Sales	(34) 2.4	(29) 1.9
									4.4	3.0
									2.7	5.7
								% Officers', Directors' Owners' Comp/Sales	(14) 3.7	(14) 9.2
									11.0	15.6
	10378M	20349M	32219M	259534M	240786M	399015M		Net Sales ($)	458803M	424666M
	2679M	10548M	13471M	75369M	161524M	109526M		Total Assets ($)	176495M	126725M

© RMA 2007

M = $ thousand   MM = $ million
See Pages 11 through 21 for Explanation of Ratios and Data

Comparative Historical Data   ## Current Data Sorted by Sales

					Type of Statement						
4		2		4	Unqualified					1	4
3		3		1	Reviewed				1		
2		10		5	Compiled		4		1		
11		6		13	Tax Returns	6	7				
10		7		8	Other	1		1			3
4/1/04-		4/1/05-		4/1/06-			3 (4/1-9/30/06)		28 (10/1/06-3/31/07)		
3/31/05		3/31/06		3/31/07							
ALL		ALL		ALL		0-1MM	1-3MM	3-5MM	5-10MM	10-25MM	25MM & OVER
30		28		31	NUMBER OF STATEMENTS	7	13	1	2	1	7
%		%		%	ASSETS	%	%	%	%	%	%
9.6		12.4		19.7	Cash & Equivalents		32.2				
9.7		12.2		8.4	Trade Receivables (net)		3.5				
24.0		24.4		17.0	Inventory		9.6				
3.1		3.7		2.2	All Other Current		1.1				
46.5		52.6		47.4	Total Current		46.5				
38.6		34.6		39.2	Fixed Assets (net)		38.1				
5.7		6.3		7.2	Intangibles (net)		6.3				
9.3		6.5		6.2	All Other Non-Current		9.1				
100.0		100.0		100.0	Total		100.0				
					LIABILITIES						
10.5		16.0		10.1	Notes Payable-Short Term		.2				
4.2		3.7		4.0	Cur. Mat.-L.T.D.		4.6				
14.8		13.4		11.7	Trade Payables		8.2				
.3		.4		.1	Income Taxes Payable		.0				
9.6		9.4		11.1	All Other Current		6.0				
39.3		42.9		37.0	Total Current		18.9				
33.8		21.9		29.9	Long-Term Debt		39.4				
.7		.2		.0	Deferred Taxes		.0				
19.1		16.7		.6	All Other Non-Current		.0				
7.1		18.3		32.6	Net Worth		41.6				
100.0		100.0		100.0	Total Liabilties & Net Worth		100.0				
					INCOME DATA						
100.0		100.0		100.0	Net Sales		100.0				
50.6M		45.8		49.0	Gross Profit		52.9				
50.4		42.3		40.0	Operating Expenses		38.1				
.2		3.5		8.9	Operating Profit		14.8				
1.2		.7		1.2	All Other Expenses (net)		1.2				
-1.0		2.8		7.8	Profit Before Taxes		13.6				
					RATIOS						
2.4		2.1		3.3			6.0				
1.3		1.4		1.4	Current		3.3				
.7		1.0		.9			1.3				
1.2		1.2		1.8			5.6				
.5		.6		.7	Quick		1.7				
.1		.2		.3			.5				
0	UND	0	UND	0	UND		0	UND			
1	353.5	4	84.7	0	UND	Sales/Receivables	0	UND			
19	18.9	21	17.0	9	39.3		1	289.7			
16	23.2	24	15.4	8	47.2		2	160.3			
54	6.8	50	7.3	35	10.5	Cost of Sales/Inventory	10	37.0			
99	3.7	89	4.1	59	6.2		33	11.1			
9	38.5	6	56.2	0	UND		0	UND			
22	16.7	20	18.4	9	39.7	Cost of Sales/Payables	8	47.2			
60	6.1	47	7.8	39	9.4		23	15.7			
10.6		11.2		7.7			4.5				
37.5		26.9		44.4	Sales/Working Capital		16.1				
-35.0		NM		-56.2			NM				
	11.5		13.1		13.4						
(28)	2.3	(25)	3.4	(26)	3.1	EBIT/Interest					
	-.6		1.3		1.4						
					Net Profit + Depr., Dep., Amort./Cur. Mat. L/T/D						
.4		.4		.3			.2				
1.5		1.6		1.1	Fixed/Worth		.6				
-11.6		NM		25.1			1.9				
.9		1.2		.4			.2				
2.4		3.3		1.5	Debt/Worth		.6				
-25.2		NM		92.0			1.4				
	51.9		46.1		84.5			89.5			
(22)	19.6	(21)	26.2	(24)	38.4	% Profit Before Taxes/Tangible Net Worth	(11)	75.4			
	5.5		5.9		2.4			15.5			
11.4		15.0		39.7			62.4				
4.3		6.0		10.7	% Profit Before Taxes/Total Assets		37.2				
-2.7		1.1		1.0			10.7				
24.3		36.8		56.9			157.7				
6.2		8.4		5.9	Sales/Net Fixed Assets		6.2				
4.2		4.7		2.8			3.3				
4.0		4.0		4.4			6.1				
2.8		2.9		2.3	Sales/Total Assets		2.2				
1.7		1.8		1.6			1.9				
	.7		.9		.8						
(28)	2.5	(20)	2.0	(23)	2.0	% Depr., Dep., Amort./Sales					
	4.5		3.7		4.3						
			2.6		2.3						
		(15)	3.9	(11)	4.0	% Officers', Directors' Owners' Comp/Sales					
			8.0		8.2						
529042M		691134M		962281M	Net Sales ($)	4154M	22799M	3774M	16505M	15714M	899335M
237813M		218982M		373117M	Total Assets ($)	1922M	9666M	1639M	8362M	5109M	346419M

M = $ thousand   MM = $ million
See Pages 11 through 21 for Explanation of Ratios and Data

Current Data Sorted by Assets — Comparative Historical Data

	0-500M	500M-2MM	2-10MM	10-50MM	50-100MM	100-250MM	Type of Statement	4/1/02-3/31/03 ALL	4/1/03-3/31/04 ALL
	1		3	5	1	2	Unqualified	11	12
	2	3	12	1			Reviewed	11	15
	10	8	6				Compiled	14	26
	75	35	3				Tax Returns	39	55
	22	14	11	7	2		Other	38	41
	30 (4/1-9/30/06)			193 (10/1/06-3/31/07)					
NUMBER OF STATEMENTS	110	60	35	13	3	2		113	149
	%	%	%	%	%	%	**ASSETS**	%	%
	16.1	9.9	7.5	7.5			Cash & Equivalents	12.0	13.6
	2.6	7.8	14.9	4.7			Trade Receivables (net)	8.1	8.0
	13.0	16.3	25.2	17.3			Inventory	21.6	20.4
	3.5	2.7	5.0	3.7			All Other Current	1.4	2.4
	35.1	36.7	52.5	33.3			Total Current	43.1	44.5
	41.0	43.6	33.2	34.3			Fixed Assets (net)	40.4	37.3
	14.8	10.3	10.2	26.9			Intangibles (net)	9.4	10.6
	9.0	9.4	4.1	5.5			All Other Non-Current	7.1	7.6
	100.0	100.0	100.0	100.0			Total	100.0	100.0
							LIABILITIES		
	7.7	6.2	11.3	5.7			Notes Payable-Short Term	4.8	7.6
	4.5	7.9	3.9	7.2			Cur. Mat.-L.T.D.	3.4	5.4
	10.6	15.7	18.5	13.3			Trade Payables	14.1	12.6
	.2	.0	.1	.2			Income Taxes Payable	.1	.3
	19.6	11.0	9.3	10.5			All Other Current	12.4	13.5
	42.6	40.8	43.1	36.9			Total Current	34.9	39.4
	28.4	39.5	19.9	21.8			Long-Term Debt	29.8	29.0
	.0	.1	.1	1.4			Deferred Taxes	.2	.2
	21.4	3.1	3.8	17.6			All Other Non-Current	7.4	7.5
	7.5	16.5	33.0	22.3			Net Worth	27.7	23.9
	100.0	100.0	100.0	100.0			Total Liabilities & Net Worth	100.0	100.0
							INCOME DATA		
	100.0	100.0	100.0	100.0			Net Sales	100.0	100.0
	60.8	44.8	35.8	47.4			Gross Profit	43.7	44.2
	57.5	42.4	31.1	41.7			Operating Expenses	39.4	40.6
	3.3	2.4	4.7	5.7			Operating Profit	4.2	3.6
	.9	1.5	1.1	1.6			All Other Expenses (net)	1.9	.8
	2.4	.9	3.7	4.1			Profit Before Taxes	2.3	2.8
							RATIOS		
	2.8	1.8	2.0	1.6			Current	2.1	2.3
	1.2	1.0	1.2	1.1				1.4	1.3
	.4	.4	.6	.5				.8	.5
	1.6	1.2	1.0	.7			Quick	1.1	1.2
(107)	.5	.4	.5	.3			(112)	.6	.5
	.1	.2	.2	.1				.3	.2
	0 UND	0 UND	1 270.0	1 331.0			Sales/Receivables	0 UND	0 UND
	0 UND	1 316.1	8 43.8	2 192.8				2 166.5	1 514.7
	0 UND	10 37.3	29 12.5	13 28.0				13 28.2	9 40.3
	6 63.4	9 41.0	11 34.1	16 23.3			Cost of Sales/Inventory	10 36.3	9 40.8
	12 31.1	17 21.7	32 11.4	27 13.5				21 17.0	21 17.6
	33 11.2	42 8.7	86 4.2	106 3.4				55 6.7	55 6.7
	0 UND	1 280.3	11 32.0	21 17.6			Cost of Sales/Payables	7 51.6	5 70.8
	3 142.3	16 23.1	24 15.0	51 7.2				19 18.8	16 22.1
	31 11.9	33 11.1	48 7.5	57 6.5				36 10.3	39 9.3
	16.5	16.4	10.5	14.8			Sales/Working Capital	12.8	11.5
	204.3	380.3	44.2	54.9				43.5	54.1
	-14.6	-12.2	-19.2	-13.5				-59.3	-18.3
	10.6	8.9	6.5	5.3			EBIT/Interest	7.4	10.0
(72)	2.5	(57) 3.3	(32) 3.1	2.2			(87) 1.8	(127) 2.7
	-.4	.6	1.1	1.1				.6	.6
							Net Profit + Depr., Dep., Amort./Cur. Mat. L/T/D	36.4	3.7
								(10) 3.1 (17) 1.6	
								1.7	.7
	.6	.6	.3	2.7			Fixed/Worth	.5	.5
	5.0	3.6	1.5	-6.2				1.6	1.6
	-1.6	-3.5	17.8	-.4				11.0	UND
	.9	1.4	1.4	3.0			Debt/Worth	1.0	1.1
	30.0	4.1	2.6	-11.6				2.4	3.0
	-3.2	-5.8	19.3	-2.3				104.3	-104.0
	188.3	53.0	104.3				% Profit Before Taxes/Tangible Net Worth	60.5	58.9
(60)	56.2	(38) 29.4	(29) 28.3				(86) 27.5	(111) 25.6
	7.3	13.7	11.1					1.0	8.1
	36.5	14.8	21.2	9.0			% Profit Before Taxes/Total Assets	19.5	17.5
	11.3	4.4	6.5	3.9				5.2	6.6
	-6.0	-2.6	.4	1.3				-1.1	-1.2
	36.7	28.5	26.5	13.4			Sales/Net Fixed Assets	26.0	26.6
	13.4	6.5	14.1	8.5				8.9	9.8
	4.8	2.9	5.7	4.8				4.1	4.6
	6.2	4.7	5.4	3.5			Sales/Total Assets	5.2	4.9
	3.8	2.5	3.5	2.2				2.9	3.0
	2.2	1.6	1.7	1.1				1.9	1.9
	1.5	.7	.6	1.4			% Depr., Dep., Amort./Sales	1.1	1.1
(74)	2.3	(56) 2.5	(30) 1.3	1.9			(91) 2.3	(128) 2.1
	4.3	4.5	2.4	2.9				4.6	5.2
	3.0	1.1	.8				% Officers', Directors' Owners' Comp/Sales	1.7	1.3
(49)	5.9	(31) 2.1	(12) 1.3				(49) 3.2	(58) 3.6
	10.7	3.3	2.6					7.1	6.9
	98899M	200304M	639633M	862597M	385343M	388865M	Net Sales ($)	3984586M	8270538M
	21422M	60258M	164057M	323369M	161406M	284620M	Total Assets ($)	1305885M	1823912M

M = $ thousand   MM = $ million
See Pages 11 through 21 for Explanation of Ratios and Data

Comparative Historical Data   Current Data Sorted by Sales

				Type of Statement						
12	8	12		Unqualified	1	1			2	8
10	13	18		Reviewed	1	3		4	7	3
20	19	24		Compiled	7	6	2	5	2	2
67	90	113		Tax Returns	74	24	6	7	1	1
35	41	56		Other	16	10	6	10	5	9
4/1/04-	4/1/05-	4/1/06-				30 (4/1-9/30/06)			193 (10/1/06-3/31/07)	
3/31/05	3/31/06	3/31/07			0-1MM	1-3MM	3-5MM	5-10MM	10-25MM	25MM & OVER
ALL	ALL	ALL								
144	171	223		NUMBER OF STATEMENTS	99	44	14	26	17	23
%	%	%		ASSETS	%	%	%	%	%	%
11.5	13.8	12.8		Cash & Equivalents	14.7	12.3	13.6	10.8	5.9	12.2
7.4	6.8	6.1		Trade Receivables (net)	1.5	5.5	11.5	13.4	17.1	7.5
15.6	17.3	16.0		Inventory	8.9	19.7	13.3	29.7	22.6	20.3
3.0	2.3	3.5		All Other Current	4.1	2.2	.8	4.3	4.2	4.1
37.5	40.2	38.4		Total Current	29.2	39.7	39.1	58.2	49.8	44.1
41.7	37.2	39.8		Fixed Assets (net)	44.9	40.2	46.2	27.3	28.2	36.0
11.7	15.7	13.8		Intangibles (net)	17.0	11.7	8.9	4.4	17.5	14.6
9.1	6.9	8.0		All Other Non-Current	8.9	8.5	5.9	10.1	4.5	5.3
100.0	100.0	100.0		Total	100.0	100.0	100.0	100.0	100.0	100.0
				LIABILITIES						
10.0	8.9	7.5		Notes Payable-Short Term	6.9	11.6	7.0	3.1	15.3	2.1
5.8	5.7	5.4		Cur. Mat.-L.T.D.	5.4	6.9	2.6	5.2	3.3	6.1
12.4	16.0	13.3		Trade Payables	8.0	13.9	23.2	19.4	20.2	17.3
.2	.4	.2		Income Taxes Payable	.2	.1	.0	.1	.0	.6
12.0	16.4	14.9		All Other Current	22.4	7.6	8.6	10.4	10.1	9.4
40.5	47.3	41.4		Total Current	42.9	40.1	41.4	38.2	49.0	35.5
29.5	26.1	29.8		Long-Term Debt	33.6	26.9	30.6	33.9	18.6	22.0
.3	.2	.2		Deferred Taxes	.0	.0	.6	.0	.1	1.3
13.8	10.9	13.0		All Other Non-Current	21.0	8.0	6.9	3.9	3.1	10.1
15.9	15.5	15.5		Net Worth	2.5	25.0	20.4	23.9	29.2	31.1
100.0	100.0	100.0		Total Liabilties & Net Worth	100.0	100.0	100.0	100.0	100.0	100.0
				INCOME DATA						
100.0	100.0	100.0		Net Sales	100.0	100.0	100.0	100.0	100.0	100.0
51.5	50.2	51.3		Gross Profit	62.2	52.5	45.9	35.8	36.2	34.4
47.1	45.9	47.8		Operating Expenses	59.1	48.4	43.2	32.3	30.8	31.2
4.4	4.3	3.5		Operating Profit	3.1	4.1	2.7	3.5	5.4	3.1
1.5	1.1	1.2		All Other Expenses (net)	1.6	.9	1.5	.4	1.2	.4
3.0	3.1	2.3		Profit Before Taxes	1.5	3.2	1.2	3.1	4.2	2.7
				RATIOS						
2.0	2.1	2.0			2.5	2.1	1.3	6.1	1.6	1.8
1.1	1.1	1.2		Current	.8	1.2	1.1	1.7	.8	1.4
.5	.4	.4			.3	.6	.7	.9	.5	1.1
1.2	1.2	1.2			1.5	1.5	1.2	1.7	.9	1.2
.6	.5 (220)	.5		Quick	(96) .3	.5	.6	.8	.4	.5
.2	.1	.1			.1	.1	.3	.3	.1	.1
0 UND	0 UND	0 UND			0 UND	0 UND	0 UND	0 UND	0 UND	2 237.5
1 413.6	0 UND	0 UND		Sales/Receivables	0 UND	0 UND	10 35.7	2 161.3	7 49.4	3 122.1
8 43.4	6 64.3	5 70.2			0 UND	3 110.3	30 12.2	31 11.6	29 12.7	8 43.8
8 44.6	6 56.9	7 49.7			6 64.8	7 49.5	4 100.9	9 40.2	7 52.1	14 25.2
14 25.7	16 23.0	16 23.2		Cost of Sales/Inventory	12 30.8	17 21.1	16 22.6	24 15.2	16 23.2	24 15.3
39 9.3	39 9.4	45 8.1			27 13.3	43 6.8	54 6.8	73 5.0	62 6.9	62 5.9
4 92.9	3 141.0	0 UND			0 UND	0 876.6	15 24.9	8 48.5	13 28.4	13 27.3
20 18.6	18 20.3	13 27.3		Cost of Sales/Payables	0 966.0	16 23.1	38 9.6	20 18.3	24 15.0	26 14.0
40 9.2	43 8.6	35 10.4			28 13.2	43 8.5	94 3.9	37 9.9	61 5.9	46 7.9
19.4	19.1	15.9			16.5	14.5	29.7	10.4	13.8	14.8
105.3	223.5	126.8		Sales/Working Capital	-83.0	143.4	156.6	25.7	-103.6	33.1
-18.9	-13.6	-15.8			-9.7	-18.8	-52.5	-276.9	-11.1	150.1
8.0	8.5	8.3			6.9	10.2	6.0	13.3	5.6	16.0
(118) 3.4	(133) 3.1	(177) 2.8		EBIT/Interest	(66) 1.0	(39) 3.4	2.6	(22) 3.7	(15) 3.9	(21) 2.8
1.2	.8	.6			-.7	1.3	.0	1.6	1.2	1.2
15.9	6.3	3.0		Net Profit + Depr., Dep.,						
(15) 2.5	(17) 1.5	(14) 1.9		Amort./Cur. Mat. L/T/D						
1.1	.7	1.2								
.7	.7	.6			.8	.6	.7	.2	.2	.6
2.0	3.3	3.9		Fixed/Worth	UND	3.9	8.5	.6	2.2	3.0
-2.4	-1.4	-1.9			-1.3	-2.9	-5.1	1.7	-1.5	-1.6
1.0	1.0	1.2			1.4	.8	1.5	.7	1.9	.9
3.1	5.9	7.2		Debt/Worth	-15.8	6.2	21.2	2.0	5.5	5.4
-5.5	-3.7	-3.8			-2.6	-6.9	-9.5	3.9	-4.4	-3.5
88.5	95.8	117.6		% Profit Before Taxes/Tangible	154.2	61.8		74.8	57.5	85.4
(97) 31.3	(103) 32.4	(135) 34.7		Net Worth	(47) 57.7	(29) 35.9	(23) 26.2	(12) 22.7	(15) 34.7	
11.4	13.9	9.8			7.6	11.1		11.6	11.2	9.8
22.1	23.7	23.4		% Profit Before Taxes/Total	33.3	22.9	13.9	20.5	19.0	16.3
7.8	7.8	6.7		Assets	4.9	10.1	2.3	7.2	5.6	6.6
.6	-.7	-1.8			-7.1	.7	-6.1	3.0	2.3	1.9
22.2	35.0	27.7			22.7	32.7	14.8	103.8	58.9	15.6
11.2	15.0	11.2		Sales/Net Fixed Assets	6.7	13.9	6.3	22.6	20.9	13.6
4.3	5.1	3.9			2.9	5.2	3.4	7.1	7.9	5.7
5.5	6.4	5.1			4.4	5.7	4.8	6.8	5.7	5.4
3.3	3.3	3.2		Sales/Total Assets	2.7	3.8	2.5	4.1	3.7	3.2
2.0	1.9	1.8			1.5	2.3	2.1	1.9	2.4	2.2
1.0	.7	1.2			1.8	.6	1.2	.3	.6	.8
(122) 2.1	(142) 1.9	(175) 2.1		% Depr., Dep., Amort./Sales	(70) 3.3	(38) 2.2	(11) 2.1	(24) .9	(12) 1.2	(20) 1.6
5.0	4.2	4.1			6.1	3.2	4.7	1.7	2.7	2.4
1.5	2.4	1.3		% Officers', Directors'	2.9	2.1		.5		
(56) 3.4	(80) 4.1	(94) 3.0		Owners' Comp/Sales	(47) 5.4	(19) 3.3		(12) 1.3		
8.6	7.3	8.2			11.9	4.8		3.0		
9690089M	4335941M	2575641M		Net Sales ($)	49621M	83682M	54236M	185385M	270664M	1932053M
2054859M	1219144M	1015132M		Total Assets ($)	24741M	33045M	21131M	58511M	102046M	775658M

M = $ thousand   MM = $ million
See Pages 11 through 21 for Explanation of Ratios and Data

Current Data Sorted by Assets

Comparative Historical Data

						Type of Statement		
	2	5	4		3	Unqualified	12	11
	8	7	4			Reviewed	23	23
23	22	9	1			Compiled	67	67
73	74	10	1	1		Tax Returns	107	130
8	20	17	4	2	1	Other	49	48
	53 (4/1-9/30/06)			245 (10/1/06-3/31/07)			4/1/02-3/31/03	4/1/03-3/31/04
0-500M	500M-2MM	2-10MM	10-50MM	50-100MM	100-250MM		ALL	ALL
104	126	48	13	3	4	NUMBER OF STATEMENTS	258	279
%	%	%	%	%	%	ASSETS	%	%
13.8	11.7	9.7	6.3			Cash & Equivalents	11.9	10.5
.9	2.0	4.2	7.1			Trade Receivables (net)	2.0	2.0
49.0	45.2	48.6	45.7			Inventory	48.5	50.2
1.5	2.7	2.0	1.1			All Other Current	1.0	1.1
65.2	61.6	64.5	60.1			Total Current	63.4	63.8
15.6	16.5	21.3	17.3			Fixed Assets (net)	18.2	17.8
15.7	14.2	7.9	10.5			Intangibles (net)	12.2	11.1
3.5	7.6	6.3	12.1			All Other Non-Current	6.1	7.3
100.0	100.0	100.0	100.0			Total	100.0	100.0
						LIABILITIES		
9.4	5.3	9.2	9.2			Notes Payable-Short Term	8.1	8.9
4.9	2.5	3.0	1.3			Cur. Mat.-L.T.D.	3.5	2.9
12.4	21.6	22.8	23.8			Trade Payables	20.6	20.2
.5	.1	.2	.1			Income Taxes Payable	.2	.5
11.1	12.7	13.6	9.9			All Other Current	10.4	10.8
38.3	42.1	48.7	44.3			Total Current	42.8	43.3
22.8	24.9	13.0	14.8			Long-Term Debt	20.6	23.1
.0	.5	.1	.0			Deferred Taxes	.0	.0
7.7	6.1	6.1	4.0			All Other Non-Current	9.3	8.2
31.2	26.5	32.1	37.0			Net Worth	27.2	25.4
100.0	100.0	100.0	100.0			Total Liabilities & Net Worth	100.0	100.0
						INCOME DATA		
100.0	100.0	100.0	100.0			Net Sales	100.0	100.0
23.4	23.8	24.4	24.8			Gross Profit	23.0	23.3
22.1	20.8	21.7	21.3			Operating Expenses	20.9	21.7
1.4	3.0	2.7	3.5			Operating Profit	2.1	1.6
-.5	.5	.1	.4			All Other Expenses (net)	.1	-.3
1.9	2.5	2.6	3.0			Profit Before Taxes	2.0	1.9
						RATIOS		
6.1	3.3	2.3	1.7				3.2	3.0
2.4	1.5	1.5	1.4			Current	1.6	1.6
1.2	1.0	1.0	.9				1.0	1.0
1.3	.8	.6	.4				.8	.8
(103) .3	(125) .3	.3	.2			Quick	(254) .3	(275) .3
.1	.1	.1	.2				.1	.1
0 UND	0 UND	0 UND	0 999.8				0 UND	0 UND
0 UND	0 UND	1 418.7	4 94.9			Sales/Receivables	0 UND	0 UND
0 UND	1 621.4	4 85.6	7 54.2				1 288.4	2 208.0
31 11.9	42 8.7	46 7.9	56 6.5				38 9.7	37 9.9
55 6.7	62 5.9	67 5.5	72 5.1			Cost of Sales/Inventory	53 6.9	55 6.6
76 4.8	83 4.4	85 4.3	104 3.5				72 5.1	80 4.6
0 UND	6 60.2	15 24.5	18 19.9				0 852.8	1 495.0
2 147.9	23 15.6	30 12.1	33 11.1			Cost of Sales/Payables	19 19.1	19 19.2
27 13.5	45 8.1	39 9.3	60 6.0				37 9.8	39 9.3
6.8	8.5	9.6	9.9				9.6	9.0
16.8	15.4	15.5	16.4			Sales/Working Capital	17.8	19.3
68.5	127.6	NM	-135.5				486.0	441.2
7.1	7.9	15.3	7.8				9.0	8.0
(74) 2.7	(105) 3.5	(43) 3.6	(12) 5.4			EBIT/Interest	(209) 3.7	(231) 3.1
-.2	1.1	1.3	3.3				1.3	1.0
						Net Profit + Depr., Dep.,	5.5	4.7
						Amort./Cur. Mat. L/T/D	(31) 3.5	(24) 2.4
							1.1	.9
.1	.2	.3	.2				.2	.2
.6	.8	.7	.7			Fixed/Worth	.8	.9
-1.1	-1.6	4.0	2.0				-3.9	-3.5
.5	1.0	1.0	1.2				1.2	1.2
2.9	4.0	2.5	2.5			Debt/Worth	3.3	3.7
-4.8	-4.8	15.3	18.4				-15.1	-17.1
46.4	50.8	41.1	72.1			% Profit Before Taxes/Tangible	66.0	66.8
(65) 13.7	(83) 22.9	(37) 15.5	(12) 38.3			Net Worth	(180) 23.6	(198) 30.8
-3.5	6.4	5.8	21.0				7.4	8.0
13.8	16.6	14.6	12.5			% Profit Before Taxes/Total	15.6	14.2
5.2	6.7	5.0	8.3			Assets	6.3	5.7
-2.3	.6	1.4	5.2				.9	.6
230.8	115.3	53.1	76.9				130.6	111.1
45.0	40.5	21.8	30.9			Sales/Net Fixed Assets	37.8	39.3
18.1	15.9	10.2	10.2				14.3	14.7
6.1	4.8	4.1	3.8				5.7	5.4
4.3	3.2	3.2	3.2			Sales/Total Assets	4.0	3.9
2.7	2.4	2.5	2.0				2.7	2.8
.3	.3	.3	.3				.4	.3
(71) 1.0	(100) .7	(43) .8	(11) .8			% Depr., Dep., Amort./Sales	(196) .8	(218) .8
1.9	1.7	1.2	1.7				1.6	1.4
2.7	1.3	1.3				% Officers', Directors'	1.6	1.6
(61) 3.5	(78) 2.2	(18) 1.8				Owners' Comp/Sales	(141) 2.7	(158) 2.4
5.0	3.6	2.3					3.9	4.1
123908M	461050M	703389M	968671M	385871M	2349804M	Net Sales ($)	2716956M	2481219M
27527M	124387M	197599M	294609M	197161M	762971M	Total Assets ($)	825839M	699740M

© RMA 2007

M = $ thousand   MM = $ million
See Pages 11 through 21 for Explanation of Ratios and Data

Comparative Historical Data | Current Data Sorted by Sales

8	10	14	Type of Statement						
8	10	14	Unqualified		1	1		3	9
25	22	19	Reviewed			1		7	3
50	50	55	Compiled	8	19	10	13	3	2
131	121	158	Tax Returns	43	74	19	17	4	1
45	47	52	Other	5	13	7	7	14	6
4/1/04-3/31/05	4/1/05-3/31/06	4/1/06-3/31/07			53 (4/1-9/30/06)		245 (10/1/06-3/31/07)		
ALL	ALL	ALL		0-1MM	1-3MM	3-5MM	5-10MM	10-25MM	25MM & OVER
259	250	298	NUMBER OF STATEMENTS	56	107	38	45	31	21
%	%	%	**ASSETS**	%	%	%	%	%	%
11.7	10.6	11.7	Cash & Equivalents	13.0	12.8	11.0	11.1	11.0	6.6
2.0	1.8	2.5	Trade Receivables (net)	.9	1.3	1.1	3.1	5.3	9.5
48.7	47.9	46.8	Inventory	38.7	48.2	49.3	55.3	44.8	41.7
1.8	1.8	2.0	All Other Current	2.5	1.2	2.9	1.5	4.6	1.0
64.3	62.1	63.0	Total Current	55.1	63.5	64.3	71.0	65.7	58.8
17.0	17.9	17.1	Fixed Assets (net)	21.7	15.0	14.7	15.2	21.2	18.8
10.7	13.5	13.5	Intangibles (net)	18.6	16.9	12.7	6.1	5.3	12.0
8.0	6.5	6.3	All Other Non-Current	4.6	4.6	8.3	7.8	7.8	10.4
100.0	100.0	100.0	Total	100.0	100.0	100.0	100.0	100.0	100.0
			LIABILITIES						
8.3	7.4	7.7	Notes Payable-Short Term	5.6	8.0	5.2	10.9	8.1	9.1
3.2	3.6	3.3	Cur. Mat.-L.T.D.	5.7	3.1	2.4	2.8	2.7	2.0
21.5	17.8	18.5	Trade Payables	7.4	16.6	26.4	24.2	25.4	21.1
.1	.1	.2	Income Taxes Payable	.0	.5	.1	.1	.2	.3
11.0	11.5	12.0	All Other Current	8.0	15.5	9.7	10.2	13.4	10.6
44.1	40.5	41.8	Total Current	26.7	43.6	43.7	48.2	49.9	43.0
20.3	22.1	21.6	Long-Term Debt	28.9	24.5	20.7	15.9	14.9	10.6
.3	.0	.2	Deferred Taxes	.0	.5	.1	.1	.2	.3
8.4	8.4	6.7	All Other Non-Current	9.5	7.4	2.9	5.5	5.5	6.4
27.1	29.0	29.8	Net Worth	34.8	24.0	32.6	30.4	29.5	39.8
100.0	100.0	100.0	Total Liabilties & Net Worth	100.0	100.0	100.0	100.0	100.0	100.0
			INCOME DATA						
100.0	100.0	100.0	Net Sales	100.0	100.0	100.0	100.0	100.0	100.0
22.7	22.9	23.8	Gross Profit	26.1	23.4	22.1	22.9	23.6	24.6
20.8	21.4	21.4	Operating Expenses	23.9	21.0	19.8	20.7	21.0	21.7
1.9	1.4	2.4	Operating Profit	2.2	2.4	2.3	2.2	2.7	2.9
-.3	-.1	.1	All Other Expenses (net)	.4	.0	-.3	.0	.1	.4
2.2	1.6	2.3	Profit Before Taxes	1.9	2.4	2.6	2.2	2.6	2.5
			RATIOS						
2.7	3.3	3.4		7.6	5.3	2.8	2.5	2.2	1.9
1.6	1.8	1.6	Current	2.4	1.5	1.7	1.5	1.4	1.4
1.0	1.0	1.1		1.2	1.0	1.0	1.1	.9	.9
.7	.8	.8		1.5	1.1	.7	.6	.7	.6
(251) .3	(249) .3	(296) .3	Quick	(55) .4	(106) .3	.3	.3	.3	.3
.1	.1	.1		.2	.1	.1	.1	.2	.2
0 UND	0 UND	0 UND		0 UND	0 UND	0 UND	0 UND	0 UND	0 924.4
0 UND	0 UND	0 UND	Sales/Receivables	0 UND	0 UND	0 UND	1 999.8	1 320.2	4 94.9
1 277.0	1 400.8	1 335.1		0 UND	1 999.8	1 329.3	3 124.1	6 57.9	13 28.4
38 9.7	38 9.5	40 9.0		39 9.3	34 10.8	43 8.4	52 7.0	38 9.6	51 7.2
55 6.6	57 6.4	59 6.1	Cost of Sales/Inventory	60 6.1	59 6.2	55 6.7	69 5.3	52 7.0	60 6.1
80 4.6	79 4.6	82 4.4		90 4.6	84 4.3	71 5.1	86 4.3	77 4.7	83 4.4
5 68.9	2 206.3	1 350.6		0 UND	0 UND	8 45.6	12 31.4	19 18.9	15 23.8
23 15.7	21 17.6	21 17.7	Cost of Sales/Payables	0 UND	16 22.4	25 14.4	24 15.2	31 11.9	32 11.4
40 9.2	34 10.7	39 9.3		19 18.8	39 9.5	43 8.6	43 8.4	43 8.5	47 7.8
9.0	8.5	8.4		5.0	7.1	10.8	9.4	12.6	9.6
18.4	16.8	16.3	Sales/Working Capital	10.7	16.8	18.1	15.1	18.0	16.4
320.9	370.9	106.3		59.8	999.8	368.4	68.3	-133.6	-135.5
14.0	8.2	8.0		5.6	5.3	12.4	8.2	26.0	8.9
(206) 3.6	(206) 3.7	(240) 3.5	EBIT/Interest	(45) 2.5	(74) 2.4	(33) 4.6	(42) 3.7	(28) 5.4	(18) 5.2
1.3	1.3	1.0		-.4	.4	1.3	1.2	3.0	2.6
3.9	4.2	11.4	Net Profit + Depr., Dep.,						
(26) 2.0	(21) 1.5	(19) 3.7	Amort./Cur. Mat. L/T/D						
1.1	.6	1.0							
.1	.1	.2		.1	.1	.2	.1	.5	.3
.5	.8	.7	Fixed/Worth	1.5	1.0	.8	.3	.8	.7
-3.1	-4.0	-2.0		-1.0	-.8	-2.6	2.5	2.5	2.4
.9	.8	.9		.5	.9	.8	.8	.9	.7
2.8	3.5	3.1	Debt/Worth	3.5	4.5	3.1	2.5	2.3	2.5
-9.4	-12.8	-7.0		-4.3	-3.3	-10.8	NM	17.0	18.5
50.0	43.0	46.7	% Profit Before Taxes/Tangible	58.8	56.7	50.7	42.7	46.3	45.2
(179) 29.2	(172) 20.1	(203) 18.6	Net Worth	(34) 17.5	(68) 20.2	(24) 18.3	(34) 16.8	(24) 20.2	(19) 21.2
12.0	7.8	5.9		5.9	-3.4	-5.2	7.0	5.7	10.9
15.5	11.4	14.2	% Profit Before Taxes/Total	13.7	13.2	17.9	14.7	16.8	10.7
6.6	5.6	6.3	Assets	5.4	5.0	7.9	4.2	6.7	8.3
1.0	1.0	.2		-1.9	-2.2	1.1	.7	2.8	3.6
119.3	137.6	115.3		138.4	186.1	149.0	132.3	55.8	67.6
42.4	39.0	36.1	Sales/Net Fixed Assets	24.1	43.6	50.3	38.4	22.9	32.6
14.9	14.3	13.9		7.3	17.7	21.8	19.6	10.3	11.5
5.3	5.2	5.0		4.2	4.9	5.1	5.1	6.2	4.2
3.9	3.8	3.5	Sales/Total Assets	2.5	3.5	4.3	4.0	3.9	3.2
2.8	2.7	2.5		1.9	2.5	3.2	3.1	2.5	2.2
.4	.3	.3		.8	.3	.3	.2	.2	.3
(197) .8	(180) .8	(230) .8	% Depr., Dep., Amort./Sales	(37) 1.6	(81) .7	(28) .6	(38) .7	(29) .7	(17) .7
1.4	1.4	1.6		3.1	1.8	1.1	1.3	1.0	1.4
1.6	1.5	1.5		2.6	1.7	1.4	1.3		
(139) 2.0	(134) 2.5	(162) 2.8	% Officers', Directors' Owners' Comp/Sales	(29) 3.9	(70) 2.9	(19) 2.1	(30) 2.2		
4.5	4.4	4.2		5.9	4.2	3.7	2.9		
3325535M	4450747M	4992693M	Net Sales ($)	37460M	188114M	143465M	314656M	515353M	3793645M
857499M	1279135M	1604254M	Total Assets ($)	16877M	59341M	38954M	84350M	152323M	1252409M

M = $ thousand   MM = $ million
See Pages 11 through 21 for Explanation of Ratios and Data

Current Data Sorted by Assets | Comparative Historical Data

						Type of Statement		
		3	6	1	2	Unqualified	12	23
	11	12	4			Reviewed	23	22
6	44	22	1			Compiled	79	87
42	73	20				Tax Returns	68	79
17	25	27		4	4	Other	61	60
0-500M	500M-2MM	2-10MM	10-50MM	50-100MM	100-250MM		4/1/02-3/31/03 ALL	4/1/03-3/31/04 ALL
	70 (4/1-9/30/06)		261 (10/1/06-3/31/07)					
65	153	84	18	5	6	NUMBER OF STATEMENTS	243	271
%	%	%	%	%	%	ASSETS	%	%
12.4	12.2	10.5	7.1			Cash & Equivalents	11.6	10.5
21.8	26.1	30.7	27.4			Trade Receivables (net)	23.6	24.9
42.4	35.3	27.9	27.4			Inventory	39.8	37.4
3.0	2.4	2.6	3.6			All Other Current	3.0	2.4
79.6	76.0	71.7	65.6			Total Current	78.0	75.2
13.8	11.0	13.5	15.1			Fixed Assets (net)	12.6	13.8
2.4	5.7	7.9	12.2			Intangibles (net)	3.9	4.6
4.2	7.3	6.9	7.0			All Other Non-Current	5.6	6.5
100.0	100.0	100.0	100.0			Total	100.0	100.0
						LIABILITIES		
5.6	9.2	11.1	13.4			Notes Payable-Short Term	8.5	7.4
4.3	3.9	3.6	2.1			Cur. Mat.-L.T.D.	2.9	3.8
32.0	25.1	22.2	21.9			Trade Payables	24.3	25.3
.0	.1	.4	.0			Income Taxes Payable	.2	.3
6.3	7.6	5.9	7.5			All Other Current	7.4	9.0
48.3	45.9	43.2	44.9			Total Current	43.4	45.8
16.7	16.3	16.3	8.7			Long-Term Debt	14.1	13.9
.0	.1	.1	.3			Deferred Taxes	.1	.1
11.7	5.2	3.1	9.2			All Other Non-Current	3.7	6.0
23.3	32.5	37.2	36.9			Net Worth	38.8	34.1
100.0	100.0	100.0	100.0			Total Liabilties & Net Worth	100.0	100.0
						INCOME DATA		
100.0	100.0	100.0	100.0			Net Sales	100.0	100.0
25.4	23.7	26.6	23.1			Gross Profit	25.4	26.6
21.8	21.7	23.8	22.6			Operating Expenses	21.7	23.3
3.5	2.0	2.8	.5			Operating Profit	3.8	3.3
.2	.1	.2	-.3			All Other Expenses (net)	.1	.2
3.3	1.8	2.6	.8			Profit Before Taxes	3.7	3.1
						RATIOS		
3.1	2.7	2.8	2.4				3.0	2.7
1.7	1.9	1.7	1.5			Current	1.9	1.8
1.1	1.3	1.2	1.1				1.3	1.2
1.4	1.5	1.5	1.2				1.5	1.4
.7	.9	.9	.7			Quick	.8	.7
.4	.6	.6	.5				.5	.5
0 UND	9 38.6	16 23.3	18 20.4				8 44.1	10 36.9
12 29.4	18 20.4	24 15.5	26 14.1			Sales/Receivables	16 23.1	18 20.4
20 18.3	25 14.4	36 10.0	43 8.4				26 14.2	26 14.1
21 17.8	22 16.3	22 16.7	24 15.4				25 14.8	25 14.6
31 11.9	31 11.6	31 11.6	41 9.0			Cost of Sales/Inventory	35 10.6	36 10.2
43 8.5	43 8.5	43 8.5	59 6.2				50 7.2	49 7.4
11 32.6	12 29.6	15 24.9	17 21.4				14 26.1	16 23.5
21 17.3	19 19.5	24 15.5	35 10.3			Cost of Sales/Payables	21 17.2	22 16.2
36 10.3	34 10.9	35 10.5	45 8.2				31 11.9	34 10.6
11.7	9.9	9.6	8.7				9.3	9.6
22.0	15.8	15.7	15.4			Sales/Working Capital	14.4	14.0
89.3	33.1	27.9	42.2				29.9	42.3
27.0	11.1	11.2	18.9				21.0	19.3
(39) 4.3	(119) 3.9	(78) 3.8	(15) 2.4			EBIT/Interest	(201) 6.8	(219) 6.0
1.3	1.1	2.3	1.2				3.1	2.5
	2.8	4.1				Net Profit + Depr., Dep.,	10.1	5.9
	(16) 1.2	(15) 1.5				Amort./Cur. Mat. L/T/D	(43) 1.9	(54) 2.1
	.6	1.2					1.0	1.5
.1	.1	.2	.2				.1	.1
.3	.3	.4	.5			Fixed/Worth	.3	.4
12.9	2.1	1.5	1.1				.7	1.2
1.0	.7	.9	.9				.7	.8
2.6	2.3	1.9	2.4			Debt/Worth	1.7	2.0
NM	31.1	8.9	13.5				4.9	7.3
147.6	63.8	58.2	42.7				77.9	64.2
(49) 59.5	(123) 19.8	(68) 18.1	(16) 14.5			% Profit Before Taxes/Tangible Net Worth	(221) 37.0	(229) 28.2
15.1	5.2	7.3	6.7				13.8	12.3
27.2	16.8	15.5	11.9				25.7	20.0
12.0	7.2	6.5	4.0			% Profit Before Taxes/Total Assets	13.1	9.8
2.9	.8	2.4	.6				5.4	3.5
215.1	183.6	74.9	52.9				127.2	129.0
94.7	67.9	43.7	39.6			Sales/Net Fixed Assets	54.5	47.4
33.8	34.7	21.6	12.4				25.7	23.4
8.7	6.6	5.3	3.8				6.6	5.9
6.9	5.2	4.0	3.1			Sales/Total Assets	5.0	4.8
4.4	4.0	3.2	2.4				3.9	3.8
.2	.2	.4	.6				.3	.4
(49) .4	(115) .4	(71) .6	.9			% Depr., Dep., Amort./Sales	(202) .6	(214) .7
1.0	.9	1.0	1.2				.9	1.1
.9	2.0	1.2				% Officers', Directors'	1.7	1.6
(40) 3.2	(105) 3.0	(35) 2.4				Owners' Comp/Sales	(133) 3.2	(139) 2.9
5.6	4.9	4.0					6.1	4.9
146258M	923738M	1462522M	1121643M	1035506M	3574552M	Net Sales ($)	8911436M	7189290M
21510M	169208M	354085M	361111M	317841M	893442M	Total Assets ($)	1658825M	1885664M

© RMA 2007

M = $ thousand   MM = $ million
See Pages 11 through 21 for Explanation of Ratios and Data

Comparative Historical Data | Current Data Sorted by Sales

Type of Statement									
Unqualified	14	19	12					4	8
Reviewed	23	22	27				8	11	8
Compiled	72	64	73	1	13	15	27	13	4
Tax Returns	77	97	135	5	35	40	34	19	2
Other	74	96	84	6	13	12	13	18	22
	4/1/04-3/31/05	4/1/05-3/31/06	4/1/06-3/31/07	70 (4/1-9/30/06)			261 (10/1/06-3/31/07)		
	ALL	ALL	ALL	0-1MM	1-3MM	3-5MM	5-10MM	10-25MM	25MM & OVER
NUMBER OF STATEMENTS	260	298	331	12	61	67	82	65	44
ASSETS	%	%	%	%	%	%	%	%	%
Cash & Equivalents	12.1	11.6	11.3	18.6	9.9	12.4	11.8	11.7	8.0
Trade Receivables (net)	23.7	24.5	26.2	18.8	20.0	24.0	28.8	31.7	27.6
Inventory	37.7	36.6	34.6	25.4	38.6	35.9	36.5	29.3	33.8
All Other Current	2.4	2.6	2.6	6.6	3.4	1.7	1.8	3.6	1.7
Total Current	75.9	75.3	74.7	69.3	72.0	74.0	78.9	76.3	71.2
Fixed Assets (net)	13.4	13.3	12.8	21.6	17.0	9.7	9.5	12.2	15.9
Intangibles (net)	4.3	5.7	6.1	2.7	3.4	9.8	6.2	4.6	7.0
All Other Non-Current	6.4	5.7	6.4	6.3	7.5	6.6	5.4	6.9	5.9
Total	100.0	100.0	100.0	100.0	100.0	100.0	100.0	100.0	100.0
LIABILITIES									
Notes Payable-Short Term	8.4	10.0	9.4	15.0	5.3	5.7	11.6	10.1	14.2
Cur. Mat.-L.T.D.	3.0	3.5	3.7	5.6	3.4	4.2	4.9	2.8	2.0
Trade Payables	22.5	24.5	25.5	12.4	26.2	23.3	26.4	29.0	24.3
Income Taxes Payable	.1	.1	.2	.0	.2	.1	.1	.4	.2
All Other Current	8.0	7.3	7.0	6.8	5.2	7.5	7.1	7.8	7.8
Total Current	42.1	45.5	45.8	39.9	40.3	40.9	50.1	50.0	48.5
Long-Term Debt	14.3	16.0	15.9	18.7	17.8	21.0	15.8	12.9	9.5
Deferred Taxes	.1	.1	.1	.0	.0	.1	.1	.2	.1
All Other Non-Current	5.9	5.7	6.2	19.1	11.2	5.7	3.3	2.7	6.9
Net Worth	37.6	32.7	32.0	22.3	30.7	32.4	30.7	34.1	35.0
Total Liabilities & Net Worth	100.0	100.0	100.0	100.0	100.0	100.0	100.0	100.0	100.0
INCOME DATA									
Net Sales	100.0	100.0	100.0	100.0	100.0	100.0	100.0	100.0	100.0
Gross Profit	25.8	25.8	24.9	40.7	26.6	25.7	22.2	23.5	24.4
Operating Expenses	22.8	23.2	22.6	32.4	23.3	23.5	21.0	20.5	23.5
Operating Profit	3.1	2.5	2.4	8.3	3.3	2.1	1.3	3.0	.8
All Other Expenses (net)	.0	.2	.1	.7	.3	-.1	.3	.2	-.2
Profit Before Taxes	3.1	2.3	2.2	7.6	3.0	2.3	1.0	2.8	1.0
RATIOS									
Current	3.1	3.1	2.7	4.5	3.5	2.9	2.5	2.4	1.9
	2.0	1.8	1.8	2.3	2.0	1.9	1.8	1.7	1.5
	1.3	1.3	1.2	1.0	1.2	1.3	1.3	1.2	1.1
Quick	1.6	1.6	1.4	2.9	1.7	1.6	1.4	1.4	1.1
	.8	(297) .9	.9	1.4	.7	.9	.9	.9	.7
	.5	.5	.5	.2	.3	.6	.5	.6	.4
Sales/Receivables	9 41.2	10 38.1	10 38.0	0 UND	1 249.6	8 45.5	13 29.0	12 29.4	14 25.2
	16 22.6	18 20.6	19 19.6	22 16.7	15 24.5	17 21.9	20 17.9	22 16.9	22 16.7
	26 14.2	26 14.3	28 13.2	49 7.5	24 15.2	26 13.8	25 14.4	33 10.9	33 11.1
Cost of Sales/Inventory	26 14.1	23 15.9	22 16.5	0 UND	26 13.9	21 17.7	24 15.1	15 24.2	25 14.6
	35 10.4	34 10.8	32 11.5	42 8.8	38 9.7	31 11.6	30 12.2	26 14.0	37 9.9
	48 7.6	49 7.4	44 8.2	107 3.4	51 7.2	45 8.0	38 9.6	38 9.6	56 6.6
Cost of Sales/Payables	11 32.7	13 29.0	13 27.4	8 44.8	14 25.7	9 40.2	13 28.2	14 25.2	19 19.0
	19 18.8	20 18.5	21 17.0	14 26.7	22 16.8	17 21.7	20 18.3	21 17.4	31 11.9
	33 11.1	32 11.3	36 10.3	78 4.7	37 9.8	35 10.6	34 10.7	34 10.6	43 8.4
Sales/Working Capital	8.8	9.3	10.1	4.9	7.7	9.9	11.1	11.2	11.8
	13.6	14.6	16.3	12.3	14.1	15.7	17.0	17.4	18.7
	35.5	38.6	44.0	-121.1	83.7	36.4	32.1	60.7	48.8
EBIT/Interest	18.9	14.2	12.2		17.4	10.4	9.8	18.0	15.8
	(216) 6.5	(243) 4.8	(261) 3.9		(43) 4.6	(47) 3.8	(66) 2.7	(58) 5.2	(40) 2.4
	2.2	1.9	1.3		2.1	.9	.8	2.8	1.4
Net Profit + Depr., Dep., Amort./Cur. Mat. L/T/D	7.9	5.2	4.1				2.4	4.1	16.5
	(39) 3.8	(42) 1.8	(43) 1.4			(10) 1.3	(11) 1.5	(13) 1.7	
	1.3	1.2	.8				.6	.8	.9
Fixed/Worth	.1	.1	.1	.0	.1	.1	.1	.1	.3
	.3	.4	.4	.6	.5	.3	.3	.3	.5
	.8	1.9	2.4	19.9	5.6	5.4	7.1	2.0	1.2
Debt/Worth	.7	.8	.9	.6	.8	.6	.7	.9	1.3
	1.7	1.9	2.3	13.4	2.4	2.6	2.1	1.8	2.4
	5.5	9.4	25.1	NM	16.2	123.2	NM	10.0	6.1
% Profit Before Taxes/Tangible Net Worth	58.3	68.6	73.4		108.6	86.6	43.8	76.2	54.3
	(227) 26.1	(244) 27.8	(265) 21.4		(50) 43.8	(52) 21.1	(62) 16.9	(52) 30.0	(40) 15.2
	9.3	9.6	6.8		6.5	6.6	3.3	12.3	5.8
% Profit Before Taxes/Total Assets	20.4	20.2	16.7	51.4	20.3	15.2	14.0	20.7	10.9
	9.6	9.0	7.2	15.1	9.7	7.1	5.8	10.5	3.7
	2.4	2.3	1.0	4.5	2.0	.5	.2	4.4	.8
Sales/Net Fixed Assets	109.4	125.9	136.4	158.2	108.1	231.4	164.0	111.8	48.8
	50.7	60.2	51.4	26.1	48.0	82.3	75.9	52.9	34.2
	24.9	26.5	24.4	6.1	18.8	34.9	35.0	28.5	16.8
Sales/Total Assets	6.3	6.4	6.6	3.8	6.4	7.1	6.6	6.8	5.1
	4.8	4.9	4.7	2.4	4.5	5.3	5.2	5.2	3.9
	3.6	3.5	3.5	1.4	3.4	3.4	4.3	3.8	3.0
% Depr., Dep., Amort./Sales	.3	.3	.3		.2	.1	.2	.4	.5
	(204) .6	(239) .5	(263) .5		(53) .5	(49) .4	(59) .4	(55) .6	(41) .7
	1.1	1.0	.9		1.1	1.1	.9	.8	.9
% Officers', Directors' Owners' Comp/Sales	1.5	1.7	1.7		1.6	1.8	2.0	1.5	
	(129) 2.9	(156) 3.1	(181) 3.0		(34) 3.2	(48) 3.4	(55) 3.0	(32) 2.3	
	5.2	5.2	4.9		6.1	5.3	4.8	3.4	
Net Sales ($)	6970063M	7393566M	8264219M	8709M	129237M	253567M	587422M	1005166M	6280118M
Total Assets ($)	1705895M	2048709M	2117197M	5776M	34710M	64431M	121925M	233680M	1656675M

© RMA 2007

M = $ thousand   MM = $ million

See Pages 11 through 21 for Explanation of Ratios and Data

Current Data Sorted by Assets   Comparative Historical Data

0-500M	500M-2MM	2-10MM	10-50MM	50-100MM	100-250MM		4/1/02-3/31/03 ALL	4/1/03-3/31/04 ALL
						Type of Statement		
			3	1	2	Unqualified	4	1
			2			Reviewed	7	4
2	1	1			1	Compiled	12	10
9	7	4		1		Tax Returns	7	8
1	1	3				Other	10	14
	7 (4/1-9/30/06)		32 (10/1/06-3/31/07)					
12	9	8	5	2	3	**NUMBER OF STATEMENTS**	40	37
%	%	%	%	%	%	**ASSETS**	%	%
11.3						Cash & Equivalents	13.8	13.5
14.9						Trade Receivables (net)	15.1	13.1
44.2						Inventory	36.4	41.6
6.8						All Other Current	1.7	3.5
77.2						Total Current	67.0	71.6
7.6						Fixed Assets (net)	23.7	20.4
5.4						Intangibles (net)	5.3	2.6
9.8						All Other Non-Current	4.0	5.4
100.0						Total	100.0	100.0
						LIABILITIES		
40.2						Notes Payable-Short Term	7.8	15.9
1.3						Cur. Mat.-L.T.D.	3.3	3.5
17.2						Trade Payables	18.4	20.8
.0						Income Taxes Payable	.1	.1
15.6						All Other Current	14.1	8.4
74.3						Total Current	43.6	48.7
9.6						Long-Term Debt	16.7	17.6
.0						Deferred Taxes	.4	.0
4.7						All Other Non-Current	9.3	2.9
11.4						Net Worth	29.9	30.7
100.0						Total Liabilities & Net Worth	100.0	100.0
						INCOME DATA		
100.0						Net Sales	100.0	100.0
43.7						Gross Profit	46.3	45.2
42.5						Operating Expenses	39.4	39.7
1.3						Operating Profit	6.9	5.5
-.1						All Other Expenses (net)	1.2	.8
1.4						Profit Before Taxes	5.7	4.7
						RATIOS		
6.0							2.4	2.6
2.0						Current	1.6	1.5
.5							1.1	1.1
2.3							1.4	1.4
(11) .5						Quick	.5	.4
.2							.2	.2
0 UND							0 UND	0 UND
0 UND						Sales/Receivables	16 22.2	15 24.7
13 29.2							35 10.5	24 15.1
0 UND							53 6.9	52 7.0
70 5.2						Cost of Sales/Inventory	70 5.2	85 4.3
133 2.7							126 2.9	166 2.2
0 UND							17 21.1	7 53.7
9 40.1						Cost of Sales/Payables	45 8.0	39 9.2
43 8.4							58 6.2	66 5.5
6.1							5.1	8.8
24.8						Sales/Working Capital	14.2	14.0
-23.1							102.7	81.2
							8.5	8.9
						EBIT/Interest	(33) 3.4	(32) 2.8
							1.2	-1.0
							6.2	14.9
						Net Profit + Depr., Dep., Amort./Cur. Mat. L/T/D	(10) 3.0	(10) 3.9
							1.5	.2
.0							.2	.2
.1						Fixed/Worth	.7	.6
NM							5.4	1.3
.3							1.5	.9
2.1						Debt/Worth	2.4	2.7
-3.4							12.8	5.3
							57.8	54.3
						% Profit Before Taxes/Tangible Net Worth	(32) 31.4	(34) 20.6
							10.9	-8.8
36.0							31.0	19.2
1.4						% Profit Before Taxes/Total Assets	6.2	6.1
-.2							.8	-5.1
UND							47.8	40.8
170.2						Sales/Net Fixed Assets	19.1	21.8
34.3							7.5	7.3
10.2							3.8	4.0
5.4						Sales/Total Assets	2.7	2.7
2.4							1.9	1.8
							.6	.6
						% Depr., Dep., Amort./Sales	(37) 1.6	(29) 1.1
							2.8	1.9
							1.9	1.4
						% Officers', Directors' Owners' Comp/Sales	(22) 2.8	(19) 2.0
							8.5	2.9
12702M	25808M	72946M	227570M	265095M	1228085M	Net Sales ($)	1222654M	268304M
2508M	11115M	29103M	89016M	118379M	541382M	Total Assets ($)	574402M	94998M

© RMA 2007

M = $ thousand   MM = $ million
See Pages 11 through 21 for Explanation of Ratios and Data

Comparative Historical Data　　　　　Current Data Sorted by Sales

			Type of Statement						
4	5	6	Unqualified				1		5
2	1	2	Reviewed						2
5	6	4	Compiled	2	1		1		
10	8	20	Tax Returns	6	6	3	3	2	
8	14	7	Other	1			2	1	2
4/1/04-	4/1/05-	4/1/06-			7 (4/1-9/30/06)		32 (10/1/06-3/31/07)		
3/31/05	3/31/06	3/31/07							
ALL	ALL	ALL		0-1MM	1-3MM	3-5MM	5-10MM	10-25MM	25MM & OVER
29	34	39	NUMBER OF STATEMENTS	9	8	3	6	4	9
%	%	%	ASSETS	%	%	%	%	%	%
6.9	4.5	8.1	Cash & Equivalents						
17.5	17.3	17.5	Trade Receivables (net)						
38.6	47.9	45.3	Inventory						
4.5	3.0	4.0	All Other Current						
67.5	72.7	74.8	Total Current						
21.9	13.3	14.0	Fixed Assets (net)						
5.2	5.9	3.9	Intangibles (net)						
5.4	8.1	7.4	All Other Non-Current						
100.0	100.0	100.0	Total						
			LIABILITIES						
11.4	17.3	19.8	Notes Payable-Short Term						
3.0	1.5	3.3	Cur. Mat.-L.T.D.						
18.7	23.0	20.8	Trade Payables						
.1	.2	.4	Income Taxes Payable						
6.6	7.0	9.9	All Other Current						
39.8	49.0	54.3	Total Current						
15.9	16.8	13.9	Long-Term Debt						
.7	.0	.0	Deferred Taxes						
4.0	7.2	10.4	All Other Non-Current						
39.5	27.0	21.4	Net Worth						
100.0	100.0	100.0	Total Liabilties & Net Worth						
			INCOME DATA						
100.0	100.0	100.0	Net Sales						
39.2	40.8	42.6	Gross Profit						
34.5	36.3	39.5	Operating Expenses						
4.7	4.6	3.2	Operating Profit						
.6	1.1	1.1	All Other Expenses (net)						
4.1	3.5	2.1	Profit Before Taxes						
			RATIOS						
4.5	3.8	3.1							
1.5	1.4	1.5	Current						
1.3	1.1	1.0							
1.2	.8	.9							
.4	.3 (38)	.5	Quick						
.2	.2	.2							

												Current Data								
0	UND	3	121.9	0	UND	Sales/Receivables														
18	20.5	19	18.9	10	35.3															
46	8.0	53	6.9	32	11.3															
45	8.1	70	5.2	46	8.0	Cost of Sales/Inventory														
103	3.5	122	3.0	89	4.1															
167	2.2	209	1.7	194	1.9															
13	28.2	21	17.6	9	42.8	Cost of Sales/Payables														
31	11.7	42	8.8	37	10.0															
56	6.5	125	2.9	83	4.4															

4.4		5.9		4.5		
11.8		12.4		15.3	Sales/Working Capital	
31.6		27.5		89.0		
13.9		7.0		5.7		
5.3	(21)	2.8	(30)	3.3	(30) EBIT/Interest	
3.0		1.8		1.2		
					Net Profit + Depr., Dep., Amort./Cur. Mat. L/T/D	
.1		.1		.0		
.5		.4		.3	Fixed/Worth	
1.6		2.9		5.4		
.5		1.4		.8		
1.5		3.6		3.0	Debt/Worth	
6.5		23.3		-7.5		
40.9		32.7		46.8	% Profit Before Taxes/Tangible Net Worth	
24.1	(25)	21.2	(28)	26.4	(28)	
12.6		6.8		13.9		
13.0		10.9		14.6	% Profit Before Taxes/Total Assets	
9.3		4.8		5.0		
4.3		2.4		.4		
76.1		108.4		192.0	Sales/Net Fixed Assets	
23.7		38.6		73.3		
5.1		11.6		16.1		
3.6		3.2		5.1	Sales/Total Assets	
2.5		2.5		2.6		
1.8		1.8		1.7		
.3		.3		.3	% Depr., Dep., Amort./Sales	
.8	(25)	.6	(29)	.8	(27)	
2.8		.9		1.7		
1.4		1.5		1.5	% Officers', Directors' Owners' Comp/Sales	
2.0	(15)	2.5	(19)	1.9	(19)	
8.5		5.6		5.1		

639546M	813463M	1832206M	Net Sales ($)	4598M	14018M	11026M	46264M	55570M	1700730M
413249M	380099M	791503M	Total Assets ($)	5281M	3687M	2922M	21865M	19497M	738251M

M = $ thousand　　MM = $ million
See Pages 11 through 21 for Explanation of Ratios and Data

Current Data Sorted by Assets   Comparative Historical Data

Type of Statement	0-500M	500M-2MM	2-10MM	10-50MM	50-100MM	100-250MM		4/1/02-3/31/03 ALL	4/1/03-3/31/04 ALL
Unqualified				2		2		4	6
Reviewed	1	1	3					6	3
Compiled	2	5	3					13	16
Tax Returns	15	3						29	19
Other	1	2	4	1		1		13	17
		7 (4/1-9/30/06)		39 (10/1/06-3/31/07)					
NUMBER OF STATEMENTS	19	11	10	3		3		65	61
	%	%	%	%	%	%	ASSETS	%	%
Cash & Equivalents	19.7	16.9	5.3					10.6	12.8
Trade Receivables (net)	8.7	13.8	18.8					11.1	14.0
Inventory	34.7	38.1	22.0					33.5	29.1
All Other Current	1.3	.2	2.2					1.9	2.9
Total Current	64.4	69.0	48.3	DATA	NOT	AVAILABLE		57.1	58.8
Fixed Assets (net)	19.5	17.7	33.1					25.5	22.3
Intangibles (net)	9.0	5.3	8.1					6.8	12.4
All Other Non-Current	7.2	8.0	10.4					10.6	6.5
Total	100.0	100.0	100.0					100.0	100.0
							LIABILITIES		
Notes Payable-Short Term	5.7	7.6	9.2					5.7	4.2
Cur. Mat.-L.T.D.	5.4	1.9	6.9					6.5	5.8
Trade Payables	20.4	22.3	19.5					19.4	15.6
Income Taxes Payable	.0	.0	.1					.1	.4
All Other Current	24.0	8.6	6.6					10.8	11.1
Total Current	55.6	40.4	42.2					42.6	37.2
Long-Term Debt	43.6	16.4	37.0					25.4	22.9
Deferred Taxes	.0	.0	.3					.1	.2
All Other Non-Current	10.9	4.5	8.9					8.6	4.7
Net Worth	-10.1	38.6	11.7					23.2	35.1
Total Liabilities & Net Worth	100.0	100.0	100.0					100.0	100.0
							INCOME DATA		
Net Sales	100.0	100.0	100.0					100.0	100.0
Gross Profit	61.6	57.0	41.6					52.0	54.8
Operating Expenses	55.1	46.4	38.4					45.6	47.4
Operating Profit	6.5	10.6	3.2					6.4	7.4
All Other Expenses (net)	1.6	.9	1.8					1.3	.8
Profit Before Taxes	4.9	9.7	1.5					5.1	6.5
							RATIOS		
Current	2.7	3.1	1.7					2.5	2.7
	1.5	2.2	1.4					1.5	1.6
	.8	1.1	.8					.8	1.1
Quick	1.5	2.3						.8	1.2
	(18) .7	.9						.4	.7
	.1	.3						.2	.3
Sales/Receivables	0 UND	0 UND	10 37.0					0 UND	1 522.5
	2 161.0	7 49.0	19 19.3					5 66.7	8 48.3
	10 34.9	38 9.6	35 10.4					16 23.1	34 10.8
Cost of Sales/Inventory	41 8.9	43 8.4	23 15.8					48 7.6	28 13.0
	66 5.5	128 2.8	49 7.4					85 4.3	77 4.7
	88 4.2	196 1.9	56 6.5					112 3.3	132 2.8
Cost of Sales/Payables	5 67.3	22 16.7	22 16.7					10 35.6	13 28.4
	27 13.5	28 12.9	34 10.9					33 10.9	33 11.1
	57 6.4	108 3.4	58 6.3					61 6.0	57 6.4
Sales/Working Capital	10.9	5.0	16.6					7.9	6.2
	28.6	6.7	40.6					22.0	15.3
	-16.9	146.9	-23.6					-63.9	72.5
EBIT/Interest	7.2		10.0					8.7	18.9
	(12) 1.1		1.8					(54) 3.8	(49) 5.5
	.0		-.9					.4	1.4
Net Profit + Depr., Dep., Amort./Cur. Mat. L/T/D									
Fixed/Worth	.0	.0	.4					.2	.2
	.4	.3	5.2					1.2	.7
	-.5	1.6	-3.2					-3.3	22.4
Debt/Worth	.8	.7	4.7					1.1	.5
	3.3	1.3	8.7					2.7	1.5
	-2.4	5.8	-6.9					-8.0	UND
% Profit Before Taxes/Tangible Net Worth	605.6							45.9	85.5
	(11) 42.9							(40) 22.5	(47) 33.9
	-3.7							-4.2	6.2
% Profit Before Taxes/Total Assets	40.5	46.5	13.3					16.3	22.6
	12.6	15.2	3.8					7.9	9.1
	-1.5	4.3	-7.2					-2.5	1.0
Sales/Net Fixed Assets	177.0	302.2	39.3					63.1	49.7
	48.3	28.4	9.7					17.4	14.9
	14.7	4.9	5.4					6.7	7.2
Sales/Total Assets	6.0	4.5	4.0					4.7	5.3
	4.7	2.2	3.1					2.9	2.7
	3.2	1.6	2.4					1.9	1.9
% Depr., Dep., Amort./Sales	.7		.8					.7	.6
	(10) 1.2		1.8					(53) 1.2	(40) 1.7
	2.0		2.4					2.3	3.7
% Officers', Directors' Owners' Comp/Sales								2.8	2.2
								(34) 7.1	(34) 6.2
								14.3	9.9
Net Sales ($)	15187M	39235M	117117M	72737M		671035M		1961848M	885572M
Total Assets ($)	3775M	11339M	36826M	35687M		464305M		575206M	539594M

M = $ thousand   MM = $ million
See Pages 11 through 21 for Explanation of Ratios and Data

Comparative Historical Data | Current Data Sorted by Sales

4/1/04-3/31/05 ALL	4/1/05-3/31/06 ALL	4/1/06-3/31/07 ALL	Type of Statement	0-1MM	1-3MM	3-5MM	5-10MM	10-25MM	25MM & OVER
4	1	4	Unqualified					1	3
5	1	5	Reviewed	1	1		1	2	
6	9	10	Compiled	1	5	2	1	1	
23	24	18	Tax Returns	12	4		1	1	
20	20	9	Other		2	1	2	3	1
				7 (4/1-9/30/06)			39 (10/1/06-3/31/07)		
58	55	46	**NUMBER OF STATEMENTS**	14	12	3	5	8	4
%	%	%	**ASSETS**	%	%	%	%	%	%
9.9	13.9	13.8	Cash & Equivalents	22.7	14.2				
12.4	11.5	11.9	Trade Receivables (net)	2.8	17.8				
29.6	29.8	29.7	Inventory	38.0	31.3				
1.5	1.4	2.0	All Other Current	.0	2.2				
53.4	56.6	57.4	Total Current	63.5	65.6				
26.0	24.0	23.6	Fixed Assets (net)	19.2	20.5				
8.8	6.5	11.3	Intangibles (net)	8.4	9.0				
11.9	12.8	7.8	All Other Non-Current	9.1	5.0				
100.0	100.0	100.0	Total	100.0	100.0				
			LIABILITIES						
7.6	6.5	6.9	Notes Payable-Short Term	1.2	10.4				
4.8	8.3	4.8	Cur. Mat.-L.T.D.	5.9	2.9				
13.5	14.9	20.3	Trade Payables	21.2	22.7				
.1	.1	.0	Income Taxes Payable	.0	.0				
9.0	16.9	15.0	All Other Current	30.5	7.8				
35.0	46.7	47.0	Total Current	58.8	43.8				
20.0	22.2	34.1	Long-Term Debt	41.0	30.9				
.4	.2	.1	Deferred Taxes	.0	.0				
5.6	13.9	8.3	All Other Non-Current	9.2	10.3				
39.0	17.0	10.6	Net Worth	-9.1	15.0				
100.0	100.0	100.0	Total Liabilties & Net Worth	100.0	100.0				
			INCOME DATA						
100.0	100.0	100.0	Net Sales	100.0	100.0				
54.1	52.2	57.1	Gross Profit	61.0	59.4				
48.0	47.0	50.1	Operating Expenses	53.1	53.8				
6.1	5.2	7.1	Operating Profit	7.9	5.6				
1.2	1.6	1.5	All Other Expenses (net)	1.7	.7				
4.9	3.6	5.5	Profit Before Taxes	6.1	5.0				
			RATIOS						
2.9	2.5	2.6	Current	2.7	3.9				
1.7	1.5	1.5		1.4	2.5				
1.0	.8	.8		.8	1.0				
1.4	1.4	1.4	Quick	1.3	2.1				
(57) .7	(53) .6	(44) .8		(13) .5	1.3				
.3	.2	.3		.1	.4				
3 121.7	2 167.1	0 UND	Sales/Receivables	0 UND	4 96.2				
9 42.8	8 47.0	9 41.3		0 UND	12 31.1				
20 18.3	19 18.9	22 16.7		5 71.9	37 9.8				
44 8.4	47 7.7	41 8.9	Cost of Sales/Inventory	37 10.0	48 7.5				
77 4.8	74 4.9	64 5.7		68 5.3	94 3.9				
128 2.9	140 2.6	99 3.7		98 3.7	167 2.2				
10 36.2	6 59.0	19 19.3	Cost of Sales/Payables	12 30.9	4 102.3				
28 13.2	32 11.5	31 11.7		27 13.5	34 10.6				
60 6.1	52 7.0	77 4.7		49 7.4	126 2.9				
8.4	6.7	8.9	Sales/Working Capital	14.1	5.2				
14.0	14.4	27.3		39.8	8.0				
-107.1	-20.4	-18.4		-16.7	NM				
12.0	10.9	13.5	EBIT/Interest		66.2				
(44) 4.1	(44) 4.0	(37) 2.5			5.7				
.9	.5	.5			2.1				
			Net Profit + Depr., Dep., Amort./Cur. Mat. L/T/D						
.3	.1	.2	Fixed/Worth	.0	.1				
.8	.9	1.2		.3	.9				
4.0	UND	-1.1		-.8	-.5				
.6	1.0	1.0	Debt/Worth	.7	.6				
1.9	6.3	5.9		2.4	3.8				
11.5	-20.9	-4.2		-3.7	-3.1				
74.1	78.3	115.4	% Profit Before Taxes/Tangible Net Worth						
(49) 30.3	(39) 31.9	(29) 49.4							
2.3	6.1	9.5							
23.1	24.4	26.1	% Profit Before Taxes/Total Assets	75.9	19.6				
9.6	9.7	7.3		11.8	10.9				
.7	1.1	-.4		-1.6	2.6				
34.8	50.8	93.3	Sales/Net Fixed Assets	UND	270.9				
14.3	17.4	25.5		49.3	15.8				
7.7	7.7	7.5		23.3	7.1				
4.1	3.4	5.3	Sales/Total Assets	7.4	4.5				
2.7	2.8	3.2		4.8	2.4				
1.9	1.9	2.2		3.1	1.7				
.8	.8	.8	% Depr., Dep., Amort./Sales						
(47) 1.8	(45) 1.5	(32) 1.6							
3.2	2.9	2.5							
2.5	2.4	2.2	% Officers', Directors' Owners' Comp/Sales						
(29) 4.5	(23) 4.6	(22) 7.0							
13.6	8.5	15.8							
773618M	1080128M	915311M	Net Sales ($)	7508M	20841M	9215M	38915M	123738M	715094M
380825M	435705M	551932M	Total Assets ($)	2006M	8581M	4095M	20541M	40521M	476188M

© RMA 2007

M = $ thousand   MM = $ million
See Pages 11 through 21 for Explanation of Ratios and Data

Current Data Sorted by Assets   Comparative Historical Data

						Type of Statement		
1	3	18	45	14	12	Unqualified	31	49
2	10	39	52	4		Reviewed	47	54
51	56	51	19	1	1	Compiled	101	152
169	156	41	5		5	Tax Returns	134	221
48	79	54	46	13	14	Other	113	126
	140 (4/1-9/30/06)			869 (10/1/06-3/31/07)			4/1/02-3/31/03	4/1/03-3/31/04
0-500M	500M-2MM	2-10MM	10-50MM	50-100MM	100-250MM		ALL	ALL
271	304	203	167	32	32	NUMBER OF STATEMENTS	426	602
%	%	%	%	%	%	ASSETS	%	%
16.3	9.5	11.0	10.0	9.3	8.7	Cash & Equivalents	9.9	11.4
5.7	5.6	10.3	10.1	6.0	8.1	Trade Receivables (net)	6.8	5.9
35.5	14.1	11.6	11.7	10.3	16.7	Inventory	19.4	21.0
2.9	2.1	3.1	2.4	4.9	2.9	All Other Current	2.5	1.8
60.4	31.3	36.0	34.2	30.5	36.4	Total Current	38.7	40.0
24.5	55.2	54.1	55.4	60.2	56.7	Fixed Assets (net)	47.8	46.6
11.0	8.8	4.3	2.9	4.4	2.4	Intangibles (net)	6.1	6.3
4.1	4.7	5.5	7.5	4.9	4.5	All Other Non-Current	7.4	7.1
100.0	100.0	100.0	100.0	100.0	100.0	Total	100.0	100.0
						LIABILITIES		
6.9	3.9	3.0	3.2	3.5	9.5	Notes Payable-Short Term	3.6	3.6
2.5	2.6	3.3	4.4	2.9	2.5	Cur. Mat.-L.T.D.	3.8	3.5
21.8	11.6	18.5	21.0	17.1	17.1	Trade Payables	15.4	15.3
.1	.1	.4	.2	.1	.0	Income Taxes Payable	.2	.3
18.3	7.7	8.7	7.6	9.8	9.8	All Other Current	8.1	8.5
49.6	25.9	33.9	36.4	33.4	38.9	Total Current	31.1	31.2
22.0	51.5	40.7	29.4	39.7	32.6	Long-Term Debt	37.5	37.2
.0	.0	.2	.8	.6	.6	Deferred Taxes	.2	.2
18.6	7.9	4.2	3.2	5.2	4.3	All Other Non-Current	10.0	12.1
9.9	14.6	21.0	30.3	21.1	23.7	Net Worth	21.2	19.2
100.0	100.0	100.0	100.0	100.0	100.0	Total Liabilities & Net Worth	100.0	100.0
						INCOME DATA		
100.0	100.0	100.0	100.0	100.0	100.0	Net Sales	100.0	100.0
12.9	13.3	11.6	11.6	12.5	10.7	Gross Profit	17.1	16.2
12.9	12.2	10.9	10.6	11.5	9.7	Operating Expenses	16.1	15.5
.0	1.1	.7	1.0	1.0	1.0	Operating Profit	1.0	.7
-.4	.5	.3	-.1	.0	.3	All Other Expenses (net)	-.1	-.2
.4	.6	.4	1.1	1.0	.7	Profit Before Taxes	1.2	.9
						RATIOS		
3.7	2.8	1.7	1.3	1.2	1.3		2.4	2.4
1.5	1.4	1.1	1.0	.9	.8	Current	1.3	1.3
.9	.8	.7	.7	.7	.6		.8	.8
1.4	1.2	1.1	.8	.7	.7		1.0	1.0
(266) .6	.5	.6	.5	.4	.5	Quick	(423) .5	(599) .5
.2	.2	.3	.4	.3	.2		.2	.2
0 UND	0 UND	1 650.6	3 133.5	2 182.9	1 356.9		0 UND	0 UND
0 999.8	0 999.8	3 113.7	4 82.6	3 111.0	3 105.1	Sales/Receivables	2 176.0	2 241.6
2 151.6	3 129.7	8 48.5	7 51.8	7 54.8	5 69.3		5 70.7	4 87.8
5 79.3	6 65.7	4 89.6	5 75.5	5 74.3	5 68.8		8 48.4	7 50.4
8 46.6	8 43.1	6 57.1	7 49.2	9 42.5	8 44.1	Cost of Sales/Inventory	12 30.7	10 35.4
13 27.7	13 27.2	10 35.3	10 35.3	11 33.9	11 31.9		17 21.2	16 22.4
1 535.8	0 999.8	5 79.8	10 36.7	9 40.6	8 44.4		3 126.2	3 134.4
4 87.6	5 77.7	10 37.1	13 28.4	12 31.4	13 29.2	Cost of Sales/Payables	10 37.1	8 43.9
8 46.3	11 33.7	14 26.0	16 22.5	16 22.6	18 20.4		17 21.7	15 24.6
35.2	28.6	36.6	83.0	93.2	79.0		29.8	28.9
94.9	84.5	257.6	-455.0	-283.5	-93.4	Sales/Working Capital	86.2	86.9
-351.7	-122.9	-53.3	-62.6	-54.3	-43.8		-78.2	-88.3
3.1	3.2	4.3	5.0	3.0	5.1		3.8	4.9
(134) 1.1	(269) 1.7	(185) 1.4	(160) 2.3	(31) 1.6	(30) 2.3	EBIT/Interest	(343) 1.8	(473) 2.0
-1.8	.8	.4	1.3	.5	1.3		.6	.9
	8.3	4.6	8.5			Net Profit + Depr., Dep.,	3.1	3.4
	(11) 3.2	(31) 2.7	(51) 3.5			Amort./Cur. Mat. L/T/D	(70) 1.8	(77) 2.0
	2.6	1.5	1.4				.8	1.0
.1	1.5	1.2	1.3	1.6	1.0		.8	.8
1.3	12.0	3.3	2.1	2.7	2.1	Fixed/Worth	2.9	2.6
-1.1	-5.2	43.4	4.4	10.7	9.7		32.0	-77.1
1.3	2.4	1.7	1.5	1.4	.8		1.6	1.4
9.1	18.0	5.1	2.8	2.5	2.3	Debt/Worth	4.1	3.9
-4.0	-7.6	141.5	6.3	12.3	16.1		206.4	-49.3
99.0	49.5	38.3	28.3	19.8	31.3	% Profit Before Taxes/Tangible	55.7	48.3
(161) 36.4	(176) 23.7	(155) 15.5	(158) 16.9	(29) 9.8	(28) 20.1	Net Worth	(323) 17.8	(436) 18.7
5.2	5.9	-.2	4.0	-5.8	5.8		3.2	3.3
16.7	7.9	7.6	7.6	6.1	9.0	% Profit Before Taxes/Total	10.1	10.7
4.5	3.3	2.0	4.4	2.9	2.9	Assets	3.5	3.9
-6.3	-1.2	-1.8	.6	-1.9	1.6		-.5	-.3
728.4	32.8	27.2	20.0	10.5	11.8		46.7	54.5
113.4	7.8	11.9	10.0	7.0	8.4	Sales/Net Fixed Assets	9.7	11.7
28.8	3.6	3.8	6.2	4.6	5.8		4.0	4.7
25.1	8.5	9.2	8.5	6.0	7.2		8.8	10.4
15.8	4.5	5.2	5.8	4.9	5.2	Sales/Total Assets	5.0	5.3
8.5	2.6	2.8	4.0	3.0	3.9		2.8	3.1
.2	.6	.6	.6	1.0	.8		.8	.7
(175) .5	(259) 1.1	(188) 1.0	(163) .9	(29) 1.2	(18) 1.2	% Depr., Dep., Amort./Sales	(367) 1.3	(500) 1.3
1.0	2.1	1.8	1.4	1.7	1.5		2.2	2.2
.5	.5	.2	.1				.6	.6
(148) 1.1	(132) 1.0	(60) .6	(45) .3			% Officers', Directors' Owners' Comp/Sales	(186) 1.2	(296) 1.2
2.0	2.0	.9	.5				2.3	2.2
968765M	2132643M	6826090M	25079312M	11133819M	36042098M	Net Sales ($)	14422843M	21648159M
63097M	329137M	958383M	3814380M	2315472M	5043036M	Total Assets ($)	3391229M	5099025M

M = $ thousand   MM = $ million
See Pages 11 through 21 for Explanation of Ratios and Data

Comparative Historical Data   Current Data Sorted by Sales

Type of Statement	4/1/04-3/31/05 ALL	4/1/05-3/31/06 ALL	4/1/06-3/31/07 ALL	0-1MM	1-3MM	3-5MM	5-10MM	10-25MM	25MM & OVER
Unqualified	67	68	93		2	2	1	7	81
Reviewed	48	71	107	2	2	2	8	9	84
Compiled	109	133	179	7	26	41	27	24	54
Tax Returns	165	215	376	25	112	100	73	38	28
Other	129	153	254	7	37	48	45	25	92
				140 (4/1-9/30/06)			869 (10/1/06-3/31/07)		
NUMBER OF STATEMENTS	518	640	1009	41	179	193	154	103	339
ASSETS	%	%	%	%	%	%	%	%	%
Cash & Equivalents	9.1	11.1	11.7	7.9	10.8	10.7	12.6	15.8	11.5
Trade Receivables (net)	7.0	7.4	7.4	3.1	3.8	4.2	5.2	8.9	12.2
Inventory	18.2	20.7	18.9	24.7	22.7	25.1	16.5	19.3	13.7
All Other Current	2.2	2.6	2.7	1.9	2.1	2.2	2.4	4.8	2.8
Total Current	36.5	41.7	40.7	37.6	39.4	42.2	36.7	48.7	40.2
Fixed Assets (net)	50.4	46.6	47.0	46.2	47.8	41.9	49.4	41.6	50.1
Intangibles (net)	5.5	5.6	7.2	11.4	8.7	13.1	7.9	3.8	3.2
All Other Non-Current	7.6	6.1	5.2	4.8	4.1	2.8	5.9	5.8	6.5
Total	100.0	100.0	100.0	100.0	100.0	100.0	100.0	100.0	100.0
LIABILITIES									
Notes Payable-Short Term	4.5	3.6	4.6	8.3	3.2	6.8	3.9	4.0	4.0
Cur. Mat.-L.T.D.	3.5	3.0	3.0	1.8	2.5	3.0	2.6	3.2	3.6
Trade Payables	15.3	17.2	17.7	9.5	10.4	16.1	15.2	19.7	23.8
Income Taxes Payable	.1	.2	.2	.0	.0	.0	.1	.1	.4
All Other Current	9.1	9.3	10.9	17.0	10.8	11.9	12.4	8.5	9.6
Total Current	32.6	33.3	36.3	36.7	27.0	37.9	34.3	35.5	41.4
Long-Term Debt	39.7	36.6	36.8	38.1	44.9	38.1	48.7	31.6	27.7
Deferred Taxes	.4	.5	.2	.0	.0		.1	.3	.5
All Other Non-Current	9.2	10.3	9.0	14.3	14.2	13.8	9.3	5.6	3.9
Net Worth	18.1	19.4	17.7	11.0	14.0	10.2	7.7	27.0	26.5
Total Liabilties & Net Worth	100.0	100.0	100.0	100.0	100.0	100.0	100.0	100.0	100.0
INCOME DATA									
Net Sales	100.0	100.0	100.0	100.0	100.0	100.0	100.0	100.0	100.0
Gross Profit	14.7	13.4	12.5	26.7	14.2	11.7	11.9	12.1	10.6
Operating Expenses	13.9	12.5	11.7	26.9	13.4	11.0	11.0	11.7	9.8
Operating Profit	.9	.8	.7	-.2	.8	.7	.9	.4	.7
All Other Expenses (net)	.1	.1	.1	-.3	.5	.3	.4	-.3	-.1
Profit Before Taxes	.8	.8	.6	.1	.3	.4	.5	.7	.8

RATIOS

Ratio	Hist 04-05	Hist 05-06	Hist 06-07	0-1MM	1-3MM	3-5MM	5-10MM	10-25MM	25MM & OVER
Current	2.1	2.5	2.1	2.2	5.7	3.4	2.3	2.2	1.3
	1.2	1.3	1.2	1.2	2.0	1.5	1.2	1.5	1.0
	.8	.8	.7	.6	.8	.7	.6	1.0	.7
Quick	.9	1.1	1.0	1.1	1.6	1.4	1.0	1.2	.8
	(512) .5	(634) .6	(1004) .5	(178) .2	.6	(190) .4	(153) .5	.8	.5
	.2	.3	.2	.1	.1	.2	.2	.3	.3
Sales/Receivables	0 999.8	0 UND	0 UND	0 UND	0 UND	0 UND	0 UND	0 999.8	2 163.0
	2 169.4	2 212.5	2 223.1	0 UND	0 UND	0 999.8	1 615.5	2 152.3	4 84.2
	6 65.1	5 73.8	5 76.7	3 112.8	2 229.6	2 162.9	3 131.2	5 72.1	7 51.0
Cost of Sales/Inventory	7 54.2	6 63.1	5 75.5	8 43.1	8 46.6	6 63.6	4 96.2	4 98.8	4 81.1
	9 38.6	9 40.9	8 47.1	30 12.0	12 29.8	8 45.2	6 62.2	7 53.2	7 52.5
	14 26.8	13 27.9	12 30.8	45 8.1	19 19.2	11 32.2	9 41.6	11 32.4	10 36.5
Cost of Sales/Payables	3 132.2	2 203.8	2 168.0	0 UND	0 UND	1 486.2	1 285.2	4 87.6	9 40.1
	9 42.4	8 46.8	7 49.9	5 76.9	3 138.6	4 91.5	5 74.7	7 48.8	12 29.9
	14 25.9	14 26.1	13 28.8	18 20.8	9 42.6	9 44.4	9 40.5	13 28.1	16 23.4
Sales/Working Capital	36.8	31.5	37.6	21.6	21.3	38.3	45.3	32.7	79.6
	133.8	104.7	163.6	64.7	42.1	90.3	193.3	68.6	-402.8
	-90.7	-131.8	-85.0	-26.2	-87.5	-126.2	-70.0	-999.8	-62.6
EBIT/Interest	4.2	4.7	4.0	3.0	2.4	2.8	3.0	6.6	5.3
	(428) 1.9	(514) 2.1	(809) 1.7	(23) .7	(126) 1.4	(137) 1.6	(124) 1.4	(84) 1.9	(315) 2.3
	1.0	1.0	.7	-.9	.5	.3	.5	.8	1.0
Net Profit + Depr., Dep., Amort./Cur. Mat. L/T/D	3.2	3.3	5.3				4.0	4.1	5.4
	(81) 1.8	(85) 2.0	(107) 3.0			(10) 2.5	(10) 3.2	(82) 3.0	
	1.2	1.3	1.7				1.2	2.2	1.7
Fixed/Worth	1.0	.8	.9	.4	.4	.8	.7	.6	1.1
	2.7	2.7	3.2	6.6	6.6	10.7	8.0	2.1	2.2
	60.5	30.4	-14.5	-3.1	-4.2	-2.1	-3.7	26.2	5.3
Debt/Worth	1.6	1.6	1.6	2.5	2.3	2.5	1.9	1.0	1.5
	4.2	4.2	5.6	13.1	15.5	34.8	18.8	3.2	3.2
	122.9	565.8	-16.0	-3.8	-5.8	-5.0	-5.4	58.8	8.5
% Profit Before Taxes/Tangible Net Worth	36.5	54.0	44.8	93.2	69.8	93.1	48.7	40.7	33.1
	(393) 14.0	(482) 23.9	(707) 19.2	(26) 23.7	(102) 21.6	(106) 36.1	(87) 29.3	(80) 13.9	(306) 17.1
	2.9	6.0	3.6	-7.7	5.6	5.8	.9	-1.5	4.0
% Profit Before Taxes/Total Assets	8.5	11.3	9.4	10.7	8.8	11.4	10.8	13.6	8.0
	3.2	4.5	3.3	2.4	2.7	3.7	2.1	3.4	4.0
	.0	.3	-1.3	-9.8	-2.2	-3.2	-2.7	-.7	.2
Sales/Net Fixed Assets	35.4	69.6	68.9	67.7	140.3	237.7	98.6	69.4	28.4
	10.1	12.3	14.6	10.7	10.1	27.2	14.1	20.2	13.2
	4.9	5.7	5.3	1.5	3.2	4.9	4.4	7.6	7.0
Sales/Total Assets	9.4	11.9	12.8	5.8	12.0	20.7	16.5	14.8	10.4
	5.4	6.1	6.3	3.0	4.2	7.6	7.2	8.8	6.8
	3.2	3.7	3.5	1.2	2.5	3.4	3.5	4.5	4.6
% Depr., Dep., Amort./Sales	.8	.5	.5	1.1	.5	.5	.5	.3	.5
	(440) 1.2	(529) 1.0	(832) .9	(30) 2.0	(131) 1.1	(144) 1.0	(127) 1.0	(89) .6	(311) .9
	1.9	1.5	1.5	4.5	2.3	1.8	1.7	1.3	1.2
% Officers', Directors' Owners' Comp/Sales	.5	.4	.4	2.0	.7	.4	.5	.4	.1
	(221) .9	(250) .8	(398) .8	(18) 2.5	(92) 1.3	(89) .9	(61) .9	(39) .8	(99) .4
	1.8	1.6	1.7	6.8	2.3	1.5	1.4	1.1	.7
Net Sales ($)	29616598M	48476855M	82182727M	27865M	371104M	770445M	1062154M	1575261M	78375898M
Total Assets ($)	6200972M	7344544M	12523505M	20097M	107706M	165569M	214673M	286078M	11729382M

© RMA 2007   M = $ thousand   MM = $ million
See Pages 11 through 21 for Explanation of Ratios and Data

Current Data Sorted by Assets   Comparative Historical Data

Type of Statement	0-500M	500M-2MM	2-10MM	10-50MM	50-100MM	100-250MM		4/1/02-3/31/03 ALL	4/1/03-3/31/04 ALL
Unqualified	1	1	3	25	10	6		78	91
Reviewed	2	4	27	18	2	1		92	99
Compiled	8	16	17	7	1			156	194
Tax Returns	57	32	15	2				168	205
Other	6	21	29	22	6	2		183	152
	64 (4/1-9/30/06)			277 (10/1/06-3/31/07)					
NUMBER OF STATEMENTS	74	74	91	74	19	9		677	741

ASSETS	%	%	%	%	%	%		%	%
Cash & Equivalents	18.3	6.8	11.1	9.3	7.5			9.6	12.1
Trade Receivables (net)	6.4	7.3	10.9	13.1	16.8			7.5	7.9
Inventory	25.8	12.5	11.2	11.4	9.6			15.1	16.7
All Other Current	1.1	2.1	2.2	2.3	1.6			2.4	2.8
Total Current	51.6	28.7	35.4	36.2	35.6			34.6	39.4
Fixed Assets (net)	27.2	56.2	51.8	54.6	53.7			53.7	47.7
Intangibles (net)	11.1	8.3	3.6	3.6	4.9			4.4	6.2
All Other Non-Current	10.1	6.9	9.2	5.7	5.8			7.2	6.7
Total	100.0	100.0	100.0	100.0	100.0			100.0	100.0

LIABILITIES									
Notes Payable-Short Term	5.5	3.6	4.0	5.0	3.4			4.6	4.1
Cur. Mat.-L.T.D.	2.9	4.4	4.8	5.0	3.7			3.9	3.4
Trade Payables	21.1	12.6	19.0	20.5	19.7			14.8	15.4
Income Taxes Payable	.1	.0	.1	.2	.2			.1	.2
All Other Current	15.7	6.2	7.5	6.9	6.5			10.1	11.1
Total Current	45.1	26.8	35.4	37.6	33.4			33.6	34.1
Long-Term Debt	23.2	50.4	34.3	31.8	27.2			38.8	37.6
Deferred Taxes	.0	.0	.3	.6	.8			.4	.3
All Other Non-Current	13.0	11.3	3.2	3.1	3.4			6.5	8.2
Net Worth	18.6	11.4	26.8	26.9	35.2			20.7	19.9
Total Liabilities & Net Worth	100.0	100.0	100.0	100.0	100.0			100.0	100.0

INCOME DATA									
Net Sales	100.0	100.0	100.0	100.0	100.0			100.0	100.0
Gross Profit	17.2	12.5	12.1	11.4	10.0			17.8	16.0
Operating Expenses	15.4	10.9	10.8	10.4	7.4			16.9	14.9
Operating Profit	1.8	1.6	1.3	1.0	2.6			.9	1.2
All Other Expenses (net)	.0	1.1	.1	.1	.3			.2	.1
Profit Before Taxes	1.8	.5	1.1	.9	2.3			.7	1.1

RATIOS									
Current	9.3	3.1	1.5	1.3	1.3			1.8	2.1
	1.4	1.3	1.0	.9	1.1			1.1	1.2
	.8	.7	.7	.7	.8			.7	.8
Quick	1.9	1.3	1.0	.7	.9			.9	1.1
	.7	.6	.6	.5	.7		(673) .5	(737) .5
	.3	.2	.3	.3	.5			.2	.3
Sales/Receivables	0 UND	0 UND	1 321.0	3 137.0	3 121.9		1 535.9	0 945.0
	0 999.8	1 555.8	4 103.5	5 76.6	9 38.6		3 126.6	2 149.4
	3 112.2	4 97.5	7 53.3	9 41.6	13 28.5		7 52.1	6 56.6
Cost of Sales/Inventory	4 91.1	4 89.9	4 92.9	5 80.3	4 91.5		7 54.2	6 59.3
	7 49.9	7 50.0	6 56.4	7 52.2	7 55.4		10 35.8	9 40.3
	12 30.8	13 28.7	10 36.2	10 35.0	11 32.0		15 24.8	15 25.1
Cost of Sales/Payables	0 UND	0 786.5	6 57.4	9 39.2	10 38.2		4 84.2	3 110.9
	4 103.8	6 60.1	9 39.0	14 27.0	12 29.2		11 32.8	10 37.0
	12 29.8	11 32.8	14 25.3	17 20.9	17 21.4		17 21.3	15 23.9
Sales/Working Capital	43.4	33.6	58.7	77.6	56.8			36.4	31.7
	95.9	117.3	-999.8	-160.4	356.8			281.9	135.4
	-217.4	-58.9	-64.0	-59.4	-115.8			-47.0	-77.9
EBIT/Interest	7.7	4.3	4.7	4.6	6.1			3.6	4.4
	(38) 2.2	(65) 1.5	(88) 1.8	(73) 2.4	3.3		(592) 1.7	(620) 2.0
	.4	.1	1.1	1.1	1.5			.4	1.0
Net Profit + Depr., Dep., Amort./Cur. Mat. L/T/D			6.0	3.1				3.9	4.1
			(18) 2.0	(23) 2.1			(100) 1.7	(110) 2.1
			1.3	1.7				1.1	1.2
Fixed/Worth	.1	1.6	1.0	1.3	1.1			1.1	.9
	1.4	13.4	2.5	2.2	1.9			2.8	2.5
	-2.8	-3.9	7.4	5.8	2.7			57.7	-33.5
Debt/Worth	1.4	2.2	1.4	1.7	1.6			1.6	1.6
	7.9	20.4	3.8	3.2	2.2			4.0	4.0
	-5.2	-8.5	9.7	6.8	3.1			90.4	-31.6
% Profit Before Taxes/Tangible Net Worth	105.5	48.5	32.4	35.9	32.3			34.1	44.0
	(46) 37.4	(43) 30.4	(74) 14.7	(65) 15.6	(18) 21.5		(514) 12.8	(537) 18.5
	6.4	10.4	2.8	5.6	9.3			-.5	5.7
% Profit Before Taxes/Total Assets	26.4	9.7	8.8	8.6	10.7			7.6	9.8
	7.6	2.9	3.0	4.1	5.0			2.4	3.9
	-.7	-3.2	.5	.4	1.4			-2.2	.3
Sales/Net Fixed Assets	476.9	23.0	25.3	21.1	19.3			21.4	37.3
	81.5	7.1	13.4	9.1	8.7			8.0	10.2
	20.5	4.1	4.9	6.3	4.8			4.0	4.5
Sales/Total Assets	24.0	7.7	9.6	8.7	7.4			7.6	9.3
	14.1	4.5	5.9	5.8	4.9			4.2	4.8
	7.8	2.7	3.4	3.8	3.6			2.6	3.0
% Depr., Dep., Amort./Sales	.3	.7	.6	.6	.7			1.0	.7
	(51) .6	(65) 1.0	(86) .9	(73) 1.0	1.0		(602) 1.6	(640) 1.3
	1.4	1.7	1.5	1.4	1.3			2.4	2.1
% Officers', Directors', Owners' Comp/Sales	.8	.4	.3	.2				.5	.5
	(49) 1.4	(33) 1.1	(36) .4	(22) .4			(265) 1.3	(295) 1.2
	2.4	2.0	1.0	.8				2.5	2.3
Net Sales ($)	247945M	518869M	3299987M	11196284M	7933552M	6508041M		35663735M	39432358M
Total Assets ($)	18304M	82013M	441658M	1659698M	1320918M	1337152M		8588246M	8559978M

M = $ thousand   MM = $ million
See Pages 11 through 21 for Explanation of Ratios and Data

© RMA 2007

Comparative Historical Data　　　　　　　　　　Current Data Sorted by Sales

4/1/04-3/31/05 ALL	4/1/05-3/31/06 ALL	4/1/06-3/31/07 ALL	Type of Statement	0-1MM	1-3MM	3-5MM	5-10MM	10-25MM	25MM & OVER
70	49	46	Unqualified	1				2	42
95	79	54	Reviewed		3	2	3	5	41
95	87	49	Compiled	1	8	9	8	10	13
195	168	106	Tax Returns	8	36	22	21	11	8
132	168	86	Other	1	5	8	16	11	45
					64 (4/1-9/30/06)			277 (10/1/06-3/31/07)	
587	551	341	NUMBER OF STATEMENTS	11	52	42	48	39	149
%	%	%	**ASSETS**	%	%	%	%	%	%
11.3	12.6	11.1	Cash & Equivalents	16.6	10.8	11.7	13.1	8.8	10.5
8.4	8.5	9.9	Trade Receivables (net)	7.2	5.2	3.9	9.8	9.5	13.7
16.6	15.6	14.6	Inventory	12.5	21.0	13.3	13.8	15.5	12.8
2.0	2.6	1.9	All Other Current	.9	.6	3.2	1.7	1.8	2.3
38.4	39.2	37.5	Total Current	37.2	37.5	32.2	38.4	35.6	39.3
47.0	48.2	48.3	Fixed Assets (net)	38.7	44.7	47.3	47.4	50.6	50.2
7.8	6.5	6.3	Intangibles (net)	14.1	8.8	12.1	5.1	6.4	3.7
6.8	6.0	7.8	All Other Non-Current	10.0	9.0	8.4	9.1	7.5	6.8
100.0	100.0	100.0	Total	100.0	100.0	100.0	100.0	100.0	100.0
			LIABILITIES						
4.1	4.7	4.4	Notes Payable-Short Term	20.7	2.6	2.3	3.8	5.3	4.4
3.1	3.3	4.2	Cur. Mat.-L.T.D.	4.5	3.0	5.3	5.2	3.3	4.3
14.8	17.3	18.3	Trade Payables	8.3	12.5	16.3	15.5	18.1	22.6
.1	.1	.1	Income Taxes Payable	.2	.0	.0	.1	.1	.2
11.1	10.0	8.8	All Other Current	30.7	9.9	8.1	7.6	8.7	7.5
33.2	35.4	35.9	Total Current	64.3	28.1	32.1	32.2	35.5	38.9
35.5	35.7	34.5	Long-Term Debt	42.4	41.2	41.6	36.7	40.0	27.5
.4	.2	.3	Deferred Taxes	.0	.0	.1	.1	.3	.5
7.1	9.4	7.1	All Other Non-Current	3.9	9.7	13.2	5.1	12.1	4.0
23.8	19.3	22.2	Net Worth	-10.7	20.9	13.1	25.9	12.2	29.0
100.0	100.0	100.0	Total Liabilities & Net Worth	100.0	100.0	100.0	100.0	100.0	100.0
			INCOME DATA						
100.0	100.0	100.0	Net Sales	100.0	100.0	100.0	100.0	100.0	100.0
14.4	14.4	12.9	Gross Profit	43.8	16.2	11.7	12.6	11.6	10.3
13.4	12.8	11.5	Operating Expenses	35.2	14.7	10.6	10.6	10.5	9.4
.9	1.6	1.5	Operating Profit	8.6	1.5	1.1	2.0	1.2	1.0
-.1	.3	.3	All Other Expenses (net)	2.2	.6	.5	.4	.4	.0
1.1	1.4	1.2	Profit Before Taxes	6.4	.9	.5	1.6	.7	1.0
			RATIOS						
2.1	2.1	1.8	Current	11.2	7.4	3.0	2.4	1.5	1.3
1.1	1.2	1.0		1.4	1.5	1.4	1.3	1.0	1.0
.8	.8	.7		.5	.8	.7	.6	.8	.7
1.0	1.2	1.0	Quick	3.5	1.4	1.3	1.5	.9	.8
(586) .6	(550) .6	.6		1.1	.8	.4	.7	.5	.6
.3	.3	.3		.3	.3	.1	.2	.3	.4
0　999.8	0　999.8	0　999.8	Sales/Receivables	0　UND	0　UND	0　UND	0　UND	0　923.7	3　139.2
2　169.8	2　149.9	3　120.2		1　432.0	0　UND	0　999.8	2　193.0	4　92.9	4　81.3
6　63.2	6　59.6	7　53.9		5　69.7	4　88.2	1　275.6	4　84.7	9　41.9	9　42.9
5　66.4	5　75.7	4　89.3	Cost of Sales/Inventory	9　42.1	7　54.6	4　93.7	3　106.4	4　92.9	4　91.8
8　43.3	7　48.9	7　52.5		19　19.4	10　37.8	7　49.9	5　70.7	7　50.5	6　59.4
14　26.6	12　30.5	11　32.9		37　10.0	16　23.3	10　36.6	8　47.1	11　33.8	10　35.8
2　157.1	3　107.2	4　99.6	Cost of Sales/Payables	0　UND	0　UND	1　725.5	1　429.5	5　79.9	9　41.3
9　41.5	9　38.9	9　39.9		2　165.0	4　94.5	5　77.3	8　45.7	9　41.2	12　29.3
14　25.8	15　24.5	14　25.4		26　14.1	9　38.6	12　30.5	11　33.4	14　25.3	16　22.6
38.0	34.4	48.6	Sales/Working Capital	11.1	27.3	45.4	45.1	69.3	79.4
166.4	147.1	580.0		78.0	64.6	119.8	128.4	-999.8	-336.9
-80.4	-78.9	-67.7		-9.5	-95.0	-81.1	-51.5	-64.4	-68.9
5.0	5.7	4.7	EBIT/Interest		2.9	3.1	6.5	3.4	5.8
(480) 2.1	(455) 2.4	(292) 2.1			(35) 1.6	(36) 1.2	(36) 2.8	(32) 1.5	(146) 2.9
1.1	1.2	1.0			.7	.2	1.4	.9	1.2
3.9	4.3	4.6	Net Profit + Depr., Dep., Amort./Cur. Mat. L/T/D						5.0
(86) 2.2	(71) 2.2	(57) 2.3						(46)	2.4
1.3	1.4	1.6							1.7
.9	.8	1.0	Fixed/Worth	.3	.4	.8	.3	1.9	1.1
2.5	2.6	2.5		8.9	6.7	8.0	2.8	5.2	2.0
51.3	38.5	UND		-.6	-12.9	-1.9	-28.5	-9.2	4.0
1.6	1.5	1.7	Debt/Worth	1.1	2.1	2.3	1.2	2.9	1.6
3.8	3.7	4.1		9.7	12.0	11.8	3.8	8.5	2.7
UND	UND	-252.0		-1.9	-8.4	-4.8	-21.4	-11.4	6.6
40.7	49.2	45.8	% Profit Before Taxes/Tangible Net Worth		90.0	47.5	101.5	40.4	34.3
(442) 18.5	(415) 23.5	(254) 20.1		(33) 27.3	(23) 25.5	(34) 31.2	(24) 16.2	(134) 15.8	
4.7	9.8	5.8			4.1	4.1	10.8	4.9	3.4
9.7	11.1	10.5	% Profit Before Taxes/Total Assets	36.4	10.7	10.6	20.8	8.9	8.8
4.1	5.2	4.3		11.1	4.6	1.2	6.4	3.0	4.1
.4	1.1	.2		-.6	-1.9	-2.9	2.3	-.2	.5
46.0	44.6	41.2	Sales/Net Fixed Assets	252.0	120.3	65.7	140.6	25.7	27.5
11.8	11.6	13.0		48.4	11.4	16.4	11.7	13.9	12.6
5.1	4.8	5.7		1.1	4.0	4.3	4.7	5.0	7.9
9.7	10.1	11.2	Sales/Total Assets	14.4	12.5	13.3	16.3	10.8	10.0
5.6	5.8	6.0		7.3	5.1	7.0	5.4	6.7	6.5
3.3	3.3	3.6		.7	2.6	2.9	3.5	3.7	4.4
.6	.6	.6	% Depr., Dep., Amort./Sales		.4	.6	.5	.6	.6
(484) 1.2	(458) 1.0	(300) .9		(43) 1.0	(35) 1.1	(42) 1.0	(33) .9	(142) .9	
1.8	1.7	1.4			1.9	1.7	1.9	1.5	1.2
.5	.4	.3	% Officers', Directors' Owners' Comp/Sales		1.1	.5	.6	.3	.2
(219) 1.0	(212) .9	(142) .8		(31) 2.0	(19) 1.2	(25) .8	(18)	(45) .3	
1.9	1.9	1.8			2.5	1.9	1.3	1.0	.6
34869353M	56564921M	29704678M	Net Sales ($)	6702M	107205M	165018M	351687M	639438M	28434628M
7110471M	8015447M	4859743M	Total Assets ($)	3548M	26949M	35569M	70839M	142025M	4580813M

© RMA 2007

M = $ thousand　　MM = $ million

See Pages 11 through 21 for Explanation of Ratios and Data

Current Data Sorted by Assets

Comparative Historical Data

Type of Statement							9	14
Unqualified							9	14
Reviewed							19	14
Compiled							23	35
Tax Returns							15	21
Other							20	21

	17 (4/1-9/30/06)		58 (10/1/06-3/31/07)				4/1/02-3/31/03	4/1/03-3/31/04
0-500M	500M-2MM	2-10MM	10-50MM	50-100MM	100-250MM		ALL	ALL
21	18	23	9	1	3	**NUMBER OF STATEMENTS**	86	105

%	%	%	%	%	%		%	%
						ASSETS		
9.1	12.0	14.5				Cash & Equivalents	10.9	13.8
9.4	12.2	11.9				Trade Receivables (net)	8.6	6.5
63.5	47.7	40.1				Inventory	48.8	51.1
.7	2.1	2.6				All Other Current	1.4	2.2
82.7	73.9	69.0				Total Current	69.7	73.6
10.3	20.5	22.2				Fixed Assets (net)	20.7	19.8
1.4	1.9	1.4				Intangibles (net)	2.3	.8
5.8	3.7	7.4				All Other Non-Current	7.4	5.7
100.0	100.0	100.0				Total	100.0	100.0
						LIABILITIES		
22.3	10.5	7.7				Notes Payable-Short Term	7.8	10.2
5.4	1.4	2.4				Cur. Mat.-L.T.D.	2.7	2.4
25.8	18.6	26.0				Trade Payables	16.5	25.8
.4	.0	.0				Income Taxes Payable	.2	.6
10.7	7.8	8.4				All Other Current	10.9	11.8
64.7	38.3	44.5				Total Current	38.0	50.8
25.2	9.5	22.7				Long-Term Debt	17.4	11.6
.0	.0	.4				Deferred Taxes	.1	.2
16.6	5.4	2.7				All Other Non-Current	5.2	4.0
-6.7	46.8	29.8				Net Worth	39.3	33.4
100.0	100.0	100.0				Total Liabilties & Net Worth	100.0	100.0
						INCOME DATA		
100.0	100.0	100.0				Net Sales	100.0	100.0
45.9	48.2	48.3				Gross Profit	45.8	44.5
44.0	43.3	44.5				Operating Expenses	43.9	41.5
2.0	4.9	3.8				Operating Profit	1.9	2.9
1.2	.5	.1				All Other Expenses (net)	.6	.6
.8	4.3	3.7				Profit Before Taxes	1.3	2.3
						RATIOS		
3.4	4.0	2.3				Current	3.3	2.4
2.1	2.2	1.7					2.1	1.6
1.1	1.3	1.3					1.3	1.1
.9	2.2	1.1				Quick	1.1	.8
.4	.4	.7					.4 (104)	.3
.1	.1	.2					.2	.1
0 UND	0 UND	0 999.8				Sales/Receivables	0 UND	0 UND
2 181.0	12 30.8	14 27.0					4 98.9	3 139.5
16 22.5	24 15.3	36 10.1					20 18.2	12 31.3
96 3.8	85 4.3	88 4.2				Cost of Sales/Inventory	90 4.0	84 4.3
160 2.3	133 2.7	128 2.9					134 2.7	129 2.8
218 1.7	223 1.6	191 1.9					194 1.9	216 1.7
26 13.9	16 22.8	52 7.1				Cost of Sales/Payables	16 22.8	33 10.9
40 9.0	40 9.1	76 4.8					40 9.2	58 6.3
67 5.5	113 3.2	117 3.1					61 6.0	99 3.7
4.6	4.2	5.4				Sales/Working Capital	3.9	4.9
6.5	5.5	10.2					6.6	9.2
211.6	14.9	17.4					19.7	43.8
7.9	18.1	21.2				EBIT/Interest	6.5	7.8
(19) 1.7	(16) 9.4	(19) 5.2					(75) 1.6	(80) 2.2
-.5	1.7	-.3					-.8	.6
						Net Profit + Depr., Dep., Amort./Cur. Mat. L/T/D	4.5	15.1
							(19) .5	(17) 1.2
							-1.1	.6
.1	.1	.1				Fixed/Worth	.2	.2
.3	.4	.4					.4	.4
-3.2	1.2	1.4					.9	1.4
.5	.4	.7				Debt/Worth	.7	.8
3.9	1.2	1.2					1.3	1.7
-14.1	3.6	3.8					4.3	5.0
36.3	22.2	39.1				% Profit Before Taxes/Tangible Net Worth	25.5	28.6
(14) 22.4	(17) 8.0	(20) 20.4					(77) 8.0	(91) 9.4
-12.4	4.2	3.3					-3.1	2.1
15.3	16.4	13.7				% Profit Before Taxes/Total Assets	8.7	10.0
4.2	6.0	5.3					1.4	3.2
-9.4	1.2	-1.9					-4.6	.0
198.8	52.4	95.5				Sales/Net Fixed Assets	48.4	52.3
41.7	15.8	13.7					16.3	19.6
16.4	6.0	5.3					7.8	9.3
3.3	3.3	2.8				Sales/Total Assets	3.1	3.2
2.5	2.3	2.4					2.4	2.3
2.1	2.0	1.7					1.8	1.7
.2	.4	.5				% Depr., Dep., Amort./Sales	.6	.5
(15) .5	(14) .9	(19) 1.3					(75) 1.4	(84) 1.3
1.2	1.6	2.3					2.3	2.1
4.7	2.3	5.2				% Officers', Directors' Owners' Comp/Sales	3.5	2.9
(18) 9.1	(13) 4.9	(11) 6.3					(48) 6.0	(61) 5.0
13.6	8.6	8.6					9.8	8.5
16499M	55955M	255411M	394737M	183030M	1147397M	Net Sales ($)	3169188M	1927539M
6016M	22364M	109185M	167113M	75191M	403144M	Total Assets ($)	1231664M	799246M

© RMA 2007

M = $ thousand   MM = $ million
See Pages 11 through 21 for Explanation of Ratios and Data

Comparative Historical Data | Current Data Sorted by Sales

Type of Statement	10 / 9 / 37 / 12 / 23	9 / 7 / 21 / 13 / 31	6 / 13 / 13 / 16 / 27	0-1MM	1-3MM	3-5MM	5-10MM	10-25MM	25MM & OVER
Unqualified							1	2	3
Reviewed					2	2	1	7	1
Compiled				5	5	2	1		
Tax Returns				7	4	3	1		1
Other				3	6	5	4	3	6
	4/1/04-3/31/05 ALL	4/1/05-3/31/06 ALL	4/1/06-3/31/07 ALL	17 (4/1-9/30/06)			58 (10/1/06-3/31/07)		
NUMBER OF STATEMENTS	91	81	75	15	17	12	8	12	11
ASSETS	%	%	%	%	%	%	%	%	%
Cash & Equivalents	10.5	12.6	10.6	6.7	17.0	9.0		11.3	8.8
Trade Receivables (net)	6.5	5.7	10.0	7.9	15.0	12.9		4.9	5.3
Inventory	56.8	50.6	50.1	67.0	42.4	54.7		50.9	49.1
All Other Current	1.0	2.7	1.7	.9	.4	1.0		2.0	1.7
Total Current	74.7	71.6	72.4	82.5	74.9	77.7		69.1	64.9
Fixed Assets (net)	18.6	20.1	19.1	11.8	18.2	13.4		17.6	26.0
Intangibles (net)	.6	1.2	2.2	1.9	.8	2.7		2.7	4.8
All Other Non-Current	6.1	7.1	6.3	4.1	6.1	6.1		10.6	4.2
Total	100.0	100.0	100.0	100.0	100.0	100.0		100.0	100.0
LIABILITIES									
Notes Payable-Short Term	13.4	11.1	13.9	29.7	7.6	7.2		12.3	12.3
Cur. Mat.-L.T.D.	2.3	1.9	2.9	6.3	1.4	3.8		1.6	1.5
Trade Payables	21.6	18.9	23.1	29.1	15.3	25.9		20.6	25.3
Income Taxes Payable	.9	.1	.1	.5	.1	.0		.0	.0
All Other Current	10.9	11.0	8.7	12.0	6.6	6.7		10.2	9.0
Total Current	49.1	43.1	48.6	77.7	30.9	43.7		44.7	48.1
Long-Term Debt	11.4	12.3	18.4	26.7	18.7	6.7		28.3	5.7
Deferred Taxes	.1	.0	.1	.0	.0	.0		.0	.1
All Other Non-Current	2.7	4.6	7.4	14.6	10.4	5.5		2.6	5.9
Net Worth	36.8	40.0	25.4	-19.2	39.9	44.2		24.4	40.2
Total Liabilties & Net Worth	100.0	100.0	100.0	100.0	100.0	100.0		100.0	100.0
INCOME DATA									
Net Sales	100.0	100.0	100.0	100.0	100.0	100.0		100.0	100.0
Gross Profit	44.6	47.5	45.7	45.6	48.8	44.3		44.5	41.2
Operating Expenses	42.7	44.7	42.3	44.8	43.4	40.2		43.0	38.1
Operating Profit	1.9	2.8	3.4	.8	5.3	4.1		1.5	3.1
All Other Expenses (net)	.2	.1	.5	1.2	.7	.0		-.3	.7
Profit Before Taxes	1.7	2.7	2.8	-.3	4.7	4.1		1.8	2.4
RATIOS									
Current	2.7 / 1.8 / 1.2	2.6 / 1.9 / 1.2	3.2 / 1.8 / 1.2	3.8 / 2.0 / 1.0	3.7 / 3.0 / 1.7	3.6 / 1.9 / 1.2		2.4 / 1.6 / 1.1	1.8 / 1.3 / 1.1
Quick	.7 / .2 / .1	.8 / .3 / .1	1.1 / .3 / .1	.5 / .3 / .1	2.3 / 1.1 / .3	1.0 / .3 / .1		.8 / .2 / .1	.4 / .2 / .1
Sales/Receivables	0 UND / 1 244.2 / 11 34.5	0 UND / 3 145.5 / 14 26.4	0 UND / 5 68.6 / 22 16.5	0 UND / 4 95.3 / 11 32.0	1 429.6 / 10 34.8 / 42 8.7	0 UND / 8 44.0 / 21 17.3		1 288.2 / 4 96.2 / 16 23.2	0 UND / 4 82.4 / 10 38.1
Cost of Sales/Inventory	96 3.8 / 145 2.5 / 228 1.6	91 4.0 / 141 2.6 / 232 1.6	84 4.4 / 148 2.5 / 209 1.7	148 2.5 / 172 2.1 / 209 1.7	78 4.7 / 164 2.2 / 231 1.6	93 3.9 / 137 2.7 / 210 1.7		84 4.3 / 115 3.2 / 226 1.6	72 5.0 / 101 3.6 / 156 2.3
Cost of Sales/Payables	30 12.1 / 45 8.2 / 72 5.1	30 12.3 / 49 7.4 / 81 4.5	33 11.2 / 50 7.3 / 89 4.1	27 13.7 / 40 9.0 / 62 5.8	16 22.2 / 39 9.3 / 116 3.1	20 18.3 / 54 6.8 / 118 3.1		35 10.4 / 52 7.1 / 70 5.2	39 9.3 / 72 5.1 / 84 4.4
Sales/Working Capital	4.8 / 8.7 / 30.2	4.1 / 7.6 / 36.1	4.7 / 7.5 / 26.3	4.6 / 6.6 / 566.0	3.2 / 5.0 / 8.5	4.0 / 6.8 / 17.6		5.7 / 9.6 / 100.4	6.7 / 26.3 / 66.6
EBIT/Interest	12.1 / (74) 2.2 / -.1	8.4 / (66) 3.1 / .0	11.5 / (65) 2.7 / .8	7.6 / (14) 2.0 / -1.4	19.0 / (14) 2.3 / .7	13.5 / (11) 8.9 / 1.9			
Net Profit + Depr., Dep., Amort./Cur. Mat. L/T/D	3.7 / (13) .4 / -.3								
Fixed/Worth	.1 / .4 / 1.1	.1 / .4 / 1.2	.1 / .4 / 1.4	.2 / .4 / -5.9	.1 / .3 / 5.7	.0 / .2 / .8		.1 / .3 / 8.0	.4 / .7 / 1.1
Debt/Worth	.6 / 1.1 / 4.7	.6 / 1.2 / 3.6	.7 / 1.8 / 5.6	.5 / 3.9 / -13.5	.4 / 1.7 / 19.8	.5 / 1.4 / 3.8		.5 / 1.0 / 20.4	1.1 / 1.5 / 4.3
% Profit Before Taxes/Tangible Net Worth	33.5 / (78) 9.7 / -.1	29.8 / (74) 11.7 / .4	33.3 / (63) 13.1 / 2.4	36.3 / (10) 20.1 / -12.4	27.1 / (14) 16.0 / 5.1	32.1 / (11) 6.5 / 2.0		26.1 / (10) 8.7 / -.2	32.2 / 13.7 / -.9
% Profit Before Taxes/Total Assets	13.3 / 2.6 / -1.8	12.0 / 4.6 / -.3	14.5 / 5.3 / -.1	15.1 / 3.4 / -11.2	16.4 / 5.9 / .8	13.0 / 5.3 / 1.2		12.2 / 4.4 / -.2	8.1 / 6.0 / -.1
Sales/Net Fixed Assets	44.2 / 18.7 / 9.7	41.3 / 16.6 / 7.9	71.3 / 16.6 / 8.0	159.0 / 29.9 / 14.3	65.3 / 20.6 / 4.3	524.8 / 35.9 / 13.3		92.2 / 17.1 / 13.3	22.6 / 10.8 / 6.8
Sales/Total Assets	3.5 / 2.6 / 1.9	3.0 / 2.4 / 1.6	3.2 / 2.4 / 1.8	3.0 / 2.3 / 2.0	3.2 / 2.2 / 1.2	3.2 / 2.3 / 1.8		4.1 / 2.6 / 1.4	3.2 / 2.9 / 2.4
% Depr., Dep., Amort./Sales	.6 / (69) 1.0 / 1.9	.5 / (70) 1.1 / 1.7	.4 / (61) 1.1 / 1.6	.4 / (11) .7 / 1.2	.2 / (14) .5 / 1.6			.4 / (11) 1.4 / 1.9	.5 / (10) 1.2 / 1.8
% Officers', Directors' Owners' Comp/Sales	2.2 / (47) 5.5 / 8.7	3.6 / (49) 5.6 / 7.9	2.6 / (46) 6.5 / 11.4	4.6 / (12) 11.8 / 15.6	4.1 / (13) 7.5 / 9.1				
Net Sales ($)	2355426M	3064975M	2053029M	9007M	28659M	46088M	62203M	194868M	1712204M
Total Assets ($)	941066M	1388097M	783013M	3516M	18205M	20014M	35646M	92524M	613108M

© RMA 2007

M = $ thousand   MM = $ million
See Pages 11 through 21 for Explanation of Ratios and Data

Current Data Sorted by Assets   Comparative Historical Data

Type of Statement

	0-500M	500M-2MM	2-10MM	10-50MM	50-100MM	100-250MM		4/1/02-3/31/03 ALL	4/1/03-3/31/04 ALL
Unqualified	1	1	3	6	2	4		24	20
Reviewed		4	6			1		17	24
Compiled	5	3	2					21	34
Tax Returns	14	9	4					12	18
Other	6	7	9	7	3	1		29	22
	21 (4/1-9/30/06)			77 (10/1/06-3/31/07)				4/1/02-3/31/03	4/1/03-3/31/04
NUMBER OF STATEMENTS	26	24	24	13	5	6		103	118

0-500M %	500M-2MM %	2-10MM %	10-50MM %	50-100MM %	100-250MM %	Item	4/1/02-3/31/03 ALL %	4/1/03-3/31/04 ALL %
						ASSETS		
14.2	13.5	12.5	17.5			Cash & Equivalents	12.2	12.7
3.2	9.9	12.0	6.3			Trade Receivables (net)	6.9	7.7
65.4	50.3	46.5	39.3			Inventory	47.1	44.6
.7	3.9	2.7	3.5			All Other Current	2.4	1.8
83.5	77.6	73.7	66.6			Total Current	68.6	66.7
15.0	16.0	16.2	27.7			Fixed Assets (net)	21.1	22.7
.1	2.9	.5	.5			Intangibles (net)	3.3	3.0
1.4	3.5	9.6	5.2			All Other Non-Current	6.9	7.6
100.0	100.0	100.0	100.0			Total	100.0	100.0
						LIABILITIES		
14.1	8.4	11.1	7.5			Notes Payable-Short Term	10.0	8.4
11.5	5.1	1.4	.4			Cur. Mat.-L.T.D.	2.8	4.8
5.0	16.2	26.6	26.2			Trade Payables	19.1	18.8
.2	.1	.6	.4			Income Taxes Payable	.5	.5
7.0	10.2	9.3	12.2			All Other Current	9.7	11.9
37.9	40.0	49.1	46.7			Total Current	42.0	44.3
18.9	12.2	4.3	6.0			Long-Term Debt	10.9	14.2
.0	.5	.1	.2			Deferred Taxes	.1	.1
4.9	4.5	3.3	2.8			All Other Non-Current	3.9	8.3
38.4	42.8	43.2	44.3			Net Worth	43.2	33.0
100.0	100.0	100.0	100.0			Total Liabilities & Net Worth	100.0	100.0
						INCOME DATA		
100.0	100.0	100.0	100.0			Net Sales	100.0	100.0
44.2	44.6	45.1	46.3			Gross Profit	42.0	41.2
41.2	38.8	42.9	44.4			Operating Expenses	38.3	39.2
3.0	5.8	2.1	1.9			Operating Profit	3.7	2.0
2.6	.8	.2	2.0			All Other Expenses (net)	.6	.8
.4	5.0	1.9	-.2			Profit Before Taxes	3.1	1.2
						RATIOS		
15.9	6.6	2.3	2.2				2.6	2.5
4.9	2.1	1.6	1.5			Current	1.7	1.7
1.1	1.2	.9	.9				1.2	1.0
3.3	2.1	.9	1.4				.9	1.0
(25) .5	.5	.3	.3			Quick	.3	.4
.1	.1	.1	.2				.1	.1
0 UND	0 UND	0 983.7	0 UND				0 UND	0 UND
0 UND	1 687.5	3 109.2	4 83.1			Sales/Receivables	3 142.0	2 239.2
2 150.2	33 11.2	23 15.9	23 16.0				11 34.4	12 30.2
90 4.1	70 5.2	54 6.7	61 6.0				66 5.5	48 7.6
133 2.7	102 3.6	96 3.8	109 3.4			Cost of Sales/Inventory	106 3.5	99 3.7
221 1.6	211 1.7	169 2.2	121 3.0				151 2.4	148 2.5
0 UND	13 27.8	27 13.6	41				24 15.5	16 22.5
1 262.2	26 13.9	49 7.5	61 6.0			Cost of Sales/Payables	37 10.0	34 10.6
20 18.4	59 6.1	91 4.0	86 4.3				56 6.5	56 6.5
3.6	6.5	5.7	4.2				5.2	5.7
6.0	10.5	11.1	14.8			Sales/Working Capital	9.9	13.1
NM	28.1	-115.4	-262.6				48.5	NM
24.8	37.6	21.8	19.6				21.7	8.6
(18) 2.3	(21) 7.4	(22) 6.2	(10) 3.0			EBIT/Interest	(88) 3.8	(104) 2.5
-3.0	-.1	1.1	-2.2				1.1	-.3
						Net Profit + Depr., Dep.,	16.4	8.1
						Amort./Cur. Mat. L/T/D	(21) 2.5	(20) 2.0
							-.4	.6
.0	.1	.1	.2				.3	.3
.2	.4	.3	.3			Fixed/Worth	.5	.6
1.5	.9	.8	1.6				1.0	4.5
.2	.5	.6	.5				.6	.7
1.1	1.4	1.2	1.2			Debt/Worth	1.1	1.4
NM	3.5	3.4	2.6				2.5	24.2
71.6	75.4	41.3	12.8			% Profit Before Taxes/Tangible	34.4	25.7
(20) 31.0	(21) 25.9	(23) 10.0	(12) -1.4			Net Worth	(92) 11.3	(94) 11.4
-13.3	1.0	1.5	-11.3				3.3	-1.1
34.7	25.4	15.4	17.0			% Profit Before Taxes/Total	13.8	10.4
8.1	11.1	4.6	1.5			Assets	5.5	3.3
-20.2	-3.1	-.1	-4.0				.4	-2.2
208.5	68.0	143.6	48.9				41.1	33.3
38.7	30.3	30.3	9.5			Sales/Net Fixed Assets	16.3	17.8
13.1	7.7	10.7	5.4				8.4	7.8
4.5	4.8	4.0	4.2				3.7	4.1
3.5	2.8	3.4	2.9			Sales/Total Assets	2.6	2.6
2.2	2.0	2.3	1.6				1.9	1.9
.3	.4	.2	.9				.6	.7
(18) .8	(16) .7	(20) .8	(11) 2.4			% Depr., Dep., Amort./Sales	(81) 1.1	(93) 1.3
2.1	1.2	1.5	3.9				2.0	2.3
5.1	3.7	1.1				% Officers', Directors'	2.3	2.8
(15) 7.4	(12) 4.8	(15) 1.7				Owners' Comp/Sales	(47) 4.6	(52) 4.8
11.6	7.0	4.3					6.8	7.4
17843M	70061M	406728M	809321M	1130673M	2284169M	Net Sales ($)	5888365M	6287443M
5650M	22391M	119976M	285719M	393728M	927151M	Total Assets ($)	2599071M	2660875M

M = $ thousand   MM = $ million
See Pages 11 through 21 for Explanation of Ratios and Data

Comparative Historical Data

Current Data Sorted by Sales

			Type of Statement						
12	13	17	Unqualified	2	1			2	12
17	12	11	Reviewed		1	3		2	3
21	20	10	Compiled	4	3	1	2		
17	13	27	Tax Returns	11	9	4	2	1	
26	32	33	Other	6	3	4		7	13
4/1/04-3/31/05 ALL	4/1/05-3/31/06 ALL	4/1/06-3/31/07 ALL		21 (4/1-9/30/06)			77 (10/1/06-3/31/07)		
				0-1MM	1-3MM	3-5MM	5-10MM	10-25MM	25MM & OVER
93	90	98	NUMBER OF STATEMENTS	23	16	13	6	12	28
%	%	%	ASSETS	%	%	%	%	%	%
13.4	14.4	14.4	Cash & Equivalents	9.4	18.2	13.3		12.6	18.7
6.2	6.1	8.5	Trade Receivables (net)	2.8	9.9	6.2		10.9	11.6
46.6	49.3	49.6	Inventory	63.5	58.2	52.4		47.4	33.2
2.0	2.6	2.5	All Other Current	1.8	.7			2.7	3.3
68.2	72.4	75.1	Total Current	77.5	87.0	76.7		73.6	66.8
21.1	19.5	17.4	Fixed Assets (net)	18.9	10.2	16.3		18.3	20.8
1.8	1.9	1.8	Intangibles (net)	.2	1.9	2.9		.3	3.6
8.9	6.2	5.6	All Other Non-Current	3.5	.9	4.2		7.8	8.8
100.0	100.0	100.0	Total	100.0	100.0	100.0		100.0	100.0
			LIABILITIES						
12.5	10.6	10.7	Notes Payable-Short Term	15.5	7.8	10.8		10.2	9.0
2.8	1.8	4.8	Cur. Mat.-L.T.D.	16.2	1.3	2.2		1.9	.6
17.8	19.2	17.1	Trade Payables	5.9	14.3	18.1		29.4	20.4
.4	.5	.3	Income Taxes Payable	.3	.0	.1		.5	.5
11.5	12.9	10.0	All Other Current	6.5	11.5	6.9		12.7	12.7
45.0	45.1	42.8	Total Current	44.4	34.9	38.1		54.6	43.2
10.9	8.6	10.7	Long-Term Debt	22.5	4.9	14.6		5.1	6.1
.2	.2	.2	Deferred Taxes	.0	.0	.8		.1	.4
4.9	8.3	4.1	All Other Non-Current	2.1	7.4	6.7		4.5	3.4
39.1	37.8	42.1	Net Worth	31.0	52.9	39.8		35.8	46.9
100.0	100.0	100.0	Total Liabilties & Net Worth	100.0	100.0	100.0		100.0	100.0
			INCOME DATA						
100.0	100.0	100.0	Net Sales	100.0	100.0	100.0		100.0	100.0
42.6	44.6	43.1	Gross Profit	45.3	42.7	49.9		45.3	38.3
40.1	41.9	39.5	Operating Expenses	42.4	36.6	49.0		44.1	34.3
2.5	2.7	3.5	Operating Profit	2.9	6.1	.9		1.2	4.0
.8	.6	1.2	All Other Expenses (net)	2.8	.9	.3		.3	.9
1.7	2.0	2.3	Profit Before Taxes	.1	5.2	.6		.8	3.1
			RATIOS						
3.0	2.6	5.3	Current	15.0	9.4	4.7		2.0	2.5
1.6	1.7	1.9		3.2	4.9	2.1		1.6	1.5
1.1	1.3	1.1		.9	1.2	1.3		1.0	1.0
1.0	.9	1.5	Quick	3.3	3.3	1.1		1.0	1.7
.4	.4	(97) .4		(22) .2	.8	.6		.3	.6
.1	.1	.1		.1	.1	.2		.1	.2
0 UND	0 UND	0 UND	Sales/Receivables	0 UND	0 UND	0 UND		0 UND	1 446.2
1 251.3	0 786.6	2 235.2		0 UND	0 UND	0 999.8		1 590.8	3 111.4
9 40.7	6 65.3	16 23.3		4 82.8	31 11.6	8 46.3		31 11.9	30 12.1
59 6.1	65 5.7	66 5.5	Cost of Sales/Inventory	93 3.9	71 5.2	73 5.0		66 5.5	45 8.1
99 3.7	99 3.7	100 3.6		138 2.7	115 3.2	96 3.8		96 3.8	69 5.3
151 2.4	186 2.0	155 2.3		255 1.4	210 1.7	256 1.4		127 2.9	103 3.6
13 27.2	18 19.8	9 41.9	Cost of Sales/Payables	0 UND	2 188.7	11 32.7		31 11.7	18 20.6
32 11.3	35 10.4	30 12.3		3 119.0	23 16.0	32 11.5		49 7.5	41 8.9
53 6.9	65 5.6	60 6.0		60 6.1	49 7.4	75 4.9		95 3.8	56 6.6
5.3	5.7	4.6	Sales/Working Capital	3.2	3.8	6.6		7.7	4.5
12.4	9.8	9.3		6.1	6.3	9.0		15.6	14.6
.45.1	24.6	75.6		-41.4	16.0	14.7		NM	NM
13.3	27.6	23.4	EBIT/Interest	22.0	103.5	13.1		29.1	31.3
(76) 4.0	(70) 3.8	(80) 4.3		(19) 2.1	(10) 5.4	(12) 1.5		(11) 3.2	(22) 12.3
1.7	.1	-.5		-2.9	-.9	-4.3		-.6	1.6
12.2	25.6	8.4	Net Profit + Depr., Dep., Amort./Cur. Mat. L/T/D						
(16) 2.1	(13) 2.7	(13) 2.4							
1.1	1.0	.1							
.2	.2	.1	Fixed/Worth	.1	.0	.1		.1	.1
.5	.4	.3		.4	.1	.4		.4	.4
.9	.9	.9		3.1	.8	.8		1.9	.8
.7	.6	.5	Debt/Worth	.2	.2	.7		.8	.5
1.5	1.5	1.3		2.0	.8	2.0		1.3	1.6
3.3	3.8	3.2		-9.7	3.2	6.5		10.7	2.8
46.8	40.5	45.5	% Profit Before Taxes/Tangible Net Worth	71.5	55.9	90.1		43.7	41.6
(84) 18.4	(79) 9.8	(86) 19.3		(17) 36.3	(13) 25.4	2.3		(11) 9.1	(26) 12.6
4.8	-2.5	-.2		-20.4	9.2	-16.2		-8.1	.3
16.7	16.5	21.9	% Profit Before Taxes/Total Assets	34.1	23.2	22.2		14.2	18.5
6.2	5.2	7.1		5.2	11.5	1.0		2.7	8.8
1.3	-1.7	-4.2		-24.4	-3.0	-9.7		-7.0	1.2
43.7	49.8	88.2	Sales/Net Fixed Assets	51.5	178.9	61.5		95.1	79.5
20.4	19.2	26.1		22.5	42.8	35.1		23.2	14.3
8.5	9.2	7.8		7.1	22.2	7.6		10.7	6.4
4.0	4.1	4.3	Sales/Total Assets	4.3	3.9	5.5		4.2	4.2
2.7	2.8	3.1		2.5	3.4	3.4		3.7	3.0
2.1	1.9	2.0		1.5	2.3	1.6		3.1	1.9
.6	.5	.4	% Depr., Dep., Amort./Sales	.3	.1			.4	.3
(68) 1.1	(69) 1.1	(72) .9		(16) 1.2	(12) .6			(11) .8	(20) 1.9
2.1	1.9	2.0		2.4	1.1			1.0	2.8
2.1	2.2	1.9	% Officers', Directors' Owners' Comp/Sales	3.4					
(37) 4.5	(33) 4.4	(45) 4.7		(13) 7.0					
6.4	6.8	7.5		11.4					
4881158M	4440743M	4718795M	Net Sales ($)	11642M	29974M	49351M	44966M	202047M	4380815M
1889216M	1636060M	1754615M	Total Assets ($)	5496M	10537M	18687M	17252M	64669M	1637974M

© RMA 2007

M = $ thousand   MM = $ million
See Pages 11 through 21 for Explanation of Ratios and Data

Current Data Sorted by Assets   Comparative Historical Data

0-500M	500M-2MM	2-10MM	10-50MM	50-100MM	100-250MM	Type of Statement	4/1/02-3/31/03 ALL	4/1/03-3/31/04 ALL
		1	2	1	3	Unqualified	6	11
3	6	5	2			Reviewed	14	14
2	5	3	1			Compiled	19	16
11	4	4				Tax Returns	12	17
3	3	2	7	2	2	Other	23	19
	17 (4/1-9/30/06)		55 (10/1/06-3/31/07)					
19	18	15	12	3	5	NUMBER OF STATEMENTS	74	77
%	%	%	%	%	%	ASSETS	%	%
11.7	12.7	8.6	9.1			Cash & Equivalents	10.0	11.0
7.3	4.3	3.4	5.4			Trade Receivables (net)	5.4	3.0
56.7	58.3	62.8	49.6			Inventory	49.5	52.7
1.3	1.3	.8	1.6			All Other Current	4.4	2.6
77.0	76.7	75.6	65.7			Total Current	69.4	69.3
17.1	12.0	19.0	27.9			Fixed Assets (net)	19.2	21.3
2.8	.7	.0	.7			Intangibles (net)	3.1	2.8
3.1	10.7	5.3	5.7			All Other Non-Current	8.4	6.6
100.0	100.0	100.0	100.0			Total	100.0	100.0
						LIABILITIES		
14.1	6.9	3.6	7.1			Notes Payable-Short Term	14.2	12.5
4.1	.8	3.6	4.2			Cur. Mat.-L.T.D.	3.3	3.2
13.4	21.9	14.1	16.8			Trade Payables	18.3	18.6
.0	.9	.1	.0			Income Taxes Payable	.2	.2
17.6	11.5	7.0	10.2			All Other Current	10.2	12.7
49.2	42.0	28.5	38.3			Total Current	46.2	47.1
17.8	16.0	9.9	8.6			Long-Term Debt	14.4	15.1
.0	.0	.0	.1			Deferred Taxes	.1	.0
8.5	6.7	.0	7.0			All Other Non-Current	5.3	8.1
24.5	35.4	61.7	46.0			Net Worth	34.0	29.7
100.0	100.0	100.0	100.0			Total Liabilities & Net Worth	100.0	100.0
						INCOME DATA		
100.0	100.0	100.0	100.0			Net Sales	100.0	100.0
39.7	43.0	38.1	44.4			Gross Profit	42.9	43.1
38.5	42.1	34.2	44.1			Operating Expenses	40.4	40.8
1.3	.9	4.0	.3			Operating Profit	2.5	2.3
1.6	.1	-.1	-1.1			All Other Expenses (net)	-.2	.1
-.3	.8	4.1	1.4			Profit Before Taxes	2.7	2.2
						RATIOS		
13.4	3.4	4.2	2.8			Current	2.6	2.9
1.6	1.8	3.2	1.5				1.8	1.7
1.0	1.1	1.8	1.3				1.1	1.0
1.4	.7	1.0	.5			Quick	.6	.7
.4	.2	.4	.2				.3	.2
.2	.1	.2	.1				.1	.0
0 UND	0 UND	0 UND	1 462.8			Sales/Receivables	0 UND	0 UND
0 UND	1 433.3	3 140.7	2 200.3				2 192.5	1 567.0
6 60.4	8 45.3	9 40.7	18 19.9				8 47.4	3 104.6
69 5.3	74 5.0	83 4.4	76 4.8			Cost of Sales/Inventory	55 6.6	85 4.3
117 3.1	93 3.9	112 3.3	121 3.0				112 3.2	131 2.8
182 2.0	257 1.4	183 2.0	170 2.1				190 1.9	189 1.9
0 UND	16 23.2	3 140.8	12 31.4			Cost of Sales/Payables	18 20.0	20 18.0
15 24.2	49 7.5	18 19.7	41 9.0				35 10.4	34 10.8
34 10.7	73 5.0	47 7.8	66 5.6				60 6.1	54 6.8
4.8	4.8	4.6	5.4			Sales/Working Capital	5.7	5.3
9.4	11.5	7.5	12.2				11.4	11.6
-542.8	37.4	9.7	28.4				74.8	106.9
2.9	29.3	16.2	6.3			EBIT/Interest	16.2	10.9
(12) 1.3	(15) 3.2	7.4	(10) 3.6				(65) 4.5	(61) 2.5
-4.4	-.2	2.7	-2.1				1.1	-1.2
						Net Profit + Depr., Dep., Amort./Cur. Mat. L/T/D	12.2	4.5
							(18) 2.5	(17) 1.3
							.9	.5
.1	.1	.1	.4			Fixed/Worth	.1	.1
1.5	.4	.2	.7				.5	.4
-1.5	.5	-.5	1.1				1.2	1.4
.3	.9	.3	.7			Debt/Worth	.6	.7
3.7	1.1	.7	1.3				1.2	1.3
-7.2	3.2	1.4	2.4				3.1	4.5
53.9	39.3	26.0	36.7			% Profit Before Taxes/Tangible Net Worth	39.9	44.4
(13) 15.7	(17) 2.7	11.8	12.7				(66) 10.4	(63) 17.9
4.5	-20.1	4.6	-9.3				1.8	-2.4
11.8	13.2	17.4	16.2			% Profit Before Taxes/Total Assets	15.4	16.7
5.9	1.6	6.2	4.0				4.6	6.0
-16.6	-2.4	2.4	-4.1				.3	-2.9
62.8	90.9	29.4	22.0			Sales/Net Fixed Assets	51.4	46.7
23.0	38.1	16.6	9.9				16.3	18.0
11.8	16.6	11.1	6.2				9.6	8.4
4.2	4.7	3.5	4.7			Sales/Total Assets	3.8	3.7
2.8	3.1	2.9	2.6				2.6	2.5
2.2	2.2	2.1	1.8				2.1	2.0
.5	.4	.4	.9			% Depr., Dep., Amort./Sales	.6	.7
(16) .7	(15) .8	(13) .5	(11) 1.3				(59) 1.4	(67) 1.4
1.5	1.1	.9	2.3				2.0	2.2
3.6						% Officers', Directors' Owners' Comp/Sales	2.4	2.0
(11) 7.8							(33) 4.2	(31) 4.8
11.1							10.4	11.5
16541M	68838M	163877M	850842M	383481M	2131388M	Net Sales ($)	4825866M	2444685M
5693M	22008M	52424M	268473M	191852M	869770M	Total Assets ($)	1176618M	775885M

M = $ thousand   MM = $ million
See Pages 11 through 21 for Explanation of Ratios and Data

Comparative Historical Data					Current Data Sorted by Sales					
	8	12	7	**Type of Statement**					1	6
	7	12	16	Unqualified	1	5	1	6	2	1
	16	19	11	Reviewed	1	4	3	2	2	1
	17	18	19	Compiled	1	4	2	3	1	
	24	17	19	Tax Returns	9	4		3	2	
	4/1/04-3/31/05	4/1/05-3/31/06	4/1/06-3/31/07	Other	1	3	1	2	1	11
	ALL	ALL	ALL		**17 (4/1-9/30/06)**			**55 (10/1/06-3/31/07)**		
					0-1MM	1-3MM	3-5MM	5-10MM	10-25MM	25MM & OVER
	72	78	72	**NUMBER OF STATEMENTS**	12	16	6	13	7	18
	%	%	%	**ASSETS**	%	%	%	%	%	%
	12.5	13.7	11.6	Cash & Equivalents	11.4	11.3		13.9		11.9
	4.0	4.8	5.1	Trade Receivables (net)	3.9	9.5		2.8		4.2
	54.5	49.8	55.8	Inventory	57.4	57.4		52.8		47.7
	1.5	1.4	1.5	All Other Current	1.3	1.4		1.4		2.5
	72.4	69.7	74.0	Total Current	74.0	79.6		70.8		66.3
	19.0	21.7	18.1	Fixed Assets (net)	18.3	12.9		21.0		25.2
	2.1	2.2	2.2	Intangibles (net)	4.3	.6		.3		5.1
	6.5	6.5	5.7	All Other Non-Current	3.4	6.9		7.8		3.5
	100.0	100.0	100.0	Total	100.0	100.0		100.0		100.0
				LIABILITIES						
	12.6	8.5	8.7	Notes Payable-Short Term	20.0	8.5		1.8		8.5
	2.5	3.4	3.0	Cur. Mat.-L.T.D.	.0	5.0		4.5		4.0
	17.0	15.1	16.5	Trade Payables	13.7	19.8		9.6		17.1
	.2	.3	.3	Income Taxes Payable	.0	.8		.1		.2
	7.1	9.6	12.2	All Other Current	14.9	13.8		9.1		12.4
	39.3	36.8	40.8	Total Current	48.6	47.9		25.1		42.2
	14.4	17.1	14.0	Long-Term Debt	15.1	24.9		12.0		13.0
	.1	.1	.0	Deferred Taxes	.0	.0		.0		.0
	3.9	5.3	5.6	All Other Non-Current	13.4	4.0		.1		6.6
	42.3	40.7	39.6	Net Worth	22.8	23.2		62.9		38.1
	100.0	100.0	100.0	Total Liabilities & Net Worth	100.0	100.0		100.0		100.0
				INCOME DATA						
	100.0	100.0	100.0	Net Sales	100.0	100.0		100.0		100.0
	43.3	42.7	41.1	Gross Profit	41.6	39.4		42.4		43.8
	39.3	40.7	39.2	Operating Expenses	40.9	38.4		38.5		41.2
	4.1	2.0	2.0	Operating Profit	.7	1.1		3.9		2.6
	.2	.1	.4	All Other Expenses (net)	1.4	1.2		-.4		.2
	3.9	1.9	1.6	Profit Before Taxes	-.7	-.1		4.2		2.4
				RATIOS						
	3.1	3.7	3.8		11.7	7.1		5.6		2.6
	1.9	2.1	1.8	Current	1.6	1.4		3.4		1.5
	1.4	1.3	1.3		1.0	1.1		1.8		1.2
	.7	1.2	.9		.9	1.3		1.8		.6
	(71) .3	(77) .4	.3	Quick	.4	.3		.5		.4
	.1	.1	.2		.1	.1		.2		.1
	0 UND	0 UND	0 UND		0 UND	0 UND		0 UND		0 UND
	0 UND	1 373.7	1 277.1	Sales/Receivables	2 240.3	1 685.6		2 194.0		1 277.1
	4 93.5	8 46.4	8 43.4		9 42.0	12 29.7		5 74.6		8 46.1
	89 4.1	82 4.5	75 4.8		70 5.2	77 4.8		71 5.1		73 5.0
	126 2.9	117 3.1	115 3.2	Cost of Sales/Inventory	126 2.9	160 2.3		100 3.6		121 3.0
	214 1.7	209 1.7	187 1.9		238 1.5	257 1.4		167 2.2		139 2.6
	19 19.5	16 22.6	10 35.4		0 UND	16 22.5		4 98.7		16 22.9
	35 10.5	28 13.0	24 15.1	Cost of Sales/Payables	8 48.2	40 14.0		17 21.1		41 9.0
	62 5.9	53 6.9	59 6.2		48 7.6	63 5.8		40 9.1		70 5.2
	4.4	4.3	5.0		4.9	4.0		4.5		6.1
	8.4	8.0	8.8	Sales/Working Capital	8.3	13.7		6.9		12.8
	18.0	18.1	22.9		NM	57.2		10.3		29.9
	11.4	10.7	11.9			3.3		22.7		6.3
	(64) 3.5	(68) 2.5	(58) 3.0	EBIT/Interest		(12) 1.2		11.8		(15) 4.0
	1.1	.8	.3			-2.0		.1		.8
	4.4	5.5	3.9	Net Profit + Depr., Dep.,						
	(16) 2.5	(17) 1.9	(19) 2.6	Amort./Cur. Mat. L/T/D						
	1.1	1.2	1.2							
	.1	.1	.2		.2	.1		.2		.5
	.3	.3	.5	Fixed/Worth	1.6	.4		.3		.8
	1.0	1.0	1.4		-.9	1.3		.5		1.9
	.6	.6	.6		.6	.9		.3		.8
	1.1	1.1	1.3	Debt/Worth	10.8	1.9		.7		1.7
	2.3	4.2	4.2		-13.6	18.4		1.1		4.8
	48.8	37.1	41.1	% Profit Before Taxes/Tangible		44.5		33.9		38.2
	(65) 14.0	(69) 12.2	(63) 12.1	Net Worth		(13) 11.1		15.8		(16) 19.3
	2.8	.0	-3.2			-20.1		-1.3		-19.7
	20.8	15.0	14.1	% Profit Before Taxes/Total	11.7	10.4		20.0		16.8
	5.2	3.0	4.9	Assets	2.7	2.8		10.3		5.3
	1.3	-.9	-1.8		-14.3	-10.2		-.7		-1.8
	47.2	50.4	46.4		62.4	70.7		32.6		18.5
	19.3	15.9	17.1	Sales/Net Fixed Assets	24.8	25.7		16.6		10.5
	9.5	7.5	9.9		9.8	12.0		13.6		8.5
	3.6	3.5	3.9		3.4	4.3		3.8		4.0
	2.8	2.4	2.7	Sales/Total Assets	2.6	2.5		2.9		2.6
	1.9	1.8	2.1		1.9	1.9		2.3		2.1
	.6	.6	.5			.5		.4		1.0
	(57) 1.1	(64) 1.1	(61) .8	% Depr., Dep., Amort./Sales		(15) .8		(12) .7		(15) 1.2
	1.5	1.9	1.3			1.1		1.1		2.3
	2.2	3.2	2.0			1.4				
	(33) 5.6	(29) 7.0	(30) 3.8	% Officers', Directors'		(10) 2.8				
	7.7	11.7	8.3	Owners' Comp/Sales		10.5				
	2296916M	3627082M	3614967M	Net Sales ($)	7296M	29127M	22291M	97767M	135701M	3322785M
	740782M	1382919M	1410220M	Total Assets ($)	3027M	12360M	7528M	33405M	63011M	1290889M

M = $ thousand   MM = $ million
See Pages 11 through 21 for Explanation of Ratios and Data

RETAIL—Clothing Accessories Stores NAICS 448150 (SIC 5611, 5632, 5699)

Current Data Sorted by Assets | **Comparative Historical Data**

0-500M	500M-2MM	2-10MM	10-50MM	50-100MM	100-250MM	Type of Statement	4/1/02-3/31/03 ALL	4/1/03-3/31/04 ALL
						Unqualified	2	2
						Reviewed	6	9
						Compiled	10	12
						Tax Returns	8	10
2	2	4		2		Other	9	5
2	8	6		5				
9	7	2						
3	6	4			3			
	8 (4/1-9/30/06)		57 (10/1/06-3/31/07)					
16	23	16	7		3	**NUMBER OF STATEMENTS**	35	38
%	%	%	%	%	%	**ASSETS**	%	%
28.4	11.7	9.5				Cash & Equivalents	15.6	12.1
14.6	10.8	15.0				Trade Receivables (net)	15.0	13.4
29.7	51.3	46.2				Inventory	49.7	46.1
1.5	1.0	4.0				All Other Current	3.1	1.4
74.2	74.8	74.8				Total Current	83.3	73.0
12.0	11.6	15.0				Fixed Assets (net)	11.8	18.0
2.7	3.2	.7				Intangibles (net)	.8	2.1
11.0	10.4	9.5				All Other Non-Current	4.0	7.0
100.0	100.0	100.0				Total	100.0	100.0
						LIABILITIES		
8.8	10.3	13.1				Notes Payable-Short Term	10.7	12.0
.7	1.2	.4				Cur. Mat.-L.T.D.	2.3	4.1
19.4	22.3	25.5				Trade Payables	23.5	20.3
.1	.5	.0				Income Taxes Payable	.1	.2
16.5	12.6	8.2				All Other Current	11.0	9.5
45.4	46.9	47.3				Total Current	47.6	46.1
17.9	7.2	8.4				Long-Term Debt	13.2	13.2
.0	.2	.0				Deferred Taxes	.1	.1
1.9	12.0	7.3				All Other Non-Current	4.6	7.5
34.7	33.7	36.9				Net Worth	34.5	33.1
100.0	100.0	100.0				Total Liabilties & Net Worth	100.0	100.0
						INCOME DATA		
100.0	100.0	100.0				Net Sales	100.0	100.0
43.2	43.3	44.6				Gross Profit	46.6	48.4
42.4	41.7	40.6				Operating Expenses	43.7	43.6
.8	1.6	4.0				Operating Profit	3.0	4.8
.2	.5	.7				All Other Expenses (net)	.4	.8
.6	1.2	3.3				Profit Before Taxes	2.5	4.0
						RATIOS		
2.8	6.1	2.2					3.7	2.3
1.9	2.5	1.8				Current	1.7	1.7
1.2	1.2	1.2					1.2	1.2
1.4	1.6	.9					1.1	1.0
.9	.3	.4				Quick	.6	.4
.3	.1	.1					.3	.2
0 UND	0 UND	0 UND					0 999.8	0 UND
5 77.8	0 999.8	12 30.0				Sales/Receivables	14 26.7	7 49.7
27 13.4	23 15.8	41 9.0					45 8.1	34 10.6
2 150.4	67 5.4	78 4.7					70 5.2	58 6.3
35 10.4	110 3.3	112 3.2				Cost of Sales/Inventory	163 2.2	118 3.1
89 4.1	218 1.7	257 1.4					245 1.5	218 1.7
2 149.8	12 30.6	53 6.8					22 16.5	23 16.2
31 11.9	34 10.8	68 5.4				Cost of Sales/Payables	53 6.9	58 6.3
55 6.6	71 5.1	107 3.4					117 3.1	102 3.6
6.7	3.9	5.0					3.9	5.3
22.0	7.1	7.3				Sales/Working Capital	7.7	8.6
52.8	25.1	18.6					22.1	47.9
20.6	12.7	42.1					18.9	14.9
(13) 5.5	(17) 3.4	3.0				EBIT/Interest	(29) 2.8	(34) 5.6
-9.6	.3	1.2					-.3	1.5
						Net Profit + Depr., Dep., Amort./Cur. Mat. L/T/D		
.0	.2	.1					.1	.1
.3	.3	.2				Fixed/Worth	.4	.4
1.9	1.4	1.7					.6	1.4
.7	.7	.6					.6	.6
1.5	2.1	1.3				Debt/Worth	1.2	1.7
7.6	35.3	10.7					3.0	3.5
167.6	54.7	29.2					30.7	53.4
(14) 58.6	(19) 14.2	(14) 13.5				% Profit Before Taxes/Tangible Net Worth	(31) 6.7	(32) 14.4
-.5	4.1	1.5					-3.7	1.8
40.8	22.6	12.4					15.0	16.6
10.5	6.0	3.6				% Profit Before Taxes/Total Assets	3.6	8.4
-6.6	-3.4	.4					-1.9	.5
UND	105.4	56.6					76.8	46.9
61.1	23.6	35.7				Sales/Net Fixed Assets	25.5	20.0
16.5	19.0	14.8					12.6	10.3
6.5	4.1	2.6					4.2	3.9
4.3	2.9	2.0				Sales/Total Assets	2.6	2.7
2.9	1.4	1.6					1.5	1.9
	.2	.4					.3	.6
	(19) .9	(15) .7				% Depr., Dep., Amort./Sales	(26) 1.0	(32) 1.3
	1.6	1.4					2.2	1.8
	2.0	1.3					3.3	2.9
	(15) 2.6	(10) 2.8				% Officers', Directors' Owners' Comp/Sales	(19) 5.9	(20) 4.7
	8.0	8.1					9.2	8.1
15956M	67951M	147189M	373177M		914038M	Net Sales ($)	228341M	241121M
3715M	24678M	71723M	181514M		443903M	Total Assets ($)	84298M	102693M

M = $ thousand   MM = $ million
See Pages 11 through 21 for Explanation of Ratios and Data

Comparative Historical Data | Current Data Sorted by Sales

Type of Statement	4/1/04-3/31/05 ALL	4/1/05-3/31/06 ALL	4/1/06-3/31/07 ALL		0-1MM	1-3MM	3-5MM	5-10MM	10-25MM	25MM & OVER
Unqualified	5	5	2							2
Reviewed	9	14	8			2	1	4	1	
Compiled	13	8	16		3	2	5	4	2	
Tax Returns	22	12	18		6	9	2	4	1	
Other	22	18	21		1	7	1	1	4	7
					8 (4/1-9/30/06)		57 (10/1/06-3/31/07)			
NUMBER OF STATEMENTS	71	57	65		10	20	9	9	8	9
ASSETS	%	%	%		%	%	%	%	%	%
Cash & Equivalents	10.5	11.6	15.4		19.4	18.3				
Trade Receivables (net)	12.8	12.0	12.6		7.0	14.0				
Inventory	48.1	46.1	42.7		43.6	42.8				
All Other Current	1.7	3.6	2.3		2.4	.2				
Total Current	73.1	73.3	73.0		72.5	75.3				
Fixed Assets (net)	17.8	16.8	13.1		10.6	15.9				
Intangibles (net)	3.7	3.4	4.2		.6	4.7				
All Other Non-Current	5.4	6.5	9.6		16.4	4.1				
Total	100.0	100.0	100.0		100.0	100.0				
LIABILITIES										
Notes Payable-Short Term	13.0	13.2	9.9		7.6	8.4				
Cur. Mat.-L.T.D.	3.3	1.6	.8		2.0	.4				
Trade Payables	20.5	18.3	20.8		15.9	21.3				
Income Taxes Payable	.2	.1	.2		.0	.1				
All Other Current	12.1	8.8	12.3		17.9	11.7				
Total Current	49.1	42.1	44.1		43.4	41.8				
Long-Term Debt	12.9	12.0	10.6		21.9	11.6				
Deferred Taxes	.1	.2	.1		.1	.0				
All Other Non-Current	5.9	10.1	7.4		4.0	8.9				
Net Worth	31.9	35.6	37.8		30.6	37.7				
Total Liabilities & Net Worth	100.0	100.0	100.0		100.0	100.0				
INCOME DATA										
Net Sales	100.0	100.0	100.0		100.0	100.0				
Gross Profit	47.4	47.7	45.1		48.3	40.8				
Operating Expenses	43.5	42.8	41.7		51.2	38.0				
Operating Profit	4.0	4.9	3.5		-2.9	2.8				
All Other Expenses (net)	.7	1.4	.6		.4	.6				
Profit Before Taxes	3.3	3.5	2.9		-3.3	2.2				
RATIOS										
Current	2.3	3.2	2.9		3.0	3.4				
	1.6	1.7	2.0		2.0	2.1				
	1.1	1.3	1.3		1.2	1.2				
Quick	1.1	1.1	1.3		.8	1.8				
	.4	.5	.6		.6	.7				
	.1	.1	.2		.1	.1				
Sales/Receivables	0 UND	0 UND	0 UND		0 UND	0 UND				
	4 92.2	3 117.9	3 109.2		0 UND	1 684.4				
	37 9.8	37 9.9	36 10.2		24 15.3	39 9.4				
Cost of Sales/Inventory	63 5.8	68 5.4	58 6.3		28 13.0	32 11.4				
	106 3.4	104 3.5	107 3.4		73 5.0	124 2.9				
	173 2.1	219 1.7	215 1.7		248 1.5	216 1.7				
Cost of Sales/Payables	19 19.0	19 19.5	21 17.7		0 UND	9 40.6				
	45 8.1	34 10.9	50 7.3		13 27.1	40 9.2				
	65 5.6	75 4.8	75 4.9		62 5.9	63 5.8				
Sales/Working Capital	6.8	4.5	5.1		5.3	4.2				
	11.9	9.4	7.4		13.9	7.9				
	73.5	19.9	24.1		NM	48.2				
EBIT/Interest	13.8	8.8	22.0			20.7				
	(62) 4.6	(44) 4.6	(56) 4.1			(13) 3.4				
	1.3	1.4	.7			.3				
Net Profit + Depr., Dep., Amort./Cur. Mat. L/T/D	3.8									
	(11) .9									
	.5									
Fixed/Worth	.2	.1	.1		.0	.0				
	.5	.3	.2		.3	.3				
	2.5	.9	1.4		NM	1.3				
Debt/Worth	.8	-.5	.7		.6	.7				
	2.1	1.3	1.4		2.3	1.5				
	8.1	3.4	7.4		NM	5.7				
% Profit Before Taxes/Tangible Net Worth	74.2	55.7	66.3			127.9				
	(63) 30.4	(50) 14.8	(56) 18.3			(18) 16.0				
	7.5	5.5	4.3			3.5				
% Profit Before Taxes/Total Assets	18.7	15.4	23.5		19.7	24.1				
	6.6	7.3	6.1		-.2	6.0				
	1.1	.9	-.1		-20.3	-2.4				
Sales/Net Fixed Assets	62.7	72.9	107.8		UND	UND				
	24.5	21.0	26.8		29.7	40.4				
	9.6	11.3	14.8		13.7	17.7				
Sales/Total Assets	3.9	3.7	3.9		5.2	4.3				
	3.0	2.7	2.6		2.9	2.4				
	2.1	1.7	1.6		2.0	1.4				
% Depr., Dep., Amort./Sales	.5	.6	.4			.3				
	(53) 1.1	(43) .9	(50) .9			(15) .9				
	1.9	1.6	1.5			2.8				
% Officers', Directors' Owners' Comp/Sales	2.7	2.5	2.2			2.0				
	(35) 4.8	(27) 3.8	(33) 4.4			(11) 7.7				
	7.5	13.4	9.2			17.2				
Net Sales ($)	1121606M	1333393M	1518311M		5220M	33441M	33593M	66053M	107845M	1272159M
Total Assets ($)	533587M	659028M	725533M		2086M	19817M	15423M	25809M	59033M	603365M

© RMA 2007

M = $ thousand　　MM = $ million
See Pages 11 through 21 for Explanation of Ratios and Data

Current Data Sorted by Assets   Comparative Historical Data

						Type of Statement		
1	1	4	7			Unqualified	14	22
4	4	15	1			Reviewed	21	19
3	14	7				Compiled	27	47
31	21	4				Tax Returns	35	35
7	16	12	9			Other	43	33
	27 (4/1-9/30/06)		130 (10/1/06-3/31/07)				4/1/02-3/31/03	4/1/03-3/31/04
0-500M	500M-2MM	2-10MM	10-50MM	50-100MM	100-250MM		ALL	ALL
42	56	42	17			NUMBER OF STATEMENTS	140	156
%	%	%	%	%	%	ASSETS	%	%
12.4	8.9	8.0	7.4			Cash & Equivalents	11.8	10.5
9.6	8.7	10.6	8.2	D	D	Trade Receivables (net)	10.3	12.9
56.4	53.1	48.5	44.9	A	A	Inventory	43.0	45.5
1.4	3.1	1.6	3.3	T	T	All Other Current	2.5	2.8
79.8	73.9	68.7	63.8	A	A	Total Current	67.6	71.7
12.4	17.9	22.2	22.8			Fixed Assets (net)	23.2	19.1
2.2	1.8	4.1	7.2	N	N	Intangibles (net)	3.5	3.1
5.6	6.4	5.0	6.1	O	O	All Other Non-Current	5.7	6.1
100.0	100.0	100.0	100.0	T	T	Total	100.0	100.0
						LIABILITIES		
19.0	14.6	11.1	13.5	A	A	Notes Payable-Short Term	9.1	11.4
3.1	1.7	2.7	5.1	V	V	Cur. Mat.-L.T.D.	4.8	2.5
20.6	15.6	22.7	15.7	A	A	Trade Payables	17.5	20.3
.0	.2	.3	1.2	I	I	Income Taxes Payable	.5	.3
12.1	12.1	10.4	7.5	L	L	All Other Current	10.1	14.0
54.8	44.3	47.2	42.9	A	A	Total Current	42.1	48.5
11.9	11.1	13.3	13.9	B	B	Long-Term Debt	22.3	14.2
.0	.0	.5	.0	L	L	Deferred Taxes	.0	.2
3.9	4.5	3.7	3.3	E	E	All Other Non-Current	12.6	8.9
29.4	40.1	35.2	40.0			Net Worth	23.0	28.2
100.0	100.0	100.0	100.0			Total Liabilities & Net Worth	100.0	100.0
						INCOME DATA		
100.0	100.0	100.0	100.0			Net Sales	100.0	100.0
48.5	45.1	45.6	45.8			Gross Profit	44.3	43.5
42.5	40.1	41.7	42.7			Operating Expenses	39.1	39.3
6.0	5.0	3.8	3.1			Operating Profit	5.2	4.1
.6	1.2	.2	1.9			All Other Expenses (net)	1.3	.6
5.4	3.8	3.6	1.2			Profit Before Taxes	3.9	3.5
						RATIOS		
3.8	3.3	2.6	2.1				2.8	2.5
1.8	2.1	1.4	1.4			Current	1.8	1.6
1.1	1.1	1.1	1.2				1.2	1.2
1.2	.7	.7	.5				1.0	.9
(41) .5	.2	.3	.3			Quick	.4	.4
.1	.1	.1	.1				.1	.2
0 UND	0 UND	0 999.8	1 285.6				0 UND	0 UND
0 UND	1 294.0	4 90.6	3 115.2			Sales/Receivables	2 207.1	4 87.0
20 17.9	25 14.6	22 16.3	33 11.1				27 13.3	37 10.0
65 5.6	72 5.1	80 4.6	83 4.4				58 6.3	65 5.6
129 2.8	134 2.7	119 3.1	112 3.3			Cost of Sales/Inventory	112 3.3	119 3.1
178 2.1	195 1.9	224 1.6	186 2.0				184 2.0	191 1.9
3 105.4	13 28.0	23 15.9	29 12.5				14 25.3	16 22.3
28 13.1	32 11.4	45 8.1	42 8.8			Cost of Sales/Payables	37 9.8	37 9.8
56 6.5	54 6.8	97 3.8	61 6.0				59 6.1	69 5.3
5.2	3.9	5.2	6.3				5.1	5.1
10.6	7.0	14.1	13.8			Sales/Working Capital	9.2	9.2
NM	54.5	122.5	70.4				35.0	24.5
24.0	12.7	10.0	10.9				8.9	9.8
(33) 5.0	(47) 2.6	(40) 4.7	(16) 3.3			EBIT/Interest	(129) 3.8	(135) 3.5
.8	1.4	1.9	1.9				1.4	1.2
		14.2					3.8	5.5
		(11) 3.9				Net Profit + Depr., Dep., Amort./Cur. Mat. L/T/D	(23) 2.6	(33) 3.1
		1.1					.6	.8
.1	.1	.2	.2				.2	.1
.2	.3	.7	.5			Fixed/Worth	.5	.5
6.9	1.1	2.6	2.1				1.8	1.4
.3	.6	1.0	.9				.7	.8
1.4	1.5	2.1	2.2			Debt/Worth	1.8	1.7
NM	5.8	5.7	4.2				6.6	5.3
149.0	46.5	56.9	65.7				51.5	51.8
(32) 60.0	(51) 15.6	(36) 27.6	(15) 32.6			% Profit Before Taxes/Tangible Net Worth	(123) 24.3	(136) 24.5
7.5	2.8	4.8	12.2				5.7	6.3
38.4	15.5	17.2	16.6				19.1	16.7
13.9	5.6	6.6	8.2			% Profit Before Taxes/Total Assets	8.4	6.9
.0	.4	1.5	1.6				1.4	1.1
88.3	72.1	33.6	27.4				53.3	57.4
41.3	27.3	16.2	15.3			Sales/Net Fixed Assets	16.6	18.8
21.7	11.3	6.4	6.8				7.5	8.1
4.3	3.5	3.5	3.1				3.6	3.5
3.3	2.7	2.6	2.0			Sales/Total Assets	2.5	2.5
2.5	1.8	1.6	1.8				1.6	1.6
.2	.3	.6	.6				.7	.6
(30) .7	(42) .8	(38) 1.1	(15) 2.0			% Depr., Dep., Amort./Sales	(111) 1.1	(122) 1.2
1.7	1.3	2.0	2.8				1.8	2.0
4.3	3.1	1.4					2.9	2.5
(21) 6.2	(32) 4.7	(24) 2.5				% Officers', Directors' Owners' Comp/Sales	(70) 5.0	(72) 4.6
9.8	6.6	5.3					9.1	9.2
38522M	151183M	483373M	1020109M			Net Sales ($)	3272591M	3527876M
11574M	56511M	195500M	438301M			Total Assets ($)	1489348M	1374743M

M = $ thousand   MM = $ million
See Pages 11 through 21 for Explanation of Ratios and Data

Comparative Historical Data			Type of Statement	Current Data Sorted by Sales					
14	11	12	Unqualified		1	1		4	6
22	23	21	Reviewed	1	4	2	5	7	2
29	25	24	Compiled	2	13		7	2	
48	50	56	Tax Returns	20	26	5	1	4	
44	40	44	Other	4	14	4	7	7	8
4/1/04-3/31/05	4/1/05-3/31/06	4/1/06-3/31/07		27 (4/1-9/30/06)			130 (10/1/06-3/31/07)		
ALL	ALL	ALL		0-1MM	1-3MM	3-5MM	5-10MM	10-25MM	25MM & OVER
157	149	157	NUMBER OF STATEMENTS	27	58	12	20	24	16
%	%	%	ASSETS	%	%	%	%	%	%
8.3	9.0	9.5	Cash & Equivalents	11.8	10.0	7.6	8.0	8.8	7.8
12.6	10.9	9.4	Trade Receivables (net)	5.5	11.8	8.3	6.4	12.2	8.1
50.0	48.9	51.9	Inventory	55.9	54.6	44.1	52.8	49.1	44.2
1.4	1.9	2.2	All Other Current	1.2	2.8	2.1	1.1	2.2	3.3
72.3	70.7	73.0	Total Current	74.3	79.2	62.1	68.2	72.2	63.4
19.2	20.9	18.1	Fixed Assets (net)	15.3	15.1	19.5	24.6	18.9	23.6
3.2	3.3	3.1	Intangibles (net)	3.0	1.5	6.3	1.3	4.9	6.5
5.3	5.0	5.8	All Other Non-Current	7.4	4.2	12.2	5.9	3.9	6.5
100.0	100.0	100.0	Total	100.0	100.0	100.0	100.0	100.0	100.0
			LIABILITIES						
14.7	13.1	14.7	Notes Payable-Short Term	20.0	14.4	17.2	11.9	11.8	13.3
2.6	3.2	2.7	Cur. Mat.-L.T.D.	1.9	2.8	.0	2.5	3.8	4.1
20.1	20.3	18.8	Trade Payables	14.3	19.5	13.4	20.1	27.0	14.6
.3	.2	.3	Income Taxes Payable	.0	.2	.0	.4	.3	1.3
9.6	10.2	11.1	All Other Current	12.2	10.0	19.5	9.9	10.1	10.0
47.3	46.9	47.7	Total Current	48.4	46.9	50.1	44.8	53.0	43.2
14.4	21.2	12.2	Long-Term Debt	12.5	10.6	15.7	15.9	10.5	12.9
.1	.1	.1	Deferred Taxes	.0	.0	1.6	.1	.0	.0
4.6	9.5	4.0	All Other Non-Current	3.9	5.5	.1	4.3	2.7	3.5
33.7	22.3	35.9	Net Worth	35.1	37.0	32.6	34.8	33.8	40.3
100.0	100.0	100.0	Total Liabilities & Net Worth	100.0	100.0	100.0	100.0	100.0	100.0
			INCOME DATA						
100.0	100.0	100.0	Net Sales	100.0	100.0	100.0	100.0	100.0	100.0
44.5	46.6	46.2	Gross Profit	51.4	43.7	49.3	46.9	42.8	48.3
40.0	42.3	41.4	Operating Expenses	44.1	38.9	46.2	42.9	39.0	44.5
4.5	4.2	4.7	Operating Profit	7.3	4.8	3.0	4.0	3.8	3.8
.4	.7	.8	All Other Expenses (net)	1.1	1.0	-.2	1.2	-.1	1.5
4.1	3.5	3.9	Profit Before Taxes	6.2	3.8	3.2	2.8	3.8	2.3
			RATIOS						
3.0	2.9	3.0		3.5	3.7	2.4	2.5	2.0	2.1
1.7	1.8	1.6	Current	1.8	2.2	1.4	1.4	1.3	1.4
1.1	1.3	1.1		1.1	1.3	.7	1.1	.9	1.1
1.0	1.0	.7		1.1	1.2	.4	.5	.7	.6
.4	.4 (156)	.3	Quick	.2	(57) .5	.1	.2	.3	.3
.1	.1	.1		.1	.2	.1	.1	.1	.2
0 UND	0 UND	0 UND		0 UND	0 UND	0 UND	0 UND	0 999.8	1 306.7
5 71.4	3 120.8	2 196.0	Sales/Receivables	0 UND	4 104.0	0 UND	1 294.7	4 90.6	3 119.0
30 12.2	29 12.5	25 14.8		6 57.1	30 12.3	6 66.1	15 24.3	39 9.5	25 14.5
63 5.8	65 5.7	74 4.9		74 4.9	69 5.3	73 5.0	77 4.7	69 5.3	81 4.5
132 2.8	132 2.8	125 2.9	Cost of Sales/Inventory	157 2.3	139 2.6	118 3.1	162 2.3	103 3.5	112 3.3
200 1.8	208 1.8	191 1.9		295 1.2	182 2.0	134 2.7	215 1.7	144 2.5	203 1.8
20 18.5	20 18.6	14 25.8		8 46.9	10 37.8	13 29.0	18 20.8	28 12.8	21 17.1
40 9.0	37 9.8	37 10.0	Cost of Sales/Payables	32 11.3	32 11.4	25 14.5	43 8.6	50 7.3	37 9.8
70 5.2	69 5.3	59 6.2		92 4.0	55 6.7	46 8.0	67 5.4	90 4.0	54 6.8
5.2	4.7	4.9		4.7	4.0	7.8	4.9	7.3	6.7
9.7	9.4	10.1	Sales/Working Capital	8.7	5.6	22.6	10.8	16.1	16.4
45.1	26.0	56.7		52.3	16.9	-15.7	56.8	NM	91.7
17.4	12.7	11.6		31.0	11.7	20.3	7.8	11.2	11.6
(137) 4.7	(134) 4.4	(136) 3.8	EBIT/Interest	(19) 5.0	(52) 2.9	(10) 5.6	(18) 3.0	(22) 6.4	(15) 3.1
1.5	1.0	1.4		-.2	1.1	2.1	1.7	2.4	1.9
3.5	6.8	6.3	Net Profit + Depr., Dep.,						
(19) 1.5	(16) 2.3	(19) 3.7	Amort./Cur. Mat. L/T/D						
.0	1.2	1.1							
.1	.1	.1		.1	.1	.2	.2	.2	.3
.5	.4	.4	Fixed/Worth	.2	.2	.5	.7	.7	.6
1.6	1.9	1.6		1.5	1.0	-1.3	1.5	3.0	2.2
.7	.8	.6		.3	.5	.6	.9	1.1	.9
1.9	2.1	1.8	Debt/Worth	1.4	1.5	1.5	2.2	2.1	2.4
6.7	8.7	6.0		16.8	5.3	-5.4	3.8	8.1	4.3
52.1	52.7	69.3	% Profit Before Taxes/Tangible	153.4	46.3		44.8	86.6	65.7
(131) 22.5	(122) 27.9	(134) 27.2	Net Worth	(21) 79.8	(52) 14.8		(18) 31.0	(20) 47.5	(15) 31.1
8.7	7.5	4.0		2.0	2.3		5.4	18.1	7.2
20.9	19.4	19.4	% Profit Before Taxes/Total	38.4	18.1	15.5	14.4	22.2	14.5
7.7	8.8	6.8	Assets	17.6	4.9	3.8	6.5	14.1	7.0
1.0	.2	.9		-.7	.2	.5	1.3	4.1	.9
61.1	62.5	65.6		116.2	80.7	56.2	29.0	49.8	25.3
20.8	20.0	25.4	Sales/Net Fixed Assets	28.3	32.5	22.7	11.6	18.7	14.5
8.5	9.4	10.3		10.0	14.3	6.3	6.8	8.9	9.4
3.5	3.6	3.7		3.8	3.4	4.4	3.7	4.1	3.6
2.5	2.6	2.8	Sales/Total Assets	2.3	2.8	3.1	2.3	3.0	2.2
1.9	1.8	1.8		1.3	1.9	2.4	1.6	2.0	1.7
.5	.5	.4		.4	.2		.4	.5	.9
(128) 1.1	(118) 1.1	(125) 1.0	% Depr., Dep., Amort./Sales	(18) 1.3	(44) .6		(17) 1.1	(23) .9	(14) 1.9
2.0	2.0	1.9		2.7	1.3		2.0	1.8	2.6
2.3	2.3	2.2	% Officers', Directors'	4.2	3.3		2.0	1.0	
(80) 4.9	(81) 5.2	(79) 4.5	Owners' Comp/Sales	(17) 6.2	(31) 5.5		(14) 2.6	(11) 2.0	
9.1	8.1	6.5		13.8	6.7		4.3	6.0	
3299378M	3891456M	1693187M	Net Sales ($)	16277M	101569M	46563M	139984M	381828M	1006966M
1043604M	1359770M	701886M	Total Assets ($)	7367M	50489M	21112M	63294M	135697M	423927M

© RMA 2007   M = $ thousand   MM = $ million
See Pages 11 through 21 for Explanation of Ratios and Data

Current Data Sorted by Assets | Comparative Historical Data

				7	1	2	Type of Statement		7	7
	1	3	3				Unqualified			
4	3	4	1				Reviewed		15	11
12	4	1				1	Compiled		25	19
7	7	10	4	2	2		Tax Returns		12	25
	18 (4/1-9/30/06)		61 (10/1/06-3/31/07)				Other		18	15
									4/1/02-3/31/03	4/1/03-3/31/04
0-500M	500M-2MM	2-10MM	10-50MM	50-100MM	100-250MM				ALL	ALL
23	15	18	15	3	5		NUMBER OF STATEMENTS		77	77
%	%	%	%	%	%		ASSETS		%	%
13.7	3.0	7.8	9.6				Cash & Equivalents		7.3	10.7
8.7	1.6	5.5	4.9				Trade Receivables (net)		4.5	5.5
68.5	81.2	64.9	57.8				Inventory		64.8	61.5
.7	.7	2.5	2.7				All Other Current		3.5	1.1
91.6	86.5	80.6	74.9				Total Current		80.1	78.8
5.0	8.1	15.4	14.8				Fixed Assets (net)		11.4	13.5
2.1	2.9	.8	2.3				Intangibles (net)		1.5	2.5
1.4	2.5	3.3	8.0				All Other Non-Current		7.0	5.3
100.0	100.0	100.0	100.0				Total		100.0	100.0
							LIABILITIES			
15.8	13.9	20.8	5.5				Notes Payable-Short Term		8.6	12.9
1.2	5.9	2.7	4.0				Cur. Mat.-L.T.D.		3.6	2.6
26.6	21.4	25.9	20.2				Trade Payables		21.0	19.2
.0	.0	.0	.4				Income Taxes Payable		.1	.2
15.0	9.7	3.3	11.3				All Other Current		7.7	12.0
58.7	51.0	52.8	41.3				Total Current		41.0	46.8
17.1	13.6	14.8	16.9				Long-Term Debt		14.0	9.1
.0	.0	.0	.0				Deferred Taxes		.1	.1
3.7	7.3	6.1	1.6				All Other Non-Current		7.1	5.0
20.5	28.2	26.3	40.1				Net Worth		37.9	39.0
100.0	100.0	100.0	100.0				Total Liabilities & Net Worth		100.0	100.0
							INCOME DATA			
100.0	100.0	100.0	100.0				Net Sales		100.0	100.0
43.8	45.2	41.8	40.6				Gross Profit		40.8	43.7
40.8	43.3	38.6	36.5				Operating Expenses		38.2	40.2
3.1	2.0	3.1	4.0				Operating Profit		2.6	3.5
1.6	.8	.7	.4				All Other Expenses (net)		.5	.9
1.5	1.2	2.4	3.6				Profit Before Taxes		2.1	2.7
							RATIOS			
4.3	2.2	2.5	3.7						3.5	3.1
2.2	1.8	1.8	2.2				Current		2.1	1.9
1.3	1.4	1.3	1.3						1.4	1.2
1.2	.1	.3	1.2						.6	.8
.2	.1	.1	.3				Quick		.2	.2
.1	.0	.0	.1						.0	.0
0	UND	0	UND	0	UND	0	UND			Sales/Receivables		0	UND	0	UND
0	UND	0	UND	0	UND	1	248.7			Sales/Receivables		1	453.6	0	739.4
12	30.3	1	268.1	2	161.8	4	92.5					4	89.2	2	167.2

0-500M		500M-2MM		2-10MM		10-50MM					ALL		ALL	
0	UND	0	UND	0	UND	0	UND		Sales/Receivables		0	UND	0	UND
0	UND	0	UND	0	UND	1	248.7				1	453.6	0	739.4
12	30.3	1	268.1	2	161.8	4	92.5				4	89.2	2	167.2
84	4.4	195	1.9	93	3.9	115	3.2		Cost of Sales/Inventory		109	3.3	101	3.6
149	2.4	210	1.7	206	1.8	138	2.6				178	2.1	177	2.1
264	1.4	247	1.5	243	1.5	204	1.8				282	1.3	256	1.4
19	19.3	41	8.8	31	11.9	29	12.7		Cost of Sales/Payables		30	12.2	21	17.0
39	9.3	55	6.6	56	6.5	40	9.0				49	7.5	38	9.6
75	4.9	71	5.1	98	3.7	66	5.5				83	4.4	71	5.2
	2.5		5.1		4.0		3.7		Sales/Working Capital			3.0		3.7
	6.1		6.7		8.6		5.6					5.2		6.5
	21.5		11.3		18.1		23.6					15.8		18.4
	7.9		3.8		8.9		5.2		EBIT/Interest			8.2		8.4
(20)	1.8		1.1	(17)	2.9	(13)	2.6			(60)	2.1	(58)	3.9
	-.5		.3		1.2		.8					.6		.9
									Net Profit + Depr., Dep., Amort./Cur. Mat. L/T/D			6.0		3.8
										(19)	1.6	(12)	2.2
											.6		1.0
	.0		.1		.1		.2		Fixed/Worth			.1		.1
	.2		.3		.3		.3					.3		.2
	1.7		6.8		.8		.8					.6		.8
	.8		1.3		.9		.6		Debt/Worth			.6		.6
	2.5		2.7		1.5		1.3					1.5		1.6
	16.1		150.5		3.8		3.7					6.0		4.2
	75.7		15.0		31.7		26.9		% Profit Before Taxes/Tangible Net Worth			40.4		41.0
(18)	30.2	(13)	1.9	(16)	14.4	(14)	19.4			(69)	8.9	(68)	15.2
	.4		-9.5		2.1		2.4					.2		.4
	21.6		3.7		10.8		13.2		% Profit Before Taxes/Total Assets			13.0		17.2
	5.1		.3		5.3		4.5					2.9		6.0
	-4.1		-1.6		.6		2.2					-.7		-.7
	508.0		86.0		79.8		34.5		Sales/Net Fixed Assets			44.0		61.6
	123.5		63.5		23.5		21.6					28.7		23.7
	36.8		20.6		10.0		9.4					14.4		13.1
	4.3		3.1		3.9		3.1		Sales/Total Assets			3.1		3.1
	2.7		2.7		2.2		2.4					2.2		2.3
	1.7		2.0		1.8		1.8					1.6		1.7
	.3		.3		.5		.7		% Depr., Dep., Amort./Sales			.6		.6
(11)	.7	(12)	.6	(15)	.5		1.0			(68)	1.0	(58)	.9
	.7		.8		1.6		1.3					1.4		1.5
	4.6		2.0		1.4				% Officers', Directors' Owners' Comp/Sales			2.2		2.1
(18)	7.0	(11)	4.9	(10)	2.0					(40)	3.9	(44)	3.9
	12.3		8.2		7.7							8.5		8.5
17811M	47920M	210415M	782854M	439697M	1893009M		Net Sales ($)		1794793M	1676790M
5916M	17030M	77759M	330330M	242723M	888414M		Total Assets ($)		797386M	886145M

M = $ thousand   MM = $ million
See Pages 11 through 21 for Explanation of Ratios and Data

Comparative Historical Data | Current Data Sorted by Sales

4/1/04-3/31/05 ALL	4/1/05-3/31/06 ALL	4/1/06-3/31/07 ALL	Type of Statement	0-1MM	1-3MM	3-5MM	5-10MM	10-25MM	25MM & OVER
10	7	10	Unqualified					1	10
11	11	7	Reviewed					2	3
15	9	12	Compiled	3	4	1	2	1	1
10	24	18	Tax Returns	8	6	2	2		1
22	24	32	Other	5	5	4	6	4	8
				0-1MM	18 (4/1-9/30/06) 1-3MM	3-5MM	61 (10/1/06-3/31/07) 5-10MM	10-25MM	25MM & OVER
68	75	79	**NUMBER OF STATEMENTS**	16	15	7	10	8	23
%	%	%	**ASSETS**	%	%	%	%	%	%
12.1	9.5	9.8	Cash & Equivalents	10.9	11.9		6.3		11.4
4.4	4.1	5.9	Trade Receivables (net)	11.5	1.2		5.1		6.0
61.9	61.9	65.5	Inventory	68.2	70.5		68.1		54.9
1.2	2.8	1.6	All Other Current	.7	.8		1.4		2.5
79.5	78.3	82.8	Total Current	91.3	84.4		80.8		74.8
14.0	13.1	11.3	Fixed Assets (net)	4.4	10.8		11.0		16.5
2.6	2.1	2.6	Intangibles (net)	2.6	2.4		1.5		4.3
3.8	6.5	3.4	All Other Non-Current	1.7	2.4		6.7		4.4
100.0	100.0	100.0	Total	100.0	100.0		100.0		100.0
			LIABILITIES						
11.1	11.2	14.0	Notes Payable-Short Term	11.9	15.5		27.8		7.0
3.4	4.2	2.9	Cur. Mat.-L.T.D.	1.7	5.4		1.2		2.5
21.2	21.6	22.8	Trade Payables	24.3	24.5		19.7		20.7
.1	.2	.1	Income Taxes Payable	.0	.0		.0		.3
7.3	13.4	10.1	All Other Current	18.6	8.3		6.7		10.1
43.1	50.5	49.8	Total Current	56.5	53.8		55.4		40.6
11.0	13.6	15.2	Long-Term Debt	14.9	19.9		26.2		13.4
.2	.1	.0	Deferred Taxes	.0	.0		.0		.1
5.3	8.5	4.3	All Other Non-Current	5.4	4.2		5.3		1.8
40.3	27.3	30.6	Net Worth	23.3	22.1		13.0		44.1
100.0	100.0	100.0	Total Liabilities & Net Worth	100.0	100.0		100.0		100.0
			INCOME DATA						
100.0	100.0	100.0	Net Sales	100.0	100.0		100.0		100.0
42.0	43.3	42.2	Gross Profit	44.0	45.3		45.2		39.0
38.9	42.2	38.7	Operating Expenses	40.4	42.6		42.0		34.2
3.1	1.1	3.5	Operating Profit	3.6	2.7		3.2		4.8
.6	.7	.9	All Other Expenses (net)	1.9	.6		1.2		.5
2.6	.5	2.6	Profit Before Taxes	1.7	2.1		2.0		4.2
			RATIOS						
3.1	2.8	2.9	Current	9.0	2.4		2.8		3.7
2.0	1.6	2.0		2.4	1.9		1.7		2.2
1.3	1.1	1.3		1.5	1.2		1.3		1.1
.8	.6	.8	Quick	1.7	.9		.2		1.2
(67) .3	(73) .2	.1		.2	.1		.2		.2
.1	.1	.1		.0	.1		.0		.1
0 UND	0 UND	0 UND	Sales/Receivables	0 UND	0 UND		0 UND		0 UND
1 355.2	1 378.1	1 558.5		0 UND	0 UND		1 539.2		2 151.3
3 110.7	6 58.7	4 92.5		23 16.1	1 369.2		9 42.1		6 62.9
92 4.0	115 3.2	109 3.3	Cost of Sales/Inventory	90 4.1	139 2.6		127 2.9		78 4.7
163 2.2	176 2.1	184 2.0		164 2.2	203 1.8		184 2.0		137 2.7
243 1.5	249 1.5	232 1.6		331 1.1	221 1.7		244 1.5		197 1.9
30 12.3	27 13.4	26 13.9	Cost of Sales/Payables	13 27.9	41 8.8		33 11.0		24 15.5
41 8.8	47 7.7	44 8.2		38 9.7	51 7.1		56 6.5		38 9.5
70 5.2	72 5.1	73 5.0		70 5.2	90 4.0		89 4.1		58 6.2
4.2	4.0	3.7	Sales/Working Capital	2.4	5.1		3.7		3.7
6.4	7.0	6.3		4.2	7.2		6.4		5.6
15.4	37.5	20.0		10.2	37.6		25.6		33.0
9.6	5.5	7.6	EBIT/Interest	5.8	15.3		3.7		20.2
(58) 3.0	(67) 2.1	(73) 2.5		(13) 1.7	(14) 3.8		2.2		(21) 3.7
1.3	.8	.4		-1.5	.3		.7		1.6
4.7	4.1	13.4	Net Profit + Depr., Dep., Amort./Cur. Mat. L/T/D						
(11) 1.5	(10) 2.4	(14) 3.0							
.5	.2	1.4							
.1	.1	.1	Fixed/Worth	.0	.1		.1		.2
.3	.3	.3		.2	.3		.3		.4
.8	2.0	.9		NM	6.8		.6		1.2
.5	.6	.8	Debt/Worth	.4	1.1		.9		.6
1.4	2.4	1.9		2.1	3.9		1.6		1.1
3.1	8.5	5.1		NM	150.5		120.3		3.7
33.1	27.4	33.0	% Profit Before Taxes/Tangible Net Worth	56.7	100.8				34.4
(60) 10.2	(60) 9.2	(68) 14.4		(12) 30.2	(12) 16.5				(21) 21.4
1.5	1.2	.7		2.3	-.8				6.5
14.1	9.1	11.5	% Profit Before Taxes/Total Assets	25.3	17.4		7.0		19.3
4.2	1.6	3.8		4.4	3.7		1.3		4.9
.6	-2.5	-1.0		-8.8	-3.6		-1.2		2.5
70.9	74.1	107.0	Sales/Net Fixed Assets	822.8	186.4		173.0		33.7
21.2	24.4	34.5		115.3	54.6		44.4		21.6
11.4	11.9	14.2		37.0	26.3		8.0		9.1
3.3	3.2	3.5	Sales/Total Assets	3.7	4.3		4.0		2.9
2.4	2.3	2.4		2.0	2.6		2.0		2.4
1.9	1.7	1.8		1.6	2.0		1.6		1.8
.6	.5	.5	% Depr., Dep., Amort./Sales				.2		.7
(48) .9	(61) .9	(60) .7			(11)		.5		(22) 1.1
1.5	1.5	1.3					.8		1.4
1.9	2.1	1.9	% Officers', Directors' Owners' Comp/Sales	3.3	4.7				
(35) 4.0	(43) 4.1	(45) 4.7		(12) 5.5	(11) 10.9				
9.6	9.4	9.0		13.8	10.9				
2388712M	1892433M	3391706M	Net Sales ($)	8206M	23615M	25692M	70007M	129788M	3134398M
1079116M	914077M	1562172M	Total Assets ($)	3718M	9425M	13176M	43014M	40480M	1452359M

M = $ thousand   MM = $ million
See Pages 11 through 21 for Explanation of Ratios and Data

Current Data Sorted by Assets — Comparative Historical Data

Type of Statement	0-500M	500M-2MM	2-10MM	10-50MM	50-100MM	100-250MM		4/1/02-3/31/03 ALL	4/1/03-3/31/04 ALL
Unqualified			1	10		1		20	22
Reviewed		5	21	18		1		47	41
Compiled	13	28	22	3				81	98
Tax Returns	20	34	23	1		1		72	78
Other	5	21	19	14	6	5		48	73
	80 (4/1-9/30/06)			192 (10/1/06-3/31/07)					
NUMBER OF STATEMENTS	38	88	86	46	6	8		268	312

	0-500M	500M-2MM	2-10MM	10-50MM	50-100MM	100-250MM		268	312
ASSETS	%	%	%	%	%	%		%	%
Cash & Equivalents	8.4	8.8	5.5	3.6				7.7	7.8
Trade Receivables (net)	7.6	6.0	7.5	11.0				8.7	7.9
Inventory	68.0	70.4	70.5	65.6				65.9	67.8
All Other Current	1.2	.8	1.5	1.2				2.0	1.8
Total Current	85.2	86.0	84.9	81.4				84.3	85.2
Fixed Assets (net)	9.7	9.4	10.4	12.2				10.3	10.0
Intangibles (net)	2.7	.8	1.0	1.1				1.1	1.0
All Other Non-Current	2.4	3.8	3.7	5.3				4.2	3.7
Total	100.0	100.0	100.0	100.0				100.0	100.0
LIABILITIES									
Notes Payable-Short Term	13.0	12.6	13.7	18.1				11.1	12.0
Cur. Mat.-L.T.D.	4.2	2.0	1.9	2.6				2.8	2.8
Trade Payables	21.0	22.7	25.1	22.5				19.0	21.8
Income Taxes Payable	.1	.2	.1	.0				.1	.2
All Other Current	15.9	5.5	9.8	10.5				9.3	9.3
Total Current	54.2	42.9	50.5	53.7				42.4	46.1
Long-Term Debt	14.7	9.0	8.9	7.4				12.2	9.1
Deferred Taxes	.0	.0	.1	.1				.1	.1
All Other Non-Current	5.4	7.8	3.8	5.4				4.5	6.0
Net Worth	25.6	40.3	36.7	33.3				40.8	38.7
Total Liabilities & Net Worth	100.0	100.0	100.0	100.0				100.0	100.0
INCOME DATA									
Net Sales	100.0	100.0	100.0	100.0				100.0	100.0
Gross Profit	44.1	43.3	40.9	44.4				44.8	44.5
Operating Expenses	40.5	38.1	35.4	41.7				40.2	40.3
Operating Profit	3.6	5.2	5.4	2.7				4.5	4.2
All Other Expenses (net)	1.4	1.3	1.7	.7				1.1	1.0
Profit Before Taxes	2.2	3.9	3.8	2.0				3.4	3.2
RATIOS									
Current	3.5 / 1.9 / 1.3	3.9 / 2.0 / 1.5	2.3 / 1.6 / 1.3	2.1 / 1.5 / 1.2				3.3 / 2.0 / 1.5	2.9 / 2.0 / 1.4
Quick	.8 / .3 / .1	.6 / .2 / .1	.5 / .2 / .1	.5 / .2 / .1				(267) .7 / .3 / .1	(309) .6 / .3 / .1
Sales/Receivables	0 UND / 0 UND / 5 69.1	0 UND / 3 113.7 / 15 24.5	0 999.8 / 7 48.8 / 25 14.4	2 173.3 / 15 24.6 / 42 8.6				2 202.6 / 9 41.3 / 27 13.6	0 741.2 / 6 65.2 / 23 15.7
Cost of Sales/Inventory	98 3.7 / 190 1.9 / 292 1.2	199 1.8 / 290 1.3 / 414 .9	189 1.9 / 312 1.2 / 404 .9	242 1.5 / 308 1.2 / 374 1.0				190 1.9 / 296 1.2 / 401 .9	193 1.9 / 293 1.2 / 397 .9
Cost of Sales/Payables	5 67.0 / 40 9.1 / 107 3.4	38 9.6 / 69 5.3 / 132 2.8	55 6.6 / 92 4.0 / 145 2.5	55 6.6 / 84 4.3 / 160 2.3				36 10.2 / 71 5.1 / 120 3.1	43 8.5 / 82 4.5 / 137 2.7
Sales/Working Capital	3.0 / 6.2 / 24.1	2.3 / 4.2 / 6.6	2.4 / 5.0 / 8.8	3.4 / 5.5 / 10.1				2.3 / 3.7 / 6.8	2.8 / 4.3 / 6.9
EBIT/Interest	6.5 / (30) 2.6 / -.1	6.4 / (77) 2.6 / 1.2	7.8 / (82) 3.2 / 1.3	4.4 / (42) 1.6 / .6				6.8 / (245) 2.7 / 1.2	9.5 / (287) 3.7 / 1.2
Net Profit + Depr., Dep., Amort./Cur. Mat. L/T/D		4.0 / (12) 1.0 / .7	2.0 / (12) 1.2 / .3	3.7 / (14) 1.5 / .6				3.4 / (63) 1.4 / .4	5.9 / (59) 2.3 / .9
Fixed/Worth	.0 / .2 / 1.2	.1 / .1 / .6	.0 / .2 / .6	.2 / .4 / .7				.1 / .2 / .5	.1 / .2 / .5
Debt/Worth	.6 / 2.0 / NM	.7 / 1.6 / 3.3	1.1 / 1.8 / 3.5	1.1 / 1.7 / 4.3				.7 / 1.4 / 3.2	.7 / 1.6 / 3.6
% Profit Before Taxes/Tangible Net Worth	62.9 / (29) 12.2 / .5	31.1 / (79) 11.1 / 3.3	25.7 / (82) 10.9 / 3.3	21.0 / (41) 8.6 / -.8				22.8 / (248) 10.2 / 1.4	27.2 / (291) 11.2 / 2.3
% Profit Before Taxes/Total Assets	16.2 / 6.0 / -.6	10.3 / 4.2 / .7	8.5 / 4.7 / .6	7.6 / 1.8 / -1.3				9.7 / 3.7 / .7	10.0 / 4.2 / .6
Sales/Net Fixed Assets	251.4 / 82.1 / 20.6	73.0 / 30.5 / 11.1	71.6 / 25.2 / 11.6	31.7 / 13.3 / 8.8				68.0 / 25.1 / 9.9	59.1 / 21.0 / 10.9
Sales/Total Assets	3.8 / 2.5 / 1.6	2.0 / 1.6 / 1.2	2.0 / 1.5 / 1.1	1.8 / 1.5 / 1.1				2.0 / 1.5 / 1.2	2.1 / 1.6 / 1.2
% Depr., Dep., Amort./Sales	.3 / (25) .5 / 1.4	.3 / (70) .8 / 1.7	.4 / (72) .7 / 1.3	.5 / (44) 1.2 / 2.1				.5 / (230) .9 / 1.5	.5 / (255) .9 / 1.6
% Officers', Directors' Owners' Comp/Sales	4.0 / (26) 8.0 / 10.9	4.3 / (55) 6.5 / 9.0	2.6 / (54) 3.8 / 5.6	1.5 / (14) 2.8 / 7.1				3.2 / (165) 5.7 / 9.3	3.3 / (176) 5.7 / 9.9
Net Sales ($)	32379M	175907M	565282M	1481318M	525810M	1994761M		2669230M	3684724M
Total Assets ($)	11315M	103409M	364299M	975216M	414072M	1338139M		1688615M	2398164M

M = $ thousand   MM = $ million
See Pages 11 through 21 for Explanation of Ratios and Data

Comparative Historical Data   **Current Data Sorted by Sales**

Type of Statement									
	4/1/04–3/31/05 ALL	4/1/05–3/31/06 ALL	4/1/06–3/31/07 ALL	0-1MM	1-3MM	3-5MM	5-10MM	10-25MM	25MM & OVER
Unqualified	22	16	12					4	8
Reviewed	48	42	45		8	8	4	16	9
Compiled	85	72	66	13	23	10	12	7	1
Tax Returns	74	68	79	20	36	8	10	3	2
Other	44	77	70	7	16	11	10	7	19
				80 (4/1–9/30/06)			192 (10/1/06–3/31/07)		
NUMBER OF STATEMENTS	273	275	272	40	83	37	36	37	39
ASSETS	%	%	%	%	%	%	%	%	%
Cash & Equivalents	6.5	6.3	6.8	7.6	7.6	8.7	6.3	4.5	5.1
Trade Receivables (net)	7.7	7.9	8.1	4.2	7.1	8.6	7.0	13.4	9.6
Inventory	69.1	69.5	68.5	72.2	69.2	67.4	70.3	67.4	63.6
All Other Current	.9	.6	1.2	1.0	1.0	1.3	1.9	.5	1.6
Total Current	84.2	84.3	84.5	84.9	84.9	86.1	85.4	85.7	80.0
Fixed Assets (net)	10.2	9.4	10.3	11.8	9.0	9.9	9.8	9.4	13.5
Intangibles (net)	1.1	1.1	1.3	.8	2.0	.3	1.1	1.4	1.5
All Other Non-Current	4.5	5.2	3.8	2.4	4.2	3.7	3.7	3.5	4.9
Total	100.0	100.0	100.0	100.0	100.0	100.0	100.0	100.0	100.0
LIABILITIES									
Notes Payable-Short Term	12.5	14.6	14.2	9.0	15.2	10.5	15.5	16.3	17.5
Cur. Mat.-L.T.D.	2.3	2.7	2.3	2.9	2.5	2.9	.8	2.5	1.7
Trade Payables	23.9	21.6	22.9	17.2	23.0	27.2	26.4	23.9	20.7
Income Taxes Payable	.2	.2	.1	.1	.1	.2	.1	.1	.3
All Other Current	8.5	8.2	9.4	13.3	6.5	11.6	8.8	8.3	10.8
Total Current	47.4	47.3	48.9	42.5	47.2	52.4	51.6	51.1	51.0
Long-Term Debt	11.2	9.5	9.5	14.9	10.2	8.4	7.8	5.5	8.9
Deferred Taxes	.2	.2	.0	.0	.0	.1	.0	.2	.0
All Other Non-Current	4.5	6.6	5.6	6.4	8.0	4.6	2.5	5.1	3.8
Net Worth	36.7	36.4	36.0	36.2	34.6	34.5	38.1	38.1	36.4
Total Liabilities & Net Worth	100.0	100.0	100.0	100.0	100.0	100.0	100.0	100.0	100.0
INCOME DATA									
Net Sales	100.0	100.0	100.0	100.0	100.0	100.0	100.0	100.0	100.0
Gross Profit	43.7	43.6	42.7	46.7	43.2	41.4	39.1	42.2	42.5
Operating Expenses	39.7	39.4	38.1	41.8	38.4	36.9	33.3	38.4	39.0
Operating Profit	4.0	4.3	4.6	4.9	4.8	4.5	5.8	3.7	3.5
All Other Expenses (net)	1.1	1.1	1.3	1.4	1.7	1.2	1.4	.7	.8
Profit Before Taxes	2.9	3.1	3.3	3.6	3.1	3.3	4.4	3.0	2.7
RATIOS									
Current	2.7	2.8	2.6	6.8	2.6	2.6	2.3	2.3	2.5
	1.8	1.8	1.7	2.3	1.8	1.6	1.6	1.7	1.5
	1.4	1.4	1.3	1.6	1.4	1.3	1.3	1.4	1.2
Quick	.5	.5	.6	.8	.5	.6	.4	.6	.5
	(270) .2	(274) .2	.2	.3	.2	.2	.2	.3	.2
	.1	.1	.1	.0	.1	.1	.0	.1	.1
Sales/Receivables	1 657.0	0 UND	0 UND	0 UND	0 UND	0 UND	0 UND	2 184.7	2 221.7
	5 69.2	6 64.6	5 67.7	0 UND	5 77.2	8 47.1	6 57.8	20 18.5	10 36.1
	21 17.2	24 15.5	22 16.8	3 130.8	21 17.5	22 16.5	17 21.8	60 6.1	40 9.1
Cost of Sales/Inventory	198 1.8	203 1.8	189 1.9	188 1.9	194 1.9	185 2.0	159 2.3	217 1.7	183 2.0
	290 1.3	292 1.3	290 1.3	295 1.2	287 1.3	299 1.2	254 1.4	285 1.3	271 1.3
	386 .9	388 .9	374 1.0	434 .8	449 .8	381 1.0	358 1.0	332 1.1	366 1.3
Cost of Sales/Payables	45 8.1	36 10.1	40 9.1	14 25.5	38 9.6	48 7.6	43 8.5	61 6.0	39 9.4
	83 4.4	69 5.3	77 4.7	62 5.8	72 5.1	81 4.5	91 4.0	80 4.5	64 5.7
	137 2.7	125 2.9	132 2.8	122 3.0	140 2.6	159 2.3	124 2.9	120 2.9	127 2.9
Sales/Working Capital	2.7	2.8	2.6	1.9	2.3	3.0	2.9	3.0	3.9
	4.8	4.6	4.8	3.0	4.3	4.8	6.2	4.7	6.3
	8.2	8.0	8.1	6.5	7.3	8.3	10.7	8.2	9.8
EBIT/Interest	8.1	6.6	6.4	7.2	4.6	6.5	8.9	7.6	6.2
	(251) 3.0	(254) 2.6	(243) 2.6	(31) 2.6	(75) 2.0	(33) 3.5	(34) 3.2	2.9	(33) 2.4
	1.3	1.1	1.1	.0	1.0	1.4	1.6	.7	.8
Net Profit + Depr., Dep., Amort./Cur. Mat. L/T/D	5.4	6.5	3.3		4.0			1.5	21.0
	(57) 1.8	(47) 2.2	(43) 1.3		(12) 1.2		(10) .9	2.8	(10) 2.8
	1.0	.9	.6		.5			.1	1.3
Fixed/Worth	.1	.1	.1	.0	.1	.1	.1	.1	.2
	.3	.2	.2	.2	.2	.2	.2	.3	.4
	.5	.5	.6	.8	.7	.6	.5	.6	.6
Debt/Worth	.9	.9	.9	.2	.9	1.0	1.2	.8	1.1
	1.8	1.7	1.8	1.5	1.9	1.9	1.6	1.7	1.8
	3.7	4.0	3.7	3.7	4.3	5.3	3.2	3.8	4.1
% Profit Before Taxes/Tangible Net Worth	26.7	26.5	29.5	45.2	29.8	28.3	28.4	23.8	30.5
	(249) 13.3	(254) 10.6	(244) 11.2	(34) 13.3	(71) 9.1	(35) 9.7	(34) 11.0	(35) 12.0	(35) 14.4
	4.1	2.3	3.0	1.3	2.0	4.0	5.1	-1.5	4.2
% Profit Before Taxes/Total Assets	10.4	9.8	10.7	15.4	8.6	8.6	11.1	9.9	13.0
	4.1	3.2	4.4	5.8	3.7	5.0	5.2	3.1	4.1
	.7	.2	.5	.1	.5	1.2	1.6	-.9	.0
Sales/Net Fixed Assets	60.4	89.3	71.8	152.9	83.7	80.8	71.4	62.2	22.9
	22.9	26.3	24.6	40.2	31.8	35.2	29.5	14.5	11.5
	11.4	11.5	10.7	7.5	12.7	12.0	14.3	10.8	8.7
Sales/Total Assets	2.1	2.1	2.1	2.4	2.1	2.2	2.4	2.0	2.0
	1.6	1.6	1.6	1.6	1.6	1.6	1.8	1.5	1.6
	1.2	1.2	1.2	1.0	1.1	1.2	1.4	1.2	1.1
% Depr., Dep., Amort./Sales	.5	.4	.4	.5	.3	.3	.2	.5	.6
	(212) 1.0	(220) .8	(224) .8	(27) 1.0	(67) .6	(32) .4	(28) .7	(34) .9	(36) 1.3
	1.7	1.6	1.6	2.3	1.4	1.5	1.4	1.5	2.1
% Officers', Directors' Owners' Comp/Sales	2.9	3.0	3.1	5.6	3.9	3.0	2.2	2.2	
	(152) 5.4	(152) 5.6	(152) 5.3	(26) 8.0	(53) 6.2	(26) 3.9	(22) 3.7	(18) 3.2	
	9.2	8.8	8.3	10.9	8.7	7.9	6.2	4.8	
Net Sales ($)	5347650M	4749367M	4775457M	24119M	152598M	139778M	261020M	591585M	3606357M
Total Assets ($)	3259238M	3186932M	3206450M	16661M	113512M	89707M	156598M	425001M	2404971M

See Pages 11 through 21 for Explanation of Ratios and Data

Current Data Sorted by Assets   Comparative Historical Data

0-500M	500M-2MM	2-10MM	10-50MM	50-100MM	100-250MM	Type of Statement	ALL 4/1/02-3/31/03	ALL 4/1/03-3/31/04
		6	4	1	2	Unqualified	26	19
3	13	24				Reviewed	45	47
10	32	31				Compiled	84	103
47	37	11			1	Tax Returns	56	102
15	39	37	10	2	6	Other	74	71
	68 (4/1-9/30/06)		263 (10/1/06-3/31/07)					
75	121	109	14	3	9	**NUMBER OF STATEMENTS**	285	342
%	%	%	%	%	%	**ASSETS**	%	%
11.1	9.3	8.6	5.5			Cash & Equivalents	7.1	8.4
3.6	9.6	7.3	8.0			Trade Receivables (net)	8.8	6.9
61.4	58.0	58.1	47.8			Inventory	60.1	60.0
1.9	1.0	1.8	2.3			All Other Current	1.1	1.8
78.0	78.0	75.7	63.6			Total Current	77.0	77.1
15.8	13.1	16.1	24.1			Fixed Assets (net)	15.1	15.8
1.4	4.3	1.7	7.8			Intangibles (net)	3.5	3.4
4.7	4.6	6.4	4.5			All Other Non-Current	4.4	3.7
100.0	100.0	100.0	100.0			Total	100.0	100.0
						LIABILITIES		
21.7	11.7	11.0	24.5			Notes Payable-Short Term	13.0	14.2
3.0	2.6	2.4	1.1			Cur. Mat.-L.T.D.	3.4	2.7
26.0	23.2	25.7	18.7			Trade Payables	24.8	23.6
.2	.2	.2	.0			Income Taxes Payable	.2	.2
10.7	7.2	8.6	8.5			All Other Current	9.2	9.2
61.5	44.9	47.8	52.8			Total Current	50.7	49.9
20.9	12.1	12.2	17.4			Long-Term Debt	12.9	13.7
.0	.1	.3	.0			Deferred Taxes	.1	.1
18.8	6.2	3.7	5.8			All Other Non-Current	6.4	7.8
-1.3	36.6	36.0	24.0			Net Worth	29.9	28.5
100.0	100.0	100.0	100.0			Total Liabilities & Net Worth	100.0	100.0
						INCOME DATA		
100.0	100.0	100.0	100.0			Net Sales	100.0	100.0
40.0	36.5	36.9	33.5			Gross Profit	36.2	37.5
38.6	33.5	33.5	31.4			Operating Expenses	34.2	35.3
1.4	3.0	3.4	2.1			Operating Profit	2.0	2.1
1.6	1.6	.8	2.7			All Other Expenses (net)	.9	.6
-.2	1.4	2.6	-.6			Profit Before Taxes	1.1	1.5
						RATIOS		
2.3	2.8	2.2	1.6			Current	2.5	2.5
1.5	1.8	1.5	1.2				1.6	1.6
1.0	1.3	1.2	1.0				1.1	1.2
.5	.8	.6	.5			Quick	.7	.6
(74) .2	.3	(108) .2	.2				(283) .2	(336) .2
.1	.1	.1	.0				.1	.1
0 UND	0 UND	0 999.8	1 247.1			Sales/Receivables	0 999.8	0 UND
0 UND	4 95.6	2 166.5	3 127.6				3 115.8	2 168.4
5 80.1	20 18.2	14 26.1	9 39.9				14 25.8	11 33.8
74 4.9	88 4.2	104 3.5	60 6.1			Cost of Sales/Inventory	88 4.2	91 4.0
134 2.7	131 2.8	154 2.4	90 4.1				133 2.7	138 2.6
221 1.6	235 1.6	199 1.8	133 2.7				189 1.9	211 1.7
12 31.2	23 16.1	36 10.0	26 14.3			Cost of Sales/Payables	27 13.7	21 17.0
46 7.9	49 7.4	54 6.7	39 9.5				49 7.4	47 7.8
97 3.8	79 4.6	90 4.1	62 5.8				81 4.5	78 4.7
4.4	4.3	5.7	13.6			Sales/Working Capital	5.5	5.3
14.1	7.3	9.2	40.4				10.3	9.5
-175.0	15.5	24.4	-69.4				34.1	28.4
4.2	8.2	6.6	6.3			EBIT/Interest	6.6	7.8
(58) 1.2	(109) 2.4	(97) 3.1	(12) 1.3				(259) 2.1	(305) 2.3
-1.2	.9	1.5	.9				.9	.7
	5.5	5.8				Net Profit + Depr., Dep., Amort./Cur. Mat. L/T/D	10.6	6.8
	(10) 2.7	(29) 2.5					(48) 2.1	(57) 2.3
	.7	1.2					.9	.8
.1	.1	.1	.3			Fixed/Worth	.1	.1
1.0	.2	.4	1.1				.4	.4
-1.2	.8	1.1	9.6				1.3	2.3
2.1	.8	.9	2.1			Debt/Worth	1.0	.9
10.3	1.6	1.9	5.0				2.3	2.3
-4.8	4.7	3.8	34.4				8.0	10.0
113.4	29.5	32.5	43.0			% Profit Before Taxes/Tangible Net Worth	29.6	30.1
(45) 35.1	(106) 9.6	(99) 13.9	(12) 20.8				(242) 11.9	(289) 12.9
1.1	.9	3.8	-14.6				.9	-.2
15.4	10.1	10.7	12.5			% Profit Before Taxes/Total Assets	8.8	10.0
1.3	3.3	4.4	3.5				3.2	2.8
-7.9	-.5	1.2	-.3				-.2	-1.2
166.0	81.0	48.5	77.3			Sales/Net Fixed Assets	60.9	72.5
35.7	35.7	23.8	23.1				27.3	26.6
11.6	12.5	10.5	7.2				12.9	10.7
4.4	3.4	2.9	3.9			Sales/Total Assets	3.4	3.4
3.0	2.5	2.2	2.9				2.5	2.5
2.0	1.6	1.7	1.6				1.9	1.8
.7	.4	.4	.3			% Depr., Dep., Amort./Sales	.5	.5
(46) 1.1	(100) .8	(102) .7	(12) .6				(246) .9	(295) 1.0
2.1	1.4	1.4	3.8				1.8	1.8
2.8	2.2	1.8				% Officers', Directors' Owners' Comp/Sales	2.2	2.2
(48) 5.2	(74) 3.2	(47) 2.8					(147) 4.3	(206) 4.1
8.4	5.7	6.0					7.6	6.8
60306M	377877M	1061550M	721375M	478409M	3335595M	Net Sales ($)	4865446M	5641272M
18582M	141673M	460525M	258095M	250036M	1681035M	Total Assets ($)	2131079M	2572444M

© RMA 2007

M = $ thousand   MM = $ million
See Pages 11 through 21 for Explanation of Ratios and Data

Comparative Historical Data / Current Data Sorted by Sales

4/1/04-3/31/05 ALL	4/1/05-3/31/06 ALL	4/1/06-3/31/07 ALL	Type of Statement	0-1MM	1-3MM	3-5MM	5-10MM	10-25MM	25MM & OVER
20	11	13	Unqualified				1	6	6
47	37	40	Reviewed	3	3	7	13	13	1
91	53	73	Compiled	8	23	13	20	9	
80	81	96	Tax Returns	39	30	16	8	2	1
63	96	109	Other	18	25	14	20	15	17
					68 (4/1-9/30/06)		263 (10/1/06-3/31/07)		
301	278	331	NUMBER OF STATEMENTS	68	81	50	62	45	25
%	%	%	ASSETS	%	%	%	%	%	%
8.4	8.0	9.0	Cash & Equivalents	10.8	7.8	13.4	10.2	4.8	4.4
8.1	7.3	7.3	Trade Receivables (net)	2.5	6.1	10.2	9.7	10.0	7.3
59.4	59.7	57.8	Inventory	62.0	59.9	54.3	54.7	61.3	48.2
1.2	1.8	1.6	All Other Current	2.6	.8	1.3	1.5	1.5	2.0
77.1	76.7	75.7	Total Current	77.9	74.5	79.2	76.2	77.7	61.9
16.0	15.9	15.9	Fixed Assets (net)	15.6	15.6	15.1	14.9	14.0	24.9
2.3	2.8	3.2	Intangibles (net)	3.0	4.5	2.3	1.5	2.2	7.2
4.6	4.5	5.2	All Other Non-Current	3.3	5.4	3.4	7.4	6.1	6.0
100.0	100.0	100.0	Total	100.0	100.0	100.0	100.0	100.0	100.0
			LIABILITIES						
16.8	15.5	14.0	Notes Payable-Short Term	25.0	11.3	7.8	11.4	11.8	16.2
2.5	2.8	2.5	Cur. Mat.-L.T.D.	3.7	2.7	2.4	1.5	1.5	1.1
22.9	25.2	24.3	Trade Payables	21.1	24.4	27.6	22.6	30.2	19.3
.2	.2	.2	Income Taxes Payable	.1	.2	.1	.3	.1	.2
8.3	9.1	8.6	All Other Current	8.9	6.3	6.9	11.4	10.1	9.5
50.7	52.8	49.6	Total Current	58.7	44.9	44.8	47.2	54.7	46.4
16.8	13.2	14.9	Long-Term Debt	22.7	17.9	9.0	10.8	7.1	20.2
.1	.1	.2	Deferred Taxes	.0	.0	.5	.1	.1	.5
7.3	8.5	8.2	All Other Non-Current	14.3	12.2	4.7	3.7	3.2	5.4
25.0	25.3	27.1	Net Worth	4.1	25.0	41.0	38.1	34.9	27.6
100.0	100.0	100.0	Total Liabilities & Net Worth	100.0	100.0	100.0	100.0	100.0	100.0
			INCOME DATA						
100.0	100.0	100.0	Net Sales	100.0	100.0	100.0	100.0	100.0	100.0
37.6	38.2	37.3	Gross Profit	42.4	36.1	36.1	36.6	36.2	33.1
35.2	36.4	34.4	Operating Expenses	40.5	33.8	33.7	32.0	34.0	28.3
2.4	1.8	2.8	Operating Profit	1.9	2.3	2.4	4.6	2.3	4.8
.7	1.0	1.4	All Other Expenses (net)	3.1	1.3	.7	.7	.8	1.8
1.7	.8	1.4	Profit Before Taxes	-1.2	.9	1.7	3.9	1.5	3.1
			RATIOS						
2.5	2.3	2.4	Current	2.7	2.7	3.0	2.2	1.9	1.9
1.6	1.6	1.6		1.5	1.7	1.8	1.6	1.5	1.5
1.2	1.1	1.1		1.0	1.3	1.2	1.3	1.2	1.0
.7	.5	.6	Quick	.5	.5	1.2	.7	.5	.4
(297) .2	(274) .2	(328) .2		.1	(80) .2	.5	(44) .3	.2	(24) .1
.1	.1	.1		.0	.1	.1	.1	.1	.1
0 UND	0 UND	0 UND	Sales/Receivables	0 UND	0 UND	0 999.8	0 999.8	1 454.4	2 204.2
2 173.2	2 149.9	2 174.1		0 UND	2 166.1	2 210.3	3 121.0	3 109.8	3 120.4
13 27.6	14 26.7	14 25.3		5 75.2	18 20.6	20 18.4	21 17.8	15 24.7	6 62.9
94 3.9	98 3.7	90 4.1	Cost of Sales/Inventory	103 3.5	108 3.4	84 4.4	76 4.8	92 4.0	65 5.6
141 2.6	150 2.4	134 2.7		168 2.2	150 2.4	128 2.9	117 3.1	122 3.0	109 3.3
206 1.8	202 1.8	199 1.8		302 1.2	242 1.5	193 1.9	184 2.0	169 2.2	147 2.5
21 17.5	27 13.7	25 14.7	Cost of Sales/Payables	7 52.9	24 15.2	30 12.3	24 15.4	41 8.8	25 14.7
42 8.8	53 6.9	50 7.3		48 7.6	55 6.6	51 7.1	44 8.3	53 6.8	44 8.3
77 4.7	87 4.2	84 4.3		117 3.1	83 4.4	97 3.8	82 4.4	77 4.8	64 5.7
4.8	5.7	4.9	Sales/Working Capital	3.9	4.2	4.5	6.5	7.9	9.4
9.1	10.3	9.6		9.7	7.9	7.3	9.2	14.5	15.9
30.9	41.1	35.5		UND	15.7	43.1	17.8	32.1	-545.3
7.9	6.4	6.4	EBIT/Interest	2.2	6.3	8.2	15.6	5.9	6.5
(270) 2.9	(248) 2.4	(287) 2.4		(51) 1.1	(73) 1.8	(41) 2.5	(58) 3.9	(42) 3.3	(22) 3.2
1.1	.4	1.0		-1.1	-.1	1.2	1.7	1.3	1.0
5.2	13.2	6.0	Net Profit + Depr., Dep., Amort./Cur. Mat. L/T/D				9.9	8.1	
(50) 2.1	(35) 4.5	(43) 2.5					(14) 2.8	(12) 3.1	
.7	1.1	1.0					2.3	1.5	
.1	.2	.1	Fixed/Worth	.1	.1	.1	.1	.1	.4
.4	.5	.4		.7	.6	.2	.3	.3	1.1
2.8	2.3	1.6		-3.6	49.1	.8	.9	1.0	9.5
1.0	1.0	1.0	Debt/Worth	2.1	1.0	.6	.9	.9	1.6
2.5	2.7	2.3		8.1	2.3	1.6	1.5	1.9	3.0
17.1	13.8	10.3		-5.6	175.0	3.5	3.1	3.6	13.8
41.1	37.3	41.1	% Profit Before Taxes/Tangible Net Worth	105.0	39.3	19.2	46.4	27.2	42.4
(241) 16.3	(229) 14.2	(271) 14.7		(44) 15.3	(62) 13.0	(45) 5.9	(57) 21.0	(42) 14.0	(21) 24.6
3.4	-2.2	2.3		-6.9	-2.4	1.4	6.4	1.6	5.4
10.4	10.5	11.4	% Profit Before Taxes/Total Assets	12.5	10.8	6.4	18.0	7.5	12.5
3.7	3.0	4.0		.6	3.3	2.9	7.1	4.4	6.4
-.1	-2.2	-.2		-8.3	-3.5	.2	1.8	.3	.3
76.0	65.5	75.2	Sales/Net Fixed Assets	195.3	75.4	74.9	58.5	57.5	77.6
26.3	26.5	27.8		31.1	24.4	29.1	30.3	32.4	15.5
11.8	10.6	11.2		8.7	11.2	12.3	11.4	17.4	6.6
3.4	3.3	3.4	Sales/Total Assets	3.8	3.2	3.3	3.7	3.6	3.2
2.5	2.5	2.4		2.3	2.1	2.4	2.6	2.8	2.4
1.8	1.7	1.7		1.3	1.5	1.8	1.9	2.1	1.7
.5	.5	.4	% Depr., Dep., Amort./Sales	.8	.4	.3	.3	.4	.3
(239) 1.0	(227) .8	(267) .9		(41) 1.4	(62) .9	(43) .7	(59) .6	(43) .7	(19) 1.1
1.8	1.6	1.6		2.8	1.7	1.3	1.4	1.1	2.5
2.4	2.0	2.0	% Officers', Directors' Owners' Comp/Sales	2.9	2.3	2.2	1.6	1.8	
(173) 4.6	(131) 3.9	(175) 3.5		(41) 5.7	(44) 3.6	(32) 3.2	(35) 2.5	(17) 2.6	
6.5	6.6	6.5		9.5	5.5	5.8	5.1	10.6	
4265462M	4165929M	6035112M	Net Sales ($)	35816M	146993M	193835M	442594M	678346M	4537528M
2092804M	1809951M	2809946M	Total Assets ($)	22202M	92807M	90453M	177570M	257068M	2169846M

© RMA 2007   M = $ thousand   MM = $ million
See Pages 11 through 21 for Explanation of Ratios and Data

Current Data Sorted by Assets   Comparative Historical Data

0-500M	500M-2MM	2-10MM	10-50MM	50-100MM	100-250MM	Type of Statement	ALL 4/1/02-3/31/03	ALL 4/1/03-3/31/04
	1	2			1	Unqualified	2	4
	1	3	3			Reviewed	6	4
2	4	1			1	Compiled	11	13
5	10	3		1		Tax Returns	14	19
8	5	5	1		2	Other	18	13
	7 (4/1-9/30/06)		51 (10/1/06-3/31/07)					
15	21	14	3	2	3	NUMBER OF STATEMENTS	51	53
%	%	%	%	%	%	ASSETS	%	%
9.3	14.7	5.4				Cash & Equivalents	11.5	10.6
7.2	4.7	13.2				Trade Receivables (net)	5.8	6.4
67.7	54.6	44.9				Inventory	58.9	56.3
.4	.7	5.4				All Other Current	2.8	2.8
84.5	74.8	68.8				Total Current	79.0	76.2
12.0	14.5	21.2				Fixed Assets (net)	11.3	14.8
2.8	5.7	1.4				Intangibles (net)	4.3	1.9
.7	5.0	8.5				All Other Non-Current	5.4	7.1
100.0	100.0	100.0				Total	100.0	100.0
						LIABILITIES		
10.1	8.7	12.0				Notes Payable-Short Term	12.7	9.6
8.2	2.3	2.1				Cur. Mat.-L.T.D.	3.8	2.6
21.2	26.8	17.9				Trade Payables	19.7	15.5
.0	.1	2.2				Income Taxes Payable	.2	.3
4.8	5.6	6.5				All Other Current	21.1	16.2
44.4	43.4	40.7				Total Current	57.5	44.3
33.8	25.7	19.3				Long-Term Debt	16.5	24.7
.0	.0	1.1				Deferred Taxes	.1	.1
2.8	10.0	6.6				All Other Non-Current	5.0	8.9
19.0	20.9	32.4				Net Worth	20.9	22.1
100.0	100.0	100.0				Total Liabilities & Net Worth	100.0	100.0
						INCOME DATA		
100.0	100.0	100.0				Net Sales	100.0	100.0
45.4	43.6	45.0				Gross Profit	43.1	40.7
47.0	39.4	40.7				Operating Expenses	40.6	37.8
-1.6	4.2	4.3				Operating Profit	2.6	2.9
2.0	1.8	.6				All Other Expenses (net)	1.2	.9
-3.6	2.4	3.7				Profit Before Taxes	1.4	2.0
						RATIOS		
6.1	3.4	3.0				Current	2.8	3.5
2.3	2.1	1.6					1.5	2.1
1.0	1.3	1.2					1.1	1.3
1.4	.9	.8				Quick	.6	.8
(14) .4	.4	.4					.3	(52) .4
.1	.2	.1					.0	.1
0 UND	0 UND	3 123.0				Sales/Receivables	0 UND	0 UND
0 UND	0 999.8	11 32.7					1 420.0	0 999.8
3 141.7	6 57.6	32 11.6					7 54.8	5 74.7
65 5.6	64 5.7	71 5.1				Cost of Sales/Inventory	87 4.2	90 4.1
143 2.6	114 3.2	151 2.4					129 2.8	125 2.9
328 1.1	180 2.0	201 1.8					216 1.7	175 2.1
0 UND	13 27.2	24 15.1				Cost of Sales/Payables	13 27.1	8 48.3
23 16.2	44 8.2	47 7.7					30 12.2	26 13.8
73 5.0	79 4.6	72 5.0					53 6.9	45 8.1
4.7	5.2	4.6				Sales/Working Capital	5.3	5.3
9.0	6.9	7.9					13.6	8.0
205.0	96.6	25.4					57.1	15.8
5.4	5.0	3.9				EBIT/Interest	6.3	7.6
(13) .3	(19) 2.5	2.3					(46) 2.5	(45) 3.4
-2.1	1.1	1.7					.7	1.4
						Net Profit + Depr., Dep., Amort./Cur. Mat. L/T/D		
.1	.1	.1				Fixed/Worth	.1	.1
.5	.3	.3					.5	.3
-.7	2.0	1.7					7.8	1.4
.8	1.3	1.0				Debt/Worth	1.4	.8
8.4	4.9	1.5					3.6	2.9
-24.7	44.1	7.6					-28.3	21.9
	83.2	42.2				% Profit Before Taxes/Tangible Net Worth	51.3	38.0
	(17) 27.9	(12) 22.4					(38) 18.3	(42) 15.8
	10.5	7.1					1.1	3.4
14.0	11.2	9.0				% Profit Before Taxes/Total Assets	12.2	11.8
-.6	6.3	5.6					5.9	7.0
-14.5	.6	2.1					-1.8	.1
141.7	221.7	58.5				Sales/Net Fixed Assets	59.0	60.0
45.6	54.5	15.7					32.8	31.8
25.1	16.9	4.6					15.7	15.7
5.8	4.1	3.2				Sales/Total Assets	3.7	3.6
3.7	3.1	1.7					2.7	2.9
1.5	1.7	1.5					1.9	2.2
	.5	.8				% Depr., Dep., Amort./Sales	.7	.5
	(15) .9	(10) 1.3					(35) 1.1	(42) 1.0
	1.7	2.8					1.8	1.6
	2.0					% Officers', Directors' Owners' Comp/Sales	1.8	1.9
	(13) 2.6						(27) 3.5	(26) 3.5
	5.3						5.1	5.2
18422M	59620M	149540M	109781M	208523M	1246597M	Net Sales ($)	1061765M	1353803M
3730M	20462M	62323M	49500M	125340M	659699M	Total Assets ($)	500519M	598381M

© RMA 2007

M = $ thousand   MM = $ million
See Pages 11 through 21 for Explanation of Ratios and Data

Comparative Historical Data | Current Data Sorted by Sales

Type of Statement	4/1/04-3/31/05 ALL	4/1/05-3/31/06 ALL	4/1/06-3/31/07 ALL	0-1MM	1-3MM	3-5MM	5-10MM	10-25MM	25MM & OVER
Unqualified	6	4	4			1	1	1	1
Reviewed	2	5	7		1	1	1	2	2
Compiled	12	12	8	1	2	1	1	1	1
Tax Returns	21	14	18	4	7	5	2	2	
Other	10	14	21	8	4	1	2	2	4
	4/1/04-3/31/05	4/1/05-3/31/06	4/1/06-3/31/07	7 (4/1-9/30/06)			51 (10/1/06-3/31/07)		
NUMBER OF STATEMENTS	51	49	58	13	14	9	8	8	8
ASSETS	%	%	%	%	%	%	%	%	%
Cash & Equivalents	10.5	11.1	10.3	6.9	13.1				
Trade Receivables (net)	4.5	5.7	7.9	3.5	6.5				
Inventory	62.0	60.3	55.6	63.1	54.8				
All Other Current	1.3	1.5	2.0	.5	.1				
Total Current	78.3	78.5	75.8	74.1	74.5				
Fixed Assets (net)	12.4	15.1	16.0	14.8	17.6				
Intangibles (net)	2.9	3.6	3.6	10.5	2.0				
All Other Non-Current	6.4	2.8	4.5	.6	5.9				
Total	100.0	100.0	100.0	100.0	100.0				
LIABILITIES									
Notes Payable-Short Term	15.1	14.8	10.1	10.6	8.4				
Cur. Mat.-L.T.D.	4.2	3.3	3.7	4.3	7.6				
Trade Payables	12.1	14.1	21.1	21.3	14.9				
Income Taxes Payable	.0	.6	.8	.0	.0				
All Other Current	7.2	11.9	6.3	4.8	4.3				
Total Current	38.7	44.7	41.9	41.0	35.2				
Long-Term Debt	21.7	23.5	26.0	40.5	30.6				
Deferred Taxes	.1	.2	.3	.0	.0				
All Other Non-Current	6.3	9.0	6.9	11.4	4.0				
Net Worth	33.3	22.7	25.0	7.1	30.1				
Total Liabilities & Net Worth	100.0	100.0	100.0	100.0	100.0				
INCOME DATA									
Net Sales	100.0	100.0	100.0	100.0	100.0				
Gross Profit	40.2	44.4	44.0	49.4	43.1				
Operating Expenses	36.5	42.2	41.3	49.5	39.4				
Operating Profit	3.7	2.2	2.6	-.2	3.7				
All Other Expenses (net)	.9	1.2	1.6	3.3	1.6				
Profit Before Taxes	2.8	1.0	1.1	-3.5	2.0				
RATIOS									
Current	4.6	4.1	3.7	6.4	4.6				
	2.4	1.9	2.0	1.4	2.4				
	1.2	1.3	1.2	.8	1.5				
Quick	1.1	1.0	1.0	1.4	.9				
	.4	(57) .5	.4	.2	(13) .5				
	.1	.1	.1	.1	.2				
Sales/Receivables	0 UND	0 UND	0 UND	0 UND	0 UND				
	0 999.8	0 999.8	1 297.1	0 UND	0 UND				
	5 73.5	11 33.0	14 25.8	4 103.1	0 824.8				
Cost of Sales/Inventory	81 4.5	86 4.2	74 5.0	116 3.1	69 5.3				
	122 3.0	137 2.7	131 2.8	201 1.8	151 2.4				
	197 1.9	240 1.5	215 1.7	472 .8	231 1.6				
Cost of Sales/Payables	2 219.9	15 23.9	14 25.9	0 UND	3 119.9				
	16 22.3	34 10.8	40 9.1	40 9.2	23 15.8				
	38 9.6	49 7.5	70 5.2	134 2.7	70 5.2				
Sales/Working Capital	5.0	3.9	4.6	3.2	4.4				
	8.6	7.1	7.4	7.8	6.2				
	30.1	17.7	31.0	NM	10.1				
EBIT/Interest	15.3	4.5	4.1	2.0	5.6				
	(45) 4.1	(43) 1.8	(52) 2.1	(12) .4	3.1				
	1.4	.4	1.0	-.8	1.5				
Net Profit + Depr., Dep., Amort./Cur. Mat. L/T/D									
Fixed/Worth	.1	.1	.1	.1	.1				
	.2	.9	.4	-22.7	.4				
	3.8	-24.3	3.0	-.5	1.3				
Debt/Worth	.6	1.0	1.0	1.2	1.2				
	2.1	4.6	3.2	-25.4	3.2				
	39.3	-33.9	81.4	-3.6	10.4				
% Profit Before Taxes/Tangible Net Worth	69.3	43.2	68.1		82.9				
	(41) 30.5	(36) 13.6	(45) 23.5		(13) 27.9				
	7.1	.1	6.7		6.7				
% Profit Before Taxes/Total Assets	20.6	9.5	10.4	8.3	12.2				
	9.4	2.5	5.1	-.6	6.6				
	1.8	-2.8	.0	-10.5	1.6				
Sales/Net Fixed Assets	82.2	74.7	88.4	118.3	102.1				
	31.3	32.6	36.5	41.1	52.0				
	14.0	15.6	10.0	12.4	7.8				
Sales/Total Assets	4.2	3.6	3.9	3.8	3.2				
	3.1	2.4	2.5	1.5	2.4				
	1.9	1.6	1.5	1.0	1.8				
% Depr., Dep., Amort./Sales	.7	.4	.5		.4				
	(37) 1.1	(39) .8	(40) .9		(12) .7				
	1.5	1.5	1.7		2.1				
% Officers', Directors' Owners' Comp/Sales	1.5	3.9	1.9						
	(27) 4.3	(23) 7.1	(27) 3.1						
	5.5	10.9	6.7						
Net Sales ($)	1343677M	2578830M	1792483M	7170M	27241M	31554M	53359M	83260M	1589899M
Total Assets ($)	630509M	1042095M	921054M	4379M	13206M	10429M	22754M	38306M	831980M

© RMA 2007

M = $ thousand   MM = $ million

See Pages 11 through 21 for Explanation of Ratios and Data

Current Data Sorted by Assets　　　　　　Comparative Historical Data

	0-500M	500M-2MM	2-10MM	10-50MM	50-100MM	100-250MM	Type of Statement	4/1/02-3/31/03 ALL	4/1/03-3/31/04 ALL
			1			1	Unqualified	9	8
		2	15	2			Reviewed	21	19
	3	9	7	1			Compiled	33	34
	3	12	5	1			Tax Returns	7	19
	4	6	7	3			Other	24	23
		26 (4/1-9/30/06)		56 (10/1/06-3/31/07)					
NUMBER OF STATEMENTS	10	29	35	7		1		94	103

	0-500M %	500M-2MM %	2-10MM %	10-50MM %	50-100MM %	100-250MM %		4/1/02-3/31/03 ALL %	4/1/03-3/31/04 ALL %
ASSETS									
Cash & Equivalents	12.0	6.7	3.1					7.5	6.5
Trade Receivables (net)	2.2	11.1	13.3	D				13.5	14.8
Inventory	60.5	64.6	56.6	A				58.4	55.9
All Other Current	.4	.9	4.7	T				2.6	3.1
Total Current	75.1	83.3	77.6	A				82.0	80.3
Fixed Assets (net)	15.3	12.0	14.3					12.2	14.9
Intangibles (net)	9.1	.6	1.4	N				1.0	1.0
All Other Non-Current	.4	4.1	6.7	O				4.8	3.8
Total	100.0	100.0	100.0	T				100.0	100.0
LIABILITIES				A					
Notes Payable-Short Term	13.8	21.7	25.9	V				16.3	20.1
Cur. Mat.-L.T.D.	1.8	6.5	5.0	A				3.5	3.5
Trade Payables	6.2	16.7	13.1	I				20.3	14.8
Income Taxes Payable	.0	.0	.4	L				.4	.3
All Other Current	3.4	7.5	8.4	A				11.3	8.9
Total Current	25.2	52.4	52.7	B				51.7	47.6
Long-Term Debt	30.7	11.6	7.4	L				8.7	13.8
Deferred Taxes	.0	.0	.5	E				.2	.3
All Other Non-Current	10.6	3.6	3.5					2.9	5.2
Net Worth	33.5	32.5	35.9					36.5	33.0
Total Liabilities & Net Worth	100.0	100.0	100.0					100.0	100.0
INCOME DATA									
Net Sales	100.0	100.0	100.0					100.0	100.0
Gross Profit	43.7	40.8	44.1					42.6	44.2
Operating Expenses	38.1	38.6	42.0					39.6	42.7
Operating Profit	5.7	2.1	2.1					3.0	1.6
All Other Expenses (net)	2.4	2.2	1.4					.6	.8
Profit Before Taxes	3.2	-.1	.7					2.4	.8
RATIOS									
Current	9.6	2.2	1.9					2.5	2.6
	4.0	1.6	1.6					1.7	1.8
	2.2	1.3	1.1					1.4	1.3
Quick	2.9	.6	.5					.8	.9
	.4	(28) .2	.2					.3	.3
	.2	.1	.1					.2	.1
Sales/Receivables	0 UND	6 59.6	7 48.9					4 83.0	5 80.6
	1 374.8	14 26.1	12 30.7					12 29.8	13 28.5
	8 46.8	25 14.6	41 8.9					30 12.2	37 9.8
Cost of Sales/Inventory	70 5.2	144 2.5	158 2.3					112 3.2	132 2.8
	160 2.3	225 1.6	189 1.9					197 1.9	210 1.7
	418 .9	391 .9	270 1.4					248 1.5	262 1.4
Cost of Sales/Payables	0 UND	21 17.4	22 16.8					21 17.4	16 22.9
	12 29.7	42 8.7	39 9.5					45 8.1	43 8.5
	34 10.8	111 3.3	69 5.3					72 5.1	67 5.5
Sales/Working Capital	2.3	3.9	3.5					4.3	3.9
	3.9	6.7	6.6					6.4	5.5
	11.9	10.8	44.0					11.4	14.2
EBIT/Interest		2.5	2.9					7.7	5.6
		(27) 1.4	1.4					(84) 3.1	(97) 2.1
		.0	.3					1.5	1.0
Net Profit + Depr., Dep., Amort./Cur. Mat. L/T/D			1.8					5.0	2.9
		(12)	.2					(30) 2.6	(33) 1.4
			-.3					.9	.4
Fixed/Worth	.1	.1	.1					.1	.1
	.6	.3	.3					.3	.3
	NM	.6	.9					.5	.9
Debt/Worth	.7	1.1	1.0					.8	1.0
	2.0	2.5	1.8					1.7	2.1
	NM	5.1	4.5					2.7	4.4
% Profit Before Taxes/Tangible Net Worth		16.4	15.5					23.1	24.1
		(27) 5.3	(33) 5.3					(88) 10.2	(93) 8.6
		-12.2	-8.2					3.9	.5
% Profit Before Taxes/Total Assets	22.2	5.5	4.2					8.0	7.2
	5.4	1.4	2.0					3.9	2.5
	.5	-4.6	-2.7					1.2	.0
Sales/Net Fixed Assets	181.4	113.5	40.0					62.7	55.8
	23.5	20.1	21.0					25.5	21.8
	10.8	11.7	10.0					13.6	9.3
Sales/Total Assets	4.6	2.7	2.3					2.6	2.6
	2.5	1.8	1.8					2.1	1.8
	1.3	1.2	1.4					1.5	1.3
% Depr., Dep., Amort./Sales		.5	.5					.5	.7
		(21) .8	(31) 1.0					(73) .9	(85) 1.2
		1.9	2.0					1.8	2.5
% Officers', Directors' Owners' Comp/Sales		2.2	1.5					3.3	2.3
		(19) 3.4	(12) 1.9					(44) 5.3	(54) 4.9
		5.4	4.6					8.3	7.9
Net Sales ($)	6466M	66094M	314771M	225125M		45520M		1356408M	1188535M
Total Assets ($)	2593M	32434M	166451M	125205M		114876M		697829M	715699M

© RMA 2007

M = $ thousand　　MM = $ million
See Pages 11 through 21 for Explanation of Ratios and Data

Comparative Historical Data / Current Data Sorted by Sales

Type of Statement	4/1/04-3/31/05 ALL	4/1/05-3/31/06 ALL	4/1/06-3/31/07 ALL	0-1MM	1-3MM	3-5MM	5-10MM	10-25MM	25MM & OVER
Unqualified	9	2	2				1		1
Reviewed	24	25	19	4	8	3	10	4	2
Compiled	23	19	20	5	8	3	3	2	
Tax Returns	22	17	21	6	3	3	3	2	
Other	19	27	20			1	4	4	2
				26 (4/1-9/30/06)			56 (10/1/06-3/31/07)		
NUMBER OF STATEMENTS	97	90	82	15	19	10	21	12	5

ASSETS

	%	%	%	%	%	%	%	%	%
Cash & Equivalents	7.0	5.9	5.3	8.6	7.8	4.8	2.8	4.0	
Trade Receivables (net)	14.1	13.5	13.7	5.3	8.8	17.8	10.9	25.5	
Inventory	55.9	60.6	58.2	60.8	67.0	56.2	53.6	55.8	
All Other Current	2.1	2.3	2.7	.4	1.2	.2	7.2	1.7	
Total Current	79.1	82.3	79.9	75.1	84.8	79.4	74.5	87.0	
Fixed Assets (net)	14.9	11.8	13.1	17.4	10.3	13.9	16.5	6.5	
Intangibles (net)	1.1	1.2	2.0	6.2	.9	1.6	.6	1.8	
All Other Non-Current	4.9	4.7	5.1	1.3	4.0	5.2	8.4	4.8	
Total	100.0	100.0	100.0	100.0	100.0	100.0	100.0	100.0	

LIABILITIES

Notes Payable-Short Term	17.2	17.5	22.6	13.1	29.4	14.1	24.7	27.7	
Cur. Mat.-L.T.D.	3.8	2.7	4.7	7.9	3.1	9.5	2.0	5.5	
Trade Payables	15.5	18.9	13.6	8.5	14.3	17.2	13.9	17.5	
Income Taxes Payable	.4	.2	.2	.0	.0	.4	.4	.1	
All Other Current	11.2	11.1	7.4	3.1	9.0	3.7	10.5	8.6	
Total Current	48.1	50.3	48.5	32.7	55.9	44.9	51.5	59.4	
Long-Term Debt	12.3	12.1	12.5	25.7	13.3	6.4	8.3	3.8	
Deferred Taxes	.3	.2	.2	.0	.0	.1	.4	.7	
All Other Non-Current	4.1	8.5	5.0	9.1	1.5	4.8	5.2	5.6	
Net Worth	35.1	28.9	33.8	32.5	29.3	43.8	34.6	30.5	
Total Liabilties & Net Worth	100.0	100.0	100.0	100.0	100.0	100.0	100.0	100.0	

INCOME DATA

Net Sales	100.0	100.0	100.0	100.0	100.0	100.0	100.0	100.0	
Gross Profit	41.6	41.2	42.5	48.1	40.2	40.7	44.2	36.3	
Operating Expenses	39.4	38.4	39.8	39.7	41.3	37.7	42.8	34.0	
Operating Profit	2.2	2.8	2.7	8.4	-1.1	3.0	1.4	2.4	
All Other Expenses (net)	.7	1.3	2.0	4.3	1.0	1.3	1.5	1.5	
Profit Before Taxes	1.5	1.5	.7	4.2	-2.1	1.7	-.1	.8	

RATIOS

Current	2.3	2.2	2.3	4.0	2.1	2.8	1.9	1.8	
	1.7	1.7	1.7	2.4	1.6	1.8	1.5	1.5	
	1.2	1.3	1.3	1.7	1.2	1.2	1.0	1.3	
Quick	.8	.7	.8	.8	.4	1.3	.4	1.1	
	.3	.3 (81)	.3	(14) .4	.2	.3	.2	.7	
	.1	.1	.1	.1	.1	.2	.1	.1	
Sales/Receivables	6 61.0	5 73.0	5 71.5	0 UND	6 62.5	7 53.0	6 61.1	9 41.4	
	16 23.2	14 26.7	13 29.1	3 104.5	13 28.8	26 13.9	10 37.5	32 11.5	
	36 10.3	29 12.4	34 10.6	20 17.9	18 19.9	44 8.4	33 10.9	147 2.5	
Cost of Sales/Inventory	131 2.8	133 2.7	134 2.7	123 3.0	162 2.3	85 4.3	151 2.4	119 3.1	
	195 1.9	180 2.0	192 1.9	276 1.3	196 1.9	209 1.7	189 1.9	138 2.6	
	273 1.3	265 1.4	277 1.3	602 .6	278 1.3	310 1.2	233 1.6	208 1.8	
Cost of Sales/Payables	14 25.2	19 19.3	19 18.8	9 40.6	23 16.1	16 22.3	23 15.7	18 20.1	
	39 9.4	44 8.3	36 10.1	17 21.1	42 8.7	34 10.7	44 8.3	37 9.8	
	81 4.5	77 4.7	76 4.8	107 3.4	77 4.7	50 7.3	90 4.1	74 4.9	
Sales/Working Capital	3.9	3.6	3.6	2.3	4.1	3.4	5.5	3.6	
	6.3	6.4	6.1	3.1	5.9	8.3	6.6	5.7	
	18.3	14.4	11.5	8.1	13.1	12.9	NM	14.4	
EBIT/Interest	5.1	3.4	2.6	3.5	1.8	11.8	2.2	3.8	
	(90) 1.7	(85) 1.6	(77) 1.4	(13) 1.9	(16) 1.0	2.1	1.1	1.6	
	.8	.8	.4	1.1	-.4	-.3	.4	1.1	
Net Profit + Depr., Dep., Amort./Cur. Mat. L/T/D	4.5	3.2	2.1						
	(29) 1.2	(18) .9	(20) .4						
	.3	.1	-.3						
Fixed/Worth	.1	.1	.1	.1	.2	.1	.2	.1	
	.3	.3	.3	.6	.3	.2	.3	.1	
	.7	.8	.8	3.0	.7	.8	1.0	1.7	
Debt/Worth	1.0	1.3	1.0	1.2	1.1	.7	1.0	1.1	
	2.0	2.2	2.1	2.3	2.6	1.4	2.1	3.3	
	4.0	6.3	4.6	9.0	11.5	2.6	5.4	17.7	
% Profit Before Taxes/Tangible Net Worth	24.4	19.9	16.5	80.1	12.3	26.2	12.3	14.4	
	(92) 7.4	(82) 7.0	(76) 5.3	(13) 8.1	(17) 4.8	13.3	(20) 2.0	(11) 5.3	
	.5	-2.1	-8.5	-6.1	-12.2	-21.3	-6.8	2.0	
% Profit Before Taxes/Total Assets	6.6	5.2	5.7	14.1	3.5	12.4	3.8	7.7	
	1.9	1.9	1.8	3.2	.3	5.4	.7	2.2	
	-.4	-.7	-2.4	.0	-4.2	-6.1	-2.1	.3	
Sales/Net Fixed Assets	50.9	64.4	50.3	104.5	87.8	346.9	55.8	97.5	
	16.9	24.3	21.8	17.2	25.0	20.4	16.9	30.3	
	8.4	13.9	11.3	5.2	11.8	5.2	9.4	23.3	
Sales/Total Assets	2.2	2.8	2.6	2.7	2.4	3.3	2.5	2.8	
	1.8	1.9	1.8	1.3	1.8	1.6	2.0	1.9	
	1.4	1.3	1.3	.5	1.3	1.4	1.4	1.2	
% Depr., Dep., Amort./Sales	.7	.5	.5		.4		.6	.4	
	(75) 1.3	(78) .8 (65)	1.0		(15) .8		(19) 1.0	(10) .9	
	2.0	1.6	2.0		2.0		3.0	1.5	
% Officers', Directors' Owners' Comp/Sales	2.4	2.3	2.0		2.1				
	(53) 4.8	(47) 3.6 (40)	3.2		(12) 2.5				
	7.1	7.2	6.1		5.3				
Net Sales ($)	1883357M	1020790M	657976M	8003M	35782M	39544M	151248M	201430M	221969M
Total Assets ($)	1015955M	651658M	441559M	7365M	21577M	20752M	86513M	118641M	186711M

M = $ thousand   MM = $ million
See Pages 11 through 21 for Explanation of Ratios and Data

Current Data Sorted by Assets   Comparative Historical Data

0-500M	500M-2MM	2-10MM	10-50MM	50-100MM	100-250MM	Type of Statement	4/1/02-3/31/03 ALL	4/1/03-3/31/04 ALL
1	1	3	4		1	Unqualified	15	13
	2	5	2			Reviewed	11	8
1	7	3	1			Compiled	14	19
7	6	1				Tax Returns	12	15
4	3	6	5	1		Other	23	26
	22 (4/1-9/30/06)		41 (10/1/06-3/31/07)					
13	19	18	11	1	1	NUMBER OF STATEMENTS	75	81
%	%	%	%	%	%	ASSETS	%	%
21.5	9.6	9.7	12.4			Cash & Equivalents	12.0	12.1
12.3	6.2	8.5	5.7			Trade Receivables (net)	7.6	7.0
42.2	56.9	46.6	38.7			Inventory	46.7	46.9
1.3	.7	3.4	2.0			All Other Current	2.7	2.9
77.3	73.4	68.1	58.8			Total Current	68.9	69.0
16.2	17.7	27.0	31.8			Fixed Assets (net)	22.3	21.1
.9	2.4	1.4	3.8			Intangibles (net)	1.9	2.0
5.6	6.5	3.5	5.6			All Other Non-Current	7.0	7.9
100.0	100.0	100.0	100.0			Total	100.0	100.0
						LIABILITIES		
22.9	19.4	5.3	10.2			Notes Payable-Short Term	6.2	5.3
.7	.9	4.4	2.4			Cur. Mat.-L.T.D.	2.4	2.4
14.3	28.6	23.4	16.2			Trade Payables	26.5	24.4
.0	.0	.7	.1			Income Taxes Payable	.2	.1
9.8	15.9	9.7	14.7			All Other Current	11.4	14.7
47.7	64.8	43.5	43.6			Total Current	46.8	46.9
5.1	11.3	12.4	5.4			Long-Term Debt	16.1	14.1
.0	.0	1.1	.0			Deferred Taxes	.2	.1
12.7	3.6	2.6	9.9			All Other Non-Current	4.9	6.4
34.5	20.2	40.5	41.1			Net Worth	32.0	32.5
100.0	100.0	100.0	100.0			Total Liabilities & Net Worth	100.0	100.0
						INCOME DATA		
100.0	100.0	100.0	100.0			Net Sales	100.0	100.0
48.3	36.1	40.1	36.8			Gross Profit	39.2	40.4
48.3	35.4	36.1	37.6			Operating Expenses	35.6	38.7
.0	.7	3.9	-.8			Operating Profit	3.6	1.8
.7	.8	.9	1.7			All Other Expenses (net)	.9	1.1
-.7	-.1	3.1	-2.6			Profit Before Taxes	2.7	.7
						RATIOS		
14.4	2.4	1.9	3.2			Current	2.7	2.7
2.3	1.1	1.6	1.7				1.6	1.5
1.0	.8	1.3	1.0				1.0	1.0
13.2	.4	.6	1.7			Quick	.9	.7
.5	.2	.4	.4				.4	.3
.0	.1	.2	.2				.1	.2
0 UND	1 475.2	2 236.7	2 221.4			Sales/Receivables	0 UND	0 999.8
3 111.0	3 118.4	9 40.1	4 91.8				3 128.3	3 120.6
12 30.0	10 36.1	15 23.8	14 27.0				11 33.1	12 31.5
11 34.7	70 5.2	47 7.7	84 4.3			Cost of Sales/Inventory	65 5.7	68 5.4
102 3.6	103 3.5	118 3.1	89 4.1				92 4.0	102 3.6
385 .9	158 2.3	146 2.5	113 3.2				125 2.9	144 2.5
0 UND	15 23.6	31 11.9	23 16.1			Cost of Sales/Payables	26 14.2	14 26.8
12 30.0	43 8.6	57 6.4	33 11.2				44 8.4	42 8.8
111 3.3	89 4.1	77 4.8	46 8.0				74 4.9	80 4.6
3.8	5.9	7.4	5.4			Sales/Working Capital	6.1	6.5
7.6	26.7	10.0	10.2				11.2	11.9
NM	-17.4	25.7	-191.6				112.1	189.6
	4.1	24.6				EBIT/Interest	20.4	11.4
	(17) 1.7	3.7					(67) 3.9	(70) 3.2
	.6	2.0					.3	.5
						Net Profit + Depr., Dep., Amort./Cur. Mat. L/T/D	14.4	5.9
							(12) 2.9	(14) 1.8
							.5	1.1
.0	.1	.4	.3			Fixed/Worth	.3	.2
.3	2.4	.7	.6				.7	.5
54.7	-.7	1.1	1.8				3.1	66.8
.1	.6	.6	.4			Debt/Worth	.7	.6
.6	7.0	1.4	.9				2.4	1.8
270.5	-6.9	2.7	2.0				11.2	165.6
56.4	18.7	27.6				% Profit Before Taxes/Tangible Net Worth	67.1	32.5
(11) 14.3	(12) 3.5	(17) 13.6					(64) 16.9	(63) 9.6
-11.0	-1.6	2.4					2.9	1.5
28.4	4.5	12.2	5.7			% Profit Before Taxes/Total Assets	13.9	8.4
3.4	1.0	4.0	4.3				5.5	2.5
-10.2	-4.3	1.2	-.1				-1.3	-1.3
348.5	81.2	30.5	20.9			Sales/Net Fixed Assets	46.7	66.2
21.2	32.9	7.5	7.4				13.4	20.4
7.8	10.4	5.5	3.5				6.7	6.6
4.4	3.8	3.4	2.8			Sales/Total Assets	3.7	4.1
2.3	2.9	2.6	2.0				2.8	2.8
1.5	2.3	1.9	1.8				2.1	1.8
	.7	1.0	1.1			% Depr., Dep., Amort./Sales	.8	.6
	(15) 1.0	1.5	1.5				(64) 1.4	(67) 1.5
	1.2	2.9	2.2				2.1	2.5
	1.8					% Officers', Directors', Owners' Comp/Sales	1.6	2.3
	(10) 3.3						(28) 4.8	(26) 3.4
	7.1						8.4	9.0
9519M	59829M	248353M	468635M	151148M	309228M	Net Sales ($)	2128066M	1311580M
3011M	19471M	92016M	218074M	67284M	145014M	Total Assets ($)	1038295M	602563M

Comparative Historical Data — Current Data Sorted by Sales

			Type of Statement	0-1MM	1-3MM	3-5MM	5-10MM	10-25MM	25MM & OVER
14	12	10	Unqualified	1		1		3	5
8	7	9	Reviewed		2	1	1	2	3
14	12	11	Compiled	1	3	3	1	3	
15	9	14	Tax Returns	9	3	1		1	
21	24	19	Other	2	3	1	4	3	6
4/1/04-3/31/05 ALL	4/1/05-3/31/06 ALL	4/1/06-3/31/07 ALL		22 (4/1-9/30/06)			41 (10/1/06-3/31/07)		
72	64	63	**NUMBER OF STATEMENTS**	13	11	7	6	12	14
%	%	%	**ASSETS**	%	%	%	%	%	%
9.6	9.0	12.6	Cash & Equivalents	20.8	5.4			11.2	11.2
6.8	6.7	7.9	Trade Receivables (net)	7.3	12.6			7.3	7.9
49.8	51.9	47.1	Inventory	48.0	48.4			40.4	40.0
2.4	3.2	2.0	All Other Current	1.3	.2			2.9	3.0
68.7	70.7	69.5	Total Current	77.4	66.7			61.8	62.0
23.1	20.5	22.8	Fixed Assets (net)	15.6	25.9			33.7	27.1
2.2	1.2	2.3	Intangibles (net)	1.7	2.9			.8	5.3
6.0	7.6	5.3	All Other Non-Current	5.3	4.6			3.7	5.5
100.0	100.0	100.0	Total	100.0	100.0			100.0	100.0
			LIABILITIES						
11.0	11.4	13.9	Notes Payable-Short Term	22.7	19.0			3.3	8.1
4.8	2.6	2.1	Cur. Mat.-L.T.D.	1.1	1.2			2.6	4.8
22.2	25.8	21.8	Trade Payables	19.3	20.4			18.9	20.5
.1	.1	.3	Income Taxes Payable	.0	.0			.7	.3
14.7	11.6	12.4	All Other Current	12.7	11.6			11.3	13.5
52.8	51.4	50.4	Total Current	55.9	52.1			36.8	47.3
12.5	9.6	9.0	Long-Term Debt	8.4	16.0			11.4	3.1
.1	.2	.3	Deferred Taxes	.0	.0			1.0	.5
8.1	11.0	6.7	All Other Non-Current	13.9	3.2			.0	12.3
26.4	27.8	33.5	Net Worth	21.9	28.7			50.8	36.8
100.0	100.0	100.0	Total Liabilities & Net Worth	100.0	100.0			100.0	100.0
			INCOME DATA						
100.0	100.0	100.0	Net Sales	100.0	100.0			100.0	100.0
43.3	40.4	40.5	Gross Profit	43.7	46.2			37.7	40.6
41.0	38.4	39.1	Operating Expenses	45.7	40.7			36.1	40.4
2.3	2.0	1.3	Operating Profit	-2.0	5.5			1.6	.2
.6	.9	1.0	All Other Expenses (net)	.9	1.5			.6	1.6
1.7	1.1	.4	Profit Before Taxes	-2.9	4.0			1.0	-1.4
			RATIOS						
2.7	2.3	2.8	Current	6.7	4.0			2.7	2.9
1.5	1.6	1.6		1.9	1.1			1.7	1.6
.9	1.2	1.0		.8	.8			1.2	1.0
.9	.6	.7	Quick	4.7	.7			.7	.9
.3	.3	.3		.2	.3			.4	.4
.1	.1	.1		.0	.0			.3	.1
0 964.9	1 280.7	1 311.1	Sales/Receivables	0 UND	0 UND			1 396.5	2 176.6
3 143.2	4 103.2	3 107.2		3 118.4	3 112.6			5 71.1	4 91.8
10 34.9	14 26.1	13 27.3		7 52.6	34 10.8			13 27.1	24 14.9
76 4.8	79 4.6	69 5.3	Cost of Sales/Inventory	18 20.1	53 6.8			47 7.7	83 4.4
113 3.2	108 3.4	103 3.5		187 1.9	104 3.5			89 4.1	106 3.4
194 1.9	167 2.2	162 2.2		385 .9	158 2.3			132 2.8	133 2.7
25 14.9	30 12.2	15 23.6	Cost of Sales/Payables	0 UND	6 57.0			23 16.0	25 14.8
44 8.3	44 8.3	46 8.0		57 6.4	36 10.1			38 9.6	39 9.5
70 5.2	85 4.3	82 4.4		129 2.8	90 4.0			58 6.3	90 4.0
5.8	6.4	5.9	Sales/Working Capital	3.8	6.2			7.4	5.7
11.7	9.8	10.3		7.6	30.9			10.0	10.5
-85.9	30.4	-191.6		-20.1	-24.2			45.4	-157.2
10.7	9.0	11.3	EBIT/Interest		10.4			42.1	9.5
(59) 2.0	(55) 2.3	(53) 3.0			(10) 3.1			4.5	(11) 3.7
.9	.2	1.0			-.1			-.4	1.0
12.8	9.2	9.4	Net Profit + Depr., Dep., Amort./Cur. Mat. L/T/D						
(12) 5.0	(12) 3.9	(11) 3.8							
1.7	.5	1.7							
.3	.2	.2	Fixed/Worth	.0	.4			.4	.4
.7	.5	.6		.3	2.4			.7	.5
7.1	3.0	4.7		56.8	-.8			1.0	NM
.7	.6	.5	Debt/Worth	.6	.6			.5	.3
1.8	1.6	1.6		7.0	3.1			.8	1.1
29.2	11.6	100.8		405.8	-13.9			2.2	NM
33.8	28.2	24.3	% Profit Before Taxes/Tangible Net Worth	47.5				24.2	13.8
(57) 11.7	(51) 8.8	(51) 8.8		(11) 5.3				11.0	(11) 6.9
1.9	.1	1.2		-55.0				-1.1	2.9
11.1	8.9	9.2	% Profit Before Taxes/Total Assets	8.9	12.1			10.1	6.0
3.7	4.2	3.6		.4	3.6			4.3	4.4
-.7	-.4	-1.3		-10.2	-4.3			-.7	1.0
33.1	40.7	47.5	Sales/Net Fixed Assets	UND	47.5			22.9	22.9
15.5	20.6	16.7		21.2	16.8			7.4	10.8
7.0	6.5	6.0		6.8	5.1			4.1	5.5
3.5	3.5	3.6	Sales/Total Assets	3.1	4.4			3.8	3.3
2.4	2.4	2.4		1.7	2.9			2.6	2.2
1.8	1.8	1.9		1.2	2.3			2.0	1.9
.9	.5	.9	% Depr., Dep., Amort./Sales		1.0			1.1	1.1
(61) 1.4	(52) 1.0	(54) 1.3			(10) 1.3			1.6	1.5
2.1	1.9	2.3			3.0			2.6	2.4
1.8	2.5	1.9	% Officers', Directors' Owners' Comp/Sales						
(23) 3.8	(15) 4.2	(23) 4.0							
8.3	7.0	6.4							
1292820M	1401615M	1246712M	Net Sales ($)	6621M	24730M	26103M	42119M	176975M	970164M
559509M	679312M	544870M	Total Assets ($)	3917M	11309M	9588M	14861M	70308M	434887M

M = $ thousand   MM = $ million
See Pages 11 through 21 for Explanation of Ratios and Data

Current Data Sorted by Assets   **Comparative Historical Data**

0-500M	500M-2MM	2-10MM	10-50MM	50-100MM	100-250MM	Type of Statement	ALL	ALL
		2	4		1	Unqualified	17	19
	1	2	3			Reviewed	11	6
2	3	2	1			Compiled	9	9
	4	1	1			Tax Returns	9	3
	2	2	7	1	2	Other	17	13
	7 (4/1-9/30/06)		34 (10/1/06-3/31/07)				4/1/02-3/31/03	4/1/03-3/31/04
2	10	9	16	1	3	NUMBER OF STATEMENTS	63	50
%	%	%	%	%	%	**ASSETS**	%	%
	8.4		10.1			Cash & Equivalents	10.0	12.3
	20.2		4.8			Trade Receivables (net)	8.4	7.5
	47.7		45.2			Inventory	36.4	40.2
	.0		2.5			All Other Current	3.0	2.6
	76.3		62.6			Total Current	57.8	62.5
	17.2		23.0			Fixed Assets (net)	29.3	21.3
	1.0		6.7			Intangibles (net)	3.4	3.8
	5.5		7.7			All Other Non-Current	9.5	12.4
	100.0		100.0			Total	100.0	100.0
						LIABILITIES		
	4.9		11.9			Notes Payable-Short Term	7.8	6.8
	2.0		1.8			Cur. Mat.-L.T.D.	1.7	2.7
	21.2		18.0			Trade Payables	14.5	15.3
	.6		.9			Income Taxes Payable	.2	.5
	12.8		6.7			All Other Current	10.0	8.2
	41.5		39.3			Total Current	34.2	33.4
	35.1		11.9			Long-Term Debt	18.1	13.9
	.6		.6			Deferred Taxes	1.0	.3
	7.0		.4			All Other Non-Current	4.2	2.3
	15.8		47.8			Net Worth	42.4	50.1
	100.0		100.0			Total Liabilities & Net Worth	100.0	100.0
						INCOME DATA		
	100.0		100.0			Net Sales	100.0	100.0
	39.7		36.8			Gross Profit	36.4	36.0
	38.6		34.1			Operating Expenses	32.1	32.2
	1.1		2.7			Operating Profit	4.3	3.7
	.9		.1			All Other Expenses (net)	.6	.3
	.3		2.6			Profit Before Taxes	3.7	3.5
						RATIOS		
	3.6		4.9			Current	3.5	3.4
	2.2		2.0				1.9	2.1
	1.4		.9				1.3	1.3
	1.0		1.6			Quick	1.2	1.1
	.3		.5				(62) .5	.6
	.1		.1				.2	.2
0	UND	0	UND			Sales/Receivables	1 487.8	0 775.3
1	550.1	6	61.8				4 82.4	3 130.0
29	12.7	19	19.4				18 20.3	15 23.8
9	41.1	62	5.9			Cost of Sales/Inventory	34 10.7	48 7.6
141	2.6	121	3.0				81 4.5	97 3.8
306	1.2	196	1.9				161 2.3	138 2.6
16	22.8	15	23.8			Cost of Sales/Payables	9 41.3	12 31.2
48	7.7	39	9.4				30 12.3	31 11.9
52	7.0	67	5.5				45 8.1	46 7.9
	4.1		3.2			Sales/Working Capital	5.0	3.8
	6.0		7.6				8.6	8.8
	NM		-60.3				69.8	19.8
			5.8			EBIT/Interest	11.9	11.1
		(13)	3.0				(53) 4.4	(38) 4.7
			.8				1.5	1.4
						Net Profit + Depr., Dep.,	15.0	7.6
						Amort./Cur. Mat. L/T/D	(13) 4.5	(13) 2.2
							2.7	.6
	.0		.2			Fixed/Worth	.2	.1
	.3		.6				.6	.4
	-39.6		3.8				1.7	.8
	.9		.4			Debt/Worth	.5	.3
	4.1		1.5				1.3	1.0
	-55.2		10.7				3.3	3.0
			30.8			% Profit Before Taxes/Tangible	30.8	27.5
		(15)	11.3			Net Worth	(54) 14.0	(46) 11.6
			3.9				3.1	.4
	12.2		9.5			% Profit Before Taxes/Total	12.8	11.8
	3.3		4.4			Assets	5.2	5.4
	-1.8		2.4				1.5	-1.6
	UND		26.8			Sales/Net Fixed Assets	34.2	49.1
	39.7		15.4				10.0	15.4
	12.9		5.4				4.5	8.4
	4.4		2.9			Sales/Total Assets	3.8	3.6
	2.6		2.0				2.1	2.4
	1.6		1.2				1.3	1.6
			.8			% Depr., Dep., Amort./Sales	.6	.5
		(14)	1.2				(53) 1.2	(46) 1.1
			2.9				2.6	2.2
						% Officers', Directors'	1.9	2.4
						Owners' Comp/Sales	(21) 4.4	(18) 5.3
							10.3	11.0
7514M	31564M	90060M	911583M	101228M	1981425M	Net Sales ($)	4351867M	3779178M
482M	10873M	46622M	386276M	90531M	496184M	Total Assets ($)	2200177M	1427884M

© RMA 2007

M = $ thousand   MM = $ million
See Pages 11 through 21 for Explanation of Ratios and Data

Comparative Historical Data | Current Data Sorted by Sales

Type of Statement

4/1/04-3/31/05 ALL	4/1/05-3/31/06 ALL	4/1/06-3/31/07 ALL	Type of Statement	0-1MM	1-3MM	3-5MM	5-10MM	10-25MM	25MM & OVER
13	7	7	Unqualified			1	1	1	5
6	6	6	Reviewed					3	2
7	9	8	Compiled			1	2	2	
3		6	Tax Returns	1	2	1			1
14	15	14	Other		4	1	3	3	7
					7 (4/1-9/30/06)		34 (10/1/06-3/31/07)		
43	37	41	NUMBER OF STATEMENTS	1	6	4	6	9	15

ASSETS (%)

4/1/04-3/31/05	4/1/05-3/31/06	4/1/06-3/31/07	ASSETS	0-1MM	1-3MM	3-5MM	5-10MM	10-25MM	25MM & OVER
11.5	15.5	9.9	Cash & Equivalents						6.8
14.1	9.4	11.8	Trade Receivables (net)						6.8
36.2	32.8	46.0	Inventory						46.7
1.4	2.2	1.6	All Other Current						2.7
63.2	60.0	69.3	Total Current						62.9
20.0	23.3	21.1	Fixed Assets (net)						25.8
3.3	8.3	3.8	Intangibles (net)						5.6
13.5	8.4	5.7	All Other Non-Current						5.7
100.0	100.0	100.0	Total						100.0

LIABILITIES

4/1/04-3/31/05	4/1/05-3/31/06	4/1/06-3/31/07	LIABILITIES	0-1MM	1-3MM	3-5MM	5-10MM	10-25MM	25MM & OVER
7.2	8.7	10.0	Notes Payable-Short Term						13.2
1.5	3.7	1.9	Cur. Mat.-L.T.D.						1.7
19.1	15.7	18.9	Trade Payables						21.4
.8	.3	.5	Income Taxes Payable						.8
8.6	11.4	8.5	All Other Current						8.5
37.2	39.7	39.9	Total Current						45.6
9.1	18.0	22.3	Long-Term Debt						14.1
1.0	.5	.4	Deferred Taxes						.3
4.2	6.7	4.5	All Other Non-Current						4.8
48.5	35.0	33.0	Net Worth						35.1
100.0	100.0	100.0	Total Liabilities & Net Worth						100.0

INCOME DATA

4/1/04-3/31/05	4/1/05-3/31/06	4/1/06-3/31/07	INCOME DATA	0-1MM	1-3MM	3-5MM	5-10MM	10-25MM	25MM & OVER
100.0	100.0	100.0	Net Sales						100.0
35.9	37.1	37.4	Gross Profit						35.9
32.0	34.3	35.7	Operating Expenses						34.5
3.9	2.8	1.7	Operating Profit						1.4
-.5	.8	.6	All Other Expenses (net)						.6
4.4	2.0	1.1	Profit Before Taxes						.8

RATIOS

4/1/04-3/31/05	4/1/05-3/31/06	4/1/06-3/31/07	RATIOS	0-1MM	1-3MM	3-5MM	5-10MM	10-25MM	25MM & OVER
3.6	2.6	3.7	Current						2.9
1.7	1.6	2.0	Current						1.6
1.3	1.1	1.3	Current						.8
1.5	1.4	1.1	Quick						1.0
.7	.5	.4	Quick						.2
.3	.2	.1	Quick						.1
1 426.2	0 UND	0 UND	Sales/Receivables						0 UND
8 45.6	2 151.3	4 86.3	Sales/Receivables						4 99.3
32 11.5	16 22.4	21 17.2	Sales/Receivables						17 22.1
38 9.6	9 39.2	52 7.1	Cost of Sales/Inventory						52 7.0
78 4.7	60 6.1	118 3.1	Cost of Sales/Inventory						115 3.2
125 2.9	115 3.2	197 1.9	Cost of Sales/Inventory						157 2.3
11 33.3	11 33.1	18 20.4	Cost of Sales/Payables						17 22.1
29 12.4	26 14.3	42 8.7	Cost of Sales/Payables						43 8.5
52 7.0	44 8.4	62 5.9	Cost of Sales/Payables						72 5.1
3.8	6.7	4.0	Sales/Working Capital						4.0
10.2	13.2	6.6	Sales/Working Capital						21.1
26.7	74.7	39.2	Sales/Working Capital						-31.0
21.7	17.5	5.4	EBIT/Interest						5.1
(35) 5.4	(33) 3.0	(34) 2.8	EBIT/Interest						(13) 2.7
2.0	1.3	1.4	EBIT/Interest						1.0
17.5	12.9	6.3	Net Profit + Depr., Dep., Amort./Cur. Mat. L/T/D						
(11) 4.1	(10) 4.6	(10) 3.3	Net Profit + Depr., Dep., Amort./Cur. Mat. L/T/D						
2.0	2.9	.9	Net Profit + Depr., Dep., Amort./Cur. Mat. L/T/D						
.2	.2	.2	Fixed/Worth						.3
.4	.6	.5	Fixed/Worth						.6
.9	NM	3.6	Fixed/Worth						5.3
.2	.9	.7	Debt/Worth						.6
1.3	1.9	1.7	Debt/Worth						2.4
3.7	NM	13.0	Debt/Worth						29.7
41.4	30.2	33.0	% Profit Before Taxes/Tangible Net Worth						60.1
(41) 14.4	(28) 15.2	(35) 11.3	% Profit Before Taxes/Tangible Net Worth						(14) 10.1
1.0	2.4	4.2	% Profit Before Taxes/Tangible Net Worth						4.2
14.8	13.1	10.4	% Profit Before Taxes/Total Assets						4.5
4.5	6.0	4.4	% Profit Before Taxes/Total Assets						3.9
.7	.7	1.6	% Profit Before Taxes/Total Assets						2.1
50.0	80.7	75.4	Sales/Net Fixed Assets						22.6
16.9	22.2	18.3	Sales/Net Fixed Assets						12.5
10.7	5.4	7.1	Sales/Net Fixed Assets						6.7
3.9	4.6	4.0	Sales/Total Assets						4.5
2.7	3.0	2.2	Sales/Total Assets						2.5
1.6	1.7	1.6	Sales/Total Assets						1.8
.5	.3	.4	% Depr., Dep., Amort./Sales						.8
(42) 1.0	(33) .9	(33) .9	% Depr., Dep., Amort./Sales						(13) 1.3
1.6	2.0	2.2	% Depr., Dep., Amort./Sales						2.2
1.5	2.7	3.7	% Officers', Directors' Owners' Comp/Sales						
(15) 4.9	(12) 4.2	(14) 4.5	% Officers', Directors' Owners' Comp/Sales						
8.8	7.0	7.7	% Officers', Directors' Owners' Comp/Sales						
3590825M	3631239M	3123374M	Net Sales ($)	713M	9464M	17444M	42896M	142757M	2910100M
1119411M	1141378M	1030968M	Total Assets ($)	171M	9163M	4158M	31388M	80568M	905520M

© RMA 2007

M = $ thousand   MM = $ million
See Pages 11 through 21 for Explanation of Ratios and Data

RETAIL—All Other General Merchandise Stores NAICS 452990 (SIC 5331, 5399, 5531)

	Current Data Sorted by Assets							Comparative Historical Data	
		1	1	6	2	3	**Type of Statement**		
			15	7			Unqualified	17	18
	8	6	7	2			Reviewed	24	23
	18	18	8				Compiled	39	54
	11	14	12			3	Tax Returns	39	47
		28 (4/1-9/30/06)		119 (10/1/06-3/31/07)			Other	39	50
								4/1/02-3/31/03	4/1/03-3/31/04
	0-500M	500M-2MM	2-10MM	10-50MM	50-100MM	100-250MM		ALL	ALL
	37	39	43	20	2	6	**NUMBER OF STATEMENTS**	158	192
	%	%	%	%	%	%	**ASSETS**	%	%
	17.3	12.8	9.6	8.9			Cash & Equivalents	10.2	10.2
	6.1	9.5	6.9	8.0			Trade Receivables (net)	7.8	7.1
	51.5	38.5	49.1	35.5			Inventory	48.2	45.0
	.5	2.3	3.6	4.8			All Other Current	2.7	3.3
	75.5	63.1	69.2	57.3			Total Current	68.9	65.6
	15.5	30.1	20.8	34.6			Fixed Assets (net)	22.1	25.1
	6.4	1.7	1.6	3.0			Intangibles (net)	2.2	2.9
	2.7	5.1	8.4	5.1			All Other Non-Current	6.8	6.4
	100.0	100.0	100.0	100.0			Total	100.0	100.0
							LIABILITIES		
	6.6	5.6	18.6	5.2			Notes Payable-Short Term	9.4	10.6
	5.0	2.5	1.0	3.3			Cur. Mat.-L.T.D.	2.3	2.4
	17.3	22.3	21.0	12.5			Trade Payables	17.0	16.4
	.1	.1	.2	.2			Income Taxes Payable	.3	.3
	15.9	13.9	10.4	8.4			All Other Current	8.3	10.8
	45.0	44.4	51.3	29.6			Total Current	37.3	40.4
	22.1	23.9	12.2	21.7			Long-Term Debt	21.0	18.4
	.0	.0	.2	.2			Deferred Taxes	.1	.2
	16.5	11.1	6.4	2.0			All Other Non-Current	7.7	10.5
	16.4	20.6	29.9	46.5			Net Worth	33.8	30.5
	100.0	100.0	100.0	100.0			Total Liabilties & Net Worth	100.0	100.0
							INCOME DATA		
	100.0	100.0	100.0	100.0			Net Sales	100.0	100.0
	42.1	41.8	38.1	38.1			Gross Profit	38.2	38.2
	37.6	39.5	36.1	31.1			Operating Expenses	35.3	35.1
	4.4	2.3	2.0	7.0			Operating Profit	2.9	3.1
	1.4	.9	.1	1.1			All Other Expenses (net)	.5	.7
	3.0	1.4	2.0	5.9			Profit Before Taxes	2.4	2.5
							RATIOS		
	3.2	4.4	2.5	4.5				3.9	3.2
	1.8	1.7	1.6	1.6			Current	2.1	1.8
	1.4	1.2	1.1	1.1				1.3	1.1
	1.2	1.5	.7	1.2				1.0	.9
	.5	.6	.2	.7			Quick	.3	.4
	.1	.1	.1	.2				.1	.1
	0 UND	0 UND	0 999.8	1 519.2				0 UND	0 UND
	0 UND	3 123.8	2 183.8	3 121.4			Sales/Receivables	2 218.6	1 281.8
	2 172.1	19 18.8	11 32.9	36 10.1				8 47.1	8 46.8
	40 9.0	25 14.8	47 7.7	57 6.5				41 8.9	34 10.9
	96 3.8	78 4.7	109 3.4	90 4.1			Cost of Sales/Inventory	104 3.5	87 4.2
	212 1.7	189 1.9	188 1.9	141 2.6				168 2.2	148 2.5
	2 162.6	6 59.6	14 25.2	15 25.1				10 36.6	10 34.9
	14 25.4	22 17.0	27 13.4	30 12.3			Cost of Sales/Payables	28 12.9	28 13.1
	52 7.0	48 7.7	51 7.1	54 6.8				48 7.6	44 8.3
	5.2	5.7	6.4	4.2				4.5	5.3
	9.5	9.5	9.1	7.9			Sales/Working Capital	9.7	12.8
	34.6	44.5	80.3	148.9				29.8	62.2
	13.3	4.0	6.3	8.9				7.1	9.2
	(32) 2.7	(30) 1.2	(42) 3.4	(19) 3.7			EBIT/Interest	(130) 2.9	(160) 3.5
	1.1	.3	1.5	1.7				.8	1.4
							Net Profit + Depr., Dep.,	10.3	6.8
							Amort./Cur. Mat. L/T/D	(23) 4.2	(30) 2.4
								1.0	1.0
	.1	.3	.2	.2				.2	.2
	.6	1.1	.4	.9			Fixed/Worth	.5	.6
	NM	-138.3	1.8	1.8				1.9	2.0
	.8	.8	.8	.5				.7	.8
	8.0	2.4	1.6	1.6			Debt/Worth	2.0	1.9
	-15.3	-154.0	6.0	2.4				6.3	6.1
	76.1	34.7	31.6	38.0			% Profit Before Taxes/Tangible	48.8	35.6
	(25) 31.7	(28) 7.9	(38) 17.1	(19) 27.2			Net Worth	(137) 15.4	(165) 19.9
	7.6	-11.9	7.6	5.4				2.3	5.6
	20.1	10.6	13.6	16.4			% Profit Before Taxes/Total	17.3	13.5
	8.3	.5	4.8	5.7			Assets	4.8	6.2
	.4	-4.6	1.4	2.0				-.4	1.3
	123.3	38.3	47.7	21.1				57.2	43.0
	29.4	11.9	25.5	7.6			Sales/Net Fixed Assets	21.5	19.4
	10.2	5.0	10.5	2.8				9.7	7.0
	6.0	4.2	4.7	2.5				4.2	4.3
	3.1	3.0	2.7	2.2			Sales/Total Assets	2.9	2.8
	2.2	1.6	1.9	1.5				2.0	2.0
	.5	.5	.5	.6				.7	.6
	(23) 1.0	(35) 1.2	(41) .7	(19) 1.2			% Depr., Dep., Amort./Sales	(131) 1.2	(159) 1.2
	2.5	1.7	1.6	2.5				1.9	2.2
	3.6	2.9	1.3				% Officers', Directors'	1.6	1.7
	(14) 6.7	(22) 5.1	(19) 1.7				Owners' Comp/Sales	(78) 4.1	(87) 3.5
	10.5	8.6	2.7					7.7	7.0
	40363M	125370M	647565M	865934M	171811M	3151608M	Net Sales ($)	5267248M	7597695M
	8938M	43541M	190920M	432504M	147108M	974327M	Total Assets ($)	2014509M	2383558M

M = $ thousand   MM = $ million
See Pages 11 through 21 for Explanation of Ratios and Data

Comparative Historical Data				**Current Data Sorted by Sales**					

4/1/04-3/31/05 ALL	4/1/05-3/31/06 ALL	4/1/06-3/31/07 ALL	Type of Statement	0-1MM	1-3MM	3-5MM	5-10MM	10-25MM	25MM & OVER
11	15	12	Unqualified				1	2	9
15	19	23	Reviewed		2	1	2	11	7
34	26	23	Compiled	4	6	4	3	1	5
48	54	44	Tax Returns	13	14	7	7	3	
39	40	45	Other	8	12	4	6	8	7
				28 (4/1-9/30/06)			119 (10/1/06-3/31/07)		
147	154	147	NUMBER OF STATEMENTS	25	34	16	19	25	28
%	%	%	**ASSETS**	%	%	%	%	%	%
8.7	10.8	12.9	Cash & Equivalents	12.6	16.5	9.6	15.5	9.3	12.1
5.6	6.8	7.3	Trade Receivables (net)	1.0	9.3	11.9	9.6	8.0	5.6
53.7	47.4	43.6	Inventory	54.2	40.5	39.7	47.1	44.0	37.7
2.4	2.6	2.5	All Other Current	.3	2.3	1.2	1.9	3.8	4.7
70.4	67.7	66.4	Total Current	68.2	68.6	62.4	74.1	65.1	60.1
20.7	22.3	24.4	Fixed Assets (net)	19.4	26.5	27.5	20.3	22.0	29.4
3.3	3.8	3.4	Intangibles (net)	8.0	1.8	3.1	1.6	2.1	4.0
5.6	6.3	5.8	All Other Non-Current	4.3	3.1	7.0	4.0	10.7	6.4
100.0	100.0	100.0	Total	100.0	100.0	100.0	100.0	100.0	100.0
			LIABILITIES						
11.0	9.0	9.4	Notes Payable-Short Term	5.2	4.7	18.8	12.2	7.8	12.9
2.9	1.9	2.7	Cur. Mat.-L.T.D.	4.5	2.4	5.3	.9	1.9	2.0
14.5	16.2	19.1	Trade Payables	15.4	23.7	9.3	16.7	21.3	21.9
.2	.2	.1	Income Taxes Payable	.2	.1	.0	.0	.4	.1
10.0	12.4	12.3	All Other Current	14.2	17.5	14.4	10.6	7.2	8.9
38.5	39.7	43.6	Total Current	39.5	48.4	47.9	40.4	38.5	45.8
19.3	19.0	19.6	Long-Term Debt	26.7	19.5	29.6	14.2	16.3	14.1
.1	.2	.1	Deferred Taxes	.0	.0	.1	.1	.2	.1
10.8	7.2	9.4	All Other Non-Current	16.9	13.4	13.4	8.4	2.4	2.6
31.3	34.0	27.3	Net Worth	16.9	18.6	9.0	36.9	42.6	37.3
100.0	100.0	100.0	Total Liabilities & Net Worth	100.0	100.0	100.0	100.0	100.0	100.0
			INCOME DATA						
100.0	100.0	100.0	Net Sales	100.0	100.0	100.0	100.0	100.0	100.0
39.0	39.3	40.3	Gross Profit	48.8	41.3	35.6	34.0	43.5	35.8
35.6	36.8	36.6	Operating Expenses	42.9	39.0	36.7	31.5	37.7	30.6
3.4	2.4	3.7	Operating Profit	5.9	2.3	-1.2	2.5	5.8	5.2
.7	.8	.8	All Other Expenses (net)	2.4	.4	1.6	-.2	1.0	.0
2.7	1.7	2.9	Profit Before Taxes	3.5	1.8	-2.7	2.7	4.8	5.2
			RATIOS						
4.2	3.5	2.9	Current	3.0	8.2	2.8	2.6	3.0	2.8
1.9	2.0	1.7		1.8	1.9	1.7	2.0	1.6	1.5
1.2	1.2	1.2		1.2	1.2	1.3	1.4	1.1	1.0
.9	1.1	1.1	Quick	.6	2.3	1.3	1.0	1.0	.8
(144) .3	(153) .4	.4		.3	.7	.7	.5	.2	.4
.1	.1	.1		.1	.1	.1	.1	.1	.2
0 UND	0 UND	0 UND	Sales/Receivables	0 UND	0 UND	2 232.9	0 UND	0 862.1	0 UND
1 322.0	1 246.8	1 324.0		0 UND	0 UND	9 40.9	2 170.3	2 147.6	2 199.8
5 68.5	9 40.3	10 36.5		0 UND	12 29.6	30 12.1	16 22.2	9 40.5	8 43.4
58 6.3	65 5.6	40 9.2	Cost of Sales/Inventory	85 4.3	26 14.1	31 11.7	23 16.1	31 11.9	39 9.3
121 3.0	112 3.3	89 4.1		155 2.4	78 4.7	104 3.5	84 4.4	79 4.6	59 6.1
227 1.6	173 2.1	168 2.2		302 1.2	209 1.7	197 1.9	153 2.4	154 2.4	117 3.1
5 78.2	10 36.3	8 43.6	Cost of Sales/Payables	0 UND	4 85.0	4 102.5	5 72.1	18 19.8	21 17.6
26 13.8	25 14.7	23 15.8		20 18.3	13 28.5	15 23.9	16 22.1	32 11.3	32 11.2
44 8.2	43 8.4	51 7.1		58 6.3	60 6.1	43 8.5	64 5.7	54 6.7	58 6.3
3.9	4.8	5.5	Sales/Working Capital	4.1	5.2	4.8	6.9	6.9	6.0
9.7	8.7	9.7		8.7	8.7	9.3	8.9	9.8	15.0
34.4	25.5	45.4		UND	41.1	26.9	35.5	75.1	247.4
8.5	7.5	6.7	EBIT/Interest	5.9	6.8	3.5	4.0	12.2	10.8
(128) 2.9	(125) 2.9	(129) 2.7		(22) 2.8	(28) 2.1	(14) 1.2	(16) 1.7	(24) 3.9	(25) 4.0
.2	1.4	1.1		1.4	.9	-1.2	.5	2.1	1.6
11.3	9.0	10.0	Net Profit + Depr., Dep., Amort./Cur. Mat. L/T/D						
(21) 2.4	(29) 3.2	(19) 2.9							
.6	1.9	1.6							
.1	.2	.2	Fixed/Worth	.1	.4	.1	.1	.2	.2
.5	.5	.7		.7	1.1	1.0	.5	.3	.9
3.7	3.0	3.9		-123.7	-104.6	-1.1	1.8	.8	1.9
.9	.7	.7	Debt/Worth	.8	.7	1.1	.8	.5	.6
2.2	1.8	2.0		9.4	7.0	2.4	1.7	1.0	1.6
7.9	14.7	21.5		-18.4	-16.9	-3.3	4.8	4.4	3.5
38.9	33.0	38.2	% Profit Before Taxes/Tangible Net Worth	76.1	38.3	10.7	34.4	58.4	39.5
(122) 18.2	(124) 13.9	(116) 18.7		(17) 21.9	(23) 25.5	(10) 5.9	(18) 16.0	(23) 21.8	(25) 20.2
2.6	2.6	4.8		7.6	-1.1	-12.7	-1.5	15.0	4.7
12.8	13.0	15.6	% Profit Before Taxes/Total Assets	18.6	13.6	4.6	9.9	16.7	17.0
4.3	4.4	4.8		6.9	1.7	.7	4.8	8.4	4.8
-1.4	-.1	.0		1.6	-1.4	-9.9	-.8	2.9	1.7
58.3	39.2	46.3	Sales/Net Fixed Assets	73.0	39.3	46.0	74.6	55.0	27.1
24.2	18.1	20.1		21.8	15.9	22.3	31.1	25.5	10.6
8.3	8.6	7.3		7.6	5.6	5.5	9.6	11.1	5.2
4.1	3.9	4.2	Sales/Total Assets	3.1	4.2	3.9	5.3	4.7	4.6
2.6	2.6	2.6		2.5	2.9	2.4	3.0	2.8	2.5
1.6	1.7	1.9		1.3	1.6	1.2	2.1	2.1	2.0
.6	.5	.5	% Depr., Dep., Amort./Sales	.5	.8	.3	.3	.6	.5
(122) 1.1	(142) 1.0	(123) 1.0		(17) 1.0	(26) 1.2	.9	(18) .7	(22) .8	(24) 1.1
1.8	1.9	1.7		3.4	1.8	2.4	1.7	1.2	1.6
2.0	2.3	1.7	% Officers', Directors' Owners' Comp/Sales		3.2		1.4		
(64) 3.6	(69) 4.2	(61) 3.9		(18) 7.9		(13) 2.4			
6.3	8.2	8.3			14.5		5.8		
8256660M	7210071M	5002651M	Net Sales ($)	13137M	62303M	59821M	133550M	413741M	4320099M
1589551M	2457693M	1797338M	Total Assets ($)	8035M	27198M	34588M	48799M	174010M	1504708M

© RMA 2007

M = $ thousand   MM = $ million
See Pages 11 through 21 for Explanation of Ratios and Data

RETAIL—Florists   NAICS 453110   (SIC 5992)

Current Data Sorted by Assets   **Comparative Historical Data**

						Type of Statement		
						Unqualified	1	3
						Reviewed	2	5
	3	4	1			Compiled	26	28
6	3	4				Tax Returns	34	23
27	4	4			2	Other	12	13
8	2	4	1				4/1/02-3/31/03	4/1/03-3/31/04
	23 (4/1-9/30/06)		46 (10/1/06-3/31/07)				ALL	ALL
0-500M	500M-2MM	2-10MM	10-50MM	50-100MM	100-250MM			
41	12	12	2		2	NUMBER OF STATEMENTS	75	72

0-500M	500M-2MM	2-10MM	10-50MM	50-100MM	100-250MM		ALL	ALL
%	%	%	%	%	%	ASSETS	%	%
11.8	7.2	10.1				Cash & Equivalents	13.6	7.0
12.1	8.4	18.2				Trade Receivables (net)	12.9	15.9
22.3	16.7	21.6				Inventory	22.6	22.7
1.1	.6	7.7				All Other Current	2.3	2.0
47.3	32.9	57.5				Total Current	51.4	47.7
38.8	42.7	28.4	D A T A N O T			Fixed Assets (net)	36.7	37.7
8.9	10.2	3.9				Intangibles (net)	6.7	5.4
5.0	14.3	10.2	A V A I L A B L E			All Other Non-Current	5.2	9.3
100.0	100.0	100.0				Total	100.0	100.0
						LIABILITIES		
9.7	2.9	7.3				Notes Payable-Short Term	8.7	9.9
6.1	4.6	2.2				Cur. Mat.-L.T.D.	7.1	4.3
17.2	10.0	10.5				Trade Payables	19.6	20.3
.0	.1	.0				Income Taxes Payable	.2	.1
19.1	6.6	8.4				All Other Current	12.8	13.4
52.1	24.2	28.5				Total Current	48.3	48.0
43.5	42.0	9.5				Long-Term Debt	37.8	33.6
.0	.4	.2				Deferred Taxes	.1	.2
16.6	5.8	5.0				All Other Non-Current	5.8	2.6
-12.3	27.6	56.9				Net Worth	7.9	15.6
100.0	100.0	100.0				Total Liabilities & Net Worth	100.0	100.0
						INCOME DATA		
100.0	100.0	100.0				Net Sales	100.0	100.0
55.5	48.2	52.0				Gross Profit	51.8	51.4
55.0	45.8	49.7				Operating Expenses	50.9	49.9
.4	2.4	2.3				Operating Profit	.9	1.5
2.4	1.7	-.7				All Other Expenses (net)	.7	.6
-2.0	.8	3.0				Profit Before Taxes	.3	1.0

RATIOS

0-500M	500M-2MM	2-10MM					ALL	ALL
2.8	2.4	3.2					2.2	1.8
1.2	1.8	2.0				Current	1.2	1.0
.5	.8	1.5					.7	.6
1.2	1.5	2.0					1.2	1.1
.5	.6	.8				Quick	.6	.4
.2	.3	.7					.3	.3
0 UND	8 44.5	15 24.8					4 102.3	9 39.7
9 42.0	13 28.9	28 12.8				Sales/Receivables	14 25.7	15 23.9
16 23.0	20 17.9	68 5.4					23 16.2	23 16.0
15 23.7	23 16.2	21 17.6					23 15.8	17 20.9
45 8.1	67 5.4	75 4.8				Cost of Sales/Inventory	44 8.3	40 9.1
104 3.5	118 3.1	101 3.6					83 4.4	77 4.7
0 UND	22 16.8	19 18.8					19 18.8	22 16.2
17 21.8	36 10.3	37 9.8				Cost of Sales/Payables	40 9.1	34 10.8
77 4.8	50 7.2	42 8.8					61 6.0	62 5.9
10.5	7.5	3.8					10.7	14.4
70.5	17.2	9.4				Sales/Working Capital	45.4	UND
-12.2	-30.8	20.5					-17.8	-16.5
5.4	2.5	9.1					5.9	8.2
(36) 1.5	1.1	(10) 1.7				EBIT/Interest	(69) 2.4	(61) 1.7
-.4	.6	-.6					.4	-1.2
						Net Profit + Depr., Dep.,	3.0	
						Amort./Cur. Mat. L/T/D	(11) 2.3	
							2.0	
1.0	.8	.2					.6	.6
-5.4	2.0	.6				Fixed/Worth	3.3	1.7
-.5	-2.4	1.0					-1.4	-2.3
2.1	.6	.4					1.2	1.2
-12.5	3.4	.8				Debt/Worth	5.5	5.9
-2.3	-4.6	1.6					-3.4	-5.1
47.9		14.9				% Profit Before Taxes/Tangible	55.6	57.6
(17) 30.4		6.8				Net Worth	(47) 12.9	(47) 12.7
-.5		.1					1.4	-13.0
16.6	4.1	10.7				% Profit Before Taxes/Total	14.2	14.0
4.3	.6	4.5				Assets	4.7	3.6
-9.1	-2.2	.0					-3.1	-6.3
18.1	18.4	31.7					30.3	26.6
10.1	3.6	8.2				Sales/Net Fixed Assets	10.5	13.5
4.9	3.0	5.9					4.4	4.4
5.2	2.2	3.0					4.8	4.9
3.2	1.9	2.2				Sales/Total Assets	3.1	3.2
1.9	1.4	1.7					2.1	2.0
1.4	1.6	.7					1.2	1.2
(35) 2.2	(11) 2.5	1.8				% Depr., Dep., Amort./Sales	(62) 2.4	(64) 2.0
4.9	3.0	2.3					4.2	3.4
3.3	3.0						3.8	4.4
(20) 5.6	(10) 5.2					% Officers', Directors' Owners' Comp/Sales	(47) 5.6	(36) 6.0
10.1	7.9						9.5	10.0
26336M	24901M	123424M	79185M		1604715M	Net Sales ($)	2627300M	2622449M
7954M	12701M	50548M	39026M		260542M	Total Assets ($)	648150M	990427M

M = $ thousand   MM = $ million
See Pages 11 through 21 for Explanation of Ratios and Data

Comparative Historical Data | Current Data Sorted by Sales

			Type of Statement	0-1MM	1-3MM	3-5MM	5-10MM	10-25MM	25MM & OVER
1			Unqualified	7	2	2	2	1	1
7	6	8	Reviewed	22	2	1		3	2
14	17	13	Compiled	6	9		2	1	1
38	29	33	Tax Returns		5				
14	19	15	Other						
4/1/04-3/31/05 ALL	4/1/05-3/31/06 ALL	4/1/06-3/31/07 ALL		23 (4/1-9/30/06)			46 (10/1/06-3/31/07)		
74	71	69	NUMBER OF STATEMENTS	35	18	3	4	5	4
%	%	%	**ASSETS**	%	%	%	%	%	%
11.4	9.4	10.8	Cash & Equivalents	10.1	12.0				
14.7	12.2	13.0	Trade Receivables (net)	11.7	10.7				
21.3	23.6	20.9	Inventory	24.4	14.3				
1.9	.9	2.2	All Other Current	1.1	.7				
49.3	46.0	46.9	Total Current	47.2	37.8				
36.4	35.3	37.9	Fixed Assets (net)	37.6	41.1				
6.0	9.6	7.9	Intangibles (net)	8.7	10.2				
8.3	9.0	7.2	All Other Non-Current	6.5	11.0				
100.0	100.0	100.0	Total	100.0	100.0				
			LIABILITIES						
9.9	16.6	8.2	Notes Payable-Short Term	8.9	7.0				
10.6	10.7	4.9	Cur. Mat.-L.T.D.	6.6	4.2				
20.9	15.8	14.5	Trade Payables	17.5	12.6				
.1	.1	.0	Income Taxes Payable	.0	.0				
11.0	10.7	14.4	All Other Current	16.7	14.7				
52.5	53.9	42.1	Total Current	49.7	38.4				
29.2	34.7	35.4	Long-Term Debt	46.2	37.5				
.1	.1	.3	Deferred Taxes	.0	.3				
11.9	8.2	12.0	All Other Non-Current	18.6	5.6				
6.2	3.2	10.3	Net Worth	-14.5	18.3				
100.0	100.0	100.0	Total Liabilities & Net Worth	100.0	100.0				
			INCOME DATA						
100.0	100.0	100.0	Net Sales	100.0	100.0				
56.3	56.7	53.3	Gross Profit	56.3	48.2				
54.9	53.6	52.1	Operating Expenses	55.8	46.8				
1.4	3.0	1.2	Operating Profit	.5	1.4				
.0	1.2	1.6	All Other Expenses (net)	2.4	1.4				
1.4	1.9	-.3	Profit Before Taxes	-1.9	-.1				
			RATIOS						
2.3	2.2	2.6	Current	3.0	2.2				
1.1	1.1	1.7		1.2	1.5				
.6	.6	.7		.4	.7				
1.4	1.2	1.4	Quick	1.2	1.3				
(73) .5	.5	.6		.5	.5				
.3	.2	.2		.1	.3				
6 62.4	4 85.1	6 60.9	Sales/Receivables	5 67.1	7 51.3				
14 26.0	10 35.1	11 33.7		9 39.4	11 34.1				
23 15.9	20 18.4	24 15.2		16 22.2	21 17.5				
18 20.7	19 19.4	20 18.3	Cost of Sales/Inventory	31 11.6	10 37.1				
47 7.8	46 8.0	56 6.5		56 6.5	26 14.0				
81 4.5	97 3.8	105 3.5		114 3.2	97 3.8				
24 15.2	6 56.4	2 197.8	Cost of Sales/Payables	0 UND	0 UND				
39 9.2	23 15.7	29 12.4		21 17.3	28 13.1				
62 5.9	54 6.7	59 6.2		80 4.6	52 7.0				
10.7	10.6	8.8	Sales/Working Capital	7.0	11.7				
45.6	80.4	22.1		61.5	31.2				
-21.5	-17.0	-24.7		-11.2	-27.4				
6.9	7.7	4.9	EBIT/Interest	5.7	2.5				
(63) 1.5	(58) 2.2	(61) 1.5		(31) 1.5	(16) .8				
-1.4	.2	.3		.4	-.6				
1.6			Net Profit + Depr., Dep., Amort./Cur. Mat. L/T/D						
(11) .7									
.2									
.6	.6	.7	Fixed/Worth	.8	1.0				
1.7	1.9	1.8		-8.0	-6.5				
-2.5	-2.1	-1.1		-.5	-.9				
.7	.6	.9	Debt/Worth	2.3	.6				
4.0	5.3	2.9		-27.0	-29.2				
-5.3	-5.1	-3.2		-2.3	-3.1				
44.7	64.1	36.3	% Profit Before Taxes/Tangible Net Worth	49.3					
(48) 9.6	(46) 13.4	(40) 10.3		(16) 32.4					
-12.4	-6.2	.1		12.2					
16.1	12.9	12.6	% Profit Before Taxes/Total Assets	16.5	5.5				
3.7	4.2	3.5		4.3	-.5				
-4.0	-3.2	-3.6		-4.3	-6.6				
20.4	30.2	18.1	Sales/Net Fixed Assets	16.7	21.8				
12.2	11.9	8.9		8.8	11.4				
5.6	5.4	4.0		4.3	3.5				
5.0	5.4	4.5	Sales/Total Assets	4.6	5.3				
3.4	3.1	2.5		2.8	2.2				
1.9	1.8	1.7		1.5	1.7				
1.3	1.1	1.3	% Depr., Dep., Amort./Sales	1.5	1.4				
(65) 2.5	(57) 1.7	(61) 2.1		(30) 2.4	(16) 2.1				
3.9	2.6	3.3		5.1	2.7				
4.1	2.3	3.1	% Officers', Directors' Owners' Comp/Sales	3.2	3.9				
(40) 6.8	(42) 4.5	(36) 5.3		(15) 4.8	(14) 6.0				
10.8	8.4	9.4		10.3	7.4				
1811572M	1685102M	1858561M	Net Sales ($)	15849M	32298M	13345M	28670M	84499M	1683900M
386800M	544503M	370771M	Total Assets ($)	6668M	14921M	7796M	13414M	28404M	299568M

M = $ thousand   MM = $ million
See Pages 11 through 21 for Explanation of Ratios and Data

Current Data Sorted by Assets   Comparative Historical Data

0-500M	500M-2MM	2-10MM	10-50MM	50-100MM	100-250MM	Type of Statement	4/1/02-3/31/03 ALL	4/1/03-3/31/04 ALL
2		3	5	1		Unqualified	4	9
1	9	13				Reviewed	15	23
2	13	8	7			Compiled	39	43
17	17	7	1			Tax Returns	31	25
3	12	13	2		1	Other	27	21
	32 (4/1-9/30/06)		98 (10/1/06-3/31/07)					
25	51	44	8	2		NUMBER OF STATEMENTS	116	121
%	%	%	%	%	%	ASSETS	%	%
11.5	6.9	10.6				Cash & Equivalents	8.3	9.6
27.9	34.1	31.9				Trade Receivables (net)	28.8	27.4
28.5	29.2	26.2				Inventory	36.0	33.6
1.6	3.4	2.2				All Other Current	2.0	2.0
69.5	73.5	71.0				Total Current	75.0	72.6
16.1	13.1	20.0				Fixed Assets (net)	14.7	15.3
5.4	4.6	2.5				Intangibles (net)	4.8	4.0
8.9	8.8	6.5				All Other Non-Current	5.4	8.0
100.0	100.0	100.0				Total	100.0	100.0
						LIABILITIES		
19.0	12.0	10.6				Notes Payable-Short Term	13.8	12.8
19.6	3.7	3.4				Cur. Mat.-L.T.D.	4.2	6.2
26.7	26.1	17.2				Trade Payables	24.9	23.4
.1	.0	.3				Income Taxes Payable	.2	.3
9.9	13.1	12.2				All Other Current	10.4	10.3
75.4	54.9	43.7				Total Current	53.6	53.0
12.4	9.7	11.8				Long-Term Debt	16.3	15.0
.0	.2	.2				Deferred Taxes	.1	.1
14.1	3.3	4.6				All Other Non-Current	5.0	5.1
-1.9	31.9	39.7				Net Worth	25.1	26.9
100.0	100.0	100.0				Total Liabilities & Net Worth	100.0	100.0
						INCOME DATA		
100.0	100.0	100.0				Net Sales	100.0	100.0
36.9	36.5	38.5				Gross Profit	37.7	38.0
36.1	34.4	36.4				Operating Expenses	36.1	35.7
.8	2.1	2.1				Operating Profit	1.6	2.3
1.0	.3	.1				All Other Expenses (net)	.4	.5
-.2	1.8	2.0				Profit Before Taxes	1.2	1.8
						RATIOS		
2.0	2.1	2.7				Current	1.9	2.0
1.5	1.4	1.6					1.5	1.5
.8	1.0	1.3					1.1	1.1
1.3	1.2	1.4				Quick	1.1	1.1
.8	.9	1.0					.7	.7
.2	.5	.6					.4	.4
7 55.9	27 13.5	27 13.6				Sales/Receivables	10 36.8	16 22.3
22 16.9	33 10.9	35 10.6					28 13.0	27 13.3
33 11.0	52 7.0	50 7.3					39 9.4	37 9.9
7 54.4	18 20.5	26 13.8				Cost of Sales/Inventory	22 16.8	21 17.6
30 12.3	46 7.9	48 7.5					57 6.4	59 6.2
77 4.7	90 4.0	100 3.7					114 3.2	98 3.7
8 47.9	20 18.3	17 21.6				Cost of Sales/Payables	20 18.7	19 19.4
34 10.9	37 9.9	26 13.8					33 11.2	32 11.3
47 7.8	70 5.2	40 9.2					52 7.0	50 7.2
12.3	7.0	6.1				Sales/Working Capital	9.5	7.2
18.4	17.5	11.7					14.8	15.0
-37.2	443.4	24.5					62.6	122.2
5.3	8.9	8.4				EBIT/Interest	6.4	5.6
(19) 2.0	(45) 2.9	(38) 2.2					(109) 2.5	(113) 2.3
-2.7	.8	1.2					-.8	.6
						Net Profit + Depr., Dep., Amort./Cur. Mat. L/T/D	2.5	2.0
							(22) 1.4	(26) 1.2
							.3	.5
.1	.1	.1				Fixed/Worth	.2	.2
.5	.4	.3					.5	.4
-.9	1.3	1.4					4.4	2.2
.9	.8	.8				Debt/Worth	1.2	1.1
2.7	2.4	1.4					3.0	2.4
-4.6	7.7	3.7					33.7	8.7
113.5	53.5	29.8				% Profit Before Taxes/Tangible Net Worth	45.2	38.1
(15) 18.1	(43) 16.2	(39) 7.5					(92) 19.3	(101) 15.7
-4.9	2.5	1.8					-1.9	.1
17.6	10.3	12.0				% Profit Before Taxes/Total Assets	9.9	9.6
3.7	3.3	2.4					4.2	3.4
-7.7	-.8	.9					-3.5	-.7
81.5	111.8	45.8				Sales/Net Fixed Assets	76.8	65.4
40.4	42.3	19.5					37.8	34.1
19.7	17.7	8.4					18.9	15.8
7.4	4.6	4.1				Sales/Total Assets	5.1	5.0
5.2	3.3	3.0					3.6	3.6
3.0	2.1	2.1					2.6	2.5
.7	.4	.7				% Depr., Dep., Amort./Sales	.5	.7
(16) 1.1	(36) .7	(42) 1.0					(98) 1.0	(97) 1.0
1.4	2.1	2.8					1.8	2.0
4.5	1.9	2.3				% Officers', Directors' Owners' Comp/Sales	1.4	2.6
(19) 6.9	(31) 3.3	(20) 3.8					(67) 4.1	(66) 4.5
11.2	5.5	6.0					7.2	7.6
33466M	216687M	609824M	619832M	283905M		Net Sales ($)	2400636M	1132458M
7211M	60463M	201141M	140035M	131271M		Total Assets ($)	595314M	518896M

Data not available for 10-50MM, 50-100MM, and 100-250MM asset size categories (noted in original as "DATA NOT AVAILABLE").

M = $ thousand   MM = $ million
See Pages 11 through 21 for Explanation of Ratios and Data

Comparative Historical Data   Current Data Sorted by Sales

			Type of Statement						
3	8	11	Unqualified	1	1	4		4	5
25	16	23	Reviewed		5	4	5	9	
36	17	23	Compiled	3	4	6	4	4	2
26	26	42	Tax Returns	5	20	6	5	4	2
22	25	31	Other	1	7	5	9	9	4
4/1/04-3/31/05 ALL	4/1/05-3/31/06 ALL	4/1/06-3/31/07 ALL		32 (4/1-9/30/06)			98 (10/1/06-3/31/07)		
				0-1MM	1-3MM	3-5MM	5-10MM	10-25MM	25MM & OVER
112	92	130	NUMBER OF STATEMENTS	10	37	21	19	30	13
%	%	%	**ASSETS**	%	%	%	%	%	%
8.9	6.7	8.8	Cash & Equivalents	3.8	12.4	9.5	5.1	9.4	5.8
30.8	37.8	32.6	Trade Receivables (net)	19.7	26.8	27.4	44.6	34.1	46.1
33.6	28.9	27.8	Inventory	31.1	25.9	28.1	32.0	27.3	24.7
2.4	1.8	2.6	All Other Current	2.1	3.8	2.0	1.0	2.9	1.8
75.8	75.2	71.8	Total Current	56.7	68.9	67.1	82.8	73.7	78.4
14.2	16.4	16.4	Fixed Assets (net)	17.7	16.4	21.5	9.8	18.3	12.4
4.0	2.8	4.0	Intangibles (net)	13.8	4.0	4.4	1.0	2.6	3.8
6.1	5.7	7.8	All Other Non-Current	11.8	10.7	7.1	6.4	5.4	5.3
100.0	100.0	100.0	Total	100.0	100.0	100.0	100.0	100.0	100.0
			LIABILITIES						
14.2	14.1	12.8	Notes Payable-Short Term	32.0	8.9	8.8	14.7	14.5	9.1
3.1	3.4	6.8	Cur. Mat.-L.T.D.	31.6	7.4	5.0	1.6	3.6	4.2
27.2	23.9	23.3	Trade Payables	22.2	21.5	24.5	27.1	19.3	31.2
.1	.1	.2	Income Taxes Payable	.2	.0	.3	.1	.2	.4
11.2	12.9	12.3	All Other Current	13.8	13.0	8.8	11.9	13.5	12.6
55.8	54.4	55.4	Total Current	99.8	50.7	47.4	55.5	51.1	57.5
16.2	13.4	11.3	Long-Term Debt	22.7	10.3	15.6	5.0	10.0	11.1
.1	.2	.2	Deferred Taxes	.0	.0	.7	.1	.0	.6
6.6	5.4	5.8	All Other Non-Current	7.8	9.4	2.4	6.0	-4.5	2.5
21.3	26.6	27.2	Net Worth	-30.4	29.6	33.8	33.4	34.4	28.4
100.0	100.0	100.0	Total Liabilities & Net Worth	100.0	100.0	100.0	100.0	100.0	100.0
			INCOME DATA						
100.0	100.0	100.0	Net Sales	100.0	100.0	100.0	100.0	100.0	100.0
35.8	35.6	37.4	Gross Profit	43.2	39.4	35.2	34.0	38.8	32.8
34.7	33.6	35.5	Operating Expenses	46.7	36.6	31.8	32.4	37.0	30.2
1.1	2.1	2.0	Operating Profit	-3.5	2.8	3.3	1.6	1.8	2.6
.2	.2	.4	All Other Expenses (net)	2.1	.1	.5	-.1	.6	.2
.9	1.9	1.6	Profit Before Taxes	-5.6	2.7	2.8	1.6	1.2	2.5
			RATIOS						
2.2	2.1	2.3	Current	2.3	2.3	2.1	2.8	2.4	2.4
1.5	1.4	1.5		1.4	1.7	1.4	1.4	1.4	1.3
1.0	1.1	1.1		.4	1.0	.9	1.1	1.0	1.2
1.1	1.2	1.3	Quick	.6	1.6	1.2	1.2	1.2	1.4
.7	.9	.9		.3	.9	.7	1.0	.9	1.1
.4	.5	.5		.1	.5	.4	.6	.5	.6
19 19.7	28 13.2	23 16.1	Sales/Receivables	12 31.2	17 21.6	14 26.3	33 11.2	25 14.5	28 13.0
31 11.6	34 10.7	33 11.0		28 13.2	31 11.8	31 11.9	34 10.6	33 10.9	38 9.5
41 9.0	44 8.3	48 7.6		54 6.8	52 7.0	40 9.0	48 7.6	47 7.7	51 7.1
23 15.8	19 19.7	21 17.8	Cost of Sales/Inventory	26 13.9	14 25.2	15 24.3	24 15.3	23 16.1	9 40.3
49 7.4	46 7.9	46 8.0		83 4.4	47 7.8	46 7.9	40 9.1	46 7.9	36 10.1
106 3.4	78 4.7	90 4.6		241 1.5	118 3.1	99 3.7	73 5.0	89 4.1	79 4.6
23 16.0	21 17.6	18 20.2	Cost of Sales/Payables	10 34.9	12 29.6	18 20.0	20 18.5	17 21.3	22 16.4
36 10.2	30 12.1	31 11.8		59 6.2	31 11.8	30 12.3	33 11.2	27 13.5	39 9.3
59 6.2	44 8.3	52 7.0		175 2.1	60 6.1	58 6.3	44 8.2	39 9.4	47 7.8
7.4	7.9	7.7	Sales/Working Capital	9.5	7.0	7.8	6.1	8.0	9.7
17.0	17.2	14.6		17.8	13.8	17.5	21.9	13.9	25.0
640.0	58.3	97.7		-2.9	NM	-64.8	43.1	NM	46.8
5.8	9.3	8.2	EBIT/Interest	6.4	9.3	7.5	10.9	4.9	14.9
(105) 2.7	(88) 2.5	(112) 2.5		.3	(27) 3.1	(19) 2.3	(16) 3.0	(28) 2.2	(12) 8.9
1.0	1.0	.9		-2.0	.0	1.0	.9	1.2	2.6
4.6	4.4	3.2	Net Profit + Depr., Dep.,						
(24) 2.6	(21) 1.6	(22) 1.5	Amort./Cur. Mat. L/T/D						
1.2	.9	1.0							
.2	.2	.1	Fixed/Worth	.1	.1	.2	.1	.2	.1
.5	.5	.4		1.0	.5	.6	.3	.4	.3
3.1	15.6	2.9		.0	-3.7	3.6	.8	1.6	44.3
1.4	1.0	.8	Debt/Worth	.8	.8	.9	.9	.8	.9
3.0	2.6	2.0		2.1	1.8	3.2	1.7	1.6	1.8
28.2	128.6	8.6		-1.4	-21.5	6.5	7.1	7.8	105.9
34.4	30.7	37.0	% Profit Before Taxes/Tangible		53.5	45.5	47.5	30.3	29.8
(91) 10.7	(71) 10.0	(105) 11.8	Net Worth		(27) 15.5	(18) 18.3	(18) 9.3	(25) 7.5	(11) 25.6
.0	.0	1.9			.1	5.5	1.2	1.9	8.8
7.9	9.9	10.8	% Profit Before Taxes/Total	4.0	15.1	7.3	9.9	9.6	16.3
3.2	4.0	3.3	Assets	-2.1	5.4	3.9	3.1	2.4	9.5
.0	.0	.0		-26.9	-2.2	.4	.0	1.0	3.0
74.5	73.0	75.7	Sales/Net Fixed Assets	150.0	69.9	102.5	94.1	46.4	107.9
36.4	34.4	35.6		71.9	33.6	19.0	42.3	20.4	47.6
16.0	14.0	13.6		8.2	16.9	8.0	34.4	9.8	18.2
4.9	5.5	4.7	Sales/Total Assets	5.0	5.2	4.5	5.3	4.2	6.6
3.3	3.7	3.3		2.1	2.9	3.2	4.3	3.4	3.8
2.4	2.7	2.3		1.0	1.8	2.2	3.4	2.5	2.6
.6	.4	.5	% Depr., Dep., Amort./Sales		.7	.6	.4	.7	.4
(93) 1.0	(82) .8	(104) 1.0			(30) 1.1	(14) 2.5	(15) .8	(28) .9	.6
1.8	1.7	1.9			2.0	4.3	1.1	1.6	1.3
2.0	2.0	2.2	% Officers', Directors'		4.4	1.3	1.9	2.4	
(59) 4.0	(51) 3.8	(73) 4.2	Owners' Comp/Sales		(24) 5.5	(14) 2.5	(10) 3.0	(13) 3.1	
5.8	6.8	7.1			9.8	4.1	6.4	4.9	
990342M	1885602M	1763714M	Net Sales ($)	6659M	67418M	88624M	127641M	479419M	993953M
358801M	587469M	540121M	Total Assets ($)	4221M	28689M	37603M	32508M	159178M	277922M

Current Data Sorted by Assets   Comparative Historical Data

0-500M	500M-2MM	2-10MM	10-50MM	50-100MM	100-250MM	Type of Statement	4/1/02-3/31/03 ALL	4/1/03-3/31/04 ALL
1	2	2	2	1	1	Unqualified	16	9
	2	9	1			Reviewed	20	23
10	7	12	3		1	Compiled	67	63
44	24	2			1	Tax Returns	45	52
10	20	15	6	1	1	Other	50	44
	24 (4/1-9/30/06)		154 (10/1/06-3/31/07)					
65	55	40	12	2	4	**NUMBER OF STATEMENTS**	198	191
%	%	%	%	%	%	**ASSETS**	%	%
13.3	12.3	10.0	12.7			Cash & Equivalents	13.5	12.2
6.8	6.6	12.0	16.0			Trade Receivables (net)	6.4	9.1
50.4	46.7	40.5	33.4			Inventory	46.8	49.5
3.1	.9	3.1	3.8			All Other Current	1.5	2.0
73.6	66.5	65.6	65.9			Total Current	68.1	72.7
13.7	21.0	25.0	27.4			Fixed Assets (net)	21.8	19.0
4.6	4.0	2.2	3.3			Intangibles (net)	4.2	3.8
8.1	8.6	7.1	3.5			All Other Non-Current	5.8	4.4
100.0	100.0	100.0	100.0			Total	100.0	100.0
						LIABILITIES		
11.0	8.6	6.8	15.9			Notes Payable-Short Term	10.4	13.0
2.9	1.7	3.3	2.5			Cur. Mat.-L.T.D.	4.8	4.1
14.7	16.2	19.2	15.1			Trade Payables	17.1	17.7
.1	.0	.6	.1			Income Taxes Payable	.2	.3
16.0	10.4	10.5	6.5			All Other Current	12.1	10.3
44.8	36.9	40.4	40.0			Total Current	44.6	45.4
22.6	16.2	17.0	11.8			Long-Term Debt	19.8	20.0
.0	.1	.1	.0			Deferred Taxes	.1	.1
10.2	9.5	9.9	9.3			All Other Non-Current	7.4	12.2
22.5	37.3	32.7	38.9			Net Worth	28.1	22.4
100.0	100.0	100.0	100.0			Total Liabilities & Net Worth	100.0	100.0
						INCOME DATA		
100.0	100.0	100.0	100.0			Net Sales	100.0	100.0
48.7	50.5	49.0	47.8			Gross Profit	46.7	44.8
44.9	45.1	45.4	45.8			Operating Expenses	43.7	42.7
3.8	5.4	3.6	2.0			Operating Profit	3.0	2.1
.7	.6	.5	2.1			All Other Expenses (net)	1.0	1.0
3.1	4.8	3.1	-.1			Profit Before Taxes	2.0	1.1
						RATIOS		
4.9	4.1	2.8	2.6			Current	3.1	3.0
2.6	2.0	1.6	1.7				1.6	1.8
1.2	1.4	1.1	1.2				1.1	1.2
1.0	1.9	1.0	1.4			Quick	.9	1.0
.3	(54) .4	.5	.8				(195) .4	(190) .4
.1	.1	.2	.2				.1	.1
0 UND	0 UND	0 UND	0 UND			Sales/Receivables	0 UND	0 UND
0 UND	0 UND	6 62.2	9 42.3				0 UND	0 999.8
3 140.0	6 60.9	29 12.7	32 11.3				5 77.5	7 53.2
45 8.1	94 3.9	66 5.5	66 5.6			Cost of Sales/Inventory	75 4.9	69 5.3
119 3.1	138 2.6	102 3.6	164 2.2				128 2.8	130 2.8
237 1.5	221 1.7	180 2.0	233 1.6				212 1.7	196 1.9
0 UND	9 38.8	22 16.3	32 11.4			Cost of Sales/Payables	11 31.8	11 32.1
16 23.4	39 9.3	44 8.4	50 7.3				34 10.6	30 12.3
54 6.8	76 4.8	85 4.3	72 5.0				66 5.5	68 5.4
3.9	3.7	4.9	3.5			Sales/Working Capital	4.6	5.1
7.8	8.4	12.2	6.0				9.6	9.0
43.8	17.4	63.2	15.6				37.6	38.0
6.4	12.4	8.5	12.7			EBIT/Interest	7.3	6.4
(50) 2.2	(47) 3.0	(38) 2.7	(11) 2.6				(176) 2.3	(174) 2.1
.1	1.0	1.0	1.1				.2	-.4
						Net Profit + Depr., Dep., Amort./Cur. Mat. L/T/D	5.8	7.4
							(29) 2.0	(23) 2.0
							.2	.6
.0	.2	.3	.2			Fixed/Worth	.2	.2
.4	.8	.6	.3				.7	.7
-1.3	2.1	2.1	2.1				4.0	11.8
.5	.6	.8	.6			Debt/Worth	.8	.9
2.4	1.5	2.0	1.6				2.1	2.7
-7.7	10.2	6.4	4.3				17.8	-999.8
70.1	37.9	47.4	40.8			% Profit Before Taxes/Tangible Net Worth	48.4	40.5
(46) 20.3	(46) 15.9	(36) 15.0	(11) 24.1				(165) 16.1	(143) 11.7
1.0	1.4	1.0	1.2				-1.5	-2.5
21.9	20.4	15.2	18.5			% Profit Before Taxes/Total Assets	15.2	14.2
5.4	7.5	5.3	3.8				3.8	3.0
-4.4	.2	.3	-.8				-2.0	-3.5
103.9	42.0	36.9	60.4			Sales/Net Fixed Assets	36.4	62.8
46.9	19.1	20.9	13.8				14.9	25.3
17.8	8.4	6.9	2.8				7.6	10.0
4.8	3.4	3.8	2.8			Sales/Total Assets	3.1	3.8
2.8	2.2	2.8	1.7				2.4	2.6
1.9	1.6	1.9	.9				1.7	1.8
.3	.4	.7				% Depr., Dep., Amort./Sales	.8	.7
(38) 1.1	(42) .8	(38) 1.3					(162) 1.4	(153) 1.2
1.9	1.9	2.3					2.4	2.1
4.4	2.6	2.5				% Officers', Directors' Owners' Comp/Sales	2.5	2.5
(33) 6.1	(35) 5.6	(14) 3.5					(90) 4.5	(96) 4.4
9.0	7.6	8.6					7.6	7.4
54149M	153845M	563772M	421769M	414918M	2330141M	Net Sales ($)	4433152M	3535106M
15761M	59203M	196650M	229566M	137469M	655443M	Total Assets ($)	1910570M	1444149M

M = $ thousand   MM = $ million
See Pages 11 through 21 for Explanation of Ratios and Data

Comparative Historical Data / Current Data Sorted by Sales

16	12	8	Type of Statement						
			Unqualified	2				2	4
18	14	13	Reviewed	2	2	1	1	7	2
48	25	33	Compiled	8	8	3	5	6	3
61	68	71	Tax Returns	37	24	6	1	2	1
39	46	53	Other	9	14	6	8	9	7
4/1/04-3/31/05	4/1/05-3/31/06	4/1/06-3/31/07		**24 (4/1-9/30/06)**			**154 (10/1/06-3/31/07)**		
ALL	ALL	ALL		0-1MM	1-3MM	3-5MM	5-10MM	10-25MM	25MM & OVER
182	165	178	**NUMBER OF STATEMENTS**	54	50	16	15	26	17
%	%	%	**ASSETS**	%	%	%	%	%	%
11.8	14.8	12.7	Cash & Equivalents	12.8	14.3	8.7	4.3	14.4	16.0
6.9	6.0	8.4	Trade Receivables (net)	5.5	4.4	12.2	19.5	9.0	15.3
49.0	45.4	45.7	Inventory	48.2	46.4	52.5	39.9	41.7	40.9
2.4	1.8	2.5	All Other Current	2.9	1.5	2.9	1.7	2.8	4.0
70.1	68.0	69.3	Total Current	69.4	66.6	76.2	65.3	67.9	76.1
19.8	22.4	19.5	Fixed Assets (net)	16.4	21.7	16.0	23.4	24.1	16.3
4.0	2.9	3.6	Intangibles (net)	5.0	3.9	3.8	3.5	.9	2.7
6.1	6.6	7.5	All Other Non-Current	9.1	7.9	4.0	7.8	7.2	4.9
100.0	100.0	100.0	Total	100.0	100.0	100.0	100.0	100.0	100.0
			LIABILITIES						
12.0	12.8	9.5	Notes Payable-Short Term	10.9	9.3	7.5	12.1	4.5	12.4
3.5	4.0	2.5	Cur. Mat.-L.T.D.	2.6	1.7	3.9	2.1	4.2	1.2
16.7	18.2	16.1	Trade Payables	12.7	16.0	18.8	20.1	16.4	20.3
.5	.2	.2	Income Taxes Payable	.2	.0		1.0	.3	.1
9.9	14.4	12.2	All Other Current	19.1	9.0	4.2	12.3	10.3	9.9
42.6	49.6	40.4	Total Current	45.5	36.1	34.4	47.5	35.8	43.8
17.6	20.1	18.1	Long-Term Debt	25.5	14.1	26.1	15.5	15.4	5.7
.1	.0	.0	Deferred Taxes	.0	.1	.0	.1	.1	.0
14.4	9.8	9.6	All Other Non-Current	13.7	5.7	7.5	8.5	9.6	10.7
25.4	20.5	31.8	Net Worth	15.3	44.0	32.0	28.4	39.1	39.8
100.0	100.0	100.0	Total Liabilities & Net Worth	100.0	100.0	100.0	100.0	100.0	100.0
			INCOME DATA						
100.0	100.0	100.0	Net Sales	100.0	100.0	100.0	100.0	100.0	100.0
47.7	50.8	49.1	Gross Profit	50.5	49.7	48.9	46.9	50.0	44.3
45.9	47.6	44.9	Operating Expenses	48.0	44.2	40.9	42.9	47.4	38.5
1.8	3.2	4.3	Operating Profit	2.4	5.5	8.0	4.1	2.6	5.7
1.0	.9	.7	All Other Expenses (net)	.6	.9	.5	1.7	.4	.6
.8	2.3	3.5	Profit Before Taxes	1.9	4.6	7.5	2.3	2.2	5.1
			RATIOS						
3.4	3.0	4.0	Current	4.9	4.6	3.8	2.2	3.2	2.9
2.0	1.7	2.0		2.2	2.5	1.8	1.3	2.1	1.5
1.2	1.1	1.3		1.1	1.3	1.5	1.0	1.4	1.2
.9	1.0	1.2	Quick	.9	1.7	1.9	.9	1.4	1.8
(181) .4	(164) .3	(177) .4		.3	(49) .6	.4	.3	.6	.7
.1	.1	.1		.1	.1	.0	.1	.2	.3
0 UND	0 UND	0 UND	Sales/Receivables	0 UND	0 UND	0 UND	0 UND	0 UND	0 UND
1 537.3	0 UND	0 UND		0 UND	0 UND	0 UND	11 32.4	6 65.3	6 65.6
7 52.2	5 68.0	10 35.0		7 51.6	2 236.6	23 15.7	45 8.0	11 34.6	24 15.4
66 5.5	58 6.3	57 6.4	Cost of Sales/Inventory	47 7.8	86 4.2	25 14.6	55 6.6	63 5.8	41 8.9
129 2.8	125 2.9	122 3.0		146 2.5	137 2.7	111 3.3	99 3.7	118 3.1	75 4.8
215 1.7	212 1.7	209 1.7		257 1.4	221 1.7	245 1.5	184 2.0	183 2.0	127 2.9
13 28.3	12 30.8	8 43.8	Cost of Sales/Payables	0 UND	7 52.0	7 51.2	41 9.0	20 18.6	20 17.8
32 11.2	39 9.4	36 10.0		22 16.7	24 15.2	43 8.4	48 7.6	38 9.6	45 8.1
58 6.3	68 5.4	71 5.1		54 6.8	78 4.7	72 5.1	74 4.9	68 5.4	55 6.7
4.7	4.7	4.1	Sales/Working Capital	3.0	4.0	4.9	8.7	3.8	4.9
8.5	9.4	8.2		5.6	8.3	9.2	17.4	6.1	12.6
32.7	99.5	27.5		47.2	21.5	15.7	88.8	28.9	20.7
7.0	6.7	10.1	EBIT/Interest	4.0	7.5	22.6	4.1	15.6	17.1
(158) 3.2	(141) 2.5	(152) 2.8		(42) 1.4	(43) 3.0	(13) 6.1	(14) 1.7	(24) 4.0	(16) 7.8
.0	.2	.9		-.5	1.1	-.1	1.0	1.1	3.1
17.0	4.0	7.7	Net Profit + Depr., Dep., Amort./Cur. Mat. L/T/D						
(22) 3.4	(19) 1.5	(19) 1.6							
.4	.6	.4							
.2	.2	.1	Fixed/Worth	.1	.1	.1	.3	.2	.2
.6	.7	.4		.9	.4	.4	.9	.4	.3
8.7	8.3	2.4		-.9	1.1	NM	3.5	.9	.9
.8	.9	.6	Debt/Worth	.6	.4	.5	1.5	.7	.5
2.2	2.5	1.7		2.9	1.1	2.0	2.1	1.6	1.2
-48.8	52.0	9.2		-5.9	3.8	NM	46.5	5.9	4.2
39.9	50.7	45.3	% Profit Before Taxes/Tangible Net Worth	48.8	39.6	73.7	95.8	55.3	48.5
(136) 16.0	(130) 17.3	(145) 18.5		(36) 13.1	(44) 15.9	(12) 30.0	(13) 8.4	(25) 17.8	(15) 30.3
.2	1.7	1.4		-7.4	1.9	-5.2	1.1	-.8	20.9
13.4	17.3	19.8	% Profit Before Taxes/Total Assets	18.0	18.8	29.0	10.5	22.3	22.8
4.8	4.2	6.4		3.7	7.5	9.4	3.3	7.0	13.5
-4.1	-1.7	.2		-4.7	.7	-1.3	.4	.0	5.3
51.5	51.8	66.7	Sales/Net Fixed Assets	86.9	54.3	81.1	96.5	36.6	56.7
21.8	19.9	24.3		32.3	21.6	42.5	22.7	19.3	35.3
8.3	6.3	9.7		13.0	8.0	17.8	12.2	6.6	13.3
3.6	3.5	3.6	Sales/Total Assets	3.1	3.5	4.4	3.8	3.9	4.3
2.7	2.6	2.6		2.2	2.2	3.4	3.2	2.7	3.1
1.8	1.7	1.8		1.5	1.7	2.4	1.8	2.0	2.4
.6	.6	.6	% Depr., Dep., Amort./Sales	.5	.4		.4	.7	.8
(153) 1.4	(135) 1.2	(131) 1.1		(32) 1.5	(38) 1.0		(14) 1.0	(24) 1.1	(14) 1.0
2.5	2.4	1.9		2.3	1.9		1.5	2.2	2.1
2.2	2.3	2.8	% Officers', Directors' Owners' Comp/Sales	4.9	3.9			2.3	
(94) 4.7	(80) 5.2	(88) 5.7		(26) 6.5	(31) 5.7		(10) 3.0		
8.7	7.6	8.4		9.8	8.5			10.2	
3854273M	4243484M	3938594M	Net Sales ($)	26247M	94402M	62066M	103128M	416389M	3236362M
1605501M	1894125M	1294092M	Total Assets ($)	14206M	45365M	24645M	61505M	178338M	970033M

M = $ thousand   MM = $ million
See Pages 11 through 21 for Explanation of Ratios and Data

Current Data Sorted by Assets   Comparative Historical Data

						Type of Statement		
	1					Unqualified	4	10
						Reviewed	5	3
	10	7				Compiled	23	26
13	10	5	1			Tax Returns	15	33
7	8	4	3	1		Other	20	24
	11 (4/1-9/30/06)		72 (10/1/06-3/31/07)				4/1/02-3/31/03	4/1/03-3/31/04
0-500M	500M-2MM	2-10MM	10-50MM	50-100MM	100-250MM		ALL	ALL
20	32	21	8	1	1	**NUMBER OF STATEMENTS**	67	96
%	%	%	%	%	%	**ASSETS**	%	%
17.5	8.2	12.5				Cash & Equivalents	9.8	7.5
6.5	14.0	17.3				Trade Receivables (net)	14.1	11.9
34.4	39.7	32.2				Inventory	41.5	44.2
1.3	4.2	4.0				All Other Current	7.2	4.5
59.8	66.2	66.0				Total Current	72.6	68.0
17.6	25.1	20.8				Fixed Assets (net)	20.5	21.1
9.9	1.5	2.9				Intangibles (net)	1.9	4.1
12.7	7.2	10.4				All Other Non-Current	5.0	6.7
100.0	100.0	100.0				Total	100.0	100.0
						LIABILITIES		
5.9	11.9	13.0				Notes Payable-Short Term	17.6	11.9
7.6	2.8	1.0				Cur. Mat.-L.T.D.	1.2	2.6
7.3	11.9	4.7				Trade Payables	6.2	8.7
.0	.3	.4				Income Taxes Payable	.1	.0
29.3	48.7	9.0				All Other Current	10.2	7.8
50.1	75.6	28.2				Total Current	35.4	31.0
17.6	20.0	11.7				Long-Term Debt	14.4	21.4
.0	.0	.0				Deferred Taxes	.0	.0
5.1	9.6	7.3				All Other Non-Current	8.5	9.6
27.2	-5.2	52.8				Net Worth	41.7	38.0
100.0	100.0	100.0				Total Liabilities & Net Worth	100.0	100.0
						INCOME DATA		
100.0	100.0	100.0				Net Sales	100.0	100.0
55.1	57.1	58.6				Gross Profit	55.7	54.2
51.8	51.8	51.7				Operating Expenses	48.0	48.1
3.2	5.4	6.8				Operating Profit	7.7	6.1
1.3	2.0	1.2				All Other Expenses (net)	2.1	1.1
1.9	3.4	5.6				Profit Before Taxes	5.5	4.9
						RATIOS		
5.7	3.2	11.2				Current	8.3	7.9
1.9	1.7	3.2					3.8	2.4
.8	.8	1.2					1.4	1.2
1.4	1.0	3.1				Quick	3.8	2.5
.5	.4	.8					(63) 1.1	.5
.1	.1	.1					.2	.1
0 UND	0 UND	0 UND				Sales/Receivables	0 UND	0 UND
1 686.8	10 37.9	8 45.5					11 34.5	8 47.1
6 64.2	36 10.2	79 4.6					59 6.1	49 7.4
63 5.8	52 7.0	18 20.4				Cost of Sales/Inventory	70 5.2	74 5.0
97 3.7	167 2.2	117 3.1					165 2.2	166 2.2
175 2.1	365 1.0	231 1.6					332 1.1	349 1.0
0 UND	11 33.4	0 UND				Cost of Sales/Payables	0 UND	2 229.9
3 120.3	30 12.3	17 22.1					11 34.1	15 24.5
41 9.0	74 4.9	51 7.2					47 7.8	44 8.3
4.2	2.7	1.8				Sales/Working Capital	1.8	2.2
11.2	6.7	5.3					2.9	4.6
-100.6	-28.4	NM					10.1	40.9
20.7	8.8	8.7				EBIT/Interest	10.6	10.5
(15) 3.0	(30) 2.5	(18) 1.9					(59) 3.8	(86) 3.4
-.7	-.5	.9					1.7	1.2
						Net Profit + Depr., Dep., Amort./Cur. Mat. L/T/D		
.1	.2	.0				Fixed/Worth	.1	.1
.4	1.8	.2					.2	.4
-1.5	-.9	1.2					1.1	1.7
.2	1.3	.3				Debt/Worth	.3	.7
1.2	3.2	.9					1.0	1.6
-5.3	-5.9	2.6					4.2	5.9
56.9	62.4	34.5				% Profit Before Taxes/Tangible Net Worth	33.6	45.7
(13) 30.6	(22) 36.6	(20) 19.0					(59) 16.8	(84) 14.4
10.4	19.6	.8					8.5	3.2
30.2	17.2	17.6				% Profit Before Taxes/Total Assets	16.7	15.3
6.7	8.2	5.2					8.0	7.5
-3.8	-4.1	.1					2.2	.7
43.1	54.3	82.1				Sales/Net Fixed Assets	51.2	51.2
21.5	21.5	20.0					15.9	16.5
9.1	8.0	7.7					6.9	6.6
3.7	3.9	3.3				Sales/Total Assets	2.2	2.9
2.8	2.2	1.3					1.5	1.8
1.6	1.2	.8					1.0	1.2
.3	.4	.3				% Depr., Dep., Amort./Sales	.4	.6
(16) 1.1	(25) 1.0	(18) .8					(51) 1.2	(74) 1.5
2.9	2.9	1.3					2.5	2.5
3.7	1.4	3.1				% Officers', Directors' Owners' Comp/Sales	3.3	2.9
(10) 5.4	(15) 3.7	(13) 4.5					(32) 9.1	(45) 6.4
9.2	7.3	18.8					11.5	9.1
16644M	84329M	249036M	378446M	87715M	256791M	Net Sales ($)	1064743M	1466037M
5974M	31633M	95667M	164628M	53435M	178861M	Total Assets ($)	672696M	881940M

M = $ thousand   MM = $ million
See Pages 11 through 21 for Explanation of Ratios and Data

Comparative Historical Data				Current Data Sorted by Sales					
			Type of Statement						
4	7	8	Unqualified	1	1	1	2	2	3
2	5	6	Reviewed			1	1	2	
12	18	17	Compiled	2	4	6	2	2	1
41	22	29	Tax Returns	16	8	2	1	1	2
20	34	23	Other	5	9	1	2	2	4
4/1/04-3/31/05 ALL	4/1/05-3/31/06 ALL	4/1/06-3/31/07 ALL		11 (4/1-9/30/06)			72 (10/1/06-3/31/07)		
				0-1MM	1-3MM	3-5MM	5-10MM	10-25MM	25MM & OVER
79	86	83	**NUMBER OF STATEMENTS**	24	22	11	8	8	10
%	%	%	**ASSETS**	%	%	%	%	%	%
14.1	11.9	11.1	Cash & Equivalents	14.7	8.8	5.9			4.9
8.8	9.8	13.8	Trade Receivables (net)	9.4	16.0	19.7			14.6
39.3	37.3	35.6	Inventory	36.1	41.2	39.2			38.9
2.3	5.6	3.2	All Other Current	2.2	3.5	2.5			2.5
64.5	64.6	63.7	Total Current	62.4	69.5	67.3			61.0
23.5	23.9	21.9	Fixed Assets (net)	23.6	16.3	22.1			20.6
3.0	4.4	5.4	Intangibles (net)	7.6	1.5	.3			14.3
9.1	7.1	9.0	All Other Non-Current	6.4	12.8	10.3			4.1
100.0	100.0	100.0	Total	100.0	100.0	100.0			100.0
			LIABILITIES						
16.9	15.5	12.1	Notes Payable-Short Term	6.1	10.6	14.1			18.9
4.3	2.6	3.2	Cur. Mat.-L.T.D.	7.6	2.5	1.4			.4
7.5	8.6	8.7	Trade Payables	7.4	6.3	10.9			11.3
.1	.1	.3	Income Taxes Payable	.3	.4	.3			
25.0	12.5	28.7	All Other Current	28.9	26.6	41.9			6.2
53.8	39.2	52.9	Total Current	50.2	46.3	68.7			37.1
18.3	16.7	16.4	Long-Term Debt	23.7	14.9	13.0			9.8
.0	.0	.1	Deferred Taxes	.0	.0	.1			.3
17.5	8.5	7.2	All Other Non-Current	11.2	8.6	5.4			3.5
10.5	35.6	23.4	Net Worth	14.9	30.1	12.8			49.3
100.0	100.0	100.0	Total Liabilties & Net Worth	100.0	100.0	100.0			100.0
			INCOME DATA						
100.0	100.0	100.0	Net Sales	100.0	100.0	100.0			100.0
50.0	46.9	55.8	Gross Profit	59.4	56.4	55.0			46.0
45.1	41.8	50.4	Operating Expenses	54.1	50.4	50.2			40.6
4.9	5.0	5.4	Operating Profit	5.3	6.0	4.7			5.5
.6	.9	1.6	All Other Expenses (net)	2.6	1.8	.8			.9
4.3	4.1	3.8	Profit Before Taxes	2.7	4.3	4.0			4.6
			RATIOS						
4.3	4.5	4.2		3.0	7.5	4.2			8.1
2.0	2.0	2.0	Current	1.7	2.6	1.6			2.1
1.0	1.1	.9		.8	1.6	.5			.5
1.6	1.2	1.4		1.4	1.5	2.0			1.7
(78) .5	(85) .6	.5	Quick	.5	.6	.3			.6
.1	.1	.1		.1	.3	.1			.1
0 UND	0 UND	0 UND		0 UND	0 UND	0 999.8			0 UND
2 202.5	0 UND	6 63.3	Sales/Receivables	1 322.5	5 68.3	20 18.2			1 263.1
20 18.5	25 14.5	56 6.5		37 9.9	74 4.9	56 6.5			66 5.6
37 9.9	29 12.7	50 7.3		86 4.2	64 5.7	35 10.4			25 14.8
103 3.6	89 4.1	116 3.1	Cost of Sales/Inventory	217 1.7	146 2.5	164 2.2			58 6.3
241 1.5	153 2.4	261 1.4		444 .8	225 1.6	249 1.5			135 2.7
0 UND	0 UND	3 127.8		0 UND	1 479.5	16 22.9			4 87.6
9 41.0	10 36.4	17 22.1	Cost of Sales/Payables	13 28.2	9 41.5	28 13.0			13 29.0
35 10.5	31 11.7	48 7.6		91 4.0	40 9.1	48 7.6			36 10.0
3.0	3.3	3.2		2.8	2.2	2.1			5.0
12.0	9.7	6.3	Sales/Working Capital	7.3	5.1	6.3			13.3
-311.1	146.0	-96.5		-89.8	13.1	-9.6			-19.0
14.9	6.9	9.2		13.9	13.1				
(64) 6.8	(75) 3.8	(71) 2.0	EBIT/Interest	(22) 2.5	(18) 4.2				
2.1	1.3	-.2		-.2	.7				
			Net Profit + Depr., Dep., Amort./Cur. Mat. L/T/D						
.1	.1	.1		.1	.1	.0			.1
.5	.5	.4	Fixed/Worth	1.8	.2	.7			.3
6.0	2.6	6.1		-1.5	2.8	-1.4			NM
.5	.6	.5		.9	.2	.2			.3
1.8	1.5	1.4	Debt/Worth	3.2	1.3	2.8			1.0
53.5	8.5	UND		-5.3	13.3	-5.5			NM
62.8	49.9	47.0	% Profit Before Taxes/Tangible Net Worth	64.8	53.0				
(60) 26.5	(70) 19.7	(63) 25.6		(16) 32.3	(19) 24.2				
5.2	5.6	8.0		5.7	9.9				
22.1	15.9	17.8	% Profit Before Taxes/Total Assets	19.2	24.2	16.4			21.3
9.9	6.1	7.0		3.0	9.7	5.2			12.1
.5	1.0	-1.1		-3.8	1.8	-6.8			-.7
75.4	84.0	49.6	Sales/Net Fixed Assets	49.0	46.3	94.3			176.4
17.8	23.1	19.3		17.5	28.8	16.1			13.9
6.6	6.7	8.7		4.7	10.4	5.9			11.6
4.5	3.8	3.5	Sales/Total Assets	2.3	3.5	4.0			8.0
2.4	2.6	1.9		1.4	2.3	2.4			1.7
1.2	1.3	1.2		1.0	1.2	1.0			1.5
.6	.6	.3	% Depr., Dep., Amort./Sales	.4	.2				
(60) 1.3	(68) 1.3	(67) 1.0		(18) 1.3	(17) .6				
2.7	2.5	2.3		3.4	1.6				
2.6	2.0	2.7	% Officers', Directors' Owners' Comp/Sales	5.0	1.7				
(34) 6.3	(38) 4.5	(40) 4.6		(13) 7.3	(14) 3.6				
12.5	7.5	9.8		9.9	8.0				
596561M	1036318M	1072961M	Net Sales ($)	14806M	42127M	43195M	48916M	130527M	793390M
298255M	481740M	530198M	Total Assets ($)	11196M	27569M	24208M	27547M	66726M	372952M

© RMA 2007

M = $ thousand   MM = $ million
See Pages 11 through 21 for Explanation of Ratios and Data

Current Data Sorted by Assets

Comparative Historical Data

Type of Statement	0-500M	500M-2MM	2-10MM	10-50MM	50-100MM	100-250MM		4/1/02-3/31/03 ALL	4/1/03-3/31/04 ALL
Unqualified									1
Reviewed			1	1					1
Compiled		2	1	1	1			1	3
Tax Returns	13	1	4					6	5
Other	1	1	4					6	3
		7 (4/1-9/30/06)		25 (10/1/06-3/31/07)					
NUMBER OF STATEMENTS	15	4	11	2				13	13
	%	%	%	%	%	%	**ASSETS**	%	%
	13.4		7.1				Cash & Equivalents	10.7	10.4
	4.8		17.4	D	D		Trade Receivables (net)	9.7	8.5
	53.9		49.7	A	A		Inventory	49.1	40.4
	.1		2.4	T	T		All Other Current	1.8	.4
	72.2		76.6	A	A		Total Current	71.2	59.6
	17.3		17.6				Fixed Assets (net)	17.0	31.3
	2.0		1.5	N	N		Intangibles (net)	6.8	3.4
	8.5		4.3	O	O		All Other Non-Current	5.0	5.7
	100.0		100.0	T	T		Total	100.0	100.0
				A	A	**LIABILITIES**		
	5.2		17.2	V	V	Notes Payable-Short Term	4.2	12.0
	.0		1.5	A	A	Cur. Mat.-L.T.D.	3.9	2.5
	15.6		27.2	I	I	Trade Payables	14.8	15.8
	.0		.0	L	L	Income Taxes Payable	.7	.3
	14.5		11.1	A	A	All Other Current	8.7	4.6
	35.3		56.9	B	B	Total Current	32.4	35.2
	27.9		12.3	L	L	Long-Term Debt	25.2	15.9
	.0		.0	E	E	Deferred Taxes	.0	.0
	50.8		1.0			All Other Non-Current	6.8	1.6
	-14.0		29.8			Net Worth	35.5	47.4
	100.0		100.0			Total Liabilities & Net Worth	100.0	100.0
						INCOME DATA		
	100.0		100.0			Net Sales	100.0	100.0
	40.4		35.6			Gross Profit	35.9	40.4
	40.5		31.6			Operating Expenses	34.7	34.5
	-.1		4.0			Operating Profit	1.2	5.9
	1.0		.8			All Other Expenses (net)	-.5	.3
	-1.1		3.2			Profit Before Taxes	1.7	5.6
						RATIOS		
	3.8		3.7				4.5	2.9
	2.8		1.4			Current	3.0	1.9
	1.4		.9				1.4	1.1
	.5		1.7				1.8	1.4
	.2		.4			Quick	.5	.6
	.1		.2				.2	.1
	0 UND		0 UND				0 UND	0 UND
	0 UND		7 56.1			Sales/Receivables	4 102.0	1 382.5
	0 UND		24 15.5				21 17.2	20 17.9
	54 6.8		42 8.8				53 6.9	44 8.2
	74 5.0		64 5.7			Cost of Sales/Inventory	81 4.5	54 6.8
	107 3.4		69 5.3				140 2.6	111 3.3
	15 24.4		20 18.7				6 60.8	4 103.9
	21 17.7		44 8.3			Cost of Sales/Payables	19 18.7	18 20.4
	24 15.2		63 5.8				40 9.2	37 9.8
	8.5		8.8				4.2	8.0
	10.8		14.3			Sales/Working Capital	8.7	11.5
	17.8		-126.5				15.1	NM
	5.4						15.1	13.3
	(12) 2.4					EBIT/Interest	(12) 2.8	(11) 6.3
	-3.9						1.2	1.8
						Net Profit + Depr., Dep., Amort./Cur. Mat. L/T/D		
	.0		.2				.1	.1
	.6		.6			Fixed/Worth	.4	.7
	-3.6		3.5				NM	1.5
	.3		.6				.4	.5
	11.1		2.3			Debt/Worth	1.6	1.3
	-5.9		7.2				NM	2.5
						% Profit Before Taxes/Tangible Net Worth	116.8	59.5
							(10) 17.0	18.7
							.7	8.7
	16.8		23.5				14.2	15.8
	3.7		9.0			% Profit Before Taxes/Total Assets	7.5	6.7
	-4.4		.2				.2	1.8
	999.8		57.0				62.7	83.3
	40.2		26.7			Sales/Net Fixed Assets	25.7	16.1
	12.8		22.3				13.5	4.8
	7.6		6.0				4.9	4.4
	4.9		4.7			Sales/Total Assets	3.8	3.3
	3.7		2.5				2.1	1.8
	.7						.8	
	(10) .9					% Depr., Dep., Amort./Sales	(10) 1.0	
	2.0						3.5	
						% Officers', Directors' Owners' Comp/Sales		
	18319M	19448M	182107M	146472M			Net Sales ($)	739319M	74900M
	3956M	4050M	43485M	39932M			Total Assets ($)	148142M	20513M

M = $ thousand   MM = $ million
See Pages 11 through 21 for Explanation of Ratios and Data

Comparative Historical Data | Current Data Sorted by Sales

4/1/04-3/31/05 ALL	4/1/05-3/31/06 ALL	4/1/06-3/31/07 ALL	Type of Statement	0-1MM	1-3MM	3-5MM	5-10MM	10-25MM	25MM & OVER
	3	2	Unqualified						2
3	4	3	Reviewed				1	2	
3	5	4	Compiled	1			1	1	1
9	9	17	Tax Returns	4	9		1	3	
7	5	6	Other	1	1	1	1	1	1
					7 (4/1-9/30/06)		25 (10/1/06-3/31/07)		
22	26	32	**NUMBER OF STATEMENTS**	6	10	1	4	7	4
%	%	%	**ASSETS**	%	%	%	%	%	%
10.2	8.6	12.8	Cash & Equivalents		17.3				
3.7	5.0	9.0	Trade Receivables (net)		6.8				
55.7	55.0	51.2	Inventory		53.6				
1.5	2.2	1.1	All Other Current		.0				
71.2	70.8	74.0	Total Current		77.7				
21.0	22.1	17.3	Fixed Assets (net)		8.2				
4.3	.7	2.7	Intangibles (net)		4.0				
3.5	6.4	6.0	All Other Non-Current		10.1				
100.0	100.0	100.0	Total		100.0				
			LIABILITIES						
5.4	11.5	10.6	Notes Payable-Short Term		.0				
3.4	1.9	.9	Cur. Mat.-L.T.D.		.7				
28.4	30.0	19.8	Trade Payables		15.9				
.6	.0	.0	Income Taxes Payable		.0				
14.5	12.7	11.6	All Other Current		10.8				
52.3	56.1	42.9	Total Current		27.4				
25.2	16.6	19.9	Long-Term Debt		25.3				
.0	.3	.0	Deferred Taxes		.0				
4.7	2.8	24.7	All Other Non-Current		27.6				
17.7	24.3	12.5	Net Worth		19.7				
100.0	100.0	100.0	Total Liabilties & Net Worth		100.0				
			INCOME DATA						
100.0	100.0	100.0	Net Sales		100.0				
41.1	34.1	37.3	Gross Profit		37.7				
35.2	32.7	35.2	Operating Expenses		36.6				
5.9	1.4	2.0	Operating Profit		1.1				
1.0	.9	.8	All Other Expenses (net)		.8				
4.9	.5	1.2	Profit Before Taxes		.2				
			RATIOS						
3.0	2.0	3.7			3.7				
1.3	1.3	2.4	Current		3.0				
.9	.9	1.2			2.4				
.6	.6	.9			1.0				
.2	(25) .2	.4	Quick		.3				
.1	.1	.1			.2				
0 UND	0 UND	0 UND		0 UND					
2 221.9	2 182.2	0 UND	Sales/Receivables	0 UND					
10 35.3	6 64.2	6 61.5		0 UND					
51 7.1	55 6.7	50 7.4		51 7.1					
71 5.2	66 5.6	65 5.6	Cost of Sales/Inventory	65 5.6					
184 2.0	84 4.4	82 4.4		77 4.7					
19 19.1	13 27.9	13 27.3		17 22.1					
37 9.8	29 12.4	23 16.2	Cost of Sales/Payables	21 17.6					
76 4.8	52 7.0	41 8.9		24 15.5					
8.4	14.4	8.5			9.0				
32.9	34.0	12.8	Sales/Working Capital		10.7				
-120.0	-121.2	63.2			15.5				
36.8	20.5	7.4							
(18) 2.9	(24) 2.1	(26) 3.4	EBIT/Interest						
.9	1.0	1.0							
			Net Profit + Depr., Dep., Amort./Cur. Mat. L/T/D						
.4	.3	.1			.0				
1.5	.8	.6	Fixed/Worth		.8				
-1.1	NM	NM			-2.8				
1.3	.7	.6			.3				
4.6	2.3	2.6	Debt/Worth		12.5				
-4.5	NM	-131.4			-20.3				
85.7	54.6	49.4							
(14) 25.0	(20) 14.2	(23) 20.0	% Profit Before Taxes/Tangible Net Worth						
-1.5	8.2	4.3							
34.0	17.5	16.7			17.3				
7.4	5.8	7.0	% Profit Before Taxes/Total Assets		2.0				
-.1	.6	-1.1			-7.6				
80.6	56.0	103.6			UND				
17.0	25.1	37.3	Sales/Net Fixed Assets		57.3				
8.8	11.8	22.2			39.9				
6.2	6.0	5.9			7.6				
4.1	4.8	4.8	Sales/Total Assets		5.6				
2.3	3.2	2.9			4.1				
.5	.6	.5							
(20) .9	(22) 1.1	(25) .9	% Depr., Dep., Amort./Sales						
2.1	1.7	1.3							
1.8	1.7	1.4							
(10) 3.4	(12) 3.6	(10) 2.9	% Officers', Directors' Owners' Comp/Sales						
10.9	7.1	10.5							
182931M	316195M	366346M	Net Sales ($)	3777M	16257M	3192M	30282M	113470M	199368M
42380M	92463M	91423M	Total Assets ($)	1254M	3294M	663M	10704M	25604M	49904M

© RMA 2007

M = $ thousand   MM = $ million
See Pages 11 through 21 for Explanation of Ratios and Data

Current Data Sorted by Assets   Comparative Historical Data

Type of Statement

Type	0-500M	500M-2MM	2-10MM	10-50MM		4/1/02-3/31/03 ALL	4/1/03-3/31/04 ALL
Unqualified				4		7	3
Reviewed		5	2	2		12	13
Compiled	7	20	25	1		71	76
Tax Returns	4	20	6	1		18	33
Other	3	10	11	3		24	22

15 (4/1-9/30/06)   109 (10/1/06-3/31/07)

Columns: 0-500M, 500M-2MM, 2-10MM, 10-50MM (10/1/06-3/31/07); 50-100MM and 100-250MM marked **DATA NOT AVAILABLE**.

0-500M	500M-2MM	2-10MM	10-50MM	50-100MM	100-250MM		4/1/02-3/31/03 ALL	4/1/03-3/31/04 ALL
14	55	44	11			**NUMBER OF STATEMENTS**	132	147
%	%	%	%	%	%	**ASSETS**	%	%
19.3	9.4	8.7	4.5			Cash & Equivalents	9.1	8.5
6.4	6.3	9.5	14.9			Trade Receivables (net)	7.0	8.4
42.8	61.6	67.2	42.4			Inventory	54.7	57.7
1.0	4.6	1.6	2.0			All Other Current	3.5	3.1
69.5	82.0	86.9	63.8			Total Current	74.2	77.7
27.0	12.8	8.7	25.9			Fixed Assets (net)	16.9	15.0
.0	1.0	.9	.3			Intangibles (net)	1.1	.8
3.5	4.1	3.5	10.0			All Other Non-Current	7.7	6.5
100.0	100.0	100.0	100.0			Total	100.0	100.0
						LIABILITIES		
53.0	43.3	36.4	35.1			Notes Payable-Short Term	36.0	39.4
7.3	1.5	5.3	1.4			Cur. Mat.-L.T.D.	2.1	2.8
5.7	6.1	6.6	5.6			Trade Payables	4.3	9.2
.0	.1	.3	.1			Income Taxes Payable	.1	.1
14.6	14.6	12.3	7.3			All Other Current	11.5	12.5
80.6	65.7	60.9	49.5			Total Current	54.0	64.0
5.9	7.6	5.4	20.1			Long-Term Debt	11.0	10.7
.0	.0	.0	.4			Deferred Taxes	.0	.0
2.3	3.0	3.3	1.8			All Other Non-Current	5.9	6.3
11.3	23.8	30.3	28.2			Net Worth	29.0	18.9
100.0	100.0	100.0	100.0			Total Liabilities & Net Worth	100.0	100.0
						INCOME DATA		
100.0	100.0	100.0	100.0			Net Sales	100.0	100.0
30.3	23.8	20.8	29.7			Gross Profit	24.6	24.7
23.9	19.7	18.4	27.1			Operating Expenses	22.7	22.5
6.4	4.1	2.3	2.6			Operating Profit	1.9	2.3
2.7	.8	.4	2.0			All Other Expenses (net)	.7	.5
3.7	3.4	2.0	.6			Profit Before Taxes	1.3	1.7
						RATIOS		
1.3	1.6	2.3	2.2				2.1	1.6
.9	1.2	1.3	1.4			Current	1.3	1.2
.4	1.0	1.1	.9				1.0	1.0
.5	.4	.7	.9				.6	.5
.3	.2	(43) .3	.2			Quick	(146) .2	.2
.0	.1	.1	.0				.1	.1
0 UND	0 UND	1 715.3	3 119.4				0 999.8	0 UND
0 UND	2 202.2	8 45.1	41 9.0			Sales/Receivables	5 68.6	5 80.0
12 30.6	12 31.1	32 11.5	124 2.9				17 21.1	21 17.2
0 UND	85 4.3	111 3.3	54 6.8				84 4.3	82 4.5
48 7.5	141 2.6	157 2.3	180 2.0			Cost of Sales/Inventory	135 2.7	128 2.9
163 2.2	208 1.8	196 1.9	306 1.2				179 2.0	178 2.0
0 UND	0 UND	1 312.4	5 70.1				0 UND	1 618.0
0 UND	3 120.8	3 113.8	30 12.2			Cost of Sales/Payables	3 104.3	4 93.5
7 48.8	11 34.6	9 40.6	70 5.2				11 32.3	17 22.1
30.1	6.6	4.8	3.0				5.4	6.2
UND	14.9	9.6	10.5			Sales/Working Capital	12.3	19.9
-12.6	124.0	28.7	-33.5				105.0	UND
2.4	3.3	7.0	5.1				4.1	4.4
(11) 1.7	(53) 2.1	(43) 2.2	(10) 3.1			EBIT/Interest	(120) 1.6	(127) 1.8
.0	.6	.9	.2				.5	.8
							5.1	2.0
						Net Profit + Depr., Dep., Amort./Cur. Mat. L/T/D	(11) 1.1	(13) 1.6
							-.6	.3
.2	.1	.1	.4				.2	.2
4.7	.4	.3	.6			Fixed/Worth	.4	.5
-5.9	1.9	.7	1.9				1.7	2.1
1.7	1.6	.8	1.4				1.1	1.7
179.6	3.5	3.3	2.2			Debt/Worth	2.9	4.0
-11.0	39.1	8.8	6.9				7.9	13.9
	45.5	52.8	25.0				37.3	52.2
(46)	16.0	(42) 20.5	(10) 13.2			% Profit Before Taxes/Tangible Net Worth	(115) 9.0	(123) 11.9
	-2.4	1.6	-.4				-1.7	-.5
19.5	13.2	11.6	9.0				7.5	8.9
4.5	4.0	4.0	3.6			% Profit Before Taxes/Total Assets	2.1	2.7
-2.5	-2.2	-.3	-1.5				-1.2	-.9
UND	102.5	147.5	13.6				68.0	54.7
45.3	41.1	32.3	5.4			Sales/Net Fixed Assets	21.6	23.3
6.5	10.4	15.6	2.4				8.8	11.4
5.2	2.8	2.5	1.6				2.8	2.9
3.3	2.1	1.9	1.1			Sales/Total Assets	2.0	2.1
1.8	1.7	1.4	.6				1.4	1.4
	.2	.3					.4	.4
(47)	.4	(33) .5				% Depr., Dep., Amort./Sales	(116) .8	(124) .9
	.9	.8					1.5	1.5
	1.7	1.0					1.4	1.5
(30)	2.8	(24) 1.4				% Officers', Directors' Owners' Comp/Sales	(67) 2.3	(61) 2.7
	3.6	2.7					4.9	4.3
12747M	158039M	350591M	258344M			Net Sales ($)	617452M	677366M
3329M	67257M	166505M	245415M			Total Assets ($)	512830M	453855M

© RMA 2007

M = $ thousand   MM = $ million
See Pages 11 through 21 for Explanation of Ratios and Data

Comparative Historical Data

Current Data Sorted by Sales

			Type of Statement						
5	5	4	Unqualified					3	1
16	11	9	Reviewed		1	3		3	1
55	42	53	Compiled	5	15	17	11	4	1
59	31	31	Tax Returns	5	13	7	4	1	1
23	31	27	Other	3	7	5	5		
4/1/04-3/31/05	4/1/05-3/31/06	4/1/06-3/31/07		15 (4/1-9/30/06)			109 (10/1/06-3/31/07)		
ALL	ALL	ALL		0-1MM	1-3MM	3-5MM	5-10MM	10-25MM	25MM & OVER
158	120	124	**NUMBER OF STATEMENTS**	13	36	32	23	16	4
%	%	%	**ASSETS**	%	%	%	%	%	%
10.3	9.8	9.8	Cash & Equivalents	18.3	8.3	10.2	11.5	4.8	
8.4	9.7	8.2	Trade Receivables (net)	4.6	6.8	7.2	12.9	9.4	
57.8	56.8	59.8	Inventory	45.0	61.1	62.6	60.4	63.9	
2.5	2.4	2.9	All Other Current	1.3	4.3	3.4	2.2	1.1	
79.0	78.8	80.7	Total Current	69.3	80.5	83.4	87.0	79.2	
13.8	14.4	14.1	Fixed Assets (net)	27.6	15.5	11.0	6.2	14.3	
.5	.2	.8	Intangibles (net)	.0	1.4	.6	.6	1.1	
6.7	6.6	4.4	All Other Non-Current	3.2	2.6	5.0	6.3	5.4	
100.0	100.0	100.0	Total	100.0	100.0	100.0	100.0	100.0	
			LIABILITIES						
39.8	34.7	41.2	Notes Payable-Short Term	56.6	44.8	41.7	38.6	27.0	
1.9	1.7	3.5	Cur. Mat.-L.T.D.	4.6	2.6	.9	4.7	8.7	
6.5	5.7	6.2	Trade Payables	2.0	6.7	5.7	9.1	6.0	
.1	.1	.1	Income Taxes Payable	.0	.1	.0	.0	.8	
11.3	13.2	13.2	All Other Current	18.3	9.0	15.1	14.4	14.1	
59.6	55.4	64.2	Total Current	81.4	63.2	63.4	66.8	56.5	
10.1	10.6	7.7	Long-Term Debt	7.3	9.3	4.5	8.6	5.8	
.0	.0	.0	Deferred Taxes	.0	.0	.0	.1	.1	
4.7	6.6	2.9	All Other Non-Current	3.9	1.2	2.9	3.2	6.0	
25.6	27.4	25.1	Net Worth	7.4	26.2	29.2	21.4	31.6	
100.0	100.0	100.0	Total Liabilities & Net Worth	100.0	100.0	100.0	100.0	100.0	
			INCOME DATA						
100.0	100.0	100.0	Net Sales	100.0	100.0	100.0	100.0	100.0	
24.0	24.8	24.0	Gross Profit	31.3	24.7	21.9	21.3	24.9	
21.1	20.2	20.4	Operating Expenses	25.7	21.6	19.0	18.7	19.4	
2.9	4.5	3.6	Operating Profit	5.6	3.0	2.9	2.6	5.5	
.5	1.2	1.0	All Other Expenses (net)	3.1	.6	.7	.1	1.6	
2.4	3.3	2.7	Profit Before Taxes	2.6	2.4	2.2	2.4	3.9	
			RATIOS						
1.7	2.3	1.7	Current	1.2	1.7	1.7	1.9	2.1	
1.2	1.4	1.2		.9	1.3	1.2	1.3	1.6	
1.0	1.0	1.0		.3	1.0	1.1	1.0	1.1	
.6	.7	.5	Quick	.5	.4	.6	.8	.8	
(156) .3	(118) .3	(123) .2		.1	.2	.3	.3	(15) .3	
.1	.1	.1		.0	.1	.1	.1	.1	
0 999.8	0 UND	0 UND	Sales/Receivables	0 UND	0 UND	1 411.6	1 505.1	0 UND	
6 64.9	9 42.2	4 100.2		0 UND	1 308.6	7 51.8	8 47.3	3 109.9	
23 16.2	24 15.5	22 16.8		9 38.6	13 27.4	25 14.5	35 10.4	21 17.2	
92 4.0	91 4.0	85 4.3	Cost of Sales/Inventory	0 UND	89 4.1	88 4.1	93 3.9	61 6.0	
135 2.7	130 2.8	142 2.6		118 3.1	164 2.2	161 2.3	144 2.5	114 3.2	
188 1.9	213 1.7	201 1.8		292 1.3	216 1.7	223 1.6	184 2.0	146 2.5	
1 314.9	1 417.4	0 UND	Cost of Sales/Payables	0 UND	0 UND	1 312.4	0 UND	2 222.4	
4 89.9	4 101.7	4 100.4		4 89.4	2 154.5	3 123.5	4 99.6	7 49.2	
11 34.1	13 27.3	11 34.4		11 34.7	10 35.7	9 40.5	12 31.4	30 12.2	
6.3	4.9	5.7	Sales/Working Capital	47.3	5.2	6.1	6.6	6.3	
14.0	11.3	13.5		-16.0	15.1	10.0	14.4	10.0	
544.5	59.9	121.9		-5.1	121.9	23.9	82.5	30.3	
4.9	4.3	5.1	EBIT/Interest	2.0	2.8	5.9	6.1	6.6	
(136) 1.9	(112) 2.2	(117) 2.1		(10) .8	(35) 1.6	(31) 2.4	(21) 2.1	2.7	
.8	1.3	.8		.0	.4	.6	1.3	1.1	
2.4			Net Profit + Depr., Dep., Amort./Cur. Mat. L/T/D						
(11) 1.9									
.4									
.2	.1	.1	Fixed/Worth	.4	.1	.1	.1	.1	
.4	.4	.4		UND	.4	.3	.3	.4	
1.1	1.2	1.6		-2.6	2.1	.8	.7	.5	
1.4	1.4	1.4	Debt/Worth	3.2	1.4	1.5	2.1	1.1	
3.4	2.8	3.5		UND	4.0	2.6	5.9	2.5	
12.4	9.5	16.7		-10.5	32.8	6.1	10.8	7.0	
32.4	57.4	50.3	% Profit Before Taxes/Tangible Net Worth		43.9	34.3	64.4	75.5	
(133) 13.8	(104) 15.6	(107) 18.1			(31) 9.5	(28) 14.8	(21) 26.1	20.6	
1.3	4.1	1.3			-23.5	-2.0	14.1	4.7	
8.1	10.8	12.0	% Profit Before Taxes/Total Assets	7.6	13.8	12.9	11.6	12.9	
2.3	4.4	4.1		3.0	3.0	3.7	5.5	7.6	
-.4	.6	-.7		-4.2	-4.5	-.7	1.0	.9	
65.2	62.4	111.6	Sales/Net Fixed Assets	UND	60.7	88.0	126.3	289.3	
25.9	30.5	32.8		14.7	31.8	26.4	65.0	29.7	
11.5	10.8	9.7		4.1	9.5	11.0	21.3	8.2	
2.9	2.8	2.7	Sales/Total Assets	2.8	2.7	2.7	2.7	3.7	
2.1	2.0	2.0		1.8	1.9	2.0	2.0	2.2	
1.6	1.4	1.6		1.0	1.7	1.5	1.6	1.3	
.3	.3	.3	% Depr., Dep., Amort./Sales		.2	.2	.3	.2	
(134) .8	(97) .6	(96) .5			(32) .6	(28) .5	(17) .4	(11) .3	
1.4	1.2	1.0			.9	.7	1.0	1.2	
1.7	1.5	1.2	% Officers', Directors' Owners' Comp/Sales		2.0	1.2	1.0		
(91) 2.7	(67) 2.6	(59) 2.5			(19) 3.3	(14) 2.6	(15) 1.4		
3.8	4.1	3.5			4.6	3.0	1.9		
777100M	666493M	779721M	Net Sales ($)	5947M	73631M	125653M	162189M	248219M	164082M
463894M	438567M	482506M	Total Assets ($)	4560M	38195M	73954M	118236M	141152M	106409M

M = $ thousand   MM = $ million
See Pages 11 through 21 for Explanation of Ratios and Data

Current Data Sorted by Assets | **Comparative Historical Data**

	0-500M	500M-2MM	2-10MM	10-50MM	50-100MM	100-250MM		4/1/02-3/31/03 ALL	4/1/03-3/31/04 ALL
Type of Statement									
Unqualified		4	9	9	8	6		36	40
Reviewed		6	39	7				53	53
Compiled	21	29	35	4	1	2		92	137
Tax Returns	73	56	18	2	1			102	137
Other	23	37	53	28		9		102	124
	79 (4/1-9/30/06)			409 (10/1/06-3/31/07)					
NUMBER OF STATEMENTS	117	132	154	50	18	17		385	491
ASSETS	%	%	%	%	%	%		%	%
Cash & Equivalents	16.2	10.7	8.3	7.2	15.2	5.2		9.7	10.3
Trade Receivables (net)	11.4	16.1	23.4	22.1	19.6	19.4		15.0	16.0
Inventory	38.4	41.0	37.1	38.1	19.9	33.7		40.3	41.1
All Other Current	1.2	1.5	3.1	4.2	7.1	5.3		2.4	3.0
Total Current	67.3	69.2	71.8	71.6	61.8	63.6		67.3	70.4
Fixed Assets (net)	23.3	20.7	19.6	16.7	22.6	19.4		23.8	21.3
Intangibles (net)	5.5	3.4	3.6	5.8	4.2	12.0		3.0	3.0
All Other Non-Current	3.8	6.7	5.0	5.9	11.4	5.0		5.8	5.4
Total	100.0	100.0	100.0	100.0	100.0	100.0		100.0	100.0
LIABILITIES									
Notes Payable-Short Term	14.1	15.4	12.8	17.1	6.2	12.4		12.1	13.9
Cur. Mat.-L.T.D.	4.2	2.5	2.5	2.1	.7	.7		3.7	3.3
Trade Payables	18.6	17.3	19.9	18.1	22.6	18.2		19.9	19.0
Income Taxes Payable	.0	.5	.5	.4	.4	2.0		.2	.3
All Other Current	18.5	9.9	10.9	13.6	8.1	18.6		11.0	11.0
Total Current	55.4	45.6	46.6	51.2	38.0	51.9		46.9	47.6
Long-Term Debt	24.1	19.4	12.4	14.4	18.7	16.6		18.7	17.3
Deferred Taxes	.0	.1	.2	.2	.7	.7		.2	.2
All Other Non-Current	17.5	5.4	5.3	8.4	3.4	12.7		6.8	6.0
Net Worth	2.9	29.5	35.5	25.8	39.2	18.1		27.5	28.9
Total Liabilties & Net Worth	100.0	100.0	100.0	100.0	100.0	100.0		100.0	100.0
INCOME DATA									
Net Sales	100.0	100.0	100.0	100.0	100.0	100.0		100.0	100.0
Gross Profit	48.8	39.6	34.8	31.8	37.3	39.5		40.6	40.7
Operating Expenses	45.6	37.0	31.5	27.5	29.8	32.8		36.9	36.9
Operating Profit	3.2	2.6	3.3	4.3	7.5	6.7		3.6	3.8
All Other Expenses (net)	1.6	.5	.7	2.0	.0	1.9		1.0	.6
Profit Before Taxes	1.7	2.1	2.6	2.3	7.5	4.8		2.7	3.2
RATIOS									
	3.5	2.9	2.3	2.0	3.8	2.1		2.2	2.6
Current	1.5	1.7	1.6	1.3	1.4	1.4		1.5	1.5
	.8	1.1	1.1	1.1	1.2	1.0		1.1	1.1
	1.2	1.3	1.1	.9	1.6	1.0		1.0	1.1
Quick	.5	.5	(153) .6	.6	.9	.5		(383) .5	(490) .5
	.2	.2	.3	.3	.7	.2		.2	.2
	0 UND	1 292.8	5 66.5	8 43.8	8 48.1	5 79.6		0 886.2	1 346.0
Sales/Receivables	3 106.7	11 34.3	23 16.0	29 12.7	41 9.0	43 8.5		8 45.5	12 31.3
	19 19.2	32 11.4	42 8.7	60 6.1	67 5.5	59 6.1		30 12.0	32 11.4
	25 14.6	29 12.5	30 12.3	28 12.9	48 7.6	66 5.6		31 11.6	30 12.3
Cost of Sales/Inventory	60 6.0	71 5.1	69 5.3	93 3.9	65 5.6	133 2.7		76 4.8	76 4.8
	142 2.6	128 2.9	127 2.9	164 2.2	125 2.9	237 1.5		144 2.5	150 2.4
	0 UND	5 70.6	18 19.9	16 22.1	33 11.1	31 11.6		13 27.9	10 36.9
Cost of Sales/Payables	20 17.9	27 13.4	33 11.2	35 10.4	71 5.1	51 7.1		34 10.9	31 12.0
	53 6.9	46 8.0	60 6.1	56 6.5	115 3.2	72 5.1		62 5.9	60 6.1
	5.5	6.0	5.5	6.5	2.3	4.7		7.0	6.2
Sales/Working Capital	27.3	11.1	12.8	10.8	11.3	12.0		14.5	13.7
	-40.8	56.2	67.3	65.0	52.7	131.8		122.7	72.1
	8.3	7.6	8.5	11.2	15.2	7.7		7.7	11.2
EBIT/Interest	(88) 1.8	(114) 2.6	(146) 2.7	(48) 2.6	(15) 3.6	(15) 2.5		(340) 3.0	(416) 3.4
	-1.2	.9	1.2	1.1	.7	.4		.9	1.1
			11.7	7.5				7.7	6.8
Net Profit + Depr., Dep., Amort./Cur. Mat. L/T/D		(28) 3.7	(10) 2.8					(61) 1.8	(69) 2.7
			1.6	.0				.8	1.0
	.2	.1	.1	.2	.1	.3		.2	.2
Fixed/Worth	1.1	.5	.5	.4	.4	.9		.7	.6
	-1.0	2.9	1.5	2.2	1.2	4.5		4.1	2.5
	1.1	.8	.9	1.1	1.0	1.7		1.0	.8
Debt/Worth	5.2	2.6	2.1	3.4	1.7	6.4		2.4	2.4
	-4.9	12.0	4.4	7.0	4.4	NM		13.1	12.9
	88.3	48.4	42.0	43.4	64.8	37.5		45.0	49.0
% Profit Before Taxes/Tangible Net Worth	(70) 24.7	(106) 17.4	(144) 16.2	(42) 15.4	(16) 20.2	(13) 27.4		(308) 16.3	(400) 20.2
	.0	3.2	2.5	3.2	5.9	-40.2		1.7	4.3
	18.3	14.8	14.3	11.4	28.6	17.9		13.8	16.5
% Profit Before Taxes/Total Assets	4.0	5.3	4.4	4.0	4.8	7.3		5.0	5.6
	-8.6	-.2	.6	.4	.0	.1		.0	.3
	93.4	78.7	59.0	41.4	67.6	34.9		44.9	61.6
Sales/Net Fixed Assets	29.5	30.6	22.2	18.9	11.8	11.6		21.9	25.5
	8.3	9.6	8.8	10.2	4.0	7.2		8.6	9.5
	5.3	4.4	4.1	3.3	2.2	2.5		4.4	4.4
Sales/Total Assets	3.3	3.0	2.5	2.1	1.7	2.0		2.9	2.8
	2.2	1.9	1.8	1.6	1.0	1.2		1.9	1.9
	.5	.4	.6	.5	.6	1.3		.7	.6
% Depr., Dep., Amort./Sales	(85) 1.2	(94) 1.1	(131) 1.1	(43) .9	(14) 2.8	(11) 1.8		(318) 1.3	(385) 1.3
	3.0	2.2	2.3	2.2	3.6	2.7		2.7	2.5
	3.7	2.5	1.2					2.3	1.9
% Officers', Directors' Owners' Comp/Sales	(65) 7.6	(68) 3.7	(70) 2.4					(194) 4.4	(241) 4.0
	11.9	5.2	4.1					8.0	6.9
Net Sales ($)	112965M	511333M	2189213M	2775999M	2418918M	6033881M		7836384M	7075161M
Total Assets ($)	28917M	142051M	666073M	1091235M	1353207M	2906077M		3363516M	3125457M

© RMA 2007

M = $ thousand   MM = $ million
See Pages 11 through 21 for Explanation of Ratios and Data

Comparative Historical Data | Current Data Sorted by Sales

			Type of Statement						
36	35	36	Unqualified		4	2	3	5	22
51	63	52	Reviewed	1	2	4	14	18	13
124	96	89	Compiled	15	18	15	17	19	5
138	189	152	Tax Returns	51	54	23	8	11	5
109	194	159	Other	21	26	15	17	34	46
4/1/04-3/31/05 ALL	4/1/05-3/31/06 ALL	4/1/06-3/31/07 ALL		79 (4/1-9/30/06)			409 (10/1/06-3/31/07)		
				0-1MM	1-3MM	3-5MM	5-10MM	10-25MM	25MM & OVER
458	577	488	NUMBER OF STATEMENTS	88	104	59	59	87	91
%	%	%	ASSETS	%	%	%	%	%	%
10.4	10.8	10.9	Cash & Equivalents	13.5	12.2	13.4	8.4	8.2	9.3
15.5	17.6	18.1	Trade Receivables (net)	10.1	12.2	17.2	21.6	24.0	25.3
39.9	38.5	37.8	Inventory	36.2	40.6	45.6	37.1	37.7	31.7
2.6	2.8	2.6	All Other Current	1.3	1.9	1.2	2.4	2.8	5.2
68.5	69.7	69.4	Total Current	61.1	67.0	77.4	69.6	72.7	71.5
21.4	20.7	20.6	Fixed Assets (net)	29.3	21.7	14.0	20.4	17.8	17.9
4.1	4.2	4.6	Intangibles (net)	5.4	4.6	4.3	4.2	3.3	5.3
6.1	5.3	5.5	All Other Non-Current	4.2	6.8	4.2	5.8	6.2	5.4
100.0	100.0	100.0	Total	100.0	100.0	100.0	100.0	100.0	100.0
			LIABILITIES						
12.8	12.8	14.0	Notes Payable-Short Term	14.7	13.9	14.8	13.4	14.7	12.6
4.1	3.0	2.7	Cur. Mat.-L.T.D.	2.6	4.4	2.3	3.2	2.4	1.2
19.3	19.7	18.7	Trade Payables	13.7	17.0	19.9	17.8	22.0	22.4
.2	.4	.4	Income Taxes Payable	.0	.0	1.1	.5	.4	.9
12.3	11.8	12.9	All Other Current	18.0	12.8	10.8	9.0	11.7	13.1
48.7	47.8	48.8	Total Current	49.0	48.2	49.0	43.8	51.3	50.1
15.4	18.0	17.7	Long-Term Debt	23.5	21.4	19.0	18.4	9.7	14.1
.2	.2	.2	Deferred Taxes	.0	.1	.1	.5	.1	.4
6.4	7.5	8.7	All Other Non-Current	19.1	7.8	4.0	5.6	6.3	7.2
29.3	26.6	24.6	Net Worth	8.4	22.5	28.0	31.7	32.7	28.2
100.0	100.0	100.0	Total Liabilities & Net Worth	100.0	100.0	100.0	100.0	100.0	100.0
			INCOME DATA						
100.0	100.0	100.0	Net Sales	100.0	100.0	100.0	100.0	100.0	100.0
40.0	39.5	39.4	Gross Profit	50.6	43.3	37.1	39.2	34.2	30.6
36.2	35.4	35.9	Operating Expenses	47.9	40.7	33.4	36.0	30.2	26.1
3.8	4.1	3.5	Operating Profit	2.7	2.7	3.7	3.2	4.1	4.6
.5	1.0	1.0	All Other Expenses (net)	2.4	.6	.6	.1	1.3	.7
3.3	3.1	2.5	Profit Before Taxes	.3	2.1	3.1	3.1	2.7	3.9
			RATIOS						
2.4	2.6	2.4	Current	3.8	2.6	2.7	2.6	2.1	2.2
1.5	1.5	1.5		1.7	1.6	1.7	1.6	1.5	1.3
1.0	1.1	1.0		.9	1.0	1.2	1.0	1.1	1.1
1.0	1.1	1.1	Quick	1.3	1.2	1.2	1.3	1.0	1.1
(456) .5	(574) .6	(487) .6		.5	.5	.6	.7	.6	(90) .7
.2	.2	.2		.1	.2	.2	.3	.3	.3
1 272.3	2 190.4	2 199.1	Sales/Receivables	0 UND	0 UND	1 695.8	5 74.1	7 51.4	6 58.0
12 31.3	14 26.1	16 23.1		6 62.0	8 44.0	4 83.5	23 16.1	25 14.5	25 14.5
31 11.8	38 9.7	39 9.3		25 14.7	27 13.7	30 12.0	40 9.1	52 7.0	54 6.7
33 11.0	26 13.8	29 12.5	Cost of Sales/Inventory	28 13.0	32 11.4	30 12.1	31 12.0	34 10.6	16 23.3
77 4.8	75 4.9	70 5.2		87 4.2	81 4.5	81 4.5	70 5.2	54 6.7	58 6.3
137 2.7	138 2.6	137 2.7		249 1.5	157 2.3	114 3.2	137 2.7	112 3.3	133 2.7
11 34.0	11 34.2	11 34.2	Cost of Sales/Payables	1 340.6	7 50.2	2 168.8	19 19.1	20 18.6	18 20.0
31 11.8	31 11.7	31 11.8		22 16.6	29 12.5	23 15.7	34 10.6	34 10.7	34 10.8
57 6.4	58 6.3	57 6.4		54 6.8	62 5.9	52 7.0	49 7.4	60 6.1	59 6.2
6.4	5.7	5.5	Sales/Working Capital	3.9	5.3	5.7	5.3	7.4	6.6
15.9	12.4	13.5		14.8	14.2	8.8	12.2	13.3	19.0
128.2	62.0	195.3		-37.2	-374.4	26.0	93.4	39.3	78.0
11.0	9.3	8.3	EBIT/Interest	4.9	6.2	11.8	6.1	10.7	14.9
(383) 4.6	(501) 3.5	(426) 2.6		(65) 1.0	(89) 2.1	(53) 4.2	(55) 2.3	(83) 3.0	(81) 3.3
1.4	1.2	.9		-1.2	-.1	1.1	1.4	1.4	1.1
7.7	7.4	10.1	Net Profit + Depr., Dep., Amort./Cur. Mat. L/T/D				23.8	5.3	17.3
(67) 2.7	(79) 2.4	(54) 3.4					(11) 6.1	(13) 2.9	(20) 6.5
1.3	1.3	1.3					1.1	1.3	2.1
.2	.2	.2	Fixed/Worth	.3	.2	.1	.2	.2	.1
.6	.6	.6		1.1		.4	.5	.5	.6
2.8	2.5	2.9		-2.0	-11.4	2.1	1.6	1.5	1.5
.9	1.0	1.0	Debt/Worth	.8	1.0	.8	1.0	.9	1.2
2.4	2.6	2.7		3.9	3.3	2.4	2.1	2.0	2.6
10.0	10.0	12.1		-4.9	-21.4	10.6	7.7	4.5	6.9
53.7	56.1	46.8	% Profit Before Taxes/Tangible Net Worth	49.8	40.0	57.3	42.2	40.4	58.5
(380) 21.6	(480) 22.1	(391) 18.8		(58) 10.9	(75) 18.8	(48) 22.7	(52) 17.9	(78) 16.9	(80) 24.7
5.4	5.3	2.5		-8.3	2.5	3.3	1.9	2.7	8.2
16.8	15.1	15.2	% Profit Before Taxes/Total Assets	12.7	14.6	22.1	9.2	15.1	19.2
6.5	6.0	4.6		2.0	3.8	7.1	4.6	5.2	6.3
.8	.6	-.2		-7.6	-3.4	.7	.6	1.1	.5
64.3	66.6	67.2	Sales/Net Fixed Assets	50.3	71.9	100.1	50.3	58.9	70.1
22.5	26.7	24.6		14.4	28.8	42.6	20.6	25.9	24.4
9.1	9.1	8.8		2.9	6.6	16.6	9.1	12.0	10.1
4.3	4.2	4.2	Sales/Total Assets	3.3	4.3	4.8	3.6	4.5	5.0
2.9	2.8	2.7		2.0	2.9	3.6	2.5	3.0	2.5
1.9	1.8	1.8		1.2	1.8	2.2	1.9	2.1	1.7
.6	.5	.5	% Depr., Dep., Amort./Sales	.5	.7	.4	.7	.4	.5
(361) 1.2	(457) 1.0	(378) 1.1		(65) 1.6	(78) 1.2	(40) 1.1	(46) 2.1	(75) 1.0	(74) .8
2.3	2.0	2.5		7.8	2.5	1.7	3.3	1.7	2.1
2.0	1.6	1.9	% Officers', Directors' Owners' Comp/Sales	5.9	2.4	2.2	1.2	1.2	1.3
(222) 3.8	(259) 3.7	(214) 3.8		(40) 8.5	(61) 3.9	(33) 3.8	(28) 2.8	(36) 1.7	(16) 2.4
7.4	7.3	8.0		13.0	7.7	4.9	5.7	3.4	4.6
6813630M	15439132M	14042309M	Net Sales ($)	49449M	178854M	228196M	410406M	1388547M	11786857M
3042530M	6067119M	6187560M	Total Assets ($)	36369M	99017M	76862M	168612M	589270M	5217430M

M = $ thousand   MM = $ million
See Pages 11 through 21 for Explanation of Ratios and Data

Current Data Sorted by Assets   Comparative Historical Data

Type of Statement

	0-500M	500M-2MM	2-10MM	10-50MM	50-100MM	100-250MM		4/1/02-3/31/03 ALL	4/1/03-3/31/04 ALL
Unqualified				3	1	4			1
Reviewed			4						
Compiled		1	1	1					
Tax Returns		1	1	4					3
Other	3	4	4	11	2	4			5
	0-500M	500M-2MM	8 (4/1-9/30/06) 2-10MM	37 (10/1/06-3/31/07) 10-50MM	50-100MM	100-250MM			
NUMBER OF STATEMENTS	3	6	10	15	3	8			9

Historical columns (4/1/02-3/31/03 ALL): **DATA NOT AVAILABLE**

	0-500M %	500M-2MM %	2-10MM %	10-50MM %	50-100MM %	100-250MM %		4/1/02-3/31/03 ALL %	4/1/03-3/31/04 ALL %
ASSETS									
Cash & Equivalents			10.0	13.8					
Trade Receivables (net)			19.5	12.6					
Inventory			50.6	31.0					
All Other Current			6.0	7.7					
Total Current			86.1	65.1					
Fixed Assets (net)			9.7	14.4					
Intangibles (net)			2.0	10.9					
All Other Non-Current			2.2	9.6					
Total			100.0	100.0					
LIABILITIES									
Notes Payable-Short Term			22.3	7.5					
Cur. Mat.-L.T.D.			.5	1.1					
Trade Payables			27.1	18.1					
Income Taxes Payable			.0	.2					
All Other Current			23.0	16.3					
Total Current			73.0	43.4					
Long-Term Debt			4.9	12.8					
Deferred Taxes			.0	.1					
All Other Non-Current			.5	1.3					
Net Worth			21.6	42.5					
Total Liabilties & Net Worth			100.0	100.0					
INCOME DATA									
Net Sales			100.0	100.0					
Gross Profit			33.9	40.4					
Operating Expenses			34.6	38.6					
Operating Profit			-.8	1.8					
All Other Expenses (net)			1.2	.1					
Profit Before Taxes			-1.9	1.7					

RATIOS

Ratio	2-10MM	10-50MM
Current	1.6	2.2
	1.4	1.5
	.9	1.0
Quick	.7	1.1
	.5	.6
	.2	.2
Sales/Receivables	(2) 219.1	(4) 96.3
	(15) 25.0	(8) 47.1
	(34) 10.6	(23) 15.8
Cost of Sales/Inventory	(31) 11.8	(22) 16.5
	(107) 3.4	(89) 4.1
	(166) 2.2	(121) 3.0
Cost of Sales/Payables	(25) 14.4	(23) 15.8
	(50) 7.2	(30) 12.2
	(73) 5.0	(65) 5.6
Sales/Working Capital	7.5	7.2
	18.3	13.1
	-252.5	999.8
EBIT/Interest		20.6
		(12) 4.3
		-6.9
Net Profit + Depr., Dep., Amort./Cur. Mat. L/T/D		
Fixed/Worth	.1	.2
	.3	.3
	NM	1.8
Debt/Worth	1.8	.6
	2.4	1.3
	NM	4.1
% Profit Before Taxes/Tangible Net Worth		27.9
		(14) 17.1
		-14.1
% Profit Before Taxes/Total Assets	4.5	12.3
	-4.6	6.3
	-16.2	-4.2
Sales/Net Fixed Assets	117.2	50.7
	72.0	33.8
	34.0	24.5
Sales/Total Assets	4.7	4.9
	2.6	2.6
	2.6	1.9
% Depr., Dep., Amort./Sales		.6
		(14) .9
		1.6
% Officers', Directors' Owners' Comp/Sales		

	0-500M	500M-2MM	2-10MM	10-50MM	50-100MM	100-250MM		4/1/03-3/31/04 ALL
Net Sales ($)	5313M	36991M	153501M	1040838M	385088M	3363970M		98287M
Total Assets ($)	839M	7870M	42976M	328873M	205273M	1484272M		39038M

M = $ thousand   MM = $ million
See Pages 11 through 21 for Explanation of Ratios and Data

Comparative Historical Data   Current Data Sorted by Sales

4/1/04-3/31/05 ALL	4/1/05-3/31/06 ALL	4/1/06-3/31/07 ALL	Type of Statement	0-1MM	1-3MM	3-5MM	5-10MM	10-25MM	25MM & OVER
4	6	8	Unqualified						8
2	5	4	Reviewed				2	2	2
4	5	3	Compiled				3		1
7	5	8	Tax Returns						
9	16	22	Other	1	3	1	3	3	16
				8 (4/1-9/30/06)			37 (10/1/06-3/31/07)		
26	37	45	NUMBER OF STATEMENTS	1	3	1	8	5	27
%	%	%	**ASSETS**	%	%	%	%	%	%
12.6	11.6	13.5	Cash & Equivalents						11.1
17.0	12.7	13.4	Trade Receivables (net)						17.3
38.3	40.8	40.7	Inventory						31.3
2.2	7.6	5.5	All Other Current						8.0
70.0	72.7	73.1	Total Current						67.8
11.2	10.2	13.4	Fixed Assets (net)						14.5
6.6	9.3	8.5	Intangibles (net)						12.1
12.2	7.9	5.0	All Other Non-Current						5.6
100.0	100.0	100.0	Total						100.0
			LIABILITIES						
14.2	11.4	11.8	Notes Payable-Short Term						9.0
2.1	3.7	1.8	Cur. Mat.-L.T.D.						1.4
20.7	26.2	21.7	Trade Payables						19.4
.3	.2	.3	Income Taxes Payable						.4
8.5	16.0	14.4	All Other Current						16.1
45.9	57.5	50.0	Total Current						46.3
9.4	11.9	13.0	Long-Term Debt						17.5
.3	.1	.2	Deferred Taxes						.3
20.1	11.8	3.4	All Other Non-Current						2.6
24.3	18.7	33.4	Net Worth						33.3
100.0	100.0	100.0	Total Liabilities & Net Worth						100.0
			INCOME DATA						
100.0	100.0	100.0	Net Sales						100.0
41.9	40.7	39.6	Gross Profit						40.1
37.6	39.7	36.0	Operating Expenses						37.1
4.3	1.0	3.6	Operating Profit						3.0
.2	1.0	.8	All Other Expenses (net)						.9
4.1	.0	2.9	Profit Before Taxes						2.1
			RATIOS						
3.3	2.0	2.2	Current						2.1
1.5	1.3	1.5							1.5
1.0	1.0	1.0							1.2
1.2	.7	1.0	Quick						1.1
.7	.3	.5							.6
.3	.2	.2							.2
2 233.0	1 314.5	1 279.4	Sales/Receivables						4 96.3
12 29.9	8 47.4	6 65.2							8 47.0
27 13.5	15 23.6	22 16.6							31 11.7
40 9.0	29 12.5	42 8.7	Cost of Sales/Inventory						22 16.5
63 5.8	74 4.9	89 4.1							91 4.0
96 3.8	107 3.4	130 2.8							125 2.9
17 21.8	26 14.1	25 14.8	Cost of Sales/Payables						28 13.0
28 12.9	37 9.9	40 9.1							40 9.2
60 6.1	56 6.5	62 5.9							65 5.6
8.3	9.6	7.2	Sales/Working Capital						7.2
13.9	16.8	14.2							13.6
NM	-304.9	586.1							31.3
17.8	3.2	10.6	EBIT/Interest						11.0
(22) 7.9	(32) 1.1	(38) 3.4							(25) 3.4
2.1	-5.0	-2.2							-1.8
		39.2	Net Profit + Depr., Dep.,						20.1
	(13) 7.4	7.4	Amort./Cur. Mat. L/T/D						(11) 7.4
		4.1							3.8
.1	.2	.2	Fixed/Worth						.2
.4	.5	.4							.5
NM	-7.0	1.4							1.1
.7	1.4	1.2	Debt/Worth						1.3
2.2	2.7	2.2							2.1
NM	-27.1	5.7							4.8
79.6	36.2	51.6	% Profit Before Taxes/Tangible						34.8
(20) 40.7	(26) 5.2	(40) 18.2	Net Worth						(25) 16.3
4.2	-7.9	-9.4							-7.5
25.0	16.7	21.7	% Profit Before Taxes/Total						14.4
13.2	.5	6.3	Assets						6.1
1.8	-6.8	-4.4							-1.1
107.9	85.0	92.9	Sales/Net Fixed Assets						48.9
32.7	43.1	33.8							26.1
23.0	22.5	16.7							13.1
5.2	4.7	4.9	Sales/Total Assets						4.9
3.5	3.4	2.7							2.6
2.6	2.4	2.0							1.9
.6	.5	.5	% Depr., Dep., Amort./Sales						.6
(18) .8	(30) .7	(39) .7							(26) 1.2
1.4	1.3	1.5							1.7
	3.5	2.1	% Officers', Directors'						
	(10) 5.8	(15) 4.2	Owners' Comp/Sales						
	7.1	6.1							
1284298M	3385202M	4985701M	Net Sales ($)	626M	6848M	4034M	64742M	82560M	4826891M
498638M	1444331M	2070103M	Total Assets ($)	129M	1389M	718M	21234M	32700M	2013933M

M = $ thousand   MM = $ million
See Pages 11 through 21 for Explanation of Ratios and Data

Current Data Sorted by Assets

Comparative Historical Data

						Type of Statement		
		8	12	5	9	Unqualified	44	48
	4	11	4	1		Reviewed	28	20
2	2	10	2			Compiled	24	34
10	8	4				Tax Returns	9	12
3	7	19	15	6	3	Other	51	36
	38 (4/1-9/30/06)		107 (10/1/06-3/31/07)				4/1/02-3/31/03	4/1/03-3/31/04
0-500M	500M-2MM	2-10MM	10-50MM	50-100MM	100-250MM		ALL	ALL
15	21	52	33	12	12	NUMBER OF STATEMENTS	156	150
%	%	%	%	%	%	ASSETS	%	%
25.1	13.3	8.7	15.6	5.6	6.0	Cash & Equivalents	11.9	12.4
13.1	12.0	13.0	14.5	8.4	8.8	Trade Receivables (net)	13.7	12.6
33.4	42.9	44.4	33.4	36.9	43.5	Inventory	41.2	40.1
3.7	3.7	4.9	4.9	4.3	6.2	All Other Current	4.8	6.0
75.3	71.9	71.0	68.4	55.2	64.5	Total Current	71.6	71.1
10.1	18.2	14.0	11.1	24.1	14.0	Fixed Assets (net)	14.3	15.8
3.0	1.4	5.4	10.8	13.9	19.9	Intangibles (net)	5.5	5.5
11.5	8.6	9.6	9.6	6.8	1.6	All Other Non-Current	8.6	7.6
100.0	100.0	100.0	100.0	100.0	100.0	Total	100.0	100.0
						LIABILITIES		
26.6	10.4	11.5	9.0	8.8	5.6	Notes Payable-Short Term	9.0	12.0
1.7	1.2	3.0	2.6	2.3	.7	Cur. Mat.-L.T.D.	5.6	3.7
33.7	24.1	31.0	25.3	21.0	19.0	Trade Payables	23.5	23.1
.0	.0	.3	.4	.6	.8	Income Taxes Payable	.3	.3
16.8	11.0	17.4	13.9	14.6	14.2	All Other Current	12.7	12.6
78.8	46.7	63.2	51.3	47.3	40.2	Total Current	51.1	51.7
10.4	11.6	8.3	11.1	16.6	20.7	Long-Term Debt	9.8	9.0
.0	.0	.1	.2	2.0	1.8	Deferred Taxes	.2	.2
1.9	13.5	9.4	1.3	7.3	6.9	All Other Non-Current	4.0	4.0
8.9	28.2	19.0	36.2	26.8	30.4	Net Worth	34.9	35.1
100.0	100.0	100.0	100.0	100.0	100.0	Total Liabilities & Net Worth	100.0	100.0
						INCOME DATA		
100.0	100.0	100.0	100.0	100.0	100.0	Net Sales	100.0	100.0
41.9	42.6	43.5	43.6	48.8	41.9	Gross Profit	44.2	44.3
41.6	39.9	41.8	40.5	43.6	39.1	Operating Expenses	40.3	41.6
.3	2.8	1.6	3.1	5.2	2.8	Operating Profit	4.0	2.7
2.3	.7	.2	.4	1.4	1.0	All Other Expenses (net)	.6	.5
-2.0	2.1	1.4	2.7	3.8	1.7	Profit Before Taxes	3.4	2.2
						RATIOS		
2.8	3.4	1.8	2.5	1.6	1.9		2.6	2.4
1.5	1.5	1.3	1.3	1.2	1.5	Current	1.6	1.5
1.0	1.0	.9	1.0	.9	1.4		1.1	1.1
1.5	1.0	.6	1.2	.6	1.0		1.2	1.1
.3	.4	(51) .2	.5	.2	.2	Quick	.4 (149)	.5
.0	.1	.1	.1	.1	.1		.1	.1
0 UND	0 755.4	1 291.9	2 227.3	1 696.9	1 360.5		3 120.2	2 154.3
0 UND	6 61.9	5 77.8	10 37.4	4 81.3	5 73.6	Sales/Receivables	10 36.3	8 47.5
10 36.4	22 16.8	14 26.1	15 24.0	14 26.4	12 31.3		25 14.6	22 16.9
0 UND	44 8.2	39 9.4	28 13.2	76 4.8	69 5.3		50 7.4	48 7.5
66 5.5	71 5.1	71 5.2	82 4.4	103 3.5	94 3.9	Cost of Sales/Inventory	88 4.2	80 4.5
103 3.5	110 3.3	128 2.9	102 3.6	168 2.2	129 2.8		126 2.9	124 2.9
0 UND	16 23.3	20 18.1	23 16.0	36 10.1	32 11.4		26 14.3	23 15.8
7 53.3	42 8.6	47 7.8	42 8.6	46 7.9	39 9.4	Cost of Sales/Payables	39 9.4	42 8.6
40 9.2	53 6.9	74 5.0	68 5.4	79 4.6	54 6.8		62 5.9	66 5.6
9.2	6.3	10.9	5.8	12.4	6.2		7.4	6.6
53.8	11.8	26.3	25.4	34.0	13.6	Sales/Working Capital	13.2	14.2
-132.5	NM	-44.6	NM	-55.1	18.0		57.3	66.8
	10.9	28.0	35.2	13.7	10.5		19.6	17.0
(18) 3.4	(46) 5.9	(28) 8.8	(11) 5.8	(11) 2.9		EBIT/Interest	(135) 6.3	(137) 4.3
.7	.3	2.4	1.9	.4			1.9	.8
						Net Profit + Depr., Dep.,	8.2	9.7
						Amort./Cur. Mat. L/T/D	(27) 3.2 (38) 3.2	
							1.2	.7
.0	.1	.1	.2	.7	.3		.1	.2
.2	.4	.5	.5	1.3	.9	Fixed/Worth	.4	.4
-1.7	3.6	1.6	1.9	NM	-.9		1.2	1.1
.6	.6	.9	.9	1.3	1.4		.8	.8
4.2	2.7	3.2	2.1	4.8	2.8	Debt/Worth	2.1	2.0
-3.1	31.2	NM	15.9	NM	-7.9		5.7	4.7
54.9	87.5	59.4	95.2			% Profit Before Taxes/Tangible	67.9	42.1
(10) 20.2	(17) 31.4	(39) 24.8	(27) 26.8			Net Worth	(133) 31.5	(131) 22.3
-21.4	.0	5.9	9.8				11.9	1.6
24.6	14.0	21.1	19.0	16.1	12.3	% Profit Before Taxes/Total	20.0	15.9
11.7	7.0	6.9	11.2	11.5	5.5	Assets	9.0	7.2
-11.6	-1.6	-3.1	3.0	2.4	.5		2.0	-.6
UND	175.0	119.3	54.2	20.2	55.3		67.1	64.0
175.1	28.5	54.6	29.4	12.0	20.5	Sales/Net Fixed Assets	30.6	30.0
38.0	10.7	20.9	20.3	8.2	10.1		15.1	11.2
20.9	6.0	5.4	4.4	3.7	4.2		4.4	4.5
5.5	4.0	4.2	2.8	2.7	2.4	Sales/Total Assets	3.0	3.0
2.8	2.5	3.1	2.2	1.8	1.6		2.2	2.2
	.5	.4	.5	1.1	.5		.5	.5
(14) .8	(41) .7	(26) 1.2	(11) 1.4	(10) .8		% Depr., Dep., Amort./Sales	(121) .9	(125) 1.0
1.1	1.1	1.7	1.9	1.7			1.7	1.6
	.9						1.6	1.5
(15) 2.0						% Officers', Directors'	(41) 3.5	(53) 3.7
3.4						Owners' Comp/Sales	6.9	7.4
21822M	111845M	1140731M	2771169M	2231087M	5203181M	Net Sales ($)	12560259M	11705218M
3494M	27689M	263114M	794468M	858728M	1883019M	Total Assets ($)	4694180M	4365339M

M = $ thousand   MM = $ million
See Pages 11 through 21 for Explanation of Ratios and Data

Comparative Historical Data | Current Data Sorted by Sales

Type of Statement	4/1/04-3/31/05 ALL	4/1/05-3/31/06 ALL	4/1/06-3/31/07 ALL	0-1MM	1-3MM	3-5MM	5-10MM	10-25MM	25MM & OVER
Unqualified	38	38	34					6	28
Reviewed	22	17	20		3	3	4		10
Compiled	14	10	16		3	1	2	7	3
Tax Returns	15	18	22	6	4	4	1	7	
Other	34	60	53		4	2	6	11	30
				38 (4/1-9/30/06)			**107 (10/1/06-3/31/07)**		
NUMBER OF STATEMENTS	123	143	145	6	14	10	13	31	71
	%	%	%	%	%	%	%	%	%
ASSETS									
Cash & Equivalents	12.9	13.6	12.2		15.9	17.0	16.1	7.7	10.5
Trade Receivables (net)	13.8	13.9	12.5		12.3	11.0	13.8	15.5	11.7
Inventory	42.1	37.6	39.9		41.7	40.2	31.8	44.2	39.4
All Other Current	4.6	4.7	4.7		4.1	1.2	6.9	4.1	5.5
Total Current	73.4	69.8	69.1		73.9	69.4	68.6	71.6	67.0
Fixed Assets (net)	13.9	14.4	14.4		11.8	14.9	17.2	13.1	14.4
Intangibles (net)	4.3	8.1	7.7		4.7	7.6	2.6	8.8	9.4
All Other Non-Current	8.4	7.7	8.8		9.6	8.1	11.5	6.5	9.2
Total	100.0	100.0	100.0		100.0	100.0	100.0	100.0	100.0
LIABILITIES									
Notes Payable-Short Term	12.4	9.4	11.6		18.4	4.7	8.7	13.7	8.7
Cur. Mat.-L.T.D.	1.8	3.0	2.3		.4	3.2	1.6	2.8	2.2
Trade Payables	26.2	26.1	27.2		13.3	30.3	20.7	32.7	26.9
Income Taxes Payable	.2	.3	.3		.0	.0	.0	.0	.6
All Other Current	12.0	13.3	15.1		9.0	15.0	15.1	14.9	15.9
Total Current	52.7	51.9	56.5		41.0	53.2	46.1	64.2	54.3
Long-Term Debt	10.4	13.1	11.3		9.0	15.2	16.4	12.1	9.7
Deferred Taxes	.2	.2	.4		.0	.0	.0	.1	.7
All Other Non-Current	3.8	7.0	7.0		2.0	.8	5.3	7.8	6.0
Net Worth	32.9	27.8	24.8		48.0	30.8	32.2	15.9	29.3
Total Liabilities & Net Worth	100.0	100.0	100.0		100.0	100.0	100.0	100.0	100.0
INCOME DATA									
Net Sales	100.0	100.0	100.0		100.0	100.0	100.0	100.0	100.0
Gross Profit	38.8	41.6	43.5		46.0	46.6	40.4	40.3	45.0
Operating Expenses	35.7	38.7	41.2		43.6	43.8	35.7	39.4	42.1
Operating Profit	3.1	2.9	2.4		2.4	2.8	4.6	.9	2.9
All Other Expenses (net)	.2	.6	.7		.7	.0	.9	.6	.5
Profit Before Taxes	2.8	2.3	1.7		1.7	2.9	3.7	.3	2.4
RATIOS									
Current	2.8	2.3	2.2		6.0	2.8	2.5	2.2	1.9
	1.4	1.4	1.3		1.7	1.7	1.4	1.3	1.2
	1.1	1.0	1.0		1.2	.7	1.0	.9	.9
Quick	1.1	1.0	.8		4.6	1.7	1.2	.7	.9
	.5	.5	(144) .3		.4	.4	.5	.3	(70) .2
	.1	.1	.1		.1	.2	.1	.1	.1
Sales/Receivables	2 240.3	2 227.0	1 438.6		0 UND	1 381.3	0 834.5	2 229.4	1 244.5
	6 58.6	6 60.2	5 71.3		1 274.5	7 49.0	6 57.4	7 52.4	5 71.3
	30 12.2	22 16.8	14 25.3		19 18.9	23 15.9	26 13.9	15 25.1	14 27.0
Cost of Sales/Inventory	31 11.6	40 9.1	44 8.4		56 6.5	15 24.8	21 17.2	41 8.8	48 7.7
	76 4.8	74 4.9	78 4.7		79 4.6	84 4.3	46 8.0	70 5.2	88 4.2
	124 2.9	119 3.1	121 3.0		130 2.8	277 1.3	77 4.7	99 3.7	127 2.9
Cost of Sales/Payables	22 16.5	21 17.5	20 18.2		0 UND	5 71.5	10 35.4	16 22.4	31 11.6
	34 10.7	42 8.7	42 8.6		17 21.9	49 7.4	28 13.2	38 9.7	46 8.0
	61 6.0	68 5.3	61 5.9		47 7.8	72 5.0	56 6.6	52 7.1	72 5.1
Sales/Working Capital	6.8	6.8	7.6		6.9	5.4	5.6	10.6	8.2
	15.5	19.1	21.8		18.0	10.4	22.6	17.6	28.0
	70.2	237.9	-132.0		56.4	-16.3	NM	-127.7	-62.5
EBIT/Interest	22.4	15.6	17.2		9.3		13.5	17.6	26.3
	(103) 6.2	(122) 5.5	(122) 5.1		(10) 1.6		(12) 6.5	(27) 2.7	(61) 6.4
	2.0	1.2	1.0		-.5		.4	1.3	1.9
Net Profit + Depr., Dep., Amort./Cur. Mat. L/T/D	7.9	13.7	15.9						9.7
	(26) 5.2	(23) 7.0	(21) 6.9						(15) 5.4
	2.8	1.7	2.4						2.3
Fixed/Worth	.1	.2	.1		.0	.1	.1	.1	.2
	.3	.5	.5		.2	.3	.5	.7	.6
	1.0	4.0	2.7		NM	NM	NM	-2.8	2.4
Debt/Worth	.9	.8	.9		.1	.5	1.0	.9	1.3
	2.0	2.7	2.9		1.0	3.2	2.1	3.3	2.8
	5.6	20.1	42.6		NM	NM	NM	-25.7	26.0
% Profit Before Taxes/Tangible Net Worth	48.3	66.7	62.0		47.5		130.0	67.1	61.9
	(107) 23.9	(110) 24.5	(110) 27.9		(11) 6.3		(10) 64.9	(23) 21.6	(55) 30.1
	4.9	5.6	6.3		-17.9		30.3	13.8	11.5
% Profit Before Taxes/Total Assets	18.0	18.0	17.5		14.3	23.8	30.7	11.0	17.9
	7.4	7.7	7.9		3.4	7.2	14.8	4.6	9.9
	1.8	.2	-.4		-6.8	.4	.2	-3.1	1.0
Sales/Net Fixed Assets	88.4	89.0	95.7		206.7	109.5	61.1	127.0	79.2
	38.9	36.7	37.4		45.1	50.9	26.8	44.0	30.2
	12.3	14.0	17.2		19.2	10.7	14.4	28.9	14.0
Sales/Total Assets	5.1	4.8	5.3		5.7	8.2	5.9	5.5	4.4
	3.3	3.0	3.5		3.8	2.7	4.0	4.3	3.4
	2.2	2.3	2.6		2.4	1.5	3.0	3.0	2.3
% Depr., Dep., Amort./Sales	.4	.5	.5				.5	.3	.6
	(100) .8	(109) .8	(109) .8				(10) .8	(24) .7	(58) 1.0
	1.4	1.4	1.5				1.1	1.2	1.8
% Officers', Directors', Owners' Comp/Sales	1.1	1.3	1.8						
	(40) 2.4	(35) 3.2	(34) 3.2						
	5.5	5.2	6.3						
Net Sales ($)	10415017M	13141263M	11479835M	3016M	28406M	41103M	92912M	539516M	10774882M
Total Assets ($)	3790794M	4634463M	3830512M	2129M	9160M	18268M	25759M	140392M	3634804M

Current Data Sorted by Assets								Comparative Historical Data	

							Type of Statement		
							Unqualified	10	12
1	3	5	3				Reviewed	23	23
2	11	16	4				Compiled	29	44
13	11	14					Tax Returns	15	22
2	11	3	5				Other	33	32
	30 (4/1-9/30/06)	9	83 (10/1/06-3/31/07)					4/1/02-3/31/03	4/1/03-3/31/04
0-500M	500M-2MM	2-10MM	10-50MM	50-100MM	100-250MM			ALL	ALL
18	36	47	12				**NUMBER OF STATEMENTS**	110	133
%	%	%	%	%	%		**ASSETS**	%	%
8.9	9.8	10.0	7.3				Cash & Equivalents	8.1	9.1
1.6	5.5	8.1	10.4	D	D		Trade Receivables (net)	7.2	6.6
12.5	19.4	16.1	12.5	A	A		Inventory	15.4	16.5
.5	4.1	1.2	2.0	T	T		All Other Current	3.1	1.7
23.5	38.8	35.4	32.1	A	A		Total Current	33.8	34.0
57.4	47.2	50.3	53.3				Fixed Assets (net)	52.4	53.7
11.2	6.7	6.4	10.8	N	N		Intangibles (net)	6.6	4.9
7.9	7.3	7.8	3.8	O	O		All Other Non-Current	7.2	7.4
100.0	100.0	100.0	100.0	T	T		Total	100.0	100.0
				A	A		**LIABILITIES**		
7.2	8.6	6.3	8.3	V	V		Notes Payable-Short Term	7.0	10.8
18.1	7.0	8.9	6.0	A	A		Cur. Mat.-L.T.D.	8.2	10.2
10.5	15.4	12.4	14.2	I	I		Trade Payables	12.6	13.2
.2	.0	.1	.2	L	L		Income Taxes Payable	.3	.2
8.0	5.2	7.1	16.9	A	A		All Other Current	9.7	8.2
44.0	36.3	34.8	45.6	B	B		Total Current	37.8	42.7
63.0	28.6	24.0	24.2	L	L		Long-Term Debt	31.7	29.4
.0	.0	.3	1.3	E	E		Deferred Taxes	.8	.5
3.5	9.0	8.8	21.0				All Other Non-Current	9.3	10.0
-10.5	26.1	32.2	8.0	E	E		Net Worth	20.4	17.4
100.0	100.0	100.0	100.0				Total Liabilties & Net Worth	100.0	100.0
							INCOME DATA		
100.0	100.0	100.0	100.0				Net Sales	100.0	100.0
44.2	43.5	50.7	44.9				Gross Profit	46.7	47.1
40.5	39.2	47.3	41.1				Operating Expenses	44.8	46.0
3.7	4.3	3.4	3.8				Operating Profit	1.9	1.1
.9	.9	1.4	2.7				All Other Expenses (net)	.5	.5
2.7	3.3	2.0	1.1				Profit Before Taxes	1.3	.6
							RATIOS		
1.5	1.7	1.6	.9					1.5	1.4
.9	1.0	.8	.7				Current	.9	.9
.3	.5	.6	.6					.6	.5
.5	.8	.8	.6					.7	.7
.3	.4	.4	.4				Quick	(109) .4	(131) .3
.1	.2	.3	.2					.2	.1
0 UND	0 UND	2 154.4	8 48.0					1 342.1	0 991.3
0 UND	2 194.6	7 49.6	12 30.9				Sales/Receivables	4 94.0	3 128.6
2 211.3	13 27.4	19 19.1	19 19.0					12 29.4	10 35.1
0 UND	14 26.0	22 16.3	18 20.8					24 15.2	21 17.4
20 18.0	27 13.7	35 10.4	30 12.2				Cost of Sales/Inventory	35 10.6	33 11.1
34 10.7	45 8.1	53 6.9	43 8.5					47 7.7	51 7.1
0 UND	3 106.1	17 22.1	25 14.8					12 30.0	13 28.7
1 404.7	25 14.5	34 10.9	30 12.0				Cost of Sales/Payables	27 13.6	27 13.3
24 15.3	42 8.7	46 7.9	41 9.0					46 8.0	47 7.7
48.7	16.0	11.7	-135.8					29.8	34.9
NM	846.3	-58.6	-25.4				Sales/Working Capital	-93.3	-43.6
-15.3	-14.2	-17.9	-10.0					-17.7	-12.2
3.9	7.8	3.5	3.4					3.6	3.8
(17) 1.3	(32) 2.3	(46) 1.8	2.5				EBIT/Interest	(106) 1.6	(128) 1.3
-.3	1.0	.5	.8					.2	-.4
								3.3	2.8
							Net Profit + Depr., Dep., Amort./Cur. Mat. L/T/D	(24) 1.8	(24) 1.4
								1.2	.9
1.3	.7	1.0	2.4					1.2	1.2
NM	1.8	2.8	15.2				Fixed/Worth	2.7	3.0
-1.2	-6.2	8.4	-10.8					-16.7	-8.8
1.2	.9	1.5	2.1					1.4	1.3
NM	2.3	3.1	20.8				Debt/Worth	4.4	3.7
-2.5	-19.2	13.6	-21.5					-27.6	-18.0
	38.4	24.7						26.2	35.7
	(25) 20.9	(40) 8.4					% Profit Before Taxes/Tangible Net Worth	(77) 7.6	(95) 6.7
	.8	-19.6						-4.7	-8.1
17.5	16.7	8.8	8.4					8.2	7.6
7.3	6.8	2.5	6.0				% Profit Before Taxes/Total Assets	2.0	1.2
-6.1	.0	-2.8	-.9					-2.9	-4.0
12.4	16.1	7.7	7.9					9.5	9.0
8.1	8.7	5.8	5.3				Sales/Net Fixed Assets	5.0	5.2
4.4	4.4	3.5	3.5					3.5	3.4
5.4	4.4	3.5	3.7					4.2	4.0
3.4	3.2	2.7	2.9				Sales/Total Assets	2.9	2.9
2.8	2.3	1.8	1.7					1.9	1.9
3.3	2.2	3.2	3.1					3.6	3.8
(16) 4.6	(33) 3.7	(43) 4.2	4.3				% Depr., Dep., Amort./Sales	(104) 5.4	(121) 5.4
8.2	6.4	7.4	6.6					7.6	8.3
4.0	1.2	.8						1.5	1.8
(11) 4.8	(19) 2.8	(15) 2.8					% Officers', Directors' Owners' Comp/Sales	(50) 4.0	(56) 4.0
6.0	4.4	3.7						5.4	7.3
19992M	125788M	655374M	718542M				Net Sales ($)	1466779M	2092648M
5080M	37136M	232218M	260855M				Total Assets ($)	792182M	1185522M

M = $ thousand   MM = $ million
See Pages 11 through 21 for Explanation of Ratios and Data

Comparative Historical Data　　　　　Current Data Sorted by Sales

			Type of Statement						
9	4	8	Unqualified	1			1	3	4
21	16	24	Reviewed	1	8	2	2	10	9
27	23	27	Compiled	1	14	7	9	2	2
12	20	27	Tax Returns	9	14	3	1	1	
25	37	27	Other	1	7	3	3		6
4/1/04- 3/31/05	4/1/05- 3/31/06	4/1/06- 3/31/07			30 (4/1-9/30/06)			83 (10/1/06-3/31/07)	
ALL	ALL	ALL		0-1MM	1-3MM	3-5MM	5-10MM	10-25MM	25MM & OVER
94	100	113	**NUMBER OF STATEMENTS**	12	29	15	16	22	19
%	%	%	**ASSETS**	%	%	%	%	%	%
9.0	10.3	9.4	Cash & Equivalents	9.1	6.9	17.2	12.8	8.7	5.5
7.3	7.2	6.5	Trade Receivables (net)	1.8	4.3	4.3	7.1	8.9	11.4
16.5	15.9	16.2	Inventory	5.1	15.8	19.1	19.1	19.7	15.1
1.8	2.3	2.1	All Other Current	1.5	2.8	2.2	2.5	.6	2.7
34.6	35.7	34.3	Total Current	17.4	29.8	42.7	41.5	37.9	34.7
53.2	49.9	50.8	Fixed Assets (net)	56.9	55.6	46.5	47.1	46.1	51.3
5.4	6.8	7.8	Intangibles (net)	17.1	6.2	6.9	3.3	6.5	10.1
6.7	7.7	7.2	All Other Non-Current	8.6	8.4	3.8	8.1	9.5	3.9
100.0	100.0	100.0	Total	100.0	100.0	100.0	100.0	100.0	100.0
			LIABILITIES						
12.8	9.1	7.4	Notes Payable-Short Term	2.5	8.6	10.1	9.0	6.5	6.3
8.6	7.5	9.5	Cur. Mat.-L.T.D.	22.8	7.7	5.6	7.8	10.4	7.0
15.2	15.1	13.2	Trade Payables	10.1	8.4	17.0	12.7	16.4	16.5
.2	.1	.1	Income Taxes Payable	.0	.1	.0	.0	.0	.4
10.5	14.8	7.7	All Other Current	5.7	5.6	5.3	5.1	8.4	15.1
47.3	46.6	37.9	Total Current	41.1	30.4	38.1	34.6	41.8	45.3
28.5	28.1	31.7	Long-Term Debt	77.8	37.9	17.8	25.2	20.7	22.3
.5	.3	.3	Deferred Taxes	.0	.0	.0	.0	.6	.9
7.0	10.0	9.3	All Other Non-Current	6.1	8.6	4.4	8.8	9.9	16.1
16.7	15.0	20.9	Net Worth	-24.9	23.1	39.7	31.4	27.1	15.5
100.0	100.0	100.0	Total Liabilities & Net Worth	100.0	100.0	100.0	100.0	100.0	100.0
			INCOME DATA						
100.0	100.0	100.0	Net Sales	100.0	100.0	100.0	100.0	100.0	100.0
48.7	46.8	46.7	Gross Profit	48.4	46.2	46.4	47.9	45.6	47.1
47.4	44.8	43.0	Operating Expenses	40.4	40.5	42.9	46.6	43.7	44.3
1.3	2.0	3.8	Operating Profit	8.0	5.6	3.5	1.3	1.8	2.8
.3	.3	1.3	All Other Expenses (net)	2.0	1.9	.7	-.1	2.2	.7
.9	1.7	2.4	Profit Before Taxes	6.1	3.7	2.8	1.4	-.4	2.1
			RATIOS						
1.1	1.8	1.5	Current	2.2	1.6	1.9	1.5	1.6	.8
.8	.8	.8		.7	1.1	1.1	1.1	.8	.7
.5	.5	.5		.2	.5	.6	.6	.5	.6
.6	.7	.7	Quick	1.2	.6	1.3	.6	1.0	.5
(93) .3	.4	.4		.3	.3	.5	.5	.3	.4
.1	.1	.2		.1	.1	.2	.3	.2	.2
1 275.9	1 440.4	0 768.5	Sales/Receivables	0 UND	0 UND	0 999.8	1 377.0	3 144.4	7 48.7
5 69.1	4 84.5	5 71.0		0 UND	2 229.5	2 192.2	8 47.2	6 56.6	12 30.2
14 26.5	13 28.2	14 26.6		1 433.5	14 25.9	9 39.7	19 18.9	13 28.0	18 19.8
21 17.1	19 19.3	19 19.1	Cost of Sales/Inventory	0 UND	18 20.2	13 28.4	26 14.0	24 15.1	21 17.4
32 11.5	29 12.4	31 11.7		7 55.9	31 11.9	24 14.9	33 11.2	37 9.8	31 11.7
48 7.7	44 8.3	46 8.0		22 16.8	42 8.7	104 3.5	48 7.5	50 7.3	41 8.9
17 21.0	8 46.5	9 42.0	Cost of Sales/Payables	0 UND	1 415.6	0 999.8	15 24.0	22 16.7	25 14.7
32 11.4	27 13.5	26 14.1		0 UND	15 24.7	16 23.4	33 11.1	29 12.4	35 10.3
47 7.8	45 8.2	42 8.8		49 7.5	36 10.2	62 5.9	45 8.1	46 8.0	42 8.8
92.3	23.7	23.6	Sales/Working Capital	21.2	13.9	15.9	15.6	23.8	-58.6
-52.9	-54.7	-105.9		-98.0	801.0	60.8	161.9	-36.9	-34.9
-12.3	-11.5	-16.5		-9.2	-12.4	-21.0	-21.0	-14.4	-16.5
4.7	4.2	3.9	EBIT/Interest	3.5	4.5	12.6	3.8	3.2	3.4
(91) 1.5	(90) 1.3	(107) 1.9		(11) 2.7	(28) 2.3	(13) 2.5	(14) 1.4	1.0	2.3
-.1	.0	.7		1.2	.7	1.0	.3	-.7	1.0
3.1	2.6	2.6	Net Profit + Depr., Dep., Amort./Cur. Mat. L/T/D						
(23) 1.9	(12) 1.8	(13) 2.2							
1.3	.8	1.1							
1.1	1.0	1.3	Fixed/Worth	2.9	1.0	.9	.7	1.0	1.8
2.2	3.2	3.0		NM	2.9	1.6	1.8	2.9	5.0
-23.8	-6.2	-13.9		-.4	-6.1	13.3	5.1	NM	34.6
1.3	1.3	1.3	Debt/Worth	2.9	.9	.5	1.0	1.4	2.2
2.8	4.5	3.3		NM	2.3	2.2	2.2	4.2	8.8
-47.2	-9.3	-27.6		-1.5	-8.2	14.9	6.8	NM	61.5
24.8	38.7	36.4	% Profit Before Taxes/Tangible Net Worth		56.3	74.9	14.7	18.9	47.0
(69) 6.5	(72) 12.4	(82) 12.6		(19) 20.9	(12) 18.5	(13) 3.8	(17) .0	(15) 23.1	
-4.1	-1.8	-6.6			.3	.1	-32.4	-32.5	4.7
7.2	9.8	10.6	% Profit Before Taxes/Total Assets	15.7	17.3	18.5	8.6	6.1	8.7
2.0	1.9	4.3		8.0	8.2	3.9	1.5	-.3	6.3
-4.0	-3.0	-1.4		2.1	-2.4	-.1	-4.2	-5.0	.1
9.3	10.9	9.6	Sales/Net Fixed Assets	11.7	9.6	17.1	10.8	10.8	8.0
6.3	6.5	6.5		8.1	4.9	5.7	5.7	6.8	6.9
3.7	3.8	4.3		1.9	3.1	3.1	4.5	4.9	4.8
4.2	4.3	4.1	Sales/Total Assets	3.9	4.1	4.8	3.5	4.5	4.0
3.3	3.1	3.0		2.6	2.8	3.5	2.7	2.9	3.5
2.2	2.1	2.2		1.5	1.7	2.5	1.8	2.5	2.7
3.1	3.2	3.1	% Depr., Dep., Amort./Sales	2.8	3.5	1.9	3.0	3.1	3.1
(90) 4.6	(91) 3.8	(104) 4.3		(11) 5.1	(25) 4.7	(14) 3.4	4.4	(20) 3.7	(18) 3.9
6.8	5.6	6.7		8.4	10.1	5.8	6.3	4.3	6.4
2.1	2.1	1.5	% Officers', Directors' Owners' Comp/Sales		1.9				
(41) 3.8	(47) 4.1	(46) 3.2			(20) 3.5				
7.1	7.0	5.2			5.7				
1320645M	1152762M	1519696M	Net Sales ($)	6810M	59933M	60221M	115803M	350402M	926527M
611864M	586358M	535289M	Total Assets ($)	5822M	31406M	21926M	51030M	112939M	312166M

© RMA 2007

M = $ thousand　　MM = $ million
See Pages 11 through 21 for Explanation of Ratios and Data

Current Data Sorted by Assets   Comparative Historical Data

Type of Statement	0-500M	500M-2MM	2-10MM	10-50MM	50-100MM	100-250MM		4/1/02-3/31/03 ALL	4/1/03-3/31/04 ALL
Unqualified			7	15	6	2		44	33
Reviewed	3	24	61	16	2			99	96
Compiled	9	31	25	5				65	90
Tax Returns	12	21	2		1			34	30
Other	5	9	22	9	2	5		32	33
	139 (4/1-9/30/06)			155 (10/1/06-3/31/07)					
NUMBER OF STATEMENTS	29	85	117	45	11	7		274	282

ASSETS	%	%	%	%	%	%		%	%
Cash & Equivalents	17.0	18.5	14.3	11.2	11.7			12.7	14.7
Trade Receivables (net)	19.5	26.3	28.7	30.2	24.4			25.0	26.4
Inventory	13.2	11.8	12.8	11.7	11.5			10.5	9.4
All Other Current	.9	1.9	2.1	2.6	2.4			3.1	2.9
Total Current	50.6	58.5	57.9	55.7	50.0			51.3	53.4
Fixed Assets (net)	24.8	21.6	26.5	30.1	29.3			32.0	29.5
Intangibles (net)	16.1	11.9	8.8	8.2	9.6			7.3	8.0
All Other Non-Current	8.4	8.0	6.8	6.0	11.1			9.5	9.1
Total	100.0	100.0	100.0	100.0	100.0			100.0	100.0

LIABILITIES									
Notes Payable-Short Term	10.7	10.2	9.4	8.9	5.2			8.6	7.9
Cur. Mat.-L.T.D.	7.7	4.9	3.7	4.9	2.7			5.1	4.1
Trade Payables	29.9	15.4	16.1	23.0	18.8			16.1	15.4
Income Taxes Payable	.1	.0	.2	.5	.0			.1	.2
All Other Current	20.0	26.1	23.1	18.2	27.2			18.6	18.1
Total Current	68.4	56.7	52.4	55.6	53.9			48.6	45.6
Long-Term Debt	24.4	14.9	15.2	18.4	28.1			18.9	18.0
Deferred Taxes	.0	.2	.5	.5	.0			.6	.5
All Other Non-Current	2.5	9.0	4.7	2.9	4.0			4.3	5.4
Net Worth	4.7	19.3	27.2	22.6	14.0			27.6	30.6
Total Liabilities & Net Worth	100.0	100.0	100.0	100.0	100.0			100.0	100.0

INCOME DATA									
Net Sales	100.0	100.0	100.0	100.0	100.0			100.0	100.0
Gross Profit	15.5	17.7	18.1	15.4	16.4			23.1	21.7
Operating Expenses	14.4	17.0	16.3	13.5	15.1			22.2	20.0
Operating Profit	1.1	.6	1.8	1.9	1.3			.8	1.8
All Other Expenses (net)	.2	.3	.1	.5	.6			.1	.0
Profit Before Taxes	.9	.4	1.7	1.4	.7			.7	1.7

RATIOS									
	1.7	1.5	1.5	1.3	1.2			1.5	1.8
Current	1.1	1.0	1.0	1.0	1.0			1.1	1.1
	.6	.7	.8	.8	.9			.8	.9
	1.6	1.2	1.1	.9	.8			1.1	1.4
Quick	.6	.8	.8	.7	.7			.8	.8
	.3	.5	.5	.5	.6			.5	.6
	1 333.7	10 35.5	13 28.4	11 32.2	13 27.3			12 30.3	13 28.7
Sales/Receivables	8 45.1	17 20.9	21 17.7	22 16.9	20 18.7			22 16.8	21 17.0
	15 23.9	26 14.1	30 12.2	34 10.8	24 14.9			33 10.9	33 11.0
	1 612.9	4 97.3	4 81.9	4 82.9	6 61.9			5 76.9	4 93.7
Cost of Sales/Inventory	4 95.4	8 47.2	9 39.3	9 40.5	12 30.7			11 34.2	9 42.5
	12 30.9	14 25.2	21 17.4	15 28.4	13 28.4			20 18.6	15 23.8
	0 UND	6 58.3	9 40.4	10 35.7	10 34.9			11 34.8	9 42.6
Cost of Sales/Payables	5 73.7	12 30.8	14 26.5	14 25.6	15 25.2			17 21.5	14 25.4
	12 29.8	19 19.0	20 17.9	21 17.8	18 20.0			26 14.2	22 16.5
	36.6	26.6	27.7	29.6	70.9			18.9	16.5
Sales/Working Capital	491.7	999.8	625.4	999.8	-485.3			137.2	90.1
	-19.3	-27.6	-47.3	-32.5	-29.7			-29.9	-58.4
	8.5	3.8	6.2	5.2	2.7			4.5	7.9
EBIT/Interest	(24) 2.5	(81) 1.5	(113) 2.2	(44) 2.5	2.1			(253) 1.7	(262) 3.2
	.2	-.8	1.0	1.4	1.2			.1	1.5
		4.7	4.2	2.7				2.8	4.9
Net Profit + Depr., Dep., Amort./Cur. Mat. L/T/D		(13) 2.9	(41) 1.8	(18) 2.0				(93) 1.9	(94) 2.3
		1.5	1.2	1.0				.8	1.4
	.3	.4	.6	.5	1.5			.5	.5
Fixed/Worth	4.5	2.4	1.4	1.9	3.7			1.4	1.3
	-.7	-1.0	9.9	-10.7	14.8			9.2	6.1
	1.9	1.6	1.5	2.5	3.8			1.3	1.1
Debt/Worth	13.7	11.1	4.3	4.7	9.6			3.1	2.9
	-3.7	-5.6	31.6	-44.2	33.2			29.6	15.9
	40.9	26.1	35.7	46.3				22.3	42.0
% Profit Before Taxes/Tangible Net Worth	(17) 5.5	(50) 7.9	(90) 13.3	(31) 21.0				(216) 8.6	(225) 17.0
	.0	-4.5	1.7	13.6				-1.9	5.1
	13.6	5.9	8.2	8.3	6.2			5.8	10.2
% Profit Before Taxes/Total Assets	2.8	1.1	2.9	5.6	2.1			1.9	4.4
	-4.4	-3.4	.1	1.4	1.1			-2.5	1.3
	173.0	50.1	43.6	52.2	35.8			25.1	30.4
Sales/Net Fixed Assets	67.0	30.1	19.9	21.7	15.3			14.0	16.9
	10.4	15.6	11.2	8.6	11.7			7.4	8.7
	17.7	6.8	5.9	8.0	7.9			5.1	5.6
Sales/Total Assets	9.8	5.1	4.3	4.9	6.0			3.6	3.9
	3.8	3.7	3.1	2.8	2.9			2.7	3.0
	.2	.7	.7	.5	.4			1.1	1.0
% Depr., Dep., Amort./Sales	(17) .9	(66) 1.1	(113) 1.1	(41) 1.0	(10) 1.0			(260) 1.8	(261) 1.5
	1.8	2.0	1.7	2.1	1.7			2.8	2.5
	1.6	1.0	.7					1.3	1.0
% Officers', Directors' Owners' Comp/Sales	(12) 2.5	(56) 2.4	(65) 1.5					(144) 2.7	(139) 2.3
	3.4	3.5	2.9					4.8	4.5
Net Sales ($)	85053M	539242M	2719406M	4421020M	4334508M	3827632M		9141961M	10788597M
Total Assets ($)	8164M	97920M	529267M	804432M	785378M	978478M		2676901M	3070118M

M = $ thousand   MM = $ million
See Pages 11 through 21 for Explanation of Ratios and Data

Comparative Historical Data | Current Data Sorted by Sales

				Type of Statement						
36		31	30	Unqualified					4	26
98		89	106	Reviewed	3	3	6	24	36	34
69		61	70	Compiled		9	12	24	15	10
31		31	36	Tax Returns	1	11	13	8	1	2
49		63	52	Other	2	3	3	10	15	19
4/1/04-3/31/05		4/1/05-3/31/06	4/1/06-3/31/07			139 (4/1-9/30/06)			155 (10/1/06-3/31/07)	
ALL		ALL	ALL		0-1MM	1-3MM	3-5MM	5-10MM	10-25MM	25MM & OVER
283		275	294	NUMBER OF STATEMENTS	6	26	34	66	71	91
%		%	%	ASSETS	%	%	%	%	%	%
12.7		16.5	14.9	Cash & Equivalents	18.5	16.3	20.0	14.1		10.6
28.0		29.5	27.3	Trade Receivables (net)	19.7	24.7	22.6	32.7		30.0
11.2		11.1	12.4	Inventory	13.8	10.6	13.6	12.1		12.1
2.1		2.2	2.2	All Other Current	1.1	.9	1.7	1.7		3.6
53.9		59.3	56.8	Total Current	53.1	52.5	58.0	60.6		56.4
29.7		26.4	25.7	Fixed Assets (net)	21.6	21.0	22.8	25.6		30.0
7.9		6.6	10.3	Intangibles (net)	13.5	19.7	11.7	8.1		6.9
8.5		7.7	7.2	All Other Non-Current	11.7	6.8	7.6	5.7		6.7
100.0		100.0	100.0	Total	100.0	100.0	100.0	100.0		100.0
				LIABILITIES						
9.3		10.7	9.8	Notes Payable-Short Term	14.9	9.6	7.1	11.2		9.5
4.8		4.6	4.6	Cur. Mat.-L.T.D.	7.4	7.8	3.7	3.8		3.9
16.8		18.2	18.2	Trade Payables	20.3	19.5	14.4	16.3		21.7
.1		.2	.2	Income Taxes Payable	.0	.1	.1	.2		.2
17.7		17.5	22.8	All Other Current	26.3	18.6	33.1	22.9		16.3
48.8		51.2	55.6	Total Current	68.9	55.7	58.4	54.4		51.7
18.1		15.7	17.0	Long-Term Debt	18.5	19.5	14.7	15.9		17.1
.6		.5	.4	Deferred Taxes	.2	.1	.1	.4		.8
5.6		6.3	5.5	All Other Non-Current	12.4	7.6	4.7	5.3		3.7
26.9		26.4	21.6	Net Worth	.0	17.2	22.1	24.1		26.7
100.0		100.0	100.0	Total Liabilties & Net Worth	100.0	100.0	100.0	100.0		100.0
				INCOME DATA						
100.0		100.0	100.0	Net Sales	100.0	100.0	100.0	100.0		100.0
20.6		17.8	17.1	Gross Profit	21.0	17.6	19.2	18.6		13.0
19.8		16.5	15.7	Operating Expenses	20.1	16.8	18.3	16.3		11.7
.8		1.3	1.4	Operating Profit	.9	.8	.9	2.2		1.3
-.1		.1	.2	All Other Expenses (net)	.8	.3	.0	.1		.3
.8		1.2	1.1	Profit Before Taxes	.2	.5	.9	2.2		1.0
				RATIOS						
1.6		1.6	1.4		1.5	1.7	1.5	1.6		1.4
1.1		1.1	1.0	Current	.9	1.0	.9	1.0		1.1
.8		.9	.8		.6	.6	.7	.9		.9
1.2		1.2	1.1		1.3	1.5	1.2	1.1		1.0
.8		.9	.7	Quick	.7	.7	.7	.8		.7
.6		.6	.5		.3	.3	.4	.6		.6

13	29.0	13	28.7	10	35.4	Sales/Receivables	10	36.2	3	114.8	10	36.8	15	25.1	10	37.6
23	16.2	24	15.5	19	19.4		15	24.5	15	24.9	18	20.0	24	15.2	19	19.6
34	10.9	32	11.4	28	13.0		25	14.4	25	14.7	27	13.6	35	10.6	26	13.8
4	86.7	4	89.4	4	88.4	Cost of Sales/Inventory	6	65.5	3	121.2	4	96.5	5	80.0	4	90.5
10	37.9	8	44.8	8	44.0		12	29.7	7	54.8	8	45.7	9	41.2	8	47.9
17	21.9	15	24.1	15	24.4		26	14.0	11	32.4	19	19.0	19	19.3	13	28.6
8	43.7	9	40.6	4	47.7	Cost of Sales/Payables	4	94.5	4	88.9	6	56.4	4	43.4	10	37.9
15	25.1	15	24.8	13	27.4		8	45.2	12	30.1	14	25.8	13	27.3	13	27.2
24	15.1	23	15.9	19	19.0		16	22.1	21	17.7	21	17.0	20	18.6	18	20.5
	22.4		19.6		26.9	Sales/Working Capital		23.0		20.4		26.9		26.1		32.6
	104.8		89.2		564.1			-58.5		NM		-65.0		350.9		194.7
	-47.3		-56.8		-35.8			-14.3		-26.6		-18.7		-59.6		-105.3
	5.9		6.7		5.2	EBIT/Interest		8.1		7.9		4.2		5.5		5.3
(256)	2.8	(260)	2.4	(280)	2.1		(23)	1.1	(32)	2.2	(62)	1.7	(70)	2.0	(89)	2.4
	1.2		1.1		.8			-.7		1.1		-.6		.7		1.4
	3.5		3.6		3.7	Net Profit + Depr., Dep., Amort./Cur. Mat. L/T/D						4.5		3.6		4.1
(92)	1.7	(93)	1.9	(80)	2.0						(17)	2.2	(25)	1.8	(36)	2.0
	1.0		1.0		1.2								1.0		1.1		1.3
	.5		.5		.5	Fixed/Worth		.4		.2		.5		.6		.7
	1.5		1.2		1.9			-1.7		3.7		2.8		1.4		1.7
	6.5		5.8		-7.0			-.4		-.6		-1.1		26.3		3.7
	1.4		1.4		1.8	Debt/Worth		1.7		1.6		2.0		1.8		1.8
	3.3		3.5		5.3			-12.5		89.6		9.0		5.0		3.8
	23.5		19.8		-19.9			-3.1		-2.7		-6.2		-580.2		15.2
	34.0		45.1		35.2	% Profit Before Taxes/Tangible Net Worth		36.3		33.6		28.2		40.1		37.7
(228)	11.6	(221)	15.1	(204)	13.7		(10)	20.8	(19)	10.9	(42)	7.9	(53)	10.8	(75)	14.8
	1.0		2.9		2.3			-.1		5.5		-16.1		.5		6.8
	7.9		8.2		7.6	% Profit Before Taxes/Total Assets		12.2		7.7		6.3		7.0		9.0
	3.6		3.2		2.9			.8		3.3		2.0		2.0		4.5
	.2		.1		-.3			-6.7		.4		-2.5		-1.1		1.1
	35.2		44.1		51.0	Sales/Net Fixed Assets		49.7		233.0		56.8		43.5		51.0
	18.9		20.2		26.0			28.5		43.1		28.6		24.9		21.5
	9.3		10.8		11.6			12.3		15.2		12.4		11.2		12.0
	6.2		6.5		6.9	Sales/Total Assets		5.2		9.5		6.5		6.3		8.0
	4.2		4.4		4.8			3.9		5.6		4.2		4.6		5.5
	3.1		3.1		3.3			3.0		3.2		2.8		3.3		4.0
	.9		.7		.6	% Depr., Dep., Amort./Sales		.8		.6		.7		.7		.5
(249)	1.4	(254)	1.1	(254)	1.1		(22)	1.7	(19)	1.3	(57)	1.1	(68)	1.2	(85)	.9
	2.3		1.9		1.8			2.6		2.7		1.9		1.8		1.3
	.9		.9		.7	% Officers', Directors' Owners' Comp/Sales		1.8		.7		1.5		.6		.3
(164)	2.0	(135)	1.6	(146)	1.7		(14)	2.9	(18)	2.2	(39)	2.5	(45)	1.3	(29)	.8
	4.7		3.2		3.1			3.7		3.8		3.3		2.7		1.6
9549444M		12785794M	15926861M	Net Sales ($)	1854M	59452M	137824M	484038M	1161593M	14082100M
2777300M		2933965M	3203639M	Total Assets ($)	869M	15858M	29748M	137114M	287023M	2733027M

M = $ thousand   MM = $ million
See Pages 11 through 21 for Explanation of Ratios and Data

	Current Data Sorted by Assets							Comparative Historical Data	
							Type of Statement		
			2	12	2	2	Unqualified	9	16
	1	6	14	5			Reviewed	21	25
	2	10	10	1		1	Compiled	17	27
	9	11	3				Tax Returns	6	18
	1		8	7	1	1	Other	16	17
	42 (4/1-9/30/06)			67 (10/1/06-3/31/07)				4/1/02-3/31/03	4/1/03-3/31/04
	0-500M	500M-2MM	2-10MM	10-50MM	50-100MM	100-250MM		ALL	ALL
	13	27	37	25	3	4	**NUMBER OF STATEMENTS**	69	103
	%	%	%	%	%	%	**ASSETS**	%	%
	20.3	9.2	9.5	4.0			Cash & Equivalents	8.3	9.3
	29.2	24.7	24.8	20.4			Trade Receivables (net)	19.0	21.1
	25.8	12.1	10.1	10.4			Inventory	9.8	10.8
	.4	2.8	3.8	3.2			All Other Current	2.4	2.1
	75.7	48.8	48.2	37.9			Total Current	39.5	43.3
	19.5	42.0	40.4	48.5			Fixed Assets (net)	46.5	42.1
	2.4	3.1	4.6	7.6			Intangibles (net)	7.4	6.9
	2.4	6.1	6.8	5.9			All Other Non-Current	6.6	7.7
	100.0	100.0	100.0	100.0			Total	100.0	100.0
							LIABILITIES		
	9.4	13.6	6.1	8.1			Notes Payable-Short Term	5.9	7.4
	8.0	5.9	3.7	5.0			Cur. Mat.-L.T.D.	5.0	6.1
	37.9	22.6	15.2	11.9			Trade Payables	13.9	14.7
	.0	.6	.1	.1			Income Taxes Payable	.1	.3
	4.8	13.0	9.0	7.6			All Other Current	8.3	10.2
	60.0	55.7	34.1	32.7			Total Current	33.2	38.8
	25.0	24.3	21.9	26.0			Long-Term Debt	21.3	22.7
	.0	.1	.1	2.2			Deferred Taxes	1.4	1.1
	9.1	6.3	4.8	3.6			All Other Non-Current	5.0	7.4
	5.9	13.5	39.1	35.6			Net Worth	39.1	30.0
	100.0	100.0	100.0	100.0			Total Liabilties & Net Worth	100.0	100.0
							INCOME DATA		
	100.0	100.0	100.0	100.0			Net Sales	100.0	100.0
	24.6	30.2	27.5	30.2			Gross Profit	39.9	36.3
	23.8	27.5	25.5	26.1			Operating Expenses	36.6	33.2
	.9	2.7	2.0	4.1			Operating Profit	3.2	3.0
	-1.2	1.4	.4	1.4			All Other Expenses (net)	.2	.4
	2.0	1.3	1.6	2.7			Profit Before Taxes	3.0	2.6
							RATIOS		
	4.6	1.5	2.1	1.7				2.1	1.9
	2.0	.8	1.4	1.1			Current	1.4	1.2
	.9	.6	1.1	.9				.8	.8
	3.6	1.2	1.5	1.1				1.5	1.3
	1.0	.6	1.1	.7			Quick	.8	.8
	.6	.3	.8	.6				.4	.5
	7 54.6	**14** 26.8	**16** 22.4	**20** 18.2				**15** 24.3	**16** 22.9
	23 16.2	**27** 13.5	**35** 10.4	**23** 15.6			Sales/Receivables	**27** 13.5	**27** 13.7
	29 12.5	**46** 8.0	**45** 8.1	**37** 10.0				**43** 8.5	**42** 8.7
	7 51.0	**5** 69.0	**7** 49.9	**10** 36.1				**15** 24.8	**8** 44.6
	13 28.1	**16** 23.1	**12** 30.4	**20** 18.6			Cost of Sales/Inventory	**24** 15.3	**21** 17.1
	24 15.5	**36** 10.1	**25** 14.4	**32** 11.4				**43** 8.4	**43** 8.5
	5 74.7	**12** 31.0	**12** 31.3	**12** 29.2				**15** 23.9	**13** 27.7
	22 16.3	**32** 11.4	**25** 14.8	**21** 17.2			Cost of Sales/Payables	**27** 13.3	**30** 12.2
	56 6.5	**58** 6.3	**37** 10.0	**33** 10.9				**47** 7.8	**48** 7.6
	7.5	32.0	8.7	14.6				9.1	12.3
	24.6	-18.3	22.6	69.3			Sales/Working Capital	26.2	47.7
	-231.9	-8.1	131.5	-87.1				-37.8	-30.7
	8.9	5.8	7.2	8.9				7.4	9.6
	(10) 5.7	(26) 1.9	(36) 2.5	2.5			EBIT/Interest	(60) 2.8	(90) 3.1
	-.1	.1	.4	1.5				.8	1.3
				2.8				3.3	4.4
				(11) 1.8			Net Profit + Depr., Dep., Amort./Cur. Mat. L/T/D	(27) 2.4	(28) 2.5
				1.2				1.6	1.6
	.2	.7	.6	.9				.7	.6
	.5	5.2	1.2	2.1			Fixed/Worth	1.5	1.8
	-.4	-2.8	2.2	3.8				3.1	5.2
	.3	1.8	.8	1.4				.8	1.1
	3.9	10.3	1.7	2.5			Debt/Worth	1.9	2.6
	-3.6	-7.1	3.8	5.9				5.1	13.0
		39.3	26.0	41.2				38.1	41.8
		(16) 11.0	(34) 6.9	(24) 28.1			% Profit Before Taxes/Tangible Net Worth	(62) 15.0	(84) 19.3
		-5.7	-1.9	8.1				5.4	8.3
	30.6	12.0	7.2	12.1				10.2	11.1
	6.0	2.4	1.5	5.8			% Profit Before Taxes/Total Assets	4.6	5.7
	-36.5	-3.7	-1.5	2.0				-.3	1.1
	109.2	27.1	11.7	7.7				7.8	11.2
	48.4	5.4	6.9	3.8			Sales/Net Fixed Assets	4.7	5.4
	11.1	3.6	3.0	2.6				2.6	2.6
	11.9	5.3	3.6	3.4				3.0	3.2
	5.9	2.5	2.4	2.0			Sales/Total Assets	2.1	2.1
	3.5	2.0	1.6	1.5				1.6	1.5
		1.5	1.6	1.5				3.3	2.4
		(24) 4.2	(35) 2.9	3.2			% Depr., Dep., Amort./Sales	(63) 5.1	(94) 4.4
		5.2	4.1	4.7				6.5	6.3
		1.7	1.1					1.7	.9
		(17) 2.8	(14) 2.3				% Officers', Directors' Owners' Comp/Sales	(29) 3.5	(39) 3.0
		3.9	4.7					5.9	6.0
	26238M	129885M	530092M	1746090M	451611M	863595M	Net Sales ($)	1187733M	2594680M
	3858M	35358M	170671M	600039M	236104M	556444M	Total Assets ($)	712847M	1163755M

M = $ thousand MM = $ million

See Pages 11 through 21 for Explanation of Ratios and Data

Comparative Historical Data | Current Data Sorted by Sales

Current Data period spans: **42 (4/1-9/30/06)** and **67 (10/1/06-3/31/07)**

4/1/04-3/31/05 ALL	4/1/05-3/31/06 ALL	4/1/06-3/31/07 ALL	Type of Statement	0-1MM	1-3MM	3-5MM	5-10MM	10-25MM	25MM & OVER
17	18	18	Unqualified					3	15
21	19	26	Reviewed	1	2	3	6	9	5
23	27	24	Compiled		4	8	4	4	4
14	11	23	Tax Returns	3	10	5	4		1
17	22	18	Other	1		1	4	2	10
92	97	109	**NUMBER OF STATEMENTS**	5	16	17	18	18	35
%	%	%	**ASSETS**	%	%	%	%	%	%
8.6	9.7	9.0	Cash & Equivalents		13.2	10.0	9.5	9.2	4.5
20.6	22.8	23.5	Trade Receivables (net)		24.9	19.0	22.1	29.4	23.1
12.1	12.4	12.5	Inventory		16.9	20.5	10.3	5.9	11.4
2.6	5.3	2.9	All Other Current		2.4	3.3	2.2	4.5	2.8
44.0	50.2	47.9	Total Current		57.4	52.8	44.1	49.0	41.9
42.2	38.0	41.2	Fixed Assets (net)		36.5	37.7	38.7	39.9	46.3
5.8	5.6	5.3	Intangibles (net)		2.2	5.2	5.7	3.2	8.3
8.0	6.1	5.7	All Other Non-Current		3.9	4.3	11.5	7.9	3.6
100.0	100.0	100.0	Total		100.0	100.0	100.0	100.0	100.0
			LIABILITIES						
6.5	7.3	8.7	Notes Payable-Short Term		11.0	10.5	14.5	3.8	7.5
4.3	4.5	5.0	Cur. Mat.-L.T.D.		12.1	4.2	3.9	4.7	3.2
15.1	17.3	18.5	Trade Payables		36.3	19.2	14.6	17.4	14.1
.1	.4	.3	Income Taxes Payable		.3	.0	.7	.0	.3
10.4	9.8	8.9	All Other Current		11.6	11.8	6.8	13.1	6.0
36.5	39.3	41.3	Total Current		71.3	45.7	40.4	39.0	31.1
23.0	20.9	24.6	Long-Term Debt		20.1	33.9	22.9	20.1	24.7
1.3	1.0	.9	Deferred Taxes		.0	.2	.2	.0	2.7
8.4	8.4	5.4	All Other Non-Current		11.0	7.4	5.0	4.8	3.0
30.9	30.3	27.8	Net Worth		-2.4	12.7	31.4	36.1	38.5
100.0	100.0	100.0	Total Liabilities & Net Worth		100.0	100.0	100.0	100.0	100.0
			INCOME DATA						
100.0	100.0	100.0	Net Sales		100.0	100.0	100.0	100.0	100.0
35.2	31.5	28.8	Gross Profit		30.3	29.5	31.4	27.0	25.4
32.4	29.0	26.0	Operating Expenses		29.8	26.9	30.6	23.0	22.3
2.8	2.5	2.8	Operating Profit		.5	2.6	.7	4.0	3.1
.5	.3	.8	All Other Expenses (net)		.6	.9	.2	.5	1.2
2.3	2.2	2.0	Profit Before Taxes		-.1	1.7	.5	3.5	1.9
			RATIOS						
2.0	2.1	2.0			2.7	2.1	1.9	1.8	1.9
1.3	1.3	1.3	Current		.8	1.4	1.4	1.4	1.3
.9	.9	.8			.4	.7	1.0	.7	1.0
1.3	1.3	1.4			1.5	1.3	1.4	1.4	1.1
.8	.8	.9	Quick		.4	.7	1.0	1.2	.8
.5	.5	.6			.2	.4	.7	.4	.6
16 22.3	16 22.3	16 22.4			6 58.5	12 31.4	17 21.6	15 23.9	19 18.9
28 13.1	28 12.9	26 14.3	Sales/Receivables		33 11.1	23 16.2	31 11.8	28 13.0	24 15.3
41 8.9	44 8.4	41 8.9			47 7.7	37 9.8	48 7.7	42 8.7	36 10.1
10 37.6	10 36.2	7 51.2			7 51.4	8 46.2	5 75.0	3 126.2	9 41.4
20 18.3	21 17.7	16 23.1	Cost of Sales/Inventory		16 23.2	19 18.8	13 27.1	12 30.7	19 19.3
36 10.0	39 9.4	31 11.9			39 9.3	30 12.0	38 9.6	19 19.5	31 11.7
15 24.1	15 24.9	12 31.5			26 14.0	8 43.0	15 23.9	11 31.8	11 32.6
27 13.7	27 13.4	25 14.8	Cost of Sales/Payables		49 7.4	27 13.7	29 12.4	17 21.3	19 18.9
47 7.8	43 8.5	42 8.7			74 5.0	40 9.2	44 8.3	33 10.9	29 12.5
12.8	10.2	10.1			13.8	14.7	9.5	13.0	10.2
37.2	24.7	43.4	Sales/Working Capital		-17.4	86.3	29.8	30.4	32.2
-45.7	-71.1	-49.6			-5.5	-11.5	NM	-21.5	-492.9
6.4	6.9	7.1			7.3	5.7	3.2	8.6	8.1
(87) 3.2	(89) 2.6	(104) 2.5	EBIT/Interest		(15) .5	(16) 2.4	1.8	(16) 3.9	2.5
1.2	1.5	.9			-1.6	.5	.4	2.5	1.5
5.8	4.1	6.0							6.2
(30) 2.1	(33) 2.0	(24) 1.9	Net Profit + Depr., Dep., Amort./Cur. Mat. L/T/D						(15) 2.0
1.3	1.2	1.0							1.2
.6	.5	.7			.1	1.0	.7	.6	.8
1.7	1.6	1.9	Fixed/Worth		NM	5.2	1.6	1.4	1.9
8.4	4.3	6.5			-3.4	-1.4	12.5	2.3	3.4
.7	1.2	1.1			.7	1.7	.7	1.3	1.2
2.5	2.5	2.6	Debt/Worth		-26.2	9.7		2.1	2.4
20.2	9.4	12.8			-7.4	-4.8	21.1	3.6	3.8
27.7	33.0	32.2				47.9	32.1	42.4	33.4
(72) 13.4	(80) 15.5	(88) 16.0	% Profit Before Taxes/Tangible Net Worth			(10) 6.7	(15) 6.4	(17) 10.3	(34) 24.0
2.1	4.0	2.4				1.3	.1	1.0	4.1
9.8	9.4	11.5			9.2	16.1	7.0	9.2	11.4
4.0	4.0	3.4	% Profit Before Taxes/Total Assets		-2.3	2.4	1.1	5.1	5.8
.5	.5	-.9			-20.9	-1.5	-1.6	-1.0	1.3
10.1	18.0	20.0			44.7	93.3	11.4	20.6	16.9
6.0	6.7	5.8	Sales/Net Fixed Assets		7.1	5.2	7.4	7.6	4.5
2.9	3.8	3.2			3.4	3.4	3.0	2.9	2.9
3.2	3.5	4.1			4.8	4.8	4.2	5.8	3.8
2.3	2.5	2.5	Sales/Total Assets		2.7	2.2	2.0	2.7	2.3
1.6	1.7	1.7			2.0	1.8	1.5	1.8	1.6
2.3	1.9	1.6			1.9	2.1	1.2	1.8	1.1
(86) 4.1	(90) 3.5	(99) 3.2	% Depr., Dep., Amort./Sales		(11) 4.4	(15) 4.1	2.8	(17) 2.8	(34) 2.9
6.0	4.5	4.6			5.4	5.0	4.5	4.1	4.3
1.6	1.1	1.3			2.8				
(36) 3.3	(40) 2.6	(45) 2.8	% Officers', Directors' Owners' Comp/Sales		(12) 3.4				
6.1	4.3	4.4			5.3				
2042257M	2494275M	3747511M	Net Sales ($)	3757M	31394M	67326M	114653M	283683M	3246698M
969332M	1037985M	1602474M	Total Assets ($)	2684M	12168M	28545M	56857M	116940M	1385280M

M = $ thousand   MM = $ million
See Pages 11 through 21 for Explanation of Ratios and Data

Current Data Sorted by Assets / Comparative Historical Data

0-500M	500M-2MM	2-10MM	10-50MM	50-100MM	100-250MM	Type of Statement	4/1/02-3/31/03 ALL	4/1/03-3/31/04 ALL
1		5	6	1	2	Unqualified	7	12
1	2	8	2			Reviewed	8	8
6	12	12			1	Compiled	8	23
41	26	11	3	1	1	Tax Returns	17	29
16	22	14	9		3	Other	18	25
	26 (4/1-9/30/06)		180 (10/1/06-3/31/07)					
65	62	50	20	2	7	**NUMBER OF STATEMENTS**	58	97
%	%	%	%	%	%	**ASSETS**	%	%
20.9	11.9	7.6	15.2			Cash & Equivalents	10.9	13.1
18.1	30.5	23.9	23.2			Trade Receivables (net)	19.4	27.3
21.8	25.2	28.4	22.3			Inventory	21.5	22.8
3.8	2.2	3.4	4.0			All Other Current	5.2	5.2
64.6	69.7	63.3	64.8			Total Current	57.1	68.4
20.2	17.0	21.9	23.4			Fixed Assets (net)	22.6	19.4
5.4	3.6	4.6	5.8			Intangibles (net)	10.9	5.3
9.8	9.7	10.2	6.0			All Other Non-Current	9.3	6.8
100.0	100.0	100.0	100.0			Total	100.0	100.0
						LIABILITIES		
19.5	10.2	17.3	7.6			Notes Payable-Short Term	14.8	15.0
1.5	3.4	4.7	1.4			Cur. Mat.-L.T.D.	7.2	2.4
16.5	20.7	16.2	16.4			Trade Payables	20.2	23.7
.1	.4	.4	.3			Income Taxes Payable	.2	.5
12.5	12.5	10.2	17.5			All Other Current	14.4	14.2
50.1	47.2	48.6	43.2			Total Current	56.8	55.8
18.0	17.8	15.5	21.3			Long-Term Debt	14.4	12.2
.0	.0	.2	.3			Deferred Taxes	.4	.3
8.6	6.4	3.3	6.0			All Other Non-Current	9.2	8.5
23.4	28.6	32.3	29.3			Net Worth	19.2	23.2
100.0	100.0	100.0	100.0			Total Liabilties & Net Worth	100.0	100.0
						INCOME DATA		
100.0	100.0	100.0	100.0			Net Sales	100.0	100.0
49.2	36.9	41.2	52.7			Gross Profit	45.3	41.0
43.1	31.9	34.4	44.0			Operating Expenses	42.1	36.0
6.0	5.0	6.8	8.6			Operating Profit	3.2	5.0
.2	.5	.9	2.0			All Other Expenses (net)	.8	.9
5.8	4.4	5.9	6.6			Profit Before Taxes	2.4	4.1
						RATIOS		
4.0	2.5	2.1	2.0			Current	2.3	2.5
1.4	1.5	1.4	1.3				1.0	1.4
.7	1.0	.9	1.1				.6	.9
2.3	1.5	1.2	1.6			Quick	.9	1.5
.8	.9	(49) .7	.8				.6	.8
.3	.5	.2	.2				.3	.4
0 UND	8 43.2	5 75.9	2 193.3			Sales/Receivables	4 86.2	8 47.8
2 156.0	28 13.0	24 15.3	12 30.6				23 16.1	23 16.1
32 11.5	55 6.6	56 6.6	77 4.7				36 10.2	51 7.1
0 UND	9 39.7	17 21.3	20 18.0			Cost of Sales/Inventory	14 26.1	9 39.6
13 27.3	32 11.5	49 7.5	54 6.8				43 8.4	33 10.9
54 6.7	54 6.7	95 3.9	137 2.7				86 4.2	83 4.4
0 UND	9 40.3	5 67.6	18 19.9			Cost of Sales/Payables	17 21.8	16 22.9
7 51.6	27 13.7	33 10.9	28 12.8				36 10.1	36 10.1
41 8.8	48 7.6	61 6.0	109 3.4				58 6.3	74 4.9
10.8	9.6	6.1	6.5			Sales/Working Capital	11.0	6.8
40.7	17.0	12.1	14.5				NM	20.0
-83.6	-137.2	-36.4	46.0				-15.3	-83.4
18.8	16.8	14.4	10.2			EBIT/Interest	13.9	23.8
(43) 7.0	(57) 5.0	(47) 4.3	(15) 1.6				(44) 6.4	(81) 5.0
1.9	1.7	1.4	.9				1.2	1.7
						Net Profit + Depr., Dep., Amort./Cur. Mat. L/T/D		15.2
							(18)	5.7
								1.7
.0	.1	.2	.3			Fixed/Worth	.5	.1
.5	.4	.7	1.0				2.1	.8
UND	4.7	5.4	5.6				-2.3	76.5
.4	1.3	1.1	1.0			Debt/Worth	1.1	.9
3.7	2.8	2.7	2.4				9.7	3.4
-47.0	31.0	16.6	18.7				-10.1	640.9
177.5	114.7	94.4	70.4			% Profit Before Taxes/Tangible Net Worth	145.7	84.3
(48) 84.8	(50) 40.6	(42) 41.2	(17) 26.0				(40) 40.9	(74) 37.4
30.2	11.3	8.1	1.1				9.5	14.7
54.4	22.2	18.7	22.4			% Profit Before Taxes/Total Assets	21.8	21.6
21.1	6.8	6.4	4.9				8.3	8.8
7.2	1.5	1.4	.2				.5	1.9
978.4	246.5	49.8	69.0			Sales/Net Fixed Assets	60.5	106.5
72.1	38.3	24.2	13.0				25.6	33.2
14.5	11.3	9.5	5.5				8.9	11.0
8.3	5.9	3.7	2.6			Sales/Total Assets	4.9	4.6
4.7	3.5	2.7	2.0				3.1	3.1
2.9	2.6	1.5	1.6				2.2	2.0
.4	.4	.4	.5			% Depr., Dep., Amort./Sales	.8	.4
(32) 1.2	(43) .8	(40) .9	(18) 1.1				(43) 1.3	(70) 1.2
2.9	2.6	2.2	1.8				3.1	2.9
2.2	1.6	1.6				% Officers', Directors' Owners' Comp/Sales	2.3	1.5
(39) 6.7	(34) 4.2	(23) 3.0					(21) 3.5	(49) 4.0
10.0	7.6	6.0					12.2	7.7
75147M	252096M	586841M	1270670M	235482M	3384523M	Net Sales ($)	2169160M	2566658M
12503M	61334M	194089M	515406M	122285M	1209492M	Total Assets ($)	981605M	927219M

© RMA 2007

M = $ thousand   MM = $ million
See Pages 11 through 21 for Explanation of Ratios and Data

Comparative Historical Data | Current Data Sorted by Sales

	4/1/04-3/31/05 ALL	4/1/05-3/31/06 ALL	4/1/06-3/31/07 ALL	Type of Statement	0-1MM	1-3MM	3-5MM	5-10MM	10-25MM	25MM & OVER
	11	9	15	Unqualified	1	1		1	1	11
	11	14	13	Reviewed		1	2	3	4	3
	24	28	31	Compiled			11	5	4	2
	40	45	82	Tax Returns	4	5	11	5	4	1
	32	53	65	Other	19	27	19	10	6	13
					15	11	9	11	11	
					26 (4/1-9/30/06)			**180 (10/1/06-3/31/07)**		
	118	149	206	**NUMBER OF STATEMENTS**	39	45	41	30	21	30
	%	%	%	**ASSETS**	%	%	%	%	%	%
	14.0	12.6	14.1	Cash & Equivalents	17.2	14.5	17.8	7.0	11.6	12.9
	22.3	21.7	24.0	Trade Receivables (net)	22.5	19.4	30.4	31.8	24.0	16.4
	26.1	22.6	24.6	Inventory	25.0	22.1	23.2	27.9	23.4	27.5
	2.2	3.7	3.3	All Other Current	4.1	2.4	2.9	2.0	5.1	4.2
	64.7	60.5	66.0	Total Current	68.7	58.4	74.3	68.8	64.0	61.0
	21.2	25.0	19.8	Fixed Assets (net)	22.8	20.4	14.4	18.7	19.5	24.0
	6.8	6.6	4.9	Intangibles (net)	3.4	5.1	3.5	5.5	6.0	7.0
	7.3	7.9	9.3	All Other Non-Current	5.1	16.1	7.7	7.0	10.5	8.0
	100.0	100.0	100.0	Total	100.0	100.0	100.0	100.0	100.0	100.0
				LIABILITIES						
	14.5	16.1	15.2	Notes Payable-Short Term	19.6	15.6	12.4	15.5	19.6	9.1
	3.2	5.3	2.8	Cur. Mat.-L.T.D.	2.7	1.5	2.7	4.2	5.9	1.4
	23.7	17.6	17.9	Trade Payables	14.4	16.6	21.7	17.0	16.2	21.1
	.2	.2	.3	Income Taxes Payable	.2	.1	.7	.0	.2	.5
	10.8	12.2	12.6	All Other Current	12.0	13.0	12.4	10.4	11.9	16.1
	52.4	51.3	48.8	Total Current	48.8	46.9	49.9	47.2	53.8	48.2
	19.6	21.0	18.1	Long-Term Debt	18.6	19.1	15.8	19.9	9.6	23.0
	.1	.2	.1	Deferred Taxes	.0	.0	.0	.0	.6	.3
	6.4	8.1	6.2	All Other Non-Current	6.3	10.4	5.3	5.3	3.1	4.0
	21.5	19.5	26.9	Net Worth	26.4	23.6	29.0	27.7	33.0	24.5
	100.0	100.0	100.0	Total Liabilities & Net Worth	100.0	100.0	100.0	100.0	100.0	100.0
				INCOME DATA						
	100.0	100.0	100.0	Net Sales	100.0	100.0	100.0	100.0	100.0	100.0
	42.5	43.7	43.5	Gross Profit	52.5	48.2	38.7	31.9	38.4	46.1
	37.9	38.6	37.2	Operating Expenses	45.0	41.7	33.5	24.8	35.7	38.9
	4.6	5.1	6.2	Operating Profit	7.5	6.5	5.2	7.1	2.6	7.1
	.9	1.1	.7	All Other Expenses (net)	.7	.4	.7	.7	.5	1.1
	3.7	4.0	5.6	Profit Before Taxes	6.8	6.1	4.5	6.4	2.2	6.1
				RATIOS						
	2.8	2.2	2.5	Current	3.4	3.8	2.9	1.7	2.1	2.1
	1.7	1.3	1.4		1.4	1.4	1.5	1.6	1.0	1.3
	.9	.8	.9		1.0	.6	1.0	1.1	.9	1.1
	1.8	1.4	1.4	Quick	1.9	1.9	1.8	1.4	1.2	1.1
(117)	.8	(148) .8	(205) .8		.7	.8	1.0	.9	.7	(29) .6
	.3	.2	.3		.3	.3	.5	.4	.2	.2
	2 216.0	2 229.8	1 306.8	Sales/Receivables	0 UND	0 UND	10 36.4	5 71.3	6 60.8	2 213.6
	21 17.1	21 17.7	19 19.7		29 12.6	4 82.8	28 13.3	31 11.9	25 14.6	6 60.4
	44 8.3	46 7.9	46 7.9		48 7.7	30 12.2	58 6.3	58 6.3	43 8.5	36 10.1
	17 21.8	8 43.8	6 58.0	Cost of Sales/Inventory	0 UND	0 UND	4 84.6	10 36.6	9 40.4	21 17.3
	41 8.9	41 9.0	34 10.6		39 9.3	24 15.4	24 15.0	43 8.5	32 11.2	50 7.3
	92 4.0	70 5.2	71 5.2		77 4.7	81 4.5	50 7.3	56 6.6	69 5.3	116 3.2
	17 22.0	9 41.6	4 94.6	Cost of Sales/Payables	0 UND	0 UND	10 35.4	9 39.8	2 169.5	22 16.6
	31 12.0	25 14.4	27 13.3		20 18.4	18 19.8	29 12.4	24 15.5	31 12.0	30 12.2
	52 7.0	58 6.3	56 6.5		64 5.7	46 8.0	66 5.5	39 9.5	85 4.3	58 6.3
	6.4	8.7	8.0	Sales/Working Capital	5.2	11.2	6.4	8.2	7.0	8.1
	18.1	16.9	18.7		17.8	39.8	13.8	14.2	151.1	18.9
	-53.7	-49.7	-118.1		UND	-83.0	NM	64.2	-33.6	134.7
	21.5	22.2	15.1	EBIT/Interest	11.8	24.0	15.3	10.1	36.8	12.9
(100)	3.4	(126) 4.8	(170) 5.2		(24) 6.6	(37) 7.0	(37) 5.8	(27) 2.5	(20) 2.7	(25) 2.3
	1.1	1.2	1.5		1.8	1.5	2.8	1.5	-.8	1.1
	6.7	4.5	4.5	Net Profit + Depr., Dep., Amort./Cur. Mat. L/T/D						
(18)	2.6	(14) 1.2	(21) 2.1							
	.9	.3	1.4							
	.2	.1	.1	Fixed/Worth	.0	.1	.1	.1	.2	.2
	.7	.8	.7		.5	.8	.3	.1	1.0	.9
	-5.1	-9.8	11.9		UND	UND	5.6	10.4	3.9	11.5
	.8	.9	1.0	Debt/Worth	.7	.5	.9	1.4	.8	.8
	2.8	3.0	2.7		2.0	3.7	2.8	3.0	5.3	2.3
	-14.1	-22.4	122.3		UND	-30.5	32.1	62.5	19.4	265.2
	71.8	100.8	114.2	% Profit Before Taxes/Tangible Net Worth	114.9	198.3	120.2	102.4	76.1	68.6
(84)	30.2	(109) 37.1	(162) 49.2		(30) 60.5	(33) 83.7	(33) 42.5	(24) 57.5	(18) 31.6	(24) 32.4
	2.6	19.2	12.0		11.8	23.5	11.7	11.7	-2.0	3.6
	23.7	26.5	30.3	% Profit Before Taxes/Total Assets	37.7	52.5	22.4	21.5	13.5	25.3
	5.0	10.7	11.2		15.0	21.1	11.9	4.7	2.1	11.4
	.1	.6	2.0		4.2	2.7	3.6	1.3	-3.0	1.2
	95.2	75.5	156.2	Sales/Net Fixed Assets	UND	215.7	183.6	109.6	83.1	52.6
	25.6	19.2	33.4		32.7	33.6	45.5	34.4	22.6	19.0
	10.4	7.0	10.6		5.4	10.9	19.6	10.2	10.4	9.8
	4.9	4.4	5.9	Sales/Total Assets	3.9	8.1	6.6	4.4	4.4	4.2
	3.5	3.1	3.4		2.8	4.9	3.4	3.3	2.9	2.5
	1.9	2.1	2.2		1.3	2.6	2.2	2.6	2.3	1.9
	.5	.7	.4	% Depr., Dep., Amort./Sales	.8	.4	.2	.4	.4	.4
(89)	1.3	(109) 1.4	(139) .9		(20) 2.0	(23) 1.9	(30) .5	(24) .8	(17) .9	(25) .9
	2.6	4.2	2.3		4.2	3.9	1.2	1.7	3.1	1.6
	1.9	1.8	1.7	% Officers', Directors' Owners' Comp/Sales	2.6	1.8	1.6	1.6	2.1	
(54)	4.5	(71) 6.4	(100) 4.4		(19) 6.5	(25) 6.7	(26) 4.9	(17) 2.8	(11) 3.4	
	8.7	10.5	7.9		13.8	12.4	7.5	5.3	4.1	
	2939674M	4023945M	5804759M	Net Sales ($)	19287M	83071M	163231M	206727M	335082M	4997361M
	1158924M	1383855M	2115109M	Total Assets ($)	8605M	25278M	58383M	89332M	117211M	1816300M

© RMA 2007

M = $ thousand   MM = $ million
See Pages 11 through 21 for Explanation of Ratios and Data

TRANSPORTATION AND
WAREHOUSING

Current Data Sorted by Assets | Comparative Historical Data

Type of Statement

Type of Statement	0-500M	500M-2MM	2-10MM	10-50MM	50-100MM	100-250MM		4/1/02-3/31/03 ALL	4/1/03-3/31/04 ALL
Unqualified			1	5	2	3		12	7
Reviewed		1	2	2				3	4
Compiled		2	1	1				8	8
Tax Returns		2	4	8				5	4
Other	2		12		5	5		18	12
		8 (4/1-9/30/06)	50 (10/1/06-3/31/07)						
NUMBER OF STATEMENTS	2	5	20	16	7	8		46	35
ASSETS	%	%	%	%	%	%		%	%
Cash & Equivalents			13.3	14.5				13.7	9.4
Trade Receivables (net)			14.0	19.3				12.4	12.9
Inventory			5.2	8.5				6.7	10.0
All Other Current			6.2	4.0				2.2	5.0
Total Current			38.7	46.3				35.0	37.3
Fixed Assets (net)			46.1	40.4				51.9	50.4
Intangibles (net)			3.2	4.9				2.6	2.0
All Other Non-Current			12.0	8.4				10.5	10.2
Total			100.0	100.0				100.0	100.0
LIABILITIES									
Notes Payable-Short Term			3.8	4.6				4.4	3.6
Cur. Mat.-L.T.D.			8.4	3.1				6.1	7.1
Trade Payables			7.3	20.1				8.8	8.9
Income Taxes Payable			.0	.4				.8	.2
All Other Current			12.3	15.5				13.2	11.9
Total Current			31.9	43.7				33.3	31.7
Long-Term Debt			43.6	21.4				25.2	34.1
Deferred Taxes			.1	.3				1.3	2.2
All Other Non-Current			5.9	7.0				12.4	7.9
Net Worth			18.5	27.5				27.9	24.2
Total Liabilities & Net Worth			100.0	100.0				100.0	100.0
INCOME DATA									
Net Sales			100.0	100.0				100.0	100.0
Gross Profit									
Operating Expenses			93.9	98.9				100.7	96.8
Operating Profit			6.1	1.1				-.7	3.2
All Other Expenses (net)			4.7	.8				1.8	2.4
Profit Before Taxes			1.4	.3				-2.5	.8
RATIOS									
Current			1.8	1.2				1.7	2.1
			1.1	1.0				1.0	1.2
			.6	.8				.6	.6
Quick			1.6	.8				1.2	1.2
			.8	.6				.7	.6
			.5	.6				.3	.2
Sales/Receivables			13 28.4	13 28.5				9 40.1	9 39.0
			27 13.3	20 18.2				25 14.8	25 14.8
			41 8.8	34 10.8				38 9.6	45 8.1
Cost of Sales/Inventory									
Cost of Sales/Payables									
Sales/Working Capital			7.6	32.1				13.4	5.1
			233.2	-571.5				NM	51.9
			-12.8	-17.6				-8.0	-8.7
EBIT/Interest			6.0	4.4				3.0	7.6
			(18) 2.4	(12) 1.7				(42) 1.1	(31) 2.5
			1.3	1.1				-3.4	.5
Net Profit + Depr., Dep., Amort./Cur. Mat. L/T/D								2.4	
								(16) 1.3	
								.3	
Fixed/Worth			.9	.7				.8	.7
			3.2	2.1				1.2	1.4
			-4.8	8.1				21.4	-10.9
Debt/Worth			1.0	1.7				.8	.9
			6.2	2.6				1.6	1.8
			-14.8	15.5				27.4	-12.6
% Profit Before Taxes/Tangible Net Worth			61.0	57.7				34.6	29.5
			(14) 25.7	(13) 32.7				(36) 5.5	(26) 13.1
			-3.0	10.7				-14.7	5.2
% Profit Before Taxes/Total Assets			15.0	13.6				8.6	10.9
			4.8	5.5				.8	4.2
			-.2	.3				-7.6	-1.5
Sales/Net Fixed Assets			16.7	23.6				6.8	9.2
			3.1	4.2				2.5	3.1
			1.8	1.6				1.3	1.3
Sales/Total Assets			2.4	4.6				2.9	2.8
			1.5	2.2				1.5	1.4
			1.0	.9				.8	.8
% Depr., Dep., Amort./Sales			1.5	.9				2.3	1.3
			(19) 2.7	(15) 5.1				(42) 5.5	(27) 6.8
			10.0	7.1				11.8	12.3
% Officers', Directors' Owners' Comp/Sales								1.3	
								(13) 4.7	
								18.3	
Net Sales ($)	4169M	9395M	208253M	743864M	1239357M	2469397M		3130512M	2641536M
Total Assets ($)	849M	5740M	111179M	303853M	498222M	1173038M		1889746M	1375708M

Comparative Historical Data | Current Data Sorted by Sales

Hist 1	Hist 2	Hist 3	Type of Statement	0-1MM	1-3MM	3-5MM	5-10MM	10-25MM	25MM & OVER
16	9	11	Unqualified					4	7
7	2	4	Reviewed				1	2	1
2	4	3	Compiled			2			1
4	8	6	Tax Returns	2	1	2			
24	31	34	Other	2	2	3	1	9	18
4/1/04-3/31/05 ALL	4/1/05-3/31/06 ALL	4/1/06-3/31/07 ALL				8 (4/1-9/30/06)		50 (10/1/06-3/31/07)	
53	54	58	NUMBER OF STATEMENTS	4	3	7	2	15	27
%	%	%	ASSETS	%	%	%	%	%	%
11.8	13.1	14.0	Cash & Equivalents					14.0	13.7
12.4	14.7	16.3	Trade Receivables (net)					13.5	20.8
4.1	4.6	4.9	Inventory					6.5	5.8
4.3	5.1	5.1	All Other Current					8.3	4.0
32.6	37.4	40.4	Total Current					42.3	44.4
54.0	50.2	44.4	Fixed Assets (net)					40.9	41.1
1.9	2.6	5.0	Intangibles (net)					4.8	5.8
11.5	9.8	10.3	All Other Non-Current					12.0	8.7
100.0	100.0	100.0	Total					100.0	100.0
			LIABILITIES						
5.3	12.2	4.1	Notes Payable-Short Term					3.7	4.5
4.9	6.3	4.8	Cur. Mat.-L.T.D.					6.7	2.7
12.9	13.1	14.1	Trade Payables					7.2	23.1
.0	.2	.2	Income Taxes Payable					.2	.2
11.9	17.5	16.3	All Other Current					16.7	18.7
35.1	49.3	39.5	Total Current					34.5	49.3
48.0	39.7	39.7	Long-Term Debt					37.1	31.0
.6	.3	.1	Deferred Taxes					.4	.1
8.5	6.8	5.0	All Other Non-Current					9.9	2.2
7.8	3.9	15.8	Net Worth					18.2	17.4
100.0	100.0	100.0	Total Liabilities & Net Worth					100.0	100.0
			INCOME DATA						
100.0	100.0	100.0	Net Sales					100.0	100.0
			Gross Profit						
91.5	91.2	95.3	Operating Expenses					92.3	98.9
8.5	8.8	4.7	Operating Profit					7.7	1.1
3.0	4.2	3.3	All Other Expenses (net)					2.1	1.4
5.5	4.6	1.4	Profit Before Taxes					5.6	-.2
			RATIOS						
1.7	1.5	1.5	Current					1.7	1.1
1.0	.9	1.0	Current					1.1	.9
.6	.6	.7	Current					.8	.7
1.4	1.4	1.0	Quick					1.0	1.0
.8	.6	.7	Quick					.8	.6
.4	.3	.5	Quick					.6	.5
7 52.2	1 352.6	12 30.3	Sales/Receivables					15 24.3	12 29.7
15 24.8	17 22.0	21 17.5	Sales/Receivables					18 19.7	22 16.9
37 10.0	30 12.0	34 10.6	Sales/Receivables					31 11.8	42 8.6
			Cost of Sales/Inventory						
			Cost of Sales/Payables						
11.9	12.5	15.8	Sales/Working Capital					8.8	43.1
113.8	-76.5	-571.5	Sales/Working Capital					28.8	-54.3
-8.7	-8.6	-14.9	Sales/Working Capital					-10.8	-16.1
12.8	7.7	5.0	EBIT/Interest					2.8	5.5
(49) 2.9	(47) 1.7	(48) 2.3	EBIT/Interest					2.3	(23) 2.5
.6	-.6	.8	EBIT/Interest					1.2	-.8
		3.4	Net Profit + Depr., Dep., Amort./Cur. Mat. L/T/D						
		(14) .5	Net Profit + Depr., Dep., Amort./Cur. Mat. L/T/D						
		-2.1	Net Profit + Depr., Dep., Amort./Cur. Mat. L/T/D						
1.1	1.1	.9	Fixed/Worth					.9	.8
2.3	10.5	2.5	Fixed/Worth					3.9	2.3
-7.1	-4.3	-14.1	Fixed/Worth					-3.7	-198.6
1.1	2.1	1.7	Debt/Worth					1.4	1.7
3.6	23.4	4.4	Debt/Worth					10.1	4.0
-16.0	-8.3	-29.2	Debt/Worth					-9.3	-349.0
97.9	61.5	60.9	% Profit Before Taxes/Tangible Net Worth						62.6
(38) 30.0	(29) 34.4	(40) 32.5	% Profit Before Taxes/Tangible Net Worth					(19)	33.0
6.9	-3.2	1.3	% Profit Before Taxes/Tangible Net Worth						21.5
16.4	15.1	14.6	% Profit Before Taxes/Total Assets					14.4	14.2
6.3	3.1	4.8	% Profit Before Taxes/Total Assets					4.4	6.7
-4.0	-3.7	-.9	% Profit Before Taxes/Total Assets					.6	-4.3
7.3	15.7	16.6	Sales/Net Fixed Assets					18.9	23.3
2.1	3.5	3.9	Sales/Net Fixed Assets					3.3	6.2
1.4	1.2	1.7	Sales/Net Fixed Assets					1.6	3.3
2.6	3.6	3.3	Sales/Total Assets					2.4	4.0
1.3	2.0	1.9	Sales/Total Assets					1.5	2.7
.7	.8	1.1	Sales/Total Assets					.9	1.7
1.9	1.4	1.6	% Depr., Dep., Amort./Sales					1.5	.9
(41) 4.6	(41) 3.3	(50) 4.2	% Depr., Dep., Amort./Sales					4.3	(23) 2.5
13.2	11.0	6.8	% Depr., Dep., Amort./Sales					6.2	6.6
1.2	1.3	2.2	% Officers', Directors' Owners' Comp/Sales						
(10) 4.8	(14) 2.2	(15) 3.0	% Officers', Directors' Owners' Comp/Sales						
12.3	12.8	7.5	% Officers', Directors' Owners' Comp/Sales						
2767322M	2914524M	4674435M	Net Sales ($)	1380M	4343M	28101M	14991M	225544M	4400076M
1643369M	1538019M	2092881M	Total Assets ($)	6665M	6787M	19257M	10727M	166366M	1883079M

M = $ thousand   MM = $ million
See Pages 11 through 21 for Explanation of Ratios and Data

Current Data Sorted by Assets | Comparative Historical Data

0-500M	500M-2MM	2-10MM	10-50MM	50-100MM	100-250MM	Type of Statement	4/1/02-3/31/03 ALL	4/1/03-3/31/04 ALL
	1	2	11	1	3	Unqualified	16	19
	1	8	2			Reviewed	13	13
	2	11				Compiled	16	25
2	10					Tax Returns	13	7
4	14	17	16	1	2	Other	36	47
	20 (4/1-9/30/06)		88 (10/1/06-3/31/07)					
6	28	38	29	2	5	**NUMBER OF STATEMENTS**	94	111

0-500M	500M-2MM	2-10MM	10-50MM	50-100MM	100-250MM		4/1/02-3/31/03 ALL	4/1/03-3/31/04 ALL
%	%	%	%	%	%	**ASSETS**	%	%
	20.4	9.4	5.9			Cash & Equivalents	7.4	10.2
	18.1	17.4	17.3			Trade Receivables (net)	17.5	17.6
	2.9	8.8	20.0			Inventory	8.1	7.0
	5.6	2.9	4.8			All Other Current	4.0	6.0
	47.0	38.5	47.9			Total Current	37.1	40.7
	37.0	43.8	45.6			Fixed Assets (net)	51.4	50.6
	4.7	4.2	.9			Intangibles (net)	1.4	2.2
	11.3	13.4	5.6			All Other Non-Current	10.0	6.5
	100.0	100.0	100.0			Total	100.0	100.0
						LIABILITIES		
	6.5	11.4	5.5			Notes Payable-Short Term	9.2	10.5
	4.7	6.8	8.6			Cur. Mat.-L.T.D.	6.3	7.5
	14.6	10.0	10.0			Trade Payables	9.8	9.7
	.3	.2	.0			Income Taxes Payable	.5	.6
	8.6	8.2	9.1			All Other Current	8.1	10.6
	34.7	36.7	33.1			Total Current	33.8	38.8
	37.3	41.1	34.9			Long-Term Debt	40.9	40.8
	.3	.6	1.1			Deferred Taxes	1.1	1.1
	6.3	9.7	2.7			All Other Non-Current	3.0	8.8
	21.3	11.9	28.2			Net Worth	21.2	10.4
	100.0	100.0	100.0			Total Liabilties & Net Worth	100.0	100.0
						INCOME DATA		
	100.0	100.0	100.0			Net Sales	100.0	100.0
						Gross Profit		
	94.1	93.5	92.5			Operating Expenses	94.1	94.2
	5.9	6.5	7.5			Operating Profit	5.9	5.8
	1.9	2.8	2.9			All Other Expenses (net)	2.1	3.6
	4.0	3.8	4.6			Profit Before Taxes	3.7	2.1
						RATIOS		
	2.8	1.7	2.6			Current	1.9	2.1
	1.3	1.0	1.2				1.1	1.3
	.5	.6	1.0				.8	.8
	1.8	1.4	1.6			Quick	1.3	1.4
	1.2	.6	.7				(93) .7	.7
	.4	.4	.4				.4	.3
	1 359.4	15 25.0	17 21.0			Sales/Receivables	17 21.9	15 24.3
	14 26.7	28 12.9	37 10.0				27 13.3	28 13.0
	32 11.3	36 10.2	60 6.0				37 9.8	44 8.2
						Cost of Sales/Inventory		
						Cost of Sales/Payables		
	12.3	12.1	5.6			Sales/Working Capital	10.1	6.4
	33.5	173.1	16.9				40.3	25.4
	-17.4	-14.8	NM				-23.2	-19.0
	9.4	6.8	5.0			EBIT/Interest	5.3	5.9
	(21) 1.5	(34) 2.7	(27) 3.4				(85) 2.2	(91) 2.0
	-.7	.7	1.7				.9	.0
						Net Profit + Depr., Dep., Amort./Cur. Mat. L/T/D	4.1	5.0
							(23) 2.7	(26) 1.7
							1.1	1.2
	.2	.6	1.0			Fixed/Worth	1.0	1.1
	1.2	2.0	1.7				2.9	2.9
	-4.9	270.6	3.1				NM	-5.8
	.7	1.4	1.2			Debt/Worth	1.3	1.7
	2.8	2.7	2.4				4.2	4.4
	-7.0	281.4	8.3				NM	-13.2
	63.4	52.0	36.0			% Profit Before Taxes/Tangible Net Worth	50.3	33.9
	(18) 34.6	(30) 22.9	(26) 17.0				(71) 25.8	(74) 13.1
	-6.6	1.2	9.7				5.3	4.9
	20.8	18.1	11.2			% Profit Before Taxes/Total Assets	11.9	8.1
	5.6	5.9	7.0				5.2	3.2
	-10.7	-.6	2.6				-.2	-3.1
	68.5	32.6	11.4			Sales/Net Fixed Assets	8.4	8.5
	9.0	5.6	2.6				2.7	2.6
	3.2	1.5	1.8				1.2	1.4
	5.7	3.1	2.7			Sales/Total Assets	2.7	2.7
	2.7	1.6	1.5				1.5	1.6
	1.5	1.0	.9				.9	1.0
	1.1	1.0	1.6			% Depr., Dep., Amort./Sales	2.2	2.9
	(17) 4.9	(30) 3.6	(23) 9.3				(82) 5.0	(94) 6.1
	10.4	10.5	10.6				9.6	13.2
	2.5					% Officers', Directors' Owners' Comp/Sales	1.9	2.9
	(12) 3.7						(32) 3.4	(24) 4.7
	4.2						8.3	7.1
4771M	112368M	387115M	940142M	322203M	695778M	Net Sales ($)	1569853M	3378255M
1752M	32270M	183668M	579098M	115296M	711117M	Total Assets ($)	1197104M	2140098M

M = $ thousand   MM = $ million
See Pages 11 through 21 for Explanation of Ratios and Data

Comparative Historical Data | **Current Data Sorted by Sales**

Current data groupings: **20 (4/1-9/30/06)** covers 0-1MM, 1-3MM, 3-5MM · **88 (10/1/06-3/31/07)** covers 5-10MM, 10-25MM, 25MM & OVER

4/1/04-3/31/05 ALL	4/1/05-3/31/06 ALL	4/1/06-3/31/07 ALL	Type of Statement	0-1MM	1-3MM	3-5MM	5-10MM	10-25MM	25MM & OVER
22	16	18	Unqualified				2	5	11
13	6	11	Reviewed			1	4	4	2
11	13	13	Compiled		2	5	4	2	
16	8	12	Tax Returns	4	5	2		1	
44	50	54	Other	6	6	6	13	13	10
106	93	108	**NUMBER OF STATEMENTS**	10	13	14	23	25	23
%	%	%	**ASSETS**	%	%	%	%	%	%
9.6	8.3	11.3	Cash & Equivalents	10.3	9.1	21.5	11.5	8.9	9.4
15.0	20.4	17.2	Trade Receivables (net)	12.4	3.0	16.6	22.7	16.7	22.6
10.5	9.1	9.7	Inventory	3.5	2.3	3.7	15.7	12.8	10.8
4.4	3.4	4.8	All Other Current	3.0	5.5	2.2	2.7	5.8	7.7
39.5	41.3	43.0	Total Current	29.3	19.9	44.0	52.6	44.2	50.4
50.2	45.7	42.7	Fixed Assets (net)	49.5	57.9	43.1	29.9	46.2	40.1
3.4	1.9	3.7	Intangibles (net)	10.3	1.9	4.1	4.7	.2	4.4
6.9	11.2	10.6	All Other Non-Current	11.2	20.4	8.8	12.8	9.4	5.1
100.0	100.0	100.0	Total	100.0	100.0	100.0	100.0	100.0	100.0
			LIABILITIES						
6.1	7.0	8.6	Notes Payable-Short Term	.0	17.3	1.9	12.6	10.0	6.1
5.4	7.2	6.7	Cur. Mat.-L.T.D.	8.1	6.8	7.7	7.2	5.7	5.8
8.8	12.8	11.0	Trade Payables	5.7	7.9	11.5	13.1	9.5	14.4
.4	.1	.4	Income Taxes Payable	.0	1.1	.2	.6	.1	.3
11.3	8.3	8.3	All Other Current	4.9	1.7	4.0	9.2	11.8	11.4
32.2	35.5	34.9	Total Current	18.7	34.9	25.3	42.5	37.1	38.0
40.9	41.6	40.5	Long-Term Debt	87.5	68.3	40.3	26.0	31.1	29.1
1.5	.8	.7	Deferred Taxes	1.1	1.4	.0	.3	.8	1.0
6.2	4.5	6.3	All Other Non-Current	7.2	6.6	6.1	7.8	7.1	3.5
19.2	17.6	17.6	Net Worth	-14.2	-11.2	28.3	23.3	23.9	28.3
100.0	100.0	100.0	Total Liabilities & Net Worth	100.0	100.0	100.0	100.0	100.0	100.0
			INCOME DATA						
100.0	100.0	100.0	Net Sales	100.0	100.0	100.0	100.0	100.0	100.0
			Gross Profit						
94.0	93.9	94.0	Operating Expenses	84.4	99.3	93.3	93.8	93.5	96.4
6.0	6.1	6.0	Operating Profit	15.6	.7	6.7	6.2	6.5	3.6
2.5	3.0	2.8	All Other Expenses (net)	11.4	2.7	1.3	1.5	1.4	3.0
3.5	3.0	3.2	Profit Before Taxes	4.2	-2.1	5.4	4.7	5.1	.6
			RATIOS						
1.9	2.2	2.3		8.8	1.4	4.3	2.3	2.6	2.0
1.2	1.4	1.2	Current	2.0	.5	1.8	1.2	1.1	1.3
.7	.8	.8		.3	.3	.8	.9	.7	1.0
1.2	1.7	1.5		8.0	1.0	2.9	1.4	1.7	1.5
.7	.8	.8	Quick	1.4	.4	1.4	.7	.6	.9
.4	.4	.4		.2	.2	.6	.4	.4	.5
15 24.6	17 20.9	12 30.0		0 UND	0 UND	0 UND	16 22.4	23 15.8	18 20.2
26 14.0	28 13.3	28 12.9	Sales/Receivables	24 15.3	5 70.7	24 15.4	28 13.0	31 11.9	32 11.5
42 8.8	44 8.2	43 8.6		60 6.1	14 26.7	45 8.1	42 8.6	45 8.1	47 7.7
			Cost of Sales/Inventory						
			Cost of Sales/Payables						
6.4	6.3	8.2		4.1	31.5	7.7	7.9	6.2	8.2
26.9	29.8	36.7	Sales/Working Capital	48.1	-15.6	20.6	39.6	68.8	17.5
-24.8	-27.3	-25.3		-2.8	-6.5	-31.1	-62.3	-21.5	212.2
7.3	6.2	5.6			3.3	6.1	12.7	5.1	5.0
(95) 2.0	(86) 2.3	(93) 2.8	EBIT/Interest	(12) .5	(11) 1.5	(19) 3.6	(23) 2.6	(22) 3.3	
.7	1.0	.6			-.7	.1	1.7	.9	1.2
3.6	5.0	3.6							
(33) 2.0	(17) 3.6	(15) 1.7	Net Profit + Depr., Dep., Amort./Cur. Mat. L/T/D						
1.3	1.9	1.1							
.9	.8	.7		.3	.9	.2	.3	1.0	1.0
2.1	1.6	1.7	Fixed/Worth	3.4	2.7	2.0	1.0	1.4	1.7
NM	7.7	26.5		-1.3	-2.8	NM	3.4	3.1	999.8
1.4	1.3	1.2		1.3	.6	.8	1.6	1.2	1.1
4.2	3.1	3.0	Debt/Worth	NM	2.9	2.2	2.9	2.4	4.2
-150.4	56.3	40.6		-2.1	-4.8	NM	8.7	6.7	999.8
53.9	59.1	45.4				55.2	73.1	35.7	39.9
(79) 18.3	(72) 17.2	(83) 22.6	% Profit Before Taxes/Tangible Net Worth		(11) 26.5	(19) 33.6	(22) 20.0	(18) 17.0	
3.4	2.8	3.4				-18.4	18.3	4.7	-4.3
8.8	12.8	14.2		15.0	12.9	27.5	18.7	12.1	17.6
3.3	5.1	6.1	% Profit Before Taxes/Total Assets	2.1	-1.3	4.1	7.3	5.6	6.9
-1.8	.0	-1.3		-14.7	-15.2	-5.7	1.2	-.4	2.4
8.7	15.0	19.4		UND	6.3	30.4	69.5	10.3	19.2
2.9	3.6	4.6	Sales/Net Fixed Assets	2.4	3.0	6.0	15.9	2.2	9.7
1.4	1.6	1.8		.8	1.8	1.8	2.6	1.7	2.4
2.5	3.3	3.1		2.2	2.7	4.0	4.7	3.2	3.0
1.4	1.6	1.8	Sales/Total Assets	1.0	1.9	1.9	1.8	1.6	2.5
.8	.8	1.0		.3	1.0	1.2	1.0	1.0	1.5
2.5	1.3	1.2				1.9	.6	1.3	.8
(90) 6.7	(73) 5.4	(78) 3.8	% Depr., Dep., Amort./Sales		(10) 3.2	(16) 1.4	(21) 5.1	(16) 2.8	
10.4	12.5	10.4				9.0	9.7	10.5	8.0
1.7	1.2	2.0							
(24) 3.3	(18) 2.7	(26) 3.7	% Officers', Directors' Owners' Comp/Sales						
7.0	6.4	5.2							
3416867M	4592461M	2462377M	Net Sales ($)	5191M	29089M	54924M	160328M	393242M	1819603M
2579745M	2392497M	1623201M	Total Assets ($)	8494M	20609M	32186M	113126M	312112M	1136674M

M = $ thousand   MM = $ million
See Pages 11 through 21 for Explanation of Ratios and Data

Current Data Sorted by Assets   Comparative Historical Data

0-500M	500M-2MM	2-10MM	10-50MM	50-100MM	100-250MM	Type of Statement	4/1/02-3/31/03 ALL	4/1/03-3/31/04 ALL
		7	3	1	1	Unqualified		4
	1	8	3			Reviewed		8
	3	3	1			Compiled	1	4
2	3					Tax Returns		5
2	7	7	3		1	Other		8
	6 (4/1-9/30/06)		50 (10/1/06-3/31/07)					
4	14	25	10	1	2	NUMBER OF STATEMENTS	1	29
%	%	%	%	%	%	**ASSETS**	%	%
	7.7	2.7	7.8			Cash & Equivalents		6.1
	8.1	18.3	7.7			Trade Receivables (net)		8.1
	5.9	15.8	5.8			Inventory		5.9
	8.7	2.3	1.1			All Other Current		1.8
	30.3	39.1	22.3			Total Current		22.0
	54.5	48.9	64.0			Fixed Assets (net)		63.7
	1.4	3.2	1.0			Intangibles (net)		.5
	13.7	8.8	12.7			All Other Non-Current		13.9
	100.0	100.0	100.0			Total		100.0
						LIABILITIES		
	11.1	6.9	.4			Notes Payable-Short Term		7.8
	4.7	4.2	5.8			Cur. Mat.-L.T.D.		3.1
	5.7	17.0	6.4			Trade Payables		7.3
	.0	.0	.3			Income Taxes Payable		.9
	7.6	21.0	10.0			All Other Current		10.9
	29.1	49.1	23.0			Total Current		30.0
	53.7	32.8	38.8			Long-Term Debt		37.9
	.0	.4	.0			Deferred Taxes		.5
	15.6	5.2	7.8			All Other Non-Current		5.7
	1.6	12.4	30.5			Net Worth		25.9
	100.0	100.0	100.0			Total Liabilities & Net Worth		100.0
						INCOME DATA		
	100.0	100.0	100.0			Net Sales		100.0
						Gross Profit		
	91.2	98.2	96.3			Operating Expenses		100.5
	8.8	1.8	3.7			Operating Profit		-.5
	4.9	4.6	3.3			All Other Expenses (net)		2.2
	4.0	-2.8	.4			Profit Before Taxes		-2.7
						RATIOS		
	2.3	1.8	1.4					1.3
	.9	.9	.8			Current		.7
	.6	.4	.4					.3
	1.5	.8	1.0					1.0
	.6	.4	.7			Quick		.6
	.2	.2	.2					.1
	0 UND	10 36.4	8 48.6					2 165.3
	5 71.0	22 16.6	30 12.2			Sales/Receivables		10 36.7
	20 18.5	40 9.0	42 8.6					41 8.9
						Cost of Sales/Inventory		
						Cost of Sales/Payables		
	12.0	13.6	26.0					17.8
	-189.2	-46.3	-29.7			Sales/Working Capital		-27.5
	-12.9	-5.2	-4.5					-6.7
	18.8	2.8						5.9
	(11) 1.3	(24) .2				EBIT/Interest		(24) .8
	.6	-1.2						-1.1
						Net Profit + Depr., Dep., Amort./Cur. Mat. L/T/D		
	.4	.8	1.2					1.0
	3.1	2.2	3.6			Fixed/Worth		1.7
	-2.4	13.5	13.3					3.9
	1.3	1.2	1.0					.9
	4.8	2.7	3.3			Debt/Worth		1.5
	-4.9	23.1	22.8					3.8
		33.9						24.0
		(21) 1.4				% Profit Before Taxes/Tangible Net Worth		(24) 1.8
		-14.1						-10.2
	20.5	2.9	8.4					7.6
	2.9	-1.7	2.7			% Profit Before Taxes/Total Assets		-.6
	-3.1	-8.5	-2.6					-6.1
	13.1	18.8	4.7					5.3
	2.7	2.6	1.7			Sales/Net Fixed Assets		1.3
	1.2	.8	.3					.6
	2.4	2.9	1.7					2.1
	1.4	1.5	.7			Sales/Total Assets		.7
	.9	.6	.3					.5
	1.5	1.0	3.6					3.3
	(11) 5.5	(23) 6.3	5.8			% Depr., Dep., Amort./Sales		(27) 7.1
	23.2	11.8	9.5					9.0
						% Officers', Directors' Owners' Comp/Sales		
4879M	29039M	240586M	187718M	229642M	490150M	Net Sales ($)	506M	93319M
1158M	16959M	131037M	163575M	53823M	400845M	Total Assets ($)	996M	105106M

© RMA 2007

M = $ thousand   MM = $ million
See Pages 11 through 21 for Explanation of Ratios and Data

Comparative Historical Data

Current Data Sorted by Sales

					Type of Statement						
	7		10	12	Unqualified			5	2	1	4
	5		9	12	Reviewed		3	2	2	4	1
	6		3	7	Compiled		4	1	1	1	
	11		2	5	Tax Returns		2				
	14		18	20	Other	3	7	2	4	3	2
	4/1/04-		4/1/05-	4/1/06-		2					
	3/31/05		3/31/06	3/31/07			6 (4/1-9/30/06)		50 (10/1/06-3/31/07)		
	ALL		ALL	ALL		0-1MM	1-3MM	3-5MM	5-10MM	10-25MM	25MM & OVER
	43		42	56	NUMBER OF STATEMENTS	5	16	10	9	9	7
	%		%	%	ASSETS	%	%	%	%	%	%
	8.2		6.4	6.4	Cash & Equivalents		7.3	6.7			
	9.9		12.9	14.5	Trade Receivables (net)		9.1	11.6			
	3.3		5.8	10.5	Inventory		4.6	10.4			
	3.2		2.4	4.5	All Other Current		7.9	.5			
	24.7		27.5	35.9	Total Current		28.9	29.2			
	70.2		56.6	52.1	Fixed Assets (net)		50.5	67.6			
	1.3		2.7	2.1	Intangibles (net)		.9	1.6			
	3.9		13.3	9.9	All Other Non-Current		19.7	1.7			
	100.0		100.0	100.0	Total		100.0	100.0			
					LIABILITIES						
	4.5		4.7	7.4	Notes Payable-Short Term		13.2	2.3			
	3.7		2.6	4.4	Cur. Mat.-L.T.D.		3.3	6.6			
	7.9		10.2	13.8	Trade Payables		14.8	7.2			
	.1		.2	.2	Income Taxes Payable		.0	.3			
	4.7		8.3	15.5	All Other Current		4.9	40.5			
	21.0		26.0	41.3	Total Current		36.2	56.9			
	36.0		33.9	36.1	Long-Term Debt		48.3	43.0			
	.4		1.3	.3	Deferred Taxes		.0	.0			
	11.4		4.8	9.9	All Other Non-Current		14.7	10.3			
	31.2		34.0	12.4	Net Worth		.7	-10.2			
	100.0		100.0	100.0	Total Liabilities & Net Worth		100.0	100.0			
					INCOME DATA						
	100.0		100.0	100.0	Net Sales		100.0	100.0			
					Gross Profit						
	93.6		93.5	97.2	Operating Expenses		95.4	98.0			
	6.4		6.5	2.8	Operating Profit		4.6	2.0			
	4.9		2.9	4.2	All Other Expenses (net)		4.8	4.5			
	1.5		3.5	-1.4	Profit Before Taxes		-.1	-2.5			
					RATIOS						
	2.2		2.0	1.8			2.0	1.4			
	1.0		1.0	.9	Current		.7	.6			
	.5		.5	.5			.5	.4			
	1.7		1.5	.9			1.5	.7			
	.8		.6	.5	Quick		.4	.5			
	.3		.3	.2			.3	.3			
3	117.6	8	47.6	6	62.8		0	UND	15	24.3	
16	23.5	20	18.2	19	19.5	Sales/Receivables	7	54.6	31	11.9	
37	9.8	48	7.6	38	9.6		19	19.5	60	6.1	
					Cost of Sales/Inventory						
					Cost of Sales/Payables						
	10.4		10.5	12.9			20.0	27.1			
	117.8		NM	-60.1	Sales/Working Capital		-52.6	-7.6			
	-10.4		-12.9	-6.6			-9.6	-5.1			
	4.9		4.4	6.2			5.2	2.9			
(38)	1.5	(35)	1.5	(51)	.7	EBIT/Interest	(14)	.4	.4		
	-.8		.7	-1.0			-5.1	-.4			
				7.9		Net Profit + Depr., Dep.,						
			(13)	1.0		Amort./Cur. Mat. L/T/D						
				-1.2								
	1.2		1.1	.7			.4	3.0			
	2.1		1.8	2.5	Fixed/Worth		1.4	5.3			
	12.3		7.4	20.0			-2.3	NM			
	.6		.9	1.2			.8	2.3			
	2.0		1.9	3.1	Debt/Worth		4.8	5.0			
	11.8		13.0	UND			-4.3	NM			
	15.4		30.5	32.2	% Profit Before Taxes/Tangible		29.7				
(35)	1.9	(35)	4.9	(43)	8.2	Net Worth	(10)	1.9			
	-8.7		-7.0	-6.8			-8.7				
	4.1		9.4	8.5			8.1	1.1			
	.4		1.4	-1.2	% Profit Before Taxes/Total		-2.3	-1.6			
	-3.5		-2.1	-8.6	Assets		-11.0	-7.0			
	5.5		5.0	13.4			14.0	5.9			
	1.2		1.5	2.6	Sales/Net Fixed Assets		2.5	.8			
	.6		.7	.9			1.3	.6			
	3.7		2.2	2.6			2.1	1.5			
	.8		.8	1.4	Sales/Total Assets		1.3	.6			
	.5		.5	.6			.8	.4			
	5.4		2.2	1.5			2.8	5.8			
(35)	7.7	(37)	8.0	(47)	5.5	% Depr., Dep., Amort./Sales	(12)	8.5	8.4		
	11.3		10.1	12.1			14.7	12.0			
	3.0			1.7	% Officers', Directors'						
(17)	11.3		(13)	3.4	Owners' Comp/Sales						
	27.2			8.1							
	591935M		1010524M	1182014M	Net Sales ($)	2326M	28677M	39464M	58706M	148702M	904139M
	487092M		975905M	767397M	Total Assets ($)	8543M	31842M	64033M	67468M	65602M	529909M

M = $ thousand   MM = $ million
See Pages 11 through 21 for Explanation of Ratios and Data

Current Data Sorted by Assets   Comparative Historical Data

0-500M	500M-2MM	2-10MM	10-50MM	50-100MM	100-250MM	Type of Statement	4/1/02-3/31/03 ALL	4/1/03-3/31/04 ALL
		2	11	4	3	Unqualified	17	20
1	1	1	1			Reviewed	6	2
2		1	3			Compiled	3	8
1	1					Tax Returns	2	1
		10	9	3	3	Other	17	21
	3 (4/1-9/30/06)		58 (10/1/06-3/31/07)					
4	6	14	24	7	6	NUMBER OF STATEMENTS	45	52
%	%	%	%	%	%		%	%

ASSETS

0-500M	500M-2MM	2-10MM	10-50MM	50-100MM	100-250MM		4/1/02-3/31/03 ALL	4/1/03-3/31/04 ALL
		11.9	10.7			Cash & Equivalents	7.0	7.6
		22.8	13.1			Trade Receivables (net)	8.7	10.1
		1.7	1.3			Inventory	2.5	3.4
		9.0	4.9			All Other Current	3.1	3.9
		45.4	30.0			Total Current	21.4	25.0
		34.0	63.0			Fixed Assets (net)	66.0	64.3
		3.3	.3			Intangibles (net)	4.1	3.3
		17.4	6.7			All Other Non-Current	8.6	7.4
		100.0	100.0			Total	100.0	100.0

LIABILITIES

0-500M	500M-2MM	2-10MM	10-50MM	50-100MM	100-250MM		4/1/02-3/31/03 ALL	4/1/03-3/31/04 ALL
		1.9	3.8			Notes Payable-Short Term	5.4	5.6
		3.0	5.1			Cur. Mat.-L.T.D.	5.1	3.0
		6.0	11.2			Trade Payables	7.6	7.1
		1.6	.2			Income Taxes Payable	.5	.2
		6.4	9.8			All Other Current	8.8	6.2
		18.9	30.1			Total Current	27.4	22.1
		17.1	28.6			Long-Term Debt	32.8	28.0
		.5	2.1			Deferred Taxes	6.1	5.1
		2.4	8.2			All Other Non-Current	10.4	10.6
		61.1	30.9			Net Worth	23.3	34.1
		100.0	100.0			Total Liabilities & Net Worth	100.0	100.0

INCOME DATA

0-500M	500M-2MM	2-10MM	10-50MM	50-100MM	100-250MM		4/1/02-3/31/03 ALL	4/1/03-3/31/04 ALL
		100.0	100.0			Net Sales	100.0	100.0
						Gross Profit		
		79.5	86.3			Operating Expenses	84.5	85.8
		20.5	13.7			Operating Profit	15.5	14.2
		.3	-.4			All Other Expenses (net)	4.0	2.1
		20.2	14.1			Profit Before Taxes	11.6	12.1

RATIOS

0-500M	500M-2MM	2-10MM	10-50MM	50-100MM	100-250MM		4/1/02-3/31/03 ALL	4/1/03-3/31/04 ALL
		5.3	1.5			Current	1.7	2.0
		2.4	.9				.8	1.0
		1.2	.7				.5	.6
		3.6	1.1			Quick	1.1	1.4
		1.9	.7				.6	.7
		1.0	.4				.3	.4
		15 24.5	35 10.3			Sales/Receivables	18 20.3	18 20.6
		40 9.2	50 7.3				39 9.5	38 9.7
		69 5.3	72 5.1				60 6.1	55 6.7
						Cost of Sales/Inventory		
						Cost of Sales/Payables		
		3.4	7.8			Sales/Working Capital	8.6	6.2
		9.5	-44.4				-19.3	138.4
		148.0	-6.1				-6.1	-9.1
		42.5	9.0			EBIT/Interest	8.8	9.2
		10.2	(22) 3.3				(44) 3.9	(50) 3.7
		2.2	2.1				1.4	2.3
			4.1			Net Profit + Depr., Dep.,	3.0	13.2
			(13) 1.5			Amort./Cur. Mat. L/T/D	(17) 2.1	(19) 4.5
			1.3				1.3	2.2
		.2	1.0			Fixed/Worth	1.4	1.2
		.7	3.2				2.8	1.9
		1.1	5.6				9.7	5.2
		.1	.9			Debt/Worth	1.4	1.0
		.5	4.0				3.2	2.0
		1.3	6.6				10.7	5.8
		33.0	56.6			% Profit Before Taxes/Tangible	46.1	38.7
		(13) 13.9	(23) 27.4			Net Worth	(39) 25.7	(46) 20.9
		7.5	14.0				9.6	13.2
		16.7	14.7			% Profit Before Taxes/Total	13.4	11.8
		11.9	10.2			Assets	5.4	6.1
		3.8	3.0				.7	3.5
		65.0	1.5			Sales/Net Fixed Assets	2.5	2.1
		3.7	1.0				.9	1.1
		2.0	.5				.5	.5
		1.8	.8			Sales/Total Assets	1.2	1.1
		1.4	.6				.7	.7
		.5	.4				.4	.3
		1.1	4.6			% Depr., Dep., Amort./Sales	4.8	4.2
		(13) 5.4	9.1				(43) 7.1	(48) 7.1
		12.7	12.7				11.5	12.0
						% Officers', Directors' Owners' Comp/Sales		
2427M	18424M	81466M	579938M	279219M	984367M	Net Sales ($)	1303836M	1592257M
798M	5761M	59221M	540288M	527180M	963813M	Total Assets ($)	1687835M	1874041M

M = $ thousand   MM = $ million
See Pages 11 through 21 for Explanation of Ratios and Data

Comparative Historical Data

Current Data Sorted by Sales

			Type of Statement						
19	23	20	Unqualified		1	1	2	8	8
7	5	4	Reviewed		2		1	1	
8	4	6	Compiled	2		1	2	1	
3	6	2	Tax Returns	1	1		1		
30	24	29	Other	1	5	2	9	7	5
4/1/04- 3/31/05 ALL	4/1/05- 3/31/06 ALL	4/1/06- 3/31/07 ALL		0-1MM	1-3MM 3 (4/1-9/30/06)	3-5MM	5-10MM	10-25MM 58 (10/1/06-3/31/07)	25MM & OVER
67	62	61	NUMBER OF STATEMENTS	4	9	4	14	17	13
%	%	%	**ASSETS**	%	%	%	%	%	%
9.2	8.8	9.0	Cash & Equivalents				10.8	6.0	9.2
14.2	17.2	17.8	Trade Receivables (net)				17.1	17.6	17.0
3.2	4.4	1.3	Inventory				1.7	1.6	1.0
2.0	4.2	5.3	All Other Current				6.3	5.6	1.9
28.7	34.6	33.4	Total Current				35.9	30.8	29.0
57.9	53.2	54.5	Fixed Assets (net)				53.1	62.1	59.7
1.6	2.7	3.6	Intangibles (net)				3.1	1.0	2.3
11.8	9.5	8.5	All Other Non-Current				7.9	6.1	9.0
100.0	100.0	100.0	Total				100.0	100.0	100.0
			LIABILITIES						
3.1	5.6	5.8	Notes Payable-Short Term				5.0	2.9	3.3
3.1	3.3	3.4	Cur. Mat.-L.T.D.				5.5	5.2	1.4
9.9	11.4	10.6	Trade Payables				13.5	8.1	7.5
1.0	.4	.5	Income Taxes Payable				1.7	.2	.3
9.3	9.6	9.2	All Other Current				4.0	8.6	17.4
26.4	30.3	29.5	Total Current				29.6	25.0	29.9
24.9	23.4	28.4	Long-Term Debt				22.1	31.2	22.2
2.7	3.9	2.6	Deferred Taxes				1.9	3.4	5.9
8.7	6.3	6.2	All Other Non-Current				9.1	3.5	9.3
37.3	36.2	33.3	Net Worth				37.3	36.9	32.8
100.0	100.0	100.0	Total Liabilties & Net Worth				100.0	100.0	100.0
			INCOME DATA						
100.0	100.0	100.0	Net Sales				100.0	100.0	100.0
			Gross Profit						
86.7	85.6	84.8	Operating Expenses				86.2	86.0	90.5
13.3	14.4	15.2	Operating Profit				13.8	14.0	9.5
2.1	1.3	1.2	All Other Expenses (net)				-.5	1.9	.1
11.2	13.0	14.0	Profit Before Taxes				14.3	12.1	9.4
			RATIOS						
2.1	2.2	1.7	Current				1.9	1.6	1.4
1.0	1.1	1.0					.9	.9	1.0
.7	.7	.7					.7	.7	.8
1.6	1.6	1.4	Quick				1.6	1.3	1.1
.8	.8	.9					.7	.7	.9
.6	.5	.5					.2	.5	.7
29 12.8	19 19.0	31 11.6	Sales/Receivables				22 16.7	36 10.0	41 8.8
46 7.9	56 6.5	45 8.2					48 7.7	50 7.4	48 7.7
60 6.1	75 4.9	64 5.7					88 4.2	67 5.4	64 5.7
			Cost of Sales/Inventory						
			Cost of Sales/Payables						
7.9	5.1	10.6	Sales/Working Capital				7.4	10.6	16.6
232.3	45.7	486.8					-31.0	-55.5	125.6
-16.9	-9.5	-12.2					-2.9	-11.4	-45.4
16.4	23.4	12.9	EBIT/Interest				39.4	7.7	30.2
(58) 6.5	(55) 5.9	(55) 3.8					3.4	(16) 2.6	(10) 10.0
2.8	1.5	2.1					2.0	1.9	2.1
5.4	10.1	8.8	Net Profit + Depr., Dep., Amort./Cur. Mat. L/T/D					3.5	
(20) 2.5	(19) 3.9	(24) 2.4					(10)	1.5	
1.3	2.2	1.4						1.3	
.9	.9	.8	Fixed/Worth				.8	.9	1.2
1.7	1.8	1.9					2.8	1.9	3.1
3.1	4.0	5.5					5.8	5.1	4.0
.9	.9	.7	Debt/Worth				.6	.7	1.2
2.2	1.9	3.0					3.1	1.8	3.3
4.4	6.6	6.3					7.4	5.4	4.2
62.5	54.7	51.9	% Profit Before Taxes/Tangible Net Worth				46.4	46.3	50.4
(66) 22.7	(56) 22.5	(56) 27.2					(13) 23.6	26.1	(12) 31.3
8.5	10.3	8.5					4.7	7.6	10.4
15.2	15.6	15.8	% Profit Before Taxes/Total Assets				15.4	15.7	16.4
8.1	9.0	8.8					9.2	8.1	10.7
2.9	2.0	3.1					3.2	2.9	4.5
4.1	5.1	4.4	Sales/Net Fixed Assets				5.0	1.9	2.9
1.3	1.5	1.4					1.2	1.1	1.2
.7	.6	.7					.4	.8	.8
1.3	1.6	1.8	Sales/Total Assets				1.5	1.2	1.7
.8	.8	.8					.7	.7	.9
.5	.4	.4					.3	.6	.6
3.1	3.4	3.7	% Depr., Dep., Amort./Sales				3.6	5.0	2.9
(57) 6.7	(56) 6.9	(57) 7.3					9.1	8.8	(12) 4.1
11.5	10.2	11.1					12.5	11.2	5.4
			% Officers', Directors' Owners' Comp/Sales						
1851939M	1316210M	1945841M	Net Sales ($)	1313M	18038M	14982M	93562M	275449M	1542497M
2134356M	1568645M	2097061M	Total Assets ($)	5407M	18418M	79888M	203207M	397604M	1392537M

M = $ thousand   MM = $ million
See Pages 11 through 21 for Explanation of Ratios and Data

Current Data Sorted by Assets / Comparative Historical Data

Type of Statement	0-500M	500M-2MM	2-10MM	10-50MM	50-100MM	100-250MM		4/1/02-3/31/03 ALL	4/1/03-3/31/04 ALL
Unqualified			3	9	8	10		29	27
Reviewed			2	5				2	4
Compiled			3	2				17	18
Tax Returns			3					4	2
Other	1	1	15	14	3	9		22	21
	1	1	19 (4/1-9/30/06)	75 (10/1/06-3/31/07)					
NUMBER OF STATEMENTS	2	6	26	30	11	19		74	72
	%	%	%	%	%	%		%	%
ASSETS									
Cash & Equivalents			9.0	9.5	4.1	4.4		7.8	7.4
Trade Receivables (net)			17.5	16.4	11.1	10.6		15.8	16.1
Inventory			.5	1.8	2.2	1.3		2.2	1.7
All Other Current			3.0	2.2	1.1	2.5		1.9	4.3
Total Current			29.9	29.9	18.5	18.9		27.6	29.5
Fixed Assets (net)			64.1	58.0	72.1	70.3		59.4	62.6
Intangibles (net)			2.0	3.3	4.6	1.4		2.2	2.5
All Other Non-Current			3.9	8.8	4.8	9.4		10.8	5.4
Total			100.0	100.0	100.0	100.0		100.0	100.0
LIABILITIES									
Notes Payable-Short Term			8.5	3.7	6.5	.7		3.5	2.3
Cur. Mat.-L.T.D.			4.8	4.3	4.7	3.1		6.6	6.4
Trade Payables			5.7	10.0	6.4	4.0		10.1	7.0
Income Taxes Payable			.9	.1	.0	.3		.6	.2
All Other Current			6.2	6.8	7.0	4.3		6.6	6.9
Total Current			26.1	24.9	24.6	12.4		27.5	22.9
Long-Term Debt			33.6	33.5	35.8	34.9		43.6	35.1
Deferred Taxes			.3	2.2	3.9	6.0		2.8	2.6
All Other Non-Current			1.0	4.7	1.0	3.9		3.6	5.5
Net Worth			39.0	34.7	34.7	42.7		22.6	33.9
Total Liabilties & Net Worth			100.0	100.0	100.0	100.0		100.0	100.0
INCOME DATA									
Net Sales			100.0	100.0	100.0	100.0		100.0	100.0
Gross Profit									
Operating Expenses			80.7	82.9	77.5	74.6		90.7	90.5
Operating Profit			19.3	17.1	22.5	25.4		9.3	9.5
All Other Expenses (net)			3.9	2.8	8.2	5.0		3.9	3.1
Profit Before Taxes			15.4	14.3	14.3	20.4		5.5	6.3
RATIOS									
Current			2.6	2.2	1.3	1.8		1.8	2.0
			1.4	1.2	.9	1.3		1.0	1.2
			.5	.4	.4	.8		.5	.6
Quick			2.3	1.5	1.1	1.3		1.8	1.6
			1.3	.8	.7	1.1		.8	1.0
			.5	.4	.4	.6		.4	.4
Sales/Receivables			14 25.5	22 16.5	7 55.0	27 13.6		14 25.8	19 18.9
			38 9.7	38 9.5	42 8.8	48 7.6		38 9.5	39 9.3
			67 5.4	66 5.6	47 7.8	81 4.5		57 6.4	61 6.0
Cost of Sales/Inventory									
Cost of Sales/Payables									
Sales/Working Capital			6.5	5.8	14.5	7.4		9.8	7.6
			25.0	38.7	-95.5	19.8		-123.6	28.4
			-9.8	-5.4	-5.7	-51.3		-8.8	-12.1
EBIT/Interest			11.5	20.1	14.4	23.0		5.3	6.4
			(22) 5.8	(26) 5.5	(10) 3.8	(18) 5.9		(71) 2.2	(63) 2.4
			2.0	2.7	3.2	2.3		1.1	1.4
Net Profit + Depr., Dep., Amort./Cur. Mat. L/T/D								2.1	2.0
								(21) 1.5	(17) 1.3
								1.0	.9
Fixed/Worth			1.1	.6	1.2	1.0		1.1	1.2
			1.9	1.8	2.3	2.3		2.4	2.0
			4.2	7.0	7.1	4.9		4.2	4.9
Debt/Worth			.9	1.0	.8	.8		1.2	1.0
			1.8	2.6	1.7	2.2		2.9	2.2
			4.3	8.5	10.4	4.7		9.0	6.2
% Profit Before Taxes/Tangible Net Worth			56.8	55.3	62.2	48.5		32.6	32.7
			(24) 30.4	(26) 38.2	(10) 37.2	29.8		(65) 17.1	(66) 14.9
			7.4	18.9	28.0	21.1		2.6	6.4
% Profit Before Taxes/Total Assets			20.2	19.4	20.3	25.7		9.0	8.0
			11.2	10.1	8.5	9.9		4.4	3.8
			2.6	5.3	6.9	4.6		.0	1.9
Sales/Net Fixed Assets			3.7	3.6	2.9	1.3		5.0	4.1
			1.9	1.5	1.6	1.0		1.5	1.4
			.9	.8	.3	.7		.7	.7
Sales/Total Assets			1.9	1.4	1.5	.9		1.9	1.8
			1.4	.8	.9	.7		.9	1.0
			.6	.5	.3	.6		.5	.5
% Depr., Dep., Amort./Sales			2.9	2.1	3.2	4.5		3.1	3.0
			(24) 4.9	(28) 5.7	5.6	(10) 6.1		(69) 7.2	(62) 7.5
			9.8	13.1	23.2	9.6		11.0	11.6
% Officers', Directors' Owners' Comp/Sales								3.3	2.3
								(14) 6.3	(12) 4.0
								9.3	11.5
Net Sales ($)	1569M	16883M	240521M	746203M	842376M	2166423M		2228680M	2796605M
Total Assets ($)	422M	9519M	158852M	702341M	798059M	2836407M		2818566M	3472287M

M = $ thousand   MM = $ million

See Pages 11 through 21 for Explanation of Ratios and Data

Comparative Historical Data | Current Data Sorted by Sales

Type of Statement

4/1/04-3/31/05	4/1/05-3/31/06	4/1/06-3/31/07	Type of Statement	0-1MM	1-3MM	3-5MM	5-10MM	10-25MM	25MM & OVER
32	22	30	Unqualified		2		2	6	20
6	8	7	Reviewed		1		1	4	1
11	9	9	Compiled		2	4		3	
5	1	5	Tax Returns	1	2	1	1		
21	38	43	Other	1	4	4	7	11	17
ALL	ALL	ALL		19 (4/1-9/30/06)			75 (10/1/06-3/31/07)		

4/1/04-3/31/05 ALL	4/1/05-3/31/06 ALL	4/1/06-3/31/07 ALL		0-1MM	1-3MM	3-5MM	5-10MM	10-25MM	25MM & OVER
75	78	94	**NUMBER OF STATEMENTS**	1	11	9	11	24	38
%	%	%	**ASSETS**	%	%	%	%	%	%
7.7	9.0	8.2	Cash & Equivalents		12.8		10.4	8.9	6.4
16.3	19.2	14.8	Trade Receivables (net)		11.7		16.5	13.3	17.3
1.8	1.6	1.5	Inventory		2.0		.1	.8	2.3
3.4	3.4	2.5	All Other Current		.7		2.3	2.9	2.1
29.1	33.3	27.0	Total Current		27.2		29.3	25.9	28.0
59.8	56.3	62.9	Fixed Assets (net)		56.2		55.8	67.2	63.2
2.8	2.2	2.4	Intangibles (net)		.0		8.4	.9	3.0
8.4	8.3	7.7	All Other Non-Current		16.6		6.5	6.0	5.7
100.0	100.0	100.0	Total		100.0		100.0	100.0	100.0
			LIABILITIES						
3.1	4.6	5.1	Notes Payable-Short Term		5.0		11.3	2.0	4.7
5.7	4.8	4.5	Cur. Mat.-L.T.D.		4.1		4.9	4.6	3.5
5.8	8.7	7.4	Trade Payables		9.8		3.2	9.4	8.2
.1	.6	.3	Income Taxes Payable		.0		.7	.0	.2
7.0	7.5	6.3	All Other Current		5.8		4.3	7.0	7.4
21.7	26.2	23.7	Total Current		24.8		24.5	23.1	23.9
31.5	30.3	34.4	Long-Term Debt		30.3		27.6	36.4	32.9
3.0	2.8	2.5	Deferred Taxes		1.5		.1	1.3	4.7
5.4	6.3	2.8	All Other Non-Current		2.6		3.4	3.2	3.2
38.4	34.5	36.6	Net Worth		40.8		44.4	36.0	35.2
100.0	100.0	100.0	Total Liabilities & Net Worth		100.0		100.0	100.0	100.0
			INCOME DATA						
100.0	100.0	100.0	Net Sales		100.0		100.0	100.0	100.0
			Gross Profit						
87.8	84.5	80.8	Operating Expenses		67.6		84.1	79.8	82.6
12.2	15.5	19.2	Operating Profit		32.4		15.9	20.2	17.4
1.6	1.7	4.2	All Other Expenses (net)		11.9		3.9	5.9	1.4
10.5	13.8	15.0	Profit Before Taxes		20.4		12.0	14.3	16.0
			RATIOS						
2.0	2.5	2.1	Current		3.0		2.8	1.7	2.0
1.3	1.3	1.1			.8		.9	1.0	1.3
.6	.8	.5			.5		.4	.6	.8
1.8	2.1	1.8	Quick		3.0		2.7	1.5	1.5
1.1	1.0	.9			.8		.9	.9	1.1
.6	.6	.5			.2		.2	.5	.6
25 14.6	31 11.9	18 20.5	Sales/Receivables		0 UND		7 50.1	8 45.1	32 11.4
41 8.9	44 8.2	39 9.2			32 11.5		37 9.8	32 11.5	46 8.0
63 5.8	83 4.4	63 5.8			113 3.2		52 7.1	53 6.9	73 5.0
			Cost of Sales/Inventory						
			Cost of Sales/Payables						
7.4	4.4	7.2	Sales/Working Capital		3.0		6.5	9.2	8.3
25.7	17.6	38.1			-17.3		-85.2	279.6	17.5
-25.8	-26.0	-11.3			-5.1		-3.5	-9.2	-46.8
5.9	9.8	16.7	EBIT/Interest					20.5	18.9
(66) 3.2	(70) 4.9	(83) 5.1						(21) 5.8	(37) 6.7
1.7	2.8	2.3						2.2	2.7
3.6	4.0	4.5	Net Profit + Depr., Dep., Amort./Cur. Mat. L/T/D						5.8
(19) 1.9	(26) 1.9	(23) 2.2						(15) 2.5	
1.4	1.2	1.2							2.0
.9	1.0	1.0	Fixed/Worth		.5		.6	1.1	1.1
1.8	1.7	1.9			1.0		2.1	1.8	2.2
4.0	3.7	5.1			7.9		4.2	3.7	5.2
.8	.9	.9	Debt/Worth		.1		.5	1.0	.9
1.5	1.9	2.0			2.5		1.7	1.5	2.4
4.7	4.1	5.0			8.5		4.0	3.6	5.2
53.2	44.2	51.8	% Profit Before Taxes/Tangible Net Worth		62.5		45.5	70.2	51.1
(66) 16.9	(70) 28.5	(85) 33.7			(10) 21.7		(10) 30.8	(22) 34.8	(34) 37.2
6.1	17.0	16.9			6.6		8.7	16.7	28.5
11.2	17.3	20.6	% Profit Before Taxes/Total Assets		12.3		21.3	21.2	24.5
6.5	11.1	9.8			7.4		7.8	9.2	13.3
2.8	5.3	4.4			.8		1.8	5.0	6.8
3.2	3.7	3.3	Sales/Net Fixed Assets		2.5		3.4	3.6	3.3
1.3	1.7	1.6			1.0		1.8	1.4	1.6
.8	.9	.8			.4		1.6	.7	1.0
1.7	1.8	1.5	Sales/Total Assets		1.0		1.4	1.5	2.0
.9	1.1	.9			.4		1.4	.8	1.0
.5	.6	.6			.2		.5	.6	.7
4.1	3.2	2.7	% Depr., Dep., Amort./Sales		6.2		4.4	2.3	2.5
(62) 7.2	(63) 5.8	(81) 5.4			(10) 10.7		5.5	(22) 5.7	(29) 4.5
11.2	9.0	10.3			30.9		10.0	19.4	7.2
2.0	.7	.8	% Officers', Directors' Owners' Comp/Sales						
(15) 4.8	(12) 3.8	(23) 2.8							
9.4	5.1	10.0							
2699812M	3294626M	4013975M	Net Sales ($)	354M	19711M	36027M	84044M	353123M	3520716M
3265991M	3442710M	4505600M	Total Assets ($)	235M	179158M	56646M	95243M	592930M	3581388M

© RMA 2007

M = $ thousand   MM = $ million
See Pages 11 through 21 for Explanation of Ratios and Data

Current Data Sorted by Assets | Comparative Historical Data

						Type of Statement		
1	8	16	36	10	10	Unqualified	62	63
8	27	105	48	1	2	Reviewed	211	214
39	105	88	4		1	Compiled	243	301
96	87	26	4		1	Tax Returns	163	194
48	114	113	54	5	3	Other	237	253
	163 (4/1-9/30/06)		897 (10/1/06-3/31/07)				4/1/02-3/31/03	4/1/03-3/31/04
0-500M	500M-2MM	2-10MM	10-50MM	50-100MM	100-250MM		ALL	ALL
192	341	348	146	16	17	NUMBER OF STATEMENTS	916	1025
%	%	%	%	%	%	ASSETS	%	%
18.8	9.6	8.1	8.5	3.4	4.6	Cash & Equivalents	10.2	10.7
22.3	29.7	27.8	24.8	21.1	20.2	Trade Receivables (net)	28.1	28.5
1.7	1.5	1.6	1.6	.7	.9	Inventory	1.9	1.5
4.3	4.0	4.1	2.8	2.9	4.7	All Other Current	4.8	4.6
47.1	44.9	41.6	37.7	28.2	30.5	Total Current	45.1	45.3
39.1	44.4	46.3	52.3	58.6	54.6	Fixed Assets (net)	43.2	42.4
2.8	2.0	2.9	3.7	5.6	5.8	Intangibles (net)	2.7	2.9
10.9	8.7	9.2	6.3	7.6	9.2	All Other Non-Current	9.0	9.3
100.0	100.0	100.0	100.0	100.0	100.0	Total	100.0	100.0
						LIABILITIES		
14.0	10.0	6.8	5.4	7.3	5.6	Notes Payable-Short Term	9.5	8.9
11.3	7.1	8.4	8.8	6.5	8.4	Cur. Mat.-L.T.D.	8.8	10.0
12.7	11.1	11.7	9.2	8.1	8.3	Trade Payables	10.9	11.2
.1	.2	.4	.3	.1	.2	Income Taxes Payable	.3	.2
24.9	9.0	7.2	7.5	5.4	7.8	All Other Current	9.7	11.3
63.0	37.4	34.4	31.1	27.5	30.4	Total Current	39.3	41.7
40.2	29.4	26.3	30.8	38.5	39.9	Long-Term Debt	25.8	26.3
.0	.4	1.2	1.9	2.2	5.1	Deferred Taxes	.9	.8
7.5	4.8	3.7	2.1	3.4	4.4	All Other Non-Current	3.7	5.4
-10.7	28.0	34.4	34.1	28.5	20.2	Net Worth	30.4	25.7
100.0	100.0	100.0	100.0	100.0	100.0	Total Liabilities & Net Worth	100.0	100.0
						INCOME DATA		
100.0	100.0	100.0	100.0	100.0	100.0	Net Sales	100.0	100.0
						Gross Profit		
95.9	95.4	95.0	93.8	90.5	94.2	Operating Expenses	96.2	95.9
4.1	4.6	5.0	6.2	9.5	5.8	Operating Profit	3.8	4.1
.7	1.4	1.0	1.3	2.0	1.0	All Other Expenses (net)	1.3	.9
3.5	3.2	4.0	4.9	7.5	4.8	Profit Before Taxes	2.5	3.2
						RATIOS		
2.2	2.7	1.9	1.9	1.3	1.6		2.0	2.0
.9	1.3	1.1	1.2	1.1	1.0	Current	1.2	1.2
.4	.6	.8	.7	.6	.9		.7	.7
2.0	2.4	1.7	1.7	1.1	1.4		1.7	1.7
.8 (339)	1.1	1.0	1.0	.9	.9	Quick	1.0	1.0
.3	.6	.6	.6	.6	.6		.6	.6
0 UND	15 23.5	25 14.8	30 12.1	32 11.3	35 10.5		18 20.5	18 20.1
4 85.9	29 12.7	35 10.3	37 9.8	38 9.6	43 8.5	Sales/Receivables	34 10.8	33 11.0
28 13.0	40 9.1	47 7.8	49 7.4	57 6.4	53 6.9		46 7.9	46 8.0
						Cost of Sales/Inventory		
						Cost of Sales/Payables		
18.0	11.5	12.9	13.2	20.4	20.1		12.2	12.1
-383.5	37.4	61.3	47.6	524.4	171.2	Sales/Working Capital	53.4	61.9
-14.0	-21.0	-25.8	-21.3	-15.1	-43.2		-26.5	-23.1
9.4	8.1	7.4	7.1	4.9	6.7		5.5	6.4
(142) 2.5	(296) 2.6	(328) 2.9	(138) 3.7	3.1	(16) 2.5	EBIT/Interest	(822) 2.1	(917) 2.5
.3	.8	1.3	1.9	1.4	1.6		.6	1.0
	3.6	3.0	3.6				3.1	2.8
	(46) 1.7	(104) 1.7	(57) 1.7			Net Profit + Depr., Dep., Amort./Cur. Mat. L/T/D	(245) 1.5	(234) 1.5
	1.1	1.1	1.2				1.0	1.0
.3	.5	.7	1.1	1.4	.8		.6	.5
1.8	1.6	1.7	1.9	2.9	2.7	Fixed/Worth	1.4	1.5
-1.6	11.7	3.6	3.7	6.8	9.8		4.0	5.5
1.0	.8	.9	1.3	1.5	1.5		.9	.9
10.8	2.6	2.4	2.3	3.4	4.2	Debt/Worth	2.2	2.5
-3.2	19.5	6.0	5.2	7.7	11.8		7.7	13.8
137.6	56.4	45.6	48.7	34.6	31.5		38.5	41.6
(113) 37.4	(267) 22.6	(312) 19.3	(135) 27.2	(14) 22.9	(14) 22.8	% Profit Before Taxes/Tangible Net Worth	(778) 13.5	(825) 14.8
3.6	3.8	4.5	12.4	11.0	11.7		-.8	1.8
35.3	17.1	14.3	15.0	13.7	16.1		11.6	12.8
7.2	6.2	5.8	7.9	7.8	4.3	% Profit Before Taxes/Total Assets	3.9	4.6
-4.2	.2	1.0	2.7	1.7	2.0		-1.2	.0
199.4	21.8	11.3	7.2	5.7	14.6		18.9	20.0
16.9	8.7	5.2	3.4	2.2	3.1	Sales/Net Fixed Assets	7.3	7.5
6.7	3.8	3.2	1.9	1.8	1.8		3.3	3.6
10.0	4.9	3.5	2.7	1.8	3.4		4.3	4.6
6.1	3.3	2.5	1.9	1.6	1.5	Sales/Total Assets	2.8	2.9
2.8	2.1	1.8	1.3	1.1	1.2		1.8	1.9
.8	1.9	2.3	2.6	2.5			2.2	2.3
(127) 3.2	(293) 4.2	(330) 4.5	(142) 5.5	(11) 3.9		% Depr., Dep., Amort./Sales	(805) 4.5	(864) 4.8
8.7	8.3	7.0	8.4	6.2			8.6	8.2
2.4	1.8	1.2	.7				2.0	1.8
(101) 4.6	(161) 3.3	(117) 2.2	(28) 1.7			% Officers', Directors' Owners' Comp/Sales	(379) 3.5	(433) 3.6
10.7	6.1	4.2	2.6				6.8	6.7
329836M	1441122M	4445799M	9935336M	1825173M	8193127M	Net Sales ($)	17213891M	16526700M
46034M	379261M	1652660M	3121046M	1118421M	2757217M	Total Assets ($)	5894201M	5744381M

M = $ thousand   MM = $ million

See Pages 11 through 21 for Explanation of Ratios and Data

© RMA 2007

Comparative Historical Data | Current Data Sorted by Sales

76	74	81	Type of Statement	2	3	2	5	20	49
232	208	191	Unqualified / Reviewed	6	15	16	37	65	52
263	245	237	Compiled	23	59	41	60	48	6
236	211	214	Tax Returns	59	65	41	31	14	4
314	363	337	Other	29	71	41	69	71	56
4/1/04-3/31/05 ALL	4/1/05-3/31/06 ALL	4/1/06-3/31/07 ALL		163 (4/1-9/30/06)			897 (10/1/06-3/31/07)		
				0-1MM	1-3MM	3-5MM	5-10MM	10-25MM	25MM & OVER
1121	1101	1060	NUMBER OF STATEMENTS	119	213	141	202	218	167
%	%	%	ASSETS	%	%	%	%	%	%
10.4	9.9	10.4	Cash & Equivalents	19.5	11.4	10.2	8.0	8.4	8.5
27.5	28.0	26.8	Trade Receivables (net)	13.1	22.1	28.5	32.3	30.0	30.3
1.7	1.8	1.6	Inventory	1.2	2.2	1.4	1.5	1.3	1.7
4.1	4.5	3.9	All Other Current	3.7	3.5	3.9	4.5	3.6	4.3
43.7	44.2	42.7	Total Current	37.6	39.2	44.0	46.2	43.3	44.8
43.7	45.1	45.6	Fixed Assets (net)	51.9	46.9	43.5	41.6	46.3	44.8
2.6	2.8	2.8	Intangibles (net)	2.3	2.1	2.7	3.6	2.3	3.7
10.1	7.8	8.9	All Other Non-Current	8.1	11.8	9.7	8.6	8.1	6.7
100.0	100.0	100.0	Total	100.0	100.0	100.0	100.0	100.0	100.0
			LIABILITIES						
9.6	9.1	8.9	Notes Payable-Short Term	15.1	10.0	8.8	7.7	7.4	6.8
8.9	8.8	8.5	Cur. Mat.-L.T.D.	8.6	10.1	7.2	7.6	9.4	7.4
11.3	11.9	11.2	Trade Payables	8.6	10.3	10.7	13.1	12.3	11.1
.3	.3	.3	Income Taxes Payable	.1	.2	.1	.4	.3	.4
10.7	10.3	11.0	All Other Current	21.3	10.6	11.2	9.5	8.0	9.8
40.7	40.4	39.9	Total Current	53.7	41.2	38.0	38.2	37.4	35.5
30.6	29.8	30.8	Long-Term Debt	41.7	37.7	30.6	25.8	26.9	25.8
1.0	1.0	.9	Deferred Taxes	.1	.4	.6	.8	1.3	2.0
5.1	3.9	4.5	All Other Non-Current	11.1	3.9	4.5	4.0	3.3	3.0
22.6	25.0	23.8	Net Worth	-6.6	16.8	26.2	31.2	31.2	33.8
100.0	100.0	100.0	Total Liabilities & Net Worth	100.0	100.0	100.0	100.0	100.0	100.0
			INCOME DATA						
100.0	100.0	100.0	Net Sales	100.0	100.0	100.0	100.0	100.0	100.0
			Gross Profit						
95.6	95.2	95.0	Operating Expenses	89.0	95.1	96.7	96.5	96.2	94.6
4.4	4.8	5.0	Operating Profit	11.0	4.9	3.3	3.5	3.8	5.4
1.0	1.1	1.1	All Other Expenses (net)	4.6	1.1	.3	.4	.8	.7
3.4	3.7	3.8	Profit Before Taxes	6.4	3.8	3.0	3.2	3.0	4.7
			RATIOS						
2.0	2.0	2.1	Current	2.1	2.9	2.3	2.3	1.8	1.8
1.1	1.2	1.1	Current	.9	1.1	1.1	1.2	1.1	1.2
.7	.7	.7	Current	.2	.5	.7	.8	.7	.8
1.7	1.7	1.9	Quick	1.9	2.4	2.2	2.1	1.7	1.6
1.0	1.0 (1058)	1.0	Quick	.7	.9 (212)	1.1	1.1 (201)	1.0	1.1
.6	.6	.6	Quick	.2	.4	.6	.6	.6	.7
14 26.8	17 22.1	16 23.5	Sales/Receivables	0 UND	1 695.1	17 21.2	24 15.4	25 14.7	31 11.7
34 10.9	33 11.1	31 11.7	Sales/Receivables	1 500.0	25 14.8	28 13.0	33 11.1	35 10.5	37 9.9
45 8.0	46 8.0	43 8.4	Sales/Receivables	30 12.2	40 9.0	41 8.9	46 7.9	44 8.2	47 7.8
			Cost of Sales/Inventory						
			Cost of Sales/Payables						
13.5	13.3	13.2	Sales/Working Capital	8.6	11.0	13.8	11.9	15.3	14.2
84.5	60.8	75.6	Sales/Working Capital	-43.2	134.0	76.8	43.8	72.8	46.3
-19.8	-29.0	-22.0	Sales/Working Capital	-7.3	-14.5	-25.7	-38.2	-25.6	-41.8
7.4	8.3	7.5	EBIT/Interest	6.2	6.3	5.7	9.3	6.4	10.0
(1006) 3.0	(1009) 3.4	(936) 3.0	EBIT/Interest	(84) 2.4	(180) 2.0	(122) 2.7	(184) 3.2	(204) 2.7	(162) 4.2
1.1	1.2	1.1	EBIT/Interest	.7	.5	.8	1.1	1.5	1.9
3.0	3.1	3.2	Net Profit + Depr., Dep., Amort./Cur. Mat. L/T/D		4.2	3.6	3.1	2.6	4.3
(260) 1.6	(251) 1.6	(217) 1.7	Net Profit + Depr., Dep., Amort./Cur. Mat. L/T/D		(18) 2.4	(22) 1.6	(41) 1.4	(72) 1.6	(63) 1.9
1.0	1.0	1.1	Net Profit + Depr., Dep., Amort./Cur. Mat. L/T/D		1.0	1.1	.9	1.1	1.2
.6	.7	.7	Fixed/Worth	.7	.6	.6	.6	.7	.7
1.7	1.6	1.8	Fixed/Worth	4.3	1.8	1.7	1.7	1.7	1.6
8.2	6.4	6.6	Fixed/Worth	-2.5	UND	10.7	5.3	3.7	3.1
1.1	1.1	1.0	Debt/Worth	.8	.8	1.0	.8	1.2	1.2
2.6	2.6	2.7	Debt/Worth	9.5	3.3	2.4	2.5	2.6	2.3
17.2	12.4	13.7	Debt/Worth	-4.4	-42.1	16.2	8.4	6.1	5.2
52.0	54.6	53.6	% Profit Before Taxes/Tangible Net Worth	95.0	66.2	72.8	45.4	53.2	49.1
(897) 21.2	(904) 23.8	(855) 23.5	% Profit Before Taxes/Tangible Net Worth	(72) 16.9	(157) 24.6	(112) 22.8	(162) 18.8	(198) 24.2	(154) 28.8
5.6	7.5	5.3	% Profit Before Taxes/Tangible Net Worth	2.1	3.4	3.3	4.8	5.4	15.1
13.5	16.5	16.2	% Profit Before Taxes/Total Assets	18.7	17.7	16.4	16.8	14.3	16.6
5.8	6.7	6.6	% Profit Before Taxes/Total Assets	5.4	5.5	6.3	7.3	6.7	8.8
.2	.8	.6	% Profit Before Taxes/Total Assets	-2.1	-1.2	-.3	1.1	1.3	2.8
18.3	18.9	18.2	Sales/Net Fixed Assets	28.1	18.1	23.8	18.0	16.0	18.2
6.8	6.9	6.6	Sales/Net Fixed Assets	5.1	6.8	9.0	8.3	5.6	5.7
3.4	3.1	3.2	Sales/Net Fixed Assets	1.3	3.0	3.8	4.2	3.2	2.6
4.5	4.7	4.6	Sales/Total Assets	4.6	5.3	5.2	4.7	4.4	4.3
2.8	2.9	2.8	Sales/Total Assets	2.2	2.8	3.5	3.1	2.8	2.5
1.8	1.9	1.8	Sales/Total Assets	.8	1.7	2.1	2.1	1.9	1.6
2.1	1.8	2.0	% Depr., Dep., Amort./Sales	4.2	2.7	1.8	1.8	1.9	1.5
(930) 4.5	(940) 4.2	(907) 4.4	% Depr., Dep., Amort./Sales	(87) 9.3	(166) 6.0	(126) 4.1	(181) 3.8	(207) 4.4	(140) 3.0
8.3	7.8	7.7	% Depr., Dep., Amort./Sales	23.5	10.3	7.1	6.1	6.9	6.0
1.7	1.5	1.6	% Officers', Directors' Owners' Comp/Sales	3.7	2.6	1.9	1.3	1.0	.8
(469) 3.2	(428) 3.2	(411) 3.0	% Officers', Directors' Owners' Comp/Sales	(45) 9.7	(102) 4.4	(75) 2.9	(81) 2.3	(77) 2.0	(31) 2.0
6.0	6.3	6.2	% Officers', Directors' Owners' Comp/Sales	16.5	8.1	4.7	4.4	3.6	3.5
19662727M	24261087M	26170393M	Net Sales ($)	58196M	404908M	550638M	1459908M	3375382M	20321361M
7888477M	9146205M	9074639M	Total Assets ($)	62760M	219298M	204730M	605020M	1415750M	6567081M

© RMA 2007

M = $ thousand   MM = $ million
See Pages 11 through 21 for Explanation of Ratios and Data

Current Data Sorted by Assets   Comparative Historical Data

Type of Statement	0-500M	500M-2MM	2-10MM	10-50MM	50-100MM	100-250MM	4/1/02-3/31/03 ALL	4/1/03-3/31/04 ALL
Unqualified	3	5	21	77	32	38	189	194
Reviewed	2	21	146	109	2	1	229	260
Compiled	28	101	144	26	2	2	263	362
Tax Returns	62	72	28	7		1	89	131
Other	37	91	163	122	25	26	295	339
		215 (4/1-9/30/06)		1,179 (10/1/06-3/31/07)				
NUMBER OF STATEMENTS	132	290	502	341	61	68	1065	1286
ASSETS	%	%	%	%	%	%	%	%
Cash & Equivalents	16.6	11.1	7.6	6.4	4.5	5.5	7.3	7.8
Trade Receivables (net)	22.8	32.0	29.8	25.0	21.1	20.0	28.3	28.4
Inventory	1.4	1.5	1.0	1.3	1.4	1.0	1.7	1.5
All Other Current	4.7	4.6	4.5	3.9	3.8	3.5	4.3	4.2
Total Current	45.5	49.2	42.9	36.5	30.9	30.1	41.6	41.9
Fixed Assets (net)	41.8	39.5	47.2	54.5	60.3	59.7	47.6	46.9
Intangibles (net)	1.2	1.8	1.5	1.6	3.6	4.5	2.3	2.2
All Other Non-Current	11.5	9.5	8.4	7.3	5.3	5.8	8.5	9.0
Total	100.0	100.0	100.0	100.0	100.0	100.0	100.0	100.0
LIABILITIES								
Notes Payable-Short Term	14.5	8.3	7.8	7.1	4.4	2.5	8.7	9.3
Cur. Mat.-L.T.D.	11.0	8.7	10.1	10.4	9.9	8.1	11.0	10.6
Trade Payables	11.9	11.9	8.9	8.8	5.6	6.2	10.6	10.6
Income Taxes Payable	.2	.1	.3	.4	.2	.0	.2	.3
All Other Current	19.5	11.6	9.3	8.2	9.9	10.0	10.9	11.5
Total Current	57.1	40.6	36.3	34.8	29.9	26.8	41.4	42.2
Long-Term Debt	44.8	28.1	28.6	31.0	34.2	34.9	26.7	26.9
Deferred Taxes	.2	.4	1.0	2.4	2.5	4.4	1.9	1.7
All Other Non-Current	10.4	3.9	3.1	2.4	2.1	4.3	3.7	4.5
Net Worth	-12.4	27.1	30.9	29.4	31.3	29.6	26.3	24.6
Total Liabilities & Net Worth	100.0	100.0	100.0	100.0	100.0	100.0	100.0	100.0
INCOME DATA								
Net Sales	100.0	100.0	100.0	100.0	100.0	100.0	100.0	100.0
Gross Profit								
Operating Expenses	95.9	94.5	95.1	95.2	95.9	94.0	96.5	96.4
Operating Profit	4.1	5.5	4.9	4.8	4.1	6.0	3.5	3.6
All Other Expenses (net)	1.8	1.0	1.2	1.0	.9	1.9	1.5	1.1
Profit Before Taxes	2.2	4.5	3.7	3.7	3.2	4.1	2.0	2.5
RATIOS								
Current	2.3	2.0	1.7	1.3	1.4	1.3	1.5	1.6
	1.0	1.3	1.1	1.0	1.0	1.0	1.0	1.0
	.4	.8	.7	.7	.7	.7	.7	.6
Quick	1.9	1.8	1.5	1.2	1.2	1.2	1.3	1.4
	.9	1.1	1.0	.8	.9	.9	(1063) .8	(1285) .9
	.4	.6	.6	.6	.5	.6	.5	.5
Sales/Receivables	0 UND	14 26.1	24 15.2	30 12.2	30 12.0	30 12.1	24 15.0	23 15.8
	11 31.9	27 13.6	33 11.1	36 10.1	35 10.3	38 9.5	35 10.6	34 10.8
	26 13.8	37 9.9	43 8.5	46 8.0	44 8.3	45 8.2	43 8.4	43 8.5
Cost of Sales/Inventory								
Cost of Sales/Payables								
Sales/Working Capital	20.1	15.7	16.2	24.2	27.3	20.7	20.3	17.7
	UND	46.5	68.0	-372.0	-999.8	-187.8	UND	352.1
	-17.8	-40.7	-25.2	-20.1	-15.7	-25.1	-18.6	-18.2
EBIT/Interest	8.4	7.2	6.1	4.5	4.0	6.0	4.5	5.5
	(103) 1.7	(255) 3.3	(476) 2.5	(326) 2.6	(60) 2.3	(65) 2.8	(996) 2.0	(1185) 2.5
	-.5	1.2	1.2	1.6	1.3	1.9	.7	1.0
Net Profit + Depr., Dep., Amort./Cur. Mat. L/T/D		4.4	2.4	2.0	4.9		2.1	2.4
		(45) 1.8	(150) 1.4	(153) 1.3	(22) 1.9		(330) 1.3	(355) 1.4
		1.2	1.0	1.0	1.4		.8	.9
Fixed/Worth	.4	.4	.7	1.3	1.5	1.2	.8	.8
	3.2	1.3	1.7	2.2	2.2	2.7	1.9	1.9
	-2.0	7.4	3.7	4.2	3.7	5.4	5.2	5.1
Debt/Worth	1.5	1.1	1.2	1.5	1.4	1.2	1.2	1.2
	20.4	2.4	2.6	3.0	2.5	3.2	2.7	2.6
	-4.1	15.4	5.4	6.0	4.4	5.9	9.0	9.0
% Profit Before Taxes/Tangible Net Worth	122.8	73.8	43.1	39.3	35.9	37.8	33.6	38.3
	(76) 42.0	(237) 32.6	(451) 18.4	(329) 20.9	(57) 17.4	(60) 27.5	(912) 12.7	(1088) 15.9
	5.0	8.5	3.5	9.7	4.6	15.4	.4	3.1
% Profit Before Taxes/Total Assets	25.3	17.7	12.8	9.2	9.5	10.1	8.6	10.6
	5.2	7.7	5.1	4.9	3.9	5.9	3.4	4.1
	-6.9	.8	.8	2.1	1.2	3.9	-.9	-.1
Sales/Net Fixed Assets	162.9	41.5	14.8	6.7	4.2	4.9	14.2	15.3
	14.8	11.0	5.4	3.4	2.5	2.5	5.6	6.1
	5.0	4.9	3.1	2.2	2.1	1.9	2.9	3.1
Sales/Total Assets	9.4	5.8	4.1	2.8	2.2	2.3	4.2	4.2
	5.0	4.1	2.8	2.0	1.8	1.6	2.6	2.7
	2.8	2.4	1.9	1.5	1.5	1.4	1.8	1.8
% Depr., Dep., Amort./Sales	1.4	1.2	1.9	3.0	3.2	1.0	2.3	2.0
	(74) 4.9	(230) 3.3	(465) 4.7	(329) 5.9	(47) 5.9	(12) 2.2	(928) 5.3	(1082) 5.0
	9.8	7.5	7.5	9.1	7.5	3.6	9.0	8.6
% Officers', Directors' Owners' Comp/Sales	1.6	1.6	1.1	.8		2.2	1.4	1.3
	(56) 3.3	(121) 2.8	(186) 2.1	(84) 1.3		(16) 6.2	(382) 2.5	(422) 2.4
	7.9	4.7	4.0	4.1		33.0	5.6	5.0
Net Sales ($)	229964M	1564078M	7819130M	18185206M	8255133M	23716015M	43081407M	46794198M
Total Assets ($)	33963M	340808M	2503241M	7890751M	4067548M	10920380M	18285617M	20034250M

M = $ thousand   MM = $ million
See Pages 11 through 21 for Explanation of Ratios and Data

Comparative Historical Data

Current Data Sorted by Sales

4/1/04-3/31/05 ALL	4/1/05-3/31/06 ALL	4/1/06-3/31/07 ALL	Type of Statement	0-1MM	1-3MM	3-5MM	5-10MM	10-25MM	25MM & OVER
217	197	176	Unqualified	2	5	1	5	17	146
256	257	281	Reviewed	3	4	18	34	111	111
286	286	303	Compiled	20	30	48	84	86	35
146	171	170	Tax Returns	38	43	28	31	22	8
337	525	464	Other	28	42	54	69	93	178
				215 (4/1-9/30/06)		1,179 (10/1/06-3/31/07)			
1242	1436	1394	NUMBER OF STATEMENTS	91	124	149	223	329	478
%	%	%	ASSETS	%	%	%	%	%	%
8.4	8.5	8.6	Cash & Equivalents	14.2	10.4	11.9	8.5	8.6	6.2
30.4	29.5	27.6	Trade Receivables (net)	12.6	23.4	25.6	29.6	29.7	29.7
1.6	1.2	1.2	Inventory	1.4	1.8	.9	1.0	1.1	1.4
3.6	4.0	4.3	All Other Current	3.2	5.5	3.9	4.9	3.9	4.3
44.0	43.2	41.7	Total Current	31.4	41.0	42.3	44.1	43.3	41.6
45.1	47.0	48.1	Fixed Assets (net)	58.1	45.9	43.7	46.1	47.9	49.1
1.8	1.9	1.8	Intangibles (net)	1.0	1.8	1.9	1.9	1.1	2.3
9.1	7.9	8.4	All Other Non-Current	9.5	11.2	12.0	8.0	7.6	7.0
100.0	100.0	100.0	Total	100.0	100.0	100.0	100.0	100.0	100.0
			LIABILITIES						
8.7	7.6	8.0	Notes Payable-Short Term	11.0	9.9	6.3	7.8	8.2	7.3
10.5	9.9	9.8	Cur. Mat.-L.T.D.	9.6	11.3	11.2	9.9	9.9	9.1
11.1	10.4	9.5	Trade Payables	4.5	9.0	10.1	9.3	9.7	10.3
.2	.3	.3	Income Taxes Payable	.2	.1	.2	.2	.3	.4
10.2	10.2	10.5	All Other Current	13.5	14.9	11.8	9.9	8.2	10.3
40.8	38.4	38.1	Total Current	38.7	45.2	39.6	37.1	36.3	37.3
27.5	29.8	31.2	Long-Term Debt	47.3	40.0	31.6	30.3	28.3	28.1
1.6	1.4	1.4	Deferred Taxes	.3	.1	.9	.7	1.2	2.5
4.5	4.0	3.8	All Other Non-Current	10.0	4.9	5.0	3.2	2.8	2.9
25.6	26.4	25.6	Net Worth	3.7	9.8	22.9	28.7	31.4	29.3
100.0	100.0	100.0	Total Liabilities & Net Worth	100.0	100.0	100.0	100.0	100.0	100.0
			INCOME DATA						
100.0	100.0	100.0	Net Sales	100.0	100.0	100.0	100.0	100.0	100.0
			Gross Profit						
95.5	95.0	95.1	Operating Expenses	83.5	93.0	96.1	95.7	96.7	96.1
4.5	5.0	4.9	Operating Profit	16.5	7.0	3.9	4.3	3.3	3.9
.9	1.0	1.2	All Other Expenses (net)	6.7	2.2	.7	.4	.5	.9
3.6	4.0	3.7	Profit Before Taxes	9.8	4.7	3.2	3.9	2.8	3.1
			RATIOS						
1.7	1.7	1.7	Current	2.7	2.1	1.9	1.7	1.7	1.5
1.1	1.1	1.1		1.0	1.0	1.1	1.2	1.1	1.0
.7	.8	.7		.3	.5	.6	.8	.8	.8
1.5	1.5	1.5	Quick	2.4	1.4	1.7	1.5	1.5	1.2
(1240) .9	1.0	.9		1.0	.8	.9	1.0	1.0	.9
.6	.6	.6		.2	.4	.5	.7	.7	.6
24 15.3	23 15.6	23 16.1	Sales/Receivables	0 UND	4 100.1	14 26.6	22 16.3	24 15.0	30 12.2
35 10.3	34 10.6	32 11.2		0 UND	22 16.5	27 13.7	31 11.8	34 10.8	36 10.1
45 8.2	44 8.2	42 8.7		33 11.1	39 9.4	36 10.1	42 8.7	42 8.8	44 8.3
			Cost of Sales/Inventory						
			Cost of Sales/Payables						
17.3	15.9	18.1	Sales/Working Capital	11.0	18.0	14.8	17.3	18.5	21.9
116.3	84.4	124.0		UND	-399.4	109.4	55.1	65.9	182.5
-24.4	-28.4	-24.5		-7.3	-14.2	-20.3	-27.2	-30.2	-29.0
8.1	7.7	6.0	EBIT/Interest	7.3	7.2	6.1	6.0	6.5	5.7
(1149) 3.3	(1315) 3.5	(1285) 2.6		(64) 2.6	(107) 1.8	(131) 2.4	(211) 2.9	(311) 2.5	(461) 2.9
1.5	1.7	1.3		1.0	.6	.9	1.2	1.3	1.7
2.4	2.9	2.3	Net Profit + Depr., Dep., Amort./Cur. Mat. L/T/D			2.7	2.2	2.2	2.5
(363) 1.4	(393) 1.5	(379) 1.5			(32) 1.5	(51) 1.6	(104) 1.3	(180) 1.5	
1.0	1.1	1.0				.9	1.1	1.0	1.1
.8	.8	.8	Fixed/Worth	.9	.8	.5	.6	.8	1.0
1.6	1.8	1.9		3.3	2.7	1.5	1.5	1.7	2.0
4.5	4.5	4.8		37.0	-10.1	18.5	4.1	3.6	4.1
1.2	1.2	1.3	Debt/Worth	1.2	1.4	1.1	1.2	1.2	1.4
2.6	2.8	2.8		5.1	7.1	2.4	2.3	2.6	2.9
8.2	7.6	7.8		-22.9	-18.2	42.6	5.6	4.9	6.0
47.7	56.0	46.5	% Profit Before Taxes/Tangible Net Worth	95.3	68.2	58.8	50.9	39.3	43.1
(1079) 22.6	(1249) 28.1	(1210) 22.5		(66) 35.8	(87) 23.7	(116) 24.5	(193) 19.2	(302) 20.8	(446) 23.9
7.3	10.4	7.2		9.2	.5	2.4	3.3	6.7	11.2
12.4	14.8	13.4	% Profit Before Taxes/Total Assets	20.4	15.6	17.7	14.2	12.8	11.2
6.2	7.0	5.5		5.3	3.5	6.3	5.8	5.4	5.7
1.4	2.4	1.1		.0	-2.8	-.1	.7	1.3	2.1
16.3	17.3	16.2	Sales/Net Fixed Assets	12.1	29.8	27.5	18.9	15.2	13.6
6.1	5.8	5.3		3.6	7.3	7.1	7.6	5.5	4.2
3.2	3.0	2.7		.7	2.8	3.8	3.3	3.2	2.4
4.3	4.4	4.4	Sales/Total Assets	3.4	5.3	4.9	4.6	4.6	3.8
2.8	2.8	2.7		1.8	3.1	3.3	3.0	2.9	2.2
1.9	1.8	1.7		.6	1.5	2.0	2.0	2.0	1.7
2.0	1.9	1.9	% Depr., Dep., Amort./Sales	6.7	2.7	2.2	1.8	1.9	1.5
(1021) 4.4	(1191) 4.6	(1157) 4.9		(57) 12.6	(90) 5.7	(121) 5.3	(194) 4.7	(306) 4.8	(389) 4.3
7.8	7.7	8.2		29.1	11.3	9.0	7.3	7.5	7.1
1.2	1.1	1.1	% Officers', Directors' Owners' Comp/Sales	3.8	1.7	1.7	1.3	1.0	.7
(443) 2.5	(465) 2.2	(468) 2.3		(20) 7.0	(58) 3.0	(64) 2.7	(90) 2.8	(136) 1.8	(100) 1.5
5.5	5.0	4.8		12.5	6.4	4.5	4.5	3.6	6.0
49796622M	61743652M	59769526M	Net Sales ($)	43360M	244510M	585220M	1639894M	5265391M	51991151M
20413885M	25270395M	25756691M	Total Assets ($)	61770M	170154M	286285M	813278M	2133939M	22291265M

© RMA 2007

M = $ thousand   MM = $ million
See Pages 11 through 21 for Explanation of Ratios and Data

Current Data Sorted by Assets | Comparative Historical Data

	0-500M	500M-2MM	2-10MM	10-50MM	50-100MM	100-250MM	Type of Statement	4/1/02-3/31/03 ALL	4/1/03-3/31/04 ALL
Unqualified			1	9	7	9	Unqualified	10	13
Reviewed	1	2	11	6		1	Reviewed	6	13
Compiled	2	6	13	5			Compiled	8	8
Tax Returns	2	4	4	1			Tax Returns	2	4
Other	5	6	9	13	5	6	Other	24	15
	19 (4/1-9/30/06)			109 (10/1/06-3/31/07)				50	53
	10	18	38	34	12	16	NUMBER OF STATEMENTS	50	53
	%	%	%	%	%	%	ASSETS	%	%
	12.2	7.5	11.4	7.9	2.9	4.5	Cash & Equivalents	5.8	8.3
	25.4	33.0	31.6	26.4	21.4	19.4	Trade Receivables (net)	29.2	29.7
	2.5	1.5	3.0	.9	.8	.5	Inventory	.7	1.4
	2.5	3.3	1.9	3.8	3.1	4.5	All Other Current	4.5	4.7
	42.6	45.3	47.9	39.2	28.2	28.9	Total Current	40.2	44.1
	43.4	36.0	40.8	51.9	61.2	61.5	Fixed Assets (net)	51.3	46.6
	9.0	4.4	2.3	3.4	6.2	5.5	Intangibles (net)	.9	1.0
	5.1	14.3	9.0	5.5	4.4	4.1	All Other Non-Current	7.6	8.3
	100.0	100.0	100.0	100.0	100.0	100.0	Total	100.0	100.0
							LIABILITIES		
	16.6	9.5	3.9	5.3	3.5	.6	Notes Payable-Short Term	7.5	13.3
	6.6	8.8	10.3	13.3	9.2	6.9	Cur. Mat.-L.T.D.	10.1	7.1
	10.7	10.6	10.2	9.2	5.1	5.1	Trade Payables	9.8	9.8
	.0	.1	.1	.3	.1	.0	Income Taxes Payable	.1	.1
	26.8	13.3	8.2	8.3	8.8	11.6	All Other Current	10.3	8.5
	60.8	42.3	32.6	36.3	26.6	24.1	Total Current	37.8	38.8
	51.5	32.9	24.9	24.1	40.7	36.2	Long-Term Debt	22.4	29.1
	.0	.0	1.4	3.2	2.2	2.5	Deferred Taxes	2.6	1.5
	.0	5.2	1.2	1.2	2.8	2.9	All Other Non-Current	1.9	4.9
	-12.3	19.6	39.9	35.2	27.6	34.3	Net Worth	35.3	25.7
	100.0	100.0	100.0	100.0	100.0	100.0	Total Liabilities & Net Worth	100.0	100.0
							INCOME DATA		
	100.0	100.0	100.0	100.0	100.0	100.0	Net Sales	100.0	100.0
							Gross Profit		
	94.0	99.4	96.0	94.4	95.3	94.7	Operating Expenses	95.2	95.8
	6.0	.6	4.0	5.6	4.7	5.3	Operating Profit	4.8	4.2
	.7	2.2	.6	1.5	1.0	1.7	All Other Expenses (net)	1.2	.6
	5.3	-1.7	3.4	4.1	3.7	3.6	Profit Before Taxes	3.6	3.6
							RATIOS		
	4.0	2.3	2.1	1.5	1.4	1.8	Current	1.7	1.9
	1.1	1.0	1.3	1.2	1.0	1.3		1.1	1.2
	.3	.7	.9	.9	.6	.9		.7	.7
	3.9	1.9	2.1	1.4	1.1	1.5	Quick	1.5	1.5
	.8	.9	1.2	1.0	.8	1.1		1.0	1.0
	.2	.6	.8	.7	.5	.6		.6	.6
	0 UND	10 37.9	25 14.7	29 12.6	33 11.1	36 10.1	Sales/Receivables	31 11.8	31 11.9
	10 37.4	29 12.6	35 10.6	39 9.4	36 10.2	38 9.6		37 10.0	37 9.9
	29 12.7	34 10.9	40 9.2	49 7.4	42 8.8	43 8.5		45 8.1	47 7.8
							Cost of Sales/Inventory		
							Cost of Sales/Payables		
	16.0	18.2	13.9	15.4	28.9	13.0	Sales/Working Capital	19.2	14.0
	524.2	-232.1	32.4	56.6	NM	37.1		86.3	58.6
	-10.5	-22.5	-97.4	-44.6	-15.3	-93.1		-20.4	-23.2
		4.6	5.6	4.6	4.0	6.6	EBIT/Interest	5.8	5.4
	(15) 1.9	(32) 2.6	(29) 3.0	(11) 3.4		4.7		(47) 2.9	(50) 2.8
	-.5	1.9	2.1	.2		2.3		1.0	1.6
			2.1	1.9			Net Profit + Depr., Dep., Amort./Cur. Mat. L/T/D	2.3	2.3
		(15) 1.4	(22) 1.4					(12) 1.2	(17) 1.5
		.9	.9					.9	1.1
	1.8	.3	.3	1.0	2.2	1.0	Fixed/Worth	.8	.8
	-22.3	2.1	1.6	1.5	3.1	1.9		1.7	1.5
	-.4	-2.4	2.5	3.2	4.5	12.3		3.4	2.8
	3.3	.8	.8	1.2	2.2	1.0	Debt/Worth	1.1	1.0
	-31.8	3.4	2.1	1.9	3.2	1.9		1.7	1.8
	-2.6	-6.1	3.5	4.5	4.4	18.0		4.4	5.7
		55.2	48.3	33.9	36.0	34.6	% Profit Before Taxes/Tangible Net Worth	24.6	32.9
	(11) 23.9	(37) 25.6	(32) 18.2	(10) 27.0	(13) 22.7			(49) 14.6	(49) 14.2
		10.1	7.7	10.0	2.8	15.7		.2	5.3
	36.3	16.5	15.7	10.8	9.4	12.3	% Profit Before Taxes/Total Assets	7.6	8.1
	16.0	4.1	6.0	5.6	6.5	9.6		4.1	4.1
	.0	-9.4	2.2	3.7	-1.0	5.1		.0	1.8
	134.3	157.2	29.5	8.8	4.5	5.2	Sales/Net Fixed Assets	11.8	13.7
	15.8	12.3	8.3	3.4	2.5	2.7		4.4	5.8
	4.3	4.8	4.4	2.2	1.8	1.8		2.5	3.4
	8.7	5.7	4.8	3.4	2.7	2.4	Sales/Total Assets	3.5	4.3
	5.5	3.6	3.2	2.0	1.6	1.6		2.1	2.7
	2.8	2.5	2.4	1.5	1.4	1.4		1.6	1.7
		.4	1.6	2.8			% Depr., Dep., Amort./Sales	2.1	1.7
		(15) 2.6	(34) 4.0	5.8				(36) 5.2	(42) 4.8
		6.4	6.3	7.9				9.0	7.9
			1.1				% Officers', Directors' Owners' Comp/Sales	.5	.5
			(19) 3.4					(12) 1.3	(18) 3.1
			4.5					4.8	5.4
	17661M	89476M	679369M	2449866M	1749674M	4814814M	Net Sales ($)	4629554M	3593112M
	3201M	19481M	197065M	845960M	869808M	2734906M	Total Assets ($)	2555358M	1683743M

M = $ thousand   MM = $ million

See Pages 11 through 21 for Explanation of Ratios and Data

Comparative Historical Data   Current Data Sorted by Sales

			Type of Statement						
18	30	26	Unqualified				4	9	26
15	14	21	Reviewed		1		4	11	7
22	17	26	Compiled	1	3	2	2	1	5
7	7	11	Tax Returns		4	3	1	1	1
30	26	44	Other	6	2	2	1	8	25
4/1/04-3/31/05 ALL	4/1/05-3/31/06 ALL	4/1/06-3/31/07 ALL		0-1MM	19 (4/1-9/30/06) 1-3MM	3-5MM	109 (10/1/06-3/31/07) 5-10MM	10-25MM	25MM & OVER
92	94	128	NUMBER OF STATEMENTS	7	10	7	11	29	64
%	%	%		%	%	%	%	%	%
			ASSETS						
7.4	7.7	8.3	Cash & Equivalents		13.9		5.5	9.9	8.0
30.0	28.4	27.5	Trade Receivables (net)		21.7		32.6	34.0	25.8
1.5	1.1	1.7	Inventory		3.9		6.1	.5	1.3
5.3	5.1	3.1	All Other Current		4.5		2.7	3.1	3.4
44.2	42.2	40.6	Total Current		43.9		46.9	47.5	38.6
48.4	50.6	47.8	Fixed Assets (net)		35.0		42.0	40.4	51.1
1.4	1.7	4.2	Intangibles (net)		6.9		2.9	.5	5.5
5.9	5.5	7.5	All Other Non-Current		14.1		8.2	11.5	4.9
100.0	100.0	100.0	Total		100.0		100.0	100.0	100.0
			LIABILITIES						
6.7	4.4	5.6	Notes Payable-Short Term		.9		6.1	5.0	3.5
8.9	9.1	10.1	Cur. Mat.-L.T.D.		13.4		6.1	13.9	8.8
8.0	9.3	8.9	Trade Payables		12.3		9.3	11.6	8.1
.2	.5	.1	Income Taxes Payable		.1		.0	.1	.2
7.6	10.4	10.9	All Other Current		27.3		7.9	9.5	10.7
31.4	33.7	35.5	Total Current		54.0		29.5	40.1	31.2
29.4	31.3	30.8	Long-Term Debt		61.9		21.7	26.9	27.7
2.0	1.7	1.8	Deferred Taxes		.0		1.6	2.0	2.4
2.3	2.5	2.0	All Other Non-Current		.2		9.9	1.1	1.9
35.0	30.8	29.9	Net Worth		-16.1		37.3	30.0	36.8
100.0	100.0	100.0	Total Liabilties & Net Worth		100.0		100.0	100.0	100.0
			INCOME DATA						
100.0	100.0	100.0	Net Sales		100.0		100.0	100.0	100.0
			Gross Profit						
96.1	95.3	95.7	Operating Expenses		98.0		97.7	96.9	95.5
3.9	4.7	4.3	Operating Profit		2.0		2.3	3.1	4.5
.2	1.2	1.3	All Other Expenses (net)		1.0		-.2	.6	1.0
3.6	3.5	3.1	Profit Before Taxes		1.0		2.5	2.5	3.5
			RATIOS						
2.0	1.7	1.7			1.8		2.2	1.9	1.7
1.3	1.1	1.2	Current		1.1		1.3	1.3	1.2
.9	.9	.8			.3		.9	.9	.9
1.5	1.6	1.6			1.6		2.2	1.9	1.5
1.1	1.0	1.0	Quick		.8		1.1	1.1	1.0
.8	.7	.7			.3		.9	.7	.7

							Sales/Receivables					
28	13.0	24	14.9	26	14.3	0	UND		26	14.2	25	14.5	30	12.2
38	9.7	35	10.4	35	10.4	15	23.6		32	11.3	32	11.3	37	9.8
43	8.5	43	8.6	42	8.7	26	13.8		46	8.0	39	9.4	43	8.5

						Sales/Receivables	0-1MM	1-3MM	3-5MM	5-10MM	10-25MM	25MM & OVER
						Cost of Sales/Inventory						
						Cost of Sales/Payables						
12.7		17.8		15.9		Sales/Working Capital		17.0		15.7	17.7	14.0
34.0		62.4		48.1				524.2		27.7	46.8	47.1
-61.9		-62.5		-48.8				-16.6		-82.1	-44.1	-60.3
	9.6		6.8		5.6	EBIT/Interest		9.2		6.3	5.2	5.7
(83)	3.7	(79)	3.6	(111)	3.0			2.4	(10)	2.0	(26) 2.5	(56) 3.4
	1.9		2.2		1.7			-.2		1.8	1.5	2.3
	2.2		2.6		2.1	Net Profit + Depr., Dep.,					2.2	2.0
(29)	1.4	(28)	1.4	(45)	1.4	Amort./Cur. Mat. L/T/D				(16)	1.4	(23) 1.5
	1.1		1.0		.9						.9	1.1
	.7		1.0		.9							
	1.4		2.0		1.9	Fixed/Worth		.6		.2	.6	1.0
	3.2		3.6		4.5			-18.7		1.6	1.9	1.6
	.9		1.1		1.1			-.4		3.0	3.6	3.7
	1.7		2.4		2.4	Debt/Worth		3.2		.6	1.3	1.0
	4.6		4.7		8.8			-28.4		2.4	2.2	2.1
								-2.0		4.2	7.3	4.3
	35.5		49.4		43.7	% Profit Before Taxes/Tangible				34.8	50.0	37.1
(88)	19.1	(87)	28.2	(107)	23.6	Net Worth			(10)	25.5	(27) 29.3	(57) 22.7
	7.6		12.5		10.1					7.4	7.4	14.4
	11.6		13.9		13.1	% Profit Before Taxes/Total		22.7		15.0	12.4	12.9
	6.4		7.4		6.0	Assets		6.1		3.4	5.7	6.9
	2.4		3.8		2.9			-9.4		1.9	2.2	4.1
	11.0		10.6		16.3	Sales/Net Fixed Assets		134.3		23.6	29.5	8.3
	5.3		5.1		5.1			13.1		8.5	9.1	3.8
	3.2		2.7		2.6			5.3		3.7	4.2	2.1
	4.1		3.8		4.1	Sales/Total Assets		6.2		4.7	5.2	3.4
	2.7		2.7		2.6			4.7		3.2	3.2	2.1
	1.9		1.8		1.6			3.2		2.4	2.2	1.5
	2.5		2.5		1.7	% Depr., Dep., Amort./Sales				.3	3.1	1.8
(72)	4.1	(70)	4.5	(98)	4.6					1.7	(25) 5.2	(45) 5.0
	7.2		7.1		7.0					4.4	8.0	6.5
	1.2		1.0		1.5	% Officers', Directors'					1.0	1.7
(33)	2.8	(24)	2.0	(36)	3.6	Owners' Comp/Sales				(14)	2.0	(13) 3.8
	5.8		4.0		5.3						4.1	12.6
5715600M		7101392M		9800860M		Net Sales ($)	5345M	20066M	27089M	78161M	523966M	9146233M
2795939M		3477605M		4670421M		Total Assets ($)	6520M	4619M	43924M	26440M	195942M	4392976M

M = $ thousand   MM = $ million
See Pages 11 through 21 for Explanation of Ratios and Data

Current Data Sorted by Assets   Comparative Historical Data

							Type of Statement		
		2	1	3		4	Unqualified	1	4
	2	7	20	4			Reviewed	11	18
	7	8	9				Compiled	8	10
	13	11	3				Tax Returns	2	5
	2	21	13	10		1	Other	7	11
		16 (4/1-9/30/06)		125 (10/1/06-3/31/07)				4/1/02-3/31/03	4/1/03-3/31/04
	0-500M	500M-2MM	2-10MM	10-50MM	50-100MM	100-250MM		ALL	ALL
	24	49	46	17	1	4	NUMBER OF STATEMENTS	29	48
	%	%	%	%	%	%	ASSETS	%	%
	11.1	9.3	8.4	5.1			Cash & Equivalents	8.1	12.1
	18.5	29.7	31.7	39.4			Trade Receivables (net)	30.8	30.3
	.3	.5	.7	2.0			Inventory	1.4	1.7
	3.5	5.3	6.4	7.7			All Other Current	6.4	5.8
	33.3	44.8	47.1	54.2			Total Current	46.7	49.9
	48.0	38.3	36.5	35.4			Fixed Assets (net)	36.2	34.8
	1.7	2.7	2.5	4.3			Intangibles (net)	1.6	.7
	17.0	14.2	13.9	6.2			All Other Non-Current	15.5	14.6
	100.0	100.0	100.0	100.0			Total	100.0	100.0
							LIABILITIES		
	12.0	5.8	7.2	12.3			Notes Payable-Short Term	6.4	7.5
	8.9	6.9	6.0	4.6			Cur. Mat.-L.T.D.	5.7	5.5
	9.8	8.6	8.3	15.5			Trade Payables	8.9	9.0
	.2	.2	.4	.1			Income Taxes Payable	.1	.2
	9.0	9.8	8.7	7.7			All Other Current	7.6	12.6
	39.9	31.3	30.5	40.1			Total Current	28.7	34.8
	30.2	32.9	23.5	20.9			Long-Term Debt	29.1	25.0
	.2	.0	1.9	.8			Deferred Taxes	.5	.4
	8.1	16.8	2.9	5.6			All Other Non-Current	5.9	8.5
	21.7	19.0	41.1	32.6			Net Worth	35.8	31.3
	100.0	100.0	100.0	100.0			Total Liabilties & Net Worth	100.0	100.0
							INCOME DATA		
	100.0	100.0	100.0	100.0			Net Sales	100.0	100.0
							Gross Profit		
	92.4	95.9	96.8	96.6			Operating Expenses	97.3	92.0
	7.6	4.1	3.2	3.4			Operating Profit	2.7	8.0
	2.3	3.3	.5	.1			All Other Expenses (net)	2.2	3.6
	5.3	.9	2.7	3.3			Profit Before Taxes	.5	4.4
							RATIOS		
	2.0	3.9	1.8	1.9				2.6	2.9
	1.0	1.6	1.3	1.2			Current	1.7	1.6
	.3	.9	1.1	1.1				1.0	.8
	2.0	3.4	1.7	1.5				2.4	2.5
	.8	1.3	1.2	1.0			Quick	1.4	1.2
	.1	.8	1.0	.9				.8	.7
0	UND	13 28.1	27 13.6	42 8.6				25 14.4	19 19.3
7	51.8	31 11.7	42 8.7	56 6.5			Sales/Receivables	38 9.7	35 10.4
25	14.5	52 7.0	58 6.3	68 5.3				53 6.8	48 7.6
							Cost of Sales/Inventory		
							Cost of Sales/Payables		
	28.8	7.9	12.6	8.8				7.5	7.2
	NM	21.7	20.4	26.2			Sales/Working Capital	14.3	21.4
	-11.2	-89.5	82.4	80.0				NM	-37.2
	16.5	5.8	4.4	7.0				9.2	7.6
	(23) 4.9	(39) 2.7	(43) 1.9	(15) 2.7			EBIT/Interest	(25) 1.9	(42) 2.9
	2.0	.8	.8	1.4				-.1	.9
			3.5						7.1
			(22) 1.6				Net Profit + Depr., Dep., Amort./Cur. Mat. L/T/D		(10) 3.9
			1.2						1.3
	.4	.5	.4	.7				.4	.4
	1.7	1.2	1.1	2.0			Fixed/Worth	.7	.6
	66.8	508.1	1.7	3.7				4.4	3.5
	1.0	.8	1.0	1.5				.7	.7
	2.9	2.7	1.6	3.4			Debt/Worth	1.6	1.4
	113.4	516.0	2.5	8.2				11.3	5.6
	119.6	42.8	27.6	78.8			% Profit Before Taxes/Tangible Net Worth	40.7	34.9
	(19) 37.2	(38) 23.6	(45) 11.8	(16) 19.8				(24) 11.0	(43) 11.2
	7.2	-.6	-.3	4.1				.8	-.3
	31.0	16.0	8.7	8.3			% Profit Before Taxes/Total Assets	9.0	9.9
	12.4	3.8	3.6	4.6				1.8	4.7
	4.0	-1.3	.0	1.5				-2.8	-.1
	52.0	22.9	19.1	15.3			Sales/Net Fixed Assets	22.8	27.0
	15.9	8.5	6.9	8.9				9.5	10.8
	3.1	4.4	4.1	4.5				4.3	6.4
	5.9	3.9	3.1	3.1			Sales/Total Assets	4.4	3.8
	3.4	3.1	2.5	2.7				2.8	3.0
	2.3	2.3	1.6	1.9				1.8	2.4
	1.6	2.1	1.7	1.5			% Depr., Dep., Amort./Sales	1.5	1.7
	(17) 4.4	(39) 3.3	(42) 2.8	(16) 2.1				(24) 2.6	(44) 3.7
	11.6	4.8	5.2	5.1				4.2	5.5
	3.6	2.7	1.0				% Officers', Directors' Owners' Comp/Sales		3.3
	(13) 7.3	(19) 5.4	(18) 3.2						(15) 5.1
	9.7	10.6	6.2						12.3
	24133M	150557M	517794M	906218M	79839M	979046M	Net Sales ($)	272993M	365286M
	5643M	51177M	216410M	364366M	52931M	526769M	Total Assets ($)	129279M	141118M

M = $ thousand   MM = $ million

See Pages 11 through 21 for Explanation of Ratios and Data

Comparative Historical Data				Current Data Sorted by Sales					
			Type of Statement						
9	7	10	Unqualified		1	1	1	1	6
30	24	33	Reviewed	1	6	3	11	8	4
18	21	24	Compiled	4	5	8	3	4	
11	13	27	Tax Returns	13	4	5	3	2	
14	40	47	Other	4	11	7	7	9	9
4/1/04-3/31/05 ALL	**4/1/05-3/31/06 ALL**	**4/1/06-3/31/07 ALL**			**16 (4/1-9/30/06)**		**125 (10/1/06-3/31/07)**		
				0-1MM	**1-3MM**	**3-5MM**	**5-10MM**	**10-25MM**	**25MM & OVER**
82	105	141	**NUMBER OF STATEMENTS**	22	27	24	25	24	19
%	%	%	**ASSETS**	%	%	%	%	%	%
9.5	9.0	9.0	Cash & Equivalents	9.4	12.6	9.0	6.3	9.0	7.1
32.0	33.1	29.5	Trade Receivables (net)	16.3	24.0	29.6	26.3	41.0	42.5
.5	.8	.7	Inventory	.2	.3	.8	.7	.7	2.2
4.3	3.5	5.6	All Other Current	3.1	4.8	4.3	9.3	4.9	7.2
46.3	46.3	44.9	Total Current	29.0	41.7	43.7	42.6	55.5	58.9
36.2	39.6	38.9	Fixed Assets (net)	57.9	36.7	34.3	40.5	34.8	29.0
1.9	2.5	2.9	Intangibles (net)	2.2	1.7	7.0	.6	.4	6.1
15.6	11.6	13.3	All Other Non-Current	10.9	19.8	15.0	16.3	9.3	6.0
100.0	100.0	100.0	Total	100.0	100.0	100.0	100.0	100.0	100.0
			LIABILITIES						
6.9	8.8	8.1	Notes Payable-Short Term	6.9	7.3	9.3	6.4	7.0	13.0
4.5	5.8	6.7	Cur. Mat.-L.T.D.	9.4	4.6	9.7	5.9	4.8	5.9
12.2	11.5	9.7	Trade Payables	7.9	6.5	10.0	7.8	11.2	16.6
.3	.4	.3	Income Taxes Payable	.3	.1	.6	.5	.1	.1
11.1	11.0	9.2	All Other Current	4.2	9.2	14.5	10.4	6.1	10.4
34.9	37.5	33.9	Total Current	28.7	27.6	44.2	30.9	29.1	45.9
20.8	25.4	27.7	Long-Term Debt	47.5	29.0	21.2	28.3	19.0	21.3
1.1	.8	.8	Deferred Taxes	.2	.0	.1	2.8	1.1	.7
3.2	3.9	8.9	All Other Non-Current	8.5	26.2	2.8	4.5	3.3	5.5
40.0	32.4	28.7	Net Worth	15.1	17.2	31.8	33.6	47.6	26.5
100.0	100.0	100.0	Total Liabilties & Net Worth	100.0	100.0	100.0	100.0	100.0	100.0
			INCOME DATA						
100.0	100.0	100.0	Net Sales	100.0	100.0	100.0	100.0	100.0	100.0
			Gross Profit						
92.9	94.1	95.6	Operating Expenses	87.7	98.9	95.4	97.3	96.9	96.7
7.1	5.9	4.4	Operating Profit	12.3	1.1	4.6	2.7	3.1	3.3
3.0	.6	1.8	All Other Expenses (net)	9.4	.6	-.3	.6	.2	.8
4.0	5.3	2.6	Profit Before Taxes	2.9	.5	5.0	2.1	3.0	2.5
			RATIOS						
2.1	1.7	2.2		1.5	4.2	1.6	1.8	3.5	1.7
1.2	1.3	1.3	Current	1.0	2.4	1.0	1.4	1.5	1.2
.8	1.0	1.0		.2	1.0	.7	1.2	1.2	1.1
1.7	1.6	1.9		1.4	3.7	1.5	1.8	3.2	1.4
1.1	1.1	1.1	Quick	.9	2.1	1.0	1.2	1.4	1.0
.7	.8	.8		.2	.6	.6	.8	1.1	.9
21 17.8	**23** 16.2	**20** 18.2		**0** UND	**11** 32.1	**20** 18.1	**24** 15.0	**34** 10.8	**43** 8.6
39 9.4	**41** 9.0	**34** 10.6	Sales/Receivables	**7** 54.4	**25** 14.6	**31** 11.7	**35** 10.4	**44** 8.3	**54** 6.7
53 6.9	**55** 6.6	**55** 6.6		**34** 10.7	**44** 8.2	**47** 7.7	**56** 6.5	**67** 5.5	**68** 5.3
			Cost of Sales/Inventory						
			Cost of Sales/Payables						
9.8	12.6	11.1		30.7	7.9	14.9	15.0	6.6	11.6
46.4	32.6	34.6	Sales/Working Capital	NM	13.5	NM	22.3	14.0	35.5
-61.4	-199.7	-339.2		-6.0	-85.7	-31.2	75.9	78.0	77.8
8.3	7.6	5.8		6.4	9.1	8.6	4.4	16.6	5.8
(66) 3.2	(92) 3.6	(125) 2.4	EBIT/Interest	(16) 3.0	(23) 2.4	(22) 3.0	1.9	(21) 2.4	(18) 2.5
1.2	2.1	1.2		1.8	.8	.7	.5	1.7	1.4
4.2	3.4	3.3					2.9	5.6	
(27) 2.0	(34) 2.2	(36) 1.6	Net Profit + Depr., Dep., Amort./Cur. Mat. L/T/D				(10) 1.5	(12) 2.1	
1.5	1.3	1.1					1.0	1.4	
.2	.6	.5		.7	.2	.7	.4	.3	.6
.8	1.4	1.2	Fixed/Worth	1.8	1.2	1.3	1.2	.8	1.8
2.0	3.9	3.7		87.9	-8.9	13.7	2.2	1.5	3.3
.7	1.2	1.0		1.1	.3	.6	1.2	.5	2.4
1.7	2.7	2.1	Debt/Worth	2.9	3.3	2.0	1.7	1.5	3.4
3.7	7.1	7.2		NM	-22.0	28.1	3.3	2.3	9.6
29.7	62.0	42.8		98.8	45.1	39.0	54.6	33.5	78.0
(74) 11.1	(91) 24.8	(122) 15.4	% Profit Before Taxes/Tangible Net Worth	(17) 34.3	(20) 18.2	(19) 15.8	15.0	11.8	(17) 20.3
2.9	7.7	2.5		6.5	-1.3	.3	-1.1	5.0	8.5
10.2	15.7	11.9		13.3	27.3	17.2	9.8	11.4	10.1
4.1	7.3	4.7	% Profit Before Taxes/Total Assets	8.5	3.8	6.3	3.3	4.5	4.9
.9	2.6	.7		1.8	-1.1	-.5	-.5	1.7	1.5
28.7	19.4	21.2		12.9	26.0	20.4	14.9	23.7	21.5
10.5	9.6	8.5	Sales/Net Fixed Assets	4.0	9.1	9.7	6.8	10.2	9.1
4.2	4.1	4.3		.8	4.3	6.4	3.9	4.5	5.4
4.2	4.5	3.8		3.4	4.5	4.0	3.3	4.3	3.1
3.0	2.8	2.7	Sales/Total Assets	2.3	2.9	3.2	2.7	2.7	2.7
1.8	1.7	1.9		.7	2.6	2.1	1.6	2.1	2.1
1.3	1.7	1.7		4.4	2.0	1.8	1.9	1.5	1.5
(69) 2.9	(90) 2.6	(118) 3.2	% Depr., Dep., Amort./Sales	(17) 10.5	(20) 3.3	(21) 3.0	(23) 3.6	(19) 1.8	(18) 2.2
5.2	5.6	5.4		20.4	4.8	4.6	6.0	3.7	3.4
2.3	1.9	2.3			3.4		1.1	.9	
(21) 2.8	(30) 2.7	(54) 4.4	% Officers', Directors' Owners' Comp/Sales		(13) 5.4		(11) 1.7	(10) 3.9	
5.0	5.6	8.8			11.3		5.4	7.1	
2384644M	1954156M	2657587M	Net Sales ($)	11624M	53960M	90634M	178688M	394028M	1928653M
906803M	922417M	1217296M	Total Assets ($)	10773M	17726M	81151M	88786M	148424M	870436M

M = $ thousand MM = $ million

See Pages 11 through 21 for Explanation of Ratios and Data

Current Data Sorted by Assets   Comparative Historical Data

	0-500M	500M-2MM	2-10MM	10-50MM	50-100MM	100-250MM		4/1/02-3/31/03 ALL	4/1/03-3/31/04 ALL
Type of Statement									
Unqualified	1	1	3	5	1			3	1
Reviewed	3	4	12	12	1			6	20
Compiled	3	8	16	3				8	17
Tax Returns	20	19	5	1				5	20
Other	13	12	16	10	2			10	13
		26 (4/1-9/30/06)		145 (10/1/06-3/31/07)					
NUMBER OF STATEMENTS	40	44	52	31	4			32	71
	%	%	%	%	%	%	**ASSETS**	%	%
Cash & Equivalents	18.9	15.5	9.3	4.4				8.4	13.6
Trade Receivables (net)	20.4	22.6	22.4	23.0				21.9	19.8
Inventory	.8	2.4	2.1	6.2				1.8	.7
All Other Current	8.3	4.1	4.1	4.9				5.4	4.0
Total Current	48.4	44.6	37.9	38.6				37.4	38.1
Fixed Assets (net)	39.3	46.6	52.1	51.5				54.1	53.3
Intangibles (net)	2.4	.2	2.7	5.6				1.4	1.0
All Other Non-Current	9.9	8.6	7.2	4.3				7.1	7.7
Total	100.0	100.0	100.0	100.0				100.0	100.0
							LIABILITIES		
Notes Payable-Short Term	12.3	10.4	5.1	8.1				18.1	8.1
Cur. Mat.-L.T.D.	6.1	8.1	8.7	8.4				6.1	11.8
Trade Payables	11.4	10.5	9.0	10.6				11.8	10.1
Income Taxes Payable	.1	.3	.7	.5				.3	1.0
All Other Current	10.2	7.1	6.0	6.9				4.9	7.3
Total Current	40.0	36.3	29.4	34.5				41.2	38.3
Long-Term Debt	27.6	28.3	32.0	26.7				26.2	33.4
Deferred Taxes	.0	.1	.5	1.7				1.1	.9
All Other Non-Current	6.0	4.6	1.9	3.1				4.7	3.7
Net Worth	26.4	30.7	36.2	34.0				26.8	23.8
Total Liabilities & Net Worth	100.0	100.0	100.0	100.0				100.0	100.0
							INCOME DATA		
Net Sales	100.0	100.0	100.0	100.0				100.0	100.0
Gross Profit									
Operating Expenses	95.9	93.4	93.8	92.9				97.9	96.8
Operating Profit	4.1	6.6	6.2	7.1				2.1	3.2
All Other Expenses (net)	.7	.9	1.1	.8				1.2	.7
Profit Before Taxes	3.4	5.6	5.1	6.3				.9	2.5
							RATIOS		
Current	4.3	2.8	2.1	1.5				1.9	1.6
	1.6	1.2	1.4	1.2				1.2	1.1
	.4	.7	.7	1.0				.6	.6
Quick	3.2	2.8	1.7	1.2				1.6	1.4
	1.2	1.0	1.2	1.0				1.0 (70)	.9
	.3	.6	.6	.5				.3	.5
Sales/Receivables	0 UND	7 49.6	17 21.7	26 13.9				10 37.3	2 167.8
	16 22.9	25 14.8	28 13.0	33 11.1				30 12.3	22 16.8
	33 11.0	37 9.8	49 7.4	52 7.1				46 7.9	37 9.8
Cost of Sales/Inventory									
Cost of Sales/Payables									
Sales/Working Capital	11.8	9.8	12.6	17.9				12.1	24.9
	31.5	59.8	33.7	40.4				36.6	104.2
	-19.4	-22.0	-28.9	328.6				-16.3	-19.8
EBIT/Interest	10.7	6.8	9.1	7.8				7.0	9.2
	(33) 1.7	(36) 2.9	(50) 3.5	(30) 5.2				(30) 1.7	(66) 2.9
	-2.4	1.1	2.0	2.6				.2	1.0
Net Profit + Depr., Dep., Amort./Cur. Mat. L/T/D			4.2	5.8					3.5
		(17) 2.1	(11) 3.2					(13) 1.3	
		1.3	1.7					1.1	
Fixed/Worth	.3	.4	.7	1.2				.8	.8
	1.6	1.5	1.6	1.6				1.7	2.3
	-8.7	4.4	3.4	3.7				17.3	10.1
Debt/Worth	.4	1.1	.7	1.3				.6	1.1
	2.2	2.1	2.3	2.3				2.1	2.5
	-32.4	6.7	5.5	6.1				20.1	24.8
% Profit Before Taxes/Tangible Net Worth	86.3	75.3	67.3	57.3				42.4	63.6
	(29) 22.7	(39) 32.1	(46) 30.6	(29) 29.7				(25) 9.1	(59) 22.6
	-10.3	5.3	12.5	15.1				.1	2.6
% Profit Before Taxes/Total Assets	28.5	23.8	21.5	13.8				9.8	13.6
	7.4	6.6	6.5	8.3				2.4	5.7
	-10.1	.8	3.2	4.1				-2.8	.5
Sales/Net Fixed Assets	43.0	16.6	9.8	7.7				15.9	13.8
	12.4	6.5	4.9	3.5				3.6	6.0
	4.3	3.1	2.1	2.2				2.1	3.2
Sales/Total Assets	7.0	4.2	3.6	2.7				3.7	5.0
	4.1	2.8	2.4	2.1				2.2	3.1
	2.2	2.2	1.5	1.5				1.1	2.0
% Depr., Dep., Amort./Sales	2.5	2.3	1.9	1.9				2.3	2.9
	(18) 7.0	(38) 4.5	(48) 6.4	(30) 4.5				(30) 6.9	(65) 6.2
	12.4	7.3	9.8	7.8				14.7	10.6
% Officers', Directors' Owners' Comp/Sales	1.9	1.2	.9	.6				2.2	1.6
	(19) 4.9	(25) 3.2	(15) 2.0	(10) 1.2				(11) 5.1	(31) 3.1
	12.7	5.6	3.2	4.2				6.4	6.1
Net Sales ($)	46912M	167304M	612835M	1535103M	338177M			273315M	513206M
Total Assets ($)	10333M	46767M	240364M	637711M	231268M			126832M	174196M

(Note: columns 50-100MM and 100-250MM in the ASSETS, LIABILITIES, INCOME DATA and RATIOS sections are marked "DATA NOT AVAILABLE".)

M = $ thousand   MM = $ million
See Pages 11 through 21 for Explanation of Ratios and Data

© RMA 2007

Comparative Historical Data   **Current Data Sorted by Sales**

			Type of Statement						
3	11	11	Unqualified	1	3		1	4	5
22	28	32	Reviewed	2		2	5	11	9
29	30	30	Compiled		8	5	8	5	4
27	33	45	Tax Returns	11	20	3	5	5	1
26	52	53	Other	9	13	5	8	7	11
4/1/04-3/31/05 ALL	4/1/05-3/31/06 ALL	4/1/06-3/31/07 ALL		26 (4/1-9/30/06)			145 (10/1/06-3/31/07)		
				0-1MM	1-3MM	3-5MM	5-10MM	10-25MM	25MM & OVER
107	154	171	NUMBER OF STATEMENTS	23	44	15	27	32	30
%	%	%	ASSETS	%	%	%	%	%	%
13.4	11.3	12.1	Cash & Equivalents	19.1	15.6	13.6	10.3	8.7	5.8
19.4	23.7	22.1	Trade Receivables (net)	16.9	17.3	25.2	22.7	28.7	24.2
.8	1.4	2.6	Inventory	.1	1.4	3.1	2.5	2.9	5.9
4.9	3.9	5.2	All Other Current	6.3	7.0	2.7	5.0	3.0	5.4
38.5	40.4	42.0	Total Current	42.3	41.3	44.5	40.4	43.3	41.3
49.9	47.9	47.9	Fixed Assets (net)	45.4	49.9	40.4	48.6	50.8	46.6
2.6	1.6	2.6	Intangibles (net)	2.4	1.2	.4	2.6	1.1	7.8
9.0	10.2	7.5	All Other Non-Current	9.8	7.6	14.8	8.3	4.9	4.2
100.0	100.0	100.0	Total	100.0	100.0	100.0	100.0	100.0	100.0
			LIABILITIES						
8.1	7.7	8.7	Notes Payable-Short Term	7.4	10.2	17.4	5.0	5.4	10.2
9.3	7.6	7.8	Cur. Mat.-L.T.D.	5.5	8.8	7.4	9.1	7.5	7.7
10.3	11.2	10.3	Trade Payables	9.4	9.7	10.5	9.5	12.1	10.3
.4	.3	.4	Income Taxes Payable	.0	.2	.5	.0	1.2	.4
6.9	7.0	7.4	All Other Current	12.3	5.5	6.4	4.8	8.0	8.7
34.9	33.9	34.6	Total Current	34.6	34.3	42.2	28.4	34.3	37.3
41.3	34.8	29.2	Long-Term Debt	25.3	36.0	17.4	35.7	27.0	24.9
.7	.9	.5	Deferred Taxes	.0	.1	.0	.8	.6	1.5
5.3	6.5	4.0	All Other Non-Current	5.0	7.0	1.6	1.8	2.4	3.4
17.8	23.9	31.6	Net Worth	35.1	22.5	38.9	33.3	35.8	32.9
100.0	100.0	100.0	Total Liabilities & Net Worth	100.0	100.0	100.0	100.0	100.0	100.0
			INCOME DATA						
100.0	100.0	100.0	Net Sales	100.0	100.0	100.0	100.0	100.0	100.0
			Gross Profit						
94.6	95.1	94.0	Operating Expenses	87.8	96.1	95.0	96.0	92.6	95.0
5.4	4.9	6.0	Operating Profit	12.2	3.9	5.0	4.0	7.4	5.0
.7	.8	1.0	All Other Expenses (net)	4.8	.1	-.6	.6	.5	1.0
4.6	4.1	5.0	Profit Before Taxes	7.4	3.8	5.5	3.3	6.9	4.1
			RATIOS						
2.7	2.3	2.2		2.9	4.6	2.5	2.1	2.1	1.5
1.4	1.2	1.3	Current	1.0	1.3	1.3	1.6	1.2	1.2
.7	.7	.7		.3	.6	.7	.8	.8	1.0
2.2	2.1	1.7		2.6	3.6	2.2	1.8	1.6	1.2
1.1 (153)	1.0	1.1	Quick	1.0	1.0	1.2	1.3	1.1	1.0
.5	.5	.6		.3	.4	.7	.6	.6	.6
3 108.6	9 41.3	11 34.1		0 UND	0 UND	6 57.5	15 23.6	19 19.3	26 14.1
24 15.2	24 15.2	27 13.3	Sales/Receivables	19 19.6	22 16.9	27 13.3	24 15.1	33 11.2	32 11.3
40 9.2	40 9.1	41 8.9		44 8.2	37 9.9	47 7.7	38 9.6	56 6.5	42 8.7
			Cost of Sales/Inventory						
			Cost of Sales/Payables						
10.6	15.2	12.4		7.7	12.1	9.0	10.8	14.7	22.3
32.5	51.7	39.0	Sales/Working Capital	159.0	34.0	35.5	20.8	40.2	55.1
-24.5	-21.5	-25.1		-4.6	-19.9	-27.1	-16.3	-42.8	NM
8.5	8.6	8.3		11.0	8.0	9.7	6.0	16.3	8.7
(95) 3.6	(135) 4.0	(153) 3.3	EBIT/Interest	(16) 1.4	(38) 2.6	(13) 4.3	3.3	(30) 4.6	(29) 4.4
.8	1.0	1.5		-4.1	.8	1.5	1.3	3.2	1.9
2.7	2.9	3.4						5.5	4.0
(18) 1.3	(34) 1.5	(41) 2.0	Net Profit + Depr., Dep., Amort./Cur. Mat. L/T/D				(10)	3.1 (15)	2.8
.8	1.2	1.2						2.0	1.3
.8	.7	.7		.2	.8	.1	.7	.6	1.1
1.8	1.7	1.6	Fixed/Worth	1.6	2.8	1.3	1.5	1.7	1.4
15.0	5.8	5.1		-45.3	31.4	2.5	3.5	3.2	4.3
1.0	1.0	.9		.4	.8	.8	.9	.9	1.2
2.2	2.4	2.3	Debt/Worth	2.1	3.2	1.6	2.8	2.2	2.5
20.3	10.6	7.8		-46.8	35.3	2.8	6.3	6.0	8.9
73.2	70.0	67.7		64.7	77.1	63.2	50.8	84.2	50.2
(86) 23.4	(127) 30.8	(146) 29.2	% Profit Before Taxes/Tangible Net Worth	(17) 18.4	(35) 41.3	(13) 18.9	(24) 26.8	(31) 50.8	(26) 30.3
4.7	10.9	9.6		-10.3	6.7	4.6	5.6	10.8	18.6
18.1	19.3	20.2		21.9	23.8	20.2	14.1	25.7	13.2
7.4	8.6	7.4	% Profit Before Taxes/Total Assets	4.4	5.6	8.2	5.7	12.3	7.7
.6	.4	1.8		-12.9	.1	1.9	1.3	3.9	3.5
12.3	15.5	13.7		37.0	14.2	17.9	9.2	15.7	10.2
5.5	6.4	6.0	Sales/Net Fixed Assets	4.2	7.3	9.0	5.5	4.3	5.5
3.0	3.0	2.7		2.1	3.1	3.8	2.6	2.2	2.8
4.8	4.1	4.2		3.2	5.0	6.2	3.8	4.5	3.5
2.9	2.8	2.6	Sales/Total Assets	1.7	3.2	2.8	2.4	2.6	2.3
1.7	1.8	1.7		1.4	2.2	2.2	1.6	1.5	1.7
3.5	3.0	2.3			3.4	2.2	2.2	1.5	1.7
(89) 7.0	(127) 5.2	(138) 5.7	% Depr., Dep., Amort./Sales		(36) 5.8	(11) 4.3	(25) 6.2	(28) 6.5	(29) 3.8
11.2	9.1	9.0			9.7	8.6	9.0	8.9	6.4
1.5	1.3	1.1			1.9			1.3	
(43) 3.3	(57) 2.6	(69) 3.0	% Officers', Directors' Owners' Comp/Sales		(23) 3.8		(16) 2.2		
4.8	4.7	5.4			4.9			6.4	
866585M	2038114M	2700331M	Net Sales ($)	9873M	84101M	59842M	202379M	504293M	1839843M
478935M	844023M	1166443M	Total Assets ($)	9719M	32436M	30029M	94481M	228780M	770998M

© RMA 2007

M = $ thousand   MM = $ million
See Pages 11 through 21 for Explanation of Ratios and Data

Current Data Sorted by Assets

Comparative Historical Data

						Type of Statement		
1	1	1	17	3	6	Unqualified	6	11
1	3	22	11	1		Reviewed	5	10
4	8	9	3			Compiled	8	12
3	3	3				Tax Returns	2	6
5	8	16	22	1	4	Other	21	21
	22 (4/1-9/30/06)		134 (10/1/06-3/31/07)				4/1/02-3/31/03	4/1/03-3/31/04
0-500M	500M-2MM	2-10MM	10-50MM	50-100MM	100-250MM		ALL	ALL
14	23	51	53	5	10	NUMBER OF STATEMENTS	32	60
%	%	%	%	%	%	**ASSETS**	%	%
16.4	14.3	7.4	8.4		1.6	Cash & Equivalents	4.2	7.3
29.4	37.3	24.3	22.0		14.2	Trade Receivables (net)	36.4	24.4
.6	1.4	.7	1.6		.9	Inventory	2.0	2.1
2.2	3.5	4.2	3.6		4.0	All Other Current	5.4	4.3
48.7	56.6	36.6	35.6		20.7	Total Current	47.9	38.1
40.2	33.6	50.4	55.9		68.2	Fixed Assets (net)	42.9	51.6
.2	1.5	2.0	2.3		2.8	Intangibles (net)	2.1	2.8
10.9	8.3	10.9	6.1		8.3	All Other Non-Current	7.0	7.5
100.0	100.0	100.0	100.0		100.0	Total	100.0	100.0
						LIABILITIES		
7.1	7.8	7.3	5.7		1.9	Notes Payable-Short Term	4.3	5.4
17.5	6.8	10.0	12.3		12.0	Cur. Mat.-L.T.D.	8.3	8.7
12.5	14.8	5.6	7.3		4.6	Trade Payables	16.5	10.0
.0	.1	.0	.6		.0	Income Taxes Payable	.6	.1
15.3	10.5	9.6	7.2		6.7	All Other Current	16.4	10.6
52.4	40.0	32.4	33.1		25.2	Total Current	46.2	34.8
28.6	16.1	29.0	30.0		38.9	Long-Term Debt	18.3	33.4
1.3	.2	1.0	3.4		8.8	Deferred Taxes	2.1	1.8
9.6	.6	6.1	3.2		.9	All Other Non-Current	8.8	6.3
8.2	43.1	31.5	30.2		26.2	Net Worth	24.7	23.6
100.0	100.0	100.0	100.0		100.0	Total Liabilties & Net Worth	100.0	100.0
						INCOME DATA		
100.0	100.0	100.0	100.0		100.0	Net Sales	100.0	100.0
						Gross Profit		
98.1	93.2	94.9	95.4		95.0	Operating Expenses	96.9	97.1
1.9	6.8	5.1	4.6		5.0	Operating Profit	3.1	2.9
-.8	.6	.4	.8		1.3	All Other Expenses (net)	.3	.9
2.7	6.2	4.8	3.8		3.6	Profit Before Taxes	2.8	2.0
						RATIOS		
2.0	2.3	1.8	1.6		1.0		1.6	1.6
1.3	1.2	1.1	1.0		.9	Current	1.2	1.1
.6	.9	.7	.8		.6		.7	.7
1.8	1.9	1.5	1.4		.7		1.2	1.3
1.2	1.1	.9	.9		.6	Quick	1.0	.9
.4	.8	.6	.6		.5		.6	.5

													Sales/Receivables				
0	UND	25	14.4	20	18.3	29	12.7			26	13.9		Sales/Receivables	22	16.3	18	20.2
17	21.8	37	10.0	34	10.9	35	10.5			32	11.5			34	10.8	32	11.4
34	10.8	42	8.7	44	8.2	40	9.1			38	9.7			56	6.5	40	9.0

Cost of Sales/Inventory

Cost of Sales/Payables

26.9		13.4		15.8		15.4			349.2	Sales/Working Capital	16.9	20.8
66.9		40.8		172.4		346.3			-44.3		74.1	63.4
-41.3		-144.0		-23.6		-35.5			-14.6		-40.9	-21.6
	15.2		13.9		7.7		5.0		3.1	EBIT/Interest		5.9		4.3
(10)	4.7	(17)	7.6	(49)	3.1		2.9		2.6		(30)	2.8	(57)	2.4
	.6		2.5		1.1		1.7		2.0			.4		1.3
					2.9		1.6			Net Profit + Depr., Dep., Amort./Cur. Mat. L/T/D				2.6
		(13)			1.1	(28)	1.3						(14)	1.6
					.9		1.1							1.2
	.2		.0		.8		1.3		2.6	Fixed/Worth		.7		1.0
	2.2		.9		1.6		2.0		3.1			2.0		2.6
	-1.0		1.8		3.5		3.9		4.9			4.6		6.6
	1.3		.5		1.0		1.5		2.3	Debt/Worth		1.1		1.3
	2.9		1.6		2.1		2.9		3.5			3.0		3.5
	-4.0		4.3		5.4		5.5		5.2			20.3		10.9
	88.8		66.3		49.3		44.2		29.8	% Profit Before Taxes/Tangible Net Worth		67.7		40.2
(10)	50.0		31.9	(46)	22.0	(52)	22.9		26.7		(27)	17.8	(52)	17.8
	-3.4		5.5		2.8		10.9		22.5			6.0		5.1
	29.0		28.9		14.1		9.8		6.5	% Profit Before Taxes/Total Assets		12.5		10.3
	20.7		12.3		7.3		4.9		5.0			4.7		4.0
	2.5		2.3		.2		2.8		3.9			-1.3		.4
	274.6		183.6		9.6		6.2		3.0	Sales/Net Fixed Assets		25.8		9.9
	11.5		7.9		4.1		3.3		1.9			6.4		4.7
	3.1		6.4		2.8		2.2		1.7			3.2		2.7
	11.6		5.3		3.2		2.9		1.9	Sales/Total Assets		4.8		3.9
	5.7		3.7		2.4		1.9		1.5			3.1		2.6
	2.1		2.7		1.6		1.5		1.2			2.0		1.7
	.2		2.3		2.8		3.6			% Depr., Dep., Amort./Sales		1.7		2.9
(11)	1.1	(17)	4.1	(50)	5.2	(50)	6.0				(25)	4.6	(49)	6.4
	8.1		6.9		8.5		8.3					11.6		11.4
					1.4					% Officers', Directors' Owners' Comp/Sales				1.3
		(20)			3.7								(22)	2.9
					4.8									9.3

26633M	115221M	661994M	2828484M	630275M	2267137M	Net Sales ($)	1524924M	1981982M
4028M	29791M	242394M	1274406M	299536M	1452724M	Total Assets ($)	537376M	814504M

M = $ thousand   MM = $ million
See Pages 11 through 21 for Explanation of Ratios and Data

Comparative Historical Data

Current Data Sorted by Sales

			Type of Statement						
20	32	29	Unqualified			1	2	2	24
17	26	38	Reviewed		4	1	6	13	14
18	20	24	Compiled	3	4	5	8	3	1
8	10	9	Tax Returns	1	1	3	3	1	
25	43	56	Other	2	4	8	6	13	23
4/1/04- 3/31/05	4/1/05- 3/31/06	4/1/06- 3/31/07			22 (4/1-9/30/06)		134 (10/1/06-3/31/07)		
ALL	ALL	ALL		0-1MM	1-3MM	3-5MM	5-10MM	10-25MM	25MM & OVER
88	131	156	NUMBER OF STATEMENTS	6	13	18	25	32	62
%	%	%	ASSETS	%	%	%	%	%	%
7.2	7.7	9.3	Cash & Equivalents		21.8	12.9	8.0	7.1	7.2
25.1	25.1	25.4	Trade Receivables (net)		24.9	22.5	30.1	23.7	26.0
1.2	1.0	1.1	Inventory		.7	1.5	.9	.8	1.4
4.3	4.6	3.7	All Other Current		5.2	4.4	4.0	1.4	4.4
37.9	38.4	39.5	Total Current		52.6	41.4	43.0	33.1	39.0
51.9	51.0	50.1	Fixed Assets (net)		31.3	48.2	44.4	56.5	52.0
3.0	3.0	2.0	Intangibles (net)		.1	1.2	3.8	1.8	2.2
7.2	7.6	8.5	All Other Non-Current		15.9	9.1	8.8	8.6	6.8
100.0	100.0	100.0	Total		100.0	100.0	100.0	100.0	100.0
			LIABILITIES						
8.6	7.6	6.3	Notes Payable-Short Term		8.8	5.4	6.8	5.6	6.6
9.7	11.3	11.0	Cur. Mat.-L.T.D.		9.6	7.6	8.4	12.2	11.0
7.4	7.7	8.1	Trade Payables		10.0	9.6	8.5	7.9	7.3
.1	.2	.2	Income Taxes Payable		.0	.0	.0	.0	.6
10.3	8.4	9.3	All Other Current		12.3	14.4	8.7	4.9	10.6
36.0	35.2	35.0	Total Current		40.8	37.0	32.4	30.7	36.1
29.7	28.6	27.9	Long-Term Debt		18.0	25.6	26.0	33.3	27.2
3.3	2.6	2.4	Deferred Taxes		1.0	.1	.1	1.5	4.8
5.1	2.7	4.1	All Other Non-Current		9.6	1.6	1.7	7.7	2.9
25.8	30.9	30.6	Net Worth		30.7	35.8	39.8	26.8	29.0
100.0	100.0	100.0	Total Liabilties & Net Worth		100.0	100.0	100.0	100.0	100.0
			INCOME DATA						
100.0	100.0	100.0	Net Sales		100.0	100.0	100.0	100.0	100.0
			Gross Profit						
97.6	94.8	95.0	Operating Expenses		92.4	93.3	96.0	94.6	95.5
2.4	5.2	5.0	Operating Profit		7.6	6.7	4.0	5.4	4.5
.4	.8	.5	All Other Expenses (net)		-2.0	.5	.4	1.3	.7
2.0	4.5	4.5	Profit Before Taxes		9.5	6.2	3.6	4.1	3.8
			RATIOS						
1.6	1.4	1.7			3.9	1.6	2.1	1.8	1.4
1.0	1.0	1.1	Current		1.4	1.0	1.2	1.0	1.0
.7	.7	.8			.6	.5	1.0	.8	.8
1.3	1.3	1.4			3.9	1.2	1.7	1.6	1.2
.8	.9	.9	Quick		1.2	.8	1.1	.9	.9
.6	.6	.6			.4	.4	.7	.7	.6

							Sales/Receivables					
24	15.4	23	15.7	23	15.7	8	45.5	2	229.8	26	13.8	24	15.1	28	12.8
34	10.8	34	10.8	34	10.8	31	11.6	20	18.1	37	10.0	34	10.9	35	10.6
41	8.9	44	8.4	43	8.6	42	8.8	31	11.7	48	7.5	43	8.5	41	8.8

			Cost of Sales/Inventory						

			Cost of Sales/Payables						

21.9	20.9	17.2	Sales/Working Capital		4.2	20.4	11.6	16.2	17.6
661.6	115.9	93.4			55.0	NM	50.7	NM	480.5
-25.2	-22.6	-37.5			-38.4	-19.4	NM	-33.5	-38.3

						EBIT/Interest				
	5.8		6.6		7.5		14.0		8.3		6.6		5.5
(83)	3.2	(123)	3.7	(143)	3.1			(15)	7.5	(23)	4.0	(31)	3.1	(61)	2.9
	1.3		2.2		1.7				1.0		1.6		1.5		1.9

				Net Profit + Depr., Dep., Amort./Cur. Mat. L/T/D					
	1.3		1.9		2.2						1.8		2.0
(28)	1.1	(54)	1.3	(50)	1.4					(11)	1.0	(30)	1.4
	.8		.8		1.0						.9		1.1

1.4	1.1	1.0	Fixed/Worth	.1	.3	.5	1.2	1.3
2.5	1.9	1.9		1.0	1.4	1.5	2.1	2.2
6.5	4.1	3.5		NM	3.2	2.8	3.5	3.9

1.6	1.2	1.2	Debt/Worth	.4	1.1	.6	1.1	1.6
3.2	2.6	2.6		1.3	2.0	2.1	2.8	3.0
10.1	5.3	5.1		NM	3.3	5.2	4.8	5.6

						% Profit Before Taxes/Tangible Net Worth				
	42.9		52.2		50.6		61.8		69.8		61.8		49.3		48.7
(75)	20.7	(117)	26.7	(146)	26.4	(10)	21.2	(16)	28.2	21.3	(30)	21.8	(60)	28.3
	2.9		13.5		11.2		4.8		7.6		3.6		7.4		16.2

11.3	14.2	15.5	% Profit Before Taxes/Total Assets	27.0	25.2	12.5	14.8	13.2
5.2	7.2	6.7		14.1	13.1	9.1	6.5	6.1
.4	3.4	2.5		2.8	.1	.9	2.1	3.4

10.4	10.2	9.0	Sales/Net Fixed Assets	206.0	36.9	10.7	6.4	7.1
4.6	4.6	4.3		9.8	6.2	6.3	3.2	4.2
2.6	2.4	2.5		3.1	2.6	2.8	2.2	2.3

3.7	3.6	3.4	Sales/Total Assets	5.7	5.3	3.5	2.8	3.2
2.5	2.3	2.3		3.7	2.7	2.7	2.1	2.1
1.7	1.6	1.6		.6	1.7	1.6	1.6	1.5

						% Depr., Dep., Amort./Sales				
	2.2		2.5		2.7		.6		2.5		2.9		3.7		2.3
(68)	3.8	(113)	5.1	(133)	5.1	(12)	5.5	(14)	4.2	(21)	5.7	(31)	5.8	(50)	4.9
	8.4		7.7		8.2		10.3		7.3		8.0		8.9		6.5

						% Officers', Directors' Owners' Comp/Sales				
	1.3		1.3		1.1						1.1		
(28)	2.5	(36)	2.6	(43)	3.0					(11)	4.1		
	6.5		5.7		4.5						5.8		

4600714M	6787084M	6529744M	Net Sales ($)	3623M	24357M	74337M	185940M	534911M	5706576M
2144474M	3321642M	3302879M	Total Assets ($)	1616M	14170M	29442M	93221M	285999M	2878431M

M = $ thousand   MM = $ million
See Pages 11 through 21 for Explanation of Ratios and Data

Current Data Sorted by Assets   Comparative Historical Data

0-500M	500M-2MM	2-10MM	10-50MM	50-100MM	100-250MM	Type of Statement	4/1/02-3/31/03 ALL	4/1/03-3/31/04 ALL
		2	2			Unqualified	3	3
	2	3	2			Reviewed	2	5
4	4	2				Compiled	10	8
4	2	1		1		Tax Returns	9	9
5	2	5	6	2		Other	9	8
	9 (4/1-9/30/06)		40 (10/1/06-3/31/07)					
13	10	13	10	3		NUMBER OF STATEMENTS	33	33
%	%	%	%	%	%	ASSETS	%	%
9.3	9.9	10.3	6.6			Cash & Equivalents	14.3	9.2
19.7	23.4	17.6	9.3			Trade Receivables (net)	19.7	26.5
.9	.5	.3	.7			Inventory	1.0	2.1
1.9	1.8	2.1	1.5			All Other Current	6.0	8.4
31.8	35.7	30.3	18.1			Total Current	41.0	46.2
41.0	46.9	34.9	39.3			Fixed Assets (net)	35.0	29.3
15.2	7.0	13.8	12.4			Intangibles (net)	13.6	10.1
12.0	10.4	21.0	30.2			All Other Non-Current	10.4	14.4
100.0	100.0	100.0	100.0			Total	100.0	100.0
						LIABILITIES		
42.2	7.0	5.0	8.6			Notes Payable-Short Term	10.0	6.7
2.5	8.1	4.9	4.3			Cur. Mat.-L.T.D.	4.7	9.4
10.8	4.9	11.3	3.1			Trade Payables	9.1	10.7
.9	.4	.5	.0			Income Taxes Payable	2.2	1.2
20.9	8.2	8.7	11.8			All Other Current	11.7	11.4
77.4	28.6	30.5	27.8			Total Current	37.6	39.5
20.4	32.2	21.3	33.2			Long-Term Debt	21.8	25.9
.0	1.1	.0	3.8			Deferred Taxes	.2	1.1
2.2	5.8	4.3	4.4			All Other Non-Current	5.8	10.5
-.1	32.2	43.9	30.8			Net Worth	34.5	23.1
100.0	100.0	100.0	100.0			Total Liabilities & Net Worth	100.0	100.0
						INCOME DATA		
100.0	100.0	100.0	100.0			Net Sales	100.0	100.0
						Gross Profit		
95.3	95.7	93.8	82.0			Operating Expenses	88.8	88.4
4.7	4.3	6.2	18.0			Operating Profit	11.2	11.6
1.7	4.4	1.5	8.8			All Other Expenses (net)	2.7	4.4
3.0	-.1	4.7	9.2			Profit Before Taxes	8.5	7.2
						RATIOS		
.9	1.7	1.5	1.8				2.0	2.6
.3	.9	1.1	.9			Current	1.0	1.5
.1	.7	.5	.3				.7	.6
.8	1.7	1.4	1.7				1.7	1.9
.3	.8	1.1	.8			Quick	1.0	1.1
.1	.6	.4	.2				.4	.3
0 UND	0 UND	1 505.1	2 199.5				3 105.9	8 48.4
19 19.3	27 13.3	29 12.8	30 12.3			Sales/Receivables	18 20.0	36 10.1
52 7.0	65 5.7	47 7.8	55 6.7				44 8.3	63 5.8
						Cost of Sales/Inventory		
						Cost of Sales/Payables		
NM	12.3	14.8	11.4				8.8	8.0
-15.7	-58.6	76.8	-85.6			Sales/Working Capital	235.5	16.2
-4.2	-14.8	-14.9	-9.3				-16.6	-13.9
		35.5					21.8	12.4
		6.8				EBIT/Interest	(29) 7.5	(25) 4.2
		1.5					2.3	1.2
						Net Profit + Depr., Dep., Amort./Cur. Mat. L/T/D		
.6	1.0	.6	.7				.5	.4
6.1	1.6	.8	4.7			Fixed/Worth	1.7	1.9
-1.2	NM	-5.4	-6.4				NM	-7.2
1.5	1.2	.5	2.1				1.8	1.5
87.5	1.8	2.0	11.1			Debt/Worth	3.1	3.6
-2.0	NM	-8.2	-11.1				NM	-13.1
							116.4	78.8
						% Profit Before Taxes/Tangible Net Worth	(25) 40.4	(22) 46.8
							23.4	18.4
17.4	5.2	21.6	16.7				27.6	21.7
1.2	-.9	13.0	8.5			% Profit Before Taxes/Total Assets	11.2	9.5
-14.5	-4.1	.5	4.0				3.9	1.7
54.9	10.0	31.1	5.8				17.6	32.6
15.5	3.3	8.3	3.6			Sales/Net Fixed Assets	8.5	8.7
5.5	1.5	3.6	2.6				4.4	4.2
11.4	3.7	3.2	2.0				3.9	3.8
3.2	1.6	1.8	1.3			Sales/Total Assets	2.2	2.2
1.3	.8	1.1	.9				1.3	1.3
		1.8					1.9	2.0
		(10) 5.6				% Depr., Dep., Amort./Sales	(28) 4.7	(27) 4.6
		11.3					12.9	9.3
							3.1	5.5
						% Officers', Directors' Owners' Comp/Sales	(19) 4.7	(17) 8.7
							12.1	10.4
9265M	19740M	144257M	354494M	293883M		Net Sales ($)	344949M	201552M
2870M	9659M	64706M	242707M	224011M		Total Assets ($)	233419M	162483M

(100-250MM column: DATA NOT AVAILABLE)

M = $ thousand   MM = $ million
See Pages 11 through 21 for Explanation of Ratios and Data

Comparative Historical Data / Current Data Sorted by Sales

			Type of Statement						
4		4	Unqualified	1	2	1	2	2	2
9	5	8	Reviewed		2			2	
7	13	10	Compiled	2	5	1	1	1	
12	15	7	Tax Returns	4	3				
7	14	20	Other	5	1	2	1	6	5
4/1/04- 3/31/05	4/1/05- 3/31/06	4/1/06- 3/31/07		9 (4/1-9/30/06)			40 (10/1/06-3/31/07)		
ALL	ALL	ALL		0-1MM	1-3MM	3-5MM	5-10MM	10-25MM	25MM & OVER
39	47	49	NUMBER OF STATEMENTS	12	11	4	4	11	7
%	%	%	ASSETS	%	%	%	%	%	%
13.1	12.7	9.4	Cash & Equivalents	11.1	5.8			8.1	
15.7	15.6	16.9	Trade Receivables (net)	20.0	23.3			16.0	
1.4	2.1	.6	Inventory	.8	.6			.2	
7.1	8.7	2.0	All Other Current	1.3	3.1			1.5	
37.2	39.1	29.0	Total Current	33.1	32.8			25.8	
40.0	31.7	39.0	Fixed Assets (net)	43.4	44.4			29.5	
7.0	10.9	12.3	Intangibles (net)	12.5	6.7			17.3	
15.8	18.3	19.7	All Other Non-Current	11.0	16.1			27.5	
100.0	100.0	100.0	Total	100.0	100.0			100.0	
			LIABILITIES						
4.7	3.3	15.7	Notes Payable-Short Term	30.3	20.8			1.5	
5.2	14.4	5.0	Cur. Mat.-L.T.D.	3.4	5.5			4.3	
7.5	9.2	7.7	Trade Payables	10.8	4.9			8.1	
.2	.2	.5	Income Taxes Payable	1.3	.0			.1	
18.4	13.7	13.2	All Other Current	17.4	13.9			9.1	
36.1	40.9	42.0	Total Current	63.3	45.2			23.0	
29.8	23.5	26.3	Long-Term Debt	32.3	29.0			22.1	
.0	.3	1.0	Deferred Taxes	.0	1.0			3.4	
7.7	4.8	3.9	All Other Non-Current	5.1	3.9			5.5	
26.4	30.6	26.8	Net Worth	-.7	20.9			46.0	
100.0	100.0	100.0	Total Liabilties & Net Worth	100.0	100.0			100.0	
			INCOME DATA						
100.0	100.0	100.0	Net Sales	100.0	100.0			100.0	
			Gross Profit						
92.0	87.9	91.3	Operating Expenses	93.0	89.1			86.6	
8.0	12.1	8.7	Operating Profit	7.0	10.9			13.4	
2.9	4.2	3.8	All Other Expenses (net)	4.7	8.0			2.6	
5.1	7.9	4.9	Profit Before Taxes	2.3	3.0			10.8	
			RATIOS						
2.1	2.1	1.4		1.3	2.6			2.1	
.8	1.1	.9	Current	.6	.8			1.1	
.4	.5	.3		.2	.2			.5	
1.2	1.8	1.3		1.3	2.5			2.0	
.7	.8	.7	Quick	.3	.6			1.1	
.3	.3	.3		.1	.2			.4	
0 UND	0 UND	1 505.1		0 UND	0 UND			20 17.9	
16 22.7	8 44.6	26 13.9	Sales/Receivables	25 14.8	22 16.4			29 12.8	
31 11.9	33 11.0	51 7.2		84 4.3	60 6.1			55 6.6	
			Cost of Sales/Inventory						
			Cost of Sales/Payables						
14.7	13.5	15.6		32.6	11.2			12.6	
-199.0	51.7	-33.3	Sales/Working Capital	-17.5	-22.3			76.8	
-12.7	-16.8	-9.7		-4.0	-14.3			-30.9	
19.2	10.3	9.5						35.3	
(28) 3.6	(35) 3.8	(41) 3.1	EBIT/Interest					(10) 4.7	
-.2	2.0	.6						2.7	
5.8	2.2	2.8	Net Profit + Depr., Dep.,						
(12) 2.1	(12) 1.6	(14) 1.7	Amort./Cur. Mat. L/T/D						
1.5	1.0	.7							
.4	.2	.7		.7	.5			.7	
1.4	1.1	2.1	Fixed/Worth	3.1	5.4			2.0	
-41.2	3.3	-5.4		-1.1	-2.5			-7.3	
1.3	1.0	1.0		1.8	1.0			.3	
2.9	3.4	2.8	Debt/Worth	5.1	5.0			2.7	
-53.7	19.0	-9.5		-1.8	-6.6			-12.5	
99.3	67.0	57.3	% Profit Before Taxes/Tangible						
(28) 42.3	(36) 34.0	(34) 19.4	Net Worth						
5.2	21.6	3.2							
20.6	20.9	15.9	% Profit Before Taxes/Total	8.4	6.7			23.7	
9.4	9.7	5.1	Assets	-.9	1.3			15.4	
-2.6	2.9	-1.8		-13.8	-3.6			3.3	
21.5	104.0	17.9		41.8	46.6			16.8	
6.5	16.6	4.9	Sales/Net Fixed Assets	5.5	15.5			4.9	
4.0	3.4	2.9		1.9	1.3			2.7	
3.9	6.6	3.5		2.9	5.1			2.9	
2.4	2.4	1.8	Sales/Total Assets	1.3	3.5			1.8	
1.2	1.2	1.1		.9	.7			1.1	
3.4	1.9	2.2							
(25) 5.2	(33) 3.9	(37) 5.4	% Depr., Dep., Amort./Sales						
12.9	8.3	10.2							
2.0	3.5	2.3	% Officers', Directors'						
(18) 5.3	(24) 5.1	(15) 4.2	Owners' Comp/Sales						
17.0	8.5	13.0							
1019686M	620523M	821639M	Net Sales ($)	5648M	18910M	16934M	24605M	192903M	562639M
486920M	340979M	543953M	Total Assets ($)	4351M	24829M	14167M	14977M	193943M	291686M

© RMA 2007

M = $ thousand   MM = $ million
See Pages 11 through 21 for Explanation of Ratios and Data

Current Data Sorted by Assets							Comparative Historical Data	
						Type of Statement		
		1	3			Unqualified	3	
		2				Reviewed	1	
	2					Compiled	3	1
5	3					Tax Returns	6	7
1	2	7	5	1		Other	1	4
	6 (4/1-9/30/06)		26 (10/1/06-3/31/07)				4/1/02-3/31/03 ALL	4/1/03-3/31/04 ALL
0-500M	500M-2MM	2-10MM	10-50MM	50-100MM	100-250MM			
6	7	10	8	1		NUMBER OF STATEMENTS	14	12
%	%	%	%	%	%	**ASSETS**	%	%
		7.2			DATA NOT AVAILABLE	Cash & Equivalents	8.4	11.7
		22.3				Trade Receivables (net)	7.0	6.9
		.0				Inventory	.0	.0
		.8				All Other Current	.3	1.8
		30.3				Total Current	15.6	20.4
		57.8				Fixed Assets (net)	75.8	72.6
		5.1				Intangibles (net)	1.4	.1
		6.7				All Other Non-Current	7.2	6.9
		100.0				Total	100.0	100.0
						LIABILITIES		
		5.9				Notes Payable-Short Term	9.9	10.8
		6.7				Cur. Mat.-L.T.D.	17.2	15.4
		3.5				Trade Payables	4.5	3.8
		.6				Income Taxes Payable	.0	.0
		5.7				All Other Current	5.3	18.7
		22.4				Total Current	37.0	48.7
		42.9				Long-Term Debt	43.5	41.9
		.9				Deferred Taxes	.3	.4
		1.9				All Other Non-Current	9.6	5.1
		31.9				Net Worth	9.7	3.9
		100.0				Total Liabilties & Net Worth	100.0	100.0
						INCOME DATA		
		100.0				Net Sales	100.0	100.0
						Gross Profit		
		94.0				Operating Expenses	95.9	98.5
		6.0				Operating Profit	4.1	1.5
		2.1				All Other Expenses (net)	3.6	1.1
		4.0				Profit Before Taxes	.5	.4
						RATIOS		
		4.6					1.5	1.2
		1.1				Current	.3	.4
		.7					.1	.1
		4.5					1.5	1.2
		1.1				Quick	.3	.3
		.7					.0	.1
		19 18.9					0 UND	0 UND
		21 17.7				Sales/Receivables	0 UND	7 50.8
		33 11.1					16 23.3	14 26.3
						Cost of Sales/Inventory		
						Cost of Sales/Payables		
		24.6					21.9	NM
		NM				Sales/Working Capital	-10.2	-11.0
		-25.6					-3.4	-7.6
							5.5	4.8
						EBIT/Interest	1.8	(11) .8
							1.4	-3.1
						Net Profit + Depr., Dep., Amort./Cur. Mat. L/T/D		
		.9					1.3	2.8
		4.0				Fixed/Worth	3.9	4.9
		NM					-3.1	-5.6
		.7					.6	2.0
		5.5				Debt/Worth	5.8	5.1
		NM					-4.2	-8.9
						% Profit Before Taxes/Tangible Net Worth		
		18.2					19.3	22.1
		9.0				% Profit Before Taxes/Total Assets	4.2	-1.2
		1.6					1.7	-12.9
		9.8					4.1	7.3
		3.4				Sales/Net Fixed Assets	2.0	5.7
		2.1					1.2	1.9
		4.0					2.5	5.2
		2.3				Sales/Total Assets	1.7	3.8
		1.7					1.0	1.7
		4.9					9.2	
		8.3				% Depr., Dep., Amort./Sales	(12) 12.5	
		9.9					23.2	
								3.1
						% Officers', Directors' Owners' Comp/Sales		(10) 4.8
								11.0
6517M	29630M	108189M	401438M	71485M		Net Sales ($)	44570M	20171M
1123M	7248M	39998M	180832M	53247M		Total Assets ($)	25650M	6250M

M = $ thousand MM = $ million

See Pages 11 through 21 for Explanation of Ratios and Data

Comparative Historical Data

Current Data Sorted by Sales

			Type of Statement						
6	7	4	Unqualified					2	2
4	2	2	Reviewed				2		
6	5	2	Compiled				1	1	
9	5	8	Tax Returns	4	4				
6	10	16	Other	2	1	2	2	4	5
4/1/04-	4/1/05-	4/1/06-			6 (4/1-9/30/06)		26 (10/1/06-3/31/07)		
3/31/05	3/31/06	3/31/07		0-1MM	1-3MM	3-5MM	5-10MM	10-25MM	25MM & OVER
ALL	ALL	ALL							
31	29	32	NUMBER OF STATEMENTS	6	5	2	5	7	7
%	%	%	ASSETS	%	%	%	%	%	%
17.6	12.5	10.1	Cash & Equivalents						
12.5	13.1	18.7	Trade Receivables (net)						
2.5	2.3	1.8	Inventory						
3.0	2.4	2.9	All Other Current						
35.7	30.3	33.4	Total Current						
54.5	52.1	53.2	Fixed Assets (net)						
4.4	10.5	6.0	Intangibles (net)						
5.4	7.1	7.3	All Other Non-Current						
100.0	100.0	100.0	Total						
			LIABILITIES						
8.1	6.4	9.3	Notes Payable-Short Term						
9.2	12.1	11.5	Cur. Mat.-L.T.D.						
3.7	3.8	6.9	Trade Payables						
.0	.0	.3	Income Taxes Payable						
10.8	7.5	8.8	All Other Current						
31.8	29.8	36.8	Total Current						
54.1	35.0	64.2	Long-Term Debt						
.0	.7	1.2	Deferred Taxes						
11.5	8.7	4.1	All Other Non-Current						
2.5	25.9	-6.2	Net Worth						
100.0	100.0	100.0	Total Liabilties & Net Worth						
			INCOME DATA						
100.0	100.0	100.0	Net Sales						
			Gross Profit						
94.1	95.2	94.8	Operating Expenses						
5.9	4.8	5.2	Operating Profit						
3.0	.9	1.7	All Other Expenses (net)						
2.9	4.0	3.5	Profit Before Taxes						
			RATIOS						
2.5	2.6	1.7							
1.0	1.0	1.1	Current						
.4	.6	.4							
2.4	2.2	1.6							
.8	.8	.8	Quick						
.3	.4	.4							
0 UND	0 UND	0 UND							
11 32.3	18 20.3	21 17.7	Sales/Receivables						
33 11.0	50 7.4	35 10.3							
			Cost of Sales/Inventory						
			Cost of Sales/Payables						
9.1	7.8	15.6							
215.3	-278.6	NM	Sales/Working Capital						
-7.3	-11.1	-12.5							
8.4	6.9	6.4							
(29) 2.3	(27) 3.2	(30) 2.5	EBIT/Interest						
-1.1	.7	1.8							
			Net Profit + Depr., Dep., Amort./Cur. Mat. L/T/D						
.7	1.0	1.1							
4.5	2.8	5.5	Fixed/Worth						
-2.6	-2.7	-2.2							
.6	1.1	1.4							
8.5	2.1	7.5	Debt/Worth						
-4.2	-5.6	-5.9							
107.8	65.1	80.4							
(21) 9.3	(21) 22.1	(21) 37.2	% Profit Before Taxes/Tangible Net Worth						
1.6	7.5	15.3							
10.9	15.3	15.7							
2.4	6.5	8.8	% Profit Before Taxes/Total Assets						
-2.5	-1.9	2.6							
11.0	9.7	18.3							
4.3	5.4	4.3	Sales/Net Fixed Assets						
1.6	1.9	2.1							
4.0	3.7	5.1							
1.7	2.1	2.2	Sales/Total Assets						
1.0	1.1	1.5							
3.4	1.3	2.3							
(25) 7.4	(22) 6.2	(27) 7.3	% Depr., Dep., Amort./Sales						
16.1	15.9	10.8							
2.3	3.9	2.1							
(13) 3.7	(11) 6.4	(15) 4.4	% Officers', Directors' Owners' Comp/Sales						
6.7	10.2	13.3							
249772M	554242M	617259M	Net Sales ($)	3217M	10220M	7995M	34457M	107814M	453556M
109349M	387833M	282448M	Total Assets ($)	1865M	3553M	6429M	12009M	63099M	195493M

M = $ thousand   MM = $ million
See Pages 11 through 21 for Explanation of Ratios and Data

Current Data Sorted by Assets							Comparative Historical Data	
						Type of Statement		
	2	3	9	2		Unqualified	10	11
	12	30	8			Reviewed	43	45
4	13	15	4			Compiled	32	45
1	4	3				Tax Returns	13	14
2	7	10	12			Other	16	13
	59 (4/1-9/30/06)		82 (10/1/06-3/31/07)				4/1/02-3/31/03	4/1/03-3/31/04
0-500M	500M-2MM	2-10MM	10-50MM	50-100MM	100-250MM		ALL	ALL
7	38	61	33	2		**NUMBER OF STATEMENTS**	114	128
%	%	%	%	%	%	**ASSETS**	%	%
	13.0	13.1	9.2		DATA NOT AVAILABLE	Cash & Equivalents	10.9	10.2
	10.7	10.6	13.0			Trade Receivables (net)	9.1	11.1
	.8	3.2	4.1			Inventory	2.5	1.6
	2.6	5.5	3.3			All Other Current	1.9	3.4
	27.0	32.4	29.5			Total Current	24.3	26.3
	60.8	55.3	62.1			Fixed Assets (net)	64.2	62.3
	2.7	2.2	1.0			Intangibles (net)	2.3	2.4
	9.5	10.2	7.4			All Other Non-Current	9.2	9.0
	100.0	100.0	100.0			Total	100.0	100.0
						LIABILITIES		
	3.1	4.9	6.5			Notes Payable-Short Term	5.6	5.7
	13.4	11.6	12.2			Cur. Mat.-L.T.D.	12.7	12.7
	3.8	3.0	5.5			Trade Payables	3.5	3.9
	.0	.4	.6			Income Taxes Payable	.3	.2
	6.1	6.4	7.7			All Other Current	11.4	8.9
	26.4	26.3	32.6			Total Current	33.5	31.4
	37.9	24.4	30.9			Long-Term Debt	31.7	31.1
	.9	1.4	2.5			Deferred Taxes	1.7	2.2
	5.0	3.4	5.4			All Other Non-Current	2.4	3.8
	29.8	44.6	28.7			Net Worth	30.6	31.4
	100.0	100.0	100.0			Total Liabilties & Net Worth	100.0	100.0
						INCOME DATA		
	100.0	100.0	100.0			Net Sales	100.0	100.0
						Gross Profit		
	91.8	94.2	91.8			Operating Expenses	93.3	93.2
	8.2	5.8	8.2			Operating Profit	6.7	6.8
	2.0	1.2	2.2			All Other Expenses (net)	2.6	2.3
	6.2	4.6	6.0			Profit Before Taxes	4.2	4.5
						RATIOS		
	1.9	2.3	1.3				1.2	1.5
	.9	1.1	.9			Current	.7	.8
	.4	.6	.5				.4	.4
	1.7	1.8	1.1				1.0	1.2
	.8	.8	.8			Quick	.6	.6
	.3	.3	.5				.3	.3
	0 UND	**5** 75.3	**18** 19.7				**5** 77.5	**5** 80.6
	16 23.4	**17** 21.5	**29** 12.8			Sales/Receivables	**13** 27.4	**20** 18.7
	28 13.3	**33** 11.0	**42** 8.6				**27** 13.5	**32** 11.4
						Cost of Sales/Inventory		
						Cost of Sales/Payables		
	12.9	10.4	17.7				39.1	25.0
	-160.2	66.8	-57.3			Sales/Working Capital	-26.3	-41.7
	-9.7	-10.9	-8.8				-7.8	-8.1
	6.5	6.8	6.1				4.3	5.3
	2.6	(57) 2.9	(32) 3.2			EBIT/Interest	(106) 2.5	(118) 2.4
	1.1	1.2	1.7				1.2	1.4
	3.2	2.2	1.5				2.8	2.4
	(10) 1.8	(22) 1.6	(15) 1.4			Net Profit + Depr., Dep., Amort./Cur. Mat. L/T/D	(37) 1.3	(42) 1.5
	1.1	1.2	1.1				1.0	1.1
	.8	.8	1.2				1.2	1.1
	1.7	1.5	1.9			Fixed/Worth	2.3	2.2
	3.9	2.4	3.4				6.5	7.1
	.8	.6	1.5				1.2	1.0
	1.5	1.4	2.0			Debt/Worth	2.3	2.2
	5.5	2.9	4.4				7.6	9.4
	53.9	39.4	35.3				41.4	36.7
	(33) 20.0	(59) 15.1	(29) 18.5			% Profit Before Taxes/Tangible Net Worth	(99) 17.4	(108) 17.9
	4.8	1.9	14.1				6.7	7.7
	14.8	13.9	10.6				10.6	10.8
	4.0	5.9	6.1			% Profit Before Taxes/Total Assets	5.4	5.5
	.7	.7	4.5				1.0	1.9
	6.3	4.1	4.0				3.7	4.5
	2.8	2.9	1.9			Sales/Net Fixed Assets	2.2	2.5
	1.5	2.0	1.2				1.6	1.6
	2.4	2.1	1.9				2.2	2.3
	1.9	1.7	1.4			Sales/Total Assets	1.5	1.6
	1.3	1.3	1.0				1.1	1.1
	6.9	7.6	7.4				7.9	7.9
	(37) 13.5	(59) 9.3	(28) 11.5			% Depr., Dep., Amort./Sales	(111) 11.9	(120) 11.3
	20.1	12.3	14.0				15.0	15.9
	2.5	1.5	.7				2.8	2.1
	(19) 5.0	(35) 3.3	(15) 1.1			% Officers', Directors' Owners' Comp/Sales	(74) 5.1	(70) 4.4
	8.2	7.7	2.4				9.2	9.2
6864M	**107735M**	**447964M**	**1024952M**	**182802M**		Net Sales ($)	**997760M**	**1091983M**
1931M	**51772M**	**248887M**	**661844M**	**138799M**		Total Assets ($)	**711077M**	**768595M**

M = $ thousand MM = $ million

See Pages 11 through 21 for Explanation of Ratios and Data

Comparative Historical Data | | Type of Statement | ## Current Data Sorted by Sales

			Type of Statement						
13	18	16	Unqualified	1	6	1	3	2	10
50	50	50	Reviewed			11	19	12	1
31	24	36	Compiled	5	11	8	6	3	3
11	13	8	Tax Returns	2	4	1	1		
12	31	31	Other	1	7	2	8	8	5
4/1/04- 3/31/05	4/1/05- 3/31/06	4/1/06- 3/31/07			59 (4/1-9/30/06)		82 (10/1/06-3/31/07)		
ALL	ALL	ALL		0-1MM	1-3MM	3-5MM	5-10MM	10-25MM	25MM & OVER
117	136	141	NUMBER OF STATEMENTS	9	28	23	37	25	19
%	%	%	ASSETS	%	%	%	%	%	%
9.9	11.6	12.7	Cash & Equivalents		11.9	14.0	16.3	6.3	12.5
10.4	12.2	11.2	Trade Receivables (net)		6.5	9.2	13.3	10.8	19.2
1.6	2.4	2.7	Inventory		.6	1.5	1.9	4.7	7.7
2.7	3.4	4.0	All Other Current		3.2	3.1	6.7	2.4	4.1
24.6	29.5	30.6	Total Current		22.1	27.8	38.1	24.2	43.6
63.3	59.3	58.2	Fixed Assets (net)		63.8	58.6	51.4	66.6	45.9
2.4	1.9	1.9	Intangibles (net)		2.9	2.5	1.1	2.0	2.0
9.7	9.4	9.3	All Other Non-Current		11.1	11.1	9.3	7.2	8.5
100.0	100.0	100.0	Total		100.0	100.0	100.0	100.0	100.0
			LIABILITIES						
5.0	5.6	5.0	Notes Payable-Short Term		2.8	8.4	3.6	6.1	6.0
13.6	13.3	12.2	Cur. Mat.-L.T.D.		15.5	12.7	9.8	13.6	10.3
4.0	5.2	3.8	Trade Payables		2.6	2.8	4.6	3.5	7.0
.3	.5	.3	Income Taxes Payable		.0	.0	.2	1.2	.4
6.4	8.2	7.0	All Other Current		4.7	7.5	9.5	3.6	8.9
29.3	32.9	28.3	Total Current		25.6	31.4	27.6	27.9	32.6
31.7	28.2	29.7	Long-Term Debt		42.8	23.5	22.5	31.7	24.9
1.6	1.8	1.4	Deferred Taxes		1.3	.4	2.3	1.8	1.6
3.4	6.0	4.5	All Other Non-Current		4.7	3.6	2.6	3.7	7.7
34.0	31.1	36.0	Net Worth		25.7	41.0	45.0	34.9	33.2
100.0	100.0	100.0	Total Liabilities & Net Worth		100.0	100.0	100.0	100.0	100.0
			INCOME DATA						
100.0	100.0	100.0	Net Sales		100.0	100.0	100.0	100.0	100.0
			Gross Profit						
94.2	93.8	93.1	Operating Expenses		91.8	97.5	93.3	93.9	92.5
5.8	6.2	6.9	Operating Profit		8.2	2.5	6.7	6.1	7.5
2.1	2.0	1.6	All Other Expenses (net)		2.6	.2	1.0	2.1	1.4
3.7	4.3	5.3	Profit Before Taxes		5.7	2.3	5.7	4.0	6.1
			RATIOS						
1.4	1.8	1.7			1.8	1.6	2.3	1.4	.1.8
.8	.9	1.0	Current		.8	1.0	1.1	.7	1.3
.4	.4	.5			.3	.5	.8	.4	.9
1.2	1.5	1.4			1.0	1.5	2.0	1.2	1.5
(116) .7	.8	.8	Quick		.7	.7	1.0	.6	.9
.4	.3	.4			.2	.3	.5	.2	.6
4 92.3	7 51.3	6 63.5		0 UND	9 41.3	4 85.8	12 29.8	23 16.1	
17 20.9	20 17.9	18 20.1	Sales/Receivables	11 31.8	17 21.5	19 19.7	21 17.0	33 11.1	
33 11.2	36 10.0	32 11.4		25 14.9	30 12.3	37 10.0	36 10.2	44 8.3	
			Cost of Sales/Inventory						
			Cost of Sales/Payables						
18.6	12.1	12.1			17.6	12.5	7.5	18.2	11.7
-50.5	-108.1	-339.4	Sales/Working Capital		-33.4	-339.4	47.9	-23.0	25.0
-9.3	-8.1	-10.8			-8.5	-7.5	-25.2	-6.6	-61.5
4.5	5.7	6.6			5.7	4.5	10.5	4.4	11.4
(109) 2.6	(125) 2.2	(135) 2.9	EBIT/Interest		2.6	2.1	(35) 4.5	(24) 2.0	(18) 3.6
1.3	1.0	1.5			1.1	1.1	1.6	1.1	2.8
1.6	1.5	2.1					3.4	1.7	
(46) 1.2	(48) 1.1	(50) 1.5	Net Profit + Depr., Dep., Amort./Cur. Mat. L/T/D			(17) 1.6	(12) 1.4		
1.0	.8	1.2					1.2	.8	
1.3	1.1	1.0			1.1	.8	.7	1.4	1.0
2.1	1.9	1.7	Fixed/Worth		2.4	1.2	1.6	2.2	1.2
4.4	4.3	3.2			7.2	3.0	2.1	4.5	2.1
1.1	1.2	.8			.7	.8	.7	1.3	.8
1.9	2.1	1.7	Debt/Worth		2.2	1.2	1.3	1.9	1.9
4.7	5.6	4.1			8.6	3.8	2.9	4.4	2.5
29.0	40.3	41.2			47.2	32.6	45.4	27.2	50.4
(107) 14.1	(118) 11.4	(129) 17.7	% Profit Before Taxes/Tangible Net Worth	(23) 16.8	(21) 6.8	23.5	(23) 17.2	(17) 20.9	
3.2	.9	5.5			5.5	.5	5.6	1.9	16.1
9.7	11.2	12.3			11.3	9.2	17.9	9.4	13.9
4.9	2.9	6.0	% Profit Before Taxes/Total Assets		4.2	3.4	10.1	4.7	8.6
.8	-.2	1.7			.9	.3	2.4	.6	5.4
4.0	5.3	4.7			3.9	4.2	6.3	2.9	7.7
2.1	2.7	2.9	Sales/Net Fixed Assets		2.6	2.7	3.7	1.7	3.7
1.4	1.6	1.6			1.4	2.0	2.4	1.2	2.5
2.2	2.4	2.2			2.0	2.0	2.7	1.7	3.0
1.4	1.6	1.7	Sales/Total Assets		1.6	1.7	2.0	1.3	1.8
1.0	1.1	1.2			.9	1.1	1.5	.9	1.5
7.6	7.4	7.2			10.4	7.6	3.7	9.0	4.5
(114) 10.8	(128) 10.0	(132) 9.9	% Depr., Dep., Amort./Sales		14.8	9.4	(35) 8.3	(23) 12.2	(15) 7.4
15.0	14.5	14.0			20.1	12.3	9.6	14.3	9.1
2.3	1.4	1.2			3.6	1.7	1.4	1.2	.7
(62) 4.4	(68) 3.2	(71) 3.3	% Officers', Directors' Owners' Comp/Sales	(15) 4.9	(11) 5.2	(22) 4.1	(11) 2.6	(10) 1.0	
8.9	6.6	7.0			7.7	10.7	7.6	4.2	2.1
1145768M	1700915M	1770317M	Net Sales ($)	6220M	50305M	92908M	261688M	357899M	1001297M
866740M	1147153M	1103233M	Total Assets ($)	8907M	40894M	62621M	144968M	301225M	544618M

© RMA 2007

M = $ thousand   MM = $ million
See Pages 11 through 21 for Explanation of Ratios and Data

Current Data Sorted by Assets							Comparative Historical Data	
						Type of Statement		
		3	3	1		Unqualified	5	7
	2	17	5			Reviewed	17	25
4	4	10	2	1		Compiled	27	26
3	9	9				Tax Returns	12	12
	10	24	7	4		Other	24	19
27 (4/1-9/30/06)			91 (10/1/06-3/31/07)				**4/1/02-3/31/03 ALL**	**4/1/03-3/31/04 ALL**
0-500M	**500M-2MM**	**2-10MM**	**10-50MM**	**50-100MM**	**100-250MM**			
7	25	63	17	6		**NUMBER OF STATEMENTS**	85	89
%	%	%	%	%	%	**ASSETS**	%	%
	7.1	5.7	8.2		DATA NOT AVAILABLE	Cash & Equivalents	8.1	8.0
	8.4	9.4	7.2			Trade Receivables (net)	8.4	9.0
	1.6	2.2	1.1			Inventory	1.3	2.0
	3.5	3.3	2.0			All Other Current	3.5	5.1
	20.6	20.7	18.4			Total Current	21.2	24.1
	65.8	71.2	75.6			Fixed Assets (net)	69.5	64.6
	2.1	.7	.4			Intangibles (net)	1.8	3.4
	11.5	7.4	5.6			All Other Non-Current	7.5	7.9
	100.0	100.0	100.0			Total	100.0	100.0
						LIABILITIES		
	5.4	2.7	3.2			Notes Payable-Short Term	4.4	6.3
	13.7	12.2	9.3			Cur. Mat.-L.T.D.	14.0	10.6
	7.5	3.6	3.6			Trade Payables	5.9	6.2
	.6	.3	1.0			Income Taxes Payable	.3	.4
	10.3	7.2	3.4			All Other Current	8.4	8.3
	37.5	26.0	20.5			Total Current	33.0	31.9
	68.3	53.9	34.4			Long-Term Debt	52.9	44.9
	.0	2.4	2.3			Deferred Taxes	1.3	1.5
	3.0	4.6	4.9			All Other Non-Current	8.6	6.6
	-8.9	13.1	37.9			Net Worth	4.3	15.2
	100.0	100.0	100.0			Total Liabilties & Net Worth	100.0	100.0
						INCOME DATA		
	100.0	100.0	100.0			Net Sales	100.0	100.0
						Gross Profit		
	94.3	93.0	92.2			Operating Expenses	94.7	97.0
	5.7	7.0	7.8			Operating Profit	5.3	3.0
	3.3	3.0	4.4			All Other Expenses (net)	3.3	2.3
	2.4	3.9	3.4			Profit Before Taxes	2.0	.7
						RATIOS		
	.8	1.3	2.3				1.3	1.3
	.4	.8	1.5			Current	.7	.8
	.2	.6	.3				.3	.4
	.8	.9	1.7				1.0	1.0
	(23) .4	(61) .6	.9			Quick	.4	(88) .5
	.1	.3	.2				.2	.3
	0 UND	**9** 42.2	**12** 30.6				**3** 126.2	**6** 65.9
	8 48.0	**15** 24.3	**27** 13.4			Sales/Receivables	**12** 30.2	**15** 25.0
	17 22.0	**38** 9.7	**39** 9.4				**24** 15.3	**25** 14.5
						Cost of Sales/Inventory		
						Cost of Sales/Payables		
	-45.8	41.3	7.8				61.0	29.2
	-11.2	-21.6	15.2			Sales/Working Capital	-19.7	-25.9
	-5.0	-8.6	-5.2				-6.8	-7.9
	3.3	4.8	5.2				2.8	3.6
	(22) 1.7	(57) 2.1	(15) 3.0			EBIT/Interest	(82) 1.4	(87) 1.3
	.7	1.1	1.4				-.1	-.5
		1.8					1.9	1.8
		(23) 1.2				Net Profit + Depr., Dep., Amort./Cur. Mat. L/T/D	(30) 1.3	(27) 1.3
		.9					1.0	.9
	4.4	1.8	1.5				2.0	1.6
	-24.1	3.5	2.0			Fixed/Worth	3.5	4.3
	-1.7	165.5	4.7				-6.7	-25.8
	6.2	1.9	1.1				1.8	1.7
	-30.5	4.7	1.7			Debt/Worth	3.7	5.5
	-4.2	329.4	4.6				-11.9	-62.9
	104.9	38.4	21.5				38.0	34.4
	(11) 12.1	(48) 21.1	13.8			% Profit Before Taxes/Tangible Net Worth	(58) 13.6	(65) 6.1
	-1.1	8.7	2.8				.9	-6.2
	11.3	9.9	8.6				8.2	6.3
	5.1	3.6	5.2			% Profit Before Taxes/Total Assets	2.0	1.7
	-.3	.8	.9				-3.1	-3.8
	4.7	2.8	1.5				3.9	5.7
	2.8	1.8	1.1			Sales/Net Fixed Assets	2.2	2.4
	1.7	1.2	.9				1.3	1.4
	3.1	2.0	1.1				2.4	2.7
	1.9	1.3	.9			Sales/Total Assets	1.5	1.6
	1.2	.8	.7				1.0	1.1
	5.3	6.0	7.9				5.9	5.2
	(22) 11.4	(59) 9.0	(15) 11.4			% Depr., Dep., Amort./Sales	(80) 9.8	(82) 8.6
	21.3	14.7	14.9				14.2	12.9
	2.4	1.3					1.5	2.1
	(11) 3.0	(26) 2.6				% Officers', Directors' Owners' Comp/Sales	(29) 2.8	(35) 3.1
	7.4	6.8					8.6	7.5
22338M	**69672M**	**480647M**	**273050M**	**439308M**		Net Sales ($)	**602158M**	**723307M**
1872M	**28966M**	**321948M**	**306084M**	**435845M**		Total Assets ($)	**438034M**	**471795M**

M = $ thousand MM = $ million

See Pages 11 through 21 for Explanation of Ratios and Data

Comparative Historical Data | Current Data Sorted by Sales

4/1/04-3/31/05 ALL	4/1/05-3/31/06 ALL	4/1/06-3/31/07 ALL	Type of Statement	0-1MM	1-3MM	3-5MM	5-10MM	10-25MM	25MM & OVER
7	9	7	Unqualified		2	2	1	4	2
18	25	24	Reviewed		6	6	11	7	2
14	17	21	Compiled	1	6	6	3	3	2
18	11	21	Tax Returns	3	7	5	3		
22	43	45	Other	3	9	8	6	10	5
					27 (4/1-9/30/06)		91 (10/1/06-3/31/07)		
79	105	118	**NUMBER OF STATEMENTS**	7	24	21	31	24	11
%	%	%	**ASSETS**	%	%	%	%	%	%
8.1	7.8	6.9	Cash & Equivalents		5.8	7.3	7.5	6.0	9.7
8.7	10.8	9.4	Trade Receivables (net)		7.5	7.4	9.1	13.5	14.1
1.9	2.3	1.9	Inventory		1.4	2.8	1.7	2.7	1.3
3.0	3.2	3.4	All Other Current		4.9	2.5	4.4	2.3	3.3
21.7	24.1	21.7	Total Current		19.7	20.1	22.7	24.6	28.3
67.2	65.2	69.1	Fixed Assets (net)		71.6	73.9	68.1	64.7	59.7
1.9	3.1	1.5	Intangibles (net)		1.0	2.3	.8	.5	5.9
9.1	7.6	7.8	All Other Non-Current		7.8	3.7	8.4	10.2	6.1
100.0	100.0	100.0	Total		100.0	100.0	100.0	100.0	100.0
			LIABILITIES						
8.4	6.1	3.6	Notes Payable-Short Term		1.2	6.0	.5	7.1	2.6
11.9	10.2	11.8	Cur. Mat.-L.T.D.		17.0	11.6	11.2	10.4	4.8
5.3	7.3	4.8	Trade Payables		3.9	5.7	4.4	5.1	4.1
.4	.3	.5	Income Taxes Payable		.0	.8	.5	.2	1.7
8.7	8.3	8.5	All Other Current		8.9	10.3	11.1	6.9	3.7
34.7	32.2	29.2	Total Current		31.1	34.4	27.9	29.6	16.8
46.6	50.3	55.7	Long-Term Debt		85.7	59.5	42.5	35.8	32.6
1.6	1.6	1.6	Deferred Taxes		.9	2.7	1.9	1.2	2.3
6.1	5.5	4.1	All Other Non-Current		3.6	5.7	2.3	6.2	3.7
11.1	10.5	9.4	Net Worth		-21.3	-2.4	25.4	27.2	44.6
100.0	100.0	100.0	Total Liabilities & Net Worth		100.0	100.0	100.0	100.0	100.0
			INCOME DATA						
100.0	100.0	100.0	Net Sales		100.0	100.0	100.0	100.0	100.0
			Gross Profit						
97.0	93.6	93.6	Operating Expenses		95.7	92.1	94.7	96.9	92.8
3.0	6.4	6.4	Operating Profit		4.3	7.9	5.3	3.1	7.2
2.1	2.5	3.0	All Other Expenses (net)		3.2	3.1	.9	2.3	.8
.9	3.8	3.4	Profit Before Taxes		1.1	4.8	4.4	.8	6.4
			RATIOS						
1.0	1.3	1.4	Current		1.2	1.2	1.3	1.5	2.9
.6	.7	.7			.7	.6	.7	.9	1.7
.3	.4	.4			.3	.3	.6	.3	1.1
1.0	.9	1.1	Quick		1.0	.8	1.0	1.0	2.8
.4	.5 (114)	.6		(23) .6	(19) .5	.6	.7	1.3	
.2	.3	.3			.0	.2	.3	.2	.8
6 62.4	8 46.9	7 53.0	Sales/Receivables	0 UND	1 409.6	9 39.3	12 31.7	21 17.4	
11 32.9	16 23.1	13 27.6		7 50.2	9 41.7	20 18.4	15 24.9	35 10.5	
33 11.0	27 13.5	33 11.2		16 23.3	19 19.0	35 10.5	39 9.3	57 6.4	
			Cost of Sales/Inventory						
			Cost of Sales/Payables						
110.8	35.5	24.2	Sales/Working Capital		67.1	NM	39.9	20.7	7.3
-15.2	-29.3	-27.1			-20.8	-10.8	-21.6	-43.8	12.4
-6.6	-8.0	-7.5			-5.8	-5.2	-8.9	-5.7	33.7
3.2	4.1	4.7	EBIT/Interest		3.3	4.2	6.0	2.8	9.4
(76) 1.7	(99) 2.4	(105) 2.2		(20) 1.1	(20) 2.0	(29) 3.0	(22) 1.6	(10) 5.3	
-.2	1.3	1.1			-.4	1.1	1.8	-.3	3.1
1.7	1.7	2.0	Net Profit + Depr., Dep., Amort./Cur. Mat. L/T/D				2.6		
(25) 1.2	(36) 1.3	(34) 1.3				(12) 1.2			
.6	.9	1.1					.9		
1.6	1.7	1.8	Fixed/Worth		6.4	8.2	1.5	1.6	1.0
4.3	3.7	4.0			NM	40.3	2.3	2.2	1.7
-7.6	-12.1	-11.2			-1.6	-2.8	4.3	10.0	2.1
1.6	1.7	1.8	Debt/Worth		6.8	10.6	1.1	1.3	.7
4.2	3.6	5.6			NM	51.1	2.1	2.3	1.8
-9.4	-20.5	-13.5			-3.2	-4.4	4.4	11.8	2.2
29.5	56.4	35.5	% Profit Before Taxes/Tangible Net Worth		54.3	387.8	36.1	23.6	25.7
(55) 6.9	(74) 22.7	(84) 16.8		(12) 9.2	(11) 39.2	(27) 22.4	(21) 13.8	(10) 16.6	
-8.4	4.9	5.8			-3.1	16.9	11.8	-7.7	11.7
6.7	11.0	9.9	% Profit Before Taxes/Total Assets		9.7	15.8	11.7	6.7	8.6
2.0	4.0	5.1			1.0	8.2	6.2	3.1	7.0
-3.4	.3	.6			-11.1	.6	1.8	-3.9	5.1
4.3	4.5	3.1	Sales/Net Fixed Assets		3.1	4.0	2.8	4.3	2.6
2.4	2.1	1.9			1.8	1.7	2.2	2.6	1.9
1.3	1.3	1.2			1.0	1.2	1.5	1.1	1.4
2.3	2.4	2.2	Sales/Total Assets		1.9	2.6	2.1	2.4	1.3
1.5	1.4	1.3			1.2	1.6	1.4	1.9	1.2
1.1	1.0	.8			.8	.8	1.0	.9	.8
4.9	4.8	6.1	% Depr., Dep., Amort./Sales		10.3	5.2	6.0	4.9	5.2
(75) 8.6	(100) 7.7	(108) 9.5		(21) 14.9	(18) 10.2	(30) 8.5	(22) 8.9	(10) 6.8	
14.4	12.5	14.9			23.4	12.4	11.5	15.1	8.5
1.1	1.5	1.4	% Officers', Directors', Owners' Comp/Sales			2.2	1.2		
(29) 3.4	(41) 2.9	(45) 3.0			(10) 2.7	(15) 2.8			
6.0	5.3	6.8				5.9	6.0		
714145M	1733376M	1285015M	Net Sales ($)	3390M	48367M	78787M	228232M	332680M	593559M
509091M	1280996M	1094715M	Total Assets ($)	8842M	63937M	65746M	157350M	264853M	533987M

© RMA 2007 M = $ thousand   MM = $ million
See Pages 11 through 21 for Explanation of Ratios and Data

Current Data Sorted by Assets

Comparative Historical Data

						Type of Statement			
1	2	12	6		3	Unqualified		27	24
1	4	7	2			Reviewed		11	15
4	6	3				Compiled		18	25
9	11	2				Tax Returns		15	21
4	6	13	7		1	Other		23	30
	23 (4/1-9/30/06)		81 (10/1/06-3/31/07)					4/1/02-3/31/03	4/1/03-3/31/04
0-500M	500M-2MM	2-10MM	10-50MM	50-100MM	100-250MM			ALL	ALL
19	29	37	15		4	NUMBER OF STATEMENTS		94	115
%	%	%	%	%	%	ASSETS		%	%
19.7	13.5	12.7	10.9			Cash & Equivalents		14.5	12.3
17.2	18.9	27.5	31.7			Trade Receivables (net)		24.2	23.3
1.5	.1	1.0	.1			Inventory		.6	1.9
5.1	5.3	4.6	7.6			All Other Current		3.4	4.6
43.5	37.8	45.8	50.4			Total Current		42.7	42.1
40.1	47.0	39.3	35.6			Fixed Assets (net)		42.6	44.6
10.0	6.2	2.9	2.1			Intangibles (net)		6.6	5.2
6.4	9.0	12.0	11.9			All Other Non-Current		8.1	8.1
100.0	100.0	100.0	100.0			Total		100.0	100.0
						LIABILITIES			
9.5	4.9	8.0	7.5			Notes Payable-Short Term		8.5	11.9
7.5	15.1	10.5	5.6			Cur. Mat.-L.T.D.		8.1	8.5
19.2	7.1	10.5	14.8			Trade Payables		5.7	6.8
.1	.0	.4	.2			Income Taxes Payable		1.0	.7
24.2	8.2	11.9	12.1			All Other Current		12.6	15.4
60.6	35.3	41.3	40.1			Total Current		36.0	43.5
33.7	31.1	15.4	17.5			Long-Term Debt		25.6	27.5
.0	.0	.7	.4			Deferred Taxes		.4	.8
22.0	9.7	4.9	.9			All Other Non-Current		5.0	6.5
-16.3	23.9	37.5	41.1			Net Worth		33.1	21.7
100.0	100.0	100.0	100.0			Total Liabilties & Net Worth		100.0	100.0
						INCOME DATA			
100.0	100.0	100.0	100.0			Net Sales		100.0	100.0
						Gross Profit			
98.5	94.8	95.9	91.6			Operating Expenses		94.5	94.7
1.5	5.2	4.1	8.4			Operating Profit		5.5	5.3
.9	1.0	.6	2.3			All Other Expenses (net)		2.3	2.8
.6	4.1	3.4	6.1			Profit Before Taxes		3.2	2.5
						RATIOS			
3.7	2.3	2.4	2.3					2.5	2.6
1.1	1.1	1.4	1.5			Current		1.4	1.1
.3	.6	.6	1.0					.8	.5
1.6	2.2	2.3	2.2					2.5	2.2
1.0	.9	1.0	1.0			Quick		1.2	.9
.2	.4	.5	.7					.7	.3
0 UND	0 UND	23 16.1	19 19.5				11 32.1	2 207.7
6 60.5	11 32.5	35 10.3	42 8.6			Sales/Receivables	39 9.3	25 14.3
33 11.1	46 7.9	49 7.4	66 5.5				64 5.7	57 6.4
						Cost of Sales/Inventory			
						Cost of Sales/Payables			
10.1	16.3	9.8	8.1					7.5	8.5
125.4	100.1	23.2	31.2			Sales/Working Capital		26.6	73.2
-13.1	-18.5	-17.5	-157.5					-27.1	-14.3
19.1	7.8	14.2	10.7					8.6	6.0
(14) 1.5	(27) 3.0	(32) 5.6	(13) 6.5			EBIT/Interest	(85) 2.9	(101) 1.8
-.8	-.4	1.3	2.2					.9	.3
						Net Profit + Depr., Dep.,		5.5	2.9
		1.3	2.2			Amort./Cur. Mat. L/T/D	(24) 1.6	(24) 1.1
								.9	.6
.4	.8	.5	.4					.5	.5
1.9	2.7	.9	.8			Fixed/Worth		1.0	1.6
-2.1	-4.8	2.6	1.8					3.5	86.6
.4	1.0	.6	.4					.7	.7
6.2	3.3	1.3	2.0			Debt/Worth		1.6	2.8
-2.7	-11.4	5.8	10.9					7.3	133.3
121.6	95.7	53.3	91.7					44.4	40.0
(11) 56.2	(18) 51.4	(32) 24.1	28.9			% Profit Before Taxes/Tangible Net Worth	(80) 12.8	(87) 9.6
1.6	-1.7	8.7	12.7					1.6	-5.5
45.6	30.9	14.6	20.5					15.0	15.3
4.2	8.7	8.7	9.7			% Profit Before Taxes/Total Assets		5.1	3.4
-9.1	-1.2	.4	4.9					-.1	-2.8
38.1	15.9	17.3	33.9					10.7	12.3
16.9	8.1	8.2	5.8			Sales/Net Fixed Assets		5.7	6.8
5.9	4.3	3.4	3.7					2.7	3.2
7.9	4.6	4.0	4.2					3.1	3.9
4.5	3.1	2.7	2.1			Sales/Total Assets		2.1	2.4
2.8	2.4	1.6	1.8					1.5	1.6
.8	2.7	2.1	.4					3.2	3.7
(13) 4.4	(25) 4.4	(33) 4.0	(13) 3.6			% Depr., Dep., Amort./Sales	(85) 6.5	(97) 5.8
9.9	8.7	5.2	8.6					10.9	8.9
	1.4							3.0	2.5
	(15) 4.3					% Officers', Directors' Owners' Comp/Sales	(40) 5.5	(38) 4.7
	7.9							10.5	10.5
48436M	125915M	537174M	736719M		748084M	Net Sales ($)		1518633M	1350314M
5588M	34769M	194632M	253529M		585339M	Total Assets ($)		727442M	637383M

© RMA 2007

M = $ thousand   MM = $ million
See Pages 11 through 21 for Explanation of Ratios and Data

Comparative Historical Data | **Current Data Sorted by Sales**

4/1/04-3/31/05 ALL	4/1/05-3/31/06 ALL	4/1/06-3/31/07 ALL	Type of Statement	0-1MM	1-3MM	3-5MM	5-10MM	10-25MM	25MM & OVER
24	21	24	Unqualified		3	2	4	6	9
14	7	14	Reviewed	1	1	3	4	4	2
23	19	13	Compiled	1	6		1	4	1
20	22	22	Tax Returns	4	10	2		5	1
24	35	31	Other	3	2	1	8	7	10
					23 (4/1-9/30/06)		81 (10/1/06-3/31/07)		
105	104	104	NUMBER OF STATEMENTS	8	22	9	25	19	21
%	%	%	**ASSETS**	%	%	%	%	%	%
10.8	12.3	13.8	Cash & Equivalents		19.0		13.5	10.6	12.6
25.0	23.1	23.4	Trade Receivables (net)		18.8		18.0	27.4	35.8
1.3	2.3	.8	Inventory		.6		.5	1.0	1.0
4.3	3.6	5.2	All Other Current		2.9		5.6	3.9	5.7
41.4	41.3	43.2	Total Current		41.2		37.6	42.8	55.1
42.1	42.0	41.3	Fixed Assets (net)		42.8		49.4	42.6	26.9
4.7	6.2	5.7	Intangibles (net)		6.8		3.0	5.7	5.2
11.8	10.6	9.8	All Other Non-Current		9.1		10.0	8.8	12.8
100.0	100.0	100.0	Total		100.0		100.0	100.0	100.0
			LIABILITIES						
9.8	11.2	7.8	Notes Payable-Short Term		9.2		6.9	6.2	13.2
12.1	9.2	10.2	Cur. Mat.-L.T.D.		14.8		13.1	6.6	4.6
9.9	8.9	11.5	Trade Payables		11.1		6.9	8.0	15.9
.5	.4	.2	Income Taxes Payable		.1		.2	.2	.5
10.2	9.9	13.0	All Other Current		17.6		7.5	14.6	14.1
42.4	39.6	42.7	Total Current		52.8		34.6	35.6	48.4
26.8	29.5	23.6	Long-Term Debt		33.0		23.1	26.6	10.8
.5	.3	.5	Deferred Taxes		.0		.5	.7	1.1
6.6	9.9	8.8	All Other Non-Current		11.2		5.4	1.6	1.9
23.6	20.6	24.4	Net Worth		3.0		36.3	35.5	37.7
100.0	100.0	100.0	Total Liabilities & Net Worth		100.0		100.0	100.0	100.0
			INCOME DATA						
100.0	100.0	100.0	Net Sales		100.0		100.0	100.0	100.0
			Gross Profit						
96.1	97.1	94.8	Operating Expenses		97.1		93.9	91.8	92.7
3.9	2.9	5.2	Operating Profit		2.9		6.1	8.2	7.3
1.4	1.0	1.2	All Other Expenses (net)		.7		.8	2.4	1.0
2.5	1.9	3.9	Profit Before Taxes		2.2		5.3	5.7	6.3
			RATIOS						
2.4	2.0	2.4	Current		1.7		2.6	2.4	1.8
1.1	1.2	1.2			1.1		1.3	2.0	1.2
.7	.6	.6			.3		.5	.6	.9
2.3	1.8	2.2	Quick		1.6		2.5	2.3	1.8
1.0	.9	1.0			1.1		.8	1.4	1.1
.5	.4	.5			.2		.5	.5	.7
7 51.5	0 UND	6 65.2	Sales/Receivables	0 UND		2 213.6	15 23.8	27 13.4	
34 10.6	23 15.8	27 13.4		25 14.8		18 19.9	30 12.0	39 9.3	
56 6.5	51 7.2	48 7.6		37 9.9		48 7.7	50 7.4	59 6.2	
			Cost of Sales/Inventory						
			Cost of Sales/Payables						
10.1	12.9	10.7	Sales/Working Capital		18.1		13.5	9.0	11.9
66.1	40.0	38.6			99.3		50.3	13.0	32.6
-16.0	-21.7	-19.6			-12.5		-17.6	-22.4	-76.4
5.9	5.8	11.8	EBIT/Interest		9.8		12.2	14.5	13.5
(97) 2.1	(99) 2.1	(90) 4.2		(21) 1.6		(23) 3.5	(16) 6.1	(19) 7.7	
-.3	.2	1.2			-1.7		1.5	1.3	1.9
2.1	3.0	3.2	Net Profit + Depr., Dep., Amort./Cur. Mat. L/T/D						
(25) .5	(17) 1.7	(17) 2.1							
.2	.6	.8							
.8	.7	.5	Fixed/Worth		1.0		.6	.5	.2
1.5	1.5	1.3			NM		1.3	.9	.9
104.5	-8.1	74.5			-.6		124.0	10.4	1.7
.9	.9	.6	Debt/Worth		1.3		1.0	.4	1.0
2.4	3.5	2.4			NM		1.8	1.0	2.2
645.0	-16.9	173.2			-3.0		164.5	16.4	7.7
50.6	56.2	76.9	% Profit Before Taxes/Tangible Net Worth		76.9		67.2	59.9	84.0
(80) 10.3	(73) 19.2	(79) 31.0		(11) 48.8		(20) 29.1	(16) 23.7	(20) 30.7	
-1.1	3.1	7.7			.0		7.6	13.1	12.5
11.3	14.2	24.4	% Profit Before Taxes/Total Assets		32.9		24.0	20.5	18.4
3.3	5.1	8.7			2.2		8.7	11.1	9.7
-3.2	-2.0	.2			-8.6		1.7	.6	4.6
12.8	20.1	18.5	Sales/Net Fixed Assets		18.4		13.7	17.5	71.7
7.6	8.3	9.8			9.1		7.6	8.8	13.0
3.3	3.9	3.8			3.5		3.7	3.5	5.8
4.1	4.3	4.5	Sales/Total Assets		4.6		4.7	4.5	4.8
2.4	2.8	2.9			3.4		3.3	2.7	3.1
1.5	1.8	1.9			2.2		1.8	1.5	2.0
3.0	2.7	1.9	% Depr., Dep., Amort./Sales		1.6		2.6	1.7	.3
(82) 5.6	(83) 5.1	(86) 4.2		(17) 4.2		(23) 4.4	(17) 3.8	(17) 2.2	
8.2	8.4	6.6			8.0		5.1	5.4	4.4
2.3	3.6	1.3	% Officers', Directors' Owners' Comp/Sales		2.0				
(37) 4.8	(41) 6.1	(30) 3.8		(10) 5.8					
10.6	9.8	8.2			11.6				
2933410M	1451323M	2196328M	Net Sales ($)	2910M	44368M	34085M	181877M	327257M	1605831M
829536M	804547M	1073857M	Total Assets ($)	2012M	18757M	15133M	71410M	143974M	822571M

Current Data Sorted by Assets | Comparative Historical Data

Type of Statement	0-500M	500M-2MM	2-10MM	10-50MM	50-100MM	100-250MM		4/1/02-3/31/03 ALL	4/1/03-3/31/04 ALL
Unqualified			1	2	2	1		2	2
Reviewed			1	1				1	3
Compiled		3						2	3
Tax Returns	1	1	8	1				6	2
Other		3	3			2		2	5
	1	4 (4/1-9/30/06)		26 (10/1/06-3/31/07)					
NUMBER OF STATEMENTS	1	7	13	4	2	3		13	15

	0-500M %	500M-2MM %	2-10MM %	10-50MM %	50-100MM %	100-250MM %		4/1/02-3/31/03 ALL %	4/1/03-3/31/04 ALL %
ASSETS									
Cash & Equivalents			7.2					6.3	12.0
Trade Receivables (net)			18.4					2.4	10.3
Inventory			4.3					6.0	3.2
All Other Current			3.0					2.6	.6
Total Current			32.9					17.2	26.2
Fixed Assets (net)			54.4					69.2	44.6
Intangibles (net)			4.8					1.0	7.9
All Other Non-Current			7.8					12.5	21.3
Total			100.0					100.0	100.0
LIABILITIES									
Notes Payable-Short Term			8.9					3.4	7.9
Cur. Mat.-L.T.D.			4.7					11.8	11.9
Trade Payables			5.2					4.0	9.9
Income Taxes Payable			.0					.2	.1
All Other Current			3.4					5.8	11.9
Total Current			22.2					25.3	41.7
Long-Term Debt			34.7					41.9	34.0
Deferred Taxes			.9					.5	.8
All Other Non-Current			14.7					2.4	6.8
Net Worth			27.5					29.9	16.8
Total Liabilities & Net Worth			100.0					100.0	100.0
INCOME DATA									
Net Sales			100.0					100.0	100.0
Gross Profit									
Operating Expenses			89.6					85.1	96.8
Operating Profit			10.4					14.9	3.2
All Other Expenses (net)			3.8					5.6	2.8
Profit Before Taxes			6.6					9.3	.5

RATIOS

Ratio	2-10MM		4/1/02-3/31/03 ALL		4/1/03-3/31/04 ALL	
Current	3.4		1.3		1.4	
	1.3		.6		.6	
	.9		.1		.3	
Quick	2.1		.6		1.4	
	1.1		.2		.3	
	.4		.1		.1	
Sales/Receivables	0 UND		0 UND		0 UND	
	14 26.3		3 135.9		12 30.4	
	46 8.0		6 56.6		37 9.8	
Cost of Sales/Inventory						
Cost of Sales/Payables						
Sales/Working Capital	6.5		57.0		30.7	
	33.2		-17.4		-6.8	
	NM		-7.9		-2.8	
EBIT/Interest	4.2		5.7		2.7	
	(12) 2.2		(12) 1.9		(12) 1.2	
	1.3		1.2		.0	
Net Profit + Depr., Dep., Amort./Cur. Mat. L/T/D						
Fixed/Worth	.8		1.1		1.4	
	1.9		2.3		3.1	
	NM		4.6		-2.9	
Debt/Worth	1.3		1.0		3.7	
	2.8		2.0		12.0	
	NM		5.1		-10.0	
% Profit Before Taxes/Tangible Net Worth	89.1		40.5			
	(10) 28.3		(11) 7.5			
	11.4		2.1			
% Profit Before Taxes/Total Assets	14.5		19.3		8.6	
	4.9		2.2		1.5	
	1.1		.6		-4.7	
Sales/Net Fixed Assets	22.5		5.9		9.3	
	3.6		2.2		5.2	
	.8		.6		1.3	
Sales/Total Assets	2.9		3.3		2.3	
	1.9		1.7		1.5	
	.6		.5		.7	
% Depr., Dep., Amort./Sales	1.2		2.8		3.1	
	(10) 6.9		(11) 12.3		(12) 5.8	
	12.7		18.1		9.1	
% Officers', Directors' Owners' Comp/Sales						

	0-500M	500M-2MM	2-10MM	10-50MM	50-100MM	100-250MM		4/1/02-3/31/03 ALL	4/1/03-3/31/04 ALL
Net Sales ($)	689M	29423M	136651M	208607M	99695M	347613M		354841M	129082M
Total Assets ($)	259M	7366M	62679M	103027M	146761M	524696M		151310M	118849M

M = $ thousand   MM = $ million
See Pages 11 through 21 for Explanation of Ratios and Data

Comparative Historical Data | Current Data Sorted by Sales

4/1/04-3/31/05 ALL	4/1/05-3/31/06 ALL	4/1/06-3/31/07 ALL	Type of Statement	0-1MM	1-3MM	3-5MM	5-10MM	10-25MM	25MM & OVER
6	5	6	Unqualified					3	3
4	1	2	Reviewed			1			1
6	2	3	Compiled	1		1		1	
6	5	4	Tax Returns	1	3				
8	8	15	Other	1	2	3	2	3	4
					4 (4/1-9/30/06)			26 (10/1/06-3/31/07)	
30	**21**	**30**	**NUMBER OF STATEMENTS**	3	5	5	2	7	8
%	%	%	**ASSETS**	%	%	%	%	%	%
10.7	11.4	7.6	Cash & Equivalents						
5.1	6.1	16.2	Trade Receivables (net)						
3.2	5.6	5.4	Inventory						
2.0	1.2	3.7	All Other Current						
21.0	24.3	32.8	Total Current						
58.8	58.3	53.2	Fixed Assets (net)						
3.8	6.4	4.5	Intangibles (net)						
16.3	10.9	9.5	All Other Non-Current						
100.0	100.0	100.0	Total						
			LIABILITIES						
8.1	11.6	6.5	Notes Payable-Short Term						
5.4	4.7	4.9	Cur. Mat.-L.T.D.						
6.8	3.2	5.0	Trade Payables						
.0	.0	.0	Income Taxes Payable						
9.9	9.0	9.8	All Other Current						
30.3	28.5	26.3	Total Current						
40.3	32.2	31.8	Long-Term Debt						
.5	.2	.7	Deferred Taxes						
11.6	11.0	8.3	All Other Non-Current						
17.4	28.2	32.9	Net Worth						
100.0	100.0	100.0	Total Liabilities & Net Worth						
			INCOME DATA						
100.0	100.0	100.0	Net Sales						
			Gross Profit						
88.1	92.9	88.3	Operating Expenses						
11.9	7.1	11.7	Operating Profit						
4.6	2.2	3.8	All Other Expenses (net)						
7.3	4.9	7.9	Profit Before Taxes						
			RATIOS						
1.7	2.5	2.3	Current						
.6	1.0	1.2							
.2	.3	.8							
1.1	1.8	1.6	Quick						
.3	.6	1.1							
.1	.1	.4							
0 UND	0 UND	2 242.6	Sales/Receivables						
1 366.2	4 88.5	18 20.7							
10 34.8	22 16.4	43 8.6							
			Cost of Sales/Inventory						
			Cost of Sales/Payables						
24.4	18.5	11.6	Sales/Working Capital						
-16.4	-74.3	39.6							
-5.1	-4.3	-23.0							
4.0	9.3	11.8	EBIT/Interest						
(22) 2.0	(17) 2.9	(27) 3.2							
.0	1.1	1.7							
			Net Profit + Depr., Dep., Amort./Cur. Mat. L/T/D						
1.3	1.3	1.1	Fixed/Worth						
3.5	2.5	2.2							
-2.5	NM	4.1							
1.1	1.2	.8	Debt/Worth						
3.0	2.7	2.8							
-6.9	NM	14.9							
29.0	64.9	79.1	% Profit Before Taxes/Tangible Net Worth						
(20) 15.3	(16) 17.1	(25) 24.3							
.2	-16.2	14.8							
12.0	18.2	17.6	% Profit Before Taxes/Total Assets						
4.0	4.7	8.9							
-.2	.1	3.4							
9.0	9.4	13.4	Sales/Net Fixed Assets						
2.5	3.3	3.6							
.9	.6	1.4							
3.6	2.2	2.9	Sales/Total Assets						
1.5	1.0	1.9							
.6	.5	.8							
3.6	2.7	1.0	% Depr., Dep., Amort./Sales						
(24) 5.8	(17) 6.6	(21) 5.0							
11.2	11.9	10.4							
2.5		2.9	% Officers', Directors' Owners' Comp/Sales						
(10) 5.5		(12) 4.6							
11.2		13.2							
375640M	352802M	822678M	Net Sales ($)	1512M	7772M	19143M	18777M	122828M	652646M
340236M	538757M	844788M	Total Assets ($)	3468M	10253M	12644M	9290M	90323M	718810M

© RMA 2007

M = $ thousand   MM = $ million
See Pages 11 through 21 for Explanation of Ratios and Data

Current Data Sorted by Assets | Comparative Historical Data

0-500M	500M-2MM	2-10MM	10-50MM	50-100MM	100-250MM	Type of Statement		
1	1	2	6	4	2	Unqualified	19	18
	1	4	5			Reviewed	11	13
2	3	3	2			Compiled	22	23
	6	4	1			Tax Returns	13	13
2	10	14	13		4	Other	49	44
	18 (4/1-9/30/06)		72 (10/1/06-3/31/07)				4/1/02-3/31/03 ALL	4/1/03-3/31/04 ALL
5	21	27	27	4	6	**NUMBER OF STATEMENTS**	114	111
%	%	%	%	%	%	**ASSETS**	%	%
	17.4	14.3	7.4			Cash & Equivalents	6.7	7.1
	14.2	22.9	20.7			Trade Receivables (net)	17.1	20.3
	13.6	13.1	14.9			Inventory	12.7	14.3
	3.4	5.1	4.0			All Other Current	3.4	3.9
	48.6	55.3	47.1			Total Current	39.8	45.5
	38.6	27.6	41.7			Fixed Assets (net)	44.0	44.4
	4.0	4.2	2.3			Intangibles (net)	7.4	5.3
	8.8	13.0	9.0			All Other Non-Current	8.9	4.8
	100.0	100.0	100.0			Total	100.0	100.0
						LIABILITIES		
	8.0	6.4	6.4			Notes Payable-Short Term	10.5	12.6
	2.6	1.7	7.2			Cur. Mat.-L.T.D.	5.1	6.3
	15.3	11.3	8.8			Trade Payables	10.2	11.0
	.4	.3	.4			Income Taxes Payable	.3	.1
	6.7	15.3	16.5			All Other Current	10.4	14.7
	33.0	35.0	39.3			Total Current	36.4	44.7
	40.3	24.0	24.5			Long-Term Debt	31.8	28.2
	.1	.1	1.3			Deferred Taxes	.5	.7
	10.8	3.0	7.7			All Other Non-Current	6.9	7.2
	15.7	38.0	27.2			Net Worth	24.4	19.2
	100.0	100.0	100.0			Total Liabilities & Net Worth	100.0	100.0
						INCOME DATA		
	100.0	100.0	100.0			Net Sales	100.0	100.0
						Gross Profit		
	95.9	94.2	97.7			Operating Expenses	92.1	97.6
	4.1	5.8	2.3			Operating Profit	7.9	2.4
	1.0	.5	1.6			All Other Expenses (net)	4.0	2.2
	3.1	5.3	.8			Profit Before Taxes	3.9	.1
						RATIOS		
	2.2	2.3	2.0				1.9	1.9
	1.4	1.5	1.3			Current	1.2	1.2
	1.1	1.0	.8				.5	.8
	1.4	1.7	1.1				1.4	1.2
	1.0	1.0	.7			Quick	.6 (110)	.7
	.5	.5	.4				.2	.3
	1 688.6	13 28.5	13 28.5				12 30.5	18 19.9
	13 27.8	28 13.0	36 10.2			Sales/Receivables	26 13.8	31 11.8
	25 14.6	51 7.2	55 6.6				42 8.7	46 7.9
						Cost of Sales/Inventory		
						Cost of Sales/Payables		
	10.8	8.4	8.8				10.6	9.0
	26.8	15.6	26.7			Sales/Working Capital	38.4	27.8
	83.7	-949.0	-19.8				-10.0	-30.5
	10.3	19.2	4.5				6.5	5.9
	(18) 3.6	(21) 4.5	(25) 1.9			EBIT/Interest	(101) 2.2	(101) 2.3
	.6	1.6	.2				.9	-.2
						Net Profit + Depr., Dep.,	4.0	5.6
						Amort./Cur. Mat. L/T/D	(17) 2.3	(18) 2.1
							1.3	.8
	.7	.1	.8				.6	.7
	1.9	.8	1.8			Fixed/Worth	2.1	1.9
	NM	1.7	-9.2				-42.9	29.9
	1.8	1.0	.9				1.0	1.3
	4.9	1.4	3.5			Debt/Worth	3.7	3.3
	NM	5.0	-15.2				-19.8	55.7
	86.3	61.7	41.4			% Profit Before Taxes/Tangible	52.7	34.1
	(16) 32.9	(24) 38.2	(19) 23.2			Net Worth	(84) 21.9	(84) 11.6
	5.9	11.6	1.0				3.8	-3.5
	16.4	23.3	10.7			% Profit Before Taxes/Total	13.1	8.8
	5.1	9.3	4.1			Assets	4.1	2.3
	-.5	2.1	-2.0				-.9	-4.4
	37.8	40.0	16.6				16.3	17.0
	5.7	10.1	6.8			Sales/Net Fixed Assets	4.1	4.4
	3.4	3.6	2.5				1.5	1.8
	3.6	2.9	2.9				2.8	3.1
	2.7	2.3	2.3			Sales/Total Assets	1.4	1.7
	2.0	1.5	1.5				.8	1.0
	1.0	1.1	.8				1.5	1.6
	(18) 2.0	(20) 2.4	(24) 2.2			% Depr., Dep., Amort./Sales	(102) 3.5	(100) 3.3
	5.7	3.7	7.1				6.7	7.2
	1.5						1.4	2.4
	(10) 2.4					% Officers', Directors' Owners' Comp/Sales	(38) 3.0	(31) 4.4
	6.2						7.7	10.1
4546M	77879M	302819M	1275724M	206718M	797183M	Net Sales ($)	2105563M	2843563M
934M	25343M	123732M	629047M	274732M	1059671M	Total Assets ($)	2089035M	2128222M

M = $ thousand   MM = $ million
See Pages 11 through 21 for Explanation of Ratios and Data

Comparative Historical Data | | | Type of Statement | | Current Data Sorted by Sales

			Type of Statement	1	2	4		9
22	21	16	Unqualified		2			5
11	14	10	Reviewed		2		3	
29	20	10	Compiled	3	1	1	3	
7	11	11	Tax Returns		4	5	1	1
40	47	43	Other	2	8	9	6	15
4/1/04-3/31/05 ALL	4/1/05-3/31/06 ALL	4/1/06-3/31/07 ALL			18 (4/1-9/30/06)	72 (10/1/06-3/31/07)		
				0-1MM	1-3MM	3-5MM	5-10MM	10-25MM	25MM & OVER

			NUMBER OF STATEMENTS	0-1MM	1-3MM	3-5MM	5-10MM	10-25MM	25MM & OVER
109	113	90		6	13	8	20	13	30
%	%	%	**ASSETS**	%	%	%	%	%	%
9.9	9.8	14.4	Cash & Equivalents	12.6	17.1		16.7	9.0	
19.1	21.4	18.6	Trade Receivables (net)	10.8	14.2		26.1	23.5	
10.2	13.6	12.4	Inventory	11.9	9.8		11.1	15.8	
4.3	3.4	3.9	All Other Current	2.5	7.3		1.2	4.3	
43.5	48.1	49.3	Total Current	37.7	48.4		55.1	52.6	
42.8	40.7	36.3	Fixed Assets (net)	45.9	35.0		34.5	31.7	
5.2	4.7	4.6	Intangibles (net)	1.5	5.9		2.2	7.0	
8.5	6.5	9.8	All Other Non-Current	14.9	10.7		8.2	8.7	
100.0	100.0	100.0	Total	100.0	100.0		100.0	100.0	
			LIABILITIES						
6.5	7.8	5.9	Notes Payable-Short Term	7.1	7.7		1.9	6.7	
6.7	4.2	3.6	Cur. Mat.-L.T.D.	2.3	1.2		4.7	6.1	
10.6	14.1	12.6	Trade Payables	20.8	11.4		14.8	11.1	
.7	.3	.4	Income Taxes Payable	.0	.0		.4	.7	
10.1	11.5	13.8	All Other Current	9.2	8.5		13.1	18.1	
34.6	37.9	36.4	Total Current	39.4	28.7		34.9	42.6	
30.5	30.3	28.2	Long-Term Debt	36.7	25.2		19.8	25.7	
.9	.5	.5	Deferred Taxes	.0	.0		.5	1.2	
7.0	7.2	6.9	All Other Non-Current	6.2	4.2		1.4	9.4	
26.9	24.0	27.9	Net Worth	17.7	41.9		44.3	21.1	
100.0	100.0	100.0	Total Liabilities & Net Worth	100.0	100.0		100.0	100.0	
			INCOME DATA						
100.0	100.0	100.0	Net Sales	100.0	100.0		100.0	100.0	
			Gross Profit						
91.0	94.0	94.7	Operating Expenses	94.5	94.6		93.5	94.9	
9.0	6.0	5.3	Operating Profit	5.5	5.4		6.5	5.1	
4.0	2.5	1.7	All Other Expenses (net)	-.5	2.7		-.2	2.1	
4.9	3.4	3.6	Profit Before Taxes	6.0	2.7		6.8	3.0	
			RATIOS						
2.2	2.3	2.1		1.8	3.3		1.9	1.9	
1.4	1.3	1.3	Current	1.1	1.6		1.4	1.2	
.9	1.0	.9		.9	.9		1.2	.8	
1.6	1.6	1.3		1.2	2.9		1.5	1.1	
.9	.9	.9	Quick	.8	1.0		1.1	.7	
.5	.5	.5		.4	.5		.9	.5	
15 23.9	16 23.4	10 37.7		0 UND		11 34.3	12 31.6	21 17.0	
29 12.7	28 13.1	26 14.0	Sales/Receivables	8 45.6		22 16.5	37 10.0	37 9.9	
45 8.1	44 8.4	50 7.3		22 16.9		50 7.3	53 6.9	59 6.2	
			Cost of Sales/Inventory						
			Cost of Sales/Payables						
6.8	8.6	8.9		15.4	4.8		8.5	10.3	
17.9	19.6	23.2	Sales/Working Capital	56.2	16.3		17.5	28.7	
-88.2	-139.9	-100.8		-198.1	-313.6		40.6	-21.0	
9.7	10.2	7.8		9.2	14.8		18.8	4.5	
(95) 3.9	(100) 3.4	(74) 2.4	EBIT/Interest	(11) 4.4	(14) 1.7	(12) 8.8	(28) 2.2	
1.6	.9	.7		.6	-1.4		1.9	1.0	
6.9	11.1	3.8						5.9	
(24) 2.8	(25) 3.4	(16) 2.0	Net Profit + Depr., Dep., Amort./Cur. Mat. L/T/D				(10) 2.6	
1.1	1.5	1.3						.9	
.7	.7	.4		.8	.1		.2	.8	
1.5	1.5	1.4	Fixed/Worth	1.9	.9		.7	3.3	
NM	-11.4	UND		39.9	2.7		1.9	-3.8	
1.0	.9	.9		1.4	.4		1.0	1.4	
2.8	2.6	3.3	Debt/Worth	3.4	1.8		1.4	7.9	
NM	-35.2	UND		NM	5.4		3.1	-10.7	
57.4	49.4	55.5		106.4	39.4		54.9	53.9	
(82) 29.1	(82) 20.4	(69) 22.7	% Profit Before Taxes/Tangible Net Worth	(10) 59.9	(17) 21.8		44.1	(19) 24.2	
9.2	.5	4.3		-4.5	.6		7.3	10.0	
17.8	18.5	14.4		17.7	18.3		27.4	10.9	
6.3	4.6	4.2	% Profit Before Taxes/Total Assets	14.0	2.7		8.9	4.2	
1.9	-.4	-.1		-2.3	-1.5		1.7	1.0	
17.3	18.9	31.3		17.3	43.9		36.8	18.9	
5.2	6.6	6.0	Sales/Net Fixed Assets	4.6	8.5		10.1	7.4	
1.7	2.6	3.3		3.0	3.2		2.9	4.7	
3.2	3.3	3.3		3.4	2.7		3.4	3.0	
1.9	2.3	2.3	Sales/Total Assets	2.2	1.8		2.4	2.4	
.8	1.3	1.4		1.3	1.0		1.8	1.6	
1.4	1.1	1.1			1.7		1.0	.8	
(91) 3.1	(100) 2.1	(71) 2.4	% Depr., Dep., Amort./Sales		(15) 3.5	(11) 2.1	(25) 2.0	
7.3	6.5	5.3			12.1		8.0	2.9	
2.0	2.1	1.5							
(32) 4.6	(27) 3.7	(21) 2.5	% Officers', Directors' Owners' Comp/Sales					
9.9	9.0	5.7							
2245941M	3495008M	2664869M	Net Sales ($)	3397M	29558M	30503M	137854M	200458M	2263099M
1809331M	2002254M	2113459M	Total Assets ($)	2315M	44659M	25493M	263794M	291221M	1485977M

© RMA 2007

M = $ thousand   MM = $ million
See Pages 11 through 21 for Explanation of Ratios and Data

Current Data Sorted by Assets

Comparative Historical Data

0-500M	500M-2MM	2-10MM	10-50MM	50-100MM	100-250MM	Type of Statement	4/1/02-3/31/03 ALL	4/1/03-3/31/04 ALL
	1	3	5	1	1	Unqualified	1	8
	3	2	1		1	Reviewed	1	5
2	3	5	1			Compiled	3	4
3						Tax Returns	1	2
2	1	7	9		1	Other	4	6
	5 (4/1-9/30/06)		47 (10/1/06-3/31/07)					
7	8	17	16	1	3	**NUMBER OF STATEMENTS**	10	25
%	%	%	%	%	%	**ASSETS**	%	%
		9.0	8.7			Cash & Equivalents	7.7	7.5
		18.2	19.5			Trade Receivables (net)	13.1	17.4
		23.7	12.0			Inventory	15.9	22.2
		4.5	4.0			All Other Current	5.0	6.3
		55.3	44.2			Total Current	41.7	53.3
		35.0	40.2			Fixed Assets (net)	50.9	39.7
		4.4	4.9			Intangibles (net)	1.0	2.1
		5.3	10.8			All Other Non-Current	6.3	4.8
		100.0	100.0			Total	100.0	100.0
						LIABILITIES		
		7.8	6.9			Notes Payable-Short Term	4.4	14.4
		8.2	2.8			Cur. Mat.-L.T.D.	6.3	4.3
		20.5	12.7			Trade Payables	8.1	9.6
		.2	.2			Income Taxes Payable	.0	.0
		14.1	8.3			All Other Current	6.7	10.7
		50.8	31.0			Total Current	25.5	39.0
		17.5	35.2			Long-Term Debt	29.8	26.8
		.4	1.0			Deferred Taxes	.2	.6
		5.5	3.7			All Other Non-Current	13.6	6.2
		25.8	29.2			Net Worth	30.9	27.4
		100.0	100.0			Total Liabilties & Net Worth	100.0	100.0
						INCOME DATA		
		100.0	100.0			Net Sales	100.0	100.0
						Gross Profit		
		99.2	92.8			Operating Expenses	93.6	95.9
		.8	7.2			Operating Profit	6.4	4.1
		3.9	1.5			All Other Expenses (net)	3.7	2.4
		-3.0	5.7			Profit Before Taxes	2.7	1.8
						RATIOS		
		1.7	2.6				2.2	2.2
		1.2	1.4			Current	1.6	1.5
		.7	.7				1.3	1.1
		1.2	1.8				1.1	1.3
		.7	.8			Quick	.9	.6
		.2	.4				.6	.4
		9 41.1	18 20.6				4 84.9	15 24.1
		21 17.8	26 13.9			Sales/Receivables	22 16.3	36 10.3
		41 8.9	52 7.0				38 9.6	57 6.5
						Cost of Sales/Inventory		
						Cost of Sales/Payables		
		8.3	7.2				11.2	4.8
		29.3	15.6			Sales/Working Capital	14.7	13.5
		-14.6	NM				34.0	46.2
		12.8	9.9				7.8	5.5
		(13) 3.5	3.3			EBIT/Interest	1.0	(21) 2.9
		2.3	1.6				-.6	-.4
						Net Profit + Depr., Dep., Amort./Cur. Mat. L/T/D		
		.6	.7				.5	.2
		1.4	1.7			Fixed/Worth	1.6	1.7
		NM	NM				5.4	10.8
		1.4	1.1				.8	1.0
		3.3	1.7			Debt/Worth	2.6	3.7
		NM	NM				5.1	16.6
		39.7	62.1					41.1
		(13) 20.3	(12) 23.6			% Profit Before Taxes/Tangible Net Worth		(22) 11.8
		15.0	3.3					-14.3
		12.9	20.2				13.2	10.2
		5.5	7.6			% Profit Before Taxes/Total Assets	.0	3.6
		-.1	1.0				-3.5	-2.9
		29.4	21.9				37.9	19.9
		10.3	5.9			Sales/Net Fixed Assets	2.2	6.5
		4.2	2.0				1.3	1.4
		3.6	2.9				2.9	2.6
		2.4	1.6			Sales/Total Assets	1.4	1.5
		1.6	1.2				1.0	.8
		1.1	.9				1.2	1.0
		(14) 2.6	(15) 2.3			% Depr., Dep., Amort./Sales	3.3	3.0
		6.7	4.1				5.4	6.0
						% Officers', Directors' Owners' Comp/Sales		
9559M	23738M	222048M	752943M	105752M	349887M	Net Sales ($)	130443M	595538M
1053M	9200M	81793M	411884M	65586M	395289M	Total Assets ($)	42624M	423689M

M = $ thousand   MM = $ million
See Pages 11 through 21 for Explanation of Ratios and Data

Comparative Historical Data | | | | Current Data Sorted by Sales

			Type of Statement	0-1MM	1-3MM	3-5MM	5-10MM	10-25MM	25MM & OVER
4	10	11	Unqualified			1	2	2	6
3	2	7	Reviewed		2	1	2	1	1
3	2	11	Compiled	3		3	1	3	1
9	3	3	Tax Returns	2		1			
11	9	20	Other	1	3	1	3	2	10
4/1/04-3/31/05 ALL	4/1/05-3/31/06 ALL	4/1/06-3/31/07 ALL			5 (4/1-9/30/06)		47 (10/1/06-3/31/07)		
30	26	52	NUMBER OF STATEMENTS	6	5	7	8	8	18
%	%	%	**ASSETS**	%	%	%	%	%	%
18.2	11.8	13.3	Cash & Equivalents						9.5
15.7	19.0	19.4	Trade Receivables (net)						24.2
15.1	14.4	17.5	Inventory						15.9
3.2	2.6	4.1	All Other Current						4.9
52.1	47.8	54.3	Total Current						54.5
34.5	40.5	35.3	Fixed Assets (net)						30.6
1.7	5.4	3.4	Intangibles (net)						4.8
11.8	6.2	7.0	All Other Non-Current						10.1
100.0	100.0	100.0	Total						100.0
			LIABILITIES						
12.1	11.3	13.1	Notes Payable-Short Term						6.2
5.8	3.9	6.1	Cur. Mat.-L.T.D.						2.3
10.5	14.7	16.4	Trade Payables						16.5
.2	.6	.3	Income Taxes Payable						.3
9.5	18.2	17.5	All Other Current						15.6
38.0	48.9	53.4	Total Current						40.8
29.4	31.1	34.0	Long-Term Debt						28.1
.0	.2	.4	Deferred Taxes						.8
4.0	8.0	7.3	All Other Non-Current						4.0
28.5	11.8	4.9	Net Worth						26.3
100.0	100.0	100.0	Total Liabilties & Net Worth						100.0
			INCOME DATA						
100.0	100.0	100.0	Net Sales						100.0
			Gross Profit						
92.8	94.2	95.2	Operating Expenses						94.1
7.2	5.8	4.8	Operating Profit						5.9
.9	1.7	2.4	All Other Expenses (net)						1.0
6.3	4.1	2.4	Profit Before Taxes						4.9
			RATIOS						
3.3	1.6	1.7							1.9
1.3	1.3	1.1	Current						1.5
1.0	.8	.6							.9
2.3	1.3	1.5							1.7
.9	.8	.7	Quick						.9
.4	.4	.3							.4
2 242.2	**8** 45.1	**11** 33.5							**16** 22.7
23 16.2	**30** 12.0	**21** 17.1	Sales/Receivables						**31** 11.8
37 10.0	**46** 7.9	**43** 8.5							**55** 6.6
			Cost of Sales/Inventory						
			Cost of Sales/Payables						
7.7	9.7	8.2							5.9
24.4	27.2	26.1	Sales/Working Capital						11.6
-144.3	-39.4	-15.0							NM
14.8	10.0	10.4							12.8
(24) 4.2	(25) 4.8	(46) 3.2	EBIT/Interest					(17)	4.1
.4	2.2	1.0							1.6
		21.2	Net Profit + Depr., Dep.,						
	(13) 5.4		Amort./Cur. Mat. L/T/D						
		1.8							
.2	1.0	.6							.6
1.0	1.6	1.4	Fixed/Worth						1.4
3.3	NM	-11.5							-22.4
1.0	1.4	1.4							1.2
2.1	2.3	3.2	Debt/Worth						1.7
5.7	NM	-21.3							-35.2
51.9	52.5	43.4	% Profit Before Taxes/Tangible						70.0
(25) 25.7	(20) 26.6	(38) 23.2	Net Worth					(13)	27.9
4.5	12.2	9.2							7.1
16.4	14.0	12.7	% Profit Before Taxes/Total						13.8
8.0	9.4	5.7	Assets						6.5
-.2	2.0	-1.1							1.7
41.4	24.0	32.1							23.5
11.2	5.2	10.3	Sales/Net Fixed Assets						10.3
2.4	2.6	3.4							3.1
5.2	3.5	3.5							3.1
2.1	1.8	2.5	Sales/Total Assets						1.6
1.1	1.3	1.4							1.2
1.1	1.0	.9							.8
(23) 2.8	(24) 2.8	(44) 2.3	% Depr., Dep., Amort./Sales					(16)	2.4
4.8	4.6	4.0							3.8
2.0		3.8	% Officers', Directors'						
(13) 4.1		(11) 5.7	Owners' Comp/Sales						
7.0		20.6							
560753M	1121762M	1463927M	Net Sales ($)	2634M	9277M	27633M	61239M	150776M	1212368M
272123M	684902M	964805M	Total Assets ($)	6844M	5495M	8093M	32643M	89267M	822463M

© RMA 2007

M = $ thousand   MM = $ million
See Pages 11 through 21 for Explanation of Ratios and Data

Current Data Sorted by Assets							Comparative Historical Data	
						Type of Statement		
	1	6	9	4	6	Unqualified	16	31
	3	7	3			Reviewed	9	10
	3	3	2			Compiled	8	9
2						Tax Returns	3	3
1	4	9	15	2	2	Other	16	22
	18 (4/1-9/30/06)		64 (10/1/06-3/31/07)				4/1/02-3/31/03 ALL	4/1/03-3/31/04 ALL
0-500M	500M-2MM	2-10MM	10-50MM	50-100MM	100-250MM			
3	11	25	29	6	8	NUMBER OF STATEMENTS	52	75
%	%	%	%	%	%	**ASSETS**	%	%
	18.8	8.6	12.9			Cash & Equivalents	9.3	10.6
	33.3	24.6	22.5			Trade Receivables (net)	24.0	21.0
	2.0	2.8	1.6			Inventory	3.8	1.8
	2.2	5.4	4.1			All Other Current	3.9	5.4
	56.3	41.4	41.0			Total Current	40.9	38.8
	36.2	41.9	46.7			Fixed Assets (net)	47.3	48.2
	.0	1.3	3.7			Intangibles (net)	2.0	2.3
	7.5	15.4	8.5			All Other Non-Current	9.7	10.6
	100.0	100.0	100.0			Total	100.0	100.0
						LIABILITIES		
	5.1	5.3	1.9			Notes Payable-Short Term	4.8	4.6
	4.0	6.5	4.9			Cur. Mat.-L.T.D.	4.5	6.1
	10.5	13.1	9.9			Trade Payables	10.2	8.8
	.0	.8	.2			Income Taxes Payable	.3	.1
	6.5	9.2	11.7			All Other Current	10.8	9.7
	26.2	34.8	28.7			Total Current	30.6	29.4
	18.8	20.5	28.3			Long-Term Debt	21.5	24.1
	2.6	.2	1.1			Deferred Taxes	1.5	1.3
	1.9	10.7	2.8			All Other Non-Current	7.2	7.2
	50.6	33.8	39.1			Net Worth	39.2	38.0
	100.0	100.0	100.0			Total Liabilties & Net Worth	100.0	100.0
						INCOME DATA		
	100.0	100.0	100.0			Net Sales	100.0	100.0
						Gross Profit		
	71.2	89.3	85.9			Operating Expenses	90.2	88.4
	28.8	10.7	14.1			Operating Profit	9.8	11.6
	3.5	1.3	1.9			All Other Expenses (net)	3.1	3.1
	25.3	9.4	12.2			Profit Before Taxes	6.7	8.5
						RATIOS		
	10.4	1.5	2.2				2.3	2.6
	2.7	1.1	1.3			Current	1.3	1.4
	1.6	.9	1.0				.9	.9
	10.4	1.4	1.9				2.0	1.9
	2.6	1.0	1.1			Quick	1.2	1.2
	1.1	.5	.7				.6	.6
	30 12.1	**31** 11.8	**32** 11.6				**28** 13.1	**24** 15.5
	47 7.8	**37** 9.8	**43** 8.5			Sales/Receivables	**48** 7.6	**43** 8.6
	64 5.7	**54** 6.7	**71** 5.1				**63** 5.8	**60** 6.1
						Cost of Sales/Inventory		
						Cost of Sales/Payables		
	3.0	10.1	6.1				5.9	7.1
	6.5	75.3	24.1			Sales/Working Capital	17.2	16.3
	17.2	-56.7	-98.2				-27.8	-51.0
		9.3	14.0				11.5	9.9
		(20) 6.7	(26) 7.1			EBIT/Interest	(45) 3.4	(63) 3.8
		2.4	3.7				1.1	1.6
							7.0	3.4
						Net Profit + Depr., Dep., Amort./Cur. Mat. L/T/D	(14) 1.5	(25) 2.4
							.4	1.0
	.1	.4	.7				.5	.5
	.5	1.0	1.3			Fixed/Worth	1.4	1.1
	2.5	2.1	2.5				2.6	3.1
	.1	.8	.9				.9	.8
	.9	1.5	1.8			Debt/Worth	2.1	1.7
	3.7	7.2	3.6				4.8	4.7
	84.9	51.3	68.3				30.7	47.5
	(10) 62.7	(21) 26.3	(28) 46.2			% Profit Before Taxes/Tangible Net Worth	(49) 18.2	(69) 18.8
	50.0	18.5	20.6				1.7	4.1
	64.1	21.0	19.4				11.3	11.4
	22.7	11.6	11.3			% Profit Before Taxes/Total Assets	4.1	5.8
	16.0	3.5	8.7				.4	1.3
	81.4	15.6	10.1				9.9	12.1
	4.8	3.3	2.5			Sales/Net Fixed Assets	3.2	4.1
	1.0	1.8	1.2				1.2	.9
	4.7	2.2	2.3				2.7	2.5
	1.3	1.8	1.4			Sales/Total Assets	1.3	1.5
	.6	1.0	.7				.8	.6
		1.5	2.2				2.7	2.4
		(21) 5.7	4.5			% Depr., Dep., Amort./Sales	(45) 4.4	(65) 4.9
		9.7	6.0				9.7	8.6
								1.1
						% Officers', Directors' Owners' Comp/Sales		(12) 2.6
								6.1
23591M	42738M	238048M	1117658M	793646M	2425574M	Net Sales ($)	2214874M	3894837M
993M	16946M	125310M	657070M	549528M	1345814M	Total Assets ($)	1832275M	3042784M

M = $ thousand MM = $ million

See Pages 11 through 21 for Explanation of Ratios and Data

Comparative Historical Data　　　　　　　　　　　Current Data Sorted by Sales

	4/1/04-3/31/05 ALL	4/1/05-3/31/06 ALL	4/1/06-3/31/07 ALL	0-1MM	1-3MM	3-5MM	5-10MM	10-25MM	25MM & OVER
Type of Statement					18 (4/1-9/30/06)		64 (10/1/06-3/31/07)		
Unqualified	26	26	26		4		3	3	16
Reviewed	8	10	13	1	1	1	3	4	3
Compiled	6	6	8		2	1	4	1	
Tax Returns	2	5	2		1			1	
Other	20	35	33	1	4	1	7	8	12
NUMBER OF STATEMENTS	62	82	82	2	12	3	17	17	31
ASSETS	%	%	%	%	%	%	%	%	%
Cash & Equivalents	12.7	11.1	11.6		16.9		7.7	16.8	8.9
Trade Receivables (net)	20.1	24.3	24.1		22.3		24.6	26.1	25.5
Inventory	1.1	2.2	2.0		2.4		.2	.4	1.8
All Other Current	6.1	4.5	3.7		1.5		5.4	2.7	4.4
Total Current	40.1	42.2	41.4		43.1		37.9	46.0	40.5
Fixed Assets (net)	46.4	45.2	44.4		43.4		45.9	38.8	47.1
Intangibles (net)	2.9	3.3	2.7		2.2		2.5	.3	2.6
All Other Non-Current	10.5	9.3	11.5		11.3		13.7	14.8	9.7
Total	100.0	100.0	100.0		100.0		100.0	100.0	100.0
LIABILITIES									
Notes Payable-Short Term	2.7	4.7	5.4		3.1		4.0	12.3	3.4
Cur. Mat.-L.T.D.	5.1	4.9	4.8		6.2		6.0	2.6	4.7
Trade Payables	12.0	11.7	10.4		9.2		7.8	14.8	10.8
Income Taxes Payable	.1	.4	.4		.3		1.2	.2	.1
All Other Current	13.0	9.7	10.6		16.7		6.6	9.9	12.3
Total Current	32.9	31.5	31.6		35.5		25.6	39.9	31.3
Long-Term Debt	25.8	23.2	22.8		15.4		24.9	19.0	22.5
Deferred Taxes	1.1	1.3	1.4		.0		1.9	.0	2.7
All Other Non-Current	6.1	5.3	4.9		4.6		5.6	10.4	2.5
Net Worth	34.0	38.7	39.2		44.4		42.0	30.7	41.0
Total Liabilities & Net Worth	100.0	100.0	100.0		100.0		100.0	100.0	100.0
INCOME DATA									
Net Sales	100.0	100.0	100.0		100.0		100.0	100.0	100.0
Gross Profit									
Operating Expenses	87.2	87.2	85.7		79.4		86.0	85.3	90.8
Operating Profit	12.8	12.8	14.3		20.6		14.0	14.7	9.2
All Other Expenses (net)	2.8	1.9	2.1		3.0		.9	1.9	1.5
Profit Before Taxes	9.9	10.9	12.2		17.5		13.1	12.7	7.7
RATIOS									
Current	2.1	2.1	2.3		11.5		2.2	2.7	2.0
	1.3	1.4	1.3		1.5		1.1	1.3	1.2
	.8	.9	.9		.3		1.0	.8	.9
Quick	1.7	2.0	2.0		11.4		2.0	2.6	1.5
	1.0	1.1	1.1		1.2		1.1	1.2	1.1
	.6	.6	.6		.2		.8	.8	.6
Sales/Receivables	24　15.3	28　13.2	30　12.1	2　172.1		33　11.0	28　12.9	33　11.1	
	41　8.8	45　8.1	39　9.3	44　8.3		49　7.4	35　10.3	41　9.0	
	58　6.3	65　5.6	59　6.2	67　5.4		74　4.9	46　8.0	48　7.6	
Cost of Sales/Inventory									
Cost of Sales/Payables									
Sales/Working Capital	7.3	6.2	6.8		3.1		8.1	6.1	12.4
	22.4	18.4	24.0		5.2		44.2	20.3	25.7
	-25.6	-46.9	-68.0		-2.6		-373.5	-60.0	-68.0
EBIT/Interest	8.6	15.4	11.0				11.0	13.5	14.0
	(49) 4.4	(72) 6.5	(68) 7.3				(16) 7.9	(15) 7.6	(28) 6.9
	2.3	3.2	3.6				4.0	3.6	3.5
Net Profit + Depr., Dep., Amort./Cur. Mat. L/T/D	3.5	8.1	7.9						5.4
	(14) 2.6	(20) 4.2	(21) 3.3						(13) 3.0
	1.9	2.2	2.6						2.6
Fixed/Worth	.6	.5	.5		.3		.6	.1	.6
	1.4	1.2	1.1		.8		1.0	.9	1.3
	3.9	2.4	2.5		NM		1.9	2.2	2.4
Debt/Worth	.9	.8	.7		.1		.6	.9	.8
	2.3	1.6	1.5		.9		1.4	2.3	1.6
	4.7	4.0	3.8		NM		1.7	8.6	2.8
% Profit Before Taxes/Tangible Net Worth	48.2	69.4	63.5				56.3	95.4	63.0
	(55) 24.4	(74) 28.4	(73) 36.7				(15) 49.4	(15) 46.8	(30) 29.5
	12.8	13.5	19.7				24.1	26.3	17.3
% Profit Before Taxes/Total Assets	15.6	21.1	22.3		42.5		23.8	26.7	17.3
	8.0	10.3	12.6		11.4		20.4	15.2	11.3
	3.2	3.1	7.8		.4		10.3	9.1	7.4
Sales/Net Fixed Assets	13.2	13.8	12.8		21.3		6.0	110.0	11.5
	3.3	3.7	3.4		2.0		3.2	3.6	3.6
	.9	1.0	1.3		1.0		1.8	1.6	1.3
Sales/Total Assets	2.8	2.7	2.3		2.0		2.0	4.6	2.5
	1.3	1.6	1.6		.8		1.6	1.8	1.8
	.6	.7	.7		.6		1.0	.9	.9
% Depr., Dep., Amort./Sales	2.3	2.1	2.1		2.1		2.9	.2	2.1
	(54) 4.7	(72) 4.6	(70) 4.3		(10) 6.7		(15) 5.7	(15) 3.0	(26) 3.9
	10.1	9.2	7.0		14.3		9.1	5.1	6.1
% Officers', Directors' Owners' Comp/Sales			2.6						
		(11) 3.4							
			7.1						
Net Sales ($)	4148119M	4310832M	4641255M	998M	22516M	12994M	143043M	283369M	4178335M
Total Assets ($)	3144303M	3070004M	2695661M	2841M	29944M	15945M	124481M	224429M	2298021M

© RMA 2007　　　　　M = $ thousand　　　MM = $ million
See Pages 11 through 21 for Explanation of Ratios and Data

Current Data Sorted by Assets							Type of Statement	Comparative Historical Data	
		1	2	3	4		Unqualified	16	14
	1	5	4	1			Reviewed	6	16
2	6	7	3				Compiled	25	21
1		2	1				Tax Returns	9	12
	5	8	9	4	2		Other	29	22
	16 (4/1-9/30/06)		55 (10/1/06-3/31/07)					4/1/02-3/31/03	4/1/03-3/31/04
0-500M	500M-2MM	2-10MM	10-50MM	50-100MM	100-250MM			ALL	ALL
3	12	23	19	8	6		NUMBER OF STATEMENTS	85	85
%	%	%	%	%	%		ASSETS	%	%
	20.9	14.9	13.5				Cash & Equivalents	7.9	8.4
	14.7	20.7	22.8				Trade Receivables (net)	16.1	16.3
	.0	3.9	.9				Inventory	.5	.5
	13.4	5.7	1.6				All Other Current	3.5	3.7
	49.0	45.1	38.8				Total Current	28.1	28.9
	43.3	43.9	54.4				Fixed Assets (net)	63.3	62.1
	1.5	.7	1.8				Intangibles (net)	.6	.3
	6.2	10.2	5.0				All Other Non-Current	8.1	8.8
	100.0	100.0	100.0				Total	100.0	100.0
							LIABILITIES		
	2.0	7.5	1.9				Notes Payable-Short Term	4.1	3.5
	3.8	6.5	3.5				Cur. Mat.-L.T.D.	9.1	6.4
	4.8	7.1	14.8				Trade Payables	7.4	5.6
	.4	.5	.3				Income Taxes Payable	.1	.1
	13.8	6.7	6.0				All Other Current	5.9	7.4
	24.7	28.3	26.5				Total Current	26.6	23.0
	15.9	31.7	29.0				Long-Term Debt	42.8	38.4
	.1	.5	.9				Deferred Taxes	1.6	1.5
	1.7	4.9	1.6				All Other Non-Current	5.6	3.9
	57.7	34.5	42.0				Net Worth	23.3	33.1
	100.0	100.0	100.0				Total Liabilities & Net Worth	100.0	100.0
							INCOME DATA		
	100.0	100.0	100.0				Net Sales	100.0	100.0
							Gross Profit		
	75.8	81.1	89.5				Operating Expenses	91.1	90.1
	24.2	18.9	10.5				Operating Profit	8.9	9.9
	1.4	2.9	1.6				All Other Expenses (net)	3.9	4.3
	22.8	16.1	8.9				Profit Before Taxes	5.0	5.6
							RATIOS		
	4.5	3.6	2.3					1.8	2.9
	2.3	1.9	1.6				Current	1.0	1.3
	1.3	1.0	1.0					.5	.6
	2.3	2.4	2.1					1.5	2.3
	1.5	1.5	1.3				Quick	.9	1.0
	.8	1.0	1.0					.4	.5
	0 UND	4 91.7	30 12.3					16 23.0	17 22.0
	2 229.3	27 13.4	48 7.7				Sales/Receivables	41 9.0	45 8.2
	33 11.0	66 5.6	67 5.4					68 5.4	72 5.0
							Cost of Sales/Inventory		
							Cost of Sales/Payables		
	6.6	6.3	7.0					8.1	5.7
	12.7	11.0	12.9				Sales/Working Capital	157.7	26.5
	33.3	-342.3	137.8					-11.0	-9.8
	44.4	9.0	11.4					3.7	4.9
	(11) 7.6	(20) 4.6	(18) 7.6				EBIT/Interest	(81) 2.0	(76) 2.9
	3.4	2.2	2.6					1.0	1.2
							Net Profit + Depr., Dep.,	3.5	4.2
							Amort./Cur. Mat. L/T/D	(25) 1.4	(23) 2.0
								.8	1.1
	.2	.7	.7					1.4	1.1
	.6	1.2	1.6				Fixed/Worth	2.4	2.1
	1.9	3.4	2.1					11.2	3.8
	.2	1.0	1.0					1.3	1.3
	.5	2.2	1.7				Debt/Worth	2.7	1.9
	2.9	5.1	2.5					19.4	5.4
	84.0	105.2	45.9				% Profit Before Taxes/Tangible	31.2	34.4
	47.1	(22) 37.6	33.6				Net Worth	(69) 14.4	(76) 15.5
	14.1	16.8	15.6					3.1	4.7
	46.6	30.1	22.1				% Profit Before Taxes/Total	8.2	11.6
	16.0	15.3	10.7				Assets	3.6	4.6
	6.9	4.8	3.8					1.0	
	44.6	6.4	5.2					3.5	4.1
	8.0	3.3	2.2				Sales/Net Fixed Assets	1.9	1.5
	1.7	2.0	1.2					.8	.7
	5.7	2.2	2.0					2.1	1.8
	1.8	1.5	1.4				Sales/Total Assets	1.0	1.1
	1.1	1.1	.9					.5	.5
		2.3	1.5					4.0	3.7
		(22) 4.6	(17) 7.0				% Depr., Dep., Amort./Sales	(81) 8.5	(82) 7.7
		6.8	10.7					12.3	16.5
							% Officers', Directors'	2.8	1.7
							Owners' Comp/Sales	(21) 6.1	(19) 4.8
								10.4	10.4
4777M	53601M	207971M	582183M	534851M	670280M		Net Sales ($)	1422254M	1349410M
1173M	13500M	130354M	360450M	594038M	954222M		Total Assets ($)	1718827M	1604422M

M = $ thousand   MM = $ million
See Pages 11 through 21 for Explanation of Ratios and Data

Comparative Historical Data / Current Data Sorted by Sales

4/1/04-3/31/05 ALL	4/1/05-3/31/06 ALL	4/1/06-3/31/07 ALL	Type of Statement	0-1MM	1-3MM	3-5MM	5-10MM	10-25MM	25MM & OVER
21	16	10	Unqualified					3	7
12	11	11	Reviewed		2			3	2
17	17	18	Compiled	3	1	2	5	5	2
4	3	4	Tax Returns	1	1	1			1
19	44	28	Other	1	3	2	5	8	9
				16 (4/1-9/30/06)			55 (10/1/06-3/31/07)		
73	91	71	**NUMBER OF STATEMENTS**	5	7	5	14	19	21
%	%	%	**ASSETS**	%	%	%	%	%	%
10.1	11.4	14.8	Cash & Equivalents				17.1	17.1	12.2
14.5	17.1	18.0	Trade Receivables (net)				18.0	19.6	21.2
.4	.7	1.9	Inventory				.2	4.7	2.1
3.0	3.6	4.9	All Other Current				7.7	3.1	1.5
28.1	32.8	39.6	Total Current				42.9	44.6	37.0
62.0	55.0	51.8	Fixed Assets (net)				48.1	48.5	53.8
.9	1.6	1.6	Intangibles (net)				2.7	.0	3.5
9.0	10.7	6.9	All Other Non-Current				6.3	6.9	5.7
100.0	100.0	100.0	Total				100.0	100.0	100.0
			LIABILITIES						
3.9	4.0	3.5	Notes Payable-Short Term				5.5	5.9	1.8
9.0	6.1	4.6	Cur. Mat.-L.T.D.				4.9	2.7	3.7
5.9	9.2	8.4	Trade Payables				5.1	10.6	13.2
.2	.3	.6	Income Taxes Payable				.7	.2	1.0
6.9	6.1	7.0	All Other Current				6.5	9.6	5.7
25.9	25.8	24.1	Total Current				22.6	29.1	25.4
41.3	35.3	27.4	Long-Term Debt				32.5	25.2	24.0
1.3	1.7	1.2	Deferred Taxes				.9	.0	3.1
5.9	2.7	5.8	All Other Non-Current				1.7	3.7	1.3
25.6	34.5	41.5	Net Worth				42.2	42.0	46.2
100.0	100.0	100.0	Total Liabilities & Net Worth				100.0	100.0	100.0
			INCOME DATA						
100.0	100.0	100.0	Net Sales				100.0	100.0	100.0
			Gross Profit						
86.6	84.4	83.2	Operating Expenses				83.7	87.9	87.1
13.4	15.6	16.8	Operating Profit				16.3	12.1	12.9
3.8	2.9	2.1	All Other Expenses (net)				1.6	1.3	1.5
9.6	12.8	14.7	Profit Before Taxes				14.7	10.7	11.4
			RATIOS						
2.0	2.5	2.4					3.4	2.3	2.3
1.2	1.4	1.7	Current				2.2	1.7	1.3
.6	.8	1.0					1.3	1.0	1.0
1.7	2.2	2.1					3.0	2.2	1.7
.9	1.2	1.3	Quick				1.8	1.3	1.1
.5	.5	.8					.9	1.0	.8
26 14.1	25 14.8	20 18.1					0 UND	24 15.1	36 10.2
44 8.2	40 9.1	41 8.9	Sales/Receivables				50 7.3	41 8.9	43 8.4
65 5.6	56 6.5	58 6.3					60 6.1	69 5.3	65 5.7
			Cost of Sales/Inventory						
			Cost of Sales/Payables						
7.4	5.4	6.6					5.6	7.7	6.4
33.4	18.4	13.0	Sales/Working Capital				9.9	12.9	13.7
-9.4	-19.6	-846.0					NM	175.3	NM
6.0	10.8	9.7					9.5	8.4	32.1
(66) 3.4	(82) 5.3	(65) 6.3	EBIT/Interest		(12) 4.5	(16) 6.7			7.5
1.7	2.3	2.9					3.1	1.8	3.5
3.4	4.3	5.9							19.3
(19) 1.8	(22) 2.2	(24) 3.1	Net Profit + Depr., Dep., Amort./Cur. Mat. L/T/D					(12)	4.4
1.3	1.6	1.9							2.2
1.0	.8	.7					.5	.8	.7
2.0	1.6	1.3	Fixed/Worth				1.6	1.3	1.2
4.9	2.9	2.5					3.0	2.0	2.1
1.3	1.0	.6					.6	.9	.6
1.9	1.7	1.6	Debt/Worth				1.8	1.7	1.3
6.8	3.9	3.2					4.1	3.3	2.4
40.1	46.0	63.8					82.9	54.5	41.2
(61) 17.6	(84) 27.2	(69) 34.4	% Profit Before Taxes/Tangible Net Worth				51.2	(18) 30.5	33.3
7.6	10.9	16.0					16.8	10.0	14.6
12.3	16.3	23.3					30.4	23.7	17.6
5.1	8.4	11.1	% Profit Before Taxes/Total Assets				15.9	9.5	10.7
1.3	3.5	4.8					4.5	2.9	3.0
3.2	5.2	6.4					7.7	8.0	5.0
1.4	2.3	2.3	Sales/Net Fixed Assets				3.0	3.2	1.6
.7	1.3	1.2					1.9	1.9	.9
1.6	2.2	2.1					2.5	2.4	2.1
.9	1.3	1.3	Sales/Total Assets				1.4	1.6	.9
.5	.8	.8					1.1	1.3	.7
3.2	2.9	2.5					2.9	.9	2.5
(63) 8.9	(82) 7.2	(63) 5.7	% Depr., Dep., Amort./Sales				5.3	(16) 5.0	(19) 5.7
13.6	10.5	8.2					7.1	8.2	7.1
1.9	1.8	1.4							
(17) 2.9	(20) 4.4	(13) 4.6	% Officers', Directors' Owners' Comp/Sales						
10.6	12.4	9.4							
1500475M	2551927M	2053663M	Net Sales ($)	3306M	11395M	19534M	107109M	329362M	1582957M
1800107M	2630176M	2053737M	Total Assets ($)	2962M	20034M	14146M	90823M	234671M	1691101M

© RMA 2007

M = $ thousand   MM = $ million

See Pages 11 through 21 for Explanation of Ratios and Data

Current Data Sorted by Assets   Comparative Historical Data

0-500M	500M-2MM	2-10MM	10-50MM	50-100MM	100-250MM	Type of Statement	4/1/02-3/31/03 ALL	4/1/03-3/31/04 ALL
		6	1	2	2	Unqualified	16	19
	1	5	2	1		Reviewed	10	9
	3	2	2			Compiled	11	15
4	1	1				Tax Returns	2	8
2	2	9	9		4	Other	24	17
	8 (4/1-9/30/06)		51 (10/1/06-3/31/07)					
6	7	23	14	3	6	NUMBER OF STATEMENTS	63	68
%	%	%	%	%	%	**ASSETS**	%	%
		14.0	6.6			Cash & Equivalents	9.2	15.2
		26.5	25.2			Trade Receivables (net)	19.7	13.9
		2.5	2.6			Inventory	3.2	2.8
		8.4	3.1			All Other Current	5.2	5.0
		51.4	37.5			Total Current	37.4	36.8
		43.3	51.3			Fixed Assets (net)	50.6	52.5
		.6	1.5			Intangibles (net)	3.6	3.3
		4.7	9.7			All Other Non-Current	8.3	7.4
		100.0	100.0			Total	100.0	100.0
						LIABILITIES		
		5.7	5.1			Notes Payable-Short Term	6.1	4.5
		6.0	6.6			Cur. Mat.-L.T.D.	7.1	6.8
		13.9	16.3			Trade Payables	7.4	5.9
		.2	.0			Income Taxes Payable	.2	.2
		11.4	9.1			All Other Current	7.2	7.0
		37.2	37.1			Total Current	27.9	24.3
		22.7	22.1			Long-Term Debt	24.6	31.5
		.0	2.2			Deferred Taxes	1.1	.7
		.8	1.6			All Other Non-Current	4.7	8.1
		39.3	37.0			Net Worth	41.6	35.4
		100.0	100.0			Total Liabilities & Net Worth	100.0	100.0
						INCOME DATA		
		100.0	100.0			Net Sales	100.0	100.0
						Gross Profit		
		84.8	82.6			Operating Expenses	86.3	85.9
		15.2	17.4			Operating Profit	13.7	14.1
		2.5	1.1			All Other Expenses (net)	3.8	2.6
		12.8	16.3			Profit Before Taxes	10.0	11.6
						RATIOS		
		2.5	3.2				2.2	3.1
		1.4	1.2			Current	1.3	1.4
		.8	.5				.6	.8
		1.7	3.0				1.7	2.3
		1.1	.9			Quick	1.0	1.0
		.4	.4				.5	.5
		3 127.6	31 11.8				18 20.8	16 22.9
		45 8.2	61 6.0			Sales/Receivables	50 7.2	44 8.3
		56 6.6	84 4.4				72 5.1	68 5.3
						Cost of Sales/Inventory		
						Cost of Sales/Payables		
		5.8	5.6				5.0	5.1
		13.8	400.4			Sales/Working Capital	15.7	15.3
		-22.0	-7.8				-16.9	-20.5
		24.8	19.9				7.2	6.3
		(18) 8.5	3.9			EBIT/Interest	(53) 3.7	(56) 3.5
		3.4	.2				1.3	1.0
							3.5	
						Net Profit + Depr., Dep., Amort./Cur. Mat. L/T/D	(13) 2.2	
							1.1	
		.2	.8				.8	.7
		1.0	1.8			Fixed/Worth	1.3	1.7
		3.7	5.3				2.8	4.5
		.5	.7				.6	.7
		1.6	2.5			Debt/Worth	1.5	1.7
		5.0	19.2				4.5	5.1
		121.9	56.4				35.7	33.3
		(21) 59.2	(13) 33.6			% Profit Before Taxes/Tangible Net Worth	(57) 14.3	(60) 12.1
		18.1	-16.6				4.6	4.3
		35.5	21.3				11.5	11.0
		11.6	6.9			% Profit Before Taxes/Total Assets	6.7	4.2
		4.7	-3.0				.2	.0
		16.1	8.7				8.6	9.6
		5.6	1.5			Sales/Net Fixed Assets	2.6	1.7
		1.7	.9				1.0	.7
		3.0	2.3				2.6	1.7
		1.7	.9			Sales/Total Assets	1.2	.9
		1.0	.6				.5	.5
		1.5	1.6				2.5	2.6
		(21) 3.1	4.3			% Depr., Dep., Amort./Sales	(52) 6.7	(56) 6.1
		8.8	7.2				11.8	12.1
							2.3	2.9
						% Officers', Directors' Owners' Comp/Sales	(14) 3.9	(15) 4.7
							5.8	9.3
3386M	18646M	231542M	532267M	162337M	1047562M	Net Sales ($)	2284734M	2054811M
1641M	7491M	112751M	320129M	216657M	881706M	Total Assets ($)	1619047M	2075418M

M = $ thousand   MM = $ million
See Pages 11 through 21 for Explanation of Ratios and Data

Comparative Historical Data			Type of Statement	Current Data Sorted by Sales					
11	9	11	Unqualified	1			1	3	6
7	9	9	Reviewed		1	2	4	1	1
15	9	7	Compiled		2	1	2		2
4	3	6	Tax Returns	3	3				
25	28	26	Other	2	3		7	6	8
4/1/04-3/31/05 ALL	4/1/05-3/31/06 ALL	4/1/06-3/31/07 ALL		8 (4/1-9/30/06)			51 (10/1/06-3/31/07)		
				0-1MM	1-3MM	3-5MM	5-10MM	10-25MM	25MM & OVER
62	58	59	**NUMBER OF STATEMENTS**	6	9	3	14	10	17
%	%	%	**ASSETS**	%	%	%	%	%	%
9.7	13.8	11.6	Cash & Equivalents				13.7	11.3	7.9
18.2	18.0	22.7	Trade Receivables (net)				22.7	21.8	33.4
2.4	1.9	3.8	Inventory				2.5	1.3	2.1
4.9	3.9	5.0	All Other Current				7.5	8.9	2.3
35.3	37.6	43.1	Total Current				46.2	43.3	45.8
54.4	53.2	47.3	Fixed Assets (net)				47.3	48.4	39.4
2.9	2.6	3.1	Intangibles (net)				1.2	1.5	4.0
7.5	6.6	6.5	All Other Non-Current				5.2	6.7	10.8
100.0	100.0	100.0	Total				100.0	100.0	100.0
			LIABILITIES						
4.3	5.4	5.1	Notes Payable-Short Term				2.5	1.3	5.2
7.2	5.5	5.5	Cur. Mat.-L.T.D.				7.0	8.9	2.6
5.6	8.0	12.2	Trade Payables				9.1	10.6	19.3
.5	.2	.2	Income Taxes Payable				.2	.1	.4
9.8	7.5	14.2	All Other Current				9.3	4.1	14.1
27.5	26.6	37.3	Total Current				28.2	25.1	41.7
32.6	34.9	25.9	Long-Term Debt				16.6	25.3	18.4
1.0	1.0	1.2	Deferred Taxes				.0	1.1	3.4
3.3	3.3	1.7	All Other Non-Current				.1	3.1	2.3
35.6	34.2	34.0	Net Worth				55.1	45.5	34.2
100.0	100.0	100.0	Total Liabilities & Net Worth				100.0	100.0	100.0
			INCOME DATA						
100.0	100.0	100.0	Net Sales				100.0	100.0	100.0
			Gross Profit						
83.6	83.9	83.6	Operating Expenses				80.1	80.0	86.1
16.4	16.1	16.4	Operating Profit				19.9	20.0	13.9
3.0	3.9	1.9	All Other Expenses (net)				-.1	1.9	.8
13.4	12.2	14.5	Profit Before Taxes				20.1	18.1	13.1
			RATIOS						
2.5	2.6	1.9					4.5	4.7	1.5
1.4	1.7	1.3	Current				1.5	1.6	1.3
.7	.9	.6					.7	.6	1.0
1.9	2.3	1.6					3.6	3.4	1.4
1.1	1.3	.9	Quick				1.1	1.3	1.0
.5	.7	.4					.4	.4	.9
13 28.7	4 99.3	8 45.9					6 66.3	0 UND	43 8.4
44 8.4	47 7.7	45 8.2	Sales/Receivables				44 8.4	61 5.9	52 7.0
80 4.5	77 4.7	75 4.9					58 6.3	83 4.4	82 4.5
			Cost of Sales/Inventory						
			Cost of Sales/Payables						
7.0	4.8	7.0					2.4	3.8	9.9
20.2	8.8	27.3	Sales/Working Capital				12.3	9.3	27.3
-14.7	-30.1	-9.8					-18.6	-14.6	NM
12.6	10.2	18.4					17.2	35.5	18.7
(56) 4.0	(50) 5.3	(52) 4.4	EBIT/Interest				(12) 8.5	7.1	(15) 4.1
2.1	2.3	1.2					6.1	.9	2.9
	3.5	3.5							
	(15) 2.9	(11) 2.3	Net Profit + Depr., Dep., Amort./Cur. Mat. L/T/D						
	1.8	1.6							
.7	.8	.6					.2	.4	.7
1.4	1.6	1.5	Fixed/Worth				.8	1.1	1.1
4.8	6.9	10.5					1.5	5.3	2.2
.7	.9	.8					.4	.7	.9
1.8	1.9	1.8	Debt/Worth				.7	1.3	1.9
5.8	10.4	13.4					1.7	7.5	4.6
41.7	90.6	74.3					117.9	65.8	143.8
(52) 23.8	(49) 38.3	(50) 41.4	% Profit Before Taxes/Tangible Net Worth				38.4	36.5	(15) 28.8
8.5	14.5	16.3					15.8	-20.4	14.1
13.8	19.2	31.7					42.7	39.8	21.3
6.8	8.7	9.4	% Profit Before Taxes/Total Assets				19.2	16.9	8.7
3.1	4.0	1.6					6.9	-.4	3.8
6.1	6.4	12.1					26.3	9.8	22.8
2.1	2.2	3.2	Sales/Net Fixed Assets				2.4	2.2	7.0
.7	.9	1.3					.9	.9	1.5
2.1	2.1	2.3					3.0	1.8	3.4
1.2	1.1	1.5	Sales/Total Assets				1.4	1.0	1.8
.4	.7	.9					.7	.6	1.0
2.6	1.7	1.6					2.2		1.1
(57) 8.6	(55) 4.4	(55) 4.4	% Depr., Dep., Amort./Sales				(13) 4.3		2.9
14.4	11.8	7.3					8.6		4.5
2.9	2.7	1.5							
(16) 4.0	(11) 4.3	(13) 4.4	% Officers', Directors' Owners' Comp/Sales						
7.3	12.3	8.2							
1043501M	1507424M	1995740M	Net Sales ($)	2833M	16649M	11260M	101638M	135255M	1728105M
869495M	1436346M	1540375M	Total Assets ($)	5154M	12977M	8561M	101000M	201181M	1211502M

© RMA 2007

M = $ thousand   MM = $ million
See Pages 11 through 21 for Explanation of Ratios and Data

Current Data Sorted by Assets | **Comparative Historical Data**

	0-500M	500M-2MM	2-10MM	10-50MM	50-100MM	100-250MM	Type of Statement	4/1/02-3/31/03 ALL	4/1/03-3/31/04 ALL
Unqualified								8	5
Reviewed		1		3	2			15	8
Compiled	9	10	2	1	1			37	40
Tax Returns	27	21	1	1	1			38	48
Other	18	18	8	7	1			38	43
		22 (4/1-9/30/06)		111 (10/1/06-3/31/07)					
NUMBER OF STATEMENTS	54	50	11	13	5			136	144
	%	%	%	%	%	%	**ASSETS**	%	%
Cash & Equivalents	16.2	11.4	8.8	7.9				10.7	12.2
Trade Receivables (net)	12.9	11.8	10.8	7.9				12.9	12.6
Inventory	14.9	8.2	12.1	8.2				13.6	16.0
All Other Current	6.4	1.6	2.4	2.2				3.3	3.5
Total Current	50.3	33.1	34.1	26.2				40.5	44.3
Fixed Assets (net)	39.0	53.9	56.5	48.3				45.5	40.3
Intangibles (net)	3.2	6.2	3.5	9.7				6.2	7.8
All Other Non-Current	7.5	6.9	5.9	15.8				7.8	7.6
Total	100.0	100.0	100.0	100.0				100.0	100.0
							LIABILITIES		
Notes Payable-Short Term	11.3	3.9	8.6	7.7				7.8	12.7
Cur. Mat.-L.T.D.	4.9	9.1	5.2	6.8				6.6	6.2
Trade Payables	12.1	6.8	7.3	8.4				11.3	11.7
Income Taxes Payable	.1	.0	.0	.0				.2	.3
All Other Current	22.9	4.1	3.7	8.6				19.0	12.3
Total Current	51.3	23.9	24.7	31.5				44.8	43.2
Long-Term Debt	38.3	43.4	44.9	34.1				36.6	29.6
Deferred Taxes	.0	.1	.0	.7				.2	.1
All Other Non-Current	6.9	7.1	4.4	8.8				6.8	21.4
Net Worth	3.5	25.6	26.0	24.9				11.6	5.8
Total Liabilties & Net Worth	100.0	100.0	100.0	100.0				100.0	100.0
							INCOME DATA		
Net Sales	100.0	100.0	100.0	100.0				100.0	100.0
Gross Profit									
Operating Expenses	95.6	93.9	91.1	88.0				95.4	94.5
Operating Profit	4.4	6.1	8.9	12.0				4.6	5.5
All Other Expenses (net)	.6	1.8	3.5	2.7				2.5	2.2
Profit Before Taxes	3.8	4.3	5.4	9.3				2.1	3.3
							RATIOS		
Current	4.2	2.7	1.9	1.6				2.6	2.1
	1.4	1.1	1.2	1.0				1.2	1.1
	.5	.7	.6	.3				.5	.6
Quick	2.4	1.7	1.3	1.4				1.5	1.3
	.8	.8	.6	.4				.6	.6
	.3	.5	.4	.1				.2	.3
Sales/Receivables	0 UND	4 101.3	2 172.6	4 84.9				1 374.7	0 UND
	2 195.4	10 35.2	15 24.0	18 20.5				8 44.2	7 49.3
	16 22.2	22 16.4	22 16.3	34 10.8				26 14.2	30 12.3
Cost of Sales/Inventory									
Cost of Sales/Payables									
Sales/Working Capital	14.1	10.9	13.2	13.5				10.9	13.0
	78.1	136.5	21.7	662.5				69.9	95.4
	-22.0	-23.3	-10.3	-5.6				-17.4	-19.2
EBIT/Interest	7.7	9.4		7.4				7.8	6.6
	(43) 3.8	(48) 3.7		(12) 3.1				(116) 2.2	(119) 2.6
	1.0	1.6		2.0				.6	.7
Net Profit + Depr., Dep., Amort./Cur. Mat. L/T/D								3.1	2.7
								(14) 1.9	(14) 1.7
								.9	1.1
Fixed/Worth	.4	.9	.8	1.1				.7	.6
	1.3	2.6	4.3	3.1				2.3	2.4
	-5.0	NM	11.7	NM				-4.5	-3.5
Debt/Worth	1.1	1.2	1.4	1.4				1.2	1.3
	13.1	3.1	4.6	3.2				4.3	7.0
	-4.6	NM	14.9	NM				-10.5	-8.1
% Profit Before Taxes/Tangible Net Worth	129.3	61.2		61.0				63.2	64.4
	(29) 42.0	(38) 35.0		(10) 47.2				(94) 19.8	(92) 21.2
	11.2	16.7		33.7				4.3	2.2
% Profit Before Taxes/Total Assets	31.6	18.2	8.1	19.9				16.8	12.8
	11.7	10.4	2.7	7.8				4.2	4.2
	-.5	3.0	-2.0	3.9				-1.2	-.8
Sales/Net Fixed Assets	100.1	11.0	14.3	8.9				21.2	31.4
	17.1	5.0	4.8	2.3				9.1	9.4
	4.7	2.3	1.2	1.3				2.4	2.6
Sales/Total Assets	9.3	3.6	3.3	1.8				4.8	4.7
	5.2	2.3	2.4	1.1				2.8	2.5
	2.8	1.6	.8	.8				1.4	1.3
% Depr., Dep., Amort./Sales	1.1	1.7	2.1	1.1				1.4	1.1
	(28) 5.6	(45) 5.1	(10) 4.5	(12) 3.7				(121) 2.7	(113) 3.4
	11.7	9.0	9.6	7.1				6.9	8.3
% Officers', Directors', Owners' Comp/Sales	3.1	2.4						2.6	2.5
	(30) 5.6	(27) 3.3						(65) 4.4	(69) 4.5
	8.3	6.0						9.2	7.1
Net Sales ($)	72250M	138570M	107567M	334009M	517669M			1030257M	1035562M
Total Assets ($)	13106M	50828M	55960M	273741M	376540M			531101M	578889M

Note: Columns 50-100MM and 100-250MM in the Current Data section are marked "DATA NOT AVAILABLE."

M = $ thousand   MM = $ million
See Pages 11 through 21 for Explanation of Ratios and Data

	Comparative Historical Data			Type of Statement	Current Data Sorted by Sales					
	11	7	6	Unqualified			1	1	1	3
	12	8	1	Reviewed						1
	28	31	23	Compiled	6	9	4	2	1	1
	64	49	51	Tax Returns	19	19	7	4	1	1
	28	63	52	Other	7	25	4	3	8	5
	4/1/04-3/31/05	4/1/05-3/31/06	4/1/06-3/31/07		22 (4/1-9/30/06)			111 (10/1/06-3/31/07)		
	ALL	ALL	ALL		0-1MM	1-3MM	3-5MM	5-10MM	10-25MM	25MM & OVER
	143	158	133	NUMBER OF STATEMENTS	32	53	16	10	11	11
	%	%	%	ASSETS	%	%	%	%	%	%
	10.0	12.3	13.1	Cash & Equivalents	11.1	16.9	8.8	12.8	3.7	16.4
	12.8	12.1	11.9	Trade Receivables (net)	10.2	12.5	13.3	13.0	7.9	15.0
	14.9	12.8	11.0	Inventory	8.3	13.5	10.8	8.4	9.6	10.0
	2.6	3.1	3.7	All Other Current	4.8	4.1	.8	1.8	4.2	4.6
	40.3	40.3	39.7	Total Current	34.5	47.0	33.6	36.1	25.4	46.0
	47.2	43.0	46.5	Fixed Assets (net)	54.1	39.4	58.5	47.6	60.0	26.2
	5.4	7.8	6.1	Intangibles (net)	5.2	6.2	.3	.9	8.1	19.5
	7.1	8.8	7.8	All Other Non-Current	6.3	7.4	7.6	15.4	6.5	8.3
	100.0	100.0	100.0	Total	100.0	100.0	100.0	100.0	100.0	100.0
				LIABILITIES						
	9.2	9.5	7.6	Notes Payable-Short Term	14.5	4.1	5.2	11.9	6.9	4.4
	7.7	7.1	6.6	Cur. Mat.-L.T.D.	7.5	7.0	7.0	4.3	4.9	4.8
	10.1	10.5	9.0	Trade Payables	8.4	9.8	11.8	6.3	6.7	7.8
	.2	.2	.1	Income Taxes Payable	.0	.0	.1	.0	.0	.4
	9.4	8.3	12.5	All Other Current	12.9	18.2	2.7	5.8	6.6	10.5
	36.6	35.6	35.8	Total Current	43.3	39.1	26.9	28.4	25.1	27.9
	36.8	39.5	39.6	Long-Term Debt	52.8	37.8	36.9	33.4	35.3	23.5
	.2	.1	.1	Deferred Taxes	.0	.0	.0	.0	.0	1.0
	14.7	9.5	7.0	All Other Non-Current	5.2	7.5	8.2	6.2	10.5	5.9
	11.8	15.2	17.5	Net Worth	-1.3	15.5	28.0	32.1	29.1	41.7
	100.0	100.0	100.0	Total Liabilties & Net Worth	100.0	100.0	100.0	100.0	100.0	100.0
				INCOME DATA						
	100.0	100.0	100.0	Net Sales	100.0	100.0	100.0	100.0	100.0	100.0
				Gross Profit						
	93.2	92.2	93.7	Operating Expenses	91.0	95.5	95.1	92.3	94.2	91.8
	6.8	7.8	6.3	Operating Profit	9.0	4.5	4.9	7.7	5.8	8.2
	2.8	2.8	1.5	All Other Expenses (net)	4.3	.4	.7	1.7	-.5	1.9
	4.0	5.0	4.8	Profit Before Taxes	4.7	4.1	4.3	5.9	6.2	6.3
				RATIOS						
	2.2	2.2	2.6		3.8	3.1	1.7	4.4	1.9	2.4
	1.2	1.2	1.3	Current	.9	1.2	1.3	1.5	1.0	1.5
	.5	.7	.6		.3	.6	.9	1.0	.4	1.4
	1.5	1.5	1.8		2.1	2.2	1.6	3.9	.8	2.1
(140)	.6	.7	.7	Quick	.6	.7	1.1	1.0	.4	1.3
	.2	.4	.3		.2	.3	.6	.6	.3	.3

											Sales/Receivables												
0	UND	1	482.6	1	382.4		0	UND	1	280.8	1	479.4	0	UND	3	121.0	12	30.6				
9	41.8	8	47.0	10	38.3		4	90.2	7	49.9	11	31.8	11	32.6	16	22.6	19	18.9				
31	11.8	28	12.9	22	16.4		24	15.0	19	18.7	22	16.7	39	9.4	30	12.1	48	7.6				

	Comparative Historical Data				Current Data Sorted by Sales					
				Cost of Sales/Inventory						
				Cost of Sales/Payables						
	12.4	15.2	11.6	Sales/Working Capital	9.2	10.0	30.8	13.1	16.8	5.1
	46.1	41.2	76.4		UND	79.8	122.9	27.8	662.5	11.1
	-18.7	-22.1	-21.8		-7.4	-21.8	NM	NM	-8.7	27.3

							EBIT/Interest								
	8.9		11.8		7.7		5.3		9.6		10.5		5.2	18.0
(123)	3.0	(138)	4.4	(115)	3.5	(26)	1.8	(46)	4.5	(15)	3.8	(10) 3.1	(10) 2.6
	.3		1.4		1.3		.3		1.2		2.6		1.3	1.4

						Net Profit + Depr., Dep., Amort./Cur. Mat. L/T/D					
	29.3		3.1								
(16)	3.0	(14)	2.0								
	2.1		1.3								

						Fixed/Worth					
	.6	.6	.6		.9	.4	1.1	.6	1.1	.3
	2.4	2.1	2.4		12.2	1.5	2.0	1.5	2.5	.8
	-9.4	-14.3	-9.4		-4.9	-8.6	NM	6.7	4.8	-2.7

						Debt/Worth					
	1.2	1.2	1.2		1.7	1.1	1.2	1.0	1.4	.5
	4.6	3.8	3.6		UND	6.1	1.8	3.0	2.8	2.8
	-11.8	-10.7	-11.0		-6.3	-5.7	NM	12.5	5.2	-11.4

							% Profit Before Taxes/Tangible Net Worth							
	91.3		112.1		74.9		47.0		120.5		48.4		70.5	
(102)	29.4	(112)	50.2	(90)	39.7	(17)	20.0	(34)	51.4	(12)	29.2	(10) 44.2	
	4.5		13.5		13.9		11.0		15.1		10.0		-1.2	

						% Profit Before Taxes/Total Assets					
	17.7	24.6	21.2		17.8	27.1	20.5	18.4	16.1	26.5
	4.2	10.3	8.5		4.3	11.8	11.4	10.3	7.8	7.7
	-1.6	1.4	1.1		-5.5	1.1	5.3	3.0	-.3	3.8

						Sales/Net Fixed Assets					
	18.4	21.9	21.2		13.4	60.3	20.4	11.5	14.3	23.8
	6.8	8.0	6.2		3.9	11.0	9.4	4.9	2.3	8.4
	2.5	2.7	3.1		1.4	4.3	3.2	2.3	1.4	3.7

						Sales/Total Assets					
	4.4	4.9	4.8		3.6	6.2	9.0	4.0	3.3	3.2
	2.6	2.5	2.8		2.3	3.1	4.4	3.3	1.5	1.6
	1.4	1.3	1.6		.9	2.2	2.4	1.7	1.0	1.1

							% Depr., Dep., Amort./Sales							
	1.7		1.3		1.7		3.1		1.1		.9			1.1
(107)	4.5	(123)	3.7	(100)	4.7	(24)	8.0	(33)	5.1	(14)	4.6		2.5
	9.7		6.5		8.7		17.1		9.4		5.8			4.4

							% Officers', Directors' Owners' Comp/Sales					
	2.4		2.3		2.5		4.0		3.1				
(76)	4.2	(65)	4.7	(66)	3.9	(11)	5.4	(32)	5.8				
	7.8		10.3		7.7		8.9		8.3				

				Net Sales ($)						
	4050300M	2663382M	1170065M		18224M	96658M	60226M	64289M	170352M	760316M
	1574481M	949418M	770175M	Total Assets ($)	18017M	35017M	15721M	65624M	124344M	511452M

© RMA 2007

M = $ thousand   MM = $ million
See Pages 11 through 21 for Explanation of Ratios and Data

Current Data Sorted by Assets   Comparative Historical Data

0-500M	500M-2MM	2-10MM	10-50MM	50-100MM	100-250MM	Type of Statement	4/1/02-3/31/03 ALL	4/1/03-3/31/04 ALL
		1	2			Unqualified	1	5
2	2	8	5	3	2	Reviewed	12	16
		4				Compiled	3	12
8	4	2	1			Tax Returns	8	8
2	10	5	5			Other	12	21
	11 (4/1-9/30/06)		55 (10/1/06-3/31/07)					
12	16	20	13	3	2	NUMBER OF STATEMENTS	36	62
%	%	%	%	%	%	ASSETS	%	%
8.8	9.2	8.1	9.7			Cash & Equivalents	9.1	10.7
15.2	31.8	26.6	19.4			Trade Receivables (net)	28.4	18.2
.5	12.4	9.4	11.4			Inventory	5.7	7.6
5.4	4.9	3.4	3.1			All Other Current	.9	5.3
29.9	58.4	47.5	43.6			Total Current	44.1	41.9
54.2	34.4	38.8	46.6			Fixed Assets (net)	36.4	42.9
7.0	.8	8.1	4.3			Intangibles (net)	3.3	3.8
8.9	6.4	5.5	5.5			All Other Non-Current	16.1	11.4
100.0	100.0	100.0	100.0			Total	100.0	100.0
						LIABILITIES		
9.7	12.7	6.3	8.1			Notes Payable-Short Term	13.0	8.8
13.7	5.6	6.7	6.7			Cur. Mat.-L.T.D.	4.9	5.9
9.3	25.8	17.6	5.5			Trade Payables	14.3	7.2
.2	.2	.0	.0			Income Taxes Payable	.0	.2
6.9	9.2	12.7	8.3			All Other Current	23.8	9.1
39.9	53.6	43.4	28.6			Total Current	56.1	31.1
28.7	22.0	20.5	24.8			Long-Term Debt	39.4	27.1
.0	.5	.2	1.3			Deferred Taxes	.6	1.1
4.5	.8	10.5	1.2			All Other Non-Current	6.5	8.6
26.9	23.1	25.4	44.1			Net Worth	-2.6	32.1
100.0	100.0	100.0	100.0			Total Liabilities & Net Worth	100.0	100.0
						INCOME DATA		
100.0	100.0	100.0	100.0			Net Sales	100.0	100.0
						Gross Profit		
86.9	97.2	91.0	85.2			Operating Expenses	88.4	88.9
13.1	2.8	9.0	14.8			Operating Profit	11.6	11.1
4.2	1.7	4.0	4.4			All Other Expenses (net)	7.2	5.1
8.9	1.1	5.1	10.4			Profit Before Taxes	4.4	5.9
						RATIOS		
1.3	2.9	1.9	1.7				2.0	3.0
.5	1.7	1.1	1.4			Current	1.0	1.2
.4	.9	.6	.9				.5	.8
1.2	2.2	1.3	1.6				2.0	1.8
.5	1.0	.8	.9			Quick	.8	.9
.3	.5	.4	.4				.4	.5
0 UND	0 UND	2 175.1	2 158.4				0 UND	3 114.6
0 UND	23 16.0	33 11.2	35 10.4			Sales/Receivables	33 11.0	27 13.4
55 6.7	43 8.6	49 7.5	54 6.8				46 8.0	41 8.9
						Cost of Sales/Inventory		
						Cost of Sales/Payables		
85.5	7.2	11.5	8.8				9.0	8.8
-10.0	22.2	96.5	17.9			Sales/Working Capital	151.2	32.4
-4.0	-84.0	-17.5	-52.0				-14.7	-31.8
	4.4	10.6	13.1				8.1	9.7
(12) 3.6	(17) 2.6	(11) 5.2				EBIT/Interest	(22) 3.2	(47) 2.5
	-12.1	1.2	2.3				1.7	1.3
								2.3
						Net Profit + Depr., Dep., Amort./Cur. Mat. L/T/D	(16) 1.2	
								.4
.5	.4	.4	.3				.2	.4
3.3	1.2	1.9	1.1			Fixed/Worth	1.2	1.4
NM	29.8	-10.8	2.4				28.6	5.2
.5	.7	1.1	.9				1.0	.7
3.1	3.3	4.4	1.4			Debt/Worth	4.0	2.7
NM	72.9	-26.2	2.6				-20.2	8.4
	78.4	83.4	35.6				69.2	23.6
(13) 17.2	(14) 24.6	26.7				% Profit Before Taxes/Tangible Net Worth	(26) 16.9	(51) 12.5
	-2.4	11.5	14.3				6.3	2.6
36.4	18.2	17.6	13.1				13.8	8.2
15.6	4.5	6.5	9.7			% Profit Before Taxes/Total Assets	5.6	3.5
-1.7	-3.0	1.0	4.4				1.1	.9
25.4	132.4	76.3	25.7				139.2	32.6
2.8	26.3	6.2	8.3			Sales/Net Fixed Assets	11.3	5.1
.6	3.7	2.2	.8				2.7	1.5
2.3	6.8	4.4	3.6				4.3	3.4
1.7	3.0	2.0	2.2			Sales/Total Assets	2.7	1.9
.5	2.3	1.1	.6				1.4	1.0
	.6	.4	.8				.6	1.4
(12) 1.4	3.3	(12) 4.3				% Depr., Dep., Amort./Sales	(28) 3.1	(50) 3.8
	6.9	10.8	14.0				13.1	10.7
							1.4	1.0
						% Officers', Directors' Owners' Comp/Sales	(10) 8.0	(15) 2.8
							23.2	7.6
6458M	80868M	269478M	706446M	793244M	596602M	Net Sales ($)	534847M	2020796M
3963M	16542M	85908M	313251M	241453M	334117M	Total Assets ($)	227142M	728661M

© RMA 2007

M = $ thousand   MM = $ million
See Pages 11 through 21 for Explanation of Ratios and Data

Comparative Historical Data   Current Data Sorted by Sales

	4/1/04-3/31/05 ALL	4/1/05-3/31/06 ALL	4/1/06-3/31/07 ALL	0-1MM	1-3MM	3-5MM	5-10MM	10-25MM	25MM & OVER
Type of Statement						11 (4/1-9/30/06)		55 (10/1/06-3/31/07)	
Unqualified	4	6	10			2	1		7
Reviewed	9	9	15	4		1	1	6	3
Compiled	3	13	4			1	1		3
Tax Returns	9	16	15	10	2	2	1		
Other	13	17	22	3	3	4	2	5	4
NUMBER OF STATEMENTS	38	61	66	17	5	10	6	11	17
ASSETS	%	%	%	%	%	%	%	%	%
Cash & Equivalents	11.0	11.7	9.6	7.0		11.3		7.7	14.3
Trade Receivables (net)	28.6	28.7	24.0	11.6		21.4		38.1	29.3
Inventory	5.8	9.2	8.7	.6		22.8		7.7	11.3
All Other Current	4.2	2.8	3.9	4.0		4.0		8.9	2.4
Total Current	49.6	52.4	46.3	23.1		59.5		62.4	57.4
Fixed Assets (net)	38.9	35.0	42.0	69.3		30.6		32.5	32.2
Intangibles (net)	4.4	2.5	5.0	1.3		.3		1.5	3.9
All Other Non-Current	7.1	10.1	6.7	6.3		9.6		3.6	6.4
Total	100.0	100.0	100.0	100.0		100.0		100.0	100.0
LIABILITIES									
Notes Payable-Short Term	9.1	11.3	9.1	6.3		4.5		13.8	8.7
Cur. Mat.-L.T.D.	4.3	7.5	7.5	10.5		8.6		7.0	5.1
Trade Payables	12.6	13.3	15.5	5.9		11.3		19.4	16.0
Income Taxes Payable	.2	.1	.1	.2		.0		.0	.1
All Other Current	13.0	8.9	10.0	4.3		7.5		15.6	11.2
Total Current	39.2	41.1	42.2	27.1		31.8		55.8	41.2
Long-Term Debt	28.8	26.2	23.0	36.5		17.8		20.4	15.0
Deferred Taxes	.5	.1	.5	.0		1.0		1.6	.2
All Other Non-Current	4.9	4.9	4.7	4.2		3.2		3.0	2.0
Net Worth	26.7	27.7	29.5	32.1		46.1		19.2	41.6
Total Liabilties & Net Worth	100.0	100.0	100.0	100.0		100.0		100.0	100.0
INCOME DATA									
Net Sales	100.0	100.0	100.0	100.0		100.0		100.0	100.0
Gross Profit									
Operating Expenses	90.3	89.7	91.0	75.3		90.0		96.0	95.4
Operating Profit	9.7	10.3	9.0	24.7		10.0		4.0	4.6
All Other Expenses (net)	3.5	2.5	3.1	10.8		-.1		1.2	-.3
Profit Before Taxes	6.3	7.8	5.9	14.0		10.1		2.7	4.8
RATIOS									
Current	2.1	2.0	1.9	2.3		2.5		1.6	1.6
	1.2	1.3	1.1	.6		2.0		1.1	1.2
	.8	.7	.7	.4		1.5		.8	.9
Quick	1.6	1.6	1.5	2.2		1.9		1.3	1.5
	1.0	1.0	.8	.5		1.1		.9	.9
	.7	.5	.4	.2		.5		.7	.6
Sales/Receivables	9 40.7	0 UND	0 UND	0 UND		0 UND		15 24.6	23 15.8
	33 11.2	32 11.5	26 13.9	0 UND		25 14.7		33 11.2	33 11.2
	45 8.1	50 7.3	48 7.6	43 8.5		58 6.3		49 7.4	49 7.4
Cost of Sales/Inventory									
Cost of Sales/Payables									
Sales/Working Capital	13.0	11.8	11.0	22.2		4.6		12.2	12.8
	36.8	27.3	96.5	-12.1		8.2		151.6	38.3
	-47.3	-17.1	-17.8	-4.3		11.9		-33.2	-103.9
EBIT/Interest	6.6	11.7	9.0					3.5	14.5
	(29) 3.9	(54) 5.8	(51) 3.5					(10) 2.4	(15) 9.1
	1.8	2.3	1.2					-3.5	2.2
Net Profit + Depr., Dep., Amort./Cur. Mat. L/T/D			6.3						
		(14)	2.1						
			1.2						
Fixed/Worth	.3	.3	.4	1.2		.3		.4	.2
	1.4	1.1	1.5	2.4		.4		2.0	.5
	9.5	3.8	4.4	29.2		1.7		3.3	1.5
Debt/Worth	1.1	1.0	1.1	.6		.4		2.0	.9
	2.6	2.7	2.3	2.5		1.3		5.4	1.7
	29.3	7.9	10.2	48.5		2.2		12.1	3.4
% Profit Before Taxes/Tangible Net Worth	43.2	94.7	55.9	74.1		62.9			50.1
	(30) 26.7	(51) 32.6	(54) 25.2	(14) 23.0		19.6			30.6
	12.0	19.2	8.8	5.4		8.4			13.9
% Profit Before Taxes/Total Assets	11.1	20.8	18.5	31.4		19.3		8.5	22.6
	7.1	11.1	6.0	2.7		9.0		4.5	9.8
	3.6	3.2	1.5	-.1		4.4		-3.6	3.0
Sales/Net Fixed Assets	45.9	54.2	38.0	7.0		31.1		92.8	104.5
	8.9	10.8	8.0	.8		6.4		27.0	9.0
	2.1	2.6	2.2	.4		3.1		3.6	3.5
Sales/Total Assets	4.9	4.5	4.2	2.0		2.8		8.8	4.9
	2.9	2.3	2.3	.7		2.2		4.5	3.2
	1.3	1.6	.9	.4		.9		2.2	1.9
% Depr., Dep., Amort./Sales	.8	1.1	.7	6.6				.3	.2
	(28) 2.5	(50) 3.1	(56) 3.3	(14) 13.1				.7	(14) 2.1
	7.1	6.1	10.1	28.3				7.4	4.3
% Officers', Directors' Owners' Comp/Sales	2.8	2.0	1.6						
	(13) 5.3	(29) 4.3	(21) 3.5						
	8.9	11.0	5.0						
Net Sales ($)	639136M	1296516M	2453096M	8815M	10015M	38041M	37986M	174495M	2183744M
Total Assets ($)	236366M	576277M	995234M	23694M	8994M	29979M	14292M	73286M	844989M

M = $ thousand   MM = $ million
See Pages 11 through 21 for Explanation of Ratios and Data

TRANSPORTATION—Freight Transportation Arrangement NAICS 488510 (SIC 4731)

		Current Data Sorted by Assets					Comparative Historical Data	

Type of Statement

						Type of Statement		
3	2	11	22	8	12	Unqualified	35	44
2	12	45	23		1	Reviewed	59	65
12	19	27	7	1		Compiled	56	74
16	20	11				Tax Returns	31	35
16	29	41	35	6	4	Other	79	84
	62 (4/1-9/30/06)		323 (10/1/06-3/31/07)				4/1/02-3/31/03	4/1/03-3/31/04
0-500M	500M-2MM	2-10MM	10-50MM	50-100MM	100-250MM		ALL	ALL
49	82	135	87	15	17	NUMBER OF STATEMENTS	260	302
%	%	%	%	%	%	ASSETS	%	%
26.5	13.8	10.0	9.0	10.9	12.9	Cash & Equivalents	8.3	9.2
38.7	52.5	55.5	49.5	25.2	32.4	Trade Receivables (net)	48.5	49.0
.0	.8	1.3	2.5	4.3	.3	Inventory	1.6	1.1
7.8	5.5	7.4	4.8	4.8	2.1	All Other Current	5.3	5.7
73.1	72.5	74.3	65.8	45.1	47.8	Total Current	63.7	65.0
16.2	16.7	16.0	20.0	37.6	32.0	Fixed Assets (net)	23.8	24.0
1.4	2.0	2.6	6.3	11.1	13.4	Intangibles (net)	3.5	3.4
9.3	8.7	7.0	7.9	6.2	6.8	All Other Non-Current	9.0	7.6
100.0	100.0	100.0	100.0	100.0	100.0	Total	100.0	100.0
						LIABILITIES		
19.1	9.8	11.8	8.8	7.1	2.2	Notes Payable-Short Term	10.9	11.3
3.1	1.8	3.6	3.0	4.1	3.0	Cur. Mat.-L.T.D.	6.5	5.3
22.6	29.8	33.7	26.5	9.3	15.8	Trade Payables	24.2	26.9
.2	.2	.3	.2	.1	.3	Income Taxes Payable	.3	.3
22.7	8.8	15.5	11.5	20.0	11.0	All Other Current	13.6	16.1
67.7	50.3	64.9	50.1	40.5	32.3	Total Current	55.5	59.9
11.2	12.4	8.7	13.3	18.8	21.7	Long-Term Debt	14.0	12.5
.0	.1	.2	.5	1.7	2.4	Deferred Taxes	.7	.7
7.3	3.0	3.3	3.1	1.8	5.3	All Other Non-Current	4.5	4.2
13.8	34.0	22.9	33.1	37.2	38.4	Net Worth	25.2	22.7
100.0	100.0	100.0	100.0	100.0	100.0	Total Liabilties & Net Worth	100.0	100.0
						INCOME DATA		
100.0	100.0	100.0	100.0	100.0	100.0	Net Sales	100.0	100.0
						Gross Profit		
92.2	95.2	95.5	94.2	92.7	93.9	Operating Expenses	96.6	96.2
7.8	4.8	4.5	5.8	7.3	6.1	Operating Profit	3.4	3.8
.0	1.3	.2	1.0	2.0	1.0	All Other Expenses (net)	.7	.7
7.8	3.4	4.3	4.8	5.3	5.1	Profit Before Taxes	2.7	3.1
						RATIOS		
2.7	2.4	1.6	1.6	1.6	1.8		1.6	1.5
1.3	1.4	1.1	1.3	1.0	1.4	Current	1.2	1.1
.6	1.0	1.0	1.0	.6	1.2		.9	.9
2.7	2.2	1.5	1.4	1.3	1.7		1.5	1.4
1.2	1.2	1.1	1.2	.9	1.4	Quick	1.1	1.0
.4	.9	.8	.9	.4	1.0		.7	.7

0	UND	22	16.2	29	12.4	32	11.3	29	12.6	39	9.3		Sales/Receivables	26	13.8	27	13.5

0 UND	22 16.2	29 12.4	32 11.3	29 12.6	39 9.3	Sales/Receivables	26 13.8	27 13.5
19 19.4	33 11.2	41 8.8	46 7.9	38 9.7	44 8.3		38 9.6	41 9.0
45 8.1	44 8.3	63 5.8	67 5.5	53 6.8	49 7.5		55 6.6	53 6.9
						Cost of Sales/Inventory		
						Cost of Sales/Payables		
13.5	12.4	12.9	12.0	10.7	11.6	Sales/Working Capital	17.0	17.2
72.2	28.7	46.5	22.9	28.7	18.2		52.6	51.8
-65.8	461.5	-220.4	229.2	-12.4	43.9		-71.7	-54.0
57.1	28.8	16.4	20.3	11.5	46.9	EBIT/Interest	13.6	15.8
(25) 7.8	(62) 9.5	(113) 5.0	(79) 5.7	3.2	10.6		(226) 3.4	(265) 4.7
1.8	1.3	1.9	2.4	1.9	1.7		1.2	1.3
	10.4	9.0	14.5			Net Profit + Depr., Dep., Amort./Cur. Mat. L/T/D	4.9	9.5
	(10) 4.0	(30) 2.5	(31) 4.3				(63) 1.7	(67) 2.3
	2.5	.8	1.8				.8	1.3
.0	.1	.1	.1	.3	.5	Fixed/Worth	.2	.2
.1	.3	.5	.3	1.5	.9		.6	.7
3.9	1.1	1.9	1.9	2.8	3.1		2.7	3.9
.8	.7	1.5	1.4	1.1	1.3	Debt/Worth	1.4	1.6
2.3	2.8	4.2	3.1	2.4	1.9		2.9	3.4
-25.7	11.4	9.2	7.7	17.0	7.9		7.3	10.4
127.9	119.8	55.2	59.9	38.3	50.4	% Profit Before Taxes/Tangible Net Worth	52.9	52.6
(36) 60.1	(71) 34.0	(115) 32.3	(80) 32.9	(13) 19.2	(14) 34.9		(218) 18.5	(249) 26.3
10.2	10.8	11.8	16.2	-6.6	24.6		4.9	6.0
47.4	24.2	16.5	15.3	9.0	16.9	% Profit Before Taxes/Total Assets	13.1	14.6
18.6	9.1	7.2	7.5	6.7	10.4		5.0	5.5
3.1	1.2	1.9	3.0	2.7	2.0		.6	.8
UND	394.3	255.9	146.6	24.7	50.9	Sales/Net Fixed Assets	110.9	112.8
380.8	70.3	50.5	38.6	5.1	6.3		32.4	35.3
32.6	18.6	12.2	9.0	1.9	2.9		8.2	7.5
14.5	8.2	6.5	5.5	2.6	3.4	Sales/Total Assets	6.0	6.5
6.5	5.7	4.1	3.3	1.5	1.7		4.1	4.4
4.0	3.2	2.2	1.5	1.0	1.2		2.3	2.2
.2	.1	.2	.3	.9		% Depr., Dep., Amort./Sales	.3	.3
(20) .4	(60) .4	(117) .5	(76) .6	(13) 5.4			(223) .8	(245) .9
2.1	1.7	1.8	2.1	6.6			3.3	3.1
1.0	1.1	1.0	.8			% Officers', Directors' Owners' Comp/Sales	1.2	1.4
(15) 2.1	(32) 2.4	(38) 1.6	(16) 1.8				(85) 3.2	(90) 3.0
4.8	3.5	3.3	4.1				5.7	5.8
119593M	592376M	3082957M	6309389M	2091897M	6190574M	Net Sales ($)	6450077M	8711936M
11096M	97146M	700212M	1764205M	1095265M	2805005M	Total Assets ($)	2086731M	3272862M

© RMA 2007

M = $ thousand   MM = $ million
See Pages 11 through 21 for Explanation of Ratios and Data

Comparative Historical Data / Current Data Sorted by Sales

			Type of Statement						
50	53	58	Unqualified	3	1	3	1	9	41
73	65	83	Reviewed	2	2	3	13	24	39
59	58	66	Compiled	5	8	14	10	15	14
40	46	47	Tax Returns	8	11	6	12	8	2
94	139	131	Other	9	13	10	20	27	52
4/1/04-3/31/05 ALL	4/1/05-3/31/06 ALL	4/1/06-3/31/07 ALL		62 (4/1-9/30/06)			323 (10/1/06-3/31/07)		
				0-1MM	1-3MM	3-5MM	5-10MM	10-25MM	25MM & OVER
316	361	385	**NUMBER OF STATEMENTS**	27	35	36	56	83	148
%	%	%	**ASSETS**	%	%	%	%	%	%
10.5	10.9	12.8	Cash & Equivalents	19.4	19.9	20.8	10.7	11.1	9.8
48.7	50.6	49.2	Trade Receivables (net)	36.1	43.7	49.2	46.3	48.7	54.2
1.5	1.5	1.4	Inventory	.0	3.1	.7	2.6	.4	1.5
6.2	6.2	6.1	All Other Current	6.4	7.6	3.9	7.1	7.5	5.2
66.9	69.3	69.5	Total Current	61.9	74.3	74.6	66.7	67.7	70.7
22.0	19.5	18.6	Fixed Assets (net)	31.2	19.2	14.7	14.4	22.4	16.7
3.7	4.2	4.0	Intangibles (net)	1.7	.8	1.5	5.2	3.1	5.8
7.4	7.0	7.8	All Other Non-Current	5.2	5.8	9.2	13.7	6.9	6.8
100.0	100.0	100.0	Total	100.0	100.0	100.0	100.0	100.0	100.0
			LIABILITIES						
12.0	10.4	11.0	Notes Payable-Short Term	8.5	15.1	8.7	16.7	11.6	8.6
4.2	2.9	3.0	Cur. Mat.-L.T.D.	3.4	4.3	1.8	2.1	3.6	3.0
26.3	28.2	28.1	Trade Payables	17.6	26.7	25.8	25.1	29.8	31.0
.2	.3	.2	Income Taxes Payable	.0	.3	.4	.2	.1	.3
13.8	13.0	14.1	All Other Current	18.3	19.0	12.3	9.4	16.7	12.9
56.5	54.8	56.4	Total Current	47.8	65.3	49.0	53.5	61.8	55.7
13.5	12.1	11.8	Long-Term Debt	25.0	14.8	9.3	11.0	11.9	9.6
.5	.5	.4	Deferred Taxes	.2	.0	.1	.1	.2	.8
6.8	4.8	3.7	All Other Non-Current	12.9	1.8	3.9	3.3	3.1	3.0
22.7	27.8	27.7	Net Worth	14.1	18.1	37.8	32.1	23.0	30.9
100.0	100.0	100.0	Total Liabilties & Net Worth	100.0	100.0	100.0	100.0	100.0	100.0
			INCOME DATA						
100.0	100.0	100.0	Net Sales	100.0	100.0	100.0	100.0	100.0	100.0
			Gross Profit						
95.5	95.2	94.5	Operating Expenses	85.8	94.4	88.4	96.3	95.1	96.7
4.5	4.8	5.5	Operating Profit	14.2	5.6	11.6	3.7	4.9	3.3
.7	.9	.7	All Other Expenses (net)	4.7	-.6	.6	.8	.3	.5
3.8	4.0	4.7	Profit Before Taxes	9.5	6.2	11.0	2.9	4.5	2.8
			RATIOS						
1.7	1.8	1.8		3.2	2.7	3.5	1.9	1.8	1.6
1.2	1.2	1.2	Current	1.7	1.3	1.4	1.2	1.2	1.3
.9	1.0	1.0		.7	.8	1.1	.8	1.0	1.0
1.6	1.6	1.7		3.2	1.8	3.1	1.7	1.6	1.4
1.1	1.1	1.2	Quick	1.5	1.1	1.3	1.1	1.1	1.2
.7	.9	.9		.6	.5	1.0	.6	.9	.9
27 13.6	26 14.1	27 13.3		2 214.3	1 469.3	25 14.8	21 17.2	27 13.5	32 11.4
43 8.6	40 9.2	39 9.4	Sales/Receivables	53 6.9	31 11.7	42 8.7	33 11.1	37 9.8	42 8.8
56 6.6	54 6.7	56 6.5		182 2.0	55 6.6	140 2.6	49 7.5	49 7.4	53 6.9
			Cost of Sales/Inventory						
			Cost of Sales/Payables						
13.4	14.1	12.3		3.0	6.4	5.5	11.5	14.5	16.4
36.5	33.3	32.3	Sales/Working Capital	13.3	50.2	13.7	37.4	35.4	34.0
-81.5	999.8	-409.6		-7.4	-39.8	58.9	-68.1	671.9	-999.8
17.2	23.3	22.0		69.0	21.7	36.4	12.2	23.8	20.9
(266) 5.8	(291) 5.9	(311) 6.0	EBIT/Interest	(10) 6.4	(22) 6.0	(24) 9.6	(47) 4.3	(71) 5.0	(137) 7.6
2.7	2.0	1.9		.6	.8	2.0	1.3	2.0	2.3
15.2	5.5	10.4						6.6	9.6
(71) 3.0	(76) 2.8	(86) 3.7	Net Profit + Depr., Dep., Amort./Cur. Mat. L/T/D				(14) 4.1	(55) 3.6
1.7	1.7	1.6						1.3	1.8
.2	.1	.1		.0	.0	.1	.1	.1	.1
.5	.5	.4	Fixed/Worth	.2	.3	.2	.4	.7	.4
3.0	1.9	2.1		11.0	2.8	1.0	1.7	2.5	1.8
1.4	1.2	1.2		.7	1.0	.4	1.1	1.3	1.4
2.9	3.2	3.1	Debt/Worth	1.8	2.4	2.6	3.7	3.6	2.9
12.9	8.1	9.8		-12.6	80.4	9.1	28.4	13.3	7.5
65.5	71.7	75.1		55.5	106.0	142.6	75.5	94.7	52.7
(256) 31.5	(314) 32.3	(329) 33.1	% Profit Before Taxes/Tangible Net Worth	(19) 18.2	(27) 21.3	(34) 59.0	(49) 32.8	(71) 37.5	(129) 31.8
10.7	11.5	11.6		4.7	8.7	17.6	9.6	17.1	13.5
15.9	18.6	18.6		20.8	36.2	29.6	19.6	20.0	15.5
7.7	7.7	8.4	% Profit Before Taxes/Total Assets	4.9	8.9	13.6	6.0	9.5	8.0
2.4	1.9	2.2		.0	1.0	2.4	.9	3.2	2.7
163.1	207.9	257.6		UND	UND	137.7	371.4	217.2	270.0
45.8	55.1	52.3	Sales/Net Fixed Assets	15.0	53.5	31.4	44.5	40.4	74.4
9.7	11.6	10.1		6.2	7.0	15.6	15.3	7.2	15.9
6.2	6.8	6.5		4.1	11.1	6.0	8.2	7.6	6.5
4.2	4.5	4.3	Sales/Total Assets	1.5	4.0	3.1	4.8	3.9	4.9
2.0	2.2	1.9		.3	1.4	.9	1.7	2.2	2.8
.3	.2	.2		1.8	.3	.2	.3	.1	.2
(247) .7	(262) .6	(294) .5	% Depr., Dep., Amort./Sales	(14) 5.9	(20) .8	(27) .7	(41) .8	(74) .7	(118) .4
2.8	2.2	2.1		16.2	2.3	2.7	1.9	2.8	.9
1.1	1.1	1.0		1.3	2.2	1.0		.9	.7
(116) 2.5	(123) 2.1	(104) 2.0	% Officers', Directors' Owners' Comp/Sales		(11) 4.6	(15) 2.8	(18) 2.4	(28) 1.2	(29) 1.3
5.5	4.1	3.7			8.9	6.1	4.2	3.1	2.4
11324946M	17679755M	18386786M	Net Sales ($)	12603M	64444M	144502M	426980M	1368686M	16369571M
4301073M	5420085M	6472929M	Total Assets ($)	14169M	47620M	117748M	182142M	575337M	5535913M

M = $ thousand   MM = $ million
See Pages 11 through 21 for Explanation of Ratios and Data

Current Data Sorted by Assets						Type of Statement	Comparative Historical Data	
	2	3	3	2	1	Unqualified	5	5
	2	3	2			Reviewed	11	15
1	4	2	1			Compiled	7	8
3	3					Tax Returns	7	10
2	8	9	2		1	Other	21	18
0-500M	16 (4/1-9/30/06) 500M-2MM	2-10MM	38 (10/1/06-3/31/07) 10-50MM	50-100MM	100-250MM		4/1/02-3/31/03 ALL	4/1/03-3/31/04 ALL
6	19	17	8	2	2	NUMBER OF STATEMENTS	51	56
%	%	%	%	%	%	**ASSETS**	%	%
	4.7	8.1				Cash & Equivalents	10.4	9.7
	36.9	43.3				Trade Receivables (net)	31.3	31.7
	9.8	7.5				Inventory	13.0	14.2
	6.8	2.3				All Other Current	1.9	2.7
	58.2	61.2				Total Current	56.7	58.3
	27.5	24.6				Fixed Assets (net)	33.6	31.9
	4.0	2.8				Intangibles (net)	4.8	5.0
	10.3	11.4				All Other Non-Current	4.9	4.8
	100.0	100.0				Total	100.0	100.0
						LIABILITIES		
	11.3	12.6				Notes Payable-Short Term	9.3	7.2
	8.0	1.1				Cur. Mat.-L.T.D.	6.2	5.1
	13.7	17.4				Trade Payables	18.8	17.4
	.3	.2				Income Taxes Payable	.3	.2
	14.0	19.6				All Other Current	9.0	10.1
	47.3	51.0				Total Current	43.7	40.0
	16.0	10.7				Long-Term Debt	20.4	20.3
	.1	.3				Deferred Taxes	.0	.0
	14.3	3.2				All Other Non-Current	3.2	7.6
	22.3	34.9				Net Worth	32.7	32.2
	100.0	100.0				Total Liabilties & Net Worth	100.0	100.0
						INCOME DATA		
	100.0	100.0				Net Sales	100.0	100.0
						Gross Profit		
	95.3	95.0				Operating Expenses	94.7	94.7
	4.7	5.0				Operating Profit	5.3	5.3
	1.4	1.3				All Other Expenses (net)	1.2	1.5
	3.4	3.7				Profit Before Taxes	4.1	3.8
						RATIOS		
	2.1	2.0					2.0	2.4
	1.3	1.2				Current	1.4	1.4
	.8	.9					.9	1.0
	1.6	1.7					1.3	2.0
	1.2	1.0				Quick	.9	.9
	.5	.8					.6	.6
	35 10.3	48 7.7					20 18.5	26 14.0
	49 7.5	66 5.6				Sales/Receivables	39 9.4	45 8.2
	62 5.9	77 4.7					56 6.5	70 5.2
						Cost of Sales/Inventory		
						Cost of Sales/Payables		
	8.1	7.4					11.6	7.8
	19.9	31.3				Sales/Working Capital	22.7	18.2
	-35.8	-60.9					-55.4	NM
	12.6	15.7					11.1	10.5
	(18) 2.9	(15) 5.9				EBIT/Interest	(43) 3.7	(46) 4.7
	.7	2.1					1.8	1.7
						Net Profit + Depr., Dep., Amort./Cur. Mat. L/T/D	21.6	17.6
							(11) 3.2	(11) 5.3
							1.3	1.4
	.3	.2					.3	.2
	1.5	.6				Fixed/Worth	1.2	1.2
	2.7	1.1					3.3	2.9
	1.1	.8					.7	.9
	3.0	1.7				Debt/Worth	2.3	2.6
	10.8	4.7					6.3	10.4
	88.6	47.2					48.6	54.9
	(15) 37.3	(15) 14.2				% Profit Before Taxes/Tangible Net Worth	(44) 30.7	(49) 28.6
	22.8	8.0					7.2	9.6
	29.5	13.6					19.8	18.1
	12.2	7.5				% Profit Before Taxes/Total Assets	8.3	8.0
	1.6	1.9					2.1	1.3
	40.5	31.8					35.8	30.5
	16.5	10.6				Sales/Net Fixed Assets	10.0	11.7
	5.2	5.7					4.2	5.2
	3.9	3.1					4.0	3.6
	2.5	2.3				Sales/Total Assets	2.9	2.9
	1.6	1.2					2.1	1.5
	.8	.8					.9	.9
	(15) 2.9	(16) 2.0				% Depr., Dep., Amort./Sales	(43) 1.8	(42) 1.6
	5.4	5.0					4.3	4.7
	2.8						1.9	2.9
	(10) 7.8					% Officers', Directors' Owners' Comp/Sales	(24) 4.7	(24) 4.8
	15.8						7.7	8.0
8853M	72251M	213187M	477594M	279241M	488689M	Net Sales ($)	766659M	748312M
1129M	24769M	85252M	193112M	125483M	319880M	Total Assets ($)	289558M	395474M

M = $ thousand   MM = $ million
See Pages 11 through 21 for Explanation of Ratios and Data

Comparative Historical Data | Current Data Sorted by Sales

					Type of Statement						
	7		12		11	Unqualified			3	1	1	6
	12		10		7	Reviewed		1	2	2	1	1
	10		6		8	Compiled	1	2	2	2		1
	9		7		6	Tax Returns	2	2	1	1		
	21		16		22	Other	3	2	2	3	5	4
	4/1/04- 3/31/05 ALL		4/1/05- 3/31/06 ALL		4/1/06- 3/31/07 ALL		0-1MM	16 (4/1-9/30/06) 1-3MM	3-5MM	38 (10/1/06-3/31/07) 5-10MM	10-25MM	25MM & OVER
	59		51		54	NUMBER OF STATEMENTS	6	7	11	11	7	12
	%		%		%	ASSETS	%	%	%	%	%	%
	11.5		10.3		9.1	Cash & Equivalents			8.3	15.3		13.6
	30.4		28.5		37.6	Trade Receivables (net)			40.9	38.0		35.3
	11.3		10.6		9.6	Inventory			8.7	8.0		16.9
	4.4		5.5		4.6	All Other Current			2.9	5.0		2.8
	57.5		54.9		60.9	Total Current			60.8	66.3		68.6
	32.9		33.6		24.1	Fixed Assets (net)			22.4	23.6		18.3
	3.1		2.5		3.9	Intangibles (net)			1.1	.0		7.2
	6.5		9.1		11.1	All Other Non-Current			15.7	10.1		5.9
	100.0		100.0		100.0	Total			100.0	100.0		100.0
					LIABILITIES						
	11.4		8.3		13.1	Notes Payable-Short Term			5.1	28.6		6.8
	3.8		4.4		5.6	Cur. Mat.-L.T.D.			4.6	3.0		2.5
	18.4		14.7		24.2	Trade Payables			16.0	15.3		17.5
	.1		.4		.4	Income Taxes Payable			.0	.6		1.0
	10.9		13.4		18.8	All Other Current			16.9	21.9		22.3
	44.7		41.2		62.1	Total Current			42.6	69.4		50.1
	18.7		21.6		14.5	Long-Term Debt			8.2	7.1		15.1
	.1		.0		.1	Deferred Taxes			.0	.0		.1
	15.1		9.4		7.7	All Other Non-Current			21.4	1.3		5.7
	21.5		27.8		15.5	Net Worth			27.7	22.3		29.0
	100.0		100.0		100.0	Total Liabilties & Net Worth			100.0	100.0		100.0
					INCOME DATA						
	100.0		100.0		100.0	Net Sales			100.0	100.0		100.0
					Gross Profit						
	95.1		93.6		94.8	Operating Expenses			94.9	96.7		93.2
	4.9		6.4		5.2	Operating Profit			5.1	3.3		6.8
	1.4		1.6		1.1	All Other Expenses (net)			-.2	1.2		.4
	3.5		4.8		4.1	Profit Before Taxes			5.3	2.1		6.4
					RATIOS						
	2.6		2.1		2.0				2.1	2.4		1.9
	1.3		1.3		1.2	Current			1.5	1.1		1.4
	.9		.9		.8				1.2	.7		1.0
	1.8		1.4		1.4				1.5	1.8		1.3
	.9		.8		.9	Quick			1.2	.8		.9
	.6		.5		.5				.8	.5		.7
28	12.9	25	14.5	33	11.0				46	7.9	29	12.4			29	12.6
41	8.9	44	8.4	52	7.1	Sales/Receivables			62	5.9	52	7.0			49	7.4
56	6.5	57	6.4	68	5.4				105	3.5	70	5.2			62	5.9
					Cost of Sales/Inventory						
					Cost of Sales/Payables						
	6.5		8.0		7.8				5.9	5.3		6.9
	29.4		21.4		31.0	Sales/Working Capital			9.5	53.3		17.3
	-76.1		-60.9		-41.0				27.6	-19.8		63.1
	9.8		31.4		10.0					23.8		6.7
(51)	3.4	(44)	2.6	(48)	4.5	EBIT/Interest				3.2	(11)	5.4
	.4		.4		1.3					-1.2		4.1
	15.1		51.9		10.3							
(14)	2.5	(13)	1.4	(10)	3.4	Net Profit + Depr., Dep., Amort./Cur. Mat. L/T/D						
	-.1		.5		2.1							
	.3		.3		.2				.1	.6		.2
	1.1		1.1		.7	Fixed/Worth			.4	.9		.6
	4.5		9.3		2.4				2.2	1.7		2.8
	1.1		.9		1.1				.7	.7		1.3
	2.8		2.5		2.9	Debt/Worth			1.6	4.0		3.5
	11.6		15.7		31.0				3.0	10.8		54.7
	65.4		60.7		67.1				64.2			87.0
(48)	29.8	(41)	22.7	(42)	26.4	% Profit Before Taxes/Tangible Net Worth		(10)	25.0		(10)	38.4
	1.4		4.5		11.2				5.5			20.1
	18.6		27.2		16.9				32.9	13.9		13.9
	5.3		3.9		8.7	% Profit Before Taxes/Total Assets			6.8	7.5		11.3
	-2.1		-1.6		1.6				1.4	-8.0		5.2
	27.0		32.0		40.9				22.7	54.9		59.8
	11.1		11.7		16.1	Sales/Net Fixed Assets			14.5	16.6		16.4
	5.8		5.0		5.6				5.3	8.3		8.8
	3.7		3.6		3.4				2.5	6.4		3.1
	2.9		2.7		2.5	Sales/Total Assets			2.3	3.3		2.7
	1.8		1.6		1.7				1.2	2.3		2.0
	1.2		1.0		.8				.7			.3
(50)	2.6	(47)	1.9	(44)	1.8	% Depr., Dep., Amort./Sales		(10)	3.7		(11)	1.1
	5.2		3.9		4.7				5.4			2.3
	1.4		1.7		1.6							
(25)	3.3	(20)	5.7	(20)	4.5	% Officers', Directors' Owners' Comp/Sales						
	6.2		10.2		11.7							
	973238M		1327867M		1539815M	Net Sales ($)	3850M	13402M	43728M	80893M	140743M	1257199M
	419964M		537120M		749625M	Total Assets ($)	1473M	7812M	25072M	31302M	51304M	632662M

Current Data Sorted by Assets   Comparative Historical Data

						Type of Statement		
	3	6	8	5	7	Unqualified	20	20
	2	8	9		1	Reviewed	22	23
6	8	7		1		Compiled	25	40
8	8	3	1			Tax Returns	18	32
4	12	16	8		3	Other	34	45
	21 (4/1-9/30/06)		113 (10/1/06-3/31/07)				4/1/02- 3/31/03	4/1/03- 3/31/04
0-500M	500M-2MM	2-10MM	10-50MM	50-100MM	100-250MM		ALL	ALL
18	33	40	26	6	11	NUMBER OF STATEMENTS	119	160
%	%	%	%	%	%	ASSETS	%	%
20.2	14.5	8.1	12.9		2.6	Cash & Equivalents	9.5	9.1
28.5	27.8	38.8	27.4		21.7	Trade Receivables (net)	29.5	29.9
4.0	5.5	9.7	2.3		5.4	Inventory	6.1	4.5
6.6	1.0	4.7	4.7		9.5	All Other Current	4.7	4.8
59.3	48.7	61.3	47.3		39.2	Total Current	49.8	48.3
29.1	41.1	28.3	41.9		46.4	Fixed Assets (net)	38.6	39.5
.9	2.1	4.7	5.0		11.0	Intangibles (net)	3.3	4.8
10.7	8.1	5.7	5.8		3.4	All Other Non-Current	8.3	7.3
100.0	100.0	100.0	100.0		100.0	Total	100.0	100.0
						LIABILITIES		
4.0	8.5	10.9	3.6		6.8	Notes Payable-Short Term	12.3	9.9
7.3	5.6	5.3	5.5		9.3	Cur. Mat.-L.T.D.	8.4	8.1
8.0	11.4	15.2	11.2		6.1	Trade Payables	15.9	13.0
.0	.2	.3	.2		.2	Income Taxes Payable	.3	.3
21.9	16.6	12.1	17.0		13.8	All Other Current	12.7	12.0
41.2	42.3	43.8	37.5		36.3	Total Current	49.6	43.3
24.3	19.8	17.1	19.8		29.5	Long-Term Debt	27.3	25.0
.0	.3	.6	1.7		1.1	Deferred Taxes	.6	.5
11.7	9.2	2.1	3.2		3.6	All Other Non-Current	5.6	8.4
22.8	28.5	36.3	37.8		29.5	Net Worth	16.8	22.8
100.0	100.0	100.0	100.0		100.0	Total Liabilities & Net Worth	100.0	100.0
						INCOME DATA		
100.0	100.0	100.0	100.0		100.0	Net Sales	100.0	100.0
						Gross Profit		
93.8	93.9	90.7	89.1		91.4	Operating Expenses	92.4	95.7
6.2	6.1	9.3	10.9		8.6	Operating Profit	7.6	4.3
-.5	2.8	.5	2.0		4.2	All Other Expenses (net)	2.6	1.3
6.7	3.2	8.8	8.8		4.4	Profit Before Taxes	5.1	3.0
						RATIOS		
4.4	2.6	1.9	1.4		1.9		1.7	1.7
2.2	1.4	1.4	1.1		1.1	Current	1.2	1.1
.4	.8	1.0	.9		.6		.6	.7
4.0	2.4	1.6	1.3		1.0		1.4	1.5
1.6	1.2	1.1	1.0		.7	Quick	.9	.9
.2	.5	.7	.7		.3		.4	.5
0 UND	0 UND	23 15.9	29 12.7		41 8.9		9 42.6	18 20.8
10 35.5	27 13.7	39 9.5	38 9.6		46 8.0	Sales/Receivables	31 11.8	33 11.2
30 12.1	53 6.9	64 5.7	55 6.6		54 6.8		52 7.0	52 7.0
						Cost of Sales/Inventory		
						Cost of Sales/Payables		
11.3	12.0	8.3	8.6		11.7		10.9	12.3
43.1	36.9	17.9	46.6		42.3	Sales/Working Capital	48.0	56.0
-24.3	-17.9	614.3	-85.9		-8.1		-16.6	-19.2
31.1	12.6	13.0	29.8		9.0		8.8	12.2
(10) 4.7	(22) 3.4	(27) 5.9	(21) 3.5		6.8	EBIT/Interest	(98) 2.7	(144) 2.7
-.5	1.0	1.3	2.0		1.4		1.0	1.0
			2.9				3.8	5.7
		(11) 1.3				Net Profit + Depr., Dep., Amort./Cur. Mat. L/T/D	(19) 1.5	(34) 2.5
		1.1					.6	1.3
.0	.2	.1	.6		.7		.6	.6
1.0	1.0	.8	1.3		1.6	Fixed/Worth	1.3	1.5
-7.5	66.2	1.8	2.7		9.3		21.3	14.6
.5	.6	1.1	1.2		2.0		1.2	1.5
2.1	2.5	2.0	2.5		3.4	Debt/Worth	3.0	3.3
-38.6	86.2	5.1	6.2		9.9		166.3	59.8
132.9	71.4	58.0	56.4			% Profit Before Taxes/Tangible Net Worth	56.2	53.9
(12) 44.6	(26) 24.1	(36) 31.9	(24) 24.4				(91) 20.7	(125) 23.4
5.8	8.5	18.0	9.6				5.4	4.3
57.8	18.7	23.5	14.6		18.6	% Profit Before Taxes/Total Assets	13.8	17.6
19.9	7.5	13.0	7.2		12.6		5.3	3.9
-2.6	1.2	2.1	3.9		2.7		.4	-.1
UND	70.7	170.5	17.2		19.6	Sales/Net Fixed Assets	39.8	32.9
119.8	8.3	11.2	5.7		5.6		8.6	8.1
8.2	3.8	4.6	2.7		1.3		2.5	3.2
7.7	5.1	4.3	3.5		3.3	Sales/Total Assets	4.9	4.3
5.1	2.7	2.9	2.0		2.0		2.5	2.9
3.2	2.0	1.6	1.0		.8		1.3	1.6
.3	.8	.5	1.2			% Depr., Dep., Amort./Sales	1.1	1.4
(12) 1.8	(27) 2.9	(27) 1.6	(22) 4.2				(94) 3.4	(127) 4.0
9.9	7.6	3.6	6.6				9.6	9.8
	2.2	.8				% Officers', Directors' Owners' Comp/Sales	1.6	1.8
	(12) 4.5	(10) 1.9					(35) 3.3	(55) 3.1
	8.4	10.0					5.6	5.8
32587M	153062M	621670M	1485741M	645224M	4126253M	Net Sales ($)	2811780M	3099768M
4730M	37145M	176491M	622645M	404363M	1885378M	Total Assets ($)	1581152M	1428162M

© RMA 2007

M = $ thousand   MM = $ million
See Pages 11 through 21 for Explanation of Ratios and Data

Comparative Historical Data | Current Data Sorted by Sales

Type of Statement	4/1/04-3/31/05 ALL	4/1/05-3/31/06 ALL	4/1/06-3/31/07 ALL	0-1MM	1-3MM	3-5MM	5-10MM	10-25MM	25MM & OVER
				21 (4/1-9/30/06)			113 (10/1/06-3/31/07)		
Unqualified	25	19	29		1	2	3	5	18
Reviewed	26	23	20	1	1	5	2		11
Compiled	25	18	22	3	8	2	4	4	1
Tax Returns	17	24	20	5	8	1	3	3	
Other	48	63	43	3	7	8			12
NUMBER OF STATEMENTS	141	147	134	12	25	13	22	20	42
ASSETS	%	%	%	%	%	%	%	%	%
Cash & Equivalents	11.4	10.7	11.5	16.6	13.1	17.2	11.3	13.4	6.5
Trade Receivables (net)	31.4	29.6	30.1	15.4	25.2	32.4	34.8	32.7	32.7
Inventory	4.6	5.2	5.7	5.9	5.0	3.8	9.8	7.3	3.8
All Other Current	4.6	3.9	4.3	7.1	1.3	7.6	1.8	3.4	6.0
Total Current	51.9	49.3	51.6	45.0	44.6	61.0	57.8	56.8	49.0
Fixed Assets (net)	36.1	38.3	37.3	49.2	44.5	28.3	32.0	28.6	39.4
Intangibles (net)	4.4	5.4	4.3	.4	2.3	1.2	1.3	8.2	7.3
All Other Non-Current	7.6	7.0	6.8	5.4	8.6	9.5	8.9	6.4	4.3
Total	100.0	100.0	100.0	100.0	100.0	100.0	100.0	100.0	100.0
LIABILITIES									
Notes Payable-Short Term	8.3	10.2	7.6	8.0	8.8	1.5	8.0	11.0	6.8
Cur. Mat.-L.T.D.	6.7	8.2	5.9	5.2	6.8	4.4	4.9	7.0	6.2
Trade Payables	13.1	12.3	11.4	4.5	7.0	16.4	15.8	11.5	12.2
Income Taxes Payable	.3	.4	.2	.0	.1	.0	.7	.0	.1
All Other Current	17.5	13.0	15.4	9.6	21.2	14.2	14.7	12.5	15.6
Total Current	45.8	44.1	40.5	27.2	43.9	36.4	44.1	42.1	40.9
Long-Term Debt	20.4	26.6	20.5	29.9	26.6	12.2	16.7	18.8	19.6
Deferred Taxes	1.1	.9	.7	.0	.4	.4	.9	.5	1.2
All Other Non-Current	6.2	6.1	5.5	9.6	13.2	1.1	4.5	1.2	3.5
Net Worth	26.5	22.4	32.8	33.3	15.9	50.3	33.7	37.3	34.8
Total Liabilties & Net Worth	100.0	100.0	100.0	100.0	100.0	100.0	100.0	100.0	100.0
INCOME DATA									
Net Sales	100.0	100.0	100.0	100.0	100.0	100.0	100.0	100.0	100.0
Gross Profit									
Operating Expenses	94.1	92.2	91.7	84.5	93.8	87.8	94.0	93.2	91.9
Operating Profit	5.9	7.8	8.3	15.5	6.2	12.2	6.0	6.8	8.1
All Other Expenses (net)	1.5	2.1	1.6	4.8	1.3	.8	1.2	.3	2.0
Profit Before Taxes	4.4	5.7	6.7	10.7	4.8	11.4	4.9	6.5	6.1
RATIOS									
Current	1.9	2.0	2.3	3.9	3.1	3.2	1.8	1.8	1.6
	1.1	1.2	1.3	1.4	1.4	2.2	1.3	1.1	1.1
	.8	.8	.8	.7	.6	1.0	1.0	.7	.9
Quick	1.6	1.6	1.7	2.0	2.8	3.2	1.4	1.8	1.4
	.9	1.0	1.0	1.2	1.1	1.2	1.0	1.0	.9
	.6	.6	.6	.4	.4	.6	.6	.6	.6
Sales/Receivables	21 17.7	20 18.7	14 26.7	0 UND	0 UND	22 16.7	20 18.6	14 26.3	26 14.1
	39 9.5	39 9.3	32 11.3	2 147.8	29 12.6	26 14.0	40 9.0	38 9.7	42 8.8
	57 6.4	54 6.8	53 6.9	29 12.8	44 8.2	67 5.4	62 5.9	61 6.0	52 7.0
Cost of Sales/Inventory									
Cost of Sales/Payables									
Sales/Working Capital	11.9	10.1	9.9	4.2	11.9	4.7	9.2	12.9	16.1
	66.4	49.8	36.8	45.3	33.8	8.1	27.9	83.2	72.1
	-38.5	-21.9	-34.7	NM	-9.6	NM	NM	-39.8	-52.9
EBIT/Interest	12.3	8.3	12.5		15.1		11.0	41.2	8.6
	(119) 4.4	(126) 4.1	(96) 3.7		(19) 2.8	(13) 4.5	(18) 5.9		(36) 3.4
	1.3	1.6	1.4		.0		.7	1.8	1.5
Net Profit + Depr., Dep., Amort./Cur. Mat. L/T/D	5.2	4.2	4.5						5.9
	(31) 2.4	(23) 1.9	(25) 2.1					(15)	2.1
	1.1	1.0	1.0						1.1
Fixed/Worth	.4	.5	.2	.0	.8	.0	.1	.1	.5
	1.1	1.5	1.0	1.9	2.0	.3	.5	1.2	1.1
	3.9	13.2	3.4	4.6	-2.8	1.1	2.2	3.1	4.2
Debt/Worth	1.2	1.4	.9	.9	.7	.3	1.0	1.2	1.6
	2.7	3.8	2.2	3.3	3.1	.5	2.0	2.1	2.5
	7.0	64.2	7.2	75.9	-16.6	2.8	5.5	11.4	6.8
% Profit Before Taxes/Tangible Net Worth	57.7	71.3	62.0	39.0	106.1	52.8	72.7	72.4	58.4
	(114) 20.9	(116) 31.0	(113) 29.7	(10) 22.3	(16) 24.1	(12) 40.5	(20) 35.4	(17) 29.4	(38) 30.0
	8.5	15.7	10.6	.0	11.5	11.4	14.7	13.1	9.9
% Profit Before Taxes/Total Assets	14.7	17.5	21.4	20.0	30.2	45.1	23.0	21.8	15.4
	6.9	8.6	9.2	7.5	7.0	24.8	12.3	7.5	8.6
	1.2	2.5	2.2	.0	-1.5	5.3	.6	2.7	2.7
Sales/Net Fixed Assets	46.7	35.6	76.3	234.6	13.1	375.8	180.2	169.1	35.1
	10.4	7.3	8.5	6.4	6.9	8.8	37.4	8.8	7.4
	3.3	3.1	3.7	.4	3.8	4.1	3.6	5.9	3.1
Sales/Total Assets	4.2	3.9	4.5	3.2	4.8	6.0	4.2	4.5	4.7
	2.8	2.4	2.6	1.4	2.3	2.7	2.7	3.2	2.6
	1.4	1.3	1.4	.3	2.0	1.4	1.3	1.8	1.4
% Depr., Dep., Amort./Sales	1.1	1.1	.7		1.8		.3	.4	.7
	(109) 3.6	(119) 3.4	(101) 2.9		(20) 5.7	(14) 1.2	(17) 1.6		(33) 2.8
	8.1	7.5	6.1		9.4		4.8	4.9	4.9
% Officers', Directors' Owners' Comp/Sales	1.7	1.5	1.5		2.6				
	(42) 3.0	(39) 3.5	(32) 3.0		(11) 5.4				
	5.9	7.0	9.7		16.5				
Net Sales ($)	4379334M	4431944M	7064537M	5489M	53580M	50953M	157552M	311058M	6485905M
Total Assets ($)	2460249M	2532607M	3130752M	8937M	38651M	23077M	98298M	200857M	2760932M

© RMA 2007 M = $ thousand MM = $ million
See Pages 11 through 21 for Explanation of Ratios and Data

Current Data Sorted by Assets

Comparative Historical Data

0-500M	500M-2MM 12 (4/1-9/30/06)	2-10MM	10-50MM 77 (10/1/06-3/31/07)	50-100MM	100-250MM	Type of Statement	4/1/02-3/31/03 ALL	4/1/03-3/31/04 ALL
	1	3	4	1		Unqualified	8	15
	3	9	1			Reviewed	13	14
2	8	4	1			Compiled	10	12
10	9					Tax Returns	15	15
10	8	13	2			Other	19	20
22	29	29	8	1		**NUMBER OF STATEMENTS**	65	76
%	%	%	%	%	%	**ASSETS**	%	%
16.9	12.4	6.6				Cash & Equivalents	6.6	9.8
24.7	25.4	44.7				Trade Receivables (net)	37.3	34.9
1.5	.1	3.4				Inventory	1.9	1.9
3.2	9.4	3.9				All Other Current	5.0	5.2
46.2	47.3	58.6				Total Current	50.8	51.8
26.4	35.4	25.5				Fixed Assets (net)	31.4	32.0
22.9	3.5	5.5				Intangibles (net)	6.7	7.9
4.5	13.8	10.4				All Other Non-Current	11.1	8.3
100.0	100.0	100.0				Total	100.0	100.0
						LIABILITIES		
22.0	10.7	14.6				Notes Payable-Short Term	13.2	11.0
22.2	11.4	6.4				Cur. Mat.-L.T.D.	6.3	9.6
3.7	6.2	10.5				Trade Payables	15.4	11.7
.0	.3	.2				Income Taxes Payable	1.0	.3
13.9	12.2	14.3				All Other Current	11.5	15.3
61.7	40.8	45.9				Total Current	47.3	48.0
38.4	26.8	17.1				Long-Term Debt	20.8	20.5
.0	.6	.4				Deferred Taxes	.8	.7
20.0	1.7	4.6				All Other Non-Current	6.1	6.2
-20.1	30.0	32.0				Net Worth	24.9	24.6
100.0	100.0	100.0				Total Liabilities & Net Worth	100.0	100.0
						INCOME DATA		
100.0	100.0	100.0				Net Sales	100.0	100.0
						Gross Profit		
95.5	92.5	95.0				Operating Expenses	96.2	95.7
4.5	7.5	5.0				Operating Profit	3.8	4.3
2.2	2.0	.6				All Other Expenses (net)	1.4	1.5
2.3	5.5	4.4				Profit Before Taxes	2.5	2.8
						RATIOS		
2.4	3.2	2.1					1.6	1.8
1.4	1.3	1.2				Current	1.2	1.1
.3	.8	.8					.7	.7
2.1	2.6	2.0					1.5	1.5
1.1	1.0	1.2				Quick	1.0	.9
.3	.3	.7					.6	.6
0 UND	0 UND	26 14.3					25 14.5	20 18.6
4 102.4	17 22.0	36 10.1				Sales/Receivables	34 10.6	33 11.2
25 14.9	37 10.0	43 8.5					45 8.1	42 8.6
						Cost of Sales/Inventory		
						Cost of Sales/Payables		
11.3	9.4	12.1					17.5	18.1
115.9	44.7	53.9				Sales/Working Capital	62.3	98.0
-20.8	-53.4	-36.3					-21.6	-32.3
9.6	17.2	16.6					9.4	10.7
(19) 3.9	(23) 6.6	(28) 6.3				EBIT/Interest	(60) 2.6	(68) 4.0
-.3	1.3	3.1					.6	1.1
						Net Profit + Depr., Dep.,	4.4	13.7
						Amort./Cur. Mat. L/T/D	(15) 2.5	(18) 5.2
							.5	1.4
.3	.3	.2					.6	.5
-2.8	.8	.9				Fixed/Worth	1.5	1.4
-.1	NM	4.1					-10.8	-12.6
1.1	.5	1.0					1.0	1.1
-6.5	1.9	2.9				Debt/Worth	3.8	3.9
-1.5	NM	7.9					-13.6	-90.1
	66.0	86.4				% Profit Before Taxes/Tangible	69.9	82.7
	(22) 21.3	(25) 43.5				Net Worth	(46) 21.0	(55) 32.2
	1.5	22.0					-1.4	6.1
43.2	33.4	24.6				% Profit Before Taxes/Total	17.3	17.9
16.7	8.1	10.8				Assets	6.0	8.3
-14.0	-1.8	3.6					-1.1	.8
157.0	80.9	115.5					55.1	49.1
32.8	14.5	34.2				Sales/Net Fixed Assets	14.6	18.6
16.1	4.4	5.8					8.0	5.8
12.7	6.1	6.5					5.5	6.0
6.3	3.8	4.8				Sales/Total Assets	4.1	4.6
3.0	2.1	2.2					2.6	2.7
.7	.9	.6					1.0	.7
(13) 1.6	(26) 3.1	(22) 1.4				% Depr., Dep., Amort./Sales	(57) 2.0	(63) 1.5
4.7	7.2	2.6					4.9	4.8
3.4	2.0	2.4				% Officers', Directors'	2.9	1.6
(11) 6.1	(17) 2.7	(11) 3.1				Owners' Comp/Sales	(36) 4.5	(36) 3.6
10.9	5.3	6.2					6.7	6.0
53855M	156183M	579843M	781345M	202430M		Net Sales ($)	1736132M	2130664M
5507M	33899M	135793M	166629M	75653M		Total Assets ($)	886343M	959984M

(Middle columns 10-50MM, 50-100MM, 100-250MM marked "DATA NOT AVAILABLE" for the ratio and percentage rows.)

M = $ thousand   MM = $ million
See Pages 11 through 21 for Explanation of Ratios and Data

Comparative Historical Data   Current Data Sorted by Sales

	4/1/04-3/31/05 ALL	4/1/05-3/31/06 ALL	4/1/06-3/31/07 ALL	Type of Statement	0-1MM	1-3MM	3-5MM	5-10MM	10-25MM	25MM & OVER
	14	12	9	Unqualified		1			4	4
	13	12	13	Reviewed		2		2	5	4
	16	16	15	Compiled			3	4	4	1
	15	13	19	Tax Returns	4	4	5	5	1	
	37	45	33	Other	5	6	6	2	9	5
						12 (4/1-9/30/06)			77 (10/1/06-3/31/07)	
	95	98	89	NUMBER OF STATEMENTS	9	16	14	13	23	14
	%	%	%	ASSETS	%	%	%	%	%	%
	8.1	9.2	11.2	Cash & Equivalents		14.9	10.0	15.6	7.7	5.2
	38.2	39.0	31.6	Trade Receivables (net)		28.5	22.3	35.3	37.9	49.9
	.9	1.1	1.6	Inventory		1.0	.1	3.8	2.3	.4
	6.1	5.0	6.0	All Other Current		12.1	2.7	3.8	7.0	6.3
	53.3	54.3	50.4	Total Current		56.6	35.0	58.4	54.8	61.8
	29.6	26.1	29.3	Fixed Assets (net)		35.2	38.0	23.7	29.2	17.8
	7.6	9.5	9.5	Intangibles (net)		4.0	7.8	3.9	5.4	7.1
	9.5	10.0	10.8	All Other Non-Current		4.1	19.1	14.0	10.6	13.4
	100.0	100.0	100.0	Total		100.0	100.0	100.0	100.0	100.0
				LIABILITIES						
	13.5	14.8	14.8	Notes Payable-Short Term		10.8	9.9	23.4	12.4	16.4
	7.4	5.3	11.9	Cur. Mat.-L.T.D.		9.9	10.3	32.5	8.9	5.1
	11.7	13.6	8.2	Trade Payables		6.6	4.3	4.9	8.3	21.8
	.2	.2	.2	Income Taxes Payable		.0	.6	.0	.2	.5
	12.8	16.0	14.0	All Other Current		13.5	6.1	15.8	15.1	21.5
	45.6	49.9	49.1	Total Current		40.8	31.1	76.7	44.9	65.4
	18.5	20.6	25.3	Long-Term Debt		41.1	25.4	26.1	22.1	9.8
	.7	.9	.4	Deferred Taxes		.0	.8	.5	.7	.4
	11.1	5.3	8.3	All Other Non-Current		3.7	.6	1.4	3.5	13.3
	24.0	23.3	16.9	Net Worth		14.4	42.1	-4.6	28.9	11.1
	100.0	100.0	100.0	Total Liabilities & Net Worth		100.0	100.0	100.0	100.0	100.0
				INCOME DATA						
	100.0	100.0	100.0	Net Sales		100.0	100.0	100.0	100.0	100.0
				Gross Profit						
	96.6	96.4	94.7	Operating Expenses		90.3	95.9	97.2	95.2	98.6
	3.4	3.6	5.3	Operating Profit		9.7	4.1	2.8	4.8	1.4
	.8	.7	1.4	All Other Expenses (net)		2.9	.0	.3	.1	.7
	2.6	2.9	3.9	Profit Before Taxes		6.8	4.1	2.5	4.7	.7
				RATIOS						
	1.9	1.9	2.2	Current		4.3	2.8	2.5	2.1	1.5
	1.2	1.2	1.2			1.7	1.1	1.0	1.2	1.1
	.8	.9	.7			.8	.6	.8	1.1	.6
	1.6	1.8	2.0	Quick		3.4	1.9	2.1	1.9	1.4
	1.0	1.1	1.0			1.4	.8	1.0	1.1	.9
	.7	.6	.5			.4	.2	.5	.9	.5
23	16.1	18 20.6	5 75.0	Sales/Receivables	0 UND	0 UND	0 UND		23 15.6	23 16.0
34	10.8	33 11.1	27 13.5		19 19.3	22 16.4	22 16.6		33 11.1	35 10.6
41	8.9	44 8.3	38 9.5		45 8.1	43 8.5	40 9.0		40 9.2	39 9.4
				Cost of Sales/Inventory						
				Cost of Sales/Payables						
	18.1	14.8	11.6	Sales/Working Capital		8.2	13.5	23.9	12.8	23.9
	70.3	81.7	67.3			29.8	NM	391.7	49.7	101.2
	-38.5	-88.0	-35.3			-33.7	-31.4	-41.8	107.6	-22.1
	9.1	9.6	14.5	EBIT/Interest		15.9	27.0	7.3	18.9	11.5
(84)	3.1	(84) 3.4	(79) 5.0		(14) 5.6	(13) 9.9	(10) 4.2	(22) 5.7		(13) 5.9
	.9	.7	1.3			2.8	2.9	-.1	2.0	1.0
	4.2	9.1	6.5	Net Profit + Depr., Dep., Amort./Cur. Mat. L/T/D						
(13)	2.7	(18) 3.3	(14) 2.1							
	.7	1.1	.9							
	.4	.2	.3	Fixed/Worth		.4	.6	.1	.2	.3
	1.7	1.1	1.1			2.1	.9	.3	1.0	1.8
	33.1	16.5	-2.4			-1.5	3.3	-5.1	7.4	-.3
	1.3	1.2	1.0	Debt/Worth		.3	.5	1.0	.9	2.1
	3.5	3.6	2.9			3.5	1.9	1.5	2.3	6.2
	-45.4	-50.2	-5.9			-6.1	6.1	-8.6	9.7	-3.2
	74.4	74.2	78.7	% Profit Before Taxes/Tangible Net Worth		64.5	103.7		105.2	
(71)	34.8	(72) 32.2	(62) 36.2		(10) 57.3	(12) 33.7		(18) 35.9		
	10.7	7.4	10.3			17.9	5.9		17.1	
	19.6	21.5	27.8	% Profit Before Taxes/Total Assets		41.0	39.7	25.9	27.2	15.9
	6.9	7.0	9.1			20.7	8.9	7.7	11.8	9.9
	-.2	-.5	-.4			3.1	5.3	-5.4	2.2	-.9
	60.4	88.0	89.7	Sales/Net Fixed Assets		78.0	54.5	167.5	80.0	80.4
	24.5	31.2	27.8			12.3	11.4	94.4	33.0	45.2
	7.4	11.6	5.8			3.5	4.6	19.9	4.0	23.3
	6.9	6.5	6.9	Sales/Total Assets		5.8	7.3	12.3	6.4	8.1
	4.6	4.6	4.5			3.2	3.8	5.3	5.2	5.3
	2.8	2.4	2.4			2.0	2.0	3.7	2.3	3.8
	.7	.6	.7	% Depr., Dep., Amort./Sales		.8	.5	.1	.8	.7
(76)	1.9	(77) 1.3	(69) 1.7		(12) 1.8	(13) 1.6	(10) 1.1	(17) 1.7		(12) 1.1
	4.1	3.5	4.8			7.0	5.5	4.3	4.2	2.3
	3.0	2.5	2.4	% Officers', Directors' Owners' Comp/Sales			2.3			
(39)	4.0	(40) 4.1	(40) 3.8			(12) 2.9				
	6.9	7.1	6.4				5.1			
	2381908M	3127542M	1773656M	Net Sales ($)	3113M	31787M	57503M	93580M	395628M	1192045M
	824134M	964124M	417481M	Total Assets ($)	1807M	10158M	19092M	19144M	115793M	251487M

© RMA 2007

M = $ thousand   MM = $ million

See Pages 11 through 21 for Explanation of Ratios and Data

Current Data Sorted by Assets — Comparative Historical Data

0-500M	500M-2MM	2-10MM	10-50MM	50-100MM	100-250MM	Type of Statement	4/1/02-3/31/03 ALL	4/1/03-3/31/04 ALL
	7	10	9	8	5	Unqualified	26	30
1	9	28	10			Reviewed	61	54
8	23	26	10			Compiled	68	108
20	26	19	1	1		Tax Returns	60	66
8	28	41	24	4	3	Other	118	126
	44 (4/1-9/30/06)			285 (10/1/06-3/31/07)				
37	93	124	54	13	8	NUMBER OF STATEMENTS	333	384
%	%	%	%	%	%	ASSETS	%	%
12.4	8.8	7.0	11.1	6.3		Cash & Equivalents	8.4	9.6
20.9	19.8	22.2	18.8	21.4		Trade Receivables (net)	16.3	17.9
2.7	1.4	3.8	3.7	2.7		Inventory	2.0	2.3
7.1	3.5	2.1	3.8	.7		All Other Current	2.3	4.3
43.2	33.4	35.1	37.4	31.1		Total Current	29.0	34.0
33.6	54.6	50.3	48.8	47.8		Fixed Assets (net)	60.5	54.7
6.7	1.5	4.0	7.1	9.1		Intangibles (net)	2.5	3.0
16.5	10.5	10.6	6.7	11.9		All Other Non-Current	8.0	8.4
100.0	100.0	100.0	100.0	100.0		Total	100.0	100.0
						LIABILITIES		
19.7	5.6	8.0	4.9	6.8		Notes Payable-Short Term	5.0	5.8
3.2	4.2	3.9	3.5	5.9		Cur. Mat.-L.T.D.	5.0	4.7
26.3	7.6	8.3	8.1	7.8		Trade Payables	6.6	7.3
.1	.1	.4	.2	.1		Income Taxes Payable	.2	.1
13.5	9.2	8.5	8.8	7.0		All Other Current	9.9	10.7
62.8	26.7	29.2	25.4	27.6		Total Current	26.6	28.7
20.5	38.5	32.7	32.1	30.4		Long-Term Debt	42.5	37.6
.0	.0	.5	.5	.6		Deferred Taxes	.3	.3
5.4	5.5	3.4	5.2	3.8		All Other Non-Current	5.2	7.0
11.4	29.2	34.2	36.7	37.8		Net Worth	25.3	26.4
100.0	100.0	100.0	100.0	100.0		Total Liabilties & Net Worth	100.0	100.0
						INCOME DATA		
100.0	100.0	100.0	100.0	100.0		Net Sales	100.0	100.0
						Gross Profit		
87.6	81.7	84.6	87.3	91.7		Operating Expenses	81.2	84.1
12.4	18.3	15.4	12.7	8.3		Operating Profit	18.8	15.9
2.4	6.8	7.8	4.2	2.9		All Other Expenses (net)	10.0	8.0
10.0	11.5	7.6	8.5	5.4		Profit Before Taxes	8.8	7.9
						RATIOS		
2.3	2.9	1.8	3.0	2.0			2.4	2.4
1.1	1.1	1.2	1.6	1.2		Current	1.1	1.2
.5	.4	.4	1.0	.9			.5	.6
2.3	2.1	1.7	2.5	1.9			1.8	1.8
.9	.9	.9	1.3	1.1		Quick	1.0	.9
.3	.3	.4	.8	.8			.3	.4
0 UND	0 UND	13 28.7	30 12.0	35 10.4			0 UND	2 201.5
10 35.8	22 16.7	33 11.1	43 8.5	49 7.5		Sales/Receivables	26 14.0	26 13.8
38 9.5	38 9.5	51 7.2	60 6.1	67 5.4			43 8.4	44 8.2
						Cost of Sales/Inventory		
						Cost of Sales/Payables		
15.2	10.3	9.5	4.1	8.6			9.1	9.1
147.4	59.8	43.2	9.8	24.9		Sales/Working Capital	48.3	42.5
-8.0	-10.0	-7.6	NM	-414.7			-9.3	-11.3
14.0	12.5	11.6	10.1	5.5			6.2	7.8
(23) 6.9	(68) 5.0	(98) 2.8	(44) 3.4	(12) 3.3		EBIT/Interest	(223) 3.1	(273) 2.9
2.0	1.7	1.0	1.8	1.2			1.2	1.1
		2.8	5.8				5.4	6.5
	(27) 1.1	1.1	(18) 3.2			Net Profit + Depr., Dep., Amort./Cur. Mat. L/T/D	(59) 2.4	(54) 2.2
		.8	1.3				1.3	1.1
.2	.5	.5	.6	1.0			.8	.7
.9	1.7	1.6	1.8	1.3		Fixed/Worth	2.3	2.4
4.0	5.0	6.4	4.3	3.5			11.8	16.5
.7	.7	.9	1.0	.9			1.1	1.0
2.3	2.3	2.1	2.3	2.3		Debt/Worth	2.6	3.1
NM	8.4	8.6	6.0	6.0			28.8	30.2
116.8	62.1	32.9	44.6	48.5			45.8	52.2
(28) 36.5	(74) 19.9	(107) 17.8	(50) 19.1	(12) 15.8		% Profit Before Taxes/Tangible Net Worth	(267) 19.1	(303) 21.5
4.0	6.6	2.7	5.9	11.3			3.1	3.3
31.0	22.1	11.0	13.1	14.1			12.5	12.1
12.8	7.1	4.3	6.9	6.7		% Profit Before Taxes/Total Assets	5.0	4.4
.7	1.0	.1	1.9	1.1			.3	.1
146.3	15.1	13.3	10.0	4.0			9.8	14.1
12.7	2.3	4.5	2.0	2.4		Sales/Net Fixed Assets	1.7	2.6
4.8	.4	.4	.7	.8			.3	.4
7.0	3.3	2.9	2.0	1.8			2.9	3.0
2.8	1.3	1.3	1.0	.9		Sales/Total Assets	1.0	1.2
1.3	.3	.3	.3	.5			.3	.3
1.6	2.2	1.8	2.0	2.5			2.8	2.2
(20) 2.3	(76) 5.4	(116) 3.7	(51) 5.0	6.0		% Depr., Dep., Amort./Sales	(294) 5.4	(329) 5.4
7.3	11.0	11.3	7.8	7.4			13.5	12.9
2.9	2.6	1.7					2.5	2.0
(11) 8.5	(25) 4.7	(24) 5.3				% Officers', Directors' Owners' Comp/Sales	(98) 6.1	(99) 5.2
13.0	15.3	12.3					11.9	10.0
34487M	240542M	1091429M	1630368M	1994926M	1530419M	Net Sales ($)	4510483M	5285461M
9842M	110836M	603842M	1207084M	911630M	1112333M	Total Assets ($)	3180936M	4040969M

M = $ thousand   MM = $ million

See Pages 11 through 21 for Explanation of Ratios and Data

Comparative Historical Data / Current Data Sorted by Sales

			Type of Statement						
42	39	39	Unqualified	2	4	2	5	5	21
44	56	48	Reviewed	4	8	5	18	12	1
56	59	67	Compiled	20	18	6	9	11	3
97	70	67	Tax Returns	40	13	5	3	4	2
108	108	108	Other	17	19	10	18	22	22
4/1/04-3/31/05 ALL	4/1/05-3/31/06 ALL	4/1/06-3/31/07 ALL		44 (4/1-9/30/06)			285 (10/1/06-3/31/07)		
				0-1MM	1-3MM	3-5MM	5-10MM	10-25MM	25MM & OVER
347	332	329	NUMBER OF STATEMENTS	83	62	28	53	54	49
%	%	%	ASSETS	%	%	%	%	%	%
8.7	9.8	8.7	Cash & Equivalents	6.0	10.3	7.7	9.8	11.1	7.8
17.9	21.3	20.6	Trade Receivables (net)	4.7	14.8	25.0	29.8	33.8	27.9
2.2	3.4	3.0	Inventory	1.0	2.9	.8	5.0	3.4	5.2
2.7	2.8	3.3	All Other Current	4.2	2.3	4.7	2.7	4.2	1.9
31.5	37.3	35.6	Total Current	15.9	30.3	38.2	47.3	52.6	42.7
55.5	49.4	49.6	Fixed Assets (net)	69.5	56.7	38.3	39.9	37.4	37.3
2.8	3.1	4.4	Intangibles (net)	4.2	2.7	3.9	3.3	1.5	11.3
10.1	10.1	10.5	All Other Non-Current	10.4	10.3	19.6	9.5	8.5	8.6
100.0	100.0	100.0	Total	100.0	100.0	100.0	100.0	100.0	100.0
			LIABILITIES						
6.6	8.2	8.0	Notes Payable-Short Term	9.9	7.0	6.3	9.9	5.1	8.0
4.7	4.6	3.9	Cur. Mat.-L.T.D.	3.3	4.3	5.4	3.1	4.7	3.4
8.4	10.6	10.0	Trade Payables	3.4	14.5	11.7	8.8	13.3	12.3
.2	.4	.2	Income Taxes Payable	.1	.1	.1	.8	.2	.2
11.4	9.8	9.2	All Other Current	5.7	7.8	10.6	12.1	11.0	11.3
31.4	33.6	31.4	Total Current	22.3	33.9	34.2	34.7	34.3	35.2
42.1	34.9	33.0	Long-Term Debt	51.1	36.6	24.0	25.9	21.4	23.1
.4	.4	.4	Deferred Taxes	.0	.0	.8	.3	.9	.7
3.9	4.6	4.5	All Other Non-Current	4.1	1.5	2.7	7.2	6.1	5.5
22.3	26.6	30.7	Net Worth	22.5	28.0	38.2	31.9	37.4	35.4
100.0	100.0	100.0	Total Liabilties & Net Worth	100.0	100.0	100.0	100.0	100.0	100.0
			INCOME DATA						
100.0	100.0	100.0	Net Sales	100.0	100.0	100.0	100.0	100.0	100.0
			Gross Profit						
82.2	83.5	84.8	Operating Expenses	70.7	79.9	91.0	93.6	93.7	92.1
17.8	16.5	15.2	Operating Profit	29.3	20.1	9.0	6.4	6.3	7.9
8.6	6.3	6.1	All Other Expenses (net)	15.4	6.5	4.1	1.4	.5	2.3
9.2	10.3	9.1	Profit Before Taxes	13.9	13.5	4.9	4.9	5.7	5.7
			RATIOS						
2.1	2.2	2.2		1.8	2.1	1.9	3.9	2.9	1.9
1.1	1.2	1.2	Current	.6	1.1	1.2	1.4	1.6	1.3
.5	.7	.6		.1	.4	.8	.8	1.0	.9
1.6	1.9	2.0		1.4	1.9	1.9	3.1	2.6	1.6
.9	(331) 1.0	.9	Quick	.5	.9	1.1	1.1	1.2	1.1
.4	.5	.4		.1	.3	.5	.7	.8	.8
0 UND	0 UND	9 41.5		0 UND	9 40.2	17 21.3	25 14.8	29 12.6	34 10.6
29 12.7	33 11.0	31 11.9	Sales/Receivables	0 UND	26 14.0	30 12.2	35 10.4	42 8.8	45 8.2
46 7.9	48 7.6	49 7.4		12 29.2	47 7.8	49 7.4	54 6.8	52 7.0	59 6.2
			Cost of Sales/Inventory						
			Cost of Sales/Payables						
10.2	8.1	7.9		15.6	6.7	10.6	5.9	6.3	8.8
75.5	34.5	38.8	Sales/Working Capital	-13.4	57.6	45.5	19.8	15.8	24.9
-8.4	-16.1	-13.4		-3.3	-7.6	-24.5	-27.6	NM	-57.4
8.8	12.4	10.8		8.0	7.4	9.2	12.0	14.6	10.1
(250) 3.5	(249) 3.5	(252) 3.5	EBIT/Interest	(39) 3.2	(47) 4.0	(25) 3.1	(46) 2.4	(51) 3.9	(44) 4.5
1.5	1.9	1.5		1.9	1.7	.6	1.2	1.5	1.8
4.8	4.2	4.9					2.6	5.2	11.4
(54) 2.0	(56) 2.0	(64) 2.0	Net Profit + Depr., Dep., Amort./Cur. Mat. L/T/D			(12) 2.0	(16) 1.5	(23) 4.4
1.0	1.0	.9					.8	.9	1.7
.7	.6	.5		1.4	.5	.3	.4	.4	.6
2.6	1.9	1.6	Fixed/Worth	3.2	1.5	1.2	1.2	.9	1.3
19.2	7.5	4.7		32.5	3.6	3.0	4.7	2.2	3.9
1.0	1.0	.9		1.0	.7	.6	.8	.8	1.0
3.6	2.7	2.3	Debt/Worth	3.0	1.8	3.1	2.0	1.7	2.6
30.5	14.4	7.3		302.5	6.1	4.1	7.0	3.8	9.9
48.6	57.9	47.6	% Profit Before Taxes/Tangible Net Worth	35.7	66.8	57.6	33.9	58.2	62.6
(277) 23.5	(276) 26.6	(279) 19.0		(63) 15.5	(53) 18.8	(26) 29.4	(46) 14.4	(48) 25.9	(43) 25.6
8.1	9.3	5.3		.8	5.0	-1.0	5.0	8.6	12.0
12.3	15.6	14.1	% Profit Before Taxes/Total Assets	10.2	20.1	14.3	15.0	21.4	14.8
5.5	7.0	6.2		4.7	6.7	8.1	4.2	9.0	9.8
1.3	1.8	.9		.0	1.6	-.6	1.1	1.2	2.9
12.5	18.7	14.5		1.7	12.3	23.4	16.2	19.4	26.7
2.4	4.4	3.8	Sales/Net Fixed Assets	.3	1.5	10.6	8.2	9.6	4.7
.4	.5	.6		.2	.5	1.3	2.0	3.0	1.9
2.9	3.2	3.0		.8	2.0	5.0	3.7	3.7	3.2
1.1	1.5	1.4	Sales/Total Assets	.3	1.0	2.2	2.2	2.2	1.8
.3	.4	.4		.2	.3	.9	.9	1.4	1.0
2.2	1.7	2.0		7.4	2.5	1.5	1.8	1.4	1.1
(308) 6.0	(292) 4.3	(284) 4.3	% Depr., Dep., Amort./Sales	(65) 12.2	(55) 7.3	(23) 2.3	(47) 3.2	(49) 2.7	(45) 2.5
13.3	10.3	9.8		21.4	10.2	4.4	6.1	5.4	5.9
2.6	2.1	2.2		7.9	3.5		1.7		
(92) 6.3	(88) 4.5	(70) 4.8	% Officers', Directors' Owners' Comp/Sales	(18) 12.7	(19) 5.3		(10) 2.8		
11.3	9.6	12.4		15.2	9.2		10.3		
5257714M	5914032M	6522171M	Net Sales ($)	32924M	115435M	110225M	380816M	919643M	4963128M
3345323M	3627011M	3955567M	Total Assets ($)	113009M*	210002M	101010M	343395M	552336M	2635815M

M = $ thousand   MM = $ million
See Pages 11 through 21 for Explanation of Ratios and Data

Current Data Sorted by Assets / Comparative Historical Data

0-500M	500M-2MM	2-10MM	10-50MM	50-100MM	100-250MM	Type of Statement	4/1/02-3/31/03 ALL	4/1/03-3/31/04 ALL
	2	5	9	2	3	Unqualified	18	25
	2	8	3			Reviewed	24	20
2	7	12	3		1	Compiled	24	34
2	1		1			Tax Returns	6	8
4	7	11	10	5	4	Other	27	39
	16 (4/1-9/30/06)		88 (10/1/06-3/31/07)					
8	19	36	26	7	8	NUMBER OF STATEMENTS	99	126
%	%	%	%	%	%	**ASSETS**	%	%
	12.1	11.5	5.4			Cash & Equivalents	7.1	6.8
	30.1	16.4	7.7			Trade Receivables (net)	14.9	13.8
	.6	2.6	4.8			Inventory	2.6	2.4
	4.4	2.2	3.3			All Other Current	3.4	5.1
	47.2	32.8	21.2			Total Current	28.0	28.1
	41.2	59.4	67.7			Fixed Assets (net)	61.3	63.9
	4.7	3.4	.6			Intangibles (net)	3.4	2.9
	6.9	4.4	10.4			All Other Non-Current	7.3	5.0
	100.0	100.0	100.0			Total	100.0	100.0
						LIABILITIES		
	4.7	1.7	6.4			Notes Payable-Short Term	5.1	4.1
	6.2	5.2	4.0			Cur. Mat.-L.T.D.	5.4	4.6
	11.7	5.6	3.7			Trade Payables	6.9	5.3
	.0	.2	.1			Income Taxes Payable	.1	.2
	18.4	9.8	3.9			All Other Current	9.6	7.7
	41.1	22.6	18.1			Total Current	27.2	21.8
	12.6	38.8	40.6			Long-Term Debt	38.5	39.1
	.1	.4	.9			Deferred Taxes	.7	.5
	9.4	2.7	3.4			All Other Non-Current	3.9	5.4
	36.8	35.4	37.0			Net Worth	29.7	33.2
	100.0	100.0	100.0			Total Liabilities & Net Worth	100.0	100.0
						INCOME DATA		
	100.0	100.0	100.0			Net Sales	100.0	100.0
						Gross Profit		
	91.6	88.5	82.6			Operating Expenses	84.4	89.8
	8.4	11.5	17.4			Operating Profit	15.6	10.2
	6.4	4.7	5.4			All Other Expenses (net)	7.9	5.9
	2.0	6.8	11.9			Profit Before Taxes	7.7	4.2
						RATIOS		
	2.2	2.8	1.5			Current	2.5	2.3
	1.1	1.7	1.1				1.2	1.3
	.9	.8	.8				.7	.7
	2.0	2.8	1.4			Quick	1.8	1.8
	1.0	1.5	.8				.9	.9
	.6	.7	.4				.6	.5
	24 15.1	23 15.6	23 16.2			Sales/Receivables	21 17.1	26 14.1
	33 10.9	37 9.9	43 8.6				35 10.3	36 10.2
	53 6.9	50 7.3	48 7.6				48 7.7	51 7.1
						Cost of Sales/Inventory		
						Cost of Sales/Payables		
	11.0	7.2	9.5			Sales/Working Capital	9.5	7.6
	42.0	15.1	79.4				45.9	32.3
	-38.8	-31.1	-20.2				-13.6	-20.1
	9.9	13.8	4.8			EBIT/Interest	5.9	5.1
	(14) 2.0	(30) 2.6	(24) 2.3				(81) 2.3	(105) 2.5
	-.1	.8	1.4				1.1	1.3
						Net Profit + Depr., Dep., Amort./Cur. Mat. L/T/D	3.2	3.3
							(25) 2.5 (28) 2.3	
							1.7	1.7
	.6	.8	1.1			Fixed/Worth	1.1	1.1
	1.1	1.7	1.9				2.6	2.3
	7.0	5.6	4.1				6.5	6.7
	.5	.8	1.0			Debt/Worth	.9	1.1
	2.0	1.6	2.2				2.7	2.2
	16.3	5.3	5.8				7.3	9.5
	34.5	47.4	18.8			% Profit Before Taxes/Tangible Net Worth	29.4	31.0
	(17) 12.9	(31) 22.8	11.9				(83) 17.4	(107) 12.1
	-.4	3.5	6.0				4.3	3.5
	9.5	19.7	6.5			% Profit Before Taxes/Total Assets	11.5	7.7
	2.2	7.7	4.3				4.7	3.7
	-.3	-.3	1.6				.2	.4
	14.3	7.1	1.3			Sales/Net Fixed Assets	4.3	4.6
	5.5	1.5	.6				1.3	1.2
	2.0	.7	.4				.6	.5
	2.9	2.4	.8			Sales/Total Assets	2.2	2.0
	2.2	.9	.4				.8	.8
	1.0	.6	.3				.4	.4
	1.2	3.0	8.2			% Depr., Dep., Amort./Sales	4.1	4.3
	(18) 2.5	(30) 6.7	(25) 10.5				(94) 8.1	(116) 8.9
	5.8	11.9	15.3				13.4	13.4
		4.2				% Officers', Directors' Owners' Comp/Sales	3.1	3.1
		(10) 5.7					(26) 4.1	(40) 4.7
		9.3					10.5	9.2
12491M	54764M	257232M	353378M	461902M	2487110M	Net Sales ($)	2088507M	2401727M
2166M	23770M	184000M	609337M	470728M	1403866M	Total Assets ($)	1932700M	2504425M

M = $ thousand   MM = $ million
See Pages 11 through 21 for Explanation of Ratios and Data

Comparative Historical Data | Current Data Sorted by Sales

			Type of Statement					
24	22	21	Unqualified	2	4	5	4	6
18	15	13	Reviewed	1 5	1	2	4	
20	19	25	Compiled	3 6	3	7	4	2
3	4	4	Tax Returns	2		2		
22	42	41	Other	3 9	5	7	7	10
4/1/04-3/31/05 ALL	4/1/05-3/31/06 ALL	4/1/06-3/31/07 ALL		0-1MM	16 (4/1-9/30/06) 1-3MM 3-5MM	88 (10/1/06-3/31/07) 5-10MM 10-25MM		25MM & OVER
87	102	104	**NUMBER OF STATEMENTS**	7 24	15	21	19	18
%	%	%	**ASSETS**	% %	%	%	%	%
8.6	8.3	10.6	Cash & Equivalents	15.9	10.7	7.3	7.4	9.3
15.6	18.6	18.1	Trade Receivables (net)	20.2	20.8	12.5	20.9	14.2
2.5	3.7	2.8	Inventory	.0	4.6	1.9	6.0	3.7
3.6	3.0	2.7	All Other Current	3.1	1.3	2.4	2.4	3.3
30.3	33.5	34.3	Total Current	39.2	37.4	24.2	36.6	30.5
62.2	57.2	57.2	Fixed Assets (net)	53.6	46.8	65.9	57.5	63.5
1.2	2.9	2.5	Intangibles (net)	4.3	1.2	3.0	2.4	1.5
6.3	6.4	6.0	All Other Non-Current	2.8	14.6	6.9	3.5	4.4
100.0	100.0	100.0	Total	100.0	100.0	100.0	100.0	100.0
			LIABILITIES					
7.5	5.9	5.8	Notes Payable-Short Term	11.4	7.4	1.7	2.8	2.7
6.2	5.5	4.7	Cur. Mat.-L.T.D.	4.9	4.3	6.0	4.4	3.0
6.8	7.7	6.5	Trade Payables	3.4	7.0	3.3	9.8	7.8
.3	.3	.2	Income Taxes Payable	.2	.0	.3	.2	.1
6.0	4.7	14.1	All Other Current	12.5	10.3	7.2	7.7	3.7
26.8	24.1	31.2	Total Current	32.4	29.0	18.5	24.9	17.4
39.0	34.7	32.3	Long-Term Debt	26.0	31.7	38.7	34.9	33.8
.5	1.0	.7	Deferred Taxes	.3	.1	.6	.8	1.9
3.5	5.4	4.4	All Other Non-Current	3.0	9.8	2.2	.5	5.6
30.0	34.8	31.4	Net Worth	38.4	29.3	40.0	38.9	41.3
100.0	100.0	100.0	Total Liabilities & Net Worth	100.0	100.0	100.0	100.0	100.0
			INCOME DATA					
100.0	100.0	100.0	Net Sales	100.0	100.0	100.0	100.0	100.0
			Gross Profit					
85.6	86.4	87.0	Operating Expenses	88.4	78.0	85.1	92.6	85.4
14.4	13.6	13.0	Operating Profit	11.6	22.0	14.9	7.4	14.6
5.7	5.1	5.7	All Other Expenses (net)	4.5	12.8	4.5	2.4	5.9
8.7	8.4	7.3	Profit Before Taxes	7.2	9.1	10.4	5.0	8.6
			RATIOS					
2.2	2.2	2.2	Current	2.0	2.8	2.0	1.7	3.1
1.3	1.4	1.4		1.2	2.1	1.2	1.3	2.0
.6	.9	.9		.7	.9	.8	1.0	1.1
1.8	2.1	2.0	Quick	2.0	2.8	1.7	1.6	2.7
1.0	1.2	1.1		.9	1.9	1.1	1.0	1.6
.4	.7	.6		.5	.3	.5	.6	.8
19 18.8	23 15.6	23 15.6	Sales/Receivables	13 27.3	15 24.9	20 18.1	36 10.1	25 14.7
33 11.1	34 10.7	38 9.5		39 9.3	29 12.6	34 10.6	43 8.4	43 8.4
48 7.6	49 7.4	52 7.1		52 7.0	75 4.8	46 8.0	53 6.9	50 7.4
			Cost of Sales/Inventory					
			Cost of Sales/Payables					
6.2	6.8	7.3	Sales/Working Capital	9.1	5.3	9.7	10.8	4.7
22.4	19.8	20.0		47.0	22.9	38.6	16.1	11.9
-12.9	-77.1	-35.4		-11.6	-38.8	-25.2	-198.8	NM
5.1	6.4	8.2	EBIT/Interest	7.1	14.5	6.3	14.9	8.1
(76) 2.7	(87) 2.7	(88) 2.4		(18) 2.0	(11) 3.9	(18) 1.8	3.8	(17) 2.9
1.6	1.3	1.1		-.6	1.1	1.3	1.2	1.7
4.0	4.7	4.2	Net Profit + Depr., Dep., Amort./Cur. Mat. L/T/D					
(19) 3.2	(24) 2.0	(20) 1.6						
2.1	1.2	1.0						
.9	.8	.8	Fixed/Worth	.5	.6	1.2	.8	.7
2.0	1.7	1.7		1.3	1.9	1.7	1.1	2.1
4.7	4.7	4.0		5.4	6.5	4.4	5.2	3.4
1.3	.9	1.0	Debt/Worth	.6	1.0	1.0	.9	.7
2.5	2.2	1.8		1.3	3.5	1.7	2.1	1.8
6.5	7.0	5.7		8.9	7.9	4.6	5.7	3.3
26.4	34.8	30.8	% Profit Before Taxes/Tangible Net Worth	43.8	46.2	27.1	36.6	20.3
(78) 15.6	(90) 14.8	(96) 15.2		(20) 18.1	(14) 20.0	(20) 13.0	14.7	12.5
4.7	5.8	4.9		.4	.9	5.2	6.1	6.7
7.5	11.2	11.8	% Profit Before Taxes/Total Assets	15.5	9.5	10.8	18.0	9.1
3.6	4.9	5.0		5.5	4.7	6.4	6.1	4.9
1.0	.9	.5		-1.1	.1	1.6	.9	2.5
5.3	7.7	7.1	Sales/Net Fixed Assets	12.1	8.2	2.9	7.3	6.4
1.0	1.7	1.3		1.5	1.3	1.7	1.3	1.0
.5	.5	.6		.6	.7	.5	.6	.5
2.3	3.1	2.6	Sales/Total Assets	2.9	2.7	1.8	3.2	2.6
.8	1.0	.8		.9	.6	.8	.9	.7
.4	.5	.4		.5	.3	.4	.5	.4
2.9	2.6	3.0	% Depr., Dep., Amort./Sales	2.1	1.8	3.0	2.3	4.0
(80) 10.6	(94) 7.1	(90) 8.3		(18) 8.8	7.8	(20) 6.3	(17) 6.3	(14) 9.2
15.1	12.1	11.8		13.7	17.1	11.8	10.4	12.0
3.2	1.5	2.4	% Officers', Directors' Owners' Comp/Sales					
(21) 4.3	(33) 4.7	(30) 5.4						
6.5	8.2	9.3						
2717333M	3756261M	3626877M	Net Sales ($)	4428M	41760M	58195M	142290M	315518M	3064686M
2304872M	2717163M	2693867M	Total Assets ($)	5896M	59218M	115150M	227687M	390661M	1895255M

© RMA 2007

M = $ thousand   MM = $ million
See Pages 11 through 21 for Explanation of Ratios and Data

Current Data Sorted by Assets | | | | | Comparative Historical Data

0-500M	500M-2MM	2-10MM	10-50MM	50-100MM	100-250MM	Type of Statement	4/1/02-3/31/03 ALL	4/1/03-3/31/04 ALL
	4	11	13	3	1	Unqualified	29	27
	10	18	5			Reviewed	22	26
	2	8	2			Compiled	11	14
3	4	1				Tax Returns	5	9
2	3	1	7		1	Other	18	9
	61 (4/1-9/30/06)		38 (10/1/06-3/31/07)					
5	23	39	27	4	1	**NUMBER OF STATEMENTS**	85	85
%	%	%	%	%	%	**ASSETS**	%	%
	11.6	7.0	7.7			Cash & Equivalents	7.3	8.8
	18.3	17.9	17.5			Trade Receivables (net)	17.3	15.1
	14.5	25.6	24.6			Inventory	20.0	20.0
	7.0	4.6	7.7			All Other Current	6.5	6.1
	51.5	55.0	57.5			Total Current	51.1	49.9
	41.1	40.4	35.3			Fixed Assets (net)	40.9	43.1
	.1	.8	.3			Intangibles (net)	1.3	1.3
	7.3	3.7	6.9			All Other Non-Current	6.7	5.7
	100.0	100.0	100.0			Total	100.0	100.0
						LIABILITIES		
	16.9	19.1	22.5			Notes Payable-Short Term	13.9	16.1
	2.2	3.5	4.4			Cur. Mat.-L.T.D.	4.1	5.1
	12.2	8.0	9.2			Trade Payables	10.1	10.1
	.1	.2	.5			Income Taxes Payable	.2	.2
	9.5	9.0	8.1			All Other Current	9.4	11.4
	40.8	39.8	44.8			Total Current	37.7	42.9
	14.9	17.2	17.1			Long-Term Debt	17.4	17.2
	1.4	1.2	1.0			Deferred Taxes	.8	.8
	1.2	2.2	2.9			All Other Non-Current	1.6	2.7
	41.7	39.5	34.2			Net Worth	42.4	36.5
	100.0	100.0	100.0			Total Liabilities & Net Worth	100.0	100.0
						INCOME DATA		
	100.0	100.0	100.0			Net Sales	100.0	100.0
						Gross Profit		
	91.6	90.0	92.4			Operating Expenses	89.3	93.2
	8.4	10.0	7.6			Operating Profit	10.7	6.8
	1.0	1.5	.8			All Other Expenses (net)	1.5	1.1
	7.5	8.4	6.8			Profit Before Taxes	9.2	5.7
						RATIOS		
	2.3	1.9	2.0				2.0	1.7
	1.2	1.3	1.2			Current	1.2	1.2
	.9	1.1	1.1				.9	1.0
	1.0	1.2	1.3				1.4	1.1
	.7	.6	.5			Quick	.6	.5
	.2	.3	.3				.2	.2
	9 42.3	8 43.9	13 27.1				8 46.3	5 77.7
	20 17.8	23 16.1	28 13.0			Sales/Receivables	19 19.4	13 27.3
	42 8.7	45 8.0	70 5.2				40 9.0	38 9.6
						Cost of Sales/Inventory		
						Cost of Sales/Payables		
	8.6	7.8	3.8				8.5	13.8
	30.3	17.8	15.2			Sales/Working Capital	31.9	35.2
	-70.9	37.6	102.9				-102.0	UND
	7.4	12.1	6.5				7.4	6.0
	(22) 2.2	(38) 3.5	(26) 2.4			EBIT/Interest	(82) 3.1	(84) 2.5
	1.3	1.8	1.8				1.7	.7
		7.3	11.2				7.2	5.6
		(14) 4.1	(16) 2.9			Net Profit + Depr., Dep., Amort./Cur. Mat. L/T/D	(28) 1.6	(27) 2.7
		2.6	1.4				.8	.2
	.5	.5	.5				.5	.6
	1.1	1.0	1.0			Fixed/Worth	1.0	1.0
	2.6	1.6	1.9				1.8	1.7
	.5	.6	1.1				.6	.7
	1.4	1.9	2.0			Debt/Worth	1.5	1.5
	4.5	3.4	5.2				3.0	3.9
	40.0	35.2	31.4				30.0	23.0
	13.7	(37) 16.2	(25) 18.0			% Profit Before Taxes/Tangible Net Worth	(81) 11.1	(78) 9.1
	5.1	7.1	10.1				4.9	-.3
	12.4	11.2	7.5				11.0	9.3
	4.5	6.7	4.4			% Profit Before Taxes/Total Assets	4.3	2.9
	1.5	1.8	3.3				1.8	-1.1
	24.0	14.6	11.3				15.2	15.4
	8.0	7.6	6.0			Sales/Net Fixed Assets	6.0	6.7
	2.2	3.1	2.1				2.0	2.0
	4.0	3.4	2.8				3.7	4.0
	2.1	2.5	1.3			Sales/Total Assets	2.0	2.4
	1.2	1.1	.7				.9	.8
	.6	.7	1.2				1.1	1.0
	2.0	(38) 1.4	2.2			% Depr., Dep., Amort./Sales	(84) 2.0	(82) 1.6
	2.9	3.1	4.4				5.0	4.2
		.5					1.4	1.7
		(10) 1.3				% Officers', Directors' Owners' Comp/Sales	(23) 3.2	(19) 2.5
		3.1					4.9	5.7
4917M	99733M	412639M	1037838M	1398263M	318149M	Net Sales ($)	3018576M	2753223M
888M	30714M	176941M	561892M	290091M	136607M	Total Assets ($)	1149262M	1063441M

© RMA 2007

M = $ thousand   MM = $ million
See Pages 11 through 21 for Explanation of Ratios and Data

Comparative Historical Data | Current Data Sorted by Sales

Type of Statement									
	29	29	32	Unqualified		3		4	11	14

Full data table:

	Hist 1	Hist 2	Hist 3	0-1MM	1-3MM	3-5MM	5-10MM	10-25MM	25MM & OVER
Type of Statement									
Unqualified	29	29	32		3		4	11	14
Reviewed	21	26	33	2	5	4	12	8	2
Compiled	8	6	12	1	2	3	3	1	2
Tax Returns	7	4	8	3	2	1		2	
Other	8	15	14	2	1	1	1	4	5
	4/1/04-3/31/05 ALL	4/1/05-3/31/06 ALL	4/1/06-3/31/07 ALL	\[61 (4/1-9/30/06)\]			\[38 (10/1/06-3/31/07)\]		
NUMBER OF STATEMENTS	73	80	99	8	13	9	20	26	23
ASSETS	%	%	%	%	%	%	%	%	%
Cash & Equivalents	11.9	11.8	9.4		6.7		9.0	11.3	4.1
Trade Receivables (net)	13.4	16.3	17.8		14.9		20.4	18.5	20.2
Inventory	21.0	21.0	22.6		19.2		20.3	22.5	36.5
All Other Current	7.8	5.8	5.8		5.9		7.6	4.8	5.9
Total Current	54.1	54.9	55.7		46.6		57.3	57.1	66.7
Fixed Assets (net)	38.6	40.1	37.8		43.7		38.2	36.0	26.6
Intangibles (net)	.6	.4	.4		.1		1.2	.3	.3
All Other Non-Current	6.8	4.6	6.1		9.5		3.3	6.5	6.4
Total	100.0	100.0	100.0		100.0		100.0	100.0	100.0
LIABILITIES									
Notes Payable-Short Term	16.3	13.8	24.5		23.2		19.2	16.4	27.8
Cur. Mat.-L.T.D.	3.8	3.4	3.4		1.9		3.3	3.2	4.1
Trade Payables	8.1	13.3	9.5		8.1		6.7	11.8	11.8
Income Taxes Payable	.1	.2	.2		.1		.4	.3	.2
All Other Current	12.0	10.3	10.9		7.9		8.8	11.0	8.5
Total Current	40.3	41.0	48.4		41.3		38.4	42.8	52.5
Long-Term Debt	14.4	14.9	15.4		22.1		14.4	16.7	13.9
Deferred Taxes	1.0	.9	1.1		1.5		2.1	.5	1.2
All Other Non-Current	1.4	2.1	2.0		.6		3.1	.8	1.3
Net Worth	42.9	41.1	33.1		34.6		42.0	39.2	31.0
Total Liabilties & Net Worth	100.0	100.0	100.0		100.0		100.0	100.0	100.0
INCOME DATA									
Net Sales	100.0	100.0	100.0		100.0		100.0	100.0	100.0
Gross Profit									
Operating Expenses	91.9	89.7	91.0		89.1		95.0	93.1	96.5
Operating Profit	8.1	10.3	9.0		10.9		5.0	6.9	3.5
All Other Expenses (net)	.4	1.2	1.6		1.9		.7	.7	.0
Profit Before Taxes	7.7	9.1	7.4		9.0		4.3	6.2	3.5
RATIOS									
Current	2.3	1.9	1.9		1.4		2.0	2.1	1.5
	1.2	1.2	1.2		1.2		1.6	1.3	1.2
	1.1	1.1	1.1		.7		1.1	1.0	1.1
Quick	1.5	1.2	1.1		.9		1.5	1.1	.7
	.6	.6	.5		.4		1.0	.6	.5
	.3	.3	.2		.2		.3	.4	.2
Sales/Receivables	5 76.6	8 46.3	9 39.7		13 28.8		10 37.4	8 45.8	13 27.1
	11 33.3	17 21.4	23 16.1		27 13.7		23 15.6	24 15.5	21 17.7
	33 11.1	40 9.2	45 8.0		61 6.0		63 5.8	40 9.2	37 9.9
Cost of Sales/Inventory									
Cost of Sales/Payables									
Sales/Working Capital	8.6	9.4	8.5		7.9		6.1	8.6	10.8
	27.2	22.1	20.6		20.6		12.7	23.4	24.8
	152.8	65.8	116.1		-13.6		39.0	327.8	46.8
EBIT/Interest	10.8	9.8	8.8		5.7		7.9	23.4	5.1
	(68) 3.4	(75) 4.5	(92) 2.9		1.9		3.3	(25) 3.7	(21) 2.6
	1.4	1.8	1.7		.9		1.8	1.3	2.2
Net Profit + Depr., Dep., Amort./Cur. Mat. L/T/D	6.0	6.3	12.0				18.7		11.2
	(20) 2.8	(26) 2.5	(36) 3.4				(10) 5.8		(12) 3.6
	.2	1.7	1.7				1.5		2.8
Fixed/Worth	.5	.5	.5		.7		.6	.4	.4
	.9	.9	1.0		1.4		1.0	.8	.9
	1.5	1.6	1.8		3.2		1.6	1.8	1.7
Debt/Worth	.5	.5	.7		.6		.5	.6	1.4
	1.4	1.7	2.0		4.2		2.5	1.6	2.4
	3.5	4.1	4.5		5.8		3.3	3.7	5.2
% Profit Before Taxes/Tangible Net Worth	26.3	40.6	35.1		36.9		20.5	34.5	35.2
	(70) 13.1	(76) 18.3	(92) 16.9		11.4		(24) 14.7	(22) 17.5	19.2
	3.2	6.3	7.6		-.5		7.4	7.5	11.3
% Profit Before Taxes/Total Assets	11.0	15.4	11.1		10.7		9.6	14.0	8.2
	4.5	5.5	5.0		2.9		3.9	5.5	5.0
	.9	1.7	2.2		-.2		3.1	1.5	3.5
Sales/Net Fixed Assets	20.7	18.6	15.5		7.6		10.5	19.4	16.7
	9.5	7.3	7.6		3.3		7.4	10.8	11.3
	3.0	1.8	3.0		2.0		3.8	3.8	6.3
Sales/Total Assets	4.2	3.8	3.7		1.9		2.8	4.4	4.4
	2.9	2.5	2.1		1.5		2.3	3.0	2.7
	1.1	1.0	1.0		1.0		.9	1.4	2.0
% Depr., Dep., Amort./Sales	.9	.6	.8		1.3		1.0	.6	.7
	(69) 1.4	(77) 1.8	(94) 1.8		2.4		1.6	(25) 1.3	(21) 1.3
	2.9	3.6	3.4		4.6		2.9	3.0	2.0
% Officers', Directors' Owners' Comp/Sales	2.2	.8	.9						
	(10) 3.1	(11) 1.4	(19) 2.0						
	5.3	3.7	4.9						
Net Sales ($)	3303471M	4896411M	3271539M	3141M	25311M	34521M	142071M	396172M	2670323M
Total Assets ($)	1060515M	1376793M	1197133M	6879M	22635M	26909M	132150M	209848M	798712M

© RMA 2007   M = $ thousand   MM = $ million
See Pages 11 through 21 for Explanation of Ratios and Data

Current Data Sorted by Assets   Comparative Historical Data

0-500M	500M-2MM	2-10MM	10-50MM	50-100MM	100-250MM	Type of Statement	4/1/02-3/31/03 ALL	4/1/03-3/31/04 ALL
		2	5		1	Unqualified	10	5
	3	11				Reviewed	15	19
1	6	4	2			Compiled	6	31
7	5	2				Tax Returns	7	14
6	2	12	4		1	Other	12	21
	9 (4/1-9/30/06)		65 (10/1/06-3/31/07)					
14	16	31	11		2	NUMBER OF STATEMENTS	50	90
%	%	%	%	%	%	ASSETS	%	%
12.8	6.5	10.4	13.6			Cash & Equivalents	8.5	10.7
8.2	8.2	26.2	15.8			Trade Receivables (net)	29.0	19.5
13.5	8.3	3.1	1.9			Inventory	5.4	2.8
.9	2.9	1.5	8.1			All Other Current	2.3	4.0
35.4	25.9	41.3	39.4			Total Current	45.2	36.9
54.0	64.9	45.6	50.3			Fixed Assets (net)	43.3	49.5
4.6	2.3	7.4	.2			Intangibles (net)	5.3	4.6
6.0	6.9	5.7	10.2			All Other Non-Current	6.2	9.0
100.0	100.0	100.0	100.0			Total	100.0	100.0
						LIABILITIES		
19.7	5.1	7.9	10.2			Notes Payable-Short Term	12.5	7.6
4.6	4.2	2.9	3.5			Cur. Mat.-L.T.D.	5.4	3.9
9.6	3.2	9.5	6.1			Trade Payables	12.3	7.2
.0	.0	1.2	.1			Income Taxes Payable	.1	.2
12.8	8.9	7.3	6.0			All Other Current	12.2	10.9
46.7	21.3	28.8	26.0			Total Current	42.5	29.8
31.4	47.8	30.7	30.3			Long-Term Debt	24.3	29.6
.0	.1	.7	.0			Deferred Taxes	.7	.4
8.1	.0	3.4	2.9			All Other Non-Current	3.8	6.0
13.9	30.8	36.4	40.8			Net Worth	28.7	34.2
100.0	100.0	100.0	100.0			Total Liabilities & Net Worth	100.0	100.0
						INCOME DATA		
100.0	100.0	100.0	100.0			Net Sales	100.0	100.0
						Gross Profit		
80.3	75.2	81.3	78.6			Operating Expenses	87.6	85.9
19.7	24.8	18.7	21.4			Operating Profit	12.4	14.1
3.9	13.9	7.3	3.4			All Other Expenses (net)	6.1	6.5
15.8	10.9	11.4	17.9			Profit Before Taxes	6.3	7.6
						RATIOS		
2.0	2.1	3.2	3.2				2.6	2.5
1.1	.9	1.6	1.5			Current	1.3	1.2
.3	.5	.8	1.2				.6	.7
1.3	1.6	2.7	3.1				1.5	1.9
.5	.5	1.3	1.3			Quick	.9	1.0
.2	.2	.7	.4				.5	.5
0 UND	0 UND	19 19.4	0 UND				25 14.4	5 72.3
1 535.1	4 90.2	40 9.1	39 9.4			Sales/Receivables	44 8.2	36 10.0
25 14.4	35 10.6	53 6.8	66 5.5				50 7.4	56 6.5
						Cost of Sales/Inventory		
						Cost of Sales/Payables		
9.7	7.1	8.8	6.1				8.2	6.5
NM	-81.5	17.0	10.2			Sales/Working Capital	31.1	27.7
-7.6	-5.8	-43.5	17.1				-10.8	-12.4
31.9		30.2	23.0				10.7	12.4
(11) 9.7		(24) 6.6	(10) 5.3			EBIT/Interest	(42) 2.3	(65) 3.0
.1		2.3	4.0				.3	1.3
							2.9	1.6
						Net Profit + Depr., Dep., Amort./Cur. Mat. L/T/D	(11) 2.1	(12) 1.2
							.7	1.0
.9	.7	.4	.6				.5	.5
3.7	5.4	.8	1.0			Fixed/Worth	2.4	2.1
-1.2	-46.3	7.3	1.9				10.2	10.0
1.0	.4	.5	.7				.9	.7
3.1	4.8	1.4	1.1			Debt/Worth	3.0	2.1
-3.9	-48.2	8.8	5.8				24.4	15.0
	77.0	50.1	62.0				54.1	56.3
	(11) 16.0	(25) 28.6	(10) 23.8			% Profit Before Taxes/Tangible Net Worth	(39) 27.7	(78) 21.3
	6.0	13.6	10.8				4.6	6.2
62.6	14.4	17.7	23.2				16.3	12.4
15.2	4.9	5.9	12.1			% Profit Before Taxes/Total Assets	4.4	5.3
-7.3	1.2	3.4	4.9				-1.9	.4
35.7	6.1	18.5	5.1				36.0	11.1
12.8	.6	5.0	2.0			Sales/Net Fixed Assets	7.0	2.8
.5	.2	.8	1.5				.7	.7
6.2	2.1	3.2	1.3				3.9	2.7
3.5	.4	1.7	1.0			Sales/Total Assets	2.2	1.2
.4	.2	.4	.7				.6	.5
1.1	3.3	1.4	-1.9				1.3	1.8
(10) 2.7	9.1	(30) 3.6	4.7			% Depr., Dep., Amort./Sales	(44) 3.0	(76) 6.5
13.1	17.9	8.6	8.1				10.9	12.3
							3.6	2.4
						% Officers', Directors' Owners' Comp/Sales	(18) 6.1	(20) 4.2
							12.4	11.6
17194M	15129M	337778M	227219M		228828M	Net Sales ($)	1170686M	1025539M
4085M	17554M	142764M	205346M		283541M	Total Assets ($)	482118M	826930M

(Columns 50-100MM and 100-250MM under ASSETS/LIABILITIES/INCOME/RATIOS: DATA NOT AVAILABLE)

M = $ thousand   MM = $ million
See Pages 11 through 21 for Explanation of Ratios and Data

Comparative Historical Data | Current Data Sorted by Sales

			Type of Statement						
6	10	8	Unqualified	1				4	3
15	21	14	Reviewed	3	1	1	5	4	
15	13	13	Compiled	5	4		3	1	
19	17	14	Tax Returns	10	4				
28	28	25	Other	4	6	1	3	8	3
4/1/04-3/31/05	4/1/05-3/31/06	4/1/06-3/31/07			9 (4/1-9/30/06)			65 (10/1/06-3/31/07)	
ALL	ALL	ALL		0-1MM	1-3MM	3-5MM	5-10MM	10-25MM	25MM & OVER
83	89	74	**NUMBER OF STATEMENTS**	23	15	2	11	17	6
%	%	%	**ASSETS**	%	%	%	%	%	%
12.3	9.9	10.3	Cash & Equivalents	3.4	19.5		12.7	9.8	
16.9	19.5	16.8	Trade Receivables (net)	1.9	13.3		17.0	36.1	
3.5	3.6	6.0	Inventory	7.9	9.3		.1	6.6	
2.1	2.2	3.0	All Other Current	1.4	1.9		1.1	5.2	
34.9	35.2	36.1	Total Current	14.6	44.0		30.8	57.6	
52.3	50.6	52.7	Fixed Assets (net)	78.2	39.6		51.3	33.6	
6.1	6.8	4.6	Intangibles (net)	3.4	3.9		14.6	.6	
6.8	7.3	6.6	All Other Non-Current	3.7	12.4		3.3	8.1	
100.0	100.0	100.0	Total	100.0	100.0		100.0	100.0	
			LIABILITIES						
9.8	6.8	9.6	Notes Payable-Short Term	1.5	25.6		6.2	11.7	
4.5	4.2	3.5	Cur. Mat.-L.T.D.	4.3	2.8		5.7	2.6	
7.8	7.4	7.5	Trade Payables	.4	11.8		5.0	11.9	
.3	.5	.5	Income Taxes Payable	.0	.0		.3	2.1	
13.3	5.1	8.6	All Other Current	6.0	13.8		9.3	7.1	
35.9	24.0	29.8	Total Current	12.1	54.0		26.4	35.4	
37.5	34.7	34.5	Long-Term Debt	62.3	22.9		37.8	14.5	
.5	.4	.6	Deferred Taxes	.1	.2		1.1	.3	
3.9	4.0	3.6	All Other Non-Current	4.7	.6		1.2	6.8	
22.2	37.0	31.6	Net Worth	20.8	22.3		33.4	43.0	
100.0	100.0	100.0	Total Liabilities & Net Worth	100.0	100.0		100.0	100.0	
			INCOME DATA						
100.0	100.0	100.0	Net Sales	100.0	100.0		100.0	100.0	
			Gross Profit						
83.1	85.0	79.2	Operating Expenses	61.6	83.7		90.0	89.8	
16.9	15.0	20.8	Operating Profit	38.4	16.3		10.0	10.2	
6.9	7.8	7.4	All Other Expenses (net)	19.4	2.8		3.4	1.4	
10.0	7.2	13.4	Profit Before Taxes	18.9	13.5		6.6	8.8	
			RATIOS						
1.9	2.6	2.8		1.9	4.1		2.5	3.2	
1.0	1.4	1.3	Current	.9	1.2		1.3	1.6	
.5	.7	.6		.4	.3		.8	1.3	
1.6	2.2	2.1		1.2	3.9		2.5	2.9	
.9	1.0	1.1	Quick	.5	.9		1.2	1.5	
.4	.5	.4		.1	.3		.7	.5	
0 UND	3 123.3	0 UND		0 UND	0 UND		19 19.4	25 14.5	
29 12.8	34 10.9	27 13.3	Sales/Receivables	0 UND	13 27.9		40 9.1	50 7.4	
42 8.6	52 7.0	50 7.3		20 18.5	37 9.8		53 6.8	63 5.8	
			Cost of Sales/Inventory						
			Cost of Sales/Payables						
11.0	6.6	8.6		8.8	5.7		17.0	8.2	
127.1	22.7	18.6	Sales/Working Capital	-58.7	58.7		33.9	11.0	
-8.5	-15.7	-13.0		-4.9	-12.6		-25.3	16.6	
9.8	8.4	24.8		14.8	32.8			16.2	
(69) 3.4	(64) 2.9	(56) 6.0	EBIT/Interest	(11) 5.8	(12) 10.1		(16) 4.8		
1.4	1.3	2.3		1.7	1.9			2.5	
6.0	4.7	9.0	Net Profit + Depr., Dep.,						
(21) 2.2	(22) 3.0	(14) 4.6	Amort./Cur. Mat. L/T/D						
1.3	1.4	1.4							
.7	.8	.6		2.0	.2		.7	.2	
1.8	1.5	1.5	Fixed/Worth	5.9	2.7		6.4	.7	
17.2	15.4	NM		-10.6	-1.6		-4.2	1.2	
1.1	.7	.7		1.1	.3		.5	.7	
2.6	1.7	1.9	Debt/Worth	5.2	4.2		6.8	1.1	
88.6	23.4	NM		-15.9	-4.3		-6.7	1.9	
57.5	37.9	53.1	% Profit Before Taxes/Tangible	32.6	58.2			57.5	
(65) 29.6	(72) 20.3	(56) 25.6	Net Worth	(14) 16.8	(10) 24.5		(16) 26.9		
10.0	5.1	12.8		5.2	12.4			11.9	
18.0	15.2	21.5	% Profit Before Taxes/Total	11.8	40.9		13.1	28.7	
5.0	4.5	8.6	Assets	5.1	13.8		5.4	12.8	
1.2	.8	1.7		.9	1.0		.9	3.9	
12.8	12.3	15.1		.6	35.3		6.1	34.8	
3.6	2.8	3.1	Sales/Net Fixed Assets	.3	10.0		5.0	11.7	
.5	.5	.5		.2	3.9		2.3	2.2	
2.8	2.8	3.1		.4	5.0		2.5	4.3	
1.7	1.2	1.3	Sales/Total Assets	.3	2.6		1.7	2.5	
.5	.4	.3		.2	1.3		.9	1.1	
1.7	1.8	1.9		7.7	1.4		2.7	1.1	
(75) 4.3	(84) 4.6	(69) 4.2	% Depr., Dep., Amort./Sales	(22) 13.2	(11) 3.2		3.8	2.1	
10.2	10.2	11.6		19.0	6.3		7.8	4.6	
2.1	1.4	3.2	% Officers', Directors'						
(23) 6.6	(26) 5.1	(16) 6.4	Owners' Comp/Sales						
13.7	13.2	12.6							
1407724M	1584104M	826148M	Net Sales ($)	9908M	25276M	6971M	77671M	277636M	428686M
826404M	1215426M	653290M	Total Assets ($)	37201M	29650M	5714M	67494M	156149M	357082M

© RMA 2007

M = $ thousand   MM = $ million

See Pages 11 through 21 for Explanation of Ratios and Data

INFORMATION

Current Data Sorted by Assets | Comparative Historical Data

	0-500M	500M-2MM	2-10MM	10-50MM	50-100MM	100-250MM	Type of Statement	4/1/02-3/31/03 ALL	4/1/03-3/31/04 ALL
		3	6	6	2	6	Unqualified	27	27
	2	7	10	1			Reviewed	13	20
		3	2				Compiled	12	16
	3	7	2	1			Tax Returns	9	8
	2	2	10	10	6	5	Other	28	26
		21 (4/1-9/30/06)		75 (10/1/06-3/31/07)					
NUMBER OF STATEMENTS	7	22	30	18	8	11		89	97
	%	%	%	%	%	%	**ASSETS**	%	%
		18.9	16.4	13.3		7.2	Cash & Equivalents	14.6	13.3
		31.6	22.9	18.5		14.9	Trade Receivables (net)	20.7	20.7
		4.2	5.8	3.4		2.4	Inventory	3.3	3.5
		2.9	1.6	3.1		1.8	All Other Current	2.7	3.9
		57.6	46.7	38.2		26.3	Total Current	41.3	41.5
		19.7	34.1	25.2		22.3	Fixed Assets (net)	33.6	26.6
		12.6	9.0	23.2		46.7	Intangibles (net)	15.6	17.9
		10.1	10.2	13.4		4.7	All Other Non-Current	9.5	14.0
		100.0	100.0	100.0		100.0	Total	100.0	100.0
							LIABILITIES		
		2.7	4.6	3.7		.0	Notes Payable-Short Term	3.1	4.4
		6.8	4.6	2.0		2.5	Cur. Mat.-L.T.D.	4.7	5.5
		11.5	9.3	5.7		5.4	Trade Payables	8.1	7.3
		.1	.1	.0		.2	Income Taxes Payable	.4	.4
		11.3	10.8	14.6		7.1	All Other Current	12.6	12.0
		32.4	29.3	26.0		15.2	Total Current	28.9	29.7
		25.3	30.5	13.1		35.2	Long-Term Debt	26.3	30.8
		.1	.7	.4		1.8	Deferred Taxes	.6	.7
		8.1	9.7	11.6		7.8	All Other Non-Current	7.8	6.4
		34.1	29.8	48.9		39.9	Net Worth	36.4	32.4
		100.0	100.0	100.0		100.0	Total Liabilities & Net Worth	100.0	100.0
							INCOME DATA		
		100.0	100.0	100.0		100.0	Net Sales	100.0	100.0
		54.9	47.1	49.7		49.7	Gross Profit	52.8	50.3
		47.7	41.5	42.9		36.4	Operating Expenses	46.2	42.8
		7.2	5.6	6.8		13.3	Operating Profit	6.6	7.5
		.3	1.0	.5		9.1	All Other Expenses (net)	1.8	2.7
		6.9	4.6	6.3		4.2	Profit Before Taxes	4.8	4.9
							RATIOS		
		3.6	2.3	2.3		2.3		2.7	2.8
		1.8	1.6	1.3		1.1	Current	1.4	1.5
		1.0	1.1	1.0		.9		.9	.9
		3.2	2.0	1.9		2.3		2.3	2.1
		1.7	1.2	1.0		1.0	Quick	1.2	1.1
		.9	.8	.7		.7		.8	.7
		25 14.5	32 11.5	31 11.7		37 10.0		30 12.0	31 11.9
		36 10.1	42 8.6	34 10.6		48 7.6	Sales/Receivables	36 10.1	37 9.9
		45 8.2	51 7.2	41 8.8		51 7.1		48 7.6	45 8.1
		0 UND	5 77.2	6 60.3		0 UND		0 UND	0 UND
		9 40.6	16 22.4	12 29.2		4 98.2	Cost of Sales/Inventory	8 44.3	8 43.5
		19 19.2	28 13.0	27 13.4		14 26.5		20 18.7	19 19.3
		14 26.4	13 27.4	12 30.7		17 21.1		14 26.1	13 28.7
		27 13.6	19 19.2	18 20.2		27 13.7	Cost of Sales/Payables	22 16.9	22 16.6
		40 9.0	47 7.8	35 10.5		48 7.6		51 7.2	42 8.6
		4.3	8.3	8.9		6.0		6.8	6.6
		14.9	14.8	22.1		50.4	Sales/Working Capital	23.4	16.3
		-786.1	53.1	-217.0		-34.7		-51.1	-60.8
		15.4	8.0	39.9				9.6	7.8
		(18) 4.9	(27) 2.7	(14) 4.5			EBIT/Interest	(74) 3.7	(84) 3.2
		2.5	1.8	1.9				1.1	1.5
							Net Profit + Depr., Dep.,	8.5	3.3
							Amort./Cur. Mat. L/T/D	(20) 2.0	(30) 1.4
								1.3	.7
		.1	.4	.3		.8		.6	.5
		.5	1.1	1.1		-2.9	Fixed/Worth	2.1	1.1
		32.4	5.1	-10.6		-.1		-4.0	NM
		.4	.8	.5		1.1		.5	.8
		2.0	1.7	1.5		-5.5	Debt/Worth	2.4	2.6
		NM	9.4	-17.0		-1.7		-9.2	NM
		72.7	49.0	35.6			% Profit Before Taxes/Tangible	43.0	67.9
		(17) 34.6	(26) 17.7	(13) 18.7			Net Worth	(61) 15.9	(73) 18.8
		1.3	4.0	3.5				1.3	2.5
		27.6	13.7	15.2		17.3	% Profit Before Taxes/Total	16.1	17.7
		12.4	4.0	6.9		6.0	Assets	7.7	6.3
		2.1	2.1	3.2		-1.5		.8	1.2
		77.7	12.7	22.3		17.7		13.1	20.1
		31.3	6.9	6.3		5.5	Sales/Net Fixed Assets	5.8	6.0
		9.5	3.0	3.6		3.1		3.1	3.8
		3.7	2.4	2.0		1.6		2.4	2.4
		2.8	1.9	1.4		.8	Sales/Total Assets	1.7	1.7
		2.0	1.5	1.1		.6		1.1	1.0
		.8	1.6	1.9				2.1	1.9
		(18) 1.7	(29) 3.8	(17) 2.6			% Depr., Dep., Amort./Sales	(79) 3.8	(86) 3.9
		2.8	5.6	3.8				6.2	6.2
		4.1					% Officers', Directors'	3.8	2.1
		(10) 7.0					Owners' Comp/Sales	(22) 7.3	(25) 4.8
		10.3						16.5	8.2
	8314M	72078M	384746M	803919M	674864M	2042916M	Net Sales ($)	1952200M	2374547M
	1573M	25321M	155601M	452587M	522479M	1908413M	Total Assets ($)	1645529M	2225799M

M = $ thousand   MM = $ million
See Pages 11 through 21 for Explanation of Ratios and Data

Comparative Historical Data   Current Data Sorted by Sales

4/1/04-3/31/05 ALL	4/1/05-3/31/06 ALL	4/1/06-3/31/07 ALL	Type of Statement	0-1MM	1-3MM	3-5MM	5-10MM	10-25MM	25MM & OVER
27	26	23	Unqualified			3	2	5	13
19	20	20	Reviewed	1	5	4	6	4	
11	8	5	Compiled		2	2	2	1	
10	12	13	Tax Returns	2	6	3	4	2	
16	33	35	Other	1	1	1	4	8	20
					21 (4/1-9/30/06)		75 (10/1/06-3/31/07)		
83	99	96	**NUMBER OF STATEMENTS**	4	14	13	13	19	33
%	%	%	**ASSETS**	%	%	%	%	%	%
11.9	10.2	14.5	Cash & Equivalents		16.8	16.3	18.6	14.1	12.3
22.1	23.0	23.8	Trade Receivables (net)		31.8	26.6	31.0	18.7	16.8
4.3	4.4	3.9	Inventory		3.1	3.4	6.9	5.3	2.6
2.1	2.7	2.6	All Other Current		1.8	2.9	2.3	1.4	3.3
40.4	40.2	44.7	Total Current		53.5	49.3	58.7	39.5	35.0
24.9	26.9	26.4	Fixed Assets (net)		19.2	26.6	22.2	36.8	26.6
23.3	19.8	18.8	Intangibles (net)		11.8	5.7	8.7	19.6	29.6
11.4	13.1	10.1	All Other Non-Current		15.5	18.4	10.4	4.1	8.7
100.0	100.0	100.0	Total		100.0	100.0	100.0	100.0	100.0
			LIABILITIES						
3.2	4.5	4.2	Notes Payable-Short Term		7.1	4.7	6.5	4.6	1.0
5.2	4.8	4.0	Cur. Mat.-L.T.D.		8.9	4.5	3.4	3.8	2.4
10.4	11.1	8.3	Trade Payables		8.2	12.3	12.9	6.9	5.6
.1	.1	.1	Income Taxes Payable		.2	.0	.3	.0	.1
11.2	9.8	13.5	All Other Current		21.3	14.6	13.3	9.3	11.7
30.1	30.3	30.1	Total Current		45.8	36.1	36.3	24.6	20.8
31.7	28.6	26.0	Long-Term Debt		36.5	15.8	10.8	34.8	23.4
.2	.5	.8	Deferred Taxes		.0	.0	1.0	.6	1.5
12.7	9.5	13.0	All Other Non-Current		11.1	12.9	6.3	8.5	17.0
25.3	31.0	30.2	Net Worth		6.6	35.2	45.6	31.5	37.4
100.0	100.0	100.0	Total Liabilties & Net Worth		100.0	100.0	100.0	100.0	100.0
			INCOME DATA						
100.0	100.0	100.0	Net Sales		100.0	100.0	100.0	100.0	100.0
46.4	48.4	51.5	Gross Profit		61.9	55.4	44.3	47.1	50.6
39.4	41.8	44.3	Operating Expenses		54.5	49.7	38.8	39.8	41.4
7.0	6.5	7.2	Operating Profit		7.5	5.7	5.5	7.3	9.2
1.8	.7	1.6	All Other Expenses (net)		.5	-.5	-.2	1.6	3.6
5.1	5.8	5.6	Profit Before Taxes		7.0	6.2	5.7	5.7	5.6
			RATIOS						
2.0	2.1	2.4			3.1	3.3	2.9	2.3	2.3
1.3	1.5	1.5	Current		1.5	1.3	1.7	1.9	1.3
.9	1.0	1.0			.9	.8	1.1	1.0	1.0
1.5	1.8	2.1			2.4	3.0	2.6	2.0	1.9
1.0	1.1	1.2	Quick		1.5	.9	1.3	1.4	1.0
.7	.7	.8			.8	.7	.7	.8	.8
30 12.2	31 11.8	32 11.4			35 10.5	24 15.2	29 12.4	31 11.6	34 10.8
37 9.9	38 9.7	37 9.8	Sales/Receivables		41 8.9	32 11.3	38 9.5	35 10.4	37 9.9
45 8.1	45 8.1	47 7.7			55 6.7	44 8.3	60 6.1	46 8.0	49 7.4
0 UND	0 UND	0 796.7			0 UND	0 UND	0 UND	6 58.3	3 141.8
7 53.1	10 36.9	9 42.3	Cost of Sales/Inventory		6 60.8	7 52.3	9 42.5	21 17.2	8 45.4
21 17.6	21 17.3	22 16.7			28 13.2	18 20.4	26 14.1	29 12.7	20 18.7
14 26.6	13 28.8	14 26.9			7 52.3	17 21.5	13 27.7	14 27.0	16 23.0
26 14.1	23 15.9	22 16.3	Cost of Sales/Payables		18 20.7	36 10.1	26 14.2	18 20.3	22 16.5
46 8.0	49 7.5	42 8.7			40 9.0	65 5.6	51 7.2	28 13.0	46 8.0
10.1	8.6	8.6			4.0	13.4	7.6	8.6	9.7
26.8	18.7	16.4	Sales/Working Capital		17.4	30.5	14.7	12.8	21.6
-34.7	-186.6	-300.0			-112.9	-49.4	50.4	-275.6	NM
9.8	12.6	10.9			8.5	16.9		18.0	20.7
(75) 4.3	(88) 3.8	(81) 3.8	EBIT/Interest		(12) 4.3	(11) 3.5		(18) 3.9	(27) 4.4
2.0	1.5	1.9			2.4	1.0		1.8	1.9
3.8	4.1	3.6							2.5
(20) 1.8	(24) 2.0	(25) 1.8	Net Profit + Depr., Dep., Amort./Cur. Mat. L/T/D					(13) 2.2	
.7	1.2	1.0							.7
.6	.6	.3			.2	.4	.2	.4	.6
2.5	1.5	1.3	Fixed/Worth		.8	2.2	.6	1.5	2.0
-.7	-2.3	-4.5			NM	-2.8	1.3	10.7	-.6
1.2	.9	.7			.6	.4	.6	.7	1.0
3.8	3.4	2.4	Debt/Worth		3.0	2.3	1.9	1.2	2.8
-4.4	-13.7	-8.9			-1.8	-25.6	4.1	16.6	-2.6
59.0	57.9	46.6			57.6		66.6	50.4	40.2
(53) 23.8	(67) 24.6	(67) 20.4	% Profit Before Taxes/Tangible Net Worth		(10) 21.5		(12) 17.4	(16) 25.3	(19) 25.4
6.7	9.9	4.2			6.9		5.2	8.3	8.2
14.9	16.0	17.2			16.2	37.9	23.4	15.7	18.1
7.1	7.2	7.3	% Profit Before Taxes/Total Assets		11.9	9.6	5.8	7.4	6.3
1.8	.9	2.1			3.8	.3	2.3	2.9	1.9
28.5	22.0	33.1			78.3	84.8	38.4	10.8	13.4
8.9	7.0	8.7	Sales/Net Fixed Assets		22.9	12.4	10.8	4.8	5.4
4.4	3.6	3.7			6.0	5.8	6.8	3.2	3.3
2.7	2.7	2.7			3.8	3.3	3.4	2.0	1.9
1.8	1.8	1.9	Sales/Total Assets		2.1	2.4	2.8	1.7	1.4
1.2	1.2	1.3			1.4	2.0	1.2	1.4	.8
1.4	1.6	1.5			.7	.8	.9	1.7	2.4
(65) 3.5	(88) 3.0	(83) 3.0	% Depr., Dep., Amort./Sales		(11) 2.2	(11) 2.4	(12) 1.7	3.7	(28) 3.6
5.7	4.9	4.8			5.2	4.2	3.1	5.3	4.4
1.8	2.2	4.1							
(25) 5.1	(21) 3.3	(22) 7.7	% Officers', Directors' Owners' Comp/Sales						
8.7	9.2	12.5							
2220706M	2959460M	3986837M	Net Sales ($)	2998M	26396M	52057M	93776M	255360M	3556250M
1837317M	2503187M	3065974M	Total Assets ($)	823M	15372M	21172M	53355M	163506M	2811746M

M = $ thousand   MM = $ million
See Pages 11 through 21 for Explanation of Ratios and Data

Current Data Sorted by Assets / Comparative Historical Data

0-500M	500M-2MM	2-10MM	10-50MM	50-100MM	100-250MM	Type of Statement	4/1/02-3/31/03 ALL	4/1/03-3/31/04 ALL
	1	5	13	2	4	Unqualified	23	27
	4	7	7	1		Reviewed	15	25
	5	3	1			Compiled	20	27
7	2	3	1			Tax Returns	5	11
3	7	12	10		2	Other	28	26
	18 (4/1-9/30/06)		82 (10/1/06-3/31/07)					
10	19	30	32	3	6	NUMBER OF STATEMENTS	91	116
%	%	%	%	%	%	**ASSETS**	%	%
19.1	12.1	21.1	10.1			Cash & Equivalents	13.7	12.9
19.9	41.2	29.1	20.3			Trade Receivables (net)	26.6	31.0
9.0	5.4	6.7	7.6			Inventory	6.2	5.3
10.1	5.8	3.4	3.5			All Other Current	6.4	4.3
58.1	64.6	60.3	41.5			Total Current	52.9	53.5
7.7	12.4	14.9	17.3			Fixed Assets (net)	19.5	19.2
16.3	14.0	13.1	29.8			Intangibles (net)	16.5	15.4
17.8	9.0	11.6	11.4			All Other Non-Current	11.2	11.9
100.0	100.0	100.0	100.0			Total	100.0	100.0
						LIABILITIES		
20.5	19.0	8.7	4.0			Notes Payable-Short Term	4.5	8.1
9.2	2.8	4.2	6.2			Cur. Mat.-L.T.D.	5.7	5.2
13.5	21.2	13.9	8.9			Trade Payables	13.9	14.4
.8	.1	.2	.6			Income Taxes Payable	.5	.4
18.6	19.1	20.9	17.3			All Other Current	22.5	17.4
62.6	62.3	48.0	37.0			Total Current	47.2	45.5
60.8	25.5	11.6	30.6			Long-Term Debt	21.6	20.3
.0	.2	.0	.7			Deferred Taxes	.6	.3
3.5	3.7	16.4	19.1			All Other Non-Current	13.1	18.9
-26.8	8.5	24.1	12.6			Net Worth	17.5	14.9
100.0	100.0	100.0	100.0			Total Liabilities & Net Worth	100.0	100.0
						INCOME DATA		
100.0	100.0	100.0	100.0			Net Sales	100.0	100.0
74.8	47.4	49.8	47.1			Gross Profit	46.9	47.9
71.8	43.1	41.9	38.9			Operating Expenses	41.7	41.7
3.0	4.3	7.9	8.2			Operating Profit	5.2	6.3
1.8	3.4	.7	2.5			All Other Expenses (net)	1.8	1.2
1.2	.9	7.2	5.7			Profit Before Taxes	3.4	5.1
						RATIOS		
1.9	1.6	2.0	1.6			Current	1.9	2.2
1.1	.9	1.4	1.2				1.2	1.3
.2	.7	.9	.7				.7	.8
1.4	1.1	1.4	1.3			Quick	1.3	1.7
.9	.8	1.1	.8				1.1	1.0
.1	.6	.6	.5				.6	.6
0 UND	32 11.4	24 15.3	37 9.9			Sales/Receivables	26 14.2	30 12.2
0 UND	44 8.3	36 10.3	43 8.6				41 9.0	42 8.7
62 5.9	62 5.9	55 6.6	53 6.8				55 6.7	61 6.0
0 UND	0 UND	0 UND	8 46.3			Cost of Sales/Inventory	0 UND	0 UND
0 UND	0 UND	0 UND	23 15.6				6 57.6	6 65.6
91 4.0	4 89.4	20 18.4	35 10.3				22 16.5	18 20.2
0 UND	12 30.6	13 27.5	15 24.4			Cost of Sales/Payables	19 19.5	17 21.0
0 UND	26 13.8	24 15.4	31 11.9				31 11.9	29 12.6
83 4.4	61 6.0	59 6.2	62 5.9				66 5.6	67 5.5
14.0	7.2	8.3	9.1			Sales/Working Capital	7.8	7.4
93.6	-89.4	19.8	20.8				27.2	24.6
-22.2	-13.5	-43.2	-11.7				-18.0	-17.6
	9.3	40.7	7.4			EBIT/Interest	15.1	16.6
	(15) 2.2	(27) 7.2	(29) 4.6				(75) 3.5	(96) 4.3
	-1.7	2.7	.9				.2	1.1
			4.9			Net Profit + Depr., Dep., Amort./Cur. Mat. L/T/D	4.3	5.5
			(11) 2.1				(15) 1.6	(24) 3.0
			1.1				.3	1.3
.0	.2	.2	.7			Fixed/Worth	.3	.3
1.0	1.3	1.0	-1.5				1.2	1.3
-.1	-.4	-1.2	-.1				-.3	-.5
.9	2.6	1.0	1.7			Debt/Worth	1.4	1.2
NM	7.0	3.5	-7.3				4.5	5.4
-1.4	-3.3	-5.5	-1.8				-4.3	-5.7
	80.2	96.0	58.2			% Profit Before Taxes/Tangible Net Worth	82.5	79.2
	(11) 44.5	(21) 56.8	(14) 18.5				(58) 23.1	(75) 27.4
	17.9	25.7	6.8				.9	6.5
40.9	26.8	25.7	16.5			% Profit Before Taxes/Total Assets	18.2	20.8
8.9	5.5	13.9	5.6				7.4	7.9
-8.1	-9.0	3.6	-.1				-2.0	.7
UND	86.3	70.4	34.3			Sales/Net Fixed Assets	47.6	50.7
40.1	33.6	35.0	16.8				18.6	21.7
26.7	27.1	17.3	6.9				8.8	6.7
5.7	4.5	3.4	1.9			Sales/Total Assets	3.3	3.7
3.6	3.4	2.6	1.5				2.2	2.1
2.4	1.9	1.9	1.1				1.4	1.4
	.4	.7	1.5			% Depr., Dep., Amort./Sales	1.2	.8
	(15) .7	(24) .9	(22) 2.0				(72) 1.8	(85) 1.5
	3.3	1.7	4.0				3.4	3.5
			2.7			% Officers', Directors' Owners' Comp/Sales	3.5	3.2
		(10) 3.1					(25) 5.5	(39) 5.7
		4.2					7.1	8.8
5863M	77239M	346677M	1040521M	404849M	487337M	Net Sales ($)	2023688M	2220669M
1693M	22803M	138380M	749682M	187244M	1079895M	Total Assets ($)	1594281M	1429058M

M = $ thousand   MM = $ million

See Pages 11 through 21 for Explanation of Ratios and Data

Comparative Historical Data | Current Data Sorted by Sales

4/1/04-3/31/05 ALL	4/1/05-3/31/06 ALL	4/1/06-3/31/07 ALL	Type of Statement	0-1MM	1-3MM	3-5MM	5-10MM	10-25MM	25MM & OVER
29	26	25	Unqualified			2	3	9	11
24	17	19	Reviewed		1	2	3	6	7
12	20	9	Compiled		1	2	4	1	1
10	8	13	Tax Returns	6	3		1	1	2
26	35	34	Other	4	5	1	4	15	5
					18 (4/1-9/30/06)		82 (10/1/06-3/31/07)		
101	106	100	**NUMBER OF STATEMENTS**	10	10	7	15	32	26
%	%	%	**ASSETS**	%	%	%	%	%	%
14.8	15.0	15.7	Cash & Equivalents	19.1	4.3		22.4	17.6	14.0
25.4	29.3	26.3	Trade Receivables (net)	14.5	41.8		30.7	23.4	20.7
6.4	6.7	6.8	Inventory	9.1	10.1		6.2	4.8	7.6
3.8	4.1	4.5	All Other Current	10.0	9.0		1.9	4.9	2.7
50.3	55.1	53.3	Total Current	52.7	65.2		61.2	50.7	45.0
15.8	13.9	13.7	Fixed Assets (net)	7.5	15.2		9.5	11.9	17.7
21.6	20.0	21.6	Intangibles (net)	24.8	11.1		17.1	24.6	26.9
12.3	11.0	11.4	All Other Non-Current	14.9	8.6		12.3	12.8	10.5
100.0	100.0	100.0	Total	100.0	100.0		100.0	100.0	100.0
			LIABILITIES						
9.6	8.2	9.7	Notes Payable-Short Term	20.5	18.4		4.9	8.9	4.7
4.0	3.6	4.8	Cur. Mat.-L.T.D.	9.4	1.9		3.9	5.7	3.6
11.0	15.2	13.1	Trade Payables	11.8	13.9		22.2	11.4	9.7
.3	.4	.4	Income Taxes Payable	.8	.0		.4	.1	.8
16.7	16.8	19.5	All Other Current	15.8	16.2		19.2	22.0	17.7
41.5	44.1	47.5	Total Current	58.3	50.4		50.8	48.1	36.4
20.0	15.9	26.6	Long-Term Debt	71.3	16.3		20.7	24.9	22.2
.5	.4	.4	Deferred Taxes	.3	.0		.0	.3	1.1
19.5	26.5	12.3	All Other Non-Current	3.5	5.7		11.6	18.7	13.7
18.5	13.1	13.2	Net Worth	-33.4	27.6		16.9	8.0	26.5
100.0	100.0	100.0	Total Liabilties & Net Worth	100.0	100.0		100.0	100.0	100.0
			INCOME DATA						
100.0	100.0	100.0	Net Sales	100.0	100.0		100.0	100.0	100.0
49.7	49.2	51.7	Gross Profit	77.7	47.5		45.4	47.9	52.7
43.7	41.9	44.4	Operating Expenses	74.6	42.4		36.3	40.0	43.7
6.0	7.3	7.2	Operating Profit	3.1	5.1		9.1	7.9	9.0
1.0	1.6	2.2	All Other Expenses (net)	7.4	1.3		1.6	2.2	1.3
5.0	5.7	5.0	Profit Before Taxes	-4.3	3.8		7.6	5.7	7.7
			RATIOS						
2.2	2.3	1.8	Current	1.9	2.5		2.8	1.6	1.8
1.5	1.3	1.2		.9	1.2		1.4	1.2	1.3
.8	.9	.7		.2	.8		.8	.7	.7
1.9	1.7	1.3	Quick	1.4	1.1		2.2	1.3	1.3
1.1	1.1	1.0		.7	.8		1.2	1.1	.9
.7	.6	.6		.1	.6		.5	.5	.6
25 14.7	26 13.8	30 12.3	Sales/Receivables	0 UND	38 9.6		16 22.8	30 12.1	36 10.2
38 9.6	42 8.7	41 8.9		0 UND	57 6.5		35 10.3	40 9.1	44 8.4
51 7.2	62 5.9	62 5.9		54 6.8	82 4.5		46 8.0	52 7.1	72 5.0
0 UND	0 UND	0 UND	Cost of Sales/Inventory	0 UND	0 UND		0 UND	0 UND	9 40.2
9 42.6	7 49.3	8 44.6		0 UND	0 UND		0 UND	7 55.7	25 14.4
28 12.8	24 15.1	29 12.7		91 4.0	16 23.0		20 18.4	22 16.4	37 9.8
15 24.4	18 20.2	15 25.0	Cost of Sales/Payables	0 UND	11 34.3		7 52.7	15 24.1	17 21.4
25 14.4	37 9.8	30 12.0		0 UND	24 15.1		20 17.9	28 12.8	45 8.1
49 7.5	63 5.8	69 5.3		90 4.0	48 7.6		47 7.8	60 6.1	76 4.8
7.0	7.2	8.7	Sales/Working Capital	14.0	3.9		4.8	12.4	8.0
21.0	21.5	24.7		NM	40.5		20.6	23.8	20.8
-23.7	-24.9	-13.7		-9.1	-12.7		-16.2	-9.1	-18.9
15.7	22.3	13.6	EBIT/Interest				63.2	9.7	28.3
(89) 6.0	(94) 4.4	(85) 4.4					(14) 6.8	(28) 4.3	(22) 6.4
1.5	.6	.9					.7	1.1	.9
9.1	10.7	15.5	Net Profit + Depr., Dep., Amort./Cur. Mat. L/T/D						24.8
(21) 2.5	(28) 4.4	(24) 3.2						(13)	2.8
1.7	1.2	1.1							1.3
.3	.2	.2	Fixed/Worth	.0	.1		.1	.3	.4
2.2	1.4	1.4		NM	1.1		1.2	7.9	NM
-.3	-.2	-.1		-.1	-.5		-.5	-.1	-.2
1.3	1.2	1.3	Debt/Worth	.9	1.2		.9	1.8	1.2
13.9	9.2	8.2		-3.4	3.3		4.6	20.4	NM
-2.7	-2.6	-2.2		-1.3	-5.7		-2.8	-1.8	-2.1
70.8	86.2	78.5	% Profit Before Taxes/Tangible Net Worth				53.3	101.7	58.8
(54) 32.9	(56) 45.8	(55) 35.6					(10) 36.0	(17) 56.8	(13) 35.6
11.7	17.5	13.8					22.0	10.0	15.6
22.0	22.8	20.7	% Profit Before Taxes/Total Assets	22.7	15.7		24.3	23.9	18.5
9.6	8.6	8.0		2.1	5.5		5.6	11.9	9.4
1.8	-1.2	-.1		-11.7	-10.3		-.1	1.1	-.1
48.2	63.4	63.4	Sales/Net Fixed Assets	UND	109.0		69.9	75.8	31.0
22.0	30.9	29.7		34.6	32.4		61.9	31.2	18.3
10.3	11.7	11.1		26.7	7.3		27.1	13.5	7.3
3.2	3.3	3.4	Sales/Total Assets	5.7	2.4		4.3	3.1	2.0
2.2	2.2	2.0		3.5	1.9		2.8	2.0	1.6
1.5	1.5	1.3		.9	1.5		1.7	1.2	.8
1.0	.5	.7	% Depr., Dep., Amort./Sales				.5	.8	1.6
(77) 1.6	(81) 1.1	(72) 1.4					(14) .7	(19) 1.4	(19) 1.8
3.3	2.5	3.2					1.2	3.5	3.4
3.2	3.6	3.0	% Officers', Directors' Owners' Comp/Sales						
(33) 4.3	(31) 5.2	(28) 4.3							
8.3	10.3	11.7							
2547790M	3030258M	2362486M	Net Sales ($)	5186M	19174M	27724M	113387M	546477M	1650538M
1878720M	2636418M	2179697M	Total Assets ($)	2215M	12598M	11456M	59378M	420781M	1673269M

© RMA 2007

M = $ thousand   MM = $ million
See Pages 11 through 21 for Explanation of Ratios and Data

Current Data Sorted by Assets   Comparative Historical Data

Type of Statement

	0-500M	500M-2MM	2-10MM	10-50MM	50-100MM	100-250MM		4/1/02-3/31/03 ALL	4/1/03-3/31/04 ALL
Unqualified		1	7	13	5	4		39	32
Reviewed	1	3	13	8				21	24
Compiled	2	4	5					12	12
Tax Returns	1	4	4					8	8
Other		4	14	13	2	2		29	26
	31 (4/1-9/30/06)			79 (10/1/06-3/31/07)					
NUMBER OF STATEMENTS	4	16	43	34	7	6		109	102

	0-500M %	500M-2MM %	2-10MM %	10-50MM %	50-100MM %	100-250MM %		ALL %	ALL %
ASSETS									
Cash & Equivalents		13.9	7.8	11.2				9.0	10.2
Trade Receivables (net)		34.3	27.3	17.4				27.8	30.0
Inventory		39.8	32.8	23.3				24.5	27.9
All Other Current		2.6	3.8	3.2				4.0	3.5
Total Current		90.6	71.7	55.1				65.4	71.6
Fixed Assets (net)		3.6	9.4	16.7				14.9	14.0
Intangibles (net)		1.2	10.9	11.0				9.8	6.2
All Other Non-Current		4.6	8.0	17.3				9.9	8.3
Total		100.0	100.0	100.0				100.0	100.0
LIABILITIES									
Notes Payable-Short Term		6.4	16.7	8.6				14.6	11.5
Cur. Mat.-L.T.D.		1.4	2.8	2.2				3.8	2.2
Trade Payables		23.8	16.8	10.1				16.7	17.4
Income Taxes Payable		.0	.3	.5				.4	.8
All Other Current		14.2	11.6	9.5				13.7	14.0
Total Current		45.9	48.2	30.9				49.2	45.9
Long-Term Debt		4.0	7.8	13.8				15.7	8.7
Deferred Taxes		.0	.3	.6				.3	.1
All Other Non-Current		7.3	3.6	8.9				10.0	8.6
Net Worth		42.8	40.1	45.9				24.9	36.7
Total Liabilities & Net Worth		100.0	100.0	100.0				100.0	100.0
INCOME DATA									
Net Sales		100.0	100.0	100.0				100.0	100.0
Gross Profit		51.6	53.8	59.2				51.3	47.3
Operating Expenses		44.7	51.0	52.2				46.6	41.5
Operating Profit		6.9	2.8	7.0				4.7	5.7
All Other Expenses (net)		.1	1.1	.8				1.5	1.1
Profit Before Taxes		6.7	1.6	6.2				3.2	4.6

RATIOS

Ratio	0-500M	500M-2MM	2-10MM	10-50MM	50-100MM	100-250MM	ALL	ALL
Current		2.9	2.7	3.0			2.3	2.5
		1.9	1.6	2.0			1.5	1.6
		1.5	1.2	1.3			1.1	1.1
Quick		1.5	1.6	1.5			1.5	1.5
		1.0	.7	.9			.9	1.0
		.8	.4	.5			.5	.6
Sales/Receivables		23 15.7	37 9.8	25 14.4			39 9.4	45 8.2
		48 7.6	58 6.3	49 7.4			56 6.5	66 5.5
		61 6.0	84 4.3	73 5.0			84 4.3	109 3.3
Cost of Sales/Inventory		39 9.3	64 5.7	113 3.2			28 13.2	57 6.4
		147 2.5	165 2.2	183 2.0			117 3.1	142 2.6
		257 1.4	313 1.2	264 1.8			182 2.0	202 1.8
Cost of Sales/Payables		18 20.1	32 11.5	32 11.5			22 16.3	30 12.0
		42 8.6	61 6.0	55 6.6			55 6.6	63 5.8
		101 3.6	139 2.6	108 3.4			96 3.8	119 3.1
Sales/Working Capital		2.7	3.0	2.7			3.6	3.0
		4.0	7.8	4.9			7.1	6.4
		9.8	23.0	13.7			52.5	37.2
EBIT/Interest		6.6	9.6	6.6			8.5	9.8
		(12) 1.9	(39) 2.5	(27) 3.5			(94) 3.4	(90) 4.6
		-1.3	1.1	2.4			.7	1.9
Net Profit + Depr., Dep., Amort./Cur. Mat. L/T/D							4.1	17.4
							(25) 2.0	(26) 3.5
							.6	1.6
Fixed/Worth		.0	.1	.1			.1	.1
		.0	.2	.3			.5	.3
		.1	.6	2.7			2.5	1.0
Debt/Worth		.6	.9	.6			.8	.8
		1.1	1.6	1.3			1.8	1.7
		3.8	8.0	5.4			26.2	4.9
% Profit Before Taxes/Tangible Net Worth		83.9	47.0	27.7			38.2	43.8
		(14) 8.8	(39) 17.2	(29) 15.8			(85) 13.4	(89) 21.6
		-5.4	.3	7.8			.1	4.0
% Profit Before Taxes/Total Assets		25.1	10.2	12.1			12.6	13.0
		6.2	2.8	7.5			5.3	5.4
		-3.0	-.4	2.4			-.1	1.1
Sales/Net Fixed Assets		777.3	59.3	32.0			37.2	53.8
		148.6	27.5	12.5			18.3	27.0
		43.4	14.2	3.8			7.8	8.7
Sales/Total Assets		3.3	2.1	1.7			2.2	2.0
		2.1	1.7	1.2			1.6	1.4
		1.5	1.1	.8			1.2	1.1
% Depr., Dep., Amort./Sales			.7	.9			.9	.6
		(30) 1.4	(29) 1.8				(85) 1.8	(81) 1.3
		2.7	3.4				3.0	3.1
% Officers', Directors' Owners' Comp/Sales			2.8				3.7	1.6
		(13) 5.5					(27) 6.5	(28) 5.4
		10.4					11.9	11.2
Net Sales ($)	3244M	58910M	396690M	987868M	631717M	976920M	3564503M	3406644M
Total Assets ($)	682M	22568M	231307M	824302M	543174M	972810M	2702952M	2675873M

M = $ thousand   MM = $ million
See Pages 11 through 21 for Explanation of Ratios and Data

Comparative Historical Data | Current Data Sorted by Sales

	4/1/04-3/31/05 ALL	4/1/05-3/31/06 ALL	4/1/06-3/31/07 ALL	Type of Statement	0-1MM	1-3MM	3-5MM	5-10MM	10-25MM	25MM & OVER
	33	19	30	Unqualified		2	2	3	5	18
	27	23	25	Reviewed	1	2	3	7	8	4
	7	9	9	Compiled		2	4	1	2	
	8	8	10	Tax Returns	1	6		2	1	
	32	36	36	Other	2	3	4	3	13	11
						31 (4/1-9/30/06)			79 (10/1/06-3/31/07)	
	107	95	110	**NUMBER OF STATEMENTS**	4	15	13	16	29	33
	%	%	%	**ASSETS**	%	%	%	%	%	%
	11.4	10.4	12.0	Cash & Equivalents		12.5	9.7	13.3	7.3	13.7
	26.8	27.2	24.0	Trade Receivables (net)		27.8	21.0	26.0	27.8	20.0
	26.2	27.9	29.2	Inventory		34.5	33.3	29.0	28.8	23.3
	3.1	4.4	3.5	All Other Current		4.3	1.6	4.3	3.7	3.6
	67.6	69.9	68.7	Total Current		79.1	65.6	72.6	67.6	60.6
	13.6	11.8	10.5	Fixed Assets (net)		2.6	9.1	8.4	14.2	13.7
	8.3	9.5	10.8	Intangibles (net)		4.8	17.5	13.5	7.7	13.6
	10.5	8.9	10.0	All Other Non-Current		13.5	7.7	5.5	10.6	12.1
	100.0	100.0	100.0	Total		100.0	100.0	100.0	100.0	100.0
				LIABILITIES						
	10.0	7.9	10.3	Notes Payable-Short Term		10.5	15.3	11.4	14.5	4.8
	2.5	3.6	2.3	Cur. Mat.-L.T.D.		1.2	2.5	1.3	3.3	2.4
	15.4	15.3	14.9	Trade Payables		18.1	14.1	10.1	20.6	11.1
	.8	.6	.3	Income Taxes Payable		.0	.1	.3	.2	.7
	14.9	14.0	11.5	All Other Current		15.7	19.3	11.3	7.5	11.4
	43.6	41.5	39.3	Total Current		45.6	51.3	34.4	46.0	30.5
	10.8	9.2	9.2	Long-Term Debt		7.2	6.1	12.4	7.6	12.3
	.6	.9	.5	Deferred Taxes		.0	.3	.5	.4	1.0
	15.0	8.1	6.2	All Other Non-Current		4.7	5.4	6.0	7.2	6.3
	30.0	40.3	44.8	Net Worth		42.5	36.8	46.7	38.8	50.0
	100.0	100.0	100.0	Total Liabilities & Net Worth		100.0	100.0	100.0	100.0	100.0
				INCOME DATA						
	100.0	100.0	100.0	Net Sales		100.0	100.0	100.0	100.0	100.0
	49.8	50.7	54.5	Gross Profit		54.5	53.7	63.1	51.4	53.8
	44.0	45.0	49.0	Operating Expenses		52.2	50.5	57.5	45.6	46.9
	5.9	5.7	5.5	Operating Profit		2.2	3.3	5.6	5.8	6.8
	1.0	1.6	.9	All Other Expenses (net)		.3	1.2	1.2	1.4	.6
	4.9	4.1	4.6	Profit Before Taxes		1.9	2.1	4.4	4.4	6.2
				RATIOS						
	2.6	2.7	3.0	Current		2.9	1.9	4.6	2.3	3.3
	1.8	1.8	1.9			2.1	1.5	2.9	1.5	2.1
	1.2	1.1	1.2			1.0	1.2	1.6	1.1	1.3
	1.5	1.5	1.8	Quick		1.8	1.0	3.1	1.2	2.1
	1.0	.9	1.0			1.1	.7	1.7	.7	1.0
	.6	.5	.5			.3	.5	.7	.5	.5
37	9.9 / 37	9.9 / 31	11.6	Sales/Receivables	24	15.4 / 21	17.5 / 36	10.3 / 39	9.5 / 31	11.8
56	6.5 / 58	6.3 / 54	6.8		51	7.1 / 41	8.8 / 59	6.2 / 63	5.8 / 53	6.9
84	4.3 / 83	4.4 / 74	4.9		123	3.0 / 59	6.2 / 79	4.6 / 80	4.6 / 73	5.0
46	8.0 / 61	6.0 / 75	4.9	Cost of Sales/Inventory	47	7.8 / 28	13.0 / 52	7.0 / 47	7.8 / 90	4.0
133	2.7 / 145	2.5 / 161	2.3		237	1.5 / 144	2.5 / 198	1.8 / 162	2.3 / 139	2.6
215	1.7 / 236	1.5 / 266	1.4		392	.9 / 281	1.3 / 308	1.2 / 199	1.8 / 207	1.8
26	13.9 / 31	11.9 / 30	12.3	Cost of Sales/Payables	10	37.6 / 16	23.4 / 40	9.1 / 31	11.7 / 34	10.8
52	7.0 / 56	6.5 / 55	6.6		45	8.1 / 35	10.5 / 70	5.2 / 60	6.1 / 54	6.7
97	3.8 / 110	3.3 / 119	3.1		167	2.2 / 123	3.0 / 111	3.3 / 135	2.7 / 117	3.1
	2.8	3.1	2.7	Sales/Working Capital		2.6	5.0	2.4	3.9	2.3
	4.9	5.7	5.8			3.8	6.8	3.1	12.2	5.8
	23.0	25.3	15.5			158.2	48.4	7.9	23.2	13.8
	11.1	11.5	7.0	EBIT/Interest		3.0	5.6	10.8	9.3	16.1
(96)	5.0 / (80)	3.9 / (91)	3.2		(11) 1.4	1.3	(12) 3.6	2.9	(25) 5.5	
	2.0	.6	1.4			.0	-1.1	1.9	1.7	2.7
	12.4	7.6	5.1	Net Profit + Depr., Dep., Amort./Cur. Mat. L/T/D						
(28)	2.5 / (22)	1.9 / (20)	2.5							
	1.3	.4	1.7							
	.1	.1	.1	Fixed/Worth		.0	.0	.0	.1	.1
	.2	.2	.2			.0	.2	.2	.2	.3
	1.1	1.2	1.1			.1	-.7	1.7	2.6	NM
	.7	.8	.6	Debt/Worth		.5	.9	.7	.8	.5
	1.5	2.1	1.3			1.1	1.4	1.6	2.0	.9
	8.2	8.8	7.7			7.6	-7.8	4.4	13.0	NM
	46.3	36.3	34.0	% Profit Before Taxes/Tangible Net Worth		13.4		43.9	53.8	27.7
(89)	19.0 / (79)	12.4 / (93)	13.5			(13) 4.4	(14) 13.2	(28) 25.1		(25) 14.7
	3.7	1.2	2.2			-.9		-6.7	7.1	8.0
	16.0	12.5	12.1	% Profit Before Taxes/Total Assets		6.2	17.3	15.6	11.6	12.1
	7.4	5.2	5.0			1.8	.8	4.0	4.4	7.6
	1.4	.0	1.2			-.5	-4.5	-4.2	1.8	3.9
	67.0	80.1	76.1	Sales/Net Fixed Assets		899.7	354.3	87.9	50.7	41.0
	28.1	25.5	26.4			73.4	38.9	34.2	22.7	12.5
	6.7	11.1	12.0			17.1	15.4	13.5	9.1	6.1
	2.1	2.0	2.0	Sales/Total Assets		2.6	2.3	2.1	2.2	1.6
	1.6	1.5	1.5			1.4	1.8	1.4	1.7	1.1
	1.1	1.1	1.0			.6	1.1	1.0	1.4	1.0
	.5	.8	.7	% Depr., Dep., Amort./Sales				.6	.7	1.0
(83)	1.1 / (66)	1.5 / (75)	1.5				(11) 1.3	(23) 1.6	(24) 1.9	
	2.1	3.1	2.8					2.6	2.8	3.9
	2.7	3.3	2.1	% Officers', Directors' Owners' Comp/Sales						
(30)	5.8 / (27)	5.7 / (29)	5.3							
	11.4	14.4	13.1							
	3362801M	3564416M	3055349M	Net Sales ($)	1351M	35924M	52875M	119614M	456594M	2388991M
	2698386M	2724927M	2594843M	Total Assets ($)	1236M	44491M	37872M	105045M	311546M	2094653M

© RMA 2007

M = $ thousand   MM = $ million
See Pages 11 through 21 for Explanation of Ratios and Data

Current Data Sorted by Assets

Comparative Historical Data

				2	1	1	Type of Statement		
				2			Unqualified	7	5
1	1	3					Reviewed	6	6
	1	1					Compiled	10	7
3	1	1	1				Tax Returns	5	2
	5	2		1		1	Other	9	11
	3 (4/1-9/30/06)		24 (10/1/06-3/31/07)					4/1/02-3/31/03	4/1/03-3/31/04
								ALL	ALL
0-500M	500M-2MM	2-10MM	10-50MM	50-100MM	100-250MM		NUMBER OF STATEMENTS	37	31
4	8	7	5	1	2				
%	%	%	%	%	%		ASSETS	%	%
							Cash & Equivalents	13.0	12.6
							Trade Receivables (net)	31.3	28.8
							Inventory	5.9	6.0
							All Other Current	1.6	2.6
							Total Current	51.8	50.1
							Fixed Assets (net)	33.2	35.2
							Intangibles (net)	6.5	7.9
							All Other Non-Current	8.5	6.8
							Total	100.0	100.0
							LIABILITIES		
							Notes Payable-Short Term	10.1	9.7
							Cur. Mat.-L.T.D.	4.8	6.7
							Trade Payables	11.5	12.3
							Income Taxes Payable	.1	.4
							All Other Current	17.0	24.3
							Total Current	43.4	53.4
							Long-Term Debt	18.7	20.4
							Deferred Taxes	.2	.4
							All Other Non-Current	10.9	10.7
							Net Worth	26.8	15.2
							Total Liabilties & Net Worth	100.0	100.0
							INCOME DATA		
							Net Sales	100.0	100.0
							Gross Profit		
							Operating Expenses	94.4	94.9
							Operating Profit	5.6	5.1
							All Other Expenses (net)	2.7	2.4
							Profit Before Taxes	2.9	2.7
							RATIOS		
								2.5	1.4
							Current	1.5	1.0
								.9	.5
								2.0	1.2
							Quick	1.3	.8
								.6	.5
								32 11.5	24 15.3
							Sales/Receivables	43 8.5	52 7.1
								56 6.5	70 5.2
							Cost of Sales/Inventory		
							Cost of Sales/Payables		
								6.6	12.7
							Sales/Working Capital	14.9	-307.4
								-82.0	-13.0
								12.3	6.9
							EBIT/Interest	(33) 2.5	(25) 2.3
								.0	.5
									5.6
							Net Profit + Depr., Dep., Amort./Cur. Mat. L/T/D	(11) 1.9	
									.9
								.4	.9
							Fixed/Worth	1.4	2.1
								6.9	6.2
								1.0	1.9
							Debt/Worth	2.6	4.6
								25.4	15.6
								51.8	68.3
							% Profit Before Taxes/Tangible Net Worth	(31) 31.8	(26) 38.1
								-1.6	7.5
								21.2	14.2
							% Profit Before Taxes/Total Assets	6.9	4.9
								-1.3	-3.1
								23.3	21.7
							Sales/Net Fixed Assets	7.9	7.7
								4.4	3.9
								3.8	3.4
							Sales/Total Assets	2.3	2.1
								1.7	1.3
								1.3	3.1
							% Depr., Dep., Amort./Sales	(29) 3.1	(21) 4.8
								5.7	8.6
								3.9	4.6
							% Officers', Directors' Owners' Comp/Sales	(19) 5.8	(11) 7.3
								11.3	10.0
3328M	40315M	131297M	412932M	93930M	798950M		Net Sales ($)	369160M	642771M
538M	9317M	39437M	136278M	55931M	310968M		Total Assets ($)	243606M	417495M

M = $ thousand   MM = $ million
See Pages 11 through 21 for Explanation of Ratios and Data

© RMA 2007

Comparative Historical Data | Current Data Sorted by Sales

4/1/04-3/31/05 ALL	4/1/05-3/31/06 ALL	4/1/06-3/31/07 ALL	Type of Statement	0-1MM	1-3MM	3-5MM	5-10MM	10-25MM	25MM & OVER
4	5	4	Unqualified				2		4
5	4	7	Reviewed		1		1	1	4
1	5	2	Compiled	1		1	1		
	3	5	Tax Returns	3			2		2
10	8	9	Other	1					
				3 (4/1-9/30/06)			24 (10/1/06-3/31/07)		
20	25	27	**NUMBER OF STATEMENTS**	5	2	2	6	2	10
%	%	%	**ASSETS**	%	%	%	%	%	%
12.8	10.2	6.4	Cash & Equivalents						3.1
37.8	35.8	40.1	Trade Receivables (net)						35.1
3.0	2.9	3.3	Inventory						7.1
.9	3.6	5.2	All Other Current						12.0
54.4	52.6	54.9	Total Current						57.3
24.2	23.1	31.5	Fixed Assets (net)						31.0
9.0	11.8	6.9	Intangibles (net)						6.7
12.3	12.5	6.8	All Other Non-Current						4.9
100.0	100.0	100.0	Total						100.0
			LIABILITIES						
8.7	8.5	8.2	Notes Payable-Short Term						5.6
3.2	4.1	2.2	Cur. Mat.-L.T.D.						3.9
17.8	24.1	15.4	Trade Payables						10.9
.2	.1	.0	Income Taxes Payable						.0
20.8	43.5	21.4	All Other Current						26.1
50.8	80.4	47.2	Total Current						46.5
23.7	11.8	26.1	Long-Term Debt						28.8
.1	.0	.1	Deferred Taxes						.2
8.3	11.7	10.8	All Other Non-Current						17.5
17.1	-3.8	15.7	Net Worth						6.9
100.0	100.0	100.0	Total Liabilities & Net Worth						100.0
			INCOME DATA						
100.0	100.0	100.0	Net Sales						100.0
			Gross Profit						
93.9	92.1	98.6	Operating Expenses						96.7
6.1	7.9	1.4	Operating Profit						3.3
1.1	1.1	2.5	All Other Expenses (net)						6.0
5.0	6.8	-1.1	Profit Before Taxes						-2.7
			RATIOS						
1.9	1.4	1.9	Current						1.6
1.0	1.0	1.4							1.4
.6	.5	.7							.9
1.9	1.3	1.7	Quick						1.3
.9	.8	1.2							1.0
.5	.4	.6							.6
43 8.5	26 14.0	20 17.9	Sales/Receivables						20 18.1
54 6.7	44 8.2	53 6.9							34 10.7
95 3.8	70 5.2	71 5.2							70 5.2
			Cost of Sales/Inventory						
			Cost of Sales/Payables						
11.1	20.4	11.3	Sales/Working Capital						7.9
UND	-97.5	34.8							22.9
-13.7	-9.2	-40.2							-107.9
16.5	38.5	16.9	EBIT/Interest						
(17) 7.6	(21) 12.0	(22) 4.5							
2.7	1.9	-.2							
			Net Profit + Depr., Dep., Amort./Cur. Mat. L/T/D						
.4	.7	.5	Fixed/Worth						.4
1.8	1.5	1.5							1.3
-2.5	-1.0	-2.5							-.6
1.4	1.2	.7	Debt/Worth						1.0
3.9	9.4	4.5							3.4
-11.6	-4.3	-4.8							-2.6
67.9	176.3	30.1	% Profit Before Taxes/Tangible Net Worth						
(14) 44.2	(17) 36.8	(18) 19.0							
17.7	15.5	-1.2							
20.9	28.8	17.0	% Profit Before Taxes/Total Assets						18.3
10.0	9.8	3.2							9.2
1.0	6.1	-13.7							-7.0
19.5	41.4	32.4	Sales/Net Fixed Assets						23.1
14.2	18.4	15.4							15.7
6.3	8.1	5.0							6.5
2.9	5.7	5.9	Sales/Total Assets						5.8
2.1	2.8	3.4							3.2
1.0	2.0	1.9							1.9
1.3	1.1	1.0	% Depr., Dep., Amort./Sales						
(18) 3.6	(21) 2.1	(21) 1.8							
4.7	3.6	4.3							
	3.2	1.4	% Officers', Directors' Owners' Comp/Sales						
	(11) 5.3	(11) 8.5							
	10.5	9.8							
421168M	643217M	1480752M	Net Sales ($)	3959M	4374M	7525M	35387M	23545M	1405962M
385475M	391988M	552469M	Total Assets ($)	1412M	5340M	1316M	21602M	5057M	517742M

© RMA 2007

M = $ thousand   MM = $ million
See Pages 11 through 21 for Explanation of Ratios and Data

Current Data Sorted by Assets | **Comparative Historical Data**

Type of Statement		
Unqualified	16	23
Reviewed	14	21
Compiled	6	17
Tax Returns	4	9
Other	30	23

0-500M	500M-2MM 19 (4/1-9/30/06)	2-10MM	10-50MM 55 (10/1/06-3/31/07)	50-100MM	100-250MM		4/1/02-3/31/03 ALL	4/1/03-3/31/04 ALL
1/3/6	1/2/2/9	4/10/3/1/5	10/3/3	1	4/3	NUMBER OF STATEMENTS		
10	17	23	16	1	7		70	93
%	%	%	%	%	%	**ASSETS**	%	%
12.5	12.9	12.2	13.1			Cash & Equivalents	11.6	11.4
44.5	30.8	31.5	28.0			Trade Receivables (net)	29.4	27.4
13.8	13.8	14.8	10.9			Inventory	15.0	15.0
1.2	3.7	3.1	6.3			All Other Current	4.9	6.3
72.0	61.2	61.5	58.4			Total Current	60.9	60.1
8.7	18.5	19.7	24.5			Fixed Assets (net)	22.8	20.8
7.8	7.5	9.9	10.9			Intangibles (net)	9.6	9.1
11.5	12.8	8.9	6.3			All Other Non-Current	6.7	10.1
100.0	100.0	100.0	100.0			Total	100.0	100.0
						LIABILITIES		
30.8	11.5	8.6	3.0			Notes Payable-Short Term	9.6	10.0
3.3	4.4	5.6	2.8			Cur. Mat.-L.T.D.	5.7	3.3
28.0	13.0	12.7	14.1			Trade Payables	18.0	15.5
.0	.0	.3	.4			Income Taxes Payable	.3	.4
19.8	16.5	17.5	21.5			All Other Current	23.4	18.5
81.9	45.4	44.7	41.8			Total Current	57.1	47.7
17.6	21.0	16.1	13.6			Long-Term Debt	12.6	18.2
.0	.0	1.1	1.1			Deferred Taxes	.4	.4
37.4	7.3	8.6	13.0			All Other Non-Current	18.9	14.8
-36.7	26.3	29.6	30.5			Net Worth	11.1	18.9
100.0	100.0	100.0	100.0			Total Liabilities & Net Worth	100.0	100.0
						INCOME DATA		
100.0	100.0	100.0	100.0			Net Sales	100.0	100.0
55.9	52.9	45.1	50.6			Gross Profit	47.4	47.3
47.9	47.8	38.9	43.2			Operating Expenses	42.4	41.5
7.9	5.2	6.2	7.4			Operating Profit	5.0	5.8
5.4	.9	1.0	.7			All Other Expenses (net)	.7	.7
2.5	4.2	5.2	6.7			Profit Before Taxes	4.3	5.1
						RATIOS		
1.7	3.6	2.4	3.2			Current	2.0	2.4
1.1	1.7	1.5	1.8				1.2	1.3
.6	.8	1.0	.9				.9	.9
1.7	2.2	2.2	1.9			Quick	1.5	1.4
.8	1.4	1.0	1.0				.8	.9
.4	.6	.7	.6				.5	.5
0 UND	17 21.8	36 10.2	59 6.2			Sales/Receivables	24 15.1	27 13.7
50 7.3	35 10.4	51 7.1	64 5.7				46 8.0	45 8.0
55 6.6	49 7.4	80 4.6	71 5.1				63 5.8	68 5.4
0 UND	0 UND	9 41.0	9 39.6			Cost of Sales/Inventory	0 UND	1 381.6
21 17.3	18 20.8	38 9.6	31 11.9				20 18.3	19 19.0
38 9.6	81 4.5	113 3.2	67 5.4				106 3.4	90 4.1
0 UND	2 211.0	20 18.5	35 10.5			Cost of Sales/Payables	19 19.3	19 19.3
35 10.4	17 22.1	31 11.9	63 5.8				38 9.6	40 9.1
62 5.9	70 5.2	61 5.9	103 3.5				88 4.2	77 4.8
13.4	5.4	4.2	3.7			Sales/Working Capital	6.7	5.6
NM	14.8	8.5	8.0				21.5	16.7
-37.3	-30.1	339.5	NM				-49.2	-24.7
	7.6	6.8	46.5			EBIT/Interest	13.7	16.8
(14) 3.1	(17) 4.2	(14) 4.3					(59) 3.9	(85) 4.4
1.5	1.1	1.1					1.0	1.3
						Net Profit + Depr., Dep., Amort./Cur. Mat. L/T/D	3.3	3.1
							(20) 2.0	(21) 1.4
							.9	.7
.0	.1	.2	.3			Fixed/Worth	.2	.3
.2	1.3	.6	1.1				.9	1.3
.0	18.9	3.7	-1.7				NM	-2.4
1.1	.9	.9	.9			Debt/Worth	1.0	1.1
NM	9.4	2.1	2.1				3.1	4.3
-2.0	37.5	41.1	-6.7				NM	-9.0
	143.7	57.5				% Profit Before Taxes/Tangible Net Worth	80.9	55.3
(14) 60.3	(18) 41.1						(53) 33.5	(65) 21.3
12.7	.0						10.0	2.7
76.3	21.7	17.6	23.6			% Profit Before Taxes/Total Assets	26.2	19.1
8.7	9.0	9.6	5.5				8.2	5.3
-33.0	2.9	.6	.3				1.5	.9
UND	113.2	53.9	26.0			Sales/Net Fixed Assets	31.2	34.6
352.5	33.3	13.6	9.8				14.2	13.8
80.0	9.2	6.3	2.9				6.8	6.6
16.2	3.8	2.2	2.2			Sales/Total Assets	2.8	2.8
5.8	2.7	1.9	1.6				2.0	1.9
2.5	2.3	1.3	1.2				1.4	1.5
	1.3	.6	1.9			% Depr., Dep., Amort./Sales	1.1	.9
(11) 2.1	(15) 1.9	(15) 4.2					(57) 2.4	(80) 2.3
3.5	4.4	5.8					5.3	4.0
						% Officers', Directors' Owners' Comp/Sales	2.2	3.0
							(15) 6.1	(31) 6.6
							8.5	9.6
21715M	61808M	248247M	701270M	39527M	1698301M	Net Sales ($)	1983914M	2283126M
2083M	19796M	130554M	419062M	53955M	1150601M	Total Assets ($)	1196940M	1405203M

M = $ thousand   MM = $ million
See Pages 11 through 21 for Explanation of Ratios and Data

Comparative Historical Data / Current Data Sorted by Sales

4/1/04-3/31/05 ALL	4/1/05-3/31/06 ALL	4/1/06-3/31/07 ALL	Type of Statement	0-1MM	1-3MM	3-5MM	5-10MM	10-25MM	25MM & OVER
					19 (4/1-9/30/06)		55 (10/1/06-3/31/07)		
23	16	20	Unqualified		1		1	4	14
22	16	15	Reviewed	1			7	4	3
6	8	6	Compiled		2	2	2		
11	6	7	Tax Returns		2	2	1	1	
26	31	26	Other	4	7	3	3	3	6
88	77	74	**NUMBER OF STATEMENTS**	5	12	8	14	12	23
%	%	%	**ASSETS**	%	%	%	%	%	%
11.1	14.6	13.5	Cash & Equivalents		8.4		16.7	9.2	15.0
28.2	31.9	29.8	Trade Receivables (net)		42.9		32.2	36.2	20.6
13.1	11.4	13.0	Inventory		13.5		13.8	12.6	11.5
4.6	7.4	4.2	All Other Current		1.6		3.9	3.2	7.2
57.0	65.4	60.6	Total Current		66.3		66.6	61.2	54.3
23.9	20.9	18.6	Fixed Assets (net)		11.5		21.6	23.5	20.4
11.2	4.9	11.0	Intangibles (net)		6.0		2.6	11.6	16.9
7.9	8.8	9.8	All Other Non-Current		16.2		9.2	3.7	8.3
100.0	100.0	100.0	Total		100.0		100.0	100.0	100.0
			LIABILITIES						
8.0	8.9	10.8	Notes Payable-Short Term		26.9		12.8	6.0	4.3
3.8	2.0	4.9	Cur. Mat.-L.T.D.		1.3		6.0	4.8	7.0
16.1	16.1	14.6	Trade Payables		25.4		13.8	15.4	12.7
.5	.5	.2	Income Taxes Payable		.0		.3	.3	.3
15.5	14.5	18.9	All Other Current		18.3		16.1	16.9	22.3
43.9	42.0	49.3	Total Current		72.0		49.0	43.3	46.6
16.1	13.4	17.3	Long-Term Debt		20.3		13.6	23.0	14.8
.5	.4	.6	Deferred Taxes		.0		.4	1.5	1.1
11.5	11.0	12.6	All Other Non-Current		26.2		7.9	6.1	11.7
28.0	33.2	20.2	Net Worth		-18.5		29.2	26.1	25.9
100.0	100.0	100.0	Total Liabilties & Net Worth		100.0		100.0	100.0	100.0
			INCOME DATA						
100.0	100.0	100.0	Net Sales		100.0		100.0	100.0	100.0
44.1	47.8	52.1	Gross Profit		54.9		52.5	45.3	54.5
37.5	41.5	45.7	Operating Expenses		49.0		46.5	37.4	48.2
6.6	6.2	6.4	Operating Profit		5.9		6.0	7.8	6.3
2.1	.5	1.4	All Other Expenses (net)		.9		.7	1.5	.6
4.5	5.8	5.0	Profit Before Taxes		4.9		5.3	6.3	5.7
			RATIOS						
2.2	3.1	2.4	Current		2.4		2.6	2.4	2.3
1.4	1.6	1.5			1.6		1.4	1.5	1.6
1.0	1.2	.9			.6		.9	1.2	.8
1.6	2.2	1.8	Quick		2.0		2.2	1.4	1.5
.9	1.2	.9			1.2		.8	1.0	.9
.6	.7	.6			.5		.6	.7	.6
32 11.4	28 13.2	29 12.4	Sales/Receivables		17 21.9		26 14.2	38 9.7	24 15.5
50 7.3	52 7.0	47 7.7			48 7.6		43 8.6	58 6.3	56 6.6
70 5.2	65 5.6	66 5.5			69 5.3		82 4.5	79 4.6	64 5.7
2 203.8	0 UND	3 134.1	Cost of Sales/Inventory		0 UND		0 UND	0 UND	4 81.1
20 18.1	23 15.7	27 13.7			11 34.1		27 13.4	19 19.2	38 9.5
74 4.9	68 5.3	72 5.0			74 4.9		115 3.2	94 3.9	71 5.1
19 18.9	19 18.9	21 17.7	Cost of Sales/Payables		3 130.2		14 25.4	22 16.3	41 8.8
34 10.7	38 9.5	43 8.6			26 13.9		38 9.6	60 6.1	60 6.1
66 5.5	77 4.7	75 4.9			86 4.3		65 5.6	70 5.2	87 4.2
6.8	5.2	5.1	Sales/Working Capital		5.8		3.9	5.6	4.3
18.8	11.5	14.0			14.9		31.5	13.1	12.4
-529.4	47.7	-44.6			-17.2		-30.2	27.8	-10.6
10.4	13.4	7.3	EBIT/Interest				8.7	53.1	6.8
(80) 3.3	(59) 5.1	(61) 3.3					(11) 7.3	(10) 4.2	(20) 3.6
.6	.9	1.1					1.6	1.0	1.1
10.6	14.0	14.3	Net Profit + Depr., Dep., Amort./Cur. Mat. L/T/D						
(26) 2.0	(15) 2.7	(14) 2.6							
.9	1.7	1.4							
.4	.2	.2	Fixed/Worth		.0		.4	.2	.3
.9	.7	.8			.3		.7	.8	7.9
NM	4.9	-1.9			NM		NM	3.4	-1.0
.9	.6	1.0	Debt/Worth		1.2		.8	1.1	1.2
2.3	1.9	3.1			9.0		7.3	2.2	25.5
-8.6	30.3	-13.1			-4.0		NM	6.4	-4.8
52.6	58.8	79.1	% Profit Before Taxes/Tangible Net Worth				123.7	58.4	58.3
(64) 17.3	(59) 21.8	(51) 42.8					(11) 56.4	(10) 41.1	(12) 20.5
3.8	7.4	8.3					38.7	-.1	1.6
11.8	24.0	18.5	% Profit Before Taxes/Total Assets		19.1		23.8	18.5	14.4
5.2	8.7	7.8			7.1		13.3	8.4	5.9
-1.2	.5	.4			-18.3		3.0	.3	.3
39.7	52.0	91.2	Sales/Net Fixed Assets		UND		101.2	32.6	18.4
10.3	16.2	15.4			131.7		23.1	16.0	9.4
5.2	7.2	7.7			25.5		8.9	5.1	5.3
2.8	2.9	2.8	Sales/Total Assets		5.7		5.0	2.4	2.2
1.8	2.1	2.1			2.7		2.0	2.1	1.4
1.3	1.5	1.3			2.4		1.3	1.9	1.1
1.6	.8	1.3	% Depr., Dep., Amort./Sales				.5		1.8
(68) 3.0	(61) 2.4	(48) 2.5					(10) 1.2	(19)	3.1
5.0	4.1	4.6					3.4		5.3
2.1	3.5	4.1	% Officers', Directors' Owners' Comp/Sales						
(20) 4.6	(28) 6.5	(15) 6.2							
8.6	7.7	12.7							
2585257M	1858926M	2770868M	Net Sales ($)	2561M	23357M	29076M	103739M	177264M	2434871M
1789303M	1310264M	1776051M	Total Assets ($)	1108M	9757M	16378M	50892M	88656M	1609260M

M = $ thousand   MM = $ million
See Pages 11 through 21 for Explanation of Ratios and Data

INFORMATION—Software Publishers NAICS 511210 (SIC 7372)

Current Data Sorted by Assets | **Comparative Historical Data**

Type of Statement	0-500M	500M-2MM	2-10MM	10-50MM	50-100MM	100-250MM	4/1/02-3/31/03 ALL	4/1/03-3/31/04 ALL
Unqualified		2	12	15	6	11	50	38
Reviewed		1	9	2			20	21
Compiled	1	6	5				17	22
Tax Returns	6	2	1				13	17
Other	8	17	14	20	11	12	60	63
	41 (4/1-9/30/06)			120 (10/1/06-3/31/07)				
NUMBER OF STATEMENTS	15	28	41	37	17	23	160	161

ASSETS	%	%	%	%	%	%	%	%
Cash & Equivalents	25.9	17.2	19.7	25.5	20.3	26.5	22.6	25.2
Trade Receivables (net)	38.2	38.5	43.5	29.4	19.6	19.5	33.0	32.9
Inventory	1.9	3.8	3.0	1.7	.2	1.4	3.2	2.7
All Other Current	2.3	4.2	3.1	5.1	7.1	7.8	5.5	5.0
Total Current	68.2	63.6	69.3	61.8	47.3	55.2	64.3	65.9
Fixed Assets (net)	20.2	15.7	12.0	8.4	8.8	5.9	15.0	13.7
Intangibles (net)	4.6	15.7	12.2	22.6	36.0	31.5	11.7	11.3
All Other Non-Current	7.0	5.1	6.5	7.2	8.0	7.4	9.0	9.1
Total	100.0	100.0	100.0	100.0	100.0	100.0	100.0	100.0

LIABILITIES								
Notes Payable-Short Term	16.0	11.1	5.3	5.2	1.8	.3	9.4	14.2
Cur. Mat.-L.T.D.	.0	3.2	6.6	2.9	1.3	1.3	3.2	2.9
Trade Payables	13.1	17.8	9.5	9.0	5.0	8.7	10.0	9.2
Income Taxes Payable	1.6	.3	.7	.8	1.0	.3	1.5	2.1
All Other Current	9.8	33.6	24.8	32.6	24.6	23.1	27.7	30.3
Total Current	40.5	65.9	46.8	50.5	33.7	33.7	51.8	58.7
Long-Term Debt	6.7	8.3	4.4	10.2	20.1	11.5	11.8	9.7
Deferred Taxes	.0	.2	.1	.4	.7	.5	.4	.3
All Other Non-Current	8.9	31.7	22.6	10.3	13.2	10.8	12.1	11.1
Net Worth	43.8	-6.1	26.1	28.5	32.3	43.5	23.9	20.3
Total Liabilties & Net Worth	100.0	100.0	100.0	100.0	100.0	100.0	100.0	100.0

INCOME DATA								
Net Sales	100.0	100.0	100.0	100.0	100.0	100.0	100.0	100.0
Gross Profit								
Operating Expenses	92.9	97.5	94.5	98.4	90.2	96.9	97.7	94.1
Operating Profit	7.1	2.5	5.5	1.6	9.8	3.1	2.3	5.9
All Other Expenses (net)	.4	1.9	.9	1.2	1.4	1.4	1.2	1.5
Profit Before Taxes	6.6	.7	4.6	.4	8.5	1.7	1.1	4.3

RATIOS								
Current	8.7	2.1	3.6	1.9	1.9	2.8	2.2	2.5
	4.4	1.0	1.7	1.4	1.3	1.4	1.4	1.5
	1.5	.6	1.0	.9	1.1	1.1	1.0	.9
Quick	8.7	1.8	3.2	1.9	1.6	2.5	2.1	2.1
	4.4	.9	1.4	1.3	1.3	1.2	1.2	1.3
	1.4	.4	1.0	.8	.8	.9	.8	.7
Sales/Receivables	16 22.3	27 13.7	52 7.0	49 7.4	32 11.5	60 6.1	35 10.3	35 10.5
	39 9.3	48 7.6	73 5.0	69 5.3	76 4.8	71 5.1	58 6.3	54 6.8
	67 5.5	67 5.5	94 3.9	105 3.5	94 3.9	91 4.0	81 4.5	79 4.6
Cost of Sales/Inventory								
Cost of Sales/Payables								
Sales/Working Capital	3.9	8.1	4.4	3.2	3.9	2.0	4.8	3.9
	8.8	156.6	7.6	6.3	8.4	6.6	11.6	13.3
	35.0	-15.7	83.3	-20.9	27.9	24.1	UND	-70.7
EBIT/Interest		16.6	69.4	15.3	6.2	29.2	16.1	33.9
		(22) 2.9	(32) 7.5	(26) 2.0	(13) 2.7	(13) 2.2	(126) 3.8	(122) 6.4
		-2.0	-1.8	-8.4	-.4	-2.7	-1.7	.9
Net Profit + Depr., Dep., Amort./Cur. Mat. L/T/D							7.5	25.0
							(26) 3.7	(17) 5.3
							1.0	1.9
Fixed/Worth	.1	.2	.1	.1	.1	.1	.1	.1
	.3	1.3	.3	.9	.4	.1	.6	.4
	-3.9	-.1	NM	-.8	-.2	-6.7	-10.0	5.6
Debt/Worth	.1	1.0	.5	1.5	1.1	.9	.8	.7
	.3	7.1	1.4	15.5	2.7	2.6	2.5	1.9
	-11.2	-1.6	NM	-5.5	-1.7	-8.0	-28.5	35.7
% Profit Before Taxes/Tangible Net Worth	55.2	126.8	68.4	91.2	41.1	22.7	57.7	62.1
	(11) 29.0	(18) 28.5	(31) 36.5	(25) 24.4	(11) 15.2	(16) 3.6	(118) 20.2	(122) 22.4
	.0	1.4	3.6	-24.0	-3.6	-85.4	-4.8	1.4
% Profit Before Taxes/Total Assets	52.3	22.9	22.0	15.5	13.7	12.8	16.9	20.1
	19.5	7.9	8.7	1.6	3.2	.7	4.6	7.6
	.0	-12.7	-.2	-8.1	-.2	-10.7	-4.8	-2.7
Sales/Net Fixed Assets	79.9	104.3	52.2	44.6	25.8	36.1	40.2	46.8
	30.8	32.7	28.1	25.6	17.0	21.0	20.0	25.8
	11.2	13.0	16.7	13.0	10.4	9.4	9.8	13.2
Sales/Total Assets	6.1	4.8	3.0	1.7	1.0	1.0	3.3	3.5
	3.5	3.1	1.9	1.4	.8	.8	1.8	2.1
	2.6	2.0	1.2	.8	.6	.5	1.2	1.3
% Depr., Dep., Amort./Sales		.8	.7	1.0	2.0	1.3	1.2	.9
		(20) 2.6	(30) 1.5	(23) 1.5	(10) 4.1	(14) 2.7	(96) 2.2	(103) 2.1
		3.7	2.8	3.8	6.6	4.5	4.6	3.7
% Officers', Directors' Owners' Comp/Sales							2.4	4.7
							(49) 7.2	(36) 6.8
							14.3	15.8
Net Sales ($)	18164M	112846M	435366M	1198363M	1218909M	3159149M	5938529M	8110173M
Total Assets ($)	4311M	36292M	197535M	814195M	1276571M	3676728M	4998408M	5022127M

M = $ thousand   MM = $ million
See Pages 11 through 21 for Explanation of Ratios and Data

Comparative Historical Data | Current Data Sorted by Sales

Current Data date ranges: **41 (4/1-9/30/06)** covers the 0-1MM and 1-3MM columns; **120 (10/1/06-3/31/07)** covers the 3-5MM through 25MM & OVER columns.

	4/1/04-3/31/05 ALL	4/1/05-3/31/06 ALL	4/1/06-3/31/07 ALL	0-1MM	1-3MM	3-5MM	5-10MM	10-25MM	25MM & OVER
Type of Statement									
Unqualified	40	46	46			3	4	13	26
Reviewed	12	14	12			4	5	2	1
Compiled	10	10	12	1	2	4	5		
Tax Returns	7	10	9	4	2	1	1	1	
Other	47	83	82	3	14	8	9	16	32
NUMBER OF STATEMENTS	116	163	161	8	18	20	24	32	59
	%	%	%		%	%	%	%	%
ASSETS									
Cash & Equivalents	26.4	26.5	22.2		21.4	15.4	21.0	21.7	25.6
Trade Receivables (net)	32.4	33.3	32.9		38.7	30.6	43.0	38.2	25.1
Inventory	2.9	3.0	2.2		.1	4.7	3.0	2.3	1.5
All Other Current	4.6	4.4	4.8		1.4	8.6	1.3	3.7	6.8
Total Current	66.2	67.3	62.1		61.5	59.3	68.2	66.0	59.0
Fixed Assets (net)	11.8	10.8	11.4		21.1	17.1	13.3	6.6	7.2
Intangibles (net)	14.1	14.4	19.7		11.4	15.2	14.0	19.1	27.2
All Other Non-Current	7.8	7.6	6.8		6.0	8.4	4.5	8.3	6.5
Total	100.0	100.0	100.0		100.0	100.0	100.0	100.0	100.0
LIABILITIES									
Notes Payable-Short Term	8.4	6.4	6.2		12.1	6.7	11.7	2.5	3.0
Cur. Mat.-L.T.D.	2.0	2.4	3.2		3.0	1.8	2.8	6.8	2.4
Trade Payables	7.9	10.3	10.6		14.4	9.8	12.9	10.5	8.7
Income Taxes Payable	1.0	1.3	.7		.0	.0	.5	.4	1.1
All Other Current	31.3	25.6	26.5		12.2	38.7	25.5	26.0	28.5
Total Current	50.5	46.0	47.1		41.7	57.1	53.4	46.2	43.8
Long-Term Debt	8.9	9.9	9.3		9.2	6.5	8.4	8.3	12.0
Deferred Taxes	2.1	.6	.3		.0		.3	.5	.4
All Other Non-Current	16.4	21.6	17.4		48.5	10.3	8.8	26.2	10.4
Net Worth	22.1	21.9	25.8		.7	26.1	29.1	18.9	33.4
Total Liabilties & Net Worth	100.0	100.0	100.0		100.0	100.0	100.0	100.0	100.0
INCOME DATA									
Net Sales	100.0	100.0	100.0		100.0	100.0	100.0	100.0	100.0
Gross Profit									
Operating Expenses	92.9	93.5	95.7		100.7	96.0	93.8	94.3	95.6
Operating Profit	7.1	6.5	4.3		-.7	4.0	6.2	5.7	4.4
All Other Expenses (net)	.6	1.2	1.2		1.3	2.1	1.2	.3	1.3
Profit Before Taxes	6.5	5.3	3.2		-2.1	1.9	4.9	5.4	3.1
RATIOS									
Current	3.0	3.2	2.9		6.0	3.3	4.7	2.9	1.9
	1.6	1.6	1.5		1.6	1.3	1.2	1.9	1.4
	1.1	1.0	1.0		.8	.8	.8	1.1	1.0
Quick	2.8	2.9	2.4		5.9	2.9	4.2	2.5	1.6
	1.4	1.4	1.3		1.6	1.1	1.2	1.7	1.2
	.9	.8	.8		.8	.4	.8	1.0	.9
Sales/Receivables	40 9.1	40 9.2	42 8.6		25 14.8	12 30.0	39 9.3	52 7.0	50 7.3
	62 5.9	64 5.7	67 5.4		61 6.0	52 7.1	63 5.8	78 4.7	68 5.3
	81 4.5	89 4.1	86 4.3		75 4.9	80 4.6	84 4.3	99 3.7	91 4.0
Cost of Sales/Inventory									
Cost of Sales/Payables									
Sales/Working Capital	3.5	3.3	3.9		4.4	4.7	4.6	3.6	3.4
	8.3	8.5	8.6		12.7	16.3	28.9	6.3	8.4
	451.7	177.0	-110.3		-43.9	-66.9	-25.3	39.3	111.3
EBIT/Interest	32.6	45.0	15.8		10.3	18.3	70.5	72.5	8.1
	(88) 6.8	(121) 10.7	(112) 3.3		(11) 3.4	(15) 7.9	(21) 6.2	(23) 7.4	(39) 2.7
	1.3	1.0	-1.8		-1.2	-2.8	-.7	-8.7	-1.8
Net Profit + Depr., Dep., Amort./Cur. Mat. L/T/D	48.1	22.6	7.8						10.2
	(18) 7.6	(27) 11.1	(23) .9					(13) .9	.9
	2.5	3.2	-2.4						-7.9
Fixed/Worth	.1	.1	.1		.2	.2	.1	.1	.1
	.4	.4	.4		1.1	.5	.9	.2	.4
	-1.7	-.8	-.8		-.1	NM	-2.5	-1.1	-.7
Debt/Worth	.6	.9	.9		.2	.6	.5	.9	1.2
	2.0	2.4	2.6		2.0	1.8	6.9	2.2	3.0
	-10.6	-10.2	-6.0		-1.9	NM	-12.7	-6.9	-4.5
% Profit Before Taxes/Tangible Net Worth	66.3	81.8	57.5		35.0	51.0	80.1	91.4	40.9
	(83) 26.2	(112) 23.6	(112) 21.9		(11) 10.9	(15) 34.1	(17) 38.2	(23) 47.2	(40) 7.9
	3.7	2.5	-2.3		-2.0	3.6	4.1	-1.8	-34.3
% Profit Before Taxes/Total Assets	21.0	22.8	19.5		29.7	21.7	18.0	26.8	12.6
	10.3	8.3	5.5		7.9	10.5	5.7	14.2	2.6
	.6	-1.8	-4.7		-6.6	-6.3	-4.5	-3.7	-4.9
Sales/Net Fixed Assets	52.5	51.4	50.2		53.8	75.1	59.6	58.6	36.7
	24.6	25.4	25.4		29.9	17.3	28.3	32.3	24.5
	12.7	13.0	12.9		11.0	8.4	14.4	14.8	12.9
Sales/Total Assets	3.3	2.9	2.8		5.6	3.5	4.6	2.6	1.7
	1.7	1.8	1.6		2.9	2.0	2.5	1.6	1.0
	1.2	1.0	.9		1.6	1.3	1.1	1.0	.7
% Depr., Dep., Amort./Sales	1.2	.8	.9			.9	.5	.9	1.1
	(69) 2.2	(106) 1.7	(105) 2.0			(17) 1.5	(17) 1.1	(20) 1.7	(36) 2.3
	4.0	3.4	4.1			3.6	4.1	2.6	4.0
% Officers', Directors' Owners' Comp/Sales	2.1	2.8	3.5						
	(23) 6.0	(28) 10.5	(22) 12.7						
	13.0	15.4	24.2						
Net Sales ($)	6180595M	6061833M	6142797M	4331M	35933M	77925M	177070M	533831M	5313707M
Total Assets ($)	4593052M	5726262M	6005632M	3717M	19580M	55920M	100486M	443974M	5381955M

© RMA 2007   M = $ thousand   MM = $ million
See Pages 11 through 21 for Explanation of Ratios and Data

Current Data Sorted by Assets | Comparative Historical Data

0-500M	500M-2MM	2-10MM	10-50MM	50-100MM	100-250MM	Type of Statement	4/1/02-3/31/03 ALL	4/1/03-3/31/04 ALL
		4		1		Unqualified	14	16
	4	16	5		3	Reviewed	27	30
4	13	8	3			Compiled	25	30
10	8	4				Tax Returns	22	29
11	12	15	9	2	5	Other	30	32
	27 (4/1-9/30/06)		110 (10/1/06-3/31/07)				4/1/02-3/31/03 ALL	4/1/03-3/31/04 ALL
0-500M	500M-2MM	2-10MM	10-50MM	50-100MM	100-250MM	NUMBER OF STATEMENTS		
25	37	47	17	3	8		118	137
%	%	%	%	%	%	**ASSETS**	%	%
24.6	12.7	13.9	14.5			Cash & Equivalents	13.3	14.1
15.3	32.4	29.9	19.3			Trade Receivables (net)	25.9	25.5
1.2	2.5	4.1	1.0			Inventory	5.6	4.8
4.8	8.1	2.6	2.8			All Other Current	3.7	3.5
46.0	55.8	50.5	37.5			Total Current	48.5	47.8
35.7	33.3	34.1	43.8			Fixed Assets (net)	31.4	37.0
5.7	3.5	8.0	4.9			Intangibles (net)	7.1	5.1
12.6	7.4	7.4	13.9			All Other Non-Current	13.0	10.0
100.0	100.0	100.0	100.0			Total	100.0	100.0
						LIABILITIES		
48.2	14.6	6.4	9.5			Notes Payable-Short Term	16.3	12.2
4.4	9.5	8.0	4.8			Cur. Mat.-L.T.D.	8.5	6.0
13.7	8.4	14.1	5.9			Trade Payables	15.2	15.8
.0	.8	.9	.8			Income Taxes Payable	.9	.4
31.6	13.4	16.7	9.1			All Other Current	17.4	19.4
97.9	46.6	46.0	30.0			Total Current	58.3	53.8
28.5	13.7	14.5	34.1			Long-Term Debt	21.9	20.1
.0	.4	1.1	.3			Deferred Taxes	.7	.5
9.4	13.4	5.8	45.4			All Other Non-Current	8.9	8.5
-35.8	25.9	32.6	-9.8			Net Worth	10.1	17.1
100.0	100.0	100.0	100.0			Total Liabilities & Net Worth	100.0	100.0
						INCOME DATA		
100.0	100.0	100.0	100.0			Net Sales	100.0	100.0
						Gross Profit		
91.4	93.4	93.1	80.7			Operating Expenses	95.1	94.6
8.6	6.6	6.9	19.3			Operating Profit	4.9	5.4
1.5	1.3	2.2	3.9			All Other Expenses (net)	2.0	2.2
7.1	5.3	4.6	15.4			Profit Before Taxes	2.8	3.3
						RATIOS		
1.2	2.3	1.6	4.3			Current	1.7	2.0
.5	1.5	1.1	1.5				1.0	1.1
.3	.7	.7	.8				.5	.6
1.2	2.0	1.6	4.3			Quick	1.4	1.6
.5	1.1	.9	1.2				.8	.9
.2	.5	.7	.6				.4	.5
0 UND	20 18.3	27 13.5	17 21.4			Sales/Receivables	19 19.2	17 20.9
6 59.3	37 9.9	44 8.3	58 6.3				43 8.4	37 9.7
34 10.9	65 5.6	64 5.7	76 4.8				62 5.9	59 6.2
						Cost of Sales/Inventory		
						Cost of Sales/Payables		
101.3	7.0	10.2	5.6			Sales/Working Capital	8.7	9.3
-19.8	23.5	76.6	49.3				NM	110.0
-5.8	-14.8	-21.0	-20.3				-10.6	-12.4
3.8	10.2	15.0	9.7			EBIT/Interest	5.1	11.0
(19) 1.9	(29) 3.5	(43) 5.7	(16) 3.6				(93) 1.7	(119) 3.1
-.4	-3.5	1.1	2.0				-.7	-.1
		3.0				Net Profit + Depr., Dep., Amort./Cur. Mat. L/T/D	5.1	5.3
		(18) 2.1					(36) 1.9	(26) 2.2
		1.1					1.0	1.0
.5	.2	.7	.5			Fixed/Worth	.4	.5
2.0	.7	1.2	3.2				1.5	1.3
-.7	3.0	4.8	-4.2				15.6	6.5
1.4	.6	1.1	.6			Debt/Worth	1.2	1.0
3.3	1.5	2.0	6.6				3.8	2.8
-1.9	6.3	20.9	-3.0				NM	31.3
218.0	74.6	84.4	93.7			% Profit Before Taxes/Tangible Net Worth	62.8	54.0
(15) 57.4	(30) 37.3	(39) 26.6	(10) 68.2				(89) 11.3	(107) 20.3
3.2	-4.1	3.1	22.1				1.3	1.7
51.1	33.5	14.8	47.5			% Profit Before Taxes/Total Assets	13.2	15.9
4.7	11.4	7.4	12.4				3.3	5.4
-2.6	-7.5	.0	5.3				-4.6	-4.4
62.5	35.0	18.8	10.4			Sales/Net Fixed Assets	31.5	31.6
17.3	12.2	6.6	3.0				10.0	8.1
5.6	4.5	4.3	1.6				4.2	3.2
7.0	4.1	2.7	2.1			Sales/Total Assets	3.5	3.7
3.6	2.8	2.2	1.3				2.1	2.3
1.8	2.0	1.7	.9				1.4	1.4
1.7	1.8	2.3	3.1			% Depr., Dep., Amort./Sales	2.0	2.1
(14) 4.2	(24) 4.0	(41) 4.5	(14) 6.0				(92) 4.8	(103) 4.5
7.2	8.0	8.6	11.6				9.3	10.4
6.9	4.4	3.8				% Officers', Directors' Owners' Comp/Sales	4.8	4.3
(16) 13.8	(19) 10.2	(17) 4.9					(52) 8.5	(63) 8.4
18.4	13.0	8.3					11.6	15.1
21512M	133474M	497795M	643676M	181085M	1203827M	Net Sales ($)	1579040M	1732238M
5435M	40580M	194495M	412628M	242812M	1073175M	Total Assets ($)	1312505M	1531232M

M = $ thousand   MM = $ million
See Pages 11 through 21 for Explanation of Ratios and Data

Comparative Historical Data & Current Data Sorted by Sales

			Type of Statement						
9	12	13	Unqualified				2	3	8
19	12	23	Reviewed			8	8	7	
17	17	25	Compiled	4	9	2	4	4	2
23	19	22	Tax Returns	8	7	4	2	1	
36	52	54	Other	11	9	5	5	11	13
4/1/04-3/31/05	4/1/05-3/31/06	4/1/06-3/31/07		0-1MM	1-3MM	3-5MM	5-10MM	10-25MM	25MM & OVER
ALL	ALL	ALL		27 (4/1-9/30/06)			110 (10/1/06-3/31/07)		
104	112	137	NUMBER OF STATEMENTS	23	25	19	21	26	23
%	%	%	ASSETS	%	%	%	%	%	%
14.1	12.5	14.9	Cash & Equivalents	21.2	17.0	7.8	16.5	13.7	12.3
25.8	28.2	26.2	Trade Receivables (net)	12.0	28.3	31.5	29.3	33.1	23.2
4.2	4.7	2.9	Inventory	1.0	1.1	4.6	2.4	4.6	4.0
4.4	5.7	4.6	All Other Current	5.6	5.2	3.9	7.9	2.3	2.9
48.5	51.2	48.6	Total Current	39.8	51.6	47.7	56.1	53.6	42.4
37.5	35.6	35.5	Fixed Assets (net)	42.5	33.3	36.4	31.2	33.6	36.2
3.9	4.8	6.8	Intangibles (net)	4.3	7.4	9.3	4.3	6.7	9.1
10.1	8.5	9.1	All Other Non-Current	13.5	7.6	6.6	8.4	6.1	12.3
100.0	100.0	100.0	Total	100.0	100.0	100.0	100.0	100.0	100.0
			LIABILITIES						
15.3	16.0	16.3	Notes Payable-Short Term	49.5	8.8	23.9	5.9	3.3	8.9
5.4	5.1	6.7	Cur. Mat.-L.T.D.	7.4	6.9	9.6	8.6	6.5	1.7
12.3	13.3	11.5	Trade Payables	13.2	7.1	12.6	10.5	13.9	12.1
.3	.6	.6	Income Taxes Payable	.0	1.1	.8	.2	.1	1.5
13.6	12.7	16.8	All Other Current	26.0	17.6	10.5	17.1	18.6	9.8
47.0	47.7	51.9	Total Current	96.1	41.5	57.3	42.4	42.5	34.0
21.3	21.2	22.0	Long-Term Debt	31.0	18.4	16.1	17.2	15.2	34.0
.7	.4	.7	Deferred Taxes	.0	.1	.4	1.5	.9	1.6
12.7	12.6	15.3	All Other Non-Current	7.5	9.1	13.9	11.7	7.0	43.7
18.4	18.1	10.0	Net Worth	-34.6	30.8	12.3	27.2	34.4	-13.2
100.0	100.0	100.0	Total Liabilties & Net Worth	100.0	100.0	100.0	100.0	100.0	100.0
			INCOME DATA						
100.0	100.0	100.0	Net Sales	100.0	100.0	100.0	100.0	100.0	100.0
			Gross Profit						
93.8	91.9	92.0	Operating Expenses	82.3	96.0	98.5	94.3	92.2	89.8
6.2	8.1	8.0	Operating Profit	17.7	4.0	1.5	5.7	7.8	10.2
1.6	1.7	2.4	All Other Expenses (net)	2.9	2.3	1.2	2.0	1.3	4.3
4.6	6.5	5.6	Profit Before Taxes	14.7	1.7	.3	3.6	6.5	6.0
			RATIOS						
2.6	2.4	1.9		1.2	2.8	1.4	4.8	1.8	2.9
1.2	1.2	1.1	Current	.4	1.4	1.0	1.2	1.2	1.4
.7	.8	.7		.3	.6	.7	.9	.8	.9
1.9	2.0	1.8		1.2	2.8	1.1	2.2	1.8	2.3
1.1	1.0	.9	Quick	.4	1.2	.9	1.1	.8	1.2
.4	.6	.5		.2	.6	.5	.7	.7	.8
16 22.5	21 17.0	15 24.8		0 UND	15 24.4	25 14.8	35 10.3	22 16.4	26 14.2
39 9.4	43 8.5	42 8.7	Sales/Receivables	6 59.3	42 8.7	43 8.5	44 8.3	44 8.3	61 6.0
59 6.2	66 5.6	65 5.6		38 9.6	52 7.0	73 5.0	61 6.0	69 5.3	89 4.1
			Cost of Sales/Inventory						
			Cost of Sales/Payables						
9.0	7.6	8.1		5.3	7.1	20.5	5.8	8.8	4.6
39.8	40.3	76.6	Sales/Working Capital	-15.7	15.9	84.4	14.9	53.6	18.3
-22.7	-25.7	-17.0		-2.5	-14.1	-14.1	-61.7	-21.5	-32.0
11.8	18.4	10.3		3.6	9.0	8.6	12.2	17.6	9.7
(82) 4.0	(100) 4.2	(118) 2.9	EBIT/Interest	(16) 1.6	(20) 2.1	(17) 1.4	(19) 3.2	(24) 8.0	(22) 2.6
1.0	.9	.7		-.4	-2.7	-3.5	.7	2.1	.8
7.9	5.3	5.3						22.6	
(14) 2.9	(23) 2.1	(26) 2.1	Net Profit + Depr., Dep., Amort./Cur. Mat. L/T/D					(12) 2.8	
.7	1.3	1.1						1.4	
.4	.4	.4		.2	.2	.6	.3	.6	.4
1.5	1.1	1.5	Fixed/Worth	2.1	1.1	2.8	1.2	1.1	2.5
9.0	6.5	28.2		-.9	2.7	-.5	22.1	5.6	116.0
1.1	.9	1.1		.6	.5	1.1	1.2	1.0	2.8
2.6	2.5	3.0	Debt/Worth	3.2	2.3	3.5	2.4	1.8	16.3
22.5	140.1	-15.5		-1.7	5.6	-7.0	31.4	31.3	-2.3
96.4	81.8	91.5	% Profit Before Taxes/Tangible Net Worth	193.1	76.9	81.3	59.6	91.5	108.7
(86) 33.0	(85) 44.3	(101) 36.1		(14) 49.8	(20) 15.8	(13) 27.7	(17) 23.8	(21) 47.1	(16) 85.7
2.2	13.3	3.9		3.5	-5.5	-18.6	1.5	23.0	14.9
26.7	30.4	26.1	% Profit Before Taxes/Total Assets	50.0	29.3	29.4	17.7	27.0	47.4
7.4	9.1	8.4		10.3	4.0	3.0	8.4	12.4	5.9
.2	.4	-1.3		-3.8	-8.1	-9.4	-.9	1.9	-.2
21.6	33.6	29.4		25.8	34.4	12.9	25.7	26.3	100.9
8.1	8.7	8.5	Sales/Net Fixed Assets	7.3	22.5	8.5	10.1	6.4	6.5
3.9	3.3	3.3		1.2	4.2	6.0	3.7	3.3	1.5
3.9	4.4	3.6		5.4	4.1	3.6	3.1	4.2	2.3
2.6	2.3	2.3	Sales/Total Assets	2.3	2.7	2.3	2.3	2.4	1.2
1.4	1.5	1.4		.8	1.9	1.7	1.8	1.7	.7
1.7	1.2	2.1		1.8	2.5	1.8	2.6	2.1	1.1
(71) 4.1	(76) 3.8	(95) 4.4	% Depr., Dep., Amort./Sales	(15) 5.2	(13) 6.1	(15) 2.8	(17) 5.2	(24) 3.2	(11) 3.1
7.1	8.8	8.4		9.8	9.4	5.4	9.5	8.4	6.6
1.8	5.3	4.1		10.1	5.3	4.5			
(39) 9.5	(50) 7.5	(53) 8.7	% Officers', Directors' Owners' Comp/Sales	(13) 13.8	(13) 11.5	(10) 8.5			
18.1	13.2	14.9		18.2	16.7	13.0			
1442922M	1882579M	2681369M	Net Sales ($)	11099M	49823M	74632M	141217M	384591M	2020007M
1193620M	1623825M	1969125M	Total Assets ($)	9364M	25741M	34178M	80650M	184770M	1634422M

© RMA 2007

M = $ thousand   MM = $ million
See Pages 11 through 21 for Explanation of Ratios and Data

Current Data Sorted by Assets   Comparative Historical Data

	0-500M	500M-2MM	2-10MM	10-50MM	50-100MM	100-250MM	Type of Statement		
		1	5	7	2	4	Unqualified	27	23
		1	3	5	2	1	Reviewed	10	14
	1	2	10	4	1		Compiled	21	15
	7	8	3	11	5		Tax Returns	11	14
	5	6	16				Other	32	34
		13 (4/1-9/30/06)		97 (10/1/06-3/31/07)				4/1/02-3/31/03 ALL	4/1/03-3/31/04 ALL
	13	18	37	27	10	5	**NUMBER OF STATEMENTS**	101	100
	%	%	%	%	%	%	**ASSETS**	%	%
	37.5	14.8	6.5	8.0	5.5		Cash & Equivalents	14.0	14.8
	2.6	.5	1.7	1.5	1.1		Trade Receivables (net)	1.8	1.0
	1.6	.7	.7	.5	1.0		Inventory	1.1	.9
	4.3	.0	1.2	2.2	1.0		All Other Current	1.4	3.2
	46.1	16.0	10.1	12.1	8.6		Total Current	18.3	19.9
	33.3	62.9	78.8	71.7	84.1		Fixed Assets (net)	71.7	68.5
	2.6	4.1	4.0	7.1	5.5		Intangibles (net)	2.1	3.6
	18.0	17.0	7.2	9.0	1.8		All Other Non-Current	7.9	8.0
	100.0	100.0	100.0	100.0	100.0		Total	100.0	100.0
							LIABILITIES		
	29.3	.2	2.4	1.7	1.5		Notes Payable-Short Term	3.0	2.6
	1.7	2.0	3.4	6.4	3.5		Cur. Mat.-L.T.D.	5.6	4.7
	7.5	15.6	5.0	4.1	5.4		Trade Payables	6.9	6.6
	.0	.0	.2	.1	.1		Income Taxes Payable	.1	.3
	23.0	22.2	5.8	6.2	4.7		All Other Current	10.8	10.8
	61.5	40.0	16.7	18.5	15.2		Total Current	26.4	24.9
	23.7	40.3	47.2	45.8	58.1		Long-Term Debt	47.2	38.6
	.0	.1	.0	.3	.3		Deferred Taxes	.3	.3
	23.2	20.4	9.2	7.1	7.8		All Other Non-Current	7.3	10.5
	-7.8	-.9	26.8	28.4	18.6		Net Worth	18.8	25.7
	100.0	100.0	100.0	100.0	100.0		Total Liabilities & Net Worth	100.0	100.0
							INCOME DATA		
	100.0	100.0	100.0	100.0	100.0		Net Sales	100.0	100.0
							Gross Profit		
	92.6	93.2	80.1	90.0	87.7		Operating Expenses	86.5	89.4
	7.4	6.8	19.9	10.0	12.3		Operating Profit	13.5	10.6
	7.6	2.0	9.8	4.4	9.2		All Other Expenses (net)	5.7	3.7
	-.2	4.8	10.2	5.6	3.1		Profit Before Taxes	7.8	7.0
							RATIOS		
	2.7	7.0	1.3	1.2	.9			2.2	1.8
	1.1	.6	.5	.7	.4		Current	.7	.9
	.5	.2	.2	.3	.2			.3	.3
	2.6	6.2	1.1	.9	.7			1.6	1.6
	.9	.6	.4	.6	.3		Quick	.5	.6
	.4	.2	.2	.2	.2			.2	.3
	0 UND	0 UND	0 UND	0 UND	0 UND			0 UND	0 UND
	0 UND	0 UND	0 UND	0 999.8	2 146.4		Sales/Receivables	0 UND	0 UND
	0 UND	0 UND	0 UND	2 204.2	4 98.3			1 267.3	1 252.7
							Cost of Sales/Inventory		
							Cost of Sales/Payables		
	21.7	19.6	24.0	48.8	NM			13.6	12.2
	46.0	-59.1	-16.5	-37.9	-11.2		Sales/Working Capital	-24.6	-60.6
	-19.5	-7.2	-7.1	-5.1	-5.3			-7.2	-8.4
		4.5	2.6	4.1				5.5	6.3
		(13) 2.0	(25) 1.7	(24) 2.2			EBIT/Interest	(81) 2.5	(89) 2.9
		.9	.5	.9				1.3	1.5
								4.9	3.2
							Net Profit + Depr., Dep., Amort./Cur. Mat. L/T/D	(17) 1.7	(21) 1.8
								1.3	1.4
	.4	1.0	1.7	1.9	3.7			1.9	1.7
	UND	NM	3.1	3.2	4.1		Fixed/Worth	4.2	3.4
	-1.1	-2.7	33.2	13.3	NM			24.2	8.9
	.4	1.0	1.2	1.6	3.1			1.5	1.4
	-30.0	-11.7	2.4	3.8	3.7		Debt/Worth	4.3	3.0
	-2.8	-3.3	34.8	38.4	NM			30.5	9.9
			38.0	56.1			% Profit Before Taxes/Tangible Net Worth	58.8	47.8
		(31)	12.7	(24) 12.8				(80) 32.6	(86) 26.3
			-5.4	-1.3				8.4	8.5
	26.2	7.6	8.4	9.8	6.6		% Profit Before Taxes/Total Assets	13.6	14.3
	-.5	3.8	3.4	3.3	1.9			6.0	5.7
	-20.5	-.2	-2.1	-.4	.3			1.4	2.0
	99.3	9.0	2.3	1.9	1.4			3.5	4.4
	17.3	2.4	.8	1.0	.9		Sales/Net Fixed Assets	1.3	1.4
	6.3	.9	.4	.7	.6			.8	.9
	7.0	3.2	1.2	1.3	1.0			1.9	2.1
	3.8	1.3	.7	.9	.7		Sales/Total Assets	1.0	1.0
	2.3	.8	.3	.5	.5			.7	.7
		2.8	5.8	4.7	5.4			3.9	4.8
		(15) 5.5	(33) 7.9	6.2	10.3		% Depr., Dep., Amort./Sales	(90) 6.5	(91) 6.4
		6.4	12.3	9.3	13.4			9.9	9.0
								2.4	2.0
							% Officers', Directors' Owners' Comp/Sales	(18) 3.0	(25) 4.0
								5.2	7.7
	10674M	42321M	172968M	655427M	536276M	1005266M	Net Sales ($)	2390260M	2758562M
	2842M	22017M	187495M	691433M	707365M	878495M	Total Assets ($)	2541116M	2165123M

M = $ thousand   MM = $ million
See Pages 11 through 21 for Explanation of Ratios and Data

Comparative Historical Data   Current Data Sorted by Sales

			Type of Statement	0-1MM	1-3MM	3-5MM	5-10MM	10-25MM	25MM & OVER
18	17	19	Unqualified	1		1	3	4	10
12	10	12	Reviewed	3		1	1	2	5
13	15	18	Compiled	3	5	4	1	3	2
11	11	18	Tax Returns	7	9		2		
48	45	43	Other	6	9	8	6	6	8
4/1/04-3/31/05	4/1/05-3/31/06	4/1/06-3/31/07			13 (4/1-9/30/06)		97 (10/1/06-3/31/07)		
ALL	ALL	ALL							
102	98	110	**NUMBER OF STATEMENTS**	20	23	14	13	15	25
%	%	%	**ASSETS**	%	%	%	%	%	%
12.1	12.2	11.9	Cash & Equivalents	19.3	15.7	8.0	10.3	5.0	9.7
1.2	1.7	1.5	Trade Receivables (net)	3.6	.5	.3	.8	1.2	1.7
1.1	1.0	.8	Inventory	.7	.6	.6	1.1	.8	.8
1.1	2.3	1.5	All Other Current	3.1	1.3	.1	.5	.3	2.6
15.5	17.1	15.7	Total Current	26.7	18.2	9.0	12.8	7.3	14.9
72.2	74.3	69.7	Fixed Assets (net)	59.9	66.8	74.6	64.7	77.1	75.4
2.8	2.8	4.7	Intangibles (net)	3.4	1.5	6.7	6.0	8.7	4.7
9.5	5.8	9.9	All Other Non-Current	10.0	13.6	9.7	16.5	6.9	5.0
100.0	100.0	100.0	Total	100.0	100.0	100.0	100.0	100.0	100.0
			LIABILITIES						
4.9	2.2	4.9	Notes Payable-Short Term	21.0	.5	1.7	1.1	1.4	1.8
4.2	4.6	3.7	Cur. Mat.-L.T.D.	2.3	1.8	3.0	4.3	9.4	3.1
5.2	6.7	6.9	Trade Payables	2.4	10.2	3.1	9.3	4.7	9.6
.3	.1	.1	Income Taxes Payable	.0	.0	.5	.0	.1	.0
7.2	12.7	10.5	All Other Current	15.2	12.2	14.7	6.1	6.5	7.3
21.7	26.3	26.0	Total Current	40.9	24.7	22.9	20.9	22.1	21.8
44.4	42.3	44.6	Long-Term Debt	44.4	40.7	44.6	47.2	42.5	48.1
.2	.2	.1	Deferred Taxes	.0	.0	.2	.1	.2	.3
6.8	7.2	12.5	All Other Non-Current	15.4	9.9	10.3	16.0	3.4	17.5
26.9	24.0	16.9	Net Worth	-.3	24.7	22.0	15.7	31.9	12.3
100.0	100.0	100.0	Total Liabilities & Net Worth	100.0	100.0	100.0	100.0	100.0	100.0
			INCOME DATA						
100.0	100.0	100.0	Net Sales	100.0	100.0	100.0	100.0	100.0	100.0
			Gross Profit						
89.0	90.1	87.4	Operating Expenses	74.0	90.8	92.7	82.9	92.7	91.1
11.0	9.9	12.6	Operating Profit	26.0	9.2	7.3	17.1	7.3	8.9
4.7	5.8	6.6	All Other Expenses (net)	13.9	5.1	6.4	5.1	4.8	4.0
6.3	4.1	6.1	Profit Before Taxes	12.1	4.1	.9	12.1	2.6	4.9
			RATIOS						
2.0	1.5	1.3	Current	1.9	3.5	1.4	.8	.8	1.3
.7	.6	.7		.9	.7	.5	.4	.3	.9
.2	.3	.2		.2	.4	.3	.2	.1	.4
1.6	1.3	1.1	Quick	1.7	3.4	1.3	.7	.6	.9
.5	.5	.5		.7	.7	.4	.3	.2	.6
.2	.2	.2		.1	.3	.2	.2	.1	.3
0 UND	0 UND	0 UND	Sales/Receivables	0 UND	0 UND	0 UND	0 UND	0 UND	0 UND
0 UND	0 UND	0 UND		0 UND	0 UND	0 UND	0 UND	0 UND	0 UND
3 143.6	3 122.1	2 200.8		0 UND	0 999.8	2 185.4	3 108.0	0 999.8	3 125.5
			Cost of Sales/Inventory						
			Cost of Sales/Payables						
13.6	23.1	28.7	Sales/Working Capital	22.0	12.4	18.8	-59.1	-42.5	34.4
-30.9	-18.0	-29.1		-63.4	-68.8	-26.1	-16.3	-8.6	-43.6
-7.7	-5.4	-7.1		-3.2	-8.6	-8.6	-3.9	-5.0	-8.5
6.3	3.8	3.1	EBIT/Interest	4.2	2.6	4.1		2.4	4.4
(84) 3.0	(77) 1.9	(84) 1.8		(12) .9	(16) 1.2	(10) 1.9		(13) 1.3	2.6
1.4	.9	.9		-.7	.4	.5		-.1	1.4
2.8	2.9	2.8	Net Profit + Depr., Dep., Amort./Cur. Mat. L/T/D						
(13) 1.8	(11) 1.4	(14) 1.9							
1.3	.7	1.2							
1.5	1.5	1.7	Fixed/Worth	1.5	.8	2.2	1.3	2.3	2.4
3.0	3.4	3.8		62.7	2.7	3.5	2.7	5.3	3.8
10.1	14.5	-17.2		-6.2	-15.7	NM	33.6	13.1	-7.0
1.2	1.1	1.6	Debt/Worth	1.8	.5	1.2	1.0	1.6	2.0
3.1	3.4	3.8		UND	4.3	2.9	2.3	4.6	3.8
11.0	19.6	-16.7		-7.4	-14.3	NM	34.6	14.5	-9.0
41.7	35.5	40.7	% Profit Before Taxes/Tangible Net Worth	24.4	67.0	41.6	87.8	51.0	29.9
(86) 21.9	(78) 10.7	(80) 12.3		(11) 9.3	(16) 12.9	(11) 33.7	(11) 16.6	(14) 8.0	(17) 22.4
7.6	.8	-.9		-10.7	-9.5	-6.4	-.3	-4.1	6.5
11.9	7.4	8.5	% Profit Before Taxes/Total Assets	8.0	12.3	8.6	18.8	8.4	10.5
5.6	2.8	3.1		1.4	2.7	2.3	3.9	1.4	6.4
1.2	-.8	-.6		-3.6	-1.5	-5.0	-.2	-.7	1.7
3.1	3.7	3.3	Sales/Net Fixed Assets	15.3	8.2	2.8	6.1	2.0	2.7
1.2	1.0	1.1		.9	1.2	.8	1.5	1.5	1.3
.7	.6	.6		.3	.5	.6	.6	.6	1.0
1.7	1.7	2.0	Sales/Total Assets	2.6	2.7	1.2	3.4	1.7	2.0
.9	.8	.8		.6	.8	.7	1.0	1.0	1.0
.5	.5	.5		.2	.5	.5	.4	.5	.7
4.4	4.2	3.9	% Depr., Dep., Amort./Sales	2.3	3.6	4.1	3.6	5.0	4.3
(85) 7.4	(88) 6.9	(96) 6.5		(17) 10.3	(17) 6.8	(12) 7.0	(14) 5.6	(22) 6.1	5.7
9.9	10.2	10.6		16.1	11.8	10.0	13.8	9.8	9.4
2.4	2.5	2.4	% Officers', Directors' Owners' Comp/Sales						
(18) 4.3	(23) 4.7	(24) 3.6							
5.8	6.1	7.2							
2403946M	1894652M	2422932M	Net Sales ($)	9956M	44542M	51271M	88676M	241886M	1986601M
2783879M	2355137M	2489647M	Total Assets ($)	28175M	67641M	81616M	186675M	312988M	1812552M

M = $ thousand   MM = $ million
See Pages 11 through 21 for Explanation of Ratios and Data

Current Data Sorted by Assets   Comparative Historical Data

						Type of Statement		
		1	1	1	1	Unqualified	7	8
	1	2				Reviewed	6	4
1	1	1				Compiled	10	7
2	3	2				Tax Returns	4	6
2	2	7	2		1	Other	17	11
	3 (4/1-9/30/06)		28 (10/1/06-3/31/07)				4/1/02-3/31/03	4/1/03-3/31/04
0-500M	500M-2MM	2-10MM	10-50MM	50-100MM	100-250MM		ALL	ALL
5	7	13	3	2	1	NUMBER OF STATEMENTS	44	36
%	%	%	%	%	%	**ASSETS**	%	%
		15.3				Cash & Equivalents	11.5	9.6
		32.6				Trade Receivables (net)	22.1	23.4
		3.0				Inventory	7.6	7.3
		1.9				All Other Current	3.0	1.4
		52.8				Total Current	44.2	41.7
		35.8				Fixed Assets (net)	46.2	47.4
		7.2				Intangibles (net)	4.5	1.7
		4.3				All Other Non-Current	5.1	9.2
		100.0				Total	100.0	100.0
						LIABILITIES		
		8.5				Notes Payable-Short Term	14.2	13.1
		5.6				Cur. Mat.-L.T.D.	7.8	5.1
		12.8				Trade Payables	10.7	8.9
		.9				Income Taxes Payable	.4	.1
		9.1				All Other Current	11.2	10.5
		36.9				Total Current	44.4	37.6
		15.9				Long-Term Debt	16.6	20.8
		.0				Deferred Taxes	.5	.3
		12.5				All Other Non-Current	5.6	12.2
		34.7				Net Worth	32.9	29.1
		100.0				Total Liabilties & Net Worth	100.0	100.0
						INCOME DATA		
		100.0				Net Sales	100.0	100.0
						Gross Profit		
		90.9				Operating Expenses	96.6	91.4
		9.1				Operating Profit	3.4	8.6
		1.4				All Other Expenses (net)	1.3	3.4
		7.7				Profit Before Taxes	2.0	5.2
						RATIOS		
		3.2					1.6	1.9
		1.4				Current	.9	1.3
		1.0					.6	.8
		3.1					1.3	1.5
		1.4				Quick	.7	1.0
		.8					.5	.6
	31	11.8					17 21.6	28 13.0
	58	6.3				Sales/Receivables	40 9.2	44 8.3
	63	5.8					58 6.3	65 5.6
						Cost of Sales/Inventory		
						Cost of Sales/Payables		
		8.0					10.3	8.0
		12.1				Sales/Working Capital	-46.5	25.1
		NM					-10.1	-18.0
		16.9					7.5	19.3
	(12)	6.9				EBIT/Interest	(40) 2.2	(31) 2.2
		1.9					.4	1.1
							3.2	8.3
						Net Profit + Depr., Dep., Amort./Cur. Mat. L/T/D	(14) 1.7	(11) 4.9
							.8	1.8
		.5					.9	.8
		1.6				Fixed/Worth	1.7	2.1
		5.5					9.6	6.2
		.9					.8	.8
		2.3				Debt/Worth	2.6	2.7
		13.9					19.8	12.2
		60.5					46.5	70.0
	(11)	45.9				% Profit Before Taxes/Tangible Net Worth	(36) 13.5	(31) 20.9
		29.5					-7.1	1.0
		24.6					13.0	22.9
		16.3				% Profit Before Taxes/Total Assets	3.6	6.5
		4.7					-2.3	.3
		15.6					8.9	9.8
		6.6				Sales/Net Fixed Assets	5.3	5.3
		4.1					2.2	1.9
		2.8					3.0	3.0
		2.6				Sales/Total Assets	1.9	2.0
		1.5					1.0	1.0
		2.0					4.6	5.3
		5.6				% Depr., Dep., Amort./Sales	(36) 9.0	(26) 8.3
		6.7					15.8	12.6
							7.9	6.1
						% Officers', Directors' Owners' Comp/Sales	(14) 9.9	(13) 9.6
							16.5	14.0
10925M	30577M	167052M	58145M	91609M	71781M	Net Sales ($)	496261M	1841194M
1850M	7085M	75267M	36863M	143340M	181395M	Total Assets ($)	364354M	753361M

M = $ thousand   MM = $ million
See Pages 11 through 21 for Explanation of Ratios and Data

Comparative Historical Data

Current Data Sorted by Sales

4/1/04-3/31/05 ALL	4/1/05-3/31/06 ALL	4/1/06-3/31/07 ALL	Type of Statement	0-1MM	1-3MM	3-5MM	5-10MM	10-25MM	25MM & OVER
8	4	4	Unqualified					1	3
6	6	3	Reviewed				1	1	
5	4	3	Compiled			1	1	1	
7	6	7	Tax Returns		2	2	2	2	
8	14	14	Other		2	2	1	9	
					3 (4/1-9/30/06)			28 (10/1/06-3/31/07)	
34	34	31	NUMBER OF STATEMENTS		4	5	5	14	3
%	%	%	ASSETS	%	%	%	%	%	%
14.3	15.8	19.9	Cash & Equivalents					15.7	
26.8	30.2	28.9	Trade Receivables (net)					30.0	
7.9	7.3	3.3	Inventory					2.4	
3.4	5.2	2.0	All Other Current					2.0	
52.3	58.6	54.1	Total Current					50.0	
41.1	32.7	31.7	Fixed Assets (net)					29.5	
2.7	4.7	6.6	Intangibles (net)					12.6	
3.8	4.1	7.5	All Other Non-Current					7.9	
100.0	100.0	100.0	Total					100.0	
			LIABILITIES						
7.4	7.6	12.4	Notes Payable-Short Term					7.6	
4.8	4.7	3.9	Cur. Mat.-L.T.D.					3.7	
10.7	10.3	12.0	Trade Payables					11.3	
.2	.5	.4	Income Taxes Payable					.2	
9.5	8.6	9.6	All Other Current					9.9	
32.7	31.6	38.3	Total Current					32.6	
19.1	13.6	8.2	Long-Term Debt					13.6	
.5	.0	.0	Deferred Taxes					.0	
12.4	10.3	13.1	All Other Non-Current					11.3	
35.3	44.5	40.3	Net Worth					42.4	
100.0	100.0	100.0	Total Liabilities & Net Worth					100.0	
			INCOME DATA						
100.0	100.0	100.0	Net Sales					100.0	
			Gross Profit						
92.7	90.3	95.4	Operating Expenses					91.4	
7.3	9.7	4.6	Operating Profit					8.6	
1.1	1.8	.4	All Other Expenses (net)					.7	
6.2	7.9	4.2	Profit Before Taxes					7.9	
			RATIOS						
2.7	4.5	3.0	Current					3.4	
1.6	2.1	1.3						1.4	
1.0	1.0	.8						.9	
1.9	3.6	2.9	Quick					3.2	
1.2	2.1	1.1						1.4	
.8	.8	.7						.8	
24 15.4	26 14.1	30 12.1	Sales/Receivables					46 8.0	
38 9.6	42 8.7	43 8.4						60 6.0	
61 6.0	61 6.0	63 5.8						64 5.7	
			Cost of Sales/Inventory						
			Cost of Sales/Payables						
5.3	5.2	7.5	Sales/Working Capital					5.4	
11.2	13.1	22.5						11.8	
-436.6	NM	-70.5						-80.4	
36.8	34.3	16.2	EBIT/Interest					17.5	
(33) 5.6	(25) 3.7	(25) 8.1						(11) 4.2	
1.4	.4	1.3						1.6	
7.3			Net Profit + Depr., Dep., Amort./Cur. Mat. L/T/D						
(12) 3.3									
2.1									
.6	.2	.2	Fixed/Worth					.2	
1.3	.6	.7						.8	
3.2	7.1	3.4						NM	
.6	.3	.6	Debt/Worth					.6	
1.4	1.3	1.5						1.5	
6.2	8.7	6.6						NM	
51.5	69.5	60.5	% Profit Before Taxes/Tangible Net Worth					53.1	
(28) 30.5	(30) 25.1	(27) 39.1						(11) 40.5	
7.6	.2	6.3						20.3	
22.8	23.2	23.5	% Profit Before Taxes/Total Assets					24.0	
10.1	8.4	13.9						15.1	
1.1	.3	2.3						4.7	
16.1	31.0	38.6	Sales/Net Fixed Assets					22.9	
6.4	7.5	9.0						6.7	
2.8	4.3	4.6						3.5	
3.3	3.9	3.9	Sales/Total Assets					2.8	
2.4	2.6	2.6						2.1	
1.3	1.4	1.5						1.4	
4.0	2.6	2.7	% Depr., Dep., Amort./Sales					2.5	
(24) 6.7	(27) 6.2	(23) 5.6						5.3	
11.3	9.3	7.4						7.0	
4.2		2.2	% Officers', Directors' Owners' Comp/Sales						
(12) 7.5		(14) 5.9							
10.1		17.7							
493136M	509150M	430089M	Net Sales ($)		5074M	17723M	33127M	198266M	175899M
385886M	454908M	445800M	Total Assets ($)		1688M	3063M	12885M	143436M	284728M

(For the Current Data columns 0-1MM through 5-10MM: DATA NOT AVAILABLE)

Current Data Sorted by Assets   Comparative Historical Data

	0-500M	500M-2MM	2-10MM	10-50MM	50-100MM	100-250MM	Type of Statement	4/1/02-3/31/03 ALL	4/1/03-3/31/04 ALL
Unqualified		2	2						1
Reviewed		1	3					3	1
Compiled		2	3						
Tax Returns	2	2	2	1	1	1			2
Other	1	3	6	1	1	.		1	4
		6 (4/1-9/30/06)		30 (10/1/06-3/31/07)					
NUMBER OF STATEMENTS	3	10	16	4	2	1		4	8
	%	%	%	%	%	%	**ASSETS**	%	%
		15.2	15.7				Cash & Equivalents		
		22.8	28.7				Trade Receivables (net)		
		3.6	14.4				Inventory		
		1.2	4.8				All Other Current		
		42.9	63.6				Total Current		
		40.5	26.0				Fixed Assets (net)		
		4.1	5.7				Intangibles (net)		
		12.6	4.7				All Other Non-Current		
		100.0	100.0				Total		
							LIABILITIES		
		10.8	10.3				Notes Payable-Short Term		
		3.0	1.9				Cur. Mat.-L.T.D.		
		18.3	7.0				Trade Payables		
		.3	.7				Income Taxes Payable		
		13.6	12.6				All Other Current		
		46.0	32.6				Total Current		
		15.3	25.6				Long-Term Debt		
		.0	.0				Deferred Taxes		
		8.9	1.7				All Other Non-Current		
		29.9	40.1				Net Worth		
		100.0	100.0				Total Liabilties & Net Worth		
							INCOME DATA		
		100.0	100.0				Net Sales		
							Gross Profit		
		78.8	90.5				Operating Expenses		
		21.2	9.5				Operating Profit		
		8.1	3.7				All Other Expenses (net)		
		13.1	5.8				Profit Before Taxes		
							RATIOS		
		1.6	3.6				Current		
		.8	1.7						
		.3	1.1						
		1.4	2.1				Quick		
		.7	1.1						
		.2	.7						
	0	UND	8	46.7			Sales/Receivables		
	16	22.7	43	8.4					
	48	7.5	82	4.5					
							Cost of Sales/Inventory		
							Cost of Sales/Payables		
		12.1	3.7				Sales/Working Capital		
		-473.7	6.2						
		-4.8	49.2						
			63.5				EBIT/Interest		
		(14)	17.1						
			1.4						
							Net Profit + Depr., Dep., Amort./Cur. Mat. L/T/D		
		.2	.1				Fixed/Worth		
		1.9	.2						
		NM	8.8						
		.9	.4				Debt/Worth		
		1.8	1.4						
		NM	10.1						
			88.9				% Profit Before Taxes/Tangible Net Worth		
		(14)	55.3						
			13.3						
		8.9	33.2				% Profit Before Taxes/Total Assets		
		2.8	8.8						
		-3.8	2.1						
		58.9	109.2				Sales/Net Fixed Assets		
		15.4	22.6						
		3.3	3.1						
		3.7	3.3				Sales/Total Assets		
		2.7	1.6						
		.4	1.2						
			.5				% Depr., Dep., Amort./Sales		
		(15)	1.7						
			4.5						
							% Officers', Directors' Owners' Comp/Sales		
	1232M	109159M	180714M	259340M	371609M	204680M	Net Sales ($)	13776M	18812M
	352M	12588M	91403M	114384M	171770M	112396M	Total Assets ($)	20316M	16122M

M = $ thousand   MM = $ million

See Pages 11 through 21 for Explanation of Ratios and Data

Comparative Historical Data | Current Data Sorted by Sales

4/1/04-3/31/05 ALL	4/1/05-3/31/06 ALL	4/1/06-3/31/07 ALL	Type of Statement	0-1MM	1-3MM	3-5MM	5-10MM	10-25MM	25MM & OVER
2	1	6	Unqualified		1		1	2	2
4	3	4	Reviewed		1	1	1	1	1
2	1	5	Compiled	2		2	1		
6		9	Tax Returns	3	1		1	1	4
5	4	12	Other	2	1		3	3	1
				6 (4/1-9/30/06)			30 (10/1/06-3/31/07)		
19	9	36	NUMBER OF STATEMENTS	7	4	3	9	6	7
%	%	%	ASSETS	%	%	%	%	%	%
13.9		20.7	Cash & Equivalents						
34.8		23.3	Trade Receivables (net)						
5.2		8.3	Inventory						
2.2		3.2	All Other Current						
56.0		55.4	Total Current						
29.4		32.2	Fixed Assets (net)						
.9		3.7	Intangibles (net)						
13.7		8.7	All Other Non-Current						
100.0		100.0	Total						
			LIABILITIES						
18.6		15.2	Notes Payable-Short Term						
2.8		1.8	Cur. Mat.-L.T.D.						
11.3		9.0	Trade Payables						
.4		.4	Income Taxes Payable						
14.1		17.8	All Other Current						
47.1		44.2	Total Current						
25.9		17.8	Long-Term Debt						
2.3		.0	Deferred Taxes						
6.5		3.9	All Other Non-Current						
18.1		34.0	Net Worth						
100.0		100.0	Total Liabilities & Net Worth						
			INCOME DATA						
100.0		100.0	Net Sales						
			Gross Profit						
93.2		85.6	Operating Expenses						
6.8		14.4	Operating Profit						
.2		4.9	All Other Expenses (net)						
6.6		9.6	Profit Before Taxes						
			RATIOS						
1.7		2.7	Current						
1.3		1.5							
.5		.7							
1.7		1.8	Quick						
1.0		1.1							
.5		.4							
0 UND		0 UND	Sales/Receivables						
52 7.0		22 16.4							
97 3.8		75 4.9							
			Cost of Sales/Inventory						
			Cost of Sales/Payables						
7.2		4.1	Sales/Working Capital						
20.2		13.1							
-26.6		-47.7							
29.7		54.6	EBIT/Interest						
(18) 2.6		(29) 21.2							
.6		1.1							
			Net Profit + Depr., Dep., Amort./Cur. Mat. L/T/D						
.1		.1	Fixed/Worth						
1.2		.4							
-3.0		5.8							
.9		.4	Debt/Worth						
3.4		1.4							
-5.1		7.9							
72.7		69.0	% Profit Before Taxes/Tangible Net Worth						
(14) 40.7		(30) 40.3							
2.7		9.7							
30.9		33.5	% Profit Before Taxes/Total Assets						
10.8		7.6							
-.5		1.6							
54.9		56.0	Sales/Net Fixed Assets						
18.2		12.3							
7.4		3.3							
5.5		3.5	Sales/Total Assets						
3.3		1.8							
1.6		1.1							
.6		.6	% Depr., Dep., Amort./Sales						
(15) 1.8		(29) 1.8							
3.8		4.6							
2.5		3.2	% Officers', Directors' Owners' Comp/Sales						
(10) 4.2		(15) 4.2							
9.6		9.1							
101968M	46953M	1126734M	Net Sales ($)	2872M	8433M	12642M	72090M	83034M	947663M
55830M	46052M	502893M	Total Assets ($)	8006M	4946M	10817M	49871M	80205M	349048M

M = $ thousand   MM = $ million
See Pages 11 through 21 for Explanation of Ratios and Data

Current Data Sorted by Assets   Comparative Historical Data

Type of Statement

0-500M	500M-2MM	2-10MM	10-50MM	50-100MM	100-250MM	Type of Statement	4/1/02-3/31/03 ALL	4/1/03-3/31/04 ALL
	5	5	14	8	3	Unqualified	38	29
2	3	6	1			Reviewed	19	12
1	7	3				Compiled	32	20
1	3	3				Tax Returns	4	11
3	7	12	7	3	1	Other	36	35
	15 (4/1-9/30/06)		83 (10/1/06-3/31/07)					
0-500M	500M-2MM	2-10MM	10-50MM	50-100MM	100-250MM			
7	25	29	22	11	4	**NUMBER OF STATEMENTS**	129	107

Financial Data

0-500M	500M-2MM	2-10MM	10-50MM	50-100MM	100-250MM		4/1/02-3/31/03 ALL	4/1/03-3/31/04 ALL
%	%	%	%	%	%	**ASSETS**	%	%
	21.7	11.6	14.8	8.1		Cash & Equivalents	10.0	10.7
	17.0	12.5	10.2	11.6		Trade Receivables (net)	15.8	17.0
	.1	.0	.8	1.0		Inventory	.2	.3
	5.1	2.3	2.4	1.4		All Other Current	3.2	3.7
	43.9	26.5	28.2	22.1		Total Current	29.2	31.6
	23.7	25.1	26.7	17.8		Fixed Assets (net)	27.2	27.6
	20.2	37.8	32.0	48.3		Intangibles (net)	30.7	28.7
	12.2	10.7	13.1	11.8		All Other Non-Current	12.9	12.1
	100.0	100.0	100.0	100.0		Total	100.0	100.0
						LIABILITIES		
	.7	6.8	4.3	1.4		Notes Payable-Short Term	2.6	2.9
	2.5	5.0	2.4	1.7		Cur. Mat.-L.T.D.	8.2	6.7
	3.8	2.5	2.8	8.3		Trade Payables	4.5	4.0
	.0	.1	.2	.2		Income Taxes Payable	.2	.0
	5.4	3.5	3.4	2.9		All Other Current	11.8	7.3
	12.5	18.0	13.1	14.5		Total Current	27.3	21.0
	45.8	43.4	27.0	28.4		Long-Term Debt	43.2	40.6
	.1	.3	.7	5.0		Deferred Taxes	.6	.4
	5.6	7.1	10.3	16.7		All Other Non-Current	10.5	15.5
	36.1	31.2	48.8	35.3		Net Worth	18.4	22.6
	100.0	100.0	100.0	100.0		Total Liabilities & Net Worth	100.0	100.0
						INCOME DATA		
	100.0	100.0	100.0	100.0		Net Sales	100.0	100.0
						Gross Profit		
	86.7	90.4	85.6	85.3		Operating Expenses	87.7	88.0
	13.3	9.6	14.4	14.7		Operating Profit	12.3	12.0
	2.2	6.0	2.5	7.6		All Other Expenses (net)	5.6	5.5
	11.1	3.6	11.9	7.2		Profit Before Taxes	6.7	6.5
						RATIOS		
	7.6	4.1	7.0	3.3			3.7	3.9
	3.5	1.7	3.4	2.0		Current	1.6	2.0
	1.9	.9	1.9	1.2			.9	1.0
	7.6	3.9	6.7	3.1			3.4	3.4
	3.4	1.7	3.3	1.5		Quick	1.5	1.8
	1.3	.7	1.5	1.1			.8	.9
0 UND		38 9.7	38 9.7	45 8.1			41 8.8	42 8.7
37 9.8		48 7.7	57 6.4	55 6.7		Sales/Receivables	56 6.5	56 6.5
63 5.8		61 6.0	67 5.5	58 6.3			67 5.4	70 5.2
						Cost of Sales/Inventory		
						Cost of Sales/Payables		
	2.8	3.9	2.9	4.5			4.5	4.4
	6.0	12.5	4.7	11.0		Sales/Working Capital	11.1	7.9
	20.3	-37.1	11.8	28.4			-52.8	-999.8
	12.5	3.3	19.7				7.0	6.9
	(19) 2.4	(24) 1.9	(17) 4.9			EBIT/Interest	(113) 2.1	(87) 3.3
	.0	.4	1.6				.7	.7
							6.1	3.2
						Net Profit + Depr., Dep., Amort./Cur. Mat. L/T/D	(19) 1.9	(15) 1.7
							1.2	.6
	.1	.9	.4	1.1			.7	.7
	.6	-2.6	1.2	210.8		Fixed/Worth	-4.7	17.3
	-1.2	-.4	-1.8	-.1			-.5	-.5
	.2	1.9	.2	1.1			1.1	1.1
	1.7	-4.8	1.9	312.0		Debt/Worth	-9.1	25.5
	-2.7	-1.8	-7.4	-1.4			-2.1	-2.0
	96.6	147.2	48.7				61.6	75.9
	(16) 41.0	(11) 44.6	(15) 18.9			% Profit Before Taxes/Tangible Net Worth	(58) 27.8	(55) 31.3
	5.6	7.6	6.5				1.4	6.8
	30.9	11.7	13.3	10.5			15.8	17.0
	9.0	4.5	6.3	7.4		% Profit Before Taxes/Total Assets	4.7	6.8
	-2.1	-3.0	2.0	-.7			-1.0	-1.1
	26.4	6.8	4.7	11.1			9.3	9.0
	6.9	2.8	3.3	3.8		Sales/Net Fixed Assets	3.7	4.1
	3.7	2.2	1.8	2.4			2.3	2.2
	1.9	1.2	1.0	.7			1.5	1.4
	1.6	.8	.5	.6		Sales/Total Assets	.9	.9
	.9	.5	.4	.4			.6	.6
	.8	2.9	3.5				3.5	2.4
	(18) 4.2	(28) 5.0	(21) 5.3			% Depr., Dep., Amort./Sales	(117) 5.5	(99) 5.0
	9.4	9.8	7.8				9.1	8.5
							3.9	4.2
						% Officers', Directors' Owners' Comp/Sales	(30) 7.2	(25) 9.1
							12.7	11.9
3924M	44643M	123276M	378387M	560680M	254804M	Net Sales ($)	1405108M	1106436M
2487M	27827M	142385M	531531M	832554M	550623M	Total Assets ($)	2444652M	1714655M

M = $ thousand   MM = $ million
See Pages 11 through 21 for Explanation of Ratios and Data

Comparative Historical Data | Current Data Sorted by Sales

Type of Statement	4/1/04-3/31/05 ALL	4/1/05-3/31/06 ALL	4/1/06-3/31/07 ALL		0-1MM	1-3MM	3-5MM	5-10MM	10-25MM	25MM & OVER
Unqualified	32	30	35		1	4	4	7	7	12
Reviewed	12	11	11		2	6	2		1	
Compiled	12	13	12		3	7		2		
Tax Returns	4	7	7		1	6				
Other	42	40	33		6	9	2	6	4	6
						15 (4/1-9/30/06)		83 (10/1/06-3/31/07)		
NUMBER OF STATEMENTS	102	101	98		13	32	8	15	12	18
ASSETS	%	%	%		%	%	%	%	%	%
Cash & Equivalents	13.6	11.2	16.4		36.7	13.7		17.9	8.4	11.8
Trade Receivables (net)	17.0	14.6	12.9		12.4	15.1		11.0	10.0	13.6
Inventory	.2	.3	.3		.0	.1		.0	.0	1.6
All Other Current	3.1	3.2	2.8		.6	4.9		3.3	.6	2.4
Total Current	33.9	29.3	32.4		49.7	33.7		32.2	19.0	29.4
Fixed Assets (net)	25.3	23.5	23.6		21.8	25.1		23.1	21.0	21.8
Intangibles (net)	30.0	33.4	32.4		21.3	31.0		37.9	44.1	35.2
All Other Non-Current	10.8	13.8	11.7		7.2	10.2		6.8	15.9	13.6
Total	100.0	100.0	100.0		100.0	100.0		100.0	100.0	100.0
LIABILITIES										
Notes Payable-Short Term	1.9	2.6	3.3		.2	6.1		6.8	.4	.9
Cur. Mat.-L.T.D.	5.4	3.9	2.9		.3	3.6		4.8	2.0	1.9
Trade Payables	3.7	3.1	3.5		3.3	2.8		1.9	3.3	6.5
Income Taxes Payable	.3	.1	.1		.1	.1		.0	.1	.4
All Other Current	6.3	9.5	4.6		11.5	3.2		2.4	2.9	5.3
Total Current	17.5	19.2	14.4		15.4	15.8		15.9	8.7	15.0
Long-Term Debt	37.4	43.9	38.0		44.6	48.1		28.5	30.6	28.5
Deferred Taxes	.5	1.7	.8		.0	.1		.0	.6	3.9
All Other Non-Current	10.6	12.1	8.9		7.3	4.2		16.4	6.6	13.0
Net Worth	34.1	23.1	37.9		32.6	31.7		39.1	53.5	39.7
Total Liabilities & Net Worth	100.0	100.0	100.0		100.0	100.0		100.0	100.0	100.0
INCOME DATA										
Net Sales	100.0	100.0	100.0		100.0	100.0		100.0	100.0	100.0
Gross Profit										
Operating Expenses	85.4	89.0	86.2		84.7	86.1		86.1	88.9	85.4
Operating Profit	14.6	11.0	13.8		15.3	13.9		13.9	11.1	14.6
All Other Expenses (net)	4.9	5.0	4.8		4.0	5.3		3.7	8.8	5.1
Profit Before Taxes	9.7	6.0	9.0		11.3	8.6		10.2	2.3	9.5
RATIOS										
Current	3.4	4.8	6.6		17.7	6.7		6.7	7.2	3.5
	2.2	2.0	2.5		5.1	3.0		3.9	1.9	2.0
	1.2	1.1	1.2		.9	1.2		1.3	1.1	1.2
Quick	3.3	4.6	5.3		17.4	6.1		6.4	7.1	3.3
	1.7	1.8	2.1		5.1	2.3		3.9	1.8	1.7
	1.0	.9	1.1		.8	.8		1.3	1.0	1.1
Sales/Receivables	44 8.2	40 9.0	30 12.1		0 UND	1 253.1		29 12.4	46 8.0	43 8.4
	53 6.9	52 7.0	48 7.5		42 8.8	49 7.5		53 6.9	61 6.0	54 6.8
	65 5.6	66 5.5	64 5.7		63 5.8	64 5.7		70 5.2	65 5.6	60 6.1
Cost of Sales/Inventory										
Cost of Sales/Payables										
Sales/Working Capital	3.6	3.9	3.0		1.5	2.9		2.6	4.0	4.3
	7.1	7.6	6.5		2.5	7.1		4.9	10.8	6.6
	29.5	72.5	23.6		NM	43.9		16.5	NM	23.4
EBIT/Interest	7.9	5.3	7.0			4.7		6.1	105.7	8.7
	(87) 3.9	(77) 2.8	(73) 2.7		(26) 1.2		(10) 2.8	(10) 3.6	(14) 4.2	
	1.6	1.3	.5			.1		2.0	1.2	1.7
Net Profit + Depr., Dep., Amort./Cur. Mat. L/T/D	3.6	4.5	5.8							
	(19) 1.3	(21) 2.0	(16) 2.4							
	1.1	1.1	1.4							
Fixed/Worth	.5	.5	.4		.0	.4		.2	.6	.5
	3.3	-7.5	2.4		.5	-2.3		-6.7	1.6	1.9
	-.7	-.4	-.5		-2.8	-.4		-.5	-.2	-3.0
Debt/Worth	.8	.8	.6		.0	.5		.2	.3	1.1
	7.9	-15.2	11.0		1.0	-5.6		-16.0	3.3	7.4
	-2.4	-1.9	-1.9		-4.3	-1.8		-1.8	-2.0	-5.4
% Profit Before Taxes/Tangible Net Worth	73.4	58.5	93.2			94.3				110.9
	(52) 20.9	(49) 26.5	(55) 29.3		(14) 39.0				(12) 40.8	
	4.6	8.9	7.2			1.5				10.1
% Profit Before Taxes/Total Assets	15.7	13.4	17.8		23.7	18.4		10.7	10.2	11.8
	7.2	5.9	6.0		3.0	3.1		6.5	3.6	8.8
	2.1	.9	-1.9		-15.4	-3.0		3.3	-2.7	1.8
Sales/Net Fixed Assets	9.3	11.5	8.3		33.3	9.7		6.7	6.8	6.9
	4.4	4.2	4.3		4.9	4.2		3.9	3.8	3.8
	2.4	2.2	2.4		3.1	2.2		1.9	2.3	2.7
Sales/Total Assets	1.4	1.4	1.4		1.7	1.6		1.3	1.2	1.3
	.9	.9	.8		1.3	.9		.8	.7	.7
	.5	.5	.5		.6	.5		.5	.3	.5
% Depr., Dep., Amort./Sales	2.3	3.0	2.7			2.7		.9	3.5	2.4
	(90) 4.8	(91) 4.8	(82) 5.0		(28) 5.4		5.0	5.0	(15) 3.5	
	8.7	8.2	8.7			9.6		9.0	6.8	6.7
% Officers', Directors' Owners' Comp/Sales	2.6	3.0	2.9			3.4				
	(22) 5.3	(17) 7.8	(16) 5.2		(11) 4.9					
	12.9	15.5	7.7			10.1				
Net Sales ($)	1106127M	1193402M	1365714M		7098M	62100M	30402M	113990M	191921M	960203M
Total Assets ($)	1892755M	2043083M	2087407M		7525M	80667M	44254M	175598M	506767M	1272596M

M = $ thousand   MM = $ million
See Pages 11 through 21 for Explanation of Ratios and Data

Current Data Sorted by Assets / Comparative Historical Data

	0-500M	500M-2MM	2-10MM	10-50MM	50-100MM	100-250MM	4/1/02-3/31/03 ALL	4/1/03-3/31/04 ALL
Type of Statement								
Unqualified		1	10	18	5	5	39	42
Reviewed			5	2			9	9
Compiled		2		2	1		3	9
Tax Returns		3	2				4	4
Other		2	17	9	3	2	22	19
		33 (4/1-9/30/06)		56 (10/1/06-3/31/07)				
NUMBER OF STATEMENTS		8	34	31	9	7	77	83
ASSETS	%	%	%	%	%	%	%	%
Cash & Equivalents	DATA NOT AVAILABLE		10.1	13.1			9.7	11.3
Trade Receivables (net)			9.5	9.6			12.9	13.5
Inventory			.1	1.4			1.2	.5
All Other Current			2.7	4.1			5.3	7.2
Total Current			22.5	28.1			29.0	32.4
Fixed Assets (net)			52.8	48.2			44.1	41.0
Intangibles (net)			12.9	6.6			14.6	16.2
All Other Non-Current			11.9	17.1			12.3	10.4
Total			100.0	100.0			100.0	100.0
LIABILITIES								
Notes Payable-Short Term			5.7	3.2			9.5	4.4
Cur. Mat.-L.T.D.			2.7	3.1			6.0	8.5
Trade Payables			4.3	3.9			5.4	5.5
Income Taxes Payable			.0	.3			.0	.1
All Other Current			19.8	4.7			8.8	8.9
Total Current			32.5	15.3			29.6	27.4
Long-Term Debt			15.7	21.3			28.8	28.4
Deferred Taxes			.6	.7			.4	.2
All Other Non-Current			9.9	3.0			5.2	8.5
Net Worth			41.3	59.7			36.0	35.4
Total Liabilities & Net Worth			100.0	100.0			100.0	100.0
INCOME DATA								
Net Sales			100.0	100.0			100.0	100.0
Gross Profit								
Operating Expenses			94.0	90.7			92.6	92.0
Operating Profit			6.0	9.3			7.4	8.0
All Other Expenses (net)			1.3	.3			5.1	5.0
Profit Before Taxes			4.6	8.9			2.4	3.0
RATIOS								
Current			2.7	3.7			2.8	2.7
			1.5	1.5			1.3	1.6
			.3	1.2			.7	.9
Quick			2.3	3.7			1.7	2.1
			1.1	1.1			1.0	1.2
			.2	.7			.5	.6
Sales/Receivables			**16** 22.9	**27** 13.3			**22** 16.7	**23** 16.1
			48 7.7	**38** 9.6			**56** 6.5	**55** 6.6
			63 5.8	**68** 5.4			**70** 5.2	**71** 5.1
Cost of Sales/Inventory								
Cost of Sales/Payables								
Sales/Working Capital			4.7	2.7			4.6	4.3
			16.2	7.9			14.1	10.8
			-2.5	37.0			-15.7	-32.6
EBIT/Interest			10.5	10.2			4.6	7.8
			(24) 2.5	(27) 4.8			(60) 2.3	(66) 2.9
			-.3	-.2			.3	.3
Net Profit + Depr., Dep., Amort./Cur. Mat. L/T/D							2.8	2.1
							(12) 1.5	(10) 1.4
							1.0	.8
Fixed/Worth			.7	.6			.7	.7
			1.1	.9			1.4	1.8
			NM	1.7			-3.5	-2.0
Debt/Worth			.3	.2			.4	.3
			1.1	.7			2.1	2.0
			NM	2.1			-7.0	-3.9
% Profit Before Taxes/Tangible Net Worth			30.9	23.5			21.1	27.5
			(26) 9.5	(29) 10.5			(53) 2.9	(55) 9.1
			.8	1.7			-10.4	-.4
% Profit Before Taxes/Total Assets			12.0	8.4			9.2	9.5
			2.9	5.7			2.3	2.5
			-1.5	-.5			-2.8	-1.9
Sales/Net Fixed Assets			3.7	2.6			3.7	4.1
			1.4	1.5			2.1	2.1
			.6	.8			1.3	1.3
Sales/Total Assets			1.1	1.0			1.2	1.3
			.7	.6			.9	.8
			.4	.4			.6	.5
% Depr., Dep., Amort./Sales			6.1	4.7			5.2	6.1
			(32) 11.0	(30) 9.1			(68) 8.3	(78) 8.1
			14.0	12.6			14.3	13.7
% Officers', Directors' Owners' Comp/Sales							1.8	1.9
							(11) 5.6	(15) 5.7
							8.8	27.6
Net Sales ($)		15723M	179256M	602330M	476370M	613206M	1486458M	1982516M
Total Assets ($)		9312M	190929M	796032M	646153M	1018226M	2291395M	2475541M

M = $ thousand MM = $ million

See Pages 11 through 21 for Explanation of Ratios and Data

| Comparative Historical Data | | | | | Current Data Sorted by Sales | | | | | |

Type of Statement

46		40		39	Unqualified		4	4	8	10	13
4		3		7	Reviewed		2	1	1	2	1
3		3		5	Compiled		1	1	1	2	
1		3		5	Tax Returns	2	1	1	1		
15		27		33	Other	4	9	2	3	9	6

4/1/04-3/31/05 ALL	4/1/05-3/31/06 ALL	4/1/06-3/31/07 ALL		33 (4/1-9/30/06)		56 (10/1/06-3/31/07)		
			0-1MM	1-3MM	3-5MM	5-10MM	10-25MM	25MM & OVER
69	76	89	**NUMBER OF STATEMENTS**	6	17	9	14	23	20

%	%	%	ASSETS	%	%	%	%	%	%
13.6	11.0	10.8	Cash & Equivalents		12.5		12.9	10.1	8.2
12.1	11.6	11.4	Trade Receivables (net)		9.8		6.8	12.3	14.6
.6	2.2	.6	Inventory		.1		.3	1.4	.7
5.0	5.4	3.0	All Other Current		1.4		5.8	3.9	3.6
31.3	30.3	25.8	Total Current		23.9		25.8	27.7	27.1
44.9	36.5	45.9	Fixed Assets (net)		60.3		49.0	43.3	33.7
10.8	16.4	12.1	Intangibles (net)		10.7		1.5	10.1	17.8
13.1	16.8	16.2	All Other Non-Current		5.1		23.7	19.0	21.4
100.0	100.0	100.0	Total		100.0		100.0	100.0	100.0

			LIABILITIES						
3.3	5.9	4.1	Notes Payable-Short Term		12.0		1.9	3.8	.6
3.2	2.3	2.4	Cur. Mat.-L.T.D.		2.1		3.4	2.5	1.8
4.5	6.2	4.0	Trade Payables		1.8		6.1	4.9	4.5
.3	.0	.1	Income Taxes Payable		.0		.0	.5	.0
7.9	14.6	11.8	All Other Current		13.7		6.8	9.3	6.9
19.1	29.1	22.4	Total Current		29.6		18.1	21.0	13.9
26.0	31.1	24.4	Long-Term Debt		25.4		19.4	18.3	27.3
.5	.4	.7	Deferred Taxes		.0		1.8	.8	1.1
10.3	13.2	10.6	All Other Non-Current		4.3		2.9	10.8	17.8
44.1	26.2	41.9	Net Worth		40.8		57.8	49.2	39.9
100.0	100.0	100.0	Total Liabilties & Net Worth		100.0		100.0	100.0	100.0

			INCOME DATA						
100.0	100.0	100.0	Net Sales		100.0		100.0	100.0	100.0
			Gross Profit						
93.5	94.9	91.1	Operating Expenses		95.3		93.4	90.4	88.4
6.5	5.1	8.9	Operating Profit		4.7		6.6	9.6	11.6
2.1	4.7	2.5	All Other Expenses (net)		2.5		-1.9	2.3	4.9
4.4	.4	6.4	Profit Before Taxes		2.2		8.5	7.3	6.7

			RATIOS						
3.0	3.0	3.4			5.4		5.1	2.6	3.9
1.7	1.6	1.6	Current		1.7		1.7	1.2	2.5
.9	.8	.8			.5		1.0	.9	1.0
2.6	2.8	2.6			5.0		4.2	2.4	3.8
1.2	1.1	1.2	Quick		1.6		1.2	1.0	1.4
.7	.5	.6			.3		.8	.5	.8

							Sales/Receivables						
12	30.4	14	25.4	25	14.4		12	29.6	11	31.9	29	12.6	31	11.9
44	8.3	49	7.4	47	7.7		55	6.6	32	11.4	52	7.1	56	6.6
64	5.7	67	5.5	66	5.5		72	5.1	63	5.8	74	5.0	71	5.1

			Cost of Sales/Inventory						

			Cost of Sales/Payables						

			Sales/Working Capital						
3.9	4.0	3.5			2.4		3.1	4.7	3.3
8.7	9.1	10.5			13.7		7.5	19.6	5.8
-31.2	-20.5	-29.9			-10.3		NM	-33.9	124.8

				EBIT/Interest								
	14.3		4.9		9.2			7.8		16.5	8.0	9.6
(58)	3.1	(56)	1.4	(72)	3.0		(13)	.7	(12)	1.9	(21)	4.8	(17)	3.6
	.7		-1.1		-.2			-4.7		-.6	1.1	1.2

				Net Profit + Depr., Dep., Amort./Cur. Mat. L/T/D						
			23.3							
		(14)	2.2							
			.7							

			Fixed/Worth						
.6	.7	.6			.9		.4	.6	.4
1.1	1.1	1.1			1.7		.9	1.0	.8
5.1	-.8	5.3			-2.6		2.3	1.8	-1.0

			Debt/Worth						
.4	.4	.2			.2		.1	.3	.2
1.3	2.0	1.2			1.1		.5	1.2	1.7
11.2	-2.9	18.0			-10.1		3.8	2.6	-4.0

				% Profit Before Taxes/Tangible Net Worth								
	18.5		15.5		28.0			17.8		22.0	29.7	24.6
(57)	3.5	(51)	2.5	(69)	9.6		(12)	7.4	(13)	4.8	(21)	15.3	(14)	6.3
	-5.5		-6.8		.3			-10.4		-1.7	4.5	-.8

			% Profit Before Taxes/Total Assets						
10.2	6.1	10.1			6.1		8.2	10.9	9.1
2.4	.9	4.1			2.4		1.3	5.7	4.0
-1.0	-4.1	-.7			-6.6		-3.9	.8	.4

			Sales/Net Fixed Assets						
3.7	4.8	3.6			1.7		2.5	3.8	4.6
1.8	2.3	1.6			.8		1.4	2.6	2.5
1.1	1.2	.9			.6		.7	1.2	1.4

			Sales/Total Assets						
1.2	1.1	1.1			.8		1.0	1.5	1.3
.8	.8	.7			.5		.6	.8	.8
.5	.4	.4			.4		.4	.5	.5

				% Depr., Dep., Amort./Sales								
	5.5		6.4		5.3			7.3		4.4	4.6	4.5
(61)	8.5	(63)	9.8	(86)	9.4			12.0		10.6	(22)	8.6	6.7
	13.2		15.2		13.1			16.8		12.2	12.2	12.0

			% Officers', Directors' Owners' Comp/Sales						

1851002M	1527201M	1886885M	Net Sales ($)	3561M	36568M	34070M	101389M	374418M	1336879M
2463699M	2492695M	2660652M	Total Assets ($)	15495M	74798M	43540M	193335M	593402M	1740082M

© RMA 2007   **M = $ thousand   MM = $ million**
See Pages 11 through 21 for Explanation of Ratios and Data

Current Data Sorted by Assets   Comparative Historical Data

Type of Statement

	0-500M	500M-2MM	2-10MM	10-50MM	50-100MM	100-250MM		4/1/02-3/31/03 ALL	4/1/03-3/31/04 ALL
Unqualified			6	8	3	8		23	21
Reviewed		3	1	3				12	10
Compiled	1	1	3	2				6	10
Tax Returns	1	4	2	5				15	15
Other	2	5	5		7	2		23	10
		10 (4/1-9/30/06)		62 (10/1/06-3/31/07)					
NUMBER OF STATEMENTS	4	13	17	18	10	10		79	66

	0-500M	500M-2MM	2-10MM	10-50MM	50-100MM	100-250MM		4/1/02-3/31/03 ALL	4/1/03-3/31/04 ALL
ASSETS	%	%	%	%	%	%		%	%
Cash & Equivalents		11.3	12.5	15.2	11.5	5.9		10.1	7.8
Trade Receivables (net)		27.8	24.5	13.1	7.3	5.8		15.9	14.4
Inventory		6.0	8.3	4.5	2.4	1.1		3.8	3.5
All Other Current		5.4	.9	11.1	.6	1.4		3.6	3.9
Total Current		50.5	46.2	43.8	21.7	14.2		33.4	29.6
Fixed Assets (net)		38.6	34.7	33.1	40.0	32.6		43.7	46.5
Intangibles (net)		3.3	11.8	14.5	29.7	48.2		14.6	13.4
All Other Non-Current		7.6	7.3	8.6	8.6	5.0		8.3	10.4
Total		100.0	100.0	100.0	100.0	100.0		100.0	100.0
LIABILITIES									
Notes Payable-Short Term		14.4	4.2	6.5	.0	.0		5.4	8.6
Cur. Mat.-L.T.D.		3.1	1.5	4.1	2.2	1.9		7.3	5.8
Trade Payables		18.7	31.4	23.7	4.3	5.1		9.9	9.8
Income Taxes Payable		.0	.6	.8	.0	.1		.4	.5
All Other Current		2.5	7.7	14.6	6.3	5.3		11.9	11.0
Total Current		38.7	45.4	49.7	12.8	12.4		34.9	35.7
Long-Term Debt		22.0	14.0	26.4	52.5	46.6		37.3	30.5
Deferred Taxes		.0	.6	.8	1.2	4.8		.7	1.1
All Other Non-Current		8.1	42.6	1.4	14.2	2.0		11.1	14.6
Net Worth		31.2	-2.5	21.7	19.2	34.1		16.0	18.1
Total Liabilties & Net Worth		100.0	100.0	100.0	100.0	100.0		100.0	100.0
INCOME DATA									
Net Sales		100.0	100.0	100.0	100.0	100.0		100.0	100.0
Gross Profit									
Operating Expenses		95.8	94.1	91.1	96.2	92.9		94.9	92.8
Operating Profit		4.2	5.9	8.9	3.8	7.1		5.1	7.2
All Other Expenses (net)		.9	3.1	4.3	13.1	9.5		4.2	2.8
Profit Before Taxes		3.2	2.8	4.5	-9.3	-2.4		1.0	4.4
RATIOS									
Current		3.3	1.8	1.1	2.4	1.0		1.5	1.4
		1.0	1.4	.8	.8	.7		.8	.7
		.7	.9	.4	.4	.6		.4	.2
Quick		2.0	1.4	.9	2.0	.7		1.3	.9
		.8	1.1	.5	.7	.6		.6	.5
		.6	.4	.2	.4	.5		.3	.2
Sales/Receivables		9 41.0	15 24.1	6 59.7	6 62.7	20 18.0		8 44.8	8 43.4
		30 12.0	33 11.0	8 44.9	23 15.7	38 9.5		23 15.6	18 19.8
		62 5.9	47 7.7	28 13.0	78 4.7	48 7.6		43 8.6	39 9.4
Cost of Sales/Inventory									
Cost of Sales/Payables									
Sales/Working Capital		23.0	10.3	148.1	2.7	NM		14.4	29.0
		170.3	18.5	-17.7	-166.0	-14.0		-32.7	-16.2
		-37.2	NM	-7.6	-10.6	-10.6		-6.5	-4.6
EBIT/Interest		11.5	42.8	16.0		2.9		(66) 4.9	(58) 6.1
		(12) 3.6	(14) 4.5	(15) 3.3		1.1		1.8	2.4
		.3	2.1	1.4		-.4		.2	.5
Net Profit + Depr., Dep., Amort./Cur. Mat. L/T/D								(13) 9.5	(12) 2.3
								2.6	1.5
								2.1	1.1
Fixed/Worth		.5	.4	.8	14.4	-11.8		.9	.8
		1.2	2.4	3.7	-6.0	-1.5		9.2	7.4
		5.9	-181.0	-3.1	-1.3	-.7		-1.5	-4.6
Debt/Worth		1.1	1.7	3.1	40.0	-15.9		2.0	2.2
		2.3	3.0	11.2	-9.7	-4.1		13.7	13.8
		13.7	-188.6	-21.0	-3.5	-2.1		-3.9	-5.9
% Profit Before Taxes/Tangible Net Worth		104.7	52.9	173.3				48.2	72.5
		(11) 27.7	(12) 26.1	(10) 55.7				(42) 19.7	(37) 34.0
		-1.0	8.6	6.5				.8	4.6
% Profit Before Taxes/Total Assets		33.4	15.7	25.3	2.9	3.7		14.3	13.7
		5.4	8.9	17.9	-2.9	.7		1.9	3.6
		-3.9	1.7	1.1	-9.5	-7.3		-3.6	-3.0
Sales/Net Fixed Assets		31.0	26.6	40.8	3.6	2.4		13.9	12.6
		10.0	12.7	11.8	1.2	1.2		3.1	3.5
		4.3	1.0	1.1	.6	.7		1.0	1.0
Sales/Total Assets		6.5	3.5	3.9	1.0	.5		2.7	3.5
		3.4	1.7	1.3	.4	.3		1.3	1.3
		2.3	.6	.7	.3	.2		.5	.5
% Depr., Dep., Amort./Sales		1.3	.6	.9				3.0	4.3
		(11) 3.1	(15) 2.4	(17) 3.8				(64) 9.9	(54) 11.1
		7.6	13.2	18.0				21.6	20.6
% Officers', Directors' Owners' Comp/Sales								2.8	2.3
								(32) 4.6	(24) 4.1
								6.9	5.8
Net Sales ($)	5445M	58742M	186189M	1009178M	408643M	860618M		2612018M	967640M
Total Assets ($)	690M	14113M	68411M	493151M	711347M	1522988M		2542347M	1261352M

M = $ thousand MM = $ million
See Pages 11 through 21 for Explanation of Ratios and Data

Comparative Historical Data   **Current Data Sorted by Sales**

Hist 1	Hist 2	Hist 3	Type of Statement	0-1MM	1-3MM	3-5MM	5-10MM	10-25MM	25MM & OVER
32	22	25	Unqualified	1	2	2	2	6	12
9	11	7	Reviewed		1		2	1	3
3	1	7	Compiled	1		1	2	1	2
8	17	7	Tax Returns	1		1	4	1	
19	26	26	Other		7	3	1	6	9
4/1/04-3/31/05 ALL	4/1/05-3/31/06 ALL	4/1/06-3/31/07 ALL			10 (4/1-9/30/06)			62 (10/1/06-3/31/07)	
				0-1MM	1-3MM	3-5MM	5-10MM	10-25MM	25MM & OVER
71	77	72	**NUMBER OF STATEMENTS**	3	10	7	11	15	26
%	%	%	**ASSETS**	%	%	%	%	%	%
10.4	9.3	13.0	Cash & Equivalents		8.8		11.3	7.6	16.3
19.4	20.5	15.9	Trade Receivables (net)		19.9		21.5	9.6	16.4
3.5	3.9	5.1	Inventory		2.1		12.4	2.9	4.3
3.0	4.7	5.1	All Other Current		3.1		2.9	1.6	7.5
36.3	38.4	39.1	Total Current		33.8		48.2	21.7	44.4
40.0	40.2	35.5	Fixed Assets (net)		49.0		35.0	37.0	26.8
17.2	13.8	17.8	Intangibles (net)		4.9		10.6	28.6	23.7
6.5	7.6	7.6	All Other Non-Current		12.3		6.2	12.7	5.1
100.0	100.0	100.0	Total		100.0		100.0	100.0	100.0
			LIABILITIES						
9.1	7.0	8.9	Notes Payable-Short Term		11.9		10.6	2.0	3.8
5.7	3.2	2.5	Cur. Mat.-L.T.D.		3.5		1.8	3.6	2.3
9.4	13.3	18.1	Trade Payables		13.1		20.8	24.2	20.6
.5	.6	.4	Income Taxes Payable		.0		.8	.1	.6
9.1	9.1	8.6	All Other Current		5.7		1.8	7.9	12.3
33.8	33.3	38.5	Total Current		34.2		35.8	37.7	39.6
28.1	25.6	28.7	Long-Term Debt		22.1		21.9	39.2	29.0
2.1	2.1	1.2	Deferred Taxes		.0		.1	4.0	.9
12.7	14.6	14.1	All Other Non-Current		22.5		51.3	5.1	4.8
23.3	24.5	17.5	Net Worth		21.2		-9.1	14.0	25.7
100.0	100.0	100.0	Total Liabilities & Net Worth		100.0		100.0	100.0	100.0
			INCOME DATA						
100.0	100.0	100.0	Net Sales		100.0		100.0	100.0	100.0
			Gross Profit						
89.4	93.0	93.1	Operating Expenses		94.9		95.4	91.4	94.2
10.6	7.0	6.9	Operating Profit		5.1		4.6	8.6	5.8
4.2	2.9	5.1	All Other Expenses (net)		4.0		2.8	8.8	5.6
6.4	4.1	1.8	Profit Before Taxes		1.2		1.8	-.2	.2
			RATIOS						
1.6	1.7	1.4	Current		1.2		2.0	1.0	1.4
1.0	1.1	1.0			1.0		1.2	.6	.9
.4	.6	.6			.6		.7	.4	.7
1.3	1.2	1.3	Quick		1.2		1.4	.9	1.2
.7	.7	.7			.8		.7	.5	.6
.3	.4	.5			.4		.5	.3	.5
13 27.6	11 32.3	7 51.2	Sales/Receivables		0 UND		7 51.8	7 50.5	8 44.0
32 11.3	25 14.4	25 14.4			37 9.8		12 30.1	18 20.4	29 12.6
48 7.6	48 7.6	47 7.8			64 5.7		39 9.4	30 12.1	48 7.6
			Cost of Sales/Inventory						
			Cost of Sales/Payables						
13.4	12.5	15.0	Sales/Working Capital		70.4		10.7	-315.5	23.9
-406.7	120.3	-314.5			212.5		34.0	-9.5	-49.8
-5.9	-12.9	-11.3			-15.8		-23.0	-7.0	-14.6
14.1	10.4	8.0	EBIT/Interest					3.0	11.6
(65) 3.8	(63) 1.9	(61) 2.6						(13) 2.6	(23) 2.9
.9	-.4	.4						1.1	.0
4.6	19.6	7.2	Net Profit + Depr., Dep., Amort./Cur. Mat. L/T/D						
(14) 3.4	(16) 3.3	(11) 3.6							
1.6	1.9	2.1							
.6	.7	.6	Fixed/Worth		.6		.5	1.5	.8
2.9	2.9	5.7			2.8		5.0	-9.2	-18.3
-2.8	-5.6	-2.9			-260.9		-.8	-.7	-1.7
1.8	1.2	2.1	Debt/Worth		1.6		2.1	1.6	3.0
6.8	4.1	11.9			6.8		4.6	-10.6	-29.4
-4.1	-9.0	-5.3			-272.5		-3.9	-2.0	-5.1
71.2	57.6	98.0	% Profit Before Taxes/Tangible Net Worth						126.9
(41) 32.0	(53) 23.9	(40) 31.4							(12) 44.4
17.8	-1.7	7.0							11.0
18.2	20.2	20.6	% Profit Before Taxes/Total Assets		6.7		26.9	15.5	21.1
6.4	5.0	4.3			1.4		8.9	2.6	4.8
-.6	-1.8	-3.2			-3.8		.0	-.1	-4.7
23.1	30.2	23.2	Sales/Net Fixed Assets		12.4		26.6	23.5	25.9
2.1	4.4	5.3			6.0		17.1	1.1	6.6
.9	.9	1.1			.9		4.6	.9	1.4
2.9	4.0	3.4	Sales/Total Assets		3.0		6.3	1.3	3.9
.9	1.6	1.4			1.5		3.2	.6	1.1
.4	.5	.5			.7		1.6	.2	.4
1.3	1.3	1.3	% Depr., Dep., Amort./Sales				.7	2.6	.9
(54) 11.1	(58) 8.7	(59) 6.2					(10) 2.6	(14) 18.0	(20) 3.6
22.7	21.7	17.5					11.4	21.1	12.8
1.7	1.4	1.6	% Officers', Directors' Owners' Comp/Sales						
(21) 4.1	(25) 3.1	(20) 3.1							
8.5	10.1	4.1							
2136155M	2139019M	2528815M	Net Sales ($)	1627M	18515M	27958M	91293M	284887M	2104535M
2540032M	2208241M	2810700M	Total Assets ($)	2570M	16909M	18781M	72180M	638457M	2061803M

M = $ thousand   MM = $ million
See Pages 11 through 21 for Explanation of Ratios and Data

Current Data Sorted by Assets　　　　　　　Comparative Historical Data

Type of Statement	0-500M	500M-2MM	2-10MM	10-50MM	50-100MM	100-250MM		4/1/02-3/31/03 ALL	4/1/03-3/31/04 ALL
Unqualified	6	5	28	62	19	17		64	60
Reviewed	3		16	3				14	14
Compiled	2	6	3	2				20	31
Tax Returns	2	10	4					6	13
Other	5	10	12	21	8	7		57	49
		37 (4/1-9/30/06)		214 (10/1/06-3/31/07)					
NUMBER OF STATEMENTS	15	34	63	88	27	24		161	167
ASSETS	%	%	%	%	%	%		%	%
Cash & Equivalents	25.8	14.7	10.7	12.3	9.4	5.1		13.1	12.9
Trade Receivables (net)	13.9	29.3	23.1	13.7	11.4	7.8		23.8	23.3
Inventory	6.7	6.9	5.0	3.1	5.1	1.5		6.4	6.5
All Other Current	.6	4.0	2.7	1.6	2.2	2.5		4.5	4.8
Total Current	47.0	55.0	41.6	30.6	28.0	16.8		47.9	47.5
Fixed Assets (net)	26.9	25.8	42.9	50.4	52.8	54.5		35.7	35.3
Intangibles (net)	7.5	6.3	4.3	7.7	10.8	19.8		6.7	7.5
All Other Non-Current	18.6	12.9	11.2	11.2	8.4	8.9		9.7	9.7
Total	100.0	100.0	100.0	100.0	100.0	100.0		100.0	100.0
LIABILITIES									
Notes Payable-Short Term	6.5	12.9	4.4	2.0	1.5	1.6		7.2	6.8
Cur. Mat.-L.T.D.	1.6	10.1	4.2	3.6	2.4	3.3		3.8	4.0
Trade Payables	7.2	26.6	13.4	9.1	6.3	4.1		15.1	13.4
Income Taxes Payable	1.4	.3	.9	.4	.3	.9		.3	.5
All Other Current	10.3	10.0	9.5	9.1	6.8	7.0		18.7	15.5
Total Current	26.9	59.9	32.4	24.2	17.4	17.0		45.1	40.3
Long-Term Debt	14.0	17.2	19.4	29.9	27.0	44.1		20.9	21.7
Deferred Taxes	.0	.0	1.2	1.9	1.3	1.5		1.4	1.4
All Other Non-Current	3.4	6.8	3.2	4.2	19.5	5.5		7.2	6.9
Net Worth	55.7	16.1	43.8	39.9	34.7	31.9		25.4	29.7
Total Liabilities & Net Worth	100.0	100.0	100.0	100.0	100.0	100.0		100.0	100.0
INCOME DATA									
Net Sales	100.0	100.0	100.0	100.0	100.0	100.0		100.0	100.0
Gross Profit									
Operating Expenses	89.8	97.8	90.4	85.9	91.0	82.7		89.7	92.4
Operating Profit	10.2	2.2	9.6	14.1	9.0	17.3		10.3	7.6
All Other Expenses (net)	1.2	1.6	1.4	2.4	1.8	5.6		3.4	2.0
Profit Before Taxes	9.0	.7	8.2	11.7	7.2	11.8		6.8	5.7
RATIOS									
Current	14.1	1.6	2.5	2.0	2.4	1.4		2.3	2.3
	1.8	1.0	1.3	1.2	1.8	1.1		1.2	1.3
	.9	.5	.8	.8	1.1	.8		.8	.8
Quick	14.1	1.3	2.1	1.7	2.0	1.1		1.8	1.9
	1.3	.9	1.1	1.1	1.4	.8		(160) .9	1.0
	.6	.3	.5	.6	.8	.4		.6	.5
Sales/Receivables	0 UND	6　65.7	28　12.8	28　12.9	28　13.0	32　11.6		29　12.8	22　16.7
	32　11.4	31　11.6	44　8.3	40　9.2	43　8.5	40　9.1		42　8.6	38　9.5
	41　8.9	51　7.2	63　5.8	57　6.4	55　6.6	54　6.8		57　6.4	58　6.3
Cost of Sales/Inventory									
Cost of Sales/Payables									
Sales/Working Capital	4.3	13.7	5.5	4.7	3.6	12.2		5.8	4.8
	13.7	NM	15.2	19.1	5.3	17.1		23.8	26.7
	-56.6	-8.2	-28.8	-25.4	37.0	-17.4		-17.4	-24.9
EBIT/Interest		13.8	15.6	8.8	8.3	6.1		7.1	10.5
		(26) 4.2	(56) 4.3	(78) 4.0	(23) 2.1	(19) 4.0		(140) 3.5	(147) 3.4
		-.5	1.4	1.7	1.1	1.8		.6	1.0
Net Profit + Depr., Dep., Amort./Cur. Mat. L/T/D			7.8	4.8	14.2			5.5	6.9
			(22) 2.6	(49) 2.6	(14) 4.3			(54) 2.7	(40) 3.3
			1.1	1.9	1.5			1.8	1.5
Fixed/Worth	.2	.2	.3	.8	.8	1.7		.4	.5
	.6	1.1	.9	1.5	2.1	4.4		1.3	1.3
	1.8	-1.2	2.0	3.5	-10.4	-32.3		5.6	8.1
Debt/Worth	.1	1.6	.5	.7	.5	1.7		1.0	.7
	.8	3.4	1.2	1.7	1.9	4.5		2.3	2.3
	4.9	-41.9	3.3	4.3	-22.2	-41.4		18.9	19.1
% Profit Before Taxes/Tangible Net Worth	79.7	100.5	45.2	30.1	21.9	83.0		61.1	54.5
	(13) 30.3	(25) 40.4	(55) 15.3	(76) 16.7	(20) 13.1	(17) 27.6		(126) 17.8	(129) 19.6
	3.1	-1.5	5.5	5.9	3.7	11.4		4.0	4.3
% Profit Before Taxes/Total Assets	34.3	17.9	12.4	14.2	9.6	10.3		15.3	13.8
	11.5	7.0	6.1	6.5	4.9	6.2		6.5	6.3
	.0	-2.3	1.3	2.3	.1	.7		.7	1.1
Sales/Net Fixed Assets	39.4	204.8	24.6	7.6	1.9	1.1		24.3	25.1
	12.3	22.2	2.3	.9	.8	.8		6.1	6.9
	3.9	4.8	.8	.6	.6	.7		.9	1.0
Sales/Total Assets	4.3	4.6	2.2	1.7	1.3	.7		3.6	2.9
	2.0	3.0	1.1	.5	.4	.5		1.6	1.7
	1.0	1.6	.5	.4	.4	.4		.5	.5
% Depr., Dep., Amort./Sales	1.3	1.0	3.0	6.1	14.0			1.6	1.2
	(12) 3.9	(23) 1.9	(58) 11.8	(81) 16.6	(21) 19.6			(133) 6.8	(133) 5.3
	15.9	5.4	19.6	21.9	24.7			18.5	16.2
% Officers', Directors', Owners' Comp/Sales		1.1	1.6					2.6	3.9
		(14) 4.3	(13) 3.0					(23) 4.4	(32) 7.6
		8.0	4.9					11.7	8.9
Net Sales ($)	10303M	150461M	503198M	2288045M	1629720M	2468015M		4411090M	4191959M
Total Assets ($)	3675M	33864M	355192M	2078728M	1960312M	3939324M		4385696M	4414003M

M = $ thousand　　MM = $ million
See Pages 11 through 21 for Explanation of Ratios and Data

Comparative Historical Data   Current Data Sorted by Sales

4/1/04-3/31/05 ALL	4/1/05-3/31/06 ALL	4/1/06-3/31/07 ALL	Type of Statement	0-1MM	1-3MM	3-5MM	5-10MM	10-25MM	25MM & OVER
159	144	137	Unqualified	9	17	15	27	25	44
18	13	22	Reviewed		2	5	7	3	5
16	17	13	Compiled	4	4	2	2	1	
8	14	16	Tax Returns	1	9	3	1	2	
64	78	63	Other	4	6	6	11	11	25
					37 (4/1-9/30/06)		214 (10/1/06-3/31/07)		
265	266	251	**NUMBER OF STATEMENTS**	18	38	31	48	42	74
%	%	%	**ASSETS**	%	%	%	%	%	%
13.8	11.8	12.0	Cash & Equivalents	19.8	11.5	7.0	13.3	13.1	11.0
12.5	15.2	17.4	Trade Receivables (net)	9.9	18.0	19.9	15.5	15.1	20.3
4.0	4.5	4.4	Inventory	1.4	11.2	2.0	1.5	4.2	4.5
3.6	4.1	2.3	All Other Current	.6	2.6	3.5	2.9	.9	2.5
33.9	35.7	36.0	Total Current	31.7	43.3	32.3	33.2	33.3	38.3
46.1	46.1	44.4	Fixed Assets (net)	39.8	41.7	46.2	47.6	51.5	40.2
8.8	6.9	8.2	Intangibles (net)	12.2	2.1	5.3	4.9	7.4	14.0
11.2	11.4	11.4	All Other Non-Current	16.2	12.8	16.1	14.2	7.9	7.5
100.0	100.0	100.0	Total	100.0	100.0	100.0	100.0	100.0	100.0
			LIABILITIES						
3.5	3.5	4.2	Notes Payable-Short Term	4.5	10.7	2.5	3.4	3.0	2.9
4.2	4.4	4.4	Cur. Mat.-L.T.D.	4.3	5.8	2.9	5.7	5.5	2.7
8.3	10.9	11.7	Trade Payables	6.3	13.9	13.2	7.8	10.3	14.4
.5	.7	.6	Income Taxes Payable	1.2	.3	.3	.7	1.0	.5
7.2	9.8	8.9	All Other Current	6.5	10.5	6.2	7.6	7.2	11.8
23.7	29.3	29.8	Total Current	22.7	41.1	25.0	25.2	27.0	32.3
27.1	27.2	25.6	Long-Term Debt	30.8	17.4	28.9	25.5	23.4	28.6
1.2	1.0	1.3	Deferred Taxes	.0	1.1	1.8	1.4	1.0	1.5
7.2	6.4	6.0	All Other Non-Current	6.4	5.0	4.0	5.1	4.3	8.8
40.7	36.2	37.3	Net Worth	40.0	35.3	40.3	42.8	44.3	28.8
100.0	100.0	100.0	Total Liabilities & Net Worth	100.0	100.0	100.0	100.0	100.0	100.0
			INCOME DATA						
100.0	100.0	100.0	Net Sales	100.0	100.0	100.0	100.0	100.0	100.0
			Gross Profit						
85.8	87.5	89.1	Operating Expenses	89.8	91.4	88.9	87.0	87.7	90.1
14.2	12.5	10.9	Operating Profit	10.2	8.6	11.1	13.0	12.3	9.9
3.7	3.3	2.2	All Other Expenses (net)	4.0	2.1	3.8	1.8	.9	2.1
10.4	9.2	8.7	Profit Before Taxes	6.2	6.5	7.4	11.2	11.4	7.8
			RATIOS						
2.4	2.3	2.1		8.0	2.8	2.7	1.9	2.2	1.8
1.5	1.3	1.3	Current	1.3	1.3	1.3	1.3	1.3	1.2
1.0	.9	.8		.6	.5	.9	.9	.8	.8
1.9	1.7	1.7		8.0	1.9	2.2	1.7	1.9	1.4
1.1	1.0	1.1	Quick	1.1	1.0	1.2	1.1	1.1	1.0
.6	.6	.6		.5	.3	.8	.6	.7	.6
(18) 20.8	(17) 21.5	(27) 13.7		(9) 39.3	(16) 22.1	(28) 12.8	(30) 12.0	(26) 14.2	(28) 13.2
(32) 11.4	(31) 11.6	(40) 9.2	Sales/Receivables	(38) 9.7	(40) 9.1	(51) 7.2	(44) 8.2	(35) 10.3	(39) 9.4
(45) 8.0	(46) 7.9	(56) 6.6		(44) 8.2	(60) 6.1	(75) 4.9	(68) 5.4	(50) 7.3	(51) 7.2
			Cost of Sales/Inventory						
			Cost of Sales/Payables						
3.5	4.5	5.3		2.6	4.8	5.5	4.1	5.5	7.4
11.8	14.0	17.8	Sales/Working Capital	16.1	14.9	15.8	16.3	15.3	26.9
-351.7	-52.5	-25.6		-11.1	-6.6	-28.7	-32.4	-30.5	-23.3
7.4	8.4	9.9			21.6	12.9	9.7	11.2	9.4
(243) 4.0	(236) 3.5	(210) 4.0	EBIT/Interest	(34) 4.8	(28) 3.3	(39) 5.1	(36) 3.7	(64) 3.9	
1.9	1.6	1.6			1.1	1.2	1.9	2.1	1.7
6.1	5.2	5.2			6.7	3.7	5.8	5.3	6.0
(123) 3.3	(116) 3.3	(92) 2.6	Net Profit + Depr., Dep., Amort./Cur. Mat. L/T/D	(13) 2.6	(11) 2.0	(25) 2.4	(17) 2.9	(24) 2.7	
2.2	2.2	1.6			1.8	1.0	1.6	1.8	1.6
.7	.7	.6		.2	.5	.6	.6	.8	.8
1.4	1.4	1.5	Fixed/Worth	1.6	1.0	1.4	1.3	1.4	2.2
3.4	3.5	4.4		-5.7	2.1	4.3	2.1	3.5	-10.2
.7	.8	.7		.1	.6	.6	.8	.5	1.4
1.5	1.6	1.9	Debt/Worth	2.0	1.5	1.5	1.6	1.5	3.5
4.9	5.4	8.0		-9.9	7.1	6.1	2.7	4.1	-26.4
30.0	37.7	45.2		32.4	56.1	30.5	45.3	26.1	76.8
(225) 13.9	(221) 14.1	(206) 17.7	% Profit Before Taxes/Tangible Net Worth	(13) 8.9	(34) 15.2	(27) 6.1	(45) 19.8	(33) 16.4	(54) 25.2
5.0	5.3	5.4		-6.2	3.6	-2.9	5.1	9.6	10.8
10.9	12.4	12.9		15.9	12.8	9.4	14.0	12.2	14.2
5.8	5.4	6.3	% Profit Before Taxes/Total Assets	4.1	6.5	4.3	6.5	6.6	7.5
1.9	1.4	1.3		-6.1	.5	.6	2.0	3.6	1.7
8.5	12.5	16.9		12.5	26.5	13.6	6.1	9.5	24.5
1.1	1.1	1.3	Sales/Net Fixed Assets	3.5	2.3	1.1	1.1	.9	2.7
.7	.7	.7		.7	.7	.5	.6	.6	.8
1.6	2.3	2.2		2.1	2.9	2.2	1.7	2.0	2.8
.6	.6	.7	Sales/Total Assets	1.1	.9	.5	.5	.6	1.3
.4	.4	.4		.4	.4	.3	.4	.4	.5
5.5	2.2	3.0		4.4	1.3	4.0	8.6	8.8	.8
(226) 16.4	(229) 15.3	(200) 14.8	% Depr., Dep., Amort./Sales	(14) 16.3	(32) 13.2	(29) 14.8	(45) 17.0	(36) 16.7	(44) 4.0
22.2	20.9	20.9		20.5	23.1	19.9	21.9	23.9	17.0
3.8	3.4	1.4			2.6				
(26) 7.4	(35) 5.6	(38) 3.7	% Officers', Directors' Owners' Comp/Sales	(11) 6.0					
11.4	10.6	7.4			8.5				
7847637M	6029367M	7049742M	Net Sales ($)	7807M	77061M	124129M	358171M	671724M	5810850M
9033637M	8835663M	8371095M	Total Assets ($)	27171M	128029M	239248M	902395M	1040858M	6033394M

© RMA 2007

M = $ thousand   MM = $ million
See Pages 11 through 21 for Explanation of Ratios and Data

Current Data Sorted by Assets   Comparative Historical Data

	0-500M	500M-2MM	2-10MM	10-50MM	50-100MM	100-250MM		ALL 4/1/02-3/31/03	ALL 4/1/03-3/31/04
		16 (4/1-9/30/06)		82 (10/1/06-3/31/07)			**Type of Statement**		
Unqualified			4	12	4	8		25	26
Reviewed		1	9	2				10	9
Compiled	1	4	5			1		15	24
Tax Returns	6	5	3					5	13
Other	3	11	8	9	2			29	30
NUMBER OF STATEMENTS	10	21	29	23	6	9		84	102
	%	%	%	%	%	%	**ASSETS**	%	%
	19.5	10.0	14.2	12.3			Cash & Equivalents	12.6	12.3
	11.8	23.6	25.5	20.5			Trade Receivables (net)	15.4	18.6
	22.6	17.1	12.3	7.5			Inventory	14.1	13.0
	.8	1.9	8.4	2.9			All Other Current	3.8	3.1
	54.6	52.6	60.3	43.1			Total Current	45.9	47.0
	22.7	38.5	27.4	39.3			Fixed Assets (net)	35.9	34.3
	.0	3.7	4.6	8.3			Intangibles (net)	6.5	9.4
	22.7	5.2	7.6	9.3			All Other Non-Current	11.8	9.3
	100.0	100.0	100.0	100.0			Total	100.0	100.0
							LIABILITIES		
	16.3	8.6	9.1	1.7			Notes Payable-Short Term	10.6	9.8
	9.8	7.9	3.2	4.5			Cur. Mat.-L.T.D.	5.3	6.7
	6.3	14.4	18.6	15.6			Trade Payables	17.0	16.3
	.0	.0	.3	.2			Income Taxes Payable	.5	.1
	28.5	7.7	19.1	12.8			All Other Current	12.9	12.8
	60.8	38.5	50.2	34.6			Total Current	46.2	45.8
	25.1	32.5	21.2	20.0			Long-Term Debt	24.8	24.5
	.0	.0	.2	.3			Deferred Taxes	1.1	.6
	8.9	6.8	3.0	4.2			All Other Non-Current	4.0	4.8
	5.0	22.2	25.4	41.0			Net Worth	23.9	24.3
	100.0	100.0	100.0	100.0			Total Liabilties & Net Worth	100.0	100.0
							INCOME DATA		
	100.0	100.0	100.0	100.0			Net Sales	100.0	100.0
							Gross Profit		
	93.0	96.2	93.9	90.5			Operating Expenses	93.0	90.3
	7.0	3.8	6.1	9.5			Operating Profit	7.0	9.7
	.6	.5	2.7	2.2			All Other Expenses (net)	1.8	2.9
	6.5	3.4	3.3	7.3			Profit Before Taxes	5.1	6.8
							RATIOS		
	5.9	2.0	2.5	2.0				1.8	2.2
	2.2	1.3	1.0	1.3			Current	1.3	1.2
	.2	.9	.7	.7				.7	.6
	3.9	1.5	1.9	1.8				1.3	1.7
	1.0	.8	.7	.9			Quick	.7	.8
	.2	.4	.5	.6				.4	.3
	0 UND	14 26.8	19 19.7	31 11.8				18 19.8	17 20.9
	0 UND	28 12.9	41 8.9	40 9.0			Sales/Receivables	32 11.3	30 12.3
	27 13.3	49 7.5	60 6.1	55 6.7				44 8.3	45 8.2
							Cost of Sales/Inventory		
							Cost of Sales/Payables		
	7.6	15.4	6.4	5.3				7.6	7.9
	28.3	29.7	192.8	15.5			Sales/Working Capital	27.3	28.9
	-17.0	-98.8	-16.0	-23.6				-17.0	-12.9
		5.7	14.4	16.3				6.5	8.8
		(20) 2.5	(26) 5.3	(20) 6.2			EBIT/Interest	(75) 2.3	(92) 3.0
		.3	1.4	1.5				.4	.5
								10.5	7.2
							Net Profit + Depr., Dep., Amort./Cur. Mat. L/T/D	(25) 1.6	(19) 2.4
								.6	.2
	.1	.7	.4	.6				.5	.5
	1.1	1.5	1.1	1.2			Fixed/Worth	1.3	1.7
	-.5	-34.9	5.4	4.1				18.5	-87.1
	.8	1.1	.6	.7				.8	1.3
	4.9	4.5	6.3	2.1			Debt/Worth	2.7	2.6
	-6.4	-45.3	16.4	24.3				NM	-107.2
		252.5	58.0	48.1				51.0	65.1
		(15) 35.4	(24) 31.5	(19) 24.2			% Profit Before Taxes/Tangible Net Worth	(63) 11.4	(75) 24.3
		-7.1	12.7	6.1				.6	.9
	51.1	16.2	18.0	21.7				14.6	15.6
	18.8	7.2	5.6	6.7			% Profit Before Taxes/Total Assets	3.8	4.7
	4.2	-3.8	1.3	1.4				-.7	-1.9
	276.0	32.2	27.6	14.8				23.1	28.4
	125.2	5.0	12.0	6.7			Sales/Net Fixed Assets	6.2	8.9
	14.4	3.4	4.8	.9				1.3	1.9
	21.3	3.6	3.3	2.8				3.1	3.2
	4.8	2.7	2.4	1.1			Sales/Total Assets	1.8	1.9
	3.1	1.5	1.0	.6				.6	.7
		1.2	1.4	1.8				1.7	1.2
		3.8	(25) 2.2	(21) 3.7			% Depr., Dep., Amort./Sales	(68) 3.7	(88) 4.3
		8.3	6.8	16.1				13.8	11.1
								3.3	3.4
							% Officers', Directors' Owners' Comp/Sales	(21) 6.5	(33) 7.1
								13.8	14.8
	14023M	72163M	327154M	972467M	642980M	1815019M	Net Sales ($)	1681690M	1665469M
	2164M	23618M	131485M	544766M	423226M	1542848M	Total Assets ($)	1611769M	1455659M

M = $ thousand   MM = $ million
See Pages 11 through 21 for Explanation of Ratios and Data

Comparative Historical Data

Current Data Sorted by Sales

4/1/04-3/31/05 ALL	4/1/05-3/31/06 ALL	4/1/06-3/31/07 ALL	Type of Statement	0-1MM	1-3MM	3-5MM	5-10MM	10-25MM	25MM & OVER
37	26	28	Unqualified			2	4	4	18
7	8	12	Reviewed			3	4	2	3
12	6	10	Compiled	1	2	3	2	2	
8	11	15	Tax Returns	5	4	3	2	1	
30	42	33	Other	3	6	5	4	6	9
				16 (4/1-9/30/06)			82 (10/1/06-3/31/07)		
94	93	98	**NUMBER OF STATEMENTS**	9	12	16	16	15	30
%	%	%	**ASSETS**	%	%	%	%	%	%
14.2	14.6	13.6	Cash & Equivalents		14.9	9.7	9.5	14.6	15.0
18.1	21.6	20.2	Trade Receivables (net)		15.9	24.3	23.6	20.7	21.0
9.5	9.5	12.3	Inventory		15.9	15.4	14.6	7.3	9.9
3.6	3.7	3.8	All Other Current		2.5	2.6	1.1	9.4	4.6
45.4	49.3	50.0	Total Current		49.2	51.9	48.8	52.1	50.5
34.8	35.7	34.6	Fixed Assets (net)		32.3	36.2	37.3	27.6	34.2
8.7	7.1	6.0	Intangibles (net)		4.5	4.7	8.3	3.7	8.8
11.2	7.9	9.5	All Other Non-Current		14.1	7.2	5.6	16.7	6.4
100.0	100.0	100.0	Total		100.0	100.0	100.0	100.0	100.0
			LIABILITIES						
4.2	6.9	6.7	Notes Payable-Short Term		15.9	5.7	11.9	5.7	1.4
6.0	3.1	5.0	Cur. Mat.-L.T.D.		4.2	8.4	4.0	1.6	3.3
14.1	18.1	14.3	Trade Payables		12.0	14.9	11.3	22.3	16.7
.1	.5	.2	Income Taxes Payable		.0	.2	.1	.3	.2
12.0	11.8	14.4	All Other Current		25.0	10.6	10.0	17.3	15.7
36.4	40.3	40.5	Total Current		57.0	39.7	37.2	47.1	37.3
23.4	28.3	25.2	Long-Term Debt		25.5	22.2	32.8	15.9	20.0
.7	.7	.5	Deferred Taxes		.0	.0	.0	.4	1.3
8.2	10.8	7.1	All Other Non-Current		6.2	3.8	3.6	13.6	6.0
31.3	19.9	26.8	Net Worth		11.2	34.4	26.4	23.0	35.5
100.0	100.0	100.0	Total Liabilties & Net Worth		100.0	100.0	100.0	100.0	100.0
			INCOME DATA						
100.0	100.0	100.0	Net Sales		100.0	100.0	100.0	100.0	100.0
			Gross Profit						
94.1	93.0	92.5	Operating Expenses		100.0	93.3	93.0	92.3	91.1
5.9	7.0	7.5	Operating Profit		.0	6.7	7.0	7.7	8.9
1.5	2.4	1.8	All Other Expenses (net)		1.1	1.3	.8	1.7	1.0
4.4	4.6	5.8	Profit Before Taxes		-1.1	5.5	6.2	6.0	7.9
			RATIOS						
2.4	2.3	2.2	Current		1.9	2.2	3.2	2.1	1.8
1.3	1.2	1.3			1.5	1.3	1.2	1.0	1.3
.8	.8	.8			.6	.9	.7	.6	.9
1.6	1.8	1.6	Quick		1.0	1.9	1.8	1.1	1.5
.9	.9	.8			.9	.7	.7	.8	.8
.5	.5	.5			.4	.4	.5	.5	.6
17 21.0	18 20.5	18 20.2	Sales/Receivables		0 UND	23 15.9	17 21.2	15 24.9	28 12.9
32 11.3	34 10.6	33 11.0			20 18.0	32 11.3	42 8.6	36 10.1	39 9.4
47 7.7	50 7.3	54 6.8			43 8.4	77 4.7	58 6.3	54 6.8	51 7.2
			Cost of Sales/Inventory						
			Cost of Sales/Payables						
6.8	6.7	7.2	Sales/Working Capital		16.5	6.0	8.5	5.3	9.8
24.0	26.0	28.2			33.0	22.6	32.9	192.8	26.8
-27.6	-30.4	-19.6			-15.7	-17.2	-11.3	-20.0	-40.8
13.0	19.1	13.3	EBIT/Interest		12.2	14.9	7.2	16.2	15.4
(85) 2.6	(74) 4.6	(85) 4.0			3.1	3.8	(15) 2.4	(13) 4.1	(24) 6.4
-.6	1.7	1.5			.3	-1.6	1.1	1.4	3.8
11.4	7.2	11.1	Net Profit + Depr., Dep.,						
(18) 1.9	(15) 2.8	(13) 2.9	Amort./Cur. Mat. L/T/D						
1.1	.9	1.8							
.4	.5	.5	Fixed/Worth		.5	.5	.5	.1	.5
1.6	1.7	1.3			1.2	1.2	1.8	1.1	1.3
14.7	UND	24.5			-2.2	24.6	6.3	4.0	14.3
.7	.9	.9	Debt/Worth		.8	.6	1.1	.9	.9
2.7	5.2	4.0			4.9	2.5	4.2	6.3	3.7
52.4	UND	89.9			-5.7	62.8	11.1	-25.8	47.9
52.8	81.6	80.7	% Profit Before Taxes/Tangible			235.1	44.7	58.2	154.6
(73) 24.5	(70) 29.1	(76) 34.5	Net Worth			(13) 31.6	(13) 16.4	(11) 33.6	(25) 45.8
2.1	7.3	12.0				.2	4.9	16.4	24.7
20.2	17.6	20.9	% Profit Before Taxes/Total		23.2	27.8	20.4	10.9	22.4
5.8	6.5	6.8	Assets		5.6	12.3	4.7	5.6	8.8
-5.7	.4	1.7			-4.0	-7.8	.4	.7	4.5
33.7	31.9	31.0	Sales/Net Fixed Assets		214.7	29.9	24.0	77.2	21.7
6.9	12.1	8.6			11.7	6.5	11.2	11.1	11.5
1.3	1.5	2.0			3.1	3.8	1.4	2.8	1.2
2.9	3.6	3.5	Sales/Total Assets		15.4	3.5	3.1	4.0	3.5
1.8	2.1	2.2			3.0	2.2	2.4	2.2	1.6
.7	.9	.8			1.5	1.2	.8	.6	.6
1.5	1.1	1.3	% Depr., Dep., Amort./Sales			1.3	1.6	.8	1.3
(78) 5.0	(74) 2.1	(77) 3.2				3.2	3.0	(12) 3.3	(18) 2.4
15.0	10.4	9.1				6.7	9.8	11.2	9.0
2.1	3.3	3.6	% Officers', Directors'						
(24) 5.0	(27) 6.2	(24) 7.2	Owners' Comp/Sales						
8.8	13.7	10.8							
2257025M	3441127M	3843806M	Net Sales ($)	5765M	23877M	62333M	128069M	240166M	3383596M
1849864M	1637280M	2668107M	Total Assets ($)	8741M	8381M	43856M	90819M	309278M	2207032M

M = $ thousand   MM = $ million
See Pages 11 through 21 for Explanation of Ratios and Data

Current Data Sorted by Assets

Comparative Historical Data

							Type of Statement				
							Unqualified		29		29
	4	7	11	2	3		Reviewed		16		18
1	4	11	2				Compiled		18		15
2	8	4					Tax Returns		11		13
9	6	1					Other		50		52
6	12	14	14	2	4				4/1/02-		4/1/03-
	11 (4/1-9/30/06)		116 (10/1/06-3/31/07)						3/31/03		3/31/04
0-500M	500M-2MM	2-10MM	10-50MM	50-100MM	100-250MM				ALL		ALL
18	34	37	27	4	7		NUMBER OF STATEMENTS		124		127
%	%	%	%	%	%		ASSETS		%		%
22.6	16.6	12.9	15.5				Cash & Equivalents		10.9		12.0
32.5	34.2	40.1	26.7				Trade Receivables (net)		31.1		31.7
12.3	7.8	9.3	7.3				Inventory		6.0		6.7
6.4	3.2	5.8	4.7				All Other Current		3.6		4.8
73.7	61.8	68.1	54.2				Total Current		51.6		55.2
12.9	18.4	20.2	25.5				Fixed Assets (net)		28.8		28.0
.3	13.0	7.6	9.8				Intangibles (net)		10.6		7.8
13.0	6.7	4.2	10.5				All Other Non-Current		9.0		8.9
100.0	100.0	100.0	100.0				Total		100.0		100.0
							LIABILITIES				
11.0	7.0	10.3	4.8				Notes Payable-Short Term		7.1		12.3
19.1	2.5	1.6	2.2				Cur. Mat.-L.T.D.		5.3		4.6
20.1	26.7	21.1	15.1				Trade Payables		13.7		18.9
1.1	.1	.7	.6				Income Taxes Payable		.4		.7
12.2	19.4	16.1	16.1				All Other Current		15.3		15.9
63.6	55.7	49.9	38.8				Total Current		41.7		52.5
28.9	25.9	9.2	15.0				Long-Term Debt		21.8		18.8
.0	.1	.1	.8				Deferred Taxes		.6		.6
7.0	7.8	11.2	5.7				All Other Non-Current		4.4		8.2
.4	10.5	29.6	39.8				Net Worth		31.4		20.0
100.0	100.0	100.0	100.0				Total Liabilties & Net Worth		100.0		100.0
							INCOME DATA				
100.0	100.0	100.0	100.0				Net Sales		100.0		100.0
							Gross Profit				
85.9	88.1	93.6	86.9				Operating Expenses		95.1		93.8
14.1	11.9	6.4	13.1				Operating Profit		4.9		6.2
6.2	1.8	1.4	3.1				All Other Expenses (net)		1.8		1.8
7.8	10.1	5.0	10.0				Profit Before Taxes		3.1		4.4
							RATIOS				
2.6	2.4	2.2	2.5						2.2		1.7
1.8	1.3	1.5	1.4				Current		1.2		1.2
1.0	.9	.9	.9						.8		.8
2.1	2.1	1.7	2.1						1.7		1.4
1.2	(33) 1.1	1.2	.9				Quick		1.0		.9
.6	.7	.7	.7						.6		.5
0 UND	4 99.0	33 11.1	29 12.5					29	12.7	24	15.5
20 18.7	34 10.8	51 7.1	55 6.7				Sales/Receivables	53	6.9	48	7.6
47 7.7	55 6.6	75 4.9	63 5.8					71	5.1	69	5.3
							Cost of Sales/Inventory				
							Cost of Sales/Payables				
5.9	10.1	5.5	5.4						7.8		9.0
38.5	47.6	11.0	11.7				Sales/Working Capital		18.9		38.8
-322.9	-41.7	-67.8	-40.0						-23.7		-22.1
8.7	38.4	26.4	37.0						8.2		12.6
(10) 3.5	(26) 13.4	(32) 3.2	(20) 7.6				EBIT/Interest	(109)	2.3	(113)	4.1
-.4	.8	-.2	2.8						-.6		1.0
									6.8		5.7
							Net Profit + Depr., Dep., Amort./Cur. Mat. L/T/D	(22)	2.0	(24)	2.8
									.4		1.6
.1	.1	.1	.3						.4		.4
.4	.5	.5	1.1				Fixed/Worth		1.0		1.4
-2.0	-.4	7.0	3.2						454.5		36.1
.7	.6	1.2	.9						.8		1.3
4.5	4.2	3.5	3.0				Debt/Worth		3.0		2.9
-18.5	-3.1	23.1	10.6						488.7		64.3
132.6	202.7	60.6	69.4				% Profit Before Taxes/Tangible Net Worth		67.5		56.8
(12) 77.3	(21) 96.7	(30) 31.0	(22) 34.1					(94)	22.6	(96)	22.8
59.1	15.2	14.1	16.2						-5.5		.9
74.1	46.0	18.9	19.6				% Profit Before Taxes/Total Assets		14.5		18.2
35.1	23.8	6.1	9.8						4.8		4.8
1.3	-.9	-4.0	6.1						-4.0		-.9
UND	123.6	67.2	20.1						25.5		32.3
60.4	32.8	20.4	10.5				Sales/Net Fixed Assets		9.9		11.3
28.3	16.6	6.8	3.1						4.0		3.8
12.4	5.1	4.1	2.5						3.1		3.7
5.0	3.7	2.3	1.5				Sales/Total Assets		2.2		2.2
2.1	2.7	1.6	.8						1.2		1.1
.3	.4	.7	.9						1.6		1.3
(11) .6	(24) .9	(31) 1.3	(25) 2.8				% Depr., Dep., Amort./Sales	(100)	3.7	(99)	3.4
2.6	2.1	3.1	6.8						6.8		7.0
	1.4	2.7							2.7		1.8
	(13) 2.8	(13) 5.8					% Officers', Directors' Owners' Comp/Sales	(46)	5.9	(27)	4.9
	8.9	12.7							10.2		7.4
26549M	178345M	442872M	1029226M	359123M	1202242M		Net Sales ($)		4277337M		4144350M
3814M	40049M	179827M	626986M	256645M	1076839M		Total Assets ($)		2852199M		3160925M

© RMA 2007

M = $ thousand MM = $ million
See Pages 11 through 21 for Explanation of Ratios and Data

Comparative Historical Data | Current Data Sorted by Sales

4/1/04-3/31/05 ALL	4/1/05-3/31/06 ALL	4/1/06-3/31/07 ALL	Type of Statement	0-1MM	1-3MM	3-5MM	5-10MM	10-25MM	25MM & OVER
31	34	27	Unqualified	1		1	6	7	12
22	22	18	Reviewed	1	1	3	5	8	
13	10	14	Compiled	4	1	3	4	2	
18	15	16	Tax Returns	5	3	2	5	1	
53	47	52	Other	4	8	4	8	14	14
				11 (4/1-9/30/06)		**116 (10/1/06-3/31/07)**			
137	128	127	**NUMBER OF STATEMENTS**	15	13	13	28	32	26
%	%	%	**ASSETS**	%	%	%	%	%	%
14.2	12.9	16.0	Cash & Equivalents	23.0	18.9	14.0	15.3	13.8	15.0
32.2	35.4	32.8	Trade Receivables (net)	27.4	13.4	29.6	42.6	37.0	31.7
7.5	8.3	8.9	Inventory	13.3	3.7	12.9	9.5	7.6	8.1
4.5	5.3	4.6	All Other Current	5.3	1.6	7.9	2.7	6.1	4.1
58.4	61.9	62.3	Total Current	69.0	37.6	64.5	70.0	64.6	58.9
26.9	23.6	20.9	Fixed Assets (net)	11.0	23.0	23.9	20.2	20.6	25.0
4.8	6.4	8.8	Intangibles (net)	11.4	22.9	5.5	5.1	8.3	6.6
9.9	8.1	7.9	All Other Non-Current	8.6	16.5	6.1	4.7	6.5	9.5
100.0	100.0	100.0	Total	100.0	100.0	100.0	100.0	100.0	100.0
			LIABILITIES						
13.8	10.9	7.9	Notes Payable-Short Term	10.9	10.2	7.6	9.0	6.4	5.6
5.6	5.8	4.6	Cur. Mat.-L.T.D.	22.0	3.8	2.6	2.4	1.7	2.1
16.9	20.0	20.3	Trade Payables	19.3	9.7	15.9	22.6	27.1	17.8
.7	.8	.5	Income Taxes Payable	.0	.0	.1	.8	1.0	.5
15.8	14.2	16.3	All Other Current	19.4	18.9	10.7	15.0	13.1	21.1
52.8	51.8	49.7	Total Current	71.6	42.6	36.9	49.9	49.3	47.1
14.6	13.7	18.9	Long-Term Debt	52.6	27.8	19.8	9.2	10.3	15.5
.6	.5	.3	Deferred Taxes	.0	.0	.2	.2	.5	.7
9.4	9.3	7.9	All Other Non-Current	10.2	2.8	11.7	13.6	6.5	2.9
22.6	24.6	23.3	Net Worth	-34.5	26.8	31.5	27.2	33.5	33.8
100.0	100.0	100.0	Total Liabilties & Net Worth	100.0	100.0	100.0	100.0	100.0	100.0
			INCOME DATA						
100.0	100.0	100.0	Net Sales	100.0	100.0	100.0	100.0	100.0	100.0
			Gross Profit						
93.0	94.1	89.2	Operating Expenses	83.9	82.8	93.8	93.2	87.0	91.7
7.0	5.9	10.8	Operating Profit	16.1	17.2	6.2	6.8	13.0	8.3
1.3	1.2	2.5	All Other Expenses (net)	7.7	5.6	2.2	1.8	.9	.9
5.7	4.7	8.3	Profit Before Taxes	8.4	11.6	4.0	5.0	12.1	7.4
			RATIOS						
1.9	1.9	2.3		3.4	2.1	2.8	2.2	2.6	2.1
1.2	1.3	1.5	Current	1.0	1.3	1.9	1.5	1.3	1.4
.9	.9	.9		.3	.3	1.4	1.0	.9	.9
1.6	1.6	1.9		2.3	2.2	2.2	1.9	1.7	1.8
.9	1.0 (126)	1.2	Quick	(12) 1.0	1.3	1.3	1.1	1.2	1.0
.6	.6	.7		.3	.4	.7	.7	.7	.6
26 13.8	25 14.6	22 16.3		7 51.8	0 UND	5 77.5	24 15.3	31 11.7	30 12.0
48 7.7	49 7.5	43 8.4	Sales/Receivables	32 11.5	1 363.8	33 10.9	47 7.8	50 7.3	54 6.7
66 5.5	72 5.1	64 5.7		91 4.0	25 14.4	54 6.8	64 5.7	72 5.1	74 4.9
			Cost of Sales/Inventory						
			Cost of Sales/Payables						
7.8	7.1	6.0		3.3	12.5	5.6	7.6	6.0	5.6
27.2	18.1	15.3	Sales/Working Capital	441.5	49.6	12.2	14.3	13.2	18.1
-58.0	-95.6	-56.8		-9.5	-7.9	65.9	727.5	-76.3	-35.7
14.8	14.0	21.7			28.0	17.5	32.4	60.0	13.4
(113) 5.4	(110) 4.7	(99) 5.1	EBIT/Interest		(10) 8.2	(11) 2.7	(23) 5.9	(22) 8.0	(24) 4.7
.5	.8	1.1			.8	.1	-.3	1.5	2.8
10.5	4.1	7.5							
(30) 3.2	(23) 2.3	(14) 2.3	Net Profit + Depr., Dep., Amort./Cur. Mat. L/T/D						
1.8	1.4	.9							
.3	.2	.2		.0	.0	.1	.3	.2	.3
.9	.9	.6	Fixed/Worth	.9	.4	.5	.8	.5	.8
4.5	6.1	11.2		-.4	NM	-6.3	2.2	3.0	3.4
1.1	1.0	.9		.8	.6	.5	1.0	.9	1.0
2.5	3.0	3.1	Debt/Worth	-36.0	7.8	1.3	3.1	2.9	2.7
14.0	33.8	-36.0		-1.6	-2.2	-17.6	13.3	10.0	15.3
80.0	72.1	93.7					108.8	79.1	80.9
(112) 34.5	(102) 30.9	(94) 48.0	% Profit Before Taxes/Tangible Net Worth				(24) 52.3	(26) 45.6	(21) 31.5
10.7	2.8	17.9					10.2	19.3	17.9
23.2	21.2	31.3		50.0	50.3	35.0	41.9	28.8	16.2
8.4	6.6	10.3	% Profit Before Taxes/Total Assets	6.0	15.3	8.6	13.2	13.2	7.5
-.8	-.4	2.3		-1.9	1.5	-1.4	-1.6	2.4	3.0
51.2	54.3	63.8		UND	168.7	58.3	67.7	63.3	40.5
18.6	15.2	20.7	Sales/Net Fixed Assets	32.9	32.1	20.7	20.7	19.5	15.6
4.6	6.1	7.0		12.4	10.5	7.7	7.0	7.6	6.0
3.6	3.5	4.5		2.9	5.8	4.3	4.9	4.8	2.9
2.6	2.6	2.4	Sales/Total Assets	2.0	2.8	3.3	3.5	2.3	1.8
1.6	1.7	1.4		.9	.5	2.3	1.8	1.3	.9
.9	.6	.6				.6	.4	.6	.9
(108) 2.2	(96) 1.9	(96) 1.2	% Depr., Dep., Amort./Sales			(11) 1.1	(25) 1.2	(28) 1.1	(18) 1.3
5.7	4.3	3.7				3.7	3.5	3.5	4.4
2.2	3.1	2.5					2.1	1.2	
(34) 6.2	(32) 6.9	(36) 4.6	% Officers', Directors' Owners' Comp/Sales				(12) 5.1	(10) 2.7	
13.3	11.7	10.8					10.5	6.8	
3773621M	4392232M	3238357M	Net Sales ($)	6816M	26599M	50768M	199205M	518786M	2436183M
2234503M	2509890M	2184160M	Total Assets ($)	4754M	62279M	28416M	87033M	324950M	1676728M

© RMA 2007

M = $ thousand   MM = $ million
See Pages 11 through 21 for Explanation of Ratios and Data

Current Data Sorted by Assets   Comparative Historical Data

	0-500M	500M-2MM	2-10MM	10-50MM	50-100MM	100-250MM	Type of Statement		4/1/02-3/31/03	4/1/03-3/31/04
		4	6	2	2	4	Unqualified		20	21
		1	6				Reviewed		5	11
	2		4				Compiled		5	12
	7	4					Tax Returns		7	5
	9	11	10	9	4		Other		28	28
		8 (4/1-9/30/06)		77 (10/1/06-3/31/07)					ALL	ALL
	18	20	26	11	6	4	NUMBER OF STATEMENTS		65	77
	%	%	%	%	%	%	ASSETS		%	%
	29.2	13.3	20.7	22.6			Cash & Equivalents		17.3	16.3
	17.6	24.5	25.6	40.3			Trade Receivables (net)		37.2	30.2
	.4	1.9	.9	1.3			Inventory		1.8	3.2
	5.9	4.4	3.4	7.5			All Other Current		5.1	4.3
	53.2	44.1	50.6	71.7			Total Current		61.4	53.9
	29.2	43.4	28.2	21.2			Fixed Assets (net)		18.9	25.0
	9.0	2.1	11.4	2.9			Intangibles (net)		14.0	13.5
	8.5	10.5	9.8	4.2			All Other Non-Current		5.7	7.7
	100.0	100.0	100.0	100.0			Total		100.0	100.0
							LIABILITIES			
	17.7	20.0	11.5	3.9			Notes Payable-Short Term		17.5	13.9
	3.1	4.1	3.1	2.1			Cur. Mat.-L.T.D.		6.6	6.7
	43.0	14.8	12.3	9.3			Trade Payables		13.8	12.7
	.1	.4	.1	.6			Income Taxes Payable		.5	.2
	25.1	33.0	23.0	18.0			All Other Current		20.9	18.6
	89.0	72.3	50.2	33.9			Total Current		59.3	52.1
	22.9	15.7	11.6	28.3			Long-Term Debt		11.9	16.4
	.0	.0	.0	.0			Deferred Taxes		.6	.9
	9.2	12.4	13.5	.5			All Other Non-Current		7.7	9.7
	-21.2	-.5	24.7	37.3			Net Worth		20.4	20.9
	100.0	100.0	100.0	100.0			Total Liabilities & Net Worth		100.0	100.0
							INCOME DATA			
	100.0	100.0	100.0	100.0			Net Sales		100.0	100.0
							Gross Profit			
	94.9	101.8	91.3	90.0			Operating Expenses		94.3	93.4
	5.1	-1.8	8.7	10.0			Operating Profit		5.7	6.6
	1.9	1.8	1.5	1.2			All Other Expenses (net)		1.0	2.4
	3.2	-3.5	7.2	8.8			Profit Before Taxes		4.7	4.2
							RATIOS			
	2.5	2.3	2.2	2.9					2.6	2.3
	.7	1.1	1.2	2.4			Current		1.3	1.2
	.4	.4	.6	1.5					.6	.8
	1.3	2.3	2.0	2.8					2.3	2.0
	.6	1.0	1.2	2.3			Quick		1.2	1.1
	.2	.3	.3	1.3					.5	.7
0	UND	8	46.6	6	56.3	40	9.1	Sales/Receivables	30	12.3	23	16.0
2	179.0	21	17.7	30	12.2	61	6.0		55	6.6	42	8.6
36	10.2	50	7.3	65	5.6	76	4.8		68	5.4	67	5.5
							Cost of Sales/Inventory			
							Cost of Sales/Payables			
	36.3	15.8	6.3	6.0					5.3	6.6
	-16.5	96.5	41.3	6.8			Sales/Working Capital		15.3	35.0
	-5.2	-6.6	-7.7	11.8					-9.2	-25.7
	11.5	12.8	34.4						40.5	17.6
(11)	1.4	(17)	-1.3	(24)	4.5		EBIT/Interest	(49)	4.0	(62)	5.7
	.2	-16.4	1.0						.0	1.2
							Net Profit + Depr., Dep., Amort./Cur. Mat. L/T/D			26.8
									(12)	2.5
										.9
	.4	.7	.2	.1					.1	.2
	7.6	1.5	1.1	.3			Fixed/Worth		.9	1.0
	-.3	-1.6	-2.5	.5					-.6	-10.7
	2.3	.7	.8	.5					.8	.9
	38.8	2.9	3.0	.7			Debt/Worth		3.0	2.2
	-2.8	-4.6	-4.8	1.4					-3.6	-13.3
	124.9	95.6	125.5	48.6			% Profit Before Taxes/Tangible Net Worth		109.0	66.2
(10)	29.9	(13)	39.7	(17)	63.9	(10)	31.3		(42)	31.0	(55)	32.6
	-61.5	-114.8	20.7	13.2					2.1	6.2
	67.5	26.7	37.9	24.2			% Profit Before Taxes/Total Assets		24.4	22.0
	8.6	-6.6	10.1	15.1					6.4	11.3
	-3.1	-35.7	.3	6.8					-2.1	1.3
	596.0	21.6	22.2	41.6			Sales/Net Fixed Assets		50.3	37.5
	14.8	7.3	11.7	15.8					19.7	13.6
	4.8	4.6	4.3	5.1					7.9	7.2
	7.8	4.4	3.4	3.2			Sales/Total Assets		3.9	3.3
	3.4	2.8	1.9	2.9					2.3	2.3
	1.7	2.0	1.3	1.8					1.1	1.3
		2.2	1.9						.8	1.3
	(16)	5.4	(21)	3.8			% Depr., Dep., Amort./Sales	(48)	2.4	(54)	2.8
		9.2	8.8						6.8	5.8
							% Officers', Directors' Owners' Comp/Sales		3.5	4.6
								(11)	10.6	(16)	10.3
									17.8	17.9
	18538M	93317M	310262M	631373M	422881M	594035M	Net Sales ($)		1781868M	2719341M
	4667M	23479M	141132M	251242M	432878M	724772M	Total Assets ($)		1744960M	2293677M

M = $ thousand   MM = $ million
See Pages 11 through 21 for Explanation of Ratios and Data

Comparative Historical Data   Current Data Sorted by Sales

Type of Statement	4/1/04-3/31/05 ALL	4/1/05-3/31/06 ALL	4/1/06-3/31/07 ALL	0-1MM	1-3MM	3-5MM	5-10MM	10-25MM	25MM & OVER
Unqualified	18	19	18		2	1	3	4	8
Reviewed	6	8	7		1	2	1	2	1
Compiled	5	5	6		3		2	1	
Tax Returns	13	10	11	6	2	3			
Other	21	36	43	7	8	5	4	4	15
	ALL	ALL	ALL	8 (4/1-9/30/06)			77 (10/1/06-3/31/07)		
NUMBER OF STATEMENTS	63	78	85	13	16	11	10	11	24
ASSETS	%	%	%	%	%	%	%	%	%
Cash & Equivalents	15.0	20.3	20.2	28.1	14.6	15.8	16.8	35.9	15.7
Trade Receivables (net)	28.4	27.4	24.2	17.9	14.2	16.3	36.0	30.5	30.3
Inventory	2.0	4.3	1.3	.6	2.8	.7	.9	.2	1.6
All Other Current	2.8	4.9	5.4	.0	9.7	3.6	1.4	5.3	7.9
Total Current	48.1	56.8	51.1	46.7	41.3	36.4	55.2	71.9	55.4
Fixed Assets (net)	27.1	20.5	29.9	38.9	42.1	34.8	31.6	12.2	22.0
Intangibles (net)	13.4	11.7	10.4	8.7	5.3	6.9	7.4	11.6	17.0
All Other Non-Current	11.4	11.0	8.7	5.7	11.3	21.9	5.8	4.2	5.7
Total	100.0	100.0	100.0	100.0	100.0	100.0	100.0	100.0	100.0
LIABILITIES									
Notes Payable-Short Term	13.0	13.6	13.2	15.3	13.4	30.3	10.0	13.3	5.5
Cur. Mat.-L.T.D.	6.8	3.9	3.0	2.3	3.4	5.7	3.5	2.6	2.0
Trade Payables	13.6	10.9	18.2	54.6	11.3	14.5	15.9	14.8	7.3
Income Taxes Payable	.2	.5	.3	.0	.7	.1	.2	.0	.4
All Other Current	17.9	23.4	26.0	28.6	14.5	46.5	28.7	23.8	22.9
Total Current	51.5	52.2	60.8	100.9	43.2	97.1	58.1	54.5	38.1
Long-Term Debt	22.8	16.2	18.7	28.7	20.4	10.8	10.4	9.2	23.5
Deferred Taxes	.9	.8	.1	.0	.0	.0	.0	.0	.3
All Other Non-Current	11.8	12.1	10.4	4.9	14.1	22.1	13.4	4.4	7.0
Net Worth	13.1	18.7	10.1	-34.4	22.4	-30.0	18.1	31.9	31.2
Total Liabilities & Net Worth	100.0	100.0	100.0	100.0	100.0	100.0	100.0	100.0	100.0
INCOME DATA									
Net Sales	100.0	100.0	100.0	100.0	100.0	100.0	100.0	100.0	100.0
Gross Profit									
Operating Expenses	91.6	97.7	95.2	95.5	97.7	104.4	89.8	90.6	93.7
Operating Profit	8.4	2.3	4.8	4.5	2.3	-4.4	10.2	9.4	6.3
All Other Expenses (net)	2.9	1.5	2.0	3.3	1.6	2.5	.4	.1	2.7
Profit Before Taxes	5.5	.8	2.8	1.1	.7	-6.9	9.8	9.3	3.6
RATIOS									
Current	2.2	3.1	2.4	1.0	2.7	1.2	2.3	4.8	2.7
	1.1	1.5	1.2	.6	1.1	.8	1.5	1.7	1.8
	.5	.8	.5	.1	.5	.2	.4	1.2	.8
Quick	2.0	2.5	2.0	1.0	1.6	1.1	2.3	4.6	2.6
	.9	1.3	1.0	.6	.5	.6	1.4	1.4	1.4
	.4	.6	.3	.1	.3	.2	.3	1.1	.7
Sales/Receivables	6 62.7	17 22.1	6 56.9	0 UND	2 184.8	6 62.9	12 30.3	10 34.9	42 8.6
	42 8.8	46 7.9	29 12.6	8 43.7	10 36.7	7 48.8	59 6.2	28 13.2	60 6.1
	64 5.7	73 5.0	64 5.7	37 9.8	27 13.4	40 9.1	70 5.2	65 5.6	73 5.0
Cost of Sales/Inventory									
Cost of Sales/Payables									
Sales/Working Capital	6.3	5.1	7.7	NM	15.0	79.4	6.1	5.9	6.0
	57.7	11.2	69.4	-13.9	205.8	-14.3	14.0	11.5	9.8
	-7.8	-19.8	-7.3	-3.9	-8.6	-2.8	-6.4	39.7	-13.5
EBIT/Interest	12.0	15.8	13.5		29.3	2.8			11.8
	(53) 4.1	(54) 3.0	(65) 2.1	(13) 2.9	.8			(16) 2.1	
	.7	-1.5	-.4		-5.2	-13.0			-.2
Net Profit + Depr., Dep., Amort./Cur. Mat. L/T/D		14.5	46.1						
		(13) 3.1	(12) 6.9						
		.5	4.0						
Fixed/Worth	.2	.2	.2	.6	.7	.9	.2	.1	.2
	2.9	.7	1.2	11.5	1.8	-5.3	2.1	.2	.6
	-.6	-3.7	-1.3	-2.3	-1.6	-1.1	-1.6	-.9	-1.1
Debt/Worth	.9	.6	.8	6.6	.7	1.5	.7	.2	.6
	3.9	3.6	3.3	45.2	2.7	-25.0	14.2	1.7	1.7
	-5.9	-9.5	-3.8	-2.8	-4.1	-3.8	-3.1	-3.5	-3.4
% Profit Before Taxes/Tangible Net Worth	65.3	64.5	108.5		78.9				56.5
	(40) 24.9	(55) 27.9	(53) 37.6	(10) 29.2				(15) 36.3	
	1.7	-9.5	3.0	-20.2					10.9
% Profit Before Taxes/Total Assets	21.0	20.5	28.6	51.5	26.9	7.5	38.9	63.4	24.0
	4.2	4.4	6.8	1.5	.9	-.2	22.0	18.0	5.5
	-.7	-9.2	-7.1	-4.0	-19.4	-48.8	-3.5	8.5	-6.5
Sales/Net Fixed Assets	53.2	34.0	34.7	UND	39.5	22.0	22.0	121.2	34.7
	15.1	16.6	12.2	5.9	6.4	6.3	9.4	22.0	15.2
	4.2	7.5	4.9	1.5	2.2	4.6	6.0	11.1	8.6
Sales/Total Assets	3.6	3.0	3.6	6.6	5.1	3.2	4.0	5.1	3.2
	2.6	2.1	2.2	2.1	2.5	2.1	2.4	2.4	2.0
	1.6	1.3	1.3	.7	1.5	1.1	1.6	1.9	.9
% Depr., Dep., Amort./Sales	.9	1.6	1.8		3.1				1.5
	(40) 3.2	(52) 3.4	(61) 3.8	(14) 5.7			(17) 3.4		
	7.6	6.5	7.9	12.1					6.7
% Officers', Directors' Owners' Comp/Sales	3.4	2.9	1.5						
	(20) 7.2	(15) 7.9	(16) 4.8						
	11.7	16.2	17.5						
Net Sales ($)	1290130M	2270709M	2070406M	6102M	34401M	40723M	65911M	183867M	1739402M
Total Assets ($)	1025408M	1543934M	1578170M	3026M	22774M	28018M	29920M	79025M	1415407M

M = $ thousand   MM = $ million
See Pages 11 through 21 for Explanation of Ratios and Data

INFORMATION—Data Processing, Hosting, and Related Services NAICS 518210 (SIC 7374, 7379, 7389)

Current Data Sorted by Assets							Comparative Historical Data	
						Type of Statement		
2	2	16	19	11	13	Unqualified	50	45
1	6	15	1			Reviewed	22	27
	5	7			1	Compiled	20	41
10	16	3		1		Tax Returns	21	21
13	37	46	20	9	7	Other	60	54
	48 (4/1-9/30/06)		213 (10/1/06-3/31/07)				4/1/02-3/31/03 ALL	4/1/03-3/31/04 ALL
0-500M	500M-2MM	2-10MM	10-50MM	50-100MM	100-250MM			
26	66	87	40	21	21	**NUMBER OF STATEMENTS**	173	188
%	%	%	%	%	%	**ASSETS**	%	%
28.4	16.5	12.3	20.2	12.5	18.3	Cash & Equivalents	16.5	16.7
29.1	40.7	32.0	28.2	26.6	15.4	Trade Receivables (net)	36.3	33.4
5.2	4.3	3.5	1.2	2.0	1.6	Inventory	3.6	4.6
7.8	3.0	3.0	5.7	6.7	16.2	All Other Current	4.1	4.9
70.5	64.5	50.8	55.3	47.8	51.4	Total Current	60.5	59.7
19.7	20.2	26.6	22.7	10.0	11.5	Fixed Assets (net)	19.9	20.4
5.3	5.1	11.5	14.0	28.1	29.9	Intangibles (net)	8.8	9.3
4.5	10.2	11.1	8.1	14.0	7.2	All Other Non-Current	10.8	10.5
100.0	100.0	100.0	100.0	100.0	100.0	Total	100.0	100.0
						LIABILITIES		
7.8	22.1	7.5	3.2	5.0	3.2	Notes Payable-Short Term	11.1	10.1
5.1	3.4	3.9	3.5	1.7	2.4	Cur. Mat.-L.T.D.	4.8	4.3
15.1	16.8	12.7	10.7	17.7	10.2	Trade Payables	14.3	12.1
.0	1.4	.8	1.0	.0	.4	Income Taxes Payable	.8	.7
24.1	14.9	16.2	19.5	13.3	20.3	All Other Current	17.5	18.8
52.2	58.7	41.2	37.8	37.7	36.5	Total Current	48.6	46.0
34.1	19.1	12.8	24.6	19.3	14.2	Long-Term Debt	14.2	12.6
.0	.0	1.0	.7	1.0	.9	Deferred Taxes	.7	.5
8.6	9.1	10.8	5.0	12.8	16.2	All Other Non-Current	7.6	10.0
5.2	13.1	34.1	31.8	29.2	32.1	Net Worth	29.0	30.9
100.0	100.0	100.0	100.0	100.0	100.0	Total Liabilities & Net Worth	100.0	100.0
						INCOME DATA		
100.0	100.0	100.0	100.0	100.0	100.0	Net Sales	100.0	100.0
						Gross Profit		
91.9	91.4	93.2	93.0	93.8	95.6	Operating Expenses	95.5	94.8
8.1	8.6	6.8	7.0	6.2	4.4	Operating Profit	4.5	5.2
1.6	2.1	2.4	2.4	2.5	.7	All Other Expenses (net)	1.0	1.3
6.6	6.5	4.4	4.7	3.7	3.7	Profit Before Taxes	3.4	3.9
						RATIOS		
5.1	2.6	2.0	2.2	2.5	2.9		2.0	2.3
1.4	1.3	1.4	1.2	1.3	1.4	Current	1.4	1.4
.9	.7	.8	1.0	.8	1.0		.9	.9
3.4	2.1	1.8	2.0	2.1	2.5		1.9	2.1
1.2	1.2	1.1	1.1	1.0	1.3	Quick	1.2	1.1
.5	.7	.7	.7	.7	.4		.7	.7

														Sales/Receivables				
0	UND	22	16.5	33	11.2	38	9.6	26	13.8	21	17.0		30	12.1	27	13.4
23	15.7	41	8.8	53	6.9	55	6.6	50	7.3	56	6.6		46	7.9	44	8.2
50	7.2	65	5.6	70	5.2	68	5.4	74	4.9	93	3.9		66	5.6	64	5.7

0-500M		500M-2MM		2-10MM		10-50MM		50-100MM		100-250MM			ALL		ALL	
												Cost of Sales/Inventory				
												Cost of Sales/Payables				
	9.2		7.6		7.6		6.8		4.7		1.9			7.1		7.7
	34.1		19.7		19.1		14.5		16.5		6.4	Sales/Working Capital		18.8		22.3
	-406.7		-23.5		-32.7		NM		-33.3		-36.9			-62.6		-76.5
	7.8		31.2		11.0		16.5		7.1		28.9			12.1		17.1
(16)	2.4	(52)	5.5	(72)	3.9	(34)	2.7	(17)	2.9	(17)	7.2	EBIT/Interest	(147)	4.0	(153)	5.2
	-4.6		.3		.5		.4		.3		-1.0			1.0		1.1
				(18)	6.8	(11)	14.1					Net Profit + Depr., Dep.,	(41)	8.1	(47)	10.0
					3.5		2.0					Amort./Cur. Mat. L/T/D		2.8		4.3
					1.2		1.1							1.2		1.6
	.1		.2		.2		.2		.4		.2			.2		.2
	.6		.7		.9		.8		1.2		1.1	Fixed/Worth		.7		.7
	-.7		-2.8		5.4		-4.3		-.2		-.2			2.6		4.6
	.4		.8		.9		.9		2.4		.9			1.0		.9
	2.4		3.1		1.9		2.8		15.0		3.8	Debt/Worth		1.9		2.0
	-2.3		-9.3		35.9		-15.7		-3.3		-3.6			13.9		14.2
	209.9		105.7		59.3		77.0		59.5		67.6	% Profit Before Taxes/Tangible		63.4		59.2
(17)	39.6	(46)	54.4	(66)	26.1	(29)	34.1	(11)	46.8	(13)	14.5	Net Worth	(142)	22.2	(146)	27.4
	8.7		11.8		5.3		.3		6.2		-9.6			3.3		4.5
	50.4		33.1		21.9		17.5		10.7		11.4	% Profit Before Taxes/Total		18.0		18.5
	19.3		13.4		7.6		5.9		4.7		3.6	Assets		6.9		7.1
	-1.2		-2.7		-.5		-.7		-4.7		-6.5			.3		.3
	320.1		104.4		36.8		53.6		73.1		35.9			40.8		52.4
	56.2		32.2		15.1		10.3		19.4		11.2	Sales/Net Fixed Assets		16.2		20.2
	18.1		10.6		4.2		3.6		7.1		6.0			8.0		9.9
	10.0		4.2		2.9		2.0		2.4		1.2			3.7		4.1
	5.2		3.1		2.0		1.5		1.3		.8	Sales/Total Assets		2.4		2.5
	3.3		1.6		1.1		1.2		.8		.3			1.6		1.4
	.6		.5		1.1		1.7		.6					.9		1.0
(13)	1.1	(38)	1.4	(66)	3.1	(31)	3.4	(13)	3.1			% Depr., Dep., Amort./Sales	(126)	2.1	(135)	2.4
	2.1		3.6		7.9		8.4		5.3					4.8		5.5
	5.3		3.8		2.8							% Officers', Directors'		4.4		3.0
(13)	9.1	(24)	8.3	(16)	3.9							Owners' Comp/Sales	(52)	7.2	(53)	6.9
	13.6		13.5		5.4									14.6		16.1
61141M		222903M		1013858M		1446010M		3554763M		2959002M		Net Sales ($)	4280818M		4958372M	
5816M		71217M		443267M		814469M		1594539M		3359958M		Total Assets ($)	2528155M		2868958M	

M = $ thousand   MM = $ million
See Pages 11 through 21 for Explanation of Ratios and Data

Comparative Historical Data | Current Data Sorted by Sales

	Comparative Historical Data			Type of Statement	Current Data Sorted by Sales					
	48	49	63	Unqualified	1		5	9	11	37
	26	18	23	Reviewed		3	2	7	9	2
	19	15	13	Compiled	1	2	3	4	2	1
	15	17	30	Tax Returns	7	11	9	1	1	1
	80	94	132	Other	15	15	22	28	21	31
	4/1/04-	4/1/05-	4/1/06-		48 (4/1-9/30/06)			213 (10/1/06-3/31/07)		
	3/31/05	3/31/06	3/31/07							
	ALL	ALL	ALL		0-1MM	1-3MM	3-5MM	5-10MM	10-25MM	25MM & OVER
NUMBER OF STATEMENTS	188	193	261		24	31	41	49	44	72
	%	%	%	ASSETS	%	%	%	%	%	%
Cash & Equivalents	18.9	16.6	16.7		26.3	14.3	18.0	13.1	15.0	17.2
Trade Receivables (net)	32.5	32.1	31.6		21.8	32.4	34.6	31.8	36.4	29.6
Inventory	3.2	4.4	3.2		2.7	6.1	3.7	2.0	4.5	2.0
All Other Current	4.0	5.1	5.3		7.1	3.3	3.0	1.9	3.6	10.1
Total Current	58.7	58.3	56.7		57.8	56.1	59.2	48.8	59.5	58.8
Fixed Assets (net)	20.5	19.7	21.1		27.1	26.4	25.5	24.0	20.7	12.8
Intangibles (net)	10.7	12.3	12.5		7.8	7.4	9.2	12.4	7.2	21.3
All Other Non-Current	10.1	9.6	9.7		7.2	10.1	6.1	14.7	12.7	7.1
Total	100.0	100.0	100.0		100.0	100.0	100.0	100.0	100.0	100.0
				LIABILITIES						
Notes Payable-Short Term	12.4	8.7	10.0		7.0	12.2	19.6	12.4	7.6	4.4
Cur. Mat.-L.T.D.	4.7	5.0	3.5		3.3	4.4	4.1	5.1	3.3	2.0
Trade Payables	14.3	12.8	13.9		13.6	8.6	15.2	14.4	17.2	13.2
Income Taxes Payable	.3	.6	.8		.1	2.1	.5	.7	.4	.9
All Other Current	17.9	17.0	17.3		22.5	11.1	17.3	17.5	13.0	20.6
Total Current	49.5	44.0	45.5		46.5	38.5	56.9	50.2	41.6	41.1
Long-Term Debt	13.8	13.5	19.0		46.6	22.2	17.1	14.5	19.3	12.4
Deferred Taxes	.6	.4	.6		.0	.6	1.2	.5	.4	.7
All Other Non-Current	7.4	12.0	9.9		6.8	14.7	6.0	13.1	9.0	9.3
Net Worth	28.7	30.1	25.0		.1	24.0	18.8	21.8	29.7	36.6
Total Liabilties & Net Worth	100.0	100.0	100.0		100.0	100.0	100.0	100.0	100.0	100.0
				INCOME DATA						
Net Sales	100.0	100.0	100.0		100.0	100.0	100.0	100.0	100.0	100.0
Gross Profit										
Operating Expenses	95.2	93.3	92.8		81.1	92.8	94.2	94.1	95.8	93.2
Operating Profit	4.8	6.7	7.2		18.9	7.2	5.8	5.9	4.2	6.8
All Other Expenses (net)	.9	1.4	2.1		7.1	1.4	.9	1.9	2.0	1.6
Profit Before Taxes	3.9	5.3	5.1		11.8	5.8	4.9	4.0	2.2	5.2
				RATIOS						
Current	2.1	2.5	2.4		3.8	2.8	2.2	2.3	2.3	2.4
	1.3	1.4	1.3		1.5	1.4	1.2	1.2	1.3	1.4
	.8	.9	.9		.5	.9	.7	.7	1.0	1.0
Quick	1.8	2.1	2.1		3.8	1.8	1.8	2.1	2.1	2.1
	1.1	1.1	1.1		1.1	1.3	1.0	1.0	1.1	1.1
	.7	.7	.7		.3	.6	.6	.6	.8	.8
Sales/Receivables	29 12.8	29 12.5	26 13.8		0 UND	18 19.9	24 15.5	27 13.4	35 10.4	33 11.2
	48 7.7	47 7.8	48 7.6		32 11.5	43 8.6	38 9.6	48 7.6	55 6.7	56 6.5
	71 5.1	71 5.1	68 5.3		51 7.2	70 5.2	59 6.2	70 5.2	63 5.8	75 4.8
Cost of Sales/Inventory										
Cost of Sales/Payables										
Sales/Working Capital	6.9	6.3	7.2		4.5	9.5	7.8	7.7	7.0	4.8
	21.8	17.3	17.5		18.8	19.5	23.3	37.2	14.9	14.9
	-29.7	-92.4	-39.2		-4.4	-86.8	-20.5	-13.2	253.4	640.9
EBIT/Interest	20.2	18.3	14.5		19.6	31.7	14.4	7.4	11.7	25.7
	(156) 5.0	(152) 5.6	(208) 3.6		(13) 3.0	(29) 4.0	(32) 3.1	(37) 3.4	(38) 2.8	(59) 6.9
	.8	1.3	.4		-4.5	.6	-1.2	-1.0	1.1	.6
Net Profit + Depr., Dep., Amort./Cur. Mat. L/T/D	8.8	12.8	10.3						9.9	14.1
	(42) 3.4	(44) 4.1	(45) 3.3				(10) 3.6		(15) 2.0	
	1.6	1.7	1.2						2.0	1.1
Fixed/Worth	.2	.2	.2		.2	.2	.3	.2	.1	.2
	.6	.7	.9		14.3	1.3	1.4	1.0	.5	.8
	7.2	4.6	-1.7		-.9	-.9	-1.8	-1.8	NM	-.6
Debt/Worth	.9	.8	.9		.5	.6	.9	.7	1.0	1.0
	2.2	2.4	2.8		31.6	1.7	3.0	2.5	2.0	2.8
	168.7	30.5	-7.7		-2.5	-7.1	-12.2	-6.2	NM	-8.2
% Profit Before Taxes/Tangible Net Worth	65.3	74.4	73.2		266.1	135.1	80.0	73.2	47.3	78.5
	(144) 25.7	(149) 28.9	(182) 32.7		(14) 60.1	(21) 21.6	(29) 29.2	(34) 32.2	(33) 27.0	(51) 46.8
	5.5	8.7	6.0		19.0	5.4	3.3	8.7	5.0	6.4
% Profit Before Taxes/Total Assets	17.3	23.5	22.3		38.0	33.0	31.1	23.8	15.8	17.7
	7.5	9.7	8.3		11.6	11.3	11.1	10.1	4.9	9.0
	-.5	1.6	-.9		-6.0	-.6	-1.6	-10.2	1.0	-.1
Sales/Net Fixed Assets	45.7	49.9	63.5		128.8	78.3	53.7	89.7	35.0	57.2
	18.4	19.2	18.4		12.2	25.8	20.3	23.0	16.9	17.7
	6.6	7.8	6.4		4.2	10.8	5.9	5.2	4.9	8.3
Sales/Total Assets	3.7	3.6	3.5		4.4	4.2	4.2	3.6	3.3	2.4
	2.3	2.3	2.0		1.9	3.0	2.5	2.2	2.2	1.5
	1.3	1.4	1.1		.9	1.3	1.7	1.1	1.3	1.0
% Depr., Dep., Amort./Sales	1.3	.8	.9		1.5	1.1	.5	1.1	.7	.7
	(126) 2.9	(141) 2.1	(169) 2.6		(11) 2.7	(21) 1.7	(25) 1.8	(32) 3.3	(37) 2.7	(43) 2.1
	6.6	4.1	5.9		10.3	3.8	9.3	6.6	6.5	4.5
% Officers', Directors' Owners' Comp/Sales	2.6	3.0	3.4			4.3	3.6			
	(47) 6.0	(41) 6.5	(59) 5.8			(14) 7.9	(16) 8.9			
	9.2	13.0	11.3			12.4	11.5			
Net Sales ($)	7172828M	5234794M	9257677M		12290M	60286M	159619M	333587M	717170M	7974725M
Total Assets ($)	3564384M	3564105M	6289266M		11223M	31351M	98420M	200304M	541575M	5406393M

M = $ thousand   MM = $ million
See Pages 11 through 21 for Explanation of Ratios and Data

FINANCE AND INSURANCE

FINANCE—Credit Card Issuing NAICS 522210 (SIC 6021, 6022, 6141)

Current Data Sorted by Assets   **Comparative Historical Data**

0-500M	500M-2MM	2-10MM	10-50MM	50-100MM	100-250MM	Type of Statement	4/1/02-3/31/03 ALL	4/1/03-3/31/04 ALL
		3	3	3	4	Unqualified	13	11
	1	2	1			Reviewed	4	5
	1	1	2			Compiled	2	5
2	1	1				Tax Returns	1	1
1	4	4		2	2	Other	4	13
	8 (4/1-9/30/06)		32 (10/1/06-3/31/07)					
3	7	11	7	6	6	**NUMBER OF STATEMENTS**	24	35
%	%	%	%	%	%	**ASSETS**	%	%
		7.5				Cash & Equivalents	2.7	11.4
		56.4				Trade Receivables (net)	70.2	53.2
		1.3				Inventory	.0	2.7
		14.3				All Other Current	18.8	15.3
		79.6				Total Current	91.7	82.7
		9.1				Fixed Assets (net)	1.6	5.4
		4.8				Intangibles (net)	.7	2.6
		6.5				All Other Non-Current	5.9	9.3
		100.0				Total	100.0	100.0
						LIABILITIES		
		29.2				Notes Payable-Short Term	30.2	30.3
		3.8				Cur. Mat.-L.T.D.	10.7	4.0
		1.4				Trade Payables	.9	5.1
		.1				Income Taxes Payable	.0	.0
		14.8				All Other Current	16.0	11.1
		49.2				Total Current	57.8	50.5
		9.4				Long-Term Debt	3.9	9.6
		.0				Deferred Taxes	.0	.2
		19.1				All Other Non-Current	7.3	7.2
		22.3				Net Worth	30.9	32.6
		100.0				Total Liabilities & Net Worth	100.0	100.0
						INCOME DATA		
		100.0				Net Sales	100.0	100.0
						Gross Profit		
		60.7				Operating Expenses	75.0	77.1
		39.3				Operating Profit	25.0	22.9
		24.6				All Other Expenses (net)	14.1	11.0
		14.7				Profit Before Taxes	10.9	11.9
						RATIOS		
		2.7					2.4	2.6
		1.6				Current	1.5	1.7
		1.2					1.2	1.4
		1.7					2.3	2.2
		1.2				Quick	1.4	1.5
		.4					1.0	.5
	13	28.2					333 1.1	7 51.9
	1071	.3				Sales/Receivables	865 .4	480 .8
	2000	.2					1578 .2	1155 .3
						Cost of Sales/Inventory		
						Cost of Sales/Payables		
		.4					.6	.6
		.8				Sales/Working Capital	1.2	1.2
		13.2					2.4	4.5
							3.5	4.6
						EBIT/Interest	(17) 1.6	(25) 2.8
							.9	1.5
						Net Profit + Depr., Dep., Amort./Cur. Mat. L/T/D		
		.0					.0	.0
		.1				Fixed/Worth	.0	.1
		1.0					.1	.3
		1.9					1.8	1.1
		4.8				Debt/Worth	2.8	2.3
		17.5					4.7	9.3
							36.0	39.1
						% Profit Before Taxes/Tangible Net Worth	(23) 14.6	(33) 16.7
							-.8	5.2
		5.2					6.3	6.9
		2.4				% Profit Before Taxes/Total Assets	2.2	4.0
		.1					-.1	2.4
		407.0					196.8	118.3
		20.8				Sales/Net Fixed Assets	40.6	30.3
		5.6					18.7	15.2
		.3					.4	1.3
		.2				Sales/Total Assets	.3	.4
		.1					.2	.2
							.3	.6
						% Depr., Dep., Amort./Sales	(19) .8	(25) 1.6
							1.2	2.3
								3.7
						% Officers', Directors' Owners' Comp/Sales	(14) 10.4	
								26.8
3621M	14453M	36774M	77417M	123555M	422847M	Net Sales ($)	183100M	429621M
544M	8199M	55070M	179474M	436255M	810388M	Total Assets ($)	470816M	1046428M

© RMA 2007

M = $ thousand   MM = $ million
See Pages 11 through 21 for Explanation of Ratios and Data

Comparative Historical Data / Current Data Sorted by Sales

			Type of Statement	0-1MM	1-3MM	3-5MM	5-10MM	10-25MM	25MM & OVER
9	8	13	Unqualified	3			4	5	1
3	1	4	Reviewed	2	1		1	1	
3	2	4	Compiled	1			1	2	
4	1	4	Tax Returns	4				1	
9	4	15	Other	6	1	1	1	3	3
4/1/04-3/31/05 ALL	4/1/05-3/31/06 ALL	4/1/06-3/31/07 ALL		8 (4/1-9/30/06)			32 (10/1/06-3/31/07)		
28	16	40	**NUMBER OF STATEMENTS**	13	5	1	6	11	4
%	%	%	**ASSETS**	%	%	%	%	%	%
9.2	7.3	9.4	Cash & Equivalents	9.8				3.6	
44.8	59.2	53.6	Trade Receivables (net)	58.6				48.3	
6.7	.6	.4	Inventory	1.1				.0	
11.7	1.8	10.8	All Other Current	15.5				17.9	
72.5	68.8	74.2	Total Current	85.0				69.8	
6.0	8.1	7.2	Fixed Assets (net)	4.7				7.7	
3.7	2.2	2.9	Intangibles (net)	3.0				3.5	
17.9	20.9	15.6	All Other Non-Current	7.3				19.0	
100.0	100.0	100.0	Total	100.0				100.0	
			LIABILITIES						
27.4	19.1	24.4	Notes Payable-Short Term	21.9				30.3	
4.5	.6	1.2	Cur. Mat.-L.T.D.	3.2				.3	
3.9	4.1	2.7	Trade Payables	1.7				2.2	
.3	.0	.1	Income Taxes Payable	.0				.1	
9.9	13.0	11.0	All Other Current	13.0				7.7	
45.9	36.9	39.3	Total Current	39.8				40.7	
13.7	13.7	12.7	Long-Term Debt	6.9				22.5	
.4	.9	.0	Deferred Taxes	.0				.1	
9.9	10.6	9.1	All Other Non-Current	8.4				7.3	
30.0	38.0	38.9	Net Worth	44.9				29.4	
100.0	100.0	100.0	Total Liabilities & Net Worth	100.0				100.0	
			INCOME DATA						
100.0	100.0	100.0	Net Sales	100.0				100.0	
			Gross Profit						
72.8	72.1	63.5	Operating Expenses	61.4				58.3	
27.2	27.9	36.5	Operating Profit	38.6				41.7	
9.0	8.3	13.3	All Other Expenses (net)	18.4				14.9	
18.2	19.6	23.1	Profit Before Taxes	20.2				26.7	
			RATIOS						
2.3	3.8	3.5	Current	8.2				3.7	
1.6	2.0	2.0		2.0				1.3	
1.1	1.2	1.2		1.2				.8	
1.9	3.7	2.7	Quick	4.7				2.1	
1.1	1.9	1.5		1.7				.9	
.2	1.2			.6				.1	
0 UND	85 4.3	0 UND	Sales/Receivables	0 UND				0 UND	
217 1.7	657 .6	523 .7		626 .6				134 2.7	
989 .4	1184 .3	1306 .3		2000 .2				2000 .2	
			Cost of Sales/Inventory						
			Cost of Sales/Payables						
.6	.6	.6	Sales/Working Capital	.5				.8	
2.1	1.0	1.3		.7				1.3	
15.9	4.7	8.6		2.3				-12.9	
6.0		24.6	EBIT/Interest						
(20) 3.4		(24) 4.5							
2.0		3.4							
			Net Profit + Depr., Dep., Amort./Cur. Mat. L/T/D						
.0	.0	.0	Fixed/Worth	.0				.0	
.0	.0	.0		.0				.1	
.1	.2	.4		.2				1.4	
.9	.6	.6	Debt/Worth	.3				1.1	
2.3	2.0	1.8		1.3				3.3	
7.3	7.6	5.7		5.4				15.6	
45.5	36.0	45.7	% Profit Before Taxes/Tangible Net Worth	28.5					
(27) 25.7	19.8	(37) 20.0		(12) 15.3					
6.5	6.5	6.5		-3.6					
9.4	10.0	13.6	% Profit Before Taxes/Total Assets	7.9				21.7	
5.0	3.9	5.2		5.2				5.2	
2.3	.9	2.1		-.1				3.2	
646.9	UND	355.7	Sales/Net Fixed Assets	UND				131.9	
74.3	82.3	37.1		108.3				45.9	
15.1	11.3	12.1		8.7				24.2	
1.1	.5	.9	Sales/Total Assets	.7				.9	
.4	.2	.3		.3				.2	
.2	.2	.1		.1				.1	
1.0		.5	% Depr., Dep., Amort./Sales						
(16) 1.4		(21) .9							
2.9		4.1							
3.0			% Officers', Directors' Owners' Comp/Sales						
(12) 6.7									
17.9									
182097M	231436M	678667M	Net Sales ($)	6592M	8455M	3298M	44202M	190706M	425414M
348312M	670581M	1489930M	Total Assets ($)	35981M	66437M	1596M	134120M	773421M	478375M

© RMA 2007

M = $ thousand   MM = $ million
See Pages 11 through 21 for Explanation of Ratios and Data

Current Data Sorted by Assets   **Comparative Historical Data**

	0-500M	500M-2MM	2-10MM	10-50MM	50-100MM	100-250MM		4/1/02-3/31/03 ALL	4/1/03-3/31/04 ALL
Type of Statement									
Unqualified		5	11	35	13	15		23	37
Reviewed	1	3	13	17		1		4	17
Compiled	1	8	11	3				3	14
Tax Returns	6	7	8	1				5	8
Other		7	24	19	6	8		6	21
		28 (4/1-9/30/06)		195 (10/1/06-3/31/07)					
NUMBER OF STATEMENTS	8	30	67	75	19	24		41	97
	%	%	%	%	%	%		%	%
ASSETS									
Cash & Equivalents		10.6	8.0	7.8	1.7	4.3		8.4	7.6
Trade Receivables (net)		29.4	49.9	54.3	55.1	42.5		37.0	47.4
Inventory		5.7	3.5	4.5	3.6	.1		2.4	2.4
All Other Current		5.6	5.6	5.6	16.9	16.4		15.2	11.8
Total Current		51.3	66.9	72.2	77.3	63.3		63.0	69.2
Fixed Assets (net)		31.9	18.9	11.6	10.3	7.5		7.7	14.4
Intangibles (net)		.1	1.3	.6	.2	1.2		2.3	1.3
All Other Non-Current		16.7	12.9	15.6	12.2	28.0		26.9	15.0
Total		100.0	100.0	100.0	100.0	100.0		100.0	100.0
LIABILITIES									
Notes Payable-Short Term		26.2	27.4	27.6	42.5	29.9		31.3	28.4
Cur. Mat.-L.T.D.		1.9	6.0	7.3	4.3	5.0		7.3	6.4
Trade Payables		4.5	5.2	3.6	1.5	1.9		3.9	3.6
Income Taxes Payable		.1	.0	.2	.6	.1		.3	.3
All Other Current		5.5	7.9	8.5	7.6	10.4		4.8	7.2
Total Current		38.2	46.5	47.2	56.5	47.3		47.6	45.9
Long-Term Debt		22.5	15.9	23.7	19.7	24.8		19.2	20.6
Deferred Taxes		.7	.0	.5	.4	.6		.3	.4
All Other Non-Current		9.7	7.8	6.8	8.1	11.1		11.4	9.4
Net Worth		28.9	29.7	21.7	15.3	16.2		21.5	23.7
Total Liabilities & Net Worth		100.0	100.0	100.0	100.0	100.0		100.0	100.0
INCOME DATA									
Net Sales		100.0	100.0	100.0	100.0	100.0		100.0	100.0
Gross Profit									
Operating Expenses		75.2	72.7	64.8	64.3	57.4		66.7	70.1
Operating Profit		24.8	27.3	35.2	35.7	42.6		33.3	29.9
All Other Expenses (net)		11.9	11.6	18.5	17.9	22.8		19.3	15.3
Profit Before Taxes		12.9	15.7	16.6	17.8	19.8		14.0	14.7
RATIOS									
Current		3.0	2.4	2.2	1.9	1.7		2.1	2.4
		1.6	1.5	1.3	1.3	1.3		1.3	1.4
		.6	1.0	1.1	1.1	1.1		1.0	1.0
Quick		2.5	2.2	2.0	1.9	1.4		1.9	2.4
		1.0	1.3	1.2	1.2	1.0		1.1	1.3
		.1	.4	.9	.1	.1		.1	.5
Sales/Receivables		0 UND	12 31.6	13 28.3	23 15.7	2 179.3		0 UND	15 23.6
		16 23.3	228 1.6	726 .5	907 .4	155 2.4		151 2.4	392 .9
		834 .4	920 .4	1572 .2	1809 .2	1373 .3		840 .4	1000 .4
Cost of Sales/Inventory									
Cost of Sales/Payables									
Sales/Working Capital		.6	1.1	.6	.6	.6		.9	.6
		4.5	3.8	2.0	1.3	1.5		1.9	1.5
		-22.5	98.2	17.6	2.3	7.7		48.2	35.2
EBIT/Interest		4.7	5.1	3.6	3.8			5.2	5.4
		(21) 1.9	(41) 3.0	(35) 2.6	(11) 2.1			(22) 2.8	(58) 2.5
		1.0	2.0	1.7	1.1			1.5	1.1
Net Profit + Depr., Dep., Amort./Cur. Mat. L/T/D									
Fixed/Worth		.0	.0	.0	.0	.0		.0	.0
		.2	.1	.1	.0	.1		.1	.1
		2.1	.4	.4	.1	.7		.7	.5
Debt/Worth		.8	1.2	2.5	3.2	3.7		2.0	1.6
		4.1	3.3	5.1	5.1	5.1		5.1	3.4
		39.2	7.0	10.2	10.8	10.1		19.5	8.4
% Profit Before Taxes/Tangible Net Worth		45.7	38.9	35.5	41.2	40.0		40.5	32.8
		(26) 9.7	(62) 26.6	(74) 23.5	(17) 22.0	(23) 22.4		(38) 20.2	(90) 17.0
		1.1	9.6	10.9	14.3	13.2		7.6	3.0
% Profit Before Taxes/Total Assets		8.1	11.8	7.7	6.8	7.3		6.4	7.0
		2.4	5.4	3.2	3.6	2.9		1.9	2.7
		.0	1.4	1.5	.8	1.6		.7	.8
Sales/Net Fixed Assets		UND	210.1	100.4	83.3	112.5		239.4	96.5
		21.0	47.3	44.0	33.8	18.7		38.9	27.0
		.7	8.2	10.9	9.6	6.1		6.6	4.9
Sales/Total Assets		.8	1.0	.4	.3	.3		.4	.5
		.4	.4	.3	.2	.2		.2	.3
		.2	.2	.2	.1	.1		.1	.2
% Depr., Dep., Amort./Sales		.6	.4	.5	.5	1.2		.6	.7
		(19) 6.7	(46) .9	(48) 1.3	(14) 1.0	(15) 1.8		(29) 1.4	(66) 1.7
		54.9	21.0	2.7	1.4	8.7		4.6	17.9
% Officers', Directors' Owners' Comp/Sales			3.6	2.2				8.8	4.1
			(20) 6.8	(21) 7.4				(11) 15.3	(27) 10.9
			12.9	12.8				33.3	20.5
Net Sales ($)	2223M	52636M	282702M	1431785M	694757M	1314511M		228813M	591818M
Total Assets ($)	1931M	33558M	367656M	1849140M	1343846M	3865093M		1050420M	1512431M

M = $ thousand   MM = $ million
See Pages 11 through 21 for Explanation of Ratios and Data

Comparative Historical Data | Current Data Sorted by Sales

			Type of Statement						
38	48	79	Unqualified	6	17	5	16	21	14
25	29	35	Reviewed	7	12	5	5	2	4
14	13	23	Compiled	9	3	2	2	6	1
17	14	22	Tax Returns	13	6	1	2		
28	50	64	Other	13	13	7	13	10	8
4/1/04-3/31/05 ALL	4/1/05-3/31/06 ALL	4/1/06-3/31/07 ALL		0-1MM	1-3MM	3-5MM	5-10MM	10-25MM	25MM & OVER
				28 (4/1-9/30/06)			195 (10/1/06-3/31/07)		
122	154	223	**NUMBER OF STATEMENTS**	48	51	20	38	39	27
%	%	%	**ASSETS**	%	%	%	%	%	%
7.4	7.2	7.2	Cash & Equivalents	6.3	5.8	7.1	6.9	6.9	12.5
49.7	49.1	47.5	Trade Receivables (net)	37.0	51.1	59.7	52.1	48.9	41.6
2.5	4.6	3.8	Inventory	3.1	2.8	.8	3.9	3.2	9.9
7.8	8.0	7.6	All Other Current	4.9	4.6	1.8	14.4	9.5	9.9
67.4	68.9	66.1	Total Current	51.4	64.3	69.3	77.4	68.5	73.9
10.7	12.7	17.3	Fixed Assets (net)	28.2	20.4	11.2	7.2	16.4	12.2
1.7	1.3	.8	Intangibles (net)	.1	.2	4.9	.4	.2	1.2
20.2	17.1	15.8	All Other Non-Current	20.3	15.1	14.5	15.0	15.0	12.7
100.0	100.0	100.0	Total	100.0	100.0	100.0	100.0	100.0	100.0
			LIABILITIES						
32.1	30.3	29.0	Notes Payable-Short Term	28.2	26.8	28.0	33.0	28.8	29.8
5.2	5.2	5.5	Cur. Mat.-L.T.D.	3.5	8.5	4.6	4.4	6.7	3.7
3.1	3.1	3.9	Trade Payables	1.6	2.9	4.1	7.5	3.0	5.5
.1	.1	.1	Income Taxes Payable	.0	.1	.1	.2	.1	.3
5.9	9.4	8.2	All Other Current	8.6	5.8	5.5	9.8	6.7	13.6
46.4	48.1	46.6	Total Current	42.0	44.1	42.2	54.9	45.4	52.9
16.7	17.6	21.8	Long-Term Debt	28.5	20.6	30.2	17.1	22.4	11.6
.6	.4	.4	Deferred Taxes	.4	.0	.6	.2	.7	.5
9.3	8.0	7.9	All Other Non-Current	7.5	8.9	2.1	5.1	11.7	9.4
26.9	26.0	23.3	Net Worth	21.6	26.3	24.8	22.7	19.8	25.6
100.0	100.0	100.0	Total Liabilities & Net Worth	100.0	100.0	100.0	100.0	100.0	100.0
			INCOME DATA						
100.0	100.0	100.0	Net Sales	100.0	100.0	100.0	100.0	100.0	100.0
			Gross Profit						
71.9	72.0	67.9	Operating Expenses	66.3	63.4	65.8	68.9	68.5	78.2
28.1	28.0	32.1	Operating Profit	33.7	36.6	34.2	31.1	31.5	21.8
10.8	12.1	15.7	All Other Expenses (net)	15.9	18.2	16.6	12.8	18.4	9.7
17.3	15.9	16.5	Profit Before Taxes	17.8	18.4	17.5	18.3	13.1	12.1
			RATIOS						
2.4	2.3	2.3		2.4	2.4	2.2	1.6	2.5	2.0
1.4	1.3	1.3	Current	1.3	1.4	1.6	1.3	1.3	1.4
1.0	1.0	1.1		.3	1.0	1.1	1.1	1.1	1.2
2.2	1.9	2.1		2.3	2.4	2.1	1.3	2.3	1.9
1.3	(152) 1.2	1.2	Quick	1.0	1.2	1.4	1.1	1.2	1.2
.6	.5	.4		.1	.6	1.1	.4	.6	.2
17 21.2	15 24.6	8 44.9		0 UND	12 31.6	13 28.7	26 14.0	16 23.5	11 33.2
379 1.0	386 .9	281 1.3	Sales/Receivables	68 5.4	543 .7	976 .4	450 .8	77 4.8	42 8.6
1216 .3	1212 .3	1217 .3		1390 .3	1447 .3	1723 .2	1045 .3	991 .4	328 1.1
			Cost of Sales/Inventory						
			Cost of Sales/Payables						
.8	.7	.7		.5	.5	.9	1.0	1.0	1.4
1.6	2.5	2.3	Sales/Working Capital	4.5	1.6	2.3	2.5	2.3	9.2
22.5	203.9	24.2		-2.5	98.2	5.0	7.6	12.8	21.7
4.9	5.4	4.4		5.6	4.2	12.0	8.8	3.6	3.4
(73) 2.7	(96) 2.8	(122) 2.7	EBIT/Interest	(24) 2.4	(24) 3.1	(13) 2.6	(16) 3.3	(24) 2.3	(21) 2.9
1.3	1.6	1.7		1.3	1.3	1.8	1.5	1.6	1.8
		8.0	Net Profit + Depr., Dep.,						
	(19)	.9	Amort./Cur. Mat. L/T/D						
		.1							
.0	.0	.0		.0	.0	.0	.0	.0	.0
.1	.1	.1	Fixed/Worth	.0	.0	.0	.1	.1	.1
.6	.5	.8		5.1	.7	.4	.3	.7	.8
1.7	1.6	2.0		1.3	1.8	2.0	2.2	3.0	2.1
3.9	3.9	4.8	Debt/Worth	5.5	4.7	4.1	5.0	5.3	3.4
10.0	10.6	9.7		73.7	7.4	8.5	-9.9	8.9	5.1
39.1	39.9	41.8	% Profit Before Taxes/Tangible	62.5	32.4	104.1	34.3	37.8	47.9
(114) 19.0	(143) 23.5	(208) 22.7	Net Worth	(39) 16.4	(49) 17.9	(19) 31.0	26.4	(38) 21.5	(25) 27.0
6.0	7.4	10.1		4.5	3.8	14.6	16.3	12.9	12.4
8.4	9.6	8.6	% Profit Before Taxes/Total	5.7	9.8	9.2	9.5	8.6	10.8
3.3	3.8	3.7	Assets	2.6	3.9	3.4	4.2	3.0	6.0
1.1	1.3	1.4		1.0	.8	.7	1.9	1.5	3.1
170.5	291.5	185.8		UND	105.8	891.1	103.6	69.5	185.8
37.1	38.4	39.5	Sales/Net Fixed Assets	45.7	40.1	50.6	40.2	21.1	54.0
7.8	7.0	5.7		.8	3.3	11.4	11.4	2.5	12.5
.6	.7	.6		.4	.4	1.0	.7	.8	3.9
.3	.3	.3	Sales/Total Assets	.2	.3	.3	.3	.3	1.1
.2	.2	.2		.1	.2	.2	.2	.1	.3
.7	.6	.5		2.6	.5	.7	.3	.4	.4
(72) 1.3	(96) 1.4	(147) 1.3	% Depr., Dep., Amort./Sales	(24) 26.5	(37) 1.4	(12) 1.2	(30) 1.0	(29) 1.2	(15) 1.3
4.1	7.9	7.3		58.3	23.8	1.7	1.8	5.9	2.1
5.5	6.3	3.8	% Officers', Directors'	5.4	5.5		2.0	3.8	
(34) 11.9	(34) 9.7	(59) 8.6	Owners' Comp/Sales	(11) 18.5	(17) 11.2		(10) 6.8	(10) 11.9	
22.0	19.6	15.7		25.1	20.8		17.7	14.0	
1175257M	2000600M	3778614M	Net Sales ($)	21583M	99753M	77683M	287750M	615412M	2676433M
2009049M	3760896M	7461224M	Total Assets ($)	120457M	484331M	371328M	1110102M	2503622M	2871384M

M = $ thousand   MM = $ million
See Pages 11 through 21 for Explanation of Ratios and Data

Current Data Sorted by Assets   Comparative Historical Data

	0-500M	500M-2MM	2-10MM	10-50MM	50-100MM	100-250MM		4/1/02-3/31/03 ALL	4/1/03-3/31/04 ALL
Type of Statement									
Unqualified	2	2	20	30	10	17		64	71
Reviewed		17	9	10				32	29
Compiled	4	9	9	2				25	35
Tax Returns	7	8	6	4				15	15
Other	3	9	21	26	6	14		73	55
	43 (4/1-9/30/06)			*193 (10/1/06-3/31/07)*					
NUMBER OF STATEMENTS	16	28	73	72	16	31		209	205
ASSETS	%	%	%	%	%	%		%	%
Cash & Equivalents	21.6	12.3	6.2	5.2	6.8	10.4		6.3	8.4
Trade Receivables (net)	14.4	61.7	58.8	68.7	64.3	64.2		63.7	63.3
Inventory	.1	.0	1.4	.9	1.3	1.1		2.8	2.4
All Other Current	32.8	4.8	9.4	9.9	13.6	6.0		11.3	7.3
Total Current	68.9	78.8	75.8	84.7	85.9	81.6		84.2	81.4
Fixed Assets (net)	22.7	10.2	4.5	6.0	5.0	6.4		4.8	6.4
Intangibles (net)	2.8	2.6	1.9	1.8	3.1	2.5		1.7	1.4
All Other Non-Current	5.6	8.4	17.9	7.6	6.0	9.6		9.3	10.7
Total	100.0	100.0	100.0	100.0	100.0	100.0		100.0	100.0
LIABILITIES									
Notes Payable-Short Term	31.0	31.5	37.3	39.1	31.0	30.3		35.6	35.2
Cur. Mat.-L.T.D.	1.1	1.3	1.5	3.7	.9	3.3		3.7	2.5
Trade Payables	2.7	4.1	1.3	1.4	5.7	2.9		2.5	2.6
Income Taxes Payable	.0	.3	.3	.2	.0	.1		.2	.1
All Other Current	5.1	7.7	8.0	7.4	13.9	13.8		11.2	8.6
Total Current	39.9	44.9	48.4	51.8	51.5	50.4		53.2	49.0
Long-Term Debt	9.3	15.9	11.6	12.5	13.3	12.7		10.4	10.2
Deferred Taxes	.0	.0	.1	.0	.0	.2		.0	.0
All Other Non-Current	17.7	8.4	10.8	9.5	8.8	10.2		9.5	10.7
Net Worth	33.6	30.7	29.1	26.2	26.3	26.5		26.9	30.1
Total Liabilities & Net Worth	100.0	100.0	100.0	100.0	100.0	100.0		100.0	100.0
INCOME DATA									
Net Sales	100.0	100.0	100.0	100.0	100.0	100.0		100.0	100.0
Gross Profit									
Operating Expenses	88.7	75.2	69.2	69.8	69.7	71.7		73.9	72.6
Operating Profit	11.3	24.8	30.8	30.2	30.3	28.3		26.1	27.4
All Other Expenses (net)	-1.8	8.3	17.3	14.1	10.6	9.9		12.0	10.3
Profit Before Taxes	13.1	16.5	13.4	16.1	19.7	18.4		14.1	17.1
RATIOS									
Current	8.4	2.6	2.5	2.4	2.6	3.4		2.6	2.8
	2.1	1.9	1.5	1.4	1.5	1.6		1.5	1.5
	1.3	1.2	1.1	1.3	1.1	1.2		1.1	1.2
Quick	3.0	2.6	2.4	2.4	2.4	2.6		2.3	2.4
	1.5	1.8	1.4	1.4	1.5	1.4		1.3	1.4
	.2	1.2	.8	.8	.9	1.1		1.0	1.1
Sales/Receivables	0 UND	142 2.6	54 6.8	135 2.7	108 3.4	120 3.0		92 4.0	95 3.8
	0 UND	223 1.6	604 .6	1019 .4	864 .4	573 .6		633 .6	746 .5
	7 53.6	866 .4	1342 .3	1492 .2	1302 .3	1008 .4		1297 .3	1260 .3
Cost of Sales/Inventory									
Cost of Sales/Payables									
Sales/Working Capital	1.0	.9	.6	.6	.6	.8		.7	.8
	1.7	2.2	1.5	1.1	1.2	2.4		1.5	1.5
	32.0	10.9	6.9	2.8	6.0	3.9		5.3	4.0
EBIT/Interest	4.9	4.3	6.0	8.6	4.9	7.6		6.2	7.1
	(10) 2.5	(20) 2.4	(39) 2.3	(37) 3.2	(11) 4.0	(22) 3.0		(142) 2.6	(144) 3.1
	.8	1.5	1.5	1.7	1.9	2.3		1.7	1.8
Net Profit + Depr., Dep., Amort./Cur. Mat. L/T/D								19.0	7.9
								(22) 3.6	(17) .6
								.7	.1
Fixed/Worth	.0	.0	.0	.0	.0	.0		.0	.0
	.1	.1	.0	.1	.1	.1		.1	.1
	UND	1.5	.2	.3	.3	.4		.3	.3
Debt/Worth	.4	.9	1.4	1.6	2.4	1.4		1.5	1.4
	1.8	3.9	3.6	4.0	3.9	3.4		4.0	3.3
	UND	10.0	9.6	16.6	8.3	13.1		10.1	7.7
% Profit Before Taxes/Tangible Net Worth	51.2	65.9	33.1	42.6	54.6	49.4		48.3	44.6
	(13) 16.7	(26) 20.0	(67) 13.6	(66) 25.5	(15) 32.4	(29) 36.5		(194) 21.1	(196) 23.8
	5.1	6.3	4.4	9.0	11.4	17.7		6.9	9.6
% Profit Before Taxes/Total Assets	11.6	10.7	7.7	9.4	9.2	10.7		8.7	11.0
	3.7	5.5	3.0	3.7	6.7	7.8		3.8	5.1
	.2	3.1	.3	1.7	2.7	2.9		1.2	2.2
Sales/Net Fixed Assets	UND	169.1	200.1	72.2	61.0	60.4		115.7	103.7
	21.9	27.7	42.4	25.5	26.7	16.5		30.1	29.8
	6.5	12.9	13.6	9.6	5.9	9.6		11.7	11.8
Sales/Total Assets	5.5	1.6	.6	.6	.6	1.2		.8	.8
	.9	.7	.3	.3	.3	.4		.3	.3
	.3	.3	.2	.2	.2	.2		.2	.2
% Depr., Dep., Amort./Sales		.8	.4	.7	.8	.8		.5	.7
		(17) 1.6	(54) .9	(52) 1.1	(13) 1.4	(17) 1.6		(133) 1.2	(140) 1.3
		3.0	1.8	2.2	2.0	3.1		2.6	2.7
% Officers', Directors' Owners' Comp/Sales		7.3	4.7	4.3				3.7	2.5
		(10) 12.6	(15) 12.1	(14) 10.5				(53) 8.8	(37) 8.7
		24.8	22.0	23.9				19.4	15.2
Net Sales ($)	7541M	41334M	181255M	785730M	633275M	3522364M		2669274M	3435391M
Total Assets ($)	2666M	31964M	396022M	1638199M	1160925M	4906338M		4468946M	4823262M

M = $ thousand   MM = $ million
See Pages 11 through 21 for Explanation of Ratios and Data

Comparative Historical Data — Current Data Sorted by Sales

Type of Statement	4/1/04-3/31/05 ALL	4/1/05-3/31/06 ALL	4/1/06-3/31/07 ALL	0-1MM	1-3MM	3-5MM	5-10MM	10-25MM	25MM & OVER
Unqualified	82	62	81	10	11	12	13	13	22
Reviewed	29	28	27	3	15	4	4	1	
Compiled	35	25	24	14	7	2	1		
Tax Returns	23	19	25	13	4	3	4	1	
Other	67	75	79	13	21	7	5	11	22
				43 (4/1-9/30/06)			193 (10/1/06-3/31/07)		
NUMBER OF STATEMENTS	236	209	236	53	58	28	27	26	44
ASSETS	%	%	%	%	%	%	%	%	%
Cash & Equivalents	9.5	10.9	8.3	10.7	6.4	5.8	4.9	11.6	9.4
Trade Receivables (net)	62.4	62.4	60.2	45.1	67.8	64.9	62.6	61.3	63.5
Inventory	1.1	.6	.9	.1	.5	2.8	1.2	1.2	1.1
All Other Current	7.9	7.4	10.4	16.3	8.2	12.6	12.3	8.7	4.7
Total Current	80.9	81.3	79.8	72.1	82.8	86.0	81.1	82.8	78.7
Fixed Assets (net)	5.9	6.4	7.1	10.4	2.8	3.2	12.3	3.6	10.2
Intangibles (net)	1.7	1.4	2.1	1.3	2.6	1.3	.4	3.2	3.6
All Other Non-Current	11.5	10.8	10.9	16.2	11.7	9.5	6.2	10.3	7.5
Total	100.0	100.0	100.0	100.0	100.0	100.0	100.0	100.0	100.0
LIABILITIES									
Notes Payable-Short Term	35.8	32.9	35.4	39.7	31.5	44.9	44.6	33.3	24.9
Cur. Mat.-L.T.D.	2.5	2.6	2.3	2.0	2.1	1.3	3.1	3.1	2.6
Trade Payables	1.7	2.7	2.3	1.3	1.8	2.4	1.6	1.5	4.8
Income Taxes Payable	.1	.2	.2	.2	.4	.0	.0	.4	.1
All Other Current	8.8	11.0	8.8	4.2	10.0	9.4	12.2	10.1	9.3
Total Current	48.9	49.4	48.9	47.4	45.8	58.1	61.6	48.4	41.6
Long-Term Debt	10.4	11.4	12.5	12.7	11.1	9.7	16.2	10.7	14.6
Deferred Taxes	.1	.1	.1	.0	.0	.0	.0	.1	.1
All Other Non-Current	10.4	10.1	10.4	10.9	13.7	9.8	4.8	9.5	9.8
Net Worth	30.3	28.9	28.2	29.2	29.3	22.4	17.4	31.2	33.9
Total Liabilties & Net Worth	100.0	100.0	100.0	100.0	100.0	100.0	100.0	100.0	100.0
INCOME DATA									
Net Sales	100.0	100.0	100.0	100.0	100.0	100.0	100.0	100.0	100.0
Gross Profit									
Operating Expenses	73.6	71.3	71.8	71.0	68.0	74.3	73.6	67.2	77.6
Operating Profit	26.4	28.7	28.2	29.0	32.0	25.7	26.4	32.8	22.4
All Other Expenses (net)	10.7	13.8	12.5	14.6	15.1	14.4	13.2	9.7	6.9
Profit Before Taxes	15.7	14.9	15.7	14.4	16.9	11.3	13.2	23.1	15.5
RATIOS									
Current	2.8	3.2	2.6	2.9	2.6	1.8	1.6	2.5	4.1
	1.6	1.5	1.5	1.7	1.7	1.4	1.3	1.5	2.1
	1.2	1.2	1.2	1.1	1.3	1.1	1.0	1.2	1.3
Quick	2.4	2.9	2.4	2.7	2.5	1.5	1.6	2.3	3.8
	1.5	1.4	1.4	1.4	1.5	1.2	1.2	1.4	2.0
	1.1	1.1	1.1	.7	1.2	1.1	.4	1.2	1.3
Sales/Receivables	92 4.0	110 3.3	102 3.6	0 UND	212 1.7	66 5.6	34 10.6	90 4.1	108 3.4
	799 .5	725 .5	556 .7	258 1.4	910 .4	996 .4	616 .6	540 .7	187 2.0
	1280 .3	1342 .3	1337 .3	1324 .3	1503 .2	1492 .2	1398 .3	1362 .3	868 .4
Cost of Sales/Inventory									
Cost of Sales/Payables									
Sales/Working Capital	.6	.7	.7	.6	.5	.6	1.0	.7	.9
	1.3	1.5	1.4	1.4	.9	1.2	1.8	1.2	2.6
	3.5	4.5	5.0	12.0	3.8	4.9	27.2	3.9	5.2
EBIT/Interest	6.3	7.5	5.8	3.9	8.2	5.2	4.6	19.1	9.1
	(163) 2.5	(133) 2.8	(139) 2.9	(24) 2.3	(30) 2.9	(15) 2.9	(18) 2.2	(16) 3.8	(36) 3.0
	1.5	1.3	1.6	1.3	1.7	1.3	1.0	2.0	2.1
Net Profit + Depr., Dep., Amort./Cur. Mat. L/T/D	2.7	2.2	7.0						
	(17) .9	(14) .5	(15) 2.3						
	.3	.1	.3						
Fixed/Worth	.0	.0	.0	.0	.0	.0	.0	.0	.0
	.1	.1	.1	.0	.0	.1	.1	.1	.3
	.3	.3	.4	.7	.1	.7	.3	.2	.7
Debt/Worth	1.3	1.3	1.3	.7	1.4	1.6	2.3	1.3	.7
	3.3	3.6	3.6	3.9	3.5	4.4	4.2	3.5	2.9
	9.3	7.6	10.8	15.2	9.7	26.4	11.6	11.3	7.4
% Profit Before Taxes/Tangible Net Worth	46.0	43.9	44.0	49.4	33.4	66.6	37.9	67.6	50.6
	(221) 19.4	(194) 17.9	(216) 21.5	(47) 11.8	(54) 16.4	(26) 17.4	(25) 25.8	(24) 39.0	(40) 36.9
	5.6	4.8	7.6	3.8	7.4	7.0	12.5	11.8	18.7
% Profit Before Taxes/Total Assets	10.0	11.3	9.4	6.4	7.9	5.6	7.1	13.1	15.7
	3.8	3.9	4.3	3.4	3.8	2.4	3.1	6.5	9.3
	1.2	.6	1.5	.7	1.6	1.0	1.0	3.0	4.7
Sales/Net Fixed Assets	119.2	98.1	97.6	UND	132.3	122.9	58.0	65.5	47.7
	27.8	26.6	27.9	36.3	41.1	24.3	23.3	22.4	16.0
	10.9	11.8	10.8	10.8	15.7	10.0	8.3	8.1	7.8
Sales/Total Assets	.7	.8	.9	.6	.5	.7	1.0	.9	1.5
	.3	.3	.3	.3	.3	.3	.4	.3	.8
	.2	.2	.2	.2	.2	.2	.2	.2	.4
% Depr., Dep., Amort./Sales	.6	.6	.6	.7	.5	.3	.8	.6	.9
	(159) 1.6	(141) 1.6	(161) 1.1	(30) 1.2	(41) 1.0	(23) 1.1	(22) 1.2	(17) .8	(28) 1.9
	2.8	2.6	2.3	4.0	1.9	2.4	1.8	1.4	3.6
% Officers', Directors' Owners' Comp/Sales	5.5	6.7	6.5	14.2	6.8				
	(53) 13.1	(47) 12.6	(48) 12.3	(12) 19.1	(15) 12.5				
	26.6	21.5	22.9	25.2	23.7				
Net Sales ($)	3575833M	4045526M	5171499M	24684M	111679M	106363M	195531M	395448M	4337794M
Total Assets ($)	5620529M	7259289M	8136114M	111285M	426842M	408134M	621589M	1561610M	5006654M

M = $ thousand   MM = $ million
See Pages 11 through 21 for Explanation of Ratios and Data

Current Data Sorted by Assets   Comparative Historical Data

						Type of Statement		
10	41	144	147	39	40	Unqualified	225	427
4	1	5	11	2		Reviewed	15	12
3	10	10	4			Compiled	22	25
21	6	15	2		2	Tax Returns	29	28
17	22	36	47	12	12	Other	72	75
	80 (4/1-9/30/06)		583 (10/1/06-3/31/07)				4/1/02-3/31/03	4/1/03-3/31/04
0-500M	500M-2MM	2-10MM	10-50MM	50-100MM	100-250MM		ALL	ALL
55	80	210	211	53	54	NUMBER OF STATEMENTS	363	567
%	%	%	%	%	%	ASSETS	%	%
53.6	27.9	16.9	9.0	8.4	5.8	Cash & Equivalents	16.5	19.7
3.6	12.3	23.9	42.9	43.4	47.6	Trade Receivables (net)	23.9	34.8
.4	1.2	4.7	8.9	7.1	4.4	Inventory	10.0	6.3
8.2	18.1	31.9	17.5	25.3	16.9	All Other Current	23.3	18.3
65.7	59.6	77.4	78.3	84.1	74.8	Total Current	73.6	79.0
19.5	18.0	6.8	3.9	3.1	4.3	Fixed Assets (net)	8.6	7.1
3.8	1.8	2.0	.9	2.2	1.5	Intangibles (net)	3.0	2.2
11.0	20.7	13.8	16.8	10.5	19.4	All Other Non-Current	14.8	11.7
100.0	100.0	100.0	100.0	100.0	100.0	Total	100.0	100.0
						LIABILITIES		
18.9	25.5	41.3	32.9	31.8	29.8	Notes Payable-Short Term	43.9	29.3
.7	1.9	1.2	1.7	.1	1.6	Cur. Mat.-L.T.D.	3.5	1.6
5.3	5.8	9.6	25.0	27.6	24.0	Trade Payables	2.8	19.2
.0	.2	.2	.2	.1	.3	Income Taxes Payable	.5	.4
13.5	12.2	7.7	8.1	7.9	6.7	All Other Current	10.4	10.5
38.4	45.7	60.0	67.9	67.5	62.4	Total Current	61.1	61.0
6.2	9.4	5.7	8.4	9.5	15.5	Long-Term Debt	9.4	6.2
.0	.2	.3	.2	.5	.2	Deferred Taxes	.2	.3
3.7	1.1	2.9	3.1	2.3	2.6	All Other Non-Current	2.2	2.2
51.8	43.7	31.2	20.4	20.2	19.3	Net Worth	27.1	30.4
100.0	100.0	100.0	100.0	100.0	100.0	Total Liabilties & Net Worth	100.0	100.0
						INCOME DATA		
100.0	100.0	100.0	100.0	100.0	100.0	Net Sales	100.0	100.0
						Gross Profit		
91.9	85.4	79.8	75.4	73.9	64.6	Operating Expenses	76.0	77.0
8.1	14.6	20.2	24.6	26.1	35.4	Operating Profit	24.0	23.0
.9	5.5	11.7	15.1	13.0	17.0	All Other Expenses (net)	6.0	5.4
7.2	9.0	8.4	9.5	13.1	18.5	Profit Before Taxes	18.0	17.7
						RATIOS		
11.1	2.4	1.6	1.4	1.4	1.4		1.8	1.6
3.9	1.3	1.2	1.1	1.1	1.1	Current	1.1	1.2
1.4	.9	1.0	1.0	1.0	1.0		1.0	1.1
11.0	1.6	1.3	1.2	1.1	1.2		1.4	1.3
3.7	.8	.7	1.0	1.0	1.0	Quick	.8	1.1
1.2	.3	.1	.1	.3	.1		.1	.3
0 UND	0 UND	0 UND	4 90.7	7 51.4	3 105.4		0 UND	0 UND
0 UND	1 277.9	11 33.2	107 3.4	151 2.4	601 .6	Sales/Receivables	14 27.0	21 17.6
3 117.8	15 24.6	181 2.0	696 .5	888 .4	2000 .2		203 1.8	446 .8
						Cost of Sales/Inventory		
						Cost of Sales/Payables		
3.5	2.5	2.0	1.8	1.3	.8		2.2	2.4
9.2	15.7	6.1	7.2	4.1	2.9	Sales/Working Capital	5.7	5.2
81.0	-45.0	21.9	33.6	10.2	10.3		48.0	16.8
15.0	6.1	2.7	2.9	3.8	9.2		9.6	8.5
(26) 7.1	(57) 1.1	(144) 1.3	(120) 1.3	(31) 1.6	(24) 3.5	EBIT/Interest	(234) 3.7	(415) 3.9
.7	-.8	.7	.8	1.0	1.2		1.9	2.1
		12.2	4.3			Net Profit + Depr., Dep.,	24.2	97.2
	(27) 2.3	(23) .7				Amort./Cur. Mat. L/T/D	(30) 4.9	(55) 17.3
		-5.2	-3.0				.6	3.5
.0	.0	.0	.0	.1	.0		.0	.0
.2	.2	.1	.1	.1	.0	Fixed/Worth	.1	.1
.7	.8	.3	.4	.2	.2		.4	.3
.1	.5	1.3	3.1	4.1	2.5		1.5	1.4
.3	1.7	3.2	7.5	8.0	6.1	Debt/Worth	5.5	3.8
2.3	3.2	6.2	13.8	13.4	11.8		12.9	8.2
67.7	39.3	24.9	28.9	34.0	37.3	% Profit Before Taxes/Tangible	64.7	78.4
(47) 33.0	(75) 6.5	(203) 6.9	(209) 11.1	(50) 14.6	(52) 16.1	Net Worth	(341) 33.6	(542) 45.2
-12.8	-13.9	-7.0	-2.4	.4	4.1		11.6	17.3
50.8	16.3	6.2	4.6	6.4	6.1	% Profit Before Taxes/Total	11.9	17.7
23.0	2.2	1.6	1.5	1.7	3.2	Assets	4.8	8.2
-11.3	-4.7	-1.4	-.5	-.1	.4		1.7	3.0
197.8	102.9	102.4	99.3	55.0	115.5		80.3	88.2
56.8	20.2	34.7	36.0	28.0	66.8	Sales/Net Fixed Assets	31.4	34.8
20.4	8.7	13.2	18.9	16.2	17.7		14.2	16.0
10.2	2.4	1.1	.8	.6	.3		1.1	1.2
3.8	1.1	.5	.3	.4	.2	Sales/Total Assets	.3	.6
2.1	.5	.3	.2	.2	.1		.2	.3
.5	.6	.6	.5	.7	.3		.6	.4
(37) .8	(60) 1.5	(147) 1.1	(155) 1.1	(35) 1.1	(35) .6	% Depr., Dep., Amort./Sales	(245) 1.1	(424) .8
1.5	2.6	1.9	1.8	1.7	1.1		1.9	1.3
8.6	5.3	1.6	1.7	1.0	.8		7.3	3.7
(19) 13.9	(28) 10.5	(70) 5.1	(75) 3.7	(13) 1.5	(10) 5.8	% Officers', Directors' Owners' Comp/Sales	(89) 12.4	(183) 9.1
22.5	15.4	11.9	7.4	4.2	18.4		24.0	16.6
45205M	175194M	1191151M	3537073M	2106181M	3351507M	Net Sales ($)	4891252M	17971648M
10798M	98689M	1096664M	4933186M	3678398M	9010968M	Total Assets ($)	10790081M	17170549M

M = $ thousand   MM = $ million
See Pages 11 through 21 for Explanation of Ratios and Data

Comparative Historical Data   Current Data Sorted by Sales

Hist 1	Hist 2	Hist 3	Type of Statement	0-1MM	1-3MM	3-5MM	5-10MM	10-25MM	25MM & OVER
390	381	421	Unqualified	36	87	57	81	92	68
14	17	23	Reviewed	8	8	4	1	1	1
16	21	27	Compiled	13	9	1	1	2	1
53	52	46	Tax Returns	29	11	3	1	1	2
75	139	146	Other	31	40	15	19	21	20
4/1/04-3/31/05 ALL	4/1/05-3/31/06 ALL	4/1/06-3/31/07 ALL		80 (4/1-9/30/06)			583 (10/1/06-3/31/07)		
				0-1MM	1-3MM	3-5MM	5-10MM	10-25MM	25MM & OVER
548	610	663	NUMBER OF STATEMENTS	117	155	80	102	117	92
%	%	%	ASSETS	%	%	%	%	%	%
16.4	17.5	17.2	Cash & Equivalents	29.3	19.7	14.6	14.6	8.9	12.9
38.7	36.3	30.4	Trade Receivables (net)	15.3	22.6	23.3	33.3	47.2	44.0
5.2	5.2	5.4	Inventory	1.4	5.3	4.7	6.0	9.2	5.9
16.2	15.5	21.9	All Other Current	14.5	23.4	35.2	25.5	18.9	17.1
76.4	74.4	74.9	Total Current	60.6	71.1	77.9	79.4	84.3	80.0
7.5	8.6	7.8	Fixed Assets (net)	13.0	7.6	6.8	6.8	4.1	8.2
2.0	1.7	1.7	Intangibles (net)	3.3	1.5	1.3	1.2	.6	2.5
14.1	15.3	15.6	All Other Non-Current	23.1	19.8	14.0	12.6	10.9	9.4
100.0	100.0	100.0	Total	100.0	100.0	100.0	100.0	100.0	100.0
			LIABILITIES						
29.2	29.3	33.2	Notes Payable-Short Term	28.9	36.6	43.9	33.7	37.6	17.2
1.2	1.2	1.4	Cur. Mat.-L.T.D.	1.1	2.0	3.1	1.4	.3	.4
25.9	22.1	16.3	Trade Payables	2.7	5.6	6.8	21.3	28.3	38.9
.2	.2	.2	Income Taxes Payable	.1	.1	.2	.1	.2	.5
6.7	6.5	8.8	All Other Current	10.1	8.5	8.8	9.2	7.4	9.0
63.2	59.3	59.8	Total Current	43.0	52.7	62.8	65.7	73.9	65.9
6.7	6.5	8.1	Long-Term Debt	10.3	11.6	5.9	7.4	5.3	6.0
.2	.3	.2	Deferred Taxes	.2	.1	.4	.3	.1	.4
2.8	3.0	2.7	All Other Non-Current	3.3	4.4	2.1	1.7	1.7	2.1
27.1	30.9	29.1	Net Worth	43.3	31.2	28.7	24.9	19.0	25.6
100.0	100.0	100.0	Total Liabilties & Net Worth	100.0	100.0	100.0	100.0	100.0	100.0
			INCOME DATA						
100.0	100.0	100.0	Net Sales	100.0	100.0	100.0	100.0	100.0	100.0
			Gross Profit						
79.1	78.4	78.4	Operating Expenses	71.3	74.8	79.1	85.4	81.0	81.7
20.9	21.6	21.6	Operating Profit	28.7	25.2	20.9	14.6	19.0	18.3
7.7	8.8	11.7	All Other Expenses (net)	13.0	15.4	11.1	8.5	11.1	8.7
13.2	12.8	9.9	Profit Before Taxes	15.7	9.8	9.8	6.1	7.9	9.7
			RATIOS						
1.5	1.7	1.7	Current	4.9	2.3	1.5	1.5	1.2	1.4
1.2	1.2	1.2		1.6	1.3	1.1	1.2	1.1	1.1
1.0	1.1	1.0		1.0	1.0	1.0	1.0	1.0	1.0
1.3	1.4	1.4	Quick	4.3	1.6	1.3	1.3	1.1	1.2
1.1	1.1	1.0		1.1	.8	.5	1.0	1.0	1.0
.3	.3	.1		.2	.1	.1	.1	.1	.6
0 UND	0 UND	0 UND	Sales/Receivables	0 UND	0 UND	0 884.3	0 UND	3 112.4	9 42.6
70 5.2	28 12.9	15 24.1		0 UND	4 98.6	14 25.2	20 18.0	158 2.3	65 5.6
661 .6	541 .7	429 .9		96 3.8	239 1.5	197 1.9	423 .9	710 .5	501 .7
			Cost of Sales/Inventory						
			Cost of Sales/Payables						
2.2	2.2	2.0	Sales/Working Capital	1.2	1.4	2.3	2.2	3.2	4.1
5.3	6.4	6.4		5.8	3.6	6.1	6.5	7.5	10.2
19.4	23.7	33.6		-27.7	45.4	17.8	16.9	19.9	89.4
6.6	4.6	3.7	EBIT/Interest	8.6	5.2	2.4	2.2	3.1	5.1
(409) 2.3	(419) 2.1	(402) 1.4		(46) 2.9	(89) 1.3	(52) 1.3	(72) 1.4	(75) 1.3	(68) 1.5
1.2	1.1	.7		.0	.2	.9	.7	1.0	.7
23.7	17.6	11.9	Net Profit + Depr., Dep., Amort./Cur. Mat. L/T/D		2.9		12.1	17.4	34.8
(52) 7.3	(56) 4.2	(66) 2.1			(12) -3.5		(16) 1.6	(15) 2.1	(13) 5.5
1.8	.4	-1.4			-14.8		-.6	-3.3	.5
.0	.0	.0	Fixed/Worth	.0	.0	.0	.0	.1	.1
.1	.1	.1		.0	.1	.1	.1	.1	.2
.3	.4	.4		.4	.3	.4	.3	.3	.6
1.7	1.2	1.4	Debt/Worth	.2	1.2	1.3	2.0	3.4	1.8
4.6	4.0	4.1		1.4	3.2	4.7	4.1	7.6	5.2
9.4	8.5	9.9		4.5	9.7	9.1	7.6	12.6	12.0
45.7	46.3	33.0	% Profit Before Taxes/Tangible Net Worth	33.0	34.2	31.7	23.2	32.9	47.0
(525) 19.5	(591) 18.7	(636) 10.4		(108) 8.8	(145) 11.9	(79) 10.6	(100) 7.7	(116) 10.5	(88) 17.3
5.0	3.1	-4.0		-1.6	-2.3	.8	-10.8	-4.3	-13.0
9.0	9.7	7.0	% Profit Before Taxes/Total Assets	15.4	6.1	5.2	4.6	6.0	10.9
3.5	3.5	1.8		2.7	1.5	1.6	1.7	1.0	3.2
.7	.5	-.7		-1.0	-1.3	-.1	-1.9	-.6	-1.2
84.4	81.2	105.1	Sales/Net Fixed Assets	UND	237.3	75.1	48.9	65.5	77.8
32.0	31.3	36.0		56.8	38.2	30.7	26.8	36.8	41.6
14.2	14.3	15.3		9.1	13.7	15.5	13.4	20.3	19.3
.9	1.3	1.3	Sales/Total Assets	2.1	1.0	1.2	1.1	1.0	2.5
.5	.5	.5		.4	.4	.5	.5	.6	.8
.2	.2	.2		.1	.1	.2	.3	.2	.4
.5	.5	.5	% Depr., Dep., Amort./Sales	.6	.6	.4	.6	.6	.4
(376) 1.0	(437) 1.0	(469) 1.1		(64) 1.5	(96) 1.2	(59) 1.0	(85) 1.1	(93) 1.0	(72) .7
1.7	1.6	1.9		3.0	2.4	1.6	1.8	1.6	1.4
2.5	2.5	2.0	% Officers', Directors' Owners' Comp/Sales	6.2	4.9	5.2	3.1	1.4	.5
(170) 6.2	(184) 6.3	(215) 5.2		(33) 12.7	(42) 10.2	(19) 13.1	(42) 4.7	(47) 2.7	(32) .9
14.9	15.3	12.5		21.1	14.1	19.5	6.7	5.7	2.6
12095713M	10491280M	10406311M	Net Sales ($)	58467M	288595M	308533M	738002M	1905113M	7107601M
17345928M	16313259M	18828703M	Total Assets ($)	263674M	1228385M	1137456M	2157302M	6242596M	7799290M

M = $ thousand   MM = $ million
See Pages 11 through 21 for Explanation of Ratios and Data

Current Data Sorted by Assets | Comparative Historical Data

0-500M	500M-2MM	2-10MM	10-50MM	50-100MM	100-250MM	Type of Statement	4/1/02-3/31/03 ALL	4/1/03-3/31/04 ALL
	4	1	12	1	3	Unqualified	13	12
		1	1			Reviewed		2
1		1	2			Compiled		2
1	5	3				Tax Returns	1	3
1		3	2			Other	3	5
	15 (4/1-9/30/06)		27 (10/1/06-3/31/07)					
3	10	8	17	1	3	**NUMBER OF STATEMENTS**	17	24
%	%	%	%	%	%	**ASSETS**	%	%
	20.0		13.0			Cash & Equivalents	20.5	28.5
	31.9		42.7			Trade Receivables (net)	16.1	22.0
	.0		.3			Inventory	7.4	.3
	11.1		7.0			All Other Current	14.2	9.0
	63.0		63.0			Total Current	58.2	59.8
	22.9		20.3			Fixed Assets (net)	17.3	16.0
	.3		.9			Intangibles (net)	.1	2.2
	13.8		15.7			All Other Non-Current	24.4	21.9
	100.0		100.0			Total	100.0	100.0
						LIABILITIES		
	10.3		33.2			Notes Payable-Short Term	23.0	14.0
	.8		2.9			Cur. Mat.-L.T.D.	4.0	2.5
	3.8		7.0			Trade Payables	6.3	5.0
	.0		.2			Income Taxes Payable	.0	.1
	2.0		8.8			All Other Current	8.4	11.7
	16.8		52.0			Total Current	41.6	33.3
	20.5		15.0			Long-Term Debt	12.1	11.8
	.0		.1			Deferred Taxes	.0	.1
	8.6		2.4			All Other Non-Current	8.8	6.5
	54.1		30.5			Net Worth	37.5	48.3
	100.0		100.0			Total Liabilities & Net Worth	100.0	100.0
						INCOME DATA		
	100.0		100.0			Net Sales	100.0	100.0
						Gross Profit		
	59.5		68.4			Operating Expenses	78.5	81.2
	40.5		31.6			Operating Profit	21.5	18.8
	4.6		19.6			All Other Expenses (net)	12.8	4.1
	35.9		12.0			Profit Before Taxes	8.7	14.7
						RATIOS		
	12.1		1.9				2.7	4.3
	2.8		1.3			Current	1.3	2.0
	1.7		1.0				1.0	.9
	4.9		1.8				1.4	3.2
	2.8		1.2			Quick	.8	1.9
	1.5		.9				.3	.7
	0 UND		4 88.9				0 UND	1 337.9
	0 UND		61 6.0			Sales/Receivables	13 28.9	19 19.7
645 .6		1521 .2				121 3.0	132 2.8	
						Cost of Sales/Inventory		
						Cost of Sales/Payables		
	.4		1.3				1.3	1.6
	1.4		4.1			Sales/Working Capital	6.3	8.3
	9.0		NM				-26.3	NM
							11.9	8.1
						EBIT/Interest	(11) 4.4	(16) 2.7
							-2.7	.6
						Net Profit + Depr., Dep., Amort./Cur. Mat. L/T/D		
	.0		.0				.0	.0
	.1		.0			Fixed/Worth	.1	.0
	2.8		.9				.9	1.4
	.1		1.0				.5	.5
	.9		3.8			Debt/Worth	2.6	1.2
	2.6		17.1				5.2	4.2
			71.7				43.2	19.9
			15.9			% Profit Before Taxes/Tangible Net Worth	(16) 9.9	(23) 8.4
			8.6				-5.1	2.7
	15.8		8.1				6.9	10.6
	10.2		4.2			% Profit Before Taxes/Total Assets	3.1	5.4
	5.0		.7				-3.5	-.1
	UND		UND				UND	UND
	28.8		56.7			Sales/Net Fixed Assets	35.7	61.5
	2.3		2.6				1.5	4.3
	1.1		1.4				1.1	2.5
	.3		.4			Sales/Total Assets	.3	.8
	.2		.1				.2	.2
							.7	.8
						% Depr., Dep., Amort./Sales	(12) 2.2	(12) 1.4
							5.1	4.1
						% Officers', Directors' Owners' Comp/Sales		
2468M	8349M	10351M	424919M	9647M	152156M	Net Sales ($)	181237M	514370M
544M	11247M	36223M	405105M	77658M	491392M	Total Assets ($)	620572M	282591M

M = $ thousand   MM = $ million
See Pages 11 through 21 for Explanation of Ratios and Data

Comparative Historical Data / Current Data Sorted by Sales

			Type of Statement						
11	20	21	Unqualified	2	8		5	3	3
1	3	2	Reviewed		1				1
2	2	4	Compiled	1	1	1	1		
6	1	9	Tax Returns	9					
7	8	6	Other	3	1		1		1
4/1/04-3/31/05 ALL	4/1/05-3/31/06 ALL	4/1/06-3/31/07 ALL		0-1MM	15 (4/1-9/30/06) 1-3MM	3-5MM	27 (10/1/06-3/31/07) 5-10MM	10-25MM	25MM & OVER
27	34	42	NUMBER OF STATEMENTS	15	10	2	7	3	5
%	%	%	ASSETS	%	%	%	%	%	%
20.9	24.2	18.0	Cash & Equivalents	13.2	19.8				
39.7	29.4	37.5	Trade Receivables (net)	31.7	49.3				
3.4	8.4	.7	Inventory	.0	.0				
10.3	5.3	8.3	All Other Current	11.6	11.1				
74.3	67.3	64.4	Total Current	56.6	80.3				
5.5	17.1	21.7	Fixed Assets (net)	21.3	15.1				
.5	1.3	.5	Intangibles (net)	.2	.1				
19.8	14.3	13.4	All Other Non-Current	21.9	4.5				
100.0	100.0	100.0	Total	100.0	100.0				
			LIABILITIES						
31.0	21.1	21.3	Notes Payable-Short Term	16.3	39.1				
1.5	4.2	1.4	Cur. Mat.-L.T.D.	.5	.4				
4.3	5.8	4.7	Trade Payables	.1	7.3				
.0	.0	.1	Income Taxes Payable	.0	.0				
7.5	8.1	7.0	All Other Current	4.6	5.2				
44.4	39.3	34.6	Total Current	21.4	52.0				
20.3	15.9	23.6	Long-Term Debt	28.8	11.4				
.0	.0	.0	Deferred Taxes	.0	.0				
3.0	5.6	5.4	All Other Non-Current	8.9	4.3				
32.3	39.1	36.4	Net Worth	40.9	32.3				
100.0	100.0	100.0	Total Liabilities & Net Worth	100.0	100.0				
			INCOME DATA						
100.0	100.0	100.0	Net Sales	100.0	100.0				
			Gross Profit						
67.6	76.1	64.5	Operating Expenses	49.9	69.1				
32.4	23.9	35.5	Operating Profit	50.1	30.9				
16.7	9.7	16.9	All Other Expenses (net)	14.7	25.8				
15.7	14.2	18.6	Profit Before Taxes	35.4	5.2				
			RATIOS						
3.8	3.9	4.0		11.0	2.1				
1.6	1.8	1.8	Current	3.3	1.5				
1.1	1.1	1.2		1.2	1.2				
3.8	3.9	3.9		4.6	2.0				
1.4	1.1	1.8	Quick	3.3	1.5				
.2	.4	1.1		1.2	.9				
0 UND	2 161.6	0 UND		0 UND	0 UND				
246 1.5	24 15.3	32 11.6	Sales/Receivables	11 31.9	35 10.4				
1556 .2	446 .8	1139 .3		1105 .3	1916 .2				
			Cost of Sales/Inventory						
			Cost of Sales/Payables						
.3	.7	.5		.3	1.0				
1.2	6.6	2.5	Sales/Working Capital	1.3	4.3				
20.1	116.6	32.2		23.7	15.0				
11.6	9.1	8.2							
(15) 2.8	(20) 4.1	(18) 4.5	EBIT/Interest						
1.5	1.8	1.4							
			Net Profit + Depr., Dep., Amort./Cur. Mat. L/T/D						
.0	.0	.0		.0	.0				
.1	.1	.1	Fixed/Worth	.0	.1				
.5	1.3	1.5		2.1	8.3				
.9	.5	.8		.8	.7				
3.9	1.4	2.1	Debt/Worth	1.3	2.6				
12.7	7.8	17.1		5.8	371.1				
35.6	42.7	48.7	% Profit Before Taxes/Tangible	49.3					
(23) 11.1	(32) 18.7	(40) 15.5	Net Worth	35.9					
2.2	7.8	7.8		8.2					
8.2	10.0	9.9	% Profit Before Taxes/Total	14.9	6.1				
2.5	5.6	4.2	Assets	7.4	3.4				
.8	1.0	1.3		1.7	-.4				
UND	UND	UND		UND	UND				
59.3	50.1	29.3	Sales/Net Fixed Assets	38.5	35.0				
18.7	4.2	3.0		2.9	6.0				
.7	2.1	.8		.3	2.0				
.2	.8	.3	Sales/Total Assets	.2	.4				
.1	.2	.1		.2	.1				
1.1	.7	.7							
(15) 1.2	(16) 1.9	(22) 1.6	% Depr., Dep., Amort./Sales						
3.1	3.9	4.2							
10.4		1.5	% Officers', Directors'						
(10) 15.2		(11) 4.5	Owners' Comp/Sales						
28.7		13.1							
151089M	1068881M	607890M	Net Sales ($)	6242M	19375M	7875M	58064M	47324M	469010M
834322M	925355M	1022169M	Total Assets ($)	58904M	86357M	40049M	306159M	279266M	251434M

Current Data Sorted by Assets   Comparative Historical Data

0-500M	500M-2MM	2-10MM	10-50MM	50-100MM	100-250MM		ALL 4/1/02-3/31/03	ALL 4/1/03-3/31/04
						Type of Statement		
5	3	31	55	15	13	Unqualified	116	119
	5	18	9		1	Reviewed	40	43
2	6	13	5	2		Compiled	29	29
9	8	9	2			Tax Returns	21	32
4	10	27	27	13	8	Other	84	86
	46 (4/1-9/30/06)		252 (10/1/06-3/31/07)					
20	32	98	98	28	22	**NUMBER OF STATEMENTS**	290	309
%	%	%	%	%	%	**ASSETS**	%	%
24.6	11.0	10.5	8.1	3.2	4.3	Cash & Equivalents	7.8	10.3
21.8	33.0	45.2	52.2	60.8	56.0	Trade Receivables (net)	45.3	43.0
11.7	4.4	2.7	1.3	3.7	1.0	Inventory	3.7	3.2
10.2	13.7	9.8	14.8	8.8	15.6	All Other Current	12.5	10.5
68.3	62.1	68.1	76.4	76.5	77.0	Total Current	69.3	67.0
9.9	20.1	11.6	7.6	2.2	2.3	Fixed Assets (net)	9.2	11.8
3.9	5.8	1.6	2.3	5.7	1.1	Intangibles (net)	1.8	1.1
17.8	12.0	18.7	13.7	15.6	19.7	All Other Non-Current	19.6	20.1
100.0	100.0	100.0	100.0	100.0	100.0	Total	100.0	100.0
						LIABILITIES		
19.0	20.4	28.9	32.8	31.8	30.0	Notes Payable-Short Term	30.5	29.9
7.8	3.0	4.9	3.0	5.4	3.1	Cur. Mat.-L.T.D.	4.0	3.6
4.2	4.5	5.1	3.8	4.2	2.9	Trade Payables	2.7	3.0
.5	.0	.2	.2	.0	.1	Income Taxes Payable	.2	.4
14.2	16.5	9.6	9.9	12.1	12.5	All Other Current	10.8	9.9
45.6	44.4	48.8	49.8	53.5	48.5	Total Current	48.2	46.9
11.7	24.1	14.6	16.3	22.9	26.7	Long-Term Debt	18.1	18.2
.6	.0	.2	.2	.0	.0	Deferred Taxes	.4	.4
9.7	7.2	12.0	8.3	5.0	2.6	All Other Non-Current	7.1	7.9
32.4	24.3	24.4	25.4	18.6	22.1	Net Worth	26.2	26.6
100.0	100.0	100.0	100.0	100.0	100.0	Total Liabilities & Net Worth	100.0	100.0
						INCOME DATA		
100.0	100.0	100.0	100.0	100.0	100.0	Net Sales	100.0	100.0
						Gross Profit		
88.5	67.6	69.8	63.8	53.3	50.3	Operating Expenses	68.0	66.9
11.5	32.4	30.2	36.2	46.7	49.7	Operating Profit	32.0	33.1
7.0	16.4	14.5	16.5	26.1	28.0	All Other Expenses (net)	16.1	13.7
4.5	16.0	15.7	19.6	20.6	21.7	Profit Before Taxes	15.8	19.4
						RATIOS		
3.1	7.0	2.1	2.5	2.7	3.9		2.4	2.6
1.3	1.4	1.4	1.4	1.4	1.7	Current	1.3	1.3
.9	.8	1.0	1.1	1.1	1.1		1.0	1.0
2.9	5.2	1.8	2.2	1.7	3.8		1.9	1.9
1.1	1.2	1.2	1.3	1.3	1.1	Quick	1.2	1.2
.2	.3	.5	.7	1.0	.4		.4	.4
0 UND	0 UND	6 60.3	15 24.5	12 30.0	0 UND		14 26.1	3 136.1
0 UND	33 11.2	172 2.1	836 .4	1536 .2	1683 .2	Sales/Receivables	302 1.2	245 1.5
78 4.7	448 .8	948 .4	1778 .2	2000 .2	2000 .1		1418 .3	1450 .3
						Cost of Sales/Inventory		
						Cost of Sales/Payables		
2.5	1.1	.8	.5	.4	.4		.6	.5
7.2	2.1	2.2	1.0	1.1	1.7	Sales/Working Capital	1.5	1.9
NM	-28.4	-175.9	5.1	9.9	4.8		34.3	NM
	3.9	7.5	4.7	5.6			5.5	7.4
	(13) .9	(61) 2.5	(43) 2.3	(11) 2.8		EBIT/Interest	(149) 2.6	(177) 3.0
	-.6	1.2	1.3	1.7			1.4	1.6
			1.7			Net Profit + Depr., Dep.,	12.2	8.3
		(10) .4				Amort./Cur. Mat. L/T/D	(18) 3.1	(18) 1.0
			.1				.6	.2
.0	.0	.0	.0	.0	.0		.0	.0
.1	.1	.1	.0	.1	.0	Fixed/Worth	.0	.0
UND	2.3	.8	.2	.3	.1		.4	.5
.3	1.8	1.4	2.1	2.5	2.4		1.5	1.6
3.0	4.3	3.6	3.3	6.4	5.4	Debt/Worth	4.2	3.8
UND	37.7	13.5	7.8	36.6	15.5		9.4	8.8
82.3	44.1	42.1	32.8	35.4	25.1	% Profit Before Taxes/Tangible	40.8	39.8
(15) 14.3	(26) 17.6	(85) 19.6	(91) 18.3	(23) 27.2	(21) 13.5	Net Worth	(270) 15.0	(286) 18.7
.0	-.8	-7.4	6.9	11.6	10.0		4.3	7.3
13.2	7.3	9.7	6.9	6.6	4.2	% Profit Before Taxes/Total	7.5	8.3
4.7	4.0	3.3	3.3	3.9	3.0	Assets	2.7	3.9
-5.2	-1.4	.8	1.2	2.1	1.5		.8	1.3
UND	UND	776.2	157.7	225.8	999.8		165.1	227.6
136.8	50.3	33.1	42.8	42.0	53.7	Sales/Net Fixed Assets	40.1	36.7
31.1	3.0	9.6	10.9	13.6	18.8		8.4	8.4
3.7	.9	.8	.4	.3	.1		.5	.6
1.1	.3	.4	.2	.2	.1	Sales/Total Assets	.2	.2
.4	.1	.2	.1	.1	.1		.1	.1
	.6	.8	.8	.7	.5		.6	.7
	(15) 1.3	(69) 1.6	(59) 1.2	(19) .9	(13) 1.4	% Depr., Dep., Amort./Sales	(184) 1.4	(193) 1.7
	22.7	3.1	3.1	1.2	2.8		3.4	3.5
		7.4	5.3			% Officers', Directors'	4.1	4.0
	(21) 10.9	(14) 6.6				Owners' Comp/Sales	(47) 9.5	(58) 10.5
	22.3	19.3					18.5	26.5
10499M	59054M	510374M	959602M	748990M	1258681M	Net Sales ($)	3401660M	3195381M
4119M	37180M	546562M	2361333M	1963874M	3415464M	Total Assets ($)	8172679M	8755121M

Comparative Historical Data			Type of Statement	Current Data Sorted by Sales					
143	103	122	Unqualified	14	28	13	34	19	14
41	26	33	Reviewed	8	14	5	2	3	1
24	16	26	Compiled	10	9	2	2	1	2
23	22	28	Tax Returns	17	7	2	2		2
93	116	89	Other	21	16	6	16	18	11
4/1/04-3/31/05 ALL	4/1/05-3/31/06 ALL	4/1/06-3/31/07 ALL		46 (4/1-9/30/06)			252 (10/1/06-3/31/07)		
				0-1MM	1-3MM	3-5MM	5-10MM	10-25MM	25MM & OVER
324	283	298	NUMBER OF STATEMENTS	70	74	28	54	44	28
%	%	%	ASSETS	%	%	%	%	%	%
10.8	8.4	9.6	Cash & Equivalents	11.8	8.5	7.0	10.6	7.9	10.3
45.9	47.2	46.9	Trade Receivables (net)	34.0	49.2	58.7	55.5	55.2	31.4
3.1	2.6	3.0	Inventory	3.7	3.0	1.8	1.0	3.3	5.9
10.3	10.7	12.2	All Other Current	13.0	11.9	8.7	10.6	11.1	19.4
70.1	68.9	71.7	Total Current	62.5	72.6	76.2	77.6	77.4	66.9
11.4	12.2	9.5	Fixed Assets (net)	11.0	10.0	9.9	7.7	8.7	9.0
1.3	1.1	2.8	Intangibles (net)	3.1	1.5	.7	1.9	4.1	7.0
17.2	17.7	16.1	All Other Non-Current	23.5	15.9	13.2	12.8	9.7	17.1
100.0	100.0	100.0	Total	100.0	100.0	100.0	100.0	100.0	100.0
			LIABILITIES						
29.5	28.1	29.0	Notes Payable-Short Term	26.7	30.7	36.1	30.5	29.5	19.0
4.0	5.3	4.2	Cur. Mat.-L.T.D.	5.0	3.9	4.7	5.3	3.6	1.6
4.6	3.9	4.3	Trade Payables	2.6	2.4	2.4	5.5	6.4	9.9
.3	.3	.2	Income Taxes Payable	.2	.1	.0	.3	.3	.1
8.0	8.7	11.2	All Other Current	9.6	8.4	12.8	9.0	16.8	16.4
46.4	46.2	48.9	Total Current	44.0	45.5	56.0	50.6	56.6	47.1
21.4	20.3	17.7	Long-Term Debt	18.2	16.8	14.0	17.7	20.2	18.2
.3	.3	.2	Deferred Taxes	.4	.0	.0	.2	.4	.0
7.2	8.2	8.8	All Other Non-Current	10.9	8.9	6.0	5.0	6.0	17.4
24.8	25.0	24.5	Net Worth	26.4	28.8	24.0	26.6	16.8	17.3
100.0	100.0	100.0	Total Liabilties & Net Worth	100.0	100.0	100.0	100.0	100.0	100.0
			INCOME DATA						
100.0	100.0	100.0	Net Sales	100.0	100.0	100.0	100.0	100.0	100.0
			Gross Profit						
68.4	66.2	65.9	Operating Expenses	60.2	64.1	75.9	62.9	61.9	86.6
31.6	33.8	34.1	Operating Profit	39.8	35.9	24.1	37.1	38.1	13.4
13.2	15.6	17.0	All Other Expenses (net)	19.8	18.5	14.9	15.4	19.7	6.5
18.5	18.2	17.2	Profit Before Taxes	20.0	17.4	9.2	21.7	18.4	6.9
			RATIOS						
3.3	2.9	2.6	Current	3.4	3.0	1.8	2.5	2.3	3.6
1.4	1.4	1.4		1.4	1.4	1.5	1.4	1.4	1.3
1.0	1.1	1.1		1.0	1.1	1.2	1.1	1.0	1.0
2.8	2.6	2.2	Quick	2.7	2.6	1.7	2.3	2.1	1.3
1.3	(282) 1.3	1.2		1.2	1.3	1.3	1.3	1.1	.9
.6	.5	.5		.2	.8	.5	.7	.5	.5
11 34.3	8 45.6	5 77.8	Sales/Receivables	0 UND	26 14.3	25 14.7	30 12.3	19 19.1	3 116.8
287 1.3	291 1.3	227 1.6		30 12.0	373 1.0	845 .4	851 .4	368 1.0	16 22.3
1576 .2	1542 .2	1436 .3		1091 .3	1599 .2	1437 .3	1778 .2	1745 .2	105 3.5
			Cost of Sales/Inventory						
			Cost of Sales/Payables						
.5	.5	.6	Sales/Working Capital	.7	.5	.6	.5	.7	3.0
1.7	1.4	1.8		2.1	1.1	1.2	1.4	2.2	9.4
34.0	16.9	12.2		16.8	7.9	12.7	4.7	15.3	574.1
6.1	5.4	6.0	EBIT/Interest	6.9	4.2	3.2	8.6	7.0	8.0
(176) 3.2	(150) 2.9	(141) 2.5		(20) 1.7	(35) 2.5	(17) 2.1	(21) 2.6	(24) 3.7	(24) 2.8
1.6	1.4	1.1		.7	1.1	.9	1.3	1.6	.9
4.2	4.1	3.1	Net Profit + Depr., Dep., Amort./Cur. Mat. L/T/D						
(26) 2.2	(26) 1.3	(22) 1.1							
.4	.1	.3							
.0	.0	.0	Fixed/Worth	.0	.0	.0	.0	.0	.1
.1	.0	.0		.0	.0	.0	.1	.1	.4
.5	.5	.4		.4	.3	.3	.4	.2	-.6
1.7	1.8	1.7	Debt/Worth	1.8	1.6	1.5	1.5	2.5	1.5
3.8	3.7	4.0		4.2	3.0	4.1	4.2	4.7	5.2
9.6	10.2	12.6		15.6	8.4	14.1	12.0	12.3	-9.6
38.3	32.7	36.7	% Profit Before Taxes/Tangible Net Worth	48.3	28.6	35.6	34.7	52.7	38.9
(298) 20.5	(263) 20.0	(261) 19.2		(63) 14.0	(67) 16.7	(24) 11.4	(51) 23.5	(38) 28.8	(18) 24.7
7.4	7.7	7.2		2.8	7.1	1.2	11.3	18.8	-1.2
7.7	7.0	7.9	% Profit Before Taxes/Total Assets	7.3	6.4	6.2	8.0	10.2	12.7
3.6	3.5	3.4		2.7	3.6	1.8	3.8	3.9	4.9
1.4	1.1	1.0		.1	1.1	-.5	1.5	2.1	-1.0
177.7	288.0	510.1	Sales/Net Fixed Assets	UND	999.8	313.5	152.1	105.2	120.0
32.9	35.7	46.9		122.2	30.1	34.6	48.3	32.3	49.3
6.5	7.9	11.7		13.8	8.3	12.8	8.8	18.4	11.8
.7	.5	.6	Sales/Total Assets	.4	.5	.6	.4	1.0	2.6
.2	.2	.3		.2	.2	.3	.2	.3	1.6
.1	.1	.1		.1	.1	.2	.1	.1	.9
.7	.6	.7	% Depr., Dep., Amort./Sales	.7	.9	.6	.7	.7	.4
(206) 1.6	(181) 1.4	(181) 1.3		(26) 1.3	(45) 1.5	(20) 1.2	(34) 1.0	(32) 1.2	(24) 1.0
3.8	4.2	2.7		22.9	2.9	2.4	4.1	1.9	2.8
2.3	3.1	6.1	% Officers', Directors' Owners' Comp/Sales	10.2	7.8				
(57) 9.2	(44) 8.8	(54) 10.8		(15) 25.1	(16) 10.8				
18.6	17.7	25.2		35.3	22.5				
7427386M	4405958M	3547200M	Net Sales ($)	28822M	142047M	101780M	396384M	699722M	2178445M
10029244M	8214479M	8328532M	Total Assets ($)	204040M	736493M	467325M	2074961M	3059420M	1786293M

M = $ thousand   MM = $ million
See Pages 11 through 21 for Explanation of Ratios and Data

Current Data Sorted by Assets   Comparative Historical Data

						Type of Statement		
5	15	38	32	8	7	Unqualified	60	90
	1	1	2			Reviewed	7	7
5	2	6	2	1		Compiled	6	22
18	9	4	2			Tax Returns	11	24
22	16	19	17	3	4	Other	19	36
	30 (4/1-9/30/06)		207 (10/1/06-3/31/07)				4/1/02-3/31/03	4/1/03-3/31/04
0-500M	500M-2MM	2-10MM	10-50MM	50-100MM	100-250MM		ALL	ALL
50	43	68	53	12	11	NUMBER OF STATEMENTS	103	179
%	%	%	%	%	%	ASSETS	%	%
49.7	27.5	17.2	13.1	11.5	6.9	Cash & Equivalents	20.5	24.2
10.0	21.7	27.6	32.5	17.9	15.2	Trade Receivables (net)	24.2	20.5
.0	1.7	8.7	4.9	15.6	17.4	Inventory	5.0	3.0
3.0	11.8	18.3	24.7	22.3	20.5	All Other Current	23.9	18.8
62.7	62.8	71.8	75.2	67.3	60.0	Total Current	73.6	66.5
23.0	20.1	10.8	6.9	5.9	13.2	Fixed Assets (net)	13.0	14.1
2.7	1.4	.9	3.5	11.5	.3	Intangibles (net)	1.2	1.1
11.6	15.8	16.6	14.4	15.3	26.4	All Other Non-Current	12.2	18.4
100.0	100.0	100.0	100.0	100.0	100.0	Total	100.0	100.0
						LIABILITIES		
17.0	20.8	42.9	51.1	42.8	53.0	Notes Payable-Short Term	37.3	31.3
4.2	1.4	.8	1.8	.5	1.8	Cur. Mat.-L.T.D.	2.9	3.7
3.7	4.3	4.1	3.2	3.0	2.3	Trade Payables	4.3	3.6
2.5	.0	.3	.2	.1	.1	Income Taxes Payable	.8	.2
10.6	9.8	10.9	11.8	12.9	6.7	All Other Current	9.3	11.9
38.0	36.3	59.0	68.1	59.1	63.8	Total Current	54.6	50.8
10.5	9.5	11.3	9.4	11.0	16.7	Long-Term Debt	9.6	7.8
.0	.2	.2	.2	.1	.0	Deferred Taxes	.2	.1
5.6	1.7	3.1	2.7	2.0	2.0	All Other Non-Current	2.4	3.8
45.9	52.3	26.4	19.6	27.7	17.5	Net Worth	33.2	37.6
100.0	100.0	100.0	100.0	100.0	100.0	Total Liabilties & Net Worth	100.0	100.0
						INCOME DATA		
100.0	100.0	100.0	100.0	100.0	100.0	Net Sales	100.0	100.0
						Gross Profit		
88.3	87.6	80.0	76.0	87.2	73.7	Operating Expenses	75.7	79.3
11.7	12.4	20.0	24.0	12.8	26.3	Operating Profit	24.3	20.7
2.8	3.2	7.6	10.1	5.8	18.2	All Other Expenses (net)	5.2	3.7
8.9	9.2	12.4	13.8	7.0	8.2	Profit Before Taxes	19.1	16.9
						RATIOS		
4.9	7.9	1.4	1.4	2.1	1.3		2.3	2.5
2.8	2.1	1.1	1.1	1.0	1.0	Current	1.3	1.2
.9	1.1	1.0	1.0	.9	.2		1.0	1.0
4.9	6.7	1.2	1.2	1.1	.6		1.7	2.1
2.8	1.6	.8	.9	.3	.1	Quick	1.0	1.0
.8	.6	.2	.1	.1	.0		.1	.3
0 UND	0 UND	0 UND	1 617.9	7 51.7	0 UND		0 UND	0 UND
0 UND	6 62.1	11 33.3	18 19.9	21 17.4	12 29.3	Sales/Receivables	9 41.5	5 79.0
4 82.2	52 7.0	281 1.3	562 .6	83 4.4	23 15.6		97 3.8	66 5.6
						Cost of Sales/Inventory		
						Cost of Sales/Payables		
6.8	3.2	2.3	.8	4.2	2.2		1.5	3.0
14.6	10.5	6.4	7.0	22.0	21.1	Sales/Working Capital	7.4	11.7
-111.6	47.5	-44.0	NM	-30.3	-.5		36.7	-310.7
37.5	20.6	5.0	8.5	4.1			9.8	33.2
(28) 9.9	(31) 1.1	(50) 1.6	(36) 2.0	(10) 1.8		EBIT/Interest	(69) 4.7	(111) 5.0
-1.8	-.9	.5	1.0	1.2			2.7	2.2
						Net Profit + Depr., Dep.,	18.7	49.0
						Amort./Cur. Mat. L/T/D	(12) 5.3	(11) 9.0
							1.9	5.0
.0	.0	.0	.0	.1	.1		.0	.0
.3	.2	.1	.2	.2	.1	Fixed/Worth	.1	.2
1.3	1.0	.7	.7	1.1	1.3		.4	.5
.2	.2	2.0	2.9	1.9	3.2		.9	.5
.5	.9	4.8	7.2	8.4	10.6	Debt/Worth	2.7	2.6
2.6	2.4	7.1	13.1	19.2	71.6		10.2	7.7
113.8	33.7	47.4	50.7	19.1	27.5	% Profit Before Taxes/Tangible	77.7	92.1
(43) 61.5	(42) 6.3	(67) 16.0	(49) 15.3	(10) 14.1	13.1	Net Worth	(99) 32.7	(170) 39.1
-2.7	-4.2	-2.9	1.9	-1.3	-35.9		15.5	12.9
66.0	23.1	10.3	5.8	6.7	6.1	% Profit Before Taxes/Total	17.0	33.3
40.5	4.3	3.9	2.2	2.0	1.6	Assets	6.9	9.5
-2.2	-1.6	-.3	-.2	.4	-.5		2.6	2.5
173.7	157.8	81.8	59.8	109.4	82.9		107.7	83.6
40.0	33.7	24.2	30.4	21.0	23.2	Sales/Net Fixed Assets	30.1	31.1
14.4	9.4	9.5	14.1	9.5	13.1		16.6	16.3
8.3	5.2	1.1	.8	1.0	.7		2.5	3.6
5.2	2.6	.6	.4	.4	.3	Sales/Total Assets	.6	1.3
3.4	1.0	.4	.2	.2	.1		.2	.4
.3	.4	.6	.6				.5	.5
(26) .6	(30) .9	(50) 1.3	(37) 1.2			% Depr., Dep., Amort./Sales	(70) 1.0	(130) .8
1.2	2.2	1.9	1.8				1.6	1.5
7.0	1.4	1.4				% Officers', Directors'	5.5	4.8
(24) 13.6	(18) 7.5	(13) 3.0				Owners' Comp/Sales	(25) 14.2	(46) 8.7
21.6	12.3	8.6					24.3	17.2
50142M	139701M	353602M	1442763M	1343629M	4644827M	Net Sales ($)	790544M	3443591M
9623M	46023M	348511M	1216530M	893764M	1775574M	Total Assets ($)	2085669M	3657573M

M = $ thousand   MM = $ million
See Pages 11 through 21 for Explanation of Ratios and Data

Comparative Historical Data / Current Data Sorted by Sales

4/1/04-3/31/05 ALL	4/1/05-3/31/06 ALL	4/1/06-3/31/07 ALL	Type of Statement	30 (4/1-9/30/06) 0-1MM	1-3MM	3-5MM	207 (10/1/06-3/31/07) 5-10MM	10-25MM	25MM & OVER
88	86	105	Unqualified	10	26	18	17	22	12
7	9	4	Reviewed	2	1		1		
17	13	16	Compiled	7	3	3	1		2
31	42	31	Tax Returns	14	13	2	2		
46	62	81	Other	22	22	8	10	9	10
189	212	237	NUMBER OF STATEMENTS	55	65	31	31	31	24
%	%	%	**ASSETS**	%	%	%	%	%	%
24.0	23.7	24.2	Cash & Equivalents	37.5	24.2	26.0	22.7	8.1	14.5
19.2	19.0	22.8	Trade Receivables (net)	18.3	22.3	29.0	25.8	24.3	21.0
6.3	4.7	5.5	Inventory	1.8	5.5	5.4	4.6	8.4	11.7
18.3	19.7	15.6	All Other Current	6.0	12.9	13.2	24.7	25.3	24.3
67.8	67.1	68.2	Total Current	63.6	64.8	73.6	77.8	66.2	71.6
16.1	15.0	14.0	Fixed Assets (net)	17.2	15.0	10.4	12.2	10.4	15.9
1.7	1.1	2.4	Intangibles (net)	2.3	2.0	.2	1.6	7.2	1.8
14.4	16.7	15.3	All Other Non-Current	17.0	18.2	15.8	8.4	16.2	10.8
100.0	100.0	100.0	Total	100.0	100.0	100.0	100.0	100.0	100.0
			LIABILITIES						
31.2	29.4	35.7	Notes Payable-Short Term	21.0	33.0	32.7	48.9	55.0	38.7
3.7	2.4	1.9	Cur. Mat.-L.T.D.	2.1	2.1	.7	1.5	1.0	3.9
3.8	4.1	3.7	Trade Payables	1.0	4.2	4.0	4.0	1.6	10.3
.4	.2	.7	Income Taxes Payable	2.3	.1	.5	.0	.3	.3
13.3	9.7	10.7	All Other Current	8.1	9.4	14.0	12.8	9.9	14.8
52.4	45.6	52.7	Total Current	34.6	48.8	51.9	67.2	67.8	67.8
10.7	13.1	10.6	Long-Term Debt	17.3	7.4	14.0	4.1	11.4	7.4
.1	.2	.1	Deferred Taxes	.0	.1	.0	.2	.4	.3
1.9	4.4	3.2	All Other Non-Current	2.4	6.8	1.4	2.2	1.0	1.4
34.9	36.7	33.3	Net Worth	45.8	36.9	32.6	26.2	19.4	23.1
100.0	100.0	100.0	Total Liabilities & Net Worth	100.0	100.0	100.0	100.0	100.0	100.0
			INCOME DATA						
100.0	100.0	100.0	Net Sales	100.0	100.0	100.0	100.0	100.0	100.0
			Gross Profit						
86.4	82.4	82.3	Operating Expenses	70.5	86.1	90.7	79.1	82.0	92.6
13.6	17.6	17.7	Operating Profit	29.5	13.9	9.3	20.9	18.0	7.4
4.3	4.9	6.7	All Other Expenses (net)	10.2	5.6	2.8	6.7	9.5	3.7
9.3	12.8	11.0	Profit Before Taxes	19.3	8.3	6.5	14.2	8.5	3.7
			RATIOS						
2.5	3.1	2.6		5.9	3.1	3.0	1.4	1.3	1.2
1.2	1.4	1.2	Current	2.6	1.3	1.2	1.1	1.0	1.0
1.0	1.0	1.0		1.1	.9	1.1	1.0	.9	.9
2.0	2.7	2.4		5.9	2.7	2.8	1.4	1.0	1.0
(188) 1.0	1.1	1.0	Quick	2.3	1.0	1.1	.6	.3	.5
.2	.2	.3		1.0	.4	.3	.1	.1	.1
0 UND	0 UND	0 UND		0 UND	0 UND	0 UND	0 UND	6 64.5	5 71.0
6 64.3	6 60.5	8 44.8	Sales/Receivables	0 UND	3 106.9	14 26.3	6 62.1	18 19.9	13 28.3
55 6.6	70 5.2	110 3.3		111 3.3	98 3.7	499 .7	130 2.8	201 1.8	29 12.7
			Cost of Sales/Inventory						
			Cost of Sales/Payables						
3.6	2.4	3.1		1.5	3.1	2.1	3.8	7.0	9.3
12.8	8.3	11.0	Sales/Working Capital	6.6	10.1	7.8	7.6	29.0	23.0
197.5	71.8	-155.0		53.1	-59.6	45.1	26.0	-12.9	-62.5
17.1	7.9	10.6		34.5	10.0	13.4	7.8	8.4	5.0
(138) 3.2	(138) 2.8	(161) 1.8	EBIT/Interest	(26) 6.4	(46) 1.6	(18) 1.6	(26) 2.2	(24) 1.7	(21) 1.6
1.1	1.3	.7		1.5	.1	-.1	1.0	.9	.5
12.4	2.5	15.4							
(13) .5	(18) .5	(14) 2.0	Net Profit + Depr., Dep., Amort./Cur. Mat. L/T/D						
.2	-.1	-1.6							
.1	.0	.0		.0	.0	.0	.0	.1	.2
.2	.2	.2	Fixed/Worth	.1	.2	.2	.1	.4	.3
.8	.7	.9		.7	1.1	.6	.8	1.3	1.9
.7	.6	.7		.2	.7	.9	2.0	4.0	1.4
2.7	2.4	3.0	Debt/Worth	.9	2.4	3.8	3.7	6.7	8.1
8.9	7.0	8.1		3.6	6.3	6.8	7.6	16.1	20.2
63.8	64.4	56.4		98.3	48.3	33.5	79.2	46.3	27.6
(179) 22.2	(201) 26.4	(222) 16.2	% Profit Before Taxes/Tangible Net Worth	(51) 19.2	(60) 12.5	(30) 17.2	(30) 31.7	(29) 11.7	(22) 12.6
1.9	5.6	-2.1		3.7	-18.1	1.2	5.1	-13.0	-44.6
21.4	19.6	16.7		55.1	19.3	10.5	22.5	8.8	7.2
4.7	6.2	4.0	% Profit Before Taxes/Total Assets	7.0	3.7	2.5	6.6	1.6	2.0
.4	1.2	-.6		1.3	-2.6	.3	.8	-.7	-5.6
94.9	84.6	105.7		UND	88.5	62.8	114.1	48.6	54.9
26.0	29.3	33.2	Sales/Net Fixed Assets	49.3	30.2	24.4	30.3	26.8	33.1
11.8	10.7	12.3		7.2	11.6	13.2	13.8	9.2	15.5
4.5	3.7	3.6		5.2	4.0	3.1	2.6	1.7	9.4
1.1	1.1	.9	Sales/Total Assets	1.9	1.0	.6	.8	.8	1.0
.4	.3	.4		.2	.4	.3	.4	.3	.4
.4	.5	.5		.4	.4	.6	.4	.6	.6
(136) 1.0	(152) 1.0	(156) 1.1	% Depr., Dep., Amort./Sales	(27) .9	(45) 1.0	(24) 1.1	(21) 1.1	(23) 1.2	(16) 1.2
2.1	1.9	1.8		1.9	1.9	1.6	1.7	1.9	1.9
5.3	3.9	2.7		5.2	5.0				
(64) 12.4	(59) 7.7	(65) 9.5	% Officers', Directors' Owners' Comp/Sales	(17) 12.7	(26) 10.7				
17.4	16.9	13.8		15.0	14.4				
4884116M	5790103M	7974664M	Net Sales ($)	30158M	121992M	120915M	203504M	503838M	6994257M
3166232M	3708835M	4290025M	Total Assets ($)	110203M	253254M	336296M	400956M	1225594M	1963722M

M = $ thousand   MM = $ million
See Pages 11 through 21 for Explanation of Ratios and Data

Current Data Sorted by Assets

Comparative Historical Data

						Type of Statement		
	2	5	4	1	3	Unqualified	4	13
	2	3				Reviewed	3	3
	1	1				Compiled	1	1
						Tax Returns	1	
3	1	7	4	4	2	Other	9	10
	7 (4/1-9/30/06)		36 (10/1/06-3/31/07)				4/1/02-3/31/03	4/1/03-3/31/04
0-500M	500M-2MM	2-10MM	10-50MM	50-100MM	100-250MM		ALL	ALL
3	6	16	5	5	5	NUMBER OF STATEMENTS	18	27
%	%	%	%	%	%	ASSETS	%	%
		33.5				Cash & Equivalents	36.8	25.2
		14.9				Trade Receivables (net)	18.9	21.3
		4.6				Inventory	1.9	1.3
		14.4				All Other Current	7.6	9.7
		67.4				Total Current	65.2	57.4
		18.7				Fixed Assets (net)	17.7	17.8
		3.2				Intangibles (net)	5.7	15.0
		10.8				All Other Non-Current	11.4	9.8
		100.0				Total	100.0	100.0
						LIABILITIES		
		12.2				Notes Payable-Short Term	11.7	14.4
		5.0				Cur. Mat.-L.T.D.	.7	1.5
		16.4				Trade Payables	7.0	12.0
		1.8				Income Taxes Payable	.1	.8
		20.0				All Other Current	27.9	24.7
		55.5				Total Current	47.4	53.4
		15.3				Long-Term Debt	6.1	5.2
		.1				Deferred Taxes	.2	.8
		3.0				All Other Non-Current	7.9	7.2
		26.2				Net Worth	38.4	33.5
		100.0				Total Liabilties & Net Worth	100.0	100.0
						INCOME DATA		
		100.0				Net Sales	100.0	100.0
						Gross Profit		
		94.9				Operating Expenses	91.5	88.6
		5.1				Operating Profit	8.5	11.4
		2.3				All Other Expenses (net)	.6	2.4
		2.9				Profit Before Taxes	7.9	9.0
						RATIOS		
		1.8					3.6	1.3
		1.0				Current	1.2	1.2
		.8					.9	.9
		1.3					2.8	1.3
		.9				Quick	1.1	.9
		.6					.7	.6
	2	161.8					0 UND	1 271.0
	32	11.6				Sales/Receivables	23 16.0	27 13.5
	71	5.1					72 5.1	75 4.8
						Cost of Sales/Inventory		
						Cost of Sales/Payables		
		5.8					2.9	4.7
		177.7				Sales/Working Capital	10.3	27.6
		-14.9					-143.8	-73.1
		21.5					35.5	29.8
	(10)	1.4				EBIT/Interest	(14) 8.4	(24) 10.4
		.3					1.6	2.4
								79.3
						Net Profit + Depr., Dep., Amort./Cur. Mat. L/T/D		(11) 23.0
								9.1
		.2					.3	.3
		.6				Fixed/Worth	.6	.6
		6.4					1.4	2.4
		1.1					.6	1.9
		2.7				Debt/Worth	1.8	3.3
		19.5					9.5	9.3
		51.3					53.8	73.0
	(13)	3.7				% Profit Before Taxes/Tangible Net Worth	(17) 29.0	(22) 50.1
		-15.2					15.1	16.7
		23.8					17.4	18.8
		.7				% Profit Before Taxes/Total Assets	7.1	8.7
		-2.8					1.4	3.2
		29.0					34.5	31.1
		8.2				Sales/Net Fixed Assets	13.9	16.8
		5.0					6.0	4.9
		2.6					4.0	1.9
		2.0				Sales/Total Assets	1.3	1.2
		.7					1.0	.7
		1.3					1.8	1.8
	(14)	2.6				% Depr., Dep., Amort./Sales	(16) 3.1	(20) 2.3
		5.6					4.3	6.3
						% Officers', Directors' Owners' Comp/Sales		
4028M	9665M	140111M	198142M	342432M	642622M	Net Sales ($)	268196M	1985667M
1034M	7907M	77808M	130930M	385413M	798415M	Total Assets ($)	232808M	1117485M

M = $ thousand   MM = $ million
See Pages 11 through 21 for Explanation of Ratios and Data

Comparative Historical Data / Current Data Sorted by Sales

Type of Statement									
	9	11	15		2	2	2	3	6
Unqualified									
	2	2	5	1	2	1		1	
Reviewed									
	3	1	2	2					
Compiled									
Tax Returns			3						
	8	18	21	2	3		5	4	7
Other									
	4/1/04-3/31/05 ALL	4/1/05-3/31/06 ALL	4/1/06-3/31/07 ALL	0-1MM	1-3MM 7 (4/1-9/30/06)	3-5MM	5-10MM 36 (10/1/06-3/31/07)	10-25MM	25MM & OVER
NUMBER OF STATEMENTS	22	35	43	5	7	3	7	8	13
ASSETS	%	%	%	%	%	%	%	%	%
Cash & Equivalents	30.6	32.9	36.1						38.0
Trade Receivables (net)	12.1	22.3	18.0						14.2
Inventory	.3	.7	1.8						.2
All Other Current	12.0	10.1	14.1						13.4
Total Current	55.0	66.0	70.0						65.8
Fixed Assets (net)	16.9	8.5	16.7						21.2
Intangibles (net)	15.2	11.3	3.7						7.4
All Other Non-Current	12.8	14.1	9.6						5.7
Total	100.0	100.0	100.0						100.0
LIABILITIES									
Notes Payable-Short Term	9.7	6.1	11.1						6.8
Cur. Mat.-L.T.D.	2.8	2.5	3.9						.8
Trade Payables	7.9	11.7	10.8						7.0
Income Taxes Payable	.6	.7	.9						.7
All Other Current	28.1	20.4	24.4						32.7
Total Current	49.1	41.4	51.1						48.0
Long-Term Debt	8.1	24.2	22.5						25.8
Deferred Taxes	.2	.4	.1						.3
All Other Non-Current	9.3	5.6	3.3						2.4
Net Worth	33.3	28.5	23.0						23.5
Total Liabilties & Net Worth	100.0	100.0	100.0						100.0
INCOME DATA									
Net Sales	100.0	100.0	100.0						100.0
Gross Profit									
Operating Expenses	93.4	88.2	89.4						92.3
Operating Profit	6.6	11.8	10.6						7.7
All Other Expenses (net)	.8	2.6	4.4						4.9
Profit Before Taxes	5.9	9.2	6.1						2.8
RATIOS									
Current	1.4	3.1	4.1						3.5
	1.1	1.5	1.2						1.1
	1.0	1.0	1.0						.9
Quick	1.3	2.8	1.7						1.6
	1.0	1.2	1.1						1.0
	.6	.9	.7						.7
Sales/Receivables	2 204.3	3 107.9	2 211.7						3 132.7
	18 20.5	41 8.9	30 12.1						56 6.6
	39 9.4	85 4.3	73 5.0						69 5.3
Cost of Sales/Inventory									
Cost of Sales/Payables									
Sales/Working Capital	6.8	3.2	3.1						3.0
	35.9	6.0	9.0						9.2
	NM	72.8	-354.3						-189.1
EBIT/Interest	25.5	34.0	13.0						11.9
	(17) 2.8	(29) 7.7	(27) 2.8						(10) 6.3
	1.7	1.4	1.0						.3
Net Profit + Depr., Dep., Amort./Cur. Mat. L/T/D	64.9		26.5						
	(10) 16.5		(11) 16.9						
	4.4		2.8						
Fixed/Worth	.2	.1	.1						.3
	.6	.2	.4						.5
	3.6	.9	1.3						-217.9
Debt/Worth	1.3	.6	.7						.7
	4.2	2.7	2.9						2.9
	33.8	10.6	7.0						-435.4
% Profit Before Taxes/Tangible Net Worth	65.4	84.3	49.5						
	(18) 26.4	(29) 45.3	(35) 15.1						
	12.5	11.4	3.3						
% Profit Before Taxes/Total Assets	7.6	23.4	14.1						12.8
	4.0	11.3	3.5						4.7
	2.0	2.7	.3						-8.7
Sales/Net Fixed Assets	36.3	36.8	35.6						16.2
	15.3	22.2	13.1						12.3
	5.0	10.9	5.7						5.5
Sales/Total Assets	2.6	2.1	2.1						1.9
	1.3	1.2	1.4						1.4
	.7	.7	.6						.6
% Depr., Dep., Amort./Sales	1.5	1.6	1.2						1.6
	(15) 2.4	(26) 2.5	(31) 2.2						(11) 4.1
	4.6	4.6	5.0						6.3
% Officers', Directors' Owners' Comp/Sales			1.6						
		(16)	3.4						
			12.9						
Net Sales ($)	1606805M	2354444M	1337000M	2713M	13651M	11043M	53120M	126679M	1129794M
Total Assets ($)	794503M	1609309M	1401507M	7299M	17733M	35828M	101077M	81985M	1157585M

| Current Data Sorted by Assets | | | | | | | Comparative Historical Data | |

						Type of Statement		
1	2	7	14	5	4	Unqualified	14	24
	2	4			1	Reviewed	5	4
5	5	4				Compiled	4	15
2	2	5				Tax Returns	3	5
7	7	12			4	Other	13	18
	9 (4/1-9/30/06)		86 (10/1/06-3/31/07)				4/1/02-3/31/03 ALL	4/1/03-3/31/04 ALL
0-500M	500M-2MM	2-10MM	10-50MM	50-100MM	100-250MM			
8	18	32	21	7	9	**NUMBER OF STATEMENTS**	39	66
%	%	%	%	%	%	**ASSETS**	%	%
41.1	27.3	26.2				Cash & Equivalents	47.2	33.0
27.7	32.4	25.9				Trade Receivables (net)	16.2	15.7
3.0	2.4	4.0				Inventory	.2	3.0
4.7	2.4	13.4				All Other Current	9.4	6.3
76.5	64.5	69.5				Total Current	73.0	58.0
15.0	8.6	8.3				Fixed Assets (net)	11.7	12.8
1.1	4.8	4.5				Intangibles (net)	5.0	7.1
7.4	22.2	17.7				All Other Non-Current	10.3	22.1
100.0	100.0	100.0				Total	100.0	100.0
						LIABILITIES		
21.9	27.8	21.4				Notes Payable-Short Term	18.1	19.3
1.5	1.4	1.1				Cur. Mat.-L.T.D.	3.4	1.0
10.3	3.0	16.3				Trade Payables	8.4	8.3
.0	.0	.1				Income Taxes Payable	.2	.5
16.4	9.2	13.7				All Other Current	9.1	20.3
50.1	41.6	52.7				Total Current	39.2	49.4
22.3	12.8	12.7				Long-Term Debt	8.7	13.6
.1	.2	.2				Deferred Taxes	.0	.3
5.3	11.7	3.1				All Other Non-Current	10.9	10.1
22.4	33.6	31.3				Net Worth	41.2	26.5
100.0	100.0	100.0				Total Liabilties & Net Worth	100.0	100.0
						INCOME DATA		
100.0	100.0	100.0				Net Sales	100.0	100.0
						Gross Profit		
83.7	71.1	78.6				Operating Expenses	80.9	80.4
16.3	28.9	21.4				Operating Profit	19.1	19.6
5.7	11.8	9.6				All Other Expenses (net)	5.9	3.8
10.6	17.1	11.8				Profit Before Taxes	13.3	15.8
						RATIOS		
6.9	3.3	2.3					3.6	2.1
1.4	1.6	1.4				Current	1.9	1.3
1.0	1.0	1.1					1.2	.9
5.6	3.3	2.0					3.4	1.5
1.4	1.6	1.1				Quick	1.6	1.1
1.0	1.0	.6					1.0	.6
0 UND	0 UND	10 36.4					0 UND	0 UND
18 20.0	35 10.5	60 6.1				Sales/Receivables	1 488.5	2 234.9
149 2.5	803 .5	310 1.2					51 7.2	74 4.9
						Cost of Sales/Inventory		
						Cost of Sales/Payables		
2.2	.7	1.1					1.9	3.0
11.3	2.7	2.4				Sales/Working Capital	3.6	8.7
NM	84.1	15.9					8.8	-13.7
104.3	45.5	5.7					10.3	16.3
(13) 8.3	(17) 6.5	(17) 2.6				EBIT/Interest	(27) 6.5	(50) 6.8
1.8	1.3	1.6					2.2	1.3
						Net Profit + Depr., Dep., Amort./Cur. Mat. L/T/D		
.1	.0	.0					.0	.0
.2	.1	.2				Fixed/Worth	.2	.4
.9	.6	.5					.7	3.2
.6	1.3	1.0					.8	1.3
2.6	2.8	4.0				Debt/Worth	1.9	3.5
9.1	8.4	9.8					4.3	12.3
157.4	48.8	37.6				% Profit Before Taxes/Tangible Net Worth	57.3	62.2
(16) 63.0	(29) 16.9	(19) 21.0					(38) 30.4	(56) 23.5
4.0	.6	14.0					16.2	7.6
44.9	20.5	10.6				% Profit Before Taxes/Total Assets	18.2	14.8
18.7	4.5	5.5					11.6	6.1
.6	.4	1.5					2.4	1.1
96.6	UND	73.3				Sales/Net Fixed Assets	92.6	78.1
28.3	37.1	29.2					17.6	12.3
11.1	10.9	6.5					7.0	4.4
3.1	1.5	1.3				Sales/Total Assets	1.6	1.5
1.8	.7	.7					1.1	.8
1.3	.1	.2					.5	.3
.6	.4	1.1				% Depr., Dep., Amort./Sales	.9	1.4
(11) 1.9	(18) 1.5	(18) 1.9					(28) 2.4	(43) 3.5
2.6	3.0	3.7					4.7	5.7
		2.4				% Officers', Directors' Owners' Comp/Sales	10.0	7.8
	(12) 6.9						(14) 18.7	(20) 17.5
		13.1					23.3	27.3
2708M	86313M	145804M	380792M	280256M	2731494M	Net Sales ($)	461249M	1195059M
1330M	25771M	159105M	452174M	551134M	1546196M	Total Assets ($)	655797M	1646767M

© RMA 2007

M = $ thousand   MM = $ million
See Pages 11 through 21 for Explanation of Ratios and Data

Comparative Historical Data   Current Data Sorted by Sales

	4/1/04-3/31/05 ALL	4/1/05-3/31/06 ALL	4/1/06-3/31/07 ALL	0-1MM	1-3MM	3-5MM	5-10MM	10-25MM	25MM & OVER
					9 (4/1-9/30/06)			86 (10/1/06-3/31/07)	
Type of Statement									
Unqualified	19	27	33	4	7	4	3	4	11
Reviewed	3	4	7		2		2	2	1
Compiled	15	6	14	9	3			2	
Tax Returns	8	11	9	4	1	1	2	1	
Other	25	43	32	4	7	4	3	8	6
NUMBER OF STATEMENTS	70	91	95	21	20	9	10	17	18
	%	%	%	%	%	%	%	%	%
ASSETS									
Cash & Equivalents	33.2	28.5	31.0	32.3	24.3		43.9	43.9	22.3
Trade Receivables (net)	17.2	23.4	26.9	24.4	42.4		8.4	17.7	28.8
Inventory	1.8	4.1	3.0	.7	2.7		7.6	5.0	3.1
All Other Current	10.8	8.9	8.7	6.0	6.3		1.2	10.5	11.6
Total Current	63.1	64.9	69.6	63.4	75.7		61.0	77.1	65.8
Fixed Assets (net)	13.3	12.6	12.1	13.5	7.2		18.9	11.7	15.3
Intangibles (net)	6.5	7.2	4.0	.3	.7		9.4	1.6	9.3
All Other Non-Current	17.2	15.3	14.2	22.8	16.4		10.7	9.6	9.6
Total	100.0	100.0	100.0	100.0	100.0		100.0	100.0	100.0
LIABILITIES									
Notes Payable-Short Term	23.1	15.9	23.8	36.7	27.1		12.4	18.8	9.1
Cur. Mat.-L.T.D.	2.3	3.6	1.2	.0	.6		3.5	1.4	2.2
Trade Payables	7.3	7.0	8.2	.6	8.6		14.3	12.9	12.9
Income Taxes Payable	.4	.4	.1	.0	.0		.0	.1	.4
All Other Current	18.3	15.3	13.3	8.1	13.5		7.9	16.1	18.3
Total Current	51.4	42.3	46.7	45.4	49.9		38.1	49.3	42.8
Long-Term Debt	17.6	18.8	16.7	19.1	18.0		18.5	9.0	23.3
Deferred Taxes	.2	.6	.2	.0	.1		.8	.3	.1
All Other Non-Current	9.7	10.5	7.5	16.5	4.3		8.4	.4	4.7
Net Worth	21.2	27.8	29.0	19.1	27.7		34.3	40.9	29.1
Total Liabilities & Net Worth	100.0	100.0	100.0	100.0	100.0		100.0	100.0	100.0
INCOME DATA									
Net Sales	100.0	100.0	100.0	100.0	100.0		100.0	100.0	100.0
Gross Profit									
Operating Expenses	84.7	85.0	77.8	66.5	74.1		88.2	89.1	83.2
Operating Profit	15.3	15.0	22.2	33.5	25.9		11.8	10.9	16.8
All Other Expenses (net)	5.2	4.6	8.7	16.7	7.2		5.0	3.0	5.0
Profit Before Taxes	10.1	10.4	13.4	16.9	18.6		6.8	7.9	11.7
RATIOS									
Current	2.4	4.0	3.1	13.8	2.5		4.2	4.7	2.4
	1.3	1.7	1.6	1.8	1.5		1.2	1.5	1.6
	.9	1.0	1.0	.8	1.0		1.0	1.1	1.1
Quick	1.8	3.9	3.1	9.7	2.3		4.1	4.7	1.9
	(69) 1.1	1.4	1.4	1.8	1.4		1.1	1.4	1.1
	.6	.8	.9	.8	.9		1.0	1.0	.6
Sales/Receivables	0 UND	0 UND	0 UND	0 UND	19 19.2		0 UND	0 UND	6 65.8
	7 49.5	38 9.6	23 15.5	3 120.0	156 2.3		0 UND	10 35.1	46 7.9
	95 3.8	126 2.9	155 2.4	689 .5	472 .8		33 11.1	43 8.4	123 3.0
Cost of Sales/Inventory									
Cost of Sales/Payables									
Sales/Working Capital	2.6	2.0	2.0	.5	.8		2.2	2.2	3.1
	8.8	4.6	3.9	2.9	3.0		21.3	6.1	8.8
	-22.9	47.7	50.2	-10.3	45.4		160.5	82.4	NM
EBIT/Interest	18.6	13.1	11.5		32.2			33.7	13.9
	(52) 4.3	(59) 4.5	(62) 4.3		(13) 2.8		(12) 3.8	(15) 3.9	
	2.1	1.3	1.7		1.4			1.4	2.2
Net Profit + Depr., Dep., Amort./Cur. Mat. L/T/D			5.1						
		(12) 2.0							
			.7						
Fixed/Worth	.1	.1	.0	.0	.0		.1	.1	.0
	.3	.3	.2	.2	.1		.5	.2	.6
	2.9	1.3	1.0	4.7	.2		2.6	.5	5.5
Debt/Worth	.8	.8	1.0	1.4	.5		1.6	.6	1.2
	5.0	2.9	3.1	4.3	2.4		3.4	1.6	3.2
	30.2	10.6	9.1	27.5	4.2		9.2	5.7	27.3
% Profit Before Taxes/Tangible Net Worth	57.8	58.3	70.0	50.6	64.1			39.2	164.6
	(55) 32.5	(78) 21.8	(84) 28.5	(17) 23.7	(19) 28.3			(16) 19.5	(15) 71.8
	7.2	5.8	6.8	3.4	3.2			6.6	23.6
% Profit Before Taxes/Total Assets	15.5	19.2	22.8	23.1	19.9		25.2	18.3	24.1
	5.6	7.1	5.7	3.0	5.6		17.1	8.8	15.7
	.9	.8	1.3	.1	1.0		.0	1.0	2.5
Sales/Net Fixed Assets	95.5	84.2	102.8	UND	115.2		30.8	72.4	71.7
	13.9	19.4	24.8	48.0	35.6		18.2	30.7	12.4
	4.1	8.4	7.5	4.4	12.2		9.8	13.5	4.2
Sales/Total Assets	2.1	1.8	1.8	1.4	1.6		2.7	4.3	1.8
	1.0	1.1	1.0	.2	.9		1.1	1.4	1.5
	.5	.4	.2	.1	.2		.7	.6	.9
% Depr., Dep., Amort./Sales	1.2	.7	.9		.4		1.4	.6	.6
	(48) 3.8	(68) 1.6	(65) 1.9		(11) 1.6		1.9	(15) 1.3	(13) 2.9
	6.7	3.1	4.0		2.0		4.5	2.4	5.7
% Officers', Directors' Owners' Comp/Sales	5.8	6.4	4.6	12.9					
	(23) 15.4	(27) 13.0	(28) 12.4	(10) 19.4					
	18.2	22.7	20.9	38.7					
Net Sales ($)	1053753M	1937107M	3627367M	9135M	39051M	36028M	67223M	257816M	3218114M
Total Assets ($)	1642497M	2412667M	2735710M	56035M	83366M	193591M	139699M	277117M	1985902M

M = $ thousand   MM = $ million
See Pages 11 through 21 for Explanation of Ratios and Data

Current Data Sorted by Assets   Comparative Historical Data

						Type of Statement		
	5	6	20	5	6	Unqualified	7	16
	2	1				Reviewed	1	1
	4					Compiled		4
3	1					Tax Returns		1
1						Other	2	6
	16 (4/1-9/30/06)	3	5 6	2	54 (10/1/06-3/31/07)		4/1/02-3/31/03	4/1/03-3/31/04
0-500M	500M-2MM	2-10MM	10-50MM	50-100MM	100-250MM		ALL	ALL
4	8	17	27	7	7	NUMBER OF STATEMENTS	16	28
%	%	%	%	%	%		%	%
						ASSETS		
		34.8	34.1			Cash & Equivalents	30.1	31.6
		17.9	23.4			Trade Receivables (net)	23.1	11.3
		9.8	12.0			Inventory	.0	4.8
		8.8	4.7			All Other Current	12.6	12.9
		71.3	74.2			Total Current	65.8	60.5
		14.9	8.1			Fixed Assets (net)	21.4	14.8
		7.7	2.2			Intangibles (net)	6.0	7.1
		6.1	15.5			All Other Non-Current	6.9	17.6
		100.0	100.0			Total	100.0	100.0
						LIABILITIES		
		14.2	12.1			Notes Payable-Short Term	21.9	14.8
		1.4	1.7			Cur. Mat.-L.T.D.	.4	.5
		10.3	19.6			Trade Payables	18.9	6.3
		.3	.2			Income Taxes Payable	.2	.1
		20.9	16.3			All Other Current	10.9	23.5
		47.1	49.8			Total Current	52.3	45.2
		8.4	2.6			Long-Term Debt	12.4	7.7
		.7	.1			Deferred Taxes	.0	.6
		1.6	1.8			All Other Non-Current	3.5	8.2
		42.2	45.8			Net Worth	31.8	38.3
		100.0	100.0			Total Liabilties & Net Worth	100.0	100.0
						INCOME DATA		
		100.0	100.0			Net Sales	100.0	100.0
						Gross Profit		
		87.2	75.6			Operating Expenses	84.8	86.6
		12.8	24.4			Operating Profit	15.2	13.4
		1.5	3.1			All Other Expenses (net)	6.0	1.3
		11.4	21.3			Profit Before Taxes	9.2	12.1
						RATIOS		
		2.1	3.1				2.7	2.9
		1.4	1.2			Current	1.4	1.3
		1.1	1.0				.7	.9
		2.0	2.7				2.3	2.2
		1.3	1.1			Quick	1.1	1.0
		.6	.3				.4	.4
	0	UND	0 UND				0 UND	0 930.7
	19	19.1	36 10.2			Sales/Receivables	29 12.8	22 16.7
	71	5.1	133 2.8				66 5.5	54 6.7
						Cost of Sales/Inventory		
						Cost of Sales/Payables		
		3.2	1.9				2.7	2.2
		6.9	3.2			Sales/Working Capital	7.2	7.8
		32.6	73.0				-57.2	NM
			999.8				35.9	63.0
		(11)	36.4			EBIT/Interest	(12) 2.6	(17) 4.4
			.4				.4	.8
						Net Profit + Depr., Dep., Amort./Cur. Mat. L/T/D		
		.0	.0				.0	.1
		.1	.0			Fixed/Worth	.6	.3
		.7	.3				2.7	1.0
		.8	.4				.7	.4
		1.8	1.3			Debt/Worth	2.5	1.7
		9.2	7.2				13.0	9.2
		75.4	49.0				60.4	81.3
		19.9	(25) 20.9			% Profit Before Taxes/Tangible Net Worth	(13) 32.3	(24) 19.7
		6.7	4.3				-16.0	-1.9
		17.7	33.3				11.3	26.0
		5.1	9.2			% Profit Before Taxes/Total Assets	5.8	5.1
		.6	.2				-1.4	-.6
		98.5	164.2				77.5	43.4
		42.0	58.7			Sales/Net Fixed Assets	28.2	18.6
		18.5	29.4				8.0	6.4
		3.9	1.3				3.1	2.8
		2.2	.5			Sales/Total Assets	1.3	1.0
		.9	.2				.3	.4
		.4	.4				1.1	1.1
		(15) .8	(17) .4			% Depr., Dep., Amort./Sales	(14) 1.7	(21) 1.9
		2.3	1.5				13.0	7.6
						% Officers', Directors' Owners' Comp/Sales		
3760M	37971M	251103M	977140M	378484M	1029190M	Net Sales ($)	618912M	686452M
1169M	9927M	103322M	639167M	442124M	1150384M	Total Assets ($)	456850M	760566M

M = $ thousand   MM = $ million
See Pages 11 through 21 for Explanation of Ratios and Data

Comparative Historical Data | | | Current Data Sorted by Sales

Hist 1	Hist 2	Hist 3	Type of Statement	0-1MM	1-3MM	3-5MM	5-10MM	10-25MM	25MM & OVER
14	22	42	Unqualified	2	5	5	7	9	14
	1	4	Reviewed				3		1
1		4	Compiled		1	1	1	1	
3		3	Tax Returns	1	2		1		
7	7	17	Other	3			3		6
4/1/04-3/31/05 ALL	4/1/05-3/31/06 ALL	4/1/06-3/31/07 ALL		16 (4/1-9/30/06)			54 (10/1/06-3/31/07)		
25	30	70	NUMBER OF STATEMENTS	6	8	6	14	15	21
%	%	%	ASSETS	%	%	%	%	%	%
39.7	27.7	38.0	Cash & Equivalents				26.0	34.4	36.9
15.3	14.6	17.6	Trade Receivables (net)				17.4	21.1	25.1
1.9	5.3	8.9	Inventory				8.2	26.2	2.6
12.9	18.0	9.6	All Other Current				9.6	2.8	12.3
69.8	65.6	74.1	Total Current				61.2	84.4	76.8
11.1	16.5	10.6	Fixed Assets (net)				15.9	5.2	10.4
7.0	6.1	3.8	Intangibles (net)				4.4	6.1	4.1
12.1	11.9	11.5	All Other Non-Current				18.5	4.3	8.7
100.0	100.0	100.0	Total				100.0	100.0	100.0
			LIABILITIES						
5.0	18.4	9.9	Notes Payable-Short Term				13.5	11.3	2.5
1.6	.7	1.1	Cur. Mat.-L.T.D.				3.0	1.2	.2
10.1	10.5	17.2	Trade Payables				9.6	23.8	14.0
.3	.1	.2	Income Taxes Payable				.2	.4	.0
20.3	21.0	17.5	All Other Current				9.3	17.9	27.4
37.3	50.8	45.9	Total Current				35.6	54.6	44.1
10.6	3.5	5.5	Long-Term Debt				7.2	2.2	4.2
.2	.0	.3	Deferred Taxes				.1	.2	.2
4.1	4.7	3.0	All Other Non-Current				4.5	.9	1.8
47.7	40.9	45.4	Net Worth				52.5	42.2	49.7
100.0	100.0	100.0	Total Liabilties & Net Worth				100.0	100.0	100.0
			INCOME DATA						
100.0	100.0	100.0	Net Sales				100.0	100.0	100.0
			Gross Profit						
84.9	88.7	77.2	Operating Expenses				82.0	79.7	77.5
15.1	11.3	22.8	Operating Profit				18.0	20.3	22.5
.3	-.2	3.0	All Other Expenses (net)				3.1	.6	2.0
14.8	11.5	19.8	Profit Before Taxes				14.8	19.6	20.5
			RATIOS						
4.0	2.5	2.9	Current				3.2	2.9	2.8
2.1	1.5	1.3					2.1	1.3	1.8
1.1	1.1	1.1					1.2	1.1	1.1
4.0	2.4	2.0	Quick				3.1	1.6	2.5
1.3	1.2	1.1					1.1	1.2	1.2
.7	.6	.6					.7	.3	.9
5 73.9	0 UND	0 UND	Sales/Receivables				0 UND	3 121.3	0 UND
12 29.4	13 29.2	12 30.5					9 38.4	48 7.6	34 10.7
45 8.1	40 9.0	79 4.6					57 6.4	133 2.8	84 4.3
			Cost of Sales/Inventory						
			Cost of Sales/Payables						
2.5	3.2	2.8	Sales/Working Capital				3.3	1.5	3.1
4.5	8.9	4.8					6.6	3.2	5.0
305.2	80.0	28.9					26.9	13.1	19.4
86.2	55.7	177.5	EBIT/Interest						999.8
(16) 11.8	(22) 13.9	(36) 6.4						(15) 66.8	
3.9	2.9	2.3							3.0
			Net Profit + Depr., Dep., Amort./Cur. Mat. L/T/D						
.0	.1	.0	Fixed/Worth				.0	.0	.0
.2	.2	.1					.1	.1	.1
.6	1.2	.3					.7	.3	.2
.4	.6	.4	Debt/Worth				.4	.5	.4
1.6	1.4	1.5					1.2	3.0	.8
3.8	7.2	4.7					1.5	5.9	3.4
119.1	64.4	69.3	% Profit Before Taxes/Tangible Net Worth				44.1	66.9	112.9
(21) 27.8	(27) 29.3	(67) 26.5					19.8	(14) 30.1	41.2
6.9	4.4	6.2					.4	3.9	25.1
51.4	19.5	35.5	% Profit Before Taxes/Total Assets				15.7	48.3	67.5
11.0	11.8	7.2					6.8	6.3	24.4
1.8	1.5	1.9					.1	1.1	5.8
146.7	85.4	157.3	Sales/Net Fixed Assets				95.4	164.2	148.5
61.9	36.1	54.7					58.6	37.7	40.3
19.5	11.6	24.4					5.0	24.6	25.6
3.4	4.1	2.6	Sales/Total Assets				4.5	2.6	3.7
1.6	1.4	1.0					1.0	.9	1.6
.6	.6	.3					.5	.5	.6
.4	.4	.4	% Depr., Dep., Amort./Sales				.4	.4	.3
(15) .7	(22) .8	(51) .6		(11) .6		(11) .7			(17) .8
3.4	1.8	1.5					5.2	1.9	1.2
		8.7	% Officers', Directors' Owners' Comp/Sales						
		(15) 16.6							
		33.6							
639377M	891319M	2677648M	Net Sales ($)	3084M	15184M	25359M	100624M	256924M	2276473M
635104M	1326424M	2346093M	Total Assets ($)	60055M	65065M	133931M	143005M	342680M	1601357M

M = $ thousand   MM = $ million
See Pages 11 through 21 for Explanation of Ratios and Data

Current Data Sorted by Assets							Comparative Historical Data	

0-500M	500M-2MM	2-10MM	10-50MM	50-100MM	100-250MM	Type of Statement	4/1/02-3/31/03 ALL	4/1/03-3/31/04 ALL
3	8	21	17	8	7	Unqualified	60	50
	1					Reviewed	4	2
3	2	3	3			Compiled	19	16
7	4		3			Tax Returns	25	21
7	7	10	10	3	6	Other	28	34
	26 (4/1-9/30/06)		107 (10/1/06-3/31/07)					
20	22	37	30	11	13	NUMBER OF STATEMENTS	136	123
%	%	%	%	%	%	ASSETS	%	%
30.7	33.3	38.3	42.1	50.5	49.3	Cash & Equivalents	31.0	32.5
20.2	11.4	18.3	15.4	24.4	20.3	Trade Receivables (net)	18.1	15.4
2.9	.4	2.3	2.5	3.8	2.4	Inventory	4.5	6.1
9.6	12.4	10.3	10.1	6.3	13.8	All Other Current	11.9	9.4
63.3	57.4	69.3	70.1	85.0	85.8	Total Current	65.5	63.4
21.5	17.9	7.5	5.4	2.9	1.4	Fixed Assets (net)	18.0	15.9
.1	7.0	6.4	3.6	2.8	2.1	Intangibles (net)	2.8	2.7
15.1	17.6	16.9	20.9	9.3	10.7	All Other Non-Current	13.7	17.9
100.0	100.0	100.0	100.0	100.0	100.0	Total	100.0	100.0
						LIABILITIES		
16.7	18.5	1.5	4.9	18.0	9.3	Notes Payable-Short Term	20.6	15.6
.6	.6	3.4	.2	1.4	1.2	Cur. Mat.-L.T.D.	5.0	1.7
10.9	7.7	15.3	12.5	8.7	21.8	Trade Payables	10.9	12.2
.0	.8	1.0	1.8	.0	.6	Income Taxes Payable	.2	.4
29.1	24.4	22.9	24.5	26.3	32.7	All Other Current	22.1	22.0
57.3	52.0	44.1	44.0	54.6	65.6	Total Current	58.9	52.0
2.9	14.2	5.0	2.4	2.4	9.5	Long-Term Debt	13.3	15.3
.0	.0	.0	.2	.1	.0	Deferred Taxes	.1	.1
8.3	1.5	3.6	5.9	6.1	1.5	All Other Non-Current	6.3	4.7
31.8	32.3	47.2	47.6	36.9	23.5	Net Worth	21.3	27.9
100.0	100.0	100.0	100.0	100.0	100.0	Total Liabilities & Net Worth	100.0	100.0
						INCOME DATA		
100.0	100.0	100.0	100.0	100.0	100.0	Net Sales	100.0	100.0
						Gross Profit		
81.1	95.2	92.0	74.4	75.2	75.8	Operating Expenses	84.4	81.2
18.9	4.8	8.0	25.6	24.8	24.2	Operating Profit	15.6	18.8
-.2	.2	1.8	5.2	3.4	7.0	All Other Expenses (net)	1.9	4.0
19.2	4.6	6.2	20.4	21.4	17.3	Profit Before Taxes	13.6	14.8
						RATIOS		
2.6	3.0	3.1	2.8	2.0	1.5		2.7	3.1
1.4	1.5	2.0	1.7	1.6	1.2	Current	1.3	1.5
.3	.5	1.4	1.2	1.3	1.1		.8	.9
2.6	2.7	2.4	2.5	1.9	1.3		1.9	2.5
1.2	1.1	1.6	1.6	1.4	1.1	Quick	(135) 1.1	1.0
.2	.4	1.1	.5	1.1	.9		.4	.4
0 UND	0 UND	4 94.0	4 99.6	0 UND	1 642.7		0 UND	0 UND
0 UND	0 UND	17 21.1	19 19.6	8 44.6	156 2.3	Sales/Receivables	10 38.3	8 43.2
11 33.0	13 29.0	42 8.7	45 8.0	200 1.8	231 1.6		65 5.6	50 7.4
						Cost of Sales/Inventory		
						Cost of Sales/Payables		
8.0	4.5	3.5	2.4	.5	1.3		3.1	2.5
32.3	24.0	8.6	5.0	3.5	3.2	Sales/Working Capital	10.7	10.1
-69.2	-12.3	27.8	60.4	13.2	6.2		-59.5	-141.5
	6.0	70.5	136.1		26.3		17.4	25.5
	(15) 2.9	(21) 15.5	(16) 15.5		(10) 7.7	EBIT/Interest	(95) 3.8	(76) 6.0
	-1.6	2.5	4.1		2.4		1.5	1.5
						Net Profit + Depr., Dep., Amort./Cur. Mat. L/T/D		3.9
								(10) .6
								-.2
.0	.0	.0	.0	.0	.0		.0	.0
.2	.2	.1	.1	.1	.1	Fixed/Worth	.2	.1
1.8	2.3	.2	.3	.3	.2		2.1	1.5
.6	.5	.4	.5	.8	1.8		.7	.4
1.8	1.7	.9	1.0	2.2	6.4	Debt/Worth	3.0	2.0
17.3	NM	2.6	3.1	12.9	19.4		23.8	11.4
885.0	51.3	60.1	67.9	79.2	32.4		83.9	59.6
(18) 162.1	(17) 1.9	(34) 31.8	(28) 36.7	46.9	(11) 16.7	% Profit Before Taxes/Tangible Net Worth	(111) 23.6	(102) 22.9
40.9	-7.3	6.0	23.3	10.1	5.9		2.9	3.7
261.5	25.4	32.3	34.1	45.8	15.9		26.6	24.2
60.6	2.6	14.5	14.2	14.7	2.9	% Profit Before Taxes/Total Assets	4.6	6.0
9.7	-5.3	3.0	5.2	5.5	.3		.8	.6
UND	398.0	154.5	89.9	411.3	UND		107.8	211.5
78.3	32.7	55.6	34.8	52.6	28.7	Sales/Net Fixed Assets	36.0	47.6
19.4	17.1	20.5	17.1	21.9	19.4		15.0	15.1
19.1	5.0	4.7	1.9	1.7	.8		5.7	4.6
5.9	2.7	2.3	1.2	.8	.5	Sales/Total Assets	2.0	1.5
2.8	1.5	.8	.6	.2	.1		.7	.5
	.3	.3	.4				.7	.5
	(15) .7	(28) .8	(22) .7			% Depr., Dep., Amort./Sales	(98) 1.3	(80) 1.0
	1.7	1.3	1.1				2.5	2.3
								9.7
						% Officers', Directors' Owners' Comp/Sales	(44) 25.6	(28) 23.3
								36.2
39040M	79632M	721037M	1128045M	1568830M	1880223M	Net Sales ($)	8625396M	4213009M
3895M	24575M	226150M	704407M	848397M	2433840M	Total Assets ($)	4396194M	2258028M

M = $ thousand   MM = $ million

See Pages 11 through 21 for Explanation of Ratios and Data

Comparative Historical Data | | | | ## Current Data Sorted by Sales

			Type of Statement						
55	53	64	Unqualified	4	11	4	8	11	26
6	4	1	Reviewed	1					
9	12	11	Compiled	2	4	2	1	1	1
16	16	14	Tax Returns	6	3	1	2	1	1
29	66	43	Other	2	6	3	7	10	15
4/1/04-	4/1/05-	4/1/06-			26 (4/1-9/30/06)			107 (10/1/06-3/31/07)	
3/31/05	3/31/06	3/31/07							
ALL	ALL	ALL		0-1MM	1-3MM	3-5MM	5-10MM	10-25MM	25MM & OVER
115	151	133	**NUMBER OF STATEMENTS**	15	24	10	18	23	43
%	%	%	**ASSETS**	%	%	%	%	%	%
32.3	37.3	39.3	Cash & Equivalents	31.5	30.9	16.2	46.3	41.7	47.9
18.4	15.9	17.5	Trade Receivables (net)	7.3	14.4	20.2	15.0	21.0	21.2
5.4	6.0	2.3	Inventory	.0	8.2	.4	1.0	.0	1.9
11.2	10.3	10.5	All Other Current	17.4	14.4	11.4	8.5	10.5	6.7
67.3	69.6	69.5	Total Current	56.1	67.9	48.1	70.8	73.2	77.6
10.2	13.3	9.9	Fixed Assets (net)	27.8	7.9	14.8	9.8	6.3	5.5
2.5	5.3	4.2	Intangibles (net)	3.4	1.2	6.5	10.0	4.4	3.1
20.0	11.9	16.4	All Other Non-Current	12.7	23.0	30.6	9.5	16.1	13.8
100.0	100.0	100.0	Total	100.0	100.0	100.0	100.0	100.0	100.0
			LIABILITIES						
9.0	10.3	9.5	Notes Payable-Short Term	20.3	18.8	.6	4.1	4.8	7.3
2.3	1.5	1.4	Cur. Mat.-L.T.D.	1.0	.6	.0	1.3	2.0	2.0
11.5	12.2	12.9	Trade Payables	11.9	8.0	6.7	16.0	9.0	18.1
.4	.5	.9	Income Taxes Payable	.0	.1	1.6	1.0	.4	1.7
24.2	21.6	25.7	All Other Current	39.5	22.3	27.3	11.7	30.5	25.6
47.4	46.1	50.3	Total Current	72.8	49.8	36.2	34.1	46.8	54.8
11.7	7.3	5.8	Long-Term Debt	6.9	9.9	.3	6.7	8.5	2.7
.5	.2	.1	Deferred Taxes	.0	.1	.0	.0	.0	.1
7.8	5.3	4.5	All Other Non-Current	2.9	9.7	4.8	2.0	3.5	3.6
32.6	41.2	39.3	Net Worth	17.7	30.6	58.7	57.2	41.2	38.8
100.0	100.0	100.0	Total Liabilties & Net Worth	100.0	100.0	100.0	100.0	100.0	100.0
			INCOME DATA						
100.0	100.0	100.0	Net Sales	100.0	100.0	100.0	100.0	100.0	100.0
			Gross Profit						
78.6	82.9	83.9	Operating Expenses	86.7	83.6	82.4	87.3	78.7	84.9
21.4	17.1	16.1	Operating Profit	13.3	16.4	17.6	12.7	21.3	15.1
3.3	1.5	2.6	All Other Expenses (net)	5.2	4.5	1.1	2.3	4.9	-.1
18.1	15.5	13.4	Profit Before Taxes	8.0	11.9	16.5	10.4	16.4	15.1
			RATIOS						
3.1	3.3	2.7		1.2	5.9	8.1	3.2	2.6	1.9
1.7	1.7	1.6	Current	1.0	2.6	1.4	2.1	1.9	1.5
1.1	1.1	1.1		.2	.9	.4	1.5	1.2	1.2
2.3	2.8	2.3		1.0	3.3	6.4	3.2	2.5	1.7
1.1	1.3	1.4	Quick	.5	2.0	1.0	1.8	1.7	1.4
.5	.6	.7		.1	.4	.3	1.1	1.1	1.0
0 UND	0 UND	0 UND		0 UND	0 UND	0 UND	0 UND	8 44.9	3 128.6
15 24.6	13 28.4	11 33.7	Sales/Receivables	0 UND	8 45.0	4 89.7	17 21.9	28 12.9	12 31.7
75 4.8	64 5.7	41 8.9		0 UND	27 13.5	21 17.3	49 7.4	76 4.8	80 4.6
			Cost of Sales/Inventory						
			Cost of Sales/Payables						
2.4	2.3	2.9		2.1	2.3	1.0	2.8	1.5	3.5
5.8	4.9	7.3	Sales/Working Capital	851.0	6.7	NM	7.2	5.9	7.2
65.5	43.1	43.7		-5.1	NM	-29.6	22.3	33.6	26.2
38.7	32.9	38.6			11.9			123.0	74.9
(66) 12.1	(79) 7.4	(76) 9.0	EBIT/Interest		(13) 2.9		(12) 23.8	(29) 12.7
2.9	3.2	2.8			.2			2.9	4.1
	16.3		Net Profit + Depr., Dep.,						
	(10) 3.4		Amort./Cur. Mat. L/T/D						
	.6								
.0	.0	.0		.1	.0	.0	.0	.0	.0
.1	.1	.1	Fixed/Worth	.3	.1	.0	.2	.1	.1
.4	.4	.4		2.7	.3	1.9	.3	.4	.2
.4	.4	.6		1.6	.3	.2	.3	.5	.8
1.3	1.3	1.4	Debt/Worth	17.3	1.8	1.0	.8	1.5	1.2
5.2	7.3	6.2		51.1	12.3	2.5	2.5	17.1	3.4
62.0	44.4	71.2	% Profit Before Taxes/Tangible	466.7	95.7		68.7	102.2	67.9
(102) 21.0	(131) 19.7	(119) 32.4	Net Worth	(13) 24.6	(20) 14.8		(17) 22.1	(20) 29.7	(40) 48.1
6.7	5.7	9.6		1.9	.4		3.3	7.4	26.6
31.3	25.6	38.1	% Profit Before Taxes/Total	54.2	35.4	387.1	29.3	50.8	35.1
7.6	8.8	13.4	Assets	3.3	5.7	31.6	7.6	14.8	14.7
1.6	1.9	2.5		-.1	.3	-.9	2.1	.3	8.5
178.6	206.6	162.2		59.0	556.7	236.7	83.2	82.7	163.9
54.2	53.7	40.8	Sales/Net Fixed Assets	21.7	58.4	104.6	26.7	38.5	49.8
19.6	18.1	21.4		3.0	19.9	55.6	17.4	14.9	22.8
3.0	3.1	4.5		4.4	4.0	20.9	5.6	3.3	5.0
1.3	1.3	1.9	Sales/Total Assets	1.7	1.9	2.3	2.0	1.3	1.7
.5	.6	.7		.1	.4	.5	.9	.6	.8
.6	.4	.4			.4		.5	.9	.2
(69) 1.0	(98) .9	(90) .8	% Depr., Dep., Amort./Sales	(17) .7		(13) .8	(14) 1.2	(33) .5
1.8	1.7	1.4			1.4		1.5	2.3	1.1
5.1	3.9	7.6	% Officers', Directors'						
(32) 13.3	(38) 19.7	(24) 17.8	Owners' Comp/Sales						
27.8	35.6	25.8							
1812371M	4344279M	5416807M	Net Sales ($)	5238M	49673M	39525M	131334M	387598M	4803439M
2319724M	3942561M	4241264M	Total Assets ($)	88800M	88440M	70264M	143440M	906190M	2944130M

Current Data Sorted by Assets / Comparative Historical Data

0-500M	500M-2MM	2-10MM	10-50MM	50-100MM	100-250MM		1	2
						Type of Statement		
		2	6	2	3	Unqualified		
		2	1			Reviewed		
1		2	2			Compiled		2
1	3	2				Tax Returns	4	2
3	2	3	10		4	Other	3	4
	4 (4/1-9/30/06)	45 (10/1/06-3/31/07)					4/1/02-3/31/03 ALL	4/1/03-3/31/04 ALL
5	5	11	19	2	7	**NUMBER OF STATEMENTS**	8	10
%	%	%	%	%	%	**ASSETS**	%	%
		33.2	19.0			Cash & Equivalents		6.1
		17.9	16.9			Trade Receivables (net)		19.5
		2.4	16.3			Inventory		7.8
		6.9	5.8			All Other Current		6.0
		60.4	58.0			Total Current		39.3
		14.3	19.0			Fixed Assets (net)		33.8
		.0	2.3			Intangibles (net)		2.4
		25.3	20.7			All Other Non-Current		24.5
		100.0	100.0			Total		100.0
						LIABILITIES		
		3.0	18.9			Notes Payable-Short Term		14.5
		.5	3.7			Cur. Mat.-L.T.D.		3.6
		6.5	5.0			Trade Payables		2.0
		.0	.3			Income Taxes Payable		.0
		6.1	15.5			All Other Current		4.1
		16.1	43.4			Total Current		24.3
		10.0	29.2			Long-Term Debt		34.3
		.0	.1			Deferred Taxes		.0
		10.6	2.3			All Other Non-Current		5.4
		63.3	25.1			Net Worth		36.1
		100.0	100.0			Total Liabilities & Net Worth		100.0
						INCOME DATA		
		100.0	100.0			Net Sales		100.0
						Gross Profit		
		55.2	59.5			Operating Expenses		59.1
		44.8	40.5			Operating Profit		40.9
		1.3	11.0			All Other Expenses (net)		23.4
		43.5	29.5			Profit Before Taxes		17.5
						RATIOS		
		8.8	2.4					10.2
		3.3	1.1			Current		1.2
		2.4	.8					.1
		5.8	1.0					9.6
		3.3	.8			Quick		.7
		1.9	.2					.1
		0 UND	0 UND				0 UND	
		20 18.5	23 15.8			Sales/Receivables		
		39 9.4	155 2.4				57 6.4	
						Cost of Sales/Inventory		
						Cost of Sales/Payables		
		.3	1.7					.5
		4.9	10.5			Sales/Working Capital		7.4
		9.3	-27.7					-2.6
			24.5					
			(11) 8.6			EBIT/Interest		
			2.9					
						Net Profit + Depr., Dep., Amort./Cur. Mat. L/T/D		
		.0	.0					.0
		.0	.1			Fixed/Worth		.1
		.2	.9					1.9
		.2	1.8					1.3
		.4	5.4			Debt/Worth		1.8
		1.1	10.4					3.2
		135.7	53.5					39.1
		20.9	(17) 33.3			% Profit Before Taxes/Tangible Net Worth		11.6
		9.9	21.1					3.3
		42.5	14.1					5.7
		20.6	3.9			% Profit Before Taxes/Total Assets		3.7
		4.7	2.4					1.1
		999.8	999.8					UND
		36.2	69.9			Sales/Net Fixed Assets		14.9
		1.1	1.7					.3
		3.6	.7					.3
		.8	.2			Sales/Total Assets		.2
		.1	.2					.1
			.6					
			(12) 2.0			% Depr., Dep., Amort./Sales		
			11.6					
						% Officers', Directors' Owners' Comp/Sales		
997M	42136M	68899M	448378M	756420M	1413803M	Net Sales ($)	30161M	18616M
1491M	4887M	47559M	462456M	140096M	1204903M	Total Assets ($)	93272M	78583M

M = $ thousand   MM = $ million
See Pages 11 through 21 for Explanation of Ratios and Data

Comparative Historical Data   **Current Data Sorted by Sales**

			Type of Statement						
5	5	13	Unqualified			1	8		4
2	1	3	Reviewed	1		1		2	
	2	5	Compiled	2	1	1		1	
1		6	Tax Returns	4	1		1		
9	8	22	Other	5	2	1	4	4	6
4/1/04-3/31/05	4/1/05-3/31/06	4/1/06-3/31/07			4 (4/1-9/30/06)			45 (10/1/06-3/31/07)	
ALL	ALL	ALL		0-1MM	1-3MM	3-5MM	5-10MM	10-25MM	25MM & OVER
17	16	49	**NUMBER OF STATEMENTS**	12	4	3	13	7	10
%	%	%	**ASSETS**	%	%	%	%	%	%
15.9	24.5	26.2	Cash & Equivalents	32.3			32.0		21.8
13.0	18.8	16.0	Trade Receivables (net)	6.4			27.1		21.5
7.9	4.3	10.5	Inventory	8.3			8.2		17.4
5.6	3.3	9.4	All Other Current	15.1			3.5		12.7
42.3	50.9	62.0	Total Current	62.1			70.8		73.3
21.0	15.6	15.9	Fixed Assets (net)	17.4			7.7		11.0
.2	1.0	1.2	Intangibles (net)	.0			3.2		.4
36.5	32.5	21.0	All Other Non-Current	20.5			18.4		15.3
100.0	100.0	100.0	Total	100.0			100.0		100.0
			LIABILITIES						
22.3	29.1	11.6	Notes Payable-Short Term	11.6			14.0		12.5
3.4	.8	2.2	Cur. Mat.-L.T.D.	2.9			1.8		.2
5.8	6.9	8.0	Trade Payables	1.4			7.7		22.3
2.2	.1	.3	Income Taxes Payable	.0			.3		.2
8.6	7.4	11.1	All Other Current	4.7			21.0		16.8
42.4	44.4	33.2	Total Current	20.4			44.9		52.0
16.2	10.9	21.5	Long-Term Debt	18.1			12.5		11.2
.1	.0	.0	Deferred Taxes	.0			.0		.0
7.1	9.5	5.4	All Other Non-Current	1.5			7.3		8.0
34.2	35.2	39.9	Net Worth	60.0			35.2		28.9
100.0	100.0	100.0	Total Liabilities & Net Worth	100.0			100.0		100.0
			INCOME DATA						
100.0	100.0	100.0	Net Sales	100.0			100.0		100.0
			Gross Profit						
57.6	68.6	61.7	Operating Expenses	36.6			64.1		84.4
42.4	31.4	38.3	Operating Profit	63.4			35.9		15.6
8.1	10.8	8.9	All Other Expenses (net)	12.6			8.3		6.3
34.3	20.6	29.3	Profit Before Taxes	50.8			27.6		9.4
			RATIOS						
3.1	4.2	4.3		11.6			3.7		6.8
.8	1.2	2.0	Current	2.7			1.6		1.1
.5	.7	1.1		1.2			1.1		1.0
3.1	4.0	4.2		5.4			3.7		2.8
.6	.9	1.0	Quick	2.5			1.4		.7
.2	.7	.6		.6			.9		.1
0 UND	0 UND	0 UND		0 UND			24 15.0		1 364.6
0 UND	10 37.4	20 18.5	Sales/Receivables	0 UND			45 8.0		13 27.3
32 11.4	26 14.0	47 7.7		0 UND			181 2.0		43 8.4
			Cost of Sales/Inventory						
			Cost of Sales/Payables						
7.9	3.6	1.2		.2			1.6		8.9
-38.1	15.1	5.4	Sales/Working Capital	1.1			4.1		27.8
-5.5	-12.8	28.4		25.8			7.0		415.3
12.5		21.9							
(10) 6.1		(26) 7.2	EBIT/Interest						
4.0		2.9							
			Net Profit + Depr., Dep., Amort./Cur. Mat. L/T/D						
.0	.0	.0		.0			.0		.0
.2	.1	.0	Fixed/Worth	.0			.0		.1
1.7	.6	.6		.6			.2		.7
.6	.1	.5		.2			.8		1.3
1.5	3.0	1.9	Debt/Worth	.5			4.2		7.1
NM	NM	7.3		2.2			7.3		9.5
48.7	107.6	54.6	% Profit Before Taxes/Tangible	37.5			102.1		96.0
(13) 26.4	(12) 23.7	(47) 26.6	Net Worth	16.0			45.7		25.8
12.9	13.5	9.9		6.8			25.9		7.6
24.5	18.3	25.8	% Profit Before Taxes/Total	29.9			38.6		37.9
14.2	6.7	6.5	Assets	8.0			9.7		3.6
2.8	.6	2.3		4.1			2.9		1.1
UND	UND	UND		UND			UND		999.8
43.5	485.4	69.9	Sales/Net Fixed Assets	UND			86.9		536.3
4.6	15.3	2.2		.7			18.3		5.6
3.0	2.7	1.5		.7			2.0		9.0
.4	.4	.3	Sales/Total Assets	.2			.4		5.9
.2	.1	.2		.1			.2		.3
		.5							
	(31)	1.6	% Depr., Dep., Amort./Sales						
		9.0							
		.9							
	(11)	7.2	% Officers', Directors' Owners' Comp/Sales						
		23.5							
416885M	246980M	2730633M	Net Sales ($)	4300M	6144M	11736M	103170M	119923M	2485360M
362785M	331805M	1861392M	Total Assets ($)	34725M	30808M	56597M	344869M	421793M	972600M

© RMA 2007

M = $ thousand   MM = $ million
See Pages 11 through 21 for Explanation of Ratios and Data

Current Data Sorted by Assets

Comparative Historical Data

						Type of Statement				
1	3	1	4	1		Unqualified			7	8
		1	1			Reviewed			4	3
		1				Compiled			3	1
		2				Tax Returns				1
	2		1			Other			8	12
	1		2		1				4/1/02-	4/1/03-
	4 (4/1-9/30/06)		22 (10/1/06-3/31/07)						3/31/03	3/31/04
0-500M	500M-2MM	2-10MM	10-50MM	50-100MM	100-250MM				ALL	ALL
1	6	8	8	2	1	NUMBER OF STATEMENTS			22	25
%	%	%	%	%	%	ASSETS			%	%
						Cash & Equivalents			15.8	17.0
						Trade Receivables (net)			40.6	40.2
						Inventory			11.6	6.8
						All Other Current			16.7	12.1
						Total Current			84.7	76.1
						Fixed Assets (net)			6.6	13.0
						Intangibles (net)			.6	3.6
						All Other Non-Current			8.1	7.2
						Total			100.0	100.0
						LIABILITIES				
						Notes Payable-Short Term			10.5	10.2
						Cur. Mat.-L.T.D.			.4	.5
						Trade Payables			36.0	33.5
						Income Taxes Payable			.1	.1
						All Other Current			10.6	6.5
						Total Current			57.6	50.8
						Long-Term Debt			6.2	4.1
						Deferred Taxes			.1	.1
						All Other Non-Current			.7	2.6
						Net Worth			35.5	42.4
						Total Liabilties & Net Worth			100.0	100.0
						INCOME DATA				
						Net Sales			100.0	100.0
						Gross Profit				
						Operating Expenses			90.1	94.3
						Operating Profit			9.9	5.7
						All Other Expenses (net)			-.4	-.3
						Profit Before Taxes			10.3	6.0
						RATIOS				
									1.9	2.1
						Current			1.3	1.4
									1.1	1.1
									1.4	1.7
						Quick			1.1	1.1
									.7	.8
							21	17.2	18	20.0
						Sales/Receivables	38	9.6	44	8.3
							69	5.3	72	5.1
						Cost of Sales/Inventory				
						Cost of Sales/Payables				
									3.0	5.4
						Sales/Working Capital			13.6	20.8
									28.9	37.8
									37.5	33.0
						EBIT/Interest	(14)	6.7	(20)	9.5
									2.1	2.4
						Net Profit + Depr., Dep., Amort./Cur. Mat. L/T/D				
									.0	.0
						Fixed/Worth			.1	.2
									.6	.6
									1.0	.7
						Debt/Worth			2.4	1.5
									5.6	4.4
									50.0	52.0
						% Profit Before Taxes/Tangible Net Worth			26.4	(23) 23.6
									5.7	15.0
									21.2	19.9
						% Profit Before Taxes/Total Assets			4.7	10.4
									1.8	4.6
									999.8	800.7
						Sales/Net Fixed Assets			107.6	132.2
									54.7	12.2
									7.1	6.3
						Sales/Total Assets			2.6	2.3
									1.4	1.6
									.1	.4
						% Depr., Dep., Amort./Sales	(13)	.3	(16)	1.5
									.9	3.4
						% Officers', Directors' Owners' Comp/Sales				
36M	23762M	191076M	563893M	106969M	804165M	Net Sales ($)			1616331M	1227437M
127M	6800M	37644M	148875M	123782M	141855M	Total Assets ($)			846646M	430897M

M = $ thousand   MM = $ million
See Pages 11 through 21 for Explanation of Ratios and Data

Comparative Historical Data

			Type of Statement						
8	12	10	Unqualified	2	2			1	5
1	2	2	Reviewed						2
1		2	Compiled		1			1	
2	2	3	Tax Returns					2	
8	16	9	Other	1		1	1	3	4
4/1/04-3/31/05 ALL	4/1/05-3/31/06 ALL	4/1/06-3/31/07 ALL		0-1MM	4 (4/1-9/30/06) 1-3MM	3-5MM	5-10MM	22 (10/1/06-3/31/07) 10-25MM	25MM & OVER
20	32	26	**NUMBER OF STATEMENTS**	3	3	1	1	7	11

Current Data Sorted by Sales

%	%	%		%	%	%	%	%	%
			ASSETS						
26.5	29.7	20.0	Cash & Equivalents						13.2
29.6	37.2	40.3	Trade Receivables (net)						49.1
7.7	8.7	10.1	Inventory						11.9
16.5	5.1	10.5	All Other Current						10.5
80.3	80.6	80.9	Total Current						84.7
6.8	8.0	10.6	Fixed Assets (net)						6.0
.4	1.5	.9	Intangibles (net)						1.8
12.5	9.9	7.5	All Other Non-Current						7.5
100.0	100.0	100.0	Total						100.0
			LIABILITIES						
10.9	8.9	20.0	Notes Payable-Short Term						22.9
.3	.3	1.0	Cur. Mat.-L.T.D.						.4
26.6	27.8	22.4	Trade Payables						26.5
.1	.0	.1	Income Taxes Payable						.0
7.7	11.4	9.6	All Other Current						5.7
45.6	48.4	53.0	Total Current						55.5
3.3	3.5	5.7	Long-Term Debt						4.1
.0	.0	.0	Deferred Taxes						.0
.5	5.9	5.9	All Other Non-Current						10.2
50.6	42.2	35.4	Net Worth						30.2
100.0	100.0	100.0	Total Liabilties & Net Worth						100.0
			INCOME DATA						
100.0	100.0	100.0	Net Sales						100.0
			Gross Profit						
86.5	90.3	90.8	Operating Expenses						88.6
13.5	9.7	9.2	Operating Profit						11.4
.4	-.9	-.4	All Other Expenses (net)						.2
13.0	10.5	9.6	Profit Before Taxes						11.3
			RATIOS						
5.6	3.7	4.1							4.1
1.6	1.6	1.3	Current						1.6
1.1	1.1	1.0							1.0
3.9	2.3	3.9							3.8
1.1	1.4	1.0	Quick						.9
.5	1.0	.6							.7
3 112.1	24 15.0	25 14.6						29 12.5	
30 12.1	37 9.7	35 10.6	Sales/Receivables					34 10.7	
47 7.8	45 8.0	62 5.9						50 7.3	
			Cost of Sales/Inventory						
			Cost of Sales/Payables						
2.8	3.9	3.4							3.4
8.7	11.7	13.3	Sales/Working Capital						21.9
38.8	34.0	214.6							603.5
55.8	22.9	30.8							9.3
(16) 12.3	(25) 4.7	(23) 3.8	EBIT/Interest						3.0
4.0	2.6	2.3							2.0
			Net Profit + Depr., Dep., Amort./Cur. Mat. L/T/D						
.0	.0	.0							.0
.0	.0	.0	Fixed/Worth						.1
.1	.2	.7							.7
.2	.4	.8							.9
1.6	1.8	3.7	Debt/Worth						5.7
3.4	8.5	10.4							34.2
90.6	54.1	81.3							88.0
45.4	(31) 22.3	(25) 46.5	% Profit Before Taxes/Tangible Net Worth					(10) 47.7	
6.6	11.1	16.4							22.6
42.0	19.5	23.4							12.8
19.5	5.1	6.8	% Profit Before Taxes/Total Assets						7.1
1.7	1.6	2.4							2.4
999.8	999.8	UND							999.8
276.6	332.0	360.1	Sales/Net Fixed Assets						313.1
18.3	29.2	10.4							17.3
4.9	6.1	5.2							7.7
3.0	3.2	2.7	Sales/Total Assets						4.1
.8	1.4	1.0							1.6
.0	.0	.0							.0
(12) .1	(19) .1	(16) .1	% Depr., Dep., Amort./Sales					(10) .1	
1.5	1.4	2.0							1.6
	.7								
	(10) 1.6		% Officers', Directors' Owners' Comp/Sales						
	22.7								
1533211M	2047308M	1689901M	Net Sales ($)	893M	5895M	3876M	7860M	108297M	1563080M
413342M	768809M	459083M	Total Assets ($)	1550M	6986M	980M	2403M	43057M	404107M

M = $ thousand   MM = $ million
See Pages 11 through 21 for Explanation of Ratios and Data

Current Data Sorted by Assets   **Comparative Historical Data**

Date groupings: 20 (4/1-9/30/06) applies to 500M-2MM; 153 (10/1/06-3/31/07) applies to 10-50MM. Historical columns are 4/1/02-3/31/03 ALL and 4/1/03-3/31/04 ALL.

Type of Statement	0-500M	500M-2MM	2-10MM	10-50MM	50-100MM	100-250MM	4/1/02-3/31/03 ALL	4/1/03-3/31/04 ALL
Unqualified	1	1	7	18	9	4	33	28
Reviewed	1	2	5	6	1	2	23	28
Compiled	1	2	5	3	1		24	46
Tax Returns	5	13	4	1			28	40
Other	9	16	23	23	3	8	62	94
NUMBER OF STATEMENTS	16	34	44	51	14	14	170	236
ASSETS	%	%	%	%	%	%	%	%
Cash & Equivalents	28.1	8.8	10.0	17.7	12.8	11.8	13.0	10.9
Trade Receivables (net)	13.6	18.8	17.0	20.9	14.7	14.8	11.0	11.7
Inventory	6.7	4.2	4.6	6.1	6.1	6.6	6.8	5.1
All Other Current	12.2	5.0	7.6	6.2	1.7	8.7	5.9	7.2
Total Current	60.6	36.9	39.2	50.8	35.3	42.0	36.6	34.9
Fixed Assets (net)	22.0	42.1	26.8	15.4	16.8	24.0	38.9	39.5
Intangibles (net)	7.1	.8	5.3	3.6	5.7	5.9	4.8	4.6
All Other Non-Current	10.3	20.3	28.7	30.2	42.2	28.1	19.7	21.0
Total	100.0	100.0	100.0	100.0	100.0	100.0	100.0	100.0
LIABILITIES								
Notes Payable-Short Term	21.9	17.2	17.2	15.3	13.6	21.6	15.5	17.7
Cur. Mat.-L.T.D.	11.6	4.8	1.2	3.5	1.5	5.2	3.0	3.2
Trade Payables	5.8	5.6	6.7	6.6	4.2	2.5	6.5	3.5
Income Taxes Payable	.0	.3	.0	.1	.0	.0	.2	.2
All Other Current	12.1	8.7	8.4	12.6	15.7	12.3	7.3	9.7
Total Current	51.4	36.5	33.6	38.1	35.0	41.6	32.6	34.3
Long-Term Debt	14.5	34.0	25.4	14.3	20.9	19.6	36.2	28.7
Deferred Taxes	.0	.0	.1	.2	.3	.3	.2	.2
All Other Non-Current	17.5	4.7	4.7	6.0	1.7	5.4	5.4	6.3
Net Worth	16.5	24.8	36.3	41.4	42.2	33.2	25.7	30.5
Total Liabilities & Net Worth	100.0	100.0	100.0	100.0	100.0	100.0	100.0	100.0
INCOME DATA								
Net Sales	100.0	100.0	100.0	100.0	100.0	100.0	100.0	100.0
Gross Profit								
Operating Expenses	92.2	60.8	68.4	64.5	60.6	75.3	68.0	62.6
Operating Profit	7.8	39.2	31.6	35.5	39.4	24.7	32.0	37.4
All Other Expenses (net)	3.2	18.6	16.1	12.9	11.9	11.8	14.5	13.8
Profit Before Taxes	4.6	20.6	15.4	22.6	27.5	13.0	17.5	23.6
RATIOS								
Current	5.2	3.7	1.9	2.1	1.6	1.5	2.3	3.0
	2.2	.8	1.3	1.2	1.2	1.2	1.2	1.1
	.4	.1	.5	.6	.3	.5	.6	.2
Quick	2.7	2.8	1.4	1.6	1.4	1.3	1.8	2.0
	1.6	.5	.7	.7	.5	.4	.8	.6
	.3	.0	.1	.3	.2	.0	.2	.1
Sales/Receivables	0 UND	0 UND	0 UND	0 UND	0 UND	0 UND	0 UND	0 UND
	0 UND	0 UND	3 108.1	26 13.9	27 13.7	14 26.3	1 635.0	1 723.0
	26 13.8	72 5.1	62 5.8	74 4.9	57 6.4	159 2.3	31 11.9	32 11.3
Cost of Sales/Inventory								
Cost of Sales/Payables								
Sales/Working Capital	5.2	3.5	2.8	1.4	3.4	.8	2.7	2.7
	15.8	-82.8	29.2	10.3	22.1	4.9	22.0	25.9
	-26.6	-4.4	-6.0	-9.1	-1.1	-7.6	-5.5	-3.0
EBIT/Interest			11.5	9.8	13.0	62.2	10.9	10.8
		(15) 6.6	(20) 4.0	(28) 4.2		(10) 23.4	(96) 3.6	(132) 4.1
		2.3	.2	1.9		2.6	1.6	1.8
Net Profit + Depr., Dep., Amort./Cur. Mat. L/T/D				3.5			6.9	8.3
				(10) 2.2			(19) 2.2	(12) 3.9
				.8			.6	1.4
Fixed/Worth	.0	.0	.0	.0	.0	.0	.0	.0
	.6	1.0	.2	.1	.2	.4	1.0	1.3
	NM	7.0	2.1	.7	2.9	5.9	10.2	4.9
Debt/Worth	.3	.9	.7	.5	1.2	1.2	1.0	.9
	1.0	3.3	2.5	1.6	1.8	3.1	3.9	2.4
	NM	14.9	5.7	14.0	3.7	14.1	NM	33.3
% Profit Before Taxes/Tangible Net Worth	127.5	85.1	56.5	70.4	68.4	13.3	51.5	50.7
	(12) 27.6	(28) 25.6	(39) 16.4	(45) 14.2	(13) 13.0	(13) 7.9	(128) 15.7	(191) 18.8
	3.6	3.2	4.9	1.0	7.7	-3.0	3.7	5.6
% Profit Before Taxes/Total Assets	61.9	31.0	13.7	17.0	15.0	5.2	11.2	13.4
	24.2	9.7	6.1	4.1	4.9	1.7	3.7	4.9
	1.6	.3	1.0	.1	2.6	-.4	.4	1.7
Sales/Net Fixed Assets	UND	UND	390.2	UND	UND	37.0	86.3	76.8
	39.5	11.9	19.9	20.5	17.3	3.9	5.5	5.2
	21.9	.2	2.6	3.4	5.0	.5	.3	.3
Sales/Total Assets	11.6	2.5	2.3	1.3	1.1	.6	1.0	.9
	5.9	.4	.3	.4	.6	.1	.3	.3
	1.8	.2	.1	.1	.1	.1	.1	.1
% Depr., Dep., Amort./Sales		1.5	.6	.6		1.5	1.5	1.2
		(18) 10.4	(24) 2.4	(32) 2.2		(10) 5.2	(124) 5.3	(160) 7.9
		21.3	14.1	3.8		16.3	14.5	18.8
% Officers', Directors' Owners' Comp/Sales							1.5	1.5
							(31) 8.3	(26) 5.4
							14.0	14.4
Net Sales ($)	18082M	67076M	235252M	1079692M	676152M	802788M	2562717M	2654025M
Total Assets ($)	3736M	40208M	220403M	1078749M	1013529M	1865273M	3444784M	3810731M

© RMA 2007

M = $ thousand   MM = $ million
See Pages 11 through 21 for Explanation of Ratios and Data

Comparative Historical Data   Current Data Sorted by Sales

4/1/04-3/31/05 ALL	4/1/05-3/31/06 ALL	4/1/06-3/31/07 ALL	Type of Statement	0-1MM	1-3MM	3-5MM	5-10MM	10-25MM	25MM & OVER
51	41	39	Unqualified	4	5	1	6	10	13
15	15	17	Reviewed	3	6	1	1	3	3
20	22	12	Compiled	4	5		1	1	1
37	50	23	Tax Returns	16	4			2	1
75	109	82	Other	23	17	6		10	8
				20 (4/1-9/30/06)			153 (10/1/06-3/31/07)		
198	237	173	**NUMBER OF STATEMENTS**	50	37	8	26	26	26
%	%	%	**ASSETS**	%	%	%	%	%	%
15.6	15.0	14.1	Cash & Equivalents	8.9	17.5	15.0	15.0	14.3	14.5
13.4	13.5	17.8	Trade Receivables (net)	11.5	20.8		11.2	22.5	26.7
5.3	6.5	5.5	Inventory	3.3	4.7		4.6	6.9	11.8
6.0	6.3	6.7	All Other Current	9.6	7.7		4.4	9.0	1.8
40.3	41.4	44.1	Total Current	33.3	50.7		35.1	52.8	54.8
31.5	30.6	25.0	Fixed Assets (net)	36.6	17.6		31.3	20.0	17.8
4.2	3.4	4.2	Intangibles (net)	2.3	.9		8.6	5.1	8.0
24.1	24.6	26.8	All Other Non-Current	27.7	30.8		25.1	22.1	19.4
100.0	100.0	100.0	Total	100.0	100.0		100.0	100.0	100.0
			LIABILITIES						
18.5	16.0	17.2	Notes Payable-Short Term	15.9	23.6		7.4	23.4	13.4
3.3	3.8	3.9	Cur. Mat.-L.T.D.	5.2	5.8		1.2	2.6	3.4
7.0	5.0	5.8	Trade Payables	1.2	3.8		8.5	9.6	12.0
.0	.5	.1	Income Taxes Payable	.0	.0		.0	.5	.1
13.9	13.5	10.9	All Other Current	5.1	11.9		8.4	12.2	17.1
42.7	38.7	37.9	Total Current	27.5	45.1		25.5	48.3	46.0
21.9	22.9	22.0	Long-Term Debt	32.7	17.9		25.4	14.6	16.0
.1	.2	.1	Deferred Taxes	.0	.1		.0	.3	.3
5.5	8.6	6.1	All Other Non-Current	4.5	9.3		8.2	4.4	5.1
29.8	29.5	33.9	Net Worth	35.4	27.6		41.0	32.4	32.7
100.0	100.0	100.0	Total Liabilties & Net Worth	100.0	100.0		100.0	100.0	100.0
			INCOME DATA						
100.0	100.0	100.0	Net Sales	100.0	100.0		100.0	100.0	100.0
			Gross Profit						
65.0	66.3	67.9	Operating Expenses	52.8	73.1		67.8	73.4	85.3
35.0	33.7	32.1	Operating Profit	47.2	26.9		32.2	26.6	14.7
11.4	9.2	13.8	All Other Expenses (net)	28.6	9.6		7.0	9.1	2.4
23.6	24.5	18.3	Profit Before Taxes	18.6	17.3		25.2	17.4	12.3
			RATIOS						
2.4	3.6	2.1		4.5	2.3		6.7	1.7	1.5
1.1	1.2	1.2	Current	1.3	1.0		2.0	1.2	1.2
.3	.4	.5		.3	.3		.7	1.0	1.0
2.1	2.5	1.6		2.9	1.9		3.5	1.2	1.2
.7	.7	.7	Quick	.4	.8		.8	.6	.9
.1	.1	.2		.0	.1		.4	.2	.5
0 UND	0 UND	0 UND		0 UND	0 UND		0 UND	0 UND	14 25.6
0 999.8	3 128.4	9 42.7	Sales/Receivables	0 UND	2 227.7		5 80.2	29 12.5	38 9.6
47 7.8	36 10.2	66 5.5		92 4.0	67 5.5		22 16.7	98 3.7	72 5.1
			Cost of Sales/Inventory						
			Cost of Sales/Payables						
2.3	2.1	2.6		1.0	2.5		1.9	4.6	9.1
43.0	23.8	13.4	Sales/Working Capital	8.5	19.1		13.3	11.4	12.7
-4.2	-6.1	-7.1		-1.5	-4.3		-23.5	NM	NM
19.1	15.6	14.2		7.3	14.2		42.9	7.3	30.4
(102) 6.3	(131) 5.9	(87) 4.4	EBIT/Interest	(10) 5.1	(23) 5.6	(14) 4.3	(14) 4.5	(23) 4.2
1.5	1.9	2.0		.5	2.0		2.2	1.9	2.3
2.7	6.9	4.7							
(14) .9	(20) 2.9	(18) 1.6	Net Profit + Depr., Dep., Amort./Cur. Mat. L/T/D						
.3	1.0	1.1							
.0	.0	.0		.0	.0		.1	.0	.1
.5	.4	.2	Fixed/Worth	.1	.1		.6	.4	.3
3.3	3.6	2.6		4.4	1.0		13.8	2.4	3.2
.7	.5	.6		.5	.3		.7	1.1	1.6
2.3	2.0	1.9	Debt/Worth	3.1	1.0		1.7	3.4	1.9
12.8	13.7	8.3		9.9	18.5		15.9	7.7	15.0
53.4	64.9	64.3		21.6	137.9		86.0	141.8	91.8
(164) 19.6	(195) 22.9	(150) 14.1	% Profit Before Taxes/Tangible Net Worth	(45) 5.9	(31) 23.7	(21) 37.7	(23) 15.2	(23) 39.4
3.8	7.5	3.2		.7	.7		11.6	7.9	13.4
14.8	18.8	21.6		5.5	32.0		27.6	45.5	22.2
5.6	7.6	5.1	% Profit Before Taxes/Total Assets	1.5	8.1		12.9	5.5	8.4
1.1	1.6	.6		.1	.0		4.9	1.2	2.1
493.1	381.4	UND		UND	UND		64.0	124.2	159.8
18.3	16.3	21.3	Sales/Net Fixed Assets	12.7	60.9		11.3	18.7	14.9
.5	.7	2.5		.2	9.3		.8	3.2	3.7
1.6	2.0	1.9		.3	4.2		2.7	2.0	3.7
.3	.4	.4	Sales/Total Assets	.1	.4		.8	1.1	1.3
.1	.2	.1		.1	.2		.3	.1	.8
.9	1.0	.9		9.7	.9		.9	.8	.5
(126) 3.0	(139) 2.8	(102) 2.5	% Depr., Dep., Amort./Sales	(21) 16.6	(18) 1.4	(17) 2.9	(19) 2.2	(23) 1.6
16.5	11.3	10.2		23.1	9.8		10.9	3.5	3.3
5.5	1.1	1.4							
(24) 11.5	(29) 12.2	(23) 8.1	% Officers', Directors' Owners' Comp/Sales						
21.0	29.6	26.4							
2496576M	3102242M	2879042M	Net Sales ($)	19606M	69344M	33822M	197508M	401773M	2156989M
4694534M	5062352M	4221898M	Total Assets ($)	203002M	312854M	203488M	563942M	1201189M	1737423M

© RMA 2007

M = $ thousand   MM = $ million
See Pages 11 through 21 for Explanation of Ratios and Data

Current Data Sorted by Assets   Comparative Historical Data

0-500M	500M-2MM	2-10MM	10-50MM	50-100MM	100-250MM	Type of Statement	4/1/02-3/31/03 ALL	4/1/03-3/31/04 ALL
2	4	12	13	4	3	Unqualified	9	15
1	1	2	1			Reviewed	2	1
1	2	6	2			Compiled	6	9
12	8	4	1			Tax Returns	2	18
4	11	11	10	4	4	Other	13	22
	14 (4/1-9/30/06)		109 (10/1/06-3/31/07)					
20	26	35	27	8	7	NUMBER OF STATEMENTS	32	65
%	%	%	%	%	%	ASSETS	%	%
25.1	24.0	26.2	36.2			Cash & Equivalents	17.3	18.5
7.8	15.5	18.6	11.9			Trade Receivables (net)	9.7	10.7
2.3	.0	.0	.4			Inventory	1.1	.2
2.1	3.6	5.2	9.5			All Other Current	5.9	5.3
37.3	43.1	50.1	58.0			Total Current	34.1	34.8
33.1	29.6	14.4	9.8			Fixed Assets (net)	30.2	34.3
7.2	8.0	10.9	7.3			Intangibles (net)	2.5	2.8
22.5	19.4	24.7	25.0			All Other Non-Current	33.2	28.2
100.0	100.0	100.0	100.0			Total	100.0	100.0
						LIABILITIES		
46.6	18.3	6.0	7.8			Notes Payable-Short Term	22.1	18.2
7.0	2.8	2.0	.6			Cur. Mat.-L.T.D.	5.3	3.2
6.0	3.2	4.5	3.8			Trade Payables	4.4	4.4
.5	.0	2.4	.2			Income Taxes Payable	.1	.3
45.7	20.3	14.8	8.7			All Other Current	10.2	23.8
105.9	44.7	29.7	21.1			Total Current	42.1	49.9
21.4	41.8	14.8	8.4			Long-Term Debt	19.8	35.2
.1	.0	.0	.5			Deferred Taxes	.1	.2
5.2	7.3	8.3	10.0			All Other Non-Current	6.2	9.3
-32.5	6.2	47.1	60.0			Net Worth	31.8	5.5
100.0	100.0	100.0	100.0			Total Liabilties & Net Worth	100.0	100.0
						INCOME DATA		
100.0	100.0	100.0	100.0			Net Sales	100.0	100.0
						Gross Profit		
81.9	78.4	71.1	59.0			Operating Expenses	74.3	76.7
18.1	21.6	28.9	41.0			Operating Profit	25.7	23.3
1.8	8.0	5.3	3.1			All Other Expenses (net)	8.2	9.7
16.4	13.5	23.6	37.9			Profit Before Taxes	17.5	13.5
						RATIOS		
2.2	1.8	4.2	8.7				3.0	2.6
.4	1.0	1.4	2.8			Current	1.3	1.3
.1	.4	.7	1.9				.2	.2
2.2	1.8	4.2	8.7				2.5	2.0
.3	1.0	1.2	2.6			Quick	.6	.9
.1	.3	.7	1.3				.1	.2
0 UND	0 UND	0 UND	0 UND				0 UND	0 UND
0 UND	0 UND	14 26.8	17 21.8			Sales/Receivables	0 UND	1 636.6
3 119.3	21 17.3	53 6.8	91 4.0				21 17.5	29 12.5
						Cost of Sales/Inventory		
						Cost of Sales/Payables		
88.3	17.4	3.3	.6				7.1	6.1
-27.7	UND	8.3	2.6			Sales/Working Capital	59.1	46.8
-6.1	-4.9	-24.2	5.3				-3.0	-8.3
29.3	10.9	49.3	36.7				21.0	20.0
(14) 6.2	(17) 6.2	(19) 14.6	(12) 17.3			EBIT/Interest	(22) 4.6	(36) 5.6
-1.3	2.8	1.1	7.8				1.5	2.0
						Net Profit + Depr., Dep., Amort./Cur. Mat. L/T/D		
.1	.1	.0	.0				.0	.1
-5.6	2.2	.1	.1			Fixed/Worth	.4	.9
-.2	79.1	1.9	.5				3.3	6.2
.7	1.2	.3	.1				.4	.8
-3.3	6.5	1.0	.8			Debt/Worth	1.5	2.5
-2.0	UND	21.6	3.2				8.5	NM
	134.7	126.3	102.3			% Profit Before Taxes/Tangible	72.6	74.7
(21) 33.4	(28) 30.2	(25) 15.6				Net Worth	(27) 10.2	(49) 16.0
5.0	2.6	7.1					2.7	5.4
51.1	22.6	57.9	22.1			% Profit Before Taxes/Total	20.2	33.5
20.0	4.6	9.6	12.0			Assets	4.5	7.2
-25.1	.2	1.6	4.0				.1	1.0
247.4	109.7	284.0	UND				310.3	109.7
52.6	29.2	52.6	48.5			Sales/Net Fixed Assets	25.4	15.1
18.3	3.7	18.8	8.0				.5	.5
20.3	7.2	2.6	1.4				2.9	4.1
7.2	2.6	1.6	.5			Sales/Total Assets	1.0	2.1
2.0	.2	.4	.1				.2	.2
.2	.7	.4	.6				1.1	1.7
(11) 1.1	(22) 1.5	(23) .9	(16) 1.3			% Depr., Dep., Amort./Sales	(21) 5.0	(42) 3.2
4.2	6.1	2.5	3.9				13.7	16.6
						% Officers', Directors'		10.3
						Owners' Comp/Sales		(12) 19.8
								30.9
54380M	99864M	318716M	665044M	154289M	328432M	Net Sales ($)	798043M	1268619M
4026M	30589M	172534M	763657M	577593M	1096477M	Total Assets ($)	470421M	600455M

M = $ thousand   MM = $ million

See Pages 11 through 21 for Explanation of Ratios and Data

Comparative Historical Data / Current Data Sorted by Sales

			Type of Statement						
8	24	38	Unqualified	3	8	3	10	7	7
2	5	5	Reviewed		1		2		2
3	10	11	Compiled	5	2	3	1		
10	16	25	Tax Returns	14	6	2	3		
25	30	44	Other	7	6	5		12	6
4/1/04-3/31/05 ALL	4/1/05-3/31/06 ALL	4/1/06-3/31/07 ALL		14 (4/1-9/30/06)			109 (10/1/06-3/31/07)		
				0-1MM	1-3MM	3-5MM	5-10MM	10-25MM	25MM & OVER
48	85	123	**NUMBER OF STATEMENTS**	29	23	13	24	19	15
%	%	%	**ASSETS**	%	%	%	%	%	%
15.4	19.5	29.2	Cash & Equivalents	21.1	30.2	28.5	36.3	24.4	38.9
16.0	13.4	13.8	Trade Receivables (net)	3.6	16.3	15.7	12.8	24.7	15.5
1.3	1.5	.5	Inventory	.0	2.1	.0	.0	.0	.8
7.1	6.0	6.7	All Other Current	8.6	1.4	1.6	9.4	7.2	11.0
39.7	40.3	50.2	Total Current	33.2	50.0	45.9	58.5	56.3	66.3
31.8	25.6	18.1	Fixed Assets (net)	25.9	19.6	13.2	13.6	19.5	10.5
5.4	7.1	7.6	Intangibles (net)	6.7	4.6	14.0	6.3	9.7	8.1
23.1	26.9	24.0	All Other Non-Current	34.2	25.8	27.0	21.6	14.5	15.1
100.0	100.0	100.0	Total	100.0	100.0	100.0	100.0	100.0	100.0
			LIABILITIES						
19.5	18.3	16.8	Notes Payable-Short Term	17.2	39.6	5.2	16.3	8.5	2.6
4.7	4.7	2.5	Cur. Mat.-L.T.D.	1.0	6.7	3.9	1.4	.4	2.1
4.0	3.4	4.0	Trade Payables	1.6	5.4	4.0	2.8	6.5	5.6
.5	.2	.8	Income Taxes Payable	.0	3.8	.2	.0	.4	2.1
15.6	21.9	18.6	All Other Current	19.2	10.3	9.1	29.6	21.5	17.1
44.5	48.4	42.8	Total Current	39.0	65.8	22.4	50.1	37.2	27.7
42.8	29.2	20.2	Long-Term Debt	25.7	19.2	18.2	35.0	4.9	8.8
.4	.2	.1	Deferred Taxes	.0	.1	.0	.0	.2	.7
7.8	8.3	7.1	All Other Non-Current	5.2	3.8	9.4	5.6	8.3	14.6
4.5	13.9	29.8	Net Worth	30.1	11.2	50.0	9.3	49.4	48.2
100.0	100.0	100.0	Total Liabilties & Net Worth	100.0	100.0	100.0	100.0	100.0	100.0
			INCOME DATA						
100.0	100.0	100.0	Net Sales	100.0	100.0	100.0	100.0	100.0	100.0
			Gross Profit						
69.7	68.7	68.3	Operating Expenses	53.0	76.4	75.4	75.0	66.5	70.6
30.3	31.3	31.7	Operating Profit	47.0	23.6	24.6	25.0	33.5	29.4
10.9	9.1	6.1	All Other Expenses (net)	13.5	10.1	8.4	1.3	.1	-1.2
19.4	22.2	25.6	Profit Before Taxes	33.5	13.4	16.2	23.7	33.4	30.6
			RATIOS						
3.0	3.3	4.7	Current	5.2	5.1	29.7	2.5	3.5	7.6
1.2	1.6	1.8		1.0	1.8	1.4	1.3	2.2	2.8
.6	.6	.7		.2	.3	.8	.8	.9	1.9
1.9	2.9	4.7	Quick	5.2	5.1	20.0	2.2	3.3	6.5
1.0	1.2	1.4		.6	1.5	1.4	1.3	2.1	2.2
.4	.3	.5		.1	.3	.8	.6	.6	1.1
0 UND	0 UND	0 UND	Sales/Receivables	0 UND	0 UND	0 UND	0 UND	0 UND	9 41.7
1 613.3	0 999.8	4 89.7		0 UND	5 79.9	22 16.9	8 43.9	26 14.1	17 21.8
52 7.1	32 11.5	39 9.4		0 UND	41 8.9	54 6.8	24 15.3	89 4.1	44 8.3
			Cost of Sales/Inventory						
			Cost of Sales/Payables						
4.8	4.0	1.8	Sales/Working Capital	1.0	1.7	1.2	1.7	2.0	2.2
18.1	15.4	8.3		UND	83.8	20.0	24.3	7.0	4.1
-19.7	-13.6	-24.2		-3.3	-6.7	-58.9	-51.3	-843.8	9.1
21.1	24.5	23.6	EBIT/Interest	14.0	14.8	7.8		430.3	303.0
(27) 4.7	(51) 8.6	(67) 9.6		(15) 4.9	(13) 1.6	(10) 2.2		(10) 64.4	(10) 31.3
1.6	2.1	2.8		2.8	.2	-1.8		9.2	15.1
			Net Profit + Depr., Dep., Amort./Cur. Mat. L/T/D						
.0	.1	.0	Fixed/Worth	.0	.0	.0	.0	.0	.1
.5	.4	.2		.0	.2	.2	.2	.1	.2
5.9	5.1	3.6		37.2	-1.2	2.4	3.1	1.9	2.9
.5	.5	.4	Debt/Worth	.2	.3	.4	.7	.4	.2
2.7	1.8	1.5		1.0	2.1	1.3	2.4	1.4	1.0
NM	26.6	39.0		98.8	-3.0	8.9	UND	17.9	339.2
89.4	80.7	108.8	% Profit Before Taxes/Tangible Net Worth	54.5	26.1	15.6	165.1	249.5	267.8
(36) 22.8	(68) 24.8	(97) 21.6		(23) 16.1	(15) 3.7	(11) 10.4	(19) 23.8	(17) 111.6	(12) 74.2
3.6	9.7	4.0		2.2	-3.1	-5.2	4.8	17.5	23.0
21.8	30.0	33.0	% Profit Before Taxes/Total Assets	15.6	17.3	11.3	55.1	71.5	70.4
7.8	7.8	10.2		4.0	2.4	3.0	10.6	22.1	33.5
.9	1.9	1.9		1.1	-3.2	-1.4	2.3	7.1	14.0
59.4	82.0	999.8	Sales/Net Fixed Assets	UND	UND	191.1	999.8	85.6	72.9
21.2	33.7	48.8		219.0	37.0	43.9	88.7	48.8	30.3
2.2	5.7	14.9		.4	18.0	5.7	26.5	39.3	10.8
3.3	3.9	3.3	Sales/Total Assets	1.2	6.1	2.9	8.2	3.3	2.4
.8	1.7	1.3		.1	1.0	1.8	2.2	2.3	1.5
.2	.2	.2		.1	.2	.6	.4	.5	.4
1.0	.6	.4	% Depr., Dep., Amort./Sales	3.4	.4	.6	.2	.4	1.0
(32) 2.5	(58) 1.6	(77) 1.2		(13) 15.4	(13) 1.0	(10) 1.3	(16) .5	(12) .7	(13) 1.4
11.4	4.7	3.4		26.2	3.9	3.8	2.3	1.7	2.6
	9.2	10.5	% Officers', Directors' Owners' Comp/Sales						
	(20) 20.8	(25) 23.3							
	34.3	34.5							
484755M	4059594M	1620725M	Net Sales ($)	14532M	41595M	52957M	179180M	301888M	1030573M
837218M	1466326M	2644876M	Total Assets ($)	203020M	252425M	160833M	581041M	562570M	884987M

© RMA 2007

M = $ thousand   MM = $ million
See Pages 11 through 21 for Explanation of Ratios and Data

Current Data Sorted by Assets   Comparative Historical Data

0-500M	500M-2MM	2-10MM	10-50MM	50-100MM	100-250MM		4/1/02-3/31/03 ALL	4/1/03-3/31/04 ALL
						Type of Statement		
3	11	5	10	2	5	Unqualified	30	27
	1	4	2			Reviewed	5	5
4	2	3	1			Compiled	16	19
15	12	3				Tax Returns	9	19
13	16	9	10	4	2	Other	35	39
	12 (4/1-9/30/06)		125 (10/1/06-3/31/07)					
35	42	24	23	6	7	**NUMBER OF STATEMENTS**	95	109
%	%	%	%	%	%	**ASSETS**	%	%
49.6	24.9	24.8	27.8			Cash & Equivalents	27.8	27.9
4.9	15.5	28.7	26.5			Trade Receivables (net)	22.3	25.2
.0	.9	.0	.6			Inventory	1.0	2.5
2.6	9.7	5.1	6.7			All Other Current	4.2	4.0
57.1	51.0	58.6	61.6			Total Current	55.2	59.6
20.8	22.4	10.7	11.8			Fixed Assets (net)	23.7	16.1
6.0	6.6	6.5	9.6			Intangibles (net)	6.8	7.5
16.2	20.0	24.2	17.1			All Other Non-Current	14.3	16.9
100.0	100.0	100.0	100.0			Total	100.0	100.0
						LIABILITIES		
19.5	9.5	7.7	5.6			Notes Payable-Short Term	17.8	16.6
6.9	2.5	1.6	5.9			Cur. Mat.-L.T.D.	3.8	6.3
2.8	5.6	4.5	5.9			Trade Payables	7.1	5.6
.0	.3	.3	.2			Income Taxes Payable	1.1	.6
20.4	15.3	17.5	16.3			All Other Current	25.3	24.0
49.6	33.1	31.7	33.9			Total Current	55.1	53.1
28.6	14.9	13.6	12.0			Long-Term Debt	9.1	14.5
.0	.1	1.9	.6			Deferred Taxes	.4	.2
18.3	3.6	4.5	8.6			All Other Non-Current	6.6	5.5
3.5	48.2	48.3	44.9			Net Worth	28.9	26.7
100.0	100.0	100.0	100.0			Total Liabilities & Net Worth	100.0	100.0
						INCOME DATA		
100.0	100.0	100.0	100.0			Net Sales	100.0	100.0
						Gross Profit		
82.3	83.5	82.2	67.0			Operating Expenses	82.0	81.5
17.7	16.5	17.8	33.0			Operating Profit	18.0	18.5
2.5	4.5	-.1	5.5			All Other Expenses (net)	4.2	1.9
15.2	12.0	17.9	27.5			Profit Before Taxes	13.8	16.6
						RATIOS		
3.4	5.7	4.8	5.1				3.0	3.5
1.4	1.7	2.3	1.9			Current	1.6	1.3
.7	.6	1.0	1.2				.6	.7
3.0	4.4	4.7	4.9				2.9	3.0
1.4	1.5	2.0	1.6			Quick	1.3	1.2
.7	.5	.8	.7				.6	.5
0 UND	0 UND	1 416.8	16 22.6				0 UND	0 UND
0 UND	8 46.7	36 10.2	40 9.1			Sales/Receivables	17 21.0	26 14.2
1 487.0	31 11.6	76 4.8	85 4.3				63 5.7	76 4.8
						Cost of Sales/Inventory		
						Cost of Sales/Payables		
15.6	5.0	2.7	2.2				4.9	3.5
233.5	18.4	7.7	4.8			Sales/Working Capital	16.8	12.5
-93.8	-23.7	125.2	17.6				-22.4	-20.3
76.3	54.7	59.9	342.3				83.8	30.8
(25) 11.2	(24) 9.6	(16) 20.4	(15) 14.3			EBIT/Interest	(65) 14.8	(73) 7.7
5.1	.8	7.7	1.6				1.3	2.9
							25.3	22.0
						Net Profit + Depr., Dep., Amort./Cur. Mat. L/T/D	(10) 7.9	(14) 3.3
							.2	.8
.0	.1	.0	.0				.1	.1
.5	.3	.2	.2			Fixed/Worth	.5	.2
7.7	2.5	.5	1.4				4.6	2.1
.3	.3	.3	.5				.5	.6
3.2	1.3	1.3	1.3			Debt/Worth	1.5	2.3
-3.4	6.8	6.5	6.1				15.6	34.1
396.0	133.5	118.9	152.6				97.6	94.1
(24) 141.2	(38) 75.6	(22) 37.1	(20) 68.8			% Profit Before Taxes/Tangible Net Worth	(72) 55.0	(84) 32.4
32.8	10.8	10.1	15.7				10.6	5.6
226.3	66.1	26.9	48.6				52.6	50.3
113.7	21.8	11.2	24.4			% Profit Before Taxes/Total Assets	18.0	14.5
14.9	2.1	3.4	4.3				2.0	3.6
477.0	115.7	149.7	78.8				72.7	79.9
91.8	39.6	39.5	25.0			Sales/Net Fixed Assets	25.8	30.6
35.1	9.5	14.9	10.3				8.8	17.6
19.8	5.3	3.9	2.2				6.2	5.3
9.0	2.9	2.2	1.5			Sales/Total Assets	2.5	2.4
4.7	1.9	1.1	.2				1.5	1.0
.4	.4	.3	.5				.8	.9
(18) .9	(25) .9	(14) 1.4	(18) 1.6			% Depr., Dep., Amort./Sales	(71) 1.4	(68) 1.5
1.9	2.0	2.4	5.2				2.3	2.5
20.6	7.5						6.7	11.9
(15) 26.1	(18) 16.7					% Officers', Directors' Owners' Comp/Sales	(25) 13.6	(36) 20.8
33.2	34.4						26.3	
50979M	185213M	256977M	766505M	186495M	909908M	Net Sales ($)	2232944M	2033253M
5669M	50886M	108251M	516035M	424629M	1165109M	Total Assets ($)	1786634M	1877597M

M = $ thousand   MM = $ million
See Pages 11 through 21 for Explanation of Ratios and Data

Comparative Historical Data | Current Data Sorted by Sales

4/1/04-3/31/05 ALL	4/1/05-3/31/06 ALL	4/1/06-3/31/07 ALL	Type of Statement	0-1MM	1-3MM	3-5MM	5-10MM	10-25MM	25MM & OVER
30	23	36	Unqualified	2	6	5	4	7	12
7	8	7	Reviewed		1		4	2	
8	10	10	Compiled	1	5		4		
21	21	30	Tax Returns	14	9	2	3	2	
37	54	54	Other	6	16	6	12	6	8
				12 (4/1-9/30/06)			125 (10/1/06-3/31/07)		
103	116	137	**NUMBER OF STATEMENTS**	23	37	13	27	17	20
%	%	%	**ASSETS**	%	%	%	%	%	%
29.0	24.2	30.2	Cash & Equivalents	30.4	36.2	35.9	24.8	26.0	26.0
26.6	23.6	18.9	Trade Receivables (net)	4.9	11.8	18.8	23.0	28.1	34.6
1.0	2.2	.5	Inventory	.0	.0	.0	1.4	.3	.9
3.5	9.3	6.2	All Other Current	4.7	10.0	10.5	3.8	3.6	3.4
60.1	59.2	55.7	Total Current	40.1	58.1	65.2	53.0	57.9	65.0
16.5	17.3	16.7	Fixed Assets (net)	25.6	17.1	14.6	16.0	12.4	11.7
6.9	10.9	7.0	Intangibles (net)	9.0	2.6	4.4	11.1	8.9	7.5
16.5	12.6	20.6	All Other Non-Current	25.3	22.2	15.9	19.9	20.8	15.8
100.0	100.0	100.0	Total	100.0	100.0	100.0	100.0	100.0	100.0
			LIABILITIES						
14.1	20.0	11.9	Notes Payable-Short Term	15.6	14.4	24.0	6.7	8.0	5.1
6.7	6.5	4.2	Cur. Mat.-L.T.D.	2.1	5.8	2.3	5.1	4.4	3.4
4.8	5.9	4.3	Trade Payables	2.7	4.5	6.9	4.0	2.4	6.5
.4	.4	.2	Income Taxes Payable	.0	.0	.3	.4	.0	.2
18.6	15.4	17.2	All Other Current	17.4	17.7	6.6	15.1	25.8	18.7
44.7	48.1	37.8	Total Current	37.7	42.4	40.2	31.5	40.6	33.9
15.4	22.5	17.5	Long-Term Debt	49.4	9.6	12.7	12.6	13.6	8.4
.2	.6	.5	Deferred Taxes	.0	.0	.0	.9	1.7	.6
8.7	8.4	8.2	All Other Non-Current	1.6	18.8	7.7	1.4	4.9	8.6
31.0	20.4	36.1	Net Worth	11.4	29.2	39.3	53.7	39.3	48.4
100.0	100.0	100.0	Total Liabilities & Net Worth	100.0	100.0	100.0	100.0	100.0	100.0
			INCOME DATA						
100.0	100.0	100.0	Net Sales	100.0	100.0	100.0	100.0	100.0	100.0
			Gross Profit						
82.5	80.8	78.0	Operating Expenses	69.1	81.0	89.2	87.1	72.0	68.1
17.5	19.2	22.0	Operating Profit	30.9	19.0	10.8	12.9	28.0	31.9
3.3	2.5	3.4	All Other Expenses (net)	10.9	4.1	1.2	-.1	2.6	.4
14.3	16.7	18.6	Profit Before Taxes	20.0	14.8	9.6	12.9	25.4	31.5
			RATIOS						
3.5	3.0	4.6	Current	1.8	11.5	3.6	5.9	2.6	5.0
1.8	1.5	1.6		1.4	1.5	1.8	1.8	1.6	1.8
1.0	.8	.7		.5	.7	.8	.7	.7	.9
3.3	2.8	4.2	Quick	1.8	8.7	3.6	5.9	2.6	4.8
1.6	1.3	1.4		1.3	1.4	1.7	1.8	1.5	1.8
.8	.5	.5		.4	.3	.7	.7	.6	.8
0 UND	0 UND	0 UND	Sales/Receivables	0 UND	0 UND	0 UND	0 999.8	0 771.9	16 22.3
20 18.1	17 21.7	10 35.2		0 UND	1 487.0	2 176.3	11 34.4	26 13.8	37 9.7
81 4.5	64 5.7	41 8.9		22 16.8	23 16.2	72 5.1	79 4.6	56 6.5	98 3.7
			Cost of Sales/Inventory						
			Cost of Sales/Payables						
3.8	4.6	4.2	Sales/Working Capital	8.1	3.8	3.8	4.5	4.7	3.6
13.0	14.0	17.6		43.7	17.1	8.5	19.5	23.1	6.2
-557.6	-46.0	-33.2		-26.0	-16.7	-270.6	-29.5	-27.8	NM
32.1	27.9	64.8	EBIT/Interest	33.7	81.4		48.4	92.3	407.9
(71) 7.6	(84) 12.1	(89) 14.3		(14) 6.6	(24) 12.8		(16) 27.0	(12) 27.3	(14) 30.5
2.5	2.6	3.7		2.6	3.6		7.6	1.3	10.3
16.5	11.7	7.9	Net Profit + Depr., Dep., Amort./Cur. Mat. L/T/D						
(10) 7.2	(10) 4.6	(12) 2.4							
2.0	1.5	1.0							
.0	.1	.0	Fixed/Worth	.0	.0	.1	.0	.0	.1
.2	.4	.2		.4	.1	.3	.1	.1	.1
2.1	3.7	2.2		-60.0	1.8	1.3	3.5	NM	1.3
.6	.7	.3	Debt/Worth	.4	.2	.5	.2	.5	.3
1.8	2.3	1.7		3.2	2.2	1.7	1.1	3.2	1.1
9.0	-25.3	11.1		-3.3	6.3	9.7	9.9	NM	16.4
105.5	139.2	138.5	% Profit Before Taxes/Tangible Net Worth	253.6	159.3	111.6	120.1	176.3	200.9
(84) 31.3	(86) 37.4	(114) 62.5		(16) 99.0	(33) 56.7	(11) 66.2	(24) 43.0	(13) 49.5	(17) 77.9
10.3	13.3	13.3		2.8	10.7	60.8	11.8	10.8	44.6
42.2	55.4	86.6	% Profit Before Taxes/Total Assets	156.3	116.0	62.5	97.2	71.1	51.5
15.0	16.2	20.5		16.7	20.3	22.3	14.6	11.9	32.3
3.6	4.1	4.7		5.0	3.4	.1	3.0	1.8	13.6
144.3	105.6	171.9	Sales/Net Fixed Assets	477.0	259.5	145.7	132.1	278.5	144.7
42.5	42.7	42.4		41.9	49.0	44.7	54.9	39.6	29.6
15.5	15.9	14.7		12.0	19.6	11.9	15.7	14.7	14.6
5.2	5.3	5.5	Sales/Total Assets	9.2	8.4	5.3	6.9	4.9	3.0
2.4	2.6	2.7		2.4	3.9	2.8	3.5	2.7	2.1
1.2	1.3	1.1		.2	1.3	2.2	1.4	1.0	1.0
.7	.6	.4	% Depr., Dep., Amort./Sales		.4		.6	.4	.5
(64) 1.3	(76) 1.1	(78) 1.1		(23) .8		(15) 1.0	(12) 1.2	(14) .9	
2.6	2.4	2.3			1.9		1.7	1.9	3.8
14.6	10.6	9.1	% Officers', Directors' Owners' Comp/Sales		15.4		6.2		
(39) 22.9	(27) 16.8	(45) 21.7		(14) 26.1		(12) 13.3			
33.4	30.3	31.4			37.5		31.2		
2190545M	3459984M	2356077M	Net Sales ($)	10690M	69208M	52955M	192424M	266236M	1764564M
1885734M	1699756M	2270579M	Total Assets ($)	21174M	163404M	21850M	269887M	432481M	1361783M

Current Data Sorted by Assets   Comparative Historical Data

0-500M	500M-2MM	2-10MM	10-50MM	50-100MM	100-250MM	Type of Statement		
	1	5	5	2	3	Unqualified	16	11
2	1					Reviewed	3	2
1		1		1		Compiled	6	10
1		1			2	Tax Returns	4	1
	1	12	5	1		Other	15	25
	11 (4/1-9/30/06)		34 (10/1/06-3/31/07)				4/1/02-3/31/03 ALL	4/1/03-3/31/04 ALL
0-500M	**500M-2MM**	**2-10MM**	**10-50MM**	**50-100MM**	**100-250MM**	NUMBER OF STATEMENTS	44	49
4	3	19	10	4	5			
%	%	%	%	%	%	ASSETS	%	%
		24.6	18.9			Cash & Equivalents	21.5	26.0
		13.5	31.6			Trade Receivables (net)	12.2	13.7
		.6	.0			Inventory	.7	2.4
		3.7	1.5			All Other Current	5.3	6.8
		42.4	51.9			Total Current	39.7	48.9
		30.8	22.6			Fixed Assets (net)	34.0	23.5
		7.9	2.4			Intangibles (net)	5.6	5.7
		18.9	23.1			All Other Non-Current	20.7	21.8
		100.0	100.0			Total	100.0	100.0
						LIABILITIES		
		1.6	8.5			Notes Payable-Short Term	9.8	9.2
		3.7	5.0			Cur. Mat.-L.T.D.	2.0	.9
		10.6	1.5			Trade Payables	5.9	5.5
		.0	.6			Income Taxes Payable	.8	.6
		7.3	17.1			All Other Current	12.5	16.5
		23.0	32.6			Total Current	31.0	32.7
		19.7	17.0			Long-Term Debt	14.9	18.4
		.0	2.0			Deferred Taxes	.2	.7
		5.2	3.2			All Other Non-Current	5.4	6.2
		52.1	45.1			Net Worth	48.6	42.0
		100.0	100.0			Total Liabilities & Net Worth	100.0	100.0
						INCOME DATA		
		100.0	100.0			Net Sales	100.0	100.0
						Gross Profit		
		69.2	55.1			Operating Expenses	76.5	78.0
		30.8	44.9			Operating Profit	23.5	22.0
		6.9	20.6			All Other Expenses (net)	6.7	4.0
		23.9	24.3			Profit Before Taxes	16.7	18.0
						RATIOS		
		5.4	10.7				5.1	7.4
		2.2	3.4			Current	1.4	2.2
		.6	.9				.7	1.0
		5.4	10.5				3.1	6.4
		2.0	3.4			Quick	1.0	2.0
		.6	.9				.3	.4
		0 UND	0 UND				0 UND	0 UND
		14 26.3	50 7.3			Sales/Receivables	15 25.0	25 14.8
		43 8.4	200 1.8				39 9.4	43 8.5
						Cost of Sales/Inventory		
						Cost of Sales/Payables		
		2.3	.7				2.5	1.7
		5.3	2.4			Sales/Working Capital	34.6	5.1
		-9.1	NM				-10.4	NM
							30.8	11.4
						EBIT/Interest	(23) 5.4	(28) 3.9
							2.6	2.0
						Net Profit + Depr., Dep., Amort./Cur. Mat. L/T/D		
		.0	.0				.1	.0
		.3	.1			Fixed/Worth	.7	.2
		2.4	.9				1.7	2.3
		.2	.5				.4	.3
		1.0	1.2			Debt/Worth	.8	1.0
		9.1	7.3				5.6	15.0
		53.1					32.8	50.2
		(16) 16.7				% Profit Before Taxes/Tangible Net Worth	(40) 14.3	(42) 16.1
		6.8					5.2	6.6
		16.9	10.6				11.1	18.2
		8.7	3.3			% Profit Before Taxes/Total Assets	4.8	6.1
		1.4	1.4				1.3	1.2
		420.0	UND				31.8	48.2
		20.9	57.5			Sales/Net Fixed Assets	12.0	19.7
		.3	.5				.3	.6
		2.0	1.1				2.0	1.9
		.4	.2			Sales/Total Assets	.6	.6
		.2	.1				.2	.2
		.7					1.6	1.1
		(12) 2.8				% Depr., Dep., Amort./Sales	(35) 3.1	(34) 2.2
		11.6					16.5	12.3
						% Officers', Directors' Owners' Comp/Sales		
4988M	25267M	113521M	91963M	103265M	1864424M	Net Sales ($)	717600M	725624M
954M	5264M	94527M	235222M	249873M	1023188M	Total Assets ($)	924996M	1145099M

M = $ thousand   MM = $ million
See Pages 11 through 21 for Explanation of Ratios and Data

Comparative Historical Data | Current Data Sorted by Sales

4/1/04-3/31/05 ALL	4/1/05-3/31/06 ALL	4/1/06-3/31/07 ALL	Type of Statement	0-1MM	1-3MM	3-5MM	5-10MM	10-25MM	25MM & OVER
12	8	16	Unqualified		4	3	2	3	4
3	2	3	Reviewed		2			1	
	3	1	Compiled					1	
5	2	4	Tax Returns	2				1	
23	24	21	Other	6	5	2	3	2	2
				11 (4/1-9/30/06)			34 (10/1/06-3/31/07)		
43	39	45	NUMBER OF STATEMENTS	8	11	5	5	10	6
%	%	%	ASSETS	%	%	%	%	%	%
30.3	22.9	28.8	Cash & Equivalents		21.4			31.4	
14.6	13.6	16.6	Trade Receivables (net)		8.2			33.5	
.8	2.3	.6	Inventory		.2			1.1	
3.1	6.0	4.8	All Other Current		1.8			3.3	
48.8	44.8	50.8	Total Current		31.7			69.4	
27.3	25.1	24.5	Fixed Assets (net)		38.5			25.8	
5.7	6.5	6.9	Intangibles (net)		6.6			2.5	
18.2	23.6	17.8	All Other Non-Current		23.2			2.4	
100.0	100.0	100.0	Total		100.0			100.0	
			LIABILITIES						
5.9	16.0	3.5	Notes Payable-Short Term		4.9			3.2	
2.3	1.1	3.1	Cur. Mat.-L.T.D.		1.0			2.5	
4.8	3.9	6.3	Trade Payables		1.6			21.0	
.6	.1	.1	Income Taxes Payable		.0			.0	
11.5	17.0	10.9	All Other Current		1.9			5.9	
25.2	38.3	24.0	Total Current		9.4			32.5	
22.6	15.5	14.6	Long-Term Debt		17.6			7.9	
1.0	.7	.5	Deferred Taxes		.0			2.0	
5.0	9.1	3.3	All Other Non-Current		3.8			2.4	
46.3	36.5	57.7	Net Worth		69.2			55.2	
100.0	100.0	100.0	Total Liabilties & Net Worth		100.0			100.0	
			INCOME DATA						
100.0	100.0	100.0	Net Sales		100.0			100.0	
			Gross Profit						
69.0	71.1	65.6	Operating Expenses		69.5			74.3	
31.0	28.9	34.4	Operating Profit		30.5			25.7	
9.1	8.1	7.9	All Other Expenses (net)		5.5			5.2	
21.9	20.8	26.5	Profit Before Taxes		25.0			20.5	
			RATIOS						
5.8	8.5	14.6	Current		21.1			6.2	
2.3	3.5	2.3			5.4			2.0	
.6	1.2	1.1			1.7			1.1	
5.3	7.8	14.4	Quick		20.8			5.3	
1.9	2.0	2.2			5.4			2.0	
.6	.5	.7			1.7			1.0	
0 UND	0 UND	0 UND	Sales/Receivables		0 UND			0 UND	
9 42.2	17 21.0	0 UND			0 UND			27 13.4	
64 5.7	48 7.7	41 8.9			27 13.5			55 6.6	
			Cost of Sales/Inventory						
			Cost of Sales/Payables						
.5	1.1	1.9	Sales/Working Capital		.8			2.6	
3.9	5.4	4.9			2.4			9.5	
-11.9	20.4	UND			18.0			NM	
12.7	11.0	14.5	EBIT/Interest						
(21) 4.3	(19) 5.0	(15) 6.9							
2.0	1.0	3.6							
			Net Profit + Depr., Dep., Amort./Cur. Mat. L/T/D						
.0	.0	.0	Fixed/Worth		.1			.0	
.2	.2	.2			.3			.3	
3.1	1.2	1.0			.9			1.1	
.2	.2	.1	Debt/Worth		.0			.4	
1.3	.5	.7			.3			.7	
10.2	6.0	3.4			1.4			3.2	
40.1	17.4	43.8	% Profit Before Taxes/Tangible Net Worth		50.8				
(38) 16.8	(32) 7.2	(40) 19.4			(10) 12.3				
4.0	1.3	6.8			3.3				
11.6	12.3	22.1	% Profit Before Taxes/Total Assets		16.9			30.1	
4.6	4.6	8.7			8.7			11.6	
1.7	.0	2.1			1.6			1.4	
74.4	UND	UND	Sales/Net Fixed Assets		50.5			UND	
7.0	27.1	37.0			.8			30.7	
.7	1.3	1.0			.3			3.2	
1.3	1.8	2.4	Sales/Total Assets		1.7			3.3	
.3	.5	.9			.3			1.9	
.1	.1	.1			.1			.7	
1.1	.8	.6	% Depr., Dep., Amort./Sales		.4				
(26) 3.4	(21) 3.7	(25) 2.0			(10) 3.8				
16.7	8.3	11.5			18.0				
			% Officers', Directors' Owners' Comp/Sales						
446860M	687746M	2203428M	Net Sales ($)	4860M	20095M	21595M	34013M	151900M	1970965M
1369424M	1125745M	1609028M	Total Assets ($)	48309M	137717M	109269M	70608M	342091M	901034M

M = $ thousand   MM = $ million
See Pages 11 through 21 for Explanation of Ratios and Data

Current Data Sorted by Assets | Comparative Historical Data

0-500M	500M-2MM	2-10MM	10-50MM	50-100MM	100-250MM	Type of Statement	4/1/02-3/31/03 ALL	4/1/03-3/31/04 ALL
		1	7	2	1	Unqualified	5	8
	1					Reviewed	2	1
1	1	3			1	Compiled	1	1
2	1	1	1		1	Tax Returns	1	4
3	4	7	8	2	2	Other	7	7
			5 (4/1-9/30/06)	45 (10/1/06-3/31/07)				
6	7	12	16	4	5	NUMBER OF STATEMENTS	16	21
%	%	%	%	%	%	**ASSETS**	%	%
		21.5	29.0			Cash & Equivalents	28.7	18.9
		21.8	13.2			Trade Receivables (net)	9.7	10.9
		8.3	.1			Inventory	2.5	1.1
		5.3	8.1			All Other Current	6.4	8.0
		56.9	50.4			Total Current	47.2	38.9
		22.4	12.6			Fixed Assets (net)	40.0	41.1
		3.2	.6			Intangibles (net)	5.1	5.4
		17.4	36.3			All Other Non-Current	7.6	14.5
		100.0	100.0			Total	100.0	100.0
						LIABILITIES		
		12.1	24.7			Notes Payable-Short Term	13.5	18.6
		8.7	.0			Cur. Mat.-L.T.D.	2.4	5.0
		7.5	4.4			Trade Payables	3.0	1.9
		.2	.3			Income Taxes Payable	.0	.0
		7.9	5.3			All Other Current	4.9	10.6
		36.5	34.8			Total Current	23.9	36.0
		23.5	17.2			Long-Term Debt	29.9	38.0
		.0	.8			Deferred Taxes	.4	.1
		3.1	.2			All Other Non-Current	2.0	3.1
		36.9	47.0			Net Worth	43.8	22.8
		100.0	100.0			Total Liabilties & Net Worth	100.0	100.0
						INCOME DATA		
		100.0	100.0			Net Sales	100.0	100.0
						Gross Profit		
		71.2	65.0			Operating Expenses	57.1	61.1
		28.8	35.0			Operating Profit	42.9	38.9
		12.6	20.7			All Other Expenses (net)	21.8	28.1
		16.1	14.3			Profit Before Taxes	21.1	10.8
						RATIOS		
		3.4	8.2				4.9	1.9
		1.6	1.9			Current	1.8	.9
		.7	.6				.5	.1
		2.7	7.3				2.4	1.6
		1.3	1.6			Quick	1.0	.6
		.3	.3				.3	.0
		0 UND	0 UND				0 UND	0 UND
		15 24.3	1 327.2			Sales/Receivables	0 UND	4 86.4
		138 2.6	89 4.1				30 12.1	41 8.8
						Cost of Sales/Inventory		
						Cost of Sales/Payables		
		2.1	.2				.4	1.5
		16.9	1.4			Sales/Working Capital	3.3	-16.4
		NM	NM				-10.6	-2.7
						EBIT/Interest		
						Net Profit + Depr., Dep., Amort./Cur. Mat. L/T/D		
		.0	.0				.0	.2
		.2	.0			Fixed/Worth	.7	1.4
		1.3	.2				3.5	11.4
		.7	.6				.5	1.0
		3.3	1.3			Debt/Worth	1.5	4.2
		6.1	2.8				5.5	12.9
		148.2	14.7				(15) 37.2	(17) 30.1
		22.6	6.0			% Profit Before Taxes/Tangible Net Worth	31.2	11.1
		9.0	-1.4				6.5	-1.5
		56.3	6.2				13.7	6.9
		4.0	2.7			% Profit Before Taxes/Total Assets	4.4	2.0
		2.0	-.9				1.1	-.5
		UND	UND				UND	41.1
		29.6	39.4			Sales/Net Fixed Assets	8.1	2.3
		5.3	12.3				.2	.2
		4.0	.3				.7	.9
		.6	.1			Sales/Total Assets	.1	.1
		.2	.1				.1	.1
							(10) 2.1	(15) 2.2
						% Depr., Dep., Amort./Sales	9.7	12.8
							18.0	23.3
						% Officers', Directors' Owners' Comp/Sales		
5069M	9121M	106579M	103653M	130193M	68242M	Net Sales ($)	154027M	673380M
1324M	7737M	58805M	450854M	278600M	737563M	Total Assets ($)	560843M	853299M

M = $ thousand   MM = $ million
See Pages 11 through 21 for Explanation of Ratios and Data

Comparative Historical Data | **Current Data Sorted by Sales**

4/1/04- 3/31/05 ALL	4/1/05- 3/31/06 ALL	4/1/06- 3/31/07 ALL	Type of Statement	0-1MM	1-3MM	3-5MM	5-10MM	10-25MM	25MM & OVER
8	11	11	Unqualified		2	3	3	1	2
	1	1	Reviewed		1			1	
	2	6	Compiled		2		2	1	1
2	2	6	Tax Returns	3	1	1		1	
11	20	26	Other	9	7	2	4	3	1
				5 (4/1-9/30/06)		45 (10/1/06-3/31/07)			
21	36	50	**NUMBER OF STATEMENTS**	12	13	6	9	6	4
%	%	%	**ASSETS**	%	%	%	%	%	%
27.1	18.1	28.3	Cash & Equivalents	11.9	43.0				
11.9	18.4	13.8	Trade Receivables (net)	12.9	15.9				
2.8	4.5	2.1	Inventory	.7	.0				
10.6	4.0	5.2	All Other Current	2.0	4.4				
52.4	44.9	49.5	Total Current	27.4	63.3				
24.0	23.3	20.5	Fixed Assets (net)	43.7	11.0				
1.2	4.1	3.7	Intangibles (net)	.5	8.7				
22.4	27.8	26.3	All Other Non-Current	28.3	16.9				
100.0	100.0	100.0	Total	100.0	100.0				
			LIABILITIES						
13.1	10.0	15.1	Notes Payable-Short Term	18.9	13.3				
1.5	.6	2.4	Cur. Mat.-L.T.D.	1.1	1.2				
4.9	3.2	3.7	Trade Payables	.7	.9				
.1	.8	.1	Income Taxes Payable	.0	.2				
10.3	19.9	8.0	All Other Current	9.2	11.5				
29.9	34.4	29.3	Total Current	29.9	27.1				
19.2	35.0	26.5	Long-Term Debt	58.4	15.3				
.7	.4	.4	Deferred Taxes	.0	.0				
2.2	7.5	.9	All Other Non-Current	.2	2.4				
48.0	22.7	42.8	Net Worth	11.5	55.1				
100.0	100.0	100.0	Total Liabilities & Net Worth	100.0	100.0				
			INCOME DATA						
100.0	100.0	100.0	Net Sales	100.0	100.0				
			Gross Profit						
64.1	71.9	67.4	Operating Expenses	60.3	72.7				
35.9	28.1	32.6	Operating Profit	39.7	27.3				
14.8	12.5	16.0	All Other Expenses (net)	30.2	10.4				
21.1	15.6	16.7	Profit Before Taxes	9.5	16.9				
			RATIOS						
4.6	3.9	5.1		3.9	9.0				
1.4	1.6	1.9	Current	.7	1.9				
.6	.4	.8		.3	.6				
4.3	2.8	3.9		2.8	8.5				
1.4	1.1	1.6	Quick	.6	1.8				
.2	.2	.4		.2	.5				
0 UND	0 UND	0 UND		0 UND	0 UND				
0 UND	21 17.8	1 276.7	Sales/Receivables	0 UND	0 UND				
43 8.4	61 6.0	52 7.0		22 17.0	25 14.4				
			Cost of Sales/Inventory						
			Cost of Sales/Payables						
1.6	1.5	.4		.6	.5				
5.1	13.9	4.9	Sales/Working Capital	-28.0	4.5				
-4.9	-10.9	-45.1		-1.3	-51.7				
53.0	28.1	33.3							
(11) 16.0	(16) 6.7	(20) 6.4	EBIT/Interest						
3.7	2.7	-.9							
			Net Profit + Depr., Dep., Amort./Cur. Mat. L/T/D						
.0	.0	.0		.0	.0				
.3	.3	.1	Fixed/Worth	1.9	.0				
1.3	4.5	1.1		NM	.3				
.4	.5	.4		.7	.2				
1.9	2.2	1.4	Debt/Worth	4.1	1.2				
4.6	15.7	4.8		NM	4.1				
42.4	24.8	32.3			65.2				
(30) 10.7	(46) 13.9	12.3	% Profit Before Taxes/Tangible Net Worth		(12) 21.0				
3.4	5.3	1.8			1.2				
15.4	16.9	21.4		4.4	49.5				
3.9	5.5	3.3	% Profit Before Taxes/Total Assets	.9	4.2				
1.9	1.2	.3		-3.9	.7				
UND	123.9	UND		UND	UND				
11.1	25.8	33.1	Sales/Net Fixed Assets	1.0	228.7				
4.6	4.0	1.1		.2	38.0				
1.9	2.1	1.4		.6	3.8				
.4	.9	.2	Sales/Total Assets	.2	1.1				
.1	.1	.1		.1	.1				
.8	.6	1.1							
(14) 2.0	(20) 1.7	(29) 2.1	% Depr., Dep., Amort./Sales						
16.5	9.7	10.4							
			% Officers', Directors' Owners' Comp/Sales						
788728M	1174650M	422857M	Net Sales ($)	5383M	23560M	23459M	63419M	86700M	220336M
1158001M	1666040M	1534883M	Total Assets ($)	59431M	136424M	223886M	486052M	320903M	308187M

M = $ thousand   MM = $ million
See Pages 11 through 21 for Explanation of Ratios and Data

Current Data Sorted by Assets							Comparative Historical Data	

Type of Statement

0-500M	500M-2MM	2-10MM	10-50MM	50-100MM	100-250MM	Type of Statement	4/1/02-3/31/03 ALL	4/1/03-3/31/04 ALL
1		5	20	12	10	Unqualified	49	53
1	1	1			1	Reviewed	3	4
4	2	2				Compiled	2	9
4	3	9	6	7	8	Tax Returns	2	2
		21 (4/1-9/30/06)	76 (10/1/06-3/31/07)			Other	23	24
0-500M	500M-2MM	2-10MM	10-50MM	50-100MM	100-250MM	NUMBER OF STATEMENTS	79	92
10	6	17	26	19	19			
%	%	%	%	%	%	ASSETS	%	%
34.3		32.4	45.8	32.6	47.7	Cash & Equivalents	35.9	41.8
4.4		23.5	17.7	13.4	10.0	Trade Receivables (net)	20.0	17.4
.0		2.6	.6	.4	.3	Inventory	1.4	1.5
2.7		2.3	2.5	10.1	2.4	All Other Current	6.0	5.6
41.4		60.7	66.7	56.5	60.4	Total Current	63.3	66.4
25.8		16.2	15.9	16.6	11.4	Fixed Assets (net)	11.1	12.3
7.3		8.9	5.4	12.3	9.2	Intangibles (net)	6.4	8.3
25.5		14.2	12.1	14.6	19.0	All Other Non-Current	19.2	13.0
100.0		100.0	100.0	100.0	100.0	Total	100.0	100.0
						LIABILITIES		
27.8		5.8	.5	.8	.4	Notes Payable-Short Term	4.0	4.4
.0		1.2	1.5	2.5	1.9	Cur. Mat.-L.T.D.	1.3	2.0
3.7		9.9	10.1	14.6	10.4	Trade Payables	18.0	16.8
.0		.1	.5	.2	.2	Income Taxes Payable	.5	.4
27.2		24.6	33.0	23.2	36.2	All Other Current	25.1	24.7
58.7		41.6	45.6	41.3	49.1	Total Current	48.9	48.3
6.1		20.5	9.0	10.8	9.9	Long-Term Debt	9.5	10.2
.0		.0	.2	.3	.8	Deferred Taxes	.4	.3
6.0		2.5	7.9	5.9	8.6	All Other Non-Current	7.7	7.5
29.2		35.4	37.3	41.8	31.7	Net Worth	33.4	33.8
100.0		100.0	100.0	100.0	100.0	Total Liabilities & Net Worth	100.0	100.0
						INCOME DATA		
100.0		100.0	100.0	100.0	100.0	Net Sales	100.0	100.0
						Gross Profit		
98.6		89.6	97.1	96.9	97.3	Operating Expenses	94.2	94.5
1.4		10.4	2.9	3.1	2.7	Operating Profit	5.8	5.5
-1.0		1.1	-1.5	.0	-.4	All Other Expenses (net)	1.1	-.3
2.4		9.3	4.5	3.2	3.1	Profit Before Taxes	4.7	5.8
						RATIOS		
2.0		3.6	2.7	1.9	2.1		1.7	2.1
.6		1.3	1.6	1.3	1.2	Current	1.3	1.5
.1		.9	1.2	1.1	.9		1.0	1.1
1.7		2.9	2.7	1.6	2.0		1.5	1.9
.5		1.2	1.5	1.0	1.2	Quick	1.2	1.4
.1		.8	1.1	.7	.8		.8	.9
0 UND		3 118.0	7 51.2	3 127.7	6 63.1		6 64.9	5 74.2
0 UND		26 14.2	16 23.2	22 17.0	18 20.2	Sales/Receivables	17 21.5	16 23.4
0 897.1		40 9.1	51 7.2	29 12.6	37 10.0		41 8.9	40 9.2
						Cost of Sales/Inventory		
						Cost of Sales/Payables		
NM		7.0	4.5	8.3	5.1		7.5	5.7
-114.9		26.8	12.9	19.5	17.5	Sales/Working Capital	16.9	11.1
-17.1		-42.6	35.8	47.1	-67.2		-103.7	124.7
		39.1	23.0	9.3			14.5	34.7
		(12) 9.8	(12) 13.3	(10) 5.5		EBIT/Interest	(43) 7.4	(54) 11.0
		2.1	5.7	.9			1.8	2.8
							7.1	16.6
						Net Profit + Depr., Dep., Amort./Cur. Mat. L/T/D	(14) 3.2	(11) 2.6
							1.1	1.5
.1		.2	.0	.0	.0		.1	.0
1.9		.4	.3	.3	.2	Fixed/Worth	.2	.3
UND		2.3	1.1	12.6	1.2		.8	1.1
.6		.7	.6	.6	.9		1.3	.9
3.3		3.2	1.3	1.7	1.4	Debt/Worth	2.8	2.0
UND		12.7	2.9	16.3	13.0		9.0	10.8
		160.9	40.1	54.3	26.8		48.6	54.8
		(15) 83.4	(24) 22.2	(17) 16.2	(15) 13.2	% Profit Before Taxes/Tangible Net Worth	(72) 16.7	(81) 28.1
		39.8	11.0	1.4	3.4		3.1	8.7
212.3		38.4	13.6	12.8	15.7		13.0	18.7
31.9		17.4	10.2	8.8	3.1	% Profit Before Taxes/Total Assets	5.3	7.6
-36.9		3.3	4.1	.5	-.8		.7	1.9
UND		125.0	145.8	184.8	999.8		294.7	284.2
125.5		25.1	19.5	41.0	45.0	Sales/Net Fixed Assets	44.3	34.5
17.6		11.8	6.1	12.1	10.0		16.3	12.9
29.1		4.1	3.5	4.1	3.3		4.3	4.3
7.8		3.4	2.6	2.4	2.4	Sales/Total Assets	2.7	2.7
4.7		2.3	1.1	1.4	1.0		.9	1.4
		.4	.3	.3			.5	.4
		(14) 1.2	(18) 1.5	(13) .8		% Depr., Dep., Amort./Sales	(50) 1.2	(59) 1.3
		2.0	3.0	5.7			3.7	3.4
							3.4	2.0
						% Officers', Directors' Owners' Comp/Sales	(10) 6.7	(11) 10.4
							31.1	33.0
29193M	17748M	308436M	1880272M	3274213M	7606988M	Net Sales ($)	12259703M	14514486M
2294M	6273M	94144M	675148M	1234039M	3277628M	Total Assets ($)	4950434M	5658996M

Comparative Historical Data | Current Data Sorted by Sales

			Type of Statement						
47	32	48	Unqualified	1	1			5	41
4			Reviewed						
4	1	4	Compiled		2		1		1
5	2	8	Tax Returns	2	1	2	1	2	
37	46	37	Other	2	5	1	1	7	21
4/1/04-3/31/05	4/1/05-3/31/06	4/1/06-3/31/07			21 (4/1-9/30/06)		76 (10/1/06-3/31/07)		
ALL	ALL	ALL		0-1MM	1-3MM	3-5MM	5-10MM	10-25MM	25MM & OVER
97	81	97	NUMBER OF STATEMENTS	4	9	4	3	14	63
%	%	%	ASSETS	%	%	%	%	%	%
39.9	41.5	37.9	Cash & Equivalents					26.4	43.0
13.8	13.4	15.3	Trade Receivables (net)					21.1	15.3
.7	1.9	1.0	Inventory					2.6	.6
6.2	9.1	3.9	All Other Current					3.7	4.4
60.6	65.8	58.1	Total Current					53.8	63.4
14.1	15.6	16.4	Fixed Assets (net)					22.2	15.1
10.2	6.3	9.4	Intangibles (net)					9.4	7.7
15.1	12.2	16.0	All Other Non-Current					14.6	13.9
100.0	100.0	100.0	Total					100.0	100.0
			LIABILITIES						
5.5	2.2	5.6	Notes Payable-Short Term					6.8	.5
2.0	1.8	1.9	Cur. Mat.-L.T.D.					1.2	2.0
11.8	12.3	10.8	Trade Payables					6.7	12.4
.3	.2	.2	Income Taxes Payable					.3	.3
23.4	24.2	28.3	All Other Current					24.9	31.8
43.0	40.8	46.8	Total Current					40.0	47.1
9.5	9.9	12.4	Long-Term Debt					12.7	10.0
.4	.2	.3	Deferred Taxes					.0	.4
7.7	8.7	7.9	All Other Non-Current					6.9	6.7
39.5	40.3	32.7	Net Worth					40.4	35.9
100.0	100.0	100.0	Total Liabilities & Net Worth					100.0	100.0
			INCOME DATA						
100.0	100.0	100.0	Net Sales					100.0	100.0
			Gross Profit						
91.4	94.3	96.2	Operating Expenses					96.6	96.3
8.6	5.7	3.8	Operating Profit					3.4	3.7
.4	.0	-.1	All Other Expenses (net)					-1.1	-.3
8.2	5.7	3.9	Profit Before Taxes					4.5	4.1
			RATIOS						
2.8	3.2	2.2	Current					2.4	2.3
1.4	1.7	1.3						1.5	1.4
1.0	1.2	.9						.8	1.1
2.5	2.4	2.0	Quick					2.2	1.9
1.2	1.4	1.2						1.2	1.3
.8	1.0	.8						.7	.9
5 70.2	4 85.7	3 108.7	Sales/Receivables					4 99.9	6 63.3
15 24.3	15 24.2	16 23.2						25 14.8	18 20.2
43 8.6	41 8.9	39 9.4						45 8.0	37 10.0
			Cost of Sales/Inventory						
			Cost of Sales/Payables						
4.3	3.2	6.6	Sales/Working Capital					5.1	5.8
14.1	9.0	19.8						18.3	17.6
-138.2	18.3	-55.5						-155.2	47.1
25.8	14.7	12.9	EBIT/Interest						22.3
(42) 9.5	(38) 5.6	(52) 5.1						(31)	8.3
4.6	1.5	1.5							2.2
		20.8	Net Profit + Depr., Dep.,						20.8
	(12) 6.3	6.3	Amort./Cur. Mat. L/T/D					(12)	6.3
		1.8							1.8
.0	.0	.1	Fixed/Worth					.2	.0
.2	.2	.4						.7	.3
2.3	1.0	3.1						2.0	1.2
.7	.6	.8	Debt/Worth					.6	.8
1.7	1.7	2.0						2.7	1.4
7.4	6.3	14.6						4.4	3.6
73.3	51.0	71.0	% Profit Before Taxes/Tangible					144.6	48.3
(82) 26.9	(77) 21.3	(81) 23.1	Net Worth					41.9	(55) 21.9
9.7	3.2	6.2						9.1	5.4
19.8	13.8	18.9	% Profit Before Taxes/Total					35.6	15.2
9.4	6.4	8.2	Assets					6.6	9.6
3.0	1.5	.6						2.7	.7
275.4	304.2	165.1	Sales/Net Fixed Assets					89.7	207.0
46.2	33.7	38.9						15.2	39.3
12.0	6.0	10.3						5.6	11.3
4.0	4.0	4.1	Sales/Total Assets					4.0	3.8
2.0	2.1	3.0						2.6	2.8
.9	.9	1.5						1.1	1.6
.4	.4	.4	% Depr., Dep., Amort./Sales					.6	.3
(67) 1.3	(54) 1.8	(65) 1.0						(12) 1.5	(40) .9
3.1	4.7	2.7						2.9	2.7
2.2		6.9	% Officers', Directors'						
(15) 4.8		(12) 17.3	Owners' Comp/Sales						
9.9		38.6							
11583004M	13067491M	13116850M	Net Sales ($)	3132M	18024M	16522M	19387M	222957M	12836828M
5245937M	5087041M	5289526M	Total Assets ($)	972M	7491M	39227M	14910M	162850M	5064076M

© RMA 2007

M = $ thousand   MM = $ million

See Pages 11 through 21 for Explanation of Ratios and Data

Current Data Sorted by Assets | Comparative Historical Data

						Type of Statement		
1		8	13	7	7	Unqualified	16	13
	1	1				Reviewed	2	5
2	2	2	2			Compiled	6	11
5	2					Tax Returns		6
1	2	4	8	9	5	Other	26	23
	7 (4/1-9/30/06)		75 (10/1/06-3/31/07)				4/1/02-3/31/03	4/1/03-3/31/04
0-500M	500M-2MM	2-10MM	10-50MM	50-100MM	100-250MM		ALL	ALL
9	7	15	23	16	12	NUMBER OF STATEMENTS	50	58
%	%	%	%	%	%	ASSETS	%	%
		39.9	50.7	53.4	50.8	Cash & Equivalents	38.5	35.3
		22.1	7.5	8.5	4.2	Trade Receivables (net)	21.7	21.3
		.0	.1	.1	.0	Inventory	.2	.0
		3.8	13.5	9.2	7.0	All Other Current	8.3	9.9
		65.8	71.8	71.3	61.9	Total Current	68.6	66.6
		8.0	2.7	1.5	.9	Fixed Assets (net)	6.6	6.8
		7.0	.3	1.4	.4	Intangibles (net)	5.8	7.1
		19.2	25.1	25.7	36.8	All Other Non-Current	19.0	19.5
		100.0	100.0	100.0	100.0	Total	100.0	100.0
						LIABILITIES		
		8.4	3.1	.1	6.2	Notes Payable-Short Term	5.8	6.4
		1.3	.2	.1	.2	Cur. Mat.-L.T.D.	.6	3.5
		22.9	9.1	9.7	9.7	Trade Payables	21.7	15.8
		1.1	1.0	.5	.7	Income Taxes Payable	.2	.4
		25.0	22.6	40.7	22.7	All Other Current	24.5	33.9
		58.7	36.1	51.1	39.5	Total Current	53.0	60.0
		30.3	9.8	.5	.7	Long-Term Debt	6.6	4.7
		.1	.1	.0	.0	Deferred Taxes	.0	.0
		4.5	14.3	15.3	25.9	All Other Non-Current	13.1	11.0
		6.4	39.7	33.1	33.9	Net Worth	27.3	24.3
		100.0	100.0	100.0	100.0	Total Liabilties & Net Worth	100.0	100.0
						INCOME DATA		
		100.0	100.0	100.0	100.0	Net Sales	100.0	100.0
						Gross Profit		
		89.3	83.1	86.6	81.3	Operating Expenses	93.9	93.2
		10.7	16.9	13.4	18.7	Operating Profit	6.1	6.8
		.2	-2.4	-3.8	-3.3	All Other Expenses (net)	.1	-1.3
		10.5	19.3	17.2	22.0	Profit Before Taxes	6.0	8.1
						RATIOS		
		1.5	5.2	2.3	5.7		2.2	1.6
		1.1	1.9	1.4	2.0	Current	1.3	1.2
		.8	1.4	.9	.8		.9	.8
		1.5	5.2	2.3	5.0		1.6	1.4
		1.1	1.7	1.2	1.7	Quick	1.2	1.0
		.8	1.0	.7	.7		.7	.6
		0 UND	0 UND	6 63.3	3 120.3		20 18.1	10 37.0
		37 10.0	23 15.7	54 6.7	18 20.5	Sales/Receivables	58 6.3	48 7.6
		63 5.8	72 5.1	89 4.1	64 5.7		136 2.7	97 3.7
						Cost of Sales/Inventory		
						Cost of Sales/Payables		
		3.0	.8	.9	1.0		1.6	2.0
		10.0	1.3	2.2	1.2	Sales/Working Capital	7.0	17.3
		-33.9	3.2	-6.9	-13.9		-13.7	-15.4
		21.7					20.2	27.1
		(10) 12.9				EBIT/Interest	(25) 7.1	(32) 13.9
		1.0					2.1	5.4
						Net Profit + Depr., Dep., Amort./Cur. Mat. L/T/D		
		.0	.0	.0	.0		.0	.0
		.4	.0	.0	.0	Fixed/Worth	.1	.1
		-17.5	.1	.1	.1		.5	.7
		1.3	1.0	1.4	1.1		1.9	1.7
		3.3	1.3	2.4	2.2	Debt/Worth	3.2	2.7
		-286.2	3.2	3.2	5.7		7.3	15.4
		71.4	25.8	29.9	34.1		42.7	58.4
		(11) 35.5	(22) 15.3	21.7	(11) 23.6	% Profit Before Taxes/Tangible Net Worth	(45) 17.9	(48) 22.1
		8.8	9.3	14.3	11.3		.9	9.9
		27.0	11.0	12.5	11.9		9.0	13.6
		6.6	5.6	6.1	7.1	% Profit Before Taxes/Total Assets	3.7	6.0
		2.3	2.5	4.7	4.0		.5	1.8
		UND	UND	689.7	UND		313.3	219.2
		39.2	47.9	47.4	119.8	Sales/Net Fixed Assets	26.9	50.8
		19.7	16.3	22.0	26.6		11.1	19.5
		3.2	.6	.7	.5		.9	1.6
		1.1	.5	.5	.4	Sales/Total Assets	.6	.9
		.4	.3	.2	.3		.4	.5
				.6			.6	.5
			(12) 1.7			% Depr., Dep., Amort./Sales	(24) 1.8	(28) 1.2
			3.2				3.0	3.2
								11.2
						% Officers', Directors' Owners' Comp/Sales		(14) 16.4
								30.9
7090M	20761M	138678M	307702M	635722M	824599M	Net Sales ($)	1676326M	1466964M
1486M	9199M	81129M	644346M	1273346M	2018064M	Total Assets ($)	2734355M	2667977M

M = $ thousand   MM = $ million
See Pages 11 through 21 for Explanation of Ratios and Data

Comparative Historical Data   Current Data Sorted by Sales

			Type of Statement						
29	29	36	Unqualified	2	6	1	5	10	12
2	5	2	Reviewed				1	1	
5	6	8	Compiled	1	3		2	2	
1	1	7	Tax Returns	4	3				
29	26	29	Other	1	1	2	3	9	13
4/1/04-3/31/05	4/1/05-3/31/06	4/1/06-3/31/07		7 (4/1-9/30/06)			75 (10/1/06-3/31/07)		
ALL	ALL	ALL		0-1MM	1-3MM	3-5MM	5-10MM	10-25MM	25MM & OVER
66	67	82	NUMBER OF STATEMENTS	8	13	3	11	22	25
%	%	%	ASSETS	%	%	%	%	%	%
51.9	45.9	45.8	Cash & Equivalents		40.3		40.6	56.6	45.7
13.2	15.6	11.1	Trade Receivables (net)		9.5		19.3	10.7	9.9
.1	.0	.1	Inventory		.0		.0	.1	.1
8.1	7.3	8.7	All Other Current		2.5		15.8	8.3	8.4
73.3	68.9	65.8	Total Current		52.3		75.7	75.7	64.0
4.9	6.1	5.8	Fixed Assets (net)		12.5		2.0	2.8	2.8
2.9	5.8	3.5	Intangibles (net)		11.8		.6	.5	1.1
19.0	19.2	24.9	All Other Non-Current		23.5		21.7	21.0	32.1
100.0	100.0	100.0	Total		100.0		100.0	100.0	100.0
			LIABILITIES						
4.2	3.9	7.2	Notes Payable-Short Term		4.8		8.9	3.9	3.0
.7	.9	1.3	Cur. Mat.-L.T.D.		.6		.8	.1	.3
15.0	15.3	14.5	Trade Payables		26.5		15.0	9.1	12.0
.3	.4	.7	Income Taxes Payable		.1		1.7	.4	1.1
30.5	28.2	25.9	All Other Current		24.4		23.1	27.6	29.8
50.7	48.7	49.7	Total Current		56.5		49.5	41.1	46.2
4.5	14.7	14.7	Long-Term Debt		18.3		15.8	15.9	1.8
.3	.3	.1	Deferred Taxes		.1		.0	.0	.0
14.1	11.3	18.3	All Other Non-Current		9.4		3.2	17.7	18.3
30.4	25.0	17.3	Net Worth		15.7		31.4	25.3	33.7
100.0	100.0	100.0	Total Liabilities & Net Worth		100.0		100.0	100.0	100.0
			INCOME DATA						
100.0	100.0	100.0	Net Sales		100.0		100.0	100.0	100.0
			Gross Profit						
89.5	87.6	85.9	Operating Expenses		86.0		79.3	86.2	86.8
10.5	12.4	14.1	Operating Profit		14.0		20.7	13.8	13.2
-1.2	.2	-1.8	All Other Expenses (net)		2.5		-1.9	-4.6	-2.4
11.7	12.1	15.8	Profit Before Taxes		11.5		22.6	18.5	15.6
			RATIOS						
1.9	1.9	2.3			1.6		2.0	5.3	2.7
1.4	1.4	1.5	Current		1.2		1.5	2.0	1.5
1.1	1.1	.9			.5		1.1	1.3	.7
1.7	1.8	2.2			1.5		2.0	4.2	2.1
1.3	1.3	1.3	Quick		1.2		1.3	1.8	1.2
1.0	1.0	.8			.5		.8	1.1	.7
0 UND	5 77.4	0 UND			0 UND		20 18.7	0 UND	6 58.1
32 11.3	47 7.7	23 15.8	Sales/Receivables		0 UND		76 4.8	26 14.1	37 9.9
93 3.9	103 3.5	64 5.7			26 14.1		121 3.0	55 6.6	69 5.3
			Cost of Sales/Inventory						
			Cost of Sales/Payables						
1.3	1.6	1.1			2.2		1.1	.8	1.1
3.2	5.1	3.7	Sales/Working Capital		10.0		4.8	1.2	3.3
34.9	34.6	-43.1			-15.1		12.6	5.8	-10.9
26.5	36.9	73.3							
(25) 15.0	(36) 14.7	(32) 12.9	EBIT/Interest						
4.2	1.4	2.9							
			Net Profit + Depr., Dep., Amort./Cur. Mat. L/T/D						
.0	.0	.0			.0		.0	.0	.0
.0	.1	.0	Fixed/Worth		.0		.0	.0	.0
.2	.4	.4			NM		.1	.1	.1
1.2	1.5	1.1			2.0		.9	1.0	1.2
2.2	2.4	2.3	Debt/Worth		4.0		1.8	1.4	2.1
5.5	3.8	4.4			-22.5		7.1	3.3	3.0
56.0	42.5	44.7					56.9	34.7	47.0
(60) 18.0	(61) 18.4	(70) 22.0	% Profit Before Taxes/Tangible Net Worth				(10) 21.5	(20) 18.2	(23) 23.6
9.9	7.1	12.5					11.4	10.3	15.5
11.8	13.3	13.6			7.0		14.6	13.1	13.6
5.2	6.2	6.0	% Profit Before Taxes/Total Assets		3.4		7.5	5.9	8.9
2.9	1.4	2.8			2.4		2.0	5.2	4.2
UND	UND	UND			UND		UND	UND	592.4
100.4	36.6	67.6	Sales/Net Fixed Assets		33.4		285.0	148.6	45.7
21.3	11.6	22.1			17.1		16.3	33.4	22.2
1.0	1.4	1.4			2.3		1.1	.9	.8
.6	.6	.5	Sales/Total Assets		.7		.5	.5	.5
.4	.3	.4			.3		.2	.3	.4
.5	.5	.6						.2	.5
(26) .9	(37) 1.4	(39) 1.2	% Depr., Dep., Amort./Sales					(10) 1.1	(11) .6
2.7	2.4	2.5						2.2	2.1
	9.1	4.2							
	(14) 16.0	(13) 10.9	% Officers', Directors' Owners' Comp/Sales						
	25.1	23.9							
1630558M	1693000M	1934552M	Net Sales ($)	4545M	25648M	12236M	76079M	335103M	1480941M
3525629M	3370705M	4027570M	Total Assets ($)	5660M	83398M	7345M	274105M	854517M	2802545M

© RMA 2007

M = $ thousand   MM = $ million
See Pages 11 through 21 for Explanation of Ratios and Data

FINANCE—Direct Title Insurance Carriers NAICS 524127 (SIC 6361)

Current Data Sorted by Assets | **Comparative Historical Data**

0-500M	500M-2MM	2-10MM	10-50MM	50-100MM	100-250MM	Type of Statement	ALL 4/1/02-3/31/03	ALL 4/1/03-3/31/04
	2	11	8	2	2	Unqualified	32	18
1	2	2				Reviewed	1	1
2	3	1	1			Compiled	6	7
8	3	2				Tax Returns	10	6
3	8	13	12	6		Other	23	33
		12 (4/1-9/30/06)		80 (10/1/06-3/31/07)				
14	18	29	21	8	2	**NUMBER OF STATEMENTS**	72	65
%	%	%	%	%	%	**ASSETS**	%	%
40.0	47.6	36.3	40.0			Cash & Equivalents	41.8	37.2
9.6	6.1	5.7	6.1			Trade Receivables (net)	6.8	7.0
.0	.0	1.9	2.0			Inventory	1.4	.5
9.6	11.8	4.4	11.7			All Other Current	6.0	7.8
59.2	65.6	48.4	59.8			Total Current	56.0	52.5
16.1	20.8	19.2	21.9			Fixed Assets (net)	22.8	19.2
5.8	5.6	9.2	3.9			Intangibles (net)	4.5	5.2
18.9	8.1	23.2	14.5			All Other Non-Current	16.7	23.0
100.0	100.0	100.0	100.0			Total	100.0	100.0
						LIABILITIES		
11.4	5.5	6.8	5.9			Notes Payable-Short Term	2.2	8.2
.3	.8	1.3	4.7			Cur. Mat.-L.T.D.	2.5	3.2
8.7	11.1	8.6	8.1			Trade Payables	9.4	9.4
.0	.0	1.2	.1			Income Taxes Payable	1.1	1.1
14.7	23.5	21.5	18.0			All Other Current	21.1	23.3
35.0	40.8	39.4	36.9			Total Current	36.3	45.3
24.2	6.3	7.0	13.3			Long-Term Debt	13.3	7.6
.0	.0	.8	.7			Deferred Taxes	.5	.6
4.1	6.5	13.0	6.0			All Other Non-Current	4.7	6.0
36.7	46.4	39.9	43.1			Net Worth	45.2	40.5
100.0	100.0	100.0	100.0			Total Liabilities & Net Worth	100.0	100.0
						INCOME DATA		
100.0	100.0	100.0	100.0			Net Sales	100.0	100.0
						Gross Profit		
88.7	87.8	97.8	94.4			Operating Expenses	87.3	83.6
11.3	12.2	2.2	5.6			Operating Profit	12.7	16.4
-.1	.1	-1.2	-1.1			All Other Expenses (net)	-.2	1.5
11.4	12.1	3.4	6.7			Profit Before Taxes	12.9	15.0
						RATIOS		
17.7	2.8	1.9	3.0			Current	2.9	2.0
1.4	1.5	1.3	2.3				1.6	1.4
.6	1.0	1.0	1.2				1.0	.8
17.6	2.8	1.8	2.9			Quick	2.5	1.8
.8	1.4	1.2	2.0				(71) 1.3	1.1
.5	.8	.7	.7				.7	.6
0 UND	0 UND	2 189.0	2 158.7			Sales/Receivables	0 UND	0 UND
0 UND	0 999.8	6 65.4	6 65.2				5 75.5	4 81.7
6 61.4	7 51.6	11 33.3	17 21.2				12 30.2	11 34.3
						Cost of Sales/Inventory		
						Cost of Sales/Payables		
10.8	7.6	5.6	3.3			Sales/Working Capital	5.4	7.6
56.3	28.0	19.7	6.3				12.9	28.3
-19.2	999.8	NM	29.9				250.5	-57.8
	48.0	20.6	210.2			EBIT/Interest	48.8	66.6
	(11) 9.4	(18) 5.8	(15) 23.3				(41) 15.8	(40) 18.5
	-1.1	-5.9	1.4				2.7	4.5
						Net Profit + Depr., Dep., Amort./Cur. Mat. L/T/D	16.0	22.6
							(15) 2.9	(15) 10.3
							1.7	3.9
.1	.1	.2	.2			Fixed/Worth	.1	.1
.5	.6	.5	.3				.4	.6
NM	2.1	.9	2.4				.9	1.3
.3	.3	.5	.4			Debt/Worth	.5	.6
2.6	1.1	1.3	.8				1.1	1.5
NM	24.6	7.2	6.4				4.3	4.1
420.3	167.2	119.6	36.2			% Profit Before Taxes/Tangible Net Worth	117.7	106.6
(11) 90.2	(16) 56.9	(26) 39.3	(18) 14.2				(64) 59.0	(57) 61.8
22.2	6.3	-30.7	-4.3				21.2	31.6
111.8	62.6	28.0	26.3			% Profit Before Taxes/Total Assets	49.2	50.5
59.6	16.0	6.2	6.5				17.7	26.1
4.0	.0	-20.1	-3.2				6.0	8.1
309.7	227.2	33.2	23.3			Sales/Net Fixed Assets	37.1	42.6
59.3	23.9	20.4	12.1				14.8	19.4
22.8	8.4	5.9	7.5				8.0	11.1
8.6	4.6	3.7	2.5			Sales/Total Assets	3.9	5.2
4.4	3.2	2.0	2.0				2.5	2.7
2.3	1.8	.9	1.2				1.5	1.5
	.8	1.5	1.5			% Depr., Dep., Amort./Sales	.9	.9
	(10) 2.2	(23) 2.2	(16) 2.1				(58) 1.5	(45) 1.3
	3.4	3.0	3.5				2.1	1.9
5.9						% Officers', Directors' Owners' Comp/Sales	4.7	3.9
(10) 11.5							(21) 15.1	(12) 9.8
20.3							33.1	20.3
24442M	59348M	344601M	1447574M	1250627M	574343M	Net Sales ($)	1648101M	3024670M
3829M	19858M	139265M	564590M	618921M	346696M	Total Assets ($)	964655M	1311922M

M = $ thousand   MM = $ million

See Pages 11 through 21 for Explanation of Ratios and Data

Comparative Historical Data / Current Data Sorted by Sales

4/1/04-3/31/05 ALL	4/1/05-3/31/06 ALL	4/1/06-3/31/07 ALL	Type of Statement	0-1MM	1-3MM	3-5MM	5-10MM	10-25MM	25MM & OVER
24	16	25	Unqualified		4	3	2	8	8
4	4	5	Reviewed	1	1		1	2	
4	3	7	Compiled	1	5				1
13	16	13	Tax Returns	5	3	3	2		
32	29	42	Other	1	6	5	5	8	17
					12 (4/1-9/30/06)		80 (10/1/06-3/31/07)		
77	68	92	**NUMBER OF STATEMENTS**	8	19	11	10	18	26
%	%	%	**ASSETS**	%	%	%	%	%	%
36.6	39.5	40.0	Cash & Equivalents		43.4	44.6	46.3	34.9	42.5
6.3	6.6	6.2	Trade Receivables (net)		7.1	7.1	1.5	7.9	5.3
.2	.0	1.1	Inventory		.4	.0	.0	5.0	.0
10.1	6.5	8.9	All Other Current		16.3	9.5	9.1	2.7	9.4
53.2	52.7	56.2	Total Current		67.2	61.3	56.9	50.5	57.1
20.3	23.6	19.0	Fixed Assets (net)		11.0	18.5	23.4	21.5	17.5
5.6	7.1	7.2	Intangibles (net)		9.0	5.6	3.2	6.6	8.0
20.9	16.6	17.6	All Other Non-Current		12.7	14.7	16.4	21.4	17.4
100.0	100.0	100.0	Total		100.0	100.0	100.0	100.0	100.0
			LIABILITIES						
10.0	5.5	6.5	Notes Payable-Short Term		3.1	8.5	9.5	9.5	.6
1.9	2.4	1.8	Cur. Mat.-L.T.D.		.5	.8	1.0	2.0	3.7
8.7	9.8	8.9	Trade Payables		7.4	9.2	7.8	11.9	9.5
.6	.3	.4	Income Taxes Payable		.2	.2	.1	1.6	.2
28.5	25.5	20.7	All Other Current		30.5	11.9	17.0	16.8	24.0
49.7	43.5	38.3	Total Current		41.7	30.5	35.5	41.8	38.0
14.3	17.8	10.7	Long-Term Debt		8.7	7.1	5.7	5.2	8.4
.5	.5	.5	Deferred Taxes		.1	.1	.0	1.2	.7
6.7	4.0	8.3	All Other Non-Current		6.5	7.3	21.6	7.2	8.0
28.8	34.2	42.2	Net Worth		43.0	55.0	37.1	44.6	44.9
100.0	100.0	100.0	Total Liabilities & Net Worth		100.0	100.0	100.0	100.0	100.0
			INCOME DATA						
100.0	100.0	100.0	Net Sales		100.0	100.0	100.0	100.0	100.0
			Gross Profit						
90.1	88.7	94.4	Operating Expenses		86.3	93.1	97.4	98.1	100.6
9.9	11.3	5.6	Operating Profit		13.7	6.9	2.6	1.9	-.6
-.1	1.2	-1.2	All Other Expenses (net)		-.2	.2	-.5	-2.1	-3.6
10.0	10.1	6.8	Profit Before Taxes		13.9	6.7	3.1	4.0	3.0
			RATIOS						
2.7	2.1	2.6			8.2	4.2	5.7	1.8	2.7
1.3	1.3	1.5	Current		1.6	2.5	1.5	1.2	1.6
1.0	.7	1.0			1.2	1.3	1.0	.8	1.1
2.1	2.0	2.4			3.7	4.1	5.6	1.7	2.5
1.3	1.1 (91)	1.3	Quick		1.2	2.1	1.5	1.0 (25)	1.4
.6	.6	.6			.6	1.0	.8	.6	.8
0 UND	0 999.8	0 968.5			0 UND	0 UND	0 UND	2 187.4	3 111.9
4 87.6	5 74.4	4 92.6	Sales/Receivables		2 173.8	5 67.4	1 592.6	8 43.3	5 70.9
11 33.0	9 40.4	12 30.0			13 27.5	15 24.4	3 125.9	14 25.7	13 28.6
			Cost of Sales/Inventory						
			Cost of Sales/Payables						
7.0	6.6	6.2			4.1	3.8	9.2	12.0	4.7
24.6	25.5	19.1	Sales/Working Capital		25.3	7.2	27.4	25.3	8.5
-282.5	-51.5	999.8			60.1	8.4	283.1	-49.7	64.2
102.0	34.2	38.4			42.8			42.6	184.8
(50) 19.4	(50) 11.9	(58) 9.2	EBIT/Interest		(13) 4.4		(10) 8.3	(16) 24.2	
6.3	2.6	-.3			-.6		-.3	-10.6	
21.0	13.9	28.9							
(13) 6.0	(11) 5.4	(16) 4.6	Net Profit + Depr., Dep., Amort./Cur. Mat. L/T/D						
1.6	2.7	.5							
.2	.3	.1			.0	.1	.1	.3	.1
.6	.7	.4	Fixed/Worth		.3	.2	.7	.5	.3
1.9	6.7	1.3			.8	.8	1.6	1.4	1.5
.6	.8	.5			.3	.3	.2	.6	.6
1.5	2.4	1.0	Debt/Worth		1.9	.8	1.0	1.2	.9
36.1	17.7	7.4			27.3	7.3	16.8	5.1	4.2
92.0	115.4	88.9			324.5	174.0		101.8	36.2
(59) 42.7	(54) 46.4	(80) 31.8	% Profit Before Taxes/Tangible Net Worth		(16) 37.5	61.0	(17) 49.6	(22) 10.7	
16.3	11.1	-5.0			.0	1.9	-24.7	-19.4	
43.8	35.6	34.3			59.0	60.2	45.0	36.4	21.8
17.8	15.4	9.3	% Profit Before Taxes/Total Assets		6.1	21.1	16.0	11.9	5.1
2.5	2.9	-4.2			.0	1.7	-6.9	-9.6	-9.8
38.7	41.3	52.4			238.4	98.2	417.6	32.6	34.7
17.4	15.2	18.8	Sales/Net Fixed Assets		33.9	33.6	9.3	19.0	14.9
9.4	8.6	8.6			9.2	4.1	5.4	8.0	9.9
5.1	4.0	4.0			4.4	5.7	4.6	4.0	3.2
2.7	2.2	2.3	Sales/Total Assets		2.2	1.0	3.7	2.7	2.2
1.3	1.0	1.3			.7	.7	1.5	1.7	1.4
1.1	1.2	1.3			.9			1.6	1.4
(51) 1.6	(52) 1.6	(62) 2.0	% Depr., Dep., Amort./Sales		(11) 1.2		(17) 2.2	(17) 2.0	
2.8	3.0	3.0			3.0		3.1	2.7	
4.8	4.1	4.3							
(20) 11.4	(15) 9.1	(21) 9.0	% Officers', Directors' Owners' Comp/Sales						
23.8	23.3	17.8							
4068266M	3050891M	3700935M	Net Sales ($)	3205M	37380M	41577M	74594M	283207M	3260972M
1916524M	1513298M	1693159M	Total Assets ($)	2369M	48721M	42243M	40503M	119690M	1439633M

M = $ thousand   MM = $ million
See Pages 11 through 21 for Explanation of Ratios and Data

Current Data Sorted by Assets   Comparative Historical Data

0-500M	500M-2MM	2-10MM	10-50MM	50-100MM	100-250MM		4/1/02-3/31/03 ALL	4/1/03-3/31/04 ALL
						Type of Statement		
1	2	6	8	6	9	Unqualified	25	25
1	1		1			Reviewed		4
		1				Compiled	5	5
1			1			Tax Returns	1	9
2	5	4	5	3	5	Other	25	24
	9 (4/1-9/30/06)		53 (10/1/06-3/31/07)					
5	10	11	13	9	14	**NUMBER OF STATEMENTS**	56	67
%	%	%	%	%	%	**ASSETS**	%	%
46.4	54.1	55.1			43.5	Cash & Equivalents	42.3	40.6
12.9	12.3	5.3			5.6	Trade Receivables (net)	20.4	16.6
.0	.0	.4			.0	Inventory	.2	.0
11.6	1.7	5.0			7.5	All Other Current	8.4	12.2
70.8	68.0	65.8			56.7	Total Current	71.3	69.5
12.2	6.6	4.5			1.1	Fixed Assets (net)	8.8	9.3
6.5	13.2	10.9			13.5	Intangibles (net)	5.2	1.8
10.6	12.1	18.8			28.7	All Other Non-Current	14.7	19.3
100.0	100.0	100.0			100.0	Total	100.0	100.0
						LIABILITIES		
7.8	3.6	.0			2.2	Notes Payable-Short Term	2.6	4.6
5.5	3.5				2.6	Cur. Mat.-L.T.D.	2.1	2.0
20.6	13.7	11.2			13.0	Trade Payables	19.1	20.0
.1	1.1	.2			2.0	Income Taxes Payable	.9	1.0
17.6	19.7	28.0			44.3	All Other Current	43.4	29.3
51.6	41.7	39.5			64.2	Total Current	68.1	56.8
9.6	16.0	3.7			8.5	Long-Term Debt	8.6	8.6
.0	.4	.1			.4	Deferred Taxes	.2	.0
4.5	4.5	17.8			9.1	All Other Non-Current	6.0	10.2
34.2	37.5	38.8			17.7	Net Worth	17.1	24.4
100.0	100.0	100.0			100.0	Total Liabilties & Net Worth	100.0	100.0
						INCOME DATA		
100.0	100.0	100.0			100.0	Net Sales	100.0	100.0
						Gross Profit		
80.2	88.3	87.4			83.8	Operating Expenses	86.5	89.0
19.8	11.7	12.6			16.2	Operating Profit	13.5	11.0
.5	-.3	-2.1			1.1	All Other Expenses (net)	1.8	1.2
19.2	12.0	14.7			15.1	Profit Before Taxes	11.7	9.8
						RATIOS		
5.8	4.6	3.0			1.5		1.8	2.1
1.0	1.2	1.5			.9	Current	1.1	1.3
.8	1.1	1.2			.3		.8	.8
5.5	4.5	2.9			1.5		1.6	2.0
.8	1.2	1.5			.9	Quick	1.0	1.1
.6	1.0	1.0			.2		.5	.5
0 UND	0 UND	1 335.9			11 32.1		0 787.0	2 216.0
3 106.5	1 321.7	9 42.7			35 10.5	Sales/Receivables	40 9.2	22 16.4
19 18.9	82 4.5	28 12.9			64 5.7		127 2.9	100 3.7
						Cost of Sales/Inventory		
						Cost of Sales/Payables		
2.9	1.2	1.6			2.5		2.1	1.6
NM	6.1	2.5			NM	Sales/Working Capital	8.7	10.9
-7.5	495.8	16.3			-1.2		-8.9	-7.8
							24.9	38.6
						EBIT/Interest	(23) 3.3	(31) 7.2
							1.3	2.2
						Net Profit + Depr., Dep., Amort./Cur. Mat. L/T/D		
.1	.0	.0			.0		.0	.0
.3	.1	.0			.0	Fixed/Worth	.2	.1
-1.7	.7	.5			-.1		2.6	.6
.5	.8	1.4			2.0		1.3	1.1
2.7	4.2	2.1			9.1	Debt/Worth	2.9	2.9
-15.4	9.1	4.9			-5.8		116.5	13.0
		41.8			70.7		83.4	45.4
		(12) 27.5			(10) 44.0	% Profit Before Taxes/Tangible Net Worth	(44) 22.3	(56) 18.6
		13.8			8.8		4.4	4.4
74.7	31.8	13.8			12.9		15.2	12.3
19.7	10.5	5.7			5.7	% Profit Before Taxes/Total Assets	5.6	3.9
.3	4.0	3.0			1.4		1.3	.7
217.4	UND	UND			UND		899.4	UND
46.5	83.9	121.8			150.5	Sales/Net Fixed Assets	28.1	43.5
17.5	20.2	21.9			43.0		13.6	16.5
6.3	3.0	1.5			.7		1.8	2.1
1.4	.7	.7			.5	Sales/Total Assets	.6	.6
.6	.6	.4			.2		.4	.4
							.6	1.0
						% Depr., Dep., Amort./Sales	(29) 1.8	(30) 1.8
							2.4	3.5
								6.9
						% Officers', Directors' Owners' Comp/Sales		(18) 14.5
								27.2
5203M	48259M	160261M	309145M	627831M	1338735M	Net Sales ($)	1639878M	2284991M
1246M	13045M	53955M	320413M	625041M	2353793M	Total Assets ($)	2254791M	3174501M

M = $ thousand   MM = $ million
See Pages 11 through 21 for Explanation of Ratios and Data

Comparative Historical Data | ## Current Data Sorted by Sales

29	16	32	Type of Statement						
29	16	32	Unqualified	1	4		5	4	18
3	1	3	Reviewed		2	1			
2	6	1	Compiled					1	
3	4	2	Tax Returns	1			1		
28	22	24	Other	5	3	2	1	4	9
4/1/04-3/31/05 ALL	4/1/05-3/31/06 ALL	4/1/06-3/31/07 ALL		0-1MM	9 (4/1-9/30/06) 1-3MM	3-5MM	53 (10/1/06-3/31/07) 5-10MM	10-25MM	25MM & OVER
65	49	62	NUMBER OF STATEMENTS	7	9	3	7	9	27
%	%	%		%	%	%	%	%	%
			ASSETS						
39.1	43.9	47.9	Cash & Equivalents						49.1
16.5	16.1	9.4	Trade Receivables (net)						8.5
.8	.9	.1	Inventory						.1
7.4	4.4	5.7	All Other Current						7.6
63.7	65.4	63.2	Total Current						65.3
8.4	10.9	7.9	Fixed Assets (net)						3.3
3.4	5.6	11.7	Intangibles (net)						13.9
24.4	18.1	17.2	All Other Non-Current						17.5
100.0	100.0	100.0	Total						100.0
			LIABILITIES						
3.9	9.5	3.3	Notes Payable-Short Term						1.3
1.0	6.2	4.0	Cur. Mat.-L.T.D.						2.1
16.3	18.7	13.4	Trade Payables						13.2
.3	.8	.7	Income Taxes Payable						1.0
30.5	21.2	27.7	All Other Current						35.7
52.0	56.4	49.1	Total Current						53.3
9.5	13.5	8.8	Long-Term Debt						6.5
.1	.2	.2	Deferred Taxes						.3
17.0	10.1	10.1	All Other Non-Current						12.6
21.4	19.8	31.7	Net Worth						27.3
100.0	100.0	100.0	Total Liabilties & Net Worth						100.0
			INCOME DATA						
100.0	100.0	100.0	Net Sales						100.0
			Gross Profit						
87.5	86.4	86.1	Operating Expenses						88.1
12.5	13.6	13.9	Operating Profit						11.9
2.4	.8	.0	All Other Expenses (net)						-.2
10.1	12.8	13.8	Profit Before Taxes						12.1
			RATIOS						
2.6	2.4	2.4							1.7
1.4	1.3	1.2	Current						1.2
.8	.8	.8							.8
2.4	2.1	2.1							1.7
1.2	1.3	1.1	Quick						1.1
.7	.6	.7							.8
0 / 898.7	0 / UND	0 / UND							7 / 53.3
23 / 16.1	19 / 19.6	11 / 32.7	Sales/Receivables						20 / 18.4
81 / 4.5	75 / 4.9	63 / 5.8							62 / 5.9
			Cost of Sales/Inventory						
			Cost of Sales/Payables						
1.3	1.7	2.4							2.3
8.7	9.8	10.3	Sales/Working Capital						11.2
-17.7	-23.1	-7.5							-5.3
39.5	11.3	34.5							24.3
(36) 8.1	(24) 6.1	(35) 8.9	EBIT/Interest						(15) 7.1
1.6	2.3	4.2							5.3
			Net Profit + Depr., Dep., Amort./Cur. Mat. L/T/D						
.0	.0	.0							.0
.1	.1	.1	Fixed/Worth						.1
1.5	2.6	2.2							-.1
1.2	1.8	1.0							1.8
3.6	3.4	3.0	Debt/Worth						2.6
85.1	UND	26.7							-8.5
51.9	90.4	59.5							51.4
(51) 15.8	(38) 23.7	(48) 36.7	% Profit Before Taxes/Tangible Net Worth						(20) 27.4
4.7	9.7	11.9							9.7
10.2	20.2	19.1							14.0
2.6	5.9	8.1	% Profit Before Taxes/Total Assets						7.8
.9	2.1	1.9							2.0
UND	UND	UND							999.8
44.4	57.1	64.6	Sales/Net Fixed Assets						60.0
16.1	17.2	21.7							22.7
1.6	2.2	2.2							1.2
.7	.7	.7	Sales/Total Assets						.7
.3	.3	.5							.5
.9	.6	.5							
(31) 1.3	(21) 1.6	(26) 1.2	% Depr., Dep., Amort./Sales						
3.2	2.7	1.6							
		4.8							
	(10) 18.5		% Officers', Directors' Owners' Comp/Sales						
		31.4							
2433792M	1828411M	2489434M	Net Sales ($)	4533M	16250M	13660M	47064M	141358M	2266569M
3225390M	1816606M	3367493M	Total Assets ($)	5559M	27005M	21702M	65878M	344284M	2903065M

© RMA 2007   M = $ thousand   MM = $ million
See Pages 11 through 21 for Explanation of Ratios and Data

Current Data Sorted by Assets   Comparative Historical Data

						Type of Statement		
	8	34	46	15	16	Unqualified	120	110
11	25	57	22	2		Reviewed	107	116
27	51	33	2		1	Compiled	145	159
105	101	30	4	1	1	Tax Returns	172	231
51	56	70	50	11	9	Other	206	230
	137 (4/1-9/30/06)		702 (10/1/06-3/31/07)				4/1/02-3/31/03	4/1/03-3/31/04
0-500M	500M-2MM	2-10MM	10-50MM	50-100MM	100-250MM		ALL	ALL
194	241	224	124	29	27	NUMBER OF STATEMENTS	750	846
%	%	%	%	%	%	ASSETS	%	%
30.5	23.6	31.9	36.5	34.3	36.6	Cash & Equivalents	28.7	30.3
8.9	19.8	25.1	21.2	24.6	16.1	Trade Receivables (net)	22.3	21.0
.0	.2	.2	.8	.3	.1	Inventory	.2	.3
6.9	4.3	4.3	7.3	7.0	7.5	All Other Current	4.4	5.1
46.4	47.9	61.5	65.9	66.3	60.3	Total Current	55.6	56.6
22.2	15.6	11.8	8.1	6.1	5.5	Fixed Assets (net)	14.0	13.8
14.3	20.4	13.4	11.6	9.3	22.2	Intangibles (net)	14.3	15.1
17.1	16.0	13.4	14.5	18.3	12.0	All Other Non-Current	16.1	14.5
100.0	100.0	100.0	100.0	100.0	100.0	Total	100.0	100.0
						LIABILITIES		
25.2	9.7	6.2	4.8	1.0	1.4	Notes Payable-Short Term	9.8	10.3
6.5	3.6	2.3	1.7	1.0	1.3	Cur. Mat.-L.T.D.	4.4	3.7
13.5	18.7	30.1	25.6	27.3	18.0	Trade Payables	25.4	25.1
.6	.3	.2	.3	.4	.3	Income Taxes Payable	.4	.4
20.4	16.4	19.1	24.6	25.5	24.1	All Other Current	18.9	19.0
66.2	48.8	57.8	57.0	55.2	45.1	Total Current	58.8	58.5
25.4	25.0	13.1	8.1	5.5	9.9	Long-Term Debt	19.5	19.3
.0	.1	.3	.6	.2	1.2	Deferred Taxes	.3	.2
10.2	5.9	4.4	5.3	3.2	16.7	All Other Non-Current	6.5	6.7
-1.8	20.2	24.5	29.0	35.9	27.2	Net Worth	14.9	15.2
100.0	100.0	100.0	100.0	100.0	100.0	Total Liabilties & Net Worth	100.0	100.0
						INCOME DATA		
100.0	100.0	100.0	100.0	100.0	100.0	Net Sales	100.0	100.0
						Gross Profit		
86.3	86.7	88.1	88.0	87.7	86.4	Operating Expenses	89.2	88.4
13.7	13.3	11.9	12.0	12.3	13.6	Operating Profit	10.8	11.6
1.2	2.8	.8	.5	-2.6	3.2	All Other Expenses (net)	1.7	1.3
12.6	10.5	11.0	11.4	14.9	10.4	Profit Before Taxes	9.0	10.3
						RATIOS		
1.8	1.6	1.4	1.6	1.5	1.5		1.4	1.4
.8	1.0	1.0	1.1	1.2	1.3	Current	1.0	1.0
.3	.5	.8	.9	.9	1.1		.7	.6
1.3	1.5	1.3	1.5	1.4	1.5		1.3	1.3
.7	(240) .9	1.0	1.0	1.0	1.1	Quick	(749) 1.0	1.0
.2	.4	.7	.7	.7	.6		.5	.5
0 UND	0 UND	8 47.0	22 16.8	21 17.2	18 20.8		1 308.0	0 UND
0 UND	13 28.1	45 8.2	55 6.7	97 3.8	47 7.8	Sales/Receivables	31 11.6	25 14.8
8 43.0	59 6.2	107 3.4	119 3.1	160 2.3	172 2.1		99 3.7	81 4.5
						Cost of Sales/Inventory		
						Cost of Sales/Payables		
24.9	10.0	6.9	3.6	2.4	1.7		8.5	8.7
-82.7	687.0	45.8	18.4	9.8	7.3	Sales/Working Capital	179.3	88.9
-10.0	-8.9	-13.7	-16.2	-42.2	39.5		-10.2	-14.2
24.9	13.3	23.0	42.6	84.9	69.1		15.6	24.4
(137) 6.8	(183) 4.5	(165) 9.8	(88) 10.7	(18) 24.3	(20) 10.4	EBIT/Interest	(578) 4.8	(635) 6.5
1.7	1.9	3.2	3.8	11.0	1.7		1.7	2.3
		3.1	6.8	17.2		Net Profit + Depr., Dep.,	5.7	6.2
	(28) 2.2	(37) 3.0	(22) 4.4			Amort./Cur. Mat. L/T/D	(139) 2.2	(118) 2.4
	.9	1.8	2.4				.8	1.1
.1	.1	.1	.1	.0	.0		.2	.1
1.1	1.0	.6	.4	.2	.4	Fixed/Worth	.8	.8
-.6	-.4	-5.2	3.5	2.3	1.9		-1.0	-.7
.9	1.3	1.9	1.8	1.2	2.3		1.8	2.2
22.9	6.6	6.9	3.8	2.4	11.8	Debt/Worth	9.3	11.4
-2.4	-3.0	-26.0	48.9	18.7	-18.7		-5.9	-4.8
406.5	106.0	87.7	82.1	79.0	94.2	% Profit Before Taxes/Tangible	103.0	129.6
(109) 89.9	(152) 29.1	(162) 39.6	(96) 32.6	(26) 34.7	(20) 23.4	Net Worth	(486) 35.8	(530) 45.2
24.2	7.2	12.7	10.3	16.7	6.4		8.3	13.2
93.9	24.3	19.3	14.0	12.0	15.0	% Profit Before Taxes/Total	18.6	23.5
25.7	9.5	8.2	7.9	8.4	3.3	Assets	6.9	8.5
2.7	2.3	2.6	2.5	4.7	.9		1.7	2.1
451.2	139.9	87.7	70.3	44.0	160.4		63.4	85.1
56.6	27.6	26.2	28.0	15.2	20.2	Sales/Net Fixed Assets	22.8	28.0
16.1	11.8	12.1	13.6	7.6	8.5		11.0	12.5
10.4	2.9	2.0	1.3	.9	.7		2.7	3.0
4.5	1.8	1.3	.9	.7	.5	Sales/Total Assets	1.4	1.5
2.5	1.0	.9	.6	.4	.3		.8	.9
.5	.9	.8	.9	.7	.6		1.0	.9
(85) 1.3	(154) 1.9	(168) 1.4	(87) 1.7	(22) 1.8	(17) 1.3	% Depr., Dep., Amort./Sales	(513) 2.0	(541) 1.9
2.8	3.2	2.4	2.6	2.6	2.4		3.5	3.3
9.1	7.1	7.4	2.7			% Officers', Directors'	7.3	7.6
(131) 16.2	(138) 14.0	(79) 13.7	(29) 5.1			Owners' Comp/Sales	(348) 15.4	(409) 14.9
25.4	22.9	23.4	16.4				25.4	25.0
245848M	607945M	1789589M	3603997M	2445681M	4528036M	Net Sales ($)	13792945M	11758010M
40901M	261797M	1071482M	2637638M	2075629M	4208886M	Total Assets ($)	9239460M	10163077M

M = $ thousand   MM = $ million
See Pages 11 through 21 for Explanation of Ratios and Data

Comparative Historical Data | Current Data Sorted by Sales

4/1/04-3/31/05 ALL	4/1/05-3/31/06 ALL	4/1/06-3/31/07 ALL	Type of Statement	137 (4/1-9/30/06) 0-1MM	1-3MM	3-5MM	702 (10/1/06-3/31/07) 5-10MM	10-25MM	25MM & OVER
116	130	119	Unqualified	4	10	8	20	31	46
117	107	117	Reviewed	11	28	21	26	23	8
131	101	114	Compiled	24	43	23	16	4	4
224	222	242	Tax Returns	103	81	26	15	13	4
230	280	247	Other	47	54	32	40	41	33
818	840	839	NUMBER OF STATEMENTS	189	216	110	117	112	95
%	%	%	ASSETS	%	%	%	%	%	%
30.2	31.0	30.1	Cash & Equivalents	24.3	28.4	30.3	31.9	36.2	36.4
20.0	19.0	18.9	Trade Receivables (net)	11.8	18.4	23.8	25.9	19.1	19.8
.2	.2	.2	Inventory	.0	.1	.4	.2	.7	.3
5.1	6.0	5.5	All Other Current	3.7	5.9	5.8	4.6	6.9	7.7
55.6	56.2	54.9	Total Current	39.9	52.8	60.4	62.6	62.9	64.2
13.7	13.1	14.3	Fixed Assets (net)	23.7	13.5	12.2	10.5	10.5	9.3
15.9	15.5	15.5	Intangibles (net)	19.0	18.4	11.4	12.4	12.3	14.4
14.8	15.2	15.3	All Other Non-Current	17.4	15.3	16.1	14.5	14.3	12.0
100.0	100.0	100.0	Total	100.0	100.0	100.0	100.0	100.0	100.0
			LIABILITIES						
10.0	12.7	11.1	Notes Payable-Short Term	18.0	12.4	12.0	9.2	6.2	1.1
4.2	3.4	3.5	Cur. Mat.-L.T.D.	6.4	4.2	2.0	2.0	1.8	1.5
23.0	21.5	21.8	Trade Payables	9.1	23.1	27.6	29.1	25.7	24.0
.3	.4	.4	Income Taxes Payable	.6	.2	.4	.2	.3	.4
18.6	18.8	19.8	All Other Current	15.3	16.5	18.4	24.3	23.5	27.8
56.0	56.7	56.5	Total Current	49.4	56.5	60.4	64.9	57.6	54.8
20.8	17.7	18.2	Long-Term Debt	30.1	21.6	14.7	13.2	9.9	7.2
.3	.2	.3	Deferred Taxes	.0	.2	.1	.4	.4	.6
6.7	5.7	6.7	All Other Non-Current	8.7	7.3	3.9	5.8	6.4	5.8
16.1	19.6	18.3	Net Worth	11.8	14.4	21.0	15.6	25.8	31.5
100.0	100.0	100.0	Total Liabilities & Net Worth	100.0	100.0	100.0	100.0	100.0	100.0
			INCOME DATA						
100.0	100.0	100.0	Net Sales	100.0	100.0	100.0	100.0	100.0	100.0
			Gross Profit						
88.4	88.4	87.2	Operating Expenses	79.7	88.0	91.3	90.5	87.9	90.6
11.6	11.6	12.8	Operating Profit	20.3	12.0	8.7	9.5	12.1	9.4
1.2	1.3	1.4	All Other Expenses (net)	4.8	1.5	-.1	-.1	-.2	-.2
10.3	10.2	11.4	Profit Before Taxes	15.6	10.5	8.8	9.6	12.3	9.6
			RATIOS						
1.6	1.7	1.5	Current	1.6	1.7	1.6	1.4	1.4	1.5
1.0	1.1	1.0		.9	1.0	1.1	1.0	1.1	1.2
.7	.7	.6		.3	.5	.8	.8	.8	1.0
1.4	1.5	1.4	Quick	1.5	1.4	1.5	1.3	1.3	1.4
1.0 (839)	1.0 (838)	1.0		.8 (215)	.9	1.0	1.0	1.0	1.0
.5	.5	.5		.2	.4	.6	.7	.7	.7
0 UND	0 UND	0 UND	Sales/Receivables	0 UND	0 UND	1 264.4	10 36.6	10 38.4	16 23.5
22 16.6	22 16.4	19 19.5		0 UND	9 39.3	34 10.8	46 7.9	39 9.5	40 9.2
74 4.9	74 4.9	75 4.9		23 15.7	55 6.7	100 3.6	96 3.8	94 3.9	105 3.5
			Cost of Sales/Inventory						
			Cost of Sales/Payables						
8.6	7.6	8.0	Sales/Working Capital	14.2	9.4	7.7	10.4	5.0	5.6
111.1	54.4	93.1		-79.2	398.3	32.2	197.5	31.4	20.7
-12.3	-12.3	-12.0		-6.3	-9.0	-15.9	-16.5	-23.5	-40.0
25.5	24.3	21.6	EBIT/Interest	11.8	19.7	36.5	19.8	34.5	80.6
(608) 7.4	(612) 7.3	(611) 7.4		(129) 4.7	(161) 5.4	(76) 8.1	(90) 7.7	(85) 13.0	(70) 16.9
2.3	2.6	2.5		2.0	1.9	2.2	2.1	4.6	4.9
5.9	6.7	6.6	Net Profit + Depr., Dep., Amort./Cur. Mat. L/T/D	3.7	3.4		4.8	12.6	20.6
(127) 2.5	(116) 2.9	(107) 2.7		(12) 2.5	(28) 1.7		(16) 3.7	(20) 5.5	(24) 5.6
1.3	1.1	1.4		1.2	.9		2.1	2.7	2.0
.1	.1	.1	Fixed/Worth	.0	.1	.1	.1	.1	.1
.8	.6	.6		1.5	.7	.6	.6	.4	.5
-.8	-1.1	-1.2		-.5	-.5	-2.2	-1.4	7.4	3.4
1.8	1.6	1.6	Debt/Worth	1.1	1.4	1.2	2.1	1.9	1.8
8.2	5.3	6.8		13.8	6.4	4.4	10.4	4.1	3.6
-5.8	-5.8	-6.6		-2.4	-2.7	-17.2	-8.4	46.9	35.7
120.1	116.0	119.2	% Profit Before Taxes/Tangible Net Worth	213.5	100.9	98.8	143.5	121.0	102.9
(524) 41.7	(560) 38.5	(565) 39.7		(112) 48.7	(134) 29.9	(77) 35.1	(81) 39.7	(86) 54.9	(75) 42.3
12.9	11.7	12.0		7.2	6.9	11.5	8.1	18.4	14.2
23.6	24.7	25.4	% Profit Before Taxes/Total Assets	40.0	28.2	25.2	24.9	21.1	15.2
8.7	8.9	10.0		11.9	10.2	8.0	7.1	11.6	9.2
2.3	2.3	2.5		2.2	2.3	3.0	1.5	3.9	2.8
97.1	98.0	111.3	Sales/Net Fixed Assets	460.3	168.8	109.9	96.1	69.5	54.1
30.9	30.3	28.8		21.1	35.7	28.4	33.9	38.3	21.2
12.6	13.3	12.5		6.9	14.8	15.2	15.3	15.9	10.1
3.2	3.4	3.1	Sales/Total Assets	4.1	3.4	3.8	2.7	2.6	2.3
1.6	1.7	1.6		1.8	1.9	1.8	1.5	1.3	1.0
.9	.9	.9		.7	1.1	1.2	.9	.9	.7
.8	.7	.7	% Depr., Dep., Amort./Sales	1.0	.6	.7	.8	.7	.7
(518) 1.8	(520) 1.5	(533) 1.5		(94) 2.2	(127) 1.5	(73) 1.4	(81) 1.5	(85) 1.3	(73) 1.6
2.9	2.7	2.7		6.0	2.9	2.4	2.2	2.3	2.5
7.8	7.3	7.1	% Officers', Directors' Owners' Comp/Sales	9.3	8.2	7.1	5.1	3.2	.8
(383) 15.3	(372) 13.9	(382) 14.6		(111) 15.6	(127) 16.1	(55) 14.1	(46) 11.8	(28) 6.2	(15) 5.4
24.1	22.7	23.1		25.4	25.8	22.2	18.5	17.5	11.0
11511230M	13006005M	13221096M	Net Sales ($)	98143M	391080M	426942M	838553M	1770383M	9695995M
9771664M	11528431M	10296333M	Total Assets ($)	109682M	374325M	330779M	1051778M	1729083M	6700686M

M = $ thousand   MM = $ million
See Pages 11 through 21 for Explanation of Ratios and Data

Current Data Sorted by Assets — **Comparative Historical Data**

0-500M	500M-2MM 10 (4/1-9/30/06)	2-10MM	10-50MM 36 (10/1/06-3/31/07)	50-100MM	100-250MM	Type of Statement	4/1/02-3/31/03 ALL	4/1/03-3/31/04 ALL
	1	4	9	2	2	Unqualified	2	5
	1					Reviewed		2
1	2	1				Compiled	4	1
1		1				Tax Returns	2	
2	4	5	7	1	2	Other	4	8
4	8	11	16	3	4	**NUMBER OF STATEMENTS**	12	16
%	%	%	%	%	%	**ASSETS**	%	%
		26.7	36.1			Cash & Equivalents	28.7	23.6
		32.2	13.2			Trade Receivables (net)	21.1	17.3
		.0	.0			Inventory	.1	1.2
		7.8	15.2			All Other Current	11.5	10.4
		66.7	64.5			Total Current	61.5	52.5
		12.6	15.8			Fixed Assets (net)	19.4	20.7
		8.2	9.0			Intangibles (net)	6.0	9.9
		12.6	10.7			All Other Non-Current	13.1	16.9
		100.0	100.0			Total	100.0	100.0
						LIABILITIES		
		15.1	1.9			Notes Payable-Short Term	5.2	13.6
		1.2	2.8			Cur. Mat.-L.T.D.	1.8	1.8
		16.4	14.6			Trade Payables	15.8	10.9
		.0	1.1			Income Taxes Payable	1.2	.4
		34.1	32.6			All Other Current	16.6	30.8
		66.7	53.0			Total Current	40.5	57.4
		19.3	7.4			Long-Term Debt	10.8	5.3
		.0	1.0			Deferred Taxes	1.3	.0
		2.7	6.8			All Other Non-Current	1.9	13.7
		11.3	31.8			Net Worth	45.4	23.5
		100.0	100.0			Total Liabilties & Net Worth	100.0	100.0
						INCOME DATA		
		100.0	100.0			Net Sales	100.0	100.0
						Gross Profit		
		96.7	94.3			Operating Expenses	92.7	95.5
		3.3	5.7			Operating Profit	7.3	4.5
		-1.5	-1.4			All Other Expenses (net)	.9	-.4
		4.8	7.0			Profit Before Taxes	6.5	5.0
						RATIOS		
		2.0	2.1			Current	3.7	2.0
		1.2	1.2				1.5	1.2
		.5	.7				1.0	.4
		1.5	1.7			Quick	2.7	1.6
		1.2	.9				1.3	.8
		.4	.6				.5	.1
		10 38.3	16 22.6			Sales/Receivables	7 49.4	9 41.1
		31 11.8	29 12.4				21 17.4	25 14.5
		75 4.9	45 8.1				42 8.7	36 10.1
						Cost of Sales/Inventory		
						Cost of Sales/Payables		
		11.9	5.3			Sales/Working Capital	5.3	7.5
		53.2	30.9				31.5	28.6
		-4.6	-8.1				NM	-8.1
			18.6			EBIT/Interest		21.4
			(10) 4.2					(14) 4.7
			.9					-3.9
						Net Profit + Depr., Dep., Amort./Cur. Mat. L/T/D		
		.1	.2			Fixed/Worth	.1	.4
		.4	.6				.4	1.1
		-.4	3.7				1.0	-2.5
		1.2	1.0			Debt/Worth	.4	1.0
		3.2	4.4				1.5	7.1
		-4.2	15.2				3.9	-5.1
			46.7			% Profit Before Taxes/Tangible Net Worth	73.2	41.1
			(13) 19.8				(11) 42.8	(11) 11.3
			7.3				19.8	6.1
		39.2	20.7			% Profit Before Taxes/Total Assets	20.7	13.8
		5.7	7.1				13.4	2.9
		-6.2	.8				5.0	-.1
		62.5	36.2			Sales/Net Fixed Assets	62.8	30.9
		25.7	16.5				29.9	12.4
		18.4	5.0				13.7	8.1
		4.2	2.4			Sales/Total Assets	5.0	2.6
		1.8	1.8				2.8	2.1
		1.4	.9				2.4	1.0
			1.4			% Depr., Dep., Amort./Sales	.8	1.5
			(15) 2.4				(10) 1.4	(15) 2.1
			3.2				2.9	3.9
						% Officers', Directors' Owners' Comp/Sales		
8774M	67690M	104855M	654642M	299831M	975444M	Net Sales ($)	198303M	407475M
1316M	9204M	45826M	362864M	220852M	659266M	Total Assets ($)	280442M	344560M

M = $ thousand   MM = $ million
See Pages 11 through 21 for Explanation of Ratios and Data

Comparative Historical Data			Type of Statement	**Current Data Sorted by Sales**					
7	11	18	Unqualified			1	2	5	10
	4	1	Reviewed					1	1
2	3	4	Compiled		1	1	1		
4	3	2	Tax Returns		1	1			
11	10	21	Other	1	2	2	5	3	8
4/1/04-3/31/05 ALL	4/1/05-3/31/06 ALL	4/1/06-3/31/07 ALL		0-1MM	1-3MM 10 (4/1-9/30/06)	3-5MM	5-10MM	10-25MM 36 (10/1/06-3/31/07)	25MM & OVER
24	31	46	NUMBER OF STATEMENTS	1	4	5	8	9	19
%	%	%	ASSETS	%	%	%	%	%	%
28.3	25.1	28.6	Cash & Equivalents						23.0
23.5	24.2	19.9	Trade Receivables (net)						18.6
.7	1.3	.0	Inventory						.0
9.1	7.1	9.1	All Other Current						11.4
61.5	57.7	57.6	Total Current						53.0
13.9	11.8	17.0	Fixed Assets (net)						15.6
5.6	14.2	12.9	Intangibles (net)						20.5
19.0	16.2	12.5	All Other Non-Current						11.0
100.0	100.0	100.0	Total						100.0
			LIABILITIES						
14.2	7.2	11.0	Notes Payable-Short Term						8.1
2.3	2.7	2.5	Cur. Mat.-L.T.D.						4.1
17.6	10.2	12.4	Trade Payables						11.9
.2	.0	.4	Income Taxes Payable						.8
33.9	26.2	33.7	All Other Current						32.5
68.1	46.4	59.9	Total Current						57.4
11.4	11.4	17.3	Long-Term Debt						12.2
.1	.5	.7	Deferred Taxes						1.7
13.7	8.3	7.3	All Other Non-Current						7.4
6.7	33.4	14.7	Net Worth						21.4
100.0	100.0	100.0	Total Liabilities & Net Worth						100.0
			INCOME DATA						
100.0	100.0	100.0	Net Sales						100.0
			Gross Profit						
94.2	91.7	93.9	Operating Expenses						93.1
5.8	8.3	6.1	Operating Profit						6.9
.6	.7	-.6	All Other Expenses (net)						.3
5.3	7.6	6.8	Profit Before Taxes						6.6
			RATIOS						
1.3	1.9	2.0	Current						1.8
1.0	1.3	1.1							1.1
.8	.9	.5							.6
1.2	1.7	1.6	Quick						1.6
.9	1.1	.8							.8
.5	.6	.4							.4
9 38.5	14 26.3	8 46.5	Sales/Receivables						16 23.0
27 13.5	33 11.0	28 13.3							30 12.0
41 8.9	51 7.1	49 7.5							39 9.4
			Cost of Sales/Inventory						
			Cost of Sales/Payables						
20.8	6.3	8.0	Sales/Working Capital						7.5
NM	26.0	93.2							59.7
-14.3	-23.5	-7.2							-7.2
45.1	33.8	18.3	EBIT/Interest						18.8
(22) 18.4	(20) 8.4	(31) 6.3							(13) 4.8
.6	2.6	1.3							1.2
		9.0	Net Profit + Depr., Dep., Amort./Cur. Mat. L/T/D						
		(13) 2.9							
		.9							
.3	.1	.2	Fixed/Worth						.5
.6	.6	.8							2.2
NM	-12.6	-1.1							-.3
1.3	1.1	1.2	Debt/Worth						1.6
4.2	2.0	7.0							10.2
NM	-48.5	-5.1							-4.2
83.2	70.2	117.4	% Profit Before Taxes/Tangible Net Worth						129.4
(18) 31.7	(23) 43.3	(30) 34.2							(12) 31.3
5.8	9.2	11.5							5.7
23.9	22.6	24.9	% Profit Before Taxes/Total Assets						18.3
10.7	10.1	8.0							6.4
.4	2.7	.3							.1
43.6	43.6	52.7	Sales/Net Fixed Assets						38.0
23.7	27.1	23.0							14.2
12.5	10.6	8.6							8.3
4.0	3.4	3.7	Sales/Total Assets						2.8
2.9	1.9	2.0							2.0
1.5	1.2	1.0							1.1
1.2	1.1	1.2	% Depr., Dep., Amort./Sales						1.3
(22) 2.2	(27) 1.6	(34) 2.0							(17) 2.8
3.2	3.2	3.0							3.8
			% Officers', Directors' Owners' Comp/Sales						
1213358M	1664934M	2111236M	Net Sales ($)	872M	6651M	19396M	53947M	129193M	1901177M
528078M	921167M	1299328M	Total Assets ($)	1182M	3352M	14619M	51525M	74434M	1154216M

FINANCE—Open-End Investment Funds NAICS 525910 (SIC 6722)

Current Data Sorted by Assets							Comparative Historical Data	
1	4	5	10	2	5	**Type of Statement**		
	1	2				Unqualified	16	14
	2	1				Reviewed	2	7
6	2	2	1			Compiled	6	16
3	7	9	4	1	3	Tax Returns	9	8
	9 (4/1-9/30/06)		62 (10/1/06-3/31/07)			Other	23	18
							4/1/02-	4/1/03-
							3/31/03	3/31/04
0-500M	500M-2MM	2-10MM	10-50MM	50-100MM	100-250MM		ALL	ALL
10	16	19	15	3	8	**NUMBER OF STATEMENTS**	56	63
%	%	%	%	%	%	**ASSETS**	%	%
36.7	10.7	17.5	31.2			Cash & Equivalents	20.8	19.1
1.9	16.9	17.7	12.8			Trade Receivables (net)	4.9	7.3
.0	.4	4.5	3.4			Inventory	.0	2.2
2.3	7.4	6.8	5.8			All Other Current	7.1	6.4
40.8	35.5	46.5	53.2			Total Current	32.8	35.1
29.5	26.2	23.9	15.5			Fixed Assets (net)	38.7	29.4
6.5	.0	6.9	12.3			Intangibles (net)	5.5	6.4
23.2	38.3	22.8	19.0			All Other Non-Current	23.1	29.2
100.0	100.0	100.0	100.0			Total	100.0	100.0
						LIABILITIES		
4.0	17.8	3.3	.7			Notes Payable-Short Term	11.9	11.6
.0	4.3	4.2	2.9			Cur. Mat.-L.T.D.	2.0	1.8
7.9	6.8	5.9	3.7			Trade Payables	3.9	3.6
.0	.1	.7	.0			Income Taxes Payable	.1	.2
46.9	14.3	12.7	8.9			All Other Current	14.0	16.4
58.8	43.3	26.8	16.2			Total Current	31.9	33.5
16.4	11.6	14.0	23.8			Long-Term Debt	35.0	25.2
.0	.0	.0	.2			Deferred Taxes	.0	.3
22.5	.3	6.5	4.2			All Other Non-Current	3.8	5.4
2.3	44.9	52.7	55.6			Net Worth	29.2	35.6
100.0	100.0	100.0	100.0			Total Liabilties & Net Worth	100.0	100.0
						INCOME DATA		
100.0	100.0	100.0	100.0			Net Sales	100.0	100.0
						Gross Profit		
88.5	76.0	67.9	50.7			Operating Expenses	65.8	65.5
11.5	24.0	32.1	49.3			Operating Profit	34.2	34.5
1.7	-.5	5.8	4.1			All Other Expenses (net)	10.9	10.0
9.8	24.5	26.2	45.3			Profit Before Taxes	23.3	24.4
						RATIOS		
6.1	4.5	8.9	999.8				2.7	3.8
1.5	.9	3.3	3.4			Current	1.1	1.0
.6	.2	1.1	.5				.2	.3
6.1	2.7	8.9	999.8				2.3	2.5
1.2	.7	2.1	3.3			Quick	.9	.7
.5	.2	.5	.5				.1	.2
0 UND	0 UND	0 UND	0 UND				0 UND	0 UND
0 UND	0 UND	11 32.5	5 76.7			Sales/Receivables	0 UND	0 UND
0 UND	44 8.4	36 10.2	79 4.6				15 24.2	20 18.1
						Cost of Sales/Inventory		
						Cost of Sales/Payables		
15.5	16.7	2.2	.1				3.2	3.4
66.9	-38.8	4.2	4.9			Sales/Working Capital	55.3	161.9
-196.6	-8.0	19.2	-3.2				-4.5	-3.0
			47.0				19.1	40.3
	(11) 4.0					EBIT/Interest	(35) 4.6	(34) 7.9
			.7				1.0	3.8
						Net Profit + Depr., Dep., Amort./Cur. Mat. L/T/D		
.0	.0	.0	.0				.0	.0
.8	.3	.2	.1			Fixed/Worth	1.4	.5
-.7	.9	1.0	10.2				12.3	5.7
.2	.1	.2	.0				.6	.4
1.1	1.0	1.0	.4			Debt/Worth	1.8	1.7
-2.2	12.9	2.9	10.7				11.6	7.2
	246.5	59.4	115.0				50.5	42.4
(15) 58.4	(16) 24.6	(13) 23.5				% Profit Before Taxes/Tangible Net Worth	(44) 16.5	(52) 19.6
	4.0	4.8	10.9				4.5	3.6
334.0	42.7	33.9	14.3				15.4	20.3
5.0	18.6	10.1	11.8			% Profit Before Taxes/Total Assets	5.6	5.1
-20.4	1.3	.9	9.0				1.3	2.0
UND	443.3	999.8	UND				54.4	93.8
26.9	31.2	22.8	49.3			Sales/Net Fixed Assets	13.1	18.3
11.4	5.8	1.3	4.8				.3	.4
16.6	3.3	1.9	2.1				1.9	2.3
5.6	1.6	1.0	.2			Sales/Total Assets	.4	.3
4.1	.3	.2	.1				.1	.1
		.7					1.7	1.0
	(11) 1.7					% Depr., Dep., Amort./Sales	(36) 4.5	(41) 2.4
	10.6						17.3	13.5
							5.9	4.5
						% Officers', Directors' Owners' Comp/Sales	(10) 17.5	(14) 5.8
							27.0	23.0
15761M	44145M	89387M	317308M	66986M	8244163M	Net Sales ($)	1082698M	762058M
2300M	19360M	84236M	320120M	200089M	1471553M	Total Assets ($)	1360188M	1655011M

M = $ thousand   MM = $ million
See Pages 11 through 21 for Explanation of Ratios and Data

Comparative Historical Data				**Current Data Sorted by Sales**					
16	26	27	**Type of Statement** Unqualified		8	6	2	7	4
6	2	3	Reviewed		1		1	1	
9	5	3	Compiled	1	2				
7	7	11	Tax Returns	6	2	1	1		1
31	39	27	Other	10	2	5	4	2	4
4/1/04- 3/31/05 ALL	4/1/05- 3/31/06 ALL	4/1/06- 3/31/07 ALL			9 (4/1-9/30/06)		62 (10/1/06-3/31/07)		
				0-1MM	1-3MM	3-5MM	5-10MM	10-25MM	25MM & OVER
69	79	71	**NUMBER OF STATEMENTS**	17	15	12	8	10	9
%	%	%	**ASSETS**	%	%	%	%	%	%
21.4	16.6	23.9	Cash & Equivalents	19.5	28.0	33.5		10.1	
12.7	13.6	13.2	Trade Receivables (net)	11.6	7.9	10.6		24.0	
2.4	3.1	2.6	Inventory	1.7	.5	.0		2.4	
12.8	7.5	5.5	All Other Current	1.5	3.6	7.2		2.9	
49.3	40.8	45.3	Total Current	34.3	40.0	51.3		39.5	
23.3	22.0	20.6	Fixed Assets (net)	35.4	16.2	25.8		12.1	
6.0	6.8	6.8	Intangibles (net)	1.8	7.6	5.2		.8	
21.4	30.4	27.3	All Other Non-Current	28.5	36.2	17.7		47.7	
100.0	100.0	100.0	Total	100.0	100.0	100.0		100.0	
			LIABILITIES						
7.2	12.7	7.7	Notes Payable-Short Term	7.4	4.0	9.6		14.6	
2.0	3.5	2.8	Cur. Mat.-L.T.D.	1.1	.5	7.1		.7	
6.5	2.8	5.2	Trade Payables	.0	2.5	9.4		7.4	
.1	.2	.2	Income Taxes Payable	.0	.1	.0		.0	
15.2	7.2	16.0	All Other Current	33.1	7.5	12.8		15.4	
31.0	26.5	31.9	Total Current	41.5	14.6	39.0		38.1	
14.9	21.9	15.9	Long-Term Debt	24.7	11.2	9.4		15.8	
.0	.2	.0	Deferred Taxes	.0	.0	.2		.0	
7.8	8.3	6.6	All Other Non-Current	17.0	.4	.6		4.5	
46.2	43.2	45.6	Net Worth	16.7	73.9	50.9		41.6	
100.0	100.0	100.0	Total Liabilities & Net Worth	100.0	100.0	100.0		100.0	
			INCOME DATA						
100.0	100.0	100.0	Net Sales	100.0	100.0	100.0		100.0	
			Gross Profit						
67.1	56.6	65.4	Operating Expenses	64.2	57.4	68.9		67.7	
32.9	43.4	34.6	Operating Profit	35.8	42.6	31.1		32.3	
6.4	6.5	4.0	All Other Expenses (net)	6.7	1.2	4.5		9.7	
26.4	36.9	30.6	Profit Before Taxes	29.1	41.5	26.6		22.6	
			RATIOS						
4.3	6.6	10.5		14.6	217.3	15.8		2.2	
1.6	1.4	1.8	Current	1.9	1.6	1.4		.8	
.7	.4	.5		.1	.9	.4		.2	
2.8	5.4	8.9		12.3	216.8	15.8		2.2	
.8	.9	1.4	Quick	1.9	1.0	1.2		.5	
.3	.2	.3		.1	.9	.2		.2	
0 UND	0 UND	0 UND		0 UND	0 UND	0 UND		0 UND	
6 63.3	1 256.3	4 86.3	Sales/Receivables	0 UND	0 UND	5 67.1		30 12.2	
47 7.7	90 4.1	36 10.1		8 43.0	47 7.8	36 10.1		45 8.2	
			Cost of Sales/Inventory						
			Cost of Sales/Payables						
2.8	2.2	2.5		1.6	.4	2.5		10.8	
10.9	11.2	19.2	Sales/Working Capital	19.5	16.7	NM		NM	
-16.8	-5.9	-10.3		-4.7	-37.9	-4.6		-1.0	
48.3	187.7	37.7							
(40) 7.0	(48) 9.3	(35) 6.7	EBIT/Interest						
1.5	3.2	2.2							
			Net Profit + Depr., Dep., Amort./Cur. Mat. L/T/D						
.0	.0	.0		.0	.0	.0		.0	
.2	.0	.2	Fixed/Worth	.8	.0	.3		.3	
2.0	1.4	1.9		NM	.8	9.2		1.9	
.2	.2	.1		.4	.0	.1		.9	
1.2	.9	1.1	Debt/Worth	1.4	.0	.8		1.4	
5.0	5.4	8.3		-8.8	.9	10.1		29.2	
57.7	79.6	114.2	% Profit Before Taxes/Tangible Net Worth	40.0	229.1	93.4			
(60) 16.3	(71) 32.0	(60) 24.0		(12) 7.4	10.0	(10) 32.6			
1.5	11.0	5.2		2.4	-2.8	11.3			
21.8	31.5	33.9	% Profit Before Taxes/Total Assets	11.2	42.8	38.6		14.1	
6.3	11.6	10.1		4.7	7.0	16.3		5.1	
.2	3.0	1.2		.0	-1.7	4.8		.4	
680.8	UND	UND		UND	UND	UND		UND	
42.5	53.4	32.0	Sales/Net Fixed Assets	32.4	66.9	24.4		24.4	
3.9	5.6	10.7		.2	12.5	3.1		9.2	
2.5	1.7	2.6		3.4	1.7	3.3		2.4	
1.0	.5	1.0	Sales/Total Assets	.2	1.0	1.6		.5	
.1	.2	.2		.1	.1	.1		.1	
1.0	1.0	.6							
(38) 2.4	(35) 3.1	(37) 1.7	% Depr., Dep., Amort./Sales						
10.9	10.2	6.6							
1.7	5.9	3.7	% Officers', Directors' Owners' Comp/Sales						
(14) 3.6	(14) 13.2	(10) 10.2							
21.2	34.9	38.3							
930528M	2402034M	8777750M	Net Sales ($)	7951M	29632M	45732M	55474M	158816M	8480145M
1345866M	2546462M	2097658M	Total Assets ($)	35264M	144895M	135776M	43210M	808352M	930161M

M = $ thousand   MM = $ million
See Pages 11 through 21 for Explanation of Ratios and Data

Current Data Sorted by Assets   Comparative Historical Data

	0-500M	500M-2MM	2-10MM	10-50MM	50-100MM	100-250MM		4/1/02-3/31/03 ALL	4/1/03-3/31/04 ALL
Type of Statement									
Unqualified	1	2	6	2	1	3		20	30
Reviewed		5		3	2		2	13	7
Compiled	1	1	6	2				21	24
Tax Returns	8	9	6	2				30	35
Other		5	15	12	3	4		30	28
	10	17	38	21	4	9	**NUMBER OF STATEMENTS**	114	124
	%	%	%	%	%	%	**ASSETS**	%	%
	19.6	17.2	10.9	6.3			Cash & Equivalents	10.0	8.6
	.0	2.4	7.0	1.6			Trade Receivables (net)	6.1	4.1
	.0	.0	5.1	10.3			Inventory	2.6	4.1
	.0	6.3	2.0	6.5			All Other Current	1.3	4.9
	19.7	26.0	25.0	24.7			Total Current	19.9	21.6
	65.8	66.9	56.6	45.0			Fixed Assets (net)	66.3	65.8
	8.8	.4	7.0	6.2			Intangibles (net)	2.9	1.9
	5.7	6.7	11.4	24.1			All Other Non-Current	10.9	10.7
	100.0	100.0	100.0	100.0			Total	100.0	100.0
							LIABILITIES		
	12.3	7.4	4.2	7.2			Notes Payable-Short Term	6.8	6.0
	2.6	6.9	2.3	2.7			Cur. Mat.-L.T.D.	4.3	4.1
	.6	.2	2.1	1.1			Trade Payables	1.9	2.3
	.0	.0	.0	.0			Income Taxes Payable	.1	.0
	25.0	7.3	3.9	3.3			All Other Current	4.0	8.4
	40.6	21.9	12.5	14.2			Total Current	17.1	20.9
	84.7	62.2	45.0	35.4			Long-Term Debt	52.6	50.9
	.0	.0	.0	.0			Deferred Taxes	.1	.4
	.4	1.1	4.0	4.7			All Other Non-Current	4.9	5.1
	-25.7	14.8	38.4	45.7			Net Worth	25.2	22.7
	100.0	100.0	100.0	100.0			Total Liabilties & Net Worth	100.0	100.0
							INCOME DATA		
	100.0	100.0	100.0	100.0			Net Sales	100.0	100.0
							Gross Profit		
	54.5	63.9	58.4	51.4			Operating Expenses	59.6	56.5
	45.5	36.1	41.6	48.6			Operating Profit	40.4	43.5
	16.7	26.2	17.0	10.7			All Other Expenses (net)	24.4	18.8
	28.8	10.0	24.5	37.9			Profit Before Taxes	15.9	24.7
							RATIOS		
	3.5	4.2	5.9	4.4				3.7	3.8
	.6	1.1	2.1	2.2			Current	1.2	1.2
	.1	.3	.4	.5				.3	.4
	3.5	3.2	5.4	2.2				2.8	2.3
	.6	1.1	.9 (20)	.8			Quick	1.0	.8
	.1	.2	.3	.2				.3	.3
	0 UND	0 UND	0 UND	0 UND				0 UND	0 UND
	0 UND	0 UND	0 UND	0 UND			Sales/Receivables	0 UND	0 UND
	0 UND	0 UND	34 10.8	9 40.3				18 20.1	13 28.4
							Cost of Sales/Inventory		
							Cost of Sales/Payables		
	8.2	2.8	2.1	2.0				2.4	2.7
	UND	63.0	8.0	4.8			Sales/Working Capital	26.9	27.1
	-1.2	-2.5	-4.5	-7.4				-4.8	-3.8
			26.1	8.1				10.1	7.1
		(16)	7.0	(12) 4.9			EBIT/Interest	(40) 3.7	(58) 3.9
			2.7	1.3				.8	1.9
							Net Profit + Depr., Dep., Amort./Cur. Mat. L/T/D		
	3.4	.4	.2	.0				1.1	1.1
	UND	2.0	2.2	1.1			Fixed/Worth	3.5	2.6
	-1.2	7.9	6.9	5.8				22.8	12.8
	2.6	1.1	.6	.1				1.1	1.1
	UND	3.8	2.8	1.5			Debt/Worth	3.6	3.0
	-2.3	31.4	8.3	127.4				30.6	14.6
		26.5	45.2	39.9				30.4	34.5
	(15)	9.3 (34)	16.0 (18)	17.0			% Profit Before Taxes/Tangible Net Worth	(90) 10.2	(100) 13.1
		-1.5	4.6	2.1				.3	5.7
	75.1	11.3	9.2	9.9				6.7	8.9
	12.5	3.6	3.5	3.4			% Profit Before Taxes/Total Assets	2.1	4.2
	4.9	-.1	1.7	1.2				.0	1.4
	2.7	10.3	11.3	UND				.9	1.6
	.9	.3	.3	.3			Sales/Net Fixed Assets	.3	.3
	.2	.1	.1	.1				.1	.2
	1.5	.7	.4	.6				.3	.4
	.4	.2	.2	.1			Sales/Total Assets	.2	.2
	.1	.1	.1	.1				.1	.1
		4.2	1.2	1.0				8.6	8.7
	(11)	12.8 (29)	9.8 (12)	10.1			% Depr., Dep., Amort./Sales	(93) 14.5	(98) 13.0
		16.6	18.3	16.1				21.8	20.5
									.9
							% Officers', Directors' Owners' Comp/Sales	(11)	6.9
									12.7
	1755M	15316M	102954M	230035M	106307M	804695M	Net Sales ($)	712817M	1414742M
	2836M	15441M	185634M	522751M	267348M	1580613M	Total Assets ($)	3082546M	3422905M

5 (4/1-9/30/06)   94 (10/1/06-3/31/07)

Comparative Historical Data | Current Data Sorted by Sales

				Type of Statement						
27		24	15	Unqualified	6	3		1	2	3
7		6	10	Reviewed	3	3			2	2
9		10	10	Compiled	4	5	1			
35		29	25	Tax Returns	20	2		2		1
41		51	39	Other	15	9	4	1	3	7
4/1/04-3/31/05 ALL		4/1/05-3/31/06 ALL	4/1/06-3/31/07 ALL		0-1MM	5 (4/1-9/30/06) 1-3MM	3-5MM	94 (10/1/06-3/31/07) 5-10MM	10-25MM	25MM & OVER
119		120	99	NUMBER OF STATEMENTS	48	22	5	4	7	13
%		%	%	ASSETS	%	%	%	%	%	%
8.2		9.4	12.4	Cash & Equivalents	10.5	16.5				10.9
4.5		8.9	4.9	Trade Receivables (net)	2.9	.7				6.5
4.6		4.5	4.8	Inventory	.0	2.8				18.9
1.8		3.9	3.5	All Other Current	3.1	2.7				7.7
19.1		26.7	25.5	Total Current	16.4	22.7				44.1
66.2		58.4	56.4	Fixed Assets (net)	68.8	48.5				41.9
3.0		2.7	6.2	Intangibles (net)	7.4	5.3				9.8
11.7		12.2	11.9	All Other Non-Current	7.4	23.5				4.2
100.0		100.0	100.0	Total	100.0	100.0				100.0
				LIABILITIES						
9.2		6.6	6.7	Notes Payable-Short Term	5.7	5.5				11.0
2.1		2.9	3.2	Cur. Mat.-L.T.D.	4.0	1.9				5.0
1.4		2.3	1.5	Trade Payables	.7	1.1				3.6
.0		.3	.0	Income Taxes Payable	.0	.0				.1
5.0		6.9	6.2	All Other Current	6.9	5.1				2.9
17.7		19.0	17.6	Total Current	17.4	13.6				22.6
42.9		46.1	49.2	Long-Term Debt	65.6	35.7				36.0
.2		.0	.0	Deferred Taxes	.0	.0				.0
5.6		2.8	2.9	All Other Non-Current	2.8	3.5				2.6
33.6		32.0	30.3	Net Worth	14.3	47.3				38.7
100.0		100.0	100.0	Total Liabilties & Net Worth	100.0	100.0				100.0
				INCOME DATA						
100.0		100.0	100.0	Net Sales	100.0	100.0				100.0
				Gross Profit						
56.7		55.6	59.2	Operating Expenses	53.2	57.1				80.1
43.3		44.4	40.8	Operating Profit	46.8	42.9				19.9
14.1		18.4	18.2	All Other Expenses (net)	23.9	17.0				9.2
29.2		26.0	22.6	Profit Before Taxes	22.9	25.9				10.7
				RATIOS						
2.6		4.0	4.6		4.0	5.9				4.2
1.0		1.1	1.6	Current	1.1	2.2				1.2
.3		.3	.4		.2	.4				.6
1.9		2.1	2.9		2.5	5.9				.8
.6		.8	(98) .8	Quick	.6	1.3				.6
.2		.1	.2		.1	.3				.2
0 UND	0 UND	0 UND		0 UND	0 UND			0 989.2
0 UND	0 UND	0 UND	Sales/Receivables	0 UND	0 UND			6 57.9
13 29.2	10 36.2	16 23.1		11 32.7	8 45.8			30 12.1
				Cost of Sales/Inventory						
				Cost of Sales/Payables						
4.1		2.8	2.4		2.1	1.6				3.3
166.0		39.5	10.7	Sales/Working Capital	UND	5.1				13.1
-2.0		-4.2	-3.1		-1.8	-4.4				-9.7
9.0		9.2	8.8		6.8	11.7				
(56) 4.4	(53) 3.6	(45) 3.5	EBIT/Interest	(18) 3.5	(11) 3.4				
2.5		1.7	2.1		2.3	1.0				
				Net Profit + Depr., Dep., Amort./Cur. Mat. L/T/D						
.8		.3	.3		1.1	.1				.2
2.3		1.9	2.0	Fixed/Worth	4.3	1.0				1.1
7.2		5.4	8.4		60.7	5.6				4.4
.8		.8	.7		1.2	.2				1.0
2.9		2.7	2.8	Debt/Worth	5.0	1.8				2.2
11.7		8.7	34.7		UND	16.5				24.1
35.5		33.4	37.6		23.5	43.6				127.4
(101) 15.8	(103) 15.9	(83) 11.2	% Profit Before Taxes/Tangible Net Worth	(37) 9.3	(20) 6.5			(11) 18.4
4.5		4.9	3.1		1.9	-1.2				4.2
9.7		11.5	9.6		10.0	8.2				8.0
4.4		5.5	3.5	% Profit Before Taxes/Total Assets	3.3	3.5				2.3
1.4		1.5	1.0		.8	-.8				1.3
2.3		19.6	10.0		1.3	11.1				23.6
.2		.4	.3	Sales/Net Fixed Assets	.2	.4				4.9
.1		.1	.1		.1	.2				.3
.4		.5	.7		.3	.4				2.1
.2		.2	.2	Sales/Total Assets	.1	.1				1.0
.1		.1	.1		.1	.1				.2
6.5		4.6	3.2		8.3	2.3				.9
(89) 14.6	(83) 11.6	(69) 11.2	% Depr., Dep., Amort./Sales	(32) 12.9	(17) 10.2			(11) 5.3
21.3		22.2	18.2		21.0	17.8				19.2
5.1		1.3	1.0							
(11) 10.2	(16) 4.8	(11) 1.1	% Officers', Directors' Owners' Comp/Sales						
23.4		12.0	6.5							
1295968M		854485M	1261062M	Net Sales ($)	16944M	37257M	18284M	27840M	109646M	1051091M
3347279M		2857225M	2574623M	Total Assets ($)	148079M	293770M	162149M	114090M	381850M	1474685M

M = $ thousand   MM = $ million
See Pages 11 through 21 for Explanation of Ratios and Data

Current Data Sorted by Assets   Comparative Historical Data

						Type of Statement		
1	1	8	8	1	7	Unqualified	8	8
	1	2	2			Reviewed	5	5
2	2	2	3			Compiled	4	5
10	9	5	4			Tax Returns	8	10
5	7	9	11	1	.6	Other	11	17
	11 (4/1-9/30/06)		96 (10/1/06-3/31/07)				4/1/02-3/31/03	4/1/03-3/31/04
0-500M	500M-2MM	2-10MM	10-50MM	50-100MM	100-250MM		ALL	ALL
18	20	26	28	2	13	NUMBER OF STATEMENTS	36	45
%	%	%	%	%	%	ASSETS	%	%
39.4	17.4	16.2	30.9		33.5	Cash & Equivalents	16.8	18.9
15.8	18.9	18.7	13.8		9.5	Trade Receivables (net)	15.6	12.2
3.8	.9	5.4	2.5		.6	Inventory	1.9	1.7
6.9	22.7	7.4	7.1		.5	All Other Current	7.4	9.5
66.0	59.9	47.7	54.3		44.1	Total Current	41.8	42.3
17.0	19.9	23.0	8.7		4.7	Fixed Assets (net)	36.5	28.5
9.2	10.8	5.4	.3		4.9	Intangibles (net)	4.4	4.6
7.9	9.5	23.8	36.7		46.3	All Other Non-Current	17.3	24.6
100.0	100.0	100.0	100.0		100.0	Total	100.0	100.0
						LIABILITIES		
11.5	7.4	7.8	7.4		23.5	Notes Payable-Short Term	21.6	12.5
3.4	1.4	1.8	7.0		.8	Cur. Mat.-L.T.D.	4.9	6.9
3.6	1.9	6.0	6.1		1.1	Trade Payables	5.5	4.7
.5	.0	.0	.3		.6	Income Taxes Payable	.2	.0
38.9	18.9	11.3	10.6		17.7	All Other Current	14.4	10.4
57.9	29.6	26.8	31.4		43.6	Total Current	46.5	34.5
17.6	22.9	21.0	9.7		4.9	Long-Term Debt	18.5	18.8
.4	.0	.0	.0		.7	Deferred Taxes	.9	.4
5.9	24.4	5.8	4.2		1.0	All Other Non-Current	1.1	2.1
18.2	23.1	46.3	54.7		49.8	Net Worth	33.0	44.2
100.0	100.0	100.0	100.0		100.0	Total Liabilties & Net Worth	100.0	100.0
						INCOME DATA		
100.0	100.0	100.0	100.0		100.0	Net Sales	100.0	100.0
						Gross Profit		
71.1	69.2	71.6	50.2		53.2	Operating Expenses	68.8	62.0
28.9	30.8	28.4	49.8		46.8	Operating Profit	31.2	38.0
4.5	8.0	8.1	21.6		8.7	All Other Expenses (net)	12.9	8.1
24.3	22.9	20.3	28.1		38.1	Profit Before Taxes	18.3	29.9
						RATIOS		
8.1	5.4	3.0	6.0		5.7		3.1	2.8
1.1	2.1	1.9	1.7		.8	Current	1.3	1.0
.6	.9	1.0	1.0		.1		.4	.5
3.1	3.6	2.9	5.5		5.5		2.7	2.4
.9	1.1	1.6	1.1		.8	Quick	.9	.7
.3	.2	.7	.4		.1		.2	.2
0 UND	0 UND	0 UND	0 UND		0 UND		0 UND	0 UND
0 UND	0 UND	4 88.2	1 504.8		0 UND	Sales/Receivables	2 238.2	0 UND
76 4.8	74 4.9	101 3.6	137 2.7		49 7.5		44 8.3	50 7.3
						Cost of Sales/Inventory		
						Cost of Sales/Payables		
3.8	.9	1.6	.5		2.1		2.1	4.8
539.4	3.0	5.4	2.2		-7.6	Sales/Working Capital	8.2	221.0
-7.5	UND	NM	-151.5		-.4		-6.3	-2.3
46.5	20.5	16.2	17.5				14.9	24.2
(12) 11.3	(12) 4.9	(16) 6.8	(13) 7.9			EBIT/Interest	(22) 5.2	(28) 7.8
3.7	1.9	1.4	1.8				.7	3.2
						Net Profit + Depr., Dep., Amort./Cur. Mat. L/T/D		
.0	.0	.0	.0		.0		.1	.0
.1	.1	.2	.0		.0	Fixed/Worth	1.1	.2
-11.9	2.9	1.7	.6		.4		7.3	1.6
.4	.7	.4	.1		.0		.5	.4
2.5	2.5	1.7	.6		2.0	Debt/Worth	2.0	.8
-5.2	NM	11.9	7.6		11.2		10.6	8.6
218.1	58.7	80.7	31.5		30.6	% Profit Before Taxes/Tangible	33.8	83.5
(12) 62.5	(15) 8.6	(25) 20.1	(25) 6.4		(12) 12.7	Net Worth	(32) 14.8	(40) 38.8
52.5	4.8	.3	.7		4.5		.3	9.1
160.5	9.5	12.2	10.5		11.8	% Profit Before Taxes/Total	14.8	29.0
39.6	4.9	6.2	3.1		2.5	Assets	3.5	6.7
16.0	.9	.2	.2		1.5		.2	4.0
UND	UND	103.8	UND		UND		61.0	127.8
70.6	27.7	30.0	UND		UND	Sales/Net Fixed Assets	12.1	16.1
18.4	4.8	1.1	7.9		5.6		.2	.7
5.8	1.4	1.7	.6		.5		2.3	2.3
2.6	.4	.5	.1		.1	Sales/Total Assets	.4	.6
.9	.1	.1	.1		.1		.1	.1
		.3	.6				1.1	1.2
	(14) 2.5	(10) 1.2				% Depr., Dep., Amort./Sales	(22) 3.6	(29) 3.1
	12.4	5.9					18.7	15.0
						% Officers', Directors' Owners' Comp/Sales		
16214M	17554M	149328M	345729M	17287M	1030011M	Net Sales ($)	311797M	250539M
5070M	23525M	134735M	658962M	151746M	2197259M	Total Assets ($)	609972M	749735M

M = $ thousand   MM = $ million
See Pages 11 through 21 for Explanation of Ratios and Data

Comparative Historical Data   Current Data Sorted by Sales

			Type of Statement						
11	16	26	Unqualified	5	3	3	7	3	5
2	3	5	Reviewed	1	3	1			
2	6	9	Compiled	5	1		2	1	
10	15	28	Tax Returns	19	8		1		
18	30	39	Other	12	10	1	4	6	6
4/1/04-3/31/05 ALL	4/1/05-3/31/06 ALL	4/1/06-3/31/07 ALL		0-1MM	11 (4/1-9/30/06) 1-3MM	3-5MM	96 (10/1/06-3/31/07) 5-10MM	10-25MM	25MM & OVER
43	70	107	NUMBER OF STATEMENTS	42	25	5	14	10	11
%	%	%	ASSETS	%	%	%	%	%	%
26.3	26.7	26.0	Cash & Equivalents	31.6	12.8		18.2	39.0	29.0
11.8	11.2	16.4	Trade Receivables (net)	15.3	14.3		31.1	11.2	16.2
3.6	3.7	2.8	Inventory	1.9	1.0		7.7	.0	8.4
9.6	11.0	9.1	All Other Current	11.4	8.5		9.1	2.2	11.2
51.2	52.6	54.4	Total Current	60.2	36.5		66.2	52.4	64.7
20.9	23.7	15.0	Fixed Assets (net)	19.2	13.4		9.5	5.7	13.7
2.7	2.1	5.6	Intangibles (net)	5.6	8.8		4.8	5.7	1.1
25.3	21.7	25.1	All Other Non-Current	14.9	41.3		19.6	36.2	20.5
100.0	100.0	100.0	Total	100.0	100.0		100.0	100.0	100.0
			LIABILITIES						
26.9	19.2	11.3	Notes Payable-Short Term	10.2	4.6		24.3	14.3	15.5
2.7	.8	3.2	Cur. Mat.-L.T.D.	1.7	8.2		1.6	1.7	.4
7.3	6.2	4.2	Trade Payables	1.6	1.7		7.3	6.6	13.8
.2	.5	.3	Income Taxes Payable	.0	.0		.7	1.1	.5
12.4	12.8	17.7	All Other Current	19.8	17.2		21.1	8.8	21.9
49.4	39.4	36.6	Total Current	33.3	31.7		55.0	32.6	52.2
14.2	15.5	15.5	Long-Term Debt	22.5	8.7		18.7	4.7	13.9
.5	.4	.2	Deferred Taxes	.0	.0		.6	.0	.9
3.5	7.2	8.2	All Other Non-Current	8.0	14.9		4.9	6.4	1.9
32.4	37.6	39.6	Net Worth	36.3	44.6		20.9	56.3	31.1
100.0	100.0	100.0	Total Liabilties & Net Worth	100.0	100.0		100.0	100.0	100.0
			INCOME DATA						
100.0	100.0	100.0	Net Sales	100.0	100.0		100.0	100.0	100.0
			Gross Profit						
67.0	61.8	62.2	Operating Expenses	62.1	52.5		72.5	47.1	86.3
33.0	38.2	37.8	Operating Profit	37.9	47.5		27.5	52.9	13.7
10.3	15.2	11.8	All Other Expenses (net)	9.7	22.8		14.4	6.3	1.9
22.7	23.0	26.0	Profit Before Taxes	28.2	24.8		13.1	46.5	11.7
			RATIOS						
2.7	3.2	5.3		6.8	3.8		1.9	63.6	2.0
1.5	1.2	1.5	Current	2.6	1.6		1.0	2.1	1.1
.5	.8	.8		1.0	.6		.9	.2	1.0
2.1	2.1	3.1		5.1	3.3		1.7	63.4	1.4
(42) 1.0	1.0	1.1	Quick	1.4	1.1		.9	1.9	.9
.1	.2	.3		.3	.1		.5	.1	.6
0 UND	0 UND	0 UND		0 UND	0 UND		0 UND	0 UND	0 UND
2 180.3	0 UND	0 UND	Sales/Receivables	0 UND	4 86.2		11 33.4	0 UND	30 12.3
30 12.2	45 8.2	87 4.2		87 4.2	81 4.5		166 2.2	33 10.9	78 4.7
			Cost of Sales/Inventory						
			Cost of Sales/Payables						
2.4	2.3	1.3		.3	1.7		2.6	1.3	3.4
13.5	6.4	5.1	Sales/Working Capital	3.0	5.3		NM	11.2	11.1
-11.6	-11.3	-8.4		-124.8	-6.2		-28.8	-.3	-8.9
32.0	19.4	28.4		13.0	24.6		20.9		
(26) 8.7	(36) 5.4	(61) 7.9	EBIT/Interest	(20) 5.3	(14) 13.7		(10) 6.8		
2.0	.6	2.5		1.6	2.7		.7		
			Net Profit + Depr., Dep., Amort./Cur. Mat. L/T/D						
.0	.0	.0		.0	.0		.0	.0	.0
.2	.2	.1	Fixed/Worth	.0	.2		.1	.1	.4
3.0	3.8	.9		2.3	1.9		3.2	.2	.6
.4	.5	.2		.3	.0		1.0	.4	.8
1.1	1.8	1.8	Debt/Worth	1.8	1.5		9.1	.8	2.8
10.7	11.5	13.7		12.6	506.8		NM	3.6	20.8
87.0	93.2	58.9		58.9	77.0		47.1		116.6
(33) 27.9	(60) 23.3	(91) 15.6	% Profit Before Taxes/Tangible Net Worth	(36) 17.3	(20) 10.6		(11) 17.6		(10) 27.1
5.1	2.0	3.2		1.6	1.9		-.9		-5.5
29.4	19.3	18.8		23.5	12.3		20.8	35.0	20.3
7.1	4.0	5.6	% Profit Before Taxes/Total Assets	4.9	5.6		3.0	11.8	5.5
.8	.7	1.3		.5	.9		.5	5.3	1.5
296.7	UND	UND		UND	UND		999.8	UND	UND
21.6	34.8	61.5	Sales/Net Fixed Assets	109.6	43.6		144.5	127.5	8.4
6.0	2.4	7.4		3.4	15.5		7.8	7.4	5.3
3.6	1.5	1.5		1.0	1.6		2.2	1.6	4.0
1.0	.4	.4	Sales/Total Assets	.2	.2		.7	.4	1.0
.1	.1	.1		.1	.1		.2	.1	.3
1.0	.9	.6		2.2					
(28) 2.7	(39) 2.6	(47) 2.7	% Depr., Dep., Amort./Sales	(17) 6.8					
6.1	11.7	8.7		24.4					
		3.2	% Officers', Directors' Owners' Comp/Sales						
	(13)	8.5							
		19.2							
346015M	818645M	1576123M	Net Sales ($)	16471M	45515M	21215M	89711M	184087M	1219124M
618801M	2051117M	3171297M	Total Assets ($)	159163M	420158M	175175M	316795M	914643M	1185363M

M = $ thousand   MM = $ million
See Pages 11 through 21 for Explanation of Ratios and Data

REAL ESTATE AND RENTAL AND LEASING

REAL ESTATE—Lessors of Residential Buildings and Dwellings NAICS 531110 (SIC 6513, 6514, 6531)

	Current Data Sorted by Assets						Comparative Historical Data	
Type of Statement								
Unqualified	2	64	124	36	11	12	154	203
Reviewed	1	5	20	18	1		55	89
Compiled	23	61	67	19	1	1	118	223
Tax Returns	178	401	247	31		2	390	623
Other	58	135	174	56	9	9	234	307
	122 (4/1-9/30/06)			1,644 (10/1/06-3/31/07)			4/1/02-3/31/03 ALL	4/1/03-3/31/04 ALL
	0-500M	500M-2MM	2-10MM	10-50MM	50-100MM	100-250MM		
NUMBER OF STATEMENTS	262	666	632	160	21	25	951	1445
	%	%	%	%	%	%	%	%
ASSETS								
Cash & Equivalents	14.4	5.8	4.9	6.8	9.3	4.6	7.9	7.6
Trade Receivables (net)	2.9	1.8	2.7	4.1	6.8	9.8	2.8	2.5
Inventory	3.4	2.3	3.8	5.8	13.3	8.2	1.8	2.8
All Other Current	3.3	1.7	3.0	2.8	9.0	2.7	2.9	3.3
Total Current	24.0	11.5	14.4	19.5	38.3	25.3	15.4	16.1
Fixed Assets (net)	68.4	80.0	76.9	66.7	43.3	51.1	74.5	73.8
Intangibles (net)	2.3	1.4	1.5	1.8	1.1	.5	1.9	1.4
All Other Non-Current	5.3	7.1	7.1	12.0	17.3	23.0	8.2	8.7
Total	100.0	100.0	100.0	100.0	100.0	100.0	100.0	100.0
LIABILITIES								
Notes Payable-Short Term	10.9	4.4	5.1	9.8	9.0	6.1	6.4	5.5
Cur. Mat.-L.T.D.	7.1	4.3	2.6	2.5	3.3	1.6	5.0	3.7
Trade Payables	2.8	1.3	1.7	2.5	6.7	1.2	1.8	1.8
Income Taxes Payable	.1	.0	.0	.0	.0	.1	.1	.1
All Other Current	11.5	5.1	5.3	7.1	5.7	11.4	6.4	8.4
Total Current	32.4	15.2	14.7	21.9	24.7	20.4	19.9	19.5
Long-Term Debt	79.5	67.1	65.9	53.9	37.4	47.0	74.8	69.1
Deferred Taxes	.0	.0	.1	.1	.1	.0	.1	.1
All Other Non-Current	3.1	3.2	3.8	3.1	7.9	9.2	3.0	5.1
Net Worth	-15.1	14.5	15.4	21.0	30.0	23.3	2.3	6.2
Total Liabilities & Net Worth	100.0	100.0	100.0	100.0	100.0	100.0	100.0	100.0
INCOME DATA								
Net Sales	100.0	100.0	100.0	100.0	100.0	100.0	100.0	100.0
Gross Profit								
Operating Expenses	70.4	67.9	71.5	74.6	76.8	76.6	69.5	72.5
Operating Profit	29.6	32.1	28.5	25.4	23.2	23.4	30.5	27.5
All Other Expenses (net)	16.4	22.8	23.8	19.2	7.8	9.2	20.6	19.0
Profit Before Taxes	13.1	9.3	4.7	6.2	15.4	14.2	9.8	8.5
RATIOS								
Current	2.0	1.8	2.3	2.4	2.7	2.8	1.9	2.0
	.7	.6	.8	.8	1.4	.8	.8	.7
	.2	.1	.2	.2	.8	.4	.2	.2
Quick	1.5	1.4	1.5	1.3	1.9	2.2	1.5	1.3
	(261) .5	.4	(630) .4	.5	.7	.4	(950) .5	(1442) .4
	.1	.1	.1	.1	.2	.2	.1	.1
Sales/Receivables	0 UND	0 UND	0 UND	0 UND	5 76.7	0 UND	0 UND	0 UND
	0 UND	0 UND	0 UND	1 313.9	19 18.8	11 33.0	0 UND	0 UND
	0 UND	1 362.9	5 79.6	15 23.6	37 10.0	40 9.1	3 133.8	3 115.1
Cost of Sales/Inventory								
Cost of Sales/Payables								
Sales/Working Capital	12.3	13.0	5.2	4.9	1.5	3.7	8.3	8.2
	-21.8	-13.4	-21.9	-32.8	9.7	-19.7	-23.8	-17.7
	-3.6	-2.8	-3.3	-2.4	-42.3	-3.8	-3.4	-3.5
EBIT/Interest	8.1	5.2	4.4	6.3	19.7	13.8	5.6	5.3
	(121) 3.2	(239) 2.5	(229) 2.2	(61) 2.4	(15) 3.0	(16) 5.0	(399) 2.6	(603) 2.4
	1.5	1.3	1.2	1.1	1.1	2.2	1.3	1.2
Net Profit + Depr., Dep., Amort./Cur. Mat. L/T/D		10.3	4.2				7.7	3.1
		(12) 2.1	(17) 1.6				(31) 2.7	(38) 1.1
		1.5	.9				1.1	.5
Fixed/Worth	1.3	2.0	1.9	1.2	.2	.3	1.8	1.8
	5.9	5.6	5.4	4.0	1.3	2.5	6.0	5.9
	-3.5	-52.0	-38.6	-81.4	4.1	52.9	-15.4	-17.4
Debt/Worth	1.0	1.7	1.8	1.6	1.1	1.1	1.6	1.7
	7.7	6.2	5.7	6.0	2.0	3.6	6.6	6.8
	-4.0	-43.9	-42.0	-60.7	8.4	58.2	-18.0	-19.5
% Profit Before Taxes/Tangible Net Worth	82.2	29.1	19.5	23.6	25.7	34.0	35.7	34.7
	(160) 23.6	(480) 8.7	(454) 5.7	(118) 7.0	(18) 12.0	(20) 16.7	(650) 10.0	(990) 8.8
	1.7	-2.9	-4.5	-.2	.8	10.7	-.7	-3.4
% Profit Before Taxes/Total Assets	22.1	6.8	4.2	4.2	10.9	6.8	8.0	7.1
	6.6	2.0	1.0	1.4	2.6	3.2	2.3	2.0
	-.2	-.9	-1.5	-.6	.1	1.3	-.6	-1.2
Sales/Net Fixed Assets	4.5	.5	.5	1.2	29.1	6.9	.9	.9
	.7	.2	.2	.3	.9	.7	.3	.3
	.2	.1	.1	.1	.3	.3	.2	.2
Sales/Total Assets	1.6	.4	.3	.4	.5	.5	.5	.5
	.5	.2	.2	.2	.4	.3	.2	.2
	.2	.1	.1	.1	.2	.2	.2	.1
% Depr., Dep., Amort./Sales	4.1	10.8	10.3	6.1	1.3	2.2	9.0	9.1
	(210) 12.1	(596) 17.3	(544) 18.5	(124) 14.3	(19) 4.8	(17) 10.0	(827) 16.9	(1251) 16.7
	22.3	25.3	27.5	23.5	12.3	13.9	24.1	25.2
% Officers', Directors' Owners' Comp/Sales	3.2	2.6	2.3	4.1			3.7	4.2
	(32) 9.4	(77) 6.2	(68) 5.2	(23) 8.5			(101) 5.7	(194) 6.9
	17.0	12.2	10.8	26.4			11.2	13.1
Net Sales ($)	100840M	377391M	1132584M	1530052M	775428M	1705864M	6268280M	6484580M
Total Assets ($)	72857M	775657M	2791712M	3096164M	1440273M	4180371M	6976600M	10533338M

© RMA 2007

M = $ thousand   MM = $ million
See Pages 11 through 21 for Explanation of Ratios and Data

Comparative Historical Data | Current Data Sorted by Sales

			Type of Statement						
240	204	249	Unqualified	144	41	18	11	17	18
80	56	45	Reviewed	13	9	4	8	5	6
159	140	172	Compiled	113	34	16	4	4	1
713	686	859	Tax Returns	709	114	14	12	5	5
343	400	441	Other	247	105	27	19	22	21
4/1/04-3/31/05 ALL	4/1/05-3/31/06 ALL	4/1/06-3/31/07 ALL		122 (4/1-9/30/06)		1,644 (10/1/06-3/31/07)			
				0-1MM	1-3MM	3-5MM	5-10MM	10-25MM	25MM & OVER
1535	1486	1766	NUMBER OF STATEMENTS	1226	303	79	54	53	51
%	%	%	ASSETS	%	%	%	%	%	%
7.2	7.2	6.9	Cash & Equivalents	5.7	8.0	11.4	13.3	10.6	10.4
2.6	2.1	2.7	Trade Receivables (net)	1.2	3.6	4.8	6.6	12.4	14.4
2.7	3.0	3.5	Inventory	1.4	5.2	6.7	15.0	14.2	15.4
2.5	2.7	2.6	All Other Current	1.7	3.1	8.6	6.8	7.8	3.3
15.1	15.0	15.7	Total Current	10.0	19.9	31.5	41.8	45.0	43.5
74.7	75.6	75.2	Fixed Assets (net)	83.6	65.3	54.1	42.2	38.3	36.7
1.6	1.3	1.6	Intangibles (net)	1.2	2.9	1.8	2.3	2.1	1.3
8.6	8.1	7.6	All Other Non-Current	5.2	11.9	12.6	13.8	14.7	18.4
100.0	100.0	100.0	Total	100.0	100.0	100.0	100.0	100.0	100.0
			LIABILITIES						
6.4	5.6	6.2	Notes Payable-Short Term	4.1	9.1	12.5	14.5	15.5	9.7
3.8	3.3	3.9	Cur. Mat.-L.T.D.	4.3	3.3	3.0	3.9	1.1	2.0
1.7	1.9	1.9	Trade Payables	1.0	2.3	3.5	4.2	7.5	9.4
.1	.1	.0	Income Taxes Payable	.0	.0	.2	.0	.1	.0
6.6	5.4	6.4	All Other Current	5.5	7.1	7.6	8.1	15.4	10.7
18.5	16.3	18.4	Total Current	15.0	21.9	26.8	30.7	39.6	31.8
70.8	71.0	66.7	Long-Term Debt	72.4	65.6	44.8	42.4	31.5	32.1
.0	.0	.0	Deferred Taxes	.0	.1	.0	.2	.2	.1
3.2	3.8	3.5	All Other Non-Current	3.3	3.7	1.5	4.3	7.0	6.5
7.5	9.0	11.3	Net Worth	9.3	8.7	26.8	22.5	21.8	29.5
100.0	100.0	100.0	Total Liabilties & Net Worth	100.0	100.0	100.0	100.0	100.0	100.0
			INCOME DATA						
100.0	100.0	100.0	Net Sales	100.0	100.0	100.0	100.0	100.0	100.0
			Gross Profit						
73.6	71.5	70.4	Operating Expenses	67.1	73.2	80.0	84.9	85.2	87.7
26.4	28.5	29.6	Operating Profit	32.9	26.8	20.0	15.1	14.8	12.3
19.3	21.8	21.5	All Other Expenses (net)	25.8	15.7	10.9	5.6	4.0	3.9
7.1	6.6	8.1	Profit Before Taxes	7.1	11.0	9.0	9.4	10.8	8.4
			RATIOS						
1.9	2.2	2.0		1.8	2.3	2.9	3.0	2.8	3.0
.7	.8	.7	Current	.5	.9	1.2	1.3	1.3	1.1
.2	.2	.2		.1	.3	.5	.6	.7	.6
1.4	1.5	1.4		1.4	1.7	1.7	1.7	1.5	1.3
.4 (1483)	.5 (1763)	.4	Quick	(1223) .4	.6	.7	.5	.6	.5
.1	.1	.1		.1	.1	.2	.1	.2	.2
0 UND	0 UND	0 UND		0 UND	0 UND	0 UND	0 UND	2 188.7	0 999.8
0 UND	0 UND	0 UND	Sales/Receivables	0 UND	0 UND	0 999.8	1 274.1	17 22.1	15 24.9
3 108.6	3 106.0	4 102.0		1 454.5	6 56.8	8 46.1	12 29.8	39 9.3	38 9.7
			Cost of Sales/Inventory						
			Cost of Sales/Payables						
9.5	7.3	7.6		10.1	5.3	7.2	4.5	4.8	4.6
-16.5	-36.1	-19.7	Sales/Working Capital	-9.6	-142.9	54.3	24.2	12.4	87.0
-3.3	-3.4	-3.1		-2.5	-5.1	-9.0	-13.8	-15.2	-12.2
5.0	6.7	5.4		4.6	5.4	8.4	6.3	12.0	16.3
(656) 2.4	(584) 2.8	(681) 2.5	EBIT/Interest	(368) 2.5	(155) 2.5	(42) 2.6	(41) 2.5	(40) 3.0	(35) 5.3
1.1	1.2	1.3		1.3	1.4	1.1	1.5	1.0	1.7
3.7	3.4	3.2		3.5					
(38) 1.6	(32) 1.4	(41) 1.7	Net Profit + Depr., Dep., Amort./Cur. Mat. L/T/D	(19) 1.9					
.5	.5	.8		1.1					
1.9	1.8	1.7		2.2	1.4	.4	.4	.2	.1
6.4	6.0	5.4	Fixed/Worth	6.2	6.7	1.9	1.8	1.1	.9
-20.5	-19.0	-26.7		-30.0	-6.8	15.2	NM	4.2	3.7
1.8	1.8	1.6		1.8	1.7	.7	1.3	1.0	1.0
7.4	6.7	6.1	Debt/Worth	6.2	9.2	2.9	3.2	3.4	2.9
-22.6	-21.5	-27.5		-27.9	-10.4	22.2	NM	20.1	9.5
35.0	31.6	28.8		24.3	35.6	72.3	53.8	68.6	47.4
(1061) 8.9	(1035) 8.7	(1250) 8.8	% Profit Before Taxes/Tangible Net Worth	(869) 5.2	(190) 13.1	(63) 14.1	(41) 19.1	(44) 19.3	(43) 15.6
-4.2	-4.7	-2.8		-5.1	.6	4.3	5.0	2.4	10.4
6.8	6.7	6.6		5.5	8.6	13.7	11.0	12.0	11.6
1.8	1.4	1.8	% Profit Before Taxes/Total Assets	1.2	3.1	2.9	4.0	2.7	4.1
-1.3	-1.4	-1.0		-1.5	.0	-.2	.7	.2	1.5
.8	.7	.7		.4	2.1	31.0	33.3	34.9	50.1
.3	.2	.2	Sales/Net Fixed Assets	.2	.4	.7	3.1	3.1	5.7
.1	.1	.1		.1	.2	.2	.6	.9	.7
.5	.4	.5		.3	.8	1.8	2.7	2.5	2.9
.2	.2	.2	Sales/Total Assets	.2	.3	.5	.7	1.0	.7
.1	.1	.1		.1	.2	.2	.3	.3	.4
9.3	9.6	8.7		12.5	4.7	1.9	.5	.6	1.1
(1335) 17.3	(1288) 16.9	(1510) 16.7	% Depr., Dep., Amort./Sales	(1090) 19.3	(246) 11.1	(59) 7.9	(44) 1.7	(36) 3.3	(35) 3.6
26.4	26.4	25.2		27.8	19.1	17.7	10.2	8.1	10.0
4.4	2.9	2.8		3.8	2.1	2.7	1.6		
(217) 6.6	(174) 6.1	(203) 6.7	% Officers', Directors' Owners' Comp/Sales	(92) 8.9	(53) 5.4	(25) 4.6	(18) 4.2		
13.3	13.1	13.2		16.5	8.7	11.2	14.8		
8791979M	4538349M	5622159M	Net Sales ($)	394087M	524310M	307652M	368064M	801643M	3226403M
9290165M	10807055M	12357034M	Total Assets ($)	2316189M	2064263M	874779M	693266M	1784145M	4624392M

© RMA 2007

M = $ thousand   MM = $ million
See Pages 11 through 21 for Explanation of Ratios and Data

Current Data Sorted by Assets   Comparative Historical Data

						Type of Statement		
3	29	82	74	28	25	Unqualified	183	179
11	59	137	61	5	9	Reviewed	217	253
74	291	345	75	3	2	Compiled	559	931
522	1749	1092	106	5	5	Tax Returns	1645	2273
130	443	679	196	28	18	Other	743	1026
	274 (4/1-9/30/06)		6,012 (10/1/06-3/31/07)				4/1/02-3/31/03 ALL	4/1/03-3/31/04 ALL
0-500M	500M-2MM	2-10MM	10-50MM	50-100MM	100-250MM	NUMBER OF STATEMENTS	ALL	ALL
740	2571	2335	512	69	59		3347	4662
%	%	%	%	%	%	**ASSETS**	%	%
10.0	4.4	4.1	5.5	6.7	5.5	Cash & Equivalents	5.4	5.6
3.2	1.2	1.8	3.3	4.6	5.2	Trade Receivables (net)	1.9	2.0
1.0	.8	1.6	3.2	6.1	4.2	Inventory	1.3	1.3
2.5	1.5	1.5	2.0	2.7	2.3	All Other Current	1.7	2.7
16.7	7.9	9.0	14.0	20.1	17.2	Total Current	10.2	11.6
75.3	86.1	83.2	74.4	62.4	66.6	Fixed Assets (net)	82.7	80.7
1.8	1.5	1.6	1.5	3.9	4.2	Intangibles (net)	1.5	1.5
6.1	4.5	6.2	10.2	13.6	12.0	All Other Non-Current	5.6	6.2
100.0	100.0	100.0	100.0	100.0	100.0	Total	100.0	100.0
						LIABILITIES		
8.9	3.9	3.7	4.4	5.7	4.6	Notes Payable-Short Term	4.7	5.2
6.7	4.4	4.1	3.6	2.1	2.4	Cur. Mat.-L.T.D.	5.3	4.4
3.4	.8	1.0	2.3	2.7	4.3	Trade Payables	1.4	1.4
.0	.0	.1	.1	.1	.7	Income Taxes Payable	.0	.0
10.2	3.7	3.8	4.7	6.7	5.1	All Other Current	5.0	6.1
29.2	12.9	12.7	15.1	17.3	17.0	Total Current	16.5	17.1
62.9	69.5	65.6	57.6	40.4	51.0	Long-Term Debt	65.5	61.6
.0	.0	.1	.3	.4	.4	Deferred Taxes	.1	.1
3.3	2.4	2.6	3.1	2.4	4.4	All Other Non-Current	2.9	5.4
4.6	15.2	19.1	24.0	39.5	27.2	Net Worth	15.0	15.8
100.0	100.0	100.0	100.0	100.0	100.0	Total Liabilties & Net Worth	100.0	100.0
						INCOME DATA		
100.0	100.0	100.0	100.0	100.0	100.0	Net Sales	100.0	100.0
						Gross Profit		
51.5	45.9	50.1	57.8	65.5	70.2	Operating Expenses	51.1	52.9
48.5	54.1	49.9	42.2	34.5	29.8	Operating Profit	48.9	47.1
21.9	30.9	30.4	23.5	14.2	15.8	All Other Expenses (net)	26.8	24.2
26.6	23.2	19.4	18.7	20.3	14.0	Profit Before Taxes	22.1	22.8
						RATIOS		
1.7	1.8	1.9	2.0	2.3	1.7		1.7	2.0
.6	.5	.6	.8	1.1	.9	Current	.5	.6
.2	.1	.1	.2	.4	.5		.1	.1
1.4	1.4	1.4	1.4	1.4	1.1		1.3	1.4
.5	.4 (2331)	.4	.5	.5	.6	Quick	(3344) .4 (4658) .4	
.1	.1	.1	.1	.2	.3		.1	.1
0 UND	0 UND	0 UND	0 UND	0 UND	0 UND		0 UND	0 UND
0 UND	0 UND	0 UND	0 999.8	8 44.9	14 26.4	Sales/Receivables	0 UND	0 UND
0 UND	0 UND	1 280.0	15 24.5	27 13.4	48 7.6		2 209.5	1 247.4
						Cost of Sales/Inventory		
						Cost of Sales/Payables		
15.4	11.3	8.3	6.1	4.4	7.9		10.6	7.4
-15.2	-8.4	-10.2	-25.8	273.5	-34.3	Sales/Working Capital	-9.3	-10.9
-3.2	-2.3	-2.2	-2.3	-4.1	-3.6		-2.3	-2.3
8.3	7.5	6.9	7.7	11.4	5.0		6.6	6.5
(269) 4.5	(667) 4.5	(584) 3.7	(176) 3.4	(34) 4.4	(33) 2.7	EBIT/Interest	(1086) 3.8	(1681) 3.7
2.8	2.7	1.8	1.6	2.3	1.5		2.1	2.0
3.1	3.6	3.2	3.4	6.4			3.2	3.4
(10) 1.9	(49) 1.6	(121) 1.7	(61) 1.5	(15) 2.2		Net Profit + Depr., Dep., Amort./Cur. Mat. L/T/D	(181) 1.4	(203) 1.5
1.2	1.0	1.1	.9	1.3			.7	.9
1.7	2.6	2.3	1.7	1.0	1.3		2.3	2.1
4.8	5.5	5.6	4.2	2.1	2.8	Fixed/Worth	5.4	5.1
-44.1	108.3	42.0	14.4	4.2	7.5		81.0	57.2
1.4	2.0	1.9	1.6	.7	1.2		1.9	1.8
5.3	5.3	5.4	4.3	1.8	2.8	Debt/Worth	5.2	5.1
-23.2	121.4	48.5	16.2	6.4	7.6		95.0	79.3
58.1	40.4	33.7	34.5	19.2	23.8		41.8	41.8
(530) 22.8	(1969) 18.2	(1825) 15.2	(439) 13.4	(61) 9.1	(49) 12.9	% Profit Before Taxes/Tangible Net Worth	(2574) 19.2	(3610) 18.6
8.5	6.0	4.3	3.9	4.4	3.2		6.4	6.2
16.8	8.8	6.4	6.4	7.9	6.2		8.7	8.5
6.9	3.8	2.9	2.6	3.6	2.7	% Profit Before Taxes/Total Assets	4.0	4.0
2.0	.8	.5	.5	1.2	.2		.9	.8
1.0	.3	.3	.4	2.2	.7		.4	.4
.3	.2	.2	.2	.3	.3	Sales/Net Fixed Assets	.2	.2
.2	.1	.1	.1	.2	.2		.1	.1
.7	.3	.2	.3	.4	.4		.3	.3
.2	.2	.2	.2	.2	.2	Sales/Total Assets	.2	.2
.2	.1	.1	.1	.1	.1		.1	.1
7.0	11.1	12.2	10.6	6.7	7.5		10.9	10.9
(628) 13.4	(2409) 16.2	(2161) 17.8	(466) 16.7	(60) 13.4	(48) 12.6	% Depr., Dep., Amort./Sales	(3126) 16.3	(4317) 16.4
19.1	22.8	24.5	23.7	20.7	18.8		22.6	23.4
4.9	3.0	2.7	1.7	1.3			3.2	3.3
(68) 8.1	(149) 5.9	(176) 5.6	(48) 4.3	(10) 8.1		% Officers', Directors' Owners' Comp/Sales	(247) 6.5	(386) 6.5
17.8	15.9	12.5	16.0	29.0			12.0	13.5
236121M	1005704M	2921210M	4300065M	2994497M	4708092M	Net Sales ($)	10075875M	14093877M
220183M	2934276M	9860548M	10444021M	4730192M	9914877M	Total Assets ($)	22819860M	28533740M

M = $ thousand   MM = $ million
See Pages 11 through 21 for Explanation of Ratios and Data

Comparative Historical Data | Current Data Sorted by Sales

4/1/04-3/31/05 ALL	4/1/05-3/31/06 ALL	4/1/06-3/31/07 ALL	Type of Statement	0-1MM	1-3MM	3-5MM	5-10MM	10-25MM	25MM & OVER
201	198	241	Unqualified	64	42	25	27	33	50
265	232	282	Reviewed	140	69	21	18	18	16
774	665	790	Compiled	580	140	30	22	13	5
2486	2476	3479	Tax Returns	3147	259	34	19	14	6
1114	1330	1494	Other	1013	267	74	57	47	36
				274 (4/1-9/30/06)	6,012 (10/1/06-3/31/07)				
4840	4901	6286	**NUMBER OF STATEMENTS**	4944	777	184	143	125	113
%	%	%	**ASSETS**	%	%	%	%	%	%
5.8	5.4	5.1	Cash & Equivalents	4.4	6.0	9.6	9.0	10.1	11.6
2.0	2.0	1.9	Trade Receivables (net)	.9	2.4	5.3	10.5	14.5	14.6
1.4	1.4	1.4	Inventory	.5	2.1	4.9	8.4	10.1	13.7
1.6	1.7	1.7	All Other Current	1.5	1.9	3.0	2.7	3.6	4.7
10.8	10.5	10.1	Total Current	7.2	12.4	22.8	30.5	38.3	44.6
81.2	81.3	82.3	Fixed Assets (net)	86.5	76.9	65.1	54.5	45.8	42.9
1.6	1.7	1.6	Intangibles (net)	1.4	2.3	2.0	1.9	3.3	3.5
6.3	6.4	5.9	All Other Non-Current	5.0	8.4	10.1	13.1	12.6	9.0
100.0	100.0	100.0	Total	100.0	100.0	100.0	100.0	100.0	100.0
			LIABILITIES						
4.5	4.8	4.5	Notes Payable-Short Term	4.1	5.0	5.7	5.9	8.1	9.1
4.4	3.9	4.4	Cur. Mat.-L.T.D.	4.6	4.1	4.3	3.5	3.4	2.5
1.3	1.3	1.4	Trade Payables	.6	2.1	3.9	6.0	8.1	10.5
.1	.0	.1	Income Taxes Payable	.0	.1	.1	.6	.1	.5
4.3	4.9	4.6	All Other Current	3.9	5.5	9.5	9.2	10.6	11.4
14.5	15.0	15.0	Total Current	13.3	16.7	23.5	25.1	30.3	34.0
65.6	64.8	65.8	Long-Term Debt	68.4	67.5	45.9	43.9	36.7	32.3
.1	.1	.1	Deferred Taxes	.0	.1	.1	.3	.4	.8
3.3	3.2	2.6	All Other Non-Current	2.4	3.8	-2.5	4.6	3.4	
16.5	16.9	16.5	Net Worth	15.8	12.0	28.0	28.6	28.0	29.5
100.0	100.0	100.0	Total Liabilities & Net Worth	100.0	100.0	100.0	100.0	100.0	100.0
			INCOME DATA						
100.0	100.0	100.0	Net Sales	100.0	100.0	100.0	100.0	100.0	100.0
			Gross Profit						
52.2	51.1	49.5	Operating Expenses	45.0	59.5	67.5	74.3	80.1	83.9
47.8	48.9	50.5	Operating Profit	55.0	40.5	32.5	25.7	19.9	16.1
23.5	25.3	28.7	All Other Expenses (net)	32.1	21.5	13.8	9.2	6.8	5.2
24.4	23.6	21.7	Profit Before Taxes	22.9	19.0	18.8	16.5	13.1	10.9
			RATIOS						
1.9	1.9	1.8	Current	1.7	2.1	3.0	2.7	2.2	2.0
.6	.6	.6		.5	.7	.8	1.4	1.3	1.2
.2	.2	.1		.1	.2	.3	.6	.8	.8
1.5	1.5	1.4	Quick	1.3	1.5	1.7	2.0	1.4	1.3
(4834) .4	(4897) .4	(6282) .4		(4940) .4	.4	.6	.8	.9	.7
.1	.1	.1		.1	.1	.2	.2	.3	.4
0 UND	0 UND	0 UND	Sales/Receivables	0 UND	0 UND	0 UND	0 UND	3 105.1	3 130.7
0 UND	0 UND	0 UND		0 UND	0 UND	1 247.3	8 44.4	19 19.5	23 15.8
1 447.5	0 999.8	0 UND		0 UND	6 60.4	21 17.2	31 11.8	45 8.0	50 7.3
			Cost of Sales/Inventory						
			Cost of Sales/Payables						
8.0	8.3	9.3	Sales/Working Capital	11.4	7.1	7.0	5.1	5.9	7.8
-11.8	-13.1	-10.7		-7.9	-19.6	-33.6	27.1	20.9	25.0
-2.4	-2.6	-2.3		-2.1	-2.9	-3.7	-8.6	-35.0	-34.2
7.2	7.7	7.5	EBIT/Interest	7.1	6.8	11.5	10.7	11.5	11.0
(1806) 4.1	(1591) 4.0	(1763) 4.1		(1086) 4.4	(317) 3.2	(100) 4.5	(85) 3.5	(89) 3.8	(86) 3.8
2.3	2.3	2.2		2.7	1.6	1.6	1.4	1.4	1.7
4.1	3.2	3.5	Net Profit + Depr., Dep., Amort./Cur. Mat. L/T/D	2.7	3.8	2.3	3.8	6.5	10.7
(197) 1.8	(214) 1.6	(265) 1.7		(117) 1.5	(62) 1.9	(14) 1.0	(27) 2.1	(17) 2.7	(28) 3.1
.9	1.0	1.0		.9	1.1	.2	.9	1.6	1.2
2.2	2.2	2.3	Fixed/Worth	2.6	1.9	1.1	.4	.4	.5
5.0	5.1	5.2		5.8	5.1	2.9	2.2	1.5	1.3
56.8	57.1	53.4		74.6	-100.8	13.8	6.4	4.1	3.5
1.7	1.8	1.8	Debt/Worth	2.0	1.6	1.0	1.0	1.0	1.1
4.9	5.1	5.2		5.6	5.5	3.2	2.5	2.7	2.6
71.8	67.3	67.3		93.5	-89.7	16.4	8.0	7.4	6.6
42.2	43.8	37.9	% Profit Before Taxes/Tangible Net Worth	35.9	43.6	44.2	36.8	58.6	47.5
(3751) 19.0	(3815) 19.0	(4873) 16.7		(3818) 16.4	(573) 17.8	(152) 16.6	(127) 15.9	(103) 18.7	(100) 21.3
7.0	6.6	5.2		5.0	5.5	6.7	4.2	4.6	9.0
8.7	8.7	8.1	% Profit Before Taxes/Total Assets	7.5	8.9	14.1	10.4	17.1	13.2
4.2	3.9	3.5		3.3	3.7	4.6	5.4	6.0	5.2
1.2	.9	.7		.6	.8	1.2	1.1	1.2	2.0
.4	.4	.3	Sales/Net Fixed Assets	.3	.6	4.7	12.8	29.3	36.4
.2	.2	.2		.2	.3	.4	1.2	3.0	4.6
.1	.1	.1		.1	.2	.2	.2	.4	.5
.3	.3	.3	Sales/Total Assets	.2	.4	1.5	2.3	2.4	3.1
.2	.2	.2		.2	.2	.3	.4	.8	1.3
.1	.1	.1		.1	.1	.2	.2	.2	.3
11.3	10.7	10.8	% Depr., Dep., Amort./Sales	12.3	8.6	4.3	1.2	.9	.5
(4448) 16.8	(4465) 16.3	(5772) 16.5		(4583) 17.4	(712) 14.8	(158) 11.4	(124) 7.3	(100) 5.9	(95) 2.7
24.0	23.1	23.0		23.8	21.2	19.8	17.3	12.5	8.7
2.4	3.1	2.8	% Officers', Directors' Owners' Comp/Sales	3.3	3.8	1.8	1.9	1.7	.5
(379) 5.9	(378) 6.5	(458) 6.4		(210) 6.6	(125) 8.0	(35) 4.5	(38) 4.2	(35) 4.6	(15) 1.6
12.8	15.3	14.9		15.8	15.8	9.3	10.6	10.8	12.5
15300174M	18004325M	16165689M	Net Sales ($)	1519744M	1302840M	712815M	1006826M	1950254M	9673210M
29594442M	32625013M	38104097M	Total Assets ($)	9981301M	6728503M	3010995M	3443035M	4889113M	10051150M

© RMA 2007

M = $ thousand   MM = $ million
See Pages 11 through 21 for Explanation of Ratios and Data

Current Data Sorted by Assets   Comparative Historical Data

0-500M	500M-2MM	2-10MM	10-50MM	50-100MM	100-250MM	Type of Statement	4/1/02-3/31/03 ALL	4/1/03-3/31/04 ALL
1	1		1		1	Unqualified		4
1	2	2	2	1		Reviewed	1	1
4	11	8	2		1	Compiled	10	13
20	49	33	1			Tax Returns	29	60
12	24	17	5	4		Other	10	28
	7 (4/1-9/30/06)		196 (10/1/06-3/31/07)					
38	87	60	11	5	2	NUMBER OF STATEMENTS	50	106
%	%	%	%	%	%	**ASSETS**	%	%
21.1	3.4	3.4	5.3			Cash & Equivalents	4.4	6.2
2.5	2.0	.8	.3			Trade Receivables (net)	.1	2.0
2.9	1.0	.9	.1			Inventory	.0	.2
1.7	3.1	1.8	1.5			All Other Current	1.7	1.0
28.2	9.5	6.8	7.3			Total Current	6.2	9.4
63.2	85.0	85.0	78.9			Fixed Assets (net)	89.5	82.2
.5	1.6	1.4	.5			Intangibles (net)	1.9	2.1
8.0	3.9	6.8	13.3			All Other Non-Current	2.3	6.3
100.0	100.0	100.0	100.0			Total	100.0	100.0
						LIABILITIES		
9.1	10.0	5.5	.8			Notes Payable-Short Term	2.4	1.5
4.6	6.3	2.6	1.4			Cur. Mat.-L.T.D.	5.5	5.5
1.9	1.0	.8	.2			Trade Payables	.3	1.0
.0	.0	.0	.0			Income Taxes Payable	.0	.0
33.6	3.1	1.4	4.6			All Other Current	3.5	3.8
49.2	20.3	10.4	7.0			Total Current	11.7	11.8
65.7	65.3	71.6	69.3			Long-Term Debt	74.7	74.9
.0	.0	.0	.0			Deferred Taxes	.0	.0
10.3	2.1	2.7	4.6			All Other Non-Current	8.1	9.4
-25.3	12.3	15.3	19.1			Net Worth	5.5	3.9
100.0	100.0	100.0	100.0			Total Liabilities & Net Worth	100.0	100.0
						INCOME DATA		
100.0	100.0	100.0	100.0			Net Sales	100.0	100.0
						Gross Profit		
73.3	59.4	63.1	60.9			Operating Expenses	59.2	67.4
26.7	40.6	36.9	39.1			Operating Profit	40.8	32.6
9.7	22.9	23.2	31.1			All Other Expenses (net)	25.5	19.1
17.0	17.8	13.8	8.0			Profit Before Taxes	15.3	13.5
						RATIOS		
2.8	3.3	2.4	4.4			Current	3.0	3.5
.9	.6	.6	1.0				.5	.8
.2	.2	.2	.5				.2	.2
2.6	1.4	2.1	1.5			Quick	1.6	3.1
.6	.5	.5	.6				.3	.7
.2	.1	.2	.1				.1	.1
0 UND	0 UND	0 UND	0 UND			Sales/Receivables	0 UND	0 UND
0 UND	0 UND	0 UND	0 UND				0 UND	0 UND
0 UND	0 UND	2 218.4	12 30.5				0 UND	1 432.1
						Cost of Sales/Inventory		
						Cost of Sales/Payables		
17.5	13.9	13.7	6.0			Sales/Working Capital	8.5	11.1
-101.8	-18.8	-13.8	-49.5				-9.2	-73.0
-7.8	-2.2	-4.2	-2.4				-2.9	-3.8
4.8	4.4	6.3				EBIT/Interest	6.1	5.2
(13) 2.7	(34) 3.3	(18) 2.8					(16) 3.7	(49) 2.6
1.5	2.2	1.0					2.0	1.5
						Net Profit + Depr., Dep., Amort./Cur. Mat. L/T/D		
1.1	2.8	2.5	1.9			Fixed/Worth	2.9	2.6
-10.1	6.5	7.0	3.4				9.9	7.0
-.6	-11.9	NM	999.8				-15.3	-13.4
.8	2.2	1.7	1.9			Debt/Worth	2.3	2.6
-11.4	6.2	6.2	9.2				10.5	7.0
-2.7	-14.0	NM	999.8				-16.3	-15.4
60.1	42.3	40.0				% Profit Before Taxes/Tangible Net Worth	51.7	45.4
(16) 43.8	(62) 19.3	(45) 10.7					(33) 16.7	(69) 13.8
13.9	8.9	2.9					7.9	3.3
40.5	8.8	5.0	2.9			% Profit Before Taxes/Total Assets	8.9	8.2
11.7	4.4	2.5	.4				3.5	3.3
2.0	2.0	-.1	-1.3				.6	.0
18.7	.4	.4	.3			Sales/Net Fixed Assets	.4	.6
2.8	.3	.2	.2				.3	.3
.4	.2	.1	.1				.2	.2
6.1	.4	.3	.2			Sales/Total Assets	.4	.4
1.2	.2	.2	.2				.3	.2
.3	.2	.1	.1				.2	.2
2.0	9.6	9.7				% Depr., Dep., Amort./Sales	10.1	10.2
(30) 5.7	(81) 14.0	(54) 14.1					(47) 14.1	(100) 16.2
13.0	19.1	22.9					18.9	21.4
						% Officers', Directors' Owners' Comp/Sales		4.8
							(17)	9.9
								16.8
22203M	42488M	63436M	34792M	79023M	102145M	Net Sales ($)	60200M	145761M
9089M	97653M	217881M	211525M	276212M	401187M	Total Assets ($)	210527M	426932M

Comparative Historical Data | Current Data Sorted by Sales

4/1/04-3/31/05 ALL	4/1/05-3/31/06 ALL	4/1/06-3/31/07 ALL	Type of Statement	0-1MM	1-3MM	3-5MM	5-10MM	10-25MM	25MM & OVER
2	4	4	Unqualified	2	1				1
7	5	8	Reviewed	2	4	1		1	1
13	17	26	Compiled	20	4	1			1
64	68	103	Tax Returns	90	11		2		
26	39	62	Other	43	10	1	5	2	1
					7 (4/1-9/30/06)		196 (10/1/06-3/31/07)		
112	133	203	**NUMBER OF STATEMENTS**	157	29	4	7	3	3
%	%	%	**ASSETS**	%	%	%	%	%	%
8.7	7.2	6.9	Cash & Equivalents	7.4	3.3				
1.9	3.2	1.6	Trade Receivables (net)	.5	4.0				
.7	.6	1.3	Inventory	.6	1.7				
1.4	1.0	2.3	All Other Current	1.7	4.3				
12.7	12.0	12.1	Total Current	10.2	13.3				
78.0	78.3	80.4	Fixed Assets (net)	83.2	78.5				
2.2	2.1	1.2	Intangibles (net)	1.1	2.0				
7.1	7.5	6.2	All Other Non-Current	5.5	6.2				
100.0	100.0	100.0	Total	100.0	100.0				
			LIABILITIES						
8.2	7.7	7.8	Notes Payable-Short Term	9.0	2.7				
7.0	3.4	4.5	Cur. Mat.-L.T.D.	4.9	2.6				
1.3	1.9	1.1	Trade Payables	.4	1.6				
.0	.0	.0	Income Taxes Payable	.0	.0				
3.8	4.7	8.4	All Other Current	7.2	16.8				
20.3	17.7	21.8	Total Current	21.5	23.7				
69.9	66.0	67.2	Long-Term Debt	70.5	59.8				
.1	.0	.0	Deferred Taxes	.0	.0				
2.6	5.2	3.9	All Other Non-Current	3.8	4.8				
7.2	11.1	7.0	Net Worth	4.2	11.7				
100.0	100.0	100.0	Total Liabilties & Net Worth	100.0	100.0				
			INCOME DATA						
100.0	100.0	100.0	Net Sales	100.0	100.0				
			Gross Profit						
65.7	65.4	63.7	Operating Expenses	60.7	73.3				
34.3	34.6	36.3	Operating Profit	39.3	26.7				
16.5	20.3	20.6	All Other Expenses (net)	22.3	15.2				
17.8	14.3	15.7	Profit Before Taxes	17.0	11.5				
			RATIOS						
1.7	2.5	3.0	Current	2.8	2.3				
.5	.8	.7		.6	.8				
.2	.2	.2		.2	.2				
1.3	2.0	1.9	Quick	2.4	1.3				
.4	.6	.5		.5	.5				
.1	.2	.1		.1	.1				
0 UND	0 UND	0 UND	Sales/Receivables	0 UND	0 UND				
0 UND	0 UND	0 UND		0 UND	0 UND				
1 390.1	5 69.3	1 373.0		0 UND	10 34.9				
			Cost of Sales/Inventory						
			Cost of Sales/Payables						
14.3	10.6	12.2	Sales/Working Capital	13.1	23.2				
-13.2	-40.0	-24.2		-18.7	-40.6				
-2.3	-4.1	-3.7		-3.3	-3.5				
5.3	5.9	4.8	EBIT/Interest	4.9	3.1				
(63) 3.3	(56) 3.0	(71) 3.1		(48) 3.3	(15) 1.9				
2.1	1.6	1.7		2.4	.4				
			Net Profit + Depr., Dep., Amort./Cur. Mat. L/T/D						
2.1	2.3	2.2	Fixed/Worth	2.7	1.9				
5.4	8.6	6.7		7.4	7.8				
-32.5	-9.7	-10.0		-8.9	-4.1				
1.6	2.1	1.8	Debt/Worth	2.2	1.1				
5.6	8.3	6.9		6.9	7.4				
-34.6	-11.3	-11.8		-10.6	-6.2				
39.7	57.2	47.3	% Profit Before Taxes/Tangible Net Worth	43.4	58.5				
(81) 21.5	(81) 20.8	(137) 16.1		(104) 15.7	(20) 20.5				
3.9	7.6	4.8		4.8	6.3				
10.4	8.0	9.0	% Profit Before Taxes/Total Assets	8.9	12.1				
4.9	3.8	3.9		3.9	4.0				
.7	.3	.9		1.1	-.6				
.7	.6	.6	Sales/Net Fixed Assets	.5	1.2				
.3	.3	.3		.3	.5				
.2	.2	.2		.2	.2				
.5	.4	.5	Sales/Total Assets	.4	.9				
.3	.2	.2		.2	.3				
.2	.2	.2		.2	.2				
9.0	9.0	7.8	% Depr., Dep., Amort./Sales	9.0	6.8				
(102) 13.9	(116) 13.5	(180) 13.2		(140) 14.0	(24) 12.9				
19.1	18.4	19.2		19.7	20.7				
5.1	3.4	2.9	% Officers', Directors' Owners' Comp/Sales	3.2					
(20) 9.4	(30) 9.1	(26) 7.9		(17) 9.3					
12.5	14.7	13.0		13.8					
221844M	263992M	344087M	Net Sales ($)	55260M	46705M	17130M	51170M	46414M	127408M
459810M	710041M	1213547M	Total Assets ($)	233638M	161590M	116335M	85585M	158831M	457568M

M = $ thousand   MM = $ million
See Pages 11 through 21 for Explanation of Ratios and Data

Current Data Sorted by Assets   ## Comparative Historical Data

Type of Statement	0-500M	500M-2MM	2-10MM	10-50MM	50-100MM	100-250MM	4/1/02-3/31/03 ALL	4/1/03-3/31/04 ALL
Unqualified	2	12	32	35	8	9	95	81
Reviewed	7	26	56	28	3	5	110	127
Compiled	33	100	118	37	2		293	425
Tax Returns	133	387	273	33	1	4	582	816
Other	53	146	215	88	15	14	387	510
		106 (4/1-9/30/06)		1,769 (10/1/06-3/31/07)				
NUMBER OF STATEMENTS	228	671	694	221	29	32	1467	1959
ASSETS	%	%	%	%	%	%	%	%
Cash & Equivalents	14.0	5.2	5.0	4.7	7.8	9.5	5.4	5.9
Trade Receivables (net)	3.9	1.5	2.5	2.9	8.0	6.4	2.3	2.2
Inventory	2.4	1.5	2.7	6.7	9.6	13.5	1.7	2.5
All Other Current	2.6	2.2	1.9	2.9	3.7	2.5	2.7	3.3
Total Current	22.9	10.3	12.1	17.2	29.1	31.9	12.1	14.0
Fixed Assets (net)	69.5	82.8	80.1	68.0	54.2	56.1	79.5	77.5
Intangibles (net)	2.5	1.4	1.6	1.2	1.8	2.0	1.9	1.5
All Other Non-Current	5.0	5.5	6.1	13.6	14.9	10.0	6.5	7.1
Total	100.0	100.0	100.0	100.0	100.0	100.0	100.0	100.0
LIABILITIES								
Notes Payable-Short Term	8.0	4.4	3.6	5.9	11.8	5.5	5.0	5.7
Cur. Mat.-L.T.D.	4.0	5.3	3.8	3.8	2.5	1.9	5.0	4.9
Trade Payables	5.4	.9	1.4	2.6	3.8	7.0	1.4	1.7
Income Taxes Payable	.0	.0	.1	.0	.5	.2	.0	.1
All Other Current	15.9	3.8	4.0	5.1	6.7	5.5	6.9	6.7
Total Current	33.3	14.5	12.8	17.3	25.2	20.1	18.3	19.1
Long-Term Debt	54.4	61.7	60.2	50.8	38.3	44.1	62.0	58.4
Deferred Taxes	.0	.0	.0	.4	1.0	.1	.1	.1
All Other Non-Current	5.5	4.0	3.5	4.3	6.0	8.4	3.4	5.1
Net Worth	6.8	19.9	23.5	27.2	29.5	27.2	16.2	17.3
Total Liabilities & Net Worth	100.0	100.0	100.0	100.0	100.0	100.0	100.0	100.0
INCOME DATA								
Net Sales	100.0	100.0	100.0	100.0	100.0	100.0	100.0	100.0
Gross Profit								
Operating Expenses	56.9	52.7	51.7	59.3	70.7	79.4	55.2	55.4
Operating Profit	43.1	47.3	48.3	40.7	29.3	20.6	44.8	44.6
All Other Expenses (net)	16.8	26.3	27.5	22.1	15.0	12.5	24.4	21.8
Profit Before Taxes	26.3	21.0	20.8	18.6	14.2	8.1	20.4	22.8
RATIOS								
Current	1.8	1.5	2.0	2.4	2.9	3.3	1.9	2.0
	.6	.6	.7	.9	1.3	1.4	.6	.7
	.2	.2	.2	.2	.7	.5	.2	.2
Quick	1.5	1.1	1.5	1.4	1.6	1.5	1.3	1.3
	.4	(670) .4	(693) .5	(220) .3	.5	.9	(1466) .4	(1957) .4
	.1	.1	.1	.0	.2	.1	.1	.1
Sales/Receivables	0 UND	0 UND	0 UND	0 UND	1 340.6	0 844.4	0 UND	0 UND
	0 UND	0 UND	0 UND	0 UND	15 24.3	9 39.4	0 UND	0 UND
	0 UND	0 UND	5 67.2	11 32.3	49 7.4	27 13.3	2 165.0	1 440.5
Cost of Sales/Inventory								
Cost of Sales/Payables								
Sales/Working Capital	9.0	11.9	5.5	3.7	2.4	3.1	9.4	7.7
	-16.9	-10.4	-14.3	-40.3	16.6	13.4	-13.2	-14.1
	-4.2	-2.7	-2.9	-2.2	-4.3	-5.1	-2.4	-2.3
EBIT/Interest	9.4	7.0	6.6	9.2	9.3	19.7	6.3	7.3
	(100) 4.3	(227) 4.0	(203) 3.9	(98) 3.7	(15) 2.4	(21) 5.4	(515) 3.5	(796) 3.9
	2.7	2.0	2.1	1.5	1.0	2.0	1.8	1.9
Net Profit + Depr., Dep., Amort./Cur. Mat. L/T/D		2.2	3.8	5.6			3.2	3.0
		(20) 1.5	(33) 1.8	(28) 2.9			(92) 1.5	(90) 1.6
		.6	.9	1.3			.7	.8
Fixed/Worth	1.1	2.0	1.7	1.1	1.0	.4	1.9	1.8
	3.3	4.7	4.1	2.7	2.2	2.6	4.7	4.5
	-28.5	34.7	21.8	7.2	4.8	25.1	65.8	55.1
Debt/Worth	1.0	1.5	1.4	1.0	1.6	1.1	1.5	1.5
	3.4	4.3	3.8	3.4	2.9	6.3	4.6	4.6
	-12.8	44.0	22.3	8.3	5.3	45.4	85.7	67.1
% Profit Before Taxes/Tangible Net Worth	78.5	41.1	33.0	27.7	47.6	42.9	39.0	41.1
	(160) 27.6	(530) 16.2	(562) 14.8	(196) 11.5	(27) 18.3	(25) 15.7	(1121) 17.2	(1520) 18.8
	11.2	3.1	4.9	1.9	7.9	-.7	4.3	5.3
% Profit Before Taxes/Total Assets	26.5	9.5	7.7	7.9	14.8	9.0	9.1	9.6
	9.6	4.0	3.2	2.8	4.9	3.0	3.8	4.1
	2.5	.3	.5	.3	.8	-1.2	.6	.8
Sales/Net Fixed Assets	6.7	.4	.3	.8	9.5	12.9	.5	.5
	.5	.2	.2	.2	.5	.8	.2	.2
	.2	.1	.1	.1	.2	.2	.1	.1
Sales/Total Assets	2.0	.3	.2	.3	.9	1.5	.4	.3
	.4	.2	.2	.2	.3	.3	.2	.2
	.2	.1	.1	.1	.1	.2	.1	.1
% Depr., Dep., Amort./Sales	4.2	9.3	10.0	7.2	2.9	3.7	10.4	10.0
	(179) 10.7	(625) 16.0	(629) 17.2	(196) 14.9	(24) 7.6	(20) 12.3	(1354) 16.5	(1772) 16.7
	17.5	23.5	24.8	23.3	17.7	19.3	24.1	24.6
% Officers', Directors' Owners' Comp/Sales	2.4	3.5	2.0	1.9			4.0	3.0
	(33) 10.5	(62) 7.3	(58) 5.8	(25) 5.4			(138) 8.0	(190) 6.0
	20.0	16.3	9.9	9.1			17.5	14.4
Net Sales ($)	96279M	291692M	1104498M	2078497M	1434521M	6636154M	4046792M	6817868M
Total Assets ($)	63492M	796150M	2915781M	4476063M	1987950M	5535130M	8522017M	11064906M

© RMA 2007

M = $ thousand   MM = $ million
See Pages 11 through 21 for Explanation of Ratios and Data

Comparative Historical Data / Current Data Sorted by Sales

Hist 1	Hist 2	Hist 3			Type of Statement	0-1MM	1-3MM	3-5MM	5-10MM	10-25MM	25MM & OVER
97	79	98			Unqualified	31	20	9	11	14	13
109	90	125			Reviewed	58	27	8	14	10	8
319	262	290			Compiled	214	53	10	6	5	2
875	679	831			Tax Returns	703	85	26	8	5	4
476	536	531			Other	321	109	23	22	28	28
4/1/04-3/31/05	4/1/05-3/31/06	4/1/06-3/31/07				106 (4/1-9/30/06)			1,769 (10/1/06-3/31/07)		
ALL	ALL	ALL									
1876	1646	1875			**NUMBER OF STATEMENTS**	1327	294	76	61	62	55
%	%	%			**ASSETS**	%	%	%	%	%	%
6.3	6.2	6.2			Cash & Equivalents	5.3	7.4	7.9	12.6	8.4	10.1
2.6	3.2	2.5			Trade Receivables (net)	1.1	3.1	3.4	8.1	14.4	13.2
2.5	2.6	3.0			Inventory	.8	4.5	9.2	9.8	14.1	19.7
2.5	2.6	2.3			All Other Current	2.1	2.2	2.1	4.1	4.2	3.2
14.0	14.7	14.0			Total Current	9.3	17.1	22.6	34.7	41.2	46.1
77.3	75.8	77.5			Fixed Assets (net)	84.2	70.3	63.9	49.6	45.2	43.0
1.5	1.8	1.6			Intangibles (net)	1.3	2.4	2.8	2.1	1.9	2.3
7.3	7.7	6.9			All Other Non-Current	5.3	10.2	10.8	13.6	11.7	8.6
100.0	100.0	100.0			Total	100.0	100.0	100.0	100.0	100.0	100.0
					LIABILITIES						
6.2	6.0	4.8			Notes Payable-Short Term	4.0	5.4	6.4	7.0	11.8	8.5
4.9	4.1	4.3			Cur. Mat.-L.T.D.	4.6	4.2	3.1	3.2	2.2	2.7
1.8	2.3	2.0			Trade Payables	.9	2.7	2.8	4.3	8.2	12.7
.1	.0	.0			Income Taxes Payable	.0	.0	.0	.2	.5	.3
6.1	6.3	5.6			All Other Current	4.5	8.1	8.0	8.0	8.8	8.0
19.0	18.8	16.7			Total Current	14.1	20.4	20.3	22.7	31.5	32.3
60.4	58.8	58.3			Long-Term Debt	61.7	59.0	42.1	39.0	39.0	37.1
.1	.1	.1			Deferred Taxes	.0	.1	.1	.4	.9	.2
3.8	4.8	4.1			All Other Non-Current	3.7	5.1	3.5	4.2	5.5	7.5
16.7	17.5	20.8			Net Worth	20.4	15.4	34.0	33.8	23.2	23.0
100.0	100.0	100.0			Total Liabilities & Net Worth	100.0	100.0	100.0	100.0	100.0	100.0
					INCOME DATA						
100.0	100.0	100.0			Net Sales	100.0	100.0	100.0	100.0	100.0	100.0
					Gross Profit						
56.6	56.0	54.3			Operating Expenses	48.1	62.5	69.5	74.6	80.6	87.0
43.4	44.0	45.7			Operating Profit	51.9	37.5	30.5	25.4	19.4	13.0
20.6	22.2	24.7			All Other Expenses (net)	29.0	18.7	13.8	8.1	7.2	5.0
22.9	21.8	21.0			Profit Before Taxes	22.9	18.7	16.7	17.3	12.2	8.1
					RATIOS						
1.9	2.1	2.0				1.7	2.4	1.9	4.0	2.3	2.7
.6	.7	.7			Current	.5	.8	1.0	1.7	1.3	1.4
.1	.2	.2				.2	.2	.4	.8	.7	.8
1.3	1.5	1.3				1.3	1.7	1.2	2.8	1.8	1.1
(1874) .4	(1644) .4	(1872) .4			Quick	(1326) .4	(293) .4	(75) .5	.9	.8	.8
.1	.1	.1				.1	.1	.1	.3	.1	.3
0 UND	0 UND	0 UND				0 UND	0 UND	0 UND	0 UND	2 217.8	1 378.2
0 UND	0 UND	0 UND			Sales/Receivables	0 UND	0 UND	0 UND	3 132.7	15 24.1	11 34.7
1 485.1	3 131.4	2 163.0				0 UND	9 41.5	11 32.8	30 12.1	48 7.7	37 9.8
					Cost of Sales/Inventory						
					Cost of Sales/Payables						
7.8	7.2	6.9				8.7	6.0	13.9	1.8	4.4	4.5
-10.7	-15.5	-14.1			Sales/Working Capital	-9.2	-19.7	650.3	6.5	15.7	14.3
-2.1	-2.7	-3.0				-2.6	-3.2	-5.7	-25.6	-12.3	-37.8
7.2	7.5	7.4				7.0	6.0	6.5	11.2	12.6	11.9
(817) 3.8	(659) 3.7	(664) -4.0			EBIT/Interest	(353) 4.2	(131) 3.5	(46) 3.5	(45) 3.2	(45) 3.3	(44) 5.4
1.8	1.8	2.0				2.4	1.5	1.6	1.4	1.7	1.6
3.0	4.2	5.1			Net Profit + Depr., Dep.,	2.0	5.3	5.2		8.5	22.8
(90) 1.5	(91) 2.0	(99) 2.0			Amort./Cur. Mat. L/T/D	(38) 1.5	(19) 2.3	(10) 2.5	(13) 3.0	(11) 8.5	
.7	.9	.8				.8	.4	.8		1.4	1.8
1.9	1.8	1.7				1.9	1.6	.9	.5	.4	.3
4.4	4.5	3.9			Fixed/Worth	4.2	4.7	2.3	1.4	1.8	1.3
48.4	54.9	22.0				24.7	NM	9.1	5.9	5.1	6.0
1.6	1.6	1.3				1.4	1.7	.6	.5	1.3	1.0
4.4	4.5	3.8			Debt/Worth	3.8	5.2	2.5	2.4	3.4	2.8
64.3	65.7	31.5				31.9	-156.1	11.3	8.6	10.0	7.8
41.5	42.2	38.7			% Profit Before Taxes/Tangible	35.4	48.9	33.9	36.9	47.9	52.0
(1457) 18.6	(1275) 18.6	(1500) 15.8			Net Worth	(1063) 14.8	(219) 19.3	(64) 15.8	(53) 12.9	(55) 23.1	(46) 28.0
5.7	6.2	4.0				3.6	4.2	3.8	5.2	7.9	13.1
9.1	9.4	9.5			% Profit Before Taxes/Total	8.6	10.4	11.5	11.7	13.6	16.4
4.3	3.9	3.8			Assets	3.5	3.6	5.8	4.3	5.8	7.7
.8	.8	.5				.4	.6	.6	.7	1.7	2.3
.5	.6	.5				.3	1.0	6.6	13.2	28.9	15.7
.2	.2	.2			Sales/Net Fixed Assets	.2	.3	.7	.8	2.8	5.3
.1	.1	.1				.1	.2	.2	.4	.5	.9
.3	.4	.3				.2	.6	1.4	1.4	2.2	2.7
.2	.2	.2			Sales/Total Assets	.2	.2	.3	.4	.9	1.4
.1	.1	.1				.1	.1	.2	.2	.3	.5
10.0	8.5	8.3				10.7	7.0	2.2	1.7	1.2	.9
(1677) 16.9	(1466) 15.7	(1673) 15.8			% Depr., Dep., Amort./Sales	(1214) 17.1	(250) 13.9	(65) 7.7	(53) 6.2	(50) 3.1	(41) 3.0
24.8	23.8	23.5				24.8	21.5	19.8	14.1	8.7	6.3
2.8	3.0	2.6			% Officers', Directors'	3.1	4.9	1.4	4.5	.6	
(176) 6.5	(154) 6.2	(184) 6.3			Owners' Comp/Sales	(74) 8.0	(53) 7.6	(22) 3.0	(12) 8.0	(15) 1.7	
12.1	13.0	12.2				14.4	17.7	7.3	12.0	4.2	
5248882M	5282831M	11641641M			Net Sales ($)	446179M	489867M	286916M	426769M	958761M	9033149M
11190706M	11422374M	15774566M			Total Assets ($)	2811727M	2319505M	1164468M	1334767M	2484634M	5659465M

Current Data Sorted by Assets   Comparative Historical Data

						Type of Statement		
2	8	30	18	6	5	Unqualified	97	101
4	17	19	10	2	1	Reviewed	93	84
31	31	33	16	1		Compiled	148	193
153	125	80	12	1	1	Tax Returns	342	469
87	94	104	42	8	7	Other	279	294
	82 (4/1-9/30/06)		866 (10/1/06-3/31/07)				4/1/02-3/31/03	4/1/03-3/31/04
0-500M	500M-2MM	2-10MM	10-50MM	50-100MM	100-250MM		ALL	ALL
277	275	266	98	18	14	NUMBER OF STATEMENTS	959	1141
%	%	%	%	%	%	ASSETS	%	%
32.4	14.1	12.6	14.4	26.2	12.4	Cash & Equivalents	16.5	18.5
6.9	8.5	7.9	9.9	9.2	11.9	Trade Receivables (net)	7.3	6.2
3.5	3.0	8.3	10.6	6.2	3.9	Inventory	2.9	4.4
8.4	7.0	5.9	6.2	17.3	4.1	All Other Current	5.5	5.6
51.2	32.6	34.7	41.1	58.9	32.3	Total Current	32.2	34.8
29.5	51.2	45.9	37.5	21.4	54.7	Fixed Assets (net)	48.3	45.3
6.6	4.8	4.8	5.9	7.0	3.4	Intangibles (net)	4.8	4.5
12.7	11.4	14.6	15.5	12.7	9.5	All Other Non-Current	14.8	15.5
100.0	100.0	100.0	100.0	100.0	100.0	Total	100.0	100.0
						LIABILITIES		
17.6	11.1	10.0	15.3	17.3	3.8	Notes Payable-Short Term	10.4	9.8
5.9	2.8	3.3	2.3	.9	3.1	Cur. Mat.-L.T.D.	4.0	4.0
6.8	3.7	4.6	6.1	7.2	3.9	Trade Payables	4.4	4.3
.2	.1	.3	.1	.1	.0	Income Taxes Payable	.2	.2
29.8	11.3	13.4	9.9	12.1	4.9	All Other Current	15.5	17.7
60.3	29.0	31.6	33.7	37.5	15.8	Total Current	34.5	36.1
18.4	38.2	38.9	30.4	20.4	52.1	Long-Term Debt	35.6	35.3
.0	.0	.1	.4	.1	.6	Deferred Taxes	.2	.2
12.8	6.2	6.1	3.0	1.7	2.2	All Other Non-Current	6.3	5.6
8.5	26.6	23.3	32.5	40.3	29.3	Net Worth	23.5	22.8
100.0	100.0	100.0	100.0	100.0	100.0	Total Liabilties & Net Worth	100.0	100.0
						INCOME DATA		
100.0	100.0	100.0	100.0	100.0	100.0	Net Sales	100.0	100.0
						Gross Profit		
88.8	74.4	75.1	75.2	73.6	82.4	Operating Expenses	76.4	77.4
11.2	25.6	24.9	24.8	26.4	17.6	Operating Profit	23.6	22.6
2.4	12.6	12.2	7.2	10.8	13.1	All Other Expenses (net)	10.9	9.5
8.9	13.0	12.7	17.6	15.5	4.6	Profit Before Taxes	12.7	13.1
						RATIOS		
3.0	2.4	2.4	2.1	2.2	3.4		2.1	2.5
1.2	.9	1.0	1.2	1.3	1.6	Current	1.0	1.0
.4	.3	.4	.5	1.1	1.0		.3	.3
2.5	1.7	1.5	1.4	1.8	2.4		1.7	1.8
(276) .9	.6	.6	.7	.8	1.1	Quick	(955) .7	(1140) .6
.2	.2	.1	.2	.3	.6		.2	.1
0 UND	0 UND	0 UND	0 UND	0 UND	1 473.7		0 UND	0 UND
0 UND	0 UND	1 410.0	2 146.2	4 98.8	17 21.1	Sales/Receivables	0 UND	0 UND
1 368.8	12 31.6	13 27.6	20 18.6	37 9.9	68 5.4		10 35.9	7 55.0
						Cost of Sales/Inventory		
						Cost of Sales/Payables		
16.6	9.2	6.2	3.9	3.0	2.9		10.5	8.0
219.5	-150.6	145.6	32.3	11.5	11.4	Sales/Working Capital	-245.2	536.7
-19.8	-7.1	-6.3	-11.7	68.7	NM		-5.5	-5.5
19.4	12.7	14.2	28.2	41.2			14.6	15.0
(157) 4.0	(153) 4.1	(164) 4.2	(69) 5.8	(11) 12.5		EBIT/Interest	(538) 4.4	(657) 4.5
.6	1.4	1.3	1.9	3.9			1.7	1.7
		6.9	2.9	4.7		Net Profit + Depr., Dep.,	8.1	7.7
	(10) 3.8	(22) 1.6	(11) 3.4			Amort./Cur. Mat. L/T/D	(76) 2.6	(84) 3.0
		1.0	.5	.3			1.0	1.2
.1	.3	.4	.2	.0	.6		.4	.3
.9	2.8	1.8	.9	.2	5.0	Fixed/Worth	1.8	1.7
-51.0	19.2	31.6	3.8	2.0	NM		32.0	20.2
.7	.8	1.2	.9	1.2	.9		.9	1.0
3.1	3.4	3.7	2.2	2.0	7.2	Debt/Worth	3.2	3.2
-6.1	101.1	NM	6.4	5.6	NM		80.4	51.2
337.2	68.8	67.8	52.6	69.8	22.7	% Profit Before Taxes/Tangible	76.4	83.3
(196) 87.8	(213) 24.1	(200) 25.2	(88) 27.9	(16) 29.9	(11) 8.1	Net Worth	(753) 25.2	(892) 28.9
13.3	6.1	4.9	8.3	13.1	.5		7.5	6.6
70.4	16.9	12.6	15.9	25.5	9.9	% Profit Before Taxes/Total	18.7	19.8
15.9	6.2	4.4	6.6	12.4	.4	Assets	6.2	6.5
-.5	.6	.0	1.4	4.4	-.7		.9	.8
261.0	35.3	44.3	29.6	170.5	9.4		34.4	44.4
48.0	4.2	5.0	6.5	36.9	2.2	Sales/Net Fixed Assets	5.3	7.4
13.5	.3	.2	.5	.6	.2		.3	.3
14.5	3.4	2.4	2.5	3.4	1.3		4.0	3.9
5.8	1.0	.6	.7	1.9	.9	Sales/Total Assets	.8	.9
2.2	.2	.2	.2	.2	.2		.2	.2
.4	.9	.9	.7	.9	1.7		1.1	1.1
(153) .9	(205) 4.9	(218) 4.2	(75) 2.1	(14) 1.6	(11) 3.4	% Depr., Dep., Amort./Sales	(773) 4.4	(886) 3.9
2.2	13.6	16.4	11.2	6.5	26.0		15.9	15.7
4.3	1.9	1.8	.8				2.7	2.8
(107) 9.5	(61) 4.0	(53) 4.2	(16) 3.9			% Officers', Directors'	(249) 7.2	(312) 7.0
20.4	9.9	10.5	25.6			Owners' Comp/Sales	16.9	15.1
465378M	747473M	2240450M	3425237M	7666684M	2295301M	Net Sales ($)	10822623M	15572980M
55369M	301017M	1243086M	2039092M	1263731M	2137603M	Total Assets ($)	8423473M	9809390M

M = $ thousand   MM = $ million
See Pages 11 through 21 for Explanation of Ratios and Data

Comparative Historical Data | | Type of Statement | Current Data Sorted by Sales

			Type of Statement						
85	91	69	Unqualified	15	5	5	8	13	23
70	45	53	Reviewed	14	11	5	6	5	12
121	117	112	Compiled	36	42	11	10	11	2
446	408	372	Tax Returns	217	70	30	29	17	9
316	412	342	Other	95	90	28	49	34	46
4/1/04-3/31/05 ALL	4/1/05-3/31/06 ALL	4/1/06-3/31/07 ALL		82 (4/1-9/30/06)		866 (10/1/06-3/31/07)			
				0-1MM	1-3MM	3-5MM	5-10MM	10-25MM	25MM & OVER
1038	1073	948	**NUMBER OF STATEMENTS**	377	218	79	102	80	92
%	%	%	**ASSETS**	%	%	%	%	%	%
20.1	20.0	19.3	Cash & Equivalents	16.0	21.2	27.8	18.8	18.3	22.1
6.3	6.9	8.1	Trade Receivables (net)	3.6	9.0	9.8	11.9	12.5	14.8
6.4	6.4	5.5	Inventory	3.5	5.2	5.4	10.2	10.0	5.4
4.7	4.8	7.2	All Other Current	5.6	6.0	9.8	10.7	9.6	7.9
37.5	38.1	40.0	Total Current	28.7	41.4	52.7	51.6	50.4	50.2
43.6	43.1	41.4	Fixed Assets (net)	57.2	39.5	27.5	24.0	24.5	27.3
4.8	5.1	5.4	Intangibles (net)	3.7	5.0	8.3	4.4	7.7	10.3
14.1	13.6	13.1	All Other Non-Current	10.3	14.1	11.5	20.0	17.4	12.2
100.0	100.0	100.0	Total	100.0	100.0	100.0	100.0	100.0	100.0
			LIABILITIES						
12.0	12.6	13.1	Notes Payable-Short Term	10.1	15.7	10.5	20.4	15.0	12.4
3.1	3.2	3.8	Cur. Mat.-L.T.D.	5.2	3.2	2.1	2.3	3.8	2.4
4.3	4.0	5.2	Trade Payables	3.0	4.9	5.6	6.2	6.8	12.3
.1	.1	.1	Income Taxes Payable	.0	.2	.4	.2	.1	.1
16.4	16.0	17.1	All Other Current	18.8	15.0	14.0	19.3	16.4	15.6
35.8	35.9	39.3	Total Current	37.1	38.9	32.7	48.4	42.2	42.8
35.8	33.9	31.7	Long-Term Debt	44.8	25.1	20.6	22.9	18.4	24.3
.1	.2	.1	Deferred Taxes	.0	.0	.1	.2	.1	.3
4.7	4.8	7.6	All Other Non-Current	7.2	10.8	5.4	6.2	5.9	6.7
23.6	25.1	21.3	Net Worth	10.9	25.1	41.3	22.3	33.4	25.8
100.0	100.0	100.0	Total Liabilities & Net Worth	100.0	100.0	100.0	100.0	100.0	100.0
			INCOME DATA						
100.0	100.0	100.0	Net Sales	100.0	100.0	100.0	100.0	100.0	100.0
			Gross Profit						
76.1	75.6	79.0	Operating Expenses	66.9	81.6	88.0	89.8	90.1	93.0
23.9	24.4	21.0	Operating Profit	33.1	18.4	12.0	10.2	9.9	7.0
8.7	8.9	8.9	All Other Expenses (net)	17.8	5.0	2.5	2.2	1.9	.7
15.2	15.5	12.1	Profit Before Taxes	15.3	13.5	9.5	8.0	8.0	6.3
			RATIOS						
2.8	3.1	2.5		2.8	2.5	3.2	2.8	2.3	2.1
1.1	1.2	1.1	Current	.8	1.2	1.7	1.2	1.2	1.2
.4	.4	.4		.2	.5	.9	.5	.8	.8
1.9	2.0	1.8		1.8	2.0	2.1	1.6	1.7	1.7
.7 (1072)	.8 (947)	.7	Quick	(376) .5	.9	1.1	.5	.7	1.0
.1	.2	.2		.1	.2	.4	.1	.3	.5
0 UND	0 UND	0 UND		0 UND	0 UND	0 UND	0 UND	0 999.8	1 405.8
0 UND	0 UND	0 UND	Sales/Receivables	0 UND	0 UND	0 805.2	2 189.1	3 118.3	5 70.8
6 61.0	7 54.7	10 36.0		1 324.8	18 20.1	6 58.2	14 25.9	16 23.5	31 11.8
			Cost of Sales/Inventory						
			Cost of Sales/Payables						
7.1	6.5	8.0		6.1	8.3	8.6	7.6	9.9	15.4
129.7	65.9	144.5	Sales/Working Capital	-36.0	151.1	45.9	110.3	42.5	59.9
-9.0	-10.2	-11.1		-3.3	-16.0	-61.3	-26.6	-81.6	-94.3
18.8	26.7	16.7		8.9	12.9	19.4	20.4	27.4	27.8
(610) 5.6	(625) 5.3	(563) 4.3	EBIT/Interest	(156) 4.0	(135) 3.7	(50) 5.8	(79) 4.0	(65) 6.8	(78) 6.0
2.2	1.8	1.3		1.7	.6	2.2	-.1	1.2	1.6
6.7	6.3	4.6				4.5			17.4
(68) 2.7	(55) 2.4	(56) 1.8	Net Profit + Depr., Dep., Amort./Cur. Mat. L/T/D		(17) 1.6	1.6			(18) 3.8
1.1	.5	.6			.5	.5			1.5
.2	.2	.2		.7	.2	.1	.1	.2	.2
1.7	1.5	1.6	Fixed/Worth	3.5	1.3	.5	.8	.5	.8
14.0	14.1	21.5		-104.2	13.6	3.2	69.6	15.0	3.8
1.0	.8	.9		1.3	.7	.7	.8	1.0	1.0
3.4	2.8	3.1	Debt/Worth	4.7	2.4	1.8	4.9	2.2	2.2
40.8	27.0	297.1		-19.0	17.9	8.8	135.3	156.6	9.4
100.0	100.0	89.9		71.8	104.8	115.0	108.5	85.9	71.0
(823) 35.3	(850) 37.3	(724) 31.7	% Profit Before Taxes/Tangible Net Worth	(267) 19.8	(173) 35.7	(70) 52.8	(78) 40.0	(64) 37.1	(72) 33.5
10.5	10.4	6.5		2.8	7.3	19.4	5.8	9.3	18.7
24.7	32.5	23.3		13.9	37.9	39.5	25.9	31.4	24.5
8.1	8.2	6.9	% Profit Before Taxes/Total Assets	4.2	7.4	14.6	6.4	9.9	10.1
1.6	1.6	.3		-.4	1.1	3.2	-1.0	.6	3.8
72.3	58.5	71.3		32.6	80.9	180.1	112.4	103.7	51.8
9.3	10.2	14.7	Sales/Net Fixed Assets	.6	17.1	43.7	34.2	37.6	23.7
.3	.3	.4		.2	1.0	8.2	11.7	8.9	9.0
4.3	4.5	5.2		2.0	5.6	10.6	9.6	7.7	6.5
1.1	1.3	1.7	Sales/Total Assets	.3	2.0	3.5	2.8	3.7	3.7
.2	.2	.3		.2	.4	1.5	1.1	1.6	2.1
1.0	.7	.7		2.9	.8	.4	.4	.4	.6
(736) 3.9	(765) 2.9	(676) 2.2	% Depr., Dep., Amort./Sales	(260) 11.2	(145) 2.2	(57) .8	(74) .8	(65) .9	(75) 1.1
16.1	14.0	11.4		19.6	7.7	3.0	2.3	1.6	1.8
2.5	2.4	2.2		7.5	3.8	1.8	1.4	1.2	.6
(280) 6.1	(251) 5.9	(245) 5.7	% Officers', Directors' Owners' Comp/Sales	(74) 12.3	(60) 7.6	(26) 3.7	(37) 3.0	(23) 2.9	(25) 1.4
15.6	12.7	14.0		23.6	12.9	6.1	5.2	4.4	19.0
15311908M	17951321M	16840523M	Net Sales ($)	146325M	395566M	308838M	729353M	1281717M	13978724M
8287913M	10533386M	7039898M	Total Assets ($)	523025M	686508M	293974M	773493M	1197696M	3565202M

© RMA 2007

M = $ thousand   MM = $ million
See Pages 11 through 21 for Explanation of Ratios and Data

Current Data Sorted by Assets   Comparative Historical Data

0-500M	500M-2MM	2-10MM	10-50MM	50-100MM	100-250MM	Type of Statement	4/1/02-3/31/03 ALL	4/1/03-3/31/04 ALL
1	4	8	7	1	2	Unqualified	5	8
1	1	5	1			Reviewed	3	2
5	6	2	2			Compiled	7	7
21	20	19	3	1		Tax Returns	16	39
17	19	19	8		1	Other	10	35
	26 (4/1-9/30/06)		148 (10/1/06-3/31/07)					
45	50	53	21	2	3	**NUMBER OF STATEMENTS**	41	91
%	%	%	%	%	%	**ASSETS**	%	%
36.6	17.8	10.2	4.6			Cash & Equivalents	18.7	14.3
9.2	6.3	5.3	2.9			Trade Receivables (net)	6.1	4.6
1.2	7.5	3.0	15.5			Inventory	10.1	5.6
7.1	6.0	4.5	5.3			All Other Current	11.2	5.1
54.0	37.5	23.0	28.3			Total Current	46.1	29.6
25.8	41.5	57.8	48.0			Fixed Assets (net)	43.4	53.5
3.4	3.3	2.8	.7			Intangibles (net)	4.4	4.4
16.8	17.6	16.4	23.0			All Other Non-Current	6.1	12.5
100.0	100.0	100.0	100.0			Total	100.0	100.0
						LIABILITIES		
7.7	11.7	10.7	12.5			Notes Payable-Short Term	12.1	17.0
1.9	7.0	4.9	1.5			Cur. Mat.-L.T.D.	4.1	3.3
6.3	5.2	2.8	1.6			Trade Payables	2.6	4.1
.0	.0	.1	.0			Income Taxes Payable	.0	.1
21.1	11.7	8.4	7.2			All Other Current	13.4	10.0
37.0	35.6	26.9	22.8			Total Current	32.2	34.4
17.1	34.3	42.6	41.5			Long-Term Debt	38.5	46.2
.0	.0	.0	.0			Deferred Taxes	.0	.0
7.9	3.1	2.8	3.4			All Other Non-Current	2.0	2.8
38.0	27.1	27.7	32.3			Net Worth	27.3	16.6
100.0	100.0	100.0	100.0			Total Liabilities & Net Worth	100.0	100.0
						INCOME DATA		
100.0	100.0	100.0	100.0			Net Sales	100.0	100.0
						Gross Profit		
85.8	80.4	81.1	76.3			Operating Expenses	80.3	74.8
14.2	19.6	18.9	23.7			Operating Profit	19.7	25.2
1.6	9.4	13.4	12.1			All Other Expenses (net)	8.3	14.4
12.5	10.3	5.5	11.5			Profit Before Taxes	11.5	10.8
						RATIOS		
5.1	3.9	1.8	2.9			Current	4.2	2.5
2.1	1.1	.9	1.3				1.8	1.1
.6	.2	.2	.5				.7	.3
4.1	3.1	1.1	1.5			Quick	2.9	1.6
1.4	.5	.7	.3				.6	.5
.4	.1	.1	.1				.1	.1
0 UND	0 UND	0 UND	0 UND			Sales/Receivables	0 UND	0 UND
0 UND	0 UND	2 230.6	6 57.2				0 UND	0 UND
14 26.7	7 55.0	22 16.9	21 17.5				15 23.7	10 38.2
						Cost of Sales/Inventory		
						Cost of Sales/Payables		
10.4	3.0	8.7	3.4			Sales/Working Capital	3.1	7.6
25.4	93.9	-31.5	19.5				17.4	65.1
-33.7	-3.8	-4.7	-4.8				-27.8	-6.0
7.8	15.7	10.3	21.4			EBIT/Interest	22.3	59.1
(21) 2.2	(25) 4.5	(26) 3.8	(11) 2.9				(21) 3.7	(46) 3.5
-2.6	-.2	.3	1.1				1.5	1.8
						Net Profit + Depr., Dep., Amort./Cur. Mat. L/T/D		
.0	.2	.9	.3			Fixed/Worth	.1	.5
.5	1.7	2.7	2.6				1.3	3.7
3.2	NM	30.1	11.6				8.2	-113.8
.2	.6	.8	.6			Debt/Worth	.6	1.0
.5	3.3	3.3	3.8				3.2	6.0
16.3	-120.7	877.5	17.5				193.9	-127.0
551.3	90.0	27.5	31.8			% Profit Before Taxes/Tangible Net Worth	89.5	108.5
(37) 49.1	(37) 26.2	(41) 8.9	(18) 9.7				(32) 18.9	(68) 31.7
.4	7.5	-3.3	-8.6				4.4	10.1
113.8	17.3	9.0	6.6			% Profit Before Taxes/Total Assets	46.2	19.4
13.5	6.8	2.3	1.6				7.0	4.4
-5.0	-1.9	-1.6	-.5				.0	.3
UND	98.4	10.3	15.7			Sales/Net Fixed Assets	45.3	22.2
127.0	4.6	.5	1.6				18.3	1.3
7.5	.2	.2	.2				.2	.2
10.2	1.9	1.1	.6			Sales/Total Assets	4.0	2.7
3.4	.6	.3	.5				.8	.5
.8	.2	.1	.1				.2	.2
.9	1.3	1.6	1.6			% Depr., Dep., Amort./Sales	1.0	2.5
(20) 2.6	(36) 11.2	(40) 10.3	(17) 6.4				(29) 4.8	(64) 12.7
6.8	20.0	21.3	17.3				20.4	19.7
3.3						% Officers', Directors' Owners' Comp/Sales	2.9	7.1
(11) 11.1							(12) 9.4	(15) 8.6
13.6							14.9	17.8
38920M	85034M	208621M	283055M	13100M	208904M	Net Sales ($)	127604M	351077M
9277M	56775M	215559M	459812M	106114M	469274M	Total Assets ($)	212617M	617598M

© RMA 2007

M = $ thousand   MM = $ million
See Pages 11 through 21 for Explanation of Ratios and Data

Comparative Historical Data | Current Data Sorted by Sales

			Type of Statement						
12	25	23	Unqualified	7	4	2	3	4	3
2	11	8	Reviewed	3	1		2	2	
7	20	15	Compiled	5	5	2	2	2	1
38	66	64	Tax Returns	46	6	2	7	3	
29	59	64	Other	31	17	5	7	7	2
4/1/04-3/31/05	4/1/05-3/31/06	4/1/06-3/31/07		26 (4/1-9/30/06)			148 (10/1/06-3/31/07)		
ALL	ALL	ALL		0-1MM	1-3MM	3-5MM	5-10MM	10-25MM	25MM & OVER
88	181	174	**NUMBER OF STATEMENTS**	92	33	11	16	16	6
%	%	%	**ASSETS**	%	%	%	%	%	%
12.6	15.2	18.4	Cash & Equivalents	18.6	19.1	26.3	21.2	10.0	
5.9	6.7	6.4	Trade Receivables (net)	5.1	6.8	4.5	9.5	10.4	
5.1	3.1	5.2	Inventory	2.8	5.1	8.1	8.3	9.9	
4.3	6.6	5.7	All Other Current	5.1	5.5	10.9	3.4	5.9	
27.8	31.6	35.8	Total Current	31.7	36.5	49.8	42.5	36.1	
53.7	50.2	43.5	Fixed Assets (net)	50.2	40.2	30.4	34.5	37.0	
3.6	4.4	3.2	Intangibles (net)	3.6	.5	7.6	.1	3.2	
14.9	13.8	17.5	All Other Non-Current	14.5	22.8	12.2	22.9	23.6	
100.0	100.0	100.0	Total	100.0	100.0	100.0	100.0	100.0	
			LIABILITIES						
10.3	10.7	10.1	Notes Payable-Short Term	8.6	12.7	7.5	14.3	10.3	
3.5	3.3	4.2	Cur. Mat.-L.T.D.	4.9	5.5	1.9	1.7	2.6	
3.3	5.1	4.2	Trade Payables	3.5	4.2	5.6	7.1	4.8	
.2	1.4	.0	Income Taxes Payable	.0	.0	.0	.0	.2	
8.4	11.8	12.3	All Other Current	10.0	13.8	13.8	10.0	22.2	
25.6	32.2	30.9	Total Current	27.0	36.2	28.8	33.1	40.1	
48.3	53.1	33.9	Long-Term Debt	38.5	31.1	32.8	19.6	30.4	
.1	.1	.0	Deferred Taxes	.0	.0	.0	.0	.0	
4.2	5.3	4.3	All Other Non-Current	5.8	2.5	.0	1.9	4.1	
21.8	9.2	30.9	Net Worth	28.6	30.2	38.3	45.3	25.3	
100.0	100.0	100.0	Total Liabilities & Net Worth	100.0	100.0	100.0	100.0	100.0	
			INCOME DATA						
100.0	100.0	100.0	Net Sales	100.0	100.0	100.0	100.0	100.0	
			Gross Profit						
79.7	77.5	81.8	Operating Expenses	76.6	87.1	90.0	82.4	90.0	
20.3	22.5	18.2	Operating Profit	23.4	12.9	10.0	17.6	10.0	
10.8	12.5	8.8	All Other Expenses (net)	12.8	8.8	.5	1.7	2.1	
9.5	10.0	9.4	Profit Before Taxes	10.6	4.2	9.5	15.9	7.9	
			RATIOS						
1.7	3.0	3.4		3.6	4.5	4.6	2.9	2.3	
.7	1.0	1.1	Current	1.0	.8	1.9	1.2	1.4	
.4	.3	.4		.2	.3	.9	.5	.7	
1.4	2.2	2.7		3.2	2.4	4.6	2.9	1.2	
(87) .5	.5	.7	Quick	.8	.5	1.3	.8	.7	
.2	.1	.1		.1	.1	.3	.3	.2	
0 UND	0 UND	0 UND		0 UND	0 UND	0 UND	0 UND	0 UND	
1 443.6	0 UND	0 UND	Sales/Receivables	0 UND	0 999.8	3 137.0	1 615.2	12 30.9	
15 24.2	17 21.5	17 21.6		6 60.0	16 23.0	19 19.6	24 15.5	30 12.1	
			Cost of Sales/Inventory						
			Cost of Sales/Payables						
9.1	5.0	5.1		3.8	10.3	3.5	4.3	6.7	
-31.7	-102.8	66.4	Sales/Working Capital	NM	-59.4	35.7	40.9	29.4	
-5.1	-4.7	-6.1		-3.6	-2.8	-52.0	-31.0	-11.1	
6.7	16.0	9.5		6.0	9.8		27.1	18.1	
(45) 2.7	(95) 5.0	(85) 3.4	EBIT/Interest	(34) 3.1	(18) 1.1		(10) 7.2	(13) 4.3	
.5	1.4	.2		-.2	-4.6		1.4	1.0	
			Net Profit + Depr., Dep., Amort./Cur. Mat. L/T/D						
.6	.3	.2		.2	.3	.0	.2	.3	
2.5	3.4	1.6	Fixed/Worth	2.3	1.3	.2	.8	2.8	
527.5	-16.9	25.1		51.9	58.9	2.6	1.8	43.3	
1.2	1.1	.4		.4	.5	.2	.5	.9	
4.2	5.2	2.6	Debt/Worth	3.3	2.2	3.3	.9	5.2	
UND	-12.1	176.1		709.7	707.9	-6.9	5.8	55.9	
65.1	70.2	67.1		57.0	49.4		137.4	62.1	
(68) 22.1	(120) 25.7	(136) 14.0	% Profit Before Taxes/Tangible Net Worth	(71) 10.3	(26) 8.4		(14) 19.7	(13) 20.1	
-4.9	3.2	.0		-1.3	-16.2		10.6	-5.6	
12.3	18.7	15.1		12.6	10.6	70.2	51.4	20.5	
3.7	3.6	3.9	% Profit Before Taxes/Total Assets	3.2	1.6	34.7	9.6	7.5	
-.9	-.3	-1.4		-1.6	-9.3	.0	1.5	-.7	
19.6	34.3	78.1		113.5	78.2	UND	86.6	39.6	
.9	2.3	4.7	Sales/Net Fixed Assets	.6	9.8	18.3	7.8	7.8	
.2	.2	.3		.2	.5	5.2	1.3	1.0	
1.5	2.3	2.4		1.2	3.7	4.9	4.5	4.9	
.5	.7	.6	Sales/Total Assets	.3	.9	2.9	1.3	.9	
.2	.2	.2		.1	.3	1.1	.5	.6	
3.0	1.4	1.4		3.2	.9		1.8	.4	
(64) 10.1	(121) 8.1	(118) 6.8	% Depr., Dep., Amort./Sales	(62) 14.9	(20) 4.2		(11) 3.0	(15) 1.5	
21.5	18.4	18.7		26.7	12.0		10.3	6.0	
3.6	5.0	2.8	% Officers', Directors' Owners' Comp/Sales	4.4					
(20) 6.5	(40) 12.2	(31) 5.5		(12) 8.8					
16.8	19.8	11.8		16.3					
883259M	1653078M	837634M	Net Sales ($)	36447M	56066M	43557M	112493M	233254M	355817M
712376M	1300951M	1316811M	Total Assets ($)	132972M	144790M	35538M	206417M	444509M	352585M

M = $ thousand   MM = $ million
See Pages 11 through 21 for Explanation of Ratios and Data

Current Data Sorted by Assets

Comparative Historical Data

						Type of Statement		
						Unqualified		
1	2	2	6	2	2	Reviewed	2	1
4	2	10	3	1	1	Compiled	5	11
16	11	13	2			Tax Returns	8	25
11	36	12	1			Other	13	18
	19	24	5	2			4/1/02-	4/1/03-
	14 (4/1-9/30/06)		174 (10/1/06-3/31/07)				3/31/03	3/31/04
0-500M	500M-2MM	2-10MM	10-50MM	50-100MM	100-250MM		ALL	ALL
32	70	61	17	5	3	NUMBER OF STATEMENTS	28	59
%	%	%	%	%	%	ASSETS	%	%
14.4	6.1	6.9	7.9			Cash & Equivalents	12.2	10.0
10.2	4.0	5.4	3.0			Trade Receivables (net)	6.0	1.3
1.9	.9	4.2	8.2			Inventory	.1	2.9
2.2	4.1	4.2	3.7			All Other Current	11.0	1.4
28.7	15.0	20.6	22.8			Total Current	29.3	15.7
57.3	76.3	63.6	51.6			Fixed Assets (net)	57.6	67.3
7.6	.2	4.5	3.3			Intangibles (net)	3.0	4.3
6.4	8.4	11.2	22.3			All Other Non-Current	10.0	12.7
100.0	100.0	100.0	100.0			Total	100.0	100.0
						LIABILITIES		
7.9	3.4	7.9	2.5			Notes Payable-Short Term	12.6	10.0
3.3	4.7	3.7	1.5			Cur. Mat.-L.T.D.	11.8	7.3
5.2	1.7	4.2	1.7			Trade Payables	2.9	.9
.0	.0	.2	.0			Income Taxes Payable	.0	.0
8.8	7.3	4.6	10.5			All Other Current	15.0	6.3
25.3	17.1	20.5	16.1			Total Current	42.4	24.5
43.1	57.5	54.8	46.2			Long-Term Debt	59.6	49.3
.0	.0	.1	.0			Deferred Taxes	.0	.0
2.8	1.5	6.0	1.8			All Other Non-Current	21.2	8.9
28.8	23.9	18.5	35.8			Net Worth	-23.2	17.2
100.0	100.0	100.0	100.0			Total Liabilities & Net Worth	100.0	100.0
						INCOME DATA		
100.0	100.0	100.0	100.0			Net Sales	100.0	100.0
						Gross Profit		
68.5	51.6	59.4	65.2			Operating Expenses	66.9	61.5
31.5	48.4	40.6	34.8			Operating Profit	33.1	38.5
14.4	26.9	21.3	13.4			All Other Expenses (net)	18.2	21.5
17.1	21.6	19.3	21.4			Profit Before Taxes	14.9	17.0
						RATIOS		
3.5	3.0	1.9	5.8				1.9	1.6
1.2	.6	.9	.8			Current	.5	.6
.3	.2	.2	.2				.2	.1
2.5	2.7	1.6	.9				1.2	1.3
1.1	.4	.6	.6			Quick	(27) .4	.4
.2	.1	.1	.1				.1	.1
0 UND	0 UND	0 UND	0 UND				0 UND	0 UND
0 UND	0 UND	0 UND	1 714.6			Sales/Receivables	0 UND	0 UND
5 70.2	2 147.2	11 32.8	9 38.5				17 21.4	2 235.2
						Cost of Sales/Inventory		
						Cost of Sales/Payables		
5.9	9.8	4.7	1.6				6.2	9.1
65.1	-9.4	-27.5	-13.1			Sales/Working Capital	-15.3	-8.1
-6.5	-3.3	-3.8	-2.9				-2.8	-1.5
67.5	6.6	8.2					7.2	6.2
(11) 5.3	(24) 4.1	(25) 3.2				EBIT/Interest	(13) 2.5	(25) 4.5
3.5	2.7	1.2					-1.4	1.4
						Net Profit + Depr., Dep., Amort./Cur. Mat. L/T/D		
.4	1.7	1.2	.1				1.7	1.5
2.0	4.3	5.1	1.3			Fixed/Worth	7.1	3.1
16.1	22.6	-515.8	NM				-6.9	14.9
.7	1.2	1.5	.4				3.1	1.2
3.9	3.9	5.0	5.3			Debt/Worth	17.0	3.5
27.1	33.7	-526.2	NM				-10.6	20.3
129.0	39.3	46.2	10.4			% Profit Before Taxes/Tangible Net Worth	124.8	35.6
(27) 43.5	(59) 21.3	(45) 15.1	(13) 3.0				(17) 21.6	(47) 18.1
5.2	2.4	.3	.7				.3	2.9
31.1	12.1	8.9	3.2			% Profit Before Taxes/Total Assets	18.4	8.6
5.8	3.0	3.9	1.0				5.5	3.9
.4	.1	.0	.7				-.3	.7
15.3	.5	7.3	14.6				16.7	2.1
1.9	.2	.2	1.0			Sales/Net Fixed Assets	.7	.3
.2	.1	.1	.2				.2	.1
2.8	.3	.6	.5				2.8	.5
.8	.2	.2	.2			Sales/Total Assets	.4	.2
.2	.1	.1	.1				.2	.1
1.7	5.4	3.2	2.5				3.2	7.5
(24) 8.8	(63) 14.4	(51) 11.7	(13) 14.2			% Depr., Dep., Amort./Sales	(20) 12.8	(53) 16.9
20.2	20.8	19.4	34.3				18.6	23.0
						% Officers', Directors' Owners' Comp/Sales		3.5
								(13) 8.3
								18.3
14387M	50566M	186727M	190226M	303786M	276450M	Net Sales ($)	355842M	275561M
9757M	80592M	260884M	416249M	355380M	473301M	Total Assets ($)	201341M	532877M

M = $ thousand   MM = $ million
See Pages 11 through 21 for Explanation of Ratios and Data

Comparative Historical Data				Current Data Sorted by Sales					
			Type of Statement						
3	2	14	Unqualified	1	5	1	2	2	3
4	7	18	Reviewed	7	2	1	2	2	4
15	12	30	Compiled	21	5	1	2	2	
34	40	65	Tax Returns	59	4	1	1	1	
38	42	61	Other	36	12	3	5	4	1
4/1/04- 3/31/05 ALL	4/1/05- 3/31/06 ALL	4/1/06- 3/31/07 ALL		14 (4/1-9/30/06)			174 (10/1/06-3/31/07)		
				0-1MM	1-3MM	3-5MM	5-10MM	10-25MM	25MM & OVER
94	103	188	**NUMBER OF STATEMENTS**	124	28	7	10	11	8
%	%	%	**ASSETS**	%	%	%	%	%	%
8.0	7.8	8.3	Cash & Equivalents	6.4	11.1		10.3	20.0	
2.9	5.9	5.8	Trade Receivables (net)	1.6	12.3		21.0	16.6	
5.0	3.1	3.4	Inventory	2.4	.4		6.0	14.0	
3.4	3.6	3.7	All Other Current	1.0	6.7		13.6	11.1	
19.3	20.4	21.2	Total Current	11.4	30.5		50.8	61.7	
69.7	69.1	65.4	Fixed Assets (net)	78.7	47.2		30.3	24.3	
2.7	2.2	3.3	Intangibles (net)	1.5	9.4		8.2	.7	
8.3	8.3	10.1	All Other Non-Current	8.4	12.9		10.7	13.3	
100.0	100.0	100.0	Total	100.0	100.0		100.0	100.0	
			LIABILITIES						
7.7	7.1	5.5	Notes Payable-Short Term	5.3	3.0		8.2	2.7	
3.5	4.3	3.7	Cur. Mat.-L.T.D.	3.2	2.6		11.4	6.8	
4.7	2.7	3.5	Trade Payables	.9	4.9		9.8	17.4	
.0	.1	.1	Income Taxes Payable	.0	.0		.4	.1	
7.7	7.0	7.2	All Other Current	3.4	14.9		18.4	13.9	
23.7	21.2	19.9	Total Current	12.9	25.4		48.2	40.8	
63.5	63.8	52.4	Long-Term Debt	60.6	41.4		46.7	16.3	
.0	.1	.0	Deferred Taxes	.0	.2		.0	.0	
2.1	5.9	3.3	All Other Non-Current	3.2	4.0		5.3	.3	
10.6	9.0	24.3	Net Worth	23.3	29.1		-.2	42.6	
100.0	100.0	100.0	Total Liabilties & Net Worth	100.0	100.0		100.0	100.0	
			INCOME DATA						
100.0	100.0	100.0	Net Sales	100.0	100.0		100.0	100.0	
			Gross Profit						
66.9	62.8	59.6	Operating Expenses	48.2	76.2		88.6	90.9	
33.1	37.2	40.4	Operating Profit	51.8	23.8		11.4	9.1	
19.0	22.4	20.8	All Other Expenses (net)	28.3	8.9		4.1	2.5	
14.1	14.8	19.6	Profit Before Taxes	23.5	14.9		7.3	6.5	
			RATIOS						
1.9	2.9	2.9		3.1	3.8		2.3	2.0	
.6	.6	.9	Current	.7	.9		1.1	1.4	
.2	.2	.2		.1	.6		.6	1.0	
1.3	1.6	1.9		2.0	2.6		1.5	1.6	
.4	.5	.6	Quick	.5	.8		.6	1.1	
.1	.1	.1		.1	.2		.4	.3	
0 UND	0 UND	0 UND		0 UND	0 UND		3 134.7	4 84.7	
0 UND	0 UND	0 UND	Sales/Receivables	0 UND	2 180.2		24 15.4	23 15.6	
6 58.4	12 29.8	9 41.5		0 UND	18 19.9		67 5.5	38 9.7	
			Cost of Sales/Inventory						
			Cost of Sales/Payables						
12.1	4.2	5.1		5.7	4.3		5.9	4.8	
-12.4	-11.3	-40.4	Sales/Working Capital	-13.0	-547.9		NM	25.6	
-3.0	-3.5	-3.5		-2.7	-6.7		-23.0	182.9	
5.0	7.2	9.2		7.5	34.1			96.3	
(36) 2.5	(42) 3.7	(74) 4.0	EBIT/Interest	(33) 4.5	(13) 3.3			(10) 2.7	
1.2	1.5	1.9		3.1	1.8			.7	
		5.6	Net Profit + Depr., Dep.,						
	(10) 1.5	Amort./Cur. Mat. L/T/D							
		.0							
1.8	1.2	1.0		1.6	.3		.4	.1	
5.5	3.9	3.9	Fixed/Worth	5.0	3.7		NM	.8	
-25.6	40.2	30.3		38.9	21.9		-.3	1.2	
1.8	1.3	1.2		1.2	.4		1.7	.4	
6.3	3.7	4.7	Debt/Worth	4.8	4.9		NM	1.9	
-27.4	77.7	45.2		53.3	34.4		-2.8	4.8	
43.9	40.1	45.2	% Profit Before Taxes/Tangible	40.8	96.0			71.3	
(65) 22.2	(79) 16.9	(151) 17.8	Net Worth	(101) 20.0	(23) 15.1			8.1	
6.9	.0	1.7		1.4	3.0			-9.2	
8.6	11.6	10.5	% Profit Before Taxes/Total	9.1	16.5		29.3	21.6	
3.3	3.9	3.5	Assets	2.9	5.2		11.5	4.2	
.3	-.2	.3		.1	1.1		-.3	-1.1	
2.2	5.5	6.2		.4	19.1		77.1	123.9	
.3	.2	.3	Sales/Net Fixed Assets	.2	6.3		19.1	21.9	
.2	.1	.1		.1	.3		3.5	3.3	
.7	.8	.8		.3	2.6		5.1	4.5	
.2	.2	.2	Sales/Total Assets	.1	.6		2.4	3.7	
.1	.1	.1		.1	.2		.8	.4	
6.0	5.5	2.5		8.8	1.2			.2	
(78) 14.9	(80) 14.3	(159) 11.9	% Depr., Dep., Amort./Sales	(108) 16.4	(20) 4.8			2.4	
23.3	22.7	20.3		20.9	14.0			5.7	
2.1		3.0		3.0					
(16) 8.4	(18) 9.7	% Officers', Directors'	(10) 8.3						
19.9		17.0	Owners' Comp/Sales	14.8					
298131M	780246M	1022142M	Net Sales ($)	38506M	46999M	24049M	70125M	179024M	663439M
737610M	797541M	1596163M	Total Assets ($)	284184M	164719M	65482M	79883M	246631M	755264M

M = $ thousand   MM = $ million
See Pages 11 through 21 for Explanation of Ratios and Data

Current Data Sorted by Assets | Comparative Historical Data

Type of Statement	0-500M	500M-2MM	2-10MM	10-50MM	50-100MM	100-250MM		4/1/02-3/31/03 ALL	4/1/03-3/31/04 ALL
Unqualified	5	8	26	28	11	13		7	20
Reviewed	3	2	10	9	5	3		5	14
Compiled	10	31	32	9	1			9	21
Tax Returns	107	203	196	36	3	2		41	142
Other	48	82	134	79	14	12		22	74
	81 (4/1-9/30/06)		1,041 (10/1/06-3/31/07)						
NUMBER OF STATEMENTS	173	326	398	161	34	30		84	271

ASSETS	%	%	%	%	%	%		%	%
Cash & Equivalents	28.2	9.1	6.9	7.1	5.7	10.4		11.3	13.7
Trade Receivables (net)	8.3	4.6	4.1	6.0	5.4	3.8		7.8	7.9
Inventory	5.2	17.9	24.9	26.4	32.6	14.4		14.6	16.9
All Other Current	4.4	5.7	4.1	7.4	4.1	5.7		8.7	4.3
Total Current	46.1	37.3	39.9	46.9	47.8	34.3		42.4	42.9
Fixed Assets (net)	39.6	47.0	43.1	31.8	26.9	26.8		42.8	41.9
Intangibles (net)	2.8	2.6	1.8	2.4	4.5	.9		1.5	1.4
All Other Non-Current	11.6	13.1	15.3	18.9	20.8	38.1		13.4	13.9
Total	100.0	100.0	100.0	100.0	100.0	100.0		100.0	100.0

LIABILITIES									
Notes Payable-Short Term	14.7	15.0	15.9	19.8	26.7	13.8		19.9	16.4
Cur. Mat.-L.T.D.	2.7	3.9	3.2	1.5	1.9	1.0		3.8	5.2
Trade Payables	7.5	3.5	1.9	2.9	2.4	3.3		3.0	3.1
Income Taxes Payable	.1	.0	.1	.0	.1	.1		.1	.1
All Other Current	19.8	11.3	8.0	8.7	14.7	7.5		7.5	9.3
Total Current	44.8	33.8	29.1	32.9	45.8	25.7		34.2	34.1
Long-Term Debt	33.7	36.7	39.1	37.0	27.0	26.5		35.1	34.2
Deferred Taxes	.0	.0	.0	.4	.4	.7		.1	.1
All Other Non-Current	5.3	6.8	3.5	3.2	2.2	4.6		5.3	5.2
Net Worth	16.2	22.7	28.3	26.5	24.7	42.6		25.3	26.4
Total Liabilities & Net Worth	100.0	100.0	100.0	100.0	100.0	100.0		100.0	100.0

INCOME DATA									
Net Sales	100.0	100.0	100.0	100.0	100.0	100.0		100.0	100.0
Gross Profit									
Operating Expenses	78.2	69.9	72.1	76.5	75.8	71.4		75.1	73.5
Operating Profit	21.8	30.1	27.9	23.5	24.2	28.6		24.9	26.5
All Other Expenses (net)	8.8	15.2	12.8	10.0	6.9	6.5		11.5	10.3
Profit Before Taxes	13.0	14.9	15.1	13.5	17.3	22.1		13.4	16.2

RATIOS									
Current	3.2	3.1	3.5	2.7	1.6	2.6		3.6	3.2
	1.1	1.0	1.2	1.4	1.1	1.3		1.3	1.1
	.3	.2	.5	.8	.4	1.0		.5	.4
Quick	2.2	1.4	1.4	1.5	.7	1.4		1.6	1.5
	.8	.2	(396) .3	.3	.1	.3		.6	.5
	.2	.0	.0	.0	.0	.1		.1	.1
Sales/Receivables	0 UND	0 UND	0 UND	0 UND	0 UND	0 UND		0 UND	0 UND
	0 UND	0 UND	0 UND	0 953.4	1 698.0	5 69.4		0 UND	0 UND
	3 145.0	2 160.6	9 42.2	23 15.9	8 43.5	21 17.2		18 20.6	6 58.9
Cost of Sales/Inventory									
Cost of Sales/Payables									
Sales/Working Capital	9.4	3.7	1.8	1.5	3.1	2.6		2.7	4.0
	201.1	230.2	16.3	9.1	19.3	6.5		21.0	33.1
	-7.4	-3.5	-5.0	-18.3	-5.5	NM		-10.0	-4.1
EBIT/Interest	10.0	10.9	8.6	19.7	38.6	44.4		15.0	12.4
	(78) 3.8	(156) 4.0	(198) 3.5	(97) 3.6	(18) 4.1	(22) 3.5		(43) 3.3	(148) 4.9
	.6	1.2	1.3	2.0	1.8	1.5		1.1	1.6
Net Profit + Depr., Dep., Amort./Cur. Mat. L/T/D									6.8
								(10)	2.4
									.2
Fixed/Worth	.0	.0	.0	.0	.0	.0		.1	.0
	1.2	1.7	1.1	.5	.8	.3		1.6	1.1
	23.2	14.8	5.0	3.7	2.3	1.8		4.7	5.4
Debt/Worth	.5	1.2	1.0	1.4	1.3	.5		1.5	1.1
	2.7	4.5	3.3	4.7	4.4	1.9		3.7	3.2
	-142.1	47.5	19.8	19.8	14.6	4.9		18.2	16.2
% Profit Before Taxes/Tangible Net Worth	242.4	74.0	61.8	49.5	50.8	40.0		72.4	86.9
	(128) 49.1	(255) 23.9	(335) 19.5	(142) 19.9	(31) 21.3	(29) 19.2		(71) 17.1	(233) 28.5
	7.1	4.2	4.1	2.3	9.6	4.9		1.1	6.8
% Profit Before Taxes/Total Assets	57.4	14.4	11.5	8.5	12.0	15.0		15.3	18.5
	9.8	4.3	3.6	3.2	4.3	4.7		3.4	5.2
	-.8	.1	.3	.4	1.7	1.3		.2	.8
Sales/Net Fixed Assets	UND	212.9	170.2	558.2	521.4	41.4		36.8	246.4
	23.3	2.7	2.5	15.1	12.9	5.2		6.0	6.6
	.8	.2	.2	.4	1.4	.5		.3	.2
Sales/Total Assets	6.8	1.4	.9	.8	1.2	.7		1.7	2.0
	2.4	.5	.3	.4	.5	.4		.5	.5
	.5	.1	.1	.1	.2	.2		.2	.2
% Depr., Dep., Amort./Sales	1.0	1.3	1.4	.2	.1	.9		1.2	.9
	(86) 4.7	(190) 9.9	(229) 7.3	(89) 1.3	(21) 1.9	(20) 2.9		(57) 4.1	(169) 6.0
	18.3	17.3	18.0	10.3	9.8	9.7		13.0	17.8
% Officers', Directors' Owners' Comp/Sales	5.1	2.5	1.2	1.1				3.7	3.2
	(41) 14.0	(62) 5.9	(53) 3.8	(24) 2.8				(20) 5.7	(50) 5.7
	23.9	15.2	10.2	5.2				19.5	17.9
Net Sales ($)	141342M	429881M	1642426M	2359201M	2953952M	2231662M		1189726M	3680975M
Total Assets ($)	42582M	370685M	1854543M	3524859M	2326394M	4088684M		907569M	2325955M

M = $ thousand   MM = $ million
See Pages 11 through 21 for Explanation of Ratios and Data

Comparative Historical Data

Current Data Sorted by Sales

			Type of Statement						
27	55	91	Unqualified	15	23	4	12	11	26
15	25	32	Reviewed	4	6	6	6	3	7
41	52	83	Compiled	38	16	8	7	13	1
228	325	547	Tax Returns	323	116	33	41	23	11
110	227	369	Other	137	100	28	38	36	30
4/1/04-3/31/05 ALL	4/1/05-3/31/06 ALL	4/1/06-3/31/07 ALL		81 (4/1-9/30/06)			1,041 (10/1/06-3/31/07)		
				0-1MM	1-3MM	3-5MM	5-10MM	10-25MM	25MM & OVER
421	684	1122	NUMBER OF STATEMENTS	517	261	79	104	86	75
%	%	%	ASSETS	%	%	%	%	%	%
12.5	12.0	10.9	Cash & Equivalents	10.2	12.5	11.1	10.4	8.9	12.6
5.6	6.5	5.2	Trade Receivables (net)	3.1	7.6	5.9	6.9	6.5	7.4
14.7	16.3	20.0	Inventory	10.6	24.4	32.6	31.9	29.2	28.5
5.6	4.1	5.1	All Other Current	3.6	5.6	6.7	7.2	8.1	6.4
38.4	38.9	41.2	Total Current	27.4	50.1	56.3	56.4	52.8	54.9
45.0	43.2	41.1	Fixed Assets (net)	57.2	30.7	22.3	25.4	28.3	22.7
1.5	2.5	2.3	Intangibles (net)	2.3	1.9	3.1	3.0	1.6	3.1
15.0	15.4	15.4	All Other Non-Current	13.1	17.3	18.3	15.2	17.3	19.3
100.0	100.0	100.0	Total	100.0	100.0	100.0	100.0	100.0	100.0
			LIABILITIES						
14.1	16.9	16.3	Notes Payable-Short Term	13.0	18.9	18.9	18.9	19.9	19.7
4.9	3.2	3.0	Cur. Mat.-L.T.D.	3.4	2.5	4.7	3.9	.6	1.9
4.6	4.0	3.4	Trade Payables	2.1	3.7	5.8	5.4	4.2	5.6
.1	.1	.1	Income Taxes Payable	.0	.0	.4	.1	.1	.1
11.4	10.0	11.0	All Other Current	9.5	12.0	12.2	7.7	17.1	15.1
35.1	34.2	33.9	Total Current	28.0	37.1	41.9	35.9	41.8	42.3
37.7	36.5	36.6	Long-Term Debt	45.8	31.0	20.3	35.8	22.6	26.8
.1	.1	.1	Deferred Taxes	.0	.0	.0	.0	.7	.5
4.9	5.2	4.7	All Other Non-Current	5.3	4.1	6.7	3.8	3.2	3.1
22.2	23.9	24.8	Net Worth	20.9	27.7	31.1	24.4	31.7	27.3
100.0	100.0	100.0	Total Liabilties & Net Worth	100.0	100.0	100.0	100.0	100.0	100.0
			INCOME DATA						
100.0	100.0	100.0	Net Sales	100.0	100.0	100.0	100.0	100.0	100.0
			Gross Profit						
72.9	74.0	73.1	Operating Expenses	63.6	79.8	81.6	80.1	83.5	85.1
27.1	26.0	26.9	Operating Profit	36.4	20.2	18.4	19.9	16.5	14.9
9.8	10.9	12.1	All Other Expenses (net)	20.7	7.4	2.2	4.1	2.8	1.9
17.4	15.1	14.7	Profit Before Taxes	15.7	12.8	16.2	15.8	13.8	13.0
			RATIOS						
3.0	3.9	3.1		3.0	3.9	4.6	4.3	2.8	2.0
1.1	1.2	1.2	Current	1.0	1.4	1.2	1.4	1.4	1.3
.4	.3	.4		.2	.6	.8	1.0	.7	1.0
1.6	2.1	1.5		1.7	1.6	1.3	1.2	1.7	1.0
(419) .4	(682) .4	(1120) .3	Quick	.4	.4	(78) .4	(103) .3	.2	.3
.1	.1	.1		.1	.1	.1	.0	.0	.1
0 UND	0 UND	0 UND		0 UND	0 UND	0 UND	0 UND	0 UND	0 UND
0 UND	0 UND	0 UND	Sales/Receivables	0 UND	0 UND	1 414.4	0 864.7	0 999.8	3 132.3
5 67.4	8 45.4	8 47.7		1 275.8	25 14.7	6 57.2	15 23.6	12 30.2	14 26.0
			Cost of Sales/Inventory						
			Cost of Sales/Payables						
3.4	3.4	2.7		3.2	1.9	2.4	1.9	2.9	4.6
58.4	25.5	24.1	Sales/Working Capital	-127.5	12.8	24.1	8.9	11.0	16.0
-4.4	-5.5	-5.1		-2.6	-10.0	-38.7	-72.6	-19.4	-144.1
15.5	23.9	10.9		9.3	6.9	15.9	17.1	27.1	37.7
(239) 4.8	(382) 5.3	(569) 3.8	EBIT/Interest	(178) 4.1	(156) 2.6	(51) 4.7	(69) 4.9	(56) 4.5	(59) 4.1
1.6	1.8	1.3		1.3	.6	1.5	1.4	2.3	1.9
7.0	12.5	2.9							
(16) 1.4	(17) 3.3	(21) 1.4	Net Profit + Depr., Dep., Amort./Cur. Mat. L/T/D						
.4	1.9	.4							
.1	.1	.0		.3	.0	.0	.0	.0	.0
1.6	1.5	1.1	Fixed/Worth	2.8	.5	.4	.3	.2	.4
8.7	9.5	6.5		20.3	4.1	2.3	2.3	2.5	1.8
1.1	1.0	1.0		1.1	.9	.9	.9	1.0	1.2
4.2	3.9	3.8	Debt/Worth	4.6	3.6	3.1	3.0	2.5	2.6
17.5	24.7	26.1		98.8	27.0	14.2	19.2	10.5	8.0
81.3	79.5	71.8		46.0	77.3	96.3	100.0	96.0	65.6
(351) 27.1	(559) 30.5	(920) 22.0	% Profit Before Taxes/Tangible Net Worth	(398) 12.3	(215) 24.6	(69) 37.8	(91) 48.6	(79) 44.4	(68) 25.0
6.4	5.3	4.2		.9	2.7	11.4	13.1	13.9	13.3
15.0	16.4	13.5		8.6	14.4	20.6	29.0	21.4	19.4
5.5	5.0	4.1	% Profit Before Taxes/Total Assets	2.2	3.6	7.3	8.6	7.6	7.7
.7	.4	.2		-.5	.0	1.4	2.1	3.1	1.9
63.9	76.2	273.3		22.6	UND	999.8	999.8	734.3	309.8
2.4	3.7	5.3	Sales/Net Fixed Assets	.3	17.6	44.2	26.2	30.3	22.0
.2	.3	.3		.1	1.0	3.5	1.9	3.8	2.6
1.6	1.6	1.4		.5	2.1	2.1	2.0	3.2	2.4
.4	.5	.5	Sales/Total Assets	.2	.6	1.0	.9	1.1	1.0
.2	.2	.2		.1	.2	.6	.5	.6	.5
1.2	.8	.9		6.8	.5	.4	.2	.3	.1
(275) 7.2	(420) 4.4	(635) 5.6	% Depr., Dep., Amort./Sales	(326) 14.5	(116) 2.2	(35) .6	(59) 1.1	(48) .9	(51) .5
18.0	16.5	16.9		22.2	8.1	4.6	2.5	2.3	3.5
2.3	2.3	2.1		5.3	2.7	2.2	1.1	1.1	
(70) 7.4	(139) 4.6	(184) 5.4	% Officers', Directors' Owners' Comp/Sales	(61) 13.8	(59) 7.0	(12) 4.0	(24) 2.3	(22) 1.9	
15.4	12.0	14.4		22.4	14.7	9.0	8.9	3.6	
2906899M	6046473M	9758464M	Net Sales ($)	190783M	471225M	311869M	753802M	1376104M	6654681M
3639712M	8234480M	12207747M	Total Assets ($)	1052789M	1475733M	521001M	1273580M	2292641M	5592003M

M = $ thousand   MM = $ million
See Pages 11 through 21 for Explanation of Ratios and Data

Current Data Sorted by Assets   Comparative Historical Data

						Type of Statement		
	1	4	10	1	4	Unqualified	13	23
	2	6	5			Reviewed	38	30
3	5	11	5			Compiled	27	35
9	6	5		3		Tax Returns	16	21
4	10	9	7		2	Other	46	42
	18 (4/1-9/30/06)		94 (10/1/06-3/31/07)				4/1/02-3/31/03	4/1/03-3/31/04
0-500M	500M-2MM	2-10MM	10-50MM	50-100MM	100-250MM		ALL	ALL
16	24	35	27	4	6	NUMBER OF STATEMENTS	140	151
%	%	%	%	%	%	ASSETS	%	%
6.9	6.5	9.0	4.7			Cash & Equivalents	8.1	8.4
1.7	8.1	7.7	4.2			Trade Receivables (net)	4.5	6.0
13.5	14.6	16.7	12.9			Inventory	19.3	8.0
4.7	7.4	2.1	15.0			All Other Current	4.4	11.9
26.8	36.7	35.5	36.8			Total Current	36.3	34.3
68.9	50.1	57.0	50.3			Fixed Assets (net)	56.7	56.6
4.4	2.6	1.9	2.8			Intangibles (net)	3.0	2.8
.1	10.6	5.6	10.1			All Other Non-Current	4.0	6.3
100.0	100.0	100.0	100.0			Total	100.0	100.0
						LIABILITIES		
25.2	25.6	26.0	47.3			Notes Payable-Short Term	32.0	31.4
12.4	8.1	6.8	5.1			Cur. Mat.-L.T.D.	8.4	7.5
14.4	3.0	6.7	1.8			Trade Payables	4.6	5.2
.0	.1	.0	.3			Income Taxes Payable	.2	.1
26.7	11.2	5.8	4.0			All Other Current	6.8	5.3
78.7	48.0	45.3	58.6			Total Current	51.9	49.5
63.2	28.1	28.2	22.7			Long-Term Debt	26.8	28.0
.0	.1	.2	1.7			Deferred Taxes	.5	.6
6.9	1.5	2.7	1.0			All Other Non-Current	3.3	4.3
-48.8	22.3	23.6	16.0			Net Worth	17.4	17.5
100.0	100.0	100.0	100.0			Total Liabilties & Net Worth	100.0	100.0
						INCOME DATA		
100.0	100.0	100.0	100.0			Net Sales	100.0	100.0
						Gross Profit		
88.6	95.9	94.1	91.7			Operating Expenses	96.6	94.6
11.4	4.1	5.9	8.3			Operating Profit	3.4	5.4
5.3	1.5	3.1	8.0			All Other Expenses (net)	1.5	1.6
6.1	2.6	2.8	.3			Profit Before Taxes	1.8	3.8
						RATIOS		
.9	2.4	1.4	1.2				1.2	1.4
.3	.7	.4	.6			Current	.7	.6
.1	.2	.2	.1				.2	.2
.5	.6	.5	.3				.5	.6
.1	.2	.3	.1			Quick	(138) .2	(150) .2
.0	.1	.1	.1				.1	.1
0 UND	1 374.0	4 88.3	8 46.6				5 80.5	5 68.8
0 UND	6 58.1	10 36.8	15 24.1			Sales/Receivables	11 32.6	11 33.3
5 68.0	26 14.1	23 15.6	24 15.1				23 15.8	28 12.9
						Cost of Sales/Inventory		
						Cost of Sales/Payables		
-358.3	8.3	6.4	5.2				10.5	10.6
-3.8	-15.0	-11.9	-7.8			Sales/Working Capital	-12.4	-17.2
-.9	-3.7	-2.2	-1.0				-2.3	-2.5
11.3	3.0	2.2	1.4				3.2	3.3
(14) 2.4	(20) 1.5	(33) 1.3	(25) 1.1			EBIT/Interest	(122) 1.6	(133) 1.7
.8	1.0	1.0	.6				1.0	1.1
						Net Profit + Depr., Dep., Amort./Cur. Mat. L/T/D	11.3	14.8
							(13) 1.2	(14) 1.7
							.9	.6
6.9	.6	.5	.3				.9	.8
-1.6	2.9	2.8	4.0			Fixed/Worth	4.2	2.5
-.9	8.0	8.9	13.2				13.5	7.0
8.6	1.2	1.8	3.5				2.7	1.8
-3.4	4.7	5.3	8.7			Debt/Worth	5.5	4.2
-2.3	12.7	12.4	38.9				19.0	11.1
	30.7	33.4	24.8			% Profit Before Taxes/Tangible Net Worth	36.9	26.8
	(21) 2.3	(33) 8.7	(23) 4.7				(115) 14.7	(133) 14.5
	.0	-.1	-11.3				2.2	2.4
17.9	10.1	5.0	3.0			% Profit Before Taxes/Total Assets	6.0	7.0
10.3	.5	1.7	.3				2.2	2.1
-1.4	.0	-.1	-1.5				-.8	.3
5.2	26.7	9.4	17.6				11.0	11.3
1.8	2.4	1.4	1.5			Sales/Net Fixed Assets	1.6	1.6
.7	1.2	.8	.7				.7	.7
2.9	2.1	1.7	.9				1.4	1.5
1.1	1.1	.8	.6			Sales/Total Assets	.8	.7
.6	.6	.5	.5				.5	.5
7.7	4.8	9.3	14.9			% Depr., Dep., Amort./Sales	10.6	11.9
(14) 32.9	(20) 12.7	(27) 22.3	(16) 34.3				(101) 29.6	(106) 27.8
43.3	24.0	39.0	41.3				42.7	39.1
	2.0	1.5	1.4			% Officers', Directors' Owners' Comp/Sales	2.2	2.3
	(11) 3.6	(15) 3.9	(11) 2.8				(47) 3.8	(59) 3.6
	6.8	8.9	4.4				5.9	7.5
7408M	43887M	217684M	554368M	389346M	755710M	Net Sales ($)	1740640M	1420052M
3595M	27097M	163350M	581599M	323581M	786226M	Total Assets ($)	1788557M	1910056M

M = $ thousand   MM = $ million
See Pages 11 through 21 for Explanation of Ratios and Data

Comparative Historical Data			Type of Statement	Current Data Sorted by Sales					
24	20	20	Unqualified	1	1	1	5	6	6
23	24	13	Reviewed	1	3	2	2	4	1
25	29	24	Compiled	5	6	6	4	3	
13	15	20	Tax Returns	11	6	1	2		
39	39	35	Other	6	6	7	4	3	9
4/1/04-3/31/05 ALL	4/1/05-3/31/06 ALL	4/1/06-3/31/07 ALL		18 (4/1-9/30/06) 0-1MM	1-3MM	3-5MM	94 (10/1/06-3/31/07) 5-10MM	10-25MM	25MM & OVER
124	127	112	**NUMBER OF STATEMENTS**	24	22	17	17	16	16
%	%	%	**ASSETS**	%	%	%	%	%	%
10.9	7.4	6.7	Cash & Equivalents	6.6	7.6	5.5	4.5	11.0	5.2
6.5	5.7	5.8	Trade Receivables (net)	3.1	3.9	5.7	6.4	6.7	11.3
14.2	13.3	15.1	Inventory	7.7	21.6	14.3	23.9	11.7	12.0
9.5	8.9	8.8	All Other Current	6.5	2.9	3.9	5.2	15.8	22.6
41.1	35.3	36.5	Total Current	24.0	36.0	29.4	40.0	45.2	51.1
49.4	53.4	53.7	Fixed Assets (net)	64.7	58.9	56.4	46.2	48.9	39.8
2.7	3.9	3.1	Intangibles (net)	3.4	1.1	5.1	2.9	1.6	5.2
6.8	7.4	6.7	All Other Non-Current	8.1	3.9	9.1	10.9	4.3	3.9
100.0	100.0	100.0	Total	100.0	100.0	100.0	100.0	100.0	100.0
			LIABILITIES						
33.6	32.2	32.2	Notes Payable-Short Term	20.5	32.2	24.2	37.9	43.4	40.8
6.3	6.7	7.1	Cur. Mat.-L.T.D.	12.7	8.2	7.6	1.4	7.9	2.0
8.2	9.3	5.6	Trade Payables	9.8	2.9	5.7	2.6	4.1	7.3
.1	.2	.1	Income Taxes Payable	.0	.1	.0	.2	.0	.3
7.6	6.3	9.5	All Other Current	19.1	5.3	11.6	3.9	6.4	7.7
55.8	54.7	54.5	Total Current	62.1	48.8	49.2	46.0	61.9	58.1
22.0	26.1	31.8	Long-Term Debt	45.3	38.8	30.8	28.4	15.4	23.1
.7	.7	.5	Deferred Taxes	.1	.2	.6	.9	1.0	.9
2.2	4.3	2.7	All Other Non-Current	3.0	3.7	4.9	.5	.6	3.0
19.3	14.2	10.4	Net Worth	-10.5	8.6	14.5	24.0	21.2	14.9
100.0	100.0	100.0	Total Liabilities & Net Worth	100.0	100.0	100.0	100.0	100.0	100.0
			INCOME DATA						
100.0	100.0	100.0	Net Sales	100.0	100.0	100.0	100.0	100.0	100.0
			Gross Profit						
93.4	93.1	92.8	Operating Expenses	91.1	94.3	93.6	92.1	93.2	93.0
6.6	6.9	7.2	Operating Profit	8.9	5.7	6.4	7.9	6.8	7.0
1.9	2.9	4.4	All Other Expenses (net)	4.2	2.2	6.0	6.5	4.1	4.0
4.7	4.0	2.8	Profit Before Taxes	4.7	3.5	.3	1.4	2.6	3.0
			RATIOS						
1.4	1.3	1.3		.9	1.8	1.3	2.5	1.4	1.3
1.0	.8	.6	Current	.2	.6	.4	1.0	1.0	1.1
.2	.2	.2		.0	.2	.2	.3	.2	.7
.8	.6	.5		.5	.5	.4	.5	.8	.6
(123) .3	.2	.2	Quick	.1	.2	.2	.3	.2	.2
.1	.1	.1		.0	.1	.1	.1	.1	.1
4 91.2	4 90.9	3 121.3		0 UND	0 UND	3 142.1	6 64.7	8 46.2	6 57.8
12 30.0	12 31.3	10 37.9	Sales/Receivables	1 310.0	5 78.7	9 41.2	17 21.7	14 26.6	21 17.7
25 14.5	24 15.3	23 15.6		21 17.5	13 27.9	23 15.6	23 15.6	27 13.7	27 13.7
			Cost of Sales/Inventory						
			Cost of Sales/Payables						
9.7	18.6	8.4		-338.2	5.9	7.7	5.9	4.8	9.7
-55.3	-20.7	-12.7	Sales/Working Capital	-4.6	-13.1	-8.7	-271.2	NM	63.2
-2.6	-2.2	-2.2		-.9	-2.5	-1.9	-3.0	-1.1	-11.1
4.3	3.2	2.3		3.0	3.0	2.0	2.7	2.3	1.7
(103) 1.6	(113) 1.7	(101) 1.2	EBIT/Interest	(20) 1.9	(19) 1.4	1.2	(16) 1.2	(14) 1.2	(15) 1.4
1.1	1.1	.9		.9	.9	1.0	.9	.9	1.1
	20.0	3.6	Net Profit + Depr., Dep.,						
(11)	5.8	(11) 1.6	Amort./Cur. Mat. L/T/D						
	1.1	.6							
.3	.7	.6		1.5	1.3	1.2	.3	.1	.4
2.7	3.6	3.8	Fixed/Worth	5.3	5.0	4.4	3.0	2.4	2.6
8.6	14.4	15.0		-1.4	22.6	14.9	13.8	11.2	9.7
1.8	2.0	2.2		1.2	3.7	4.2	1.4	2.4	2.3
4.5	5.3	7.2	Debt/Worth	10.1	6.0	9.7	5.3	5.0	9.0
15.6	32.5	38.9		-3.1	133.7	32.4	88.7	15.1	33.4
34.1	36.1	25.7	% Profit Before Taxes/Tangible	12.5	43.3	27.8	21.5	27.2	27.4
(104) 16.7	(104) 14.8	(91) 7.3	Net Worth	(15) 5.0	(18) 13.4	(15) 8.7	(14) 4.7	(15) 8.2	(14) 10.2
3.8	3.7	.0		.0	-1.7	-.3	-10.1	-8.7	5.0
7.0	6.9	7.4	% Profit Before Taxes/Total	12.0	9.9	5.0	5.4	3.6	3.5
2.3	2.6	1.6	Assets	2.7	1.3	1.3	.6	1.5	2.4
.4	.5	-.5		-.9	-.5	.0	-1.2	-1.1	.2
26.8	15.9	17.3		2.5	15.4	8.5	8.6	24.3	24.9
2.4	2.0	2.0	Sales/Net Fixed Assets	1.0	2.1	1.0	4.2	2.5	15.6
.9	.8	.8		.7	1.3	.7	.9	.7	1.5
1.7	1.7	1.8		1.0	2.2	1.9	2.6	1.0	1.9
.9	.8	.8	Sales/Total Assets	.7	1.1	.7	.9	.6	1.1
.5	.5	.5		.5	.8	.5	.5	.5	.7
8.3	5.1	9.7		19.8	4.7	10.7	4.7		
(76) 24.0	(88) 18.7	(79) 20.1	% Depr., Dep., Amort./Sales	(19) 36.8	(19) 11.8	(13) 31.5	(13) 17.8		
36.9	35.0	39.0		40.7	22.3	42.0	38.9		
2.3	1.9	1.7			2.9				
(42) 4.1	(50) 3.7	(41) 3.6	% Officers', Directors' Owners' Comp/Sales		(13) 3.9				
7.3	7.2	6.8			7.9				
1935333M	2368035M	1968403M	Net Sales ($)	10945M	42574M	65682M	123037M	235857M	1490308M
2177094M	2300971M	1885448M	Total Assets ($)	16896M	43874M	92235M	151188M	325828M	1255427M

M = $ thousand   MM = $ million
See Pages 11 through 21 for Explanation of Ratios and Data

Current Data Sorted by Assets   Comparative Historical Data

Type of Statement	0-500M	500M-2MM	2-10MM	10-50MM	50-100MM	100-250MM	4/1/02-3/31/03 ALL	4/1/03-3/31/04 ALL
Unqualified			3	15	4	6	16	21
Reviewed	1	3	9	13	1	2	14	33
Compiled	2	4	13	5	1		23	43
Tax Returns	6	3	1	1			11	11
Other	2	11	13	14	1		34	34
		31 (4/1-9/30/06)		102 (10/1/06-3/31/07)				
NUMBER OF STATEMENTS	11	21	39	48	6	8	98	142
ASSETS	%	%	%	%	%	%	%	%
Cash & Equivalents	12.9	10.1	5.4	3.5			5.3	6.3
Trade Receivables (net)	2.2	5.3	7.4	13.6			7.6	5.9
Inventory	7.0	15.6	11.9	3.4			8.2	7.4
All Other Current	6.9	1.8	4.5	12.7			5.7	8.3
Total Current	29.1	32.8	29.3	33.2			26.7	27.8
Fixed Assets (net)	63.5	56.4	51.1	38.9			51.6	52.9
Intangibles (net)	.0	.3	2.5	2.6			.5	.9
All Other Non-Current	7.4	10.5	17.1	25.3			21.2	18.4
Total	100.0	100.0	100.0	100.0			100.0	100.0
LIABILITIES								
Notes Payable-Short Term	12.6	15.9	21.2	14.3			17.6	14.8
Cur. Mat.-L.T.D.	14.4	9.2	7.9	7.9			9.4	9.8
Trade Payables	4.8	2.7	7.3	5.9			4.1	2.5
Income Taxes Payable	.0	.0	.0	.5			.4	.4
All Other Current	33.3	4.6	6.7	3.0			6.9	4.9
Total Current	65.1	32.4	43.0	31.6			38.3	32.4
Long-Term Debt	19.9	38.6	38.6	45.9			39.8	46.3
Deferred Taxes	.7	.2	.3	1.3			.7	1.3
All Other Non-Current	4.5	3.6	3.8	4.2			5.1	4.0
Net Worth	9.7	25.2	14.2	17.0			16.1	16.0
Total Liabilities & Net Worth	100.0	100.0	100.0	100.0			100.0	100.0
INCOME DATA								
Net Sales	100.0	100.0	100.0	100.0			100.0	100.0
Gross Profit								
Operating Expenses	89.0	86.0	88.7	82.8			88.5	87.8
Operating Profit	11.0	14.0	11.3	17.2			11.5	12.2
All Other Expenses (net)	7.3	3.9	5.5	9.3			6.3	7.7
Profit Before Taxes	3.7	10.0	5.8	7.9			5.1	4.6
RATIOS								
Current	1.7	5.2	1.3	2.2			1.5	2.2
	.3	.6	.6	1.1			.9	1.1
	.1	.1	.2	.3			.2	.4
Quick	.8	3.8	.8	1.1			1.1	1.5
	.2	.3	.2	.5			.3	.5
	.0	.0	.1	.1			.1	.1
Sales/Receivables	0 UND	0 UND	3 112.9	5 80.1			6 60.5	3 126.7
	0 UND	4 82.0	10 37.3	26 14.2			16 23.0	14 25.3
	26 14.3	14 26.5	19 19.2	127 2.9			35 10.3	42 8.7
Cost of Sales/Inventory								
Cost of Sales/Payables								
Sales/Working Capital	7.9	6.4	9.3	2.6			8.8	5.1
	-9.3	-8.6	-18.8	16.0			-24.7	29.0
	-.6	-2.0	-1.5	-7.4			-1.6	-2.9
EBIT/Interest		3.8	3.0	2.0			2.8	2.5
		(20) 2.1	(33) 1.4	(34) 1.3			(77) 1.6	(114) 1.5
		1.4	1.1	1.2			1.1	1.1
Net Profit + Depr., Dep., Amort./Cur. Mat. L/T/D								4.3
							(17) 1.2	
							.3	
Fixed/Worth	1.0	.1	1.1	.1			.3	.7
	2.4	2.0	3.8	2.0			2.4	3.2
	-33.8	5.3	19.0	7.3			8.5	10.3
Debt/Worth	1.0	1.2	3.2	4.5			2.1	3.3
	2.3	2.8	7.6	7.9			5.7	6.9
	-39.4	14.5	37.0	15.4			19.6	22.2
% Profit Before Taxes/Tangible Net Worth		30.0	56.2	40.8			31.5	23.2
	(19) 17.1	(32) 19.5	(46) 13.8				(84) 11.9	(125) 11.6
		9.2	2.6	7.8			3.7	2.7
% Profit Before Taxes/Total Assets	24.4	7.1	6.2	2.9			4.0	3.1
	2.4	5.0	1.8	1.4			2.0	1.4
	-1.5	2.3	.5	.7			.2	.1
Sales/Net Fixed Assets	3.6	519.8	17.0	57.6			23.4	16.3
	1.1	.8	1.3	2.5			1.4	1.0
	.6	.6	.5	.5			.5	.6
Sales/Total Assets	1.5	1.0	1.6	.5			.9	.7
	.6	.5	.6	.4			.5	.5
	.4	.4	.3	.3			.3	.3
% Depr., Dep., Amort./Sales		49.9	5.3	3.9			11.6	12.1
	(14) 58.4	(32) 29.0	(30) 45.5				(69) 36.0	(111) 35.8
		73.2	55.2	64.3			59.2	66.0
% Officers', Directors' Owners' Comp/Sales			1.0	3.8			1.3	1.4
			(14) 3.0	(11) 5.1			(30) 3.1	(41) 4.7
			8.2	6.9			5.2	7.8
Net Sales ($)	5736M	39354M	280205M	487394M	134842M	505582M	1574265M	1414953M
Total Assets ($)	2483M	22474M	187119M	1188642M	476003M	1256253M	2149498M	2757795M

M = $ thousand   MM = $ million
See Pages 11 through 21 for Explanation of Ratios and Data

Comparative Historical Data

Current Data Sorted by Sales

	4/1/04-3/31/05 ALL	4/1/05-3/31/06 ALL	4/1/06-3/31/07 ALL	Type of Statement	31 (4/1-9/30/06) 0-1MM	1-3MM	3-5MM	102 (10/1/06-3/31/07) 5-10MM	10-25MM	25MM & OVER
27	26	28	Unqualified			5	5	11	7
31	40	29	Reviewed	5	4	4	9	5	2
26	29	24	Compiled	6	9	5	2	1	1
13	15	11	Tax Returns	7	2		1	1	
40	36	41	Other	14	4	5	8	9	1
137	146	133	NUMBER OF STATEMENTS	32	19	19	25	27	11
%	%	%	**ASSETS**	%	%	%	%	%	%
6.7	6.9	6.0	Cash & Equivalents	8.8	6.6	3.6	4.9	6.0	3.2
8.5	10.2	8.9	Trade Receivables (net)	1.8	4.1	5.5	17.3	11.3	19.5
4.5	7.8	7.9	Inventory	3.9	17.1	3.9	4.0	9.3	16.2
9.7	5.0	7.5	All Other Current	1.2	13.7	1.5	12.9	12.3	1.0
29.4	29.9	30.3	Total Current	15.8	41.5	14.5	39.2	38.8	39.9
49.7	45.4	48.8	Fixed Assets (net)	70.9	43.5	60.1	30.0	34.1	53.0
.6	2.1	1.7	Intangibles (net)	.3	.2	4.1	3.6	1.8	.2
20.3	22.6	19.1	All Other Non-Current	13.0	14.9	21.3	27.3	25.3	6.8
100.0	100.0	100.0	Total	100.0	100.0	100.0	100.0	100.0	100.0
			LIABILITIES						
16.7	16.3	16.6	Notes Payable-Short Term	14.4	24.1	11.4	16.8	15.7	20.5
8.4	8.6	8.4	Cur. Mat.-L.T.D.	10.9	9.5	13.2	2.4	8.8	3.4
3.9	5.0	5.2	Trade Payables	.5	3.5	.7	7.3	10.4	12.3
.2	.3	.3	Income Taxes Payable	.0	.0	.5	.1	.5	1.0
4.2	3.9	6.7	All Other Current	12.8	8.7	2.3	2.4	3.8	9.4
33.5	34.0	37.2	Total Current	38.6	45.9	28.1	29.1	39.2	46.4
49.0	46.7	40.7	Long-Term Debt	34.2	40.3	51.1	52.8	37.6	22.6
.9	.8	.8	Deferred Taxes	.8	.1	1.5	.4	1.2	.4
2.9	4.8	4.4	All Other Non-Current	4.6	4.2	7.2	1.6	3.0	9.3
13.7	13.7	16.9	Net Worth	21.7	9.4	12.1	16.1	18.9	21.3
100.0	100.0	100.0	Total Liabilties & Net Worth	100.0	100.0	100.0	100.0	100.0	100.0
			INCOME DATA						
100.0	100.0	100.0	Net Sales	100.0	100.0	100.0	100.0	100.0	100.0
			Gross Profit						
86.4	85.9	84.9	Operating Expenses	83.2	84.9	83.9	88.4	81.5	92.2
13.6	14.1	15.1	Operating Profit	16.8	15.1	16.1	11.6	18.5	7.8
8.0	7.8	7.7	All Other Expenses (net)	7.0	7.6	12.0	5.8	8.7	4.3
5.6	6.3	7.4	Profit Before Taxes	9.9	7.5	4.1	5.8	9.8	3.5
			RATIOS						
2.5	2.2	1.8	Current	2.8	2.2	2.0	4.1	1.8	1.2
1.1	1.0	1.0		.3	1.1	.5	1.1	1.2	.9
.3	.3	.2		.1	.2	.2	.4	.3	.3
1.5	1.6	1.1	Quick	1.4	.8	.9	2.1	1.2	.9
.6	.4	.3		.2	.2	.5	.7	.2	.4
.1	.1	.1		.0	.1	.1	.2	.1	.2
3 143.9	2 181.7	2 199.5	Sales/Receivables	0 UND	1 354.1	11 32.3	3 135.5	2 185.3	6 56.9
14 25.3	12 29.9	12 31.1		4 81.3	5 76.3	27 13.4	11 33.5	18 20.7	15 24.5
38 9.5	43 8.4	36 10.3		25 14.7	18 20.1	53 6.8	65 5.6	68 5.4	32 11.5
			Cost of Sales/Inventory						
			Cost of Sales/Payables						
4.9	5.4	4.0	Sales/Working Capital	7.0	2.1	3.1	4.3	3.7	30.6
43.8	59.0	-275.8		-3.1	11.0	-5.4	19.1	20.2	-97.7
-2.6	-2.8	-1.9		-1.2	-1.5	-1.1	-17.7	-6.6	-10.3
3.0	3.2	3.2	EBIT/Interest	3.6	2.5	1.4	3.2	11.4	
(106) 1.6	(111) 1.6	(101) 1.5		(26) 2.3	(14) 1.3	(15) 1.2	(18) 1.4	(19) 1.6	
1.1	1.1	1.2		1.6	1.1	1.0	1.2	1.2	
1.3	1.4	1.6	Net Profit + Depr., Dep., Amort./Cur. Mat. L/T/D						
(12) 1.0	(15) 1.0	(13) .7							
.2	.2	.3							
.3	.1	.2	Fixed/Worth	1.4	.1	1.2	.0	.0	1.6
3.2	2.8	2.6		2.5	2.3	6.8	1.6	.7	2.2
12.0	13.0	8.1		6.6	18.3	31.6	7.3	7.0	11.4
3.4	3.4	3.0	Debt/Worth	1.2	2.2	6.0	5.1	3.3	1.9
9.0	9.5	6.7		4.3	7.6	9.5	10.9	6.7	3.4
34.8	33.4	17.3		8.0	118.4	34.3	19.2	13.8	13.2
35.0	34.0	38.8	% Profit Before Taxes/Tangible Net Worth	30.4	37.9	38.5	38.5	52.6	
(122) 12.7	(122) 16.9	(119) 15.7		(28) 17.7	(15) 19.2	(16) 10.7	(24) 11.8	23.1	
2.8	5.7	8.3		7.8	4.2	-4.9	8.3	11.9	
3.0	4.1	5.1	% Profit Before Taxes/Total Assets	6.8	5.4	2.1	2.7	7.8	4.8
1.1	1.7	2.0		3.3	1.7	1.2	1.3	2.1	2.7
.2	.5	.8		1.7	.3	-.2	.7	1.2	.5
26.7	92.3	29.9	Sales/Net Fixed Assets	1.1	268.1	12.0	76.4	145.1	135.8
1.3	1.5	1.1		.7	1.3	.8	4.3	10.9	1.1
.5	.6	.5		.4	.5	.3	.8	.6	.6
.7	.8	.7	Sales/Total Assets	.6	.6	.6	.8	.8	10.1
.4	.5	.5		.5	.5	.3	.5	.5	1.0
.3	.3	.3		.3	.3	.2	.3	.3	.4
13.6	2.2	8.0	% Depr., Dep., Amort./Sales	45.0	21.3	36.8	4.7	.5	
(91) 39.6	(103) 26.8	(90) 39.9		(27) 56.1	(13) 36.4	(15) 59.4	(17) 9.6	(14) 3.8	
68.4	57.1	63.7		69.4	71.3	63.8	56.8	8.3	
1.2	1.0	1.1	% Officers', Directors' Owners' Comp/Sales					1.0	
(34) 4.1	(36) 3.5	(29) 3.8						(10) 3.9	
7.1	5.9	6.4						5.8	
1245250M	1602702M	1453113M	Net Sales ($)	13981M	35890M	73483M	181527M	443564M	704668M
2705330M	3365730M	3132974M	Total Assets ($)	46003M	92694M	272469M	527886M	1260153M	933769M

© RMA 2007

M = $ thousand   MM = $ million
See Pages 11 through 21 for Explanation of Ratios and Data

Current Data Sorted by Assets   Comparative Historical Data

						Type of Statement		
		10	20	11	20	Unqualified	49	56
1	6	21	23	3	1	Reviewed	63	50
4	15	17	8			Compiled	34	49
16	12	10	1			Tax Returns	10	19
6	23	30	26	5	6	Other	70	76
	52 (4/1-9/30/06)		243 (10/1/06-3/31/07)				4/1/02-3/31/03 ALL	4/1/03-3/31/04 ALL
0-500M	500M-2MM	2-10MM	10-50MM	50-100MM	100-250MM	NUMBER OF STATEMENTS	226	250
27	56	88	78	19	27			
%	%	%	%	%	%	**ASSETS**	%	%
22.7	10.9	6.7	6.1	4.3	4.1	Cash & Equivalents	6.9	8.7
3.4	13.6	11.1	11.7	7.4	7.4	Trade Receivables (net)	11.7	10.5
6.7	8.7	11.2	9.0	11.1	3.1	Inventory	8.3	8.7
5.1	7.5	2.7	2.8	3.7	5.9	All Other Current	3.9	4.4
37.9	40.7	31.8	29.6	26.4	20.5	Total Current	30.8	32.3
58.1	46.2	61.5	60.0	63.1	63.5	Fixed Assets (net)	58.3	55.4
.0	.8	1.7	1.5	.6	2.1	Intangibles (net)	.7	1.1
4.0	12.3	5.0	8.9	9.8	13.9	All Other Non-Current	10.2	11.2
100.0	100.0	100.0	100.0	100.0	100.0	Total	100.0	100.0
						LIABILITIES		
8.0	16.8	9.9	9.2	16.3	6.7	Notes Payable-Short Term	9.2	11.9
10.9	6.8	10.2	12.2	10.2	10.0	Cur. Mat.-L.T.D.	13.0	11.9
2.5	9.6	4.8	3.4	4.4	3.3	Trade Payables	4.1	5.6
.0	.1	.3	.3	.1	.6	Income Taxes Payable	.3	.4
28.1	4.8	9.3	6.6	3.3	3.3	All Other Current	7.0	6.0
49.5	38.3	34.4	31.7	34.3	23.8	Total Current	33.6	35.8
61.2	28.3	34.2	38.2	35.3	49.1	Long-Term Debt	34.5	31.8
.0	.2	.7	2.9	2.2	4.5	Deferred Taxes	1.7	2.0
8.8	5.2	3.6	4.7	.6	1.7	All Other Non-Current	3.4	4.1
-19.5	27.9	27.0	22.5	27.5	20.9	Net Worth	26.9	26.4
100.0	100.0	100.0	100.0	100.0	100.0	Total Liabilties & Net Worth	100.0	100.0
						INCOME DATA		
100.0	100.0	100.0	100.0	100.0	100.0	Net Sales	100.0	100.0
						Gross Profit		
86.6	78.0	85.7	88.6	91.7	87.8	Operating Expenses	87.5	88.0
13.4	22.0	14.3	11.4	8.3	12.2	Operating Profit	12.5	12.0
2.5	4.1	2.4	4.9	1.2	6.0	All Other Expenses (net)	5.7	4.1
11.0	17.9	11.9	6.5	7.1	6.2	Profit Before Taxes	6.8	7.9
						RATIOS		
4.8	3.1	1.8	1.3	1.2	1.7		1.5	1.4
.8	1.2	1.0	.9	.9	.9	Current	.9	.9
.3	.5	.4	.5	.4	.6		.5	.4
1.0	1.4	1.0	.9	.6	.7		1.0	1.0
.5	.5	.4	.5	.3	.5	Quick	.5	.5
.2	.2	.2	.3	.2	.3		.2	.2
0 UND	0 UND	0 UND	15 24.3	16 23.4	29 12.5		6 60.8	1 624.3
0 UND	4 87.8	26 14.1	28 13.2	34 10.6	36 10.2	Sales/Receivables	29 12.5	26 14.3
5 72.7	33 11.2	43 8.5	49 7.4	40 9.2	48 7.5		49 7.4	45 8.2
						Cost of Sales/Inventory		
						Cost of Sales/Payables		
14.3	5.1	8.6	16.5	51.5	11.8		10.2	10.2
-38.9	52.3	-151.3	-33.8	-28.4	-17.3	Sales/Working Capital	-30.8	-38.2
-2.3	-4.5	-3.4	-3.6	-5.6	-6.9		-5.1	-4.7
8.7	7.2	6.4	2.7	3.8	2.6		3.8	4.5
(22) 1.5	(44) 4.2	(79) 2.6	(70) 1.9	(18) 2.3	(24) 1.8	EBIT/Interest	(191) 1.6	(216) 2.2
-2.2	1.9	1.1	1.3	1.4	1.6		1.0	1.2
		1.7	1.9				1.8	1.9
	(12) 1.3	(31) 1.3				Net Profit + Depr., Dep., Amort./Cur. Mat. L/T/D	(56) 1.3	(59) 1.3
		.8	.9				.9	.9
.9	.4	.9	1.6	1.7	1.8		.9	1.0
4.4	1.8	2.2	2.9	3.1	2.9	Fixed/Worth	2.4	2.2
-2.3	17.4	5.4	5.8	4.2	5.9		5.7	5.9
1.6	1.4	.9	2.2	2.0	2.9		1.4	1.3
18.8	3.3	3.3	4.4	4.1	4.1	Debt/Worth	3.3	3.4
-4.7	23.0	10.8	8.4	5.8	6.6		7.2	9.0
121.1	100.7	42.9	31.9	25.1	20.9		28.4	28.3
(14) 18.5	(45) 29.5	(75) 17.4	(72) 16.9	20.8	(26) 14.9	% Profit Before Taxes/Tangible Net Worth	(203) 10.5	(219) 12.8
-12.2	12.6	5.8	6.0	3.9	12.7		1.4	4.0
42.8	20.8	14.0	7.4	8.1	5.6		7.5	8.1
6.6	10.8	4.5	3.5	3.4	2.8	% Profit Before Taxes/Total Assets	2.4	3.2
-4.2	3.6	.5	1.1	.5	1.7		.1	.8
6.6	11.9	4.2	3.6	3.7	1.5		5.1	6.2
2.7	2.0	1.2	1.2	1.3	.9	Sales/Net Fixed Assets	1.3	1.5
1.0	.6	.5	.6	.5	.6		.7	.7
4.0	3.0	2.0	1.4	1.5	.9		1.7	1.9
1.5	.8	.9	.7	.9	.5	Sales/Total Assets	.8	.8
.6	.5	.4	.4	.5	.4		.4	.4
5.6	5.4	5.6	7.6	1.6			7.4	4.7
(17) 15.1	(43) 24.4	(82) 19.9	(69) 15.2	(11) 16.6		% Depr., Dep., Amort./Sales	(194) 24.0	(209) 20.8
72.8	51.1	43.0	34.7	28.5			41.3	44.0
	4.1	1.8	.5				1.4	1.1
	(10) 9.0	(20) 4.6	(13) 1.3			% Officers', Directors' Owners' Comp/Sales	(51) 4.0	(54) 2.6
	18.1	7.8	3.0				7.6	6.5
16701M	137564M	580819M	1834345M	1507076M	2538386M	Net Sales ($)	4354868M	5035189M
6360M	64558M	458168M	1849977M	1362410M	3827266M	Total Assets ($)	4256520M	4880729M

M = $ thousand   MM = $ million
See Pages 11 through 21 for Explanation of Ratios and Data

Comparative Historical Data | | | | **Current Data Sorted by Sales** | | | | |

Hist 1	Hist 2	Hist 3	Type of Statement	0-1MM	1-3MM	3-5MM	5-10MM	10-25MM	25MM & OVER
57	53	61	Unqualified	2	7	1	3	8	40
51	48	55	Reviewed	6	7	8	9	13	12
45	47	44	Compiled	9	12	5	11	6	1
26	41	39	Tax Returns	24	4	6	3	2	
72	94	96	Other	19	14	9	12	25	17
4/1/04-3/31/05 ALL	4/1/05-3/31/06 ALL	4/1/06-3/31/07 ALL		52 (4/1-9/30/06)			243 (10/1/06-3/31/07)		
251	283	295	NUMBER OF STATEMENTS	60	44	29	38	54	70
%	%	%	ASSETS	%	%	%	%	%	%
7.5	7.6	8.4	Cash & Equivalents	14.6	8.1	6.9	7.0	8.4	4.8
12.5	10.0	10.4	Trade Receivables (net)	4.3	5.9	11.2	16.2	15.8	10.9
7.3	9.1	9.0	Inventory	2.2	2.4	2.4	19.2	14.7	11.8
3.7	3.2	4.2	All Other Current	3.5	9.1	3.0	2.1	3.4	4.1
31.0	29.9	32.1	Total Current	24.6	25.5	23.5	44.5	42.3	31.6
58.4	59.5	58.2	Fixed Assets (net)	64.2	64.6	68.8	43.4	49.9	59.0
1.2	1.5	1.3	Intangibles (net)	.5	2.8	1.7	.4	1.5	1.2
9.4	9.2	8.5	All Other Non-Current	10.8	7.0	6.0	11.7	6.3	8.2
100.0	100.0	100.0	Total	100.0	100.0	100.0	100.0	100.0	100.0
			LIABILITIES						
12.0	11.4	11.0	Notes Payable-Short Term	11.0	7.4	5.9	16.8	11.4	11.7
12.6	11.7	10.1	Cur. Mat.-L.T.D.	10.5	12.8	11.7	7.8	8.8	9.9
5.5	5.1	5.0	Trade Payables	1.3	1.9	2.9	10.8	7.9	5.4
.3	.2	.3	Income Taxes Payable	.0	.3	.3	.1	.5	.3
5.9	7.5	8.5	All Other Current	15.4	4.2	7.4	4.6	12.7	4.8
36.3	36.0	34.8	Total Current	38.2	26.6	28.1	40.0	41.4	32.1
37.0	37.9	38.0	Long-Term Debt	47.3	41.4	34.8	35.0	28.9	38.0
1.7	1.7	1.6	Deferred Taxes	.1	1.0	1.6	1.0	2.1	3.1
3.2	4.1	4.3	All Other Non-Current	8.6	2.0	4.4	4.5	3.9	2.2
21.8	20.3	21.2	Net Worth	5.7	29.0	31.1	19.5	23.7	24.6
100.0	100.0	100.0	Total Liabilities & Net Worth	100.0	100.0	100.0	100.0	100.0	100.0
			INCOME DATA						
100.0	100.0	100.0	Net Sales	100.0	100.0	100.0	100.0	100.0	100.0
			Gross Profit						
90.3	85.8	85.7	Operating Expenses	74.8	78.6	85.1	91.3	91.4	92.2
9.7	14.2	14.3	Operating Profit	25.2	21.4	14.9	8.7	8.6	7.8
3.4	4.1	3.6	All Other Expenses (net)	6.6	3.3	2.5	3.0	2.3	3.1
6.4	10.1	10.7	Profit Before Taxes	18.6	18.0	12.4	5.7	6.3	4.8
			RATIOS						
1.6	1.3	1.5	Current	2.6	2.5	1.7	1.8	1.5	1.2
.9	.8	.9		.6	.8	.4	1.2	1.1	1.0
.4	.4	.4		.3	.3	.2	.5	.6	.6
1.1	.9	1.0	Quick	1.5	1.2	1.5	1.1	1.0	.7
.5	.5	.5		.5	.4	.3	.4	.5	.5
.2	.2	.2		.1	.2	.1	.2	.3	.3
1 311.2	0 UND	0 UND	Sales/Receivables	0 UND	0 UND	0 UND	10 36.4	14 26.6	19 19.5
27 13.5	24 15.2	22 16.5		0 UND	12 29.3	16 22.4	30 12.2	28 13.0	32 11.5
46 8.0	41 8.8	42 8.8		17 22.1	49 7.5	40 9.2	45 8.1	43 8.5	42 8.7
			Cost of Sales/Inventory						
			Cost of Sales/Payables						
10.3	14.3	11.3	Sales/Working Capital	7.0	4.9	15.7	7.8	9.6	19.6
-56.0	-25.7	-55.3		-6.9	-21.9	-5.4	52.3	74.1	-297.5
-4.0	-4.0	-4.3		-1.6	-2.4	-1.9	-6.4	-8.1	-9.1
3.7	4.6	4.5	EBIT/Interest	5.0	6.8	6.9	6.6	3.2	2.8
(222) 2.0	(250) 2.7	(257) 2.3		(48) 2.9	(36) 4.2	(27) 3.2	(34) 1.7	(47) 2.0	(65) 1.9
1.2	1.5	1.3		1.0	1.0	1.3	1.2	1.3	1.5
1.9	2.0	1.8	Net Profit + Depr., Dep., Amort./Cur. Mat. L/T/D					1.8	2.1
(53) 1.1	(67) 1.4	(52) 1.3						(16) 1.4	(16) 1.1
1.0	1.0	.9						.9	1.0
1.3	1.2	1.1	Fixed/Worth	1.1	1.1	1.2	.2	.6	1.6
2.7	2.6	2.6		3.3	3.1	4.1	2.4	1.9	3.0
8.2	10.1	6.1		-14.2	29.6	12.9	11.6	3.9	4.4
1.8	1.8	1.8	Debt/Worth	1.6	1.4	.8	2.1	1.7	2.3
4.1	4.2	3.9		4.0	3.5	3.2	5.9	3.6	4.1
16.2	15.2	10.3		-15.1	30.8	13.9	13.0	6.4	5.8
31.2	51.2	38.7	% Profit Before Taxes/Tangible Net Worth	49.7	71.7	40.7	40.5	42.0	26.6
(209) 16.5	(237) 22.8	(251) 17.7		(41) 17.5	(35) 19.6	(24) 22.8	(33) 16.8	(51) 16.6	(67) 17.7
6.5	10.0	8.0		6.2	4.8	3.9	8.8	4.9	10.9
7.8	10.8	11.0	% Profit Before Taxes/Total Assets	12.9	16.7	25.8	10.6	10.5	6.2
3.1	4.8	4.0		5.7	6.8	8.1	2.5	3.8	3.5
.8	1.7	1.1		.4	.2	1.5	.9	1.0	1.7
4.5	5.5	4.7	Sales/Net Fixed Assets	2.4	2.8	2.9	85.0	9.4	4.0
1.4	1.4	1.3		.8	.7	1.0	4.6	2.2	1.7
.6	.6	.6		.5	.4	.4	.8	.9	.9
1.8	1.9	1.6	Sales/Total Assets	.8	1.0	1.6	3.2	2.2	1.8
.8	.8	.8		.5	.5	.7	1.1	1.2	1.0
.4	.5	.4		.3	.3	.3	.5	.6	.7
6.8	5.3	6.5	% Depr., Dep., Amort./Sales	13.7	19.6	14.2	1.4	5.2	2.0
(201) 19.2	(225) 18.1	(228) 17.2		(48) 32.6	(37) 40.3	(26) 27.8	(31) 11.0	(46) 11.2	(40) 8.0
38.8	38.1	42.5		61.8	60.5	61.8	30.3	24.1	13.6
1.3	1.7	1.3	% Officers', Directors' Owners' Comp/Sales	8.5				1.0	.4
(43) 6.4	(51) 4.2	(55) 3.5		(10) 13.3				(11) 2.8	(11) 1.5
13.4	8.6	8.3		19.8				6.7	2.5
4351599M	7106126M	6614891M	Net Sales ($)	28086M	71491M	115250M	281791M	840322M	5277951M
4754164M	6837364M	7568739M	Total Assets ($)	70662M	183499M	219830M	403176M	1196426M	5495146M

© RMA 2007

M = $ thousand   MM = $ million
See Pages 11 through 21 for Explanation of Ratios and Data

Current Data Sorted by Assets

Comparative Historical Data

Type of Statement	0-500M	500M-2MM	2-10MM	10-50MM	50-100MM	100-250MM	4/1/02-3/31/03 ALL	4/1/03-3/31/04 ALL
Unqualified	4	2	6	7			7	13
Reviewed		10	8	4			11	16
Compiled	6	8	8	1			20	34
Tax Returns	1	7	7	1			17	16
Other				5	2	1	23	26
	0-500M	12 (4/1-9/30/06) 500M-2MM	2-10MM	76 (10/1/06-3/31/07) 10-50MM	50-100MM	100-250MM		
NUMBER OF STATEMENTS	11	27	29	18	2	1	78	105
ASSETS	%	%	%	%	%	%	%	%
Cash & Equivalents	13.0	6.5	7.4	6.9			6.5	6.3
Trade Receivables (net)	2.4	14.4	18.5	12.1			10.7	12.6
Inventory	3.6	14.2	15.8	11.0			11.7	10.5
All Other Current	.2	.9	3.9	9.2			3.6	4.0
Total Current	19.2	35.9	45.6	39.3			32.5	33.5
Fixed Assets (net)	68.3	50.7	37.3	36.5			54.6	45.8
Intangibles (net)	.8	3.8	5.9	9.7			1.5	4.5
All Other Non-Current	11.8	9.6	11.2	14.5			11.5	16.2
Total	100.0	100.0	100.0	100.0			100.0	100.0
LIABILITIES								
Notes Payable-Short Term	8.5	25.0	19.1	16.0			17.1	13.1
Cur. Mat.-L.T.D.	10.9	7.4	6.5	7.8			13.3	9.0
Trade Payables	3.0	6.8	9.8	8.4			3.9	8.0
Income Taxes Payable	.0	.0	.4	.2			.2	.1
All Other Current	3.7	7.0	7.3	4.9			5.2	6.9
Total Current	26.1	46.2	43.1	37.3			39.8	37.2
Long-Term Debt	34.5	24.8	14.5	22.6			37.4	35.7
Deferred Taxes	.0	.0	.5	2.4			.7	.5
All Other Non-Current	5.9	10.6	9.6	2.9			5.0	11.1
Net Worth	33.5	18.3	32.3	34.8			17.2	15.5
Total Liabilities & Net Worth	100.0	100.0	100.0	100.0			100.0	100.0
INCOME DATA								
Net Sales	100.0	100.0	100.0	100.0			100.0	100.0
Gross Profit								
Operating Expenses	89.5	92.2	94.2	83.4			86.6	84.9
Operating Profit	10.5	7.8	5.8	16.6			13.4	15.1
All Other Expenses (net)	2.9	4.6	1.9	4.3			7.1	7.6
Profit Before Taxes	7.6	3.2	3.9	12.3			6.3	7.5
RATIOS								
Current	3.1	2.0	3.1	1.5			1.5	1.6
	.5	1.1	1.4	1.0			.7	.9
	.2	.5	.6	.7			.3	.3
Quick	3.1	1.5	1.7	.8			.8	.9
	.4	.7	.6	.5			.3	.5
	.1	.0	.1	.2			.1	.1
Sales/Receivables	0 UND	0 UND	1 467.6	3 113.8			0 UND	0 UND
	0 UND	1 301.7	22 17.0	23 15.8			10 38.1	11 33.0
	12 30.5	36 10.2	42 8.7	48 7.6			34 10.8	36 10.2
Cost of Sales/Inventory								
Cost of Sales/Payables								
Sales/Working Capital	12.2	8.0	5.9	4.9			6.9	10.3
	-17.6	66.9	17.5	410.1			-19.2	-42.8
	-6.9	-3.9	-6.7	-8.4			-3.4	-6.3
EBIT/Interest	8.9	8.7	6.4	10.3			4.4	4.1
	(25) 1.7	(25) 2.4	(15) 3.2	3.8			(66) 2.0	(79) 1.7
	-.7	.0	.5	2.5			.5	.5
Net Profit + Depr., Dep., Amort./Cur. Mat. L/T/D							2.2	3.9
							(10) 1.5	(16) 2.0
							.2	1.4
Fixed/Worth	.9	.7	.3	.4			1.0	.6
	2.1	2.8	1.0	.9			2.6	2.5
	10.6	-3.8	6.4	8.5			59.9	16.1
Debt/Worth	1.0	.6	.5	1.0			1.5	1.6
	1.5	4.7	2.3	4.2			4.5	4.6
	11.2	-5.1	9.5	17.6			114.1	46.1
% Profit Before Taxes/Tangible Net Worth	112.0	51.0	41.6	43.7			42.7	36.5
	(10) 8.9	(18) 30.8	(23) 31.1	(16) 31.3			(60) 13.8	(81) 14.8
	-23.6	4.4	8.6	15.7			-1.9	2.1
% Profit Before Taxes/Total Assets	38.2	11.9	13.7	15.9			8.6	9.2
	3.6	6.9	6.8	8.3			2.2	2.9
	-13.8	-1.7	-2.8	3.4			-2.1	-.5
Sales/Net Fixed Assets	6.4	10.0	15.8	21.9			6.2	14.4
	1.5	3.0	9.2	3.6			2.5	3.1
	1.4	1.9	2.6	.8			.7	1.2
Sales/Total Assets	2.2	2.4	3.0	2.0			2.1	2.2
	1.5	1.8	2.1	1.5			1.1	1.2
	.6	1.0	1.1	.4			.4	.4
% Depr., Dep., Amort./Sales	8.6	5.4	1.0	4.1			8.9	4.7
	(10) 16.3	(22) 13.9	(23) 6.1	(12) 12.2			(63) 17.5	(75) 14.6
	34.5	26.2	29.6	42.3			38.8	35.2
% Officers', Directors' Owners' Comp/Sales			1.9				4.4	3.1
		(11)	3.3				(24) 6.2	(42) 6.9
			7.3				12.7	14.8
Net Sales ($)	8582M	58950M	286042M	460371M	133707M	20723M	402941M	593313M
Total Assets ($)	3013M	34313M	129841M	350910M	141938M	199490M	562564M	637933M

Comparative Historical Data　　　　　　　　　　Current Data Sorted by Sales

10	7	15	Type of Statement		2	2	3	5	3
14	15	14	Reviewed		3	1	2	4	4
25	22	23	Compiled	5	7	2	6	3	
15	14	15	Tax Returns	6	7	1		1	
23	18	21	Other	3	5	1	5	5	2
4/1/04-3/31/05 ALL	4/1/05-3/31/06 ALL	4/1/06-3/31/07 ALL		0-1MM	12 (4/1-9/30/06) 1-3MM	3-5MM	76 (10/1/06-3/31/07) 5-10MM	10-25MM	25MM & OVER
87	76	88	**NUMBER OF STATEMENTS**	14	24	7	16	18	9
%	%	%	**ASSETS**	%	%	%	%	%	%
8.8	7.0	7.6	Cash & Equivalents	12.7	6.2		5.6	9.3	
10.7	15.1	13.6	Trade Receivables (net)	5.3	9.5		14.5	22.8	
11.8	10.4	12.3	Inventory	2.4	15.2		11.7	9.0	
4.8	3.3	4.7	All Other Current	3.6	2.5		7.1	8.4	
36.0	35.9	38.2	Total Current	24.0	33.2		39.0	49.5	
45.7	48.7	44.4	Fixed Assets (net)	59.7	48.4		51.5	27.8	
4.3	3.7	5.3	Intangibles (net)	.5	6.7		3.6	7.3	
14.0	11.7	12.2	All Other Non-Current	15.9	11.7		5.9	15.5	
100.0	100.0	100.0	Total	100.0	100.0		100.0	100.0	
			LIABILITIES						
12.0	15.0	18.5	Notes Payable-Short Term	8.1	24.3		15.4	16.1	
10.1	9.4	7.7	Cur. Mat.-L.T.D.	6.2	9.0		8.6	1.8	
4.9	7.3	7.5	Trade Payables	1.4	7.2		4.8	10.0	
.1	.2	.2	Income Taxes Payable	.0	.0		.3	.5	
7.2	7.5	7.1	All Other Current	2.1	8.8		4.9	12.5	
34.1	39.3	41.0	Total Current	17.9	49.2		34.0	41.0	
33.8	31.5	22.3	Long-Term Debt	35.1	28.4		23.0	13.4	
.5	.1	.7	Deferred Taxes	.0	.0		.5	1.6	
7.2	5.2	7.8	All Other Non-Current	13.2	11.1		10.1	2.9	
24.4	23.9	28.2	Net Worth	33.9	11.3		32.4	41.1	
100.0	100.0	100.0	Total Liabilties & Net Worth	100.0	100.0		100.0	100.0	
			INCOME DATA						
100.0	100.0	100.0	Net Sales	100.0	100.0		100.0	100.0	
			Gross Profit						
86.1	86.5	90.4	Operating Expenses	79.0	96.5		90.1	91.0	
13.9	13.5	9.6	Operating Profit	21.0	3.5		9.9	9.0	
5.2	3.8	3.6	All Other Expenses (net)	6.0	4.9		4.6	1.8	
8.7	9.7	6.0	Profit Before Taxes	15.0	-1.4		5.3	7.2	
			RATIOS						
2.0	1.7	2.2		3.4	1.7		2.5	4.0	
1.1	1.1	1.0	Current	1.6	.8		1.0	1.4	
.5	.4	.5		.4	.2		.5	.7	
1.1	1.4	1.3		2.7	.8		1.9	2.8	
.5	.6	.5	Quick	1.4	.3		.3	1.0	
.2	.2	.1		.2	.0		.1	.1	
0 UND	0 UND	0 UND		0 UND	0 UND		3 145.8	3 116.7	
9 40.8	12 29.3	12 29.3	Sales/Receivables	0 UND	1 317.9		31 11.6	23 15.6	
35 10.5	44 8.3	37 9.7		2 187.4	26 14.2		43 8.5	57 6.5	
			Cost of Sales/Inventory						
			Cost of Sales/Payables						
5.9	12.5	6.7		4.9	8.1		6.7	4.6	
25.4	96.7	111.0	Sales/Working Capital	13.9	-67.7		NM	13.9	
-13.0	-9.2	-7.1		-7.6	-3.2		-15.0	-69.4	
4.9	9.8	7.4		6.2	5.0		14.1	86.2	
(73) 2.0	(67) 2.3	(77) 2.5	EBIT/Interest	(13) 1.4	(23) 2.4		(13) 2.7	(13) 4.1	
-.5	1.2	.9		-.1	-1.0		.9	1.7	
4.7		3.5	Net Profit + Depr., Dep.,						
(12) 1.8		(16) 1.6	Amort./Cur. Mat. L/T/D						
.6		.3							
.6	.6	.4		.5	.5		.7	.2	
2.2	1.9	1.6	Fixed/Worth	2.5	5.9		1.8	.5	
14.3	12.2	10.6		10.6	-1.8		3.7	1.2	
1.5	.9	.6		.8	1.0		.6	.3	
4.3	2.8	2.8	Debt/Worth	1.7	8.6		2.3	1.9	
18.4	72.4	21.3		15.1	-4.0		8.6	16.2	
48.0	54.9	45.2	% Profit Before Taxes/Tangible	58.4	39.7		46.8	46.3	
(71) 14.5	(59) 22.1	(70) 30.9	Net Worth	(12) 10.1	(14) 11.9		(15) 31.9	(16) 38.6	
3.3	8.0	8.8		-12.4	3.7		15.7	18.1	
10.0	19.7	13.9	% Profit Before Taxes/Total	9.6	10.5		32.0	23.3	
3.9	5.3	6.1	Assets	2.4	4.8		7.3	8.9	
-2.9	.9	.5		-5.4	-14.4		1.4	1.8	
14.3	10.3	15.2		3.1	11.4		8.8	36.4	
4.1	3.5	4.3	Sales/Net Fixed Assets	1.5	3.6		3.9	10.8	
1.6	1.8	1.8		.7	1.7		1.3	6.4	
2.4	2.6	2.4		1.6	2.1		2.8	3.1	
1.6	1.6	1.8	Sales/Total Assets	.7	1.4		1.9	2.3	
.5	.8	.8		.3	.9		.8	1.2	
4.7	6.4	3.4		14.0	2.5		6.1	.4	
(64) 13.3	(59) 10.3	(67) 11.3	% Depr., Dep., Amort./Sales	(12) 21.9	(21) 8.7		(15) 9.0	(11) 3.2	
24.4	27.1	28.9		59.1	26.8		22.9	15.8	
3.5	2.2	2.1	% Officers', Directors'						
(31) 11.4	(34) 4.1	(26) 4.9	Owners' Comp/Sales						
16.9	9.2	8.1							
648649M	739293M	968375M	Net Sales ($)	5970M	46570M	27333M	115580M	281800M	491122M
698628M	538453M	859505M	Total Assets ($)	10345M	61741M	30849M	117965M	408523M	230082M

© RMA 2007　　　M = $ thousand　　MM = $ million
See Pages 11 through 21 for Explanation of Ratios and Data

Current Data Sorted by Assets   **Comparative Historical Data**

						Type of Statement		
						Unqualified	3	10
						Reviewed	2	2
16	1	2				Compiled	9	8
1	2					Tax Returns	11	7
2	2		2		1	Other	14	7
	2 (4/1-9/30/06)		30 (10/1/06-3/31/07)				4/1/02-3/31/03	4/1/03-3/31/04
0-500M	500M-2MM	2-10MM	10-50MM	50-100MM	100-250MM		ALL	ALL
19	7	4	1		1	**NUMBER OF STATEMENTS**	39	34
%	%	%	%	%	%	**ASSETS**	%	%
12.6						Cash & Equivalents	14.5	14.2
.0						Trade Receivables (net)	2.5	3.7
29.6						Inventory	16.7	12.3
.0						All Other Current	2.1	.8
42.2						Total Current	35.8	31.1
21.0						Fixed Assets (net)	44.3	39.4
21.4						Intangibles (net)	13.3	19.9
15.3						All Other Non-Current	6.6	9.6
100.0						Total	100.0	100.0
						LIABILITIES		
.0						Notes Payable-Short Term	5.0	6.4
13.8						Cur. Mat.-L.T.D.	6.5	4.4
14.6						Trade Payables	15.6	13.5
.0						Income Taxes Payable	.0	.1
20.1						All Other Current	10.6	14.2
48.5						Total Current	37.6	38.5
33.5						Long-Term Debt	31.4	24.3
.0						Deferred Taxes	.0	.3
5.5						All Other Non-Current	8.5	3.3
12.5						Net Worth	22.6	33.7
100.0						Total Liabilities & Net Worth	100.0	100.0
						INCOME DATA		
100.0						Net Sales	100.0	100.0
						Gross Profit		
94.8						Operating Expenses	95.1	92.2
5.2						Operating Profit	4.9	7.8
1.9						All Other Expenses (net)	.4	1.3
3.2						Profit Before Taxes	4.5	6.5
						RATIOS		
1.1						Current	1.9	1.9
.9							1.0	.9
.6							.5	.5
.5						Quick	.7	1.1
.2							.4	.4
.1							.2	.2
0 UND						Sales/Receivables	0 UND	0 UND
0 UND							0 UND	1 253.5
0 UND							4 83.6	7 49.7
						Cost of Sales/Inventory		
						Cost of Sales/Payables		
43.8						Sales/Working Capital	13.1	16.3
-31.1							-200.4	-67.2
-7.2							-13.1	-12.2
9.3						EBIT/Interest	14.5	11.1
(15) 2.5							(26) 5.4	(28) 5.6
-.8							2.9	-.8
						Net Profit + Depr., Dep., Amort./Cur. Mat. L/T/D		
1.3						Fixed/Worth	.5	.9
-1.2							1.9	2.0
-.4							-3.1	-6.0
2.4						Debt/Worth	.9	.7
-4.9							3.6	2.8
-2.3							-6.9	-9.0
						% Profit Before Taxes/Tangible Net Worth	97.4	55.3
							(25) 44.8	(23) 40.3
							20.9	20.7
25.7						% Profit Before Taxes/Total Assets	26.5	22.4
6.8							12.5	10.0
-16.9							4.4	.9
17.7						Sales/Net Fixed Assets	14.6	19.0
13.3							7.4	6.2
9.4							3.2	2.4
2.6						Sales/Total Assets	3.4	4.7
2.1							2.5	1.8
1.7							1.2	1.1
1.8						% Depr., Dep., Amort./Sales	1.2	3.4
(17) 2.3							(22) 3.1	(21) 8.5
4.1							18.8	18.3
						% Officers', Directors' Owners' Comp/Sales	3.1	
							(16) 6.5	
							23.3	
10020M	18192M	49085M	14764M		43370M	Net Sales ($)	1781445M	756192M
4643M	6500M	14476M	10566M		229260M	Total Assets ($)	677903M	702539M

(Columns 500M-2MM, 2-10MM, 10-50MM, 50-100MM, 100-250MM in the Current Data section are marked "DATA NOT AVAILABLE.")

M = $ thousand   MM = $ million
See Pages 11 through 21 for Explanation of Ratios and Data

Comparative Historical Data						Type of Statement	Current Data Sorted by Sales					
	4		2			Unqualified				3		
	5		5		3	Reviewed						
	5		18		18	Compiled	16	2				
	13		2		3	Tax Returns	2	1				
	15		6		8	Other	2		2	1	1	2
	4/1/04-3/31/05 ALL		4/1/05-3/31/06 ALL		4/1/06-3/31/07 ALL		0-1MM	2 (4/1-9/30/06) 1-3MM	3-5MM	30 (10/1/06-3/31/07) 5-10MM	10-25MM	25MM & OVER
	42		33		32	NUMBER OF STATEMENTS	20	3	2	4	1	2
	%		%		%	ASSETS	%	%	%	%	%	%
	12.7		13.9		12.0	Cash & Equivalents	13.4					
	4.4		4.1		2.6	Trade Receivables (net)	.0					
	14.5		27.6		22.6	Inventory	28.1					
	3.4		2.5		2.5	All Other Current	.0					
	35.0		48.1		39.6	Total Current	41.6					
	37.5		26.3		33.0	Fixed Assets (net)	23.5					
	13.7		17.3		15.6	Intangibles (net)	20.4					
	13.8		8.3		11.8	All Other Non-Current	14.6					
	100.0		100.0		100.0	Total	100.0					
						LIABILITIES						
	9.3		2.4		.8	Notes Payable-Short Term	.0					
	4.5		11.5		11.8	Cur. Mat.-L.T.D.	13.6					
	17.9		17.3		16.6	Trade Payables	13.8					
	.0		.0		.1	Income Taxes Payable	.0					
	11.8		10.9		16.8	All Other Current	19.2					
	43.6		42.1		46.2	Total Current	46.6					
	24.0		34.5		32.2	Long-Term Debt	34.3					
	.7		.0		.5	Deferred Taxes	.0					
	2.0		4.9		4.5	All Other Non-Current	5.2					
	29.6		18.5		16.6	Net Worth	13.9					
	100.0		100.0		100.0	Total Liabilties & Net Worth	100.0					
						INCOME DATA						
	100.0		100.0		100.0	Net Sales	100.0					
						Gross Profit						
	88.9		92.7		92.5	Operating Expenses	92.4					
	11.1		7.3		7.5	Operating Profit	7.6					
	1.1		1.6		2.2	All Other Expenses (net)	2.2					
	10.0		5.7		5.3	Profit Before Taxes	5.4					
						RATIOS						
	1.6		2.0		1.1		1.2					
	.8		1.3		.8	Current	.9					
	.4		.7		.6		.6					
	.9		.8		.5		.5					
	.4		.4		.3	Quick	.2					
	.2		.2		.2		.1					
0	UND	0	UND	0	UND		0	UND				
0	UND	0	UND	0	UND	Sales/Receivables	0	UND				
6	63.6	6	61.1	1	266.9		0	UND				
						Cost of Sales/Inventory						
						Cost of Sales/Payables						
	9.1		7.9		44.3		28.5					
	-50.4		33.9		-28.4	Sales/Working Capital	NM					
	-9.4		-11.9		-7.3		-8.2					
	24.0		6.3		7.6		8.8					
(33)	7.7	(29)	2.7	(27)	3.9	EBIT/Interest	(16)	3.2				
	2.3		.2		1.8		-.4					
						Net Profit + Depr., Dep., Amort./Cur. Mat. L/T/D						
	.7		.8		1.3		1.3					
	2.0		-12.6		NM	Fixed/Worth	-1.7					
	-11.4		-.6		-.4		-.4					
	1.3		.9		1.5		1.8					
	3.0		-15.1		NM	Debt/Worth	-7.1					
	-26.9		-3.0		-3.4		-2.5					
	110.8		73.4		65.0	% Profit Before Taxes/Tangible Net Worth						
(29)	52.6	(16)	47.5	(16)	37.2							
	19.3		19.1		13.8							
	31.4		20.7		23.3		25.7					
	16.1		8.3		9.0	% Profit Before Taxes/Total Assets	8.1					
	4.0		-1.4		2.3		-14.5					
	21.1		18.5		17.6		17.6					
	8.0		8.9		10.7	Sales/Net Fixed Assets	12.8					
	3.3		4.5		5.8		9.3					
	3.4		2.8		3.0		2.5					
	2.3		1.7		2.1	Sales/Total Assets	2.1					
	1.5		1.3		1.7		1.7					
	2.1		1.4		1.9		1.8					
(20)	6.9	(25)	2.0	(28)	3.2	% Depr., Dep., Amort./Sales	(18)	2.3				
	13.2		5.0		4.9		4.0					
	3.7					% Officers', Directors' Owners' Comp/Sales						
(18)	5.6											
	7.9											
	1232949M		339690M		135431M	Net Sales ($)	10424M	5316M	6526M	27778M	14764M	70623M
	435086M		177092M		265445M	Total Assets ($)	5390M	2008M	2181M	9829M	10566M	235471M

M = $ thousand   MM = $ million
See Pages 11 through 21 for Explanation of Ratios and Data

Current Data Sorted by Assets   Comparative Historical Data

	0-500M	500M-2MM	2-10MM	10-50MM	50-100MM	100-250MM	Type of Statement	4/1/02-3/31/03 ALL	4/1/03-3/31/04 ALL
							Unqualified	11	10
		1	2	3		2	Reviewed	15	17
	1	8	3				Compiled	9	17
		4	3				Tax Returns	14	15
	4		7	3			Other	24	24
	4		8	7	1				
			6 (4/1-9/30/06)	55 (10/1/06-3/31/07)					
NUMBER OF STATEMENTS	9	13	23	13	1	2		73	83

ASSETS

	0-500M %	500M-2MM %	2-10MM %	10-50MM %	50-100MM %	100-250MM %		ALL %	ALL %
Cash & Equivalents		7.5	7.2	5.6				8.1	8.6
Trade Receivables (net)		21.1	24.9	24.9				30.0	27.9
Inventory		9.3	11.0	8.5				11.4	9.1
All Other Current		1.6	.9	2.3				2.8	3.5
Total Current		39.4	44.1	41.3				52.4	49.1
Fixed Assets (net)		51.1	48.9	47.5				40.4	40.4
Intangibles (net)		4.4	2.7	6.2				2.2	1.7
All Other Non-Current		5.0	4.2	5.0				5.1	8.8
Total		100.0	100.0	100.0				100.0	100.0

LIABILITIES

	0-500M	500M-2MM	2-10MM	10-50MM	50-100MM	100-250MM		ALL	ALL
Notes Payable-Short Term		12.1	11.4	9.6				10.2	6.9
Cur. Mat.-L.T.D.		6.8	7.5	7.8				9.2	6.7
Trade Payables		13.7	11.0	8.6				10.4	12.1
Income Taxes Payable		.0	.0	.7				1.2	.7
All Other Current		3.8	6.2	6.4				7.7	7.3
Total Current		36.4	36.1	33.2				38.7	33.8
Long-Term Debt		27.9	27.5	29.5				24.1	29.4
Deferred Taxes		.0	.7	.5				.7	1.2
All Other Non-Current		3.2	3.3	5.1				5.3	7.1
Net Worth		32.5	32.5	31.7				31.2	28.5
Total Liabilties & Net Worth		100.0	100.0	100.0				100.0	100.0

INCOME DATA

	0-500M	500M-2MM	2-10MM	10-50MM	50-100MM	100-250MM		ALL	ALL
Net Sales		100.0	100.0	100.0				100.0	100.0
Gross Profit									
Operating Expenses		91.4	92.0	85.1				90.2	89.0
Operating Profit		8.6	8.0	14.9				9.8	11.0
All Other Expenses (net)		2.0	2.8	3.9				4.2	3.6
Profit Before Taxes		6.5	5.2	10.9				5.5	7.3

RATIOS

	0-500M	500M-2MM	2-10MM	10-50MM	50-100MM	100-250MM		ALL	ALL
Current		1.6	2.2	2.4				2.6	2.5
		1.0	1.3	1.4				1.5	1.4
		.3	.8	.7				1.0	.9
Quick		1.4	1.9	1.4				1.8	1.9
		.6	.9	1.0				1.0	1.1
		.3	.4	.6				.5	.6
Sales/Receivables		0 UND	25 14.6	20 18.2				14 25.5	30 12.1
		23 15.8	66 5.5	68 5.4				57 6.4	51 7.1
		63 5.8	77 4.8	83 4.4				91 4.0	78 4.7
Cost of Sales/Inventory									
Cost of Sales/Payables									
Sales/Working Capital		12.3	7.6	3.5				5.3	4.2
		-294.2	26.6	11.0				10.1	11.4
		-13.3	-15.7	-11.8				NM	-46.8
EBIT/Interest		15.9	6.4	7.4				7.4	10.3
		(10) 3.3	(20) 2.3	(11) 1.8				(61) 2.6	(70) 3.9
		1.2	.6	.5				1.0	1.3
Net Profit + Depr., Dep., Amort./Cur. Mat. L/T/D								6.5	9.7
								(16) 1.6	(19) 2.3
								1.1	1.2
Fixed/Worth		.8	.6	.9				.4	.4
		2.3	1.5	1.5				1.2	1.1
		20.3	3.4	14.4				4.3	5.4
Debt/Worth		.9	.9	1.2				1.0	1.0
		1.8	2.2	2.7				2.2	2.3
		36.6	3.7	24.9				7.4	10.7
% Profit Before Taxes/Tangible Net Worth		99.1	41.7	58.5				35.0	44.7
		(11) 22.3	(21) 18.8	(11) 18.4				(61) 17.8	(69) 24.8
		2.0	-1.0	-4.8				1.7	7.1
% Profit Before Taxes/Total Assets		26.4	13.1	12.0				14.0	16.2
		9.0	4.9	3.6				5.0	6.6
		1.7	-1.1	-1.8				-.3	.9
Sales/Net Fixed Assets		9.8	7.9	5.4				14.2	10.9
		4.8	3.9	2.4				5.0	4.8
		2.8	2.4	1.2				1.5	1.3
Sales/Total Assets		2.8	2.2	1.9				2.2	2.3
		2.2	1.4	1.0				1.6	1.6
		1.8	1.0	.7				.8	.6
% Depr., Dep., Amort./Sales		5.1	4.1	3.9				3.3	1.8
		(12) 7.9	(21) 10.6	6.7				(65) 7.6	(74) 7.3
		15.2	30.6	13.9				23.1	21.3
% Officers', Directors' Owners' Comp/Sales								3.5	3.8
								(25) 7.5	(26) 6.7
								18.1	
Net Sales ($)	4936M	33872M	197405M	354086M	111446M	145526M		1214826M	1856903M
Total Assets ($)	2479M	13186M	109165M	275593M	93303M	215847M		903282M	1277565M

M = $ thousand   MM = $ million
See Pages 11 through 21 for Explanation of Ratios and Data

Comparative Historical Data / Current Data Sorted by Sales

		Comparative Historical Data				Current Data Sorted by Sales				
	4/1/04-3/31/05 ALL	4/1/05-3/31/06 ALL	4/1/06-3/31/07 ALL	Type of Statement	0-1MM	1-3MM	3-5MM	5-10MM	10-25MM	25MM & OVER
	12	6	8	Unqualified			2		2	4
	17	14	12	Reviewed	1	1	2	4	3	2
	9	6	7	Compiled	2	3	1		1	
	5	5	8	Tax Returns	4	2	2			
	23	24	26	Other	5	2	7	4	5	3
					6 (4/1-9/30/06)			55 (10/1/06-3/31/07)		
	66	55	61	NUMBER OF STATEMENTS	12	8	12	9	11	9
	%	%	%	ASSETS	%	%	%	%	%	%
	11.3	7.4	8.1	Cash & Equivalents	10.2		8.2		5.9	
	22.8	25.8	21.5	Trade Receivables (net)	4.7		12.8		27.1	
	8.2	8.4	9.1	Inventory	5.3		12.8		7.1	
	2.9	1.9	2.8	All Other Current	5.9		1.3		3.9	
	45.2	43.5	41.5	Total Current	26.1		35.2		44.0	
	43.9	44.1	47.9	Fixed Assets (net)	61.8		56.2		48.1	
	3.0	5.8	5.5	Intangibles (net)	5.8		1.9		5.5	
	8.0	6.5	5.0	All Other Non-Current	6.2		6.7		2.5	
	100.0	100.0	100.0	Total	100.0		100.0		100.0	
				LIABILITIES						
	9.5	9.4	11.0	Notes Payable-Short Term	8.8		14.4		10.4	
	8.8	8.3	6.8	Cur. Mat.-L.T.D.	3.0		5.1		12.4	
	8.2	10.6	10.0	Trade Payables	3.3		10.7		12.2	
	.7	.7	.2	Income Taxes Payable	.0		.0		.8	
	7.1	6.3	6.4	All Other Current	5.5		5.6		3.8	
	34.3	35.4	34.3	Total Current	20.7		35.8		39.7	
	27.9	24.8	32.1	Long-Term Debt	52.7		26.8		27.0	
	1.0	.9	.4	Deferred Taxes	.0		.5		1.0	
	5.0	4.8	3.5	All Other Non-Current	1.8		1.7		.6	
	31.9	34.1	29.7	Net Worth	24.8		35.1		31.7	
	100.0	100.0	100.0	Total Liabilties & Net Worth	100.0		100.0		100.0	
				INCOME DATA						
	100.0	100.0	100.0	Net Sales	100.0		100.0		100.0	
				Gross Profit						
	85.1	87.6	90.1	Operating Expenses	98.4		83.0		88.8	
	14.9	12.4	9.9	Operating Profit	1.6		17.0		11.2	
	4.1	3.3	2.9	All Other Expenses (net)	2.1		4.5		4.2	
	10.7	9.1	7.0	Profit Before Taxes	-.5		12.5		7.0	
				RATIOS						
	2.9	2.0	1.9	Current	5.0		1.7		2.2	
	1.5	1.2	1.2		.9		1.1		1.0	
	.8	.8	.7		.6		.3		.6	
	2.2	1.6	1.5	Quick	3.3		1.3		1.5	
	1.2	1.0	.9		.6		.6		.6	
	.5	.5	.5		.2		.3		.4	
0	UND	29 12.4	2 182.2	Sales/Receivables	0 UND		0 UND		42 8.6	
46	8.0	54 6.7	45 8.1		0 UND		23 15.8		68 5.4	
66	5.5	77 4.7	72 5.1		18 19.8		66 5.5		84 4.3	
				Cost of Sales/Inventory						
				Cost of Sales/Payables						
	5.8	5.5	5.2	Sales/Working Capital	6.0		4.1		3.4	
	16.3	16.1	53.8		-33.0		NM		-999.8	
	-16.4	-17.3	-17.5		-18.3		-10.9		-6.2	
	11.1	8.8	7.4	EBIT/Interest			8.0			
(61)	4.6	(49) 3.7	(51) 2.7				(11) 3.3			
	1.7	1.5	.5				1.8			
	4.5	4.3	3.0	Net Profit + Depr., Dep., Amort./Cur. Mat. L/T/D						
(17)	2.4	(15) 2.6	(14) 1.6							
	1.3	1.2	.8							
	.5	.7	.8	Fixed/Worth	.7		.9		.9	
	1.4	1.3	1.5		3.1		2.0		1.6	
	6.0	4.3	4.9		NM		4.2		5.6	
	.9	.9	1.0	Debt/Worth	.4		1.1		1.5	
	2.3	2.1	2.3		2.6		2.0		2.6	
	8.2	5.6	7.0		NM		4.8		6.1	
	69.7	58.4	49.5	% Profit Before Taxes/Tangible Net Worth			44.4		51.8	
(56)	34.8	(48) 20.5	(51) 18.8				21.3		(10) 20.5	
	14.9	6.3	2.0				17.1		-21.6	
	23.3	15.4	13.8	% Profit Before Taxes/Total Assets	6.4		15.6		13.9	
	9.6	5.9	5.0		-3.1		8.7		5.0	
	2.0	1.4	-1.6		-12.9		2.4		-2.8	
	9.4	7.6	7.7	Sales/Net Fixed Assets	16.5		8.6		6.0	
	4.0	4.6	4.2		1.2		2.7		3.1	
	1.4	2.0	1.9		.2		.7		1.8	
	2.4	2.3	2.2	Sales/Total Assets	1.9		2.4		2.1	
	1.7	1.6	1.7		1.0		1.3		1.7	
	.8	1.0	1.0		.2		.6		1.0	
	4.9	4.8	3.9	% Depr., Dep., Amort./Sales			4.7		4.8	
(55)	9.1	(49) 7.3	(53) 6.9				(11) 6.9		6.4	
	19.2	13.5	15.4				46.1		16.6	
	2.4	5.0	3.9	% Officers', Directors' Owners' Comp/Sales						
(21)	4.7	(22) 7.4	(18) 8.7							
	14.6	15.8	17.9							
	1771352M	674553M	847271M	Net Sales ($)	5353M	14222M	43113M	58899M	167204M	558480M
	741848M	605191M	709573M	Total Assets ($)	11579M	9881M	60269M	35113M	222134M	370597M

Current Data Sorted by Assets   Comparative Historical Data

	0-500M	500M-2MM	2-10MM	10-50MM	50-100MM	100-250MM	Type of Statement	4/1/02-3/31/03 ALL	4/1/03-3/31/04 ALL
							Unqualified		
	1	10	2	2			Reviewed	2	4
	2	2	1				Compiled	3	6
	2	4	2	4			Tax Returns	5	4
			2				Other	3	5
		9 (4/1-9/30/06)		25 (10/1/06-3/31/07)					
NUMBER OF STATEMENTS	5	16	7	6				13	19
	%	%	%	%	%	%	ASSETS	%	%
		7.3			DATA	DATA	Cash & Equivalents	12.8	8.2
		9.1			NOT	NOT	Trade Receivables (net)	19.7	23.3
		18.8			AVAILABLE	AVAILABLE	Inventory	5.5	6.3
		3.7					All Other Current	2.2	1.2
		39.0					Total Current	40.2	39.0
		53.3					Fixed Assets (net)	52.3	54.4
		3.1					Intangibles (net)	2.7	.9
		4.6					All Other Non-Current	4.8	5.8
		100.0					Total	100.0	100.0
							LIABILITIES		
		19.2					Notes Payable-Short Term	18.6	17.0
		8.6					Cur. Mat.-L.T.D.	8.1	9.9
		7.8					Trade Payables	7.4	8.5
		.0					Income Taxes Payable	.0	.1
		10.9					All Other Current	11.2	6.3
		46.5					Total Current	45.3	41.9
		26.5					Long-Term Debt	19.6	16.6
		.1					Deferred Taxes	.0	1.2
		21.9					All Other Non-Current	8.6	14.8
		5.0					Net Worth	26.5	25.5
		100.0					Total Liabilties & Net Worth	100.0	100.0
							INCOME DATA		
		100.0					Net Sales	100.0	100.0
							Gross Profit		
		98.1					Operating Expenses	95.6	89.6
		1.9					Operating Profit	4.4	10.4
		4.5					All Other Expenses (net)	2.7	5.3
		-2.6					Profit Before Taxes	1.7	5.1
							RATIOS		
		1.6						1.8	2.0
		.8					Current	1.1	1.0
		.3						.4	.4
		.5						1.4	1.7
	(15)	.4					Quick	.9	.7
		.2						.2	.2
	0	UND						5 66.5	5 70.6
	8	44.0					Sales/Receivables	25 14.9	23 15.8
	36	10.3						63 5.8	40 9.1
							Cost of Sales/Inventory		
							Cost of Sales/Payables		
		20.4						9.5	9.1
		-25.9					Sales/Working Capital	50.1	-93.6
		-2.8						-3.3	-5.1
		3.0						2.8	9.1
	(14)	1.2					EBIT/Interest	(12) 1.6	(15) 2.4
		-.4						.5	-.3
							Net Profit + Depr., Dep., Amort./Cur. Mat. L/T/D		
		1.7						.8	.6
		5.1					Fixed/Worth	1.9	1.3
		-5.2						66.8	5.5
		1.3						1.1	.9
		6.0					Debt/Worth	2.7	1.7
		-14.3						85.6	26.8
								209.1	65.4
							% Profit Before Taxes/Tangible Net Worth	(11) 6.0	(17) 11.9
								1.0	-3.5
		4.7						7.7	19.1
		.8					% Profit Before Taxes/Total Assets	2.0	4.0
		-6.2						-.3	-3.4
		12.4						6.0	16.2
		3.0					Sales/Net Fixed Assets	5.0	2.7
		.7						1.9	1.8
		2.5						2.8	2.9
		1.4					Sales/Total Assets	2.2	1.6
		.6						1.1	1.1
		4.9						3.5	2.0
	(12)	10.0					% Depr., Dep., Amort./Sales	8.0	(17) 15.3
		51.5						29.9	35.2
							% Officers', Directors' Owners' Comp/Sales		
	11393M	26137M	65717M	220690M			Net Sales ($)	38070M	152004M
	1575M	16113M	35405M	174872M			Total Assets ($)	24228M	68636M

© RMA 2007

M = $ thousand   MM = $ million

See Pages 11 through 21 for Explanation of Ratios and Data

Comparative Historical Data / Current Data Sorted by Sales

Type of Statement	4/1/04-3/31/05 ALL	4/1/05-3/31/06 ALL	4/1/06-3/31/07 ALL	0-1MM	1-3MM	3-5MM	5-10MM	10-25MM	25MM & OVER
Unqualified		1	2						
Reviewed	6	4	2					2	2
Compiled	6	10	12	4	4	3	1		2
Tax Returns	4	8	6	4		1		1	
Other	8	7	12	2	3	1	1	3	2
	4/1/04-3/31/05 ALL	4/1/05-3/31/06 ALL	4/1/06-3/31/07 ALL	\	9 (4/1-9/30/06)			25 (10/1/06-3/31/07)	
NUMBER OF STATEMENTS	24	30	34	10	7	5	2	6	4

	%	%	%	%	%	%	%	%	%
ASSETS									
Cash & Equivalents	9.1	9.2	9.7	9.2					
Trade Receivables (net)	19.1	10.6	12.2	2.4					
Inventory	12.2	8.6	16.0	11.5					
All Other Current	2.2	1.2	3.4	5.1					
Total Current	42.6	29.6	41.3	28.2					
Fixed Assets (net)	45.9	62.4	50.3	70.4					
Intangibles (net)	7.2	2.9	3.3	.7					
All Other Non-Current	4.4	5.1	5.2	.7					
Total	100.0	100.0	100.0	100.0					
LIABILITIES									
Notes Payable-Short Term	31.9	18.8	19.8	3.1					
Cur. Mat.-L.T.D.	15.6	6.4	9.0	12.9					
Trade Payables	15.0	6.8	8.9	3.0					
Income Taxes Payable	.1	.1	.0	.0					
All Other Current	7.2	5.0	13.7	1.5					
Total Current	70.0	37.0	51.4	20.5					
Long-Term Debt	25.3	27.3	23.9	43.0					
Deferred Taxes	.4	.5	.2	.0					
All Other Non-Current	8.3	11.8	11.2	13.7					
Net Worth	-4.0	23.5	13.3	22.9					
Total Liabilities & Net Worth	100.0	100.0	100.0	100.0					
INCOME DATA									
Net Sales	100.0	100.0	100.0	100.0					
Gross Profit									
Operating Expenses	93.0	87.1	96.8	92.6					
Operating Profit	7.0	12.9	3.2	7.4					
All Other Expenses (net)	1.2	5.4	3.0	6.7					
Profit Before Taxes	5.9	7.5	.3	.7					
RATIOS									
Current	1.4	1.4	1.3	4.8					
	1.1	.7	.7	1.3					
	.3	.3	.4	.3					
Quick	1.2	1.1	.8	2.0					
	.5	.4	(33) .4	.4					
	.2	.2	.2	.2					
Sales/Receivables	7 49.6	0 UND	0 UND	0 UND					
	30 12.0	17 21.4	10 37.3	0 UND					
	44 8.3	33 11.0	35 10.4	11 32.8					
Cost of Sales/Inventory									
Cost of Sales/Payables									
Sales/Working Capital	12.8	21.4	14.8	3.9					
	NM	-24.0	-25.6	NM					
	-5.5	-2.6	-5.7	-1.7					
EBIT/Interest	7.0	3.4	4.8	5.1					
	(22) 3.1	(24) 2.0	(31) 2.0	1.7					
	-.3	-.5	.3	-2.2					
Net Profit + Depr., Dep., Amort./Cur. Mat. L/T/D									
Fixed/Worth	1.0	1.0	1.5	1.8					
	1.5	2.3	3.0	3.1					
	NM	31.1	-9.6	-72.8					
Debt/Worth	1.2	.9	1.6	1.4					
	2.5	1.8	4.9	3.4					
	NM	49.1	-89.4	-130.1					
% Profit Before Taxes/Tangible Net Worth	31.9	36.1	37.6						
	(18) 20.9	(24) 8.0	(24) 12.9						
	8.7	-.5	-5.5						
% Profit Before Taxes/Total Assets	11.2	10.5	6.8	8.0					
	6.1	3.6	2.3	2.3					
	-2.3	-5.5	-2.9	-4.6					
Sales/Net Fixed Assets	11.9	5.2	9.6	4.6					
	4.9	2.5	3.4	1.4					
	1.8	.7	1.5	.3					
Sales/Total Assets	2.8	2.3	2.7	1.5					
	1.6	1.6	1.5	.8					
	1.1	.6	.9	.3					
% Depr., Dep., Amort./Sales	5.4	5.1	4.9						
	(18) 11.8	(25) 12.5	(26) 10.1						
	20.0	24.8	17.8						
% Officers', Directors' Owners' Comp/Sales		3.9	2.7						
		(10) 6.6	(15) 7.6						
		11.6	15.4						
Net Sales ($)	994357M	215595M	323937M	5604M	11153M	16717M	14311M	91072M	185080M
Total Assets ($)	245739M	152819M	227965M	7330M	5871M	12520M	2010M	73318M	126916M

M = $ thousand   MM = $ million
See Pages 11 through 21 for Explanation of Ratios and Data

Current Data Sorted by Assets   Comparative Historical Data

	0-500M	500M-2MM	2-10MM	10-50MM	50-100MM	100-250MM		4/1/02-3/31/03 ALL	4/1/03-3/31/04 ALL
		22 (4/1-9/30/06)		121 (10/1/06-3/31/07)			**Type of Statement**		
			1	5		4	Unqualified		
	1	3	7	3	2	1	Reviewed	3	4
	4	10	6				Compiled	3	7
	17	13	4	1			Tax Returns	4	14
	9	23	17	7	5		Other	6	7
	31	49	35	16	7	5	**NUMBER OF STATEMENTS**	16	32
	%	%	%	%	%	%	**ASSETS**	%	%
	11.8	8.5	5.4	5.3			Cash & Equivalents	4.1	4.8
	7.8	8.4	7.0	7.6			Trade Receivables (net)	10.4	10.0
	7.2	6.1	14.7	15.3			Inventory	16.2	10.3
	4.5	2.0	4.6	4.9			All Other Current	1.0	1.8
	31.3	25.0	31.8	33.0			Total Current	31.7	26.8
	62.2	69.5	59.1	36.7			Fixed Assets (net)	57.4	63.7
	4.1	2.2	2.3	5.7			Intangibles (net)	3.9	4.1
	2.4	3.3	6.8	24.5			All Other Non-Current	7.1	5.3
	100.0	100.0	100.0	100.0			Total	100.0	100.0
							LIABILITIES		
	12.5	6.1	11.3	20.8			Notes Payable-Short Term	22.2	11.7
	10.7	10.2	12.0	6.6			Cur. Mat.-L.T.D.	15.6	7.1
	3.9	5.9	4.5	3.4			Trade Payables	4.2	7.0
	.2	.1	.3	.3			Income Taxes Payable	.0	.0
	17.2	4.7	3.8	5.2			All Other Current	3.9	3.9
	44.5	27.0	32.0	36.4			Total Current	45.9	29.7
	24.7	40.7	34.3	32.4			Long-Term Debt	25.0	46.5
	.0	.0	.6	2.0			Deferred Taxes	.1	.3
	13.5	14.5	6.4	1.2			All Other Non-Current	13.3	9.9
	17.2	17.8	26.7	27.9			Net Worth	15.7	13.6
	100.0	100.0	100.0	100.0			Total Liabilities & Net Worth	100.0	100.0
							INCOME DATA		
	100.0	100.0	100.0	100.0			Net Sales	100.0	100.0
							Gross Profit		
	87.8	83.0	84.1	79.7			Operating Expenses	93.7	91.8
	12.2	17.0	15.9	20.3			Operating Profit	6.3	8.2
	4.1	5.4	4.4	9.6			All Other Expenses (net)	4.2	4.5
	8.1	11.7	11.4	10.7			Profit Before Taxes	2.1	3.7
							RATIOS		
	2.2	2.0	2.0	1.6				1.6	1.5
	.3	1.0	.8	1.2			Current	.7	.9
	.2	.3	.4	.6				.2	.5
	1.4	1.5	.8	1.0				.6	.8
	.2	.7	(34) .4	.4			Quick	.2	.5
	.1	.2	.0	.1				.1	.1
	0 UND	0 UND	0 999.8	0 UND				0 UND	0 UND
	6 59.8	12 30.9	13 28.9	24 15.4			Sales/Receivables	7 50.6	19 19.1
	18 20.4	29 12.6	31 11.6	37 9.8				41 8.9	47 7.8
							Cost of Sales/Inventory		
							Cost of Sales/Payables		
	17.8	8.8	6.3	6.8				NM	14.4
	-12.7	999.8	-39.2	32.3			Sales/Working Capital	-13.7	-24.5
	-2.8	-9.4	-5.3	-3.0				-4.5	-7.5
	11.3	5.3	4.8	3.7				7.7	4.6
	(24) 3.9	(44) 3.1	(33) 2.6	(11) 2.8			EBIT/Interest	(15) 2.8	(30) 2.1
	-.5	.6	1.8	1.1				-1.2	-1.4
							Net Profit + Depr., Dep., Amort./Cur. Mat. L/T/D		
	1.1	1.8	.9	.1				1.1	1.4
	3.4	4.3	1.9	1.3			Fixed/Worth	2.8	5.6
	-3.0	NM	-309.1	5.8				143.7	196.2
	.5	1.8	1.1	1.6				.5	1.0
	4.7	4.6	2.9	5.3			Debt/Worth	3.4	5.8
	-4.1	NM	-399.1	8.2				345.8	315.9
	178.9	102.1	36.7	31.6				37.1	74.5
	(19) 38.1	(37) 34.1	(26) 18.5	(14) 21.9			% Profit Before Taxes/Tangible Net Worth	(13) 8.3	(25) 25.4
	.0	13.2	9.2	12.0				-49.0	-3.3
	29.3	16.1	13.4	8.3				8.7	9.1
	13.5	7.6	6.7	3.3			% Profit Before Taxes/Total Assets	2.6	4.1
	-7.6	.9	3.0	1.8				-11.6	-10.4
	7.1	2.9	10.2	25.3				9.2	3.8
	4.1	2.1	2.1	3.9			Sales/Net Fixed Assets	2.6	2.0
	2.4	1.0	.7	1.5				1.4	1.1
	3.8	1.8	1.9	1.2				2.5	2.3
	2.3	1.3	1.3	.6			Sales/Total Assets	1.4	1.1
	1.3	.7	.6	.2				1.0	.9
	4.0	9.7	3.7	.5				2.2	9.3
	(27) 8.3	(48) 16.6	(28) 16.3	(13) 11.9			% Depr., Dep., Amort./Sales	(15) 6.4	15.2
	21.3	25.7	35.4	19.6				20.7	21.0
	3.2	2.3							3.2
	(11) 8.8	(22) 5.2					% Officers', Directors' Owners' Comp/Sales		(13) 6.3
	23.7	6.3							8.9
	19759M	68063M	200813M	302757M	360011M	753521M	Net Sales ($)	133971M	143433M
	8151M	51372M	140117M	378796M	488623M	741538M	Total Assets ($)	119493M	144675M

M = $ thousand   MM = $ million
See Pages 11 through 21 for Explanation of Ratios and Data

Comparative Historical Data

Current Data Sorted by Sales

			Type of Statement	0-1MM	1-3MM	3-5MM	5-10MM	10-25MM	25MM & OVER
4	4	10	Unqualified				3	3	4
5	6	17	Reviewed	2	5	1	3	3	3
8	14	20	Compiled	8	5	2	4	1	
14	17	35	Tax Returns	20	11	2	1		1
10	15	61	Other	22	19	3	5	6	6
4/1/04-3/31/05 ALL	4/1/05-3/31/06 ALL	4/1/06-3/31/07 ALL		22 (4/1-9/30/06)			121 (10/1/06-3/31/07)		
41	56	143	NUMBER OF STATEMENTS	52	40	8	16	13	14
%	%	%	ASSETS	%	%	%	%	%	%
8.5	9.0	7.6	Cash & Equivalents	7.8	9.3		8.5	6.8	2.0
9.9	5.7	8.4	Trade Receivables (net)	5.5	9.4		7.4	12.3	13.2
10.5	9.1	9.0	Inventory	6.1	6.6		19.8	11.4	9.9
1.5	1.9	3.5	All Other Current	5.0	3.3		1.2	4.7	2.0
30.4	25.8	28.5	Total Current	24.4	28.6		36.9	35.2	27.2
59.1	67.0	60.6	Fixed Assets (net)	68.3	66.0		44.8	36.9	58.9
1.7	1.6	3.3	Intangibles (net)	3.2	1.6		2.5	9.3	5.8
8.8	5.7	7.5	All Other Non-Current	4.1	3.8		15.8	18.6	8.1
100.0	100.0	100.0	Total	100.0	100.0		100.0	100.0	100.0
			LIABILITIES						
11.6	13.0	10.8	Notes Payable-Short Term	10.3	5.9		13.0	18.2	18.6
8.6	8.2	9.7	Cur. Mat.-L.T.D.	8.7	12.7		8.3	12.1	4.9
7.3	5.3	4.6	Trade Payables	4.6	4.7		5.6	3.8	5.3
.3	.1	.2	Income Taxes Payable	.2	.1		.6	.4	.0
7.5	6.5	7.2	All Other Current	8.9	7.6		4.2	6.6	6.2
35.2	33.1	32.7	Total Current	32.8	30.8		31.6	41.1	35.0
42.2	39.1	34.7	Long-Term Debt	34.1	36.7		35.2	21.6	34.4
.2	.4	.5	Deferred Taxes	.2	.1		.6	2.5	.9
3.4	6.2	9.7	All Other Non-Current	15.8	9.3		5.9	4.2	1.7
19.0	21.2	22.4	Net Worth	17.2	23.1		26.8	30.6	28.1
100.0	100.0	100.0	Total Liabilities & Net Worth	100.0	100.0		100.0	100.0	100.0
			INCOME DATA						
100.0	100.0	100.0	Net Sales	100.0	100.0		100.0	100.0	100.0
			Gross Profit						
92.3	84.8	84.4	Operating Expenses	79.6	83.9		91.4	85.9	92.0
7.7	15.2	15.6	Operating Profit	20.4	16.1		8.6	14.1	8.0
4.3	6.4	5.5	All Other Expenses (net)	7.6	4.9		2.3	5.9	4.9
3.4	8.8	10.1	Profit Before Taxes	12.9	11.2		6.3	8.1	3.1
			RATIOS						
1.8	1.9	1.8	Current	2.0	2.2		3.0	1.7	1.2
1.0	1.0	1.0		.7	.9		.9	1.2	1.0
.3	.3	.3		.1	.4		.7	.4	.6
1.3	1.4	1.1	Quick	1.3	1.3		1.0	1.3	1.0
.6	.7	(142) .6		.2	.6	(15)	.7	.5	.7
.2	.2	.1		.1	.2		.3	.1	.3
0 UND	0 UND	0 UND	Sales/Receivables	0 UND	0 UND		0 760.7	1 277.1	17 21.0
16 22.5	4 98.9	14 26.9		8 46.0	8 43.0		14 27.0	27 13.7	38 9.6
32 11.3	24 15.5	33 11.0		29 12.6	24 14.9		27 13.7	56 6.5	54 6.7
			Cost of Sales/Inventory						
			Cost of Sales/Payables						
12.5	8.7	8.9	Sales/Working Capital	6.6	9.6		5.5	4.9	18.0
566.0	UND	-302.6		-33.0	-102.1		NM	40.6	NM
-6.3	-6.4	-4.3		-2.3	-6.3		-11.0	-2.5	-7.0
6.1	8.1	5.3	EBIT/Interest	6.0	7.9		3.8	5.1	3.8
(37) 1.9	(45) 2.6	(122) 2.8		(40) 2.7	(36) 3.6	(15) 2.2	(10) 2.9		2.0
.6	-.5	1.0		.0	1.4		1.8	1.2	.8
		5.5	Net Profit + Depr., Dep., Amort./Cur. Mat. L/T/D						
		(14) 2.0							
		1.5							
1.0	1.2	1.2	Fixed/Worth	1.5	1.3		.3	.2	1.2
2.1	4.4	2.8		6.2	2.6		1.2	1.4	2.3
19.8	-105.0	-405.5		-8.0	9.1		NM	-2.6	5.9
.9	1.2	1.2	Debt/Worth	1.3	1.0		.9	1.7	1.2
3.3	4.5	4.0		6.5	2.9		2.8	4.8	3.6
27.8	-233.0	-852.0		-11.7	17.0		NM	-12.8	8.3
42.2	45.4	66.4	% Profit Before Taxes/Tangible Net Worth	84.9	140.0		37.8		23.5
(33) 14.8	(41) 16.6	(107) 22.3		(37) 19.6	(31) 32.5	(12) 22.9		(12) 14.1
-5.6	.5	9.8		7.1	12.8		7.5		-.1
10.9	13.7	15.5	% Profit Before Taxes/Total Assets	15.4	24.5		12.7	17.6	9.5
4.6	3.8	6.9		6.0	7.7		6.3	4.9	3.0
-2.1	-2.3	1.1		-2.8	1.7		3.1	2.0	-.9
5.9	4.5	5.7	Sales/Net Fixed Assets	4.1	5.6		21.1	41.4	6.5
3.0	2.3	2.4		1.6	2.5		5.7	3.4	1.5
1.6	1.3	1.1		.5	1.5		1.3	2.1	.8
2.7	2.3	2.2	Sales/Total Assets	2.1	2.3		2.4	2.0	1.7
1.7	1.4	1.3		.9	1.6		1.8	1.1	1.1
.9	.7	.6		.4	1.1		.8	.3	.5
8.0	7.7	7.5	% Depr., Dep., Amort./Sales	8.3	7.5		3.7	1.2	
(35) 10.5	(47) 10.0	(121) 13.2		(47) 18.8	(38) 13.0	(12) 12.5	(12) 11.5	
18.1	17.3	25.6		33.2	19.4		24.8	30.9	
3.5	4.3	1.8	% Officers', Directors' Owners' Comp/Sales	2.9	2.3				
(20) 6.0	(23) 7.8	(46) 4.5		(17) 5.5	(14) 6.0				
8.7	14.6	7.0		14.6	6.8				
252895M	708440M	1704924M	Net Sales ($)	28206M	68874M	29568M	115522M	191024M	1271730M
202415M	426245M	1808597M	Total Assets ($)	40194M	81386M	35147M	167588M	375500M	1108782M

© RMA 2007

M = $ thousand   MM = $ million
See Pages 11 through 21 for Explanation of Ratios and Data

Current Data Sorted by Assets | Comparative Historical Data

Type of Statement

						Type of Statement	2	6
1	1	1	1	4	4	Unqualified	2	6
	2	3	2	1		Reviewed	5	5
	5	3	3			Compiled	8	8
4	2	2			3	Tax Returns	5	2
	8 (4/1-9/30/06)	7	3			Other	4	8
			45 (10/1/06-3/31/07)				4/1/02-3/31/03	4/1/03-3/31/04
0-500M	500M-2MM	2-10MM	10-50MM	50-100MM	100-250MM		ALL	ALL
5	10	16	9	6	7	NUMBER OF STATEMENTS	24	29
%	%	%	%	%	%	**ASSETS**	%	%
	7.1	12.3				Cash & Equivalents	8.4	13.1
	9.4	16.1				Trade Receivables (net)	14.3	11.5
	10.3	2.8				Inventory	1.6	1.2
	8.6	4.7				All Other Current	3.1	4.3
	35.3	35.9				Total Current	27.4	30.1
	63.4	46.7				Fixed Assets (net)	69.4	66.4
	.1	2.5				Intangibles (net)	.3	.1
	1.2	15.0				All Other Non-Current	2.9	3.4
	100.0	100.0				Total	100.0	100.0
						LIABILITIES		
	8.4	3.1				Notes Payable-Short Term	2.9	4.4
	4.8	7.9				Cur. Mat.-L.T.D.	11.0	8.2
	2.0	12.0				Trade Payables	10.4	9.0
	.0	.0				Income Taxes Payable	.4	.4
	4.6	14.4				All Other Current	4.1	4.1
	19.8	37.5				Total Current	28.8	26.1
	68.9	26.4				Long-Term Debt	42.7	39.6
	.4	.2				Deferred Taxes	1.9	1.9
	8.5	2.4				All Other Non-Current	3.0	3.0
	2.3	33.5				Net Worth	23.6	29.3
	100.0	100.0				Total Liabilties & Net Worth	100.0	100.0
						INCOME DATA		
	100.0	100.0				Net Sales	100.0	100.0
						Gross Profit		
	81.6	85.8				Operating Expenses	85.4	82.3
	18.4	14.2				Operating Profit	14.6	17.7
	18.1	6.6				All Other Expenses (net)	4.1	4.8
	.3	7.6				Profit Before Taxes	10.5	12.9
						RATIOS		
	5.1	1.4				Current	1.5	1.6
	1.3	.9					1.0	1.0
	.1	.3					.5	.3
	3.9	1.3				Quick	1.3	1.2
	.7	.5					.7	.8
	.0	.1					.3	.2
	0 UND	0 UND				Sales/Receivables	18 20.2	6 65.9
	0 UND	8 45.3					35 10.3	29 12.8
	27 13.6	45 8.0					60 6.1	52 7.1
						Cost of Sales/Inventory		
						Cost of Sales/Payables		
	1.1	11.1				Sales/Working Capital	9.3	8.3
	21.5	-122.6					NM	-175.7
	-1.8	-7.3					-6.2	-3.0
		16.5				EBIT/Interest	7.8	7.4
	(11)	9.9					(21) 3.5	(22) 3.6
		1.1					.8	1.6
						Net Profit + Depr., Dep., Amort./Cur. Mat. L/T/D		
	.5	.3				Fixed/Worth	1.2	.7
	7.5	1.6					2.1	2.1
	NM	10.3					3.6	4.2
	2.3	.8				Debt/Worth	1.0	1.0
	7.3	2.3					2.3	1.7
	NM	10.2					4.3	6.2
		62.6				% Profit Before Taxes/Tangible Net Worth	65.2	47.6
	(13)	15.3					(20) 23.4	(26) 17.5
		.3					10.3	3.7
	3.4	13.7				% Profit Before Taxes/Total Assets	10.9	11.1
	.6	4.3					6.9	4.0
	-4.6	-.1					-1.6	.0
	5.2	19.9				Sales/Net Fixed Assets	2.0	2.6
	.7	3.9					1.1	.7
	.1	.3					.5	.4
	1.1	3.3				Sales/Total Assets	1.4	1.4
	.3	1.2					.8	.5
	.1	.2					.5	.3
		1.6				% Depr., Dep., Amort./Sales	4.8	5.0
	(12)	9.4					(21) 17.2	(22) 11.3
		48.6					33.5	35.4
						% Officers', Directors' Owners' Comp/Sales		
1099M	6928M	99947M	278168M	163665M	722009M	Net Sales ($)	395243M	357948M
1567M	10635M	58898M	212485M	489719M	1038325M	Total Assets ($)	467615M	614239M

M = $ thousand   MM = $ million
See Pages 11 through 21 for Explanation of Ratios and Data

Comparative Historical Data

Current Data Sorted by Sales

			Type of Statement						
6	8	11	Unqualified	1	1			2	7
4	6	7	Reviewed	3		1	1	2	
10	8	8	Compiled	2			3	2	
5	2	7	Tax Returns	5	1	1			1
7	7	20	Other	8	2	1	1	6	2
4/1/04-3/31/05	4/1/05-3/31/06	4/1/06-3/31/07			8 (4/1-9/30/06)		45 (10/1/06-3/31/07)		
ALL	ALL	ALL		0-1MM	1-3MM	3-5MM	5-10MM	10-25MM	25MM & OVER
32	31	53	NUMBER OF STATEMENTS	19	4	3	5	12	10
%	%	%	ASSETS	%	%	%	%	%	%
11.6	7.0	8.0	Cash & Equivalents	8.5				7.7	4.7
14.8	15.7	14.6	Trade Receivables (net)	7.8				20.6	22.7
2.7	4.2	6.3	Inventory	7.0				.9	7.8
4.1	5.7	4.1	All Other Current	6.0				.4	2.4
33.2	32.5	33.1	Total Current	29.3				29.6	37.6
61.2	55.3	51.0	Fixed Assets (net)	62.2				60.4	41.9
.4	2.6	1.7	Intangibles (net)	2.4				2.9	.4
5.2	9.6	14.2	All Other Non-Current	6.2				7.2	20.0
100.0	100.0	100.0	Total	100.0				100.0	100.0
			LIABILITIES						
5.9	8.9	6.1	Notes Payable-Short Term	6.4				2.2	10.6
5.8	3.6	6.6	Cur. Mat.-L.T.D.	9.9				5.6	4.7
10.2	8.3	7.4	Trade Payables	1.5				12.4	14.5
.0	.2	.1	Income Taxes Payable	.0				.0	.3
5.6	9.3	7.5	All Other Current	4.1				6.9	5.7
27.6	30.3	27.7	Total Current	21.9				27.2	35.8
47.4	32.0	38.8	Long-Term Debt	52.0				36.5	21.0
2.6	2.2	.9	Deferred Taxes	.2				2.2	1.2
7.0	5.5	7.7	All Other Non-Current	9.0				1.1	10.6
15.3	30.0	25.0	Net Worth	16.8				33.0	31.4
100.0	100.0	100.0	Total Liabilities & Net Worth	100.0				100.0	100.0
			INCOME DATA						
100.0	100.0	100.0	Net Sales	100.0				100.0	100.0
			Gross Profit						
90.8	85.4	80.5	Operating Expenses	79.2				73.0	90.8
9.2	14.6	19.5	Operating Profit	20.8				27.0	9.2
5.2	7.7	10.3	All Other Expenses (net)	16.5				8.9	2.3
4.0	6.9	9.2	Profit Before Taxes	4.3				18.1	7.0
			RATIOS						
2.0	2.6	1.7		3.6				1.6	1.6
1.1	1.1	1.1	Current	1.3				1.0	1.2
.3	.4	.4		.2				.4	.9
1.9	1.6	1.4		2.2				1.6	1.4
.8	.7	.7	Quick	.8				.7	.9
.3	.1	.2		.1				.4	.2
8 46.6	12 30.9	0 UND		0 UND				13 28.2	26 14.0
35 10.4	34 10.9	22 16.4	Sales/Receivables	0 UND				52 7.0	43 8.5
69 5.3	71 5.1	68 5.4		39 9.4				84 4.3	74 4.9
			Cost of Sales/Inventory						
			Cost of Sales/Payables						
7.3	6.0	4.6		2.7				12.1	7.3
108.0	116.2	38.3	Sales/Working Capital	9.4				105.5	28.1
-3.9	-4.7	-3.3		-1.8				-4.5	NM
5.2	10.0	9.9							
(26) 1.8	(26) 3.7	(34) 3.1	EBIT/Interest						
.0	1.5	1.4							
			Net Profit + Depr., Dep., Amort./Cur. Mat. L/T/D						
.8	1.1	.7		.2				1.4	.8
2.2	1.9	1.8	Fixed/Worth	3.5				2.1	1.2
6.8	4.4	7.7		-105.2				4.1	2.0
.9	1.1	.9		.6				1.1	.9
2.9	2.3	2.8	Debt/Worth	4.0				1.8	1.8
30.8	11.2	11.4		-114.9				4.4	8.3
40.0	27.2	41.7		18.7				48.3	
(26) 14.4	(27) 13.5	(44) 14.3	% Profit Before Taxes/Tangible Net Worth	(14) 6.5				(11) 17.1	
.9	2.7	4.0		-10.7				8.0	
8.6	11.2	12.1		7.1				21.7	15.0
2.6	4.4	3.5	% Profit Before Taxes/Total Assets	.5				8.1	6.8
-3.6	-.2	.2		-5.0				3.5	3.2
5.5	4.8	10.0		2.9				8.6	10.1
1.0	1.0	1.2	Sales/Net Fixed Assets	.4				.7	2.0
.4	.5	.4		.2				.2	.7
1.4	1.3	1.3		.5				3.1	1.8
.7	.6	.5	Sales/Total Assets	.2				.6	.9
.4	.3	.2		.1				.2	.4
4.5	3.8	2.9		20.2				5.5	
(27) 19.6	(25) 15.3	(42) 16.9	% Depr., Dep., Amort./Sales	(17) 47.5				(11) 14.4	
36.4	27.8	47.8		67.8				32.1	
			% Officers', Directors' Owners' Comp/Sales						
804173M	736198M	1271816M	Net Sales ($)	6293M	7120M	12121M	35476M	189176M	1021630M
901558M	1234151M	1811629M	Total Assets ($)	25221M	38381M	45146M	26702M	545794M	1130385M

M = $ thousand   MM = $ million
See Pages 11 through 21 for Explanation of Ratios and Data

Current Data Sorted by Assets   Comparative Historical Data

0-500M	500M-2MM	2-10MM	10-50MM	50-100MM	100-250MM	Type of Statement	ALL	ALL
2	3	12	30	10	9	Unqualified	37	46
2	8	47	34	2	2	Reviewed	54	69
7	18	23	10			Compiled	54	63
20	18	15	3		1	Tax Returns	24	35
7	22	39	37	5	7	Other	69	79
	65 (4/1-9/30/06)		328 (10/1/06-3/31/07)				4/1/02-3/31/03	4/1/03-3/31/04
38	69	136	114	17	19	NUMBER OF STATEMENTS	238	292
%	%	%	%	%	%	**ASSETS**	%	%
10.7	9.1	6.7	4.9	4.9	4.2	Cash & Equivalents	6.5	7.7
8.0	12.0	16.6	15.4	15.8	16.2	Trade Receivables (net)	16.4	15.7
4.2	5.7	9.6	15.1	5.9	17.5	Inventory	9.1	9.6
8.8	2.7	2.7	2.3	1.9	2.7	All Other Current	2.9	3.3
31.6	29.5	35.6	37.6	28.5	40.6	Total Current	35.0	36.3
62.7	62.5	58.4	55.8	62.4	51.6	Fixed Assets (net)	57.4	55.1
.2	2.0	1.5	1.2	5.6	1.0	Intangibles (net)	1.9	1.3
5.5	6.0	4.5	5.5	3.6	6.9	All Other Non-Current	5.8	7.3
100.0	100.0	100.0	100.0	100.0	100.0	Total	100.0	100.0
						LIABILITIES		
16.8	7.1	10.7	9.7	13.8	8.3	Notes Payable-Short Term	10.9	12.1
20.1	10.6	10.5	10.5	5.1	4.1	Cur. Mat.-L.T.D.	11.6	10.9
5.9	3.6	6.3	5.6	10.5	11.3	Trade Payables	5.9	5.7
.3	.2	.4	.3	.0	.4	Income Taxes Payable	.3	.2
4.3	7.6	5.3	4.4	5.7	7.4	All Other Current	5.5	7.7
47.3	29.1	33.1	30.5	35.0	31.5	Total Current	34.2	36.5
37.8	36.3	31.5	33.5	40.8	33.2	Long-Term Debt	30.6	31.3
.0	.1	1.0	1.7	.5	.6	Deferred Taxes	1.2	.9
10.2	2.5	4.2	2.0	1.8	2.3	All Other Non-Current	3.9	5.0
4.7	32.0	30.1	32.3	21.9	32.4	Net Worth	30.2	26.2
100.0	100.0	100.0	100.0	100.0	100.0	Total Liabilties & Net Worth	100.0	100.0
						INCOME DATA		
100.0	100.0	100.0	100.0	100.0	100.0	Net Sales	100.0	100.0
						Gross Profit		
88.0	82.7	83.7	85.5	82.4	82.9	Operating Expenses	89.9	89.7
12.0	17.3	16.3	14.5	17.6	17.1	Operating Profit	10.1	10.3
3.3	3.2	4.2	2.5	5.1	2.9	All Other Expenses (net)	4.3	3.3
8.6	14.1	12.1	12.0	12.5	14.2	Profit Before Taxes	5.8	7.0
						RATIOS		
2.6	2.1	1.6	1.7	1.8	1.8	Current	1.8	1.8
.6	1.0	1.1	1.2	1.1	1.2		1.1	1.1
.1	.4	.6	.7	.7	.9		.5	.5
1.2	1.6	1.4	1.2	1.6	1.1	Quick	1.3	1.2
.2	.7	.7	.7	.9	.8		.7	.7
.0	.3	.3	.3	.5	.3		.3	.3
0 UND	0 UND	19 19.2	33 11.1	38 9.6	35 10.5	Sales/Receivables	25 14.7	12 30.7
0 UND	30 12.3	44 8.4	56 6.5	62 5.9	43 8.5		48 7.6	45 8.1
33 11.2	54 6.8	69 5.3	69 5.3	67 5.5	79 4.6		72 5.1	68 5.3
						Cost of Sales/Inventory		
						Cost of Sales/Payables		
6.4	8.1	7.1	6.3	8.6	8.1	Sales/Working Capital	6.7	6.6
-10.9	112.6	40.9	19.9	23.7	18.7		51.1	75.9
-2.3	-3.5	-6.1	-10.4	-41.4	-29.4		-6.6	-4.6
5.8	8.0	7.1	5.9	6.5	6.6	EBIT/Interest	3.5	5.3
(34) 2.4	(63) 3.9	(130) 3.3	(106) 3.0	(16) 3.4	(16) 3.6		(216) 2.0	(256) 2.0
.9	1.6	1.5	2.0	1.9	2.2		.6	.6
		3.5	3.2			Net Profit + Depr., Dep., Amort./Cur. Mat. L/T/D	2.0	2.3
		(30) 1.4	(42) 1.3				(67) 1.4	(63) 1.5
		1.2	1.1				.8	1.1
1.0	1.0	1.1	1.0	1.6	.8	Fixed/Worth	1.0	.9
5.8	2.2	2.2	1.9	2.3	1.5		2.0	2.0
-3.2	7.9	4.1	3.5	6.8	2.6		5.5	4.7
1.1	.9	1.6	1.3	1.8	1.4	Debt/Worth	1.2	1.2
6.3	2.3	2.6	2.7	2.7	2.1		2.6	2.4
-4.8	11.6	5.4	5.0	8.0	4.1		7.4	6.8
175.6	65.4	58.6	44.4	48.8	42.9	% Profit Before Taxes/Tangible Net Worth	32.4	30.4
(25) 23.5	(58) 23.8	(125) 29.8	(113) 27.0	(15) 39.1	29.0		(216) 11.8	(252) 14.0
12.0	7.2	10.6	16.0	10.1	18.5		-1.5	.5
16.8	20.0	17.3	13.2	16.6	10.8	% Profit Before Taxes/Total Assets	7.5	9.1
6.7	7.8	7.9	7.4	7.1	7.2		3.1	3.3
-.6	1.2	1.9	3.7	2.3	5.5		-1.5	-1.1
5.4	3.8	3.8	3.7	3.7	8.2	Sales/Net Fixed Assets	4.0	4.7
2.4	1.4	1.6	1.5	1.2	2.0		1.7	1.8
1.2	.7	.7	.9	.8	.7		.8	.8
2.3	1.6	1.6	1.4	1.1	1.6	Sales/Total Assets	1.5	1.6
1.4	1.0	1.0	.9	.8	1.0		1.0	1.0
.8	.5	.5	.7	.5	.5		.6	.6
13.4	9.5	7.4	6.0	3.1		% Depr., Dep., Amort./Sales	7.2	6.3
(30) 33.4	(56) 21.2	(124) 12.6	(101) 10.4	(12) 10.8			(215) 13.8	(254) 14.1
52.5	44.5	28.0	18.8	22.1			28.7	24.2
4.6	3.2	2.7	1.3			% Officers', Directors' Owners' Comp/Sales	2.4	2.3
(10) 12.0	(17) 5.7	(47) 4.7	(21) 5.1				(69) 4.4	(78) 4.6
19.1	9.9	6.2	8.6				10.1	9.4
18971M	88616M	734911M	2934827M	1088760M	3252962M	Net Sales ($)	3640683M	4330117M
9636M	81686M	670663M	2823192M	1179207M	2949779M	Total Assets ($)	4216745M	4746214M

© RMA 2007

M = $ thousand   MM = $ million
See Pages 11 through 21 for Explanation of Ratios and Data

Comparative Historical Data / Current Data Sorted by Sales

				Type of Statement						
45	48		66	Unqualified	3	5	4	6	14	34
79	63		95	Reviewed	9	14	11	19	24	18
52	67		58	Compiled	17	16	8	9	5	3
40	41		57	Tax Returns	30	11	8	4	3	1
80	117		117	Other	22	19	12	16	24	24
4/1/04-3/31/05 ALL	4/1/05-3/31/06 ALL		4/1/06-3/31/07 ALL		65 (4/1-9/30/06)			328 (10/1/06-3/31/07)		
					0-1MM	1-3MM	3-5MM	5-10MM	10-25MM	25MM & OVER
296	336		393	NUMBER OF STATEMENTS	81	65	43	54	70	80
%	%		%	**ASSETS**	%	%	%	%	%	%
6.9	8.1		6.8	Cash & Equivalents	7.6	9.6	7.4	6.2	5.5	4.8
16.2	15.2		14.5	Trade Receivables (net)	6.2	15.3	12.3	17.4	18.3	18.4
10.0	11.3		10.2	Inventory	2.5	5.6	7.6	13.0	14.1	17.8
2.1	1.8		3.1	All Other Current	6.4	2.2	4.5	1.1	1.9	2.4
35.1	36.5		34.7	Total Current	22.7	32.7	31.7	37.6	39.8	43.4
56.1	56.3		58.6	Fixed Assets (net)	70.6	61.2	61.3	53.1	55.6	49.3
1.3	1.7		1.5	Intangibles (net)	.7	1.7	1.1	3.3	.9	1.8
7.5	5.5		5.2	All Other Non-Current	6.0	4.4	5.9	6.0	3.8	5.5
100.0	100.0		100.0	Total	100.0	100.0	100.0	100.0	100.0	100.0
				LIABILITIES						
10.1	10.6		10.4	Notes Payable-Short Term	9.1	8.7	10.1	10.3	11.0	12.6
8.9	8.9		10.9	Cur. Mat.-L.T.D.	16.9	10.0	12.4	9.2	9.6	6.9
6.9	6.7		6.0	Trade Payables	3.5	4.3	5.4	5.4	7.7	9.2
.3	.4		.3	Income Taxes Payable	.2	.3	.1	.6	.4	.2
6.4	5.2		5.5	All Other Current	4.8	7.0	4.4	6.2	4.3	6.1
32.6	31.7		33.0	Total Current	34.4	30.4	32.5	31.8	33.0	35.1
33.3	34.4		34.0	Long-Term Debt	40.5	37.3	34.4	29.5	30.5	30.7
1.2	1.0		.9	Deferred Taxes	.2	.6	1.0	1.3	2.0	.6
4.1	3.1		3.6	All Other Non-Current	5.7	2.6	1.5	6.3	2.0	3.2
28.8	29.7		28.4	Net Worth	19.2	29.1	30.6	31.1	32.6	30.4
100.0	100.0		100.0	Total Liabilities & Net Worth	100.0	100.0	100.0	100.0	100.0	100.0
				INCOME DATA						
100.0	100.0		100.0	Net Sales	100.0	100.0	100.0	100.0	100.0	100.0
				Gross Profit						
88.7	84.4		84.4	Operating Expenses	78.4	82.1	84.4	87.9	86.9	87.6
11.3	15.6		15.6	Operating Profit	21.6	17.9	15.6	12.1	13.1	12.4
2.5	3.1		3.4	All Other Expenses (net)	5.2	5.8	3.5	1.1	2.1	2.5
8.7	12.5		12.2	Profit Before Taxes	16.4	12.2	12.1	11.0	10.9	9.9
				RATIOS						
1.8	2.0		1.8		1.7	2.1	1.6	1.8	1.7	1.8
1.1	1.3		1.1	Current	.5	1.1	.9	1.3	1.2	1.3
.6	.6		.6		.2	.5	.6	.7	.7	.9
1.4	1.5		1.4		.9	1.7	1.5	1.4	1.3	1.3
.8	.8		.7	Quick	.3	.8	.6	.8	.8	.8
.3	.3		.3		.1	.3	.3	.3	.5	.3
20 18.0	8 45.1	17	21.0		0 UND	5 73.3	26 14.3	31 11.8	36 10.1	33 11.0
49 7.4	43 8.5	42	8.7	Sales/Receivables	0 UND	41 9.0	38 9.6	52 7.0	64 5.7	46 8.0
73 5.0	73 5.0	66	5.6		34 10.8	67 5.5	56 6.6	69 5.3	82 4.4	68 5.3
				Cost of Sales/Inventory						
				Cost of Sales/Payables						
6.2	6.1		7.0		7.0	7.0	7.5	6.9	6.9	6.9
30.5	21.2		50.5	Sales/Working Capital	-6.3	57.3	-27.1	20.2	27.2	13.7
-8.0	-7.5		-6.2		-1.9	-5.9	-4.3	-11.3	-11.1	-42.5
6.4	6.9		6.6		6.4	7.1	5.5	7.4	9.4	5.8
(257) 2.7	(300) 3.4	(365)	3.3	EBIT/Interest	(72) 3.6	(59) 2.5	(41) 2.6	3.4	(66) 3.5	(73) 3.1
1.2	2.1		1.7		1.3	1.1	1.2	1.8	2.0	2.0
2.4	2.6		3.5	Net Profit + Depr., Dep.,			3.5	2.0	4.2	3.7
(69) 1.5	(69) 1.8	(89)	1.5	Amort./Cur. Mat. L/T/D		(10) 1.3	(15) 1.4	(24) 1.2	(24) 2.8
.9	1.1		1.1				1.0	1.1	.9	1.3
.9	1.0		1.1		1.5	1.0	1.6	1.0	.8	1.5
2.1	1.9		2.1	Fixed/Worth	3.2	2.1	2.3	2.1	2.0	1.8
5.3	4.2		4.7		42.7	6.9	4.7	4.2	3.5	2.9
1.3	1.2		1.3		1.1	1.1	1.6	1.3	1.2	1.6
2.6	2.3		2.6	Debt/Worth	3.1	2.5	3.0	2.8	2.5	2.4
6.5	6.0		6.2		42.4	7.7	6.1	5.1	5.3	4.5
37.4	45.3		51.8	% Profit Before Taxes/Tangible	71.6	65.5	54.5	65.0	51.8	42.9
(259) 19.6	(295) 26.2	(355)	27.2	Net Worth	(64) 27.6	(53) 23.9	(41) 24.0	(49) 34.1	29.2	(78) 29.2
5.5	11.8		12.5		11.1	7.1	4.6	15.3	18.0	13.0
11.6	14.8		15.3	% Profit Before Taxes/Total	17.3	18.8	13.7	17.8	15.1	12.8
4.5	7.9		7.3	Assets	7.1	5.7	6.7	8.3	8.4	6.9
.8	2.4		2.5		1.2	-.2	1.0	3.3	4.1	3.0
5.2	4.8		4.1		2.3	4.2	3.1	4.3	5.8	7.7
2.0	1.6		1.6	Sales/Net Fixed Assets	1.1	1.2	1.6	2.1	1.5	2.6
.8	.8		.8		.4	.6	.9	1.1	.9	1.2
1.6	1.6		1.5		1.3	1.6	1.6	1.6	1.4	1.7
1.0	1.0		1.0	Sales/Total Assets	.6	.8	1.0	1.2	1.0	1.2
.6	.5		.6		.3	.4	.7	.7	.7	.8
5.9	5.3		6.7		21.0	9.3	8.3	5.9	5.8	2.6
(254) 12.9	(288) 12.7	(327)	13.5	% Depr., Dep., Amort./Sales	(66) 41.2	(57) 22.9	(38) 14.2	(50) 10.6	(61) 10.8	(55) 6.5
24.1	28.5		28.0		54.7	43.5	23.0	16.6	18.4	10.8
1.9	1.7		2.4		4.2	4.6	2.7	2.9	1.4	.9
(74) 3.7	(80) 4.6	(99)	5.1	% Officers', Directors'	(11) 15.4	(22) 6.2	(21) 4.6	(20) 5.0	(12) 2.1	(13) 1.8
8.6	7.9		8.7	Owners' Comp/Sales	21.7	11.1	6.1	6.4	8.2	5.9
4523285M	5737614M		8119047M	Net Sales ($)	40782M	118486M	170215M	369948M	1111978M	6307638M
4547909M	5345099M		7714163M	Total Assets ($)	77528M	182589M	231846M	416853M	1263558M	5541789M

M = $ thousand   MM = $ million
See Pages 11 through 21 for Explanation of Ratios and Data

REAL ESTATE—Office Machinery and Equipment Rental and Leasing NAICS 532420 (SIC 7359, 7377)

Current Data Sorted by Assets | Comparative Historical Data

Type of Statement	0-500M	500M-2MM	2-10MM	10-50MM	50-100MM	100-250MM		4/1/02-3/31/03 ALL	4/1/03-3/31/04 ALL
Unqualified			3	10	4	5		12	14
Reviewed		1	5	2				9	9
Compiled	4	8	6					4	15
Tax Returns	8	10	10	1				5	11
Other	1	13	17	4	4	1		18	20
	13 (4/1-9/30/06)			104 (10/1/06-3/31/07)					
NUMBER OF STATEMENTS	13	32	41	17	8	6		48	69

ASSETS	%	%	%	%	%	%		%	%
Cash & Equivalents	14.7	9.2	4.5	9.7				9.4	6.6
Trade Receivables (net)	15.5	19.2	12.9	21.4				21.8	18.2
Inventory	11.5	6.6	11.0	6.4				5.1	5.7
All Other Current	2.3	2.8	6.3	10.5				3.1	8.3
Total Current	44.0	37.8	34.8	48.0				39.4	38.8
Fixed Assets (net)	44.7	53.9	42.3	37.8				43.3	43.6
Intangibles (net)	2.6	2.3	1.1	1.3				1.5	1.9
All Other Non-Current	8.7	6.0	21.8	12.9				15.8	15.7
Total	100.0	100.0	100.0	100.0				100.0	100.0

LIABILITIES									
Notes Payable-Short Term	11.3	15.3	13.5	16.3				13.6	13.4
Cur. Mat.-L.T.D.	11.1	10.6	7.3	19.0				15.1	13.2
Trade Payables	26.3	7.2	8.2	9.4				7.9	5.8
Income Taxes Payable	.5	.1	.4	.2				.2	.1
All Other Current	11.6	6.1	5.8	8.2				6.8	5.7
Total Current	60.7	39.3	35.2	53.0				43.7	38.2
Long-Term Debt	82.3	23.9	35.2	19.9				27.4	26.1
Deferred Taxes	.0	.0	.2	.8				.4	.3
All Other Non-Current	7.7	10.9	8.3	10.5				7.0	7.7
Net Worth	-50.6	25.9	21.1	15.8				21.5	27.8
Total Liabilties & Net Worth	100.0	100.0	100.0	100.0				100.0	100.0

INCOME DATA									
Net Sales	100.0	100.0	100.0	100.0				100.0	100.0
Gross Profit									
Operating Expenses	74.7	74.5	78.9	79.3				87.0	82.1
Operating Profit	25.3	25.5	21.1	20.7				13.0	17.9
All Other Expenses (net)	13.7	5.1	13.3	10.9				10.0	8.8
Profit Before Taxes	11.6	20.4	7.8	9.8				3.1	9.1

RATIOS									
Current	1.3	1.7	1.7	1.4				1.7	1.6
	.8	.8	1.0	1.1				.7	1.0
	.3	.2	.4	.3				.3	.4
Quick	1.0	1.5	.9	1.1				1.2	1.1
	.5	.5	.5	.4				.6	.5
	.2	.2	.1	.1				.3	.1
Sales/Receivables	0 UND	0 UND	5 68.6	8 43.3				5 74.8	0 UND
	0 UND	27 13.5	33 11.1	25 14.6				29 12.6	22 16.6
	31 11.8	61 6.0	47 7.7	50 7.2				67 5.5	56 6.6
Cost of Sales/Inventory									
Cost of Sales/Payables									
Sales/Working Capital	22.4	4.0	11.0	2.6				6.3	10.3
	-18.9	-16.2	-102.0	38.4				-15.1	-56.9
	-6.2	-2.4	-6.0	-1.9				-3.1	-3.4
EBIT/Interest		21.1	5.2	2.9				2.8	4.9
		(27) 5.6	(33) 2.0	(12) 2.0				(40) 1.3	(50) 2.3
		1.3	1.2	1.2				-1.4	1.0
Net Profit + Depr., Dep., Amort./Cur. Mat. L/T/D									3.0
								(10) 1.8	
									.5
Fixed/Worth	.7	.7	.1	.1				.4	.4
	16.2	1.7	1.6	.9				1.8	1.4
	-.4	18.8	4.0	12.6				5.3	3.3
Debt/Worth	1.5	.7	1.5	2.6				1.9	1.3
	32.8	5.3	3.9	6.2				3.2	3.8
	-4.3	30.4	21.1	21.0				10.9	10.9
% Profit Before Taxes/Tangible Net Worth		100.4	35.4	46.8				39.4	43.6
		(26) 48.4	(34) 21.4	(15) 25.4				(42) 10.3	(62) 14.0
		15.0	12.4	3.6				-7.2	2.2
% Profit Before Taxes/Total Assets	38.8	27.3	8.5	8.2				4.4	8.9
	8.3	12.2	3.1	3.2				1.4	2.5
	-.4	1.8	.6	.8				-6.0	.1
Sales/Net Fixed Assets	79.5	18.7	36.7	100.9				15.9	13.0
	13.9	2.2	4.7	6.4				3.8	3.5
	1.2	.6	.9	.9				.8	.9
Sales/Total Assets	6.2	2.0	1.9	1.4				2.2	1.7
	2.5	.9	.6	.7				.9	.8
	.5	.3	.4	.2				.5	.2
% Depr., Dep., Amort./Sales		3.7	2.3	1.0				4.3	6.0
		(24) 23.9	(34) 9.5	(12) 4.5				(36) 16.8	(49) 14.8
		67.3	41.3	50.4				60.0	49.7
% Officers', Directors', Owners' Comp/Sales			4.2					3.0	2.2
			(14) 6.3					(15) 7.8	(17) 10.2
			18.6					16.1	23.4
Net Sales ($)	11070M	48572M	273312M	316650M	233983M	215442M		832804M	2458878M
Total Assets ($)	3090M	39309M	207930M	355001M	553013M	950559M		865207M	1150273M

© RMA 2007

M = $ thousand   MM = $ million
See Pages 11 through 21 for Explanation of Ratios and Data

Comparative Historical Data | Current Data Sorted by Sales

24	23	22	Type of Statement	0-1MM	1-3MM	3-5MM	5-10MM	10-25MM	25MM & OVER
24	23	22	Unqualified	1		1	6	9	5
11	10	8	Reviewed	4	2			1	1
15	8	18	Compiled	3	10	3	2		
16	16	29	Tax Returns	16	7	2	2	1	1
23	30	40	Other	7	10	7	5	4	7
4/1/04-3/31/05 ALL	4/1/05-3/31/06 ALL	4/1/06-3/31/07 ALL		13 (4/1-9/30/06)			104 (10/1/06-3/31/07)		
89	87	117	NUMBER OF STATEMENTS	31	29	13	15	15	14
%	%	%	**ASSETS**	%	%	%	%	%	%
7.4	7.5	7.3	Cash & Equivalents	13.3	3.6	5.1	7.5	5.4	5.8
16.1	19.0	18.8	Trade Receivables (net)	9.6	15.0	16.8	37.2	21.2	26.8
8.7	5.2	8.5	Inventory	.0	13.5	5.5	3.3	18.7	14.5
7.1	6.5	6.4	All Other Current	5.7	5.9	13.2	1.2	7.1	7.8
39.4	38.3	41.1	Total Current	28.6	38.1	40.5	49.2	52.4	54.9
41.4	43.8	40.2	Fixed Assets (net)	51.4	43.0	51.3	37.9	32.8	9.6
1.5	1.8	1.9	Intangibles (net)	.0	3.5	2.7	.8	.7	4.6
17.7	16.1	16.8	All Other Non-Current	20.0	15.4	5.4	12.1	14.2	30.8
100.0	100.0	100.0	Total	100.0	100.0	100.0	100.0	100.0	100.0
			LIABILITIES						
12.6	10.7	14.9	Notes Payable-Short Term	20.0	14.8	2.9	15.2	10.0	20.2
13.9	12.3	10.9	Cur. Mat.-L.T.D.	11.5	8.9	9.1	15.1	17.5	3.3
6.4	6.7	9.5	Trade Payables	2.2	12.2	10.5	9.3	16.7	11.2
.1	.3	.3	Income Taxes Payable	.1	.5	.2	.6	.5	.3
6.4	8.8	6.6	All Other Current	4.9	9.7	4.0	6.0	6.8	7.3
39.5	38.8	42.2	Total Current	38.7	46.0	26.7	46.2	51.5	42.3
28.3	31.5	34.4	Long-Term Debt	52.5	31.3	40.3	25.7	26.5	12.5
.3	.4	.3	Deferred Taxes	.0	.0	.1	.7	.6	.7
9.3	7.1	9.9	All Other Non-Current	6.9	13.6	3.7	11.5	4.3	18.6
22.7	22.2	13.3	Net Worth	1.8	9.0	29.1	15.9	17.1	25.9
100.0	100.0	100.0	Total Liabilties & Net Worth	100.0	100.0	100.0	100.0	100.0	100.0
			INCOME DATA						
100.0	100.0	100.0	Net Sales	100.0	100.0	100.0	100.0	100.0	100.0
			Gross Profit						
83.9	76.0	76.3	Operating Expenses	57.5	80.6	81.6	81.0	87.4	86.8
16.1	24.0	23.7	Operating Profit	42.5	19.4	18.4	19.0	12.6	13.2
5.5	7.8	11.6	All Other Expenses (net)	18.0	11.7	6.7	10.1	9.0	6.1
10.6	16.3	12.1	Profit Before Taxes	24.5	7.7	11.7	8.9	3.6	7.1
			RATIOS						
1.6	1.7	1.5		1.4	1.4	4.1	2.2	1.2	1.8
1.1	1.0	1.0	Current	.6	.7	1.5	1.0	1.0	1.3
.3	.4	.4		.1	.3	.3	.4	.6	1.0
1.1	1.4	1.1		1.3	.7	1.9	2.0	.6	1.4
.6	.5	.5	Quick	.5	.4	.6	1.0	.5	.8
.2	.2	.2		.0	.2	.1	.4	.2	.2
1 559.5	3 112.2	0 UND		0 UND	11 32.3	0 UND	27 13.4	13 28.1	22 16.8
27 13.6	32 11.4	28 13.0	Sales/Receivables	0 UND	28 13.2	30 12.1	37 9.8	33 11.1	40 9.0
50 7.3	73 5.0	55 6.6		61 5.9	42 8.7	66 5.5	1086 .3	56 6.5	46 7.9
			Cost of Sales/Inventory						
			Cost of Sales/Payables						
6.3	5.3	5.6		3.6	17.2	3.6	2.0	8.7	3.5
70.5	438.7	-95.8	Sales/Working Capital	-11.2	-13.8	13.2	232.3	96.0	14.9
-3.6	-3.1	-3.7		-2.1	-3.7	-3.1	-6.9	-4.6	NM
6.6	9.5	7.2		10.8	5.9	25.2	12.1	3.5	3.5
(72) 2.3	(68) 2.9	(89) 2.4	EBIT/Interest	(20) 2.9	(22) 1.9	(11) 4.1	(11) 2.2	(13) 2.2	(12) 2.3
1.1	1.7	1.2		1.2	1.0	1.1	1.3	1.2	1.8
1.9	2.3	5.0	Net Profit + Depr., Dep.,						
(10) .8	(12) 1.5	(15) 2.2	Amort./Cur. Mat. L/T/D						
.3	1.0	.8							
.2	.1	.1		.1	.2	.5	.1	.2	.0
1.6	1.6	1.2	Fixed/Worth	1.3	2.7	1.8	1.5	.8	.1
3.4	4.0	10.7		21.2	NM	81.9	12.5	3.8	.6
1.7	1.8	1.5		1.0	2.6	.7	2.2	2.8	1.4
3.8	4.2	5.6	Debt/Worth	9.4	6.2	2.7	5.1	5.6	4.0
11.9	13.1	31.1		33.3	-97.2	92.1	24.5	13.1	13.5
59.0	64.7	52.7	% Profit Before Taxes/Tangible	69.8	77.1	56.3	42.5	34.0	28.6
(81) 19.0	(77) 27.1	(97) 23.7	Net Worth	(26) 24.4	(21) 29.9	(11) 47.4	(13) 20.6	(14) 18.3	(12) 13.8
4.3	12.6	10.7		10.7	11.0	12.4	11.9	1.2	5.4
9.9	12.2	11.7	% Profit Before Taxes/Total	14.6	15.0	27.0	9.4	10.9	8.7
4.2	5.2	4.4	Assets	4.5	4.5	7.7	4.2	2.8	3.6
.4	2.1	.9		1.1	.1	1.3	.9	.5	1.5
35.3	35.1	43.3		16.7	71.6	55.7	36.5	36.0	220.1
4.4	3.4	6.8	Sales/Net Fixed Assets	1.0	8.5	1.1	5.7	7.6	43.0
1.1	.9	.9		.5	1.1	.7	1.4	3.5	8.8
2.2	1.7	1.9		.6	2.6	2.1	2.0	2.4	3.0
.8	.7	.7	Sales/Total Assets	.4	1.0	.7	.7	1.7	.9
.3	.3	.3		.2	.4	.5	.2	.4	.4
1.0	2.5	1.6		4.3	.8		1.8	.7	
(64) 11.6	(63) 14.6	(84) 8.5	% Depr., Dep., Amort./Sales	(24) 43.2	(18) 17.1		(14) 3.5	(11) 3.7	
37.5	39.6	50.1		67.4	53.7		28.8	5.2	
2.2	1.7	2.4	% Officers', Directors'						
(24) 5.8	(22) 3.9	(28) 6.2	Owners' Comp/Sales						
16.2	11.0	14.5							
1028432M	827702M	1099029M	Net Sales ($)	12269M	55588M	48241M	113372M	253234M	616325M
1281574M	1654118M	2108902M	Total Assets ($)	43050M	104116M	80424M	329591M	575587M	976134M

© RMA 2007

M = $ thousand   MM = $ million
See Pages 11 through 21 for Explanation of Ratios and Data

Current Data Sorted by Assets   Comparative Historical Data

		5	15	40	15	12	**Type of Statement**		
	7	13	38	28	1		Unqualified	76	74
	18	43	34	9	1		Reviewed	95	104
	40	54	18	3			Compiled	121	165
	12	51	72	39	7	11	Tax Returns	89	85
		87 (4/1-9/30/06)		499 (10/1/06-3/31/07)			Other	170	176
								4/1/02- 3/31/03	4/1/03- 3/31/04
	0-500M	500M-2MM	2-10MM	10-50MM	50-100MM	100-250MM		ALL	ALL
	77	166	177	119	24	23	NUMBER OF STATEMENTS	551	604
	%	%	%	%	%	%	ASSETS	%	%
	13.5	9.9	8.0	5.6	3.9	5.3	Cash & Equivalents	7.8	7.8
	6.9	14.4	15.2	22.7	19.5	23.5	Trade Receivables (net)	13.2	13.4
	4.4	7.0	8.8	5.6	12.9	6.8	Inventory	8.0	8.5
	4.4	2.3	3.0	6.4	1.0	9.6	All Other Current	4.8	5.5
	29.1	33.7	35.0	40.3	37.3	45.3	Total Current	33.8	35.3
	61.2	55.5	56.2	41.1	47.9	29.1	Fixed Assets (net)	54.9	52.4
	1.2	3.4	2.9	2.5	1.1	2.2	Intangibles (net)	2.6	2.7
	8.5	7.4	6.0	16.1	13.7	23.5	All Other Non-Current	8.7	9.6
	100.0	100.0	100.0	100.0	100.0	100.0	Total	100.0	100.0
							LIABILITIES		
	15.7	7.9	9.3	8.8	16.7	17.7	Notes Payable-Short Term	12.3	11.1
	12.5	8.8	7.7	9.7	5.3	6.7	Cur. Mat.-L.T.D.	10.7	9.2
	5.2	6.4	6.4	6.7	6.3	4.4	Trade Payables	5.3	5.7
	.0	.2	.6	.1	.6	.6	Income Taxes Payable	.4	.3
	19.0	6.1	7.4	5.8	4.1	3.3	All Other Current	8.1	7.7
	52.4	29.5	31.4	31.1	33.0	32.6	Total Current	36.8	33.9
	38.7	34.2	29.9	34.5	35.0	36.5	Long-Term Debt	32.8	31.6
	.0	.6	1.0	1.0	2.1	1.3	Deferred Taxes	.6	.7
	7.9	4.4	4.8	4.1	2.9	3.2	All Other Non-Current	6.4	7.2
	1.1	31.2	32.8	29.4	27.0	26.4	Net Worth	23.3	26.6
	100.0	100.0	100.0	100.0	100.0	100.0	Total Liabilities & Net Worth	100.0	100.0
							INCOME DATA		
	100.0	100.0	100.0	100.0	100.0	100.0	Net Sales	100.0	100.0
							Gross Profit		
	75.4	77.7	82.7	78.4	77.6	73.8	Operating Expenses	85.0	85.1
	24.6	22.3	17.3	21.6	22.4	26.2	Operating Profit	15.0	14.9
	5.5	5.5	5.4	8.4	10.3	14.5	All Other Expenses (net)	7.2	5.5
	19.1	16.9	11.9	13.2	12.1	11.7	Profit Before Taxes	7.8	9.3
							RATIOS		
	1.9	2.8	2.2	2.2	2.6	2.7		1.7	2.2
	.8	1.1	1.1	1.1	1.1	1.1	Current	.9	1.1
	.2	.5	.4	.8	.5	.7		.4	.5
	1.3	2.0	1.5	1.6	1.6	1.7		1.1	1.3
	.4	.7	.8	.8	.5	.8	Quick	(550) .5 (603) .6	
	.2	.3	.3	.4	.2	.4		.2	.2
	0 UND	0 UND	4 91.5	23 16.1	8 45.0	7 54.4		0 UND	0 UND
	0 UND	19 19.4	30 12.1	49 7.4	50 7.3	53 6.9	Sales/Receivables	21 17.2	23 16.0
	26 14.2	49 7.5	53 6.9	99 3.7	82 4.5	85 4.3		51 7.1	51 7.1
							Cost of Sales/Inventory		
							Cost of Sales/Payables		
	9.0	6.2	7.1	4.3	5.1	.6		7.6	6.0
	-29.3	78.9	50.9	31.2	35.7	15.5	Sales/Working Capital	-124.2	78.8
	-4.3	-5.7	-6.0	-12.5	-4.8	-7.4		-4.2	-5.2
	14.1	10.0	8.6	6.0	4.4	11.0		5.3	7.0
	(62) 5.9	(141) 4.3	(155) 3.4	(90) 2.8	(17) 3.3	(12) 4.0	EBIT/Interest	(442) 2.2 (508) 2.6	
	1.1	1.7	1.6	1.9	2.2	2.8		.9	1.0
		8.9	5.3	2.1				2.8	4.1
		(17) 2.9	(34) 3.4	(27) 1.1			Net Profit + Depr., Dep., Amort./Cur. Mat. L/T/D	(93) 1.9 (101) 1.9	
		1.5	1.5	.9				1.2	.9
	1.0	.8	.8	.1	.1	.1		.8	.6
	4.4	2.0	1.8	1.3	1.5	.9	Fixed/Worth	2.0	1.7
	-34.5	6.7	5.7	3.5	5.3	2.7		8.2	6.7
	.8	.8	.8	1.4	1.5	1.2		1.2	1.0
	6.5	2.2	2.3	2.8	4.1	5.2	Debt/Worth	3.2	2.8
	-43.8	10.9	8.4	7.2	8.9	11.3		11.9	10.5
	164.0	74.5	60.0	36.5	47.1	30.5		34.7	42.1
	(53) 66.7	(136) 35.1	(152) 28.9	(114) 25.1	20.7	(22) 20.1	% Profit Before Taxes/Tangible Net Worth	(463) 14.7 (502) 15.7	
	13.1	12.0	11.6	12.5	10.4	11.5		2.1	3.2
	47.2	20.5	16.3	9.9	8.6	9.3		10.0	12.8
	14.6	10.9	8.8	4.9	6.0	2.6	% Profit Before Taxes/Total Assets	3.6	4.4
	.0	3.1	2.5	2.3	1.6	1.5		-.3	.1
	6.7	5.4	5.5	20.9	28.1	15.7		7.2	7.8
	2.2	2.2	2.1	3.3	2.5	4.7	Sales/Net Fixed Assets	2.2	2.3
	1.0	.6	.7	.9	.5	.8		.7	.8
	2.5	2.1	1.8	1.4	1.4	.9		1.9	1.9
	1.2	1.1	1.2	.6	.5	.2	Sales/Total Assets	.9	1.0
	.6	.4	.5	.2	.2	.1		.4	.4
	6.9	6.6	4.7	1.9	1.0	1.0		6.1	5.3
	(61) 19.3	(146) 13.9	(158) 12.0	(99) 8.8	(15) 6.7	(12) 3.8	% Depr., Dep., Amort./Sales	(480) 14.6 (515) 14.5	
	45.5	36.9	32.6	19.7	22.9	7.3		38.9	35.6
	3.9	3.9	1.8	1.4				2.6	2.8
	(20) 7.3	(49) 6.0	(49) 3.6	(28) 3.5			% Officers', Directors' Owners' Comp/Sales	(154) 6.2 (170) 5.4	
	12.4	9.1	8.0	8.9				10.8	9.8
	35200M	283856M	1065434M	2548571M	1480663M	1849692M	Net Sales ($)	5763993M	5534936M
	20514M	190112M	821340M	2624773M	1735071M	3317079M	Total Assets ($)	6424267M	6827433M

© RMA 2007

M = $ thousand   MM = $ million
See Pages 11 through 21 for Explanation of Ratios and Data

Comparative Historical Data / Current Data Sorted by Sales

Hist 1	Hist 2	Hist 3	Type of Statement	0-1MM	1-3MM	3-5MM	5-10MM	10-25MM	25MM & OVER
95	80	87	Unqualified	6	7	5	16	24	29
95	101	87	Reviewed	12	24	8	14	19	10
155	110	105	Compiled	42	24	15	16	6	2
84	124	115	Tax Returns	64	31	14	3	2	1
151	227	192	Other	39	52	18	33	29	21
4/1/04-3/31/05 ALL	4/1/05-3/31/06 ALL	4/1/06-3/31/07 ALL		87 (4/1-9/30/06)			499 (10/1/06-3/31/07)		
580	642	586	NUMBER OF STATEMENTS	163	138	60	82	80	63
%	%	%	ASSETS	%	%	%	%	%	%
7.6	9.4	8.5	Cash & Equivalents	9.9	9.2	7.1	9.5	6.3	6.4
14.0	15.6	15.9	Trade Receivables (net)	8.0	13.7	15.8	25.0	23.8	19.2
7.3	7.5	7.2	Inventory	2.6	7.1	8.1	7.6	10.5	13.4
5.5	4.8	3.9	All Other Current	3.1	4.3	4.3	4.4	3.2	4.4
34.4	37.3	35.4	Total Current	23.6	34.3	35.3	46.6	43.9	43.4
52.1	50.7	52.2	Fixed Assets (net)	65.9	52.6	54.9	38.7	41.4	44.4
2.7	2.6	2.6	Intangibles (net)	2.3	2.2	2.5	4.7	1.4	3.4
10.8	9.5	9.8	All Other Non-Current	8.2	10.9	7.2	10.1	13.3	8.8
100.0	100.0	100.0	Total	100.0	100.0	100.0	100.0	100.0	100.0
			LIABILITIES						
11.1	11.0	10.3	Notes Payable-Short Term	10.6	9.3	10.3	9.5	12.0	10.4
11.0	9.5	8.9	Cur. Mat.-L.T.D.	11.1	8.5	9.3	8.6	6.8	6.8
5.8	6.9	6.2	Trade Payables	3.3	5.8	4.7	8.6	8.3	10.3
.3	.3	.3	Income Taxes Payable	.2	.4	.2	.4	.4	.5
8.8	9.7	7.9	All Other Current	11.7	5.0	4.6	8.2	8.0	7.3
37.0	37.4	33.7	Total Current	36.9	29.0	29.0	35.2	35.5	35.3
32.7	31.9	33.7	Long-Term Debt	41.3	36.1	30.8	28.2	26.4	27.9
.9	.7	.8	Deferred Taxes	.3	1.1	.7	.5	1.4	1.4
5.3	4.8	4.8	All Other Non-Current	3.8	8.0	4.4	4.5	3.1	3.6
24.1	25.1	27.0	Net Worth	17.8	25.7	35.1	31.5	33.6	31.9
100.0	100.0	100.0	Total Liabilties & Net Worth	100.0	100.0	100.0	100.0	100.0	100.0
			INCOME DATA						
100.0	100.0	100.0	Net Sales	100.0	100.0	100.0	100.0	100.0	100.0
			Gross Profit						
84.4	81.0	78.9	Operating Expenses	68.4	77.8	81.8	86.5	83.6	89.4
15.6	19.0	21.1	Operating Profit	31.6	22.2	18.2	13.5	16.4	10.6
4.9	5.0	6.6	All Other Expenses (net)	9.6	6.8	4.7	4.5	6.3	3.4
10.7	14.0	14.5	Profit Before Taxes	22.0	15.4	13.5	8.9	10.1	7.2
			RATIOS						
1.8	1.9	2.3		1.7	3.8	2.8	2.5	2.1	1.6
1.0	1.1	1.1	Current	.7	1.1	1.2	1.2	1.2	1.1
.4	.5	.5		.3	.5	.6	.8	.9	.8
1.2	1.4	1.6		1.2	2.4	1.8	2.2	1.7	1.1
(578) .5	(640) .7	.7	Quick	.4	.7	.8	1.0	.8	.8
.2	.3	.3		.2	.3	.3	.4	.4	.4
0 UND	0 UND	0 UND		0 UND	0 UND	9 42.1	18 19.7	20 18.6	27 13.4
26 14.2	26 13.8	28 13.1	Sales/Receivables	0 UND	21 17.3	36 10.2	40 9.0	46 8.0	43 8.4
52 7.1	52 7.1	60 6.1		41 9.0	54 6.8	55 6.7	72 5.0	78 4.7	63 5.8
			Cost of Sales/Inventory						
			Cost of Sales/Payables						
7.0	6.7	6.0		6.8	3.9	5.1	5.1	6.7	8.8
664.4	58.2	55.9	Sales/Working Capital	-12.3	71.3	19.8	24.6	31.1	42.8
-4.8	-6.7	-6.1		-2.4	-4.8	-12.5	-15.1	-35.7	-16.0
6.3	8.6	8.5		9.1	8.1	8.3	10.2	11.4	6.2
(474) 2.8	(535) 3.7	(477) 3.6	EBIT/Interest	(124) 3.8	(113) 3.3	(55) 3.6	(68) 4.0	(61) 4.5	(56) 3.3
1.2	1.7	1.7		1.2	1.5	1.7	1.9	2.0	2.1
4.1	4.3	4.5		4.2	6.4	6.2	5.0	3.5	4.6
(94) 1.9	(96) 2.0	(91) 2.2	Net Profit + Depr., Dep., Amort./Cur. Mat. L/T/D	(13) 1.7	(15) 2.5	(11) 2.8	(13) 3.2	(19) 2.1	(20) 2.1
1.3	1.1	1.1		1.5	.9	.8	1.9	1.1	1.0
.8	.7	.7		1.2	.6	.7	.4	.3	.6
2.0	1.7	1.7	Fixed/Worth	3.5	1.6	1.5	1.4	1.2	1.5
8.5	6.7	5.7		459.6	10.0	3.8	3.1	2.4	4.2
1.2	1.2	1.0		.9	.9	.9	.9	1.1	1.3
3.4	2.8	2.7	Debt/Worth	3.6	2.8	1.8	2.5	2.6	2.6
15.9	10.4	10.8		654.0	14.7	5.7	9.9	5.5	6.6
43.2	57.6	62.2		100.0	54.7	68.9	47.7	47.5	40.8
(476) 20.1	(539) 27.0	(501) 29.7	% Profit Before Taxes/Tangible Net Worth	(124) 35.3	(114) 28.6	(57) 35.7	(69) 25.7	(77) 28.8	(60) 27.2
6.1	9.9	12.2		9.4	12.5	11.7	12.1	14.6	9.8
12.1	18.2	16.5		20.1	15.1	21.6	14.5	16.7	11.8
5.0	7.0	7.2	% Profit Before Taxes/Total Assets	7.5	7.0	7.8	7.6	8.3	6.3
.9	2.0	2.1		.8	1.7	2.5	2.6	2.4	2.4
8.2	9.1	7.1		2.5	6.9	5.5	27.1	11.6	8.9
2.4	2.5	2.4	Sales/Net Fixed Assets	1.0	2.4	2.4	5.3	3.8	3.1
.8	.9	.8		.4	.7	1.2	1.7	1.8	1.3
1.9	2.1	1.8		1.1	1.8	1.8	2.5	2.1	2.3
1.0	1.1	1.0	Sales/Total Assets	.5	.8	1.3	1.4	1.4	1.3
.4	.5	.4		.3	.3	.5	.5	.5	.7
4.7	4.0	4.6		13.3	4.7	5.3	2.6	1.0	2.2
(467) 13.6	(527) 11.8	(491) 12.1	% Depr., Dep., Amort./Sales	(143) 34.2	(119) 12.7	(52) 10.7	(65) 6.8	(66) 6.6	(46) 5.7
37.4	31.9	32.1		52.4	32.9	25.5	17.4	11.5	10.1
3.0	2.6	2.6		6.0	4.2	1.3	2.4	1.2	
(146) 5.8	(141) 5.1	(149) 5.3	% Officers', Directors' Owners' Comp/Sales	(27) 9.7	(43) 6.3	(22) 3.5	(29) 3.6	(21) 2.1	
10.4	8.6	8.9		17.2	8.8	7.2	7.4	7.0	
6585124M	8216844M	7263416M	Net Sales ($)	68384M	264069M	234063M	570979M	1347062M	4778859M
7600657M	9089430M	8708889M	Total Assets ($)	149082M	592145M	400089M	869229M	2581228M	4117116M

M = $ thousand   MM = $ million
See Pages 11 through 21 for Explanation of Ratios and Data

Current Data Sorted by Assets   Comparative Historical Data

						Type of Statement		
1	2	3	9	2	1	Unqualified	22	12
1	1			1		Reviewed	1	2
1	1	3				Compiled	1	1
1	9	1	1		1	Tax Returns	3	7
3	6	7	7	1	1	Other	9	10
	12 (4/1-9/30/06)		52 (10/1/06-3/31/07)				4/1/02-3/31/03	4/1/03-3/31/04
0-500M	500M-2MM	2-10MM	10-50MM	50-100MM	100-250MM		ALL	ALL
7	19	14	17	4	3	**NUMBER OF STATEMENTS**	36	32
%	%	%	%	%	%	**ASSETS**	%	%
	7.8	7.0	19.6			Cash & Equivalents	22.1	14.8
	6.7	5.5	16.2			Trade Receivables (net)	13.8	18.3
	2.0	1.7	3.9			Inventory	4.9	3.5
	1.7	9.2	5.2			All Other Current	6.5	7.8
	18.2	23.5	44.9			Total Current	47.2	44.4
	72.9	54.0	22.6			Fixed Assets (net)	28.1	35.3
	2.9	2.7	19.0			Intangibles (net)	12.0	6.1
	5.9	19.9	13.5			All Other Non-Current	12.6	14.2
	100.0	100.0	100.0			Total	100.0	100.0
						LIABILITIES		
	.8	2.7	3.0			Notes Payable-Short Term	4.2	15.4
	2.6	4.6	3.4			Cur. Mat.-L.T.D.	2.9	4.2
	5.6	4.8	13.1			Trade Payables	12.4	10.4
	1.7	.0	.0			Income Taxes Payable	2.7	.1
	10.4	9.5	11.5			All Other Current	11.4	20.3
	21.2	21.7	31.1			Total Current	33.7	50.3
	57.6	44.6	22.6			Long-Term Debt	22.6	20.6
	.0	.0	1.1			Deferred Taxes	.8	.9
	5.2	5.5	3.1			All Other Non-Current	10.1	5.9
	16.0	28.2	42.1			Net Worth	32.9	22.2
	100.0	100.0	100.0			Total Liabilities & Net Worth	100.0	100.0
						INCOME DATA		
	100.0	100.0	100.0			Net Sales	100.0	100.0
						Gross Profit		
	65.5	79.2	83.2			Operating Expenses	85.7	73.5
	34.5	20.8	16.8			Operating Profit	14.3	26.5
	18.4	16.3	-.6			All Other Expenses (net)	2.9	5.0
	16.1	4.5	17.5			Profit Before Taxes	11.4	21.4
						RATIOS		
	9.3	15.8	2.8				3.0	1.7
	1.0	1.1	1.6			Current	1.6	1.1
	.1	.6	.7				.7	.6
	2.8	4.9	2.4				2.7	1.5
	1.0	.8	1.3			Quick	1.3	.8
	.1	.3	.5				.5	.3
	0 UND	0 UND	18 20.5				6 63.8	0 UND
	0 UND	1 393.2	29 12.7			Sales/Receivables	23 16.0	27 13.5
	15 24.2	14 26.4	42 8.8				44 8.4	57 6.4
						Cost of Sales/Inventory		
						Cost of Sales/Payables		
	5.3	2.2	4.2				4.1	9.8
	-336.0	NM	7.7			Sales/Working Capital	9.8	54.9
	-1.2	-6.5	-11.0				-15.2	-4.1
			15.0				32.9	62.5
		(16) 6.7				EBIT/Interest	(28) 6.8	(27) 15.7
			2.3				2.8	4.9
						Net Profit + Depr., Dep., Amort./Cur. Mat. L/T/D		
	1.3	.2	.3				.2	.3
	45.3	2.2	1.1			Fixed/Worth	1.0	1.2
	-12.3	NM	NM				NM	8.4
	1.1	.8	.6				.6	.8
	51.6	2.7	2.2			Debt/Worth	2.3	3.0
	-14.2	NM	NM				NM	13.0
	143.9	37.5	73.4				61.7	113.5
	(11) 37.2	(11) 22.9	(13) 42.0			% Profit Before Taxes/Tangible Net Worth	(27) 24.6	(25) 47.8
	2.9	-23.1	18.7				10.5	20.9
	13.4	19.5	26.2				20.6	29.8
	2.5	3.3	14.4			% Profit Before Taxes/Total Assets	6.7	12.7
	.4	-1.2	6.3				3.0	4.9
	2.2	31.9	20.4				30.9	33.1
	.4	1.5	5.6			Sales/Net Fixed Assets	14.7	7.6
	.2	.2	2.2				1.6	1.2
	1.6	2.0	1.4				2.9	2.3
	.3	.6	1.0			Sales/Total Assets	1.1	1.0
	.1	.2	.7				.6	.5
	1.3	1.6	.8				1.4	.7
	(14) 10.2	(12) 8.7	(13) 2.9			% Depr., Dep., Amort./Sales	(27) 2.9	(27) 2.4
	19.4	23.3	4.2				4.6	6.0
						% Officers', Directors' Owners' Comp/Sales		
5534M	25395M	89849M	469321M	354892M	139185M	Net Sales ($)	1158123M	484139M
1988M	22353M	73364M	361735M	248998M	602269M	Total Assets ($)	771850M	626239M

Comparative Historical Data | Current Data Sorted by Sales

15	18	18	Type of Statement / Unqualified	1	1	2	4	5	5
3	4	3	Reviewed	1	1				1
3	3	5	Compiled	3		1			1
8	4	13	Tax Returns	10		1	1		1
15	13	25	Other	5	9	2		5	4
4/1/04-3/31/05 ALL	4/1/05-3/31/06 ALL	4/1/06-3/31/07 ALL		0-1MM	12 (4/1-9/30/06) 1-3MM	3-5MM	5-10MM	52 (10/1/06-3/31/07) 10-25MM	25MM & OVER
44	42	64	NUMBER OF STATEMENTS	20	11	6	5	10	12
%	%	%	ASSETS	%	%	%	%	%	%
11.3	14.5	13.4	Cash & Equivalents	6.0	19.2			15.2	19.8
13.1	14.3	12.2	Trade Receivables (net)	2.0	6.1			21.2	22.9
2.9	4.8	2.0	Inventory	.0	.2			2.5	4.8
5.1	5.8	5.9	All Other Current	1.8	15.7			2.5	10.1
32.5	39.4	33.5	Total Current	9.9	41.2			41.5	57.5
45.1	41.3	45.6	Fixed Assets (net)	70.7	50.3			18.4	22.7
8.4	8.8	9.0	Intangibles (net)	7.9	.2			19.4	14.4
14.0	10.6	11.9	All Other Non-Current	11.6	8.3			20.6	5.4
100.0	100.0	100.0	Total	100.0	100.0			100.0	100.0
			LIABILITIES						
4.3	6.3	3.0	Notes Payable-Short Term	.8	1.3			3.1	6.0
4.1	5.3	5.4	Cur. Mat.-L.T.D.	2.1	9.9			7.3	6.7
8.2	10.3	8.4	Trade Payables	1.6	9.1			16.6	10.3
.2	.0	.5	Income Taxes Payable	.0	.0			.0	.0
9.8	11.9	11.9	All Other Current	8.8	6.4			8.8	17.7
26.7	33.8	29.2	Total Current	13.2	26.6			35.8	40.6
42.2	43.0	41.3	Long-Term Debt	73.6	50.0			13.2	23.1
.9	.9	.5	Deferred Taxes	.0				1.9	1.1
10.0	6.1	6.3	All Other Non-Current	5.4	3.3			7.1	11.9
20.2	16.2	22.8	Net Worth	7.8	20.0			42.0	23.4
100.0	100.0	100.0	Total Liabilties & Net Worth	100.0	100.0			100.0	100.0
			INCOME DATA						
100.0	100.0	100.0	Net Sales	100.0	100.0			100.0	100.0
			Gross Profit						
78.9	83.2	78.0	Operating Expenses	66.3	74.8			80.8	88.4
21.1	16.8	22.0	Operating Profit	33.7	25.2			19.2	11.6
7.8	6.7	10.5	All Other Expenses (net)	22.9	12.2			1.3	3.7
13.4	10.1	11.4	Profit Before Taxes	10.8	13.0			18.0	7.9
			RATIOS						
1.9	2.1	3.2	Current	10.2	20.2			2.0	2.7
1.1	1.1	1.2		.9	2.0			1.2	1.1
.6	.6	.4		.1	.7			.4	.8
1.4	1.4	2.1	Quick	7.8	20.9			1.9	2.0
.7	.7 (63)	1.0		.8 (10)	1.6			1.2	1.0
.3	.4	.3		.1	.7			.4	.4
0 999.8	0 UND	0 UND	Sales/Receivables	0 UND	0 UND			19 19.5	8 45.5
14 25.5	18 20.0	11 33.7		0 UND	4 97.4			33 11.1	26 14.0
32 11.3	34 10.7	35 10.3		22 16.9	15 24.2			53 6.9	102 3.6
			Cost of Sales/Inventory						
			Cost of Sales/Payables						
11.7	7.3	4.8	Sales/Working Capital	1.9	.4			6.8	4.7
54.8	52.0	25.5		-83.2	14.4			10.5	6.5
-12.6	-14.1	-7.5		-2.4	-11.0			-7.8	NM
21.4	18.6	11.4	EBIT/Interest						55.2
(36) 6.0	(28) 5.3	(43) 5.0							(10) 4.1
3.1	1.4	1.5							1.9
	15.3	21.2	Net Profit + Depr., Dep., Amort./Cur. Mat. L/T/D						
	(12) 6.9	(11) 6.2							
	2.1	1.7							
.4	.6	.5	Fixed/Worth	6.2	.4			.4	.2
2.5	2.6	3.2		NM	1.1			1.0	2.2
8.3	-18.5	-8.2		-3.1	483.7			NM	-2.2
1.6	1.6	.9	Debt/Worth	5.9	.6			.8	1.3
3.8	4.8	9.7		NM	.9			2.9	12.6
8.7	-43.0	-11.8		-5.1	516.3			NM	-6.5
80.3	54.6	72.6	% Profit Before Taxes/Tangible Net Worth	213.5					
(36) 47.4	(30) 28.3	(43) 36.9		(10) 30.2					
19.6	5.0	2.0		-1.6					
19.2	10.4	17.7	% Profit Before Taxes/Total Assets	9.7	22.2			24.9	6.8
9.1	5.7	6.3		1.1	1.5			18.4	6.3
3.6	1.2	.1		-1.0	-.4			14.5	3.9
17.5	17.9	18.6	Sales/Net Fixed Assets	1.0	20.0			92.7	36.2
4.2	3.6	2.6		.3	.7			8.5	12.8
.5	.5	.3		.2	.2			5.4	2.8
2.8	2.5	2.0	Sales/Total Assets	.5	3.6			1.9	2.7
1.1	1.3	.7		.2	.5			1.2	1.0
.4	.4	.2		.1	.1			.9	.6
1.2	1.4	.8	% Depr., Dep., Amort./Sales	7.9					.5
(39) 5.1	(36) 5.8	(50) 4.2		(15) 13.1					(10) 1.9
13.1	12.1	13.4		21.0					3.6
		1.5	% Officers', Directors' Owners' Comp/Sales						
		(10) 6.8							
		25.4							
1012531M	905100M	1084176M	Net Sales ($)	6349M	14830M	24790M	33297M	190294M	814616M
804772M	722104M	1310707M	Total Assets ($)	29550M	291246M	30333M	28435M	154731M	776412M

M = $ thousand   MM = $ million
See Pages 11 through 21 for Explanation of Ratios and Data

PROFESSIONAL, SCIENTIFIC, AND TECHNICAL SERVICES

Current Data Sorted by Assets   Comparative Historical Data

	0-500M	500M-2MM	2-10MM	10-50MM	50-100MM	100-250MM	Type of Statement	4/1/02-3/31/03 ALL	4/1/03-3/31/04 ALL
	7	10	19	43	12	19	Unqualified	82	100
	8	32	79	62	2	4	Reviewed	181	182
	76	74	74	15		1	Compiled	275	365
	297	141	62	12	3	2	Tax Returns	348	459
	197	205	202	107	17	19	Other	604	639
		117 (4/1-9/30/06)		1,684 (10/1/06-3/31/07)					
	585	462	436	239	34	45	NUMBER OF STATEMENTS	1490	1745
	%	%	%	%	%	%	ASSETS	%	%
	35.1	31.8	26.8	32.1	33.1	39.8	Cash & Equivalents	30.0	31.8
	7.6	13.5	24.5	21.3	14.2	13.1	Trade Receivables (net)	17.3	15.8
	.6	.8	2.3	2.8	1.5	1.0	Inventory	1.5	1.2
	11.9	14.8	13.0	11.2	14.0	8.5	All Other Current	12.4	13.0
	55.2	61.0	66.6	67.4	62.7	62.3	Total Current	61.2	61.9
	24.2	22.0	18.4	21.5	31.4	28.6	Fixed Assets (net)	24.9	23.6
	4.7	2.7	1.2	1.3	.9	2.4	Intangibles (net)	1.8	2.0
	16.0	14.3	13.8	9.8	4.9	6.7	All Other Non-Current	12.1	12.5
	100.0	100.0	100.0	100.0	100.0	100.0	Total	100.0	100.0
							LIABILITIES		
	46.2	23.0	14.0	7.1	6.3	12.2	Notes Payable-Short Term	24.6	25.4
	7.9	3.8	2.7	2.5	2.9	1.8	Cur. Mat.-L.T.D.	5.8	5.2
	3.2	2.4	3.3	3.1	2.6	1.2	Trade Payables	2.9	3.1
	.1	.2	1.0	.7	1.6	.1	Income Taxes Payable	.4	.6
	45.2	31.6	24.8	21.3	14.6	15.1	All Other Current	30.9	31.4
	102.6	60.9	45.8	34.8	28.0	30.4	Total Current	64.6	65.7
	20.2	13.1	11.6	11.8	10.5	11.3	Long-Term Debt	12.9	12.6
	.0	.0	.7	.3	.0	.5	Deferred Taxes	.4	.4
	8.5	5.8	6.5	7.1	6.0	9.7	All Other Non-Current	6.4	6.2
	-31.3	20.1	35.4	46.1	55.3	48.1	Net Worth	15.8	15.1
	100.0	100.0	100.0	100.0	100.0	100.0	Total Liabilties & Net Worth	100.0	100.0
							INCOME DATA		
	100.0	100.0	100.0	100.0	100.0	100.0	Net Sales	100.0	100.0
							Gross Profit		
	84.2	83.0	78.1	69.5	70.4	65.4	Operating Expenses	81.8	82.6
	15.8	17.0	21.9	30.5	29.6	34.6	Operating Profit	18.2	17.4
	.8	1.5	1.7	1.7	1.5	1.0	All Other Expenses (net)	1.1	1.1
	15.0	15.5	20.2	28.8	28.1	33.6	Profit Before Taxes	17.1	16.3
							RATIOS		
	1.3	2.1	3.6	6.0	7.8	10.1		2.8	3.0
	.7	1.0	1.5	2.3	3.7	4.1	Current	1.2	1.2
	.3	.6	1.0	1.2	1.3	1.9		.6	.6
	1.0	1.8	2.8	4.7	6.6	8.2		2.3	2.2
(584)	.5	.8 (434)	1.1	1.8	3.2	3.9	Quick (1488)	.9 (1743)	.9
	.1	.3	.6	.9	.9	1.2		.4	.3
0	UND	0 UND	0 UND	0 UND	0 UND	0 UND	0 UND	0 UND	
0	UND	0 UND	9 40.5	8 47.8	3 107.3	4 92.8	Sales/Receivables 0 UND	0 UND	
0	UND	8 46.5	63 5.8	62 5.9	35 10.4	18 20.0	26 13.8	21 17.6	
							Cost of Sales/Inventory		
							Cost of Sales/Payables		
	75.9	16.4	5.7	4.5	5.1	4.4		8.1	9.0
	-54.0	247.6	19.9	9.8	9.7	7.2	Sales/Working Capital	63.3	83.3
	-14.0	-18.3	-139.3	41.6	34.2	12.3		-27.8	-26.8
	49.1	68.3	105.3	239.2	140.0	123.4		92.9	102.4
(449)	10.0	9.4 (359)	16.7 (346)	74.7 (207)	72.6 (26)	75.6 (39)	EBIT/Interest (1240)	15.9 (1439)	16.0
	1.0	1.3	1.9	7.6	12.3	14.9		1.6	1.4
		10.1	7.1	17.0				5.9	7.0
	(26)	2.9 (47)	1.5 (29)	3.3			Net Profit + Depr., Dep., Amort./Cur. Mat. L/T/D (110)	2.1 (118)	2.5
		1.6	.8	1.3				1.1	1.1
	.2	.2	.1	.2	.3	.2		.2	.2
	3.6	.9	.4	.4	.5	.5	Fixed/Worth	.8	.8
	-.4	-14.6	2.7	.9	1.1	.9		-29.8	-4.3
	1.5	.9	.6	.3	.3	.1		.6	.6
	-33.5	4.1	1.7	.9	.5	.5	Debt/Worth	2.6	2.8
	-2.3	-27.4	8.9	3.2	2.1	2.2		-28.1	-13.6
	882.9	446.4	324.6	313.7	372.4	217.3		319.3	326.7
(281)	191.1	92.6 (333)	100.9 (365)	183.5 (225)	187.4 (30)	163.0 (41)	% Profit Before Taxes/Tangible Net Worth (1082)	100.8 (1228)	113.2
	34.3	10.1	13.0	34.7	115.7	132.7		13.5	15.0
	218.3	128.9	136.2	170.9	213.5	145.9		135.6	135.9
	46.6	17.3	28.2	93.0	122.9	106.3	% Profit Before Taxes/Total Assets	29.0	28.6
	-.4	1.3	1.8	10.5	48.9	63.8		.9	1.0
	351.5	107.4	66.4	34.2	26.6	22.2		65.8	85.1
	77.3	42.1	32.1	21.6	14.2	12.5	Sales/Net Fixed Assets	29.8	35.2
	30.5	20.5	16.7	13.0	10.5	8.5		14.9	17.7
	19.9	9.4	5.8	4.8	5.5	4.0		9.0	10.1
	9.7	4.6	3.1	3.2	3.6	3.0	Sales/Total Assets	4.6	5.1
	4.7	2.5	1.9	2.0	2.8	2.2		2.5	2.7
	.3	.4	.6	.8	.8	1.3		.8	.7
(288)	.6	.8 (304)	1.0 (355)	1.3 (207)	1.3 (26)	1.4 (31)	% Depr., Dep., Amort./Sales (1114)	1.3 (1197)	1.2
	1.2	1.4	1.5	1.8	1.8	1.8		2.0	1.9
	13.4	12.2	11.7	6.0		12.9		13.5	14.0
(310)	25.4	23.2 (232)	25.8 (149)	20.4 (75)		25.8 (17)	% Officers', Directors' Owners' Comp/Sales (702)	24.8 (863)	25.4
	35.1	36.6	34.8	34.0		32.0		35.7	36.8
	1458507M	3320134M	8690299M	24798983M	10848230M	24667020M	Net Sales ($)	47477283M	75062906M
	120887M	508709M	2043380M	5135842M	2407968M	6811293M	Total Assets ($)	11504472M	14194758M

M = $ thousand   MM = $ million
See Pages 11 through 21 for Explanation of Ratios and Data

Comparative Historical Data | | | Current Data Sorted by Sales

			Type of Statement						
102	75	110	Unqualified	3	7	1	9	11	79
190	164	187	Reviewed		7	12	24	65	79
242	234	240	Compiled	21	56	42	52	47	22
441	420	517	Tax Returns	133	174	57	67	56	30
598	763	747	Other	76	145	80	140	121	185
4/1/04-3/31/05	4/1/05-3/31/06	4/1/06-3/31/07		117 (4/1-9/30/06)			1,684 (10/1/06-3/31/07)		
ALL	ALL	ALL		0-1MM	1-3MM	3-5MM	5-10MM	10-25MM	25MM & OVER
1573	1656	1801	NUMBER OF STATEMENTS	233	389	192	292	300	395
%	%	%	ASSETS	%	%	%	%	%	%
31.7	33.6	31.9	Cash & Equivalents	32.7	32.4	32.1	28.5	30.5	34.6
16.4	15.1	15.3	Trade Receivables (net)	7.0	11.0	15.9	19.3	20.8	16.9
1.2	1.2	1.4	Inventory	.2	1.1	1.0	2.2	2.5	1.2
12.9	12.2	12.8	All Other Current	9.5	14.8	14.7	15.2	12.0	10.5
62.1	62.1	61.4	Total Current	49.3	59.3	63.7	65.2	65.8	63.2
22.3	21.5	22.1	Fixed Assets (net)	26.6	19.3	18.3	18.8	21.8	26.9
2.2	2.1	2.8	Intangibles (net)	6.8	3.9	3.2	1.4	1.4	1.0
13.3	14.3	13.8	All Other Non-Current	17.3	17.5	14.8	14.6	11.0	8.9
100.0	100.0	100.0	Total	100.0	100.0	100.0	100.0	100.0	100.0
			LIABILITIES						
26.1	23.1	25.6	Notes Payable-Short Term	39.0	39.9	32.2	26.4	13.2	9.4
5.9	4.9	4.6	Cur. Mat.-L.T.D.	3.6	6.1	8.5	4.4	3.2	3.0
2.8	3.1	3.0	Trade Payables	4.3	3.0	2.3	2.8	3.2	2.4
.7	.6	.5	Income Taxes Payable	.0	.1	.5	1.0	.6	.6
29.5	29.6	32.3	All Other Current	42.7	34.9	38.0	32.9	30.0	22.1
64.9	61.2	65.9	Total Current	89.6	83.9	81.5	67.6	50.2	37.5
14.3	14.4	14.8	Long-Term Debt	24.0	17.3	15.1	10.6	12.5	11.6
.5	.4	.2	Deferred Taxes	.0	.1	.3	.5	.3	.2
5.0	5.5	7.1	All Other Non-Current	9.0	8.8	7.2	6.7	6.3	5.1
15.3	18.4	11.9	Net Worth	-22.7	-10.2	-4.1	14.6	30.7	45.7
100.0	100.0	100.0	Total Liabilities & Net Worth	100.0	100.0	100.0	100.0	100.0	100.0
			INCOME DATA						
100.0	100.0	100.0	Net Sales	100.0	100.0	100.0	100.0	100.0	100.0
			Gross Profit						
80.8	80.4	79.7	Operating Expenses	80.8	84.2	83.6	84.3	79.1	69.9
19.2	19.6	20.3	Operating Profit	19.2	15.8	16.4	15.7	20.9	30.1
1.0	1.4	1.3	All Other Expenses (net)	4.0	.8	.8	.5	.7	1.7
18.2	18.2	18.9	Profit Before Taxes	15.3	15.0	15.6	15.2	20.2	28.4
			RATIOS						
3.0	3.2	2.8		1.6	1.7	2.2	2.2	3.6	5.4
1.1	1.2	1.2	Current	.7	.9	1.0	1.1	1.5	2.0
.6	.7	.6		.2	.4	.5	.6	.9	1.1
2.3	2.6	2.2		1.1	1.2	1.3	1.7	2.7	4.7
(1568) .9	(1652) 1.0	(1798) .9	Quick	.5 (388) .6		.7 (291) .9		1.2 (394) 1.6	
.3	.4	.3		.1	.2	.2	.3	.5	.8
0 UND	0 UND	0 UND		0 UND	0 UND	0 UND	0 UND	0 UND	0 UND
0 UND	0 UND	0 UND	Sales/Receivables	0 UND	0 UND	0 UND	0 UND	3 110.3	4 89.9
24 15.4	17 20.9	17 21.9		0 UND	3 115.5	13 27.6	48 7.6	46 8.0	16 22.4
			Cost of Sales/Inventory						
			Cost of Sales/Payables						
8.8	8.7	9.1		26.1	22.5	17.0	7.2	6.9	6.4
72.8	69.1	92.1	Sales/Working Capital	-22.0	-63.7	-743.4	81.5	27.4	19.0
-25.4	-34.1	-25.2		-6.0	-14.0	-20.6	-30.9	-132.9	208.7
124.3	110.9	94.1		28.9	46.1	50.3	68.1	174.0	199.2
(1269) 20.3	(1332) 19.8	(1426) 16.8	EBIT/Interest	(157) 6.0	(305) 9.6	(157) 9.4	(237) 10.0	(249) 30.6	(321) 74.6
2.2	2.0	1.9		.3	.9	1.1	1.4	2.6	9.7
9.5	5.6	10.4			7.1		6.2	11.2	22.8
(108) 2.6	(97) 1.8	(117) 2.1	Net Profit + Depr., Dep., Amort./Cur. Mat. L/T/D		(12) 1.2		(16) 1.9	(29) 2.4	(50) 3.5
1.1	.9	1.0			-3.9		-.7	1.3	1.3
.2	.1	.2		.1	.1	.1	.1	.2	.3
.7	.6	.7	Fixed/Worth	1.7	1.4	1.0	.7	.5	.5
-16.7	7.0	-12.8		-.8	-.5	-.6	-9.0	4.3	1.1
.6	.6	.6		1.6	1.3	1.0	.9	.6	.3
2.7	2.3	2.9	Debt/Worth	56.3	29.6	7.2	3.1	1.6	.9
-23.3	-327.7	-15.6		-2.6	-3.3	-4.2	-34.6	13.9	3.2
376.5	368.6	402.5		458.1	439.1	681.5	328.7	361.6	402.9
(1128) 133.8	(1237) 134.2	(1275) 139.5	% Profit Before Taxes/Tangible Net Worth	(127) 116.9	(214) 107.5	(113) 101.7	(210) 92.1	(244) 112.5	(367) 197.7
17.9	20.4	20.1		27.8	11.3	14.5	10.5	16.5	60.7
152.9	148.0	162.4		93.8	139.4	184.1	126.1	167.7	206.2
39.0	39.5	40.5	% Profit Before Taxes/Total Assets	21.3	28.7	22.2	18.5	48.3	124.6
2.1	2.0	2.0		-2.0	-.5	1.4	1.5	3.4	14.9
99.6	110.5	103.3		320.1	224.5	238.5	120.8	75.4	36.3
36.0	38.0	37.9	Sales/Net Fixed Assets	41.7	55.8	66.4	51.9	37.7	22.0
18.3	18.5	17.8		12.1	23.2	30.4	24.8	19.9	13.2
9.4	9.7	9.7		6.9	11.1	15.4	11.3	10.0	7.2
4.6	4.8	4.6	Sales/Total Assets	3.3	4.8	6.1	4.6	5.1	4.4
2.5	2.5	2.5		1.5	2.6	2.5	2.5	2.6	3.0
.7	.5	.5		.5	.3	.3	.4	.5	.7
(1038) 1.2	(1124) 1.0	(1211) .9	% Depr., Dep., Amort./Sales	(111) 1.2	(202) .7	(111) .7	(201) .7	(246) .9	(340) 1.2
1.8	1.6	1.5		5.1	1.3	1.3	1.3	1.5	1.6
12.0	12.7	11.9		12.4	13.7	11.7	13.5	10.4	6.7
(742) 23.6	(777) 25.2	(791) 23.9	% Officers', Directors' Owners' Comp/Sales	(95) 21.7	(214) 25.5	(105) 21.9	(136) 26.4	(129) 24.7	(112) 24.5
35.4	35.4	35.1		31.0	36.7	33.1	35.6	36.8	35.2
52413705M	66951783M	73783173M	Net Sales ($)	118783M	730252M	762124M	2110736M	4862809M	65198469M
13723291M	14414017M	17028079M	Total Assets ($)	84511M	278489M	216900M	656553M	1445377M	14346249M

M = $ thousand   MM = $ million
See Pages 11 through 21 for Explanation of Ratios and Data

Current Data Sorted by Assets   **Comparative Historical Data**

						Type of Statement		
1	1	5	4			Unqualified	6	6
1	1	1				Reviewed	8	5
2	5	5				Compiled	12	20
13	10	4	2			Tax Returns	11	25
9	10	10	7		1	Other	21	28
	3 (4/1-9/30/06)		89 (10/1/06-3/31/07)				4/1/02-3/31/03	4/1/03-3/31/04
0-500M	500M-2MM	2-10MM	10-50MM	50-100MM	100-250MM		ALL	ALL
26	27	25	13		1	NUMBER OF STATEMENTS	58	84
%	%	%	%	%	%	ASSETS	%	%
33.3	39.8	25.8	37.1			Cash & Equivalents	35.0	33.5
4.5	9.6	18.5	6.4			Trade Receivables (net)	11.2	8.5
.0	.2	.0	.0			Inventory	.0	1.4
7.8	5.1	5.3	9.0			All Other Current	9.4	6.6
45.6	54.7	49.6	52.5			Total Current	55.6	49.9
22.3	23.8	20.6	17.4			Fixed Assets (net)	23.3	26.7
10.6	14.5	8.7	.5			Intangibles (net)	10.1	7.0
21.6	7.0	21.1	29.6			All Other Non-Current	11.0	16.4
100.0	100.0	100.0	100.0			Total	100.0	100.0
						LIABILITIES		
42.0	1.2	10.0	12.2			Notes Payable-Short Term	8.4	10.1
1.3	1.6	1.0	1.9			Cur. Mat.-L.T.D.	4.4	1.9
4.4	8.5	6.3	6.8			Trade Payables	10.7	6.6
.6	.2	.5	.7			Income Taxes Payable	.1	.8
42.7	24.0	19.8	23.2			All Other Current	30.3	19.1
91.0	35.5	37.6	44.9			Total Current	53.9	38.6
16.8	18.3	13.7	9.2			Long-Term Debt	15.2	15.6
.0	.0	1.5	.7			Deferred Taxes	.0	.2
.2	3.4	4.7	6.6			All Other Non-Current	4.2	6.8
-8.1	42.8	42.4	38.5			Net Worth	26.6	38.8
100.0	100.0	100.0	100.0			Total Liabilities & Net Worth	100.0	100.0
						INCOME DATA		
100.0	100.0	100.0	100.0			Net Sales	100.0	100.0
						Gross Profit		
90.5	87.5	93.1	88.2			Operating Expenses	86.7	82.0
9.5	12.5	6.9	11.8			Operating Profit	13.3	18.0
.0	.6	-.4	-1.6			All Other Expenses (net)	2.3	1.7
9.5	11.9	7.3	13.4			Profit Before Taxes	11.0	16.3
						RATIOS		
2.1	3.2	2.7	1.3				2.9	2.2
1.0	1.4	1.4	1.0			Current	1.3	1.4
.2	1.0	.6	.7				.9	.9
2.1	3.1	2.3	1.3				2.4	2.1
.7	1.4	1.3	1.0			Quick	1.1	1.1
.2	.7	.5	.6				.7	.5
0 UND	0 UND	2 180.8	0 UND				0 UND	0 UND
0 UND	0 999.8	8 44.8	9 41.3			Sales/Receivables	1 356.1	0 UND
0 UND	8 45.2	25 14.7	16 22.6				23 15.8	13 28.1
						Cost of Sales/Inventory		
						Cost of Sales/Payables		
18.2	7.8	6.6	9.7				9.3	8.0
NM	20.2	15.0	83.9			Sales/Working Capital	22.8	29.6
-9.4	-103.8	-18.7	-17.6				-33.3	-57.9
15.8	34.8	9.1					47.3	60.2
(16) 6.5	(20) 6.0	(18) 3.7				EBIT/Interest	(40) 16.5	(59) 24.0
2.4	.8	.1					2.3	9.1
						Net Profit + Depr., Dep., Amort./Cur. Mat. L/T/D		
.0	.1	.1	.1				.3	.2
.5	.5	.4	.4			Fixed/Worth	.7	.6
-1.7	3.0	3.2	1.2				16.1	3.5
.4	.7	.4	.7				.6	.7
3.2	1.8	2.7	1.7			Debt/Worth	2.4	1.7
-8.1	215.2	10.7	9.4				161.2	9.8
172.2	277.3	60.7	92.6			% Profit Before Taxes/Tangible Net Worth	208.6	214.0
(17) 78.9	(22) 74.2	(22) 15.7	(12) 26.4				(45) 66.1	(72) 88.2
15.8	25.7	-1.0	1.3				18.9	37.0
67.1	54.5	14.8	31.6			% Profit Before Taxes/Total Assets	53.3	71.1
32.8	19.5	5.5	11.2				18.8	27.7
4.1	1.5	-1.6	.3				4.2	12.6
255.3	68.4	65.2	37.0			Sales/Net Fixed Assets	40.0	38.8
34.6	27.7	16.7	14.3				17.2	18.0
15.2	7.6	5.0	7.8				9.7	7.9
8.4	6.1	2.5	2.7			Sales/Total Assets	4.1	4.9
3.8	2.4	1.7	1.1				2.6	2.8
2.4	1.0	1.0	.6				1.4	1.4
.6	.7	.8	.7			% Depr., Dep., Amort./Sales	1.1	1.0
(13) 1.1	(18) 2.0	(17) 1.7	(11) 1.6				(42) 1.9	(56) 2.0
2.5	5.1	3.9	2.5				2.8	3.1
5.0	5.6					% Officers', Directors' Owners' Comp/Sales	7.1	6.0
(11) 14.4	(11) 8.7						(28) 13.0	(34) 9.8
18.7	20.2						24.0	18.6
27091M	101607M	287427M	623646M		60826M	Net Sales ($)	1632585M	551753M
5795M	28463M	138983M	324564M		214635M	Total Assets ($)	532624M	270503M

M = $ thousand   MM = $ million
See Pages 11 through 21 for Explanation of Ratios and Data

Comparative Historical Data | Current Data Sorted by Sales

			Type of Statement						
15	5	11	Unqualified	1	1	1	3	4	1
3	1	3	Reviewed	1	2				
15	13	12	Compiled	3	3	2	2	2	
29	23	29	Tax Returns	14	7	5	1	2	
27	33	37	Other	5	6	3	8	7	8
4/1/04-	4/1/05-	4/1/06-			3 (4/1-9/30/06)		89 (10/1/06-3/31/07)		
3/31/05	3/31/06	3/31/07							
ALL	ALL	ALL		0-1MM	1-3MM	3-5MM	5-10MM	10-25MM	25MM & OVER
89	75	92	**NUMBER OF STATEMENTS**	24	19	11	14	15	9
%	%	%	**ASSETS**	%	%	%	%	%	%
35.2	32.9	33.5	Cash & Equivalents	30.9	36.5	36.8	38.5	30.3	
8.2	9.6	10.1	Trade Receivables (net)	3.9	7.2	8.9	18.8	15.9	
.1	.0	.1	Inventory	.0	.0	.5	.0	.0	
8.3	6.4	6.5	All Other Current	3.8	10.4	10.3	4.0	5.5	
51.9	49.0	50.2	Total Current	38.5	54.2	56.5	61.3	51.7	
21.9	21.3	21.4	Fixed Assets (net)	28.5	16.0	14.7	21.9	23.5	
8.3	8.2	9.7	Intangibles (net)	14.7	15.0	11.4	1.0	5.9	
18.0	21.5	18.7	All Other Non-Current	18.3	14.8	17.4	15.8	19.0	
100.0	100.0	100.0	Total	100.0	100.0	100.0	100.0	100.0	
			LIABILITIES						
13.3	17.1	16.7	Notes Payable-Short Term	35.4	15.5	8.9	7.1	12.7	
1.6	2.5	1.7	Cur. Mat.-L.T.D.	1.2	1.7	.8	1.2	1.6	
7.2	7.3	6.4	Trade Payables	7.6	2.7	3.1	6.7	9.4	
.7	.5	.5	Income Taxes Payable	.7	.0	.3	.9	.2	
20.9	24.3	27.9	All Other Current	45.7	21.8	24.2	19.4	22.3	
43.8	51.6	53.2	Total Current	90.4	41.8	37.2	35.3	46.1	
14.7	21.5	15.6	Long-Term Debt	25.5	14.2	9.6	12.8	10.9	
.2	.8	.5	Deferred Taxes	.0	.0	.0	2.6	.0	
7.1	11.2	3.3	All Other Non-Current	.6	4.2	4.7	.7	4.1	
34.3	14.8	27.4	Net Worth	-16.7	39.7	48.5	48.6	38.9	
100.0	100.0	100.0	Total Liabilties & Net Worth	100.0	100.0	100.0	100.0	100.0	
			INCOME DATA						
100.0	100.0	100.0	Net Sales	100.0	100.0	100.0	100.0	100.0	
			Gross Profit						
88.8	88.3	90.2	Operating Expenses	85.1	85.5	98.6	93.3	91.1	
11.2	11.7	9.8	Operating Profit	14.9	14.5	1.4	6.7	8.9	
1.1	1.7	-.1	All Other Expenses (net)	2.6	.3	-3.0	.0	-2.5	
10.1	10.0	10.0	Profit Before Taxes	12.3	14.2	4.4	6.7	11.4	
			RATIOS						
2.2	2.8	2.2		1.8	3.2	3.6	3.2	1.9	
1.2	1.0	1.2	Current	.9	1.4	1.9	2.0	1.2	
.8	.5	.6		.1	.6	1.0	.8	.6	
2.1	2.8	2.2		1.8	3.1	3.2	3.0	1.8	
1.1	.9	1.1	Quick	.8	1.1	1.7	1.9	1.2	
.6	.4	.4		.1	.4	.6	.7	.4	
0 UND	0 UND	0 UND		0 UND	0 UND	0 UND	1 262.9	2 149.6	
1 482.8	0 UND	2 189.6	Sales/Receivables	0 UND	0 UND	4 100.9	5 71.9	7 50.9	
15 24.1	14 26.7	17 21.4		0 UND	8 45.3	18 20.7	20 18.1	25 14.7	
			Cost of Sales/Inventory						
			Cost of Sales/Payables						
7.7	9.8	8.6		22.3	6.4	9.5	7.0	7.3	
30.0	668.6	33.2	Sales/Working Capital	-78.6	15.8	12.1	33.2	30.8	
-51.2	-16.4	-19.6		-11.6	-26.6	35.6	-36.9	-8.9	
61.5	17.3	17.0		10.0	29.4				
(60) 12.3	(47) 6.3	(63) 5.8	EBIT/Interest	(16) 5.9	(14) 6.5				
1.9	.6	.6		2.4	1.0				
			Net Profit + Depr., Dep., Amort./Cur. Mat. L/T/D						
.1	.1	.1		.0	.0	.1	.1	.3	
.5	.5	.5	Fixed/Worth	1.9	.3	.4	.3	.6	
6.1	10.6	3.7		NM	-11.4	.9	1.7	3.0	
.5	.8	.6		1.4	.3	.2	.3	.7	
1.9	2.6	2.3	Debt/Worth	11.0	2.7	2.0	.9	3.5	
119.5	-102.4	24.9		-9.3	-13.7	10.4	7.4	9.3	
122.5	139.9	118.5		203.8	155.2		95.5	140.7	
(68) 37.0	(56) 57.1	(74) 51.9	% Profit Before Taxes/Tangible Net Worth	(17) 78.9	(13) 68.4		(12) 26.8	(14) 66.8	
9.2	11.2	3.1		8.6	13.2		2.0	6.7	
36.9	35.0	45.3		39.2	54.5	28.1	54.3	48.9	
10.5	12.2	12.8	% Profit Before Taxes/Total Assets	12.3	15.4	3.6	8.1	14.3	
1.2	.9	.6		.6	8.0	-3.6	-1.6	1.5	
99.3	99.3	75.4		281.8	307.5	67.6	100.3	35.0	
20.5	21.8	23.7	Sales/Net Fixed Assets	25.4	29.8	26.5	32.9	14.3	
11.7	11.0	8.4		7.3	12.4	7.6	16.8	5.3	
5.2	5.2	4.2		4.3	4.0	4.0	7.4	3.2	
2.5	2.8	2.3	Sales/Total Assets	2.2	2.3	2.4	3.6	2.1	
1.0	1.0	1.0		.7	1.2	1.6	.8	1.5	
1.0	.8	.7		.4	.9		.6	1.2	
(59) 1.9	(47) 1.3	(60) 1.7	% Depr., Dep., Amort./Sales	(11) 1.2	(11) 2.0		(12) 1.0	(11) 2.1	
3.1	2.7	3.7		5.1	3.5		1.8	4.5	
3.6	6.2	3.6		7.0	4.4				
(29) 7.4	(29) 8.8	(31) 7.7	% Officers', Directors' Owners' Comp/Sales	(10) 11.0	(10) 7.9				
15.2	20.9	16.4		20.1	15.0				
1136314M	1211631M	1100597M	Net Sales ($)	12490M	31404M	43291M	98521M	248057M	666834M
665617M	467011M	712440M	Total Assets ($)	10321M	30084M	26282M	86936M	131935M	426882M

Current Data Sorted by Assets

Comparative Historical Data

	0-500M	500M-2MM	2-10MM	10-50MM	50-100MM	100-250MM	Type of Statement	4/1/02-3/31/03 ALL	4/1/03-3/31/04 ALL
	3	5	7	2	5		Unqualified	22	23
	3	1	1		2		Reviewed	11	13
32	39	24	6	2	2		Compiled	112	144
110	28	6	1	4			Tax Returns	85	140
129	147	150	34	10	12		Other	382	418
	204 (4/1-9/30/06)		559 (10/1/06-3/31/07)						
271	220	186	49	18	19	NUMBER OF STATEMENTS	612	738
%	%	%	%	%	%	ASSETS	%	%
26.2	12.2	12.6	15.5	13.6	7.3	Cash & Equivalents	13.1	14.4
18.2	38.5	40.5	37.8	39.2	33.9	Trade Receivables (net)	36.4	34.7
1.4	7.2	5.6	2.5	1.9	.0	Inventory	4.5	4.2
5.5	6.0	9.2	12.4	5.6	6.5	All Other Current	6.7	7.1
51.3	63.9	67.9	68.2	60.3	47.8	Total Current	60.7	60.4
22.7	16.5	16.1	15.2	20.0	10.4	Fixed Assets (net)	19.2	18.2
11.4	9.4	7.1	5.2	10.4	24.7	Intangibles (net)	8.6	10.1
14.6	10.2	9.0	11.4	9.4	17.1	All Other Non-Current	11.5	11.4
100.0	100.0	100.0	100.0	100.0	100.0	Total	100.0	100.0
						LIABILITIES		
24.1	12.6	9.8	8.5	11.3	7.8	Notes Payable-Short Term	18.3	20.0
6.8	3.0	2.6	2.2	6.0	5.5	Cur. Mat.-L.T.D.	5.2	4.8
4.7	3.5	3.5	7.1	4.3	6.2	Trade Payables	3.2	3.5
.1	.5	1.0	.2	.3	.1	Income Taxes Payable	.6	.5
21.8	14.6	15.3	18.8	15.8	25.1	All Other Current	19.2	19.0
57.5	34.3	32.2	36.8	37.7	44.7	Total Current	46.4	47.8
20.7	16.2	13.5	10.3	17.1	21.6	Long-Term Debt	16.5	19.2
.0	.2	.7	.0	.2	.0	Deferred Taxes	.4	.2
9.7	4.8	7.5	6.7	17.0	7.8	All Other Non-Current	7.2	7.2
12.0	44.5	46.1	46.2	28.1	25.9	Net Worth	29.6	25.5
100.0	100.0	100.0	100.0	100.0	100.0	Total Liabilties & Net Worth	100.0	100.0
						INCOME DATA		
100.0	100.0	100.0	100.0	100.0	100.0	Net Sales	100.0	100.0
						Gross Profit		
82.8	83.2	83.7	81.9	75.1	80.4	Operating Expenses	86.7	85.9
17.2	16.8	16.3	18.1	24.9	19.6	Operating Profit	13.3	14.1
1.1	2.1	2.2	2.0	1.9	2.3	All Other Expenses (net)	2.2	2.0
16.0	14.8	14.1	16.1	23.0	17.3	Profit Before Taxes	11.1	12.1
						RATIOS		
2.9	4.3	4.6	3.8	4.2	2.9	Current	3.3	3.2
1.3	2.0	2.2	2.4	2.2	1.5		1.8	1.7
.4	1.1	1.4	1.3	1.0	.4		1.0	.8
2.4	3.3	3.7	3.1	3.9	2.7	Quick	2.8	2.6
(270) 1.1	1.5	(185) 1.7	1.9	1.9	1.4		1.4	1.3
.4	.8	1.0	1.1	.6	.3		.7	.6
0 UND	26 13.9	45 8.2	41 8.9	33 11.1	17 21.8	Sales/Receivables	18 20.1	0 UND
0 UND	53 6.9	61 6.0	66 5.6	52 7.0	61 5.9		50 7.3	46 7.9
36 10.1	74 4.9	85 4.3	90 4.1	129 2.8	75 4.9		80 4.6	78 4.7
						Cost of Sales/Inventory		
						Cost of Sales/Payables		
11.2	4.9	4.1	3.5	3.3	6.6	Sales/Working Capital	5.3	5.7
96.6	9.0	6.4	6.0	5.1	10.2		10.9	11.9
-18.2	59.9	13.9	14.7	NM	-19.6		-172.1	-72.0
26.8	35.0	42.4	100.7	31.4	45.8	EBIT/Interest	29.0	36.1
(193) 8.4	(184) 6.3	(158) 10.6	(39) 21.7	(17) 13.1	(15) 21.3		(507) 7.2	(617) 8.5
2.3	2.1	2.5	4.1	2.7	1.2		1.8	2.0
	4.7	12.3				Net Profit + Depr., Dep.,	4.7	3.6
	(10) 1.6	(13) 3.1				Amort./Cur. Mat. L/T/D	(42) 1.8	(48) 1.2
	.5	1.5					.8	.8
.1	.1	.1	.1	.1	.2	Fixed/Worth	.1	.1
.8	.3	.3	.3	.5	.4		.4	.4
-2.5	1.4	.9	.6	-1.2	-.2		4.3	16.9
.6	.3	.4	.4	.4	.5	Debt/Worth	.6	.6
3.8	1.3	1.2	.9	3.7	1.1		1.7	2.0
-3.8	9.6	4.2	2.1	-6.4	-7.9		37.3	-80.8
554.3	139.2	112.9	128.4	147.2	174.0	% Profit Before Taxes/Tangible Net Worth	121.4	140.4
(168) 163.2	(180) 50.1	(167) 37.6	(45) 77.4	(12) 85.5	(13) 124.1		(478) 42.9	(548) 53.8
42.5	8.3	10.3	35.4	15.0	90.3		6.8	7.8
129.0	59.8	56.7	65.9	77.0	70.3	% Profit Before Taxes/Total Assets	49.7	60.3
43.5	16.3	11.2	24.3	34.8	54.3		13.0	17.2
9.4	2.9	3.1	6.5	2.4	3.0		1.3	1.6
569.5	90.8	37.9	37.3	28.5	65.4	Sales/Net Fixed Assets	49.6	64.1
39.2	30.6	21.4	18.7	15.7	17.7		24.6	27.8
13.6	15.6	12.5	12.3	11.8	12.1		14.1	14.3
9.5	3.9	3.0	2.8	3.0	3.0	Sales/Total Assets	4.2	4.6
5.1	2.7	2.3	2.1	2.0	2.3		2.8	3.0
2.9	1.8	1.7	1.7	1.1	1.5		1.9	2.0
.9	.9	1.2	1.2	1.5		% Depr., Dep., Amort./Sales	1.2	1.1
(139) 1.6	(138) 1.5	(151) 1.7	(41) 1.6	(15) 2.6			(424) 1.9	(494) 1.8
2.9	2.4	2.4	2.6	3.4			2.8	2.7
14.0	14.1	14.4	8.2			% Officers', Directors' Owners' Comp/Sales	14.8	13.7
(151) 22.8	(105) 24.6	(80) 26.3	(19) 20.2				(322) 24.4	(382) 23.7
32.6	33.9	32.0	29.0				32.9	31.4
316063M	729579M	1997152M	4759258M	4612048M	7602825M	Net Sales ($)	13192649M	13953421M
52743M	239970M	828741M	983795M	1234900M	3087720M	Total Assets ($)	3614046M	4265219M

M = $ thousand   MM = $ million
See Pages 11 through 21 for Explanation of Ratios and Data

Comparative Historical Data   Current Data Sorted by Sales

22 / 11 / 118 / 160 / 458	21 / 5 / 109 / 141 / 444	22 / 5 / 105 / 149 / 482	Type of Statement	1st group	2nd group				
			Unqualified		1	2	2	5	12
			Reviewed			2	1	1	1
			Compiled	22	34	11	23	6	9
			Tax Returns	74	48	14	7	2	4
			Other	104	103	64	91	68	52
4/1/04-3/31/05 ALL	4/1/05-3/31/06 ALL	4/1/06-3/31/07 ALL		204 (4/1-9/30/06)		559 (10/1/06-3/31/07)			
				0-1MM	1-3MM	3-5MM	5-10MM	10-25MM	25MM & OVER
769	720	763	**NUMBER OF STATEMENTS**	200	186	93	124	82	78
%	%	%	**ASSETS**	%	%	%	%	%	%
15.5	16.3	17.4	Cash & Equivalents	21.9	17.3	17.3	14.6	15.3	12.8
32.6	33.4	31.6	Trade Receivables (net)	18.2	29.0	36.4	41.2	41.2	41.3
4.0	3.9	4.1	Inventory	1.9	4.9	7.5	4.5	4.9	2.7
6.3	6.3	7.0	All Other Current	5.1	5.6	8.5	9.3	8.7	8.3
58.4	59.9	60.2	Total Current	47.1	56.8	69.7	69.6	70.1	65.1
18.4	17.9	18.4	Fixed Assets (net)	26.2	18.3	12.0	15.4	14.6	15.3
10.1	9.2	9.7	Intangibles (net)	11.8	11.7	8.2	7.2	4.0	11.1
13.0	13.0	11.7	All Other Non-Current	14.9	13.2	10.1	7.7	11.3	8.5
100.0	100.0	100.0	Total	100.0	100.0	100.0	100.0	100.0	100.0
			LIABILITIES						
18.9	17.0	15.6	Notes Payable-Short Term	21.1	19.6	16.5	8.3	8.4	9.8
4.6	4.1	4.4	Cur. Mat.-L.T.D.	4.3	6.8	3.4	3.6	2.2	3.4
3.4	3.8	4.2	Trade Payables	3.5	2.6	4.1	6.1	4.9	6.6
.8	.6	.5	Income Taxes Payable	.2	.3	1.4	.4	.7	.2
19.2	18.2	17.9	All Other Current	18.7	16.7	20.1	17.2	14.4	21.0
46.9	43.8	42.5	Total Current	47.8	46.0	45.5	35.6	30.5	40.8
18.0	18.5	16.9	Long-Term Debt	25.7	19.0	10.1	10.4	12.3	12.8
.2	.3	.2	Deferred Taxes	.0	.1	.0	.8	.6	.1
8.0	8.8	7.7	All Other Non-Current	9.8	7.3	5.3	7.5	8.3	5.9
26.9	28.7	32.6	Net Worth	16.8	27.5	39.1	45.8	48.3	40.4
100.0	100.0	100.0	Total Liabilities & Net Worth	100.0	100.0	100.0	100.0	100.0	100.0
			INCOME DATA						
100.0	100.0	100.0	Net Sales	100.0	100.0	100.0	100.0	100.0	100.0
			Gross Profit						
85.4	84.5	82.8	Operating Expenses	78.1	85.6	86.4	85.6	83.1	79.5
14.6	15.5	17.2	Operating Profit	21.9	14.4	13.6	14.4	16.9	20.5
1.3	1.9	1.8	All Other Expenses (net)	3.1	1.3	.7	1.3	2.5	.8
13.3	13.7	15.4	Profit Before Taxes	18.9	13.2	12.9	13.1	14.3	19.7
			RATIOS						
3.0	3.8	3.9	Current	3.0	3.8	3.3	5.0	4.7	3.9
1.6	1.7	1.8		1.3	1.6	1.5	2.3	2.5	2.2
.8	.9	1.0		.4	.7	1.1	1.4	1.5	1.3
2.5	3.0	3.1	Quick	2.5	3.0	2.5	4.3	3.6	3.6
(768) 1.3	(719) 1.4	(761) 1.4		(198) 1.1	1.3	1.3	1.7	1.9	1.9
.6	.7	.7		.4	.6	.7	1.0	1.2	1.1
0 UND	0 UND	0 UND	Sales/Receivables	0 UND	0 UND	9 40.5	33 11.1	42 8.8	38 9.5
43 8.6	42 8.6	45 8.1		3 131.1	40 9.0	50 7.3	57 6.4	57 6.5	63 5.8
72 5.1	72 5.1	71 5.1		45 8.1	70 5.2	73 5.0	82 4.4	69 5.3	82 4.4
			Cost of Sales/Inventory						
			Cost of Sales/Payables						
6.1	5.4	5.2	Sales/Working Capital	6.8	5.7	5.5	4.3	4.2	4.5
13.6	12.2	11.5		59.2	25.0	10.5	7.3	6.4	7.2
-50.0	-116.4	-189.7		-13.1	-48.6	60.6	18.4	15.2	14.3
35.6	38.6	35.4	EBIT/Interest	24.9	26.0	36.7	35.1	72.2	62.5
(620) 9.1	(584) 10.2	(606) 8.9		(134) 7.0	(153) 8.0	(79) 7.0	(108) 8.5	(69) 14.2	(63) 21.7
2.4	2.3	2.4		2.4	2.2	2.0	2.4	2.6	4.1
6.0	7.5	7.6	Net Profit + Depr., Dep., Amort./Cur. Mat. L/T/D						
(41) 2.2	(35) 2.4	(36) 2.4							
1.4	.7	1.1							
.1	.1	.1	Fixed/Worth	.1	.1	.0	.1	.1	.1
.4	.3	.4		1.1	.4	.2	.3	.3	.3
9.6	4.6	3.1		-2.6	19.3	1.0	1.2	.6	.6
.7	.5	.5	Debt/Worth	.6	.4	.5	.4	.4	.4
1.9	1.7	1.7		5.5	2.0	1.7	1.1	.8	1.0
-212.2	189.4	125.3		-5.2	-13.1	7.7	4.8	1.8	3.5
146.1	150.5	173.8	% Profit Before Taxes/Tangible Net Worth	490.4	219.2	195.1	133.3	127.5	139.3
(575) 55.7	(548) 62.8	(585) 77.6		(125) 117.3	(134) 64.7	(79) 35.6	(106) 50.3	(76) 59.7	(65) 86.9
10.7	13.7	14.0		43.3	10.9	5.8	11.6	12.2	43.1
64.2	67.2	75.7	% Profit Before Taxes/Total Assets	92.4	78.7	73.1	68.0	63.1	75.0
17.2	19.4	23.0		30.1	21.7	14.0	12.2	16.9	46.0
3.1	3.5	4.2		7.2	3.7	1.7	2.8	4.7	7.3
80.3	75.5	78.5	Sales/Net Fixed Assets	170.7	172.9	107.7	53.6	34.9	43.6
28.4	31.1	26.7		20.7	30.9	35.6	26.4	22.7	18.4
14.0	14.6	13.4		8.2	15.0	22.2	15.4	17.1	12.6
4.7	4.7	4.6	Sales/Total Assets	6.5	6.2	5.0	3.7	3.4	3.4
3.0	2.9	2.9		3.0	3.2	3.2	2.7	2.7	2.6
2.0	1.9	1.9		1.4	2.1	2.2	2.0	2.2	1.8
1.1	1.0	1.0	% Depr., Dep., Amort./Sales	1.1	1.0	.9	1.0	1.1	1.2
(480) 1.7	(460) 1.7	(493) 1.6		(106) 2.3	(113) 1.6	(55) 1.5	(91) 1.5	(71) 1.5	(57) 1.6
2.6	2.5	2.6		4.6	2.7	2.1	2.4	2.0	2.3
16.0	14.6	13.9	% Officers', Directors' Owners' Comp/Sales	14.3	11.9	12.6	16.0	16.8	9.0
(414) 24.5	(347) 23.2	(366) 24.6		(101) 21.5	(96) 24.1	(48) 28.0	(58) 26.1	(34) 26.9	(29) 24.4
32.8	33.3	32.7		30.4	34.0	35.5	32.6	33.0	33.6
14367324M	18628290M	20016925M	Net Sales ($)	101692M	345594M	368748M	894393M	1278526M	17027972M
4358538M	5241910M	6427869M	Total Assets ($)	72778M	198984M	141486M	393847M	767493M	4853281M

Current Data Sorted by Assets   Comparative Historical Data

Type of Statement	0-500M	500M-2MM	2-10MM	10-50MM	50-100MM	100-250MM	4/1/02-3/31/03 ALL	4/1/03-3/31/04 ALL
Unqualified	2		1	1	3	2	4	1
Reviewed		1	1					
Compiled	1	4	2			1	5	5
Tax Returns	29	10	1	1			2	8
Other	19	25	20	8	1	3	5	16
		16 (4/1-9/30/06)		120 (10/1/06-3/31/07)				
NUMBER OF STATEMENTS	51	40	25	10	7	3	16	30
ASSETS	%	%	%	%	%	%	%	%
Cash & Equivalents	30.5	13.8	21.3	12.3			13.6	16.4
Trade Receivables (net)	11.5	32.4	36.0	43.2			35.2	24.7
Inventory	.0	3.7	6.2	5.1			1.0	1.5
All Other Current	7.6	1.3	9.2	1.7			6.6	7.6
Total Current	49.6	51.2	72.6	62.3			56.4	50.3
Fixed Assets (net)	24.3	26.1	10.7	5.7			24.2	19.8
Intangibles (net)	9.2	9.1	11.7	3.6			7.5	12.7
All Other Non-Current	16.9	13.5	4.9	28.4			11.9	17.1
Total	100.0	100.0	100.0	100.0			100.0	100.0
LIABILITIES								
Notes Payable-Short Term	15.8	13.1	15.0	22.1			19.3	11.1
Cur. Mat.-L.T.D.	2.2	4.6	3.6	1.8			8.4	2.1
Trade Payables	4.3	9.3	7.4	2.3			10.7	5.2
Income Taxes Payable	.2	1.2	1.0	.0			.0	.2
All Other Current	28.5	15.6	24.2	21.4			14.9	17.6
Total Current	51.0	43.8	51.2	47.6			53.3	36.2
Long-Term Debt	21.9	14.7	5.5	13.5			13.4	22.1
Deferred Taxes	.0	.0	.7	.2			.1	.8
All Other Non-Current	4.5	7.4	3.4	15.5			10.9	4.8
Net Worth	22.5	34.1	39.1	23.2			22.3	36.1
Total Liabilties & Net Worth	100.0	100.0	100.0	100.0			100.0	100.0
INCOME DATA								
Net Sales	100.0	100.0	100.0	100.0			100.0	100.0
Gross Profit								
Operating Expenses	85.3	88.0	90.9	80.0			90.2	89.9
Operating Profit	14.7	12.0	9.1	20.0			9.8	10.1
All Other Expenses (net)	1.2	2.5	.2	8.1			2.5	1.3
Profit Before Taxes	13.5	9.5	8.9	11.9			7.3	8.8
RATIOS								
Current	4.9	2.0	2.4	5.5			1.9	2.6
	1.3	1.1	1.5	1.7			1.1	1.6
	.4	.7	1.0	1.0			.7	1.0
Quick	3.6	1.8	1.8	5.3			1.3	2.6
	.9	1.0	1.2	1.6			.8	1.2
	.2	.6	.7	.8			.6	.6
Sales/Receivables	0 UND	5 80.9	24 15.5	11 33.3			4 85.7	0 UND
	0 UND	33 10.9	46 7.9	57 6.4			52 7.0	37 9.9
	22 16.9	63 5.7	96 3.8	166 2.2			70 5.2	58 6.3
Cost of Sales/Inventory								
Cost of Sales/Payables								
Sales/Working Capital	8.2	8.9	6.6	2.6			9.8	6.5
	101.0	68.3	11.0	10.7			NM	24.2
	-20.5	-18.5	NM	NM			-17.8	UND
EBIT/Interest	23.5	30.0	22.2				15.5	17.2
	(28) 3.7	(32) 8.2	(18) 5.6				(12) 5.0	(22) 4.6
	.4	2.1	1.0				-.5	1.6
Net Profit + Depr., Dep., Amort./Cur. Mat. L/T/D								
Fixed/Worth	.0	.1	.1	.1			.1	.1
	.5	.5	.3	.1			.8	.7
	-4.7	3.0	4.3	NM			NM	-2.3
Debt/Worth	.3	.7	.7	1.3			1.9	.5
	3.1	2.1	2.6	8.0			3.9	2.3
	-6.2	NM	38.2	NM			NM	-5.7
% Profit Before Taxes/Tangible Net Worth	157.2	85.0	129.1				265.8	66.7
	(34) 78.8	(30) 39.7	(20) 52.2				(12) 28.3	(19) 40.3
	7.8	8.7	21.6				-5.4	1.9
% Profit Before Taxes/Total Assets	93.6	35.7	26.2	15.4			25.3	35.8
	37.4	10.8	11.1	8.0			3.8	14.2
	.5	2.0	2.9	1.0			-16.8	1.7
Sales/Net Fixed Assets	UND	64.5	61.2	71.5			148.1	173.1
	47.7	15.8	29.9	31.9			17.1	39.5
	11.1	6.6	13.2	11.1			6.3	6.1
Sales/Total Assets	12.6	4.4	3.0	2.9			3.8	3.6
	4.3	2.9	2.4	1.2			2.5	2.5
	2.2	1.8	1.3	.2			1.7	1.7
% Depr., Dep., Amort./Sales	1.0	1.0	.9				1.9	1.6
	(22) 1.7	(26) 1.3	(16) 1.3				(10) 2.8	(15) 2.4
	4.5	4.3	3.7				6.0	4.7
% Officers', Directors' Owners' Comp/Sales	4.7	5.8	2.0					8.3
	(21) 8.8	(14) 10.7	(11) 9.0					(10) 22.0
	19.6	19.0	19.6					30.9
Net Sales ($)	58782M	173873M	528119M	620425M	1848724M	879613M	306327M	107761M
Total Assets ($)	9578M	44263M	98052M	250590M	495238M	515456M	188513M	44878M

M = $ thousand   MM = $ million
See Pages 11 through 21 for Explanation of Ratios and Data

Comparative Historical Data / Current Data Sorted by Sales

Type of Statement

			Type of Statement						
1	7	9	Unqualified		1	1	1	2	4
1	3	2	Reviewed				2		
6	6	8	Compiled	1	2	3		1	1
11	15	42	Tax Returns	24	11	4		1	1
24	37	75	Other	19	16	6	18	8	8
4/1/04-3/31/05	4/1/05-3/31/06	4/1/06-3/31/07				16 (4/1-9/30/06)			
ALL	ALL	ALL		0-1MM	1-3MM		120 (10/1/06-3/31/07)		25MM & OVER
						3-5MM	5-10MM	10-25MM	

Data

4/1/04-3/31/05 ALL	4/1/05-3/31/06 ALL	4/1/06-3/31/07 ALL		0-1MM	1-3MM	3-5MM	5-10MM	10-25MM	25MM & OVER
43	68	136	**NUMBER OF STATEMENTS**	44	30	14	21	11	16
%	%	%	**ASSETS**	%	%	%	%	%	%
15.7	23.7	21.3	Cash & Equivalents	28.2	24.7	14.5	6.5	25.3	18.0
27.0	29.6	25.5	Trade Receivables (net)	11.1	22.7	22.3	53.8	26.0	35.7
1.1	3.2	2.8	Inventory	.0	2.4	5.8	3.7	6.6	4.5
6.6	5.8	5.9	All Other Current	4.4	5.6	12.3	3.3	6.6	8.0
50.4	62.3	55.4	Total Current	43.8	55.3	55.0	67.3	64.6	66.2
20.8	15.3	20.0	Fixed Assets (net)	27.3	16.9	36.3	9.9	13.2	9.7
9.5	11.4	9.9	Intangibles (net)	8.2	15.2	3.1	9.5	8.9	11.9
19.3	10.9	14.6	All Other Non-Current	20.7	12.5	5.6	13.4	13.3	12.2
100.0	100.0	100.0	Total	100.0	100.0	100.0	100.0	100.0	100.0
			LIABILITIES						
14.9	13.6	14.9	Notes Payable-Short Term	8.5	15.7	31.4	24.9	7.4	8.5
3.2	4.8	3.1	Cur. Mat.-L.T.D.	2.3	4.6	4.5	2.9	2.4	1.6
7.5	7.5	6.0	Trade Payables	3.4	10.8	3.5	8.2	7.5	2.7
.3	.2	.6	Income Taxes Payable	.2	.0	1.5	2.4	.0	.2
11.4	19.4	22.3	All Other Current	30.1	17.8	19.0	14.4	20.7	23.7
37.2	45.5	46.9	Total Current	44.5	49.0	59.9	52.7	38.0	36.8
29.2	10.3	15.0	Long-Term Debt	15.5	21.3	28.9	5.4	2.6	10.6
.3	.1	.2	Deferred Taxes	.0	.0	.4	.6	.1	.2
7.8	14.5	6.8	All Other Non-Current	8.1	4.4	1.2	7.2	10.1	9.9
25.4	29.6	31.1	Net Worth	31.9	25.3	9.6	34.2	49.2	42.5
100.0	100.0	100.0	Total Liabilities & Net Worth	100.0	100.0	100.0	100.0	100.0	100.0
			INCOME DATA						
100.0	100.0	100.0	Net Sales	100.0	100.0	100.0	100.0	100.0	100.0
			Gross Profit						
83.5	86.6	86.2	Operating Expenses	83.7	90.9	85.2	85.1	90.0	83.8
16.5	13.4	13.8	Operating Profit	16.3	9.1	14.8	14.9	10.0	16.2
2.3	2.2	1.9	All Other Expenses (net)	2.5	.4	1.3	4.3	1.1	1.0
14.2	11.2	11.9	Profit Before Taxes	13.8	8.7	13.5	10.6	8.9	15.2
			RATIOS						
4.5	3.8	2.9	Current	3.1	2.3	6.8	2.4	4.9	3.2
1.8	1.4	1.4		1.0	1.0	1.5	1.5	2.1	1.7
.8	1.0	.7		.4	.4	.5	1.0	1.0	1.2
4.2	3.0	2.3	Quick	2.8	2.1	4.8	2.1	4.9	2.8
1.4	1.2	1.1		.9	1.0	.9	1.1	1.7	1.3
.7	.8	.6		.2	.3	.3	.8	.7	.9
0 UND	0 UND	0 UND	Sales/Receivables	0 UND	0 UND	0 UND	41 8.9	4 89.8	27 13.6
18 20.0	37 9.9	25 14.5		0 UND	19 19.2	17 21.8	73 5.0	25 14.6	44 8.3
64 5.7	79 4.6	56 6.5		27 13.5	54 6.7	51 7.2	104 3.5	46 8.0	81 4.5
			Cost of Sales/Inventory						
			Cost of Sales/Payables						
4.6	5.3	7.3	Sales/Working Capital	7.4	9.7	13.1	5.5	5.9	4.9
18.8	15.9	32.0		NM	71.3	47.2	10.3	21.2	15.0
-98.5	-369.9	-23.1		-18.2	-15.0	-18.4	NM	-999.8	87.7
29.4	37.0	23.7	EBIT/Interest	6.9	16.3	25.1	30.8		99.7
(33) 8.2	(47) 12.0	(92) 5.9		(23) 2.2	(22) 3.6	(12) 9.5	(17) 11.5	(11) 5.8	
2.3	2.4	1.5		-.6	2.0	2.9	2.4		1.2
		3.8	Net Profit + Depr., Dep., Amort./Cur. Mat. L/T/D						
	(10)	1.5							
		-1.2							
.1	.1	.1	Fixed/Worth	.0	.1	.0	.1	.1	.1
.6	.5	.4		.5	.9	1.4	.2	.3	.3
-1.5	UND	6.4		UND	-.7	-3.6	.8	3.0	.5
.5	.6	.5	Debt/Worth	.4	.7	.7	1.1	.2	.7
2.8	3.1	2.6		1.9	7.9	2.5	2.8	2.1	1.7
-6.8	UND	-21.5		-16.1	-3.8	-14.2	37.1	9.3	7.5
186.4	157.9	109.7	% Profit Before Taxes/Tangible Net Worth	145.7	92.2	117.5	120.0		120.1
(27) 73.4	(52) 91.6	(100) 62.1		(31) 66.7	(19) 39.2	(10) 85.1	(17) 26.8	(14) 79.8	
23.2	29.4	11.9		2.6	16.3	8.7	10.5		22.8
57.9	56.3	50.7	% Profit Before Taxes/Total Assets	67.8	32.4	102.2	28.1	51.0	63.1
25.3	18.9	14.3		21.3	11.6	37.3	8.4	23.0	19.7
7.2	4.9	2.2		.0	4.6	2.2	2.0	1.8	5.9
46.2	88.9	92.1	Sales/Net Fixed Assets	224.3	52.0	412.3	61.9	86.6	165.4
23.7	34.3	28.3		20.6	17.1	22.7	29.9	45.7	40.5
11.5	12.8	10.9		6.7	9.3	5.4	16.9	21.1	12.1
4.6	5.9	5.0	Sales/Total Assets	5.6	4.3	8.8	3.3	18.1	6.0
2.8	2.4	2.8		2.6	2.6	4.2	2.6	3.9	2.5
1.5	1.3	1.6		1.3	1.8	2.8	.9	2.4	1.6
1.3	.8	.9	% Depr., Dep., Amort./Sales	1.0	1.0		.8		.2
(25) 2.5	(44) 1.6	(79) 1.3		(18) 2.7	(22) 1.6		(15) .9	(11) 1.1	
3.8	3.3	3.5		7.8	4.0		1.4		1.3
5.9	9.4	5.2	% Officers', Directors' Owners' Comp/Sales	6.1	5.0				
(14) 17.6	(29) 16.0	(49) 9.0		(18) 10.4	(11) 8.8				
29.1	31.7	18.9		27.1	18.3				
586331M	3419110M	4109536M	Net Sales ($)	19719M	57804M	60259M	153446M	180243M	3638065M
279848M	1607894M	1413177M	Total Assets ($)	13017M	28073M	16603M	184158M	128221M	1043105M

M = $ thousand   MM = $ million
See Pages 11 through 21 for Explanation of Ratios and Data

Current Data Sorted by Assets

Comparative Historical Data

						Type of Statement		
1	1	7	19	3	5	Unqualified	34	36
2	17	57	24	2		Reviewed	74	87
18	34	29	2			Compiled	84	102
60	24	6	1			Tax Returns	51	83
37	47	56	32	3	5	Other	115	122
	51 (4/1-9/30/06)		441 (10/1/06-3/31/07)				4/1/02-3/31/03	4/1/03-3/31/04
0-500M	500M-2MM	2-10MM	10-50MM	50-100MM	100-250MM		ALL	ALL
118	123	155	78	8	10	NUMBER OF STATEMENTS	358	430
%	%	%	%	%	%	ASSETS	%	%
28.6	12.8	7.1	9.0		14.0	Cash & Equivalents	10.3	14.2
19.0	49.1	58.1	55.0		44.4	Trade Receivables (net)	49.2	45.0
.3	2.3	3.3	2.0		2.4	Inventory	1.7	1.7
6.7	5.2	6.0	12.0		8.1	All Other Current	6.5	5.7
54.6	69.4	74.5	77.9		68.8	Total Current	67.7	66.7
25.6	19.8	16.1	13.7		17.4	Fixed Assets (net)	20.1	20.7
5.8	1.7	1.9	1.1		5.1	Intangibles (net)	2.2	2.0
13.9	9.1	7.5	7.3		8.6	All Other Non-Current	10.0	10.6
100.0	100.0	100.0	100.0		100.0	Total	100.0	100.0
						LIABILITIES		
34.8	12.7	8.6	6.3		1.1	Notes Payable-Short Term	19.0	18.0
6.2	3.1	2.7	2.7		3.3	Cur. Mat.-L.T.D.	3.9	4.2
8.6	14.2	17.9	15.1		16.5	Trade Payables	17.4	15.1
.3	2.2	2.9	3.3		1.1	Income Taxes Payable	1.8	1.8
31.0	12.9	15.1	23.1		30.3	All Other Current	20.3	19.9
80.9	45.2	47.1	50.5		52.3	Total Current	62.4	59.0
15.2	9.6	9.1	6.8		6.4	Long-Term Debt	11.8	11.9
.0	1.0	1.7	1.9		.3	Deferred Taxes	1.8	1.4
6.9	4.8	3.4	3.6		2.8	All Other Non-Current	4.1	5.0
-3.1	39.4	38.6	37.3		38.2	Net Worth	19.9	22.8
100.0	100.0	100.0	100.0		100.0	Total Liabilities & Net Worth	100.0	100.0
						INCOME DATA		
100.0	100.0	100.0	100.0		100.0	Net Sales	100.0	100.0
						Gross Profit		
93.8	91.2	92.2	91.4		88.3	Operating Expenses	97.0	95.2
6.2	8.8	7.8	8.6		11.7	Operating Profit	3.0	4.8
.1	.8	1.6	1.4		.0	All Other Expenses (net)	1.1	1.0
6.2	8.0	6.3	7.2		11.8	Profit Before Taxes	2.0	3.8
						RATIOS		
2.3	3.4	2.2	2.1		1.5	Current	2.1	2.2
.9	1.7	1.6	1.5		1.3		1.4	1.4
.2	1.1	1.2	1.2		1.1		1.0	1.0
2.2	3.1	2.0	1.9		1.3	Quick	1.8	2.0
.7	1.5	1.4	1.2		1.0		1.2 (429) 1.2	
.2	.9	1.0	1.0		1.0		.8	.8
0 UND	35 10.5	65 5.6	74 4.9		61 5.9	Sales/Receivables	39 9.2	0 UND
0 UND	63 5.8	90 4.1	94 3.9		98 3.7		72 5.1	65 5.6
26 14.2	93 3.9	108 3.4	115 3.2		140 2.6		103 3.6	97 3.8
						Cost of Sales/Inventory		
						Cost of Sales/Payables		
15.0	5.8	5.3	4.5		6.9	Sales/Working Capital	6.6	6.6
-175.3	11.9	9.2	9.1		10.6		14.4	18.2
-14.0	93.0	20.1	30.9		17.1		-527.3	-196.0
23.7	27.5	36.8	45.2			EBIT/Interest	17.3	24.0
(81) 8.2	(95) 11.0	(136) 10.9	(66) 16.7				(291) 4.0	(340) 5.3
1.5	1.9	2.8	5.0				-.7	.0
	4.3	7.0	8.4			Net Profit + Depr., Dep., Amort./Cur. Mat. L/T/D	3.9	4.6
	(18) 2.3	(36) 2.4	(30) 2.2				(89) 1.8	(90) 1.8
	.6	1.1	1.3				.2	.4
.2	.1	.2	.1		.2	Fixed/Worth	.2	.2
1.3	.4	.3	.3		.4		.5	.4
-.8	1.4	.7	.7		.5		1.8	1.8
.9	.4	.9	1.0		1.2	Debt/Worth	1.0	.8
9.9	1.4	1.7	1.8		2.3		2.1	2.1
-3.6	5.1	3.6	3.4		4.1		9.9	9.1
234.4	78.7	62.1	50.6		88.9	% Profit Before Taxes/Tangible Net Worth	46.0	60.9
(69) 72.7	(105) 35.8	(146) 29.5	(76) 30.5		42.0		(295) 14.9	(360) 18.8
4.0	10.6	6.4	15.7		27.4		-1.4	-.6
65.8	34.1	24.9	22.6		46.9	% Profit Before Taxes/Total Assets	15.7	27.5
26.3	15.6	10.9	10.7		11.2		3.5	5.3
-1.1	2.0	1.6	4.7		6.0		-4.6	-1.2
140.4	38.6	42.4	38.6		26.2	Sales/Net Fixed Assets	44.7	54.3
44.7	22.4	22.0	22.0		20.4		25.0	27.9
20.7	12.5	12.7	15.3		16.3		13.7	15.6
14.3	4.0	3.1	2.6		3.1	Sales/Total Assets	4.0	4.7
7.6	2.9	2.5	2.1		1.8		2.7	2.9
4.2	2.2	1.9	1.7		1.3		2.1	2.2
.4	.9	.9	.9			% Depr., Dep., Amort./Sales	1.0	.9
(60) .8	(91) 1.3	(130) 1.3	(71) 1.3				(297) 1.5 (342) 1.4	
1.5	2.0	1.9	1.8				2.2	2.2
7.5	6.2	4.0	2.2			% Officers', Directors' Owners' Comp/Sales	6.6	6.5
(87) 13.2	(58) 12.6	(55) 7.5	(20) 8.7				(142) 11.1 (183) 11.7	
18.4	19.3	12.8	14.7				19.7	19.3
227743M	454547M	1861947M	3921500M	1368132M	5019413M	Net Sales ($)	12067603M	9225549M
26354M	136532M	734178M	1559179M	526702M	1751953M	Total Assets ($)	3025405M	3051202M

© RMA 2007

M = $ thousand   MM = $ million
See Pages 11 through 21 for Explanation of Ratios and Data

Comparative Historical Data | | | | Current Data Sorted by Sales | | | | | |

			Type of Statement						
29	40	36	Unqualified	1		2	2	4	27
87	74	102	Reviewed		6	9	25	40	22
85	84	83	Compiled	7	21	21	18	12	4
68	83	91	Tax Returns	23	37	12	10	8	1
139	163	180	Other	22	44	26	22	28	38
4/1/04-3/31/05	4/1/05-3/31/06	4/1/06-3/31/07		51 (4/1-9/30/06)			441 (10/1/06-3/31/07)		
ALL	ALL	ALL		0-1MM	1-3MM	3-5MM	5-10MM	10-25MM	25MM & OVER
408	444	492	**NUMBER OF STATEMENTS**	53	108	70	77	92	92
%	%	%	**ASSETS**	%	%	%	%	%	%
11.9	14.1	14.4	Cash & Equivalents	23.2	19.4	16.6	9.1	8.7	11.7
48.5	46.8	45.5	Trade Receivables (net)	25.9	31.0	47.1	56.1	57.3	51.9
1.9	2.2	2.1	Inventory	.5	1.7	3.7	2.3	2.6	1.4
5.3	6.2	7.0	All Other Current	5.6	5.9	4.5	6.5	8.8	9.8
67.6	69.3	69.0	Total Current	55.2	58.1	72.0	73.9	77.4	74.8
20.1	18.5	18.8	Fixed Assets (net)	28.1	23.8	15.7	17.3	14.5	15.6
2.6	2.2	2.8	Intangibles (net)	5.1	3.7	3.6	2.3	1.1	1.8
9.7	10.1	9.4	All Other Non-Current	11.7	14.4	8.7	6.4	7.0	7.8
100.0	100.0	100.0	Total	100.0	100.0	100.0	100.0	100.0	100.0
			LIABILITIES						
17.3	15.0	15.3	Notes Payable-Short Term	41.4	22.6	12.1	10.9	7.3	5.8
3.2	3.3	3.6	Cur. Mat.-L.T.D.	5.6	2.4	4.4	5.3	2.8	2.7
15.7	15.9	14.2	Trade Payables	6.3	13.2	15.9	14.1	17.8	15.1
2.3	2.1	2.1	Income Taxes Payable	.8	.4	3.0	2.5	3.5	2.6
20.6	18.3	20.4	All Other Current	30.3	19.5	13.3	16.6	18.5	26.0
59.0	54.6	55.6	Total Current	84.4	58.0	48.8	49.3	49.8	52.2
12.3	10.7	10.3	Long-Term Debt	21.7	13.8	6.9	7.1	7.2	7.9
1.2	1.0	1.1	Deferred Taxes	.0	.6	.8	1.7	2.0	1.3
3.7	5.9	4.6	All Other Non-Current	8.1	5.2	4.8	3.7	3.5	3.8
23.7	27.8	28.4	Net Worth	-14.1	22.5	38.8	38.2	37.5	34.8
100.0	100.0	100.0	Total Liabilties & Net Worth	100.0	100.0	100.0	100.0	100.0	100.0
			INCOME DATA						
100.0	100.0	100.0	Net Sales	100.0	100.0	100.0	100.0	100.0	100.0
			Gross Profit						
94.4	92.6	92.1	Operating Expenses	88.5	91.5	92.5	93.8	93.5	91.9
5.6	7.4	7.9	Operating Profit	11.5	8.5	7.5	6.2	6.5	8.1
1.1	.8	.9	All Other Expenses (net)	2.7	.6	.2	.7	.4	1.5
4.5	6.7	6.9	Profit Before Taxes	8.9	7.9	7.2	5.4	6.0	6.7
			RATIOS						
2.2	2.3	2.3		2.6	2.4	4.0	2.6	2.1	1.9
1.3	1.5	1.5	Current	1.2	1.3	1.5	1.7	1.6	1.3
.9	1.0	1.0		.3	.6	1.0	1.2	1.2	1.1
1.9	2.1	2.1		2.6	2.2	3.3	2.5	2.0	1.6
1.2 (443)	1.3	1.3	Quick	1.0	1.1	1.4	1.5	1.3	1.2
.8	.8	.8		.2	.3	.9	1.0	1.0	.9
24 14.9	11 31.9	21 17.3		0 UND	0 UND	30 12.4	55 6.7	65 5.6	68 5.4
73 5.0	73 5.0	70 5.2	Sales/Receivables	2 187.5	31 11.9	62 5.8	80 4.6	93 3.9	83 4.4
108 3.4	105 3.5	98 3.7		66 5.6	78 4.7	93 3.9	106 3.4	110 3.3	111 3.3
			Cost of Sales/Inventory						
			Cost of Sales/Payables						
6.7	6.1	6.4		9.4	7.8	5.7	5.3	5.4	5.9
15.9	14.0	13.1	Sales/Working Capital	52.3	41.2	14.9	9.0	9.7	12.6
-119.4	-212.9	999.8		-8.7	-13.9	NM	28.1	22.4	33.1
25.0	47.0	31.2		26.5	19.8	34.8	40.8	38.3	44.9
(340) 6.9	(371) 11.3	(392) 11.2	EBIT/Interest	(35) 11.0	(83) 8.2	(53) 10.0	(59) 12.1	(85) 11.8	(77) 16.5
1.1	2.8	2.6		1.7	1.5	2.7	3.4	2.8	4.5
5.9	6.8	6.5					7.2	5.5	7.3
(84) 2.3	(90) 2.8	(96) 2.7	Net Profit + Depr., Dep., Amort./Cur. Mat. L/T/D			(11) 4.3	(31) 1.9	(37) 2.6	
1.0	1.1	1.3					2.0	.8	1.4
.2	.1	.2		.2	.2	.1	.1	.2	.2
.5	.4	.4	Fixed/Worth	1.1	.6	.3	.4	.3	.4
3.1	1.4	1.5		-.4	NM	1.2	1.9	.7	.8
.9	.8	.8		.8	.6	.5	.6	.9	1.2
2.5	2.1	1.9	Debt/Worth	3.9	1.9	1.5	1.4	1.8	2.0
15.9	7.0	5.6		-3.0	NM	9.2	10.8	4.3	3.6
67.1	74.8	73.7		118.7	98.0	105.5	64.3	61.4	51.4
(335) 23.0	(372) 36.3	(413) 35.2	% Profit Before Taxes/Tangible Net Worth	(33) 38.6	(81) 44.8	(58) 41.6	(67) 39.9	(85) 27.8	(89) 31.8
3.1	13.2	10.8		-4.8	8.9	13.1	12.9	7.0	15.5
24.1	31.1	31.5		56.2	44.5	41.3	28.2	24.9	21.6
7.3	11.7	12.4	% Profit Before Taxes/Total Assets	14.6	16.5	15.2	15.5	9.9	10.4
.0	2.6	2.3		-3.8	1.7	2.9	2.3	1.6	4.7
51.1	56.0	48.8		67.7	71.7	85.1	45.4	44.7	36.6
29.3	28.5	25.6	Sales/Net Fixed Assets	22.8	28.9	32.7	22.9	23.4	22.2
15.4	15.5	14.3		9.6	13.0	20.7	15.1	14.6	15.7
4.4	4.6	4.2		6.8	7.7	4.6	3.7	3.4	2.8
2.8	2.9	2.8	Sales/Total Assets	4.0	3.7	3.2	2.8	2.6	2.2
2.1	2.0	2.0		2.0	2.4	2.3	2.3	2.0	1.9
.8	.7	.8		.9	.6	.8	.8	.8	.9
(319) 1.4	(352) 1.2	(362) 1.3	% Depr., Dep., Amort./Sales	(26) 1.4	(70) 1.3	(47) 1.1	(62) 1.4	(79) 1.3	(78) 1.3
2.0	1.9	1.9		3.3	1.9	1.7	1.9	1.8	1.8
6.1	6.5	5.4		9.8	7.3	4.0	4.3	3.9	2.3
(161) 10.1	(205) 10.9	(223) 10.5	% Officers', Directors' Owners' Comp/Sales	(31) 17.2	(65) 11.8	(38) 9.4	(40) 8.9	(26) 7.3	(23) 8.2
17.7	18.5	18.0		25.1	18.5	14.5	15.2	18.4	13.6
6974255M	6777216M	12853282M	Net Sales ($)	31396M	207580M	280472M	555520M	1415167M	10363147M
2543183M	3047333M	4734898M	Total Assets ($)	18076M	85309M	105929M	204817M	573417M	3747350M

M = $ thousand   MM = $ million
See Pages 11 through 21 for Explanation of Ratios and Data

Current Data Sorted by Assets | Comparative Historical Data

0-500M	500M-2MM	2-10MM	10-50MM	50-100MM	100-250MM		8 / 4/1/02-3/31/03 ALL	10 / 4/1/03-3/31/04 ALL
						Type of Statement		
1		4	2			Unqualified	8	10
2	8	21	5	1		Reviewed	55	41
5	25	8	1			Compiled	41	48
21	17					Tax Returns	48	50
14	20	20			2	Other	57	58
	21 (4/1-9/30/06)		161 (10/1/06-3/31/07)					
43	70	53	13	1	2	**NUMBER OF STATEMENTS**	209	207
%	%	%	%	%	%	**ASSETS**	%	%
10.7	12.1	8.4	8.0			Cash & Equivalents	10.3	8.7
21.9	32.2	43.3	41.1			Trade Receivables (net)	31.1	32.7
2.4	10.0	8.5	6.1			Inventory	8.2	8.9
2.6	2.4	4.5	2.9			All Other Current	4.6	2.6
37.7	56.7	64.7	58.1			Total Current	54.1	52.8
46.5	36.3	27.8	31.3			Fixed Assets (net)	38.2	36.3
4.0	1.6	2.8	7.7			Intangibles (net)	2.1	2.8
11.7	5.4	4.7	2.9			All Other Non-Current	5.6	8.1
100.0	100.0	100.0	100.0			Total	100.0	100.0
						LIABILITIES		
29.3	9.7	11.6	8.7			Notes Payable-Short Term	12.9	15.3
8.2	5.6	5.3	5.8			Cur. Mat.-L.T.D.	6.3	7.2
10.0	15.4	13.5	14.2			Trade Payables	11.4	11.6
.0	.3	2.0	.9			Income Taxes Payable	1.0	.5
7.1	8.8	10.8	15.0			All Other Current	8.5	10.9
54.7	39.9	43.2	44.6			Total Current	40.1	45.5
36.3	24.0	16.0	16.3			Long-Term Debt	22.9	21.2
.0	.3	1.3	2.9			Deferred Taxes	1.0	.9
3.9	7.5	3.6	10.8			All Other Non-Current	4.7	5.9
5.1	28.3	35.9	25.4			Net Worth	31.3	26.6
100.0	100.0	100.0	100.0			Total Liabilties & Net Worth	100.0	100.0
						INCOME DATA		
100.0	100.0	100.0	100.0			Net Sales	100.0	100.0
						Gross Profit		
94.9	94.2	94.3	95.4			Operating Expenses	95.4	95.2
5.1	5.8	5.7	4.6			Operating Profit	4.6	4.8
1.4	1.4	1.2	1.0			All Other Expenses (net)	1.2	1.0
3.7	4.4	4.5	3.6			Profit Before Taxes	3.4	3.8
						RATIOS		
2.4	2.6	2.1	1.9			Current	2.4	2.4
.9	1.5	1.4	1.3				1.5	1.3
.2	1.0	1.1	.9				1.0	.8
1.9	1.9	1.8	1.8			Quick	2.0	1.7
.7	1.1	1.2	1.2				(208) 1.1	1.0
.2	.7	.9	.7				.6	.5
0 UND	12 30.1	42 8.6	48 7.7			Sales/Receivables	10 35.9	14 26.9
11 34.0	34 10.8	54 6.8	61 6.0				39 9.3	37 9.9
31 11.7	62 5.9	74 5.0	88 4.2				64 5.7	63 5.8
						Cost of Sales/Inventory		
						Cost of Sales/Payables		
16.3	6.8	7.4	6.5			Sales/Working Capital	7.9	8.6
-82.0	20.3	13.6	10.1				20.4	25.2
-13.3	-289.2	40.1	-53.4				-472.0	-38.0
12.0	10.8	11.1	18.6			EBIT/Interest	9.6	9.0
(39) 4.0	(63) 4.1	(50) 3.1	6.1				(185) 3.2	(184) 3.3
.7	1.3	1.5	2.2				1.2	1.0
		4.9				Net Profit + Depr., Dep., Amort./Cur. Mat. L/T/D	3.5	4.0
		(17) 2.1					(46) 2.1	(40) 2.1
		1.4					1.0	.8
.5	.5	.4	.5			Fixed/Worth	.5	.5
2.7	1.1	.9	1.8				1.0	1.1
-6.9	3.5	1.7	2.2				3.1	6.6
.8	1.1	1.0	1.6			Debt/Worth	.8	.8
3.0	2.3	2.2	3.6				2.0	1.9
-11.5	14.7	3.8	4.8				5.3	24.1
138.7	70.1	57.2	63.9			% Profit Before Taxes/Tangible Net Worth	60.0	55.2
(29) 38.7	(58) 22.7	(48) 27.9	(12) 13.8				(185) 19.9	(166) 24.0
3.9	5.0	6.6	11.1				2.9	4.5
33.2	20.9	16.8	16.7			% Profit Before Taxes/Total Assets	18.8	17.3
9.8	8.7	7.7	5.1				6.7	7.1
.0	.4	2.0	2.6				.5	.3
24.8	20.8	27.9	21.6			Sales/Net Fixed Assets	16.1	19.6
12.5	9.6	12.5	8.2				8.5	9.2
6.1	4.5	6.4	2.6				5.4	5.3
7.8	3.7	3.5	2.8			Sales/Total Assets	3.9	4.0
4.2	2.7	2.9	2.4				2.9	2.9
2.8	1.9	2.1	1.4				2.1	2.1
1.3	1.6	1.2	1.5			% Depr., Dep., Amort./Sales	2.1	1.8
(31) 2.7	(56) 2.9	(49) 2.2	(10) 2.8				(177) 3.6	(173) 3.2
4.9	5.3	3.4	4.2				5.2	5.2
3.5	2.1	1.9				% Officers', Directors' Owners' Comp/Sales	2.8	3.2
(26) 6.9	(45) 5.7	(19) 3.9					(109) 5.5	(112) 5.9
17.1	9.0	7.6					11.5	10.2
54536M	215119M	625133M	453442M	86943M	665860M	Net Sales ($)	2790350M	4995040M
10735M	77111M	219473M	229861M	61159M	335154M	Total Assets ($)	1142933M	1816224M

M = $ thousand   MM = $ million
See Pages 11 through 21 for Explanation of Ratios and Data

Comparative Historical Data | | | | **Current Data Sorted by Sales**

Hist 1	Hist 2	Hist 3	Type of Statement	0-1MM	1-3MM	3-5MM	5-10MM	10-25MM	25MM & OVER
14	11	7	Unqualified	1			1	2	3
38	37	37	Reviewed		9	5	6	11	6
35	41	39	Compiled	5	13	10	7	3	1
48	54	38	Tax Returns	11	19	6		2	
50	63	61	Other	9	16	10	12	8	6
4/1/04-3/31/05 ALL	4/1/05-3/31/06 ALL	4/1/06-3/31/07 ALL		21 (4/1-9/30/06)			161 (10/1/06-3/31/07)		
185	206	182	NUMBER OF STATEMENTS	26	57	31	26	26	16
%	%	%	**ASSETS**	%	%	%	%	%	%
10.5	10.6	10.3	Cash & Equivalents	12.0	11.9	10.3	9.3	8.1	7.2
31.6	29.5	33.3	Trade Receivables (net)	10.5	29.3	37.9	43.0	46.2	39.3
9.0	7.3	7.3	Inventory	6.8	6.6	8.0	11.3	7.3	3.2
3.2	2.8	3.0	All Other Current	3.6	2.8	1.2	5.2	3.1	3.1
54.4	50.2	54.0	Total Current	32.9	50.6	57.4	68.7	64.7	52.8
34.1	37.5	36.5	Fixed Assets (net)	54.6	38.2	34.7	25.3	26.5	38.8
3.7	3.7	3.0	Intangibles (net)	2.3	3.5	1.9	1.2	4.5	4.9
7.8	8.6	6.5	All Other Non-Current	10.3	7.6	6.1	4.8	4.4	3.5
100.0	100.0	100.0	Total	100.0	100.0	100.0	100.0	100.0	100.0
			LIABILITIES						
14.5	13.7	14.7	Notes Payable-Short Term	27.9	14.4	13.3	11.3	13.4	4.9
6.5	5.1	6.2	Cur. Mat.-L.T.D.	6.1	7.5	5.9	4.0	5.5	7.0
11.4	13.6	13.3	Trade Payables	6.3	12.7	17.5	13.2	16.7	13.1
.5	.5	.8	Income Taxes Payable	.0	.0	1.2	1.2	2.1	1.0
10.5	11.9	9.4	All Other Current	8.0	7.5	9.1	9.6	12.7	13.9
43.4	45.0	44.4	Total Current	48.3	42.1	47.1	39.3	50.4	39.9
22.0	27.3	24.0	Long-Term Debt	53.7	26.7	16.0	12.2	12.3	19.5
.7	.4	.7	Deferred Taxes	.0	.2	.3	1.6	1.6	1.6
4.1	4.4	5.7	All Other Non-Current	7.1	4.3	6.0	7.9	6.9	2.2
30.0	22.8	25.2	Net Worth	-9.1	26.6	30.6	39.0	28.8	36.8
100.0	100.0	100.0	Total Liabilities & Net Worth	100.0	100.0	100.0	100.0	100.0	100.0
			INCOME DATA						
100.0	100.0	100.0	Net Sales	100.0	100.0	100.0	100.0	100.0	100.0
			Gross Profit						
94.9	93.2	94.4	Operating Expenses	92.0	94.9	96.5	93.3	95.1	93.4
5.1	6.8	5.6	Operating Profit	8.0	5.1	3.5	6.7	4.9	6.6
.9	1.7	1.3	All Other Expenses (net)	4.7	1.0	-.2	1.0	1.1	.5
4.2	5.1	4.3	Profit Before Taxes	3.3	4.1	3.7	5.7	3.8	6.2
			RATIOS						
2.1	2.2	2.2	Current	3.7	2.5	2.3	3.1	1.8	1.9
1.3	1.2	1.3		1.2	1.3	1.2	1.6	1.2	1.4
.8	.8	.9		.3	.6	.9	1.2	.9	.9
1.8	1.7	1.8	Quick	1.4	2.2	2.0	2.7	1.6	1.7
1.0	1.0	1.1		.7	1.0	1.1	1.2	1.1	1.2
.5	.5	.6		.2	.5	.7	.9	.8	.9
11 32.6	4 96.5	13 27.6	Sales/Receivables	0 UND	8 48.2	19 19.2	36 10.0	32 11.3	46 8.0
35 10.4	34 10.8	40 9.2		9 38.5	29 12.6	46 8.0	62 5.9	50 7.3	55 6.6
61 6.0	62 5.9	63 5.8		27 13.3	58 6.3	67 5.4	80 4.6	63 5.8	79 4.6
			Cost of Sales/Inventory						
			Cost of Sales/Payables						
8.5	9.9	7.9	Sales/Working Capital	4.9	7.8	8.7	5.3	11.6	8.8
24.1	42.9	22.9		122.4	37.1	33.3	9.0	26.2	18.6
-45.2	-36.6	-80.2		-10.8	-24.1	-38.7	23.8	-112.6	-89.8
12.5	17.2	11.7	EBIT/Interest	4.2	10.2	16.9	22.2	11.3	21.3
(167) 5.0	(184) 4.8	(168) 4.1		(21) 1.5	(53) 3.5	(29) 7.6	(24) 2.7	(25) 4.7	8.1
1.5	1.3	1.4		-1.1	1.4	2.2	.5	1.8	5.0
5.8	2.6	3.2	Net Profit + Depr., Dep., Amort./Cur. Mat. L/T/D					7.9	
(36) 2.2	(27) 1.6	(32) 1.7						(11) 1.7	
1.4	1.2	1.3						1.3	
.4	.6	.5	Fixed/Worth	.8	.5	.4	.3	.5	.4
1.0	1.4	1.2		13.6	1.1	1.2	.8	.9	1.3
4.0	11.6	4.0		-1.5	17.0	2.7	1.8	1.8	2.1
.9	1.1	1.1	Debt/Worth	.8	1.0	1.2	.4	1.3	1.4
2.3	2.7	2.4		13.9	2.3	1.7	2.1	2.4	2.7
10.1	21.7	13.9		-3.6	32.6	11.8	5.0	4.2	4.1
54.4	86.5	65.7	% Profit Before Taxes/Tangible Net Worth	63.0	68.0	100.4	67.0	59.5	65.3
(150) 27.6	(162) 34.5	(150) 26.0		(15) 14.0	(45) 20.9	(28) 29.4	(24) 23.9	(22) 32.5	49.6
8.3	11.5	7.2		3.8	3.9	11.3	-.9	9.0	13.1
21.7	25.1	21.7	% Profit Before Taxes/Total Assets	16.7	22.1	23.6	35.4	17.3	24.1
9.3	9.3	8.3		2.2	8.3	11.0	9.3	8.8	11.9
1.8	.9	1.8		-4.9	1.7	3.4	.3	2.3	3.7
25.4	20.8	23.6	Sales/Net Fixed Assets	12.6	24.2	30.6	39.9	30.4	16.5
12.2	10.3	11.5		5.3	11.8	8.9	12.6	14.1	7.6
6.1	5.3	5.3		1.5	5.4	5.6	6.2	9.6	3.1
5.3	4.5	3.9	Sales/Total Assets	4.4	4.5	3.9	3.5	4.3	3.3
2.9	3.0	3.0		1.9	3.3	3.0	2.8	3.3	2.4
2.0	2.0	2.0		.8	2.0	2.2	2.1	2.7	1.6
1.6	1.8	1.4	% Depr., Dep., Amort./Sales	2.3	1.4	1.1	1.4	1.1	1.5
(141) 3.3	(167) 3.1	(147) 2.6		(18) 4.6	(45) 2.9	(26) 2.2	(22) 2.2	(25) 2.1	(11) 2.8
4.3	4.7	4.6		11.1	5.7	3.3	3.7	3.4	3.9
2.7	2.9	2.5	% Officers', Directors' Owners' Comp/Sales	3.6	3.4	2.2	2.9		
(103) 5.2	(118) 5.7	(91) 5.7		(15) 7.8	(32) 3.2	(21) 3.2	(11) 5.7		
10.0	9.3	9.6		19.5	11.1	6.8	9.6		
5751114M	3071016M	2101033M	Net Sales ($)	14650M	113196M	118932M	188906M	409127M	1256222M
1694112M	1326309M	933493M	Total Assets ($)	12218M	41771M	42223M	85162M	134254M	617865M

© RMA 2007

M = $ thousand   MM = $ million
See Pages 11 through 21 for Explanation of Ratios and Data

	Current Data Sorted by Assets							Comparative Historical Data	
							Type of Statement		
	1	16	77	109	25	23	Unqualified	226	218
	9	61	190	59		1	Reviewed	327	344
	38	97	90	11		1	Compiled	242	313
	124	94	25	2		5	Tax Returns	139	169
	58	162	183	101	15	14	Other	364	408
		202 (4/1-9/30/06)		1,389 (10/1/06-3/31/07)				4/1/02-3/31/03	4/1/03-3/31/04
	0-500M	500M-2MM	2-10MM	10-50MM	50-100MM	100-250MM		ALL	ALL
	230	430	565	282	40	44	**NUMBER OF STATEMENTS**	1298	1452
	%	%	%	%	%	%	**ASSETS**	%	%
	26.4	13.4	9.6	9.8	15.3	11.6	Cash & Equivalents	11.5	12.0
	22.9	46.7	55.0	48.7	42.0	37.0	Trade Receivables (net)	46.6	46.0
	2.0	4.8	4.5	4.1	1.7	2.3	Inventory	3.7	3.7
	5.4	4.5	7.2	10.6	13.3	15.6	All Other Current	7.5	8.1
	56.8	69.4	76.3	73.2	72.4	66.4	Total Current	69.3	69.8
	28.7	20.3	15.0	15.6	10.2	14.8	Fixed Assets (net)	19.7	19.5
	3.2	2.2	2.2	4.1	7.9	11.0	Intangibles (net)	2.6	2.6
	11.3	8.1	6.4	7.1	9.5	7.9	All Other Non-Current	8.4	8.1
	100.0	100.0	100.0	100.0	100.0	100.0	Total	100.0	100.0
							LIABILITIES		
	34.3	11.4	10.0	7.0	4.4	11.0	Notes Payable-Short Term	14.2	15.7
	6.3	2.8	2.6	2.6	1.3	6.0	Cur. Mat.-L.T.D.	3.5	4.0
	8.3	10.5	11.2	11.9	14.2	13.5	Trade Payables	11.0	10.9
	.5	.7	2.6	3.7	3.5	2.1	Income Taxes Payable	2.0	1.8
	21.1	12.9	15.3	19.8	28.3	25.4	All Other Current	17.1	16.6
	70.5	38.3	41.8	45.1	51.7	58.1	Total Current	47.9	48.9
	21.2	12.1	8.4	9.4	6.1	14.1	Long-Term Debt	11.4	11.0
	.2	.8	1.4	1.5	.4	.4	Deferred Taxes	1.6	1.7
	10.6	4.6	3.5	3.5	7.8	6.8	All Other Non-Current	4.9	5.5
	-2.3	44.3	45.0	40.4	33.9	20.7	Net Worth	34.2	32.8
	100.0	100.0	100.0	100.0	100.0	100.0	Total Liabilties & Net Worth	100.0	100.0
							INCOME DATA		
	100.0	100.0	100.0	100.0	100.0	100.0	Net Sales	100.0	100.0
							Gross Profit		
	93.5	91.1	92.2	92.6	96.3	96.5	Operating Expenses	96.1	95.6
	6.5	8.9	7.8	7.4	3.7	3.5	Operating Profit	3.9	4.4
	1.1	1.3	1.4	1.7	.4	.7	All Other Expenses (net)	.8	.9
	5.4	7.6	6.5	5.7	3.3	2.8	Profit Before Taxes	3.1	3.6
							RATIOS		
	3.0	3.9	3.1	2.2	1.7	1.8		2.6	2.7
	1.2	2.1	1.8	1.6	1.3	1.3	Current	1.6	1.6
	.4	1.2	1.3	1.3	1.1	1.1		1.1	1.2
	2.4	3.6	2.6	1.9	1.3	1.3		2.2	2.2
(229)	1.0	1.8	1.6	1.3	1.1	.9	Quick	1.3	1.3
	.3	1.0	1.1	.9	.7	.7		.9	.9
0 UND		35 10.3	56 6.6	60 6.1	50 7.3	47 7.8		42 8.7	41 9.0
0 UND		58 6.3	76 4.8	77 4.7	71 5.1	62 5.9	Sales/Receivables	69 5.3	67 5.4
44 8.3		91 4.0	100 3.6	98 3.7	87 4.2	98 3.7		96 3.8	94 3.9
							Cost of Sales/Inventory		
							Cost of Sales/Payables		
	11.8	5.2	4.6	5.1	8.1	7.3		5.5	5.4
	87.0	8.8	7.4	8.3	13.5	12.1	Sales/Working Capital	10.5	10.1
	-26.4	30.8	17.0	15.6	28.1	70.3		42.0	41.2
	20.6	29.9	30.2	30.4	21.5	16.4		15.8	19.7
(168)	5.4	(348) 7.6	(471) 8.5	(240) 9.7	(28) 9.5	6.4	EBIT/Interest	(1127) 4.7	(1221) 5.5
	.0	1.9	2.7	3.0	2.8	2.8		.8	1.2
		3.8	10.0	7.8	19.6	5.5	Net Profit + Depr., Dep.,	5.8	6.0
		(50) 2.0	(142) 4.6	(111) 3.4	(14) 5.9	(19) 3.2	Amort./Cur. Mat. L/T/D	(378) 2.2	(382) 2.4
		.9	1.8	1.4	2.5	2.1		1.0	1.1
	.1	.1	.1	.1	.2	.3		.2	.2
	1.0	.3	.3	.3	.3	.6	Fixed/Worth	.4	.4
	-1.5	1.1	.6	.8	.8	1.5		1.1	1.1
	.6	.4	.6	.9	1.5	2.0		.7	.7
	3.7	1.1	1.3	1.5	2.8	4.1	Debt/Worth	1.6	1.6
	-4.8	3.5	2.7	3.0	6.2	9.3		4.3	4.4
	196.8	73.8	53.4	48.7	63.7	58.1	% Profit Before Taxes/Tangible	45.6	47.7
(152)	86.0	(383) 35.1	(537) 28.6	(262) 28.0	(38) 33.2	(36) 38.4	Net Worth	(1161) 19.0	(1266) 20.3
	15.2	11.4	11.7	13.1	17.6	20.9		2.5	3.1
	71.4	35.8	24.8	17.1	16.7	12.4	% Profit Before Taxes/Total	17.2	18.7
	23.3	13.7	11.4	9.9	9.6	7.3	Assets	6.2	6.8
	-5.8	2.7	3.8	3.9	5.0	2.9		-.1	.4
	126.9	58.8	53.7	42.5	51.0	41.5		43.8	52.8
	38.1	21.5	23.2	19.6	29.4	22.3	Sales/Net Fixed Assets	20.4	22.8
	17.5	11.1	13.2	10.0	17.9	11.0		11.4	11.4
	13.4	4.1	3.2	2.7	2.7	2.9		3.6	3.8
	6.5	2.9	2.5	2.2	2.1	2.2	Sales/Total Assets	2.6	2.7
	3.8	2.1	2.0	1.8	1.6	1.6		2.0	1.9
	.5	.7	.8	.8	.6	.8		1.0	.9
(129)	1.3	(326) 1.5	(489) 1.4	(255) 1.5	(31) 1.1	(37) 1.4	% Depr., Dep., Amort./Sales	(1109) 1.8	(1178) 1.7
	2.6	2.8	2.3	2.2	1.7	2.0		2.9	2.8
	6.5	4.2	2.4	1.6			% Officers', Directors'	4.5	4.8
(140)	11.8	(176) 7.7	(146) 5.4	(45) 5.0			Owners' Comp/Sales	(480) 8.7	(503) 9.1
	19.3	13.1	10.6	12.6				15.7	15.7
	404287M	1668742M	6870114M	13444754M	6314506M	21408977M	Net Sales ($)	320027741M	39316018M
	51673M	504740M	2612372M	6036749M	2830637M	7245564M	Total Assets ($)	12962236M	14185757M

M = $ thousand   MM = $ million
See Pages 11 through 21 for Explanation of Ratios and Data

Comparative Historical Data / Current Data Sorted by Sales

			Type of Statement	0-1MM	1-3MM	3-5MM	5-10MM	10-25MM	25MM & OVER
227	220	251	Unqualified		10	9	20	58	154
342	298	320	Reviewed	4	24	45	89	103	55
230	224	237	Compiled	26	47	57	59	39	9
199	173	250	Tax Returns	48	101	46	34	14	7
406	549	533	Other	39	104	67	97	101	125
4/1/04-3/31/05 ALL	4/1/05-3/31/06 ALL	4/1/06-3/31/07 ALL		202 (4/1-9/30/06)			1,389 (10/1/06-3/31/07)		
1404	1464	1591	**NUMBER OF STATEMENTS**	117	286	224	299	315	350
%	%	%	**ASSETS**	%	%	%	%	%	%
11.8	13.2	13.3	Cash & Equivalents	18.3	18.8	12.4	12.4	11.7	10.0
47.0	47.1	46.2	Trade Receivables (net)	25.8	35.7	48.0	49.8	53.5	50.6
3.9	4.0	4.0	Inventory	1.6	4.5	4.6	5.5	3.6	3.2
7.2	7.3	7.2	All Other Current	5.2	4.3	5.5	6.7	7.9	11.1
69.9	71.6	70.7	Total Current	50.9	63.3	70.5	74.4	76.7	74.9
18.3	17.8	18.4	Fixed Assets (net)	37.1	23.8	18.6	16.3	13.9	13.3
2.9	2.9	3.1	Intangibles (net)	3.4	2.4	2.4	2.9	2.4	4.8
9.0	7.6	7.8	All Other Non-Current	8.6	10.4	8.4	6.4	7.1	7.0
100.0	100.0	100.0	Total	100.0	100.0	100.0	100.0	100.0	100.0
			LIABILITIES						
15.4	13.9	13.3	Notes Payable-Short Term	21.4	22.1	15.1	9.9	9.8	8.1
3.9	3.5	3.3	Cur. Mat.-L.T.D.	5.2	4.3	2.7	3.1	2.4	3.0
11.4	11.7	10.9	Trade Payables	8.7	8.5	10.1	10.7	12.1	13.1
1.7	1.9	2.0	Income Taxes Payable	.2	.4	1.6	2.0	2.5	3.6
16.6	16.2	16.9	All Other Current	12.3	14.6	17.0	12.6	18.7	22.3
49.0	47.1	46.3	Total Current	47.9	49.9	46.4	38.3	45.6	50.1
12.7	12.1	11.5	Long-Term Debt	30.6	15.0	13.0	7.6	7.8	7.9
1.3	1.1	1.0	Deferred Taxes	.1	.3	1.2	1.6	1.3	1.1
5.2	5.7	5.0	All Other Non-Current	13.1	6.1	4.0	5.1	2.3	4.4
31.8	34.0	36.2	Net Worth	8.3	28.6	35.4	47.4	43.1	36.5
100.0	100.0	100.0	Total Liabilities & Net Worth	100.0	100.0	100.0	100.0	100.0	100.0
			INCOME DATA						
100.0	100.0	100.0	Net Sales	100.0	100.0	100.0	100.0	100.0	100.0
			Gross Profit						
94.3	93.2	92.4	Operating Expenses	82.6	92.1	93.5	92.7	93.1	94.2
5.7	6.8	7.6	Operating Profit	17.4	7.9	6.5	7.3	6.9	5.8
1.0	1.0	1.3	All Other Expenses (net)	7.4	1.1	.5	.7	.6	1.1
4.7	5.8	6.3	Profit Before Taxes	10.0	6.8	6.0	6.6	6.3	4.6
			RATIOS						
2.7	2.8	3.0		3.6	4.0	3.6	3.7	2.6	2.1
1.6	1.7	1.7	Current	1.3	1.9	2.0	2.1	1.7	1.5
1.1	1.2	1.2		.4	.9	1.2	1.3	1.3	1.2
2.4	2.5	2.6		3.3	3.5	2.9	3.2	2.2	1.8
(1403) 1.3	1.4 (1590)	1.5	Quick	1.2 (285)	1.5	1.7	1.7	1.4	1.2
.9	.9	.9		.3	.7	1.0	1.1	1.0	.9
43 8.4	43 8.6	41 8.8		0 UND	0 UND	36 10.1	47 7.8	53 6.9	57 6.4
70 5.2	70 5.2	66 5.5	Sales/Receivables	10 36.7	49 7.5	65 5.6	69 5.3	74 4.9	73 5.0
97 3.7	93 3.9	93 3.9		66 5.5	84 4.3	97 3.8	96 3.8	99 3.7	91 4.0
			Cost of Sales/Inventory						
			Cost of Sales/Payables						
5.4	5.2	5.3		6.4	5.4	4.8	4.6	5.3	6.0
9.9	9.7	9.4	Sales/Working Capital	37.7	11.5	8.5	7.4	8.4	10.2
39.0	28.8	30.5		-14.4	-119.8	32.4	17.2	19.7	20.0
22.9	29.2	27.9		15.9	18.1	27.8	35.8	41.9	24.8
(1176) 7.1	(1241) 8.0	(1299) 8.1	EBIT/Interest	(68) 5.1	(225) 5.6	(182) 6.7	(263) 9.9	(263) 9.8	(298) 9.1
1.7	2.4	2.2		-.5	.7	1.9	2.7	2.9	3.2
7.5	8.2	8.4			3.0	6.9	9.6	9.6	8.2
(338) 2.9	(313) 2.7	(343) 3.4	Net Profit + Depr., Dep., Amort./Cur. Mat. L/T/D		(14) 1.9	(30) 3.2	(70) 4.0	(83) 3.6	(141) 3.7
1.1	1.3	1.5			.0	1.4	1.4	1.5	1.8
.1	.1	.1		.2	.1	.1	.1	.1	.2
.3	.3	.3	Fixed/Worth	1.1	.5	.3	.3	.3	.3
1.1	1.1	1.0		-28.9	3.6	1.1	.6	.6	.8
.7	.7	.6		.6	.5	.5	.4	.6	1.0
1.6	1.6	1.5	Debt/Worth	3.1	1.6	1.2	1.1	1.3	1.9
5.0	4.3	4.2		-12.2	15.1	4.7	2.6	2.7	4.1
53.2	65.8	64.6		145.0	88.7	65.7	56.6	57.6	52.1
(1219) 25.2	(1299) 30.7	(1408) 31.5	% Profit Before Taxes/Tangible Net Worth	(83) 24.0	(231) 40.4	(196) 30.2	(278) 33.3	(297) 29.1	(323) 31.3
6.6	10.6	12.9		7.1	9.6	11.3	12.8	13.2	14.6
20.7	26.2	27.3		32.6	39.4	32.6	30.0	27.0	17.1
8.3	11.2	11.5	% Profit Before Taxes/Total Assets	7.6	15.0	12.1	13.7	11.6	10.1
1.4	2.4	3.0		-1.6	.5	2.4	4.3	4.2	4.0
54.0	59.1	56.8		59.4	65.8	55.4	50.7	62.0	52.5
24.1	24.5	24.0	Sales/Net Fixed Assets	16.6	23.5	26.6	23.8	25.0	25.7
12.4	12.3	12.5		2.7	10.3	12.5	13.4	14.1	12.4
3.6	3.6	3.7		5.2	5.6	4.3	3.6	3.4	3.0
2.6	2.6	2.6	Sales/Total Assets	2.6	3.1	2.8	2.7	2.6	2.4
1.9	2.0	2.0		.8	1.9	2.0	2.1	2.0	1.9
.9	.8	.7		1.3	.8	.7	.8	.7	.7
(1108) 1.6	(1178) 1.4	(1267) 1.4	% Depr., Dep., Amort./Sales	(68) 3.6	(183) 1.7	(187) 1.4	(249) 1.5	(269) 1.3	(311) 1.2
2.6	2.3	2.4		12.2	3.3	2.4	2.4	2.2	1.9
4.1	3.9	3.6		10.4	5.5	4.0	3.9	1.8	1.4
(498) 7.8	(454) 7.8	(516) 7.9	% Officers', Directors' Owners' Comp/Sales	(48) 14.3	(143) 9.7	(97) 7.4	(89) 6.2	(89) 3.9	(50) 7.1
15.0	14.0	15.1		22.2	16.8	12.3	12.8	8.9	16.0
34649297M	42299877M	50111380M	Net Sales ($)	60235M	552243M	886343M	2206129M	4943945M	41462485M
14089585M	16675594M	19281735M	Total Assets ($)	63147M	243803M	347976M	875927M	2081445M	15669437M

M = $ thousand   MM = $ million
See Pages 11 through 21 for Explanation of Ratios and Data

Current Data Sorted by Assets

Comparative Historical Data

						Type of Statement		
		1	1	1	1	Unqualified	5	4
		4	4	1		Reviewed	12	6
1	7	6	1		1	Compiled	16	20
11	9	3	1			Tax Returns	20	17
9		5		2		Other	25	35
	11 (4/1-9/30/06)		59 (10/1/06-3/31/07)				4/1/02-3/31/03	4/1/03-3/31/04
0-500M	500M-2MM	2-10MM	10-50MM	50-100MM	100-250MM		ALL	ALL
21	21	19	5	2	2	NUMBER OF STATEMENTS	78	82
%	%	%	%	%	%	ASSETS	%	%
26.1	16.5	10.9				Cash & Equivalents	14.3	16.9
19.1	34.8	43.9				Trade Receivables (net)	33.2	33.1
.1	.3	4.9				Inventory	2.3	2.8
6.4	2.8	8.3				All Other Current	4.5	5.6
51.7	54.3	67.9				Total Current	54.4	58.5
39.3	35.0	18.5				Fixed Assets (net)	35.5	29.7
2.1	.6	4.1				Intangibles (net)	2.8	3.7
6.9	10.1	9.4				All Other Non-Current	7.4	8.2
100.0	100.0	100.0				Total	100.0	100.0
						LIABILITIES		
27.8	14.5	10.4				Notes Payable-Short Term	10.7	17.3
6.2	3.5	4.4				Cur. Mat.-L.T.D.	5.5	4.9
5.4	10.9	8.3				Trade Payables	5.1	10.2
.2	.6	2.1				Income Taxes Payable	1.5	1.2
11.6	10.9	13.7				All Other Current	9.9	11.3
51.1	40.5	38.9				Total Current	32.7	44.9
31.3	19.6	7.9				Long-Term Debt	22.8	19.1
.0	.2	.2				Deferred Taxes	.4	.7
8.3	4.2	2.3				All Other Non-Current	6.0	4.5
9.3	35.5	50.7				Net Worth	38.1	30.8
100.0	100.0	100.0				Total Liabilties & Net Worth	100.0	100.0
						INCOME DATA		
100.0	100.0	100.0				Net Sales	100.0	100.0
						Gross Profit		
97.5	88.3	92.1				Operating Expenses	93.2	92.0
2.5	11.7	7.9				Operating Profit	6.8	8.0
.9	3.4	.4				All Other Expenses (net)	.9	1.3
1.6	8.4	7.5				Profit Before Taxes	5.9	6.7
						RATIOS		
2.2	3.2	2.3					4.5	5.3
.9	1.5	1.9				Current	1.9	2.1
.5	.7	1.3					1.0	.9
2.2	3.1	2.0					4.4	4.0
.9	1.4	1.3				Quick	1.5 (81)	1.7
.4	.7	1.0					.8	.9
0 UND	19 19.0	48 7.6					0 UND	0 UND
0 UND	48 7.6	66 5.6				Sales/Receivables	62 5.9	58 6.3
39 9.3	89 4.1	109 3.4					85 4.3	96 3.8
						Cost of Sales/Inventory		
						Cost of Sales/Payables		
17.5	5.1	5.2					5.4	4.8
-933.0	10.9	9.3				Sales/Working Capital	10.6	10.8
-12.9	-18.4	14.0					-87.9	-570.4
7.6	45.2	31.9					16.5	25.6
(20) 1.4	(18) 9.4	(17) 10.2				EBIT/Interest	(73) 4.4	(71) 5.6
-.5	1.9	1.7					.6	.6
						Net Profit + Depr., Dep.,	5.9	10.9
						Amort./Cur. Mat. L/T/D	(19) 2.8	(13) 2.1
							1.1	1.4
.4	.2	.2					.3	.2
1.9	.5	.3				Fixed/Worth	.9	.6
-.9	3.6	.7					2.2	1.7
1.1	.4	.4					.6	.5
2.9	1.4	1.1				Debt/Worth	1.6	1.6
-3.9	7.1	1.9					5.2	4.1
158.2	76.0	79.5				% Profit Before Taxes/Tangible	77.4	84.8
(11) 35.0	(19) 32.8	(18) 41.5				Net Worth	(70) 21.4	(71) 33.7
10.6	10.2	1.5					4.7	5.8
27.0	29.1	30.1				% Profit Before Taxes/Total	33.8	34.7
3.6	15.0	17.2				Assets	9.7	10.5
-11.9	2.9	-.2					-.1	.9
54.0	26.9	42.2					17.4	26.7
17.3	9.2	24.1				Sales/Net Fixed Assets	10.6	15.9
8.6	4.5	10.0					4.8	7.5
8.5	3.3	3.4					4.0	4.4
4.6	2.5	2.3				Sales/Total Assets	2.5	2.8
2.7	1.6	1.6					1.6	1.9
	2.4	1.4					2.5	2.1
	(11) 3.8	(15) 1.8				% Depr., Dep., Amort./Sales	(68) 3.8	(62) 3.2
	6.1	2.6					6.2	5.7
6.9	6.4					% Officers', Directors'	7.7	7.4
(13) 15.4	(11) 11.1					Owners' Comp/Sales	(33) 13.1	(38) 11.2
19.4	16.1						16.1	15.0
23442M	49937M	207668M	190641M	109272M	1209225M	Net Sales ($)	509371M	1523279M
4624M	19980M	77118M	100819M	120654M	405823M	Total Assets ($)	248521M	667436M

© RMA 2007

M = $ thousand   MM = $ million
See Pages 11 through 21 for Explanation of Ratios and Data

Comparative Historical Data				Current Data Sorted by Sales					
7	3	4	**Type of Statement** Unqualified	1		1			2
13	15	9	Reviewed		1	2	3	2	1
15	18	8	Compiled	1			4	1	2
23	19	22	Tax Returns	8	9	3		1	1
26	34	27	Other	8	9	2	1	3	4
4/1/04- 3/31/05 ALL	4/1/05- 3/31/06 ALL	4/1/06- 3/31/07 ALL		0-1MM	11 (4/1-9/30/06) 1-3MM	3-5MM	59 (10/1/06-3/31/07) 5-10MM	10-25MM	25MM & OVER
84	89	70	**NUMBER OF STATEMENTS**	18	19	8	8	7	10
%	%	%	**ASSETS**	%	%	%	%	%	%
14.5	13.9	16.5	Cash & Equivalents	20.8	23.4				10.2
32.5	35.2	33.1	Trade Receivables (net)	24.8	19.8				42.1
2.0	3.1	1.7	Inventory	.1	.4				1.7
5.1	5.1	5.7	All Other Current	2.5	7.6				5.7
54.1	57.2	57.0	Total Current	48.3	51.1				59.6
29.0	28.8	30.2	Fixed Assets (net)	45.2	36.2				23.9
3.8	4.7	4.6	Intangibles (net)	2.3	2.9				12.8
13.1	9.3	8.2	All Other Non-Current	4.3	9.8				3.6
100.0	100.0	100.0	Total	100.0	100.0				100.0
			LIABILITIES						
20.0	16.4	17.0	Notes Payable-Short Term	24.1	12.9				12.2
4.7	4.2	4.5	Cur. Mat.-L.T.D.	3.3	6.4				2.2
4.9	5.2	8.2	Trade Payables	5.7	6.5				7.3
1.8	1.4	.9	Income Taxes Payable	.0	.6				.2
12.1	11.4	11.3	All Other Current	9.5	11.6				6.8
43.5	38.6	41.8	Total Current	42.6	38.1				28.6
25.2	20.2	19.6	Long-Term Debt	29.3	26.6				13.4
.9	.5	.5	Deferred Taxes	.0	.2				1.9
4.5	8.3	5.4	All Other Non-Current	6.4	7.7				5.6
26.0	32.4	32.7	Net Worth	21.7	27.4				50.6
100.0	100.0	100.0	Total Liabilities & Net Worth	100.0	100.0				100.0
			INCOME DATA						
100.0	100.0	100.0	Net Sales	100.0	100.0				100.0
			Gross Profit						
93.3	90.9	92.0	Operating Expenses	89.5	97.5				85.3
6.7	9.1	8.0	Operating Profit	10.5	2.5				14.7
.9	.9	1.6	All Other Expenses (net)	4.0	.2				.9
5.9	8.2	6.4	Profit Before Taxes	6.6	2.3				13.8
			RATIOS						
3.6	4.2	2.6	Current	3.6	2.8				3.8
1.8	1.7	1.5		1.1	1.5				1.6
1.0	1.0	.9		.5	.4				1.2
2.9	3.4	2.5	Quick	3.4	2.5				3.4
1.5	1.6	1.2		1.1	1.4				1.5
.7	.8	.8		.5	.3				1.0
0 UND	0 UND	0 UND	Sales/Receivables	0 UND	0 UND			42	8.8
56 6.5	55 6.7	50 7.2		0 UND	14 27.0			61	6.0
80 4.6	98 3.7	93 3.9		98 3.7	48 7.6			119	3.1
			Cost of Sales/Inventory						
			Cost of Sales/Payables						
5.4	5.4	6.8	Sales/Working Capital	6.3	7.5				3.8
12.3	9.4	13.5		NM	22.0				9.1
NM	104.6	-51.7		-7.6	-29.1				48.1
28.2	23.3	30.2	EBIT/Interest	11.4	33.4				159.1
(77) 4.7	(81) 8.1	(64) 5.2		(15) 4.5	(16) 4.8				8.6
1.0	1.5	1.0		-.5	.2				3.2
6.3	2.1	21.4	Net Profit + Depr., Dep., Amort./Cur. Mat. L/T/D						
(12) 2.0	(17) 1.5	(14) 4.3							
1.0	1.0	1.7							
.2	.3	.3	Fixed/Worth	.4	.3				.3
.7	.7	.6		13.5	.5				.8
4.2	4.2	NM		-1.6	4.7				-10.4
.4	.5	.5	Debt/Worth	.8	.4				.3
1.5	1.7	1.3		14.3	1.4				.8
30.8	7.4	NM		-6.2	5.4				-95.0
65.8	87.0	87.7	% Profit Before Taxes/Tangible Net Worth	138.9	56.9				
(65) 26.2	(72) 31.0	(53) 40.1		(11) 57.6	(15) 28.5				
6.4	13.3	9.6		10.6	-2.2				
28.4	38.3	28.7	% Profit Before Taxes/Total Assets	33.3	25.4				75.8
10.1	12.2	11.0		6.7	6.3				20.9
.3	1.6	-.4		-12.2	-1.5				6.5
39.5	25.1	33.2	Sales/Net Fixed Assets	39.7	39.1				21.9
15.7	12.7	12.2		9.1	10.6				10.3
6.8	6.1	6.5		1.9	5.9				6.1
4.5	3.9	4.4	Sales/Total Assets	4.5	7.7				5.3
2.6	2.6	2.5		2.5	3.4				2.0
2.0	1.7	1.6		1.0	2.1				1.5
1.6	1.7	1.5	% Depr., Dep., Amort./Sales						
(60) 2.6	(65) 2.7	(42) 2.5							
4.9	5.6	5.5							
6.7	6.0	6.0	% Officers', Directors' Owners' Comp/Sales		5.0				
(44) 10.3	(32) 9.7	(32) 10.4			(13) 8.5				
15.8	15.8	16.1			16.1				
561481M	1597000M	1790185M	Net Sales ($)	9643M	38522M	30176M	54524M	118257M	1539063M
246610M	664301M	729018M	Total Assets ($)	5705M	14351M	15552M	25032M	97106M	571272M

© RMA 2007

M = $ thousand   MM = $ million
See Pages 11 through 21 for Explanation of Ratios and Data

Current Data Sorted by Assets   Comparative Historical Data

						Type of Statement		
	3	11	12	3	2	Unqualified	26	23
1	11	26	8			Reviewed	45	43
4	17	9	1			Compiled	28	40
16	9	3				Tax Returns	16	29
9	18	25	12		1	Other	52	51
	38 (4/1-9/30/06)		163 (10/1/06-3/31/07)				4/1/02-3/31/03	4/1/03-3/31/04
0-500M	500M-2MM	2-10MM	10-50MM	50-100MM	100-250MM		ALL	ALL
30	58	74	33	3	3	NUMBER OF STATEMENTS	167	186
%	%	%	%	%	%	ASSETS	%	%
14.9	11.1	9.9	11.7			Cash & Equivalents	10.2	11.6
24.9	35.0	36.0	37.7			Trade Receivables (net)	36.7	36.3
4.1	1.8	5.7	1.5			Inventory	2.4	3.9
4.8	3.5	3.4	3.8			All Other Current	4.1	3.8
48.8	51.4	55.0	54.7			Total Current	53.4	55.5
36.8	36.7	33.6	35.8			Fixed Assets (net)	36.9	33.8
4.8	4.0	5.8	5.0			Intangibles (net)	4.2	4.7
9.7	8.0	5.6	4.4			All Other Non-Current	5.5	6.0
100.0	100.0	100.0	100.0			Total	100.0	100.0
						LIABILITIES		
19.9	11.5	9.0	3.2			Notes Payable-Short Term	9.4	8.5
6.9	4.7	4.8	3.2			Cur. Mat.-L.T.D.	6.0	4.9
17.2	9.0	7.9	6.9			Trade Payables	8.5	8.4
.2	.2	.9	.4			Income Taxes Payable	.6	.6
13.2	9.5	13.2	12.3			All Other Current	10.1	11.8
57.4	34.9	35.7	25.9			Total Current	34.7	34.2
25.1	16.9	13.4	22.0			Long-Term Debt	21.3	21.1
.0	.7	.9	.3			Deferred Taxes	1.1	1.3
17.4	8.7	2.3	3.4			All Other Non-Current	4.3	6.7
.1	38.8	47.8	48.3			Net Worth	38.6	36.8
100.0	100.0	100.0	100.0			Total Liabilities & Net Worth	100.0	100.0
						INCOME DATA		
100.0	100.0	100.0	100.0			Net Sales	100.0	100.0
						Gross Profit		
91.8	90.8	90.2	90.1			Operating Expenses	92.4	90.9
8.2	9.2	9.8	9.9			Operating Profit	7.6	9.1
1.2	1.9	1.6	.8			All Other Expenses (net)	1.6	2.3
7.0	7.3	8.2	9.1			Profit Before Taxes	5.9	6.8
						RATIOS		
1.9	2.7	2.7	4.4				2.7	2.9
.9	1.6	1.6	2.1			Current	1.6	1.6
.4	1.0	1.0	1.4				1.1	1.1
1.8	2.4	2.3	4.1				2.3	2.5
.7	1.4	1.4	1.8			Quick	1.4	1.5
.3	1.0	.8	1.3				.9	.9
0 UND	36 10.0	48 7.6	62 5.9				44 8.3	41 9.0
27 13.6	54 6.8	71 5.1	74 4.9			Sales/Receivables	68 5.4	60 6.1
52 7.1	78 4.7	89 4.1	102 3.6				87 4.2	78 4.7
						Cost of Sales/Inventory		
						Cost of Sales/Payables		
19.3	6.3	5.1	3.6				5.3	5.4
-152.6	14.4	11.6	6.7			Sales/Working Capital	12.1	11.5
-11.0	NM	NM	15.6				55.6	55.6
14.3	25.9	15.4	34.0				11.9	13.8
(26) 4.7	(50) 5.2	(66) 5.4	(30) 6.1			EBIT/Interest	(153) 4.0	(161) 3.9
1.1	1.8	2.4	2.9				1.5	1.4
		5.1	12.9			Net Profit + Depr., Dep.,	6.2	7.6
	(28) 2.6	(16) 4.6				Amort./Cur. Mat. L/T/D	(61) 2.5	(56) 2.4
		1.6	2.5				1.4	1.6
.9	.4	.5	.4				.4	.4
3.0	.9	.8	1.0			Fixed/Worth	1.0	.9
-1.1	2.3	1.4	1.5				2.0	2.2
1.0	.6	.7	.3				.7	.7
25.2	1.3	1.3	1.3			Debt/Worth	1.6	1.8
-4.0	4.0	2.7	2.8				4.4	4.0
226.1	74.7	48.8	48.8			% Profit Before Taxes/Tangible	51.1	51.3
(17) 69.4	(49) 30.3	(72) 29.6	(31) 31.0			Net Worth	(149) 21.4	(167) 25.0
1.6	12.5	10.5	11.6				5.8	3.9
72.5	29.8	20.0	26.1			% Profit Before Taxes/Total	19.7	20.7
22.2	8.9	10.9	12.4			Assets	7.4	8.4
-1.4	3.6	3.6	6.5				1.3	1.1
35.6	13.2	11.9	8.8				11.0	14.8
9.9	7.0	6.6	5.5			Sales/Net Fixed Assets	6.6	7.6
7.5	3.7	3.8	3.2				3.4	3.9
5.0	2.9	2.5	2.2				2.8	3.0
3.5	2.4	1.9	1.8			Sales/Total Assets	2.0	2.1
2.8	1.6	1.3	1.3				1.5	1.5
.8	1.5	2.0	2.9				2.4	2.0
(24) 2.2	(48) 3.0	(69) 3.8	4.1			% Depr., Dep., Amort./Sales	(153) 3.8	(165) 4.0
5.2	5.1	5.5	5.7				7.2	6.6
6.4	4.5	3.8	1.2			% Officers', Directors'	3.2	3.5
(17) 10.5	(20) 9.7	(16) 5.1	(10) 2.7			Owners' Comp/Sales	(56) 6.3	(69) 6.6
12.9	12.9	6.2	11.6				10.2	14.8
31114M	159858M	632472M	1118888M	326576M	331623M	Net Sales ($)	2369848M	2266432M
7887M	65058M	359378M	648114M	235512M	463832M	Total Assets ($)	1554297M	1477116M

© RMA 2007

M = $ thousand   MM = $ million
See Pages 11 through 21 for Explanation of Ratios and Data

Comparative Historical Data | | | | Current Data Sorted by Sales

			Type of Statement						
30	27	31	Unqualified	1	1	3	5	10	11
49	43	46	Reviewed		5	9	17	9	6
30	29	31	Compiled	3	10	8	8	2	
22	28	28	Tax Returns	9	14	3	2		
57	89	65	Other	13	13	7	11	11	8
4/1/04- 3/31/05 ALL	4/1/05- 3/31/06 ALL	4/1/06- 3/31/07 ALL		0-1MM	38 (4/1-9/30/06) 1-3MM	3-5MM	163 (10/1/06-3/31/07) 5-10MM	10-25MM	25MM & OVER
188	216	201	NUMBER OF STATEMENTS	26	43	30	43	34	25
%	%	%	ASSETS	%	%	%	%	%	%
11.9	11.0	11.6	Cash & Equivalents	13.0	11.7	12.8	10.9	9.0	13.2
35.3	36.1	33.9	Trade Receivables (net)	18.2	33.6	34.7	37.5	40.3	35.3
4.1	4.4	3.5	Inventory	3.4	2.4	4.5	4.7	3.9	2.1
3.8	4.0	3.7	All Other Current	2.6	4.9	2.5	4.0	3.8	3.7
55.0	55.5	52.8	Total Current	37.3	52.5	54.5	57.1	57.0	54.3
33.8	35.2	35.2	Fixed Assets (net)	47.2	34.9	34.7	31.3	31.7	35.6
5.1	3.4	5.3	Intangibles (net)	4.4	4.5	4.9	5.9	6.4	5.4
6.1	5.9	6.7	All Other Non-Current	11.1	8.0	5.8	5.7	4.9	4.7
100.0	100.0	100.0	Total	100.0	100.0	100.0	100.0	100.0	100.0
			LIABILITIES						
8.2	12.5	10.5	Notes Payable-Short Term	11.5	17.4	7.5	8.3	11.1	4.2
5.0	4.8	4.7	Cur. Mat.-L.T.D.	8.5	4.6	3.1	5.7	3.5	3.0
8.5	11.6	9.4	Trade Payables	11.4	13.0	7.6	6.5	10.2	7.2
.4	.5	.5	Income Taxes Payable	.0	.2	.7	1.1	.4	.5
12.3	14.7	12.0	All Other Current	8.8	11.8	9.4	15.2	12.6	12.4
34.4	44.2	37.1	Total Current	40.1	47.0	28.2	36.8	37.9	27.4
20.1	19.1	17.5	Long-Term Debt	31.8	17.7	13.9	12.4	12.2	22.3
1.3	.9	.6	Deferred Taxes	.0	.2	1.2	.9	.8	.4
7.0	8.2	6.6	All Other Non-Current	11.8	16.2	1.0	2.9	2.7	3.2
37.3	27.5	38.2	Net Worth	16.3	19.0	55.7	46.9	46.4	46.7
100.0	100.0	100.0	Total Liabilties & Net Worth	100.0	100.0	100.0	100.0	100.0	100.0
			INCOME DATA						
100.0	100.0	100.0	Net Sales	100.0	100.0	100.0	100.0	100.0	100.0
			Gross Profit						
91.4	91.2	90.4	Operating Expenses	82.9	92.5	93.7	89.2	93.8	88.0
8.6	8.8	9.6	Operating Profit	17.1	7.5	6.3	10.8	6.2	12.0
2.2	2.5	1.5	All Other Expenses (net)	4.8	1.5	.7	1.4	.2	.7
6.4	6.3	8.2	Profit Before Taxes	12.3	6.0	5.6	9.4	6.0	11.3
			RATIOS						
3.2	2.8	2.7		2.0	2.4	3.1	2.7	2.4	4.0
1.6	1.5	1.5	Current	.8	1.2	2.1	1.6	1.5	2.1
1.1	1.1	1.0		.4	.7	1.2	1.1	1.1	1.3
2.7	2.4	2.5		1.8	1.6	3.0	2.3	2.0	3.6
(187) 1.4	1.3	1.4	Quick	.8	1.1	2.0	1.4	1.3	1.8
.9	.8	.8		.4	.6	1.2	.9	.8	1.1
40 9.1	40 9.2	38 9.6		0 UND	8 45.8	38 9.6	48 7.6	55 6.6	64 5.7
60 6.1	62 5.9	63 5.8	Sales/Receivables	29 12.4	45 8.1	60 6.1	71 5.2	74 4.9	73 5.0
79 4.6	85 4.3	83 4.4		56 6.6	67 5.5	83 4.4	93 3.9	87 4.2	87 4.2
			Cost of Sales/Inventory						
			Cost of Sales/Payables						
5.3	5.2	5.8		10.5	6.5	4.9	6.5	5.2	3.6
11.3	12.5	13.2	Sales/Working Capital	-66.2	44.6	8.5	12.0	8.9	6.7
48.6	76.7	-175.5		-6.2	-59.1	29.2	51.2	NM	17.9
17.6	15.5	18.6		9.3	18.3	20.1	32.4	32.0	27.7
(167) 4.9	(183) 5.4	(176) 5.4	EBIT/Interest	(18) 3.7	(39) 7.4	(26) 4.3	(40) 7.6	(32) 5.6	(21) 6.4
1.2	1.2	2.2		1.9	1.6	1.2	2.2	2.8	2.1
7.8	7.2	5.5	Net Profit + Depr., Dep., Amort./Cur. Mat. L/T/D			5.2	6.9	10.4	
(56) 3.3	(60) 3.1	(53) 2.9				(17) 2.7	(14) 2.5	(14) 3.9	
1.7	1.8	1.9				1.2	1.7	2.5	
.4	.4	.5		.6	.8	.4	.4	.4	.3
.9	.9	.9	Fixed/Worth	2.4	1.3	.7	.8	.8	.8
1.9	2.7	2.0		-3.4	-8.8	1.1	1.8	1.2	2.0
.7	.6	.6		.6	1.0	.3	.5	.8	.3
1.7	1.7	1.4	Debt/Worth	3.0	3.3	.9	1.2	1.7	1.2
4.1	6.5	3.8		-7.3	-28.7	1.6	3.1	2.7	4.3
51.0	56.9	61.1	% Profit Before Taxes/Tangible Net Worth	69.1	100.8	39.5	76.1	46.4	49.0
(168) 22.5	(179) 27.3	(174) 30.9		(17) 30.3	(32) 44.4	(29) 12.8	(41) 40.7	(32) 29.6	(23) 35.2
6.7	7.6	11.4		8.3	13.7	4.7	13.4	12.1	17.6
19.2	23.5	26.7	% Profit Before Taxes/Total Assets	28.4	42.3	26.0	32.1	20.0	26.1
8.4	9.6	11.3		8.9	12.6	6.2	11.6	11.0	12.7
1.1	.6	3.7		.7	3.8	2.5	3.6	5.5	7.6
14.7	14.4	12.2	Sales/Net Fixed Assets	12.9	16.2	10.6	12.1	11.9	10.4
7.2	6.8	6.8		6.9	9.2	5.9	7.6	5.7	5.3
3.8	3.8	4.0		2.0	5.8	4.5	4.4	3.6	3.0
2.8	2.9	2.8	Sales/Total Assets	3.2	4.1	2.7	2.8	2.4	2.2
2.1	2.1	2.2		2.1	2.8	2.2	2.1	2.0	1.8
1.4	1.5	1.4		1.3	2.0	1.6	1.3	1.5	1.1
2.2	1.8	1.9	% Depr., Dep., Amort./Sales	2.2	1.2	1.8	1.9	1.9	2.7
(165) 3.8	(188) 3.6	(179) 3.5		(21) 4.8	(34) 2.4	(27) 3.5	(40) 3.9	(33) 3.3	(24) 4.1
6.1	5.7	5.2		9.4	4.9	5.0	6.1	5.3	5.2
3.5	2.8	4.0	% Officers', Directors' Owners' Comp/Sales		4.7		4.5	3.4	
(63) 6.2	(69) 5.5	(63) 6.2		(20) 10.2	(10) 5.8	(10) 3.9			
10.1	10.6	11.2		12.0	10.8	5.8			
2724507M	2628896M	2600531M	Net Sales ($)	15516M	84103M	116584M	305475M	563176M	1515677M
1707238M	1617157M	1779781M	Total Assets ($)	11922M	41092M	67376M	187745M	318549M	1153097M

M = $ thousand   MM = $ million
See Pages 11 through 21 for Explanation of Ratios and Data

Current Data Sorted by Assets   Comparative Historical Data

	0-500M	500M-2MM	2-10MM	10-50MM	50-100MM	100-250MM	Type of Statement	4/1/02-3/31/03 ALL	4/1/03-3/31/04 ALL
		8 (4/1-9/30/06)			51 (10/1/06-3/31/07)				
		1	1	2			Unqualified		2
		1	2				Reviewed	1	2
	2	4	4				Compiled	2	6
	10	6	1		1	1	Tax Returns	4	13
	3	12	6	1	1	1	Other	5	12
NUMBER OF STATEMENTS	15	24	14	3	1	2		12	35
ASSETS	%	%	%	%	%	%		%	%
Cash & Equivalents	32.5	8.4	18.3					32.2	20.1
Trade Receivables (net)	12.9	32.2	25.7					25.3	20.4
Inventory	17.8	14.1	21.3					23.0	18.5
All Other Current	.8	10.6	15.6					4.4	6.3
Total Current	64.0	65.3	81.0					84.9	65.4
Fixed Assets (net)	22.6	20.2	12.7					12.0	17.3
Intangibles (net)	3.2	3.1	.0					.3	4.8
All Other Non-Current	10.2	11.4	6.3					2.8	12.5
Total	100.0	100.0	100.0					100.0	100.0
LIABILITIES									
Notes Payable-Short Term	8.4	11.3	8.7					2.2	11.3
Cur. Mat.-L.T.D.	7.1	2.4	.9					.8	1.8
Trade Payables	9.9	15.6	14.4					15.8	15.7
Income Taxes Payable	.0	.9	.1					.0	.1
All Other Current	44.6	20.5	37.9					41.6	34.1
Total Current	70.1	50.7	62.0					60.4	63.0
Long-Term Debt	13.8	21.2	5.3					4.6	13.4
Deferred Taxes	.0	.0	2.7					.0	.7
All Other Non-Current	21.2	4.3	3.3					.0	5.5
Net Worth	-5.1	23.7	26.8					34.9	17.5
Total Liabilties & Net Worth	100.0	100.0	100.0					100.0	100.0
INCOME DATA									
Net Sales	100.0	100.0	100.0					100.0	100.0
Gross Profit									
Operating Expenses	99.2	93.8	94.1					94.7	95.1
Operating Profit	.8	6.2	5.9					5.3	4.9
All Other Expenses (net)	.6	1.6	.1					.1	.4
Profit Before Taxes	.2	4.6	5.8					5.3	4.5
RATIOS									
Current	1.8	2.4	1.8					2.5	1.5
	1.3	1.3	1.4					1.6	1.1
	.7	.7	1.0					1.0	.8
Quick	1.3	1.5	1.3					2.3	1.0
	.8	.7	.6					1.0	.6
	.2	.3	.4					.4	.3
Sales/Receivables	0 UND	11 33.4	6 57.0					12 31.1	0 UND
	3 126.3	28 12.9	32 11.3					21 17.3	19 19.6
	22 16.8	48 7.7	71 5.1					44 8.3	57 6.4
Cost of Sales/Inventory									
Cost of Sales/Payables									
Sales/Working Capital	20.8	9.4	5.0					7.3	13.5
	50.8	18.5	12.7					11.1	76.1
	-44.4	-13.2	-443.8					NM	-33.7
EBIT/Interest	22.4	11.0	179.9						21.5
	(10) 9.4	(19) 1.7	(12) 13.4					(28)	2.6
	-2.6	-5.2	2.8						-1.4
Net Profit + Depr., Dep., Amort./Cur. Mat. L/T/D									
Fixed/Worth	.2	.3	.2					.1	.3
	.6	1.2	.5					.4	1.3
	-.4	-3.9	.8					1.1	-2.4
Debt/Worth	1.0	.7	1.0					.6	2.0
	-27.8	9.5	4.2					1.7	6.9
	-3.2	-10.9	15.6					7.9	-31.3
% Profit Before Taxes/Tangible Net Worth		105.3	82.4					110.0	131.4
	(16) 78.9	(13) 53.4						(11) 17.0	(24) 41.0
		6.3	12.2					-.3	2.1
% Profit Before Taxes/Total Assets	18.9	26.2	19.5					36.3	31.5
	3.6	7.9	9.6					7.5	1.8
	-6.5	-16.2	1.1					-.8	-4.2
Sales/Net Fixed Assets	903.9	45.0	49.6					180.0	90.7
	36.4	29.9	23.3					41.4	32.8
	9.8	12.6	9.1					11.0	13.8
Sales/Total Assets	10.3	4.0	3.8					5.3	4.9
	6.2	3.3	2.1					2.7	2.7
	3.6	2.6	1.1					2.2	2.1
% Depr., Dep., Amort./Sales		.4	.5					.3	.5
	(19) 1.1	(12) 1.1						(11) 1.0	(24) 1.1
		1.5	1.6					1.5	2.2
% Officers', Directors' Owners' Comp/Sales	1.7	3.8							2.7
	(10) 6.7	(10) 5.6							(23) 5.0
	12.8	7.2							14.4
Net Sales ($)	28038M	77413M	142724M	132789M	1167310M	1353734M		404830M	174727M
Total Assets ($)	3273M	22974M	58477M	51936M	80624M	289968M		85276M	81486M

© RMA 2007

M = $ thousand   MM = $ million

See Pages 11 through 21 for Explanation of Ratios and Data

Comparative Historical Data   Current Data Sorted by Sales

			Type of Statement						
2	3	4	Unqualified		1			1	2
2	5	3	Reviewed			1	2		
6	6	10	Compiled	2	1	4	1	1	1
15	7	19	Tax Returns	3	9	4	1		2
12	13	23	Other	3	7	4	3	4	2
4/1/04-3/31/05	4/1/05-3/31/06	4/1/06-3/31/07		0-1MM	8 (4/1-9/30/06) 1-3MM	3-5MM	5-10MM	51 (10/1/06-3/31/07) 10-25MM	25MM & OVER
ALL	ALL	ALL							
37	34	59	NUMBER OF STATEMENTS	8	18	13	7	6	7
%	%	%	ASSETS	%	%	%	%	%	%
14.7	17.0	18.7	Cash & Equivalents		23.2	13.0			
22.4	27.8	25.4	Trade Receivables (net)		20.9	32.3			
22.2	21.9	16.1	Inventory		17.9	12.3			
3.9	3.3	9.0	All Other Current		8.2	13.4			
63.2	70.1	69.2	Total Current		70.1	71.0			
21.9	15.5	18.7	Fixed Assets (net)		19.2	14.7			
3.8	5.2	3.2	Intangibles (net)		2.7	4.2			
11.2	9.2	8.9	All Other Non-Current		8.0	10.2			
100.0	100.0	100.0	Total		100.0	100.0			
			LIABILITIES						
20.7	10.8	9.7	Notes Payable-Short Term		4.7	15.4			
1.2	2.0	3.3	Cur. Mat.-L.T.D.		6.2	1.0			
15.6	15.8	13.2	Trade Payables		11.1	11.0			
.3	.3	.5	Income Taxes Payable		.9	.1			
33.0	21.5	32.6	All Other Current		40.0	30.6			
70.8	50.4	59.2	Total Current		62.8	58.1			
10.5	17.3	14.2	Long-Term Debt		20.2	9.5			
.2	.0	.7	Deferred Taxes		.0	2.8			
11.2	6.4	10.6	All Other Non-Current		2.5	4.0			
7.3	26.0	15.3	Net Worth		14.5	25.6			
100.0	100.0	100.0	Total Liabilties & Net Worth		100.0	100.0			
			INCOME DATA						
100.0	100.0	100.0	Net Sales		100.0	100.0			
			Gross Profit						
94.8	94.1	95.1	Operating Expenses		95.2	97.2			
5.2	5.9	4.9	Operating Profit		4.8	2.8			
1.5	1.1	1.0	All Other Expenses (net)		.8	.1			
3.7	4.8	3.9	Profit Before Taxes		4.0	2.8			
			RATIOS						
1.8	2.5	2.2			2.3	2.5			
1.2	1.4	1.3	Current		1.3	1.5			
.5	.9	.8			.8	.8			
1.0	1.6	1.3			1.1	1.9			
.6	.8	.8	Quick		.8	.6			
.2	.4	.3			.3	.3			
2 202.7	9 39.2	3 126.3		0 UND	0 UND				
18 20.1	31 11.9	22 16.8	Sales/Receivables	18 20.7	30 12.2				
42 8.8	63 5.8	45 8.1		34 10.6	62 5.9				
			Cost of Sales/Inventory						
			Cost of Sales/Payables						
7.2	7.6	8.0			6.3	9.4			
58.2	15.1	24.7	Sales/Working Capital		46.2	20.8			
-8.9	-34.3	-44.9			-36.9	-11.9			
27.2	16.1	35.6			36.6	150.0			
(25) 3.8	(28) 4.8	(46) 3.9	EBIT/Interest		(13) 3.9	(12) 3.6			
.7	1.6	-.7			-3.7	-4.6			
			Net Profit + Depr., Dep., Amort./Cur. Mat. L/T/D						
.2	.2	.2			.1	.3			
1.5	.5	.6	Fixed/Worth		1.0	.5			
-1.1	NM	-3.9			-1.2	NM			
1.7	1.1	1.0			.7	.7			
5.6	3.8	5.5	Debt/Worth		5.4	12.4			
-7.5	NM	-8.6			-5.9	NM			
83.7	117.0	94.3			99.8	346.0			
(24) 23.2	(26) 59.2	(40) 59.2	% Profit Before Taxes/Tangible Net Worth		(10) 71.6	(10) 65.2			
7.3	4.6	8.2			14.0	-30.0			
20.1	24.6	22.3			16.7	24.9			
4.5	12.3	9.5	% Profit Before Taxes/Total Assets		7.0	3.6			
.7	1.9	-3.5			-9.6	-16.3			
53.8	87.8	103.2			109.5	78.5			
24.9	29.8	27.6	Sales/Net Fixed Assets		22.4	31.5			
9.0	15.1	11.7			11.5	10.9			
4.5	4.6	5.0			6.7	5.0			
2.5	3.0	3.5	Sales/Total Assets		3.5	3.4			
1.8	2.0	2.1			2.6	1.7			
.6	.5	.4			.4				
(26) 1.0	(26) .9	(39) .9	% Depr., Dep., Amort./Sales		(12) 1.0				
2.4	1.9	1.5			1.8				
2.8	2.8	2.9			3.3				
(23) 5.5	(20) 5.2	(30) 6.5	% Officers', Directors' Owners' Comp/Sales		(10) 4.6				
7.6	6.7	9.6			8.4				
1391137M	1165476M	2902008M	Net Sales ($)	4449M	35757M	51972M	46032M	78365M	2685433M
185187M	227238M	507252M	Total Assets ($)	3487M	11884M	22027M	12224M	29069M	428561M

M = $ thousand   MM = $ million
See Pages 11 through 21 for Explanation of Ratios and Data

PROFESSIONAL SERVICES—Graphic Design Services NAICS 541430 (SIC 7336)

	Current Data Sorted by Assets							Comparative Historical Data	
1	1	8	6	3	1	Type of Statement			
1	1	8	6	3	1	Unqualified		19	14
1	4	14	3			Reviewed		26	29
10	14	14	1		1	Compiled		38	41
20	6	8	1		1	Tax Returns		16	28
13	24	20	18	6	5	Other		61	62
	49 (4/1-9/30/06)		155 (10/1/06-3/31/07)					4/1/02-3/31/03 ALL	4/1/03-3/31/04 ALL
0-500M	500M-2MM	2-10MM	10-50MM	50-100MM	100-250MM				
45	49	64	29	9	8	NUMBER OF STATEMENTS		160	174
%	%	%	%	%	%	ASSETS		%	%
15.5	16.0	11.8	17.2			Cash & Equivalents		12.2	13.8
29.8	31.0	31.7	22.8			Trade Receivables (net)		34.9	33.4
4.5	6.5	9.4	5.8			Inventory		6.8	8.3
4.7	3.3	2.3	7.1			All Other Current		3.2	3.1
54.6	56.9	55.2	52.9			Total Current		57.2	58.6
36.3	27.4	36.0	31.0			Fixed Assets (net)		28.7	29.0
1.7	6.6	2.7	6.5			Intangibles (net)		6.0	4.9
7.4	9.2	6.1	9.6			All Other Non-Current		8.1	7.4
100.0	100.0	100.0	100.0			Total		100.0	100.0
						LIABILITIES			
23.1	12.8	9.4	7.6			Notes Payable-Short Term		14.6	15.4
11.1	4.8	11.9	2.3			Cur. Mat.-L.T.D.		6.1	5.7
11.3	12.9	13.5	9.8			Trade Payables		14.6	13.8
.0	.7	.1	1.0			Income Taxes Payable		.5	.3
27.1	10.7	10.7	19.0			All Other Current		14.4	12.7
72.7	42.0	45.7	39.7			Total Current		50.2	47.9
36.7	18.3	18.9	19.3			Long-Term Debt		18.1	17.8
.0	.8	.9	.6			Deferred Taxes		.4	.9
6.0	3.8	5.1	9.9			All Other Non-Current		3.7	7.2
-15.4	35.1	29.5	30.4			Net Worth		27.6	26.2
100.0	100.0	100.0	100.0			Total Liabilities & Net Worth		100.0	100.0
						INCOME DATA			
100.0	100.0	100.0	100.0			Net Sales		100.0	100.0
						Gross Profit			
96.1	95.6	93.2	95.5			Operating Expenses		95.7	95.1
3.9	4.4	6.8	4.5			Operating Profit		4.3	4.9
1.1	.8	2.3	.8			All Other Expenses (net)		1.5	.9
2.8	3.6	4.4	3.7			Profit Before Taxes		2.8	4.0
						RATIOS			
1.9	3.0	2.7	1.9					2.3	2.6
1.0	1.3	1.5	1.4			Current		1.3	1.4
.5	.9	1.0	1.1					.8	1.0
1.5	2.7	2.2	1.7					1.9	2.2
.8	1.0	1.1	1.1			Quick		1.0	1.1
.3	.6	.6	.8					.6	.7
0 UND	14 25.5	33 11.1	24 15.4					30 12.2	28 12.9
25 14.3	41 9.0	52 7.0	55 6.7			Sales/Receivables		46 8.0	46 8.0
45 8.1	60 6.1	64 5.7	65 5.6					68 5.3	64 5.7
						Cost of Sales/Inventory			
						Cost of Sales/Payables			
16.2	6.6	5.6	7.5					7.7	7.4
UND	35.9	15.9	14.6			Sales/Working Capital		20.2	18.7
-14.2	-38.5	NM	NM					-29.4	UND
8.0	23.7	6.0	6.8					6.7	14.9
(34) 2.4	(43) 6.6	(58) 2.8	(25) 3.0			EBIT/Interest		(131) 2.3	(150) 2.7
.3	1.8	1.1	.6					-1.1	.1
		3.5						4.2	3.7
		(11) 1.5				Net Profit + Depr., Dep., Amort./Cur. Mat. L/T/D		(30) 1.5	(29) 2.0
		1.3						.8	1.2
.6	.2	.4	.5					.3	.3
5.0	1.0	1.1	1.2			Fixed/Worth		.9	.8
-1.8	6.2	3.8	7.2					4.0	3.8
.9	.7	.6	1.1					.8	.8
5.6	2.6	1.9	3.4			Debt/Worth		2.1	2.1
-6.0	13.0	8.2	20.8					10.9	9.3
99.2	84.9	38.4	39.0					56.2	69.8
(28) 32.3	(40) 29.5	(56) 14.4	(26) 9.9			% Profit Before Taxes/Tangible Net Worth		(131) 14.5	(146) 21.5
-3.3	6.9	2.9	-2.0					-6.9	-.5
30.8	27.6	13.8	8.4					15.3	21.1
6.4	9.9	4.6	4.6			% Profit Before Taxes/Total Assets		3.9	3.4
-3.3	1.6	.5	-.3					-5.4	-1.3
47.4	58.5	14.3	17.2					27.5	30.8
18.3	14.0	6.8	6.5			Sales/Net Fixed Assets		11.3	12.7
7.7	5.1	3.4	3.0					5.5	5.4
7.5	4.7	3.0	2.4					3.9	3.7
4.3	2.9	2.1	1.7			Sales/Total Assets		2.6	2.6
3.0	1.9	1.6	1.1					1.7	1.8
.9	.7	1.3	1.5					1.1	1.2
(35) 1.9	(34) 1.6	(60) 2.6	(27) 3.3			% Depr., Dep., Amort./Sales		(129) 2.8	(145) 2.6
3.1	5.8	5.7	4.6					5.4	4.9
6.9	3.8	2.8						5.0	4.7
(25) 9.6	(25) 6.9	(23) 4.9				% Officers', Directors' Owners' Comp/Sales		(65) 8.3	(69) 8.4
15.4	13.0	10.3						14.9	18.5
58069M	209250M	854788M	1521623M	762952M	3934411M	Net Sales ($)		2099526M	3697087M
11054M	55133M	267637M	607189M	583887M	1550064M	Total Assets ($)		1087583M	1582350M

M = $ thousand   MM = $ million
See Pages 11 through 21 for Explanation of Ratios and Data

Comparative Historical Data | Current Data Sorted by Sales

					Type of Statement						
	11		16		20	Unqualified	1	2	1	4	7	6
	31		22		22	Reviewed	1	1	3	9	6	2
	36		35		40	Compiled	5	11	8	7	7	2
	37		23		36	Tax Returns	10	12	5	5	1	3
	65		58		86	Other	10	20	7	13	14	22
	4/1/04-3/31/05 ALL		4/1/05-3/31/06 ALL		4/1/06-3/31/07 ALL		0-1MM	49 (4/1-9/30/06) 1-3MM	3-5MM	5-10MM	155 (10/1/06-3/31/07) 10-25MM	25MM & OVER
	180		154		204	NUMBER OF STATEMENTS	26	46	24	38	35	35
	%		%		%	ASSETS	%	%	%	%	%	%
	13.6		12.5		14.6	Cash & Equivalents	16.0	12.1	16.0	11.4	16.8	17.0
	31.5		34.3		29.0	Trade Receivables (net)	23.9	28.1	33.5	36.2	27.5	24.6
	8.6		7.9		6.7	Inventory	3.1	4.8	5.7	11.0	9.5	5.5
	2.4		2.9		3.8	All Other Current	7.2	2.8	2.8	2.0	4.1	5.1
	56.0		57.6		54.2	Total Current	50.2	47.7	58.0	60.6	57.8	52.2
	32.1		30.3		32.8	Fixed Assets (net)	41.0	36.2	29.0	32.6	31.0	27.1
	5.8		4.8		4.8	Intangibles (net)	1.2	5.8	3.7	2.2	4.0	10.7
	6.1		7.4		8.2	All Other Non-Current	7.6	10.3	9.3	4.6	7.2	10.0
	100.0		100.0		100.0	Total	100.0	100.0	100.0	100.0	100.0	100.0
						LIABILITIES						
	16.5		11.5		12.7	Notes Payable-Short Term	24.3	11.6	11.3	9.7	13.9	8.3
	7.6		6.1		8.0	Cur. Mat.-L.T.D.	11.6	6.1	4.4	7.0	3.0	16.1
	14.2		14.3		11.8	Trade Payables	8.2	10.3	14.3	14.6	13.4	9.7
	.5		.4		.4	Income Taxes Payable	.0	.0	.7	.6	.1	.9
	15.0		13.7		15.3	All Other Current	14.3	21.0	9.4	11.3	13.7	18.7
	53.8		45.9		48.1	Total Current	58.3	49.1	40.1	43.3	44.2	53.8
	22.7		21.2		23.4	Long-Term Debt	44.2	29.8	11.9	18.9	14.7	21.0
	.3		.3		.6	Deferred Taxes	.0	.7	.9	.7	.6	.8
	8.2		8.7		6.3	All Other Non-Current	7.2	6.1	7.9	3.2	5.1	9.4
	15.0		23.9		21.6	Net Worth	-9.8	14.4	39.2	33.9	35.4	15.0
	100.0		100.0		100.0	Total Liabilities & Net Worth	100.0	100.0	100.0	100.0	100.0	100.0
						INCOME DATA						
	100.0		100.0		100.0	Net Sales	100.0	100.0	100.0	100.0	100.0	100.0
						Gross Profit						
	93.9		94.4		94.9	Operating Expenses	90.9	95.0	94.9	95.8	96.7	95.4
	6.1		5.6		5.1	Operating Profit	9.1	5.0	5.1	4.2	3.3	4.6
	2.0		1.6		1.4	All Other Expenses (net)	4.8	1.4	.4	.9	.5	1.0
	4.1		4.0		3.7	Profit Before Taxes	4.3	3.6	4.7	3.4	2.8	3.6
						RATIOS						
	2.0		2.4		2.5		2.7	1.9	3.0	2.3	2.9	2.6
	1.2		1.4		1.4	Current	1.3	1.3	1.6	1.3	1.5	1.4
	.8		.9		.9		.5	.6	.9	1.0	1.2	.9
	1.6		2.0		2.2		2.0	1.8	2.7	1.9	2.7	1.8
	.9		1.2		1.1	Quick	.9	.9	1.5	1.1	1.1	1.2
	.6		.7		.6		.3	.6	.6	.8	.7	.7
20	18.0	28	12.8	19	18.8		0 UND	16 23.2	20 18.6	41 9.0	29 12.5	20 18.1
41	8.9	46	7.9	45	8.1	Sales/Receivables	26 13.9	38 9.6	46 8.0	53 6.8	49 7.5	55 6.7
61	6.0	62	5.9	61	6.0		66 5.5	50 7.3	62 5.9	64 5.7	63 5.8	65 5.6
						Cost of Sales/Inventory						
						Cost of Sales/Payables						
	8.4		7.6		7.0		9.5	15.0	4.9	6.7	6.6	6.3
	31.6		15.9		19.5	Sales/Working Capital	30.4	78.9	17.2	23.1	13.3	14.6
	-21.8		-83.0		-53.9		-7.9	-15.3	-46.8	130.6	67.4	-90.4
	11.5		17.7		9.0		8.9	7.1	30.4	7.7	10.5	10.8
(156)	3.3	(134)	3.5	(174)	3.4	EBIT/Interest	(19) 1.3	(40) 3.2	(19) 4.7	(36) 4.7	(30) 2.5	(30) 3.9
	.7		.9		.9		.5	.8	1.2	1.4	.5	1.1
	4.2		5.2		7.8							
(27)	2.2	(26)	1.9	(31)	2.3	Net Profit + Depr., Dep., Amort./Cur. Mat. L/T/D						
	1.4		.7		1.3							
	.4		.4		.4		.6	.5	.1	.5	.4	.4
	1.4		1.0		1.2	Fixed/Worth	2.4	2.5	.5	1.0	.6	1.9
	UND		7.7		9.2		UND	-5.5	NM	2.5	4.5	9.2
	1.0		1.0		.8		.8	.8	.4	.9	.6	1.1
	4.0		3.2		2.6	Debt/Worth	4.1	4.2	1.2	2.5	1.7	3.8
	UND		24.5		26.3		UND	-11.8	NM	6.3	8.7	38.5
	65.3		90.1		52.6		113.4	54.6	60.1	52.8	39.6	56.0
(136)	33.8	(119)	24.8	(162)	20.0	% Profit Before Taxes/Tangible Net Worth	(21) 22.0	(30) 10.2	(18) 25.5	(35) 29.9	(31) 10.0	(27) 21.2
	5.0		6.1		1.7		-1.7	-5.9	-1.1	5.2	1.7	2.5
	21.5		22.2		17.0		33.2	19.2	30.7	14.2	9.1	14.8
	4.6		6.5		6.2	% Profit Before Taxes/Total Assets	3.4	5.8	10.0	6.9	3.1	6.7
	-1.2		.0		-.1		-3.8	-2.0	-.4	2.2	-.5	1.1
	33.8		35.1		33.3		20.8	43.4	52.2	29.6	15.9	31.5
	12.9		11.2		9.9	Sales/Net Fixed Assets	11.9	12.2	13.5	8.5	6.5	9.8
	5.1		5.7		4.3		3.2	3.9	4.7	5.4	3.7	4.9
	4.3		3.7		3.9		4.6	4.8	4.9	3.7	3.3	2.9
	2.8		2.5		2.5	Sales/Total Assets	2.9	3.1	2.9	2.5	2.1	2.2
	1.7		2.0		1.6		1.3	1.5	1.7	1.8	1.2	1.4
	1.1		1.2		1.2		1.7	.7	1.1	.8	1.5	1.4
(144)	2.7	(127)	2.6	(168)	2.5	% Depr., Dep., Amort./Sales	(19) 2.7	(36) 2.0	(17) 1.5	(35) 2.6	(33) 2.6	(28) 2.4
	5.9		4.4		4.7		7.2	6.1	4.4	4.5	4.9	3.7
	3.5		4.0		3.7		9.1	6.2	4.6	2.1		
(82)	6.6	(72)	6.5	(81)	7.3	% Officers', Directors' Owners' Comp/Sales	(11) 11.5	(24) 7.9	(12) 10.1	(17) 4.0		
	10.6		9.9		13.8		20.6	13.6	13.9	6.0		
	1852209M		2094622M		7341093M	Net Sales ($)	14126M	84985M	94968M	270601M	584532M	6291881M
	968908M		833215M		3074964M	Total Assets ($)	11935M	55698M	36904M	114138M	429515M	2426774M

Current Data Sorted by Assets   Comparative Historical Data

Type of Statement (number of statements)

Type of Statement	0-500M	500M-2MM	2-10MM	10-50MM	50-100MM	100-250MM	4/1/02-3/31/03 ALL	4/1/03-3/31/04 ALL
Unqualified	1	9	43	35	6	13	64	71
Reviewed	4	22	47	5			66	50
Compiled	8	29	13	1	1		55	71
Tax Returns	36	35	15	3			35	52
Other	27	57	94	49	13	8	113	150
	77 (4/1-9/30/06)			497 (10/1/06-3/31/07)				
NUMBER OF STATEMENTS	76	152	212	93	20	21	333	394

ASSETS (%)

	0-500M	500M-2MM	2-10MM	10-50MM	50-100MM	100-250MM	4/1/02-3/31/03 ALL	4/1/03-3/31/04 ALL
Cash & Equivalents	31.8	18.8	15.9	20.2	21.9	23.7	17.0	20.4
Trade Receivables (net)	29.0	50.7	49.5	32.5	22.1	23.6	42.5	40.3
Inventory	2.6	2.2	1.7	2.2	4.3	3.1	2.6	3.4
All Other Current	4.8	4.3	4.3	6.2	3.6	6.2	4.7	4.4
Total Current	68.2	76.0	71.4	61.1	51.8	56.5	66.8	68.5
Fixed Assets (net)	17.4	11.6	10.6	14.4	9.0	13.1	15.1	14.2
Intangibles (net)	4.6	4.9	8.8	16.2	29.6	22.6	8.4	7.6
All Other Non-Current	9.9	7.5	9.2	8.2	9.5	7.8	9.7	9.7
Total	100.0	100.0	100.0	100.0	100.0	100.0	100.0	100.0

LIABILITIES

	0-500M	500M-2MM	2-10MM	10-50MM	50-100MM	100-250MM	4/1/02-3/31/03 ALL	4/1/03-3/31/04 ALL
Notes Payable-Short Term	36.2	14.2	9.4	8.8	8.2	3.3	14.9	12.2
Cur. Mat.-L.T.D.	3.2	1.5	2.2	2.3	.6	1.6	5.9	3.5
Trade Payables	9.0	12.5	12.4	8.8	5.0	8.9	13.6	13.3
Income Taxes Payable	.2	.5	.6	.8	1.6	.3	.7	.7
All Other Current	23.1	22.3	25.4	29.0	16.5	17.7	21.2	23.7
Total Current	71.7	51.0	49.9	49.7	31.9	31.9	56.5	53.3
Long-Term Debt	22.3	7.2	8.7	9.8	12.9	7.0	11.7	9.7
Deferred Taxes	.2	.6	.6	.4	1.2	.5	.9	.8
All Other Non-Current	31.9	7.7	9.8	8.8	7.1	6.4	7.7	11.2
Net Worth	-26.1	33.5	31.0	31.4	46.9	54.2	23.2	24.9
Total Liabilties & Net Worth	100.0	100.0	100.0	100.0	100.0	100.0	100.0	100.0

INCOME DATA

	0-500M	500M-2MM	2-10MM	10-50MM	50-100MM	100-250MM	4/1/02-3/31/03 ALL	4/1/03-3/31/04 ALL
Net Sales	100.0	100.0	100.0	100.0	100.0	100.0	100.0	100.0
Gross Profit								
Operating Expenses	94.9	95.4	93.8	93.7	92.4	96.3	95.8	95.0
Operating Profit	5.1	4.6	6.2	6.3	7.6	3.7	4.2	5.0
All Other Expenses (net)	1.1	.8	.9	.8	.4	-.3	.9	1.2
Profit Before Taxes	4.0	3.8	5.4	5.5	7.2	4.0	3.3	3.8

RATIOS

	0-500M	500M-2MM	2-10MM	10-50MM	50-100MM	100-250MM	4/1/02-3/31/03 ALL	4/1/03-3/31/04 ALL
Current	3.2	3.6	2.3	2.1	3.1	3.2	2.8	2.7
	1.6	1.5	1.5	1.3	1.7	2.1	1.5	1.6
	.6	1.0	1.0	.9	1.2	1.3	.9	1.0
Quick	3.1	3.2	2.3	1.9	2.8	3.0	2.6	2.5
	1.3	1.4	1.4	1.1	1.5	1.6	1.3	1.4
	.4	.9	.9	.7	.8	1.0	.8	.8
Sales/Receivables	0 UND	37 10.0	46 7.9	37 9.8	41 8.9	51 7.2	32 11.5	31 11.8
	12 31.0	56 6.5	65 5.6	61 6.0	75 4.9	71 5.1	51 7.2	52 7.1
	42 8.8	73 5.0	84 4.3	85 4.3	98 3.7	86 4.2	73 5.0	71 5.2
Cost of Sales/Inventory								
Cost of Sales/Payables								
Sales/Working Capital	11.7	6.5	5.5	4.6	2.3	2.4	6.0	5.7
	38.1	14.5	12.7	11.9	5.8	5.4	14.7	12.5
	-24.8	400.1	816.2	-30.4	16.2	20.3	-63.9	UND
EBIT/Interest	24.2	24.9	40.6	29.5	18.6	50.4	21.2	29.8
	(54) 4.5	(117) 5.4	(174) 8.6	(75) 7.9	(12) 4.9	(19) 5.3	(265) 5.2	(305) 5.7
	-1.3	.6	1.9	1.7	3.6	-2.0	.5	.4
Net Profit + Depr., Dep., Amort./Cur. Mat. L/T/D		26.4	27.0	26.1			8.2	16.3
		(12) 8.6	(28) 4.0	(19) 6.4			(48) 3.8	(47) 5.7
		.8	1.0	1.8			.8	1.4
Fixed/Worth	.0	.1	.1	.1	.1	.1	.1	.1
	.5	.3	.3	.5	.5	.2	.3	.4
	-.6	1.2	1.4	-3.6	NM	.7	4.0	1.8
Debt/Worth	.7	.6	.8	1.1	.9	.3	.6	.8
	5.6	1.8	2.0	3.3	2.3	1.1	2.0	1.8
	-3.0	7.7	10.8	-31.4	NM	3.3	81.9	11.5
% Profit Before Taxes/Tangible Net Worth	91.7	77.7	73.4	92.9	45.9	40.7	67.1	71.9
	(45) 55.6	(126) 39.7	(170) 39.3	(66) 43.1	(15) 23.2	(18) 15.2	(256) 31.1	(310) 29.9
	7.4	7.4	14.6	16.0	5.9	1.1	3.9	3.4
% Profit Before Taxes/Total Assets	57.1	31.6	20.6	18.2	15.8	12.8	25.3	25.4
	18.4	11.6	13.1	9.9	8.9	4.7	8.1	7.8
	-14.8	1.3	2.2	1.5	3.3	-.7	-3.7	-1.3
Sales/Net Fixed Assets	540.8	140.4	111.7	49.5	22.1	52.5	69.5	72.7
	67.2	49.8	46.5	23.6	16.7	10.6	29.1	29.1
	25.2	23.9	17.2	9.6	11.1	4.7	14.8	15.0
Sales/Total Assets	10.5	4.8	3.8	2.3	1.2	1.4	4.4	4.5
	5.8	3.6	2.6	1.6	.9	1.1	3.0	2.8
	3.6	2.5	1.7	1.1	.7	.7	1.9	1.7
% Depr., Dep., Amort./Sales	.2	.4	.4	1.1	1.5		.7	.8
	(37) .6	(94) .8	(145) 1.0	(60) 2.1	(14) 2.8		(228) 1.5	(249) 1.7
	1.3	1.8	2.3	3.8	5.8		2.9	3.2
% Officers', Directors' Owners' Comp/Sales	5.3	4.3	2.0	3.1			3.5	4.1
	(38) 12.1	(59) 7.7	(50) 5.4	(10) 6.2			(109) 6.6	(110) 8.2
	20.1	10.4	9.4	14.2			13.4	12.7
Net Sales ($)	136646M	658299M	2505845M	4352034M	1858232M	4737082M	7770564M	8097479M
Total Assets ($)	18075M	175589M	936303M	2002424M	1423168M	3052419M	3093676M	4566447M

© RMA 2007

M = $ thousand   MM = $ million
See Pages 11 through 21 for Explanation of Ratios and Data

Comparative Historical Data | Current Data Sorted by Sales

79 / 55 / 61 / 46 / 163 (Hist 1)	70 / 55 / 28 / 55 / 208 (Hist 2)	107 / 78 / 51 / 90 / 248 (Hist 3)	Type of Statement	0-1MM	1-3MM	3-5MM	5-10MM	10-25MM	25MM & OVER
79	70	107	Unqualified	1	3	8	17	35	44
55	55	78	Reviewed	1	11	6	31	19	10
61	28	51	Compiled	5	17	12	12	4	1
46	55	90	Tax Returns	13	36	14	18	5	4
163	208	248	Other	17	31	27	63	55	55
4/1/04-3/31/05 ALL	4/1/05-3/31/06 ALL	4/1/06-3/31/07 ALL		77 (4/1-9/30/06)			497 (10/1/06-3/31/07)		
404	416	574	**NUMBER OF STATEMENTS**	36	98	67	141	118	114
%	%	%	**ASSETS**	%	%	%	%	%	%
19.9	20.9	20.0	Cash & Equivalents	19.3	26.3	21.7	18.7	16.2	19.2
42.4	42.3	42.4	Trade Receivables (net)	26.8	37.3	47.0	46.5	48.0	38.4
3.4	2.7	2.2	Inventory	2.6	2.3	2.2	2.2	1.6	2.4
4.6	5.1	4.7	All Other Current	5.9	5.0	5.8	4.0	3.7	5.3
70.3	71.0	69.3	Total Current	54.7	70.9	76.6	71.3	69.6	65.4
12.5	12.4	12.4	Fixed Assets (net)	21.9	13.6	12.4	10.5	11.7	11.7
8.5	9.2	9.6	Intangibles (net)	8.3	7.0	4.7	8.9	10.0	15.8
8.7	7.3	8.6	All Other Non-Current	15.2	8.5	6.3	9.2	8.7	7.2
100.0	100.0	100.0	Total	100.0	100.0	100.0	100.0	100.0	100.0
			LIABILITIES						
12.7	13.9	13.8	Notes Payable-Short Term	34.8	24.9	12.4	9.3	9.6	8.6
3.1	3.8	2.1	Cur. Mat.-L.T.D.	1.4	1.8	1.3	2.9	2.2	1.8
12.2	12.7	11.0	Trade Payables	10.2	10.6	8.1	11.5	12.5	11.2
.9	1.2	.6	Income Taxes Payable	.0	.2	1.1	.4	.7	1.0
21.3	21.6	24.3	All Other Current	19.9	24.4	21.8	25.5	24.9	24.6
50.1	53.2	51.8	Total Current	66.3	61.8	44.7	49.6	50.0	47.3
9.1	8.7	10.4	Long-Term Debt	23.1	11.7	11.1	9.4	6.9	9.5
.9	.5	.5	Deferred Taxes	.7	.7	.3	.5	.7	.4
10.2	10.7	11.8	All Other Non-Current	10.5	27.1	9.2	10.0	8.0	6.6
29.7	26.9	25.6	Net Worth	-.6	-1.2	34.7	30.4	34.5	36.2
100.0	100.0	100.0	Total Liabilities & Net Worth	100.0	100.0	100.0	100.0	100.0	100.0
			INCOME DATA						
100.0	100.0	100.0	Net Sales	100.0	100.0	100.0	100.0	100.0	100.0
			Gross Profit						
94.2	93.9	94.4	Operating Expenses	94.3	95.4	91.0	95.5	93.9	94.7
5.8	6.1	5.6	Operating Profit	5.7	4.6	9.0	4.5	6.1	5.3
.7	.8	.8	All Other Expenses (net)	3.1	.9	.6	.8	.3	.6
5.0	5.3	4.8	Profit Before Taxes	2.6	3.7	8.4	3.7	5.8	4.7
			RATIOS						
2.7	2.8	2.9	Current	2.0	4.4	3.3	2.7	2.1	2.8
1.6	1.6	1.5		1.0	1.4	1.8	1.5	1.5	1.5
1.0	1.0	1.0		.5	.8	1.3	1.0	1.0	1.1
2.4	2.6	2.6	Quick	1.8	3.7	3.1	2.6	2.0	2.2
1.3	1.4	1.4		1.0	1.3	1.6	1.4	1.3	1.4
.9	.8	.9		.3	.6	1.1	.8	1.0	.9
32 11.5	34 10.7	35 10.4	Sales/Receivables	0 UND	16 23.1	33 11.0	39 9.3	41 8.8	46 7.9
54 6.7	56 6.6	58 6.3		20 18.1	47 7.8	63 5.8	59 6.2	61 6.0	63 5.8
74 4.9	83 4.4	78 4.7		69 5.3	72 5.0	84 4.3	80 4.6	78 4.7	84 4.4
			Cost of Sales/Inventory						
			Cost of Sales/Payables						
5.9	5.4	5.9	Sales/Working Capital	10.7	5.5	4.3	6.3	7.0	3.8
14.4	10.8	13.9		UND	17.0	10.6	14.0	16.5	11.8
438.1	UND	-220.9		-8.8	-25.7	24.2	-271.6	NM	87.5
40.9	37.9	29.5	EBIT/Interest	9.0	7.2	62.7	26.6	41.6	43.5
(306) 6.8	(312) 6.9	(451) 6.3		(23) .5	(72) 2.9	(50) 8.7	(115) 6.0	(99) 12.3	(92) 8.3
1.7	1.6	1.3		-2.8	-1.9	3.3	-1.2	3.1	2.6
16.6	20.1	26.1	Net Profit + Depr., Dep., Amort./Cur. Mat. L/T/D				35.5	37.5	12.6
(47) 6.8	(62) 5.9	(70) 6.3				(13) 3.1	(25) 3.1	(21) 6.4	
1.9	1.1	1.2					.1	1.1	2.1
.1	.1	.1	Fixed/Worth	.0	.1	.1	.1	.1	.1
.3	.3	.3		.7	.4	.3	.2	.3	.3
1.9	3.0	2.9		NM	-1.6	1.0	9.3	1.2	5.5
.6	.7	.8	Debt/Worth	1.0	.6	.6	.7	1.0	.8
1.9	2.2	2.2		7.2	2.8	1.5	2.2	2.3	2.2
15.2	69.9	41.5		-3.9	-5.4	7.3	41.4	8.8	83.6
75.6	74.0	78.6	% Profit Before Taxes/Tangible Net Worth	69.2	80.5	87.7	75.0	97.7	72.8
(315) 36.1	(313) 37.3	(440) 39.1		(24) 19.4	(68) 39.1	(55) 40.3	(108) 35.3	(98) 42.5	(87) 36.7
11.9	12.8	11.5		-56.6	4.2	19.9	7.5	19.6	14.4
27.4	27.4	25.1	% Profit Before Taxes/Total Assets	17.6	33.2	35.9	25.7	25.1	17.4
10.1	10.9	11.4		2.4	8.2	19.2	11.2	13.1	11.2
1.6	1.9	1.3		-24.8	.0	6.5	-1.4	3.8	3.1
102.7	103.2	113.5	Sales/Net Fixed Assets	293.3	153.8	107.6	111.3	88.1	109.1
37.7	37.3	42.1		54.7	43.4	46.6	56.5	35.0	28.7
17.1	16.4	16.1		12.9	18.8	23.5	19.7	16.0	10.0
4.5	4.2	4.3	Sales/Total Assets	5.7	5.1	4.8	4.3	4.4	3.6
2.9	2.8	2.8		3.5	3.1	2.6	2.9	2.8	1.8
1.7	1.7	1.6		1.5	2.2	1.9	1.9	1.7	1.1
.5	.5	.4	% Depr., Dep., Amort./Sales	.4	.4	.6	.4	.5	.4
(234) 1.3	(279) 1.2	(359) 1.1		(16) .9	(51) 1.0	(37) 1.4	(98) .9	(87) 1.2	(70) 1.5
3.0	2.4	2.5		3.7	1.7	4.0	2.0	2.3	3.1
3.8	3.5	3.7	% Officers', Directors' Owners' Comp/Sales	10.5	5.5	3.7	3.3	1.9	1.3
(112) 7.2	(128) 8.1	(160) 7.2		(15) 19.0	(45) 8.5	(22) 7.9	(41) 6.0	(23) 4.3	(14) 2.0
12.4	13.6	12.8		30.5	15.1	9.6	8.5	8.3	11.2
10290534M	10859526M	14248138M	Net Sales ($)	21633M	194612M	269952M	1014168M	1875384M	10872389M
5414987M	6190434M	7607978M	Total Assets ($)	14412M	74921M	187892M	505424M	922163M	5903166M

© RMA 2007

M = $ thousand   MM = $ million
See Pages 11 through 21 for Explanation of Ratios and Data

Current Data Sorted by Assets   Comparative Historical Data

	0-500M	500M-2MM	2-10MM	10-50MM	50-100MM	100-250MM	Type of Statement	4/1/02-3/31/03 ALL	4/1/03-3/31/04 ALL
	1	7	52	44	8	13	Unqualified	129	103
	3	24	39	11			Reviewed	70	64
	9	23	24	1		1	Compiled	41	81
	22	30	14		14		Tax Returns	33	40
	25	64	86	38		7	Other	158	144
		82 (4/1-9/30/06)		478 (10/1/06-3/31/07)					
	60	148	215	94	22	21	NUMBER OF STATEMENTS	431	432
	%	%	%	%	%	%	ASSETS	%	%
	20.0	14.0	13.5	14.4	15.1	19.2	Cash & Equivalents	17.5	16.1
	37.2	49.3	52.4	45.8	27.7	28.2	Trade Receivables (net)	43.8	45.1
	3.6	6.1	6.6	5.5	4.8	6.3	Inventory	6.4	4.8
	4.7	3.3	4.6	7.1	5.9	5.9	All Other Current	5.2	5.7
	65.5	72.8	77.1	72.8	53.5	59.6	Total Current	72.8	71.7
	13.5	14.8	9.6	9.2	10.2	9.0	Fixed Assets (net)	14.0	13.9
	5.5	4.1	5.8	10.0	31.4	24.2	Intangibles (net)	6.4	7.7
	15.5	8.3	7.4	8.0	4.9	7.2	All Other Non-Current	6.8	6.7
	100.0	100.0	100.0	100.0	100.0	100.0	Total	100.0	100.0
							LIABILITIES		
	28.2	16.5	11.0	11.5	5.0	1.2	Notes Payable-Short Term	15.8	15.7
	11.3	3.2	3.4	.9	1.3	3.2	Cur. Mat.-L.T.D.	3.1	3.0
	17.0	15.3	19.6	16.9	10.7	14.4	Trade Payables	16.5	18.6
	.0	.7	.5	1.1	.3	.8	Income Taxes Payable	.5	.8
	19.5	13.9	18.8	21.4	23.4	19.0	All Other Current	20.5	21.4
	76.1	49.6	53.2	51.8	40.7	38.6	Total Current	56.3	59.5
	19.4	9.6	8.2	7.5	17.5	5.8	Long-Term Debt	7.3	12.3
	.0	.6	.2	.2	1.3	.8	Deferred Taxes	.5	.5
	11.5	6.6	7.6	5.7	9.3	7.8	All Other Non-Current	7.1	8.2
	-6.9	33.6	30.9	34.9	31.2	47.1	Net Worth	28.7	19.6
	100.0	100.0	100.0	100.0	100.0	100.0	Total Liabilities & Net Worth	100.0	100.0
							INCOME DATA		
	100.0	100.0	100.0	100.0	100.0	100.0	Net Sales	100.0	100.0
							Gross Profit		
	92.8	93.7	94.5	94.9	95.2	98.3	Operating Expenses	95.7	95.8
	7.2	6.3	5.5	5.1	4.8	1.7	Operating Profit	4.3	4.2
	1.4	1.6	.8	.1	1.3	1.0	All Other Expenses (net)	.6	.9
	5.8	4.7	4.8	4.9	3.5	.7	Profit Before Taxes	3.7	3.2
							RATIOS		
	2.7	2.9	2.2	2.1	1.7	2.8		2.3	2.2
	1.3	1.5	1.4	1.6	1.2	1.8	Current	1.4	1.3
	.4	1.0	1.1	1.0	1.1	1.1		1.0	1.0
	2.2	2.3	1.9	1.8	1.6	2.5		2.0	1.8
(59)	1.1	1.3	1.3	1.2	1.0	1.1	Quick	1.2	1.1
	.4	.9	.9	.8	.9	.8		.7	.8
	0 UND	31 11.8	46 8.0	55 6.7	50 7.2	46 8.0		36 10.3	35 10.5
	31 11.9	47 7.8	63 5.8	66 5.5	70 5.2	72 5.1	Sales/Receivables	57 6.5	56 6.5
	60 6.1	75 4.9	84 4.4	90 4.1	85 4.3	90 4.1		78 4.7	76 4.8
							Cost of Sales/Inventory		
							Cost of Sales/Payables		
	9.2	7.2	6.3	5.7	7.1	3.2		6.7	7.1
	30.1	14.2	12.7	9.7	16.4	7.4	Sales/Working Capital	14.4	17.6
	-11.1	999.8	41.5	95.3	110.2	24.2		-130.1	-146.6
	13.3	19.4	24.5	26.5	9.7	41.3		23.5	20.8
(48)	3.4	(121) 5.0	(176) 5.9	(72) 10.0	(16) 3.7	(17) 3.8	EBIT/Interest	(362) 5.6	(362) 5.6
	.3	.5	1.4	3.2	1.5	-30.4		1.2	1.2
		5.2	14.9	25.9				29.6	15.3
		(11) 1.8	(32) 3.3	(21) 6.3			Net Profit + Depr., Dep., Amort./Cur. Mat. L/T/D	(64) 6.6	(68) 2.9
		.2	.4	.4				1.8	.7
	.1	.1	.1	.1	.1	.1		.1	.1
	.5	.4	.2	.3	.7	.2	Fixed/Worth	.4	.4
	-.7	1.9	1.4	1.1	-.4	.8		1.9	3.5
	.7	.7	.9	1.0	1.3	.5		.9	.9
	4.0	2.0	2.0	2.1	5.1	1.4	Debt/Worth	2.2	3.0
	-2.9	10.5	6.2	9.9	-2.3	6.0		10.6	74.0
	197.4	79.6	67.7	71.2	75.2	49.3		65.8	65.7
(37)	52.1	(121) 36.1	(175) 37.9	(79) 36.5	(15) 20.9	(18) 24.4	% Profit Before Taxes/Tangible Net Worth	(349) 33.5	(329) 30.6
	26.5	11.2	12.2	17.8	-9.4	7.1		4.5	5.3
	50.2	23.7	23.1	19.4	8.0	11.1		22.0	17.8
	14.3	10.1	9.4	11.0	6.3	4.3	% Profit Before Taxes/Total Assets	8.0	8.3
	-2.4	.0	1.7	5.1	1.6	1.9		.3	.5
	251.7	122.6	125.5	93.5	84.9	53.7		75.2	88.5
	60.1	48.1	59.8	42.3	31.8	29.7	Sales/Net Fixed Assets	32.3	35.4
	22.1	19.0	24.3	20.0	19.9	10.6		15.9	15.0
	6.7	4.8	3.9	3.3	2.6	1.9		4.1	4.5
	4.5	3.6	3.0	2.2	1.5	1.5	Sales/Total Assets	3.0	2.9
	3.0	2.4	2.0	1.5	.9	.9		1.9	1.9
	.4	.4	.4	.4	.4	1.0		.6	.6
(36)	.9	(97) .9	(162) .8	(72) .9	(10) 1.5	(13) 2.3	% Depr., Dep., Amort./Sales	(318) 1.3	(294) 1.3
	3.4	2.0	1.5	2.2	2.2	3.1		2.5	2.4
	7.2	2.8	1.7					3.2	2.6
(29)	12.2	(57) 5.0	(43) 4.4				% Officers', Directors' Owners' Comp/Sales	(118) 5.9	(101) 6.4
	15.0	9.8	7.8					13.7	12.9
	72772M	609734M	3051766M	5037948M	3187849M	6254826M	Net Sales ($)	11206330M	10013023M
	15077M	168591M	1012753M	1992600M	1546077M	3473692M	Total Assets ($)	5921584M	5429026M

© RMA 2007

M = $ thousand   MM = $ million
See Pages 11 through 21 for Explanation of Ratios and Data

Comparative Historical Data / Current Data Sorted by Sales

	99/98/125 group			Type of Statement	82 (4/1-9/30/06)			478 (10/1/06-3/31/07)		
				Unqualified	2	2	3	20	32	66
				Reviewed	3	9	3	24	26	12
				Compiled	5	13	9	17	11	3
				Tax Returns	11	22	13	11	9	
				Other	15	35	29	43	49	63
	4/1/04-3/31/05 ALL	4/1/05-3/31/06 ALL	4/1/06-3/31/07 ALL		0-1MM	1-3MM	3-5MM	5-10MM	10-25MM	25MM & OVER
	99	98	125	(Unqualified)						
	65	67	77	(Reviewed)						
	55	50	58	(Compiled)						
	37	46	66	(Tax Returns)						
	178	186	234	(Other)						
NUMBER OF STATEMENTS	434	447	560		36	81	57	115	127	144
	%	%	%	**ASSETS**	%	%	%	%	%	%
Cash & Equivalents	16.0	15.4	14.8		16.9	16.4	13.3	17.1	13.0	13.5
Trade Receivables (net)	45.4	48.8	47.0		32.4	38.8	45.9	48.7	54.6	47.6
Inventory	5.2	4.4	5.9		3.7	6.6	8.9	4.6	6.4	5.3
All Other Current	5.4	5.2	4.8		1.8	5.5	2.2	4.6	5.1	5.9
Total Current	71.9	73.8	72.4		54.9	67.3	70.4	75.1	79.2	72.3
Fixed Assets (net)	12.6	11.9	11.4		22.2	15.5	13.7	10.9	9.1	7.8
Intangibles (net)	7.6	6.9	7.7		5.7	4.1	8.3	5.4	5.3	14.0
All Other Non-Current	7.9	7.4	8.5		17.3	13.1	7.6	8.6	6.4	5.9
Total	100.0	100.0	100.0		100.0	100.0	100.0	100.0	100.0	100.0
				LIABILITIES						
Notes Payable-Short Term	16.3	15.5	13.8		26.0	17.2	20.2	12.7	11.2	9.3
Cur. Mat.-L.T.D.	3.2	2.3	3.7		6.2	7.6	5.0	4.7	1.9	1.2
Trade Payables	16.9	16.7	17.2		17.5	13.7	16.4	15.3	18.1	20.1
Income Taxes Payable	.7	.8	.6		.5	.3	.4	.9	.3	.9
All Other Current	21.8	17.7	18.2		17.6	16.2	12.7	18.6	19.7	20.0
Total Current	59.0	53.0	53.4		67.8	55.1	54.7	52.2	51.1	51.4
Long-Term Debt	10.7	8.2	9.9		28.5	13.8	8.5	7.4	8.0	7.2
Deferred Taxes	.6	.4	.3		.1	.2	.5	.5	.1	.5
All Other Non-Current	7.1	8.2	7.5		7.3	10.6	10.5	5.9	7.1	6.3
Net Worth	22.6	30.2	28.8		-3.7	20.4	25.8	34.0	33.6	34.6
Total Liabilities & Net Worth	100.0	100.0	100.0		100.0	100.0	100.0	100.0	100.0	100.0
				INCOME DATA						
Net Sales	100.0	100.0	100.0		100.0	100.0	100.0	100.0	100.0	100.0
Gross Profit										
Operating Expenses	95.1	94.3	94.3		82.0	94.4	95.0	94.2	96.1	95.7
Operating Profit	4.9	5.7	5.7		18.0	5.6	5.0	5.8	3.9	4.3
All Other Expenses (net)	.8	.9	1.0		6.8	.8	.9	.5	.3	.7
Profit Before Taxes	4.1	4.8	4.7		11.2	4.9	4.1	5.3	3.6	3.7
				RATIOS						
Current	2.2	2.4	2.2		2.1	2.6	2.9	2.5	2.6	2.0
	1.3	1.5	1.5		1.2	1.4	1.4	1.5	1.5	1.5
	1.0	1.1	1.0		.3	.9	.8	1.1	1.2	1.1
Quick	1.9	2.1	2.0		2.0	2.1	2.6	2.3	2.2	1.8
	1.1	1.3	(559) 1.2		1.0 (80)	1.1	1.0	1.3	1.3	1.3
	.8	.9	.8		.2	.6	.7	.9	.9	.9
Sales/Receivables	38 9.6	41 8.9	38 9.7		0 UND	15 24.1	30 12.1	35 10.3	50 7.3	49 7.5
	55 6.6	62 5.9	59 6.2		28 12.8	51 7.2	42 8.8	54 6.8	65 5.6	64 5.7
	77 4.7	82 4.5	79 4.6		67 5.4	76 4.8	76 4.8	79 4.6	84 4.3	82 4.5
Cost of Sales/Inventory										
Cost of Sales/Payables										
Sales/Working Capital	6.7	6.4	6.4		7.8	6.5	7.0	6.3	6.0	6.8
	16.9	13.5	13.1		24.9	15.6	22.3	12.0	11.4	12.6
	301.6	101.8	98.3		-5.5	-94.7	-25.2	91.7	34.1	44.7
EBIT/Interest	31.8	21.7	22.4		11.7	16.5	9.8	16.4	31.9	30.0
	(356) 7.7	(355) 5.9	(450) 5.7		(26) 4.8	(63) 4.2	(51) 2.3	(92) 5.5	(101) 7.6	(117) 8.8
	1.7	1.6	1.3		1.5	-.7	-1.4	1.3	1.7	2.2
Net Profit + Depr., Dep., Amort./Cur. Mat. L/T/D	19.0	21.9	15.8					11.5	14.8	36.4
	(66) 2.9	(69) 5.8	(75) 3.2					(21) 1.8	(17) .9	(31) 7.4
	1.2	2.1	.3					.2	-2.2	1.6
Fixed/Worth	.1	.1	.1		.1	.1	.1	.1	.1	.1
	.3	.3	.3		1.6	.5	.5	.2	.2	.2
	2.1	1.6	1.9		-1.4	-4.1	-.4	.8	.9	1.0
Debt/Worth	.9	.9	.8		1.1	.8	.8	.7	.7	1.0
	2.5	2.4	2.1		3.4	2.1	3.0	2.0	1.9	2.2
	20.3	14.6	15.8		-4.7	-29.7	-6.2	6.8	5.3	13.7
% Profit Before Taxes/Tangible Net Worth	68.6	73.5	73.4		97.9	78.7	60.1	85.7	68.9	73.4
	(343) 36.6	(367) 34.2	(445) 36.0		(24) 38.8	(59) 41.9	(39) 30.3	(97) 39.7	(109) 38.2	(117) 34.1
	10.8	9.6	13.7		24.2	8.8	9.2	12.8	10.6	16.9
% Profit Before Taxes/Total Assets	20.3	22.2	22.2		42.8	28.4	21.9	26.4	23.0	17.3
	9.8	9.4	9.5		11.0	9.9	6.6	11.2	11.6	8.6
	1.8	1.3	1.6		2.5	-3.2	-7.0	.9	3.0	2.6
Sales/Net Fixed Assets	97.5	115.3	121.4		214.3	111.4	152.4	101.2	115.2	122.3
	43.8	39.5	50.4		38.8	40.4	41.2	49.3	58.8	58.4
	16.5	18.4	20.6		8.7	14.0	26.8	20.3	21.3	23.1
Sales/Total Assets	4.2	4.2	4.3		4.5	4.3	4.7	4.7	4.0	3.9
	3.0	3.1	3.0		2.9	3.0	3.5	3.2	3.1	2.4
	1.9	1.8	1.8		1.1	1.8	2.1	2.1	2.1	1.5
% Depr., Dep., Amort./Sales	.5	.4	.4		.5	.4	.6	.4	.4	.3
	(285) 1.1	(307) 1.1	(390) .9		(21) 3.6	(52) 1.0	(30) 1.1	(90) .9	(98) .8	(99) .8
	2.6	2.0	2.0		5.9	2.2	3.2	1.8	1.6	2.0
% Officers', Directors' Owners' Comp/Sales	3.8	3.0	2.9		11.8	4.4	2.8	2.3	1.5	
	(98) 7.2	(116) 5.7	(135) 5.6		(13) 13.0	(37) 7.5	(23) 4.9	(31) 4.8	(23) 3.9	
	16.0	11.6	11.5		18.1	13.3	9.3	6.1	6.3	
Net Sales ($)	13531050M	12836455M	18214895M		19612M	147611M	227065M	841014M	2010825M	14968768M
Total Assets ($)	6737616M	6765232M	8208790M		13935M	64101M	86402M	378995M	800640M	6864717M

© RMA 2007

M = $ thousand   MM = $ million
See Pages 11 through 21 for Explanation of Ratios and Data

Current Data Sorted by Assets　　　　　　Comparative Historical Data

0-500M	500M-2MM	2-10MM	10-50MM	50-100MM	100-250MM	Type of Statement			4/1/02-3/31/03 ALL	4/1/03-3/31/04 ALL
4	3	36	28	5	5	Unqualified			65	61
2	16	34	4		1	Reviewed			42	44
6	22	12	1			Compiled			47	75
53	36	11	1	1		Tax Returns			48	65
36	54	71	28	2	5	Other			118	126
	48 (4/1-9/30/06)		429 (10/1/06-3/31/07)							
101	131	164	62	8	11	NUMBER OF STATEMENTS			320	371
%	%	%	%	%	%	ASSETS			%	%
27.0	17.5	12.5	16.6		29.9	Cash & Equivalents			12.9	15.7
26.9	45.9	52.3	39.5		26.7	Trade Receivables (net)			46.0	43.5
3.5	6.8	5.4	6.7		.4	Inventory			3.6	4.8
7.0	2.4	4.5	5.0		3.0	All Other Current			3.8	3.8
64.3	72.6	74.7	67.8		60.0	Total Current			66.4	67.8
21.2	15.8	11.9	13.9		14.3	Fixed Assets (net)			18.8	16.5
5.0	5.4	5.5	10.0		16.0	Intangibles (net)			6.8	6.0
9.5	6.2	7.8	8.4		9.8	All Other Non-Current			8.1	9.7
100.0	100.0	100.0	100.0		100.0	Total			100.0	100.0
						LIABILITIES				
33.9	14.8	10.7	9.7		1.0	Notes Payable-Short Term			19.1	16.4
3.1	2.4	2.3	4.3		1.6	Cur. Mat.-L.T.D.			4.3	3.3
11.0	16.8	18.5	16.6		10.0	Trade Payables			16.0	14.1
.6	.2	.9	.3		.6	Income Taxes Payable			.6	.7
19.4	16.3	19.5	17.2		17.2	All Other Current			20.6	18.4
68.0	50.5	52.0	48.1		30.4	Total Current			60.7	52.9
21.5	10.3	8.1	10.2		5.7	Long-Term Debt			11.6	10.6
.2	.2	.5	.1		.4	Deferred Taxes			.7	.7
19.5	8.2	7.6	11.5		11.6	All Other Non-Current			8.2	8.9
-9.2	30.8	31.8	30.0		52.0	Net Worth			18.8	26.9
100.0	100.0	100.0	100.0		100.0	Total Liabilties & Net Worth			100.0	100.0
						INCOME DATA				
100.0	100.0	100.0	100.0		100.0	Net Sales			100.0	100.0
						Gross Profit				
91.6	94.9	94.4	92.3		95.8	Operating Expenses			95.5	94.9
8.4	5.1	5.6	7.7		4.2	Operating Profit			4.5	5.1
2.2	1.4	1.0	1.0		-.8	All Other Expenses (net)			1.3	1.1
6.3	3.8	4.6	6.7		5.0	Profit Before Taxes			3.2	4.0
						RATIOS				
3.7	3.1	2.2	2.1		3.2				1.9	2.5
1.2	1.5	1.5	1.3		1.8	Current			1.3	1.5
.6	1.0	1.1	1.0		1.1				.8	.9
3.3	2.4	2.0	1.9		3.1				1.8	2.2
(100) 1.0	1.4	1.3	1.1		1.8	Quick			(370) 1.1	1.2
.4	.8	.8	.8		.9				.7	.7
0 UND	30 12.1	46 7.9	47 7.7		38 9.5				29 12.4	28 13.2
10 36.5	47 7.7	67 5.5	63 5.8		87 4.2	Sales/Receivables			48 7.6	50 7.4
43 8.5	63 5.8	86 4.2	80 4.6		93 3.9				66 5.5	73 5.0
						Cost of Sales/Inventory				
						Cost of Sales/Payables				
9.7	7.7	6.8	5.3		1.3				9.7	7.4
57.8	16.9	12.3	12.4		4.4	Sales/Working Capital			24.8	15.7
-23.1	-663.6	77.0	NM		33.0				-36.1	-120.3
22.1	12.3	29.4	25.6						15.7	22.2
(71) 5.2	(100) 4.9	(127) 5.3	(48) 5.1			EBIT/Interest			(266) 3.6	(294) 4.8
-.5	1.6	1.5	1.8						.7	1.0
		5.0	42.8						9.8	6.7
	(25) 2.6	(12) 4.3				Net Profit + Depr., Dep., Amort./Cur. Mat. L/T/D			(59) 3.0	(44) 2.0
		.2	1.5						1.1	.5
.1	.1	.1	.2		.1				.2	.1
1.3	.4	.3	.6		.2	Fixed/Worth			.6	.4
-.6	3.1	1.9	9.6		.9				13.2	3.0
.8	.7	.9	1.1		.5				1.1	.7
24.2	2.7	2.0	4.1		1.2	Debt/Worth			2.8	2.1
-3.2	18.5	13.1	87.6		3.4				71.5	17.5
314.4	75.6	61.2	74.6		35.5				73.1	74.5
(54) 84.4	(104) 34.3	(135) 33.5	(48) 39.5		(10) 22.7	% Profit Before Taxes/Tangible Net Worth			(244) 28.9	(295) 27.3
28.2	7.2	10.5	12.1		-11.7				7.2	3.5
56.6	30.2	21.5	18.6		17.1				21.2	24.1
18.5	9.6	9.8	6.9		5.5	% Profit Before Taxes/Total Assets			7.5	8.2
-.1	1.3	1.6	2.4		-2.6				-1.7	.2
388.0	117.2	126.3	67.8		44.6				71.3	83.7
52.5	35.9	50.2	23.1		12.5	Sales/Net Fixed Assets			34.8	34.5
19.3	12.5	19.3	11.1		11.0				13.6	13.0
11.0	4.9	4.1	2.9		2.4				4.7	4.7
5.6	3.8	2.9	2.0		1.0	Sales/Total Assets			3.5	3.2
3.2	2.6	1.9	1.4		.6				2.4	2.1
.5	.3	.4	.4						.7	.5
(52) .9	(93) 1.1	(119) .8	(54) 1.2			% Depr., Dep., Amort./Sales			(241) 1.3	(261) 1.2
1.7	2.7	1.9	3.1						2.9	2.7
5.2	4.1	1.7							4.0	3.3
(54) 8.9	(52) 7.4	(43) 3.2				% Officers', Directors' Owners' Comp/Sales			(103) 7.3	(109) 6.0
19.0	12.5	5.7							11.0	11.4
162404M	584947M	2245186M	3134232M	1044733M	1968030M	Net Sales ($)			13319093M	7229200M
24355M	146414M	760840M	1465925M	626879M	1641794M	Total Assets ($)			3375205M	4250448M

© RMA 2007

M = $ thousand　　MM = $ million
See Pages 11 through 21 for Explanation of Ratios and Data

Comparative Historical Data

Current Data Sorted by Sales

			Type of Statement						
61	68	81	Unqualified	5	3	2	8	22	41
61	51	57	Reviewed		5	11	18	18	5
50	37	41	Compiled	3	12	12	4	9	1
62	87	102	Tax Returns	29	32	16	15	8	2
163	185	196	Other	17	37	24	43	40	35
4/1/04-	4/1/05-	4/1/06-		48 (4/1-9/30/06)			429 (10/1/06-3/31/07)		
3/31/05	3/31/06	3/31/07							
ALL	ALL	ALL		0-1MM	1-3MM	3-5MM	5-10MM	10-25MM	25MM & OVER
397	428	477	**NUMBER OF STATEMENTS**	54	89	65	88	97	84
%	%	%	**ASSETS**	%	%	%	%	%	%
17.5	17.0	17.9	Cash & Equivalents	26.6	20.4	16.2	16.9	15.6	14.7
42.5	43.9	42.5	Trade Receivables (net)	18.7	37.6	41.8	46.8	54.0	45.9
4.9	4.9	5.5	Inventory	5.2	5.4	6.5	4.7	5.4	5.8
3.7	4.3	4.4	All Other Current	10.4	2.4	2.0	5.2	4.3	3.9
68.6	70.1	70.3	Total Current	60.9	65.8	66.5	73.6	79.3	70.3
16.1	14.0	15.4	Fixed Assets (net)	23.2	18.5	19.7	12.4	10.4	12.6
7.3	7.1	6.3	Intangibles (net)	7.3	7.3	5.4	5.0	3.9	9.3
7.9	8.9	8.0	All Other Non-Current	8.5	8.3	8.4	9.0	6.3	7.7
100.0	100.0	100.0	Total	100.0	100.0	100.0	100.0	100.0	100.0
			LIABILITIES						
17.6	13.5	16.4	Notes Payable-Short Term	30.1	16.2	20.8	16.8	11.3	9.5
3.0	3.1	2.8	Cur. Mat.-L.T.D.	4.5	2.3	3.2	2.1	2.2	3.1
14.7	16.2	15.8	Trade Payables	7.5	12.8	15.4	16.2	21.5	17.7
1.2	.7	.6	Income Taxes Payable	1.0	.2	.0	1.3	.4	.4
19.3	19.2	18.4	All Other Current	14.9	16.2	24.0	20.6	16.3	18.6
55.7	52.7	53.9	Total Current	58.0	47.8	63.5	57.0	51.7	49.4
14.3	13.7	11.8	Long-Term Debt	25.0	18.7	7.9	7.0	7.6	9.0
.4	.3	.4	Deferred Taxes	.0	.3	.2	.1	1.0	.2
9.0	11.1	11.1	All Other Non-Current	16.1	18.2	9.5	8.9	6.6	9.2
20.7	22.2	22.8	Net Worth	.9	15.1	18.8	27.0	33.1	32.1
100.0	100.0	100.0	Total Liabilties & Net Worth	100.0	100.0	100.0	100.0	100.0	100.0
			INCOME DATA						
100.0	100.0	100.0	Net Sales	100.0	100.0	100.0	100.0	100.0	100.0
			Gross Profit						
93.3	93.7	93.6	Operating Expenses	87.0	94.5	94.9	94.7	94.5	93.6
6.7	6.3	6.4	Operating Profit	13.0	5.5	5.1	5.3	5.5	6.4
1.1	1.0	1.3	All Other Expenses (net)	4.8	1.2	1.2	.7	.5	1.0
5.7	5.3	5.1	Profit Before Taxes	8.1	4.3	3.9	4.7	5.0	5.4
			RATIOS						
2.4	2.6	2.6		4.5	3.2	2.3	3.1	2.0	2.1
1.4	1.4	1.5	Current	1.4	1.5	1.4	1.4	1.5	1.4
1.0	1.0	1.0		.5	.9	.9	.9	1.1	1.0
2.1	2.2	2.2		4.0	2.4	2.2	2.6	1.9	2.0
1.2	1.3	(476) 1.2	Quick	(53) .9	1.2	1.2	1.1	1.4	1.2
.8	.8	.8		.2	.7	.7	.7	1.0	.8
25 14.4	29 12.7	29 12.6		0 UND	13 27,7	27 13.3	34 10.7	43 8.5	47 7.7
51 7.1	54 6.8	52 7.0	Sales/Receivables	11 32.1	44 8.2	52 7.0	55 6.7	61 6.0	59 6.2
72 5.1	74 5.0	76 4.8		46 7.9	60 6.1	75 4.9	80 4.5	80 4.6	80 4.6
			Cost of Sales/Inventory						
			Cost of Sales/Payables						
7.1	6.9	6.9		4.4	6.9	10.3	6.7	7.0	6.5
17.8	15.9	16.3	Sales/Working Capital	20.8	20.9	22.8	17.6	12.9	12.5
-468.3	-169.7	-241.5		-11.7	-104.8	-36.0	-45.9	32.7	NM
23.3	29.1	17.7		7.4	12.8	14.3	25.6	19.0	44.0
(309) 6.2	(350) 7.3	(360) 5.1	EBIT/Interest	(33) 2.8	(67) 5.0	(53) 4.8	(68) 5.8	(74) 5.1	(65) 7.9
1.9	1.8	1.4		-.9	.9	1.5	2.0	1.7
13.7	18.1	19.4						18.6	59.7
(51) 4.4	(41) 4.8	(46) 3.5	Net Profit + Depr., Dep., Amort./Cur. Mat. L/T/D				(15) 3.0	(14) 9.9
1.2	.9	.8						-.4	1.8
.1	.1	.1		.2	.1	.2	.1	.1	.1
.4	.3	.4	Fixed/Worth	5.1	.5	1.0	.4	.2	.3
UND	13.3	22.2		-.6	-1.3	-2.8	UND	1.3	3.8
.9	.8	.9		.4	.8	.8	.7	.9	1.0
2.7	2.5	2.9	Debt/Worth	23.1	3.2	2.7	2.9	2.0	2.5
-113.2	UND	-125.4		-4.0	-5.9	-10.4	UND	5.5	20.5
72.4	82.0	75.4	% Profit Before Taxes/Tangible Net Worth	299.7	94.3	74.9	62.4	58.6	75.6
(295) 40.7	(321) 40.5	(357) 37.4		(30) 60.1	(60) 62.2	(47) 38.7	(67) 36.4	(87) 29.7	(66) 40.1
14.4	12.7	11.7		12.5	13.2	6.1	13.8	11.8	12.7
25.9	29.7	26.6	% Profit Before Taxes/Total Assets	47.5	32.7	24.8	26.5	20.3	23.4
11.3	11.1	10.3		11.9	13.3	6.7	11.7	8.3	10.8
2.2	1.2	1.2		-1.6	.7	.6	1.9	2.1	1.5
101.0	148.1	118.5	Sales/Net Fixed Assets	118.6	123.2	75.9	129.6	155.8	105.7
39.3	48.9	41.0		17.7	31.4	31.9	51.7	65.0	38.9
15.5	16.3	15.2		6.9	15.6	12.1	25.6	22.0	12.8
4.5	4.7	4.8	Sales/Total Assets	5.9	5.9	4.9	4.9	4.7	3.6
3.2	3.3	3.2		2.3	4.0	3.6	3.2	3.3	2.6
2.0	2.1	2.0		1.0	2.3	1.9	2.3	2.2	1.7
.5	.3	.4	% Depr., Dep., Amort./Sales	1.1	.4	.5	.3	.3	.4
(266) 1.2	(291) .9	(330) 1.0		(29) 2.1	(54) 1.1	(47) 1.1	(60) .7	(74) .8	(66) .9
2.5	2.6	2.3		5.8	2.4	3.1	1.8	1.6	2.2
4.2	2.9	3.3	% Officers', Directors' Owners' Comp/Sales	6.2	5.8	3.7	2.2	1.7	
(111) 7.3	(129) 6.6	(152) 6.0		(28) 12.2	(40) 9.1	(25) 4.8	(29) 4.1	(24) 2.9	
14.4	11.2	12.6		23.6	14.2	8.1	8.0	5.7	
8793460M	9965407M	9139532M	Net Sales ($)	28474M	175542M	256686M	630899M	1529948M	6517983M
4910996M	5655571M	4666207M	Total Assets ($)	21056M	70272M	99734M	250253M	627568M	3597324M

© RMA 2007

M = $ thousand   MM = $ million
See Pages 11 through 21 for Explanation of Ratios and Data

Current Data Sorted by Assets | Comparative Historical Data

Type of Statement									
		9	45	33	11	16	Unqualified	107	100
	4	17	42	7			Reviewed	73	65
	12	19	19	2			Compiled	53	86
	47	26	15	3			Tax Returns	60	65
	36	66	74	37	6	5	Other	144	150
		78 (4/1-9/30/06)		473 (10/1/06-3/31/07)				4/1/02-3/31/03 ALL	4/1/03-3/31/04 ALL
	0-500M	500M-2MM	2-10MM	10-50MM	50-100MM	100-250MM			
	99	137	195	82	17	21	NUMBER OF STATEMENTS	427	466

ASSETS	%	%	%	%	%	%		%	%
Cash & Equivalents	35.4	18.5	13.2	17.0	17.3	10.6		17.6	18.3
Trade Receivables (net)	21.8	38.3	44.4	41.1	29.0	29.6		39.0	35.8
Inventory	.6	2.9	3.9	2.6	1.3	8.1		2.3	3.5
All Other Current	10.0	5.5	6.3	6.7	4.5	6.5		7.4	6.4
Total Current	67.9	65.2	67.8	67.4	52.2	54.8		66.3	63.9
Fixed Assets (net)	15.3	16.8	17.1	12.4	9.5	13.4		17.2	17.2
Intangibles (net)	5.6	4.4	5.2	9.7	34.0	25.3		5.2	6.2
All Other Non-Current	11.2	13.5	9.8	10.6	4.3	6.5		11.2	12.7
Total	100.0	100.0	100.0	100.0	100.0	100.0		100.0	100.0

LIABILITIES									
Notes Payable-Short Term	24.1	11.7	10.5	6.3	5.7	4.2		14.7	12.4
Cur. Mat.-L.T.D.	2.2	3.4	2.7	3.1	3.5	3.0		4.0	3.4
Trade Payables	7.6	10.2	12.1	14.4	9.3	8.6		12.9	12.6
Income Taxes Payable	.5	.9	.7	1.0	1.3	1.2		.8	.7
All Other Current	33.4	19.5	17.5	22.2	27.7	16.2		20.0	20.4
Total Current	67.8	45.7	43.4	46.9	47.6	33.1		52.3	49.5
Long-Term Debt	12.5	10.8	14.4	10.4	11.2	22.8		12.6	13.8
Deferred Taxes	.2	.3	.3	.8	2.2	1.1		.8	.7
All Other Non-Current	6.4	6.8	5.8	6.5	16.0	5.0		8.2	9.0
Net Worth	13.1	36.3	36.1	35.4	22.9	38.1		26.0	26.9
Total Liabilities & Net Worth	100.0	100.0	100.0	100.0	100.0	100.0		100.0	100.0

INCOME DATA									
Net Sales	100.0	100.0	100.0	100.0	100.0	100.0		100.0	100.0
Gross Profit									
Operating Expenses	86.6	90.4	90.7	90.8	93.9	89.9		93.3	93.0
Operating Profit	13.4	9.6	9.3	9.2	6.1	10.1		6.7	7.0
All Other Expenses (net)	1.4	1.3	1.8	2.5	2.1	3.1		2.7	1.1
Profit Before Taxes	12.0	8.3	7.5	6.7	4.0	7.1		4.0	5.9

RATIOS									
Current	3.7	4.1	3.2	2.3	1.4	2.5		2.6	2.5
	1.2	1.6	1.5	1.4	1.1	1.6		1.5	1.4
	.5	1.0	1.1	1.0	.8	1.1		.9	.9
Quick	3.6	3.4	2.5	2.0	1.2	1.9		2.2	2.1
	1.0	1.4	1.3	1.2	.9	1.1	(426)	1.3	1.2
	.4	.7	.8	.8	.7	.8		.8	.7

Sales/Receivables															
	0	UND	13	28.3	24	15.0	43	8.5	48	7.6	47	7.8	20	18.5	14	26.1
	0	UND	42	8.7	49	7.4	67	5.4	72	5.1	68	5.4	50	7.3	48	7.6
	34	10.8	63	5.8	77	4.7	93	3.9	94	3.9	81	4.5	78	4.7	71	5.1

Cost of Sales/Inventory

Cost of Sales/Payables

Sales/Working Capital									
	12.5	6.0	5.5	4.7	14.9	4.5		5.9	6.8
	105.7	14.6	13.8	10.7	91.3	8.3		13.5	20.0
	-40.3	NM	65.6	NM	-12.1	78.5		-169.6	-79.5

EBIT/Interest														
		41.8		23.8		41.7		26.6		15.9		17.4		19.5		24.4
	(63)	11.6	(99)	5.5	(161)	9.4	(61)	9.7	(14)	3.8	(18)	5.3	(325)	5.4	(353)	5.3
		1.8		1.1		2.0		2.1		1.6		3.0		.6		1.4

Net Profit + Depr., Dep., Amort./Cur. Mat. L/T/D								
			8.8	12.7				6.9	10.0
		(31)	2.1	(16) 5.8			(82)	2.1	(72) 3.6
			.5	1.3				.9	1.4

Fixed/Worth									
	.0	.1	.1	.1	.4	.2		.1	.1
	.3	.3	.3	.3	-.5	.5		.4	.5
	10.0	1.5	2.4	1.7	-.1	-1.7		4.1	3.6

Debt/Worth									
	.4	.5	.6	1.1	3.1	1.2		.7	.8
	2.1	1.8	1.9	2.4	-4.6	4.8		2.1	2.3
	-30.8	10.5	7.5	12.2	-1.6	-5.8		32.9	20.7

% Profit Before Taxes/Tangible Net Worth											
		382.1		77.3		74.6		68.8		74.8		63.0		79.4
	(73)	83.4	(114)	41.0	(162)	31.7	(70)	34.7	(14)	53.3	(331)	27.8	(366)	30.4
		18.1		6.3		8.8		13.7		18.0		1.0		5.9

% Profit Before Taxes/Total Assets									
	123.5	36.9	31.3	20.0	11.2	12.8		22.1	22.1
	38.4	12.1	11.0	8.9	9.3	9.3		7.5	9.7
	2.6	1.1	2.0	3.0	1.9	5.9		-1.5	1.2

Sales/Net Fixed Assets									
	UND	139.1	94.4	88.2	44.7	48.2		86.8	94.9
	124.8	40.5	39.5	33.5	25.5	11.6		32.4	32.1
	35.9	12.8	11.1	12.6	18.8	6.6		13.0	12.6

Sales/Total Assets									
	16.4	4.4	3.9	3.2	2.1	1.9		4.6	4.3
	5.9	3.0	2.8	2.1	1.4	1.5		2.8	2.7
	3.1	2.0	1.8	1.2	1.1	1.2		1.7	1.7

% Depr., Dep., Amort./Sales														
		.4		.4		.5		.7		1.4		1.1		.7		.6
	(42)	.7	(93)	1.0	(154)	1.0	(58)	1.2	(12)	2.6	(14)	2.4	(308)	1.6	(334)	1.5
		1.4		2.3		2.0		2.1		3.6		3.2		2.8		2.7

% Officers', Directors' Owners' Comp/Sales								
		7.8		5.0		1.0		3.4		3.4
	(49)	15.3	(45)	9.9	(43)	3.5	(124)	7.2	(124)	8.3
		23.2		14.7		6.4		17.3		17.9

	0-500M	500M-2MM	2-10MM	10-50MM	50-100MM	100-250MM			
Net Sales ($)	183843M	502067M	2585593M	3757271M	1969682M	5299223M		14679577M	15248388M
Total Assets ($)	21126M	154912M	843919M	1736703M	1313290M	3300301M		6044206M	5960291M

© RMA 2007

M = $ thousand   MM = $ million
See Pages 11 through 21 for Explanation of Ratios and Data

Comparative Historical Data | Current Data Sorted by Sales

			Type of Statement						
106	98	114	Unqualified	2	8	4	17	30	53
79	75	70	Reviewed	1	11	7	17	30	4
62	59	52	Compiled	6	14	11	14	4	3
70	74	91	Tax Returns	35	27	11	9	6	3
160	212	224	Other	28	46	23	41	40	46
4/1/04-3/31/05 ALL	4/1/05-3/31/06 ALL	4/1/06-3/31/07 ALL		78 (4/1-9/30/06) 0-1MM	1-3MM	3-5MM	473 (10/1/06-3/31/07) 5-10MM	10-25MM	25MM & OVER
477	518	551	**NUMBER OF STATEMENTS**	72	106	56	98	110	109
%	%	%	**ASSETS**	%	%	%	%	%	%
16.5	17.7	19.1	Cash & Equivalents	25.0	20.6	21.0	22.8	13.4	15.1
37.3	37.3	37.3	Trade Receivables (net)	13.5	32.4	38.8	37.8	49.2	44.5
3.3	3.3	3.0	Inventory	.1	4.2	2.4	3.6	3.0	3.2
4.3	4.9	6.8	All Other Current	13.3	6.1	6.2	6.2	4.9	5.9
61.5	63.1	66.1	Total Current	52.0	63.3	68.5	70.5	70.5	68.7
18.0	17.1	15.6	Fixed Assets (net)	25.9	16.2	13.9	14.8	14.8	10.8
7.2	6.7	7.4	Intangibles (net)	8.3	4.5	6.3	5.9	5.6	13.3
13.3	13.1	10.8	All Other Non-Current	13.8	15.9	11.3	8.8	9.0	7.2
100.0	100.0	100.0	Total	100.0	100.0	100.0	100.0	100.0	100.0
			LIABILITIES						
14.9	15.0	12.2	Notes Payable-Short Term	16.9	15.8	10.1	13.8	11.5	6.1
4.3	3.6	2.9	Cur. Mat.-L.T.D.	4.0	3.0	3.3	2.4	2.2	2.9
11.9	11.1	10.9	Trade Payables	1.9	9.1	13.2	9.9	14.6	14.7
.7	.7	.8	Income Taxes Payable	.4	.5	.6	.5	.5	1.2
19.8	19.0	21.8	All Other Current	22.9	22.9	21.5	18.7	19.9	24.9
51.5	49.5	48.6	Total Current	46.1	51.3	48.7	46.3	48.7	49.8
15.6	13.4	12.8	Long-Term Debt	19.9	16.2	10.3	12.7	7.4	11.5
.5	.5	.4	Deferred Taxes	.4	.4	.1	.2	.3	1.1
8.7	8.2	6.5	All Other Non-Current	4.0	10.6	5.0	6.4	5.0	6.7
23.7	28.4	31.6	Net Worth	29.6	21.5	35.9	34.4	38.6	30.9
100.0	100.0	100.0	Total Liabilities & Net Worth	100.0	100.0	100.0	100.0	100.0	100.0
			INCOME DATA						
100.0	100.0	100.0	Net Sales	100.0	100.0	100.0	100.0	100.0	100.0
			Gross Profit						
92.4	90.4	90.0	Operating Expenses	75.5	91.4	92.8	90.8	93.4	92.6
7.6	9.6	10.0	Operating Profit	24.5	8.6	7.2	9.2	6.6	7.4
1.4	1.3	1.8	All Other Expenses (net)	5.9	1.3	.5	.9	1.4	1.3
6.2	8.2	8.3	Profit Before Taxes	18.7	7.3	6.7	8.3	5.2	6.2
			RATIOS						
2.6	3.0	3.1		6.3	3.8	3.5	3.8	2.3	2.0
1.4	1.6	1.5	Current	1.4	1.6	1.6	1.6	1.5	1.4
.9	.9	.9		.4	.9	1.0	1.1	1.1	1.0
2.3	2.5	2.4		4.5	3.1	3.2	2.9	2.1	1.7
1.2	1.3	1.2	Quick	.7	1.3	1.3	1.4	1.3	1.2
.7	.7	.7		.2	.6	.7	.9	.8	.8
13	28.8	10	36.0	11	34.4	Sales/Receivables	0 UND	0 UND	14 25.2	20 18.4	30 12.2	46 8.0

H1		H2		H3			C1	C2	C3	C4	C5	C6
13	28.8	10	36.0	11	34.4	Sales/Receivables	0 UND	0 UND	14 25.2	20 18.4	30 12.2	46 8.0
47	7.7	47	7.7	45	8.0		0 UND	34 10.8	41 9.0	44 8.3	57 6.4	67 5.5
71	5.1	78	4.7	73	5.0		35 10.4	61 6.0	69 5.3	68 5.4	89 4.1	84 4.3

			Category						
			Cost of Sales/Inventory						
			Cost of Sales/Payables						
6.4	5.4	6.0	Sales/Working Capital	3.6	5.3	5.9	5.4	7.3	6.6
21.1	15.8	16.2		151.7	18.7	15.1	11.9	15.0	15.4
-86.2	-107.9	-147.9		-10.7	-50.7	778.6	84.4	86.9	-216.8
27.8	30.2	34.4	EBIT/Interest	38.3	17.7	40.8	36.0	40.0	36.5
(371) 6.6	(390) 7.3	(416) 7.9		(44) 8.6	(77) 3.7	(42) 9.0	(74) 10.6	(92) 9.5	(87) 9.4
1.3	1.7	1.8		1.6	.8	2.6	2.1	1.8	2.8
12.3	12.1	9.0	Net Profit + Depr., Dep., Amort./Cur. Mat. L/T/D				17.9	19.7	11.2
(70) 4.2	(64) 3.7	(70) 2.8				(10) 1.3	(19) 5.8	(29) 2.8	
1.2	1.1	.5					.3	1.0	.8
.1	.1	.1	Fixed/Worth	.0	.0	.0	.1	.1	.1
.5	.3	.3		.5	.4	.3	.3	.3	.4
8.8	2.0	2.6		18.6	6.3	1.2	1.9	.9	5.3
.7	.6	.7	Debt/Worth	.3	.7	.5	.5	.6	1.3
2.5	2.0	2.1		2.0	2.4	1.3	1.7	1.8	3.5
UND	25.3	17.9		-74.4	41.0	14.8	8.0	5.0	38.3
77.9	84.9	83.4	% Profit Before Taxes/Tangible Net Worth	206.1	89.3	77.3	91.9	62.4	77.6
(359) 32.1	(407) 38.2	(441) 39.5		(53) 45.5	(82) 38.0	(46) 30.9	(81) 48.4	(93) 30.6	(86) 48.1
5.3	12.3	10.8		11.9	3.0	8.0	6.9	12.7	16.6
27.0	30.6	34.4	% Profit Before Taxes/Total Assets	93.2	34.9	44.9	44.0	30.1	20.4
10.5	12.9	11.9		15.6	11.8	10.2	17.2	11.8	9.3
.5	1.8	2.2		1.5	.2	3.6	2.6	2.9	3.9
76.5	108.8	129.2	Sales/Net Fixed Assets	UND	190.9	161.5	95.0	104.7	103.0
33.8	38.3	42.4		24.0	52.2	49.5	39.4	42.6	39.4
12.4	15.6	12.9		3.9	14.3	20.0	13.6	19.1	15.0
4.6	4.5	4.4	Sales/Total Assets	5.4	5.1	5.1	4.2	4.5	3.5
2.9	2.8	2.8		1.9	2.8	3.4	3.0	3.0	2.3
1.8	1.7	1.7		.5	1.5	2.3	2.4	2.1	1.5
.7	.5	.5	% Depr., Dep., Amort./Sales	.8	.4	.5	.4	.5	.7
(336) 1.3	(363) 1.1	(373) 1.0		(33) 2.0	(61) 1.1	(38) .8	(77) 1.0	(88) .9	(76) 1.2
2.5	2.4	2.1		7.6	2.6	2.0	1.7	2.0	2.1
4.6	3.5	3.6	% Officers', Directors' Owners' Comp/Sales	8.0	6.8	3.3	2.6	1.6	.6
(140) 7.5	(137) 7.8	(145) 8.4		(34) 16.3	(39) 12.0	(20) 8.8	(19) 4.0	(23) 3.9	(10) 8.5
17.5	18.3	16.2		27.0	16.9	14.0	8.4	6.0	10.8
10818394M	14969586M	14297679M	Net Sales ($)	36895M	204519M	224636M	727951M	1759160M	11344518M
5392635M	6683542M	7370251M	Total Assets ($)	68384M	135087M	91254M	289220M	899713M	5886593M

M = $ thousand   MM = $ million
See Pages 11 through 21 for Explanation of Ratios and Data

Current Data Sorted by Assets   Comparative Historical Data

0-500M	500M-2MM	2-10MM	10-50MM	50-100MM	100-250MM	Type of Statement	4/1/02-3/31/03 ALL	4/1/03-3/31/04 ALL
	5	12	10	1	1	Unqualified	9	13
1	5	10	2			Reviewed	4	5
6	6	5				Compiled	12	13
12	9	2	1			Tax Returns	10	11
14	18	18	11	3	1	Other	37	36
	26 (4/1-9/30/06)		127 (10/1/06-3/31/07)					
33	43	47	24	4	2	**NUMBER OF STATEMENTS**	72	78
%	%	%	%	%	%	**ASSETS**	%	%
30.7	19.4	19.7	10.7			Cash & Equivalents	13.6	13.4
31.5	46.7	42.6	47.0			Trade Receivables (net)	48.6	47.8
.3	.3	.1	.5			Inventory	.0	.0
5.8	4.5	5.8	5.2			All Other Current	6.4	6.7
68.3	70.9	68.2	63.5			Total Current	68.6	68.0
13.6	11.7	13.2	6.4			Fixed Assets (net)	11.1	13.5
6.3	4.4	4.7	20.9			Intangibles (net)	6.3	5.1
11.8	13.0	13.9	9.3			All Other Non-Current	14.0	13.4
100.0	100.0	100.0	100.0			Total	100.0	100.0
						LIABILITIES		
21.7	19.3	15.8	7.3			Notes Payable-Short Term	20.5	30.4
7.1	1.0	2.4	2.4			Cur. Mat.-L.T.D.	4.7	6.8
13.7	7.5	5.3	9.8			Trade Payables	7.6	10.6
.2	.4	1.8	.9			Income Taxes Payable	.0	.5
9.4	33.5	26.4	27.6			All Other Current	21.3	18.9
52.1	61.7	51.7	48.0			Total Current	54.2	67.1
38.4	11.5	11.8	10.3			Long-Term Debt	6.2	11.0
.0	.0	.8	.4			Deferred Taxes	.7	.7
4.9	3.6	7.1	7.0			All Other Non-Current	11.1	7.5
4.6	23.3	28.7	34.2			Net Worth	27.8	13.7
100.0	100.0	100.0	100.0			Total Liabilities & Net Worth	100.0	100.0
						INCOME DATA		
100.0	100.0	100.0	100.0			Net Sales	100.0	100.0
						Gross Profit		
90.1	96.5	94.5	99.0			Operating Expenses	97.5	95.3
9.9	3.5	5.5	1.0			Operating Profit	2.5	4.7
2.5	1.3	1.3	1.2			All Other Expenses (net)	.9	1.0
7.5	2.2	4.1	-.2			Profit Before Taxes	1.6	3.7
						RATIOS		
5.3	2.4	2.0	1.6				2.5	1.9
1.4	1.2	1.3	1.2			Current	1.5	1.2
.8	1.0	1.0	.9				1.0	.8
3.5	2.4	1.5	1.5				2.2	1.9
1.1	1.2	1.2	1.1			Quick	1.3	1.1
.7	.6	.8	.7				.8	.6
0 UND	3 127.9	33 11.2	39 9.3				18 19.8	22 16.6
3 124.7	31 11.9	55 6.6	50 7.3			Sales/Receivables	46 8.0	36 10.0
30 12.0	43 8.6	78 4.7	72 5.1				60 6.1	56 6.6
						Cost of Sales/Inventory		
						Cost of Sales/Payables		
11.7	15.0	7.1	13.6				9.7	11.5
63.8	54.6	22.5	28.1			Sales/Working Capital	20.3	102.2
-66.9	-177.1	-153.7	NM				NM	-34.5
36.3	12.1	8.7	17.8				19.6	27.0
(26) 5.4	(35) 4.1	(38) 2.9	(22) 4.9			EBIT/Interest	(55) 4.0	(63) 4.6
.0	1.2	1.0	-.8				-1.3	1.1
						Net Profit + Depr., Dep., Amort./Cur. Mat. L/T/D		
.0	.0	.1	.1				.1	.1
.6	.3	.5	.2			Fixed/Worth	.3	.3
-13.0	2.3	4.5	-3.2				1.3	4.2
1.0	1.1	1.0	1.5				.8	1.0
9.1	5.1	3.2	3.2			Debt/Worth	1.7	3.0
-3.9	14.5	26.4	-9.1				11.4	UND
599.9	127.1	56.2	74.5				56.1	81.7
(21) 79.5	(34) 43.1	(38) 28.3	(16) 29.8			% Profit Before Taxes/Tangible Net Worth	(56) 21.2	(59) 30.6
8.7	7.4	8.5	12.2				-3.1	3.1
81.7	25.8	15.3	16.9				18.6	22.0
25.7	7.9	6.8	6.4			% Profit Before Taxes/Total Assets	5.9	6.9
.0	.7	.2	-3.3				-5.1	-.2
377.6	533.4	201.1	145.4				136.3	201.1
99.1	138.3	43.8	81.2			Sales/Net Fixed Assets	54.4	62.4
44.1	38.6	16.3	28.4				26.2	26.2
14.3	10.3	5.0	6.1				6.0	6.8
7.5	7.2	2.8	3.4			Sales/Total Assets	4.4	5.0
4.4	3.6	1.3	1.8				2.5	3.3
.3	.1	.1	.2				.4	.4
(15) .6	(29) .2	(38) .5	(16) .5			% Depr., Dep., Amort./Sales	(49) 1.0	(49) .7
1.1	1.0	1.5	1.2				1.6	1.2
6.3	.9	2.8					1.6	1.7
(12) 9.6	(11) 2.5	(10) 4.3				% Officers', Directors' Owners' Comp/Sales	(28) 4.3	(26) 6.5
13.1	12.2	20.7					11.3	11.4
59305M	690531M	1386371M	2809320M	1066585M	113525M	Net Sales ($)	1966811M	4633613M
6937M	50069M	233754M	549722M	289540M	221029M	Total Assets ($)	698363M	1038069M

Comparative Historical Data | Current Data Sorted by Sales

				Type of Statement						
19		15	29	Unqualified	1		4	7	4	13
12		15	18	Reviewed		2	1	3	8	4
19		21	17	Compiled	2	3	4	3	4	1
13		13	24	Tax Returns	5	11	2	2	2	.2
42		42	65	Other	5	11	5	12	11	21
4/1/04-3/31/05 ALL		4/1/05-3/31/06 ALL	4/1/06-3/31/07 ALL		0-1MM	26 (4/1-9/30/06) 1-3MM	3-5MM	5-10MM	127 (10/1/06-3/31/07) 10-25MM	25MM & OVER
105		106	153	NUMBER OF STATEMENTS	13	27	16	27	29	41
%		%	%	ASSETS	%	%	%	%	%	%
15.1		16.7	20.2	Cash & Equivalents	36.0	25.8	22.1	16.2	8.8	21.6
48.2		49.5	41.3	Trade Receivables (net)	18.4	31.1	38.3	53.3	52.5	40.5
.1		.4	.2	Inventory	.0	.3	.1	.5	.0	.3
5.7		6.3	5.5	All Other Current	6.1	4.9	2.8	3.7	9.3	5.2
69.0		72.9	67.2	Total Current	60.4	62.2	63.4	73.7	70.6	67.6
14.6		9.0	12.0	Fixed Assets (net)	17.3	12.8	22.1	7.5	13.9	7.4
6.0		7.9	8.4	Intangibles (net)	7.3	8.4	.1	9.0	7.8	11.9
10.4		10.2	12.4	All Other Non-Current	15.0	16.6	14.3	9.7	7.7	13.2
100.0		100.0	100.0	Total	100.0	100.0	100.0	100.0	100.0	100.0
				LIABILITIES						
27.6		26.9	16.1	Notes Payable-Short Term	13.2	13.9	22.9	21.2	21.4	8.7
3.2		2.9	3.1	Cur. Mat.-L.T.D.	8.8	4.6	.6	1.7	3.3	1.8
9.0		9.7	8.4	Trade Payables	8.6	14.0	5.2	7.1	6.5	8.3
.3		.5	.8	Income Taxes Payable	.0	.4	.0	.5	1.3	1.6
18.1		28.3	24.7	All Other Current	10.8	19.6	17.5	23.6	17.4	41.0
58.2		68.3	53.1	Total Current	41.4	52.6	46.2	54.0	49.9	61.4
10.4		7.6	17.8	Long-Term Debt	75.9	21.9	13.7	9.2	8.9	10.2
.2		.3	.3	Deferred Taxes	.0	.1	.0	.0	1.4	.1
8.1		9.3	6.1	All Other Non-Current	4.7	8.1	2.6	3.2	8.1	7.1
23.1		14.5	22.7	Net Worth	-22.0	17.3	37.4	33.5	31.6	21.2
100.0		100.0	100.0	Total Liabilities & Net Worth	100.0	100.0	100.0	100.0	100.0	100.0
				INCOME DATA						
100.0		100.0	100.0	Net Sales	100.0	100.0	100.0	100.0	100.0	100.0
				Gross Profit						
93.6		93.2	95.0	Operating Expenses	84.0	91.6	95.2	98.8	96.2	97.4
6.4		6.8	5.0	Operating Profit	16.0	8.4	4.8	1.2	3.8	2.6
.7		1.3	1.6	All Other Expenses (net)	5.1	2.3	-.4	1.3	.7	1.5
5.7		5.5	3.4	Profit Before Taxes	10.8	6.1	5.2	-.1	3.1	1.1
				RATIOS						
2.0		2.0	2.1		3.8	3.0	1.9	3.0	3.5	1.5
1.4		1.4	1.3	Current	1.6	1.1	1.5	1.4	1.3	1.2
.9		.9	.9		.9	.7	1.0	.8	1.1	.8
1.7		1.7	2.0		2.4	2.7	1.9	2.7	2.9	1.4
1.2		1.3	1.2	Quick	1.3	1.1	1.3	1.3	1.1	1.1
.8		.8	.7		.8	.5	1.0	.7	.9	.7
16	23.5	17	21.2	5	68.6					

Sales/Receivables row:

					0 UND	0 UND	8 47.7	21 17.1	29 12.7	2 181.6
16 23.5	17 21.2	5 68.6		Sales/Receivables	0 UND	0 UND	8 47.7	21 17.1	29 12.7	2 181.6
39 9.4	42 8.7	38 9.7			3 124.7	27 13.6	35 10.3	41 8.9	46 7.9	43 8.5
55 6.7	62 5.9	60 6.0			29 12.7	55 6.6	68 5.4	61 6.0	72 5.1	55 6.7
				Cost of Sales/Inventory						
				Cost of Sales/Payables						
12.6	10.5	10.8			6.5	11.1	10.2	7.5	7.9	19.1
29.8	24.4	30.0		Sales/Working Capital	15.9	56.1	20.9	20.8	25.5	112.6
-113.2	-49.9	-90.6			-67.5	-19.2	NM	-28.0	552.0	-83.1
18.8	21.5	11.5			39.3	7.5	27.7	8.8	7.9	17.2
(83) 6.0	(88) 7.5	(127) 4.0		EBIT/Interest	(10) 4.1	(19) 4.3	(14) 4.1	(23) 1.8	(28) 2.5	(33) 5.8
1.6	1.8	.9			.7	-1.7	.9	-1.1	1.4	1.1
		19.9	17.8							
	(12) 5.5	(17) 3.5		Net Profit + Depr., Dep., Amort./Cur. Mat. L/T/D						
	1.6	-1.6								
.1	.0	.1			.0	.0	.1	.0	.1	.1
.3	.2	.3		Fixed/Worth	1.2	.8	.4	.2	.7	.3
NM	.8	UND			UND	-10.0	1.5	4.6	-4.3	-2.2
1.0	1.1	1.1			1.9	.9	.7	.8	.7	1.8
2.4	2.4	4.4		Debt/Worth	32.0	7.9	2.3	1.9	2.9	4.6
-30.1	-327.3	-44.9			-1.7	-7.1	5.5	-76.6	-28.7	-22.0
84.7	86.8	108.5		% Profit Before Taxes/Tangible Net Worth		186.8	127.7	57.2	75.2	107.8
(77) 33.3	(79) 46.8	(112) 31.3			(17) 52.5	23.6	(20) 19.5	(21) 28.6	(30) 31.3	
9.7	12.9	8.3				-2.6	4.4	-2.0	8.4	18.2
24.4	33.8	23.3		% Profit Before Taxes/Total Assets	54.2	71.9	47.3	23.2	15.6	16.0
11.2	14.5	7.8			21.6	13.8	6.3	2.9	7.1	7.6
1.5	3.3	-.1			4.1	-2.2	.5	-3.6	2.4	.5
247.3	441.4	283.6		Sales/Net Fixed Assets	259.5	382.8	118.4	282.3	195.1	489.4
77.9	83.9	78.9			62.1	62.6	36.2	112.8	75.3	110.3
21.9	33.5	30.8			20.5	36.4	21.7	36.4	28.0	51.2
7.7	7.4	8.6		Sales/Total Assets	5.6	9.0	8.2	8.2	8.2	18.9
4.9	4.8	4.6			3.8	4.6	3.7	4.3	4.9	6.0
3.1	2.6	2.3			1.5	2.2	1.4	1.8	2.4	3.3
.3	.2	.2		% Depr., Dep., Amort./Sales		.2	.6	.1	.1	.1
(77) .6	(71) .6	(102) .5			(15) .8	(10) 1.0	(19) .4	(24) .4	(28) .3	
1.1	1.4	1.2				2.1	2.7	1.5	1.0	.7
2.3	2.0	2.3		% Officers', Directors' Owners' Comp/Sales		8.5				
(32) 6.1	(30) 4.3	(34) 7.1			(10) 11.8					
8.8	8.9	12.6			16.7					
1592981M	2377561M	6125637M		Net Sales ($)	6895M	51353M	64969M	201353M	472610M	5328457M
382673M	538347M	1351051M		Total Assets ($)	6961M	22746M	29575M	85972M	246758M	959039M

M = $ thousand   MM = $ million
See Pages 11 through 21 for Explanation of Ratios and Data

PROFESSIONAL SERVICES—Marketing Consulting Services NAICS 541613 (SIC 8742)

Current Data Sorted by Assets · **Comparative Historical Data**

	0-500M	500M-2MM	2-10MM	10-50MM	50-100MM	100-250MM	4/1/02-3/31/03 ALL	4/1/03-3/31/04 ALL
Type of Statement		11 (4/1-9/30/06)		94 (10/1/06-3/31/07)				
Unqualified	1	2		7	2	3	2	6
Reviewed			5	3			3	3
Compiled	3	2	5	1			3	3
Tax Returns	4	5	1				3	5
Other	10	17	17	10	3	4	9	18
NUMBER OF STATEMENTS	18	24	30	21	5	7	20	35
	%	%	%	%	%	%	%	%
ASSETS								
Cash & Equivalents	27.2	17.9	9.7	18.7			16.1	15.1
Trade Receivables (net)	25.3	39.3	44.4	33.1			38.1	43.3
Inventory	.7	3.2	6.5	2.9			2.1	3.1
All Other Current	1.1	6.4	8.8	7.0			7.9	3.5
Total Current	54.4	66.8	69.4	61.6			64.2	65.0
Fixed Assets (net)	10.9	17.0	13.1	10.7			12.9	15.4
Intangibles (net)	5.5	2.6	8.3	21.1			5.7	8.2
All Other Non-Current	29.2	13.6	9.2	6.6			17.1	11.4
Total	100.0	100.0	100.0	100.0			100.0	100.0
LIABILITIES								
Notes Payable-Short Term	37.8	15.9	14.1	5.4			6.0	11.9
Cur. Mat.-L.T.D.	.8	1.2	2.0	1.1			1.9	3.2
Trade Payables	16.4	16.2	23.1	13.5			9.6	13.7
Income Taxes Payable	.0	.0	.5	1.9			.0	.4
All Other Current	37.3	10.0	17.9	15.0			27.8	12.7
Total Current	92.3	43.3	57.8	36.9			45.3	41.9
Long-Term Debt	27.6	13.8	5.6	7.1			13.6	11.3
Deferred Taxes	.0	.0	.0	.0			.2	.3
All Other Non-Current	2.7	7.0	13.2	6.8			4.8	9.2
Net Worth	-22.6	35.8	23.4	49.2			36.1	37.3
Total Liabilities & Net Worth	100.0	100.0	100.0	100.0			100.0	100.0
INCOME DATA								
Net Sales	100.0	100.0	100.0	100.0			100.0	100.0
Gross Profit								
Operating Expenses	90.2	90.1	96.2	88.9			88.0	93.7
Operating Profit	9.8	9.9	3.8	11.1			12.0	6.3
All Other Expenses (net)	.9	1.3	.8	1.2			.9	1.1
Profit Before Taxes	8.9	8.6	3.0	9.9			11.1	5.3
RATIOS								
Current	2.0	2.7	2.2	3.5			4.7	3.1
	.5	1.4	1.2	1.7			1.7	1.9
	.3	.8	.8	1.0			.8	1.1
Quick	1.7	2.7	1.8	2.7			3.4	2.6
	.5	1.3	.9	1.5			1.2	1.4
	.2	.5	.7	.9			.6	.8
Sales/Receivables	0 UND	26 14.0	31 11.9	36 10.1			14 26.8	40 9.2
	2 167.8	45 8.0	46 8.0	54 6.8			33 11.0	54 6.8
	68 5.4	72 5.1	64 5.7	84 4.4			65 5.6	66 5.5
Cost of Sales/Inventory								
Cost of Sales/Payables								
Sales/Working Capital	587.3	7.0	9.6	3.9			7.6	5.4
	-29.1	17.5	37.0	7.7			23.9	13.7
	-8.6	-63.1	-21.2	NM			-20.8	51.7
EBIT/Interest	10.5	7.7	23.1	170.0			55.7	30.1
	(13) 3.2	(17) 2.3	(26) 3.8	(16) 13.2			(13) 28.8	(26) 6.5
	-.8	-2.1	-3.7	3.2			6.0	.6
Net Profit + Depr., Dep., Amort./Cur. Mat. L/T/D								
Fixed/Worth	.1	.1	.3	.1			.0	.1
	2.9	.3	.7	.2			.2	.4
	-.1	40.5	-.8	1.1			3.0	-3.9
Debt/Worth	1.6	.6	1.5	.5			.3	.7
	-10.9	1.9	3.7	1.3			1.2	1.8
	-2.3	46.5	-9.8	7.4			-13.1	-23.9
% Profit Before Taxes/Tangible Net Worth		108.8	90.9	92.1			136.5	125.7
	(19) 53.7	(20) 46.9	(18) 50.4				(14) 45.5	(25) 32.9
	20.9	-16.0	27.5				22.3	1.0
% Profit Before Taxes/Total Assets	73.3	36.3	31.1	28.8			46.9	28.9
	21.5	12.1	8.3	18.5			25.1	12.8
	2.6	-4.4	-5.9	4.5			7.4	-2.7
Sales/Net Fixed Assets	UND	120.4	103.3	66.6			248.1	80.7
	122.0	46.2	36.3	28.3			33.6	45.3
	26.8	8.6	15.9	9.4			21.8	14.7
Sales/Total Assets	14.2	4.5	4.4	2.5			5.5	4.3
	4.8	3.1	3.2	1.8			3.9	2.8
	2.8	1.9	2.3	1.3			1.9	2.1
% Depr., Dep., Amort./Sales		.4	.5	.6			.4	.5
	(10) .8	(27) .8	(18) 1.4				(10) 1.7	(20) 1.3
	1.8	2.5	3.0				2.8	2.8
% Officers', Directors' Owners' Comp/Sales		2.8						5.4
	(12) 7.0						(13) 13.0	
	14.8						6.6	
Net Sales ($)	28396M	79432M	532375M	745576M	684958M	1711080M	343561M	466655M
Total Assets ($)	3643M	23999M	153793M	379452M	352041M	1269019M	211967M	206717M

M = $ thousand   MM = $ million
See Pages 11 through 21 for Explanation of Ratios and Data

Comparative Historical Data | Current Data Sorted by Sales

				Type of Statement						
	8	11	15	Unqualified		1			3	11
	5	6	8	Reviewed				1	4	3
	6	9	11	Compiled				3	3	
	7	10	10	Tax Returns	1	2	2	3	3	
	19	31	61	Other	2	4	3	1	1	
					8	14	3	7	12	17
	4/1/04-	4/1/05-	4/1/06-			11 (4/1-9/30/06)		94 (10/1/06-3/31/07)		
	3/31/05	3/31/06	3/31/07		0-1MM	1-3MM	3-5MM	5-10MM	10-25MM	25MM & OVER
	ALL	ALL	ALL							
	45	67	105	NUMBER OF STATEMENTS	11	21	8	11	23	31
	%	%	%	ASSETS	%	%	%	%	%	%
	12.9	15.6	16.7	Cash & Equivalents	18.4	18.7		10.1	16.2	13.3
	40.4	39.8	35.9	Trade Receivables (net)	32.6	29.3		45.2	41.3	37.1
	7.2	8.1	4.2	Inventory	4.3	1.5		4.8	6.7	4.7
	4.0	3.9	6.1	All Other Current	3.0	7.2		3.1	5.2	9.7
	64.5	67.4	62.9	Total Current	58.2	56.8		63.2	69.3	64.8
	16.0	15.4	13.1	Fixed Assets (net)	7.8	19.0		9.1	12.7	11.6
	9.9	7.8	11.3	Intangibles (net)	.3	9.7		20.8	5.8	18.9
	9.6	9.5	12.7	All Other Non-Current	33.7	14.5		6.9	12.2	4.8
	100.0	100.0	100.0	Total	100.0	100.0		100.0	100.0	100.0
				LIABILITIES						
	19.1	16.1	15.5	Notes Payable-Short Term	47.9	23.3		17.3	8.3	5.7
	2.5	2.4	1.6	Cur. Mat.-L.T.D.	.8	2.0		2.9	1.5	1.7
	23.0	21.6	17.7	Trade Payables	7.8	24.4		19.2	20.1	17.1
	.3	.4	.6	Income Taxes Payable	.0	.0		.0	.7	1.4
	18.5	15.7	18.6	All Other Current	29.7	13.4		15.0	18.8	15.3
	63.3	56.2	54.0	Total Current	86.2	63.1		54.4	49.3	41.2
	10.4	10.6	12.2	Long-Term Debt	6.0	14.6		9.1	3.3	8.0
	.4	.4	.2	Deferred Taxes	.0	.0		.0	.1	.5
	16.2	15.2	8.8	All Other Non-Current	2.2	9.3		11.8	9.3	10.2
	9.8	17.6	24.9	Net Worth	5.6	12.9		24.7	38.0	40.1
	100.0	100.0	100.0	Total Liabilties & Net Worth	100.0	100.0		100.0	100.0	100.0
				INCOME DATA						
	100.0	100.0	100.0	Net Sales	100.0	100.0		100.0	100.0	100.0
				Gross Profit						
	94.7	93.6	92.0	Operating Expenses	83.5	92.1		94.4	95.2	91.7
	5.3	6.4	8.0	Operating Profit	16.5	7.9		5.6	4.8	8.3
	1.8	1.6	1.1	All Other Expenses (net)	1.6	2.0		2.4	-.3	1.2
	3.5	4.9	6.8	Profit Before Taxes	14.9	6.0		3.2	5.0	7.1
				RATIOS						
	1.8	2.0	2.2		2.0	1.9		1.7	2.6	2.5
	1.1	1.2	1.4	Current	.8	1.1		.9	1.6	1.5
	.7	.9	.8		.5	.5		.6	1.1	1.0
	1.6	1.7	1.9		2.0	1.8		1.4	2.1	2.2
	.9	1.0	1.1	Quick	.5	.9		.8	1.2	1.4
	.5	.7	.6		.3	.3		.5	.8	.9
29	12.5	22 16.6	29 12.8	Sales/Receivables	13 28.4	24 15.0	44 8.3	37 9.9	40 9.1	
47	7.8	48 7.7	49 7.4		28 13.0	43 8.5	67 5.4	46 8.0	54 6.8	
75	4.9	65 5.6	69 5.3		88 4.2	68 5.4	92 4.0	66 5.5	63 5.8	
				Cost of Sales/Inventory						
				Cost of Sales/Payables						
	10.3	6.9	6.7	Sales/Working Capital	158.7	7.7		8.7	4.9	4.9
	38.4	30.9	21.7		-40.9	96.1		-29.5	21.5	9.9
	-16.4	-38.7	-33.4		-3.4	-12.3		-8.6	44.0	128.6
	22.4	34.0	16.2	EBIT/Interest		6.4		4.4	28.8	46.7
(39)	4.8	(56) 6.3	(82) 3.4		(16) 2.8		(10) 2.3	(16) 12.7	(26) 6.5	
	-.2	1.2	.0			-.3		.9	-2.6	2.2
			73.2	Net Profit + Depr., Dep.,						
		(14)	18.6	Amort./Cur. Mat. L/T/D						
			1.1							
	.2	.2	.1	Fixed/Worth	.0	.3		.1	.1	.1
	1.3	.7	.4		.1	1.4		-2.4	.4	.3
	-1.5	-1.2	-1.1		-.3	-.7		-.1	3.7	1.6
	1.8	.8	.9	Debt/Worth	.3	2.0		1.7	.6	.7
	12.3	5.8	3.3		-51.5	6.3		-21.4	1.6	2.1
	-7.4	-6.6	-8.1		-2.7	-3.5		-3.8	6.6	10.8
	129.1	111.9	95.2	% Profit Before Taxes/Tangible		97.9			69.5	114.6
(29)	58.3	(47) 40.6	(71) 48.5	Net Worth	(13) 48.8			(18) 42.8	(25) 52.2	
	23.1	15.5	20.6			19.5			12.9	21.4
	27.5	26.9	28.7	% Profit Before Taxes/Total	93.5	23.7		13.4	34.7	26.5
	7.9	9.2	11.8	Assets	20.4	15.2		3.9	18.0	10.8
	-6.7	1.6	.7		-11.9	1.7		.6	-3.3	2.7
	60.2	156.6	104.2	Sales/Net Fixed Assets	UND	92.4		96.5	69.2	88.5
	29.0	33.1	38.4		247.3	31.2		36.1	34.3	26.7
	18.1	12.3	14.6		17.5	10.2		15.1	16.2	10.6
	4.8	4.5	4.2	Sales/Total Assets	5.1	4.3		4.6	4.2	3.1
	3.0	3.3	2.8		2.6	3.2		2.4	3.2	2.2
	1.6	1.9	1.8		2.0	1.8		1.4	1.6	1.4
	1.0	.5	.5	% Depr., Dep., Amort./Sales					.6	.6
(29)	1.4	(46) 1.2	(71) 1.1					(21) 1.1	(24) 1.3	
	2.0	2.7	2.6						2.7	2.8
	5.5	4.3	2.7	% Officers', Directors'		2.5				
(10)	9.3	(22) 8.1	(31) 4.7	Owners' Comp/Sales	(11) 6.0					
	14.4	16.2	10.2			15.3				
	1987165M	8719190M	3781817M	Net Sales ($)	7189M	41647M	29818M	79622M	408390M	3215151M
	1109054M	1780237M	2181947M	Total Assets ($)	3130M	19732M	6390M	53615M	179569M	1919511M

M = $ thousand   MM = $ million
See Pages 11 through 21 for Explanation of Ratios and Data

Current Data Sorted by Assets | Comparative Historical Data

Type of Statement	0-500M	500M-2MM	2-10MM	10-50MM	50-100MM	100-250MM		4/1/02-3/31/03 ALL	4/1/03-3/31/04 ALL
Unqualified		1	5	3	2	2		3	9
Reviewed	1	1	3					16	8
Compiled	2	7	2	1				9	12
Tax Returns	2				1			1	4
Other	4	9	10	7	3	2		8	18
		14 (4/1-9/30/06)		54 (10/1/06-3/31/07)					
NUMBER OF STATEMENTS	9	18	20	11	6	4		37	51

0-500M	500M-2MM	2-10MM	10-50MM	50-100MM	100-250MM		4/1/02-3/31/03 ALL	4/1/03-3/31/04 ALL
%	%	%	%	%	%	**ASSETS**	%	%
	14.6	10.1	9.1			Cash & Equivalents	8.1	10.7
	49.1	46.2	46.1			Trade Receivables (net)	48.5	41.7
	6.1	10.6	3.3			Inventory	.2	.5
	2.9	4.0	2.7			All Other Current	6.2	5.2
	72.8	70.9	61.3			Total Current	63.0	58.1
	15.3	17.2	20.1			Fixed Assets (net)	23.3	25.6
	4.4	2.8	9.9			Intangibles (net)	3.0	7.1
	7.6	9.1	8.7			All Other Non-Current	10.7	9.2
	100.0	100.0	100.0			Total	100.0	100.0
						LIABILITIES		
	21.0	14.6	3.8			Notes Payable-Short Term	11.8	9.7
	1.9	7.2	3.2			Cur. Mat.-L.T.D.	3.3	5.8
	20.0	15.1	16.0			Trade Payables	29.3	26.9
	.2	1.2	1.2			Income Taxes Payable	.3	.2
	20.2	15.5	13.1			All Other Current	12.6	15.3
	63.2	53.6	37.4			Total Current	57.3	57.9
	3.6	15.0	12.7			Long-Term Debt	9.2	13.3
	.3	.6	.1			Deferred Taxes	.9	1.0
	2.1	3.2	4.9			All Other Non-Current	1.9	2.2
	30.9	27.6	44.9			Net Worth	30.6	25.6
	100.0	100.0	100.0			Total Liabilities & Net Worth	100.0	100.0
						INCOME DATA		
	100.0	100.0	100.0			Net Sales	100.0	100.0
						Gross Profit		
	95.1	94.8	96.3			Operating Expenses	93.9	96.3
	4.9	5.2	3.7			Operating Profit	6.1	3.7
	.0	.0	.7			All Other Expenses (net)	.9	.9
	4.9	5.2	3.0			Profit Before Taxes	5.2	2.8
						RATIOS		
	2.4	1.9	2.3				1.3	1.4
	1.6	1.6	1.6			Current	1.1	1.1
	.8	.8	1.4				.8	.7
	2.1	1.8	2.0				1.3	1.2
	1.2	1.1	1.6			Quick	1.0	1.0
	.6	.6	1.4				.6	.7
	30 12.1	25 14.3	41 9.0				27 13.3	24 15.1
	44 8.2	42 8.8	59 6.2			Sales/Receivables	35 10.3	39 9.2
	58 6.3	70 5.2	67 5.5				61 6.0	51 7.1
						Cost of Sales/Inventory		
						Cost of Sales/Payables		
	8.6	9.4	6.9				17.2	14.6
	16.3	27.4	14.6			Sales/Working Capital	87.3	55.7
	-21.6	-40.6	32.6				-61.3	-23.6
	44.6	6.3	53.4				36.8	19.1
	(14) 3.2	(15) 2.3	(10) 15.3			EBIT/Interest	(32) 8.0	(45) 5.2
	1.0	1.2	2.2				1.6	1.7
						Net Profit + Depr., Dep.,	15.2	21.2
						Amort./Cur. Mat. L/T/D	(11) 9.8	(11) 3.4
							2.1	.9
	.1	.1	.1				.1	.2
	.3	.6	.3			Fixed/Worth	.7	.8
	NM	1.6	1.3				1.6	6.6
	.5	1.2	.6				1.4	1.3
	1.4	3.9	1.4			Debt/Worth	3.3	3.2
	NM	10.0	4.5				6.0	10.7
	91.7	100.3	35.7			% Profit Before Taxes/Tangible	76.0	62.7
	(14) 33.8	(18) 33.6	(10) 25.8			Net Worth	(33) 34.9	(42) 22.4
	9.1	22.4	15.5				13.9	-2.1
	46.4	16.1	15.7			% Profit Before Taxes/Total	25.6	19.4
	9.4	8.5	11.5			Assets	9.4	6.0
	1.0	2.3	4.3				2.4	.2
	153.5	145.1	83.8				127.2	96.8
	50.4	60.5	39.6			Sales/Net Fixed Assets	54.6	21.7
	13.7	8.1	9.5				7.6	7.6
	5.8	6.4	7.2				5.5	5.6
	3.7	3.4	3.1			Sales/Total Assets	4.0	3.4
	2.8	2.4	1.7				2.4	1.3
	.2	.2					.4	.5
	(13) .6	(16) .4				% Depr., Dep., Amort./Sales	(31) 1.0	(37) 1.1
	2.2	3.5					2.4	4.5
						% Officers', Directors'	2.8	1.7
						Owners' Comp/Sales	(13) 4.1 (15) 7.7	
							8.9	19.6
24441M	93965M	378819M	958691M	4858239M	1518925M	Net Sales ($)	998107M	1579899M
1620M	19935M	82460M	233376M	425344M	713270M	Total Assets ($)	473645M	714540M

© RMA 2007

M = $ thousand   MM = $ million
See Pages 11 through 21 for Explanation of Ratios and Data

Comparative Historical Data | | Current Data Sorted by Sales

4/1/04-3/31/05 ALL	4/1/05-3/31/06 ALL	4/1/06-3/31/07 ALL	Type of Statement	0-1MM	1-3MM	3-5MM	5-10MM	10-25MM	25MM & OVER
11	9	13	Unqualified				2	2	9
8	17	5	Reviewed		1		1	1	1
13	11	12	Compiled		3	3	2	3	1
2	3	3	Tax Returns	2					1
21	32	35	Other	2	5	4	6	7	11
					14 (4/1-9/30/06)			54 (10/1/06-3/31/07)	
55	72	68	**NUMBER OF STATEMENTS**	4	9	8	11	13	23
%	%	%	**ASSETS**	%	%	%	%	%	%
8.9	9.6	10.2	Cash & Equivalents				12.9	13.2	10.2
47.6	49.0	43.0	Trade Receivables (net)				58.0	35.6	43.9
2.7	4.7	5.4	Inventory				5.6	.3	4.6
6.0	4.3	6.3	All Other Current				3.2	2.2	3.8
65.2	67.6	64.9	Total Current				79.6	51.2	62.4
19.5	17.1	17.7	Fixed Assets (net)				15.6	26.3	17.1
4.3	5.7	8.1	Intangibles (net)				.8	11.7	12.4
10.9	9.6	9.4	All Other Non-Current				4.0	10.9	8.0
100.0	100.0	100.0	Total				100.0	100.0	100.0
			LIABILITIES						
12.0	12.6	12.6	Notes Payable-Short Term				10.6	25.1	5.3
3.1	7.0	5.4	Cur. Mat.-L.T.D.				3.0	3.0	2.6
22.3	21.2	17.1	Trade Payables				21.8	7.6	17.4
.1	.3	.6	Income Taxes Payable				.0	1.9	.7
13.9	13.1	15.0	All Other Current				16.8	10.7	14.5
51.3	54.3	50.8	Total Current				52.3	48.4	40.4
11.0	12.1	12.1	Long-Term Debt				10.7	13.5	16.0
.8	1.0	.6	Deferred Taxes				.9	.2	1.1
2.9	6.4	3.6	All Other Non-Current				1.3	1.8	5.2
33.9	26.3	33.0	Net Worth				34.8	36.3	37.2
100.0	100.0	100.0	Total Liabilities & Net Worth				100.0	100.0	100.0
			INCOME DATA						
100.0	100.0	100.0	Net Sales				100.0	100.0	100.0
			Gross Profit						
95.7	95.7	96.0	Operating Expenses				93.2	95.1	96.1
4.3	4.3	4.0	Operating Profit				6.8	4.9	3.9
.5	.8	.3	All Other Expenses (net)				.4	.7	.5
3.8	3.6	3.7	Profit Before Taxes				6.4	4.1	3.4
			RATIOS						
1.6	2.1	2.3	Current				2.7	1.8	2.1
1.2	1.3	1.5					2.0	1.7	1.4
.9	1.0	.9					.8	.6	1.2
1.4	1.9	1.9	Quick				2.3	1.7	2.0
1.1	1.2	1.3					2.0	1.6	1.4
.7	.8	.7					.7	.6	.9
35 10.4	33 11.1	27 13.4	Sales/Receivables				43 8.4	26 14.1	27 13.6
51 7.1	47 7.8	44 8.3					65 5.6	40 9.2	46 7.9
77 4.7	72 5.0	63 5.8					74 4.9	53 6.9	73 5.0
			Cost of Sales/Inventory						
			Cost of Sales/Payables						
11.1	8.6	8.5	Sales/Working Capital				5.7	9.8	7.1
33.4	29.4	19.9					18.4	16.3	22.0
-86.4	895.6	-174.0					-17.1	-75.9	48.8
20.3	15.5	21.8	EBIT/Interest					23.0	33.9
(43) 7.3	(62) 6.1	(53) 4.9					(11) 2.1	(20) 11.8	
1.8	2.1	1.4						-1.4	2.3
	7.1	38.0	Net Profit + Depr., Dep., Amort./Cur. Mat. L/T/D						
	(21) 2.9	(13) 3.0							
	1.0	1.7							
.1	.1	.1	Fixed/Worth				.1	.1	.2
.4	.3	.4					.5	.9	.4
1.4	1.5	3.9					3.5	2.8	4.1
1.0	.9	.9	Debt/Worth				.5	1.0	1.3
2.1	2.3	2.9					5.4	3.9	2.9
5.8	6.7	16.0					10.2	15.9	16.3
56.1	67.0	91.8	% Profit Before Taxes/Tangible Net Worth				106.1	98.9	38.7
(48) 24.7	(59) 27.0	(56) 30.9					(10) 85.6	(11) 28.2	(18) 29.6
4.3	11.1	10.2					34.4	17.4	10.8
19.9	18.8	20.9	% Profit Before Taxes/Total Assets				45.4	39.8	15.7
7.0	9.1	8.8					16.2	12.1	8.8
.8	2.9	2.2					2.8	-6.5	3.3
181.8	201.4	157.3	Sales/Net Fixed Assets				115.5	175.6	153.1
43.7	37.2	46.4					66.8	42.2	41.0
11.5	10.7	9.6					8.0	5.6	10.0
5.6	5.2	6.4	Sales/Total Assets				4.7	7.9	8.1
3.8	3.3	3.5					3.3	3.6	3.3
1.3	2.1	2.2					2.5	2.0	1.6
.4	.3	.3	% Depr., Dep., Amort./Sales				.2		.3
(37) .9	(49) .9	(45) .6					(10) .4	(15)	.5
3.7	2.8	2.7					2.9		2.5
3.6	1.6	.8	% Officers', Directors' Owners' Comp/Sales						
(20) 10.1	(21) 3.6	(16) 2.7							
16.1	6.2	4.8							
2031273M	3217610M	7833080M	Net Sales ($)	1615M	18676M	29946M	84383M	190920M	7507540M
719482M	1173345M	1476005M	Total Assets ($)	261M	5598M	15921M	26704M	73706M	1353815M

© RMA 2007

M = $ thousand   MM = $ million
See Pages 11 through 21 for Explanation of Ratios and Data

Current Data Sorted by Assets   Comparative Historical Data

	0-500M	500M-2MM	2-10MM	10-50MM	50-100MM	100-250MM		4/1/02-3/31/03 ALL	4/1/03-3/31/04 ALL
Type of Statement									
Unqualified	3	5	37	31	5	5		58	56
Reviewed	2	9	47	3		1		40	36
Compiled	10	23	10	2				38	69
Tax Returns	23	17	8					28	38
Other	24	34	56	31	7	8		102	86
	58 (4/1-9/30/06)		343 (10/1/06-3/31/07)						
NUMBER OF STATEMENTS	62	88	158	67	12	14		266	285
	%	%	%	%	%	%		%	%
ASSETS									
Cash & Equivalents	25.8	17.4	15.2	12.5	9.9	26.1		16.3	14.5
Trade Receivables (net)	27.3	44.4	50.9	42.2	36.5	30.3		43.6	46.0
Inventory	1.8	2.7	2.7	1.6	1.6	1.5		2.0	2.4
All Other Current	9.3	5.2	7.2	10.7	4.6	9.9		5.0	5.4
Total Current	64.2	69.7	76.0	67.0	52.6	67.7		66.9	68.3
Fixed Assets (net)	19.0	18.3	12.9	16.2	9.7	7.2		20.1	17.7
Intangibles (net)	2.4	3.7	3.5	5.3	25.1	14.0		5.5	3.7
All Other Non-Current	14.4	8.3	7.5	11.5	12.6	11.1		7.6	10.3
Total	100.0	100.0	100.0	100.0	100.0	100.0		100.0	100.0
LIABILITIES									
Notes Payable-Short Term	35.8	11.9	11.9	8.4	12.1	3.4		16.1	15.3
Cur. Mat.-L.T.D.	7.1	2.6	3.3	1.9	1.6	1.1		3.8	3.4
Trade Payables	11.2	12.8	14.5	14.6	11.8	15.1		12.3	14.5
Income Taxes Payable	1.2	.8	1.8	.9	.2	.8		.7	.8
All Other Current	21.3	12.9	20.6	18.7	16.6	23.4		23.4	18.4
Total Current	76.5	40.9	52.0	44.6	42.4	43.9		56.3	52.4
Long-Term Debt	17.5	13.3	8.4	10.2	9.8	14.8		11.9	11.4
Deferred Taxes	.0	.6	.9	.9	1.2	.3		.6	.6
All Other Non-Current	7.7	8.2	5.3	7.3	19.0	2.8		6.5	8.1
Net Worth	-1.7	37.0	33.4	36.8	28.4	38.2		24.8	27.5
Total Liabilties & Net Worth	100.0	100.0	100.0	100.0	100.0	100.0		100.0	100.0
INCOME DATA									
Net Sales	100.0	100.0	100.0	100.0	100.0	100.0		100.0	100.0
Gross Profit									
Operating Expenses	88.9	90.3	92.0	93.0	91.8	92.9		94.3	92.4
Operating Profit	11.1	9.7	8.0	7.0	8.2	7.1		5.7	7.6
All Other Expenses (net)	1.2	1.4	1.8	.8	1.2	-.3		1.0	1.3
Profit Before Taxes	9.9	8.2	6.2	6.2	7.0	7.4		4.7	6.3
RATIOS									
Current	3.3	2.9	2.4	2.3	1.4	2.5		2.5	2.3
	1.1	1.8	1.4	1.6	1.2	1.5		1.4	1.5
	.6	1.1	1.1	1.1	1.1	1.2		1.0	1.0
Quick	2.7	2.5	2.0	2.1	1.2	2.2		2.2	2.1
	1.0	1.5	1.3	1.3	1.1	1.3		1.2	1.3
	.3	.9	.9	.9	.9	.7		.8	.8
Sales/Receivables	0 UND	28 13.2	44 8.2	38 9.6	34 10.7	36 10.1		29 12.8	28 12.8
	0 UND	54 6.8	66 5.5	66 5.5	61 6.0	47 7.8		53 6.8	59 6.2
	47 7.8	80 4.6	94 3.9	95 3.8	101 3.6	90 4.0		86 4.3	92 4.0
Cost of Sales/Inventory									
Cost of Sales/Payables									
Sales/Working Capital	11.6	5.4	5.9	4.8	10.2	3.1		6.4	6.1
	86.3	8.9	12.1	9.4	28.7	7.6		14.8	11.7
	-25.8	69.2	58.9	28.1	44.8	16.2		-142.2	-170.9
EBIT/Interest	45.0	21.3	27.0	37.5		141.0		22.0	26.8
	(43) 7.4	(65) 4.5	(129) 8.9	(56) 11.5		(10) 9.6		(211) 5.2	(232) 5.9
	2.2	1.3	1.3	4.8		2.9		1.6	1.4
Net Profit + Depr., Dep., Amort./Cur. Mat. L/T/D			9.8	23.6				9.9	7.0
			(29) 2.9	(22) 4.3				(45) 4.4	(61) 2.5
			1.2	1.6				1.3	1.1
Fixed/Worth	.0	.1	.1	.1	.1	.1		.2	.1
	.4	.2	.2	.4	1.1	.3		.4	.4
	6.3	2.5	.9	1.0	-.3	NM		2.2	2.4
Debt/Worth	.7	.6	.8	.7	3.1	.6		.8	.7
	3.8	1.8	1.9	1.8	8.3	1.8		1.9	1.9
	-5.0	5.8	5.6	7.5	-2.9	NM		10.2	11.0
% Profit Before Taxes/Tangible Net Worth	244.2	74.9	61.1	83.8		79.3		71.5	74.2
	(44) 111.2	(74) 49.5	(141) 30.2	(60) 29.7		(11) 41.0		(216) 29.3	(228) 30.2
	27.0	12.5	9.6	13.2		14.7		6.3	7.1
% Profit Before Taxes/Total Assets	90.0	35.4	24.9	18.5	10.6	22.0		21.9	26.7
	26.7	14.8	8.7	8.8	3.6	8.8		8.3	9.5
	4.7	4.0	2.0	3.8	-3.8	3.2		.8	.8
Sales/Net Fixed Assets	620.6	93.7	93.0	57.8	249.9	62.6		63.4	91.0
	116.9	39.0	40.3	20.1	36.6	29.0		27.3	30.3
	18.3	13.9	19.9	9.2	15.3	11.3		12.2	12.3
Sales/Total Assets	13.0	4.1	3.7	3.0	3.1	2.3		4.3	4.3
	5.4	3.0	2.7	2.2	1.6	1.6		2.8	2.8
	2.9	1.9	1.9	1.0	.8	.9		1.9	1.9
% Depr., Dep., Amort./Sales	.3	.6	.4	.7				.8	.8
	(37) .7	(63) 1.2	(126) .9	(54) 1.4				(197) 1.6	(215) 1.6
	2.1	2.2	1.9	3.0				3.3	3.0
% Officers', Directors' Owners' Comp/Sales	5.5	4.3	2.7	2.1				3.8	3.9
	(27) 10.7	(29) 6.6	(34) 4.8	(10) 12.4				(79) 9.4	(82) 9.2
	23.2	10.3	13.6	35.9				20.2	17.1
Net Sales ($)	119565M	340263M	2263801M	3699081M	1988329M	6831691M		4831284M	6320753M
Total Assets ($)	14919M	106425M	770906M	1395334M	854358M	2215714M		2219688M	2648950M

M = $ thousand   MM = $ million
See Pages 11 through 21 for Explanation of Ratios and Data

Comparative Historical Data

Current Data Sorted by Sales

Hist 4/1/04-3/31/05 ALL	Hist 4/1/05-3/31/06 ALL	Hist 4/1/06-3/31/07 ALL	Type of Statement	0-1MM	1-3MM	3-5MM	5-10MM	10-25MM	25MM & OVER
42	60	86	Unqualified	2	4	6	14	23	37
56	58	62	Reviewed	1	4	6	17	27	7
39	40	45	Compiled	8	15	6	11	3	2
41	38	48	Tax Returns	13	22	4	6	3	
105	147	160	Other	14	21	16	28	39	42
4/1/04-3/31/05 ALL	4/1/05-3/31/06 ALL	4/1/06-3/31/07 ALL		58 (4/1-9/30/06)			343 (10/1/06-3/31/07)		
283	343	401	**NUMBER OF STATEMENTS**	38	66	38	76	95	88
%	%	%	**ASSETS**	%	%	%	%	%	%
17.6	15.6	17.1	Cash & Equivalents	18.0	26.6	15.2	16.8	13.1	14.9
44.7	44.4	43.2	Trade Receivables (net)	15.6	32.6	50.5	49.8	50.2	46.8
1.8	3.0	2.3	Inventory	1.2	2.3	2.9	2.9	2.5	1.8
5.6	6.5	7.7	All Other Current	12.2	6.8	5.8	4.9	7.5	9.8
69.7	69.5	70.3	Total Current	47.1	68.3	74.3	74.4	73.3	73.3
14.5	16.4	15.3	Fixed Assets (net)	29.3	19.8	14.3	11.4	13.9	11.2
4.0	4.9	4.7	Intangibles (net)	2.9	2.8	3.2	7.1	2.9	7.5
11.7	9.2	9.7	All Other Non-Current	20.8	9.1	8.2	7.2	9.8	8.0
100.0	100.0	100.0	Total	100.0	100.0	100.0	100.0	100.0	100.0
			LIABILITIES						
16.5	14.8	14.7	Notes Payable-Short Term	37.6	16.4	11.2	9.8	13.3	10.8
2.6	3.8	3.4	Cur. Mat.-L.T.D.	6.9	5.7	3.9	1.6	2.2	2.6
14.6	14.7	13.6	Trade Payables	9.5	9.2	10.0	15.3	15.9	16.2
1.2	.9	1.2	Income Taxes Payable	1.1	.9	.2	1.5	2.2	.7
17.8	16.0	18.7	All Other Current	13.5	21.7	11.7	19.0	17.1	23.1
52.8	50.1	51.6	Total Current	68.5	53.8	36.9	47.3	50.8	53.4
10.0	12.9	11.5	Long-Term Debt	25.8	15.5	10.1	8.4	9.1	8.1
.8	.7	.7	Deferred Taxes	.7	.4	.7	.2	1.0	1.0
5.5	6.3	6.9	All Other Non-Current	4.3	10.7	11.1	4.5	5.6	7.1
30.9	30.0	29.3	Net Worth	.7	19.6	41.2	39.6	33.6	30.5
100.0	100.0	100.0	Total Liabilties & Net Worth	100.0	100.0	100.0	100.0	100.0	100.0
			INCOME DATA						
100.0	100.0	100.0	Net Sales	100.0	100.0	100.0	100.0	100.0	100.0
			Gross Profit						
92.3	91.3	91.3	Operating Expenses	82.5	88.2	90.2	92.8	95.1	92.6
7.7	8.7	8.7	Operating Profit	17.5	11.8	9.8	7.2	4.9	7.4
1.9	1.3	1.4	All Other Expenses (net)	5.2	1.0	1.4	.6	1.1	.9
5.8	7.4	7.3	Profit Before Taxes	12.3	10.7	8.4	6.6	3.8	6.5
			RATIOS						
2.6	2.5	2.5		3.0	3.1	3.8	2.5	2.3	2.0
1.5	1.5	1.5	Current	1.0	1.5	2.4	1.6	1.4	1.4
1.1	1.1	1.0		.3	.9	1.3	1.1	1.1	1.1
2.4	2.2	2.2		1.8	2.8	3.2	2.4	1.9	1.8
1.3	(342) 1.3	1.3	Quick	.6	1.4	1.8	1.4	1.2	1.2
.9	.9	.8		.3	.7	1.1	.9	.9	.9
30 12.2	22 16.7	27 13.5		0 UND	0 UND	34 10.7	38 9.6	41 9.0	41 8.9
58 6.2	58 6.3	57 6.5	Sales/Receivables	0 UND	32 11.5	57 6.4	70 5.2	63 5.8	60 6.1
88 4.1	89 4.1	88 4.1		58 6.3	65 5.6	90 4.1	96 3.8	87 4.2	92 4.0
			Cost of Sales/Inventory						
			Cost of Sales/Payables						
6.0	5.7	5.7		7.4	5.3	4.5	5.6	6.7	5.2
15.3	12.7	12.6	Sales/Working Capital	UND	16.9	7.4	8.8	13.7	11.9
127.5	81.1	97.7		-2.8	-39.1	43.5	82.7	39.1	44.8
26.8	24.0	27.4		62.0	21.9	12.1	34.3	20.1	46.0
(220) 7.6	(274) 7.4	(312) 7.0	EBIT/Interest	(27) 6.1	(48) 3.6	(24) 4.5	(59) 13.4	(83) 5.1	(71) 11.3
1.5	1.7	1.8		-.5	1.4	2.1	2.3	1.1	3.5
9.7	5.4	11.3					15.5	6.8	20.2
(44) 3.3	(57) 2.6	(65) 3.7	Net Profit + Depr., Dep., Amort./Cur. Mat. L/T/D			(11) 4.3	(17) 2.7	(30) 5.6
1.4	1.2	1.4					2.5	1.2	1.4
.1	.1	.1		.0	.1	.1	.1	.1	.1
.3	.3	.3	Fixed/Worth	.5	.4	.2	.2	.3	.4
1.1	2.1	1.4		6.8	UND	1.2	1.2	.9	1.1
.7	.7	.7		1.0	.5	.5	.6	.8	.9
1.9	2.0	1.9	Debt/Worth	3.4	2.2	1.4	1.7	1.8	2.4
6.1	12.2	10.8		-70.8	UND	3.7	5.4	6.5	10.4
74.0	85.3	79.4		156.7	149.9	66.2	70.4	55.7	84.9
(240) 36.5	(284) 36.8	(338) 38.3	% Profit Before Taxes/Tangible Net Worth	(28) 52.4	(50) 56.1	(33) 22.5	(67) 36.7	(83) 25.6	(77) 48.1
6.5	8.9	12.4		1.3	21.1	14.9	11.4	5.0	18.6
28.4	27.2	29.6		64.9	55.2	38.9	33.7	22.4	23.9
9.6	9.4	10.7	% Profit Before Taxes/Total Assets	7.9	14.8	12.1	14.6	8.1	10.4
.5	1.6	3.3		-5.2	4.0	4.8	5.2	1.0	3.8
125.2	98.7	107.5		383.8	235.4	71.0	95.2	98.6	76.8
42.2	37.0	38.7	Sales/Net Fixed Assets	22.5	39.5	37.5	48.6	30.8	38.9
19.3	15.2	14.8		4.9	13.6	17.3	22.2	13.9	14.7
4.4	4.2	4.1		4.6	5.5	4.8	3.5	3.9	3.8
3.0	2.8	2.8	Sales/Total Assets	2.3	2.9	3.2	2.8	2.7	2.8
1.9	1.8	1.8		.4	1.7	1.9	2.1	2.0	1.7
.5	.5	.4		1.0	.3	.8	.3	.3	.5
(198) 1.2	(258) 1.3	(295) 1.1	% Depr., Dep., Amort./Sales	(21) 2.2	(45) 1.0	(32) 1.1	(52) 1.0	(76) 1.1	(69) .9
2.3	2.3	2.2		9.5	2.4	2.6	1.8	2.0	2.0
3.8	3.1	3.2		7.1	4.7	4.5	2.7	1.4	5.3
(91) 7.5	(96) 6.5	(103) 6.8	% Officers', Directors' Owners' Comp/Sales	(10) 13.5	(25) 10.1	(17) 6.8	(19) 4.9	(22) 3.7	(10) 13.9
16.5	18.0	16.3		33.7	15.2	10.7	12.2	8.8	35.9
6473172M	11121142M	15242730M	Net Sales ($)	20513M	133634M	151484M	547055M	1536905M	12853139M
2847191M	4172270M	5357656M	Total Assets ($)	34168M	88978M	67365M	240659M	733700M	4192786M

M = $ thousand   MM = $ million
See Pages 11 through 21 for Explanation of Ratios and Data

PROFESSIONAL SERVICES—Environmental Consulting Services NAICS 541620 (SIC 8999)

| Current Data Sorted by Assets | | | | | | | Comparative Historical Data | |

Type of Statement

0-500M	500M-2MM	2-10MM	10-50MM	50-100MM	100-250MM	Type of Statement	4/1/02-3/31/03 ALL	4/1/03-3/31/04 ALL
	2	5	7	1		Unqualified	1	5
1	5	11	1			Reviewed	5	12
1	7	6				Compiled	2	8
10	5	1				Tax Returns	4	8
5	8	10	7	1		Other	7	15
	8 (4/1-9/30/06)			86 (10/1/06-3/31/07)				
17	27	33	15	2		NUMBER OF STATEMENTS	19	48

(50-100MM and 100-250MM columns below marked: DATA NOT AVAILABLE)

Main Data

0-500M	500M-2MM	2-10MM	10-50MM			Label	4/1/02-3/31/03 ALL %	4/1/03-3/31/04 ALL %
%	%	%	%	%	%	**ASSETS**	%	%
29.0	4.9	9.0	4.8			Cash & Equivalents	10.8	13.1
23.4	51.9	55.2	55.9			Trade Receivables (net)	48.1	50.5
4.2	1.1	2.4	1.3			Inventory	1.1	1.0
5.9	4.2	5.8	6.3			All Other Current	4.8	5.0
62.6	62.1	72.5	68.3			Total Current	64.8	69.7
31.3	26.7	19.0	17.1			Fixed Assets (net)	27.5	19.8
4.6	5.0	2.1	8.6			Intangibles (net)	.6	3.4
1.5	6.2	6.4	6.0			All Other Non-Current	7.1	7.1
100.0	100.0	100.0	100.0			Total	100.0	100.0
						LIABILITIES		
29.2	15.2	8.1	13.3			Notes Payable-Short Term	6.2	14.6
5.9	2.8	2.5	3.6			Cur. Mat.-L.T.D.	4.2	3.4
8.2	17.6	12.5	14.3			Trade Payables	22.6	18.3
.0	.5	.8	4.6			Income Taxes Payable	1.8	.7
16.5	11.4	13.2	17.3			All Other Current	10.9	10.4
59.8	47.5	37.2	53.1			Total Current	45.6	47.4
26.9	20.3	9.1	14.1			Long-Term Debt	13.9	10.2
.1	.2	1.2	1.0			Deferred Taxes	.2	.2
6.1	2.5	3.1	3.0			All Other Non-Current	2.0	7.9
7.1	29.5	49.4	28.8			Net Worth	38.4	34.2
100.0	100.0	100.0	100.0			Total Liabilties & Net Worth	100.0	100.0
						INCOME DATA		
100.0	100.0	100.0	100.0			Net Sales	100.0	100.0
						Gross Profit		
91.8	93.0	92.3	95.0			Operating Expenses	96.2	94.9
8.2	7.0	7.7	5.0			Operating Profit	3.8	5.1
.3	3.2	.8	2.2			All Other Expenses (net)	1.1	.6
7.9	3.8	6.9	2.7			Profit Before Taxes	2.7	4.5
						RATIOS		
2.2	1.6	3.6	1.6			Current	2.0	3.2
1.3	1.4	2.1	1.4				1.6	1.6
.6	1.1	1.4	1.0				.9	1.0
2.0	1.6	3.3	1.4			Quick	1.9	2.4
1.0	1.3	1.6	1.0				1.4	1.4
.4	.8	1.1	.9				.7	.9
0 UND	46 7.9	70 5.2	71 5.2			Sales/Receivables	38 9.6	41 8.8
0 UND	69 5.3	93 3.9	80 4.6				65 5.6	81 4.5
49 7.5	88 4.2	114 3.2	115 3.2				93 3.9	99 3.7
						Cost of Sales/Inventory		
						Cost of Sales/Payables		
13.7	11.0	3.9	7.3			Sales/Working Capital	8.5	4.8
117.6	20.1	5.2	15.1				13.6	9.5
-28.2	87.6	9.6	67.5				-359.8	797.0
28.6	12.3	39.0	10.1			EBIT/Interest	17.5	15.2
(14) 7.9	(21) 6.0	(31) 10.7	2.9				(14) 6.0	(37) 5.5
1.1	2.0	4.4	1.7				-.7	1.3
						Net Profit + Depr., Dep., Amort./Cur. Mat. L/T/D		18.9
							(14)	8.5
								1.1
.1	.3	.2	.3			Fixed/Worth	.2	.2
2.0	.6	.3	.5				.5	.4
-1.6	1.6	.7	2.3				1.6	1.6
1.4	1.1	.6	1.5			Debt/Worth	.9	.7
2.8	2.2	1.2	3.5				1.4	1.8
-3.2	4.9	1.8	8.7				4.4	6.2
526.0	61.4	47.6	25.4			% Profit Before Taxes/Tangible Net Worth	80.6	60.9
(11) 178.8	(23) 41.8	(32) 26.6	(13) 18.2				(18) 24.2	(44) 27.2
24.8	11.6	12.2	10.2				5.5	10.7
145.1	30.5	22.8	7.8			% Profit Before Taxes/Total Assets	37.7	18.1
37.6	12.4	13.9	5.2				6.7	11.0
4.4	3.5	3.5	2.1				1.4	2.5
341.8	48.8	26.7	36.8			Sales/Net Fixed Assets	54.1	47.0
56.8	16.2	17.1	17.8				15.8	26.7
7.8	10.0	11.0	7.2				9.3	10.4
16.1	3.7	2.8	2.8			Sales/Total Assets	5.1	3.6
5.9	2.6	2.3	2.5				2.6	2.5
2.9	1.8	1.6	1.1				2.0	2.0
	.9	.8	1.1			% Depr., Dep., Amort./Sales	1.0	1.2
	(23) 1.6	(29) 1.3	(14) 2.1				(14) 2.5	(37) 1.9
	3.7	2.9	4.7				3.5	3.2
7.4	3.1	2.5				% Officers', Directors' Owners' Comp/Sales	3.6	4.3
(12) 12.9	(10) 9.1	(14) 6.1					(14) 9.3	(17) 6.5
20.7	12.9	10.5					21.6	19.0
25423M	88014M	296755M	668307M	531194M		Net Sales ($)	110386M	254586M
3947M	32270M	132379M	332062M	104543M		Total Assets ($)	46390M	108849M

© RMA 2007

M = $ thousand   MM = $ million

See Pages 11 through 21 for Explanation of Ratios and Data

Comparative Historical Data | Current Data Sorted by Sales

Type of Statement									
				Unqualified			2	3	2	8
	6	6	15	Reviewed	1	4	3	4	6	
	15	11	18	Compiled	1	4	5	3	1	
	3	8	14	Tax Returns	5	8		3		
	9	5	16	Other	4	8	5	5	6	7
	17	23	31			8 (4/1-9/30/06)		86 (10/1/06-3/31/07)		
	4/1/04-3/31/05	4/1/05-3/31/06	4/1/06-3/31/07		0-1MM	1-3MM	3-5MM	5-10MM	10-25MM	25MM & OVER
	ALL	ALL	ALL							

	ALL	ALL	ALL	NUMBER OF STATEMENTS	0-1MM	1-3MM	3-5MM	5-10MM	10-25MM	25MM & OVER
	50	53	94		11	20	15	18	15	15
	%	%	%	**ASSETS**	%	%	%	%	%	%
	9.6	9.6	11.1	Cash & Equivalents	11.1	22.7	5.3	11.0	4.1	8.7
	48.1	49.4	48.3	Trade Receivables (net)	22.1	35.2	65.0	47.6	62.3	55.0
	1.0	1.6	2.1	Inventory	.0	4.3	2.9	2.2	1.3	.8
	5.3	7.8	5.3	All Other Current	7.0	1.7	6.4	7.8	6.1	4.2
	64.0	68.4	66.9	Total Current	40.3	64.0	79.6	68.6	73.8	68.7
	24.7	23.1	22.9	Fixed Assets (net)	47.3	23.8	15.4	23.8	16.5	16.9
	3.5	3.2	4.4	Intangibles (net)	11.1	2.3	1.8	4.2	5.7	3.5
	7.8	5.4	5.8	All Other Non-Current	1.3	9.9	3.2	3.3	3.9	10.9
	100.0	100.0	100.0	Total	100.0	100.0	100.0	100.0	100.0	100.0
				LIABILITIES						
	15.0	12.6	14.9	Notes Payable-Short Term	25.6	17.5	18.7	7.0	13.1	11.0
	4.1	2.8	3.3	Cur. Mat.-L.T.D.	1.6	6.2	1.6	3.5	3.0	2.8
	16.1	11.3	13.3	Trade Payables	7.4	9.3	19.3	15.4	12.3	15.4
	.6	1.5	1.1	Income Taxes Payable	.0	.6	.2	1.1	.1	4.7
	12.4	11.5	14.5	All Other Current	5.5	17.1	13.6	14.2	11.7	21.6
	48.1	39.7	47.2	Total Current	40.1	50.7	53.4	41.2	40.2	55.5
	19.2	12.5	16.1	Long-Term Debt	41.4	19.6	7.9	14.4	8.7	10.7
	.9	.5	.7	Deferred Taxes	.0	.1	.3	2.2	.1	1.0
	7.7	2.5	3.4	All Other Non-Current	1.6	5.7	1.0	3.1	5.1	2.8
	24.1	44.9	32.6	Net Worth	16.9	23.9	37.3	39.1	46.0	30.1
	100.0	100.0	100.0	Total Liabilties & Net Worth	100.0	100.0	100.0	100.0	100.0	100.0
				INCOME DATA						
	100.0	100.0	100.0	Net Sales	100.0	100.0	100.0	100.0	100.0	100.0
				Gross Profit						
	93.7	93.1	92.7	Operating Expenses	76.7	96.6	95.8	94.9	91.3	95.1
	6.3	6.9	7.3	Operating Profit	23.3	3.4	4.2	5.1	8.7	4.9
	2.4	.8	1.6	All Other Expenses (net)	7.4	.7	.8	.3	1.6	1.0
	3.8	6.1	5.6	Profit Before Taxes	15.9	2.7	3.4	4.8	7.1	3.9
				RATIOS						
	1.9	2.7	2.2	Current	9.1	2.1	2.0	2.3	2.9	1.6
	1.4	1.7	1.5		1.4	1.3	1.5	1.6	1.8	1.3
	1.1	1.2	1.1		1.2	1.0	1.3	1.3	1.2	1.0
	1.5	2.4	1.8	Quick	9.1	2.1	2.0	1.7	2.7	1.4
	1.3	1.6	1.3		1.2	1.2	1.4	1.4	1.5	1.0
	1.0	1.0	.9		.7	.7	1.0	1.1	1.1	.9
(49)	7.5	(48) 7.6	(46) 7.9	Sales/Receivables	(0) UND	(0) UND	(77) 4.7	(49) 7.5	(71) 5.1	(48) 7.5
(76)	4.8	(74) 4.9	(75) 4.9		(27) 13.5	(43) 8.5	(82) 4.4	(65) 5.6	(96) 3.8	(80) 4.6
(101)	3.6	(103) 3.5	(100) 3.6		(51) 7.1	(88) 4.2	(116) 3.2	(94) 3.9	(119) 3.1	(108) 3.4
				Cost of Sales/Inventory						
				Cost of Sales/Payables						
	7.7	5.1	6.0	Sales/Working Capital	2.6	11.9	4.8	4.7	4.5	8.2
	15.4	9.8	13.9		17.7	73.4	10.6	9.6	6.9	18.5
	63.5	33.1	72.5		87.6	-89.8	14.5	21.5	18.8	587.4
	13.4	26.0	23.6	EBIT/Interest	25.7	13.1	33.8	105.1	25.7	15.4
(40)	4.7	(48) 7.3	(82) 6.2		(10) 6.1	(15) 2.8	(13) 11.4	(16) 10.5	(14) 4.7	(14) 6.1
	1.0	2.5	2.2		1.1	-1.9	2.6	4.5	1.6	2.7
		8.1	11.8	Net Profit + Depr., Dep., Amort./Cur. Mat. L/T/D						
		(13) 2.2	(18) 3.2							
		1.4	1.0							
	.3	.3	.2	Fixed/Worth	.5	.1	.2	.3	.1	.2
	.6	.4	.5		2.7	.6	.4	.5	.3	.4
	2.0	.9	1.7		5.3	1.9	.6	2.6	1.2	1.1
	1.0	.5	1.0	Debt/Worth	1.5	.7	1.1	.7	.6	1.4
	2.0	1.6	1.9		2.8	1.8	1.8	1.5	1.4	2.4
	5.4	3.1	5.0		-3.6	6.2	3.9	8.3	3.6	5.9
	41.1	49.7	61.9	% Profit Before Taxes/Tangible Net Worth		168.1	80.9	48.0	49.5	58.8
(44)	17.0	(51) 22.1	(81) 28.5			(16) 43.2	(14) 47.1	(15) 28.5	(14) 20.5	(14) 22.5
	-3.7	9.0	13.2			20.8	11.4	9.1	13.4	10.6
	19.4	21.6	24.8	% Profit Before Taxes/Total Assets	37.6	53.0	22.5	31.5	23.6	14.0
	5.7	8.6	10.5		14.4	13.2	13.4	10.9	7.7	7.4
	-.9	3.5	3.1		2.8	1.7	4.3	2.7	2.8	2.1
	51.8	30.3	48.2	Sales/Net Fixed Assets	233.5	86.9	35.0	23.0	32.6	41.9
	17.9	15.0	18.3		4.6	42.9	17.9	14.0	17.1	30.0
	5.9	7.3	10.4		.4	7.9	12.2	12.7	8.0	14.8
	3.5	3.1	3.5	Sales/Total Assets	2.7	6.6	3.5	3.9	3.1	3.3
	2.6	2.5	2.6		1.5	3.3	2.3	2.7	2.4	2.8
	1.8	2.0	1.8		.3	1.8	2.0	2.2	1.8	2.4
	.8	1.1	.9	% Depr., Dep., Amort./Sales		.8	.5	1.0	.9	.4
(39)	2.2	(43) 2.0	(73) 1.7			(14) 1.5	(13) 1.6	(13) 1.3	(14) 2.0	(13) 1.2
	3.2	2.8	3.2			3.7	2.4	2.9	5.2	2.3
	1.9	6.6	3.6	% Officers', Directors' Owners' Comp/Sales		3.4		5.7		
(16)	6.1	(18) 13.1	(37) 9.2			(12) 10.1		(10) 9.8		
	19.3	20.8	14.4			13.7		14.9		
	393838M	664285M	1609693M	Net Sales ($)	6631M	35550M	58998M	127066M	213265M	1168183M
	181965M	269200M	605201M	Total Assets ($)	7966M	16300M	29032M	46463M	121436M	384004M

© RMA 2007

M = $ thousand   MM = $ million
See Pages 11 through 21 for Explanation of Ratios and Data

Current Data Sorted by Assets / Comparative Historical Data

Type of Statement	0-500M	500M-2MM	2-10MM	10-50MM	50-100MM	100-250MM		4/1/02-3/31/03 ALL	4/1/03-3/31/04 ALL
Unqualified		3	7	6	3	2		1	6
Reviewed		2	8					4	9
Compiled	4	5	6					7	9
Tax Returns	9	6	2			1		2	7
Other	9	13	17	9	4	3		11	17
		14 (4/1-9/30/06)		105 (10/1/06-3/31/07)					
NUMBER OF STATEMENTS	22	29	40	15	8	5		25	48
ASSETS	%	%	%	%	%	%		%	%
Cash & Equivalents	18.4	15.7	12.7	17.3				10.9	17.8
Trade Receivables (net)	30.5	44.9	50.5	49.1				36.8	36.2
Inventory	5.6	1.4	2.6	1.1				7.5	3.9
All Other Current	4.1	6.5	6.9	4.4				3.3	9.0
Total Current	58.7	68.4	72.6	71.9				58.6	67.0
Fixed Assets (net)	23.1	17.1	14.6	18.1				34.1	23.9
Intangibles (net)	8.1	6.3	5.0	4.9				1.5	4.1
All Other Non-Current	10.2	8.1	7.8	5.1				5.9	5.0
Total	100.0	100.0	100.0	100.0				100.0	100.0
LIABILITIES									
Notes Payable-Short Term	31.1	12.5	8.6	4.6				17.4	21.4
Cur. Mat.-L.T.D.	4.2	4.4	3.4	.7				7.5	5.6
Trade Payables	10.9	16.8	18.1	10.2				12.2	14.4
Income Taxes Payable	.0	1.4	.8	2.4				.8	.2
All Other Current	27.8	27.0	14.5	21.3				17.9	13.9
Total Current	74.1	62.2	45.4	39.2				55.9	55.5
Long-Term Debt	15.1	21.5	4.5	11.7				22.3	13.3
Deferred Taxes	3.4	.6	.4	.3				.5	.5
All Other Non-Current	9.2	7.8	4.6	4.7				.4	3.6
Net Worth	-1.8	7.8	45.0	44.0				20.9	27.2
Total Liabilities & Net Worth	100.0	100.0	100.0	100.0				100.0	100.0
INCOME DATA									
Net Sales	100.0	100.0	100.0	100.0				100.0	100.0
Gross Profit									
Operating Expenses	84.9	94.0	91.6	88.7				95.3	96.9
Operating Profit	15.1	6.0	8.4	11.3				4.7	3.1
All Other Expenses (net)	2.2	1.2	.3	.5				2.6	.4
Profit Before Taxes	12.8	4.8	8.1	10.9				2.0	2.6
RATIOS									
Current	2.4	2.2	3.3	2.6				1.7	2.0
	1.4	1.3	1.7	1.9				1.1	1.2
	.3	.8	1.2	1.5				.8	.9
Quick	2.0	2.0	3.1	2.5				1.6	1.7
	1.0	1.1	1.4	1.9				.9	1.0
	.3	.6	1.0	1.4				.6	.6
Sales/Receivables	0 UND	10 36.3	39 9.4	61 5.9				33 11.2	31 11.9
	12 30.9	43 8.5	67 5.5	87 4.2				55 6.6	52 7.1
	44 8.3	72 5.1	82 4.5	114 3.2				87 4.2	70 5.2
Cost of Sales/Inventory									
Cost of Sales/Payables									
Sales/Working Capital	10.5	9.9	4.7	3.4				15.0	8.0
	32.0	51.8	10.2	6.1				63.4	25.9
	-23.3	-17.6	27.9	10.6				-15.3	-33.9
EBIT/Interest	23.1	9.1	41.3	220.0				7.6	9.7
	(18) 9.8	(19) 5.0	(34) 19.6	(11) 86.9				(22) 2.5	(36) 3.9
	.7	1.0	9.3	6.3				-.3	1.3
Net Profit + Depr., Dep., Amort./Cur. Mat. L/T/D									
Fixed/Worth	.1	.2	.1	.1				.3	.2
	.2	.8	.3	.2				1.4	.8
	-1.9	-.7	.7	1.2				NM	2.2
Debt/Worth	.6	1.2	.5	.7				1.5	.9
	2.5	3.3	1.5	1.3				2.8	2.6
	-4.4	-6.8	2.8	2.6				-46.4	7.5
% Profit Before Taxes/Tangible Net Worth	999.8	71.1	66.8	68.2				41.9	75.3
	(14) 149.2	(19) 33.2	(35) 36.6	(14) 51.0				(18) 20.7	(41) 20.2
	45.8	.0	19.7	21.4				-6.8	.1
% Profit Before Taxes/Total Assets	93.6	35.4	29.5	35.3				10.5	17.0
	28.8	12.7	18.4	22.3				4.5	4.5
	4.7	-.4	6.7	4.1				-6.3	-.1
Sales/Net Fixed Assets	421.5	133.4	85.6	92.2				18.1	59.2
	52.6	50.7	34.9	32.1				9.8	13.4
	18.1	15.1	12.3	5.6				5.2	7.2
Sales/Total Assets	8.7	5.7	3.7	3.0				3.2	3.5
	5.9	3.5	2.8	2.0				2.3	2.6
	2.9	2.2	2.0	1.0				1.5	1.7
% Depr., Dep., Amort./Sales	.2	.6	.5	.3				1.6	1.8
	(15) 1.1	(21) .9	(30) 1.2	(10) 1.1				(19) 2.7	(34) 2.9
	1.5	3.8	1.9	2.0				5.5	4.6
% Officers', Directors' Owners' Comp/Sales	2.4		1.1					1.6	4.5
	(13) 5.0		(12) 1.3					(11) 4.9	(18) 7.8
	11.3		4.8					11.3	17.2
Net Sales ($)	41434M	152361M	540525M	921914M	1596607M	1070232M		167223M	372082M
Total Assets ($)	5817M	34052M	183630M	379999M	670426M	700487M		80411M	169057M

M = $ thousand   MM = $ million
See Pages 11 through 21 for Explanation of Ratios and Data

Comparative Historical Data   Current Data Sorted by Sales

4/1/04-3/31/05 ALL	4/1/05-3/31/06 ALL	4/1/06-3/31/07 ALL	Type of Statement	0-1MM	1-3MM	3-5MM	5-10MM	10-25MM	25MM & OVER
9	8	21	Unqualified		2	1	3	5	10
8	8	10	Reviewed		1	1	1	6	1
9	14	15	Compiled	1	6	4	2	2	
9	12	18	Tax Returns	6	3	3	3	2	1
21	29	55	Other	2	10	6	11	10	16
					14 (4/1-9/30/06)		105 (10/1/06-3/31/07)		
56	71	119	**NUMBER OF STATEMENTS**	9	22	15	20	25	28
%	%	%	**ASSETS**	%	%	%	%	%	%
15.0	14.5	14.3	Cash & Equivalents		17.3	18.3	11.6	14.3	10.2
41.3	47.4	43.6	Trade Receivables (net)		34.1	36.4	51.8	47.3	51.4
3.7	5.5	3.0	Inventory		2.0	5.7	1.8	4.0	3.1
4.6	4.3	5.6	All Other Current		3.0	12.8	7.3	4.7	3.4
64.6	71.7	66.5	Total Current		56.3	73.3	72.4	70.2	68.1
16.1	14.0	17.2	Fixed Assets (net)		23.2	16.0	20.4	15.5	10.7
6.6	3.6	7.9	Intangibles (net)		12.8	3.1	1.2	5.5	13.6
12.7	10.7	8.4	All Other Non-Current		7.7	7.6	6.0	8.8	7.6
100.0	100.0	100.0	Total		100.0	100.0	100.0	100.0	100.0
			LIABILITIES						
13.9	15.5	13.4	Notes Payable-Short Term		12.0	38.4	12.3	9.1	7.7
1.6	2.5	3.2	Cur. Mat.-L.T.D.		3.6	3.3	3.1	3.1	1.6
10.3	13.5	14.1	Trade Payables		9.5	8.3	18.8	19.2	13.0
.7	1.0	1.0	Income Taxes Payable		.0	1.6	1.8	.6	1.6
18.0	17.1	21.8	All Other Current		16.4	38.9	21.8	14.9	23.8
44.6	49.5	53.6	Total Current		41.6	90.6	57.8	46.8	47.7
13.9	12.6	13.3	Long-Term Debt		11.3	28.0	15.6	5.2	10.5
1.0	.8	1.0	Deferred Taxes		.0	1.1	.0	.6	.6
6.7	4.1	7.0	All Other Non-Current		2.7	5.9	8.8	5.2	8.5
33.9	32.9	25.0	Net Worth		44.4	-25.6	17.7	42.1	32.6
100.0	100.0	100.0	Total Liabilities & Net Worth		100.0	100.0	100.0	100.0	100.0
			INCOME DATA						
100.0	100.0	100.0	Net Sales		100.0	100.0	100.0	100.0	100.0
			Gross Profit						
93.1	94.0	90.4	Operating Expenses		90.6	89.5	93.1	93.0	91.5
6.9	6.0	9.6	Operating Profit		9.4	10.5	6.9	7.0	8.5
1.4	.7	1.0	All Other Expenses (net)		2.3	.9	.2	.0	.9
5.5	5.3	8.6	Profit Before Taxes		7.1	9.6	6.7	7.0	7.6
			RATIOS						
2.8	3.4	2.3	Current		5.6	2.2	2.2	2.5	2.1
1.8	1.6	1.6			2.4	1.2	1.7	1.6	1.5
.9	1.1	1.0			.8	.9	1.0	1.1	1.1
2.4	2.4	2.2	Quick		5.3	1.7	2.0	1.8	2.0
1.6	1.4	1.4			2.3	1.0	1.4	1.4	1.4
.8	.8	.8			.8	.3	1.0	.9	.9
24 15.3	33 11.1	24 15.1	Sales/Receivables	0 UND	0 UND	30 12.2	29 12.6	62 5.8	
46 7.9	59 6.2	61 6.0		35 10.4	39 9.2	64 5.7	65 5.6	89 4.1	
76 4.8	94 3.9	89 4.1		55 6.7	78 4.7	99 3.7	74 4.9	96 3.8	
			Cost of Sales/Inventory						
			Cost of Sales/Payables						
5.0	5.4	5.8	Sales/Working Capital		4.8	9.1	4.4	5.8	6.2
11.5	11.1	13.4			16.1	15.1	11.5	16.3	10.3
-96.8	70.4	800.0			-187.3	-30.0	220.6	111.8	73.3
41.5	35.3	31.6	EBIT/Interest		35.9	12.0	19.0	28.2	162.4
(42) 15.6	(54) 6.8	(93) 11.1		(18) 13.1	(10) 7.4	(15) 14.4	(22) 16.6	(21) 13.4	
5.9	1.7	3.8			3.3	.6	4.4	4.0	4.0
5.4		4.7	Net Profit + Depr., Dep.,						
(12) 2.9	(11) 2.9	2.9	Amort./Cur. Mat. L/T/D						
1.1		1.0							
.1	.1	.1	Fixed/Worth		.1	.0	.2	.1	.1
.3	.2	.3			.3	.4	.4	.3	.3
1.7	.9	2.8			1.6	-6.2	-.7	1.0	-4.3
.6	.5	.9	Debt/Worth		.3	1.2	.9	.7	1.0
1.2	1.6	2.1			1.0	2.8	1.6	1.5	2.3
6.7	3.7	UND			2.9	-11.6	-6.3	4.5	-16.5
84.5	80.7	92.8	% Profit Before Taxes/Tangible		140.8	51.5	59.7	69.0	86.9
(47) 35.4	(63) 37.7	(90) 44.3	Net Worth	(19) 36.6	(10) 29.8	(14) 39.0	(22) 42.0	(20) 53.6	
11.2	9.4	19.9			9.6	14.8	15.2	19.9	28.5
26.5	28.4	35.3	% Profit Before Taxes/Total		43.1	35.6	37.8	28.3	35.4
12.1	12.7	18.8	Assets		21.3	14.0	14.6	19.8	16.5
2.5	3.5	3.9			1.8	.0	5.2	5.7	4.5
80.8	106.4	86.3	Sales/Net Fixed Assets		95.8	621.4	57.9	98.1	85.8
37.7	43.1	37.8			39.1	74.3	36.3	37.8	40.4
14.3	16.3	12.1			8.0	12.9	11.9	20.1	16.5
5.4	4.6	4.7	Sales/Total Assets		7.5	5.6	5.4	4.7	3.7
3.1	2.8	3.0			2.9	3.5	3.1	3.3	2.1
1.7	1.7	1.9			1.5	2.9	2.0	2.4	1.5
.7	.5	.5	% Depr., Dep., Amort./Sales		.7		.5	.3	.4
(38) 1.5	(42) 1.2	(87) 1.1		(14) 1.5		(17) .9	(18) .8	(21) 1.0	
2.8	2.3	1.9			5.6		2.1	1.4	1.4
3.0	4.0	1.4	% Officers', Directors'						
(16) 7.0	(18) 9.1	(35) 5.0	Owners' Comp/Sales						
12.1	14.5	9.0							
1127979M	2200426M	4323073M	Net Sales ($)	5187M	47174M	57703M	145744M	387912M	3679353M
683758M	1199106M	1974411M	Total Assets ($)	2387M	32167M	27608M	53538M	127042M	1731669M

M = $ thousand   MM = $ million
See Pages 11 through 21 for Explanation of Ratios and Data

Current Data Sorted by Assets							Comparative Historical Data	

Type of Statement

0-500M	500M-2MM	2-10MM	10-50MM	50-100MM	100-250MM	Type of Statement	70	62
2	5	30	32	13	14	Unqualified	70	62
	3	7	5	1		Reviewed	27	17
4	1	5	2			Compiled	16	25
8	6	5		7	4	Tax Returns	12	18
6	23	25	21			Other	48	43
	71 (4/1-9/30/06)		158 (10/1/06-3/31/07)				4/1/02-3/31/03 ALL	4/1/03-3/31/04 ALL
20	38	72	60	21	18	NUMBER OF STATEMENTS	173	165
%	%	%	%	%	%	ASSETS	%	%
33.5	18.7	15.1	19.2	7.4	23.5	Cash & Equivalents	16.0	19.1
24.3	36.0	36.1	26.7	19.7	16.0	Trade Receivables (net)	30.7	30.4
2.9	5.0	5.9	3.7	1.3	3.0	Inventory	3.5	2.3
8.5	3.6	5.7	5.7	6.5	5.4	All Other Current	7.5	6.8
69.3	63.3	62.8	55.4	35.0	47.9	Total Current	57.6	58.7
25.8	25.0	25.3	30.2	30.9	28.6	Fixed Assets (net)	26.3	26.0
.9	3.9	2.8	3.6	9.0	5.5	Intangibles (net)	5.1	4.9
4.0	7.9	9.1	10.9	25.1	18.0	All Other Non-Current	10.9	10.4
100.0	100.0	100.0	100.0	100.0	100.0	Total	100.0	100.0
						LIABILITIES		
44.8	8.4	6.0	5.0	2.8	4.4	Notes Payable-Short Term	8.0	7.5
1.6	2.9	3.7	2.3	2.1	.8	Cur. Mat.-L.T.D.	2.6	1.8
16.6	15.9	12.9	10.1	6.5	8.5	Trade Payables	9.2	10.2
2.6	.5	.6	1.4	.7	.0	Income Taxes Payable	.4	.5
29.4	11.3	20.4	15.6	14.6	17.2	All Other Current	16.5	17.4
94.9	39.1	43.7	34.5	26.6	31.0	Total Current	36.7	37.4
4.7	15.1	10.5	13.0	24.0	15.0	Long-Term Debt	12.6	12.7
.0	.4	.2	.0	2.0	.2	Deferred Taxes	.8	.6
12.7	12.2	6.5	7.4	5.8	8.8	All Other Non-Current	6.7	6.3
-12.4	33.2	39.1	45.0	41.6	45.0	Net Worth	43.2	43.0
100.0	100.0	100.0	100.0	100.0	100.0	Total Liabilities & Net Worth	100.0	100.0
						INCOME DATA		
100.0	100.0	100.0	100.0	100.0	100.0	Net Sales	100.0	100.0
						Gross Profit		
95.6	93.8	93.0	95.1	94.5	95.7	Operating Expenses	94.4	94.8
4.4	6.2	7.0	4.9	5.5	4.3	Operating Profit	5.6	5.2
1.1	1.0	1.3	.4	2.4	-1.0	All Other Expenses (net)	2.1	.5
3.3	5.1	5.7	4.5	3.2	5.4	Profit Before Taxes	3.4	4.7
						RATIOS		
1.8	2.6	2.9	2.9	1.9	3.5		2.8	3.7
1.0	1.8	1.7	1.7	1.1	1.7	Current	1.6	1.7
.6	1.1	1.2	1.1	.8	1.1		1.2	1.1
1.7	2.4	2.3	2.7	1.6	2.5		2.4	3.0
.9	1.4	1.3	1.3	.8	1.6	Quick	1.4	1.4
.4	.9	.8	.8	.7	.9		.9	.9
0 UND	23 16.1	36 10.0	24 15.1	33 11.0	40 9.2		32 11.4	31 11.9
13 29.0	49 7.5	53 6.9	56 6.5	47 7.8	53 6.9	Sales/Receivables	56 6.6	52 7.0
40 9.2	76 4.8	79 4.6	85 4.3	74 5.0	73 5.0		81 4.5	76 4.8
						Cost of Sales/Inventory		
						Cost of Sales/Payables		
18.3	7.4	4.4	3.7	8.0	2.6		4.7	4.3
UND	13.5	10.1	7.5	20.9	9.2	Sales/Working Capital	9.0	8.7
-15.1	NM	40.5	33.5	-21.9	NM		29.9	34.1
19.5	15.8	15.8	17.0	16.7	13.3		16.6	28.3
(15) 2.8	(26) 6.7	(56) 7.1	(38) 6.1	(15) 3.3	(13) 5.2	EBIT/Interest	(134) 4.9	(118) 5.1
-1.5	3.8	1.3	-1.4	.7	1.5		1.1	1.1
		9.6					10.7	7.4
	(15) 2.6					Net Profit + Depr., Dep., Amort./Cur. Mat. L/T/D	(38) 3.9	(27) 2.6
		.1					2.6	2.1
.1	.1	.2	.1	.3	.4		.2	.2
1.4	.6	.5	.6	1.1	.7	Fixed/Worth	.5	.5
-.6	2.0	1.2	1.4	3.8	1.5		1.2	1.4
1.2	.9	.5	.6	.6	.4		.5	.5
10.6	2.3	1.1	1.2	3.2	1.3	Debt/Worth	1.2	1.1
-4.2	5.6	2.5	2.6	5.9	4.2		3.4	3.1
736.7	90.6	45.6	34.7	26.1	11.3		37.4	37.7
(12) 109.2	(33) 39.4	(67) 31.0	(55) 13.5	(18) 10.4	(15) 6.5	% Profit Before Taxes/Tangible Net Worth	(152) 18.7	(145) 14.0
-37.2	4.9	2.8	.3	-.9	4.1		2.5	.8
69.4	37.2	20.7	16.1	9.1	6.1		18.3	17.0
8.4	13.0	10.7	5.1	3.4	3.4	% Profit Before Taxes/Total Assets	5.4	5.5
-19.0	1.0	-.2	-1.2	-.5	1.0		-.5	-.1
153.1	51.1	46.1	22.1	20.0	12.5		26.7	32.1
34.1	20.3	14.5	7.1	4.7	1.8	Sales/Net Fixed Assets	11.0	12.9
14.7	5.1	4.5	1.7	1.1	1.2		3.8	4.2
12.4	3.9	3.1	2.1	1.8	1.5		3.0	3.1
5.1	2.5	2.3	1.2	1.1	.8	Sales/Total Assets	2.0	2.0
2.8	1.8	1.2	.7	.4	.5		1.0	1.1
	1.0	1.0	1.8	1.7	1.4		1.5	1.2
	(26) 1.7	(59) 2.1	(46) 4.0	(19) 3.8	(16) 3.7	% Depr., Dep., Amort./Sales	(150) 2.5	(134) 2.5
	3.2	3.7	9.0	11.2	6.9		5.1	5.0
		2.5					6.2	3.5
	(14)	4.9				% Officers', Directors' Owners' Comp/Sales	(33) 10.8	(39) 10.6
		16.5					22.6	16.4
20515M	134393M	827123M	2598276M	1827992M	3266659M	Net Sales ($)	5478217M	5203175M
4559M	43836M	343121M	1399954M	1524023M	2940204M	Total Assets ($)	4124902M	3780004M

M = $ thousand   MM = $ million
See Pages 11 through 21 for Explanation of Ratios and Data

Comparative Historical Data / Current Data Sorted by Sales

			Type of Statement						
64	70	96	Unqualified	2	3	7	14	21	49
21	26	16	Reviewed	1	2	3	5	3	2
16	11	12	Compiled	3	2	1	3	3	
7	10	19	Tax Returns	5	6	6	2		
66	92	86	Other	5	17	9	12	19	24
4/1/04-3/31/05 ALL	4/1/05-3/31/06 ALL	4/1/06-3/31/07 ALL		71 (4/1-9/30/06)			158 (10/1/06-3/31/07)		
				0-1MM	1-3MM	3-5MM	5-10MM	10-25MM	25MM & OVER
174	209	229	**NUMBER OF STATEMENTS**	16	30	26	36	46	75
%	%	%	**ASSETS**	%	%	%	%	%	%
20.0	20.9	18.4	Cash & Equivalents	25.5	16.6	22.2	16.9	14.3	19.4
30.2	28.9	29.5	Trade Receivables (net)	17.1	29.9	29.5	30.5	32.7	29.6
4.7	4.1	4.3	Inventory	3.5	6.4	6.7	4.1	3.2	3.5
6.0	5.4	5.6	All Other Current	11.6	2.1	1.9	3.6	6.5	7.5
60.9	59.3	57.8	Total Current	57.8	55.0	60.3	55.2	56.7	60.0
24.0	25.5	27.3	Fixed Assets (net)	25.8	38.3	23.7	29.9	26.5	23.8
5.3	4.7	3.8	Intangibles (net)	.0	1.3	3.2	4.8	4.6	4.8
9.8	10.5	11.1	All Other Non-Current	16.4	5.4	12.8	10.0	12.2	11.4
100.0	100.0	100.0	Total	100.0	100.0	100.0	100.0	100.0	100.0
			LIABILITIES						
7.5	5.5	9.1	Notes Payable-Short Term	45.6	11.9	6.6	4.6	6.5	4.9
1.9	2.0	2.6	Cur. Mat.-L.T.D.	1.1	3.6	2.9	2.5	3.1	2.3
10.0	10.4	12.1	Trade Payables	11.1	15.4	11.5	12.5	10.5	11.9
.6	.5	.9	Income Taxes Payable	1.3	1.2	.5	.0	.8	1.4
16.8	16.4	17.7	All Other Current	30.2	8.9	11.6	11.8	25.6	18.5
36.8	34.8	42.4	Total Current	89.2	41.0	33.2	31.4	46.5	39.0
10.9	12.8	13.0	Long-Term Debt	2.7	20.9	15.3	17.6	8.1	12.0
.4	.2	.4	Deferred Taxes	2.6	.0	.6	.3	.1	.1
6.5	8.1	8.3	All Other Non-Current	12.4	11.9	12.8	4.2	10.1	5.4
45.3	44.0	35.9	Net Worth	-7.0	26.1	38.1	46.5	35.2	43.5
100.0	100.0	100.0	Total Liabilties & Net Worth	100.0	100.0	100.0	100.0	100.0	100.0
			INCOME DATA						
100.0	100.0	100.0	Net Sales	100.0	100.0	100.0	100.0	100.0	100.0
			Gross Profit						
95.5	95.3	94.3	Operating Expenses	95.7	93.4	95.9	89.8	94.5	95.7
4.5	4.7	5.7	Operating Profit	4.3	6.6	4.1	10.2	5.5	4.3
.5	1.0	.9	All Other Expenses (net)	1.9	1.8	.2	1.7	1.5	-.2
4.0	3.7	4.8	Profit Before Taxes	2.4	4.8	3.9	8.5	4.0	4.5
			RATIOS						
3.1	3.2	2.7		1.7	2.6	2.6	3.0	2.9	2.5
1.8	1.7	1.6	Current	.9	1.5	1.7	1.6	1.7	1.5
1.2	1.1	1.0		.6	.9	1.3	1.2	1.1	1.1
2.5	2.7	2.2		1.6	2.5	2.3	2.8	2.2	2.1
1.4	1.5	1.3	Quick	.7	1.1	1.5	1.4	1.3	1.2
.9	.9	.8		.3	.6	.9	.8	.9	.7
33 11.0	31 11.8	29 12.5		0 UND	22 16.8	24 15.2	35 10.6	28 13.0	40 9.2
55 6.6	52 7.0	49 7.4	Sales/Receivables	13 27.1	50 7.3	41 8.9	50 7.3	50 7.3	55 6.6
79 4.6	83 4.4	78 4.7		46 7.9	80 4.6	79 4.6	82 4.4	75 4.9	81 4.5
			Cost of Sales/Inventory						
			Cost of Sales/Payables						
4.1	3.7	4.7		16.5	5.0	4.8	3.0	5.0	3.9
8.5	8.2	11.8	Sales/Working Capital	-58.7	14.3	8.9	9.3	11.5	10.8
29.8	46.0	108.0		-7.6	-61.3	19.4	42.4	44.1	76.2
39.5	21.8	14.7			9.2	19.1	17.2	18.7	19.0
(115) 8.8	(141) 5.2	(163) 6.0	EBIT/Interest		(26) 5.7	(19) 3.3	(23) 7.6	(34) 6.3	(52) 6.6
.5	.9	1.1			.5	-2.1	2.9	.4	1.6
11.7	7.0	9.5							19.8
(25) 4.7	(29) 3.1	(33) 2.8	Net Profit + Depr., Dep., Amort./Cur. Mat. L/T/D					(13) 5.7	
1.8	.9	1.0							2.4
.2	.2	.2		.0	.6	.1	.2	.2	.1
.5	.5	.7	Fixed/Worth	.6	1.3	.6	.6	.6	.5
1.4	1.4	1.8		-3.9	-5.4	1.9	1.3	1.2	1.5
.4	.5	.6		.8	.5	.7	.7	.6	.6
1.1	1.2	1.5	Debt/Worth	5.5	2.3	1.7	1.2	1.2	1.6
3.2	3.3	4.7		-8.3	-10.3	5.9	2.8	2.5	3.6
46.2	43.0	46.3		205.6	75.1	60.1	60.4	45.6	32.2
(153) 17.1	(188) 13.4	(200) 20.3	% Profit Before Taxes/Tangible Net Worth	(11) 17.7	(22) 30.8	(24) 24.8	(34) 23.0	(40) 23.8	(69) 19.4
.7	.5	1.8		-1.1	-4.3	-2.0	4.9	.8	3.3
16.9	16.1	17.6		25.7	27.6	20.9	19.7	21.4	14.0
7.5	5.2	6.5	% Profit Before Taxes/Total Assets	1.2	10.4	4.1	9.9	8.3	5.9
-1.0	-.3	-.1		-20.7	-3.7	-2.8	.6	-3.1	1.2
30.0	25.4	36.0		UND	25.3	31.9	22.6	34.9	41.1
12.2	10.5	11.3	Sales/Net Fixed Assets	58.2	5.6	11.9	9.6	10.7	10.8
4.0	3.0	2.8		22.3	2.3	3.8	1.3	4.3	2.1
2.8	2.6	3.0		11.7	3.6	3.2	3.0	2.9	2.5
1.7	1.8	1.9	Sales/Total Assets	2.3	1.9	1.9	1.9	2.2	1.5
1.0	1.0	1.0		.8	1.2	.9	.7	1.0	1.0
1.3	1.3	1.1			1.5	1.1	1.4	1.3	.9
(131) 2.0	(176) 3.0	(175) 2.4	% Depr., Dep., Amort./Sales		(20) 3.6	(22) 2.1	(26) 2.7	(38) 2.2	(62) 2.6
5.3	5.8	5.7			7.2	4.9	5.3	7.1	4.7
2.6	2.6	2.5							
(25) 3.8	(38) 8.5	(36) 7.5	% Officers', Directors' Owners' Comp/Sales						
11.3	17.6	18.0							
7115953M	8100642M	8674958M	Net Sales ($)	8362M	55466M	98818M	261827M	721369M	7529116M
5236653M	6628474M	6255697M	Total Assets ($)	82696M	37162M	146641M	306705M	606755M	5075738M

© RMA 2007

M = $ thousand   MM = $ million
See Pages 11 through 21 for Explanation of Ratios and Data

Current Data Sorted by Assets / Comparative Historical Data

Type of Statement	0-500M	500M-2MM	2-10MM	10-50MM	50-100MM	100-250MM		4/1/02-3/31/03 ALL	4/1/03-3/31/04 ALL
Unqualified		1	3	9	1	3		6	9
Reviewed		1	3	1				3	1
Compiled	1	2	1	1				1	3
Tax Returns	3		1					1	
Other	1	2	8	4	4	2		9	5
		16 (4/1-9/30/06)		36 (10/1/06-3/31/07)					
NUMBER OF STATEMENTS	5	6	16	15	5	5		20	18
ASSETS	%	%	%	%	%	%		%	%
Cash & Equivalents			26.5	34.0				18.1	11.8
Trade Receivables (net)			42.2	24.3				38.1	35.8
Inventory			.4	.5				2.7	1.9
All Other Current			6.2	8.0				11.8	14.2
Total Current			75.4	66.8				70.6	63.6
Fixed Assets (net)			16.8	14.2				17.5	22.3
Intangibles (net)			2.9	6.1				2.8	5.2
All Other Non-Current			4.9	12.8				9.1	8.9
Total			100.0	100.0				100.0	100.0
LIABILITIES									
Notes Payable-Short Term			5.4	1.1				10.5	14.3
Cur. Mat.-L.T.D.			.9	1.7				2.7	1.7
Trade Payables			10.9	4.7				7.9	8.0
Income Taxes Payable			.1	.2				.8	.1
All Other Current			24.2	19.3				28.1	28.0
Total Current			41.4	27.0				50.1	52.1
Long-Term Debt			7.8	9.2				11.2	9.8
Deferred Taxes			.0	.3				.4	1.6
All Other Non-Current			3.4	6.8				2.7	9.2
Net Worth			47.3	56.7				35.6	27.4
Total Liabilties & Net Worth			100.0	100.0				100.0	100.0
INCOME DATA									
Net Sales			100.0	100.0				100.0	100.0
Gross Profit									
Operating Expenses			89.3	91.3				96.4	93.1
Operating Profit			10.7	8.7				3.6	6.9
All Other Expenses (net)			.6	-.6				4.1	2.4
Profit Before Taxes			10.1	9.4				-.5	4.5
RATIOS									
Current			4.1	3.7				2.6	1.8
			2.0	2.4				1.8	1.3
			1.1	1.7				1.1	.9
Quick			3.7	3.0				2.1	1.4
			2.0	2.0				1.6	1.0
			1.0	1.2				.8	.6
Sales/Receivables			14 25.5	17 21.4				37 9.8	21 17.6
			56 6.5	48 7.7				59 6.2	58 6.3
			87 4.2	86 4.3				90 4.0	85 4.3
Cost of Sales/Inventory									
Cost of Sales/Payables									
Sales/Working Capital			4.1	2.1				4.9	7.2
			9.0	3.8				7.4	12.3
			156.6	6.1				30.8	-56.4
EBIT/Interest			34.0	145.0				20.3	15.3
			(15) 8.0	(10) 15.2				(15) 3.6	(15) 7.6
			1.1	5.3				-2.6	1.3
Net Profit + Depr., Dep., Amort./Cur. Mat. L/T/D									
Fixed/Worth			.1	.0				.1	.3
			.3	.1				.3	.8
			1.1	.7				.9	3.2
Debt/Worth			.4	.4				.7	1.3
			.9	.7				1.1	3.2
			3.0	1.4				2.6	18.7
% Profit Before Taxes/Tangible Net Worth			60.6	34.0				26.0	79.4
			(14) 28.8	(13) 13.6				(17) 6.1	(15) 13.3
			2.0	6.1				-9.3	-12.2
% Profit Before Taxes/Total Assets			26.0	18.5				12.7	19.1
			10.9	9.7				2.3	4.1
			.4	3.3				-5.6	-4.0
Sales/Net Fixed Assets			75.1	108.7				39.1	41.1
			31.8	28.0				27.0	29.9
			7.8	3.3				10.6	6.3
Sales/Total Assets			3.2	1.5				3.5	3.3
			2.7	1.2				2.6	2.5
			1.7	.9				1.4	1.2
% Depr., Dep., Amort./Sales			.4	.6				.8	.7
			(15) 1.4	(10) 2.3				(18) 1.4	(16) 1.2
			2.6	4.5				2.4	4.3
% Officers', Directors' Owners' Comp/Sales									
Net Sales ($)	17436M	44396M	219297M	483152M	295870M	935161M		720046M	625900M
Total Assets ($)	1134M	8316M	82426M	388608M	387207M	944036M		759488M	480803M

M = $ thousand   MM = $ million
See Pages 11 through 21 for Explanation of Ratios and Data

Comparative Historical Data				Current Data Sorted by Sales					
			Type of Statement						
9	17	17	Unqualified			1	2	6	8
	1	5	Reviewed		1		1	1	2
2	3	5	Compiled	1			3	1	
2	3	4	Tax Returns				1	1	
6	13	21	Other		2	3	5	4	9
4/1/04-3/31/05 ALL	4/1/05-3/31/06 ALL	4/1/06-3/31/07 ALL		0-1MM	16 (4/1-9/30/06) 1-3MM	3-5MM	5-10MM	36 (10/1/06-3/31/07) 10-25MM	25MM & OVER
19	34	52	NUMBER OF STATEMENTS	1	3	4	12	13	19
%	%	%	ASSETS	%	%	%	%	%	%
19.3	20.1	23.6	Cash & Equivalents				22.9	27.8	23.4
31.6	32.5	30.2	Trade Receivables (net)				35.5	29.2	25.4
.6	.8	.5	Inventory				.4	.1	1.0
3.8	8.6	7.7	All Other Current				17.6	9.5	3.4
55.3	62.0	62.0	Total Current				76.3	66.6	53.2
20.5	20.7	20.2	Fixed Assets (net)				13.5	14.5	25.2
6.4	7.5	8.1	Intangibles (net)				2.2	2.7	12.9
17.9	9.8	9.7	All Other Non-Current				8.0	16.2	8.7
100.0	100.0	100.0	Total				100.0	100.0	100.0
			LIABILITIES						
15.3	3.5	14.4	Notes Payable-Short Term				18.4	2.6	.2
1.4	1.0	1.2	Cur. Mat.-L.T.D.				.4	1.4	1.9
10.7	8.5	8.6	Trade Payables				7.6	7.5	7.7
.0	.0	.1	Income Taxes Payable				.0	.1	.3
24.8	17.8	25.3	All Other Current				18.4	26.4	20.1
52.2	30.9	49.6	Total Current				44.9	38.0	30.2
13.7	11.7	11.7	Long-Term Debt				4.4	9.5	16.3
.0	.0	.2	Deferred Taxes				.1	.0	.4
4.3	5.0	5.4	All Other Non-Current				5.3	4.4	8.2
29.8	52.3	33.1	Net Worth				45.5	48.0	44.9
100.0	100.0	100.0	Total Liabilties & Net Worth				100.0	100.0	100.0
			INCOME DATA						
100.0	100.0	100.0	Net Sales				100.0	100.0	100.0
			Gross Profit						
93.0	96.2	92.4	Operating Expenses				93.6	94.3	92.3
7.0	3.8	7.6	Operating Profit				6.4	5.7	7.7
.6	-.1	.4	All Other Expenses (net)				.6	-1.4	.8
6.3	4.0	7.2	Profit Before Taxes				5.8	7.1	6.9
			RATIOS						
2.9	3.6	2.6	Current				7.5	4.0	2.4
1.6	1.9	1.8					2.2	1.7	2.0
1.0	1.4	1.0					.8	1.1	.9
2.2	2.9	2.4	Quick				7.2	3.4	2.0
1.3	1.6	1.3					1.6	1.2	1.8
.8	1.2	.9					.7	1.0	.8
7 49.9	22 16.4	18 20.2	Sales/Receivables				4 83.4	7 49.0	39 9.4
55 6.7	58 6.3	53 6.9					40 9.2	46 8.0	64 5.7
92 4.0	91 4.0	75 4.9					98 3.7	67 5.4	70 5.2
			Cost of Sales/Inventory						
			Cost of Sales/Payables						
4.3	3.8	3.6	Sales/Working Capital				1.8	3.3	4.1
6.5	6.7	8.3					10.9	6.5	7.9
-999.8	20.0	-134.7					NM	110.8	-100.3
28.3	52.4	26.7	EBIT/Interest					34.0	98.6
(18) 4.2	(25) 10.8	(43) 6.8						(11) 8.9	(15) 16.0
-.8	1.1	1.1						.8	1.4
			Net Profit + Depr., Dep., Amort./Cur. Mat. L/T/D						
.2	.1	.1	Fixed/Worth				.0	.0	.1
.5	.3	.4					.2	.4	.6
1.2	.7	2.7					1.9	.9	4.5
.6	.5	.5	Debt/Worth				.3	.3	.7
2.1	1.0	.9					1.4	.7	1.0
4.4	3.0	9.1					4.1	3.9	9.2
34.4	100.0	49.5	% Profit Before Taxes/Tangible Net Worth				46.3	49.6	87.8
(15) 12.7	(31) 21.5	(42) 15.2				(11) 15.1		(11) 21.8	(16) 12.6
2.3	1.3	2.2					7.2	5.7	-.7
13.6	27.4	19.3	% Profit Before Taxes/Total Assets				22.8	31.9	16.2
6.6	10.0	6.9					9.3	6.0	8.2
-2.0	.2	.2					2.1	1.6	.2
56.8	47.5	102.6	Sales/Net Fixed Assets				87.6	101.5	43.0
19.2	23.4	24.1					32.8	46.9	4.9
1.8	3.4	4.2					19.6	8.8	2.3
4.9	2.8	3.2	Sales/Total Assets				3.8	3.1	1.6
2.2	1.7	1.7					2.7	2.0	1.2
.6	1.0	1.1					1.2	1.2	.8
1.2	1.0	.6	% Depr., Dep., Amort./Sales				.4	.2	2.8
(14) 2.0	(26) 1.5	(40) 2.3				(10) .8		(11) 1.5	(15) 3.7
3.8	3.4	4.3					2.6	2.5	6.2
		3.8	% Officers', Directors' Owners' Comp/Sales						
	(16)	8.7							
		28.3							
759442M	1414289M	1995312M	Net Sales ($)	969M	6134M	14501M	94085M	223086M	1656537M
754168M	1340232M	1811727M	Total Assets ($)	410M	2851M	7771M	75707M	192280M	1532708M

M = $ thousand   MM = $ million
See Pages 11 through 21 for Explanation of Ratios and Data

Current Data Sorted by Assets   Comparative Historical Data

Type of Statement	0-500M	500M-2MM	2-10MM	10-50MM	50-100MM	100-250MM		4/1/02-3/31/03 ALL	4/1/03-3/31/04 ALL
Unqualified		1	15	10		5		17	24
Reviewed	5	14	45	12				76	79
Compiled	10	36	20	4				62	98
Tax Returns	37	24	9	2				54	57
Other	21	53	57	22	3	3		104	123
		61 (4/1-9/30/06)		347 (10/1/06-3/31/07)					
NUMBER OF STATEMENTS	73	128	146	50	3	8		313	381
	%	%	%	%	%	%		%	%
ASSETS									
Cash & Equivalents	24.4	11.8	12.6	17.5				16.7	16.0
Trade Receivables (net)	31.0	49.7	51.8	53.7				45.5	46.8
Inventory	1.4	3.5	4.5	2.8				2.9	2.9
All Other Current	7.2	4.0	3.4	5.4				4.4	4.8
Total Current	63.9	69.1	72.3	79.3				69.6	70.4
Fixed Assets (net)	20.9	17.0	15.4	8.3				18.1	14.7
Intangibles (net)	4.5	4.1	5.7	8.2				3.9	4.4
All Other Non-Current	10.7	9.8	6.6	4.2				8.4	10.4
Total	100.0	100.0	100.0	100.0				100.0	100.0
LIABILITIES									
Notes Payable-Short Term	26.3	12.4	8.5	3.7				12.6	14.2
Cur. Mat.-L.T.D.	11.0	2.7	2.0	.9				4.5	3.1
Trade Payables	20.5	29.2	36.1	31.1				32.5	32.7
Income Taxes Payable	.2	.5	.5	.4				.5	.4
All Other Current	25.9	13.5	18.3	30.2				22.2	19.2
Total Current	83.8	58.3	65.4	66.3				72.3	69.7
Long-Term Debt	23.3	11.1	9.0	3.1				11.2	8.5
Deferred Taxes	.1	.5	.2	.1				.6	.3
All Other Non-Current	11.7	4.9	5.7	5.4				3.8	4.7
Net Worth	-19.0	25.2	19.8	25.1				12.1	16.7
Total Liabilities & Net Worth	100.0	100.0	100.0	100.0				100.0	100.0
INCOME DATA									
Net Sales	100.0	100.0	100.0	100.0				100.0	100.0
Gross Profit									
Operating Expenses	95.6	95.0	94.5	94.6				96.6	96.2
Operating Profit	4.4	5.0	5.5	5.4				3.4	3.8
All Other Expenses (net)	1.4	1.1	1.9	-.1				.9	1.0
Profit Before Taxes	3.0	3.9	3.6	5.5				2.6	2.9
RATIOS									
Current	2.2	2.0	1.6	1.4				1.6	1.6
	1.1	1.2	1.1	1.1				1.1	1.1
	.4	.9	.9	.9				.8	.8
Quick	1.8	1.7	1.5	1.2				1.4	1.4
	1.0	1.0 (145)	1.0	1.0				1.0	1.0
	.4	.8	.8	.8				.7	.7
Sales/Receivables	0 UND	30 12.1	38 9.5	45 8.0				28 13.0	29 12.6
	18 20.8	46 8.0	56 6.5	68 5.4				47 7.8	52 7.0
	44 8.3	63 5.8	92 4.0	100 3.7				71 5.2	76 4.8
Cost of Sales/Inventory									
Cost of Sales/Payables									
Sales/Working Capital	16.9	14.1	12.2	10.4				14.1	13.0
	143.8	46.2	38.1	36.5				88.8	93.0
	-19.6	-32.7	-37.5	-53.9				-32.1	-24.8
EBIT/Interest	13.2	18.3	24.2	109.8				16.8	19.3
	(53) 2.1	(107) 4.4	(117) 7.4	(38) 16.3				(257) 4.3	(304) 4.8
	-1.9	1.1	2.1	5.4				.3	-.7
Net Profit + Depr., Dep., Amort./Cur. Mat. L/T/D			8.9					7.7	8.5
		(34) 2.8						(50) 2.0	(52) 3.7
			.4					.4	.7
Fixed/Worth	.1	.2	.3	.1				.3	.2
	1.4	.7	.8	.5				.8	.6
	-.4	2.8	90.5	2.3				-11.8	46.8
Debt/Worth	1.7	.9	1.6	2.3				1.6	1.7
	33.0	3.2	5.7	5.9				4.6	4.9
	-2.2	22.7	NM	20.5				-57.4	-42.9
% Profit Before Taxes/Tangible Net Worth	183.3	112.8	87.2	94.4				77.6	87.5
	(39) 51.3	(102) 34.6	(110) 38.0	(40) 54.7				(228) 27.7	(282) 27.5
	7.1	7.9	11.5	19.3				3.6	2.5
% Profit Before Taxes/Total Assets	42.1	24.0	17.7	17.4				17.0	16.4
	12.5	7.3	7.6	7.1				5.2	4.5
	-11.1	1.4	1.3	2.1				-.5	-1.1
Sales/Net Fixed Assets	227.4	86.7	75.8	143.0				74.7	97.9
	73.5	33.0	31.8	43.2				34.0	39.5
	23.8	17.3	15.3	25.4				13.7	17.6
Sales/Total Assets	9.0	5.3	4.1	4.3				5.1	5.1
	5.9	3.9	2.9	2.9				3.7	3.5
	3.4	2.6	2.1	1.9				2.4	2.2
% Depr., Dep., Amort./Sales	.4	.5	.4	.4				.6	.5
	(41) .7	(100) .9	(122) 1.0	(42) .7				(260) 1.2	(299) 1.1
	1.8	1.7	1.9	1.5				2.4	2.3
% Officers', Directors' Owners' Comp/Sales	6.1	3.3	1.9					3.1	2.8
	(42) 8.8	(66) 5.4	(49) 3.6					(141) 6.1	(150) 7.4
	14.1	10.7	9.0					11.0	12.9
Net Sales ($)	117419M	629521M	2229313M	2851048M	576894M	947959M		7297368M	10158644M
Total Assets ($)	16274M	147203M	679789M	989366M	196407M	1262140M		1914921M	3183787M

M = $ thousand   MM = $ million
See Pages 11 through 21 for Explanation of Ratios and Data

Comparative Historical Data | Current Data Sorted by Sales

Hist 4/1/04-3/31/05	Hist 4/1/05-3/31/06	Hist 4/1/06-3/31/07	Type of Statement	0-1MM	1-3MM	3-5MM	5-10MM	10-25MM	25MM & OVER
32	20	31	Unqualified			2	4	10	15
72	57	76	Reviewed	3	6	5	16	28	18
74	58	70	Compiled	7	14	16	15	13	5
74	56	72	Tax Returns	21	23	9	14	2	3
125	159	159	Other	10	33	16	29	41	30
ALL	ALL	ALL		61 (4/1-9/30/06)			347 (10/1/06-3/31/07)		
377	350	408	**NUMBER OF STATEMENTS**	41	76	48	78	94	71
%	%	%	**ASSETS**	%	%	%	%	%	%
18.1	15.4	14.9	Cash & Equivalents	23.3	14.1	10.0	14.0	13.5	17.0
45.1	45.9	47.2	Trade Receivables (net)	24.4	41.1	52.2	48.4	56.3	50.5
3.5	4.1	3.6	Inventory	1.2	2.7	4.2	3.0	5.5	3.6
4.0	4.5	4.5	All Other Current	8.8	4.6	3.4	5.2	3.1	3.6
70.8	69.8	70.2	Total Current	57.6	62.5	69.7	70.5	78.4	74.8
16.6	16.1	15.8	Fixed Assets (net)	30.6	19.3	15.4	16.8	11.2	8.8
4.4	5.0	5.9	Intangibles (net)	6.0	5.9	3.3	4.6	4.3	11.4
8.3	9.0	8.1	All Other Non-Current	5.7	12.4	11.6	8.1	6.1	5.0
100.0	100.0	100.0	Total	100.0	100.0	100.0	100.0	100.0	100.0
			LIABILITIES						
13.4	11.0	12.1	Notes Payable-Short Term	20.7	20.4	15.3	10.3	7.7	4.2
3.5	2.3	3.7	Cur. Mat.-L.T.D.	7.8	7.5	4.0	2.7	1.3	1.0
30.8	29.2	30.3	Trade Payables	13.4	25.0	32.1	31.1	36.5	35.6
.4	.6	.4	Income Taxes Payable	.4	.1	.6	.4	.7	.2
18.5	19.1	19.8	All Other Current	15.1	22.1	15.0	19.0	16.9	27.9
66.6	62.1	66.3	Total Current	57.5	75.1	67.1	63.6	63.0	68.9
13.9	9.8	11.8	Long-Term Debt	40.1	11.8	10.9	10.4	5.4	6.0
.3	.2	.3	Deferred Taxes	.1	.1	1.0	.2	.3	.1
6.7	9.0	6.6	All Other Non-Current	5.0	14.4	1.8	4.4	4.9	7.1
12.5	18.8	15.0	Net Worth	-2.7	-1.4	19.2	21.5	26.5	17.8
100.0	100.0	100.0	Total Liabilties & Net Worth	100.0	100.0	100.0	100.0	100.0	100.0
			INCOME DATA						
100.0	100.0	100.0	Net Sales	100.0	100.0	100.0	100.0	100.0	100.0
			Gross Profit						
95.1	94.1	94.6	Operating Expenses	88.3	96.3	95.3	95.7	94.8	94.7
4.9	5.9	5.4	Operating Profit	11.7	3.7	4.7	4.3	5.2	5.3
.9	.9	1.3	All Other Expenses (net)	7.9	1.1	.7	.5	.3	.6
4.0	5.0	4.0	Profit Before Taxes	3.8	2.6	4.1	3.7	4.9	4.7
			RATIOS						
1.7	1.8	1.7		3.0	1.5	1.5	1.6	1.9	1.3
1.2	1.1	1.1	Current	1.2	1.0	1.1	1.1	1.2	1.1
.9	.8	.8		.6	.6	.8	.9	.9	.9
1.6	1.6	1.5		2.6	1.4	1.5	1.5	1.7	1.2
1.1	1.0 (407)	1.0	Quick	1.2 (75)	.9	1.0	1.0	1.1	1.0
.7	.7	.7		.5	.4	.7	.7	.8	.8
29 12.8	29 12.4	30 12.2		0 UND	18 20.4	34 10.7	33 11.2	39 9.5	35 10.5
46 8.0	48 7.6	48 7.6	Sales/Receivables	4 95.8	43 8.4	54 6.7	54 6.8	55 6.7	50 7.2
72 5.1	74 5.0	73 5.0		49 7.5	60 6.1	82 4.5	78 4.7	85 4.3	73 5.0
			Cost of Sales/Inventory						
			Cost of Sales/Payables						
11.9	10.7	13.6		8.0	15.4	11.3	16.6	10.1	18.7
46.0	36.7	50.4	Sales/Working Capital	44.8	-343.9	48.3	33.5	34.3	81.3
-31.5	-37.2	-31.5		-9.1	-19.1	-31.0	-43.9	-69.0	-37.2
23.8	34.6	23.4		3.0	8.4	22.1	22.0	49.1	51.6
(296) 7.1	(272) 8.8	(323) 5.5	EBIT/Interest	(23) 1.0	(66) 2.6	(42) 6.0	(68) 8.5	(71) 11.3	(53) 9.8
1.6	1.6	1.3		-1.8	-2.8	2.5	1.1	2.9	2.3
19.6	11.2	7.6					10.2	5.8	10.5
(45) 4.3	(54) 3.5	(51) 2.6	Net Profit + Depr., Dep., Amort./Cur. Mat. L/T/D			(12) 6.1	(21) 2.1	(14) 3.1	
1.4	1.3	1.1				.0	.6	1.2	
.2	.2	.2		.0	.3	.2	.2	.2	.2
.5	.6	.8	Fixed/Worth	2.3	1.2	.8	.6	.5	.8
5.7	5.8	-47.3		-.6	-.6	NM	3.7	3.7	-8.7
1.4	1.6	1.5		1.3	1.5	1.2	1.4	1.1	3.7
4.7	4.4	5.7	Debt/Worth	33.0	6.7	3.8	4.2	5.0	6.0
271.3	71.3	-59.3		-3.1	-3.9	NM	68.2	29.5	-145.5
89.3	100.7	98.9		46.7	151.1	104.1	135.1	94.9	95.1
(286) 40.8	(271) 51.9	(296) 45.0	% Profit Before Taxes/Tangible Net Worth	(23) 14.5	(49) 50.9	(36) 34.2	(61) 34.2	(76) 49.0	(51) 57.9
9.2	16.2	11.5		.0	7.7	7.6	13.0	17.2	18.1
21.0	24.1	23.2		30.2	27.5	23.3	23.9	23.5	16.3
8.1	9.2	7.3	% Profit Before Taxes/Total Assets	1.6	5.9	9.2	7.3	10.3	6.0
.5	1.6	.8		-4.6	-15.4	2.1	.2	2.1	2.1
106.2	87.2	93.4		UND	112.7	73.1	76.0	85.7	149.1
40.0	37.7	36.7	Sales/Net Fixed Assets	47.6	31.2	33.8	31.3	44.5	46.2
15.3	15.1	17.8		8.6	14.4	16.4	15.4	25.5	26.2
4.9	4.9	5.1		6.1	5.9	4.7	5.4	4.8	4.8
3.5	3.4	3.5	Sales/Total Assets	3.3	3.1	3.6	3.6	3.4	3.7
2.2	2.2	2.4		1.5	2.3	2.4	2.5	2.6	2.3
.4	.5	.4		1.5	.4	.5	.5	.3	.3
(278) 1.1	(275) 1.0	(313) .9	% Depr., Dep., Amort./Sales	(21) 3.0	(58) .7	(39) 1.0	(59) 1.0	(80) .8	(56) .7
2.1	1.9	1.8		13.9	1.8	2.1	1.7	1.3	1.4
3.2	3.4	3.0		6.3	5.5	3.2	3.2	2.1	.5
(143) 6.4	(152) 6.6	(167) 6.1	% Officers', Directors' Owners' Comp/Sales	(21) 13.3	(37) 7.5	(31) 5.3	(34) 5.3	(30) 3.4	(14) 1.8
11.8	11.6	11.4		18.6	11.0	13.7	9.6	6.9	3.4
6387069M	6795109M	7352154M	Net Sales ($)	21539M	159625M	181498M	558024M	1512716M	4918752M
2142470M	2400901M	3291179M	Total Assets ($)	17852M	58549M	68649M	207995M	532977M	2405157M

© RMA 2007   M = $ thousand   MM = $ million
See Pages 11 through 21 for Explanation of Ratios and Data

Current Data Sorted by Assets | Comparative Historical Data

						Type of Statement		
	2	12	2		5	Unqualified	11	6
	6	7	2			Reviewed	8	11
1	6	3	1		1	Compiled	18	20
7	3	2				Tax Returns	8	8
6	12	11	3	1		Other	25	24
	18 (4/1-9/30/06)		75 (10/1/06-3/31/07)				4/1/02-3/31/03	4/1/03-3/31/04
0-500M	500M-2MM	2-10MM	10-50MM	50-100MM	100-250MM		ALL	ALL
14	29	35	8	1	6	NUMBER OF STATEMENTS	70	69
%	%	%	%	%	%	ASSETS	%	%
27.0	16.6	14.7				Cash & Equivalents	15.0	13.7
8.7	52.1	51.0				Trade Receivables (net)	45.5	47.2
.0	.7	4.8				Inventory	2.8	2.9
3.2	3.5	4.7				All Other Current	4.7	3.4
39.0	72.9	75.2				Total Current	67.9	67.2
35.2	14.8	11.5				Fixed Assets (net)	18.7	20.3
7.5	2.7	2.5				Intangibles (net)	4.7	2.9
18.3	9.5	10.8				All Other Non-Current	8.6	9.6
100.0	100.0	100.0				Total	100.0	100.0
						LIABILITIES		
19.2	18.0	12.1				Notes Payable-Short Term	10.7	20.2
20.3	3.1	1.6				Cur. Mat.-L.T.D.	3.5	2.6
2.6	13.2	20.2				Trade Payables	18.8	16.5
.0	.9	.9				Income Taxes Payable	.8	1.5
15.9	17.7	17.0				All Other Current	24.8	22.0
58.1	52.8	51.8				Total Current	58.6	62.8
43.8	9.9	4.8				Long-Term Debt	11.2	12.8
.0	.6	.7				Deferred Taxes	.5	.4
13.8	14.1	8.9				All Other Non-Current	7.0	6.9
-15.6	22.7	33.8				Net Worth	22.7	17.1
100.0	100.0	100.0				Total Liabilties & Net Worth	100.0	100.0
						INCOME DATA		
100.0	100.0	100.0				Net Sales	100.0	100.0
						Gross Profit		
91.2	93.7	95.2				Operating Expenses	96.2	94.2
8.8	6.3	4.8				Operating Profit	3.8	5.8
.2	.5	.0				All Other Expenses (net)	1.0	1.6
8.7	5.8	4.8				Profit Before Taxes	2.8	4.2
						RATIOS		
2.7	2.7	2.2				Current	2.1	1.8
1.2	1.5	1.5					1.4	1.3
.4	1.1	1.0					.9	.9
2.4	2.7	1.9				Quick	1.8	1.8
.7	1.4	1.3					1.2	1.1
.3	1.1	.8					.8	.7
0 UND	37 9.9	43 8.6				Sales/Receivables	28 12.9	30 12.1
0 UND	53 6.9	68 5.4					51 7.1	55 6.6
3 113.5	83 4.4	81 4.5					73 5.0	77 4.7
						Cost of Sales/Inventory		
						Cost of Sales/Payables		
32.1	4.9	6.8				Sales/Working Capital	8.1	9.1
UND	11.9	12.2					17.6	18.2
-22.2	89.0	-227.8					-76.1	-29.9
21.0	18.4	32.1				EBIT/Interest	15.0	24.8
(11) 8.0	(24) 8.3	(29) 6.7					(50) 4.9	(57) 5.8
1.0	1.8	1.3					.6	1.1
						Net Profit + Depr., Dep., Amort./Cur. Mat. L/T/D	6.2	12.3
							(11) 1.3	(13) 6.2
							-.4	1.5
.3	.2	.1				Fixed/Worth	.2	.1
.8	.5	.2					.5	.5
-.2	2.2	1.8					6.0	5.5
.1	1.0	.8				Debt/Worth	1.2	1.1
2.9	2.0	2.0					2.5	2.3
-1.8	10.9	12.0					22.6	87.1
	81.0	89.9				% Profit Before Taxes/Tangible Net Worth	57.6	69.4
	(24) 34.6	(29) 43.8					(58) 16.8	(53) 22.4
	1.8	12.3					-2.6	4.5
142.6	38.2	25.4				% Profit Before Taxes/Total Assets	19.9	22.0
79.6	8.7	8.0					3.7	7.5
7.5	.4	.7					-2.1	.3
189.3	76.8	81.6				Sales/Net Fixed Assets	70.5	60.2
46.2	28.8	42.5					27.8	35.1
16.1	14.4	29.1					12.3	14.1
26.7	3.9	4.0				Sales/Total Assets	4.4	4.8
14.5	3.1	2.7					3.2	3.1
6.0	2.0	2.1					2.3	2.4
	.5	.5				% Depr., Dep., Amort./Sales	.7	.8
	(22) 1.2	(31) .9					(55) 1.3	(51) 1.4
	1.7	1.5					2.2	2.3
						% Officers', Directors' Owners' Comp/Sales	5.8	5.6
							(34) 12.0	(34) 10.0
							21.4	20.7
39199M	122513M	582507M	317528M	40375M	1926829M	Net Sales ($)	998349M	2072571M
3184M	36897M	172336M	161834M	62618M	1057011M	Total Assets ($)	424373M	657913M

M = $ thousand   MM = $ million

See Pages 11 through 21 for Explanation of Ratios and Data

Comparative Historical Data | Current Data Sorted by Sales

Periods: 18 (4/1-9/30/06) and 75 (10/1/06-3/31/07)

	4/1/04-3/31/05 ALL	4/1/05-3/31/06 ALL	4/1/06-3/31/07 ALL	0-1MM	1-3MM	3-5MM	5-10MM	10-25MM	25MM & OVER
Type of Statement									
Unqualified	10	8	21		2	2	1	6	10
Reviewed	13	9	15		4	3	4	3	1
Compiled	12	18	12		1	3	3	4	1
Tax Returns	8	16	12		3	4	5		
Other	33	33	33	3	7	7	4	5	7
NUMBER OF STATEMENTS	76	84	93	3	17	19	17	18	19
	%	%	%	%	%	%	%	%	%
ASSETS									
Cash & Equivalents	11.0	20.8	18.8		19.7	18.6	18.7	10.4	24.5
Trade Receivables (net)	41.2	42.6	40.8		24.5	46.1	41.7	53.1	38.9
Inventory	2.5	1.3	2.5		.9	.4	5.1	4.4	2.1
All Other Current	5.8	3.4	4.8		3.3	4.0	5.9	8.3	3.5
Total Current	60.5	68.1	66.9		48.3	69.1	71.4	76.2	69.0
Fixed Assets (net)	20.6	19.9	17.4		34.3	14.7	9.3	13.9	14.0
Intangibles (net)	5.7	4.0	4.3		5.8	2.2	5.2	2.0	6.7
All Other Non-Current	13.1	7.9	11.5		11.6	14.0	14.0	7.8	10.3
Total	100.0	100.0	100.0		100.0	100.0	100.0	100.0	100.0
LIABILITIES									
Notes Payable-Short Term	14.1	19.7	13.2		28.8	12.1	11.5	10.5	4.3
Cur. Mat.-L.T.D.	4.2	4.0	6.1		16.3	4.4	.7	2.5	7.4
Trade Payables	13.5	11.0	13.9		3.1	12.4	13.4	25.4	15.3
Income Taxes Payable	1.0	1.1	.7		1.0	.1	1.0	.9	.8
All Other Current	15.8	20.4	19.1		15.1	21.5	15.7	18.0	26.5
Total Current	48.6	56.2	52.9		64.4	50.5	42.3	57.4	54.2
Long-Term Debt	18.2	9.9	12.8		45.9	8.0	3.3	6.4	4.2
Deferred Taxes	.0	.1	.6		.1	.0	.9	1.2	.6
All Other Non-Current	7.3	7.2	11.4		6.1	23.8	6.2	8.0	12.3
Net Worth	26.0	26.6	22.3		-16.5	17.7	47.3	27.0	28.6
Total Liabilties & Net Worth	100.0	100.0	100.0		100.0	100.0	100.0	100.0	100.0
INCOME DATA									
Net Sales	100.0	100.0	100.0		100.0	100.0	100.0	100.0	100.0
Gross Profit									
Operating Expenses	93.6	93.0	93.2		96.0	94.0	92.4	91.6	92.9
Operating Profit	6.4	7.0	6.8		4.0	6.0	7.6	8.4	7.1
All Other Expenses (net)	1.3	1.7	1.0		1.9	.6	-.1	.0	2.7
Profit Before Taxes	5.0	5.3	5.7		2.2	5.4	7.7	8.4	4.4
RATIOS									
Current	2.7	2.4	2.3		3.3	1.7	3.4	1.9	2.7
	1.3	1.5	1.5		1.2	1.5	1.5	1.3	1.3
	.9	.9	.9		.3	1.0	1.3	.9	.9
Quick	2.4	2.3	1.9		2.8	1.6	3.2	1.8	2.7
	1.2	1.4	1.3		.7	1.4	1.4	1.1	1.1
	.7	.7	.8		.2	1.0	.9	.7	.8
Sales/Receivables	24 15.0	15 24.1	31 11.6	0 UND	45 8.1	21 17.6	42 8.7	35 10.3	
	53 6.8	47 7.7	53 6.9	12 31.4	68 5.4	53 6.9	68 5.4	43 8.6	
	76 4.8	73 5.0	79 4.6	71 5.1	81 4.5	81 4.5	84 4.4	65 5.6	
Cost of Sales/Inventory									
Cost of Sales/Payables									
Sales/Working Capital	6.0	7.5	6.8		4.6	9.3	7.6	6.6	7.6
	20.3	18.0	12.8		471.8	11.6	19.9	12.4	13.2
	-179.5	-76.5	-158.6		-10.2	150.7	255.1	-49.0	-136.1
EBIT/Interest	36.4	32.8	28.5		13.3	13.7	46.9	42.9	47.1
	(62) 6.5	(63) 7.0	(75) 7.8		(14) 7.9	(14) 9.2	(13) 3.3	(16) 8.7	(16) 29.6
	2.2	2.0	1.2		.1	2.7	1.1	3.2	-3.1
Net Profit + Depr., Dep., Amort./Cur. Mat. L/T/D	27.2	18.2	28.1						
	(12) 3.4	(11) 1.6	(17) 2.9						
	-.1	1.1	.5						
Fixed/Worth	.2	.1	.1		.3	.1	.1	.1	.2
	.5	.5	.4		1.4	.4	.1	.6	.4
	1.7	3.4	2.6		-.2	1.6	.6	2.4	-.3
Debt/Worth	.7	.7	.8		.7	.9	.3	1.9	.5
	2.1	1.9	2.0		1.2	2.5	1.1	2.6	2.0
	10.4	17.2	13.6		-2.1	11.6	2.9	16.2	-5.9
% Profit Before Taxes/Tangible Net Worth	84.3	99.6	88.8		95.4	76.4	94.5	155.8	76.1
	(66) 19.1	(70) 41.5	(73) 43.8		(11) 7.3	(15) 24.9	(15) 44.0	(16) 62.6	(13) 56.4
	3.6	1.1	9.3		-16.0	7.5	3.0	17.8	20.6
% Profit Before Taxes/Total Assets	22.2	34.4	39.3		92.8	43.9	46.3	23.5	21.5
	8.9	8.6	10.0		8.7	7.2	19.4	12.0	9.9
	1.2	.1	.5		-6.4	1.9	.4	5.5	-7.0
Sales/Net Fixed Assets	62.0	78.0	80.4		79.9	79.3	195.2	63.0	57.1
	29.2	33.2	36.4		14.9	42.8	81.6	36.6	28.2
	14.2	15.7	16.2		7.1	20.9	28.8	23.9	18.4
Sales/Total Assets	4.9	5.4	4.6		9.7	3.9	6.0	3.7	4.7
	3.1	3.5	2.7		2.3	3.1	3.5	2.6	3.1
	2.1	2.3	1.8		1.5	2.4	2.0	2.0	1.6
% Depr., Dep., Amort./Sales	1.0	.7	.5		.9	.5	.4	.5	.7
	(51) 1.4	(66) 1.2	(75) 1.1		(12) 1.8	(15) 1.1	(12) .7	(17) .9	(18) 1.3
	2.3	2.1	2.1		2.9	1.4	1.1	2.2	2.4
% Officers', Directors' Owners' Comp/Sales	8.4	6.3	6.0						
	(28) 12.6	(40) 9.1	(28) 14.7						
	24.4	16.8	23.3						
Net Sales ($)	5027346M	3411858M	3028951M	2604M	35458M	72856M	131932M	257997M	2528104M
Total Assets ($)	708650M	808127M	1493880M	1153M	29354M	26284M	42979M	107839M	1286271M

M = $ thousand   MM = $ million
See Pages 11 through 21 for Explanation of Ratios and Data

Current Data Sorted by Assets | Comparative Historical Data

	0-500M	500M-2MM 6 (4/1-9/30/06)	2-10MM	10-50MM 5 (10/1/06-3/31/07)	50-100MM	100-250MM		4/1/02-3/31/03 ALL	4/1/03-3/31/04 ALL
Type of Statement									
Unqualified		1	3	3	1	2		3	4
Reviewed		2	4	2				10	8
Compiled	2	3	2					15	11
Tax Returns	5	2	7					5	13
Other	5	8	14	5		1		14	17
NUMBER OF STATEMENTS	12	16	30	10	1	3		47	53
	%	%	%	%	%	%		%	%
ASSETS									
Cash & Equivalents	7.4	5.9	7.5	4.1				7.8	7.3
Trade Receivables (net)	16.2	17.9	31.5	18.6				21.8	21.9
Inventory	9.2	9.0	7.7	14.5				5.1	5.9
All Other Current	.2	3.8	4.2	2.3				3.4	3.6
Total Current	33.1	36.6	50.9	39.5				38.0	38.6
Fixed Assets (net)	49.3	42.3	40.0	36.0				48.2	47.6
Intangibles (net)	3.6	6.5	3.6	13.9				4.4	6.7
All Other Non-Current	14.0	14.7	5.5	10.6				9.4	7.1
Total	100.0	100.0	100.0	100.0				100.0	100.0
LIABILITIES									
Notes Payable-Short Term	15.3	9.6	8.9	15.0				5.3	9.8
Cur. Mat.-L.T.D.	5.0	6.9	7.9	6.9				6.9	5.7
Trade Payables	9.1	10.8	11.7	6.9				11.9	10.8
Income Taxes Payable	.0	.0	.0	.1				.0	.2
All Other Current	9.9	4.1	12.9	12.9				10.9	11.2
Total Current	39.3	31.4	41.5	41.9				35.0	37.7
Long-Term Debt	32.5	22.2	38.5	20.8				31.4	31.0
Deferred Taxes	.0	.0	.0	.7				.0	.1
All Other Non-Current	7.7	4.2	9.3	4.8				5.1	18.3
Net Worth	20.5	42.1	10.7	31.8				28.4	12.8
Total Liabilities & Net Worth	100.0	100.0	100.0	100.0				100.0	100.0
INCOME DATA									
Net Sales	100.0	100.0	100.0	100.0				100.0	100.0
Gross Profit									
Operating Expenses	75.3	83.1	87.5	86.8				86.3	92.8
Operating Profit	24.7	16.9	12.5	13.2				13.7	7.2
All Other Expenses (net)	11.8	2.4	4.4	2.2				4.3	4.1
Profit Before Taxes	12.9	14.6	8.1	11.1				9.4	3.1
RATIOS									
Current	1.1	2.4	1.9	1.3				2.0	1.8
	.7	1.3	1.3	1.2				1.0	1.0
	.1	.7	.9	.6				.5	.6
Quick	1.0	1.5	1.6	1.0				1.6	1.4
	.6	.9	1.1	.6				.8	.9
	.1	.3	.4	.4				.5	.4
Sales/Receivables	0 UND	0 UND	31 11.7	33 11.2				21 17.1	19 19.1
	4 94.2	22 16.7	55 6.6	39 9.4				41 9.0	37 9.8
	29 12.7	47 7.8	72 5.1	61 6.0				53 6.9	54 6.8
Cost of Sales/Inventory									
Cost of Sales/Payables									
Sales/Working Capital	NM	8.5	9.0	16.5				8.0	11.1
	-44.2	24.3	27.3	27.0				227.7	UND
	-8.9	-19.3	-42.6	-12.6				-15.2	-13.4
EBIT/Interest		27.3	10.9	6.8				6.8	8.9
		(14) 9.4	(27) 4.6	4.3				(40) 2.9	(45) 3.3
		1.9	1.3	1.6				1.1	.4
Net Profit + Depr., Dep., Amort./Cur. Mat. L/T/D									
Fixed/Worth	.7	.3	.2	.8				.4	.8
	3.1	.8	1.9	1.9				1.3	2.4
	-3.3	2.2	-30.2	NM				23.1	-5.9
Debt/Worth	.7	.7	1.2	1.3				.9	1.2
	3.4	1.1	3.3	3.9				2.1	4.7
	-4.4	2.3	-57.2	NM				254.0	-11.5
% Profit Before Taxes/Tangible Net Worth		69.7	81.5					32.3	50.8
		(13) 38.5	(21) 40.4					(36) 14.3	(35) 26.6
		14.5	22.7					-.4	6.9
% Profit Before Taxes/Total Assets	50.4	24.7	20.2	19.7				15.3	14.3
	26.4	13.7	10.1	6.7				6.4	6.1
	1.4	7.2	.7	2.8				.1	-2.4
Sales/Net Fixed Assets	56.9	20.9	56.1	61.2				14.3	18.4
	8.7	5.2	7.0	5.7				2.6	4.7
	.8	.9	.9	.9				.9	.8
Sales/Total Assets	4.1	3.4	3.0	2.6				3.4	3.3
	1.9	1.8	2.0	.9				1.2	1.9
	.8	.8	.7	.5				.6	.7
% Depr., Dep., Amort./Sales		.6	.6					2.3	2.0
		(10) 6.7	(24) 2.0					(40) 5.1	(48) 7.2
		14.4	11.1					14.7	15.2
% Officers', Directors' Owners' Comp/Sales			2.7					3.7	6.2
			(13) 3.6					(16) 9.6	(20) 9.9
			5.0					12.5	15.8
Net Sales ($)	8023M	49329M	268776M	287680M	146934M	730901M		320380M	257741M
Total Assets ($)	3356M	19416M	136655M	166217M	56383M	607207M		344187M	194285M

© RMA 2007

M = $ thousand   MM = $ million
See Pages 11 through 21 for Explanation of Ratios and Data

Comparative Historical Data | Current Data Sorted by Sales

4/1/04-3/31/05 ALL	4/1/05-3/31/06 ALL	4/1/06-3/31/07 ALL	Type of Statement	0-1MM	1-3MM	3-5MM	5-10MM	10-25MM	25MM & OVER
					6 (4/1-9/30/06)			66 (10/1/06-3/31/07)	
4	4	10	Unqualified				3	1	6
11	11	8	Reviewed		1		2	4	1
11	8	7	Compiled	3	1	1	2		
10	12	14	Tax Returns	7	3	2		2	
20	18	33	Other	7	8	3		8	2
56	53	72	**NUMBER OF STATEMENTS**	17	13	6	12	15	9
%	%	%	**ASSETS**	%	%	%	%	%	%
8.9	8.6	7.0	Cash & Equivalents	4.7	6.1		6.2	9.1	
26.2	27.2	23.9	Trade Receivables (net)	7.8	12.3		29.4	44.5	
7.2	8.6	8.9	Inventory	1.8	8.4		10.8	13.4	
4.3	2.5	3.0	All Other Current	.8	6.8		.8	4.6	
46.6	46.9	42.9	Total Current	15.1	33.6		47.2	71.6	
40.1	37.6	40.7	Fixed Assets (net)	71.5	37.5		41.1	18.2	
4.6	5.9	6.9	Intangibles (net)	1.4	12.1		3.7	6.6	
8.7	9.6	9.6	All Other Non-Current	12.0	16.8		8.0	3.7	
100.0	100.0	100.0	Total	100.0	100.0		100.0	100.0	
			LIABILITIES						
12.5	20.0	11.2	Notes Payable-Short Term	8.9	13.0		6.2	12.1	
5.8	4.4	6.7	Cur. Mat.-L.T.D.	5.4	8.4		12.3	3.3	
12.8	14.8	10.5	Trade Payables	4.2	4.5		16.5	17.5	
.1	.0	.0	Income Taxes Payable	.0	.0		.1	.0	
17.0	13.2	10.3	All Other Current	6.3	10.0		7.1	16.7	
48.1	52.4	38.7	Total Current	24.9	36.0		42.2	49.6	
24.1	24.1	31.6	Long-Term Debt	43.3	25.1		21.8	20.7	
.1	.2	.1	Deferred Taxes	.0	.0		.6	.0	
5.7	9.1	6.9	All Other Non-Current	1.8	5.3		6.6	14.6	
21.9	14.2	22.6	Net Worth	30.1	33.6		28.8	15.1	
100.0	100.0	100.0	Total Liabilties & Net Worth	100.0	100.0		100.0	100.0	
			INCOME DATA						
100.0	100.0	100.0	Net Sales	100.0	100.0		100.0	100.0	
			Gross Profit						
90.5	90.8	84.3	Operating Expenses	70.6	84.3		92.0	92.3	
9.5	9.2	15.7	Operating Profit	29.4	15.7		8.0	7.7	
1.7	2.1	4.8	All Other Expenses (net)	13.7	1.9		3.2	1.2	
7.8	7.1	10.9	Profit Before Taxes	15.7	13.9		4.8	6.5	
			RATIOS						
1.6	1.4	1.7	Current	1.2	1.9		1.9	1.9	
1.0	1.0	1.2		.7	.9		1.3	1.4	
.7	.5	.7		.1	.6		1.0	1.1	
1.1	1.3	1.3	Quick	1.2	1.4		1.5	1.5	
.8	.7	.9		.5	.7		1.0	1.2	
.4	.4	.4		.1	.1		.8	.7	
7 52.5	20 18.2	17 22.0	Sales/Receivables	0 UND	0 UND		30 12.3	46 7.9	
43 8.5	39 9.3	38 9.7		0 UND	17 21.1		40 9.0	58 6.3	
71 5.2	69 5.3	62 5.9		30 12.1	60 6.1		67 5.5	73 5.0	
			Cost of Sales/Inventory						
			Cost of Sales/Payables						
9.3	16.6	10.3	Sales/Working Capital	47.3	9.3		10.3	8.0	
200.3	199.5	37.0		-26.4	-64.0		22.8	17.0	
-12.7	-7.8	-22.8		-2.4	-12.2		100.3	27.9	
9.5	15.4	12.2	EBIT/Interest	13.0	15.2		10.9	16.7	
(47) 3.0	(48) 3.7	(61) 5.0		(10) 6.7	(11) 6.4		(11) 4.4	(14) 7.5	
.4	1.2	1.6		-.9	3.7		1.5	3.4	
			Net Profit + Depr., Dep., Amort./Cur. Mat. L/T/D						
.4	.3	.5	Fixed/Worth	1.0	.7		.1	.1	
1.6	1.2	1.4		1.9	1.4		1.5	.3	
11.2	NM	-38.7		-5.2	5.3		NM	1.4	
1.1	1.5	1.0	Debt/Worth	.5	1.0		1.0	.8	
4.2	4.0	2.8		1.1	1.7		3.4	1.6	
NM	-10.2	-61.8		-6.8	17.4		NM	25.3	
77.3	93.2	81.8	% Profit Before Taxes/Tangible Net Worth	65.0	83.2			68.4	
(42) 27.2	(37) 33.9	(52) 41.3		(11) 42.9	(11) 38.5			(12) 38.2	
9.4	11.3	15.3		3.5	15.0			20.6	
19.1	17.6	24.7	% Profit Before Taxes/Total Assets	33.8	21.8		12.6	28.3	
6.9	7.0	10.2		12.6	13.1		7.7	17.6	
.4	.4	2.5		-3.7	6.7		1.3	4.8	
29.6	39.9	43.9	Sales/Net Fixed Assets	2.6	26.5		100.1	59.4	
4.8	7.7	5.6		.7	5.3		6.8	52.3	
1.0	1.2	1.0		.3	.7		.8	8.0	
2.9	3.5	2.8	Sales/Total Assets	1.6	2.3		3.1	3.6	
1.7	1.6	1.7		.7	1.3		2.1	2.7	
.8	.7	.7		.2	.6		.6	1.8	
2.2	1.0	.7	% Depr., Dep., Amort./Sales	5.1			.4	.4	
(47) 7.9	(43) 3.7	(53) 4.6		(11) 12.6			(11) 4.8	(11) .7	
13.5	11.7	12.1		20.0			15.5	1.9	
4.5	3.5	2.7	% Officers', Directors' Owners' Comp/Sales						
(23) 8.5	(21) 5.7	(21) 4.0							
12.2	8.8	6.3							
453722M	580102M	1491643M	Net Sales ($)	7286M	22514M	23487M	83727M	220219M	1134410M
277712M	375265M	989234M	Total Assets ($)	15776M	29746M	14897M	65544M	114185M	749086M

M = $ thousand   MM = $ million
See Pages 11 through 21 for Explanation of Ratios and Data

Current Data Sorted by Assets | Comparative Historical Data

0-500M	500M-2MM	2-10MM	10-50MM	50-100MM	100-250MM		ALL 4/1/02-3/31/03	ALL 4/1/03-3/31/04
		5	10	1	1	**Type of Statement**		
1	5	12	2			Unqualified	26	18
1	7	10	2			Reviewed	31	27
5	4	2				Compiled	20	35
5	10	10	17	2	1	Tax Returns	14	14
	14 (4/1-9/30/06)		99 (10/1/06-3/31/07)			Other	47	43
12	26	39	31	3	2	**NUMBER OF STATEMENTS**	138	137
%	%	%	%	%	%	**ASSETS**	%	%
15.1	11.0	9.5	14.3			Cash & Equivalents	18.6	15.0
30.5	49.8	36.5	40.9			Trade Receivables (net)	35.2	36.2
.4	2.9	4.9	4.5			Inventory	3.6	3.6
11.4	1.7	3.5	3.6			All Other Current	2.2	2.8
57.4	65.5	54.5	63.2			Total Current	59.5	57.6
26.7	20.5	36.0	20.9			Fixed Assets (net)	27.4	26.1
6.3	3.1	3.6	8.7			Intangibles (net)	5.0	7.2
9.5	10.8	5.8	7.1			All Other Non-Current	8.0	9.1
100.0	100.0	100.0	100.0			Total	100.0	100.0
						LIABILITIES		
14.1	11.8	7.9	5.5			Notes Payable-Short Term	8.6	11.4
12.8	2.9	5.9	3.0			Cur. Mat.-L.T.D.	6.1	4.6
12.3	17.7	17.7	24.2			Trade Payables	19.6	20.0
.0	.0	.0	.3			Income Taxes Payable	.2	.8
17.9	17.0	17.5	21.9			All Other Current	19.3	19.3
57.1	49.5	49.0	54.9			Total Current	53.7	56.0
44.1	10.6	18.2	13.7			Long-Term Debt	16.2	18.2
.0	.2	.7	.1			Deferred Taxes	.2	.3
17.6	.9	1.6	2.7			All Other Non-Current	6.8	7.5
-18.7	38.9	30.5	28.7			Net Worth	23.1	18.0
100.0	100.0	100.0	100.0			Total Liabilities & Net Worth	100.0	100.0
						INCOME DATA		
100.0	100.0	100.0	100.0			Net Sales	100.0	100.0
						Gross Profit		
97.0	93.1	91.8	96.8			Operating Expenses	96.5	95.0
3.0	6.9	8.2	3.2			Operating Profit	3.5	5.0
1.5	.4	2.4	.2			All Other Expenses (net)	1.8	1.2
1.5	6.5	5.8	3.0			Profit Before Taxes	1.7	3.8
						RATIOS		
1.7	1.8	1.5	1.5				1.9	1.6
1.0	1.3	1.1	1.2			Current	1.1	1.0
.7	1.0	.7	.9				.8	.8
1.3	1.7	1.3	1.4				1.7	1.5
.8	1.1	.8	1.0			Quick	1.0	.9
.6	.9	.6	.8				.7	.7
0 UND	41 8.9	30 12.1	36 10.2				31 11.9	24 15.2
21 17.4	53 6.9	50 7.2	59 6.2			Sales/Receivables	47 7.8	46 8.0
40 9.0	68 5.4	72 5.1	75 4.9				61 5.9	66 5.5
						Cost of Sales/Inventory		
						Cost of Sales/Payables		
33.8	11.6	13.7	10.5				8.8	13.3
NM	23.4	111.2	37.2			Sales/Working Capital	45.2	102.8
-18.9	-474.2	-20.9	-33.2				-22.7	-25.8
21.1	14.9	17.6	19.9				14.8	16.7
(11) 3.1	(24) 3.9	(34) 5.4	(27) 5.0			EBIT/Interest	(121) 3.5	(119) 3.3
-1.1	.7	1.1	1.4				1.1	.4
			12.8				4.0	3.4
			(12) 3.7			Net Profit + Depr., Dep., Amort./Cur. Mat. L/T/D	(35) 1.4	(32) 1.4
			1.7				.5	.7
.9	.2	.7	.5				.4	.3
-1.7	.5	1.4	1.1			Fixed/Worth	1.0	1.2
-.3	1.0	3.2	-145.3				5.5	-9.3
1.2	1.1	.8	1.7				1.1	1.2
-6.4	2.0	3.0	4.3			Debt/Worth	3.5	4.2
-2.0	3.6	7.3	-195.6				20.3	-34.4
	82.9	75.4	85.5				63.0	78.4
	(24) 36.8	(33) 50.9	(23) 40.1			% Profit Before Taxes/Tangible Net Worth	(110) 20.5	(100) 27.6
	1.7	2.8	4.4				2.3	5.5
66.1	32.3	35.3	16.7				16.0	22.4
10.1	10.1	8.7	8.2			% Profit Before Taxes/Total Assets	4.1	7.1
-16.7	.4	.9	.9				-4.1	-.2
52.0	47.0	15.4	27.6				20.1	34.1
19.7	26.2	7.9	13.2			Sales/Net Fixed Assets	10.9	14.0
11.5	12.4	4.4	6.5				6.0	7.2
8.8	4.4	3.7	3.4				4.0	4.3
5.3	3.7	2.9	2.3			Sales/Total Assets	2.4	2.7
3.4	2.2	1.9	1.7				1.9	2.0
	.8	1.4	.8				1.4	1.0
	(20) 2.1	(37) 2.4	(29) 1.7			% Depr., Dep., Amort./Sales	(122) 3.4	(118) 2.4
	2.9	4.8	3.6				5.8	4.1
	2.1	1.9					2.7	3.3
	(11) 5.3	(19) 3.4				% Officers', Directors' Owners' Comp/Sales	(62) 4.8	(52) 6.3
	12.8	6.4					8.6	10.5
20215M	121169M	516746M	1801571M	211698M	255786M	Net Sales ($)	2586025M	2450920M
3057M	31853M	179159M	671164M	200378M	300624M	Total Assets ($)	1243681M	1197720M

M = $ thousand   MM = $ million
See Pages 11 through 21 for Explanation of Ratios and Data

Comparative Historical Data

Current Data Sorted by Sales

	4/1/04-3/31/05 ALL	4/1/05-3/31/06 ALL	4/1/06-3/31/07 ALL	Type of Statement	0-1MM	1-3MM	3-5MM	5-10MM	10-25MM	25MM & OVER
	15	9	17	Unqualified	1		3	4	4	9
	27	19	20	Reviewed		3	1	7	7	2
	14	11	20	Compiled		4		6	7	3
	13	12	11	Tax Returns	2		2	1	1	1
	31	34	45	Other	3	7	2	12	2	19
						14 (4/1-9/30/06)			99 (10/1/06-3/31/07)	
100		85	113	**NUMBER OF STATEMENTS**	6	14	8	30	21	34
	%	%	%	**ASSETS**	%	%	%	%	%	%
	13.6	13.5	11.7	Cash & Equivalents		13.2		8.3	13.5	13.3
	37.1	37.2	39.0	Trade Receivables (net)		44.0		42.1	40.1	35.0
	3.3	5.2	3.7	Inventory		1.1		4.5	3.9	4.6
	4.6	5.2	3.9	All Other Current		11.1		2.6	2.6	3.7
	58.6	61.1	58.4	Total Current		69.4		57.5	60.0	56.5
	26.2	27.0	27.1	Fixed Assets (net)		23.1		30.5	27.8	25.4
	5.1	4.4	6.8	Intangibles (net)		2.5		4.4	6.3	11.1
	10.1	7.4	7.7	All Other Non-Current		5.0		7.5	5.8	7.0
	100.0	100.0	100.0	Total		100.0		100.0	100.0	100.0
				LIABILITIES						
	11.0	10.1	8.5	Notes Payable-Short Term		6.7		8.9	8.5	4.6
	4.4	5.0	5.1	Cur. Mat.-L.T.D.		7.2		4.7	5.9	3.5
	18.1	16.7	18.6	Trade Payables		13.7		18.1	21.2	20.8
	.3	.2	.1	Income Taxes Payable		.1		.0	.0	.3
	20.5	19.1	19.2	All Other Current		16.9		19.6	20.0	21.5
	54.3	51.0	51.5	Total Current		44.5		51.2	55.7	50.8
	21.5	15.4	18.6	Long-Term Debt		18.6		15.3	15.7	16.6
	.4	.4	.3	Deferred Taxes		.3		.7	.2	.1
	6.9	6.3	3.4	All Other Non-Current		15.8		1.6	1.7	2.0
	16.7	27.0	26.3	Net Worth		20.8		31.2	26.7	30.5
	100.0	100.0	100.0	Total Liabilities & Net Worth		100.0		100.0	100.0	100.0
				INCOME DATA						
	100.0	100.0	100.0	Net Sales		100.0		100.0	100.0	100.0
				Gross Profit						
	93.8	92.8	94.0	Operating Expenses		88.8		97.2	94.0	94.2
	6.2	7.2	6.0	Operating Profit		11.2		2.8	6.0	5.8
	1.7	1.3	1.3	All Other Expenses (net)		.6		.5	.5	.8
	4.5	5.9	4.7	Profit Before Taxes		10.6		2.3	5.5	5.0
				RATIOS						
	1.8	1.9	1.5	Current		3.3		1.5	1.5	1.5
	1.0	1.2	1.1			1.6		1.1	1.1	1.2
	.8	.8	.9			.9		.7	.9	.9
	1.6	1.7	1.3	Quick		3.2		1.4	1.4	1.3
	.9	1.0	1.0			1.2		.9	.9	1.0
	.6	.6	.7			.8		.6	.8	.7
28 / 13.2		28 / 13.1	26 / 13.9	Sales/Receivables		21 / 17.8		37 / 9.9	31 / 11.9	24 / 15.1
50 / 7.3		44 / 8.2	50 / 7.2			48 / 7.7		60 / 6.1	48 / 7.6	49 / 7.4
68 / 5.4		71 / 5.2	68 / 5.4			59 / 6.1		79 / 4.6	66 / 5.5	61 / 6.0
				Cost of Sales/Inventory						
				Cost of Sales/Payables						
	10.3	10.7	13.7	Sales/Working Capital		7.0		17.6	13.7	11.8
	120.0	27.1	82.8			20.2		83.7	97.1	63.7
	-24.7	-35.2	-26.1			-57.9		-16.7	-29.7	-39.1
	28.5	17.2	16.3	EBIT/Interest		40.1		12.2	22.5	18.1
(88)	4.6	(77) 6.6	(101) 4.6		(12)	9.8	(26)	2.8 (19)	7.0 (32)	5.2
	1.6	2.7	1.1			1.0		.4	2.3	2.1
	5.3	6.1	8.2	Net Profit + Depr., Dep., Amort./Cur. Mat. L/T/D						9.5
(28)	2.1	(20) 2.5	(27) 3.3						(15)	3.3
	.9	1.3	1.5							1.6
	.3	.3	.5	Fixed/Worth		.1		.5	.7	.6
	1.3	1.3	1.1			.7		1.0	2.1	1.1
	16.1	8.3	8.1			-2.1		2.9	NM	-109.9
	1.2	1.4	1.2	Debt/Worth		.6		.9	2.3	1.2
	3.6	4.0	3.1			1.6		2.9	5.4	3.0
	41.6	25.0	36.6			-6.3		5.9	NM	-152.3
	85.7	104.7	83.8	% Profit Before Taxes/Tangible Net Worth		116.4		74.4	86.9	88.8
(76)	35.3	(72) 50.9	(86) 42.7		(10)	71.1	(26)	34.4 (16)	51.8 (25)	45.9
	8.7	18.1	3.7			23.3		-4.4	26.3	15.9
	24.5	27.8	27.2	% Profit Before Taxes/Total Assets		59.5		17.4	36.7	20.9
	5.7	11.6	8.4			27.0		3.6	10.2	11.1
	.9	4.4	.8			2.6		-2.5	2.4	3.1
	44.1	37.3	31.5	Sales/Net Fixed Assets		49.5		26.2	39.9	25.8
	16.4	14.6	13.6			19.7		7.7	11.4	11.7
	6.0	6.4	6.2			9.9		4.6	5.6	8.1
	4.3	3.8	4.2	Sales/Total Assets		7.0		4.0	4.6	3.7
	2.8	2.9	3.0			4.0		2.7	3.3	3.0
	1.9	2.1	1.8			1.8		1.7	2.0	1.8
	1.0	.7	1.2	% Depr., Dep., Amort./Sales		.9		1.4	.7	1.3
(86)	2.3	(72) 1.9	(97) 2.3		(10)	2.2	(29)	2.8 (19)	1.9 (32)	2.4
	4.6	4.1	4.2			3.2		4.8	4.6	3.7
	1.9	1.4	1.8	% Officers', Directors' Owners' Comp/Sales				2.2		
(35)	5.9	(34) 5.1	(43) 4.8				(16)	5.5		
	10.7	9.1	8.1					9.2		
1642873M		1539863M	2927185M	Net Sales ($)	2548M	28432M	28925M	212713M	339193M	2315374M
791426M		737029M	1386235M	Total Assets ($)	3721M	9451M	8317M	114388M	123803M	1126555M

M = $ thousand   MM = $ million
See Pages 11 through 21 for Explanation of Ratios and Data

Current Data Sorted by Assets / Comparative Historical Data

Type of Statement	0-500M	500M-2MM	2-10MM	10-50MM	50-100MM	100-250MM		4/1/02-3/31/03 ALL	4/1/03-3/31/04 ALL
Unqualified			5	7				14	11
Reviewed		4	5	2				9	11
Compiled		2	4	1				9	23
Tax Returns		4	10	5				12	12
Other		3						20	27
Period label		8 (4/1-9/30/06)		45 (10/1/06-3/31/07)					
NUMBER OF STATEMENTS	1	13	24	15				64	84

(Columns 50-100MM and 100-250MM: DATA NOT AVAILABLE)

	0-500M %	500M-2MM %	2-10MM %	10-50MM %	50-100MM %	100-250MM %		ALL %	ALL %
ASSETS									
Cash & Equivalents		18.5	13.7	16.7				14.2	13.9
Trade Receivables (net)		28.5	27.9	36.7				33.3	36.3
Inventory		7.2	10.8	12.4				6.2	5.4
All Other Current		1.4	8.6	5.5				9.2	5.8
Total Current		55.8	61.0	71.3				62.9	61.5
Fixed Assets (net)		33.4	21.8	12.8				23.0	23.1
Intangibles (net)		1.1	9.1	10.0				5.8	5.1
All Other Non-Current		9.8	8.1	6.0				8.2	10.3
Total		100.0	100.0	100.0				100.0	100.0
LIABILITIES									
Notes Payable-Short Term		14.0	6.9	5.2				24.1	18.1
Cur. Mat.-L.T.D.		3.1	3.6	4.7				9.0	6.9
Trade Payables		14.2	16.0	20.7				17.7	20.6
Income Taxes Payable		.4	.5	.0				.3	.2
All Other Current		13.8	19.2	20.2				16.7	24.6
Total Current		45.5	46.2	50.7				67.9	70.5
Long-Term Debt		16.1	12.6	10.4				15.3	16.1
Deferred Taxes		.4	.5	.0				.1	.1
All Other Non-Current		.3	3.6	12.6				6.5	7.1
Net Worth		37.7	37.1	26.3				10.3	6.2
Total Liabilties & Net Worth		100.0	100.0	100.0				100.0	100.0
INCOME DATA									
Net Sales		100.0	100.0	100.0				100.0	100.0
Gross Profit									
Operating Expenses		95.6	89.6	92.7				95.4	96.8
Operating Profit		4.4	10.4	7.3				4.6	3.2
All Other Expenses (net)		.5	1.7	1.6				1.7	1.1
Profit Before Taxes		3.9	8.8	5.6				2.8	2.0

RATIOS

Ratio	0-500M	500M-2MM	2-10MM	10-50MM	50-100MM	100-250MM		ALL	ALL
Current		5.2	2.5	2.3				1.7	2.1
		1.3	1.1	1.5				1.1	1.2
		.8	.8	.8				.7	.8
Quick		4.5	2.0	2.0				1.3	1.7
		.8	.9	.9				.8	1.0
		.6	.5	.5				.5	.6
Sales/Receivables	0 UND		9 39.7	22 16.4				17 22.0	29 12.8
	26 13.8		34 10.6	42 8.7				44 8.3	44 8.3
	54 6.8		61 5.9	78 4.7				65 5.6	62 5.9
Cost of Sales/Inventory									
Cost of Sales/Payables									
Sales/Working Capital		11.3	6.8	5.1				11.9	8.3
		89.9	34.6	13.0				49.8	28.0
		-20.1	-29.6	-23.2				-19.6	-32.9
EBIT/Interest			16.3	32.4				18.2	11.7
		(19) 4.1		(13) 6.0				(58) 5.1	(64) 3.5
			1.4	-.5				1.5	-2.6
Net Profit + Depr., Dep., Amort./Cur. Mat. L/T/D								10.0	6.5
								(13) 2.0	(13) 3.3
								.7	.4
Fixed/Worth		.3	.2	.1				.3	.2
		.7	.7	.5				1.2	.7
		29.9	1.8	-.5				-4.4	-2.8
Debt/Worth		.5	.8	.5				1.1	1.0
		1.7	2.0	2.6				7.8	3.5
		32.9	17.2	-3.6				-13.4	-17.6
% Profit Before Taxes/Tangible Net Worth		88.9	127.1	66.1				90.6	71.7
	(11) 24.5		(19) 19.6	(10) 38.7				(47) 43.6	(58) 28.1
		12.8	7.6	18.3				9.6	.5
% Profit Before Taxes/Total Assets		36.0	27.8	26.7				19.9	15.8
		10.0	8.4	14.9				9.6	5.0
		-3.7	2.2	.2				1.4	-6.4
Sales/Net Fixed Assets		22.7	70.8	74.9				46.1	75.8
		20.5	18.1	29.9				23.3	22.3
		8.7	7.7	10.4				9.6	8.5
Sales/Total Assets		4.7	3.8	3.9				5.5	4.4
		4.3	2.5	2.4				3.4	2.9
		2.8	1.7	1.8				1.8	1.7
% Depr., Dep., Amort./Sales		.9	.4	.4				.6	.6
	(12) 2.0		(20) 1.3	(11) .6				(54) 2.1	(65) 1.8
		5.7	2.8	3.3				4.2	3.5
% Officers', Directors' Owners' Comp/Sales								3.2	3.2
								(25) 5.1	(32) 5.1
								9.3	12.8
Net Sales ($)	969M	86334M	345098M	819550M				2958499M	2086754M
Total Assets ($)	101M	17026M	130246M	308415M				1136651M	882390M

© RMA 2007

M = $ thousand   MM = $ million
See Pages 11 through 21 for Explanation of Ratios and Data

Comparative Historical Data | Current Data Sorted by Sales

			Type of Statement						
4	10	12	Unqualified				1	2	7
9	8	11	Reviewed				1	4	2
9	8	7	Compiled			1	1	4	1
7	12	4	Tax Returns	1		1	2	2	1
29	32	19	Other	1	2	2	2	1	6
4/1/04-	4/1/05-	4/1/06-		1			2	1	
3/31/05	3/31/06	3/31/07			8 (4/1-9/30/06)		45 (10/1/06-3/31/07)		
ALL	ALL	ALL		0-1MM	1-3MM	3-5MM	5-10MM	10-25MM	25MM & OVER
58	70	53	NUMBER OF STATEMENTS	3	2	5	12	15	16
%	%	%	ASSETS	%	%	%	%	%	%
12.5	13.2	15.9	Cash & Equivalents				17.2	18.1	15.8
36.0	43.7	31.1	Trade Receivables (net)				25.0	37.4	34.1
7.3	5.9	10.2	Inventory				10.3	18.3	7.4
5.0	5.0	5.8	All Other Current				10.0	4.5	7.1
60.8	67.9	63.1	Total Current				62.5	78.3	64.4
22.5	19.1	22.0	Fixed Assets (net)				23.0	12.1	20.8
8.5	6.0	7.2	Intangibles (net)				4.4	1.9	8.4
8.2	7.0	7.7	All Other Non-Current				10.1	7.7	6.4
100.0	100.0	100.0	Total				100.0	100.0	100.0
			LIABILITIES						
7.9	9.4	8.0	Notes Payable-Short Term				5.0	10.7	3.7
3.8	2.4	3.8	Cur. Mat.-L.T.D.				1.9	1.4	4.2
21.9	18.1	16.9	Trade Payables				23.0	16.5	19.0
.2	.2	.4	Income Taxes Payable				.4	.6	.3
18.8	17.2	19.0	All Other Current				22.8	16.2	18.9
52.7	47.4	48.1	Total Current				53.1	45.4	46.1
18.3	16.1	14.4	Long-Term Debt				8.7	9.6	16.2
.2	.3	.4	Deferred Taxes				.6	.7	.0
5.5	3.5	5.3	All Other Non-Current				.0	2.9	13.5
23.3	32.7	31.9	Net Worth				37.6	41.4	24.2
100.0	100.0	100.0	Total Liabilities & Net Worth				100.0	100.0	100.0
			INCOME DATA						
100.0	100.0	100.0	Net Sales				100.0	100.0	100.0
			Gross Profit						
93.2	93.6	91.9	Operating Expenses				98.5	91.1	92.4
6.8	6.4	8.1	Operating Profit				1.5	8.9	7.6
1.5	1.4	1.4	All Other Expenses (net)				.3	.6	1.3
5.3	4.9	6.8	Profit Before Taxes				1.2	8.3	6.3
			RATIOS						
1.8	2.6	2.5					2.0	5.4	2.7
1.3	1.4	1.3	Current				.9	1.4	1.6
.9	1.0	.8					.7	1.1	.9
1.4	2.4	2.1					1.6	2.8	2.2
1.0	1.1	.9	Quick				.6	1.1	1.3
.7	.8	.5					.5	.5	.7
18 20.3	30 12.0	16 22.4				8 47.2	25 14.4	14 26.2	
45 8.2	53 6.9	36 10.3	Sales/Receivables			25 14.8	56 6.6	34 10.7	
61 6.0	73 5.0	58 6.3				45 8.1	79 4.6	64 5.7	
			Cost of Sales/Inventory						
			Cost of Sales/Payables						
8.7	6.5	6.9					10.6	4.4	8.5
23.1	14.8	34.5	Sales/Working Capital				-78.1	7.0	23.4
-80.7	UND	-24.7					-25.6	46.7	-30.0
24.1	22.5	20.7					33.8	32.2	
(46) 5.9	(56) 6.1	(41) 5.0	EBIT/Interest			(12) 3.6	(14) 17.7		
1.5	2.1	1.2					.6	3.9	
14.6	6.1								
(12) 4.5	(14) 3.7		Net Profit + Depr., Dep.,						
3.5	1.2		Amort./Cur. Mat. L/T/D						
.2	.2	.2					.3	.1	.2
.7	.6	.7	Fixed/Worth				.7	.2	.9
-7.3	2.0	NM					-1.4	.7	-.5
1.3	.9	.7					.5	.5	.6
2.4	2.3	2.3	Debt/Worth				1.3	1.7	2.1
-352.5	13.6	NM					-13.2	5.7	-5.5
80.0	63.8	82.9	% Profit Before Taxes/Tangible					62.7	119.3
(43) 34.1	(57) 30.6	(40) 27.9	Net Worth				(14) 28.4	(11) 59.8	
11.8	6.1	12.4						5.2	29.4
22.6	21.6	28.5	% Profit Before Taxes/Total				11.8	20.2	43.3
8.6	9.7	9.3	Assets				4.5	9.3	19.2
2.3	1.6	1.3					1.3	2.0	1.3
94.6	82.6	60.7					22.8	48.8	74.7
26.9	24.5	22.2	Sales/Net Fixed Assets				21.2	30.4	31.3
10.2	9.3	9.0					8.1	10.4	10.4
4.8	3.9	4.3					4.5	2.5	4.7
3.0	2.9	2.6	Sales/Total Assets				3.8	2.4	3.7
1.9	2.2	1.8					2.7	1.6	2.3
.5	.5	.5					.7	.5	.3
(45) 1.6	(56) 1.3	(43) 1.3	% Depr., Dep., Amort./Sales			(11) 1.1	(12) 1.4	(13) .7	
2.9	3.1	3.1					1.7	3.1	2.8
2.6	3.0	2.3							
(25) 3.8	(23) 4.9	(14) 3.4	% Officers', Directors'						
8.0	8.1	6.3	Owners' Comp/Sales						
1074057M	1929407M	1251951M	Net Sales ($)	2524M	4532M	22757M	87725M	234464M	899949M
460726M	561008M	455788M	Total Assets ($)	6898M	1712M	19658M	26923M	128121M	272476M

M = $ thousand   MM = $ million
See Pages 11 through 21 for Explanation of Ratios and Data

Current Data Sorted by Assets   Comparative Historical Data

Type of Statement	0-500M	500M-2MM	2-10MM	10-50MM	50-100MM	100-250MM		4/1/02-3/31/03 ALL	4/1/03-3/31/04 ALL
Unqualified			4	4	1			6	3
Reviewed		2	6	1				9	12
Compiled	3	7	3	2				16	16
Tax Returns	7	12						8	7
Other	8	9	18	11	4	1		14	19
	0-500M	14 (4/1-9/30/06) 500M-2MM	2-10MM	89 (10/1/06-3/31/07) 10-50MM	50-100MM	100-250MM			
NUMBER OF STATEMENTS	18	30	31	18	5	1		53	57
ASSETS	%	%	%	%	%	%		%	%
Cash & Equivalents	31.7	14.6	11.3	18.6				15.3	8.3
Trade Receivables (net)	31.7	38.5	40.2	32.6				35.6	42.2
Inventory	7.1	11.7	15.4	8.2				23.0	20.5
All Other Current	2.0	4.5	3.3	9.6				1.9	1.1
Total Current	72.5	69.4	70.2	69.1				75.8	72.1
Fixed Assets (net)	24.7	15.3	14.4	15.6				15.5	18.1
Intangibles (net)	.8	7.2	6.3	10.8				1.1	3.0
All Other Non-Current	2.0	8.0	9.2	4.5				7.6	6.8
Total	100.0	100.0	100.0	100.0				100.0	100.0
LIABILITIES									
Notes Payable-Short Term	30.4	12.1	14.8	8.2				15.5	19.6
Cur. Mat.-L.T.D.	15.2	2.3	3.4	3.0				3.5	2.9
Trade Payables	23.2	13.6	28.7	16.1				19.1	21.7
Income Taxes Payable	.6	.1	.2	1.4				.6	.2
All Other Current	25.5	16.2	15.5	19.2				10.5	9.6
Total Current	94.9	44.3	62.6	47.9				49.1	54.1
Long-Term Debt	34.7	19.2	11.8	16.2				10.0	14.3
Deferred Taxes	.0	.0	.3	.7				.1	.2
All Other Non-Current	6.9	5.4	4.3	5.6				9.4	4.2
Net Worth	-36.5	31.1	20.9	29.6				31.5	27.1
Total Liabilities & Net Worth	100.0	100.0	100.0	100.0				100.0	100.0
INCOME DATA									
Net Sales	100.0	100.0	100.0	100.0				100.0	100.0
Gross Profit									
Operating Expenses	93.8	88.3	94.9	89.2				94.3	96.5
Operating Profit	6.2	11.7	5.1	10.8				5.7	3.5
All Other Expenses (net)	1.4	1.8	1.4	2.1				1.1	1.3
Profit Before Taxes	4.8	9.9	3.7	8.7				4.6	2.2
RATIOS									
Current	2.3	3.9	1.7	2.2				3.7	2.1
	1.5	1.5	1.1	1.4				1.8	1.4
	.6	.8	.9	1.1				1.1	1.1
Quick	2.0	2.1	1.1	1.5				2.0	1.4
	1.2	1.2	.8	1.2				1.2	1.0
	.3	.7	.6	.6				.6	.7
Sales/Receivables	0 UND	19 18.8	38 9.6	25 14.6				28 13.3	24 15.3
	23 15.8	37 9.9	49 7.5	50 7.3				34 10.6	48 7.7
	47 7.8	66 5.5	69 5.3	69 5.3				53 6.9	67 5.5
Cost of Sales/Inventory									
Cost of Sales/Payables									
Sales/Working Capital	14.4	6.2	12.3	6.0				4.5	6.8
	23.4	21.6	66.9	15.9				8.7	16.6
	-28.3	-55.8	-25.6	36.2				92.7	89.2
EBIT/Interest	7.0	47.3	10.4	28.2				15.2	7.5
	(14) 1.3	(25) 7.1	(28) 2.9	(14) 5.5				(46) 2.5	(51) 2.7
	-6.3	2.9	1.2	1.9				-.3	1.0
Net Profit + Depr., Dep., Amort./Cur. Mat. L/T/D									
Fixed/Worth	.2	.1	.3	.1				.1	.1
	.7	.3	1.1	.4				.2	.4
	-.4	3.0	-1.1	3.8				2.0	2.7
Debt/Worth	1.4	.6	1.9	1.3				.5	1.2
	3.4	2.7	5.4	3.5				2.1	2.4
	-8.3	15.0	-8.5	34.1				11.8	6.5
% Profit Before Taxes/Tangible Net Worth	252.0	90.0	70.7	94.7				48.9	38.5
	(13) 15.5	(24) 28.9	(21) 17.6	(15) 35.8				(42) 19.4	(48) 10.6
	-4.8	19.2	3.0	17.1				2.5	-.8
% Profit Before Taxes/Total Assets	73.4	40.6	14.9	19.6				20.2	10.6
	3.2	15.0	1.9	9.6				6.3	2.3
	-6.0	4.9	.2	5.5				-.9	-1.9
Sales/Net Fixed Assets	109.4	82.7	90.4	136.7				177.7	98.5
	64.1	43.1	36.4	34.3				44.9	44.2
	36.9	15.1	13.5	10.8				14.3	15.7
Sales/Total Assets	13.8	4.7	3.6	2.9				4.3	4.3
	5.4	3.3	2.8	2.5				3.1	3.3
	3.3	2.6	2.0	1.7				1.9	2.0
% Depr., Dep., Amort./Sales		.4	.8	.5				.4	.3
		(24) 1.1	(25) 1.2	(13) 1.2				(42) .9	(50) .7
		1.8	2.6	5.1				2.6	2.1
% Officers', Directors' Owners' Comp/Sales	5.5	3.5	2.4					1.7	1.7
	(11) 9.7	(14) 5.4	(14) 3.5					(27) 4.4	(28) 3.8
	16.8	8.1	7.5					7.4	6.4
Net Sales ($)	24790M	123765M	412850M	1033082M	908235M	196104M		618630M	670617M
Total Assets ($)	4132M	34852M	146088M	424294M	311066M	196566M		308307M	283946M

M = $ thousand   MM = $ million
See Pages 11 through 21 for Explanation of Ratios and Data

Comparative Historical Data — Current Data Sorted by Sales

04-05	05-06	06-07		0-1MM	1-3MM	3-5MM	5-10MM	10-25MM	25MM & OVER
			Type of Statement						
4	7	9	Unqualified	1		1	1	3	5
9	10	9	Reviewed		7		3	4	1
11	14	15	Compiled			2	1	3	1
9	8	19	Tax Returns	6	3	6	4		
12	24	51	Other	6	4	4	12	9	16
4/1/04-3/31/05 ALL	4/1/05-3/31/06 ALL	4/1/06-3/31/07 ALL		14 (4/1-9/30/06)			89 (10/1/06-3/31/07)		
45	63	103	**NUMBER OF STATEMENTS**	13	14	13	21	19	23
%	%	%	**ASSETS**	%	%	%	%	%	%
14.7	10.7	16.9	Cash & Equivalents	20.0	23.2	23.4	10.9	13.7	15.9
35.5	38.1	37.0	Trade Receivables (net)	30.8	32.7	29.4	43.1	37.3	41.8
19.8	16.4	12.0	Inventory	5.6	6.8	17.3	18.0	9.9	11.8
5.1	3.1	4.6	All Other Current	2.0	2.6	8.4	2.5	2.7	8.7
75.2	68.4	70.6	Total Current	58.4	65.3	78.5	74.5	63.7	78.2
14.9	19.2	16.4	Fixed Assets (net)	28.8	24.1	12.0	11.6	18.6	9.8
2.8	6.3	6.7	Intangibles (net)	4.5	4.4	8.5	2.3	12.5	7.5
7.1	6.1	6.3	All Other Non-Current	8.3	6.2	1.1	11.6	5.2	4.4
100.0	100.0	100.0	Total	100.0	100.0	100.0	100.0	100.0	100.0
			LIABILITIES						
16.9	17.8	15.3	Notes Payable-Short Term	24.8	29.3	11.7	12.9	10.9	9.0
4.9	3.4	5.0	Cur. Mat.-L.T.D.	18.8	4.2	1.5	3.1	4.3	2.0
16.6	19.4	20.3	Trade Payables	24.8	13.3	10.5	22.6	20.3	25.7
.3	.5	.4	Income Taxes Payable	.0	.8	.2	.0	.3	1.1
23.4	14.6	18.2	All Other Current	7.0	23.9	27.7	13.3	18.1	20.3
62.1	55.6	59.3	Total Current	75.5	71.6	51.5	52.0	53.9	58.1
8.6	14.6	18.3	Long-Term Debt	44.4	24.7	12.9	19.5	8.1	9.9
.4	.3	.3	Deferred Taxes	.0	.0	.0	.2	.7	.5
9.1	7.3	5.3	All Other Non-Current	9.7	2.4	9.9	3.2	3.5	5.3
19.8	22.1	16.9	Net Worth	-29.5	1.4	25.7	25.2	33.7	26.2
100.0	100.0	100.0	Total Liabilities & Net Worth	100.0	100.0	100.0	100.0	100.0	100.0
			INCOME DATA						
100.0	100.0	100.0	Net Sales	100.0	100.0	100.0	100.0	100.0	100.0
			Gross Profit						
95.1	95.6	91.6	Operating Expenses	80.5	90.8	93.3	95.2	92.6	93.2
4.9	4.4	8.4	Operating Profit	19.5	9.2	6.7	4.8	7.4	6.8
1.5	1.7	1.6	All Other Expenses (net)	5.6	.4	.7	1.3	.9	1.5
3.3	2.7	6.8	Profit Before Taxes	13.9	8.8	6.0	3.5	6.5	5.3
			RATIOS						
1.7	2.1	2.2	Current	2.2	3.5	5.4	2.9	1.7	2.2
1.4	1.3	1.4		.9	1.5	1.4	1.7	1.1	1.5
1.0	.9	.9		.4	1.0	.8	1.0	.8	1.1
1.4	1.4	1.5	Quick	1.8	3.2	1.8	1.9	1.2	1.3
.9	.9	1.0		.6	1.3	1.1	1.0	.9	1.1
.5	.5	.6		.3	.8	.6	.6	.6	.8
27 13.3	32 11.3	23 16.2	Sales/Receivables	0 UND	0 UND	0 UND	24 15.4	45 8.0	26 14.1
43 8.6	42 8.6	46 8.0		45 8.1	34 10.6	34 10.7	38 9.7	54 6.8	51 7.1
64 5.7	65 5.6	68 5.4		100 3.7	49 7.5	54 6.7	67 5.5	69 5.3	71 5.2
			Cost of Sales/Inventory						
			Cost of Sales/Payables						
9.9	7.9	7.4	Sales/Working Capital	8.9	7.8	6.2	6.7	9.4	6.7
16.5	25.2	23.8		-30.2	20.9	24.8	18.5	59.1	14.5
269.4	-55.7	-63.6		-3.8	NM	-85.2	NM	-23.5	38.4
24.9	13.3	23.0	EBIT/Interest	6.3	9.0		52.3	12.6	49.2
(37) 5.3	(56) 3.9	(87) 4.1		(12) 1.6	(11) 3.2		(20) 3.6	(17) 4.2	(19) 5.7
1.3	1.0	1.5		-4.4	1.4		1.3	1.4	1.9
11.8	9.2	6.1	Net Profit + Depr., Dep., Amort./Cur. Mat. L/T/D						
(13) 3.7	(15) 4.8	(18) 3.3							
1.7	1.6	1.2							
.1	.1	.1	Fixed/Worth	.2	.1	.1	.1	.1	.1
.4	.5	.5		1.2	.6	.3	.5	1.1	.3
13.4	18.9	4.7		-2.0	-3.7	NM	NM	3.4	2.8
1.3	1.1	1.1	Debt/Worth	.9	1.4	.2	.9	1.4	1.3
2.3	3.8	3.0		2.7	3.7	2.6	2.8	4.0	3.0
35.9	-29.9	47.2		-8.5	-8.0	NM	NM	-35.9	11.6
132.5	66.2	87.6	% Profit Before Taxes/Tangible Net Worth		130.2	160.2	219.4	56.2	89.1
(35) 24.4	(45) 23.8	(79) 30.3			(10) 37.2	(10) 57.4	(16) 25.4	(14) 19.4	(20) 46.6
3.0	3.3	12.2			2.8	17.3	6.7	1.4	25.1
30.0	21.1	25.4	% Profit Before Taxes/Total Assets	16.1	73.4	41.5	28.6	18.0	21.4
5.5	5.6	7.5		3.3	20.0	21.8	5.1	7.5	9.6
-.2	.5	1.9		-7.0	2.8	4.9	.9	.3	4.4
133.0	78.6	97.8	Sales/Net Fixed Assets	81.5	108.4	115.5	94.3	60.6	133.0
40.5	29.5	46.6		19.7	49.4	61.8	56.1	20.3	50.1
14.0	13.0	14.7		.7	19.3	27.5	18.9	10.8	14.7
4.5	4.4	4.1	Sales/Total Assets	3.9	6.9	4.9	5.6	3.3	3.7
3.4	2.9	2.9		1.9	4.1	3.8	3.3	2.5	2.7
2.5	1.9	2.1		.3	2.6	2.8	2.2	1.5	2.2
.5	.6	.6	% Depr., Dep., Amort./Sales			.5	.3	1.0	.5
(33) 1.1	(47) 1.1	(74) 1.1				(10) 1.3	(16) .7	(17) 1.2	(16) 1.0
2.5	2.2	2.2				2.0	1.6	3.4	2.2
2.5	3.2	3.0	% Officers', Directors' Owners' Comp/Sales					2.8	
(19) 4.8	(28) 6.3	(41) 4.7						(10) 5.0	
10.4	12.9	8.5						8.7	
1013219M	1512420M	2698826M	Net Sales ($)	5568M	29906M	55425M	142625M	294934M	2170368M
531773M	475983M	1116998M	Total Assets ($)	6343M	7975M	15700M	46236M	169220M	871524M

M = $ thousand   MM = $ million
See Pages 11 through 21 for Explanation of Ratios and Data

Current Data Sorted by Assets   Comparative Historical Data

0-500M	500M-2MM	2-10MM	10-50MM	50-100MM	100-250MM		4/1/02-3/31/03 ALL	4/1/03-3/31/04 ALL
						Type of Statement		
1	3	5	9	2	1	Unqualified	22	22
1	2	4	2			Reviewed	11	6
7	12	5	1			Compiled	8	17
11	2	3				Tax Returns	4	9
7	6	15	3		1	Other	29	29
	13 (4/1-9/30/06)		90 (10/1/06-3/31/07)					
27	25	32	15	2	2	**NUMBER OF STATEMENTS**	74	83
%	%	%	%	%	%	**ASSETS**	%	%
22.2	19.5	16.1	18.7			Cash & Equivalents	17.1	16.6
18.8	44.6	42.8	40.3			Trade Receivables (net)	41.2	39.6
2.6	1.2	.5	4.5			Inventory	2.2	1.3
6.2	2.1	3.4	4.8			All Other Current	3.6	5.6
49.7	67.4	62.8	68.4			Total Current	64.1	63.2
28.6	20.3	19.4	15.6			Fixed Assets (net)	21.5	19.9
3.3	1.3	7.8	6.4			Intangibles (net)	7.0	6.4
18.3	11.0	10.0	9.6			All Other Non-Current	7.3	10.5
100.0	100.0	100.0	100.0			Total	100.0	100.0
						LIABILITIES		
21.8	12.5	10.8	4.8			Notes Payable-Short Term	9.7	11.9
8.6	3.5	1.8	2.4			Cur. Mat.-L.T.D.	3.5	3.4
5.9	17.5	13.5	13.1			Trade Payables	13.2	16.6
.4	.7	.5	.7			Income Taxes Payable	1.0	.3
24.7	15.4	18.6	27.3			All Other Current	21.2	23.8
61.4	49.6	45.2	48.3			Total Current	48.7	56.0
15.1	9.9	7.8	6.9			Long-Term Debt	12.1	9.9
.0	.7	.5	.4			Deferred Taxes	.4	.3
.8	1.6	9.0	15.2			All Other Non-Current	8.1	12.5
22.7	38.3	37.6	29.2			Net Worth	30.7	21.3
100.0	100.0	100.0	100.0			Total Liabilties & Net Worth	100.0	100.0
						INCOME DATA		
100.0	100.0	100.0	100.0			Net Sales	100.0	100.0
						Gross Profit		
91.3	88.7	87.7	93.4			Operating Expenses	95.6	94.4
8.7	11.3	12.3	6.6			Operating Profit	4.4	5.6
-.7	2.2	3.0	1.1			All Other Expenses (net)	.8	1.2
9.4	9.1	9.4	5.5			Profit Before Taxes	3.5	4.5
						RATIOS		
2.8	3.4	2.4	2.3				2.0	1.8
1.2	1.8	1.5	1.5			Current	1.4	1.3
.2	.7	1.0	1.1				1.1	.9
1.9	3.2	2.3	1.9				1.8	1.7
.9	1.8	1.5	1.1			Quick	1.1	1.2
.1	.7	.9	.9				.9	.8
0 UND	19 19.0	39 9.3	37 9.8				38 9.5	31 11.9
0 UND	43 8.4	61 5.9	63 5.8			Sales/Receivables	58 6.3	61 6.0
17 21.1	58 6.3	71 5.1	79 4.6				91 4.0	74 4.9
						Cost of Sales/Inventory		
						Cost of Sales/Payables		
13.7	5.2	7.0	4.5				7.0	8.7
169.1	19.6	15.4	13.0			Sales/Working Capital	16.1	24.7
-10.9	-36.0	130.5	48.8				60.4	-85.5
13.9	33.4	19.5	23.2				22.3	31.7
(14) 3.8	(17) 9.4	(26) 8.7	(12) 7.7			EBIT/Interest	(64) 5.3	(70) 8.2
.7	2.9	1.6	3.4				1.4	1.6
							11.2	15.8
						Net Profit + Depr., Dep., Amort./Cur. Mat. L/T/D	(14) 3.1 (19) 4.2	
							.9	1.3
.0	.2	.1	.3				.3	.2
.9	.4	.4	.4			Fixed/Worth	.6	.6
-12.6	3.5	1.6	1.9				2.4	1.9
.5	.4	.9	.7				1.0	1.1
1.5	1.1	1.4	2.2			Debt/Worth	1.9	1.7
-22.9	14.5	8.2	12.8				7.2	14.6
283.9	226.1	76.8	52.7				51.9	76.0
(19) 88.7	(23) 64.1	(27) 39.1	(12) 23.3			% Profit Before Taxes/Tangible Net Worth	(61) 18.6	(69) 30.6
22.8	31.1	14.9	8.6				2.7	9.9
88.7	37.5	30.3	12.1				16.9	20.7
33.1	24.8	13.5	9.9			% Profit Before Taxes/Total Assets	7.3	10.3
6.0	4.4	3.5	6.2				.7	.6
159.6	69.4	61.4	47.3				42.0	41.2
39.6	20.7	23.2	25.2			Sales/Net Fixed Assets	18.6	21.2
14.9	11.9	9.1	11.2				8.1	11.3
14.8	4.7	3.4	4.0				3.3	3.8
7.5	3.4	2.6	2.5			Sales/Total Assets	2.5	2.6
4.3	2.4	2.0	1.9				1.8	1.9
.5	1.0	.8	.8				1.0	.9
(16) .9	(17) 1.6	(28) 1.4	1.3			% Depr., Dep., Amort./Sales	(62) 1.7	(68) 1.7
1.5	3.7	2.4	3.1				3.2	3.2
10.5	3.4	1.1					3.5	3.1
(12) 17.5	(10) 6.2	(11) 3.5				% Officers', Directors' Owners' Comp/Sales	(21) 5.8	(22) 6.1
26.6	21.6	16.4					19.7	14.1
66537M	134244M	414493M	1206052M	330807M	337858M	Net Sales ($)	2825232M	3025609M
6994M	29744M	140023M	389602M	162377M	315440M	Total Assets ($)	1323344M	1478015M

M = $ thousand   MM = $ million
See Pages 11 through 21 for Explanation of Ratios and Data

Comparative Historical Data — Current Data Sorted by Sales

			Type of Statement						
21	18	21	Unqualified	2	1	1	1	4	12
11	12	9	Reviewed		1		4	3	1
14	21	25	Compiled	2	6	8	6	1	2
20	11	16	Tax Returns	4	5	2	1	3	
35	30	32	Other	4	5	2	7	9	5
4/1/04-3/31/05 ALL	4/1/05-3/31/06 ALL	4/1/06-3/31/07 ALL		0-1MM	13 (4/1-9/30/06) 1-3MM	3-5MM	90 (10/1/06-3/31/07) 5-10MM	10-25MM	25MM & OVER
101	92	103	NUMBER OF STATEMENTS	12	18	13	20	20	20
%	%	%	ASSETS	%	%	%	%	%	%
17.8	14.6	18.7	Cash & Equivalents	24.5	18.5	26.8	14.1	14.7	18.7
35.7	41.3	36.3	Trade Receivables (net)	5.0	30.7	39.8	44.1	46.5	40.0
1.4	2.5	1.8	Inventory	5.9	.0	2.2	.5	2.5	1.2
5.7	3.8	4.1	All Other Current	11.5	3.3	1.0	3.8	1.4	5.4
60.5	62.2	60.9	Total Current	47.0	52.5	69.7	62.5	65.2	65.2
19.7	18.8	21.6	Fixed Assets (net)	37.1	21.8	27.6	16.0	19.0	16.6
8.4	7.0	5.4	Intangibles (net)	.6	1.6	.7	9.7	6.2	9.7
11.3	12.0	12.1	All Other Non-Current	15.3	24.2	2.1	11.8	9.6	8.4
100.0	100.0	100.0	Total	100.0	100.0	100.0	100.0	100.0	100.0
			LIABILITIES						
11.1	14.4	12.9	Notes Payable-Short Term	13.0	20.8	17.9	14.6	8.9	4.6
4.0	2.8	4.2	Cur. Mat.-L.T.D.	.8	9.6	8.4	3.0	1.1	2.6
15.0	11.2	12.1	Trade Payables	3.1	6.9	7.6	13.1	24.9	11.6
.3	.4	.5	Income Taxes Payable	.9	.0	1.1	.1	.8	.6
25.2	21.7	20.6	All Other Current	35.1	11.8	18.9	21.1	17.1	23.8
55.5	50.5	50.2	Total Current	52.8	49.1	54.0	51.8	52.7	43.2
17.2	16.0	10.8	Long-Term Debt	11.3	20.9	13.0	7.0	4.3	10.3
.2	.3	.4	Deferred Taxes	.0	.0	1.2	.1	.7	.6
8.5	7.9	5.9	All Other Non-Current	.0	1.0	4.5	5.8	6.9	13.9
18.6	25.3	32.6	Net Worth	35.8	29.0	27.3	35.3	35.4	32.0
100.0	100.0	100.0	Total Liabilities & Net Worth	100.0	100.0	100.0	100.0	100.0	100.0
			INCOME DATA						
100.0	100.0	100.0	Net Sales	100.0	100.0	100.0	100.0	100.0	100.0
			Gross Profit						
94.6	93.8	89.9	Operating Expenses	77.1	89.1	93.2	91.2	92.8	91.8
5.4	6.2	10.1	Operating Profit	22.9	10.9	6.8	8.8	7.2	8.2
.9	1.0	1.5	All Other Expenses (net)	2.0	.9	.7	3.3	.8	1.2
4.5	5.2	8.6	Profit Before Taxes	20.9	9.9	6.1	5.5	6.4	6.9
			RATIOS						
1.8	2.0	2.8	Current	4.6	4.6	3.0	2.0	2.1	2.7
1.3	1.2	1.5		1.5	1.3	1.7	1.4	1.4	1.6
.9	.8	.9		.1	.5	.8	.9	.7	1.1
1.6	1.6	2.3	Quick	4.1	4.6	2.7	1.9	1.9	2.4
1.1	1.0	1.3		.9	1.3	1.7	1.3	1.2	1.4
.7	.7	.8		.1	.4	.8	.8	.7	1.0
18 19.9	25 14.7	10 38.0	Sales/Receivables	0 UND	0 UND	25 14.9	36 10.0	20 18.6	38 9.6
49 7.4	51 7.2	45 8.0		0 UND	41 8.9	46 8.0	61 5.9	50 7.4	65 5.6
69 5.3	78 4.7	68 5.3		7 51.2	50 7.3	71 5.1	70 5.2	69 5.3	80 4.6
			Cost of Sales/Inventory						
			Cost of Sales/Payables						
8.2	7.5	7.2	Sales/Working Capital	5.9	8.1	5.2	7.4	11.5	5.9
32.9	28.3	22.4		220.9	93.1	13.6	28.1	24.5	14.6
-53.5	-53.6	-61.1		-9.3	-9.2	-27.6	NM	-113.7	48.2
28.1	19.2	19.7	EBIT/Interest		14.6		22.8	21.2	30.5
(81) 7.8	(76) 5.5	(73) 7.2			(12) 3.6		(14) 7.3	(16) 12.1	(17) 7.5
1.6	.7	2.2			.6		1.6	3.8	2.4
10.1	9.3	9.1	Net Profit + Depr., Dep., Amort./Cur. Mat. L/T/D						
(17) 4.0	(14) 4.1	(15) 2.8							
2.0	1.7	1.8							
.2	.2	.2	Fixed/Worth	.0	.2	.2	.1	.2	.2
.8	.4	.5		.7	.4	.5	.4	.5	.6
-3.2	2.4	3.2		1.8	NM	14.4	NM	2.1	2.9
1.0	.9	.7	Debt/Worth	.3	.3	.8	.4	.9	.7
3.4	2.7	1.7		.8	1.3	3.3	2.4	1.5	2.3
-7.5	37.7	18.5		6.9	-26.7	29.2	NM	4.7	11.2
76.4	67.1	129.4	% Profit Before Taxes/Tangible Net Worth	228.6	212.3	74.5	226.1	177.7	82.9
(71) 32.3	(71) 36.0	(84) 50.6		(11) 95.5	(13) 61.7	(11) 41.2	(15) 49.6	(18) 53.7	(16) 32.7
10.5	.0	14.9		51.6	19.3	7.6	7.3	23.5	2.7
23.7	25.6	35.7	% Profit Before Taxes/Total Assets	86.3	68.6	36.9	26.7	32.1	28.8
10.9	9.1	12.2		44.9	24.9	10.2	12.9	14.0	11.0
1.5	-1.4	4.4		9.1	-2.1	4.1	4.5	4.2	3.2
50.0	70.1	62.5	Sales/Net Fixed Assets	54.1	47.9	45.7	119.7	65.8	64.7
23.4	30.7	24.2		21.2	21.1	19.2	36.7	25.7	28.3
13.9	11.8	11.0		5.8	11.8	13.3	16.3	9.1	10.3
4.3	4.2	5.1	Sales/Total Assets	9.2	5.8	7.7	4.0	8.4	4.3
2.9	3.1	3.1		3.6	4.6	3.7	3.2	3.1	2.4
1.8	2.1	2.2		.7	2.4	2.4	2.3	2.5	1.9
.8	.7	.8	% Depr., Dep., Amort./Sales		.5	.5	.5	.8	.5
(80) 1.5	(70) 1.4	(78) 1.3			(11) 1.0	(10) 2.1	(17) 1.1	(16) 1.4	(17) 1.1
2.4	3.0	2.5			1.6	2.8	1.5	2.4	3.2
3.2	3.2	3.6	% Officers', Directors' Owners' Comp/Sales						
(32) 7.0	(34) 9.2	(35) 9.9							
14.4	16.5	24.3							
2781529M	2212489M	2489991M	Net Sales ($)	6744M	33482M	48320M	156360M	286103M	1958982M
1487430M	821844M	1044180M	Total Assets ($)	7965M	9472M	18152M	53759M	86360M	868472M

M = $ thousand   MM = $ million
See Pages 11 through 21 for Explanation of Ratios and Data

Current Data Sorted by Assets   **Comparative Historical Data**

Type of Statement

Type of Statement	0-500M	500M-2MM	2-10MM	10-50MM	50-100MM	100-250MM	4/1/02-3/31/03 ALL	4/1/03-3/31/04 ALL
Unqualified				1	2	1	2	1
Reviewed		2	3	1			7	11
Compiled		2	3				13	23
Tax Returns	5	7	5				17	18
Other	13	4					13	12
	8							

9 (4/1-9/30/06)   50 (10/1/06-3/31/07)

	0-500M	500M-2MM	2-10MM	10-50MM	50-100MM	100-250MM		
NUMBER OF STATEMENTS	26	15	11	3	3	1	52	65

Main Data

	0-500M %	500M-2MM %	2-10MM %	10-50MM %	50-100MM %	100-250MM %	4/1/02-3/31/03 ALL %	4/1/03-3/31/04 ALL %
ASSETS								
Cash & Equivalents	24.8	19.2	13.2				18.8	17.7
Trade Receivables (net)	7.8	6.0	21.8				6.6	8.2
Inventory	2.7	3.4	10.3				6.4	7.4
All Other Current	14.4	8.2	2.2				2.8	4.5
Total Current	49.7	36.7	47.6				34.6	37.7
Fixed Assets (net)	29.0	51.4	44.1				49.8	46.4
Intangibles (net)	2.9	.2	1.5				8.6	4.3
All Other Non-Current	18.3	11.7	6.8				6.9	11.6
Total	100.0	100.0	100.0				100.0	100.0
LIABILITIES								
Notes Payable-Short Term	14.1	10.4	12.8				11.3	12.4
Cur. Mat.-L.T.D.	4.5	5.5	5.6				4.6	5.0
Trade Payables	4.9	7.7	11.5				9.0	7.7
Income Taxes Payable	.3	.0	.2				.1	.2
All Other Current	27.0	8.3	14.9				12.0	13.0
Total Current	50.8	31.9	45.1				37.0	38.4
Long-Term Debt	12.4	42.9	13.1				44.0	33.8
Deferred Taxes	.0	.0	.4				.2	.0
All Other Non-Current	1.8	13.5	6.5				11.5	6.7
Net Worth	35.1	11.7	34.8				7.3	21.1
Total Liabilities & Net Worth	100.0	100.0	100.0				100.0	100.0
INCOME DATA								
Net Sales	100.0	100.0	100.0				100.0	100.0
Gross Profit								
Operating Expenses	88.5	88.0	97.2				95.3	95.7
Operating Profit	11.5	12.0	2.8				4.7	4.3
All Other Expenses (net)	.4	3.0	1.0				1.7	1.4
Profit Before Taxes	11.2	9.1	1.8				3.0	2.9
RATIOS								
Current	3.7	8.4	3.1				1.8	2.2
	.8	1.8	.9				.9	1.1
	.3	.2	.6				.6	.5
Quick	2.6	4.4	2.9				1.5	1.9
	.5	(14) 1.4	.6				.7	.5
	.1	.2	.4				.3	.2
Sales/Receivables	0 UND	0 UND	2 228.9				0 UND	0 UND
	0 UND	2 165.9	23 15.9				1 708.9	1 719.3
	27 13.6	10 38.0	76 4.8				7 53.1	8 46.1
Cost of Sales/Inventory								
Cost of Sales/Payables								
Sales/Working Capital	9.9	3.7	5.0				25.8	17.4
	-63.3	14.3	-51.2				-428.7	79.1
	-9.8	-40.6	-17.3				-27.6	-16.9
EBIT/Interest	10.8	8.3	7.9				7.5	12.4
	(16) 3.6	(12) 3.4	2.1				(44) 1.8	(59) 3.5
	-.6	-1.3	.2				.5	.6
Net Profit + Depr., Dep., Amort./Cur. Mat. L/T/D								
Fixed/Worth	.0	.5	.7				1.2	.7
	.9	1.6	1.4				2.1	1.8
	NM	-158.0	2.8				-3.8	92.3
Debt/Worth	.2	.8	.9				.9	.8
	3.9	1.8	2.0				5.0	2.6
	NM	-218.0	8.9				-6.5	120.7
% Profit Before Taxes/Tangible Net Worth	108.6	82.7	28.2				72.0	72.0
	(20) 66.3	(11) 32.7	(10) 14.3				(36) 32.2	(50) 27.4
	7.3	-1.2	-7.4				.4	-.2
% Profit Before Taxes/Total Assets	56.9	38.8	7.7				16.4	22.3
	24.6	7.3	3.3				3.1	10.6
	-.4	-1.0	-5.2				-2.9	-.9
Sales/Net Fixed Assets	258.3	10.7	12.8				17.5	21.2
	16.6	7.1	7.1				6.7	6.8
	4.8	1.0	4.5				4.0	3.4
Sales/Total Assets	6.6	3.2	4.0				4.3	5.2
	3.4	2.7	2.4				3.2	3.1
	1.7	.9	1.7				2.3	2.0
% Depr., Dep., Amort./Sales	1.5	1.8	1.6				1.6	1.5
	(15) 2.9	(13) 4.2	3.1				(44) 3.7	(49) 3.1
	4.3	9.1	3.9				5.6	5.9
% Officers', Directors' Owners' Comp/Sales	5.9						2.1	4.1
	(15) 14.5						(36) 6.4	(39) 7.1
	17.9						17.1	12.1
Net Sales ($)	16064M	43374M	114775M	159403M	508993M	291841M	1550914M	1875521M
Total Assets ($)	4378M	17669M	39723M	90821M	208607M	106568M	401252M	846879M

© RMA 2007

M = $ thousand   MM = $ million
See Pages 11 through 21 for Explanation of Ratios and Data

Comparative Historical Data | | | | Current Data Sorted by Sales

4/1/04-3/31/05 ALL	4/1/05-3/31/06 ALL	4/1/06-3/31/07 ALL	Type of Statement	0-1MM	1-3MM	3-5MM	5-10MM	10-25MM	25MM & OVER
			Unqualified						4
2	4	4	Reviewed	4	2	3		1	2
2	6	6	Compiled	13	5		4		
14	13	10	Tax Returns			2			
8	14	20	Other	7	4		5	1	2
10	24	19							
				9 (4/1-9/30/06)			50 (10/1/06-3/31/07)		
36	61	59	NUMBER OF STATEMENTS	24	11	5	9	2	8
%	%	%	**ASSETS**	%	%	%	%	%	%
16.6	21.1	20.9	Cash & Equivalents	22.0	26.6				
12.6	9.6	9.4	Trade Receivables (net)	6.3	12.0				
6.6	4.8	4.7	Inventory	2.1	6.0				
4.6	1.9	9.0	All Other Current	13.5	13.3				
40.3	37.4	44.0	Total Current	43.9	57.9				
40.6	43.5	38.9	Fixed Assets (net)	40.3	17.7				
7.0	9.6	4.4	Intangibles (net)	3.2	.2				
12.1	9.5	12.7	All Other Non-Current	12.6	24.3				
100.0	100.0	100.0	Total	100.0	100.0				
			LIABILITIES						
10.2	11.6	11.3	Notes Payable-Short Term	12.0	10.4				
4.1	11.0	4.8	Cur. Mat.-L.T.D.	4.0	5.6				
6.3	7.4	7.0	Trade Payables	2.4	9.7				
.8	.4	.3	Income Taxes Payable	.1	.6				
13.2	15.0	19.1	All Other Current	25.3	12.1				
34.6	45.4	42.4	Total Current	43.8	38.4				
30.6	28.4	20.6	Long-Term Debt	23.4	31.2				
.2	.4	.4	Deferred Taxes	.0	.0				
14.1	8.1	12.9	All Other Non-Current	2.9	6.4				
20.5	17.8	23.8	Net Worth	29.9	24.0				
100.0	100.0	100.0	Total Liabilties & Net Worth	100.0	100.0				
			INCOME DATA						
100.0	100.0	100.0	Net Sales	100.0	100.0				
			Gross Profit						
95.2	91.6	91.2	Operating Expenses	84.6	93.7				
4.8	8.4	8.8	Operating Profit	15.4	6.3				
2.2	1.6	1.5	All Other Expenses (net)	2.1	.0				
2.6	6.8	7.3	Profit Before Taxes	13.4	6.3				
			RATIOS						
2.0	1.8	3.2		4.0	16.5				
1.0	.9	1.0	Current	.9	1.8				
.5	.4	.4		.3	.4				
1.6	1.6	2.5		3.2	3.1				
.7	.6 (58)	.6	Quick	(23) .6	.8				
.2	.2	.2		.2	.1				
0 UND	0 UND	0 UND		0 UND	0 UND				
2 146.8	3 130.7	2 217.0	Sales/Receivables	0 UND	5 72.4				
43 8.4	19 19.6	25 14.6		30 12.2	25 14.6				
			Cost of Sales/Inventory						
			Cost of Sales/Payables						
9.9	16.6	5.6		4.7	5.6				
-307.0	-67.3	569.7	Sales/Working Capital	UND	15.8				
-15.7	-17.5	-16.4		-12.4	-42.4				
6.6	10.4	8.8		11.3					
(31) 2.3	(51) 4.3	(46) 3.2	EBIT/Interest	(16) 3.8					
.7	1.8	-.3		-.6					
	4.1								
	(12) 3.1		Net Profit + Depr., Dep., Amort./Cur. Mat. L/T/D						
	1.5								
.5	.9	.3		.3	.0				
1.7	1.9	1.4	Fixed/Worth	1.3	.2				
-4.1	-3.9	18.0		NM	1.6				
.6	1.0	.8		.5	.2				
2.9	2.5	2.7	Debt/Worth	5.2	1.6				
-7.5	-6.0	41.0		NM	22.8				
31.7	88.8	82.8		98.5					
(25) 10.0	(43) 31.4	(45) 31.4	% Profit Before Taxes/Tangible Net Worth	(18) 52.9					
-.3	6.4	2.1		-2.6					
17.4	28.2	29.5		41.7	68.9				
7.2	8.8	7.3	% Profit Before Taxes/Total Assets	14.8	25.0				
-.2	2.7	-1.0		-1.3	.0				
20.8	21.3	20.1		27.5	999.8				
8.0	7.6	8.4	Sales/Net Fixed Assets	7.0	37.1				
4.6	4.3	3.9		1.5	10.7				
4.1	5.9	4.3		3.9	7.4				
2.9	3.1	2.7	Sales/Total Assets	1.8	4.3				
2.1	1.8	1.5		1.0	2.7				
1.6	1.8	1.7		2.0					
(30) 3.2	(43) 2.8	(44) 3.1	% Depr., Dep., Amort./Sales	(16) 3.6					
5.7	5.7	5.0		15.2					
6.9	4.2	5.0		8.5					
(16) 11.4	(29) 9.5	(29) 9.8	% Officers', Directors' Owners' Comp/Sales	(13) 15.7					
16.3	11.6	16.4		19.0					
1171137M	1522454M	1134450M	Net Sales ($)	8675M	21451M	20998M	58817M	32389M	992120M
483512M	738968M	467766M	Total Assets ($)	7520M	7227M	7117M	27152M	6554M	412196M

M = $ thousand   MM = $ million
See Pages 11 through 21 for Explanation of Ratios and Data

Current Data Sorted by Assets   Comparative Historical Data

		1	1	1	1	Type of Statement		
		2				Unqualified		2
2	3	1				Reviewed	4	5
6	3					Compiled	7	11
	2	4		1		Tax Returns	3	6
						Other	13	8
	7 (4/1-9/30/06)			21 (10/1/06-3/31/07)			4/1/02-3/31/03	4/1/03-3/31/04
0-500M	500M-2MM	2-10MM	10-50MM	50-100MM	100-250MM		ALL	ALL
8	8	8	2	1	1	NUMBER OF STATEMENTS	27	32
%	%	%	%	%	%	ASSETS	%	%
						Cash & Equivalents	14.1	9.0
						Trade Receivables (net)	17.5	26.8
						Inventory	3.8	4.8
						All Other Current	3.6	4.7
						Total Current	38.9	45.3
						Fixed Assets (net)	44.0	42.4
						Intangibles (net)	8.2	2.3
						All Other Non-Current	8.8	9.9
						Total	100.0	100.0
						LIABILITIES		
						Notes Payable-Short Term	9.4	14.3
						Cur. Mat.-L.T.D.	5.4	7.9
						Trade Payables	11.8	15.1
						Income Taxes Payable	.8	.5
						All Other Current	20.2	13.6
						Total Current	47.8	51.4
						Long-Term Debt	19.8	22.7
						Deferred Taxes	1.3	.9
						All Other Non-Current	10.3	8.2
						Net Worth	20.8	16.8
						Total Liabilities & Net Worth	100.0	100.0
						INCOME DATA		
						Net Sales	100.0	100.0
						Gross Profit		
						Operating Expenses	96.1	97.9
						Operating Profit	3.9	2.1
						All Other Expenses (net)	1.2	1.2
						Profit Before Taxes	2.7	.9
						RATIOS		
						Current	2.2	2.0
							.8	1.1
							.4	.4
						Quick	2.2	1.7
							.6	.9
							.3	.3
						Sales/Receivables	0 UND	14 27.0
							29 12.7	41 9.0
							53 6.8	59 6.2
						Cost of Sales/Inventory		
						Cost of Sales/Payables		
						Sales/Working Capital	9.6	10.0
							-19.8	42.4
							-8.0	-10.2
						EBIT/Interest	5.6	4.6
							(21) 2.1	(26) 1.4
							-.9	-3.5
						Net Profit + Depr., Dep., Amort./Cur. Mat. L/T/D		
						Fixed/Worth	.7	.7
							2.1	1.2
							-3.5	19.9
						Debt/Worth	.8	1.1
							2.8	2.3
							-7.8	34.2
						% Profit Before Taxes/Tangible Net Worth	29.8	45.4
							(19) 11.6	(25) 6.9
							-7.6	-13.9
						% Profit Before Taxes/Total Assets	16.7	12.5
							6.5	2.4
							-4.5	-14.4
						Sales/Net Fixed Assets	10.8	16.0
							5.0	5.0
							2.8	3.8
						Sales/Total Assets	3.2	4.0
							2.2	2.4
							1.3	1.9
						% Depr., Dep., Amort./Sales	2.0	1.7
							(20) 4.6	(28) 4.2
							9.6	7.5
						% Officers', Directors' Owners' Comp/Sales	4.4	4.4
							(13) 8.0	(22) 6.8
							16.3	10.2
8170M	14288M	69729M	82990M	84720M	291841M	Net Sales ($)	113566M	157962M
2052M	7252M	38721M	66900M	84580M	106568M	Total Assets ($)	45659M	72725M

Comparative Historical Data   ## Current Data Sorted by Sales

Type of Statement									
	1	3	4		1				3
Unqualified	5	11	2		4		1	1	
Reviewed	3	7	6		6	2			
Compiled	7	5	9	3	2		3		
Tax Returns	13	6	7		7				
Other									
	4/1/04-	4/1/05-	4/1/06-		7 (4/1-9/30/06)		21 (10/1/06-3/31/07)		
	3/31/05	3/31/06	3/31/07	0-1MM	1-3MM	3-5MM	5-10MM	10-25MM	25MM & OVER
	ALL	ALL	ALL						
NUMBER OF STATEMENTS	29	32	28	3	13	2	4	2	4
	%	%	%	%	%	%	%	%	%
ASSETS									
Cash & Equivalents	10.9	11.6	12.1		11.1				
Trade Receivables (net)	22.0	27.5	26.9		23.9				
Inventory	8.5	8.5	4.8		5.2				
All Other Current	3.9	5.8	7.1		9.4				
Total Current	45.4	53.3	50.9		49.6				
Fixed Assets (net)	37.0	35.0	36.8		41.9				
Intangibles (net)	5.8	4.2	5.0		3.8				
All Other Non-Current	11.7	7.5	7.3		4.7				
Total	100.0	100.0	100.0		100.0				
LIABILITIES									
Notes Payable-Short Term	17.1	8.2	8.8		9.6				
Cur. Mat.-L.T.D.	3.5	4.8	5.1		2.6				
Trade Payables	15.3	10.1	6.9		6.6				
Income Taxes Payable	.1	.2	.9		.1				
All Other Current	16.0	12.4	11.7		11.4				
Total Current	52.0	35.7	33.5		30.3				
Long-Term Debt	23.2	15.2	20.7		27.9				
Deferred Taxes	.3	1.0	.3		.5				
All Other Non-Current	3.5	10.1	13.6		2.7				
Net Worth	21.1	37.9	31.9		38.6				
Total Liabilties & Net Worth	100.0	100.0	100.0		100.0				
INCOME DATA									
Net Sales	100.0	100.0	100.0		100.0				
Gross Profit									
Operating Expenses	96.6	97.1	88.1		87.6				
Operating Profit	3.4	2.9	11.9		12.4				
All Other Expenses (net)	1.3	1.1	3.5		1.1				
Profit Before Taxes	2.1	1.8	8.4		11.3				
RATIOS									
Current	2.0	2.5	3.9		8.5				
	1.1	1.7	1.7		2.1				
	.4	1.0	.9		1.0				
Quick	1.6	1.8	3.0		6.4				
	.6	1.2	1.4		2.1				
	.2	.7	.4		.2				
Sales/Receivables	1 275.7	19 18.9	4 95.6	0 UND					
	26 13.9	38 9.7	47 7.8	25 14.6					
	57 6.4	61 6.0	76 4.8	61 6.0					
Cost of Sales/Inventory									
Cost of Sales/Payables									
Sales/Working Capital	10.1	4.8	5.6		5.6				
	37.1	14.3	9.7		8.6				
	-13.6	UND	-94.3		UND				
EBIT/Interest	10.6	9.6	18.7		19.2				
	(28) 2.7	(27) 2.5	(23) 4.5		(11) 4.9				
	-1.4	-.1	1.8		.1				
Net Profit + Depr., Dep., Amort./Cur. Mat. L/T/D									
Fixed/Worth	.6	.4	.3		.5				
	1.7	1.0	.9		1.1				
	NM	1.7	2.3		2.3				
Debt/Worth	.9	.8	.6		.7				
	2.9	1.4	1.4		1.4				
	NM	4.5	5.4		5.2				
% Profit Before Taxes/Tangible Net Worth	46.5	34.6	76.1		90.9				
	(22) 9.8	(30) 5.9	(25) 44.1		(11) 57.5				
	-7.0	-9.5	11.4		2.8				
% Profit Before Taxes/Total Assets	23.2	12.9	37.3		76.9				
	4.8	2.4	10.5		10.8				
	-4.5	-4.4	2.4		-3.7				
Sales/Net Fixed Assets	28.2	15.6	20.5		19.5				
	9.8	6.4	6.9		6.3				
	4.9	3.5	3.8		3.4				
Sales/Total Assets	4.6	3.4	3.1		4.5				
	3.0	2.2	2.4		2.6				
	1.5	1.3	1.5		1.7				
% Depr., Dep., Amort./Sales	2.2	1.7	1.7		1.3				
	(23) 4.7	(30) 4.0	(24) 3.5		(12) 2.9				
	6.6	6.6	6.7		6.8				
% Officers', Directors' Owners' Comp/Sales	5.0	5.2	6.0						
	(17) 8.0	(16) 9.1	(10) 12.0						
	12.7	14.8	17.7						
Net Sales ($)	109533M	230949M	551738M	926M	21091M	6788M	31070M	32312M	459551M
Total Assets ($)	44029M	133548M	306073M	1012M	12006M	4460M	12825M	17722M	258048M

M = $ thousand   MM = $ million
See Pages 11 through 21 for Explanation of Ratios and Data

Current Data Sorted by Assets | Comparative Historical Data

						Type of Statement		
1	1	1	3		1	Unqualified	8	8
1	2	3	2			Reviewed	12	11
43	20	5		1	1	Compiled	70	68
117	44	7	1	1	1	Tax Returns	97	139
62	26	14	2		1	Other	54	74
	26 (4/1-9/30/06)		335 (10/1/06-3/31/07)				4/1/02-3/31/03 ALL	4/1/03-3/31/04 ALL
0-500M	500M-2MM	2-10MM	10-50MM	50-100MM	100-250MM			
224	93	30	8	2	4	NUMBER OF STATEMENTS	241	300
%	%	%	%	%	%	ASSETS	%	%
23.5	17.2	16.6				Cash & Equivalents	20.0	17.8
6.1	4.4	8.0				Trade Receivables (net)	9.8	9.3
11.4	5.3	4.4				Inventory	11.2	11.2
4.2	3.0	2.8				All Other Current	2.3	3.3
45.2	29.9	31.9				Total Current	43.3	41.5
35.5	44.0	57.8				Fixed Assets (net)	40.8	36.1
9.2	15.2	5.6				Intangibles (net)	8.6	13.7
10.1	10.9	4.7				All Other Non-Current	7.2	8.7
100.0	100.0	100.0				Total	100.0	100.0
						LIABILITIES		
10.3	5.8	3.2				Notes Payable-Short Term	8.9	7.5
5.8	4.9	3.5				Cur. Mat.-L.T.D.	5.1	6.3
12.4	4.1	8.4				Trade Payables	8.7	10.6
.6	.0	.4				Income Taxes Payable	.3	.4
15.3	7.2	4.4				All Other Current	14.7	15.2
44.4	22.0	19.9				Total Current	37.7	40.0
31.5	48.1	42.4				Long-Term Debt	27.7	31.9
.1	.1	.2				Deferred Taxes	.2	.3
10.1	3.3	3.2				All Other Non-Current	6.7	6.9
13.9	26.5	34.3				Net Worth	27.6	20.9
100.0	100.0	100.0				Total Liabilties & Net Worth	100.0	100.0
						INCOME DATA		
100.0	100.0	100.0				Net Sales	100.0	100.0
						Gross Profit		
91.7	85.5	85.4				Operating Expenses	91.5	90.5
8.3	14.5	14.6				Operating Profit	8.5	9.5
1.1	5.0	8.8				All Other Expenses (net)	2.1	2.2
7.2	9.5	5.8				Profit Before Taxes	6.4	7.3
						RATIOS		
3.2	3.8	4.0					3.1	2.6
1.3	1.4	1.2				Current	1.4	1.2
.5	.4	.7					.7	.5
2.1	2.9	3.1					2.1	1.8
(222) .8	.8	1.0				Quick	(240) .9	(298) .8
.2	.3	.5					.4	.2
0 UND	0 UND	0 UND					0 UND	0 UND
0 UND	0 UND	1 272.4				Sales/Receivables	1 246.9	1 272.5
4 87.9	6 63.1	20 18.4					11 32.2	9 40.7
						Cost of Sales/Inventory		
						Cost of Sales/Payables		
16.1	11.5	5.9					14.3	15.8
90.5	39.3	34.4				Sales/Working Capital	53.5	99.9
-29.7	-19.1	-40.0					-35.2	-24.4
25.0	13.3	9.9					12.0	17.6
(161) 6.0	(79) 5.8	(21) 4.8				EBIT/Interest	(182) 4.8	(224) 5.9
1.2	1.3	2.0					1.7	1.7
						Net Profit + Depr., Dep., Amort./Cur. Mat. L/T/D	5.9	6.5
							(16) 3.9	(12) .9
							1.9	.6
.4	.7	.7					.5	.5
1.7	5.1	2.6				Fixed/Worth	1.5	2.4
-1.1	-4.4	10.4					-12.5	-2.6
.6	1.0	.9					.5	1.0
2.4	9.6	2.2				Debt/Worth	2.3	4.0
-3.5	-5.6	16.9					-18.4	-4.6
252.2	142.8	74.0				% Profit Before Taxes/Tangible Net Worth	148.8	154.2
(142) 78.4	(61) 48.7	(25) 22.2					(174) 55.0	(196) 55.4
28.4	21.0	12.2					15.8	15.2
69.0	33.7	22.9				% Profit Before Taxes/Total Assets	44.1	42.2
25.9	12.0	6.8					18.1	17.0
3.9	1.8	2.0					2.4	2.4
63.6	24.7	13.1				Sales/Net Fixed Assets	34.3	48.8
22.6	9.1	2.9					15.8	18.0
8.9	2.4	.8					6.8	7.5
9.6	4.2	3.8				Sales/Total Assets	7.5	7.0
5.9	2.3	1.5					4.6	4.0
3.5	1.1	.5					2.2	2.3
.6	2.0	1.8				% Depr., Dep., Amort./Sales	1.2	1.1
(144) 1.5	(65) 3.1	(27) 3.1					(187) 2.3	(211) 2.3
3.2	4.9	9.0					4.2	4.6
7.4	4.8	2.1				% Officers', Directors' Owners' Comp/Sales	7.4	7.2
(150) 11.0	(56) 9.7	(11) 10.7					(154) 12.3	(194) 11.9
17.2	18.0	23.6					17.4	
285698M	246563M	206838M	378351M	909543M	2165256M	Net Sales ($)	7313822M	4658474M
47068M	86952M	107155M	225523M	149719M	595728M	Total Assets ($)	912449M	881734M

M = $ thousand   MM = $ million
See Pages 11 through 21 for Explanation of Ratios and Data

Comparative Historical Data   Current Data Sorted by Sales

			Type of Statement						
2	9	7	Unqualified	1	1		1		4
7	13	8	Reviewed	1	3		1	1	2
69	58	70	Compiled	21	35	4	6	2	2
146	174	171	Tax Returns	76	70	14	6	3	2
63	100	105	Other	35	45	12	6	4	3
4/1/04-3/31/05 ALL	4/1/05-3/31/06 ALL	4/1/06-3/31/07 ALL		26 (4/1-9/30/06)			335 (10/1/06-3/31/07)		
				0-1MM	1-3MM	3-5MM	5-10MM	10-25MM	25MM & OVER
287	354	361	NUMBER OF STATEMENTS	134	154	30	20	10	13
%	%	%	ASSETS	%	%	%	%	%	%
20.6	20.3	21.0	Cash & Equivalents	13.9	26.3	27.5	19.4	30.1	10.9
6.6	6.2	6.0	Trade Receivables (net)	4.1	6.0	9.1	8.2	7.4	14.7
12.0	10.0	9.5	Inventory	10.1	8.5	10.7	6.5	5.1	21.1
2.2	2.4	3.6	All Other Current	4.1	3.6	2.8	5.5	.7	1.2
41.4	38.9	40.1	Total Current	32.2	44.3	50.0	39.7	43.2	47.9
36.1	38.3	39.1	Fixed Assets (net)	47.4	34.1	34.0	42.1	29.6	27.1
12.5	14.4	11.1	Intangibles (net)	9.9	12.2	6.5	7.4	18.5	21.5
10.1	8.4	9.6	All Other Non-Current	10.5	9.3	9.5	10.8	8.7	3.5
100.0	100.0	100.0	Total	100.0	100.0	100.0	100.0	100.0	100.0
			LIABILITIES						
10.3	9.9	8.5	Notes Payable-Short Term	10.0	7.9	8.5	5.5	3.4	8.4
4.4	4.6	5.2	Cur. Mat.-L.T.D.	6.4	5.0	3.9	4.4	2.7	2.8
9.3	8.8	9.7	Trade Payables	11.2	7.5	13.9	9.5	11.7	10.2
.1	.2	.4	Income Taxes Payable	.7	.3	.0	.6	.0	.0
14.0	13.5	12.1	All Other Current	10.0	13.9	16.2	9.0	7.7	10.8
38.2	37.0	36.0	Total Current	38.3	34.5	42.5	29.0	25.4	32.3
34.5	36.4	36.3	Long-Term Debt	52.2	26.1	29.0	35.8	26.1	18.6
.2	.1	.1	Deferred Taxes	.0	.3	.0	.4	.0	.0
6.5	7.3	7.6	All Other Non-Current	9.7	7.0	5.8	4.7	1.3	5.4
20.7	19.2	20.1	Net Worth	-.2	32.2	22.7	30.0	47.3	43.7
100.0	100.0	100.0	Total Liabilities & Net Worth	100.0	100.0	100.0	100.0	100.0	100.0
			INCOME DATA						
100.0	100.0	100.0	Net Sales	100.0	100.0	100.0	100.0	100.0	100.0
			Gross Profit						
89.3	90.6	89.8	Operating Expenses	86.9	90.7	91.0	93.8	89.6	99.8
10.7	9.4	10.2	Operating Profit	13.1	9.3	9.0	6.2	10.4	.2
2.2	1.8	2.7	All Other Expenses (net)	6.0	1.0	.4	-.1	.5	.8
8.5	7.6	7.5	Profit Before Taxes	7.1	8.4	8.6	6.3	9.9	-.6
			RATIOS						
2.9	2.8	3.4		2.4	4.2	3.8	2.6	61.0	2.7
1.2	1.2	1.3	Current	1.0	1.5	1.9	1.2	1.2	1.2
.6	.5	.5		.3	.7	.9	.7	.7	.6
2.2	1.9	2.3		1.7	3.1	3.0	2.0	60.2	1.3
(283) .7	(359) .8	.8	Quick	(132) .5	1.0	1.1	.8	1.1	.7
.3	.3	.3		.1	.4	.5	.3	.5	.1
0 UND	0 UND	0 UND		0 UND	0 UND	0 UND	0 UND	0 UND	0 UND
0 UND	0 UND	0 UND	Sales/Receivables	0 UND	0 UND	3 124.8	2 198.1	2 224.3	2 147.0
5 79.1	5 77.0	5 75.9		7 55.3	4 98.8	11 33.0	9 38.9	4 101.7	44 8.4
			Cost of Sales/Inventory						
			Cost of Sales/Payables						
17.2	18.0	14.1		14.8	14.0	9.2	14.6	15.7	6.8
105.2	107.3	63.0	Sales/Working Capital	NM	43.0	43.7	160.0	38.7	44.0
-29.4	-28.9	-26.6		-11.4	-67.7	-255.0	-25.1	-117.4	-28.9
24.0	16.8	17.7		9.8	25.4	26.1	35.2		6.9
(224) 6.6	(270) 5.2	(272) 5.7	EBIT/Interest	(98) 3.6	(113) 6.7	(24) 11.3	(19) 7.5		(11) 2.8
1.5	2.0	1.6		.7	1.9	3.0	2.8		2.0
	3.0	2.9							
(11) 1.7	(12) 1.7		Net Profit + Depr., Dep., Amort./Cur. Mat. L/T/D						
	.8	1.0							
.5	.5	.5		.9	.4	.6	.5	.4	.4
1.9	3.0	2.1	Fixed/Worth	15.7	1.4	1.6	1.9	.7	1.2
-2.0	-1.5	-1.9		-.9	-3.3	-12.4	102.6	NM	-1.1
.7	.8	.8		1.1	.6	.7	1.0	.4	1.1
3.8	5.2	3.1	Debt/Worth	20.2	1.6	2.5	2.5	1.1	3.4
-4.8	-3.7	-4.3		-2.9	-9.6	-54.1	157.0	NM	-2.6
159.2	191.6	172.3		139.3	179.3	254.0	250.7		
(188) 73.7	(219) 60.6	(236) 57.9	% Profit Before Taxes/Tangible Net Worth	(73) 47.4	(109) 63.6	(22) 96.5	(16) 85.3		
23.1	17.5	18.9		12.7	18.0	40.9	22.2		
59.9	50.1	52.0		41.4	67.5	63.2	55.8	69.7	11.6
21.9	18.2	19.3	% Profit Before Taxes/Total Assets	12.0	25.9	31.9	16.1	34.4	7.2
1.9	2.4	2.4		-.4	10.0	5.6	10.4		2.2
55.2	48.3	43.9		30.8	60.8	42.7	35.3	29.9	32.8
19.5	18.8	15.4	Sales/Net Fixed Assets	8.3	23.1	17.4	12.3	18.6	18.3
7.9	6.4	5.5		3.2	9.9	7.9	5.8	11.2	6.7
8.0	8.4	7.5		5.8	9.2	8.0	6.0	8.4	5.1
4.8	4.7	4.3	Sales/Total Assets	3.1	5.1	5.2	4.0	4.6	3.0
2.6	2.1	2.3		1.3	3.0	3.2	2.8	2.6	1.1
.9	1.0	.8		1.2	.6	.7	1.2	.7	
(195) 1.8	(238) 1.8	(246) 2.2	% Depr., Dep., Amort./Sales	(92) 2.8	(97) 1.7	(23) 2.3	(15) 2.5	1.6	
3.2	3.3	3.8		5.9	3.7	3.2	3.4	2.2	
6.5	7.1	6.6		8.4	5.6	4.8	5.8		
(197) 11.3	(215) 11.1	(222) 10.8	% Officers', Directors' Owners' Comp/Sales	(72) 12.9	(102) 10.2	(22) 14.3	(14) 9.1		
16.4	18.1	17.5		17.4	16.5	19.0	16.0		
8688674M	12218389M	4192249M	Net Sales ($)	78445M	262050M	112177M	137058M	143829M	3458690M
915756M	2114018M	1212145M	Total Assets ($)	63907M	76384M	37665M	36039M	43255M	954895M

© RMA 2007

M = $ thousand   MM = $ million
See Pages 11 through 21 for Explanation of Ratios and Data

Current Data Sorted by Assets   Comparative Historical Data

						Type of Statement		
6	20	40	43	13	11	Unqualified	71	114
5	23	50	10	1	1	Reviewed	45	78
37	62	31	1	1	1	Compiled	69	159
127	76	29	3	1	1	Tax Returns	75	164
80	124	79	37	8	8	Other	121	191
	124 (4/1-9/30/06)		802 (10/1/06-3/31/07)				4/1/02-3/31/03	4/1/03-3/31/04
0-500M	500M-2MM	2-10MM	10-50MM	50-100MM	100-250MM		ALL	ALL
255	305	229	94	23	20	NUMBER OF STATEMENTS	381	706
%	%	%	%	%	%	**ASSETS**	%	%
23.7	15.2	12.7	12.1	17.2	10.5	Cash & Equivalents	15.6	16.2
20.7	30.4	35.6	33.5	25.0	17.1	Trade Receivables (net)	25.2	26.4
4.1	8.3	8.1	4.5	3.4	8.9	Inventory	6.3	7.1
4.6	4.3	4.9	8.0	3.3	3.5	All Other Current	4.1	4.9
53.0	58.1	61.2	58.1	48.9	40.1	Total Current	51.2	54.6
29.9	28.0	24.1	25.2	18.4	26.3	Fixed Assets (net)	33.8	31.5
5.8	3.9	4.8	7.8	15.5	12.7	Intangibles (net)	5.9	4.3
11.4	10.0	9.9	8.9	17.3	21.0	All Other Non-Current	9.1	9.6
100.0	100.0	100.0	100.0	100.0	100.0	Total	100.0	100.0
						LIABILITIES		
20.0	10.8	10.7	9.8	8.2	4.3	Notes Payable-Short Term	9.9	11.7
5.4	3.7	3.8	4.1	4.4	2.9	Cur. Mat.-L.T.D.	6.3	4.2
11.0	12.4	14.4	13.6	7.4	11.4	Trade Payables	11.3	11.5
.2	.1	.8	.7	.4	.6	Income Taxes Payable	.5	.4
29.9	13.2	13.6	14.9	10.8	16.0	All Other Current	13.6	15.6
66.6	40.3	43.4	43.1	31.2	35.3	Total Current	41.7	43.4
28.4	18.1	15.9	18.4	15.4	23.2	Long-Term Debt	23.4	20.4
.0	.1	.5	.6	.4	.9	Deferred Taxes	.4	.4
7.7	5.2	5.1	5.1	15.3	7.9	All Other Non-Current	5.1	5.8
-2.7	36.3	35.1	32.8	37.6	32.8	Net Worth	29.4	30.0
100.0	100.0	100.0	100.0	100.0	100.0	Total Liabilties & Net Worth	100.0	100.0
						INCOME DATA		
100.0	100.0	100.0	100.0	100.0	100.0	Net Sales	100.0	100.0
						Gross Profit		
91.9	90.8	92.2	88.6	74.7	90.1	Operating Expenses	92.1	91.0
8.1	9.2	7.8	11.4	25.3	9.9	Operating Profit	7.9	9.0
1.3	2.5	1.5	2.7	4.5	5.6	All Other Expenses (net)	1.9	2.1
6.8	6.6	6.3	8.7	20.8	4.2	Profit Before Taxes	6.0	6.9
						RATIOS		
2.9	2.9	2.1	2.0	2.6	3.5		2.5	2.9
1.1	1.5	1.4	1.4	1.8	1.3	Current	1.3	1.4
.4	.9	1.0	.9	.8	.9		.8	.9
2.3	2.4	1.9	1.8	2.6	2.5		2.0	2.2
.9	(304) 1.2	1.2	1.0	1.5	.8	Quick	(380) 1.0	(705) 1.1
.3	.6	.7	.7	.8	.5		.5	.6
0 UND	0 UND	28 13.1	27 13.8	12 30.1	15 23.7		2 174.9	1 504.5
1 460.4	30 12.1	50 7.3	52 7.1	53 6.9	42 8.6	Sales/Receivables	30 12.0	31 11.7
32 11.6	56 6.5	75 4.9	79 4.6	82 4.5	84 4.4		55 6.6	61 6.0
						Cost of Sales/Inventory		
						Cost of Sales/Payables		
13.4	7.9	5.8	4.4	2.3	3.3		6.9	6.7
167.4	18.8	15.7	14.3	8.6	20.0	Sales/Working Capital	26.4	21.3
-21.6	-59.1	165.6	-43.7	-18.8	NM		-33.2	-42.8
16.6	22.0	13.5	15.4	29.3	14.9		8.2	16.7
(168) 3.7	(245) 5.1	(192) 4.2	(79) 4.9	(16) 3.1	(15) 4.8	EBIT/Interest	(293) 3.4	(532) 3.7
-.4	1.7	1.0	1.7	1.9	2.5		1.0	.8
		4.0	17.1	6.5			5.2	5.3
	(21) 2.2	(40) 4.4	(23) 1.8			Net Profit + Depr., Dep., Amort./Cur. Mat. L/T/D	(58) 2.3	(82) 1.9
	.6	1.5	.4				1.1	.7
.1	.2	.1	.2	.0	.2		.3	.2
1.1	.5	.5	.7	.9	.4	Fixed/Worth	.9	.9
-3.5	2.4	2.4	3.0	-2.8	5.9		5.0	4.6
.8	.6	.8	.9	.7	1.0		.6	.6
6.0	2.0	2.1	3.1	2.0	3.6	Debt/Worth	2.2	2.2
-4.2	8.1	6.4	13.8	-11.8	190.7		16.7	17.0
232.2	78.1	62.3	63.9	60.2	50.0		56.8	66.1
(161) 87.1	(259) 38.9	(200) 29.2	(77) 21.8	(17) 21.8	(16) 17.3	% Profit Before Taxes/Tangible Net Worth	(305) 18.2	(563) 23.2
14.2	7.5	7.3	9.4	6.4	4.5		1.9	2.9
62.7	29.1	21.4	16.0	11.1	11.3		16.9	20.7
18.8	11.1	7.4	7.9	4.2	4.9	% Profit Before Taxes/Total Assets	5.5	6.9
-2.8	2.0	.4	2.1	1.7	1.1		.0	.0
218.2	61.9	61.3	57.2	178.3	31.7		43.2	50.6
37.8	21.4	16.9	11.4	8.9	7.1	Sales/Net Fixed Assets	12.2	13.4
11.2	7.4	5.1	3.5	5.1	1.6		3.3	4.2
10.9	4.6	3.2	2.7	1.5	1.8		4.0	4.5
5.4	3.1	2.3	1.6	.5	.8	Sales/Total Assets	2.5	2.5
3.3	1.8	1.4	.8	.2	.5		1.1	1.2
.6	.6	.6	.5	1.4	1.8		1.1	1.0
(136) 1.2	(229) 1.6	(190) 1.8	(85) 1.4	(16) 3.9	(16) 3.1	% Depr., Dep., Amort./Sales	(313) 2.7	(528) 2.7
2.7	3.4	4.1	4.5	7.6	8.1		5.3	5.8
5.4	3.0	1.9	.5				3.6	3.0
(137) 9.3	(122) 5.7	(75) 3.5	(22) 1.8			% Officers', Directors' Owners' Comp/Sales	(118) 6.9	(248) 6.2
17.3	12.3	6.8	5.2				14.5	12.1
402293M	1155791M	2525924M	3691692M	1403304M	3723095M	Net Sales ($)	12312939M	12961305M
60035M	326212M	1030720M	1969012M	1663023M	3027761M	Total Assets ($)	4232885M	5729741M

M = $ thousand   MM = $ million
See Pages 11 through 21 for Explanation of Ratios and Data

Comparative Historical Data　　　　　Current Data Sorted by Sales

			Type of Statement						
120	101	133	Unqualified	9	13	18	13	37	43
75	77	88	Reviewed	4	12	7	35	19	11
114	132	133	Compiled	17	49	27	26	12	2
205	209	236	Tax Returns	87	78	26	23	18	4
219	319	336	Other	45	95	53	56	45	42
4/1/04-3/31/05	4/1/05-3/31/06	4/1/06-3/31/07			124 (4/1-9/30/06)		802 (10/1/06-3/31/07)		
ALL	ALL	ALL		0-1MM	1-3MM	3-5MM	5-10MM	10-25MM	25MM & OVER
733	838	926	NUMBER OF STATEMENTS	162	247	131	153	131	102
%	%	%	ASSETS	%	%	%	%	%	%
18.5	17.7	16.6	Cash & Equivalents	20.0	17.5	15.3	15.9	16.6	11.4
27.5	28.6	28.9	Trade Receivables (net)	11.5	28.0	33.6	34.6	35.1	36.0
7.2	6.6	6.6	Inventory	3.3	5.9	9.0	7.4	7.3	8.2
4.6	4.3	4.8	All Other Current	4.2	4.1	4.4	4.9	6.7	5.9
57.9	57.3	56.9	Total Current	39.0	55.5	62.3	62.8	65.7	61.5
28.8	28.4	27.0	Fixed Assets (net)	42.6	26.9	24.0	25.0	18.7	20.1
3.8	5.2	5.5	Intangibles (net)	6.9	5.2	3.2	4.0	4.6	10.3
9.4	9.1	10.7	All Other Non-Current	11.6	12.4	10.6	8.3	11.0	8.1
100.0	100.0	100.0	Total	100.0	100.0	100.0	100.0	100.0	100.0
			LIABILITIES						
13.5	14.8	13.0	Notes Payable-Short Term	16.7	15.0	15.2	10.6	8.3	9.2
5.0	4.9	4.3	Cur. Mat.-L.T.D.	6.7	3.0	4.8	4.3	3.9	3.3
12.4	12.0	12.5	Trade Payables	6.3	11.9	13.8	14.3	14.0	17.6
.5	.4	.4	Income Taxes Payable	.1	.2	.2	.3	1.1	.9
17.3	18.6	18.1	All Other Current	31.5	15.7	15.3	14.3	13.2	18.1
48.7	50.7	48.3	Total Current	61.3	45.8	49.3	43.7	40.5	49.0
22.4	21.2	20.5	Long-Term Debt	35.3	21.5	17.2	17.9	10.8	14.8
.3	.4	.3	Deferred Taxes	.0	.1	.1	.6	.2	.7
8.6	9.1	6.2	All Other Non-Current	8.6	6.7	3.3	5.3	6.5	5.9
20.0	18.7	24.8	Net Worth	-5.2	26.0	30.2	32.5	42.0	29.4
100.0	100.0	100.0	Total Liabilties & Net Worth	100.0	100.0	100.0	100.0	100.0	100.0
			INCOME DATA						
100.0	100.0	100.0	Net Sales	100.0	100.0	100.0	100.0	100.0	100.0
			Gross Profit						
91.5	91.0	90.8	Operating Expenses	84.1	92.2	92.5	92.3	91.0	93.4
8.5	9.0	9.2	Operating Profit	15.9	7.8	7.5	7.7	9.0	6.6
1.7	1.9	2.1	All Other Expenses (net)	6.2	1.3	1.1	1.4	1.1	.9
6.9	7.1	7.1	Profit Before Taxes	9.7	6.5	6.4	6.3	7.9	5.7
			RATIOS						
2.7	2.7	2.5		2.8	3.1	2.4	2.7	2.9	1.9
1.4	1.4	1.4	Current	.9	1.5	1.4	1.5	1.6	1.4
.9	.8	.8		.2	.8	.8	1.0	1.2	.9
2.2	2.2	2.1		1.9	2.6	1.9	2.4	2.3	1.5
1.1 (837)	1.1 (925)	1.1	Quick	.7 (246)	1.2	1.1	1.2	1.4	.9
.5	.6	.5		.5	.5	.5	.5	.8	.7
1 626.3	1 402.3	1 673.4		0 UND	0 UND	12 30.1	15 24.9	16 23.3	27 13.5
30 12.1	32 11.4	33 11.0	Sales/Receivables	0 UND	28 13.3	35 10.3	40 9.2	42 8.6	53 6.9
59 6.2	58 6.3	62 5.9		22 16.3	60 6.1	69 5.3	62 5.9	70 5.2	77 4.7
			Cost of Sales/Inventory						
			Cost of Sales/Payables						
7.0	7.0	7.8		13.2	7.3	7.5	7.9	5.1	9.1
19.8	24.4	22.3	Sales/Working Capital	-55.7	21.4	18.8	18.4	14.1	22.4
-47.4	-48.1	-46.8		-6.8	-45.1	-86.1	283.8	53.6	-59.9
17.4	18.8	17.0		9.5	15.1	22.0	17.0	25.8	15.4
(557) 4.8	(668) 5.2	(715) 4.3	EBIT/Interest	(95) 2.7	(187) 3.8	(108) 5.3	(135) 4.3	(102) 8.4	(88) 5.1
1.2	1.4	1.1		-.7	.4	1.1	.9	2.3	2.1
7.0	5.8	6.5			3.9		5.6	19.4	9.6
(88) 2.8	(79) 2.2	(99) 2.4	Net Profit + Depr., Dep., Amort./Cur. Mat. L/T/D	(12) 1.7		(19) 2.2	(27) 4.8	(29) 2.2
1.1	1.0	1.0			-.8		.9	1.7	.9
.2	.2	.1		.1	.1	.2	.2	.1	.2
.8	.9	.6	Fixed/Worth	2.1	.7	.5	.6	.3	.7
6.3	11.4	4.3		-12.8	11.4	2.2	2.7	1.2	13.6
.8	.9	.7		.9	.6	.6	.9	.6	1.1
2.5	2.9	2.5	Debt/Worth	7.2	2.3	2.4	2.0	1.7	4.0
30.9	UND	28.8		-4.4	48.3	6.8	9.6	4.1	61.4
74.1	98.4	86.5		145.0	110.9	78.7	70.3	76.1	76.0
(570) 28.1	(633) 38.3	(730) 37.1	% Profit Before Taxes/Tangible Net Worth	(105) 27.3	(189) 43.1	(108) 46.7	(129) 33.5	(120) 34.4	(79) 34.5
7.4	9.7	7.9		2.8	6.7	8.9	7.6	10.0	14.8
22.2	28.6	29.4		36.5	34.5	29.4	26.7	30.2	18.9
8.8	9.6	9.6	% Profit Before Taxes/Total Assets	6.1	11.1	14.6	7.9	14.8	8.1
.5	1.2	.7		-1.0	.0	2.0	-.1	2.9	2.7
65.4	70.0	80.0		144.1	75.5	64.8	65.2	122.9	66.8
18.8	18.0	22.1	Sales/Net Fixed Assets	11.1	23.2	28.7	19.3	29.5	16.3
5.6	6.2	6.7		1.4	8.1	12.1	7.6	7.9	7.1
4.8	4.7	4.8		5.6	5.3	4.7	5.3	4.2	4.0
2.8	2.9	3.0	Sales/Total Assets	2.2	3.2	3.3	3.1	2.6	2.4
1.5	1.6	1.6		.6	1.8	2.1	1.9	1.6	1.2
.8	.7	.6		1.1	.8	.4	.7	.3	.4
(532) 1.9	(607) 1.7	(672) 1.6	% Depr., Dep., Amort./Sales	(97) 3.8	(164) 1.6	(93) 1.4	(125) 1.9	(106) 1.0	(87) 1.3
4.8	4.1	3.6		16.9	3.0	3.0	3.5	2.4	3.1
3.1	3.1	2.8		6.5	4.9	3.1	2.1	1.3	.6
(276) 6.5	(327) 6.8	(359) 6.1	% Officers', Directors' Owners' Comp/Sales	(67) 9.8	(109) 9.2	(58) 5.1	(66) 3.9	(39) 2.3	(20) 1.7
13.0	12.3	11.9		19.5	15.5	10.3	8.0	4.4	4.4
17053271M	12260241M	12902099M	Net Sales ($)	77386M	460322M	515041M	1093563M	2054798M	8700989M
6284705M	6841423M	8076763M	Total Assets ($)	87605M	398005M	314950M	571040M	1696437M	5008726M

© RMA 2007　　M = $ thousand　　MM = $ million
See Pages 11 through 21 for Explanation of Ratios and Data

MANAGEMENT OF
COMPANIES AND
ENTERPRISES

MANAGEMENT—Offices of Other Holding Companies NAICS 551112 (SIC 6719)

Current Data Sorted by Assets

Comparative Historical Data

						Type of Statement		
3	7	22	33	22	13	Unqualified	113	129
2	12	30	20	2	1	Reviewed	112	89
17	41	53	17	2		Compiled	242	277
36	115	59	10	1		Tax Returns	285	300
26	89	83	51	15	11	Other	308	307
	88 (4/1-9/30/06)		705 (10/1/06-3/31/07)				4/1/02-3/31/03	4/1/03-3/31/04
0-500M	500M-2MM	2-10MM	10-50MM	50-100MM	100-250MM		ALL	ALL
84	264	247	131	42	25	NUMBER OF STATEMENTS	1060	1102
%	%	%	%	%	%	ASSETS	%	%
16.8	6.7	6.5	8.3	12.7	5.0	Cash & Equivalents	6.4	6.0
3.9	3.5	6.4	12.3	18.6	13.4	Trade Receivables (net)	5.1	5.9
4.3	2.8	4.9	11.4	7.8	7.5	Inventory	3.9	4.1
5.2	2.2	2.9	5.0	9.0	7.6	All Other Current	3.6	4.0
30.2	15.2	20.7	37.1	48.0	33.6	Total Current	19.0	20.0
53.1	73.6	65.0	46.2	31.8	38.4	Fixed Assets (net)	69.5	66.3
2.9	2.6	2.8	3.9	8.9	12.0	Intangibles (net)	1.8	2.5
13.8	8.6	11.6	12.9	11.3	16.0	All Other Non-Current	9.7	11.1
100.0	100.0	100.0	100.0	100.0	100.0	Total	100.0	100.0
						LIABILITIES		
7.6	4.5	6.3	8.2	8.2	3.7	Notes Payable-Short Term	5.5	6.4
4.5	4.8	4.3	3.5	4.7	4.2	Cur. Mat.-L.T.D.	5.6	4.5
3.5	2.2	3.1	6.0	7.7	9.1	Trade Payables	3.2	3.4
.0	.1	.1	.2	.2	.5	Income Taxes Payable	.1	.1
18.2	4.7	6.5	9.4	15.0	10.4	All Other Current	7.4	8.2
33.7	16.3	20.2	27.3	35.8	27.9	Total Current	21.8	22.6
37.3	55.6	45.6	32.6	28.0	31.8	Long-Term Debt	51.1	47.5
.0	.0	.4	.6	.2	1.0	Deferred Taxes	.3	.3
14.7	4.3	2.5	6.0	4.9	3.8	All Other Non-Current	4.6	6.1
14.3	23.8	31.3	33.4	31.0	35.5	Net Worth	22.2	23.5
100.0	100.0	100.0	100.0	100.0	100.0	Total Liabilties & Net Worth	100.0	100.0
						INCOME DATA		
100.0	100.0	100.0	100.0	100.0	100.0	Net Sales	100.0	100.0
						Gross Profit		
66.0	52.0	60.0	73.3	80.6	76.5	Operating Expenses	58.9	59.3
34.0	48.0	40.0	26.7	19.4	23.5	Operating Profit	41.1	40.7
11.1	23.1	20.2	9.3	9.2	8.4	All Other Expenses (net)	19.4	17.8
22.9	24.9	19.8	17.4	10.2	15.1	Profit Before Taxes	21.7	22.9
						RATIOS		
4.4	2.0	1.9	2.4	2.0	1.8		1.6	2.1
1.2	.6	1.0	1.2	1.3	1.2	Current	.6	.8
.4	.2	.2	.6	.9	.6		.2	.2
2.9	1.4	1.4	1.3	1.4	1.0		1.1	1.2
(82) .8	.5	(246) .6	.7	.8	.7	Quick	.4	.4
.2	.1	.1	.2	.5	.3		.1	.1
0 UND	0 UND	0 UND	0 UND	12 30.9	4 93.4		0 UND	0 UND
0 UND	0 UND	0 UND	16 23.1	39 9.4	25 14.7	Sales/Receivables	0 UND	0 UND
0 UND	0 UND	31 11.7	53 6.8	69 5.3	57 6.4		13 27.6	14 25.5
						Cost of Sales/Inventory		
						Cost of Sales/Payables		
7.7	12.4	6.0	4.0	5.1	7.3		8.5	6.9
38.7	-19.4	-70.6	21.8	15.6	21.3	Sales/Working Capital	-10.6	-22.8
-8.9	-3.2	-2.8	-16.4	-98.5	-9.5		-2.3	-2.4
15.5	9.0	11.3	9.7	10.6	6.7		6.9	7.5
(39) 4.0	(108) 3.8	(114) 3.4	(87) 3.5	(31) 3.7	(18) 3.9	EBIT/Interest	(500) 3.6	(564) 3.8
1.9	1.7	1.5	1.5	1.2	1.5		1.5	1.7
		4.7	8.5	16.3	17.5		3.1	4.0
		(32) 2.6	(31) 1.9	(11) 3.1	(11) 2.3	Net Profit + Depr., Dep., Amort./Cur. Mat. L/T/D	(121) 1.7	(101) 1.7
		1.0	.8	-.1	.9		.8	.8
.2	1.3	.9	.5	.1	.5		1.2	1.1
1.7	4.0	3.0	1.6	1.4	2.0	Fixed/Worth	3.1	3.2
12.6	17.4	7.6	6.0	7.2	-7.1		14.0	14.5
.5	1.2	1.2	.9	1.3	1.0		1.2	1.2
2.0	4.0	2.9	2.4	2.9	2.0	Debt/Worth	3.4	3.6
32.7	80.4	8.8	8.4	13.2	-8.8		19.2	21.2
67.6	38.9	35.9	42.3	44.8	40.6		37.5	43.1
(65) 22.5	(203) 18.2	(221) 18.6	(108) 19.5	(33) 28.2	(18) 20.1	% Profit Before Taxes/Tangible Net Worth	(882) 17.8	(908) 19.4
7.5	7.3	5.9	8.3	8.6	7.3		5.1	7.6
42.9	11.3	9.7	12.1	13.3	9.2		9.4	9.7
9.2	4.8	4.2	4.8	6.0	5.8	% Profit Before Taxes/Total Assets	4.1	4.5
1.1	1.2	.9	1.8	.2	2.2		.9	1.1
29.6	.9	4.3	14.7	23.0	23.9		1.6	2.6
2.1	.2	.3	3.4	4.8	7.4	Sales/Net Fixed Assets	.3	.3
.2	.2	.1	.2	.7	1.4		.2	.2
3.9	.5	.8	1.7	2.0	1.8		.5	.6
.8	.2	.2	.7	1.2	1.2	Sales/Total Assets	.2	.2
.2	.1	.1	.1	.3	.2		.1	.1
1.5	9.4	5.1	1.2	1.1	.9		6.8	6.4
(55) 9.8	(218) 15.5	(214) 15.4	(113) 4.3	(40) 3.0	(18) 2.8	% Depr., Dep., Amort./Sales	(954) 15.1	(958) 15.1
16.9	21.9	23.8	18.1	7.6	6.8		23.2	22.9
2.3	3.1	2.3	1.9				2.1	2.4
(16) 9.0	(32) 8.8	(39) 5.7	(10) 5.5			% Officers', Directors' Owners' Comp/Sales	(110) 4.9	(126) 5.8
20.2	18.8	18.0	10.9				12.2	11.9
51585M	230062M	815734M	3971181M	3861082M	4320466M	Net Sales ($)	10963748M	15766601M
22056M	310326M	1153869M	3059884M	2890829M	3569200M	Total Assets ($)	12591682M	14660347M

M = $ thousand   MM = $ million
See Pages 11 through 21 for Explanation of Ratios and Data

Comparative Historical Data | Current Data Sorted by Sales

			Type of Statement	0-1MM	1-3MM	3-5MM	5-10MM	10-25MM	25MM & OVER
109	81	100	Unqualified	16	12	4	7	9	52
78	83	67	Reviewed	26	11	3	5	8	14
197	164	130	Compiled	82	21	7	5	11	4
318	260	221	Tax Returns	169	31	6	10	4	1
289	312	275	Other	128	51	12	29	18	37
4/1/04- 3/31/05	4/1/05- 3/31/06	4/1/06- 3/31/07		88 (4/1-9/30/06)			705 (10/1/06-3/31/07)		
ALL	ALL	ALL							
991	900	793	**NUMBER OF STATEMENTS**	421	126	32	56	50	108
%	%	%	**ASSETS**	%	%	%	%	%	%
7.0	7.4	8.2	Cash & Equivalents	6.6	8.7	8.7	12.1	9.7	11.2
6.3	7.0	7.0	Trade Receivables (net)	.9	6.7	12.7	12.0	20.1	20.7
5.3	6.0	5.5	Inventory	1.3	5.8	5.9	10.4	13.9	14.6
3.2	3.0	3.7	All Other Current	1.8	4.6	6.3	6.5	9.4	5.3
21.8	23.3	24.4	Total Current	10.6	25.8	33.7	41.1	53.2	51.9
64.6	63.6	60.9	Fixed Assets (net)	78.7	57.8	40.5	33.4	29.6	30.0
3.0	2.8	3.5	Intangibles (net)	1.4	3.6	4.0	7.9	4.9	8.6
10.6	10.2	11.2	All Other Non-Current	9.3	12.8	21.9	17.6	12.4	9.5
100.0	100.0	100.0	Total	100.0	100.0	100.0	100.0	100.0	100.0
			LIABILITIES						
7.1	6.2	6.1	Notes Payable-Short Term	4.6	7.2	9.1	7.4	8.1	8.4
3.9	3.9	4.4	Cur. Mat.-L.T.D.	4.6	4.2	4.2	6.6	3.5	3.2
3.7	4.1	3.7	Trade Payables	1.3	3.1	4.2	6.7	7.8	10.6
.1	.1	.1	Income Taxes Payable	.1	.1	.0	.1	.2	.4
6.2	6.6	8.2	All Other Current	5.0	8.9	10.7	11.7	11.9	15.2
21.0	21.0	22.6	Total Current	15.6	23.4	28.3	32.5	31.4	37.8
49.7	47.6	44.6	Long-Term Debt	56.1	44.3	28.6	23.2	32.8	21.0
.2	.2	.3	Deferred Taxes	.0	.2	1.1	.4	.3	.9
4.5	4.5	5.1	All Other Non-Current	5.1	3.2	7.1	6.4	6.8	5.4
24.5	26.6	27.5	Net Worth	23.1	28.9	34.9	37.6	28.8	34.9
100.0	100.0	100.0	Total Liabilties & Net Worth	100.0	100.0	100.0	100.0	100.0	100.0
			INCOME DATA						
100.0	100.0	100.0	Net Sales	100.0	100.0	100.0	100.0	100.0	100.0
			Gross Profit						
61.1	61.0	61.8	Operating Expenses	46.8	65.0	73.7	83.8	85.5	90.5
38.9	39.0	38.2	Operating Profit	53.2	35.0	26.3	16.2	14.5	9.5
16.1	17.4	17.5	All Other Expenses (net)	26.9	11.9	8.4	5.2	4.5	2.1
22.8	21.6	20.8	Profit Before Taxes	26.3	23.1	17.8	11.0	10.0	7.4
			RATIOS						
2.1	2.1	2.1	Current	1.8	3.0	2.6	2.6	2.6	1.9
.9	1.0	1.0		.6	1.1	1.3	1.3	1.7	1.3
.2	.3	.3		.2	.3	.5	.7	1.2	1.0
1.5	1.5	1.4	Quick	1.3	2.0	1.9	1.8	1.4	1.2
(989) .5	.6 (790)	.6		(419) .4	.6	.5	(55) .8	1.0	.8
.1	.1	.2		.1	.1	.1	.3	.6	.5
0 UND	0 UND	0 UND	Sales/Receivables	0 UND	0 UND	0 UND	0 UND	2 195.3	15 25.1
0 UND	0 UND	0 UND		0 UND	0 UND	4 89.3	12 30.6	35 10.4	39 9.4
17 21.2	23 16.0	27 13.5		0 UND	30 12.1	43 8.4	52 7.0	61 6.0	61 6.0
			Cost of Sales/Inventory						
			Cost of Sales/Payables						
5.9	5.9	6.3	Sales/Working Capital	9.9	3.8	4.0	7.7	2.9	6.2
-62.0	-212.8	UND		-10.7	140.7	17.6	31.7	7.8	20.5
-3.4	-3.6	-3.7		-2.3	-3.2	-9.8	-18.2	26.6	-141.8
7.9	9.8	10.3	EBIT/Interest	7.0	13.7	15.7	12.3	10.3	10.6
(524) 4.1	(433) 4.4	(397) 3.7		(128) 3.8	(67) 3.4	(23) 5.7	(45) 3.0	3.3	(89) 3.8
1.8	2.0	1.6		2.1	1.3	1.7	1.2	1.5	1.5
4.5	4.0	6.4	Net Profit + Depr., Dep., Amort./Cur. Mat. L/T/D	3.8	2.4		4.0		9.9
(100) 1.5	(96) 2.1	(94) 2.4		(13) 2.4	(11) 1.6		(11) 2.8	(45) 2.3	
.8	1.1	1.0		.7	1.1		1.5		1.0
1.0	.9	.9	Fixed/Worth	1.7	.5	.1	.3	.2	.4
2.9	2.8	2.6		4.2	2.2	1.0	1.0	1.5	1.1
12.4	11.3	11.0		13.8	13.1	3.3	5.3	4.5	3.6
1.2	1.1	1.1	Debt/Worth	1.2	.7	.6	.5	1.3	1.0
3.4	3.3	3.0		3.9	2.4	1.7	2.3	2.7	2.5
16.5	14.2	15.0		17.8	30.6	7.4	12.5	18.9	8.3
44.1	41.4	41.7	% Profit Before Taxes/Tangible Net Worth	33.8	64.7	28.3	79.8	67.4	60.1
(814) 19.4	(745) 19.8	(648) 18.9		(345) 16.3	(101) 20.0	(27) 12.4	(46) 31.1	(40) 31.0	(89) 25.5
6.4	6.9	6.4		5.6	8.9	5.0	6.1	17.5	13.4
10.0	10.7	11.9	% Profit Before Taxes/Total Assets	9.1	14.2	12.7	18.4	16.2	14.3
4.8	4.8	4.8		4.1	5.4	4.4	6.3	6.5	8.4
1.3	1.2	1.1		1.0	1.8	1.0	1.0	1.8	2.1
4.0	6.2	8.7	Sales/Net Fixed Assets	.3	13.7	24.3	25.8	23.5	23.5
.3	.3	.4		.2	.6	4.4	8.9	8.5	8.5
.2	.2	.2		.1	.2	.4	1.9	2.0	3.4
.8	1.2	1.4	Sales/Total Assets	.2	1.3	3.0	3.1	2.4	2.8
.2	.2	.2		.2	.3	.7	1.8	1.3	1.7
.1	.1	.1		.2	.2	.2	.6	.4	1.2
5.4	3.6	3.2	% Depr., Dep., Amort./Sales	11.8	2.5	1.2	1.5	.9	.8
(834) 14.9	(787) 13.1	(658) 12.6		(360) 17.4	(96) 13.7	(24) 3.6	(45) 2.3	(42) 3.3	(91) 2.0
23.0	21.0	20.8		24.5	22.0	18.2	5.1	6.6	4.1
2.4	1.7	2.5	% Officers', Directors' Owners' Comp/Sales	3.7	1.7	2.5	2.3		
(122) 5.5	(106) 4.9	(102) 6.7		(31) 11.1	(28) 7.0	(11) 9.0	(15) 4.3		
13.6	13.5	16.4		20.9	17.0	15.9	9.2		
13704641M	13669694M	13250110M	Net Sales ($)	139624M	221634M	126647M	405493M	807681M	11549031M
13172365M	12361076M	11006164M	Total Assets ($)	861237M	861195M	445351M	700024M	1211932M	6926425M

M = $ thousand   MM = $ million
See Pages 11 through 21 for Explanation of Ratios and Data

ADMINISTRATIVE AND SUPPORT AND WASTE MANAGEMENT AND REMEDIATION SERVICES

Current Data Sorted by Assets | **Comparative Historical Data**

0-500M	500M-2MM	2-10MM	10-50MM	50-100MM	100-250MM	Type of Statement	4/1/02-3/31/03 ALL	4/1/03-3/31/04 ALL
3	6	16	25	6	8	Unqualified	64	63
2	11	13	2			Reviewed	37	33
6	11	6			1	Compiled	26	64
25	21	7			5	Tax Returns	32	43
19	21	28	10	4		Other	87	93
	37 (4/1-9/30/06)		219 (10/1/06-3/31/07)					
55	70	70	37	10	14	NUMBER OF STATEMENTS	246	296
%	%	%	%	%	%	ASSETS	%	%
38.8	15.0	14.5	24.8	10.7	15.1	Cash & Equivalents	17.3	18.3
10.5	29.3	26.2	28.5	21.0	18.5	Trade Receivables (net)	24.3	22.8
.0	3.2	3.0	4.7	3.4	4.6	Inventory	2.7	2.7
6.3	8.6	7.3	4.0	2.4	7.0	All Other Current	7.4	8.7
55.7	56.0	51.1	62.0	37.5	45.1	Total Current	51.7	52.6
27.6	23.1	24.1	26.5	25.5	21.4	Fixed Assets (net)	26.3	23.2
3.6	2.7	7.8	5.2	22.6	17.3	Intangibles (net)	6.9	7.7
13.1	18.1	17.1	6.4	14.4	16.2	All Other Non-Current	15.2	16.5
100.0	100.0	100.0	100.0	100.0	100.0	Total	100.0	100.0
						LIABILITIES		
13.2	14.2	8.9	6.6	1.3	.5	Notes Payable-Short Term	9.9	11.0
2.5	3.3	4.0	3.4	5.9	.9	Cur. Mat.-L.T.D.	3.4	3.8
3.4	10.6	10.1	15.4	7.3	12.3	Trade Payables	11.4	10.7
1.7	.8	.5	.2	.7	.1	Income Taxes Payable	.6	.4
53.0	19.5	21.9	12.6	21.2	18.5	All Other Current	18.2	20.6
73.8	48.5	45.5	38.3	36.4	32.4	Total Current	43.6	46.4
19.0	19.6	23.2	16.2	24.7	17.5	Long-Term Debt	18.9	18.6
.0	.3	.1	.6	.5	.6	Deferred Taxes	.3	.2
1.4	5.3	7.9	5.9	12.6	8.8	All Other Non-Current	6.9	9.0
5.8	26.2	23.2	38.9	25.8	40.6	Net Worth	30.4	25.8
100.0	100.0	100.0	100.0	100.0	100.0	Total Liabilities & Net Worth	100.0	100.0
						INCOME DATA		
100.0	100.0	100.0	100.0	100.0	100.0	Net Sales	100.0	100.0
						Gross Profit		
87.5	91.2	83.4	93.4	88.6	89.8	Operating Expenses	91.3	89.3
12.5	8.8	16.6	6.6	11.4	10.2	Operating Profit	8.7	10.7
.6	2.5	4.0	.6	2.7	2.5	All Other Expenses (net)	1.4	2.3
11.9	6.2	12.6	6.0	8.8	7.7	Profit Before Taxes	7.3	8.4
						RATIOS		
7.4	2.5	2.6	3.9	1.6	2.5		2.4	2.7
1.1	1.3	1.3	1.9	1.1	1.4	Current	1.3	1.3
.2	.7	.7	1.1	.8	.8		.8	.8
7.0	1.8	1.8	3.8	1.6	2.2		2.0	2.0
.9	.9	1.1	1.3	.8	.9	Quick	1.1	1.0
.2	.5	.4	.9	.7	.6		.5	.5
0 UND	0 UND	4 102.9	30 12.3	20 17.8	22 16.6		0 UND	0 UND
0 UND	23 16.0	25 14.7	40 9.2	35 10.5	38 9.6	Sales/Receivables	26 13.8	28 13.0
4 93.5	61 6.0	65 5.6	61 6.0	68 5.4	74 5.0		55 6.6	57 6.5
						Cost of Sales/Inventory		
						Cost of Sales/Payables		
8.5	8.3	5.2	3.8	7.7	3.3		7.7	6.2
99.6	44.1	22.2	9.0	113.6	19.1	Sales/Working Capital	29.8	22.9
-22.6	-23.3	-10.9	82.1	-9.2	-28.4		-39.4	-24.5
16.7	12.6	17.1	20.4	14.7	29.8		17.3	15.3
(30) 3.5	(46) 2.9	(56) 3.8	(33) 6.3	5.8	(13) 6.2	EBIT/Interest	(183) 4.9	(203) 5.0
.0	-.6	1.6	1.3	1.4	2.3		1.4	1.5
						Net Profit + Depr., Dep.,	14.3	11.3
						Amort./Cur. Mat. L/T/D	(38) 4.4 / (37) 3.3	
							1.3	1.9
.0	.1	.1	.4	.9	.3		.2	.2
.5	.8	.9	.8	19.9	.7	Fixed/Worth	.7	.6
UND	-8.6	-2.5	2.3	-.5	-4.6		3.3	3.7
.4	.9	.9	.7	2.5	.7		.8	.8
2.3	2.9	5.4	1.7	53.7	1.9	Debt/Worth	2.4	2.5
-5.2	-34.5	-7.6	5.5	-5.1	-8.6		14.8	17.6
251.4	97.5	63.9	71.2		71.4		75.0	72.7
(40) 109.4	(51) 28.4	(46) 30.6	(32) 30.2		(10) 11.5	% Profit Before Taxes/Tangible Net Worth	(206) 30.5	(241) 29.8
22.9	3.3	9.7	6.9		2.7		6.4	7.3
121.3	32.4	22.7	23.8	21.5	10.2		20.5	20.6
33.5	6.2	9.4	7.5	5.5	5.2	% Profit Before Taxes/Total Assets	8.0	8.9
.0	-.8	2.4	.8	1.8	2.1		.7	1.2
678.0	93.9	87.2	51.4	30.1	16.4		56.4	65.9
48.3	33.5	24.3	13.4	10.1	6.7	Sales/Net Fixed Assets	15.4	18.5
13.1	8.7	5.6	5.0	1.5	2.1		5.0	5.3
13.6	4.6	3.8	3.4	2.5	1.7		4.1	4.1
6.4	3.4	1.8	2.4	1.8	.9	Sales/Total Assets	2.3	2.2
2.3	1.8	.5	1.4	.4	.7		1.1	1.1
.4	.7	.5	.6		.7		.8	1.2
(27) 1.2	(53) 1.3	(53) 2.3	(33) 1.5		(11) 2.8	% Depr., Dep., Amort./Sales	(189) 1.8	(209) 2.4
2.5	3.4	4.8	3.6		7.9		4.8	5.1
7.9	3.1	2.7					4.2	3.7
(19) 10.6	(22) 7.3	(13) 7.4				% Officers', Directors' Owners' Comp/Sales	(64) 8.6	(67) 8.6
20.7	23.3	26.3					17.5	16.8
77239M	258407M	920096M	2182886M	1207915M	2714536M	Net Sales ($)	9637337M	2071392M
11654M	76047M	336354M	882523M	759436M	2415091M	Total Assets ($)	4998292M	1507209M

M = $ thousand   MM = $ million
See Pages 11 through 21 for Explanation of Ratios and Data

Comparative Historical Data | | | | Current Data Sorted by Sales

			Type of Statement						
47	48	64	Unqualified	2	5	4	8	9	36
36	34	28	Reviewed	1	5	7	7	5	3
36	31	23	Compiled	4	5	7	6	1	
44	44	54	Tax Returns	21	15	8	7	2	1
78	116	87	Other	22	12	15	9	12	17
4/1/04-3/31/05 ALL	4/1/05-3/31/06 ALL	4/1/06-3/31/07 ALL		0-1MM	37 (4/1-9/30/06) 1-3MM	3-5MM	219 (10/1/06-3/31/07) 5-10MM	10-25MM	25MM & OVER
241	273	256	**NUMBER OF STATEMENTS**	50	42	41	37	29	57
%	%	%	**ASSETS**	%	%	%	%	%	%
20.4	18.5	21.2	Cash & Equivalents	27.1	22.0	18.3	22.5	23.1	15.9
23.5	27.4	23.4	Trade Receivables (net)	11.2	16.9	28.9	28.2	25.1	31.0
2.0	3.4	2.8	Inventory	.2	.7	3.1	4.4	2.4	5.3
7.0	7.0	6.8	All Other Current	7.2	6.9	9.1	6.5	6.7	4.7
52.8	56.2	54.1	Total Current	45.7	46.5	59.4	61.7	57.3	56.9
22.9	20.9	24.8	Fixed Assets (net)	28.9	31.9	21.1	19.9	19.6	24.6
8.6	5.8	6.2	Intangibles (net)	4.1	4.8	3.5	6.2	8.7	9.8
15.7	17.1	14.8	All Other Non-Current	21.3	16.8	16.0	12.2	14.4	8.7
100.0	100.0	100.0	Total	100.0	100.0	100.0	100.0	100.0	100.0
			LIABILITIES						
14.4	9.4	10.2	Notes Payable-Short Term	8.8	19.6	13.3	9.5	5.9	4.8
2.9	3.4	3.3	Cur. Mat.-L.T.D.	4.4	.9	3.9	4.2	2.7	3.6
10.9	12.1	9.6	Trade Payables	1.9	7.3	11.3	11.3	12.1	14.5
.4	.6	.8	Income Taxes Payable	.0	.6	3.5	.3	.1	.3
21.5	22.0	26.4	All Other Current	44.2	26.8	19.3	20.9	22.1	21.3
50.2	47.5	50.3	Total Current	59.4	55.1	51.3	46.2	43.1	44.5
19.8	15.6	20.1	Long-Term Debt	24.6	26.7	19.4	13.7	12.0	19.8
.4	.3	.3	Deferred Taxes	.0	.0	.5	.1	.1	.6
5.7	10.9	5.8	All Other Non-Current	3.9	3.1	5.0	9.2	5.7	7.7
23.9	25.7	23.6	Net Worth	12.2	15.1	23.7	30.8	39.1	27.4
100.0	100.0	100.0	Total Liabilities & Net Worth	100.0	100.0	100.0	100.0	100.0	100.0
			INCOME DATA						
100.0	100.0	100.0	Net Sales	100.0	100.0	100.0	100.0	100.0	100.0
			Gross Profit						
89.3	90.4	88.4	Operating Expenses	75.8	89.7	90.7	92.6	91.7	92.5
10.7	9.6	11.6	Operating Profit	24.2	10.3	9.3	7.4	8.3	7.5
1.8	1.7	2.2	All Other Expenses (net)	5.3	2.3	1.9	1.3	-.2	1.6
8.9	7.9	9.3	Profit Before Taxes	18.9	8.0	7.4	6.1	8.5	5.9
			RATIOS						
2.6	2.5	2.9		5.7	7.1	3.0	3.3	3.2	2.3
1.2	1.2	1.3	Current	1.2	1.1	1.4	1.4	1.4	1.2
.7	.9	.7		.2	.4	.8	1.0	.9	.9
2.3	2.0	2.1		3.4	2.1	2.4	2.2	2.7	1.9
(239) 1.1	(272) 1.0	1.0	Quick	.8	.8	1.0	1.2	1.3	1.1
.5	.6	.5		.1	.1	.6	.7	.6	.7
0 UND	0 999.8	0 UND		0 UND	0 UND	0 UND	0 UND	19 19.4	19 19.3
21 17.1	29 12.4	24 15.4	Sales/Receivables	0 UND	0 UND	28 13.0	30 12.2	39 9.5	39 9.4
56 6.5	57 6.4	56 6.5		39 9.4	21 17.0	64 5.7	54 6.8	60 6.1	63 5.8
			Cost of Sales/Inventory						
			Cost of Sales/Payables						
6.3	7.5	6.2		4.2	5.5	7.6	8.6	4.0	6.6
31.1	30.7	28.4	Sales/Working Capital	63.1	108.0	37.6	24.8	13.7	28.9
-26.4	-58.0	-29.7		-6.1	-10.2	-30.3	-637.1	-69.2	-247.9
24.5	18.8	16.2		13.1	7.0	13.1	17.0	37.7	16.7
(170) 6.2	(197) 5.7	(188) 3.9	EBIT/Interest	(26) 3.5	(32) 2.8	(26) 2.8	(27) 5.3	(25) 15.2	(52) 6.3
1.4	1.3	1.1		-.6	.3	.5	1.0	2.5	1.8
15.6	6.2	12.8							13.9
(32) 4.2	(39) 1.8	(27) 3.1	Net Profit + Depr., Dep., Amort./Cur. Mat. L/T/D					(15) 2.1	
.7	.2	.8							.6
.1	.1	.1		.0	.2	.1	.0	.1	.5
.5	.5	.9	Fixed/Worth	.9	1.2	.4	.4	.4	1.2
3.7	3.3	-12.9		UND	NM	-1.8	NM	-6.0	-9.1
.8	.8	.8		.7	.8	.6	.5	.5	1.4
2.7	2.3	3.2	Debt/Worth	1.8	4.6	2.7	3.3	1.5	4.2
15.0	29.9	-17.6		-15.2	-32.2	-9.4	NM	-19.2	-22.1
82.0	88.2	90.3	% Profit Before Taxes/Tangible Net Worth	147.1	77.2	91.5	193.6	84.6	76.5
(193) 27.6	(216) 35.3	(185) 38.2		(36) 51.7	(31) 17.7	(28) 25.3	(28) 52.6	(21) 35.4	(41) 39.6
7.8	4.6	8.2		16.9	3.3	2.9	8.9	8.1	13.8
23.2	26.8	27.9	% Profit Before Taxes/Total Assets	63.3	24.1	33.7	41.1	24.8	19.8
8.7	8.9	8.9		13.3	4.3	9.4	12.0	10.2	7.5
1.5	.1	.7		-.9	.0	.0	1.1	3.1	1.0
118.8	111.2	84.7	Sales/Net Fixed Assets	749.8	110.6	83.8	200.7	72.1	40.0
25.0	24.6	25.2		30.2	21.7	42.6	35.6	29.1	12.3
6.7	10.1	6.9		2.0	2.8	12.1	12.4	8.2	5.0
4.8	4.9	4.4	Sales/Total Assets	2.8	7.1	4.4	6.7	4.0	4.0
2.7	3.1	2.6		1.5	2.2	3.2	3.9	2.6	2.4
1.3	1.7	1.2		.7	.5	1.8	2.4	1.2	1.5
.7	.6	.6	% Depr., Dep., Amort./Sales	.8	1.1	.6	.5	.6	.5
(170) 1.7	(193) 1.5	(185) 1.8		(28) 2.1	(30) 2.4	(29) 1.1	(25) 1.5	(23) 2.1	(50) 1.5
3.5	2.6	4.0		5.3	8.0	3.0	3.1	4.7	3.5
3.5	3.5	3.5	% Officers', Directors' Owners' Comp/Sales	8.0	7.9	5.0	.6		
(68) 10.8	(67) 8.3	(57) 8.4		(12) 22.1	(18) 11.5	(11) 8.2	(10) 2.5		
16.1	17.3	22.3		37.0	17.7	27.0	7.5		
6929860M	10090361M	7361079M	Net Sales ($)	24808M	76451M	153554M	276169M	489189M	6340908M
3894695M	4728722M	4481105M	Total Assets ($)	35137M	88653M	74464M	106447M	456962M	3719442M

M = $ thousand   MM = $ million
See Pages 11 through 21 for Explanation of Ratios and Data

Current Data Sorted by Assets

Comparative Historical Data

1	2	14	12	2			Type of Statement		
	6	6	2				Unqualified	18	26
1	1	2					Reviewed	9	3
2	4		1				Compiled	5	10
4	4	8	8	2	2		Tax Returns		5
	17 (4/1-9/30/06)		67 (10/1/06-3/31/07)				Other	22	22
								4/1/02-	4/1/03-
								3/31/03	3/31/04
0-500M	500M-2MM	2-10MM	10-50MM	50-100MM	100-250MM			ALL	ALL
8	17	30	23	4	2		NUMBER OF STATEMENTS	54	66
%	%	%	%	%	%		ASSETS	%	%
	13.3	13.1	7.7				Cash & Equivalents	9.2	7.7
	42.1	44.1	49.8				Trade Receivables (net)	45.2	48.5
	4.8	.8	.5				Inventory	1.9	1.9
	.7	8.7	16.0				All Other Current	8.7	8.0
	60.9	66.7	73.9				Total Current	65.0	66.0
	20.8	21.0	19.8				Fixed Assets (net)	21.5	19.1
	6.5	3.2	2.3				Intangibles (net)	7.4	5.4
	11.8	9.0	3.9				All Other Non-Current	6.1	9.5
	100.0	100.0	100.0				Total	100.0	100.0
							LIABILITIES		
	14.0	7.2	11.2				Notes Payable-Short Term	18.5	12.9
	6.8	5.6	5.0				Cur. Mat.-L.T.D.	4.2	3.8
	11.7	16.3	15.5				Trade Payables	12.7	16.6
	.5	2.1	.4				Income Taxes Payable	.3	.6
	16.0	13.7	17.4				All Other Current	17.4	19.8
	49.2	44.8	49.5				Total Current	53.1	53.7
	18.9	10.4	14.0				Long-Term Debt	14.2	9.6
	.1	.4	.1				Deferred Taxes	.6	.3
	4.0	3.0	2.4				All Other Non-Current	4.1	4.6
	27.7	41.5	34.0				Net Worth	28.0	31.9
	100.0	100.0	100.0				Total Liabilties & Net Worth	100.0	100.0
							INCOME DATA		
	100.0	100.0	100.0				Net Sales	100.0	100.0
							Gross Profit		
	94.3	89.3	92.6				Operating Expenses	94.5	93.2
	5.7	10.7	7.4				Operating Profit	5.5	6.8
	1.3	1.1	.8				All Other Expenses (net)	2.1	1.4
	4.4	9.6	6.6				Profit Before Taxes	3.4	5.4
							RATIOS		
	3.3	2.3	2.6					2.0	1.8
	1.5	1.6	1.4				Current	1.4	1.4
	.8	1.3	1.2					1.0	1.0
	3.4	2.0	2.5					1.8	1.6
	(16) 1.3	1.4	1.1				Quick	1.1	1.1
	.7	1.1	.7					.7	.8
11 34.3	25 14.4	28 13.1						34 10.7	42 8.6
50 7.4	50 7.3	60 6.1					Sales/Receivables	56 6.5	63 5.8
65 5.6	74 4.9	91 4.0						68 5.3	77 4.7
							Cost of Sales/Inventory		
							Cost of Sales/Payables		
	5.4	5.8	6.0					9.1	7.2
	22.4	13.0	13.0				Sales/Working Capital	18.9	16.3
	-44.1	30.0	30.6					NM	NM
	16.0	27.5	22.8					19.1	20.4
	(15) 6.9	(22) 14.9	(19) 5.4				EBIT/Interest	(48) 5.4	(54) 7.5
	.2	6.1	2.4					1.9	2.0
								4.9	118.1
							Net Profit + Depr., Dep.,	(13) 1.3	(15) 6.0
							Amort./Cur. Mat. L/T/D	.3	1.7
	.1	.1	.1					.1	.1
	1.1	.1	.5				Fixed/Worth	.7	.4
	-9.3	1.4	1.1					2.5	1.4
	.8	.6	.6					.9	1.0
	3.1	1.5	2.5				Debt/Worth	3.1	2.3
	-11.8	3.1	8.8					18.0	6.7
	58.8	63.3	64.6				% Profit Before Taxes/Tangible	101.9	82.8
	(12) 34.4	(27) 37.0	(21) 36.4				Net Worth	(45) 46.5	(55) 40.2
	12.2	19.8	20.1					8.1	12.1
	15.7	25.4	17.4				% Profit Before Taxes/Total	22.4	22.4
	8.9	15.4	11.1				Assets	7.9	11.2
	-1.2	7.2	4.7					1.4	2.5
	211.8	152.4	135.6					118.8	112.0
	31.7	50.8	24.9				Sales/Net Fixed Assets	37.8	40.1
	14.5	5.1	13.0					8.7	11.7
	6.2	4.5	4.4					4.4	3.7
	3.5	3.0	2.9				Sales/Total Assets	2.7	2.7
	1.5	1.5	2.0					1.8	1.6
	.6	.4	.3					.3	.6
	(13) 1.1	(24) 1.1	(18) 1.3				% Depr., Dep., Amort./Sales	(46) 1.2	(52) 1.1
	2.3	4.0	2.1					3.8	2.5
								.8	1.1
							% Officers', Directors'	(13) 3.1	(17) 6.3
							Owners' Comp/Sales	4.6	16.6
14527M	81544M	458991M	1411022M	689221M	459568M		Net Sales ($)	2052429M	3230109M
1844M	18780M	146361M	477577M	244558M	288086M		Total Assets ($)	943924M	1510231M

M = $ thousand   MM = $ million
See Pages 11 through 21 for Explanation of Ratios and Data

Comparative Historical Data   **Current Data Sorted by Sales**

			Type of Statement	0-1MM	1-3MM	3-5MM	5-10MM	10-25MM	25MM & OVER
18	32	31	Unqualified	2	3		5	5	16
6	10	14	Reviewed	3			4	4	3
3	3	4	Compiled	1		1	1	1	
9	10	7	Tax Returns		1				1
18	25	28	Other	3	5	2	5	6	10
4/1/04-3/31/05 ALL	4/1/05-3/31/06 ALL	4/1/06-3/31/07 ALL			17 (4/1-9/30/06)		67 (10/1/06-3/31/07)		
54	80	84	NUMBER OF STATEMENTS	6	11	5	16	16	30
%	%	%	ASSETS	%	%	%	%	%	%
13.5	12.9	11.0	Cash & Equivalents		18.2		15.7	8.8	8.9
42.0	40.3	43.5	Trade Receivables (net)		30.3		40.6	52.4	51.9
2.5	2.0	1.8	Inventory		.5		.4	1.4	1.4
5.3	7.0	8.5	All Other Current		.7		3.6	16.0	12.4
63.3	62.2	64.7	Total Current		49.8		60.3	78.6	74.6
20.0	25.9	22.2	Fixed Assets (net)		35.8		21.9	15.8	14.7
2.5	4.4	3.8	Intangibles (net)		7.9		1.4	.4	3.8
14.2	7.4	9.3	All Other Non-Current		6.5		16.4	5.1	6.9
100.0	100.0	100.0	Total		100.0		100.0	100.0	100.0
			LIABILITIES						
15.6	10.9	9.5	Notes Payable-Short Term		11.2		3.9	10.5	10.4
2.7	4.9	5.1	Cur. Mat.-L.T.D.		7.7		3.0	.8	4.2
16.3	13.6	14.2	Trade Payables		7.9		16.3	15.9	16.9
.6	.9	1.0	Income Taxes Payable		.0		2.8	.7	.7
15.6	14.8	16.1	All Other Current		14.6		14.2	14.9	21.8
50.9	45.1	45.8	Total Current		41.5		40.1	42.7	54.0
14.8	15.4	14.6	Long-Term Debt		18.2		9.2	10.0	11.4
.3	.1	.2	Deferred Taxes		.0		.4	.1	.3
3.4	3.5	4.2	All Other Non-Current		8.5		8.8	1.9	2.7
30.6	35.9	35.1	Net Worth		31.8		41.5	45.3	31.5
100.0	100.0	100.0	Total Liabilities & Net Worth		100.0		100.0	100.0	100.0
			INCOME DATA						
100.0	100.0	100.0	Net Sales		100.0		100.0	100.0	100.0
			Gross Profit						
92.7	92.6	91.8	Operating Expenses		78.7		90.8	94.9	95.9
7.3	7.4	8.2	Operating Profit		21.3		9.2	5.1	4.1
2.4	2.2	1.2	All Other Expenses (net)		2.5		.3	-.4	1.1
4.9	5.3	7.0	Profit Before Taxes		18.9		8.9	5.5	3.0
			RATIOS						
1.9	2.3	2.6			4.5		3.3	3.7	1.9
1.3	1.4	1.6	Current		1.5		1.8	2.1	1.3
.9	1.0	1.2			.4		1.1	1.4	1.2
1.7	1.9	2.5			4.0		3.2	2.5	1.8
1.1	1.3 (83)	1.3	Quick		1.5		1.8	1.4	1.1
.8	.9	.9			.4		1.0	.7	.9
29 12.6	27 13.6	23 15.6		23 15.7		8 45.6	23 16.0	39 9.3
50 7.3	46 7.9	50 7.3	Sales/Receivables	50 7.3		47 7.8	43 8.5	63 5.8
72 5.1	79 4.6	69 5.3		88 4.1		95 3.8	72 5.1	74 5.0
			Cost of Sales/Inventory						
			Cost of Sales/Payables						
8.2	5.9	7.6			4.7		5.1	5.2	9.9
26.6	14.9	14.9	Sales/Working Capital		16.1		10.6	11.6	19.4
-123.8	169.0	38.2			-8.8		NM	18.7	33.1
22.2	17.6	23.0			70.0		26.8	134.2	19.5
(41) 5.9	(68) 6.2	(67) 8.7	EBIT/Interest	(10) 8.7		(11) 20.6	(12) 16.3	(26) 5.4
1.5	1.4	2.6			2.8		4.9	9.8	2.7
12.4	8.3	10.3							10.4
(15) 4.6	(12) 3.4	(20) 5.3	Net Profit + Depr., Dep., Amort./Cur. Mat. L/T/D					(11) 3.8
2.3	1.2	1.6							1.4
.1	.2	.1			.3		.1	.1	.1
.4	.6	.5	Fixed/Worth		1.1		.4	.1	.4
3.6	2.9	2.1			7.5		1.7	.5	1.4
1.0	.8	.8			1.0		.6	.6	1.4
2.4	2.5	2.1	Debt/Worth		1.8		1.4	1.1	3.0
12.6	6.5	7.1			7.5		3.3	2.2	9.9
87.3	85.2	64.2					50.2	56.0	93.2
(44) 35.6	(68) 30.6	(73) 36.4	% Profit Before Taxes/Tangible Net Worth			(14) 37.1	(14) 31.7	(28) 36.1
4.8	2.4	17.9					17.6	19.2	19.0
20.7	24.4	20.4			56.3		18.4	27.0	16.4
9.8	8.0	11.2	% Profit Before Taxes/Total Assets		27.1		12.1	15.4	8.7
.7	-.5	4.4			5.4		7.7	5.9	4.4
112.5	70.6	137.4			31.7		137.4	186.4	184.5
51.0	24.9	32.1	Sales/Net Fixed Assets		11.4		54.5	61.3	33.2
13.0	6.2	6.5			2.9		7.1	10.9	14.6
4.8	4.9	4.7			4.0		4.9	6.0	4.9
3.0	2.8	3.0	Sales/Total Assets		1.6		2.9	3.6	3.0
1.6	1.5	1.7			.6		1.4	2.5	2.3
.3	.6	.5			.8		.6	.3	.3
(45) .8	(66) 1.4	(67) 1.3	% Depr., Dep., Amort./Sales	(10) 2.0		(12) .9	(14) .7	(23) 1.1
3.2	4.4	3.7			10.3		3.2	2.7	2.0
	3.8	1.0	% Officers', Directors' Owners' Comp/Sales						
(19) 6.6	(17) 3.5								
17.3	8.8								
2830568M	2105045M	3114873M	Net Sales ($)	2482M	17546M	19988M	114791M	297287M	2662779M
1034996M	970408M	1177206M	Total Assets ($)	2073M	12950M	7463M	57015M	112665M	985040M

M = $ thousand   MM = $ million
See Pages 11 through 21 for Explanation of Ratios and Data

Current Data Sorted by Assets   Comparative Historical Data

						Type of Statement		
	5	9	15	4	1	Unqualified	50	51
1	21	40	8			Reviewed	55	57
8	24	11				Compiled	56	82
42	20	5				Tax Returns	46	49
21	41	37	24	4	3	Other	121	137
	25 (4/1-9/30/06)		321 (10/1/06-3/31/07)				4/1/02-3/31/03	4/1/03-3/31/04
0-500M	500M-2MM	2-10MM	10-50MM	50-100MM	100-250MM		ALL	ALL
72	111	102	48	8	5	NUMBER OF STATEMENTS	328	376
%	%	%	%	%	%	ASSETS	%	%
33.1	10.7	9.9	14.0			Cash & Equivalents	14.9	12.9
32.3	64.1	66.0	50.8			Trade Receivables (net)	47.8	49.9
.0	.8	.1	.2			Inventory	.3	.5
5.7	3.6	3.9	7.6			All Other Current	5.8	5.0
71.1	79.2	79.9	72.6			Total Current	68.8	68.3
12.4	6.8	7.8	9.0			Fixed Assets (net)	14.4	12.7
5.7	2.5	3.6	8.3			Intangibles (net)	6.0	7.0
10.7	11.5	8.7	10.2			All Other Non-Current	10.8	12.0
100.0	100.0	100.0	100.0			Total	100.0	100.0
						LIABILITIES		
34.9	23.1	21.2	15.3			Notes Payable-Short Term	19.7	22.2
12.4	1.9	2.0	1.5			Cur. Mat.-L.T.D.	2.4	2.6
9.6	7.9	9.4	8.2			Trade Payables	7.3	7.1
.1	.7	.6	.6			Income Taxes Payable	.9	.6
27.5	20.5	21.2	23.5			All Other Current	22.4	20.6
84.5	54.1	54.4	49.1			Total Current	52.7	53.1
17.3	5.4	6.5	7.7			Long-Term Debt	8.1	10.5
.8	.5	.3	.3			Deferred Taxes	.6	.5
15.0	5.9	2.3	5.7			All Other Non-Current	7.3	8.6
-17.6	34.2	36.5	37.2			Net Worth	31.4	27.3
100.0	100.0	100.0	100.0			Total Liabilties & Net Worth	100.0	100.0
						INCOME DATA		
100.0	100.0	100.0	100.0			Net Sales	100.0	100.0
						Gross Profit		
94.4	96.3	95.7	93.6			Operating Expenses	98.0	96.8
5.6	3.7	4.3	6.4			Operating Profit	2.0	3.2
.5	.1	1.3	.5			All Other Expenses (net)	.9	.9
5.2	3.5	3.0	5.9			Profit Before Taxes	1.2	2.3
						RATIOS		
2.2	2.9	2.2	2.1				2.3	2.6
1.3	1.6	1.4	1.3			Current	1.4	1.4
.7	1.0	1.1	1.1				.9	1.0
2.0	2.7	2.1	1.7				2.2	2.4
1.1	1.4	1.4	1.2			Quick	(327) 1.3	1.3
.6	1.0	1.0	.9				.8	.8
0 UND	28 13.1	34 10.6	34 10.8				18 20.3	15 24.5
3 129.7	39 9.4	45 8.0	43 8.6			Sales/Receivables	37 9.9	40 9.1
37 9.7	48 7.6	63 5.8	71 5.1				50 7.2	54 6.7
						Cost of Sales/Inventory		
						Cost of Sales/Payables		
17.0	11.0	10.8	11.2				11.3	10.3
99.2	22.8	22.8	24.4			Sales/Working Capital	30.0	28.8
-24.6	130.3	100.6	123.1				-251.9	-571.5
18.0	18.0	17.2	21.1				14.6	19.7
(55) 4.3	(96) 4.7	(88) 7.3	(41) 8.6			EBIT/Interest	(259) 3.3	(317) 4.2
1.0	1.6	1.8	3.0				-.8	.2
	5.1	43.3					5.3	13.9
	(12) 2.0	(11) 2.8				Net Profit + Depr., Dep., Amort./Cur. Mat. L/T/D	(26) 2.4	(39) 3.5
	1.4	1.5					.5	.4
.0	.0	.1	.1				.1	.1
.2	.1	.1	.2			Fixed/Worth	.3	.3
-.3	.5	.4	.9				2.0	2.8
.7	.8	.8	.9				.6	.8
7.9	2.0	1.8	2.2			Debt/Worth	1.7	2.0
-3.1	4.7	4.8	7.1				13.9	22.5
212.2	77.7	73.8	96.8				60.6	73.6
(39) 93.1	(95) 32.6	(90) 44.6	(41) 53.7			% Profit Before Taxes/Tangible Net Worth	(269) 22.1	(295) 25.9
39.5	11.9	10.5	20.6				-1.7	6.8
83.6	24.1	25.3	22.7				19.4	20.5
26.1	13.3	14.2	15.2			% Profit Before Taxes/Total Assets	5.3	6.4
1.5	2.8	2.7	6.5				-3.8	-1.0
UND	460.0	328.1	192.0				193.3	264.2
354.1	190.1	125.2	96.2			Sales/Net Fixed Assets	71.7	91.8
72.9	73.8	55.2	38.5				33.2	37.1
18.3	8.4	6.9	6.2				7.4	7.6
8.4	6.2	5.3	3.9			Sales/Total Assets	5.3	5.1
5.0	5.0	3.7	2.5				3.5	3.3
.1	.1	.1	.2				.2	.2
(30) .3	(68) .3	(86) .3	(36) .3			% Depr., Dep., Amort./Sales	(246) .5	(279) .4
1.2	.5	.5	.7				1.2	1.1
2.0	2.3	1.4					2.0	1.6
(37) 4.1	(47) 4.4	(35) 2.8				% Officers', Directors' Owners' Comp/Sales	(130) 3.8	(141) 3.3
12.9	6.9	5.9					7.9	6.7
174702M	985150M	2600665M	4662424M	2653563M	4085129M	Net Sales ($)	18439070M	13625838M
15525M	129981M	466676M	954447M	527987M	721116M	Total Assets ($)	2671059M	3537692M

© RMA 2007

M = $ thousand   MM = $ million
See Pages 11 through 21 for Explanation of Ratios and Data

Comparative Historical Data | Current Data Sorted by Sales

			Type of Statement						
57	49	34	Unqualified		2	3	5	24
56	57	70	Reviewed	1	6	13	23	27
47	56	43	Compiled	2	8	7	12	12	2
46	41	69	Tax Returns	13	16	15	14	9	2
123	135	130	Other	8	17	9	21	27	48
4/1/04- 3/31/05 ALL	4/1/05- 3/31/06 ALL	4/1/06- 3/31/07 ALL			25 (4/1-9/30/06)		321 (10/1/06-3/31/07)		
				0-1MM	1-3MM	3-5MM	5-10MM	10-25MM	25MM & OVER
329	338	346	**NUMBER OF STATEMENTS**	24	41	39	63	76	103
%	%	%	**ASSETS**	%	%	%	%	%	%
15.5	14.4	15.6	Cash & Equivalents	27.1	22.2	20.6	16.1	11.4	11.0
53.9	55.0	55.4	Trade Receivables (net)	26.8	44.0	50.3	59.6	64.8	59.0
.5	.4	.3	Inventory	.0	.0	.0	1.3	.2	.1
5.5	5.1	4.8	All Other Current	12.4	2.9	3.0	3.2	3.2	6.6
75.3	74.9	76.1	Total Current	66.3	69.1	73.9	80.2	79.7	76.8
8.9	8.9	8.6	Fixed Assets (net)	8.4	15.4	9.9	6.8	6.9	7.8
4.2	5.4	4.8	Intangibles (net)	5.1	5.1	3.8	3.4	4.6	5.8
11.6	10.8	10.5	All Other Non-Current	20.2	10.4	12.3	9.5	8.8	9.6
100.0	100.0	100.0	Total	100.0	100.0	100.0	100.0	100.0	100.0
			LIABILITIES						
22.5	24.1	23.7	Notes Payable-Short Term	18.7	23.2	31.9	21.7	29.0	19.1
3.3	2.2	4.2	Cur. Mat.-L.T.D.	9.1	6.5	2.0	7.4	2.6	2.3
8.1	6.7	8.7	Trade Payables	4.1	12.4	5.7	6.2	10.8	9.4
1.1	.8	.5	Income Taxes Payable	.0	.1	.2	.6	1.1	.5
21.1	22.2	22.6	All Other Current	22.6	28.5	18.8	18.0	21.6	25.1
56.1	56.0	59.7	Total Current	54.6	70.8	58.6	53.9	65.1	56.4
7.0	6.7	8.7	Long-Term Debt	11.8	18.5	8.1	9.8	6.6	5.1
.3	.3	.5	Deferred Taxes	2.3	.0	.0	.8	.2	.3
8.3	6.3	7.0	All Other Non-Current	1.6	22.8	10.0	4.7	3.2	5.2
28.3	30.8	24.1	Net Worth	29.8	-12.1	23.3	30.7	25.0	32.9
100.0	100.0	100.0	Total Liabilties & Net Worth	100.0	100.0	100.0	100.0	100.0	100.0
			INCOME DATA						
100.0	100.0	100.0	Net Sales	100.0	100.0	100.0	100.0	100.0	100.0
			Gross Profit						
96.6	96.4	95.4	Operating Expenses	84.6	95.6	96.6	97.0	95.4	96.5
3.4	3.6	4.6	Operating Profit	15.4	4.4	3.4	3.0	4.6	3.5
.5	.3	.6	All Other Expenses (net)	3.1	1.1	-.3	.6	.3	.5
2.9	3.2	3.9	Profit Before Taxes	12.3	3.3	3.7	2.5	4.3	3.0
			RATIOS						
2.4	2.6	2.3		3.7	2.7	3.2	2.9	2.0	1.9
1.5	1.5	1.4	Current	1.4	1.2	1.7	1.8	1.4	1.3
1.1	1.1	1.0		.6	.8	.9	1.1	1.0	1.1
2.3	2.5	2.1		2.2	2.7	3.2	2.7	1.8	1.7
(328) 1.4	1.4	1.3	Quick	1.1	1.1	1.7	1.7	1.3	1.2
.9	1.0	.9		.1	.6	.8	1.0	.9	.9
25 14.6	29 12.6	23 16.0		0 UND	0 UND	6 62.8	31 11.8	31 11.6	33 11.1
38 9.5	42 8.7	39 9.3	Sales/Receivables	0 UND	30 12.1	34 10.6	42 8.8	39 9.3	41 8.9
53 6.9	58 6.3	58 6.3		63 5.8	50 7.4	47 7.7	59 6.2	59 6.1	59 6.2
			Cost of Sales/Inventory						
			Cost of Sales/Payables						
11.7	10.1	12.0		8.0	13.0	12.3	10.0	12.6	13.6
22.2	20.4	25.7	Sales/Working Capital	20.0	43.8	37.7	17.3	31.9	28.4
204.7	171.4	999.8		-18.6	-29.8	-234.1	95.1	NM	153.2
19.3	20.3	17.8		23.8	9.6	51.2	21.7	17.1	14.2
(272) 6.6	(286) 6.9	(290) 5.7	EBIT/Interest	(12) 17.5	(35) 2.6	(36) 7.7	(53) 5.3	(66) 6.8	(88) 6.6
2.1	2.0	1.8		5.2	.7	-1.3	2.0	1.9	2.0
6.7	19.3	13.8						5.1	41.8
(29) 3.4	(33) 5.6	(35) 2.8	Net Profit + Depr., Dep., Amort./Cur. Mat. L/T/D				(11) 2.3	(15) 5.6
1.3	.9	1.6						1.6	2.7
.0	.1	.0		.0	.1	.0	.0	.0	.1
.2	.2	.2	Fixed/Worth	.0	.4	.1	.1	.2	.2
1.0	1.1	1.0		.9	-.2	1.4	.5	.7	.7
.8	.7	.8		.1	1.2	.3	.6	.8	1.2
1.9	1.8	2.2	Debt/Worth	1.3	3.9	2.0	1.4	2.2	2.5
9.2	9.7	12.3		-3.6	-7.2	-11.8	4.8	10.6	5.8
71.5	77.6	94.8		192.7	154.3	99.9	86.0	78.0	89.4
(272) 36.3	(279) 36.9	(273) 45.5	% Profit Before Taxes/Tangible Net Worth	(15) 61.1	(28) 65.3	(28) 26.4	(55) 35.1	(60) 52.2	(87) 41.8
10.6	10.9	16.0		34.8	20.0	9.6	11.9	27.6	13.7
25.0	24.9	28.0		60.0	32.3	51.6	27.4	33.6	20.9
11.3	10.8	14.7	% Profit Before Taxes/Total Assets	27.6	13.9	13.3	15.3	17.2	11.0
2.7	2.5	2.9		4.3	-.7	-10.0	3.4	4.4	2.9
417.1	330.0	482.8		UND	641.2	999.8	308.5	485.7	296.6
129.0	123.9	158.5	Sales/Net Fixed Assets	UND	207.9	264.2	179.4	202.6	110.6
58.2	55.2	56.8		25.7	26.6	41.9	83.1	71.5	58.2
7.7	7.6	8.1		7.2	9.2	11.7	7.7	8.5	7.5
5.7	5.4	5.9	Sales/Total Assets	4.2	5.7	6.1	5.9	6.2	5.6
4.0	3.6	4.0		2.1	4.0	4.7	4.0	4.5	3.7
.1	.2	.1			.2	.1	.1	.1	.1
(216) .3	(235) .3	(229) .3	% Depr., Dep., Amort./Sales	(24) .6	(16) .3	(45) .3	(57) .2	(80) .3
.8	.7	.6			1.7	.5	.4	.5	.6
2.2	1.9	2.1		4.2	1.3	3.1	2.2	1.4	1.3
(114) 4.6	(122) 3.7	(126) 4.0	% Officers', Directors' Owners' Comp/Sales	(12) 8.8	(19) 3.4	(20) 6.7	(29) 3.1	(27) 2.4	(19) 3.3
8.3	7.9	7.9		17.4	10.9	9.8	6.0	4.4	11.0
10584980M	16765469M	15161633M	Net Sales ($)	13378M	78727M	153858M	467774M	1191194M	13256702M
2266509M	3252448M	2815732M	Total Assets ($)	7010M	26805M	26201M	104998M	258058M	2392660M

© RMA 2007   M = $ thousand   MM = $ million
See Pages 11 through 21 for Explanation of Ratios and Data

ADMIN & WASTE MANAGEMENT SERVICES—Temporary Help Services NAICS 561320 (SIC 7363)

Current Data Sorted by Assets **Comparative Historical Data**

© RMA 2007

						Type of Statement		
1	4	27	27	5	3	Unqualified	52	42
	12	30	6	1		Reviewed	51	38
7	20	18		1		Compiled	57	83
9	12	2		1		Tax Returns	14	22
22	40	52	13	5	8	Other	88	109
	27 (4/1-9/30/06)		299 (10/1/06-3/31/07)				4/1/02-3/31/03	4/1/03-3/31/04
0-500M	500M-2MM	2-10MM	10-50MM	50-100MM	100-250MM		ALL	ALL
39	88	129	46	13	11	NUMBER OF STATEMENTS	262	294
%	%	%	%	%	%	ASSETS	%	%
18.6	14.8	11.2	11.3	20.1	12.0	Cash & Equivalents	11.7	14.7
51.7	57.4	62.2	52.5	38.3	42.9	Trade Receivables (net)	54.8	50.4
.1	.9	.5	.0	.1	.0	Inventory	.7	.9
4.7	5.9	6.7	6.9	4.5	5.7	All Other Current	6.4	6.9
75.0	78.9	80.6	70.7	62.9	60.6	Total Current	73.6	72.9
12.2	9.5	6.5	8.2	8.6	4.7	Fixed Assets (net)	9.6	10.6
4.5	1.6	3.1	12.9	23.0	30.8	Intangibles (net)	8.3	6.2
8.3	10.1	9.8	8.1	5.5	3.9	All Other Non-Current	8.5	10.2
100.0	100.0	100.0	100.0	100.0	100.0	Total	100.0	100.0
						LIABILITIES		
31.0	19.9	20.1	14.5	14.7	5.9	Notes Payable-Short Term	22.0	21.8
1.1	1.2	.9	1.4	1.4	5.0	Cur. Mat.-L.T.D.	5.3	3.3
3.5	8.1	5.7	7.5	8.2	6.2	Trade Payables	6.7	7.3
.1	.8	.4	.4	.2	.3	Income Taxes Payable	.5	.5
42.6	21.5	22.4	21.6	27.8	27.7	All Other Current	22.1	20.7
78.3	51.6	49.6	45.5	52.4	45.1	Total Current	56.5	53.7
7.4	7.9	2.8	8.1	16.3	16.1	Long-Term Debt	9.1	11.1
.6	.0	.2	.4	.5	.6	Deferred Taxes	.2	.2
16.1	8.9	3.6	4.7	6.8	4.4	All Other Non-Current	7.8	8.7
-2.4	31.6	43.8	41.4	24.0	33.8	Net Worth	26.5	26.3
100.0	100.0	100.0	100.0	100.0	100.0	Total Liabilities & Net Worth	100.0	100.0
						INCOME DATA		
100.0	100.0	100.0	100.0	100.0	100.0	Net Sales	100.0	100.0
						Gross Profit		
97.6	96.9	96.4	96.9	92.1	97.2	Operating Expenses	98.5	97.0
2.4	3.1	3.6	3.1	7.9	2.8	Operating Profit	1.5	3.0
.6	.6	.4	.4	.4	1.4	All Other Expenses (net)	.6	.7
1.8	2.5	3.2	2.7	7.5	1.3	Profit Before Taxes	.9	2.2
						RATIOS		
3.5	3.5	2.4	2.4	1.8	2.2		2.3	2.4
1.7	1.5	1.5	1.6	1.2	1.4	Current	1.5	1.5
.8	1.0	1.2	1.1	1.0	.8		1.0	1.0
3.5	3.0	2.4	2.1	1.7	2.1		2.0	2.1
1.7	1.4	1.4	1.4	1.2	1.2	Quick	1.4	1.3
.8	1.0	1.1	1.0	.8	.7		.9	.9

												Sales/Receivables				
13	27.5	24	15.3	31	11.8	35	10.6	26	14.3	44	8.2		25	14.3	22	16.7
29	12.6	39	9.3	42	8.7	48	7.7	40	9.1	50	7.4		38	9.5	37	10.0
47	7.8	53	6.9	55	6.7	56	6.5	62	5.9	58	6.3		52	7.0	51	7.2

Cost of Sales/Inventory

Cost of Sales/Payables

	11.4		11.1		9.7		11.0		13.0		12.4	Sales/Working Capital		11.1		11.0
	23.7		25.4		20.8		19.2		38.7		20.2			22.8		26.8
	-63.6		495.0		56.3		438.1		NM		-21.4			271.7		NM
	22.5		14.5		23.4		28.2		11.0		6.3	EBIT/Interest		10.9		18.9
(28)	1.8	(71)	3.9	(113)	8.8	(39)	6.3	(11)	9.7	(10)	1.7		(226)	2.6	(252)	5.1
	-3.4		1.4		3.3		3.3		1.9		.4			-.3		.9
					36.0		56.1					Net Profit + Depr., Dep., Amort./Cur. Mat. L/T/D		3.8		6.7
		(17)		(17)	4.6	(14)	8.7						(37)	1.4	(36)	2.6
					1.7		2.8							.1		.5
	.0		.0		.0		.1		.4		.2	Fixed/Worth		.1		.1
	.2		.2		.1		.3		2.7		-.6			.2		.2
	4.6		.5		.3		.9		-.2		-.1			1.0		1.2
	.4		.4		.7		1.0		4.4		1.3	Debt/Worth		.8		.9
	2.9		2.3		1.5		2.6		18.3		-17.5			2.2		2.4
	-4.0		6.7		2.7		7.5		-4.3		-3.3			11.4		11.4
	126.1		74.7		69.7		77.8					% Profit Before Taxes/Tangible Net Worth		44.9		61.0
(26)	46.7	(80)	36.4	(123)	41.8	(41)	45.5						(208)	15.9	(237)	25.4
	-16.2		5.5		16.5		21.8							-3.2		3.8
	56.7		23.9		26.4		20.5		14.5		6.2	% Profit Before Taxes/Total Assets		14.4		19.4
	11.0		9.7		16.1		11.2		8.5		3.9			4.5		6.9
	-19.7		2.1		5.3		4.1		5.1		-2.2			-3.2		-.1
	UND		575.1		441.6		207.4		162.5		103.9	Sales/Net Fixed Assets		218.9		261.0
	289.0		134.8		159.3		103.1		66.5		67.6			85.9		90.6
	65.5		54.0		66.2		33.5		26.8		40.2			38.9		42.2
	14.3		8.1		7.8		6.0		4.9		3.2	Sales/Total Assets		7.7		7.8
	7.8		5.8		5.7		4.5		3.9		2.4			5.3		5.5
	5.0		3.9		4.1		3.5		1.4		1.6			3.6		3.6
	.2		.2		.1		.1		.3			% Depr., Dep., Amort./Sales		.2		.2
(19)	.2	(60)	.3	(105)	.2	(36)	.3	(12)	.7				(202)	.5	(227)	.5
	1.0		.6		.5		.8		1.1					1.0		.9
	2.6		1.6		1.4							% Officers', Directors' Owners' Comp/Sales		1.5		1.5
(16)	5.1	(35)	5.1	(39)	2.5								(78)	2.8	(99)	3.1
	6.7		9.0		6.9									4.7		5.5
85837M	880885M	4414734M	5591081M	6019986M	4771007M	Net Sales ($)	15867483M	17053670M
9529M	108833M	548300M	1028649M	830549M	1677349M	Total Assets ($)	3939254M	3551183M

M = $ thousand   MM = $ million
See Pages 11 through 21 for Explanation of Ratios and Data

Comparative Historical Data   Current Data Sorted by Sales

Hist 1	Hist 2	Hist 3	Type of Statement	0-1MM	1-3MM	3-5MM	5-10MM	10-25MM	25MM & OVER
44	46	67	Unqualified	2	1		3	7	54
53	51	49	Reviewed		2	3	10	21	13
41	48	46	Compiled	1	8	7	12	13	5
33	27	24	Tax Returns	4	6	8	2	2	2
101	123	140	Other	9	12	9	22	33	55
4/1/04-3/31/05 ALL	4/1/05-3/31/06 ALL	4/1/06-3/31/07 ALL		27 (4/1-9/30/06)			299 (10/1/06-3/31/07)		
272	295	326	NUMBER OF STATEMENTS	16	29	27	49	76	129
%	%	%	ASSETS	%	%	%	%	%	%
14.6	14.5	13.5	Cash & Equivalents	13.6	11.5	22.7	11.1	11.5	14.0
52.6	52.5	56.7	Trade Receivables (net)	40.9	53.6	45.6	61.1	70.0	52.1
.3	.2	.4	Inventory	.2	.2	2.7	.9	.2	.0
6.0	5.5	6.1	All Other Current	16.8	5.9	4.3	4.1	2.5	8.2
73.4	72.7	76.7	Total Current	71.5	71.2	75.3	77.2	84.2	74.3
10.1	9.0	8.2	Fixed Assets (net)	15.7	9.3	15.4	8.7	6.3	6.5
6.1	7.8	6.0	Intangibles (net)	1.8	5.1	1.2	4.3	1.6	10.9
10.4	10.4	9.1	All Other Non-Current	11.0	14.4	8.1	9.8	7.9	8.2
100.0	100.0	100.0	Total	100.0	100.0	100.0	100.0	100.0	100.0
			LIABILITIES						
20.5	18.6	19.9	Notes Payable-Short Term	17.6	36.0	21.3	23.6	18.3	15.8
4.6	2.9	1.2	Cur. Mat.-L.T.D.	.5	1.3	1.7	1.2	1.1	1.3
7.7	8.8	6.5	Trade Payables	2.4	4.2	10.5	6.0	5.6	7.3
.5	.4	.5	Income Taxes Payable	.2	.8	1.2	.2	.4	.4
20.8	24.5	24.9	All Other Current	42.2	38.2	15.9	16.7	19.0	28.1
54.1	55.3	52.9	Total Current	62.8	80.6	50.6	47.7	44.4	53.0
8.6	6.1	6.4	Long-Term Debt	1.8	5.7	12.9	8.8	2.1	7.5
.2	.3	.3	Deferred Taxes	1.5	.0	.0	.1	.3	.3
5.0	7.0	6.9	All Other Non-Current	.4	22.0	18.9	4.7	3.4	4.6
32.1	31.2	33.5	Net Worth	33.4	-8.4	17.7	38.7	49.8	34.7
100.0	100.0	100.0	Total Liabilties & Net Worth	100.0	100.0	100.0	100.0	100.0	100.0
			INCOME DATA						
100.0	100.0	100.0	Net Sales	100.0	100.0	100.0	100.0	100.0	100.0
			Gross Profit						
97.3	96.6	96.6	Operating Expenses	94.8	95.5	98.7	97.0	95.6	97.1
2.7	3.4	3.4	Operating Profit	5.2	4.5	1.3	3.0	4.4	2.9
.3	.3	.5	All Other Expenses (net)	2.4	.8	.2	.5	.2	.5
2.4	3.1	2.9	Profit Before Taxes	2.8	3.7	1.1	2.6	4.3	2.4
			RATIOS						
2.3	2.1	2.6	Current	6.3	3.3	3.6	2.8	3.3	2.0
1.4	1.4	1.5		1.6	1.4	1.7	1.4	1.9	1.4
1.0	1.0	1.1		.3	.5	1.0	1.1	1.3	1.1
2.1	2.0	2.4	Quick	5.9	2.5	3.6	2.6	3.1	1.8
(271) 1.3	1.3	1.4		1.5	1.1	1.6	1.4	1.8	1.3
.9	.9	1.0		.2	.5	1.0	1.0	1.3	.9
20 17.9	24 15.3	26 13.9	Sales/Receivables	0 UND	25 14.4	17 21.9	32 11.5	35 10.4	23 15.8
38 9.7	38 9.6	42 8.8		52 7.0	38 9.7	36 10.2	42 8.6	42 8.6	40 9.2
49 7.5	51 7.1	54 6.8		163 2.2	51 7.1	53 6.9	63 5.8	55 6.6	51 7.2
			Cost of Sales/Inventory						
			Cost of Sales/Payables						
13.1	12.2	10.8	Sales/Working Capital	1.2	9.1	10.8	10.3	9.6	13.8
30.2	30.6	22.9		8.4	23.4	27.0	19.4	15.3	33.7
936.1	321.2	131.4		-7.3	-10.6	282.2	77.5	29.3	294.4
18.3	21.6	18.1	EBIT/Interest	18.7	26.4	12.9	13.2	25.8	17.7
(227) 5.2	(257) 7.1	(272) 5.9		(10) 1.7	(22) 2.7	(23) 2.7	(45) 3.9	(63) 8.7	(109) 9.1
1.5	2.6	1.9		-5.6	.5	-1.4	1.8	4.0	2.5
20.2	20.0	40.4	Net Profit + Depr., Dep., Amort./Cur. Mat. L/T/D						51.8
(26) 6.3	(43) 5.6	(39) 4.6						(24) 7.0	
3.0	.9	1.1							1.2
.1	.1	.1	Fixed/Worth	.0	.0	.1	.1	.0	.1
.2	.2	.2		.0	.1	.2	.2	.1	.2
.7	.8	.6		1.1	1.1	1.4	.8	.2	1.1
.8	.9	.7	Debt/Worth	.2	1.0	.4	.6	.5	1.4
2.2	2.3	2.0		.8	4.5	2.0	2.1	1.1	3.0
7.2	13.7	5.9		3.6	-4.3	28.6	5.8	2.2	11.3
66.9	79.8	73.2	% Profit Before Taxes/Tangible Net Worth	39.1	78.5	69.8	72.0	65.8	81.3
(230) 33.4	(242) 41.5	(282) 41.8		(14) 10.3	(19) 57.6	(24) 22.5	(43) 35.4	(74) 40.7	(108) 48.9
8.4	20.4	12.8		-12.8	4.0	-11.6	11.1	12.4	26.4
21.6	25.3	24.1	% Profit Before Taxes/Total Assets	12.5	35.0	20.4	24.9	30.3	21.3
9.7	12.5	11.8		2.5	9.5	3.2	11.1	18.5	11.3
2.1	4.5	3.0		-17.5	.6	-6.3	2.9	6.3	4.4
318.4	370.1	384.5	Sales/Net Fixed Assets	UND	UND	356.3	241.1	332.3	385.7
116.0	138.7	138.4		236.3	238.3	79.0	107.3	148.8	147.9
49.3	46.5	55.5		30.2	58.8	36.0	46.7	63.6	63.2
8.4	8.2	7.9	Sales/Total Assets	4.0	8.1	10.1	7.0	7.5	9.5
5.7	5.7	5.6		1.3	5.8	5.1	5.1	5.8	5.6
3.9	3.7	3.9		.5	2.0	3.6	3.7	4.8	3.9
.2	.1	.1	% Depr., Dep., Amort./Sales		.2	.2	.2	.1	.1
(210) .3	(220) .3	(240) .3		(15) .3	(16) .4	(40) .4	(60) .3	(101) .3	
.7	.7	.7			1.2	.7	.6	.5	.6
1.6	1.6	1.5	% Officers', Directors' Owners' Comp/Sales		4.4	2.1	1.2	1.4	.7
(99) 2.9	(92) 2.6	(100) 2.9		(13) 5.9	(14) 5.5	(19) 2.5	(31) 2.2	(19) 1.7	
4.9	4.4	6.8			13.3	7.1	7.9	6.4	3.2
15214508M	21582727M	21763530M	Net Sales ($)	9123M	54068M	110138M	366520M	1263404M	19960277M
3569548M	4124747M	4203209M	Total Assets ($)	11265M	15605M	25599M	86203M	296420M	3768117M

© RMA 2007   M = $ thousand   MM = $ million
See Pages 11 through 21 for Explanation of Ratios and Data

Current Data Sorted by Assets							Comparative Historical Data	

0-500M	500M-2MM	2-10MM	10-50MM	50-100MM	100-250MM	**Type of Statement**		
		5	3	1	1	Unqualified	7	6
	3	7	1			Reviewed	9	12
3	11	2				Compiled	17	23
12	5	2				Tax Returns	11	16
7	10	7				Other	28	34
	14 (4/1-9/30/06)		72 (10/1/06-3/31/07)				4/1/02-3/31/03 ALL	4/1/03-3/31/04 ALL
22	29	23	8	3	1	**NUMBER OF STATEMENTS**	72	91
%	%	%	%	%	%	**ASSETS**	%	%
19.1	10.0	9.6				Cash & Equivalents	10.8	12.2
23.8	34.8	28.8				Trade Receivables (net)	26.5	29.9
7.1	8.5	14.2				Inventory	9.5	9.2
7.4	1.4	1.2				All Other Current	1.8	2.6
57.4	54.8	53.9				Total Current	48.6	53.9
24.8	30.4	35.4				Fixed Assets (net)	35.8	32.2
8.8	7.4	3.9				Intangibles (net)	5.2	5.3
8.9	7.5	6.7				All Other Non-Current	10.4	8.5
100.0	100.0	100.0				Total	100.0	100.0
						LIABILITIES		
23.4	12.6	8.7				Notes Payable-Short Term	11.9	9.2
19.0	6.9	5.0				Cur. Mat.-L.T.D.	5.9	6.8
11.6	13.8	12.6				Trade Payables	14.8	15.4
.2	.1	.0				Income Taxes Payable	.2	.3
17.3	11.6	8.0				All Other Current	8.9	11.5
71.6	45.0	34.3				Total Current	41.8	43.2
44.5	22.7	20.0				Long-Term Debt	24.7	22.6
.0	.1	.1				Deferred Taxes	.5	.2
9.2	4.5	2.5				All Other Non-Current	6.1	7.2
-25.4	27.8	43.0				Net Worth	26.8	26.7
100.0	100.0	100.0				Total Liabilities & Net Worth	100.0	100.0
						INCOME DATA		
100.0	100.0	100.0				Net Sales	100.0	100.0
						Gross Profit		
88.9	93.7	92.9				Operating Expenses	96.3	94.4
11.1	6.3	7.1				Operating Profit	3.7	5.6
1.3	1.7	2.8				All Other Expenses (net)	1.6	1.4
9.8	4.6	4.3				Profit Before Taxes	2.1	4.2
						RATIOS		
3.4	1.9	2.2					2.1	2.0
1.6	1.1	1.4				Current	1.3	1.4
.5	.9	1.0					.9	1.0
1.6	1.6	1.9					1.9	1.8
1.1	.9	.8				Quick	1.0	1.2
.4	.6	.6					.6	.7
0 UND	24 15.2	38 9.7					29 12.8	31 11.7
26 13.8	36 10.2	43 8.6				Sales/Receivables	41 8.9	40 9.1
42 8.6	50 7.4	52 7.1					53 6.9	50 7.4
						Cost of Sales/Inventory		
						Cost of Sales/Payables		
6.8	12.2	6.5					11.2	7.6
64.2	36.2	12.7				Sales/Working Capital	22.4	16.1
-13.6	-58.8	-999.8					-90.4	-318.0
8.9	7.7	21.7					8.2	10.4
(15) 4.5	(27) 2.8	(21) 3.1				EBIT/Interest	(67) 2.5	(83) 5.0
.3	1.0	2.0					-.1	.9
							3.5	4.7
						Net Profit + Depr., Dep., Amort./Cur. Mat. L/T/D	(20) 2.3 (17) 2.2	
							1.0	1.0
.2	.6	.3					.6	.3
8.1	1.8	1.0				Fixed/Worth	1.3	1.2
-.4	NM	2.1					6.1	4.9
1.2	1.2	.8					1.1	1.0
22.5	3.0	1.9				Debt/Worth	2.2	2.3
-2.3	NM	3.5					13.0	8.8
288.2	79.7	56.5				% Profit Before Taxes/Tangible Net Worth	60.8	65.0
(13) 69.5	(22) 31.6	(21) 18.7					(56) 14.8	(74) 25.6
30.6	7.6	9.6					.9	3.4
47.2	20.6	19.2				% Profit Before Taxes/Total Assets	16.4	20.2
16.7	6.9	6.0					3.6	8.0
-1.5	-.2	2.0					-5.4	-.7
86.7	50.8	33.9				Sales/Net Fixed Assets	13.6	25.6
37.6	11.0	6.7					7.8	10.1
8.6	6.1	4.2					4.1	4.5
5.2	4.4	2.7				Sales/Total Assets	3.1	3.6
3.9	3.2	2.4					2.3	2.6
2.5	2.3	1.5					1.5	1.7
.9	2.2	1.4				% Depr., Dep., Amort./Sales	2.2	1.9
(13) 1.1	(21) 2.9	(22) 3.0					(63) 5.5	(72) 4.7
5.4	4.5	5.6					7.3	7.3
5.7	1.7					% Officers', Directors' Owners' Comp/Sales	3.7	3.8
(10) 7.9	(17) 5.1						(32) 6.5	(47) 5.9
14.7	6.5						11.9	9.0
17239M	126093M	240288M	279854M	229065M	205710M	Net Sales ($)	922807M	1494438M
4669M	37916M	111232M	186676M	222105M	163870M	Total Assets ($)	583415M	790678M

M = $ thousand   MM = $ million

See Pages 11 through 21 for Explanation of Ratios and Data

Comparative Historical Data | | | Current Data Sorted by Sales

			Type of Statement						
7	4	10	Unqualified			1		5	4
17	14	11	Reviewed		1	1	5	4	
20	15	16	Compiled	2	4	7	3		
25	21	19	Tax Returns	10	3	6			
27	35	30	Other	7	3	3	3	6	4
4/1/04-3/31/05 ALL	4/1/05-3/31/06 ALL	4/1/06-3/31/07 ALL		0-1MM	14 (4/1-9/30/06) 1-3MM	3-5MM	72 (10/1/06-3/31/07) 5-10MM	10-25MM	25MM & OVER
96	89	86	**NUMBER OF STATEMENTS**	19	11	18	15	15	8
%	%	%	**ASSETS**	%	%	%	%	%	%
11.3	11.6	11.7	Cash & Equivalents	11.8	25.1	12.7	7.6	8.3	
28.1	30.0	28.9	Trade Receivables (net)	21.2	25.1	25.8	42.3	34.9	
9.4	8.1	9.0	Inventory	6.5	8.3	11.0	10.8	11.3	
1.0	2.9	2.8	All Other Current	8.6	.0	2.0	1.3	.9	
50.0	52.6	52.5	Total Current	48.0	58.6	51.6	62.1	55.4	
36.6	36.2	29.3	Fixed Assets (net)	34.1	20.7	35.7	20.9	31.9	
7.3	5.7	10.5	Intangibles (net)	14.2	3.7	4.1	10.3	8.0	
6.2	5.6	7.7	All Other Non-Current	3.7	17.0	8.6	6.7	4.6	
100.0	100.0	100.0	Total	100.0	100.0	100.0	100.0	100.0	
			LIABILITIES						
9.1	11.9	13.2	Notes Payable-Short Term	20.5	17.1	14.2		8.9	
6.4	5.7	9.2	Cur. Mat.-L.T.D.	8.5	29.6	8.1	2.9	4.8	
11.9	12.1	12.0	Trade Payables	7.1	15.8	13.9	14.1	13.5	
.2	.6	.1	Income Taxes Payable	.1	.4	.1	.0	.0	
13.4	14.6	11.7	All Other Current	16.0	13.4	9.0	11.8	10.6	
40.9	44.9	46.2	Total Current	52.2	76.2	45.3	36.8	37.6	
27.0	28.4	26.9	Long-Term Debt	39.1	48.7	26.2	11.3	21.5	
.4	.4	.2	Deferred Taxes	.0	.0	.1	.1	.1	
6.9	6.0	5.7	All Other Non-Current	10.4	4.8	2.3	7.1	1.3	
24.8	20.3	21.1	Net Worth	-1.7	-29.7	26.1	44.7	39.4	
100.0	100.0	100.0	Total Liabilities & Net Worth	100.0	100.0	100.0	100.0	100.0	
			INCOME DATA						
100.0	100.0	100.0	Net Sales	100.0	100.0	100.0	100.0	100.0	
			Gross Profit						
94.5	94.2	92.0	Operating Expenses	83.9	97.1	95.5	91.8	92.6	
5.5	5.8	8.0	Operating Profit	16.1	2.9	4.5	8.2	7.4	
1.0	1.1	2.2	All Other Expenses (net)	4.9	1.5	1.2	1.6	1.5	
4.5	4.7	5.8	Profit Before Taxes	11.2	1.4	3.3	6.7	5.9	
			RATIOS						
2.1	2.3	2.1		3.1	1.8	1.9	3.2	1.9	
1.3	1.3	1.3	Current	1.5	1.1	1.1	1.7	1.4	
1.0	.9	.9		.6	.6	.8	1.1	1.0	
1.7	2.1	1.6		1.5	1.7	1.4	3.1	1.9	
1.0	1.0	.9	Quick	.9	1.1	.9	1.5	1.3	
.7	.7	.6		.4	.4	.5	.8	.7	
29 12.8	32 11.4	27 13.8		0 UND	26 13.8	22 16.4	36 10.2	40 9.2	
41 9.0	41 8.9	40 9.0	Sales/Receivables	22 16.9	31 11.7	35 10.5	47 7.7	52 7.1	
52 7.0	54 6.8	52 7.1		44 8.4	37 10.0	46 7.9	53 6.9	73 5.0	
			Cost of Sales/Inventory						
			Cost of Sales/Payables						
9.6	8.3	9.3		7.2	12.1	10.7	5.9	9.3	
26.1	23.3	25.5	Sales/Working Capital	109.7	36.2	43.7	12.4	14.1	
-166.8	-59.6	-64.9		-4.2	-14.5	-35.8	73.3	-999.8	
10.8	7.4	7.8		7.0	8.2	10.2	57.0	5.9	
(87) 3.1	(81) 4.0	(74) 3.6	EBIT/Interest	(12) 3.5	(10) 2.0	(17) 4.6	(14) 5.0	(14) 2.6	
1.2	1.4	1.5		.4	-.6	1.6	2.1	2.1	
3.8	4.7	4.5	Net Profit + Depr., Dep.,						
(18) 2.3	(15) 2.3	(19) 2.4	Amort./Cur. Mat. L/T/D						
1.1	1.4	1.5							
.6	.5	.5		.3	.2	.5	.2	.8	
1.5	1.7	1.6	Fixed/Worth	9.8	2.3	.7	.7	1.1	
15.9	12.3	12.2		-.5	-.8	-80.3	11.4	1.7	
1.0	.8	1.1		1.2	1.2	1.2	.8	1.0	
3.8	3.0	2.7	Debt/Worth	12.9	6.0	3.3	1.3	2.1	
34.2	19.8	182.8		-2.0	-4.8	-120.0	165.1	3.5	
63.6	74.2	91.5		344.1		82.5	91.3	76.3	
(75) 24.8	(69) 27.4	(66) 31.0	% Profit Before Taxes/Tangible Net Worth	(12) 114.7		(13) 34.6	(12) 35.2	(14) 24.5	
7.3	8.0	12.4		25.2		14.4	12.3	9.9	
18.1	23.8	21.0		39.8	20.2	18.3	42.9	19.2	
6.4	7.8	7.2	% Profit Before Taxes/Total Assets	9.2	4.8	8.9	9.9	6.9	
.4	1.3	1.4		-.9	-2.7	.7	1.8	4.2	
16.4	20.1	42.1		50.7	251.8	14.6	85.3	17.5	
7.0	8.6	9.8	Sales/Net Fixed Assets	14.2	59.7	8.6	14.4	6.1	
3.7	4.3	5.6		5.3	9.4	5.8	9.5	4.2	
3.2	3.7	4.0		4.8	4.5	4.3	3.7	2.9	
2.4	2.7	2.6	Sales/Total Assets	3.1	3.3	2.8	3.0	2.2	
1.6	1.9	1.7		1.6	2.0	2.1	2.4	1.5	
2.3	1.4	1.4		.9		2.0	.9	2.0	
(81) 4.2	(73) 3.5	(68) 3.0	% Depr., Dep., Amort./Sales	(11) 2.1		(17) 3.6	(12) 2.5	(14) 3.1	
6.4	6.2	5.2		9.0		4.5	3.9	4.5	
3.4	3.0	3.3				3.3			
(50) 4.9	(43) 5.9	(36) 5.8	% Officers', Directors' Owners' Comp/Sales			(10) 5.4			
9.6	11.3	8.9				6.4			
874921M	1288021M	1098249M	Net Sales ($)	9502M	19897M	73123M	120169M	210507M	665051M
473919M	649456M	726468M	Total Assets ($)	8529M	6819M	27351M	52659M	111059M	520051M

© RMA 2007

M = $ thousand   MM = $ million

See Pages 11 through 21 for Explanation of Ratios and Data

Current Data Sorted by Assets   Comparative Historical Data

						Type of Statement		
	3	13	18	4	3	Unqualified	40	38
3	5	12	2			Reviewed	21	19
4	6	8				Compiled	11	21
5	15	2		1		Tax Returns	16	18
4	6	11	14	2		Other	27	36
							4/1/02-3/31/03	4/1/03-3/31/04
0-500M	500M-2MM	2-10MM	10-50MM	50-100MM	100-250MM		ALL	ALL
11 (4/1-9/30/06)			130 (10/1/06-3/31/07)					
16	35	46	35	6	3	NUMBER OF STATEMENTS	115	132
%	%	%	%	%	%	ASSETS	%	%
38.5	23.9	18.1	17.3			Cash & Equivalents	24.6	23.3
11.1	23.7	27.9	20.4			Trade Receivables (net)	22.1	27.6
.0	.0	1.2	4.7			Inventory	1.6	.7
2.1	8.3	6.3	8.7			All Other Current	11.8	9.6
51.7	55.9	53.5	51.1			Total Current	60.2	61.2
35.2	22.7	22.7	25.0			Fixed Assets (net)	20.5	19.3
5.2	7.8	9.2	15.7			Intangibles (net)	8.1	8.1
7.9	13.6	14.6	8.2			All Other Non-Current	11.2	11.3
100.0	100.0	100.0	100.0			Total	100.0	100.0
						LIABILITIES		
21.8	11.3	9.6	13.6			Notes Payable-Short Term	13.1	14.5
18.1	9.9	5.3	6.3			Cur. Mat.-L.T.D.	7.7	5.4
3.1	11.7	13.6	9.4			Trade Payables	10.2	10.2
.0	.2	.1	.5			Income Taxes Payable	.9	.2
27.7	17.2	14.8	13.4			All Other Current	19.3	16.0
70.6	50.4	43.4	43.3			Total Current	51.2	46.2
18.0	16.4	14.1	19.2			Long-Term Debt	17.9	14.1
.0	.0	.1	.3			Deferred Taxes	.5	.3
3.8	3.3	5.2	7.0			All Other Non-Current	9.4	6.9
7.5	29.9	37.1	30.3			Net Worth	21.1	32.6
100.0	100.0	100.0	100.0			Total Liabilties & Net Worth	100.0	100.0
						INCOME DATA		
100.0	100.0	100.0	100.0			Net Sales	100.0	100.0
						Gross Profit		
92.9	93.4	93.8	84.8			Operating Expenses	90.1	88.0
7.1	6.6	6.2	15.2			Operating Profit	9.9	12.0
-.3	.7	1.3	3.8			All Other Expenses (net)	2.1	3.2
7.4	5.9	4.9	11.4			Profit Before Taxes	7.8	8.8
						RATIOS		
1.6	2.2	1.9	1.8				2.2	2.3
.8	1.2	1.2	1.2			Current	1.2	1.4
.4	.6	.7	.9				.8	.8
1.6	1.9	1.8	1.6				1.9	2.0
.7	.9	1.0	.9			Quick	1.0	1.2
.4	.4	.6	.5				.5	.6
0 UND	5 66.8	16 23.3	18 20.1				2 208.2	2 184.1
0 UND	25 14.3	29 12.5	32 11.3			Sales/Receivables	20 18.3	24 15.1
22 16.6	40 9.1	50 7.3	52 7.1				46 8.0	51 7.1
						Cost of Sales/Inventory		
						Cost of Sales/Payables		
191.6	7.7	10.2	8.8				6.9	6.3
-65.6	51.6	35.5	19.5			Sales/Working Capital	35.8	18.5
-12.5	-12.7	-30.3	-43.4				-35.7	-37.6
11.1	43.3	30.9	17.3				24.8	23.3
(13) 1.2	(29) 7.0	(42) 9.9	(32) 6.3			EBIT/Interest	(95) 5.6	(97) 4.4
-2.7	-.2	1.0	1.6				1.8	1.4
			16.5			Net Profit + Depr., Dep.,	6.5	30.8
			(10) 2.6			Amort./Cur. Mat. L/T/D	(12) 3.5	(13) 7.0
			1.6				1.7	1.2
1.0	.2	.3	.4				.2	.1
2.3	.8	.9	1.2			Fixed/Worth	.8	.5
-.8	32.0	3.5	3.8				2.8	2.5
1.0	.7	.9	1.9				.8	.9
5.3	2.3	2.3	3.1			Debt/Worth	3.6	2.2
-5.3	-50.5	15.4	22.7				19.5	11.9
	138.4	84.8	83.8			% Profit Before Taxes/Tangible	99.1	94.6
(26) 66.3	(39) 45.0	(28) 45.5				Net Worth	(89) 56.3	(107) 41.2
	11.5	14.0	8.5				9.9	11.8
59.1	46.6	31.5	20.9			% Profit Before Taxes/Total	37.3	26.2
4.0	12.1	12.9	11.0			Assets	12.7	11.4
-4.8	-2.8	.1	2.0				1.9	1.4
50.0	61.4	28.0	22.5				50.6	51.3
22.7	14.7	17.4	11.7			Sales/Net Fixed Assets	21.1	24.0
13.5	10.3	9.6	5.8				9.9	11.4
10.9	5.4	3.9	2.5				5.6	5.1
6.1	3.6	2.7	2.1			Sales/Total Assets	2.8	2.6
3.0	2.1	1.5	1.0				1.3	1.1
1.2	1.1	1.4	1.6				1.2	1.0
(11) 2.8	(23) 1.9	(38) 2.0	(28) 2.8			% Depr., Dep., Amort./Sales	(93) 1.9	(101) 1.9
4.1	4.1		3.7				3.1	3.0
	4.5					% Officers', Directors'	4.5	4.0
	(16) 7.0					Owners' Comp/Sales	(44) 7.9	(44) 8.3
	16.6						13.7	16.7
34467M	163020M	695129M	1466706M	553473M	346211M	Net Sales ($)	2635431M	3475864M
4757M	40392M	234089M	752416M	457230M	391159M	Total Assets ($)	1228924M	2368177M

M = $ thousand   MM = $ million
See Pages 11 through 21 for Explanation of Ratios and Data

Comparative Historical Data / Current Data Sorted by Sales

Comparative Historical Data					Type of Statement		Current Data Sorted by Sales					
46		30		41	Unqualified			1		3	18	19
12		22		22	Reviewed			5	1	10	5	1
13		18		18	Compiled		2	3	4	4	4	1
27		12		23	Tax Returns		4	8	5	4	1	1
41		45		37	Other		8	8	5	4	6	13
4/1/04-3/31/05 ALL		4/1/05-3/31/06 ALL		4/1/06-3/31/07 ALL			11 (4/1-9/30/06)			130 (10/1/06-3/31/07)		
						0-1MM	1-3MM	3-5MM	5-10MM	10-25MM	25MM & OVER
139		127		141	NUMBER OF STATEMENTS	6	25	15	26	34	35
%		%		%	ASSETS	%	%	%	%	%	%
26.5		21.7		21.4	Cash & Equivalents		24.5	22.3	21.7	16.9	19.7
26.2		24.8		22.8	Trade Receivables (net)		15.7	27.2	24.1	26.5	24.5
2.4		1.0		1.5	Inventory		.0	.0	3.3	3.2	.7
8.7		10.7		6.7	All Other Current		10.4	12.4	4.8	5.9	4.9
63.8		58.2		52.5	Total Current		50.6	61.9	53.9	52.5	49.8
17.1		20.9		23.5	Fixed Assets (net)		27.7	18.3	17.9	23.9	23.9
8.7		6.4		11.5	Intangibles (net)		9.7	8.2	11.4	12.1	15.6
10.3		14.5		12.6	All Other Non-Current		12.0	11.7	16.8	11.5	10.7
100.0		100.0		100.0	Total		100.0	100.0	100.0	100.0	100.0
					LIABILITIES						
12.6		15.3		11.8	Notes Payable-Short Term		15.8	8.9	10.6	13.5	5.3
4.3		4.9		7.9	Cur. Mat.-L.T.D.		15.8	9.4	6.9	4.7	6.1
9.8		11.4		10.2	Trade Payables		6.0	21.1	6.4	12.9	10.0
.3		.3		.2	Income Taxes Payable		.2	.0	.2	.1	.5
18.9		17.1		16.5	All Other Current		20.4	16.1	14.1	12.6	18.2
46.0		48.9		46.6	Total Current		58.1	55.5	38.0	43.8	40.1
13.3		15.9		17.0	Long-Term Debt		22.6	11.1	12.0	17.2	19.9
.1		.0		.2	Deferred Taxes		.0	.0	.0	.4	.3
5.2		8.2		4.8	All Other Non-Current		8.4	3.0	4.7	1.5	6.9
35.4		26.9		31.3	Net Worth		11.0	30.5	45.2	37.1	32.8
100.0		100.0		100.0	Total Liabilties & Net Worth		100.0	100.0	100.0	100.0	100.0
					INCOME DATA						
100.0		100.0		100.0	Net Sales		100.0	100.0	100.0	100.0	100.0
					Gross Profit						
88.1		87.7		90.2	Operating Expenses		89.8	96.7	89.0	91.7	87.4
11.9		12.3		9.8	Operating Profit		10.2	3.3	11.0	8.3	12.6
2.0		2.3		2.3	All Other Expenses (net)		3.5	.6	1.6	1.5	3.7
9.9		10.0		7.5	Profit Before Taxes		6.7	2.7	9.4	6.8	8.9
					RATIOS						
2.6		1.8		1.9			1.9	2.1	3.1	2.0	1.7
1.3		1.2		1.2	Current		1.0	1.3	1.4	1.2	1.2
.9		.8		.7			.5	.6	.8	.9	.9
2.1		1.6		1.7			1.8	1.9	2.5	1.7	1.7
1.1		1.0		1.0	Quick		.8	.7	1.1	1.1	1.1
.8		.6		.5			.3	.5	.6	.5	.8

10	36.9	9	41.1	9	40.1		0	UND	0	UND	9	40.9	16	23.2	19	19.4
26	13.9	27	13.5	26	13.8	Sales/Receivables	13	27.2	19	19.2	26	14.1	32	11.4	33	10.9
47	7.8	43	8.5	46	8.0		40	9.2	44	8.3	44	8.2	49	7.4	55	6.6

					Cost of Sales/Inventory					
					Cost of Sales/Payables					
4.5		7.7		8.8			7.1	7.4	7.2	10.6	11.4
19.8		36.1		45.4	Sales/Working Capital		-197.6	33.2	27.0	48.5	19.5
-170.4		-70.4		-25.2			-6.4	-15.5	-19.4	-39.8	-101.0

	36.3		23.6		20.3			22.0		19.9		16.9		21.3		26.4
(115)	9.1	(106)	7.9	(122)	6.3	EBIT/Interest	(21)	3.7	(13)	1.1	(23)	11.1	(30)	6.1	(30)	7.8
	2.6		2.5		1.0			.0		-3.8		1.5		.8		1.8
	14.1		9.6		19.7											9.4
(22)	2.9	(17)	4.8	(18)	2.6	Net Profit + Depr., Dep., Amort./Cur. Mat. L/T/D								(10)	2.6
	1.4		2.1		1.1											1.5
	.1		.3		.3			.3		.2		.2		.2		.4
	.4		.9		1.1	Fixed/Worth		1.6		1.1		.5		.9		1.2
	2.1		4.4		10.8			-.8		-7.7		2.5		3.7		2.7
	.8		.9		.9			1.1		.8		.5		.9		1.8
	1.7		2.6		2.8	Debt/Worth		10.0		4.0		2.1		2.2		3.1
	13.4		20.8		30.7			-4.3		-28.1		10.8		15.9		16.3
	80.7		110.5		89.6			62.1		110.1		107.1		84.8		104.1
(109)	39.5	(101)	56.6	(109)	47.4	% Profit Before Taxes/Tangible Net Worth	(16)	35.8	(11)	25.1	(22)	64.7	(27)	26.7	(30)	62.5
	17.4		17.0		8.6			5.4		-113.2		30.8		5.1		15.8
	27.1		30.8		30.7			21.2		30.7		53.6		28.2		19.7
	14.5		15.8		11.4	% Profit Before Taxes/Total Assets		3.5		.8		25.2		12.7		12.6
	4.2		3.9		.5			-1.4		-17.7		6.6		-.3		3.9
	60.2		40.8		38.1			33.0		57.4		39.3		50.7		24.6
	24.2		20.1		16.5	Sales/Net Fixed Assets		12.9		24.8		19.0		20.4		14.6
	11.4		10.6		8.7			7.6		11.5		12.8		8.6		7.4
	4.5		4.7		4.0			4.8		5.3		5.3		4.2		3.3
	2.8		2.8		2.6	Sales/Total Assets		2.2		3.4		3.5		2.7		2.5
	1.3		1.5		1.4			1.1		2.0		1.7		1.3		1.6
	1.0		1.2		1.4			2.7				1.2		1.4		1.5
(101)	1.7	(91)	1.9	(107)	2.1	% Depr., Dep., Amort./Sales	(15)	2.9	(21)	1.7	(29)	2.0	(29)	2.2
	2.9		3.1		3.3			5.6				2.7		2.8		2.9
	3.7		3.2		2.7												
(41)	6.3	(36)	6.5	(32)	6.2	% Officers', Directors' Owners' Comp/Sales										
	12.8		13.6		13.4												

5000663M		6294036M		3259006M	Net Sales ($)	3149M	43983M	64519M	191608M	560406M	2395341M
2587929M		2534757M		1880043M	Total Assets ($)	2363M	46634M	34192M	108470M	361019M	1327365M

© RMA 2007

M = $ thousand   MM = $ million
See Pages 11 through 21 for Explanation of Ratios and Data

Current Data Sorted by Assets / Comparative Historical Data

Type of Statement	0-500M	500M-2MM	2-10MM	10-50MM	50-100MM	100-250MM		
Unqualified	4	8	32	39	19	13	135	146
Reviewed	5	21	60	15	1		125	150
Compiled	14	36	27	6			150	236
Tax Returns	65	41	18	1		1	116	163
Other	29	73	80	38	16	12	286	340
	114 (4/1-9/30/06)			560 (10/1/06-3/31/07)			4/1/02-3/31/03 ALL	4/1/03-3/31/04 ALL
	0-500M	500M-2MM	2-10MM	10-50MM	50-100MM	100-250MM		
NUMBER OF STATEMENTS	117	179	217	99	36	26	812	1035
ASSETS	%	%	%	%	%	%	%	%
Cash & Equivalents	34.4	17.6	14.0	15.1	12.3	11.7	14.7	14.9
Trade Receivables (net)	18.3	28.7	37.1	27.9	24.6	28.8	32.8	30.6
Inventory	6.4	8.4	7.8	7.9	4.7	.9	7.1	8.1
All Other Current	4.7	4.5	4.2	6.8	7.9	11.3	4.8	5.8
Total Current	63.8	59.2	63.2	57.7	49.5	52.8	59.5	59.5
Fixed Assets (net)	22.5	27.6	22.7	23.6	20.1	14.2	25.1	26.6
Intangibles (net)	4.9	5.8	4.7	7.8	22.2	20.2	6.9	6.0
All Other Non-Current	8.7	7.4	9.4	10.8	8.2	12.8	8.6	8.0
Total	100.0	100.0	100.0	100.0	100.0	100.0	100.0	100.0
LIABILITIES								
Notes Payable-Short Term	12.2	11.6	10.5	12.9	7.1	19.8	12.6	11.3
Cur. Mat.-L.T.D.	4.2	3.1	3.0	3.3	3.6	3.2	4.9	4.3
Trade Payables	15.1	13.8	13.4	14.4	13.1	7.9	15.2	13.4
Income Taxes Payable	.4	.5	.5	.7	.7	.4	.5	.6
All Other Current	19.3	17.3	16.5	15.8	15.0	20.4	17.9	16.8
Total Current	51.3	46.3	43.8	47.0	39.5	51.7	51.2	46.5
Long-Term Debt	20.3	16.7	13.7	13.1	30.7	13.9	15.9	18.1
Deferred Taxes	.0	.2	.4	.4	.4	.2	.4	.4
All Other Non-Current	13.1	9.2	5.9	6.2	4.3	2.7	6.6	7.5
Net Worth	15.4	27.6	36.2	33.3	25.0	31.5	25.8	27.5
Total Liabilities & Net Worth	100.0	100.0	100.0	100.0	100.0	100.0	100.0	100.0
INCOME DATA								
Net Sales	100.0	100.0	100.0	100.0	100.0	100.0	100.0	100.0
Gross Profit								
Operating Expenses	90.0	89.8	89.8	90.6	90.3	87.9	93.4	92.5
Operating Profit	10.0	10.2	10.2	9.4	9.7	12.1	6.6	7.5
All Other Expenses (net)	.7	2.7	1.5	1.4	2.4	7.3	2.1	2.1
Profit Before Taxes	9.3	7.6	8.8	7.9	7.3	4.8	4.4	5.4
RATIOS								
Current	3.1	2.5	2.4	1.7	2.4	1.6	1.9	2.3
	1.3	1.4	1.4	1.2	1.2	1.2	1.2	1.3
	.8	.9	1.0	.8	1.0	.6	.8	.9
Quick	2.4	2.2	2.0	1.3	1.8	1.5	1.6	1.8
	1.1	1.2	1.3	.9	.9	.9	(810) 1.0	(1034) 1.0
	.5	.6	.8	.5	.6	.5	.6	.6
Sales/Receivables	0 UND	2 179.1	23 16.0	21 17.7	41 8.9	26 14.3	17 21.6	13 28.3
	0 UND	29 12.7	44 8.3	45 8.0	52 7.0	53 6.9	40 9.1	39 9.3
	29 12.6	50 7.3	70 5.2	68 5.3	67 5.5	108 3.4	65 5.6	61 6.0
Cost of Sales/Inventory								
Cost of Sales/Payables								
Sales/Working Capital	8.9	7.4	6.4	6.3	6.3	5.6	8.8	7.3
	38.9	23.9	13.7	28.1	20.3	12.4	30.4	21.4
	-121.2	-57.6	NM	-30.2	NM	-8.4	-33.8	-42.1
EBIT/Interest	14.1	18.1	39.9	10.0	8.5	46.8	12.9	13.5
	(67) 3.3	(138) 5.0	(168) 6.2	(79) 3.6	(30) 3.7	(21) 8.0	(672) 3.7	(851) 4.5
	.5	1.2	2.2	1.7	1.3	1.4	1.1	1.0
Net Profit + Depr., Dep., Amort./Cur. Mat. L/T/D		12.8	10.4	12.4	12.1		5.9	6.6
	(14) 5.2	(47) 3.7	(17) 2.5	(14) 6.6			(149) 2.2	(156) 2.4
	1.9	1.5	1.9	2.5			.9	.9
Fixed/Worth	.0	.2	.1	.1	.3	.3	.2	.2
	.5	.9	.6	.8	1.2	.7	.9	.8
	UND	8.4	1.9	4.9	NM	-.6	5.5	5.7
Debt/Worth	.7	1.0	.8	1.1	1.6	1.6	1.1	.9
	2.4	2.5	1.9	3.4	3.3	6.6	2.7	2.5
	-10.4	23.3	6.5	25.3	-50.4	-3.1	38.9	21.1
% Profit Before Taxes/Tangible Net Worth	203.9	89.7	74.3	61.7	49.1	54.7	66.0	72.9
	(82) 62.0	(141) 39.3	(187) 36.5	(82) 35.6	(26) 25.4	(18) 28.6	(626) 25.3	(827) 28.8
	23.3	8.9	11.2	10.5	8.4	9.6	4.2	5.3
% Profit Before Taxes/Total Assets	62.7	30.0	24.8	15.7	11.8	22.0	19.0	20.0
	16.0	8.9	11.0	6.5	5.7	4.7	6.9	7.8
	.0	1.0	3.6	1.7	1.7	1.2	.1	.2
Sales/Net Fixed Assets	UND	94.3	65.0	32.7	30.7	48.9	52.4	51.2
	55.1	23.0	19.9	12.4	9.8	11.4	16.5	16.2
	13.0	7.2	6.7	5.1	5.6	6.8	6.8	5.9
Sales/Total Assets	11.0	4.7	3.8	2.9	2.3	2.1	4.2	4.1
	5.5	3.1	2.4	2.0	1.5	1.1	2.7	2.6
	2.6	1.7	1.6	1.1	.8	.5	1.6	1.5
% Depr., Dep., Amort./Sales	.4	.5	.6	.7	1.3	.2	.9	.9
	(61) 1.3	(133) 1.6	(178) 1.6	(85) 1.9	(24) 3.1	(14) 1.0	(629) 2.1	(788) 2.3
	3.3	4.3	3.0	3.8	4.7	3.3	4.6	4.6
% Officers', Directors' Owners' Comp/Sales	4.5	2.5	1.6	1.3			3.2	2.9
	(59) 8.4	(77) 6.1	(72) 3.4	(11) 1.9			(285) 6.7	(365) 6.1
	14.3	10.5	10.1	8.7			12.1	12.1
Net Sales ($)	193026M	663308M	3052958M	4793352M	5332274M	7991738M	19760823M	29613471M
Total Assets ($)	26488M	197613M	1013310M	2023511M	2768606M	4042332M	11411081M	11992049M

© RMA 2007

M = $ thousand   MM = $ million
See Pages 11 through 21 for Explanation of Ratios and Data

Comparative Historical Data | | | Current Data Sorted by Sales

			Type of Statement	114 (4/1-9/30/06)			560 (10/1/06-3/31/07)		
142	134	115	Unqualified	5	6	3	17	25	59
149	111	102	Reviewed	4	11	15	26	33	13
144	85	83	Compiled	11	16	19	21	9	7
177	150	126	Tax Returns	48	32	20	15	8	3
330	376	248	Other	31	48	31	33	44	61
4/1/04-3/31/05 ALL	4/1/05-3/31/06 ALL	4/1/06-3/31/07 ALL		0-1MM	1-3MM	3-5MM	5-10MM	10-25MM	25MM & OVER
942	856	674	**NUMBER OF STATEMENTS**	99	113	88	112	119	143
%	%	%	**ASSETS**	%	%	%	%	%	%
15.4	15.4	18.5	Cash & Equivalents	22.5	24.9	20.9	14.9	14.9	15.0
31.6	31.8	29.3	Trade Receivables (net)	14.9	22.7	28.9	31.9	37.7	35.5
7.8	7.5	7.3	Inventory	5.2	10.9	7.6	6.2	8.5	5.6
4.6	4.7	5.2	All Other Current	3.6	5.6	4.3	5.4	5.2	6.6
59.3	59.3	60.3	Total Current	46.3	64.0	61.8	58.4	66.2	62.7
24.6	23.8	23.6	Fixed Assets (net)	40.6	21.6	20.1	27.4	19.7	16.0
6.5	7.0	7.0	Intangibles (net)	6.1	4.1	6.2	4.9	6.2	13.0
9.6	9.9	9.0	All Other Non-Current	7.0	10.3	12.0	9.3	7.9	8.3
100.0	100.0	100.0	Total	100.0	100.0	100.0	100.0	100.0	100.0
			LIABILITIES						
12.6	13.5	11.6	Notes Payable-Short Term	11.3	11.7	13.0	9.9	11.8	12.1
4.2	3.6	3.3	Cur. Mat.-L.T.D.	4.0	3.8	3.0	3.0	2.9	3.1
14.8	13.8	13.7	Trade Payables	10.9	11.2	13.0	13.9	14.8	17.1
.4	.5	.5	Income Taxes Payable	.3	.2	.8	.7	.3	.7
16.9	17.4	17.1	All Other Current	13.2	20.7	16.4	15.6	17.5	18.4
49.0	48.9	46.3	Total Current	39.7	47.8	46.1	43.2	47.2	51.5
19.1	16.0	16.5	Long-Term Debt	32.7	17.2	9.8	16.0	9.6	14.9
.3	.3	.3	Deferred Taxes	.1	.0	.6	.4	.4	.3
6.7	8.9	7.8	All Other Non-Current	11.6	9.3	13.8	5.2	3.8	5.9
24.9	26.0	29.1	Net Worth	16.0	25.7	29.7	35.1	39.0	27.4
100.0	100.0	100.0	Total Liabilties & Net Worth	100.0	100.0	100.0	100.0	100.0	100.0
			INCOME DATA						
100.0	100.0	100.0	Net Sales	100.0	100.0	100.0	100.0	100.0	100.0
			Gross Profit						
91.4	91.8	89.9	Operating Expenses	80.2	87.6	90.8	92.3	92.3	93.9
8.6	8.2	10.1	Operating Profit	19.8	12.4	9.2	7.7	7.7	6.1
1.9	2.0	1.9	All Other Expenses (net)	5.6	2.5	.3	.7	1.6	1.2
6.7	6.2	8.2	Profit Before Taxes	14.2	9.8	8.9	7.0	6.2	4.9
			RATIOS						
2.2	2.2	2.4		3.5	4.0	3.2	2.2	2.2	1.8
1.3	1.4	1.3	Current	1.4	1.4	1.4	1.4	1.4	1.2
.9	.9	.9		.6	.9	.9	1.0	1.0	.9
1.8	1.8	2.0		2.1	3.1	2.3	1.8	1.8	1.5
(941) 1.0	1.1	1.1	Quick	1.2	1.0	1.3	1.1	1.1	1.0
.6	.6	.6		.3	.4	.6	.7	.8	.6
13 27.1	13 28.3	7 53.3		0 UND	0 UND	6 63.7	18 20.6	21 17.1	29 12.6
39 9.4	42 8.7	36 10.1	Sales/Receivables	0 UND	23 16.1	32 11.2	42 8.7	43 8.4	47 7.7
60 6.1	63 5.8	59 6.2		38 9.7	45 8.2	59 6.2	61 6.0	62 5.9	68 5.4
			Cost of Sales/Inventory						
			Cost of Sales/Payables						
7.5	7.2	7.1		6.9	5.6	7.0	8.5	6.8	8.3
25.4	19.6	20.8	Sales/Working Capital	28.4	21.3	21.4	19.0	14.0	25.0
-47.0	-52.3	-113.8		-16.9	-59.5	-49.8	NM	192.4	-133.0
20.8	18.9	18.2		14.2	9.6	26.0	20.0	34.5	15.0
(742) 5.2	(694) 5.2	(503) 4.7	EBIT/Interest	(50) 3.3	(75) 3.0	(71) 6.5	(98) 5.6	(90) 6.2	(119) 4.4
1.6	1.5	1.4		-.5	.7	1.7	1.6	2.4	1.7
7.1	5.9	10.4					9.9	15.6	14.5
(126) 2.6	(113) 2.7	(99) 4.5	Net Profit + Depr., Dep., Amort./Cur. Mat. L/T/D			(25) 3.7	(24) 2.2	(36) 6.6
1.2	.8	1.9					1.3	1.1	2.6
.2	.2	.1		.1	.1	.1	.3	.1	.1
.7	.7	.7	Fixed/Worth	1.1	.5	.5	.8	.6	.7
4.3	5.2	3.4		UND	10.3	2.1	2.0	2.2	19.1
.9	1.0	.9		.8	.6	.5	.9	.8	1.5
2.6	2.7	2.5	Debt/Worth	2.7	3.2	1.9	2.2	2.1	4.1
15.9	21.2	25.4		-14.5	UND	5.7	7.3	6.5	-116.7
78.9	84.8	81.1		137.9	94.4	84.6	72.4	73.4	70.7
(751) 33.9	(675) 32.5	(536) 38.2	% Profit Before Taxes/Tangible Net Worth	(72) 46.0	(85) 36.8	(70) 39.4	(97) 34.9	(106) 37.2	(106) 42.9
9.8	7.9	10.3		6.9	11.1	10.3	8.2	10.5	13.5
23.8	24.4	26.5		34.9	41.4	30.8	24.5	25.0	19.7
8.6	8.6	9.2	% Profit Before Taxes/Total Assets	6.8	9.4	11.7	8.5	11.5	8.7
1.5	1.3	2.0		-.1	-.2	3.9	2.4	3.5	2.2
73.2	70.2	85.6		121.3	118.4	118.7	44.6	72.6	71.0
20.1	22.5	21.1	Sales/Net Fixed Assets	9.7	31.1	29.0	16.3	21.5	19.7
6.7	6.8	7.2		1.4	7.7	9.9	6.3	7.5	8.7
4.2	4.3	4.4		4.5	4.8	5.0	4.5	4.2	4.1
2.8	2.7	2.6	Sales/Total Assets	1.7	2.8	3.2	2.6	2.5	2.4
1.6	1.5	1.5		.3	1.5	1.9	1.9	1.6	1.4
.7	.7	.6		1.2	.4	.7	.7	.5	.4
(674) 1.8	(641) 1.8	(495) 1.6	% Depr., Dep., Amort./Sales	(64) 4.0	(68) 1.6	(62) 1.3	(93) 1.9	(100) 1.4	(108) 1.4
4.1	3.6	3.6		14.8	4.4	2.5	3.4	3.2	3.0
2.5	2.6	2.3		6.3	4.3	2.2	2.0	1.5	.7
(315) 5.3	(269) 5.6	(223) 5.8	% Officers', Directors' Owners' Comp/Sales	(29) 9.9	(51) 8.2	(44) 5.6	(44) 3.5	(36) 2.7	(19) 1.6
11.3	11.4	10.9		15.7	11.2	14.0	9.4	8.2	7.4
25113463M	28721801M	22026656M	Net Sales ($)	47114M	219542M	346451M	823044M	1876803M	18713702M
11854983M	12460481M	10071860M	Total Assets ($)	68443M	201093M	181942M	540044M	1262116M	7818222M

© RMA 2007   M = $ thousand   MM = $ million
See Pages 11 through 21 for Explanation of Ratios and Data

Current Data Sorted by Assets

Comparative Historical Data

						Type of Statement		
		5	8	1	2	Unqualified	14	13
	2	8	1			Reviewed	18	18
4	6	5	1			Compiled	32	35
12	6	3	1			Tax Returns	20	24
4	5	11	7	2	1	Other	41	23
	26 (4/1-9/30/06)		69 (10/1/06-3/31/07)				4/1/02-3/31/03	4/1/03-3/31/04
0-500M	500M-2MM	2-10MM	10-50MM	50-100MM	100-250MM		ALL	ALL
20	19	32	18	3	3	NUMBER OF STATEMENTS	125	113
%	%	%	%	%	%	ASSETS	%	%
36.6	27.8	28.7	22.0			Cash & Equivalents	29.1	26.7
11.3	18.8	22.1	24.1			Trade Receivables (net)	21.9	21.7
.4	3.4	2.1	.4			Inventory	.7	.6
8.1	8.2	8.8	11.3			All Other Current	4.3	4.7
56.3	58.2	61.8	57.8			Total Current	56.0	53.6
25.9	18.2	19.9	11.7			Fixed Assets (net)	19.0	20.1
7.3	13.7	6.2	8.7			Intangibles (net)	8.0	11.7
10.8	9.8	12.2	21.8			All Other Non-Current	17.0	14.5
100.0	100.0	100.0	100.0			Total	100.0	100.0
						LIABILITIES		
37.7	10.9	12.8	6.3			Notes Payable-Short Term	11.1	28.5
1.4	1.2	1.5	.8			Cur. Mat.-L.T.D.	3.4	4.2
18.1	16.1	21.2	24.5			Trade Payables	24.6	22.2
.1	.1	.3	.3			Income Taxes Payable	.5	.5
23.9	23.1	36.8	31.3			All Other Current	27.9	29.9
81.1	51.5	72.7	63.2			Total Current	67.5	85.4
12.1	13.6	10.6	3.8			Long-Term Debt	9.7	9.6
.1	.1	.1	.2			Deferred Taxes	.1	.3
6.2	18.1	1.2	7.6			All Other Non-Current	25.2	10.7
.3	16.7	15.5	25.2			Net Worth	-2.6	-6.0
100.0	100.0	100.0	100.0			Total Liabilites & Net Worth	100.0	100.0
						INCOME DATA		
100.0	100.0	100.0	100.0			Net Sales	100.0	100.0
						Gross Profit		
95.7	97.1	94.8	96.6			Operating Expenses	99.5	99.2
4.3	2.9	5.2	3.4			Operating Profit	.5	.8
-.2	.9	1.9	.0			All Other Expenses (net)	.0	.0
4.5	1.9	3.3	3.4			Profit Before Taxes	.5	.9
						RATIOS		
3.3	3.2	1.4	1.5				1.7	1.5
1.0	1.1	1.0	.9			Current	1.0	1.0
.7	.6	.6	.6				.5	.4
3.3	2.1	1.4	1.3				1.5	1.5
.9	.9	.8	.7			Quick	.9	.9
.4	.4	.3	.4				.5	.3
0 UND	2 191.4	3 109.0	4 81.7				1 362.9	1 489.0
0 UND	5 77.1	9 40.9	34 10.7			Sales/Receivables	8 43.1	7 52.3
4 87.5	22 16.9	59 6.1	55 6.7				30 12.1	26 13.9
						Cost of Sales/Inventory		
						Cost of Sales/Payables		
29.4	5.5	14.8	22.8				24.0	34.9
UND	54.7	-643.8	-74.1			Sales/Working Capital	-315.5	-269.0
-79.1	-55.5	-5.9	-7.0				-18.0	-9.5
10.5	15.8	29.2	35.6				10.2	14.4
(13) 2.8	(12) 6.4	(20) 6.3	(11) 9.3			EBIT/Interest	(82) 3.4	(83) 4.2
-2.3	1.2	1.9	1.7				-2.0	-2.8
						Net Profit + Depr., Dep.,	21.0	4.4
						Amort./Cur. Mat. L/T/D	(17) 6.1	(18) 2.2
							.7	.3
.2	.2	.1	.2				.2	.3
1.5	.7	1.0	.5			Fixed/Worth	.7	1.3
UND	-26.9	4.8	NM				-1.6	-.7
.4	1.2	1.3	1.8				1.2	1.5
3.1	7.5	4.9	4.6			Debt/Worth	4.9	6.5
UND	-130.2	NM	NM				-7.0	-3.7
109.7	170.2	68.0	75.4			% Profit Before Taxes/Tangible	39.9	53.6
(15) 47.6	(14) 29.3	(24) 25.4	(14) 42.8			Net Worth	(80) 17.8	(69) 15.4
17.4	16.0	12.9	16.5				.0	-2.8
49.3	18.1	15.6	12.6			% Profit Before Taxes/Total	12.4	14.1
9.5	4.8	5.8	7.1			Assets	4.0	5.0
-2.9	.4	1.7	2.5				-5.1	-6.6
802.4	150.0	110.9	177.9				240.1	213.0
52.8	75.3	60.4	49.8			Sales/Net Fixed Assets	55.7	40.8
15.1	12.2	13.6	9.2				15.1	16.2
34.4	8.7	7.5	4.0				13.7	15.4
9.5	3.3	2.9	2.2			Sales/Total Assets	4.4	5.5
3.4	2.0	1.6	1.4				2.0	2.4
.3	.1	.3	.3				.2	.2
(13) 1.0	(12) 1.3	(25) .7	(15) .8			% Depr., Dep., Amort./Sales	(89) .7	(87) .8
1.6	4.4	1.6	2.0				2.1	1.9
1.4							1.1	1.0
(12) 2.8						% Officers', Directors'	(50) 2.8	(45) 3.6
12.7						Owners' Comp/Sales	5.9	8.5
56747M	159794M	949705M	929704M	688959M	396903M	Net Sales ($)	3623427M	2236549M
3761M	20076M	161181M	372399M	175917M	604870M	Total Assets ($)	1147037M	732848M

© RMA 2007

M = $ thousand   MM = $ million
See Pages 11 through 21 for Explanation of Ratios and Data

Comparative Historical Data — Current Data Sorted by Sales

			Type of Statement						
16	15	16	Unqualified				2	3	11
18	11	11	Reviewed			1	4	1	5
18	14	16	Compiled	1	3	2	4	1	5
23	22	22	Tax Returns	4	8	2	1	4	3
32	30	30	Other	5	1	4	7	5	8
4/1/04-3/31/05 ALL	4/1/05-3/31/06 ALL	4/1/06-3/31/07 ALL			26 (4/1-9/30/06)			69 (10/1/06-3/31/07)	
				0-1MM	1-3MM	3-5MM	5-10MM	10-25MM	25MM & OVER
107	92	95	NUMBER OF STATEMENTS	10	12	9	18	14	32
%	%	%	**ASSETS**	%	%	%	%	%	%
30.1	35.2	29.3	Cash & Equivalents	25.4	34.0		29.5	36.8	26.1
19.7	16.4	18.7	Trade Receivables (net)	15.3	13.7		19.3	15.4	24.1
.7	.6	1.6	Inventory	.0	.1		.0	4.9	2.2
5.5	7.5	8.7	All Other Current	10.8	10.9		4.0	12.5	8.7
55.9	59.7	58.2	Total Current	51.5	58.7		52.9	69.5	61.2
20.7	15.7	18.5	Fixed Assets (net)	46.3	16.2		18.8	10.9	13.3
11.7	10.0	10.1	Intangibles (net)	1.1	15.7		6.2	9.6	11.5
11.7	14.5	13.2	All Other Non-Current	1.3	9.8		22.3	9.9	13.9
100.0	100.0	100.0	Total	100.0	100.0		100.0	100.0	100.0
			LIABILITIES						
12.3	10.1	15.6	Notes Payable-Short Term	19.4	2.4		16.0	6.9	5.8
4.6	2.8	1.2	Cur. Mat.-L.T.D.	2.8	.8		1.4	1.7	.8
20.9	18.1	20.4	Trade Payables	9.7	13.7		21.3	20.9	27.3
.5	.5	.2	Income Taxes Payable	.0	.0		.4	.4	.2
28.1	40.9	29.9	All Other Current	14.1	26.0		43.7	15.1	34.9
66.4	72.4	67.4	Total Current	45.9	42.9		82.9	44.9	69.1
13.2	9.9	9.9	Long-Term Debt	25.1	7.6		12.1	5.7	3.4
.0	.0	.1	Deferred Taxes	.0	.2		.1	.4	.0
12.1	11.7	7.8	All Other Non-Current	11.8	25.2		.6	10.7	4.8
8.3	5.8	14.8	Net Worth	16.2	24.2		4.4	38.4	22.7
100.0	100.0	100.0	Total Liabilties & Net Worth	100.0	100.0		100.0	100.0	100.0
			INCOME DATA						
100.0	100.0	100.0	Net Sales	100.0	100.0		100.0	100.0	100.0
			Gross Profit						
98.2	95.2	96.2	Operating Expenses	86.1	94.5		97.3	93.9	98.8
1.8	4.8	3.8	Operating Profit	13.9	5.5		2.7	6.1	1.2
.4	.3	1.1	All Other Expenses (net)	8.3	-.1		.3	.4	.8
1.4	4.5	2.7	Profit Before Taxes	5.6	5.6		2.4	5.7	.4
			RATIOS						
1.6	1.9	1.7	Current	3.7	3.5		1.7	3.0	1.1
1.0	1.0	1.0		1.2	1.2		.8	1.4	.9
.6	.6	.6		.5	.9		.5	.9	.6
1.5	1.6	1.6	Quick	3.7	3.1		1.7	2.2	1.0
.9	.9	.8		1.1	1.0		.8	.9	.7
.4	.4	.4		.0	.9		.4	.5	.4
1 701.8	0 816.9	1 402.9	Sales/Receivables	0 UND	0 895.9	3 127.1	0 799.6		2 176.7
7 50.2	7 53.5	7 53.1		0 UND	4 96.9	9 40.9	7 55.7		8 45.3
33 11.1	24 15.2	42 8.8		81 4.5	30 12.3	81 4.5	46 7.9		31 11.7
			Cost of Sales/Inventory						
			Cost of Sales/Payables						
25.5	14.7	23.2	Sales/Working Capital	4.2	6.9		19.5	5.1	57.2
UND	NM	-721.0		UND	282.7		-250.9	57.7	-94.1
-17.3	-14.5	-15.6		-2.0	-46.1		-5.8	-64.6	-20.7
22.8	28.5	22.1	EBIT/Interest				9.3		34.1
(76) 5.4	(57) 7.3	(59) 4.8					(11) 4.0		(21) 4.2
.5	1.5	1.0					-2.0		.1
3.4	29.4		Net Profit + Depr., Dep., Amort./Cur. Mat. L/T/D						
(12) 2.0	(11) 5.8								
.4	2.5								
.3	.2	.2	Fixed/Worth	1.5	.1		.2	.1	.2
1.2	.6	.8		4.4	.2		.5	.4	.9
-1.3	-1.0	-26.9		UND	4.6		-2.9	UND	-7.4
1.5	1.2	1.4	Debt/Worth	1.9	.3		.6	.4	1.9
4.0	4.8	5.6		4.8	4.3		5.1	5.0	5.6
-5.4	-8.1	-49.8		UND	NM		-10.2	UND	-43.4
73.5	59.8	72.4	% Profit Before Taxes/Tangible Net Worth				48.5	140.3	53.9
(72) 25.0	(61) 29.0	(70) 35.1					(13) 26.5	(11) 69.7	(23) 21.4
11.3	14.8	15.3					1.9	17.4	12.4
18.1	17.7	14.8	% Profit Before Taxes/Total Assets	14.2	55.4		16.9	19.2	11.8
6.7	6.9	5.4		4.6	6.9		6.8	11.6	4.9
.7	1.2	.4		-1.0	.8		-3.2	2.5	-.1
149.3	190.6	147.6	Sales/Net Fixed Assets	33.4	785.3		71.5	677.9	163.9
54.9	60.6	59.5		4.6	61.9		39.0	119.7	70.4
19.1	16.5	13.0		.8	12.2		12.7	17.6	30.7
15.8	8.4	8.2	Sales/Total Assets	2.2	7.8		8.7	9.5	8.7
4.4	4.2	3.3		1.1	4.0		2.9	2.5	4.1
2.3	1.4	1.6		.6	1.9		1.6	1.3	2.5
.2	.2	.3	% Depr., Dep., Amort./Sales				.6	.0	.3
(78) .6	(60) .7	(68) .8					(12) 1.5	(10) .5	(26) .5
2.0	2.0	1.7					2.7	1.7	.8
1.5	.7	1.3	% Officers', Directors' Owners' Comp/Sales						
(43) 3.4	(34) 2.3	(30) 4.4							
7.7	8.6	10.1							
5048430M	3279153M	3181812M	Net Sales ($)	4011M	22943M	34718M	131209M	222355M	2766576M
976909M	1136526M	1338204M	Total Assets ($)	11422M	11170M	11589M	55274M	129383M	1119366M

© RMA 2007

M = $ thousand   MM = $ million
See Pages 11 through 21 for Explanation of Ratios and Data

Current Data Sorted by Assets   Comparative Historical Data

0-500M	500M-2MM	2-10MM	10-50MM	50-100MM	100-250MM	Type of Statement	4/1/02-3/31/03 ALL	4/1/03-3/31/04 ALL
		4	2	2		Unqualified	7	7
	1		1			Reviewed	6	4
2	5	3	1			Compiled	13	7
3		2	1	1		Tax Returns	3	5
1	4	5	1		3	Other	12	24
	5 (4/1-9/30/06)		37 (10/1/06-3/31/07)					
6	10	14	6	3	3	NUMBER OF STATEMENTS	41	47
%	%	%	%	%	%	**ASSETS**	%	%
	13.5	19.6				Cash & Equivalents	27.7	29.7
	7.3	19.6				Trade Receivables (net)	11.2	8.5
	.0	1.5				Inventory	2.1	.8
	11.2	9.2				All Other Current	7.4	8.2
	32.0	49.9				Total Current	48.5	47.1
	60.2	33.8				Fixed Assets (net)	38.4	38.3
	.7	3.7				Intangibles (net)	2.6	4.3
	7.1	12.7				All Other Non-Current	10.5	10.4
	100.0	100.0				Total	100.0	100.0
						LIABILITIES		
	4.1	7.3				Notes Payable-Short Term	2.2	3.7
	12.2	2.9				Cur. Mat.-L.T.D.	4.8	3.6
	3.6	19.7				Trade Payables	11.1	15.2
	.0	1.1				Income Taxes Payable	.2	.1
	7.5	36.3				All Other Current	30.2	32.2
	27.3	67.2				Total Current	48.6	54.7
	42.6	23.3				Long-Term Debt	30.8	22.9
	.0	.1				Deferred Taxes	.4	.1
	15.6	3.7				All Other Non-Current	3.0	6.4
	14.4	5.7				Net Worth	17.2	15.8
	100.0	100.0				Total Liabilties & Net Worth	100.0	100.0
						INCOME DATA		
	100.0	100.0				Net Sales	100.0	100.0
						Gross Profit		
	97.2	99.6				Operating Expenses	92.8	97.1
	2.8	.4				Operating Profit	7.2	2.9
	1.5	1.1				All Other Expenses (net)	2.9	1.0
	1.3	-.7				Profit Before Taxes	4.3	1.9
						RATIOS		
	1.9	1.1					1.7	2.1
	.6	.8				Current	1.1	1.0
	.2	.5					.8	.5
	1.6	.9					1.4	1.8
	.5	.6				Quick	1.0	.9
	.2	.2					.7	.4
	0 UND	1 345.6					1 402.4	0 UND
	6 58.9	12 30.9				Sales/Receivables	8 47.6	4 96.8
	21 17.1	31 11.8					29 12.4	14 25.5
						Cost of Sales/Inventory		
						Cost of Sales/Payables		
	13.7	35.6					11.1	14.8
	-32.3	-60.1				Sales/Working Capital	36.3	-286.7
	-15.3	-4.5					-46.8	-7.8
		9.0					6.6	6.2
	(13)	1.1				EBIT/Interest	(29) 1.9	(30) 1.8
		-4.0					.2	-4.0
						Net Profit + Depr., Dep., Amort./Cur. Mat. L/T/D		
	2.1	.7					.5	.5
	5.2	2.0				Fixed/Worth	1.4	2.1
	NM	-8.6					9.2	-4.6
	2.0	2.2					1.4	1.1
	6.0	12.8				Debt/Worth	3.7	3.7
	NM	-19.7					35.4	-8.2
							68.6	76.1
						% Profit Before Taxes/Tangible Net Worth	(33) 24.2	(34) 19.7
							-1.9	-9.1
	6.3	14.6					15.8	19.4
	2.4	-.3				% Profit Before Taxes/Total Assets	3.4	4.2
	-4.5	-5.8					-1.8	-7.2
	14.6	67.5					38.1	55.8
	4.2	13.1				Sales/Net Fixed Assets	4.7	11.9
	2.5	2.5					2.0	2.1
	3.5	4.0					4.3	4.6
	2.5	2.5				Sales/Total Assets	2.0	2.3
	1.6	1.7					1.3	1.2
		.3					.5	.4
	(11)	.6				% Depr., Dep., Amort./Sales	(40) 3.7	(38) 2.2
		5.6					7.1	5.8
							2.3	
						% Officers', Directors' Owners' Comp/Sales	(10) 3.6	
							4.4	
17850M	33048M	278940M	268964M	637034M	1203334M	Net Sales ($)	913199M	1348737M
1993M	13125M	88170M	151454M	240561M	486749M	Total Assets ($)	441249M	690827M

M = $ thousand   MM = $ million
See Pages 11 through 21 for Explanation of Ratios and Data

Comparative Historical Data | Current Data Sorted by Sales

			Type of Statement		0-1MM	1-3MM	3-5MM	5-10MM	10-25MM	25MM & OVER
5	5	8	Unqualified					2		6
4	5	2	Reviewed			1			1	
13	6	6	Compiled			1		2	1	2
4	5	11	Tax Returns			6	1	2		2
13	14	15	Other			3	1	3	3	5
4/1/04-	4/1/05-	4/1/06-				5 (4/1-9/30/06)		37 (10/1/06-3/31/07)		
3/31/05	3/31/06	3/31/07								
ALL	ALL	ALL			0-1MM	1-3MM	3-5MM	5-10MM	10-25MM	25MM & OVER
39	35	42	NUMBER OF STATEMENTS			11	2	9	5	15
%	%	%	ASSETS	%	%	%	%	%	%	%
32.5	28.0	24.2	Cash & Equivalents		19.8					39.6
11.8	12.3	10.1	Trade Receivables (net)	D	7.3					14.1
1.2	.9	1.5	Inventory	A	3.8					1.3
5.1	9.8	9.3	All Other Current	T	9.5					8.6
50.5	51.1	45.2	Total Current	A	40.4					63.5
29.7	29.4	39.5	Fixed Assets (net)	N	45.6					21.5
2.6	2.0	3.9	Intangibles (net)	O	2.6					.7
17.2	17.5	11.5	All Other Non-Current	T	11.5					14.3
100.0	100.0	100.0	Total		100.0					100.0
			LIABILITIES	A						
2.1	5.9	5.4	Notes Payable-Short Term	V	8.9					2.7
5.8	7.2	4.7	Cur. Mat.-L.T.D.	A	6.2					1.0
12.2	16.9	11.1	Trade Payables	I	5.3					22.1
.2	.1	.9	Income Taxes Payable	L	.0					1.6
33.5	28.3	28.1	All Other Current	A	13.4					36.8
53.7	58.4	50.2	Total Current	B	33.7					64.1
21.9	21.3	30.1	Long-Term Debt	L	57.3					6.1
.0	.2	.0	Deferred Taxes	E	.0					.0
7.4	3.2	9.8	All Other Non-Current		16.2					1.6
16.9	16.9	9.9	Net Worth		-7.1					28.1
100.0	100.0	100.0	Total Liabilties & Net Worth		100.0					100.0
			INCOME DATA							
100.0	100.0	100.0	Net Sales		100.0					100.0
			Gross Profit							
96.3	95.6	94.0	Operating Expenses		94.4					89.1
3.7	4.4	6.0	Operating Profit		5.6					10.9
.3	1.4	.8	All Other Expenses (net)		2.4					-.6
3.4	3.0	5.2	Profit Before Taxes		3.3					11.5
			RATIOS							
1.9	1.7	1.6			3.4					1.3
1.0	.9	.8	Current		1.7					.9
.7	.5	.4			.3					.5
1.7	1.6	1.4			2.0					1.0
.9	.8	.6	Quick		1.4					.8
.6	.3	.3			.3					.3
0 UND	0 UND	0 UND			0 UND					0 UND
3 112.3	7 51.5	6 60.7	Sales/Receivables		5 72.1					5 66.8
22 16.4	25 14.6	21 17.1			21 17.3					15 24.1
			Cost of Sales/Inventory							
			Cost of Sales/Payables							
13.2	22.6	14.7			12.2					14.0
-115.3	-83.6	-32.3	Sales/Working Capital		26.9					-102.6
-19.6	-17.1	-8.0			-6.6					-8.9
15.5	16.5	8.1								
(24) 2.6	(24) 3.5	(32) 2.5	EBIT/Interest							
-.1	-.4	.2								
			Net Profit + Depr., Dep., Amort./Cur. Mat. L/T/D							
.3	.2	.8			1.4					.1
1.5	1.4	2.9	Fixed/Worth		10.9					.8
-5.2	-9.1	-3.8			-1.9					3.9
1.0	1.0	2.0			3.2					1.3
5.0	3.5	3.7	Debt/Worth		13.5					2.9
-34.8	-18.9	-30.1			-3.2					13.1
89.8	85.7	110.1	% Profit Before Taxes/Tangible Net Worth							74.6
(29) 22.4	(25) 31.4	(28) 30.0							(12)	45.2
7.9	7.9	-.9								16.6
20.4	22.7	21.3	% Profit Before Taxes/Total Assets		39.5					25.3
6.3	5.0	3.6			6.2					12.9
.6	-1.4	-2.6			-3.6					1.5
66.1	112.8	88.4	Sales/Net Fixed Assets		36.5					181.1
14.8	15.7	10.0			9.7					87.2
3.3	4.1	2.7			2.7					7.3
5.3	7.5	4.0	Sales/Total Assets		4.7					4.2
2.2	3.2	2.6			3.4					3.5
1.2	1.9	1.6			1.7					1.5
.6	.3	.4	% Depr., Dep., Amort./Sales							.1
(30) 2.6	(28) 1.5	(32) 3.5							(11)	.3
8.2	5.4	6.2								1.6
2.5	3.2		% Officers', Directors' Owners' Comp/Sales							
(11) 5.6	(10) 4.7									
12.0	7.4									
1309289M	1840307M	2439170M	Net Sales ($)		22203M	7573M	59179M	75708M		2274507M
639724M	733234M	982052M	Total Assets ($)		8845M	2702M	41056M	60118M		869331M

© RMA 2007

M = $ thousand   MM = $ million
See Pages 11 through 21 for Explanation of Ratios and Data

Current Data Sorted by Assets   Comparative Historical Data

0-500M	500M-2MM	2-10MM	10-50MM	50-100MM	100-250MM	Type of Statement	4/1/02-3/31/03 ALL	4/1/03-3/31/04 ALL
1	2	3	6	3	2	Unqualified	10	14
		1				Reviewed	3	1
2	3			1	1	Compiled	8	9
1	1	2				Tax Returns	5	6
6	3	2	2	1	1	Other	16	12
	9 (4/1-9/30/06)		31 (10/1/06-3/31/07)					
10	9	8	7	4	2	**NUMBER OF STATEMENTS**	42	42
%	%	%	%	%	%	**ASSETS**	%	%
34.3						Cash & Equivalents	16.6	20.0
10.3						Trade Receivables (net)	4.4	8.0
8.5						Inventory	6.9	2.1
11.9						All Other Current	4.2	5.4
64.9						Total Current	32.2	35.5
17.3						Fixed Assets (net)	58.8	52.5
6.2						Intangibles (net)	3.3	2.6
11.6						All Other Non-Current	5.7	9.4
100.0						Total	100.0	100.0
						LIABILITIES		
13.3						Notes Payable-Short Term	2.0	5.9
1.5						Cur. Mat.-L.T.D.	6.3	3.8
12.2						Trade Payables	5.0	5.7
.0						Income Taxes Payable	1.0	1.1
13.9						All Other Current	7.8	9.4
40.9						Total Current	22.1	25.8
6.9						Long-Term Debt	42.1	31.7
.0						Deferred Taxes	.0	.6
.4						All Other Non-Current	4.9	4.5
51.8						Net Worth	30.9	37.4
100.0						Total Liabilties & Net Worth	100.0	100.0
						INCOME DATA		
100.0						Net Sales	100.0	100.0
						Gross Profit		
90.1						Operating Expenses	83.7	85.7
9.9						Operating Profit	16.3	14.3
2.5						All Other Expenses (net)	7.7	7.4
7.4						Profit Before Taxes	8.7	6.9
						RATIOS		
4.6							6.0	7.2
2.2						Current	1.7	1.3
1.1							.7	.6
2.9							4.1	6.2
1.8						Quick	.9	.9
.5							.4	.2
0 UND							0 UND	0 UND
0 UND						Sales/Receivables	2 161.9	3 140.5
1 364.7							9 40.3	27 13.4
						Cost of Sales/Inventory		
						Cost of Sales/Payables		
5.6							3.8	2.4
39.0						Sales/Working Capital	10.3	12.0
NM							-21.2	-27.7
							6.9	8.6
						EBIT/Interest	(31) 2.2	(27) 3.7
							.7	2.0
						Net Profit + Depr., Dep., Amort./Cur. Mat. L/T/D		
.0							.8	.7
.0						Fixed/Worth	1.8	1.3
.7							11.1	4.1
.3							.5	.4
.6						Debt/Worth	2.3	1.6
NM							16.0	5.4
						% Profit Before Taxes/Tangible Net Worth	57.1	39.9
							(34) 11.7	(35) 13.7
							.5	5.2
94.4						% Profit Before Taxes/Total Assets	20.2	17.2
11.1							5.0	6.2
-16.2							.2	3.0
UND							8.3	12.3
610.4						Sales/Net Fixed Assets	2.1	1.9
11.4							.6	.8
7.7							2.8	1.8
4.3						Sales/Total Assets	1.2	1.0
1.2							.5	.5
						% Depr., Dep., Amort./Sales	2.7	2.9
							(36) 6.4	(32) 5.6
							10.5	11.3
						% Officers', Directors' Owners' Comp/Sales	4.5	2.1
							(13) 11.8	(10) 3.9
							17.2	8.4
13697M	30688M	78384M	496474M	270890M	256881M	Net Sales ($)	849836M	522091M
2646M	9385M	39333M	203529M	280438M	444576M	Total Assets ($)	775320M	591694M

M = $ thousand   MM = $ million
See Pages 11 through 21 for Explanation of Ratios and Data

Comparative Historical Data | Current Data Sorted by Sales

			Type of Statement	0-1MM	1-3MM	3-5MM	5-10MM	10-25MM	25MM & OVER
11	11	17	Unqualified	2	1	1	2	2	9
		1	Reviewed					1	
4	5	5	Compiled	2	1		2		
6	4	4	Tax Returns	2	1		1		
12	15	13	Other	2	1	3	1	2	1
4/1/04-3/31/05	4/1/05-3/31/06	4/1/06-3/31/07		9 (4/1-9/30/06)			31 (10/1/06-3/31/07)		
ALL	ALL	ALL							
33	35	40	**NUMBER OF STATEMENTS**	8	7	4	6	5	10
%	%	%	**ASSETS**	%	%	%	%	%	%
22.0	24.5	36.0	Cash & Equivalents						44.8
10.8	9.2	11.9	Trade Receivables (net)						12.4
2.2	1.8	3.2	Inventory						.8
7.0	4.6	9.4	All Other Current						9.9
42.1	40.1	60.5	Total Current						68.0
40.5	41.6	21.4	Fixed Assets (net)						11.3
1.4	1.8	3.4	Intangibles (net)						4.0
16.0	16.5	14.7	All Other Non-Current						16.8
100.0	100.0	100.0	Total						100.0
			LIABILITIES						
4.4	7.6	5.6	Notes Payable-Short Term						.7
3.2	2.5	2.6	Cur. Mat.-L.T.D.						1.5
6.7	7.9	11.3	Trade Payables						14.2
1.0	1.1	.6	Income Taxes Payable						.9
11.2	14.9	17.7	All Other Current						36.0
26.4	34.0	37.7	Total Current						53.4
22.0	21.4	8.6	Long-Term Debt						1.8
.5	.3	.6	Deferred Taxes						.2
8.3	7.1	7.6	All Other Non-Current						11.1
42.7	37.2	45.4	Net Worth						33.5
100.0	100.0	100.0	Total Liabilties & Net Worth						100.0
			INCOME DATA						
100.0	100.0	100.0	Net Sales						100.0
			Gross Profit						
85.1	86.7	89.9	Operating Expenses						98.3
14.9	13.3	10.1	Operating Profit						1.7
3.5	3.2	1.1	All Other Expenses (net)						-2.9
11.4	10.1	9.0	Profit Before Taxes						4.6
			RATIOS						
5.6	2.8	4.1	Current						1.7
1.8	1.4	1.7							1.3
.9	1.0	1.1							.8
5.1	2.5	2.5	Quick						1.6
1.0	1.3	1.5							1.2
.3	.7	.8							.8
0 UND	0 UND	0 UND	Sales/Receivables						0 UND
10 34.8	1 249.6	5 80.6							6 60.4
27 13.6	20 18.5	17 21.6							19 18.9
			Cost of Sales/Inventory						
			Cost of Sales/Payables						
2.4	3.3	2.3	Sales/Working Capital						2.7
9.4	16.9	10.8							22.3
-36.1	-403.6	125.6							-35.8
33.9	29.3	51.2	EBIT/Interest						
(25) 4.9	(25) 6.6	(27) 19.7							
1.6	1.9	4.0							
			Net Profit + Depr., Dep., Amort./Cur. Mat. L/T/D						
.2	.3	.0	Fixed/Worth						.0
1.1	1.0	.3							.3
5.3	2.5	1.0							5.9
.4	.4	.4	Debt/Worth						.9
1.1	1.4	1.1							2.2
16.1	4.1	3.3							52.8
41.3	51.2	45.5	% Profit Before Taxes/Tangible Net Worth						
(28) 11.5	(31) 16.1	(35) 15.0							
1.2	5.2	7.0							
23.7	28.0	29.4	% Profit Before Taxes/Total Assets						10.5
7.8	9.7	8.1							4.3
1.2	2.3	2.7							-4.2
38.6	29.1	244.1	Sales/Net Fixed Assets						310.8
3.1	5.5	16.5							29.8
1.2	1.1	4.2							8.8
2.0	3.1	4.5	Sales/Total Assets						5.0
1.0	1.5	1.5							1.3
.6	.7	.8							.6
.9	1.7	.7	% Depr., Dep., Amort./Sales						.7
(26) 3.3	(24) 2.5	(22) 2.5							
7.3	6.8	6.8							
3.4			% Officers', Directors' Owners' Comp/Sales						
(10) 5.2									
13.2									
471223M	659306M	1147014M	Net Sales ($)	4384M	13129M	15108M	38389M	78606M	997398M
492250M	381974M	979907M	Total Assets ($)	6272M	6540M	30147M	18796M	127955M	790197M

© RMA 2007

M = $ thousand   MM = $ million
See Pages 11 through 21 for Explanation of Ratios and Data

Current Data Sorted by Assets

Comparative Historical Data

						Type of Statement		
1			5	6	1	5	Unqualified	13	11
2	3		10	4			Reviewed	15	17
	6		6	1			Compiled	13	28
4	2		3				Tax Returns	6	3
3	9		8	6	2	2	Other	24	23

18 (4/1-9/30/06)			71 (10/1/06-3/31/07)					4/1/02-3/31/03	4/1/03-3/31/04
0-500M	500M-2MM	2-10MM	10-50MM	50-100MM	100-250MM			ALL	ALL
10	20	32	17	3	7	NUMBER OF STATEMENTS	71	82
%	%	%	%	%	%	ASSETS	%	%
24.3	14.8	7.4	7.8			Cash & Equivalents	9.7	7.9
25.1	44.7	57.2	60.4			Trade Receivables (net)	49.2	48.3
4.3	1.0	.6	1.0			Inventory	1.4	.8
2.0	7.2	1.1	3.4			All Other Current	7.0	5.8
55.7	67.8	66.3	72.8			Total Current	67.2	62.7
26.2	22.2	12.8	12.4			Fixed Assets (net)	16.0	18.2
7.6	4.9	7.8	6.8			Intangibles (net)	7.8	6.8
10.5	5.2	13.1	8.0			All Other Non-Current	8.9	12.2
100.0	100.0	100.0	100.0			Total	100.0	100.0
						LIABILITIES		
17.7	14.3	16.7	19.7			Notes Payable-Short Term	19.1	17.6
4.7	5.5	2.8	5.0			Cur. Mat.-L.T.D.	6.2	6.0
7.8	4.3	7.7	10.4			Trade Payables	6.2	7.8
.0	.1	.4	22.4			Income Taxes Payable	1.0	1.1
13.5	22.3	22.9	20.2			All Other Current	22.7	19.8
43.6	46.4	50.5	77.7			Total Current	55.3	52.3
27.3	12.7	5.5	22.4			Long-Term Debt	17.0	19.6
.0	.1	.3	.2			Deferred Taxes	.5	.7
1.2	3.7	2.5	8.7			All Other Non-Current	6.5	5.8
27.8	37.1	41.2	-9.0			Net Worth	20.8	21.7
100.0	100.0	100.0	100.0			Total Liabilties & Net Worth	100.0	100.0
						INCOME DATA		
100.0	100.0	100.0	100.0			Net Sales	100.0	100.0
						Gross Profit		
97.3	96.4	94.6	97.1			Operating Expenses	96.3	95.6
2.7	3.6	5.4	2.9			Operating Profit	3.7	4.4
.5	.2	1.2	.8			All Other Expenses (net)	.8	1.2
2.2	3.4	4.2	2.1			Profit Before Taxes	2.9	3.1
						RATIOS		
2.5	2.0	1.9	1.7				1.7	1.8
1.5	1.5	1.2	1.1			Current	1.2	1.2
.5	1.1	1.0	.8				1.0	1.0
1.9	2.0	1.8	1.7				1.5	1.6
1.3	1.2	1.2	1.1			Quick	1.1	1.1
.5	.7	.9	.7				.8	.8

0	UND	28	13.1	39	9.3	48	7.6				37	9.9	35	10.4
27	13.6	36	10.2	47	7.8	54	6.8	Sales/Receivables	42	8.7	41	8.8
61	6.0	45	8.2	58	6.2	62	5.9		55	6.6	53	6.8

Cost of Sales/Inventory

Cost of Sales/Payables

14.2	9.4	12.9	12.3	Sales/Working Capital	13.9	17.3
191.8	21.7	37.7	69.7		35.8	38.3
-167.1	130.2	-445.3	-28.6		261.3	-498.0

	17.4		9.1		10.7			9.1		7.1
(18)	5.6	(27)	3.9		2.8	EBIT/Interest	(65)	3.5	(74)	3.4
	2.2		2.5		2.1			1.1		1.4

								4.6		20.8
						Net Profit + Depr., Dep., Amort./Cur. Mat. L/T/D	(24)	1.5	(22)	2.4
								.9		1.1

.5	.2	.1	.2		.2	.2
14.8	.4	.3	1.8	Fixed/Worth	.7	.6
-.9	3.6	.5	-.7		39.0	2.9
.7	.7	.9	1.2		1.6	1.6
22.7	2.2	2.1	11.9	Debt/Worth	3.9	3.1
-7.7	9.3	3.7	-6.9		141.7	14.1

	81.0		49.1		97.8			83.9		60.2
(17)	40.5	(30)	28.1	(11)	39.3	% Profit Before Taxes/Tangible Net Worth	(54)	28.5	(67)	37.4
	8.8		12.2		23.4			12.5		10.9

64.7	23.7	17.9	17.1	% Profit Before Taxes/Total Assets	13.5	17.1
14.2	11.4	7.7	7.5		5.0	7.9
-5.3	3.7	3.3	5.0		.2	1.4
206.7	63.9	81.6	94.9	Sales/Net Fixed Assets	94.3	101.4
52.8	41.6	53.2	53.0		45.1	38.4
16.0	12.9	31.2	34.3		18.1	17.4
35.8	6.6	5.3	4.9	Sales/Total Assets	5.8	5.5
7.2	5.0	4.4	4.5		4.3	4.0
1.9	2.3	3.1	3.7		2.9	3.0

	.3		.5		.3			.5		.4
(18)	.7	(30)	.7	(14)	.5	% Depr., Dep., Amort./Sales	(53)	1.1	(63)	.9
	1.4		1.2		.9			2.2		2.3

			1.0				1.7		2.3
		(14)	2.1			% Officers', Directors' Owners' Comp/Sales	(18)	4.8	(28)	3.0
			4.3				8.6		5.2

42852M	114613M	541280M	2513225M	551691M	3196684M	Net Sales ($)	4114417M	3380297M
2972M	24395M	125286M	362238M	189639M	1270170M	Total Assets ($)	1185563M	988903M

M = $ thousand   MM = $ million
See Pages 11 through 21 for Explanation of Ratios and Data

Comparative Historical Data				Current Data Sorted by Sales					

				Type of Statement						
13	15	18	Unqualified		1		1	2	14
21	18	19	Reviewed	1	2		4	6	6
13	10	13	Compiled	1	1	2	6	2	2
7	5	9	Tax Returns	2		2	2	3	
27	49	30	Other	4		1	8	7	10
4/1/04-	4/1/05-	4/1/06-			18 (4/1-9/30/06)		71 (10/1/06-3/31/07)		
3/31/05	3/31/06	3/31/07							
ALL	ALL	ALL		0-1MM	1-3MM	3-5MM	5-10MM	10-25MM	25MM & OVER
81	97	89	**NUMBER OF STATEMENTS**	7	4	5	21	20	32
%	%	%	**ASSETS**	%	%	%	%	%	%
7.4	9.5	10.6	Cash & Equivalents				12.2	8.7	5.4
54.8	50.1	50.9	Trade Receivables (net)				50.0	59.2	60.0
.8	1.1	1.3	Inventory				.3	.7	1.0
4.0	4.4	3.4	All Other Current				3.1	1.2	3.5
67.0	65.1	66.1	Total Current				65.6	69.7	69.9
16.5	16.7	16.0	Fixed Assets (net)				18.9	11.6	9.7
4.8	6.3	7.9	Intangibles (net)				7.1	7.2	10.2
11.7	11.9	9.9	All Other Non-Current				8.3	11.5	10.2
100.0	100.0	100.0	Total				100.0	100.0	100.0
			LIABILITIES						
19.5	17.6	16.5	Notes Payable-Short Term				14.0	15.4	19.6
5.6	3.9	3.9	Cur. Mat.-L.T.D.				5.0	2.7	3.5
5.8	6.1	7.3	Trade Payables				3.4	9.7	8.5
.9	.3	4.5	Income Taxes Payable				.1	.6	12.0
21.8	22.2	21.6	All Other Current				18.1	26.5	23.6
53.6	50.2	53.8	Total Current				40.6	54.9	67.3
15.8	16.5	14.3	Long-Term Debt				8.9	7.0	17.1
.5	.6	.2	Deferred Taxes				.4	.1	.3
3.7	10.2	4.2	All Other Non-Current				2.7	.7	7.0
26.4	22.5	27.5	Net Worth				47.3	37.3	8.2
100.0	100.0	100.0	Total Liabilities & Net Worth				100.0	100.0	100.0
			INCOME DATA						
100.0	100.0	100.0	Net Sales				100.0	100.0	100.0
			Gross Profit						
96.7	94.7	95.8	Operating Expenses				96.5	96.1	96.4
3.3	5.3	4.2	Operating Profit				3.5	3.9	3.6
.4	1.0	.8	All Other Expenses (net)				.2	.5	.8
2.9	4.3	3.4	Profit Before Taxes				3.3	3.4	2.7
			RATIOS						
2.0	2.4	2.0					2.9	1.8	1.8
1.3	1.4	1.2	Current				1.4	1.3	1.2
1.0	1.0	.9					1.1	.9	.9
1.8	2.2	1.9					2.1	1.7	1.7
1.2	1.3	1.2	Quick				1.3	1.3	1.1
.9	1.0	.9					1.0	.9	.9
34 10.8	36 10.2	35 10.4					30 12.1	37 9.9	47 7.8
45 8.1	47 7.7	47 7.8	Sales/Receivables				36 10.1	45 8.0	54 6.8
63 5.8	57 6.4	59 6.2					48 7.6	58 6.2	72 5.0
			Cost of Sales/Inventory						
			Cost of Sales/Payables						
13.5	10.7	11.8					10.0	12.9	11.6
28.6	22.5	32.1	Sales/Working Capital				32.1	28.9	40.8
-999.8	290.9	-161.6					137.1	-154.1	-84.3
10.0	16.0	16.0					22.8	4.0	13.4
(75) 4.5	(83) 5.5	(79) 4.1	EBIT/Interest			(19) 9.1	(17) 3.0	4.6
1.8	2.4	2.2					4.1	2.1	2.1
11.5	6.9	10.0							30.4
(25) 4.1	(27) 2.4	(24) 2.8	Net Profit + Depr., Dep., Amort./Cur. Mat. L/T/D					(15) 2.1
1.6	1.3	1.2							1.2
.2	.2	.2					.1	.1	.2
.4	.5	.4	Fixed/Worth				.3	.2	.5
1.3	3.3	4.2					1.2	.8	-1.2
1.1	.9	1.0					.5	.9	2.4
2.7	2.6	2.8	Debt/Worth				.9	1.8	4.6
8.4	9.5	20.2					6.3	4.2	-7.9
63.2	75.1	68.5					141.8	44.2	97.8
(70) 28.0	(80) 32.3	(72) 38.1	% Profit Before Taxes/Tangible Net Worth			(20) 42.1	(17) 25.2	(23) 42.1
8.7	17.6	15.7					10.3	14.5	23.4
15.9	20.4	19.9					39.8	17.9	17.2
9.5	9.7	8.5	% Profit Before Taxes/Total Assets				15.5	5.9	7.6
2.5	4.1	3.5					5.2	3.1	4.9
94.6	104.7	85.2					53.9	151.4	103.1
50.8	50.3	45.4	Sales/Net Fixed Assets				41.6	67.0	50.3
29.3	23.4	29.2					25.9	42.2	33.2
5.6	5.5	5.6					6.8	6.8	5.0
4.3	4.2	4.5	Sales/Total Assets				5.1	5.0	4.4
3.4	3.0	2.7					3.1	3.9	3.4
.3	.4	.4					.4	.3	.3
(71) .6	(75) .8	(78) .7	% Depr., Dep., Amort./Sales			(19) .7	(18) .5	(28) .7
1.1	1.6	1.3					1.3	.9	1.1
1.4	1.1	.9						.7	
(33) 2.9	(32) 3.3	(27) 2.4	% Officers', Directors' Owners' Comp/Sales				(10) 1.9	
6.1	6.7	4.9						5.0	
3044958M	3692458M	6960345M	Net Sales ($)	4021M	8619M	19339M	155790M	335505M	6437071M
827154M	1101068M	1974700M	Total Assets ($)	6886M	2461M	5782M	33691M	77283M	1848597M

M = $ thousand   MM = $ million
See Pages 11 through 21 for Explanation of Ratios and Data

Current Data Sorted by Assets | Comparative Historical Data

Type of Statement

0-500M	500M-2MM	2-10MM	10-50MM	50-100MM	100-250MM	Type of Statement	4/1/02-3/31/03 ALL	4/1/03-3/31/04 ALL
1	1	7	7	2	1	Unqualified	24	22
1	12	34	2			Reviewed	41	44
7	14	4				Compiled	28	48
3	13	5				Tax Returns	24	22
9	13	21	10	6	5	Other	39	49
	29 (4/1-9/30/06)		149 (10/1/06-3/31/07)				4/1/02-3/31/03 ALL	4/1/03-3/31/04 ALL
21	53	71	19	8	6	NUMBER OF STATEMENTS	156	185

0-500M %	500M-2MM %	2-10MM %	10-50MM %	50-100MM %	100-250MM %		%	%
						ASSETS		
19.8	10.5	9.3	4.9			Cash & Equivalents	10.2	9.3
30.0	45.6	37.2	27.3			Trade Receivables (net)	35.5	34.1
12.1	13.6	11.1	8.0			Inventory	9.8	11.1
6.9	3.1	5.3	2.8			All Other Current	4.4	4.7
68.8	72.8	62.8	43.0			Total Current	59.8	59.2
16.3	15.6	17.9	17.2			Fixed Assets (net)	17.2	19.9
10.1	4.9	12.2	23.6			Intangibles (net)	12.9	12.4
4.8	6.7	7.1	16.2			All Other Non-Current	10.0	8.4
100.0	100.0	100.0	100.0			Total	100.0	100.0
						LIABILITIES		
15.9	11.3	11.7	9.8			Notes Payable-Short Term	17.1	13.8
4.0	7.0	3.4	5.9			Cur. Mat.-L.T.D.	7.3	5.7
16.1	15.7	17.8	13.2			Trade Payables	13.5	14.1
1.1	.2	.3	.1			Income Taxes Payable	.4	.2
26.4	15.9	18.5	16.1			All Other Current	16.9	17.6
63.6	50.1	51.6	45.0			Total Current	55.2	51.4
10.6	19.5	19.6	39.1			Long-Term Debt	20.1	25.1
.0	.2	.4	.3			Deferred Taxes	.4	.4
50.4	5.8	7.9	10.2			All Other Non-Current	6.1	8.8
-24.7	24.4	20.5	5.4			Net Worth	18.2	14.3
100.0	100.0	100.0	100.0			Total Liabilities & Net Worth	100.0	100.0
						INCOME DATA		
100.0	100.0	100.0	100.0			Net Sales	100.0	100.0
						Gross Profit		
95.0	96.1	93.6	97.2			Operating Expenses	94.4	95.3
5.0	3.9	6.4	2.8			Operating Profit	5.6	4.7
.6	.8	1.8	5.1			All Other Expenses (net)	2.8	2.2
4.4	3.2	4.6	-2.3			Profit Before Taxes	2.8	2.5
						RATIOS		
3.9	2.3	1.8	2.2				1.9	1.9
1.3	1.4	1.2	1.0			Current	1.3	1.2
.7	1.1	1.0	.4				.8	.8
2.9	1.7	1.4	1.4				1.5	1.5
.9	1.1	.9	.9			Quick	.9	.9
.4	.7	.6	.2				.5	.5
9 39.2	34 10.7	36 10.2	21 17.7			Sales/Receivables	26 13.9	27 13.4
19 19.5	45 8.2	49 7.4	37 9.8				43 8.4	43 8.5
45 8.1	72 5.0	68 5.4	84 4.4				66 5.5	60 6.1
						Cost of Sales/Inventory		
						Cost of Sales/Payables		
9.1	7.1	7.8	5.2			Sales/Working Capital	7.6	8.2
59.3	17.5	18.3	109.7				24.3	27.8
-18.7	52.8	-711.6	-6.1				-36.8	-21.1
14.2	10.7	9.2	8.0			EBIT/Interest	10.7	8.0
(15) 3.7	(49) 4.4	(64) 4.2	(18) 1.9				(136) 3.7	(170) 2.9
-6.0	1.8	.8	.1				1.4	.5
	8.0	6.8				Net Profit + Depr., Dep.,	4.2	3.3
	(14) 3.4	(22) 2.6				Amort./Cur. Mat. L/T/D	(42) 2.1	(43) 1.8
	2.5	.4					1.2	.8
.2	.2	.2	.5			Fixed/Worth	.2	.3
9.5	.5	1.0	-1.7				.6	1.1
-.3	1.9	-.8	-.1				10.9	-.8
.7	.9	1.4	3.1			Debt/Worth	1.2	1.3
48.0	1.8	4.6	-11.3				3.9	4.0
-2.6	9.9	-5.8	-2.5				-13.5	-4.2
173.0	57.7	71.5				% Profit Before Taxes/Tangible Net Worth	79.9	51.5
(11) 71.1	(46) 24.7	(47) 43.0					(115) 30.7	(120) 19.0
-34.2	6.3	11.1					5.4	1.3
48.9	18.5	19.5	8.3			% Profit Before Taxes/Total Assets	18.1	14.3
13.4	8.2	8.1	1.6				6.0	4.3
-16.6	2.1	-.5	-6.2				.3	-1.7
94.6	46.4	47.2	36.1			Sales/Net Fixed Assets	43.3	44.1
42.8	21.5	23.2	14.5				20.8	21.1
19.3	14.0	8.5	5.8				11.9	10.4
7.1	4.1	3.2	2.4			Sales/Total Assets	3.7	3.7
4.6	3.3	2.5	1.5				2.7	2.7
3.7	2.4	1.5	.9				1.5	1.7
	.9	.7	.9			% Depr., Dep., Amort./Sales	.7	.8
	(41) 1.7	(59) 1.4	(16) 3.9				(113) 1.8	(145) 1.7
	2.7	3.7	9.8				3.5	3.3
	3.9	2.6				% Officers', Directors' Owners' Comp/Sales	3.8	3.5
	(28) 5.9	(22) 4.0					(66) 7.0	(71) 6.6
	10.8	6.3					11.1	10.8
31870M	217785M	898336M	653491M	1073374M	1253385M	Net Sales ($)	2090372M	2563111M
4179M	62481M	329079M	421594M	528085M	969039M	Total Assets ($)	1722376M	1722515M

M = $ thousand   MM = $ million
See Pages 11 through 21 for Explanation of Ratios and Data

Comparative Historical Data — Current Data Sorted by Sales

4/1/04-3/31/05 ALL	4/1/05-3/31/06 ALL	4/1/06-3/31/07 ALL	Type of Statement	0-1MM	1-3MM	3-5MM	5-10MM	10-25MM	25MM & OVER
26	25	19	Unqualified		1	1	5	3	9
41	43	49	Reviewed	1	3	8	24	10	3
33	35	25	Compiled	4	10	3	5	2	1
28	24	21	Tax Returns	1	8	3	8	1	
58	51	64	Other	7	10	5	10		20
				29 (4/1-9/30/06)			**149 (10/1/06-3/31/07)**		
186	178	178	**NUMBER OF STATEMENTS**	13	32	20	52	28	33
%	%	%	**ASSETS**	%	%	%	%	%	%
9.7	9.9	9.9	Cash & Equivalents	17.1	15.7	10.7	8.3	9.1	4.4
34.4	37.5	36.2	Trade Receivables (net)	33.3	33.8	44.1	37.5	35.5	33.6
10.0	10.0	11.3	Inventory	14.1	12.6	14.2	12.1	11.0	6.5
4.1	4.2	4.5	All Other Current	6.8	3.5	3.2	5.4	4.5	4.2
58.2	61.6	62.1	Total Current	71.3	65.6	72.2	63.3	60.1	48.6
17.9	18.0	16.8	Fixed Assets (net)	16.1	18.3	16.0	16.4	18.4	15.5
14.5	11.0	12.1	Intangibles (net)	8.3	8.8	5.7	12.9	15.8	16.1
9.5	9.5	9.0	All Other Non-Current	4.3	7.2	6.1	7.4	5.8	19.7
100.0	100.0	100.0	Total	100.0	100.0	100.0	100.0	100.0	100.0
			LIABILITIES						
10.0	12.4	11.4	Notes Payable-Short Term	17.5	8.5	14.0	12.0	14.7	6.5
6.1	4.5	4.7	Cur. Mat.-L.T.D.	3.9	7.3	2.7	6.9	2.3	2.1
13.0	15.3	15.5	Trade Payables	14.8	13.9	12.3	16.5	19.8	14.3
.2	.2	.4	Income Taxes Payable	.0	.8	.3	.4	.1	.3
17.4	17.5	18.3	All Other Current	31.4	13.9	16.1	17.8	15.7	21.7
46.6	49.9	50.3	Total Current	67.5	44.3	45.3	53.7	52.7	44.9
25.9	26.2	22.9	Long-Term Debt	10.5	18.3	23.1	20.6	15.9	41.8
.3	.2	.3	Deferred Taxes	.0	.2	.3	.4	.2	.3
6.8	12.1	12.7	All Other Non-Current	57.9	11.3	7.0	11.1	6.8	7.3
20.3	11.6	13.8	Net Worth	35.9	25.8	24.2	14.2	24.4	5.8
100.0	100.0	100.0	Total Liabilties & Net Worth	100.0	100.0	100.0	100.0	100.0	100.0
			INCOME DATA						
100.0	100.0	100.0	Net Sales	100.0	100.0	100.0	100.0	100.0	100.0
			Gross Profit						
93.6	94.7	94.6	Operating Expenses	96.1	92.7	96.9	93.6	98.4	92.8
6.4	5.3	5.4	Operating Profit	3.9	7.3	3.1	6.4	1.6	7.2
2.1	2.0	2.3	All Other Expenses (net)	.4	1.9	1.4	1.4	2.7	5.3
4.3	3.2	3.0	Profit Before Taxes	3.5	5.4	1.7	5.0	-1.1	1.9
			RATIOS						
2.2	2.1	2.1	Current	3.9	2.8	2.9	1.8	1.8	1.7
1.3	1.4	1.3		1.3	1.5	1.6	1.2	1.2	1.1
.9	.9	.9		.7	1.1	1.2	.9	.8	.7
1.5	1.7	1.5	Quick	2.9	2.1	2.4	1.3	1.4	1.4
1.0	1.1	1.0		.8	1.2	1.1	.9	.9	.9
.6	.6	.6		.5	.6	.8	.6	.6	.4
31 11.9	30 12.2	27 13.7	Sales/Receivables	9 39.2	19 19.4	39 9.4	34 10.8	26 13.9	26 14.3
46 8.0	46 8.0	46 7.9		34 10.8	46 7.9	50 7.3	46 8.0	49 7.5	41 8.9
67 5.4	71 5.1	67 5.5		54 6.7	75 4.9	71 5.2	72 5.1	61 6.0	71 5.2
			Cost of Sales/Inventory						
			Cost of Sales/Payables						
7.4	7.7	7.6	Sales/Working Capital	4.5	6.0	6.2	8.7	7.9	12.6
22.5	20.8	18.7		189.4	11.8	11.6	29.1	21.7	47.6
-35.6	-37.6	-57.8		-15.0	56.2	19.6	-74.7	-26.7	-23.2
12.6	11.2	9.0	EBIT/Interest		7.9	9.5	12.9	8.5	9.9
(164) 4.7	(163) 3.4	(158) 3.6		(29) 2.9	(18) 2.4	(48) 5.3	(25) 2.1	(30) 4.0	
1.3	1.3	.8			1.7	.3	1.1	-1.0	.5
7.5	5.3	7.4	Net Profit + Depr., Dep., Amort./Cur. Mat. L/T/D				4.7		
(41) 2.4	(43) 1.8	(47) 3.2					(16) 3.0		
1.3	1.1	1.2					.3		
.3	.2	.3	Fixed/Worth	.2	.3	.1	.3	.2	.5
1.1	1.0	1.0		9.5	.6	.5	.9	1.6	7.4
-.7	-1.2	-.8		-.3	10.4	3.5	-.9	-.6	-.5
1.3	1.3	1.4	Debt/Worth	.7	.8	1.1	1.3	1.5	3.5
4.2	5.2	3.8		48.0	1.5	2.4	4.3	3.7	33.2
-5.4	-4.8	-5.1		-3.3	19.2	4.6	-4.7	-5.2	-3.4
72.6	88.2	71.4	% Profit Before Taxes/Tangible Net Worth		76.7	38.6	83.6	46.7	137.7
(122) 25.9	(113) 29.8	(118) 29.0		(25) 21.1	(16) 19.2	(35) 43.0	(17) 29.4	(18) 65.9	
6.0	8.3	6.8			6.0	2.7	11.9	-4.2	23.3
21.1	18.6	19.2	% Profit Before Taxes/Total Assets	43.0	20.2	11.6	18.9	13.5	25.3
6.9	5.5	7.2		5.6	8.0	4.5	8.1	5.7	6.6
.8	.9	-.4		-29.9	1.5	-.1	.9	-4.5	-3.1
48.9	53.6	48.7	Sales/Net Fixed Assets	63.3	47.8	67.4	37.6	52.8	62.7
22.1	27.2	21.6		34.3	18.5	22.5	23.4	23.6	17.8
11.2	11.7	11.7		13.7	11.2	11.3	11.0	11.5	11.8
3.5	4.1	3.9	Sales/Total Assets	6.5	3.6	3.8	3.8	3.9	3.5
2.6	2.7	2.6		4.1	2.3	2.7	2.8	2.6	2.2
1.5	1.7	1.6		1.9	1.8	1.8	1.8	1.6	1.2
.8	.5	.8	% Depr., Dep., Amort./Sales		1.1	.6	.8	.5	.7
(139) 1.5	(139) 1.4	(129) 1.7		(20) 2.7	(15) 1.7	(47) 1.3	(23) 1.4	(22) 1.6	
3.5	2.9	3.5			4.3	2.8	2.9	3.5	3.8
3.9	3.7	3.0	% Officers', Directors' Owners' Comp/Sales		4.4		2.9		
(74) 6.8	(63) 6.6	(60) 5.2		(16) 5.9			(21) 4.0		
11.6	11.6	9.2			12.6		7.4		
2864812M	3821909M	4128241M	Net Sales ($)	6089M	61972M	84543M	371547M	442031M	3162059M
1948266M	2102979M	2314457M	Total Assets ($)	1684M	33769M	36823M	178453M	262503M	1801225M

© RMA 2007

M = $ thousand   MM = $ million

See Pages 11 through 21 for Explanation of Ratios and Data

Current Data Sorted by Assets

Comparative Historical Data

						Type of Statement		
1	1	8	2 2			Unqualified	6	3
5	10	3	1			Reviewed	7	6
12	3	2				Compiled	9	15
10	5	5	7		1	Tax Returns	13	17
						Other	14	13
	12 (4/1-9/30/06)		66 (10/1/06-3/31/07)				4/1/02-3/31/03	4/1/03-3/31/04
0-500M	500M-2MM	2-10MM	10-50MM	50-100MM	100-250MM		ALL	ALL
28	19	18	12		1	NUMBER OF STATEMENTS	49	54
%	%	%	%	%	%	ASSETS	%	%
26.7	13.4	12.7	17.6			Cash & Equivalents	13.9	13.5
17.2	27.1	34.0	17.8			Trade Receivables (net)	20.5	19.4
1.6	1.8	6.2	4.8			Inventory	3.7	5.2
5.2	6.6	5.1	5.2			All Other Current	2.5	1.9
50.7	48.9	58.0	45.4			Total Current	40.7	39.9
29.5	33.2	33.5	33.9			Fixed Assets (net)	42.9	37.9
7.5	12.8	5.5	15.8			Intangibles (net)	7.7	8.1
12.3	5.1	3.0	4.9			All Other Non-Current	8.7	14.1
100.0	100.0	100.0	100.0			Total	100.0	100.0
						LIABILITIES		
4.5	5.4	6.7	2.4			Notes Payable-Short Term	6.9	10.9
10.5	7.1	4.1	4.2			Cur. Mat.-L.T.D.	6.5	6.7
8.2	7.7	14.1	10.5			Trade Payables	8.3	9.5
.0	.1	1.0	.2			Income Taxes Payable	.2	.2
20.8	11.5	15.5	17.1			All Other Current	15.5	17.8
44.0	31.8	41.5	34.4			Total Current	37.4	45.0
67.8	20.9	20.6	16.3			Long-Term Debt	27.4	33.2
.0	.0	.2	.1			Deferred Taxes	.5	.3
7.1	4.4	4.0	6.7			All Other Non-Current	3.1	3.2
-19.0	42.9	33.8	42.5			Net Worth	31.7	18.3
100.0	100.0	100.0	100.0			Total Liabilities & Net Worth	100.0	100.0
						INCOME DATA		
100.0	100.0	100.0	100.0			Net Sales	100.0	100.0
						Gross Profit		
93.5	93.1	92.5	93.7			Operating Expenses	92.9	93.1
6.5	6.9	7.5	6.3			Operating Profit	7.1	6.9
1.5	.6	3.6	.2			All Other Expenses (net)	1.8	2.9
5.0	6.3	3.9	6.0			Profit Before Taxes	5.3	3.9
						RATIOS		
5.1	2.5	2.4	2.1				1.9	1.4
1.6	2.0	1.4	1.3			Current	1.1	1.0
.5	.9	.9	1.2				.6	.5
5.1	2.0	1.7	1.7				1.6	1.4
1.0	1.5	1.0	1.1			Quick	1.0	.9
.4	.5	.7	.7				.6	.5
0 UND	16 23.1	26 14.2	14 26.7				11 32.1	0 UND
8 47.8	25 14.6	34 10.9	20 18.0			Sales/Receivables	22 16.9	23 15.6
27 13.3	37 9.8	49 7.5	26 14.1				29 12.4	34 10.7
						Cost of Sales/Inventory		
						Cost of Sales/Payables		
11.6	13.8	9.4	11.6				18.0	26.1
42.7	20.1	22.9	28.4			Sales/Working Capital	69.7	137.7
-28.7	-70.0	-55.4	54.7				-19.7	-14.2
29.9	124.7	16.4	50.4				18.8	14.3
(21) 5.9	(17) 8.6	(16) 4.4	(11) 8.2			EBIT/Interest	(43) 7.9	(50) 4.6
4.0	1.6	2.3	4.2				3.2	1.2
						Net Profit + Depr., Dep.,	9.8	7.9
						Amort./Cur. Mat. L/T/D	(13) 2.7	(14) 2.0
							2.3	1.5
.2	.6	.5	.5				.7	.6
1.8	1.0	1.0	1.7			Fixed/Worth	1.2	1.6
-.8	3.2	2.9	12.5				8.1	21.1
1.2	1.1	.9	.6				.9	1.6
-9.9	1.6	2.2	2.4			Debt/Worth	2.1	3.5
-2.4	4.0	4.8	28.1				16.4	33.7
166.6	98.5	47.9	112.2			% Profit Before Taxes/Tangible	97.6	118.7
(13) 139.9	(18) 57.4	(16) 20.6	(11) 41.5			Net Worth	(40) 41.5	(43) 31.4
34.8	13.2	10.7	28.0				16.9	7.4
83.3	48.1	12.5	26.1			% Profit Before Taxes/Total	24.1	24.5
26.4	17.5	6.9	14.1			Assets	14.1	9.2
6.3	1.6	1.7	6.8				4.4	.3
81.6	19.6	30.4	13.9				16.9	24.2
21.2	12.0	11.7	8.5			Sales/Net Fixed Assets	9.1	10.8
9.5	7.7	6.2	5.1				5.4	5.9
8.7	6.0	4.4	3.4				4.7	5.0
4.6	3.6	3.5	2.7			Sales/Total Assets	3.6	3.4
3.3	2.7	2.2	2.1				2.6	2.0
1.2	2.3	.7	1.8				2.3	1.8
(15) 1.9	(16) 3.4	(17) 1.8	3.6			% Depr., Dep., Amort./Sales	(44) 4.4	(47) 3.3
3.9	3.9	3.3	4.0				5.4	4.7
2.1	4.2	4.2					3.5	3.4
(19) 6.5	(16) 5.6	(10) 5.6				% Officers', Directors' Owners' Comp/Sales	(25) 6.9	(35) 8.1
10.3	12.3	7.7					13.3	13.0
39391M	93703M	227431M	782073M		469400M	Net Sales ($)	798522M	1126511M
7178M	19950M	75885M	292275M		111194M	Total Assets ($)	264689M	390524M

© RMA 2007

M = $ thousand   MM = $ million
See Pages 11 through 21 for Explanation of Ratios and Data

Comparative Historical Data / Current Data Sorted by Sales

Type of Statement

	4/1/04-3/31/05 ALL	4/1/05-3/31/06 ALL	4/1/06-3/31/07 ALL	0-1MM	1-3MM	3-5MM	5-10MM	10-25MM	25MM & OVER
Unqualified	2	1	2						2
Reviewed	9	12	12	1	1	1	2	5	3
Compiled	17	19	19		7	4	3	3	1
Tax Returns	24	17	18	3	9	1	2	2	1
Other	17	20	27	8	4	3	2	2	7

Current-data period splits: **12 (4/1-9/30/06)** covering 0-1MM / 1-3MM / 3-5MM; **66 (10/1/06-3/31/07)** covering 5-10MM / 10-25MM / 25MM & OVER.

NUMBER OF STATEMENTS	69	69	78	12	21	9	9	13	14

ASSETS (%)

Item	ALL '05	ALL '06	ALL '07	0-1MM	1-3MM	3-5MM	5-10MM	10-25MM	25MM & OVER
Cash & Equivalents	16.6	18.9	18.7	39.1	15.1			9.3	16.5
Trade Receivables (net)	20.6	20.4	23.4	10.2	22.3			37.5	17.3
Inventory	3.7	3.4	3.2	.3	1.6			4.3	7.6
All Other Current	3.3	3.6	5.4	8.8	3.0			10.4	5.1
Total Current	44.2	46.2	50.7	58.5	42.0			61.5	46.5
Fixed Assets (net)	37.2	33.3	31.8	28.3	34.9			31.5	30.5
Intangibles (net)	7.7	11.8	10.4	5.7	14.3			3.4	18.7
All Other Non-Current	10.9	8.6	7.1	7.5	8.9			3.6	4.3
Total	100.0	100.0	100.0	100.0	100.0			100.0	100.0

LIABILITIES

Item	ALL '05	ALL '06	ALL '07	0-1MM	1-3MM	3-5MM	5-10MM	10-25MM	25MM & OVER
Notes Payable-Short Term	10.7	8.3	4.9	6.7	1.5			7.0	2.5
Cur. Mat.-L.T.D.	5.4	7.6	7.1	12.9	9.7			6.1	3.6
Trade Payables	8.5	10.5	9.8	1.8	12.9			12.5	11.8
Income Taxes Payable	.5	.4	.3	.0	.1			.7	.2
All Other Current	10.4	13.7	16.5	29.7	11.0			17.3	15.0
Total Current	35.5	40.6	38.6	51.1	35.2			43.5	33.1
Long-Term Debt	29.6	17.5	37.3	75.4	60.2			17.3	18.9
Deferred Taxes	.5	.2	.1	.0	.0			.3	.1
All Other Non-Current	10.4	9.6	5.9	5.0	7.7			4.8	7.6
Net Worth	24.0	32.1	18.2	-31.5	-3.2			34.2	40.3
Total Liabilities & Net Worth	100.0	100.0	100.0	100.0	100.0			100.0	100.0

INCOME DATA

Item	ALL '05	ALL '06	ALL '07	0-1MM	1-3MM	3-5MM	5-10MM	10-25MM	25MM & OVER
Net Sales	100.0	100.0	100.0	100.0	100.0			100.0	100.0
Gross Profit									
Operating Expenses	92.9	94.6	93.3	91.8	92.4			94.3	94.2
Operating Profit	7.1	5.4	6.7	8.2	7.6			5.7	5.8
All Other Expenses (net)	1.6	.9	1.6	5.2	1.5			1.1	.3
Profit Before Taxes	5.6	4.5	5.2	3.0	6.2			4.7	5.4

RATIOS

Ratio	ALL '05	ALL '06	ALL '07	0-1MM	1-3MM	3-5MM	5-10MM	10-25MM	25MM & OVER
Current	2.6	2.0	2.6	6.5	2.9			2.5	2.2
	1.4	1.2	1.5	4.4	1.1			1.5	1.4
	.7	.7	.8	.4	.6			1.1	1.2
Quick	2.2	1.7	2.2	6.5	2.5			1.7	1.4
	1.0	1.0	1.2	4.2	1.0			1.0	1.1
	.6	.6	.7	.2	.5			.6	.8
Sales/Receivables	0 UND	12 / 29.8	6 / 63.7	0 UND	4 / 95.2			23 / 15.9	12 / 30.0
	24 / 15.1	20 / 18.6	22 / 16.3	0 UND	21 / 17.4			31 / 11.8	20 / 18.0
	34 / 10.9	28 / 12.9	33 / 11.1	19 / 18.9	31 / 11.7			47 / 7.8	27 / 13.4
Cost of Sales/Inventory									
Cost of Sales/Payables									
Sales/Working Capital	10.8	16.0	11.5	7.9	13.1			9.8	10.6
	40.3	84.5	24.3	12.9	197.7			24.9	28.4
	-26.6	-36.4	-49.0	-24.1	-28.7			133.3	70.9
EBIT/Interest	18.4	25.8	33.6		22.4			50.3	48.6
	(63) 5.7	(60) 8.1	(66) 5.1		(20) 4.3		(12) 4.1		(13) 6.4
	2.6	2.8	2.4		1.3			2.1	3.7
Net Profit + Depr., Dep., Amort./Cur. Mat. L/T/D	10.5	14.3	5.4						
	(16) 2.2	(13) 2.4	(20) 2.6						
	1.6	2.0	1.3						
Fixed/Worth	.5	.6	.5	.0	.7			.5	.5
	1.1	1.3	1.1	.7	7.6			.9	1.7
	5.5	7.6	19.1	-3.3	-.7			2.2	15.6
Debt/Worth	.6	.7	1.1	.6	1.5			.9	1.3
	1.9	2.6	2.2	-9.9	14.9			1.8	2.4
	10.0	21.6	-11.5	-1.8	-2.6			5.0	36.9
% Profit Before Taxes/Tangible Net Worth	76.4	97.7	109.5		161.8			92.5	111.3
	(56) 34.4	(56) 32.2	(58) 42.1		(12) 47.0		(12) 35.9		(12) 39.2
	11.0	9.5	17.6		13.7			15.8	22.2
% Profit Before Taxes/Total Assets	24.0	26.2	41.6	93.8	55.2			40.5	22.6
	13.7	11.8	13.8	27.3	14.0			9.2	13.4
	3.4	1.8	4.7	-1.9	1.8			5.9	6.0
Sales/Net Fixed Assets	24.9	23.3	34.8	UND	21.2			26.4	35.2
	10.4	12.3	12.6	51.5	12.5			12.9	9.2
	6.5	7.0	7.7	5.3	7.7			9.5	6.2
Sales/Total Assets	4.5	4.8	5.1	11.7	5.6			4.7	3.7
	3.8	3.7	3.7	4.0	3.7			4.4	2.8
	2.6	2.5	2.6	2.2	2.6			3.5	2.2
% Depr., Dep., Amort./Sales	1.5	1.6	1.5		1.5			1.3	1.5
	(55) 2.8	(58) 3.0	(60) 2.4		(15) 3.6			2.0	(13) 3.5
	4.9	4.1	3.9		5.7			2.8	4.0
% Officers', Directors' Owners' Comp/Sales	4.0	4.0	3.2		3.4				
	(43) 7.1	(43) 6.6	(49) 5.6		(20) 7.1				
	10.6	13.8	9.3		10.3				
Net Sales ($)	1167041M	1054367M	1611998M	7471M	32928M	37027M	62821M	192019M	1279732M
Total Assets ($)	351356M	358681M	506482M	5451M	9522M	10726M	17883M	49586M	413314M

© RMA 2007

M = $ thousand   MM = $ million
See Pages 11 through 21 for Explanation of Ratios and Data

Current Data Sorted by Assets   ## Comparative Historical Data

						Type of Statement		
	3	10	8	4	4	Unqualified	30	22
3	13	29	4			Reviewed	45	58
12	17	10				Compiled	48	57
38	20	3	1		1	Tax Returns	40	36
17	19	22	13	2	2	Other	70	66
	48 (4/1-9/30/06)		207 (10/1/06-3/31/07)				4/1/02-3/31/03	4/1/03-3/31/04
0-500M	500M-2MM	2-10MM	10-50MM	50-100MM	100-250MM		ALL	ALL
70	72	74	26	6	7	NUMBER OF STATEMENTS	233	239
%	%	%	%	%	%	ASSETS	%	%
18.2	10.2	9.5	11.9			Cash & Equivalents	11.5	12.0
24.7	39.0	46.9	44.2			Trade Receivables (net)	39.0	39.6
5.7	5.9	1.2	3.9			Inventory	2.9	2.9
6.8	5.9	4.6	3.7			All Other Current	5.1	4.2
55.5	61.0	62.1	63.7			Total Current	58.6	58.8
27.4	25.6	17.9	17.9			Fixed Assets (net)	24.7	25.0
8.1	5.8	8.8	4.7			Intangibles (net)	6.9	5.6
9.0	7.6	11.2	13.7			All Other Non-Current	9.9	10.6
100.0	100.0	100.0	100.0			Total	100.0	100.0
						LIABILITIES		
27.2	9.0	13.5	13.9			Notes Payable-Short Term	15.0	14.4
6.0	4.8	3.0	1.4			Cur. Mat.-L.T.D.	4.2	5.8
8.5	14.2	12.9	10.0			Trade Payables	12.2	11.3
.3	.3	.3	.2			Income Taxes Payable	.4	.4
24.2	11.9	16.1	21.1			All Other Current	17.1	17.2
66.1	40.2	45.7	46.5			Total Current	48.8	49.1
30.0	20.1	11.1	13.9			Long-Term Debt	15.2	14.7
.0	.9	.2	.1			Deferred Taxes	.4	.5
4.6	7.2	6.0	3.5			All Other Non-Current	5.8	6.1
-.7	31.6	36.9	35.9			Net Worth	29.9	29.6
100.0	100.0	100.0	100.0			Total Liabilties & Net Worth	100.0	100.0
						INCOME DATA		
100.0	100.0	100.0	100.0			Net Sales	100.0	100.0
						Gross Profit		
95.3	96.4	94.3	94.8			Operating Expenses	95.9	96.0
4.7	3.6	5.7	5.2			Operating Profit	4.1	4.0
.5	.0	1.3	.5			All Other Expenses (net)	1.3	.9
4.2	3.6	4.4	4.6			Profit Before Taxes	2.8	3.1
						RATIOS		
2.0	2.7	1.9	2.0				2.1	2.0
.9	1.7	1.3	1.4			Current	1.3	1.3
.5	1.0	1.0	1.0				.9	.8
1.5	2.5	1.8	1.8				1.9	1.7
(69) .8	1.4	1.3	1.2			Quick	(232) 1.1	1.1
.4	.7	.9	.9				.7	.7
0 UND	21 17.0	27 13.4	28 13.1				19 19.1	21 17.2
12 29.5	35 10.5	41 8.9	40 9.1			Sales/Receivables	32 11.5	35 10.5
33 11.2	51 7.1	58 6.3	59 6.1				47 7.8	51 7.2
						Cost of Sales/Inventory		
						Cost of Sales/Payables		
15.8	7.9	13.0	12.0				13.0	12.5
-275.7	17.5	25.6	26.9			Sales/Working Capital	40.9	34.5
-22.7	282.6	-493.6	-291.7				-80.1	-50.8
11.6	14.7	18.2	46.4				12.6	13.0
(58) 5.5	(70) 5.5	(68) 5.0	(24) 12.7			EBIT/Interest	(200) 3.4	(209) 5.0
1.3	1.2	2.0	3.2				1.3	1.9
	5.3	13.9				Net Profit + Depr., Dep.,	4.9	6.0
	(16) 1.5	(17) 4.4				Amort./Cur. Mat. L/T/D	(47) 2.1	(63) 2.5
	-.1	1.3					1.1	1.2
.3	.3	.2	.3				.3	.3
1.8	.9	.5	.5			Fixed/Worth	.7	.8
-1.0	NM	1.8	1.8				4.4	3.9
1.4	.9	1.0	.9				.9	.9
5.5	1.8	2.0	2.5			Debt/Worth	2.3	2.3
-4.1	NM	12.1	7.3				13.5	12.6
158.8	56.1	69.9	66.9			% Profit Before Taxes/Tangible	68.0	61.7
(41) 52.6	(54) 27.9	(60) 42.7	(22) 52.6			Net Worth	(184) 25.5	(192) 26.4
18.0	8.4	14.9	30.3				8.3	7.4
53.7	21.8	21.9	26.5			% Profit Before Taxes/Total	19.9	18.6
17.3	10.4	11.4	13.5			Assets	7.1	7.9
1.8	1.6	3.6	5.1				1.6	2.0
115.9	44.3	62.6	59.2				58.4	50.4
36.3	22.0	32.6	31.4			Sales/Net Fixed Assets	25.3	24.6
14.3	9.4	13.5	15.6				12.5	10.7
9.7	5.7	5.6	5.3				6.1	6.0
5.7	3.9	3.9	4.0			Sales/Total Assets	4.6	4.0
3.5	2.4	2.5	2.3				2.9	2.7
.8	.7	.6	.6				.8	.6
(40) 2.0	(62) 1.2	(64) 1.1	(23) 1.2			% Depr., Dep., Amort./Sales	(199) 1.3	(193) 1.3
3.6	2.8	2.3	1.9				2.4	2.4
4.7	2.6	1.3				% Officers', Directors'	2.9	2.6
(45) 6.9	(40) 4.0	(28) 2.4				Owners' Comp/Sales	(105) 5.5	(108) 4.6
11.2	5.7	4.1					8.5	8.0
128027M	346550M	1437781M	2808081M	946655M	4896782M	Net Sales ($)	6138646M	6095485M
15468M	80663M	348592M	551719M	364282M	1015387M	Total Assets ($)	1637198M	1737776M

© RMA 2007

M = $ thousand   MM = $ million
See Pages 11 through 21 for Explanation of Ratios and Data

Comparative Historical Data | Current Data Sorted by Sales

4/1/04-3/31/05 ALL	4/1/05-3/31/06 ALL	4/1/06-3/31/07 ALL	Type of Statement	0-1MM	1-3MM	3-5MM	5-10MM	10-25MM	25MM & OVER
42	46	29	Unqualified		1	1	4	5	18
58	47	49	Reviewed	1	4	5	10	15	14
37	25	39	Compiled	3	14	7	9	3	3
51	45	63	Tax Returns	14	34	8	2	2	3
51	85	75	Other	6	15	7	11	15	21
				48 (4/1-9/30/06)			207 (10/1/06-3/31/07)		
239	248	255	NUMBER OF STATEMENTS	24	68	28	36	40	59
%	%	%	ASSETS	%	%	%	%	%	%
11.5	11.2	12.5	Cash & Equivalents	16.2	16.6	7.5	12.2	10.1	10.6
39.8	41.7	37.4	Trade Receivables (net)	22.2	26.1	40.7	40.4	47.8	46.1
2.8	3.0	4.0	Inventory	8.4	4.1	8.3	3.6	.9	2.4
3.7	4.0	5.6	All Other Current	4.9	5.1	5.5	5.6	6.9	5.5
57.7	59.9	59.5	Total Current	51.8	52.0	62.1	61.7	65.8	64.7
23.0	20.5	22.4	Fixed Assets (net)	30.0	28.8	25.3	19.8	17.7	15.3
8.1	7.8	8.0	Intangibles (net)	8.7	9.1	5.3	8.3	5.3	9.6
11.1	11.7	10.0	All Other Non-Current	9.5	10.2	7.3	10.1	11.2	10.5
100.0	100.0	100.0	Total	100.0	100.0	100.0	100.0	100.0	100.0
			LIABILITIES						
13.5	12.9	15.4	Notes Payable-Short Term	15.1	22.0	13.4	11.4	11.1	14.4
4.3	4.1	4.0	Cur. Mat.-L.T.D.	5.7	7.3	3.4	3.0	2.9	1.4
12.7	11.9	11.6	Trade Payables	7.6	8.3	12.2	17.1	15.3	10.8
.4	.4	.3	Income Taxes Payable	.0	.2	.6	.4	.4	.2
17.5	14.9	17.9	All Other Current	30.5	14.5	17.9	12.4	16.0	21.4
48.5	44.2	49.3	Total Current	58.9	52.2	47.5	44.4	45.7	48.2
19.2	17.8	19.5	Long-Term Debt	29.4	32.6	21.8	10.0	10.5	11.2
.4	.3	.4	Deferred Taxes	.1	.5	1.2	.3	.1	.2
5.6	7.1	6.0	All Other Non-Current	5.9	4.2	7.2	6.1	9.1	5.4
26.3	30.5	24.9	Net Worth	5.6	10.5	22.3	39.2	34.7	35.1
100.0	100.0	100.0	Total Liabilities & Net Worth	100.0	100.0	100.0	100.0	100.0	100.0
			INCOME DATA						
100.0	100.0	100.0	Net Sales	100.0	100.0	100.0	100.0	100.0	100.0
			Gross Profit						
95.8	94.8	95.2	Operating Expenses	95.4	94.9	96.1	94.8	94.9	95.5
4.2	5.2	4.8	Operating Profit	4.6	5.1	3.9	5.2	5.1	4.5
.6	.5	.6	All Other Expenses (net)	.5	.6	.1	1.3	.6	.5
3.7	4.7	4.2	Profit Before Taxes	4.1	4.6	3.8	3.9	4.4	4.0
			RATIOS						
2.1	2.3	2.1	Current	6.0	2.7	2.5	2.7	1.9	1.8
1.4	1.3	1.4		1.2	1.1	1.6	1.5	1.5	1.3
.8	1.0	.9		.5	.6	1.1	.9	1.1	1.0
2.0	2.2	1.9	Quick	2.5	2.1	1.9	2.5	1.9	1.8
1.2	1.2 (254)	1.2		.9	(67) .9	1.4	1.3	1.4	1.2
.6	.8	.6		.2	.5	.7	.6	.9	.9
20 18.4	23 15.7	17 20.9	Sales/Receivables	0 UND	0 UND	22 16.6	21 17.2	23 15.9	28 13.2
33 10.9	38 9.6	32 11.3		12 30.1	27 13.4	36 10.0	33 11.1	36 10.1	41 9.0
51 7.2	55 6.7	51 7.1		36 10.1	44 8.3	59 6.2	52 7.0	57 6.4	55 6.6
			Cost of Sales/Inventory						
			Cost of Sales/Payables						
11.7	11.0	11.9	Sales/Working Capital	9.0	11.4	7.9	8.6	13.2	13.9
28.8	22.9	31.8		126.7	NM	17.5	20.2	23.9	31.8
-67.0	-461.9	-52.1		-15.0	-22.3	84.8	-48.3	172.6	-999.8
19.5	21.8	15.8	EBIT/Interest	8.4	11.5	14.9	31.2	26.4	39.7
(205) 6.6	(216) 5.4	(232) 5.6		(19) 4.9	(60) 4.7	(27) 5.3	(35) 4.9	(36) 7.6	(55) 7.9
1.9	2.1	1.7		1.0	1.2	1.9	1.7	1.9	2.8
7.0	6.7	13.1	Net Profit + Depr., Dep., Amort./Cur. Mat. L/T/D						60.6
(53) 3.0	(61) 3.5	(48) 3.3						(17)	14.9
1.3	1.6	1.2							1.6
.2	.2	.3	Fixed/Worth	.0	.5	.4	.3	.2	.2
.7	.6	.9		1.6	1.5	.8	.5	.6	.6
6.3	3.4	-22.9		-3.4	-1.6	-1.4	34.1	1.9	1.9
.9	.8	1.0	Debt/Worth	1.1	1.1	1.0	.7	1.0	1.0
2.3	2.2	2.5		2.9	5.5	1.9	1.6	2.0	2.6
24.5	10.7	-38.3		-4.6	-6.7	-6.8	259.9	12.5	12.2
67.8	73.0	74.6	% Profit Before Taxes/Tangible Net Worth	67.6	131.0	47.6	58.0	82.8	68.0
(183) 31.8	(197) 35.8	(184) 40.2		(16) 20.4	(38) 54.2	(20) 31.0	(28) 20.6	(35) 43.5	(47) 51.2
12.5	11.8	17.1		1.5	26.6	19.2	7.4	17.7	28.2
23.1	24.5	25.6	% Profit Before Taxes/Total Assets	36.4	37.3	19.9	22.0	22.9	25.5
9.3	11.5	12.2		6.2	16.9	11.3	9.3	14.4	11.8
2.7	3.6	3.2		.3	3.9	3.3	2.4	3.7	4.9
69.5	62.7	63.7	Sales/Net Fixed Assets	UND	64.4	38.7	57.6	77.7	71.8
25.2	28.7	29.6		13.8	25.9	25.3	27.4	43.0	39.1
11.4	14.1	12.3		4.9	8.3	10.7	11.7	15.7	18.5
5.9	5.9	6.1	Sales/Total Assets	4.7	8.6	4.7	5.8	6.2	5.8
4.2	4.0	4.1		3.3	4.1	3.6	4.0	4.2	4.7
2.7	2.6	2.7		1.9	2.4	2.8	2.8	2.7	3.2
.7	.6	.7	% Depr., Dep., Amort./Sales	2.1	1.2	.5	.7	.5	.5
(189) 1.5	(209) 1.2	(198) 1.2		(12) 5.1	(46) 2.4	(24) 1.1	(32) 1.2	(34) .8	(50) 1.1
2.8	2.3	2.7		9.0	4.0	2.0	1.7	1.4	2.0
2.2	2.3	2.4	% Officers', Directors' Owners' Comp/Sales	6.9	3.0	2.2		1.5	.8
(104) 4.2	(105) 4.4	(121) 4.7		(15) 11.4	(42) 5.0	(17) 4.9		(25) 2.7	(14) 2.1
7.3	7.0	7.4		18.2	7.2	6.7		4.3	6.4
7837290M	6952700M	10563876M	Net Sales ($)	10609M	123447M	108654M	260967M	615298M	9444901M
2156282M	2059043M	2376111M	Total Assets ($)	4317M	40543M	31518M	80348M	162605M	2056780M

© RMA 2007

M = $ thousand   MM = $ million
See Pages 11 through 21 for Explanation of Ratios and Data

Current Data Sorted by Assets   Comparative Historical Data

						Type of Statement		
1	5	6	11	2	1	Unqualified	17	20
4	27	50	6			Reviewed	46	52
30	37	15			1	Compiled	73	87
91	45	10	1		2	Tax Returns	98	123
30	62	49	10	4	4	Other	75	86
	48 (4/1-9/30/06)		456 (10/1/06-3/31/07)				4/1/02-3/31/03	4/1/03-3/31/04
0-500M	500M-2MM	2-10MM	10-50MM	50-100MM	100-250MM		ALL	ALL
156	176	130	28	6	8	**NUMBER OF STATEMENTS**	309	368
%	%	%	%	%	%	**ASSETS**	%	%
17.1	8.0	7.3	6.3			Cash & Equivalents	10.5	12.1
17.2	27.4	34.7	33.3			Trade Receivables (net)	22.0	22.1
3.4	7.5	6.8	6.2			Inventory	8.5	7.7
3.1	2.5	5.0	4.3			All Other Current	2.8	2.3
40.8	45.4	53.8	50.1			Total Current	43.8	44.3
47.5	45.1	36.3	43.7			Fixed Assets (net)	47.6	46.3
2.6	2.9	3.4	3.1			Intangibles (net)	2.3	2.2
9.1	6.6	6.5	3.1			All Other Non-Current	6.3	7.2
100.0	100.0	100.0	100.0			Total	100.0	100.0
						LIABILITIES		
14.3	10.5	8.9	9.1			Notes Payable-Short Term	11.9	12.5
7.1	7.6	5.6	7.5			Cur. Mat.-L.T.D.	7.5	9.1
9.8	11.9	13.2	15.1			Trade Payables	9.9	10.9
.2	.3	.5	.3			Income Taxes Payable	.3	.5
20.7	7.8	9.9	9.6			All Other Current	9.6	10.5
52.1	38.1	38.2	41.5			Total Current	39.3	43.5
43.1	32.8	21.6	20.6			Long-Term Debt	28.4	34.9
.0	.6	.9	.6			Deferred Taxes	.6	.5
8.6	3.6	1.9	6.0			All Other Non-Current	4.7	5.6
-3.9	24.9	37.4	31.3			Net Worth	27.0	15.5
100.0	100.0	100.0	100.0			Total Liabilities & Net Worth	100.0	100.0
						INCOME DATA		
100.0	100.0	100.0	100.0			Net Sales	100.0	100.0
						Gross Profit		
93.8	93.6	92.9	93.5			Operating Expenses	95.2	95.0
6.2	6.4	7.1	6.5			Operating Profit	4.8	5.0
1.3	1.6	1.8	1.5			All Other Expenses (net)	1.1	1.3
4.9	4.8	5.3	5.0			Profit Before Taxes	3.7	3.7
						RATIOS		
2.8	2.2	2.2	1.7				2.0	2.0
1.0	1.3	1.4	1.2			Current	1.2	1.1
.4	.8	1.0	.8				.7	.7
2.2	1.7	1.8	1.2				1.5	1.5
(155) .8	1.0	1.1	.9			Quick	.9	.9
.3	.6	.6	.7				.4	.5
0 UND	11 32.4	30 12.0	36 10.0				4 96.0	1 421.4
5 69.0	27 13.6	45 8.0	55 6.6			Sales/Receivables	24 15.5	22 16.3
29 12.6	49 7.4	67 5.5	82 4.5				43 8.4	45 8.2
						Cost of Sales/Inventory		
						Cost of Sales/Payables		
15.0	11.5	8.6	8.0				12.5	12.9
UND	38.5	16.6	25.1			Sales/Working Capital	49.6	73.3
-17.8	-31.1	512.3	-24.5				-26.1	-23.5
14.0	7.8	16.4	7.7				8.2	9.2
(132) 5.1	(171) 3.4	(122) 5.1	3.8			EBIT/Interest	(279) 2.8	(344) 3.5
1.2	1.1	1.6	1.4				1.0	.9
		3.6	3.2				4.2	3.5
	(30) 2.1	(35) 1.9				Net Profit + Depr., Dep., Amort./Cur. Mat. L/T/D	(62) 2.1	(59) 2.0
		1.2	1.0				1.1	1.1
.8	.7	.5	.6				.7	.7
3.9	1.8	.9	1.5			Fixed/Worth	1.6	1.9
-1.8	8.7	2.1	2.7				5.1	55.9
1.3	1.1	.9	1.9				1.0	1.2
9.3	2.6	2.4	2.7			Debt/Worth	2.2	2.9
-4.2	13.3	4.2	4.3				8.2	315.3
209.1	65.8	59.3	65.3				69.3	71.0
(99) 83.3	(138) 33.2	(127) 35.0	25.8			% Profit Before Taxes/Tangible Net Worth	(260) 19.8	(278) 22.8
19.7	11.2	10.6	5.7				3.3	1.5
47.1	20.5	23.2	16.2				20.7	25.0
16.9	8.5	10.9	7.7			% Profit Before Taxes/Total Assets	6.0	6.7
1.2	.4	2.5	.8				.0	-1.4
31.5	13.8	14.9	11.8				13.6	15.4
10.8	7.6	8.5	4.7			Sales/Net Fixed Assets	7.8	8.3
5.5	4.4	4.5	2.7				4.6	4.7
7.8	4.0	3.4	2.8				4.4	4.8
4.7	3.0	2.4	2.2			Sales/Total Assets	3.2	3.2
3.2	2.1	1.8	1.6				2.2	2.2
1.6	2.5	2.0	2.8				2.7	2.4
(116) 3.4	(148) 3.8	(119) 3.3	(27) 4.3			% Depr., Dep., Amort./Sales	(273) 4.2	(314) 4.3
6.4	5.8	5.0	7.4				7.3	7.3
3.7	2.5	1.3					2.6	2.8
(98) 7.0	(102) 4.1	(42) 3.9				% Officers', Directors' Owners' Comp/Sales	(173) 5.0	(230) 4.9
10.1	6.0	5.4					8.8	9.1
195504M	618411M	1440892M	1392700M	826315M	6135822M	Net Sales ($)	10421222M	5148008M
34925M	191208M	549907M	628659M	365773M	1361480M	Total Assets ($)	1933094M	1549961M

© RMA 2007

M = $ thousand   MM = $ million

See Pages 11 through 21 for Explanation of Ratios and Data

Comparative Historical Data / Current Data Sorted by Sales

			Type of Statement						
26	30	26	Unqualified	3	1	1	2	6	13
67	68	87	Reviewed	4	12	17	26	19	9
67	92	83	Compiled	13	34	16	11	8	1
147	131	149	Tax Returns	53	54	22	12	5	3
108	150	159	Other	22	32	41	26	17	21
4/1/04-3/31/05 ALL	4/1/05-3/31/06 ALL	4/1/06-3/31/07 ALL		48 (4/1-9/30/06)		456 (10/1/06-3/31/07)			
				0-1MM	1-3MM	3-5MM	5-10MM	10-25MM	25MM & OVER
415	471	504	NUMBER OF STATEMENTS	95	133	97	77	55	47
%	%	%	**ASSETS**	%	%	%	%	%	%
11.0	9.4	10.7	Cash & Equivalents	16.4	12.0	7.7	6.8	10.7	8.0
25.4	27.4	26.4	Trade Receivables (net)	14.5	19.3	30.2	33.4	37.4	37.7
7.0	6.6	5.8	Inventory	3.9	6.4	6.8	7.0	5.2	5.0
2.8	2.5	3.5	All Other Current	1.3	3.7	2.4	4.6	6.8	4.1
46.2	45.9	46.4	Total Current	36.2	41.4	47.1	51.9	60.1	54.8
43.6	42.5	43.4	Fixed Assets (net)	54.8	45.8	42.5	38.7	31.7	37.5
3.0	3.2	3.0	Intangibles (net)	4.3	3.1	3.1	1.8	1.7	4.0
7.1	8.4	7.1	All Other Non-Current	4.8	9.8	7.4	7.6	6.5	3.7
100.0	100.0	100.0	Total	100.0	100.0	100.0	100.0	100.0	100.0
			LIABILITIES						
12.9	11.6	11.1	Notes Payable-Short Term	10.1	13.2	11.1	9.0	11.8	9.9
7.1	7.5	6.8	Cur. Mat.-L.T.D.	5.2	7.9	7.0	8.8	5.3	5.5
11.9	10.8	11.6	Trade Payables	7.9	10.7	12.4	12.0	17.0	13.4
.3	.3	.3	Income Taxes Payable	.2	.2	.5	.4	.3	.3
8.7	11.0	12.6	All Other Current	24.8	10.0	8.2	8.8	11.0	12.1
41.0	41.2	42.4	Total Current	48.2	42.0	39.1	39.1	45.3	41.0
34.5	32.8	32.1	Long-Term Debt	48.7	39.2	29.6	22.0	16.9	17.9
.5	.4	.5	Deferred Taxes	.0	.4	.6	1.4	.2	.5
4.5	5.7	4.9	All Other Non-Current	12.2	3.1	3.8	1.9	3.1	5.0
19.5	19.9	20.0	Net Worth	-9.2	15.3	26.8	35.6	34.6	35.6
100.0	100.0	100.0	Total Liabilties & Net Worth	100.0	100.0	100.0	100.0	100.0	100.0
			INCOME DATA						
100.0	100.0	100.0	Net Sales	100.0	100.0	100.0	100.0	100.0	100.0
			Gross Profit						
95.1	94.3	93.5	Operating Expenses	89.4	94.1	95.4	94.4	94.1	93.9
4.9	5.7	6.5	Operating Profit	10.6	5.9	4.6	5.6	5.9	6.1
1.2	1.2	1.5	All Other Expenses (net)	4.2	1.2	.8	.5	.7	1.1
3.7	4.5	5.0	Profit Before Taxes	6.4	4.7	3.8	5.1	5.3	5.0
			RATIOS						
1.9	2.0	2.2		3.1	1.9	2.4	2.4	1.9	1.8
1.3	1.2	1.2	Current	1.1	1.1	1.3	1.5	1.3	1.4
.7	.6	.7		.4	.6	.8	.9	.9	.9
1.6	1.6	1.8		2.6	1.6	1.8	1.8	1.7	1.4
.9 (470)	1.0 (503)	1.0	Quick	(94) .9	.8	1.1	1.2	1.0	1.0
.5	.5	.5		.3	.3	.6	.6	.7	.8
6 56.3	8 44.5	7 53.2		0 UND	0 UND	14 26.2	20 18.4	30 12.1	40 9.0
27 13.5	34 10.9	30 12.2	Sales/Receivables	3 130.0	18 19.9	33 11.1	35 10.3	44 8.3	54 6.8
50 7.3	58 6.3	52 7.0		31 11.8	40 9.1	57 6.4	62 5.9	56 6.5	67 5.4
			Cost of Sales/Inventory						
			Cost of Sales/Payables						
12.4	10.7	11.0		14.0	13.1	9.1	8.8	12.2	9.7
32.7	34.1	38.7	Sales/Working Capital	128.0	340.4	34.4	17.2	22.6	19.1
-29.3	-32.6	-30.1		-16.2	-18.7	-38.2	-87.8	-230.1	-118.4
10.7	9.9	11.4		9.9	9.1	8.4	20.9	15.9	13.5
(377) 3.9	(438) 3.9	(465) 4.6	EBIT/Interest	(75) 4.6	(127) 3.2	(92) 3.8	(74) 6.0	(52) 5.4	(45) 5.2
1.1	1.4	1.4		.7	1.2	1.0	1.7	2.0	2.3
3.2	3.2	3.7			5.1	3.9	2.7	6.1	11.1
(56) 2.0	(91) 1.8	(83) 2.2	Net Profit + Depr., Dep., Amort./Cur. Mat. L/T/D	(14) 2.0	(21) 1.9	(18) 1.6	(12) 2.3	(14) 2.7	
1.2	1.0	1.1			1.2	1.1	1.0	1.4	1.5
.7	.7	.6		1.0	.8	.7	.5	.4	.5
1.7	1.5	1.6	Fixed/Worth	6.9	2.2	1.5	1.1	.9	1.1
114.0	32.3	7.2		-1.9	-8.8	5.8	2.7	1.8	2.2
1.2	1.1	1.2		1.9	1.2	1.0	.8	1.2	1.5
2.9	2.8	2.8	Debt/Worth	8.9	3.6	2.4	2.0	2.3	2.3
241.0	98.3	17.6		-3.4	-16.8	7.1	5.4	4.2	3.4
76.0	74.5	82.7	% Profit Before Taxes/Tangible Net Worth	133.6	87.2	73.0	66.3	78.0	55.7
(316) 29.9	(366) 33.3	(406) 35.0		(61) 55.7	(93) 31.5	(82) 33.2	(70) 36.9	(53) 37.4	29.2
6.5	8.8	11.0		11.3	9.5	10.4	13.1	10.2	11.2
24.3	23.8	27.0	% Profit Before Taxes/Total Assets	39.3	24.3	20.2	28.2	30.0	16.5
7.2	9.4	10.3		13.8	6.5	9.6	15.6	11.5	10.2
.2	1.7	1.7		-1.3	1.3	-.1	2.6	2.3	3.4
15.4	15.5	17.4		13.6	22.8	15.1	16.8	24.2	16.3
8.3	8.1	8.3	Sales/Net Fixed Assets	5.6	8.3	9.1	8.7	10.6	8.2
4.8	4.6	4.7		3.4	4.5	4.9	5.6	6.8	4.4
4.5	4.4	4.6		5.8	5.6	4.3	4.0	4.6	3.2
3.1	2.9	3.1	Sales/Total Assets	3.3	3.3	3.3	3.0	3.3	2.7
2.1	2.1	2.1		1.8	2.2	2.2	2.1	2.2	2.0
2.4	2.1	2.1		3.1	1.7	2.5	1.9	1.7	1.8
(340) 3.6	(400) 3.6	(416) 3.6	% Depr., Dep., Amort./Sales	(66) 5.3	(110) 3.6	(83) 4.0	(70) 3.1	(50) 3.2	(37) 3.0
6.1	6.0	5.7		8.8	5.6	6.1	4.4	4.7	4.7
2.9	2.9	2.7		4.2	3.6	2.6	1.3	1.0	1.4
(251) 4.9	(259) 4.6	(251) 4.7	% Officers', Directors' Owners' Comp/Sales	(51) 7.5	(75) 5.6	(60) 4.3	(30) 3.1	(23) 2.7	(12) 2.6
7.8	7.3	7.6		12.7	8.1	5.3	4.7	5.4	3.9
8352076M	7560142M	10609644M	Net Sales ($)	47928M	241452M	380307M	530748M	825705M	8583504M
2203251M	2450201M	3131952M	Total Assets ($)	28862M	93653M	139356M	203433M	295898M	2370750M

M = $ thousand   MM = $ million
See Pages 11 through 21 for Explanation of Ratios and Data

Current Data Sorted by Assets / Comparative Historical Data

0-500M	500M-2MM	2-10MM	10-50MM	50-100MM	100-250MM		4/1/02-3/31/03 ALL	4/1/03-3/31/04 ALL
						Type of Statement		
1						Unqualified	1	1
	4	1				Reviewed	3	3
2	2	1				Compiled	9	12
7	3	2			1	Tax Returns	8	12
7	3		2			Other	5	6
	3 (4/1-9/30/06)		33 (10/1/06-3/31/07)					
17	12	4	2		1	**NUMBER OF STATEMENTS**	26	34
%	%	%	%	%	%	**ASSETS**	%	%
17.8	13.2			DATA NOT AVAILABLE		Cash & Equivalents	12.7	18.2
20.0	25.2					Trade Receivables (net)	26.0	21.8
4.5	6.9					Inventory	4.4	3.2
3.8	2.8					All Other Current	7.7	3.6
46.1	48.1					Total Current	50.8	46.9
35.5	27.6					Fixed Assets (net)	30.7	30.4
8.8	9.3					Intangibles (net)	13.4	17.7
9.7	15.0					All Other Non-Current	5.1	5.1
100.0	100.0					Total	100.0	100.0
						LIABILITIES		
19.4	16.7					Notes Payable-Short Term	20.5	11.2
3.1	3.7					Cur. Mat.-L.T.D.	7.4	6.5
5.4	13.3					Trade Payables	8.2	13.8
.0	.0					Income Taxes Payable	.1	.0
6.9	5.7					All Other Current	11.5	17.2
34.8	39.4					Total Current	47.6	48.8
41.1	17.5					Long-Term Debt	22.4	27.7
.0	.0					Deferred Taxes	.1	.0
1.4	6.5					All Other Non-Current	6.9	.7
22.6	36.6					Net Worth	23.0	22.9
100.0	100.0					Total Liabilties & Net Worth	100.0	100.0
						INCOME DATA		
100.0	100.0					Net Sales	100.0	100.0
						Gross Profit		
89.7	96.1					Operating Expenses	92.5	99.3
10.3	3.9					Operating Profit	7.5	.7
1.7	-.1					All Other Expenses (net)	1.3	.9
8.7	4.1					Profit Before Taxes	6.2	-.2
						RATIOS		
2.3	2.3					Current	3.5	2.9
1.1	1.4						1.1	1.5
.6	.9						.6	.7
1.8	2.1					Quick	3.3	2.7
1.0	1.0						.7	1.2
.4	.5						.3	.5
0 UND	0 UND					Sales/Receivables	0 UND	0 UND
3 136.8	19 19.0						15 23.7	14 25.5
51 7.2	26 13.8						54 6.7	39 9.3
						Cost of Sales/Inventory		
						Cost of Sales/Payables		
7.7	10.6					Sales/Working Capital	6.8	9.3
173.0	26.8						118.6	31.7
-37.6	NM						-31.4	-41.8
22.9	12.0					EBIT/Interest	46.7	6.7
6.1	6.0						(25) 6.3	(27) 1.6
1.2	2.8						1.6	-.1
						Net Profit + Depr., Dep., Amort./Cur. Mat. L/T/D		
.4	.3					Fixed/Worth	.4	.5
9.5	.8						1.4	2.0
-3.3	1.6						-4.4	-1.7
.6	.8					Debt/Worth	.6	.7
27.6	1.5						1.8	2.9
-4.6	15.1						-10.5	-3.5
518.3	179.5					% Profit Before Taxes/Tangible Net Worth	103.3	47.0
(10) 107.8	(11) 25.5						(17) 46.9	(23) 13.9
13.9	5.0						22.1	-4.5
49.9	17.1					% Profit Before Taxes/Total Assets	57.3	12.6
15.3	12.1						19.6	1.8
1.5	3.3						2.3	-5.0
48.4	46.4					Sales/Net Fixed Assets	24.4	33.6
15.4	21.0						13.5	12.8
6.0	9.5						9.4	9.0
6.2	5.2					Sales/Total Assets	6.3	5.0
4.7	4.1						3.9	3.3
2.5	2.5						2.9	2.5
.9						% Depr., Dep., Amort./Sales	1.6	1.4
(12) 2.9							(19) 3.1	(28) 3.6
7.8							4.3	5.4
5.0						% Officers', Directors' Owners' Comp/Sales	4.4	3.9
(11) 6.0							(13) 8.9	(20) 10.3
7.7							11.7	15.9
19530M	47713M	42976M	157450M		879883M	Net Sales ($)	2964222M	2032095M
4682M	11998M	14987M	32024M		225608M	Total Assets ($)	344498M	299290M

M = $ thousand MM = $ million

See Pages 11 through 21 for Explanation of Ratios and Data

Comparative Historical Data

Current Data Sorted by Sales

Type of Statement

			Type of Statement	0-1MM	1-3MM	3-5MM	5-10MM	10-25MM	25MM & OVER
			Unqualified	1					
5	1	1	Reviewed			2	3		
11	3	5	Compiled	1	1	1	2		
12	8	5	Tax Returns	4	6		1	1	
14	8	13	Other	4	4	1	1		2
	13	12							

5	1	1							
11	3	5							
12	8	5							
14	8	13							
	13	12							

Periods: 4/1/04–3/31/05 ALL | 4/1/05–3/31/06 ALL | 4/1/06–3/31/07 ALL | | 3 (4/1–9/30/06) | | | 33 (10/1/06–3/31/07) | | |

04-05 ALL	05-06 ALL	06-07 ALL		0-1MM	1-3MM	3-5MM	5-10MM	10-25MM	25MM & OVER
42	33	36	**NUMBER OF STATEMENTS**	10	11	4	7	1	3
%	%	%	**ASSETS**	%	%	%	%	%	%
16.3	13.6	16.6	Cash & Equivalents	10.7	22.4				
21.8	22.3	25.0	Trade Receivables (net)	19.7	25.8				
6.5	7.7	5.2	Inventory	6.7	.9				
3.5	1.9	3.3	All Other Current	1.9	4.1				
48.1	45.5	50.1	Total Current	39.0	53.3				
33.9	38.6	30.2	Fixed Assets (net)	31.2	29.6				
9.3	6.2	8.5	Intangibles (net)	15.6	5.2				
8.7	9.6	11.2	All Other Non-Current	14.2	11.9				
100.0	100.0	100.0	Total	100.0	100.0				
			LIABILITIES						
10.5	10.4	16.7	Notes Payable-Short Term	23.5	19.0				
6.8	4.8	3.3	Cur. Mat.-L.T.D.	3.3	2.4				
14.7	7.6	9.4	Trade Payables	1.9	9.1				
.1	.1	.0	Income Taxes Payable	.0	.0				
9.2	10.4	6.6	All Other Current	7.0	4.7				
41.3	33.2	36.1	Total Current	35.7	35.2				
25.8	29.3	26.8	Long-Term Debt	41.1	30.1				
.2	.3	.3	Deferred Taxes	.0	.0				
4.7	4.3	3.7	All Other Non-Current	1.3	4.1				
28.0	33.0	33.1	Net Worth	21.8	30.6				
100.0	100.0	100.0	Total Liabilities & Net Worth	100.0	100.0				
			INCOME DATA						
100.0	100.0	100.0	Net Sales	100.0	100.0				
			Gross Profit						
91.8	88.8	91.3	Operating Expenses	91.4	89.6				
8.2	11.2	8.7	Operating Profit	8.6	10.4				
1.2	1.5	.8	All Other Expenses (net)	2.3	.4				
7.0	9.7	7.8	Profit Before Taxes	6.3	10.0				
			RATIOS						
2.6	3.2	2.3		2.1	7.8				
1.2	1.7	1.3	Current	1.1	1.1				
.6	.6	.8		.6	.4				
1.7	3.0	2.1		1.7	4.6				
.9	1.2	1.0	Quick	.8	1.1				
.5	.3	.5		.3	.4				
4 98.8	0 UND	0 UND		0 UND	0 UND				
24 15.1	8 43.9	19 19.0	Sales/Receivables	7 50.9	1 459.0				
40 9.2	38 9.6	47 7.8		75 4.8	49 7.5				
			Cost of Sales/Inventory						
			Cost of Sales/Payables						
8.8	6.7	8.4		6.1	6.8				
29.2	27.4	37.7	Sales/Working Capital	109.3	164.9				
-16.2	-94.0	-63.2		-37.5	-31.4				
13.1	23.9	25.4		6.6	39.8				
(39) 4.4	(30) 7.6	6.2	EBIT/Interest	2.2	7.0				
1.2	3.4	1.3		-.2	4.6				
			Net Profit + Depr., Dep., Amort./Cur. Mat. L/T/D						
.5	.5	.3		.3	.2				
1.1	1.6	1.4	Fixed/Worth	NM	1.4				
22.0	18.0	121.8		-.6	24.3				
1.0	.6	.7		.6	.5				
2.5	1.5	2.9	Debt/Worth	NM	12.7				
NM	255.0	228.2		-3.1	39.7				
111.9	153.9	183.1							
(32) 53.0	(26) 62.2	(28) 61.5	% Profit Before Taxes/Tangible Net Worth						
7.0	18.9	9.1							
32.1	48.7	31.4		17.2	96.6				
14.1	14.3	12.6	% Profit Before Taxes/Total Assets	8.6	17.0				
.4	5.3	1.9		-6.2	8.6				
22.1	21.4	46.4		39.7	74.3				
11.8	15.6	15.9	Sales/Net Fixed Assets	12.8	28.7				
4.9	8.4	7.2		4.6	8.3				
5.4	6.8	5.8		5.7	6.1				
3.1	3.6	4.3	Sales/Total Assets	2.7	5.3				
2.2	2.4	2.8		1.3	2.8				
1.1	1.3	.8							
(32) 2.4	(21) 2.1	(27) 1.9	% Depr., Dep., Amort./Sales						
5.5	3.7	4.3							
3.3	4.2	3.5							
(21) 4.4	(18) 9.4	(21) 5.0	% Officers', Directors' Owners' Comp/Sales						
9.6	14.4	7.5							
236340M	273615M	1147552M	Net Sales ($)	5649M	21915M	15412M	47902M	19341M	1037333M
83804M	90391M	289299M	Total Assets ($)	2684M	5327M	9102M	10570M	3984M	257632M

© RMA 2007

M = $ thousand   MM = $ million
See Pages 11 through 21 for Explanation of Ratios and Data

Current Data Sorted by Assets

Comparative Historical Data

							Type of Statement					
			2	4	1		Unqualified				2	4
1	3		8				Reviewed				7	8
7	5		7				Compiled				9	17
23	10		2				Tax Returns				7	22
12	8		14	1 (10/1/06-3/31/07)			Other				15	14
	17 (4/1-9/30/06)			93							4/1/02-3/31/03	4/1/03-3/31/04
0-500M	500M-2MM	2-10MM	10-50MM	50-100MM	100-250MM						ALL	ALL
43	26	33	5	3			NUMBER OF STATEMENTS				40	65
%	%	%	%	%	%		ASSETS				%	%
21.0	9.8	8.9					Cash & Equivalents				9.2	11.4
26.6	43.1	43.1				D	Trade Receivables (net)				40.0	32.0
6.1	7.8	9.1				A	Inventory				4.6	4.1
1.4	5.6	3.6				T	All Other Current				4.0	2.6
55.1	66.2	64.7				A	Total Current				57.8	50.1
26.7	27.4	22.9					Fixed Assets (net)				24.7	29.2
9.8	1.9	3.5				N	Intangibles (net)				5.6	9.8
8.4	4.5	9.0				O	All Other Non-Current				11.8	10.8
100.0	100.0	100.0				T	Total				100.0	100.0
						A	LIABILITIES					
12.6	14.5	11.5				V	Notes Payable-Short Term				18.5	10.9
5.5	3.8	4.2				A	Cur. Mat.-L.T.D.				5.6	7.4
9.9	15.2	17.7				I	Trade Payables				14.1	13.0
.1	.1	.1				L	Income Taxes Payable				.0	.1
20.9	4.2	11.4				A	All Other Current				10.6	16.7
49.0	37.8	44.9				B	Total Current				48.7	48.2
30.5	16.1	18.7				L	Long-Term Debt				19.0	19.4
.0	.2	.5				E	Deferred Taxes				.1	.2
10.6	3.2	5.0					All Other Non-Current				2.6	7.4
9.9	42.7	30.9					Net Worth				29.6	24.8
100.0	100.0	100.0					Total Liabilties & Net Worth				100.0	100.0
							INCOME DATA					
100.0	100.0	100.0					Net Sales				100.0	100.0
							Gross Profit					
89.6	93.2	91.3					Operating Expenses				97.9	96.8
10.4	6.8	8.7					Operating Profit				2.1	3.2
2.0	.5	2.6					All Other Expenses (net)				.9	.3
8.5	6.3	6.1					Profit Before Taxes				1.2	2.8
							RATIOS					
2.6	4.2	2.7									1.8	1.7
1.1	1.5	1.4					Current				1.3	1.2
.8	1.1	.9									.9	.8
2.4	3.8	1.9									1.4	1.6
1.0	1.4	1.1					Quick				1.0	1.0
.5	.6	.7									.8	.6
0 UND	28 13.1	43 8.4						25	14.4	7	51.2
25 14.5	49 7.4	58 6.3					Sales/Receivables	40	9.1	31	11.9
38 9.6	71 5.2	85 4.3						56	6.5	51	7.1
							Cost of Sales/Inventory					
							Cost of Sales/Payables					
12.3	5.9	6.0									13.0	16.5
106.7	13.5	11.7					Sales/Working Capital				34.1	76.5
-30.6	NM	-114.9									-118.8	-29.0
21.5	19.1	40.7									7.5	11.0
(33) 5.3	(24) 5.3	(30) 8.1					EBIT/Interest			(57)	2.2	2.6
1.6	2.2	1.7									.2	1.0
							Net Profit + Depr., Dep., Amort./Cur. Mat. L/T/D					6.3
										(11)	2.3	2.3
												1.6
.4	.2	.2									.3	.5
2.3	.4	.6					Fixed/Worth				.8	1.5
-1.3	2.2	1.5									21.7	-3.8
.9	.4	.7									1.2	1.0
5.2	1.1	1.9					Debt/Worth				2.2	3.1
-2.8	5.0	5.4									30.2	-25.1
247.9	66.2	57.0					% Profit Before Taxes/Tangible Net Worth				37.6	67.5
(29) 138.7	(22) 35.2	(29) 30.6								(48)	13.8	30.3
27.4	21.0	12.0									-4.2	2.8
65.6	38.7	23.1					% Profit Before Taxes/Total Assets				16.1	21.6
19.4	12.4	9.8									2.4	4.2
.5	5.4	2.3									-1.4	-.1
62.4	30.7	37.3					Sales/Net Fixed Assets				43.5	53.6
19.3	11.2	17.5									23.8	23.8
7.9	7.2	5.7									9.4	8.8
6.1	4.5	3.6					Sales/Total Assets				5.7	6.3
3.8	2.9	2.4									3.5	3.6
2.0	2.3	1.7									2.6	2.5
1.0	.6	.7					% Depr., Dep., Amort./Sales				1.1	.9
(25) 1.9	(20) 1.7	(29) 2.0						(33)		(48)	1.6	1.6
4.0	3.9	5.4									3.8	3.5
3.4	1.9	1.4					% Officers', Directors' Owners' Comp/Sales				3.3	2.4
(21) 7.4	(16) 3.6	(14) 3.5						(24)		(39)	5.6	5.4
15.4	8.4	7.7									8.4	8.8
42934M	102991M	336711M	236769M	418272M			Net Sales ($)				630759M	352022M
10478M	29075M	134958M	75898M	182819M			Total Assets ($)				233366M	123145M

© RMA 2007

M = $ thousand   MM = $ million
See Pages 11 through 21 for Explanation of Ratios and Data

Comparative Historical Data | Current Data Sorted by Sales

	4/1/04-3/31/05 ALL	4/1/05-3/31/06 ALL	4/1/06-3/31/07 ALL	Type of Statement	0-1MM	1-3MM	3-5MM	5-10MM	10-25MM	25MM & OVER
	3	3	7	Unqualified			3		3	4
	9	10	12	Reviewed	2	5	3	2	5	
	11	14	19	Compiled	6	18	3	3	2	
	20	22	35	Tax Returns	11			1	2	
	20	11	37	Other	10	7	4	3	11	2
						17 (4/1-9/30/06)		93 (10/1/06-3/31/07)		
NUMBER OF STATEMENTS	63	60	110		29	30	13	9	23	6
	%	%	%	**ASSETS**	%	%	%	%	%	%
	9.8	14.2	13.4	Cash & Equivalents	20.5	15.5	10.8		8.6	
	31.5	36.1	36.7	Trade Receivables (net)	20.1	30.7	49.4		51.9	
	7.3	7.8	7.4	Inventory	5.4	6.7	7.1		5.5	
	2.1	3.1	3.6	All Other Current	.6	4.4	3.0		5.9	
	50.8	61.1	61.1	Total Current	46.7	57.3	70.4		72.0	
	32.7	25.6	25.4	Fixed Assets (net)	31.0	32.4	23.4		13.9	
	5.4	6.8	6.1	Intangibles (net)	13.7	3.8	2.3		2.8	
	11.1	6.5	7.4	All Other Non-Current	8.6	6.5	4.0		11.3	
	100.0	100.0	100.0	Total	100.0	100.0	100.0		100.0	
				LIABILITIES						
	17.3	17.2	12.3	Notes Payable-Short Term	13.0	15.1	8.6		11.3	
	6.5	4.4	4.6	Cur. Mat.-L.T.D.	3.2	7.9	4.2		3.8	
	14.3	9.7	13.9	Trade Payables	9.1	11.5	12.0		23.0	
	.1	.1	.2	Income Taxes Payable	.1	.0	.0		.2	
	9.9	9.4	13.8	All Other Current	13.4	18.3	6.0		13.1	
	48.2	40.9	44.7	Total Current	38.8	52.8	30.9		51.3	
	25.1	23.1	22.3	Long-Term Debt	30.2	35.0	8.6		8.1	
	.7	.5	.3	Deferred Taxes	.0	.0	1.2		.5	
	6.0	11.2	7.0	All Other Non-Current	8.3	9.3	1.3		2.8	
	20.1	24.3	25.6	Net Worth	22.7	2.8	58.0		37.3	
	100.0	100.0	100.0	Total Liabilties & Net Worth	100.0	100.0	100.0		100.0	
				INCOME DATA						
	100.0	100.0	100.0	Net Sales	100.0	100.0	100.0		100.0	
				Gross Profit						
	94.4	91.9	91.3	Operating Expenses	86.3	91.5	92.6		94.3	
	5.6	8.1	8.7	Operating Profit	13.7	8.5	7.4		5.7	
	1.0	1.6	1.7	All Other Expenses (net)	4.6	.9	.0		.6	
	4.6	6.5	7.0	Profit Before Taxes	9.1	7.6	7.4		5.1	
				RATIOS						
	2.1	4.0	2.8		2.5	2.8	3.6		2.9	
	1.2	1.6	1.4	Current	1.1	1.1	1.9		1.3	
	.7	1.0	.9		.6	.7	1.5		1.0	
	1.7	3.0	2.3		2.4	2.2	3.5		1.9	
	.9	1.4	1.1	Quick	.8	.9	1.9		1.2	
	.5	.7	.7		.5	.5	1.4		.9	
	15 24.4	2 165.5	23 16.0		0 UND	0 UND	36 10.1		43 8.4	
	34 10.8	40 9.0	42 8.8	Sales/Receivables	18 20.6	32 11.4	70 5.2		56 6.5	
	60 6.1	73 5.0	67 5.4		49 7.4	53 6.9	75 4.9		75 4.8	
				Cost of Sales/Inventory						
				Cost of Sales/Payables						
	12.7	6.3	8.1		11.3	9.0	5.4		6.6	
	28.1	16.7	16.6	Sales/Working Capital	176.0	45.5	7.0		19.8	
	-25.6	253.4	-164.5		-14.7	-36.3	14.9		-192.9	
	11.0	12.1	20.0		10.5	18.3	100.9		66.8	
	(54) 4.2	(50) 3.8	(95) 5.3	EBIT/Interest	(20) 4.2	(28) 4.0	15.0		(20) 9.0	
	1.1	1.3	2.1		1.6	1.0	4.5		2.5	
	6.1		10.1							
	(10) 4.0		(11) 6.6	Net Profit + Depr., Dep., Amort./Cur. Mat. L/T/D						
	1.9		3.1							
	.5	.2	.3		.8	.4	.2		.2	
	1.0	.7	1.0	Fixed/Worth	2.6	1.3	.3		.3	
	4.6	6.9	6.7		-1.4	-3.4	.9		1.5	
	.8	.8	.7		1.0	.9	.4		.4	
	2.7	3.0	2.8	Debt/Worth	9.9	4.3	.8		2.8	
	10.2	45.3	35.7		-4.3	-4.9	1.5		5.4	
	83.8	69.6	138.7		293.1	202.2	70.5		86.0	
	(50) 24.4	(47) 28.0	(87) 47.8	% Profit Before Taxes/Tangible Net Worth	(19) 138.7	(20) 47.2	49.8		(22) 40.5	
	3.3	4.2	17.0		18.1	26.6	10.9		14.4	
	17.8	22.9	35.4		43.1	44.3	46.5		28.4	
	6.8	7.0	13.5	% Profit Before Taxes/Total Assets	14.5	14.6	15.4		11.7	
	.4	1.0	4.1		-.1	1.4	6.5		3.3	
	42.7	38.1	38.3		36.3	39.5	42.3		79.5	
	14.3	20.5	17.2	Sales/Net Fixed Assets	9.7	18.4	12.1		25.4	
	4.1	7.9	7.3		3.9	7.0	7.3		14.8	
	5.2	4.8	4.5		3.8	5.6	3.8		4.3	
	2.9	3.0	2.9	Sales/Total Assets	2.2	3.8	2.6		3.4	
	1.9	2.3	2.0		1.4	2.4	2.2		2.0	
	1.3	.8	.7		1.6	.8	.8		.3	
	(47) 2.4	(48) 1.6	(81) 1.7	% Depr., Dep., Amort./Sales	(18) 3.2	(20) 1.7	(11) 2.2		(19) 1.0	
	7.0	4.7	4.0		7.2	7.6	6.8		2.0	
	3.6	4.2	3.6		3.0	3.0			1.2	
	(31) 6.1	(30) 8.7	(53) 4.3	% Officers', Directors' Owners' Comp/Sales	(10) 9.7	(19) 6.9			(11) 2.8	
	12.0	15.0	8.8		19.8	9.1			6.6	
	346355M	353092M	1137677M	Net Sales ($)	14628M	58065M	52324M	66621M	320359M	625680M
	160962M	162412M	433228M	Total Assets ($)	12092M	21711M	20708M	26787M	120502M	231428M

© RMA 2007

M = $ thousand   MM = $ million
See Pages 11 through 21 for Explanation of Ratios and Data

Current Data Sorted by Assets | **Comparative Historical Data**

0-500M	500M-2MM	2-10MM	10-50MM	50-100MM	100-250MM	Type of Statement	4/1/02-3/31/03 ALL	4/1/03-3/31/04 ALL
		1	2			Unqualified	5	6
	2	6	3			Reviewed	1	7
2	3					Compiled		3
2	3	1	1			Tax Returns		1
3	8	8	1	1	3	Other	1	8
	10 (4/1-9/30/06)		40 (10/1/06-3/31/07)					
7	16	16	7	1	3	NUMBER OF STATEMENTS	7	25
%	%	%	%	%	%	**ASSETS**	%	%
	10.8	8.2				Cash & Equivalents		7.7
	36.7	26.8				Trade Receivables (net)		29.2
	11.0	10.5				Inventory		11.0
	1.8	2.4				All Other Current		1.9
	60.3	48.0				Total Current		49.8
	30.8	37.6				Fixed Assets (net)		27.4
	1.1	11.5				Intangibles (net)		11.9
	7.8	2.9				All Other Non-Current		10.9
	100.0	100.0				Total		100.0
						LIABILITIES		
	12.6	8.9				Notes Payable-Short Term		14.6
	3.1	3.0				Cur. Mat.-L.T.D.		6.9
	27.7	15.3				Trade Payables		21.4
	.0	.0				Income Taxes Payable		.0
	10.2	15.5				All Other Current		10.2
	53.5	42.6				Total Current		53.1
	24.9	25.3				Long-Term Debt		23.7
	.0	.0				Deferred Taxes		.4
	2.0	3.9				All Other Non-Current		6.3
	19.6	28.2				Net Worth		16.5
	100.0	100.0				Total Liabilties & Net Worth		100.0
						INCOME DATA		
	100.0	100.0				Net Sales		100.0
						Gross Profit		
	85.8	96.0				Operating Expenses		97.0
	14.2	4.0				Operating Profit		3.0
	6.3	4.0				All Other Expenses (net)		1.7
	7.8	.0				Profit Before Taxes		1.3
						RATIOS		
	1.7	1.6						1.3
	1.1	1.2				Current		1.0
	.9	.7						.5
	1.2	1.4						1.0
	.8	.9				Quick		.7
	.7	.5						.4
	33 11.2	36 10.1						26 14.0
	50 7.3	53 6.8				Sales/Receivables		36 10.3
	59 6.1	70 5.2						44 8.3
						Cost of Sales/Inventory		
						Cost of Sales/Payables		
	14.5	10.1						15.4
	69.0	33.7				Sales/Working Capital		375.6
	-86.1	-11.3						-13.2
	11.8	10.3						5.6
	(13) 3.6	(14) 3.7				EBIT/Interest		(24) 2.8
	.6	.3						-.1
						Net Profit + Depr., Dep., Amort./Cur. Mat. L/T/D		
	.2	.5						.6
	1.3	1.5				Fixed/Worth		1.2
	54.1	20.5						-3.6
	3.0	1.4						2.5
	6.3	3.7				Debt/Worth		10.7
	NM	117.4						-4.0
	95.7	99.4						101.4
	(12) 51.0	(13) 25.9				% Profit Before Taxes/Tangible Net Worth		(16) 40.1
	17.2	2.2						11.3
	14.3	15.6						16.0
	6.6	3.4				% Profit Before Taxes/Total Assets		3.6
	1.5	-1.2						-4.0
	60.2	24.1						62.7
	18.5	5.8				Sales/Net Fixed Assets		9.9
	5.2	2.3						4.0
	5.3	2.3						4.9
	2.9	2.1				Sales/Total Assets		2.8
	2.2	.9						1.9
		1.1						1.0
		(14) 2.6				% Depr., Dep., Amort./Sales		(19) 2.0
		11.3						5.3
								1.3
						% Officers', Directors' Owners' Comp/Sales		(12) 3.0
								7.0
13336M	64498M	153913M	400988M	80911M	1027350M	Net Sales ($)	416693M	456028M
1418M	20358M	84384M	151179M	74239M	356858M	Total Assets ($)	199293M	222277M

M = $ thousand MM = $ million

See Pages 11 through 21 for Explanation of Ratios and Data

Comparative Historical Data

Current Data Sorted by Sales

Type of Statement	4/1/04-3/31/05 ALL	4/1/05-3/31/06 ALL	4/1/06-3/31/07 ALL	0-1MM	1-3MM	3-5MM	5-10MM	10-25MM	25MM & OVER
Unqualified	2	4	3				1		2
Reviewed	5	10	11	1		3	1	3	3
Compiled		3	5	1		2	2		
Tax Returns	3	4	7	1	2	2	3	1	
Other	8	12	24	3	5	1	4	4	5
				10 (4/1-9/30/06)			40 (10/1/06-3/31/07)		
NUMBER OF STATEMENTS	18	33	50	6	7	8	11	8	10

	%	%	%	%	%	%	%	%	%
ASSETS									
Cash & Equivalents	9.8	8.1	10.8				9.9		.9
Trade Receivables (net)	27.2	29.1	28.7				36.4		29.7
Inventory	10.2	16.1	13.4				4.1		32.8
All Other Current	.4	1.0	3.2				4.0		1.0
Total Current	47.6	54.3	56.2				54.5		64.3
Fixed Assets (net)	37.8	33.1	33.0				37.9		31.3
Intangibles (net)	7.0	6.5	6.6				1.5		3.2
All Other Non-Current	7.6	6.1	4.1				6.0		1.2
Total	100.0	100.0	100.0				100.0		100.0
LIABILITIES									
Notes Payable-Short Term	11.7	13.9	15.0				6.5		39.7
Cur. Mat.-L.T.D.	4.2	3.9	3.5				4.1		7.6
Trade Payables	19.2	22.2	20.7				22.9		25.4
Income Taxes Payable	.1	.2	.1				.0		.3
All Other Current	7.7	7.6	12.8				18.1		5.8
Total Current	42.8	47.8	52.1				51.6		78.8
Long-Term Debt	24.3	23.3	21.7				17.4		17.3
Deferred Taxes	.6	.2	.1				.0		.4
All Other Non-Current	4.2	3.2	7.1				1.9		9.7
Net Worth	28.1	25.5	18.9				29.0		-6.1
Total Liabilties & Net Worth	100.0	100.0	100.0				100.0		100.0
INCOME DATA									
Net Sales	100.0	100.0	100.0				100.0		100.0
Gross Profit									
Operating Expenses	91.9	94.0	92.7				96.4		99.8
Operating Profit	8.1	6.0	7.3				3.6		.2
All Other Expenses (net)	3.3	2.2	4.2				.9		2.1
Profit Before Taxes	4.8	3.8	3.0				2.8		-1.9
RATIOS									
Current	1.6	1.5	1.5				2.0		1.2
	1.3	1.1	1.1				1.2		1.1
	.9	.9	.8				.8		.9
Quick	1.4	1.4	1.3				1.4		.6
	.9	.7	.8				1.0		.4
	.5	.5	.4				.8		.4
Sales/Receivables	35 10.3	27 13.4	22 16.5				0 UND		25 14.8
	44 8.2	38 9.6	43 8.4				52 7.0		43 8.5
	54 6.7	50 7.3	63 5.8				70 5.2		56 6.5
Cost of Sales/Inventory									
Cost of Sales/Payables									
Sales/Working Capital	11.6	13.7	10.7				7.0		15.3
	40.2	62.5	50.2				51.0		62.5
	-47.7	-45.1	-55.7				-83.8		-161.5
EBIT/Interest	6.0	10.7	9.9						2.8
	(17) 3.9	(27) 4.5	(41) 2.9						2.0
	-1.1	1.6	.8						.4
Net Profit + Depr., Dep., Amort./Cur. Mat. L/T/D									
Fixed/Worth	.5	.7	.4				.7		.7
	2.1	1.7	1.6				1.3		2.5
	NM	5.4	15.6				6.2		5.7
Debt/Worth	1.0	1.0	2.5				1.4		4.1
	4.2	5.5	5.1				3.2		5.4
	NM	224.4	NM				6.3		16.5
% Profit Before Taxes/Tangible Net Worth	65.4	126.3	98.8						
	(14) 31.7	(26) 42.1	(38) 37.4						
	-.8	8.3	2.8						
% Profit Before Taxes/Total Assets	12.0	18.8	14.2				16.5		5.6
	5.7	6.7	5.1				5.1		3.6
	-4.1	2.7	.6				1.0		-2.3
Sales/Net Fixed Assets	22.2	22.9	33.6				35.9		13.8
	5.4	10.0	9.5				15.4		9.5
	2.5	4.6	3.8				4.0		5.2
Sales/Total Assets	3.5	4.4	4.0				5.5		3.8
	2.1	2.6	2.2				2.9		2.0
	1.4	1.8	1.5				2.2		1.6
% Depr., Dep., Amort./Sales	1.0	1.3	1.1						1.4
	(15) 3.0	(28) 2.1	(39) 1.7						1.7
	6.1	4.6	4.0						2.9
% Officers', Directors' Owners' Comp/Sales		2.3	1.7						
		(11) 3.3	(13) 3.6						
		5.6	6.0						
Net Sales ($)	489274M	766431M	1740996M	1858M	12952M	31300M	78310M	123401M	1493175M
Total Assets ($)	264848M	380924M	688436M	7118M	4443M	20409M	28582M	63750M	564134M

M = $ thousand   MM = $ million
See Pages 11 through 21 for Explanation of Ratios and Data

Current Data Sorted by Assets | Comparative Historical Data

3 1 2 9 8	1 5 12 10	8 10 5 3 13	7 14	4 4	1 5	Type of Statement Unqualified Reviewed Compiled Tax Returns Other	8 2 7 4 21	16 8 11 7 16
	23 (4/1-9/30/06)		102 (10/1/06-3/31/07)				4/1/02- 3/31/03 ALL	4/1/03- 3/31/04 ALL
0-500M	500M-2MM	2-10MM	10-50MM	50-100MM	100-250MM			
23	28	39	21	8	6	NUMBER OF STATEMENTS	42	58
%	%	%	%	%	%	ASSETS	%	%
34.7	16.5	9.0	7.8			Cash & Equivalents	13.2	16.7
21.0	24.8	36.3	32.2			Trade Receivables (net)	31.8	30.7
3.0	10.1	13.2	6.4			Inventory	7.8	10.9
1.8	5.6	2.3	6.3			All Other Current	4.5	4.5
60.5	56.9	60.8	52.7			Total Current	57.3	62.9
25.0	28.9	28.0	37.8			Fixed Assets (net)	28.0	22.9
5.6	6.8	2.2	1.6			Intangibles (net)	9.7	5.0
9.0	7.3	9.0	7.9			All Other Non-Current	4.9	9.2
100.0	100.0	100.0	100.0			Total	100.0	100.0
						LIABILITIES		
8.8	15.3	13.8	4.0			Notes Payable-Short Term	12.1	13.4
7.6	3.2	4.1	3.6			Cur. Mat.-L.T.D.	6.0	1.6
18.2	12.2	12.3	13.3			Trade Payables	11.9	21.1
.6	.5	.0	1.7			Income Taxes Payable	1.2	.5
16.6	11.7	14.7	14.4			All Other Current	17.0	18.2
51.8	42.8	44.9	36.9			Total Current	48.3	54.8
13.0	22.1	14.6	21.0			Long-Term Debt	19.8	13.9
.7	.0	.8	.5			Deferred Taxes	.2	.4
5.9	14.5	2.5	8.1			All Other Non-Current	7.0	6.1
29.1	20.6	37.2	33.5			Net Worth	24.6	24.8
100.0	100.0	100.0	100.0			Total Liabilities & Net Worth	100.0	100.0
						INCOME DATA		
100.0	100.0	100.0	100.0			Net Sales	100.0	100.0
						Gross Profit		
94.5	95.0	92.4	88.4			Operating Expenses	91.9	92.3
5.5	5.0	7.6	11.6			Operating Profit	8.1	7.7
1.6	.7	.0	2.1			All Other Expenses (net)	3.6	.6
4.0	4.2	7.7	9.5			Profit Before Taxes	4.5	7.2
						RATIOS		
3.9	3.7	2.1	2.2				1.6	2.5
1.1	1.3	1.3	1.2			Current	1.2	1.3
.6	.9	1.0	1.0				.8	.9
3.2	2.5	1.6	1.7				1.3	1.9
1.0	1.1	1.1	.9			Quick	.9	.9
.5	.4	.6	.6				.5	.6
0 UND	0 UND	19 18.8	33 11.0				10 38.1	3 109.8
5 71.8	26 14.0	45 8.0	44 8.2			Sales/Receivables	46 8.0	31 11.7
41 8.8	47 7.8	64 5.7	67 5.5				80 4.5	59 6.1
						Cost of Sales/Inventory		
						Cost of Sales/Payables		
12.2	5.1	8.2	7.1				10.5	7.8
134.7	63.7	26.7	30.8			Sales/Working Capital	73.7	17.7
-66.7	-71.2	-116.3	NM				-23.9	-46.7
11.1	16.4	21.9	12.9				7.0	19.2
(17) 2.3	(22) 3.4	(37) 6.0	(18) 2.6			EBIT/Interest	(37) 2.8	(44) 4.6
.9	1.0	1.1	1.4				.8	1.0
						Net Profit + Depr., Dep., Amort./Cur. Mat. L/T/D	6.4	
							(10) 2.9	
							.7	
.0	.2	.1	.4				.3	.2
.6	.9	.7	1.0			Fixed/Worth	.9	.6
4.3	15.2	1.8	NM				-16.0	3.7
.8	.7	.7	.9				1.4	.8
6.5	2.7	2.0	1.8			Debt/Worth	3.3	2.0
86.0	25.2	9.2	NM				-24.6	7.7
131.3	115.5	71.5	66.5				57.5	83.3
(19) 54.3	(22) 44.3	(36) 39.9	(16) 45.0			% Profit Before Taxes/Tangible Net Worth	(30) 15.9	(46) 21.5
-9.2	7.1	10.0	22.4				4.5	3.9
28.7	28.4	26.5	33.3				23.5	25.6
11.2	8.8	11.4	9.0			% Profit Before Taxes/Total Assets	3.4	6.8
.0	.3	.2	2.3				-.2	-.3
UND	91.9	61.0	42.1				46.9	86.1
35.3	24.3	13.0	5.7			Sales/Net Fixed Assets	17.2	26.1
9.4	4.5	4.6	1.8				6.4	6.7
9.6	4.3	3.8	2.9				4.3	4.5
5.7	2.9	2.4	1.8			Sales/Total Assets	2.3	3.1
3.0	1.9	1.3	1.2				1.0	2.0
1.4	.8	.8	1.4				1.0	.7
(14) 2.6	(20) 2.5	(34) 2.2	(18) 6.2			% Depr., Dep., Amort./Sales	(33) 2.1	(44) 2.0
4.8	8.8	4.8	9.9				4.9	3.3
7.4	2.1	2.7					2.0	2.7
(11) 11.2	(19) 6.1	(14) 4.7				% Officers', Directors' Owners' Comp/Sales	(10) 4.7	(18) 6.6
15.6	11.2	9.6					9.7	11.5
34977M	110599M	500498M	1166155M	698525M	1529655M	Net Sales ($)	1315852M	1667690M
5150M	29481M	176150M	573954M	573191M	1034666M	Total Assets ($)	971413M	995676M

M = $ thousand   MM = $ million
See Pages 11 through 21 for Explanation of Ratios and Data

Comparative Historical Data

Current Data Sorted by Sales

			Type of Statement						
16	24	24	Unqualified	2	2	4		4	12
3	8	11	Reviewed		1	1	7	1	1
10	9	12	Compiled	2	3	1	2	4	
16	17	24	Tax Returns	5	14	2	2	1	
18	24	54	Other	4	7	6	8	4	25
4/1/04-	4/1/05-	4/1/06-			23 (4/1-9/30/06)		102 (10/1/06-3/31/07)		
3/31/05	3/31/06	3/31/07		0-1MM	1-3MM	3-5MM	5-10MM	10-25MM	25MM & OVER
ALL	ALL	ALL							
63	82	125	NUMBER OF STATEMENTS	13	27	14	19	14	38
%	%	%	ASSETS	%	%	%	%	%	%
14.0	15.7	15.3	Cash & Equivalents	23.7	25.0	22.0	10.8	5.6	8.8
31.7	31.4	28.9	Trade Receivables (net)	19.3	18.4	30.6	32.1	36.9	34.6
5.9	8.6	8.3	Inventory	5.3	9.4	4.6	12.2	16.8	4.7
6.0	5.4	4.3	All Other Current	5.4	1.7	3.3	.6	6.4	7.3
57.6	61.2	56.8	Total Current	53.7	54.5	60.5	55.6	65.7	55.5
28.4	24.8	28.2	Fixed Assets (net)	38.1	29.7	29.2	24.4	27.5	25.4
6.6	7.5	6.8	Intangibles (net)	2.3	5.5	3.4	7.9	2.1	11.6
7.3	6.6	8.3	All Other Non-Current	5.9	10.3	6.9	12.1	4.7	7.5
100.0	100.0	100.0	Total	100.0	100.0	100.0	100.0	100.0	100.0
			LIABILITIES						
11.0	9.6	10.5	Notes Payable-Short Term	5.4	12.7	4.6	19.1	13.7	7.4
4.3	2.7	4.2	Cur. Mat.-L.T.D.	4.3	6.7	3.5	4.9	3.1	2.8
14.2	15.1	13.3	Trade Payables	25.7	7.4	8.3	13.6	15.6	14.1
.2	1.2	.5	Income Taxes Payable	.0	.5	.0	.7	.1	1.0
13.9	12.4	14.6	All Other Current	11.9	10.8	19.2	14.4	17.9	15.6
43.6	41.0	43.2	Total Current	47.4	38.1	35.5	52.6	50.4	41.0
22.6	14.6	17.6	Long-Term Debt	20.9	20.7	14.3	14.3	16.3	17.6
.3	.8	.7	Deferred Taxes	.2	.7	.0	.0	.2	1.6
10.5	4.9	7.0	All Other Non-Current	5.4	3.9	7.4	17.5	3.0	5.8
22.9	38.7	31.6	Net Worth	27.0	36.6	42.8	15.6	30.1	34.0
100.0	100.0	100.0	Total Liabilties & Net Worth	100.0	100.0	100.0	100.0	100.0	100.0
			INCOME DATA						
100.0	100.0	100.0	Net Sales	100.0	100.0	100.0	100.0	100.0	100.0
			Gross Profit						
92.4	91.7	92.3	Operating Expenses	93.4	93.4	94.2	94.6	86.7	91.4
7.6	8.3	7.7	Operating Profit	6.6	6.6	5.8	5.4	13.3	8.6
1.4	1.1	1.0	All Other Expenses (net)	2.7	.0	.2	.3	1.5	1.5
6.2	7.3	6.7	Profit Before Taxes	3.8	6.6	5.6	5.1	11.8	7.1
			RATIOS						
2.0	2.4	2.4		2.9	3.4	4.1	2.0	2.1	2.3
1.3	1.4	1.2	Current	1.2	1.1	1.5	1.3	1.1	1.2
.9	1.0	.9		.7	.7	.9	.9	.9	1.0
1.6	1.9	1.8		1.5	3.4	2.7	1.6	1.4	1.6
1.1	(81) 1.1	1.0	Quick	1.0	1.0	1.3	1.1	1.0	1.0
.6	.7	.6		.5	.4	.9	.4	.5	.6
4 84.0	17 21.9	11 32.2		0 UND	0 UND	19 19.2	19 18.8	8 47.6	33 11.1
43 8.6	38 9.6	37 10.0	Sales/Receivables	31 11.6	11 34.3	38 9.6	37 10.0	46 7.9	50 7.3
69 5.3	63 5.8	62 5.8		49 7.5	48 7.6	89 4.1	59 6.2	65 5.6	70 5.2
			Cost of Sales/Inventory						
			Cost of Sales/Payables						
8.0	7.2	7.7		4.0	8.7	4.3	6.9	11.4	7.3
21.6	15.7	33.9	Sales/Working Capital	64.1	71.9	14.3	37.3	40.7	28.8
-25.2	-128.9	-91.1		-69.7	-66.7	-35.2	-61.9	-105.2	-321.1
18.0	29.1	16.0			9.9	38.3	61.4	25.6	11.4
(53) 6.4	(68) 7.1	(106) 3.1	EBIT/Interest	(23) 2.4	(11) 4.2	(18) 4.4	9.7	(32) 3.3	
1.6	1.9	1.1		1.2	1.1	.9	2.3	1.1	
	43.5	9.1						13.0	
	(15) 6.6	(18) 2.1	Net Profit + Depr., Dep., Amort./Cur. Mat. L/T/D					(12) 3.2	
	2.0	1.6						1.7	
.2	.1	.1		.2	.0	.1	.3	.1	.3
1.1	.7	.8	Fixed/Worth	3.2	.9	.9	.7	.7	.7
13.5	2.5	3.5		8.3	3.7	3.6	1.4	2.8	NM
1.0	.8	.8		1.6	.7	.4	.8	1.2	1.0
2.7	1.8	2.8	Debt/Worth	4.3	2.0	1.1	2.1	3.3	3.3
70.3	9.9	22.3		24.2	25.3	5.2	19.7	14.2	-155.5
82.4	91.7	89.4		117.3	79.5	39.1	124.3	95.5	88.7
(49) 34.6	(67) 38.6	(102) 40.6	% Profit Before Taxes/Tangible Net Worth	(12) 12.6	(22) 42.8	(12) 26.7	(15) 56.4	(13) 44.9	(28) 45.0
8.3	11.1	10.8		-33.2	1.5	10.0	32.0	26.0	21.5
21.9	24.5	25.8		29.6	23.1	17.5	54.6	31.7	25.2
10.8	13.3	9.0	% Profit Before Taxes/Total Assets	1.9	6.6	9.0	14.3	15.1	7.9
.7	2.4	.8		-5.3	.9	.1	.1	4.9	2.0
39.1	116.9	91.8		25.6	241.9	191.0	42.7	200.7	53.7
18.5	18.2	14.6	Sales/Net Fixed Assets	9.4	23.0	8.2	15.6	43.9	9.0
5.8	5.0	4.9		3.4	4.4	4.0	10.2	5.5	3.7
3.8	4.3	4.4		6.2	5.7	3.0	5.5	5.3	3.3
2.9	2.5	2.6	Sales/Total Assets	2.8	2.9	2.4	3.1	4.1	1.8
1.4	1.5	1.5		1.5	1.3	1.3	1.6	1.8	1.2
1.2	.6	1.1		2.4	.6	.5	1.2	.3	1.1
(45) 2.6	(63) 2.1	(93) 2.5	% Depr., Dep., Amort./Sales	(10) 3.2	(21) 2.4	(11) 2.5	(12) 2.1	(13) 1.5	(26) 3.4
5.8	4.8	6.6		9.2	10.0	9.5	4.6	4.4	8.2
2.2	3.9	2.8			6.0		3.6		
(22) 6.2	(29) 7.9	(47) 6.9	% Officers', Directors' Owners' Comp/Sales	(19) 11.2		(10) 5.4			
12.1	11.1	11.2			15.4		8.9		
3003664M	2885423M	4040409M	Net Sales ($)	5888M	49647M	56771M	144628M	209859M	3573616M
1395211M	1677487M	2392592M	Total Assets ($)	4138M	30325M	37651M	60182M	139172M	2121124M

M = $ thousand   MM = $ million
See Pages 11 through 21 for Explanation of Ratios and Data

Current Data Sorted by Assets / Comparative Historical Data

Type of Statement	0-500M	500M-2MM	2-10MM	10-50MM	50-100MM	100-250MM		4/1/02-3/31/03 ALL	4/1/03-3/31/04 ALL
Unqualified			8	9	1	3		18	28
Reviewed		9	15	6	1			21	27
Compiled	3	11	7					15	29
Tax Returns	18	16	5					11	23
Other	3	26	32	13	3	3		20	26
	24 (4/1-9/30/06)			168 (10/1/06-3/31/07)					
NUMBER OF STATEMENTS	24	62	67	28	5	6		85	133

ASSETS (%)

	0-500M	500M-2MM	2-10MM	10-50MM	50-100MM	100-250MM		Hist. '02-'03	Hist. '03-'04
Cash & Equivalents	12.8	8.3	7.5	7.7				10.4	10.3
Trade Receivables (net)	11.0	17.7	21.5	15.4				22.7	20.2
Inventory	7.2	1.7	1.4	.5				.8	2.2
All Other Current	1.9	3.3	3.1	1.9				4.5	3.9
Total Current	32.8	31.1	33.6	25.5				38.4	36.4
Fixed Assets (net)	53.9	56.5	52.3	61.4				48.7	49.5
Intangibles (net)	2.9	4.9	5.5	7.3				3.9	5.4
All Other Non-Current	10.3	7.5	8.6	5.8				9.0	8.7
Total	100.0	100.0	100.0	100.0				100.0	100.0

LIABILITIES

	0-500M	500M-2MM	2-10MM	10-50MM	50-100MM	100-250MM		Hist. '02-'03	Hist. '03-'04
Notes Payable-Short Term	9.1	6.4	5.5	3.8				11.5	10.1
Cur. Mat.-L.T.D.	4.6	11.1	7.0	10.9				10.0	9.6
Trade Payables	8.6	11.6	12.4	8.1				9.1	9.9
Income Taxes Payable	.2	.2	.1	.3				.3	.2
All Other Current	9.6	8.5	11.0	9.3				9.6	8.3
Total Current	32.0	37.8	35.9	32.4				40.5	38.0
Long-Term Debt	48.8	42.1	34.4	31.2				36.2	31.8
Deferred Taxes	.0	.3	.4	3.1				.8	.8
All Other Non-Current	22.4	9.8	8.8	4.8				6.2	6.1
Net Worth	-3.2	10.0	20.6	28.5				16.3	23.3
Total Liabilties & Net Worth	100.0	100.0	100.0	100.0				100.0	100.0

INCOME DATA

	0-500M	500M-2MM	2-10MM	10-50MM	50-100MM	100-250MM		Hist. '02-'03	Hist. '03-'04
Net Sales	100.0	100.0	100.0	100.0				100.0	100.0
Gross Profit									
Operating Expenses	95.2	91.5	91.7	92.8				92.4	94.3
Operating Profit	4.8	8.5	8.3	7.2				7.6	5.7
All Other Expenses (net)	2.5	3.1	2.2	1.9				3.9	1.7
Profit Before Taxes	2.4	5.4	6.1	5.4				3.8	4.0

RATIOS

	0-500M	500M-2MM	2-10MM	10-50MM	50-100MM	100-250MM		Hist. '02-'03	Hist. '03-'04
Current	4.2	1.4	1.5	1.1				1.9	1.7
	1.4	.8	.9	.8				1.0	1.0
	.6	.4	.5	.5				.6	.6
Quick	2.2	1.2	1.4	1.0				1.8	1.4
	1.3	.7	.8	.6				.8	.9
	.5	.3	.5	.5				.5	.5
Sales/Receivables	0 UND	2 242.7	31 12.0	29 12.7				21 17.6	19 19.7
	9 38.4	20 18.0	38 9.5	39 9.4				35 10.5	32 11.3
	31 11.7	50 7.2	57 6.4	46 7.9				47 7.8	43 8.6
Cost of Sales/Inventory									
Cost of Sales/Payables									
Sales/Working Capital	12.3	24.1	17.5	107.4				11.8	15.0
	75.1	-85.5	-75.4	-18.4				-328.0	999.8
	-60.4	-8.9	-7.8	-9.6				-17.0	-16.4
EBIT/Interest	8.1	5.7	6.3	4.5				4.4	5.4
	(19) 1.3	(60) 1.9	(62) 3.1	3.1				(74) 2.2	(119) 2.1
	.7	1.0	1.6	2.0				.6	1.0
Net Profit + Depr., Dep., Amort./Cur. Mat. L/T/D			3.1	2.9				3.1	3.3
		(14) 1.9	(12) 1.8					(22) 1.7	(34) 1.6
			1.2	1.3				1.1	.9
Fixed/Worth	1.4	1.5	1.2	1.7				.8	.8
	3.0	8.4	3.9	2.6				2.2	2.5
	-4.5	-3.7	24.1	4.8				-12.4	37.9
Debt/Worth	2.1	1.7	1.9	1.8				1.2	1.1
	5.7	10.5	5.3	3.1				3.1	3.1
	-6.6	-6.7	31.8	5.5				-16.9	112.5
% Profit Before Taxes/Tangible Net Worth	102.4	58.6	48.0	40.3				43.3	50.2
	(16) 22.5	(37) 21.3	(52) 30.0	(24) 22.0				(60) 20.6	(105) 20.6
	2.5	5.8	13.4	8.4				-.3	.5
% Profit Before Taxes/Total Assets	16.0	13.7	13.9	10.6				11.1	10.7
	3.2	4.2	7.5	6.8				3.1	4.2
	-.6	.3	2.9	2.9				-.5	.0
Sales/Net Fixed Assets	12.5	6.5	4.9	3.2				10.0	9.9
	6.5	3.9	2.9	2.1				4.8	4.1
	4.3	2.1	2.0	1.7				2.4	1.9
Sales/Total Assets	6.1	2.9	2.0	1.7				3.5	3.4
	3.4	2.0	1.6	1.4				2.3	2.1
	1.3	1.4	1.3	1.1				1.4	1.1
% Depr., Dep., Amort./Sales	2.6	4.8	4.4	6.0				4.2	4.1
	(22) 8.6	(56) 8.5	(57) 7.0	7.7				(74) 6.3	(115) 6.4
	13.3	12.3	10.3	10.6				9.4	10.9
% Officers', Directors' Owners' Comp/Sales	5.5	3.5	1.9					3.6	1.6
	(13) 7.2	(30) 5.0	(22) 5.8					(34) 5.4	(51) 4.3
	12.9	8.4	7.8					10.1	8.4
Net Sales ($)	35488M	161011M	526830M	804052M	1027369M	884036M		1135420M	2103465M
Total Assets ($)	6448M	70032M	307422M	650147M	381672M	867538M		915378M	1420958M

M = $ thousand   MM = $ million
See Pages 11 through 21 for Explanation of Ratios and Data

Comparative Historical Data | Current Data Sorted by Sales

				0-1MM	1-3MM	3-5MM	5-10MM	10-25MM	25MM & OVER
28	22	21	**Type of Statement** — Unqualified			1	5	7	8
20	28	31	Reviewed	1	3	5	7	11	4
28	18	21	Compiled	2	7	6	5	1	
20	37	39	Tax Returns	15	16	3	4	1	
35	55	80	Other	7	17	15	15	13	13
4/1/04-3/31/05 ALL	4/1/05-3/31/06 ALL	4/1/06-3/31/07 ALL				24 (4/1-9/30/06)		168 (10/1/06-3/31/07)	
131	160	192	**NUMBER OF STATEMENTS**	25	43	30	36	33	25
%	%	%	**ASSETS**	%	%	%	%	%	%
8.8	11.4	8.3	Cash & Equivalents	7.2	9.1	8.3	10.5	7.4	6.0
23.0	18.5	17.8	Trade Receivables (net)	13.3	14.0	19.6	20.1	23.0	17.0
2.3	.7	2.1	Inventory	6.9	.2	3.3	.9	2.0	1.2
2.8	2.4	2.8	All Other Current	.7	3.2	4.6	3.3	2.1	2.6
36.9	33.0	31.1	Total Current	28.1	26.4	35.7	34.7	34.5	26.8
45.5	51.3	54.9	Fixed Assets (net)	54.3	59.9	48.1	56.0	54.3	54.4
9.2	8.3	6.1	Intangibles (net)	5.8	5.3	5.0	4.7	4.8	12.6
8.5	7.4	7.9	All Other Non-Current	11.8	8.5	11.1	4.6	6.4	6.2
100.0	100.0	100.0	Total	100.0	100.0	100.0	100.0	100.0	100.0
			LIABILITIES						
9.4	9.2	5.8	Notes Payable-Short Term	13.4	4.0	5.7	3.7	6.7	3.0
9.1	8.4	8.5	Cur. Mat.-L.T.D.	4.0	9.7	10.6	7.7	9.4	8.4
11.9	10.8	11.0	Trade Payables	6.4	7.8	14.4	13.5	13.2	10.6
.4	.1	.2	Income Taxes Payable	.0	.2	.2	.2	.3	.4
7.1	7.1	9.5	All Other Current	2.2	8.9	15.7	13.5	8.3	6.1
37.9	35.7	35.0	Total Current	26.0	30.6	46.5	38.6	37.9	28.6
34.7	36.8	38.0	Long-Term Debt	50.1	50.3	31.8	33.9	25.9	34.0
1.1	1.0	.8	Deferred Taxes	.0	.0	.4	.6	1.7	2.8
9.5	6.9	10.1	All Other Non-Current	22.7	12.1	14.2	2.9	5.7	5.0
16.7	19.6	16.1	Net Worth	1.1	7.0	7.1	24.0	28.9	29.6
100.0	100.0	100.0	Total Liabilties & Net Worth	100.0	100.0	100.0	100.0	100.0	100.0
			INCOME DATA						
100.0	100.0	100.0	Net Sales	100.0	100.0	100.0	100.0	100.0	100.0
			Gross Profit						
94.3	94.1	92.3	Operating Expenses	79.2	92.7	97.2	94.7	93.8	93.0
5.7	5.9	7.7	Operating Profit	20.8	7.3	2.8	5.3	6.2	7.0
2.0	1.8	2.5	All Other Expenses (net)	6.4	2.7	1.4	1.6	1.6	1.8
3.7	4.1	5.3	Profit Before Taxes	14.4	4.6	1.3	3.7	4.6	5.2
			RATIOS						
1.5	1.6	1.5	Current	2.8	1.7	1.5	1.4	1.4	1.3
1.0	.9	.9		1.3	.8	.8	.9	.8	.9
.6	.5	.5		.5	.4	.4	.6	.6	.5
1.2	1.5	1.3	Quick	1.8	1.6	1.4	1.2	1.1	1.1
.9	.8	.8		1.3	.6	.7	.8	.7	.8
.5	.5	.5		.4	.3	.2	.5	.5	.5
25 14.5	16 22.3	15 24.0	Sales/Receivables	0 UND	0 UND	7 55.4	27 13.4	29 12.5	31 11.8
37 10.0	33 11.2	34 10.8		28 13.0	15 25.0	27 13.4	36 10.1	37 9.8	38 9.6
48 7.6	47 7.8	46 7.9		45 8.1	47 7.8	64 5.7	44 8.2	44 8.3	46 7.9
			Cost of Sales/Inventory						
			Cost of Sales/Payables						
23.6	18.2	19.3	Sales/Working Capital	11.0	25.0	17.1	20.7	24.4	23.8
-999.8	-145.7	-78.3		32.9	-37.2	-68.8	-87.1	-25.5	-67.4
-13.3	-10.3	-9.4		-5.2	-8.3	-8.0	-14.0	-9.7	-10.7
6.3	5.7	5.5	EBIT/Interest	8.4	5.8	6.4	4.7	6.0	4.4
(119) 2.7	(146) 2.6	(180) 2.5		(20) 1.6	1.9	(29) 1.8	(31) 3.0	(32) 3.8	3.2
1.1	1.1	1.1		1.0	1.0	-1.0	1.3	2.0	2.0
1.8	2.5	3.0	Net Profit + Depr., Dep., Amort./Cur. Mat. L/T/D				2.3	4.0	3.1
(40) 1.5	(35) 1.6	(43) 1.9				(11) 2.0	(10) 1.5	(15) 2.1	
.9	1.0	1.2				1.2	1.2	1.3	
1.0	1.3	1.5	Fixed/Worth	1.5	2.5	1.2	1.4	1.1	1.6
3.0	3.2	3.8		3.1	UND	12.9	2.8	2.4	2.8
-4.3	-7.8	-19.9		-4.4	-1.9	-6.2	6.1	4.2	7.0
1.7	1.7	1.9	Debt/Worth	1.8	3.4	2.0	1.8	1.8	1.8
3.7	5.0	4.8		5.1	UND	26.0	4.1	3.5	3.4
-9.3	-10.1	-37.1		-6.7	-4.9	-11.2	10.2	8.0	8.6
59.6	73.4	55.9	% Profit Before Taxes/Tangible Net Worth	53.8	74.5	54.1	42.6	63.2	44.1
(90) 26.2	(111) 29.9	(137) 25.5		(17) 14.3	(22) 30.9	(19) 12.8	(31) 30.8	(28) 28.1	(20) 22.3
8.6	8.4	9.9		3.2	12.5	-36.8	19.7	9.8	12.8
13.9	16.0	13.4	% Profit Before Taxes/Total Assets	14.5	14.4	14.2	13.9	14.8	8.4
6.0	5.8	6.5		3.7	4.2	4.0	6.7	7.5	7.1
.5	.4	1.2		.0	.4	-3.7	2.9	3.3	3.4
12.9	9.5	6.0	Sales/Net Fixed Assets	8.0	6.2	8.7	7.5	4.9	3.8
3.9	3.6	3.3		4.3	3.1	5.2	2.9	2.7	2.3
2.1	2.0	2.0		1.3	2.0	3.2	2.0	2.0	1.8
3.3	3.1	2.6	Sales/Total Assets	3.0	2.7	3.1	2.6	2.6	1.6
1.8	1.8	1.7		1.2	1.8	2.0	1.8	1.6	1.3
1.1	1.2	1.2		.6	1.3	1.5	1.3	1.3	1.0
3.4	3.4	4.7	% Depr., Dep., Amort./Sales	7.4	5.6	3.9	3.9	4.4	5.0
(109) 6.4	(137) 6.4	(172) 7.7		(21) 13.2	(37) 10.6	(27) 5.4	(33) 7.7	(31) 6.4	(23) 7.1
10.2	10.1	11.1		20.6	12.5	8.5	9.8	10.4	9.2
2.7	2.6	2.4	% Officers', Directors' Owners' Comp/Sales	5.4	3.7	1.3	2.8	.4	
(44) 5.3	(69) 4.0	(73) 5.7		(12) 7.7	(23) 5.9	(12) 3.7	(10) 7.1	(10) 2.5	
8.6	6.1	7.8		15.5	8.5	5.6	16.7	6.7	
3235298M	4879683M	3438786M	Net Sales ($)	12065M	84273M	119061M	244712M	536183M	2442492M
2398543M	2950323M	2283259M	Total Assets ($)	14167M	48470M	69834M	138425M	361137M	1651226M

M = $ thousand   MM = $ million
See Pages 11 through 21 for Explanation of Ratios and Data

Current Data Sorted by Assets

Comparative Historical Data

						Type of Statement			
		2	4		1	Unqualified		3	6
1	3	11	1			Reviewed		3	4
	3	4	1			Compiled		6	4
	3					Tax Returns		4	7
1	4	4	2	1	3	Other		6	8
	4 (4/1-9/30/06)		45 (10/1/06-3/31/07)					4/1/02-3/31/03	4/1/03-3/31/04
0-500M	500M-2MM	2-10MM	10-50MM	50-100MM	100-250MM			ALL	ALL
2	13	21	8	1	4	NUMBER OF STATEMENTS		22	29
%	%	%	%	%	%	ASSETS		%	%
	14.2	7.1				Cash & Equivalents		6.4	10.5
	30.4	25.5				Trade Receivables (net)		33.3	24.9
	2.6	1.0				Inventory		3.3	1.8
	2.9	2.8				All Other Current		5.3	4.2
	50.1	36.5				Total Current		48.4	41.5
	43.3	49.2				Fixed Assets (net)		37.4	46.0
	1.3	4.2				Intangibles (net)		5.6	4.8
	5.3	10.1				All Other Non-Current		8.7	7.8
	100.0	100.0				Total		100.0	100.0
						LIABILITIES			
	9.6	3.0				Notes Payable-Short Term		10.0	6.6
	8.2	6.8				Cur. Mat.-L.T.D.		3.4	6.2
	10.9	13.2				Trade Payables		20.9	16.8
	.1	.0				Income Taxes Payable		1.2	.0
	11.3	7.2				All Other Current		13.0	17.9
	40.2	30.2				Total Current		48.5	47.5
	25.7	21.8				Long-Term Debt		26.9	24.7
	.5	.3				Deferred Taxes		.0	.8
	8.9	3.9				All Other Non-Current		3.5	8.2
	24.7	43.8				Net Worth		21.1	18.7
	100.0	100.0				Total Liabilities & Net Worth		100.0	100.0
						INCOME DATA			
	100.0	100.0				Net Sales		100.0	100.0
						Gross Profit			
	93.9	91.2				Operating Expenses		90.4	93.1
	6.1	8.8				Operating Profit		9.6	6.9
	-.1	2.6				All Other Expenses (net)		2.5	1.2
	6.2	6.2				Profit Before Taxes		7.1	5.6
						RATIOS			
	2.7	1.5						1.8	2.7
	1.4	1.2				Current		1.1	1.3
	.8	.8						.4	.6
	2.5	1.5						1.6	2.5
	1.1	1.0				Quick		.8	.8
	.8	.6						.3	.5
24	15.4	26	14.0				16	22.8	16	22.6
35	10.4	42	8.7			Sales/Receivables	41	9.0	45	8.1
58	6.3	68	5.4				67	5.4	60	6.1
						Cost of Sales/Inventory			
						Cost of Sales/Payables			
	7.4	13.6						7.6	6.9
	17.6	47.0				Sales/Working Capital		63.1	21.5
	-56.1	-17.2						-7.2	-14.0
	17.5	11.3						13.2	12.0
(12)	5.3	(18)	7.5			EBIT/Interest	(18)	2.9	(27)	5.1
	2.9	1.1						1.4	.9
						Net Profit + Depr., Dep., Amort./Cur. Mat. L/T/D			
	.5	.7						.3	.6
	1.5	1.3				Fixed/Worth		1.0	2.1
	85.2	2.7						6.7	NM
	.8	.7						1.2	.8
	2.3	2.0				Debt/Worth		5.1	2.5
	113.8	2.5						-9.6	NM
	103.8	45.2						91.1	85.2
(11)	52.2	(20)	30.8			% Profit Before Taxes/Tangible Net Worth	(16)	34.6	(22)	30.0
	9.0	.0						14.4	4.6
	33.5	19.2						14.1	16.7
	14.3	13.1				% Profit Before Taxes/Total Assets		6.4	8.7
	6.8	.1						.9	.0
	10.9	6.7						276.0	7.5
	6.5	4.2				Sales/Net Fixed Assets		4.2	4.8
	4.4	2.4						3.5	2.3
	4.4	2.6						4.0	3.2
	3.0	2.1				Sales/Total Assets		1.8	1.9
	1.9	1.3						1.5	1.2
	1.9	2.9						2.3	3.5
	4.4	(20)	5.3			% Depr., Dep., Amort./Sales	(17)	4.3	(28)	5.3
	6.2	9.0						6.7	8.4
						% Officers', Directors' Owners' Comp/Sales			
2170M	44207M	209332M	281271M	58365M	482892M	Net Sales ($)		318829M	400706M
864M	14082M	104939M	169277M	68754M	473157M	Total Assets ($)		179453M	400970M

M = $ thousand   MM = $ million
See Pages 11 through 21 for Explanation of Ratios and Data

Comparative Historical Data

Current Data Sorted by Sales

				Type of Statement	0-1MM	1-3MM	3-5MM	5-10MM	10-25MM	25MM & OVER
	7	3	7	Unqualified	1	1			1	4
	11	12	16	Reviewed		2	2	5	6	1
	5	5	8	Compiled	1	2	1	2	2	
	7	4	3	Tax Returns	1		1	1		
	15	8	15	Other	1	1	4		4	5
	4/1/04-3/31/05 ALL	4/1/05-3/31/06 ALL	4/1/06-3/31/07 ALL		4 (4/1-9/30/06)			45 (10/1/06-3/31/07)		
	45	32	49	**NUMBER OF STATEMENTS**	4	6	8	8	13	10
	%	%	%	**ASSETS**	%	%	%	%	%	%
	9.6	10.4	9.7	Cash & Equivalents					12.5	5.1
	33.9	23.3	25.9	Trade Receivables (net)					25.6	29.6
	1.8	2.6	1.5	Inventory					1.4	1.7
	3.4	3.1	3.0	All Other Current					1.0	5.1
	48.7	39.4	40.1	Total Current					40.6	41.4
	38.8	44.4	45.7	Fixed Assets (net)					40.5	41.8
	3.6	5.9	5.6	Intangibles (net)					9.1	9.3
	8.9	10.3	8.6	All Other Non-Current					9.8	7.4
	100.0	100.0	100.0	Total					100.0	100.0
				LIABILITIES						
	6.1	6.8	4.8	Notes Payable-Short Term					2.5	2.7
	5.3	7.3	5.8	Cur. Mat.-L.T.D.					6.4	2.1
	15.2	13.1	11.3	Trade Payables					9.4	13.1
	.2	.0	.1	Income Taxes Payable					.0	.4
	11.0	8.2	9.2	All Other Current					10.8	8.8
	37.8	35.4	31.1	Total Current					29.1	27.0
	27.6	25.7	22.0	Long-Term Debt					16.6	16.8
	.6	.5	.3	Deferred Taxes					.3	.5
	4.5	11.4	5.9	All Other Non-Current					2.8	7.6
	29.5	27.0	40.6	Net Worth					51.2	48.1
	100.0	100.0	100.0	Total Liabilities & Net Worth					100.0	100.0
				INCOME DATA						
	100.0	100.0	100.0	Net Sales					100.0	100.0
				Gross Profit						
	93.6	93.3	89.6	Operating Expenses					89.7	85.3
	6.4	6.7	10.4	Operating Profit					10.3	14.7
	2.4	1.5	1.3	All Other Expenses (net)					.6	.2
	4.0	5.2	9.1	Profit Before Taxes					9.7	14.5
				RATIOS						
	2.0	1.8	1.9	Current					1.9	2.0
	1.3	1.1	1.3						1.2	1.4
	.9	.8	1.0						1.0	1.2
	1.8	1.6	1.7	Quick					1.9	1.8
	1.1	(31) .9	1.1						1.2	1.2
	.8	.6	.8						1.0	.9
	29 12.7	27 13.7	26 14.0	Sales/Receivables					27 13.3	53 6.9
	52 7.1	38 9.5	40 9.0						36 10.2	66 5.6
	68 5.4	58 6.3	64 5.7						54 6.8	86 4.2
				Cost of Sales/Inventory						
				Cost of Sales/Payables						
	8.8	16.9	9.8	Sales/Working Capital					12.9	8.4
	23.5	60.0	23.2						46.0	15.1
	-77.3	-27.8	-136.2						NM	26.6
	14.5	12.5	18.6	EBIT/Interest					20.4	
	(40) 4.2	(30) 3.0	(44) 6.4						9.1	
	.7	1.6	2.8						2.7	
	10.8		3.9	Net Profit + Depr., Dep., Amort./Cur. Mat. L/T/D						
	(10) 7.8	(14) 2.4								
	4.2	1.4								
	.4	.8	.7	Fixed/Worth					.6	.7
	1.0	1.8	1.3						1.1	1.0
	2.6	4.6	3.2						1.9	3.6
	.9	1.5	.6	Debt/Worth					.7	.3
	2.1	3.0	2.0						1.0	1.7
	5.3	8.8	5.8						2.5	5.9
	54.5	46.1	80.4	% Profit Before Taxes/Tangible Net Worth					77.8	
	(38) 20.8	(30) 16.5	(44) 39.4						(12) 30.1	
	1.1	8.6	11.2						6.4	
	16.4	20.9	25.3	% Profit Before Taxes/Total Assets					27.9	28.6
	6.0	4.8	14.1						14.7	13.3
	-.5	2.0	5.6						4.3	6.4
	16.3	11.8	6.8	Sales/Net Fixed Assets					6.7	6.8
	5.5	4.4	4.4						4.2	4.2
	2.5	3.0	2.9						3.4	1.8
	3.1	3.1	2.8	Sales/Total Assets					2.6	2.1
	2.1	2.2	1.9						2.1	1.5
	1.5	1.4	1.2						1.9	.9
	1.9	2.8	2.7	% Depr., Dep., Amort./Sales					2.7	
	(38) 5.5	(28) 5.4	(46) 4.7						4.6	
	8.6	6.8	6.9						6.1	
	1.7	2.6	1.8	% Officers', Directors' Owners' Comp/Sales						
	(22) 4.6	(13) 3.9	(18) 3.6							
	6.8	7.1	8.1							
	817966M	515355M	1078237M	Net Sales ($)	2994M	13065M	30987M	54924M	194110M	782157M
	668057M	363973M	831073M	Total Assets ($)	5131M	8357M	12787M	29879M	110484M	664435M

© RMA 2007

M = $ thousand   MM = $ million

See Pages 11 through 21 for Explanation of Ratios and Data

Current Data Sorted by Assets

Comparative Historical Data

	0-500M	500M-2MM	2-10MM	10-50MM	50-100MM	100-250MM		ALL	ALL
	1	3	10	19	2	2	**Type of Statement**		
		6	13	4	1		Unqualified	48	36
	3	5	5	3			Reviewed	49	35
	5	4	4				Compiled	37	40
	3	8	13	12	3	2	Tax Returns	32	25
							Other	52	57
		31 (4/1-9/30/06)		100 (10/1/06-3/31/07)				4/1/02-3/31/03	4/1/03-3/31/04
	12	26	45	38	6	4	**NUMBER OF STATEMENTS**	218	193
	%	%	%	%	%	%	**ASSETS**	%	%
	31.0	14.9	9.5	7.4			Cash & Equivalents	8.9	9.7
	24.8	21.4	21.7	17.8			Trade Receivables (net)	19.6	18.5
	.4	.0	3.3	3.9			Inventory	1.5	2.6
	7.1	1.9	1.6	1.6			All Other Current	2.0	4.1
	63.2	38.2	36.0	30.8			Total Current	32.0	34.8
	32.2	46.5	49.4	53.6			Fixed Assets (net)	53.8	48.8
	2.1	6.0	3.7	6.9			Intangibles (net)	5.5	7.5
	2.5	9.3	10.9	8.7			All Other Non-Current	8.6	8.9
	100.0	100.0	100.0	100.0			Total	100.0	100.0
							LIABILITIES		
	1.3	7.2	5.4	4.3			Notes Payable-Short Term	7.1	6.7
	3.1	4.8	6.0	6.5			Cur. Mat.-L.T.D.	7.5	5.0
	12.3	11.7	11.2	8.7			Trade Payables	11.9	11.8
	.0	.1	.6	.2			Income Taxes Payable	.1	.1
	13.6	6.2	8.6	8.6			All Other Current	9.2	11.0
	30.3	30.1	31.8	28.2			Total Current	35.8	34.7
	19.3	28.1	27.5	27.0			Long-Term Debt	29.1	25.3
	.0	1.0	.3	1.3			Deferred Taxes	.7	.7
	3.6	1.2	5.2	7.4			All Other Non-Current	5.7	7.4
	46.9	39.7	35.1	36.1			Net Worth	28.7	32.0
	100.0	100.0	100.0	100.0			Total Liabilities & Net Worth	100.0	100.0
							INCOME DATA		
	100.0	100.0	100.0	100.0			Net Sales	100.0	100.0
							Gross Profit		
	86.6	87.9	90.5	92.3			Operating Expenses	92.7	92.0
	13.4	12.1	9.5	7.7			Operating Profit	7.3	8.0
	.5	2.0	1.7	1.3			All Other Expenses (net)	2.8	2.3
	12.8	10.1	7.9	6.4			Profit Before Taxes	4.5	5.7
							RATIOS		
	4.0	2.3	2.1	1.6				1.4	1.7
	2.7	1.3	1.1	1.0			Current	1.0	1.1
	1.0	.9	.7	.8				.5	.6
	4.0	2.2	1.7	1.1				1.3	1.4
	2.5	1.3	1.0	.9			Quick	(217) .9	(192) .9
	.8	.8	.7	.7				.4	.5
	0 UND	0 UND	27 13.4	28 13.1				25 14.4	24 15.5
	17 22.1	34 10.6	38 9.5	38 9.6			Sales/Receivables	38 9.5	39 9.3
	48 7.7	58 6.3	57 6.4	56 6.5				59 6.1	55 6.7
							Cost of Sales/Inventory		
							Cost of Sales/Payables		
	3.8	6.0	9.5	15.7				14.1	10.5
	8.5	50.2	118.4	-942.7			Sales/Working Capital	528.4	80.3
	NM	-85.0	-21.6	-20.4				-10.6	-12.5
		18.0	11.2	10.6				6.3	8.7
		(24) 6.1	(41) 3.3	(35) 4.2			EBIT/Interest	(205) 2.6	(168) 2.9
		3.3	1.9	1.8				1.0	.9
			4.6	4.7				4.4	4.5
			(14) 2.0	(15) 1.7			Net Profit + Depr., Dep., Amort./Cur. Mat. L/T/D	(52) 1.8	(31) 2.3
			1.6	1.2				1.1	1.3
	.0	.5	.8	1.2				.9	.9
	.7	1.3	1.8	1.8			Fixed/Worth	2.2	1.9
	2.9	2.4	4.9	3.8				8.1	9.8
	.4	.7	.9	1.0				1.2	.9
	1.1	1.4	2.8	2.7			Debt/Worth	2.4	2.4
	4.0	5.7	6.9	5.2				13.1	12.6
	185.5	75.4	51.9	63.2				46.7	47.1
	70.7	(22) 33.3	(40) 29.8	(35) 27.3			% Profit Before Taxes/Tangible Net Worth	(178) 20.2	(151) 17.7
	28.2	9.8	11.1	5.2				4.4	3.1
	61.3	23.7	16.8	15.1				12.2	14.6
	22.4	13.4	6.4	6.5			% Profit Before Taxes/Total Assets	4.6	4.8
	9.6	4.0	3.0	2.0				.1	-.1
	217.0	9.2	7.4	4.8				5.9	6.2
	18.2	5.9	3.5	2.3			Sales/Net Fixed Assets	3.1	3.1
	3.9	1.8	1.7	1.3				1.8	1.6
	6.3	3.2	2.6	2.0				2.4	2.3
	2.7	2.0	1.9	1.4			Sales/Total Assets	1.7	1.5
	1.3	1.5	1.1	.8				1.1	.9
		3.3	3.3	3.9				4.1	3.5
		(21) 6.3	(44) 5.6	(36) 7.6			% Depr., Dep., Amort./Sales	(199) 7.6	(166) 7.5
		8.5	9.7	12.1				11.1	12.1
		1.4	1.1					2.1	2.6
		(10) 3.5	(14) 1.7				% Officers', Directors' Owners' Comp/Sales	(78) 3.9	(55) 4.8
		6.6	3.6					7.5	6.6
	12189M	69726M	461140M	1263760M	313450M	565141M	Net Sales ($)	3115915M	3624441M
	3708M	29084M	257544M	851445M	378980M	516989M	Total Assets ($)	2832190M	3282747M

M = $ thousand   MM = $ million
See Pages 11 through 21 for Explanation of Ratios and Data

Comparative Historical Data | Current Data Sorted by Sales

4/1/04-3/31/05 ALL	4/1/05-3/31/06 ALL	4/1/06-3/31/07 ALL	Type of Statement	0-1MM	1-3MM	3-5MM	5-10MM	10-25MM	25MM & OVER
46	37	37	Unqualified	1	4	3	6	10	13
45	36	24	Reviewed	1	3	2	6	7	5
33	10	16	Compiled	3	3	3	3	4	
16	23	13	Tax Returns	3	6	1		3	
45	63	41	Other	3	8	7	3	8	12
				31 (4/1-9/30/06)			100 (10/1/06-3/31/07)		
185	169	131	NUMBER OF STATEMENTS	11	24	16	18	32	30
%	%	%	**ASSETS**	%	%	%	%	%	%
11.4	8.6	11.7	Cash & Equivalents	27.8	15.1	12.7	12.4	8.1	5.7
18.3	18.1	20.5	Trade Receivables (net)	28.1	14.9	14.9	19.9	21.5	24.7
1.8	1.9	2.4	Inventory	.3	.2	.6	5.4	.8	5.7
2.4	3.2	2.2	All Other Current	6.0	3.0	2.0	1.2	1.8	1.5
33.8	31.9	36.8	Total Current	62.2	33.2	30.3	39.0	32.1	37.6
49.6	53.7	48.2	Fixed Assets (net)	30.2	51.7	58.1	42.6	55.5	42.1
5.7	4.5	5.1	Intangibles (net)	6.0	2.8	3.6	2.2	5.4	8.9
10.9	9.9	9.9	All Other Non-Current	1.5	12.3	8.0	16.2	6.9	11.3
100.0	100.0	100.0	Total	100.0	100.0	100.0	100.0	100.0	100.0
			LIABILITIES						
5.1	4.4	4.7	Notes Payable-Short Term	10.1	1.8	6.0	4.2	4.6	4.7
6.8	6.9	5.4	Cur. Mat.-L.T.D.	3.8	3.3	6.4	4.9	7.5	5.2
11.8	9.5	10.3	Trade Payables	12.4	5.5	11.2	14.8	9.5	11.1
.2	.1	.3	Income Taxes Payable	.0	.1	.0	1.4	.2	.2
11.6	8.4	8.9	All Other Current	13.3	7.0	5.3	6.9	7.9	12.9
35.6	29.3	29.6	Total Current	39.7	17.6	28.9	32.3	29.8	34.2
30.0	33.2	25.9	Long-Term Debt	24.3	21.5	30.7	26.5	34.4	18.0
.8	.7	.7	Deferred Taxes	.0	.4	1.1	1.2	1.1	.5
6.6	5.6	4.8	All Other Non-Current	.1	4.8	8.5	3.5	5.0	5.3
27.0	31.2	38.9	Net Worth	36.0	55.7	30.8	36.6	29.7	41.9
100.0	100.0	100.0	Total Liabilities & Net Worth	100.0	100.0	100.0	100.0	100.0	100.0
			INCOME DATA						
100.0	100.0	100.0	Net Sales	100.0	100.0	100.0	100.0	100.0	100.0
			Gross Profit						
90.0	89.4	89.7	Operating Expenses	77.5	87.4	92.3	92.8	92.1	90.3
10.0	10.6	10.3	Operating Profit	22.5	12.6	7.7	7.2	7.9	9.7
2.6	2.4	1.4	All Other Expenses (net)	4.5	.5	2.3	.3	2.2	.3
7.4	8.3	8.9	Profit Before Taxes	18.0	12.1	5.4	6.9	5.7	9.4
			RATIOS						
1.8	1.8	2.1	Current	4.0	3.3	1.6	2.3	1.7	1.8
1.1	1.1	1.1		2.2	1.9	1.1	1.1	.9	1.0
.7	.7	.8		.8	1.0	.6	.8	.7	.9
1.5	1.6	1.9	Quick	4.0	3.2	1.5	1.6	1.4	1.2
.9	.9	1.0		2.1	1.6	1.0	1.0	.9	.9
.6	.6	.7		.8	.9	.5	.7	.7	.7
26 13.8	23 15.7	25 14.7	Sales/Receivables	14 26.1	3 117.5	17 21.7	25 14.4	27 13.4	37 9.9
37 9.8	38 9.7	38 9.7		54 6.8	34 10.6	31 11.6	35 10.5	34 10.8	51 7.1
53 6.8	53 6.9	57 6.5		107 3.4	56 6.5	48 7.6	57 6.4	53 7.0	64 5.7
			Cost of Sales/Inventory						
			Cost of Sales/Payables						
8.3	10.3	8.4	Sales/Working Capital	2.2	5.7	12.2	4.3	13.9	10.5
58.8	80.1	64.1		4.8	15.1	117.8	66.3	-74.7	NM
-14.3	-16.0	-32.2		-42.3	-340.3	-34.9	-20.9	-15.2	-40.5
8.4	9.3	13.0	EBIT/Interest		18.5	13.9	12.3	6.4	26.0
(168) 4.1	(156) 3.9	(118) 5.0		(22) 11.8	(15) 3.6	(16) 3.9	(30) 2.9	(29) 5.5	
1.5	1.7	2.0			5.6	2.7	1.7	1.3	3.1
4.2	3.5	4.7	Net Profit + Depr., Dep., Amort./Cur. Mat. L/T/D					3.9	12.9
(46) 2.1	(41) 2.0	(39) 1.9					(14) 2.1	(15) 3.1	
1.2	1.4	1.4						1.4	1.3
.9	1.0	.7	Fixed/Worth	.0	.5	1.2	.5	1.2	.8
1.9	1.9	1.4		1.7	.8	1.7	1.4	2.9	1.4
9.2	6.7	3.5		4.7	1.4	94.9	3.7	8.1	2.2
.9	1.0	.8	Debt/Worth	.5	.4	1.4	.8	1.5	.9
2.5	2.4	1.9		2.0	.8	2.6	2.2	3.9	1.6
15.1	9.2	4.8		13.3	1.3	126.2	7.8	9.6	4.3
55.9	60.4	67.4	% Profit Before Taxes/Tangible Net Worth	258.0	62.9	66.9	71.4	60.2	69.1
(147) 21.5	(142) 30.5	(119) 32.5		(10) 61.4	(23) 29.3	(13) 19.7	(16) 20.3	(28) 27.0	(29) 39.4
6.7	7.1	10.2		30.1	7.9	5.1	.5	13.2	16.1
12.0	13.4	18.0	% Profit Before Taxes/Total Assets	44.8	25.1	19.7	16.1	14.6	17.9
5.2	6.5	8.3		13.4	15.4	5.0	4.8	5.8	9.6
1.0	1.6	3.1		4.2	5.3	-1.0	.6	1.6	4.6
6.8	5.1	7.3	Sales/Net Fixed Assets	200.3	7.4	4.8	16.2	6.2	6.3
2.8	2.8	3.5		17.1	3.5	3.1	3.0	2.8	4.3
1.4	1.4	1.7		1.5	1.3	.9	1.2	1.8	2.2
2.5	2.3	2.6	Sales/Total Assets	3.1	2.6	2.6	2.7	2.6	2.5
1.4	1.5	1.6		1.4	1.5	1.5	1.3	1.8	1.7
.8	.8	1.0		.7	.8	.6	.7	1.3	1.0
4.5	3.7	3.3	% Depr., Dep., Amort./Sales		4.7	6.2	2.7	3.5	2.7
(156) 7.4	(154) 6.7	(117) 6.1		(20) 7.0	7.9	(15) 5.8	6.1	(28) 5.0	
12.0	10.4	9.7			11.3	20.4	10.1	9.7	6.9
1.8	1.6	2.0	% Officers', Directors' Owners' Comp/Sales	2.0					
(42) 4.6	(46) 3.2	(36) 2.3		(12) 4.2					
7.8	5.8	5.0		9.0					
4514200M	3697022M	2685406M	Net Sales ($)	5900M	49699M	63458M	120164M	503218M	1942967M
3622630M	2796016M	2037750M	Total Assets ($)	4899M	50624M	95264M	178425M	359331M	1349207M

M = $ thousand   MM = $ million
See Pages 11 through 21 for Explanation of Ratios and Data

Current Data Sorted by Assets   Comparative Historical Data

	0-500M	500M-2MM	2-10MM	10-50MM	50-100MM	100-250MM	Type of Statement	4/1/02-3/31/03 ALL	4/1/03-3/31/04 ALL
			3	3		1	Unqualified	2	7
	1	10	13				Reviewed	2	8
	5	4	1				Compiled		3
	2	4					Tax Returns	1	3
	1	3	2		2	1	Other	5	5
		5 (4/1-9/30/06)		51 (10/1/06-3/31/07)					
NUMBER OF STATEMENTS	9	21	19	3	2	2		10	26
	%	%	%	%	%	%	**ASSETS**	%	%
		10.6	5.0				Cash & Equivalents	10.3	7.9
		48.3	47.9				Trade Receivables (net)	52.7	49.8
		3.2	4.0				Inventory	.7	2.8
		8.5	12.6				All Other Current	3.6	8.0
		70.7	69.5				Total Current	67.5	68.5
		23.9	23.8				Fixed Assets (net)	23.8	23.5
		3.0	3.3				Intangibles (net)	.0	1.5
		2.4	3.4				All Other Non-Current	8.8	6.9
		100.0	100.0				Total	100.0	100.0
							LIABILITIES		
		18.6	10.1				Notes Payable-Short Term	15.1	13.7
		4.0	4.6				Cur. Mat.-L.T.D.	3.3	2.9
		13.5	19.3				Trade Payables	12.7	15.2
		2.8	.6				Income Taxes Payable	.6	.4
		14.7	10.5				All Other Current	8.5	8.1
		53.6	45.0				Total Current	40.1	40.3
		17.9	12.7				Long-Term Debt	10.7	10.8
		.4	.6				Deferred Taxes	.0	.2
		5.9	1.0				All Other Non-Current	1.1	6.2
		22.2	40.8				Net Worth	48.1	42.8
		100.0	100.0				Total Liabilties & Net Worth	100.0	100.0
							INCOME DATA		
		100.0	100.0				Net Sales	100.0	100.0
							Gross Profit		
		95.8	94.8				Operating Expenses	88.9	95.3
		4.2	5.2				Operating Profit	11.1	4.7
		1.4	.6				All Other Expenses (net)	1.7	1.3
		2.8	4.6				Profit Before Taxes	9.5	3.4
							RATIOS		
		2.2	2.1					2.9	2.5
		1.4	1.5				Current	2.0	1.7
		1.0	1.2					1.1	1.4
		1.8	1.6					2.7	2.0
		1.2	1.2				Quick	1.9	1.5
		.8	1.0					1.0	1.0
	50	7.3	50 7.3					39 9.3	43 8.4
	78	4.7	82 4.4				Sales/Receivables	68 5.4	82 4.4
	96	3.8	100 3.7					92 4.0	107 3.4
							Cost of Sales/Inventory		
							Cost of Sales/Payables		
		10.2	6.1					5.1	6.1
		15.2	10.0				Sales/Working Capital	8.4	8.5
		157.0	31.2					NM	14.7
		9.9	8.7						10.3
		(18) 3.9	5.0				EBIT/Interest		(20) 4.6
		1.1	2.6						1.5
							Net Profit + Depr., Dep., Amort./Cur. Mat. L/T/D		
		.4	.3					.1	.2
		.7	.6				Fixed/Worth	.5	.4
		NM	1.0					.9	.9
		1.2	1.3					.5	.8
		5.2	1.6				Debt/Worth	.9	1.3
		NM	2.7					2.8	3.1
		75.4	42.9				% Profit Before Taxes/Tangible Net Worth	75.4	33.1
		(16) 49.3	23.3					41.1	(25) 10.5
		24.0	10.1					20.9	3.2
		17.5	13.8				% Profit Before Taxes/Total Assets	48.4	10.1
		9.0	9.1					20.7	3.3
		3.7	4.1					6.5	.9
		30.0	20.1					47.8	31.9
		11.1	12.4				Sales/Net Fixed Assets	16.2	13.9
		6.2	5.7					7.2	5.6
		3.4	2.8					4.1	2.9
		2.6	2.4				Sales/Total Assets	3.1	2.2
		2.1	1.8					1.3	1.8
		1.1	1.1						1.0
		(18) 1.8	1.7				% Depr., Dep., Amort./Sales		(22) 2.0
		2.4	3.6						3.5
		4.1	1.6						2.4
		(10) 5.1	(10) 2.2				% Officers', Directors' Owners' Comp/Sales		(12) 3.3
		7.4	4.1						6.9
Net Sales ($)	8201M	65909M	221312M	213642M	202561M	183654M		71112M	170830M
Total Assets ($)	2219M	24391M	89250M	72094M	133236M	403514M		23378M	77228M

Comparative Historical Data

Current Data Sorted by Sales

			Type of Statement	0-1MM	1-3MM	3-5MM	5-10MM	10-25MM	25MM & OVER
9	11	7	Unqualified		7	5	6	2	5
14	13	24	Reviewed		5			6	
4	4	10	Compiled	3		2	2		
4	4	6	Tax Returns	3		1	1		
7	7	9	Other	1	3			1	3
4/1/04-3/31/05 ALL	4/1/05-3/31/06 ALL	4/1/06-3/31/07 ALL			5 (4/1-9/30/06)		51 (10/1/06-3/31/07)		
38	39	56	NUMBER OF STATEMENTS	7	15	8	9	9	8
%	%	%	ASSETS	%	%	%	%	%	%
6.1	6.9	9.5	Cash & Equivalents		13.2				
45.8	48.8	43.4	Trade Receivables (net)		40.5				
3.2	2.8	3.1	Inventory		2.5				
8.5	11.6	10.9	All Other Current		15.5				
63.5	70.1	66.9	Total Current		71.7				
26.5	21.0	21.9	Fixed Assets (net)		25.6				
3.2	3.5	6.1	Intangibles (net)		.6				
6.8	5.4	5.1	All Other Non-Current		2.1				
100.0	100.0	100.0	Total		100.0				
			LIABILITIES						
8.4	10.8	16.1	Notes Payable-Short Term		11.1				
4.3	4.3	3.8	Cur. Mat.-L.T.D.		5.8				
16.4	17.0	16.5	Trade Payables		15.2				
.5	.4	1.3	Income Taxes Payable		3.4				
9.8	11.9	14.9	All Other Current		12.1				
39.4	44.4	52.5	Total Current		47.6				
14.0	16.7	15.2	Long-Term Debt		22.6				
.6	1.0	.6	Deferred Taxes		.0				
4.6	2.2	3.6	All Other Non-Current		7.4				
41.4	35.7	28.0	Net Worth		22.5				
100.0	100.0	100.0	Total Liabilities & Net Worth		100.0				
			INCOME DATA						
100.0	100.0	100.0	Net Sales		100.0				
			Gross Profit						
92.5	96.7	95.4	Operating Expenses		97.0				
7.5	3.3	4.6	Operating Profit		3.0				
.8	1.1	1.0	All Other Expenses (net)		1.1				
6.7	2.2	3.6	Profit Before Taxes		1.9				
			RATIOS						
2.5	2.3	1.9			2.4				
1.6	1.5	1.3	Current		1.4				
1.2	1.2	1.0			1.2				
2.3	1.9	1.5			1.5				
1.3	1.2	1.1	Quick		1.2				
1.0	.7	.7			.8				
43 8.5	46 7.9	40 9.2			23 15.5				
74 4.9	70 5.2	74 5.0	Sales/Receivables		65 5.6				
106 3.5	91 4.0	96 3.8			91 4.0				
			Cost of Sales/Inventory						
			Cost of Sales/Payables						
6.8	6.7	8.2			6.5				
10.7	9.4	17.1	Sales/Working Capital		13.7				
18.0	22.3	233.0			23.6				
18.5	12.1	9.9			9.8				
(32) 6.6	(34) 3.4	(50) 4.1	EBIT/Interest		(11) 3.7				
2.1	.6	1.8			-2.4				
	13.6	5.9							
(11) 2.7		(16) 3.0	Net Profit + Depr., Dep., Amort./Cur. Mat. L/T/D						
.8		1.0							
.3	.2	.2			.1				
.5	.4	.7	Fixed/Worth		.7				
1.4	1.4	4.7			-1.7				
.7	.8	1.3			.6				
1.8	2.3	2.4	Debt/Worth		2.2				
3.5	6.0	15.3			-4.3				
80.6	53.6	63.9			63.0				
(37) 34.4	(34) 23.1	(45) 32.1	% Profit Before Taxes/Tangible Net Worth		(11) 47.0				
6.1	2.9	11.6			16.6				
24.4	13.3	17.9			20.1				
8.6	6.3	9.0	% Profit Before Taxes/Total Assets		14.0				
1.9	-1.3	3.6			7.2				
29.4	35.6	37.5			52.9				
14.4	19.0	12.6	Sales/Net Fixed Assets		10.2				
6.6	8.4	6.6			5.9				
3.3	3.6	3.7			3.7				
2.5	2.5	2.6	Sales/Total Assets		2.9				
1.8	1.8	1.9			1.9				
1.1	.9	1.0			1.0				
(30) 2.0	(31) 1.5	(49) 1.7	% Depr., Dep., Amort./Sales		(13) 1.6				
3.6	2.9	3.6			2.7				
1.0	1.7	2.2							
(14) 2.4	(17) 3.5	(25) 4.6	% Officers', Directors' Owners' Comp/Sales						
4.2	5.4	7.5							
703461M	945641M	895279M	Net Sales ($)	5111M	32118M	33015M	59789M	134258M	630988M
477545M	464052M	724704M	Total Assets ($)	1777M	13033M	14109M	29792M	52118M	613875M

Current Data Sorted by Assets   Comparative Historical Data

Type of Statement

						Type of Statement	4/1/02-3/31/03 ALL	4/1/03-3/31/04 ALL
						Unqualified	11	9
						Reviewed	6	8
						Compiled	5	11
						Tax Returns	1	5
						Other	8	13

Statement type counts by asset size (top of current-data columns):
0-500M: 2, 1, 4, 2 · 500M-2MM: 1, 2, 2, 5 · 2-10MM: 1, 11, 3, 3, 6 · 10-50MM: 4, 2, 1, 5 · 50-100MM: 1

Dates: 9 (4/1-9/30/06)   47 (10/1/06-3/31/07)

0-500M	500M-2MM	2-10MM	10-50MM	50-100MM	100-250MM		4/1/02-3/31/03 ALL	4/1/03-3/31/04 ALL
9	10	24	12	1		NUMBER OF STATEMENTS	31	46
%	%	%	%	%	%	**ASSETS**	%	%
	8.5	9.3	7.2		D	Cash & Equivalents	7.5	5.7
	34.8	17.4	20.6		A	Trade Receivables (net)	18.5	19.8
	13.2	4.1	15.1		T	Inventory	2.4	5.8
	.0	4.1	3.3		A	All Other Current	3.1	3.4
	56.6	34.9	46.2			Total Current	31.5	34.8
	27.2	54.1	32.3		N	Fixed Assets (net)	53.7	49.2
	2.0	4.0	6.7		O	Intangibles (net)	7.3	5.3
	14.3	6.9	14.8		T	All Other Non-Current	7.6	10.8
	100.0	100.0	100.0			Total	100.0	100.0
					A	**LIABILITIES**		
	9.7	4.9	9.8		V	Notes Payable-Short Term	4.4	6.4
	3.0	5.2	6.2		A	Cur. Mat.-L.T.D.	7.3	10.7
	21.0	12.5	7.3		I	Trade Payables	8.8	12.6
	.1	.1	.2		L	Income Taxes Payable	.0	.2
	17.7	8.1	7.8		A	All Other Current	7.0	12.2
	51.5	30.9	31.3		B	Total Current	27.5	42.1
	14.7	37.5	25.4		L	Long-Term Debt	39.0	28.2
	.5	.5	.4		E	Deferred Taxes	.8	.7
	2.6	6.6	3.0			All Other Non-Current	5.2	4.5
	30.7	24.4	40.0			Net Worth	27.4	24.5
	100.0	100.0	100.0			Total Liabilties & Net Worth	100.0	100.0
						INCOME DATA		
	100.0	100.0	100.0			Net Sales	100.0	100.0
						Gross Profit		
	98.7	89.7	93.0			Operating Expenses	91.9	94.6
	1.3	10.3	7.0			Operating Profit	8.1	5.4
	.1	6.3	1.6			All Other Expenses (net)	2.5	2.8
	1.2	4.1	5.4			Profit Before Taxes	5.6	2.6
						RATIOS		
	2.0	1.7	2.1				1.7	1.4
	1.3	1.1	1.6			Current	1.0	1.0
	.7	.7	1.1				.5	.6
	1.4	1.5	1.7				1.4	1.0
	1.0	.9	1.4			Quick	1.0	.7
	.5	.4	.4				.5	.4
	18 20.6	16 22.4	22 16.4				31 11.7	24 15.3
	28 12.9	34 10.8	35 10.4			Sales/Receivables	37 9.9	36 10.2
	44 8.3	49 7.5	48 7.6				61 6.0	53 6.9
						Cost of Sales/Inventory		
						Cost of Sales/Payables		
	19.6	11.5	8.2				16.7	22.3
	39.6	59.9	14.6			Sales/Working Capital	95.5	NM
	-23.3	-18.7	54.8				-7.3	-8.5
		7.1	7.7				8.4	6.7
		(22) 2.2	(10) 2.4			EBIT/Interest	(30) 2.8	(43) 3.6
		1.5	1.2				1.2	1.5
							2.6	3.2
						Net Profit + Depr., Dep., Amort./Cur. Mat. L/T/D	(13) 1.3	(16) 1.4
							1.0	1.2
	.4	1.1	.3				1.5	1.1
	.7	2.5	1.0			Fixed/Worth	3.8	2.8
	NM	9.7	3.1				33.0	66.1
	.6	2.2	.6				1.3	.9
	4.8	4.9	2.1			Debt/Worth	5.6	4.2
	NM	15.0	5.8				39.3	107.8
		61.2	29.7				87.3	70.9
	(20)	22.1	(11) 8.5			% Profit Before Taxes/Tangible Net Worth	(24) 28.0	(36) 22.7
		9.2	6.1				9.0	6.9
	17.6	8.4	14.6				12.5	12.2
	4.9	3.6	2.8			% Profit Before Taxes/Total Assets	6.1	6.0
	-2.2	1.8	1.2				.6	.2
	173.7	5.6	18.1				8.1	11.8
	20.3	3.4	5.4			Sales/Net Fixed Assets	2.2	3.9
	8.2	1.5	2.9				1.2	1.7
	7.0	2.6	3.4				2.4	2.9
	4.6	1.7	1.8			Sales/Total Assets	1.3	1.6
	2.7	.9	1.0				.8	.9
	.2	3.6	.9				4.7	2.7
	1.2	7.2	1.9			% Depr., Dep., Amort./Sales	(28) 8.2	(40) 5.0
	3.2	11.0	5.6				10.1	7.5
								2.2
						% Officers', Directors' Owners' Comp/Sales		(12) 4.8
								8.5
11579M	56849M	202752M	795239M	210436M		Net Sales ($)	5925216M	1002267M
2269M	11454M	105539M	360520M	62680M		Total Assets ($)	606269M	885719M

(The 50-100MM and 100-250MM columns are marked **DATA NOT AVAILABLE**.)

M = $ thousand   MM = $ million
See Pages 11 through 21 for Explanation of Ratios and Data

Comparative Historical Data　　　　　　Current Data Sorted by Sales

			Type of Statement	0-1MM	1-3MM	3-5MM	5-10MM	10-25MM	25MM & OVER
6	7	6	Unqualified		1	1			4
6	10	17	Reviewed	2	4	3	5	2	1
7	7	7	Compiled		1	1	2	1	2
4	10	7	Tax Returns	1	3			3	
17	8	19	Other	2	3	2	4		5
4/1/04-3/31/05 ALL	4/1/05-3/31/06 ALL	4/1/06-3/31/07 ALL			9 (4/1-9/30/06)		47 (10/1/06-3/31/07)		
40	42	56	NUMBER OF STATEMENTS	5	11	7	11	10	12
%	%	%	ASSETS	%	%	%	%	%	%
9.7	10.1	9.7	Cash & Equivalents		13.4		12.9	9.8	6.8
16.9	23.1	22.7	Trade Receivables (net)		27.6		19.9	18.6	28.4
7.7	3.9	8.0	Inventory		3.3		6.7	15.2	14.0
5.6	4.8	4.2	All Other Current		3.6		1.3	4.1	2.9
39.9	42.0	44.5	Total Current		47.9		40.9	47.8	52.0
47.8	44.5	40.0	Fixed Assets (net)		33.5		49.1	32.2	29.7
4.2	3.5	4.8	Intangibles (net)		7.7		.4	5.2	6.7
8.2	10.1	10.6	All Other Non-Current		10.9		9.6	14.8	11.6
100.0	100.0	100.0	Total		100.0		100.0	100.0	100.0
			LIABILITIES						
4.4	7.7	9.2	Notes Payable-Short Term		17.0		3.3	5.9	13.0
7.0	5.9	4.8	Cur. Mat.-L.T.D.		4.1		5.1	5.3	4.6
12.3	17.4	13.6	Trade Payables		9.8		13.2	16.2	12.3
.5	.1	.8	Income Taxes Payable		3.5		.2	.0	.2
11.2	10.6	9.3	All Other Current		14.3		9.2	6.8	8.7
35.5	41.8	37.6	Total Current		48.7		31.0	34.2	38.7
31.3	25.0	27.8	Long-Term Debt		23.4		27.9	24.7	22.0
.5	.6	.4	Deferred Taxes		.5		.6	.0	.4
6.2	13.9	4.6	All Other Non-Current		4.8		1.1	9.6	2.1
26.6	18.8	29.6	Net Worth		22.7		39.4	31.5	36.9
100.0	100.0	100.0	Total Liabilties & Net Worth		100.0		100.0	100.0	100.0
			INCOME DATA						
100.0	100.0	100.0	Net Sales		100.0		100.0	100.0	100.0
			Gross Profit						
90.2	93.7	92.1	Operating Expenses		92.0		94.9	92.1	94.5
9.8	6.3	7.9	Operating Profit		8.0		5.1	7.9	5.5
4.3	3.3	3.7	All Other Expenses (net)		.9		1.1	1.2	1.1
5.5	3.0	4.2	Profit Before Taxes		7.1		4.0	6.7	4.4
			RATIOS						
2.2	1.6	2.1			8.3		2.3	1.9	2.0
1.3	1.0	1.2	Current		2.0		1.4	1.2	1.5
.8	.6	.7			.7		.7	1.0	.8
1.5	1.4	1.6			4.7		1.7	1.3	1.5
.9	.9	1.0	Quick		1.6		1.2	.9	1.2
.5	.5	.4			.6		.5	.4	.5
21　17.2	20　18.0	16　22.4			23　16.1		4　102.9	17　21.1	22　16.3
29　12.5	32　11.5	30　12.3	Sales/Receivables		36　10.1		24　15.5	26　14.0	39　9.4
43　8.4	47　7.8	48　7.6			65　5.6		25　14.6	41　8.9	48　7.6
			Cost of Sales/Inventory						
			Cost of Sales/Payables						
8.0	18.6	11.3			7.8		19.0	10.8	8.7
29.4	596.9	36.2	Sales/Working Capital		27.0		35.4	26.1	26.5
-17.7	-11.4	-24.6			-7.3		-28.6	NM	NM
10.3	11.7	8.9					58.8	13.8	6.8
(35)　4.6	(37)　3.5	(48)　2.5	EBIT/Interest		(10)　6.6			2.8	(10)　3.4
1.6	1.0	1.5					2.3	1.6	1.5
			Net Profit + Depr., Dep., Amort./Cur. Mat. L/T/D						
.7	.6	.4			.4		.4	.4	.3
2.1	1.7	2.0	Fixed/Worth		2.3		1.9	1.4	.8
NM	17.0	8.4			-.4		7.7	NM	3.1
.9	.9	.9			.3		.4	1.6	.8
4.0	4.0	3.1	Debt/Worth		3.3		2.2	3.1	2.7
NM	30.4	14.6			-3.5		9.9	NM	14.6
70.4	44.6	49.5					72.6		42.4
(30)　30.1	(33)　21.1	(46)　20.5	% Profit Before Taxes/Tangible Net Worth				31.8	(11)　19.5	
8.6	10.6	7.6					18.3		8.0
15.9	14.5	16.6			30.6		17.4	18.3	19.6
8.8	4.4	4.7	% Profit Before Taxes/Total Assets		8.8		6.6	5.6	2.9
1.8	.7	1.2			-4.1		4.5	1.7	1.4
8.1	15.3	21.9			177.2		24.6	24.4	21.9
4.1	6.0	5.7	Sales/Net Fixed Assets		15.1		3.7	5.3	11.4
1.9	2.1	2.9			9.3		2.6	3.9	3.5
3.0	3.9	4.0			5.7		6.3	4.4	3.9
1.6	2.4	2.6	Sales/Total Assets		3.2		2.5	2.5	3.2
1.2	1.1	1.1			.8		1.7	1.1	1.1
1.8	2.2	1.5					.9	1.4	.5
(34)　5.4	(37)　5.3	(51)　3.6	% Depr., Dep., Amort./Sales				3.1	4.3	1.7
11.2	8.9	9.2					10.5	7.6	5.3
	1.7	1.0							
(16)　3.4	(15)　2.1		% Officers', Directors' Owners' Comp/Sales						
6.1	6.6								
979604M	1196021M	1276855M	Net Sales ($)	2052M	24419M	26338M	77416M	133050M	1013580M
750006M	536600M	542462M	Total Assets ($)	3814M	16973M	24799M	31472M	78366M	387038M

© RMA 2007　　M = $ thousand　　MM = $ million
See Pages 11 through 21 for Explanation of Ratios and Data

Current Data Sorted by Assets

Comparative Historical Data

Type of Statement	1	2	6	9	5	3		14	22
Unqualified		2	6	9		3		14	22
Reviewed	1	7	7	5				19	22
Compiled	3	10	9					14	24
Tax Returns	12	16	5		1	1		6	19
Other	4	4	25	5				17	18
		23 (4/1-9/30/06)		112 (10/1/06-3/31/07)				4/1/02-3/31/03 ALL	4/1/03-3/31/04 ALL
	0-500M	500M-2MM	2-10MM	10-50MM	50-100MM	100-250MM	NUMBER OF STATEMENTS	70	105
	20	39	52	19	1	4			
	%	%	%	%	%	%	ASSETS	%	%
	20.2	11.8	9.2	9.1			Cash & Equivalents	9.2	10.4
	18.8	28.6	29.5	23.6			Trade Receivables (net)	20.9	23.3
	3.2	3.4	2.7	2.6			Inventory	1.0	2.6
	5.9	2.9	3.3	2.7			All Other Current	3.2	3.2
	48.1	46.7	44.7	38.0			Total Current	34.3	39.5
	44.3	41.6	41.8	46.4			Fixed Assets (net)	50.4	48.5
	5.1	3.4	3.8	11.0			Intangibles (net)	5.7	4.5
	2.6	8.3	9.6	4.7			All Other Non-Current	9.6	7.4
	100.0	100.0	100.0	100.0			Total	100.0	100.0
							LIABILITIES		
	16.3	9.4	5.3	4.1			Notes Payable-Short Term	4.3	8.4
	8.7	7.9	6.0	5.3			Cur. Mat.-L.T.D.	11.1	8.2
	6.2	12.5	12.3	11.8			Trade Payables	10.3	9.3
	.7	.9	1.5	.7			Income Taxes Payable	.3	.2
	10.6	6.6	9.8	5.1			All Other Current	7.4	7.2
	42.5	37.2	34.9	27.0			Total Current	33.4	33.3
	34.2	32.4	22.6	24.0			Long-Term Debt	33.9	31.5
	.3	.2	.2	.4			Deferred Taxes	.2	.5
	.8	3.4	1.4	7.4			All Other Non-Current	5.8	6.7
	22.2	26.7	41.0	41.2			Net Worth	26.7	28.0
	100.0	100.0	100.0	100.0			Total Liabilties & Net Worth	100.0	100.0
							INCOME DATA		
	100.0	100.0	100.0	100.0			Net Sales	100.0	100.0
							Gross Profit		
	89.1	93.9	93.6	95.0			Operating Expenses	91.5	93.1
	10.9	6.1	6.4	5.0			Operating Profit	8.5	6.9
	2.8	2.0	1.3	1.7			All Other Expenses (net)	3.6	2.8
	8.1	4.2	5.1	3.3			Profit Before Taxes	4.9	4.1
							RATIOS		
	4.4	2.6	2.0	1.9				2.0	2.1
	1.1	1.3	1.4	1.4			Current	1.0	1.2
	.4	.6	.9	1.0				.6	.7
	4.3	2.5	1.9	1.6				1.7	1.7
	.9	1.0	1.1	1.3			Quick	.9	1.0
	.3	.5	.6	.8				.4	.6
	0 UND	14 27.0	19 18.9	24 15.2				25 14.4	23 15.8
	18 20.4	30 12.2	45 8.1	42 8.7			Sales/Receivables	37 9.8	40 9.1
	59 6.1	59 6.2	70 5.2	71 5.1				53 6.9	61 6.0
							Cost of Sales/Inventory		
							Cost of Sales/Payables		
	7.5	8.0	7.3	10.2				9.4	10.3
	UND	52.2	18.8	21.0			Sales/Working Capital	NM	27.0
	-10.8	-20.7	-63.6	212.6				-15.4	-29.2
	29.4	15.8	14.8	6.9				7.4	10.8
	(16) 3.8	(35) 2.5	(48) 5.3	3.9			EBIT/Interest	(65) 1.9	(97) 3.6
	1.0	.6	1.2	.8				.8	1.0
			12.5					3.8	2.7
		(13) 2.2					Net Profit + Depr., Dep., Amort./Cur. Mat. L/T/D	(19) 2.0	(24) 1.7
			1.2					1.1	.6
	.4	.6	.6	1.0				.9	.9
	4.6	1.8	1.1	1.7			Fixed/Worth	1.7	1.7
	-8.2	15.3	2.1	3.1				7.9	6.1
	1.0	.8	.7	.8				.9	1.1
	5.2	3.4	1.9	1.6			Debt/Worth	2.1	2.8
	-14.8	32.1	3.4	3.9				11.5	12.3
	183.5	97.6	62.4	31.3				44.9	59.4
	(13) 74.4	(30) 27.2	(47) 34.6	(16) 13.5			% Profit Before Taxes/Tangible Net Worth	(55) 21.1	(84) 27.3
	9.9	-6.0	.9	-1.0				1.1	.0
	39.6	32.4	19.7	13.6				16.1	16.3
	5.1	7.6	9.5	5.8			% Profit Before Taxes/Total Assets	3.6	6.7
	-.2	-1.0	.0	-1.0				-1.0	-.7
	19.5	12.8	16.0	6.2				8.5	10.7
	9.1	7.6	5.9	4.1			Sales/Net Fixed Assets	3.5	4.5
	3.1	3.6	2.6	1.9				1.6	2.4
	4.7	4.7	2.6	2.2				2.7	2.9
	3.7	2.7	2.0	1.7			Sales/Total Assets	1.7	2.0
	1.9	2.0	1.1	1.2				.8	1.5
	2.8	2.4	2.6	3.6				5.3	3.8
	(14) 6.1	(33) 4.9	(44) 4.1	(18) 5.1			% Depr., Dep., Amort./Sales	(64) 8.6	(93) 7.0
	20.1	7.8	8.7	8.5				14.5	10.8
		2.3	2.4					3.9	3.0
	(23) 3.3		(19) 3.9				% Officers', Directors', Owners' Comp/Sales	(26) 6.0	(45) 5.3
		4.5	6.2					9.8	8.7
	14158M	150388M	478192M	618155M	81836M	576815M	Net Sales ($)	813362M	1111920M
	4469M	44579M	252980M	363415M	69152M	676836M	Total Assets ($)	984964M	988928M

M = $ thousand   MM = $ million
See Pages 11 through 21 for Explanation of Ratios and Data

Comparative Historical Data

Current Data Sorted by Sales

			Type of Statement						
17	18	20	Unqualified	1	1	3	1	7	7
20	31	20	Reviewed	1	4	3	1	8	3
22	14	22	Compiled	2	4	7	6	3	
21	20	33	Tax Returns	8	14	4	6	6	
34	61	40	Other	6	6	6	7	8	7
4/1/04-3/31/05 ALL	4/1/05-3/31/06 ALL	4/1/06-3/31/07 ALL		0-1MM	1-3MM 23 (4/1-9/30/06)	3-5MM	5-10MM 112 (10/1/06-3/31/07)	10-25MM	25MM & OVER
114	144	135	NUMBER OF STATEMENTS	18	29	23	21	27	17
%	%	%	ASSETS	%	%	%	%	%	%
13.5	10.8	11.6	Cash & Equivalents	17.1	12.4	10.2	11.3	10.1	9.5
23.9	27.2	26.6	Trade Receivables (net)	8.2	24.9	21.3	33.7	38.9	28.0
2.6	2.8	2.8	Inventory	3.0	2.9	.6	3.3	3.9	3.3
3.4	3.3	3.5	All Other Current	6.2	.9	5.9	2.6	3.3	3.1
43.4	44.1	44.6	Total Current	34.5	41.1	38.0	50.8	56.2	43.9
45.3	42.5	42.4	Fixed Assets (net)	56.1	46.9	47.2	35.0	33.2	37.6
2.9	5.0	5.5	Intangibles (net)	4.2	2.5	5.5	5.7	5.7	11.6
8.4	8.5	7.5	All Other Non-Current	5.1	9.6	9.2	8.4	4.9	6.9
100.0	100.0	100.0	Total	100.0	100.0	100.0	100.0	100.0	100.0
			LIABILITIES						
8.9	6.9	7.8	Notes Payable-Short Term	13.4	9.4	6.3	5.6	7.6	3.8
6.8	7.2	6.7	Cur. Mat.-L.T.D.	8.1	6.7	7.9	8.5	5.0	3.9
10.4	12.1	11.2	Trade Payables	3.0	11.7	7.6	15.4	14.5	13.6
.2	.5	1.0	Income Taxes Payable	.4	.7	.9	1.6	1.6	.9
8.4	10.3	8.4	All Other Current	7.4	8.2	11.3	7.3	7.8	8.5
34.7	36.9	35.1	Total Current	32.3	36.6	34.0	38.4	36.4	30.8
29.4	28.5	27.9	Long-Term Debt	37.4	36.3	24.7	27.1	18.1	24.0
1.5	.6	.3	Deferred Taxes	.3	.2	.2	.0	.5	.2
13.2	5.9	2.7	All Other Non-Current	.9	1.0	3.8	3.1	2.1	6.6
21.3	28.1	34.0	Net Worth	29.0	25.8	37.3	31.3	42.9	38.4
100.0	100.0	100.0	Total Liabilties & Net Worth	100.0	100.0	100.0	100.0	100.0	100.0
			INCOME DATA						
100.0	100.0	100.0	Net Sales	100.0	100.0	100.0	100.0	100.0	100.0
			Gross Profit						
91.8	89.4	93.0	Operating Expenses	91.7	92.6	94.6	94.5	92.8	91.5
8.2	10.6	7.0	Operating Profit	8.3	7.4	5.4	5.5	7.2	8.5
2.0	2.9	1.8	All Other Expenses (net)	3.0	2.9	1.0	1.0	.8	2.3
6.2	7.6	5.1	Profit Before Taxes	5.2	4.5	4.4	4.4	6.4	6.2
			RATIOS						
2.1	1.9	2.1	Current	3.7	2.6	2.7	2.2	1.9	1.9
1.3	1.3	1.4		1.4	.9	1.2	1.0	1.4	1.3
.7	.8	.8		.4	.5	.6	.8	1.2	.9
1.7	1.8	1.9	Quick	3.6	2.1	2.5	2.2	1.9	1.6
1.0	1.1	1.1		1.3	.9	1.0	.9	1.3	1.1
.6	.6	.6		.3	.4	.3	.6	1.1	.7
12 30.2	27 13.7	16 22.6	Sales/Receivables	0 UND	2 152.1	0 UND	17 21.1	37 9.9	30 12.2
36 10.1	46 7.9	38 9.5		0 UND	36 10.2	30 12.0	34 10.6	56 6.6	52 7.0
60 6.1	72 5.1	65 5.6		37 9.7	59 6.2	59 6.1	59 6.2	79 4.6	81 4.5
			Cost of Sales/Inventory						
			Cost of Sales/Payables						
7.7	7.7	7.7	Sales/Working Capital	4.2	9.1	5.4	12.8	7.8	8.8
27.8	23.9	22.9		44.2	-77.1	60.0	93.6	11.9	21.3
-20.9	-31.7	-28.3		-16.1	-11.5	-15.7	-46.8	27.8	NM
11.4	10.4	15.0	EBIT/Interest	5.2	10.6	16.0	14.8	16.2	53.2
(102) 3.6	(133) 3.9	(123) 4.1		(15) 1.2	(26) 2.7	(20) 2.1	(20) 6.4	(25) 5.9	4.2
.8	1.3	1.0		.6	.5	-.8	1.0	2.5	1.9
7.3	3.4	5.7	Net Profit + Depr., Dep., Amort./Cur. Mat. L/T/D					8.3	
(18) 2.5	(31) 2.0	(28) 2.2						(10) 2.4	
1.6	1.4	.8						1.9	
.6	.6	.6	Fixed/Worth	.8	.7	.6	.4	.5	.3
1.6	1.4	1.3		3.2	3.1	1.7	1.8	.7	1.2
15.0	7.2	6.8		-8.9	NM	7.2	UND	1.7	NM
.7	1.0	.8	Debt/Worth	.3	.8	1.0	1.1	.8	.8
2.1	2.5	2.1		3.2	3.5	1.9	2.2	1.9	1.6
27.9	24.2	8.3		-15.1	NM	7.2	UND	2.9	NM
61.4	67.0	72.6	% Profit Before Taxes/Tangible Net Worth	150.8	106.7	41.2	110.1	68.5	47.4
(90) 25.9	(111) 32.7	(109) 24.8		(12) 5.1	(22) 34.2	(19) 11.4	(17) 48.7	(26) 34.0	(13) 24.2
8.1	7.1	.6		-.6	3.0	-6.7	-5.7	16.3	11.9
18.0	20.3	22.7	% Profit Before Taxes/Total Assets	10.5	28.5	14.4	37.7	20.6	19.9
8.7	9.1	7.5		1.5	7.6	5.9	14.5	10.8	7.2
.0	1.9	-.1		-.3	-1.8	-1.3	-.5	5.8	3.3
11.6	13.4	13.5	Sales/Net Fixed Assets	11.9	12.3	9.5	39.0	18.3	12.1
5.4	5.5	6.2		3.3	5.5	4.4	8.8	7.9	5.0
2.3	2.5	3.0		.3	2.3	2.8	4.4	4.5	3.3
3.3	2.8	3.5	Sales/Total Assets	4.4	3.3	3.4	4.6	2.7	2.5
2.1	1.9	2.1		2.0	2.2	2.0	2.9	2.1	1.9
1.3	1.1	1.4		.2	1.2	1.1	1.9	1.7	1.2
3.1	2.1	2.7	% Depr., Dep., Amort./Sales	5.3	3.0	3.5	1.3	2.1	1.8
(98) 6.7	(120) 4.6	(113) 4.8		(14) 10.4	(23) 6.7	(20) 5.4	(16) 4.1	(24) 3.3	(16) 3.7
13.0	8.4	8.2		22.1	10.9	8.1	6.6	7.0	5.2
2.0	2.5	2.5	% Officers', Directors' Owners' Comp/Sales		3.5	2.6	3.3		
(46) 3.6	(51) 4.1	(53) 3.8			(11) 3.9	(12) 3.1	(12) 4.1		
7.0	8.0	6.9			7.0	7.1	6.7		
1315201M	2149817M	1919544M	Net Sales ($)	7713M	55614M	86136M	151285M	424805M	1193991M
1030014M	1873594M	1411431M	Total Assets ($)	23272M	37380M	72078M	86765M	206147M	985789M

© RMA 2007

M = $ thousand   MM = $ million
See Pages 11 through 21 for Explanation of Ratios and Data

EDUCATIONAL SERVICES

Current Data Sorted by Assets

Comparative Historical Data

0-500M	500M-2MM	2-10MM	10-50MM	50-100MM	100-250MM	Type of Statement			
33	78	290	438	126	72	Unqualified		625	631
2	17	49	16	1		Reviewed		51	53
6	11	28	6	1		Compiled		45	153
22	15	22				Tax Returns		22	36
24	52	87	63	17	4	Other		216	200
	1,369 (4/1-9/30/06)		111 (10/1/06-3/31/07)					4/1/02-3/31/03	4/1/03-3/31/04
								ALL	ALL
87	173	476	523	145	76	**NUMBER OF STATEMENTS**		959	1073
%	%	%	%	%	%	**ASSETS**		%	%
34.0	27.0	21.9	21.7	16.8	20.6	Cash & Equivalents		22.3	22.0
13.9	11.4	5.9	4.9	4.3	4.6	Trade Receivables (net)		5.9	6.1
.1	.1	.3	.2	.2	.2	Inventory		.2	.3
8.9	5.5	3.8	3.1	4.9	4.8	All Other Current		3.9	6.2
56.9	44.1	31.9	29.9	26.2	30.1	Total Current		32.3	34.5
30.8	46.6	58.2	57.1	56.1	51.5	Fixed Assets (net)		52.7	53.7
3.0	2.2	.5	.6	1.2	1.0	Intangibles (net)		.6	.7
9.3	7.2	9.5	12.4	16.5	17.4	All Other Non-Current		14.3	11.0
100.0	100.0	100.0	100.0	100.0	100.0	Total		100.0	100.0
						LIABILITIES			
7.3	6.4	2.9	1.5	1.3	1.6	Notes Payable-Short Term		3.3	2.9
2.5	2.8	2.4	2.0	1.9	2.0	Cur. Mat.-L.T.D.		1.4	1.7
16.1	6.1	2.5	2.6	1.8	2.6	Trade Payables		3.3	3.7
.2	.1	.1	.1	.0	.3	Income Taxes Payable		.1	.1
36.5	14.1	11.2	8.5	5.9	6.3	All Other Current		12.1	11.5
62.6	29.5	19.1	14.7	10.9	12.8	Total Current		20.1	19.9
18.6	23.7	28.6	28.4	34.8	36.8	Long-Term Debt		23.6	23.6
.0	.1	.0	.0	.0	.0	Deferred Taxes		.0	.1
11.7	5.5	5.9	4.5	4.0	3.4	All Other Non-Current		6.2	6.9
7.0	41.1	46.4	52.4	50.2	46.9	Net Worth		51.6	49.6
100.0	100.0	100.0	100.0	100.0	100.0	Total Liabilties & Net Worth		100.0	100.0
						INCOME DATA			
100.0	100.0	100.0	100.0	100.0	100.0	Net Sales		100.0	100.0
						Gross Profit			
98.7	94.9	93.2	91.7	90.6	92.9	Operating Expenses		94.8	94.1
1.3	5.1	6.8	8.3	9.4	7.1	Operating Profit		5.2	5.9
.5	1.8	1.7	.8	.9	.9	All Other Expenses (net)		2.9	1.2
.8	3.3	5.1	7.5	8.6	6.2	Profit Before Taxes		2.3	4.7
						RATIOS			
2.6	4.0	3.9	5.1	6.1	4.7			4.2	4.7
1.3	1.4	1.8	2.1	2.2	2.4	Current		1.9	1.8
.7	.7	.9	1.1	1.1	1.3			.9	1.0
2.5	3.4	3.5	4.6	4.8	3.4			3.6	3.6
1.0	1.2	1.5	1.7	1.8	1.9	Quick		1.6	1.4
.4	.6	.7	.9	.9	1.0			.7	.7
0 UND	0 UND	1 264.5	2 233.4	2 216.3	1 288.8		1 327.9	1 404.3
3 143.1	5 73.9	6 56.3	9 41.2	10 36.2	7 53.8	Sales/Receivables	6 62.0	6 60.7
12 29.5	22 16.8	23 16.0	33 10.9	40 9.1	39 9.3		24 15.4	24 14.9
						Cost of Sales/Inventory			
						Cost of Sales/Payables			
12.2	5.2	3.2	2.0	1.7	1.9			3.1	2.8
61.4	22.2	8.5	6.1	5.9	4.6	Sales/Working Capital		8.5	8.8
-29.4	-19.7	-34.0	37.9	58.5	14.1			-50.7	932.2
	14.5	5.3	5.9	7.0	6.7	8.7		5.6	7.4
(41) 2.3	(109) 2.0	(366) 2.2	(422) 2.9	(109) 2.8	(62) 2.4	EBIT/Interest	(635) 1.8	(722) 2.2
-.2	-.1	.6	1.1	1.5	1.3		-.3	.4
								6.5	3.3
						Net Profit + Depr., Dep., Amort./Cur. Mat. L/T/D	(13) 2.3	(16) 2.2
								2.1	.5
.2	.3	.7	.7	.6	.5			.6	.6
.8	1.2	1.3	1.1	1.0	1.4	Fixed/Worth		1.0	1.0
UND	3.3	2.5	1.9	2.5	2.4			1.8	2.0
.5	.5	.5	.4	.4	.3			.4	.4
1.8	1.5	1.1	.9	.8	1.7	Debt/Worth		.8	.9
-49.7	3.6	2.7	2.1	3.3	3.0			1.8	2.3
57.5	34.7	17.8	13.7	13.2	12.5	% Profit Before Taxes/Tangible Net Worth		12.4	13.8
(65) 11.9	(154) 15.5	(446) 6.5	(508) 5.8	(136) 6.4	(74) 6.4		(911) 2.8	(1026) 4.2
-8.5	-2.4	-1.0	.8	2.2	.4			-3.9	-2.0
19.7	13.0	7.5	6.4	6.2	5.0	% Profit Before Taxes/Total Assets		5.7	6.5
5.5	5.4	2.8	3.1	3.5	2.4			1.5	1.9
-12.0	-2.1	-.7	.4	.8	.4			-2.1	-1.2
132.0	20.1	3.0	1.4	1.2	1.7	Sales/Net Fixed Assets		2.6	3.2
26.0	4.8	1.1	.9	.8	.9			1.1	1.1
8.0	1.5	.7	.6	.6	.6			.7	.7
8.7	3.0	1.1	.7	.7	1.0	Sales/Total Assets		1.2	1.4
4.8	1.9	.7	.5	.4	.5			.6	.7
2.6	.9	.5	.4	.3	.3			.4	.4
.7	1.5	2.7	3.6	3.7	2.5	% Depr., Dep., Amort./Sales		3.0	3.1
(50) 1.5	(127) 2.6	(390) 4.4	(456) 5.4	(115) 5.6	(54) 4.9		(712) 4.9	(794) 4.9
2.9	4.3	6.1	7.4	7.5	6.8			7.0	6.9
6.4	3.7	3.6	5.6	3.8		% Officers', Directors' Owners' Comp/Sales		2.9	2.9
(26) 9.6	(34) 5.7	(59) 6.5	(39) 8.0	(14) 10.9			(123) 6.8	(144) 6.6
12.0	11.5	14.5	18.5	19.3				16.4	15.0
120407M	473880M	2579517M	8710870M	5818997M	6997019M	Net Sales ($)		14459644M	15047425M
23287M	208036M	2585415M	12620904M	10328911M	10740341M	Total Assets ($)		21018518M	21228903M

M = $ thousand   MM = $ million
See Pages 11 through 21 for Explanation of Ratios and Data

Comparative Historical Data | Current Data Sorted by Sales

			Type of Statement						
687	730	1037	Unqualified	23	149	140	251	266	208
44	57	85	Reviewed	4	31	13	27	9	1
36	36	52	Compiled	8	24	9	8	2	1
40	36	59	Tax Returns	22	27	4	5	1	
202	313	247	Other	27	71	36	46	44	23
4/1/04-3/31/05 ALL	4/1/05-3/31/06 ALL	4/1/06-3/31/07 ALL		0-1MM	1,369 (4/1-9/30/06) 1-3MM	3-5MM	5-10MM	111 (10/1/06-3/31/07) 10-25MM	25MM & OVER
1009	1172	1480	**NUMBER OF STATEMENTS**	84	302	202	337	322	233
%	%	%	**ASSETS**	%	%	%	%	%	%
22.0	22.5	22.6	Cash & Equivalents	21.6	23.3	23.0	22.2	22.3	22.4
6.9	6.1	6.5	Trade Receivables (net)	6.5	7.0	7.2	5.6	5.3	7.9
.3	.2	.2	Inventory	.1	.1	.2	.2	.2	.3
4.3	4.2	4.2	All Other Current	5.8	4.3	3.6	3.4	4.5	4.9
33.4	33.1	33.4	Total Current	34.1	34.7	34.0	31.5	32.3	35.6
54.4	53.6	54.3	Fixed Assets (net)	58.2	56.3	54.8	55.0	51.7	52.2
.8	.9	1.0	Intangibles (net)	2.0	1.1	1.7	.4	.5	1.3
11.4	12.4	11.3	All Other Non-Current	5.8	7.8	9.4	13.1	15.6	11.0
100.0	100.0	100.0	Total	100.0	100.0	100.0	100.0	100.0	100.0
			LIABILITIES						
3.0	3.1	2.8	Notes Payable-Short Term	2.5	3.9	3.4	2.8	2.0	2.5
2.5	1.7	2.2	Cur. Mat.-L.T.D.	2.8	2.6	1.9	1.9	1.7	2.9
3.6	4.2	3.7	Trade Payables	4.1	4.8	4.8	2.6	2.9	3.8
.2	.2	.1	Income Taxes Payable	.0	.1	.0	.2	.1	.2
12.1	10.7	11.3	All Other Current	14.2	14.5	12.6	9.7	9.7	9.6
21.4	19.9	20.2	Total Current	23.6	26.0	22.7	17.2	16.4	18.9
26.7	25.5	28.4	Long-Term Debt	36.5	29.6	27.9	21.7	25.1	38.5
.2	.0	.0	Deferred Taxes	.0	.0	.0	.0	.0	.0
6.8	6.0	5.4	All Other Non-Current	6.1	6.0	6.9	5.7	4.2	4.3
45.0	48.7	46.0	Net Worth	33.8	38.5	42.6	55.3	54.3	38.3
100.0	100.0	100.0	Total Liabilities & Net Worth	100.0	100.0	100.0	100.0	100.0	100.0
			INCOME DATA						
100.0	100.0	100.0	Net Sales	100.0	100.0	100.0	100.0	100.0	100.0
			Gross Profit						
93.7	93.5	92.9	Operating Expenses	93.0	94.6	93.5	92.1	91.4	93.5
6.3	6.5	7.1	Operating Profit	7.0	5.4	6.5	7.9	8.6	6.5
.6	1.0	1.2	All Other Expenses (net)	5.0	2.2	1.1	.4	.2	1.1
5.7	5.5	5.9	Profit Before Taxes	2.1	3.2	5.4	7.6	8.4	5.4
			RATIOS						
3.9	4.8	4.3		5.7	4.0	4.3	4.8	4.6	3.4
1.8	1.9	1.9	Current	2.2	1.5	1.6	2.1	2.1	2.0
.9	.9	.9		.7	.6	.9	.9	1.1	1.3
3.5	4.3	3.9		4.0	3.6	4.1	4.4	4.2	2.7
1.5 (1171)	1.6	1.6	Quick	1.5	1.2	1.5	1.7	1.7	1.6
.7	.7	.7		.6	.5	.8	.8	.9	1.0
1 296.3	1 300.3	1 316.8		0 UND	0 UND	2 201.6	2 191.7	1 269.6	2 237.8
7 51.7	7 54.1	7 53.6	Sales/Receivables	3 138.1	4 83.5	7 55.4	9 42.7	8 48.0	13 27.7
27 13.3	25 14.5	28 13.0		16 22.6	18 20.3	32 11.5	32 11.3	31 11.8	38 9.7
			Cost of Sales/Inventory						
			Cost of Sales/Payables						
3.5	3.0	2.8		2.8	3.4	2.8	2.5	2.2	3.5
9.6	8.8	8.3	Sales/Working Capital	10.6	18.2	8.0	7.5	6.4	7.6
-72.7	-68.3	-88.6		-21.6	-14.1	-44.5	-56.2	51.1	23.0
9.0	7.8	6.7		4.6	4.5	6.4	9.0	7.5	6.0
(702) 2.7	(821) 2.5 (1109)	2.6	EBIT/Interest	(49) 1.6	(216) 1.6 (148)	2.9 (256)	3.3 (247)	3.0 (193)	2.5
.7	.8	.9		.0	.1	.9	1.1	1.3	1.2
3.9	6.7	12.0	Net Profit + Depr., Dep.,						
(10) .8	(13) 4.8 (14)	3.4	Amort./Cur. Mat. L/T/D						
-.5	2.3	1.7							
.6	.6	.6		.7	.7	.7	.6	.6	.7
1.1	1.1	1.1	Fixed/Worth	1.6	1.5	1.3	1.0	.9	1.5
2.5	2.1	2.3		5.4	3.4	2.4	1.6	1.6	2.9
.4	.4	.4		.3	.5	.5	.3	.4	.7
1.0	.9	1.0	Debt/Worth	1.7	1.3	1.4	.7	.7	1.9
2.6	2.3	2.7		5.7	3.8	2.9	1.6	1.7	4.0
17.3	16.1	16.8	% Profit Before Taxes/Tangible	23.0	17.1	20.2	16.1	13.8	16.9
(938) 6.3	(1099) 5.9 (1383)	6.5	Net Worth	(71) 11.3	(271) 5.2 (191)	7.5 (322)	5.5 (312)	6.5 (216)	8.7
-.1	.0	.4		-5.6	-3.3	.8	1.0	1.1	2.2
8.1	7.3	7.6		10.6	7.8	7.3	8.8	7.2	6.3
2.6	2.8	3.1	% Profit Before Taxes/Total Assets	2.2	2.1	3.1	3.0	3.2	3.6
-.5	-.2	-.1		-2.4	-2.1	.2	.3	.6	.8
3.4	3.3	3.1		10.9	8.3	3.1	2.1	1.7	3.2
1.1	1.1	1.1	Sales/Net Fixed Assets	1.5	1.3	1.2	1.0	1.0	1.4
.7	.7	.7		.6	.7	.6	.7	.6	.8
1.4	1.4	1.2		2.1	2.2	1.3	.9	.9	1.4
.7	.6	.7	Sales/Total Assets	.9	.7	.6	.6	.5	.9
.4	.4	.4		.3	.5	.4	.4	.4	.5
3.1	2.9	2.7		1.7	2.1	3.2	3.2	3.4	2.1
(763) 4.7	(934) 4.7 (1192)	4.6	% Depr., Dep., Amort./Sales	(61) 4.3	(226) 4.1 (172)	4.5 (303)	5.4 (275)	5.0 (155)	3.4
6.8	6.9	6.5		7.8	5.8	6.5	6.9	7.2	5.0
3.9	3.3	4.1	% Officers', Directors'	6.9	4.1	2.5	2.9	5.3	4.3
(100) 7.4	(142) 6.6 (177)	7.6	Owners' Comp/Sales	(22) 9.9	(41) 6.0 (25)	6.4 (35)	6.0 (30)	8.3 (24)	11.6
12.9	12.9	16.1		14.4	11.6	11.7	18.4	17.2	29.1
14375073M	17160586M	24700690M	Net Sales ($)	53134M	585964M	797538M	2439847M	5100421M	15723786M
20271047M	25161838M	36506894M	Total Assets ($)	107172M	950349M	1498153M	4773808M	10688380M	18489032M

M = $ thousand   MM = $ million
See Pages 11 through 21 for Explanation of Ratios and Data

Current Data Sorted by Assets   Comparative Historical Data

		3	8	13	6	7	Type of Statement		
		1		1			Unqualified	32	26
			1				Reviewed	1	2
				1			Compiled	2	3
							Tax Returns		1
1	2	2	2	4	2	2	Other	11	9
	45 (4/1-9/30/06)			8 (10/1/06-3/31/07)				4/1/02-3/31/03	4/1/03-3/31/04
0-500M	500M-2MM		2-10MM	10-50MM	50-100MM	100-250MM		ALL	ALL
1	6		11	18	8	9	NUMBER OF STATEMENTS	46	41
%	%		%	%	%	%	**ASSETS**	%	%
			28.3	14.3			Cash & Equivalents	19.0	16.3
			13.4	10.6			Trade Receivables (net)	12.3	15.1
			1.9	1.1			Inventory	1.0	1.5
			3.3	3.0			All Other Current	4.2	5.8
			46.9	29.0			Total Current	36.5	38.7
			43.3	49.5			Fixed Assets (net)	46.4	45.1
			.3	1.7			Intangibles (net)	5.6	2.8
			9.6	19.8			All Other Non-Current	11.5	13.4
			100.0	100.0			Total	100.0	100.0
							LIABILITIES		
			1.2	.6			Notes Payable-Short Term	.7	.7
			1.7	2.8			Cur. Mat.-L.T.D.	2.6	2.4
			7.1	5.3			Trade Payables	3.7	4.1
			.0	.7			Income Taxes Payable	.4	.1
			9.6	14.2			All Other Current	15.7	15.8
			19.6	23.6			Total Current	23.1	23.1
			23.1	29.2			Long-Term Debt	15.7	12.7
			1.1	.3			Deferred Taxes	.1	.1
			2.9	1.4			All Other Non-Current	4.7	7.3
			53.3	45.5			Net Worth	56.4	56.7
			100.0	100.0			Total Liabilties & Net Worth	100.0	100.0
							INCOME DATA		
			100.0	100.0			Net Sales	100.0	100.0
							Gross Profit		
			94.6	95.7			Operating Expenses	90.4	91.1
			5.4	4.3			Operating Profit	9.6	8.9
			1.4	-.7			All Other Expenses (net)	2.5	1.0
			4.0	4.9			Profit Before Taxes	7.1	7.9
							RATIOS		
			12.0	2.4				3.7	3.8
			1.8	1.2			Current	1.8	2.0
			1.3	.7				1.0	1.1
			9.2	2.0				2.7	3.1
			1.7	1.0			Quick	1.4	1.6
			1.0	.6				.7	.9
			14 25.4	10 37.7				5 75.1	8 46.7
			23 16.2	19 19.0			Sales/Receivables	16 23.4	22 16.7
			88 4.1	36 10.1				35 10.5	66 5.5
							Cost of Sales/Inventory		
							Cost of Sales/Payables		
			4.5	5.6				3.3	3.3
			7.8	18.7			Sales/Working Capital	9.0	8.2
			28.7	-16.6				NM	38.7
				7.4				13.7	20.4
				(16) 4.0			EBIT/Interest	(33) 6.3	(31) 7.3
				1.9				3.2	2.2
							Net Profit + Depr., Dep., Amort./Cur. Mat. L/T/D		
			.5	.8				.7	.7
			.8	1.0			Fixed/Worth	.9	.8
			1.3	1.8				1.2	1.2
			.4	.5				.4	.4
			1.1	1.3			Debt/Worth	.9	.7
			2.0	3.7				2.3	1.8
			57.5	35.8				40.1	37.2
			3.9	10.4			% Profit Before Taxes/Tangible Net Worth	(44) 12.7	18.9
			-6.7	3.3				3.4	2.5
			19.3	15.7				13.4	14.4
			2.0	4.1			% Profit Before Taxes/Total Assets	5.6	5.1
			-3.0	2.2				2.7	.9
			8.2	5.0				6.2	7.4
			2.9	1.7			Sales/Net Fixed Assets	1.6	3.2
			1.7	.9				.9	1.1
			2.3	1.5				1.4	2.0
			1.2	.8			Sales/Total Assets	.9	1.0
			.2	.5				.5	.6
			1.6	1.8				3.3	2.3
			(10) 4.0	(17) 2.6			% Depr., Dep., Amort./Sales	(38) 4.5	(38) 3.9
			7.5	5.5				5.4	5.5
							% Officers', Directors' Owners' Comp/Sales		
2079M	15412M		75202M	536856M	435939M	1089633M	Net Sales ($)	1351832M	1181062M
302M	7037M		52009M	538238M	579460M	1534310M	Total Assets ($)	1731223M	1409686M

© RMA 2007

M = $ thousand   MM = $ million
See Pages 11 through 21 for Explanation of Ratios and Data

Comparative Historical Data / Current Data Sorted by Sales

39	32	37	Type of Statement	1	2	5	3	8	18
			Unqualified						
5	4	2	Reviewed						
	2	1	Compiled		1			1	
4	11	13	Tax Returns	1					
4/1/04-	4/1/05-	4/1/06-	Other	1	1	1	1	4	5
3/31/05	3/31/06	3/31/07			45 (4/1-9/30/06)			8 (10/1/06-3/31/07)	
ALL	ALL	ALL		0-1MM	1-3MM	3-5MM	5-10MM	10-25MM	25MM & OVER
48	49	53	NUMBER OF STATEMENTS	3	4	6	4	13	23
%	%	%	ASSETS	%	%	%	%	%	%
19.2	19.6	19.2	Cash & Equivalents					11.8	17.6
13.4	14.8	12.6	Trade Receivables (net)					11.4	10.6
1.1	.9	1.0	Inventory					.9	.9
4.1	4.1	3.2	All Other Current					1.8	3.3
37.9	39.4	36.0	Total Current					25.9	32.4
46.8	46.2	46.2	Fixed Assets (net)					48.2	48.2
2.7	.8	1.6	Intangibles (net)					1.7	2.4
12.7	13.5	16.2	All Other Non-Current					24.2	17.0
100.0	100.0	100.0	Total					100.0	100.0
			LIABILITIES						
1.9	1.3	.7	Notes Payable-Short Term					1.3	.4
1.7	1.7	2.5	Cur. Mat.-L.T.D.					2.5	2.2
3.5	4.8	4.5	Trade Payables					4.7	4.2
.3	.3	.3	Income Taxes Payable					.0	.6
14.0	11.6	11.4	All Other Current					12.5	12.9
21.3	19.6	19.3	Total Current					21.1	20.4
18.1	26.9	29.8	Long-Term Debt					25.8	23.0
.1	.1	.3	Deferred Taxes					1.1	.1
6.3	5.2	3.8	All Other Non-Current					3.8	2.8
54.2	48.1	46.7	Net Worth					48.3	53.8
100.0	100.0	100.0	Total Liabilties & Net Worth					100.0	100.0
			INCOME DATA						
100.0	100.0	100.0	Net Sales					100.0	100.0
			Gross Profit						
84.8	90.9	93.0	Operating Expenses					92.0	93.9
15.2	9.1	7.0	Operating Profit					8.0	6.1
-.3	1.7	.1	All Other Expenses (net)					-.6	-1.5
15.5	7.4	6.9	Profit Before Taxes					8.6	7.5
			RATIOS						
3.6	4.0	4.1	Current					4.0	3.2
1.6	2.1	1.8						1.5	1.7
1.0	1.3	1.1						.7	1.1
3.3	3.3	3.7	Quick					3.2	2.5
1.4	1.9	1.7						1.1	1.6
.9	1.0	.9						.6	.9

	11	33.5	10	38.2	12	31.0	Sales/Receivables	17	21.3	9	42.1
	28	12.9	27	13.7	23	16.2		22	16.5	20	18.3
	74	5.0	85	4.3	75	4.9		49	7.5	41	8.8

39 hist			Row	10-25MM	25MM & OVER
			Cost of Sales/Inventory		
			Cost of Sales/Payables		
3.3	2.7	3.5	Sales/Working Capital	4.6	3.2
7.5	5.7	7.8		11.4	8.1
269.7	23.6	34.1		-27.1	24.1
28.3	16.4	10.0	EBIT/Interest	8.1	11.8
(37) 8.1	(38) 4.9	(43) 4.0		(10) 4.1	(22) 5.9
3.4	3.1	2.0		1.8	3.0
			Net Profit + Depr., Dep., Amort./Cur. Mat. L/T/D		
.7	.6	.7	Fixed/Worth	.7	.8
.9	.8	.9		1.0	.9
1.4	1.4	1.3		2.0	1.2
.3	.5	.4	Debt/Worth	.4	.4
.7	1.1	1.1		1.8	1.1
2.4	2.6	2.1		2.8	1.6
33.7	29.0	38.1	% Profit Before Taxes/Tangible Net Worth	58.2	33.7
(46) 18.0	(48) 10.5	(52) 9.0		9.8	10.5
5.8	3.3	3.5		3.6	4.3
17.9	12.5	13.5	% Profit Before Taxes/Total Assets	17.4	12.2
6.5	5.4	4.3		5.2	4.9
2.6	1.3	2.0		2.2	3.1
7.2	6.2	5.4	Sales/Net Fixed Assets	3.9	3.4
1.7	2.1	2.2		2.2	1.5
1.1	1.0	.9		.8	1.0
1.5	1.8	1.8	Sales/Total Assets	1.6	1.4
.8	1.0	.9		1.0	.7
.5	.5	.5		.4	.5
2.2	2.0	2.0	% Depr., Dep., Amort./Sales	1.6	2.3
(42) 3.7	(43) 3.9	(49) 3.7		3.3	(22) 3.9
6.5	5.3	5.6		6.4	5.1
			% Officers', Directors' Owners' Comp/Sales		

1452489M	1365997M	2155121M	Net Sales ($)	1690M	7556M	22140M	31227M	236368M	1856140M
1766555M	1553238M	2711356M	Total Assets ($)	7029M	8788M	15223M	51426M	355157M	2273733M

Current Data Sorted by Assets   ### Comparative Historical Data

0-500M	500M-2MM	2-10MM	10-50MM	50-100MM	100-250MM		4/1/02-3/31/03 ALL	4/1/03-3/31/04 ALL
						Type of Statement		
2	13	50	183	164	185	Unqualified	494	479
	1	4		1	1	Reviewed	6	3
		1		1		Compiled	4	56
		1				Tax Returns	2	2
2	1	12	39	19	24	Other	91	92
	649 (4/1-9/30/06)		54 (10/1/06-3/31/07)					
4	15	68	222	185	209	**NUMBER OF STATEMENTS**	597	632
%	%	%	%	%	%	**ASSETS**	%	%
	26.1	21.7	15.5	12.8	16.4	Cash & Equivalents	14.4	15.0
	24.9	11.2	6.2	3.8	3.9	Trade Receivables (net)	5.1	5.6
	4.3	.9	.4	.5	.3	Inventory	.5	.6
	1.9	4.0	3.6	2.6	3.6	All Other Current	4.3	7.5
	57.2	37.8	25.8	19.7	24.3	Total Current	24.3	28.7
	30.0	43.1	50.5	48.3	44.4	Fixed Assets (net)	48.1	47.0
	3.9	2.9	1.3	1.5	1.2	Intangibles (net)	.7	.7
	8.9	16.3	22.4	30.5	30.0	All Other Non-Current	26.8	23.5
	100.0	100.0	100.0	100.0	100.0	Total	100.0	100.0
						LIABILITIES		
	2.9	3.2	2.5	1.3	.5	Notes Payable-Short Term	1.6	2.0
	2.8	2.2	1.9	1.1	1.0	Cur. Mat.-L.T.D.	1.2	1.2
	5.4	4.9	3.4	2.6	2.3	Trade Payables	3.0	3.0
	.0	.3	.0	.1	.0	Income Taxes Payable	.1	.1
	16.6	19.5	6.0	4.1	5.1	All Other Current	6.3	6.4
	27.6	30.1	13.9	9.1	8.8	Total Current	12.2	12.8
	15.6	15.4	26.7	26.5	23.2	Long-Term Debt	22.3	22.1
	.3	.1	.0	.0	.1	Deferred Taxes	.1	.1
	9.3	3.1	4.2	3.4	3.7	All Other Non-Current	4.1	4.4
	47.2	51.3	55.2	61.0	64.2	Net Worth	61.3	60.6
	100.0	100.0	100.0	100.0	100.0	Total Liabilities & Net Worth	100.0	100.0
						INCOME DATA		
	100.0	100.0	100.0	100.0	100.0	Net Sales	100.0	100.0
						Gross Profit		
	89.9	91.0	91.5	90.9	89.3	Operating Expenses	97.1	96.1
	10.1	9.0	8.5	9.1	10.7	Operating Profit	2.9	3.9
	1.0	.1	1.1	-.6	-2.2	All Other Expenses (net)	4.6	1.5
	9.1	8.9	7.4	9.7	12.9	Profit Before Taxes	-1.7	2.4
						RATIOS		
	7.3	2.8	3.8	4.0	4.3	Current	3.7	5.0
	2.3	1.7	1.7	1.9	2.0		1.9	2.1
	1.4	.9	.9	1.0	1.1		1.0	1.1
	7.3	2.7	3.1	3.3	3.6	Quick	3.1	3.1
	1.9	1.3	1.2	1.5	1.6		1.4	1.4
	1.1	.7	.5	.7	.8		.7	.7
	4 103.1	2 184.5	8 43.2	9 42.0	7 51.7	Sales/Receivables	8 47.1	8 47.4
	14 25.3	13 27.9	17 20.9	19 19.4	17 22.0		18 20.1	19 19.7
	39 9.3	30 12.3	35 10.3	33 11.1	39 9.5		41 8.9	40 9.2
						Cost of Sales/Inventory		
						Cost of Sales/Payables		
	3.1	2.7	2.7	2.9	2.1	Sales/Working Capital	2.5	1.8
	8.6	13.1	10.0	7.7	6.4		7.6	5.9
	52.9	-93.9	-35.5	-229.1	50.1		110.3	45.8
		8.3	9.4	7.7	10.0	EBIT/Interest	4.2	6.4
		(46) 4.1	(172) 2.9	(145) 4.3	(176) 5.2		(437) 1.3	(486) 2.1
		.7	1.2	2.3	2.5		-1.5	-.2
		7.5				Net Profit + Depr., Dep.,	64.1	14.8
		(10) 4.9				Amort./Cur. Mat. L/T/D	(13) 7.6	(15) 2.7
		2.0					3.0	.7
	.1	.4	.6	.6	.5	Fixed/Worth	.5	.5
	.4	.8	.9	.8	.7		.8	.8
	5.1	1.3	1.6	1.2	1.0		1.1	1.1
	.4	.3	.4	.4	.3	Debt/Worth	.3	.3
	.8	.6	.7	.6	.5		.5	.6
	18.5	1.7	1.5	1.1	.9		1.0	1.0
	76.6	23.5	14.9	11.6	11.9	% Profit Before Taxes/Tangible	5.5	7.5
	(13) 19.7	(62) 7.7	(214) 5.8	(182) 6.9	(206) 7.1	Net Worth	(591) .3	(623) 2.4
	-10.0	-.5	1.4	2.7	3.2		-4.8	-1.7
	23.7	10.8	8.2	7.3	7.4	% Profit Before Taxes/Total	3.2	4.8
	7.5	4.7	3.2	4.2	4.3	Assets	.2	1.5
	.4	-.5	.8	1.3	1.9		-3.0	-1.1
	21.2	9.1	2.0	1.3	1.2	Sales/Net Fixed Assets	1.4	1.5
	9.7	2.4	1.1	1.0	.9		.9	1.0
	3.2	1.0	.8	.8	.7		.7	.7
	4.0	1.3	.8	.6	.6	Sales/Total Assets	.7	.7
	2.0	.9	.6	.5	.4		.5	.5
	1.1	.5	.4	.4	.3		.3	.3
	1.0	2.1	3.8	4.7	4.5	% Depr., Dep., Amort./Sales	4.4	4.3
	(12) 2.9	(57) 4.1	(204) 5.2	(169) 5.7	(193) 5.6		(539) 6.0	(570) 5.8
	4.0	5.7	6.6	7.3	7.3		7.8	7.8
			5.8	3.9	5.1	% Officers', Directors'	5.0	4.7
			(23) 16.5	(25) 8.9	(24) 8.4	Owners' Comp/Sales	(74) 11.8	(73) 11.5
			28.1	16.3	14.6		24.3	22.9
8667M	50141M	419107M	4333913M	6860578M	14494971M	Net Sales ($)	19271746M	20472766M
863M	16116M	373656M	6365093M	13492204M	32235518M	Total Assets ($)	42748018M	45662964M

M = $ thousand   MM = $ million
See Pages 11 through 21 for Explanation of Ratios and Data

Comparative Historical Data | Current Data Sorted by Sales

Type of Statement									
	473	503	597	Unqualified	7	21	25	53	148	343
	3	4	6	Reviewed			2	1	2	1
	3	5	2	Compiled			1			1
	4	5	1	Tax Returns						
	81	150	97	Other	1 2	4	5	13	27	46

	4/1/04-3/31/05 ALL	4/1/05-3/31/06 ALL	4/1/06-3/31/07 ALL		0-1MM	1-3MM	3-5MM	5-10MM	10-25MM	25MM & OVER
						649 (4/1-9/30/06)			54 (10/1/06-3/31/07)	
564	667	703	**NUMBER OF STATEMENTS**	10	25	33	67	177	391

%	%	%	**ASSETS**	%	%	%	%	%	%
15.7	15.8	15.9	Cash & Equivalents	38.4	18.5	20.2	15.1	13.9	15.8
6.2	5.3	5.8	Trade Receivables (net)	3.6	15.9	9.0	6.9	5.4	4.9
.5	.6	.5	Inventory	.1	.1	.8	.9	.6	.4
3.8	3.8	3.3	All Other Current	.5	3.7	2.8	3.7	3.6	3.3
26.1	25.5	25.6	Total Current	42.6	38.1	32.8	26.7	23.6	24.5
46.9	47.7	47.0	Fixed Assets (net)	34.3	49.4	48.7	46.3	47.5	46.9
1.3	.8	1.5	Intangibles (net)	6.0	.6	1.2	2.2	1.1	1.6
25.7	26.1	25.9	All Other Non-Current	17.1	11.9	17.3	24.8	27.8	27.0
100.0	100.0	100.0	Total	100.0	100.0	100.0	100.0	100.0	100.0

			LIABILITIES						
2.0	2.1	1.7	Notes Payable-Short Term	2.2	1.9	4.9	2.5	2.4	.9
1.2	1.2	1.5	Cur. Mat.-L.T.D.	1.9	2.3	2.5	1.4	1.9	1.1
3.2	3.0	3.1	Trade Payables	2.5	3.9	3.7	2.7	3.2	3.0
.1	.1	.1	Income Taxes Payable	.0	.7	.0	.1	.0	.1
7.4	6.6	7.4	All Other Current	6.5	13.3	15.4	12.7	7.6	5.4
13.9	13.0	13.7	Total Current	13.1	22.1	26.5	19.4	15.2	10.5
23.7	24.6	24.4	Long-Term Debt	22.0	34.0	19.7	28.1	22.9	24.3
.0	.0	.1	Deferred Taxes	.0	.0	.1	.0	.0	.1
3.9	4.1	4.4	All Other Non-Current	11.1	.7	4.1	6.4	3.8	4.3
58.4	58.2	57.5	Net Worth	53.8	43.1	49.6	46.0	58.0	60.8
100.0	100.0	100.0	Total Liabilities & Net Worth	100.0	100.0	100.0	100.0	100.0	100.0

			INCOME DATA						
100.0	100.0	100.0	Net Sales	100.0	100.0	100.0	100.0	100.0	100.0
			Gross Profit						
91.7	92.2	90.7	Operating Expenses	77.5	84.3	90.9	88.4	91.4	91.5
8.3	7.8	9.3	Operating Profit	22.5	15.7	9.1	11.6	8.6	8.5
-1.7	.0	-.4	All Other Expenses (net)	2.4	5.1	4.0	3.8	-.7	-1.8
10.0	7.8	9.7	Profit Before Taxes	20.1	10.7	5.0	7.8	9.3	10.3

			RATIOS						
3.8	4.1	3.9	Current	60.3	7.4	2.5	4.5	3.9	3.8
1.9	1.9	1.8		6.4	1.6	1.5	1.9	1.7	1.9
1.0	1.0	1.0		1.3	1.0	.9	.8	.8	1.1
3.1	3.1	3.2	Quick	59.8	7.3	2.4	4.2	3.3	3.1
1.4	1.5	1.4		6.3	1.6	1.3	1.2	1.2	1.6
.7	.7	.7		1.3	.7	.5	.6	.6	.8
8 45.0	8 44.5	7 51.1	Sales/Receivables	0 UND	1 303.9	2 171.0	4 89.9	9 40.1	9 41.8
18 20.0	17 20.9	17 21.2		4 81.6	13 28.8	14 25.3	10 36.9	19 19.7	18 20.3
38 9.5	38 9.7	36 10.2		15 24.9	60 6.1	25 14.5	38 9.6	41 9.0	35 10.3
			Cost of Sales/Inventory						
			Cost of Sales/Payables						
2.8	2.6	2.7	Sales/Working Capital	.4	1.1	3.3	2.5	2.5	2.9
7.4	7.1	8.0		5.8	3.1	13.2	10.3	9.2	7.4
NM	-157.8	-171.2		38.3	-188.5	NM	-18.9	-37.0	65.7
12.2	8.1	9.1	EBIT/Interest		4.4	8.7	9.5	8.7	9.8
(446) 5.1	(514) 3.9	(548) 4.3		(12) .9	(23) 4.5	(46) 3.2	(139) 2.9	(324) 4.9	
2.1	1.4	1.9			-2.1	.5	.3	1.5	2.4
76.2	7.9	8.1	Net Profit + Depr., Dep., Amort./Cur. Mat. L/T/D						7.5
(15) 6.6	(18) 3.6	(25) 2.4						(14)	4.7
2.1	1.9	1.1							2.3
.6	.6	.5	Fixed/Worth	.2	.1	.4	.5	.5	.6
.8	.8	.8		1.0	.8	.8	.8	.8	.8
1.2	1.2	1.2		NM	4.2	1.6	2.0	1.2	1.1
.4	.3	.3	Debt/Worth	.0	.2	.4	.2	.4	.3
.6	.6	.6		.7	.6	.9	.7	.6	.6
1.1	1.2	1.2		NM	5.2	1.7	2.6	1.1	1.1
13.6	10.6	13.1	% Profit Before Taxes/Tangible Net Worth		18.0	16.2	16.7	11.9	13.2
(551) 7.6	(648) 5.2	(677) 6.9		(21) 1.5	(31) 7.4	(58) 3.7	(173) 5.4	(386) 7.6	
2.8	1.1	2.4			-1.8	1.4	-2.1	1.9	3.5
8.0	6.0	7.8	% Profit Before Taxes/Total Assets	20.3	5.4	7.9	7.8	7.5	7.8
4.6	3.2	4.1		4.1	.4	5.4	2.2	3.1	4.6
1.4	.6	1.3		-1.0	-.6	.3	-1.5	1.1	1.9
1.7	1.5	1.7	Sales/Net Fixed Assets	19.5	12.3	8.6	2.6	1.6	1.5
1.1	1.0	1.0		3.5	1.2	1.3	1.1	1.0	1.0
.8	.7	.8		.3	.5	.8	.7	.7	.8
.7	.7	.7	Sales/Total Assets	1.5	1.1	1.3	.9	.7	.7
.5	.5	.5		.7	.5	.6	.6	.5	.5
.4	.3	.4		.1	.2	.4	.3	.3	.4
4.0	4.3	4.1	% Depr., Dep., Amort./Sales		3.0	2.1	2.8	3.9	4.5
(520) 5.4	(599) 5.7	(639) 5.4		(21) 5.6	(29) 5.1	(61) 5.5	(165) 5.3	(356) 5.5	
7.1	7.5	6.9			9.9	7.0	7.0	7.2	6.6
5.2	5.1	5.1	% Officers', Directors' Owners' Comp/Sales					5.8	3.6
(58) 13.0	(83) 10.9	(79) 8.8					(17)	10.3	(51) 8.8
23.6	25.3	20.7						22.3	27.3
19056381M	22732129M	26167377M	Net Sales ($)	5994M	50391M	129741M	511221M	3101976M	22368054M
37751960M	47955587M	52483450M	Total Assets ($)	18599M	263476M	257434M	1321193M	7710713M	42912035M

M = $ thousand   MM = $ million
See Pages 11 through 21 for Explanation of Ratios and Data

Current Data Sorted by Assets   Comparative Historical Data

Type of Statement	0-500M	500M-2MM	2-10MM	10-50MM	50-100MM	100-250MM	4/1/02-3/31/03 ALL	4/1/03-3/31/04 ALL
Unqualified	1	3	12	5	3		9	14
Reviewed			1					
Compiled		1		1			3	1
Tax Returns	2	2			2	2	2	2
Other		4	3				7	5
	29 (4/1-9/30/06)			13 (10/1/06-3/31/07)				
NUMBER OF STATEMENTS	3	10	16	6	5	2	21	22
	%	%	%	%	%	%	%	%
ASSETS								
Cash & Equivalents		15.0	21.2				26.4	26.9
Trade Receivables (net)		8.7	22.8				14.0	17.4
Inventory		5.3	.4				.6	.8
All Other Current		11.2	7.2				8.0	3.5
Total Current		40.2	51.7				49.1	48.6
Fixed Assets (net)		52.4	39.4				37.6	38.1
Intangibles (net)		3.8	.4				1.3	3.1
All Other Non-Current		3.6	8.4				12.0	10.1
Total		100.0	100.0				100.0	100.0
LIABILITIES								
Notes Payable-Short Term		25.4	3.0				6.5	7.2
Cur. Mat.-L.T.D.		1.5	1.2				1.0	1.1
Trade Payables		11.7	5.8				10.1	5.7
Income Taxes Payable		.1	.1				.4	.3
All Other Current		10.6	19.1				12.8	14.5
Total Current		49.3	29.2				30.8	28.8
Long-Term Debt		18.5	16.9				19.6	23.2
Deferred Taxes		.0	.1				.0	.1
All Other Non-Current		4.3	6.2				.5	5.1
Net Worth		27.9	47.5				49.0	42.8
Total Liabilties & Net Worth		100.0	100.0				100.0	100.0
INCOME DATA								
Net Sales		100.0	100.0				100.0	100.0
Gross Profit								
Operating Expenses		101.9	97.8				99.1	97.5
Operating Profit		-1.9	2.2				.9	2.5
All Other Expenses (net)		1.3	1.2				4.6	.3
Profit Before Taxes		-3.3	1.0				-3.7	2.2
RATIOS								
Current		1.2	3.5				5.1	2.5
		.6	1.5				1.6	1.7
		.3	1.0				1.0	1.0
Quick		.7	2.8				4.6	2.5
		.3	1.4				1.6	1.5
		.2	.9				.5	.8
Sales/Receivables		0 UND	3 135.4				0 UND	2 199.3
		1 565.4	31 11.7				11 32.5	24 15.5
		9 39.6	82 4.5				42 8.7	45 8.1
Cost of Sales/Inventory								
Cost of Sales/Payables								
Sales/Working Capital		39.3	3.4				4.5	6.3
		-35.1	10.9				12.0	14.1
		-9.4	UND				NM	NM
EBIT/Interest			9.1				8.4	9.5
		(14)	1.9				(15) .5	(16) 2.0
			.1				-3.6	-3.9
Net Profit + Depr., Dep., Amort./Cur. Mat. L/T/D								
Fixed/Worth		1.0	.2				.3	.3
		1.9	.9				.8	1.0
		-25.7	1.5				1.5	1.4
Debt/Worth		.7	.5				.3	.7
		3.4	1.1				.5	1.2
		-39.1	2.9				9.4	3.9
% Profit Before Taxes/Tangible Net Worth			25.1				15.4	75.3
		(15)	3.4				(19) -3.3	1.3
			-.2				-13.5	-10.6
% Profit Before Taxes/Total Assets		22.1	6.9				10.2	15.7
		.3	2.7				-1.6	.6
		-29.7	.0				-5.6	-5.7
Sales/Net Fixed Assets		22.9	40.0				23.3	24.1
		9.7	3.8				9.4	5.5
		4.2	1.0				1.1	1.9
Sales/Total Assets		5.7	1.7				3.5	3.5
		4.1	1.3				1.5	1.6
		1.7	.6				.5	.7
% Depr., Dep., Amort./Sales			1.3				.9	1.3
		(14)	2.0				(14) 2.5	(17) 2.6
			7.4				3.4	4.1
% Officers', Directors' Owners' Comp/Sales								
Net Sales ($)	2376M	37572M	163867M	54918M	337989M	1097771M	219363M	207068M
Total Assets ($)	621M	10175M	102330M	99055M	308107M	305834M	318923M	128655M

M = $ thousand   MM = $ million
See Pages 11 through 21 for Explanation of Ratios and Data

Comparative Historical Data / Current Data Sorted by Sales

Type of Statement	12	11	24		1	2	4	7	6	4
Unqualified										
Reviewed			1					1		
Compiled	2	1	2				2			
Tax Returns	2	3	4			1	1			
Other	5	6	11		2	1	1	1		4
	4/1/04-3/31/05 ALL	4/1/05-3/31/06 ALL	4/1/06-3/31/07 ALL		0-1MM	1-3MM	3-5MM	5-10MM	10-25MM	25MM & OVER
					29 (4/1-9/30/06)			13 (10/1/06-3/31/07)		
NUMBER OF STATEMENTS	21	21	42		3	7	8	8	7	8
	%	%	%		%	%	%	%	%	%
ASSETS										
Cash & Equivalents	13.7	20.7	17.0							
Trade Receivables (net)	27.9	14.4	14.2							
Inventory	.6	2.9	2.9							
All Other Current	3.8	4.0	7.7							
Total Current	46.0	42.1	41.8							
Fixed Assets (net)	37.6	43.4	41.1							
Intangibles (net)	2.5	.2	6.3							
All Other Non-Current	14.0	14.3	10.8							
Total	100.0	100.0	100.0							
LIABILITIES										
Notes Payable-Short Term	15.5	6.2	8.3							
Cur. Mat.-L.T.D.	.4	5.1	2.8							
Trade Payables	5.2	6.8	5.9							
Income Taxes Payable	.0	.0	.1							
All Other Current	10.2	12.7	14.8							
Total Current	31.4	30.8	31.8							
Long-Term Debt	13.1	20.6	19.1							
Deferred Taxes	1.5	1.7	.1							
All Other Non-Current	31.1	33.2	5.8							
Net Worth	23.0	13.8	43.2							
Total Liabilities & Net Worth	100.0	100.0	100.0							
INCOME DATA										
Net Sales	100.0	100.0	100.0							
Gross Profit										
Operating Expenses	101.3	92.2	97.9							
Operating Profit	-1.3	7.8	2.1							
All Other Expenses (net)	.5	2.7	1.3							
Profit Before Taxes	-1.8	5.1	.8							
RATIOS										
Current	3.2	6.3	2.9							
	1.5	1.4	1.2							
	1.0	.8	.7							
Quick	2.8	3.6	2.3							
	1.3	1.2	1.0							
	.8	.5	.4							
Sales/Receivables	1 561.7	0 UND	1 356.6							
	35 10.3	3 143.7	14 26.0							
	85 4.3	40 9.1	53 6.9							
Cost of Sales/Inventory										
Cost of Sales/Payables										
Sales/Working Capital	6.1	6.0	6.0							
	20.8	12.9	22.3							
	NM	-41.9	-37.2							
EBIT/Interest	2.9	5.5	11.7							
	(19) 1.4	(17) 3.4	(34) 1.8							
	-2.9	1.4	-2.4							
Net Profit + Depr., Dep., Amort./Cur. Mat. L/T/D										
Fixed/Worth	.1	.3	.2							
	.9	1.2	1.0							
	1.3	2.2	2.4							
Debt/Worth	.5	.5	.5							
	1.1	1.4	1.2							
	3.0	4.8	6.1							
% Profit Before Taxes/Tangible Net Worth	41.6	44.3	35.3							
	(20) 6.1	(19) 8.3	(36) 6.6							
	-12.7	1.6	-.5							
% Profit Before Taxes/Total Assets	8.3	9.1	12.5							
	2.7	2.1	1.6							
	-4.1	.5	-1.6							
Sales/Net Fixed Assets	23.9	40.3	33.7							
	5.7	7.2	5.4							
	1.2	1.4	1.7							
Sales/Total Assets	3.5	4.5	2.4							
	1.4	1.7	1.3							
	.7	.9	.8							
% Depr., Dep., Amort./Sales	1.4	1.1	1.3							
	(17) 3.7	(14) 2.5	(29) 2.6							
	9.1	6.9	4.6							
% Officers', Directors' Owners' Comp/Sales										
Net Sales ($)	293532M	93348M	1694493M		1082M	12369M	30192M	62414M	91211M	1497225M
Total Assets ($)	200559M	72412M	826122M		1248M	24730M	50171M	69414M	60336M	620223M

M = $ thousand   MM = $ million
See Pages 11 through 21 for Explanation of Ratios and Data

Current Data Sorted by Assets | Comparative Historical Data

						Type of Statement		
2	10	22	15	9	8	Unqualified	35	32
1		4				Reviewed	3	
1	3	2				Compiled	4	9
7	3	1	1			Tax Returns	2	2
8	3	17	5	1		Other	16	22
	57 (4/1-9/30/06)		66 (10/1/06-3/31/07)				4/1/02-3/31/03	4/1/03-3/31/04
0-500M	500M-2MM	2-10MM	10-50MM	50-100MM	100-250MM		ALL	ALL
19	19	46	21	10	8	NUMBER OF STATEMENTS	60	65
%	%	%	%	%	%	ASSETS	%	%
31.1	27.7	18.3	24.1	17.7		Cash & Equivalents	17.8	20.3
30.4	25.1	25.5	18.6	5.6		Trade Receivables (net)	27.6	25.7
3.9	1.3	.7	1.3	.8		Inventory	2.4	1.8
6.9	3.4	2.9	1.3	3.5		All Other Current	3.4	6.4
72.3	57.6	47.4	45.4	27.6		Total Current	51.1	54.2
17.1	30.2	45.4	34.5	32.5		Fixed Assets (net)	31.6	30.0
2.8	4.3	1.5	7.4	26.2		Intangibles (net)	4.5	5.0
7.8	8.0	5.7	12.7	13.8		All Other Non-Current	12.9	10.9
100.0	100.0	100.0	100.0	100.0		Total	100.0	100.0
						LIABILITIES		
20.1	4.8	4.2	3.1	2.1		Notes Payable-Short Term	8.1	7.0
1.2	2.2	2.4	2.9	2.3		Cur. Mat.-L.T.D.	2.9	2.7
13.5	4.3	7.4	2.9	3.0		Trade Payables	9.6	6.3
.0	1.4	.2	1.0	.5		Income Taxes Payable	.4	.6
29.8	24.9	20.2	19.9	21.2		All Other Current	22.6	23.4
64.6	37.6	34.4	29.8	29.0		Total Current	43.7	40.1
5.3	10.6	18.2	17.1	24.2		Long-Term Debt	17.6	14.1
.0	.3	.3	.5	.1		Deferred Taxes	.1	.2
8.9	2.8	4.0	7.4	2.4		All Other Non-Current	10.7	7.5
21.2	48.6	43.1	45.2	44.3		Net Worth	27.9	38.1
100.0	100.0	100.0	100.0	100.0		Total Liabilities & Net Worth	100.0	100.0
						INCOME DATA		
100.0	100.0	100.0	100.0	100.0		Net Sales	100.0	100.0
						Gross Profit		
92.2	89.0	91.7	95.2	94.2		Operating Expenses	92.1	91.4
7.8	11.0	8.3	4.8	5.8		Operating Profit	7.9	8.6
.2	1.8	.3	1.4	1.6		All Other Expenses (net)	3.2	1.2
7.6	9.1	8.0	3.4	4.3		Profit Before Taxes	4.7	7.4
						RATIOS		
4.7	4.0	2.3	3.3	1.4			2.2	3.0
.9	1.3	1.4	1.5	1.1		Current	1.3	1.5
.7	.7	1.1	.9	.5			.8	.9
4.1	3.7	2.3	3.0	1.3			2.0	2.2
.8	1.1	1.3	1.5	.9		Quick	1.1	1.2
.4	.7	.9	.7	.4			.7	.7
0 UND	1 355.0	13 28.0	7 53.4	7 50.6			19 19.4	13 29.1
27 13.3	62 5.8	45 8.2	15 24.0	14 25.3		Sales/Receivables	32 11.4	32 11.4
78 4.7	105 3.5	93 3.9	62 5.9	45 8.1			93 3.9	78 4.7
						Cost of Sales/Inventory		
						Cost of Sales/Payables		
8.1	4.1	4.5	3.4	15.6			5.6	5.0
-155.5	14.5	15.5	6.6	43.0		Sales/Working Capital	14.3	12.5
-12.2	-14.6	61.1	-23.0	-6.7			-28.6	-56.5
18.3	12.4	17.0	32.1				13.9	21.7
(10) 7.4	(12) 3.7	(34) 5.0	(12) 2.9			EBIT/Interest	(45) 4.6	(45) 7.0
1.4	-3.9	1.5	1.9				.8	.1
						Net Profit + Depr., Dep.,	9.0	10.5
						Amort./Cur. Mat. L/T/D	(12) 3.1	(16) 3.2
							1.8	1.6
.0	.3	.4	.3	.8			.4	.3
.7	.7	.8	.5	NM		Fixed/Worth	1.0	.6
2.6	1.9	2.1	2.0	-.3			2.8	1.5
1.0	.6	.5	.5	.3			1.0	.3
2.5	1.5	1.5	1.4	NM		Debt/Worth	2.4	1.7
-9.8	2.6	3.7	4.5	-2.2			12.2	4.3
432.2	25.8	43.1	28.4			% Profit Before Taxes/Tangible	47.6	54.7
(14) 73.5	(18) 15.5	(43) 13.2	(18) 22.0			Net Worth	(49) 16.4	(57) 15.1
12.6	-18.4	3.6	4.7				2.4	-.4
54.0	13.3	11.5	17.7	9.9		% Profit Before Taxes/Total	15.9	22.0
30.1	5.2	6.0	3.7	3.2		Assets	6.5	7.8
3.3	-5.8	1.4	.5	-2.3			-.6	-.2
491.0	18.0	14.3	12.2	8.9			22.7	18.9
27.0	8.4	3.2	4.1	3.8		Sales/Net Fixed Assets	7.5	7.7
20.7	5.1	1.2	1.6	1.3			3.1	3.0
13.7	2.3	1.9	2.0	1.2			2.5	2.7
4.5	1.7	1.4	1.0	.7		Sales/Total Assets	1.6	1.4
3.1	.7	.7	.5	.4			.9	.9
.7	2.2	1.5	2.2				1.4	1.7
(11) 1.3	(17) 3.3	(39) 2.9	(19) 3.3			% Depr., Dep., Amort./Sales	(52) 2.3	(56) 2.6
2.2	4.0	6.5	5.9				4.6	4.7
						% Officers', Directors',	2.9	3.1
						Owners' Comp/Sales	(12) 7.7	(13) 6.8
							13.2	7.6
21660M	44206M	319123M	678692M	718544M	1681992M	Net Sales ($)	1362719M	1115152M
3491M	24520M	206512M	522993M	736809M	1272021M	Total Assets ($)	926959M	834141M

Comparative Historical Data | Current Data Sorted by Sales

			Type of Statement						
47	46	66	Unqualified	1	13	9	12	11	20
3	6	5	Reviewed		1		1	3	
4	6	6	Compiled	3	1	2			
5	7	12	Tax Returns	6	2			2	
23	30	34	Other	7	9	3	5	5	5
4/1/04-	4/1/05-	4/1/06-			57 (4/1-9/30/06)		66 (10/1/06-3/31/07)		
3/31/05	3/31/06	3/31/07							
ALL	ALL	ALL		0-1MM	1-3MM	3-5MM	5-10MM	10-25MM	25MM & OVER
82	95	123	**NUMBER OF STATEMENTS**	17	26	14	20	21	25
%	%	%	**ASSETS**	%	%	%	%	%	%
26.6	18.8	22.1	Cash & Equivalents	33.6	19.7	18.2	25.6	22.9	15.8
17.2	24.4	23.4	Trade Receivables (net)	30.7	19.2	24.5	25.0	24.4	20.2
1.3	1.1	1.4	Inventory	2.1	2.7	.8	.7	.5	1.5
2.9	2.7	3.5	All Other Current	2.6	6.3	1.6	2.1	3.8	3.1
48.0	47.0	50.5	Total Current	68.9	47.8	45.0	53.3	51.6	40.6
34.0	36.0	35.0	Fixed Assets (net)	21.0	41.0	47.2	38.3	30.9	32.0
6.8	5.0	6.3	Intangibles (net)	1.5	5.8	.5	.8	8.0	16.2
11.3	12.0	8.3	All Other Non-Current	8.6	5.3	7.2	7.6	9.6	11.2
100.0	100.0	100.0	Total	100.0	100.0	100.0	100.0	100.0	100.0
			LIABILITIES						
5.6	4.5	6.1	Notes Payable-Short Term	8.6	9.9	4.5	6.5	5.7	1.5
2.0	2.9	2.5	Cur. Mat.-L.T.D.	1.2	2.4	2.4	2.7	2.7	3.2
5.7	6.4	6.8	Trade Payables	8.4	7.6	3.4	7.8	7.5	5.7
.6	.7	.5	Income Taxes Payable	.0	.1	1.7	.1	.5	1.2
21.8	24.6	23.2	All Other Current	21.7	24.4	21.7	29.3	13.6	26.9
35.6	39.1	39.2	Total Current	39.9	44.3	33.6	46.3	29.9	38.5
16.5	17.3	15.1	Long-Term Debt	9.1	18.9	14.7	13.8	15.2	16.3
.3	.2	.3	Deferred Taxes	.0	.2	.7	.1	.1	.5
8.3	9.1	5.3	All Other Non-Current	.0	6.3	3.5	10.8	.6	8.3
39.3	34.2	40.2	Net Worth	51.0	30.2	47.4	29.1	54.1	36.5
100.0	100.0	100.0	Total Liabilities & Net Worth	100.0	100.0	100.0	100.0	100.0	100.0
			INCOME DATA						
100.0	100.0	100.0	Net Sales	100.0	100.0	100.0	100.0	100.0	100.0
			Gross Profit						
91.5	94.1	92.0	Operating Expenses	79.3	93.5	89.9	97.4	97.0	91.8
8.5	5.9	8.0	Operating Profit	20.7	6.5	10.1	2.6	3.0	8.2
1.4	.8	.9	All Other Expenses (net)	1.8	1.5	-.5	-1.4	1.6	1.7
7.1	5.1	7.1	Profit Before Taxes	18.8	5.0	10.6	4.0	1.5	6.5
			RATIOS						
3.2	2.8	2.3		25.3	2.7	2.4	1.5	2.7	1.5
1.2	1.5	1.2	Current	1.5	1.2	1.2	1.1	1.5	1.1
.9	.8	.8		.7	.6	1.1	.8	1.2	.6
3.1	2.3	2.2		23.8	2.6	2.3	1.5	2.6	1.4
1.1	1.4	1.1	Quick	1.5	1.0	1.2	1.1	1.5	.9
.8	.8	.7		.6	.5	.9	.8	1.0	.5
8 45.9	11 34.7	6 58.1		0 UND	0 UND	19 19.4	7 48.9	10 34.9	14 26.5
23 16.0	31 11.6	35 10.5	Sales/Receivables	31 11.7	16 23.3	76 4.8	21 17.3	23 15.9	41 9.0
42 8.6	73 5.0	78 4.7		81 4.5	68 5.4	118 3.1	130 2.8	66 5.5	70 5.3
			Cost of Sales/Inventory						
			Cost of Sales/Payables						
6.6	5.3	4.9		3.8	4.6	4.1	7.7	5.3	10.4
21.4	15.0	19.0	Sales/Working Capital	55.0	15.2	12.4	23.6	13.2	85.3
-45.7	-19.9	-15.4		-12.0	-10.7	NM	-18.8	47.5	-9.8
21.0	16.3	14.9			13.6	16.0	31.5	12.3	21.6
(62) 3.4	(73) 4.9	(83) 4.5	EBIT/Interest	(16) 4.0	(11) 5.2	(16) 5.4	(12) 2.5	(19) 3.1	
1.2	.8	1.5			1.5	.9	1.9	.9	1.5
13.6	37.6	3.4							2.9
(15) 3.1	(16) 2.2	(22) 1.8	Net Profit + Depr., Dep., Amort./Cur. Mat. L/T/D					(10) 1.4	
1.2	-.9	.4							-.6
.5	.4	.4		.0	.6	.6	.5	.2	.4
.9	.7	.8	Fixed/Worth	.2	.9	.9	.7	.5	1.7
2.0	2.5	2.4		2.5	2.8	1.6	4.3	1.2	-11.0
.6	.5	.6		.1	1.4	.6	.8	.3	.8
1.5	1.6	1.7	Debt/Worth	1.1	2.4	1.1	2.6	.8	3.9
4.4	5.0	5.6		7.3	9.0	1.7	5.5	3.0	-15.2
77.5	42.8	45.9		122.9	22.0	45.8	37.2	27.4	51.3
(74) 22.4	(82) 14.3	(103) 17.6	% Profit Before Taxes/Tangible Net Worth	(15) 52.0	(22) 12.4	17.1	(17) 10.0	(19) 5.6	(16) 28.8
3.4	.4	3.8		7.0	3.8	9.8	2.5	-1.8	18.0
19.7	14.3	17.5		40.7	9.9	14.2	10.2	7.3	18.7
6.5	4.2	5.2	% Profit Before Taxes/Total Assets	31.6	5.5	7.4	3.2	3.2	9.9
1.0	-.1	1.2		4.1	1.2	2.0	.7	-1.1	2.7
17.1	18.2	18.7		UND	21.9	6.1	15.1	15.6	12.4
6.8	6.2	6.9	Sales/Net Fixed Assets	27.0	8.3	3.8	2.8	8.2	5.6
2.5	1.7	2.0		15.0	.8	1.2	1.9	2.0	3.0
2.9	2.4	2.3		5.6	2.5	1.7	1.9	3.2	2.1
1.8	1.5	1.6	Sales/Total Assets	2.5	1.5	1.1	1.6	1.6	1.5
.9	.8	.7		.6	.7	.7	.8	.5	.9
1.7	1.3	1.7			1.5	1.7	.7	1.9	2.4
(70) 2.7	(83) 2.5	(99) 3.2	% Depr., Dep., Amort./Sales	(23) 3.3	3.9	(17) 2.7	(18) 3.4	(19) 3.5	
4.8	5.3	5.1			7.5	6.5	4.6	5.9	4.4
4.1	4.5	2.2							
(15) 6.5	(16) 11.0	(24) 4.0	% Officers', Directors' Owners' Comp/Sales						
18.7	21.4	14.7							
2065676M	2245161M	3464217M	Net Sales ($)	9394M	45871M	54648M	138621M	318194M	2897489M
1436703M	1608672M	2766346M	Total Assets ($)	7211M	42305M	57497M	120715M	413277M	2125341M

M = $ thousand   MM = $ million
See Pages 11 through 21 for Explanation of Ratios and Data

EDUCATION—Fine Arts Schools   NAICS 611610 (SIC 7911, 8299)

Current Data Sorted by Assets | ## Comparative Historical Data

0-500M	500M-2MM	2-10MM	10-50MM	50-100MM	100-250MM	Type of Statement	4/1/02-3/31/03 ALL	4/1/03-3/31/04 ALL
3	2	10	4		1	Unqualified	14	14
		1				Reviewed		
3						Compiled	1	4
2	1					Tax Returns	2	4
1	2	1		1		Other	7	8
	23 (4/1-9/30/06)		9 (10/1/06-3/31/07)					
9	5	12	5		1	NUMBER OF STATEMENTS	24	30
%	%	%	%	%	%	ASSETS	%	%
		13.4				Cash & Equivalents	14.2	16.6
		4.3				Trade Receivables (net)	6.5	4.0
		.6				Inventory	3.8	1.4
		1.0				All Other Current	3.5	2.2
		19.3				Total Current	27.9	24.2
		56.9				Fixed Assets (net)	53.1	55.9
		1.3				Intangibles (net)	1.0	2.5
		22.5				All Other Non-Current	18.0	17.5
		100.0				Total	100.0	100.0
						LIABILITIES		
		3.1				Notes Payable-Short Term	7.1	3.8
		.4				Cur. Mat.-L.T.D.	2.7	.9
		1.9				Trade Payables	5.0	5.3
		.0				Income Taxes Payable	.0	.0
		2.1				All Other Current	15.5	18.4
		7.5				Total Current	30.3	28.4
		15.8				Long-Term Debt	15.7	22.0
		.0				Deferred Taxes	.0	.0
		2.1				All Other Non-Current	4.9	6.9
		74.7				Net Worth	49.1	42.8
		100.0				Total Liabilties & Net Worth	100.0	100.0
						INCOME DATA		
		100.0				Net Sales	100.0	100.0
						Gross Profit		
		90.2				Operating Expenses	91.0	100.4
		9.8				Operating Profit	9.0	-.4
		-1.1				All Other Expenses (net)	2.2	.7
		11.0				Profit Before Taxes	6.8	-1.1
						RATIOS		
		4.6				Current	2.0	3.2
		2.3					.9	1.0
		1.1					.4	.6
		4.5				Quick	1.3	2.7
		2.2					.6	.8
		.9					.2	.5
		3 107.9				Sales/Receivables	0 UND	0 UND
		19 19.4					5 80.1	4 100.0
		58 6.3					22 16.9	32 11.6
						Cost of Sales/Inventory		
						Cost of Sales/Payables		
		2.6				Sales/Working Capital	6.4	8.9
		7.6					-74.8	NM
		NM					-10.0	-15.0
						EBIT/Interest	19.3	7.7
							(17) 1.5	(19) .6
							-2.6	-3.6
						Net Profit + Depr., Dep., Amort./Cur. Mat. L/T/D		
		.6				Fixed/Worth	.6	.7
		.8					1.1	1.4
		1.0					2.3	2.4
		.1				Debt/Worth	.3	.3
		.2					1.0	1.3
		.5					2.7	2.8
		25.4				% Profit Before Taxes/Tangible Net Worth	39.5	18.6
		2.6					(23) 18.1	(27) .0
		-1.6					-5.0	-10.9
		7.0				% Profit Before Taxes/Total Assets	16.0	7.8
		2.2					6.9	-.2
		-1.3					-1.8	-9.8
		1.6				Sales/Net Fixed Assets	13.7	18.1
		.9					2.5	1.4
		.7					1.3	.7
		.7				Sales/Total Assets	3.1	2.9
		.5					1.5	1.1
		.4					.7	.5
		4.8				% Depr., Dep., Amort./Sales	1.6	1.0
		(10) 6.3					(18) 3.1	(25) 4.7
		7.9					5.2	8.6
						% Officers', Directors' Owners' Comp/Sales		3.9
								(10) 8.2
								18.9
6337M	11105M	46928M	45862M		35846M	Net Sales ($)	79364M	89976M
1845M	5224M	81044M	78359M		105578M	Total Assets ($)	204386M	145962M

M = $ thousand   MM = $ million
See Pages 11 through 21 for Explanation of Ratios and Data

Comparative Historical Data | | | Type of Statement | | Current Data Sorted by Sales

18	30	20	Type of Statement Unqualified	3	4	7	4	1	1
		1	Reviewed		1				
3	1	3	Compiled	1	2				
4	6	3	Tax Returns	2	1				
6	17	5	Other	1	2		1	1	
4/1/04- 3/31/05 ALL	4/1/05- 3/31/06 ALL	4/1/06- 3/31/07 ALL			23 (4/1-9/30/06)		9 (10/1/06-3/31/07)		
				0-1MM	1-3MM	3-5MM	5-10MM	10-25MM	25MM & OVER
31	54	32	NUMBER OF STATEMENTS	7	10	7	5	2	1
%	%	%	ASSETS	%	%	%	%	%	%
12.5	19.4	19.3	Cash & Equivalents		21.6				
5.2	8.3	6.2	Trade Receivables (net)		5.0				
6.9	2.3	2.6	Inventory		7.2				
2.2	6.5	1.5	All Other Current		.2				
26.8	36.5	29.6	Total Current		34.1				
55.0	46.1	50.3	Fixed Assets (net)		49.2				
1.7	4.0	3.2	Intangibles (net)		1.1				
16.5	13.5	16.9	All Other Non-Current		15.7				
100.0	100.0	100.0	Total		100.0				
			LIABILITIES						
6.8	3.6	5.3	Notes Payable-Short Term		9.9				
2.3	1.4	.9	Cur. Mat.-L.T.D.		1.0				
3.7	4.4	2.8	Trade Payables		1.8				
.0	.0	.0	Income Taxes Payable		.0				
8.0	7.9	12.7	All Other Current		12.4				
20.8	17.3	21.7	Total Current		25.1				
23.8	21.4	24.1	Long-Term Debt		18.6				
.0	.2	.0	Deferred Taxes		.0				
11.2	1.6	1.7	All Other Non-Current		.3				
44.2	59.5	52.5	Net Worth		56.0				
100.0	100.0	100.0	Total Liabilties & Net Worth		100.0				
			INCOME DATA						
100.0	100.0	100.0	Net Sales		100.0				
			Gross Profit						
85.9	88.9	91.2	Operating Expenses		86.4				
14.1	11.1	8.8	Operating Profit		13.6				
2.5	.7	.0	All Other Expenses (net)		1.3				
11.6	10.4	8.8	Profit Before Taxes		12.3				
			RATIOS						
2.3	7.0	4.6			6.1				
1.6	2.8	1.8	Current		1.2				
.7	1.1	.7			.4				
2.3	4.6	3.5			3.6				
1.3	2.3	1.3	Quick		1.1				
.3	.6	.5			.3				
0 UND	**0** UND	**3** 134.6		**0** UND					
7 54.0	**8** 47.8	**11** 32.0	Sales/Receivables	**14** 26.5					
29 12.5	**23** 16.2	**20** 18.7		**39** 9.4					
			Cost of Sales/Inventory						
			Cost of Sales/Payables						
7.3	3.7	5.4			9.1				
11.9	8.9	11.9	Sales/Working Capital		NM				
-20.8	NM	-23.1			-12.4				
18.4	13.4	16.9							
(26) 2.5	**(34)** 3.7	**(19)** 3.5	EBIT/Interest						
.2	1.8	1.5							
			Net Profit + Depr., Dep., Amort./Cur. Mat. L/T/D						
.6	.4	.6			.2				
1.0	.8	.9	Fixed/Worth		.7				
2.1	1.7	2.1			NM				
.4	.2	.2			.1				
.8	.5	.6	Debt/Worth		.5				
3.3	1.3	3.0			NM				
34.7	33.3	40.1	% Profit Before Taxes/Tangible						
(29) 8.9	**(48)** 7.9	**(27)** 7.5	Net Worth						
.5	-1.5	-1.5							
15.9	19.2	24.3	% Profit Before Taxes/Total		50.7				
4.2	6.2	3.4	Assets		11.2				
-.2	.7	-.3			-.2				
10.3	15.0	8.8			11.4				
1.6	1.9	1.6	Sales/Net Fixed Assets		3.6				
.7	.7	.9			.8				
2.3	3.0	2.4			5.3				
1.0	.8	.9	Sales/Total Assets		1.3				
.5	.4	.4			.4				
1.6	2.3	3.6							
(24) 3.1	**(37)** 4.8	**(24)** 5.2	% Depr., Dep., Amort./Sales						
5.5	6.4	7.0							
	4.0		% Officers', Directors'						
	(11) 10.4		Owners' Comp/Sales						
	14.9								
310476M	495373M	146078M	Net Sales ($)	2952M	18554M	26088M	35479M	27159M	35846M
500257M	1067648M	272050M	Total Assets ($)	1452M	26762M	48848M	50054M	39356M	105578M

M = $ thousand   MM = $ million
See Pages 11 through 21 for Explanation of Ratios and Data

Current Data Sorted by Assets

Comparative Historical Data

Type of Statement	0-500M	500M-2MM	2-10MM	10-50MM	50-100MM	100-250MM	14	31
Unqualified	7	13	29	23	2	2	14	31
			2					1
Reviewed	2	3	4	1				2
Compiled	12	6	1				1	2
Tax Returns	4	8	12	7	1	1		
Other		102 (4/1-9/30/06)		38 (10/1/06-3/31/07)			6 4/1/02-3/31/03 ALL	7 4/1/03-3/31/04 ALL
NUMBER OF STATEMENTS	25	30	48	31	3	3	21	41
	%	%	%	%	%	%	%	%
ASSETS								
Cash & Equivalents	32.8	25.2	28.0	23.4			22.7	14.6
Trade Receivables (net)	12.3	21.5	8.4	8.8			6.6	12.6
Inventory	2.4	2.8	2.8	1.0			.3	1.2
All Other Current	3.9	1.5	4.9	4.9			5.2	6.0
Total Current	51.3	51.0	44.1	38.1			34.7	34.4
Fixed Assets (net)	26.4	36.2	43.4	41.8			48.0	50.3
Intangibles (net)	11.1	6.0	1.1	1.2			2.3	3.1
All Other Non-Current	11.1	6.8	11.4	18.9			14.9	12.2
Total	100.0	100.0	100.0	100.0			100.0	100.0
LIABILITIES								
Notes Payable-Short Term	24.2	9.0	2.1	3.0			7.3	6.3
Cur. Mat.-L.T.D.	4.3	2.8	3.6	1.9			2.0	3.2
Trade Payables	5.3	5.7	8.0	3.5			3.0	6.4
Income Taxes Payable	1.1	.1	.2	.0			.0	.0
All Other Current	21.4	16.7	12.1	12.3			11.9	15.3
Total Current	56.3	34.3	26.1	20.7			24.2	31.3
Long-Term Debt	11.5	15.9	17.4	18.6			18.0	18.1
Deferred Taxes	.0	.0	.0	.0			.0	.0
All Other Non-Current	17.9	11.9	5.8	5.6			2.9	4.6
Net Worth	14.4	37.9	50.7	55.1			54.8	45.9
Total Liabilities & Net Worth	100.0	100.0	100.0	100.0			100.0	100.0
INCOME DATA								
Net Sales	100.0	100.0	100.0	100.0			100.0	100.0
Gross Profit								
Operating Expenses	95.6	97.2	92.8	91.7			96.4	98.0
Operating Profit	4.4	2.8	7.2	8.3			3.6	2.0
All Other Expenses (net)	1.0	2.5	1.1	.4			2.2	.0
Profit Before Taxes	3.4	.3	6.1	7.9			1.4	2.0
RATIOS								
Current	1.6	6.5	5.1	3.1			3.0	2.5
	1.0	1.9	2.5	1.7			1.7	1.4
	.6	.7	1.0	1.0			.7	.8
Quick	1.5	6.0	4.5	3.1			2.4	2.2
	.7	1.4	1.7	1.3			1.3	1.1
	.3	.7	.5	.9			.6	.6
Sales/Receivables	0 UND	2 207.6	2 229.3	5 80.3			3 116.4	3 126.2
	0 UND	21 17.0	9 40.8	21 17.2			13 29.1	19 19.0
	24 15.3	49 7.5	24 15.2	36 10.2			32 11.3	45 8.0
Cost of Sales/Inventory								
Cost of Sales/Payables								
Sales/Working Capital	13.8	2.7	3.7	3.8			4.6	5.7
	202.0	11.2	9.5	7.6			23.3	16.7
	-14.2	-23.7	263.6	-406.6			-14.3	-17.8
EBIT/Interest	18.4	4.1	30.9	13.0			21.0	7.6
	(14) 5.6	(19) 1.8	(29) 3.1	(24) 5.1			(14) 4.3	(33) 3.7
	-1.5	-1.5	.4	2.0			-.9	.8
Net Profit + Depr., Dep., Amort./Cur. Mat. L/T/D								
Fixed/Worth	.0	.5	.4	.4			.6	.6
	.5	.7	.7	.8			.9	1.0
	-1.8	NM	2.3	1.2			1.3	1.8
Debt/Worth	.5	.4	.2	.3			.4	.4
	10.2	.9	1.2	.7			.7	.7
	-3.6	NM	3.1	1.5			2.1	3.0
% Profit Before Taxes/Tangible Net Worth	200.9	24.5	31.8	17.7			26.4	21.9
	(15) 60.0	(23) 10.2	(45) 11.4	5.8			7.6	(37) 6.4
	.0	-4.3	-3.8	3.2			-4.7	.5
% Profit Before Taxes/Total Assets	46.4	10.3	14.7	9.5			9.5	9.1
	12.4	3.2	6.0	3.7			5.2	2.6
	-5.0	-3.8	-1.2	1.9			-1.7	-.3
Sales/Net Fixed Assets	UND	12.8	13.6	7.2			9.5	11.2
	49.7	6.8	3.6	2.0			1.6	2.1
	10.9	3.7	1.4	.6			1.0	.8
Sales/Total Assets	9.1	3.3	2.5	1.6			1.7	2.8
	4.5	2.1	1.4	.8			.8	.9
	2.6	1.2	.6	.4			.6	.5
% Depr., Dep., Amort./Sales	.5	.9	1.1	1.7			1.5	2.0
	(15) 1.4	(25) 2.1	(35) 2.9	(28) 3.3			(20) 3.1	(36) 4.3
	2.8	2.8	6.3	7.4			4.9	6.6
% Officers', Directors' Owners' Comp/Sales	5.3	3.0						
	(12) 7.7	(11) 4.4						
	14.1	7.1						
Net Sales ($)	22047M	80894M	433161M	866585M	130289M	249682M	272756M	341404M
Total Assets ($)	5314M	38028M	245856M	748260M	228489M	362959M	329878M	459163M

M = $ thousand   MM = $ million
See Pages 11 through 21 for Explanation of Ratios and Data

Comparative Historical Data | Current Data Sorted by Sales

			Type of Statement						
27	46	76	Unqualified	7	15	9	16	21	8
4	2	2	Reviewed		1			1	
6	2	10	Compiled	4	2	1	1	1	1
7	14	19	Tax Returns	9	8	1	1		
15	18	33	Other	3	11	6	4	4	5
4/1/04-3/31/05	4/1/05-3/31/06	4/1/06-3/31/07		102 (4/1-9/30/06)			38 (10/1/06-3/31/07)		
ALL	ALL	ALL		0-1MM	1-3MM	3-5MM	5-10MM	10-25MM	25MM & OVER
59	82	140	NUMBER OF STATEMENTS	23	37	17	22	27	14
%	%	%	ASSETS	%	%	%	%	%	%
21.0	25.8	26.9	Cash & Equivalents	27.3	24.6	22.1	32.5	24.9	33.3
12.9	13.8	12.0	Trade Receivables (net)	9.0	15.4	9.0	9.1	12.4	15.2
1.8	1.6	2.3	Inventory	1.2	3.1	1.1	2.8	2.1	3.2
4.7	5.1	3.8	All Other Current	3.4	2.3	1.2	4.3	5.3	7.8
40.4	46.3	45.0	Total Current	40.9	45.5	33.3	48.6	44.6	59.4
42.3	41.0	38.1	Fixed Assets (net)	43.5	35.3	51.2	37.9	38.0	21.8
6.3	3.1	3.9	Intangibles (net)	9.0	6.2	2.5	.5	2.1	.2
11.1	9.6	13.0	All Other Non-Current	6.6	13.0	13.1	13.0	15.3	18.6
100.0	100.0	100.0	Total	100.0	100.0	100.0	100.0	100.0	100.0
			LIABILITIES						
8.6	7.6	7.6	Notes Payable-Short Term	19.7	10.4	3.5	1.5	4.8	.8
2.6	3.8	3.2	Cur. Mat.-L.T.D.	4.2	4.9	1.1	3.2	1.9	2.3
7.2	4.6	5.9	Trade Payables	3.1	4.7	4.3	6.9	7.2	11.1
.0	.1	.3	Income Taxes Payable	1.2	.2	.0	.0	.0	.0
14.3	14.9	14.5	All Other Current	11.5	14.1	14.8	16.2	13.4	20.2
32.8	31.0	31.5	Total Current	39.6	34.2	23.7	27.8	27.2	34.5
22.6	17.9	15.9	Long-Term Debt	19.9	19.5	18.3	12.4	14.9	4.3
.0	.0	.0	Deferred Taxes	.0	.0	.0	.0	.0	.0
2.7	5.6	9.8	All Other Non-Current	23.4	7.8	2.9	5.2	9.7	8.7
41.8	45.4	42.8	Net Worth	17.1	38.5	55.1	54.6	48.2	52.6
100.0	100.0	100.0	Total Liabilties & Net Worth	100.0	100.0	100.0	100.0	100.0	100.0
			INCOME DATA						
100.0	100.0	100.0	Net Sales	100.0	100.0	100.0	100.0	100.0	100.0
			Gross Profit						
94.8	93.4	94.1	Operating Expenses	89.5	97.4	89.6	93.5	96.2	95.6
5.2	6.6	5.9	Operating Profit	10.5	2.6	10.4	6.5	3.8	4.4
.7	1.5	1.2	All Other Expenses (net)	6.9	-.1	1.9	.3	-.7	-1.0
4.5	5.1	4.7	Profit Before Taxes	3.6	2.7	8.5	6.2	4.4	5.4
			RATIOS						
3.1	4.6	4.8		1.9	6.4	6.4	5.5	3.9	4.2
1.4	1.7	1.5	Current	1.2	1.5	2.0	2.2	1.5	2.2
.7	.9	.8		.3	.7	.8	1.0	1.0	1.1
3.0	3.8	3.9		1.6	4.8	5.4	4.9	3.8	3.0
1.4	1.4	1.3	Quick	.8	1.0	2.0	1.9	1.4	1.8
.4	.7	.7		.3	.6	.7	.7	.6	1.0
1 306.6	0 UND	1 513.2		0 UND	0 UND	1 257.3	1 251.9	5 67.9	13 28.4
16 23.4	13 27.5	14 26.0	Sales/Receivables	0 UND	13 28.4	12 29.7	9 40.9	21 17.2	25 14.7
44 8.3	36 10.1	34 10.6		24 15.1	45 8.1	49 7.4	23 15.5	39 9.3	35 10.5
			Cost of Sales/Inventory						
			Cost of Sales/Payables						
4.0	3.5	4.3		11.2	2.4	3.1	3.9	3.8	5.3
12.2	13.6	12.7	Sales/Working Capital	135.0	12.7	7.1	9.8	13.8	8.4
-18.2	-72.1	-32.2		-13.0	-23.5	-13.5	NM	206.2	89.6
6.7	13.3	11.4		13.7	5.3		27.0	14.8	
(47) 2.3	(56) 3.1	(91) 3.2	EBIT/Interest	(11) 1.7	(26) 2.4		(15) 5.7	(22) 5.1	
-.2	1.4	.6		-3.0	.2		2.2	1.1	
			Net Profit + Depr., Dep., Amort./Cur. Mat. L/T/D						
.4	.4	.4		.4	.4	.4	.2	.6	.2
1.2	1.0	.7	Fixed/Worth	1.1	.6	1.0	.6	.9	.4
3.7	2.1	2.3		-1.3	2.5	4.1	1.3	1.5	.5
.4	.3	.3		.3	.4	.1	.2	.5	.3
1.4	1.1	1.0	Debt/Worth	10.2	1.5	.4	.8	.8	.6
8.5	3.3	5.8		-2.7	9.1	4.4	3.1	2.5	4.5
26.4	37.3	32.9		110.5	36.0	27.8	38.6	19.4	35.2
(48) 7.6	(71) 14.2	(119) 10.8	% Profit Before Taxes/Tangible Net Worth	(15) 18.9	(29) 5.5	(16) 7.9	(21) 13.8	(24) 9.8	6.7
-.7	2.9	.0		-9.7	-4.2	-10.0	5.7	1.4	.6
9.2	15.0	14.3		36.0	11.5	9.7	12.4	14.3	24.8
3.2	5.3	5.0	% Profit Before Taxes/Total Assets	5.4	4.6	1.8	7.4	4.6	4.1
-2.1	1.0	-.4		-5.8	-2.6	-7.3	3.6	.5	2.0
18.9	22.9	19.1		67.5	19.2	6.8	17.3	7.9	58.2
3.6	4.9	5.3	Sales/Net Fixed Assets	14.2	5.7	1.4	7.5	3.8	18.3
1.3	1.5	1.5		1.1	1.4	.6	1.6	2.0	3.2
3.4	3.8	3.3		5.8	3.7	1.7	3.0	2.2	3.9
1.4	1.6	1.5	Sales/Total Assets	2.4	1.4	.7	1.9	1.6	2.3
.6	.8	.6		.6	.6	.4	.7	.8	.9
1.6	1.0	1.1		.6	1.7	1.3	.6	1.6	.7
(49) 3.1	(62) 2.4	(109) 2.5	% Depr., Dep., Amort./Sales	(17) 1.7	(28) 2.8	(14) 2.5	(17) 1.3	(23) 2.5	(10) 2.8
4.8	4.7	4.9		6.9	7.2	7.3	3.7	4.6	3.6
4.5	2.2	3.3			2.6				
(14) 6.2	(18) 5.4	(29) 6.8	% Officers', Directors' Owners' Comp/Sales		(13) 4.6				
8.8	7.6	11.2			8.0				
774980M	1580658M	1782658M	Net Sales ($)	12044M	74955M	66168M	150287M	437317M	1041887M
708792M	869619M	1628906M	Total Assets ($)	20823M	105642M	137716M	155747M	557062M	651916M

M = $ thousand   MM = $ million
See Pages 11 through 21 for Explanation of Ratios and Data

EDUCATION—Educational Support Services NAICS 611710 (SIC 8299, 8748)

Current Data Sorted by Assets | **Comparative Historical Data**

0-500M	500M-2MM	2-10MM	10-50MM	50-100MM	100-250MM	Type of Statement	4/1/02-3/31/03 ALL	4/1/03-3/31/04 ALL
7	30	71	64	21	15	Unqualified	167	153
	5	11	3			Reviewed	10	19
1	5	11	2			Compiled	21	50
7	11	7				Tax Returns	17	32
8	19	21	20			Other	88	81
	243 (4/1-9/30/06)		96 (10/1/06-3/31/07)					
23	70	121	89	21	15	**NUMBER OF STATEMENTS**	303	335
%	%	%	%	%	%	**ASSETS**	%	%
33.8	28.0	20.8	21.1	12.6	23.4	Cash & Equivalents	21.1	20.5
25.7	23.5	13.1	9.3	3.2	8.8	Trade Receivables (net)	15.0	14.6
1.2	1.8	2.3	1.9	.2	.3	Inventory	1.3	1.3
5.6	4.1	2.9	3.2	4.7	7.3	All Other Current	4.3	6.1
66.3	57.4	39.2	35.4	20.7	39.8	Total Current	41.7	42.5
20.9	30.8	48.6	43.8	45.9	36.2	Fixed Assets (net)	43.6	42.5
5.3	2.7	1.6	3.0	2.2	1.7	Intangibles (net)	1.8	2.3
7.5	9.1	10.6	17.8	31.2	22.3	All Other Non-Current	13.0	12.7
100.0	100.0	100.0	100.0	100.0	100.0	Total	100.0	100.0
						LIABILITIES		
27.9	8.9	2.5	1.6	1.0	.0	Notes Payable-Short Term	6.8	5.4
1.0	1.0	2.6	1.6	2.1	1.8	Cur. Mat.-L.T.D.	1.7	4.3
6.9	11.2	5.7	3.6	2.4	5.9	Trade Payables	6.1	6.7
	.4	.4	.1	.0	.0	Income Taxes Payable	.2	.4
37.8	16.4	13.9	11.5	8.9	14.6	All Other Current	13.3	15.0
73.6	37.9	25.0	18.4	14.5	22.3	Total Current	28.0	31.9
11.9	15.9	24.5	24.8	25.0	23.3	Long-Term Debt	22.2	20.3
.0	.0	.0	.1	.0	.2	Deferred Taxes	.2	.1
14.8	7.4	2.6	7.0	3.6	14.2	All Other Non-Current	4.7	6.4
-.3	38.8	47.8	49.7	56.9	39.9	Net Worth	44.8	41.3
100.0	100.0	100.0	100.0	100.0	100.0	Total Liabilities & Net Worth	100.0	100.0
						INCOME DATA		
100.0	100.0	100.0	100.0	100.0	100.0	Net Sales	100.0	100.0
						Gross Profit		
94.3	94.9	91.9	90.8	92.8	81.6	Operating Expenses	94.3	93.0
5.7	5.1	8.1	9.2	7.2	18.4	Operating Profit	5.7	7.0
-.1	1.4	2.2	1.6	.1	.9	All Other Expenses (net)	1.9	2.0
5.9	3.7	6.0	7.7	7.1	17.5	Profit Before Taxes	3.8	5.0
						RATIOS		
1.7	4.4	3.6	4.3	2.8	4.6	Current	3.4	4.2
1.1	1.7	1.5	1.7	1.2	2.1		1.7	1.8
.4	.9	.9	1.0	.6	1.0		.9	.8
1.5	3.6	3.2	3.5	1.9	4.6	Quick	3.0	3.4
1.0	1.5	1.3	1.4	.9	1.7		1.4	1.4
.4	.7	.7	.9	.5	.8		.8	.7
0 UND	2 226.6	2 166.1	4 86.2	0 999.8	0 854.1	Sales/Receivables	2 206.4	1 260.0
26 13.9	20 18.2	17 20.9	22 16.2	6 61.7	15 24.0		14 27.0	15 23.7
50 7.2	46 8.0	47 7.8	55 6.6	26 14.1	73 5.0		48 7.5	47 7.7
						Cost of Sales/Inventory		
						Cost of Sales/Payables		
10.6	5.2	3.6	2.4	4.4	2.7	Sales/Working Capital	4.1	3.8
63.0	13.5	14.9	7.8	26.8	4.4		12.1	10.3
-26.2	-54.4	-32.4	79.4	-9.0	99.0		-130.6	-36.5
6.7	8.2	7.1	6.7	8.3	14.0	EBIT/Interest	9.1	9.7
(11) 2.6	(39) 2.4	(82) 2.2	(66) 2.8	(15) 2.8	(10) 2.7		(206) 2.0	(226) 3.1
-.2	-.3	1.1	1.1	.5	2.2		-.5	.4
						Net Profit + Depr., Dep., Amort./Cur. Mat. L/T/D	9.9	7.8
							(16) 3.8	(14) 2.1
							1.4	.9
.1	.1	.4	.4	.3	.2	Fixed/Worth	.4	.3
.6	.5	1.2	.9	.7	1.2		.9	.9
-.5	2.2	2.4	1.8	1.7	1.9		1.8	1.8
.8	.5	.4	.4	.4	.3	Debt/Worth	.4	.5
3.4	1.2	1.2	.8	.5	1.8		1.0	1.0
-2.9	4.5	2.3	2.6	1.4	3.8		2.9	3.1
118.7	52.3	19.2	17.1	10.7	27.5	% Profit Before Taxes/Tangible Net Worth	21.7	27.7
(13) 23.9	(61) 24.8	(113) 8.6	(83) 7.9	(20) 4.8	(14) 16.4		(277) 7.1	(296) 6.6
-13.3	-2.8	.9	1.5	-.2	8.9		-2.5	-.6
61.6	20.6	9.3	7.0	4.7	16.0	% Profit Before Taxes/Total Assets	9.3	11.4
11.0	8.7	2.8	3.1	3.1	5.0		2.6	3.4
-10.4	-4.1	.0	.5	-.1	2.3		-2.1	-1.2
154.3	82.5	15.9	5.5	3.9	13.1	Sales/Net Fixed Assets	17.3	19.0
72.5	22.8	1.6	1.7	.8	1.7		3.2	3.5
21.6	3.1	.7	.8	.7	.9		.9	.9
7.9	3.9	1.8	1.3	1.0	1.0	Sales/Total Assets	2.5	2.4
3.6	2.7	.9	.7	.5	.6		1.3	1.2
2.4	1.5	.5	.4	.3	.4		.5	.5
.3	.5	1.5	2.5	2.5		% Depr., Dep., Amort./Sales	1.6	1.6
(12) .6	(47) 2.0	(89) 3.9	(71) 4.8	(17) 5.5			(241) 3.3	(259) 3.4
1.0	3.4	5.9	6.9	7.2			5.9	6.0
	3.7	1.8				% Officers', Directors' Owners' Comp/Sales	4.8	4.3
	(18) 7.7	(17) 3.1					(59) 9.0	(48) 7.6
	15.6	7.0					13.6	13.1
33555M	215540M	782437M	1930625M	1039514M	3212015M	Net Sales ($)	4589368M	4854012M
5949M	75419M	623871M	2155752M	1447765M	2213254M	Total Assets ($)	4901428M	4210279M

© RMA 2007

M = $ thousand   MM = $ million
See Pages 11 through 21 for Explanation of Ratios and Data

Comparative Historical Data				Current Data Sorted by Sales					

			Type of Statement						
155	173	208	Unqualified	11	41	35	31	43	47
18	15	19	Reviewed	1	5	1	6	5	1
24	26	19	Compiled		11	3	4		1
22	31	25	Tax Returns	8	11	2	2	2	
69	111	68	Other	7	16	10	18	11	6
4/1/04-	4/1/05-	4/1/06-			243 (4/1-9/30/06)		96 (10/1/06-3/31/07)		
3/31/05	3/31/06	3/31/07		0-1MM	1-3MM	3-5MM	5-10MM	10-25MM	25MM & OVER
ALL	ALL	ALL							
288	356	339	**NUMBER OF STATEMENTS**	27	84	51	61	61	55
%	%	%	**ASSETS**	%	%	%	%	%	%
22.4	23.6	22.8	Cash & Equivalents	31.0	23.3	24.9	22.5	19.1	20.8
15.1	12.3	14.3	Trade Receivables (net)	3.9	14.2	18.4	17.1	13.9	13.2
2.3	1.9	1.8	Inventory	1.4	1.0	.6	1.4	4.1	2.2
4.4	3.7	3.7	All Other Current	4.1	3.2	3.4	2.8	4.5	4.8
44.2	41.6	42.7	Total Current	40.4	41.6	47.2	43.8	41.7	41.0
41.1	43.5	41.1	Fixed Assets (net)	43.7	49.3	35.8	42.5	36.0	36.1
2.8	3.3	2.5	Intangibles (net)	4.1	1.9	1.5	3.3	2.0	3.2
11.9	11.6	13.7	All Other Non-Current	11.8	7.2	15.5	10.4	20.2	19.7
100.0	100.0	100.0	Total	100.0	100.0	100.0	100.0	100.0	100.0
			LIABILITIES						
4.7	4.6	5.1	Notes Payable-Short Term	12.1	7.0	5.5	4.7	3.2	.9
	3.0	1.8	Cur. Mat.-L.T.D.	2.7	1.5	.9	2.7	1.4	2.2
6.2	5.0	6.2	Trade Payables	5.4	4.7	9.4	5.9	5.1	7.3
.1	.2	.3	Income Taxes Payable	.0	.2	.9	.2	.0	.1
16.1	11.2	15.1	All Other Current	16.1	12.7	17.5	17.0	12.5	16.8
29.1	24.0	28.5	Total Current	36.2	26.1	34.3	30.5	22.3	27.4
21.8	23.4	21.9	Long-Term Debt	28.9	25.1	20.9	16.8	21.5	20.9
.1	.1	.0	Deferred Taxes	.0	.0	.0	.1	.0	.1
5.3	6.8	6.2	All Other Non-Current	8.9	6.1	5.6	3.3	7.5	7.2
43.7	45.7	43.4	Net Worth	26.1	42.8	39.2	49.3	48.6	44.4
100.0	100.0	100.0	Total Liabilties & Net Worth	100.0	100.0	100.0	100.0	100.0	100.0
			INCOME DATA						
100.0	100.0	100.0	Net Sales	100.0	100.0	100.0	100.0	100.0	100.0
			Gross Profit						
93.8	93.1	92.0	Operating Expenses	86.1	91.9	92.3	94.7	91.7	91.9
6.2	6.9	8.0	Operating Profit	13.9	8.1	7.7	5.3	8.3	8.1
.8	1.7	1.5	All Other Expenses (net)	5.1	2.1	1.1	.0	1.6	.8
5.4	5.2	6.5	Profit Before Taxes	8.9	6.0	6.6	5.3	6.6	7.4
			RATIOS						
3.2	5.0	3.8		4.1	5.1	3.0	3.3	4.2	3.0
1.6	2.0	1.6	Current	1.2	1.7	1.6	1.3	1.8	1.5
.9	.9	.9		.6	.9	.8	.9	1.0	1.0
2.7	4.1	3.3		3.3	4.7	2.9	2.7	3.3	2.3
1.3	1.6	1.3	Quick	.9	1.5	1.5	1.2	1.3	1.1
.7	.8	.7		.4	.6	.6	.8	.7	.8
2 208.6	1 469.6	2 177.0		0 UND	0 UND	6 60.3	5 69.9	3 116.6	0 999.8
15 23.6	16 23.4	19 19.0	Sales/Receivables	2 204.3	9 42.3	28 13.1	25 14.5	24 15.5	20 17.9
47 7.8	41 8.9	49 7.4		39 9.4	41 8.9	56 6.5	49 7.4	51 7.2	61 6.0
			Cost of Sales/Inventory						
			Cost of Sales/Payables						
4.3	3.3	3.7		3.1	3.5	3.5	3.6	3.5	4.4
12.3	8.7	13.0	Sales/Working Capital	28.0	10.6	9.6	20.4	11.3	13.3
-130.0	-92.5	-72.8		-4.7	-39.8	-28.9	-70.2	160.1	-427.1
13.6	8.8	6.9		4.9	6.0	7.7	11.9	7.2	9.1
(198) 3.4	(255) 2.4	(223) 2.6	EBIT/Interest	(11) 2.0	(60) 1.8	(25) 4.3	(42) 3.5	(42) 2.6	(43) 2.8
1.0	.6	1.1		1.3	-.6	1.1	1.6	1.1	1.0
37.4	5.6	12.5							
(15) 5.1	(20) 2.5	(10) 8.7	Net Profit + Depr., Dep., Amort./Cur. Mat. L/T/D						
1.6	.6	1.2							
.3	.3	.3		.1	.4	.2	.3	.3	.2
.8	.9	.9	Fixed/Worth	1.4	1.2	.6	.9	.9	.9
2.2	2.4	2.3		11.0	2.6	2.9	1.6	1.7	1.8
.4	.4	.4		.3	.5	.3	.4	.4	.5
1.1	1.0	1.2	Debt/Worth	2.1	1.3	1.1	1.1	.8	1.3
3.1	3.4	3.3		10.7	3.3	4.1	2.0	4.3	3.1
33.6	23.2	24.8		27.3	24.6	38.4	18.3	21.1	24.2
(255) 9.5	(321) 7.2	(304) 9.7	% Profit Before Taxes/Tangible Net Worth	(21) 8.3	(76) 10.6	(44) 15.5	(57) 6.8	(54) 4.7	(52) 11.9
.3	-1.3	1.1		-4.3	1.7	1.3	1.1	.4	4.9
13.1	10.6	11.0		11.8	13.0	19.5	9.3	9.4	8.9
4.3	3.2	3.5	% Profit Before Taxes/Total Assets	3.3	2.8	5.0	3.1	2.8	4.4
.1	-.8	.0		-2.1	-2.7	.6	-.3	-.4	.9
25.9	17.3	23.1		90.8	27.9	35.3	32.6	19.1	14.0
4.1	3.0	3.1	Sales/Net Fixed Assets	3.1	1.9	3.6	3.0	2.9	4.0
.9	.9	.9		.3	.7	.8	1.0	1.1	1.3
2.6	2.1	2.3		2.0	2.8	2.6	2.4	2.1	2.0
1.3	1.1	1.0	Sales/Total Assets	.9	1.0	.9	1.0	1.1	1.3
.6	.5	.5		.2	.5	.4	.6	.6	.7
1.6	1.6	1.4		1.1	1.3	1.1	1.7	1.4	1.1
(218) 3.5	(269) 3.8	(245) 3.3	% Depr., Dep., Amort./Sales	(17) 5.0	(62) 3.4	(35) 2.9	(46) 3.8	(46) 3.8	(39) 2.7
6.1	6.2	5.9		14.0	5.8	6.8	5.8	5.3	5.2
3.8	4.2	2.4			3.1		2.4		
(53) 6.7	(58) 7.3	(51) 5.1	% Officers', Directors' Owners' Comp/Sales	(16) 6.1		(11) 5.1			
14.5	14.1	11.5		10.8		8.0			
6681044M	7270552M	7213686M	Net Sales ($)	15045M	164148M	194823M	443516M	1004778M	5391376M
4045377M	6393919M	6522010M	Total Assets ($)	37723M	264537M	436743M	594476M	1319559M	3868972M

© RMA 2007

M = $ thousand   MM = $ million
See Pages 11 through 21 for Explanation of Ratios and Data

HEALTH CARE AND SOCIAL ASSISTANCE

Current Data Sorted by Assets   Comparative Historical Data

	0-500M	500M-2MM	2-10MM	10-50MM	50-100MM	100-250MM	Type of Statement	4/1/02-3/31/03 ALL	4/1/03-3/31/04 ALL
	11	15	58	81	18	16	Unqualified	163	178
	12	34	70	23	2		Reviewed	136	145
	291	209	138	13	2	4	Compiled	551	730
	770	317	106	13	7	11	Tax Returns	670	872
	312	279	266	103	19	8	Other	538	671
	384 (4/1-9/30/06)			2,824 (10/1/06-3/31/07)					
NUMBER OF STATEMENTS	1396	854	638	233	48	39		2058	2596
	%	%	%	%	%	%	ASSETS	%	%
Cash & Equivalents	35.0	23.3	14.3	13.4	17.8	23.5		25.1	26.9
Trade Receivables (net)	4.1	10.8	21.0	24.5	19.1	11.7		11.6	11.0
Inventory	.8	.9	1.4	1.9	2.6	.7		.8	.9
All Other Current	4.3	3.1	3.7	4.9	6.7	5.7		4.0	4.8
Total Current	44.3	38.1	40.4	44.7	46.2	41.6		41.6	43.5
Fixed Assets (net)	37.6	46.0	47.2	41.3	38.0	33.6		43.7	41.8
Intangibles (net)	4.0	4.8	3.1	3.5	4.3	9.3		3.9	3.7
All Other Non-Current	14.1	11.2	9.3	10.5	11.5	15.5		10.9	11.0
Total	100.0	100.0	100.0	100.0	100.0	100.0		100.0	100.0
							LIABILITIES		
Notes Payable-Short Term	32.1	14.9	10.2	5.4	22.2	4.2		23.5	22.6
Cur. Mat.-L.T.D.	9.2	7.6	6.6	7.9	5.3	4.9		8.1	9.0
Trade Payables	2.9	2.5	5.3	5.7	5.7	2.8		3.3	3.2
Income Taxes Payable	.4	.2	.5	1.3	2.1	1.9		.4	.5
All Other Current	38.2	24.2	15.8	16.0	19.8	21.5		28.6	28.1
Total Current	82.8	49.4	38.4	36.3	55.1	35.4		63.9	63.4
Long-Term Debt	31.4	33.6	33.5	29.9	40.1	35.9		31.9	32.5
Deferred Taxes	.0	.1	.3	.4	.3	.1		.3	.2
All Other Non-Current	5.0	3.7	4.0	5.5	7.1	4.4		5.7	6.3
Net Worth	-19.2	13.2	23.7	27.9	-2.8	24.2		-1.8	-2.5
Total Liabilities & Net Worth	100.0	100.0	100.0	100.0	100.0	100.0		100.0	100.0
							INCOME DATA		
Net Sales	100.0	100.0	100.0	100.0	100.0	100.0		100.0	100.0
Gross Profit									
Operating Expenses	91.3	86.5	86.2	90.2	93.3	94.0		91.0	90.1
Operating Profit	8.7	13.5	13.8	9.8	6.7	6.0		9.0	9.9
All Other Expenses (net)	.6	2.7	4.3	2.9	-.2	.8		1.9	1.6
Profit Before Taxes	8.1	10.8	9.5	6.9	6.9	5.2		7.1	8.3
							RATIOS		
Current	1.4	1.9	2.5	2.4	2.1	2.4		1.8	2.0
	.7	.8	1.1	1.3	1.3	1.5		.8	.8
	.2	.3	.5	.9	.9	.6		.3	.3
Quick	1.3	1.8	2.1	2.0	1.7	2.2		1.6	1.7
	(1391) .5	(852) .7	.9	(232) 1.1	1.1	1.3		(2054) .7	(2589) .7
	.2	.2	.4	.7	.7	.5		.2	.2
Sales/Receivables	0 UND	0 UND	0 UND	4 99.2	2 234.0	0 UND		0 UND	0 UND
	0 UND	0 UND	18 20.3	39 9.2	43 8.5	29 12.6		0 UND	0 UND
	0 UND	0 999.8	47 7.7	55 6.6	56 6.5	54 6.7		20 18.2	9 39.0
Cost of Sales/Inventory									
Cost of Sales/Payables									
Sales/Working Capital	91.7	21.9	9.3	8.5	8.1	6.7		25.2	21.9
	-77.6	-101.7	132.0	23.6	19.6	29.0		-134.9	-134.5
	-19.8	-20.1	-21.9	-54.1	-156.3	-42.7		-21.8	-20.9
EBIT/Interest	18.0	22.7	17.5	12.2	10.8	7.9		12.0	18.5
	(1008) 4.3	(694) 3.3	(519) 4.2	(197) 3.5	(43) 5.2	(35) 3.1		(1613) 2.7	(2004) 3.8
	.5	.8	1.0	1.0	2.1	.8		.7	.6
Net Profit + Depr., Dep., Amort./Cur. Mat. L/T/D	7.1	2.9	2.7	3.0	7.9			3.1	2.7
	(25) 1.3	(50) 1.9	(62) 1.5	(49) 1.6	(16) 2.9			(159) 1.7	(173) 1.6
	.4	1.2	.9	.8	1.4			1.0	.9
Fixed/Worth	.5	.7	.6	.6	.8	.6		.7	.7
	8.1	4.1	2.3	1.3	1.6	1.5		4.0	4.1
	-.9	-5.7	125.1	8.5	12.0	-1.6		-3.1	-2.1
Debt/Worth	1.5	1.3	1.0	1.0	1.7	.8		1.4	1.3
	UND	9.2	4.2	2.9	3.5	2.8		9.2	11.4
	-2.9	-9.7	374.1	14.3	49.3	-7.7		-6.4	-5.0
% Profit Before Taxes/Tangible Net Worth	444.4	228.1	126.1	50.9	78.0	58.7		160.4	213.1
	(710) 114.5	(547) 72.8	(484) 37.5	(193) 16.1	(38) 31.6	(27) 6.6		(1271) 36.1	(1549) 50.0
	12.5	8.0	3.9	1.6	12.3	1.6		.8	4.3
% Profit Before Taxes/Total Assets	90.3	50.0	30.1	13.5	19.4	22.7		38.3	46.9
	21.0	8.9	6.9	5.5	6.5	3.8		5.7	8.3
	-1.8	-.3	.0	.1	2.9	-.1		-2.6	-1.1
Sales/Net Fixed Assets	178.3	42.1	22.0	15.1	22.6	35.1		59.0	66.7
	45.9	16.6	9.6	6.8	7.2	7.6		20.8	21.7
	18.8	7.1	3.1	2.8	2.7	2.9		8.2	8.3
Sales/Total Assets	22.6	10.8	5.9	3.5	3.6	9.2		14.3	14.6
	12.2	5.7	3.1	2.4	2.4	2.1		6.8	6.8
	6.4	2.8	1.5	1.3	1.5	1.1		2.9	2.9
% Depr., Dep., Amort./Sales	.4	1.0	1.3	1.7	1.2	1.3		.9	.9
	(836) 1.0	(680) 1.9	(568) 2.5	(218) 2.9	(39) 2.7	(26) 2.8		(1627) 1.9	(1911) 1.9
	2.1	3.7	5.2	4.8	4.1	4.7		3.7	3.8
% Officers', Directors' Owners' Comp/Sales	16.3	14.3	10.7	4.6	7.8	13.0		15.4	16.8
	(949) 26.0	(472) 25.1	(207) 26.4	(58) 19.9	(17) 15.8	(17) 31.0		(1097) 26.5	(1440) 27.5
	36.0	35.6	35.4	32.1	36.4	41.3		37.0	36.8
Net Sales ($)	4031748M	6763482M	11784077M	19629468M	16700971M	51354023M		66280356M	86067410M
Total Assets ($)	286225M	884836M	2789150M	5015711M	3222444M	6401877M		10699946M	14702814M

© RMA 2007

M = $ thousand   MM = $ million
See Pages 11 through 21 for Explanation of Ratios and Data

Comparative Historical Data   Current Data Sorted by Sales

			Type of Statement						
193	191	199	Unqualified	4	12	7	32	43	101
143	114	141	Reviewed	7	13	13	20	43	45
607	611	657	Compiled	103	160	110	123	117	44
1062	1080	1224	Tax Returns	284	383	195	188	109	65
792	992	987	Other	123	198	120	180	170	196
4/1/04-3/31/05 ALL	4/1/05-3/31/06 ALL	4/1/06-3/31/07 ALL		384 (4/1-9/30/06) 0-1MM	1-3MM	3-5MM	2,824 (10/1/06-3/31/07) 5-10MM	10-25MM	25MM & OVER
2797	2988	3208	NUMBER OF STATEMENTS	521	766	445	543	482	451
%	%	%	ASSETS	%	%	%	%	%	%
27.3	26.6	25.8	Cash & Equivalents	25.0	29.6	27.6	27.3	22.8	20.0
12.1	11.1	11.1	Trade Receivables (net)	4.8	8.0	10.3	12.0	14.4	19.6
.9	.9	1.1	Inventory	.8	.7	1.0	1.4	1.1	1.5
3.4	3.7	4.0	All Other Current	3.7	4.6	2.6	3.6	4.1	4.8
43.7	42.4	41.9	Total Current	34.2	42.9	41.4	44.2	42.5	45.9
40.2	41.5	42.0	Fixed Assets (net)	47.7	38.4	43.2	41.6	43.1	39.5
4.0	3.9	4.1	Intangibles (net)	4.6	4.8	4.3	3.2	3.5	3.6
12.1	12.3	12.1	All Other Non-Current	13.5	13.9	11.0	10.9	11.0	10.9
100.0	100.0	100.0	Total	100.0	100.0	100.0	100.0	100.0	100.0
			LIABILITIES						
21.5	19.8	20.7	Notes Payable-Short Term	26.7	25.6	20.3	18.3	15.3	14.7
8.1	8.3	8.0	Cur. Mat.-L.T.D.	7.4	9.9	7.9	7.8	6.9	7.3
3.6	3.1	3.5	Trade Payables	2.4	3.0	3.1	3.5	4.3	5.5
.4	.5	.5	Income Taxes Payable	.1	.3	.5	.3	.3	1.6
28.9	28.1	27.9	All Other Current	20.7	26.4	30.7	35.0	28.9	26.7
62.6	59.9	60.7	Total Current	57.3	65.1	62.5	64.9	55.7	55.7
33.8	33.1	32.5	Long-Term Debt	40.2	37.3	31.6	30.0	25.1	27.2
.3	.3	.1	Deferred Taxes	.0	.2	.0	.1	.2	.4
4.7	5.2	4.5	All Other Non-Current	8.2	3.6	4.3	2.9	3.9	4.5
-1.5	1.5	2.2	Net Worth	-5.7	-6.1	1.6	2.1	15.0	12.2
100.0	100.0	100.0	Total Liabilties & Net Worth	100.0	100.0	100.0	100.0	100.0	100.0
			INCOME DATA						
100.0	100.0	100.0	Net Sales	100.0	100.0	100.0	100.0	100.0	100.0
			Gross Profit						
89.7	88.9	89.0	Operating Expenses	78.4	88.0	91.6	91.9	92.2	93.6
10.3	11.1	11.0	Operating Profit	21.6	12.0	8.4	8.1	7.8	6.4
1.6	1.9	2.1	All Other Expenses (net)	7.5	1.9	.8	.5	.6	.7
8.7	9.2	8.9	Profit Before Taxes	14.1	10.1	7.6	7.6	7.2	5.7
			RATIOS						
1.9	2.0	1.9		2.3	2.0	1.7	1.9	1.9	1.7
.9	.8	.9	Current	.7	.8	.8	.8	.9	1.1
.3	.3	.3		.2	.3	.3	.3	.4	.5
1.7	1.8	1.6		2.0	1.7	1.5	1.7	1.5	1.5
(2788) .8	(2982) .7	(3200) .7	Quick	(517) .6	(764) .7	.7	(542) .7	.8	(450) .9
.2	.2	.2		.2	.2	.2	.3	.3	.4
0 UND	0 UND	0 UND		0 UND	0 UND	0 UND	0 UND	0 UND	0 UND
0 UND	0 UND	0 UND	Sales/Receivables	0 UND	0 UND	0 UND	0 UND	0 UND	13 28.0
17 21.0	8 45.2	13 28.2		0 UND	0 UND	0 999.8	24 15.0	35 10.6	45 8.1
			Cost of Sales/Inventory						
			Cost of Sales/Payables						
23.7	24.0	24.2		29.6	27.1	29.8	28.1	23.9	16.0
-148.5	-137.6	-132.6	Sales/Working Capital	-52.0	-110.9	-124.9	-112.9	-167.3	185.3
-21.6	-21.6	-20.9		-7.1	-17.6	-25.0	-26.3	-29.2	-30.1
18.8	20.6	17.7		15.2	21.1	17.0	23.1	19.4	12.2
(2136) 4.1	(2337) 4.5	(2496) 3.8	EBIT/Interest	(305) 5.0	(569) 4.2	(374) 3.4	(440) 3.5	(416) 4.0	(392) 3.2
.7	1.0	.8		.9	1.0	.3	.7	.9	.9
3.5	3.4	3.3			4.4	5.6	2.8	3.2	3.8
(166) 1.6	(167) 1.6	(206) 1.7	Net Profit + Depr., Dep., Amort./Cur. Mat. L/T/D	(19) 1.1	(19) 2.1	(28) 1.7	(54) 1.6	(82) 1.8	
.9	.9	.9			.5	.5	.7	1.2	1.0
.6	.6	.6		.6	.5	.6	.6	.7	.6
3.2	3.4	3.5	Fixed/Worth	4.9	3.7	3.9	4.1	2.8	2.1
-2.2	-2.6	-3.3		-2.1	-1.6	-2.4	-3.2	-6.1	-24.4
1.2	1.2	1.3		1.1	1.2	1.4	1.2	1.2	1.3
9.0	8.8	9.2	Debt/Worth	9.7	20.0	10.4	11.8	6.7	4.9
-5.2	-5.7	-6.7		-4.1	-4.0	-5.2	-6.5	-11.8	-33.4
212.0	226.9	222.2		221.6	353.0	250.1	219.7	177.6	119.4
(1714) 53.2	(1840) 52.5	(1999) 56.3	% Profit Before Taxes/Tangible Net Worth	(319) 85.0	(438) 95.9	(266) 55.7	(334) 53.3	(315) 39.4	(327) 23.9
6.6	8.7	6.0		15.3	16.7	-.2	1.0	5.0	1.6
49.1	55.3	54.4		66.5	76.1	50.9	51.6	35.5	21.9
9.3	10.6	10.2	% Profit Before Taxes/Total Assets	17.6	18.6	10.5	8.4	7.0	5.3
-.8	.0	-.4		.5	.0	-3.4	-1.0	-.1	-.2
77.8	70.5	69.2		76.8	101.5	71.3	66.8	51.9	37.7
23.2	23.1	21.2	Sales/Net Fixed Assets	14.5	28.5	25.4	25.2	19.1	15.1
8.8	8.5	7.7		2.0	8.6	10.4	11.0	9.1	6.9
14.5	14.5	14.0		9.6	15.0	16.9	17.2	14.1	10.0
6.6	6.7	6.6	Sales/Total Assets	4.1	6.7	8.4	8.7	7.3	4.7
2.9	2.9	2.8		.9	3.1	3.8	3.6	3.2	2.5
.9	.8	.8		1.0	.6	.7	.8	.9	1.0
(1964) 1.9	(2239) 1.7	(2367) 1.8	% Depr., Dep., Amort./Sales	(324) 3.3	(509) 1.5	(331) 1.5	(412) 1.7	(409) 1.7	(382) 2.0
3.8	3.3	3.5		15.1	4.0	3.1	2.8	2.8	3.3
14.0	14.9	15.1		16.2	14.2	15.3	17.0	17.8	11.2
(1506) 25.3	(1593) 25.8	(1720) 25.8	% Officers', Directors' Owners' Comp/Sales	(258) 24.0	(489) 22.9	(270) 26.3	(301) 29.3	(230) 30.6	(172) 25.2
35.8	36.4	35.8		33.3	33.1	35.9	38.0	39.9	36.2
93139771M	69881505M	110263769M	Net Sales ($)	291353M	1462170M	1735232M	3854093M	7490906M	95430015M
13964307M	14899872M	18600243M	Total Assets ($)	307208M	631838M	493108M	995159M	1855313M	14317617M

M = $ thousand   MM = $ million
See Pages 11 through 21 for Explanation of Ratios and Data

Current Data Sorted by Assets   Comparative Historical Data

0-500M	500M-2MM	2-10MM	10-50MM	50-100MM	100-250MM	Type of Statement	4/1/02-3/31/03 ALL	4/1/03-3/31/04 ALL
						Unqualified		4
	1	6	6			Reviewed	1	1
8	4	2			1	Compiled	10	8
14	4					Tax Returns	10	14
6	4	5	3	1		Other	5	4
	16 (4/1-9/30/06)		49 (10/1/06-3/31/07)					
28	13	13	9	1	1	**NUMBER OF STATEMENTS**	26	31
%	%	%	%	%	%	**ASSETS**	%	%
32.1	18.6	17.9				Cash & Equivalents	32.5	25.2
14.5	20.2	24.7				Trade Receivables (net)	13.5	12.1
.5	4.2	.8				Inventory	.6	.1
3.7	3.7	2.7				All Other Current	3.5	3.8
50.8	46.8	46.1				Total Current	50.1	41.3
31.1	40.1	43.3				Fixed Assets (net)	37.5	44.3
7.9	4.0	.1				Intangibles (net)	7.0	5.0
10.3	9.1	10.5				All Other Non-Current	5.5	9.5
100.0	100.0	100.0				Total	100.0	100.0
						LIABILITIES		
33.7	12.3	8.4				Notes Payable-Short Term	23.5	36.4
14.9	3.3	4.2				Cur. Mat.-L.T.D.	9.2	6.1
.6	2.3	7.8				Trade Payables	2.1	4.0
.0	.9	.0				Income Taxes Payable	.0	.1
51.4	12.0	13.1				All Other Current	19.3	20.8
100.6	30.8	33.6				Total Current	54.0	67.4
28.3	20.9	22.1				Long-Term Debt	21.2	29.6
.0	.3	.0				Deferred Taxes	.0	.0
1.8	4.4	.9				All Other Non-Current	19.8	13.8
-30.6	43.6	43.4				Net Worth	5.0	-10.8
100.0	100.0	100.0				Total Liabilities & Net Worth	100.0	100.0
						INCOME DATA		
100.0	100.0	100.0				Net Sales	100.0	100.0
						Gross Profit		
83.8	76.3	93.9				Operating Expenses	83.1	87.9
16.2	23.7	6.1				Operating Profit	16.9	12.1
.8	6.7	2.2				All Other Expenses (net)	3.4	2.8
15.4	17.0	3.9				Profit Before Taxes	13.5	9.4
						RATIOS		
1.7	3.8	4.4					6.7	2.1
.7	1.1	1.5				Current	1.4	.5
.2	.4	.5					.4	.2
1.6	2.4	4.0					6.3	1.8
.6	1.1	1.5				Quick	1.1	.4
.1	.3	.5					.4	.2
0 UND	0 UND	16 23.5					0 UND	0 UND
0 UND	0 UND	52 7.0				Sales/Receivables	0 UND	0 UND
1 304.8	44 8.2	74 5.0					6 65.8	35 10.3
						Cost of Sales/Inventory		
						Cost of Sales/Payables		
29.0	7.8	3.6					10.6	11.4
-180.1	620.8	6.5				Sales/Working Capital	39.2	-41.2
-13.0	-8.4	-30.1					-23.3	-13.8
24.8	206.8						135.3	54.3
(15) 2.5	(12) 26.2					EBIT/Interest	(20) 11.0	(22) 2.9
-1.8	2.9						1.7	-.6
						Net Profit + Depr., Dep., Amort./Cur. Mat. L/T/D		
.2	.1	.2					.4	.3
3.8	1.7	1.3				Fixed/Worth	1.8	6.5
-.9	6.8	2.3					-1.6	-1.0
1.8	.4	.5					.4	1.0
UND	1.8	1.4				Debt/Worth	4.0	121.3
-2.0	7.7	3.0					-4.1	-2.4
693.3	405.1	32.6					241.1	499.1
(15) 308.4	(12) 67.1	(12) 8.7				% Profit Before Taxes/Tangible Net Worth	(15) 126.9	(16) 30.4
.0	2.7	-2.5					25.7	-6.3
267.9	62.6	8.5					118.8	76.5
67.6	39.8	1.9				% Profit Before Taxes/Total Assets	21.6	3.0
-.6	.1	-1.4					.7	-3.0
339.9	105.7	16.3					39.3	42.1
67.4	17.5	9.4				Sales/Net Fixed Assets	18.5	20.8
20.9	6.0	2.4					10.0	8.3
25.1	6.4	3.1					12.8	14.0
11.3	4.5	1.6				Sales/Total Assets	6.4	9.5
4.5	1.1	1.1					2.4	2.6
.3		.8					.7	.7
(16) 1.0		(12) 1.5				% Depr., Dep., Amort./Sales	(19) 2.1	(25) 2.4
3.1		5.7					4.8	3.5
17.4							10.8	9.5
(14) 23.9						% Officers', Directors' Owners' Comp/Sales	(16) 22.7	(14) 22.9
40.7							30.7	33.1
70558M	68954M	154636M	484956M	29377M	858908M	Net Sales ($)	1036650M	204516M
5912M	15556M	56410M	212899M	76076M	238237M	Total Assets ($)	234435M	90311M

© RMA 2007

M = $ thousand   MM = $ million
See Pages 11 through 21 for Explanation of Ratios and Data

Comparative Historical Data | | | | Current Data Sorted by Sales

			Type of Statement						
3	8	13	Unqualified		1		4	2	6
1	1		Reviewed						
12	13	15	Compiled	1	6	3	2	1	2
14	25	18	Tax Returns	6	7	1	2	2	2
8	12	19	Other	3	6	2	1		3
4/1/04-3/31/05	4/1/05-3/31/06	4/1/06-3/31/07			16 (4/1-9/30/06)		49 (10/1/06-3/31/07)		
ALL	ALL	ALL		0-1MM	1-3MM	3-5MM	5-10MM	10-25MM	25MM & OVER
38	59	65	**NUMBER OF STATEMENTS**	10	19	7	12	6	11
%	%	%	**ASSETS**	%	%	%	%	%	%
28.0	33.0	24.7	Cash & Equivalents	22.9	29.4		28.0		21.4
6.1	10.9	17.6	Trade Receivables (net)	18.2	17.3		17.9		13.4
.4	.8	2.3	Inventory	1.0	2.8		.6		6.6
5.3	7.3	3.5	All Other Current	.3	6.6		5.0		1.8
39.9	51.9	48.1	Total Current	42.4	56.1		51.5		43.1
41.2	35.0	36.3	Fixed Assets (net)	48.4	26.8		39.5		39.5
5.3	3.0	4.8	Intangibles (net)	8.9	4.2		6.5		3.5
13.6	10.1	10.9	All Other Non-Current	.3	12.9		2.4		13.9
100.0	100.0	100.0	Total	100.0	100.0		100.0		100.0
			LIABILITIES						
23.1	27.8	20.7	Notes Payable-Short Term	19.7	34.0		13.6		13.0
7.2	7.1	8.2	Cur. Mat.-L.T.D.	6.6	19.7		1.6		5.6
.8	3.1	3.3	Trade Payables	.7	1.3		2.8		5.4
.5	1.5	.2	Income Taxes Payable	.0	.0		.9		.0
35.3	33.3	29.4	All Other Current	9.6	57.9		14.3		18.6
66.9	72.9	61.8	Total Current	36.7	112.9		33.3		42.7
44.2	31.7	22.5	Long-Term Debt	65.1	15.2		23.0		13.4
.0	.0	.1	Deferred Taxes	.0	.0		.3		.0
4.4	5.7	2.5	All Other Non-Current	4.6	.5		2.6		2.4
-15.5	-10.2	13.2	Net Worth	-6.4	-28.6		40.8		41.5
100.0	100.0	100.0	Total Liabilties & Net Worth	100.0	100.0		100.0		100.0
			INCOME DATA						
100.0	100.0	100.0	Net Sales	100.0	100.0		100.0		100.0
			Gross Profit						
87.9	90.6	86.2	Operating Expenses	71.1	86.4		95.3		94.7
12.1	9.4	13.8	Operating Profit	28.9	13.6		4.7		5.3
3.9	.1	2.2	All Other Expenses (net)	12.9	-1.0		2.0		-.3
8.1	9.3	11.6	Profit Before Taxes	16.0	14.6		2.7		5.6
			RATIOS						
1.3	2.5	2.8		2.3	4.9		4.5		2.0
.7	1.1	1.1	Current	1.2	.9		2.3		.9
.2	.4	.4		.2	.2		.8		.4
1.2	2.1	2.3		2.3	2.0		3.6		1.5
.5	.8	.9	Quick	1.2	.6		2.3		.9
.2	.3	.3		.2	.1		.8		.2
0 UND	0 UND	0 UND		0 UND	0 UND		0 UND		0 UND
0 UND	0 UND	1 470.2	Sales/Receivables	0 UND	0 UND		34 10.9		22 16.4
4 88.3	8 48.2	47 7.8		48 7.5	7 52.8		65 5.6		46 8.0
			Cost of Sales/Inventory						
			Cost of Sales/Payables						
76.1	15.1	6.6		10.2	9.1		3.1		5.6
-63.6	330.5	658.3	Sales/Working Capital	NM	-458.0		28.0		-83.1
-16.3	-23.2	-20.0		-3.3	-8.1		-52.2		-26.0
9.5	65.9	28.1			117.7				
(23) 2.8	(42) 9.7	(41) 3.7	EBIT/Interest		(11) 2.0				
-2.2	.5	.2			-1.0				
			Net Profit + Depr., Dep., Amort./Cur. Mat. L/T/D						
1.0	.4	.2		.0	.1		.4		.5
7.1	2.4	1.4	Fixed/Worth	7.1	1.3		1.6		.9
-.8	-.8	16.5		NM	UND		5.0		2.3
1.7	.7	.5		1.4	.5		.5		.5
80.8	6.6	2.6	Debt/Worth	21.9	7.0		2.2		2.0
-2.6	-3.1	UND		-1.8	-2.2		7.0		2.9
552.4	173.8	310.2			644.5		120.2		81.7
(20) 44.8	(35) 52.4	(50) 24.6	% Profit Before Taxes/Tangible Net Worth		(13) 64.0		(10) 5.5		(10) 13.2
6.0	5.2	.0			-53.4		-1.6		.0
43.8	106.1	78.0		92.5	269.0		17.6		11.4
10.6	16.2	9.0	% Profit Before Taxes/Total Assets	24.0	55.3		2.6		6.7
-1.8	-.5	-.5		.8	-.8		-3.3		-.3
73.1	78.2	74.5		UND	303.0		15.7		28.9
37.5	33.2	18.7	Sales/Net Fixed Assets	10.3	32.1		11.0		6.9
10.8	10.2	4.7		.2	17.6		2.8		2.7
15.6	15.9	11.5		4.7	15.4		6.7		6.1
9.4	7.9	4.4	Sales/Total Assets	1.7	5.8		2.2		3.0
1.9	3.8	1.4		.2	4.4		1.3		.9
.8	.7	.6			.2				.8
(26) 1.2	(41) 1.3	(46) 1.3	% Depr., Dep., Amort./Sales		(12) .9				(10) 2.0
3.5	2.6	3.8			1.3				3.2
16.5	11.3	9.1							
(22) 24.2	(31) 22.5	(24) 23.2	% Officers', Directors' Owners' Comp/Sales						
35.3	31.9	38.5							
343518M	1110168M	1667389M	Net Sales ($)	4965M	31668M	29082M	80141M	94299M	1427234M
167224M	566361M	605090M	Total Assets ($)	8981M	9045M	6082M	43656M	32680M	504646M

© RMA 2007

M = $ thousand   MM = $ million

See Pages 11 through 21 for Explanation of Ratios and Data

Current Data Sorted by Assets   Comparative Historical Data

0-500M	500M-2MM	2-10MM	10-50MM	50-100MM	100-250MM	Type of Statement	4/1/02-3/31/03 ALL	4/1/03-3/31/04 ALL
2	5		5	2	3	Unqualified	13	14
5	4	2	1			Reviewed	10	17
110	54	7	1	1	7	Compiled	153	196
365	83	8	1	1	4	Tax Returns	295	403
136	44	14	1	3		Other	116	136
	77 (4/1-9/30/06)		798 (10/1/06-3/31/07)					
618	190	31	15	7	14	**NUMBER OF STATEMENTS**	587	766
%	%	%	%	%	%	**ASSETS**	%	%
23.7	13.8	13.1	18.8		6.1	Cash & Equivalents	20.4	22.3
4.2	8.4	12.1	17.0		1.6	Trade Receivables (net)	6.8	6.8
.3	.5	3.3	2.2		1.1	Inventory	.6	.4
3.4	3.2	2.2	4.9		1.8	All Other Current	2.4	2.2
31.6	25.9	30.6	42.9		10.6	Total Current	30.2	31.9
45.3	47.1	52.6	24.7		28.9	Fixed Assets (net)	47.4	45.3
13.4	20.0	7.2	15.5		40.0	Intangibles (net)	13.4	12.8
9.7	7.0	9.6	16.8		20.5	All Other Non-Current	9.0	10.0
100.0	100.0	100.0	100.0		100.0	Total	100.0	100.0
						LIABILITIES		
15.6	8.4	7.2	5.2		13.1	Notes Payable-Short Term	14.6	13.3
8.6	6.7	7.1	6.6		8.6	Cur. Mat.-L.T.D.	9.9	7.7
1.4	2.1	3.6	9.7		.9	Trade Payables	2.7	2.6
.1	.3	.7	.0		.0	Income Taxes Payable	.7	.4
25.6	10.7	17.4	60.0		8.9	All Other Current	19.8	19.0
51.4	28.2	36.1	81.5		31.4	Total Current	47.6	43.1
45.4	51.8	42.3	22.5		55.4	Long-Term Debt	42.7	41.0
.0	.1	.6	.4		1.2	Deferred Taxes	.1	.1
6.0	7.5	7.9	8.7		13.7	All Other Non-Current	5.8	5.7
-2.7	12.4	13.2	-13.2		-1.6	Net Worth	3.8	10.1
100.0	100.0	100.0	100.0		100.0	Total Liabilities & Net Worth	100.0	100.0
						INCOME DATA		
100.0	100.0	100.0	100.0		100.0	Net Sales	100.0	100.0
						Gross Profit		
87.7	87.1	87.6	95.1		89.1	Operating Expenses	89.1	88.2
12.3	12.9	12.4	4.9		10.9	Operating Profit	10.9	11.8
1.5	3.4	6.1	-.1		4.4	All Other Expenses (net)	2.3	2.2
10.8	9.5	6.3	5.0		6.5	Profit Before Taxes	8.6	9.6
						RATIOS		
2.0	2.5	1.4	1.0		1.0	Current	1.7	1.9
.7	.9	1.1	.7		.5		.7	.7
.2	.3	.5	.4		.1		.2	.3
1.7	2.1	1.4	.8		.8	Quick	1.6	1.8
(615) .6	(188) .8	.9	.6		.3		(584) .6	(763) .6
.2	.2	.4	.4		.0		.2	.2
0 UND	0 UND	0 UND	3 123.1		0 UND	Sales/Receivables	0 UND	0 UND
0 UND	0 UND	0 UND	16 22.7		0 UND		0 UND	0 UND
0 UND	0 862.0	25 14.8	22 16.4		1 267.2		0 UND	0 UND
						Cost of Sales/Inventory		
						Cost of Sales/Payables		
40.4	18.2	28.0	-999.8		NM	Sales/Working Capital	28.0	28.6
-97.0	-327.1	142.7	-37.2		-17.6		-71.1	-85.8
-17.8	-16.6	-15.4	-15.2		-10.4		-16.5	-18.4
20.4	12.5	21.8	26.6		5.7	EBIT/Interest	12.3	15.7
(467) 5.5	(160) 2.9	(25) 5.8	(11) 8.7		1.6		(483) 3.5	(606) 3.8
1.1	1.0	1.8	2.1		.8		1.0	.9
						Net Profit + Depr., Dep., Amort./Cur. Mat. L/T/D	8.4	6.0
							(27) 2.4	(26) 2.1
							1.3	.7
1.0	1.4	1.6	.6		-4.7	Fixed/Worth	1.3	1.1
27.2	41.2	5.2	2.6		-.6		17.1	10.4
-.8	-1.5	-11.8	-.6		-.3		-1.3	-1.4
1.4	2.0	2.9	1.0		-8.5	Debt/Worth	1.8	1.5
201.5	UND	9.3	6.3		-2.4		59.0	29.4
-2.4	-3.2	-21.5	-4.9		-1.7		-3.3	-3.3
454.4	146.3	98.4				% Profit Before Taxes/Tangible Net Worth	266.5	221.1
(318) 142.8	(96) 63.1	(20) 58.1					(309) 75.2	(425) 88.7
44.6	16.3	21.4					13.2	13.7
92.3	35.0	21.1	17.2		23.5	% Profit Before Taxes/Total Assets	56.9	63.0
28.8	12.5	8.3	11.5		3.7		13.5	15.5
1.6	.0	2.1	5.8		-1.8		.0	.0
44.9	21.1	18.4	29.8		24.6	Sales/Net Fixed Assets	33.0	35.0
18.1	7.3	5.2	10.2		6.5		12.8	13.9
8.1	2.7	3.3	6.1		3.7		5.9	6.5
11.8	4.0	4.3	3.5		5.8	Sales/Total Assets	9.4	8.9
6.0	2.3	3.0	2.6		2.9		4.5	4.8
3.2	1.4	1.9	1.7		.6		2.4	2.7
1.0	1.8	1.1	1.7			% Depr., Dep., Amort./Sales	1.4	1.3
(411) 2.1	(133) 4.0	(26) 2.2	(12) 2.6				(439) 2.8	(543) 2.7
4.7	7.1	4.4	3.8				5.1	5.2
13.8	10.8	3.3				% Officers', Directors' Owners' Comp/Sales	14.2	14.8
(461) 20.3	(126) 15.6	(16) 17.8					(406) 20.0	(556) 22.1
27.1	26.1	26.5					27.9	29.6
827656M	557572M	387317M	3366702M	5062619M	8357951M	Net Sales ($)	24916966M	12729832M
131346M	171886M	128172M	420187M	535379M	2424283M	Total Assets ($)	3764184M	2651934M

© RMA 2007

M = $ thousand   MM = $ million
See Pages 11 through 21 for Explanation of Ratios and Data

Comparative Historical Data

Current Data Sorted by Sales

Type of Statement

				0-1MM	1-3MM	3-5MM	5-10MM	10-25MM	25MM & OVER
15	11	17	Unqualified	2	2	1	2		10
8	12	12	Reviewed	1	6	1	1	2	1
159	148	173	Compiled	62	77	15	12	4	3
414	389	465	Tax Returns	200	196	34	20	6	9
154	203	208	Other	78	79	12	14	12	13
4/1/04-3/31/05 ALL	4/1/05-3/31/06 ALL	4/1/06-3/31/07 ALL		77 (4/1-9/30/06)			798 (10/1/06-3/31/07)		
750	763	875	**NUMBER OF STATEMENTS**	343	360	63	49	24	36
%	%	%	**ASSETS**	%	%	%	%	%	%
23.0	23.0	20.7	Cash & Equivalents	20.8	20.3	27.3	20.4	23.2	9.9
5.7	5.7	5.6	Trade Receivables (net)	4.2	5.2	6.5	10.0	12.2	11.4
.4	.4	.5	Inventory	.5	.2	.4	.3	3.8	1.8
2.4	2.0	3.4	All Other Current	3.9	2.4	5.1	4.4	2.8	4.0
31.6	31.2	30.1	Total Current	29.4	28.0	39.3	35.1	41.9	27.1
42.8	42.5	45.4	Fixed Assets (net)	45.2	46.6	46.1	48.8	40.7	33.3
15.2	16.5	15.1	Intangibles (net)	16.2	15.7	9.5	6.2	5.5	26.5
10.4	9.7	9.4	All Other Non-Current	9.1	9.7	5.1	9.9	11.9	13.0
100.0	100.0	100.0	Total	100.0	100.0	100.0	100.0	100.0	100.0
			LIABILITIES						
14.2	16.4	13.4	Notes Payable-Short Term	11.8	14.5	13.3	14.2	27.8	7.6
8.0	7.0	8.1	Cur. Mat.-L.T.D.	8.1	8.2	6.5	9.9	6.6	8.1
3.0	2.4	1.8	Trade Payables	2.3	1.0	.5	1.8	3.2	6.0
.2	.2	.2	Income Taxes Payable	.0	.1	.4	.1	2.0	.1
19.2	19.0	22.4	All Other Current	22.4	19.5	27.5	23.8	32.9	34.5
44.6	44.9	45.9	Total Current	44.6	43.4	48.3	49.8	72.4	56.3
44.2	45.3	46.5	Long-Term Debt	53.6	45.4	33.4	35.0	26.2	42.2
.1	.1	.1	Deferred Taxes	.0	.0	.0	.4	.0	.7
4.1	7.6	6.7	All Other Non-Current	5.6	7.7	2.5	6.5	9.9	14.2
7.0	2.1	.8	Net Worth	-3.8	3.6	15.9	8.4	-8.5	-13.4
100.0	100.0	100.0	Total Liabilties & Net Worth	100.0	100.0	100.0	100.0	100.0	100.0
			INCOME DATA						
100.0	100.0	100.0	Net Sales	100.0	100.0	100.0	100.0	100.0	100.0
			Gross Profit						
88.5	87.7	87.7	Operating Expenses	84.7	88.2	92.8	92.4	92.8	92.9
11.5	12.3	12.3	Operating Profit	15.3	11.8	7.2	7.6	7.2	7.1
1.8	1.9	2.1	All Other Expenses (net)	3.3	1.4	.7	.5	.7	2.7
9.7	10.4	10.2	Profit Before Taxes	11.9	10.3	6.5	7.1	6.5	4.4
			RATIOS						
2.1	2.2	2.0	Current	2.5	2.0	2.2	1.4	1.9	1.2
.8	.9	.8		.9	.7	1.0	.8	1.0	.7
.2	.3	.2		.2	.3	.5	.2	.5	.4
2.0	2.0	1.8	Quick	2.0	1.8	1.7	1.3	1.9	.9
(746) .7	(759) .8	(870) .7		(342) .7	(356) .6	.9	.7	.8	.6
.2	.2	.2		.1	.2	.3	.2	.3	.3
0 UND	0 UND	0 UND	Sales/Receivables	0 UND	0 UND	0 UND	0 UND	0 UND	0 UND
0 UND	0 UND	0 UND		0 UND	0 UND	0 UND	0 UND	0 999.8	12 30.6
0 UND	0 UND	0 UND		0 UND	0 UND	0 UND	1 554.2	22 16.4	22 16.6
			Cost of Sales/Inventory						
			Cost of Sales/Payables						
26.8	26.9	33.1	Sales/Working Capital	18.6	46.3	28.6	74.7	26.9	129.9
-99.2	-159.9	-110.5		-165.5	-84.4	-824.3	-77.4	NM	-35.1
-17.2	-18.4	-17.1		-12.1	-19.0	-53.3	-20.4	-21.5	-13.9
18.4	15.5	16.6	EBIT/Interest	12.2	21.3	20.1	29.3	26.3	9.7
(581) 4.5	(601) 5.6	(684) 4.6		(250) 4.3	(289) 5.4	(50) 4.4	(43) 6.4	(19) 6.3	(33) 2.5
1.0	1.4	1.1		1.3	1.0	.8	1.1	3.6	1.4
4.9	7.6	3.4	Net Profit + Depr., Dep., Amort./Cur. Mat. L/T/D						20.0
(18) 2.1	(18) 1.8	(27) 2.0						(10)	2.2
.5	.8	1.4							1.4
.9	1.0	1.1	Fixed/Worth	1.1	1.1	.9	1.3	1.0	2.1
10.8	29.1	36.8		-999.8	10.3	17.0	10.0	3.0	-2.0
-1.2	-1.0	-.9		-.6	-1.0	-2.1	-2.7	-3.6	-.4
1.4	1.6	1.7	Debt/Worth	2.0	1.3	.7	3.1	2.0	5.9
71.6	-304.0	243.0		-43.3	70.7	21.2	16.6	21.8	-5.7
-2.9	-2.6	-2.4		-2.2	-2.4	-6.0	-10.4		-1.7
292.6	307.8	370.0	% Profit Before Taxes/Tangible Net Worth	395.9	364.0	409.0	214.2	168.1	150.8
(394) 95.9	(381) 110.0	(447) 119.0		(167) 134.2	(188) 123.0	(37) 77.3	(28) 52.4	(14) 90.5	(13) 39.3
16.9	18.5	28.1		40.0	30.0	18.3	18.6	36.5	17.1
67.3	67.9	71.6	% Profit Before Taxes/Total Assets	68.7	81.8	69.2	46.2	33.3	14.7
18.1	25.6	21.0		23.6	24.9	21.0	13.3	17.7	7.8
.3	1.6	1.3		1.8	.2	.9	.7	4.2	1.5
38.3	37.5	37.3	Sales/Net Fixed Assets	29.6	41.3	65.7	34.0	41.0	23.8
15.3	14.4	14.2		10.6	16.4	27.9	18.5	14.3	9.4
6.9	6.6	5.7		4.2	7.6	10.1	7.7	5.6	5.6
8.9	9.2	9.2	Sales/Total Assets	6.1	10.7	17.4	13.0	7.4	5.5
4.7	4.6	4.5		3.3	5.8	8.3	6.6	4.6	2.9
2.5	2.4	2.3		1.9	2.9	3.9	4.0	3.1	1.8
1.2	1.1	1.2	% Depr., Dep., Amort./Sales	1.6	1.1	.5	1.1	.8	1.4
(491) 2.6	(510) 2.4	(594) 2.5		(230) 4.2	(240) 2.0	(43) 1.6	(37) 1.9	(19) 1.7	(25) 2.9
5.1	4.8	5.2		8.0	4.1	3.1	2.9	2.4	4.8
13.6	12.2	12.8	% Officers', Directors' Owners' Comp/Sales	11.5	13.7	13.8	14.0	2.3	14.0
(543) 21.4	(554) 19.4	(614) 19.6		(237) 18.3	(274) 17.1	(46) 25.8	(33) 28.4	(13) 17.7	(11) 21.6
28.9	27.3	26.8		25.5	25.9	34.2	37.6	28.1	31.8
13316972M	23214943M	18559817M	Net Sales ($)	225309M	582327M	237800M	318804M	359850M	16835727M
2452000M	4063470M	3811253M	Total Assets ($)	95181M	140520M	39255M	73344M	102189M	3360764M

© RMA 2007

M = $ thousand   MM = $ million

See Pages 11 through 21 for Explanation of Ratios and Data

Current Data Sorted by Assets

Comparative Historical Data

				1			Type of Statement				
							Unqualified			1	1
	12	1					Reviewed			1	
	54	6				1	Compiled			17	20
	30	9		1	1	2	Tax Returns			44	44
				2	1	Other			20	26
		5 (4/1-9/30/06)		116 (10/1/06-3/31/07)						4/1/02-3/31/03	4/1/03-3/31/04
	0-500M	500M-2MM	2-10MM	10-50MM	50-100MM	100-250MM				ALL	ALL
	96	16	1	1	3	4	NUMBER OF STATEMENTS			83	91
	%	%	%	%	%	%	ASSETS			%	%
	24.5	12.6					Cash & Equivalents			24.0	21.2
	8.6	23.9					Trade Receivables (net)			15.2	12.5
	.6	1.6					Inventory			.6	.9
	4.4	7.0					All Other Current			2.7	5.4
	38.1	45.0					Total Current			42.6	40.0
	37.4	26.1					Fixed Assets (net)			42.1	37.0
	7.3	16.5					Intangibles (net)			7.2	13.3
	17.0	12.3					All Other Non-Current			8.2	9.7
	100.0	100.0					Total			100.0	100.0
							LIABILITIES				
	26.5	12.3					Notes Payable-Short Term			36.1	20.0
	5.7	2.3					Cur. Mat.-L.T.D.			6.7	10.7
	2.6	4.1					Trade Payables			5.7	1.8
	.7	.8					Income Taxes Payable			.8	.3
	19.5	5.1					All Other Current			20.9	13.1
	55.1	24.5					Total Current			70.2	46.0
	22.6	24.7					Long-Term Debt			29.3	38.0
	.0	.0					Deferred Taxes			.3	.4
	8.1	3.4					All Other Non-Current			7.0	13.1
	14.1	47.4					Net Worth			-6.8	2.6
	100.0	100.0					Total Liabilties & Net Worth			100.0	100.0
							INCOME DATA				
	100.0	100.0					Net Sales			100.0	100.0
							Gross Profit				
	87.3	80.3					Operating Expenses			85.1	84.2
	12.7	19.7					Operating Profit			14.9	15.8
	2.1	2.3					All Other Expenses (net)			2.7	2.6
	10.5	17.4					Profit Before Taxes			12.1	13.2
							RATIOS				
	3.4	12.4								5.3	2.8
	1.0	4.9					Current			1.2	1.1
	.3	1.0								.2	.3
	3.0	12.4								3.6	2.5
	.9	2.7					Quick			1.2	1.0
	.2	.3								.2	.2
0	UND	0 UND						0	UND	0	UND
0	UND	1 458.4					Sales/Receivables	0	UND	0	UND
0	UND	165 2.2						18	20.3	0	UND
							Cost of Sales/Inventory				
							Cost of Sales/Payables				
	14.3	2.1								9.5	10.7
	UND	10.2					Sales/Working Capital			112.0	201.5
	-11.6	NM								-8.8	-23.4
	14.9	15.4								28.3	23.6
(64)	4.2	(10) 4.3					EBIT/Interest	(62)	4.5	(69) 7.5
	1.4	2.7								.7	1.0
							Net Profit + Depr., Dep., Amort./Cur. Mat. L/T/D				
	.2	.2								.4	.5
	1.3	.7					Fixed/Worth			2.0	2.6
	-5.0	12.0								-1.5	-1.1
	.5	.1								.7	1.1
	3.6	.8					Debt/Worth			5.2	11.5
	-8.5	90.3								-2.7	-3.6
	318.4	104.5								295.4	282.0
(65)	92.0	(13) 51.3					% Profit Before Taxes/Tangible Net Worth	(53)	121.0	(52) 132.5
	36.3	12.4								25.4	13.6
	80.0	55.0								104.2	96.9
	29.9	14.6					% Profit Before Taxes/Total Assets			28.5	33.9
	2.5	4.0								2.3	.7
	78.3	32.7								35.3	38.4
	16.8	12.6					Sales/Net Fixed Assets			14.7	15.3
	6.6	3.4								6.5	7.2
	8.8	1.8								8.8	7.0
	5.2	1.2					Sales/Total Assets			4.0	4.1
	2.4	.6								1.9	2.0
	.8									1.4	1.0
(51)	2.0						% Depr., Dep., Amort./Sales	(52)	2.8	(60) 2.0
	3.7									4.9	3.2
	11.0									7.9	12.0
(61)	17.6						% Officers', Directors' Owners' Comp/Sales	(50)	13.7	(66) 18.3
	25.1									25.7	28.8
	63012M	34639M	13160M	111890M	1236922M	1313334M	Net Sales ($)			706434M	1813990M
	13666M	15957M	2061M	42066M	204519M	669470M	Total Assets ($)			207685M	328800M

M = $ thousand   MM = $ million
See Pages 11 through 21 for Explanation of Ratios and Data

Comparative Historical Data

Current Data Sorted by Sales

04-05 ALL	05-06 ALL	06-07 ALL	Type of Statement	0-1MM	1-3MM	3-5MM	5-10MM	10-25MM	25MM & OVER
			Unqualified						
3	1	1	Reviewed	9	3		1	1	1
15	14	14	Compiled	52	7	1			4
53	53	64	Tax Returns	27	10	1		1	3
22	27	42	Other						
4/1/04-3/31/05	4/1/05-3/31/06	4/1/06-3/31/07		5 (4/1-9/30/06)			116 (10/1/06-3/31/07)		
93	**95**	**121**	**NUMBER OF STATEMENTS**	**88**	**20**	**2**	**1**	**2**	**8**
%	%	%	**ASSETS**	%	%	%	%	%	%
23.6	22.3	23.8	Cash & Equivalents	23.5	17.7				
8.9	8.5	10.5	Trade Receivables (net)	12.6	4.7				
2.0	.4	.7	Inventory	.6	.1				
4.8	4.7	4.5	All Other Current	3.4	9.2				
39.2	35.9	39.6	Total Current	40.1	31.8				
41.2	42.4	36.3	Fixed Assets (net)	34.8	41.4				
8.5	11.6	8.8	Intangibles (net)	8.8	9.7				
11.2	10.1	15.3	All Other Non-Current	16.2	17.2				
100.0	100.0	100.0	Total	100.0	100.0				
			LIABILITIES						
15.1	24.0	23.2	Notes Payable-Short Term	25.3	17.1				
9.6	5.4	4.9	Cur. Mat.-L.T.D.	6.4	.6				
2.5	1.2	2.8	Trade Payables	2.4	2.5				
.1	.1	.6	Income Taxes Payable	.7	.6				
23.5	20.2	16.6	All Other Current	17.8	16.3				
50.7	50.8	48.1	Total Current	52.7	37.1				
36.9	31.6	22.9	Long-Term Debt	24.2	20.1				
.3	.0	.0	Deferred Taxes	.0	.0				
4.8	9.4	7.0	All Other Non-Current	4.5	22.0				
7.2	8.2	22.0	Net Worth	18.6	20.9				
100.0	100.0	100.0	Total Liabilties & Net Worth	100.0	100.0				
			INCOME DATA						
100.0	100.0	100.0	Net Sales	100.0	100.0				
			Gross Profit						
86.7	82.8	85.7	Operating Expenses	86.2	86.3				
13.3	17.2	14.3	Operating Profit	13.8	13.7				
2.8	3.2	2.1	All Other Expenses (net)	2.4	1.7				
10.5	14.0	12.3	Profit Before Taxes	11.5	11.9				
			RATIOS						
3.7	3.5	4.4	Current	3.4	11.7				
.9	1.2	1.6		1.2	3.5				
.3	.3	.4		.3	.4				
3.3	3.5	3.6	Quick	3.1	11.1				
(92) .7	(94) 1.0	1.3		.9	2.7				
.2	.2	.2		.2	.3				
0 UND	0 UND	0 UND	Sales/Receivables	0 UND	0 UND				
0 UND	0 UND	0 UND		0 UND	0 UND				
2 173.8	0 UND	5 76.4		11 33.1	0 UND				
			Cost of Sales/Inventory						
			Cost of Sales/Payables						
8.9	10.8	10.4	Sales/Working Capital	11.1	9.8				
-399.0	207.0	88.8		122.8	46.9				
-10.7	-20.4	-16.9		-11.0	-20.4				
19.0	28.6	17.1	EBIT/Interest	19.9	10.6				
(69) 3.5	(68) 6.7	(80) 4.5		(57) 4.4	(15) 3.8				
-.2	1.2	1.8		1.3	3.0				
			Net Profit + Depr., Dep., Amort./Cur. Mat. L/T/D						
.3	.6	.2	Fixed/Worth	.2	.4				
2.7	2.5	1.1		1.3	.8				
-1.2	-1.5	-7.8		-3.9	6.2				
.7	.6	.4	Debt/Worth	.4	.2				
7.0	4.5	2.4		2.8	2.2				
-4.0	-3.3	-11.8		-8.1	UND				
265.9	435.1	247.6	% Profit Before Taxes/Tangible Net Worth	318.2	108.0				
(58) 70.8	(57) 116.4	(86) 82.2		(59) 92.0	(16) 59.0				
5.4	26.5	31.1		33.1	22.7				
58.7	85.5	80.5	% Profit Before Taxes/Total Assets	80.0	63.9				
13.8	25.8	27.9		30.1	16.2				
-4.1	1.4	3.3		2.7	4.9				
40.0	36.0	52.8	Sales/Net Fixed Assets	62.0	44.2				
16.1	13.4	16.1		16.4	12.2				
4.8	6.9	5.9		5.6	5.5				
7.5	7.5	7.8	Sales/Total Assets	7.7	8.4				
3.4	3.3	3.6		3.3	4.3				
1.8	1.8	1.9		2.0	1.8				
1.0	.7	.8	% Depr., Dep., Amort./Sales	.9					
(64) 2.3	(64) 2.4	(59) 1.8		(45) 2.1					
4.9	4.0	3.7		3.9					
12.0	10.9	10.5	% Officers', Directors' Owners' Comp/Sales	11.4	8.4				
(56) 18.1	(60) 16.6	(73) 15.4		(55) 17.6	(10) 10.7				
29.1	26.0	24.0		25.3	19.1				
650047M	1734242M	2772957M	Net Sales ($)	38403M	29931M	7041M	5862M	29574M	2662146M
152346M	264611M	947739M	Total Assets ($)	16263M	10780M	1046M	357M	3238M	916055M

M = $ thousand   MM = $ million
See Pages 11 through 21 for Explanation of Ratios and Data

Current Data Sorted by Assets   Comparative Historical Data

Type of Statement	0-500M	500M-2MM	2-10MM	10-50MM	50-100MM	100-250MM	4/1/02-3/31/03 ALL	4/1/03-3/31/04 ALL
Unqualified	1	4	1				9	5
Reviewed	1	3	1				10	9
Compiled	33	11	5	1			48	56
Tax Returns	66	19	6	1		1	65	88
Other	15	18	3	3		3	40	42
	11 (4/1-9/30/06)			185 (10/1/06-3/31/07)				
NUMBER OF STATEMENTS	116	55	16	5		4	172	200
ASSETS %	%	%	%	%	%	%	%	%
Cash & Equivalents	21.0	14.1	9.1				16.6	17.5
Trade Receivables (net)	8.1	11.9	22.2				10.2	10.9
Inventory	16.1	9.3	4.0				11.4	13.3
All Other Current	2.9	3.2	.7				2.6	2.6
Total Current	48.1	38.6	36.0				40.7	44.4
Fixed Assets (net)	33.1	40.4	52.2				44.5	40.2
Intangibles (net)	11.2	12.7	4.8				7.6	6.6
All Other Non-Current	7.6	8.3	7.0				7.2	8.9
Total	100.0	100.0	100.0				100.0	100.0
LIABILITIES								
Notes Payable-Short Term	8.9	5.8	9.1				15.6	15.2
Cur. Mat.-L.T.D.	10.5	7.1	8.4				9.1	7.0
Trade Payables	4.4	5.5	10.2				6.0	7.3
Income Taxes Payable	.4	.3	1.4				.5	.4
All Other Current	17.9	14.4	17.1				12.9	13.5
Total Current	42.1	33.1	46.3				44.0	43.4
Long-Term Debt	42.6	30.2	24.7				34.3	29.1
Deferred Taxes	.0	.0	.0				.2	.1
All Other Non-Current	8.8	8.2	1.1				4.6	11.8
Net Worth	6.6	28.5	28.0				16.8	15.5
Total Liabilties & Net Worth	100.0	100.0	100.0				100.0	100.0
INCOME DATA								
Net Sales	100.0	100.0	100.0				100.0	100.0
Gross Profit								
Operating Expenses	89.9	89.0	85.8				91.7	91.5
Operating Profit	10.1	11.0	14.2				8.3	8.5
All Other Expenses (net)	1.7	1.7	2.1				1.3	1.5
Profit Before Taxes	8.5	9.3	12.1				7.1	7.0
RATIOS								
Current	3.1	2.6	1.1				2.4	2.3
	1.6	1.3	.8				1.0	1.1
	.5	.6	.6				.4	.5
Quick	2.2	1.9	.9				1.4	1.3
	(115) .8	.8	.7				(171) .5	(198) .6
	.2	.3	.5				.2	.3
Sales/Receivables	0 UND	0 UND	0 UND				0 UND	0 UND
	0 UND	0 UND	28 13.1				0 UND	0 UND
	7 49.9	20 18.0	37 10.0				21 17.1	18 20.1
Cost of Sales/Inventory								
Cost of Sales/Payables								
Sales/Working Capital	16.2	13.7	NM				19.3	17.2
	68.3	97.6	-32.8				-612.7	221.9
	-34.9	-30.0	-18.0				-18.2	-29.1
EBIT/Interest	17.9	28.1	6.5				10.3	11.9
	(97) 4.6	(47) 3.2	(15) 5.3				(145) 3.7	(158) 3.5
	.7	.7	1.1				.9	.9
Net Profit + Depr., Dep., Amort./Cur. Mat. L/T/D							2.5	6.9
							(15) 1.4	(11) 2.6
							.8	1.3
Fixed/Worth	.6	.7	1.2				.7	.6
	3.4	3.7	2.3				2.5	2.8
	-1.3	-2.6	18.7				-2.8	-2.5
Debt/Worth	1.6	.7	1.2				1.0	1.2
	12.1	4.9	3.3				5.2	7.9
	-3.7	-17.9	34.8				-6.5	-6.1
% Profit Before Taxes/Tangible Net Worth	283.3	177.5	93.2				113.2	123.8
	(63) 93.8	(38) 56.4	(13) 33.1				(112) 44.0	(127) 49.1
	7.1	.6	20.0				4.3	2.1
% Profit Before Taxes/Total Assets	84.5	57.2	14.6				39.7	39.1
	18.4	9.8	7.8				8.6	9.2
	-.4	.0	1.1				-.9	-.8
Sales/Net Fixed Assets	73.2	28.9	12.4				23.5	39.1
	24.6	15.9	6.1				11.5	14.6
	10.6	6.0	4.5				6.5	6.9
Sales/Total Assets	12.5	6.7	4.8				7.6	7.9
	5.2	3.9	3.5				4.7	4.6
	3.2	2.7	2.0				2.7	2.8
% Depr., Dep., Amort./Sales	1.1	1.7	1.7				1.9	1.5
	(72) 2.6	(43) 2.6	2.8				(135) 3.2	(145) 2.7
	5.2	3.8	4.0				5.3	5.0
% Officers', Directors' Owners' Comp/Sales	8.2	9.5					9.9	8.8
	(90) 13.7	(36) 14.0					(108) 19.0	(131) 16.8
	24.1	21.7					28.9	25.9
Net Sales ($)	178682M	273704M	222824M	641181M		1553316M	2590254M	4551767M
Total Assets ($)	26161M	53228M	68652M	82106M		591123M	650312M	1045407M

Note: Columns for 10-50MM, 50-100MM, 100-250MM marked "DATA NOT AVAILABLE" for Assets/Liabilities/Income/Ratios sections.

M = $ thousand   MM = $ million
See Pages 11 through 21 for Explanation of Ratios and Data

Comparative Historical Data

Current Data Sorted by Sales

Type of Statement									
	4	1	6		2	1	1	1	1
Unqualified	10	6	5		1		1	3	
Reviewed	53	36	50	13	16	10	6	4	1
Compiled	87	75	93	37	37	7	6	4	2
Tax Returns	53	55	42	9	14	5	7	2	5
Other	4/1/04-3/31/05 ALL	4/1/05-3/31/06 ALL	4/1/06-3/31/07 ALL	11 (4/1-9/30/06)		185 (10/1/06-3/31/07)			
				0-1MM	1-3MM	3-5MM	5-10MM	10-25MM	25MM & OVER
NUMBER OF STATEMENTS	207	173	196	59	70	23	21	14	9
ASSETS	%	%	%	%	%	%	%	%	%
Cash & Equivalents	16.7	15.7	17.7	19.1	15.1	16.5	28.2	14.4	
Trade Receivables (net)	9.5	10.3	10.6	7.1	13.3	8.0	4.6	22.9	
Inventory	12.7	12.3	13.3	16.9	13.9	9.7	4.6	11.0	
All Other Current	2.5	2.1	2.8	3.0	2.0	2.3	3.0	.5	
Total Current	41.4	40.4	44.5	46.2	44.3	36.5	40.4	48.8	
Fixed Assets (net)	42.1	39.9	36.5	35.5	33.4	41.7	46.2	44.8	
Intangibles (net)	6.9	10.4	11.7	9.2	15.0	11.7	8.5	2.9	
All Other Non-Current	9.6	9.3	7.4	9.1	7.4	10.1	4.9	3.5	
Total	100.0	100.0	100.0	100.0	100.0	100.0	100.0	100.0	
LIABILITIES									
Notes Payable-Short Term	14.5	10.7	8.3	6.4	5.1	11.2	16.8	11.0	
Cur. Mat.-L.T.D.	9.0	6.7	8.9	9.1	9.7	11.5	7.3	7.8	
Trade Payables	6.4	6.1	5.5	3.3	5.9	5.4	4.1	10.9	
Income Taxes Payable	.4	.4	.4	.0	.5	.8	.1	2.1	
All Other Current	14.9	15.0	16.5	17.4	8.7	24.3	20.5	35.7	
Total Current	45.1	38.9	39.6	36.1	29.9	53.2	48.8	67.4	
Long-Term Debt	36.0	38.8	36.5	45.6	40.9	29.9	27.5	14.8	
Deferred Taxes	.1	.0	.1	.0	.0	.0	.0	.0	
All Other Non-Current	6.8	10.0	9.4	13.4	6.2	2.8	8.6	.9	
Net Worth	12.0	12.2	14.5	4.9	22.9	14.1	15.1	16.9	
Total Liabilties & Net Worth	100.0	100.0	100.0	100.0	100.0	100.0	100.0	100.0	
INCOME DATA									
Net Sales	100.0	100.0	100.0	100.0	100.0	100.0	100.0	100.0	
Gross Profit									
Operating Expenses	90.7	91.2	89.1	87.1	88.8	92.5	84.7	98.9	
Operating Profit	9.3	8.8	10.9	12.9	11.2	7.5	15.3	1.1	
All Other Expenses (net)	1.7	1.4	1.9	4.1	1.3	-.6	1.8	-.1	
Profit Before Taxes	7.6	7.4	8.9	8.8	9.9	8.2	13.5	1.2	
RATIOS									
Current	2.1	2.6	2.6	2.7	3.6	1.4	1.7	1.2	
	1.2	1.1	1.3	1.7	2.1	.7	1.0	.8	
	.5	.5	.6	.6	.6	.5	.5	.7	
Quick	1.4	1.6	1.9	2.5	2.6	.8	1.1	1.0	
	(204) .6	(172) .7	(195) .7	.7	1.2	.5	(20) .8	.7	
	.2	.2	.3	.2	.2	.3	.4	.4	
Sales/Receivables	0 UND	0 UND	0 UND	0 UND	0 UND	0 UND	0 UND	0 UND	
	0 UND	0 UND	0 UND	0 UND	0 UND	0 UND	0 UND	27 13.6	
	18 20.8	21 17.5	20 18.4	14 26.7	23 15.7	16 22.8	2 175.3	33 11.2	
Cost of Sales/Inventory									
Cost of Sales/Payables									
Sales/Working Capital	16.0	15.2	15.7	10.7	13.0	46.0	63.0	50.0	
	141.7	133.1	94.9	33.4	50.6	-68.9	-999.8	-50.7	
	-28.0	-23.0	-30.1	-19.1	-36.4	-23.4	-31.8	-26.7	
EBIT/Interest	16.3	23.8	16.4	16.7	33.4	11.0	40.2	6.4	
	(175) 3.6	(144) 3.3	(166) 4.1	(45) 4.7	(59) 3.3	3.3	(20) 7.8	(12) 2.7	
	.8	.8	.9	1.3	.3	.2	.6	1.0	
Net Profit + Depr., Dep., Amort./Cur. Mat. L/T/D									
Fixed/Worth	.9	.8	.7	.4	.6	.9	1.2	1.1	
	3.4	5.8	3.0	2.2	3.2	4.2	4.6	3.4	
	-2.7	-1.9	-2.6	-1.5	-1.8	-6.8	-2.2	-7.3	
Debt/Worth	1.4	1.1	1.4	1.3	.7	3.0	2.0	1.3	
	6.1	10.4	7.4	6.6	9.6	9.7	4.9	5.2	
	-8.1	-5.0	-4.7	-3.5	-3.9	-10.5	-5.0	-30.2	
% Profit Before Taxes/Tangible Net Worth	217.9	150.0	190.1	170.2	262.7	594.2	999.8		
	(135) 71.3	(103) 50.0	(119) 58.6	(37) 55.9	(39) 120.0	(16) 53.5	(14) 59.3		
	6.7	9.5	7.1	20.2	25.2	1.4	-10.3		
% Profit Before Taxes/Total Assets	53.9	47.0	57.0	37.5	89.8	49.5	127.4	9.3	
	12.9	10.1	13.4	17.5	25.7	9.8	32.7	4.3	
	.0	-.5	.0	3.4	-2.5	-3.5	-1.6	.0	
Sales/Net Fixed Assets	31.5	30.9	55.8	54.5	83.4	33.9	60.4	28.9	
	13.7	15.3	18.1	13.2	18.9	15.9	22.3	12.4	
	7.6	8.5	7.4	4.4	8.6	11.0	9.1	7.3	
Sales/Total Assets	8.8	8.6	9.1	7.7	6.9	12.9	16.6	8.9	
	4.7	4.8	4.5	2.8	4.4	6.8	7.9	5.2	
	2.8	2.6	2.7	1.9	3.3	3.3	4.9	3.8	
% Depr., Dep., Amort./Sales	1.6	1.3	1.4	2.0	1.0	2.2	1.7	1.3	
	(157) 2.8	(133) 2.2	(137) 2.6	(42) 4.3	(41) 2.1	(19) 2.9	(15) 2.3	1.7	
	4.7	4.5	4.2	7.3	3.6	3.8	3.0	3.1	
% Officers', Directors' Owners' Comp/Sales	9.5	8.0	7.8	8.3	8.7	4.7	7.6		
	(120) 17.3	(110) 16.0	(138) 13.5	(43) 11.5	(56) 15.4	(16) 11.1	(13) 16.0		
	27.9	25.2	22.9	19.6	21.8	33.5	30.6		
Net Sales ($)	4918011M	2702809M	2869707M	31852M	126932M	93076M	147431M	247927M	2222489M
Total Assets ($)	746991M	558921M	821270M	21327M	42507M	20431M	23318M	51864M	661823M

M = $ thousand   MM = $ million
See Pages 11 through 21 for Explanation of Ratios and Data

HEALTH CARE—Offices of Mental Health Practitioners (except Physicians) NAICS 621330 (SIC 8049)

Current Data Sorted by Assets   **Comparative Historical Data**

0-500M	500M-2MM	2-10MM	10-50MM	50-100MM	100-250MM	Type of Statement	4/1/02-3/31/03 ALL	4/1/03-3/31/04 ALL
2	2	10	3	.1		Unqualified	6	8
			1			Reviewed	2	3
4	1			1		Compiled	11	5
17	4	2	5			Tax Returns	12	13
9						Other	5	5
	20 (4/1-9/30/06)		47 (10/1/06-3/31/07)					
32	12	12	9	2		**NUMBER OF STATEMENTS**	36	34
%	%	%	%	%	%	**ASSETS**	%	%
38.4	24.4	22.0				Cash & Equivalents	24.9	22.1
9.8	19.4	19.9				Trade Receivables (net)	20.1	20.6
.5	1.1	.0				Inventory	.9	.9
4.0	1.3	3.4				All Other Current	4.5	5.0
52.8	46.2	45.3				Total Current	50.4	48.6
35.9	29.2	45.3				Fixed Assets (net)	32.3	36.8
1.5	8.8	1.1				Intangibles (net)	3.3	4.3
9.9	15.8	8.3				All Other Non-Current	13.9	10.3
100.0	100.0	100.0				Total	100.0	100.0
						LIABILITIES		
44.0	10.1	3.7				Notes Payable-Short Term	24.2	15.9
4.7	5.1	1.8				Cur. Mat.-L.T.D.	9.7	14.2
2.6	2.4	4.0				Trade Payables	3.8	5.1
.1	.1	1.0				Income Taxes Payable	.0	.5
28.5	12.4	11.7				All Other Current	25.2	19.8
80.0	30.1	22.4				Total Current	62.9	55.6
36.0	26.1	27.9				Long-Term Debt	40.3	17.2
.0	.0	.0				Deferred Taxes	.0	.2
4.0	3.8	2.4				All Other Non-Current	14.7	1.5
-19.9	39.9	47.3				Net Worth	-17.9	25.3
100.0	100.0	100.0				Total Liabilities & Net Worth	100.0	100.0
						INCOME DATA		
100.0	100.0	100.0				Net Sales	100.0	100.0
						Gross Profit		
93.8	87.2	99.8				Operating Expenses	92.6	92.1
6.2	12.8	.2				Operating Profit	7.4	7.9
1.3	.7	-.9				All Other Expenses (net)	-.3	1.6
4.9	12.1	1.2				Profit Before Taxes	7.7	6.3
						RATIOS		
1.8	6.6	4.3					2.9	1.9
1.2	2.2	1.9				Current	1.3	1.1
.3	1.0	1.1					.4	.3
1.7	6.6	4.3					2.3	1.7
1.1	1.7	1.9				Quick	1.1	.9
.2	.9	.9					.3	.2
0 UND	0 UND	25 14.8					0 UND	0 UND
0 UND	10 34.9	45 8.1				Sales/Receivables	0 UND	19 19.4
0 UND	47 7.8	56 6.5					65 5.6	61 6.0
						Cost of Sales/Inventory		
						Cost of Sales/Payables		
22.3	5.0	3.4					7.3	9.4
339.9	9.8	11.2				Sales/Working Capital	455.6	38.3
-40.1	NM	75.9					-22.9	-21.8
14.5	49.2	8.2					15.4	9.1
(22) 4.3	(10) 1.2	(10) 3.6				EBIT/Interest	(28) 1.4	(25) 3.0
1.5	-1.4	1.4					.8	-.7
						Net Profit + Depr., Dep., Amort./Cur. Mat. L/T/D		
.1	.2	.6					.3	.6
1.6	.6	.9				Fixed/Worth	.9	1.6
-.7	4.1	8.2					-4.3	-21.6
1.0	.3	.4					.4	.5
2.3	2.1	1.0				Debt/Worth	2.9	3.1
-4.5	4.8	13.8					-5.9	-42.7
415.1	113.4	29.0				% Profit Before Taxes/Tangible Net Worth	96.1	68.4
(20) 127.3	(10) 18.7	(11) 12.4					(24) 25.3	(23) 12.2
14.0	-28.6	3.8					-2.7	-.2
79.9	54.7	6.6				% Profit Before Taxes/Total Assets	40.5	18.0
27.5	1.6	4.2					5.2	3.7
-6.7	-8.1	.1					-.9	-1.0
383.4	60.0	6.2				Sales/Net Fixed Assets	74.0	40.4
61.7	20.5	3.4					17.3	11.7
19.5	4.4	2.8					6.4	7.3
27.5	5.1	2.1				Sales/Total Assets	13.5	8.1
10.7	3.5	1.8					4.3	3.5
3.7	.9	1.1					2.2	1.6
.5	.4	1.9				% Depr., Dep., Amort./Sales	.9	.8
(21) .7	(11) 1.5	2.6					(32) 1.8	(26) 1.8
1.5	2.3	3.1					2.4	2.9
6.4						% Officers', Directors' Owners' Comp/Sales	10.8	6.7
(18) 17.6							(17) 17.2	(16) 16.4
23.5							31.4	29.4
61413M	35239M	135519M	396080M	2269893M		Net Sales ($)	160112M	150744M
5232M	11738M	72272M	172021M	124996M		Total Assets ($)	48305M	45891M

(The 100-250MM column reads vertically: DATA NOT AVAILABLE)

M = $ thousand   MM = $ million
See Pages 11 through 21 for Explanation of Ratios and Data

Comparative Historical Data   Current Data Sorted by Sales

9	11	18	Type of Statement						
		1	Unqualified		3	2	4	5	4
			Reviewed						1
4	4	6	Compiled	3	1	1			1
14	6	21	Tax Returns	10	7	3		1	
7	8	21	Other	5	5	3	3		2
4/1/04-3/31/05	4/1/05-3/31/06	4/1/06-3/31/07		20 (4/1-9/30/06)			47 (10/1/06-3/31/07)		
ALL	ALL	ALL		0-1MM	1-3MM	3-5MM	5-10MM	10-25MM	25MM & OVER
34	29	67	NUMBER OF STATEMENTS	18	16	9	7	9	8
%	%	%	ASSETS	%	%	%	%	%	%
22.6	25.8	31.0	Cash & Equivalents	40.1	32.8				
20.6	28.1	15.4	Trade Receivables (net)	5.9	18.4				
.5	.1	.6	Inventory	.7	1.1				
6.2	6.7	4.3	All Other Current	.8	8.4				
49.9	60.8	51.2	Total Current	47.5	60.6				
38.1	29.1	36.0	Fixed Assets (net)	34.6	33.0				
2.0	.4	3.3	Intangibles (net)	4.2	3.2				
10.0	9.7	9.5	All Other Non-Current	13.7	3.2				
100.0	100.0	100.0	Total	100.0	100.0				
			LIABILITIES						
20.6	20.5	23.9	Notes Payable-Short Term	29.6	30.3				
5.1	2.6	3.8	Cur. Mat.-L.T.D.	6.7	3.5				
6.3	7.3	2.9	Trade Payables	1.3	4.3				
1.2	.0	.3	Income Taxes Payable	.0	.2				
14.3	19.8	21.8	All Other Current	31.8	18.9				
47.5	50.2	52.7	Total Current	69.4	57.1				
19.3	30.2	32.0	Long-Term Debt	44.7	38.1				
.0	.0	.1	Deferred Taxes	.0	.0				
6.9	6.4	3.2	All Other Non-Current	.0	7.9				
26.3	13.2	12.0	Net Worth	-14.1	-3.2				
100.0	100.0	100.0	Total Liabilities & Net Worth	100.0	100.0				
			INCOME DATA						
100.0	100.0	100.0	Net Sales	100.0	100.0				
			Gross Profit						
85.7	94.6	92.5	Operating Expenses	88.5	89.2				
14.3	5.4	7.5	Operating Profit	11.5	10.8				
3.0	.6	1.9	All Other Expenses (net)	2.6	2.0				
11.3	4.8	5.6	Profit Before Taxes	8.9	8.8				
			RATIOS						
3.0	3.3	3.0		1.9	8.4				
1.5	1.5	1.6	Current	1.2	1.8				
.6	.9	.9		.5	1.5				
2.7	3.1	2.3		1.8	5.7				
(33) 1.3	1.4	1.2	Quick	1.2	1.6				
.4	.8	.8		.5	1.1				
0 UND	0 UND	0 UND		0 UND	0 UND				
2 183.4	33 11.0	6 58.0	Sales/Receivables	0 UND	0 UND				
54 6.7	75 4.9	44 8.4		0 UND	21 17.4				
			Cost of Sales/Inventory						
			Cost of Sales/Payables						
8.8	7.5	8.0		20.3	6.5				
17.3	24.0	37.7	Sales/Working Capital	295.8	11.1				
-60.6	-102.4	-104.2		-13.4	103.8				
37.2	9.6	14.5		13.1	40.8				
(25) 6.2	(23) 4.8	(50) 4.0	EBIT/Interest	(10) 1.8	(13) 8.0				
.0	2.2	.9		-.8	.1				
			Net Profit + Depr., Dep., Amort./Cur. Mat. L/T/D						
.3	.5	.3		.1	.1				
1.0	1.1	.9	Fixed/Worth	4.8	.9				
UND	UND	-999.8		-.4	NM				
.6	.7	.7		1.0	.7				
3.0	2.6	2.0	Debt/Worth	8.3	2.7				
UND	UND	-999.8		-3.3	NM				
290.4	75.4	174.4		366.7	238.1				
(26) 47.6	(22) 21.1	(50) 33.4	% Profit Before Taxes/Tangible Net Worth	(11) 92.9	(12) 80.4				
9.4	7.5	4.6		-14.3	14.7				
55.3	25.9	52.1		70.1	94.6				
12.4	7.3	6.7	% Profit Before Taxes/Total Assets	10.8	37.9				
1.4	3.9	-3.8		-24.1	-4.1				
49.7	145.7	93.3		605.0	100.3				
19.6	8.8	20.8	Sales/Net Fixed Assets	49.7	39.3				
3.8	3.8	4.0		6.4	13.6				
6.2	5.5	11.2		21.6	10.9				
2.8	2.4	3.7	Sales/Total Assets	4.4	4.8				
1.6	1.7	1.8		2.2	3.4				
.8	.9	.6		.5	.6				
(29) 1.1	(19) 2.2	(53) 1.7	% Depr., Dep., Amort./Sales	(11) 1.1	(12) .8				
2.1	3.0	2.7		2.3	2.2				
11.3	2.9	5.6		17.3					
(18) 15.8	(10) 7.5	(27) 15.8	% Officers', Directors' Owners' Comp/Sales	(10) 22.5					
25.0	22.0	22.7		36.4					
218598M	167800M	2898144M	Net Sales ($)	7801M	29120M	31951M	50747M	155384M	2623141M
87615M	76604M	386259M	Total Assets ($)	3793M	19168M	10779M	27725M	92040M	232754M

M = $ thousand   MM = $ million
See Pages 11 through 21 for Explanation of Ratios and Data

Current Data Sorted by Assets | Comparative Historical Data

Type of Statement	0-500M	500M-2MM	2-10MM	10-50MM	50-100MM	100-250MM		4/1/02-3/31/03 ALL	4/1/03-3/31/04 ALL
Unqualified	1	4	9	2	3	1		17	24
Reviewed	2	2	9	1				7	16
Compiled	17	12	7	1	1			30	45
Tax Returns	64	15	2	2		1		50	58
Other	24	11	16	3	1	1		40	53
	0-500M	35 (4/1-9/30/06) 500M-2MM	2-10MM	177 (10/1/06-3/31/07) 10-50MM	50-100MM	100-250MM			
NUMBER OF STATEMENTS	108	44	43	9	5	3		144	196
ASSETS	%	%	%	%	%	%		%	%
Cash & Equivalents	31.9	15.0	11.7					21.6	21.5
Trade Receivables (net)	9.6	25.3	33.8					17.7	22.4
Inventory	1.5	.2	.6					1.1	1.4
All Other Current	2.9	6.2	4.1					5.1	3.5
Total Current	45.8	46.7	50.2					45.4	48.8
Fixed Assets (net)	32.9	33.4	37.0					41.7	35.4
Intangibles (net)	6.0	4.8	3.7					3.4	6.1
All Other Non-Current	15.3	15.1	9.2					9.5	9.6
Total	100.0	100.0	100.0					100.0	100.0
LIABILITIES									
Notes Payable-Short Term	28.1	12.4	8.0					22.5	18.4
Cur. Mat.-L.T.D.	5.7	7.7	3.2					5.3	5.9
Trade Payables	4.8	3.8	4.5					4.5	4.4
Income Taxes Payable	.0	.1	.2					.5	.4
All Other Current	29.0	20.6	14.0					26.8	21.2
Total Current	67.7	44.6	29.8					59.6	50.2
Long-Term Debt	20.8	20.1	22.7					25.2	22.5
Deferred Taxes	.0	.5	.5					.0	.2
All Other Non-Current	3.0	2.3	5.7					7.0	6.3
Net Worth	8.4	32.5	41.4					8.2	20.8
Total Liabilties & Net Worth	100.0	100.0	100.0					100.0	100.0
INCOME DATA									
Net Sales	100.0	100.0	100.0					100.0	100.0
Gross Profit									
Operating Expenses	91.2	91.3	89.5					92.3	91.6
Operating Profit	8.8	8.7	10.5					7.7	8.4
All Other Expenses (net)	.1	2.2	2.0					.9	1.6
Profit Before Taxes	8.8	6.5	8.5					6.8	6.7
RATIOS									
Current	2.2	2.4	3.1					2.4	3.0
	1.0	1.0	1.7					1.2	1.3
	.3	.3	1.1					.4	.5
Quick	2.2	2.4	2.9					2.1	2.6
	(107) .9	1.0	1.4					1.0	1.1
	.2	.1	.9					.3	.4
Sales/Receivables	0 UND	0 UND	14 26.8					0 UND	0 UND
	0 UND	0 UND	50 7.2					0 UND	2 209.3
	0 UND	60 6.1	79 4.6					44 8.3	58 6.3
Cost of Sales/Inventory									
Cost of Sales/Payables									
Sales/Working Capital	18.4	8.9	5.6					12.7	8.1
	UND	128.6	11.1					138.0	47.7
	-18.7	-17.8	74.4					-26.8	-24.8
EBIT/Interest	29.5	24.8	22.9					15.1	16.4
	(72) 8.5	(32) 3.5	(35) 6.5					(117) 3.2	(156) 4.9
	.9	1.0	2.9					-.2	.9
Net Profit + Depr., Dep., Amort./Cur. Mat. L/T/D									4.9
								(18) 2.4	
								.7	
Fixed/Worth	.2	.2	.2					.5	.4
	1.2	.6	.8					1.6	1.5
	-1.3	11.4	1.5					60.1	-7.2
Debt/Worth	.5	.6	.4					1.0	.8
	3.8	2.4	1.2					3.3	2.4
	-4.2	17.2	2.9					-59.5	-32.1
% Profit Before Taxes/Tangible Net Worth	358.6	120.0	59.5					145.5	97.2
	(71) 103.3	(36) 31.9	(39) 26.8					(106) 42.3	(138) 30.9
	13.6	-1.6	7.2					-.4	9.7
% Profit Before Taxes/Total Assets	133.8	26.3	20.0					43.2	38.2
	31.1	6.6	8.7					10.7	8.7
	.7	-.6	2.7					-3.5	-.6
Sales/Net Fixed Assets	134.1	115.1	36.1					44.5	44.8
	35.1	20.0	9.1					15.1	19.0
	16.3	3.7	3.6					6.0	6.0
Sales/Total Assets	14.3	5.7	3.6					8.9	7.5
	8.4	3.7	2.8					4.2	3.7
	3.9	1.3	1.5					2.3	1.8
% Depr., Dep., Amort./Sales	.4	.5	.8					1.0	.8
	(61) .9	(36) 1.7	(40) 1.7					(102) 2.0	(160) 1.7
	1.7	3.6	2.4					4.0	3.5
% Officers', Directors' Owners' Comp/Sales	6.8	6.4						8.9	10.3
	(65) 17.2	(19) 9.6						(73) 16.1	(99) 18.4
	25.6	14.9						26.4	29.6
Net Sales ($)	148531M	226131M	523150M	1584888M	1023525M	833424M		3473354M	6272362M
Total Assets ($)	18458M	53070M	198956M	202966M	370087M	501667M		782077M	1694191M

© RMA 2007

M = $ thousand   MM = $ million
See Pages 11 through 21 for Explanation of Ratios and Data

Comparative Historical Data | Current Data Sorted by Sales

			Type of Statement						
26	21	20	Unqualified	1	1	2	6	3	7
13	9	14	Reviewed		2	2	3	5	2
27	30	38	Compiled	12	10	4	8	3	1
68	72	84	Tax Returns	36	25	9	7	3	4
54	73	56	Other	15	15	5	9	9	4
4/1/04-3/31/05 ALL	4/1/05-3/31/06 ALL	4/1/06-3/31/07 ALL		35 (4/1-9/30/06)			177 (10/1/06-3/31/07)		
				0-1MM	1-3MM	3-5MM	5-10MM	10-25MM	25MM & OVER
188	205	212	NUMBER OF STATEMENTS	64	53	22	32	23	18
%	%	%	ASSETS	%	%	%	%	%	%
24.9	26.4	23.1	Cash & Equivalents	28.6	24.8	23.7	16.3	14.8	20.5
19.3	17.1	18.5	Trade Receivables (net)	8.2	11.2	29.8	36.2	26.9	20.7
1.2	1.1	1.0	Inventory	.7	.2	4.6	.3	1.1	1.1
2.4	4.0	3.9	All Other Current	2.1	3.3	4.9	4.9	8.3	3.8
47.8	48.5	46.5	Total Current	39.6	39.5	63.0	57.6	51.1	46.1
36.8	34.9	34.2	Fixed Assets (net)	32.9	45.1	24.4	27.2	32.8	33.2
5.3	2.9	5.8	Intangibles (net)	6.0	5.1	6.4	3.7	3.9	13.1
10.2	13.6	13.4	All Other Non-Current	21.5	10.3	6.1	11.5	12.2	7.7
100.0	100.0	100.0	Total	100.0	100.0	100.0	100.0	100.0	100.0
			LIABILITIES						
25.8	23.8	19.7	Notes Payable-Short Term	27.5	23.4	13.5	10.8	11.3	15.7
4.2	5.8	5.4	Cur. Mat.-L.T.D.	4.7	5.7	10.3	5.3	3.6	4.0
4.5	3.8	4.5	Trade Payables	5.8	2.5	7.5	4.6	3.3	4.1
.1	.2	.1	Income Taxes Payable	.0	.0	.2	.2	.2	.0
20.2	21.4	23.4	All Other Current	17.7	34.7	21.0	20.8	19.2	23.0
54.8	54.9	53.1	Total Current	55.6	66.3	52.5	41.6	37.7	46.8
25.3	23.0	20.9	Long-Term Debt	26.5	21.3	16.2	14.4	20.4	18.1
.1	.1	.3	Deferred Taxes	.0	.0	.0	1.3	.0	1.1
7.3	6.9	3.3	All Other Non-Current	1.3	5.5	2.2	4.2	5.0	1.9
12.4	15.0	22.3	Net Worth	16.6	6.9	29.1	38.4	36.9	32.2
100.0	100.0	100.0	Total Liabilties & Net Worth	100.0	100.0	100.0	100.0	100.0	100.0
			INCOME DATA						
100.0	100.0	100.0	Net Sales	100.0	100.0	100.0	100.0	100.0	100.0
			Gross Profit						
93.0	90.0	90.6	Operating Expenses	89.1	86.2	95.2	96.6	92.8	89.4
7.0	10.0	9.4	Operating Profit	10.9	13.8	4.8	3.4	7.2	10.6
1.2	1.0	1.1	All Other Expenses (net)	2.7	.3	.1	.4	.1	.9
5.8	9.0	8.4	Profit Before Taxes	8.2	13.4	4.7	3.1	7.1	9.7
			RATIOS						
2.5	3.2	2.3		2.7	2.2	3.8	2.5	2.0	2.0
1.2	1.2	1.2	Current	1.0	.8	1.8	1.5	1.4	1.2
.4	.5	.4		.3	.1	.9	.9	.9	.8
2.3	2.8	2.2		2.3	2.1	3.1	2.5	1.4	1.8
1.1	1.0 (211)	1.1	Quick	.9 (52)	.8	1.5	1.4	1.1	1.1
.4	.4	.3		.2	.1	.7	.7	.6	.5
0 UND	0 UND	0 UND		0 UND	0 UND	0 UND	2 160.6	0 UND	0 UND
0 UND	0 UND	0 UND	Sales/Receivables	0 UND	0 UND	20 17.9	37 10.0	26 14.0	24 15.1
46 8.0	42 8.8	46 7.9		0 UND	5 75.8	65 5.6	72 5.1	59 6.2	51 7.2
			Cost of Sales/Inventory						
			Cost of Sales/Payables						
10.8	9.7	10.9		12.9	14.4	5.6	7.4	10.9	5.5
91.0	65.5	77.0	Sales/Working Capital	UND	-80.4	20.1	33.5	36.7	34.1
-26.7	-24.0	-25.2		-14.0	-14.9	-127.9	-131.3	-81.3	-291.1
25.4	25.0	21.4		14.3	37.3	42.6	12.7	20.6	15.8
(154) 5.8	(155) 5.6	(153) 6.3	EBIT/Interest	(35) 7.5	(40) 6.9	(18) 11.4	(26) 2.8	(18) 5.9	(16) 5.7
.9	1.2	1.5		.2	2.2	1.1	.5	3.8	2.3
9.1		8.5							
(13) 1.9	(12) 1.6		Net Profit + Depr., Dep., Amort./Cur. Mat. L/T/D						
.7	.8								
.4	.3	.3		.1	.4	.3	.1	.1	.8
1.8	1.0	.9	Fixed/Worth	1.0	2.8	.6	.6	.8	1.1
-3.5	NM	25.6		-1.1	-3.0	4.9	1.4	1.7	-175.7
.7	.6	.5		.5	.5	.5	.6	.7	.8
3.1	2.6	2.0	Debt/Worth	2.3	5.3	1.2	1.9	1.5	2.8
-8.8	-41.4	UND		-5.1	-5.4	46.8	6.0	4.4	-202.2
107.3	149.1	194.1		170.5	373.6	80.6	62.9	202.4	71.6
(132) 26.0	(149) 43.1	(159) 33.6	% Profit Before Taxes/Tangible Net Worth	(41) 65.1	(37) 132.5	(18) 16.4	(29) 13.5	(21) 31.1	(13) 27.5
3.0	3.2	6.3		12.0	32.3	-10.0	-1.4	2.9	12.0
36.5	65.2	56.4		95.1	123.9	60.7	18.5	46.2	30.7
9.2	15.7	13.5	% Profit Before Taxes/Total Assets	14.4	32.9	13.9	6.1	9.8	11.3
-.2	.4	.8		.0	6.6	-1.6	-.6	2.9	5.5
62.6	69.6	106.6		165.0	76.1	110.9	152.6	144.6	28.1
21.2	18.7	25.1	Sales/Net Fixed Assets	32.4	21.8	37.9	27.2	17.2	12.7
7.1	5.5	7.9		10.1	6.1	13.7	8.7	5.7	5.4
9.7	9.8	9.6		10.9	12.6	11.2	4.9	7.8	5.2
4.2	4.2	4.1	Sales/Total Assets	4.1	6.0	6.2	3.5	3.7	3.0
1.9	2.1	2.0		1.7	3.0	2.1	2.3	2.9	1.5
.7	.7	.5		.6	.8	.3	.5	.2	1.7
(135) 1.6	(149) 1.6 (148)	1.6	% Depr., Dep., Amort./Sales	(31) 1.4	(41) 1.7	(18) .6	(28) 1.5	(17) 1.1	(13) 2.2
2.9	2.9	2.6		3.6	4.2	1.9	2.3	1.9	2.9
10.5	5.3	6.7		3.5	5.7	3.7	5.6		
(86) 17.0	(98) 12.7 (93)	14.2	% Officers', Directors' Owners' Comp/Sales	(35) 18.9	(27) 11.3	(10) 13.7	(10) 9.2		
26.5	21.3	26.8		29.6	18.9	24.2	16.6		
1851482M	2784050M	4339649M	Net Sales ($)	29594M	92648M	86277M	228959M	348655M	3553516M
1224847M	1063279M	1345204M	Total Assets ($)	16986M	47158M	27017M	87502M	110239M	1056302M

M = $ thousand   MM = $ million
See Pages 11 through 21 for Explanation of Ratios and Data

Current Data Sorted by Assets   Comparative Historical Data

						Type of Statement		
						Unqualified		
						Reviewed		
6						Compiled	9	2
13	5					Tax Returns	6	5
8		1				Other	1	10
	3 (4/1-9/30/06)		30 (10/1/06-3/31/07)				4/1/02-	4
							3/31/03	4/1/03-
								3/31/04
0-500M	500M-2MM	2-10MM	10-50MM	50-100MM	100-250MM		ALL	ALL
27	5	1				NUMBER OF STATEMENTS	16	21
%	%	%	%	%	%	ASSETS	%	%
34.0						Cash & Equivalents	35.2	25.8
5.1		D	D	D		Trade Receivables (net)	6.0	5.3
.1		A	A	A		Inventory	.9	.3
1.1		T	T	T		All Other Current	5.5	.2
40.4		A	A	A		Total Current	47.6	31.5
28.4						Fixed Assets (net)	35.4	36.6
12.1		N	N	N		Intangibles (net)	10.1	7.9
19.1		O	O	O		All Other Non-Current	6.9	23.9
100.0		T	T	T		Total	100.0	100.0
						LIABILITIES		
23.1		A	A	A		Notes Payable-Short Term	28.7	20.8
14.0		V	V	V		Cur. Mat.-L.T.D.	9.5	5.9
4.1		A	A	A		Trade Payables	11.5	4.5
.1		I	I	I		Income Taxes Payable	.0	1.1
28.6		L	L	L		All Other Current	34.4	31.3
69.9		A	A	A		Total Current	84.1	63.5
35.2		B	B	B		Long-Term Debt	54.9	27.8
.0		L	L	L		Deferred Taxes	.0	.0
15.2		E	E	E		All Other Non-Current	9.1	9.7
-20.2						Net Worth	-48.2	-1.0
100.0						Total Liabilities & Net Worth	100.0	100.0
						INCOME DATA		
100.0						Net Sales	100.0	100.0
						Gross Profit		
89.6						Operating Expenses	98.5	93.9
10.4						Operating Profit	1.5	6.1
.9						All Other Expenses (net)	.3	.8
9.5						Profit Before Taxes	1.2	5.2
						RATIOS		
1.4							1.5	1.4
.5						Current	.9	.5
.2							.3	.1
1.4							1.5	1.3
.5						Quick	.6	.5
.2							.2	.1
0 UND							0 UND	0 UND
0 UND						Sales/Receivables	0 UND	0 UND
0 UND							0 UND	0 UND
						Cost of Sales/Inventory		
						Cost of Sales/Payables		
14.7							82.4	47.5
-41.1						Sales/Working Capital	-177.9	-93.1
-22.2							-24.1	-9.3
13.3							5.3	5.0
(20) 4.6						EBIT/Interest	(10) 1.9	(15) 2.8
.0							-.6	.0
						Net Profit + Depr., Dep., Amort./Cur. Mat. L/T/D		
.1							.3	.7
3.5						Fixed/Worth	NM	-16.2
-.3							-1.1	-.8
1.4							.8	1.4
-74.2						Debt/Worth	-15.8	-26.4
-1.6							-2.4	-3.6
545.0								627.7
(13) 114.3						% Profit Before Taxes/Tangible Net Worth		(10) 318.9
44.6								8.6
100.0							32.8	72.4
41.6						% Profit Before Taxes/Total Assets	5.9	13.6
-1.8							-11.9	.1
212.0							94.5	84.2
40.5						Sales/Net Fixed Assets	41.6	30.0
12.6							25.8	12.8
21.1							26.5	20.8
6.0						Sales/Total Assets	9.6	8.7
3.8							6.9	4.1
.7							.9	.9
(17) 1.7						% Depr., Dep., Amort./Sales	(10) 1.9	(15) 1.5
2.9							3.3	3.2
19.0							18.4	17.4
(20) 25.1						% Officers', Directors' Owners' Comp/Sales	(11) 31.1	(19) 24.0
40.8							35.2	42.9
23489M	10574M	13210M				Net Sales ($)	19652M	37462M
3976M	5172M	5415M				Total Assets ($)	1705M	4774M

M = $ thousand   MM = $ million
See Pages 11 through 21 for Explanation of Ratios and Data

Comparative Historical Data			Type of Statement	Current Data Sorted by Sales					
1			Unqualified						
			Reviewed						
6	2	6	Compiled	2	4				
7	14	18	Tax Returns	12	5	1			
3	4	9	Other	5	3			1	
4/1/04- 3/31/05 ALL	4/1/05- 3/31/06 ALL	4/1/06- 3/31/07 ALL		0-1MM	3 (4/1-9/30/06) 1-3MM	3-5MM	30 (10/1/06-3/31/07) 5-10MM	10-25MM	25MM & OVER
17	20	33	**NUMBER OF STATEMENTS**	19	12		1	1	
%	%	%	**ASSETS**	%	%		%	%	%
29.5	20.8	29.0	Cash & Equivalents	34.2	23.7	D			D
1.8	5.0	6.6	Trade Receivables (net)	2.4	7.7	A			A
.2	.7	.1	Inventory	.1	.0	T			T
1.1	4.3	.9	All Other Current	.7	1.5	A			A
32.5	30.8	36.6	Total Current	37.4	33.0				
37.6	41.1	34.8	Fixed Assets (net)	32.9	42.3	N			N
8.3	6.4	10.1	Intangibles (net)	13.1	6.8	O			O
21.5	21.7	18.5	All Other Non-Current	16.5	17.9	T			T
100.0	100.0	100.0	Total	100.0	100.0				
			LIABILITIES			A			A
26.2	8.4	19.3	Notes Payable-Short Term	18.6	23.2	V			V
8.9	4.9	13.6	Cur. Mat.-L.T.D.	9.4	18.2	A			A
.2	1.6	3.4	Trade Payables	.6	8.2	I			I
.7	2.4	.1	Income Taxes Payable	.0	.3	L			L
27.1	18.7	23.7	All Other Current	31.1	15.4	A			A
63.0	35.9	60.1	Total Current	59.7	65.3	B			B
26.4	29.5	41.2	Long-Term Debt	55.3	23.4	L			L
.0	.0	.0	Deferred Taxes	.0	.0	E			E
10.9	.5	12.7	All Other Non-Current	21.9	.2				
-.3	34.1	-14.0	Net Worth	-37.0	11.0				
100.0	100.0	100.0	Total Liabilities & Net Worth	100.0	100.0				
			INCOME DATA						
100.0	100.0	100.0	Net Sales	100.0	100.0				
			Gross Profit						
88.7	81.4	87.2	Operating Expenses	86.1	90.1				
11.3	18.6	12.8	Operating Profit	13.9	9.9				
2.3	4.6	2.8	All Other Expenses (net)	3.1	.4				
9.0	14.0	10.1	Profit Before Taxes	10.7	9.5				
			RATIOS						
2.3	2.0	1.7		2.4	1.0				
.6	.9	.6	Current	.8	.3				
.0	.7	.2		.4	.1				
2.2	1.2	1.7		2.4	.8				
.6	.8	.6	Quick	.8	.3				
.0	.3	.2		.4	.1				
0 UND	0 UND	0 UND		0 UND	0 UND				
0 UND	0 UND	0 UND	Sales/Receivables	0 UND	0 UND				
0 UND	0 UND	0 UND		0 UND	0 UND				
			Cost of Sales/Inventory						
			Cost of Sales/Payables						
28.8	19.6	61.8		14.5	NM				
-27.3	NM	-39.4	Sales/Working Capital	-49.8	-23.6				
-8.6	-33.9	-21.5		-28.1	-20.3				
23.8	58.4	18.4		7.2	26.0				
(13) 5.4	(14) 12.1	(25) 4.6	EBIT/Interest	(12) 3.7	(11) 11.5				
-1.0	2.2	.7		.1	.6				
			Net Profit + Depr., Dep., Amort./Cur. Mat. L/T/D						
.5	.2	.1		.1	.3				
-4.0	1.3	3.5	Fixed/Worth	5.5	3.6				
-.7	4.1	-.7		-.3	-6.8				
.8	.9	1.7		2.1	1.7				
-6.5	2.6	5.6	Debt/Worth	-16.0	6.2				
-2.3	17.3	-2.3		-1.5	-3.8				
	561.8	356.1	% Profit Before Taxes/Tangible Net Worth						
	(17) 102.8	(18) 100.3							
	20.1	16.8							
65.7	82.1	86.1	% Profit Before Taxes/Total Assets	100.0	89.1				
20.8	41.0	21.3		21.3	27.0				
-10.4	5.6	.5		1.9	-1.8				
64.6	123.0	173.5	Sales/Net Fixed Assets	135.0	213.0				
18.6	13.1	30.3		28.5	39.3				
8.9	3.3	7.9		5.0	10.0				
8.3	10.5	12.9	Sales/Total Assets	12.3	23.1				
6.0	3.8	5.0		4.7	9.2				
3.6	1.8	2.3		1.9	4.7				
.7	.2	.5	% Depr., Dep., Amort./Sales	.8					
(13) 2.1	(14) 1.3	(22) 1.5		(13) 1.8					
6.3	6.9	3.4		6.8					
10.1	15.0	19.0	% Officers', Directors' Owners' Comp/Sales	19.0					
(13) 20.0	(15) 21.4	(22) 25.1		(15) 20.1					
30.0	40.4	41.9		32.1					
23242M	33563M	47273M	Net Sales ($)	9437M	17189M		7437M	13210M	
3949M	10429M	14563M	Total Assets ($)	4762M	2758M		1628M	5415M	

M = $ thousand   MM = $ million
See Pages 11 through 21 for Explanation of Ratios and Data

Current Data Sorted by Assets

Comparative Historical Data

0-500M	500M-2MM	2-10MM	10-50MM	50-100MM	100-250MM	Type of Statement	4/1/02-3/31/03 ALL	4/1/03-3/31/04 ALL
	5	12	12	1	1	Unqualified	1	10
1	3	2	2			Reviewed		4
19	14	8				Compiled	5	15
48	14	9			1	Tax Returns	12	26
25	19	21	9	1	1	Other	16	21
32 (4/1-9/30/06)			196 (10/1/06-3/31/07)					
93	55	52	23	2	3	NUMBER OF STATEMENTS	34	76
%	%	%	%	%	%	ASSETS	%	%
33.0	14.9	12.2	7.5			Cash & Equivalents	22.5	26.2
6.5	24.4	27.5	19.5			Trade Receivables (net)	22.3	20.7
3.1	2.7	2.2	1.6			Inventory	1.3	2.9
5.5	2.7	2.3	7.4			All Other Current	3.3	4.2
48.2	44.7	44.2	36.1			Total Current	49.4	54.0
31.5	40.4	45.5	50.8			Fixed Assets (net)	35.2	34.0
5.6	2.8	2.9	5.7			Intangibles (net)	4.5	3.1
14.8	12.1	7.4	7.4			All Other Non-Current	10.9	8.8
100.0	100.0	100.0	100.0			Total	100.0	100.0
						LIABILITIES		
22.4	13.6	5.1	4.0			Notes Payable-Short Term	8.2	20.4
7.9	6.6	7.8	3.0			Cur. Mat.-L.T.D.	11.8	12.2
6.2	5.0	6.6	7.2			Trade Payables	5.0	3.8
1.3	.3	.0	.4			Income Taxes Payable	.2	.1
32.3	19.2	14.0	15.6			All Other Current	20.0	26.1
70.1	44.7	33.4	30.2			Total Current	45.2	62.7
38.9	22.0	27.0	34.2			Long-Term Debt	21.3	27.8
.0	.1	.8	.7			Deferred Taxes	.0	.1
6.0	4.7	4.0	4.4			All Other Non-Current	10.8	6.8
-15.0	28.5	34.7	30.5			Net Worth	22.7	2.6
100.0	100.0	100.0	100.0			Total Liabilities & Net Worth	100.0	100.0
						INCOME DATA		
100.0	100.0	100.0	100.0			Net Sales	100.0	100.0
						Gross Profit		
87.1	89.1	86.4	93.4			Operating Expenses	92.6	93.3
12.9	10.9	13.6	6.6			Operating Profit	7.4	6.7
1.2	3.8	2.4	2.8			All Other Expenses (net)	.8	1.6
11.8	7.1	11.2	3.7			Profit Before Taxes	6.6	5.1
						RATIOS		
3.3	2.8	3.7	2.1			Current	3.0	2.5
.8	1.2	1.8	1.3				1.2	1.5
.3	.4	.6	1.0				.4	.5
2.5	2.6	3.2	1.8			Quick	2.5	2.2
(91) .7	1.1	1.5	1.0				(33) 1.2	1.2
.2	.3	.6	.7				.4	.4
0 UND	0 UND	0 UND	14 26.0			Sales/Receivables	0 UND	0 UND
0 UND	27 13.4	36 10.2	38 9.6				0 UND	6 61.9
0 UND	51 7.1	57 6.4	55 6.7				52 7.0	49 7.4
						Cost of Sales/Inventory		
						Cost of Sales/Payables		
23.8	8.3	6.1	9.0			Sales/Working Capital	15.8	7.8
-166.0	37.5	11.7	20.9				77.2	30.4
-16.4	-25.0	-16.1	-702.9				-30.3	-31.1
22.6	17.1	17.0	2.7			EBIT/Interest	11.8	12.9
(61) 3.7	(39) 5.3	(40) 3.7	(20) 1.4				(26) 2.9	(62) 2.3
.6	1.9	.8	.9				-1.3	-.8
						Net Profit + Depr., Dep., Amort./Cur. Mat. L/T/D		
.3	.4	.5	.9			Fixed/Worth	.2	.3
4.3	1.1	1.5	2.6				1.1	1.6
-.6	5.2	7.0	9.0				-15.2	-4.0
.9	.7	.5	1.1			Debt/Worth	.7	.9
24.0	2.0	1.6	2.4				2.5	2.6
-2.6	6.0	13.7	12.0				-88.6	-11.0
999.8	137.9	73.9	13.0			% Profit Before Taxes/Tangible Net Worth	110.6	105.0
(54) 152.2	(45) 56.3	(43) 13.1	(18) 7.2				(24) 33.7	(50) 20.6
44.8	9.6	.5	-.5				6.8	-3.6
130.1	36.1	28.0	4.2			% Profit Before Taxes/Total Assets	38.7	43.3
24.8	14.8	4.7	.8				8.1	4.7
4.0	.7	-.7	-.7				-2.3	-4.3
230.9	51.1	20.7	6.1			Sales/Net Fixed Assets	56.3	115.2
39.0	10.2	7.3	4.0				26.4	21.0
13.6	4.2	1.7	2.1				8.1	7.1
14.8	5.5	4.4	2.1			Sales/Total Assets	9.3	9.2
8.5	2.9	2.1	1.7				4.5	3.9
3.5	2.0	1.1	1.3				2.1	2.2
.4	1.1	1.2	1.9			% Depr., Dep., Amort./Sales	1.0	.5
(52) .8	(48) 2.3	(46) 2.6	(20) 2.9				(22) 1.5	(61) 1.8
3.3	4.5	5.6	5.0				3.3	3.2
7.6	4.4	2.1				% Officers', Directors' Owners' Comp/Sales	7.4	9.1
(49) 13.2	(15) 8.3	(16) 8.5					(11) 18.3	(39) 14.1
24.4	21.6	27.5					29.5	27.1
153188M	294499M	572423M	808606M	127001M	1030058M	Net Sales ($)	433713M	537762M
16519M	60533M	241854M	403913M	171491M	425645M	Total Assets ($)	146279M	252229M

M = $ thousand   MM = $ million
See Pages 11 through 21 for Explanation of Ratios and Data

Comparative Historical Data | Current Data Sorted by Sales

			Type of Statement						
22	21	31	Unqualified		6	2	4	11	8
2	9	8	Reviewed	1	1	1	1	1	3
17	24	41	Compiled	7	12	12	4	6	
41	42	72	Tax Returns	36	21	4	4	5	2
37	34	76	Other	17	18	9	4	16	7
4/1/04- 3/31/05 ALL	4/1/05- 3/31/06 ALL	4/1/06- 3/31/07 ALL		32 (4/1-9/30/06)			196 (10/1/06-3/31/07)		
				0-1MM	1-3MM	3-5MM	5-10MM	10-25MM	25MM & OVER
119	130	228	NUMBER OF STATEMENTS	61	58	28	22	39	20
%	%	%	ASSETS	%	%	%	%	%	%
23.7	23.8	20.9	Cash & Equivalents	32.1	19.2	16.0	20.8	12.4	14.7
18.1	19.4	17.0	Trade Receivables (net)	8.1	11.0	18.8	35.5	25.7	21.2
1.0	2.4	2.6	Inventory	3.3	2.2	2.5	2.9	2.5	1.3
4.3	3.2	4.3	All Other Current	4.5	5.6	2.3	3.0	2.1	7.9
47.1	48.7	44.6	Total Current	48.1	38.0	39.6	62.1	42.6	45.0
38.0	37.2	38.6	Fixed Assets (net)	37.9	37.3	50.7	26.1	43.1	31.7
3.6	4.2	5.2	Intangibles (net)	2.0	6.6	3.1	3.9	4.9	15.7
11.3	9.8	11.6	All Other Non-Current	12.0	18.0	6.6	7.8	9.3	7.5
100.0	100.0	100.0	Total	100.0	100.0	100.0	100.0	100.0	100.0
			LIABILITIES						
10.5	17.7	14.0	Notes Payable-Short Term	20.1	11.7	18.4	7.6	10.4	9.7
8.8	4.2	7.1	Cur. Mat.-L.T.D.	6.1	7.3	8.2	5.9	9.2	4.7
5.4	5.4	6.0	Trade Payables	7.5	3.3	4.5	9.4	6.8	6.6
.0	.6	.6	Income Taxes Payable	1.9	.2	.1	.1	.0	.4
25.6	20.7	22.7	All Other Current	23.1	19.1	13.1	26.6	27.6	31.1
50.3	48.6	50.4	Total Current	58.8	41.5	44.3	49.6	54.0	52.5
34.8	27.8	31.5	Long-Term Debt	41.5	31.8	32.9	16.6	27.5	22.5
.1	.3	.3	Deferred Taxes	.0	.5	.0	.7	.1	1.1
10.2	5.2	5.1	All Other Non-Current	5.0	8.1	4.2	1.2	3.3	6.2
4.7	18.2	12.7	Net Worth	-5.3	18.0	18.6	31.9	15.0	17.7
100.0	100.0	100.0	Total Liabilties & Net Worth	100.0	100.0	100.0	100.0	100.0	100.0
			INCOME DATA						
100.0	100.0	100.0	Net Sales	100.0	100.0	100.0	100.0	100.0	100.0
			Gross Profit						
88.7	89.3	87.8	Operating Expenses	83.2	83.9	90.0	91.4	94.8	92.9
11.3	10.7	12.2	Operating Profit	16.8	16.1	10.0	8.6	5.2	7.1
1.3	2.3	2.4	All Other Expenses (net)	4.8	2.5	1.9	1.5	-.5	1.6
10.1	8.4	9.8	Profit Before Taxes	12.0	13.5	8.0	7.1	5.7	5.5
			RATIOS						
2.7	2.2	2.7		3.8	3.6	2.7	2.1	2.1	2.0
1.5	1.2	1.2	Current	1.1	1.2	1.1	1.2	1.3	1.1
.6	.6	.5		.3	.4	.4	.9	.6	.9
2.6	2.0	2.2		3.5	2.8	2.5	2.0	2.1	1.3
1.2 (129)	1.0 (226)	1.0	Quick	(59) 1.1	1.1	1.1	1.1	1.0	.9
.4	.5	.4		.3	.2	.3	.7	.6	.7
0 UND	0 UND	0 UND		0 UND	0 UND	0 UND	0 UND	2 234.2	1 252.0
5 75.7	2 162.1	1 596.8	Sales/Receivables	0 UND	0 UND	0 UND	38 9.5	36 10.1	31 11.7
41 8.8	50 7.3	42 8.7		9 41.4	28 13.0	49 7.4	54 6.7	49 7.5	62 5.9
			Cost of Sales/Inventory						
			Cost of Sales/Payables						
9.7	10.7	10.1		18.4	7.9	6.0	7.5	9.2	10.1
36.8	130.8	76.6	Sales/Working Capital	160.3	100.4	80.1	37.8	30.0	60.1
-31.0	-22.9	-23.1		-8.5	-42.2	-20.8	-183.7	-22.3	-239.6
24.1	14.7	13.7		15.4	18.9	21.1	28.0	10.9	6.6
(93) 6.3	(96) 4.2	(164) 3.5	EBIT/Interest	(40) 3.4	(36) 5.1	(24) 5.2	(18) 2.5	(31) 2.0	(15) 2.1
1.3	.9	1.0		1.0	1.6	-1.2	1.2	.4	.2
39.1		5.3							
(10) 5.3	(12) 2.9		Net Profit + Depr., Dep., Amort./Cur. Mat. L/T/D						
1.7		1.3							
.3	.2	.4		.2	.4	.4	.2	.6	.8
1.7	1.0	1.6	Fixed/Worth	2.3	1.9	1.3	1.1	1.7	3.6
17.0	35.9	-3.0		-.9	-2.2	NM	NM	-339.3	-3.7
.8	.8	.8		.8	.6	.7	.6	1.0	1.8
2.8	2.4	2.8	Debt/Worth	5.7	2.0	1.4	2.5	2.5	9.9
-18.1	-39.0	-9.3		-4.8	-6.5	NM	NM	-14.7	-10.1
193.8	123.9	161.5		529.5	244.9	235.1	84.7	98.9	74.8
(89) 45.6	(97) 28.5	(162) 46.7	% Profit Before Taxes/Tangible Net Worth	(41) 77.4	(42) 98.8	(21) 56.3	(17) 17.7	(28) 11.1	(13) 6.1
8.1	4.0	6.7		18.6	19.8	6.9	1.9	-3.1	-3.5
58.3	35.6	46.5		54.9	95.5	69.5	33.2	17.3	5.3
9.7	11.2	10.0	% Profit Before Taxes/Total Assets	17.9	22.2	9.5	5.4	2.3	2.2
.4	.0	.3		3.8	3.2	-8.0	.6	-1.6	-2.1
54.4	75.0	62.0		105.4	123.8	19.4	386.8	23.8	34.0
14.7	15.8	13.9	Sales/Net Fixed Assets	19.1	18.2	9.3	16.8	8.7	10.4
5.7	3.4	3.9		3.3	4.0	3.8	7.9	3.4	3.8
7.7	8.6	7.4		10.7	10.7	6.4	5.7	5.5	5.8
4.0	3.7	3.5	Sales/Total Assets	3.8	3.7	3.0	3.4	3.5	2.3
2.3	1.5	1.9		2.1	1.9	1.9	1.9	1.5	1.7
.7	.9	.7		.6	.7	.6	.5	.8	.6
(90) 1.8	(94) 2.2	(170) 2.3	% Depr., Dep., Amort./Sales	(35) 2.6	(43) 2.2	(27) 2.7	(16) 1.9	(33) 2.5	(16) 1.4
4.2	4.6	4.4		6.7	5.2	3.8	2.9	3.5	2.9
6.9	8.0	5.4		6.9	7.0	5.3		2.2	
(54) 14.1	(57) 13.6	(83) 11.9	% Officers', Directors' Owners' Comp/Sales	(28) 12.8	(21) 12.1	(12) 10.4		(12) 6.3	
23.2	28.3	22.5		31.9	26.0	18.6		27.3	
3377658M	2660880M	2985775M	Net Sales ($)	33282M	108922M	109345M	154161M	622307M	1957758M
662385M	810441M	1319955M	Total Assets ($)	19929M	92779M	56828M	68672M	236364M	845383M

© RMA 2007

M = $ thousand   MM = $ million
See Pages 11 through 21 for Explanation of Ratios and Data

Current Data Sorted by Assets   Comparative Historical Data

Periods: 23 (4/1-9/30/06)   16 (10/1/06-3/31/07)

	0-500M	500M-2MM	2-10MM	10-50MM	50-100MM	100-250MM	Type of Statement	4/1/02-3/31/03 ALL	4/1/03-3/31/04 ALL
	1	3	12	5	1	1	Unqualified	14	21
				1			Reviewed	1	2
	2	3	3	5			Compiled	4	5
							Tax Returns	6	3
							Other	9	7
	3	8	15	11	1	1	**NUMBER OF STATEMENTS**	34	38
	%	%	%	%	%	%	**ASSETS**	%	%
			17.9	22.8			Cash & Equivalents	13.0	18.3
			16.4	13.7			Trade Receivables (net)	24.8	21.0
			.9	2.3			Inventory	1.2	1.6
			10.6	3.3			All Other Current	4.3	6.1
			45.8	42.1			Total Current	43.4	46.9
			36.0	37.5			Fixed Assets (net)	45.3	41.8
			.0	.1			Intangibles (net)	2.4	1.8
			18.1	20.2			All Other Non-Current	8.8	9.4
			100.0	100.0			Total	100.0	100.0
							LIABILITIES		
			.9	1.7			Notes Payable-Short Term	11.7	2.4
			1.9	2.3			Cur. Mat.-L.T.D.	5.3	3.4
			8.0	4.1			Trade Payables	9.8	8.5
			.8	.0			Income Taxes Payable	.0	.4
			13.2	4.6			All Other Current	15.5	12.1
			24.7	12.7			Total Current	42.5	26.7
			17.9	10.6			Long-Term Debt	26.2	26.0
			.0	.0			Deferred Taxes	.0	.0
			2.2	.3			All Other Non-Current	2.2	1.4
			55.1	76.4			Net Worth	29.2	45.9
			100.0	100.0			Total Liabilities & Net Worth	100.0	100.0
							INCOME DATA		
			100.0	100.0			Net Sales	100.0	100.0
							Gross Profit		
			91.3	92.2			Operating Expenses	93.4	89.5
			8.7	7.8			Operating Profit	6.6	10.5
			-.6	-.3			All Other Expenses (net)	.5	.5
			9.2	8.1			Profit Before Taxes	6.1	10.0
							RATIOS		
			4.5	5.1				2.9	2.9
			2.0	2.9			Current	1.5	1.5
			1.4	2.6				.9	1.2
			3.1	3.6				2.7	2.8
			1.6	2.7			Quick	1.3	1.4
			1.1	1.2				.5	1.1
		9	41.4	18 19.8				5 75.8	6 60.1
		28	13.2	30 12.1			Sales/Receivables	30 12.3	36 10.1
		66	5.5	72 5.1				61 6.0	57 6.4
							Cost of Sales/Inventory		
							Cost of Sales/Payables		
			3.7	2.5				6.0	5.6
			7.7	5.8			Sales/Working Capital	24.4	13.6
			14.8	10.1				-122.4	73.1
			17.2	21.7				16.1	15.5
			(11) 13.8	(10) 8.0			EBIT/Interest	(25) 3.2	(31) 3.7
			1.4	.3				.9	1.5
							Net Profit + Depr., Dep., Amort./Cur. Mat. L/T/D		
			.3	.2				.5	.5
			.6	.4			Fixed/Worth	1.1	.9
			2.1	1.0				NM	1.7
			.2	.2				.5	.7
			.5	.2			Debt/Worth	1.5	1.2
			3.6	.6				NM	3.4
			26.7	8.7			% Profit Before Taxes/Tangible Net Worth	31.6	49.5
			9.8	2.9				(26) 8.3	(37) 15.9
			2.6	.5				-1.1	1.5
			12.1	7.5			% Profit Before Taxes/Total Assets	25.5	38.5
			2.5	2.0				5.8	8.0
			1.1	.3				-.7	.8
			9.4	7.9				29.0	18.6
			4.0	3.5			Sales/Net Fixed Assets	6.0	6.2
			2.4	2.0				2.9	2.5
			2.8	1.5				4.0	4.2
			1.4	1.1			Sales/Total Assets	2.8	2.4
			.8	.9				1.6	1.5
			1.5	1.9				1.1	1.8
			2.1	3.2			% Depr., Dep., Amort./Sales	(30) 2.2	(34) 2.5
			3.7	3.5				4.0	3.7
								9.2	1.2
							% Officers', Directors' Owners' Comp/Sales	(10) 12.5	(11) 5.0
								29.3	12.8
	1939M	23056M	138200M	333476M	69231M	119665M	Net Sales ($)	468518M	652285M
	764M	9496M	82196M	255852M	88985M	105473M	Total Assets ($)	120106M	361942M

© RMA 2007

M = $ thousand   MM = $ million
See Pages 11 through 21 for Explanation of Ratios and Data

Comparative Historical Data				Current Data Sorted by Sales					
12	21	23	**Type of Statement**	2	4	3	3	8	3
			Unqualified						
2	2	1	Reviewed						
5	4	2	Compiled					1	
			Tax Returns			1	1		
9	10	13	Other	3	2	1		4	3
4/1/04-3/31/05 ALL	4/1/05-3/31/06 ALL	4/1/06-3/31/07 ALL		0-1MM	23 (4/1-9/30/06) 1-3MM	3-5MM	16 (10/1/06-3/31/07) 5-10MM	10-25MM	25MM & OVER
28	37	39	**NUMBER OF STATEMENTS**	5	6	5	4	13	6
%	%	%	**ASSETS**	%	%	%	%	%	%
18.5	19.1	18.0	Cash & Equivalents					18.3	
19.5	21.2	14.9	Trade Receivables (net)					19.0	
2.6	2.0	2.3	Inventory					2.2	
2.9	6.2	6.3	All Other Current					10.7	
43.5	48.6	41.5	Total Current					50.3	
41.6	38.2	40.9	Fixed Assets (net)					32.0	
6.4	1.9	1.8	Intangibles (net)					.1	
8.5	11.3	15.9	All Other Non-Current					17.7	
100.0	100.0	100.0	Total					100.0	
			LIABILITIES						
2.8	4.0	2.7	Notes Payable-Short Term					2.4	
6.9	4.0	1.5	Cur. Mat.-L.T.D.					2.4	
8.7	8.9	6.7	Trade Payables					10.1	
.3	.4	.3	Income Taxes Payable					.9	
7.3	10.5	9.4	All Other Current					13.8	
26.0	27.6	20.6	Total Current					29.5	
24.4	23.9	18.1	Long-Term Debt					13.8	
.0	.0	.0	Deferred Taxes					.0	
.2	.6	1.7	All Other Non-Current					2.4	
49.4	47.9	59.7	Net Worth					54.3	
100.0	100.0	100.0	Total Liabilties & Net Worth					100.0	
			INCOME DATA						
100.0	100.0	100.0	Net Sales					100.0	
			Gross Profit						
85.1	91.1	93.1	Operating Expenses					92.4	
14.9	8.9	6.9	Operating Profit					7.6	
.7	.6	.2	All Other Expenses (net)					-2.3	
14.2	8.3	6.6	Profit Before Taxes					9.9	
			RATIOS						
3.3	3.1	4.1	Current					2.8	
1.7	1.7	2.7						1.7	
1.0	1.2	1.3						1.2	
2.7	2.6	3.6	Quick					2.2	
1.6	1.4	2.0						1.6	
.8	.9	1.0						1.0	
0 UND	10 37.9	7 49.5	Sales/Receivables					14 26.5	
18 20.8	36 10.2	24 15.5						28 13.2	
65 5.6	59 6.2	62 5.9						58 6.3	
			Cost of Sales/Inventory						
			Cost of Sales/Payables						
5.7	4.6	3.7	Sales/Working Capital					4.0	
13.2	12.5	7.8						10.2	
162.0	35.3	17.5						24.1	
26.5	20.6	15.5	EBIT/Interest					26.5	
(18) 16.0	(29) 9.1	(32) 4.8						(11) 10.9	
1.9	-.9	.7						1.4	
			Net Profit + Depr., Dep., Amort./Cur. Mat. L/T/D						
.3	.3	.2	Fixed/Worth					.3	
.6	.7	.6						.4	
2.9	1.8	1.5						2.5	
.4	.4	.2	Debt/Worth					.2	
.9	1.0	.6						.6	
4.2	2.2	1.2						4.5	
45.7	22.3	26.6	% Profit Before Taxes/Tangible Net Worth					87.1	
(23) 15.6	(33) 6.6	(38) 6.6						8.7	
4.4	-4.6	.2						1.8	
41.6	15.3	8.1	% Profit Before Taxes/Total Assets					7.8	
11.5	3.3	2.5						2.5	
2.3	-3.8	-.4						.8	
17.9	22.6	9.4	Sales/Net Fixed Assets					9.7	
6.3	5.9	3.5						5.7	
3.3	3.0	2.0						3.2	
4.2	3.6	2.7	Sales/Total Assets					2.8	
2.1	2.0	1.4						1.9	
1.5	1.0	.9						1.0	
1.0	1.0	1.7	% Depr., Dep., Amort./Sales					1.3	
(26) 2.3	(32) 2.4	(36) 3.0						2.4	
3.4	3.7	3.6						3.4	
			% Officers', Directors' Owners' Comp/Sales						
199274M	523904M	685567M	Net Sales ($)	2607M	12411M	19962M	29529M	231343M	389715M
118189M	374146M	542766M	Total Assets ($)	6394M	11186M	23809M	21529M	163757M	316091M

© RMA 2007

M = $ thousand　　MM = $ million

See Pages 11 through 21 for Explanation of Ratios and Data

Current Data Sorted by Assets   Comparative Historical Data

Type of Statement

	0-500M	500M-2MM	2-10MM	10-50MM	50-100MM	100-250MM		4/1/02-3/31/03 ALL	4/1/03-3/31/04 ALL
Unqualified		9	26	24	2			8	29
Reviewed		1	1					1	2
Compiled			2	1					4
Tax Returns	3		1						5
Other	2	6	14	5				9	10
		69 (4/1-9/30/06)		28 (10/1/06-3/31/07)			**NUMBER OF STATEMENTS**		
	5	16	44	30	2			18	50

Current data columns represent asset-size categories 0-500M, 500M-2MM, 2-10MM, 10-50MM, 50-100MM, 100-250MM. "DATA NOT AVAILABLE" is printed vertically across the 50-100MM / 100-250MM columns for the common-size (%) sections.

%	%	%	%	%	%		%	%
						ASSETS		
	12.6	21.5	21.3			Cash & Equivalents	26.4	26.4
	27.9	17.7	16.8			Trade Receivables (net)	18.4	16.8
	.9	.1	.2			Inventory	.1	.2
	8.3	5.1	4.9			All Other Current	3.4	5.1
	49.6	44.3	43.3			Total Current	48.3	48.5
	46.4	44.9	48.4			Fixed Assets (net)	43.4	38.9
	.4	1.7	.7			Intangibles (net)	1.4	.8
	3.5	9.0	7.6			All Other Non-Current	6.9	11.8
	100.0	100.0	100.0			Total	100.0	100.0
						LIABILITIES		
	4.5	3.0	1.2			Notes Payable-Short Term	1.0	12.1
	2.1	1.7	4.3			Cur. Mat.-L.T.D.	1.0	2.1
	10.0	4.8	4.5			Trade Payables	6.3	6.6
	.0	.6	.1			Income Taxes Payable	.0	.2
	17.4	10.3	12.4			All Other Current	11.5	27.9
	34.0	20.4	22.6			Total Current	19.9	48.9
	25.8	19.1	26.1			Long-Term Debt	20.4	19.5
	.0	.0	.0			Deferred Taxes	.1	.1
	2.1	1.6	.8			All Other Non-Current	5.6	3.1
	38.2	58.8	50.5			Net Worth	54.1	28.3
	100.0	100.0	100.0			Total Liabilities & Net Worth	100.0	100.0
						INCOME DATA		
	100.0	100.0	100.0			Net Sales	100.0	100.0
						Gross Profit		
	95.5	94.3	95.9			Operating Expenses	98.7	97.2
	4.5	5.7	4.1			Operating Profit	1.3	2.8
	2.7	1.1	1.5			All Other Expenses (net)	1.0	.1
	1.8	4.6	2.6			Profit Before Taxes	.3	2.7
						RATIOS		
	4.1	4.2	3.9			Current	4.4	2.9
	1.9	2.1	2.3				2.8	1.7
	1.3	1.3	1.3				1.5	1.1
	3.6	3.8	3.5			Quick	4.2	2.3
	1.8	1.9	1.8				2.5	1.5
	.7	1.3	1.1				1.5	.9
	2 156.7	16 23.5	19 19.2			Sales/Receivables	12 29.3	11 32.0
	36 10.1	28 13.2	34 10.8				30 12.3	32 11.6
	55 6.7	47 7.8	52 7.0				49 7.4	43 8.5
						Cost of Sales/Inventory		
						Cost of Sales/Payables		
	7.0	4.3	3.3			Sales/Working Capital	4.4	5.7
	14.3	7.2	7.7				6.9	11.1
	39.9	19.9	32.7				15.5	55.4
		7.0	8.0			EBIT/Interest	3.8	7.0
	(34)	4.2	(29) 2.0				(14) 2.5	(35) 2.5
		1.0	.7				-.4	.3
						Net Profit + Depr., Dep., Amort./Cur. Mat. L/T/D		
	.4	.5	.6			Fixed/Worth	.3	.4
	1.0	.7	.8				.8	.9
	NM	1.3	1.8				1.7	1.9
	.6	.4	.4			Debt/Worth	.5	.5
	1.0	.7	.8				.7	1.1
	NM	1.2	1.9				1.6	4.4
	12.0	15.7	11.3			% Profit Before Taxes/Tangible Net Worth	9.1	20.2
	(12) 6.3	6.6	(29) 4.2				(17) 2.7	(43) 7.1
	-8.7	-.8	-.4				-7.1	-2.6
	7.3	9.6	5.9			% Profit Before Taxes/Total Assets	7.9	11.4
	4.1	3.4	1.4				1.6	2.9
	-3.0	-.5	-.9				-4.2	-3.1
	30.5	5.7	3.9			Sales/Net Fixed Assets	19.7	22.3
	3.9	3.5	2.3				3.0	5.7
	2.2	2.1	1.8				2.0	2.5
	4.9	2.3	1.8			Sales/Total Assets	2.3	3.1
	2.5	1.6	1.2				1.5	1.6
	1.5	1.0	1.0				1.2	1.3
	.5	1.7	2.3			% Depr., Dep., Amort./Sales	.9	1.3
	(14) 1.5	(41) 2.7	2.9				(43) 2.2	2.3
	5.3	3.7	3.8				2.6	3.3
						% Officers', Directors' Owners' Comp/Sales		
12822M	74444M	410944M	1118178M	160684M		Net Sales ($)	684728M	803204M
1425M	21384M	233505M	647061M	178676M		Total Assets ($)	237962M	568148M

M = $ thousand   MM = $ million
See Pages 11 through 21 for Explanation of Ratios and Data

Comparative Historical Data / Current Data Sorted by Sales

			Type of Statement						
31	42	61	Unqualified	2	3	7	13	23	13
5	4	1	Reviewed		1				
2	4	3	Compiled			1		1	1
	2	5	Tax Returns		2	1	2		
		2	Other	3	3	3	8	6	4
11	13	27			69 (4/1-9/30/06)		28 (10/1/06-3/31/07)		
4/1/04-	4/1/05-	4/1/06-							
3/31/05	3/31/06	3/31/07							
ALL	ALL	ALL		0-1MM	1-3MM	3-5MM	5-10MM	10-25MM	25MM & OVER
49	65	97	NUMBER OF STATEMENTS	5	9	12	23	30	18
%	%	%	ASSETS	%	%	%	%	%	%
20.2	20.0	19.7	Cash & Equivalents			25.6	20.0	19.3	19.5
19.1	19.8	19.6	Trade Receivables (net)			10.7	24.7	17.6	24.2
.2	.2	.3	Inventory			.2	.6	.1	.1
6.5	5.7	5.2	All Other Current			4.2	7.3	5.9	3.3
46.0	45.8	44.8	Total Current			40.7	52.7	42.9	47.1
42.7	42.4	45.1	Fixed Assets (net)			51.9	38.3	47.3	39.6
1.3	1.2	1.5	Intangibles (net)			.1	2.2	1.9	1.5
10.0	10.6	8.6	All Other Non-Current			7.3	6.7	7.9	11.9
100.0	100.0	100.0	Total			100.0	100.0	100.0	100.0
			LIABILITIES						
3.2	5.1	2.5	Notes Payable-Short Term			1.0	3.7	3.4	2.1
3.3	2.5	2.7	Cur. Mat.-L.T.D.			1.3	2.1	1.6	2.6
6.7	7.1	5.9	Trade Payables			1.7	6.3	7.6	7.7
.0	.1	.3	Income Taxes Payable			.0	.8	.3	.1
16.4	14.6	12.7	All Other Current			7.3	15.7	13.1	15.7
29.7	29.3	24.1	Total Current			11.4	28.6	25.9	28.2
23.0	22.1	23.8	Long-Term Debt			23.8	16.5	20.2	28.6
.0	.0	.0	Deferred Taxes			.0	.0	.0	.0
.6	5.0	2.1	All Other Non-Current			1.2	3.5	1.7	.8
46.8	43.7	49.9	Net Worth			63.6	51.4	52.2	42.5
100.0	100.0	100.0	Total Liabilties & Net Worth			100.0	100.0	100.0	100.0
			INCOME DATA						
100.0	100.0	100.0	Net Sales			100.0	100.0	100.0	100.0
			Gross Profit						
96.2	94.6	94.7	Operating Expenses			91.6	98.5	96.1	97.5
3.8	5.4	5.3	Operating Profit			8.4	1.5	3.9	2.5
.1	1.0	1.5	All Other Expenses (net)			.0	-1.1	1.0	.5
3.7	4.4	3.8	Profit Before Taxes			8.4	2.7	3.0	2.0
			RATIOS						
3.3	2.8	3.8				22.2	4.1	3.6	2.4
1.7	1.5	1.9	Current			2.3	1.9	1.8	1.6
1.2	1.0	1.3				1.5	1.3	1.3	1.1
2.9	2.4	3.3				14.9	2.7	3.0	2.2
1.5	1.4	1.8	Quick			2.2	1.8	1.7	1.5
1.0	.9	1.1				1.3	1.1	1.2	1.0
13 27.5	9 40.3	17 21.5		15 23.8	14 25.9	20 18.6	20 18.6		
24 15.0	28 13.1	31 12.0	Sales/Receivables	25 14.8	25 14.4	33 10.9	37 9.8		
56 6.6	47 7.7	51 7.1		50 7.3	51 7.2	52 7.0	54 6.8		
			Cost of Sales/Inventory						
			Cost of Sales/Payables						
4.5	7.9	4.0				1.5	5.2	4.6	6.2
12.2	16.1	10.5	Sales/Working Capital			6.6	12.9	8.0	12.2
27.1	NM	39.4				20.4	41.9	22.5	124.4
12.2	8.7	9.2					10.9	9.2	8.0
(41) 3.2	(51) 2.7	(79) 2.7	EBIT/Interest		(18) 4.5	(27) 4.8	(17) 2.0		
1.0	1.0	.7				.0	1.0	.7	
			Net Profit + Depr., Dep., Amort./Cur. Mat. L/T/D						
.6	.5	.5				.5	.4	.6	.5
.9	1.0	.8	Fixed/Worth			.7	.7	.8	.8
1.4	1.6	1.6				1.8	1.4	1.3	2.0
.5	.5	.4				.2	.6	.4	.6
1.0	1.1	.8	Debt/Worth			.6	.8	.7	1.3
2.1	3.3	1.8				1.4	1.2	1.6	2.6
21.7	26.9	13.6				28.7	12.0	15.3	12.2
(46) 9.9	(60) 8.9	(89) 6.1	% Profit Before Taxes/Tangible Net Worth		(21) 4.2	(29) 6.2	(17) 8.3		
.8	.2	-1.1				-3.0	-1.4	-.5	-1.6
11.8	11.7	8.4				23.0	7.3	9.0	6.6
5.0	3.9	3.0	% Profit Before Taxes/Total Assets			2.5	2.8	3.7	2.2
.3	-.1	-.7				-3.0	-.8	-.2	-1.1
13.8	12.4	9.2				3.6	25.9	5.4	15.7
3.8	4.1	3.3	Sales/Net Fixed Assets			2.6	5.3	2.6	3.8
2.1	2.2	2.0				.9	2.6	2.0	2.7
2.6	3.6	2.7				1.7	4.5	2.3	3.4
1.5	2.1	1.5	Sales/Total Assets			.9	1.9	1.4	1.8
1.1	1.2	1.0				.7	1.2	1.2	1.2
1.4	1.0	1.5				2.2	.7	1.6	1.1
(45) 2.7	(56) 2.2	(91) 2.7	% Depr., Dep., Amort./Sales		(20) 2.0	2.8	2.7		
3.8	3.0	3.8				4.3	3.3	3.6	3.1
		1.6	% Officers', Directors' Owners' Comp/Sales						
	(12) 6.0								
		14.2							
829134M	1117411M	1777072M	Net Sales ($)	1773M	19120M	44300M	170575M	469382M	1071922M
469461M	593617M	1082051M	Total Assets ($)	6780M	22960M	47582M	94862M	338048M	571819M

M = $ thousand   MM = $ million
See Pages 11 through 21 for Explanation of Ratios and Data

Current Data Sorted by Assets

Comparative Historical Data

Type of Statement

Type of Statement	0-500M	500M-2MM	2-10MM	10-50MM	50-100MM	100-250MM		4/1/02-3/31/03 ALL	4/1/03-3/31/04 ALL
Unqualified									
Reviewed			1	2	1			2	3
Compiled		1	1		1				
Tax Returns	4	2	4					7	4
Other	3	11	9	3	1			1	8
								22	26
	7 (4/1-9/30/06)			37 (10/1/06-3/31/07)				4/1/02-3/31/03	4/1/03-3/31/04
NUMBER OF STATEMENTS	7	14	15	5	3			32	41

(Columns 10-50MM, 50-100MM and 100-250MM: DATA NOT AVAILABLE for the percentage/ratio detail.)

	0-500M %	500M-2MM %	2-10MM %	10-50MM %	50-100MM %	100-250MM %	4/1/02-3/31/03 ALL %	4/1/03-3/31/04 ALL %
ASSETS								
Cash & Equivalents		17.3	10.1			D	15.5	15.0
Trade Receivables (net)		36.2	29.6			A	27.1	25.1
Inventory		4.4	2.8			T	2.4	2.3
All Other Current		3.2	2.6			A	2.3	3.7
Total Current		61.1	45.0				47.3	46.1
Fixed Assets (net)		35.5	44.2			N	40.6	34.8
Intangibles (net)		2.0	4.6			O	6.3	8.5
All Other Non-Current		1.4	6.2			T	5.8	10.6
Total		100.0	100.0				100.0	100.0
LIABILITIES						A		
Notes Payable-Short Term		5.9	10.6			V	13.3	8.5
Cur. Mat.-L.T.D.		12.3	2.8			A	3.6	4.1
Trade Payables		6.7	7.6			I	6.4	7.0
Income Taxes Payable		.0	.0			L	.5	.0
All Other Current		14.8	13.5			A	17.2	17.4
Total Current		39.8	34.5			B	41.0	37.0
Long-Term Debt		22.7	38.2			L	19.3	26.8
Deferred Taxes		.0	.0			E	.0	.0
All Other Non-Current		2.8	2.9				2.3	5.5
Net Worth		34.7	24.3				37.4	30.7
Total Liabilities & Net Worth		100.0	100.0				100.0	100.0
INCOME DATA								
Net Sales		100.0	100.0				100.0	100.0
Gross Profit								
Operating Expenses		94.0	78.5				88.2	89.3
Operating Profit		6.0	21.5				11.8	10.7
All Other Expenses (net)		.7	9.3				1.4	1.1
Profit Before Taxes		5.3	12.3				10.4	9.6

RATIOS

	0-500M	500M-2MM	2-10MM	10-50MM	50-100MM	100-250MM	4/1/02-3/31/03 ALL	4/1/03-3/31/04 ALL
Current		3.7	3.4				3.4	3.6
		3.0	1.4				1.9	2.1
		.9	.7				1.0	.8
Quick		3.6	3.2				3.1	3.2
		2.5	1.4				1.8	1.8
		.6	.6				.8	.7
Sales/Receivables	37	10.0	0 UND				0 UND	0 UND
	62	5.9	54 6.7				54 6.8	45 8.1
	81	4.5	81 4.5				67 5.5	68 5.4
Cost of Sales/Inventory								
Cost of Sales/Payables								
Sales/Working Capital		4.4	6.3				6.5	5.6
		6.8	10.0				14.9	13.1
		-42.2	-22.9				NM	-59.8
EBIT/Interest		49.2	23.8				42.0	43.6
	(10)	10.7	(11) 6.2				(27) 10.0	(30) 9.9
		-.4	-.7				4.0	1.7
Net Profit + Depr., Dep., Amort./Cur. Mat. L/T/D								
Fixed/Worth		.3	.6				.4	.4
		.7	1.3				.9	.8
		-4.4	29.2				6.3	2.2
Debt/Worth		.4	.4				.4	.5
		1.0	4.1				1.2	1.5
		-8.1	29.9				8.4	5.0
% Profit Before Taxes/Tangible Net Worth			164.1				128.5	102.7
		(12)	72.1				(26) 59.8	(32) 64.6
			33.7				38.0	16.7
% Profit Before Taxes/Total Assets		42.9	29.3				43.9	38.8
		15.2	6.9				21.7	16.1
		-1.1	3.5				6.3	.2
Sales/Net Fixed Assets		15.9	17.5				19.1	19.4
		9.6	4.9				7.9	11.6
		5.2	.9				3.5	3.9
Sales/Total Assets		3.3	3.0				3.8	4.1
		2.3	1.5				2.5	2.4
		1.9	.7				1.6	1.5
% Depr., Dep., Amort./Sales		1.1	1.2				1.4	1.7
		1.6	(13) 2.7				(30) 2.1	(38) 2.4
		2.3	10.1				4.4	3.8
% Officers', Directors' Owners' Comp/Sales							5.3	2.9
							(10) 7.9	(17) 7.7
							46.7	8.2
Net Sales ($)	19530M	55969M	126424M	129018M	226145M		298695M	348230M
Total Assets ($)	926M	18706M	67721M	96890M	179573M		141590M	186803M

M = $ thousand   MM = $ million
See Pages 11 through 21 for Explanation of Ratios and Data

Comparative Historical Data / Current Data Sorted by Sales

			Type of Statement						
6	6	4	Unqualified					2	2
2	6	2	Reviewed						1
3	2	1	Compiled		1		1		
9	7	10	Tax Returns				1		
15	27	27	Other	4	5	6	6	4	3
4/1/04-3/31/05	4/1/05-3/31/06	4/1/06-3/31/07			7 (4/1-9/30/06)		37 (10/1/06-3/31/07)		
ALL	ALL	ALL		0-1MM	1-3MM	3-5MM	5-10MM	10-25MM	25MM & OVER
35	48	44	NUMBER OF STATEMENTS	4	11	7	10	6	6
%	%	%	ASSETS	%	%	%	%	%	%
11.3	17.0	19.5	Cash & Equivalents		36.7		16.9		
23.4	26.1	25.4	Trade Receivables (net)		17.9		29.0		
1.8	3.5	2.7	Inventory		2.4		2.5		
3.7	2.0	3.2	All Other Current		4.1		4.0		
40.2	48.6	50.8	Total Current		61.1		52.3		
38.8	33.5	39.0	Fixed Assets (net)		31.4		37.2		
12.1	10.4	5.9	Intangibles (net)		3.9		7.1		
8.9	7.5	4.3	All Other Non-Current		3.7		3.4		
100.0	100.0	100.0	Total		100.0		100.0		
			LIABILITIES						
17.1	3.9	6.8	Notes Payable-Short Term		11.7		13.4		
4.7	4.3	8.9	Cur. Mat.-L.T.D.		12.4		17.7		
8.7	8.8	5.8	Trade Payables		7.1		5.8		
.1	.1	.6	Income Taxes Payable		2.5		.1		
21.3	16.4	23.9	All Other Current		44.7		27.8		
51.9	33.4	46.0	Total Current		78.4		64.8		
32.5	21.6	29.4	Long-Term Debt		17.2		21.6		
.1	.0	.1	Deferred Taxes		.0		.3		
2.9	5.6	6.4	All Other Non-Current		17.6		.2		
12.6	39.4	18.1	Net Worth		-13.2		13.2		
100.0	100.0	100.0	Total Liabilties & Net Worth		100.0		100.0		
			INCOME DATA						
100.0	100.0	100.0	Net Sales		100.0		100.0		
			Gross Profit						
84.8	82.9	88.0	Operating Expenses		99.2		91.4		
15.2	17.1	12.0	Operating Profit		.8		8.6		
3.0	3.1	3.5	All Other Expenses (net)		1.9		-.1		
12.1	13.9	8.5	Profit Before Taxes		-1.1		8.7		
			RATIOS						
2.5	3.8	3.6			2.8		3.7		
1.5	2.6	1.7	Current		.6		1.1		
.3	1.5	.8			.3		.6		
2.4	3.7	3.3			2.8		3.5		
1.0	2.2	1.4	Quick		.5		.8		
.3	1.2	.6			.3		.5		
0 UND	32 11.5	0 UND		0 UND		0 UND			
47 7.8	49 7.5	53 6.8	Sales/Receivables	0 UND		38 9.7			
60 6.1	77 4.7	73 5.0		81 4.5		85 4.3			
			Cost of Sales/Inventory						
			Cost of Sales/Payables						
6.2	5.0	5.6			4.1		9.2		
14.6	7.2	10.5	Sales/Working Capital		-120.3		NM		
-23.1	23.0	-66.8			-5.3		-10.9		
57.2	51.3	24.0							
(27) 17.8	(38) 10.4	(33) 7.2	EBIT/Interest						
.9	2.3	1.8							
	16.4		Net Profit + Depr., Dep.,						
	(11) 6.7		Amort./Cur. Mat. L/T/D						
	.9								
.4	.3	.6			56.0		.8		
.9	.7	2.4	Fixed/Worth		-3.0		1.8		
-4.3	2.2	-2.7			-.4		-1.4		
.6	.3	.4			74.0		1.2		
1.5	.8	5.8	Debt/Worth		-8.6		4.6		
-7.1	3.7	-7.3			-2.6		-5.5		
103.6	107.3	102.0	% Profit Before Taxes/Tangible						
(24) 55.9	(38) 49.8	(27) 50.1	Net Worth						
19.0	8.4	13.5							
44.8	46.6	28.4	% Profit Before Taxes/Total		15.6		81.3		
15.7	24.2	11.5	Assets		.7		21.3		
-.4	2.2	1.0			-13.2		3.3		
18.7	27.1	22.6			140.9		46.8		
7.6	7.6	7.1	Sales/Net Fixed Assets		19.6		6.5		
4.1	3.8	3.4			10.4		4.5		
4.3	3.6	4.3			19.0		8.1		
2.3	2.2	2.0	Sales/Total Assets		2.5		2.9		
1.6	1.1	1.3			1.7		1.4		
1.7	1.5	1.0							
(31) 2.5	(42) 2.7	(41) 2.2	% Depr., Dep., Amort./Sales						
5.0	4.2	4.4							
5.0	4.1	4.9							
(13) 7.2	(19) 8.0	(19) 8.1	% Officers', Directors' Owners' Comp/Sales						
24.2	9.7	18.7							
362596M	586061M	557086M	Net Sales ($)	2466M	19196M	30058M	67194M	108267M	329905M
153929M	412031M	363816M	Total Assets ($)	9749M	7901M	19076M	36252M	53621M	237217M

M = $ thousand   MM = $ million
See Pages 11 through 21 for Explanation of Ratios and Data

Current Data Sorted by Assets   Comparative Historical Data

						Type of Statement		
	1	15	6	1	2	Unqualified	8	13
	1	3	2			Reviewed	5	12
8	7	8				Compiled	39	55
18	17	11				Tax Returns	31	39
10	14	42	5		2	Other	28	43
	15 (4/1-9/30/06)		158 (10/1/06-3/31/07)				4/1/02-3/31/03	4/1/03-3/31/04
0-500M	500M-2MM	2-10MM	10-50MM	50-100MM	100-250MM		ALL	ALL
36	40	79	13	3	2	**NUMBER OF STATEMENTS**	111	162
%	%	%	%	%	%	**ASSETS**	%	%
35.1	19.9	13.6	10.0			Cash & Equivalents	24.1	25.0
6.1	10.8	22.3	19.7			Trade Receivables (net)	11.1	10.8
2.0	1.9	3.2	2.3			Inventory	.9	1.3
4.2	2.6	3.3	6.8			All Other Current	3.2	3.5
47.3	35.3	42.4	38.8			Total Current	39.2	40.5
37.4	50.4	46.0	53.2			Fixed Assets (net)	46.2	45.0
6.6	2.3	5.5	1.2			Intangibles (net)	5.0	5.3
8.7	12.1	6.1	6.7			All Other Non-Current	9.5	9.2
100.0	100.0	100.0	100.0			Total	100.0	100.0
						LIABILITIES		
23.1	10.1	6.5	3.1			Notes Payable-Short Term	21.7	17.5
13.6	6.7	5.0	7.4			Cur. Mat.-L.T.D.	7.7	10.4
4.0	3.8	5.3	5.6			Trade Payables	3.3	3.6
.1	.1	.0	.1			Income Taxes Payable	.5	.4
51.9	9.1	8.2	9.4			All Other Current	35.2	23.3
92.6	29.8	24.9	25.5			Total Current	68.5	55.2
34.5	31.5	30.8	23.9			Long-Term Debt	31.1	33.9
.0	.0	.0	.3			Deferred Taxes	.1	.1
2.6	3.2	.6	4.9			All Other Non-Current	11.0	6.3
-29.7	35.5	43.6	45.3			Net Worth	-10.6	4.5
100.0	100.0	100.0	100.0			Total Liabilities & Net Worth	100.0	100.0
						INCOME DATA		
100.0	100.0	100.0	100.0			Net Sales	100.0	100.0
						Gross Profit		
87.6	74.8	81.5	82.2			Operating Expenses	94.4	90.8
12.4	25.2	18.5	17.8			Operating Profit	5.6	9.2
.0	3.0	3.0	-.6			All Other Expenses (net)	.5	1.7
12.4	22.2	15.5	18.4			Profit Before Taxes	5.1	7.5
						RATIOS		
1.4	4.7	3.8	2.6				1.5	2.0
.7	.8	2.3	1.3			Current	.7	.9
.1	.3	.9	.9				.3	.4
1.3	3.4	3.4	2.0				1.3	1.8
.5	.7	1.7	1.1			Quick	.6	.9
.1	.3	.6	.6				.2	.3
0 UND	0 UND	16 22.8	29 12.6				0 UND	0 UND
0 UND	0 UND	40 9.2	34 10.7			Sales/Receivables	0 UND	0 UND
0 UND	17 21.7	61 6.0	78 4.7				26 13.9	40 9.1
						Cost of Sales/Inventory		
						Cost of Sales/Payables		
113.9	8.3	5.2	4.5				46.3	15.2
-44.8	-59.4	9.9	9.9			Sales/Working Capital	-52.4	-290.8
-21.0	-13.2	-63.9	NM				-17.9	-22.1
33.8	41.7	34.2	35.3				10.8	13.0
(24) 6.2	(33) 11.8	(68) 10.5	(11) 7.7			EBIT/Interest	(91) 3.3	(131) 3.5
.0	2.8	3.0	.8				1.0	.7
							5.6	2.9
						Net Profit + Depr., Dep., Amort./Cur. Mat. L/T/D	(11) 1.5	(13) 2.3
							.1	1.4
.7	.3	.5	.7				1.2	.9
6.7	1.5	1.3	1.1			Fixed/Worth	5.8	3.7
-.8	23.2	4.1	2.6				-1.3	-2.6
2.2	.5	.6	.5				1.8	1.2
-9.0	1.7	1.8	1.5			Debt/Worth	8.9	7.9
-2.1	22.5	5.2	3.0				-5.6	-5.5
797.6	241.8	124.0	115.8				203.0	226.6
(17) 246.5	(31) 80.0	(71) 62.4	(12) 45.8			% Profit Before Taxes/Tangible Net Worth	(67) 50.9	(104) 42.9
37.7	40.9	16.3	6.0				6.6	2.6
160.8	80.8	59.2	63.3				33.9	35.4
35.7	31.6	20.9	13.1			% Profit Before Taxes/Total Assets	6.1	7.3
.2	6.3	3.5	-.3				.0	-1.0
131.3	18.9	11.7	5.4				59.5	33.7
37.8	7.9	6.2	2.7			Sales/Net Fixed Assets	15.9	11.8
22.9	2.7	2.1	1.8				6.1	4.0
20.8	3.9	2.8	2.2				14.8	10.2
13.6	3.1	1.9	1.5			Sales/Total Assets	5.9	4.3
6.6	1.5	1.3	1.1				2.6	2.0
.5	2.7	1.8	3.5				.9	1.8
(24) .9	(31) 4.2	(71) 3.8	4.7			% Depr., Dep., Amort./Sales	(81) 1.9	(115) 2.9
1.9	7.0	6.1	8.5				5.0	6.9
15.7	4.4	1.5					4.8	9.5
(25) 22.4	(11) 9.7	(12) 6.3				% Officers', Directors' Owners' Comp/Sales	(67) 22.7	(89) 24.1
33.9	23.2	27.5					39.3	33.9
112906M	151595M	781913M	464268M	129671M	249549M	Net Sales ($)	1195773M	2800292M
7884M	47442M	348783M	292776M	220635M	284466M	Total Assets ($)	551039M	1030121M

© RMA 2007

M = $ thousand   MM = $ million
See Pages 11 through 21 for Explanation of Ratios and Data

Comparative Historical Data   Current Data Sorted by Sales

Type of Statement	4/1/04-3/31/05 ALL	4/1/05-3/31/06 ALL	4/1/06-3/31/07 ALL	0-1MM	1-3MM	3-5MM	5-10MM	10-25MM	25MM & OVER
Unqualified	19	15	25	1	1	2	7	7	7
Reviewed	20	13	6	1	1		1	1	2
Compiled	43	29	23	5	6	4	7	1	
Tax Returns	42	29	46	10	13	9	7	6	1
Other	48	62	73	3	10	15	19	21	5
				\<— 15 (4/1-9/30/06) —\>			\<— 158 (10/1/06-3/31/07) —\>		
NUMBER OF STATEMENTS	172	148	173	20	31	30	41	36	15
ASSETS	%	%	%	%	%	%	%	%	%
Cash & Equivalents	23.1	20.0	19.4	16.2	21.7	19.4	20.7	20.6	12.1
Trade Receivables (net)	11.9	15.6	15.8	1.0	14.8	12.6	20.1	23.7	13.6
Inventory	1.7	2.0	2.5	1.7	1.2	2.9	3.5	3.2	1.5
All Other Current	3.1	3.1	3.6	3.5	2.1	2.6	5.0	2.6	7.5
Total Current	39.7	40.8	41.3	22.3	39.8	37.5	49.2	50.2	34.8
Fixed Assets (net)	47.3	43.8	45.4	55.3	44.5	49.6	42.5	39.0	48.2
Intangibles (net)	5.5	6.3	5.3	8.8	3.6	4.7	4.2	4.0	11.2
All Other Non-Current	7.5	9.1	8.0	13.6	12.0	8.1	4.1	6.9	5.8
Total	100.0	100.0	100.0	100.0	100.0	100.0	100.0	100.0	100.0
LIABILITIES									
Notes Payable-Short Term	20.1	23.0	10.4	7.7	19.5	17.3	4.1	6.2	8.8
Cur. Mat.-L.T.D.	6.3	6.7	7.3	8.8	13.6	6.0	6.3	3.3	7.5
Trade Payables	3.1	4.5	4.6	2.6	3.6	4.5	5.5	5.4	5.7
Income Taxes Payable	.4	.1	.0	.1	.1	.1	.0	.0	.0
All Other Current	19.2	18.8	17.6	20.4	18.8	9.1	23.6	19.3	7.9
Total Current	49.1	53.1	40.0	39.6	55.5	37.0	39.5	34.2	30.0
Long-Term Debt	31.6	32.2	31.3	46.7	36.6	37.1	24.6	19.7	34.1
Deferred Taxes	.5	.2	.1	.0	.0	.0	.1	.0	.3
All Other Non-Current	4.2	5.6	2.1	2.0	1.9	.1	2.1	2.5	5.9
Net Worth	14.6	8.9	26.5	11.6	5.9	25.7	33.8	43.6	29.7
Total Liabilties & Net Worth	100.0	100.0	100.0	100.0	100.0	100.0	100.0	100.0	100.0
INCOME DATA									
Net Sales	100.0	100.0	100.0	100.0	100.0	100.0	100.0	100.0	100.0
Gross Profit									
Operating Expenses	83.9	87.0	81.5	69.8	83.3	81.0	83.3	82.0	88.4
Operating Profit	16.1	13.0	18.5	30.2	16.7	19.0	16.7	18.0	11.6
All Other Expenses (net)	3.7	2.2	2.2	11.6	.9	2.1	.6	-.1	2.5
Profit Before Taxes	12.3	10.8	16.3	18.6	15.9	17.0	16.2	18.1	9.1
RATIOS									
Current	2.6	2.5	3.6	1.1	5.0	2.6	3.7	4.5	2.2
	1.0	1.0	1.3	.7	.8	1.3	1.5	2.8	1.5
	.4	.4	.6	.1	.4	.5	.6	1.1	.7
Quick	2.3	2.1	3.0	.9	5.0	2.2	3.0	4.1	1.9
	.9	.9	1.2	.5	.7	1.1	1.1	2.7	1.2
	.3	.3	.4	.1	.4	.5	.4	.9	.6
Sales/Receivables	0 UND	0 UND	0 UND	0 UND	0 UND	0 UND	0 UND	15 25.0	0 UND
	0 UND	1 265.5	18 20.0	0 UND	0 UND	18 20.3	35 10.4	37 9.9	32 11.4
	43 8.6	49 7.4	51 7.2	0 UND	54 6.8	48 7.6	59 6.2	56 6.5	52 7.0
Cost of Sales/Inventory									
Cost of Sales/Payables									
Sales/Working Capital	9.9	9.5	6.2	400.5	6.4	7.2	5.7	5.2	5.6
	NM	UND	28.6	-29.0	-144.1	36.9	12.1	10.7	13.9
	-21.2	-18.4	-29.0	-11.3	-12.7	-20.0	-39.8	85.3	-31.1
EBIT/Interest	23.4	18.0	34.9	8.9	32.9	15.3	53.2	59.4	7.7
	(137) 6.8	(119) 6.5	(141) 7.7	(11) 1.7	(25) 7.5	(27) 11.2	(32) 15.5	(31) 17.5	4.3
	1.0	2.2	1.8	1.1	2.8	1.3	3.1	4.2	.3
Net Profit + Depr., Dep., Amort./Cur. Mat. L/T/D	3.6	8.1	6.2						
	(19) 2.5	(15) 3.1	(12) 2.4						
	1.4	1.2	.7						
Fixed/Worth	.8	.6	.5	1.0	.4	.8	.3	.4	1.1
	2.5	3.9	1.7	5.5	2.2	2.3	.7	.6	3.1
	-5.3	-4.7	10.1	-6.4	-2.7	-11.5	7.0	1.9	-5.5
Debt/Worth	1.0	.9	.6	1.4	.6	.9	.5	.4	1.5
	4.0	5.6	2.4	10.9	4.7	2.8	1.8	.8	4.4
	-12.7	-8.0	17.8	-7.7	-7.1	-17.4	15.8	3.0	-16.6
% Profit Before Taxes/Tangible Net Worth	196.3	166.5	192.5	178.9	442.1	228.0	337.2	125.1	151.6
	(123) 50.0	(100) 63.9	(134) 75.2	(13) 55.9	(22) 84.2	(22) 71.0	(33) 95.9	(34) 76.1	(10) 16.9
	4.8	20.0	21.2	3.3	42.1	13.8	23.4	41.6	-12.7
% Profit Before Taxes/Total Assets	49.3	43.1	66.8	40.5	88.9	59.7	93.2	75.7	24.5
	8.7	15.4	23.7	5.7	26.3	32.5	25.8	43.4	10.4
	-.2	2.7	3.8	.6	4.6	.5	4.3	12.1	-2.1
Sales/Net Fixed Assets	30.6	34.1	21.5	33.9	112.2	18.5	25.4	13.5	7.2
	10.0	11.0	7.8	7.4	12.2	5.1	8.0	8.7	3.3
	3.0	3.5	2.7	.3	2.7	1.9	3.0	5.6	1.7
Sales/Total Assets	9.6	8.7	5.4	9.9	8.9	3.9	7.5	4.6	2.7
	3.5	3.4	2.4	1.8	3.8	2.0	2.6	2.4	1.2
	1.4	1.5	1.4	.2	1.4	1.2	1.7	1.7	.7
% Depr., Dep., Amort./Sales	1.6	1.3	1.8	3.2	.8	2.1	1.7	1.6	2.8
	(139) 3.5	(119) 2.8	(144) 3.7	(14) 11.9	(26) 2.9	(26) 3.8	(31) 3.5	(32) 3.1	5.5
	7.2	5.2	6.1	20.9	8.1	6.5	5.9	4.7	8.1
% Officers', Directors' Owners' Comp/Sales	6.0	7.3	6.5		3.7	5.8	8.1		
	(75) 21.6	(49) 21.6	(50) 16.9		(12) 16.5	(10) 13.5	(11) 18.8		
	32.8	30.1	29.2		33.9	26.8	28.7		
Net Sales ($)	2008579M	1488277M	1889902M	12673M	61899M	121425M	279437M	569688M	844780M
Total Assets ($)	1104445M	664767M	1201986M	21943M	29479M	71610M	122758M	223647M	732549M

© RMA 2007

M = $ thousand   MM = $ million
See Pages 11 through 21 for Explanation of Ratios and Data

Current Data Sorted by Assets | Comparative Historical Data

	0-500M	500M-2MM	2-10MM	10-50MM	50-100MM	100-250MM	4/1/02-3/31/03 ALL	4/1/03-3/31/04 ALL
Type of Statement								
Unqualified	6	7	44	43	7	4	100	89
Reviewed		5	13	1			17	19
Compiled	6	11	15	1		1	33	45
Tax Returns	16	11	7		3	3	15	28
Other	17	22	40	15	3		64	89
	125 (4/1-9/30/06)			173 (10/1/06-3/31/07)				
NUMBER OF STATEMENTS	45	56	119	60	10	8	229	270
	%	%	%	%	%	%	%	%
ASSETS								
Cash & Equivalents	32.2	19.5	17.4	21.1	19.4		17.1	18.9
Trade Receivables (net)	11.6	21.8	21.3	20.4	10.6		21.0	20.8
Inventory	1.3	1.0	1.5	1.0	1.2		1.3	1.7
All Other Current	6.8	5.1	2.4	4.4	2.7		5.0	5.2
Total Current	52.0	47.4	42.5	46.9	33.9		44.3	46.6
Fixed Assets (net)	31.3	42.7	49.5	38.2	43.0		42.6	41.8
Intangibles (net)	6.1	5.0	1.4	5.7	11.2		3.9	3.5
All Other Non-Current	10.6	4.9	6.5	9.3	11.9		9.1	8.2
Total	100.0	100.0	100.0	100.0	100.0		100.0	100.0
LIABILITIES								
Notes Payable-Short Term	21.5	10.0	5.1	2.1	.2		7.1	7.8
Cur. Mat.-L.T.D.	8.3	6.3	5.6	2.6	1.5		8.1	5.6
Trade Payables	5.7	6.7	7.2	6.3	3.1		7.2	7.1
Income Taxes Payable	.0	.2	.3	.1	.0		.3	.4
All Other Current	20.2	13.3	11.1	12.8	14.8		15.5	15.8
Total Current	55.8	36.5	29.3	23.9	19.5		38.1	36.7
Long-Term Debt	21.3	31.4	31.4	18.8	20.1		30.4	24.6
Deferred Taxes	.0	1.6	.1	.1	.4		.2	.1
All Other Non-Current	13.3	.7	2.6	3.4	4.4		2.9	5.4
Net Worth	9.6	29.8	36.6	53.8	55.6		28.4	33.2
Total Liabilities & Net Worth	100.0	100.0	100.0	100.0	100.0		100.0	100.0
INCOME DATA								
Net Sales	100.0	100.0	100.0	100.0	100.0		100.0	100.0
Gross Profit								
Operating Expenses	91.9	85.3	85.9	93.8	95.2		91.9	89.7
Operating Profit	8.1	14.7	14.1	6.2	4.8		8.1	10.3
All Other Expenses (net)	.8	3.0	4.7	.4	.1		1.0	1.5
Profit Before Taxes	7.3	11.8	9.4	5.8	4.7		7.1	8.8
RATIOS								
Current	3.8	3.4	3.1	3.5	2.9		2.7	3.1
	1.3	1.5	1.7	2.1	1.8		1.6	1.5
	.6	.8	.9	1.3	1.1		.8	.9
Quick	2.9	2.3	2.8	3.1	2.7		2.4	2.6
	1.0	(55) 1.3	1.6	1.8	1.4		1.4	(269) 1.3
	.4	.7	.7	1.1	1.0		.7	.7
Sales/Receivables	0 UND	0 UND	16 22.1	31 12.0	27 13.5		10 38.2	1 269.6
	0 UND	17 21.3	38 9.6	41 9.0	35 10.4		39 9.4	34 10.6
	15 24.8	47 7.7	57 6.4	60 6.1	49 7.4		59 6.1	57 6.4
Cost of Sales/Inventory								
Cost of Sales/Payables								
Sales/Working Capital	15.8	8.0	5.1	4.9	4.3		5.5	6.4
	90.0	18.1	14.1	7.5	10.8		17.6	16.5
	-26.4	-28.0	-76.7	20.8	NM		-61.2	-126.6
EBIT/Interest	34.7	40.4	20.1	12.7			14.5	21.9
	(30) 12.3	(42) 8.0	(92) 5.5	(46) 3.9			(179) 3.2	(212) 5.5
	1.7	1.1	1.4	1.5			.6	1.2
Net Profit + Depr., Dep., Amort./Cur. Mat. L/T/D							8.3	6.2
							(22) 2.5	(16) 2.8
							1.3	1.3
Fixed/Worth	.3	.4	.6	.4	.4		.6	.6
	1.3	1.4	1.2	.8	1.0		1.3	1.2
	-1.0	-3.7	7.1	1.5	11.9		5.7	3.6
Debt/Worth	.4	.6	.6	.3	.4		.6	.6
	3.6	1.9	1.5	.8	1.0		1.8	1.8
	-6.4	-11.5	10.4	2.2	13.7		17.0	6.4
% Profit Before Taxes/Tangible Net Worth	384.6	113.8	64.7	24.2			60.4	95.9
	(30) 66.8	(40) 24.4	(99) 22.8	(55) 11.7			(179) 14.1	(223) 18.5
	19.8	1.1	4.2	2.0			2.4	1.9
% Profit Before Taxes/Total Assets	116.5	46.5	21.8	11.4	9.9		19.8	22.2
	21.3	7.6	7.7	5.4	4.5		6.4	7.2
	.4	-.3	.7	.4	.2		-1.1	.2
Sales/Net Fixed Assets	107.3	40.5	9.7	7.3	3.8		17.0	26.3
	27.9	7.8	3.7	3.6	2.5		5.2	5.6
	12.3	2.1	1.4	2.3	1.3		2.3	2.3
Sales/Total Assets	10.4	4.4	2.8	2.2	1.4		3.5	4.0
	6.2	2.7	1.8	1.5	.8		2.0	2.0
	2.9	1.5	.8	1.0	.6		1.1	1.2
% Depr., Dep., Amort./Sales	.7	.9	1.7	1.4	2.2		1.4	1.4
	(28) 1.3	(48) 2.7	(111) 3.9	(55) 2.4	4.5		(204) 2.6	(226) 3.1
	3.7	7.9	9.8	4.2	6.4		4.9	5.8
% Officers', Directors' Owners' Comp/Sales	8.2	5.6	3.1				4.8	4.7
	(14) 19.4	(13) 18.2	(19) 7.0				(40) 14.6	(43) 14.7
	32.0	37.2	11.0				30.4	34.9
Net Sales ($)	74428M	228020M	1300513M	2033815M	858447M	2286968M	6553622M	8739201M
Total Assets ($)	10137M	60020M	576970M	1175070M	723902M	1120571M	3490036M	3107400M

M = $ thousand   MM = $ million
See Pages 11 through 21 for Explanation of Ratios and Data

Comparative Historical Data | | | Type of Statement | ## Current Data Sorted by Sales

			Type of Statement						
91	100	111	Unqualified	4	9	6	26	30	36
19	19	19	Reviewed		2		7	6	
32	26	33	Compiled	7	10	5	7	3	1
26	27	35	Tax Returns	13	9	4	6	1	2
101	100	100	Other	14	22	13	18	17	16
4/1/04-	4/1/05-	4/1/06-			125 (4/1-9/30/06)			173 (10/1/06-3/31/07)	
3/31/05	3/31/06	3/31/07		0-1MM	1-3MM	3-5MM	5-10MM	10-25MM	25MM & OVER
ALL	ALL	ALL							
269	272	298	NUMBER OF STATEMENTS	38	52	32	64	57	55
%	%	%	ASSETS	%	%	%	%	%	%
20.3	19.2	21.1	Cash & Equivalents	16.8	23.4	12.5	20.5	23.0	25.8
19.1	19.7	19.1	Trade Receivables (net)	7.6	15.0	22.2	22.2	24.1	20.3
1.4	1.4	1.2	Inventory	1.1	.7	1.1	1.8	1.4	1.2
4.5	3.4	4.0	All Other Current	3.8	4.2	6.3	3.7	3.3	3.7
45.3	43.7	45.5	Total Current	29.3	43.2	42.1	48.3	51.8	51.1
42.1	42.8	42.8	Fixed Assets (net)	56.2	47.5	47.4	40.9	37.4	34.3
3.8	3.8	4.0	Intangibles (net)	5.9	3.0	6.5	3.6	1.5	4.9
8.7	9.7	7.7	All Other Non-Current	8.5	6.3	4.0	7.2	9.3	9.7
100.0	100.0	100.0	Total	100.0	100.0	100.0	100.0	100.0	100.0
			LIABILITIES						
7.6	6.4	7.7	Notes Payable-Short Term	19.6	13.1	5.9	3.5	3.1	5.1
5.1	6.2	5.3	Cur. Mat.-L.T.D.	4.9	8.8	7.4	5.4	2.6	3.4
7.0	6.3	6.6	Trade Payables	3.7	5.7	6.7	7.1	7.0	8.4
.3	.1	.2	Income Taxes Payable	.0	.1	.4	.4	.1	.2
16.5	12.6	13.3	All Other Current	10.9	9.7	10.0	12.9	16.2	17.7
36.5	31.5	33.1	Total Current	39.2	37.4	30.3	29.3	29.1	34.9
26.2	29.6	27.1	Long-Term Debt	48.2	34.2	29.6	24.0	17.4	18.0
.4	.1	.4	Deferred Taxes	.0	.0	2.7	.0	.2	.2
3.3	4.8	4.2	All Other Non-Current	10.3	7.2	.1	1.9	1.3	5.2
33.6	33.9	35.3	Net Worth	2.4	21.2	37.3	44.8	52.1	41.8
100.0	100.0	100.0	Total Liabilties & Net Worth	100.0	100.0	100.0	100.0	100.0	100.0
			INCOME DATA						
100.0	100.0	100.0	Net Sales	100.0	100.0	100.0	100.0	100.0	100.0
			Gross Profit						
85.6	89.2	89.1	Operating Expenses	80.3	89.9	85.7	85.7	93.4	96.1
14.4	10.8	10.9	Operating Profit	19.7	10.1	14.3	14.3	6.6	3.9
2.2	2.3	2.7	All Other Expenses (net)	14.9	2.1	1.8	.7	-.9	1.4
12.1	8.5	8.2	Profit Before Taxes	4.8	8.1	12.5	13.6	7.5	2.5
			RATIOS						
3.0	3.4	3.2		2.5	3.9	3.0	3.4	3.5	2.6
1.6	1.6	1.7	Current	.9	1.5	1.5	2.1	1.9	1.6
.9	.9	.9		.3	.5	.9	1.1	1.3	1.2
2.6	3.0	2.8		2.3	3.2	2.4	3.2	3.0	2.5
1.4	1.4 (297)	1.5	Quick	.7 (51)	1.3	1.3	2.0	1.8	1.5
.8	.7	.7		.3	.4	.7	1.0	1.2	.9
2 239.8	1 582.9	0 UND		0 UND	0 UND	20 18.1	16 23.4	29 12.5	14 25.5
37 9.7	34 10.7	33 11.2	Sales/Receivables	0 UND	12 30.1	36 10.0	38 9.7	40 9.1	33 11.2
53 6.9	56 6.6	54 6.8		25 14.8	51 7.2	58 6.3	59 6.2	55 6.6	48 7.6
			Cost of Sales/Inventory						
			Cost of Sales/Payables						
6.1	5.2	5.7		6.0	7.9	7.8	4.5	5.1	5.9
14.8	15.8	15.3	Sales/Working Capital	-128.0	27.0	18.1	10.4	10.5	14.9
-134.8	-87.7	-139.2		-4.8	-13.3	NM	90.2	31.3	43.6
28.5	19.6	22.6		28.1	18.8	40.4	31.1	34.2	10.2
(207) 7.6	(220) 5.0	(226) 5.8	EBIT/Interest	(17) 6.2	(42) 3.8	(26) 3.8	(53) 6.9	(45) 9.6	(43) 3.8
1.6	1.2	1.4		1.3	1.1	.9	2.0	2.1	.2
15.1	3.6	6.5							7.1
(15) 4.1	(16) 1.6	(19) 1.5	Net Profit + Depr., Dep., Amort./Cur. Mat. L/T/D					(10) 4.7	
2.7	1.1	.6						1.3	
.5	.4	.4		1.0	.4	.6	.4	.4	.3
1.0	1.1	1.0	Fixed/Worth	6.8	2.2	1.9	.9	.7	.9
4.0	4.4	6.2		-2.5	-4.9	37.5	2.1	1.3	2.4
.6	.5	.5		.9	.6	.8	.4	.3	.5
1.6	1.8	1.4	Debt/Worth	7.7	3.7	2.9	.9	.7	1.4
5.9	7.1	10.3		-9.2	-10.3	111.0	.9	1.7	3.4
127.0	68.1	68.4		96.4	257.9	104.1	115.4	44.8	31.4
(224) 26.3	(223) 17.0	(240) 19.6	% Profit Before Taxes/Tangible Net Worth	(25) 36.4	(35) 38.1	(26) 26.8	(55) 24.2	(53) 14.0	(46) 14.1
3.8	1.8	2.7		-6.4	3.5	.5	4.7	4.0	1.2
34.1	24.8	22.8		24.9	44.4	42.2	38.4	17.8	15.4
8.1	5.5	7.0	% Profit Before Taxes/Total Assets	3.9	12.3	10.8	8.2	7.3	4.8
1.4	.4	.2		-1.5	-1.6	.3	2.1	1.8	-2.4
21.4	17.6	18.6		25.6	32.1	12.6	16.1	10.3	23.9
5.3	5.4	5.3	Sales/Net Fixed Assets	3.0	9.1	5.1	4.3	4.7	5.9
2.4	2.5	2.3		.2	1.7	1.8	2.5	2.9	2.9
3.5	3.5	3.4		3.1	6.6	3.2	3.2	3.0	3.4
1.9	1.9	2.0	Sales/Total Assets	1.1	2.6	2.2	1.9	2.0	2.2
1.1	1.1	1.0		.2	.9	1.0	1.0	1.3	1.3
1.4	1.5	1.3		2.9	1.1	.9	1.7	1.1	1.3
(227) 3.1	(234) 2.9	(259) 3.0	% Depr., Dep., Amort./Sales	(28) 6.6	(44) 3.3	(31) 5.4	(59) 3.5	(49) 2.1	(48) 2.5
6.7	6.3	6.2		19.8	10.7	9.0	5.0	3.7	4.7
4.0	4.3	4.3			4.0		1.4		
(39) 12.7	(54) 9.2	(52) 9.0	% Officers', Directors' Owners' Comp/Sales		(10) 7.9		(11) 9.0		
21.5	27.6	27.1			23.4		31.6		
4697990M	7349342M	6782191M	Net Sales ($)	20798M	100477M	123522M	457948M	938877M	5140569M
2508475M	3522708M	3666670M	Total Assets ($)	49863M	71762M	83913M	334658M	589789M	2536685M

© RMA 2007

M = $ thousand   MM = $ million

See Pages 11 through 21 for Explanation of Ratios and Data

Current Data Sorted by Assets   Comparative Historical Data

						Type of Statement		
	2	10	26	4	9	Unqualified	29	38
	6	11	3			Reviewed	15	20
8	10	10	1			Compiled	22	38
11	8	3		1		Tax Returns	22	25
13	21	32	9	4	6	Other	66	47
	29 (4/1-9/30/06)		179 (10/1/06-3/31/07)				4/1/02-3/31/03	4/1/03-3/31/04
0-500M	500M-2MM	2-10MM	10-50MM	50-100MM	100-250MM		ALL	ALL
32	47	66	39	9	15	NUMBER OF STATEMENTS	154	168
%	%	%	%	%	%	ASSETS	%	%
23.2	16.6	13.0	15.4		8.1	Cash & Equivalents	14.2	14.7
16.0	19.6	31.1	22.3		15.0	Trade Receivables (net)	26.1	25.4
1.9	1.3	2.9	2.8		6.2	Inventory	2.9	4.4
4.1	3.1	3.3	4.3		2.2	All Other Current	2.7	4.2
45.2	40.6	50.3	44.7		31.5	Total Current	45.9	48.8
44.6	48.1	37.7	40.8		27.7	Fixed Assets (net)	38.7	34.6
3.5	3.7	7.7	4.1		29.9	Intangibles (net)	6.6	6.7
6.8	7.7	4.3	10.3		10.8	All Other Non-Current	8.7	9.9
100.0	100.0	100.0	100.0		100.0	Total	100.0	100.0
						LIABILITIES		
37.3	5.2	5.8	1.3		1.5	Notes Payable-Short Term	10.0	10.3
9.7	7.8	6.1	7.3		1.8	Cur. Mat.-L.T.D.	8.3	6.6
11.4	7.6	8.1	8.7		6.5	Trade Payables	7.6	8.2
.0	.0	.3	.2		.0	Income Taxes Payable	.8	1.2
37.6	12.7	15.0	13.0		9.6	All Other Current	12.3	13.8
96.1	33.2	35.3	30.5		19.5	Total Current	38.9	40.1
23.8	35.5	22.1	21.9		24.1	Long-Term Debt	26.9	22.2
.5	.0	.4	.3		1.8	Deferred Taxes	.4	.4
5.3	5.2	5.2	5.7		4.8	All Other Non-Current	4.0	6.1
-25.7	26.1	37.0	41.6		49.7	Net Worth	29.8	31.2
100.0	100.0	100.0	100.0		100.0	Total Liabilities & Net Worth	100.0	100.0
						INCOME DATA		
100.0	100.0	100.0	100.0		100.0	Net Sales	100.0	100.0
						Gross Profit		
88.3	88.0	88.8	92.7		86.4	Operating Expenses	89.8	91.7
11.7	12.0	11.2	7.3		13.6	Operating Profit	10.2	8.3
.6	2.5	1.6	1.0		2.6	All Other Expenses (net)	2.4	1.9
11.1	9.5	9.5	6.4		10.9	Profit Before Taxes	7.8	6.4
						RATIOS		
1.5	2.2	2.8	2.3		2.7		2.5	2.4
.6	1.1	1.5	1.5		1.3	Current	1.5	1.4
.3	.6	.9	1.0		1.1		.9	.8
1.3	2.2	2.7	1.9		1.9		2.3	2.0
.6	1.0	1.4	1.2		1.1	Quick	1.1	1.1
.2	.5	.7	.8		.7		.7	.7
0 UND	0 UND	31 11.9	34 10.8		41 9.0		10 35.5	0 UND
0 UND	28 13.2	45 8.1	46 7.9		54 6.7	Sales/Receivables	47 7.7	44 8.3
35 10.3	56 6.5	69 5.3	65 5.7		61 5.9		68 5.4	65 5.6
						Cost of Sales/Inventory		
						Cost of Sales/Payables		
22.4	8.3	6.0	4.8		4.8		6.9	7.5
-132.2	77.8	16.8	15.9		14.3	Sales/Working Capital	17.0	22.9
-18.4	-29.3	-50.0	237.8		43.5		-105.1	-32.9
26.8	21.0	21.5	11.3		12.9		15.7	15.8
(20) 8.7	(41) 3.6	(58) 8.9	(36) 6.1		3.6	EBIT/Interest	(135) 5.1	(139) 4.8
1.0	2.2	1.3	2.1		2.1		1.4	1.5
		15.3	6.0				14.0	11.6
	(10) 2.2	(13) 3.3			Net Profit + Depr., Dep.,	(29) 4.2	(17) 1.6
		.8	1.6			Amort./Cur. Mat. L/T/D	1.6	.2
.5	.6	.4	.4		.5		.4	.4
3.6	2.2	.8	.8		1.2	Fixed/Worth	1.1	1.1
-.6	-13.4	2.2	2.3		-.9		7.2	6.4
.6	1.0	.6	.7		.6		.7	.7
7.3	2.4	1.5	1.3		2.3	Debt/Worth	2.0	2.1
-2.9	-31.0	5.2	2.6		-2.6		22.7	75.7
175.2	154.6	112.3	33.0				86.2	58.1
(17) 80.5	(34) 52.8	(58) 36.6	(36) 16.9			% Profit Before Taxes/Tangible Net Worth	(122) 29.8	(128) 26.7
14.9	21.2	6.4	10.5				9.2	6.3
99.8	37.6	27.5	13.9		13.9		22.2	21.9
43.1	11.1	13.1	8.4		7.0	% Profit Before Taxes/Total Assets	8.5	7.6
-2.4	3.4	.4	1.9		2.3		1.0	1.1
78.8	22.1	21.8	10.7		16.0		17.2	24.3
20.3	7.4	6.7	5.2		2.8	Sales/Net Fixed Assets	6.3	9.8
10.1	1.8	3.1	2.0		2.1		2.8	3.0
15.3	4.4	3.3	2.5		1.4		3.2	3.8
8.0	2.6	2.2	1.4		.8	Sales/Total Assets	2.2	2.1
3.5	1.3	1.3	1.2		.7		1.4	1.3
.4	1.3	1.4	3.0				2.1	1.8
(22) 1.2	(41) 3.1	(59) 2.7	(37) 4.3			% Depr., Dep., Amort./Sales	(133) 3.7	(144) 3.8
2.6	13.1	7.1	7.1				7.3	7.1
12.2	3.2	3.1					5.0	4.3
(17) 17.5	(14) 6.9	(20) 10.3				% Officers', Directors' Owners' Comp/Sales	(41) 11.6	(50) 11.3
31.7	12.0	26.7					27.0	23.2
91918M	330889M	794921M	1657044M	975920M	2353240M	Net Sales ($)	4325226M	4346816M
7856M	57311M	351320M	988724M	663013M	2496827M	Total Assets ($)	2777437M	2994866M

M = $ thousand   MM = $ million
See Pages 11 through 21 for Explanation of Ratios and Data

Comparative Historical Data | Current Data Sorted by Sales

			Type of Statement						
46	50	51	Unqualified			1	4	14	32
25	18	20	Reviewed		2	2	5	7	4
26	20	29	Compiled	4	6	3	7	8	1
24	22	23	Tax Returns	3	8	3	4	4	1
60	95	85	Other	10	21	6	13	17	18
4/1/04-3/31/05	4/1/05-3/31/06	4/1/06-3/31/07		29 (4/1-9/30/06)			179 (10/1/06-3/31/07)		
ALL	ALL	ALL		0-1MM	1-3MM	3-5MM	5-10MM	10-25MM	25MM & OVER
181	205	208	**NUMBER OF STATEMENTS**	17	37	15	33	50	56
%	%	%	**ASSETS**	%	%	%	%	%	%
15.4	15.4	15.3	Cash & Equivalents	8.0	14.2	20.3	21.8	17.4	11.3
29.2	21.5	22.8	Trade Receivables (net)	15.6	24.1	11.3	25.6	28.1	20.9
3.3	3.0	2.5	Inventory	3.0	.5	.9	4.0	2.3	3.5
3.1	4.0	3.4	All Other Current	4.9	4.5	1.4	2.1	3.4	3.7
51.0	43.8	44.1	Total Current	31.5	43.4	34.0	53.5	51.1	39.3
35.3	40.8	41.0	Fixed Assets (net)	61.7	46.3	48.0	34.6	38.1	35.8
5.4	5.7	7.7	Intangibles (net)	4.9	3.5	12.9	5.5	4.7	13.9
8.4	9.6	7.2	All Other Non-Current	1.8	6.9	5.2	6.4	6.1	11.0
100.0	100.0	100.0	Total	100.0	100.0	100.0	100.0	100.0	100.0
			LIABILITIES						
9.0	8.6	9.1	Notes Payable-Short Term	16.1	9.5	29.3	10.3	8.4	1.3
7.0	8.4	6.9	Cur. Mat.-L.T.D.	9.4	6.6	6.5	7.5	8.1	5.0
10.5	9.2	8.5	Trade Payables	14.6	9.0	5.7	8.1	7.4	8.2
.9	.7	.2	Income Taxes Payable	.0	.0	.1	.0	.3	.3
15.7	15.6	16.8	All Other Current	11.6	15.2	29.9	22.1	14.7	14.7
43.2	42.5	41.5	Total Current	51.8	40.4	71.5	48.1	38.9	29.4
25.4	32.7	25.5	Long-Term Debt	27.4	37.8	33.3	19.1	23.1	20.5
.6	.3	.4	Deferred Taxes	.0	.5	.0	.4	.2	.9
8.7	7.5	5.1	All Other Non-Current	1.9	8.7	13.7	4.1	1.4	5.2
22.1	17.0	27.6	Net Worth	18.9	12.6	-18.6	28.4	36.5	44.0
100.0	100.0	100.0	Total Liabilities & Net Worth	100.0	100.0	100.0	100.0	100.0	100.0
			INCOME DATA						
100.0	100.0	100.0	Net Sales	100.0	100.0	100.0	100.0	100.0	100.0
			Gross Profit						
91.2	91.2	88.7	Operating Expenses	85.6	87.8	87.1	90.2	89.2	89.4
8.8	8.8	11.3	Operating Profit	14.4	12.2	12.9	9.8	10.8	10.6
1.9	1.7	1.5	All Other Expenses (net)	3.8	2.5	2.8	.9	.7	1.1
7.0	7.1	9.7	Profit Before Taxes	10.6	9.7	10.2	8.9	10.0	9.5
			RATIOS						
2.6	2.5	2.3		2.4	2.8	1.3	2.8	2.8	2.1
1.5	1.4	1.4	Current	.9	1.1	.9	1.6	1.5	1.5
.8	.7	.8		.3	.4	.3	.7	.9	1.0
2.1	2.0	2.1		1.5	2.8	1.2	2.7	2.5	1.8
1.1	1.2	1.1	Quick	.9	1.0	.8	1.1	1.4	1.3
.6	.5	.6		.3	.4	.3	.6	.8	.7
20 18.3	0 UND	0 UND		0 UND	0 UND	0 UND	0 UND	27 13.6	34 10.8
46 8.0	41 8.9	41 9.0	Sales/Receivables	38 9.6	29 12.4	0 UND	39 9.4	44 8.2	44 8.3
70 5.2	58 6.3	62 5.9		67 5.5	64 5.7	52 7.1	49 7.4	64 5.7	62 5.9
			Cost of Sales/Inventory						
			Cost of Sales/Payables						
6.4	6.2	7.1		5.3	6.0	19.1	7.9	6.2	6.6
18.2	19.9	25.7	Sales/Working Capital	-431.0	52.1	-52.1	13.6	27.2	16.5
-39.1	-31.2	-39.9		-8.0	-27.2	-4.1	-41.9	-353.6	217.5
17.1	12.8	19.4		7.2	20.5	16.8	64.1	25.1	14.7
(155) 5.1	(166) 3.7	(177) 6.0	EBIT/Interest	(12) 3.3	(27) 4.6	7.4	(30) 8.2	(42) 6.9	(51) 6.0
1.3	1.0	2.1		.3	1.9	.2	2.9	1.4	2.2
5.5	3.5	8.8							9.4
(29) 2.9	(31) 1.7	(32) 3.7	Net Profit + Depr., Dep., Amort./Cur. Mat. L/T/D						(19) 3.7
1.0	.4	1.5							1.8
.4	.4	.5		.8	.5	1.2	.3	.4	.5
1.1	1.3	1.2	Fixed/Worth	2.2	2.5	2.4	.7	.8	1.0
9.7	9.7	13.5		-41.3	-3.3	-2.4	12.2	2.4	3.1
.7	.7	.7		.3	.6	1.0	.7	.6	.9
1.9	1.8	1.8	Debt/Worth	2.1	2.4	3.9	1.2	1.6	1.4
19.3	44.9	16.9		-51.2	-9.2	-7.0	33.3	5.2	6.4
76.7	82.9	92.1	% Profit Before Taxes/Tangible Net Worth	80.5	129.8		109.7	123.8	68.8
(142) 35.6	(160) 25.9	(162) 36.0		(12) 41.3	(24) 65.9		(27) 37.7	(44) 31.0	(46) 22.0
6.4	6.0	11.2		-18.7	29.3		1.4	8.6	10.9
28.2	26.5	34.5	% Profit Before Taxes/Total Assets	54.7	43.8	48.8	48.7	29.2	19.9
8.5	8.6	10.3		11.8	12.4	6.9	13.9	9.9	7.6
.5	.1	2.1		-3.8	3.3	-2.0	2.5	1.1	2.7
24.2	18.7	20.1		18.3	19.9	19.8	46.3	26.8	11.8
9.8	7.0	7.2	Sales/Net Fixed Assets	6.0	7.4	5.9	13.5	7.6	6.2
3.5	2.9	2.7		1.0	2.1	2.1	5.1	3.0	2.7
3.7	4.0	3.7		4.4	4.3	6.3	4.1	4.7	2.7
2.4	2.1	2.2	Sales/Total Assets	2.5	2.3	1.6	2.9	2.4	1.5
1.3	1.1	1.2		.8	1.3	.7	2.1	1.4	.9
1.6	1.9	1.5		2.4	1.2	1.2	.9	1.2	.2
(148) 3.2	(159) 3.9	(174) 3.0	% Depr., Dep., Amort./Sales	(14) 5.7	(27) 3.4	(12) 5.6	(27) 1.9	(49) 2.6	(45) 3.2
6.3	7.7	6.0		28.9	14.0	18.1	3.1	5.9	4.3
5.8	3.5	4.8			5.5		3.3	4.5	
(39) 11.5	(53) 12.6	(60) 11.2	% Officers', Directors' Owners' Comp/Sales		(15) 8.3		(13) 15.3	(14) 8.0	
25.2	29.1	25.8			21.8		25.2	26.9	
4618266M	5361606M	6203932M	Net Sales ($)	11172M	65491M	58564M	231764M	810094M	5026847M
2991374M	3830099M	4565051M	Total Assets ($)	9691M	43652M	40537M	100343M	395972M	3974856M

M = $ thousand   MM = $ million
See Pages 11 through 21 for Explanation of Ratios and Data

Current Data Sorted by Assets | Comparative Historical Data

						Type of Statement		
	1	9	12		3	Unqualified	4	6
1	2	5	7	1		Reviewed	4	6
8	16	14	2			Compiled	6	9
7	12	10	1			Tax Returns	1	13
6	19	38	18	3	1	Other	12	27
	16 (4/1-9/30/06)		180 (10/1/06-3/31/07)				4/1/02-3/31/03	4/1/03-3/31/04
0-500M	500M-2MM	2-10MM	10-50MM	50-100MM	100-250MM		ALL	ALL
22	50	76	40	4	4	NUMBER OF STATEMENTS	27	61
%	%	%	%	%	%	ASSETS	%	%
34.3	16.0	12.3	6.4			Cash & Equivalents	15.2	16.9
8.2	15.2	19.4	22.1			Trade Receivables (net)	24.9	19.2
.2	1.3	.3	.8			Inventory	1.7	.3
9.2	3.2	2.9	2.7			All Other Current	2.3	6.0
52.0	35.6	35.0	32.0			Total Current	44.1	42.4
29.4	53.6	51.2	55.2			Fixed Assets (net)	41.5	44.8
4.4	3.7	5.1	7.1			Intangibles (net)	6.6	4.6
14.2	7.1	8.7	5.7			All Other Non-Current	7.9	8.2
100.0	100.0	100.0	100.0			Total	100.0	100.0
						LIABILITIES		
18.7	6.6	3.2	5.2			Notes Payable-Short Term	4.9	11.5
4.7	9.9	11.0	12.5			Cur. Mat.-L.T.D.	9.6	9.9
7.8	5.1	5.1	3.6			Trade Payables	4.2	3.6
.0	.0	.2	.7			Income Taxes Payable	.4	.0
64.3	10.3	8.5	8.0			All Other Current	6.1	18.2
95.5	31.8	28.1	30.0			Total Current	25.2	43.3
21.7	45.6	35.5	30.8			Long-Term Debt	29.6	31.1
.0	.0	.0	.4			Deferred Taxes	1.7	.2
22.6	3.5	2.6	5.8			All Other Non-Current	5.7	4.4
-39.8	19.1	33.9	32.9			Net Worth	37.8	21.0
100.0	100.0	100.0	100.0			Total Liabilties & Net Worth	100.0	100.0
						INCOME DATA		
100.0	100.0	100.0	100.0			Net Sales	100.0	100.0
						Gross Profit		
93.7	88.2	81.8	81.8			Operating Expenses	86.0	90.7
6.3	11.8	18.2	18.2			Operating Profit	14.0	9.3
.9	3.4	2.1	4.0			All Other Expenses (net)	3.4	2.1
5.3	8.4	16.1	14.2			Profit Before Taxes	10.6	7.2
						RATIOS		
2.0	3.3	2.8	1.7				3.7	2.2
.8	1.2	1.2	1.0			Current	1.7	1.2
.4	.3	.6	.6				.8	.5
1.8	2.7	2.5	1.4				2.9	2.0
.5	.9	(75) 1.2	.9			Quick	1.5	1.0
.2	.2	.6	.4				.7	.4
0 UND	0 UND	0 UND	33 10.9				31 11.9	0 UND
0 UND	0 UND	42 8.6	45 8.2			Sales/Receivables	60 6.1	37 9.9
0 UND	45 8.1	66 5.6	69 5.3				87 4.2	69 5.3
						Cost of Sales/Inventory		
						Cost of Sales/Payables		
24.3	10.0	6.5	8.1				4.6	8.0
-237.6	167.0	52.2	NM			Sales/Working Capital	10.0	47.0
-14.1	-30.3	-11.6	-11.0				-21.6	-18.1
17.9	19.0	17.1	19.2				22.7	20.1
(14) 2.7	(41) 3.8	(69) 5.9	(38) 6.5			EBIT/Interest	(21) 8.3	(49) 4.0
-.3	.5	2.5	1.7				1.6	.1
						Net Profit + Depr., Dep., Amort./Cur. Mat. L/T/D		
.0	.7	.7	.9				.3	.8
.9	3.1	1.7	2.1			Fixed/Worth	1.2	2.3
-1.9	-2.9	19.9	5.5				3.5	-11.0
.9	.5	.9	1.1				.4	1.1
NM	4.1	1.9	2.0			Debt/Worth	2.1	3.0
-1.8	-4.5	27.0	10.0				121.4	-21.5
153.2	175.0	184.0	76.8				82.9	78.5
(11) 84.3	(31) 55.3	(64) 87.7	(33) 42.3			% Profit Before Taxes/Tangible Net Worth	(21) 45.5	(45) 40.5
13.2	5.8	27.3	15.7				11.7	-.8
59.5	46.7	45.9	31.9				38.5	31.5
24.1	16.9	17.9	15.2			% Profit Before Taxes/Total Assets	12.2	7.5
-5.3	-3.0	5.9	3.6				1.5	-5.5
999.8	21.2	7.1	4.9				18.2	15.5
60.7	4.7	3.8	3.2			Sales/Net Fixed Assets	4.5	5.8
8.4	2.0	2.1	1.7				1.7	2.3
36.6	5.6	2.7	2.4				3.0	3.6
8.1	2.8	1.7	1.5			Sales/Total Assets	2.0	2.0
4.2	1.3	1.1	.9				.8	1.0
.4	2.0	4.3	5.5				2.4	2.4
(10) 1.1	(44) 6.2	(72) 7.7	(38) 9.0			% Depr., Dep., Amort./Sales	(25) 7.4	(51) 5.2
10.2	14.3	11.6	14.0				10.8	11.4
8.4	4.6	4.7	3.9				5.4	11.1
(10) 15.8	(12) 13.1	(15) 5.7	(10) 21.7			% Officers', Directors' Owners' Comp/Sales	(11) 16.2	(15) 21.5
34.5	19.7	8.4	30.3				34.4	28.7
94157M	345532M	734128M	1391570M	266884M	519800M	Net Sales ($)	344523M	956604M
5318M	56010M	347945M	888642M	294876M	622703M	Total Assets ($)	319171M	520828M

M = $ thousand   MM = $ million
See Pages 11 through 21 for Explanation of Ratios and Data

Comparative Historical Data   Current Data Sorted by Sales

4/1/04- 3/31/05 ALL	4/1/05- 3/31/06 ALL	4/1/06- 3/31/07 ALL	Type of Statement	0-1MM	1-3MM	3-5MM	5-10MM	10-25MM	25MM & OVER
14	11	25	Unqualified		1		3	10	11
10	12	16	Reviewed		1	3	3	3	6
17	24	40	Compiled	2	15	7	12	3	1
18	13	30	Tax Returns	6	9	4	5	4	2
25	55	85	Other	7	11	12	12	23	20
				16 (4/1-9/30/06)			180 (10/1/06-3/31/07)		
84	**115**	**196**	**NUMBER OF STATEMENTS**	**15**	**37**	**26**	**35**	**43**	**40**
%	%	%	**ASSETS**	%	%	%	%	%	%
14.5	13.9	14.6	Cash & Equivalents	21.3	11.5	15.6	20.4	12.2	11.9
16.6	15.5	17.2	Trade Receivables (net)	6.6	16.1	18.2	17.1	17.2	21.7
.7	.3	.6	Inventory	3.3	.4	.6	.3	.1	.8
4.3	4.1	3.6	All Other Current	5.8	3.0	1.7	5.6	3.2	3.4
36.1	33.8	36.1	Total Current	37.0	31.0	36.2	43.4	32.7	37.8
52.6	51.5	49.6	Fixed Assets (net)	50.0	58.3	45.9	42.9	51.4	47.9
2.2	6.6	5.6	Intangibles (net)	6.4	2.1	5.4	6.6	5.7	7.7
9.0	8.1	8.7	All Other Non-Current	6.6	8.6	12.5	7.1	10.3	6.6
100.0	100.0	100.0	Total	100.0	100.0	100.0	100.0	100.0	100.0
			LIABILITIES						
12.8	4.3	6.1	Notes Payable-Short Term	16.3	8.2	2.9	4.9	6.4	3.1
11.6	11.3	10.0	Cur. Mat.-L.T.D.	6.8	10.2	12.0	8.8	9.5	11.5
3.6	3.7	5.1	Trade Payables	6.1	6.8	3.6	6.6	4.4	3.5
.3	.3	.2	Income Taxes Payable	.0	.0	.1	.0	.2	.9
11.3	16.2	14.9	All Other Current	16.0	21.6	7.2	14.5	14.5	14.3
39.6	35.7	36.4	Total Current	45.2	46.8	25.8	34.8	35.0	33.3
36.6	43.2	36.1	Long-Term Debt	58.5	46.8	38.1	28.1	31.0	29.0
.1	.5	.1	Deferred Taxes	.0	.0	.0	.0	.2	.1
5.9	3.2	5.7	All Other Non-Current	6.2	6.8	11.3	2.4	3.4	6.0
17.9	17.4	21.7	Net Worth	-9.9	-.4	24.9	34.7	30.3	31.5
100.0	100.0	100.0	Total Liabilities & Net Worth	100.0	100.0	100.0	100.0	100.0	100.0
			INCOME DATA						
100.0	100.0	100.0	Net Sales	100.0	100.0	100.0	100.0	100.0	100.0
			Gross Profit						
87.5	84.9	84.5	Operating Expenses	94.7	86.0	74.8	83.7	84.5	86.4
12.5	15.1	15.5	Operating Profit	5.3	14.0	25.2	16.3	15.5	13.6
1.7	2.8	3.0	All Other Expenses (net)	5.9	4.0	4.0	1.1	1.6	3.4
10.8	12.3	12.5	Profit Before Taxes	-.5	9.9	21.2	15.2	13.9	10.2
			RATIOS						
2.0	2.0	2.5		2.0	2.7	4.2	2.9	2.5	2.3
1.0	1.0	1.1	Current	.8	.8	1.4	1.4	1.1	1.1
.4	.5	.6		.5	.4	.4	.6	.6	.8
1.9	1.9	2.0		1.6	2.6	3.7	2.2	2.1	1.3
.8 (114)	.9 (195)	1.0	Quick	.6	.8	(25) 1.4	1.4	.8	1.0
.2	.5	.4		.2	.3	.6	.6	.3	.6
0 UND	0 UND	0 UND		0 UND	0 UND	0 UND	0 UND	0 UND	2 228.7
27 13.6	32 11.3	38 9.7	Sales/Receivables	0 UND	13 28.1	46 7.9	38 9.5	33 11.1	42 8.7
63 5.8	51 7.1	57 6.4		55 6.6	76 4.8	75 4.9	55 6.6	46 7.9	55 6.7
			Cost of Sales/Inventory						
			Cost of Sales/Payables						
10.9	10.7	9.1		15.1	9.7	4.2	6.4	13.2	11.8
-586.1	-130.7	96.5	Sales/Working Capital	-37.3	-46.1	24.1	31.0	999.8	66.7
-13.5	-15.8	-14.2		-3.9	-5.6	-15.1	-35.1	-17.2	-21.0
17.1	13.6	17.3		6.3	6.9	17.5	23.0	23.2	16.7
(75) 3.5	(101) 4.4	(170) 5.3	EBIT/Interest	(13) 2.4	(29) 2.9	(22) 7.3	(31) 10.2	(39) 4.5	(36) 5.9
1.0	1.5	1.2		-.4	-.4	3.3	2.8	1.0	.8
3.4	3.4	4.1							
(10) 1.1	(17) 1.4	(12) 3.0	Net Profit + Depr., Dep., Amort./Cur. Mat. L/T/D						
.8	.8	.8							
.9	1.1	.7		.9	.8	.6	.5	.9	.8
2.2	2.9	1.9	Fixed/Worth	-13.2	3.7	1.0	1.2	1.9	1.8
NM	-8.2	NM		-2.5	-14.6	NM	18.2	9.6	NM
1.1	1.1	.9		2.2	1.1	.7	.8	1.0	.9
2.4	3.5	2.4	Debt/Worth	-10.2	7.2	1.0	2.3	1.8	2.2
-26.3	-11.4	-24.2		-2.5	-10.8	NM	28.0	13.2	NM
158.2	164.5	150.2			105.8	157.3	187.2	138.9	116.2
(62) 52.9	(75) 67.7	(144) 61.0	% Profit Before Taxes/Tangible Net Worth	(25) 55.1	(20) 62.4	(28) 132.9	(36) 64.5	(30) 45.5	
18.7	24.6	21.3			-10.9	22.2	35.1	16.2	10.3
40.1	40.6	41.4		37.6	33.2	53.0	70.5	42.5	38.1
12.3	15.7	16.2	% Profit Before Taxes/Total Assets	6.9	12.5	22.9	38.4	12.5	16.7
-.1	3.4	1.0		-11.5	-8.8	7.6	7.6	.1	.7
13.5	9.3	9.5		25.3	6.3	9.9	15.7	9.2	12.3
5.1	3.9	4.1	Sales/Net Fixed Assets	2.0	2.1	4.6	6.2	4.6	4.1
2.0	2.1	2.0		1.2	1.4	2.8	3.0	2.6	2.4
5.0	3.7	3.7		4.4	2.7	3.2	5.4	5.0	3.2
2.4	2.0	2.0	Sales/Total Assets	1.1	1.4	1.8	2.4	2.5	2.1
1.0	1.1	1.1		.7	1.0	1.1	1.4	1.3	1.2
3.5	3.5	3.6		17.1	2.8	2.6	4.0	5.2	3.0
(66) 6.1	(94) 6.8	(167) 7.7	% Depr., Dep., Amort./Sales	(10) 20.0	(33) 9.1	(24) 7.0	(31) 7.0	(36) 7.2	(33) 6.7
14.3	13.9	12.8		29.5	15.1	13.2	11.6	10.7	10.2
8.5	8.8	4.8						4.2	
(24) 20.6	(26) 19.0	(47) 9.8	% Officers', Directors' Owners' Comp/Sales					(11) 6.4	
39.5	32.6	20.5						20.5	
878843M	3972185M	3352071M	Net Sales ($)	9728M	67916M	101670M	253221M	676789M	2242747M
454050M	1686248M	2215494M	Total Assets ($)	9541M	67593M	95153M	127029M	407014M	1509164M

© RMA 2007   M = $ thousand   MM = $ million
See Pages 11 through 21 for Explanation of Ratios and Data

Current Data Sorted by Assets   Comparative Historical Data

						Type of Statement		
4	11	43	40	7	3	Unqualified	88	97
3	6	13	3			Reviewed	26	16
8	14	7	1	1	1	Compiled	31	49
38	16	3	1	1		Tax Returns	19	25
23	46	33	29	4	2	Other	70	95
	85 (4/1-9/30/06)		275 (10/1/06-3/31/07)				4/1/02-3/31/03	4/1/03-3/31/04
0-500M	500M-2MM	2-10MM	10-50MM	50-100MM	100-250MM		ALL	ALL
76	93	99	73	13	6	**NUMBER OF STATEMENTS**	234	282
%	%	%	%	%	%	**ASSETS**	%	%
33.6	11.2	16.8	22.9	16.5		Cash & Equivalents	15.9	17.7
30.8	45.9	37.5	24.9	21.6		Trade Receivables (net)	41.7	38.9
.5	1.5	2.7	.6	1.1		Inventory	3.1	2.1
4.6	1.9	4.5	3.6	6.6		All Other Current	4.3	6.0
69.5	60.5	61.5	52.1	45.8		Total Current	64.9	64.7
14.8	22.8	27.6	28.4	21.1		Fixed Assets (net)	19.6	19.4
4.5	4.4	2.2	4.9	20.6		Intangibles (net)	4.4	4.9
11.2	12.3	8.7	14.5	12.5		All Other Non-Current	11.1	10.9
100.0	100.0	100.0	100.0	100.0		Total	100.0	100.0
						LIABILITIES		
19.3	12.4	4.5	1.9	18.6		Notes Payable-Short Term	10.3	11.8
2.6	2.6	3.3	2.2	2.3		Cur. Mat.-L.T.D.	3.9	3.4
11.0	7.6	8.4	6.5	6.0		Trade Payables	9.8	7.9
.0	.3	.2	.2	.7		Income Taxes Payable	.4	.9
29.0	17.0	16.9	18.3	23.5		All Other Current	23.3	23.2
61.8	39.9	33.2	29.1	51.1		Total Current	47.6	47.1
8.6	17.7	16.5	16.5	14.7		Long-Term Debt	12.2	12.9
.0	.0	.0	.2	.5		Deferred Taxes	.3	.2
10.1	6.1	6.8	4.3	3.6		All Other Non-Current	4.2	6.6
19.5	36.2	43.5	49.9	30.1		Net Worth	35.8	33.2
100.0	100.0	100.0	100.0	100.0		Total Liabilties & Net Worth	100.0	100.0
						INCOME DATA		
100.0	100.0	100.0	100.0	100.0		Net Sales	100.0	100.0
						Gross Profit		
94.4	90.5	94.5	95.2	97.2		Operating Expenses	95.3	93.4
5.6	9.5	5.5	4.8	2.8		Operating Profit	4.7	6.6
.3	1.7	.1	-.6	.1		All Other Expenses (net)	.7	1.1
5.4	7.8	5.4	5.4	2.6		Profit Before Taxes	4.0	5.5
						RATIOS		
7.5	3.3	3.1	3.6	2.3			2.7	3.2
1.8	1.6	1.9	1.8	1.6		Current	1.6	1.7
.8	.8	1.4	1.2	1.0			1.0	1.1
6.2	3.2	2.9	3.4	2.1			2.5	2.9
1.8	1.6	1.7	1.8	1.4		Quick	1.4	1.4
.7	.7	1.2	1.1	.9			.9	.9
0 UND	28 13.0	37 9.9	36 10.2	39 9.3			33 11.1	30 12.2
17 21.9	44 8.3	47 7.8	50 7.4	52 7.0		Sales/Receivables	50 7.3	47 7.8
43 8.4	65 5.7	68 5.4	61 6.0	62 5.9			73 5.0	69 5.3
						Cost of Sales/Inventory		
						Cost of Sales/Payables		
10.6	7.0	5.1	3.4	7.0			6.3	5.4
35.1	15.9	9.6	7.7	12.8		Sales/Working Capital	13.8	11.9
-42.9	-33.3	22.3	31.7	NM			216.2	86.6
53.8	22.3	18.6	19.3	81.0			24.6	28.2
(41) 9.5	(70) 5.1	(75) 6.6	(57) 5.7	(12) 7.3		EBIT/Interest	(183) 6.6	(200) 7.2
1.1	1.2	1.8	1.7	-3.0			1.2	1.7
						Net Profit + Depr., Dep.,	18.4	11.5
						Amort./Cur. Mat. L/T/D	(25) 8.1	(27) 4.2
							2.8	2.1
.0	.1	.1	.2	.3			.1	.1
.2	.4	.5	.7	.9		Fixed/Worth	.5	.4
UND	4.3	1.5	1.4	-.3			2.2	1.4
.3	.6	.4	.4	.5			.6	.4
1.1	2.2	1.0	.8	1.0		Debt/Worth	1.6	1.3
-15.0	15.9	2.6	2.9	-2.3			9.3	6.0
237.0	102.0	53.4	24.8			% Profit Before Taxes/Tangible	65.5	60.1
(55) 85.4	(78) 48.6	(92) 19.4	(64) 12.5			Net Worth	(196) 27.1	(232) 24.3
27.5	6.3	5.1	4.2				4.7	4.0
99.8	35.8	22.4	14.6	14.7		% Profit Before Taxes/Total	23.6	23.5
27.0	15.7	8.1	7.1	4.2		Assets	10.3	10.2
-.9	1.3	2.7	1.8	-23.3			1.4	.8
UND	143.2	70.7	33.9	72.3			79.5	94.5
125.8	51.7	14.4	7.1	38.1		Sales/Net Fixed Assets	26.6	26.0
34.3	7.6	3.9	3.3	6.6			7.4	7.4
10.7	5.0	3.5	2.3	3.1			4.2	4.2
6.4	3.6	2.4	1.6	1.8		Sales/Total Assets	2.6	2.8
4.3	2.2	1.5	.9	1.0			1.7	1.7
.4	.3	.5	.9	.9			.5	.5
(34) .6	(63) .8	(85) 1.4	(65) 1.8	(11) 1.4		% Depr., Dep., Amort./Sales	(197) 1.3	(224) 1.2
1.4	3.0	2.9	3.1	2.3			2.2	2.3
5.4	2.3	2.2				% Officers', Directors'	2.8	3.5
(32) 10.5	(30) 6.0	(14) 4.4				Owners' Comp/Sales	(53) 4.4	(56) 5.6
15.7	10.9	12.2					9.2	9.0
117510M	365765M	1199213M	3015068M	3664100M	5492353M	Net Sales ($)	7717085M	5663004M
16828M	102542M	463021M	1596755M	874394M	1002119M	Total Assets ($)	3187405M	2937520M

Comparative Historical Data

Current Data Sorted by Sales

91	79	108	Type of Statement						
91	79	108	Unqualified	4	10	7	15	37	35
21	22	25	Reviewed	1	6	1	9	5	3
36	35	32	Compiled	5	9	2	6	7	3
37	38	58	Tax Returns	15	25	9	7	1	1
110	116	137	Other	13	33	14	35	16	26
4/1/04-3/31/05 ALL	4/1/05-3/31/06 ALL	4/1/06-3/31/07 ALL		85 (4/1-9/30/06)			275 (10/1/06-3/31/07)		
				0-1MM	1-3MM	3-5MM	5-10MM	10-25MM	25MM & OVER
295	290	360	NUMBER OF STATEMENTS	38	83	33	72	66	68
%	%	%	ASSETS	%	%	%	%	%	%
18.5	18.0	20.1	Cash & Equivalents	27.6	20.2	21.8	14.4	18.7	22.5
38.8	36.7	34.8	Trade Receivables (net)	21.9	36.2	40.0	41.4	34.2	31.4
1.7	2.0	1.4	Inventory	1.1	1.1	.0	3.0	1.5	.9
5.4	4.2	3.9	All Other Current	2.0	4.1	2.4	2.9	4.7	5.9
64.4	61.0	60.3	Total Current	52.6	61.7	64.3	61.7	59.1	60.6
20.6	20.5	23.5	Fixed Assets (net)	35.3	20.8	17.4	25.9	25.0	19.1
3.6	4.8	4.9	Intangibles (net)	5.3	3.5	2.0	3.5	3.8	10.2
11.4	13.7	11.4	All Other Non-Current	6.9	14.0	16.3	8.9	12.1	10.1
100.0	100.0	100.0	Total	100.0	100.0	100.0	100.0	100.0	100.0
			LIABILITIES						
10.7	10.1	9.6	Notes Payable-Short Term	19.9	14.2	11.8	6.2	4.5	5.4
3.2	2.5	2.7	Cur. Mat.-L.T.D.	4.0	2.0	1.2	4.2	2.3	2.0
10.0	8.8	8.2	Trade Payables	9.6	8.8	4.4	10.7	6.8	7.1
.3	.2	.2	Income Taxes Payable	.0	.1	.7	.1	.1	.3
20.3	21.2	20.1	All Other Current	20.9	22.5	17.2	16.7	15.8	25.9
44.5	42.6	40.7	Total Current	54.3	47.7	35.3	38.0	29.6	40.8
15.9	16.4	15.1	Long-Term Debt	19.7	16.5	13.2	16.0	13.0	12.7
.1	.1	.1	Deferred Taxes	.0	.0	.1	.0	.0	.4
6.9	7.0	6.7	All Other Non-Current	5.0	9.8	2.4	5.0	4.3	10.0
32.6	33.8	37.5	Net Worth	20.9	26.0	49.0	41.0	53.1	36.1
100.0	100.0	100.0	Total Liabilties & Net Worth	100.0	100.0	100.0	100.0	100.0	100.0
			INCOME DATA						
100.0	100.0	100.0	Net Sales	100.0	100.0	100.0	100.0	100.0	100.0
			Gross Profit						
94.8	94.1	93.8	Operating Expenses	90.5	93.0	89.5	95.1	95.2	96.1
5.2	5.9	6.2	Operating Profit	9.5	7.0	10.5	4.9	4.8	3.9
.5	.9	.4	All Other Expenses (net)	3.6	.7	.1	.3	-.8	-.2
4.7	5.1	5.7	Profit Before Taxes	5.8	6.3	10.4	4.6	5.5	4.1
			RATIOS						
3.2	3.5	3.6	Current	6.5	4.4	4.8	3.2	3.5	3.1
1.7	1.8	1.8		1.6	1.8	1.8	1.7	2.0	1.7
1.0	1.1	1.1		.4	.7	1.2	1.2	1.3	1.2
3.0	3.3	3.3	Quick	6.3	3.8	4.6	2.7	3.2	3.0
(294) 1.5	1.6	1.7		1.6	1.8	1.8	1.6	1.9	1.5
.9	.9	.9		.4	.7	1.1	1.0	1.1	1.0
28 13.1	20 17.8	23 15.7	Sales/Receivables	0 UND	1 521.0	19 19.7	33 11.2	38 9.7	34 10.7
48 7.7	46 8.0	44 8.3		16 22.4	36 10.3	41 8.9	54 6.8	48 7.6	50 7.3
71 5.1	67 5.4	62 5.9		50 7.3	56 6.5	61 6.0	69 5.3	65 5.6	59 6.1
			Cost of Sales/Inventory						
			Cost of Sales/Payables						
5.5	5.3	6.0	Sales/Working Capital	5.7	7.7	6.4	6.3	4.5	4.4
12.1	13.3	12.3		28.2	24.1	15.8	11.2	9.2	10.9
999.8	72.2	103.6		-5.4	-31.0	115.3	48.3	27.3	31.9
33.0	33.0	21.0	EBIT/Interest	4.1	31.8	56.5	15.8	14.1	42.6
(218) 7.9	(211) 9.7	(261) 5.7		(15) 1.4	(60) 5.6	(24) 10.0	(59) 4.7	(47) 6.9	(56) 8.6
1.3	1.4	1.3		-.7	1.1	2.9	.9	2.1	1.3
11.5	8.5	14.1	Net Profit + Depr., Dep., Amort./Cur. Mat. L/T/D						18.3
(25) 1.9	(28) 3.0	(19) 4.8						(13)	10.9
1.0	1.0	1.2							1.6
.1	.1	.1	Fixed/Worth	.0	.1	.0	.1	.1	.2
.5	.3	.4		.6	.3	.1	.6	.5	.4
3.3	1.8	1.9		NM	3.2	1.2	2.2	1.4	2.0
.4	.4	.4	Debt/Worth	.2	.5	.3	.6	.3	.5
1.3	1.2	1.1		2.6	2.0	.9	1.5	.8	1.0
14.9	7.7	6.4		-9.6	43.0	3.6	3.6	1.7	27.1
67.4	71.1	76.2	% Profit Before Taxes/Tangible Net Worth	100.9	131.5	160.4	57.4	45.3	44.8
(235) 24.7	(238) 23.1	(301) 27.2		(27) 12.5	(67) 50.0	(30) 66.5	(62) 19.3	(61) 14.0	(54) 20.7
6.0	5.5	5.7		-22.0	6.7	12.9	.9	5.4	5.8
26.3	25.3	28.6	% Profit Before Taxes/Total Assets	25.0	64.3	65.1	24.3	18.6	20.3
9.5	10.2	9.9		4.8	21.1	23.3	8.9	8.0	10.3
1.2	1.1	1.4		-19.0	1.0	8.1	.1	2.6	1.1
101.3	129.6	132.8	Sales/Net Fixed Assets	UND	268.4	294.2	87.8	92.4	78.2
26.7	31.1	28.5		24.8	54.5	80.9	14.3	14.8	22.6
8.1	8.0	5.8		1.1	9.0	21.0	4.1	3.8	7.7
4.9	4.8	5.0	Sales/Total Assets	5.4	7.2	6.2	4.2	3.5	3.8
2.9	2.7	2.9		2.5	4.0	3.8	3.3	2.1	2.2
1.6	1.6	1.5		.7	2.4	1.7	1.7	1.2	1.4
.4	.5	.5	% Depr., Dep., Amort./Sales	1.4	.4	.2	.5	.6	.6
(235) 1.1	(225) 1.2	(262) 1.2		(17) 2.3	(51) .9	(20) .5	(57) 1.2	(58) 1.6	(59) 1.2
2.2	2.4	2.7		7.5	5.5	3.0	2.4	2.8	2.1
2.0	2.6	2.8	% Officers', Directors' Owners' Comp/Sales	5.1	3.3	2.0			
(63) 4.0	(63) 4.8	(83) 6.8		(28) 10.6	(13) 5.9	(19) 4.9			
8.9	10.7	13.0		17.9	9.8	12.2			
5032618M	7435831M	13854009M	Net Sales ($)	18570M	165653M	131553M	518158M	1063256M	11956819M
2875906M	3066438M	4055659M	Total Assets ($)	18051M	57413M	63783M	267236M	686371M	2962805M

M = $ thousand   MM = $ million
See Pages 11 through 21 for Explanation of Ratios and Data

HEALTH CARE—Ambulance Services NAICS 621910 (SIC 4119, 4522)

Current Data Sorted by Assets | Comparative Historical Data

Type of Statement	0-500M	500M-2MM	2-10MM	10-50MM	50-100MM	100-250MM	4/1/02-3/31/03 ALL	4/1/03-3/31/04 ALL
Unqualified		2	9	4		1	8	10
Reviewed		2	5	2			4	4
Compiled	4	4	4				6	7
Tax Returns	6	4					5	6
Other	4	4	4	5	1		3	8
	14 (4/1-9/30/06)			51 (10/1/06-3/31/07)				
NUMBER OF STATEMENTS	14	16	22	11	1	1	26	35
ASSETS	%	%	%	%	%	%	%	%
Cash & Equivalents	37.5	7.6	12.6	12.3			6.4	13.3
Trade Receivables (net)	9.0	19.2	35.9	42.0			31.7	22.9
Inventory	1.3	1.3	1.9	3.0			4.0	2.7
All Other Current	4.6	4.7	1.8	6.4			2.8	2.8
Total Current	52.4	32.8	52.2	63.7			44.8	41.7
Fixed Assets (net)	42.7	56.3	38.2	31.1			43.2	48.7
Intangibles (net)	2.8	3.2	2.5	3.3			5.6	3.4
All Other Non-Current	2.0	7.7	7.1	1.8			6.4	6.1
Total	100.0	100.0	100.0	100.0			100.0	100.0
LIABILITIES								
Notes Payable-Short Term	20.4	6.3	7.1	5.8			12.5	8.9
Cur. Mat.-L.T.D.	9.2	5.2	6.3	3.3			8.3	6.4
Trade Payables	2.3	3.2	7.4	5.7			7.9	5.4
Income Taxes Payable	.0	1.7	.1	.5			.7	.7
All Other Current	16.2	7.6	5.1	7.3			10.3	9.5
Total Current	48.1	23.9	26.0	22.7			39.6	30.9
Long-Term Debt	43.2	54.0	15.7	39.4			33.0	30.5
Deferred Taxes	.3	.1	1.5	1.0			1.9	.7
All Other Non-Current	6.2	.7	3.6	1.1			5.0	8.8
Net Worth	2.2	21.2	53.3	35.9			20.4	29.0
Total Liabilties & Net Worth	100.0	100.0	100.0	100.0			100.0	100.0
INCOME DATA								
Net Sales	100.0	100.0	100.0	100.0			100.0	100.0
Gross Profit								
Operating Expenses	91.7	87.1	93.3	86.3			92.6	95.8
Operating Profit	8.3	12.9	6.7	13.7			7.4	4.2
All Other Expenses (net)	1.5	1.7	.3	1.2			3.3	1.5
Profit Before Taxes	6.8	11.2	6.4	12.5			4.2	2.8
RATIOS								
Current	15.5	3.3	3.3	5.2			1.9	3.3
	1.0	1.6	2.1	3.8			1.2	1.6
	.4	.8	1.5	1.5			.9	1.0
Quick	15.5	3.1	2.9	4.8			1.6	3.1
	.7	1.1	2.1	3.7			1.1	1.4
	.3	.5	1.3	1.4			.7	.8
Sales/Receivables	0 UND	0 UND	43 8.4	44 8.4			33 10.9	3 123.0
	0 UND	29 12.4	53 6.9	97 3.8			51 7.1	39 9.3
	6 62.6	77 4.7	77 4.8	112 3.3			88 4.2	69 5.3
Cost of Sales/Inventory								
Cost of Sales/Payables								
Sales/Working Capital	14.0	6.7	5.2	1.8			9.4	7.0
	NM	30.5	8.5	4.6			21.4	21.9
	-27.7	-30.8	16.5	9.2			-49.1	-239.0
EBIT/Interest	25.0	12.1	15.7	23.1			7.3	9.4
	(12) 5.0	(13) 3.2	(19) 4.9	(10) 9.3			(25) 3.1	(30) 3.1
	1.5	1.1	1.1	2.7			.8	.3
Net Profit + Depr., Dep., Amort./Cur. Mat. L/T/D								
Fixed/Worth	.4	.8	.3	.3			.9	.7
	1.1	1.7	.7	.7			2.3	1.3
	-29.2	7.1	1.5	2.4			7.3	2.6
Debt/Worth	.3	.5	.5	.2			1.6	.5
	3.5	3.2	.9	1.0			4.1	1.6
	-60.2	7.2	1.5	3.5			23.7	3.9
% Profit Before Taxes/Tangible Net Worth	585.5	62.2	40.6	31.0			59.9	43.9
	(10) 81.6	(14) 19.4	(21) 18.0	(10) 21.3			(21) 28.3	(31) 19.3
	6.4	12.6	7.1	12.1			-5.6	-2.6
% Profit Before Taxes/Total Assets	85.4	19.6	20.3	23.5			21.3	17.4
	13.3	6.9	8.9	11.0			4.7	8.0
	.6	2.5	.7	4.2			-1.9	-.9
Sales/Net Fixed Assets	34.5	7.0	12.1	10.3			10.3	11.0
	17.1	4.4	5.6	7.4			5.9	5.9
	7.1	3.0	3.6	2.0			1.7	3.2
Sales/Total Assets	10.3	3.2	2.8	2.2			2.6	3.4
	5.3	2.0	2.3	2.0			2.0	2.7
	2.9	1.5	1.6	.9			1.1	1.5
% Depr., Dep., Amort./Sales	.6	4.0	3.1	1.3			1.5	1.8
	(11) 2.8	6.0	(21) 4.0	2.6			(24) 4.6	(31) 5.2
	7.3	10.3	5.2	5.6			6.5	6.4
% Officers', Directors' Owners' Comp/Sales								3.0
							(10) 5.1	
							10.5	
Net Sales ($)	17435M	45703M	268164M	458619M	198246M	91416M	296196M	826464M
Total Assets ($)	3257M	19411M	100668M	253326M	94825M	102735M	149331M	342705M

M = $ thousand   MM = $ million
See Pages 11 through 21 for Explanation of Ratios and Data

Comparative Historical Data / Current Data Sorted by Sales

Type of Statement	4/1/04-3/31/05 ALL	4/1/05-3/31/06 ALL	4/1/06-3/31/07 ALL	0-1MM	1-3MM	3-5MM	5-10MM	10-25MM	25MM & OVER
					14 (4/1-9/30/06)		51 (10/1/06-3/31/07)		
Unqualified	3	8	16			3	5	4	4
Reviewed	3	7	9	1	1	1	3	3	1
Compiled	7	7	12		3	4	4		
Tax Returns	5	4	10	3	6	1			
Other	16	14	18	5	3		3		7
NUMBER OF STATEMENTS	34	40	65	9	13	9	15	7	12
ASSETS	%	%	%	%	%	%	%	%	%
Cash & Equivalents	16.9	17.3	16.4		16.0		16.2		11.9
Trade Receivables (net)	26.4	35.4	26.9		13.3		31.3		35.5
Inventory	1.5	1.1	1.8		2.3		1.9		3.0
All Other Current	3.9	2.1	4.0		9.5		1.0		7.5
Total Current	48.7	55.9	49.2		41.1		50.4		58.0
Fixed Assets (net)	41.3	36.5	42.1		46.3		39.3		31.0
Intangibles (net)	3.5	4.2	3.0		5.1		4.2		4.4
All Other Non-Current	6.6	3.5	5.7		7.5		6.1		6.6
Total	100.0	100.0	100.0		100.0		100.0		100.0
LIABILITIES									
Notes Payable-Short Term	27.8	5.4	9.4		21.7		7.4		7.4
Cur. Mat.-L.T.D.	9.9	5.5	6.0		6.3		6.0		4.2
Trade Payables	6.7	5.6	4.9		4.1		3.5		9.8
Income Taxes Payable	.1	.6	.6		.0		1.3		.7
All Other Current	10.2	5.9	9.0		13.5		5.8		11.0
Total Current	54.6	23.1	29.9		45.5		24.1		33.0
Long-Term Debt	36.6	17.3	34.9		55.4		15.0		36.0
Deferred Taxes	.0	1.0	.7		.0		2.1		.9
All Other Non-Current	6.9	2.1	3.1		7.2		2.5		1.6
Net Worth	1.9	56.5	31.3		-8.2		56.3		28.6
Total Liabilties & Net Worth	100.0	100.0	100.0		100.0		100.0		100.0
INCOME DATA									
Net Sales	100.0	100.0	100.0		100.0		100.0		100.0
Gross Profit									
Operating Expenses	95.1	93.3	90.2		94.8		91.8		90.0
Operating Profit	4.9	6.7	9.8		5.2		8.2		10.0
All Other Expenses (net)	2.7	1.7	1.1		2.8		-.3		.9
Profit Before Taxes	2.2	5.0	8.7		2.4		8.5		9.0
RATIOS									
Current	3.5	5.0	3.7		2.0		3.8		3.5
	1.5	2.6	1.9		1.0		2.2		1.8
	1.0	1.7	1.0		.9		1.0		1.2
Quick	3.5	4.9	3.5		1.7		3.7		3.5
	1.2	2.5	1.6		.8		2.1		1.5
	.9	1.6	.8		.2		1.0		.9
Sales/Receivables	0 UND	33 11.1	0 UND		0 UND		45 8.1		42 8.7
	55 6.7	56 6.6	45 8.1		0 UND		58 6.3		58 6.3
	98 3.7	72 5.1	78 4.7		57 6.4		76 4.8		93 3.9
Cost of Sales/Inventory									
Cost of Sales/Payables									
Sales/Working Capital	3.4	4.2	5.2		13.2		5.2		4.8
	10.0	7.6	10.2		601.0		7.8		9.8
	-171.6	23.8	-999.8		-183.3		182.8		23.7
EBIT/Interest	13.8	16.1	16.4		25.2		20.4		12.4
	(29) 2.3	(36) 7.1	(56) 5.1		(11) 1.9		(13) 9.2		(11) 9.1
	-4.5	2.3	1.6		.7		2.0		4.4
Net Profit + Depr., Dep., Amort./Cur. Mat. L/T/D			6.3						
		(14)	3.3						
			1.2						
Fixed/Worth	.7	.3	.4		1.1		.4		.4
	1.5	.7	1.0		3.6		.8		.8
	NM	1.2	3.0		-5.0		1.5		3.8
Debt/Worth	.6	.3	.4		1.8		.3		.7
	2.9	.7	1.1		7.5		.7		1.9
	NM	1.8	4.9		-9.1		1.5		4.2
% Profit Before Taxes/Tangible Net Worth	33.6	41.4	49.9				55.2		36.3
	(26) 15.7	(37) 15.4	(57) 19.9				(14) 34.8		(11) 19.0
	-45.2	3.5	10.8				16.5		12.4
% Profit Before Taxes/Total Assets	20.2	21.1	22.0		26.4		28.8		19.0
	5.0	8.3	8.9		6.3		17.8		8.7
	-14.0	2.5	1.9		-1.7		4.3		4.7
Sales/Net Fixed Assets	12.1	18.1	11.7		17.1		9.7		9.8
	7.6	8.5	6.0		6.0		5.9		7.7
	3.2	4.1	3.7		3.7		4.6		5.9
Sales/Total Assets	3.9	3.5	3.5		7.2		2.9		2.7
	1.8	2.4	2.2		2.3		2.3		2.2
	1.2	1.6	1.5		1.7		1.4		2.0
% Depr., Dep., Amort./Sales	2.7	2.3	2.6		2.2		3.2		1.3
	(30) 4.9	(34) 3.9	(60) 3.9		(12) 4.8		3.7		(10) 2.3
	6.9	6.8	6.6		7.3		6.2		3.5
% Officers', Directors' Owners' Comp/Sales		3.1	1.6						
	(11)	4.1	(23) 3.8						
		6.6	4.9						
Net Sales ($)	726451M	681344M	1079583M	4191M	23035M	33688M	105973M	111953M	800743M
Total Assets ($)	316707M	394122M	574222M	3473M	8854M	17061M	55300M	72527M	417007M

© RMA 2007

M = $ thousand   MM = $ million

See Pages 11 through 21 for Explanation of Ratios and Data

Current Data Sorted by Assets   Comparative Historical Data

0-500M	500M-2MM	2-10MM	10-50MM	50-100MM	100-250MM	Type of Statement	4/1/02-3/31/03 ALL	4/1/03-3/31/04 ALL
		10	13	3	2	Unqualified	13	19
	1		1			Reviewed	1	3
						Compiled	6	2
						Tax Returns		3
3	2	7	4			Other	10	11
		21 (4/1-9/30/06)	27 (10/1/06-3/31/07)					
3	3	17	18	5	2	NUMBER OF STATEMENTS	30	38
%	%	%	%	%	%	ASSETS	%	%
		20.9	19.2			Cash & Equivalents	15.9	14.1
		21.1	16.8			Trade Receivables (net)	25.2	25.4
		4.5	2.8			Inventory	2.0	2.5
		3.4	6.5			All Other Current	7.6	3.1
		49.8	45.3			Total Current	50.6	45.1
		35.1	36.5			Fixed Assets (net)	38.4	33.9
		3.7	.3			Intangibles (net)	3.3	5.4
		11.3	18.0			All Other Non-Current	7.6	15.6
		100.0	100.0			Total	100.0	100.0
						LIABILITIES		
		1.2	2.4			Notes Payable-Short Term	3.4	4.4
		1.6	1.2			Cur. Mat.-L.T.D.	1.2	2.6
		8.0	9.4			Trade Payables	7.3	9.4
		.2	.0			Income Taxes Payable	.1	.1
		8.4	5.7			All Other Current	10.2	8.6
		19.4	18.7			Total Current	22.1	25.0
		19.2	14.1			Long-Term Debt	17.8	19.0
		.0	.0			Deferred Taxes	.1	.1
		3.7	2.6			All Other Non-Current	2.8	5.7
		57.7	64.5			Net Worth	57.2	50.2
		100.0	100.0			Total Liabilties & Net Worth	100.0	100.0
						INCOME DATA		
		100.0	100.0			Net Sales	100.0	100.0
						Gross Profit		
		92.9	91.7			Operating Expenses	92.2	94.0
		7.1	8.3			Operating Profit	7.8	6.0
		-.1	-1.0			All Other Expenses (net)	1.0	.4
		7.1	9.3			Profit Before Taxes	6.8	5.6
						RATIOS		
		4.9	4.1				4.6	3.5
		2.9	2.9			Current	2.7	1.8
		1.7	1.6				1.3	1.2
		3.8	3.1				3.5	3.0
		2.1	2.5			Quick	2.0	1.7
		1.6	1.4				.9	1.1
		(25) 14.7	(33) 11.1				(29) 12.8	(35) 10.6
		40 9.2	49 7.4			Sales/Receivables	47 7.8	42 8.6
		43 8.5	61 6.0				58 6.3	52 7.0
						Cost of Sales/Inventory		
						Cost of Sales/Payables		
		3.9	3.0				2.8	5.5
		6.6	5.0			Sales/Working Capital	6.8	8.9
		14.3	12.2				31.1	42.2
		18.4	14.0				37.5	17.2
		(10) 5.8	(10) 4.9			EBIT/Interest	(21) 5.6	(23) 7.8
		3.0	2.0				1.6	2.7
						Net Profit + Depr., Dep., Amort./Cur. Mat. L/T/D		
		.2	.1				.3	.3
		.6	.6			Fixed/Worth	.6	.6
		1.5	1.3				1.8	1.3
		.2	.1				.2	.4
		.7	.5			Debt/Worth	.6	.9
		2.7	1.2				1.8	1.9
		23.4	21.8				32.1	23.7
		(16) 12.1	9.9			% Profit Before Taxes/Tangible Net Worth	(28) 10.1	(36) 10.6
		5.9	2.5				3.3	1.9
		16.5	14.8				16.1	14.1
		6.4	7.3			% Profit Before Taxes/Total Assets	8.0	5.8
		2.6	1.7				2.1	.8
		16.7	20.0				11.1	15.8
		4.2	3.6			Sales/Net Fixed Assets	5.7	4.9
		2.9	2.5				3.1	3.3
		2.4	1.8				2.7	2.8
		1.8	1.1			Sales/Total Assets	1.7	1.7
		1.1	.9				1.0	1.0
		.8	1.1				1.9	1.5
		(14) 2.5	(15) 2.5			% Depr., Dep., Amort./Sales	(24) 2.7	(33) 2.4
		3.4	3.1				3.9	4.2
						% Officers', Directors' Owners' Comp/Sales		
3369M	12219M	218957M	449922M	427861M	783208M	Net Sales ($)	1218875M	1577415M
1088M	1904M	100037M	354269M	337574M	322672M	Total Assets ($)	703289M	964381M

M = $ thousand   MM = $ million
See Pages 11 through 21 for Explanation of Ratios and Data

Comparative Historical Data | Current Data Sorted by Sales

		Comparative Historical Data		Type of Statement	0-1MM	1-3MM	3-5MM	5-10MM	10-25MM	25MM & OVER
	23	17	28	Unqualified	1			6	9	12
	1			Reviewed					1	
	1	1	1	Compiled				1		
		2	1	Tax Returns						
	10	11	18	Other	1	5		3	4	5
	4/1/04-3/31/05 ALL	4/1/05-3/31/06 ALL	4/1/06-3/31/07 ALL			21 (4/1-9/30/06)			27 (10/1/06-3/31/07)	
	35	31	48	**NUMBER OF STATEMENTS**	2	5		10	14	17
	%	%	%	**ASSETS**	%	%	%	%	%	%
	19.6	18.2	20.4	Cash & Equivalents				31.8	18.9	16.9
	21.3	19.4	21.5	Trade Receivables (net)				9.6	23.1	19.6
	4.8	3.9	5.3	Inventory				3.6	5.7	7.2
	3.5	7.7	4.6	All Other Current				8.0	4.3	4.3
	49.2	49.2	51.8	Total Current				52.9	52.0	48.0
	36.4	32.1	32.5	Fixed Assets (net)				27.9	29.1	39.9
	2.9	2.5	1.6	Intangibles (net)				5.8	.1	1.0
	11.5	16.2	14.1	All Other Non-Current				13.4	18.8	11.2
	100.0	100.0	100.0	Total				100.0	100.0	100.0
				LIABILITIES		DATA NOT AVAILABLE				
	4.0	5.1	4.2	Notes Payable-Short Term				2.1	1.3	1.4
	2.5	1.4	1.2	Cur. Mat.-L.T.D.				1.5	.7	1.8
	8.9	10.2	9.8	Trade Payables				3.8	9.0	11.8
	.0	.0	.1	Income Taxes Payable				.0	.0	.2
	12.2	10.6	7.9	All Other Current				3.8	7.5	9.9
	27.7	27.3	23.2	Total Current				11.2	18.6	25.1
	17.6	13.4	14.1	Long-Term Debt				12.4	9.4	18.8
	.0	.0	.0	Deferred Taxes				.0	.0	.0
	4.1	5.7	3.2	All Other Non-Current				5.6	1.1	4.0
	50.6	53.7	59.5	Net Worth				70.8	70.9	52.1
	100.0	100.0	100.0	Total Liabilties & Net Worth				100.0	100.0	100.0
				INCOME DATA						
	100.0	100.0	100.0	Net Sales				100.0	100.0	100.0
				Gross Profit						
	93.4	92.7	92.4	Operating Expenses				82.5	95.1	96.0
	6.6	7.3	7.6	Operating Profit				17.5	4.9	4.0
	.9	.1	-.4	All Other Expenses (net)				.4	-2.3	.3
	5.7	7.2	8.0	Profit Before Taxes				17.0	7.1	3.7
				RATIOS						
	3.6	3.9	4.3					24.1	4.4	3.3
	2.0	2.4	2.8	Current				3.6	3.1	2.4
	1.1	1.3	1.6					2.0	2.2	1.3
	3.1	3.2	3.5					13.8	3.9	2.5
	1.6	2.0	2.3	Quick				3.2	2.4	1.6
	1.0	1.0	1.4					2.0	1.7	.9
	28 13.1	25 14.7	27 13.5		0 UND		32 11.4		35 10.4	
	37 9.8	37 9.9	42 8.6	Sales/Receivables	25 14.8		40 9.2		50 7.3	
	52 7.0	50 7.3	52 7.0		44 8.3		53 6.9		60 6.1	
				Cost of Sales/Inventory						
				Cost of Sales/Payables						
	4.5	4.1	3.6					1.5	3.7	3.6
	8.7	8.9	5.3	Sales/Working Capital				5.9	4.5	5.1
	44.2	38.1	12.0					10.6	10.5	105.0
	32.7	35.8	23.4							16.1
	(25) 8.0	(23) 6.7	(31) 6.5	EBIT/Interest					(13) 3.7	
	.2	2.1	3.3							1.9
				Net Profit + Depr., Dep., Amort./Cur. Mat. L/T/D						
	.4	.4	.2					.0	.2	.4
	.7	.7	.6	Fixed/Worth				.5	.4	.7
	1.7	1.5	1.3					1.2	.7	1.4
	.2	.3	.2					.1	.1	.4
	1.0	.8	.7	Debt/Worth				.4	.3	.9
	1.9	1.7	1.4					1.2	.9	1.5
	23.8	31.7	36.4					65.3	24.4	20.9
	(33) 9.5	(30) 13.9	(47) 12.4	% Profit Before Taxes/Tangible Net Worth				10.9	14.5	(16) 8.7
	3.4	8.5	6.2					4.9	8.1	4.5
	18.6	17.6	16.5					39.0	17.3	11.5
	6.0	9.4	7.2	% Profit Before Taxes/Total Assets				5.7	9.7	4.7
	-.4	4.1	3.2					1.9	5.8	1.6
	11.1	18.3	23.2					49.2	41.6	9.1
	5.5	6.1	4.7	Sales/Net Fixed Assets				3.6	8.2	3.6
	3.4	3.4	2.7					3.0	2.5	2.8
	2.5	2.7	2.4					1.9	2.4	2.1
	1.8	2.1	1.6	Sales/Total Assets				1.1	1.6	1.7
	1.2	1.1	1.0					.7	1.0	1.2
	1.4	1.2	.7						.4	1.4
	(30) 2.1	(28) 2.3	(40) 2.5	% Depr., Dep., Amort./Sales			(11)		2.5	(16) 2.7
	2.9	2.9	3.1						3.0	3.5
				% Officers', Directors' Owners' Comp/Sales						
	961138M	899478M	1895536M	Net Sales ($)	1416M	10579M		70308M	236181M	1577052M
	689333M	607113M	1117544M	Total Assets ($)	4686M	3780M		67436M	164359M	877283M

© RMA 2007

M = $ thousand   MM = $ million
See Pages 11 through 21 for Explanation of Ratios and Data

Current Data Sorted by Assets

Comparative Historical Data

0-500M	500M-2MM	2-10MM	10-50MM	50-100MM	100-250MM	Type of Statement	4/1/02-3/31/03 ALL	4/1/03-3/31/04 ALL
2	9	44	43	7	15	Unqualified	158	139
6	6	12	1			Reviewed	23	24
6	7	10	2		1	Compiled	26	74
13	8	6	1		1	Tax Returns	35	41
7	25	31	17	5	9	Other	112	121
	94 (4/1-9/30/06)		194 (10/1/06-3/31/07)					
28	55	103	64	12	26	**NUMBER OF STATEMENTS**	354	399
%	%	%	%	%	%	**ASSETS**	%	%
28.4	14.7	15.2	16.4	20.8	12.1	Cash & Equivalents	19.1	18.1
7.9	30.4	33.4	23.4	12.3	23.5	Trade Receivables (net)	24.2	23.1
7.3	3.8	2.2	1.5	3.6	2.7	Inventory	2.0	1.8
2.0	5.5	3.3	3.5	4.6	3.4	All Other Current	4.4	6.0
45.6	54.5	54.1	44.8	41.3	41.6	Total Current	49.7	49.0
30.6	33.7	32.0	33.6	24.1	18.3	Fixed Assets (net)	36.5	34.0
3.3	6.0	4.6	6.7	18.7	21.8	Intangibles (net)	3.8	5.8
20.5	5.9	9.3	14.9	15.8	18.2	All Other Non-Current	10.1	11.3
100.0	100.0	100.0	100.0	100.0	100.0	Total	100.0	100.0
						LIABILITIES		
18.7	11.2	8.1	5.3	.3	8.6	Notes Payable-Short Term	8.5	10.1
5.2	4.0	4.1	3.7	2.0	1.2	Cur. Mat.-L.T.D.	3.6	4.0
10.5	8.0	9.9	7.4	12.1	9.1	Trade Payables	9.5	9.6
4.2	.0	.3	.3	.4	.1	Income Taxes Payable	.4	.3
24.9	19.3	16.7	10.0	13.7	10.9	All Other Current	17.3	17.3
63.5	42.6	39.0	26.7	28.5	29.9	Total Current	39.3	41.3
21.4	29.9	21.0	26.7	18.6	21.0	Long-Term Debt	21.1	21.2
.0	.1	.1	.1	.4	1.0	Deferred Taxes	.1	.3
4.2	5.5	6.0	4.1	2.8	6.2	All Other Non-Current	5.9	5.2
10.9	21.9	33.8	42.3	49.8	41.9	Net Worth	33.5	32.0
100.0	100.0	100.0	100.0	100.0	100.0	Total Liabilties & Net Worth	100.0	100.0
						INCOME DATA		
100.0	100.0	100.0	100.0	100.0	100.0	Net Sales	100.0	100.0
						Gross Profit		
89.8	87.8	90.2	91.5	82.3	91.1	Operating Expenses	93.6	92.2
10.2	12.2	9.8	8.5	17.7	8.9	Operating Profit	6.4	7.8
1.1	3.6	2.6	.3	4.2	1.2	All Other Expenses (net)	1.5	1.5
9.1	8.6	7.2	8.2	13.4	7.6	Profit Before Taxes	4.8	6.3
						RATIOS		
1.7	4.4	2.5	2.8	2.4	3.3	Current	3.0	2.7
1.1	1.9	1.7	1.7	1.4	1.4		1.5	1.5
.3	.7	1.0	1.1	1.0	1.1		.9	.9
1.6	3.5	2.3	2.3	1.6	2.3	Quick	2.7	2.4
.6	1.5	1.5	1.4	1.1	1.2		1.3	1.2
.2	.6	.8	.9	.8	1.0		.8	.8
0 UND	0 UND	26 14.1	29 12.7	0 UND	27 13.4	Sales/Receivables	11 32.4	7 52.3
0 UND	30 12.4	46 8.0	43 8.4	28 13.2	50 7.3		37 9.7	38 9.6
6 61.1	64 5.7	69 5.3	61 5.9	58 6.3	64 5.7		57 6.4	58 6.3
						Cost of Sales/Inventory		
						Cost of Sales/Payables		
52.0	5.1	6.1	4.8	5.4	6.1	Sales/Working Capital	5.8	6.0
558.4	13.6	12.6	11.7	13.8	14.9		15.2	16.7
-37.1	-56.2	-492.1	51.2	-181.7	60.3		-98.0	-152.0
96.4	15.5	14.8	10.2	12.0	5.7	EBIT/Interest	10.6	15.1
(13) 10.0	(36) 3.0	(84) 4.3	(52) 4.9	(10) 2.6	(22) 3.0		(270) 3.4	(299) 4.8
1.3	.2	1.2	1.2	-5.2	2.0		1.0	1.4
						Net Profit + Depr., Dep., Amort./Cur. Mat. L/T/D	5.0	7.0
							(32) 2.7	(35) 2.9
							1.2	1.0
.1	.2	.3	.2	.3	.5	Fixed/Worth	.4	.3
.9	1.2	.7	.8	.6	1.0		.9	.9
4.2	-12.1	3.2	2.2	3.4	-.7		3.6	3.5
.6	.5	.8	.4	.3	.9	Debt/Worth	.5	.5
3.6	2.4	1.5	1.3	1.4	3.7		1.4	1.8
-20.0	-24.6	5.9	4.4	7.6	-6.9		7.7	9.6
982.1	65.0	64.0	47.6	41.2	35.6	% Profit Before Taxes/Tangible Net Worth	39.4	54.9
(20) 144.7	(39) 27.5	(85) 20.0	(59) 12.1	(10) 1.6	(17) 11.2		(295) 13.4	(329) 15.9
1.6	4.6	2.3	3.9	-26.1	4.8		1.1	2.2
223.3	33.9	22.5	13.8	17.1	8.7	% Profit Before Taxes/Total Assets	15.0	17.7
28.2	10.0	6.7	7.0	2.9	5.2		4.9	6.6
.0	.2	-.5	2.8	-1.9	1.5		.1	.3
345.5	53.2	39.1	16.6	19.9	36.6	Sales/Net Fixed Assets	29.7	33.9
80.9	14.1	9.0	4.5	9.1	9.3		6.3	8.2
15.5	3.8	3.6	2.3	2.0	2.4		2.7	3.0
15.5	4.4	3.2	2.3	1.6	1.8	Sales/Total Assets	3.8	3.9
9.6	2.9	2.4	1.4	1.3	1.2		2.0	2.0
4.1	1.5	1.5	.9	.8	.6		1.2	1.2
.6	1.0	1.4	1.9		1.0	% Depr., Dep., Amort./Sales	1.2	1.1
(13) .7	(47) 1.7	(90) 2.3	(57) 2.8		(18) 3.3		(304) 2.6	(326) 2.6
1.3	4.5	4.7	4.3		5.6		4.4	4.8
8.2	9.3	3.9				% Officers', Directors' Owners' Comp/Sales	4.9	4.1
(11) 12.7	(13) 11.6	(16) 9.1					(67) 9.3	(78) 9.3
25.5	32.5	18.3					20.9	21.0
57368M	227543M	1220459M	2261406M	977922M	8231102M	Net Sales ($)	11645781M	16542932M
4661M	66054M	477688M	1331987M	742472M	4150133M	Total Assets ($)	5962010M	8539660M

M = $ thousand   MM = $ million
See Pages 11 through 21 for Explanation of Ratios and Data

Comparative Historical Data | Current Data Sorted by Sales

			Type of Statement						
144	118	120	Unqualified	4	8	5	21	40	42
17	14	19	Reviewed	1	2	1	4	8	3
39	42	26	Compiled	5	4	6	5	4	2
31	41	29	Tax Returns	8	10	5	3	2	1
134	166	94	Other	6	11	14	18	15	30
4/1/04-3/31/05	4/1/05-3/31/06	4/1/06-3/31/07		94 (4/1-9/30/06)			194 (10/1/06-3/31/07)		
ALL	ALL	ALL		0-1MM	1-3MM	3-5MM	5-10MM	10-25MM	25MM & OVER
365	381	288	**NUMBER OF STATEMENTS**	24	35	31	51	69	78
%	%	%	**ASSETS**	%	%	%	%	%	%
18.8	19.0	16.6	Cash & Equivalents	22.2	12.8	15.8	18.0	15.5	17.0
25.3	22.6	26.3	Trade Receivables (net)	11.5	21.6	27.3	29.0	29.7	27.9
3.0	3.4	3.0	Inventory	4.5	6.8	1.1	2.6	2.0	2.6
3.6	3.3	3.7	All Other Current	.6	3.5	5.3	3.6	3.6	4.3
50.6	48.3	49.6	Total Current	38.8	44.6	49.4	53.2	50.7	51.9
32.8	33.8	31.0	Fixed Assets (net)	46.7	35.2	30.1	30.4	32.1	23.9
5.7	6.4	7.3	Intangibles (net)	1.5	4.8	2.5	7.3	5.6	13.8
10.9	11.4	12.1	All Other Non-Current	12.9	15.4	17.9	9.1	11.5	10.4
100.0	100.0	100.0	Total	100.0	100.0	100.0	100.0	100.0	100.0
			LIABILITIES						
9.3	7.9	8.8	Notes Payable-Short Term	19.4	13.9	8.4	6.1	5.5	8.2
4.8	3.5	3.8	Cur. Mat.-L.T.D.	3.9	5.8	3.1	2.7	4.6	3.0
7.7	7.8	9.1	Trade Payables	7.6	5.4	6.6	6.0	12.8	10.8
.3	.2	.6	Income Taxes Payable	.0	.0	.0	2.4	.3	.3
16.6	16.2	15.9	All Other Current	6.8	14.5	25.0	15.9	16.5	15.1
38.8	35.6	38.1	Total Current	37.7	39.7	43.1	33.1	39.7	37.4
19.2	23.6	23.9	Long-Term Debt	31.9	27.3	22.4	19.1	23.8	23.8
.3	.2	.2	Deferred Taxes	.0	.2	.0	.0	.3	.4
7.3	7.2	5.2	All Other Non-Current	7.6	5.8	1.3	6.2	6.3	4.1
34.5	33.3	32.6	Net Worth	22.8	27.1	33.2	41.6	29.9	34.3
100.0	100.0	100.0	Total Liabilities & Net Worth	100.0	100.0	100.0	100.0	100.0	100.0
			INCOME DATA						
100.0	100.0	100.0	Net Sales	100.0	100.0	100.0	100.0	100.0	100.0
			Gross Profit						
91.3	89.5	89.7	Operating Expenses	84.5	85.4	88.1	91.2	92.8	90.3
8.7	10.5	10.3	Operating Profit	15.5	14.6	11.9	8.8	7.2	9.7
1.8	2.4	2.1	All Other Expenses (net)	10.4	1.1	3.4	1.0	.8	1.3
6.9	8.1	8.2	Profit Before Taxes	5.2	13.5	8.4	7.9	6.4	8.4
			RATIOS						
2.8	3.3	2.6		6.8	2.5	3.5	3.5	2.2	2.3
1.6	1.7	1.5	Current	1.6	1.5	1.2	1.8	1.5	1.4
1.0	1.0	1.0		.3	.9	.9	1.3	.9	1.1
2.4	2.9	2.3		6.7	2.4	3.5	2.6	2.2	1.9
1.4	1.4	1.4	Quick	.8	1.4	1.1	1.6	1.4	1.2
.9	.8	.8		.1	.3	.7	1.2	.8	1.0
9 42.8	0 819.5	8 46.4		0 UND	0 UND	0 UND	22 16.9	28 12.8	28 13.1
40 9.2	36 10.1	39 9.3	Sales/Receivables	0 UND	7 55.8	27 13.5	44 8.3	44 8.4	45 8.2
59 6.2	56 6.5	61 5.9		16 22.5	69 5.3	66 5.5	66 5.5	60 6.0	63 5.8
			Cost of Sales/Inventory						
			Cost of Sales/Payables						
6.0	5.3	6.0		3.0	4.8	6.1	5.1	7.2	6.9
14.8	13.0	14.3	Sales/Working Capital	31.8	16.7	237.6	9.6	16.3	14.0
999.8	UND	-619.1		-7.1	-20.4	-27.9	37.3	-62.6	68.2
17.1	18.5	13.0			14.9	51.6	17.2	10.2	8.5
(277) 5.5	(282) 5.3	(217) 3.9	EBIT/Interest	(30) 4.4	(20) 5.2	(42) 5.5	(53) 3.1	(64) 3.6	
1.6	1.4	1.1			1.5	1.0	1.3	.1	1.4
12.8	6.7	6.7							8.3
(33) 4.8	(30) 1.6	(24) 3.1	Net Profit + Depr., Dep., Amort./Cur. Mat. L/T/D					(18) 3.5
1.5	.4	1.9							2.1
.3	.3	.3		.3	.2	.1	.2	.3	.4
.8	.8	.8	Fixed/Worth	1.3	1.2	.8	.6	.9	.8
5.6	3.8	4.3		5.3	-14.1	10.3	1.7	6.2	3.4
.6	.5	.5		.4	.5	.4	.4	.7	.6
1.6	1.6	1.7	Debt/Worth	3.7	1.6	.9	1.4	1.6	3.4
13.9	10.1	10.8		61.7	-39.3	19.0	3.3	10.4	11.0
59.5	56.8	62.0		48.1	110.6	104.1	65.2	35.3	61.6
(292) 16.9	(309) 21.3	(230) 17.9	% Profit Before Taxes/Tangible Net Worth	(19) 13.3	(26) 46.8	(25) 25.0	(42) 19.4	(56) 10.5	(62) 22.5
4.4	4.6	3.2		-5.4	4.9	.5	4.5	.0	4.3
16.9	20.2	22.3		19.9	36.2	43.1	34.5	13.6	14.1
6.4	8.0	7.0	% Profit Before Taxes/Total Assets	4.9	15.9	13.7	8.4	6.6	7.4
1.0	.9	.8		-4.8	2.2	-.4	.2	.4	2.1
37.1	34.7	43.6		27.7	25.4	74.4	69.8	28.9	39.9
9.7	9.7	9.8	Sales/Net Fixed Assets	5.6	9.6	31.6	10.8	6.1	12.3
3.2	2.7	3.3		.3	2.2	4.4	3.0	3.8	3.5
3.9	4.1	3.6		4.4	3.0	6.4	3.3	3.3	3.4
2.1	1.9	2.2	Sales/Total Assets	1.3	1.7	3.0	2.4	2.5	1.8
1.2	1.0	1.1		.2	.9	1.8	1.3	1.2	1.1
1.1	1.1	1.3		1.1	1.2	.7	1.3	1.4	1.4
(292) 2.5	(312) 2.5	(233) 2.5	% Depr., Dep., Amort./Sales	(18) 6.4	(28) 2.1	(24) 1.5	(43) 3.3	(62) 2.2	(58) 2.6
4.7	4.5	4.6		18.9	4.5	6.2	6.2	3.3	4.6
2.1	5.6	5.4						2.0	
(62) 6.6	(73) 11.8	(48) 11.5	% Officers', Directors' Owners' Comp/Sales					(10) 4.4	
19.7	23.9	25.9						26.3	
11366537M	13216176M	12975800M	Net Sales ($)	11760M	67055M	123262M	370132M	1151238M	11252353M
7346785M	7125882M	6772995M	Total Assets ($)	23338M	81650M	109068M	293891M	790029M	5475019M

Current Data Sorted by Assets   Comparative Historical Data

0-500M	500M-2MM	2-10MM	10-50MM	50-100MM	100-250MM		4/1/02-3/31/03 ALL	4/1/03-3/31/04 ALL
						Type of Statement		
13	10	39	131	67	125	Unqualified	427	403
1	3	5	1		1	Reviewed	11	12
7	4	8	1		1	Compiled	13	60
6	5	3				Tax Returns	11	15
7	22	57	62	43	57	Other	206	193
	357 (4/1-9/30/06)		322 (10/1/06-3/31/07)					
34	44	112	195	110	184	NUMBER OF STATEMENTS	668	683
%	%	%	%	%	%	**ASSETS**	%	%
49.6	28.1	13.8	11.5	12.3	9.5	Cash & Equivalents	11.3	11.4
10.8	15.6	26.2	19.2	16.1	13.7	Trade Receivables (net)	16.8	17.6
1.5	3.1	3.0	2.5	1.9	1.6	Inventory	1.9	1.8
1.4	3.6	4.2	4.0	2.7	3.9	All Other Current	3.6	4.7
63.3	50.4	47.2	37.2	33.1	28.7	Total Current	33.5	35.5
27.2	36.9	41.0	46.5	45.1	44.1	Fixed Assets (net)	45.8	45.4
.9	1.3	2.4	2.3	1.0	2.5	Intangibles (net)	1.4	1.3
8.8	11.4	9.4	14.1	20.8	24.6	All Other Non-Current	19.3	17.8
100.0	100.0	100.0	100.0	100.0	100.0	Total	100.0	100.0
						LIABILITIES		
10.0	3.8	4.2	1.6	.7	.5	Notes Payable-Short Term	2.0	3.6
3.0	8.4	4.7	3.5	2.4	1.5	Cur. Mat.-L.T.D.	2.6	3.1
2.7	6.8	8.5	7.2	5.9	5.0	Trade Payables	5.5	6.3
.0	.0	.1	.2	.1	.0	Income Taxes Payable	.1	.2
32.7	14.0	15.8	8.2	8.6	8.6	All Other Current	11.9	11.8
48.4	33.1	33.4	20.6	17.7	15.7	Total Current	22.1	25.0
20.5	30.7	25.6	29.0	30.0	29.7	Long-Term Debt	27.6	27.6
.0	.0	.1	.1	.0	.1	Deferred Taxes	.1	.1
11.6	3.1	5.4	3.6	6.8	3.6	All Other Non-Current	3.7	5.2
19.3	33.1	35.7	46.6	45.4	50.9	Net Worth	46.6	42.1
100.0	100.0	100.0	100.0	100.0	100.0	Total Liabilities & Net Worth	100.0	100.0
						INCOME DATA		
100.0	100.0	100.0	100.0	100.0	100.0	Net Sales	100.0	100.0
						Gross Profit		
95.8	86.4	89.7	94.9	96.6	95.7	Operating Expenses	94.3	95.2
4.2	13.6	10.3	5.1	3.4	4.3	Operating Profit	5.7	4.8
.1	2.6	1.2	.6	.0	-.3	All Other Expenses (net)	1.7	1.5
4.1	11.0	9.1	4.5	3.4	4.6	Profit Before Taxes	4.0	3.2
						RATIOS		
8.3	4.2	2.3	3.0	3.0	2.7		2.7	2.8
2.3	1.9	1.5	1.9	2.2	1.9	Current	1.9	1.8
1.1	.9	1.0	1.3	1.5	1.4		1.2	1.2
8.3	3.4	2.1	2.5	2.6	2.3		2.3	2.3
2.3	1.6	1.2	1.6	1.9	1.5	Quick	1.6 (682)	1.5
1.0	.8	.8	1.1	1.2	1.1		1.0	1.0
0 UND	0 UND	29 12.8	42 8.7	42 8.7	40 9.2		42 8.7	42 8.7
7 55.2	6 60.6	45 8.0	53 6.9	51 7.1	50 7.3	Sales/Receivables	53 6.9	54 6.7
24 15.4	52 7.0	61 5.9	65 5.7	60 6.1	58 6.3		64 5.7	65 5.6
						Cost of Sales/Inventory		
						Cost of Sales/Payables		
3.0	7.1	6.3	4.2	4.1	5.1		4.8	4.7
16.9	18.1	13.8	7.6	6.6	7.9	Sales/Working Capital	7.9	8.6
NM	-94.1	UND	19.5	14.0	14.6		26.6	33.6
7.8	24.1	19.2	8.9	5.9	7.5		5.6	6.0
(12) 3.2	(31) 6.3	(92) 5.4	(183) 3.1	(107) 3.5	(175) 3.9	EBIT/Interest	(594) 2.3	(615) 2.3
1.2	.7	1.5	1.0	1.3	1.6		.5	.3
					17.1		8.7	9.7
				(12)	5.5	Net Profit + Depr., Dep., Amort./Cur. Mat. L/T/D	(27) 5.3	(26) 4.9
					3.8		2.0	1.8
.0	.2	.5	.6	.7	.6		.6	.6
.4	.8	.9	.9	.9	.8	Fixed/Worth	.9	.9
6.4	5.5	3.2	1.9	1.4	1.3		1.4	1.6
.2	.2	.6	.5	.5	.5		.5	.6
.7	1.1	1.5	1.0	1.0	.9	Debt/Worth	.9	1.1
NM	9.8	4.7	2.5	1.8	1.5		1.8	2.5
61.9	110.4	73.2	14.1	12.5	12.8	% Profit Before Taxes/Tangible Net Worth	11.3	12.9
(26) 12.1	(36) 21.5	(97) 26.5	(181) 6.9	(103) 5.7	(174) 7.5		(630) 4.5	(624) 5.1
-16.0	2.2	6.7	.6	1.3	2.3		-.6	-1.2
28.8	69.3	29.0	7.6	5.6	7.2	% Profit Before Taxes/Total Assets	5.7	5.5
4.2	6.5	8.3	3.5	3.0	4.2		2.3	2.2
-6.6	-.1	1.1	.2	.8	1.0		-.5	-1.2
UND	47.9	12.0	4.2	3.1	2.9		3.2	3.4
69.1	11.3	5.5	2.8	2.3	2.2	Sales/Net Fixed Assets	2.3	2.3
8.8	4.3	2.2	1.8	1.7	1.7		1.7	1.8
10.1	6.6	3.1	1.6	1.3	1.2		1.4	1.4
5.0	3.4	2.1	1.2	1.0	.9	Sales/Total Assets	1.1	1.0
1.5	1.7	1.2	1.0	.8	.7		.8	.8
.8	1.5	1.7	3.2	3.9	3.9	% Depr., Dep., Amort./Sales	3.9	3.7
(18) 2.0	(29) 2.6	(101) 3.6	(192) 4.3	(108) 5.0	(134) 5.1		(589) 5.2	(597) 5.0
4.5	5.1	6.1	5.6	6.3	6.1		6.3	6.3
		4.8	7.4	3.8	9.3	% Officers', Directors' Owners' Comp/Sales	5.9	6.9
	(10)	17.2	(21) 11.9	(14) 12.3	(12) 42.8		(90) 14.9	(84) 18.0
		34.3	33.5	41.0	44.4		36.2	35.8
60053M	260369M	1279393M	6554859M	9143947M	30765700M	Net Sales ($)	46812190M	47474853M
8417M	49646M	564145M	4999209M	7975813M	30009350M	Total Assets ($)	46198702M	47220859M

© RMA 2007

M = $ thousand   MM = $ million
See Pages 11 through 21 for Explanation of Ratios and Data

Comparative Historical Data | Current Data Sorted by Sales

	410	353	385	Type of Statement	18	7	8	14	71	267
	9	10	11	Unqualified	1	3	1	2	3	1
	23	21	21	Reviewed			4	9	1	3
	13	22	14	Compiled						
	200	248	248	Tax Returns	1	5	2	3	3	
	4/1/04-3/31/05 ALL	4/1/05-3/31/06 ALL	4/1/06-3/31/07 ALL	Other	8	13	14	21	43	149
					357 (4/1-9/30/06)			**322 (10/1/06-3/31/07)**		
					0-1MM	1-3MM	3-5MM	5-10MM	10-25MM	25MM & OVER
NUMBER OF STATEMENTS	655	654	679		28	32	29	49	121	420
ASSETS	%	%	%		%	%	%	%	%	%
Cash & Equivalents	11.9	12.6	14.5		43.0	25.3	14.9	19.7	14.8	11.0
Trade Receivables (net)	17.7	16.8	17.7		12.0	12.4	16.9	15.0	23.4	17.2
Inventory	2.1	2.1	2.2		.7	3.1	2.2	3.2	2.7	2.0
All Other Current	3.4	3.6	3.7		.6	1.2	3.0	5.1	4.7	3.6
Total Current	35.1	35.1	38.0		56.4	42.0	36.9	42.9	45.5	33.9
Fixed Assets (net)	44.1	44.0	43.1		31.4	38.9	49.4	44.5	40.8	44.3
Intangibles (net)	2.0	2.0	2.0		1.1	2.3	1.5	3.4	1.7	2.0
All Other Non-Current	18.9	18.9	16.8		11.3	16.7	12.2	9.2	12.0	19.8
Total	100.0	100.0	100.0		100.0	100.0	100.0	100.0	100.0	100.0
LIABILITIES										
Notes Payable-Short Term	2.4	2.5	2.1		.1	9.3	1.0	6.9	2.9	1.0
Cur. Mat.-L.T.D.	3.2	3.0	3.3		2.1	4.2	7.3	6.8	3.6	2.5
Trade Payables	6.7	6.0	6.3		2.4	6.2	5.1	5.7	7.9	6.3
Income Taxes Payable	.1	.1	.1		.0	.0	.0	.0	.1	.1
All Other Current	11.5	11.1	11.2		9.9	12.3	29.5	13.3	12.3	9.4
Total Current	23.8	22.8	23.1		14.6	32.2	43.0	32.6	26.8	19.4
Long-Term Debt	27.3	27.8	28.5		38.3	42.8	26.5	20.5	22.7	29.5
Deferred Taxes	.1	.0	.1		.0	.0	.0	.1	.1	.1
All Other Non-Current	6.2	5.1	4.8		3.6	6.1	8.2	3.3	3.9	5.0
Net Worth	42.7	44.3	43.5		43.3	18.9	22.3	43.5	46.5	46.1
Total Liabilities & Net Worth	100.0	100.0	100.0		100.0	100.0	100.0	100.0	100.0	100.0
INCOME DATA										
Net Sales	100.0	100.0	100.0		100.0	100.0	100.0	100.0	100.0	100.0
Gross Profit										
Operating Expenses	94.8	94.7	94.0		90.9	83.5	89.1	87.9	94.7	95.9
Operating Profit	5.2	5.3	6.0		9.1	16.5	10.9	12.1	5.3	4.1
All Other Expenses (net)	.7	.8	.5		6.0	4.1	.4	1.0	-.3	.0
Profit Before Taxes	4.5	4.5	5.5		3.2	12.4	10.5	11.2	5.7	4.1
RATIOS										
Current	2.6	2.9	2.9		12.6	3.3	2.9	3.1	2.9	2.8
	1.8	1.9	1.9		4.1	1.5	1.7	2.0	1.9	1.9
	1.1	1.3	1.2		1.4	.7	.8	.8	1.3	1.3
Quick	2.2	2.4	2.4		12.4	2.5	2.6	2.2	2.5	2.3
	1.5	1.6	1.6		3.9	1.2	1.3	1.6	1.5	1.6
	1.0	1.0	1.0		1.2	.4	.8	.5	1.0	1.1
Sales/Receivables	39 9.3	37 9.8	37 10.0		8 48.3	0 UND	0 UND	0 UND	42 8.7	40 9.0
	50 7.2	49 7.5	49 7.4		21 17.4	0 UND	37 9.7	22 16.5	51 7.1	51 7.2
	61 6.0	60 6.1	60 6.0		53 6.9	52 7.0	57 6.4	63 5.8	65 5.7	60 6.1
Cost of Sales/Inventory										
Cost of Sales/Payables										
Sales/Working Capital	5.3	5.0	4.9		2.2	5.7	6.9	5.1	4.5	5.0
	8.9	8.5	8.3		6.5	20.1	13.2	11.0	8.3	8.0
	33.9	24.9	27.1		16.2	-35.8	-62.7	-67.3	23.4	20.3
EBIT/Interest	7.5	8.9	8.3			4.5	21.6	22.2	9.1	7.5
	(602) 3.2	(597) 4.1	(600) 3.7		(19) 2.3	(23) 7.3	(42) 6.6	(108) 3.3	(400) 3.6	
	1.3	1.4	1.3			1.0	1.0	1.6	.9	1.3
Net Profit + Depr., Dep., Amort./Cur. Mat. L/T/D	8.4	9.9	8.0							8.1
	(35) 3.5	(28) 4.7	(30) 4.0						(21) 5.2	
	1.3	1.8	1.8							2.1
Fixed/Worth	.6	.6	.6		.0	.1	.7	.5	.5	.6
	.9	.9	.9		.5	.9	1.0	1.0	.8	.9
	1.6	1.6	1.6		1.1	7.5	8.8	3.7	1.6	1.4
Debt/Worth	.6	.5	.5		.1	.5	.3	.6	.4	.5
	1.1	1.0	1.0		.4	1.9	1.7	1.2	.9	1.0
	2.4	2.6	2.5		.9	23.5	17.0	5.1	2.8	1.9
% Profit Before Taxes/Tangible Net Worth	13.8	14.4	18.0		14.0	113.5	72.0	92.1	23.1	13.3
	(594) 7.1	(596) 7.7	(617) 8.1		(25) 5.0	(25) 28.1	(23) 27.5	(44) 23.0	(113) 8.1	(387) 7.5
	1.9	2.2	2.1		-12.8	7.3	2.2	1.3	.4	2.2
% Profit Before Taxes/Total Assets	6.7	7.1	8.6		11.1	32.2	44.4	45.6	10.1	7.3
	3.5	3.8	4.1		2.7	6.5	9.1	7.4	4.5	4.0
	.5	.7	.4		-4.5	1.1	-1.6	-.4	.1	.9
Sales/Net Fixed Assets	3.9	4.0	5.2		396.3	62.1	12.2	18.4	7.4	3.6
	2.5	2.6	2.7		3.4	10.3	3.9	5.5	3.5	2.4
	1.8	1.8	1.8		1.7	2.1	2.1	1.8	2.4	1.8
Sales/Total Assets	1.6	1.6	1.8		2.3	5.9	3.4	5.2	2.3	1.5
	1.1	1.1	1.2		1.3	1.7	1.9	2.2	1.5	1.1
	.9	.8	.9		.8	.7	1.1	1.1	1.0	.8
% Depr., Dep., Amort./Sales	3.6	3.4	3.2		3.9	1.6	2.3	2.0	2.7	3.4
	(571) 4.8	(578) 4.6	(582) 4.4		(13) 5.4	(21) 4.2	(25) 5.7	(42) 3.3	(116) 4.0	(365) 4.6
	6.1	5.9	5.8		22.6	15.2	9.5	6.4	5.3	5.8
% Officers', Directors' Owners' Comp/Sales	6.6	5.1	7.0						14.0	6.8
	(78) 18.2	(74) 15.9	(71) 14.4						(14) 33.8	(39) 11.9
	39.4	37.6	37.8						45.9	42.5
Net Sales ($)	49114864M	46447006M	48064321M		16469M	63006M	111243M	370344M	2008059M	45495200M
Total Assets ($)	47523638M	44925945M	43606580M		25022M	78903M	75493M	412435M	1598501M	41416226M

M = $ thousand   MM = $ million
See Pages 11 through 21 for Explanation of Ratios and Data

Current Data Sorted by Assets   Comparative Historical Data

0-500M	500M-2MM	2-10MM	10-50MM	50-100MM	100-250MM	Type of Statement	97	149
	1	18	69	51	90	Unqualified	97	149
		3				Reviewed		
		1	1		1	Compiled		
		1				Tax Returns		
	2	6	25	28	33	Other	17	46
	194 (4/1-9/30/06)			136 (10/1/06-3/31/07)			17 4/1/02-3/31/03 ALL	46 4/1/03-3/31/04 ALL
	3	29	95	79	124	NUMBER OF STATEMENTS	114	195
%	%	%	%	%	%	**ASSETS**	%	%
		11.8	11.7	9.6	11.0	Cash & Equivalents	9.2	9.6
		26.4	16.7	15.0	13.3	Trade Receivables (net)	16.1	16.0
		3.4	2.0	1.6	1.5	Inventory	1.6	1.6
		3.8	3.8	3.1	3.1	All Other Current	4.2	3.9
		45.3	34.2	29.3	28.9	Total Current	31.2	31.1
		43.8	45.4	43.9	44.8	Fixed Assets (net)	45.1	45.1
		.4	.5	1.1	1.1	Intangibles (net)	.7	1.0
		10.5	19.8	25.7	25.3	All Other Non-Current	23.1	22.9
		100.0	100.0	100.0	100.0	Total	100.0	100.0
						LIABILITIES		
		3.6	1.5	.3	.4	Notes Payable-Short Term	.6	.7
		4.0	3.2	3.2	1.5	Cur. Mat.-L.T.D.	1.8	2.1
		11.7	5.5	6.8	5.2	Trade Payables	6.4	6.4
		.0	.0	.0	.0	Income Taxes Payable	.0	.1
		12.7	9.4	10.2	9.1	All Other Current	8.3	7.9
		32.0	19.6	20.5	16.2	Total Current	17.0	17.2
		20.4	24.3	32.1	29.9	Long-Term Debt	27.8	26.5
		.0	.0	.0	.0	Deferred Taxes	.0	.0
		.4	3.5	4.4	5.0	All Other Non-Current	3.1	4.6
		47.2	52.6	43.0	48.9	Net Worth	52.1	51.7
		100.0	100.0	100.0	100.0	Total Liabilties & Net Worth	100.0	100.0
						INCOME DATA		
		100.0	100.0	100.0	100.0	Net Sales	100.0	100.0
						Gross Profit		
		99.1	94.2	96.5	97.2	Operating Expenses	97.4	97.2
		.9	5.8	3.5	2.8	Operating Profit	2.6	2.8
		-.8	.6	1.3	.0	All Other Expenses (net)	1.2	.2
		1.7	5.1	2.1	2.9	Profit Before Taxes	1.3	2.7
						RATIOS		
		2.8	3.0	2.3	2.6		2.6	2.9
		1.7	1.9	1.7	1.9	Current	1.9	2.1
		.9	1.3	1.2	1.3		1.4	1.5
		2.4	2.4	2.0	2.2		2.2	2.3
		1.5	1.6	1.4	1.5	Quick	1.6	1.7
		.8	.9	1.0	1.1		1.1	1.2
	40	9.0 41	9.0 42	8.8 42	8.6	Sales/Receivables	50 7.3	46 8.0
	56	6.6 52	7.0 48	7.6 49	7.4		57 6.4	53 6.8
	68	5.4 60	6.1 56	6.5 56	6.5		68 5.4	63 5.8
						Cost of Sales/Inventory		
						Cost of Sales/Payables		
		5.1	4.0	6.0	5.2		5.0	4.5
		10.2	8.6	10.0	8.4	Sales/Working Capital	7.1	7.2
		-54.8	22.5	27.3	18.2		13.1	15.3
		6.9	9.2	6.1	5.7		3.8	5.8
	(27)	2.1 (89)	4.9 (73)	2.4 (120)	3.3	EBIT/Interest	(106) 2.0	(183) 2.6
		-5.0	1.7	.7	1.1		.4	.5
						Net Profit + Depr., Dep., Amort./Cur. Mat. L/T/D		
		.6	.6	.6	.7		.7	.6
		.9	.8	.9	.9	Fixed/Worth	.8	.9
		1.7	1.4	1.5	1.2		1.2	1.2
		.5	.4	.6	.6		.5	.5
		.9	.8	1.0	1.0	Debt/Worth	.9	.9
		1.6	1.3	2.2	1.6		1.5	1.4
		12.1	11.9	10.2	10.5	% Profit Before Taxes/Tangible Net Worth	6.9	9.5
	(28)	6.5 (84)	8.0 (74)	5.8 (121)	5.6		(113) 2.8	(190) 4.1
		-13.9	2.9	-.7	1.1		-2.6	-1.5
		6.9	6.7	5.6	4.8	% Profit Before Taxes/Total Assets	3.7	4.9
		2.0	4.2	2.6	3.1		1.4	2.2
		-7.3	.8	-.6	.2		-1.3	-.9
		6.7	3.7	3.3	2.6	Sales/Net Fixed Assets	2.7	3.1
		4.2	2.7	2.5	2.1		2.1	2.2
		2.5	1.8	2.0	1.8		1.7	1.7
		2.3	1.5	1.4	1.1	Sales/Total Assets	1.1	1.3
		1.8	1.2	1.1	1.0		.9	1.0
		1.2	.9	.8	.8		.8	.7
		1.8	3.9	3.7	4.3	% Depr., Dep., Amort./Sales	4.4	4.2
		3.6 (94)	4.7	5.0 (92)	5.1		(93) 5.5	(162) 5.2
		5.0	6.2	5.7	5.8		6.6	6.3
						% Officers', Directors' Owners' Comp/Sales		7.9
								(11) 29.6
								35.7
	8409M	326386M	3120235M	6670470M	20788581M	Net Sales ($)	11248458M	17158235M
	4547M	184883M	2650313M	5789597M	20562602M	Total Assets ($)	11908435M	18585177M

(The 0-500M column is marked "DATA NOT AVAILABLE.")

© RMA 2007

M = $ thousand   MM = $ million

See Pages 11 through 21 for Explanation of Ratios and Data

Comparative Historical Data — Current Data Sorted by Sales

	Hist 1	Hist 2	Hist 3		0-1MM	1-3MM	3-5MM	5-10MM	10-25MM	25MM & OVER
Type of Statement										
Unqualified	182	152	229		1	4	4	7	25	188
Reviewed			3			1		1	1	
Compiled	1		3					1	1	1
Tax Returns	1		1					1	1	
Other	50	80	94		2		2	5	12	73
	4/1/04-3/31/05 ALL	4/1/05-3/31/06 ALL	4/1/06-3/31/07 ALL		194 (4/1-9/30/06)			136 (10/1/06-3/31/07)		
NUMBER OF STATEMENTS	234	232	330		1	7	6	14	40	262
	%	%	%		%	%	%	%	%	%
ASSETS										
Cash & Equivalents	10.8	12.0	11.1					7.2	12.1	10.7
Trade Receivables (net)	15.6	15.7	15.9					21.7	22.5	15.1
Inventory	1.8	1.9	1.9					4.0	2.5	1.7
All Other Current	3.5	3.6	3.4					5.2	2.9	3.5
Total Current	31.7	33.2	32.3					38.1	39.9	31.1
Fixed Assets (net)	45.1	44.3	44.5					52.7	44.0	43.9
Intangibles (net)	.7	.8	.9					.6	.6	1.0
All Other Non-Current	22.5	21.7	22.4					8.7	15.5	24.0
Total	100.0	100.0	100.0					100.0	100.0	100.0
LIABILITIES										
Notes Payable-Short Term	.7	.8	1.0					5.0	1.4	.5
Cur. Mat.-L.T.D.	2.3	3.0	2.6					4.8	3.5	2.4
Trade Payables	5.5	6.2	6.2					11.8	7.2	5.9
Income Taxes Payable	.0	.0	.0					.0	.0	.0
All Other Current	9.3	11.0	9.8					9.5	10.1	10.0
Total Current	17.8	21.1	19.6					31.0	22.2	18.7
Long-Term Debt	26.6	26.5	28.1					41.7	20.9	28.7
Deferred Taxes	.0	.0	.0					.0	.0	.0
All Other Non-Current	3.9	5.4	4.0					6.0	1.3	4.2
Net Worth	51.7	47.0	48.2					21.2	55.5	48.3
Total Liabilties & Net Worth	100.0	100.0	100.0					100.0	100.0	100.0
INCOME DATA										
Net Sales	100.0	100.0	100.0					100.0	100.0	100.0
Gross Profit										
Operating Expenses	96.6	96.1	96.3					96.9	97.8	96.9
Operating Profit	3.4	3.9	3.7					3.1	2.2	3.1
All Other Expenses (net)	.4	.1	.4					4.6	-1.3	.1
Profit Before Taxes	3.0	3.8	3.3					-1.4	3.4	3.0
RATIOS										
Current	2.6	2.7	2.6					3.4	3.0	2.4
	1.9	1.9	1.9					1.7	1.9	1.9
	1.3	1.4	1.3					.9	1.4	1.3
Quick	2.2	2.2	2.2					2.5	2.6	2.1
	1.5	1.6	1.5					1.4	1.7	1.5
	1.1	1.1	1.0					.7	1.2	1.0
Sales/Receivables	43 8.6	40 9.2	42 8.7					25 14.5	47 7.7	43 8.5
	52 7.0	49 7.5	50 7.4					56 6.5	53 6.9	49 7.4
	60 6.1	58 6.3	58 6.3					66 5.6	66 5.5	57 6.4
Cost of Sales/Inventory										
Cost of Sales/Payables										
Sales/Working Capital	5.1	4.9	5.1					2.1	4.0	5.8
	7.9	7.6	8.7					11.9	7.6	8.8
	17.2	16.0	21.5					-68.7	21.2	19.6
EBIT/Interest	6.4	7.4	7.1					4.5	8.9	6.3
	(220) 2.8	(220) 3.3	(312) 3.3			(13) .4	(36) 4.2			(251) 3.4
	1.3	1.8	1.1					-2.7	1.7	1.1
Net Profit + Depr., Dep., Amort./Cur. Mat. L/T/D										
Fixed/Worth	.6	.6	.6					1.5	.6	.6
	.9	.9	.9					3.5	.7	.9
	1.2	1.4	1.3					-20.8	1.2	1.3
Debt/Worth	.5	.5	.5					1.6	.3	.6
	.9	1.0	.9					5.5	.7	.9
	1.4	1.8	1.6					-30.0	1.3	1.6
% Profit Before Taxes/Tangible Net Worth	10.5	12.2	11.0					12.1	10.3	11.2
	(226) 5.5	(222) 7.1	(309) 6.2			(10) -6.3	(38) 6.8			(248) 6.2
	1.3	2.9	.9					-381.9	2.3	.9
% Profit Before Taxes/Total Assets	5.6	6.4	5.9					5.2	6.9	5.7
	2.7	3.5	3.2					-2.7	4.1	3.3
	.5	1.3	.1					-9.2	1.2	.3
Sales/Net Fixed Assets	3.1	3.4	3.4					4.6	4.9	3.3
	2.4	2.5	2.4					2.3	3.1	2.3
	1.9	1.8	1.9					.4	1.8	1.9
Sales/Total Assets	1.3	1.4	1.4					2.2	2.0	1.3
	1.0	1.0	1.1					1.2	1.3	1.1
	.8	.8	.8					.3	1.0	.9
% Depr., Dep., Amort./Sales	4.2	3.9	3.8					3.6	2.7	3.9
	(206) 5.0	(204) 4.8	(297) 4.9					6.8	4.1	(230) 4.9
	6.0	6.0	5.8					13.8	5.4	5.7
% Officers', Directors' Owners' Comp/Sales	8.2	1.8	1.6							
	(10) 16.3	(12) 10.0	(11) 20.3							
	37.4	32.4	40.8							
Net Sales ($)	19432669M	21133289M	30914081M		384M	11083M	23413M	96906M	710797M	30071498M
Total Assets ($)	19675824M	20819908M	29191942M		12304M	59040M	81173M	231445M	635522M	28172458M

	Current Data Sorted by Assets						Comparative Historical Data	
Type of Statement								
Unqualified	2	3	18	31			50	38
Reviewed								
Compiled	2	1	1				1	1
Tax Returns			2	1				4
Other		3	10	8		2	20	20
	63 (4/1-9/30/06)			21 (10/1/06-3/31/07)			4/1/02-3/31/03	4/1/03-3/31/04
	0-500M	500M-2MM	2-10MM	10-50MM	50-100MM	100-250MM	ALL	ALL
NUMBER OF STATEMENTS	4	7	31	40		2	71	63
ASSETS	%	%	%	%	%	%	%	%
Cash & Equivalents			22.0	18.6	DATA NOT AVAILABLE		13.1	17.7
Trade Receivables (net)			17.8	14.6			22.2	21.1
Inventory			.1	.8			.3	.8
All Other Current			3.8	3.9			4.8	5.0
Total Current			43.8	37.8			40.4	44.7
Fixed Assets (net)			47.8	45.4			46.9	43.7
Intangibles (net)			1.1	3.7			3.1	1.9
All Other Non-Current			7.4	13.1			9.5	9.7
Total			100.0	100.0			100.0	100.0
LIABILITIES								
Notes Payable-Short Term			3.8	2.8			3.7	3.9
Cur. Mat.-L.T.D.			1.6	3.3			3.4	1.9
Trade Payables			7.1	4.5			6.0	6.9
Income Taxes Payable			.1	.2			.0	.1
All Other Current			13.1	9.0			17.6	14.0
Total Current			25.7	19.8			30.8	26.8
Long-Term Debt			23.6	25.9			25.9	21.1
Deferred Taxes			.0	.0			.0	.4
All Other Non-Current			2.9	1.6			3.5	1.5
Net Worth			47.7	52.7			39.8	50.2
Total Liabilties & Net Worth			100.0	100.0			100.0	100.0
INCOME DATA								
Net Sales			100.0	100.0			100.0	100.0
Gross Profit								
Operating Expenses			91.0	93.8			95.3	96.4
Operating Profit			9.0	6.2			4.7	3.6
All Other Expenses (net)			4.0	.5			1.7	-.6
Profit Before Taxes			5.0	5.6			3.0	4.2
RATIOS								
Current			3.0	3.8			2.7	2.9
			1.7	1.9			1.9	2.0
			1.0	1.3			1.1	1.2
Quick			2.9	3.4			2.4	2.5
			1.5	1.6			1.5	1.8
			.9	1.0			.9	.9
Sales/Receivables			**13** 28.7	**26** 13.8			**32** 11.6	**27** 13.6
			34 10.9	**41** 8.8			**44** 8.3	**48** 7.5
			54 6.7	**54** 6.7			**58** 6.3	**64** 5.7
Cost of Sales/Inventory								
Cost of Sales/Payables								
Sales/Working Capital			5.1	3.2			4.7	4.9
			11.5	8.3			10.7	8.6
			-999.8	22.0			69.7	29.7
EBIT/Interest			5.0	7.4			5.0	9.8
			(23) 1.8	(36) 3.6			(60) 1.8	(54) 5.0
			-.8	1.4			.3	1.7
Net Profit + Depr., Dep., Amort./Cur. Mat. L/T/D								
Fixed/Worth			.5	.6			.6	.6
			1.0	.9			1.2	.9
			2.5	1.4			2.6	1.5
Debt/Worth			.5	.3			.5	.4
			1.0	.9			1.3	1.0
			3.2	2.7			4.0	2.1
% Profit Before Taxes/Tangible Net Worth			16.9	15.7			22.9	24.2
			(28) 4.8	(38) 8.1			(63) 8.6	(60) 8.4
			-4.2	1.4			-2.1	3.2
% Profit Before Taxes/Total Assets			8.1	9.4			8.5	9.2
			2.6	3.9			2.8	4.6
			-1.0	.8			-1.3	1.3
Sales/Net Fixed Assets			7.3	4.1			4.4	7.3
			3.7	2.6			3.0	3.3
			1.9	1.9			2.2	2.3
Sales/Total Assets			2.4	1.5			2.2	2.4
			1.8	1.2			1.5	1.5
			1.0	1.0			1.1	1.1
% Depr., Dep., Amort./Sales			1.7	2.1			2.0	1.8
			(28) 2.3	2.7			(64) 2.7	(55) 2.7
			3.0	3.8			3.7	3.7
% Officers', Directors' Owners' Comp/Sales								
Net Sales ($)	3214M	24006M	328516M	1150948M		3055993M	1896789M	1269551M
Total Assets ($)	902M	6123M	190771M	895694M		299489M	1495498M	954704M

M = $ thousand MM = $ million

See Pages 11 through 21 for Explanation of Ratios and Data

Comparative Historical Data   Current Data Sorted by Sales

	4/1/04-3/31/05 ALL	4/1/05-3/31/06 ALL	4/1/06-3/31/07 ALL		0-1MM	1-3MM	3-5MM	5-10MM	10-25MM	25MM & OVER
						63 (4/1-9/30/06)			**21 (10/1/06-3/31/07)**	
Type of Statement										
Unqualified	42	38	54		2	4	3	8	25	12
Reviewed	1	1								
Compiled	1	4	4			2		2		
Tax Returns	2	1	3							
Other	16	35	23		1	4		3	9	6
NUMBER OF STATEMENTS	62	79	84		3	10	3	13	36	19
	%	%	%		%	%	%	%	%	%
ASSETS										
Cash & Equivalents	18.6	15.7	20.0			23.8		13.4	21.6	22.2
Trade Receivables (net)	23.1	21.9	17.1			19.5		18.2	17.4	14.0
Inventory	.7	.6	.4			.5		.1	.2	1.5
All Other Current	3.0	2.5	3.7			3.9		5.2	3.9	2.4
Total Current	45.4	40.7	41.2			47.3		36.9	43.1	40.2
Fixed Assets (net)	44.0	43.3	46.1			43.1		56.0	42.7	45.1
Intangibles (net)	1.8	1.1	2.2			.3		.8	1.4	6.5
All Other Non-Current	8.8	14.8	10.4			9.3		6.3	12.9	8.3
Total	100.0	100.0	100.0			100.0		100.0	100.0	100.0
LIABILITIES										
Notes Payable-Short Term	5.4	3.2	3.9			3.1		7.9	3.0	.7
Cur. Mat.-L.T.D.	3.1	3.2	2.7			3.9		1.1	2.6	3.3
Trade Payables	8.1	7.1	6.3			10.5		8.3	4.7	5.9
Income Taxes Payable	.1	.0	.1			.3		.0	.2	.0
All Other Current	13.5	11.1	11.0			8.9		14.7	11.4	8.8
Total Current	30.2	24.6	24.0			26.7		32.0	21.9	18.7
Long-Term Debt	23.1	18.8	23.7			21.1		24.9	20.9	27.2
Deferred Taxes	.2	.0	.0			.0		.0	.0	.0
All Other Non-Current	5.9	4.0	2.5			6.4		2.3	1.3	3.5
Net Worth	40.7	52.6	49.7			45.7		40.9	55.9	50.6
Total Liabilities & Net Worth	100.0	100.0	100.0			100.0		100.0	100.0	100.0
INCOME DATA										
Net Sales	100.0	100.0	100.0			100.0		100.0	100.0	100.0
Gross Profit										
Operating Expenses	96.0	95.4	93.1			86.4		96.6	94.7	93.7
Operating Profit	4.0	4.6	6.9			13.6		3.4	5.3	6.3
All Other Expenses (net)	.4	1.1	1.8			6.7		.9	.5	.8
Profit Before Taxes	3.6	3.5	5.1			6.9		2.5	4.8	5.5
RATIOS										
Current	2.7	2.8	3.5			3.4		1.6	3.8	4.1
	1.5	1.8	1.8			2.0		1.1	1.9	2.8
	1.2	1.2	1.1			1.0		.7	1.3	1.3
Quick	2.6	2.5	3.0			3.4		1.6	3.4	3.6
	1.5	1.5	1.6			1.6		.9	1.8	2.7
	1.1	1.1	.9			.9		.6	1.0	1.1
Sales/Receivables	28 13.0	24 15.0	17 21.9			0 UND		14 26.0	27 13.6	17 22.1
	45 8.1	42 8.8	40 9.2			7 51.0		29 12.5	43 8.4	39 9.3
	63 5.8	58 6.3	52 7.0			46 7.9		80 4.6	57 6.4	50 7.2
Cost of Sales/Inventory										
Cost of Sales/Payables										
Sales/Working Capital	5.0	5.4	4.9			4.0		15.8	4.9	3.1
	12.0	10.1	10.7			10.0		40.6	8.3	15.7
	51.5	49.5	68.3			NM		-21.5	14.8	40.8
EBIT/Interest	19.8	14.2	6.3					3.9	10.2	5.3
	(50) 4.7	(65) 5.5	(68) 3.4					(12) 1.7	(29) 4.1	(16) 3.7
	1.1	1.9	.2					-1.5	-.1	2.6
Net Profit + Depr., Dep., Amort./Cur. Mat. L/T/D										
Fixed/Worth	.6	.5	.5			.3		.8	.5	.6
	1.0	.8	.9			1.2		1.1	.7	1.0
	2.0	1.2	1.6			1.9		4.6	1.3	1.4
Debt/Worth	.6	.4	.4			.7		.6	.3	.3
	1.2	.8	1.0			1.2		1.3	.8	.9
	3.1	2.1	2.8			5.3		5.7	1.5	2.2
% Profit Before Taxes/Tangible Net Worth	28.4	18.3	16.6			111.1		8.1	16.2	16.9
	(54) 12.7	(77) 7.7	(78) 6.1			28.3		(11) 1.7	(35) 5.6	(17) 8.4
	4.1	2.4	-.6			-4.1		-5.2	-.9	3.2
% Profit Before Taxes/Total Assets	11.2	9.6	10.6			20.1		3.0	9.4	11.7
	7.2	4.2	3.4			13.8		1.0	3.4	4.9
	.3	1.1	-.6			-1.1		-6.1	-.3	2.3
Sales/Net Fixed Assets	7.8	5.5	5.9			96.6		4.9	5.7	5.9
	3.5	3.8	3.1			4.0		2.6	3.1	3.3
	2.0	2.1	2.0			.6		1.6	2.1	2.2
Sales/Total Assets	2.8	2.3	2.2			3.6		2.3	2.0	2.5
	1.5	1.5	1.4			1.5		1.5	1.3	1.3
	1.1	1.0	1.0			.4		.9	1.1	1.0
% Depr., Dep., Amort./Sales	1.6	1.7	1.7					2.3	1.7	1.8
	(56) 2.5	(72) 2.5	(75) 2.5					2.8	(34) 2.5	(17) 2.5
	3.5	3.4	3.6					3.6	3.8	3.5
% Officers', Directors' Owners' Comp/Sales	4.0		8.4							
	(11) 9.3		(10) 15.3							
	20.5		33.8							
Net Sales ($)	1295638M	1910340M	4562677M		915M	19523M	10512M	100223M	617916M	3813588M
Total Assets ($)	949115M	1451469M	1392979M		3753M	27697M	3619M	75160M	483396M	799354M

© RMA 2007

M = $ thousand   MM = $ million
See Pages 11 through 21 for Explanation of Ratios and Data

Current Data Sorted by Assets

Comparative Historical Data

						Type of Statement		
			18	15	11	15	Unqualified	61	54
		5	1				Reviewed	3	3
			4				Compiled	11	24
	2	1					Tax Returns	10	7
	3	3					Other	45	38
	2	12	9	11	4	8		4/1/02-3/31/03	4/1/03-3/31/04
		59 (4/1-9/30/06)		65 (10/1/06-3/31/07)				ALL	ALL
	0-500M	500M-2MM	2-10MM	10-50MM	50-100MM	100-250MM	NUMBER OF STATEMENTS	130	126
	7	21	32	26	15	23			
	%	%	%	%	%	%	ASSETS	%	%
		16.9	15.4	14.9	16.5	14.8	Cash & Equivalents	15.0	11.1
		30.1	32.1	18.1	15.6	15.1	Trade Receivables (net)	20.0	21.6
		.2	.8	1.4	1.1	.9	Inventory	1.5	1.8
		.7	4.5	8.3	3.8	3.2	All Other Current	4.4	6.6
		47.9	52.9	42.6	37.1	34.0	Total Current	41.0	41.1
		34.8	29.3	44.5	38.5	30.0	Fixed Assets (net)	39.6	42.8
		4.3	2.4	1.2	.2	7.1	Intangibles (net)	5.3	3.3
		13.0	15.4	11.6	24.3	28.8	All Other Non-Current	14.1	12.7
		100.0	100.0	100.0	100.0	100.0	Total	100.0	100.0
							LIABILITIES		
		20.2	7.1	2.6	1.6	1.0	Notes Payable-Short Term	6.0	5.0
		1.4	3.4	5.8	1.2	1.6	Cur. Mat.-L.T.D.	4.0	3.7
		15.3	12.3	5.6	6.3	5.3	Trade Payables	6.5	7.2
		.0	.6	.0	.1	.0	Income Taxes Payable	.2	.1
		17.5	37.0	12.7	9.8	9.7	All Other Current	23.7	14.0
		54.3	60.4	26.7	19.0	17.6	Total Current	40.4	29.9
		24.8	18.5	25.8	18.7	23.4	Long-Term Debt	24.2	24.6
		.0	.0	.5	.0	.0	Deferred Taxes	.2	.1
		.1	2.7	2.4	2.7	6.8	All Other Non-Current	3.5	3.3
		20.8	18.5	44.6	59.7	52.1	Net Worth	31.7	42.1
		100.0	100.0	100.0	100.0	100.0	Total Liabilties & Net Worth	100.0	100.0
							INCOME DATA		
		100.0	100.0	100.0	100.0	100.0	Net Sales	100.0	100.0
							Gross Profit		
		95.2	87.5	90.2	91.2	90.7	Operating Expenses	91.4	90.9
		4.8	12.5	9.8	8.8	9.3	Operating Profit	8.6	9.1
		.5	4.8	1.9	.2	4.0	All Other Expenses (net)	2.6	1.8
		4.3	7.7	7.9	8.6	5.3	Profit Before Taxes	6.0	7.3
							RATIOS		
		2.1	1.9	2.7	4.9	3.2		2.4	2.8
		1.2	1.0	1.5	2.2	2.5	Current	1.5	1.7
		.5	.6	1.0	1.5	1.1		.8	.9
		2.0	1.6	2.0	4.1	2.7		2.2	2.2
		1.2	.9	1.3	1.9	1.8	Quick	1.3	1.3
		.5	.5	.8	1.3	.9		.6	.8
0	UND	15	24.1	37	9.7	32	11.6	42	8.8		14	26.0	23	15.6
32	11.3	48	7.7	49	7.4	51	7.2	60	6.1	Sales/Receivables	50	7.3	51	7.2
65	5.6	74	4.9	55	6.7	61	6.0	71	5.2		71	5.1	67	5.5
							Cost of Sales/Inventory		
							Cost of Sales/Payables		
		12.6	6.4	4.4	2.8	2.5		5.1	5.2
		22.8	NM	11.7	6.4	6.6	Sales/Working Capital	12.9	11.9
		-22.4	-11.0	134.8	13.7	42.0		-52.4	-53.8
		14.1	10.4	12.0	16.0	10.1		12.3	13.2
	(16)	.1	(22)	2.6	(17)	4.3	(13)	4.7	(22)	3.6	EBIT/Interest	(113)	3.3	(106)	4.0
		-3.7	1.3	.4	1.7	1.0		.3	1.1
							Net Profit + Depr., Dep., Amort./Cur. Mat. L/T/D		8.6
								(10)	4.5
									1.4
		.4	.3	.5	.4	.5		.5	.5
		1.1	1.3	.9	.6	.7	Fixed/Worth	1.1	1.0
		-.8	29.1	3.2	.8	1.6		4.4	2.7
		.5	.8	.6	.3	.3		.6	.5
		2.0	1.9	1.0	.6	.9	Debt/Worth	1.2	1.3
		-4.8	513.3	4.2	1.1	3.3		12.5	4.5
		91.0	44.6	49.0	24.3	18.0		32.1	50.7
	(13)	22.7	(25)	20.6	(24)	13.6	7.6	(21)	6.2	% Profit Before Taxes/Tangible Net Worth	(101)	8.2	(107)	9.3
		6.8	2.4	6.1	2.9	1.5		-.4	.4
		24.3	13.6	19.9	13.9	7.4		15.0	15.1
		4.6	4.2	5.9	7.3	4.3	% Profit Before Taxes/Total Assets	4.2	4.8
		-26.0	.2	1.4	2.1	.0		-1.6	.1
		55.9	41.3	8.6	4.7	5.9		14.1	8.4
		23.2	14.1	3.9	2.8	2.8	Sales/Net Fixed Assets	3.3	3.0
		6.2	4.4	1.4	1.9	1.9		1.6	1.7
		6.5	3.3	1.9	1.5	1.1		2.7	2.5
		3.0	1.9	1.2	1.2	.8	Sales/Total Assets	1.4	1.4
		1.9	.7	.8	.7	.5		.7	.8
		.3	.6	1.5	3.2	2.5		2.1	2.1
	(16)	1.6	(27)	1.6	(25)	4.1	4.5	(22)	4.2	% Depr., Dep., Amort./Sales	(108)	3.7	(113)	3.8
		3.0	3.0	6.4	6.4	4.7		6.5	6.8
							% Officers', Directors' Owners' Comp/Sales		9.6	10.4
								(14)	19.1	(11)	17.7
								33.4	31.3
	21831M	184023M	308883M	768960M	1314572M	3165646M	Net Sales ($)	5535953M	5335563M
	1476M	27002M	148772M	570183M	1146321M	3496066M	Total Assets ($)	4945298M	4687102M

M = $ thousand   MM = $ million
See Pages 11 through 21 for Explanation of Ratios and Data

© RMA 2007

Comparative Historical Data				Current Data Sorted by Sales					
			Type of Statement						
49	61	64	Unqualified	2	6	4	6	11	35
10	4	1	Reviewed	1					
9	11	7	Compiled		1	1	1	4	
10	6	6	Tax Returns	1	1	1	1	1	1
45	47	46	Other	2	4	8	7	8	17
4/1/04-3/31/05 ALL	4/1/05-3/31/06 ALL	4/1/06-3/31/07 ALL		0-1MM	59 (4/1-9/30/06) 1-3MM	3-5MM	5-10MM	65 (10/1/06-3/31/07) 10-25MM	25MM & OVER
123	129	124	**NUMBER OF STATEMENTS**	6	12	14	15	24	53
%	%	%	**ASSETS**	%	%	%	%	%	%
15.5	16.7	16.7	Cash & Equivalents	27.8	17.7	18.4	11.9	16.0	
21.6	21.3	22.5	Trade Receivables (net)	14.3	30.5	35.7	29.0	17.9	
1.1	1.2	1.0	Inventory	.1	.3	1.4	1.1	1.3	
2.7	3.9	4.3	All Other Current	.9	4.0	1.9	8.0	4.2	
40.9	43.1	44.4	Total Current	43.1	52.5	57.3	50.1	39.3	
41.3	37.9	35.4	Fixed Assets (net)	32.8	39.1	28.0	31.5	36.1	
3.6	2.9	2.9	Intangibles (net)	.8	.8	3.6	4.8	3.2	
14.2	16.2	17.3	All Other Non-Current	23.2	7.5	11.0	13.6	21.4	
100.0	100.0	100.0	Total	100.0	100.0	100.0	100.0	100.0	
			LIABILITIES						
13.7	6.0	8.2	Notes Payable-Short Term	7.0	3.4	10.5	9.2	6.4	
4.8	4.5	3.8	Cur. Mat.-L.T.D.	.8	4.0	1.4	3.0	3.2	
7.7	9.4	9.4	Trade Payables	11.5	17.4	13.4	10.5	5.9	
.9	.1	.2	Income Taxes Payable	.0	.1	.0	.7	.0	
15.8	13.6	20.3	All Other Current	22.4	17.3	18.0	40.8	10.9	
42.9	33.6	41.8	Total Current	41.7	42.3	43.3	64.3	26.5	
27.2	19.4	22.4	Long-Term Debt	24.0	18.6	27.6	17.7	20.6	
.1	.2	.1	Deferred Taxes	.8	.0	.0	.0	.1	
2.9	4.2	2.9	All Other Non-Current	.1	.8	1.3	1.6	4.4	
26.8	42.7	32.8	Net Worth	33.5	38.3	27.7	16.4	48.3	
100.0	100.0	100.0	Total Liabilities & Net Worth	100.0	100.0	100.0	100.0	100.0	
			INCOME DATA						
100.0	100.0	100.0	Net Sales	100.0	100.0	100.0	100.0	100.0	
			Gross Profit						
88.5	91.4	91.3	Operating Expenses	89.0	94.8	93.5	91.9	92.0	
11.5	8.6	8.7	Operating Profit	11.0	5.2	6.5	8.1	8.0	
3.7	1.7	2.5	All Other Expenses (net)	2.2	-.1	3.7	1.9	1.2	
7.8	6.9	6.2	Profit Before Taxes	8.8	5.3	2.9	6.2	6.8	
			RATIOS						
2.4	3.0	2.6	Current	2.0	2.2	2.8	1.8	3.1	
1.4	1.6	1.5		1.1	1.6	1.4	.9	1.8	
.7	.9	.8		.8	.8	.9	.6	1.1	
2.2	2.5	2.2	Quick	1.5	2.0	2.8	1.0	2.6	
1.2	1.4	1.2		1.0	1.5	1.4	.8	1.6	
.6	.6	.7		.5	.8	.8	.5	1.0	
8 43.8	19 19.2	14 25.2	Sales/Receivables	0 UND	16 22.4	11 34.2	33 11.0	40 9.1	
45 8.1	41 8.9	47 7.7		0 UND	42 8.6	49 7.4	47 7.7	52 7.0	
64 5.7	62 5.9	65 5.6		52 7.0	76 4.8	70 5.2	57 6.4	65 5.6	
			Cost of Sales/Inventory						
			Cost of Sales/Payables						
6.3	5.3	4.8	Sales/Working Capital	9.5	5.9	7.8	6.0	2.8	
27.2	11.8	13.7		165.9	11.3	12.5	-290.8	9.1	
-25.8	-50.1	-33.8		-11.6	-41.7	-29.6	-18.2	39.8	
13.7	14.6	10.9	EBIT/Interest		20.8			9.9	11.7
(107) 4.9	(105) 4.2	(94) 3.8			(12) 5.0			(20) 3.5	(46) 4.2
1.8	.6	.9			1.3			1.0	1.2
9.9	8.2		Net Profit + Depr., Dep., Amort./Cur. Mat. L/T/D						
(13) 1.9	(10) 4.6								
.5	2.0								
.5	.4	.4	Fixed/Worth	.1	.4	.2	.6	.4	
1.2	.8	.8		1.9	.8	.7	1.4	.7	
11.6	1.9	2.9		NM	6.1	-1.0	5.7	1.6	
.7	.5	.5	Debt/Worth	.8	.4	.2	.8	.4	
2.3	1.0	1.2		2.5	.6	3.1	1.6	.8	
24.9	3.8	8.4		NM	15.4	-5.2	22.9	2.8	
84.3	44.3	35.5	% Profit Before Taxes/Tangible Net Worth		87.0	104.1		38.7	26.5
(97) 20.0	(114) 10.1	(102) 11.2			(12) 31.7	(10) 9.2		(19) 13.7	(48) 9.2
4.5	1.0	3.7			7.8	-5.7		2.1	4.0
19.1	14.4	13.6	% Profit Before Taxes/Total Assets	13.7	25.3	11.5	11.4	11.1	
6.0	5.2	5.1		4.6	6.0	2.6	6.2	5.1	
1.3	-.8	.1		-1.3	1.4	-8.0	.1	1.6	
22.7	12.5	21.1	Sales/Net Fixed Assets	64.3	33.3	43.2	34.9	5.9	
4.3	3.9	4.8		16.0	9.4	13.6	18.0	3.2	
1.9	2.1	2.3		1.0	3.6	3.6	4.7	2.2	
3.0	2.8	2.7	Sales/Total Assets	6.0	4.2	3.8	5.4	1.8	
1.7	1.6	1.5		1.2	2.4	2.2	2.4	1.1	
.9	.8	.8		.4	.7	1.4	1.2	.8	
1.6	1.6	1.4	% Depr., Dep., Amort./Sales		.8	1.3		.7	2.1
(107) 3.3	(113) 2.8	(108) 2.8			(13) 1.8	(11) 1.7		(21) 1.8	(51) 3.8
6.5	5.1	4.9			8.5	6.7		4.0	5.0
11.0	8.1	11.2	% Officers', Directors' Owners' Comp/Sales						
(24) 19.2	(24) 21.8	(18) 22.4							
27.1	34.2	29.6							
8554561M	5406867M	5763915M	Net Sales ($)	2897M	25892M	57690M	115543M	400114M	5161779M
4375443M	5086906M	5389820M	Total Assets ($)	8232M	41842M	48285M	116268M	242564M	4932629M

© RMA 2007

M = $ thousand   MM = $ million
See Pages 11 through 21 for Explanation of Ratios and Data

Current Data Sorted by Assets

Comparative Historical Data

0-500M	500M-2MM	2-10MM	10-50MM	50-100MM	100-250MM	Type of Statement	4/1/02-3/31/03 ALL	4/1/03-3/31/04 ALL
10	34	186	201	58	60	Unqualified	490	478
4	28	74	16	1		Reviewed	103	138
18	62	67	9	1	1	Compiled	148	272
56	38	27	7	7		Tax Returns	77	89
31	121	194	115	45	20	Other	479	478
\ 436 (4/1-9/30/06) /			\ 1,048 (10/1/06-3/31/07) /					
NUMBER OF STATEMENTS								
119	283	548	348	105	81		1297	1455
%	%	%	%	%	%	**ASSETS**	%	%
21.6	12.6	10.6	10.9	9.1	11.9	Cash & Equivalents	10.5	10.4
26.2	33.6	22.9	13.1	10.1	7.7	Trade Receivables (net)	17.4	20.1
.2	.7	.4	.3	.4	1.2	Inventory	.3	.4
6.6	4.8	3.4	2.8	1.9	3.3	All Other Current	3.2	4.2
54.6	51.7	37.4	27.1	21.6	24.1	Total Current	31.4	35.1
27.8	35.2	46.6	52.9	57.0	51.2	Fixed Assets (net)	51.3	49.4
2.7	3.6	4.4	4.4	4.6	4.7	Intangibles (net)	4.6	3.1
14.9	9.6	11.7	15.6	16.8	20.0	All Other Non-Current	12.7	12.4
100.0	100.0	100.0	100.0	100.0	100.0	Total	100.0	100.0
						LIABILITIES		
8.8	7.3	5.2	1.4	1.5	.6	Notes Payable-Short Term	5.3	5.0
4.4	2.8	2.7	3.2	2.7	2.2	Cur. Mat.-L.T.D.	3.4	3.7
26.6	16.0	9.0	6.1	5.1	3.3	Trade Payables	7.4	8.3
.3	.2	.1	.1	.0	.0	Income Taxes Payable	.1	.1
45.8	28.3	16.0	10.3	7.1	7.1	All Other Current	18.0	17.7
85.9	54.6	33.1	21.1	16.3	13.2	Total Current	34.3	34.7
22.6	29.4	43.9	47.5	53.1	46.0	Long-Term Debt	45.5	41.2
.0	.1	.1	.0	.0	.1	Deferred Taxes	.1	.1
13.2	8.7	4.8	9.0	16.5	18.3	All Other Non-Current	9.6	11.3
-21.7	7.2	18.2	22.4	14.2	22.3	Net Worth	10.5	12.7
100.0	100.0	100.0	100.0	100.0	100.0	Total Liabilities & Net Worth	100.0	100.0
						INCOME DATA		
100.0	100.0	100.0	100.0	100.0	100.0	Net Sales	100.0	100.0
						Gross Profit		
95.3	92.6	88.5	90.1	94.3	92.7	Operating Expenses	90.7	91.0
4.7	7.4	11.5	9.9	5.7	7.3	Operating Profit	9.3	9.0
1.2	3.8	5.6	5.0	3.7	3.6	All Other Expenses (net)	5.6	5.2
3.5	3.6	5.8	4.9	2.1	3.7	Profit Before Taxes	3.7	3.8
						RATIOS		
1.8	1.9	2.2	2.3	2.6	3.3	Current	2.0	2.2
1.0	1.1	1.2	1.3	1.4	1.7		1.1	1.2
.4	.7	.7	.8	.9	1.0		.6	.7
1.8	1.7	2.0	2.0	2.3	2.6	Quick	1.8	1.8
.8	1.0	1.1	1.2	1.2	1.2		1.0 (1454)	1.0
.3	.6	.6	.7	.8	.9		.5	.6
0 UND	13 27.9	22 16.3	19 18.9	22 16.6	19 19.4	Sales/Receivables	12 29.6	14 25.2
6 58.9	31 11.6	38 9.7	35 10.5	34 10.8	34 10.6		31 11.9	33 10.9
24 15.2	46 8.0	53 6.8	47 7.7	43 8.5	45 8.1		46 7.9	48 7.5
						Cost of Sales/Inventory		
						Cost of Sales/Payables		
32.5	14.2	8.9	6.1	4.8	2.5	Sales/Working Capital	9.0	7.9
-314.1	96.3	39.1	20.0	16.0	12.9		55.5	37.5
-17.0	-16.9	-18.3	-32.1	-75.8	-280.8		-14.8	-16.4
17.4	12.5	6.7	3.9	2.4	3.3	EBIT/Interest	4.1	4.4
(69) 2.3	(200) 3.5	(446) 2.5	(305) 2.0	(98) 1.6	(78) 1.9		(1029) 1.8	(1154) 1.8
-1.1	.6	1.0	1.0	.8	.9		.6	.6
	7.8	10.5	8.9	2.9		Net Profit + Depr., Dep., Amort./Cur. Mat. L/T/D	5.5	3.6
	(12) 3.4	(40) 2.7	(26) 3.3	(10) .9			(97) 2.6	(89) 2.0
	1.5	1.4	1.0	.4			1.2	.8
.2	.5	.7	1.0	2.2	1.5	Fixed/Worth	1.0	.9
1.5	2.0	2.9	2.6	7.6	2.8		3.7	3.7
-.5	-2.4	-8.8	-59.8	-9.4	11.9		-5.6	-6.6
1.1	1.1	1.2	1.4	2.6	2.1	Debt/Worth	1.4	1.4
9.0	6.4	4.5	4.0	11.8	3.9		5.9	6.1
-2.5	-6.0	-15.5	-91.0	-16.2	19.0		-9.2	-11.7
189.6	80.6	62.2	32.0	26.1	22.1	% Profit Before Taxes/Tangible Net Worth	47.0	44.4
(72) 68.2	(182) 30.7	(376) 23.4	(258) 11.3	(66) 10.6	(65) 8.8		(844) 12.5	(968) 13.2
4.6	5.1	5.7	2.1	1.9	1.4		-.1	-.2
48.5	18.5	13.2	7.0	3.9	4.1	% Profit Before Taxes/Total Assets	9.8	9.0
12.3	7.0	5.2	3.0	1.7	2.4		2.6	2.6
-7.0	-2.8	.1	.2	-.8	-.4		-1.3	-1.6
264.0	41.1	15.3	3.5	2.4	2.1	Sales/Net Fixed Assets	9.2	12.4
45.1	16.1	3.2	1.6	.9	.7		2.2	2.3
15.6	3.3	1.5	.8	.5	.5		.9	.9
12.2	5.0	2.5	1.3	1.3	1.0	Sales/Total Assets	2.4	2.7
7.2	3.2	1.5	.8	.5	.4		1.1	1.2
4.4	1.5	.9	.5	.3	.3		.6	.6
.3	.5	1.2	2.2	3.9	3.9	% Depr., Dep., Amort./Sales	1.7	1.5
(84) .7	(250) 1.2	(520) 2.6	(337) 4.3	(102) 7.7	(78) 7.0		(1217) 3.6	(1353) 3.5
1.8	3.6	4.8	7.8	10.8	11.9		7.1	7.2
3.9	2.3	1.9	1.5			% Officers', Directors' Owners' Comp/Sales	2.0	2.1
(35) 5.9	(50) 3.9	(71) 4.2	(38) 3.6				(200) 4.7	(190) 4.6
9.2	7.7	6.6	12.4				10.0	9.4
195385M	1088957M	4871178M	9374145M	7211472M	8760316M	Net Sales ($)	20352214M	24244066M
26886M	329206M	2820908M	8184256M	7424815M	12306002M	Total Assets ($)	22785836M	24200363M

M = $ thousand   MM = $ million

See Pages 11 through 21 for Explanation of Ratios and Data

Comparative Historical Data

Current Data Sorted by Sales

			Type of Statement						
550	449	549	Unqualified	16	27	48	133	187	138
147	144	123	Reviewed	2	23	19	39	35	5
209	157	158	Compiled	31	41	24	38	20	4
115	124	128	Tax Returns	41	40	28	12	4	3
535	631	526	Other	51	73	57	131	109	105
4/1/04-3/31/05 ALL	4/1/05-3/31/06 ALL	4/1/06-3/31/07 ALL		436 (4/1-9/30/06)		1,048 (10/1/06-3/31/07)			
				0-1MM	1-3MM	3-5MM	5-10MM	10-25MM	25MM & OVER
1556	1505	1484	NUMBER OF STATEMENTS	141	204	176	353	355	255
%	%	%	ASSETS	%	%	%	%	%	%
11.4	12.4	11.9	Cash & Equivalents	13.9	14.6	11.8	11.2	10.9	11.1
20.8	20.2	21.2	Trade Receivables (net)	7.4	16.9	28.3	25.6	22.4	19.5
.3	.4	.5	Inventory	.0	.4	.7	.7	.4	.4
4.0	3.9	3.7	All Other Current	4.8	4.2	3.8	3.8	3.1	3.1
36.5	36.9	37.2	Total Current	26.2	36.1	44.7	41.3	36.7	34.1
47.0	46.4	45.4	Fixed Assets (net)	58.5	47.2	40.7	41.2	45.5	45.6
3.8	4.0	4.1	Intangibles (net)	3.6	4.5	2.8	4.6	3.6	5.1
12.7	12.7	13.3	All Other Non-Current	11.7	12.2	11.9	12.9	14.2	15.2
100.0	100.0	100.0	Total	100.0	100.0	100.0	100.0	100.0	100.0
			LIABILITIES						
6.3	5.6	4.5	Notes Payable-Short Term	6.2	7.3	4.5	4.3	3.9	2.3
3.1	3.1	2.9	Cur. Mat.-L.T.D.	3.4	3.1	3.0	2.7	2.6	3.3
9.7	9.8	10.5	Trade Payables	6.7	12.2	14.4	11.3	9.2	9.2
.1	.1	.1	Income Taxes Payable	.1	.2	.2	.0	.1	.1
17.8	17.9	18.3	All Other Current	15.0	22.3	25.4	21.0	14.5	13.6
37.1	36.5	36.3	Total Current	31.4	45.2	47.6	39.3	30.3	28.4
42.9	40.3	41.0	Long-Term Debt	57.7	47.0	35.7	34.4	39.9	41.6
.1	.1	.1	Deferred Taxes	.1	.0	.0	.2	.0	.0
7.7	9.0	8.8	All Other Non-Current	5.4	11.0	11.1	5.9	9.6	10.1
12.3	14.1	13.8	Net Worth	5.5	-3.2	5.5	20.3	20.2	19.9
100.0	100.0	100.0	Total Liabilities & Net Worth	100.0	100.0	100.0	100.0	100.0	100.0
			INCOME DATA						
100.0	100.0	100.0	Net Sales	100.0	100.0	100.0	100.0	100.0	100.0
			Gross Profit						
89.7	89.5	90.8	Operating Expenses	72.1	87.0	93.3	93.5	93.6	95.0
10.3	10.5	9.2	Operating Profit	27.9	13.0	6.7	6.5	6.4	5.0
4.8	5.3	4.5	All Other Expenses (net)	16.1	7.2	3.7	2.8	2.7	1.6
5.5	5.2	4.6	Profit Before Taxes	11.8	5.8	3.0	3.7	3.7	3.4
			RATIOS						
2.1	2.2	2.1	Current	2.2	2.0	2.2	2.2	2.2	2.0
1.2	1.2	1.2		.8	1.0	1.3	1.3	1.3	1.3
.7	.7	.8		.2	.5	.8	.8	.9	.9
1.8	1.9	2.0	Quick	2.0	1.8	1.9	2.0	1.9	1.8
1.0	1.1	1.1		.6	.8	1.1	1.2	1.2	1.1
.6	.6	.6		.1	.4	.7	.7	.7	.8
16 23.3	12 29.8	15 23.6	Sales/Receivables	0 UND	0 UND	14 26.4	25 14.4	28 13.1	30 12.3
32 11.5	32 11.5	34 10.9		0 UND	11 34.0	30 12.3	39 9.5	38 9.6	37 9.8
47 7.8	48 7.7	47 7.7		11 32.9	34 10.8	46 7.9	54 6.8	55 6.6	47 7.8
			Cost of Sales/Inventory						
			Cost of Sales/Payables						
8.6	8.3	8.4	Sales/Working Capital	7.1	10.4	10.9	8.6	7.4	7.7
40.9	32.5	35.6		-26.2	999.8	37.7	26.4	24.1	26.1
-18.7	-17.1	-22.2		-4.1	-12.8	-28.4	-22.9	-43.2	-74.5
5.9	6.1	5.4	EBIT/Interest	5.5	7.5	6.3	6.6	4.5	4.6
(1239) 2.5	(1189) 2.3	(1196) 2.3		(60) 1.9	(142) 2.1	(142) 1.7	(294) 2.5	(312) 2.3	(246) 2.2
.9	.9	.9		.7	.4	.5	1.1	1.0	1.2
6.1	7.9	7.4	Net Profit + Depr., Dep., Amort./Cur. Mat. L/T/D			2.8	6.8	11.7	7.0
(91) 2.9	(90) 3.1	(97) 2.8			(11) 2.0	(12) 2.6	(29) 3.5	(36) 3.1	
1.2	1.2	1.0				1.4	.7	1.1	
.8	.8	.8	Fixed/Worth	1.0	.7	.5	.7	.8	1.1
3.9	3.1	2.8		9.1	5.4	3.7	2.0	2.3	3.1
-5.9	-7.3	-8.4		-4.1	-2.6	-3.8	-28.5	-44.8	-226.9
1.4	1.4	1.3	Debt/Worth	1.5	1.3	1.2	1.1	1.3	1.9
6.7	5.1	5.0		13.1	12.4	6.4	3.6	3.3	5.9
-11.5	-12.8	-14.0		-5.2	-4.8	-7.4	-43.4	-37.5	-314.9
63.8	65.8	59.8	% Profit Before Taxes/Tangible Net Worth	61.0	79.4	66.9	61.6	51.8	52.0
(1030) 21.1	(1011) 19.9	(1019) 17.7		(85) 22.8	(116) 22.0	(107) 16.9	(257) 21.8	(264) 16.0	(190) 16.2
4.3	3.3	3.9		1.7	6.0	4.6	3.3	2.9	5.8
12.1	13.6	11.9	% Profit Before Taxes/Total Assets	14.0	15.6	14.1	13.2	10.7	8.8
4.4	4.1	3.8		3.1	4.4	3.5	4.4	3.6	3.5
-.3	-.2	-.4		-1.9	-2.6	-1.4	-.1	.2	.6
16.8	19.6	19.7	Sales/Net Fixed Assets	14.6	32.4	33.3	25.2	11.1	7.5
2.8	2.9	3.0		.8	4.3	7.6	4.0	2.4	2.4
1.0	1.0	1.1		.2	.8	1.5	1.5	1.1	1.1
2.9	3.0	3.0	Sales/Total Assets	2.1	4.8	4.8	3.2	2.5	2.2
1.3	1.4	1.3		.5	1.6	1.9	1.7	1.3	1.2
.6	.6	.6		.2	.5	.9	.9	.6	.6
1.3	1.1	1.1	% Depr., Dep., Amort./Sales	2.9	1.1	.6	.9	1.5	1.6
(1418) 3.1	(1389) 3.0	(1371) 2.9		(118) 8.3	(169) 3.3	(169) 1.6	(329) 2.3	(344) 2.9	(242) 3.4
6.7	6.6	6.3		24.4	7.4	5.1	4.4	5.9	6.8
2.3	2.5	2.2	% Officers', Directors' Owners' Comp/Sales	4.3	3.7	2.8	1.3	1.6	1.2
(221) 4.9	(211) 5.3	(206) 4.5		(19) 10.1	(40) 5.6	(32) 4.3	(49) 3.5	(45) 3.0	(21) 5.6
9.9	8.4	8.5		23.2	14.7	8.6	6.1	7.2	10.9
26731400M	27103021M	31501453M	Net Sales ($)	80254M	392316M	701714M	2581911M	5482888M	22262370M
25015291M	26872461M	31092073M	Total Assets ($)	240453M	627697M	817877M	2664352M	7371266M	19370428M

M = $ thousand   MM = $ million
See Pages 11 through 21 for Explanation of Ratios and Data

Current Data Sorted by Assets   Comparative Historical Data

Type of Statement

	0-500M	500M-2MM	2-10MM	10-50MM	50-100MM	100-250MM		17	39
Unqualified	2	11	36	18	6	5		17	39
Reviewed	2								
Compiled	4	1	4						1
Tax Returns		2	7	7		2		1	1
Other								11	6
		80 (4/1-9/30/06)		27 (10/1/06-3/31/07)				4/1/02-3/31/03 ALL	4/1/03-3/31/04 ALL
NUMBER OF STATEMENTS	8	14	47	25	6	7		29	47

ASSETS

	0-500M %	500M-2MM %	2-10MM %	10-50MM %	50-100MM %	100-250MM %		17 %	39 %
Cash & Equivalents		27.7	19.6	17.1				11.3	9.9
Trade Receivables (net)		20.9	17.0	15.7				15.1	17.5
Inventory		.0	.2	.0				.1	.2
All Other Current		3.5	2.6	1.8				3.3	6.5
Total Current		52.1	39.4	34.6				29.8	34.1
Fixed Assets (net)		44.0	49.7	54.1				56.7	53.9
Intangibles (net)		.0	1.8	1.2				2.7	1.6
All Other Non-Current		3.9	9.1	10.1				10.9	10.4
Total		100.0	100.0	100.0				100.0	100.0

LIABILITIES

	0-500M	500M-2MM	2-10MM	10-50MM	50-100MM	100-250MM		17	39
Notes Payable-Short Term		7.2	2.4	4.5				5.1	6.6
Cur. Mat.-L.T.D.		2.8	2.1	2.5				5.3	2.7
Trade Payables		5.0	5.4	8.3				5.9	5.6
Income Taxes Payable		.0	.3	.0				.4	.0
All Other Current		11.5	11.2	8.8				12.4	15.5
Total Current		26.5	21.2	24.1				29.1	30.4
Long-Term Debt		22.8	26.4	39.4				44.4	32.1
Deferred Taxes		.2	.0	.0				.0	.0
All Other Non-Current		.1	.9	2.3				3.8	4.7
Net Worth		50.4	51.5	34.3				22.6	32.8
Total Liabilities & Net Worth		100.0	100.0	100.0				100.0	100.0

INCOME DATA

	0-500M	500M-2MM	2-10MM	10-50MM	50-100MM	100-250MM		17	39
Net Sales		100.0	100.0	100.0				100.0	100.0
Gross Profit									
Operating Expenses		96.2	93.5	96.3				94.8	96.5
Operating Profit		3.8	6.5	3.7				5.2	3.5
All Other Expenses (net)		.1	1.4	1.1				4.1	1.8
Profit Before Taxes		3.8	5.1	2.6				1.0	1.7

RATIOS

	0-500M	500M-2MM	2-10MM	10-50MM	50-100MM	100-250MM		17	39
Current		9.4	3.7	2.1				1.7	1.7
		1.5	1.9	1.4				1.0	1.1
		.9	.9	.9				.9	.8
Quick		9.2	3.2	2.0				1.5	1.6
		1.5	1.8	1.3				1.0	.8
		.7	.8	.8				.6	.6
Sales/Receivables		0 UND	17 21.5	28 12.8				8 47.0	17 21.6
		15 24.5	31 11.8	41 9.0				26 14.1	34 10.8
		32 11.4	41 8.9	57 6.4				40 9.2	43 8.5
Cost of Sales/Inventory									
Cost of Sales/Payables									
Sales/Working Capital		4.2	4.7	5.9				16.3	10.8
		17.8	10.2	23.1				173.2	117.2
		-142.4	-131.9	-97.5				-57.4	-36.1
EBIT/Interest			9.4	3.6				3.2	3.7
			(38) 2.1	(19) 2.0				(27) 1.6	(42) 1.6
			.6	1.1				.8	.3
Net Profit + Depr., Dep., Amort./Cur. Mat. L/T/D									
Fixed/Worth		.4	.4	.8				1.0	.9
		.8	1.0	1.8				2.8	1.7
		2.4	2.0	7.7				14.7	3.9
Debt/Worth		.1	.5	.9				1.5	.9
		1.3	.9	1.5				5.1	2.4
		3.8	2.2	10.8				NM	13.7
% Profit Before Taxes/Tangible Net Worth		21.3	21.1	17.7				23.8	22.5
		(12) 4.1	(45) 6.0	(21) 7.2				(22) 8.2	(40) 4.8
		-5.3	.7	2.6				.8	-2.4
% Profit Before Taxes/Total Assets		9.1	10.4	5.0				4.1	4.8
		3.5	2.4	3.3				1.2	1.5
		-2.3	.1	.9				-.6	-2.3
Sales/Net Fixed Assets		28.4	7.1	3.1				5.0	5.2
		7.5	3.1	2.1				2.6	3.2
		.8	1.7	1.8				.5	1.8
Sales/Total Assets		5.0	2.3	1.6				2.2	2.8
		2.6	1.5	1.2				1.5	1.7
		.1	1.0	.9				.4	1.2
% Depr., Dep., Amort./Sales		.7	1.5	2.2				2.7	1.9
		1.5	(46) 2.5	(23) 3.1				(23) 3.9	(43) 2.7
		2.6	3.8	4.1				9.7	4.2
% Officers', Directors' Owners' Comp/Sales									
Net Sales ($)	5967M	56627M	364731M	761468M	430096M	892562M		898341M	1031530M
Total Assets ($)	1709M	16961M	220289M	558008M	406819M	986253M		819078M	643025M

M = $ thousand   MM = $ million
See Pages 11 through 21 for Explanation of Ratios and Data

Comparative Historical Data   **Current Data Sorted by Sales**

			Type of Statement		80 (4/1-9/30/06)			27 (10/1/06-3/31/07)	
51	52	78	Unqualified	8	8	8	20	15	19
4	2		Reviewed						
	3	2	Compiled	1	1				
4	2	9	Tax Returns	3	4		2		
19	11	18	Other	1			6	7	4
4/1/04-3/31/05 ALL	4/1/05-3/31/06 ALL	4/1/06-3/31/07 ALL		0-1MM	1-3MM	3-5MM	5-10MM	10-25MM	25MM & OVER
78	70	107	NUMBER OF STATEMENTS	13	13	8	28	22	23
%	%	%	ASSETS	%	%	%	%	%	%
11.9	20.9	18.8	Cash & Equivalents	16.9	30.8		14.7	16.2	16.6
17.8	19.6	16.9	Trade Receivables (net)	10.3	6.3		19.6	22.7	19.7
.1	.1	.1	Inventory	.2	.0		.2	.2	.0
7.8	3.8	2.7	All Other Current	.5	1.8		3.0	3.2	3.7
37.7	44.4	38.5	Total Current	27.9	39.0		37.5	42.3	40.0
50.1	44.7	50.0	Fixed Assets (net)	62.6	50.0		49.4	45.2	49.0
1.3	1.2	1.4	Intangibles (net)	.7	2.0		1.0	2.5	1.3
10.9	9.8	10.1	All Other Non-Current	8.9	9.1		12.1	10.1	9.7
100.0	100.0	100.0	Total	100.0	100.0		100.0	100.0	100.0
			LIABILITIES						
7.0	4.8	3.9	Notes Payable-Short Term	2.8	1.9		3.3	4.7	7.1
2.4	2.1	2.2	Cur. Mat.-L.T.D.	1.8	.6		2.3	3.4	2.5
6.2	7.7	7.0	Trade Payables	6.8	5.4		6.3	6.9	10.6
.2	.4	.2	Income Taxes Payable	.0	.0		.4	.0	.2
12.4	14.8	11.6	All Other Current	11.3	10.1		10.7	14.7	10.8
28.2	29.7	24.9	Total Current	22.7	18.0		23.0	29.8	31.2
31.7	24.3	33.5	Long-Term Debt	58.5	28.4		32.0	30.1	35.2
.0	.0	.0	Deferred Taxes	.0	.0		.1	.0	.0
6.7	5.4	1.9	All Other Non-Current	.2	2.1		2.0	1.3	3.7
33.3	40.5	39.7	Net Worth	18.6	51.5		42.8	38.8	29.9
100.0	100.0	100.0	Total Liabilties & Net Worth	100.0	100.0		100.0	100.0	100.0
			INCOME DATA						
100.0	100.0	100.0	Net Sales	100.0	100.0		100.0	100.0	100.0
			Gross Profit						
95.1	95.9	93.6	Operating Expenses	81.8	92.1		91.8	97.5	97.5
4.9	4.1	6.4	Operating Profit	18.2	7.9		8.2	2.5	2.5
2.3	.6	2.0	All Other Expenses (net)	7.5	.5		3.4	1.0	.6
2.7	3.5	4.4	Profit Before Taxes	10.7	7.4		4.8	1.5	1.9
			RATIOS						
2.4	2.7	2.6		6.3	12.1		2.7	2.2	1.6
1.3	1.5	1.6	Current	1.7	3.6		1.8	1.4	1.1
.9	.9	.9		.6	1.1		1.0	.8	.9
1.8	2.5	2.5		5.8	11.2		2.5	2.1	1.5
1.1	1.3	1.4	Quick	1.6	3.0		1.5	1.4	1.0
.7	.8	.8		.6	.7		1.0	.7	.7
14 26.1	23 15.8	14 25.6		0 UND	0 UND		22 16.8	29 12.6	33 11.0
30 12.2	35 10.5	32 11.4	Sales/Receivables	0 UND	14 26.1		34 10.9	37 10.0	52 7.0
40 9.1	49 7.5	51 7.1		0 UND	34 10.8		54 6.7	47 7.7	63 5.8
			Cost of Sales/Inventory						
			Cost of Sales/Payables						
8.0	5.7	5.2		1.9	2.2		3.8	6.3	10.1
24.4	15.1	13.4	Sales/Working Capital	19.4	8.8		11.9	23.3	66.8
-98.2	-47.9	-131.9		-9.3	NM		NM	-49.3	-32.0
5.5	8.2	5.3		7.0			11.2	6.8	5.2
(61) 1.7	(55) 2.8	(81) 2.1	EBIT/Interest	(10) 3.5		(20) 2.1	(20) 3.0	(19) 1.6	
.8	1.3	1.0		1.6			-.4	.6	.8
			Net Profit + Depr., Dep., Amort./Cur. Mat. L/T/D						
.7	.5	.5		.7	.2		.5	.6	.7
1.6	1.2	1.3	Fixed/Worth	2.0	1.3		1.2	1.2	2.0
4.7	2.7	3.3		-3.4	10.1		2.2	2.8	7.3
.8	.7	.6		.3	.1		.5	.9	1.3
2.1	1.5	1.5	Debt/Worth	1.5	.7		1.3	1.6	2.6
6.8	3.6	4.2		-4.7	9.9		2.7	4.1	10.6
21.8	24.4	18.9			32.7		21.1	22.4	12.4
(68) 6.3	(66) 7.8	(94) 6.8	% Profit Before Taxes/Tangible Net Worth		(12) 14.7		(25) 4.9	(20) 7.2	(21) 7.2
.1	1.5	.6			-4.0		-1.7	-2.3	-1.6
6.5	9.3	7.7		13.1	12.4		10.9	6.3	4.1
1.5	3.6	2.7	% Profit Before Taxes/Total Assets	4.4	1.8		2.7	3.3	2.2
-.1	.6	.1		.3	-3.7		-.5	-.9	.1
7.1	6.7	6.0		2.4	92.9		7.4	19.7	5.4
3.2	3.2	2.6	Sales/Net Fixed Assets	.9	3.5		3.1	3.1	2.5
1.8	2.2	1.6		.1	1.3		1.6	2.1	1.9
2.7	2.4	2.3		1.7	2.4		2.3	3.2	2.0
1.8	1.6	1.5	Sales/Total Assets	.2	1.1		1.6	1.7	1.5
1.0	1.0	.9		.1	.7		.8	1.2	1.1
1.7	1.4	1.7		1.5	1.3		1.6	1.4	1.7
(72) 2.8	(62) 2.3	(103) 2.6	% Depr., Dep., Amort./Sales	3.1	(12) 2.9		2.6	(21) 2.4	(21) 2.7
3.8	3.3	4.0		37.3	4.3		3.8	3.3	4.1
		3.5	% Officers', Directors' Owners' Comp/Sales						
	(16) 4.7								
		16.0							
935974M	1557869M	2511451M	Net Sales ($)	4518M	26603M	31723M	205062M	370372M	1873173M
561338M	1109416M	2190039M	Total Assets ($)	19770M	31633M	22631M	385880M	238213M	1491912M

© RMA 2007   M = $ thousand   MM = $ million
See Pages 11 through 21 for Explanation of Ratios and Data

Current Data Sorted by Assets   Comparative Historical Data

0-500M	500M-2MM	2-10MM	10-50MM	50-100MM	100-250MM	Type of Statement	4/1/02-3/31/03	4/1/03-3/31/04
3	27	76	65	8	10	Unqualified	218	184
	5		2			Reviewed	14	11
1	3	2				Compiled	9	28
2	6					Tax Returns	13	8
3	11	23	21	3		Other	63	81
	172 (4/1-9/30/06)		99 (10/1/06-3/31/07)				ALL	ALL
9	47	106	88	11	10	**NUMBER OF STATEMENTS**	317	312
%	%	%	%	%	%	**ASSETS**	%	%
	17.2	16.5	11.7	19.5	10.8	Cash & Equivalents	13.0	13.1
	17.4	18.7	17.1	12.7	13.3	Trade Receivables (net)	16.7	16.4
	.0	.2	.2	.1	.3	Inventory	.4	.3
	2.3	2.9	2.7	2.6	1.1	All Other Current	2.9	4.9
	37.0	38.3	31.6	34.9	25.5	Total Current	33.0	34.6
	55.2	50.4	54.0	38.6	47.3	Fixed Assets (net)	53.0	52.8
	1.3	1.5	2.5	6.4	1.6	Intangibles (net)	2.1	1.5
	6.5	9.9	11.9	20.1	25.6	All Other Non-Current	12.0	11.0
	100.0	100.0	100.0	100.0	100.0	Total	100.0	100.0
						LIABILITIES		
	5.3	3.1	4.5	2.9	1.8	Notes Payable-Short Term	4.8	3.5
	2.6	4.2	2.6	2.3	3.3	Cur. Mat.-L.T.D.	2.3	2.6
	5.1	5.8	4.9	12.1	5.8	Trade Payables	5.9	5.4
	.0	.2	.1	.0	.0	Income Taxes Payable	.0	.0
	19.1	12.1	10.2	7.1	4.6	All Other Current	15.6	14.1
	32.2	25.3	22.2	24.4	15.7	Total Current	28.6	25.7
	42.1	28.8	32.4	22.9	38.1	Long-Term Debt	34.2	31.3
	.0	.0	.0	.0	.0	Deferred Taxes	.4	.1
	5.0	2.3	5.4	10.6	8.4	All Other Non-Current	2.7	6.4
	20.7	43.5	40.0	42.1	37.8	Net Worth	34.1	36.5
	100.0	100.0	100.0	100.0	100.0	Total Liabilties & Net Worth	100.0	100.0
						INCOME DATA		
	100.0	100.0	100.0	100.0	100.0	Net Sales	100.0	100.0
						Gross Profit		
	92.5	95.0	95.2	98.9	98.0	Operating Expenses	96.0	95.4
	7.5	5.0	4.8	1.1	2.0	Operating Profit	4.0	4.6
	5.1	1.3	2.5	-1.3	-.1	All Other Expenses (net)	4.0	2.5
	2.4	3.7	2.3	2.4	2.1	Profit Before Taxes	.0	2.1
						RATIOS		
	2.7	2.3	2.3	2.4	2.7		2.3	2.5
	1.0	1.4	1.4	1.3	2.0	Current	1.4	1.4
	.6	1.0	.9	.9	1.0		.9	.9
	2.7	2.2	2.0	2.2	2.4		2.2	2.0
	.9	1.3	1.2	1.3	1.9	Quick	(311) 1.3	1.3
	.6	.9	.8	.7	1.0		.7	.8
	0 UND	20 18.1	29 12.6	6 56.8	32 11.3		13 27.8	13 28.5
	20 18.5	34 10.8	41 8.8	38 9.6	45 8.1	Sales/Receivables	34 10.8	31 11.6
	35 10.3	45 8.1	59 6.2	70 5.2	77 4.8		51 7.1	47 7.7
						Cost of Sales/Inventory		
						Cost of Sales/Payables		
	7.8	7.1	5.3	7.3	3.7		6.7	7.2
	-999.8	19.8	16.6	20.0	8.9	Sales/Working Capital	19.3	16.1
	-20.7	-580.4	-69.0	-40.8	NM		-43.6	-76.8
	6.9	6.3	4.3				3.7	3.9
	(33) 1.8	(83) 2.8	(81) 2.1			EBIT/Interest	(247) 1.4	(233) 1.8
	.9	.9	1.0				.3	.8
						Net Profit + Depr., Dep.,		3.5
						Amort./Cur. Mat. L/T/D	(11)	2.1
								1.0
	.6	.7	.8	.5	.6		.8	.7
	2.4	1.3	1.6	.8	.9	Fixed/Worth	1.4	1.4
	32.5	2.1	3.0	5.2	NM		4.5	4.6
	.9	.7	.8	.6	.4		.6	.6
	3.2	1.4	1.9	1.4	1.4	Debt/Worth	1.5	1.6
	-711.0	2.9	4.4	6.8	NM		5.9	6.4
	31.1	19.0	17.3			% Profit Before Taxes/Tangible	15.0	18.4
	(35) 7.9	(97) 9.1	(83) 4.9			Net Worth	(276) 2.8	(274) 4.7
	-1.1	1.2	.2				-4.9	-2.0
	11.8	9.1	4.6	10.5	6.1	% Profit Before Taxes/Total	5.2	6.5
	2.6	3.8	1.8	2.8	2.7	Assets	.8	1.6
	-.8	-.2	.1	.1	-1.8		-2.1	-1.0
	12.5	7.2	4.3	3.8	3.6		4.9	5.9
	2.9	3.1	2.2	1.8	1.7	Sales/Net Fixed Assets	2.4	2.6
	1.5	1.8	1.2	1.6	1.0		1.1	1.3
	4.2	2.4	1.8	1.3	1.2		2.2	2.2
	1.6	1.6	1.2	1.1	.9	Sales/Total Assets	1.3	1.4
	.9	1.0	.7	.7	.5		.6	.8
	1.1	1.4	1.9	2.8	2.5		2.0	2.1
	(43) 2.1	(100) 2.4	(84) 2.8	3.2	4.0	% Depr., Dep., Amort./Sales	(299) 3.2	(283) 3.4
	5.4	3.7	5.3	4.0	6.3		5.6	5.3
						% Officers', Directors'	4.4	2.4
						Owners' Comp/Sales	(40) 8.0	(32) 6.1
							15.6	14.5
9035M	157650M	1057819M	2261626M	1275821M	1201920M	Net Sales ($)	4204164M	4267103M
1991M	58420M	597100M	1667512M	747934M	1382492M	Total Assets ($)	4743203M	4628088M

M = $ thousand   MM = $ million
See Pages 11 through 21 for Explanation of Ratios and Data

Comparative Historical Data | Current Data Sorted by Sales

Type of Statement	4/1/04-3/31/05 ALL	4/1/05-3/31/06 ALL	4/1/06-3/31/07 ALL	0-1MM	1-3MM	3-5MM	5-10MM	10-25MM	25MM & OVER
Unqualified	193	170	189	10	22	19	36	57	45
Reviewed	11	9	7	1	1	1	2	2	
Compiled	14	6	6	1	3		1	1	
Tax Returns	8	13	8	1	3	1	2	1	
Other	64	86	61	7	10	5	10	21	8
				172 (4/1-9/30/06)			99 (10/1/06-3/31/07)		
NUMBER OF STATEMENTS	290	284	271	20	39	26	51	82	53
ASSETS	%	%	%	%	%	%	%	%	%
Cash & Equivalents	14.3	15.0	15.3	16.1	18.2	13.1	16.9	14.6	13.5
Trade Receivables (net)	15.2	16.2	17.5	9.2	8.4	17.9	17.2	20.3	23.4
Inventory	.2	.1	.2	.0	.3	.0	.1	.3	.3
All Other Current	2.5	4.1	2.9	1.8	3.0	1.7	1.8	4.0	3.4
Total Current	32.2	35.5	36.0	27.0	29.9	32.7	36.0	39.2	40.5
Fixed Assets (net)	55.3	52.7	51.4	65.2	61.3	57.0	52.8	45.6	43.6
Intangibles (net)	1.4	1.2	1.9	.6	1.1	.6	2.8	1.8	3.1
All Other Non-Current	11.1	10.6	10.7	7.2	7.7	9.7	8.4	13.4	12.8
Total	100.0	100.0	100.0	100.0	100.0	100.0	100.0	100.0	100.0
LIABILITIES									
Notes Payable-Short Term	3.5	5.4	4.3	8.6	2.3	4.4	4.5	3.6	4.8
Cur. Mat.-L.T.D.	2.9	2.8	3.2	1.2	2.8	2.7	4.7	3.0	3.4
Trade Payables	5.2	5.5	5.8	2.1	4.7	4.0	4.9	6.2	9.3
Income Taxes Payable	.0	.1	.1	.0	.0	.2	.0	.1	.1
All Other Current	12.5	11.8	12.8	8.8	12.3	8.7	14.2	14.5	12.6
Total Current	24.1	25.6	26.2	20.8	22.1	20.0	28.2	27.4	30.2
Long-Term Debt	34.6	31.7	32.0	26.9	54.1	31.7	25.9	28.6	28.9
Deferred Taxes	.0	.0	.0	.0	.0	.0	.1	.0	.1
All Other Non-Current	4.7	5.1	4.4	2.9	5.0	1.8	7.1	2.7	6.0
Net Worth	36.6	37.5	37.4	49.5	18.7	46.6	38.7	41.3	34.8
Total Liabilties & Net Worth	100.0	100.0	100.0	100.0	100.0	100.0	100.0	100.0	100.0
INCOME DATA									
Net Sales	100.0	100.0	100.0	100.0	100.0	100.0	100.0	100.0	100.0
Gross Profit									
Operating Expenses	94.7	95.0	94.8	82.4	92.5	97.0	95.7	96.1	97.2
Operating Profit	5.3	5.0	5.2	17.6	7.5	3.0	4.3	3.9	2.8
All Other Expenses (net)	2.2	2.3	2.4	12.6	6.2	1.1	1.1	.6	.2
Profit Before Taxes	3.1	2.7	2.8	5.0	1.3	1.9	3.1	3.2	2.7
RATIOS									
Current	2.4	2.8	2.3	2.5	2.9	2.6	2.4	2.2	2.1
	1.5	1.6	1.4	.7	1.5	1.4	1.3	1.5	1.3
	.9	1.0	.9	.2	.8	.9	.8	1.0	1.0
Quick	2.3	2.4	2.1	2.5	2.8	2.6	2.4	1.8	2.0
	1.4	1.4	1.3	.7	1.5	1.4	1.3	1.3	1.2
	.8	.8	.8	.2	.6	.9	.7	.9	.9
Sales/Receivables	10 35.7	17 21.0	18 20.5	0 UND	1 604.0	23 15.9	20 18.2	22 16.8	31 11.7
	30 12.3	34 10.8	35 10.4	0 UND	28 13.2	39 9.3	35 10.6	35 10.5	46 7.9
	45 8.1	51 7.2	50 7.3	32 11.4	41 8.8	53 6.8	45 8.1	45 8.1	73 5.0
Cost of Sales/Inventory									
Cost of Sales/Payables									
Sales/Working Capital	7.2	5.6	6.6	7.5	4.7	4.2	6.7	7.9	7.4
	18.1	14.7	20.3	-113.1	18.4	21.2	23.8	19.8	19.3
	-84.3	UND	-58.3	-3.7	-26.6	-66.3	-34.4	-502.3	-465.6
EBIT/Interest	4.9	5.7	5.1		3.4	4.0	6.5	8.0	5.2
	(226) 1.9	(229) 2.3	(222) 2.2		(30) 1.4	(19) 1.8	(45) 2.3	(70) 2.8	(49) 2.1
	.8	1.2	1.0		.8	-.6	.8	1.1	1.2
Net Profit + Depr., Dep., Amort./Cur. Mat. L/T/D		7.7	4.7						
		(11) 2.6	(15) 1.4						
		1.9	.7						
Fixed/Worth	.8	.6	.7	.6	1.1	.7	.7	.6	.7
	1.5	1.4	1.4	1.4	2.6	1.1	1.4	1.2	1.4
	3.8	3.3	3.2	3.4	-77.5	2.8	3.1	2.1	3.3
Debt/Worth	.7	.6	.8	.1	1.0	.4	.5	.6	1.2
	1.6	1.5	1.6	1.6	3.4	1.0	1.5	1.5	2.0
	4.8	4.1	4.2	3.6	-79.2	3.3	6.5	3.5	5.6
% Profit Before Taxes/Tangible Net Worth	15.4	16.0	20.0	19.6	15.2	13.2	20.0	19.5	24.0
	(251) 5.1	(251) 6.5	(238) 6.9	4.7	(27) 4.9	(23) 6.1	(41) 7.5	(79) 8.1	(48) 9.6
	-.7	1.1	.2	-4.3	.4	-1.1	-.5	1.6	.3
% Profit Before Taxes/Total Assets	6.7	6.5	7.6	8.9	5.4	5.9	9.8	7.8	6.8
	2.2	2.2	2.9	1.4	2.2	1.6	2.7	3.9	2.6
	-.5	.2	-.1	-2.4	-.5	-3.1	-.4	.5	.1
Sales/Net Fixed Assets	4.9	5.7	6.3	21.0	3.2	4.0	5.0	7.9	6.5
	2.4	2.5	2.8	.8	1.7	2.0	2.5	3.4	3.7
	1.0	1.3	1.5	.2	.6	.9	1.1	2.1	2.1
Sales/Total Assets	2.2	2.2	2.2	1.5	1.6	2.1	2.6	2.5	2.6
	1.3	1.3	1.4	.4	1.0	1.1	1.4	1.7	1.6
	.7	.7	.8	.1	.3	.6	.8	1.2	1.1
% Depr., Dep., Amort./Sales	2.0	1.7	1.5	1.8	2.3	1.8	1.6	1.4	1.5
	(264) 3.2	(264) 3.0	(254) 2.6	(12) 5.1	(36) 5.1	(25) 3.7	(50) 2.6	(80) 2.3	(51) 2.5
	5.9	5.3	4.6	49.5	8.6	6.5	4.1	3.1	3.4
% Officers', Directors' Owners' Comp/Sales	1.0	3.1	2.8						
	(22) 7.2	(33) 5.8	(20) 6.3						
	21.6	9.7	10.0						
Net Sales ($)	4039469M	4597753M	5963871M	9233M	73770M	101962M	377800M	1349425M	4051681M
Total Assets ($)	3964603M	4188300M	4455449M	34353M	178225M	110975M	438735M	899185M	2793976M

M = $ thousand   MM = $ million
See Pages 11 through 21 for Explanation of Ratios and Data

Current Data Sorted by Assets   Comparative Historical Data

	0-500M	500M-2MM	2-10MM	10-50MM	50-100MM	100-250MM	Type of Statement	4/1/02-3/31/03 ALL	4/1/03-3/31/04 ALL
	2	6	33	85	36	27	Unqualified	114	125
	4	12	11	1	1		Reviewed	22	27
	3	8	15	4			Compiled	38	59
	1	4	7	1			Tax Returns	17	15
	6	12	36	38	15	7	Other	91	97
		129 (4/1-9/30/06)		246 (10/1/06-3/31/07)					
	16	42	102	129	52	34	NUMBER OF STATEMENTS	282	323
	%	%	%	%	%	%	**ASSETS**	%	%
	18.0	10.7	11.1	9.4	8.6	13.9	Cash & Equivalents	9.5	10.1
	12.1	23.7	10.0	6.6	4.4	3.4	Trade Receivables (net)	12.6	14.4
	.0	.1	.2	.2	.1	.3	Inventory	.6	.4
	13.4	2.8	2.4	2.8	3.2	1.8	All Other Current	2.5	3.6
	43.5	37.4	23.7	19.0	16.4	19.4	Total Current	25.2	28.6
	42.4	49.3	65.9	62.2	62.3	53.4	Fixed Assets (net)	60.2	56.3
	5.5	7.3	3.1	1.9	1.5	2.7	Intangibles (net)	1.7	1.9
	8.6	5.9	7.3	16.9	19.8	24.5	All Other Non-Current	12.9	13.2
	100.0	100.0	100.0	100.0	100.0	100.0	Total	100.0	100.0
							LIABILITIES		
	5.1	9.2	2.3	2.4	1.0	.7	Notes Payable-Short Term	5.1	5.7
	3.7	2.5	2.0	2.0	1.7	1.5	Cur. Mat.-L.T.D.	3.0	4.1
	17.2	9.4	5.9	2.9	3.0	2.0	Trade Payables	5.9	7.4
	1.9	.0	.2	.0	.0	.0	Income Taxes Payable	.0	.1
	66.6	26.2	10.2	5.9	6.3	6.5	All Other Current	13.6	12.4
	94.5	47.4	20.6	13.3	11.9	10.7	Total Current	27.7	29.7
	36.8	47.7	61.6	49.8	43.9	39.2	Long-Term Debt	49.1	45.9
	.0	.1	.1	.2	.0	.4	Deferred Taxes	.3	.1
	33.0	6.0	4.3	14.6	35.0	24.6	All Other Non-Current	11.9	11.9
	-64.3	-1.3	13.4	22.0	9.1	25.0	Net Worth	11.0	12.4
	100.0	100.0	100.0	100.0	100.0	100.0	Total Liabilities & Net Worth	100.0	100.0
							INCOME DATA		
	100.0	100.0	100.0	100.0	100.0	100.0	Net Sales	100.0	100.0
							Gross Profit		
	96.0	89.0	87.1	92.3	95.2	92.3	Operating Expenses	90.0	91.8
	4.0	11.0	12.9	7.7	4.8	7.7	Operating Profit	10.0	8.2
	2.8	6.3	9.3	5.9	3.3	3.8	All Other Expenses (net)	7.3	5.0
	1.2	4.7	3.7	1.8	1.5	3.8	Profit Before Taxes	2.8	3.2
							RATIOS		
	1.6	1.9	2.2	2.7	2.4	3.7		2.0	2.2
	.8	1.1	1.2	1.7	1.5	1.5	Current	1.2	1.4
	.1	.3	.6	1.0	1.0	.5		.6	.7
	.9	1.7	1.8	2.3	2.0	3.0		1.8	1.9
	.5	1.0	1.1	1.4	1.3	1.0	Quick	1.0	1.1
	.1	.2	.5	.7	.8	.4		.4	.6
	0 UND	0 UND	1 488.5	13 27.9	14 25.5	5 67.6		4 88.3	8 44.4
	2 213.0	15 23.8	12 30.1	27 13.7	26 14.0	19 18.7	Sales/Receivables	21 17.6	26 14.0
	8 43.2	45 8.1	38 9.6	43 8.4	37 9.9	42 8.6		38 9.6	43 8.5
							Cost of Sales/Inventory		
							Cost of Sales/Payables		
	294.7	11.1	8.7	4.5	4.1	3.0		8.6	7.7
	-30.0	313.8	53.5	11.7	12.3	15.5	Sales/Working Capital	37.6	24.8
	-8.0	-6.9	-14.7	-219.8	NM	-9.6		-14.7	-24.2
		5.3	3.7	3.6	2.5	3.9		3.4	3.3
		(28) 2.2	(74) 2.0	(111) 1.7	(46) 1.4	(27) 2.3	EBIT/Interest	(233) 1.6	(265) 1.5
		1.0	1.0	.9	.8	.7		.6	.3
								5.0	4.1
							Net Profit + Depr., Dep., Amort./Cur. Mat. L/T/D	(15) 1.5	(21) 2.9
								.7	2.2
	.7	.8	1.3	1.3	2.0	1.5		1.3	1.1
	3.1	8.0	9.3	2.6	7.1	3.2	Fixed/Worth	4.0	3.6
	-.4	-2.1	-6.5	110.0	-4.2	14.7		-12.8	-22.4
	.9	1.4	1.4	1.5	2.5	1.6		1.5	1.5
	8.8	10.4	9.9	3.4	9.1	4.6	Debt/Worth	5.6	5.5
	-1.9	-6.2	-8.4	140.8	-9.2	29.5		-14.8	-26.5
	593.3	92.2	59.1	16.5	14.5	26.3		30.9	38.1
	(10) 95.6	(23) 39.0	(67) 21.8	(99) 4.5	(30) 6.0	(28) 7.1	% Profit Before Taxes/Tangible Net Worth	(195) 10.0	(229) 9.4
	4.9	16.1	2.2	-2.8	1.8	2.2		-.9	-1.8
	34.8	16.7	10.4	3.7	2.5	3.8		6.3	6.6
	17.4	4.7	3.9	1.6	.9	1.4	% Profit Before Taxes/Total Assets	1.3	1.6
	-14.7	-1.7	-.4	-.6	-.5	-.6		-1.4	-1.6
	41.2	31.3	3.2	1.7	.9	1.1		4.8	6.3
	20.3	4.1	1.0	.8	.4	.5	Sales/Net Fixed Assets	1.2	1.4
	7.4	.8	.5	.5	.3	.3		.5	.6
	9.8	4.9	1.6	.8	.5	.4		1.9	1.9
	6.4	2.4	.7	.5	.3	.3	Sales/Total Assets	.8	.8
	3.6	.7	.4	.3	.2	.2		.3	.4
	.8	.7	1.5	4.7	6.7	6.0		2.2	2.2
	(12) 1.3	(38) 2.2	(101) 5.4	(124) 7.6	(51) 10.9	(32) 9.5	% Depr., Dep., Amort./Sales	(267) 5.2	(307) 4.5
	2.2	7.0	11.3	12.1	14.6	12.6		10.5	10.0
			1.5	1.7				2.5	2.4
			(12) 4.2	(14) 8.7			% Officers', Directors' Owners' Comp/Sales	(52) 6.0	(58) 5.1
			13.4	37.9				12.5	10.9
	22425M	147222M	520369M	2200466M	2776288M	1913931M	Net Sales ($)	3702986M	4453121M
	3983M	54647M	500676M	3369265M	3761236M	4787588M	Total Assets ($)	6171342M	6742938M

© RMA 2007

M = $ thousand   MM = $ million
See Pages 11 through 21 for Explanation of Ratios and Data

Comparative Historical Data				Current Data Sorted by Sales					
			Type of Statement	6	20	7	29	87	40
144	145	189	Unqualified	6	20	7	29	87	40
24	19	29	Reviewed	4	9	8	6		2
48	30	30	Compiled	4	13	4	7	2	
23	19	13	Tax Returns	4	5		2	1	1
128	145	114	Other	9	22	9	19	35	20
4/1/04-3/31/05 ALL	4/1/05-3/31/06 ALL	4/1/06-3/31/07 ALL		129 (4/1-9/30/06)			246 (10/1/06-3/31/07)		
				0-1MM	1-3MM	3-5MM	5-10MM	10-25MM	25MM & OVER
367	358	375	**NUMBER OF STATEMENTS**	27	69	28	63	125	63
%	%	%	**ASSETS**	%	%	%	%	%	%
10.2	10.9	10.7	Cash & Equivalents	8.1	8.8	8.5	13.3	10.4	12.9
11.8	11.7	9.1	Trade Receivables (net)	2.9	3.6	15.6	18.0	6.9	10.2
.5	.4	.2	Inventory	.0	.2	.1	.1	.1	.3
2.1	2.7	3.1	All Other Current	3.1	4.2	1.3	4.0	2.0	4.3
24.7	25.7	23.1	Total Current	14.1	16.8	25.5	35.4	19.4	27.6
59.1	57.5	60.1	Fixed Assets (net)	75.7	73.0	63.1	48.4	59.0	52.1
2.2	2.2	3.0	Intangibles (net)	2.7	4.8	4.6	2.6	2.4	2.1
14.0	14.6	13.8	All Other Non-Current	7.5	5.4	6.8	13.7	19.2	18.2
100.0	100.0	100.0	Total	100.0	100.0	100.0	100.0	100.0	100.0
			LIABILITIES						
5.0	4.9	2.9	Notes Payable-Short Term	4.8	1.0	7.1	3.4	1.9	3.8
3.4	3.2	2.0	Cur. Mat.-L.T.D.	3.1	1.8	2.7	2.0	1.9	1.9
5.5	6.2	5.0	Trade Payables	1.2	4.5	8.4	9.1	3.1	5.2
.1	.0	.1	Income Taxes Payable	.0	.4	.2	.2	.0	.0
11.8	11.1	12.1	All Other Current	15.2	18.4	14.3	16.0	5.9	11.0
25.8	25.5	22.1	Total Current	24.3	26.1	32.6	30.8	12.8	22.0
52.0	47.4	50.5	Long-Term Debt	82.1	70.6	49.2	39.3	44.1	39.2
.1	.2	.1	Deferred Taxes	.0	.1	.2	.2	.2	.1
10.4	13.5	15.4	All Other Non-Current	21.5	2.6	10.9	9.4	26.5	12.6
11.6	13.4	11.9	Net Worth	-27.8	.6	7.1	20.3	16.3	26.1
100.0	100.0	100.0	Total Liabilities & Net Worth	100.0	100.0	100.0	100.0	100.0	100.0
			INCOME DATA						
100.0	100.0	100.0	Net Sales	100.0	100.0	100.0	100.0	100.0	100.0
			Gross Profit						
91.2	91.6	91.1	Operating Expenses	76.4	84.9	92.6	92.9	95.3	93.1
8.8	8.4	8.9	Operating Profit	23.6	15.1	7.4	7.1	4.7	6.9
6.1	5.5	6.2	All Other Expenses (net)	17.4	14.0	5.1	3.5	3.3	1.8
2.7	2.9	2.8	Profit Before Taxes	6.2	1.1	2.3	3.6	1.4	5.1
			RATIOS						
2.5	2.3	2.4	Current	1.5	2.2	1.7	3.1	2.5	2.0
1.2	1.3	1.3		.4	1.0	1.1	1.5	1.7	1.3
.6	.8	.7		.1	.5	.7	.7	1.1	.8
2.2	2.1	2.0	Quick	1.4	1.7	1.6	2.3	2.3	1.8
1.0	1.1	1.1		.3	.7	.9	1.3	1.5	1.1
.5	.6	.5		.1	.3	.5	.5	1.0	.6
4 97.9	6 57.6	4 83.1	Sales/Receivables	0 UND	0 844.8	2 164.5	14 26.2	14 25.4	17 21.8
22 16.9	23 16.0	22 16.4		0 UND	4 99.4	21 17.3	28 13.0	27 13.7	31 11.7
41 8.9	37 10.0	41 9.0		1 298.3	14 25.6	46 7.9	44 8.3	40 9.2	46 7.9
			Cost of Sales/Inventory						
			Cost of Sales/Payables						
6.4	7.5	5.6	Sales/Working Capital	9.1	9.6	9.0	5.1	4.3	6.4
37.7	29.8	24.5		-6.8	231.6	73.2	22.6	10.4	24.5
-15.2	-22.3	-19.6		-2.8	-9.5	-21.7	-17.3	57.4	-24.5
4.2	3.7	3.5	EBIT/Interest	3.9	3.2	3.0	5.4	3.3	3.9
(301) 1.8	(288) 1.9	(295) 1.8		(13) 1.9	(42) 1.6	(23) 2.6	(51) 2.2	(110) 1.5	(56) 2.4
.8	.8	.9		1.2	1.0	.9	.7	.9	1.2
5.4	2.9	6.7	Net Profit + Depr., Dep., Amort./Cur. Mat. L/T/D						
(16) 1.7	(14) 2.0	(12) 2.7							
1.1	1.2	1.2							
1.2	1.2	1.3	Fixed/Worth	4.1	2.3	1.9	.6	1.4	1.1
4.1	4.3	4.1		9.4	20.2	14.9	2.2	3.6	2.1
-7.4	-8.6	-8.0		-4.2	-5.0	-4.6	67.6	-5.7	5.4
1.4	1.5	1.6	Debt/Worth	3.6	2.2	.8	.9	1.7	1.6
5.8	6.2	6.5		10.7	19.3	24.8	2.4	5.2	3.1
-10.2	-14.3	-12.8		-5.3	-7.0	-7.2	107.5	-9.3	8.3
36.7	41.9	36.3	% Profit Before Taxes/Tangible Net Worth	56.8	54.4	73.2	32.3	13.0	45.0
(237) 9.7	(241) 11.7	(257) 9.5		(14) 29.1	(40) 16.5	(16) 24.1	(48) 10.5	(83) 6.0	(56) 11.7
.0	1.8	1.8		-.7	-3.6	5.8	-4.4	-.2	2.8
7.0	6.6	6.0	% Profit Before Taxes/Total Assets	6.3	7.0	6.5	11.8	2.9	6.3
2.0	2.2	1.9		3.4	.9	2.3	3.0	1.2	3.2
-.8	-.8	-.5		-2.5	-2.5	-1.4	-1.3	-.5	1.1
4.1	4.5	2.3	Sales/Net Fixed Assets	1.0	1.4	10.1	18.1	1.5	3.2
.9	1.1	.8		.4	.7	1.2	1.8	.7	1.3
.5	.5	.4		.2	.3	.5	.6	.4	.7
1.6	1.8	1.2	Sales/Total Assets	.8	.9	2.4	3.1	.8	1.6
.6	.7	.5		.4	.5	.9	.9	.4	.7
.3	.3	.3		.2	.3	.4	.4	.3	.4
2.7	2.2	2.9	% Depr., Dep., Amort./Sales	7.0	4.1	2.1	1.0	5.2	1.9
(338) 7.0	(334) 5.9	(358) 7.0		(23) 16.5	(66) 9.2	(27) 4.7	(59) 4.2	(121) 8.7	(62) 4.3
11.6	11.0	12.3		27.7	17.2	7.6	8.6	13.3	8.6
2.0	1.9	1.5	% Officers', Directors' Owners' Comp/Sales				1.8	2.4	
(65) 6.1	(58) 5.8	(45) 3.6					(10) 4.3	(14) 10.4	
13.0	12.8	15.6					19.8	21.9	
4538644M	7275730M	7580701M	Net Sales ($)	13668M	131534M	114058M	474184M	1918160M	4929097M
8891402M	10707679M	12477395M	Total Assets ($)	49470M	339316M	193427M	857369M	5654219M	5383594M

© RMA 2007

M = $ thousand   MM = $ million
See Pages 11 through 21 for Explanation of Ratios and Data

Current Data Sorted by Assets | Comparative Historical Data

1	6	23	12	4	1	Type of Statement		22	33
	1	4				Unqualified		22	33
	1	4				Reviewed		3	3
2	1	4				Compiled		5	8
8	3	1				Tax Returns		6	12
5	7	14	7	3		Other		11	16
	34 (4/1-9/30/06)		73 (10/1/06-3/31/07)					4/1/02-3/31/03 ALL	4/1/03-3/31/04 ALL
0-500M	500M-2MM	2-10MM	10-50MM	50-100MM	100-250MM				
16	18	46	19	7	1	NUMBER OF STATEMENTS		47	72
%	%	%	%	%	%	ASSETS		%	%
12.8	19.3	8.9	6.5			Cash & Equivalents		11.7	18.2
10.7	19.1	5.2	6.6			Trade Receivables (net)		9.1	9.8
.0	.1	.1	.1			Inventory		.1	.4
7.9	5.2	1.0	1.1			All Other Current		2.0	2.0
31.5	43.7	15.2	14.3			Total Current		22.9	30.5
56.4	42.6	72.6	66.6			Fixed Assets (net)		61.4	54.7
5.8	3.5	2.5	.6			Intangibles (net)		2.7	2.9
6.3	10.2	9.7	18.5			All Other Non-Current		13.0	11.9
100.0	100.0	100.0	100.0			Total		100.0	100.0
						LIABILITIES			
4.4	4.3	1.4	1.3			Notes Payable-Short Term		3.7	8.3
3.9	2.9	4.4	2.6			Cur. Mat.-L.T.D.		6.2	5.9
9.0	11.3	2.8	1.8			Trade Payables		3.9	5.7
.0	.0	.0	.0			Income Taxes Payable		.7	.3
91.7	14.7	6.0	6.4			All Other Current		4.9	17.6
108.9	33.2	14.7	12.2			Total Current		19.4	37.8
21.0	40.9	59.4	53.2			Long-Term Debt		37.4	30.3
.0	.0	.1	.0			Deferred Taxes		.0	.0
7.2	.4	7.1	8.0			All Other Non-Current		10.4	13.2
-37.2	25.5	18.7	26.5			Net Worth		32.8	18.7
100.0	100.0	100.0	100.0			Total Liabilties & Net Worth		100.0	100.0
						INCOME DATA			
100.0	100.0	100.0	100.0			Net Sales		100.0	100.0
						Gross Profit			
97.6	94.0	82.1	86.2			Operating Expenses		90.2	94.2
2.4	6.0	17.9	13.8			Operating Profit		9.8	5.8
1.1	2.3	9.9	6.3			All Other Expenses (net)		6.0	3.2
1.3	3.7	8.0	7.6			Profit Before Taxes		3.9	2.5
						RATIOS			
2.1	2.8	2.9	2.0					3.1	2.4
.5	1.5	1.1	1.1			Current		1.2	1.1
.3	1.0	.4	.6					.7	.6
1.1	2.7	2.6	2.0					2.5	2.3
.5	1.2	1.1	.9			Quick		1.2	1.0
.1	.7	.4	.5					.5	.4
0 UND	0 UND	2 232.5	2 220.6					3 135.0	1 448.4
0 UND	20 18.5	11 33.9	17 22.1			Sales/Receivables		16 22.9	12 29.2
13 27.2	33 11.0	31 11.8	45 8.2					32 11.4	32 11.5
						Cost of Sales/Inventory			
						Cost of Sales/Payables			
20.4	5.9	7.8	11.7					6.9	9.9
-57.7	28.1	97.2	133.0			Sales/Working Capital		26.9	149.4
-5.7	NM	-10.1	-14.6					-16.6	-10.1
		31.1	5.7	4.0				3.2	7.5
	(12) 1.9	(31) 1.5	(12) 2.6			EBIT/Interest	(38)	1.6	(51) 2.0
		1.2	.8	.9				.9	.5
						Net Profit + Depr., Dep., Amort./Cur. Mat. L/T/D			
1.1	.2	1.3	1.0					1.1	.7
7.0	.7	6.3	2.9			Fixed/Worth		1.8	2.0
-2.8	-5.6	-17.9	-999.8					16.4	235.8
.5	.4	1.5	.6					.9	.7
34.8	1.8	7.3	3.4			Debt/Worth		3.6	2.5
-2.7	-7.1	-23.1	-999.8					22.1	-42.5
	46.5	23.9	36.8					19.8	36.9
(13) 23.9	(32) 12.8	(14) 12.6				% Profit Before Taxes/Tangible Net Worth	(37) 7.3	(53) 15.5	
	-3.0	-8.1	1.5					3.0	1.5
24.1	18.9	8.7	8.0					7.6	13.1
5.6	6.9	1.9	2.4			% Profit Before Taxes/Total Assets		2.3	3.0
-3.0	.2	-1.2	-1.1					-.4	-2.3
28.8	28.3	1.6	1.9					3.3	10.5
9.1	11.2	.7	.9			Sales/Net Fixed Assets		.9	2.2
2.4	1.6	.3	.4					.5	.7
10.0	3.9	1.0	1.0					1.9	3.7
4.4	2.3	.6	.5			Sales/Total Assets		.6	1.4
1.6	1.0	.3	.3					.3	.5
	.4	.8	2.6	3.5				2.6	1.8
(13) 2.1	(17) 1.8	(44) 6.1	7.4			% Depr., Dep., Amort./Sales	(39) 6.6	(62) 3.8	
	3.2	4.3	11.3	10.7				10.3	8.4
						% Officers', Directors' Owners' Comp/Sales		4.4	5.7
							(10) 6.6	(16) 11.1	
								12.4	17.5
15094M	61347M	176364M	329014M	212457M	54400M	Net Sales ($)		405093M	689225M
3562M	20954M	246049M	495415M	491044M	133245M	Total Assets ($)		887969M	945352M

M = $ thousand   MM = $ million
See Pages 11 through 21 for Explanation of Ratios and Data

Comparative Historical Data | Current Data Sorted by Sales

4/1/04-3/31/05 ALL	4/1/05-3/31/06 ALL	4/1/06-3/31/07 ALL	Type of Statement	0-1MM	1-3MM	3-5MM	5-10MM	10-25MM	25MM & OVER
33	30	47	Unqualified	5	6	15	5	9	7
1	3	5	Reviewed	1	1	2	1	1	
12	6	7	Compiled	3	3		1		
7	10	12	Tax Returns	7	3	2			
25	32	36	Other	8	13		7	6	2
				34 (4/1-9/30/06)			73 (10/1/06-3/31/07)		
NUMBER OF STATEMENTS 78	81	107		24	26	19	14	15	9
%	%	%	**ASSETS**	%	%	%	%	%	%
13.4	9.7	10.7	Cash & Equivalents	9.7	11.3	11.0	11.9	12.4	
9.4	8.1	8.6	Trade Receivables (net)	3.2	8.5	11.6	9.1	10.7	
.2	.1	.1	Inventory	.0	.0	.2	.1	.1	
3.5	2.7	2.8	All Other Current	5.4	2.4	2.9	.7	1.8	
26.6	20.5	22.1	Total Current	18.3	22.3	25.7	21.8	24.9	
58.8	64.3	62.4	Fixed Assets (net)	68.2	66.4	58.2	64.3	59.4	
1.9	2.0	2.8	Intangibles (net)	4.4	4.4	2.1	1.2	.3	
12.8	13.2	12.7	All Other Non-Current	9.1	6.9	14.1	12.6	15.4	
100.0	100.0	100.0	Total	100.0	100.0	100.0	100.0	100.0	
			LIABILITIES						
12.2	3.4	2.3	Notes Payable-Short Term	1.6	2.5	3.7	1.4	2.0	
7.6	2.2	4.5	Cur. Mat.-L.T.D.	3.7	6.0	1.6	5.4	1.5	
4.4	3.7	5.0	Trade Payables	1.2	5.0	7.2	10.3	4.0	
.1	.0	.0	Income Taxes Payable	.0	.0	.1	.0	.0	
10.5	8.4	20.8	All Other Current	48.9	6.1	19.9	16.5	13.1	
34.7	17.6	32.6	Total Current	55.5	19.6	32.4	33.6	20.6	
49.2	56.0	47.5	Long-Term Debt	50.6	53.5	52.3	39.6	46.4	
.1	.0	.0	Deferred Taxes	.0	.0	.1	.0	.0	
8.1	3.9	6.4	All Other Non-Current	8.7	6.0	1.5	8.1	8.9	
7.8	22.5	13.5	Net Worth	-14.8	20.8	13.7	18.7	24.0	
100.0	100.0	100.0	Total Liabilities & Net Worth	100.0	100.0	100.0	100.0	100.0	
			INCOME DATA						
100.0	100.0	100.0	Net Sales	100.0	100.0	100.0	100.0	100.0	
			Gross Profit						
92.5	91.0	88.0	Operating Expenses	84.1	85.9	89.0	88.8	93.2	
7.5	9.0	12.0	Operating Profit	15.9	14.1	11.0	11.2	6.8	
4.5	7.2	5.9	All Other Expenses (net)	8.9	10.8	3.6	4.3	1.5	
3.0	1.8	6.2	Profit Before Taxes	7.0	3.4	7.3	6.9	5.4	
			RATIOS						
2.7	2.5	2.1	Current	4.4	2.4	1.7	1.8	2.0	
1.3	1.2	1.1		1.1	.5	1.3	1.1	1.2	
.6	.4	.4		.4	.3	.8	.6	.5	
2.2	2.2	1.9	Quick	2.8	1.9	1.7	1.8	2.0	
1.1	.8	1.0		1.0	.5	1.2	1.0	1.1	
.4	.3	.4		.2	.3	.7	.3	.5	
2 157.3	0 990.7	1 349.0	Sales/Receivables	0 UND	0 UND	6 58.0	2 219.6	13 28.3	
15 23.6	10 37.7	13 27.1		1 245.5	2 188.4	20 18.6	16 22.2	23 16.0	
29 12.7	33 11.1	32 11.3		13 27.5	17 22.0	38 9.5	42 8.7	32 11.3	
			Cost of Sales/Inventory						
			Cost of Sales/Payables						
7.0	7.5	10.4	Sales/Working Capital	10.9	7.4	9.9	12.0	8.8	
27.7	68.8	133.0		379.4	-23.2	34.5	NM	67.8	
-15.6	-10.1	-9.1		-8.6	-7.5	-49.1	-29.7	-8.3	
8.0	4.9	5.8	EBIT/Interest	2.6	8.6	1.8	21.8	3.7	
(60) 2.4	(67) 1.8	(71) 1.9		(12) 1.5	(13) 2.3	(15) 1.0	(11) 7.4	(11) 2.4	
.9	.7	.9		.7	1.1	.5	1.5	1.1	
			Net Profit + Depr., Dep., Amort./Cur. Mat. L/T/D						
1.0	1.1	1.0	Fixed/Worth	4.2	.8	.6	1.1	1.0	
1.9	2.8	5.2		9.7	8.5	2.2	2.4	3.7	
-17.4	-47.7	-17.3		-4.8	-8.3	-18.9	-3.9	83.4	
.8	.9	.8	Debt/Worth	3.5	.6	.5	.9	1.2	
2.9	6.4	5.2		14.6	NM	1.7	2.3	4.3	
-26.6	-71.8	-21.3		-6.8	-9.0	-23.7	-72.3	104.0	
40.3	41.3	33.7	% Profit Before Taxes/Tangible Net Worth	44.4	30.8	23.2	56.4	88.9	
(57) 13.1	(60) 9.6	(74) 13.4		(16) 10.2	(13) 3.9	(14) -.6	(10) 23.5	(13) 17.9	
3.2	-.6	-3.3		-12.3	-12.4	-8.7	16.0	5.6	
8.1	10.5	8.9	% Profit Before Taxes/Total Assets	7.3	8.5	8.9	22.5	10.7	
2.4	2.0	3.4		2.2	1.6	1.2	11.0	3.4	
-.6	-1.4	-1.0		-3.0	-2.7	-1.5	1.7	1.2	
7.9	2.4	5.0	Sales/Net Fixed Assets	5.3	22.1	11.2	10.6	2.6	
2.0	.8	1.4		1.2	.7	1.9	1.5	.9	
.5	.5	.5		.2	.3	.8	.7	.5	
2.8	1.4	1.8	Sales/Total Assets	3.7	2.5	1.9	2.9	1.8	
1.2	.7	.9		.9	.6	1.1	1.0	.8	
.4	.4	.4		.2	.3	.6	.5	.3	
1.8	2.9	2.0	% Depr., Dep., Amort./Sales	2.5	1.5	.8	1.5	2.7	
(70) 4.3	(77) 7.0	(101) 4.8		(22) 5.5	(22) 5.3	3.5	4.7	7.4	
10.1	11.0	9.8		14.2	14.5	8.6	8.2	11.3	
2.8	2.3	4.1	% Officers', Directors' Owners' Comp/Sales						
(20) 7.5	(15) 5.2	(17) 8.7							
15.2	8.7	12.0							
845900M	677424M	848676M	Net Sales ($)	12704M	47888M	78971M	98560M	243016M	367537M
1388608M	1368701M	1390269M	Total Assets ($)	48002M	103953M	124562M	121991M	484651M	507110M

Current Data Sorted by Assets | Comparative Historical Data

						Type of Statement		
3	12	47	34	4	2	Unqualified	23	28
2		4	1			Reviewed		
1		4				Compiled	1	5
3	5					Tax Returns	1	2
8	8	25	12	2	2	Other	5	13
	91 (4/1-9/30/06)		89 (10/1/06-3/31/07)				4/1/02-3/31/03 ALL	4/1/03-3/31/04 ALL
0-500M	500M-2MM	2-10MM	10-50MM	50-100MM	100-250MM			
17	25	80	48	6	4	NUMBER OF STATEMENTS	30	48
%	%	%	%	%	%	ASSETS	%	%
16.2	21.6	14.3	14.7			Cash & Equivalents	14.2	12.7
20.2	13.5	14.6	13.3			Trade Receivables (net)	13.5	13.2
.0	.0	.3	.1			Inventory	.1	.1
6.6	6.5	3.2	1.9			All Other Current	7.3	5.1
43.0	41.7	32.4	30.1			Total Current	35.1	31.1
43.1	50.6	57.4	53.3			Fixed Assets (net)	51.6	53.2
6.4	2.8	2.3	1.7			Intangibles (net)	1.5	3.3
7.5	4.9	7.9	14.9			All Other Non-Current	11.8	12.4
100.0	100.0	100.0	100.0			Total	100.0	100.0
						LIABILITIES		
15.5	6.7	2.6	2.5			Notes Payable-Short Term	3.3	3.8
5.7	2.8	2.9	2.0			Cur. Mat.-L.T.D.	3.5	2.4
8.7	7.6	4.9	4.0			Trade Payables	5.3	4.5
.0	.1	.0	.0			Income Taxes Payable	.0	.0
31.4	11.8	9.9	12.0			All Other Current	13.3	7.7
61.4	28.9	20.4	20.5			Total Current	25.4	18.5
29.5	27.1	37.7	37.0			Long-Term Debt	36.4	29.8
.0	.0	.0	.0			Deferred Taxes	.0	.3
34.9	2.4	3.4	3.9			All Other Non-Current	14.5	2.7
-25.7	41.6	38.5	38.5			Net Worth	23.7	48.7
100.0	100.0	100.0	100.0			Total Liabilties & Net Worth	100.0	100.0
						INCOME DATA		
100.0	100.0	100.0	100.0			Net Sales	100.0	100.0
						Gross Profit		
98.0	96.0	92.3	93.5			Operating Expenses	92.3	94.0
2.0	4.0	7.7	6.5			Operating Profit	7.7	6.0
3.2	1.1	4.1	.9			All Other Expenses (net)	4.9	1.3
-1.1	2.9	3.6	5.5			Profit Before Taxes	2.8	4.7
						RATIOS		
1.9	3.3	2.8	2.4				4.2	2.8
.6	2.1	1.7	1.5			Current	1.9	1.5
.3	.9	1.0	1.0				.9	1.0
1.4	3.3	2.7	2.3				2.4	2.7
.6	1.5	1.4	1.4			Quick	1.5	1.5
.3	.6	.7	.9				.7	.8
0 UND	0 UND	5 69.8	22 16.9				0 UND	4 96.9
4 99.5	19 19.6	29 12.7	36 10.2			Sales/Receivables	24 15.5	24 15.5
29 12.5	31 11.8	41 9.0	48 7.6				43 8.5	41 8.9
						Cost of Sales/Inventory		
						Cost of Sales/Payables		
23.5	8.0	6.2	5.1				4.7	5.8
-30.5	15.2	14.4	15.0			Sales/Working Capital	20.9	16.9
-13.5	NM	465.8	-138.0				-244.9	-324.2
5.6	15.0	7.6	8.9				2.9	7.2
(15) 3.2	(18) 2.0	(64) 2.0	(39) 2.2			EBIT/Interest	(21) 1.8	(41) 2.0
.6	-.2	1.1	.9				.6	.7
						Net Profit + Depr., Dep., Amort./Cur. Mat. L/T/D		
.4	.8	.6	.7				.6	.6
130.0	1.1	1.8	1.2			Fixed/Worth	1.3	1.1
-.3	2.8	5.9	3.4				10.6	2.7
1.2	.5	.5	.6				.4	.4
154.0	1.3	1.7	1.5			Debt/Worth	2.1	1.3
-1.8	5.6	7.5	4.0				17.9	4.1
	34.6	20.5	17.5				38.1	23.9
(23) 13.7	(68) 6.9	(44) 7.8			% Profit Before Taxes/Tangible Net Worth	(25) 6.9	(43) 6.3
	-7.9	-1.7	-.9				-.6	-.5
66.6	17.1	7.7	6.0				6.4	7.9
16.6	2.5	3.1	3.8			% Profit Before Taxes/Total Assets	2.5	3.1
-.7	-.6	.2	-.4				-.2	-.6
66.6	16.4	4.7	3.6				7.3	5.6
18.8	4.4	2.1	2.5			Sales/Net Fixed Assets	3.4	2.9
2.9	2.3	.9	1.2				1.3	1.1
9.1	3.1	1.9	1.6				2.9	2.2
4.3	2.6	1.3	1.2			Sales/Total Assets	1.6	1.4
2.0	1.4	.6	.6				.7	.7
.7	1.7	2.0	2.2				2.5	2.0
(12) 2.3	(19) 2.8	(77) 3.2	(45) 3.2			% Depr., Dep., Amort./Sales	(27) 2.9	(45) 3.6
4.6	4.3	5.9	5.0				5.0	5.2
						% Officers', Directors' Owners' Comp/Sales		
19451M	80720M	563430M	1362785M	315986M	360286M	Net Sales ($)	487322M	507689M
4509M	30684M	376050M	1035407M	488688M	541763M	Total Assets ($)	425768M	371461M

M = $ thousand MM = $ million
See Pages 11 through 21 for Explanation of Ratios and Data

Comparative Historical Data				Current Data Sorted by Sales					
32	**56**	**102**	Type of Statement						
2	1	7	Unqualified	6	17	14	17	29	19
4	4	5	Reviewed	2	2		2	1	
7	3	9	Compiled	1	1	2		1	
26	30	57	Tax Returns	2	4	2		1	
4/1/04-	4/1/05-	4/1/06-	Other	7	16	9	9	9	9
3/31/05	3/31/06	3/31/07		91 (4/1-9/30/06)			89 (10/1/06-3/31/07)		
ALL	ALL	ALL		0-1MM	1-3MM	3-5MM	5-10MM	10-25MM	25MM & OVER
71	94	180	**NUMBER OF STATEMENTS**	18	40	27	28	39	28
%	%	%	**ASSETS**	%	%	%	%	%	%
17.3	14.5	15.9	Cash & Equivalents	13.3	13.2	19.1	16.2	17.9	15.5
17.0	13.9	14.3	Trade Receivables (net)	4.4	12.4	12.9	16.8	17.4	18.1
.3	.3	.2	Inventory	.0	.0	.1	.5	.1	.2
3.2	3.9	3.7	All Other Current	1.2	6.1	4.9	1.2	3.8	3.0
37.8	32.5	34.1	Total Current	18.9	31.8	37.0	34.6	39.3	36.9
48.0	50.5	53.1	Fixed Assets (net)	74.7	56.3	52.9	56.5	43.4	44.8
2.8	4.1	3.0	Intangibles (net)	2.5	3.5	5.0	.8	2.8	3.1
11.4	12.9	9.8	All Other Non-Current	3.9	8.3	5.0	8.1	14.5	15.3
100.0	100.0	100.0	Total	100.0	100.0	100.0	100.0	100.0	100.0
			LIABILITIES						
3.9	6.1	4.3	Notes Payable-Short Term	4.4	9.3	.9	2.1	3.9	2.9
3.2	2.6	2.9	Cur. Mat.-L.T.D.	1.3	3.9	3.9	3.1	2.4	2.4
6.0	5.1	5.3	Trade Payables	1.2	6.9	4.2	3.3	5.6	8.2
.0	.0	.0	Income Taxes Payable	.0	.0	.1	.0	.0	.0
21.4	13.1	12.6	All Other Current	4.1	18.1	8.4	13.1	12.5	13.7
34.5	26.9	25.1	Total Current	11.0	38.3	17.5	21.5	24.5	27.2
26.9	34.3	35.0	Long-Term Debt	43.9	38.5	32.5	35.3	30.2	33.0
1.1	.0	.0	Deferred Taxes	.0	.0	.0	.0	.0	.0
2.6	3.8	6.5	All Other Non-Current	4.7	15.1	.7	7.4	4.1	3.5
34.9	35.0	33.4	Net Worth	40.4	8.1	49.3	35.8	41.2	36.3
100.0	100.0	100.0	Total Liabilties & Net Worth	100.0	100.0	100.0	100.0	100.0	100.0
			INCOME DATA						
100.0	100.0	100.0	Net Sales	100.0	100.0	100.0	100.0	100.0	100.0
			Gross Profit						
92.4	93.4	93.8	Operating Expenses	88.1	90.5	90.5	98.6	96.2	97.1
7.6	6.6	6.2	Operating Profit	11.9	9.5	9.5	1.4	3.8	2.9
1.2	2.0	2.5	All Other Expenses (net)	12.8	3.9	2.3	.9	.2	-.7
6.4	4.6	3.7	Profit Before Taxes	-.8	5.6	7.2	.6	3.6	3.6
			RATIOS						
4.0	2.5	2.8	Current	6.4	2.1	3.9	2.7	2.8	2.1
1.5	1.4	1.6		1.0	1.1	2.5	1.6	1.7	1.6
1.0	.7	.8		.4	.4	1.4	1.1	1.0	1.0
3.2	2.3	2.5	Quick	6.4	1.6	3.7	2.7	2.5	1.9
1.3	1.2	1.3		.8	.9	2.5	1.5	1.6	1.2
.8	.6	.7		.4	.3	.9	1.0	.7	.9
17 21.2 / 4 104.2 / 4 85.9			Sales/Receivables	0 UND / 0 UND / 2 237.4			26 13.8 / 22 16.6 / 26 13.8		
31 11.8 / 33 11.0 / 29 12.8				0 UND / 5 66.4 / 24 15.1			35 10.5 / 32 11.3 / 39 9.3		
39 9.4 / 47 7.7 / 42 8.8				12 30.7 / 30 12.0 / 39 9.4			49 7.4 / 46 7.9 / 53 6.8		
			Cost of Sales/Inventory						
			Cost of Sales/Payables						
5.7	6.3	6.3	Sales/Working Capital	4.6	12.0	3.3	6.9	5.9	8.2
15.3	21.9	16.1		NM	132.5	8.7	15.2	14.2	14.0
999.8	-25.7	-46.6		-13.1	-7.7	29.4	102.4	393.4	NM
11.9	7.4	8.4	EBIT/Interest	4.0	4.6	19.9	4.1	10.4	9.1
(45) 3.6	(75) 2.5	(145) 2.2		(12) 1.7	(30) 1.5	(20) 3.4	(25) 2.1	(35) 2.4	(23) 2.5
.9	.9	1.0		-2.1	.9	1.8	.9	.7	1.2
			Net Profit + Depr., Dep., Amort./Cur. Mat. L/T/D						
.6	.7	.6	Fixed/Worth	1.0	.9	.5	.7	.5	.6
1.2	1.4	1.5		2.9	3.2	1.0	1.6	1.1	.9
14.6	7.7	6.1		10.3	-10.0	3.4	4.9	2.4	3.3
.3	.6	.5	Debt/Worth	.4	.8	.3	.6	.7	.6
1.9	1.8	1.7		2.2	3.1	1.3	1.1	1.5	1.2
28.3	11.7	8.3		10.6	-14.6	4.5	5.3	3.9	4.9
58.8	18.9	22.4	% Profit Before Taxes/Tangible Net Worth	20.3	25.3	22.3	15.3	23.6	22.8
(59) 8.8	(77) 6.5	(153) 9.2		(17) -4.3	(28) 9.7	(23) 9.3	(24) 6.7	(35) 9.4	(26) 12.4
-.7	.3	-.9		-29.8	-1.2	4.9	-.1	-3.0	.5
15.9	9.4	9.2	% Profit Before Taxes/Total Assets	4.7	12.4	9.2	9.2	8.0	9.1
4.1	2.6	3.7		.0	4.0	5.2	3.0	3.8	4.5
-.1	-.2	-.1		-6.6	.3	1.5	-.2	-1.0	.1
13.6	6.7	5.7	Sales/Net Fixed Assets	1.6	14.5	5.3	4.7	7.0	7.6
2.7	2.3	2.6		.8	2.4	2.5	2.2	3.1	3.4
1.1	1.3	1.2		.3	.7	1.5	1.5	2.0	2.0
3.1	1.9	2.4	Sales/Total Assets	1.3	2.8	2.1	2.0	2.7	2.2
1.5	1.2	1.3		.6	1.3	1.1	1.4	1.6	1.4
.6	.7	.7		.3	.4	.7	.8	1.0	1.2
1.6	1.7	1.9	% Depr., Dep., Amort./Sales	4.1	1.2	1.8	2.1	1.5	1.8
(58) 2.8	(82) 3.0	(163) 3.2		(17) 9.5	(31) 4.1	(25) 2.9	(27) 3.2	(36) 2.9	(27) 2.4
4.9	4.7	5.2		13.9	7.5	4.9	4.2	4.0	3.3
3.1	2.8	2.9	% Officers', Directors' Owners' Comp/Sales	4.0					
(14) 8.2	(20) 6.3	(27) 6.4		(11) 5.9					
11.5	17.0	8.9		7.9					
710605M	1543686M	2702658M	Net Sales ($)	11148M	82562M	102622M	206599M	610053M	1689674M
611037M	1394853M	2477101M	Total Assets ($)	29305M	141766M	114364M	193282M	662767M	1335617M

M = $ thousand   MM = $ million
See Pages 11 through 21 for Explanation of Ratios and Data

Current Data Sorted by Assets | | | | | Comparative Historical Data

						Type of Statement		
9	40	92	70	7	5	Unqualified	76	136
2		1	1		1	Reviewed		1
3	2	2				Compiled	2	5
9	1	2				Tax Returns	4	6
7	19	29	19	5	3	Other	20	25
	224 (4/1-9/30/06)		105 (10/1/06-3/31/07)				4/1/02-3/31/03	4/1/03-3/31/04
0-500M	500M-2MM	2-10MM	10-50MM	50-100MM	100-250MM		ALL	ALL
30	62	126	90	12	9	NUMBER OF STATEMENTS	102	173
%	%	%	%	%	%	ASSETS	%	%
25.6	19.7	20.3	18.6	20.3		Cash & Equivalents	18.8	18.3
25.5	22.2	17.6	13.9	7.7		Trade Receivables (net)	15.4	18.9
.1	1.1	1.0	.2	.8		Inventory	.7	.3
2.4	4.6	3.6	2.7	1.8		All Other Current	9.0	6.3
53.5	47.6	42.5	35.4	30.7		Total Current	43.9	43.8
29.0	39.4	45.6	45.0	48.1		Fixed Assets (net)	45.6	44.1
8.1	.9	.5	.7	.5		Intangibles (net)	.2	.4
9.4	12.1	11.4	18.8	20.8		All Other Non-Current	10.2	11.6
100.0	100.0	100.0	100.0	100.0		Total	100.0	100.0
						LIABILITIES		
15.0	5.7	3.9	1.7	.9		Notes Payable-Short Term	3.7	4.4
1.0	2.8	1.4	1.2	1.1		Cur. Mat.-L.T.D.	1.9	2.0
14.6	8.4	7.1	5.4	5.2		Trade Payables	8.3	8.6
2.2	.1	.1	.0	.0		Income Taxes Payable	.0	.0
14.2	13.7	8.5	7.8	5.5		All Other Current	10.0	8.4
47.0	30.7	21.0	16.1	12.6		Total Current	23.9	23.4
38.5	17.5	16.2	20.6	27.5		Long-Term Debt	19.0	16.4
.0	.0	.0	.1	.0		Deferred Taxes	.2	.0
9.3	6.2	2.6	3.0	5.8		All Other Non-Current	4.7	4.1
5.2	45.5	60.2	60.2	54.1		Net Worth	52.3	56.0
100.0	100.0	100.0	100.0	100.0		Total Liabilities & Net Worth	100.0	100.0
						INCOME DATA		
100.0	100.0	100.0	100.0	100.0		Net Sales	100.0	100.0
						Gross Profit		
97.3	94.9	94.5	94.7	92.9		Operating Expenses	92.8	97.0
2.7	5.1	5.5	5.3	7.1		Operating Profit	7.2	3.0
.1	1.0	.3	-.6	.7		All Other Expenses (net)	2.7	.3
2.6	4.1	5.3	5.9	6.4		Profit Before Taxes	4.6	2.7
						RATIOS		
2.9	4.2	4.8	4.3	3.9			4.2	4.2
1.7	1.6	2.2	2.4	2.3		Current	1.9	2.0
1.1	1.1	1.3	1.5	1.4			1.1	1.2
2.9	3.6	4.1	3.9	3.4			2.6	3.5
1.6	1.6	1.9	2.2	2.2		Quick	1.5	1.6
1.0	.8	1.1	1.3	1.0			.8	1.0

													Sales/Receivables				

Sales/Receivables:

											Sales/Receivables				
0	UND	0	UND	12	31.4	16	23.4	9	38.9			3	118.6	13	28.3
14	25.4	24	14.9	33	11.2	40	9.1	20	18.5			28	13.2	32	11.5
41	8.8	43	8.5	49	7.5	59	6.2	35	10.4			48	7.5	50	7.3

0-500M	500M-2MM	2-10MM	10-50MM	50-100MM	100-250MM		ALL	ALL
						Cost of Sales/Inventory		
						Cost of Sales/Payables		
12.1	5.7	4.2	3.3	1.4			4.3	4.2
31.3	14.2	9.3	5.6	6.8		Sales/Working Capital	12.2	11.0
UND	NM	25.1	14.8	18.9			67.0	37.9

										EBIT/Interest				
	12.0		6.6		12.8		9.8					9.8		6.2
(15)	5.4	(29)	1.6	(86)	4.4	(75)	3.6			EBIT/Interest	(57)	2.0	(111)	1.8
	-4.9		-1.6		.2		1.8					-.7		-.4

0-500M	500M-2MM	2-10MM	10-50MM	50-100MM	100-250MM		ALL	ALL
						Net Profit + Depr., Dep., Amort./Cur. Mat. L/T/D		
.1	.1	.4	.4	.4			.4	.4
.4	.8	.8	.8	1.0		Fixed/Worth	1.0	.8
UND	2.1	1.3	1.2	1.7			1.8	1.6
.4	.4	.2	.2	.4			.2	.2
1.6	1.2	.5	.6	.9		Debt/Worth	.9	.7
-2.5	3.1	1.4	1.7	1.6			2.2	1.8

										% Profit Before Taxes/Tangible Net Worth				
	52.4		23.7		16.4		14.9		12.9			18.6		14.0
(20)	15.6	(56)	8.1	(121)	7.2	(89)	5.7		4.9	% Profit Before Taxes/Tangible Net Worth	(97)	8.9	(166)	4.0
	-4.3		-3.1		-.9		2.2		-.9			-1.9		-3.5

0-500M	500M-2MM	2-10MM	10-50MM	50-100MM	100-250MM		ALL	ALL
23.6	10.5	10.4	7.6	4.9			10.1	6.3
8.0	3.5	4.1	3.4	2.2		% Profit Before Taxes/Total Assets	2.9	1.6
-8.2	-2.3	-.8	.9	-.7			-2.2	-1.8
238.8	41.4	8.2	3.8	3.8			11.9	10.5
39.7	7.2	3.4	2.4	1.2		Sales/Net Fixed Assets	3.7	4.0
16.3	2.1	1.4	1.2	.9			1.3	1.5
9.1	3.6	2.3	1.5	1.6			2.6	2.7
5.6	2.1	1.3	1.0	.6		Sales/Total Assets	1.6	1.7
2.6	.9	.8	.6	.2			.7	.9

										% Depr., Dep., Amort./Sales				
	.4		.7		1.2		1.8		1.7			1.3		1.3
(16)	1.2	(53)	1.8	(115)	2.3	(87)	2.9	(10)	4.8	% Depr., Dep., Amort./Sales	(87)	2.3	(152)	2.2
	2.3		3.3		4.0		4.3		9.1			4.1		3.5

										% Officers', Directors' Owners' Comp/Sales				
	3.0		4.1		2.7							3.4		4.3
(11)	4.0	(10)	10.1	(11)	5.9					% Officers', Directors' Owners' Comp/Sales	(10)	7.4	(19)	6.7
	10.6		29.4		9.3							10.9		34.1

0-500M	500M-2MM	2-10MM	10-50MM	50-100MM	100-250MM		ALL	ALL
37475M	206502M	1240141M	2320621M	856894M	2046500M	Net Sales ($)	1561585M	1531419M
7532M	76252M	628174M	2047639M	888962M	1412274M	Total Assets ($)	1253918M	1153360M

M = $ thousand   MM = $ million
See Pages 11 through 21 for Explanation of Ratios and Data

Comparative Historical Data				Current Data Sorted by Sales					
111	136	223	**Type of Statement** Unqualified	14	38	31	46	56	38
3	5	5	Reviewed	2			1	1	1
3	3	7	Compiled	4	2	1			
6	8	12	Tax Returns	6	5			1	
23	43	82	Other	8	17	10	13	16	18
4/1/04- 3/31/05 ALL	4/1/05- 3/31/06 ALL	4/1/06- 3/31/07 ALL		0-1MM	224 (4/1-9/30/06) 1-3MM	3-5MM	5-10MM	105 (10/1/06-3/31/07) 10-25MM	25MM & OVER
146	195	329	**NUMBER OF STATEMENTS**	34	62	42	60	74	57
%	%	%	**ASSETS**	%	%	%	%	%	%
17.6	19.7	20.1	Cash & Equivalents	23.0	20.6	21.1	18.8	17.6	22.0
23.3	18.2	17.6	Trade Receivables (net)	12.4	14.5	17.3	17.0	21.8	19.2
.3	.6	.7	Inventory	.0	1.2	.1	1.4	.6	.6
3.6	4.6	3.6	All Other Current	1.0	3.3	5.9	5.0	2.6	3.5
44.7	43.0	42.0	Total Current	36.4	39.6	44.4	42.1	42.6	45.3
45.1	41.2	42.2	Fixed Assets (net)	49.1	44.1	39.8	43.1	42.6	36.5
.2	1.3	1.5	Intangibles (net)	2.6	3.5	.1	.2	.4	2.7
9.9	14.5	14.2	All Other Non-Current	12.0	12.7	15.6	14.6	14.5	15.5
100.0	100.0	100.0	Total	100.0	100.0	100.0	100.0	100.0	100.0
			LIABILITIES						
3.9	6.9	4.5	Notes Payable-Short Term	10.9	5.9	5.6	2.0	3.2	2.4
2.0	1.6	1.5	Cur. Mat.-L.T.D.	1.3	2.3	2.1	.9	1.3	1.3
8.1	8.0	7.4	Trade Payables	6.7	4.2	8.5	6.5	6.8	12.5
.1	.0	.2	Income Taxes Payable	.0	1.0	.1	.1	.0	.0
10.6	9.6	9.7	All Other Current	8.0	8.8	7.2	10.6	10.5	11.6
24.6	26.1	23.4	Total Current	26.9	22.3	23.6	20.1	21.8	27.8
21.5	17.3	20.2	Long-Term Debt	19.9	31.9	15.7	15.8	16.5	20.4
.0	.0	.0	Deferred Taxes	.0	.0	.0	.0	.0	.1
4.6	5.2	4.2	All Other Non-Current	4.0	5.2	2.1	3.5	5.6	3.6
49.3	51.3	52.2	Net Worth	49.1	40.7	58.6	60.5	56.0	48.1
100.0	100.0	100.0	Total Liabilties & Net Worth	100.0	100.0	100.0	100.0	100.0	100.0
			INCOME DATA						
100.0	100.0	100.0	Net Sales	100.0	100.0	100.0	100.0	100.0	100.0
			Gross Profit						
95.7	97.6	94.8	Operating Expenses	90.7	94.6	93.8	95.4	95.3	96.6
4.3	2.4	5.2	Operating Profit	9.3	5.4	6.2	4.6	4.7	3.4
.6	.6	.2	All Other Expenses (net)	4.1	-.2	-.2	.0	-.8	-.2
3.7	1.8	5.1	Profit Before Taxes	5.2	5.5	6.4	4.6	5.5	3.5
			RATIOS						
3.6	3.3	4.3		4.8	6.8	4.8	4.4	3.7	3.1
2.0	1.8	2.1	Current	1.8	2.9	2.5	2.1	2.3	1.5
1.1	1.1	1.3		.9	1.2	1.2	1.4	1.6	1.1
3.5	3.0	3.8		3.5	6.0	4.3	3.8	3.0	2.8
1.8	1.5	1.9	Quick	1.8	2.4	2.0	1.9	2.0	1.3
1.1	.9	1.1		.7	1.2	1.2	1.0	1.5	1.0
19 18.9	12 30.1	9 39.4		0 UND	0 UND	9 40.1	12 31.2	21 17.6	16 23.5
33 11.0	33 11.1	30 12.2	Sales/Receivables	11 33.4	18 20.8	27 13.5	34 10.7	36 10.0	34 10.7
52 7.1	56 6.6	51 7.1		69 5.3	37 9.9	48 7.6	53 6.9	59 6.2	57 6.4
			Cost of Sales/Inventory						
			Cost of Sales/Payables						
5.1	4.7	4.0		3.1	3.4	3.0	3.9	3.9	4.5
10.2	12.6	9.1	Sales/Working Capital	10.5	9.5	10.0	7.9	7.8	13.4
40.9	171.3	35.1		UND	60.8	43.8	24.9	16.0	109.4
8.5	10.1	9.7		3.7	9.1	5.0	15.3	16.9	8.7
(107) 2.8	(130) 2.6	(220) 3.5	EBIT/Interest	(14) .7	(35) 2.9	(25) 1.1	(44) 5.6	(55) 5.0	(47) 3.3
.7	.0	.8		-3.8	-.4	-.8	.9	2.7	1.4
			Net Profit + Depr., Dep., Amort./Cur. Mat. L/T/D						
.5	.3	.3		.1	.1	.2	.4	.4	.4
.9	.8	.8	Fixed/Worth	.9	.8	.7	.6	.8	.9
1.6	1.4	1.4		3.0	1.8	1.2	1.1	1.3	1.5
.3	.3	.2		.2	.2	.2	.2	.3	.5
.7	.7	.7	Debt/Worth	.9	.6	.3	.5	.7	.9
2.1	2.1	1.9		6.3	2.1	1.2	1.5	1.7	2.7
19.0	12.6	17.6		23.1	26.5	14.6	15.7	18.9	15.4
(137) 6.0	(182) 3.8	(306) 7.1	% Profit Before Taxes/Tangible Net Worth	(30) 3.5	(53) 4.6	(39) 7.0	(58) 8.7	(72) 7.2	(54) 7.3
-1.1	-3.7	.1		-5.0	-.8	-.9	-.3	3.0	1.3
8.6	7.1	9.6		8.2	14.6	10.5	9.6	7.9	8.0
3.1	1.8	3.7	% Profit Before Taxes/Total Assets	1.4	3.6	3.7	4.3	4.0	3.2
-.6	-2.0	-.2		-3.0	-2.4	-1.0	-.2	1.4	.5
13.4	14.1	14.2		52.7	24.3	24.8	6.8	7.9	12.8
3.5	3.7	3.4	Sales/Net Fixed Assets	2.0	3.1	5.0	2.8	3.6	3.7
1.8	1.6	1.5		.5	1.1	1.8	1.2	1.9	2.6
3.2	2.7	2.6		2.6	2.8	2.5	2.6	2.6	2.5
1.7	1.5	1.4	Sales/Total Assets	.7	1.4	1.3	1.2	1.5	1.4
.9	.7	.7		.2	.7	1.0	.6	.8	.8
1.0	1.2	1.3		1.3	1.3	1.0	1.4	1.1	1.3
(132) 2.1	(174) 2.3	(289) 2.4	% Depr., Dep., Amort./Sales	(25) 4.0	(51) 2.8	(34) 2.2	(57) 2.7	(70) 2.2	(52) 2.2
3.4	4.0	4.0		10.2	4.5	3.6	4.3	3.0	3.0
3.5	1.1	2.8		3.4					
(13) 9.7	(23) 3.7	(38) 5.7	% Officers', Directors' Owners' Comp/Sales	(15) 9.7					
13.6	7.2	10.5		16.5					
1979211M	3115810M	6708133M	Net Sales ($)	16053M	124147M	167291M	434890M	1182481M	4783271M
1506741M	2674392M	5060833M	Total Assets ($)	31363M	148842M	194807M	519560M	1106748M	3059513M

M = $ thousand   MM = $ million
See Pages 11 through 21 for Explanation of Ratios and Data

Current Data Sorted by Assets

Comparative Historical Data

0-500M	500M-2MM	2-10MM	10-50MM	50-100MM	100-250MM	Type of Statement	4/1/02-3/31/03 ALL	4/1/03-3/31/04 ALL
5	18	42	32	2	2	Unqualified	17	21
			1			Reviewed	1	
	2	2	2			Compiled		2
3	2	2	1			Tax Returns		1
5	8	9	10	1	1	Other	4	12
	102 (4/1-9/30/06)		46 (10/1/06-3/31/07)					
13	30	55	44	3	3	NUMBER OF STATEMENTS	22	36
%	%	%	%	%	%	ASSETS	%	%
26.1	21.4	19.7	20.4			Cash & Equivalents	18.8	12.3
12.3	28.0	18.2	16.8			Trade Receivables (net)	25.1	20.1
2.5	.7	.2	.6			Inventory	.0	.3
13.6	4.2	3.3	4.1			All Other Current	2.9	5.7
54.5	54.3	41.4	42.0			Total Current	46.9	38.5
33.4	39.7	45.5	51.8			Fixed Assets (net)	44.2	49.4
.4	.3	3.9	.4			Intangibles (net)	.0	5.1
11.7	5.7	9.2	5.8			All Other Non-Current	8.9	7.0
100.0	100.0	100.0	100.0			Total	100.0	100.0
						LIABILITIES		
6.4	3.3	3.2	2.3			Notes Payable-Short Term	4.4	6.3
3.0	1.2	2.2	1.9			Cur. Mat.-L.T.D.	1.7	4.3
6.2	7.4	6.8	8.2			Trade Payables	9.0	8.0
.1	.0	.0	.0			Income Taxes Payable	.0	.0
14.0	15.6	11.9	12.2			All Other Current	14.4	13.9
29.7	27.4	24.1	24.6			Total Current	29.5	32.6
18.0	11.1	23.5	26.6			Long-Term Debt	19.6	29.0
.0	.0	.3	.1			Deferred Taxes	.0	.0
12.2	3.1	1.9	3.4			All Other Non-Current	2.8	3.0
40.1	58.4	50.2	45.3			Net Worth	48.0	35.4
100.0	100.0	100.0	100.0			Total Liabilities & Net Worth	100.0	100.0
						INCOME DATA		
100.0	100.0	100.0	100.0			Net Sales	100.0	100.0
						Gross Profit		
91.5	94.3	94.2	94.9			Operating Expenses	98.7	95.9
8.5	5.7	5.8	5.1			Operating Profit	1.3	4.1
.4	-.3	.8	.5			All Other Expenses (net)	.3	4.5
8.0	6.0	5.0	4.6			Profit Before Taxes	1.0	-.4
						RATIOS		
4.8	3.6	3.0	3.0			Current	2.8	2.2
2.1	2.3	1.9	1.7				1.6	1.3
.7	1.0	1.4	1.0				.9	.9
3.3	3.5	2.8	2.8			Quick	2.7	1.9
1.6	2.0	(54) 1.8	1.5				1.5	1.1
.5	.9	1.1	.8				.8	.6
0 UND	24 15.4	13 27.6	17 21.3			Sales/Receivables	13 27.6	11 34.3
3 114.5	37 9.7	28 12.9	31 11.7				31 11.6	32 11.4
20 18.7	56 6.5	48 7.6	48 7.6				41 8.8	45 8.1
						Cost of Sales/Inventory		
						Cost of Sales/Payables		
3.9	4.7	5.0	3.9			Sales/Working Capital	8.0	8.8
10.0	10.9	9.9	10.4				18.2	32.6
-107.3	113.7	31.0	827.5				-122.0	-48.1
	19.1	12.2	8.6			EBIT/Interest	11.9	4.6
	(20) 6.3	(41) 3.5	(37) 3.7				(13) 2.3	(26) 1.8
	2.2	1.3	1.4				.3	.0
						Net Profit + Depr., Dep., Amort./Cur. Mat. L/T/D		
.3	.3	.5	.8			Fixed/Worth	.2	.7
.5	.5	1.0	1.3				.8	1.1
1.8	1.0	1.7	2.9				2.2	3.7
.3	.3	.3	.5			Debt/Worth	.4	.7
.6	.5	1.2	1.3				1.1	1.7
2.9	2.0	2.0	4.0				4.9	7.3
82.6	31.8	20.3	18.8			% Profit Before Taxes/Tangible Net Worth	19.1	14.5
(11) 28.9	(28) 14.3	(50) 9.1	(43) 8.4				9.2	(30) 6.7
8.0	5.1	1.9	4.1				-3.5	2.5
37.3	15.9	12.2	8.2			% Profit Before Taxes/Total Assets	8.1	4.9
23.6	8.8	3.6	3.8				2.0	2.4
2.9	1.9	.9	1.0				-1.1	-2.7
54.9	26.8	10.1	4.9			Sales/Net Fixed Assets	33.4	10.7
13.3	6.2	3.4	2.8				3.9	3.4
4.9	2.4	2.5	1.5				2.2	2.0
9.5	4.0	2.3	2.0			Sales/Total Assets	3.3	3.3
2.1	2.3	1.8	1.5				1.8	1.9
1.6	1.4	1.1	.8				1.6	.9
	.8	1.3	1.9			% Depr., Dep., Amort./Sales	1.1	2.5
	(25) 1.4	(52) 2.4	(42) 3.0				(18) 2.5	(30) 3.2
	3.0	3.9	4.2				3.7	5.0
						% Officers', Directors' Owners' Comp/Sales		
17250M	99895M	579483M	1555875M	190142M	355125M	Net Sales ($)	249539M	2466820M
3564M	38692M	303784M	913870M	181114M	500444M	Total Assets ($)	160325M	475430M

© RMA 2007

M = $ thousand   MM = $ million
See Pages 11 through 21 for Explanation of Ratios and Data

Comparative Historical Data   ## Current Data Sorted by Sales

			Type of Statement						
48	66	101	Unqualified	5	15	13	18	28	22
1	2	1	Reviewed						1
6	2	4	Compiled	1		2		1	
2	5	8	Tax Returns	1	4	1	1	1	1
19	19	34	Other	4	5	3	10	8	4
4/1/04-3/31/05 ALL	4/1/05-3/31/06 ALL	4/1/06-3/31/07 ALL		102 (4/1-9/30/06)			46 (10/1/06-3/31/07)		
				0-1MM	1-3MM	3-5MM	5-10MM	10-25MM	25MM & OVER
76	94	148	**NUMBER OF STATEMENTS**	11	24	17	30	38	28
%	%	%	**ASSETS**	%	%	%	%	%	%
19.5	19.2	20.5	Cash & Equivalents	19.5	21.5	26.1	20.4	17.4	20.8
19.7	18.6	19.0	Trade Receivables (net)	5.8	17.0	18.6	19.9	18.5	25.9
.5	.4	.9	Inventory	3.0	.3	.9	.0	.4	2.2
5.6	4.7	4.7	All Other Current	4.7	5.9	4.4	6.7	4.0	2.4
45.4	42.8	45.0	Total Current	32.9	44.8	50.0	47.0	40.3	51.3
43.1	45.8	44.9	Fixed Assets (net)	56.7	45.0	34.2	44.1	49.2	41.6
1.2	2.1	1.8	Intangibles (net)	.7	.3	6.8	3.3	.2	1.2
10.4	9.3	8.3	All Other Non-Current	9.7	10.0	9.1	5.5	10.3	6.0
100.0	100.0	100.0	Total	100.0	100.0	100.0	100.0	100.0	100.0
			LIABILITIES						
6.9	5.3	3.2	Notes Payable-Short Term	1.3	1.5	6.5	3.7	3.8	2.1
2.0	2.4	2.0	Cur. Mat.-L.T.D.	1.8	2.0	.8	1.5	2.7	2.4
8.4	7.7	7.2	Trade Payables	3.1	6.3	6.5	5.2	6.0	13.5
.0	.0	.0	Income Taxes Payable	.0	.1	.0	.0	.0	.0
11.9	12.2	12.7	All Other Current	10.4	9.9	13.3	16.0	12.0	13.0
29.3	27.6	25.1	Total Current	16.6	19.8	27.1	26.4	24.5	31.1
23.2	25.6	22.1	Long-Term Debt	26.8	23.2	12.3	18.9	23.4	27.0
.0	.0	.1	Deferred Taxes	.0	.0	.0	.0	.6	.0
4.7	5.0	3.7	All Other Non-Current	.2	8.2	6.7	.7	2.5	4.3
42.9	41.8	48.9	Net Worth	56.4	48.8	53.9	54.0	49.0	37.6
100.0	100.0	100.0	Total Liabilities & Net Worth	100.0	100.0	100.0	100.0	100.0	100.0
			INCOME DATA						
100.0	100.0	100.0	Net Sales	100.0	100.0	100.0	100.0	100.0	100.0
			Gross Profit						
93.2	96.5	94.4	Operating Expenses	84.1	90.9	97.4	95.0	96.0	96.9
6.8	3.5	5.6	Operating Profit	15.9	9.1	2.6	5.0	4.0	3.1
2.2	.9	.5	All Other Expenses (net)	1.4	1.2	.9	.6	-.5	.6
4.7	2.6	5.1	Profit Before Taxes	14.5	8.0	1.7	4.4	4.5	2.5
			RATIOS						
3.0	2.9	3.3		5.9	4.3	4.0	3.3	2.3	3.2
1.7	1.6	1.9	Current	2.1	2.6	2.2	2.0	1.8	1.5
1.1	.9	1.1		.3	1.5	1.1	1.1	.9	1.0
2.8	2.6	2.8		5.3	4.3	3.9	2.8	2.1	2.7
1.6	1.4 (147)	1.7	Quick	1.8	2.0	1.9	1.6 (37)	1.8	1.4
.8	.9	.9		.3	1.2	1.0	1.0	.8	1.0
7 55.3	10 36.3	13 27.5		0 UND	4 103.2	9 39.6	10 37.7	13 27.9	31 11.9
31 11.7	32 11.5	31 11.7	Sales/Receivables	17 21.8	24 15.3	25 14.4	27 13.7	32 11.4	34 10.7
47 7.7	45 8.1	48 7.6		49 7.4	44 8.3	48 7.6	46 8.0	51 7.2	53 6.9
			Cost of Sales/Inventory						
			Cost of Sales/Payables						
5.5	5.9	4.5		3.7	3.6	4.0	4.3	6.4	4.9
14.4	16.2	10.2	Sales/Working Capital	10.0	8.6	10.6	10.6	9.9	13.7
88.4	-182.1	117.9		-10.1	25.4	NM	68.2	-45.6	270.6
15.3	8.1	11.6			34.0	4.9	9.9	12.2	7.4
(53) 2.6	(70) 2.4	(110) 3.7	EBIT/Interest		(15) 9.9	(11) 2.0	(23) 3.5	(29) 3.7	(25) 2.6
.8	1.1	1.3			1.3	-1.7	-.3	1.7	1.5
			Net Profit + Depr., Dep., Amort./Cur. Mat. L/T/D						
.4	.5	.5		.4	.3	.2	.5	.6	.8
.9	1.1	1.0	Fixed/Worth	.9	.5	.7	.9	1.2	1.0
1.6	2.6	1.7		-430.0	1.4	1.6	1.6	2.1	2.8
.4	.5	.4		.1	.1	.3	.4	.4	.7
1.0	1.2	1.0	Debt/Worth	.4	.6	.5	.8	1.1	2.4
2.9	3.8	2.9		-495.0	1.9	3.5	1.6	2.4	4.7
24.1	19.2	22.7	% Profit Before Taxes/Tangible		40.6	14.9	27.2	17.5	22.4
(68) 7.3	(85) 8.9	(138) 10.7	Net Worth		(21) 14.4	(16) 6.0	(29) 12.3	(37) 8.4	(27) 10.6
-.7	.8	3.0			4.3	-3.0	-2.5	3.3	5.6
12.2	8.8	12.9	% Profit Before Taxes/Total	28.9	26.1	5.0	14.7	9.6	9.0
2.9	3.5	4.2	Assets	13.6	6.8	3.6	7.2	3.6	3.9
-.5	.3	.9		6.5	1.4	-1.0	-1.4	1.3	1.0
15.0	11.3	10.9		8.0	23.4	47.3	14.2	5.4	9.2
3.9	4.2	3.5	Sales/Net Fixed Assets	2.0	2.9	5.1	3.5	3.0	4.8
2.1	2.2	2.0		.6	1.1	3.0	2.0	1.8	2.8
3.0	2.7	2.5		1.9	3.7	2.3	3.3	2.1	3.3
1.9	1.9	1.8	Sales/Total Assets	1.5	1.5	1.8	2.1	1.8	2.0
1.1	1.3	1.1		.5	.8	.8	1.1	1.0	1.5
1.0	1.7	1.3			.9	1.1	1.2	2.0	1.1
(62) 2.4	(83) 2.7	(134) 2.5	% Depr., Dep., Amort./Sales		(20) 2.1	(14) 2.4	(29) 2.4	(35) 3.0	(27) 2.0
3.8	3.9	4.0			5.6	4.4	3.9	4.1	3.1
	2.7	2.7	% Officers', Directors'						
	(15) 4.7	(21) 5.8	Owners' Comp/Sales						
	16.7	19.6							
1868387M	1619098M	2797770M	Net Sales ($)	5948M	50320M	68445M	210812M	597115M	1865130M
743712M	988306M	1941468M	Total Assets ($)	6845M	48495M	78467M	157742M	586682M	1063237M

M = $ thousand   MM = $ million
See Pages 11 through 21 for Explanation of Ratios and Data

Current Data Sorted by Assets   Comparative Historical Data

						Type of Statement		
24	69	221	167	24	4	Unqualified	476	437
2	3	3				Reviewed	8	8
3	3	9	2			Compiled	13	51
4	3	3	3			Tax Returns	12	17
16	22	62	33	9	2	Other	131	135
	521 (4/1-9/30/06)		170 (10/1/06-3/31/07)				4/1/02- 3/31/03	4/1/03- 3/31/04
0-500M	500M-2MM	2-10MM	10-50MM	50-100MM	100-250MM		ALL	ALL
49	100	298	205	33	6	**NUMBER OF STATEMENTS**	640	648
%	%	%	%	%	%	**ASSETS**	%	%
28.4	21.9	20.1	19.0	15.6		Cash & Equivalents	18.1	17.1
19.6	19.7	18.0	14.8	7.7		Trade Receivables (net)	18.3	20.1
1.1	.7	1.8	1.1	.0		Inventory	.7	.6
5.8	6.3	5.5	4.4	6.2		All Other Current	5.2	5.7
54.8	48.7	45.5	39.3	29.5		Total Current	42.2	43.6
31.2	40.2	44.3	44.0	42.1		Fixed Assets (net)	44.1	44.3
2.8	.4	.6	1.0	2.4		Intangibles (net)	.9	.7
11.1	10.8	9.6	15.7	25.9		All Other Non-Current	12.8	11.3
100.0	100.0	100.0	100.0	100.0		Total	100.0	100.0
						LIABILITIES		
12.3	4.9	3.5	2.8	1.6		Notes Payable-Short Term	5.0	4.7
1.2	3.0	2.1	1.7	1.7		Cur. Mat.-L.T.D.	2.0	2.0
11.2	6.2	7.8	5.5	5.1		Trade Payables	6.9	7.6
.0	.2	.2	.0	.0		Income Taxes Payable	.1	.1
25.3	10.0	11.3	9.8	9.0		All Other Current	12.4	13.3
50.0	24.4	24.9	19.9	17.3		Total Current	26.4	27.7
11.8	19.2	17.5	19.9	25.0		Long-Term Debt	19.5	19.6
.0	.0	.1	.0	.0		Deferred Taxes	.0	.1
2.7	2.6	2.6	2.0	4.2		All Other Non-Current	3.7	4.9
35.4	53.8	54.9	58.3	53.4		Net Worth	50.4	47.6
100.0	100.0	100.0	100.0	100.0		Total Liabilities & Net Worth	100.0	100.0
						INCOME DATA		
100.0	100.0	100.0	100.0	100.0		Net Sales	100.0	100.0
						Gross Profit		
97.7	96.6	96.7	96.6	93.7		Operating Expenses	97.2	97.2
2.3	3.4	3.3	3.4	6.3		Operating Profit	2.8	2.8
1.3	1.0	-.1	-.3	1.6		All Other Expenses (net)	1.3	.2
1.0	2.4	3.3	3.7	4.7		Profit Before Taxes	1.5	2.6
						RATIOS		
2.8	4.4	3.9	3.3	2.5			3.3	3.1
1.5	2.0	2.1	2.0	1.7		Current	1.8	1.8
.7	1.3	1.2	1.2	1.1			1.1	1.1
2.6	3.8	3.3	2.8	2.2			2.8	2.7
1.2	1.8	1.8	1.6	1.2		Quick	1.5	1.6
.6	1.1	1.0	1.0	.8			.9	.9

0	UND	10	36.4	12	30.0	20	18.4	16	23.3		Sales/Receivables	15	23.9	14	26.2
13	28.7	26	14.1	32	11.5	37	9.8	31	11.8			33	11.1	32	11.3
34	10.8	43	8.5	48	7.5	57	6.4	55	6.6			49	7.4	49	7.5

						Cost of Sales/Inventory		

						Cost of Sales/Payables		

6.6		3.9		4.4		3.9		3.3		Sales/Working Capital	5.0	5.4
20.7		10.5		8.2		7.6		11.5			10.9	11.5
-20.7		36.5		33.3		30.7		49.5			84.7	90.3

	5.3		8.1		7.9		8.1		6.9	EBIT/Interest		6.8	8.7
(23)	-.2	(67)	2.2	(210)	2.8	(147)	3.4	(27)	2.1		(425)	1.9	(463) 2.4
	-11.8		.4		.1		1.1		.3			-.5	-.2

						Net Profit + Depr., Dep., Amort./Cur. Mat. L/T/D		

.1	.3	.4	.4	.4			.4	.4
.7	.7	.8	.8	.8		Fixed/Worth	.9	.9
2.0	1.2	1.4	1.4	1.4			1.6	1.6
.4	.3	.3	.3	.5			.3	.4
.8	.7	.7	.7	.9		Debt/Worth	.8	.9
3.9	1.4	1.7	1.4	1.5			1.9	2.2

	43.8		16.2		14.0		12.4		8.1	% Profit Before Taxes/Tangible Net Worth		16.5	15.9
(42)	-.3	(93)	6.8	(285)	4.7	(201)	5.6	(32)	3.3		(611)	3.5	(611) 4.9
	-21.9		-1.3		-1.6		.2		-.4			-5.0	-2.4

16.0	9.2	7.6	6.5	3.9		% Profit Before Taxes/Total Assets	7.6	7.8
-.2	3.4	2.3	2.8	1.0			1.6	2.3
-18.1	-.7	-.8	.1	-.1			-2.7	-1.5
140.2	26.7	10.9	5.7	3.6		Sales/Net Fixed Assets	10.8	10.4
21.0	5.6	3.9	2.9	1.9			3.6	3.8
4.6	2.2	1.8	1.5	1.1			1.8	1.9
5.7	3.4	2.5	1.7	1.2		Sales/Total Assets	2.6	2.9
2.9	1.9	1.7	1.1	.7			1.6	1.7
1.7	1.1	.9	.7	.5			.9	1.0

	.9		.9		1.2		1.4		2.2	% Depr., Dep., Amort./Sales		1.4	1.1
(30)	1.5	(84)	1.6	(269)	2.1	(195)	2.4	(32)	3.3		(563)	2.3	(586) 2.1
	5.1		3.2		3.8		3.8		4.9			3.6	3.6

	9.6				2.6		1.4			% Officers', Directors' Owners' Comp/Sales		3.2	3.8
(10)	10.7	(25)			4.8	(22)	6.3				(68)	7.2	(62) 5.9
	20.5				15.6		15.2					13.8	13.2

49158M	293196M	2914635M	6234896M	2115664M	3243749M	Net Sales ($)	9336058M	10858346M
10551M	121385M	1502895M	4201789M	2239421M	1017625M	Total Assets ($)	6824581M	7133850M

M = $ thousand   MM = $ million
See Pages 11 through 21 for Explanation of Ratios and Data

Comparative Historical Data | Current Data Sorted by Sales

				Type of Statement						
461	426	509		Unqualified	31	76	52	102	148	100
10	8	8		Reviewed	2	4		1	1	
12	6	17		Compiled	6	2	1	2	3	3
15	20	13		Tax Returns	5	2		3	1	2
125	242	144		Other	15	30	18	22	34	25
4/1/04-	4/1/05-	4/1/06-				521 (4/1-9/30/06)			170 (10/1/06-3/31/07)	
3/31/05	3/31/06	3/31/07								
ALL	ALL	ALL			0-1MM	1-3MM	3-5MM	5-10MM	10-25MM	25MM & OVER
623	702	691		**NUMBER OF STATEMENTS**	59	114	71	130	187	130
%	%	%		**ASSETS**	%	%	%	%	%	%
17.8	20.1	20.6		Cash & Equivalents	29.8	18.3	17.7	20.1	18.6	23.3
19.4	16.9	16.9		Trade Receivables (net)	11.8	13.9	12.4	16.6	20.5	19.4
.8	.9	1.4		Inventory	1.9	.6	.0	1.0	1.3	3.1
3.8	5.3	5.3		All Other Current	4.0	6.1	5.8	5.1	5.2	5.4
41.8	43.3	44.2		Total Current	47.4	38.9	36.0	42.8	45.6	51.3
45.3	43.0	42.3		Fixed Assets (net)	37.7	48.9	47.1	45.5	42.0	33.4
.8	.7	.9		Intangibles (net)	2.7	.6	.6	.7	.6	1.1
12.1	13.1	12.5		All Other Non-Current	12.2	11.5	16.4	10.9	11.8	14.2
100.0	100.0	100.0		Total	100.0	100.0	100.0	100.0	100.0	100.0
				LIABILITIES						
4.2	4.5	4.1		Notes Payable-Short Term	7.9	4.7	2.4	4.2	3.6	3.2
2.6	2.0	2.0		Cur. Mat.-L.T.D.	1.7	2.9	3.0	1.5	1.8	1.6
7.7	7.2	7.0		Trade Payables	6.7	4.2	5.0	5.7	7.7	10.9
.1	.1	.1		Income Taxes Payable	.0	.1	.2	.1	.2	.1
10.8	9.1	11.6		All Other Current	11.2	7.2	8.1	9.4	14.0	16.1
25.4	23.0	24.7		Total Current	27.5	19.2	18.6	20.9	27.2	31.9
19.8	20.0	18.2		Long-Term Debt	22.6	17.5	18.3	18.3	19.2	15.5
.0	.0	.0		Deferred Taxes	.0	.0	.0	.0	.1	.0
3.9	3.7	2.5		All Other Non-Current	3.2	2.0	1.5	2.0	2.4	3.8
50.9	53.2	54.5		Net Worth	46.7	61.2	61.5	58.8	51.2	48.7
100.0	100.0	100.0		Total Liabilties & Net Worth	100.0	100.0	100.0	100.0	100.0	100.0
				INCOME DATA						
100.0	100.0	100.0		Net Sales	100.0	100.0	100.0	100.0	100.0	100.0
				Gross Profit						
96.6	96.3	96.6		Operating Expenses	94.0	95.4	95.1	96.7	97.8	97.8
3.4	3.7	3.4		Operating Profit	6.0	4.6	4.9	3.3	2.2	2.2
.0	.6	.2		All Other Expenses (net)	2.2	.3	.5	.5	-.5	-.3
3.4	3.1	3.2		Profit Before Taxes	3.8	4.3	4.4	2.8	2.6	2.5
				RATIOS						
3.3	4.0	3.6			6.2	4.6	4.1	4.4	3.1	2.9
1.8	2.0	2.0		Current	2.0	2.7	2.3	2.1	2.0	1.6
1.1	1.2	1.2			.6	1.4	1.1	1.3	1.2	1.1
3.0	3.6	3.1			4.7	3.7	3.5	3.7	2.8	2.5
1.6	1.6	1.7		Quick	1.6	2.0	1.7	1.7	1.8	1.3
.9	1.0	1.0			.6	1.1	.9	1.0	1.1	.9

							Sales/Receivables											
13	28.0	11	32.4	13	29.0			0	UND	7	56.1	8	48.2	19	19.6	21	17.3	14	25.8
31	11.8	32	11.5	32	11.6			11	33.3	25	14.5	24	14.9	32	11.3	37	9.8	34	10.6
49	7.4	50	7.3	50	7.4			29	12.5	45	8.1	48	7.5	49	7.4	55	6.6	50	7.3

				Cost of Sales/Inventory						

				Cost of Sales/Payables						

5.1	4.1	4.2		Sales/Working Capital	3.7	2.6	3.9	4.1	4.8	5.4
12.2	9.8	9.1			12.0	5.8	9.1	8.9	8.4	13.1
158.5	44.9	36.7			-22.2	25.6	138.6	24.1	29.5	66.4

							EBIT/Interest						
	9.0		8.3		7.7				5.1		7.2		16.9		7.0		6.5		10.0
(423)	2.9	(496)	2.7	(476)	2.9			(26)	1.4	(81)	2.3	(47)	2.9	(93)	2.7	(133)	3.1	(96)	3.4
	.3		.2		.4				-6.5		-1.8		-.1		.0		1.1		1.1

							Net Profit + Depr., Dep., Amort./Cur. Mat. L/T/D						
			11.9																
		(10)	6.9																
			2.1																

.4	.4	.3		Fixed/Worth	.1	.4	.3	.3	.4	.3
.9	.8	.8			.6	.9	.8	.7	.8	.6
1.6	1.5	1.3			2.1	1.3	1.4	1.2	1.4	1.3
.3	.3	.3		Debt/Worth	.2	.2	.2	.3	.4	.4
.8	.7	.7			.6	.5	.5	.6	.8	1.0
2.1	1.9	1.6			3.1	1.0	1.3	1.7	1.6	1.9

							% Profit Before Taxes/Tangible Net Worth						
	15.8		12.7		13.6				40.0		11.2		19.3		12.4		13.4		13.4
(597)	5.9	(669)	4.5	(659)	* 4.9			(51)	2.6	(109)	3.6	(70)	6.9	(125)	3.5	(181)	5.1	(123)	5.7
	-1.9		-1.9		-.8				-7.8		-3.3		-1.8		-1.6		.0		.3

7.5	7.1	7.6		% Profit Before Taxes/Total Assets	7.6	7.7	11.6	7.0	6.5	7.3
2.6	2.3	2.5			1.0	2.4	4.7	2.2	2.3	3.1
-1.3	-1.2	-.6			-5.9	-2.9	-1.1	-.9	-.1	.1
10.8	10.8	11.9		Sales/Net Fixed Assets	43.3	8.3	8.4	9.5	9.5	19.6
3.7	3.7	3.7			5.9	2.2	3.0	3.2	4.0	5.1
1.7	1.8	1.7			.8	.9	1.0	1.6	2.2	2.8
2.6	2.5	2.4		Sales/Total Assets	3.0	1.9	2.1	2.3	2.3	3.3
1.6	1.5	1.5			1.3	1.0	1.3	1.5	1.6	1.8
.8	.8	.8			.5	.5	.6	.8	1.0	1.1

							% Depr., Dep., Amort./Sales						
	1.2		1.2		1.2				1.1		1.4		1.4		1.3		1.2		.7
(549)	2.2	(606)	2.3	(614)	2.2			(38)	3.9	(100)	2.9	(63)	2.4	(117)	2.3	(178)	1.9	(118)	1.7
	3.6		3.7		3.8				9.7		5.7		4.6		3.9		3.2		2.9

							% Officers', Directors' Owners' Comp/Sales						
	2.9		3.9		3.0				2.4						1.8		1.8		1.8
(56)	8.3	(67)	6.6	(66)	7.8					(12)	7.9			(11)	15.3	(18)	6.5	(13)	7.2
	18.7		14.5		15.4						10.5				17.8		14.2		17.7

10700001M	12295573M	14851298M		Net Sales ($)	28787M	214711M	287480M	930442M	2983256M	10406622M
6378847M	9047681M	9093666M		Total Assets ($)	41282M	358611M	380271M	927646M	2435890M	4949966M

M = $ thousand   MM = $ million
See Pages 11 through 21 for Explanation of Ratios and Data

Current Data Sorted by Assets   Comparative Historical Data

0-500M	500M-2MM	2-10MM	10-50MM	50-100MM	100-250MM	Type of Statement	4/1/02-3/31/03 ALL	4/1/03-3/31/04 ALL
	2	12	15	2	1	Unqualified	8	14
1		1				Reviewed		2
	1					Compiled		
1	3		1			Tax Returns		
						Other	4	8
	30 (4/1-9/30/06)	6	18 (10/1/06-3/31/07)					
2	6	19	18	2	1	NUMBER OF STATEMENTS	12	24
%	%	%	%	%	%		%	%
						ASSETS		
		12.0	9.8			Cash & Equivalents	7.4	13.9
		8.5	4.1			Trade Receivables (net)	17.6	12.6
		5.4	5.9			Inventory	4.5	2.3
		7.9	3.8			All Other Current	4.3	2.0
		33.9	23.5			Total Current	33.8	30.7
		47.0	48.1			Fixed Assets (net)	45.6	49.1
		.1	.7			Intangibles (net)	1.2	.2
		19.0	27.7			All Other Non-Current	19.5	19.9
		100.0	100.0			Total	100.0	100.0
						LIABILITIES		
		4.2	3.0			Notes Payable-Short Term	1.6	7.0
		3.8	8.3			Cur. Mat.-L.T.D.	3.0	1.8
		5.0	4.7			Trade Payables	7.5	4.0
		.0	.0			Income Taxes Payable	.5	.0
		7.6	2.4			All Other Current	11.7	6.2
		20.6	18.4			Total Current	24.4	19.0
		26.3	29.5			Long-Term Debt	28.6	44.7
		.0	.0			Deferred Taxes	.0	.0
		1.6	5.0			All Other Non-Current	2.4	3.2
		51.4	47.1			Net Worth	44.6	33.1
		100.0	100.0			Total Liabilities & Net Worth	100.0	100.0
						INCOME DATA		
		100.0	100.0			Net Sales	100.0	100.0
						Gross Profit		
		90.4	91.1			Operating Expenses	89.2	97.3
		9.6	8.9			Operating Profit	10.8	2.7
		1.3	4.6			All Other Expenses (net)	1.4	6.4
		8.2	4.3			Profit Before Taxes	9.4	-3.7
						RATIOS		
		3.5	3.6			Current	2.8	5.9
		1.4	1.9				1.2	1.7
		.9	.8				1.0	.7
		1.5	2.7			Quick	2.6	5.0
		1.0	1.0				.9	1.4
		.5	.6				.8	.6
	2	222.7	0 UND			Sales/Receivables	10 36.0	4 83.3
	31	11.7	21 17.0				35 10.5	22 16.8
	73	5.0	57 6.4				60 6.1	54 6.8
						Cost of Sales/Inventory		
						Cost of Sales/Payables		
		1.7	1.4			Sales/Working Capital	4.4	3.1
		11.8	5.1				34.9	10.7
		-14.0	-25.7				919.3	-17.8
		10.1	75.5			EBIT/Interest		6.9
		(14) 3.3	(10) 3.0					(11) 1.2
		.9	-.3					-3.4
						Net Profit + Depr., Dep., Amort./Cur. Mat. L/T/D		
		.4	.2			Fixed/Worth	.4	.3
		.9	1.0				1.0	1.3
		1.6	2.7				2.8	31.3
		.6	.4			Debt/Worth	.5	.3
		1.0	1.0				1.5	2.1
		1.4	3.6				4.9	86.7
		16.1	14.0			% Profit Before Taxes/Tangible Net Worth	17.7	23.2
		(18) 4.4	(16) 1.7				2.2	(19) 5.8
		-2.6	-3.4				-3.8	-3.5
		8.4	5.6			% Profit Before Taxes/Total Assets	10.6	7.0
		1.6	.7				.7	.3
		-1.0	-1.3				-2.8	-3.1
		4.3	6.0			Sales/Net Fixed Assets	9.5	16.3
		1.5	1.0				1.9	1.3
		.4	.2				.9	.4
		1.1	.6			Sales/Total Assets	1.5	2.4
		.5	.3				.8	.7
		.3	.1				.3	.2
		1.2	1.2			% Depr., Dep., Amort./Sales	.8	.7
		(17) 4.7	(16) 4.4				(11) 3.0	(22) 5.3
		8.6	14.7				5.8	16.7
						% Officers', Directors' Owners' Comp/Sales		
1309M	5781M	73922M	162263M	66704M	12839M	Net Sales ($)	291473M	334112M
463M	6959M	92440M	381708M	144439M	119901M	Total Assets ($)	402805M	267111M

Comparative Historical Data | Current Data Sorted by Sales

			Type of Statement	0-1MM	1-3MM	3-5MM	5-10MM	10-25MM	25MM & OVER
13	24	32	Unqualified	1	14		6	8	3
3	2	2	Reviewed	1				1	
1			Compiled						
	1	1	Tax Returns	1					
5	7	13	Other	3	7	2	1		
4/1/04-3/31/05	4/1/05-3/31/06	4/1/06-3/31/07			30 (4/1-9/30/06)			18 (10/1/06-3/31/07)	
ALL	ALL	ALL		0-1MM	1-3MM	3-5MM	5-10MM	10-25MM	25MM & OVER
22	34	48	NUMBER OF STATEMENTS	6	21	2	7	9	3
%	%	%	ASSETS	%	%	%	%	%	%
13.4	12.1	12.4	Cash & Equivalents		13.5				
7.1	8.7	6.8	Trade Receivables (net)		7.3				
5.3	1.7	4.6	Inventory		5.1				
2.2	4.3	5.2	All Other Current		7.0				
28.0	26.8	29.0	Total Current		32.9				
54.3	44.5	47.3	Fixed Assets (net)		45.8				
.4	.5	.8	Intangibles (net)		1.5				
17.3	28.2	22.9	All Other Non-Current		19.7				
100.0	100.0	100.0	Total		100.0				
			LIABILITIES						
6.5	2.1	7.1	Notes Payable-Short Term		8.8				
2.7	2.3	4.9	Cur. Mat.-L.T.D.		5.6				
1.9	4.5	4.4	Trade Payables		3.0				
.0	.0	.0	Income Taxes Payable		.0				
5.9	5.8	4.8	All Other Current		3.8				
17.0	14.7	21.2	Total Current		21.2				
42.3	35.3	28.2	Long-Term Debt		28.7				
.0	.0	.0	Deferred Taxes		.0				
1.3	2.1	2.7	All Other Non-Current		.8				
39.4	47.9	48.0	Net Worth		49.3				
100.0	100.0	100.0	Total Liabilities & Net Worth		100.0				
			INCOME DATA						
100.0	100.0	100.0	Net Sales		100.0				
			Gross Profit						
89.9	89.9	90.7	Operating Expenses		87.7				
10.1	10.1	9.3	Operating Profit		12.3				
7.3	4.2	2.8	All Other Expenses (net)		2.8				
2.8	5.8	6.6	Profit Before Taxes		9.5				
			RATIOS						
3.4	4.5	3.5			5.2				
1.7	1.8	1.6	Current		2.6				
1.0	1.0	.9			.9				
2.8	2.2	2.4			2.4				
1.5	1.4	1.0	Quick		1.0				
.7	.8	.5			.7				
0 UND	2 218.0	0 UND			0 UND				
26 13.8	16 22.4	21 17.0	Sales/Receivables		30 12.0				
56 6.6	45 8.1	58 6.3			86 4.2				
			Cost of Sales/Inventory						
			Cost of Sales/Payables						
3.3	2.0	2.0			1.2				
7.4	5.3	7.9	Sales/Working Capital		2.4				
37.3	-602.8	-21.8			-51.6				
3.5	3.7	7.5			20.3				
(16) 1.4	(21) 1.5	(31) 2.8	EBIT/Interest		(13) 3.6				
-1.8	.7	1.0			.6				
			Net Profit + Depr., Dep., Amort./Cur. Mat. L/T/D						
.7	.2	.3			.5				
1.3	1.0	.9	Fixed/Worth		.9				
5.6	2.4	1.8			2.8				
.6	.5	.5			.5				
1.6	.9	1.0	Debt/Worth		.9				
5.9	3.3	2.9			3.2				
11.5	14.6	15.9			15.9				
(20) 5.3	(31) 4.1	(43) 4.6	% Profit Before Taxes/Tangible Net Worth		(19) 4.6				
-1.9	-.8	-.9			-.9				
3.5	3.9	7.3			7.9				
1.6	1.4	1.6	% Profit Before Taxes/Total Assets		3.2				
-1.4	-.5	-.5			-.2				
4.7	11.9	4.9			4.0				
.8	1.2	1.5	Sales/Net Fixed Assets		1.1				
.4	.4	.4			.3				
1.2	1.0	.9			.7				
.5	.4	.4	Sales/Total Assets		.4				
.2	.2	.2			.2				
.8	1.2	1.4			1.4				
(21) 5.8	(28) 5.0	(42) 3.9	% Depr., Dep., Amort./Sales		3.3				
13.1	8.6	7.7			7.7				
			% Officers', Directors' Owners' Comp/Sales						
271188M	355761M	322818M	Net Sales ($)	2467M	37817M	8670M	50679M	130159M	93026M
383982M	517787M	745910M	Total Assets ($)	10195M	167576M	23958M	104698M	273024M	166459M

M = $ thousand   MM = $ million
See Pages 11 through 21 for Explanation of Ratios and Data

Current Data Sorted by Assets / Comparative Historical Data

						Type of Statement		
5	31	98	62	5	4	Unqualified	153	159
	3	1	1			Reviewed	1	4
	2	3	3			Compiled	7	21
3	4	2				Tax Returns	7	5
2	10	21	22	1		Other	52	54
	192 (4/1-9/30/06)		91 (10/1/06-3/31/07)				4/1/02-3/31/03 ALL	4/1/03-3/31/04 ALL
0-500M	500M-2MM	2-10MM	10-50MM	50-100MM	100-250MM			
10	50	125	88	6	4	NUMBER OF STATEMENTS	220	243
%	%	%	%	%	%	ASSETS	%	%
37.3	18.3	16.5	18.0			Cash & Equivalents	17.1	15.8
15.2	24.7	17.3	17.7			Trade Receivables (net)	20.2	19.3
.1	1.5	3.1	3.6			Inventory	2.3	2.4
20.7	5.8	4.8	2.8			All Other Current	3.6	4.8
73.3	50.3	41.7	42.1			Total Current	43.3	42.3
17.1	43.0	47.8	45.6			Fixed Assets (net)	45.4	45.4
.2	1.4	1.0	1.2			Intangibles (net)	1.1	1.2
9.4	5.2	9.5	11.2			All Other Non-Current	10.3	11.1
100.0	100.0	100.0	100.0			Total	100.0	100.0
						LIABILITIES		
1.6	7.9	3.2	2.3			Notes Payable-Short Term	4.3	5.0
.9	2.8	2.1	1.9			Cur. Mat.-L.T.D.	3.9	2.8
2.5	6.7	5.7	7.2			Trade Payables	8.2	6.7
.0	.1	.1	.0			Income Taxes Payable	.0	.0
25.5	13.4	10.1	9.4			All Other Current	11.4	11.9
30.5	31.0	21.2	20.8			Total Current	27.9	26.5
12.9	18.7	18.8	20.3			Long-Term Debt	21.9	18.4
.0	.0	.2	.0			Deferred Taxes	.0	.0
.8	8.6	2.2	2.3			All Other Non-Current	2.7	3.9
55.7	41.7	57.6	56.5			Net Worth	47.5	51.2
100.0	100.0	100.0	100.0			Total Liabilities & Net Worth	100.0	100.0
						INCOME DATA		
100.0	100.0	100.0	100.0			Net Sales	100.0	100.0
						Gross Profit		
79.7	97.5	96.3	95.6			Operating Expenses	96.5	96.2
20.3	2.5	3.7	4.4			Operating Profit	3.5	3.8
1.7	1.6	.8	-.2			All Other Expenses (net)	2.0	.9
18.6	.9	2.8	4.6			Profit Before Taxes	1.5	2.9
						RATIOS		
11.0	3.2	3.4	3.9				3.3	3.1
4.9	1.4	2.1	2.2			Current	1.8	1.9
1.0	1.0	1.2	1.5				1.1	1.2
11.0	2.8	2.9	3.4				2.8	2.6
4.8	1.3	1.7	1.8			Quick	1.6	1.5
.4	.9	1.1	1.2				1.0	.9
0 UND	8 45.1	11 32.2	17 21.4				19 18.9	17 21.7
14 25.8	31 12.0	33 11.1	31 11.7			Sales/Receivables	34 10.8	33 11.0
37 9.9	51 7.1	47 7.8	51 7.1				51 7.1	48 7.7
						Cost of Sales/Inventory		
						Cost of Sales/Payables		
4.3	6.5	4.3	3.9				5.3	5.7
6.2	13.6	10.0	8.0			Sales/Working Capital	11.3	11.6
UND	-291.2	30.6	17.3				39.8	30.0
	6.8	7.2	8.2				6.2	9.1
	(41) 2.4	(99) 3.4	(76) 3.6			EBIT/Interest	(174) 2.2	(185) 2.8
	-2.3	.5	.9				-.3	.1
						Net Profit + Depr., Dep., Amort./Cur. Mat. L/T/D		
.0	.4	.5	.4				.5	.5
.5	1.1	.9	.9			Fixed/Worth	1.0	.9
UND	2.0	1.3	1.4				1.5	1.4
.2	.5	.4	.4				.4	.4
.4	1.1	.8	.7			Debt/Worth	.8	.8
UND	2.7	1.3	1.4				1.9	1.7
UND	18.5	12.1	14.3			% Profit Before Taxes/Tangible Net Worth	14.8	18.5
19.4	(45) 3.2	(124) 5.7	7.4				(210) 4.7	(233) 4.7
1.2	-17.1	-1.5	.0				-3.8	-2.9
288.3	9.7	6.8	8.2			% Profit Before Taxes/Total Assets	7.4	9.6
10.8	2.0	2.7	3.9				2.4	3.2
1.0	-7.2	-.8	.0				-2.5	-1.4
UND	31.9	7.4	4.7			Sales/Net Fixed Assets	8.9	8.7
UND	5.9	3.2	2.6				3.9	3.5
13.6	1.9	1.8	1.9				2.3	1.9
27.2	4.2	2.4	1.9			Sales/Total Assets	2.4	2.4
3.1	2.4	1.5	1.3				1.8	1.6
2.1	1.1	1.0	.8				1.1	1.0
	1.0	1.7	1.7			% Depr., Dep., Amort./Sales	1.9	1.6
	(45) 2.3	(115) 3.1	(85) 2.7				(201) 2.7	(218) 2.9
	3.5	4.7	3.9				4.1	4.3
	2.9	2.3				% Officers', Directors' Owners' Comp/Sales	2.8	2.1
	(10) 21.0	(10) 16.6					(25) 9.0	(25) 7.0
	44.4	41.7					29.3	25.5
6638M	172310M	1129717M	3052197M	602276M	1004392M	Net Sales ($)	5010836M	4518919M
2286M	65516M	668727M	2033489M	399151M	528145M	Total Assets ($)	2340361M	2536540M

M = $ thousand   MM = $ million
See Pages 11 through 21 for Explanation of Ratios and Data

Comparative Historical Data / Current Data Sorted by Sales

			Type of Statement						
168	145	205	Unqualified	9	29	20	47	54	46
3	7	5	Reviewed		1	2		1	1
7	6	8	Compiled		2	1	1	4	
8	8	9	Tax Returns	4	3	2			
44	69	56	Other	3	8	2	14	15	14
4/1/04-	4/1/05-	4/1/06-			192 (4/1-9/30/06)		91 (10/1/06-3/31/07)		
3/31/05	3/31/06	3/31/07		0-1MM	1-3MM	3-5MM	5-10MM	10-25MM	25MM & OVER
ALL	ALL	ALL							
230	235	283	NUMBER OF STATEMENTS	16	43	27	62	74	61
%	%	%	ASSETS	%	%	%	%	%	%
17.3	16.8	17.8	Cash & Equivalents	14.7	18.7	23.0	17.1	16.4	18.2
19.5	21.7	18.7	Trade Receivables (net)	5.6	15.0	24.0	17.0	19.3	23.5
3.5	2.5	2.8	Inventory	.2	3.4	2.9	2.0	3.0	3.6
3.5	4.0	4.9	All Other Current	13.5	3.6	1.5	9.3	3.1	2.9
43.8	45.0	44.3	Total Current	34.1	40.7	51.4	45.4	41.8	48.1
43.9	44.3	45.0	Fixed Assets (net)	50.7	53.5	35.8	43.8	46.5	41.0
1.5	1.6	1.1	Intangibles (net)	.1	1.0	1.1	1.6	.9	1.1
10.8	9.1	9.7	All Other Non-Current	15.1	4.9	11.7	9.2	10.8	9.8
100.0	100.0	100.0	Total	100.0	100.0	100.0	100.0	100.0	100.0
			LIABILITIES						
4.8	5.3	3.6	Notes Payable-Short Term	2.2	5.7	6.4	3.1	3.2	2.4
4.1	2.7	2.1	Cur. Mat.-L.T.D.	1.0	2.9	2.0	2.6	1.5	2.0
7.8	7.9	6.4	Trade Payables	2.1	3.9	8.0	5.6	6.2	9.4
.1	.0	.1	Income Taxes Payable	.0	.1	.1	.1	.0	.0
13.1	11.6	11.1	All Other Current	13.4	8.1	10.3	11.7	10.3	13.4
29.9	27.6	23.2	Total Current	18.7	20.6	27.0	23.2	21.2	27.1
19.6	20.2	19.2	Long-Term Debt	24.5	25.7	12.4	17.2	20.2	17.1
.0	.0	.1	Deferred Taxes	.0	.0	.0	.5	.0	.0
2.2	4.9	3.5	All Other Non-Current	.1	1.7	6.6	5.8	1.8	4.1
48.3	47.2	53.9	Net Worth	56.7	52.0	54.0	53.3	56.8	51.7
100.0	100.0	100.0	Total Liabilties & Net Worth	100.0	100.0	100.0	100.0	100.0	100.0
			INCOME DATA						
100.0	100.0	100.0	Net Sales	100.0	100.0	100.0	100.0	100.0	100.0
			Gross Profit						
97.2	97.0	95.8	Operating Expenses	85.5	92.8	99.2	95.4	97.9	97.0
2.8	3.0	4.2	Operating Profit	14.5	7.2	.8	4.6	2.1	3.0
.2	.8	.7	All Other Expenses (net)	6.0	2.7	-.7	-.4	-.1	.4
2.6	2.2	3.5	Profit Before Taxes	8.5	4.5	1.5	4.9	2.1	2.6
			RATIOS						
2.9	4.0	3.6		10.4	6.2	7.0	3.4	3.5	2.5
1.7	1.9	2.0	Current	1.9	2.1	3.3	2.1	2.0	1.7
1.1	1.2	1.2		1.0	1.1	1.2	1.2	1.3	1.3
2.6	3.1	3.2		10.4	6.0	6.4	2.7	3.3	2.3
1.5	1.6	1.6	Quick	1.6	1.5	2.7	1.6	1.7	1.5
.9	1.0	1.0		.5	.9	1.1	1.0	1.1	1.1
17 21.4	13 27.8	13 28.6	Sales/Receivables	0 UND	9 42.4	23 16.2	10 36.7	20 18.2	17 21.4
34 10.8	34 10.8	32 11.4		1 367.9	31 11.7	37 9.8	29 12.7	34 10.6	34 10.8
46 8.0	50 7.2	49 7.5		26 14.1	57 6.4	54 6.7	42 8.6	47 7.8	54 6.7
			Cost of Sales/Inventory						
			Cost of Sales/Payables						
5.7	4.8	4.7	Sales/Working Capital	2.0	4.1	3.0	4.9	5.5	5.7
11.7	10.2	9.8		15.1	7.4	5.7	10.3	9.8	11.0
47.8	32.2	32.1		UND	131.1	17.0	30.3	28.8	31.5
11.0	9.5	7.5			7.0	7.4	7.1	7.2	14.5
(187) 3.5	(183) 2.8	(230) 3.4	EBIT/Interest	(31) 2.4	(22) 2.9	(49) 3.3	(66) 3.6	(53) 3.5	
1.1	.2	.3			-.6	-1.5	.6	1.3	.8
			Net Profit + Depr., Dep., Amort./Cur. Mat. L/T/D						
.5	.5	.4		.7	.6	.2	.4	.5	.4
.9	1.0	.9	Fixed/Worth	1.1	1.1	.5	.9	.8	.9
1.5	1.6	1.4		3.3	2.0	1.4	1.5	1.3	1.3
.5	.5	.4		.1	.3	.2	.4	.4	.5
.9	.9	.8	Debt/Worth	.6	1.0	.8	.8	.7	1.0
2.0	2.0	1.6		2.6	2.1	1.9	1.4	1.4	1.7
15.2	16.6	14.4	% Profit Before Taxes/Tangible Net Worth	42.0	18.8	13.8	12.2	13.0	17.4
(216) 6.7	(226) 6.8	(277) 6.2		.5	(42) 7.0	(25) 5.9	(60) 3.8	(73) 6.1	6.8
.6	-2.5	-1.8		-5.2	-7.0	-9.0	-1.1	-.2	-1.2
8.1	8.6	8.4	% Profit Before Taxes/Total Assets	13.0	10.3	7.6	8.2	6.3	10.3
3.4	3.5	3.4		.5	2.7	2.8	3.2	3.7	3.8
.3	-1.6	-.8		-4.1	-2.5	-4.7	-.5	-.3	-.6
9.9	10.7	9.9	Sales/Net Fixed Assets	UND	6.0	13.1	17.2	6.2	11.4
3.8	3.7	3.3		1.8	2.1	3.7	3.3	3.3	4.0
2.0	1.9	1.9		.3	1.0	1.9	2.0	2.0	2.3
2.7	2.8	2.6	Sales/Total Assets	2.5	2.2	2.5	2.7	2.5	2.8
1.5	1.7	1.6		.4	1.1	1.2	1.7	1.6	1.8
1.1	.9	1.0		.1	.6	.9	1.2	1.1	1.2
1.6	1.5	1.5	% Depr., Dep., Amort./Sales	2.2	1.9	1.5	1.1	1.5	1.4
(215) 2.5	(216) 2.7	(259) 2.7		(10) 7.6	(37) 3.4	(25) 3.2	(57) 2.7	(72) 2.6	(58) 2.3
4.1	4.0	4.1		41.5	5.6	4.3	3.9	3.5	3.9
4.1	2.1	3.1	% Officers', Directors' Owners' Comp/Sales						
(23) 9.1	(20) 7.2	(30) 9.8							
19.4	28.6	37.9							
4355786M	5022812M	5967530M	Net Sales ($)	6202M	83691M	108348M	449622M	1205979M	4113688M
2660084M	3008963M	3697314M	Total Assets ($)	21909M	103796M	114876M	322774M	915649M	2218310M

M = $ thousand   MM = $ million
See Pages 11 through 21 for Explanation of Ratios and Data

Current Data Sorted by Assets   Comparative Historical Data

Type of Statement	0-500M	500M-2MM	2-10MM	10-50MM	50-100MM	100-250MM	4/1/02-3/31/03 ALL	4/1/03-3/31/04 ALL
Unqualified	7	19	37	9	2	1	51	70
Reviewed	4	2	5				10	18
Compiled	22	14	8			1	51	82
Tax Returns	114	48	9	1	2	2	89	106
Other	44	36	17	6	1	1	61	54
	106 (4/1-9/30/06)			306 (10/1/06-3/31/07)				
NUMBER OF STATEMENTS	191	119	76	16	5	5	262	330
ASSETS	%	%	%	%	%	%	%	%
Cash & Equivalents	28.8	13.0	18.2	14.7			17.6	19.5
Trade Receivables (net)	7.5	8.0	9.9	13.6			8.9	9.2
Inventory	.4	.2	.0	.5			.1	.2
All Other Current	6.1	1.8	2.9	3.2			4.0	4.0
Total Current	43.0	22.9	31.0	32.0			30.6	32.8
Fixed Assets (net)	39.5	58.9	60.7	59.1			55.4	53.4
Intangibles (net)	8.0	8.5	2.2	1.7			5.9	4.2
All Other Non-Current	9.5	9.7	6.0	7.2			8.0	9.6
Total	100.0	100.0	100.0	100.0			100.0	100.0
LIABILITIES								
Notes Payable-Short Term	7.6	6.5	2.2	1.8			8.2	6.4
Cur. Mat.-L.T.D.	5.3	3.6	2.3	10.0			6.5	3.9
Trade Payables	3.7	4.9	6.4	8.6			5.0	6.9
Income Taxes Payable	.1	.0	.1	.0			.1	.1
All Other Current	32.7	9.2	9.6	9.5			20.7	16.7
Total Current	49.3	24.1	20.5	29.9			40.5	34.0
Long-Term Debt	30.2	49.4	37.7	38.9			34.5	39.3
Deferred Taxes	.0	.2	.1	.2			.1	.1
All Other Non-Current	13.9	6.1	2.3	8.2			15.4	9.1
Net Worth	6.6	20.1	39.3	22.7			9.5	17.5
Total Liabilities & Net Worth	100.0	100.0	100.0	100.0			100.0	100.0
INCOME DATA								
Net Sales	100.0	100.0	100.0	100.0			100.0	100.0
Gross Profit								
Operating Expenses	92.4	85.0	89.9	97.8			91.8	93.1
Operating Profit	7.6	15.0	10.1	2.2			8.2	6.9
All Other Expenses (net)	1.6	8.6	5.1	1.1			3.6	2.5
Profit Before Taxes	6.0	6.3	5.0	1.1			4.6	4.4
RATIOS								
Current	3.8	2.3	2.9	1.9			2.2	2.7
	1.0	.9	1.3	1.5			.9	1.1
	.4	.2	.8	1.0			.3	.4
Quick	3.1	2.1	2.8	1.6			2.0	2.4
	(190) .8	(118) .7	1.3	1.3			(260) .8	(329) 1.0
	.3	.1	.6	.8			.2	.3
Sales/Receivables	0 UND	0 UND	0 UND	5 77.0			0 UND	0 UND
	0 UND	0 UND	14 26.9	16 23.0			2 187.0	1 302.6
	4 92.0	19 19.7	24 15.3	29 12.7			17 21.8	16 22.2
Cost of Sales/Inventory								
Cost of Sales/Payables								
Sales/Working Capital	22.7	12.3	7.6	9.4			16.9	12.9
	UND	-51.9	27.8	23.8			-243.4	152.6
	-23.4	-8.2	-44.0	-457.3			-13.5	-16.8
EBIT/Interest	12.2	3.0	9.9	6.3			6.5	5.4
	(120) 4.7	(82) 1.5	(59) 3.3	(14) 2.9			(184) 2.6	(231) 2.5
	1.0	.3	1.4	.0			1.1	1.1
Net Profit + Depr., Dep., Amort./Cur. Mat. L/T/D							5.0	4.1
							(22) 2.0	(24) 1.7
							1.4	.6
Fixed/Worth	.3	.8	.7	1.1			.8	.7
	1.5	7.4	1.4	1.6			2.6	1.9
	-2.5	-5.6	5.0	5.5			-32.5	233.0
Debt/Worth	.5	1.4	.6	.8			.8	.8
	2.6	7.1	1.5	1.6			3.7	2.9
	-4.5	-8.3	5.8	7.0			-35.1	UND
% Profit Before Taxes/Tangible Net Worth	146.7	61.5	31.4	20.7			64.2	60.8
	(123) 58.4	(74) 30.1	(68) 11.3	(13) 6.9			(191) 21.1	(248) 17.3
	12.4	3.0	2.3	-.1			4.4	1.5
% Profit Before Taxes/Total Assets	57.5	12.6	10.0	9.9			19.6	17.2
	21.8	3.5	4.1	2.2			6.1	5.9
	1.6	-1.8	.8	-5.1			.1	.0
Sales/Net Fixed Assets	107.0	11.3	7.5	8.9			25.3	20.2
	18.6	1.9	2.2	2.2			5.6	6.2
	7.7	.8	1.0	1.8			1.4	1.5
Sales/Total Assets	11.6	2.4	3.0	3.5			5.6	5.8
	5.9	1.2	1.2	1.6			2.4	2.5
	3.1	.6	.7	1.2			1.1	1.1
% Depr., Dep., Amort./Sales	.9	1.7	1.4	1.3			1.3	1.3
	(126) 1.9	(98) 3.6	(66) 2.5	2.0			(212) 2.5	(268) 2.7
	3.1	9.8	4.5	4.7			5.2	4.4
% Officers', Directors' Owners' Comp/Sales	2.6	2.5	2.0				3.1	3.4
	(95) 5.9	(36) 4.8	(10) 4.3				(101) 5.8	(126) 6.1
	8.4	9.5	37.1				12.7	11.4
Net Sales ($)	165883M	212066M	680017M	614628M	1306041M	4761165M	3502292M	3749358M
Total Assets ($)	31566M	126321M	325653M	282796M	357732M	815689M	1410504M	1517220M

M = $ thousand   MM = $ million
See Pages 11 through 21 for Explanation of Ratios and Data

Comparative Historical Data | Current Data Sorted by Sales

				Type of Statement						
57		56	75	Unqualified	13	18	6	11	16	11
8		13	11	Reviewed	3	3	2	2	1	
54		50	45	Compiled	20	15	3	4	2	1
138		135	176	Tax Returns	110	52	7	2		5
70		99	105	Other	44	36	5	4	9	7
4/1/04-3/31/05 ALL		4/1/05-3/31/06 ALL	4/1/06-3/31/07 ALL		106 (4/1-9/30/06)			306 (10/1/06-3/31/07)		
					0-1MM	1-3MM	3-5MM	5-10MM	10-25MM	25MM & OVER
327		353	412	NUMBER OF STATEMENTS	190	124	23	23	28	24
%		%	%	ASSETS	%	%	%	%	%	%
19.5		18.3	21.5	Cash & Equivalents	22.2	20.6	17.8	26.3	20.6	21.0
8.6		9.1	8.3	Trade Receivables (net)	5.0	7.0	22.5	11.4	13.3	19.1
.3		.8	.3	Inventory	.4	.2	.0	.1	.1	.3
2.2		4.5	4.2	All Other Current	4.2	4.7	5.0	2.2	2.5	4.5
30.6		32.7	34.3	Total Current	31.8	32.6	45.3	40.0	36.5	44.9
54.3		52.7	49.7	Fixed Assets (net)	52.7	47.8	45.9	47.6	51.3	39.4
5.9		6.0	7.0	Intangibles (net)	7.1	9.6	.7	3.9	2.5	7.3
9.2		8.6	9.0	All Other Non-Current	8.4	10.0	8.1	8.5	9.6	8.5
100.0		100.0	100.0	Total	100.0	100.0	100.0	100.0	100.0	100.0
				LIABILITIES						
6.7		5.6	5.9	Notes Payable-Short Term	6.6	6.4	9.0	3.3	1.8	1.7
4.1		4.3	4.5	Cur. Mat.-L.T.D.	5.4	3.2	1.9	2.7	3.0	9.1
4.9		4.9	5.0	Trade Payables	2.7	4.0	9.9	6.1	9.8	17.2
.3		.0	.0	Income Taxes Payable	.1	.0	.0	.3	.0	.0
16.8		14.5	20.4	All Other Current	28.9	13.3	11.1	10.1	14.9	14.2
32.7		29.3	35.7	Total Current	43.6	26.9	31.9	22.5	29.5	42.3
39.6		36.0	37.3	Long-Term Debt	43.7	35.2	29.2	22.5	31.8	25.9
.1		.1	.1	Deferred Taxes	.0	.1	.1	.3	.1	.2
13.8		9.8	9.5	All Other Non-Current	10.3	11.0	1.8	5.3	5.6	10.7
13.8		24.7	17.4	Net Worth	2.3	26.7	37.0	49.4	33.0	20.9
100.0		100.0	100.0	Total Liabilties & Net Worth	100.0	100.0	100.0	100.0	100.0	100.0
				INCOME DATA						
100.0		100.0	100.0	Net Sales	100.0	100.0	100.0	100.0	100.0	100.0
				Gross Profit						
91.1		91.8	90.1	Operating Expenses	86.6	91.8	92.6	92.4	97.2	96.9
8.9		8.2	9.9	Operating Profit	13.4	8.2	7.4	7.6	2.8	3.1
3.2		3.5	4.2	All Other Expenses (net)	6.9	2.7	1.8	1.1	.4	.7
5.8		4.6	5.6	Profit Before Taxes	6.5	5.5	5.6	6.5	2.4	2.4
				RATIOS						
2.5		3.3	2.9		3.2	3.4	2.4	4.4	1.8	1.8
1.2		1.3	1.1	Current	.8	1.1	1.2	1.7	1.2	1.2
.4		.5	.4		.3	.5	.5	1.1	.9	.9
2.3		2.6	2.4		3.0	3.1	1.9	3.9	1.7	1.5
(325) 1.0	(350)	1.1	(410) .9	Quick	(188) .6	.9	1.1	1.4	1.2	1.1
.3		.3	.3		.2	.3	.3	1.1	.9	.5
0 UND	0	UND	0 UND		0 UND	0 UND	0 999.8	1 368.4	2 149.6	4 86.3
0 999.8	1	379.6	0 UND	Sales/Receivables	0 UND	0 UND	16 22.9	10 38.3	17 20.9	11 34.6
16 22.7	15	24.4	15 25.1		4 86.5	10 35.3	32 11.5	22 16.4	22 16.7	31 11.9
				Cost of Sales/Inventory						
				Cost of Sales/Payables						
16.2		12.5	15.3		18.0	15.4	10.0	7.6	13.7	17.8
153.2		60.5	228.6	Sales/Working Capital	-92.1	178.4	47.0	22.0	34.5	134.6
-24.8		-27.6	-20.3		-9.8	-28.7	-20.7	188.8	-144.4	-158.0
8.0		9.9	9.5		9.0	6.9	10.5	57.8	20.6	17.5
(242) 3.2	(256)	3.5	(281) 2.6	EBIT/Interest	(117) 2.0	(90) 2.6	(16) 2.8	(17) 9.9	(23) 4.8	(18) 3.9
.8		1.0	.9		-.1	1.2	.8	1.8	2.2	1.9
5.7		15.6	8.3							
(26) 3.1	(22)	5.0	(19) 3.6	Net Profit + Depr., Dep., Amort./Cur. Mat. L/T/D						
1.7		2.3	1.8							
.7		.6	.6		.5	.5	.3	.5	.8	.6
2.1		1.9	2.0	Fixed/Worth	3.7	1.9	1.1	.9	1.5	1.9
-22.1		-232.8	-8.1		-3.2	-5.3	5.6	2.0	3.8	-4.7
.8		.6	.7		.9	.5	.7	.2	1.0	1.0
2.9		2.1	2.7	Debt/Worth	6.4	2.4	1.5	.8	1.5	2.0
-14.6		-411.2	-10.0		-5.0	-8.1	5.6	2.6	6.6	-14.5
68.0		73.1	88.3		104.1	102.4	75.2	41.8	36.4	48.1
(231) 22.1	(264)	28.6	(283) 29.6	% Profit Before Taxes/Tangible Net Worth	(114) 44.4	(86) 33.2	(22) 27.5	(20) 17.3	(24) 10.5	(17) 16.2
2.1		3.5	4.3		4.2	2.9	10.8	9.6	2.3	3.8
24.5		25.4	28.6		36.0	32.9	20.7	17.9	14.8	18.2
7.7		7.4	8.3	% Profit Before Taxes/Total Assets	6.6	10.3	8.5	10.9	5.9	6.1
-.7		.2	.0		-1.2	.8	-.8	3.1	1.1	1.4
25.5		22.0	33.7		39.9	40.6	28.2	12.7	12.5	31.0
6.9		6.8	8.0	Sales/Net Fixed Assets	9.0	8.2	10.8	6.5	5.8	12.3
1.5		1.4	1.6		1.2	1.4	1.3	2.8	2.1	4.2
6.1		5.5	6.2		7.4	7.0	5.2	3.6	4.3	5.8
2.8		2.8	2.9	Sales/Total Assets	2.7	2.7	2.7	2.7	2.8	4.1
1.1		1.0	1.0		.9	.9	1.0	1.8	1.6	2.3
1.2		1.2	1.2		1.4	1.5	.2	1.4	1.0	.5
(259) 2.5	(282)	2.3	(311) 2.4	% Depr., Dep., Amort./Sales	(140) 3.1	(85) 2.2	(20) 1.5	(21) 1.8	(27) 1.6	(18) 1.2
4.8		4.2	4.6		8.0	4.5	3.0	3.0	2.5	3.8
2.5		3.1	2.5		2.7	2.5				
(120) 5.6	(132)	5.7	(146) 5.8	% Officers', Directors' Owners' Comp/Sales	(72) 6.1	(52) 4.7				
10.8		10.7	9.4		13.3	7.6				
4179592M		2533261M	7739800M	Net Sales ($)	101771M	208607M	85252M	166299M	436327M	6741544M
1293959M		1197786M	1939757M	Total Assets ($)	82108M	142762M	49652M	88535M	263210M	1313490M

M = $ thousand   MM = $ million
See Pages 11 through 21 for Explanation of Ratios and Data

ARTS, ENTERTAINMENT, AND RECREATION

Current Data Sorted by Assets

Comparative Historical Data

						Type of Statement		
5	7	24	27	8	3	Unqualified	57	60
1		9	2			Reviewed	16	21
4	15	6		1		Compiled	31	56
18	12	4	1			Tax Returns	38	40
17	12	16	7	1	3	Other	63	64
	106 (4/1-9/30/06)		97 (10/1/06-3/31/07)				4/1/02-3/31/03	4/1/03-3/31/04
0-500M	500M-2MM	2-10MM	10-50MM	50-100MM	100-250MM		ALL	ALL
45	46	59	37	10	6	NUMBER OF STATEMENTS	205	241
%	%	%	%	%	%	ASSETS	%	%
17.0	17.5	12.9	22.2	18.4		Cash & Equivalents	16.4	15.4
6.2	3.6	6.7	4.8	1.9		Trade Receivables (net)	6.2	5.8
4.9	2.2	3.7	.4	.5		Inventory	3.8	3.2
3.5	4.5	5.3	2.7	2.7		All Other Current	5.4	5.6
31.5	27.8	28.6	30.2	23.4		Total Current	31.9	30.0
49.0	52.2	50.9	40.8	41.9		Fixed Assets (net)	48.1	50.3
6.8	6.7	4.3	3.7	.2		Intangibles (net)	6.3	4.7
12.8	13.3	16.2	25.3	34.5		All Other Non-Current	13.7	15.0
100.0	100.0	100.0	100.0	100.0		Total	100.0	100.0
						LIABILITIES		
30.1	8.0	5.8	3.0	.4		Notes Payable-Short Term	18.9	15.4
5.3	2.9	2.3	2.6	.5		Cur. Mat.-L.T.D.	6.4	5.2
15.4	6.2	5.9	3.0	2.0		Trade Payables	8.9	6.6
.0	.1	.6	.1	.0		Income Taxes Payable	.4	.1
24.1	8.0	13.1	11.7	5.7		All Other Current	17.8	14.9
75.0	25.2	27.7	20.4	8.6		Total Current	52.4	42.2
22.4	28.8	17.4	16.0	15.3		Long-Term Debt	23.1	26.8
.0	.0	.0	.1	.1		Deferred Taxes	.0	.1
1.0	5.0	6.1	3.5	1.9		All Other Non-Current	7.6	7.8
1.6	41.0	48.8	60.0	73.8		Net Worth	16.8	23.0
100.0	100.0	100.0	100.0	100.0		Total Liabilties & Net Worth	100.0	100.0
						INCOME DATA		
100.0	100.0	100.0	100.0	100.0		Net Sales	100.0	100.0
						Gross Profit		
95.8	90.5	96.3	95.1	101.9		Operating Expenses	95.5	95.2
4.2	9.5	3.7	4.9	-1.9		Operating Profit	4.5	4.8
1.4	2.1	.9	1.1	1.2		All Other Expenses (net)	1.4	1.6
2.8	7.3	2.7	3.9	-3.1		Profit Before Taxes	3.1	3.2
						RATIOS		
1.4	2.9	2.0	2.2	12.7			1.7	2.0
.5	.8	.9	1.1	1.7		Current	.7	1.0
.2	.4	.4	.7	.8			.4	.3
1.0	2.2	1.2	1.9	10.9			1.3	1.5
.3	.7	.6	.9	1.2		Quick	.4 (238)	.7
.1	.3	.3	.4	.5			.2	.2
0 UND	0 UND	0 UND	3 124.3	0 UND			0 UND	0 UND
0 UND	0 791.5	6 65.5	6 61.9	6 56.5		Sales/Receivables	1 412.4	1 420.2
5 80.3	13 27.3	21 17.7	30 12.3	28 13.0			12 29.9	14 25.8
						Cost of Sales/Inventory		
						Cost of Sales/Payables		
96.9	8.0	9.3	3.4	3.5			12.8	11.3
-35.0	-65.2	-71.8	64.2	5.5		Sales/Working Capital	-32.4	999.8
-8.7	-9.4	-8.1	-14.1	-44.4			-11.4	-10.7
12.8	17.6	7.2	8.8				7.1	6.7
(30) 2.4	(36) 3.9	(49) 2.1	(27) 1.6			EBIT/Interest	(150) 2.2	(178) 1.8
.3	1.1	-3.3	-1.4				.2	-.3
						Net Profit + Depr., Dep.,	4.3	6.7
						Amort./Cur. Mat. L/T/D	(19) 1.5	(26) 3.0
							.3	1.0
.8	.7	.5	.2	.2			.5	.5
2.3	1.3	1.1	.6	.6		Fixed/Worth	1.5	1.4
-2.6	3.1	2.2	1.9	.9			-12.2	9.4
.6	.4	.3	.2	.1			.5	.5
3.2	1.2	1.1	.4	.3		Debt/Worth	1.6	1.5
-4.4	4.1	3.4	3.4	.6			-11.2	16.3
129.6	62.1	44.0	26.3	18.6		% Profit Before Taxes/Tangible	47.8	43.7
(29) 35.8	(37) 27.8	(53) 4.5	(35) 1.9	-2.0		Net Worth	(147) 8.1	(187) 9.4
3.6	4.4	-9.0	-2.5	-4.4			-4.1	-1.5
39.6	28.2	10.0	12.6	8.3		% Profit Before Taxes/Total	14.5	13.4
8.1	8.0	3.1	1.2	-1.6		Assets	4.0	3.1
-4.8	.3	-4.8	-1.4	-3.1			-3.7	-4.4
53.1	10.1	9.3	10.6	5.0			14.6	13.7
15.1	4.1	2.2	2.4	1.1		Sales/Net Fixed Assets	6.4	4.7
4.6	1.3	1.3	.9	.4			1.9	1.8
8.5	2.8	2.0	1.5	1.3			4.7	3.6
5.3	1.8	1.3	.7	.3		Sales/Total Assets	2.3	1.8
3.1	.9	.7	.4	.2			.9	.8
.6	1.9	1.8	1.7				1.4	1.6
(35) 1.2	(42) 3.4	(54) 3.9	(33) 3.5			% Depr., Dep., Amort./Sales	(174) 3.0	(200) 3.0
2.9	4.8	8.4	7.1				5.5	5.7
4.0	2.4	1.5				% Officers', Directors'	2.3	2.9
(18) 5.5	(17) 4.1	(11) 4.3				Owners' Comp/Sales	(56) 3.7	(79) 5.6
9.9	14.2	35.3					9.1	10.9
55259M	106343M	542029M	1245882M	598134M	319654M	Net Sales ($)	3430241M	2553264M
10158M	50154M	291130M	745176M	665847M	945142M	Total Assets ($)	2531480M	2635071M

© RMA 2007

M = $ thousand   MM = $ million
See Pages 11 through 21 for Explanation of Ratios and Data

Comparative Historical Data / Current Data Sorted by Sales

	Comparative Historical Data			Type of Statement	Current Data Sorted by Sales					
				Unqualified	4	14	10	16	16	14
				Reviewed	1	2	2	2	5	2
				Compiled	5	11	2	4	2	2
				Tax Returns	16	13	3	2	1	
				Other	13	17	5	11	6	4
	4/1/04-3/31/05 ALL	4/1/05-3/31/06 ALL	4/1/06-3/31/07 ALL		106 (4/1-9/30/06)			97 (10/1/06-3/31/07)		
					0-1MM	1-3MM	3-5MM	5-10MM	10-25MM	25MM & OVER
NUMBER OF STATEMENTS	279	208	203		39	55	22	35	30	22
	%	%	%	ASSETS	%	%	%	%	%	%
Cash & Equivalents	14.6	15.3	16.9		11.4	17.7	17.5	18.5	16.2	22.2
Trade Receivables (net)	3.9	5.2	5.2		3.9	4.3	4.8	5.7	4.6	9.7
Inventory	4.5	2.9	2.8		2.3	3.0	2.2	1.6	3.3	5.1
All Other Current	2.6	5.4	4.1		2.9	5.3	4.7	4.4	4.1	1.9
Total Current	25.5	28.8	28.9		20.5	30.2	29.2	30.1	28.3	38.9
Fixed Assets (net)	54.1	50.6	48.7		67.4	44.6	48.9	40.9	50.3	35.6
Intangibles (net)	5.8	5.3	5.0		1.9	8.9	3.9	4.3	3.9	4.3
All Other Non-Current	14.5	15.2	17.5		10.4	16.3	17.9	24.7	17.5	21.2
Total	100.0	100.0	100.0		100.0	100.0	100.0	100.0	100.0	100.0
				LIABILITIES						
Notes Payable-Short Term	4.7	6.6	10.7		28.8	12.2	4.1	3.7	3.1	3.5
Cur. Mat.-L.T.D.	5.6	3.3	3.0		5.0	2.9	1.3	3.0	2.4	2.5
Trade Payables	10.7	7.8	7.2		11.4	8.2	3.5	5.1	4.6	8.2
Income Taxes Payable	.2	.5	.2		.0	.0	.4	.1	.7	.2
All Other Current	15.1	16.6	13.5		15.5	12.5	13.9	12.1	9.4	19.7
Total Current	36.3	34.9	34.7		60.8	35.8	23.2	24.0	20.2	34.1
Long-Term Debt	31.8	25.8	21.2		32.6	17.0	13.9	19.6	23.8	18.0
Deferred Taxes	.1	.1	.0		.0	.0	.0	.0	.0	.3
All Other Non-Current	8.9	6.1	4.0		1.1	4.6	3.2	5.1	4.2	5.9
Net Worth	23.0	33.2	40.0		5.4	42.5	59.6	51.3	51.8	41.6
Total Liabilities & Net Worth	100.0	100.0	100.0		100.0	100.0	100.0	100.0	100.0	100.0
				INCOME DATA						
Net Sales	100.0	100.0	100.0		100.0	100.0	100.0	100.0	100.0	100.0
Gross Profit										
Operating Expenses	93.4	94.2	94.9		92.3	93.9	95.0	99.2	96.9	92.2
Operating Profit	6.6	5.8	5.1		7.7	6.1	5.0	.8	3.1	7.8
All Other Expenses (net)	1.9	1.5	1.3		5.6	.1	1.2	.1	-.1	1.0
Profit Before Taxes	4.7	4.3	3.8		2.1	6.0	3.8	.7	3.3	6.9
				RATIOS						
Current	1.7	2.1	2.1		1.0	2.6	4.3	2.3	1.9	2.5
	.9	.9	.9		.4	1.1	1.6	.9	1.3	1.0
	.3	.5	.4		.3	.4	.4	.6	.7	.5
Quick	1.5	1.6	1.4		.7	1.8	2.4	2.0	1.3	1.3
	(273) .5	.6	.6		.4	.5	.9	.6	.9	.8
	.2	.2	.2		.1	.2	.4	.3	.3	.5
Sales/Receivables	0 UND	0 UND	0 UND		0 UND	0 UND	0 UND	2 158.2	2 162.2	1 538.8
	0 999.8	2 179.5	3 130.6		0 UND	0 841.0	2 188.5	6 61.9	7 52.3	6 63.9
	4 87.1	13 28.9	13 29.0		12 31.2	9 41.0	15 24.5	15 24.3	32 11.4	11 33.0
Cost of Sales/Inventory										
Cost of Sales/Payables										
Sales/Working Capital	21.5	8.0	10.0		-177.5	18.1	6.5	4.6	5.9	4.7
	-78.6	-165.4	-71.8		-12.9	400.0	23.4	-87.9	23.1	NM
	-15.8	-11.5	-9.2		-5.7	-7.7	-10.5	-8.1	-39.2	-15.9
EBIT/Interest	9.4	10.3	11.8		4.0	19.3	10.7	10.6	8.5	41.1
	(213) 3.4	(154) 2.3	(153) 2.4		(29) 1.5	(40) 3.7	(16) 2.3	(28) 1.8	(24) 2.2	(16) 5.8
	.5	.0	-.1		-.3	.0	-6.3	-1.2	-1.4	.4
Net Profit + Depr., Dep., Amort./Cur. Mat. L/T/D	4.4	6.7	31.2							
	(35) 2.4	(18) 2.6	(13) 4.1							
	1.0	1.3	1.3							
Fixed/Worth	.7	.6	.4		1.1	.5	.5	.3	.4	.1
	1.7	1.2	1.2		2.2	1.2	.8	.8	1.0	.7
	-49.8	9.7	3.2		-4.8	3.2	1.6	1.7	2.2	3.7
Debt/Worth	.5	.4	.3		.7	.3	.2	.2	.4	.5
	2.5	1.7	1.1		2.2	1.2	.4	.6	1.0	1.8
	-21.3	11.8	4.2		-7.8	4.7	2.6	2.5	3.2	5.8
% Profit Before Taxes/Tangible Net Worth	66.2	51.6	48.3		33.7	75.9	42.1	20.1	35.1	84.4
	(203) 21.2	(166) 14.3	(170) 13.0		(26) 9.9	(45) 33.5	(21) 14.5	(30) .5	(29) 7.0	(19) 30.3
	1.4	-.6	-2.8		-.7	-4.5	-2.5	-3.1	-4.6	-2.6
% Profit Before Taxes/Total Assets	17.0	14.3	22.4		8.2	34.1	24.0	17.2	11.0	33.7
	6.2	3.6	3.3		.9	8.1	5.3	.6	1.3	8.1
	-1.1	-1.6	-2.2		-4.8	-4.1	-1.8	-1.4	-2.0	-1.6
Sales/Net Fixed Assets	11.7	14.1	13.5		12.6	25.5	7.9	10.8	5.6	86.5
	4.6	3.3	3.6		2.1	6.1	2.4	3.3	2.3	11.5
	2.2	1.2	1.3		.8	2.0	1.2	1.5	.8	1.6
Sales/Total Assets	4.5	3.1	3.7		5.3	4.6	2.1	2.6	1.9	7.1
	2.6	1.6	1.5		1.7	2.4	1.3	1.2	1.3	2.0
	1.2	.6	.7		.4	1.0	.8	.6	.4	.5
% Depr., Dep., Amort./Sales	1.6	1.7	1.5		1.3	.9	2.8	2.2	1.6	.5
	(238) 2.8	(171) 3.5	(179) 3.1		(32) 4.6	(48) 2.3	(20) 4.2	(33) 4.0	(27) 3.1	(19) 1.6
	4.6	6.1	5.3		11.4	3.9	7.1	7.4	6.9	4.0
% Officers', Directors' Owners' Comp/Sales	2.2	2.3	2.8		4.5	3.2				
	(111) 4.6	(53) 4.7	(55) 4.6		(13) 6.1	(19) 4.4				
	8.2	9.6	12.2		12.6	15.8				
Net Sales ($)	3878216M	2938841M	2867301M		20890M	104301M	86744M	249006M	486429M	1919931M
Total Assets ($)	2392476M	3005590M	2707607M		35595M	80085M	89264M	373844M	850586M	1278233M

M = $ thousand   MM = $ million
See Pages 11 through 21 for Explanation of Ratios and Data

Current Data Sorted by Assets							Comparative Historical Data	
						Type of Statement		
3	6	10	8	3	4	Unqualified	30	28
1		1				Reviewed		1
2	2	1				Compiled	12	10
2		1				Tax Returns	5	9
5	3	4	6	1	2	Other	26	15
	45 (4/1-9/30/06)		20 (10/1/06-3/31/07)				4/1/02-3/31/03 ALL	4/1/03-3/31/04 ALL
0-500M	500M-2MM	2-10MM	10-50MM	50-100MM	100-250MM			
13	11	17	14	4	6	**NUMBER OF STATEMENTS**	73	63
%	%	%	%	%	%	**ASSETS**	%	%
53.7	15.4	17.2	14.7			Cash & Equivalents	23.5	26.1
9.8	12.1	5.8	4.3			Trade Receivables (net)	13.3	10.3
2.4	1.0	2.8	.1			Inventory	1.6	4.4
1.4	12.3	6.3	6.7			All Other Current	4.7	6.3
67.3	40.9	32.1	25.8			Total Current	43.1	47.1
11.7	29.4	26.0	22.2			Fixed Assets (net)	27.1	21.8
1.0	.6	2.6	.2			Intangibles (net)	3.4	4.0
20.0	29.1	39.3	51.8			All Other Non-Current	26.4	27.1
100.0	100.0	100.0	100.0			Total	100.0	100.0
						LIABILITIES		
5.3	19.8	4.9	7.8			Notes Payable-Short Term	19.8	17.9
4.5	.4	1.7	.6			Cur. Mat.-L.T.D.	3.3	2.5
57.7	7.3	4.5	3.7			Trade Payables	9.5	10.7
.0	4.0	.3	.0			Income Taxes Payable	.9	1.3
32.7	9.5	8.1	6.3			All Other Current	16.7	30.3
100.1	40.9	19.4	18.3			Total Current	50.2	62.8
21.2	12.9	5.7	12.9			Long-Term Debt	9.7	19.6
.0	.0	.0	.0			Deferred Taxes	.0	.1
11.9	29.8	8.2	3.8			All Other Non-Current	7.3	12.6
-33.2	16.4	66.7	65.0			Net Worth	32.8	4.9
100.0	100.0	100.0	100.0			Total Liabilities & Net Worth	100.0	100.0
						INCOME DATA		
100.0	100.0	100.0	100.0			Net Sales	100.0	100.0
						Gross Profit		
100.4	83.2	100.0	88.9			Operating Expenses	92.4	91.8
-.4	16.8	.0	11.1			Operating Profit	7.6	8.2
-.3	1.9	-.3	4.0			All Other Expenses (net)	2.4	.8
-.1	14.9	.3	7.1			Profit Before Taxes	5.2	7.3
						RATIOS		
3.4	2.9	2.4	2.2				2.9	3.5
.6	1.5	.9	1.3			Current	1.3	1.3
.4	.4	.4	.8				.6	.4
3.0	2.2	1.4	1.9				2.8	2.3
.6	1.5	.5	.8			Quick	(72) 1.0	(62) .9
.4	.3	.1	.3				.5	.2
0 UND	0 UND	1 310.0	1 444.7				1 328.2	0 UND
4 93.8	5 80.2	8 48.4	16 23.0			Sales/Receivables	11 32.5	9 42.1
19 19.2	37 9.9	40 9.0	47 7.8				38 9.6	52 7.0
						Cost of Sales/Inventory		
						Cost of Sales/Payables		
11.1	6.4	5.8	4.1				5.7	3.9
-21.0	21.1	-147.2	31.0			Sales/Working Capital	41.1	80.7
-8.8	-4.8	-5.9	-16.3				-16.2	-10.3
		8.5	15.7				15.8	28.6
	(11)	1.8	5.1			EBIT/Interest	(37) 1.9	(36) 9.1
		-.3	-1.9				-8.9	.4
						Net Profit + Depr., Dep., Amort./Cur. Mat. L/T/D		
.1	.2	.0	.0				.0	.0
.2	.8	.1	.1			Fixed/Worth	.4	.3
-.2	-3.6	1.1	.9				1.4	4.8
.5	.2	.2	.2				.2	.4
1.8	3.7	.5	.4			Debt/Worth	.8	1.0
-2.6	-6.5	.7	.8				4.9	-10.1
		9.8	8.6			% Profit Before Taxes/Tangible Net Worth	70.1	48.8
		(13) .6	1.3				(63) 16.3	(47) 21.1
		-11.1	-3.1				-7.6	-3.0
40.9	66.6	2.6	6.9			% Profit Before Taxes/Total Assets	25.9	28.8
1.9	3.7	-.4	1.8				6.0	7.1
-12.8	.0	-8.1	-2.2				-4.9	-4.9
249.2	26.6	34.9	36.5				93.9	327.3
62.1	17.6	14.1	21.5			Sales/Net Fixed Assets	14.5	40.9
24.5	2.8	2.3	2.1				1.8	4.5
9.1	3.7	1.4	.7				4.3	4.6
2.4	1.8	1.0	.6			Sales/Total Assets	1.4	1.8
1.4	.8	.5	.4				.5	.6
		.6	1.0				.7	.3
	(16)	1.2	(11) 1.6			% Depr., Dep., Amort./Sales	(51) 1.7	(42) 1.0
		3.5	2.8				4.7	5.0
						% Officers', Directors' Owners' Comp/Sales	4.7	8.4
							(15) 11.9	(12) 10.5
							24.0	19.0
11062M	27829M	80867M	196459M	68486M	690229M	Net Sales ($)	721469M	738471M
2623M	14007M	89102M	339442M	251642M	1066278M	Total Assets ($)	1341490M	1037189M

© RMA 2007

M = $ thousand   MM = $ million

See Pages 11 through 21 for Explanation of Ratios and Data

Comparative Historical Data

Current Data Sorted by Sales

			Type of Statement						
23	22	34	Unqualified	1	9	5	7	9	3
3	2	2	Reviewed	1		1			
6	4	5	Compiled	3	1		1		
8	3	3	Tax Returns		3				
11	21	21	Other	5	5	2	2	5	2
4/1/04-3/31/05 ALL	4/1/05-3/31/06 ALL	4/1/06-3/31/07 ALL		45 (4/1-9/30/06)			20 (10/1/06-3/31/07)		
				0-1MM	1-3MM	3-5MM	5-10MM	10-25MM	25MM & OVER
51	52	65	NUMBER OF STATEMENTS	10	18	8	10	14	5
%	%	%	ASSETS	%	%	%	%	%	%
22.7	17.9	22.5	Cash & Equivalents	40.5	26.3		16.9	8.3	
15.6	12.2	7.2	Trade Receivables (net)	4.6	11.7		6.6	6.6	
5.9	2.1	1.4	Inventory	1.9	1.3		.7	3.0	
6.7	7.7	5.9	All Other Current	1.0	7.0		5.8	3.6	
50.9	40.0	37.0	Total Current	48.0	46.3		30.0	21.5	
27.0	26.7	24.7	Fixed Assets (net)	22.6	34.0		9.6	30.8	
1.7	1.2	1.2	Intangibles (net)	1.1	.3		.2	.8	
20.5	32.1	37.0	All Other Non-Current	28.2	19.4		60.2	46.9	
100.0	100.0	100.0	Total	100.0	100.0		100.0	100.0	
			LIABILITIES						
11.3	13.3	7.6	Notes Payable-Short Term	4.8	5.8		15.5	6.9	
1.5	3.5	1.6	Cur. Mat.-L.T.D.	2.3	3.6		.2	.5	
11.4	10.7	14.9	Trade Payables	51.8	15.7		7.0	2.6	
1.4	.1	.8	Income Taxes Payable	.0	2.5		.0	.3	
14.7	13.8	13.4	All Other Current	15.9	19.8		10.7	4.3	
40.4	41.6	38.2	Total Current	74.8	47.3		33.5	14.6	
15.3	10.0	12.6	Long-Term Debt	14.9	20.1		.2	16.0	
.0	.0	.0	Deferred Taxes	.0	.0		.0	.0	
6.0	7.6	10.7	All Other Non-Current	3.1	13.5		16.6	2.7	
38.2	40.8	38.5	Net Worth	7.1	19.1		49.7	66.7	
100.0	100.0	100.0	Total Liabilities & Net Worth	100.0	100.0		100.0	100.0	
			INCOME DATA						
100.0	100.0	100.0	Net Sales	100.0	100.0		100.0	100.0	
			Gross Profit						
93.2	95.2	93.3	Operating Expenses	97.5	89.9		102.7	89.5	
6.8	4.8	6.7	Operating Profit	2.5	10.1		-2.7	10.5	
.9	2.1	.8	All Other Expenses (net)	1.6	.6		-1.0	-1.1	
5.9	2.7	5.9	Profit Before Taxes	.8	9.6		-1.8	11.6	
			RATIOS						
5.2	2.8	2.8	Current	6.1	2.4		3.6	3.4	
1.4	1.3	1.2		1.0	1.2		1.0	1.5	
.7	.5	.6		.3	.6		.3	.7	
2.7	2.0	2.0	Quick	5.4	2.2		2.8	1.8	
1.0	.8	.9		.9	.6		.9	1.2	
.5	.3	.3		.2	.4		.2	.4	
2　232.0	3　141.5	1　454.9	Sales/Receivables	0　UND	0　UND		2　152.4	1　350.2	
15　24.6	18　20.4	9　40.6		0　UND	8　43.9		13　29.1	40　9.1	
50　7.3	59　6.2	38　9.7		26　14.1	28　13.0		45　8.1	79　4.6	
			Cost of Sales/Inventory						
			Cost of Sales/Payables						
4.0	5.0	4.5	Sales/Working Capital	3.7	8.5		4.1	3.5	
14.3	19.9	27.1		NM	24.4		NM	9.6	
-21.2	-6.1	-8.7		-5.9	-11.3		-4.2	-8.9	
21.7	7.1	12.6	EBIT/Interest		21.0			12.4	
(29)　2.0	(29)　1.6	(43)　4.1		(11)　4.8			(12)　6.0		
-4.6	-3.9	-.7			1.8			-4.9	
			Net Profit + Depr., Dep., Amort./Cur. Mat. L/T/D						
.0	.0	.1	Fixed/Worth	.0	.4		.0	.0	
.3	.4	.3		.1	.9		.1	.3	
4.6	1.3	1.4		.8	-2.7		UND	1.2	
.4	.3	.2	Debt/Worth	.4	.2		.2	.1	
1.0	.7	.6		1.2	.8		.4	.5	
6.0	5.0	2.7		NM	-7.5		UND	.8	
40.8	22.2	14.0	% Profit Before Taxes/Tangible Net Worth		47.5			10.6	
(42)　6.8	(43)　2.3	(54)　2.5		(13)　2.0			(13)　3.9		
-6.4	-2.7	-6.5			-6.4			-2.7	
11.0	6.9	8.2	% Profit Before Taxes/Total Assets	14.2	39.2		4.5	8.5	
3.8	.7	1.9		.7	2.4		.8	3.2	
-4.2	-4.0	-4.0		-28.3			-5.8	-1.7	
91.7	53.1	39.5	Sales/Net Fixed Assets	73.6	71.6		54.8	27.9	
21.0	13.4	16.0		24.5	11.7		24.2	3.0	
2.8	2.7	2.1		2.4	1.3		15.1	.5	
3.8	3.2	2.0	Sales/Total Assets	2.2	7.7		1.6	.6	
1.3	1.2	1.0		1.4	1.5		.8	.4	
.4	.4	.4		.9	.6		.6	.3	
.6	.9	.8	% Depr., Dep., Amort./Sales		.4			1.1	
(40)　1.3	(43)　1.5	(48)　1.3		(12)　2.3			(12)　2.4		
2.7	4.1	4.0			6.6			7.4	
4.4	7.6		% Officers', Directors' Owners' Comp/Sales						
(11)　8.1	(11)　9.4								
20.8	17.2								
487161M	863197M	1074932M	Net Sales ($)	3780M	34025M	31861M	75916M	233486M	695864M
1136788M	1386324M	1763094M	Total Assets ($)	4681M	49328M	37239M	84017M	850775M	737054M

M = $ thousand　　MM = $ million
See Pages 11 through 21 for Explanation of Ratios and Data

Current Data Sorted by Assets   Comparative Historical Data

0-500M	500M-2MM	2-10MM	10-50MM	50-100MM	100-250MM	Type of Statement	4/1/02-3/31/03 ALL	4/1/03-3/31/04 ALL
2	2	5	12	17	25	Unqualified	39	38
		5	1			Reviewed	6	8
2	1	1	1			Compiled	8	11
3	3	4				Tax Returns	4	8
1	6	11	6	4	12	Other	35	33
	56 (4/1-9/30/06)		68 (10/1/06-3/31/07)					
8	12	26	20	21	37	NUMBER OF STATEMENTS	92	98
%	%	%	%	%	%	ASSETS	%	%
	13.1	9.9	12.0	9.1	14.0	Cash & Equivalents	15.9	10.4
	9.5	6.0	12.3	16.2	10.6	Trade Receivables (net)	9.1	11.5
	4.5	.8	.8	.7	.4	Inventory	1.3	1.3
	8.1	.7	8.7	8.5	3.5	All Other Current	5.3	5.9
	35.2	17.3	33.8	34.4	28.6	Total Current	31.6	29.0
	43.5	39.0	27.9	21.8	24.0	Fixed Assets (net)	30.9	30.8
	20.1	23.8	21.1	23.3	28.0	Intangibles (net)	21.0	23.0
	1.1	19.9	17.2	20.4	19.5	All Other Non-Current	16.5	17.2
	100.0	100.0	100.0	100.0	100.0	Total	100.0	100.0
						LIABILITIES		
	8.5	4.8	25.8	14.5	10.9	Notes Payable-Short Term	6.5	10.0
	1.8	4.1	4.1	6.8	1.6	Cur. Mat.-L.T.D.	4.6	3.2
	10.7	4.8	10.3	8.8	6.0	Trade Payables	8.2	5.9
	.0	.0	.0	.7	.2	Income Taxes Payable	.9	.1
	8.7	8.2	41.7	23.0	19.6	All Other Current	22.1	17.5
	29.7	21.9	82.0	53.8	38.2	Total Current	42.3	36.7
	41.5	27.0	32.1	34.9	30.5	Long-Term Debt	36.4	33.9
	.0	.2	.2	.0	.1	Deferred Taxes	.5	.4
	8.0	4.6	25.8	41.2	23.0	All Other Non-Current	28.3	23.0
	20.8	46.3	-40.1	-29.9	8.2	Net Worth	-7.5	6.0
	100.0	100.0	100.0	100.0	100.0	Total Liabilties & Net Worth	100.0	100.0
						INCOME DATA		
	100.0	100.0	100.0	100.0	100.0	Net Sales	100.0	100.0
						Gross Profit		
	88.4	91.8	102.9	98.9	92.4	Operating Expenses	94.9	97.0
	11.6	8.2	-2.9	1.1	7.6	Operating Profit	5.1	3.0
	6.8	7.1	2.8	1.6	3.4	All Other Expenses (net)	4.9	3.7
	4.8	1.1	-5.7	-.4	4.2	Profit Before Taxes	.2	-.7
						RATIOS		
	3.0	2.2	1.1	1.3	1.2		1.8	1.6
	1.2	1.0	.6	.7	.9	Current	.8	.9
	.3	.3	.3	.4	.4		.4	.4
	2.2	2.0	1.1	1.1	1.0		1.4	1.3
	1.1	.8	.6	.5	.7	Quick	.7	.7
	.2	.2	.2	.2	.4		.3	.3
0 UND	6 63.5	8 46.9	17 21.6	23 16.2			5 77.5	9 41.2
4 88.6	19 19.6	20 18.2	34 10.7	34 10.9		Sales/Receivables	18 20.4	28 12.9
38 9.5	47 7.7	58 6.3	64 5.7	68 5.4		42 8.6	71 5.2
						Cost of Sales/Inventory		
						Cost of Sales/Payables		
	9.5	5.9	17.3	13.8	8.1		10.8	11.1
	62.4	NM	-12.0	-13.8	-40.2	Sales/Working Capital	-14.0	-105.8
	-4.9	-6.3	-2.1	-2.6	-2.4		-4.4	-4.5
		1.3	3.1	7.2	6.4		7.1	5.2
	(15)	1.0	(18) .6	(18) .5	(33) 1.3	EBIT/Interest	(65) 1.0	(75) 1.3
		-.9	-2.0	-1.8	-.3		-1.9	-1.7
						Net Profit + Depr., Dep., Amort./Cur. Mat. L/T/D		
	.9	.4	.7	.6	3.5		1.0	.9
	6.7	2.9	NM	-.9	-.8	Fixed/Worth	-2.9	-261.2
	-.9	-.6	.0	.0	-.1		-.1	-.1
	1.2	.6	.8	8.0	5.9		1.6	1.4
	12.1	3.4	NM	-2.7	-5.2	Debt/Worth	-6.0	-11.0
	-3.7	-5.5	-1.4	-1.5	-2.0		-1.7	-2.0
		19.6	24.0		99.0		65.4	12.0
	(17)	7.6	(10) 3.5		(14) 22.2	% Profit Before Taxes/Tangible Net Worth	(40) 18.3	(47) .3
		-.3	-8.6		-2.6		-.5	-13.3
	10.4	9.0	3.8	22.1	10.9		9.1	7.3
	.7	.1	-2.0	1.5	.5	% Profit Before Taxes/Total Assets	.1	.2
	-7.6	-3.0	-14.6	-16.9	-3.0		-7.4	-6.6
	79.0	22.2	109.6	148.7	45.2		42.1	24.7
	21.2	3.9	10.8	27.1	12.2	Sales/Net Fixed Assets	8.3	7.1
	.9	.3	1.7	4.5	2.5		1.4	1.8
	3.7	1.0	2.2	1.6	1.1		1.9	1.8
	1.5	.5	1.0	1.2	.8	Sales/Total Assets	1.0	.8
	.7	.3	.4	.8	.6		.5	.4
		1.7	.6	1.3	1.2		.9	1.5
	(25)	3.6	(16) 3.8	(13) 3.7	(20) 5.4	% Depr., Dep., Amort./Sales	(55) 3.0	(65) 3.0
		10.0	16.1	6.8	7.5		5.7	7.4
							1.3	4.0
						% Officers', Directors' Owners' Comp/Sales	(11) 8.5	(10) 5.9
							16.1	18.7
3844M	32115M	72595M	853834M	2371067M	4904195M	Net Sales ($)	5162353M	5017587M
2013M	16043M	126953M	563103M	1449238M	6305506M	Total Assets ($)	6290681M	6092964M

M = $ thousand   MM = $ million
See Pages 11 through 21 for Explanation of Ratios and Data

Comparative Historical Data

Current Data Sorted by Sales

			Type of Statement						
53	40	63	Unqualified	4	1	2	5	4	47
7	7	6	Reviewed		3	1	1	1	
9	6	5	Compiled	3	2				
9	9	10	Tax Returns	3	5	2			
35	41	40	Other	5	9	2	5	2	17
4/1/04-3/31/05 ALL	4/1/05-3/31/06 ALL	4/1/06-3/31/07 ALL		56 (4/1-9/30/06)			68 (10/1/06-3/31/07)		
				0-1MM	1-3MM	3-5MM	5-10MM	10-25MM	25MM & OVER
113	103	124	NUMBER OF STATEMENTS	15	20	7	11	7	64
%	%	%	ASSETS	%	%	%	%	%	%
12.1	14.7	12.5	Cash & Equivalents	15.5	8.2		19.2		12.4
10.5	9.2	10.7	Trade Receivables (net)	5.1	6.9		10.4		14.2
1.2	1.3	1.1	Inventory	1.1	2.9		.7		.6
3.1	4.0	4.9	All Other Current	.8	4.7		2.0		7.0
27.0	29.2	29.2	Total Current	22.5	22.7		32.3		34.2
32.0	35.2	30.8	Fixed Assets (net)	59.6	42.9		22.5		19.6
23.1	21.9	23.3	Intangibles (net)	8.0	18.8		21.2		27.3
18.0	13.7	16.7	All Other Non-Current	10.0	15.6		24.0		18.9
100.0	100.0	100.0	Total	100.0	100.0		100.0		100.0
			LIABILITIES						
12.7	10.9	11.9	Notes Payable-Short Term	6.5	3.1		7.0		18.9
3.4	3.0	3.5	Cur. Mat.-L.T.D.	6.3	2.0		2.2		3.3
5.7	5.8	7.4	Trade Payables	4.8	6.9		8.2		8.5
.1	.2	.2	Income Taxes Payable	.0	.0		.0		.3
21.0	20.5	19.8	All Other Current	9.3	6.2		6.7		30.1
43.0	40.4	42.7	Total Current	26.8	18.2		24.0		61.2
39.4	40.0	33.5	Long-Term Debt	46.7	38.9		24.3		33.3
.2	.3	.1	Deferred Taxes	.0	.0		.4		.1
21.3	22.2	21.4	All Other Non-Current	13.5	7.7		8.9		31.8
-3.9	-2.8	2.3	Net Worth	12.9	35.3		42.4		-26.4
100.0	100.0	100.0	Total Liabilities & Net Worth	100.0	100.0		100.0		100.0
			INCOME DATA						
100.0	100.0	100.0	Net Sales	100.0	100.0		100.0		100.0
			Gross Profit						
96.2	93.9	94.9	Operating Expenses	90.2	92.2		94.3		96.0
3.8	6.1	5.1	Operating Profit	9.8	7.8		5.7		4.0
2.2	4.6	4.2	All Other Expenses (net)	11.0	6.6		.9		2.8
1.7	1.6	.8	Profit Before Taxes	-1.2	1.2		4.8		1.2
			RATIOS						
2.1	1.7	1.7		2.8	2.3		3.2		1.1
.9	.9	.9	Current	1.3	1.1		2.3		.8
.3	.4	.4		.9	.4		.4		.4
1.5	1.6	1.4		2.8	1.9		2.9		.9
.7	.7	.8	Quick	1.2	1.1		1.7		.7
.3	.2	.3		.9	.4		.1		.3
7 49.8	3 115.3	9 40.5	Sales/Receivables	0 UND	0 UND		4 97.9		20 18.4
18 20.6	17 21.3	27 13.6		16 22.4	17 21.7		7 52.1		33 10.9
47 7.7	40 9.2	51 7.2		36 10.2	46 7.9		36 10.1		59 6.2
			Cost of Sales/Inventory						
			Cost of Sales/Payables						
10.5	9.7	9.5		9.5	6.1		2.6		23.0
-63.3	-49.2	-40.6	Sales/Working Capital	20.7	20.2		10.2		-24.5
-4.2	-5.9	-3.8		-60.0	-7.4		-6.5		-2.4
4.1	4.6	4.9			1.5				5.4
(92) 1.2	(78) 1.1	(96) 1.0	EBIT/Interest		(14) .9			(58)	.9
-4.5	-2.9	-1.4			-.1				-1.6
			Net Profit + Depr., Dep., Amort./Cur. Mat. L/T/D						
1.2	1.0	.9		.9	.3		.1		2.5
-1.6	-5.5	NM	Fixed/Worth	3.0	4.1		.6		-.4
-.1	-.1	-.2		-3.0	NM		-.3		.0
2.2	1.7	1.9		.4	1.0		.3		7.1
-5.3	-7.5	-11.4	Debt/Worth	3.0	4.5		.7		-3.0
-1.8	-2.1	-1.8		-4.3	NM		-1.7		-1.5
52.9	40.4	39.4	% Profit Before Taxes/Tangible Net Worth	10.0	76.3				114.1
(48) 11.7	(48) 10.0	(59) 7.6		(10) 5.2	(15) 2.0			(20)	33.6
-5.4	-.6	-2.9		-12.3	-5.7				10.5
10.9	11.6	10.7	% Profit Before Taxes/Total Assets	4.8	14.0		8.3		11.2
2.0	1.9	.1		-1.3	-.2		2.3		1.0
-6.4	-6.9	-7.3		-12.2	-6.6		-3.5		-12.9
32.2	39.1	45.3	Sales/Net Fixed Assets	9.5	40.0		21.8		85.9
7.3	8.7	8.5		1.5	5.7		7.1		24.0
1.8	.9	1.7		.3	.7		2.5		3.0
1.9	1.9	1.5	Sales/Total Assets	1.6	1.4		2.5		1.6
.9	1.0	.9		.8	.6		1.0		1.1
.5	.5	.5		.2	.3		.3		.7
1.4	1.4	1.2	% Depr., Dep., Amort./Sales	1.7	1.0				1.1
(79) 2.8	(74) 3.4	(88) 3.7		(13) 6.5	(16) 3.2			(37)	2.6
9.3	9.8	7.8		8.8	10.1				6.7
2.3	8.6	3.3	% Officers', Directors' Owners' Comp/Sales						
(15) 6.0	(16) 14.6	(19) 8.8							
11.5	27.3	16.3							
5651728M	6577667M	8237650M	Net Sales ($)	7069M	37167M	24397M	74596M	131554M	7962867M
6883018M	6778385M	8462856M	Total Assets ($)	27440M	78012M	54359M	159822M	491129M	7652094M

M = $ thousand   MM = $ million
See Pages 11 through 21 for Explanation of Ratios and Data

Current Data Sorted by Assets | Comparative Historical Data

0-500M	500M-2MM	2-10MM	10-50MM	50-100MM	100-250MM	Type of Statement	4/1/02-3/31/03 ALL	4/1/03-3/31/04 ALL
		3	11	6	3	Unqualified	29	17
	1	1				Reviewed	3	2
	3	1			1	Compiled	5	20
5	1	1				Tax Returns	3	3
4	4	5	4	1	2	Other	27	18
	4 (4/1-9/30/06)		49 (10/1/06-3/31/07)					
5	9	11	15	7	6	NUMBER OF STATEMENTS	67	60
%	%	%	%	%	%	**ASSETS**	%	%
		10.0	12.8			Cash & Equivalents	14.1	14.5
		9.8	5.8			Trade Receivables (net)	6.8	5.8
		3.8	2.9			Inventory	3.7	5.4
		4.6	2.4			All Other Current	3.6	5.0
		28.2	23.9			Total Current	28.1	30.6
		53.5	64.6			Fixed Assets (net)	57.3	55.6
		10.0	2.5			Intangibles (net)	2.8	6.1
		8.3	9.0			All Other Non-Current	11.8	7.8
		100.0	100.0			Total	100.0	100.0
						LIABILITIES		
		5.7	.6			Notes Payable-Short Term	4.7	6.7
		6.5	1.3			Cur. Mat.-L.T.D.	3.0	5.4
		8.6	5.9			Trade Payables	7.3	7.4
		.0	.1			Income Taxes Payable	.6	.6
		18.0	16.7			All Other Current	19.1	15.9
		38.8	24.6			Total Current	34.8	36.0
		28.4	23.0			Long-Term Debt	26.9	27.2
		.3	.1			Deferred Taxes	.2	.1
		10.5	2.3			All Other Non-Current	8.2	5.9
		22.1	50.0			Net Worth	29.9	30.9
		100.0	100.0			Total Liabilities & Net Worth	100.0	100.0
						INCOME DATA		
		100.0	100.0			Net Sales	100.0	100.0
						Gross Profit		
		100.7	94.0			Operating Expenses	94.3	95.6
		-.7	6.0			Operating Profit	5.7	4.4
		1.8	.7			All Other Expenses (net)	1.5	1.9
		-2.4	5.3			Profit Before Taxes	4.2	2.6
						RATIOS		
		1.7	1.4				1.5	1.8
		.4	1.0			Current	.9	.9
		.2	.5				.5	.3
		1.6	1.2				1.3	1.6
		(10) .3	.7			Quick	.6	.6
		.2	.5				.3	.2
		4 85.0	9 39.6				1 491.5	1 255.7
		11 32.9	13 28.3			Sales/Receivables	6 57.7	9 40.5
		25 14.6	25 14.6				26 14.2	18 20.2
						Cost of Sales/Inventory		
						Cost of Sales/Payables		
		24.5	17.5				20.6	8.5
		-6.9	174.2			Sales/Working Capital	-204.0	-53.7
		-5.7	-7.7				-9.2	-5.9
		8.9	47.2				20.3	13.3
		(10) -.2	5.9			EBIT/Interest	(60) 2.8	(53) 1.5
		-2.8	-.3				-.3	-1.6
						Net Profit + Depr., Dep.,		14.2
						Amort./Cur. Mat. L/T/D	(10) 1.3	
								.7
		1.0	.9				.9	.8
		3.0	1.3			Fixed/Worth	1.8	1.9
		-1.3	2.1				5.9	6.0
		.9	.3				.7	.7
		9.3	1.2			Debt/Worth	1.8	1.7
		-3.6	2.5				8.8	6.8
			29.8			% Profit Before Taxes/Tangible	63.5	49.8
			20.9			Net Worth	(57) 20.5	(48) 11.2
			-5.2				-4.8	-8.4
		9.9	21.7			% Profit Before Taxes/Total	22.8	20.0
		-4.4	6.3			Assets	5.9	1.9
		-10.8	-2.0				-2.8	-5.7
		15.8	3.2				5.5	7.1
		2.9	2.2			Sales/Net Fixed Assets	2.9	2.8
		1.6	.8				2.1	1.2
		2.6	2.0				2.4	2.3
		1.7	1.6			Sales/Total Assets	1.7	1.5
		1.2	.5				1.0	.7
		2.8	2.2				2.1	2.9
		(10) 4.6	3.3			% Depr., Dep., Amort./Sales	(61) 3.7	(52) 4.3
		6.6	4.8				7.1	8.3
						% Officers', Directors'	2.4	2.4
						Owners' Comp/Sales	(15) 8.3	(12) 7.5
							17.6	23.4
6261M	19317M	146109M	560925M	642429M	1179004M	Net Sales ($)	2089023M	1705853M
1080M	9005M	55521M	432737M	465858M	999008M	Total Assets ($)	1612928M	1440323M

M = $ thousand   MM = $ million
See Pages 11 through 21 for Explanation of Ratios and Data

Comparative Historical Data   ## Current Data Sorted by Sales

				Type of Statement						
	20	23	23	Unqualified				3	2	18
		1	2	Reviewed		1	1			
	4	3	5	Compiled	2			1		2
	11	15	7	Tax Returns	3	3		1		
	15	23	16	Other	2	2	1	3	3	5
	4/1/04- 3/31/05	4/1/05- 3/31/06	4/1/06- 3/31/07			4 (4/1-9/30/06)		49 (10/1/06-3/31/07)		
	ALL	ALL	ALL		0-1MM	1-3MM	3-5MM	5-10MM	10-25MM	25MM & OVER
	50	65	53	NUMBER OF STATEMENTS	7	6	2	8	5	25
	%	%	%	ASSETS	%	%	%	%	%	%
	10.5	12.5	12.8	Cash & Equivalents						11.4
	6.2	6.7	7.4	Trade Receivables (net)						7.3
	4.0	2.9	2.8	Inventory						3.1
	.9	3.7	3.4	All Other Current						5.3
	21.7	25.8	26.4	Total Current						27.2
	59.5	61.4	61.1	Fixed Assets (net)						60.9
	4.3	3.8	4.1	Intangibles (net)						3.9
	14.5	9.0	8.4	All Other Non-Current						8.0
	100.0	100.0	100.0	Total						100.0
				LIABILITIES						
	9.6	6.0	5.3	Notes Payable-Short Term						2.7
	4.7	3.8	6.0	Cur. Mat.-L.T.D.						4.8
	9.2	8.0	13.9	Trade Payables						5.3
	.1	.0	.0	Income Taxes Payable						.0
	13.9	17.1	19.4	All Other Current						14.0
	37.6	34.9	44.6	Total Current						26.8
	42.0	31.9	27.5	Long-Term Debt						19.2
	.8	.7	.2	Deferred Taxes						.3
	12.4	9.0	11.3	All Other Non-Current						9.9
	7.3	23.5	16.3	Net Worth						43.7
	100.0	100.0	100.0	Total Liabilities & Net Worth						100.0
				INCOME DATA						
	100.0	100.0	100.0	Net Sales						100.0
				Gross Profit						
	95.2	91.8	94.0	Operating Expenses						89.3
	4.8	8.2	6.0	Operating Profit						10.7
	2.9	3.7	2.1	All Other Expenses (net)						1.1
	2.0	4.6	3.9	Profit Before Taxes						9.6
				RATIOS						
	1.6	1.6	1.5							1.4
	.7	.8	.7	Current						1.1
	.3	.4	.4							.5
	1.1	1.3	1.3							1.3
	.6	.6	(52) .5	Quick						(24) .8
	.2	.3	.2							.4
	1 621.0	3 143.4	3 125.6							5 79.7
	8 46.8	8 48.2	10 35.1	Sales/Receivables						11 33.6
	18 19.8	23 15.7	23 15.6							26 13.8
				Cost of Sales/Inventory						
				Cost of Sales/Payables						
	26.9	15.9	17.3							15.3
	-33.2	-60.4	-22.9	Sales/Working Capital						170.6
	-6.1	-8.2	-6.6							-8.9
	6.0	15.0	16.0							42.3
	(44) 1.3	(55) 2.1	(47) 3.5	EBIT/Interest						(24) 7.7
	-1.1	-.1	-.3							.2
				Net Profit + Depr., Dep., Amort./Cur. Mat. L/T/D						
	1.1	1.1	1.0							.8
	2.7	2.3	2.1	Fixed/Worth						1.3
	-6.8	NM	21.1							3.3
	.9	.9	.9							.6
	3.0	3.2	2.0	Debt/Worth						1.3
	-15.5	NM	27.0							3.0
	39.3	64.1	39.9	% Profit Before Taxes/Tangible Net Worth						47.3
	(35) 9.0	(49) 20.2	(41) 18.6							(23) 27.2
	-4.0	-6.3	-4.0							-4.7
	10.0	15.4	16.8	% Profit Before Taxes/Total Assets						26.9
	.9	3.9	2.7							13.3
	-4.4	-3.8	-5.8							-1.9
	8.9	4.8	4.5							3.7
	2.3	2.6	2.5	Sales/Net Fixed Assets						2.5
	1.0	1.2	1.3							1.7
	2.4	2.7	2.5							2.2
	1.2	1.6	1.6	Sales/Total Assets						1.6
	.5	.8	.9							.9
	2.0	2.8	2.5	% Depr., Dep., Amort./Sales						2.2
	(39) 4.9	(61) 4.1	(50) 4.3							(22) 3.3
	9.5	7.6	6.8							4.5
	1.0	1.6		% Officers', Directors' Owners' Comp/Sales						
	(10) 8.0	(17) 5.5								
	14.2	12.9								
	1362966M	3694737M	2554045M	Net Sales ($)	4256M	11600M	7724M	57005M	107411M	2366049M
	1612776M	2195518M	1963209M	Total Assets ($)	4176M	6383M	4358M	58843M	117315M	1772134M

© RMA 2007   M = $ thousand   MM = $ million
See Pages 11 through 21 for Explanation of Ratios and Data

Current Data Sorted by Assets · Comparative Historical Data

Type of Statement								
7	1	12	10	7	4	Unqualified	15	10
1	4	6	1			Reviewed	11	8
1	4	2				Compiled	38	21
9	5	2				Tax Returns	55	69
7	5	2	4	1		Other	30	30

0-500M	500M-2MM	2-10MM	10-50MM	50-100MM	100-250MM		4/1/02-3/31/03 ALL	4/1/03-3/31/04 ALL
	38 (4/1-9/30/06)		56 (10/1/06-3/31/07)					
24	19	24	15	8	4	**NUMBER OF STATEMENTS**	149	138
%	%	%	%	%	%	**ASSETS**	%	%
32.9	12.5	13.2	16.7			Cash & Equivalents	7.0	6.5
6.2	10.1	8.8	5.2			Trade Receivables (net)	3.8	2.9
2.6	3.1	7.9	.6			Inventory	1.0	.4
13.6	1.1	2.6	6.8			All Other Current	1.3	2.4
55.3	26.8	32.5	29.2			Total Current	13.1	12.2
25.7	57.1	59.8	53.1			Fixed Assets (net)	77.6	77.6
5.4	2.5	1.6	2.7			Intangibles (net)	1.4	2.1
13.6	13.6	6.2	15.0			All Other Non-Current	7.8	8.1
100.0	100.0	100.0	100.0			Total	100.0	100.0
						LIABILITIES		
22.7	17.5	1.7	1.0			Notes Payable-Short Term	3.4	6.9
1.8	7.4	8.8	7.3			Cur. Mat.-L.T.D.	4.7	3.2
8.5	6.7	4.2	8.2			Trade Payables	1.4	1.8
.1	.1	.0	.0			Income Taxes Payable	.1	.0
20.8	6.3	5.3	14.5			All Other Current	3.4	3.1
53.9	37.9	20.1	30.9			Total Current	13.0	15.1
19.7	32.5	30.2	30.6			Long-Term Debt	62.1	60.4
.0	.0	.1	.1			Deferred Taxes	.1	.1
33.0	27.7	3.8	7.7			All Other Non-Current	7.2	6.8
-6.6	1.9	45.8	30.7			Net Worth	17.6	17.6
100.0	100.0	100.0	100.0			Total Liabilities & Net Worth	100.0	100.0
						INCOME DATA		
100.0	100.0	100.0	100.0			Net Sales	100.0	100.0
						Gross Profit		
88.7	74.7	82.7	96.4			Operating Expenses	52.9	57.0
11.3	25.3	17.3	3.6			Operating Profit	47.1	43.0
4.3	11.0	4.3	3.3			All Other Expenses (net)	26.1	23.5
7.0	14.3	13.1	.3			Profit Before Taxes	21.0	19.5
						RATIOS		
7.8	1.2	6.4	2.0			Current	2.9	2.7
1.7	.7	1.8	1.0				.8	.7
.5	.2	.7	.5				.2	.2
7.6	1.2	4.0	1.3			Quick	2.4	2.1
1.1	.6	1.1	.8				.5	.4
.3	.2	.4	.4				.1	.1
0 UND	0 UND	0 UND	6 57.2			Sales/Receivables	0 UND	0 UND
0 999.8	7 50.3	12 30.9	12 30.4				0 UND	0 UND
6 63.4	41 8.8	41 8.8	25 14.5				17 22.1	4 84.7
						Cost of Sales/Inventory		
						Cost of Sales/Payables		
8.1	10.0	5.1	5.3			Sales/Working Capital	5.3	7.5
46.7	-8.7	8.7	285.8				-46.7	-15.2
-15.9	-2.1	-16.9	-8.5				-2.8	-3.3
11.3	8.7	17.3	17.2			EBIT/Interest	11.0	5.8
(14) 7.2	(10) 3.7	(14) 4.0	(13) 2.0				(44) 3.3	(55) 3.0
2.3	.4	1.2	.0				2.1	1.8
						Net Profit + Depr., Dep., Amort./Cur. Mat. L/T/D		
.1	.9	.3	.5			Fixed/Worth	1.8	2.0
1.1	2.5	1.0	1.7				4.7	5.1
-.2	-257.7	6.2	4.0				39.7	-57.6
.3	.8	.2	.4			Debt/Worth	1.4	1.5
5.8	4.0	1.0	1.4				4.5	5.6
-3.2	-8.6	6.4	3.3				41.3	-63.5
145.3	111.2	49.0	13.6			% Profit Before Taxes/Tangible Net Worth	41.9	35.6
(14) 16.8	(13) 21.9	(20) 25.1	(12) 5.5				(120) 16.9	(100) 19.6
-40.9	-1.1	7.1	.0				5.1	3.2
80.2	19.0	19.6	5.7			% Profit Before Taxes/Total Assets	8.1	7.9
14.3	5.7	5.1	2.1				4.0	3.2
-14.7	-1.2	2.0	-3.7				1.4	.9
242.1	6.3	5.6	2.7			Sales/Net Fixed Assets	.6	.6
39.9	1.5	1.4	1.9				.2	.2
6.3	.3	.4	.8				.2	.2
7.7	1.8	1.8	1.6			Sales/Total Assets	.3	.4
4.4	1.0	.7	.8				.2	.2
2.1	.2	.3	.3				.1	.1
.6	1.4	2.6	3.6			% Depr., Dep., Amort./Sales	8.8	9.4
(14) 1.5	(13) 10.7	(21) 7.7	(13) 6.7				(137) 16.5	(129) 16.0
6.8	15.6	12.8	8.2				23.8	22.4
						% Officers', Directors' Owners' Comp/Sales	3.0	1.0
							(19) 8.7	(25) 7.4
							13.6	23.7
30832M	37059M	142197M	335452M	318434M	286347M	Net Sales ($)	633419M	830171M
6102M	21629M	117300M	322370M	556579M	697897M	Total Assets ($)	1933491M	1254870M

© RMA 2007

M = $ thousand   MM = $ million
See Pages 11 through 21 for Explanation of Ratios and Data

Comparative Historical Data			Type of Statement	Current Data Sorted by Sales					
16	18	41	Unqualified	6	7	5	5	8	10
5	3	11	Reviewed	2	4	2	2	1	
5	9	7	Compiled	5	2				
7	18	16	Tax Returns	7	5	1	2	1	
12	16	19	Other	7	5		2	1	4
4/1/04-3/31/05 ALL	4/1/05-3/31/06 ALL	4/1/06-3/31/07 ALL		38 (4/1-9/30/06)			56 (10/1/06-3/31/07)		
				0-1MM	1-3MM	3-5MM	5-10MM	10-25MM	25MM & OVER
45	64	94	**NUMBER OF STATEMENTS**	27	23	8	11	11	14
%	%	%	**ASSETS**	%	%	%	%	%	%
10.1	11.4	18.0	Cash & Equivalents	22.3	19.9		21.3	17.5	10.1
7.8	7.1	7.7	Trade Receivables (net)	1.9	13.0		8.6	11.0	10.4
.5	.9	3.4	Inventory	.1	2.7		2.5	12.7	.4
6.3	3.7	5.8	All Other Current	4.3	9.7		4.3	1.4	7.0
24.6	23.1	35.0	Total Current	28.6	45.3		36.6	42.6	27.8
53.2	59.1	48.9	Fixed Assets (net)	56.8	45.7		39.0	46.2	48.6
7.2	5.7	4.0	Intangibles (net)	3.8	3.1		1.0	4.2	8.4
14.9	12.1	12.2	All Other Non-Current	10.8	5.9		23.4	7.0	15.2
100.0	100.0	100.0	Total	100.0	100.0		100.0	100.0	100.0
			LIABILITIES						
8.1	8.8	9.9	Notes Payable-Short Term	8.0	22.5		9.8	6.7	.0
7.3	7.6	5.9	Cur. Mat.-L.T.D.	6.0	7.4		4.4	8.8	4.1
8.0	6.2	6.3	Trade Payables	2.1	9.2		11.5	5.4	7.9
.1	.1	.1	Income Taxes Payable	.0	.1		.1	.0	.0
11.0	8.7	11.1	All Other Current	2.3	22.6		8.9	8.7	11.4
34.5	31.4	33.2	Total Current	18.4	61.8		34.8	29.5	23.5
31.6	35.3	27.1	Long-Term Debt	46.7	15.8		20.6	13.4	27.2
.1	.1	.0	Deferred Taxes	.0	.0		.0	.3	.0
6.5	6.4	16.9	All Other Non-Current	26.0	25.1		6.5	4.4	9.6
27.4	26.8	22.8	Net Worth	8.8	-2.6		38.2	52.4	39.8
100.0	100.0	100.0	Total Liabilities & Net Worth	100.0	100.0		100.0	100.0	100.0
			INCOME DATA						
100.0	100.0	100.0	Net Sales	100.0	100.0		100.0	100.0	100.0
			Gross Profit						
80.8	77.9	85.3	Operating Expenses	74.8	83.7		90.8	101.7	87.2
19.2	22.1	14.7	Operating Profit	25.2	16.3		9.2	-1.7	12.8
7.1	9.7	5.6	All Other Expenses (net)	12.2	4.1		2.2	1.7	2.2
12.1	12.4	9.2	Profit Before Taxes	13.0	12.2		7.0	-3.5	10.7
			RATIOS						
2.3	2.2	3.5		9.0	1.8		2.9	3.0	3.5
.9	.9	1.1	Current	1.6	.7		.8	1.2	1.2
.3	.4	.5		.3	.5		.6	.5	.8
2.0	1.7	2.7		6.0	1.1		2.9	2.7	2.8
.6	.6	.8	Quick	1.3	.6		.8	.5	1.0
.1	.3	.4		.3	.2		.4	.4	.3
0 UND	0 UND	0 UND		0 UND	0 999.8		6 57.2	4 86.8	4 88.0
3 117.7	5 67.7	8 47.7	Sales/Receivables	0 UND	10 35.1		16 22.4	15 24.2	12 29.2
27 13.8	22 16.3	27 13.7		5 66.5	56 6.5		27 13.6	44 8.4	30 12.3
			Cost of Sales/Inventory						
			Cost of Sales/Payables						
4.8	8.9	6.1		5.3	47.8		6.3	7.4	3.6
-50.1	-51.9	269.1	Sales/Working Capital	15.4	-18.1		-40.6	252.3	29.0
-4.9	-4.9	-8.3		-5.9	-5.9		-10.5	-4.1	-21.7
13.6	6.8	11.1		13.8					16.1
(28) 4.1	(32) 3.1	(58) 3.8	EBIT/Interest		(17) 8.7			(11)	3.2
-1.7	1.1	.8			-.3				1.3
			Net Profit + Depr., Dep., Amort./Cur. Mat. L/T/D						
.7	.8	.4		.2	1.0		.0	.2	.3
2.0	2.0	1.4	Fixed/Worth	2.3	3.2		1.7	1.0	1.2
-11.0	24.9	NM		-6.9	-1.6		2.5	1.1	4.3
.4	.4	.3		.3	.5		.7	.4	.3
2.8	2.1	2.0	Debt/Worth	4.1	4.0		2.2	.7	1.3
-10.5	46.9	-221.4		-8.2	-3.4		7.7	2.4	3.6
41.7	47.3	51.4		81.1	64.9		65.2		52.0
(32) 21.5	(49) 16.6	(69) 13.6	% Profit Before Taxes/Tangible Net Worth	(17) 7.1	(14) 24.2		(10) 19.2	(12)	10.0
2.0	-1.7	1.1		-16.8	1.4		11.1		2.6
15.6	14.4	19.3		9.8	69.6		14.8	40.4	15.5
6.2	2.7	4.7	% Profit Before Taxes/Total Assets	3.0	19.0		9.2	3.9	5.6
-.7	-1.0	-1.3		-4.3	-2.3		3.8	-3.4	.7
28.2	7.7	32.9		31.5	80.5		109.3	46.2	26.9
1.6	.8	2.1	Sales/Net Fixed Assets	.7	4.6		2.7	3.1	1.8
.2	.2	.6		.2	1.2		2.0	.3	.8
2.6	2.0	3.0		2.6	4.6		1.9	5.1	2.1
.4	.5	1.1	Sales/Total Assets	.5	1.8		1.2	1.9	.7
.2	.2	.3		.2	.6		.4	.2	.4
4.4	3.2	1.4		4.4	1.2				2.9
(36) 9.6	(54) 8.7	(73) 6.4	% Depr., Dep., Amort./Sales	(19) 8.8	(18) 4.9			(12)	6.2
18.5	16.2	12.3		18.5	12.3				7.2
	5.8	3.4							
(11) 7.5	(18) 5.5		% Officers', Directors' Owners' Comp/Sales						
30.2	17.9								
542359M	855197M	1150321M	Net Sales ($)	11109M	44355M	32037M	80112M	171653M	811055M
1157504M	1557085M	1721877M	Total Assets ($)	27461M	44090M	99375M	144839M	295622M	1110490M

© RMA 2007

M = $ thousand   MM = $ million
See Pages 11 through 21 for Explanation of Ratios and Data

Current Data Sorted by Assets | Comparative Historical Data

Date ranges: **128 (4/1-9/30/06)** covers 500M-2MM / 2-10MM; **65 (10/1/06-3/31/07)** covers 10-50MM / 50-100MM / 100-250MM. Historical columns: **4/1/02-3/31/03 ALL** and **4/1/03-3/31/04 ALL**.

0-500M	500M-2MM	2-10MM	10-50MM	50-100MM	100-250MM		4/1/02-3/31/03 ALL	4/1/03-3/31/04 ALL
						Type of Statement		
1	6	33	60	21	18	Unqualified	89	86
		2		1		Reviewed	6	4
1	2					Compiled	7	12
2	2	3				Tax Returns	3	3
2	2	12	16	7	4	Other	39	24
6	10	50	76	29	22	**NUMBER OF STATEMENTS**	144	129
%	%	%	%	%	%	**ASSETS**	%	%
	10.0	14.3	13.1	8.7	11.8	Cash & Equivalents	12.5	14.1
	3.0	4.6	4.6	4.4	3.0	Trade Receivables (net)	4.9	4.2
	9.4	3.0	1.5	.4	2.0	Inventory	7.8	5.7
	2.5	4.9	3.2	3.5	1.9	All Other Current	4.4	6.5
	24.9	26.7	22.5	17.0	18.7	Total Current	29.5	30.5
	62.7	48.2	53.6	47.8	40.6	Fixed Assets (net)	47.6	48.9
	.4	.4	.4	.4	.9	Intangibles (net)	1.0	.7
	12.0	24.6	23.4	34.8	39.8	All Other Non-Current	21.8	19.9
	100.0	100.0	100.0	100.0	100.0	Total	100.0	100.0
						LIABILITIES		
	15.2	4.0	2.4	.9	1.9	Notes Payable-Short Term	3.7	3.6
	1.3	.9	1.0	.5	.3	Cur. Mat.-L.T.D.	1.6	1.8
	13.8	4.6	2.6	2.4	2.1	Trade Payables	5.8	5.6
	.0	.0	.3	.0	.0	Income Taxes Payable	.0	.1
	15.5	3.3	1.7	1.5	.9	All Other Current	3.4	3.1
	45.8	12.9	8.0	5.3	5.2	Total Current	14.4	14.2
	17.8	6.6	14.5	10.9	13.2	Long-Term Debt	12.9	11.4
	.0	.0	.0	.0	.0	Deferred Taxes	.0	.0
	2.8	3.1	1.7	.8	1.7	All Other Non-Current	1.9	2.2
	33.7	77.4	75.8	82.9	79.9	Net Worth	70.8	72.2
	100.0	100.0	100.0	100.0	100.0	Total Liabilities & Net Worth	100.0	100.0
						INCOME DATA		
	100.0	100.0	100.0	100.0	100.0	Net Sales	100.0	100.0
						Gross Profit		
	97.4	88.9	90.1	80.1	88.4	Operating Expenses	92.7	94.4
	2.6	11.1	9.9	19.9	11.6	Operating Profit	7.3	5.6
	2.9	1.1	.8	.2	1.6	All Other Expenses (net)	5.7	1.7
	-.3	10.0	9.1	19.7	10.1	Profit Before Taxes	1.6	3.9
						RATIOS		
	3.7	6.2	7.2	8.2	9.3		6.5	7.2
	1.5	2.8	2.7	2.9	2.1	Current	2.2	2.3
	.3	1.3	1.5	1.2	1.4		.9	1.1
	2.8	5.3	5.4	5.9	7.2		4.1	4.3
	.5	2.0	2.1	2.8	1.4	Quick	1.2	1.6
	.2	.6	.8	.6	1.0		.4	.5
	0 UND	1 570.3	3 144.6	7 55.5	12 30.9		1 436.2	1 420.7
	0 UND	8 45.7	13 28.8	20 18.6	33 11.1	Sales/Receivables	11 34.2	9 39.5
	11 33.4	26 14.2	71 5.1	109 3.3	61 6.0		45 8.1	46 8.0
						Cost of Sales/Inventory		
						Cost of Sales/Payables		
	3.9	1.9	1.3	1.1	1.5		1.8	1.3
	16.2	4.4	3.8	3.4	5.1	Sales/Working Capital	4.7	4.9
	-3.1	34.5	12.4	18.9	11.6		-55.6	50.0
		9.5	10.3	18.1	10.3		6.5	8.5
		(29) 1.8	(52) 3.2	(17) 2.2	(18) 1.5	EBIT/Interest	(79) 1.4	(69) -.4
		-6.7	.1	.0	-.9		-5.3	-5.8
						Net Profit + Depr., Dep., Amort./Cur. Mat. L/T/D		
	.9	.2	.4	.4	.3		.3	.3
	1.3	.7	.7	.6	.4	Fixed/Worth	.7	.7
	-.9	.9	.9	.8	.8		1.1	1.0
	.2	.0	.1	.1	.1		.1	.1
	1.0	.2	.2	.1	.2	Debt/Worth	.2	.2
	-4.6	.4	.5	.3	.4		.8	.7
		15.5	9.1	12.0	5.3	% Profit Before Taxes/Tangible Net Worth	8.9	8.6
		(49) 1.2	(75) 2.7	3.1	1.0		(139) .5	(125) .0
		-3.4	-2.1	-.5	-1.1		-5.9	-3.2
	3.5	8.9	6.5	9.8	4.5	% Profit Before Taxes/Total Assets	4.5	5.1
	-.3	.9	1.5	2.7	1.0		.3	-.1
	-5.1	-3.2	-2.1	-.4	-.8		-5.3	-2.7
	4.8	6.3	1.0	.8	1.0		3.6	2.3
	1.1	1.0	.5	.6	.5	Sales/Net Fixed Assets	.8	.6
	.3	.4	.4	.3	.3		.4	.4
	2.0	.8	.5	.3	.3		.7	.5
	1.0	.5	.3	.3	.2	Sales/Total Assets	.3	.3
	.2	.2	.2	.1	.1		.2	.2
		1.8	5.3	4.9	5.0	% Depr., Dep., Amort./Sales	3.4	4.0
		(42) 7.2	(72) 9.7	(25) 8.4	(19) 10.4		(116) 6.8	(109) 8.1
		10.6	15.7	14.6	16.5		12.6	13.9
						% Officers', Directors' Owners' Comp/Sales	4.0	1.4
							(25) 12.4	(15) 3.5
							27.9	22.4
3633M	9056M	170736M	748104M	494526M	766634M	Net Sales ($)	1511275M	2787292M
1901M	8800M	294525M	2019230M	1935075M	3209903M	Total Assets ($)	4050643M	4465703M

M = $ thousand   MM = $ million
See Pages 11 through 21 for Explanation of Ratios and Data

Comparative Historical Data | | Type of Statement | Current Data Sorted by Sales

Comparative Historical Data			Type of Statement	Current Data Sorted by Sales					
82	110	139	Unqualified	11	22	15	33	42	16
5	4	3	Reviewed		1			2	
6	5	3	Compiled	3					
2	4	7	Tax Returns	2	4			1	
31	42	41	Other	3	8	4	12		2
4/1/04- 3/31/05	4/1/05- 3/31/06	4/1/06- 3/31/07			128 (4/1-9/30/06)			65 (10/1/06-3/31/07)	
ALL	ALL	ALL		0-1MM	1-3MM	3-5MM	5-10MM	10-25MM	25MM & OVER
126	165	193	NUMBER OF STATEMENTS	19	35	19	45	57	18
%	%	%	ASSETS	%	%	%	%	%	%
13.8	14.9	12.5	Cash & Equivalents	10.7	11.8	14.1	10.6	15.7	8.9
4.4	4.3	4.3	Trade Receivables (net)	6.0	2.6	1.6	4.1	5.8	4.3
5.7	3.8	2.5	Inventory	7.7	1.4	4.0	.6	2.6	2.7
3.3	2.9	3.4	All Other Current	.6	2.9	5.3	5.7	2.4	3.2
27.2	26.0	22.8	Total Current	24.9	18.6	25.0	21.0	26.4	19.1
48.4	48.3	50.4	Fixed Assets (net)	58.6	56.6	50.0	48.7	47.7	42.3
1.2	.8	.5	Intangibles (net)	.2	.3	.6	.4	.3	1.8
23.1	24.9	26.4	All Other Non-Current	16.2	24.5	24.4	29.9	25.6	36.8
100.0	100.0	100.0	Total	100.0	100.0	100.0	100.0	100.0	100.0
			LIABILITIES						
9.8	5.6	3.6	Notes Payable-Short Term	5.7	6.9	4.1	3.0	1.7	1.7
1.6	1.2	.8	Cur. Mat.-L.T.D.	.5	.7	.7	.7	1.2	.6
5.3	5.0	3.9	Trade Payables	4.9	4.5	3.5	2.8	4.3	3.8
.1	.1	.1	Income Taxes Payable	.0	.0	.0	.0	.4	.0
5.3	4.8	2.9	All Other Current	3.8	4.8	.9	3.2	2.1	2.2
22.1	16.7	11.3	Total Current	14.9	16.9	9.2	9.6	9.8	8.3
10.8	13.4	11.7	Long-Term Debt	8.2	11.6	13.3	10.6	13.9	9.7
.0	.0	.0	Deferred Taxes	.0	.0	.0	.0	.0	.0
1.2	2.2	2.0	All Other Non-Current	1.3	.8	.3	2.8	2.6	2.5
66.0	67.8	75.0	Net Worth	75.7	70.8	77.2	77.0	73.7	79.4
100.0	100.0	100.0	Total Liabilities & Net Worth	100.0	100.0	100.0	100.0	100.0	100.0
			INCOME DATA						
100.0	100.0	100.0	Net Sales	100.0	100.0	100.0	100.0	100.0	100.0
			Gross Profit						
91.2	94.5	88.6	Operating Expenses	90.2	96.1	90.5	88.1	84.9	83.2
8.8	5.5	11.4	Operating Profit	9.8	3.9	9.5	11.9	15.1	16.8
.1	.5	.9	All Other Expenses (net)	1.9	1.9	1.9	.2	1.3	-2.2
8.7	5.0	10.5	Profit Before Taxes	8.0	2.0	7.7	11.7	13.8	19.0
			RATIOS						
4.4	5.6	6.5		13.2	6.0	8.1	7.4	6.8	5.2
1.8	2.3	2.5	Current	3.5	2.5	1.9	2.8	2.0	2.1
.9	1.0	1.3		1.1	1.0	1.6	1.4	1.3	1.4
3.5	4.3	5.3		13.1	5.2	5.4	4.7	5.7	4.2
1.1	1.6	1.7	Quick	2.8	1.7	1.8	1.6	1.6	1.4
.4	.5	.7		.1	.6	.5	.8	.7	.8
0 999.8	1 367.2	2 216.2		0 UND	2 162.7	0 UND	1 297.9	4 82.7	9 40.7
7 49.9	8 43.0	12 31.7	Sales/Receivables	0 UND	10 36.8	7 54.6	13 27.4	15 24.3	23 16.2
47 7.8	48 7.6	48 7.6		16 23.4	27 13.5	31 11.8	59 6.2	71 5.2	49 7.5
			Cost of Sales/Inventory						
			Cost of Sales/Payables						
2.2	1.6	1.6		2.4	2.2	.9	1.5	1.1	2.5
5.7	4.5	4.4	Sales/Working Capital	4.3	6.0	2.8	4.6	5.2	5.1
-115.4	428.3	18.6		26.9	-82.3	11.6	16.9	19.8	13.2
13.8	16.2	9.9			1.8	2.3	10.3	19.1	99.9
(78) 2.4	(103) 2.3	(129) 1.8	EBIT/Interest	(27) .3	(12) .5	(30) 4.5	(37) 4.0	(15) 5.3	
-1.5	-1.9	-.6			-6.6	-3.7	.2	.3	.7
			Net Profit + Depr., Dep., Amort./Cur. Mat. L/T/D						
.3	.3	.3		.7	.5	.6	.4	.3	.3
.7	.7	.7	Fixed/Worth	.9	.8	.7	.7	.6	.6
1.1	1.0	.9		1.0	1.0	.9	.9	.9	.9
.1	.1	.1		.0	.0	.1	.1	.1	.1
.3	.2	.2	Debt/Worth	.1	.2	.2	.2	.2	.2
.6	.7	.5		.7	.5	.5	.4	.6	.5
13.2	9.8	10.2	% Profit Before Taxes/Tangible Net Worth	10.1	2.9	10.5	10.4	11.7	9.5
(122) 2.4	(158) 1.7	(187) 2.5		(18) .8	(32) -.3	.7	(44) 2.6	(56) 4.2	5.0
-2.7	-3.0	-1.1		-3.9	-3.9	-3.7	-.9	-.6	-.5
9.0	6.7	6.8	% Profit Before Taxes/Total Assets	6.4	1.7	5.4	7.1	8.2	7.8
1.3	1.0	1.5		-.2	-.5	.7	2.1	3.2	3.8
-2.5	-2.2	-1.1		-3.6	-4.0	-3.2	-1.0	-.7	-.3
4.8	1.6	1.3		5.3	1.3	1.4	1.2	1.3	2.8
.8	.7	.7	Sales/Net Fixed Assets	.9	.6	.4	.7	.6	.9
.4	.3	.4		.2	.4	.3	.3	.4	.6
.7	.6	.6		.9	.6	.4	.6	.5	.6
.4	.3	.3	Sales/Total Assets	.2	.3	.2	.3	.3	.4
.2	.2	.2		.2	.2	.2	.2	.2	.3
4.0	3.5	4.3		2.6	2.6	4.4	4.0	5.0	3.5
(100) 8.7	(147) 8.7	(170) 8.7	% Depr., Dep., Amort./Sales	(14) 10.2	(31) 7.9	(18) 10.4	(39) 9.4	(50) 8.4	6.0
13.8	15.6	14.9		19.7	12.5	16.0	17.0	13.0	11.7
4.5	3.0	3.3	% Officers', Directors' Owners' Comp/Sales						
(13) 10.4	(21) 6.0	(21) 7.4							
30.6	19.2	22.2							
1199557M	1788903M	2192689M	Net Sales ($)	11391M	68434M	74009M	308157M	859434M	871264M
3831047M	6195582M	7469434M	Total Assets ($)	46063M	258714M	324996M	1325543M	3393414M	2120704M

M = $ thousand   MM = $ million
See Pages 11 through 21 for Explanation of Ratios and Data

Current Data Sorted by Assets | Comparative Historical Data

						Type of Statement		
		2	6	2	1	Unqualified	14	11
		5	5			Reviewed	20	22
2	4	4				Compiled	22	15
3	8	4	2			Tax Returns	17	15
1	7	7	8	1	1	Other	20	19
	10 (4/1-9/30/06)		63 (10/1/06-3/31/07)				4/1/02-3/31/03 ALL	4/1/03-3/31/04 ALL
0-500M	500M-2MM	2-10MM	10-50MM	50-100MM	100-250MM			
6	19	22	21	3	2	NUMBER OF STATEMENTS	93	82
%	%	%	%	%	%	ASSETS	%	%
	14.6	6.9	12.4			Cash & Equivalents	8.8	7.3
	1.1	.7	.7			Trade Receivables (net)	.5	.6
	.7	1.2	2.3			Inventory	2.1	2.2
	1.2	1.0	2.9			All Other Current	4.1	2.4
	17.5	9.8	18.3			Total Current	15.5	12.6
	66.5	82.2	71.6			Fixed Assets (net)	73.2	72.6
	3.8	.5	3.1			Intangibles (net)	2.7	2.4
	12.2	7.5	7.1			All Other Non-Current	8.6	12.4
	100.0	100.0	100.0			Total	100.0	100.0
						LIABILITIES		
	1.6	3.6	1.7			Notes Payable-Short Term	9.1	3.8
	2.9	5.5	4.2			Cur. Mat.-L.T.D.	6.8	9.0
	5.6	2.0	1.8			Trade Payables	2.3	2.3
	.6	.0	.0			Income Taxes Payable	.3	.0
	18.3	4.2	6.0			All Other Current	11.5	8.3
	29.0	15.3	13.8			Total Current	30.1	23.4
	42.0	39.3	37.5			Long-Term Debt	36.6	44.9
	.0	.9	1.1			Deferred Taxes	.5	1.0
	6.8	9.5	2.3			All Other Non-Current	13.2	10.7
	22.2	35.0	45.3			Net Worth	19.6	20.0
	100.0	100.0	100.0			Total Liabilities & Net Worth	100.0	100.0
						INCOME DATA		
	100.0	100.0	100.0			Net Sales	100.0	100.0
						Gross Profit		
	83.9	99.1	86.9			Operating Expenses	87.5	90.6
	16.1	.9	13.1			Operating Profit	12.5	9.4
	5.1	4.3	4.5			All Other Expenses (net)	5.9	5.7
	11.1	-3.5	8.6			Profit Before Taxes	6.6	3.7
						RATIOS		
	2.4	1.3	3.1				1.2	1.1
	1.1	.6	1.1			Current	.7	.6
	.1	.2	.2				.2	.2
	2.4	1.2	2.5				1.0	.8
	.8	.4	.5			Quick	(92) .3	.3
	.1	.1	.1				.1	.1
0 UND		0 UND	0 UND				0 UND	0 UND
0 UND		1 523.7	1 422.1			Sales/Receivables	0 UND	0 UND
0 UND		5 77.0	5 78.9				3 108.4	4 96.9
						Cost of Sales/Inventory		
						Cost of Sales/Payables		
	9.4	26.2	5.6				37.5	81.2
	181.0	-14.4	102.7			Sales/Working Capital	-27.0	-17.8
	-8.5	-5.5	-6.1				-7.0	-6.3
	5.9	2.1	9.5				4.1	3.9
(16)	1.8	(21) .7	(19) 2.3			EBIT/Interest	(74) 2.4	(70) 1.4
	.6	-1.7	1.6				.7	-.1
						Net Profit + Depr., Dep.,	3.3	3.5
						Amort./Cur. Mat. L/T/D	(16) 2.2	(17) 2.0
							1.1	1.4
	.9	1.1	.8				1.2	1.3
	3.2	4.5	3.2			Fixed/Worth	2.2	2.8
	-189.2	16.2	4.5				52.1	-56.3
	.3	.5	.4				.7	.8
	2.5	4.1	2.5			Debt/Worth	2.1	2.8
	-211.0	16.4	3.7				61.1	-63.1
	44.4	5.4	36.1			% Profit Before Taxes/Tangible	37.8	28.2
(14)	11.3	(19) 3.1	(18) 17.4			Net Worth	(71) 18.9	(59) 9.0
	.0	-18.6	5.5				2.4	-7.3
	12.4	3.1	16.7			% Profit Before Taxes/Total	13.5	8.0
	3.7	.0	5.5			Assets	5.3	1.5
	-.8	-7.3	2.4				-2.4	-5.0
	4.1	1.5	2.2				3.2	2.3
	1.9	.9	1.1			Sales/Net Fixed Assets	1.2	1.2
	.6	.5	.5				.8	.7
	2.9	1.2	1.0				1.7	1.6
	.8	.8	.8			Sales/Total Assets	.9	.9
	.3	.5	.5				.6	.6
	4.9	8.3	7.5				5.4	7.0
(17)	8.4	16.5	(20) 11.6			% Depr., Dep., Amort./Sales	(85) 10.2	(75) 12.0
	20.0	25.6	14.4				15.3	16.5
						% Officers', Directors'	3.7	2.9
						Owners' Comp/Sales	(30) 7.7	(26) 5.3
							12.8	8.9
9274M	38088M	108905M	472196M	240797M	170115M	Net Sales ($)	1025267M	1055351M
1499M	23365M	129048M	504170M	212745M	224242M	Total Assets ($)	1247857M	1411814M

© RMA 2007

M = $ thousand   MM = $ million
See Pages 11 through 21 for Explanation of Ratios and Data

Comparative Historical Data | Current Data Sorted by Sales

4/1/04-3/31/05 ALL	4/1/05-3/31/06 ALL	4/1/06-3/31/07 ALL	Type of Statement	0-1MM	1-3MM	3-5MM	5-10MM	10-25MM	25MM & OVER
11	13	11	Unqualified			2	1	4	4
16	16	10	Reviewed		2		3	3	2
15	16	10	Compiled	4	4	1	1		
15	15	17	Tax Returns	8	2	3	1	2	1
24	24	25	Other	2	1	9	4	4	5
					10 (4/1-9/30/06)		63 (10/1/06-3/31/07)		
ALL	ALL	ALL							
81	84	73	**NUMBER OF STATEMENTS**	14	9	15	10	13	12
%	%	%	**ASSETS**	%	%	%	%	%	%
11.7	9.1	11.8	Cash & Equivalents	12.2		8.7	15.5	11.2	13.4
1.2	1.4	.8	Trade Receivables (net)	.1		.6	2.0	.7	1.1
2.6	2.0	1.6	Inventory	.2		1.1	2.0	1.1	3.4
1.0	2.4	2.0	All Other Current	.0		1.9	.2	1.1	7.2
16.5	14.8	16.2	Total Current	12.5		12.4	19.7	14.1	25.0
68.7	73.7	72.8	Fixed Assets (net)	71.2		73.1	77.2	76.8	60.5
3.2	2.3	2.8	Intangibles (net)	3.2		3.4	1.5	2.4	4.6
11.5	9.2	8.2	All Other Non-Current	13.1		11.2	1.7	6.6	9.8
100.0	100.0	100.0	Total	100.0		100.0	100.0	100.0	100.0
			LIABILITIES						
11.0	6.0	2.8	Notes Payable-Short Term	3.8		1.0	2.9	4.6	1.7
5.5	4.3	3.8	Cur. Mat.-L.T.D.	1.0		4.7	7.4	4.1	2.7
4.0	5.7	2.9	Trade Payables	.2		4.8	1.5	2.1	2.8
.1	.0	.1	Income Taxes Payable	.8		.0	.0	.0	.0
14.9	14.2	11.9	All Other Current	19.0		11.7	15.0	2.7	11.1
35.6	30.2	21.6	Total Current	24.7		22.2	26.7	13.5	18.3
45.3	44.9	34.5	Long-Term Debt	31.6		32.9	43.8	39.4	9.0
.9	1.0	.7	Deferred Taxes	.0		.1	2.5	.0	2.1
10.7	8.4	8.8	All Other Non-Current	1.8		12.9	8.2	3.9	8.1
7.6	15.5	34.4	Net Worth	41.9		32.0	18.8	43.3	62.4
100.0	100.0	100.0	Total Liabilities & Net Worth	100.0		100.0	100.0	100.0	100.0
			INCOME DATA						
100.0	100.0	100.0	Net Sales	100.0		100.0	100.0	100.0	100.0
			Gross Profit						
94.3	92.6	90.2	Operating Expenses	75.4		99.0	99.6	88.5	85.7
5.7	7.4	9.8	Operating Profit	24.6		1.0	.4	11.5	14.3
4.9	5.1	4.4	All Other Expenses (net)	7.2		1.9	1.8	3.9	3.7
.8	2.3	5.4	Profit Before Taxes	17.4		-.9	-1.4	7.6	10.7
			RATIOS						
1.4	1.7	1.6	Current	3.7		1.3	1.6	2.1	7.6
.5	.8	.7		.5		.8	.5	.7	1.0
.2	.2	.2		.2		.1	.2	.2	.3
1.0	1.2	1.5	Quick	3.6		1.1	1.5	1.9	6.6
.3	.3	.4		.5		.4	.4	.3	.3
.1	.1	.1		.1		.1	.1	.2	.1
0 UND	0 UND	0 UND	Sales/Receivables	0 UND		0 UND	0 UND	0 UND	1 391.3
0 999.8	0 907.1	0 999.8		0 UND		1 618.5	1 547.3	0 999.8	2 207.1
4 101.5	3 112.5	4 103.0		0 UND		3 107.8	4 81.6	5 72.0	6 57.4
			Cost of Sales/Inventory						
			Cost of Sales/Payables						
34.6	17.9	10.8	Sales/Working Capital	4.0		22.1	30.9	7.6	3.8
-15.4	-31.2	-32.6		-12.2		-32.6	-38.2	-20.6	554.0
-3.9	-4.5	-5.7		-2.6		-8.5	-5.1	-7.3	-5.1
3.5	3.9	3.7	EBIT/Interest	6.1		21.1	2.6	9.0	8.5
(72) 1.3	(75) 1.7	(67) 1.6		(11) 2.3		(14) 1.0	1.6	2.3	(10) 2.9
-.8	.1	.4		.5		-.9	-.5	1.2	1.6
2.8	4.6	3.1	Net Profit + Depr., Dep., Amort./Cur. Mat. L/T/D						
(13) 2.0	(17) 2.5	(13) 2.3							
1.2	1.0	1.1							
1.4	1.4	1.0	Fixed/Worth	.9		1.1	1.9	1.0	.5
4.0	3.2	3.2		2.7		7.6	9.1	2.1	1.0
-3.4	-7.2	13.4		13.3		13.2	-299.5	4.5	1.8
1.2	.8	.4	Debt/Worth	.3		.3	1.1	.5	.2
5.0	3.9	2.5				7.7	15.9	1.5	.6
-6.2	-9.2	17.8		19.6		15.0	-314.2	3.7	1.5
23.3	29.5	34.9	% Profit Before Taxes/Tangible Net Worth	53.4		40.0		33.6	38.7
(57) 6.7	(60) 10.4	(61) 7.7		(12) 11.4		(14) 1.6		(11) 13.5	21.4
-5.4	-2.9	-1.2		-1.4		-22.0		3.8	4.4
6.1	9.0	10.1	% Profit Before Taxes/Total Assets	11.9		5.0	4.5	16.7	16.3
.4	3.1	3.0		3.7		.0	2.7	4.5	8.9
-6.9	-3.9	-1.8		-1.2		-7.0	-3.5	.8	2.9
4.1	2.9	2.4	Sales/Net Fixed Assets	1.1		4.1	4.7	2.1	3.4
1.6	1.2	1.1		.7		1.2	1.4	1.1	1.8
.7	.6	.6		.3		.8	.8	.5	1.0
2.0	1.8	1.4	Sales/Total Assets	.7		2.9	3.0	1.2	1.5
1.1	.9	.8		.4		.8	1.2	1.0	.8
.5	.5	.5		.3		.6	.8	.5	.8
5.7	5.8	6.2	% Depr., Dep., Amort./Sales	6.0		7.4		7.8	3.7
(74) 10.4	(79) 9.2	(68) 10.1		(13) 8.4		(14) 13.3		9.7	(10) 6.3
15.2	15.5	17.0		23.8		19.8		15.1	11.9
2.6	2.9	1.4	% Officers', Directors' Owners' Comp/Sales						
(19) 4.8	(22) 5.1	(22) 5.0							
7.4	7.7	16.8							
788459M	1136801M	1039375M	Net Sales ($)	5427M	15390M	60900M	68691M	176428M	712539M
972778M	1327912M	1095069M	Total Assets ($)	14477M	26194M	74674M	59259M	238471M	681994M

M = $ thousand   MM = $ million
See Pages 11 through 21 for Explanation of Ratios and Data

Current Data Sorted by Assets   Comparative Historical Data

						Type of Statement		
	2	6	7	2	10	Unqualified	27	30
1		3	1			Reviewed	8	11
2	1	2				Compiled	18	19
2	4	3				Tax Returns	13	21
3	5	6	12	1	5	Other	27	33
	24 (4/1-9/30/06)		54 (10/1/06-3/31/07)				4/1/02-3/31/03	4/1/03-3/31/04
0-500M	500M-2MM	2-10MM	10-50MM	50-100MM	100-250MM		ALL	ALL
8	12	20	20	3	15	NUMBER OF STATEMENTS	93	114
%	%	%	%	%	%	ASSETS	%	%
	16.4	15.1	17.8		22.6	Cash & Equivalents	15.2	16.2
	11.4	3.8	2.0		1.2	Trade Receivables (net)	2.6	3.3
	8.6	4.8	5.6		.7	Inventory	4.5	4.0
	.6	1.6	4.1		1.0	All Other Current	3.3	4.1
	37.1	25.3	29.4		25.5	Total Current	25.6	27.6
	56.5	62.3	60.1		68.4	Fixed Assets (net)	63.0	60.9
	4.3	8.2	9.3		1.6	Intangibles (net)	4.5	4.3
	2.2	4.2	1.2		4.5	All Other Non-Current	6.9	7.1
	100.0	100.0	100.0		100.0	Total	100.0	100.0
						LIABILITIES		
	4.1	5.9	3.7		.0	Notes Payable-Short Term	4.3	7.0
	7.9	10.0	13.7		1.6	Cur. Mat.-L.T.D.	8.2	8.4
	13.0	4.8	10.0		4.2	Trade Payables	4.5	4.6
	.0	.4	.0		.0	Income Taxes Payable	.2	.1
	16.1	8.8	8.1		8.9	All Other Current	8.7	6.9
	41.1	29.8	35.5		14.8	Total Current	25.9	27.0
	73.7	25.9	25.1		29.4	Long-Term Debt	30.2	30.8
	.0	.0	.3		.2	Deferred Taxes	.4	.2
	4.9	1.5	4.6		.2	All Other Non-Current	7.2	7.0
	-19.6	42.7	34.5		55.4	Net Worth	36.2	35.0
	100.0	100.0	100.0		100.0	Total Liabilties & Net Worth	100.0	100.0
						INCOME DATA		
	100.0	100.0	100.0		100.0	Net Sales	100.0	100.0
						Gross Profit		
	94.6	82.4	85.0		58.5	Operating Expenses	86.3	86.5
	5.4	17.6	15.0		41.5	Operating Profit	13.7	13.5
	2.0	2.2	5.3		1.7	All Other Expenses (net)	3.6	2.8
	3.4	15.4	9.7		39.8	Profit Before Taxes	10.1	10.7
						RATIOS		
	1.3	2.3	2.0		3.8		1.8	2.1
	.9	.8	1.2		1.7	Current	.9	.9
	.4	.4	.5		1.1		.5	.4
	1.2	1.5	1.4		3.5		1.2	1.5
	.5	.6	.7		1.3	Quick	.7 (113)	.7
	.0	.2	.4		1.1		.2	.2
1	320.2	0 UND	1 485.3		1 432.8		0 UND	0 UND
3	106.2	2 152.9	2 187.4		1 255.6	Sales/Receivables	1 704.2	1 570.8
9	38.7	19 18.8	4 86.3		6 62.3		4 97.5	4 82.2
						Cost of Sales/Inventory		
						Cost of Sales/Payables		
	42.7	11.6	9.4		7.0		21.3	10.6
	NM	-34.8	41.6		21.7	Sales/Working Capital	-82.8	-61.2
	-7.2	-9.3	-9.4		62.1		-10.1	-9.6
	3.7	21.2	7.6		122.8		11.4	13.8
(10)	1.0	(17) 2.6	(18) 2.3		(14) 35.4	EBIT/Interest	(79) 4.3	(99) 4.4
	-2.0	1.8	.1		22.7		1.1	.9
						Net Profit + Depr., Dep.,	10.6	5.0
						Amort./Cur. Mat. L/T/D	(11) 4.5	(16) 2.7
							1.7	1.5
	3.4	.8	.8		.9		.9	.8
	-15.1	1.8	1.8		1.1	Fixed/Worth	1.6	1.9
	-.9	5.2	5.2		1.5		6.2	17.0
	4.3	.7	.8		.4		.6	.6
	-20.0	1.5	1.8		.5	Debt/Worth	1.5	1.9
	-2.3	4.9	7.0		1.7		8.7	18.3
		83.9	54.9		206.8	% Profit Before Taxes/Tangible	87.2	96.7
	(17)	29.5 (17)	21.7		(13) 114.3	Net Worth	(74) 32.4	(87) 32.6
		9.1	-31.7		84.4		6.8	3.7
	26.7	41.2	25.1		94.5	% Profit Before Taxes/Total	28.5	28.7
	5.1	10.7	5.6		64.6	Assets	8.0	9.7
	-17.5	2.5	-2.1		28.8		.5	-.1
	8.3	13.1	3.1		2.9		5.2	5.5
	5.1	2.2	2.2		2.3	Sales/Net Fixed Assets	2.5	2.4
	2.3	.9	1.4		1.6		1.4	1.3
	3.7	3.1	1.9		1.8		2.4	2.4
	2.0	1.4	1.3		1.6	Sales/Total Assets	1.5	1.4
	1.6	.8	.8		1.1		1.1	1.0
	2.7	1.5	5.0				2.9	3.9
(11)	8.7	(19) 8.1	7.7			% Depr., Dep., Amort./Sales	(74) 6.7	(94) 7.2
	15.6	13.9	11.1				12.9	12.0
						% Officers', Directors'	3.4	3.1
						Owners' Comp/Sales	(24) 6.2	(38) 5.0
							11.2	10.2
8478M	33978M	335586M	585092M	288490M	4259221M	Net Sales ($)	4249972M	5418318M
2652M	12687M	114718M	400597M	265213M	2609072M	Total Assets ($)	3338542M	4593314M

© RMA 2007   M = $ thousand   MM = $ million

See Pages 11 through 21 for Explanation of Ratios and Data

Comparative Historical Data			Type of Statement	Current Data Sorted by Sales					
26	24	27	Unqualified			3	6	18	
6	8	5	Reviewed		1	1	2	1	
10	6	5	Compiled		2	1			
18	11	9	Tax Returns	2	7	2			
16	30	32	Other	5	2	2	4	8	11
4/1/04-3/31/05 ALL	4/1/05-3/31/06 ALL	4/1/06-3/31/07 ALL		24 (4/1-9/30/06)			54 (10/1/06-3/31/07)		
				0-1MM	1-3MM	3-5MM	5-10MM	10-25MM	25MM & OVER
76	79	78	NUMBER OF STATEMENTS	7	12	4	9	16	30
%	%	%	ASSETS	%	%	%	%	%	%
19.3	17.2	18.8	Cash & Equivalents		13.5			17.9	21.8
2.3	2.5	4.3	Trade Receivables (net)		7.1			2.0	1.9
3.8	3.6	4.3	Inventory		10.5			5.9	3.4
3.4	3.4	2.4	All Other Current		.5			3.3	2.3
28.8	26.7	29.8	Total Current		31.5			29.1	29.3
61.2	61.3	60.2	Fixed Assets (net)		62.5			59.0	64.5
3.5	4.3	6.2	Intangibles (net)		4.6			9.7	3.0
6.5	7.6	3.8	All Other Non-Current		1.4			2.2	3.2
100.0	100.0	100.0	Total		100.0			100.0	100.0
			LIABILITIES						
13.3	8.1	3.7	Notes Payable-Short Term		3.1			1.2	3.8
7.1	5.6	8.0	Cur. Mat.-L.T.D.		9.8			17.4	4.7
5.6	5.6	8.5	Trade Payables		9.4			6.0	7.3
.0	.3	.2	Income Taxes Payable		.0			.0	.3
12.5	9.0	10.2	All Other Current		6.5			10.9	9.5
38.5	28.6	30.5	Total Current		28.9			35.5	25.6
31.1	29.9	32.7	Long-Term Debt		66.5			21.9	21.5
.5	.1	.1	Deferred Taxes		.0			.2	.1
9.6	6.6	6.3	All Other Non-Current		3.6			1.8	5.8
20.2	34.8	30.4	Net Worth		1.1			40.6	47.1
100.0	100.0	100.0	Total Liabilties & Net Worth		100.0			100.0	100.0
			INCOME DATA						
100.0	100.0	100.0	Net Sales		100.0			100.0	100.0
			Gross Profit						
85.6	78.8	80.6	Operating Expenses		96.8			85.0	72.1
14.4	21.2	19.4	Operating Profit		3.2			15.0	27.9
2.9	3.6	2.9	All Other Expenses (net)		3.0			3.3	3.0
11.5	17.6	16.6	Profit Before Taxes		.2			11.7	24.8
			RATIOS						
1.7	2.6	2.2			2.7			4.4	2.0
.9	1.3	1.2	Current		.9			1.6	1.3
.3	.6	.5			.3			.4	.7
1.3	2.4	1.9			1.1			4.2	1.8
.7	(78) .9	.9	Quick		.3			.5	1.1
.2	.4	.4			.0			.2	.6
0 UND	0 UND	1 560.6		0 UND			0 850.0	1 475.2	
0 969.7	1 438.9	2 198.5	Sales/Receivables	3 131.9			2 187.4	1 297.8	
4 102.6	6 61.2	6 65.1		6 58.8			4 102.0	4 92.3	
			Cost of Sales/Inventory						
			Cost of Sales/Payables						
15.4	8.4	11.7			18.6			5.7	10.8
-180.1	38.3	68.9	Sales/Working Capital		NM			15.6	46.3
-10.8	-11.3	-11.4			-5.3			-9.9	-25.5
27.7	22.4	25.5		1.8			8.0	48.2	
(63) 5.0	(66) 6.3	(68) 3.8	EBIT/Interest	(11) .3			(13) 3.3	(27) 22.5	
1.3	1.3	.8		-2.3			1.3	.9	
			Net Profit + Depr., Dep., Amort./Cur. Mat. L/T/D						
.9	.9	.9		1.6			.6	.9	
2.1	1.6	1.7	Fixed/Worth	NM			1.4	1.2	
NM	3.6	NM		-3.2			2.8	2.9	
.8	.6	.5		1.2			.4	.5	
2.1	1.7	1.6	Debt/Worth	NM			1.5	1.0	
-275.3	4.1	-40.3		-4.4			2.1	3.5	
97.5	99.9	113.6	% Profit Before Taxes/Tangible Net Worth				55.5	163.3	
(56) 52.6	(65) 38.2	(58) 39.6					(13) 29.1	(26) 94.3	
24.9	11.7	10.6					8.7	25.4	
39.4	40.0	62.5	% Profit Before Taxes/Total Assets	5.7			26.5	87.8	
12.1	14.1	14.8		-2.7			15.6	46.0	
1.0	2.2	1.8		-17.5			2.5	1.9	
7.0	4.2	5.8		7.9			4.1	5.5	
2.8	2.1	2.5	Sales/Net Fixed Assets	2.5			2.4	2.4	
1.5	1.3	1.6		1.3			1.4	1.8	
3.0	1.9	2.5		3.5			2.2	2.6	
1.7	1.4	1.7	Sales/Total Assets	1.7			1.3	1.7	
1.1	.8	.9		1.1			.8	1.2	
4.1	3.9	3.6		7.0			4.7	1.5	
(58) 6.9	(65) 8.4	(64) 7.3	% Depr., Dep., Amort./Sales	10.4			6.7	(19) 5.3	
13.7	11.5	11.6		15.2			11.4	8.7	
4.1	2.4	1.4	% Officers', Directors' Owners' Comp/Sales						
(27) 6.6	(19) 4.8	(18) 2.7							
13.0	11.1	6.9							
3737049M	3275633M	5510845M	Net Sales ($)	4058M	18593M	15320M	63283M	265842M	5143749M
2553119M	2898339M	3404939M	Total Assets ($)	11509M	13460M	18045M	50309M	212098M	3099518M

M = $ thousand   MM = $ million
See Pages 11 through 21 for Explanation of Ratios and Data

ENTERTAINMENT—Casinos (except Casino Hotels) NAICS 713210 (SIC 7999)

Current Data Sorted by Assets / Comparative Historical Data

	0-500M	500M-2MM	2-10MM	10-50MM	50-100MM	100-250MM		17	33
Type of Statement									
Unqualified		2	8	13	11	17		17	33
Reviewed			2	1					
Compiled			1	1				1	1
Tax Returns	4	2						3	5
Other	2	2	14	26	7	5		12	8
		30 (4/1-9/30/06)		88 (10/1/06-3/31/07)				4/1/02-3/31/03	4/1/03-3/31/04
	0-500M	500M-2MM	2-10MM	10-50MM	50-100MM	100-250MM		ALL	ALL
NUMBER OF STATEMENTS	6	6	25	41	18	22		33	47
	%	%	%	%	%	%		%	%
ASSETS									
Cash & Equivalents			30.8	16.8	12.0	20.6		21.3	21.4
Trade Receivables (net)			1.0	.8	.8	.6		.6	.7
Inventory			1.2	.5	.5	.3		1.1	1.1
All Other Current			5.1	2.4	1.9	1.1		1.9	3.2
Total Current			38.1	20.4	15.2	22.7		25.0	26.3
Fixed Assets (net)			55.1	71.5	77.4	69.5		62.8	61.3
Intangibles (net)			2.3	2.5	2.6	5.2		9.7	7.6
All Other Non-Current			4.5	5.5	4.8	2.6		2.6	4.8
Total			100.0	100.0	100.0	100.0		100.0	100.0
LIABILITIES									
Notes Payable-Short Term			.8	9.8	.3	4.5		2.9	1.3
Cur. Mat.-L.T.D.			4.9	5.8	4.5	2.9		5.6	6.8
Trade Payables			3.8	3.4	3.7	2.2		4.3	5.1
Income Taxes Payable			.0	.0	.0	.0		.0	.0
All Other Current			13.4	8.7	8.3	11.0		10.6	10.5
Total Current			22.8	27.7	16.8	20.8		23.5	23.7
Long-Term Debt			15.6	32.8	38.0	29.6		36.0	31.2
Deferred Taxes			.3	.7	.0	.0		.0	.0
All Other Non-Current			2.5	1.2	.1	2.9		1.7	2.4
Net Worth			58.8	37.6	45.1	46.8		38.7	42.7
Total Liabilties & Net Worth			100.0	100.0	100.0	100.0		100.0	100.0
INCOME DATA									
Net Sales			100.0	100.0	100.0	100.0		100.0	100.0
Gross Profit									
Operating Expenses			76.5	72.4	70.5	63.4		69.5	76.6
Operating Profit			23.5	27.6	29.5	36.6		30.5	23.4
All Other Expenses (net)			1.9	4.4	3.5	6.0		4.1	3.0
Profit Before Taxes			21.6	23.2	25.9	30.6		26.4	20.4
RATIOS									
Current			2.8	2.1	1.2	1.8		1.7	1.8
			2.1	1.1	.9	1.2		1.0	1.1
			.9	.7	.6	.8		.7	.7
Quick			2.4	1.7	1.1	1.6		1.5	1.7
			1.5	.9	.7	1.2		.9	.9
			.7	.5	.5	.7		.6	.5
Sales/Receivables			0 UND	0 954.7	0 790.4	0 932.4		0 UND	0 999.8
			0 999.8	1 289.3	1 546.7	1 355.3		1 497.5	0 735.4
			3 136.1	3 114.2	2 166.1	3 114.2		2 176.1	2 194.7
Cost of Sales/Inventory									
Cost of Sales/Payables									
Sales/Working Capital			7.7	13.6	87.1	13.0		21.7	13.3
			37.4	71.8	-225.5	36.8		164.0	92.9
			-143.9	-20.6	-20.5	-29.6		-42.6	-24.6
EBIT/Interest			66.5	23.0	38.3	72.0		32.1	47.2
			(17) 17.3	(34) 6.9	(16) 10.3	(15) 23.6		(28) 13.0	(38) 12.3
			2.2	2.5	3.8	9.1		3.6	4.5
Net Profit + Depr., Dep., Amort./Cur. Mat. L/T/D									
Fixed/Worth			.6	.9	1.4	1.0		.9	.8
			.7	1.5	1.7	1.4		1.8	1.5
			1.7	5.6	3.1	4.0		NM	5.6
Debt/Worth			.2	.4	.7	.5		.4	.4
			.3	1.0	1.3	.8		1.4	1.0
			2.4	8.3	2.5	5.2		-340.8	5.5
% Profit Before Taxes/Tangible Net Worth			141.8	96.1	168.2	139.3		228.9	116.8
			(24) 80.7	(35) 55.3	(17) 81.1	(20) 86.3		(24) 92.5	(38) 62.0
			31.1	28.3	57.7	36.7		43.2	27.8
% Profit Before Taxes/Total Assets			84.8	59.2	51.1	73.9		75.9	51.2
			57.1	24.2	37.1	38.2		43.5	26.4
			5.5	6.6	6.5	5.8		19.2	7.8
Sales/Net Fixed Assets			8.5	2.9	2.1	2.5		5.0	6.6
			4.2	1.7	1.6	1.8		2.5	2.7
			3.1	1.2	.9	1.1		1.5	1.8
Sales/Total Assets			4.0	1.8	1.7	1.7		3.6	3.5
			2.4	1.2	1.3	1.4		1.8	1.9
			1.3	.8	.8	.6		1.2	1.4
% Depr., Dep., Amort./Sales			2.0	4.9	4.2	3.5		3.4	3.0
			(23) 4.7	(40) 6.8	6.0	(12) 5.5		(26) 4.7	(37) 5.1
			6.9	9.1	8.2	6.6		6.8	6.6
% Officers', Directors' Owners' Comp/Sales									
Net Sales ($)	17545M	27992M	426435M	1398834M	2154043M	4169378M		2241788M	3196556M
Total Assets ($)	1267M	5257M	158554M	1083180M	1293209M	3127578M		1271445M	1920651M

M = $ thousand   MM = $ million
See Pages 11 through 21 for Explanation of Ratios and Data

Comparative Historical Data				Current Data Sorted by Sales					
			Type of Statement						
39	56	51	Unqualified		2		2	10	37
2	1		Reviewed						
		3	Compiled					3	
6	4	8	Tax Returns	2	2		2	2	
18	44	56	Other		4	3	4	13	32
4/1/04-3/31/05	4/1/05-3/31/06	4/1/06-3/31/07			30 (4/1-9/30/06)			88 (10/1/06-3/31/07)	
ALL	ALL	ALL		0-1MM	1-3MM	3-5MM	5-10MM	10-25MM	25MM & OVER
65	105	118	**NUMBER OF STATEMENTS**	2	8	3	8	28	69
%	%	%	**ASSETS**	%	%	%	%	%	%
21.3	21.3	22.1	Cash & Equivalents					26.2	19.1
.9	1.0	1.0	Trade Receivables (net)					.7	.8
1.8	.7	.7	Inventory					1.1	.5
2.2	2.4	4.5	All Other Current					3.9	1.9
26.2	25.5	28.3	Total Current					31.9	22.3
64.0	68.1	63.5	Fixed Assets (net)					59.2	72.2
6.1	2.5	3.9	Intangibles (net)					5.9	1.8
3.7	3.9	4.3	All Other Non-Current					2.9	3.7
100.0	100.0	100.0	Total					100.0	100.0
			LIABILITIES						
1.7	3.0	5.0	Notes Payable-Short Term					.3	7.3
7.5	4.6	4.4	Cur. Mat.-L.T.D.					6.1	4.6
3.3	3.8	4.1	Trade Payables					3.4	3.7
.0	.1	.0	Income Taxes Payable					.0	.0
10.1	10.2	11.8	All Other Current					10.7	10.4
22.6	21.7	25.4	Total Current					20.6	26.0
31.4	28.8	28.1	Long-Term Debt					22.1	28.1
.1	.1	.3	Deferred Taxes					.5	.0
1.4	2.4	1.8	All Other Non-Current					2.2	1.5
44.6	47.1	44.4	Net Worth					54.7	44.4
100.0	100.0	100.0	Total Liabilties & Net Worth					100.0	100.0
			INCOME DATA						
100.0	100.0	100.0	Net Sales					100.0	100.0
			Gross Profit						
75.0	70.5	72.6	Operating Expenses					77.9	67.6
25.0	29.5	27.4	Operating Profit					22.1	32.4
2.8	2.8	3.6	All Other Expenses (net)					3.7	4.1
22.2	26.7	23.7	Profit Before Taxes					18.4	28.3
			RATIOS						
1.7	2.2	2.4						2.8	1.7
1.2	1.3	1.2	Current					1.8	1.0
.7	.7	.8						.9	.7
1.7	2.0	2.1						2.4	1.6
1.0	1.1	1.0	Quick					1.1	.9
.6	.6	.6						.8	.5
0 999.8	0 999.8	0 999.8						0 UND	0 954.9
1 635.5	1 403.7	1 438.8	Sales/Receivables					1 566.1	1 432.8
2 165.8	3 140.5	3 126.0						3 125.8	3 129.1
			Cost of Sales/Inventory						
			Cost of Sales/Payables						
13.6	9.9	11.9						8.0	15.4
68.4	39.4	57.7	Sales/Working Capital					39.9	145.1
-34.6	-26.2	-29.4						-83.9	-23.4
65.5	44.4	33.1						31.9	41.7
(56) 14.1	(86) 17.4	(89) 11.3	EBIT/Interest				(19) 6.0		(56) 16.7
6.7	8.0	2.9						2.5	4.8
			Net Profit + Depr., Dep., Amort./Cur. Mat. L/T/D						
.9	1.0	.9						.6	1.0
1.3	1.3	1.4	Fixed/Worth					1.1	1.5
2.9	2.4	3.6						2.7	2.9
.5	.3	.3						.2	.5
.9	.9	.9	Debt/Worth					.8	.8
4.5	2.1	4.1						3.0	2.3
139.8	151.2	124.1						104.7	150.4
(54) 79.1	(95) 78.1	(104) 78.1	% Profit Before Taxes/Tangible Net Worth				(25) 77.7		(62) 82.6
33.9	39.3	31.9						27.0	50.1
57.1	70.4	68.5						74.6	72.4
34.0	39.7	32.5	% Profit Before Taxes/Total Assets					25.6	43.3
15.1	18.8	6.6						7.2	15.2
4.4	3.5	4.6						5.0	3.2
2.4	2.1	2.1	Sales/Net Fixed Assets					3.5	1.9
1.6	1.5	1.4						1.2	1.4
2.4	2.1	2.4						2.7	2.1
1.6	1.5	1.5	Sales/Total Assets					2.0	1.4
1.2	1.1	1.0						.8	1.1
4.2	4.1	3.6						2.9	4.1
(54) 5.5	(86) 5.9	(103) 5.8	% Depr., Dep., Amort./Sales				(27) 6.5		(59) 5.8
7.0	7.8	8.1						9.3	7.2
		1.7							
		(13) 4.3	% Officers', Directors' Owners' Comp/Sales						
		16.4							
4642740M	8988011M	8194227M	Net Sales ($)	382M	15880M	12066M	51984M	482468M	7631447M
3151334M	5974141M	5669045M	Total Assets ($)	235M	19245M	30399M	168461M	486020M	4964685M

© RMA 2007

M = $ thousand   MM = $ million

See Pages 11 through 21 for Explanation of Ratios and Data

Current Data Sorted by Assets   Comparative Historical Data

						Type of Statement		
1	7	140	101	9	3	Unqualified	283	236
1	12	68	18			Reviewed	141	126
19	54	65	3			Compiled	155	247
24	35	34	5	1	1	Tax Returns	101	107
18	61	158	63	3		Other	303	285
	209 (4/1-9/30/06)		695 (10/1/06-3/31/07)				4/1/02-3/31/03	4/1/03-3/31/04
0-500M	500M-2MM	2-10MM	10-50MM	50-100MM	100-250MM		ALL	ALL
63	169	465	190	13	4	NUMBER OF STATEMENTS	983	1001
%	%	%	%	%	%	ASSETS	%	%
20.2	7.2	6.0	6.0	15.1		Cash & Equivalents	7.6	7.0
3.5	4.0	5.6	4.2	4.2		Trade Receivables (net)	5.2	4.9
8.5	2.8	1.4	1.2	1.4		Inventory	2.6	2.5
2.9	1.3	1.5	1.2	.8		All Other Current	1.4	2.9
35.1	15.3	14.6	12.7	21.4		Total Current	16.9	17.3
57.9	74.8	80.3	80.5	70.9		Fixed Assets (net)	76.9	75.0
3.8	2.7	1.5	1.2	1.8		Intangibles (net)	1.5	2.1
3.2	7.3	3.6	5.7	5.9		All Other Non-Current	4.7	5.6
100.0	100.0	100.0	100.0	100.0		Total	100.0	100.0
						LIABILITIES		
11.1	8.5	3.2	4.1	1.1		Notes Payable-Short Term	3.6	4.4
4.8	3.9	4.8	2.2	2.8		Cur. Mat.-L.T.D.	4.0	3.5
7.3	3.6	2.9	2.1	1.3		Trade Payables	3.2	4.2
.0	.6	.1	.1	.0		Income Taxes Payable	.1	.1
21.1	10.6	8.2	6.9	11.1		All Other Current	9.5	10.5
44.3	27.1	19.1	15.3	16.3		Total Current	20.3	22.7
49.0	45.0	42.5	27.3	34.2		Long-Term Debt	38.3	40.6
.0	.1	.0	.1	.0		Deferred Taxes	.1	.1
18.6	12.3	5.6	4.9	13.9		All Other Non-Current	9.6	8.6
-11.9	15.4	32.7	52.3	35.7		Net Worth	31.6	28.0
100.0	100.0	100.0	100.0	100.0		Total Liabilties & Net Worth	100.0	100.0
						INCOME DATA		
100.0	100.0	100.0	100.0	100.0		Net Sales	100.0	100.0
						Gross Profit		
98.9	93.3	96.4	99.4	98.5		Operating Expenses	97.9	98.1
1.1	6.7	3.6	.6	1.5		Operating Profit	2.1	1.9
3.4	5.3	4.5	2.4	2.1		All Other Expenses (net)	4.0	4.2
-2.3	1.4	-.9	-1.8	-.6		Profit Before Taxes	-1.9	-2.3
						RATIOS		
2.0	1.6	1.7	1.9	2.0			1.7	1.7
.9	.7	.9	1.1	1.1		Current	.9	.9
.2	.2	.5	.7	.7			.5	.4
1.4	1.2	1.4	1.5	1.9			1.4	1.3
.4	.5 (462)	.7	.9	1.0		Quick	(981) .7	(998) .6
.1	.1	.3	.5	.6			.3	.2
0 UND	0 UND	5 79.4	14 26.3	14 26.5			1 378.2	1 532.3
0 UND	1 245.0	25 14.9	30 12.2	34 10.8		Sales/Receivables	18 19.7	16 23.2
2 148.0	16 22.6	41 9.0	45 8.2	45 8.1			37 10.0	34 10.7
						Cost of Sales/Inventory		
						Cost of Sales/Payables		
22.7	15.9	10.3	7.3	7.3			11.3	12.4
-92.3	-19.2	-59.1	62.6	13.2		Sales/Working Capital	-102.5	-45.4
-7.4	-5.6	-7.7	-11.0	-24.0			-7.8	-7.1
4.3	2.3	2.1	3.3	7.0			2.1	2.0
(45) 1.6	(142) 1.0	(395) .9	(152) 1.1	(11) 1.2		EBIT/Interest	(807) .9	(793) .7
-1.0	-.2	-.2	-.6	-1.0			-.4	-.9
	3.4	7.2	4.6				3.4	3.1
(19)	1.1	(26) 2.9	(16) 3.5			Net Profit + Depr., Dep., Amort./Cur. Mat. L/T/D	(98) 1.7	(70) 1.7
	.9	1.1	2.1				.9	.4
1.1	1.5	1.3	1.0	.9			1.2	1.2
5.2	3.0	2.2	1.4	1.6		Fixed/Worth	2.0	2.2
-1.1	-15.8	7.4	2.0	-14.7			5.3	10.3
1.0	1.0	.6	.3	.6			.5	.6
6.6	2.9	1.7	.7	1.2		Debt/Worth	1.5	1.9
-2.8	-15.8	7.4	1.4	-16.7			6.0	12.9
58.9	20.6	7.2	5.1				6.2	6.2
(37) 13.0	(119) 2.8	(381) .5	(174) .6			% Profit Before Taxes/Tangible Net Worth	(816) .2	(798) -.9
-2.9	-11.4	-9.6	-2.9				-7.9	-8.9
14.8	5.3	2.8	3.2	6.9			2.6	2.5
2.7	.6	-.3	.1	.7		% Profit Before Taxes/Total Assets	-.2	-.8
-13.8	-4.0	-4.2	-2.2	-4.2			-4.2	-5.0
15.0	2.3	1.0	.7	1.3			1.3	1.3
5.4	1.2	.7	.5	.6		Sales/Net Fixed Assets	.8	.8
1.7	.7	.5	.4	.4			.5	.5
4.7	1.4	.8	.6	.9			1.0	1.0
2.7	.9	.6	.4	.4		Sales/Total Assets	.6	.6
1.4	.6	.5	.3	.3			.4	.4
2.4	5.0	7.5	9.0	5.6			7.1	7.1
(49) 4.4	(145) 7.5	(434) 9.9	(172) 11.5	12.1		% Depr., Dep., Amort./Sales	(901) 9.9	(896) 10.0
7.2	10.6	12.9	14.4	15.5			13.0	13.5
4.7	3.8	3.2	2.4				3.9	5.0
(15) 8.2	(47) 7.5	(69) 8.2	(21) 7.7			% Officers', Directors' Owners' Comp/Sales	(171) 8.0	(180) 9.7
14.3	15.3	24.5	33.8				16.4	21.4
48964M	219019M	1445242M	1893835M	935211M	560343M	Net Sales ($)	6340663M	5459001M
16880M	202179M	2310425M	3508137M	847890M	551446M	Total Assets ($)	8171972M	8448381M

M = $ thousand   MM = $ million
See Pages 11 through 21 for Explanation of Ratios and Data

Comparative Historical Data | **Current Data Sorted by Sales**

			Type of Statement						
228	236	261	Unqualified	3	44	86	90	29	9
135	94	99	Reviewed	9	42	34	12	2	
162	146	141	Compiled	51	75	11	4		
96	79	100	Tax Returns	50	38	3	5	1	3
250	278	303	Other	38	138	63	48	12	4
4/1/04-3/31/05	4/1/05-3/31/06	4/1/06-3/31/07		209 (4/1-9/30/06)		695 (10/1/06-3/31/07)			
ALL	ALL	ALL		0-1MM	1-3MM	3-5MM	5-10MM	10-25MM	25MM & OVER
871	833	904	**NUMBER OF STATEMENTS**	151	337	197	159	44	16
%	%	%	**ASSETS**	%	%	%	%	%	%
6.9	7.7	7.4	Cash & Equivalents	8.5	7.2	6.9	6.3	6.8	19.6
4.8	4.8	4.8	Trade Receivables (net)	1.5	4.3	6.7	6.9	4.5	3.6
2.6	2.5	2.1	Inventory	3.0	2.3	1.6	1.7	1.4	5.0
1.1	1.4	1.5	All Other Current	1.4	1.5	1.8	1.3	.8	1.0
15.5	16.4	15.9	Total Current	14.4	15.3	17.0	16.3	13.5	29.2
76.9	76.9	77.6	Fixed Assets (net)	78.3	77.8	78.1	77.5	76.9	61.9
2.3	2.0	1.8	Intangibles (net)	2.8	2.4	.4	1.2	2.0	2.2
5.4	4.7	4.7	All Other Non-Current	4.5	4.4	4.4	5.0	7.6	6.6
100.0	100.0	100.0	Total	100.0	100.0	100.0	100.0	100.0	100.0
			LIABILITIES						
4.7	4.1	4.9	Notes Payable-Short Term	5.3	6.2	2.7	2.4	.6	36.8
3.3	3.8	4.0	Cur. Mat.-L.T.D.	5.3	4.6	3.9	2.6	2.1	2.0
3.6	3.5	3.1	Trade Payables	2.9	3.3	3.1	3.3	1.9	4.3
.1	.1	.2	Income Taxes Payable	.7	.0	.1	.1	.2	.0
10.1	9.2	9.3	All Other Current	7.0	9.5	9.0	11.7	7.9	12.6
21.9	20.7	21.5	Total Current	21.2	23.5	18.7	20.1	12.6	55.7
39.8	38.3	40.1	Long-Term Debt	54.5	46.6	31.4	28.1	25.1	34.8
.1	.1	.1	Deferred Taxes	.1	.1	.0	.0	.6	.0
7.9	10.3	8.0	All Other Non-Current	12.4	8.4	6.5	4.5	5.7	19.3
30.3	30.5	30.3	Net Worth	11.9	21.4	43.4	47.3	56.0	-9.8
100.0	100.0	100.0	Total Liabilities & Net Worth	100.0	100.0	100.0	100.0	100.0	100.0
			INCOME DATA						
100.0	100.0	100.0	Net Sales	100.0	100.0	100.0	100.0	100.0	100.0
			Gross Profit						
98.1	98.1	96.6	Operating Expenses	90.5	96.3	100.0	98.8	97.2	97.3
1.9	1.9	3.4	Operating Profit	9.5	3.7	.0	1.2	2.8	2.7
3.7	3.5	4.1	All Other Expenses (net)	9.1	5.5	1.7	.6	-.4	1.5
-1.7	-1.6	-.7	Profit Before Taxes	.5	-1.8	-1.7	.6	3.2	1.3
			RATIOS						
1.7	1.8	1.7		2.0	1.7	1.8	1.7	1.5	1.7
.9	.9	.9	Current	.7	.8	.9	1.0	1.1	1.1
.4	.5	.5		.2	.3	.6	.6	.8	.8
1.3	1.4	1.4		1.3	1.4	1.5	1.4	1.3	1.4
.6 (832)	.7 (901)	.7	Quick	.3	.6 (334)	.8	.8	.8	1.0
.2	.3	.3		.1	.2	.4	.5	.5	.6
0 999.8	1 590.9	1 336.8		0 UND	0 993.7	18 20.4	17 21.3	15 25.1	2 163.7
15 24.1	18 20.7	18 20.2	Sales/Receivables	0 UND	11 32.4	31 11.6	31 11.8	29 12.6	10 36.2
34 10.8	35 10.5	37 9.8		6 62.5	33 10.9	44 8.3	42 8.7	42 8.6	27 13.4
			Cost of Sales/Inventory						
			Cost of Sales/Payables						
13.4	10.2	10.7		18.9	10.6	8.8	10.0	12.8	12.4
-49.0	-108.8	-80.5	Sales/Working Capital	-19.1	-34.2	-93.9	191.6	53.6	65.4
-6.5	-9.5	-8.0		-5.6	-6.2	-9.5	-12.4	-12.6	-30.5
1.9	2.1	2.3		2.1	2.0	2.0	3.0	8.3	7.0
(701) .7	(682) .7	(748) 1.0	EBIT/Interest	(113) 1.0	(286) .8	(166) .7	(131) 1.3	(38) 3.2	(14) 2.5
-.7	-.8	-.2		-.2	-.3	-.4	.2	.8	-.1
4.5	3.7	4.8	Net Profit + Depr., Dep.,	3.2	4.4	4.5	13.8		
(53) 1.6	(59) 1.7	(64) 3.0	Amort./Cur. Mat. L/T/D	(13) 1.0	(19) 2.7	(12) 3.0	(11) 4.8		
.6	.8	1.1		.7	1.1	1.1	1.8		
1.2	1.2	1.2		1.5	1.5	1.1	1.1	1.0	1.1
2.3	2.1	2.1	Fixed/Worth	4.0	2.7	1.8	1.5	1.3	1.6
11.4	8.8	7.9		-5.4	30.1	3.9	2.2	1.6	NM
.6	.6	.5		1.0	.9	.4	.4	.2	.7
1.8	1.7	1.5	Debt/Worth	3.9	2.4	1.1	.9	.7	1.2
12.6	11.3	9.3		-6.7	32.5	3.4	2.0	1.4	NM
6.6	6.5	8.3	% Profit Before Taxes/Tangible	12.9	11.8	3.8	7.0	9.2	32.2
(695) -.4	(668) -.6	(723) .9	Net Worth	(99) 3.2	(255) .3	(174) -.8	(143) 2.2	(40) 3.6	(12) 16.6
-8.4	-7.1	-6.5		-7.5	-12.0	-7.6	-2.2	-.4	4.5
2.5	3.0	3.6	% Profit Before Taxes/Total	4.6	3.6	2.2	3.8	5.9	12.5
-.6	-.7	.1	Assets	.5	-.7	-.6	.9	2.2	6.0
-4.3	-4.3	-3.8		-4.5	-4.9	-3.7	-1.7	-.8	.2
1.4	1.3	1.3		1.5	1.4	1.2	1.1	1.0	3.6
.8	.8	.7	Sales/Net Fixed Assets	.7	.7	.7	.7	.6	1.6
.5	.5	.5		.4	.5	.5	.5	.4	1.0
1.0	1.0	.9		1.2	1.0	.8	.8	.8	1.7
.6	.6	.6	Sales/Total Assets	.6	.6	.6	.6	.5	1.1
.4	.4	.4		.3	.4	.4	.5	.4	.7
6.7	6.5	7.0		6.6	6.4	7.4	7.8	8.4	4.3
(789) 9.6	(762) 9.4	(815) 9.7	% Depr., Dep., Amort./Sales	(126) 9.8	(307) 9.8	(180) 9.4	(149) 9.7	(42) 11.3	(11) 7.0
13.4	12.7	12.7		15.4	13.0	12.2	12.1	13.2	9.4
5.3	3.4	3.1	% Officers', Directors'	4.0	4.3	2.4	2.2		
(161) 9.6	(133) 7.5	(155) 7.7	Owners' Comp/Sales	(33) 7.6	(66) 8.7	(27) 8.2	(20) 6.9		
21.2	18.5	17.0		15.7	23.1	18.2	31.9		
3973357M	5198458M	5102614M	Net Sales ($)	84996M	638444M	773227M	1047846M	627944M	1930157M
6850733M	6861904M	7436957M	Total Assets ($)	194343M	1232753M	1521455M	1948792M	1365200M	1174414M

M = $ thousand   MM = $ million
See Pages 11 through 21 for Explanation of Ratios and Data

Current Data Sorted by Assets   Comparative Historical Data

		5	3	2	3	Type of Statement	9	18
	1	6	1			Unqualified	3	3
1	2	2				Reviewed		3
						Compiled		4
		3	6	2	2	Tax Returns	7	3
	25 (4/1-9/30/06)		14 (10/1/06-3/31/07)			Other	4/1/02-3/31/03	4/1/03-3/31/04
0-500M	500M-2MM	2-10MM	10-50MM	50-100MM	100-250MM		ALL	ALL
1	3	16	10	4	5	**NUMBER OF STATEMENTS**	19	31
%	%	%	%	%	%	**ASSETS**	%	%
		8.5	4.2			Cash & Equivalents	5.9	4.4
		1.2	1.2			Trade Receivables (net)	3.5	2.5
		5.7	1.8			Inventory	1.8	2.1
		3.9	2.8			All Other Current	2.6	2.1
		19.2	9.9			Total Current	13.8	11.2
		67.8	85.9			Fixed Assets (net)	78.7	75.5
		1.5	.8			Intangibles (net)	2.5	4.7
		11.4	3.4			All Other Non-Current	5.0	8.6
		100.0	100.0			Total	100.0	100.0
						LIABILITIES		
		6.0	4.4			Notes Payable-Short Term	4.4	4.2
		3.9	2.7			Cur. Mat.-L.T.D.	4.2	3.4
		9.2	2.8			Trade Payables	4.9	5.4
		.2	.3			Income Taxes Payable	.3	.1
		6.2	16.1			All Other Current	9.2	7.2
		25.6	26.2			Total Current	22.9	20.3
		26.9	10.0			Long-Term Debt	29.7	37.9
		.8	4.0			Deferred Taxes	2.2	2.5
		7.9	.8			All Other Non-Current	2.1	7.3
		38.8	59.0			Net Worth	43.0	32.1
		100.0	100.0			Total Liabilties & Net Worth	100.0	100.0
						INCOME DATA		
		100.0	100.0			Net Sales	100.0	100.0
						Gross Profit		
		92.4	97.3			Operating Expenses	92.7	94.3
		7.6	2.7			Operating Profit	7.3	5.7
		.3	.9			All Other Expenses (net)	3.2	6.5
		7.3	1.8			Profit Before Taxes	4.1	-.8
						RATIOS		
		1.8	.5				1.2	.9
		.4	.3			Current	.7	.5
		.2	.2				.3	.3
		1.2	.3				.8	.6
		.1	.2			Quick	.4	.3
		.1	.1				.1	.1
		0 999.8	1 289.9				1 459.2	0 796.0
		1 244.9	4 98.0			Sales/Receivables	2 149.1	3 143.1
		3 110.6	6 61.2				14 26.9	9 40.6
						Cost of Sales/Inventory		
						Cost of Sales/Payables		
		18.9	-9.9				48.8	-68.0
		-8.7	-8.1			Sales/Working Capital	-11.5	-11.3
		-3.9	-3.5				-6.7	-4.8
		7.8					7.7	4.9
		(15) 2.3				EBIT/Interest	(18) 2.3	(27) 1.4
		.1					1.0	-.3
								114.9
						Net Profit + Depr., Dep., Amort./Cur. Mat. L/T/D	(12)	2.6
								1.6
		.9	1.2				1.2	1.7
		2.4	1.4			Fixed/Worth	1.8	2.2
		3.3	2.0				3.1	3.8
		.3	.3				.5	1.1
		1.8	.8			Debt/Worth	1.2	1.7
		11.1	1.4				3.1	3.7
		43.3	15.5				27.2	15.0
		(14) 14.0	9.3			% Profit Before Taxes/Tangible Net Worth	(17) 10.7	(26) 2.0
		-2.5	3.6				1.9	-6.6
		23.5	10.9				10.2	5.2
		5.1	4.6			% Profit Before Taxes/Total Assets	3.9	.6
		-3.8	1.5				-.4	-3.1
		2.7	1.4				2.0	1.6
		1.4	1.0			Sales/Net Fixed Assets	.9	1.0
		1.0	.6				.7	.8
		1.7	1.3				1.5	1.2
		1.0	.9			Sales/Total Assets	.8	.8
		.8	.5				.7	.6
		6.4					7.2	8.6
		(14) 9.6				% Depr., Dep., Amort./Sales	(18) 11.1	(29) 12.7
		12.5					14.4	15.1
						% Officers', Directors' Owners' Comp/Sales		
2029M	4879M	109937M	174850M	179056M	573518M	Net Sales ($)	387370M	663971M
181M	2879M	79445M	197529M	243635M	905437M	Total Assets ($)	524327M	858141M

M = $ thousand   MM = $ million
See Pages 11 through 21 for Explanation of Ratios and Data

Comparative Historical Data　　　　　Current Data Sorted by Sales

			Type of Statement						
14	15	13	Unqualified	1	1	4	1		6
4	7	8	Reviewed	1	2	2	1		2
3	4	5	Compiled	4		1			
1		4	Tax Returns						
10	10	13	Other	1	1		3	5	3
4/1/04-3/31/05 ALL	4/1/05-3/31/06 ALL	4/1/06-3/31/07 ALL		1	25 (4/1-9/30/06)		3 14 (10/1/06-3/31/07)		
				0-1MM	1-3MM	3-5MM	5-10MM	10-25MM	25MM & OVER
32	40	39	NUMBER OF STATEMENTS	1	7	3	10	7	11
%	%	%	**ASSETS**	%	%	%	%	%	%
3.1	8.6	7.5	Cash & Equivalents				3.3		9.5
.8	1.3	1.3	Trade Receivables (net)				1.4		2.3
1.5	2.3	4.0	Inventory				9.1		1.7
4.9	2.8	3.4	All Other Current				5.0		4.6
10.3	15.1	16.3	Total Current				18.7		18.2
76.6	72.4	74.2	Fixed Assets (net)				77.1		73.0
5.1	2.4	1.5	Intangibles (net)				.5		2.4
7.9	10.1	8.0	All Other Non-Current				3.7		6.5
100.0	100.0	100.0	Total				100.0		100.0
			LIABILITIES						
5.1	5.3	8.1	Notes Payable-Short Term				2.7		.7
3.2	6.8	3.5	Cur. Mat.-L.T.D.				5.2		2.0
4.7	5.2	7.1	Trade Payables				11.3		7.2
.0	.2	.3	Income Taxes Payable				.2		.9
11.7	7.9	9.2	All Other Current				8.8		9.1
24.8	25.4	28.3	Total Current				28.2		20.0
36.1	31.9	25.7	Long-Term Debt				34.4		25.7
3.3	2.9	2.2	Deferred Taxes				.3		3.9
6.4	9.4	8.6	All Other Non-Current				5.4		7.8
29.4	30.4	35.1	Net Worth				31.8		42.7
100.0	100.0	100.0	Total Liabilities & Net Worth				100.0		100.0
			INCOME DATA						
100.0	100.0	100.0	Net Sales				100.0		100.0
			Gross Profit						
94.4	90.9	94.2	Operating Expenses				93.6		87.7
5.6	9.1	5.8	Operating Profit				6.4		12.3
4.5	6.6	.5	All Other Expenses (net)				2.5		-.3
1.2	2.5	5.3	Profit Before Taxes				4.0		12.6
			RATIOS						
.6	1.2	.9					1.9		1.3
.5	.7	.4	Current				.4		.8
.2	.4	.2					.1		.7
.3	.8	.6					.6		.8
.2	.4	.2	Quick				.1		.5
.0	.1	.1					.1		.3
0　924.7	1　721.8	1　671.9					0　UND	4　90.1	
3　131.7	3　142.3	3　112.0	Sales/Receivables				3　131.1	8　43.9	
8　46.1	10　34.8	7　48.7					4　91.5	16　23.5	
			Cost of Sales/Inventory						
			Cost of Sales/Payables						
-16.8	44.7	-113.4					NM		29.1
-6.9	-15.4	-9.9	Sales/Working Capital				-5.5		-23.8
-3.7	-6.4	-4.1					-4.0		-9.9
5.2	6.5	12.7					10.5		41.6
(29) 2.2	(35) 2.5	(36) 4.3	EBIT/Interest				4.1		6.1
.3	.0	.2					.9		4.1
12.5	11.0	14.7	Net Profit + Depr., Dep.,						
(12) 2.1	(17) 2.0	(10) 2.0	Amort./Cur. Mat. L/T/D						
.7	.9	.7							
1.6	1.5	1.1					1.2		1.1
2.1	1.9	1.9	Fixed/Worth				2.4		1.7
9.6	8.9	3.5					NM		3.5
1.2	.9	.3					.3		.8
1.6	1.7	1.5	Debt/Worth				2.3		1.4
25.2	13.4	6.6					NM		3.5
27.2	27.9	33.5	% Profit Before Taxes/Tangible						53.3
(25) 9.8	(33) 5.8	(34) 9.9	Net Worth						24.0
-3.1	-5.0	-1.1							9.0
8.0	10.4	13.2	% Profit Before Taxes/Total				11.6		17.9
2.6	3.0	4.7	Assets				4.8		11.7
-2.2	-3.1	-3.4					-.1		4.4
1.6	1.9	2.4					2.6		1.3
.9	1.0	1.2	Sales/Net Fixed Assets				1.2		1.1
.8	.7	.9					.9		.8
1.2	1.2	1.4					1.5		1.0
.8	.7	.9	Sales/Total Assets				1.1		.7
.6	.6	.7					.8		.6
9.0	6.2	5.7							
(28) 11.9	(36) 9.6	(32) 9.0	% Depr., Dep., Amort./Sales						
13.8	11.6	12.2							
		1.6	% Officers', Directors'						
	(11) 4.6		Owners' Comp/Sales						
		9.5							
791183M	1067002M	1044269M	Net Sales ($)	253M	13449M	10964M	70582M	130779M	818242M
1090547M	1499732M	1429106M	Total Assets ($)	10440M	13455M	12493M	65534M	170663M	1156521M

© RMA 2007　　　　M = $ thousand　　MM = $ million
See Pages 11 through 21 for Explanation of Ratios and Data

Current Data Sorted by Assets   Comparative Historical Data

	0-500M	500M-2MM	2-10MM	10-50MM	50-100MM	100-250MM		4/1/02-3/31/03 ALL	4/1/03-3/31/04 ALL
Type of Statement									
Unqualified	1		5	2	1			1	8
Reviewed		3	19	4				19	27
Compiled	2	22	8	2		1		31	38
Tax Returns	12	14	8					41	43
Other	6	16	22	11				39	46
		13 (4/1-9/30/06)		146 (10/1/06-3/31/07)					
NUMBER OF STATEMENTS	21	55	62	19	1	1		131	162
	%	%	%	%	%	%	**ASSETS**	%	%
	13.1	7.7	9.5	6.4			Cash & Equivalents	9.8	8.9
	12.0	8.4	5.3	2.5			Trade Receivables (net)	6.9	6.5
	17.4	14.9	10.9	8.8			Inventory	16.9	17.1
	4.3	2.1	.3	1.9			All Other Current	3.4	3.0
	46.7	33.2	26.0	19.6			Total Current	37.0	35.6
	36.4	51.7	64.2	67.6			Fixed Assets (net)	54.9	55.4
	7.5	6.1	3.4	9.3			Intangibles (net)	3.9	4.1
	9.4	9.1	6.4	3.5			All Other Non-Current	4.1	5.0
	100.0	100.0	100.0	100.0			Total	100.0	100.0
							LIABILITIES		
	10.1	7.4	6.0	7.1			Notes Payable-Short Term	9.4	13.0
	3.3	4.8	7.9	1.4			Cur. Mat.-L.T.D.	6.0	4.1
	9.0	3.2	2.4	2.2			Trade Payables	4.5	4.1
	.2	.1	.0	.1			Income Taxes Payable	.3	.1
	18.5	9.1	8.2	3.4			All Other Current	14.4	12.7
	41.2	24.6	24.6	14.2			Total Current	34.5	34.0
	26.5	41.6	54.8	64.2			Long-Term Debt	44.0	46.8
	.0	.2	.0	.0			Deferred Taxes	.1	.2
	20.3	8.0	4.0	2.2			All Other Non-Current	7.9	8.9
	12.0	25.6	16.7	19.5			Net Worth	13.6	10.0
	100.0	100.0	100.0	100.0			Total Liabilities & Net Worth	100.0	100.0
							INCOME DATA		
	100.0	100.0	100.0	100.0			Net Sales	100.0	100.0
							Gross Profit		
	89.2	87.0	86.2	84.0			Operating Expenses	89.5	88.5
	10.8	13.0	13.8	16.0			Operating Profit	10.5	11.5
	3.2	7.6	6.7	17.0			All Other Expenses (net)	6.2	5.6
	7.7	5.3	7.2	-1.0			Profit Before Taxes	4.3	5.9
							RATIOS		
	6.0	2.8	2.7	3.0				2.3	2.3
	1.4	1.4	1.2	1.1			Current	1.2	1.2
	.8	.7	.4	.8				.7	.7
	2.6	2.3	2.2	1.7				1.2	1.3
	.7	.8	.5	.7			Quick	.4	.5
	.1	.3	.2	.2				.1	.1
	0 UND	1 528.6	5 66.8	6 58.0				2 195.0	2 211.3
	5 70.8	19 19.2	18 19.8	13 27.6			Sales/Receivables	12 30.9	12 29.3
	20 18.3	41 8.9	41 8.9	42 8.7				29 12.4	30 12.3
							Cost of Sales/Inventory		
							Cost of Sales/Payables		
	10.2	5.9	4.7	4.0				7.4	5.8
	32.2	16.4	41.1	36.7			Sales/Working Capital	27.0	26.6
	-43.5	-26.4	-6.7	-16.6				-13.7	-15.3
	7.1	4.2	4.1	3.1				4.4	4.0
	(14) 1.3	(47) 1.5	(52) 1.5	(12) 1.4			EBIT/Interest	(114) 2.0	(143) 2.0
	.0	.8	.9	1.0				1.2	1.0
								5.1	3.7
							Net Profit + Depr., Dep., Amort./Cur. Mat. L/T/D	(20) 2.0	(15) 2.1
								.9	1.2
	.3	.9	1.2	1.7				1.3	1.0
	4.8	2.7	3.4	4.8			Fixed/Worth	5.0	3.6
	-1.6	-13.6	-10.0	-4.7				-8.8	-22.0
	.3	1.2	1.0	1.9				1.7	1.8
	24.2	3.7	4.3	6.0			Debt/Worth	7.4	7.2
	-3.2	-18.6	-14.8	-7.8				-11.2	-30.8
	169.2	40.8	35.5	22.2				38.8	53.2
	(11) 28.7	(40) 13.4	(44) 18.0	(14) 4.9			% Profit Before Taxes/Tangible Net Worth	(87) 21.1	(113) 23.3
	12.7	1.4	2.3	-10.5				8.2	2.2
	33.1	8.6	9.3	7.2				8.5	10.2
	6.7	3.0	2.3	1.2			% Profit Before Taxes/Total Assets	3.4	3.7
	-12.1	-.5	-.5	-1.9				.3	-.1
	36.1	6.6	1.8	1.5				6.7	6.8
	12.7	1.8	.9	.6			Sales/Net Fixed Assets	1.7	1.6
	2.7	.9	.5	.2				.8	.8
	5.2	1.7	1.0	.9				1.9	1.8
	3.4	1.0	.6	.4			Sales/Total Assets	1.0	.9
	1.4	.5	.4	.2				.6	.5
	.7	1.9	4.4	6.1				2.1	2.5
	(14) 2.0	(51) 5.8	(59) 8.1	11.4			% Depr., Dep., Amort./Sales	(121) 5.5	(145) 6.1
	11.3	11.7	11.6	17.3				11.8	13.2
		3.1	1.5					2.6	2.1
		(21) 5.9	(13) 3.4				% Officers', Directors' Owners' Comp/Sales	(50) 4.0	(58) 4.2
		9.1	8.0					8.1	8.2
	16819M	71138M	216483M	174101M	29091M	322493M	Net Sales ($)	571451M	1470371M
	5601M	60981M	290608M	363763M	69142M	236771M	Total Assets ($)	544306M	985260M

© RMA 2007

M = $ thousand   MM = $ million
See Pages 11 through 21 for Explanation of Ratios and Data

Comparative Historical Data / Current Data Sorted by Sales

Current Data date spans: 13 (4/1-9/30/06) and 146 (10/1/06-3/31/07)

	4/1/04-3/31/05 ALL	4/1/05-3/31/06 ALL	4/1/06-3/31/07 ALL	0-1MM	1-3MM	3-5MM	5-10MM	10-25MM	25MM & OVER
Type of Statement									
Unqualified	8	5	9	1	2	1	3	1	1
Reviewed	21	17	26	2	9	7	5	2	1
Compiled	40	30	34	11	15	4	3	1	
Tax Returns	32	29	35	20	11	2	1		1
Other	41	53	55	16	21	8	7	3	
NUMBER OF STATEMENTS	142	134	159	50	58	22	19	7	3
	%	%	%	%	%	%	%	%	%
ASSETS									
Cash & Equivalents	10.4	7.3	9.0	8.3	8.3	10.2	9.4		
Trade Receivables (net)	7.0	6.7	6.9	4.6	10.2	7.5	4.4		
Inventory	17.5	17.2	12.8	4.8	16.2	17.3	16.4		
All Other Current	2.2	2.6	1.7	3.5	1.0	.3	.8		
Total Current	37.2	33.9	30.3	21.1	35.7	35.2	30.9		
Fixed Assets (net)	53.8	54.3	56.8	62.6	52.2	52.3	61.4		
Intangibles (net)	3.9	5.4	5.5	7.7	4.4	5.3	2.1		
All Other Non-Current	5.1	6.4	7.4	8.5	7.7	7.2	5.5		
Total	100.0	100.0	100.0	100.0	100.0	100.0	100.0		
LIABILITIES									
Notes Payable-Short Term	10.4	8.8	7.4	2.6	8.1	11.7	7.4		
Cur. Mat.-L.T.D.	6.1	3.6	5.3	3.3	5.6	11.4	4.5		
Trade Payables	4.5	3.9	3.7	2.1	5.4	1.8	3.1		
Income Taxes Payable	.0	.6	.1	.1	.1	.0	.0		
All Other Current	15.4	9.3	9.3	7.1	15.1	4.4	4.9		
Total Current	36.4	26.2	25.8	15.2	34.2	29.4	20.0		
Long-Term Debt	45.2	52.1	47.3	46.7	45.4	33.5	53.4		
Deferred Taxes	.1	.1	.1	.0	.2	.0	.0		
All Other Non-Current	6.1	8.8	7.4	10.0	7.6	2.5	6.2		
Net Worth	12.2	12.8	19.5	28.0	12.7	34.6	20.3		
Total Liabilities & Net Worth	100.0	100.0	100.0	100.0	100.0	100.0	100.0		
INCOME DATA									
Net Sales	100.0	100.0	100.0	100.0	100.0	100.0	100.0		
Gross Profit									
Operating Expenses	89.9	88.1	86.6	81.4	90.2	87.8	87.3		
Operating Profit	10.1	11.9	13.4	18.6	9.8	12.2	12.7		
All Other Expenses (net)	4.9	7.1	7.7	11.6	5.6	7.3	6.3		
Profit Before Taxes	5.2	4.9	5.8	7.0	4.2	4.9	6.4		
RATIOS									
Current	2.4	3.1	2.8	3.1	2.7	4.0	3.1		
	1.2	1.3	1.3	1.2	1.3	1.2	1.8		
	.6	.9	.7	.6	.7	.7	1.0		
Quick	1.6	1.9	2.1	2.6	1.5	2.6	1.9		
	.5	.6	.7	.8	.7	.4	.6		
	.1	.2	.2	.2	.3	.2	.4		
Sales/Receivables	1 274.6	3 130.5	4 99.0	0 UND	6 57.4	7 52.2	5 67.2		
	11 33.3	12 31.4	16 22.2	5 67.8	23 16.0	21 17.6	18 20.4		
	30 12.1	34 10.7	40 9.1	34 10.6	48 7.6	41 9.0	29 12.4		
Cost of Sales/Inventory									
Cost of Sales/Payables									
Sales/Working Capital	7.3	4.9	6.1	8.2	6.0	4.7	5.8		
	17.8	14.2	26.7	32.2	30.5	15.9	8.6		
	-6.9	-47.5	-13.9	-6.4	-13.1	-14.7	-153.0		
EBIT/Interest	4.3	4.0	4.3	4.8	4.0	12.2	4.8		
	(111) 1.8	(111) 1.8	(126) 1.5	(29) 1.4	(54) 1.7	(18) 2.2	(16) 1.4		
	.8	1.0	.8	.0	.8	.9	.8		
Net Profit + Depr., Dep., Amort./Cur. Mat. L/T/D	2.2	3.0	3.5						
	(14) 1.6	(19) 1.4	(11) .9						
	.1	.6	.2						
Fixed/Worth	1.0	1.0	1.0	1.2	1.0	.6	1.0		
	3.7	4.5	3.4	3.5	4.3	2.0	3.0		
	-15.7	-5.8	-6.4	-11.5	-4.2	7.6	-4.5		
Debt/Worth	1.8	1.6	1.2	1.0	1.5	.8	.8		
	6.2	6.0	4.6	5.9	4.6	2.9	3.6		
	-19.3	-8.1	-11.7	-16.8	-8.6	9.6	-6.6		
% Profit Before Taxes/Tangible Net Worth	49.7	46.1	36.4	30.2	49.2	41.2	33.7		
	(102) 16.8	(87) 21.6	(111) 18.0	(34) 14.0	(39) 16.8	(19) 21.3	(13) 19.5		
	2.7	1.3	.9	1.9	3.4	-4.7	-1.7		
% Profit Before Taxes/Total Assets	9.5	8.9	9.2	11.8	8.5	14.6	9.4		
	3.6	3.8	3.2	3.1	2.6	2.7	4.0		
	-.6	-.1	-.6	-.4	-.7	-1.5	-.8		
Sales/Net Fixed Assets	7.1	5.6	4.3	2.9	8.4	10.3	2.9		
	1.6	1.5	1.5	.9	1.9	1.3	1.5		
	.7	.6	.6	.3	.6	.6	.6		
Sales/Total Assets	1.8	1.5	1.5	1.1	1.9	1.2	1.4		
	1.0	.9	.9	.5	1.0	.7	.9		
	.5	.5	.4	.2	.5	.5	.5		
% Depr., Dep., Amort./Sales	2.3	2.1	3.3	7.5	1.7	2.6	3.3		
	(128) 5.8	(127) 6.9	(145) 7.4	(41) 10.0	(54) 5.4	(21) 6.1	10.5		
	12.7	13.7	12.1	18.6	10.2	8.2	13.3		
% Officers', Directors' Owners' Comp/Sales	2.5	1.5	2.3	5.5	2.2				
	(45) 4.6	(36) 3.5	(47) 3.9	(13) 10.3	(19) 5.9				
	8.6	5.9	10.2	15.4	7.4				
Net Sales ($)	446269M	406439M	830125M	26284M	103863M	81822M	135845M	98502M	383809M
Total Assets ($)	547701M	537772M	1026866M	88582M	144662M	159969M	207439M	100499M	325715M

M = $ thousand   MM = $ million
See Pages 11 through 21 for Explanation of Ratios and Data

Current Data Sorted by Assets | Comparative Historical Data

0-500M	500M-2MM	2-10MM	10-50MM	50-100MM	100-250MM	Type of Statement	4/1/02-3/31/03 ALL	4/1/03-3/31/04 ALL
2	2	22	36	6	2	Unqualified	46	39
4	6	22	14			Reviewed	30	36
13	23	21	5	6		Compiled	58	84
53	31	15	3		1	Tax Returns	79	69
27	37	49	39	14	1	Other	101	98
	67 (4/1-9/30/06)		381 (10/1/06-3/31/07)					
99	99	129	97	20	4	**NUMBER OF STATEMENTS**	314	326
%	%	%	%	%	%	**ASSETS**	%	%
21.9	9.5	6.3	7.6	8.7		Cash & Equivalents	12.4	10.6
3.9	4.4	3.6	5.5	2.7		Trade Receivables (net)	3.9	4.8
3.6	1.8	.7	1.0	1.5		Inventory	2.0	2.0
2.2	1.9	1.4	2.4	4.5		All Other Current	2.2	3.4
31.6	17.6	12.0	16.5	17.4		Total Current	20.6	20.7
50.8	65.9	76.2	70.8	60.1		Fixed Assets (net)	65.5	66.6
7.0	6.9	2.9	3.1	7.5		Intangibles (net)	4.6	5.3
10.7	9.5	8.8	9.5	14.9		All Other Non-Current	9.3	7.4
100.0	100.0	100.0	100.0	100.0		Total	100.0	100.0
						LIABILITIES		
14.1	3.5	2.1	1.8	3.1		Notes Payable-Short Term	5.8	5.9
6.4	5.1	3.2	2.8	3.5		Cur. Mat.-L.T.D.	4.2	5.2
5.1	5.4	2.4	2.6	2.6		Trade Payables	5.2	3.9
.0	.0	.1	.1	.0		Income Taxes Payable	.2	.2
27.8	10.9	6.9	6.2	8.6		All Other Current	11.6	14.4
53.4	24.9	14.7	13.5	17.8		Total Current	27.0	29.6
32.3	45.6	47.1	39.3	29.9		Long-Term Debt	40.8	38.6
.0	.0	.1	.2	.4		Deferred Taxes	.1	.1
14.9	12.3	7.5	5.9	8.9		All Other Non-Current	9.2	12.3
-.5	17.1	30.7	41.1	43.0		Net Worth	22.9	19.4
100.0	100.0	100.0	100.0	100.0		Total Liabilties & Net Worth	100.0	100.0
						INCOME DATA		
100.0	100.0	100.0	100.0	100.0		Net Sales	100.0	100.0
						Gross Profit		
96.9	89.6	87.8	89.4	80.5		Operating Expenses	91.1	90.6
3.1	10.4	12.2	10.6	19.5		Operating Profit	8.9	9.4
2.2	4.7	8.1	4.1	3.3		All Other Expenses (net)	4.4	4.7
.9	5.7	4.1	6.5	16.1		Profit Before Taxes	4.5	4.6
						RATIOS		
2.1	1.8	1.9	2.7	4.3		Current	2.4	1.8
.7	.8	.9	1.1	1.2			.9	.7
.2	.3	.3	.5	.3			.3	.3
1.7	1.5	1.4	1.8	3.9		Quick	1.9	1.3
(98) .5	.5	.7	.8	1.0			(312) .7	(324) .5
.2	.2	.2	.4	.2			.2	.2
0 UND	0 UND	0 UND	3 116.9	2 236.8		Sales/Receivables	0 UND	0 UND
0 UND	0 999.8	4 95.7	8 43.2	4 91.4			1 503.3	1 347.5
3 130.0	11 32.5	22 16.3	24 15.1	25 14.8			11 33.3	12 29.7
						Cost of Sales/Inventory		
						Cost of Sales/Payables		
40.4	19.5	10.8	6.2	2.6		Sales/Working Capital	12.8	19.1
-63.1	-37.0	-73.8	65.3	28.6			-108.4	-39.8
-9.3	-8.6	-6.3	-12.9	-5.2			-9.2	-7.4
9.9	7.5	3.6	4.4	8.5		EBIT/Interest	6.7	7.1
(65) 2.3	(85) 2.2	(103) 1.3	(84) 2.4	2.7			(264) 2.2	(266) 2.1
-1.1	1.0	.6	1.1	1.5			.8	.8
			6.9			Net Profit + Depr., Dep., Amort./Cur. Mat. L/T/D	4.5	5.3
			(13) 3.9				(25) 2.9	(26) 2.0
			1.5				2.0	1.2
.9	1.3	1.3	1.0	.8		Fixed/Worth	1.1	1.2
4.3	3.1	2.6	1.8	1.4			2.7	2.9
-1.4	-10.8	9.2	4.3	6.3			295.5	-35.6
1.0	1.1	.8	.6	.3		Debt/Worth	.9	1.0
9.2	3.8	2.0	1.5	2.6			2.9	3.3
-3.3	-6.5	12.0	4.7	11.8			NM	-37.3
133.0	68.0	27.0	32.4	24.1		% Profit Before Taxes/Tangible Net Worth	62.4	54.4
(57) 35.9	(64) 11.4	(107) 6.8	(84) 9.7	(16) 9.4			(236) 15.0	(238) 18.1
-5.4	2.3	-2.4	.5	1.1			.6	1.4
36.8	13.0	6.7	9.4	8.2		% Profit Before Taxes/Total Assets	15.4	14.4
6.9	3.6	.8	3.9	3.3			3.9	3.7
-7.2	-.3	-1.7	.1	.6			-1.4	-1.1
26.0	5.3	1.5	1.4	2.1		Sales/Net Fixed Assets	5.4	5.3
7.9	2.1	.7	.8	1.0			2.0	1.8
3.6	.8	.5	.5	.8			.8	.7
6.8	2.2	.9	1.0	1.0		Sales/Total Assets	2.5	2.7
3.9	1.3	.6	.6	.7			1.3	1.2
1.7	.7	.4	.4	.4			.6	.5
1.9	3.6	6.1	5.4	5.4		% Depr., Dep., Amort./Sales	4.2	4.1
(76) 3.4	(78) 6.5	(119) 8.8	(88) 7.9	(18) 7.0			(281) 7.1	(295) 7.2
7.1	10.9	13.3	10.0	10.7			10.6	10.1
6.7	2.8	2.9	1.7			% Officers', Directors' Owners' Comp/Sales	3.5	4.3
(38) 9.8	(30) 5.4	(20) 4.9	(16) 3.7				(102) 7.1	(108) 7.5
16.1	10.8	8.5	7.2				13.2	13.2
87272M	166941M	490186M	2561786M	1021073M	409222M	Net Sales ($)	1940359M	2334628M
23025M	102071M	650517M	2218148M	1450450M	603578M	Total Assets ($)	1964504M	2050191M

M = $ thousand   MM = $ million
See Pages 11 through 21 for Explanation of Ratios and Data

Comparative Historical Data | | | | Current Data Sorted by Sales

			Type of Statement						
55	68	70	Unqualified	4	11	10	18	11	16
40	21	46	Reviewed	5	10	14	11	4	2
47	59	62	Compiled	17	28	7	4	5	1
80	75	103	Tax Returns	55	35	7	3	3	3
126	139	167	Other	38	45	19	23	21	21
4/1/04- 3/31/05	4/1/05- 3/31/06	4/1/06- 3/31/07		67 (4/1-9/30/06)			381 (10/1/06-3/31/07)		
ALL	ALL	ALL		0-1MM	1-3MM	3-5MM	5-10MM	10-25MM	25MM & OVER
348	362	448	**NUMBER OF STATEMENTS**	119	129	57	59	41	43
%	%	%	**ASSETS**	%	%	%	%	%	%
11.7	12.9	10.8	Cash & Equivalents	16.4	9.3	7.6	7.0	9.7	10.5
3.9	4.7	4.2	Trade Receivables (net)	2.1	4.6	4.2	5.3	4.5	7.3
1.7	2.1	1.7	Inventory	2.4	1.2	1.5	1.6	.6	2.5
2.1	3.0	2.0	All Other Current	1.6	1.7	1.2	2.5	2.8	3.8
19.4	22.7	18.8	Total Current	22.5	16.9	14.6	16.4	17.6	24.0
66.4	63.5	66.3	Fixed Assets (net)	63.9	65.7	70.4	72.0	70.6	57.3
5.0	5.4	5.2	Intangibles (net)	5.1	5.7	5.3	2.4	3.0	9.7
9.2	8.5	9.8	All Other Non-Current	8.5	11.8	9.7	9.2	8.8	8.9
100.0	100.0	100.0	Total	100.0	100.0	100.0	100.0	100.0	100.0
			LIABILITIES						
7.4	4.9	5.0	Notes Payable-Short Term	11.1	4.3	2.2	1.2	2.6	1.6
4.9	3.8	4.2	Cur. Mat.-L.T.D.	4.2	6.1	3.1	3.0	3.0	3.4
3.6	4.4	3.7	Trade Payables	3.2	3.5	2.1	7.2	3.0	3.7
.1	.1	.0	Income Taxes Payable	.0	.0	.0	.0	.1	.1
10.5	11.4	12.3	All Other Current	17.1	13.0	9.7	8.0	6.8	11.5
26.7	24.7	25.3	Total Current	35.7	26.9	17.1	19.3	15.5	20.4
38.7	38.2	40.8	Long-Term Debt	40.5	48.0	38.3	39.2	37.0	29.3
.1	.1	.1	Deferred Taxes	.0	.0	.1	.0	.1	1.0
8.9	7.3	9.9	All Other Non-Current	13.9	9.0	9.6	8.5	8.5	5.4
25.6	29.8	23.8	Net Worth	10.0	16.0	34.9	33.0	38.9	43.8
100.0	100.0	100.0	Total Liabilities & Net Worth	100.0	100.0	100.0	100.0	100.0	100.0
			INCOME DATA						
100.0	100.0	100.0	Net Sales	100.0	100.0	100.0	100.0	100.0	100.0
			Gross Profit						
90.1	91.3	90.2	Operating Expenses	90.0	91.3	90.4	91.3	85.8	90.1
9.9	8.7	9.8	Operating Profit	10.0	8.7	9.6	8.7	14.2	9.9
3.3	3.9	4.9	All Other Expenses (net)	8.9	4.2	3.4	3.1	3.3	2.2
6.6	4.8	4.8	Profit Before Taxes	1.1	4.5	6.1	5.6	10.9	7.7
			RATIOS						
2.5	2.4	2.0	Current	2.2	1.7	2.2	2.2	3.0	2.6
.8	.9	.9		.9	.6	1.1	.9	1.2	1.2
.3	.4	.3		.2	.2	.5	.4	.6	.4
2.2	2.0	1.7	Quick	1.7	1.2	1.9	1.4	2.4	1.8
(346) .6	(361) .7	(447) .7		.5 (128)	.5	.7	.6	.9	1.0
.2	.3	.2		.2	.2	.3	.3	.4	.3
0 UND	0 UND	0 UND	Sales/Receivables	0 UND	0 UND	0 UND	1 555.9	2 217.6	2 157.7
1 527.0	2 152.3	3 131.4		0 UND	0 999.8	9 39.7	7 49.4	8 43.4	8 45.5
12 31.1	16 22.6	17 21.6		3 130.0	12 29.8	28 12.8	25 14.7	24 15.2	22 16.4
			Cost of Sales/Inventory						
			Cost of Sales/Payables						
11.8	11.3	12.6	Sales/Working Capital	19.5	26.2	10.7	8.8	4.3	8.1
-59.3	-221.3	-80.3		-30.3	-35.9	188.8	-129.9	68.6	28.9
-8.2	-10.2	-8.5		-4.5	-8.6	-8.7	-11.2	-13.2	-13.0
8.3	5.5	6.2	EBIT/Interest	3.6	6.4	5.8	6.3	9.8	11.0
(298) 2.4	(282) 2.4	(361) 2.1		(76) 1.5	(108) 1.8	(47) 1.3	(53) 2.2	(37) 2.7	(40) 3.3
.9	.7	.7		-.2	.6	.7	.6	2.1	1.4
6.2	6.8	10.3	Net Profit + Depr., Dep., Amort./Cur. Mat. L/T/D						4.4
(34) 3.0	(27) 2.3	(35) 3.0						(12)	2.5
1.6	1.3	1.1							1.2
1.0	1.0	1.2	Fixed/Worth	1.2	1.2	1.3	1.2	.9	.8
2.3	2.1	2.6		4.5	3.3	2.6	1.9	2.2	1.4
NM	37.9	UND		-6.0	-4.8	6.3	5.2	15.3	4.2
.5	.7	.8	Debt/Worth	.9	1.0	.8	.7	.4	.7
2.1	1.9	2.5		6.6	3.2	2.1	1.7	1.5	1.5
NM	146.5	-112.2		-6.9	-9.5	6.3	12.6	16.5	5.3
42.6	50.8	42.5	% Profit Before Taxes/Tangible Net Worth	42.6	49.9	42.0	30.7	55.2	42.0
(261) 15.5	(278) 13.5	(331) 11.4		(75) 7.9	(86) 7.8	(51) 9.7	(49) 10.8	(33) 26.5	(37) 19.6
.6	.1	.0		-.7	-2.9	-.4	.8	6.5	1.3
16.2	12.6	11.9	% Profit Before Taxes/Total Assets	7.7	15.2	11.4	8.3	18.0	14.6
5.4	3.7	3.0		1.5	3.1	1.5	2.2	7.4	5.8
-.6	-.8	-1.1		-5.1	-1.6	-.7	-1.3	2.5	.5
5.8	6.4	5.2	Sales/Net Fixed Assets	7.7	7.2	2.3	1.9	2.7	3.0
1.9	1.6	1.3		1.7	2.2	.8	.8	.9	1.6
.8	.7	.6		.5	.7	.6	.6	.6	1.0
2.4	2.6	2.1	Sales/Total Assets	2.8	2.8	1.3	.9	1.4	1.3
1.1	1.0	.9		1.3	1.2	.6	.7	.8	1.0
.6	.5	.5		.4	.6	.5	.4	.6	.7
4.4	3.9	4.3	% Depr., Dep., Amort./Sales	3.4	3.5	3.9	5.4	5.4	4.6
(297) 6.5	(306) 6.2	(381) 7.1		(94) 8.3	(109) 6.2	(49) 8.0	(56) 7.2	(38) 7.1	(35) 5.6
9.2	9.1	10.9		13.8	10.8	11.4	8.7	9.8	7.9
3.4	3.6	3.4	% Officers', Directors' Owners' Comp/Sales	7.2	3.1				
(116) 6.6	(105) 6.8	(105) 6.7		(33) 10.9	(41) 5.2				
11.7	13.7	11.1		15.8	10.1				
6545282M	3740938M	4736480M	Net Sales ($)	56864M	223993M	222844M	417559M	631557M	3183663M
2737885M	4048797M	5047789M	Total Assets ($)	102710M	340845M	352511M	757861M	987541M	2506321M

© RMA 2007   M = $ thousand   MM = $ million
See Pages 11 through 21 for Explanation of Ratios and Data

Current Data Sorted by Assets / Comparative Historical Data

0-500M	500M-2MM	2-10MM	10-50MM	50-100MM	100-250MM		4/1/02-3/31/03 ALL	4/1/03-3/31/04 ALL
						Type of Statement		
1		1	2			Unqualified	3	5
1	6	4	1			Reviewed	21	19
6	22	5				Compiled	50	45
26	28	7				Tax Returns	34	49
8	8	5	1			Other	25	18
	42 (4/1-9/30/06)		90 (10/1/06-3/31/07)					
42	64	22	4			**NUMBER OF STATEMENTS**	133	136
%	%	%	%	%	%	**ASSETS**	%	%
16.6	11.6	12.5		DATA NOT AVAILABLE	DATA NOT AVAILABLE	Cash & Equivalents	12.3	11.0
.5	.6	.8				Trade Receivables (net)	1.3	1.2
8.0	2.4	1.7				Inventory	3.4	3.8
5.4	.7	.9				All Other Current	2.0	2.9
30.5	15.3	16.0				Total Current	19.0	18.8
50.2	68.7	68.1				Fixed Assets (net)	70.3	67.5
6.2	3.8	4.6				Intangibles (net)	4.6	4.7
13.1	12.2	11.3				All Other Non-Current	6.1	8.9
100.0	100.0	100.0				Total	100.0	100.0
						LIABILITIES		
10.6	8.3	1.3				Notes Payable-Short Term	6.2	5.9
7.4	4.5	6.0				Cur. Mat.-L.T.D.	6.8	6.2
9.2	3.6	1.9				Trade Payables	5.0	5.1
.1	.0	.0				Income Taxes Payable	.1	.4
27.2	8.3	5.9				All Other Current	20.6	14.9
54.5	24.7	15.1				Total Current	38.7	32.4
47.3	58.4	77.7				Long-Term Debt	75.8	66.0
.2	.3	.2				Deferred Taxes	.2	.1
20.5	15.5	2.5				All Other Non-Current	12.4	19.9
-22.5	1.1	4.5				Net Worth	-27.1	-18.5
100.0	100.0	100.0				Total Liabilties & Net Worth	100.0	100.0
						INCOME DATA		
100.0	100.0	100.0				Net Sales	100.0	100.0
						Gross Profit		
96.5	92.2	86.0				Operating Expenses	91.9	94.2
3.5	7.8	14.0				Operating Profit	8.1	5.8
1.1	4.7	7.2				All Other Expenses (net)	5.7	4.5
2.3	3.1	6.8				Profit Before Taxes	2.4	1.3
						RATIOS		
1.6	1.7	1.9				Current	1.4	1.3
.7	.9	1.1					.5	.6
.2	.2	.5					.2	.2
.7	1.3	1.5				Quick	.9	.8
(41) .2	.6	1.0					(131) .3	(135) .3
.0	.1	.4					.1	.1
0 UND	0 UND	0 UND				Sales/Receivables	0 UND	0 UND
0 UND	0 UND	0 UND					0 UND	0 UND
0 UND	1 311.3	3 129.0					1 265.5	1 284.6
						Cost of Sales/Inventory		
						Cost of Sales/Payables		
34.3	15.3	8.2				Sales/Working Capital	30.0	35.1
-40.8	-68.5	71.6					-20.6	-17.3
-9.6	-6.1	-13.8					-5.5	-5.5
10.5	3.7	3.5				EBIT/Interest	2.6	2.5
(32) 2.0	(61) 1.3	(21) 2.1					(111) 1.3	(122) 1.4
.3	.8	1.2					.6	.3
						Net Profit + Depr., Dep., Amort./Cur. Mat. L/T/D	3.7	3.3
							(16) 1.8	(12) 1.4
							1.2	.6
1.3	2.3	3.1				Fixed/Worth	2.6	3.0
6.8	-25.1	NM					62.7	-19.7
-.6	-3.5	-3.1					-2.1	-1.6
1.6	3.1	3.4				Debt/Worth	2.7	3.8
28.0	-36.3	NM					-66.0	-22.7
-2.6	-4.9	-5.2					-3.2	-3.3
181.8	64.6	71.3				% Profit Before Taxes/Tangible Net Worth	60.7	54.5
(23) 29.7	(30) 18.3	(11) 27.5					(66) 14.4	(62) 17.1
7.7	.8	6.2					.6	-.1
23.3	9.6	9.1				% Profit Before Taxes/Total Assets	10.7	8.0
6.6	2.3	3.5					2.2	2.2
-9.5	-.9	1.1					-2.1	-5.2
24.3	3.3	2.0				Sales/Net Fixed Assets	4.1	4.4
9.3	1.7	1.3					1.8	1.9
3.6	1.2	.9					.9	1.1
5.6	1.7	1.2				Sales/Total Assets	2.1	2.3
3.7	1.2	.9					1.3	1.2
2.1	.9	.6					.8	.7
1.1	4.6	5.5				% Depr., Dep., Amort./Sales	4.4	4.7
(35) 2.3	6.9	7.7					(124) 7.6	(129) 7.6
5.4	9.5	10.1					11.8	10.9
4.1	3.3	3.4				% Officers', Directors' Owners' Comp/Sales	4.6	4.0
(27) 7.4	(35) 5.9	(10) 5.1					(48) 6.1	(63) 6.0
13.0	12.9	9.1					11.6	7.9
33586M	87778M	64697M	76215M			Net Sales ($)	424787M	806443M
9761M	67280M	72269M	70350M			Total Assets ($)	349691M	377162M

M = $ thousand MM = $ million

See Pages 11 through 21 for Explanation of Ratios and Data

Comparative Historical Data   Current Data Sorted by Sales

			Type of Statement						
			Unqualified		1	1		2	
2	4	4	Reviewed	2	6	2	1	1	
16	15	12	Compiled	12	18	1	2		
45	44	33	Tax Returns	34	24	2	1		
46	62	61	Other	9	10	1	1	1	
26	27	22							
4/1/04- 3/31/05 ALL	4/1/05- 3/31/06 ALL	4/1/06- 3/31/07 ALL		42 (4/1-9/30/06)			90 (10/1/06-3/31/07)		
				0-1MM	1-3MM	3-5MM	5-10MM	10-25MM	25MM & OVER
135	152	132	NUMBER OF STATEMENTS	57	59	7	5	4	
%	%	%	ASSETS	%	%	%	%	%	%
14.3	12.1	13.1	Cash & Equivalents	10.9	14.8				D
1.3	1.8	.6	Trade Receivables (net)	.5	.6				A
4.4	4.9	4.1	Inventory	5.6	2.9				T
1.4	2.6	2.2	All Other Current	3.8	.9				A
21.4	21.2	20.0	Total Current	20.8	19.2				
65.9	62.6	62.9	Fixed Assets (net)	61.6	63.6				N
4.8	5.9	5.0	Intangibles (net)	6.0	4.0				O
7.9	10.3	12.1	All Other Non-Current	11.6	13.2				T
100.0	100.0	100.0	Total	100.0	100.0				
			LIABILITIES						A
4.0	4.5	7.7	Notes Payable-Short Term	6.9	9.4				V
6.4	4.7	5.7	Cur. Mat.-L.T.D.	6.5	4.9				A
5.7	6.4	5.0	Trade Payables	5.9	4.5				I
.1	.2	.1	Income Taxes Payable	.1	.0				L
11.3	12.5	13.9	All Other Current	11.5	17.6				A
27.5	28.2	32.4	Total Current	31.0	36.5				B
73.1	62.9	57.9	Long-Term Debt	59.9	52.7				L
.2	.2	.2	Deferred Taxes	.1	.2				E
19.1	22.0	14.7	All Other Non-Current	14.3	16.9				
-19.9	-13.3	-5.2	Net Worth	-5.3	-6.2				
100.0	100.0	100.0	Total Liabilties & Net Worth	100.0	100.0				
			INCOME DATA						
100.0	100.0	100.0	Net Sales	100.0	100.0				
			Gross Profit						
93.1	94.2	92.6	Operating Expenses	92.1	92.9				
6.9	5.8	7.4	Operating Profit	7.9	7.1				
4.8	3.3	4.0	All Other Expenses (net)	4.4	3.6				
2.1	2.5	3.4	Profit Before Taxes	3.5	3.5				
			RATIOS						
1.7	2.0	1.7		1.7	2.1				
.7	.8	.8	Current	.8	.8				
.3	.4	.3		.2	.2				
1.2	1.4	1.2		1.0	1.6				
(133) .4	.4	(131) .5	Quick	(56) .3	.6				
.2	.2	.1		.1	.1				
0 UND	0 UND	0 UND		0 UND	0 UND				
0 UND	0 UND	0 UND	Sales/Receivables	0 UND	0 UND				
1 292.5	1 293.4	1 422.8		0 UND	1 412.0				
			Cost of Sales/Inventory						
			Cost of Sales/Payables						
27.7	22.5	20.0		28.4	12.6				
-27.7	-51.2	-49.0	Sales/Working Capital	-47.8	-29.9				
-7.7	-10.6	-9.4		-8.8	-7.6				
4.7	3.7	3.7		3.4	5.7				
(115) 1.6	(127) 1.5	(118) 1.6	EBIT/Interest	(46) 1.5	(56) 1.7				
.6	.3	.8		.7	.9				
4.4	2.5	2.3	Net Profit + Depr., Dep.,						
(14) 1.6	(14) 1.6	(15) 1.8	Amort./Cur. Mat. L/T/D						
1.2	.9	.9							
2.4	1.6	2.2		2.2	1.9				
-23.3	NM	55.6	Fixed/Worth	13.0	-163.6				
-1.1	-1.8	-1.9		-1.4	-2.6				
3.0	2.2	2.7		2.0	3.0				
-16.4	-64.1	87.1	Debt/Worth	41.0	-284.9				
-2.5	-3.0	-3.7		-3.3	-3.7				
43.6	52.9	78.1	% Profit Before Taxes/Tangible	92.5	78.0				
(59) 8.8	(74) 14.3	(68) 22.6	Net Worth	(31) 15.5	(28) 41.4				
-4.2	.3	4.6		-3.2	11.6				
10.2	12.8	10.8	% Profit Before Taxes/Total	10.9	13.3				
2.4	2.3	3.3	Assets	2.9	3.7				
-2.8	-4.8	-1.2		-1.2	-.9				
5.1	5.9	5.9		9.2	4.7				
2.0	2.2	1.9	Sales/Net Fixed Assets	2.8	1.8				
1.0	1.4	1.3		1.0	1.3				
2.1	2.8	2.8		3.5	2.1				
1.4	1.5	1.3	Sales/Total Assets	1.5	1.3				
.7	.9	.9		.7	1.0				
4.6	3.3	3.2		2.0	3.3				
(117) 7.7	(142) 6.6	(125) 6.6	% Depr., Dep., Amort./Sales	(51) 6.6	(58) 5.9				
11.7	9.6	9.6		10.1	8.3				
2.7	4.2	3.5	% Officers', Directors'	4.1	3.2				
(64) 5.5	(65) 8.1	(74) 6.0	Owners' Comp/Sales	(33) 8.8	(35) 5.4				
10.5	11.4	12.4		13.1	7.9				
239794M	1618052M	262276M	Net Sales ($)	37746M	91002M	26191M	31122M	76215M	
240184M	570814M	219660M	Total Assets ($)	33700M	75343M	20593M	19674M	70350M	

M = $ thousand   MM = $ million
See Pages 11 through 21 for Explanation of Ratios and Data

Current Data Sorted by Assets

Comparative Historical Data

Type of Statement	0-500M	500M-2MM	2-10MM	10-50MM	50-100MM	100-250MM		4/1/02-3/31/03 ALL	4/1/03-3/31/04 ALL
Unqualified	1	3	20	21	4	11		67	81
Reviewed	1	9	19					29	31
Compiled	13	14	14	1				40	74
Tax Returns	39	31	9	1	1			62	77
Other	27	26	51	9	4	8		78	84
		79 (4/1-9/30/06)		258 (10/1/06-3/31/07)					
NUMBER OF STATEMENTS	81	83	113	32	9	19		276	347
	%	%	%	%	%	%		%	%
ASSETS									
Cash & Equivalents	23.7	13.9	14.6	12.8		16.2		13.0	12.1
Trade Receivables (net)	5.7	6.7	6.8	4.5		4.5		4.7	5.1
Inventory	8.8	5.0	5.8	3.5		1.4		5.6	5.4
All Other Current	6.6	5.3	2.8	2.9		4.1		2.7	4.0
Total Current	44.8	30.9	30.0	23.7		26.2		25.9	26.6
Fixed Assets (net)	45.7	54.1	58.2	64.5		56.5		61.2	57.8
Intangibles (net)	4.0	4.9	4.4	3.2		6.9		2.9	5.1
All Other Non-Current	5.6	10.1	7.4	8.6		10.4		10.0	10.5
Total	100.0	100.0	100.0	100.0		100.0		100.0	100.0
LIABILITIES									
Notes Payable-Short Term	20.3	5.1	3.7	5.4		1.4		9.7	8.7
Cur. Mat.-L.T.D.	9.5	3.7	5.2	3.3		9.0		4.2	5.8
Trade Payables	12.4	10.1	7.3	5.6		3.9		6.3	5.7
Income Taxes Payable	.1	.0	.1	.1		.3		.2	.1
All Other Current	25.0	19.9	9.5	5.8		11.6		12.5	13.1
Total Current	67.3	38.8	25.8	20.2		26.3		32.8	33.5
Long-Term Debt	39.5	42.5	36.3	30.2		24.5		35.4	32.8
Deferred Taxes	.0	.1	.2	.1		.9		.2	.6
All Other Non-Current	11.2	14.1	5.0	11.1		3.4		14.3	8.3
Net Worth	-18.0	4.5	32.7	38.3		45.0		17.2	24.8
Total Liabilties & Net Worth	100.0	100.0	100.0	100.0		100.0		100.0	100.0
INCOME DATA									
Net Sales	100.0	100.0	100.0	100.0		100.0		100.0	100.0
Gross Profit									
Operating Expenses	94.4	91.2	89.3	86.0		80.0		91.2	91.5
Operating Profit	5.6	8.8	10.7	14.0		20.0		8.8	8.5
All Other Expenses (net)	2.9	4.8	4.5	4.5		2.2		4.3	3.9
Profit Before Taxes	2.8	3.9	6.1	9.5		17.7		4.5	4.6
RATIOS									
Current	2.3	2.6	2.9	1.7		1.6		2.0	2.4
	.7	1.0	1.2	1.1		1.1		.9	.8
	.2	.3	.6	.5		.8		.3	.3
Quick	1.5	1.7	2.2	1.4		1.2		1.5	1.5
	.3	.6	(112) .9	.7		.8		(275) .5	(345) .5
	.1	.1	.3	.3		.3		.2	.1
Sales/Receivables	0 UND	0 UND	0 UND	1 253.3		1 672.8		0 UND	0 UND
	0 UND	0 UND	4 90.5	8 45.9		4 81.1		1 322.5	1 292.9
	0 UND	15 24.3	17 21.9	24 15.5		15 24.2		11 33.3	10 38.4
Cost of Sales/Inventory									
Cost of Sales/Payables									
Sales/Working Capital	16.5	7.0	6.0	9.7		7.7		12.6	9.9
	-39.0	-304.5	44.5	52.8		42.3		-60.6	-63.6
	-7.7	-7.8	-14.0	-7.8		-12.2		-8.4	-6.2
EBIT/Interest	8.0	4.6	6.4	6.9		24.1		7.3	8.3
	(54) 1.7	(62) 1.7	(90) 2.7	(26) 3.5		(16) 3.5		(215) 2.2	(277) 2.4
	-.3	-.3	.6	2.1		1.5		.3	.1
Net Profit + Depr., Dep., Amort./Cur. Mat. L/T/D			6.7					7.5	6.9
			(11) 2.6					(26) 3.7	(35) 3.8
			1.3					1.8	1.6
Fixed/Worth	.2	1.0	.8	.9		1.0		1.0	.9
	2.2	3.6	1.9	1.8		1.6		2.0	2.1
	-1.0	-2.2	7.1	4.1		2.7		24.2	-40.5
Debt/Worth	.9	1.2	.5	.4		.8		.7	.6
	4.9	10.0	1.6	1.5		1.8		1.9	2.5
	-2.7	-4.0	12.4	4.2		3.4		NM	-28.4
% Profit Before Taxes/Tangible Net Worth	100.0	60.4	34.4	35.3		81.7		45.2	47.7
	(49) 29.4	(47) 19.7	(95) 11.3	(27) 23.2		(18) 31.7		(207) 15.2	(254) 14.1
	5.5	5.0	-2.1	6.4		3.7		.3	-.8
% Profit Before Taxes/Total Assets	30.5	14.5	16.5	12.9		25.9		14.4	15.1
	5.7	3.7	4.6	7.8		7.3		3.0	3.4
	-9.3	-4.4	-1.2	1.2		1.0		-2.6	-2.1
Sales/Net Fixed Assets	65.8	16.6	8.3	3.4		2.9		7.2	8.1
	11.5	2.6	1.7	1.4		1.3		1.7	2.0
	2.3	1.1	.5	.9		1.2		.8	.9
Sales/Total Assets	7.0	2.6	2.2	1.3		1.6		2.4	2.5
	3.7	1.5	1.0	.9		.8		1.1	1.2
	1.8	.7	.4	.6		.6		.6	.6
% Depr., Dep., Amort./Sales	1.1	2.2	3.1	3.7		3.6		3.1	3.5
	(46) 2.8	(65) 5.9	(101) 6.4	(30) 6.0		(11) 5.1		(231) 7.4	(294) 7.3
	7.9	10.9	11.9	7.7		8.0		11.6	12.2
% Officers', Directors' Owners' Comp/Sales	4.9	3.2	1.2					2.9	3.9
	(28) 8.6	(28) 7.4	(20) 3.1					(72) 6.6	(92) 7.1
	14.9	11.9	6.8					13.9	12.5
Net Sales ($)	80000M	210707M	821480M	731535M	1090746M	3867501M		4921707M	5728054M
Total Assets ($)	18406M	91499M	518312M	751644M	692693M	2970523M		3902381M	4809774M

© RMA 2007

M = $ thousand   MM = $ million

See Pages 11 through 21 for Explanation of Ratios and Data

Comparative Historical Data | Current Data Sorted by Sales

4/1/04-3/31/05 ALL	4/1/05-3/31/06 ALL	4/1/06-3/31/07 ALL	Type of Statement	0-1MM	1-3MM	3-5MM	5-10MM	10-25MM	25MM & OVER
63	62	60	Unqualified	2	8	6	4	14	26
25	27	29	Reviewed	1	8	8		11	1
56	50	42	Compiled	16	17	2	5	2	
85	73	81	Tax Returns	51	19	2	5	3	1
76	153	125	Other	28	32	18	14	15	16
				79 (4/1-9/30/06)			258 (10/1/06-3/31/07)		
305	365	337	**NUMBER OF STATEMENTS**	98	84	36	30	45	44
%	%	%	**ASSETS**	%	%	%	%	%	%
12.4	14.9	16.6	Cash & Equivalents	15.8	14.9	16.9	17.7	17.9	19.3
4.5	6.0	6.1	Trade Receivables (net)	2.2	6.6	6.5	13.2	7.7	7.1
4.8	5.1	6.0	Inventory	4.7	5.1	9.4	4.2	10.0	5.0
3.7	2.9	4.5	All Other Current	5.8	3.0	7.6	2.2	3.5	4.8
25.4	29.0	33.2	Total Current	28.5	29.6	40.4	37.3	39.0	36.2
60.7	56.8	54.5	Fixed Assets (net)	62.0	55.9	51.5	45.4	46.8	51.6
4.7	4.8	4.5	Intangibles (net)	4.6	3.9	2.1	5.8	5.2	5.6
9.2	9.5	7.8	All Other Non-Current	5.0	10.6	6.0	11.6	9.0	6.6
100.0	100.0	100.0	Total	100.0	100.0	100.0	100.0	100.0	100.0
			LIABILITIES						
7.0	6.5	8.0	Notes Payable-Short Term	13.7	7.7	7.1	5.3	3.4	3.6
6.1	4.5	5.9	Cur. Mat.-L.T.D.	8.3	3.7	6.9	4.8	3.8	6.6
4.7	6.7	9.0	Trade Payables	6.4	7.8	10.8	8.2	15.1	9.9
.1	.2	.1	Income Taxes Payable	.1	.0	.3	.1	.0	.2
11.4	17.7	15.5	All Other Current	14.6	17.4	13.7	11.7	20.4	13.0
29.3	35.6	38.5	Total Current	43.0	36.5	38.8	30.1	42.8	33.2
35.8	37.4	37.1	Long-Term Debt	55.7	30.7	29.3	31.7	33.3	21.7
.3	.4	.2	Deferred Taxes	.1	.0	.6	.1	.2	.5
9.2	9.1	9.2	All Other Non-Current	12.8	5.9	11.1	7.8	5.7	10.2
25.4	17.5	15.1	Net Worth	-11.6	26.9	20.2	30.4	18.0	34.3
100.0	100.0	100.0	Total Liabilties & Net Worth	100.0	100.0	100.0	100.0	100.0	100.0
			INCOME DATA						
100.0	100.0	100.0	Net Sales	100.0	100.0	100.0	100.0	100.0	100.0
			Gross Profit						
91.0	89.9	90.2	Operating Expenses	90.3	91.8	95.3	92.7	88.7	82.7
9.0	10.1	9.8	Operating Profit	9.7	8.2	4.7	7.3	11.3	17.3
3.2	3.8	4.0	All Other Expenses (net)	6.7	3.7	2.2	3.2	1.5	3.1
5.8	6.4	5.8	Profit Before Taxes	3.0	4.5	2.5	4.1	9.8	14.2
			RATIOS						
2.1	2.0	2.4	Current	3.1	2.6	4.2	3.0	1.9	1.5
.9	1.0	1.1		.8	1.0	1.2	1.0	1.2	1.2
.3	.4	.4		.2	.3	.5	.5	.6	.8
1.5	1.5	1.7	Quick	2.0	1.7	2.7	2.0	1.4	1.2
(304) .5	(364) .6	(336) .6		.4	.7	.6	(29) .9	.7	.8
.1	.2	.2		.1	.1	.2	.4	.3	.5
0 UND	0 UND	0 UND	Sales/Receivables	0 UND	0 UND	0 UND	0 UND	1 334.1	1 600.0
1 429.6	1 268.3	1 303.8		0 UND	1 269.7	4 87.7	2 201.5	8 46.5	4 87.3
13 27.2	15 25.1	13 27.4		0 UND	13 28.2	15 24.5	29 12.7	16 22.4	18 19.9
			Cost of Sales/Inventory						
			Cost of Sales/Payables						
14.1	11.1	7.8	Sales/Working Capital	7.3	7.7	5.5	7.6	7.7	11.3
-88.4	-187.8	84.4		-57.9	UND	53.7	NM	44.5	48.1
-7.7	-7.8	-9.9		-6.5	-7.8	-11.3	-13.4	-17.9	-18.5
9.2	6.7	6.2	EBIT/Interest	2.7	5.0	4.6	7.1	24.6	19.8
(246) 2.6	(280) 2.2	(256) 2.4		(65) 1.0	(64) 2.2	(28) 1.9	(24) 2.8	(39) 4.2	(36) 3.4
.7	.1	.3		-.4	.4	-.2	.0	2.4	1.8
4.9	5.2	4.8	Net Profit + Depr., Dep., Amort./Cur. Mat. L/T/D						
(27) 2.0	(30) 2.3	(19) 2.6							
1.3	1.1	1.3							
.9	.9	.8	Fixed/Worth	1.0	.8	.7	.2	.6	.9
1.9	2.0	2.0		3.5	2.1	2.3	1.0	1.6	1.6
15.0	-10.7	-122.0		-1.9	20.5	-24.6	8.9	4.7	3.4
.5	.5	.7	Debt/Worth	.9	.7	.7	.6	.4	.8
2.1	2.5	2.7		5.1	2.9	3.0	1.5	1.7	2.2
23.8	-14.7	-24.7		-2.8	27.3	-10.2	16.6	21.4	4.4
50.9	53.0	52.4	% Profit Before Taxes/Tangible Net Worth	57.0	61.9	33.9	46.3	45.7	86.4
(236) 15.6	(261) 15.6	(245) 18.6		(56) 12.2	(66) 15.2	(24) 6.9	(25) 10.8	(35) 25.6	(39) 35.3
1.5	-.5	2.0		-.3	1.1	-5.3	-3.2	11.8	9.2
14.9	14.3	18.2	% Profit Before Taxes/Total Assets	15.8	18.4	13.7	12.9	20.4	34.5
4.3	3.8	5.1		1.7	4.4	3.1	4.8	9.3	8.3
-1.5	-2.8	-2.1		-4.7	-1.0	-6.4	-3.7	4.0	2.6
6.8	10.4	13.7	Sales/Net Fixed Assets	12.0	16.4	13.6	20.4	16.4	5.5
2.2	2.4	2.4		1.9	2.4	3.3	4.4	6.5	2.3
.8	.9	1.0		.6	.9	.8	1.6	1.6	1.3
2.6	2.9	3.0	Sales/Total Assets	3.1	3.2	2.6	3.3	4.1	2.2
1.3	1.3	1.5		1.2	1.5	1.4	1.7	2.1	1.2
.6	.6	.7		.5	.6	.7	1.0	.9	.8
3.4	2.9	2.4	% Depr., Dep., Amort./Sales	3.8	2.1	1.4	3.0	1.4	2.6
(243) 6.7	(285) 5.9	(261) 5.5		(65) 8.9	(66) 6.0	(31) 4.5	(25) 5.4	(41) 3.5	(33) 4.9
11.5	10.3	9.9		13.7	11.3	11.8	7.9	6.2	6.6
3.5	2.8	2.4	% Officers', Directors' Owners' Comp/Sales	5.2	4.1				
(86) 6.0	(93) 5.7	(79) 6.4		(30) 11.8	(25) 8.2				
12.9	11.8	12.0		18.9	10.3				
5076893M	8042799M	6801969M	Net Sales ($)	47298M	153009M	138234M	208671M	701636M	5553121M
4669935M	6496812M	5043077M	Total Assets ($)	80499M	183778M	127390M	159350M	546655M	3945405M

© RMA 2007

M = $ thousand   MM = $ million
See Pages 11 through 21 for Explanation of Ratios and Data

ACCOMMODATION AND FOOD SERVICES

Current Data Sorted by Assets

Comparative Historical Data

						Type of Statement		
1	11	46	44	20	18	Unqualified		
5	13	53	22	1	1	Reviewed	170	159
33	86	139	29	2	1	Compiled	172	153
137	295	348	16	1	1	Tax Returns	337	402
27	96	256	84	7	15	Other	429	603
	112 (4/1-9/30/06)		1,695 (10/1/06-3/31/07)					446 / 512
0-500M	500M-2MM	2-10MM	10-50MM	50-100MM	100-250MM		4/1/02-3/31/03 ALL	4/1/03-3/31/04 ALL
203	501	842	195	31	35	**NUMBER OF STATEMENTS**	1554	1829
%	%	%	%	%	%	**ASSETS**	%	%
25.7	7.0	6.1	6.7	10.0	11.5	Cash & Equivalents	8.6	8.2
6.1	1.8	1.6	2.3	6.2	3.1	Trade Receivables (net)	2.9	2.4
2.4	.7	.5	1.8	1.1	2.6	Inventory	1.2	1.0
5.3	1.8	1.5	2.0	2.5	4.6	All Other Current	2.2	2.1
39.5	11.3	9.7	12.8	19.8	21.8	Total Current	14.8	13.7
47.4	78.5	81.6	75.5	70.2	67.7	Fixed Assets (net)	74.4	75.8
4.6	3.2	3.5	2.9	1.1	3.1	Intangibles (net)	4.0	3.6
8.5	7.0	5.1	8.8	9.0	7.5	All Other Non-Current	6.8	7.0
100.0	100.0	100.0	100.0	100.0	100.0	Total	100.0	100.0
						LIABILITIES		
7.6	3.0	1.7	1.4	11.6	1.5	Notes Payable-Short Term	4.2	3.8
1.7	3.5	3.1	3.1	2.4	1.9	Cur. Mat.-L.T.D.	4.0	4.0
7.6	1.9	1.5	2.4	10.4	5.3	Trade Payables	3.6	3.1
.2	.0	.0	.1	.1	.1	Income Taxes Payable	.1	.1
33.0	8.2	6.1	7.6	11.6	6.2	All Other Current	11.9	10.9
50.2	16.7	12.4	14.6	36.0	14.9	Total Current	23.8	21.8
30.7	67.3	72.3	62.6	54.7	43.3	Long-Term Debt	61.8	61.6
.0	.0	.0	.2	.4	.9	Deferred Taxes	.1	.1
17.8	4.4	4.7	3.1	1.1	9.3	All Other Non-Current	7.8	7.4
1.3	11.5	10.5	19.5	7.9	31.6	Net Worth	6.5	9.1
100.0	100.0	100.0	100.0	100.0	100.0	Total Liabilities & Net Worth	100.0	100.0
						INCOME DATA		
100.0	100.0	100.0	100.0	100.0	100.0	Net Sales	100.0	100.0
						Gross Profit		
89.9	81.2	80.5	84.1	84.2	83.5	Operating Expenses	85.6	86.2
10.1	18.8	19.5	15.9	15.8	16.5	Operating Profit	14.4	13.8
4.0	11.5	12.9	10.0	5.7	5.1	All Other Expenses (net)	10.4	10.2
6.1	7.3	6.6	5.9	10.1	11.5	Profit Before Taxes	4.0	3.6
						RATIOS		
3.5	2.3	2.2	1.9	1.8	2.2	Current	1.8	1.7
1.5	.8	.9	1.0	.9	1.1		.7	.7
.4	.2	.3	.4	.4	.5		.2	.3
3.2	1.8	2.2	1.6	1.6	1.7	Quick	1.4	1.3
1.0	.6	(840) .7	.7	.8	.7		(1551) .5	(1824) .5
.2	.2	.2	.3	.3	.3		.2	.2
0 UND	0 UND	0 UND	3 116.9	5 71.7	4 94.4		0 UND	0 UND
0 UND	0 UND	4 89.1	7 48.8	10 36.0	11 33.4	Sales/Receivables	4 94.9	4 98.3
4 84.6	6 57.4	9 41.1	13 28.2	25 14.5	17 22.0		10 37.3	10 37.6
						Cost of Sales/Inventory		
						Cost of Sales/Payables		
13.0	14.9	12.4	8.7	10.8	6.7	Sales/Working Capital	18.9	18.0
57.5	-36.1	-131.7	-344.0	-56.1	120.1		-28.0	-23.1
-12.4	-6.6	-7.5	-9.1	-5.4	-8.2		-6.0	-5.5
5.7	3.3	2.8	3.1	3.6	5.5	EBIT/Interest	2.9	2.8
(97) 2.3	(382) 1.8	(674) 1.8	(161) 1.7	(29) 2.2	(32) 2.5		(1179) 1.6	(1430) 1.5
1.0	1.0	1.1	1.0	1.6	1.3		.8	.7
		3.5	7.4	3.9		Net Profit + Depr., Dep.,	4.7	3.6
	(12) 2.1	(35) 2.3	(24) 2.8			Amort./Cur. Mat. L/T/D	(121) 2.4	(97) 1.9
	1.1	1.5	1.7				1.1	.9
.3	2.5	3.5	1.9	1.3	1.5	Fixed/Worth	2.3	2.5
2.9	6.9	10.6	4.9	3.3	2.7		7.5	7.8
-3.8	-10.5	-14.4	138.3	7.7	50.6		-8.2	-11.9
.5	2.0	3.0	1.8	1.7	.9	Debt/Worth	2.2	2.4
5.4	7.1	11.5	4.7	4.4	2.3		8.5	8.5
-4.9	-13.4	-16.5	172.1	59.0	66.4		-9.9	-13.9
99.5	54.1	60.1	36.1	60.9	96.4	% Profit Before Taxes/Tangible	42.2	42.2
(128) 40.6	(327) 21.4	(540) 22.3	(147) 11.6	(25) 31.7	(28) 18.1	Net Worth	(992) 15.1	(1198) 12.8
8.2	2.8	4.3	.0	10.3	4.0		.0	-2.5
36.3	10.2	8.2	7.6	11.1	10.8	% Profit Before Taxes/Total	7.7	7.0
7.4	3.7	3.2	3.2	5.9	4.4	Assets	2.2	1.9
-.9	-.5	-.6	-.2	2.0	.1		-1.8	-2.2
43.7	1.2	.8	1.1	1.4	1.3	Sales/Net Fixed Assets	1.6	1.3
7.7	.6	.5	.6	.7	.9		.7	.6
1.7	.4	.4	.4	.5	.6		.4	.4
6.0	.9	.6	.8	.8	.8	Sales/Total Assets	1.0	.9
3.2	.5	.5	.5	.6	.6		.6	.5
1.1	.4	.3	.3	.4	.4		.4	.3
1.4	5.5	6.8	6.8	5.9	6.3	% Depr., Dep., Amort./Sales	6.3	6.9
(160) 3.4	(466) 8.4	(778) 9.5	(179) 8.8	(30) 8.4	(24) 7.9		(1424) 9.7	(1661) 10.3
7.7	12.3	13.2	12.2	12.5	11.2		13.9	14.5
2.7	3.1	2.0	1.6			% Officers', Directors'	2.5	2.9
(84) 4.5	(188) 5.3	(213) 3.9	(43) 3.2			Owners' Comp/Sales	(417) 4.8	(457) 5.0
12.1	8.4	6.2	4.7				9.5	9.1
169427M	503714M	2098837M	2567013M	2608401M	4304863M	Net Sales ($)	11037853M	10300865M
50007M	634322M	3578110M	4167454M	2115418M	5612973M	Total Assets ($)	13587228M	15285545M

Comparative Historical Data   Current Data Sorted by Sales

Type of Statement	4/1/04-3/31/05 ALL	4/1/05-3/31/06 ALL	4/1/06-3/31/07 ALL	0-1MM	1-3MM	3-5MM	5-10MM	10-25MM	25MM & OVER
Unqualified	175	114	140	7	25	11	31	22	44
Reviewed	154	100	95	11	31	23	13	13	4
Compiled	314	246	289	110	122	22	20	13	2
Tax Returns	621	705	798	420	317	32	16	9	4
Other	444	521	485	113	203	52	52	37	28
				112 (4/1-9/30/06)			1,695 (10/1/06-3/31/07)		
NUMBER OF STATEMENTS	1708	1686	1807	661	698	140	132	94	82
ASSETS	%	%	%	%	%	%	%	%	%
Cash & Equivalents	8.6	9.0	8.8	8.1	8.9	8.6	9.8	9.6	10.9
Trade Receivables (net)	2.6	2.6	2.4	1.4	2.3	3.8	3.8	3.5	5.2
Inventory	.9	.9	1.0	.5	.7	1.6	2.4	1.8	2.3
All Other Current	2.1	2.0	2.1	1.8	2.1	3.0	2.5	1.6	3.2
Total Current	14.1	14.6	14.2	11.8	14.0	17.0	18.6	16.5	21.5
Fixed Assets (net)	74.9	75.4	75.8	78.8	76.4	70.9	70.3	71.2	68.7
Intangibles (net)	3.4	3.5	3.4	3.7	3.3	3.8	2.7	4.2	2.3
All Other Non-Current	7.6	6.5	6.5	5.7	6.3	8.3	8.5	8.1	7.5
Total	100.0	100.0	100.0	100.0	100.0	100.0	100.0	100.0	100.0
LIABILITIES									
Notes Payable-Short Term	3.6	2.8	2.9	3.9	1.9	2.0	3.2	.9	6.1
Cur. Mat.-L.T.D.	4.0	3.1	3.0	2.9	2.9	3.5	4.2	2.7	2.7
Trade Payables	3.1	2.9	2.6	1.8	2.1	4.0	3.8	3.6	8.2
Income Taxes Payable	.1	.1	.1	.0	.1	.1	.1	.2	.1
All Other Current	9.8	8.6	10.0	11.4	7.8	11.5	11.6	11.1	10.1
Total Current	20.6	17.5	18.5	20.1	14.7	21.2	23.0	18.6	27.1
Long-Term Debt	62.7	64.6	64.3	64.6	67.2	58.0	64.9	64.6	47.9
Deferred Taxes	.1	.1	.1	.0	.0	.1	.1	.2	.6
All Other Non-Current	7.1	8.3	6.0	7.5	5.1	7.4	4.1	3.6	4.5
Net Worth	9.6	9.5	11.1	7.9	13.0	13.3	8.0	13.0	19.9
Total Liabilities & Net Worth	100.0	100.0	100.0	100.0	100.0	100.0	100.0	100.0	100.0
INCOME DATA									
Net Sales	100.0	100.0	100.0	100.0	100.0	100.0	100.0	100.0	100.0
Gross Profit									
Operating Expenses	85.0	82.4	82.3	80.2	82.4	81.9	87.3	86.6	85.0
Operating Profit	15.0	17.6	17.7	19.8	17.6	18.1	12.7	13.4	15.0
All Other Expenses (net)	9.5	10.2	10.9	14.6	10.1	8.5	6.6	6.9	4.4
Profit Before Taxes	5.4	7.3	6.8	5.2	7.6	9.6	6.1	6.6	10.6
RATIOS									
Current	1.9	2.4	2.3	2.8	2.4	1.9	1.8	1.7	1.8
	.7	.9	.9	.7	1.0	1.0	1.0	1.1	.9
	.3	.3	.3	.2	.3	.4	.5	.5	.4
Quick	1.6	2.0	1.9	2.3	2.0	1.6	1.6	1.4	1.6
	(1705) .5	(1680) .7	(1805) .7	.6	(697) .8	(139) .7	.7	.9	.7
	.2	.2	.2	.1	.2	.3	.3	.4	.3
Sales/Receivables	0 UND	0 UND	0 UND	0 UND	0 UND	2 166.1	3 119.3	4 89.9	4 81.6
	4 90.4	4 98.5	3 116.8	0 UND	4 91.9	5 71.4	7 50.8	8 43.6	10 35.3
	10 36.8	10 34.9	9 41.5	5 80.8	8 43.3	10 36.1	13 28.4	14 26.1	19 18.8
Cost of Sales/Inventory									
Cost of Sales/Payables									
Sales/Working Capital	15.4	13.1	12.4	14.0	11.6	13.9	9.5	13.9	8.9
	-25.6	-128.2	-135.2	-28.5	264.6	-280.5	-334.3	139.4	-58.5
	-6.1	-8.1	-7.6	-4.3	-10.3	-9.1	-9.5	-13.7	-8.6
EBIT/Interest	3.2	3.2	3.1	2.6	3.2	3.9	3.9	4.4	4.4
	(1372) 1.7	(1305) 1.8	(1375) 1.8	(408) 1.6	(566) 1.8	(118) 2.3	(118) 1.7	(89) 2.1	(76) 2.4
	.8	1.0	1.1	1.0	1.1	1.1	.8	1.3	1.5
Net Profit + Depr., Dep., Amort./Cur. Mat. L/T/D	5.6	5.2	5.2		4.1	8.4	5.9		7.4
	(82) 2.3	(76) 2.8	(78) 2.4		(18) 2.0	(10) 2.2	(19) 3.5		(14) 3.7
	1.0	1.6	1.5		1.5	1.7	1.5		1.8
Fixed/Worth	2.3	2.5	2.5	2.9	2.7	1.7	1.8	1.8	1.5
	7.9	8.0	7.2	8.9	7.7	6.4	6.1	7.8	2.5
	-11.2	-13.5	-14.4	-10.2	-19.1	-7.6	-62.7	-9.4	7.0
Debt/Worth	2.2	2.3	2.2	2.5	2.4	1.3	1.8	2.0	1.1
	8.3	9.0	7.7	9.9	7.9	7.0	6.2	9.0	2.5
	-12.4	-15.0	-15.8	-12.2	-21.2	-10.5	-26.3	-11.3	9.6
% Profit Before Taxes/Tangible Net Worth	47.5	64.0	60.6	46.9	65.5	59.1	54.4	79.9	72.9
	(1119) 16.6	(1102) 22.1	(1195) 21.2	(417) 17.6	(468) 27.1	(88) 25.6	(96) 11.5	(60) 20.8	(66) 25.6
	.3	3.1	3.5	.0	5.2	7.8	-1.3	7.8	9.1
% Profit Before Taxes/Total Assets	8.4	9.8	9.6	6.9	10.7	11.7	9.8	10.2	11.8
	2.9	3.6	3.6	2.4	4.2	5.4	3.6	4.7	5.7
	-1.3	-.5	-.4	-1.6	.0	.4	-1.0	.5	2.0
Sales/Net Fixed Assets	1.5	1.3	1.3	.8	1.2	1.9	2.1	1.9	1.8
	.7	.6	.6	.5	.6	.8	1.0	.9	1.1
	.4	.4	.4	.3	.5	.5	.6	.6	.7
Sales/Total Assets	.9	.9	.9	.6	.8	1.2	1.3	1.2	1.1
	.5	.5	.5	.4	.5	.7	.7	.8	.7
	.4	.4	.4	.3	.4	.4	.5	.5	.6
% Depr., Dep., Amort./Sales	6.3	5.5	5.8	6.3	5.9	5.5	4.3	5.6	5.2
	(1542) 9.6	(1516) 8.7	(1637) 8.8	(608) 9.9	(636) 8.9	(117) 7.8	(122) 7.6	(87) 7.2	(67) 7.3
	14.3	12.5	12.4	14.5	12.3	10.8	10.2	10.2	9.1
% Officers', Directors' Owners' Comp/Sales	2.9	2.6	2.4	3.3	2.0	1.3	2.1	1.7	
	(413) 5.0	(470) 4.7	(532) 4.3	(243) 5.2	(195) 3.5	(33) 4.0	(28) 3.7	(26) 3.6	
	9.6	8.2	7.5	8.5	6.5	5.7	6.1	4.9	
Net Sales ($)	15287265M	11128748M	12252255M	365560M	1224426M	532671M	935058M	1440267M	7754273M
Total Assets ($)	15218162M	13523906M	16158284M	1010801M	2490637M	1012229M	1400578M	2216562M	8027477M

© RMA 2007

M = $ thousand   MM = $ million
See Pages 11 through 21 for Explanation of Ratios and Data

Current Data Sorted by Assets							Comparative Historical Data	
						Type of Statement		
		1	4	1	10	Unqualified	17	19
		2				Reviewed		
		1				Compiled		
	2					Tax Returns	1	2
	1	1	11	7	9	Other	6	6
	12 (4/1-9/30/06)		38 (10/1/06-3/31/07)				**4/1/02-3/31/03 ALL**	**4/1/03-3/31/04 ALL**
0-500M	**500M-2MM**	**2-10MM**	**10-50MM**	**50-100MM**	**100-250MM**			
	3	5	15	8	19	**NUMBER OF STATEMENTS**	24	27
%	%	%	%	%	%	**ASSETS**	%	%
DATA NOT AVAILABLE			16.6		18.4	Cash & Equivalents	11.5	9.3
			1.2		1.0	Trade Receivables (net)	1.0	1.2
			.7		.4	Inventory	1.0	.2
			2.3		1.5	All Other Current	2.7	2.8
			20.9		21.2	Total Current	16.2	13.4
			72.2		67.2	Fixed Assets (net)	78.0	80.3
			5.3		8.6	Intangibles (net)	2.4	2.7
			1.6		2.9	All Other Non-Current	3.4	3.5
			100.0		100.0	Total	100.0	100.0
						LIABILITIES		
			2.0		.0	Notes Payable-Short Term	.4	.3
			5.7		3.2	Cur. Mat.-L.T.D.	4.8	6.1
			2.0		1.3	Trade Payables	4.9	1.0
			.0		.2	Income Taxes Payable	.0	.0
			10.0		10.2	All Other Current	5.5	9.3
			19.7		14.9	Total Current	15.7	16.7
			34.9		35.1	Long-Term Debt	41.7	32.9
			1.0		.6	Deferred Taxes	.4	.2
			9.2		1.4	All Other Non-Current	3.4	7.3
			35.2		48.0	Net Worth	38.8	42.8
			100.0		100.0	Total Liabilities & Net Worth	100.0	100.0
						INCOME DATA		
			100.0		100.0	Net Sales	100.0	100.0
						Gross Profit		
			76.2		74.5	Operating Expenses	83.6	85.4
			23.8		25.5	Operating Profit	16.4	14.6
			5.1		4.9	All Other Expenses (net)	4.4	3.6
			18.6		20.6	Profit Before Taxes	12.0	11.0
						RATIOS		
			2.2		2.3		1.5	1.1
			1.2		1.4	Current	1.0	.8
			.6		1.0		.6	.6
			1.8		1.9		1.0	.9
			.9		1.3	Quick	.8	.6
			.5		.7		.5	.5
			0 999.8		2 181.2		1 251.3	2 146.1
			2 185.1		3 113.4	Sales/Receivables	4 103.7	4 88.2
			4 89.9		6 61.4		6 56.8	7 49.5
						Cost of Sales/Inventory		
						Cost of Sales/Payables		
			9.2		5.1		26.2	457.0
			53.5		14.8	Sales/Working Capital	NM	-27.3
			-23.1		782.0		-16.2	-16.4
			65.5		62.5		7.5	7.1
			(12) 6.8		(15) 22.2	EBIT/Interest	(23) 4.6	(24) 3.5
			2.6		3.1		1.2	1.4
						Net Profit + Depr., Dep., Amort./Cur. Mat. L/T/D		
			1.0		1.0		1.4	1.3
			2.8		1.5	Fixed/Worth	2.6	2.0
			8.0		5.6		3.5	4.7
			.4		.3		.7	.6
			2.1		1.2	Debt/Worth	2.2	1.4
			8.4		6.8		3.5	4.1
			164.5		85.5		77.9	48.4
			(12) 59.2		(17) 43.8	% Profit Before Taxes/Tangible Net Worth	(22) 33.2	(24) 20.5
			33.6		16.2		12.8	7.1
			49.3		38.9		23.1	15.6
			19.9		10.1	% Profit Before Taxes/Total Assets	11.2	9.1
			6.0		-.1		1.8	1.3
			2.7		1.9		1.7	1.6
			1.6		1.5	Sales/Net Fixed Assets	1.3	1.2
			.9		.9		1.0	.8
			1.7		1.2		1.3	1.2
			1.2		1.0	Sales/Total Assets	1.0	1.0
			.6		.4		.7	.7
			4.5		5.7		5.3	5.5
			7.3		(10) 6.5	% Depr., Dep., Amort./Sales	(17) 6.5	(22) 7.3
			11.7		8.9		9.2	8.9
						% Officers', Directors' Owners' Comp/Sales		
	16736M	31453M	724595M	1223946M	3355063M	Net Sales ($)	2403472M	2154194M
	3858M	26522M	511735M	604658M	3183502M	Total Assets ($)	2441583M	2185727M

M = $ thousand MM = $ million

See Pages 11 through 21 for Explanation of Ratios and Data

Comparative Historical Data   ## Current Data Sorted by Sales

			Type of Statement						
17	14	16	Unqualified		1		2	2	12
1	1	2	Reviewed				1	1	
		1	Compiled			1			
1	1	2	Tax Returns	1	1			3	25
15	25	29	Other	1	1				
4/1/04-	4/1/05-	4/1/06-			12 (4/1-9/30/06)		38 (10/1/06-3/31/07)		
3/31/05	3/31/06	3/31/07							
ALL	ALL	ALL		0-1MM	1-3MM	3-5MM	5-10MM	10-25MM	25MM & OVER
34	41	50	NUMBER OF STATEMENTS	1	3		3	6	37
%	%	%	ASSETS	%	%	%	%	%	%
15.5	13.0	16.2	Cash & Equivalents						18.8
1.3	.8	1.2	Trade Receivables (net)		D				1.1
.5	.3	.7	Inventory		A				.5
2.6	3.2	2.1	All Other Current		T				2.3
20.0	17.3	20.2	Total Current		A				22.7
73.4	69.5	70.3	Fixed Assets (net)						70.0
2.9	9.1	6.8	Intangibles (net)		N				5.1
3.8	4.2	2.7	All Other Non-Current		O				2.3
100.0	100.0	100.0	Total		T				100.0
			LIABILITIES		A				
2.9	.3	1.0	Notes Payable-Short Term		V				.9
7.3	6.1	4.3	Cur. Mat.-L.T.D.		A				3.1
2.7	1.7	3.4	Trade Payables		I				1.9
.0	.1	.1	Income Taxes Payable		L				.1
8.9	9.2	10.2	All Other Current		A				11.8
21.9	17.4	19.0	Total Current		B				17.8
31.7	35.3	35.3	Long-Term Debt		L				33.1
.2	.2	.5	Deferred Taxes		E				.3
5.6	2.7	6.9	All Other Non-Current						2.6
40.5	44.4	38.2	Net Worth						46.1
100.0	100.0	100.0	Total Liabilties & Net Worth						100.0
			INCOME DATA						
100.0	100.0	100.0	Net Sales						100.0
			Gross Profit						
82.4	79.1	77.1	Operating Expenses						73.4
17.6	20.9	22.9	Operating Profit						26.6
2.2	3.8	5.2	All Other Expenses (net)						3.8
15.5	17.1	17.7	Profit Before Taxes						22.9
			RATIOS						
1.5	2.0	1.8							2.0
.8	1.2	1.2	Current						1.3
.6	.8	.7							.9
1.2	1.7	1.5							1.7
.7	1.0	1.0	Quick						1.1
.5	.6	.6							.7
1 250.2	1 422.9	1 457.0							1 380.4
3 108.4	3 143.9	3 145.2	Sales/Receivables						3 142.5
7 53.2	5 73.6	5 78.8							4 84.7
			Cost of Sales/Inventory						
			Cost of Sales/Payables						
19.5	8.9	10.4							8.9
-34.7	34.4	52.8	Sales/Working Capital						43.8
-10.6	-46.2	-37.6							-79.7
12.9	23.9	60.7							73.0
(30) 4.5	(36) 7.0	(39) 6.3	EBIT/Interest					(30) 21.9
1.4	1.9	2.5							3.3
			Net Profit + Depr., Dep., Amort./Cur. Mat. L/T/D						
1.1	1.2	1.0							1.0
1.8	1.6	1.9	Fixed/Worth						1.5
5.4	4.0	7.2							4.8
.5	.5	.5							.4
1.1	1.3	1.4	Debt/Worth						.9
5.3	5.2	7.9							5.4
70.5	80.4	97.3	% Profit Before Taxes/Tangible						116.3
(30) 28.1	(35) 40.7	(41) 48.1	Net Worth					(33) 52.0
8.3	17.9	22.5							30.0
25.3	34.5	46.2	% Profit Before Taxes/Total						52.3
11.3	14.1	18.1	Assets						22.4
1.4	3.5	3.9							7.5
2.0	2.1	2.5							2.4
1.4	1.7	1.6	Sales/Net Fixed Assets						1.7
.9	1.0	.9							1.3
1.5	1.4	1.8							1.8
1.1	1.0	1.1	Sales/Total Assets						1.2
.7	.7	.7							.8
5.1	5.8	4.4							4.5
(29) 7.3	(33) 7.6	(40) 6.6	% Depr., Dep., Amort./Sales					(27) 6.2
8.8	8.9	9.5							7.8
			% Officers', Directors' Owners' Comp/Sales						
3105212M	3798456M	5351793M	Net Sales ($)	989M	6190M		19468M	97185M	5227961M
2911676M	3472211M	4330275M	Total Assets ($)	643M	12899M		33585M	218650M	4064498M

© RMA 2007

M = $ thousand   MM = $ million
See Pages 11 through 21 for Explanation of Ratios and Data

Current Data Sorted by Assets

Comparative Historical Data

	0-500M	500M-2MM	2-10MM	10-50MM	50-100MM	100-250MM	Type of Statement	4/1/02-3/31/03 ALL	4/1/03-3/31/04 ALL
	2	1	1	3		1	Unqualified	6	4
		3	5		1		Reviewed	3	7
	5	11	1	9	1		Compiled	20	17
	10	15	9		1	2	Tax Returns	36	33
		6	6				Other	12	12
		6 (4/1-9/30/06)		78 (10/1/06-3/31/07)					
NUMBER OF STATEMENTS	17	36	22	5	3	1		77	73
	%	%	%	%	%	%	**ASSETS**	%	%
	19.4	8.4	8.4				Cash & Equivalents	7.7	7.9
	.3	3.2	1.0				Trade Receivables (net)	1.4	1.7
	3.3	7.5	6.5				Inventory	3.8	7.2
	2.0	.5	2.0				All Other Current	1.6	1.6
	25.0	19.6	17.9				Total Current	14.5	18.4
	62.3	70.1	65.1				Fixed Assets (net)	74.3	66.3
	5.6	7.4	3.7				Intangibles (net)	3.7	3.4
	7.1	2.9	13.3				All Other Non-Current	7.4	11.8
	100.0	100.0	100.0				Total	100.0	100.0
							LIABILITIES		
	3.4	5.3	7.0				Notes Payable-Short Term	6.0	7.2
	5.5	3.1	3.6				Cur. Mat.-L.T.D.	3.2	5.7
	.7	2.7	1.1				Trade Payables	.9	3.4
	.0	.0	.0				Income Taxes Payable	.1	.0
	18.2	10.9	12.5				All Other Current	10.8	12.3
	27.8	21.9	24.2				Total Current	21.0	28.6
	60.2	57.8	43.2				Long-Term Debt	56.3	54.4
	.0	.0	.0				Deferred Taxes	.1	.2
	14.1	8.9	8.9				All Other Non-Current	10.2	9.3
	-2.0	11.3	23.6				Net Worth	12.5	7.5
	100.0	100.0	100.0				Total Liabilties & Net Worth	100.0	100.0
							INCOME DATA		
	100.0	100.0	100.0				Net Sales	100.0	100.0
							Gross Profit		
	82.2	82.8	86.4				Operating Expenses	83.0	84.2
	17.8	17.2	13.6				Operating Profit	17.0	15.8
	5.7	10.2	4.9				All Other Expenses (net)	10.2	6.8
	12.1	7.0	8.7				Profit Before Taxes	6.8	9.0
							RATIOS		
	4.3	2.2	3.7					1.7	1.8
	.8	.9	.8				Current	.7	.8
	.4	.3	.2					.2	.2
	4.0	1.7	1.6					1.2	1.0
	.4	.6	.3				Quick	.4	.3
	.1	.2	.0					.1	.1
	0 UND	0 UND	0 UND					0 UND	0 UND
	0 UND	0 UND	1 625.8				Sales/Receivables	0 UND	0 UND
	0 UND	5 72.1	4 88.5					5 75.7	3 105.9
							Cost of Sales/Inventory		
							Cost of Sales/Payables		
	16.8	6.6	4.1					16.3	14.3
	-32.7	-101.4	-24.8				Sales/Working Capital	-26.0	-28.2
	-8.3	-9.0	-3.6					-5.0	-7.0
	7.3	11.8	5.9					5.4	6.0
	(12) 1.4	(28) 2.7	(18) 1.9				EBIT/Interest	(59) 1.9	(60) 2.5
	.6	1.0	.6					1.0	1.2
							Net Profit + Depr., Dep., Amort./Cur. Mat. L/T/D		
	1.4	2.3	1.0					1.7	1.4
	3.5	9.6	4.7				Fixed/Worth	4.5	5.8
	-3.2	-3.7	-4.8					-10.9	-7.9
	1.6	2.4	.5					1.4	1.5
	3.7	8.7	5.1				Debt/Worth	5.2	5.8
	-21.0	-5.8	-6.6					-14.7	-10.4
	351.0	67.4	31.7				% Profit Before Taxes/Tangible	50.3	48.6
	(12) 8.5	(21) 9.8	(15) 21.4				Net Worth	(51) 18.9	(49) 18.3
	-9.9	-3.0	.5					-1.8	2.7
	76.4	23.0	12.1				% Profit Before Taxes/Total	12.5	12.5
	2.6	2.8	4.5				Assets	3.3	6.1
	-2.3	-.7	-.4					-1.7	1.2
	15.1	4.1	2.9					2.0	3.3
	3.8	.8	.9				Sales/Net Fixed Assets	.9	1.4
	.7	.4	.5					.5	.6
	5.2	1.9	1.2					1.2	1.9
	1.3	.6	.7				Sales/Total Assets	.6	.8
	.7	.4	.4					.4	.4
	1.6	4.2	3.7					4.7	4.6
	(15) 7.5	(33) 10.0	(18) 7.1				% Depr., Dep., Amort./Sales	(72) 8.4	(68) 8.6
	23.3	16.7	13.5					15.6	15.2
		2.4					% Officers', Directors'	3.8	3.6
		(12) 6.7					Owners' Comp/Sales	(26) 7.7	(24) 7.8
		12.6						13.4	13.4
	7057M	48122M	66887M	58299M	213033M	12428M	Net Sales ($)	300691M	221518M
	4099M	38855M	86688M	118606M	283136M	107920M	Total Assets ($)	390454M	299447M

M = $ thousand   MM = $ million
See Pages 11 through 21 for Explanation of Ratios and Data

Comparative Historical Data

Current Data Sorted by Sales

Comparative Historical Data			Type of Statement	Current Data Sorted by Sales					
4	4	8	Unqualified	2	1	1	1	3	
7	5	9	Reviewed	3	1	3	1		1
22	16	18	Compiled	12	4		1	1	
44	38	34	Tax Returns	19	10	5			
16	19	15	Other	5	4	1	3	1	1
4/1/04- 3/31/05 ALL	4/1/05- 3/31/06 ALL	4/1/06- 3/31/07 ALL		6 (4/1-9/30/06)			78 (10/1/06-3/31/07)		
				0-1MM	1-3MM	3-5MM	5-10MM	10-25MM	25MM & OVER
93	82	84	NUMBER OF STATEMENTS	41	20	10	6	5	2
%	%	%	ASSETS	%	%	%	%	%	%
9.7	11.0	10.4	Cash & Equivalents	11.0	10.2	7.0			
1.9	2.9	2.2	Trade Receivables (net)	.5	3.3	5.2			
8.0	8.9	5.8	Inventory	3.5	8.0	10.1			
1.6	.9	1.4	All Other Current	1.0	.9	1.2			
21.1	23.7	19.7	Total Current	16.0	22.4	23.5			
67.6	62.9	64.4	Fixed Assets (net)	75.7	60.6	50.3			
3.5	4.3	6.4	Intangibles (net)	3.8	12.1	4.0			
7.7	9.1	9.5	All Other Non-Current	4.5	4.8	22.2			
100.0	100.0	100.0	Total	100.0	100.0	100.0			
			LIABILITIES						
13.4	14.7	5.4	Notes Payable-Short Term	4.8	4.5	6.1			
3.5	3.1	3.5	Cur. Mat.-L.T.D.	3.9	4.0	4.1			
1.9	2.5	1.8	Trade Payables	.7	3.1	3.0			
.1	.1	.0	Income Taxes Payable	.0	.0	.0			
7.6	8.8	13.1	All Other Current	8.4	17.9	22.0			
26.5	29.2	23.7	Total Current	17.9	29.5	35.2			
49.8	60.0	50.7	Long-Term Debt	71.6	36.2	36.9			
.1	.0	.0	Deferred Taxes	.0	.0	.0			
6.3	5.7	12.0	All Other Non-Current	11.5	6.6	2.2			
17.2	5.2	13.5	Net Worth	-1.0	27.6	25.7			
100.0	100.0	100.0	Total Liabilties & Net Worth	100.0	100.0	100.0			
			INCOME DATA						
100.0	100.0	100.0	Net Sales	100.0	100.0	100.0			
			Gross Profit						
83.8	85.3	84.3	Operating Expenses	80.3	89.1	86.0			
16.2	14.7	15.7	Operating Profit	19.7	10.9	14.0			
6.0	5.1	7.6	All Other Expenses (net)	11.8	3.3	2.0			
10.1	9.6	8.0	Profit Before Taxes	7.9	7.7	12.0			
			RATIOS						
2.3	2.1	2.6		2.6	2.5	3.3			
1.0	.9	.8	Current	.8	.9	.7			
.2	.3	.3		.4	.2	.1			
1.9	1.4	1.7		1.9	1.4	1.8			
(92) .6	(81) .4	.4	Quick	.6	.4	.3			
.1	.1	.2		.3	.1	.0			
0 UND	0 UND	0 UND		0 UND	0 UND	0 UND			
0 UND	0 UND	0 UND	Sales/Receivables	0 UND	2 210.0	1 695.5			
4 98.7	2 182.7	4 83.3		0 UND	15 24.8	5 74.6			
			Cost of Sales/Inventory						
			Cost of Sales/Payables						
7.4	9.9	6.6		6.8	6.5	5.4			
138.5	-133.8	-41.8	Sales/Working Capital	-43.4	-237.3	-37.5			
-6.9	-7.1	-6.3		-8.3	-4.0	-4.0			
9.1	5.3	7.8		2.6	15.8				
(74) 2.9	(67) 2.7	(65) 1.9	EBIT/Interest	(28) 1.2	(17) 2.7				
1.2	1.6	.9		.5	1.2				
11.8			Net Profit + Depr., Dep., Amort./Cur. Mat. L/T/D						
(12) 3.9									
.9									
1.2	1.0	1.2		3.2	.8	.4			
4.2	3.2	4.8	Fixed/Worth	7.2	4.0	6.1			
-42.0	-4.7	-4.0		-3.5	-4.7	-18.3			
.9	1.2	1.9		3.1	1.0	1.5			
4.9	3.6	6.0	Debt/Worth	9.6	3.7	6.2			
-34.4	-5.9	-7.1		-5.3	-6.8	-43.0			
51.2	53.6	31.5	% Profit Before Taxes/Tangible Net Worth	35.0	51.5				
(68) 19.5	(55) 25.1	(55) 11.0		(26) 6.3	(13) 13.6				
4.8	7.1	-1.3		-10.0	.3				
16.9	15.7	17.5	% Profit Before Taxes/Total Assets	6.9	21.1	42.7			
5.7	6.1	3.2		.6	4.9	13.8			
.9	1.3	-.8		-2.6	.2	1.4			
3.4	4.9	4.3	Sales/Net Fixed Assets	1.7	4.3	9.0			
1.3	1.8	1.0		.6	2.4	3.2			
.5	.7	.5		.4	.7	1.2			
1.6	2.1	1.7	Sales/Total Assets	1.1	2.0	2.4			
.8	1.1	.8		.5	1.3	1.3			
.4	.5	.4		.3	.6	.7			
4.3	3.6	3.9	% Depr., Dep., Amort./Sales	7.4	2.7				
(82) 7.8	(74) 7.1	(73) 7.5		(35) 12.8	(18) 5.7				
15.1	12.3	15.0		21.7	9.6				
3.4	3.0	3.8	% Officers', Directors' Owners' Comp/Sales	5.0	3.0				
(29) 6.8	(32) 7.8	(28) 5.9		(11) 10.2	(10) 5.9				
12.1	12.6	12.5		15.6	12.4				
300611M	236296M	405826M	Net Sales ($)	17299M	35570M	42882M	44694M	75650M	189731M
535683M	303749M	639304M	Total Assets ($)	35258M	39871M	41298M	76875M	247172M	198830M

M = $ thousand   MM = $ million
See Pages 11 through 21 for Explanation of Ratios and Data

	Current Data Sorted by Assets						Comparative Historical Data	
Type of Statement	0-500M	500M-2MM	2-10MM	10-50MM	50-100MM	100-250MM		
Unqualified		1	8	3	2	1	8	8
Reviewed		2	5				8	7
Compiled	2	3	2				11	17
Tax Returns	3	10	1				12	14
Other	3	3	6		2		8	12
		17 (4/1-9/30/06)		40 (10/1/06-3/31/07)			4/1/02-3/31/03 ALL	4/1/03-3/31/04 ALL
NUMBER OF STATEMENTS	8	19	22	3	4	1	47	58
ASSETS	%	%	%	%	%	%	%	%
Cash & Equivalents		10.6	10.9				8.8	10.2
Trade Receivables (net)		.4	2.0				1.0	3.3
Inventory		2.4	.2				1.3	1.6
All Other Current		1.0	2.1				5.1	3.6
Total Current		14.4	15.2				16.2	18.7
Fixed Assets (net)		73.3	71.2				72.3	68.1
Intangibles (net)		2.9	6.0				3.3	4.1
All Other Non-Current		9.5	7.7				8.3	9.0
Total		100.0	100.0				100.0	100.0
LIABILITIES								
Notes Payable-Short Term		3.9	2.0				13.5	13.4
Cur. Mat.-L.T.D.		4.1	4.4				4.3	3.7
Trade Payables		5.3	2.3				2.3	3.9
Income Taxes Payable		.0	.0				.0	.9
All Other Current		16.6	11.9				11.5	11.1
Total Current		30.0	20.6				31.6	33.0
Long-Term Debt		57.5	25.2				35.5	33.7
Deferred Taxes		.0	.0				.0	.1
All Other Non-Current		14.6	10.4				5.5	8.7
Net Worth		-2.1	43.8				27.3	24.5
Total Liabilties & Net Worth		100.0	100.0				100.0	100.0
INCOME DATA								
Net Sales		100.0	100.0				100.0	100.0
Gross Profit								
Operating Expenses		89.3	92.2				91.9	90.2
Operating Profit		10.7	7.8				8.1	9.8
All Other Expenses (net)		7.2	2.9				4.8	5.3
Profit Before Taxes		3.5	4.9				3.3	4.5
RATIOS								
Current		1.2	5.6				1.4	1.2
		.4	.8				.6	.7
		.2	.4				.2	.2
Quick		1.1	3.9				1.3	.9
		.2	.7				.3	.4
		.1	.2				.1	.1
Sales/Receivables	0	UND	0 UND				0 UND	0 UND
	0	UND	0 999.8				0 UND	0 UND
	1	472.5	10 36.6				2 199.3	6 60.2
Cost of Sales/Inventory								
Cost of Sales/Payables								
Sales/Working Capital		24.9	7.5				28.0	64.8
		-10.9	-65.4				-16.0	-26.4
		-3.6	-11.3				-3.8	-5.6
EBIT/Interest		8.7	6.8				(40) 5.2	(48) 5.5
	(17)	1.5	(18) 2.1				2.0	1.7
		-.1	-.2				.6	.3
Net Profit + Depr., Dep., Amort./Cur. Mat. L/T/D								
Fixed/Worth		2.5	1.2				1.2	1.4
		13.8	1.6				2.3	2.3
		-2.5	NM				-43.4	8.3
Debt/Worth		2.5	.5				.6	1.3
		14.5	1.4				1.9	3.1
		-4.2	NM				-49.8	13.4
% Profit Before Taxes/Tangible Net Worth		64.0	37.4				(35) 33.6	(45) 30.0
	(10)	5.9	(17) 10.0				10.0	10.7
		-4.5	-1.1				-3.1	.5
% Profit Before Taxes/Total Assets		12.4	9.7				12.7	8.8
		1.6	3.6				1.8	2.4
		-5.0	-1.7				-2.0	-3.5
Sales/Net Fixed Assets		3.1	1.7				4.0	3.6
		1.7	.7				1.4	1.7
		1.1	.4				.6	.8
Sales/Total Assets		2.5	1.3				2.2	1.9
		1.1	.6				1.0	1.1
		.9	.3				.5	.5
% Depr., Dep., Amort./Sales		3.7	5.4				(40) 3.5	(54) 3.6
	(17)	6.0	(18) 8.6				6.2	5.7
		7.6	15.1				10.1	9.2
% Officers', Directors' Owners' Comp/Sales							(16) 2.7	(20) 3.2
							7.3	5.6
							13.6	10.5
Net Sales ($)	5214M	25904M	97676M	22492M	124137M	47129M	85615M	272869M
Total Assets ($)	1626M	17222M	97453M	60975M	237116M	172210M	99409M	281001M

M = $ thousand   MM = $ million

See Pages 11 through 21 for Explanation of Ratios and Data

© RMA 2007

Comparative Historical Data | Current Data Sorted by Sales

			Type of Statement						
6	8	15	Unqualified	2	6		3	1	3
7	9	7	Reviewed	1	4	1	1		
11	12	7	Compiled	2	4			1	
20	9	14	Tax Returns	8	6				
14	16	14	Other	6	2	3	1		2
4/1/04-3/31/05 ALL	4/1/05-3/31/06 ALL	4/1/06-3/31/07 ALL		17 (4/1-9/30/06)		40 (10/1/06-3/31/07)			
				0-1MM	1-3MM	3-5MM	5-10MM	10-25MM	25MM & OVER
58	54	57	NUMBER OF STATEMENTS	19	22	4	5	2	5
%	%	%	ASSETS	%	%	%	%	%	%
10.5	10.0	15.2	Cash & Equivalents	17.0	12.6				
1.8	2.3	1.4	Trade Receivables (net)	.5	.9				
1.2	.8	1.1	Inventory	1.2	1.4				
1.1	2.2	1.2	All Other Current	.5	1.5				
14.6	15.3	18.9	Total Current	19.3	16.5				
74.0	67.3	65.3	Fixed Assets (net)	70.9	75.8				
1.5	5.2	5.2	Intangibles (net)	3.0	2.5				
9.9	12.2	10.7	All Other Non-Current	6.8	5.2				
100.0	100.0	100.0	Total	100.0	100.0				
			LIABILITIES						
6.2	3.6	2.1	Notes Payable-Short Term	3.6	.9				
3.0	3.8	4.6	Cur. Mat.-L.T.D.	5.1	3.2				
2.6	3.2	3.1	Trade Payables	.7	4.7				
.2	.3	.0	Income Taxes Payable	.0	.0				
8.7	7.2	13.5	All Other Current	17.8	13.6				
20.6	18.1	23.3	Total Current	27.3	22.4				
34.0	30.7	40.5	Long-Term Debt	44.4	43.7				
.1	.4	.0	Deferred Taxes	.0	.0				
10.4	9.6	11.6	All Other Non-Current	6.5	8.7				
34.8	41.3	24.6	Net Worth	21.9	25.2				
100.0	100.0	100.0	Total Liabilities & Net Worth	100.0	100.0				
			INCOME DATA						
100.0	100.0	100.0	Net Sales	100.0	100.0				
			Gross Profit						
89.9	86.4	88.2	Operating Expenses	86.0	94.2				
10.1	13.6	11.8	Operating Profit	14.0	5.8				
3.9	5.4	4.3	All Other Expenses (net)	9.4	1.6				
6.1	8.2	7.5	Profit Before Taxes	4.7	4.2				
			RATIOS						
1.3	1.7	3.7		6.8	2.1				
.5	.9	.7	Current	.6	.7				
.2	.4	.3		.2	.3				
1.2	1.6	3.2		4.5	1.4				
.3	.6	.6	Quick	.5	.6				
.1	.3	.2		.2	.1				
0 UND	0 UND	0 UND		0 UND	0 UND				
0 UND	0 UND	0 UND	Sales/Receivables	0 UND	0 UND				
3 120.7	5 74.9	8 47.7		1 257.0	7 54.7				
			Cost of Sales/Inventory						
			Cost of Sales/Payables						
24.3	26.4	8.6		7.7	10.6				
-22.2	-60.0	-42.8	Sales/Working Capital	-218.3	-21.2				
-6.0	-8.3	-10.0		-4.7	-10.2				
10.8	10.9	9.1		8.9	7.9				
(52) 2.2	(47) 2.5	(46) 1.5	EBIT/Interest	(13) 1.0	(20) 3.1				
.7	1.4	.1		-.4	.0				
	6.1								
	(11) 3.4		Net Profit + Depr., Dep., Amort./Cur. Mat. L/T/D						
	.9								
1.2	1.0	1.2		1.2	1.3				
2.1	1.7	2.5	Fixed/Worth	3.4	2.2				
6.7	4.3	-6.5		-4.6	NM				
.7	.6	.8		.5	.5				
1.8	1.6	2.8	Debt/Worth	4.2	2.1				
7.4	5.6	-10.7		-5.8	NM				
34.7	30.7	43.1		36.5	27.5				
(51) 10.5	(46) 6.7	(40) 7.4	% Profit Before Taxes/Tangible Net Worth	(13) 5.8	(17) 6.0				
2.3	.2	-1.2		-5.1	-1.0				
13.6	9.1	19.7		11.2	11.6				
2.8	2.9	2.7	% Profit Before Taxes/Total Assets	.3	2.5				
-.3	.2	-1.7		-3.3	-1.7				
2.2	2.9	3.3		4.6	2.6				
1.2	1.2	1.3	Sales/Net Fixed Assets	1.1	1.2				
.6	.7	.6		.4	.6				
1.6	1.6	1.6		1.8	1.9				
.9	.7	.7	Sales/Total Assets	.7	1.0				
.5	.4	.4		.2	.5				
4.7	3.9	4.5		5.1	3.4				
(49) 6.7	(48) 6.0	(46) 6.2	% Depr., Dep., Amort./Sales	(13) 6.8	(20) 6.2				
10.8	7.7	10.3		9.3	13.5				
4.9	4.1	3.3		2.0					
(21) 8.0	(20) 6.4	(17) 6.3	% Officers', Directors' Owners' Comp/Sales	(10) 5.6					
13.5	12.1	12.7		15.4					
227170M	266388M	322552M	Net Sales ($)	9673M	43494M	15899M	38910M	43310M	171266M
408781M	522977M	586602M	Total Assets ($)	18591M	54827M	19654M	73014M	11190M	409326M

M = $ thousand   MM = $ million
See Pages 11 through 21 for Explanation of Ratios and Data

RESTAURANT/LODGING—Full-Service Restaurants NAICS 722110 (SIC 5812)

Current Data Sorted by Assets						Type of Statement	Comparative Historical Data	
7	20	28	59	23	20	Unqualified	190	183
13	35	77	34	2	1	Reviewed	224	173
164	173	110	13	1	4	Compiled	629	649
636	315	79	13	1	9	Tax Returns	769	941
241	285	226	113	21	16	Other	775	680
	236 (4/1-9/30/06)		2,503 (10/1/06-3/31/07)				4/1/02-3/31/03	4/1/03-3/31/04
0-500M	500M-2MM	2-10MM	10-50MM	50-100MM	100-250MM		ALL	ALL
1061	828	520	232	48	50	NUMBER OF STATEMENTS	2587	2626
%	%	%	%	%	%	ASSETS	%	%
19.2	12.2	12.0	10.5	7.1	7.2	Cash & Equivalents	13.2	12.3
2.1	2.4	3.1	2.3	2.0	2.0	Trade Receivables (net)	2.6	2.8
8.8	4.7	4.0	3.1	2.8	4.2	Inventory	6.0	6.4
3.3	3.2	3.0	2.9	2.6	2.3	All Other Current	3.3	3.8
33.5	22.6	22.1	18.7	14.5	15.8	Total Current	25.1	25.3
47.1	56.1	58.0	61.0	64.7	52.0	Fixed Assets (net)	54.8	54.6
9.9	9.1	9.2	11.5	13.8	21.6	Intangibles (net)	9.8	9.8
9.6	12.1	10.7	8.7	7.0	10.7	All Other Non-Current	10.3	10.2
100.0	100.0	100.0	100.0	100.0	100.0	Total	100.0	100.0
						LIABILITIES		
7.6	3.7	3.9	2.7	3.0	4.0	Notes Payable-Short Term	5.6	5.0
4.4	3.8	4.5	5.2	4.5	3.1	Cur. Mat.-L.T.D.	5.7	5.0
12.8	8.9	7.9	7.0	9.0	6.1	Trade Payables	10.9	11.3
.1	.2	.1	.1	.1	.2	Income Taxes Payable	.2	.2
26.3	17.4	12.4	11.1	11.2	11.9	All Other Current	17.7	19.0
51.3	34.1	28.8	26.1	27.7	25.2	Total Current	40.0	40.5
27.1	39.0	39.2	41.7	38.0	52.0	Long-Term Debt	37.9	37.5
.0	.1	.1	.3	.5	1.5	Deferred Taxes	.1	.1
16.6	9.4	5.4	7.0	9.6	15.4	All Other Non-Current	10.3	11.4
5.1	17.4	26.6	24.9	24.2	5.9	Net Worth	11.7	10.5
100.0	100.0	100.0	100.0	100.0	100.0	Total Liabilties & Net Worth	100.0	100.0
						INCOME DATA		
100.0	100.0	100.0	100.0	100.0	100.0	Net Sales	100.0	100.0
59.7	60.9	60.3	59.6	53.4	56.3	Gross Profit	59.7	59.1
55.7	56.3	54.5	53.0	49.7	50.1	Operating Expenses	55.3	56.2
4.1	4.6	5.8	6.5	3.7	6.1	Operating Profit	4.4	2.9
.7	1.5	1.9	2.0	2.8	3.2	All Other Expenses (net)	1.5	1.2
3.3	3.0	3.8	4.5	1.0	2.9	Profit Before Taxes	2.9	1.7
						RATIOS		
1.9	1.5	1.4	1.2	.9	.9		1.4	1.4
.8	.7	.8	.6	.5	.5	Current	.7	.6
.3	.3	.4	.3	.3	.3		.3	.3
1.3	1.0	1.0	.8	.6	.6		.9	.8
(1050) .5	(818) .4	(516) .5	.4	.3	(48) .3	Quick	(2560) .4	(2594) .3
.1	.1	.2	.2	.2	.1		.1	.1
0 UND	0 UND	0 UND	0 UND	0 999.8	0 UND		0 UND	0 UND
0 UND	0 UND	1 540.6	1 297.3	2 175.9	2 208.7	Sales/Receivables	0 999.8	0 UND
0 999.8	2 221.8	4 97.1	4 85.2	7 55.2	6 64.3		2 213.4	2 194.1
4 81.2	6 57.6	6 59.2	6 61.5	5 66.6	7 55.9		6 58.8	6 58.7
9 40.4	11 34.0	10 37.6	10 36.5	10 37.6	11 34.6	Cost of Sales/Inventory	10 36.4	10 35.8
16 22.5	19 19.4	17 21.9	15 25.2	16 22.7	20 17.9		16 22.4	18 20.7
0 UND	5 76.8	11 33.0	15 23.6	16 22.3	9 39.3		7 55.5	6 61.4
11 33.1	21 17.4	23 15.7	27 13.5	24 15.1	24 15.1	Cost of Sales/Payables	21 17.6	21 17.7
27 13.5	39 9.4	43 8.5	47 7.8	51 7.1	46 7.9		38 9.6	39 9.3
40.0	37.1	31.1	69.1	-100.8	-77.8		53.6	54.0
-115.7	-48.6	-51.4	-24.2	-19.2	-18.5	Sales/Working Capital	-39.2	-36.6
-18.1	-12.7	-13.5	-12.3	-9.1	-10.0		-13.1	-12.2
14.0	8.8	8.1	6.6	2.7	4.9		8.1	6.9
(660) 3.9	(706) 3.0	(460) 3.0	(222) 2.8	(44) 1.5	(46) 1.9	EBIT/Interest	(2140) 2.8	(2120) 2.1
.8	.9	1.3	1.4	1.0	1.2		.9	.1
11.2	4.9	4.9	5.3	11.5	2.9		4.3	4.7
(13) 3.4	(37) 2.4	(57) 2.6	(62) 2.9	(21) 2.4	(10) 1.7	Net Profit + Depr., Dep., Amort./Cur. Mat. L/T/D	(245) 2.2	(217) 2.0
1.0	1.3	1.5	1.3	1.1	-2.1		1.3	1.1
.7	1.1	1.2	1.6	1.8	2.6		1.1	1.1
2.6	4.1	3.2	3.7	8.4	-8.8	Fixed/Worth	3.9	4.3
-1.7	-4.4	-19.0	-9.3	-4.5	-1.3		-3.2	-2.8
.7	1.0	1.1	1.3	1.7	2.9		1.1	1.2
5.3	5.7	4.1	4.3	8.3	-14.9	Debt/Worth	5.6	6.5
-3.3	-6.9	-25.1	-14.3	-6.4	-2.9		-5.4	-4.9
156.2	85.8	68.5	59.5	20.8	95.5	% Profit Before Taxes/Tangible Net Worth	86.4	73.8
(632) 60.0	(518) 33.4	(369) 31.1	(161) 28.6	(29) 11.5	(22) 25.3		(1630) 34.4	(1611) 26.1
15.9	8.7	7.6	9.7	-6.9	8.6		8.8	2.1
43.0	23.6	17.7	13.4	6.5	12.4	% Profit Before Taxes/Total Assets	22.2	17.3
15.6	8.1	7.3	7.2	1.8	4.8		7.7	4.8
.0	-.2	1.3	1.7	-1.5	1.4		-.3	-3.4
36.7	11.5	8.5	5.3	4.1	12.8		14.2	14.9
13.2	5.2	4.0	3.4	2.3	3.3	Sales/Net Fixed Assets	6.5	6.4
6.9	2.6	2.1	2.2	1.9	2.5		2.9	3.0
9.7	4.1	3.3	2.7	2.1	2.7		5.4	5.6
5.9	2.7	2.2	2.0	1.6	1.8	Sales/Total Assets	3.2	3.1
3.7	1.7	1.4	1.4	1.4	1.5		1.9	1.8
.8	1.5	1.9	2.3	3.4	1.0		1.6	1.6
(829) 1.6	(741) 2.5	(485) 2.8	(229) 3.2	(43) 4.1	(24) 3.1	% Depr., Dep., Amort./Sales	(2310) 2.8	(2295) 2.8
3.0	4.2	4.3	4.3	5.3	3.4		4.3	4.5
2.9	1.9	1.5	1.3		1.4		2.2	2.4
(560) 5.1	(324) 3.6	(187) 3.1	(41) 2.5		(15) 4.3	% Officers', Directors' Owners' Comp/Sales	(1109) 4.3	(1135) 4.6
8.7	6.6	6.2	6.7		10.3		7.9	8.1
1375907M	2625731M	5992368M	11348469M	6889755M	18699762M	Net Sales ($)	56967854M	55689509M
236656M	861395M	2322482M	5147746M	3413334M	7567158M	Total Assets ($)	21367639M	20469408M

M = $ thousand   MM = $ million
See Pages 11 through 21 for Explanation of Ratios and Data

	Comparative Historical Data			Current Data Sorted by Sales					
Type of Statement									
Unqualified	187	149	157	5	8	10	13	23	98
Reviewed	168	139	162	5	24	17	39	39	38
Compiled	525	443	465	69	201	70	56	51	18
Tax Returns	988	967	1053	346	492	111	57	23	24
Other	698	901	902	127	284	119	120	100	152
	4/1/04-3/31/05 ALL	4/1/05-3/31/06 ALL	4/1/06-3/31/07 ALL	236 (4/1-9/30/06) 0-1MM	2,503 (10/1/06-3/31/07) 1-3MM	3-5MM	5-10MM	10-25MM	25MM & OVER
NUMBER OF STATEMENTS	2566	2599	2739	552	1009	327	285	236	330
ASSETS	%	%	%	%	%	%	%	%	%
Cash & Equivalents	14.4	14.0	14.5	16.0	15.3	14.5	15.0	14.2	9.8
Trade Receivables (net)	2.6	2.6	2.4	1.4	2.1	2.7	3.8	3.6	2.8
Inventory	6.5	6.1	6.0	7.8	6.2	5.7	5.3	5.0	4.0
All Other Current	3.0	2.9	3.2	2.1	3.5	4.6	2.9	2.6	2.9
Total Current	26.4	25.6	26.1	27.4	27.1	27.6	27.1	25.4	19.5
Fixed Assets (net)	52.3	53.0	53.5	54.2	52.3	51.2	51.8	56.3	57.4
Intangibles (net)	10.6	10.7	9.9	9.6	9.8	7.6	9.5	9.5	13.7
All Other Non-Current	10.7	10.7	10.5	8.8	10.8	13.6	11.6	8.8	9.4
Total	100.0	100.0	100.0	100.0	100.0	100.0	100.0	100.0	100.0
LIABILITIES									
Notes Payable-Short Term	7.8	5.0	5.2	7.6	5.2	3.9	4.4	5.4	3.0
Cur. Mat.-L.T.D.	4.9	4.4	4.3	3.5	4.0	4.5	5.8	4.7	4.7
Trade Payables	11.1	11.1	10.0	7.4	11.1	12.9	10.2	9.0	8.5
Income Taxes Payable	.2	.3	.1	.0	.2	.1	.1	.1	.1
All Other Current	18.1	19.6	19.2	22.9	20.7	19.7	16.9	15.0	12.8
Total Current	42.1	40.3	38.8	41.4	41.2	41.1	37.4	34.4	29.1
Long-Term Debt	36.2	37.4	34.9	34.3	34.8	29.4	32.9	38.5	40.3
Deferred Taxes	.1	.1	.1	.0	.0	.0	.0	.2	.5
All Other Non-Current	10.6	11.5	11.3	18.0	11.9	10.0	7.4	2.7	9.3
Net Worth	11.0	10.7	14.9	6.3	12.1	19.5	22.2	24.3	20.7
Total Liabilities & Net Worth	100.0	100.0	100.0	100.0	100.0	100.0	100.0	100.0	100.0
INCOME DATA									
Net Sales	100.0	100.0	100.0	100.0	100.0	100.0	100.0	100.0	100.0
Gross Profit	59.0	59.2	60.0	60.3	60.0	61.7	61.7	59.3	56.7
Operating Expenses	54.9	54.6	55.2	56.9	55.5	56.2	55.7	53.5	51.4
Operating Profit	4.1	4.5	4.8	3.4	4.5	5.5	6.1	5.8	5.2
All Other Expenses (net)	1.2	1.2	1.4	1.7	1.4	.8	1.1	1.2	1.8
Profit Before Taxes	2.9	3.3	3.4	1.7	3.2	4.7	4.9	4.6	3.4
RATIOS									
Current	1.4	1.5	1.5	2.5	1.6	1.5	1.4	1.4	1.0
	.7	.7	.7	.8	.8	.8	.8	.8	.6
	.3	.3	.3	.3	.3	.3	.4	.4	.3
Quick	1.0	1.0	1.0	1.5	1.1	1.0	1.0	.9	.7
	(2538) .4	(2588) .4	(2712) .4	(546) .4	(994) .4	(326) .4	(284) .5	(235) .5	(327) .3
	.1	.1	.1	.1	.1	.1	.2	.2	.2
Sales/Receivables	0 UND	0 UND	0 UND	0 UND	0 UND	0 UND	0 UND	0 UND	0 999.8
	0 UND	0 UND	0 UND	0 UND	0 UND	0 999.8	1 601.3	1 354.7	1 280.5
	2 202.6	2 209.1	2 210.0	0 UND	1 427.0	2 148.7	3 124.0	4 84.4	4 87.4
Cost of Sales/Inventory	6 66.0	5 69.4	5 66.5	5 79.4	5 73.8	6 58.1	6 57.2	6 62.1	6 59.6
	10 37.9	10 37.9	10 37.0	12 31.3	9 39.0	10 38.0	10 35.6	9 41.0	10 36.9
	16 22.3	17 21.3	17 21.4	22 16.9	16 22.7	18 19.8	17 21.4	14 26.0	15 25.0
Cost of Sales/Payables	4 83.2	3 129.6	3 118.6	0 UND	1 327.6	9 42.6	12 31.7	11 32.0	14 26.0
	18 20.2	19 19.3	18 19.8	4 86.3	17 22.0	23 15.7	24 15.2	23 16.0	24 15.3
	36 10.0	38 9.5	36 10.1	25 14.6	33 10.9	45 8.1	43 8.6	38 9.5	42 8.7
Sales/Working Capital	55.8	40.9	40.1	30.8	41.7	36.9	37.1	47.9	NM
	-42.3	-47.5	-56.2	-90.9	-80.0	-64.1	-44.1	-54.0	-24.5
	-13.2	-13.1	-14.5	-13.7	-15.7	-14.6	-13.1	-15.7	-12.1
EBIT/Interest	9.2	8.7	9.1	6.5	9.2	13.4	12.9	9.8	6.5
	(1980) 2.9	(2020) 2.9	(2138) 3.0	(355) 1.7	(740) 2.7	(267) 4.8	(252) 4.2	(215) 3.8	(309) 2.6
	.7	.9	1.0	-.8	.8	1.9	1.5	1.6	1.4
Net Profit + Depr., Dep., Amort./Cur. Mat. L/T/D	5.3	5.3	5.3		4.6		4.9	4.1	6.1
	(190) 2.3	(190) 2.4	(200) 2.6		(32) 2.2		(21) 1.6	(34) 2.7	(100) 2.7
	1.3	1.3	1.4		1.2		.8	1.3	1.4
Fixed/Worth	1.1	1.1	1.0	.8	.9	.9	1.0	1.2	1.5
	4.3	4.5	3.4	4.5	4.0	2.4	2.4	3.3	4.4
	-2.5	-2.9	-3.8	-2.3	-3.0	-6.5	-10.8	-10.3	-4.4
Debt/Worth	1.2	1.2	1.0	.7	.9	.9	1.0	1.2	1.4
	5.9	6.5	5.1	8.3	6.6	3.1	3.2	3.9	5.4
	-4.8	-4.8	-6.1	-3.8	-9.8	-9.8	-11.5	-14.5	-6.2
% Profit Before Taxes/Tangible Net Worth	100.3	99.5	98.3	116.8	110.3	84.6	103.9	87.8	65.8
	(1567) 37.7	(1584) 39.6	(1731) 37.5	(316) 38.6	(615) 42.5	(227) 38.3	(201) 37.2	(161) 37.4	(211) 28.6
	8.1	8.4	9.8	8.3	9.7	12.6	8.5	12.1	9.3
% Profit Before Taxes/Total Assets	24.3	24.6	25.8	29.0	32.2	27.2	24.6	21.8	13.6
	7.6	7.8	9.2	7.7	10.0	12.1	12.4	9.6	6.3
	-1.1	-.3	.5	-5.7	.0	3.2	2.3	3.4	1.5
Sales/Net Fixed Assets	18.6	16.5	16.3	21.3	21.0	17.0	14.2	10.8	8.0
	7.3	6.9	6.8	7.5	8.5	7.3	5.8	5.4	4.0
	3.4	3.1	3.1	2.9	3.6	3.3	3.2	2.6	2.6
Sales/Total Assets	6.2	5.9	5.7	6.8	6.9	5.6	4.4	4.5	3.4
	3.5	3.3	3.3	3.7	3.9	3.2	2.9	2.8	2.4
	2.0	1.9	1.9	1.8	2.1	2.0	1.9	1.8	1.6
% Depr., Dep., Amort./Sales	1.4	1.3	1.3	1.1	1.1	1.2	1.2	1.7	2.2
	(2189) 2.5	(2237) 2.3	(2351) 2.4	(438) 2.4	(837) 2.2	(298) 2.3	(263) 2.3	(225) 2.5	(290) 3.0
	4.1	3.8	3.9	4.4	3.8	3.4	3.8	3.5	4.0
% Officers', Directors' Owners' Comp/Sales	2.1	2.3	2.3	3.4	2.4	2.6	1.6	1.3	1.1
	(1155) 4.0	(1097) 4.4	(1132) 4.3	(281) 5.7	(468) 4.2	(124) 4.3	(117) 2.8	(76) 2.2	(66) 3.2
	7.0	7.6	7.9	10.2	7.4	7.7	5.0	4.3	7.9
Net Sales ($)	44394445M	53335888M	46931992M	349260M	1815588M	1257116M	1994797M	3736146M	37779085M
Total Assets ($)	17140085M	18934876M	19548771M	163692M	698573M	528078M	832712M	1605361M	15720355M

M = $ thousand   MM = $ million
See Pages 11 through 21 for Explanation of Ratios and Data

Current Data Sorted by Assets   Comparative Historical Data

						Type of Statement		
1	5	14	46	13	17	Unqualified	16	54
5	12	39	19	2		Reviewed	8	57
76	64	51	9	1	2	Compiled	38	126
169	51	29	5	1	4	Tax Returns	66	198
74	79	90	61	13	10	Other	43	154
	89 (4/1-9/30/06)		873 (10/1/06-3/31/07)				4/1/02-3/31/03 ALL	4/1/03-3/31/04 ALL
0-500M	500M-2MM	2-10MM	10-50MM	50-100MM	100-250MM	NUMBER OF STATEMENTS	171	589
325	211	223	140	30	33			
%	%	%	%	%	%	ASSETS	%	%
18.9	14.2	14.2	9.4	9.0	9.2	Cash & Equivalents	12.4	13.7
.9	1.5	1.4	2.0	.8	1.9	Trade Receivables (net)	.9	1.4
5.9	2.9	2.5	2.1	2.1	3.3	Inventory	3.3	3.8
3.5	3.3	2.4	4.1	3.7	2.2	All Other Current	2.6	3.5
29.1	21.8	20.5	17.6	15.6	16.6	Total Current	19.2	22.4
49.5	56.3	55.3	55.4	64.2	54.7	Fixed Assets (net)	57.0	55.0
14.7	14.4	14.8	16.8	14.7	23.9	Intangibles (net)	14.2	12.6
6.7	7.5	9.4	10.2	5.5	4.9	All Other Non-Current	9.6	10.0
100.0	100.0	100.0	100.0	100.0	100.0	Total	100.0	100.0
						LIABILITIES		
7.7	4.6	2.8	1.4	3.1	1.9	Notes Payable-Short Term	5.6	5.8
4.9	5.5	6.0	6.3	4.4	5.3	Cur. Mat.-L.T.D.	6.0	6.8
9.4	6.8	7.6	7.4	4.6	7.8	Trade Payables	7.4	9.3
.1	.1	.1	.1	.3	.2	Income Taxes Payable	.2	.3
18.2	14.7	11.9	10.2	9.5	14.5	All Other Current	16.9	14.0
40.4	31.6	28.4	25.5	21.9	29.8	Total Current	36.1	36.4
40.6	42.9	42.3	46.1	44.6	62.3	Long-Term Debt	45.6	41.9
.0	.3	.2	.3	.6	1.4	Deferred Taxes	.2	.1
12.0	8.9	5.4	5.3	6.0	17.4	All Other Non-Current	8.3	8.7
7.0	16.3	23.7	22.7	26.9	-10.9	Net Worth	9.9	12.9
100.0	100.0	100.0	100.0	100.0	100.0	Total Liabilities & Net Worth	100.0	100.0
						INCOME DATA		
100.0	100.0	100.0	100.0	100.0	100.0	Net Sales	100.0	100.0
59.6	58.7	60.1	62.0	64.8	54.1	Gross Profit	60.3	62.1
56.0	52.8	54.6	55.5	59.0	48.4	Operating Expenses	55.6	58.1
3.5	5.9	5.4	6.5	5.8	5.7	Operating Profit	4.7	4.0
.9	2.0	1.2	2.2	2.2	2.7	All Other Expenses (net)	1.6	1.5
2.6	3.8	4.2	4.3	3.6	3.0	Profit Before Taxes	3.0	2.5
						RATIOS		
2.0	1.5	1.3	1.1	1.1	1.1		1.5	1.5
.9	.7	.6	.6	.6	.6	Current	.6	.6
.3	.2	.4	.3	.3	.3		.3	.2
1.4	1.0	1.0	.8	.8	.8		1.2	1.1
(322) .5	(209) .5	(222) .5	.3	.4	.4	Quick	(170) .4	(580) .4
.1	.1	.2	.2	.2	.2		.1	.1
0 UND	0 UND	0 UND	0 UND	0 UND	0 946.0		0 UND	0 UND
0 UND	0 UND	0 999.8	1 607.0	1 683.3	1 371.0	Sales/Receivables	0 UND	0 UND
0 UND	1 469.5	1 400.3	2 149.2	3 134.9	7 52.3		1 599.0	1 446.0
4 81.6	4 88.5	5 78.0	6 64.5	6 60.5	5 68.4		5 78.5	6 65.0
8 46.5	8 48.1	8 44.3	8 44.9	9 41.0	8 43.0	Cost of Sales/Inventory	7 49.6	9 40.6
13 28.9	12 30.1	11 32.7	11 32.5	13 27.3	14 26.2		12 31.3	12 29.4
0 UND	3 114.5	11 33.6	16 23.3	18 20.5	10 35.5		5 75.0	7 55.6
8 45.7	15 24.7	21 17.1	29 12.7	24 15.4	24 15.1	Cost of Sales/Payables	16 22.2	18 19.8
20 17.9	32 11.6	36 10.1	44 8.3	38 9.7	43 8.5		30 12.3	34 10.6
44.3	49.1	57.4	69.2	84.3	153.5		50.9	48.0
-270.5	-42.7	-32.2	-27.6	-25.3	-29.2	Sales/Working Capital	-46.5	-35.6
-18.3	-10.5	-13.9	-13.8	-11.7	-10.9		-14.1	-12.0
8.0	9.3	8.5	6.2	6.3	3.4		6.2	7.1
(219) 2.3	(192) 3.7	(207) 3.4	(136) 2.7	(27) 1.8	(31) 1.5	EBIT/Interest	(149) 2.2	(517) 2.2
.1	1.3	1.6	1.5	1.1	1.1		1.0	.6
	6.0	5.6	3.4	3.2			4.7	3.3
	(11) 2.4	(32) 1.9	(34) 1.7	(11) 2.7		Net Profit + Depr., Dep., Amort./Cur. Mat. L/T/D	(18) 2.1	(60) 1.6
	1.4	1.4	1.4	1.3			1.5	.9
1.0	1.4	1.4	1.6	2.2	3.1		1.5	1.4
6.0	5.4	4.8	10.7	5.3	-10.2	Fixed/Worth	16.2	5.9
-1.1	-2.2	-2.9	-2.7	-7.9	-.8		-2.6	-3.0
.9	1.4	1.1	1.5	1.7	4.1		1.6	1.5
11.2	5.9	6.3	11.7	6.1	-11.7	Debt/Worth	26.7	8.0
-2.9	-4.4	-6.1	-4.9	-10.2	-1.9		-4.4	-4.7
138.3	92.0	80.9	58.6	80.2	74.3		118.8	83.3
(183) 56.8	(125) 37.5	(132) 36.8	(76) 36.3	(19) 20.8	(13) 22.2	% Profit Before Taxes/Tangible Net Worth	(95) 52.6	(345) 30.4
4.5	12.1	18.7	18.4	-2.4	6.6		8.1	5.7
39.3	24.4	19.4	15.5	11.3	10.1		20.6	17.5
10.1	9.4	9.8	7.4	3.7	3.6	% Profit Before Taxes/Total Assets	5.9	6.0
-2.5	1.0	2.5	2.5	-.5	.4		-.2	-1.4
26.3	11.4	9.0	7.0	4.1	8.3		10.9	12.8
11.1	5.9	5.7	3.5	2.1	3.4	Sales/Net Fixed Assets	5.5	6.0
4.9	3.1	2.8	2.4	1.7	2.5		2.8	2.9
8.2	4.4	3.9	2.7	2.1	3.8		4.6	5.1
5.0	3.1	2.8	2.0	1.5	1.6	Sales/Total Assets	3.0	3.0
2.8	1.8	1.7	1.4	1.3	1.3		1.9	1.8
1.2	1.6	2.1	2.4	2.7	3.4		2.2	2.1
(260) 2.4	(192) 2.7	(213) 2.9	(135) 3.2	(29) 3.9	(16) 3.8	% Depr., Dep., Amort./Sales	(156) 3.5	(530) 3.2
4.8	4.2	4.0	4.3	5.0	4.1		5.0	4.6
2.8	1.9	1.4	.6				1.5	2.0
(162) 5.0	(84) 3.4	(81) 2.3	(22) 1.4			% Officers', Directors' Owners' Comp/Sales	(64) 4.0	(252) 3.7
7.9	5.5	4.4	3.8				6.9	6.2
359974M	795761M	3038143M	6712977M	4306424M	14595227M	Net Sales ($)	2941816M	7505302M
72438M	228400M	1068120M	3242393M	2153631M	5247637M	Total Assets ($)	1325349M	3802680M

© RMA 2007   M = $ thousand   MM = $ million
See Pages 11 through 21 for Explanation of Ratios and Data

Comparative Historical Data | Current Data Sorted by Sales

				Type of Statement						
32		47	96	Unqualified	1	2	2	4	15	72
37		54	77	Reviewed	2	6	2	20	26	21
115		141	203	Compiled	46	54	20	36	31	16
171		244	259	Tax Returns	119	87	14	15	16	8
150		249	327	Other	49	68	39	40	46	85
4/1/04- 3/31/05 ALL		4/1/05- 3/31/06 ALL	4/1/06- 3/31/07 ALL		89 (4/1-9/30/06)			873 (10/1/06-3/31/07)		
505		735	962	NUMBER OF STATEMENTS	0-1MM 217	1-3MM 217	3-5MM 77	5-10MM 115	10-25MM 134	25MM & OVER 202
%		%	%	ASSETS	%	%	%	%	%	%
14.1		14.6	14.8	Cash & Equivalents	15.2	18.6	15.7	14.8	14.2	10.1
1.5		1.1	1.3	Trade Receivables (net)	.9	.6	2.4	1.9	1.5	1.5
4.2		3.9	3.7	Inventory	5.0	4.3	3.3	3.0	3.0	2.6
4.0		3.3	3.2	All Other Current	2.1	4.7	3.7	3.3	3.1	2.8
23.8		23.0	23.0	Total Current	23.2	28.3	25.0	23.0	21.9	17.0
51.5		52.6	53.8	Fixed Assets (net)	56.7	48.4	54.2	52.0	54.0	57.2
14.9		15.5	15.3	Intangibles (net)	14.5	14.9	15.4	14.2	14.8	17.5
9.8		8.9	7.9	All Other Non-Current	5.7	8.3	5.4	10.7	9.4	8.3
100.0		100.0	100.0	Total	100.0	100.0	100.0	100.0	100.0	100.0
				LIABILITIES						
6.9		3.7	4.6	Notes Payable-Short Term	7.9	5.0	7.9	3.2	2.3	1.7
6.6		4.9	5.5	Cur. Mat.-L.T.D.	5.5	3.9	4.0	7.9	6.1	6.0
8.2		9.4	7.9	Trade Payables	8.0	7.8	7.1	8.1	9.5	7.2
.4		.2	.1	Income Taxes Payable	.1	.1	.0	.2	.1	.2
14.7		14.4	14.4	All Other Current	13.8	17.8	17.0	14.4	12.2	12.1
36.8		32.6	32.6	Total Current	35.2	34.5	36.1	33.7	30.2	27.3
43.3		44.9	43.2	Long-Term Debt	51.5	35.3	33.7	42.4	43.3	46.7
.1		.1	.2	Deferred Taxes	.0	.0	.7	.2	.2	.6
9.8		11.1	8.8	All Other Non-Current	13.2	9.0	7.9	6.4	5.7	7.7
10.0		11.3	15.2	Net Worth	.0	21.2	21.7	17.4	20.5	17.7
100.0		100.0	100.0	Total Liabilties & Net Worth	100.0	100.0	100.0	100.0	100.0	100.0
				INCOME DATA						
100.0		100.0	100.0	Net Sales	100.0	100.0	100.0	100.0	100.0	100.0
61.3		62.0	59.8	Gross Profit	59.3	60.7	58.9	57.4	60.2	60.9
57.5		57.4	54.8	Operating Expenses	56.1	55.2	52.5	52.3	54.7	55.1
3.8		4.5	5.1	Operating Profit	3.2	5.5	6.4	5.1	5.5	5.8
1.1		1.2	1.5	All Other Expenses (net)	2.0	1.0	1.8	1.3	1.0	1.8
2.7		3.3	3.6	Profit Before Taxes	1.2	4.5	4.5	3.8	4.5	4.0
				RATIOS						
1.6		1.5	1.5	Current	1.9	2.0	1.7	1.3	1.2	1.1
.7		.7	.7		.8	.9	.8	.6	.6	.6
.3		.3	.3		.3	.4	.2	.3	.4	.3
1.1		1.0	1.1	Quick	1.3	1.4	1.3	.9	1.0	.8
(499) .4	(724)	.4	(956) .5		(216) .4	(215) .5	(75) .6	(114) .4	.5	.4
.1		.1	.1		.1	.1	.1	.2	.2	.2
0 UND	0	UND	0 UND		0 UND	0 UND	0 UND	0 UND	0 UND	0 999.8
0 UND	0	UND	0 UND	Sales/Receivables	0 UND	0 UND	0 999.8	0 999.8	0 999.8	1 526.5
1 587.5	1	483.5	1 400.3		0 950.0	0 999.8	1 410.6	1 354.1	1 364.3	2 151.2
5 67.2	5	66.5	5 78.3		5 73.2	4 92.9	4 91.6	4 88.3	5 78.1	6 63.2
8 43.0	8	43.0	8 45.8	Cost of Sales/Inventory	10 38.1	7 49.3	8 47.0	7 50.0	8 47.2	9 42.5
12 30.0	12	30.0	12 30.9		15 23.7	11 33.0	12 31.1	11 34.4	11 34.0	12 31.5
4 83.6	3	104.3	6 65.4		0 UND	2 161.2	3 105.8	9 40.4	11 34.2	14 25.4
16 23.3	16	22.5	17 22.0	Cost of Sales/Payables	7 54.0	12 29.6	16 22.5	20 18.5	21 17.4	25 14.6
31 11.8	36	10.2	32 11.4		19 18.8	27 13.7	33 11.0	31 11.9	36 10.3	40 11.5
42.9		55.3	54.7		44.3	32.3	38.8	56.6	68.1	289.0
-48.9		-53.0	-52.7	Sales/Working Capital	-111.5	-254.8	-67.9	-31.2	-35.9	-27.8
-13.7		-15.0	-14.3		-10.7	-19.7	-12.5	-13.4	-14.9	-13.0
7.8		7.8	7.6		5.5	9.5	10.8	7.1	9.2	6.5
(427) 2.8	(607)	3.0	(812) 2.9	EBIT/Interest	(157) 1.3	(162) 3.6	(67) 4.7	(107) 3.2	(126) 4.2	(193) 2.7
1.0		1.3	1.0		-.4	1.1	1.5	1.4	1.9	1.3
3.4		2.9	4.3	Net Profit + Depr., Dep.,				2.3	6.0	5.2
(33) 1.5	(57)	1.7	(97) 2.1	Amort./Cur. Mat. L/T/D			(10) 1.4	(24) 2.3	(54) 2.2	
1.0		1.0	1.4				.4	1.6	1.5	
1.3		1.3	1.3		1.3	1.0	1.0	1.3	1.4	1.9
9.6		11.6	6.5	Fixed/Worth	14.9	3.8	8.6	5.2	3.6	14.1
-2.1		-1.9	-2.0		-1.0	-2.6	-1.5	-3.3	-2.0	-2.7
1.7		1.6	1.2		1.2	.9	.9	1.6	1.2	1.7
12.7		20.0	9.0	Debt/Worth	32.0	5.6	8.0	5.9	4.7	19.3
-3.8		-3.5	-4.0		-2.6	-5.0	-3.7	-4.9	-4.7	-4.5
107.8		115.4	98.0	% Profit Before Taxes/Tangible	100.4	141.9	71.8	105.4	86.1	76.5
(285) 39.1	(398)	42.7	(548) 38.8	Net Worth	(114) 36.9	(133) 48.1	(41) 34.3	(72) 37.2	(83) 37.4	(105) 37.1
11.5		12.6	13.4		-.1	11.0	17.1	19.0	18.7	16.6
20.6		23.5	22.9	% Profit Before Taxes/Total	23.3	35.6	24.9	17.9	22.2	16.2
7.2		8.7	8.9	Assets	4.5	13.1	11.0	9.8	12.0	6.9
.0		.9	.4		-6.7	1.5	1.4	2.2	4.2	1.5
14.4		14.1	12.4		17.1	20.0	12.2	11.6	10.9	7.6
6.8		6.4	6.1	Sales/Net Fixed Assets	5.4	8.9	6.2	7.2	6.3	4.2
3.2		3.1	2.9		2.5	4.5	3.8	3.7	3.7	2.5
5.2		5.2	5.0		5.7	7.5	4.7	4.3	4.8	3.5
3.1		3.0	3.0	Sales/Total Assets	2.9	4.1	3.2	3.2	3.1	2.2
1.9		1.8	1.8		1.7	2.2	1.9	2.0	2.1	1.5
2.0		1.7	1.8		1.5	1.2	1.5	1.8	1.8	2.4
(444) 3.2	(648)	2.9	(845) 2.9	% Depr., Dep., Amort./Sales	(177) 3.6	(181) 2.3	(69) 2.9	(109) 3.0	(126) 2.5	(183) 3.2
4.7		4.2	4.3		6.3	3.8	4.2	3.9	3.7	4.1
2.0		2.1	1.9	% Officers', Directors'	3.1	2.1	1.9	1.8	1.0	.8
(209) 4.1	(278)	3.9	(358) 3.6	Owners' Comp/Sales	(101) 5.7	(104) 4.0	(29) 2.9	(44) 2.8	(49) 1.8	(31) 2.6
6.7		6.5	6.3		10.7	5.9	5.7	4.0	2.9	5.0
7781450M		16201240M	29808506M	Net Sales ($)	125812M	391207M	301082M	820241M	2150872M	26019292M
3043631M		6456397M	12012619M	Total Assets ($)	60667M	145917M	127700M	375534M	828430M	10474371M

© RMA 2007

M = $ thousand   MM = $ million
See Pages 11 through 21 for Explanation of Ratios and Data

Current Data Sorted by Assets / Comparative Historical Data

0-500M	500M-2MM	2-10MM	10-50MM	50-100MM	100-250MM	Type of Statement	4/1/02-3/31/03 ALL	4/1/03-3/31/04 ALL
			3		4	Unqualified	1	5
	3	4				Reviewed	2	2
6	2	1	1	1		Compiled	6	8
30	10	2				Tax Returns	9	22
15	16	2	1		3	Other	2	3
0-500M	3 (4/1-9/30/06) 500M-2MM	2-10MM	101 (10/1/06-3/31/07) 10-50MM	50-100MM	100-250MM			
51	31	9	5	1	7	NUMBER OF STATEMENTS	20	40
%	%	%	%	%	%	ASSETS	%	%
15.3	8.5					Cash & Equivalents	12.1	9.2
.2	1.7					Trade Receivables (net)	2.7	2.3
5.8	2.4					Inventory	4.8	4.5
1.1	.3					All Other Current	1.9	.6
22.4	12.8					Total Current	21.4	16.6
46.0	52.1					Fixed Assets (net)	53.7	50.2
15.5	16.9					Intangibles (net)	9.8	17.4
16.1	18.1					All Other Non-Current	15.0	15.8
100.0	100.0					Total	100.0	100.0
						LIABILITIES		
11.0	12.5					Notes Payable-Short Term	1.5	5.8
8.1	4.7					Cur. Mat.-L.T.D.	9.3	6.9
4.3	6.0					Trade Payables	8.3	9.2
.3	.0					Income Taxes Payable	.1	.1
17.9	8.5					All Other Current	5.4	18.8
41.6	31.8					Total Current	24.6	40.8
34.5	41.9					Long-Term Debt	27.1	51.6
.0	.0					Deferred Taxes	.7	.2
8.6	15.2					All Other Non-Current	6.1	16.8
15.2	11.1					Net Worth	41.6	-9.3
100.0	100.0					Total Liabilities & Net Worth	100.0	100.0
						INCOME DATA		
100.0	100.0					Net Sales	100.0	100.0
						Gross Profit		
91.9	90.8					Operating Expenses	91.0	95.3
8.1	9.2					Operating Profit	9.0	4.7
.7	3.8					All Other Expenses (net)	1.7	4.2
7.4	5.3					Profit Before Taxes	7.3	.5
						RATIOS		
2.2	1.5					Current	1.3	1.0
.9	.5						.8	.5
.1	.1						.4	.3
1.8	1.3					Quick	1.0	.9
(50) .7	.5						(39) .6	.3
.1	.0						.2	.1
0 UND	0 UND					Sales/Receivables	0 UND	0 UND
0 UND	0 UND						0 UND	0 UND
0 UND	1 290.9						4 92.4	3 135.7
						Cost of Sales/Inventory		
						Cost of Sales/Payables		
30.3	39.6					Sales/Working Capital	63.1	287.4
-189.3	-31.6						-49.4	-33.5
-8.9	-9.4						-20.0	-12.5
10.0	12.1					EBIT/Interest	9.3	7.7
(33) 4.5	(28) 3.1						(18) 4.2	(29) 2.0
1.7	1.2						2.0	-2.7
						Net Profit + Depr., Dep., Amort./Cur. Mat. L/T/D		
.6	1.4					Fixed/Worth	1.2	1.1
3.3	14.2						1.7	10.5
-1.2	-1.2						4.1	-1.4
.6	1.0					Debt/Worth	.8	1.7
5.1	22.6						1.8	28.0
-3.2	-2.6						5.1	-2.5
181.5	80.0					% Profit Before Taxes/Tangible Net Worth	90.1	100.0
(30) 79.2	(17) 31.5						(17) 16.9	(22) 46.7
34.6	16.0						5.7	12.5
38.1	20.1					% Profit Before Taxes/Total Assets	45.6	20.7
19.8	7.6						12.5	7.1
5.2	1.1						2.9	-11.6
16.5	7.1					Sales/Net Fixed Assets	9.0	12.4
7.1	3.0						6.0	5.2
4.8	2.2						4.2	3.0
4.9	2.7					Sales/Total Assets	4.3	4.1
3.2	1.9						3.4	2.7
2.4	1.2						2.4	1.8
1.6	2.2					% Depr., Dep., Amort./Sales	2.2	2.5
(42) 3.5	(29) 3.7						(18) 3.4	(36) 4.0
5.2	8.4						4.5	6.8
2.1	1.9					% Officers', Directors' Owners' Comp/Sales	1.9	2.0
(19) 4.2	(10) 4.9						(14) 3.6	(24) 4.0
8.8	9.4						9.2	5.7
36473M	55210M	109145M	214633M	697861M	2837992M	Net Sales ($)	55584M	308910M
11631M	30153M	41511M	147220M	96398M	893808M	Total Assets ($)	18379M	179914M

M = $ thousand   MM = $ million
See Pages 11 through 21 for Explanation of Ratios and Data

Comparative Historical Data | Current Data Sorted by Sales

			Type of Statement						
4	5	7	Unqualified						7
1	2	7	Reviewed	1	2	2		2	
1	14	10	Compiled	5	4		1		
11	19	42	Tax Returns	26	12	1	1	2	
12	11	38	Other	16	12	3		3	4
4/1/04-3/31/05	4/1/05-3/31/06	4/1/06-3/31/07				3 (4/1-9/30/06)	101 (10/1/06-3/31/07)		
ALL	ALL	ALL		0-1MM	1-3MM	3-5MM	5-10MM	10-25MM	25MM & OVER
29	51	104	**NUMBER OF STATEMENTS**	48	30	6	2	7	11
%	%	%	**ASSETS**	%	%	%	%	%	%
7.9	10.8	11.8	Cash & Equivalents	13.9	11.1				6.3
6.4	4.1	2.5	Trade Receivables (net)	.2	.6				5.6
4.5	4.3	4.8	Inventory	5.1	2.6				4.2
1.1	3.0	1.2	All Other Current	.9	.5				4.3
19.9	22.3	20.3	Total Current	20.2	14.8				20.4
59.7	53.5	48.4	Fixed Assets (net)	49.0	46.9				51.0
7.2	14.2	15.7	Intangibles (net)	15.2	18.9				18.8
13.3	10.0	15.6	All Other Non-Current	15.6	19.3				9.9
100.0	100.0	100.0	Total	100.0	100.0				100.0
			LIABILITIES						
10.6	3.5	10.4	Notes Payable-Short Term	13.0	10.3				7.2
5.1	7.4	6.5	Cur. Mat.-L.T.D.	7.6	6.6				3.0
7.7	6.8	5.9	Trade Payables	2.9	7.6				7.1
.0	.0	.2	Income Taxes Payable	.3	.1				.0
14.8	11.5	15.3	All Other Current	15.9	11.7				21.6
38.2	29.1	38.3	Total Current	39.7	36.4				39.0
42.2	41.2	36.1	Long-Term Debt	42.9	31.9				27.7
.2	.0	.1	Deferred Taxes	.0	.0				1.0
17.4	12.4	11.8	All Other Non-Current	10.1	11.4				19.2
1.9	17.2	13.7	Net Worth	7.2	20.4				13.1
100.0	100.0	100.0	Total Liabilties & Net Worth	100.0	100.0				100.0
			INCOME DATA						
100.0	100.0	100.0	Net Sales	100.0	100.0				100.0
			Gross Profit						
94.0	93.8	92.5	Operating Expenses	90.8	92.7				95.1
6.0	6.2	7.5	Operating Profit	9.2	7.3				4.9
2.4	2.3	1.9	All Other Expenses (net)	2.3	1.4				2.9
3.6	3.9	5.6	Profit Before Taxes	6.8	5.8				2.0
			RATIOS						
1.6	1.7	1.6		2.3	1.2				1.1
.7	.8	.7	Current	1.0	.5				.5
.4	.3	.1		.1	.1				.3
.9	1.1	1.3		1.9	1.2				.7
(28) .4	.4	(103) .5	Quick	.7	(29) .5				.3
.1	.1	.1		.0	.0				.1
0 UND	0 UND	0 UND		0 UND	0 UND			0	825.4
0 UND	0 UND	0 UND	Sales/Receivables	0 UND	0 UND			3	123.4
7 53.3	2 174.1	1 284.2		0 UND	1 332.6			26	13.9
			Cost of Sales/Inventory						
			Cost of Sales/Payables						
60.6	26.7	45.8		25.3	183.3				162.1
-55.5	-67.9	-51.7	Sales/Working Capital	NM	-26.7				-43.6
-12.0	-14.3	-9.3		-8.1	-9.4				-5.9
7.1	9.6	8.4		5.3	12.9				8.4
(26) 2.6	(44) 2.8	(83) 2.7	EBIT/Interest	(32) 2.2	(25) 5.4				1.9
.7	.4	1.5		1.1	1.9				.6
			Net Profit + Depr., Dep., Amort./Cur. Mat. L/T/D						
1.3	1.2	1.0		.8	.8				1.2
3.2	13.4	6.0	Fixed/Worth	-7.9	1.5				2.2
-1.5	-1.8	-1.2		-1.3	-1.0				-.3
1.0	1.3	.9		1.0	.8				.5
12.1	16.6	10.1	Debt/Worth	-14.9	3.1				2.6
-2.9	-3.9	-3.2		-3.2	-2.2				-1.6
53.2	60.8	139.8		164.7	146.9				
(16) 24.4	(27) 33.7	(61) 56.8	% Profit Before Taxes/Tangible Net Worth	(23) 52.9	(20) 61.2				
5.3	-1.9	17.7		22.4	21.7				
25.9	23.5	24.9		24.9	36.3				22.6
9.6	8.6	8.4	% Profit Before Taxes/Total Assets	7.2	17.3				3.0
.2	-2.8	1.7		.2	5.4				-6.3
10.1	11.0	12.0		12.8	12.4				11.5
5.0	5.4	6.3	Sales/Net Fixed Assets	5.8	6.3				7.9
2.4	2.3	2.9		2.5	3.0				3.3
4.9	3.5	4.0		4.2	3.9				4.9
2.7	2.4	2.6	Sales/Total Assets	2.6	2.5				2.8
1.5	1.6	1.6		1.6	1.9				1.7
1.7	2.6	2.2		2.4	1.8				
(21) 2.9	(42) 3.7	(85) 3.7	% Depr., Dep., Amort./Sales	(40) 4.2	(27) 3.3				
4.7	6.1	5.3		7.0	4.4				
2.5	2.4	2.1		2.9	1.5				
(15) 5.3	(21) 5.1	(32) 4.4	% Officers', Directors' Owners' Comp/Sales	(15) 5.3	(12) 4.3				
8.9	7.2	8.7		10.2	5.9				
453279M	1019027M	3951314M	Net Sales ($)	26493M	47093M	22973M	13268M	110203M	3731284M
222356M	539396M	1220721M	Total Assets ($)	15920M	22172M	11547M	14017M	71789M	1085276M

© RMA 2007

M = $ thousand   MM = $ million
See Pages 11 through 21 for Explanation of Ratios and Data

Current Data Sorted by Assets

Comparative Historical Data

	0-500M	500M-2MM	2-10MM	10-50MM	50-100MM	100-250MM	Type of Statement	4/1/02-3/31/03 ALL	4/1/03-3/31/04 ALL
	2		1	1	2		Unqualified	2	1
			1				Reviewed	1	4
			2				Compiled	5	4
			1				Tax Returns	3	3
	2		2	4	2		Other	2	2
		9 (4/1-9/30/06)		29 (10/1/06-3/31/07)					
NUMBER OF STATEMENTS	4	7	18	5	4			13	14
	%	%	%	%	%	%		%	%
							ASSETS		
			17.8				Cash & Equivalents	17.0	11.7
			28.7				Trade Receivables (net)	24.2	27.4
			8.2				Inventory	9.1	5.7
			3.3				All Other Current	4.8	2.9
			58.0				Total Current	55.0	47.8
			21.8				Fixed Assets (net)	28.1	33.5
			3.3				Intangibles (net)	11.2	5.6
			16.9				All Other Non-Current	5.7	13.2
			100.0				Total	100.0	100.0
							LIABILITIES		
			7.1				Notes Payable-Short Term	7.6	8.7
			2.5				Cur. Mat.-L.T.D.	3.9	5.7
			18.8				Trade Payables	11.9	14.6
			.9				Income Taxes Payable	.5	.4
			17.1				All Other Current	16.9	20.8
			46.4				Total Current	40.9	50.1
			17.3				Long-Term Debt	18.9	28.7
			.1				Deferred Taxes	.3	1.4
			1.5				All Other Non-Current	6.1	32.8
			34.6				Net Worth	33.8	-13.0
			100.0				Total Liabilties & Net Worth	100.0	100.0
							INCOME DATA		
			100.0				Net Sales	100.0	100.0
							Gross Profit		
			96.3				Operating Expenses	97.8	96.2
			3.7				Operating Profit	2.2	3.8
			.5				All Other Expenses (net)	1.3	1.2
			3.3				Profit Before Taxes	.9	2.6
							RATIOS		
			1.8				Current	1.8	1.9
			1.3					1.2	1.3
			.8					.6	.4
			1.6				Quick	1.4	1.6
			.8					.7	1.0
			.5					.2	.2
		9	42.4				Sales/Receivables	1 639.7	2 227.6
		15	25.1					6 58.8	19 19.6
		47	7.7					35 10.5	39 9.3
							Cost of Sales/Inventory		
							Cost of Sales/Payables		
			13.7				Sales/Working Capital	16.2	14.0
			36.8					35.8	58.0
			-22.0					-19.8	-15.9
			13.8				EBIT/Interest	25.9	10.9
		(13)	5.3					(11) 3.2	2.8
			-.9					1.4	.6
							Net Profit + Depr., Dep., Amort./Cur. Mat. L/T/D		
			.2				Fixed/Worth	.1	.6
			.6					.9	11.4
			1.7					-10.5	-.6
			.6				Debt/Worth	.8	.7
			2.2					11.6	23.9
			5.5					-7.9	-3.5
			42.5				% Profit Before Taxes/Tangible Net Worth		
		(16)	27.8						
			10.3						
			16.8				% Profit Before Taxes/Total Assets	13.6	16.3
			9.4					5.0	6.4
			-3.6					-1.5	-.7
			41.9				Sales/Net Fixed Assets	UND	45.6
			21.1					28.3	15.3
			8.4					7.5	7.2
			5.8				Sales/Total Assets	7.6	5.8
			3.3					4.1	4.9
			1.7					2.3	2.8
			.4				% Depr., Dep., Amort./Sales	.3	.8
		(16)	1.6					(10) 1.7	(13) 1.8
			3.1					4.0	6.3
							% Officers', Directors' Owners' Comp/Sales		
	9839M	33351M	352737M	327212M	751797M		Net Sales ($)	198790M	166002M
	1040M	6765M	101179M	117575M	234491M		Total Assets ($)	83255M	55471M

© RMA 2007

M = $ thousand   MM = $ million
See Pages 11 through 21 for Explanation of Ratios and Data

Comparative Historical Data | Current Data Sorted by Sales

			Type of Statement						
6	9	9	Unqualified					4	5
7	4	8	Reviewed		1	1	2	1	1
3	5	4	Compiled		2		1	2	2
13	3	2	Tax Returns		1				
			Other	2	1	1	2	3	6

4/1/04-3/31/05 ALL	4/1/05-3/31/06 ALL	4/1/06-3/31/07 ALL		0-1MM	9 (4/1-9/30/06) 1-3MM	3-5MM	5-10MM	29 (10/1/06-3/31/07) 10-25MM	25MM & OVER
29	35	38	**NUMBER OF STATEMENTS**	2	5	2	5	10	14
%	%	%	**ASSETS**	%	%	%	%	%	%
8.8	10.3	13.3	Cash & Equivalents					16.8	11.3
25.7	25.9	25.3	Trade Receivables (net)					29.3	33.2
13.6	10.3	8.0	Inventory					9.0	7.9
3.5	3.1	5.2	All Other Current					1.6	5.1
51.6	49.6	51.7	Total Current					56.7	57.6
33.5	33.9	27.8	Fixed Assets (net)					17.4	23.4
2.4	3.8	4.7	Intangibles (net)					5.4	4.2
12.5	12.7	15.8	All Other Non-Current					20.5	14.9
100.0	100.0	100.0	Total					100.0	100.0
			LIABILITIES						
10.7	9.2	8.1	Notes Payable-Short Term					5.4	1.7
4.7	2.8	3.6	Cur. Mat.-L.T.D.					.9	5.1
21.8	16.1	17.7	Trade Payables					14.9	22.2
.3	.3	1.2	Income Taxes Payable					.7	2.2
14.5	16.9	17.5	All Other Current					22.6	24.4
52.0	45.2	48.1	Total Current					44.4	55.5
19.8	22.3	18.3	Long-Term Debt					15.3	17.8
.2	.2	.1	Deferred Taxes					.1	.1
5.9	5.6	11.2	All Other Non-Current					.9	12.7
22.1	26.6	22.3	Net Worth					39.2	13.9
100.0	100.0	100.0	Total Liabilities & Net Worth					100.0	100.0
			INCOME DATA						
100.0	100.0	100.0	Net Sales					100.0	100.0
			Gross Profit						
93.8	91.9	95.0	Operating Expenses					91.2	98.5
6.2	8.1	5.0	Operating Profit					8.8	1.5
1.4	3.0	1.5	All Other Expenses (net)					3.7	.2
4.8	5.1	3.5	Profit Before Taxes					5.1	1.3
			RATIOS						
1.8	1.7	1.8						2.1	1.3
1.1	1.1	1.1	Current					1.5	1.0
.4	.6	.5						.5	.8
1.2	1.2	1.4						1.7	1.1
.4	.9	.8	Quick					1.2	.8
.2	.4	.4						.4	.6
(2) 175.0	(1) 592.2	(9) 42.4						(3) 108.3	(13) 27.7
(12) 31.3	(17) 21.0	(14) 26.7	Sales/Receivables					(10) 35.1	(29) 12.6
(28) 13.2	(35) 10.4	(40) 9.1						(49) 7.5	(40) 9.1
			Cost of Sales/Inventory						
			Cost of Sales/Payables						
18.4	17.7	15.6						11.5	30.0
126.8	73.6	93.8	Sales/Working Capital					31.8	548.1
-10.5	-24.6	-20.7						-18.0	-33.3
7.5	8.9	13.8							20.3
(21) 3.3	(26) 3.2	(29) 4.1	EBIT/Interest						(12) 5.0
2.1	1.9	.6							2.8
		5.5							
	(10) 3.7		Net Profit + Depr., Dep., Amort./Cur. Mat. L/T/D						
		1.9							
.2	.2	.3						.1	.4
.9	.9	1.0	Fixed/Worth					.4	1.6
-3.0	-54.5	NM						1.5	-1.6
1.1	1.0	.7						.6	3.1
2.1	2.5	3.4	Debt/Worth					1.1	5.9
-8.4	-58.6	NM						5.9	-5.1
73.8	76.7	57.8							83.9
(20) 29.0	(26) 23.8	(29) 33.5	% Profit Before Taxes/Tangible Net Worth						(10) 54.1
10.0	9.2	11.1							34.9
14.9	13.6	14.2						16.8	13.9
9.5	8.2	9.4	% Profit Before Taxes/Total Assets					9.7	10.3
.9	1.9	-1.4						-3.6	7.8
59.1	72.1	36.4						93.9	39.8
14.0	16.1	16.9	Sales/Net Fixed Assets					21.1	17.8
7.0	4.2	7.4						8.9	11.6
6.3	5.7	5.1						5.4	5.8
4.0	3.4	3.2	Sales/Total Assets					3.3	3.6
3.3	2.2	2.1						2.0	3.1
.4	.5	.6							.4
(22) 1.2	(32) 1.7	(30) 1.8	% Depr., Dep., Amort./Sales						(12) 2.0
2.2	2.6	3.1							2.9
		1.2							
	(13) 2.5		% Officers', Directors' Owners' Comp/Sales						
		5.8							
2044319M	1501026M	1474936M	Net Sales ($)	1187M	9247M	7756M	32480M	163636M	1260630M
405831M	444114M	461050M	Total Assets ($)	494M	3664M	4799M	16834M	50454M	384805M

M = $ thousand   MM = $ million
See Pages 11 through 21 for Explanation of Ratios and Data

Current Data Sorted by Assets   Comparative Historical Data

						Type of Statement		
1	1	2	1			Unqualified		1
	1	2	2			Reviewed		4
4	7	2				Compiled	4	6
19	6	4				Tax Returns	5	12
7	7	3			1	Other	5	7
	7 (4/1-9/30/06)		63 (10/1/06-3/31/07)				4/1/02-3/31/03	4/1/03-3/31/04
0-500M	500M-2MM	2-10MM	10-50MM	50-100MM	100-250MM		ALL	ALL
31	22	13	3		1	NUMBER OF STATEMENTS	14	30
%	%	%	%	%	%	ASSETS	%	%
24.8	12.7	14.6				Cash & Equivalents	17.1	16.9
17.5	16.3	24.4				Trade Receivables (net)	8.6	10.8
4.0	3.2	3.2				Inventory	3.6	6.5
3.1	3.8	.9				All Other Current	1.9	3.7
49.4	36.1	43.0				Total Current	31.2	37.9
42.9	47.6	40.0				Fixed Assets (net)	51.2	47.4
4.3	4.6	11.6				Intangibles (net)	3.9	5.9
3.3	11.7	5.4				All Other Non-Current	13.8	8.8
100.0	100.0	100.0				Total	100.0	100.0
						LIABILITIES		
12.0	7.1	8.7				Notes Payable-Short Term	9.2	4.6
1.9	6.1	2.5				Cur. Mat.-L.T.D.	4.4	13.5
17.3	13.1	12.5				Trade Payables	18.8	18.3
1.4	2.2	.4				Income Taxes Payable	.1	.1
34.4	11.2	30.3				All Other Current	13.6	20.0
67.0	39.6	54.4				Total Current	46.2	56.5
33.1	32.9	20.3				Long-Term Debt	21.4	34.2
.0	.0	.5				Deferred Taxes	.0	.4
16.5	6.9	12.0				All Other Non-Current	29.1	26.4
-16.7	20.7	12.8				Net Worth	3.1	-17.5
100.0	100.0	100.0				Total Liabilities & Net Worth	100.0	100.0
						INCOME DATA		
100.0	100.0	100.0				Net Sales	100.0	100.0
						Gross Profit		
94.6	89.7	92.1				Operating Expenses	97.5	95.0
5.4	10.3	7.9				Operating Profit	2.5	5.0
2.6	2.6	2.4				All Other Expenses (net)	.8	3.4
2.8	7.7	5.5				Profit Before Taxes	1.7	1.6
						RATIOS		
1.5	2.5	1.6					4.5	2.7
.8	.9	1.0				Current	.6	.9
.3	.3	.3					.3	.4
1.3	2.0	1.5					4.0	2.4
.6	.7	.8				Quick	.5	.6
.3	.2	.3					.2	.3
0 UND	0 UND	0 UND					0 UND	0 UND
4 83.8	10 35.5	11 34.7				Sales/Receivables	5 68.9	2 154.8
15 24.0	30 12.2	38 9.7					15 23.6	14 26.8
						Cost of Sales/Inventory		
						Cost of Sales/Payables		
24.4	28.5	16.2					16.7	12.0
-73.3	NM	-999.8				Sales/Working Capital	-27.6	-137.4
-16.4	-10.5	-4.2					-6.5	-13.9
8.8	13.7	44.0					4.1	11.1
(21) 2.9	(18) 4.2	(11) 3.4				EBIT/Interest	(11) .4	(21) 4.9
1.3	1.4	1.7					-1.8	-7.0
						Net Profit + Depr., Dep., Amort./Cur. Mat. L/T/D		
.5	.7	.5					.9	1.1
3.4	3.0	134.9				Fixed/Worth	3.2	4.7
-1.1	-10.0	-2.5					-4.6	-1.1
.8	1.4	1.0					.9	1.7
92.0	5.8	136.7				Debt/Worth	3.7	6.3
-2.7	-13.1	-8.1					-7.2	-2.3
162.0	171.1							150.8
(16) 21.8	(16) 82.2					% Profit Before Taxes/Tangible Net Worth	(19) 61.9
15.0	29.8							21.3
31.4	45.4	23.4					15.6	30.2
9.0	11.2	7.9				% Profit Before Taxes/Total Assets	1.3	12.0
.9	1.6	3.6					-9.5	-11.6
71.6	30.0	34.8					12.6	21.9
19.2	5.6	15.5				Sales/Net Fixed Assets	6.8	9.5
6.6	1.9	2.2					4.6	3.8
14.0	6.8	3.9					4.3	6.2
6.1	2.8	3.4				Sales/Total Assets	3.6	3.6
3.2	1.6	.9					2.5	2.0
.5	2.1	.5					1.3	.9
(17) 1.2	(16) 2.5	(11) 2.8				% Depr., Dep., Amort./Sales	(13) 3.1	(25) 1.7
2.7	3.5	4.2					5.4	3.6
3.4								2.9
(17) 6.8						% Officers', Directors' Owners' Comp/Sales	(19) 4.2
9.5								6.9
36339M	86729M	151417M	69477M		596348M	Net Sales ($)	198096M	110173M
6561M	23625M	54948M	52525M		169318M	Total Assets ($)	50461M	47126M

M = $ thousand   MM = $ million
See Pages 11 through 21 for Explanation of Ratios and Data

Comparative Historical Data   ## Current Data Sorted by Sales

3	4	5	Type of Statement	0-1MM	1-3MM	3-5MM	5-10MM	10-25MM	25MM & OVER
			Unqualified		1		1	2	1
3	4	5	Reviewed		1	1	1	1	1
5	5	13	Compiled	3	5		3	1	1
9	17	29	Tax Returns	10	11	3	3	2	1
7	11	18	Other	6	8	1	1		1
4/1/04- 3/31/05 ALL	4/1/05- 3/31/06 ALL	4/1/06- 3/31/07 ALL		7 (4/1-9/30/06)		63 (10/1/06-3/31/07)			
27	41	70	NUMBER OF STATEMENTS	19	26	5	9	7	4
%	%	%	**ASSETS**	%	%	%	%	%	%
13.9	19.0	18.0	Cash & Equivalents	24.1	16.4				
19.9	16.3	18.6	Trade Receivables (net)	3.3	21.0				
5.9	6.6	4.0	Inventory	1.5	4.2				
4.2	2.3	2.9	All Other Current	5.0	2.3				
44.0	44.1	43.4	Total Current	33.9	43.9				
41.4	38.0	43.1	Fixed Assets (net)	58.8	42.9				
5.1	4.8	5.6	Intangibles (net)	5.8	4.4				
9.5	13.1	7.9	All Other Non-Current	1.4	8.8				
100.0	100.0	100.0	Total	100.0	100.0				
			LIABILITIES						
8.3	12.5	9.7	Notes Payable-Short Term	13.6	9.3				
2.6	3.0	3.4	Cur. Mat.-L.T.D.	3.1	1.4				
21.1	16.7	14.5	Trade Payables	8.1	17.2				
.0	.1	1.4	Income Taxes Payable	.0	3.4				
17.8	23.6	25.4	All Other Current	35.9	18.7				
49.9	55.8	54.3	Total Current	60.7	50.1				
19.2	39.3	30.3	Long-Term Debt	40.2	35.6				
.4	.1	.1	Deferred Taxes	.0	.1				
25.1	4.6	11.8	All Other Non-Current	23.6	6.7				
5.4	.3	3.5	Net Worth	-24.6	7.6				
100.0	100.0	100.0	Total Liabilties & Net Worth	100.0	100.0				
			INCOME DATA						
100.0	100.0	100.0	Net Sales	100.0	100.0				
			Gross Profit						
96.0	93.9	92.2	Operating Expenses	88.6	94.0				
4.0	6.1	7.8	Operating Profit	11.4	6.0				
1.0	1.6	2.5	All Other Expenses (net)	6.6	1.2				
3.0	4.5	5.3	Profit Before Taxes	4.8	4.9				
			RATIOS						
1.4	1.7	1.6		2.2	1.6				
1.0	1.0	.8	Current	.3	.8				
.5	.4	.3		.1	.5				
1.2	1.5	1.4		1.2	1.6				
.8	.7	.7	Quick	.3	.7				
.3	.3	.3		.1	.4				
0 UND	0 UND	0 UND		0 UND	0 UND				
7 49.3	5 75.7	6 61.1	Sales/Receivables	0 UND	10 36.3				
20 18.0	20 18.2	25 14.9		5 80.6	26 14.0				
			Cost of Sales/Inventory						
			Cost of Sales/Payables						
15.3	25.1	23.8		15.0	22.2				
-531.5	-257.2	-77.1	Sales/Working Capital	-20.9	-77.1				
-11.9	-20.8	-11.3		-5.0	-16.1				
8.6	12.1	10.3			7.5				
(20) 2.7	(28) 7.5	(54) 3.7	EBIT/Interest		(23) 3.3				
-1.5	1.7	1.4			1.1				
			Net Profit + Depr., Dep., Amort./Cur. Mat. L/T/D						
.7	.8	.5		.3	1.0				
2.5	2.2	3.1	Fixed/Worth	3.4	20.6				
55.6	UND	-2.5		-1.1	-1.9				
2.2	1.5	1.3		.6	1.6				
3.4	3.1	6.2	Debt/Worth	3.7	114.3				
177.0	UND	-5.7		-2.2	-4.8				
86.9	153.8	111.9	% Profit Before Taxes/Tangible Net Worth	70.3	183.7				
(21) 35.2	(31) 50.9	(44) 42.0		(12) 26.6	(15) 34.3				
10.7	24.1	15.0		10.6	11.3				
15.4	47.4	28.4	% Profit Before Taxes/Total Assets	30.0	34.7				
4.3	15.5	9.1		9.0	8.3				
-6.5	2.6	1.6		-1.9	.7				
32.3	59.2	33.4	Sales/Net Fixed Assets	27.9	35.9				
12.2	18.5	15.3		6.6	14.2				
3.1	6.5	3.6		1.6	3.8				
4.7	7.6	7.1	Sales/Total Assets	11.6	6.7				
3.4	4.8	3.8		2.6	4.3				
1.6	2.5	1.6		.9	1.9				
.6	.7	.8	% Depr., Dep., Amort./Sales	.4	1.0				
(20) 1.4	(27) 1.4	(48) 2.1		(10) 2.0	(19) 2.2				
3.1	3.1	3.5		4.9	3.5				
1.6	3.0	2.6	% Officers', Directors' Owners' Comp/Sales		2.5				
(12) 4.6	(20) 6.1	(34) 4.7			(14) 5.6				
6.5	7.5	7.9			9.0				
137790M	866114M	940310M	Net Sales ($)	9733M	49465M	19166M	67647M	91109M	703190M
46524M	230345M	306977M	Total Assets ($)	6245M	21427M	5434M	34921M	46133M	192817M

M = $ thousand   MM = $ million
See Pages 11 through 21 for Explanation of Ratios and Data

Current Data Sorted by Assets / Comparative Historical Data

	0-500M	500M-2MM	2-10MM	10-50MM	50-100MM	100-250MM		4/1/02-3/31/03 ALL	4/1/03-3/31/04 ALL
Type of Statement									
Unqualified			2			2		6	5
Reviewed	1	2	2					2	7
Compiled	12	9	3	1	1			37	41
Tax Returns	83	19	6	2	1	1		80	85
Other	20	14	7	1	1			44	38
		13 (4/1-9/30/06)		179 (10/1/06-3/31/07)					
NUMBER OF STATEMENTS	116	44	20	7	2	3		169	176
	%	%	%	%	%	%	**ASSETS**	%	%
	13.9	15.4	9.6				Cash & Equivalents	16.0	13.1
	1.0	1.2	4.4				Trade Receivables (net)	1.7	2.2
	9.5	9.2	11.4				Inventory	9.7	9.9
	4.2	1.5	7.2				All Other Current	4.0	2.4
	28.5	27.4	32.7				Total Current	31.4	27.6
	45.2	50.2	47.3				Fixed Assets (net)	48.4	50.5
	17.8	11.4	9.0				Intangibles (net)	9.6	10.2
	8.5	11.0	11.0				All Other Non-Current	10.6	11.7
	100.0	100.0	100.0				Total	100.0	100.0
							LIABILITIES		
	7.0	3.8	3.1				Notes Payable-Short Term	6.3	7.9
	1.7	5.4	3.9				Cur. Mat.-L.T.D.	2.8	5.2
	4.7	6.0	7.8				Trade Payables	7.1	9.4
	.3	.1	.1				Income Taxes Payable	.4	.5
	24.0	15.4	12.5				All Other Current	14.3	14.2
	37.7	30.7	27.3				Total Current	30.8	37.1
	29.5	35.1	42.5				Long-Term Debt	32.7	33.1
	.0	.0	.0				Deferred Taxes	.0	.1
	15.4	11.6	23.6				All Other Non-Current	15.5	13.4
	17.4	22.6	6.6				Net Worth	21.0	16.4
	100.0	100.0	100.0				Total Liabilities & Net Worth	100.0	100.0
							INCOME DATA		
	100.0	100.0	100.0				Net Sales	100.0	100.0
	58.9	58.2	58.6				Gross Profit	58.7	58.2
	55.0	51.4	52.2				Operating Expenses	53.9	55.9
	3.8	6.8	6.3				Operating Profit	4.8	2.3
	.5	2.4	2.5				All Other Expenses (net)	1.2	1.2
	3.3	4.4	3.8				Profit Before Taxes	3.5	1.1
							RATIOS		
	3.7	4.1	1.9				Current	3.5	2.5
	.8	1.0	1.2					1.2	.9
	.3	.2	.4					.5	.3
	2.1	3.1	1.1				Quick	1.8	1.5
	(112) .4	.5	.3					.6 (175)	.3
	.1	.1	.2					.1	.1
	0 UND	0 UND	0 UND				Sales/Receivables	0 UND	0 UND
	0 UND	0 UND	1 728.6					0 UND	0 UND
	0 UND	1 314.6	2 226.7					0 978.9	1 623.2
	6 56.7	9 42.9	11 33.3				Cost of Sales/Inventory	8 43.4	9 41.5
	15 24.8	19 19.3	22 16.7					18 20.4	16 23.5
	28 12.8	28 12.9	49 7.5					29 12.6	25 14.5
	0 UND	0 UND	3 111.6				Cost of Sales/Payables	0 UND	0 UND
	0 UND	14 26.0	30 12.0					8 43.7	14 26.1
	13 27.4	29 12.4	52 7.0					31 11.6	33 11.2
	20.6	9.2	19.5				Sales/Working Capital	15.6	23.4
	-244.5	NM	71.2					94.0	-279.0
	-18.0	-10.4	-12.9					-19.1	-12.2
	13.2	8.2	4.6				EBIT/Interest	7.6	6.0
	(70) 2.2	(34) 2.2	(18) 1.8					(117) 2.1	(129) 2.1
	.8	-.1	1.1					.6	-.9
							Net Profit + Depr., Dep., Amort./Cur. Mat. L/T/D		
	.8	.6	1.4				Fixed/Worth	.5	.7
	2.1	5.1	14.8					2.2	3.2
	-1.2	-1.7	-1.3					-5.0	-3.2
	.7	.4	3.4				Debt/Worth	.5	.9
	5.9	30.3	NM					3.1	4.0
	-2.6	-3.5	-3.7					-8.2	-4.9
	100.7	100.0	36.7				% Profit Before Taxes/Tangible Net Worth	67.4	82.6
	(66) 45.3	(24) 69.8	(10) 21.9					(111) 30.2	(112) 35.3
	6.6	25.5	13.1					4.7	.3
	33.5	30.9	12.6				% Profit Before Taxes/Total Assets	28.8	20.3
	9.2	7.8	3.3					6.5	6.1
	-1.3	-6.9	.9					-2.3	-5.7
	33.9	8.5	8.8				Sales/Net Fixed Assets	21.6	18.4
	11.1	4.7	4.3					7.3	7.4
	5.9	1.9	1.7					3.2	3.2
	6.9	3.1	2.9				Sales/Total Assets	4.9	5.7
	4.1	2.1	1.6					3.2	3.3
	2.4	1.3	.9					2.0	1.9
	1.1	1.4	1.6				% Depr., Dep., Amort./Sales	1.5	1.6
	(84) 1.8	(40) 2.9	(17) 2.6					(143) 2.6	(137) 3.1
	3.7	4.2	4.0					5.1	4.9
	3.0	1.1					% Officers', Directors' Owners' Comp/Sales	2.6	2.8
	(63) 4.7	(16) 2.1						(74) 6.0	(84) 5.8
	8.2	3.6						10.5	10.0
	95188M	92041M	252452M	224394M	795329M	1896956M	Net Sales ($)	805578M	1667462M
	23497M	42078M	99312M	108676M	153592M	514491M	Total Assets ($)	250562M	573966M

M = $ thousand   MM = $ million
See Pages 11 through 21 for Explanation of Ratios and Data

Comparative Historical Data   Current Data Sorted by Sales

1	2	4	Type of Statement				1 1	2	3
2	3	5	Unqualified	7	2	6	1 1	2	3
41	27	26	Reviewed	65	9	3	3	1	3
80	117	111	Compiled	15	37	5	4	2	1
49	38	46	Tax Returns		16				5
4/1/04-3/31/05 ALL	4/1/05-3/31/06 ALL	4/1/06-3/31/07 ALL	Other — 13 (4/1-9/30/06) — 179 (10/1/06-3/31/07)	0-1MM	1-3MM	3-5MM	5-10MM	10-25MM	25MM & OVER
173	187	192	NUMBER OF STATEMENTS	87	64	14	9	6	12
%	%	%	**ASSETS**	%	%	%	%	%	%
14.2	15.9	14.0	Cash & Equivalents	13.6	12.6	20.2			23.7
1.6	1.9	1.5	Trade Receivables (net)	.9	1.0	2.0			2.1
9.5	8.1	9.3	Inventory	9.0	8.1	11.0			7.9
5.0	3.3	4.0	All Other Current	3.6	4.6	2.7			6.6
30.2	29.1	28.8	Total Current	27.1	26.4	36.0			40.4
50.0	44.2	47.5	Fixed Assets (net)	46.1	48.9	47.9			52.5
10.6	15.3	14.5	Intangibles (net)	17.2	16.0	6.7			4.7
9.2	11.4	9.1	All Other Non-Current	9.5	8.7	9.5			2.5
100.0	100.0	100.0	Total	100.0	100.0	100.0			100.0
			LIABILITIES						
6.3	5.1	5.5	Notes Payable-Short Term	5.1	6.7	7.5			1.4
2.6	4.3	3.1	Cur. Mat.-L.T.D.	2.0	3.1	4.2			8.7
8.2	7.1	5.6	Trade Payables	2.8	6.6	8.6			10.0
.1	.2	.2	Income Taxes Payable	.1	.4	.2			.0
19.9	20.4	19.9	All Other Current	25.0	19.2	9.2			12.5
37.0	37.1	34.3	Total Current	35.1	36.0	29.7			32.5
36.8	27.9	32.5	Long-Term Debt	33.4	29.3	32.6			32.4
.0	.0	.0	Deferred Taxes	.0	.0	.0			.0
14.1	18.4	15.8	All Other Non-Current	18.6	13.0	5.4			26.6
12.1	16.6	17.4	Net Worth	12.8	21.7	32.2			8.4
100.0	100.0	100.0	Total Liabilties & Net Worth	100.0	100.0	100.0			100.0
			INCOME DATA						
100.0	100.0	100.0	Net Sales	100.0	100.0	100.0			100.0
59.2	58.4	58.7	Gross Profit	57.5	61.6	58.6			57.2
55.5	53.6	53.9	Operating Expenses	54.9	55.6	45.2			52.6
3.7	4.8	4.8	Operating Profit	2.6	6.0	13.4			4.6
.7	.8	1.2	All Other Expenses (net)	1.3	.8	3.1			1.6
3.0	4.1	3.6	Profit Before Taxes	1.3	5.2	10.3			3.0
			RATIOS						
3.1	3.3	3.1	Current	4.6	3.0	2.9			3.9
1.0	1.3	1.1		.8	.9	1.4			1.1
.4	.4	.3		.3	.3	.8			.6
1.8	2.1	2.0	Quick	2.5	1.1	2.6			2.7
(171) .4	(186) .6	(188) .4		(83) .4	.4	.7			.4
.1	.2	.1		.1	.1	.1			.2
0 UND	0 UND	0 UND	Sales/Receivables	0 UND	0 UND	0 UND			0 UND
0 UND	0 UND	0 UND		0 UND	0 UND	1 699.1			0 UND
1 434.0	1 596.8	1 490.7		0 UND	0 999.8	1 254.6			4 92.5
9 41.0	9 41.0	8 46.9	Cost of Sales/Inventory	8 44.8	6 60.2	8 47.6			7 50.6
16 23.2	17 21.4	16 22.5		17 21.7	15 24.8	17 21.5			12 30.9
27 13.4	26 13.8	29 12.6		31 11.6	23 15.9	24 15.3			21 17.4
0 UND	0 UND	0 UND	Cost of Sales/Payables	0 UND	0 UND	3 139.7			0 UND
8 47.4	8 44.2	3 136.8		0 UND	6 63.3	19 19.7			14 25.4
30 12.2	26 14.0	26 14.2		12 30.0	27 13.7	28 12.9			95 3.8
14.6	16.5	17.4	Sales/Working Capital	14.9	26.3	12.6			13.4
262.4	84.5	485.7		-269.0	-765.9	31.0			407.1
-17.5	-22.4	-16.7		-17.0	-14.9	-66.7			-18.4
10.5	12.5	12.5	EBIT/Interest	5.1	16.8	27.5			27.1
(119) 3.1	(127) 3.5	(133) 2.3		(53) 1.6	(45) 3.6	(10) 4.1		(10)	6.8
.8	1.0	.7		-.9	.2	1.6			.2
			Net Profit + Depr., Dep., Amort./Cur. Mat. L/T/D						
.8	.7	.8	Fixed/Worth	.8	.7	.6			.4
2.4	2.4	3.7		4.6	3.3	3.9			3.2
-4.8	-1.6	-1.5		-1.3	-1.3	-26.4			-3.4
.7	.6	.8	Debt/Worth	.7	.7	.5			1.7
2.9	3.7	5.9		28.9	3.5	4.4			4.3
-8.2	-3.5	-2.9		-2.5	-2.8	-120.9			-3.4
85.3	73.6	94.6	% Profit Before Taxes/Tangible Net Worth	60.3	154.9	144.1			
(109) 35.7	(115) 37.9	(109) 38.6		(45) 34.0	(36) 59.1	(10) 101.3			
7.0	4.6	12.6		.0	24.6	69.9			
26.3	26.8	31.3	% Profit Before Taxes/Total Assets	18.2	47.3	59.6			33.0
8.4	11.0	8.0		3.5	16.9	24.2			12.8
-1.8	-.3	-1.3		-7.6	-.6	5.7			-1.8
22.9	23.0	26.1	Sales/Net Fixed Assets	32.0	26.9	16.3			13.2
7.2	9.5	7.9		8.6	7.8	7.6			6.9
3.0	4.4	3.7		3.8	4.0	5.2			3.3
5.6	5.4	5.0	Sales/Total Assets	4.7	6.2	4.6			5.3
2.9	3.1	3.1		3.0	3.4	2.9			3.2
1.8	1.8	1.7		1.5	2.1	1.9			1.9
1.4	1.1	1.3	% Depr., Dep., Amort./Sales	1.1	1.3	.6			1.5
(136) 2.9	(157) 1.9	(152) 2.3		(64) 2.3	(52) 1.9	(13) 2.0		(10)	2.6
5.0	3.9	4.0		4.1	4.0	3.4			4.3
3.3	2.8	2.3	% Officers', Directors' Owners' Comp/Sales	2.9	2.0				
(76) 4.9	(96) 4.7	(87) 4.4		(46) 5.6	(29) 3.9				
8.7	8.3	7.2		11.7	4.6				
2329227M	3226777M	3356360M	Net Sales ($)	44910M	99936M	54531M	67980M	94136M	2994867M
334005M	823190M	941646M	Total Assets ($)	19569M	41478M	23630M	57055M	36291M	763623M

M = $ thousand   MM = $ million
See Pages 11 through 21 for Explanation of Ratios and Data

OTHER SERVICES (EXCEPT PUBLIC ADMINISTRATION)

Current Data Sorted by Assets							Comparative Historical Data	
						Type of Statement		
3		1	2			Unqualified	10	9
3	4	13	2			Reviewed	29	23
32	25	11	2	1	1	Compiled	100	121
151	43	5	1		3	Tax Returns	147	185
48	53	14			3	Other	84	98
60 (4/1-9/30/06)		367 (10/1/06-3/31/07)					4/1/02-3/31/03 ALL	4/1/03-3/31/04 ALL
0-500M	500M-2MM	2-10MM	10-50MM	50-100MM	100-250MM			
237	125	44	12	2	7	**NUMBER OF STATEMENTS**	370	436
%	%	%	%	%	%	**ASSETS**	%	%
17.8	10.9	8.2	5.4			Cash & Equivalents	14.0	13.6
11.1	12.0	13.3	12.9			Trade Receivables (net)	11.1	12.8
19.5	19.6	21.4	24.6			Inventory	20.0	19.0
2.3	1.8	2.0	2.9			All Other Current	2.3	1.8
50.7	44.3	44.9	45.8			Total Current	47.4	47.3
35.6	36.5	43.9	30.5			Fixed Assets (net)	39.7	40.1
7.0	8.5	5.1	15.3			Intangibles (net)	4.4	4.9
6.7	10.7	6.1	8.4			All Other Non-Current	8.5	7.8
100.0	100.0	100.0	100.0			Total	100.0	100.0
						LIABILITIES		
13.1	6.9	8.2	12.1			Notes Payable-Short Term	9.7	9.3
4.4	5.0	4.5	5.1			Cur. Mat.-L.T.D.	5.1	6.1
14.2	14.3	15.9	11.3			Trade Payables	12.8	17.2
.1	.2	.1	.0			Income Taxes Payable	.3	.2
17.7	9.4	10.3	7.1			All Other Current	11.8	13.2
49.5	35.9	39.0	35.5			Total Current	39.7	46.1
33.4	33.0	29.7	20.7			Long-Term Debt	28.9	35.0
.0	.1	.4	.3			Deferred Taxes	.1	.1
18.2	5.2	7.2	18.5			All Other Non-Current	7.1	8.6
-1.1	25.9	23.9	25.0			Net Worth	24.2	10.2
100.0	100.0	100.0	100.0			Total Liabilties & Net Worth	100.0	100.0
						INCOME DATA		
100.0	100.0	100.0	100.0			Net Sales	100.0	100.0
						Gross Profit		
95.4	95.5	92.5	90.7			Operating Expenses	95.8	95.0
4.6	4.5	7.5	9.3			Operating Profit	4.2	5.0
.7	1.6	3.9	4.2			All Other Expenses (net)	1.5	2.2
3.9	2.9	3.6	5.1			Profit Before Taxes	2.7	2.8
						RATIOS		
2.7	2.3	1.3	1.8				2.8	2.5
1.3	1.3	1.0	1.1			Current	1.3	1.2
.7	.8	.7	.5				.7	.6
1.6	1.2	.7	.9				1.7	1.4
(236) .7	.6	.5	.5			Quick	(368) .7	(434) .6
.2	.3	.3	.2				.3	.2
0 UND	3 116.1	5 67.2	1 258.8				0 999.8	1 617.8
3 132.4	10 35.0	13 28.6	20 18.5			Sales/Receivables	5 66.8	7 53.8
12 29.4	18 20.4	26 14.1	65 5.7				19 19.2	22 16.5
						Cost of Sales/Inventory		
						Cost of Sales/Payables		
15.0	10.3	23.6	8.0				10.9	11.5
47.6	36.5	-633.0	89.0			Sales/Working Capital	47.9	76.7
-38.8	-27.5	-26.1	-21.9				-42.9	-22.5
12.7	6.4	4.7	8.5				8.3	6.9
(178) 3.0	(103) 2.3	(40) 2.5	(10) 4.6			EBIT/Interest	(303) 2.6	(349) 2.6
.8	.0	1.5	1.4				1.0	.6
		2.0					4.9	3.6
		(11) 1.6				Net Profit + Depr., Dep., Amort./Cur. Mat. L/T/D	(36) 2.5	(43) 1.5
		1.0					.7	.7
.4	.3	.9	.4				.4	.5
2.8	1.4	1.8	22.8			Fixed/Worth	1.6	2.2
-1.0	11.7	4.7	-.6				59.0	-5.9
1.1	.9	1.8	1.5				.8	1.0
7.5	2.8	3.7	27.1			Debt/Worth	2.6	3.5
-3.1	17.8	10.7	-5.9				UND	-8.4
117.3	56.0	46.8					60.5	57.5
(133) 48.1	(97) 18.9	(38) 19.4				% Profit Before Taxes/Tangible Net Worth	(282) 19.1	(297) 21.6
7.2	1.5	9.1					1.6	2.2
43.1	12.7	7.4	26.7				19.3	18.8
9.4	4.3	3.8	12.2			% Profit Before Taxes/Total Assets	5.4	5.2
-1.8	-1.4	1.2	1.0				.0	-1.4
63.6	33.9	19.3	27.3				32.0	36.6
23.2	12.5	9.5	13.0			Sales/Net Fixed Assets	13.7	12.7
7.7	3.5	3.2	4.2				5.0	5.1
8.1	4.1	4.2	3.3				6.2	6.2
4.7	2.8	3.1	1.6			Sales/Total Assets	3.7	3.8
3.0	1.5	1.7	1.0				2.2	2.1
.7	.7	1.1	.7				1.1	1.1
(173) 1.7	(98) 1.9	(42) 1.9	2.2			% Depr., Dep., Amort./Sales	(294) 2.1	(344) 2.1
3.7	4.0	2.7	4.3				3.6	3.8
3.9	2.6	1.9					3.9	3.3
(167) 6.6	(67) 4.3	(14) 5.0				% Officers', Directors' Owners' Comp/Sales	(236) 6.5	(259) 6.6
11.8	6.4	8.4					10.3	10.4
231361M	339811M	589594M	1008934M	1928947M	2760210M	Net Sales ($)	7809240M	7119073M
48239M	116723M	188584M	275200M	129370M	1091402M	Total Assets ($)	1671912M	1571474M

M = $ thousand   MM = $ million
See Pages 11 through 21 for Explanation of Ratios and Data

Comparative Historical Data

Current Data Sorted by Sales

7	8	6	Type of Statement	1	2		1		2
31	24	23	Unqualified	4	2	1	2	8	6
103	86	72	Reviewed	30	19	10	6	4	3
190	196	203	Compiled	105	69	13	11		5
79	115	123	Tax Returns	40	48	11	12	6	6
4/1/04-3/31/05 ALL	4/1/05-3/31/06 ALL	4/1/06-3/31/07 ALL	Other		60 (4/1-9/30/06)			367 (10/1/06-3/31/07)	
				0-1MM	1-3MM	3-5MM	5-10MM	10-25MM	25MM & OVER
410	429	427	NUMBER OF STATEMENTS	180	140	35	32	18	22
%	%	%	**ASSETS**	%	%	%	%	%	%
12.8	15.6	14.3	Cash & Equivalents	14.3	15.4	17.0	13.1	8.4	8.3
13.2	12.1	11.8	Trade Receivables (net)	9.2	13.1	14.1	13.6	13.5	17.2
18.3	21.0	19.8	Inventory	14.9	22.6	25.7	24.3	24.9	21.6
2.7	2.4	2.3	All Other Current	1.9	2.9	1.5	1.3	1.0	4.8
47.0	51.2	48.1	Total Current	40.3	54.0	58.3	52.3	47.8	52.0
39.1	34.9	36.5	Fixed Assets (net)	45.5	29.2	25.9	35.6	33.4	29.2
6.2	5.7	7.5	Intangibles (net)	8.0	7.1	7.3	4.4	8.4	10.5
7.7	8.3	7.9	All Other Non-Current	6.2	9.6	8.6	7.7	10.4	8.3
100.0	100.0	100.0	Total	100.0	100.0	100.0	100.0	100.0	100.0
			LIABILITIES						
11.3	10.9	10.8	Notes Payable-Short Term	11.9	11.0	9.5	5.9	10.3	9.7
5.1	4.8	4.6	Cur. Mat.-L.T.D.	4.0	5.4	3.6	5.8	4.1	4.6
14.6	15.5	14.5	Trade Payables	9.5	18.0	16.9	17.1	22.0	20.5
.1	.1	.1	Income Taxes Payable	.1	.2	.1	.1	.3	.0
15.5	15.3	14.0	All Other Current	18.0	11.4	9.5	13.1	9.0	11.3
46.6	46.7	44.0	Total Current	43.4	45.9	39.5	42.0	45.7	46.1
36.0	30.0	32.2	Long-Term Debt	38.1	32.5	17.6	32.9	19.5	14.3
.1	.1	.1	Deferred Taxes	.0	.0	.2	.1	.9	.1
9.4	8.5	13.1	All Other Non-Current	18.0	10.8	4.3	12.7	2.2	11.9
7.9	14.7	10.6	Net Worth	.5	10.8	38.4	12.4	31.7	27.7
100.0	100.0	100.0	Total Liabilities & Net Worth	100.0	100.0	100.0	100.0	100.0	100.0
			INCOME DATA						
100.0	100.0	100.0	Net Sales	100.0	100.0	100.0	100.0	100.0	100.0
			Gross Profit						
95.6	94.7	95.0	Operating Expenses	93.0	96.0	97.7	97.7	97.1	93.9
4.4	5.3	5.0	Operating Profit	7.0	4.0	2.3	2.3	2.9	6.1
1.2	1.4	1.4	All Other Expenses (net)	2.4	.6	.9	1.2	.9	.5
3.2	3.9	3.6	Profit Before Taxes	4.6	3.4	1.4	1.0	2.0	5.6
			RATIOS						
2.3	2.5	2.5		3.3	2.2	3.0	2.3	1.2	1.4
1.1	1.4	1.3	Current	1.3	1.3	1.6	1.2	.9	1.1
.6	.7	.7		.5	.7	1.1	.8	.8	.8
1.3	1.5	1.3		1.8	1.2	1.8	1.2	.6	.7
(409) .6	(426) .7	(426) .6	Quick	(179) .7	.6	.9	.6	.4	.5
.2	.3	.3		.2	.3	.4	.3	.3	.3
1 362.9	0 UND	0 UND		0 UND	1 288.3	6 60.7	3 130.6	6 66.3	2 223.2
8 47.2	6 56.2	6 61.8	Sales/Receivables	2 158.8	8 47.8	12 31.4	9 42.8	13 28.9	14 26.3
21 17.6	18 19.8	17 21.6		14 26.8	17 21.6	25 14.6	26 14.2	22 16.5	42 8.7
			Cost of Sales/Inventory						
			Cost of Sales/Payables						
13.4	11.0	13.6		11.8	14.1	9.7	13.3	22.3	24.6
120.0	37.3	51.4	Sales/Working Capital	58.3	46.9	19.5	47.4	-90.7	121.3
-22.3	-44.7	-31.5		-17.3	-39.6	131.1	-55.6	-29.6	-51.5
7.2	8.1	7.9		8.6	9.0	5.9	6.9	4.4	10.2
(341) 2.7	(342) 2.8	(339) 2.7	EBIT/Interest	(124) 2.2	(119) 2.8	(30) 2.8	(29) 2.9	(17) 2.4	(20) 5.8
.9	.8	.8		.6	.3	.4	.5	1.6	2.4
4.3	4.3	2.7	Net Profit + Depr., Dep.,						
(42) 1.9	(29) 3.1	(24) 1.6	Amort./Cur. Mat. L/T/D						
.8	1.1	.8							
.5	.4	.4		.6	.3	.2	.7	.8	.6
2.2	1.7	2.2	Fixed/Worth	3.8	1.5	.4	2.0	1.5	2.9
-4.0	-5.6	-2.9		-1.8	-1.9	3.0	NM	2.4	-14.1
1.3	1.1	1.2		1.2	1.2	.5	1.6	1.6	1.6
5.1	3.8	5.0	Debt/Worth	11.1	4.8	1.6	4.2	4.1	4.8
-6.3	-14.8	-6.0		-3.4	-5.6	6.7	NM	7.4	-57.9
64.4	86.4	84.0	% Profit Before Taxes/Tangible	86.5	105.0	62.6	45.6	51.2	181.6
(272) 25.4	(297) 30.9	(282) 30.7	Net Worth	(106) 35.7	(92) 35.5	(28) 15.9	(24) 19.8	(16) 20.2	(16) 38.6
5.5	6.8	5.5		4.8	5.5	2.7	3.9	7.7	23.4
18.6	23.5	25.2	% Profit Before Taxes/Total	37.3	26.5	18.4	14.1	7.4	33.4
5.7	7.2	6.9	Assets	5.9	9.3	4.7	3.7	4.5	17.1
.0	.0	-.8		-2.1	-1.3	-2.5	-.1	1.2	6.7
34.3	47.4	42.5		33.2	64.9	50.0	60.2	16.6	35.2
15.0	17.5	15.7	Sales/Net Fixed Assets	12.3	26.0	23.2	17.2	13.0	16.9
5.2	7.0	5.2		2.9	7.9	10.4	5.5	7.3	10.4
6.0	6.4	5.8		5.9	6.1	4.5	6.5	4.9	5.4
3.8	3.9	3.8	Sales/Total Assets	3.6	4.2	3.7	3.6	3.6	3.5
2.2	2.4	2.2		1.5	2.8	3.0	2.6	2.4	2.2
1.3	.9	.7		1.2	.6	.6	.7	.8	1.0
(322) 2.3	(327) 1.8	(331) 1.8	% Depr., Dep., Amort./Sales	(136) 2.6	(103) 1.2	(27) 1.6	(28) 1.6	1.8	(19) 1.5
4.4	3.3	3.8		5.1	3.2	2.6	2.6	2.4	2.8
3.6	3.1	3.5		4.8	3.3	1.6	2.0		6.8
(249) 5.7	(258) 5.9	(256) 5.8	% Officers', Directors' Owners' Comp/Sales	(110) 7.9	(97) 4.9	(18) 3.5	(19) 3.1		(10) 9.6
9.5	9.5	9.7		12.7	7.5	6.3	8.6		16.4
5439138M	9574659M	6858857M	Net Sales ($)	102904M	246265M	137135M	236152M	297620M	5838781M
1608178M	2482918M	1849518M	Total Assets ($)	62285M	72249M	50299M	107330M	236411M	1320944M

M = $ thousand   MM = $ million
See Pages 11 through 21 for Explanation of Ratios and Data

Current Data Sorted by Assets / Comparative Historical Data

0-500M	500M-2MM	2-10MM	10-50MM	50-100MM	100-250MM		4/1/02-3/31/03 ALL	4/1/03-3/31/04 ALL
						Type of Statement		
1			1			Unqualified	2	3
	1	4				Reviewed	1	4
2	2	1				Compiled	8	10
9	1					Tax Returns	10	23
4	4	2	1		2	Other	12	8
7 (4/1-9/30/06)		28 (10/1/06-3/31/07)						
16	8	7	2		2	**NUMBER OF STATEMENTS**	33	48
%	%	%	%	%	%	**ASSETS**	%	%
15.0				DATA NOT AVAILABLE		Cash & Equivalents	14.0	11.6
10.9						Trade Receivables (net)	5.8	5.5
21.1						Inventory	21.7	23.1
2.7						All Other Current	2.2	3.2
49.6						Total Current	43.6	43.4
35.2						Fixed Assets (net)	41.0	36.9
10.9						Intangibles (net)	8.6	8.4
4.2						All Other Non-Current	6.8	11.4
100.0						Total	100.0	100.0
						LIABILITIES		
1.2						Notes Payable-Short Term	5.1	8.8
5.2						Cur. Mat.-L.T.D.	6.8	4.3
10.7						Trade Payables	22.3	17.7
.0						Income Taxes Payable	.1	.1
20.8						All Other Current	33.2	10.8
37.9						Total Current	67.4	41.7
33.5						Long-Term Debt	34.8	28.2
.0						Deferred Taxes	.0	.0
30.5						All Other Non-Current	.7	7.4
-1.8						Net Worth	-3.0	22.7
100.0						Total Liabilties & Net Worth	100.0	100.0
						INCOME DATA		
100.0						Net Sales	100.0	100.0
						Gross Profit		
95.8						Operating Expenses	95.1	94.7
4.2						Operating Profit	4.9	5.3
.0						All Other Expenses (net)	1.9	1.3
4.2						Profit Before Taxes	3.0	3.9
						RATIOS		
5.0							1.7	2.3
2.1						Current	.8	1.0
.9							.4	.6
2.4							.7	1.0
.8						Quick	.3	(47) .2
.3							.1	.1
1 267.0							1 377.3	0 UND
5 68.7						Sales/Receivables	2 149.1	2 172.5
10 35.0							4 91.4	7 49.9
						Cost of Sales/Inventory		
						Cost of Sales/Payables		
9.9							22.8	9.6
20.5						Sales/Working Capital	-44.4	184.3
NM							-11.5	-19.8
							6.6	5.8
						EBIT/Interest	(24) 1.7	(38) 2.5
							1.2	.6
						Net Profit + Depr., Dep., Amort./Cur. Mat. L/T/D		
.5							.6	.5
NM						Fixed/Worth	4.3	2.8
-.7							-16.5	-6.6
.8							1.3	1.3
-9.2						Debt/Worth	6.9	3.5
-2.1							-6.1	-27.9
							52.4	77.8
						% Profit Before Taxes/Tangible Net Worth	(21) 37.2	(35) 35.5
							17.1	-3.4
38.7							22.9	22.3
3.6						% Profit Before Taxes/Total Assets	4.4	3.2
-5.8							-1.7	-2.6
34.7							21.4	27.5
14.2						Sales/Net Fixed Assets	10.8	11.4
9.2							3.6	5.8
5.9							5.1	5.0
4.4						Sales/Total Assets	3.6	3.2
3.3							2.0	2.1
1.2							1.5	1.5
(13) 1.9						% Depr., Dep., Amort./Sales	(29) 2.4	(41) 2.6
3.6							3.9	4.0
							2.9	3.3
						% Officers', Directors' Owners' Comp/Sales	(17) 3.9	(32) 5.9
							7.8	9.6
13368M	22858M	93264M	85992M		79854M	Net Sales ($)	270862M	238698M
2945M	8326M	43775M	70882M		269715M	Total Assets ($)	98839M	105427M

M = $ thousand MM = $ million

See Pages 11 through 21 for Explanation of Ratios and Data

Comparative Historical Data | | | | Current Data Sorted by Sales

			Type of Statement						
3	2	2	Unqualified	1					1
5	6	5	Reviewed			1	1	3	
6	5	5	Compiled	2	1	1	1		
13	11	10	Tax Returns	6	4				
8	7	13	Other	6	1			3	3
4/1/04-3/31/05 ALL	4/1/05-3/31/06 ALL	4/1/06-3/31/07 ALL		0-1MM	7 (4/1-9/30/06) 1-3MM	3-5MM	28 (10/1/06-3/31/07) 5-10MM	10-25MM	25MM & OVER
35	31	35	**NUMBER OF STATEMENTS**	15	6	2	2	6	4
%	%	%	**ASSETS**	%	%	%	%	%	%
12.0	11.4	11.5	Cash & Equivalents	12.4					
5.9	7.5	6.6	Trade Receivables (net)	10.1					
20.6	21.0	18.1	Inventory	16.2					
4.4	1.1	2.0	All Other Current	2.9					
42.9	41.1	38.2	Total Current	41.5					
34.3	35.0	33.7	Fixed Assets (net)	44.1					
8.3	11.0	15.1	Intangibles (net)	9.5					
14.5	12.9	13.1	All Other Non-Current	4.8					
100.0	100.0	100.0	Total	100.0					
			LIABILITIES						
4.8	6.1	2.2	Notes Payable-Short Term	1.0					
5.1	2.8	4.2	Cur. Mat.-L.T.D.	6.4					
15.8	11.4	10.1	Trade Payables	5.7					
.3	.0	.0	Income Taxes Payable	.0					
24.8	20.1	16.4	All Other Current	19.8					
50.8	40.5	32.9	Total Current	32.8					
21.6	43.4	31.3	Long-Term Debt	37.8					
.1	.3	.3	Deferred Taxes	.0					
9.4	9.2	17.3	All Other Non-Current	27.6					
18.0	6.7	18.3	Net Worth	1.8					
100.0	100.0	100.0	Total Liabilties & Net Worth	100.0					
			INCOME DATA						
100.0	100.0	100.0	Net Sales	100.0					
			Gross Profit						
96.0	95.0	93.0	Operating Expenses	91.3					
4.0	5.0	7.0	Operating Profit	8.7					
2.5	2.5	3.4	All Other Expenses (net)	4.6					
1.5	2.5	3.6	Profit Before Taxes	4.1					
			RATIOS						
1.5	2.3	2.7		3.5					
1.0	1.3	1.4	Current	1.9					
.6	.8	.8		.8					
.8	1.5	1.2		2.5					
.4	.5	.6	Quick	.7					
.2	.2	.2		.2					
1 387.1	1 447.5	1 335.7		1 293.7					
3 143.5	3 123.8	3 133.5	Sales/Receivables	6 65.9					
6 56.5	8 47.8	10 37.6		17 22.0					
			Cost of Sales/Inventory						
			Cost of Sales/Payables						
12.8	14.7	12.0		9.2					
999.8	30.8	22.6	Sales/Working Capital	21.6					
-17.2	-42.9	-20.8		-24.5					
3.6	8.0	6.2							
(26) 2.0	(26) 1.8	(25) 1.5	EBIT/Interest						
1.2	1.0	-.1							
			Net Profit + Depr., Dep., Amort./Cur. Mat. L/T/D						
.6	.4	.5		.5					
1.8	2.3	5.1	Fixed/Worth	7.3					
31.9	-3.0	-.9		-.9					
1.2	1.2	.9		.8					
3.9	5.5	11.8	Debt/Worth	60.4					
-31.1	-2.8	-3.1		-2.0					
55.4	78.1	49.7	% Profit Before Taxes/Tangible Net Worth						
(26) 21.1	(22) 22.4	(21) 13.6							
-2.5	5.7	-5.2							
7.2	14.1	13.8	% Profit Before Taxes/Total Assets	13.8					
2.7	6.4	2.9		.6					
-.3	.1	-3.8		-4.8					
52.2	74.4	25.9	Sales/Net Fixed Assets	14.8					
14.8	10.3	11.1		10.3					
4.3	5.9	5.7		5.7					
5.2	5.6	4.8	Sales/Total Assets	4.9					
3.8	3.3	3.1		3.8					
2.0	2.1	1.4		2.5					
1.4	1.1	1.1	% Depr., Dep., Amort./Sales	1.6					
(24) 2.2	(25) 2.5	(29) 1.9		(12) 2.9					
3.4	3.1	3.4		4.8					
2.4	2.5	1.8	% Officers', Directors' Owners' Comp/Sales						
(24) 5.5	(20) 4.8	(18) 2.8							
7.4	6.5	5.0							
675077M	485962M	295336M	Net Sales ($)	8131M	11400M	6230M	10297M	93432M	165846M
300859M	259577M	395643M	Total Assets ($)	3434M	4441M	1416M	11738M	34017M	340597M

M = $ thousand   MM = $ million
See Pages 11 through 21 for Explanation of Ratios and Data

Current Data Sorted by Assets   Comparative Historical Data

	0-500M	500M-2MM	2-10MM	10-50MM	50-100MM	100-250MM		4/1/02-3/31/03 ALL		4/1/03-3/31/04 ALL
Type of Statement										
Unqualified			1		1			3		2
Reviewed			1					6		3
Compiled	7	8	2	1		1		15		12
Tax Returns	15	7	1					16		15
Other	6	5	4	3				7		8
		14 (4/1-9/30/06)		50 (10/1/06-3/31/07)						
NUMBER OF STATEMENTS	28	21	9	4	1	1		47		40
	%	%	%	%	%	%		%		%
ASSETS										
Cash & Equivalents	14.1	6.1						9.3		11.4
Trade Receivables (net)	15.4	19.9						17.9		16.7
Inventory	17.5	21.7						24.0		22.9
All Other Current	4.2	2.2						3.0		1.6
Total Current	51.2	49.9						54.2		52.6
Fixed Assets (net)	32.7	33.3						33.9		35.3
Intangibles (net)	7.7	4.7						4.4		4.8
All Other Non-Current	8.4	12.0						7.6		7.3
Total	100.0	100.0						100.0		100.0
LIABILITIES										
Notes Payable-Short Term	7.4	7.9						13.4		13.9
Cur. Mat.-L.T.D.	3.6	4.8						5.6		5.2
Trade Payables	14.2	15.3						16.1		12.0
Income Taxes Payable	.1	.4						.6		.0
All Other Current	29.6	6.4						30.8		11.8
Total Current	54.8	34.9						66.4		42.9
Long-Term Debt	35.9	31.8						19.6		28.2
Deferred Taxes	.0	.0						.5		.7
All Other Non-Current	14.9	9.8						10.4		6.9
Net Worth	-5.7	23.5						3.1		21.3
Total Liabilties & Net Worth	100.0	100.0						100.0		100.0
INCOME DATA										
Net Sales	100.0	100.0						100.0		100.0
Gross Profit										
Operating Expenses	98.1	92.1						95.2		94.6
Operating Profit	1.9	7.9						4.8		5.4
All Other Expenses (net)	.2	4.8						2.1		2.6
Profit Before Taxes	1.8	3.0						2.7		2.8
RATIOS										
Current	5.3	2.0						2.0		2.1
	1.2	1.3						1.3		1.3
	.5	.9						.6		.8
Quick	3.3	1.6						1.2		1.3
	.5	.6						.6		.6
	.2	.3						.1		.2
Sales/Receivables	1 284.6	4 94.5						0 999.8		0 807.5
	8 47.1	22 16.6						7 52.8		11 33.4
	25 14.9	37 9.9						41 8.8		27 13.3
Cost of Sales/Inventory										
Cost of Sales/Payables										
Sales/Working Capital	8.3	9.0						8.2		8.1
	54.6	14.4						50.5		49.8
	-31.7	-509.6						-14.3		-30.5
EBIT/Interest	5.9	6.2						9.0		5.5
	(18) 2.5	(20) 2.8						(40) 2.3		(31) 2.8
	.8	1.2						.8		.1
Net Profit + Depr., Dep., Amort./Cur. Mat. L/T/D										
Fixed/Worth	.5	.2						.3		.6
	1.4	.9						1.2		1.6
	-1.6	2.2						-30.9		-6.5
Debt/Worth	.6	1.3						.7		.9
	9.0	2.4						3.1		3.4
	-3.1	NM						-20.1		-16.9
% Profit Before Taxes/Tangible Net Worth	45.6	31.2						58.7		82.6
	(17) 21.7	(16) 18.6						(32) 13.5		(29) 16.3
	-7.3	3.0						-1.7		-5.2
% Profit Before Taxes/Total Assets	19.8	15.6						21.3		22.5
	8.1	3.9						4.8		3.5
	.2	.5						.0		-3.9
Sales/Net Fixed Assets	41.6	40.0						33.4		25.6
	17.4	17.3						13.0		9.5
	9.8	3.2						4.9		4.4
Sales/Total Assets	6.6	4.1						5.0		4.5
	4.5	2.3						2.7		3.1
	2.6	1.6						1.9		1.7
% Depr., Dep., Amort./Sales	.7	.8						1.2		1.4
	(22) 1.7	(18) 1.7						(35) 2.5		(35) 2.4
	3.3	5.8						3.8		3.8
% Officers', Directors' Owners' Comp/Sales	5.6	2.3						4.5		2.9
	(21) 6.8	(11) 5.9						(25) 7.2		(26) 6.0
	9.3	12.2						10.0		12.4
Net Sales ($)	32988M	61715M	84429M	198474M	807749M	558930M		483558M		164077M
Total Assets ($)	5704M	22421M	34179M	78454M	98153M	150693M		325397M		90202M

Comparative Historical Data   **Current Data Sorted by Sales**

Type of Statement					14 (4/1-9/30/06)		50 (10/1/06-3/31/07)			
	1	1	2	Unqualified				2		
	4	8	2	Reviewed				1		1
	15	16	19	Compiled	5	7	2	2	2	
	11	19	23	Tax Returns	11	6	4	2		3
	12	14	18	Other	5	6	1	2		2
	4/1/04-3/31/05 ALL	4/1/05-3/31/06 ALL	4/1/06-3/31/07 ALL		0-1MM	1-3MM	3-5MM	5-10MM	10-25MM	25MM & OVER
	43	58	64	**NUMBER OF STATEMENTS**	21	19	7	9	2	6
	%	%	%	**ASSETS**	%	%	%	%	%	%
	12.6	10.7	11.3	Cash & Equivalents	14.8	6.4				
	18.8	16.8	17.0	Trade Receivables (net)	11.4	17.6				
	21.0	26.5	18.8	Inventory	11.8	23.5				
	2.4	5.6	3.4	All Other Current	5.6	2.0				
	54.8	59.6	50.5	Total Current	43.6	49.5				
	30.4	29.2	35.2	Fixed Assets (net)	34.5	38.7				
	6.6	6.4	5.5	Intangibles (net)	11.8	3.3				
	8.3	4.8	8.8	All Other Non-Current	10.1	8.5				
	100.0	100.0	100.0	Total	100.0	100.0				
				LIABILITIES						
	11.5	10.0	8.0	Notes Payable-Short Term	6.0	6.8				
	5.1	4.2	4.1	Cur. Mat.-L.T.D.	5.2	3.9				
	15.7	15.5	14.1	Trade Payables	7.7	19.9				
	.1	.1	.2	Income Taxes Payable	.0	.0				
	19.6	16.2	16.8	All Other Current	9.8	36.6				
	52.0	45.9	43.2	Total Current	28.7	67.2				
	19.9	28.8	34.3	Long-Term Debt	33.0	48.1				
	.7	.5	.0	Deferred Taxes	.0	.0				
	9.4	6.6	11.2	All Other Non-Current	15.4	8.3				
	17.9	18.3	11.3	Net Worth	22.9	-23.6				
	100.0	100.0	100.0	Total Liabilities & Net Worth	100.0	100.0				
				INCOME DATA						
	100.0	100.0	100.0	Net Sales	100.0	100.0				
				Gross Profit						
	95.6	94.7	95.2	Operating Expenses	92.2	98.1				
	4.4	5.3	4.8	Operating Profit	7.8	1.9				
	.9	1.9	1.9	All Other Expenses (net)	4.6	.7				
	3.5	3.4	2.9	Profit Before Taxes	3.2	1.3				
				RATIOS						
	2.5	2.4	2.5		6.0	2.0				
	1.3	1.5	1.3	Current	1.3	1.1				
	.9	1.0	.7		.4	.4				
	1.8	1.4	1.9		5.2	1.7				
	.8	.5	.6	Quick	.5	.4				
	.3	.2	.2		.2	.2				
	3 112.9	2 197.6	2 222.8		0 UND	2 225.4				
	13 27.5	10 37.1	13 28.8	Sales/Receivables	8 46.4	9 39.7				
	27 13.5	38 9.7	28 12.9		24 15.0	33 11.1				
				Cost of Sales/Inventory						
				Cost of Sales/Payables						
	9.1	8.4	9.6		7.6	12.7				
	26.4	22.7	32.6	Sales/Working Capital	29.1	263.8				
	-78.4	NM	-69.6		-10.1	-51.7				
	10.9	13.7	7.5		6.3	4.8				
	(40) 3.9	(48) 3.8	(53) 2.9	EBIT/Interest	(13) 2.8	(16) 2.8				
	1.3	.0	1.2		.4	-.7				
				Net Profit + Depr., Dep., Amort./Cur. Mat..L/T/D						
	.4	.3	.4		.3	.5				
	.8	.8	1.4	Fixed/Worth	1.4	1.5				
	4.7	8.3	-10.4		-1.8	-1.5				
	.8	.9	.9		.4	1.8				
	2.3	2.5	2.7	Debt/Worth	7.7	3.0				
	54.6	-127.5	-11.4		-3.3	-3.5				
	90.0	44.2	40.1		22.2	41.5				
	(34) 20.9	(43) 17.2	(44) 22.0	% Profit Before Taxes/Tangible Net Worth	(12) 13.6	(12) 30.5				
	2.8	1.1	3.4		-35.7	5.5				
	18.7	17.1	18.9		18.5	18.4				
	5.8	5.8	7.4	% Profit Before Taxes/Total Assets	8.7	7.3				
	.8	-.9	.6		-2.2	-5.5				
	37.8	42.3	39.2		45.8	40.0				
	16.5	18.1	15.1	Sales/Net Fixed Assets	10.3	15.6				
	8.0	6.8	4.3		4.3	3.7				
	4.6	5.8	5.2		4.8	6.5				
	3.9	3.5	3.3	Sales/Total Assets	3.2	2.6				
	2.7	2.0	1.8		1.8	1.7				
	.8	.7	.8		1.0	.7				
	(38) 1.7	(43) 1.2	(55) 1.6	% Depr., Dep., Amort./Sales	(17) 2.3	(16) 1.8				
	2.4	2.4	3.8		4.3	4.7				
	2.9	3.2	2.3		5.9					
	(27) 4.1	(33) 5.4	(41) 5.9	% Officers', Directors' Owners' Comp/Sales	(16) 8.6					
	7.1	10.4	9.1		11.9					
	280146M	2034715M	1744285M	Net Sales ($)	11765M	35435M	25286M	66982M	37750M	1567067M
	105347M	405719M	389604M	Total Assets ($)	5735M	12473M	10033M	26281M	19001M	316081M

M = $ thousand   MM = $ million
See Pages 11 through 21 for Explanation of Ratios and Data

Current Data Sorted by Assets							Comparative Historical Data	

Type of Statement

3	5	2				Unqualified	7	5
24	25	5				Reviewed	16	14
96	32	12				Compiled	82	90
33	31	4			1	Tax Returns	85	112
		19				Other	52	68
	48 (4/1-9/30/06)		257 (10/1/06-3/31/07)	9	4		4/1/02-3/31/03	4/1/03-3/31/04
0-500M	500M-2MM	2-10MM	10-50MM	50-100MM	100-250MM		ALL	ALL
156	93	42	9	4	1	NUMBER OF STATEMENTS	242	289
%	%	%	%	%	%	**ASSETS**	%	%
15.8	13.3	9.5				Cash & Equivalents	14.1	13.9
13.3	16.7	13.7				Trade Receivables (net)	14.4	15.9
13.7	9.2	15.3				Inventory	11.1	12.5
2.8	3.0	3.8				All Other Current	2.4	2.5
45.6	42.2	42.3				Total Current	42.0	44.9
40.5	43.5	39.6				Fixed Assets (net)	42.0	39.6
4.8	2.2	9.6				Intangibles (net)	6.6	6.4
9.2	12.0	8.6				All Other Non-Current	9.5	9.1
100.0	100.0	100.0				Total	100.0	100.0
						LIABILITIES		
16.2	7.5	5.4				Notes Payable-Short Term	9.3	9.3
4.4	4.1	4.7				Cur. Mat.-L.T.D.	5.9	5.1
23.8	12.8	14.6				Trade Payables	15.2	15.1
.5	.1	.0				Income Taxes Payable	.2	.3
17.7	10.4	10.8				All Other Current	10.7	12.4
62.6	34.9	35.6				Total Current	41.3	42.2
37.4	31.1	28.6				Long-Term Debt	30.8	28.8
.0	.2	.0				Deferred Taxes	.2	.1
11.4	3.2	5.3				All Other Non-Current	7.0	9.5
-11.4	30.6	30.4				Net Worth	20.7	19.4
100.0	100.0	100.0				Total Liabilities & Net Worth	100.0	100.0
						INCOME DATA		
100.0	100.0	100.0				Net Sales	100.0	100.0
						Gross Profit		
96.1	92.6	94.6				Operating Expenses	95.8	96.0
3.9	7.4	5.4				Operating Profit	4.2	4.0
1.8	2.4	2.7				All Other Expenses (net)	1.6	1.3
2.1	5.0	2.6				Profit Before Taxes	2.6	2.7
						RATIOS		
1.7	2.5	1.8					1.9	2.1
.8	1.3	1.1				Current	1.1	1.1
.4	.8	.6					.6	.7
1.2	1.9	1.3					1.6	1.7
(155) .4	(92) .9	.6				Quick	(240) .7	(285) .7
.2	.5	.4					.3	.4
0 UND	2 232.1	9 40.0					2 205.7	1 661.9
5 67.5	15 23.6	17 21.7				Sales/Receivables	11 33.6	11 32.0
12 31.6	26 13.9	25 14.4					19 18.8	19 18.9
						Cost of Sales/Inventory		
						Cost of Sales/Payables		
27.0	12.5	10.9					17.1	14.9
-86.8	43.0	108.2				Sales/Working Capital	216.6	98.6
-17.7	-34.7	-21.1					-28.2	-33.7
8.8	11.4	9.6					9.2	8.3
(137) 2.8	(77) 3.8	(38) 3.0				EBIT/Interest	(202) 2.6	(231) 2.6
-.1	1.7	1.3					.8	.9
	5.9					Net Profit + Depr., Dep.,	4.6	5.3
	(13) 3.8					Amort./Cur. Mat. L/T/D	(33) 1.9	(26) 1.5
	.5						.9	.4
.7	.5	.5					.5	.7
4.2	1.8	1.9				Fixed/Worth	1.8	2.0
-1.1	5.9	14.3					-10.2	-20.7
1.6	.8	1.3					1.0	1.2
15.9	2.8	4.0				Debt/Worth	3.4	4.0
-2.7	14.7	22.5					-20.4	-28.9
125.7	106.7	50.7				% Profit Before Taxes/Tangible	52.6	73.3
(91) 66.7	(77) 33.3	(36) 28.4				Net Worth	(167) 25.5	(210) 23.9
6.6	11.2	11.7					1.3	1.7
35.6	21.1	14.1				% Profit Before Taxes/Total	20.8	16.8
9.4	9.4	8.1				Assets	6.3	6.0
-4.0	3.1	2.0					-1.0	-.6
49.3	28.0	27.2					27.7	31.5
19.6	10.3	7.9				Sales/Net Fixed Assets	12.0	13.7
8.1	4.3	3.0					5.1	6.5
10.1	5.3	3.9					6.1	6.4
6.1	3.4	2.4				Sales/Total Assets	4.0	4.5
4.0	1.9	1.5					2.4	2.6
.7	1.0	1.4					1.1	.9
(120) 1.5	(80) 1.6	(34) 2.1				% Depr., Dep., Amort./Sales	(216) 1.9	(242) 1.9
2.9	2.9	3.5					3.4	3.5
3.2	2.4	1.4				% Officers', Directors'	3.3	2.9
(106) 5.4	(64) 3.9	(20) 2.8				Owners' Comp/Sales	(158) 5.5	(200) 4.8
9.2	6.1	4.0					8.4	8.0
229458M	352640M	479586M	479904M	1172297M	1954747M	Net Sales ($)	6595533M	4466555M
37279M	92700M	174181M	207099M	279381M	211290M	Total Assets ($)	1424586M	967171M

M = $ thousand   MM = $ million
See Pages 11 through 21 for Explanation of Ratios and Data

Comparative Historical Data | | | | Current Data Sorted by Sales

			Type of Statement						
10	4	2	Unqualified	1					1
18	18	13	Reviewed	2	4	2	4	1	
65	41	61	Compiled	10	23	14	9	5	
132	115	133	Tax Returns	35	71	13	7	5	2
83	106	96	Other	18	36	10	12	7	13
4/1/04-3/31/05 ALL	4/1/05-3/31/06 ALL	4/1/06-3/31/07 ALL		48 (4/1-9/30/06)		257 (10/1/06-3/31/07)			
				0-1MM	1-3MM	3-5MM	5-10MM	10-25MM	25MM & OVER
308	284	305	NUMBER OF STATEMENTS	66	134	39	32	18	16
%	%	%	ASSETS	%	%	%	%	%	%
14.8	14.1	13.8	Cash & Equivalents	11.9	15.7	17.9	6.3	17.4	6.5
15.9	16.0	14.5	Trade Receivables (net)	9.6	13.9	17.1	22.0	16.3	17.1
11.3	13.0	12.8	Inventory	16.0	11.0	8.1	17.5	16.0	13.8
2.0	2.4	2.9	All Other Current	2.1	3.1	3.4	3.9	2.6	1.5
44.1	45.6	44.0	Total Current	39.6	43.7	46.5	49.6	52.4	39.0
40.3	40.5	40.7	Fixed Assets (net)	47.3	41.5	37.5	36.3	33.0	32.3
5.8	5.9	5.4	Intangibles (net)	3.7	4.8	2.4	6.3	7.1	20.6
9.8	8.0	9.9	All Other Non-Current	9.4	10.0	13.6	7.7	7.4	8.1
100.0	100.0	100.0	Total	100.0	100.0	100.0	100.0	100.0	100.0
			LIABILITIES						
8.5	13.2	11.8	Notes Payable-Short Term	17.3	11.3	9.6	6.2	11.8	9.4
5.0	4.4	4.2	Cur. Mat.-L.T.D.	3.0	4.7	5.2	4.8	3.2	3.5
18.1	17.5	18.7	Trade Payables	16.7	20.9	15.7	17.8	21.4	14.1
.5	.2	.3	Income Taxes Payable	.1	.5	.1	.3	.1	.0
14.1	15.4	14.5	All Other Current	20.0	13.8	7.7	13.9	13.0	16.9
46.2	50.8	49.4	Total Current	57.0	51.1	38.3	43.1	49.5	43.8
36.9	34.4	34.9	Long-Term Debt	47.8	36.3	22.9	23.9	11.6	46.7
.1	.1	.1	Deferred Taxes	.0	.1	.1	.3	.0	.1
7.5	11.7	8.4	All Other Non-Current	9.7	8.5	5.9	5.0	6.3	16.5
9.2	3.1	7.3	Net Worth	-14.5	4.0	32.9	27.7	32.6	-7.1
100.0	100.0	100.0	Total Liabilties & Net Worth	100.0	100.0	100.0	100.0	100.0	100.0
			INCOME DATA						
100.0	100.0	100.0	Net Sales	100.0	100.0	100.0	100.0	100.0	100.0
			Gross Profit						
95.6	94.7	94.7	Operating Expenses	91.5	95.6	95.2	95.1	96.3	96.6
4.4	5.3	5.3	Operating Profit	8.5	4.4	4.8	4.9	3.7	3.4
1.8	2.2	2.2	All Other Expenses (net)	5.5	1.5	.6	1.0	.5	2.7
2.6	3.1	3.1	Profit Before Taxes	3.0	2.9	4.2	4.0	3.2	.7
			RATIOS						
2.1	1.8	1.8		2.0	1.8	2.3	1.8	2.5	1.1
1.1	1.1	1.0	Current	.7	1.0	1.3	1.2	1.0	.9
.5	.5	.5		.3	.5	.8	.7	.8	.5
1.5	1.3	1.4		1.2	1.4	1.8	1.4	1.6	.7
.7 (283)	.6 (303)	.6	Quick	.4 (133)	.6	.9 (31)	.8	.7	.4
.3	.3	.3		.2	.3	.5	.5	.5	.3
1 321.9	2 227.6	0 999.8		0 UND	0 UND	5 72.4	10 38.2	5 78.3	12 30.7
10 37.5	11 34.4	9 39.6	Sales/Receivables	5 75.3	8 47.9	11 31.8	18 20.0	13 28.2	15 24.5
19 19.3	21 17.2	20 18.7		11 33.6	18 20.8	25 14.6	28 12.9	23 15.9	26 14.1
			Cost of Sales/Inventory						
			Cost of Sales/Payables						
15.5	15.6	18.3		17.3	23.9	11.2	20.1	18.6	157.6
110.0	156.6	UND	Sales/Working Capital	-49.2	-990.2	33.7	44.8	NM	-308.5
-22.4	-16.2	-21.0		-7.8	-22.8	-66.9	-25.4	-40.2	-13.8
8.5	8.7	9.2		5.2	9.8	10.6	10.5	32.2	3.9
(245) 2.2	(241) 2.3	(265) 3.0	EBIT/Interest	(54) 1.3	(119) 2.9	(33) 4.6	(28) 3.5	(16) 11.6	(15) 2.6
-.3	.3	1.0		-.7	.6	1.9	1.6	2.9	1.2
4.4	6.2	4.2							
(32) 1.7	(20) 2.0	(26) 1.6	Net Profit + Depr., Dep., Amort./Cur. Mat. L/T/D						
.6	.2	.6							
.6	.7	.6		.8	.7	.4	.6	.3	2.1
2.1	3.7	2.5	Fixed/Worth	4.2	3.0	1.3	1.6	1.6	-3.4
-4.9	-2.3	-4.4		-1.6	-3.0	7.3	8.7	125.2	-.5
1.1	1.4	1.4		1.7	1.3	.5	1.4	.7	7.7
4.1	8.0	5.1	Debt/Worth	9.5	5.1	2.2	2.8	3.5	-5.5
-9.0	-6.0	-7.6		-2.7	-6.0	23.9	10.4	181.1	-2.4
73.4	76.7	110.7		102.5	123.3	135.0	97.0	72.0	
(212) 25.1	(176) 31.5	(209) 39.3	% Profit Before Taxes/Tangible Net Worth	(41) 57.1	(86) 45.7	(33) 46.5	(27) 36.1	(15) 31.9	
2.4	4.5	9.1		1.6	6.0	15.4	11.5	21.7	
17.2	17.9	26.0		22.7	29.7	29.8	26.1	31.7	12.9
4.0	5.2	8.8	% Profit Before Taxes/Total Assets	3.1	9.6	9.3	11.0	9.6	5.6
-3.3	-1.2	.2		-4.2	-2.3	3.9	2.9	2.7	1.2
32.3	32.8	34.9		35.8	41.1	31.7	36.3	47.1	22.0
15.6	12.8	13.8	Sales/Net Fixed Assets	8.2	16.6	13.5	17.8	20.9	11.9
5.4	5.9	5.8		3.3	6.8	5.8	6.1	11.9	10.2
6.7	6.1	7.0		6.4	8.7	6.5	6.6	8.5	3.9
4.1	4.3	4.5	Sales/Total Assets	3.1	5.1	4.5	4.5	5.0	3.1
2.5	2.4	2.6		1.9	3.0	2.2	2.4	3.3	2.3
.8	1.1	.9		1.5	.7	1.4	.7	.9	1.3
(252) 1.8	(230) 2.0	(246) 1.6	% Depr., Dep., Amort./Sales	(43) 3.7	(112) 1.5	(35) 2.2	(27) 1.4	(15) 1.5	(14) 2.3
3.4	3.3	3.0		5.6	2.4	3.2	2.5	1.6	3.3
3.1	3.1	2.8		4.1	3.2	2.5	1.7	.7	
(190) 4.7	(172) 5.2	(193) 4.5	% Officers', Directors' Owners' Comp/Sales	(35) 7.5	(95) 4.9	(30) 3.2	(19) 3.2	(10) 1.3	
8.6	8.9	7.9		9.9	8.2	5.3	5.3	2.7	
3617605M	2549525M	4668632M	Net Sales ($)	40786M	252172M	152919M	226457M	310940M	3685358M
713850M	912493M	1001930M	Total Assets ($)	27860M	66424M	46295M	85195M	72165M	703991M

M = $ thousand   MM = $ million
See Pages 11 through 21 for Explanation of Ratios and Data

Current Data Sorted by Assets

Comparative Historical Data

		1						
1	4	4						
2	1	1						
7	3							
3	1	2		1	1			
	7 (4/1-9/30/06)		25 (10/1/06-3/31/07)					

Type of Statement

0-500M	500M-2MM	2-10MM	10-50MM	50-100MM	100-250MM		4/1/02-3/31/03 ALL	4/1/03-3/31/04 ALL
						Unqualified	8	5
						Reviewed	1	4
						Compiled	5	5
						Tax Returns	10	15
						Other	12	15
13	9	8	1	1		NUMBER OF STATEMENTS	36	44
%	%	%	%	%	%	**ASSETS**	%	%
11.4						Cash & Equivalents	9.2	10.3
18.0						Trade Receivables (net)	30.9	33.2
17.9						Inventory	14.0	17.1
2.3						All Other Current	2.8	1.6
49.7						Total Current	56.9	62.2
30.8						Fixed Assets (net)	28.5	28.1
7.2						Intangibles (net)	2.4	2.0
12.2						All Other Non-Current	12.2	7.7
100.0						Total	100.0	100.0
						LIABILITIES		
16.2						Notes Payable-Short Term	9.9	10.9
6.2						Cur. Mat.-L.T.D.	4.2	4.0
7.6						Trade Payables	21.1	21.1
.0						Income Taxes Payable	.2	.3
7.9						All Other Current	10.7	21.1
38.0						Total Current	46.1	57.4
46.2						Long-Term Debt	16.4	26.1
.0						Deferred Taxes	.1	.2
5.9						All Other Non-Current	10.3	2.1
9.9						Net Worth	27.1	14.2
100.0						Total Liabilities & Net Worth	100.0	100.0
						INCOME DATA		
100.0						Net Sales	100.0	100.0
						Gross Profit		
96.3						Operating Expenses	97.8	98.6
3.7						Operating Profit	2.2	1.4
.9						All Other Expenses (net)	.6	.7
2.8						Profit Before Taxes	1.6	.8
						RATIOS		
4.4							1.8	2.4
1.3						Current	1.4	1.4
.8							.8	.9
3.2							1.5	1.5
.8						Quick	1.1	1.0
.2							.5	.5
0 UND							19 19.7	16 22.7
7 53.1						Sales/Receivables	25 14.6	24 15.2
23 16.0							65 5.7	37 9.9
						Cost of Sales/Inventory		
						Cost of Sales/Payables		
16.1							8.4	8.5
132.7						Sales/Working Capital	22.1	22.3
-116.0							-32.5	-52.8
							13.1	30.9
						EBIT/Interest	(34) 2.0	(34) 5.1
							.3	-.1
						Net Profit + Depr., Dep., Amort./Cur. Mat. L/T/D		
.4							.4	.3
4.2						Fixed/Worth	1.1	1.2
-1.3							2.2	NM
2.5							1.1	1.1
19.3						Debt/Worth	2.1	3.4
-3.4							7.3	NM
							69.9	65.9
						% Profit Before Taxes/Tangible Net Worth	(30) 9.9	(33) 24.4
							-5.7	-1.7
66.8							17.2	24.8
9.5						% Profit Before Taxes/Total Assets	3.8	5.5
-7.2							-2.2	-4.7
48.0							28.5	28.0
15.1						Sales/Net Fixed Assets	14.7	17.9
12.9							6.1	9.8
10.7							5.0	5.2
4.2						Sales/Total Assets	2.9	3.8
2.6							2.1	2.3
1.7							1.0	1.1
(10) 2.5						% Depr., Dep., Amort./Sales	(34) 1.9	(40) 1.8
4.8							3.2	2.7
2.9							1.3	3.1
(10) 5.1						% Officers', Directors' Owners' Comp/Sales	(11) 2.7	(24) 4.6
7.7							4.8	10.0
12544M	37125M	105981M	49792M	100203M		Net Sales ($)	760557M	556689M
2804M	10397M	35986M	47921M	54927M		Total Assets ($)	353765M	285852M

(Columns 500M-2MM through 100-250MM marked: DATA NOT AVAILABLE)

M = $ thousand   MM = $ million
See Pages 11 through 21 for Explanation of Ratios and Data

Comparative Historical Data | Current Data Sorted by Sales

			Type of Statement						
6	3	1	Unqualified				1		
7	10	9	Reviewed	1	1		5	2	
11	4	4	Compiled	1	1		1		1
15	11	10	Tax Returns	6	4		1		
7	5	8	Other	2	2				2
4/1/04-3/31/05	4/1/05-3/31/06	4/1/06-3/31/07		7 (4/1-9/30/06)			25 (10/1/06-3/31/07)		
ALL	ALL	ALL		0-1MM	1-3MM	3-5MM	5-10MM	10-25MM	25MM & OVER
46	33	32	**NUMBER OF STATEMENTS**	10	8		8	3	3
%	%	%	**ASSETS**	%	%	%	%	%	%
11.1	12.7	13.0	Cash & Equivalents	7.4					
29.2	28.8	22.9	Trade Receivables (net)	9.8					
14.8	16.9	15.2	Inventory	19.9					
1.7	.9	2.6	All Other Current	.7					
56.8	59.3	53.7	Total Current	37.8		D			
31.7	28.7	29.6	Fixed Assets (net)	39.0		A			
2.1	2.4	8.5	Intangibles (net)	9.3		T			
9.3	9.7	8.1	All Other Non-Current	13.9		A			
100.0	100.0	100.0	Total	100.0					
			LIABILITIES			N			
8.5	9.1	12.2	Notes Payable-Short Term	21.1		O			
5.5	9.5	4.2	Cur. Mat.-L.T.D.	1.9		T			
19.7	18.3	14.2	Trade Payables	4.6					
.3	.1	.0	Income Taxes Payable	.0		A			
9.9	7.9	9.1	All Other Current	3.8		V			
43.8	44.8	39.7	Total Current	31.4		A			
19.7	22.4	28.2	Long-Term Debt	52.7		I			
.4	.0	.1	Deferred Taxes	.0		L			
9.4	5.6	9.4	All Other Non-Current	7.6		A			
26.7	27.2	22.7	Net Worth	8.2		B			
100.0	100.0	100.0	Total Liabilties & Net Worth	100.0		L			
			INCOME DATA			E			
100.0	100.0	100.0	Net Sales	100.0					
			Gross Profit						
97.8	96.4	98.4	Operating Expenses	97.7					
2.2	3.6	1.6	Operating Profit	2.3					
.3	.9	.8	All Other Expenses (net)	1.2					
1.9	2.6	.8	Profit Before Taxes	1.0					
			RATIOS						
2.0	2.5	3.1		6.0					
1.4	1.4	1.3	Current	1.7					
.7	1.0	.8		.6					
1.6	1.5	2.3		4.0					
.9	1.0	.7	Quick	.6					
.5	.6	.5		.1					
15 23.7	19 19.5	7 49.9		0 UND					
26 13.9	26 14.1	17 21.3	Sales/Receivables	5 69.9					
40 9.1	41 8.9	35 10.4		17 21.5					
			Cost of Sales/Inventory						
			Cost of Sales/Payables						
9.0	7.2	9.0		10.8					
34.9	17.2	30.0	Sales/Working Capital	UND					
-19.5	-402.7	-34.0		-9.5					
17.0	9.0	5.9							
(38) 6.0	(27) 1.4	(27) 2.0	EBIT/Interest						
-.6	-.3	-3.1							
			Net Profit + Depr., Dep., Amort./Cur. Mat. L/T/D						
.3	.3	.4		1.1					
1.2	.9	1.1	Fixed/Worth	5.1					
NM	8.3	-4.3		-.9					
1.0	.8	.7		3.3					
2.4	2.0	4.4	Debt/Worth	27.6					
NM	85.1	-6.8		-2.5					
59.2	26.4	75.9	% Profit Before Taxes/Tangible Net Worth						
(35) 21.0	(26) 3.3	(22) 11.7							
-8.4	-1.7	-13.8							
20.1	10.3	14.7	% Profit Before Taxes/Total Assets	17.7					
7.5	2.8	3.0		7.9					
-4.9	-2.6	-9.3		-17.9					
32.1	41.9	40.6	Sales/Net Fixed Assets	20.4					
14.5	19.3	15.0		14.0					
6.8	7.3	9.1		8.3					
5.1	4.5	6.5	Sales/Total Assets	10.0					
3.7	3.4	3.0		3.2					
2.4	2.4	2.1		1.7					
1.2	1.1	1.3	% Depr., Dep., Amort./Sales	1.7					
(38) 1.6	(29) 1.6	(26) 2.0		2.3					
3.0	2.7	2.6		3.2					
2.9	3.6	3.2	% Officers', Directors' Owners' Comp/Sales						
(24) 4.8	(18) 5.0	(15) 6.4							
9.0	8.7	9.5							
728928M	598179M	305645M	Net Sales ($)	5605M	15426M		53974M	54217M	176423M
340833M	277026M	152035M	Total Assets ($)	2334M	7037M		15789M	15967M	110908M

M = $ thousand   MM = $ million
See Pages 11 through 21 for Explanation of Ratios and Data

Current Data Sorted by Assets   Comparative Historical Data

Type of Statement	0-500M	500M-2MM	2-10MM	10-50MM	50-100MM	100-250MM	4/1/02-3/31/03 ALL	4/1/03-3/31/04 ALL
Unqualified	4		1	2		3	7	12
Reviewed		1	9	2			13	18
Compiled	36	49	13	2	1	1	70	84
Tax Returns	62	55	15	2	1	1	76	89
Other	17	37	18	6	1	2	83	91
	36 (4/1-9/30/06)			307 (10/1/06-3/31/07)				
NUMBER OF STATEMENTS	115	146	58	13	4	7	249	294
	%	%	%	%	%	%	%	%
ASSETS								
Cash & Equivalents	13.7	7.2	6.2	14.6			10.8	10.1
Trade Receivables (net)	4.6	1.5	4.2	2.2			3.0	4.0
Inventory	5.1	2.0	3.6	4.6			4.0	3.9
All Other Current	.6	2.0	.7	2.8			2.4	1.9
Total Current	24.0	12.6	14.7	24.2			20.1	19.9
Fixed Assets (net)	59.2	73.1	70.8	66.8			68.3	67.9
Intangibles (net)	6.4	9.5	7.6	5.6			6.1	6.5
All Other Non-Current	10.5	4.8	6.9	3.4			5.4	5.7
Total	100.0	100.0	100.0	100.0			100.0	100.0
LIABILITIES								
Notes Payable-Short Term	8.2	2.8	2.7	5.2			5.8	5.1
Cur. Mat.-L.T.D.	9.4	4.9	5.7	4.7			5.2	4.6
Trade Payables	7.1	3.2	4.2	4.7			5.2	4.8
Income Taxes Payable	.3	.1	.0	.0			.0	.1
All Other Current	15.5	6.3	5.9	12.0			10.3	10.6
Total Current	40.5	17.3	18.6	26.6			26.5	25.2
Long-Term Debt	57.7	68.0	57.0	44.2			54.3	56.5
Deferred Taxes	.0	.0	.0	.0			.0	.1
All Other Non-Current	15.1	10.2	7.8	3.0			6.5	8.6
Net Worth	-13.3	4.5	16.6	26.2			12.7	9.6
Total Liabilties & Net Worth	100.0	100.0	100.0	100.0			100.0	100.0
INCOME DATA								
Net Sales	100.0	100.0	100.0	100.0			100.0	100.0
Gross Profit								
Operating Expenses	90.4	86.7	87.4	84.5			86.5	88.0
Operating Profit	9.6	13.3	12.6	15.5			13.5	12.0
All Other Expenses (net)	6.5	13.4	10.7	5.4			8.4	8.5
Profit Before Taxes	3.1	.0	1.9	10.0			5.0	3.5
RATIOS								
Current	2.0	1.9	1.9	1.6			2.1	2.1
	.6	.5	.8	1.0			.8	.7
	.2	.1	.3	.4			.2	.2
Quick	1.8	1.5	1.0	1.1			1.5	1.6
	.4	.3	.5	.7			(248) .5	.5
	.1	.1	.2	.1			.1	.1
Sales/Receivables	0 UND	0 UND	0 UND	0 UND			0 UND	0 UND
	0 UND	0 UND	2 226.3	3 106.9			0 UND	0 UND
	1 366.0	1 383.5	4 91.0	13 29.0			2 213.7	3 119.6
Cost of Sales/Inventory								
Cost of Sales/Payables								
Sales/Working Capital	25.7	22.0	38.0	11.4			18.6	22.0
	-37.6	-15.1	-50.8	-999.8			-70.4	-40.4
	-6.4	-4.3	-6.7	-5.1			-5.9	-6.2
EBIT/Interest	3.8	3.0	2.3	2.2			4.6	4.1
	(86) 1.3	(95) 1.5	(45) 1.1	(10) 1.8			(186) 1.9	(218) 1.7
	.4	.6	.0	1.3			.6	.5
Net Profit + Depr., Dep., Amort./Cur. Mat. L/T/D							7.4	4.8
							(21) 1.3	(23) 2.4
							.8	1.9
Fixed/Worth	1.5	3.6	3.5	1.6			1.4	1.6
	70.3	-90.7	34.2	3.5			9.8	8.8
	-1.2	-2.9	-13.6	16.3			-7.0	-6.0
Debt/Worth	1.5	3.3	2.8	1.6			1.3	1.7
	UND	-48.0	42.9	3.7			10.1	11.6
	-2.6	-4.2	-14.7	37.9			-8.8	-7.9
% Profit Before Taxes/Tangible Net Worth	80.0	60.9	30.2	47.4			70.2	59.3
	(60) 28.3	(69) 17.7	(32) 10.4	(12) 26.7			(152) 19.8	(176) 22.2
	.3	1.0	-12.0	9.8			4.0	5.6
% Profit Before Taxes/Total Assets	16.5	7.8	3.4	8.2			11.4	9.5
	2.6	1.3	.1	4.4			3.9	3.4
	-4.1	-3.8	-5.8	-.2			-1.9	-2.9
Sales/Net Fixed Assets	23.6	2.9	3.4	2.4			5.0	5.7
	4.5	.8	.7	1.4			1.5	1.1
	1.0	.4	.3	.5			.5	.5
Sales/Total Assets	4.4	1.4	1.3	2.0			2.4	2.2
	1.9	.6	.6	.9			1.0	.8
	.8	.3	.3	.4			.5	.4
% Depr., Dep., Amort./Sales	2.2	4.3	2.3	3.1			3.3	3.6
	(87) 5.8	(124) 10.4	(52) 8.0	(12) 5.9			(217) 7.8	(262) 8.6
	15.9	22.4	15.7	14.5			18.7	20.4
% Officers', Directors' Owners' Comp/Sales	4.0	3.2	1.7				3.4	2.9
	(51) 8.5	(41) 6.7	(15) 3.7				(86) 6.8	(95) 6.0
	13.0	10.8	9.9				11.4	11.9
Net Sales ($)	66545M	182419M	269597M	622622M	327355M	2375622M	850536M	1460432M
Total Assets ($)	28971M	159857M	212358M	286719M	239513M	983555M	838415M	1250513M

© RMA 2007

M = $ thousand   MM = $ million
See Pages 11 through 21 for Explanation of Ratios and Data

Comparative Historical Data						Type of Statement	Current Data Sorted by Sales					
	8		5		13	Unqualified	1	2	2	1	1	6
	18		8		12	Reviewed	1	3	2	2	4	
	76		67		102	Compiled	64	24	7	2	3	2
	116		115		135	Tax Returns	97	31	3		2	2
	127		119		81	Other	47	12	8	5	2	7
	4/1/04-3/31/05 ALL		4/1/05-3/31/06 ALL		4/1/06-3/31/07 ALL		36 (4/1-9/30/06) 0-1MM	1-3MM	3-5MM	307 (10/1/06-3/31/07) 5-10MM	10-25MM	25MM & OVER
	345		314		343	NUMBER OF STATEMENTS	210	72	22	10	12	17
	%		%		%	ASSETS	%	%	%	%	%	%
	9.4		9.8		9.5	Cash & Equivalents	8.6	10.4	9.4	16.1	9.3	12.4
	5.1		2.3		3.1	Trade Receivables (net)	2.2	3.7	7.7	1.2	6.3	4.5
	4.0		3.7		3.5	Inventory	1.6	6.0	8.3	2.8	8.6	6.0
	1.6		1.7		1.3	All Other Current	.5	2.0	1.5	11.5	2.7	1.5
	20.1		17.5		17.3	Total Current	12.9	22.1	26.9	31.5	26.9	24.4
	66.6		66.4		67.4	Fixed Assets (net)	72.2	64.0	57.8	55.3	49.1	55.8
	6.7		8.3		8.3	Intangibles (net)	7.1	9.9	10.8	2.0	12.7	14.9
	6.6		7.8		6.9	All Other Non-Current	7.8	4.0	4.5	11.2	11.3	4.9
	100.0		100.0		100.0	Total	100.0	100.0	100.0	100.0	100.0	100.0
						LIABILITIES						
	4.0		3.0		4.7	Notes Payable-Short Term	5.2	2.3	8.7	7.8	2.2	3.3
	4.7		4.2		6.4	Cur. Mat.-L.T.D.	7.3	6.8	2.9	4.3	3.0	2.0
	4.5		5.8		5.0	Trade Payables	4.0	3.2	12.0	5.5	10.1	11.0
	.1		.2		.2	Income Taxes Payable	.2	.2	.2	.0	.0	.0
	9.4		11.1		9.5	All Other Current	9.1	6.9	19.3	9.6	8.0	14.1
	22.7		24.3		25.7	Total Current	25.8	19.4	43.2	27.2	23.3	30.4
	70.0		69.5		60.8	Long-Term Debt	68.3	57.2	46.8	33.0	35.3	34.4
	.0		.0		.0	Deferred Taxes	.0	.0	.0	.0	.0	.2
	6.7		11.3		11.1	All Other Non-Current	9.7	15.6	17.4	2.9	11.4	6.0
	.6		-5.1		2.3	Net Worth	3.9	7.7	-7.3	36.9	30.0	29.0
	100.0		100.0		100.0	Total Liabilities & Net Worth	100.0	100.0	100.0	100.0	100.0	100.0
						INCOME DATA						
	100.0		100.0		100.0	Net Sales	100.0	100.0	100.0	100.0	100.0	100.0
						Gross Profit						
	89.5		90.3		88.3	Operating Expenses	85.1	91.7	96.3	88.5	96.1	97.9
	10.5		9.7		11.7	Operating Profit	14.9	8.3	3.7	11.5	3.9	2.1
	8.0		8.4		9.9	All Other Expenses (net)	13.9	5.2	2.1	3.8	.6	1.5
	2.5		1.3		1.7	Profit Before Taxes	1.0	3.1	1.6	7.7	3.3	.6
						RATIOS						
	2.4		1.8		1.9		1.5	2.9	2.6	1.7	1.6	1.3
	.8		.6		.6	Current	.4	1.0	.9	1.0	1.1	.6
	.3		.2		.2		.1	.4	.4	.4	.7	.4
	1.8		1.2		1.3		1.3	2.3	1.8	1.3	1.0	1.0
(341)	.6	(311)	.4		.4	Quick	.3	.5	.6	.5	.7	.4
	.1		.1		.1		.1	.1	.3	.0	.4	.2
0	UND	0	UND	0	UND		0 UND	0 UND	0 999.8	1 563.2	2 164.3	0 UND
0	UND	0	UND	0	UND	Sales/Receivables	0 UND	0 972.2	2 191.1	2 166.5	5 79.4	1 259.4
4	96.4	3	145.2	2	164.0		0 UND	3 145.6	12 31.0	3 117.4	8 45.5	18 20.2
						Cost of Sales/Inventory						
						Cost of Sales/Payables						
	12.4		20.6		24.6		30.2	18.3	15.1	19.3	20.5	59.7
	-54.9		-26.3		-26.8	Sales/Working Capital	-10.9	UND	-64.1	325.3	NM	-25.9
	-7.2		-5.9		-5.2		-4.0	-13.2	-13.7	-1.7	-84.7	-8.2
	3.5		3.2		3.0		2.9	2.9	2.6		6.8	8.8
(278)	1.5	(235)	1.4	(247)	1.4	EBIT/Interest	(131) 1.3	(59) 1.4	(20) 1.4		1.8	(16) 2.2
	.2		.3		.5		.5	.5	-.5		-1.6	-1.0
	4.2		3.5		7.9	Net Profit + Depr., Dep.,						
(27)	2.3	(19)	1.4	(15)	2.4	Amort./Cur. Mat. L/T/D						
	1.3		.6		.9							
	2.2		2.5		2.1		3.3	1.2	4.2	.4	1.0	.9
	18.4		102.1		35.1	Fixed/Worth	-129.2	UND	42.9	1.4	2.6	2.0
	-2.6		-1.6		-2.9		-2.5	-2.5	-2.0	12.1	22.3	19.9
	2.0		2.8		2.2		2.9	1.5	3.4	.7	1.1	.6
	21.1		168.0		79.0	Debt/Worth	-98.4	UND	77.7	2.2	2.3	3.8
	-4.4		-3.3		-4.2		-4.0	-3.7	-3.7	11.9	32.3	-10.9
	54.4		84.1		60.0	% Profit Before Taxes/Tangible	44.6	99.4	53.1		130.9	112.9
(192)	18.4	(161)	30.1	(180)	21.8	Net Worth	(100) 13.1	(36) 38.5	(13) 22.8		(10) 18.2	(12) 28.3
	1.7		4.2		.0		-3.6	13.4	-54.5		-4.3	2.3
	9.8		8.3		8.6	% Profit Before Taxes/Total	6.5	10.8	13.3	15.6	12.6	13.6
	2.4		1.6		1.4	Assets	.3	2.7	2.4	5.1	5.3	6.7
	-3.1		-4.5		-4.3		-4.8	-3.1	-6.1	-3.5	-5.0	-12.1
	4.5		5.3		6.9		5.9	8.0	13.5	14.8	27.2	35.6
	1.2		1.4		1.3	Sales/Net Fixed Assets	.7	2.3	3.1	3.9	7.5	2.7
	.5		.5		.4		.3	.8	2.1	.5	1.4	1.3
	2.0		2.3		2.3		1.4	2.7	3.6	2.9	7.8	4.4
	.8		.9		.9	Sales/Total Assets	.6	1.3	2.0	2.0	2.4	1.6
	.4		.4		.4		.3	.8	1.1	.5	1.0	1.0
	3.8		3.6		3.2		5.9	2.0	1.2	.6	.9	2.1
(306)	9.6	(276)	8.4	(282)	8.6	% Depr., Dep., Amort./Sales	(167) 15.3	(63) 4.1	(19) 3.1	3.7	(11) 1.8	(12) 2.9
	18.5		17.9		19.5		25.0	10.3	4.9	11.2	5.1	4.1
	2.7		2.5		3.1	% Officers', Directors'	5.0	2.3				
(117)	5.9	(101)	5.3	(112)	6.3	Owners' Comp/Sales	(62) 8.8	(31) 4.5				
	11.4		10.3		10.9		13.0	9.2				
1420255M		1169169M		3844160M		Net Sales ($)	87235M	124782M	86114M	71297M	189793M	3284939M
1185632M		985594M		1910973M		Total Assets ($)	172802M	128249M	51642M	104986M	114766M	1338528M

M = $ thousand   MM = $ million
See Pages 11 through 21 for Explanation of Ratios and Data

Current Data Sorted by Assets | Comparative Historical Data

						Type of Statement		
1		1	5	1	1	Unqualified	7	4
2	2	2	1			Reviewed	6	10
8	13	6	1			Compiled	26	28
28	17	5			1	Tax Returns	25	43
13	16	7	3		1	Other	24	36
	22 (4/1-9/30/06)		113 (10/1/06-3/31/07)				4/1/02-3/31/03	4/1/03-3/31/04
0-500M	500M-2MM	2-10MM	10-50MM	50-100MM	100-250MM		ALL	ALL
52	48	21	10	1	3	NUMBER OF STATEMENTS	88	121

%	%	%	%	%	%	ASSETS	%	%
16.3	12.8	9.4	7.0			Cash & Equivalents	11.8	12.0
13.2	13.2	17.8	14.9			Trade Receivables (net)	14.8	14.5
25.3	17.4	22.2	19.1			Inventory	24.7	25.7
2.1	1.8	1.7	2.7			All Other Current	2.2	2.3
57.0	45.2	51.1	43.8			Total Current	53.5	54.4
28.1	41.0	31.4	37.3			Fixed Assets (net)	33.5	36.1
5.5	6.8	8.3	13.4			Intangibles (net)	4.2	2.7
9.5	7.1	9.2	5.4			All Other Non-Current	8.8	6.7
100.0	100.0	100.0	100.0			Total	100.0	100.0
						LIABILITIES		
9.7	9.7	10.2	2.7			Notes Payable-Short Term	8.9	11.6
3.6	4.0	2.4	3.9			Cur. Mat.-L.T.D.	5.7	5.2
14.9	12.7	13.3	12.6			Trade Payables	21.1	14.5
2.0	.1	.1	.4			Income Taxes Payable	.0	.3
15.9	8.9	6.4	7.3			All Other Current	14.0	17.2
46.1	35.3	32.3	26.9			Total Current	49.7	48.8
24.5	34.4	24.0	24.4			Long-Term Debt	32.1	31.7
.0	.0	.6	.6			Deferred Taxes	.0	.0
33.9	4.1	7.7	3.3			All Other Non-Current	18.4	11.2
-4.5	26.1	35.3	44.8			Net Worth	-.2	8.3
100.0	100.0	100.0	100.0			Total Liabilties & Net Worth	100.0	100.0
						INCOME DATA		
100.0	100.0	100.0	100.0			Net Sales	100.0	100.0
						Gross Profit		
96.3	92.1	90.0	93.2			Operating Expenses	96.6	96.1
3.7	7.9	10.0	6.8			Operating Profit	3.4	3.9
.7	3.3	3.3	1.7			All Other Expenses (net)	1.3	2.0
3.1	4.6	6.6	5.0			Profit Before Taxes	2.0	1.9
						RATIOS		
3.7	2.5	2.1	2.4				2.6	2.5
1.4	1.4	1.4	1.5			Current	1.2	1.4
.8	.8	1.1	1.0				.6	.8
1.7	1.8	1.1	1.5				1.3	1.4
(51) .8	.7	.7	.6			Quick	.5　(118)	.7
.1	.3	.5	.4				.2	.2
0　UND	0　865.1	11　33.6	0　UND				1　272.0	0　UND
3　122.3	10　36.5	20　18.4	16　23.1			Sales/Receivables	10　35.0	9　39.1
17　21.9	32　11.5	41　8.9	53　6.9				27　13.4	26　14.0
						Cost of Sales/Inventory		
						Cost of Sales/Payables		
9.9	8.6	13.3	7.9				9.7	8.9
41.6	18.2	15.2	38.2			Sales/Working Capital	40.8	23.4
-71.1	-17.1	97.7	NM				-24.9	-43.4
15.0	6.5	12.3					4.8	6.5
(39) 2.0	(40) 2.9	(19) 2.6				EBIT/Interest	(77) 2.4	(104) 2.3
-2.0	1.3	1.7					.1	-.7
						Net Profit + Depr., Dep., Amort./Cur. Mat. L/T/D		
.2	.3	.3	.5				.3	.4
1.3	1.4	1.6	1.1			Fixed/Worth	1.5	1.1
-.9	NM	NM	-2.2				-10.0	-5.9
.5	.9	.8	.3				1.6	.9
13.9	4.8	2.2	1.7			Debt/Worth	3.8	3.3
-3.2	-20.2	NM	-5.4				-11.3	-8.1
108.3	49.5	43.2					57.2	51.7
(30) 44.4	(34) 19.9	(16) 33.6				% Profit Before Taxes/Tangible Net Worth	(62) 16.8	(85) 15.6
-.4	5.3	6.4					1.8	-6.9
48.5	15.5	18.0	21.3				12.2	17.2
4.9	7.2	8.3	7.8			% Profit Before Taxes/Total Assets	3.4	3.9
-4.1	.8	2.4	3.5				-3.5	-4.0
112.2	19.7	57.8	18.9				52.1	46.6
35.5	8.3	13.6	11.3			Sales/Net Fixed Assets	16.8	15.9
10.4	2.3	3.5	2.2				5.1	5.7
8.3	3.4	3.9	2.7				5.9	6.7
5.2	2.4	2.4	2.2			Sales/Total Assets	3.3	3.3
3.4	1.3	1.4	1.4				1.8	2.0
.6	2.3	.9					1.2	1.0
(37) 1.3	(34) 3.6	(17) 2.0				% Depr., Dep., Amort./Sales	(70) 2.3	(96) 2.1
3.1	6.2	4.1					3.5	4.4
5.9	2.3						1.5	2.9
(33) 8.4	(24) 3.7					% Officers', Directors' Owners' Comp/Sales	(41) 4.9	(70) 5.5
11.4	6.0						9.9	10.0
59904M	129654M	180988M	1256014M	137004M	1439000M	Net Sales ($)	1613417M	3782464M
11032M	51241M	76112M	232573M	66888M	553590M	Total Assets ($)	456703M	769186M

M = $ thousand　　MM = $ million
See Pages 11 through 21 for Explanation of Ratios and Data

Comparative Historical Data | Current Data Sorted by Sales

4	8	9	Type of Statement						
			Unqualified		1		1		7
7	8	7	Reviewed	1	2	1	1	1	1
30	34	28	Compiled	4	13	4	5		2
44	52	51	Tax Returns	24	15	9	1	1	1
32	42	40	Other	10	11	8	3	3	3
4/1/04-3/31/05 ALL	4/1/05-3/31/06 ALL	4/1/06-3/31/07 ALL		22 (4/1-9/30/06)		113 (10/1/06-3/31/07)			
				0-1MM	1-3MM	3-5MM	5-10MM	10-25MM	25MM & OVER
117	144	135	NUMBER OF STATEMENTS	39	42	22	13	5	14
%	%	%	**ASSETS**	%	%	%	%	%	%
12.8	13.6	13.0	Cash & Equivalents	16.0	10.7	18.0	8.8		5.9
16.8	13.8	14.1	Trade Receivables (net)	6.4	15.1	20.3	17.4		17.5
21.2	17.8	21.3	Inventory	25.3	17.2	17.9	27.7		22.3
1.6	2.6	1.9	All Other Current	1.6	2.8	1.3	1.9		2.0
52.3	47.8	50.3	Total Current	49.3	45.8	57.6	55.8		47.6
30.7	38.4	34.5	Fixed Assets (net)	43.6	31.4	31.9	21.2		35.8
7.9	5.1	7.1	Intangibles (net)	4.5	9.2	3.2	9.6		11.6
9.0	8.6	8.2	All Other Non-Current	2.5	13.6	7.3	13.4		4.9
100.0	100.0	100.0	Total	100.0	100.0	100.0	100.0		100.0
			LIABILITIES						
9.9	12.4	9.2	Notes Payable-Short Term	9.8	10.8	7.0	6.6		7.1
4.8	3.1	3.6	Cur. Mat.-L.T.D.	3.8	4.6	2.2	3.2		3.1
14.7	11.1	13.4	Trade Payables	9.2	15.3	16.3	17.1		11.9
.4	.2	.9	Income Taxes Payable	2.0	.0	1.6	.1		.3
16.4	11.1	11.3	All Other Current	13.5	9.6	14.5	7.7		9.7
46.2	37.9	38.3	Total Current	38.1	40.2	41.5	34.7		32.2
29.2	31.0	28.6	Long-Term Debt	42.6	25.1	21.6	14.0		27.9
.0	.1	.1	Deferred Taxes	.0	.0	.0	1.0		.4
14.6	9.3	16.0	All Other Non-Current	30.6	16.7	1.1	14.9		2.5
10.0	21.7	16.9	Net Worth	-11.3	18.0	35.7	35.3		37.0
100.0	100.0	100.0	Total Liabilties & Net Worth	100.0	100.0	100.0	100.0		100.0
			INCOME DATA						
100.0	100.0	100.0	Net Sales	100.0	100.0	100.0	100.0		100.0
			Gross Profit						
95.1	92.0	93.6	Operating Expenses	90.3	95.5	94.8	93.7		94.5
4.9	8.0	6.4	Operating Profit	9.7	4.5	5.2	6.3		5.5
1.0	2.9	2.1	All Other Expenses (net)	4.3	1.3	1.0	1.1		1.7
3.8	5.2	4.3	Profit Before Taxes	5.4	3.2	4.2	5.2		3.8
			RATIOS						
2.6	2.2	2.5		4.0	2.2	3.9	1.9		2.0
1.4	1.4	1.4	Current	1.6	1.3	1.4	1.4		1.6
.8	.8	.9		.6	.7	.8	1.2		1.0
1.3	1.6	1.7		1.7	1.6	2.1	.9		1.2
(116) .6	.7	(134) .7	Quick	.8	(41) .7	.9	.7		.6
.3	.3	.3		.1	.3	.3	.6		.4
0 UND	1 528.4	0 UND		0 UND	0 UND	4 99.7	10 35.1		0 UND
8 42.9	9 42.0	10 35.0	Sales/Receivables	1 461.0	10 38.1	17 21.2	31 11.6		27 13.4
28 13.1	28 12.9	30 12.2		14 26.5	26 14.0	30 12.1	46 7.9		49 7.4
			Cost of Sales/Inventory						
			Cost of Sales/Payables						
12.0	10.6	9.4		8.2	10.6	7.5	11.7		8.5
34.9	26.4	26.0	Sales/Working Capital	30.1	61.0	25.9	15.0		34.7
-40.3	-44.5	-73.5		-15.9	-16.5	-66.5	38.2		NM
10.0	13.5	7.0		5.3	6.7	19.4	15.9		5.5
(101) 2.5	(118) 3.4	(110) 2.5	EBIT/Interest	(27) 2.0	(35) 1.9	(19) 3.2	(12) 2.6	(12)	3.1
-.1	1.0	1.1		.7	.8	.6	1.2		1.5
2.9	3.6	4.8	Net Profit + Depr., Dep., Amort./Cur. Mat. L/T/D						
(10) 2.4	(14) 2.9	(11) 2.9							
.8	1.3	1.0							
.4	.4	.3		.4	.3	.2	.1		.3
1.9	1.9	1.3	Fixed/Worth	5.0	1.6	.6	.8		1.1
-2.1	-7.7	-4.0		-1.4	-3.2	5.7	-8.3		-2.3
1.4	1.0	.7		1.0	.7	.5	.9		.6
6.0	4.1	4.3	Debt/Worth	44.5	5.0	2.2	1.0		2.2
-5.4	-12.8	-5.1		-2.5	-4.8	NM	-29.8		-5.1
88.3	76.9	62.8	% Profit Before Taxes/Tangible Net Worth	83.1	74.0	56.5			
(76) 30.5	(100) 32.9	(89) 27.5		(21) 37.5	(28) 19.9	(17) 23.8			
1.4	4.0	5.1		2.9	2.7	2.4			
21.8	22.8	20.1	% Profit Before Taxes/Total Assets	58.0	15.8	25.3	18.7		15.1
7.1	7.9	6.7		5.2	4.9	8.8	10.0		7.4
-5.7	-.1	.4		-.5	-1.4	-.6	.8		3.1
60.2	35.0	55.8	Sales/Net Fixed Assets	78.0	58.5	57.1	50.3		22.7
19.6	12.7	13.1		10.8	12.9	15.7	22.1		12.7
6.7	4.0	5.3		1.5	6.3	4.6	7.7		4.2
6.0	4.7	5.1	Sales/Total Assets	6.4	5.4	6.0	4.2		3.7
3.4	2.9	3.0		3.2	3.2	3.2	2.6		2.2
2.4	1.4	1.9		1.1	2.2	2.1	2.0		1.5
1.1	1.2	1.0	% Depr., Dep., Amort./Sales	.8	1.4	.9			1.2
(82) 1.9	(113) 2.0	(97) 2.3		(30) 3.9	(27) 2.9	(18) 2.3		(10)	1.6
4.1	4.2	4.2		7.5	5.8	3.4			2.5
2.3	2.7	2.9	% Officers', Directors' Owners' Comp/Sales	6.9	3.2	2.0			
(60) 4.1	(68) 5.0	(68) 6.1		(20) 9.0	(24) 5.6	(13) 3.1			
10.1	9.5	10.1		11.9	9.6	4.9			
1528085M	3410685M	3202564M	Net Sales ($)	20565M	79229M	87669M	93255M	77490M	2844356M
691448M	1193943M	991436M	Total Assets ($)	18287M	31476M	30216M	39396M	25315M	846746M

© RMA 2007

M = $ thousand   MM = $ million
See Pages 11 through 21 for Explanation of Ratios and Data

Current Data Sorted by Assets   Comparative Historical Data

Type of Statement

Type of Statement	0-500M	500M-2MM	2-10MM	10-50MM	50-100MM	100-250MM	4/1/02-3/31/03 ALL	4/1/03-3/31/04 ALL
Unqualified			1	1	1		3	5
Reviewed		2	3				6	10
Compiled	1	2					4	12
Tax Returns	4	4	3	4			4	4
Other	2	3					9	8
		4 (4/1-9/30/06)		27 (10/1/06-3/31/07)				
NUMBER OF STATEMENTS	7	11	7	5	1		26	39

Current data columns 0-500M, 2-10MM, 10-50MM, 50-100MM and 100-250MM: **DATA NOT AVAILABLE**

Item	500M-2MM %	4/1/02-3/31/03 ALL %	4/1/03-3/31/04 ALL %
ASSETS			
Cash & Equivalents	21.2	12.6	10.5
Trade Receivables (net)	42.1	43.8	37.7
Inventory	7.5	14.6	18.1
All Other Current	6.0	2.4	4.9
Total Current	76.8	73.5	71.3
Fixed Assets (net)	12.9	17.1	10.5
Intangibles (net)	1.7	3.0	5.4
All Other Non-Current	8.6	6.5	12.9
Total	100.0	100.0	100.0
LIABILITIES			
Notes Payable-Short Term	12.6	18.6	16.3
Cur. Mat.-L.T.D.	3.9	4.5	2.1
Trade Payables	20.6	19.5	17.8
Income Taxes Payable	.1	.4	.2
All Other Current	16.2	17.3	20.9
Total Current	53.4	60.4	57.3
Long-Term Debt	2.5	10.2	5.9
Deferred Taxes	.0	.0	.1
All Other Non-Current	1.1	10.0	6.3
Net Worth	43.0	19.4	30.3
Total Liabilities & Net Worth	100.0	100.0	100.0
INCOME DATA			
Net Sales	100.0	100.0	100.0
Gross Profit			
Operating Expenses	93.6	95.2	94.7
Operating Profit	6.4	4.8	5.3
All Other Expenses (net)	1.6	.9	.9
Profit Before Taxes	4.8	3.8	4.4
RATIOS			
Current	1.8	1.7	2.0
	1.2	1.4	1.4
	1.1	1.1	1.0
Quick	1.6	1.4	1.5
	1.1	1.1	.9
	.8	.7	.6
Sales/Receivables	35 10.4	25 14.9	24 15.3
	46 8.0	37 9.8	40 9.2
	51 7.2	58 6.3	54 6.8
Cost of Sales/Inventory			
Cost of Sales/Payables			
Sales/Working Capital	13.9	11.8	6.4
	16.7	17.5	14.1
	60.6	43.8	-806.3
EBIT/Interest		17.2	23.3
		(24) 3.0	(36) 8.5
		1.2	1.3
Net Profit + Depr., Dep., Amort./Cur. Mat. L/T/D			
Fixed/Worth	.1	.2	.1
	.2	.5	.4
	.5	2.6	1.2
Debt/Worth	.8	1.9	1.2
	1.7	3.7	2.9
	6.4	16.9	7.1
% Profit Before Taxes/Tangible Net Worth	111.4	56.2	62.0
	43.9	(22) 32.1	(33) 30.3
	5.6	7.6	5.1
% Profit Before Taxes/Total Assets	23.7	23.4	17.6
	7.2	6.9	9.5
	3.0	2.4	.9
Sales/Net Fixed Assets	167.3	97.0	83.1
	80.9	44.7	37.1
	12.1	17.1	21.5
Sales/Total Assets	5.9	5.6	4.5
	3.7	3.9	3.3
	2.9	3.0	1.8
% Depr., Dep., Amort./Sales		.5	.5
		(22) 1.0	(30) 1.1
		1.6	1.6
% Officers', Directors' Owners' Comp/Sales		3.8	2.7
		(15) 6.4	(17) 4.4
		12.2	8.0

	0-500M	500M-2MM	2-10MM	10-50MM	50-100MM	4/1/02-3/31/03	4/1/03-3/31/04
Net Sales ($)	13208M	45677M	78704M	252704M	26965M	305422M	523151M
Total Assets ($)	1481M	11630M	33673M	105762M	58095M	79461M	271508M

M = $ thousand   MM = $ million
See Pages 11 through 21 for Explanation of Ratios and Data

Comparative Historical Data | Current Data Sorted by Sales

Type of Statement	4/1/04-3/31/05 ALL	4/1/05-3/31/06 ALL	4/1/06-3/31/07 ALL	0-1MM	1-3MM	3-5MM	5-10MM	10-25MM	25MM & OVER
Unqualified	8	6	3					1	2
Reviewed	6	7	5		1		2	2	
Compiled	7	5	3		2		1		
Tax Returns	6	4	8	4	1	1	2		
Other	11	18	12	1	1	2	4	1	3
				4 (4/1-9/30/06)			27 (10/1/06-3/31/07)		
NUMBER OF STATEMENTS	38	40	31	5	5	3	9	4	5

ASSETS (%)

	4/1/04-3/31/05	4/1/05-3/31/06	4/1/06-3/31/07
Cash & Equivalents	9.7	14.4	20.7
Trade Receivables (net)	41.4	38.0	33.8
Inventory	17.7	11.8	9.1
All Other Current	2.8	2.1	3.9
Total Current	71.7	66.3	67.5
Fixed Assets (net)	12.9	18.2	15.7
Intangibles (net)	3.1	5.2	12.1
All Other Non-Current	12.3	10.3	4.7
Total	100.0	100.0	100.0

LIABILITIES

	4/1/04-3/31/05	4/1/05-3/31/06	4/1/06-3/31/07
Notes Payable-Short Term	23.2	14.8	10.1
Cur. Mat.-L.T.D.	1.7	2.7	6.6
Trade Payables	16.7	16.2	15.0
Income Taxes Payable	.4	.9	.1
All Other Current	18.3	11.7	22.6
Total Current	60.4	46.4	54.4
Long-Term Debt	19.2	9.2	12.3
Deferred Taxes	.5	.1	.0
All Other Non-Current	11.6	10.9	7.4
Net Worth	8.4	33.5	25.9
Total Liabilties & Net Worth	100.0	100.0	100.0

INCOME DATA

	4/1/04-3/31/05	4/1/05-3/31/06	4/1/06-3/31/07
Net Sales	100.0	100.0	100.0
Gross Profit			
Operating Expenses	97.0	92.2	93.1
Operating Profit	3.0	7.8	6.9
All Other Expenses (net)	1.9	.9	1.0
Profit Before Taxes	1.1	6.9	5.9

RATIOS

	4/1/04-3/31/05	4/1/05-3/31/06	4/1/06-3/31/07
Current	2.0	2.8	2.3
	1.7	1.5	1.3
	1.0	1.0	1.1
Quick	1.7	2.1	2.1
	1.0	1.2	1.1
	.6	.7	.7
Sales/Receivables	21 17.8	27 13.4	16 22.2
	38 9.5	42 8.8	44 8.3
	59 6.2	69 5.3	52 7.1
Cost of Sales/Inventory			
Cost of Sales/Payables			
Sales/Working Capital	7.4	6.2	7.9
	17.7	13.0	22.8
	NM	363.4	80.8
EBIT/Interest	12.4	29.6	40.0
	(33) 1.8	(33) 4.6	(27) 6.1
	.4	1.7	1.7
Net Profit + Depr., Dep., Amort./Cur. Mat. L/T/D		18.4	
		(10) 11.1	
		1.2	
Fixed/Worth	.2	.1	.2
	.5	.3	.5
	7.9	1.5	-10.9
Debt/Worth	1.1	.7	.9
	3.4	1.7	3.7
	95.3	7.4	-8.9
% Profit Before Taxes/Tangible Net Worth	48.5	83.3	117.7
	(30) 11.3	(34) 37.7	(22) 54.3
	-.9	11.2	7.6
% Profit Before Taxes/Total Assets	14.9	26.9	38.1
	2.7	9.6	13.3
	-1.0	2.9	1.2
Sales/Net Fixed Assets	106.1	133.4	131.2
	47.4	41.6	45.6
	19.6	8.2	20.5
Sales/Total Assets	5.1	4.3	5.9
	3.4	3.2	3.5
	2.6	1.8	1.9
% Depr., Dep., Amort./Sales	.5	.6	.4
	(28) 1.2	(26) 1.0	(22) .6
	2.4	1.5	1.6
% Officers', Directors' Owners' Comp/Sales	2.5	2.0	3.3
	(17) 5.9	(13) 6.2	(12) 5.0
	12.4	15.8	10.1

	4/1/04-3/31/05	4/1/05-3/31/06	4/1/06-3/31/07	0-1MM	1-3MM	3-5MM	5-10MM	10-25MM	25MM & OVER
Net Sales ($)	485101M	538238M	417258M	3405M	9523M	10400M	65294M	65176M	263460M
Total Assets ($)	255496M	293037M	210641M	1326M	3878M	3876M	20035M	44144M	137382M

M = $ thousand   MM = $ million
See Pages 11 through 21 for Explanation of Ratios and Data

Current Data Sorted by Assets   Comparative Historical Data

	0-500M	500M-2MM	2-10MM	10-50MM	50-100MM	100-250MM	Type of Statement	4/1/02-3/31/03 ALL	4/1/03-3/31/04 ALL
		1	5	6	2	2	Unqualified	22	23
	4	4	18	7			Reviewed	58	42
	19	14	8				Compiled	63	82
	9	18	2				Tax Returns	39	36
		14	12	11	2	1	Other	45	56
		26 (4/1-9/30/06)		133 (10/1/06-3/31/07)					
NUMBER OF STATEMENTS	32	51	45	24	4	3		227	239
	%	%	%	%	%	%	ASSETS	%	%
Cash & Equivalents	11.3	13.5	7.6	5.3				9.9	9.1
Trade Receivables (net)	24.2	33.8	32.6	32.1				31.9	31.4
Inventory	26.1	19.5	20.1	18.3				20.4	19.1
All Other Current	2.2	3.7	3.9	5.3				2.6	2.9
Total Current	63.8	70.6	64.2	61.0				64.8	62.6
Fixed Assets (net)	25.1	23.3	26.8	26.9				26.8	26.9
Intangibles (net)	4.7	1.7	2.1	7.6				2.1	4.0
All Other Non-Current	6.4	4.3	6.9	4.5				6.2	6.5
Total	100.0	100.0	100.0	100.0				100.0	100.0
							LIABILITIES		
Notes Payable-Short Term	18.2	11.5	13.4	13.2				13.9	13.6
Cur. Mat.-L.T.D.	4.8	2.2	5.8	4.9				6.0	4.7
Trade Payables	13.0	15.9	12.3	14.9				15.2	15.9
Income Taxes Payable	.2	.8	.3	.4				.3	.4
All Other Current	20.5	15.0	9.8	8.4				10.7	11.9
Total Current	56.8	45.4	41.6	41.7				46.1	46.5
Long-Term Debt	44.4	17.9	18.4	22.5				18.4	23.1
Deferred Taxes	.0	.2	.3	.4				.4	.3
All Other Non-Current	9.8	5.2	6.2	2.1				4.3	5.5
Net Worth	-11.0	31.4	33.5	33.2				30.9	24.5
Total Liabilities & Net Worth	100.0	100.0	100.0	100.0				100.0	100.0
							INCOME DATA		
Net Sales	100.0	100.0	100.0	100.0				100.0	100.0
Gross Profit									
Operating Expenses	92.5	96.6	91.7	93.3				94.8	94.7
Operating Profit	7.5	3.4	8.3	6.7				5.2	5.3
All Other Expenses (net)	1.5	.5	1.3	1.9				1.0	1.5
Profit Before Taxes	6.0	3.0	6.9	4.8				4.2	3.8
							RATIOS		
Current	4.2	3.3	2.8	2.0				2.6	2.4
	2.1	1.7	1.4	1.3				1.4	1.4
	1.2	1.2	1.2	1.0				1.0	1.0
Quick	2.6	2.3	1.7	1.2				1.6	1.5
	1.1	1.1	.8	.8				.9 (238)	.9
	.5	.6	.7	.6				.6	.6
Sales/Receivables	1 589.8	29 12.4	42 8.7	47 7.8				24 15.1	28 13.1
	30 12.2	42 8.7	50 7.2	53 6.9				41 9.0	43 8.4
	42 8.8	52 7.1	67 5.5	68 5.4				56 6.5	58 6.3
Cost of Sales/Inventory									
Cost of Sales/Payables									
Sales/Working Capital	7.6	6.0	5.0	5.3				6.0	6.4
	14.9	9.6	9.7	12.9				14.2	16.3
	64.1	28.9	30.7	761.2				-839.0	366.5
EBIT/Interest	8.3	15.1	9.1	7.5				9.5	8.5
	(27) 3.2	(46) 3.4	(43) 4.4	3.1				(201) 3.7	(204) 3.6
	2.1	1.0	2.0	.8				1.1	1.1
Net Profit + Depr., Dep., Amort./Cur. Mat. L/T/D				4.3				5.6	5.5
		(13)		2.1				(47) 2.3	(46) 2.3
				1.5				.4	1.0
Fixed/Worth	.4	.1	.3	.3				.3	.3
	2.1	.6	.8	1.2				.8	.9
	-.6	5.5	1.8	3.6				3.9	4.5
Debt/Worth	.7	.5	.9	1.2				.8	.9
	7.5	1.7	1.7	2.7				2.2	2.4
	-5.0	12.2	7.0	14.3				8.8	14.7
% Profit Before Taxes/Tangible Net Worth	89.4	78.2	61.0	54.7				61.8	51.1
	(20) 50.4	(42) 24.9	(39) 39.5	(21) 28.0				(193) 20.0	(189) 23.4
	28.1	7.1	13.0	-.8				2.4	5.0
% Profit Before Taxes/Total Assets	31.8	16.9	20.4	16.4				17.0	16.7
	15.0	7.4	8.4	8.5				6.0	6.6
	4.7	1.0	2.7	-.8				.4	.5
Sales/Net Fixed Assets	126.7	42.6	24.5	33.2				34.2	28.9
	23.1	15.8	10.9	8.3				13.4	13.9
	11.1	8.5	5.6	3.2				6.9	6.8
Sales/Total Assets	5.0	4.1	2.8	2.5				3.7	3.6
	3.7	3.0	2.1	2.1				2.8	2.6
	2.2	2.3	1.6	1.3				2.0	1.8
% Depr., Dep., Amort./Sales	.8	1.0	1.0	1.1				1.1	.9
	(20) 1.6	(39) 2.1	(42) 2.0	2.1				(194) 2.2	(200) 2.2
	2.8	3.7	3.2	4.5				4.2	4.1
% Officers', Directors', Owners' Comp/Sales	5.3	3.0	3.1					3.5	2.7
	(21) 7.6	(35) 7.0	(14) 4.9					(110) 5.9	(109) 5.6
	10.6	11.2	10.8					9.0	9.0
Net Sales ($)	31203M	169315M	438946M	931814M	364251M	762648M		3540893M	3238085M
Total Assets ($)	8289M	53914M	201976M	456606M	251850M	591208M		1655672M	1307647M

© RMA 2007

M = $ thousand   MM = $ million
See Pages 11 through 21 for Explanation of Ratios and Data

Comparative Historical Data | Current Data Sorted by Sales

			Type of Statement	0-1MM	1-3MM	3-5MM	5-10MM	10-25MM	25MM & OVER
23	16	16	Unqualified		1	1	1	3	10
38	35	29	Reviewed		1	5	10	8	5
50	51	26	Compiled	4	9	5	5	3	
56	33	39	Tax Returns	15	12	7	5		
73	74	49	Other	8	9	6	8	10	8
4/1/04-3/31/05 ALL	4/1/05-3/31/06 ALL	4/1/06-3/31/07 ALL		26 (4/1-9/30/06)			133 (10/1/06-3/31/07)		
				0-1MM	1-3MM	3-5MM	5-10MM	10-25MM	25MM & OVER
240	209	159	NUMBER OF STATEMENTS	27	32	24	29	24	23
%	%	%	**ASSETS**	%	%	%	%	%	%
11.0	11.5	9.9	Cash & Equivalents	11.2	13.0	10.4	10.3	7.4	5.7
29.7	30.2	30.8	Trade Receivables (net)	16.6	29.3	40.5	33.8	31.8	34.5
22.2	19.4	21.0	Inventory	29.3	21.6	16.5	16.9	19.4	22.3
2.4	2.8	3.6	All Other Current	1.9	4.8	2.6	3.0	6.7	2.5
65.3	63.9	65.3	Total Current	59.0	68.6	70.1	64.1	65.2	64.9
24.8	26.5	25.3	Fixed Assets (net)	26.6	27.1	22.9	23.8	28.4	22.2
4.4	4.8	3.8	Intangibles (net)	5.5	.4	2.0	5.3	2.9	7.3
5.5	4.8	5.7	All Other Non-Current	8.9	3.9	5.0	6.9	3.6	5.6
100.0	100.0	100.0	Total	100.0	100.0	100.0	100.0	100.0	100.0
			LIABILITIES						
12.1	12.2	13.3	Notes Payable-Short Term	20.2	11.5	9.7	13.6	12.6	11.8
4.6	4.6	4.3	Cur. Mat.-L.T.D.	5.6	1.7	2.8	7.0	3.7	4.8
14.4	16.5	14.0	Trade Payables	10.0	13.1	17.0	14.2	14.2	16.4
.4	.4	.5	Income Taxes Payable	.2	.1	1.0	.9	.4	.6
11.2	10.6	13.4	All Other Current	22.6	13.3	13.3	10.7	10.4	9.8
42.7	44.4	45.5	Total Current	58.6	39.7	43.7	46.3	41.2	43.2
21.3	21.3	24.4	Long-Term Debt	57.6	15.7	15.7	17.7	19.3	20.4
.4	.3	.3	Deferred Taxes	.0	.1	.3	.0	.7	.6
6.7	5.4	5.8	All Other Non-Current	12.4	5.8	4.9	2.2	6.5	3.0
28.9	28.6	24.0	Net Worth	28.7	38.7	35.3	33.8	32.2	32.8
100.0	100.0	100.0	Total Liabilities & Net Worth	100.0	100.0	100.0	100.0	100.0	100.0
			INCOME DATA						
100.0	100.0	100.0	Net Sales	100.0	100.0	100.0	100.0	100.0	100.0
			Gross Profit						
95.0	93.7	93.3	Operating Expenses	93.3	94.4	94.2	92.1	93.6	92.4
5.0	6.3	6.7	Operating Profit	6.7	5.6	5.8	7.9	6.4	7.6
1.2	1.3	1.4	All Other Expenses (net)	2.4	.5	.7	1.5	1.2	2.8
3.8	5.0	5.2	Profit Before Taxes	4.3	5.2	5.1	6.4	5.3	4.8
			RATIOS						
2.6	2.4	3.0		4.4	4.4	2.4	3.2	2.3	2.2
1.6	1.6	1.7	Current	2.3	1.8	1.7	1.4	1.5	1.4
1.1	1.1	1.2		.7	1.3	1.3	.9	1.2	1.0
1.7	1.6	2.0		2.5	3.0	2.0	2.4	1.2	1.9
.9	(208) 1.0	1.0	Quick	.7	1.1	1.1	.9	.9	.8
.6	.6	.6		.1	.5	.9	.6	.7	.6
26 13.9	30 12.3	32 11.4		1 711.0	24 15.4	35 10.5	33 11.1	46 8.0	43 8.5
43 8.6	44 8.3	46 7.9	Sales/Receivables	28 13.1	43 8.5	43 8.5	49 7.5	49 7.4	55 6.6
58 6.3	59 6.2	60 6.1		40 9.1	53 6.9	59 6.2	63 5.8	63 5.8	69 5.3
			Cost of Sales/Inventory						
			Cost of Sales/Payables						
6.5	6.5	5.4		3.6	4.4	7.5	6.6	5.5	5.1
13.6	11.6	11.4	Sales/Working Capital	11.4	11.5	10.7	10.2	10.9	10.6
86.1	105.6	33.8		-27.8	32.6	23.4	-89.3	37.5	-71.7
12.0	10.2	9.3		7.0	13.1	13.2	34.1	7.5	8.2
(213) 4.0	(189) 3.9	(146) 3.3	EBIT/Interest	2.6	(24) 3.4	(22) 4.7	(27) 3.0	3.4	(22) 3.4
1.1	1.6	1.6		.7	1.4	1.9	1.5	2.1	1.4
4.1	6.9	7.0	Net Profit + Depr., Dep.,					3.1	8.5
(48) 2.1	(45) 2.6	(37) 2.6	Amort./Cur. Mat. L/T/D					(10) 2.2	(11) 2.9
1.4	1.0	1.5						1.6	.4
.2	.3	.3		.5	.1	.2	.2	.5	.3
.8	.9	.8	Fixed/Worth	-673.0	.6	.6	.4	1.4	.9
4.0	5.7	4.4		-.4	2.2	1.5	4.1	2.8	3.8
.9	1.0	.9		1.5	.3	.8	.3	1.0	1.6
2.3	2.4	2.3	Debt/Worth	-732.0	1.3	1.8	1.6	2.0	2.8
30.5	23.8	15.9		-1.9	5.6	4.8	10.9	7.6	15.9
59.5	61.6	59.6	% Profit Before Taxes/Tangible	54.3	77.7	55.1	88.1	58.4	48.6
(190) 27.0	(164) 29.0	(128) 34.1	Net Worth	(13) 27.3	(28) 36.1	(22) 32.4	(25) 45.0	(20) 36.8	(20) 26.0
7.2	10.1	9.7		-1.6	7.7	11.5	8.0	19.2	8.0
18.7	18.4	19.3	% Profit Before Taxes/Total	19.3	27.5	18.0	31.9	20.1	14.7
7.3	7.9	9.3	Assets	9.0	13.4	8.3	7.4	12.2	5.7
.7	2.1	2.2		-1.6	1.7	2.8	1.0	4.0	2.7
38.2	30.3	35.1		43.6	58.4	53.9	31.3	20.7	28.2
16.5	14.3	13.9	Sales/Net Fixed Assets	14.3	17.3	16.6	15.1	9.3	13.3
6.6	5.5	7.1		6.0	7.4	7.4	8.6	3.7	6.1
3.6	3.5	3.7		3.9	4.8	4.1	3.7	2.8	2.7
2.6	2.5	2.5	Sales/Total Assets	2.1	2.8	3.2	2.5	2.2	2.1
1.8	1.7	1.8		1.4	2.1	2.2	1.7	1.5	1.6
1.0	1.1	1.0		1.0	.6	.9	1.2	1.0	.8
(185) 1.9	(169) 2.0	(131) 1.9	% Depr., Dep., Amort./Sales	(20) 2.6	(22) 1.9	(19) 1.7	(25) 2.1	(23) 2.0	(22) 1.5
3.6	3.5	3.4		5.8	3.2	3.8	3.6	2.8	2.6
3.2	2.1	3.2	% Officers', Directors'	5.5	3.1	3.8	2.7		
(101) 5.9	(86) 4.3	(73) 6.8	Owners' Comp/Sales	(18) 10.1	(18) 7.6	(17) 7.0	(14) 4.7		
9.4	9.1	10.4		12.4	9.8	12.5	8.9		
3695641M	4288362M	2698177M	Net Sales ($)	16505M	60881M	96365M	203191M	403008M	1918227M
1737741M	1724868M	1563843M	Total Assets ($)	11029M	24869M	39850M	104370M	202529M	1181196M

© RMA 2007

M = $ thousand   MM = $ million
See Pages 11 through 21 for Explanation of Ratios and Data

Current Data Sorted by Assets | Comparative Historical Data

						Type of Statement		
1		9	10	3	2	Unqualified		
2	9	23	4			Reviewed	24	26
10	21	20				Compiled	37	51
44	33	10	1	1		Tax Returns	26	56
20	32	24	1		2	Other	31	36
	64 (4/1-9/30/06)		227 (10/1/06-3/31/07)				4/1/02-3/31/03	4/1/03-3/31/04
0-500M	500M-2MM	2-10MM	10-50MM	50-100MM	100-250MM		ALL	ALL
77	95	86	24	5	4	NUMBER OF STATEMENTS	121	173
%	%	%	%	%	%	ASSETS	%	%
14.7	9.6	9.0	5.9			Cash & Equivalents	10.0	9.5
27.0	33.4	36.2	33.5			Trade Receivables (net)	30.5	29.7
13.1	20.3	21.4	21.4			Inventory	16.1	22.3
4.2	2.2	3.8	8.4			All Other Current	3.0	2.8
59.0	65.5	70.4	69.3			Total Current	59.7	64.2
29.5	25.5	23.5	23.4			Fixed Assets (net)	32.3	27.0
3.8	2.3	2.0	3.1			Intangibles (net)	2.2	3.1
7.7	6.7	4.2	4.2			All Other Non-Current	5.8	5.6
100.0	100.0	100.0	100.0			Total	100.0	100.0
						LIABILITIES		
19.2	9.4	13.4	13.8			Notes Payable-Short Term	10.9	13.2
5.9	4.7	4.4	2.7			Cur. Mat.-L.T.D.	6.5	4.7
15.9	16.9	15.5	15.7			Trade Payables	12.4	14.0
.2	.1	.4	.2			Income Taxes Payable	.3	.2
11.8	9.7	12.0	13.6			All Other Current	7.3	9.3
53.1	40.7	45.7	46.0			Total Current	37.3	41.5
38.4	23.1	16.5	14.6			Long-Term Debt	25.4	22.2
.1	.2	.4	.8			Deferred Taxes	.2	.4
8.5	5.7	3.3	3.5			All Other Non-Current	6.4	8.4
-.1	30.2	34.0	35.1			Net Worth	30.6	27.5
100.0	100.0	100.0	100.0			Total Liabilities & Net Worth	100.0	100.0
						INCOME DATA		
100.0	100.0	100.0	100.0			Net Sales	100.0	100.0
						Gross Profit		
96.4	93.0	92.8	93.6			Operating Expenses	96.8	96.4
3.6	7.0	7.2	6.4			Operating Profit	3.2	3.6
.5	1.6	1.2	.3			All Other Expenses (net)	1.2	1.1
3.0	5.4	6.0	6.1			Profit Before Taxes	2.0	2.5
						RATIOS		
3.3	2.8	2.4	2.0			Current	2.8	2.6
1.3	1.7	1.5	1.3				1.7	1.6
.6	1.1	1.2	1.2				1.1	1.1
2.2	1.7	1.6	1.2			Quick	1.9	1.8
.8	1.0	1.1	.9			(120)	1.2	1.0
.5	.7	.6	.5				.7	.6
0 UND	28 12.9	39 9.3	35 10.5			Sales/Receivables	31 11.9	23 16.2
25 14.8	41 8.9	52 7.0	54 6.8				50 7.4	41 9.0
39 9.3	54 6.8	65 5.6	71 5.1				66 5.6	60 6.1
						Cost of Sales/Inventory		
						Cost of Sales/Payables		
9.8	6.1	4.9	7.1			Sales/Working Capital	6.3	6.5
50.1	11.1	10.5	10.9				11.0	12.2
-32.4	46.0	20.2	23.7				99.6	50.8
16.0	13.5	12.1	16.3			EBIT/Interest	5.6	7.5
(63) 2.6	(81) 3.3	(77) 5.3	(23) 5.8			(108)	2.2 (157)	3.3
.5	1.4	2.2	2.8				-.4	.9
	4.5	4.7				Net Profit + Depr., Dep., Amort./Cur. Mat. L/T/D	3.5	3.4
(10) 2.0	(19) 1.9					(20)	1.7 (26)	1.8
1.3	1.4						.4	.7
.3	.2	.2	.3			Fixed/Worth	.3	.3
1.2	.8	.7	.7				1.0	.9
-1.3	3.1	1.3	1.6				5.1	3.7
.9	.9	1.0	1.1			Debt/Worth	.8	1.2
6.3	2.0	2.0	2.6				2.0	2.3
-3.4	8.5	5.5	4.6				13.2	11.0
125.3	69.2	67.5	59.7			% Profit Before Taxes/Tangible Net Worth	28.5	44.1
(51) 36.2	(79) 31.1	(78) 32.5	(23) 39.7			(98)	10.8 (139)	21.6
.0	7.8	12.8	21.5				-1.3	.5
28.1	20.4	20.8	21.9			% Profit Before Taxes/Total Assets	11.4	16.9
10.7	8.2	11.4	10.7				3.0	6.7
-1.3	1.7	4.5	5.3				-4.6	.1
48.3	33.2	37.1	28.3			Sales/Net Fixed Assets	19.4	39.3
24.9	16.0	11.9	11.0				9.4	12.8
9.9	7.6	5.8	5.1				4.5	4.9
6.1	3.9	3.1	3.1			Sales/Total Assets	3.4	3.8
4.3	2.7	2.3	2.1				2.4	2.5
3.0	2.1	1.7	1.8				1.8	1.6
.8	.9	.8	.7			% Depr., Dep., Amort./Sales	1.4	1.1
(57) 1.5	(78) 1.5	(78) 1.7	(21) 1.4			(99)	2.7 (146)	2.1
3.1	2.9	2.8	3.2				4.8	4.1
4.2	3.6	1.7				% Officers', Directors' Owners' Comp/Sales	3.8	3.0
(51) 9.0	(52) 5.3	(36) 3.0				(65)	6.8 (101)	6.2
14.0	8.5	6.2					12.7	11.0
88460M	316494M	920006M	1203544M	777477M	808304M	Net Sales ($)	674867M	931349M
18480M	107294M	377213M	489131M	349831M	552588M	Total Assets ($)	306486M	391070M

M = $ thousand   MM = $ million
See Pages 11 through 21 for Explanation of Ratios and Data

Comparative Historical Data | Current Data Sorted by Sales

4/1/04-3/31/05 ALL	4/1/05-3/31/06 ALL	4/1/06-3/31/07 ALL	Type of Statement	0-1MM	1-3MM	3-5MM	5-10MM	10-25MM	25MM & OVER
13	23	25	Unqualified	1		1	2	7	14
24	37	38	Reviewed	1	3	5	11	13	5
57	50	51	Compiled	8	16	10	10	7	
52	62	89	Tax Returns	22	38	18	7	2	2
55	69	88	Other	14	23	16	15	7	13
				64 (4/1-9/30/06)		227 (10/1/06-3/31/07)			
201	241	291	**NUMBER OF STATEMENTS**	46	80	50	45	36	34
%	%	%	**ASSETS**	%	%	%	%	%	%
10.8	9.9	10.5	Cash & Equivalents	10.4	11.5	11.2	10.6	9.4	8.1
31.5	32.0	32.5	Trade Receivables (net)	21.5	30.2	31.9	41.2	36.8	37.5
17.4	17.9	18.5	Inventory	12.0	18.0	21.5	17.7	24.9	18.7
2.5	2.7	3.7	All Other Current	5.2	2.6	4.0	1.9	3.0	6.7
62.3	62.4	65.2	Total Current	49.1	62.3	68.7	71.5	74.2	70.9
27.7	26.9	25.6	Fixed Assets (net)	34.6	29.9	22.4	22.2	21.1	17.6
2.8	3.2	3.2	Intangibles (net)	4.5	2.4	2.4	2.2	2.4	6.4
7.2	7.4	6.0	All Other Non-Current	11.8	5.4	6.5	4.2	2.3	5.1
100.0	100.0	100.0	Total	100.0	100.0	100.0	100.0	100.0	100.0
			LIABILITIES						
12.2	13.9	13.3	Notes Payable-Short Term	22.0	11.2	9.9	12.8	13.2	12.1
5.0	5.2	4.7	Cur. Mat.-L.T.D.	6.2	5.5	2.9	5.9	4.0	2.9
16.8	16.0	15.9	Trade Payables	11.7	16.7	17.3	19.1	14.8	14.8
.3	.2	.2	Income Taxes Payable	.3	.0	.1	.4	.6	.2
9.8	10.5	11.4	All Other Current	16.5	7.0	12.6	8.6	13.0	14.9
44.1	45.8	45.6	Total Current	56.7	40.5	42.9	46.8	45.5	44.8
22.3	22.0	24.6	Long-Term Debt	47.2	27.1	22.1	15.2	14.9	14.3
.4	.3	.3	Deferred Taxes	.1	.1	.2	.5	.6	.8
7.1	4.6	5.4	All Other Non-Current	5.7	9.4	3.9	4.5	2.3	2.3
26.2	27.3	24.1	Net Worth	-9.7	22.9	31.0	33.0	36.6	37.8
100.0	100.0	100.0	Total Liabilties & Net Worth	100.0	100.0	100.0	100.0	100.0	100.0
			INCOME DATA						
100.0	100.0	100.0	Net Sales	100.0	100.0	100.0	100.0	100.0	100.0
			Gross Profit						
94.3	95.4	93.8	Operating Expenses	92.2	95.5	94.6	94.1	90.6	94.1
5.7	4.6	6.2	Operating Profit	7.8	4.5	5.4	5.9	9.4	5.9
1.1	.8	1.0	All Other Expenses (net)	2.2	.7	.8	.8	1.8	-.1
4.6	3.8	5.2	Profit Before Taxes	5.6	3.8	4.6	5.2	7.6	6.0
			RATIOS						
2.6	2.2	2.5	Current	3.0	2.8	3.1	2.1	2.1	2.1
1.5	1.4	1.5		1.2	1.6	1.7	1.5	1.6	1.5
1.0	1.0	1.1		.4	1.0	1.2	1.1	1.3	1.2
1.6	1.6	1.6	Quick	2.1	1.8	1.9	1.6	1.5	1.5
(200) 1.0	1.0	1.0		.7	.9	1.1	1.0	1.2	1.0
.6	.6	.6		.2	.6	.7	.7	.6	.5
27 13.7	26 14.0	25 14.8	Sales/Receivables	0 UND	22 16.9	26 14.0	38 9.7	42 8.7	35 10.4
45 8.2	44 8.2	41 8.9		18 20.4	36 10.2	40 9.1	47 7.7	52 7.0	57 6.4
62 5.9	65 5.6	58 6.3		38 9.5	54 6.8	54 6.8	59 6.1	65 5.6	79 4.6
			Cost of Sales/Inventory						
			Cost of Sales/Payables						
6.6	7.3	6.7	Sales/Working Capital	7.4	6.4	5.9	8.5	5.0	6.7
13.3	15.2	12.7		63.1	13.3	11.0	14.9	10.8	10.3
106.7	276.5	90.2		-12.4	450.6	25.8	101.9	18.2	25.2
11.8	10.4	14.5	EBIT/Interest	13.3	11.1	14.3	15.9	31.7	16.2
(170) 3.8	(215) 3.7	(252) 4.5		(32) 2.9	(73) 3.3	(43) 2.6	(40) 5.0	(33) 7.6	(31) 5.4
.9	1.3	1.5		.6	1.2	1.1	1.9	3.4	2.8
6.3	4.0	4.9	Net Profit + Depr., Dep., Amort./Cur. Mat. L/T/D				4.1	5.9	5.9
(32) 2.5	(40) 1.6	(44) 2.2				(10) 2.1	(11) 2.6	(13) 4.1	
1.1	.8	1.4				1.4	1.6	.7	
.3	.3	.3	Fixed/Worth	.5	.4	.2	.2	.2	.3
1.0	1.0	.9		2.7	1.1	.8	.7	.6	.6
4.2	4.0	3.1		-1.0	6.8	3.1	1.3	1.1	.9
.9	1.0	1.0	Debt/Worth	1.1	.8	.8	1.1	1.1	1.0
2.6	3.0	2.3		11.3	3.1	2.1	1.7	2.0	2.0
18.3	11.2	10.3		-2.7	22.9	11.1	5.8	4.0	4.9
69.1	70.4	73.0	% Profit Before Taxes/Tangible Net Worth	100.0	86.0	51.3	69.2	74.6	63.8
(164) 27.6	(200) 29.2	(239) 33.6		(27) 33.3	(65) 31.5	(41) 17.6	(39) 33.6	(35) 42.4	(32) 39.6
4.8	7.4	10.8		14.5	7.8	4.7	14.6	20.2	16.4
22.1	20.1	22.1	% Profit Before Taxes/Total Assets	25.3	21.6	18.1	28.8	23.4	20.8
6.7	7.8	9.3		8.8	8.7	6.8	16.0	16.5	12.2
.8	.7	2.2		-.9	1.1	.6	4.4	7.2	4.9
35.6	30.3	37.1	Sales/Net Fixed Assets	40.7	36.1	31.7	39.4	44.7	41.7
13.0	14.5	14.7		13.3	14.2	14.6	21.9	14.2	21.8
5.7	6.3	7.3		5.0	6.7	7.0	9.4	6.0	7.6
3.8	4.0	4.1	Sales/Total Assets	4.9	4.5	4.1	3.9	3.2	3.3
2.5	2.7	2.8		3.5	2.9	2.5	3.1	2.4	2.6
1.7	1.7	2.0		1.7	2.1	1.6	2.3	1.7	2.0
1.0	.8	.8	% Depr., Dep., Amort./Sales	1.5	.8	.8	.9	.8	.6
(164) 1.9	(209) 1.8	(243) 1.5		(33) 3.2	(66) 1.7	(44) 1.3	(32) 1.4	(31) 1.7	1.0
3.5	3.6	2.9		5.1	2.9	2.5	2.8	2.6	2.8
3.5	3.1	3.2	% Officers', Directors' Owners' Comp/Sales	8.0	4.0	3.0	2.2	1.1	
(111) 5.2	(123) 5.7	(142) 5.5		(26) 11.8	(48) 5.8	(33) 5.4	(19) 3.5	(12) 1.8	
8.1	9.6	10.3		20.4	10.6	8.4	5.3	2.6	
2919926M	4115173M	4114285M	Net Sales ($)	26874M	143982M	201784M	313111M	535681M	2892853M
607904M	1229886M	1894537M	Total Assets ($)	18061M	56283M	95379M	104413M	239803M	1380598M

M = $ thousand   MM = $ million
See Pages 11 through 21 for Explanation of Ratios and Data

Current Data Sorted by Assets   Comparative Historical Data

0-500M	500M-2MM	2-10MM	10-50MM	50-100MM	100-250MM		4/1/02-3/31/03 ALL	4/1/03-3/31/04 ALL
						Type of Statement		
				1		Unqualified	4	4
	1	3				Reviewed	8	12
1	3	2	3			Compiled	9	12
6	3			2		Tax Returns	5	14
3	4					Other	20	11
	6 (4/1-9/30/06)		26 (10/1/06-3/31/07)					
10	11	8	3			**NUMBER OF STATEMENTS**	46	53
%	%	%	%	%	%	**ASSETS**	%	%
14.3	8.0	D	D	D	D	Cash & Equivalents	12.5	8.5
13.7	37.6	A	A	A	A	Trade Receivables (net)	38.8	39.6
18.5	10.3	T	T	T	T	Inventory	12.1	16.2
3.4	1.9	A	A	A	A	All Other Current	6.2	5.0
49.8	57.9					Total Current	69.6	69.3
30.2	32.3	N	N	N	N	Fixed Assets (net)	21.5	20.7
3.8	.8	O	O	O	O	Intangibles (net)	2.2	2.2
16.1	8.9	T	T	T	T	All Other Non-Current	6.7	7.8
100.0	100.0					Total	100.0	100.0
		A	A	A	A	**LIABILITIES**		
39.5	6.9	V	V	V	V	Notes Payable-Short Term	10.5	10.7
.8	1.8	A	A	A	A	Cur. Mat.-L.T.D.	3.4	6.0
4.5	13.0	I	I	I	I	Trade Payables	21.5	19.8
2.0	.0	L	L	L	L	Income Taxes Payable	.8	.2
9.5	12.4	A	A	A	A	All Other Current	16.8	16.0
56.3	34.1	B	B	B	B	Total Current	53.1	52.6
29.5	23.6	L	L	L	L	Long-Term Debt	8.1	14.1
.0	1.3	E	E	E	E	Deferred Taxes	.3	.5
1.3	10.4					All Other Non-Current	4.5	4.6
12.9	30.6					Net Worth	34.0	28.3
100.0	100.0					Total Liabilities & Net Worth	100.0	100.0
						INCOME DATA		
100.0	100.0					Net Sales	100.0	100.0
						Gross Profit		
93.9	93.3					Operating Expenses	96.7	97.9
6.1	6.7					Operating Profit	3.3	2.1
1.8	1.2					All Other Expenses (net)	.8	.3
4.3	5.5					Profit Before Taxes	2.5	1.8
						RATIOS		
3.2	3.8						2.2	2.2
1.1	2.1					Current	1.3	1.4
.2	1.2						1.0	1.0
2.2	2.2						1.7	1.7
.7	1.2					Quick	1.0	1.0
.0	.7						.7	.6
0 UND	25 14.9						26 13.8	33 11.2
10 36.1	52 7.1					Sales/Receivables	43 8.6	47 7.7
15 24.0	74 4.9						56 6.5	72 5.1
						Cost of Sales/Inventory		
						Cost of Sales/Payables		
14.4	6.4						9.3	8.5
UND	14.8					Sales/Working Capital	22.4	17.7
-19.0	50.7						189.8	UND
	36.9						13.0	6.1
(10)	4.9					EBIT/Interest	(38) 3.5	(45) 2.0
	.8						.9	.4
							7.9	
						Net Profit + Depr., Dep., Amort./Cur. Mat. L/T/D	(12) 3.0	
							.8	
.3	.5						.3	.3
4.5	1.1					Fixed/Worth	.6	.7
-1.1	3.2						1.6	3.7
.4	1.3						.8	1.0
82.1	3.2					Debt/Worth	1.9	2.6
-3.7	4.5						7.6	24.6
							54.5	45.1
						% Profit Before Taxes/Tangible Net Worth	(40) 14.0	(44) 8.5
							2.2	-.2
41.9	26.9						8.7	9.6
30.6	15.0					% Profit Before Taxes/Total Assets	5.0	2.1
4.6	-3.6						.6	-1.9
71.7	20.5						34.5	38.2
32.4	12.4					Sales/Net Fixed Assets	24.0	20.0
12.5	4.1						15.4	12.1
11.5	4.3						4.3	4.1
6.6	3.4					Sales/Total Assets	3.5	3.0
3.6	1.6						2.5	2.0
	1.0						1.1	1.2
	2.1					% Depr., Dep., Amort./Sales	(43) 1.7	(46) 1.9
	5.7						2.6	2.4
							3.2	3.0
						% Officers', Directors' Owners' Comp/Sales	(27) 6.2	(35) 5.1
							10.3	
13827M	32842M	108465M	87313M			Net Sales ($)	403808M	361416M
1847M	10999M	39731M	41976M			Total Assets ($)	137177M	127460M

© RMA 2007

M = $ thousand   MM = $ million
See Pages 11 through 21 for Explanation of Ratios and Data

Comparative Historical Data

Current Data Sorted by Sales

					Type of Statement						
	2		4		1	Unqualified						1
	10		5		4	Reviewed		1		1	2	
	14		8		6	Compiled		1	1	3	1	
	18		5		9	Tax Returns		4		1		
	11		14		12	Other	4	3	1		4	1
	4/1/04- 3/31/05 ALL		4/1/05- 3/31/06 ALL		4/1/06- 3/31/07 ALL		3	6 (4/1-9/30/06)	1	26 (10/1/06-3/31/07)		
							0-1MM	1-3MM	3-5MM	5-10MM	10-25MM	25MM & OVER
	55		36		32	NUMBER OF STATEMENTS	7	9	2	5	7	2
	%		%		%	ASSETS	%	%	%	%	%	%
	13.0		15.3		12.2	Cash & Equivalents						
	33.5		40.9		28.2	Trade Receivables (net)						
	18.1		9.8		13.1	Inventory						
	3.9		8.5		6.1	All Other Current						
	68.5		74.5		59.6	Total Current						
	21.6		17.7		27.1	Fixed Assets (net)						
	3.6		5.1		3.9	Intangibles (net)						
	6.3		2.7		9.4	All Other Non-Current						
	100.0		100.0		100.0	Total						
					LIABILITIES						
	9.9		14.3		18.3	Notes Payable-Short Term						
	4.8		4.2		3.4	Cur. Mat.-L.T.D.						
	20.3		19.5		10.8	Trade Payables						
	.2		.4		.9	Income Taxes Payable						
	14.6		18.1		14.2	All Other Current						
	49.8		56.5		47.5	Total Current						
	15.2		14.9		21.4	Long-Term Debt						
	.3		.4		.6	Deferred Taxes						
	7.8		3.3		4.3	All Other Non-Current						
	26.8		24.9		26.3	Net Worth						
	100.0		100.0		100.0	Total Liabilties & Net Worth						
					INCOME DATA						
	100.0		100.0		100.0	Net Sales						
					Gross Profit						
	95.3		95.1		93.9	Operating Expenses						
	4.7		4.9		6.1	Operating Profit						
	.8		.6		1.4	All Other Expenses (net)						
	3.9		4.3		4.7	Profit Before Taxes						
					RATIOS						
	2.0		2.5		3.0							
	1.5		1.6		1.3	Current						
	1.1		1.0		.9							
	1.4		1.8		2.1							
	.9		1.1		1.0	Quick						
	.5		.7		.5							
16	22.3	32	11.5	11	34.3							
35	10.4	46	7.9	26	14.1	Sales/Receivables						
62	5.9	67	5.5	60	6.1							
					Cost of Sales/Inventory						
					Cost of Sales/Payables						
	10.1		6.5		9.6							
	16.2		11.5		23.2	Sales/Working Capital						
	343.0		219.3		-33.4							
	14.5		13.2		9.4							
(45)	4.1	(33)	7.3	(28)	5.2	EBIT/Interest						
	1.6		2.5		1.7							
	5.2					Net Profit + Depr., Dep.,						
(12)	2.0					Amort./Cur. Mat. L/T/D						
	1.3											
	.4		.3		.3							
	.8		.5		1.1	Fixed/Worth						
	7.3		1.5		6.8							
	1.3		1.1		1.1							
	3.0		2.2		2.9	Debt/Worth						
	31.4		5.4		124.2							
	68.1		72.6		66.7	% Profit Before Taxes/Tangible						
(43)	34.4	(32)	41.6	(25)	46.0	Net Worth						
	10.1		11.6		21.9							
	17.1		21.4		28.8	% Profit Before Taxes/Total						
	9.4		11.3		15.0	Assets						
	2.2		4.0		2.5							
	60.2		43.6		34.9							
	21.6		22.1		15.8	Sales/Net Fixed Assets						
	12.2		13.8		8.4							
	4.6		4.0		4.5							
	3.4		3.2		3.4	Sales/Total Assets						
	2.5		2.4		2.0							
	.9		.7		.8							
(45)	2.1	(28)	1.4	(28)	2.0	% Depr., Dep., Amort./Sales						
	2.6		2.3		3.4							
	3.0		4.5		3.4	% Officers', Directors'						
(32)	6.5	(13)	6.3	(17)	5.0	Owners' Comp/Sales						
	13.0		18.9		9.3							
	474036M		540181M		242447M	Net Sales ($)	4188M	16668M	6184M	31571M	116918M	66918M
	136268M		234276M		94553M	Total Assets ($)	1536M	5555M	3889M	9210M	42734M	31629M

© RMA 2007

M = $ thousand   MM = $ million
See Pages 11 through 21 for Explanation of Ratios and Data

Current Data Sorted by Assets   Comparative Historical Data

Type of Statement	0-500M	500M-2MM	2-10MM	10-50MM	50-100MM	100-250MM		4/1/02-3/31/03 ALL	4/1/03-3/31/04 ALL
Unqualified									
Reviewed		2	4		1			2	3
Compiled	2	4	3	1				8	6
Tax Returns	3	6	2	1	1			3	9
Other	2	5	1					4	1
		8 (4/1-9/30/06)	30 (10/1/06-3/31/07)						
NUMBER OF STATEMENTS	7	17	10	2	2			17	19

	0-500M %	500M-2MM %	2-10MM %	10-50MM %	50-100MM %	100-250MM %		4/1/02-3/31/03 ALL %	4/1/03-3/31/04 ALL %
ASSETS									
Cash & Equivalents		7.5	11.1				D	16.5	22.0
Trade Receivables (net)		30.8	37.6				A	19.6	20.1
Inventory		24.8	14.0				T	22.1	16.4
All Other Current		.5	7.3				A	1.5	1.9
Total Current		63.5	70.1					59.7	60.3
Fixed Assets (net)		30.3	24.5				N	29.1	28.8
Intangibles (net)		1.6	.0				O	3.2	2.5
All Other Non-Current		4.5	5.4				T	7.9	8.4
Total		100.0	100.0					100.0	100.0
LIABILITIES							A		
Notes Payable-Short Term		9.1	7.4				V	14.9	14.7
Cur. Mat.-L.T.D.		1.9	11.5				A	4.3	16.0
Trade Payables		15.4	17.0				I	12.8	11.5
Income Taxes Payable		.9	.3				L	.1	.0
All Other Current		6.9	13.6				A	8.0	20.4
Total Current		34.2	49.8				B	40.0	62.6
Long-Term Debt		29.2	15.4				L	23.6	25.2
Deferred Taxes		.0	.2				E	.1	.0
All Other Non-Current		5.0	7.9					5.2	30.6
Net Worth		31.6	26.6					31.1	-18.5
Total Liabilities & Net Worth		100.0	100.0					100.0	100.0
INCOME DATA									
Net Sales		100.0	100.0					100.0	100.0
Gross Profit									
Operating Expenses		93.0	93.1					96.2	90.9
Operating Profit		7.0	6.9					3.8	9.1
All Other Expenses (net)		.7	.9					.4	3.1
Profit Before Taxes		6.3	5.9					3.4	6.0
RATIOS									
Current		2.6	2.1					1.8	3.3
		1.9	1.4					1.4	1.3
		1.2	1.2					1.0	.4
Quick		1.7	1.4					1.3	1.5
		1.0	1.1					.7	.6
		.8	.8					.2	.3
Sales/Receivables		14 26.6	34 10.9					0 UND	0 UND
		29 12.7	59 6.1					20 18.0	14 25.4
		64 5.7	71 5.1					34 10.7	27 13.3
Cost of Sales/Inventory									
Cost of Sales/Payables									
Sales/Working Capital		6.4	7.1					10.2	11.6
		9.8	13.8					22.8	37.5
		42.3	33.8					NM	-16.1
EBIT/Interest		22.6	15.8					14.3	15.7
		(14) 4.4	3.6					3.4	(17) 10.9
		2.1	2.0					-2.1	.6
Net Profit + Depr., Dep., Amort./Cur. Mat. L/T/D									
Fixed/Worth		.1	.3					.3	.2
		.6	1.0					.9	.7
		-11.4	1.7					NM	-1.8
Debt/Worth		.7	1.6					.9	.8
		1.1	3.0					1.9	2.8
		-28.1	7.0					NM	-4.4
% Profit Before Taxes/Tangible Net Worth		71.1	152.0					82.8	28.2
		(12) 35.9	24.7					(13) 20.1	(11) 17.3
		16.8	10.1					5.3	10.1
% Profit Before Taxes/Total Assets		26.8	36.7					22.0	69.5
		9.0	7.8					5.9	5.7
		4.1	2.5					-4.4	.4
Sales/Net Fixed Assets		43.9	39.8					78.8	34.3
		15.7	14.8					13.0	23.2
		6.1	6.8					5.6	12.8
Sales/Total Assets		3.9	3.6					5.5	7.4
		2.7	2.7					3.4	4.1
		2.4	1.7					2.0	2.5
% Depr., Dep., Amort./Sales		.6						.5	1.0
		(13) 1.9						(15) 1.7	(14) 1.6
		4.9						3.0	2.4
% Officers', Directors' Owners' Comp/Sales		3.2						2.2	
		(11) 3.6						(11) 4.3	
		9.0						7.5	
Net Sales ($)	5179M	58801M	107388M	94678M	1000616M			218597M	127283M
Total Assets ($)	1759M	19358M	39413M	34031M	138481M			102784M	38055M

M = $ thousand   MM = $ million
See Pages 11 through 21 for Explanation of Ratios and Data

Comparative Historical Data | Current Data Sorted by Sales

4/1/04-3/31/05 ALL	4/1/05-3/31/06 ALL	4/1/06-3/31/07 ALL	Type of Statement	0-1MM	1-3MM	3-5MM	5-10MM	10-25MM	25MM & OVER
			Unqualified						1
1	2	1	Reviewed		1	2	1	2	2
3	2	6	Compiled	2	4		1	1	1
4	2	10	Tax Returns	3	2	3	1		1
12	7	12	Other	3	2	2	1		1
3	7	9		1	4				
					8 (4/1-9/30/06)		30 (10/1/06-3/31/07)		
23	**20**	**38**	**NUMBER OF STATEMENTS**	**6**	**11**	**7**	**6**	**3**	**5**
%	%	%	**ASSETS**	%	%	%	%	%	%
18.9	12.7	13.1	Cash & Equivalents		16.3				
28.0	24.9	32.8	Trade Receivables (net)		25.3				
13.0	9.0	16.6	Inventory		14.2				
2.8	3.9	2.4	All Other Current		.3				
62.7	50.6	65.0	Total Current		56.1				
24.0	37.6	28.5	Fixed Assets (net)		35.5				
4.1	5.8	2.8	Intangibles (net)		2.4				
9.2	6.0	3.7	All Other Non-Current		6.0				
100.0	100.0	100.0	Total		100.0				
			LIABILITIES						
8.5	9.2	6.5	Notes Payable-Short Term		4.6				
5.5	5.5	4.8	Cur. Mat.-L.T.D.		5.1				
15.3	17.8	13.6	Trade Payables		9.6				
.5	2.4	.6	Income Taxes Payable		1.3				
8.4	10.5	10.8	All Other Current		9.0				
38.1	45.3	36.3	Total Current		29.7				
26.3	25.9	28.6	Long-Term Debt		50.4				
.5	.2	.1	Deferred Taxes		.0				
10.4	4.2	5.1	All Other Non-Current		2.4				
24.8	24.4	29.9	Net Worth		17.6				
100.0	100.0	100.0	Total Liabilties & Net Worth		100.0				
			INCOME DATA						
100.0	100.0	100.0	Net Sales		100.0				
			Gross Profit						
91.9	91.7	89.1	Operating Expenses		91.2				
8.1	8.3	10.9	Operating Profit		8.8				
1.6	2.9	1.6	All Other Expenses (net)		1.5				
6.5	5.5	9.3	Profit Before Taxes		7.4				
			RATIOS						
2.3	2.4	2.8	Current		2.9				
1.8	1.3	1.8			1.7				
1.1	.9	1.2			1.1				
2.0	1.7	2.1	Quick		2.8				
1.1	1.1	1.2			1.0				
.6	.5	.9			.8				
8 44.8	0 UND	12 30.6	Sales/Receivables		11 31.8				
25 14.8	24 15.4	39 9.4			20 17.8				
37 9.7	62 5.9	71 5.1			76 4.8				
			Cost of Sales/Inventory						
			Cost of Sales/Payables						
8.3	11.7	6.1	Sales/Working Capital		6.7				
12.3	23.1	10.1			9.8				
281.5	UND	31.0			265.7				
37.6	16.0	21.5	EBIT/Interest						
(21) 7.6	(17) 5.8	(33) 6.1							
5.0	.5	2.1							
			Net Profit + Depr., Dep., Amort./Cur. Mat. L/T/D						
.2	.5	.1	Fixed/Worth		.1				
.5	1.3	.6			1.8				
7.4	17.1	3.8			-3.9				
.7	.8	.9	Debt/Worth		.9				
2.3	2.7	1.8			4.3				
39.8	37.9	16.2			-6.6				
350.0	64.0	90.6	% Profit Before Taxes/Tangible Net Worth						
(19) 42.1	(16) 41.6	(30) 41.7							
8.8	6.2	16.9							
35.5	25.3	32.0	% Profit Before Taxes/Total Assets		45.7				
10.8	6.8	12.8			11.6				
5.3	-.3	5.0			3.2				
86.4	23.9	62.5	Sales/Net Fixed Assets		36.5				
24.8	15.2	17.1			15.7				
11.9	7.1	6.3			3.5				
7.4	6.7	4.1	Sales/Total Assets		5.2				
3.8	2.9	2.8			2.6				
2.8	2.4	2.1			2.2				
.7	1.1	.6	% Depr., Dep., Amort./Sales						
(17) 1.4	(15) 2.1	(27) 1.6							
2.3	3.4	3.4							
4.1	1.9	1.9	% Officers', Directors' Owners' Comp/Sales						
(16) 6.9	(11) 3.5	(25) 3.2							
12.3	4.5	6.2							
784174M	883156M	1266662M	Net Sales ($)	2394M	25463M	27328M	42836M	44034M	1124607M
63225M	118331M	233042M	Total Assets ($)	2240M	10037M	11009M	13062M	14616M	182078M

M = $ thousand   MM = $ million
See Pages 11 through 21 for Explanation of Ratios and Data

Current Data Sorted by Assets

Comparative Historical Data

						Type of Statement		
2			4	1		Unqualified	2	6
1	2	6	1			Reviewed	5	4
9	9	1				Compiled	16	30
61	22	4			1	Tax Returns	55	62
29	11	6		2	1	Other	36	32
	16 (4/1-9/30/06)		158 (10/1/06-3/31/07)				4/1/02-3/31/03	4/1/03-3/31/04
0-500M	500M-2MM	2-10MM	10-50MM	50-100MM	100-250MM		ALL	ALL
102	44	17	6	3	2	NUMBER OF STATEMENTS	114	134
%	%	%	%	%	%	ASSETS	%	%
23.1	15.4	14.9				Cash & Equivalents	21.8	20.4
.9	1.7	8.3				Trade Receivables (net)	3.1	2.5
15.4	8.6	10.4				Inventory	10.9	11.0
1.0	2.3	2.4				All Other Current	1.0	3.8
40.4	28.0	36.0				Total Current	36.7	37.6
43.5	48.3	44.9				Fixed Assets (net)	48.7	47.1
7.3	10.8	6.5				Intangibles (net)	6.9	7.5
8.8	12.9	12.5				All Other Non-Current	7.6	7.8
100.0	100.0	100.0				Total	100.0	100.0
						LIABILITIES		
18.9	5.1	5.3				Notes Payable-Short Term	7.1	10.5
2.7	3.3	3.3				Cur. Mat.-L.T.D.	6.6	6.8
8.2	6.3	11.6				Trade Payables	7.1	5.7
.0	.1	.0				Income Taxes Payable	.3	.2
26.4	22.3	29.8				All Other Current	23.6	19.5
56.2	37.1	49.9				Total Current	44.7	42.8
33.7	30.3	20.8				Long-Term Debt	29.4	31.1
.2	.0	.0				Deferred Taxes	.0	.0
14.7	10.7	20.2				All Other Non-Current	20.6	8.5
-4.8	21.9	9.1				Net Worth	5.3	17.6
100.0	100.0	100.0				Total Liabilities & Net Worth	100.0	100.0
						INCOME DATA		
100.0	100.0	100.0				Net Sales	100.0	100.0
						Gross Profit		
95.6	93.5	92.6				Operating Expenses	95.3	94.4
4.4	6.5	7.4				Operating Profit	4.7	5.6
.9	2.8	1.7				All Other Expenses (net)	1.2	1.3
3.5	3.6	5.7				Profit Before Taxes	3.6	4.2
						RATIOS		
1.9	1.2	1.1					1.8	2.2
.9	.8	.5				Current	.9	1.0
.3	.4	.3					.4	.5
1.0	1.0	.8					1.3	1.3
(100) .5	.3	.3				Quick	(112) .5	.6
.1	.1	.1					.2	.2
0 UND	0 UND	0 UND					0 UND	0 UND
0 UND	0 UND	1 439.8				Sales/Receivables	0 UND	0 UND
0 UND	0 999.8	4 94.1					0 999.8	1 406.3
						Cost of Sales/Inventory		
						Cost of Sales/Payables		
25.4	28.8	82.7					22.1	21.0
-140.6	-31.7	-20.7				Sales/Working Capital	-290.8	UND
-14.4	-14.1	-6.5					-13.7	-16.4
11.0	15.7	15.6					6.5	12.0
(71) 3.5	(34) 3.1	(15) 6.2				EBIT/Interest	(84) 2.3	(102) 3.5
.5	.9	1.9					.8	1.5
						Net Profit + Depr., Dep., Amort./Cur. Mat. L/T/D		
.6	1.0	1.8					1.0	.8
2.4	2.0	5.2				Fixed/Worth	5.5	2.3
-1.9	-9.0	NM					-2.9	-2.9
1.1	1.4	3.3					1.4	.8
6.5	4.1	7.8				Debt/Worth	7.3	3.8
-2.9	-6.6	NM					-5.1	-6.5
173.2	62.7	224.6					78.0	105.9
(59) 58.8	(27) 32.0	(13) 53.9				% Profit Before Taxes/Tangible Net Worth	(68) 21.4	(89) 36.8
12.1	8.7	25.4					4.7	7.8
42.2	19.5	20.2					30.3	26.9
12.2	6.8	7.2				% Profit Before Taxes/Total Assets	6.9	10.5
-2.2	.0	3.0					-.4	1.4
39.2	14.4	14.3					22.6	20.9
14.8	7.6	9.2				Sales/Net Fixed Assets	9.4	10.5
6.5	2.3	4.1					4.4	5.5
9.2	4.2	4.6					6.6	6.7
5.9	2.4	3.2				Sales/Total Assets	3.9	4.1
3.3	1.5	1.7					2.5	2.4
.6	1.9	1.3					1.2	1.0
(70) 1.4	(36) 2.6	(14) 2.0				% Depr., Dep., Amort./Sales	(91) 2.0	(112) 2.1
2.9	4.9	3.0					4.8	3.7
3.8	2.5						3.4	3.9
(53) 6.9	(22) 4.5					% Officers', Directors' Owners' Comp/Sales	(61) 5.8	(69) 7.8
12.6	5.5						11.6	13.5
99406M	141766M	209341M	221102M	516750M	650913M	Net Sales ($)	1411192M	3420298M
16915M	49560M	67257M	139446M	236853M	251399M	Total Assets ($)	478279M	713175M

M = $ thousand   MM = $ million
See Pages 11 through 21 for Explanation of Ratios and Data

Comparative Historical Data　　　　　　　　　　　　Current Data Sorted by Sales

4	5	7	Type of Statement	2				1	4
5	7	10	Unqualified	1	1		5	2	1
27	19	19	Reviewed	5	7	4	3		
49	59	88	Compiled	46	25	11	2	3	1
36	39	50	Tax Returns	22	13	3	3		3
4/1/04-3/31/05	4/1/05-3/31/06	4/1/06-3/31/07	Other		16 (4/1-9/30/06)			158 (10/1/06-3/31/07)	
ALL	ALL	ALL		0-1MM	1-3MM	3-5MM	5-10MM	10-25MM	25MM & OVER
121	129	174	NUMBER OF STATEMENTS	76	46	18	15	10	9
%	%	%	ASSETS	%	%	%	%	%	%
17.9	17.3	19.5	Cash & Equivalents	20.8	17.1	24.3	24.5	12.2	
4.8	2.7	2.1	Trade Receivables (net)	1.1	.3	4.9	6.2	3.9	
12.0	11.9	12.9	Inventory	12.6	14.4	12.5	9.3	12.8	
3.9	2.7	1.7	All Other Current	.5	2.5	1.2	2.7	4.0	
38.7	34.7	36.2	Total Current	35.0	34.2	43.0	42.7	32.9	
47.4	48.7	43.6	Fixed Assets (net)	45.6	46.6	41.6	39.1	40.2	
5.2	6.8	9.7	Intangibles (net)	10.3	7.1	5.6	9.3	13.9	
8.6	9.8	10.5	All Other Non-Current	9.1	12.0	9.9	8.9	12.9	
100.0	100.0	100.0	Total	100.0	100.0	100.0	100.0	100.0	
			LIABILITIES						
8.4	9.3	12.9	Notes Payable-Short Term	20.7	9.9	3.8	6.8	2.5	
5.1	5.3	3.2	Cur. Mat.-L.T.D.	2.6	2.7	4.9	2.7	9.1	
8.5	7.2	8.2	Trade Payables	4.4	11.0	8.2	13.2	13.3	
.1	.1	.1	Income Taxes Payable	.1	.0	.1	.2	.0	
17.8	20.3	25.4	All Other Current	17.8	34.0	27.9	36.2	21.7	
39.9	42.2	49.8	Total Current	45.7	57.6	44.9	59.1	46.7	
33.9	29.3	31.0	Long-Term Debt	38.5	32.5	24.0	14.7	12.5	
.0	.0	.0	Deferred Taxes	.3	.0	.0	.0	.0	
9.5	7.4	13.7	All Other Non-Current	14.5	13.5	12.7	6.0	28.1	
16.7	21.2	5.4	Net Worth	1.0	-3.7	18.4	20.1	12.7	
100.0	100.0	100.0	Total Liabilties & Net Worth	100.0	100.0	100.0	100.0	100.0	
			INCOME DATA						
100.0	100.0	100.0	Net Sales	100.0	100.0	100.0	100.0	100.0	
			Gross Profit						
92.9	93.7	94.1	Operating Expenses	93.4	96.0	94.4	96.3	95.4	
7.1	6.3	5.9	Operating Profit	6.6	4.0	5.6	3.7	4.6	
2.0	1.7	1.8	All Other Expenses (net)	2.5	1.0	.8	1.9	2.3	
5.1	4.6	4.0	Profit Before Taxes	4.1	3.0	4.8	1.8	2.3	
			RATIOS						
2.2	2.4	1.7		2.0	1.7	2.0	1.2	1.1	
1.1	.9	.8	Current	.9	.5	.8	1.0	.6	
.5	.4	.3		.3	.2	.5	.5	.4	
1.3	1.2	1.0		1.2	.8	1.1	1.0	.5	
(127) .6	(172) .5	.4	Quick	(74) .5	.2	.5	.5	.3	
.2	.2	.1		.2	.0	.3	.1	.1	
0 UND	0 UND	0 UND		0 UND	0 UND	0 UND	0 UND	0 UND	
0 UND	0 UND	0 UND	Sales/Receivables	0 UND	0 UND	0 UND	0 UND	999.8	2 170.6
1 588.6	0 760.3	0 UND		0 UND	0 UND	0 920.4	5 78.7	6 60.8	
			Cost of Sales/Inventory						
			Cost of Sales/Payables						
22.5	23.5	26.4		23.1	28.0	28.0	24.6	101.9	
258.9	-204.7	-52.0	Sales/Working Capital	-150.7	-35.1	-31.7	-314.7	-36.1	
-16.9	-12.4	-13.0		-12.1	-12.9	-15.8	-7.2	-5.6	
13.3	10.6	11.0		9.8	6.4	23.9	31.9	16.8	
(94) 4.7	(102) 4.2	(130) 3.5	EBIT/Interest	(51) 3.1	(33) 2.5	(16) 6.6	(12) 10.9	2.6	
1.5	.5	1.0		.9	.4	1.9	2.1	1.3	
5.5		6.3	Net Profit + Depr., Dep.,						
(15) 2.7		(11) 3.6	Amort./Cur. Mat. L/T/D						
1.3		.5							
.7	.9	.8		.8	.7	.8	.9	1.6	
2.3	2.4	2.5	Fixed/Worth	2.3	NM	1.9	1.3	5.4	
-5.8	-3.9	-2.4		-2.1	-1.3	NM	616.0	-3.2	
1.1	.7	1.3		1.0	1.3	2.4	1.3	2.7	
3.5	3.6	6.0	Debt/Worth	6.5	-43.2	3.6	5.1	7.1	
-10.8	-7.3	-4.7		-3.0	-3.1	-13.9	-14.8	-12.0	
109.2	105.0	144.2	% Profit Before Taxes/Tangible	174.2	88.5	125.2	150.2		
(87) 50.0	(92) 49.7	(105) 52.6	Net Worth	(46) 53.4	(22) 34.8	(13) 54.3	(11) 45.9		
17.2	9.8	13.5		10.5	9.2	19.1	29.6		
27.0	32.1	28.3	% Profit Before Taxes/Total	32.0	25.4	25.6	31.4	24.2	
10.7	9.1	9.9	Assets	11.4	9.4	11.4	7.1	6.4	
1.7	-1.0	-.4		-2.3	-2.2	3.5	-1.6	1.7	
17.7	17.5	26.6		26.7	40.2	20.4	33.0	23.4	
9.1	8.9	11.7	Sales/Net Fixed Assets	10.2	14.6	10.2	9.6	12.0	
3.9	4.7	5.5		4.5	4.4	5.1	6.8	8.4	
6.0	6.1	7.0		7.5	8.5	5.8	5.0	5.2	
3.4	3.6	4.1	Sales/Total Assets	4.2	4.5	2.7	4.2	4.0	
2.1	2.2	2.2		1.9	2.9	2.1	2.9	2.7	
1.1	1.0	.9		.8	.5	.7	1.0		
(106) 2.1	(108) 2.0	(123) 2.2	% Depr., Dep., Amort./Sales	(53) 2.5	(31) 1.9	(16) 2.0	(12) 2.1		
3.3	3.3	3.5		4.4	3.3	3.7	3.0		
2.5	2.9	2.9		5.6	3.0	2.6			
(52) 5.4	(63) 6.4	(82) 5.1	% Officers', Directors'	(32) 9.7	(28) 4.6	(11) 4.7			
8.5	13.7	10.1	Owners' Comp/Sales	15.3	7.1	6.5			
2012170M	1603511M	1839278M	Net Sales ($)	37212M	77834M	68683M	113911M	152330M	1389308M
846055M	576634M	761430M	Total Assets ($)	18840M	21830M	25688M	48745M	62465M	583862M

M = $ thousand　　　MM = $ million
See Pages 11 through 21 for Explanation of Ratios and Data

Current Data Sorted by Assets   Comparative Historical Data

Type of Statement	0-500M	500M-2MM	2-10MM	10-50MM	50-100MM	100-250MM	4/1/02-3/31/03 ALL	4/1/03-3/31/04 ALL
Unqualified	1		3	3		2	14	9
Reviewed	5	8	10	2			24	29
Compiled	27	51	26	2			104	130
Tax Returns	56	41	10	1			69	94
Other	23	25	25	2	2		59	55
	70 (4/1-9/30/06)			255 (10/1/06-3/31/07)				
NUMBER OF STATEMENTS	112	125	74	10	2	2	270	317
ASSETS	%	%	%	%	%	%	%	%
Cash & Equivalents	14.8	8.5	9.7	3.0			10.9	11.0
Trade Receivables (net)	20.0	15.4	9.7	5.0			15.3	15.2
Inventory	7.1	4.2	3.5	2.9			5.1	4.3
All Other Current	1.2	2.0	4.3	7.9			2.5	3.1
Total Current	43.0	30.0	27.2	18.8			33.8	33.6
Fixed Assets (net)	38.0	44.6	45.8	28.0			42.8	45.0
Intangibles (net)	8.6	12.5	7.2	6.7			8.2	7.9
All Other Non-Current	10.4	12.9	19.8	46.5			15.2	13.5
Total	100.0	100.0	100.0	100.0			100.0	100.0
LIABILITIES								
Notes Payable-Short Term	7.3	3.8	2.9	.1			6.6	4.4
Cur. Mat.-L.T.D.	5.6	3.3	3.1	5.4			4.0	4.3
Trade Payables	10.3	4.7	4.0	1.3			4.5	6.0
Income Taxes Payable	.1	.2	.4	.0			.2	.3
All Other Current	14.6	6.3	6.7	12.1			7.6	9.8
Total Current	37.9	18.3	17.2	18.9			23.0	24.7
Long-Term Debt	47.8	44.1	36.5	21.9			35.7	37.9
Deferred Taxes	.0	.2	.2	.0			.1	.1
All Other Non-Current	12.6	7.6	10.5	21.6			11.1	10.4
Net Worth	1.7	29.8	35.7	37.7			30.1	26.9
Total Liabilties & Net Worth	100.0	100.0	100.0	100.0			100.0	100.0
INCOME DATA								
Net Sales	100.0	100.0	100.0	100.0			100.0	100.0
Gross Profit								
Operating Expenses	95.6	91.2	90.7	91.2			93.8	92.3
Operating Profit	4.4	8.8	9.3	8.8			6.2	7.7
All Other Expenses (net)	1.0	2.7	3.5	4.5			2.7	3.2
Profit Before Taxes	3.3	6.0	5.8	4.3			3.4	4.5
RATIOS								
Current	3.4	4.0	3.1	1.7			3.2	3.1
	1.4	1.8	1.8	.9			1.7	1.5
	.6	.8	1.2	.5			.9	.8
Quick	3.0	3.3	2.5	.9			2.7	2.6
	1.1	1.4	1.3	.5			1.3	1.2
	.4	.6	.6	.4			.6	.6
Sales/Receivables	1 582.7	20 17.8	23 16.0	0 UND			22 16.7	17 22.0
	22 16.8	35 10.5	33 11.0	25 14.6			36 10.2	34 10.6
	41 8.8	51 7.1	45 8.2	62 5.8			50 7.3	52 7.0
Cost of Sales/Inventory								
Cost of Sales/Payables								
Sales/Working Capital	7.5	5.4	5.0	8.1			5.5	5.4
	37.0	11.8	12.2	-145.2			12.4	15.8
	-20.0	-23.9	80.5	-2.0			-58.1	-34.5
EBIT/Interest	10.3	5.0	5.6				4.8	6.0
	(82) 3.2	(112) 2.2	(64) 2.5				(221) 2.2	(279) 2.2
	.5	.9	1.3				1.0	.8
Net Profit + Depr., Dep., Amort./Cur. Mat. L/T/D		8.9	2.2				3.0	3.6
		(14) 3.0	(15) 1.5				(51) 1.9	(60) 1.6
		.8	1.3				1.2	1.1
Fixed/Worth	.6	.7	.7	.2			.6	.7
	2.9	1.7	1.4	.8			1.6	1.9
	-.8	-29.7	5.0	3.3			17.5	-146.1
Debt/Worth	.7	.8	.8	.6			.7	.8
	4.1	2.7	2.0	3.8			2.2	2.9
	-3.1	-36.9	7.4	5.4			33.2	-273.5
% Profit Before Taxes/Tangible Net Worth	60.9	47.2	20.3				31.9	37.0
	(66) 17.3	(91) 19.2	(62) 10.8				(209) 10.5	(237) 13.0
	-2.4	3.4	2.8				.7	.6
% Profit Before Taxes/Total Assets	22.9	10.6	8.8	4.7			9.6	10.5
	8.6	5.2	3.7	1.6			3.8	3.7
	-1.8	-.6	.6	-1.3			-.2	-.4
Sales/Net Fixed Assets	17.5	7.1	5.1	9.6			7.6	6.9
	9.0	3.8	2.0	3.1			3.6	3.5
	5.0	1.7	1.0	.8			2.0	1.6
Sales/Total Assets	4.1	2.0	1.4	.6			2.2	2.2
	2.8	1.3	.9	.3			1.4	1.2
	2.0	.8	.5	.3			.8	.7
% Depr., Dep., Amort./Sales	1.3	2.1	3.1				2.4	2.6
	(92) 2.6	(108) 3.6	(67) 4.1				(251) 4.3	(295) 4.7
	4.1	6.2	6.8				7.0	7.8
% Officers', Directors' Owners' Comp/Sales	8.3	7.1	4.2				7.8	6.6
	(69) 12.1	(83) 10.4	(42) 8.1				(179) 11.1	(209) 11.5
	17.2	14.9	13.6				16.4	15.8
Net Sales ($)	92857M	183354M	339114M	210368M	36464M	57793M	1252586M	1463281M
Total Assets ($)	29914M	129306M	345794M	203980M	115449M	264937M	940782M	1144457M

© RMA 2007

M = $ thousand   MM = $ million
See Pages 11 through 21 for Explanation of Ratios and Data

Comparative Historical Data | Current Data Sorted by Sales

				Type of Statement						
10	5	9		Unqualified	1		4	1	1	2
30	23	25		Reviewed	5	11	5	4		
107	93	106		Compiled	39	44	16	5	2	
99	88	108		Tax Returns	59	40	5	1	2	1
62	85	77		Other	31	25	10	7	3	1
4/1/04-3/31/05	4/1/05-3/31/06	4/1/06-3/31/07				70 (4/1-9/30/06)		255 (10/1/06-3/31/07)		
ALL	ALL	ALL			0-1MM	1-3MM	3-5MM	5-10MM	10-25MM	25MM & OVER
308	294	325		NUMBER OF STATEMENTS	135	120	40	18	8	4
%	%	%		ASSETS	%	%	%	%	%	%
10.1	10.2	10.7		Cash & Equivalents	10.2	12.8	6.7	9.7		
14.1	15.3	15.3		Trade Receivables (net)	14.2	17.8	14.1	11.5		
5.5	3.7	5.1		Inventory	6.2	3.8	5.4	3.0		
1.5	2.2	2.5		All Other Current	1.6	2.2	3.1	3.9		
31.2	31.4	33.6		Total Current	32.2	36.5	29.4	28.0		
43.9	42.7	41.7		Fixed Assets (net)	45.9	38.4	43.4	37.0		
10.0	9.9	9.7		Intangibles (net)	10.2	11.2	7.6	2.7		
15.0	15.9	15.1		All Other Non-Current	11.7	13.9	19.5	32.3		
100.0	100.0	100.0		Total	100.0	100.0	100.0	100.0		
				LIABILITIES						
5.4	5.2	4.7		Notes Payable-Short Term	5.7	4.3	3.9	1.0		
3.8	4.6	4.1		Cur. Mat.-L.T.D.	4.4	3.7	4.5	3.5		
5.9	6.7	6.3		Trade Payables	7.1	6.0	6.9	3.7		
.2	.3	.2		Income Taxes Payable	.1	.2	.2	1.0		
10.5	7.5	9.5		All Other Current	11.3	7.5	7.6	9.0		
25.9	24.2	24.8		Total Current	28.6	21.6	23.2	18.1		
41.0	39.2	42.6		Long-Term Debt	50.1	39.2	43.8	25.5		
.7	.2	.1		Deferred Taxes	.0	.2	.0	.4		
9.6	13.9	10.9		All Other Non-Current	12.5	10.0	7.1	9.3		
22.8	22.6	21.6		Net Worth	8.8	28.9	25.9	46.6		
100.0	100.0	100.0		Total Liabilities & Net Worth	100.0	100.0	100.0	100.0		
				INCOME DATA						
100.0	100.0	100.0		Net Sales	100.0	100.0	100.0	100.0		
				Gross Profit						
92.8	93.4	92.7		Operating Expenses	90.9	93.6	94.4	94.8		
7.2	6.6	7.3		Operating Profit	9.1	6.4	5.6	5.2		
2.7	2.6	2.3		All Other Expenses (net)	4.0	1.3	1.4	-.2		
4.6	4.0	5.0		Profit Before Taxes	5.0	5.1	4.2	5.4		
				RATIOS						
3.1	3.3	3.5			4.0	3.9	2.8	4.3		
1.5	1.5	1.6		Current	1.3	1.9	1.4	1.3		
.7	.7	.8			.4	1.1	.9	.8		
2.4	2.5	2.8			3.3	3.0	2.3	2.1		
1.1	1.2	1.3		Quick	.9	1.6	1.2	1.1		
.5	.5	.5			.3	.8	.5	.7		

Sales/Receivables

15	23.6	17	20.9	14	26.2	0	UND	20	18.4	24	15.0	21	17.0
32	11.5	34	10.8	31	11.9	26	14.1	34	10.7	34	10.8	33	11.2
46	8.0	48	7.6	46	7.9	47	7.8	45	8.1	51	7.1	45	8.1

Cost of Sales/Inventory

Cost of Sales/Payables

6.9	6.1	5.9		Sales/Working Capital	6.7	5.8	6.0	3.7		
15.9	18.0	16.3			36.3	12.7	11.9	24.0		
-19.0	-19.9	-27.2			-14.3	110.4	-117.8	-33.2		

						EBIT/Interest							
	5.4		5.3		6.2		6.0		6.7		5.0		8.6
(261)	2.0	(249)	2.3	(269)	2.4	(102)	1.7	(104)	2.6	(36)	2.9	(16)	2.1
	.8		.8		1.0		.6		1.2		1.4		1.1

						Net Profit + Depr., Dep., Amort./Cur. Mat. L/T/D				
	4.1		4.0		3.9			9.6		
(46)	1.9	(44)	2.0	(40)	1.7		(20)	3.0		
	.9		1.0		1.2			1.0		

.7	.7	.6		Fixed/Worth	.9	.6	.7	.4
2.2	2.0	1.7			4.6	1.6	1.3	.7
-6.7	-3.1	-5.5			-1.7	-11.3	13.3	1.7

.9	.9	.8		Debt/Worth	1.6	.7	.7	.5
3.9	3.4	2.9			6.5	2.3	2.1	1.3
-18.8	-8.7	-13.0			-3.4	-17.2	27.5	1.7

						% Profit Before Taxes/Tangible Net Worth							
	32.7		32.8		38.5		51.0		38.5		17.5		20.7
(219)	10.9	(198)	11.9	(231)	14.6	(84)	17.4	(87)	15.6	(31)	11.1		7.6
	1.0		.0		1.1		.8		-.6		3.4		.0

10.2	11.1	12.4		% Profit Before Taxes/Total Assets	12.7	16.8	8.9	11.1
3.1	2.9	4.8			4.6	6.1	4.6	2.6
.0	-1.0	-.4			-1.7	-.4	.9	.0

8.2	8.1	10.1		Sales/Net Fixed Assets	10.2	12.9	5.9	7.9
3.8	4.4	5.0			4.4	5.9	3.4	2.7
1.7	1.7	1.9			1.6	3.4	1.4	1.5

2.3	2.3	2.6		Sales/Total Assets	2.5	2.9	2.1	2.0
1.3	1.5	1.5			1.6	1.9	1.2	1.0
.7	.7	.8			.7	1.1	.6	.5

						% Depr., Dep., Amort./Sales							
	2.5		2.3		2.0		2.2		1.8		2.5		2.5
(278)	4.4	(270)	3.9	(278)	3.3	(111)	3.9	(106)	2.7	(36)	3.7	(15)	3.4
	7.4		6.3		6.0		7.9		4.7		6.6		4.1

						% Officers', Directors' Owners' Comp/Sales							
	6.9		6.9		6.9		8.0		7.3		3.4		4.7
(196)	10.9	(191)	10.7	(197)	10.4	(73)	11.4	(82)	11.5	(25)	7.6	(10)	10.8
	15.7		16.0		15.3		18.1		14.7		10.8		12.6

724245M	606298M	919950M		Net Sales ($)	79716M	202862M	156916M	128483M	105587M	246386M
898368M	655378M	1089380M		Total Assets ($)	80348M	170019M	195236M	206654M	233409M	203714M

M = $ thousand   MM = $ million
See Pages 11 through 21 for Explanation of Ratios and Data

Current Data Sorted by Assets

Comparative Historical Data

0-500M	500M-2MM	2-10MM	10-50MM	50-100MM	100-250MM	Type of Statement	4/1/02-3/31/03 ALL	4/1/03-3/31/04 ALL
	1	1	1	1	2	Unqualified	3	5
	2	1		1		Reviewed	6	3
2	3	4	1			Compiled	15	12
1	9	2	1			Tax Returns	2	14
2	1	8	6	1		Other	13	10
	12 (4/1-9/30/06)		39 (10/1/06-3/31/07)					
5	16	16	9	3	2	NUMBER OF STATEMENTS	39	44
%	%	%	%	%	%	ASSETS	%	%
	11.7	14.1				Cash & Equivalents	10.4	9.2
	14.1	13.0				Trade Receivables (net)	14.3	15.0
	3.9	18.1				Inventory	10.2	13.1
	1.8	1.2				All Other Current	1.5	3.5
	31.5	46.4				Total Current	36.5	40.8
	41.7	22.7				Fixed Assets (net)	42.2	35.2
	6.4	1.7				Intangibles (net)	6.3	7.4
	20.4	29.2				All Other Non-Current	15.0	16.7
	100.0	100.0				Total	100.0	100.0
						LIABILITIES		
	4.3	3.6				Notes Payable-Short Term	5.4	5.0
	4.0	9.7				Cur. Mat.-L.T.D.	3.2	4.3
	1.8	7.5				Trade Payables	3.8	7.7
	.1	.2				Income Taxes Payable	.3	.1
	3.5	4.9				All Other Current	7.7	6.4
	13.8	26.0				Total Current	20.4	23.5
	42.6	17.0				Long-Term Debt	35.6	25.2
	.2	.0				Deferred Taxes	.3	.3
	12.2	17.9				All Other Non-Current	9.6	14.4
	31.2	39.1				Net Worth	34.0	36.5
	100.0	100.0				Total Liabilties & Net Worth	100.0	100.0
						INCOME DATA		
	100.0	100.0				Net Sales	100.0	100.0
						Gross Profit		
	84.1	89.0				Operating Expenses	87.4	95.5
	15.9	11.0				Operating Profit	12.6	4.5
	5.7	1.6				All Other Expenses (net)	3.5	.7
	10.2	9.3				Profit Before Taxes	9.1	3.7
						RATIOS		
	8.3	6.4					3.6	3.4
	2.6	2.4				Current	1.8	2.0
	1.0	1.3					.8	1.0
	7.7	3.5					2.4	2.6
	2.2	1.7				Quick	1.2	1.3
	.9	.9					.4	.4
21	17.0	2	185.1				19	19.1	19	18.9
43	8.4	55	6.7			Sales/Receivables	35	10.4	31	11.7
108	3.4	110	3.3				79	4.6	46	7.9
						Cost of Sales/Inventory		
						Cost of Sales/Payables		
	2.3	1.3					2.3	4.5
	7.6	3.5				Sales/Working Capital	8.1	11.4
	NM	19.3					-20.2	233.6
	6.8	8.9					8.0	7.4
(13)	3.4	(11)	3.4			EBIT/Interest	(33)	2.6	(35)	4.0
	1.4	1.7					1.4	2.0
						Net Profit + Depr., Dep., Amort./Cur. Mat. L/T/D		7.2
							(11)	2.9
								2.2
	.8	.1					.4	.5
	1.3	.5				Fixed/Worth	1.5	.9
	7.8	2.5					24.2	7.4
	1.1	.2					.6	.4
	2.8	4.1				Debt/Worth	2.0	2.6
	17.8	13.0					45.5	21.0
	69.4	38.6				% Profit Before Taxes/Tangible Net Worth	27.9	36.9
(13)	21.8	(15)	13.8				(31)	12.2	(36)	14.6
	4.0	7.7					2.3	3.7
	15.8	6.2				% Profit Before Taxes/Total Assets	8.4	9.8
	6.4	4.5					4.0	3.4
	1.1	1.5					.9	1.0
	4.4	22.4					6.6	10.4
	2.3	3.6				Sales/Net Fixed Assets	2.1	5.2
	.6	1.2					1.0	2.1
	1.4	1.3					1.2	2.7
	.6	.5				Sales/Total Assets	.7	1.3
	.5	.2					.4	.6
	.8	1.4					2.6	2.0
(13)	1.3	(11)	2.3			% Depr., Dep., Amort./Sales	(32)	3.7	(40)	3.5
	8.3	3.2					5.5	6.3
						% Officers', Directors' Owners' Comp/Sales		3.8		4.1
							(16)	9.2	(24)	8.8
								16.5		13.8
2434M	15997M	52454M	77358M	100961M	431558M	Net Sales ($)	238138M	226847M
1120M	18392M	87733M	237810M	180409M	321097M	Total Assets ($)	507878M	375409M

M = $ thousand   MM = $ million
See Pages 11 through 21 for Explanation of Ratios and Data

Comparative Historical Data   Current Data Sorted by Sales

				Type of Statement						
	4		5	6	Unqualified	2				2	2
	4		4	4	Reviewed	1	1	1			1
	7		10	10	Compiled	4	2	2	2		
	8		4	13	Tax Returns	8	2	2	1		
	13		7	18	Other	4	4	4	3	3	
	4/1/04- 3/31/05		4/1/05- 3/31/06	4/1/06- 3/31/07			12 (4/1-9/30/06)		39 (10/1/06-3/31/07)		
	ALL		ALL	ALL		0-1MM	1-3MM	3-5MM	5-10MM	10-25MM	25MM & OVER
	36		30	51	NUMBER OF STATEMENTS	19	9	9	6	5	3
	%		%	%	ASSETS	%	%	%	%	%	%
	8.8		8.1	10.3	Cash & Equivalents	12.5					
	14.3		20.2	14.4	Trade Receivables (net)	14.6					
	15.0		9.2	12.8	Inventory	3.9					
	1.7		1.9	2.6	All Other Current	1.5					
	39.8		39.5	40.1	Total Current	32.4					
	36.9		39.7	32.3	Fixed Assets (net)	40.7					
	3.2		3.6	4.1	Intangibles (net)	2.5					
	20.0		17.2	23.5	All Other Non-Current	24.4					
	100.0		100.0	100.0	Total	100.0					
					LIABILITIES						
	8.8		7.0	8.4	Notes Payable-Short Term	14.1					
	4.6		3.8	4.7	Cur. Mat.-L.T.D.	4.0					
	6.0		4.1	5.4	Trade Payables	4.2					
	.2		.1	.2	Income Taxes Payable	.2					
	10.1		9.0	6.2	All Other Current	7.4					
	29.7		24.0	24.9	Total Current	29.9					
	24.2		21.4	24.5	Long-Term Debt	39.0					
	.1		.2	.1	Deferred Taxes	.3					
	10.4		15.7	18.6	All Other Non-Current	10.2					
	35.6		38.7	31.9	Net Worth	20.7					
	100.0		100.0	100.0	Total Liabilities & Net Worth	100.0					
					INCOME DATA						
	100.0		100.0	100.0	Net Sales	100.0					
					Gross Profit						
	92.2		93.6	87.9	Operating Expenses	82.1					
	7.8		6.4	12.1	Operating Profit	17.9					
	.8		.0	2.3	All Other Expenses (net)	4.6					
	7.0		6.3	9.8	Profit Before Taxes	13.3					
					RATIOS						
	3.4		3.7	8.3		10.2					
	1.7		1.8	2.5	Current	2.5					
	.7		.7	1.2		1.0					
	2.6		3.0	5.7		7.8					
	.9		1.3	1.6	Quick	1.9					
	.4		.5	.7		.8					
21	17.6	17	21.2	21	17.2		Sales/Receivables	13	28.4					
45	8.1	53	6.9	58	6.3			52	7.0					
106	3.4	134	2.7	118	3.1			118	3.1					
					Cost of Sales/Inventory						
					Cost of Sales/Payables						
	2.4		1.9	1.2		1.2					
	6.0		7.4	4.3	Sales/Working Capital	5.2					
	-16.0		-26.3	23.6		-156.0					
	15.6		14.6	8.0		5.7					
(29)	4.5	(25)	3.4	(39)	3.4	EBIT/Interest	(15)	3.4					
	1.0		.7	1.7		1.7					
				6.9	Net Profit + Depr., Dep.,						
		(11)	3.2		Amort./Cur. Mat. L/T/D						
			1.0								
	.4		.5	.4		.5					
	1.0		.9	.9	Fixed/Worth	1.0					
	5.1		10.3	4.7		10.4					
	.5		.5	.7		.6					
	2.1		1.1	3.6	Debt/Worth	4.0					
	51.0		13.2	14.2		20.3					
	36.0		22.2	51.2	% Profit Before Taxes/Tangible	50.1					
(29)	11.0	(25)	10.5	(44)	13.4	Net Worth	(15)	13.0					
	.6		1.2	4.1		3.2					
	9.9		9.9	8.5	% Profit Before Taxes/Total	13.6					
	3.9		3.0	4.4	Assets	8.3					
	-.5		-.4	1.4		1.2					
	8.3		5.8	6.1		4.6					
	3.8		2.4	2.4	Sales/Net Fixed Assets	2.1					
	1.2		1.3	1.1		.6					
	2.2		1.6	1.3		.7					
	.7		.6	.5	Sales/Total Assets	.5					
	.3		.3	.3		.3					
	1.9		1.9	1.2		.8					
(30)	4.1	(26)	3.6	(39)	2.8	% Depr., Dep., Amort./Sales	(13)	3.7					
	6.2		6.0	4.1		8.5					
	4.5			3.6	% Officers', Directors'						
(16)	9.6		(11)	7.6	Owners' Comp/Sales						
	28.5			16.1							
	218934M		468739M	680762M	Net Sales ($)	9807M	16718M	33552M	42450M	74609M	503626M
	474158M		461556M	846561M	Total Assets ($)	21598M	37294M	93753M	120760M	185512M	387644M

© RMA 2007

M = $ thousand   MM = $ million

See Pages 11 through 21 for Explanation of Ratios and Data

Current Data Sorted by Assets   Comparative Historical Data

Type of Statement	0-500M	500M-2MM	2-10MM	10-50MM	50-100MM	100-250MM		4/1/02-3/31/03 ALL	4/1/03-3/31/04 ALL
Unqualified			1	1				4	1
Reviewed			2					8	5
Compiled	4	6	4	1	1			17	16
Tax Returns	13	19	1			1		18	32
Other	7	4	3	3				14	19
	8 (4/1-9/30/06)		62 (10/1/06-3/31/07)						
NUMBER OF STATEMENTS	24	29	11	4	1	1		61	73
ASSETS	%	%	%	%	%	%		%	%
Cash & Equivalents	19.8	8.7	10.9					12.3	12.9
Trade Receivables (net)	1.4	1.3	2.9					1.7	4.3
Inventory	1.0	1.9	3.2					1.3	4.8
All Other Current	1.6	2.4	.7					5.1	1.4
Total Current	23.7	14.3	17.7					20.4	23.4
Fixed Assets (net)	57.3	74.2	65.2					65.0	62.1
Intangibles (net)	13.8	5.2	6.0					8.6	6.0
All Other Non-Current	5.1	6.3	11.1					5.9	8.5
Total	100.0	100.0	100.0					100.0	100.0
LIABILITIES									
Notes Payable-Short Term	8.8	2.1	3.8					6.9	4.3
Cur. Mat.-L.T.D.	14.0	8.0	12.0					12.1	7.3
Trade Payables	4.2	2.0	11.2					2.8	4.1
Income Taxes Payable	.0	.0	.0					.1	.1
All Other Current	8.6	7.1	6.4					8.3	5.8
Total Current	35.7	19.0	33.4					30.2	21.6
Long-Term Debt	60.5	48.9	19.1					45.0	42.0
Deferred Taxes	.0	.0	.0					.3	.3
All Other Non-Current	14.1	6.4	5.1					8.9	14.2
Net Worth	-10.2	25.6	42.4					15.7	21.8
Total Liabilities & Net Worth	100.0	100.0	100.0					100.0	100.0
INCOME DATA									
Net Sales	100.0	100.0	100.0					100.0	100.0
Gross Profit									
Operating Expenses	92.4	89.4	90.9					93.0	92.5
Operating Profit	7.6	10.6	9.1					7.0	7.5
All Other Expenses (net)	3.0	6.8	2.4					3.8	3.4
Profit Before Taxes	4.6	3.8	6.7					3.2	4.1
RATIOS									
Current	2.1	2.0	1.5					1.3	2.4
	.8	.5	.5					.6	1.1
	.2	.1	.1					.3	.5
Quick	2.1	1.7	1.1					1.1	2.0
	.6	.4	.5					.4	.7
	.2	.1	.1					.1	.3
Sales/Receivables	0 UND	0 UND	0 UND					0 UND	0 UND
	0 UND	0 UND	1 355.4					0 UND	0 UND
	0 UND	0 UND	5 66.7					2 160.0	5 74.4
Cost of Sales/Inventory									
Cost of Sales/Payables									
Sales/Working Capital	43.5	24.1	19.7					61.8	9.7
	-72.6	-21.9	-23.5					-25.9	107.8
	-11.8	-5.2	-5.0					-9.9	-14.8
EBIT/Interest	10.3	4.2						3.9	4.0
	(20) 2.6	(23) 3.0						(55) 1.8	(57) 1.4
	.1	.1						.5	.5
Net Profit + Depr., Dep., Amort./Cur. Mat. L/T/D									7.6
								(10) 2.0	
									1.1
Fixed/Worth	1.1	1.7	1.1					1.2	1.0
	2.5	4.7	1.6					4.2	3.3
	-1.1	NM	4.5					-7.2	-6.8
Debt/Worth	.5	1.2	.8					.9	.6
	8.4	3.8	1.1					5.5	2.9
	-1.8	NM	4.1					-9.0	-5.8
% Profit Before Taxes/Tangible Net Worth	61.4	88.3						60.4	32.8
	(14) 13.3	(22) 24.8						(38) 18.6	(51) 15.3
	-7.7	-7.1						.0	1.4
% Profit Before Taxes/Total Assets	54.2	15.6	16.2					18.4	14.6
	4.4	5.1	4.5					4.9	3.1
	-9.0	-2.8	.8					-.9	-1.9
Sales/Net Fixed Assets	17.3	3.6	5.8					7.1	6.6
	5.0	1.2	2.3					2.8	2.4
	2.7	.4	1.5					1.4	1.1
Sales/Total Assets	5.5	2.1	1.7					3.4	2.7
	2.4	1.0	1.4					1.7	1.6
	1.4	.4	1.3					1.1	.9
% Depr., Dep., Amort./Sales	2.8	4.9	9.2					4.7	4.0
	(16) 8.3	(28) 7.6	(10) 12.6					(52) 9.2	(67) 8.6
	13.0	19.4	15.2					16.4	14.2
% Officers', Directors' Owners' Comp/Sales	3.9	2.1						4.6	3.8
	(10) 7.2	(12) 6.1						(29) 9.2	(35) 7.3
	11.4	15.7						12.6	12.7
Net Sales ($)	13336M	42819M	77432M	140905M	100656M	361283M		647497M	494440M
Total Assets ($)	4648M	31176M	46959M	91429M	85494M	186593M		504167M	380448M

M = $ thousand   MM = $ million
See Pages 11 through 21 for Explanation of Ratios and Data

Comparative Historical Data | Current Data Sorted by Sales

						Type of Statement						
	4		3		2	Unqualified			1			1
	5		2		2	Reviewed				1	1	
	19		14		15	Compiled	7	3	2	2		1
	35		35		34	Tax Returns	21	9	2	1		1
	21		30		17	Other	9	1	2		3	1
	4/1/04- 3/31/05		4/1/05- 3/31/06		4/1/06- 3/31/07			8 (4/1-9/30/06)			62 (10/1/06-3/31/07)	
	ALL		ALL		ALL		0-1MM	1-3MM	3-5MM	5-10MM	10-25MM	25MM & OVER
	84		84		70	**NUMBER OF STATEMENTS**	37	13	7	5	4	4
	%		%		%	**ASSETS**	%	%	%	%	%	%
	11.7		11.6		12.8	Cash & Equivalents	13.7	14.0				
	1.8		2.7		1.6	Trade Receivables (net)	1.3	1.3				
	3.1		5.3		1.8	Inventory	.5	1.7				
	1.1		1.2		1.8	All Other Current	2.5	1.2				
	17.7		20.9		18.0	Total Current	18.0	18.3				
	59.3		65.5		66.8	Fixed Assets (net)	71.1	59.2				
	11.2		7.5		8.5	Intangibles (net)	6.7	15.3				
	11.8		6.1		6.6	All Other Non-Current	4.2	7.1				
	100.0		100.0		100.0	Total	100.0	100.0				
						LIABILITIES						
	7.5		5.7		5.8	Notes Payable-Short Term	5.9	2.1				
	7.4		6.3		10.7	Cur. Mat.-L.T.D.	12.9	13.1				
	2.5		4.8		4.3	Trade Payables	3.4	1.9				
	.0		.0		.0	Income Taxes Payable	.0	.0				
	11.8		6.8		7.4	All Other Current	5.6	10.0				
	29.1		23.6		28.2	Total Current	27.8	27.1				
	45.8		48.8		47.8	Long-Term Debt	54.7	58.2				
	.3		.4		.0	Deferred Taxes	.0	.0				
	10.6		7.1		8.7	All Other Non-Current	10.1	9.7				
	14.1		20.1		15.3	Net Worth	7.4	5.0				
	100.0		100.0		100.0	Total Liabilties & Net Worth	100.0	100.0				
						INCOME DATA						
	100.0		100.0		100.0	Net Sales	100.0	100.0				
						Gross Profit						
	92.8		90.5		91.1	Operating Expenses	89.1	90.9				
	7.2		9.5		8.9	Operating Profit	10.9	9.1				
	3.8		3.9		4.6	All Other Expenses (net)	7.4	1.4				
	3.4		5.6		4.3	Profit Before Taxes	3.5	7.7				
						RATIOS						
	3.1		2.9		1.7		2.0	2.0				
	.8		1.0		.5	Current	.4	1.2				
	.1		.3		.1		.1	.1				
	2.1		1.7		1.3		1.5	2.0				
	.4	(83)	.7		.5	Quick	.4	.7				
	.1		.2		.1		.1	.1				
0	UND	0	UND	0	UND		0 UND	0 UND				
0	UND	0	UND	0	UND	Sales/Receivables	0 UND	0 UND				
2	206.2	5	72.2	1	321.5		0 UND	1 437.4				
						Cost of Sales/Inventory						
						Cost of Sales/Payables						
	17.0		17.7		27.4		50.7	21.5				
	-65.1		UND		-28.5	Sales/Working Capital	-20.7	296.8				
	-5.8		-16.2		-5.9		-5.2	-14.7				
	5.7		6.9		7.3		4.2	9.8				
(74)	1.9	(73)	3.2	(58)	2.6	EBIT/Interest	(27) 2.0	(12) 3.3				
	.1		1.0		.7		.0	1.4				
	37.1											
(13)	7.6					Net Profit + Depr., Dep., Amort./Cur. Mat. L/T/D						
	1.3											
	1.1		1.1		1.2		1.5	1.3				
	5.0		3.6		3.0	Fixed/Worth	4.8	2.1				
	-3.3		-3.3		-15.8		-4.0	-76.6				
	1.1		.9		1.0		.9	1.3				
	5.9		3.1		3.9	Debt/Worth	6.2	3.1				
	-3.8		-5.9		-15.5		-5.7	-11.1				
	56.9		57.0		51.7	% Profit Before Taxes/Tangible Net Worth	49.1					
(50)	21.6	(54)	18.4	(48)	19.0		(25) 16.8					
	1.8		1.4		1.5		-8.3					
	14.3		22.1		17.9	% Profit Before Taxes/Total Assets	19.2	32.5				
	3.4		6.4		4.6		3.5	9.6				
	-3.5		-.6		-1.5		-6.2	1.6				
	5.8		5.8		5.5	Sales/Net Fixed Assets	4.5	8.5				
	2.6		2.0		2.5		1.3	3.9				
	1.2		1.2		1.0		.4	2.3				
	2.4		2.6		2.5	Sales/Total Assets	2.2	4.6				
	1.4		1.5		1.5		1.0	2.4				
	.9		.7		.8		.4	1.4				
	4.9		4.8		4.3	% Depr., Dep., Amort./Sales	6.3	2.8				
(71)	10.4	(76)	8.7	(59)	10.4		(29) 11.9	(12) 5.0				
	15.0		14.2		15.6		22.8	8.0				
	2.5		2.0		2.6	% Officers', Directors' Owners' Comp/Sales	5.0					
(46)	6.1	(34)	5.5	(31)	6.7		(11) 8.9					
	10.5		8.2		10.3		23.7					
	1998149M		684110M		736431M	Net Sales ($)	14576M	23249M	27213M	32443M	66771M	572179M
	912576M		408360M		446299M	Total Assets ($)	21225M	10869M	20991M	17115M	42386M	333713M

© RMA 2007　　　**M = $ thousand　　MM = $ million**
See Pages 11 through 21 for Explanation of Ratios and Data

Current Data Sorted by Assets

Comparative Historical Data

0-500M	500M-2MM	2-10MM	10-50MM	50-100MM	100-250MM	Type of Statement	4/1/02-3/31/03 ALL	4/1/03-3/31/04 ALL
		1	6			Unqualified	10	8
1	2	11	2			Reviewed	26	23
5	15	7	3			Compiled	53	49
32	18	5	1			Tax Returns	40	56
14	11	11	1			Other	45	37
	24 (4/1-9/30/06)		125 (10/1/06-3/31/07)					
52	47	37	13			NUMBER OF STATEMENTS	174	173
%	%	%	%	%	%	ASSETS	%	%
17.1	9.4	12.2	9.5			Cash & Equivalents	9.9	10.8
6.2	11.8	15.9	13.8			Trade Receivables (net)	9.6	9.9
2.4	2.1	4.0	4.7	D	D	Inventory	4.6	3.5
3.0	3.7	1.5	1.4	A	A	All Other Current	2.8	2.8
28.7	26.9	33.5	29.3	T	T	Total Current	26.8	27.1
49.2	50.9	46.8	47.0	A	A	Fixed Assets (net)	56.3	50.7
12.1	10.8	5.8	9.1			Intangibles (net)	6.9	10.4
9.9	11.4	13.8	14.6	N	N	All Other Non-Current	10.0	11.8
100.0	100.0	100.0	100.0	O	O	Total	100.0	100.0
				T	T	LIABILITIES		
6.7	6.0	4.3	1.2	A	A	Notes Payable-Short Term	8.1	8.1
12.2	3.9	8.1	3.7	V	V	Cur. Mat.-L.T.D.	7.5	6.6
7.3	4.5	9.4	7.4	A	A	Trade Payables	6.0	6.6
.1	.2	.1	.2	I	I	Income Taxes Payable	1.0	.1
11.0	6.9	6.9	8.1	L	L	All Other Current	9.6	11.2
37.4	21.5	28.8	20.6	A	A	Total Current	32.2	32.7
54.1	42.1	35.6	31.9	B	B	Long-Term Debt	51.3	43.8
.0	.4	.4	1.0	L	L	Deferred Taxes	.2	.2
8.4	8.6	.5	5.5	E	E	All Other Non-Current	6.1	7.5
.2	27.4	34.6	41.0			Net Worth	10.2	15.9
100.0	100.0	100.0	100.0			Total Liabilities & Net Worth	100.0	100.0
						INCOME DATA		
100.0	100.0	100.0	100.0			Net Sales	100.0	100.0
						Gross Profit		
93.1	88.8	92.0	94.3			Operating Expenses	92.5	93.3
6.9	11.2	8.0	5.7			Operating Profit	7.5	6.7
2.4	5.5	3.1	1.5			All Other Expenses (net)	3.4	3.2
4.5	5.7	4.8	4.2			Profit Before Taxes	4.2	3.5
						RATIOS		
4.5	3.5	1.6	2.9				2.0	1.8
1.0	1.4	1.1	1.2			Current	1.0	.9
.3	.9	.3	1.1				.4	.3
3.3	2.2	1.5	1.9				1.4	1.3
.9	1.1	1.0	1.0			Quick	(173) .6	.7
.1	.5	.3	.6				.3	.3
0 UND	0 UND	6 56.3	13 28.7				0 UND	0 UND
0 UND	11 34.7	15 24.2	29 12.4			Sales/Receivables	8 47.6	8 46.4
5 67.2	30 12.1	36 10.2	35 10.4				27 13.5	27 13.6
						Cost of Sales/Inventory		
						Cost of Sales/Payables		
19.5	8.1	16.7	6.0				14.3	17.8
811.9	38.6	54.1	60.9			Sales/Working Capital	-612.0	-91.9
-13.0	-73.3	-11.7	144.8				-14.4	-12.0
13.9	12.0	6.0	7.5				5.0	4.9
(36) 1.6	(38) 3.4	(35) 3.6	3.8			EBIT/Interest	(157) 2.1	(156) 2.1
.2	1.3	1.9	1.1				1.0	.7
						Net Profit + Depr., Dep., Amort./Cur. Mat. L/T/D	3.3	5.3
							(31) 1.8	(20) 2.0
							1.4	1.1
.6	.9	.6	.7				1.1	1.0
6.7	2.7	1.3	1.1			Fixed/Worth	2.9	3.0
-.9	-5.3	4.4	7.3				-5.1	-2.9
.4	1.3	1.0	.5				1.1	1.1
11.9	3.7	2.1	1.6			Debt/Worth	3.6	4.3
-2.8	-10.3	6.2	8.0				-6.6	-6.9
158.8	88.8	46.9	24.1			% Profit Before Taxes/Tangible Net Worth	39.6	48.4
(31) 85.7	(31) 40.0	(32) 24.6	(12) 15.5				(113) 18.9	(112) 17.7
23.3	16.2	12.6	2.6				2.0	1.7
56.0	17.0	11.3	11.5			% Profit Before Taxes/Total Assets	14.2	13.5
9.5	9.1	7.7	3.1				5.6	4.3
-4.1	.9	3.7	.5				.1	-.4
20.0	8.1	9.6	11.7			Sales/Net Fixed Assets	9.3	9.8
10.7	5.1	5.5	3.5				4.6	5.2
3.6	1.8	2.3	1.5				1.7	2.6
6.3	3.0	3.1	2.3			Sales/Total Assets	3.6	3.3
3.9	2.2	2.3	1.4				2.2	2.2
2.0	.9	1.2	.9				1.1	1.4
1.4	3.1	2.8	1.8			% Depr., Dep., Amort./Sales	3.4	3.1
(41) 4.2	(44) 5.3	(33) 4.4	4.3				(154) 4.8	(154) 5.0
8.6	8.2	6.9	6.3				9.0	8.1
4.8	3.4	3.4				% Officers', Directors' Owners' Comp/Sales	3.4	3.3
(35) 7.8	(23) 4.6	(18) 4.7					(82) 5.7	(96) 6.6
15.4	7.3	7.1					10.1	10.0
47873M	94448M	318003M	547969M			Net Sales ($)	1678947M	2315617M
12375M	44605M	155777M	233856M			Total Assets ($)	982496M	714308M

M = $ thousand   MM = $ million
See Pages 11 through 21 for Explanation of Ratios and Data

Comparative Historical Data | Current Data Sorted by Sales

			Type of Statement						
9	8	10	Unqualified			1	3	3	3
22	9	16	Reviewed	1	1	2	6	6	
40	33	30	Compiled	5	11	5	6	2	1
48	49	56	Tax Returns	36	15	2	2		1
46	53	37	Other	11	9	5	6	5	1
4/1/04-3/31/05	4/1/05-3/31/06	4/1/06-3/31/07			24 (4/1-9/30/06)		125 (10/1/06-3/31/07)		
ALL	ALL	ALL		0-1MM	1-3MM	3-5MM	5-10MM	10-25MM	25MM & OVER
165	152	149	**NUMBER OF STATEMENTS**	53	36	15	23	16	6
%	%	%	**ASSETS**	%	%	%	%	%	%
11.4	11.3	12.8	Cash & Equivalents	12.9	13.0	11.7	10.9	16.8	
10.6	9.8	11.0	Trade Receivables (net)	4.1	12.3	15.7	11.0	19.2	
4.4	3.7	2.9	Inventory	1.8	2.9	1.4	5.1	4.2	
3.8	2.4	2.7	All Other Current	1.6	5.8	1.9	1.7	2.0	
30.1	27.2	29.4	Total Current	20.4	34.0	30.8	28.7	42.3	
51.9	47.9	49.0	Fixed Assets (net)	57.0	46.5	44.4	47.6	43.4	
8.2	12.9	9.9	Intangibles (net)	13.7	8.9	8.3	7.1	2.8	
9.8	11.9	11.8	All Other Non-Current	8.9	10.7	16.5	16.6	11.5	
100.0	100.0	100.0	Total	100.0	100.0	100.0	100.0	100.0	
			LIABILITIES						
10.5	8.5	5.4	Notes Payable-Short Term	4.2	7.0	14.8	1.7	2.5	
7.1	6.4	7.8	Cur. Mat.-L.T.D.	9.7	8.0	5.1	7.2	6.6	
9.4	6.5	6.9	Trade Payables	5.7	4.6	7.6	7.1	13.1	
.2	.2	.2	Income Taxes Payable	.1	.1	.3	.1	.2	
8.6	11.9	8.4	All Other Current	7.6	10.4	8.4	8.0	4.8	
35.8	33.5	28.8	Total Current	27.4	30.1	36.2	24.2	27.2	
41.4	44.3	43.8	Long-Term Debt	63.9	37.8	25.6	38.0	20.2	
.3	.3	.3	Deferred Taxes	.0	.4	.2	.4	1.1	
8.2	10.1	6.2	All Other Non-Current	8.5	10.2	1.5	.6	1.9	
14.3	11.9	20.9	Net Worth	.1	21.5	36.5	36.8	49.5	
100.0	100.0	100.0	Total Liabilties & Net Worth	100.0	100.0	100.0	100.0	100.0	
			INCOME DATA						
100.0	100.0	100.0	Net Sales	100.0	100.0	100.0	100.0	100.0	
			Gross Profit						
94.1	93.2	91.6	Operating Expenses	86.9	92.6	93.4	95.9	95.1	
5.9	6.8	8.4	Operating Profit	13.1	7.4	6.6	4.1	4.9	
2.2	2.8	3.5	All Other Expenses (net)	7.3	1.5	1.6	1.6	.9	
3.7	4.0	4.9	Profit Before Taxes	5.8	5.8	5.1	2.5	4.0	
			RATIOS						
1.8	2.1	2.8		3.6	3.9	1.3	2.0	2.6	
1.0	1.0	1.2	Current	1.6	1.0	.9	1.0	1.4	
.4	.3	.6		.5	.6	.2	.4	1.1	
1.4	1.6	2.1		3.5	1.7	1.2	1.5	1.9	
.7	.8	1.0	Quick	1.3	.7	.7	1.0	1.4	
.3	.2	.4		.2	.3	.2	.3	.9	
0 UND	0 UND	0 UND		0 UND	0 UND	6 63.9	8 47.0	7 50.1	
11 33.3	7 52.6	8 45.9	Sales/Receivables	0 UND	11 32.1	19 19.1	15 24.4	32 11.4	
29 12.4	26 13.9	26 14.3		3 129.4	21 17.0	34 10.6	33 10.9	41 8.8	
			Cost of Sales/Inventory						
			Cost of Sales/Payables						
16.8	17.3	12.0		8.2	10.4	28.9	11.9	6.7	
-999.8	UND	80.1	Sales/Working Capital	80.1	NM	-34.8	241.0	18.3	
-13.0	-13.2	-24.4		-44.7	-21.0	-9.6	-11.8	76.9	
7.2	7.0	9.0		5.1	11.9	14.0	4.7	9.7	
(145) 2.2	(128) 2.7	(122) 3.3	EBIT/Interest	(34) 1.6	(31) 3.6	(14) 4.8	(22) 3.5	(15) 6.1	
.7	1.3	1.2		.8	.5	1.3	1.8	2.5	
5.7	9.4	4.0	Net Profit + Depr., Dep.,						
(21) 2.3	(10) 3.0	(13) 1.9	Amort./Cur. Mat. L/T/D						
1.3	1.9	1.3							
.9	.9	.7		.9	.9	.9	.6	.4	
2.8	2.6	2.1	Fixed/Worth	9.9	2.4	1.3	1.3	.9	
-4.0	-1.7	-8.5		-2.0	-1.6	-9.2	4.5	1.3	
.9	.9	.9		1.1	.9	1.0	.9	.5	
4.2	4.0	2.8	Debt/Worth	14.6	3.3	2.4	1.6	1.0	
-6.0	-3.7	-13.0		-3.1	-3.8	-46.4	7.3	2.3	
58.4	78.6	86.0	% Profit Before Taxes/Tangible	130.3	133.8	85.7	41.7	25.1	
(111) 21.1	(91) 21.8	(106) 31.0	Net Worth	(31) 67.4	(23) 63.8	(11) 43.9	(20) 23.5	18.3	
1.4	8.7	12.7		23.3	8.4	16.9	7.8	6.9	
18.8	17.1	23.1	% Profit Before Taxes/Total	39.4	39.6	31.7	11.9	10.0	
4.3	5.6	7.5	Assets	5.4	12.2	8.1	6.7	8.2	
-1.4	.6	1.1		-1.1	-.7	2.1	1.6	3.1	
11.6	11.3	13.7		11.1	16.9	11.8	9.1	12.3	
5.1	5.7	5.7	Sales/Net Fixed Assets	2.7	7.0	7.8	5.5	5.2	
2.3	3.0	2.2		1.2	5.0	4.1	2.9	1.8	
3.7	3.7	3.7		4.1	4.6	4.4	3.2	3.1	
2.2	2.4	2.4	Sales/Total Assets	1.5	3.0	3.0	2.2	2.2	
1.1	1.2	1.2		.8	2.2	1.2	1.4	1.1	
2.6	2.4	2.5		4.6	1.5	2.4	3.3	2.2	
(140) 4.6	(133) 4.3	(131) 4.6	% Depr., Dep., Amort./Sales	(43) 8.6	(32) 3.1	4.3	(22) 4.6	(14) 3.9	
7.7	7.2	7.3		12.7	4.7	5.7	6.5	5.4	
3.3	3.1	3.8	% Officers', Directors'	6.0	2.6		3.7		
(82) 6.2	(78) 5.6	(79) 5.7	Owners' Comp/Sales	(29) 9.3	(23) 4.6		(13) 5.3		
10.3	10.3	9.4		18.0	6.5		9.3		
2171211M	662954M	1008293M	Net Sales ($)	26282M	66922M	58311M	157632M	253800M	445346M
565389M	354234M	446613M	Total Assets ($)	23624M	24510M	32922M	86062M	150758M	128737M

M = $ thousand   MM = $ million
See Pages 11 through 21 for Explanation of Ratios and Data

Current Data Sorted by Assets | | | | Comparative Historical Data

0-500M	500M-2MM	2-10MM	10-50MM	50-100MM	100-250MM	Type of Statement	4/1/02-3/31/03 ALL	4/1/03-3/31/04 ALL
		6	6	2		Unqualified	17	19
	3	8	2			Reviewed	20	21
1	6	3	1			Compiled	15	17
1	4	2				Tax Returns	5	7
	3	14	7	1		Other	19	15
	15 (4/1-9/30/06)		55 (10/1/06-3/31/07)					
2	16	33	16	3		NUMBER OF STATEMENTS	76	79
%	%	%	%	%	%	ASSETS	%	%
	10.0	11.1	7.3			Cash & Equivalents	8.1	9.9
	22.4	20.5	16.5			Trade Receivables (net)	19.4	20.1
	4.3	8.6	12.9			Inventory	13.5	11.5
	2.9	.8	2.1			All Other Current	2.5	3.1
	39.7	41.0	38.8			Total Current	43.5	44.5
	48.2	42.1	51.5			Fixed Assets (net)	42.0	41.7
	8.7	5.4	4.4			Intangibles (net)	4.6	3.6
	3.5	11.5	5.3			All Other Non-Current	10.0	10.3
	100.0	100.0	100.0			Total	100.0	100.0
						LIABILITIES		
	9.5	5.7	5.7			Notes Payable-Short Term	8.0	6.2
	4.9	4.9	5.1			Cur. Mat.-L.T.D.	5.7	4.9
	8.9	10.1	10.4			Trade Payables	9.5	9.0
	.5	.1	.5			Income Taxes Payable	.5	.4
	6.5	9.1	8.5			All Other Current	9.5	8.9
	30.4	29.9	30.3			Total Current	33.2	29.3
	32.4	22.2	28.2			Long-Term Debt	25.9	27.5
	.6	.4	.3			Deferred Taxes	.7	.8
	2.3	6.0	2.6			All Other Non-Current	7.9	9.1
	34.3	41.5	38.7			Net Worth	32.3	33.4
	100.0	100.0	100.0			Total Liabilities & Net Worth	100.0	100.0
						INCOME DATA		
	100.0	100.0	100.0			Net Sales	100.0	100.0
						Gross Profit		
	91.4	94.6	97.0			Operating Expenses	95.5	96.8
	8.6	5.4	3.0			Operating Profit	4.5	3.2
	5.0	.3	2.2			All Other Expenses (net)	1.3	1.3
	3.6	5.1	.8			Profit Before Taxes	3.1	1.9
						RATIOS		
	2.4	2.2	1.9			Current	1.9	2.6
	1.1	1.4	1.1				1.4	1.5
	.7	1.0	.9				1.0	1.1
	1.7	1.7	1.1			Quick	1.3	1.7
	1.0	1.2	.9				1.0	1.0
	.6	.7	.5				.6	.6
	15　24.8	30　12.1	30　12.0			Sales/Receivables	27　13.7	28　13.1
	32　11.5	36　10.1	38　9.7				35　10.5	34　10.6
	39　9.5	42　8.7	46　7.9				43　8.5	41　9.0
						Cost of Sales/Inventory		
						Cost of Sales/Payables		
	10.6	8.2	6.9			Sales/Working Capital	8.6	6.7
	96.1	19.2	61.8				17.6	12.5
	-57.2	-565.7	-230.8				-366.4	73.4
	19.4	11.2	6.5			EBIT/Interest	6.8	5.8
	(14)　3.3	(29)　3.8	1.8				(72)　3.4	(74)　2.6
	-2.8	1.9	.3				1.2	.4
						Net Profit + Depr., Dep., Amort./Cur. Mat. L/T/D	5.4	2.7
							(24)　2.1	(26)　1.5
							1.2	1.0
	.7	.6	.8			Fixed/Worth	.7	.6
	2.4	1.1	1.7				1.2	1.2
	NM	2.8	3.3				2.9	2.8
	.5	.5	.8			Debt/Worth	.7	.7
	2.5	1.1	1.9				1.8	1.6
	NM	5.1	5.1				4.7	5.8
	120.0	38.7	25.1			% Profit Before Taxes/Tangible Net Worth	40.1	32.6
	(12)　26.4	(30)　13.1	7.9				(65)　18.1	(68)　11.8
	1.9	4.4	-1.9				7.9	-.7
	15.4	12.6	7.9			% Profit Before Taxes/Total Assets	13.0	12.7
	10.1	7.0	1.7				6.2	3.9
	-1.8	2.3	-.9				.8	-.9
	16.0	8.3	5.5			Sales/Net Fixed Assets	9.7	8.4
	8.4	5.2	2.5				5.4	5.4
	2.5	3.0	1.4				3.1	3.7
	3.3	2.6	2.0			Sales/Total Assets	2.5	2.6
	2.6	2.1	1.6				2.1	2.1
	1.8	1.5	.8				1.4	1.6
	2.8	2.5	3.2			% Depr., Dep., Amort./Sales	2.4	2.8
	(14)　5.3	(31)　4.3	(14)　5.2				(70)　4.1	(69)　4.0
	10.8	6.1	8.2				6.3	6.1
		4.6				% Officers', Directors' Owners' Comp/Sales	3.0	2.2
	(13)	9.4					(37)　6.1	(37)　3.4
		19.5					10.3	7.5
2000M	49367M	512198M	506603M	444190M		Net Sales ($)	1513025M	1602253M
662M	18044M	169428M	313068M	216746M		Total Assets ($)	927375M	948669M

DATA NOT AVAILABLE

M = $ thousand　　MM = $ million
See Pages 11 through 21 for Explanation of Ratios and Data

Comparative Historical Data   Current Data Sorted by Sales

4/1/04-3/31/05 ALL	4/1/05-3/31/06 ALL	4/1/06-3/31/07 ALL	Type of Statement	0-1MM	1-3MM	3-5MM	5-10MM	10-25MM	25MM & OVER
17	14	14	Unqualified	1	1	1	2	4	5
22	20	13	Reviewed		1	2	5	3	2
11	9	11	Compiled		1		5	3	2
5	4	7	Tax Returns	3		2	2		
24	32	25	Other	1	3	4	6	7	4
					15 (4/1-9/30/06)		55 (10/1/06-3/31/07)		
79	79	70	**NUMBER OF STATEMENTS**	5	6	9	20	17	13
%	%	%	**ASSETS**	%	%	%	%	%	%
9.0	8.8	9.4	Cash & Equivalents				12.9	7.5	6.0
20.9	21.3	19.7	Trade Receivables (net)				22.1	20.2	20.0
9.6	10.7	8.5	Inventory				9.2	10.1	13.9
2.2	2.1	2.0	All Other Current				.6	1.2	2.8
41.6	42.9	39.6	Total Current				44.8	39.0	42.8
44.3	45.0	46.9	Fixed Assets (net)				41.4	46.2	45.9
5.8	5.1	5.6	Intangibles (net)				4.5	7.9	2.9
8.3	7.1	8.0	All Other Non-Current				9.2	6.9	8.3
100.0	100.0	100.0	Total				100.0	100.0	100.0
			LIABILITIES						
6.8	6.9	6.9	Notes Payable-Short Term				6.9	8.5	6.4
5.6	5.9	5.4	Cur. Mat.-L.T.D.				5.0	4.8	4.0
9.6	9.6	10.0	Trade Payables				10.2	10.8	11.3
.3	.3	.3	Income Taxes Payable				.1	.1	.6
8.1	7.7	8.5	All Other Current				6.5	7.7	13.3
30.4	30.3	31.0	Total Current				28.7	31.9	35.6
25.1	20.7	27.6	Long-Term Debt				21.2	23.0	28.7
.9	.8	.4	Deferred Taxes				.6	.3	.0
8.8	6.2	5.0	All Other Non-Current				8.3	2.7	7.3
34.8	41.9	36.1	Net Worth				41.1	42.1	28.4
100.0	100.0	100.0	Total Liabilties & Net Worth				100.0	100.0	100.0
			INCOME DATA						
100.0	100.0	100.0	Net Sales				100.0	100.0	100.0
			Gross Profit						
94.8	95.6	94.9	Operating Expenses				94.2	94.8	97.6
5.2	4.4	5.1	Operating Profit				5.8	5.2	2.4
1.7	1.6	1.9	All Other Expenses (net)				.4	1.3	1.5
3.5	2.8	3.2	Profit Before Taxes				5.4	3.9	.9
			RATIOS						
2.2	2.2	2.0					2.6	2.1	2.2
1.3	1.4	1.3	Current				1.5	1.1	1.4
.9	.9	.9					1.1	.9	1.0
1.6	1.6	1.4					2.1	1.3	1.1
.9 (78)	.9	1.0	Quick				1.3	.8	.8
.7	.6	.6					.7	.6	.5
30 12.4	31 11.8	28 13.0					31 11.6	28 12.9	29 12.8
35 10.4	37 9.8	36 10.2	Sales/Receivables				36 10.2	39 9.5	36 10.2
45 8.1	45 8.1	42 8.8					45 8.2	44 8.4	38 9.6
			Cost of Sales/Inventory						
			Cost of Sales/Payables						
7.6	7.3	9.1					6.8	8.0	9.7
19.5	18.2	34.1	Sales/Working Capital				12.8	36.7	94.0
-56.9	-42.2	-63.5					NM	-53.5	NM
8.7	9.1	10.8					14.1	11.5	5.9
(71) 3.9	(74) 3.1	(64) 2.9	EBIT/Interest				(17) 5.9	2.2	1.9
1.2	1.0	1.1					2.2	.3	.6
3.1	2.9	7.2	Net Profit + Depr., Dep.,						
(26) 2.1	(22) 1.9	(17) 2.5	Amort./Cur. Mat. L/T/D						
1.2	1.1	1.3							
.7	.8	.7					.5	.6	1.1
1.2	1.1	1.3	Fixed/Worth				.9	1.4	2.2
2.9	2.5	3.6					2.7	3.2	3.3
.7	.6	.6					.5	.7	1.4
1.4	1.2	1.7	Debt/Worth				.7	1.7	4.1
5.5	3.9	6.9					5.7	4.0	7.7
35.6	31.9	31.6	% Profit Before Taxes/Tangible				32.8	52.9	26.9
(70) 19.5	(72) 14.6	(61) 13.1	Net Worth				(17) 13.1	(16) 13.6	(12) 9.2
4.1	1.7	.7					3.7	-8.8	2.9
12.7	12.3	13.1	% Profit Before Taxes/Total				14.4	12.0	10.7
6.4	4.7	5.3	Assets				7.2	5.3	1.8
.1	.0	-.1					3.0	-1.8	-2.5
8.2	8.4	8.3					13.7	6.6	8.0
4.9	4.5	4.9	Sales/Net Fixed Assets				5.1	5.2	4.7
2.8	2.6	2.5					2.6	2.5	3.1
2.7	2.6	2.7					2.8	2.2	2.8
2.0	2.0	2.1	Sales/Total Assets				2.0	2.0	2.1
1.4	1.5	1.4					1.4	1.5	1.6
3.0	2.8	2.9					2.5	3.4	2.2
(67) 3.9	(70) 4.0	(64) 4.6	% Depr., Dep., Amort./Sales				(19) 3.5	(15) 5.5	(12) 4.2
6.1	6.5	7.1					5.7	6.9	5.3
1.9	2.4	2.3	% Officers', Directors'						
(31) 4.3	(29) 4.5	(25) 4.9	Owners' Comp/Sales						
9.7	9.2	14.6							
1391073M	1637468M	1514358M	Net Sales ($)	3231M	13666M	35894M	137694M	251827M	1072046M
763499M	792296M	717948M	Total Assets ($)	9863M	14578M	19592M	83385M	152052M	438478M

1530 OTHER SERVICES—Photofinishing Laboratories (except One-Hour) NAICS 812921 (SIC 7384)

Current Data Sorted by Assets

Comparative Historical Data

Type of Statement	0-500M	500M-2MM	2-10MM	10-50MM	50-100MM	100-250MM		4/1/02-3/31/03 ALL	4/1/03-3/31/04 ALL
Unqualified			1					5	3
Reviewed			1					6	6
Compiled	2	2	4					14	7
Tax Returns	6	5	1					4	7
Other	1		7	1				19	21
	14 (4/1-9/30/06)			17 (10/1/06-3/31/07)					
NUMBER OF STATEMENTS	9	9	12	1				48	44
	%	%	%	%	%	%		%	%
ASSETS									
Cash & Equivalents			14.2					10.8	11.9
Trade Receivables (net)			25.6					24.4	25.4
Inventory			5.1	D	D			9.5	7.9
All Other Current			1.2	A	A			2.4	2.9
Total Current			46.1	T	T			47.1	48.1
Fixed Assets (net)			42.4	A	A			42.3	42.7
Intangibles (net)			3.5					3.1	2.4
All Other Non-Current			8.1	N	N			7.5	6.8
Total			100.0	O	O			100.0	100.0
LIABILITIES				T	T				
Notes Payable-Short Term			5.6					11.1	5.8
Cur. Mat.-L.T.D.			5.8	A	A			7.0	5.3
Trade Payables			10.4	V	V			10.2	11.4
Income Taxes Payable			.5	A	A			.1	.2
All Other Current			8.3	I	I			9.0	16.3
Total Current			30.6	L	L			37.3	39.0
Long-Term Debt			18.2	A	A			24.7	19.4
Deferred Taxes			1.6	B	B			.3	.2
All Other Non-Current			8.4	L	L			3.6	7.0
Net Worth			41.1	E	E			34.2	34.5
Total Liabilties & Net Worth			100.0					100.0	100.0
INCOME DATA									
Net Sales			100.0					100.0	100.0
Gross Profit									
Operating Expenses			93.0					97.2	97.3
Operating Profit			7.0					2.8	2.7
All Other Expenses (net)			3.6					1.1	.5
Profit Before Taxes			3.4					1.6	2.3
RATIOS									
Current			2.5					2.9	2.2
			1.6					1.3	1.2
			1.0					.8	.8
Quick			1.9					2.3	1.9
			1.5					.9	.9
			.8					.5	.5
Sales/Receivables			**19** 19.6					**18** 20.3	**20** 17.9
			44 8.3					**30** 12.0	**34** 10.8
			60 6.1					**55** 6.6	**52** 7.0
Cost of Sales/Inventory									
Cost of Sales/Payables									
Sales/Working Capital			7.8					7.8	8.5
			19.8					29.7	28.9
			209.1					-22.1	-29.4
EBIT/Interest			5.9					(42) 8.5	(38) 7.1
			(10) 4.6					2.4	1.9
			1.4					.6	-.1
Net Profit + Depr., Dep., Amort./Cur. Mat. L/T/D									
Fixed/Worth			.4					.6	.7
			1.7					1.3	1.2
			4.2					5.1	2.8
Debt/Worth			.5					.8	.8
			2.4					1.6	1.4
			6.1					8.2	5.0
% Profit Before Taxes/Tangible Net Worth			53.7					(40) 35.3	(37) 33.1
			18.7					16.5	6.5
			2.0					-1.4	-12.2
% Profit Before Taxes/Total Assets			12.9					16.8	12.9
			8.3					4.2	2.3
			.6					-1.4	-4.1
Sales/Net Fixed Assets			11.1					10.8	9.7
			4.7					5.3	4.5
			4.1					3.1	3.5
Sales/Total Assets			2.8					2.8	2.9
			2.4					2.2	2.1
			1.7					1.8	1.5
% Depr., Dep., Amort./Sales			2.9					(43) 2.7	(38) 3.5
			3.8					5.3	5.1
			7.1					7.3	7.6
% Officers', Directors', Owners' Comp/Sales								(25) 2.8	(26) 4.5
								5.3	7.0
								10.8	12.9
Net Sales ($)	4969M	25160M	97091M	37150M				242060M	258627M
Total Assets ($)	2575M	9515M	45482M	13908M				99725M	121262M

© RMA 2007

M = $ thousand   MM = $ million
See Pages 11 through 21 for Explanation of Ratios and Data

Comparative Historical Data   ## Current Data Sorted by Sales

						Type of Statement	0-1MM	1-3MM	3-5MM	5-10MM	10-25MM	25MM & OVER
2		3		1		Unqualified				1		
7		7		5		Reviewed		1		1		
11		4		3		Compiled	2		3		1	
3		3		8		Tax Returns	6	1	1			1
6		8		14		Other	2	1	4	5		1
							14 (4/1-9/30/06)			17 (10/1/06-3/31/07)		
4/1/04-3/31/05 ALL		4/1/05-3/31/06 ALL		4/1/06-3/31/07 ALL			0-1MM	1-3MM	3-5MM	5-10MM	10-25MM	25MM & OVER
29		25		31		NUMBER OF STATEMENTS	10	3	7	9	1	1
%		%		%		**ASSETS**	%	%	%	%	%	%
10.4		8.9		14.9		Cash & Equivalents	24.5					
30.3		28.7		18.7		Trade Receivables (net)	7.8					
6.8		8.0		6.5		Inventory	3.0					
1.4		4.8		3.6		All Other Current	7.1					
48.9		50.4		43.7		Total Current	42.4					
37.7		41.1		44.1		Fixed Assets (net)	43.9					
5.1		1.5		5.1		Intangibles (net)	7.5					
8.2		7.0		7.0		All Other Non-Current	6.2					
100.0		100.0		100.0		Total	100.0					
						LIABILITIES						
10.2		13.2		15.3		Notes Payable-Short Term	16.2					
6.5		7.2		6.1		Cur. Mat.-L.T.D.	5.2					
10.5		9.3		13.2		Trade Payables	17.9					
.2		.3		.2		Income Taxes Payable	.0					
20.0		11.1		14.3		All Other Current	22.5					
47.4		41.1		49.2		Total Current	61.7					
14.9		19.4		28.8		Long-Term Debt	42.1					
.1		1.1		.9		Deferred Taxes	.0					
6.7		14.7		18.0		All Other Non-Current	30.0					
30.9		23.6		3.0		Net Worth	-33.8					
100.0		100.0		100.0		Total Liabilties & Net Worth	100.0					
						INCOME DATA						
100.0		100.0		100.0		Net Sales	100.0					
						Gross Profit						
99.5		96.1		96.6		Operating Expenses	98.4					
.5		3.9		3.4		Operating Profit	1.6					
1.1		2.3		2.8		All Other Expenses (net)	1.1					
-.6		1.6		.7		Profit Before Taxes	.5					
						RATIOS						
1.6		3.0		1.9		Current	2.9					
1.0		1.5		1.1			1.1					
.7		.6		.7			.4					
1.4		1.8		1.8		Quick	2.4					
.8		1.0		.9			.6					
.6		.4		.5			.2					
23	16.2	18	20.8	10	35.6	Sales/Receivables	0 UND					
40	9.2	30	12.3	23	15.8		6 62.7					
58	6.3	54	6.7	46	8.0		32 11.2					
						Cost of Sales/Inventory						
						Cost of Sales/Payables						
10.8		7.0		9.1		Sales/Working Capital	11.1					
431.5		20.2		74.8			182.2					
-14.3		-11.4		-13.7			-9.7					
	9.0		11.4		5.0	EBIT/Interest						
(27)	1.6	(23)	3.4	(26)	2.0							
	-1.5		1.0		-.4							
						Net Profit + Depr., Dep., Amort./Cur. Mat. L/T/D						
.8		.7		.6		Fixed/Worth	.4					
1.2		1.2		1.8			1.6					
7.8		NM		12.3			-2.1					
1.0		1.2		1.1		Debt/Worth	.9					
2.1		2.0		2.7			11.2					
11.6		NM		28.9			-2.1					
	49.8		50.5		53.7	% Profit Before Taxes/Tangible Net Worth						
(25)	3.6	(19)	17.0	(24)	19.6							
	-26.8		5.4		2.4							
9.6		17.2		11.8		% Profit Before Taxes/Total Assets	26.0					
1.7		9.5		5.3			4.5					
-10.3		-1.9		-5.3			-55.0					
17.5		12.8		10.8		Sales/Net Fixed Assets	28.2					
7.9		5.6		4.3			3.9					
3.9		3.7		3.7			3.0					
3.1		3.8		3.3		Sales/Total Assets	2.7					
2.5		2.5		2.3			2.0					
2.1		2.0		1.6			1.2					
	2.7		2.9		3.4	% Depr., Dep., Amort./Sales						
(24)	5.5	(21)	4.6	(29)	4.6							
	7.4		6.4		7.1							
	4.1				5.1	% Officers', Directors' Owners' Comp/Sales						
(10)	5.9			(16)	7.3							
	10.7				10.6							
179407M		124936M		164370M		Net Sales ($)	5744M	6427M	26968M	69442M	18639M	37150M
74781M		54891M		71480M		Total Assets ($)	3231M	2283M	11298M	35082M	5678M	13908M

M = $ thousand   MM = $ million
See Pages 11 through 21 for Explanation of Ratios and Data

Current Data Sorted by Assets   Comparative Historical Data

Type of Statement

Type of Statement	0-500M	500M-2MM	2-10MM	10-50MM	50-100MM	100-250MM	4/1/02-3/31/03 ALL	4/1/03-3/31/04 ALL
Unqualified			1				14	8
Reviewed			3	4	1	2	5	11
Compiled	1	1	2				6	9
Tax Returns	2	6					1	9
Other	1	8	7	4	1	1	19	20
		10 (4/1-9/30/06)		35 (10/1/06-3/31/07)				
NUMBER OF STATEMENTS	4	15	13	8	2	3	45	57

Financial Data

	0-500M %	500M-2MM %	2-10MM %	10-50MM %	50-100MM %	100-250MM %		4/1/02-3/31/03 ALL %	4/1/03-3/31/04 ALL %
ASSETS									
Cash & Equivalents		28.7	13.8					12.9	14.3
Trade Receivables (net)		20.5	11.0					11.5	11.5
Inventory		.3	.0					.0	1.0
All Other Current		1.2	2.7					4.1	3.2
Total Current		50.8	27.5					28.4	30.0
Fixed Assets (net)		31.1	56.5					53.7	46.1
Intangibles (net)		4.0	5.8					7.7	8.4
All Other Non-Current		14.1	10.1					10.2	15.6
Total		100.0	100.0					100.0	100.0
LIABILITIES									
Notes Payable-Short Term		12.2	1.0					3.4	5.9
Cur. Mat.-L.T.D.		2.9	2.1					4.0	2.3
Trade Payables		9.9	5.8					6.9	6.2
Income Taxes Payable		.0	.0					.3	.5
All Other Current		14.6	16.3					17.9	18.6
Total Current		39.6	25.3					32.5	33.5
Long-Term Debt		24.4	53.4					36.6	34.1
Deferred Taxes		.0	.0					.4	.3
All Other Non-Current		4.1	8.6					8.8	10.2
Net Worth		31.8	12.8					21.7	21.9
Total Liabilities & Net Worth		100.0	100.0					100.0	100.0
INCOME DATA									
Net Sales		100.0	100.0					100.0	100.0
Gross Profit									
Operating Expenses		83.6	76.2					86.2	85.4
Operating Profit		16.4	23.8					13.8	14.6
All Other Expenses (net)		3.0	10.0					7.9	8.2
Profit Before Taxes		13.4	13.8					5.9	6.4
RATIOS									
Current		3.3	3.0					1.7	2.0
		1.4	1.1					.9	.9
		.6	.3					.6	.4
Quick		3.2	3.0					1.4	1.9
		1.2	1.0					.9	.8
		.6	.3					.5	.3
Sales/Receivables		0 UND	0 UND					1 376.0	0 UND
		4 84.0	6 59.5					10 35.6	7 53.8
		30 12.0	29 12.5					33 11.2	22 16.7
Cost of Sales/Inventory									
Cost of Sales/Payables									
Sales/Working Capital		3.2	10.4					25.7	14.3
		50.9	27.3					-86.4	-102.7
		-15.4	-5.9					-10.4	-7.5
EBIT/Interest		11.6	20.9					6.0	8.3
		(13) 6.0	(11) 2.2					(31) 2.9	(40) 2.6
		.8	1.5					.8	.3
Net Profit + Depr., Dep., Amort./Cur. Mat. L/T/D									2.3
								(10) 1.8	
								.9	
Fixed/Worth		.0	.6					1.0	.7
		.5	23.8					4.0	2.1
		-109.8	-3.2					-9.3	UND
Debt/Worth		.9	1.8					1.7	1.9
		1.6	23.2					5.4	4.0
		-57.2	-4.5					-16.7	UND
% Profit Before Taxes/Tangible Net Worth		45.5						84.2	101.4
		(10) 33.7						(31) 18.7	(43) 20.7
		3.7						-1.0	.3
% Profit Before Taxes/Total Assets		22.9	22.7					16.4	12.1
		12.5	6.5					2.7	2.9
		-.8	3.8					-.4	-.8
Sales/Net Fixed Assets		228.0	19.5					17.5	41.3
		12.8	1.8					1.2	5.9
		1.1	.3					.3	.5
Sales/Total Assets		5.9	3.6					3.5	4.7
		2.1	.8					.9	1.0
		.5	.3					.3	.3
% Depr., Dep., Amort./Sales		.4	.4					1.2	1.4
		(10) 1.1	(12) .7					(43) 4.2	(47) 3.5
		3.5	13.6					14.7	17.8
% Officers', Directors' Owners' Comp/Sales								2.6	2.1
								(14) 8.2	(15) 5.0
								17.1	8.8
Net Sales ($)	10652M	74377M	144641M	142194M	28505M	894375M		1128898M	1951651M
Total Assets ($)	1247M	20683M	68929M	143690M	107709M	492758M		1022923M	1166218M

M = $ thousand   MM = $ million
See Pages 11 through 21 for Explanation of Ratios and Data

Comparative Historical Data			Type of Statement	Current Data Sorted by Sales					
			Unqualified		1	1		2	4
			Reviewed		1			1	1
			Compiled	2	1			1	1
			Tax Returns	4	1	1	1	1	
16	13	8	Other	5	1	1	1		2
5	5	3							
6	5	4			10 (4/1-9/30/06)			35 (10/1/06-3/31/07)	
7	10	8							
14	20	22		0-1MM	1-3MM	3-5MM	5-10MM	10-25MM	25MM & OVER
4/1/04-3/31/05 ALL	4/1/05-3/31/06 ALL	4/1/06-3/31/07 ALL							
48	53	45	NUMBER OF STATEMENTS	11	11	3	5	8	7
%	%	%	ASSETS	%	%	%	%	%	%
15.6	18.1	19.1	Cash & Equivalents	19.7	17.5				
9.4	9.4	14.6	Trade Receivables (net)	14.7	2.8				
.4	1.0	.1	Inventory	.0	.0				
2.6	4.0	2.1	All Other Current	1.7	3.1				
28.0	32.5	35.9	Total Current	36.2	23.4				
48.9	48.5	48.2	Fixed Assets (net)	56.1	61.1				
8.8	4.4	7.1	Intangibles (net)	1.1	8.1				
14.3	14.6	8.7	All Other Non-Current	6.6	7.4				
100.0	100.0	100.0	Total	100.0	100.0				
			LIABILITIES						
6.2	6.9	4.3	Notes Payable-Short Term	10.7	3.1				
7.1	4.2	2.3	Cur. Mat.-L.T.D.	1.6	2.9				
4.6	6.3	7.3	Trade Payables	4.5	2.4				
.1	.1	.0	Income Taxes Payable	.0	.0				
12.9	10.4	14.1	All Other Current	10.0	9.7				
31.0	27.8	28.0	Total Current	26.8	18.0				
38.0	31.7	38.1	Long-Term Debt	37.0	54.4				
.3	.4	.4	Deferred Taxes	.0	.0				
9.3	8.1	4.8	All Other Non-Current	4.9	4.9				
21.4	32.0	28.7	Net Worth	31.4	22.6				
100.0	100.0	100.0	Total Liabilities & Net Worth	100.0	100.0				
			INCOME DATA						
100.0	100.0	100.0	Net Sales	100.0	100.0				
			Gross Profit						
80.5	80.7	77.9	Operating Expenses	66.6	67.3				
19.5	19.3	22.1	Operating Profit	33.4	32.7				
8.8	8.2	7.8	All Other Expenses (net)	6.1	16.0				
10.7	11.1	14.3	Profit Before Taxes	27.3	16.7				
			RATIOS						
1.7	2.8	3.1		5.0	3.7				
.8	1.3	1.2	Current	1.5	1.1				
.5	.6	.6		.2	.4				
1.3	2.3	2.5		4.9	3.7				
.7	1.2	1.1	Quick	1.5	.7				
.5	.5	.5		.2	.3				
0 781.5	0 UND	0 731.4		0 UND	0 UND				
10 37.6	7 55.7	8 46.5	Sales/Receivables	1 308.0	6 59.5				
23 16.0	28 13.2	27 13.5		12 29.8	36 10.2				
			Cost of Sales/Inventory						
			Cost of Sales/Payables						
26.7	5.7	7.8		3.3	7.0				
-36.7	59.3	50.9	Sales/Working Capital	9.7	27.3				
-5.3	-13.8	-10.5		-1.8	-9.1				
6.3	11.6	14.5							
(29) 1.8	(35) 4.1	(34) 5.1	EBIT/Interest						
.7	1.7	1.3							
4.8	5.7		Net Profit + Depr., Dep., Amort./Cur. Mat. L/T/D						
(13) 1.1	(11) 1.9								
.5	.5								
.7	.5	.4		.1	.4				
2.9	1.6	1.7	Fixed/Worth	2.2	3.4				
UND	23.2	-18.0		-109.8	-3.4				
1.9	.8	.9		.4	.5				
4.2	2.1	3.1	Debt/Worth	12.5	3.7				
UND	44.1	-22.4		-57.2	-5.0				
73.3	57.5	69.7	% Profit Before Taxes/Tangible Net Worth						
(36) 15.1	(43) 24.0	(28) 26.8							
5.6	6.9	4.5							
10.5	16.8	20.4	% Profit Before Taxes/Total Assets	28.0	20.2				
4.2	7.5	6.0		3.9	5.1				
.3	1.4	1.5		-.8	1.0				
19.1	23.8	31.3	Sales/Net Fixed Assets	124.0	10.2				
4.3	3.4	5.5		1.1	.6				
.3	.3	.4		.2	.2				
3.7	3.8	4.0	Sales/Total Assets	1.0	.9				
.8	1.0	.9		.5	.4				
.2	.3	.3		.2	.1				
1.4	1.7	.5	% Depr., Dep., Amort./Sales						
(42) 4.7	(48) 4.6	(36) 2.5							
12.6	14.0	6.8							
2.0	2.3	2.2	% Officers', Directors' Owners' Comp/Sales						
(16) 6.4	(16) 5.4	(14) 6.4							
9.2	12.7	14.4							
1490970M	1366270M	1294744M	Net Sales ($)	5765M	22476M	10418M	38340M	120390M	1097355M
1205670M	1153732M	835016M	Total Assets ($)	14662M	84863M	29612M	12727M	152585M	540567M

M = $ thousand   MM = $ million
See Pages 11 through 21 for Explanation of Ratios and Data

Current Data Sorted by Assets							Comparative Historical Data		
						Type of Statement			
1	5	4	9	2	4	Unqualified		14	14
1	6	12	1			Reviewed		10	13
13	21	13	1			Compiled		30	56
91	41	13		1		Tax Returns		48	53
40	39	22	5	2	2	Other		30	40
	32 (4/1-9/30/06)		317 (10/1/06-3/31/07)					4/1/02-3/31/03	4/1/03-3/31/04
0-500M	500M-2MM	2-10MM	10-50MM	50-100MM	100-250MM			ALL	ALL
146	112	64	16	5	6	**NUMBER OF STATEMENTS**		132	176
%	%	%	%	%	%	**ASSETS**		%	%
25.3	16.7	14.0	16.5			Cash & Equivalents		14.5	20.2
9.7	22.0	28.0	13.3			Trade Receivables (net)		15.6	16.0
3.2	6.8	6.8	2.6			Inventory		3.2	4.6
6.1	4.4	3.2	10.5			All Other Current		3.9	5.5
44.4	50.0	52.0	42.9			Total Current		37.3	46.3
39.9	39.1	36.9	34.0			Fixed Assets (net)		44.4	35.9
6.8	5.1	3.2	4.8			Intangibles (net)		5.0	5.1
8.9	5.9	7.9	18.3			All Other Non-Current		13.3	12.8
100.0	100.0	100.0	100.0			Total		100.0	100.0
						LIABILITIES			
19.2	9.3	8.9	14.2			Notes Payable-Short Term		11.8	13.8
6.9	4.6	3.1	1.1			Cur. Mat.-L.T.D.		7.5	3.9
6.0	8.9	8.9	7.0			Trade Payables		9.5	9.9
.2	.0	.5	.0			Income Taxes Payable		.6	.3
27.1	14.3	13.0	12.9			All Other Current		17.6	20.6
59.5	37.1	34.3	35.1			Total Current		46.9	48.5
33.3	27.7	23.1	11.3			Long-Term Debt		27.0	23.4
.0	.1	.2	.2			Deferred Taxes		.2	.2
8.2	8.1	5.6	4.7			All Other Non-Current		7.0	9.6
-1.0	27.0	36.8	48.7			Net Worth		18.9	18.3
100.0	100.0	100.0	100.0			Total Liabilities & Net Worth		100.0	100.0
						INCOME DATA			
100.0	100.0	100.0	100.0			Net Sales		100.0	100.0
						Gross Profit			
92.4	89.8	87.2	92.4			Operating Expenses		91.5	93.1
7.6	10.2	12.8	7.6			Operating Profit		8.5	6.9
1.6	3.1	2.9	.6			All Other Expenses (net)		4.4	1.8
5.9	7.0	10.0	7.0			Profit Before Taxes		4.1	5.1
						RATIOS			
2.7	3.2	2.6	2.6					2.0	2.1
1.0	1.4	1.4	1.2			Current		.9	1.1
.3	.6	.8	1.0					.4	.5
2.2	2.6	2.1	2.0					1.6	1.8
.7	.9	1.1	1.1			Quick		.7 (174)	.9
.2	.4	.6	.4					.2	.3
0 UND	0 UND	0 UND	5 69.2					0 UND	0 UND
0 UND	12 29.5	31 11.7	27 13.7			Sales/Receivables		5 78.8	7 56.0
8 44.2	43 8.5	61 6.0	50 7.4					31 11.8	36 10.1
						Cost of Sales/Inventory			
						Cost of Sales/Payables			
17.7	8.9	6.5	5.0					12.1	9.9
UND	34.5	16.2	27.6			Sales/Working Capital		-219.3	210.9
-10.5	-15.8	-52.9	NM					-9.3	-13.0
10.5	15.8	23.0	9.9					9.5	9.0
(111) 2.8	(88) 4.2	(53) 7.7	(12) 5.7			EBIT/Interest		(102) 2.9	(123) 3.0
.2	1.3	1.6	1.9					.2	-.4
		7.0							4.9
		(14) 1.8				Net Profit + Depr., Dep., Amort./Cur. Mat. L/T/D		(14)	2.6
		.8							1.1
.3	.2	.2	.2					.6	.2
2.9	2.2	.9	.8			Fixed/Worth		2.2	1.3
-1.1	UND	6.8	1.9					24.1	-34.2
.9	.8	.7	.6					1.3	.8
6.8	4.9	2.1	1.4			Debt/Worth		3.6	2.7
-2.9	-313.3	10.6	2.2					182.2	-25.5
140.7	118.2	88.5	31.5					79.3	64.7
(83) 39.2	(83) 40.3	(55) 44.3	(15) 12.8			% Profit Before Taxes/Tangible Net Worth		(101) 24.0	(127) 27.4
-2.2	10.3	11.9	3.6					1.5	2.5
43.3	30.1	36.9	13.3					17.6	22.8
10.5	9.5	10.7	5.9			% Profit Before Taxes/Total Assets		5.0	6.8
-5.0	.4	3.7	1.4					-2.4	-2.7
75.5	44.7	36.2	39.2					24.7	47.5
12.9	10.6	15.4	5.8			Sales/Net Fixed Assets		7.0	10.8
4.1	2.1	1.6	2.4					2.2	3.4
7.1	4.3	3.2	2.2					5.2	5.2
4.1	2.3	2.1	1.5			Sales/Total Assets		2.4	2.6
2.3	1.1	1.0	.8					1.1	1.1
1.0	1.1	.8	1.1					1.6	1.2
(91) 2.4	(91) 2.9	(51) 1.9	(15) 3.1			% Depr., Dep., Amort./Sales		(105) 4.1	(137) 3.3
6.0	8.0	5.8	11.2					8.6	8.0
5.4	3.0	2.0						3.6	3.9
(66) 9.7	(45) 4.9	(20) 3.3				% Officers', Directors' Owners' Comp/Sales		(59) 7.0	(64) 7.2
14.0	7.9	13.2						11.3	12.2
152183M	444800M	682727M	532512M	3303791M	1594266M	Net Sales ($)		1464036M	2486499M
31097M	126964M	283539M	334700M	335857M	974295M	Total Assets ($)		927904M	1545469M

M = $ thousand   MM = $ million
See Pages 11 through 21 for Explanation of Ratios and Data

Comparative Historical Data | Current Data Sorted by Sales

			Type of Statement						
18	24	25	Unqualified	1	3	2	3	4	12
15	17	20	Reviewed	2	4	8	6		
36	37	48	Compiled	13	17	4	7	6	1
93	94	146	Tax Returns	81	37	12	11	4	1
50	93	110	Other	38	23	15	13	13	13
4/1/04-3/31/05 ALL	4/1/05-3/31/06 ALL	4/1/06-3/31/07 ALL		32 (4/1-9/30/06)		317 (10/1/06-3/31/07)			
				0-1MM	1-3MM	3-5MM	5-10MM	10-25MM	25MM & OVER
212	265	349	**NUMBER OF STATEMENTS**	135	80	37	37	33	27
%	%	%	**ASSETS**	%	%	%	%	%	%
17.7	17.8	20.0	Cash & Equivalents	22.5	21.3	12.4	14.7	20.0	20.8
19.1	17.3	17.1	Trade Receivables (net)	5.3	15.9	24.6	36.3	37.8	18.5
5.2	5.5	5.1	Inventory	2.5	5.2	8.6	10.8	4.8	5.5
3.3	3.2	5.2	All Other Current	5.8	4.6	1.6	6.6	4.2	8.1
45.3	43.8	47.4	Total Current	36.2	46.9	47.2	68.4	66.8	52.9
38.3	39.7	38.7	Fixed Assets (net)	51.5	38.3	32.5	19.2	23.8	28.8
5.7	6.4	5.7	Intangibles (net)	6.6	6.3	3.5	4.0	2.2	8.4
10.7	10.1	8.3	All Other Non-Current	5.7	8.5	16.8	8.4	7.2	9.9
100.0	100.0	100.0	Total	100.0	100.0	100.0	100.0	100.0	100.0
			LIABILITIES						
19.8	12.0	14.3	Notes Payable-Short Term	11.0	21.0	13.5	10.3	8.5	24.4
5.9	3.4	5.1	Cur. Mat.-L.T.D.	7.5	3.1	7.4	3.6	1.7	1.6
11.0	8.7	7.4	Trade Payables	2.9	6.7	7.0	18.5	15.4	7.6
.6	.2	.2	Income Taxes Payable	.2	.1	.1	.3	.6	.2
23.1	19.1	19.3	All Other Current	19.9	23.3	11.0	21.9	15.8	17.0
60.5	43.4	46.3	Total Current	41.5	54.3	39.0	54.5	42.0	50.8
27.7	24.5	28.1	Long-Term Debt	42.8	26.3	25.0	10.2	8.8	13.0
.1	.2	.1	Deferred Taxes	.0	.1	.0	.0	.2	.5
10.7	15.7	7.4	All Other Non-Current	8.2	10.5	3.6	4.4	6.7	4.2
1.0	16.2	18.1	Net Worth	7.6	8.8	32.4	30.8	42.3	31.5
100.0	100.0	100.0	Total Liabilties & Net Worth	100.0	100.0	100.0	100.0	100.0	100.0
			INCOME DATA						
100.0	100.0	100.0	Net Sales	100.0	100.0	100.0	100.0	100.0	100.0
			Gross Profit						
92.6	91.9	90.5	Operating Expenses	88.5	92.6	88.4	91.7	93.3	92.6
7.4	8.1	9.5	Operating Profit	11.5	7.4	11.6	8.3	6.7	7.4
2.0	2.2	2.4	All Other Expenses (net)	4.6	1.2	.9	.7	.4	1.7
5.5	5.9	7.1	Profit Before Taxes	7.0	6.2	10.7	7.6	6.3	5.7
			RATIOS						
2.2	2.7	2.9		3.9	3.6	1.7	2.4	2.8	1.7
1.1	1.2	1.2	Current	1.2	1.0	1.2	1.5	1.4	1.2
.4	.5	.5		.3	.5	.6	.9	1.1	.8
1.9	2.1	2.2		3.1	2.2	1.6	1.7	2.7	1.4
.9	.9	.9	Quick	.7	.9	.8	1.1	1.3	1.1
.2	.3	.3		.1	.4	.5	.7	.8	.4
0 UND	0 UND	0 UND		0 UND	0 UND	0 UND	8 47.8	0 913.1	3 104.5
5 68.1	4 98.8	3 130.8	Sales/Receivables	0 UND	2 172.7	23 16.1	36 10.1	31 12.0	24 15.1
37 9.9	40 9.2	35 10.5		4 92.7	33 11.0	60 6.1	66 5.5	61 6.0	38 9.7
			Cost of Sales/Inventory						
			Cost of Sales/Payables						
10.8	8.5	9.0		9.8	10.2	7.8	7.2	7.3	9.0
78.0	68.0	45.8	Sales/Working Capital	167.0	377.2	35.0	21.0	17.8	39.8
-13.0	-19.1	-15.0		-6.4	-11.4	-20.7	-517.8	139.8	-43.2
14.0	20.6	12.5		7.9	10.5	21.7	17.0	40.3	10.5
(159) 3.5	(197) 4.4	(273) 3.7	EBIT/Interest	(97) 1.8	(64) 2.7	(31) 7.3	(32) 8.2	(27) 19.2	(22) 5.0
1.1	1.0	1.1		-.1	1.0	3.9	1.7	3.2	1.6
8.1	13.5	12.6	Net Profit + Depr., Dep.,						
(13) 4.3	(22) 4.1	(24) 2.6	Amort./Cur. Mat. L/T/D						
1.4	1.1	1.1							
.3	.3	.3		.7	.3	.2	.1	.1	.2
1.8	1.7	1.7	Fixed/Worth	6.4	2.4	1.0	.6	.4	.9
-2.6	-16.9	-18.8		-1.7	-8.4	2.3	3.6	1.0	7.8
.9	.8	.8		1.0	.9	.4	.7	.6	1.3
4.0	3.0	3.3	Debt/Worth	6.7	7.7	2.2	2.3	1.7	2.2
-5.8	-15.6	-15.5		-3.7	-6.7	7.3	NM	5.1	8.5
104.2	98.1	101.1	% Profit Before Taxes/Tangible	98.2	109.3	124.4	124.3	95.1	99.6
(141) 37.5	(190) 41.8	(245) 36.9	Net Worth	(79) 23.0	(50) 31.8	(33) 54.9	(28) 46.2	(32) 54.5	(23) 31.8
12.8	10.7	7.2		-5.3	4.4	29.4	13.0	14.2	2.4
29.9	30.3	33.2	% Profit Before Taxes/Total	24.6	23.3	52.9	40.5	39.8	24.5
10.2	9.5	9.3	Assets	4.7	9.0	22.2	8.9	20.4	9.6
1.5	-.2	.0		-5.6	.5	9.0	2.9	4.4	1.3
59.0	41.2	47.7		22.2	47.3	49.1	54.6	93.5	47.1
9.8	9.8	11.6	Sales/Net Fixed Assets	4.6	11.2	12.8	24.4	47.8	10.6
3.7	3.0	3.0		1.2	3.3	6.3	16.0	10.5	4.5
5.6	4.8	5.0		4.6	5.1	5.2	5.7	6.6	4.6
2.7	2.7	2.8	Sales/Total Assets	2.1	3.2	2.9	3.9	3.6	2.0
1.4	1.4	1.4		.7	1.8	1.9	2.1	1.9	1.3
1.5	.9	1.0		1.3	1.5	1.0	.7	.2	.5
(148) 3.4	(198) 2.7	(254) 2.5	% Depr., Dep., Amort./Sales	(97) 4.7	(57) 2.4	(27) 2.5	(29) 1.6	(24) 1.0	(20) 1.4
6.7	6.9	6.6		11.4	5.7	4.2	3.5	2.2	5.4
3.1	3.5	3.4	% Officers', Directors'	6.0	3.9	3.4	1.2	1.4	
(94) 6.9	(103) 6.2	(134) 6.5	Owners' Comp/Sales	(49) 10.4	(33) 7.9	(21) 5.1	(12) 3.3	(14) 2.3	
12.6	13.0	12.2		15.7	11.4	7.3	5.6	7.9	
1404606M	4778126M	6710279M	Net Sales ($)	65535M	142259M	140385M	261023M	515147M	5585930M
984866M	1701921M	2086452M	Total Assets ($)	68930M	91525M	73755M	89134M	206999M	1556109M

M = $ thousand   MM = $ million
See Pages 11 through 21 for Explanation of Ratios and Data

Current Data Sorted by Assets

Comparative Historical Data

						Type of Statement		
8	14	122	186	36	32	Unqualified	302	303
	14	73	30	5		Reviewed	101	96
12	55	128	27	1		Compiled	161	292
1	4	1	2			Tax Returns	2	7
92	246	602	218	13	17	Other	761	974
	706 (4/1-9/30/06)		1,233 (10/1/06-3/31/07)				4/1/02-3/31/03 ALL	4/1/03-3/31/04 ALL
0-500M	500M-2MM	2-10MM	10-50MM	50-100MM	100-250MM			
113	333	926	463	55	49	NUMBER OF STATEMENTS	1327	1672
%	%	%	%	%	%	ASSETS	%	%
59.0	21.0	9.7	13.3	23.1	30.4	Cash & Equivalents	16.7	16.1
3.0	1.7	1.0	2.0	7.0	7.0	Trade Receivables (net)	2.0	1.8
.2	.3	.3	.4	.3	.8	Inventory	.4	.3
2.4	1.7	.9	2.5	3.2	3.8	All Other Current	1.9	2.6
64.6	24.7	11.9	18.2	33.6	42.0	Total Current	21.1	20.9
27.8	71.6	83.4	70.8	38.2	26.0	Fixed Assets (net)	70.5	71.8
.0	.1	.3	.6	.1	.3	Intangibles (net)	.3	.2
7.6	3.6	4.4	10.4	28.1	31.7	All Other Non-Current	8.1	7.1
100.0	100.0	100.0	100.0	100.0	100.0	Total	100.0	100.0
						LIABILITIES		
8.6	3.0	2.2	1.9	3.3	2.9	Notes Payable-Short Term	2.4	2.9
.7	1.5	1.3	1.7	1.6	2.9	Cur. Mat.-L.T.D.	1.8	1.8
5.0	1.2	.8	1.4	2.1	1.5	Trade Payables	1.3	1.4
.0	.0	.0	.0	.0	.0	Income Taxes Payable	.0	.0
14.9	3.3	1.7	4.3	16.8	11.4	All Other Current	4.2	4.0
29.2	9.1	6.0	9.3	23.9	18.8	Total Current	9.7	10.1
31.2	33.6	29.7	25.6	13.4	16.7	Long-Term Debt	26.2	26.7
.0	.0	.0	.0	.0	.0	Deferred Taxes	.0	.0
3.1	2.1	1.0	2.4	6.4	6.5	All Other Non-Current	2.0	2.6
36.5	55.2	63.3	62.6	56.4	58.0	Net Worth	62.1	60.6
100.0	100.0	100.0	100.0	100.0	100.0	Total Liabilties & Net Worth	100.0	100.0
						INCOME DATA		
100.0	100.0	100.0	100.0	100.0	100.0	Net Sales	100.0	100.0
						Gross Profit		
92.3	83.1	85.3	87.9	93.2	82.1	Operating Expenses	88.0	88.0
7.7	16.9	14.7	12.1	6.8	17.9	Operating Profit	12.0	12.0
1.8	5.5	6.1	4.2	-.4	4.0	All Other Expenses (net)	5.4	4.5
5.8	11.4	8.6	7.9	7.2	13.9	Profit Before Taxes	6.6	7.4
						RATIOS		
15.3	19.8	9.1	6.9	4.1	6.0		8.9	10.8
3.5	4.4	3.0	2.6	1.9	2.7	Current	2.7	2.8
1.2	1.0	1.0	1.0	.9	1.1		.9	1.0
15.3	19.0	8.8	6.5	3.9	5.6		8.2	9.5
3.3	3.8	2.7	2.1	1.8	2.3	Quick	2.4	2.3
1.1	.9	.9	.8	.7	.9		.8	.8
0 UND	0 UND	0 UND	0 UND	5 76.3	1 342.1		0 UND	0 UND
0 UND	0 UND	0 UND	0 999.8	28 13.0	29 12.5	Sales/Receivables	0 UND	0 UND
0 UND	0 UND	0 999.8	9 40.2	89 4.1	93 3.9		4 101.3	2 177.1
						Cost of Sales/Inventory		
						Cost of Sales/Payables		
3.7	1.9	3.5	2.6	1.0	.5		2.7	2.7
8.3	7.0	8.5	7.1	3.7	3.0	Sales/Working Capital	8.0	8.3
45.2	691.9	227.5	-720.8	-46.8	38.3		-128.5	UND
5.7	5.2	4.5	5.0	5.4	5.1		3.9	4.9
(29) 1.5	(187) 2.2	(562) 2.2	(310) 2.3	(41) 2.1	(31) 2.4	EBIT/Interest	(772) 1.8	(962) 2.1
1.0	1.1	1.1	.9	-.6	1.2		.6	.9
						Net Profit + Depr., Dep., Amort./Cur. Mat. L/T/D		
.0	.8	1.0	.8	.2	.1		.7	.8
.0	1.3	1.3	1.1	.5	.3	Fixed/Worth	1.2	1.2
1.0	2.6	1.9	1.7	1.0	1.0		1.7	1.8
.1	.1	.2	.2	.2	.2		.2	.2
.4	.8	.5	.6	.6	.7	Debt/Worth	.5	.6
2.5	2.1	1.1	1.1	1.2	1.7		1.1	1.2
42.2	17.5	8.6	9.4	5.9	10.7	% Profit Before Taxes/Tangible Net Worth	9.8	10.3
(98) 9.4	(317) 6.8	(922) 2.6	(457) 2.9	(53) 3.2	5.6		(1306) 2.4	(1632) 2.9
-1.1	.4	.1	-.1	-1.8	.1		-.9	-.4
29.1	8.1	4.8	5.3	4.1	5.6	% Profit Before Taxes/Total Assets	5.7	5.9
4.6	2.9	1.6	1.9	1.4	2.4		1.4	1.7
-2.6	.1	.0	-.1	-1.3	.0		-.6	-.3
UND	1.2	.6	.9	4.0	3.3		1.0	1.0
UND	.5	.3	.4	.9	1.4	Sales/Net Fixed Assets	.5	.4
2.0	.3	.2	.3	.5	.7		.3	.3
5.3	.7	.5	.5	.5	.4		.6	.6
2.5	.4	.3	.3	.3	.2	Sales/Total Assets	.3	.4
1.0	.3	.2	.2	.2	.1		.2	.2
1.2	2.0	3.9	3.1	2.2	1.3		3.0	3.4
(20) 3.6	(120) 5.6	(351) 6.7	(307) 7.0	(46) 5.5	(38) 3.7	% Depr., Dep., Amort./Sales	(638) 6.1	(700) 6.4
6.1	9.0	10.6	10.1	8.2	5.5		9.5	10.2
5.0	10.9	6.6	3.9			% Officers', Directors' Owners' Comp/Sales	6.7	7.0
(27) 8.0	(58) 16.4	(163) 11.6	(47) 10.7				(237) 14.7	(296) 14.1
12.3	28.3	23.6	24.4				27.9	24.5
71775M	241059M	1852865M	4643408M	2428610M	4789775M	Net Sales ($)	8720228M	8315481M
25356M	410825M	4679606M	9329982M	3736470M	7217560M	Total Assets ($)	19347756M	19254346M

M = $ thousand   MM = $ million
See Pages 11 through 21 for Explanation of Ratios and Data

Comparative Historical Data | | | | Current Data Sorted by Sales

Hist 1	Hist 2	Hist 3		0-1MM	1-3MM	3-5MM	5-10MM	10-25MM	25MM & OVER
			Type of Statement						
305	324	398	Unqualified	27	68	63	96	90	54
105	92	122	Reviewed	27	51	14	21	9	
198	158	223	Compiled	94	94	23	8	4	
7	7	8	Tax Returns	3	3			2	
935	1057	1188	Other	516	422	117	60	42	31
4/1/04-3/31/05 ALL	4/1/05-3/31/06 ALL	4/1/06-3/31/07 ALL		706 (4/1-9/30/06)			1,233 (10/1/06-3/31/07)		
1550	1638	1939	**NUMBER OF STATEMENTS**	667	638	217	185	147	85
%	%	%	**ASSETS**	%	%	%	%	%	%
15.7	16.7	16.3	Cash & Equivalents	17.4	13.7	13.2	15.8	19.3	30.5
1.5	1.8	1.8	Trade Receivables (net)	.8	1.4	1.6	2.3	4.3	8.2
.5	.3	.3	Inventory	.1	.2	.2	.3	1.5	1.7
1.6	1.5	1.6	All Other Current	1.2	.8	2.5	3.1	2.6	4.4
19.4	20.4	20.1	Total Current	19.5	16.1	17.5	21.5	27.7	44.7
73.3	71.7	72.4	Fixed Assets (net)	76.8	78.5	76.5	66.9	49.7	32.3
.2	.3	.3	Intangibles (net)	.1	.2	.4	.7	.8	.4
7.0	7.7	7.3	All Other Non-Current	3.6	5.2	5.6	10.9	21.8	22.6
100.0	100.0	100.0	Total	100.0	100.0	100.0	100.0	100.0	100.0
			LIABILITIES						
2.7	3.3	2.7	Notes Payable-Short Term	3.2	2.3	2.3	1.9	2.9	4.1
1.8	1.5	1.4	Cur. Mat.-L.T.D.	1.1	1.7	1.5	1.7	1.1	2.4
1.4	1.3	1.3	Trade Payables	1.0	.8	1.1	1.8	2.7	4.6
.0	.0	.0	Income Taxes Payable	.0	.0	.0	.1	.0	.0
3.7	3.8	4.1	All Other Current	3.4	2.4	3.1	4.6	7.7	16.6
9.5	10.1	9.5	Total Current	8.7	7.2	8.0	10.1	14.4	27.6
29.0	29.8	28.7	Long-Term Debt	34.2	28.1	27.6	27.0	15.1	19.7
.0	.0	.0	Deferred Taxes	.0	.0	.0	.0	.0	.0
1.9	1.9	1.9	All Other Non-Current	1.1	1.1	1.3	3.8	3.9	8.9
59.6	58.2	59.8	Net Worth	56.0	63.5	63.1	59.1	66.7	43.8
100.0	100.0	100.0	Total Liabilities & Net Worth	100.0	100.0	100.0	100.0	100.0	100.0
			INCOME DATA						
100.0	100.0	100.0	Net Sales	100.0	100.0	100.0	100.0	100.0	100.0
			Gross Profit						
88.0	86.8	86.1	Operating Expenses	83.5	86.1	88.8	87.4	88.1	92.6
12.0	13.2	13.9	Operating Profit	16.5	13.9	11.2	12.6	11.9	7.4
4.3	4.9	5.1	All Other Expenses (net)	7.3	5.1	3.5	3.7	1.7	1.0
7.7	8.3	8.8	Profit Before Taxes	9.2	8.8	7.7	9.0	10.2	6.4
			RATIOS						
10.8	10.0	10.2	Current	17.0	10.7	9.1	7.0	4.8	3.5
2.7	2.7	3.0		3.5	3.1	3.1	2.6	2.0	2.2
1.0	1.0	1.0		1.0	1.1	1.1	1.1	.9	1.0
9.7	9.0	9.5	Quick	15.8	10.0	8.7	6.4	4.2	3.2
2.4	2.5	2.7		3.2	2.8	2.7	2.3	1.8	1.4
.8	.9	.9		.9	.9	.9	.8	.6	.7
0 UND	0 UND	0 UND	Sales/Receivables	0 UND	0 UND	0 UND	0 UND	0 UND	1 267.5
0 UND	0 UND	0 UND		0 UND	0 UND	0 UND	1 619.4	5 73.5	15 23.6
1 374.5	1 246.5	2 188.3		0 UND	0 999.8	4 81.6	8 45.0	31 11.9	57 6.4
			Cost of Sales/Inventory						
			Cost of Sales/Payables						
3.1	3.1	2.8	Sales/Working Capital	2.4	3.4	2.9	2.5	2.5	1.9
9.1	8.3	7.7		6.7	9.2	8.2	6.4	6.3	6.0
240.3	352.1	233.6		459.0	126.2	57.6	59.0	-59.2	-374.6
5.2	5.3	4.9	EBIT/Interest	3.5	5.1	4.9	6.1	7.6	9.9
(939) 2.1	(1030) 2.2	(1160) 2.2		(321) 1.8	(396) 2.3	(145) 2.4	(142) 1.9	(94) 3.8	(62) 3.9
.9	1.0	1.1		1.0	1.2	1.0	.9	1.2	.3
			Net Profit + Depr., Dep., Amort./Cur. Mat. L/T/D						
.8	.8	.8	Fixed/Worth	.9	.9	.9	.7	.2	.1
1.2	1.2	1.2		1.3	1.3	1.3	1.1	.7	.5
1.8	1.9	1.8		2.1	1.8	1.9	1.8	1.3	1.0
.2	.2	.2	Debt/Worth	.2	.2	.2	.2	.2	.4
.6	.6	.6		.6	.5	.6	.6	.4	.8
1.2	1.4	1.3		1.5	1.1	1.2	1.3	.9	1.7
10.3	10.7	10.6	% Profit Before Taxes/Tangible Net Worth	9.4	10.3	10.1	10.9	12.7	13.0
(1519) 3.0	(1600) 3.2	(1896) 3.4		(645) 2.5	(629) 3.4	(216) 3.3	(180) 4.7	(146) 4.5	(80) 7.5
-.1	.0	.1		.1	.1	-.2	.2	1.0	-1.4
5.6	5.6	5.8	% Profit Before Taxes/Total Assets	4.8	5.7	5.9	6.4	7.6	6.5
1.8	1.8	2.0		1.3	2.1	2.0	2.4	3.0	3.3
-.2	.0	.0		.0	.0	-.1	.0	.5	-1.2
.9	.9	.9	Sales/Net Fixed Assets	.6	.7	.8	1.2	3.1	7.9
.4	.4	.4		.3	.4	.5	.6	1.1	2.9
.3	.3	.3		.2	.3	.3	.4	.6	1.2
.6	.6	.5	Sales/Total Assets	.4	.5	.5	.6	.7	1.5
.3	.3	.3		.3	.3	.4	.4	.5	.6
.2	.2	.2		.2	.2	.3	.3	.3	.3
3.0	3.2	3.1	% Depr., Dep., Amort./Sales	3.9	3.8	4.7	3.9	2.2	1.2
(678) 6.3	(744) 6.6	(882) 6.3		(180) 8.0	(236) 7.1	(129) 7.3	(144) 6.3	(125) 4.3	(68) 2.7
10.2	10.4	9.9		12.1	10.9	10.5	9.6	7.4	4.6
7.0	6.1	6.3	% Officers', Directors' Owners' Comp/Sales	9.1	6.5	2.7	3.8		
(250) 14.4	(285) 12.8	(303) 11.6		(128) 12.9	(112) 10.7	(24) 5.4	(24) 9.2		
26.6	24.9	23.4		23.4	23.7	18.7	21.5		
7736228M	9911240M	14027492M	Net Sales ($)	361080M	1124167M	824610M	1264936M	2295401M	8157298M
17254534M	21736179M	25399799M	Total Assets ($)	1601179M	3781685M	2555779M	3956540M	6207180M	7297436M

M = $ thousand   MM = $ million
See Pages 11 through 21 for Explanation of Ratios and Data

Current Data Sorted by Assets   Comparative Historical Data

						Type of Statement		
1	2	5	8	3	4	Unqualified	12	15
						Reviewed		
		1		1		Compiled	1	2
	1		2			Tax Returns		
			1		1	Other	5	3
	19 (4/1-9/30/06)		15 (10/1/06-3/31/07)				4/1/02-3/31/03	4/1/03-3/31/04
0-500M	500M-2MM	2-10MM	10-50MM	50-100MM	100-250MM		ALL	ALL
1	4	9	11	4	5	NUMBER OF STATEMENTS	18	20
%	%	%	%	%	%	ASSETS	%	%
			21.5			Cash & Equivalents	36.1	36.4
			9.7			Trade Receivables (net)	8.5	1.2
			.2			Inventory	.0	.3
			5.2			All Other Current	2.2	7.2
			36.5			Total Current	46.8	45.1
			31.1			Fixed Assets (net)	19.8	23.1
			.8			Intangibles (net)	3.7	2.5
			31.6			All Other Non-Current	29.8	29.3
			100.0			Total	100.0	100.0
						LIABILITIES		
			4.6			Notes Payable-Short Term	8.2	1.1
			1.2			Cur. Mat.-L.T.D.	.5	2.2
			1.7			Trade Payables	1.9	2.7
			.0			Income Taxes Payable	.0	.0
			5.0			All Other Current	10.4	1.9
			12.6			Total Current	20.9	7.9
			17.7			Long-Term Debt	7.9	21.1
			.0			Deferred Taxes	.1	.1
			.6			All Other Non-Current	5.5	3.4
			69.1			Net Worth	65.6	67.5
			100.0			Total Liabilties & Net Worth	100.0	100.0
						INCOME DATA		
			100.0			Net Sales	100.0	100.0
						Gross Profit		
			78.7			Operating Expenses	81.5	71.7
			21.3			Operating Profit	18.5	28.3
			5.0			All Other Expenses (net)	6.5	8.4
			16.4			Profit Before Taxes	12.0	19.9
						RATIOS		
			18.7				25.7	24.4
			7.1			Current	7.9	6.0
			2.8				1.6	1.3
			18.7				25.6	24.4
			7.0			Quick	7.3	4.8
			1.6				.9	.6
		1	286.0				0 UND	0 UND
		6	60.2			Sales/Receivables	4 87.7	1 256.7
		129	2.8				24 15.1	18 20.0
						Cost of Sales/Inventory		
						Cost of Sales/Payables		
			.4				.2	.2
			2.0			Sales/Working Capital	1.1	1.2
			6.1				12.7	NM
								22.5
						EBIT/Interest	(12) 7.6	7.6
								3.2
						Net Profit + Depr., Dep., Amort./Cur. Mat. L/T/D		
			.0				.0	.0
			.1			Fixed/Worth	.2	.1
			1.0				.6	.9
			.0				.0	.0
			.7			Debt/Worth	.3	.3
			.9				1.3	1.9
			11.0				13.6	15.5
			4.9			% Profit Before Taxes/Tangible Net Worth	(16) 2.1	3.2
			.9				.2	.7
			5.6				10.3	4.6
			4.3			% Profit Before Taxes/Total Assets	2.1	2.1
			.6				.2	.4
			306.0				24.8	11.2
			34.7			Sales/Net Fixed Assets	5.9	1.6
			.3				.8	.3
			.4				.5	.2
			.3			Sales/Total Assets	.2	.1
			.1				.1	.1
							.4	.7
						% Depr., Dep., Amort./Sales	(14) 1.4	(18) 3.8
							4.1	9.2
						% Officers', Directors' Owners' Comp/Sales		
377M	2066M	46229M	82771M	50224M	86460M	Net Sales ($)	298949M	272456M
182M	3494M	39052M	257460M	345939M	598278M	Total Assets ($)	936061M	1270567M

© RMA 2007

M = $ thousand   MM = $ million
See Pages 11 through 21 for Explanation of Ratios and Data

Comparative Historical Data | Current Data Sorted by Sales

			Type of Statement						
			Unqualified	4	2	6	5	6	
			Reviewed						
			Compiled						
			Tax Returns	1				1	
			Other	2	2		1	3	1
18	19	23	(Unqualified counts, historical)						
1	1		(Reviewed)						
1		2	(Compiled)						
3	4	9	(Other)						

4/1/04-3/31/05 ALL	4/1/05-3/31/06 ALL	4/1/06-3/31/07 ALL		0-1MM	1-3MM	19 (4/1-9/30/06) 3-5MM	5-10MM	15 (10/1/06-3/31/07) 10-25MM	25MM & OVER
23	24	34	**NUMBER OF STATEMENTS**	7	4	6	6	10	1
%	%	%	**ASSETS**	%	%	%	%	%	%
23.7	34.2	33.1	Cash & Equivalents					21.1	
9.7	9.0	8.4	Trade Receivables (net)					14.8	
1.9	1.8	.4	Inventory					.0	
6.8	1.5	4.5	All Other Current					5.0	
42.1	46.5	46.4	Total Current					41.0	
30.6	25.6	25.7	Fixed Assets (net)					20.1	
.1	.2	.6	Intangibles (net)					.4	
27.2	27.8	27.3	All Other Non-Current					38.5	
100.0	100.0	100.0	Total					100.0	
			LIABILITIES						
4.0	5.2	4.2	Notes Payable-Short Term					7.9	
.5	1.0	.4	Cur. Mat.-L.T.D.					1.2	
3.8	2.8	2.4	Trade Payables					2.8	
.2	.0	.0	Income Taxes Payable					.0	
4.4	4.9	5.3	All Other Current					10.5	
13.0	13.8	12.3	Total Current					22.3	
15.8	11.0	14.7	Long-Term Debt					18.9	
.5	.0	.0	Deferred Taxes					.0	
7.7	4.8	1.1	All Other Non-Current					3.6	
63.1	70.4	71.9	Net Worth					55.2	
100.0	100.0	100.0	Total Liabilities & Net Worth					100.0	
			INCOME DATA						
100.0	100.0	100.0	Net Sales					100.0	
			Gross Profit						
71.1	75.3	68.4	Operating Expenses					91.7	
28.9	24.7	31.6	Operating Profit					8.3	
1.9	2.2	3.4	All Other Expenses (net)					4.1	
27.1	22.5	28.2	Profit Before Taxes					4.2	
			RATIOS						
28.0	16.3	14.2						10.0	
7.7	4.5	6.9	Current					3.8	
1.6	1.3	2.7						1.5	
27.9	16.3	13.8						4.2	
6.5	3.5	4.1	Quick					3.5	
1.0	1.1	1.6						1.2	
0 UND	0 UND	0 UND						0 UND	
7 53.4	11 34.4	2 236.5	Sales/Receivables					1 569.5	
49 7.4	51 7.1	20 17.9						130 2.8	
			Cost of Sales/Inventory						
			Cost of Sales/Payables						
.9	.5	.4						1.0	
1.7	1.6	1.9	Sales/Working Capital					2.2	
7.9	6.6	5.8						6.1	
36.3	42.2	75.3							
(13) 1.7	(12) 6.7	(14) 4.7	EBIT/Interest						
-5.2	2.4	2.2							
			Net Profit + Depr., Dep., Amort./Cur. Mat. L/T/D						
.0	.0	.0						.0	
.4	.2	.2	Fixed/Worth					.2	
1.8	.8	.9						3.2	
.1	.0	.0						.2	
.4	.3	.3	Debt/Worth					.8	
1.8	.7	.8						3.9	
25.6	14.2	24.4	% Profit Before Taxes/Tangible Net Worth					5.8	
10.2	3.9	6.1						2.6	
.1	1.9	2.3						.2	
11.6	7.9	11.9	% Profit Before Taxes/Total Assets					3.1	
3.5	2.9	4.8						2.3	
.0	.7	1.7						-.3	
21.5	26.6	455.8	Sales/Net Fixed Assets					256.0	
1.5	1.7	1.7						18.1	
.3	.7	.4						.2	
.6	.4	.9	Sales/Total Assets					1.2	
.3	.2	.3						.3	
.1	.1	.1						.1	
.9	.7	.6	% Depr., Dep., Amort./Sales						
(18) 2.6	(19) 2.1	(25) 2.7							
7.3	4.1	8.8							
			% Officers', Directors' Owners' Comp/Sales						
610923M	372301M	268127M	Net Sales ($)	3023M	7530M	23838M	47895M	145819M	40022M
1499284M	1137085M	1244405M	Total Assets ($)	12340M	26303M	107450M	380077M	607271M	110964M

M = $ thousand   MM = $ million

See Pages 11 through 21 for Explanation of Ratios and Data

Current Data Sorted by Assets | **Comparative Historical Data**

	0-500M	500M-2MM	2-10MM	10-50MM	50-100MM	100-250MM	4/1/02-3/31/03 ALL	4/1/03-3/31/04 ALL
Top count	7	10	27	24	3	4	30	50
Type of Statement								
Unqualified	7	10	27	24	3	4	30	50
Reviewed			1				1	
Compiled							1	
Tax Returns			1				15	16
Other	3	4	4	4	2	1		
		73 (4/1-9/30/06)		22 (10/1/06-3/31/07)				
NUMBER OF STATEMENTS	10	14	33	28	5	5	47	66
	%	%	%	%	%	%	%	%
ASSETS								
Cash & Equivalents	30.1	24.3	19.4	20.8			19.8	18.1
Trade Receivables (net)	37.5	28.2	20.4	13.1			20.0	19.8
Inventory	.0	2.0	.2	.5			1.0	1.0
All Other Current	12.7	10.2	2.6	7.8			4.6	3.6
Total Current	80.3	64.6	42.6	42.3			45.4	42.6
Fixed Assets (net)	15.1	27.9	41.0	38.7			38.9	45.2
Intangibles (net)	.3	.2	.4	.2			1.0	.5
All Other Non-Current	4.4	7.3	15.9	18.9			14.6	11.6
Total	100.0	100.0	100.0	100.0			100.0	100.0
LIABILITIES								
Notes Payable-Short Term	21.2	2.4	3.5	2.9			3.6	3.3
Cur. Mat.-L.T.D.	.3	1.1	1.9	1.8			1.7	1.1
Trade Payables	10.5	12.6	6.8	5.2			7.0	6.9
Income Taxes Payable	.0	.0	.4	.0			.0	.0
All Other Current	22.9	8.0	9.9	8.4			14.5	10.8
Total Current	54.9	24.1	22.6	18.4			26.9	22.1
Long-Term Debt	.5	6.5	19.1	20.7			16.0	19.9
Deferred Taxes	.0	.0	.3	.0			.0	.2
All Other Non-Current	3.9	1.5	1.3	2.0			3.4	2.2
Net Worth	40.7	67.9	56.8	58.9			53.7	55.5
Total Liabilities & Net Worth	100.0	100.0	100.0	100.0			100.0	100.0
INCOME DATA								
Net Sales	100.0	100.0	100.0	100.0			100.0	100.0
Gross Profit								
Operating Expenses	97.6	95.4	94.9	91.2			93.3	97.6
Operating Profit	2.4	4.6	5.1	8.8			6.7	2.4
All Other Expenses (net)	1.8	.0	-.3	1.0			2.3	.7
Profit Before Taxes	.6	4.6	5.4	7.8			4.4	1.6
RATIOS								
Current	2.5	7.5	3.6	4.9			3.1	4.3
	1.4	3.5	2.1	2.1			1.7	1.9
	1.0	1.3	1.1	1.3			1.1	1.2
Quick	2.5	4.1	3.5	4.4			2.5	4.2
	1.3	2.3	2.1	1.7			1.4	1.6
	.8	1.2	.9	1.0			.9	1.0
Sales/Receivables	0 UND	2 206.0	16 22.6	16 22.5			8 44.5	5 67.5
	18 20.8	26 13.8	38 9.7	32 11.3			32 11.6	32 11.3
	36 10.1	46 8.0	59 6.1	55 6.6			47 7.8	63 5.8
Cost of Sales/Inventory								
Cost of Sales/Payables								
Sales/Working Capital	4.5	4.1	4.4	1.9			4.1	4.1
	23.6	8.7	8.1	7.1			11.7	8.9
	UND	21.2	35.6	19.5			55.8	25.0
EBIT/Interest			12.7	9.9			6.7	7.6
		(26) 4.3	(18) 3.1				(30) 1.2	(41) 3.2
			2.2	1.4			-.9	-.3
Net Profit + Depr., Dep., Amort./Cur. Mat. L/T/D								
Fixed/Worth	.0	.1	.3	.3			.2	.4
	.2	.5	.7	.6			.6	.6
	1.2	.7	1.4	1.3			1.4	1.3
Debt/Worth	.7	.1	.3	.3			.3	.3
	1.7	.4	.6	.6			.6	.7
	6.0	1.2	1.6	1.5			1.4	1.8
% Profit Before Taxes/Tangible Net Worth	59.4	39.3	19.3	16.8			16.5	13.7
	21.7	9.3	10.8	4.4			(43) 4.9	(65) 4.0
	-25.2	-2.0	2.1	1.7			-5.1	-7.0
% Profit Before Taxes/Total Assets	21.6	16.7	10.8	11.7			5.5	6.9
	1.3	5.3	4.6	3.0			1.3	1.7
	-5.3	-1.4	1.5	.2			-3.2	-3.0
Sales/Net Fixed Assets	UND	332.2	14.8	8.3			38.6	7.6
	169.6	15.7	3.7	2.5			4.5	3.3
	12.0	5.2	2.0	1.8			1.6	1.2
Sales/Total Assets	9.0	4.1	2.1	1.4			2.4	2.4
	4.1	2.6	1.7	1.1			1.3	1.3
	1.9	1.8	1.0	.6			.8	.7
% Depr., Dep., Amort./Sales		.7	1.0	1.4			1.0	1.4
		(11) 1.5	(32) 2.0	(25) 2.7			(38) 2.3	(55) 2.7
		2.9	3.6	3.8			4.3	4.2
% Officers', Directors' Owners' Comp/Sales								
Net Sales ($)	11613M	56773M	272403M	607029M	266078M	880789M	947898M	691960M
Total Assets ($)	2634M	17444M	187698M	536793M	356448M	833340M	723533M	652983M

© RMA 2007

M = $ thousand   MM = $ million
See Pages 11 through 21 for Explanation of Ratios and Data

Comparative Historical Data　　　　　　　　　　　　　　　Current Data Sorted by Sales

68	64	75	Type of Statement	9	5	10	13	25	13
		1	Unqualified						
	1		Reviewed					1	
			Compiled						
20	9	18	Tax Returns				1		
1	1	1	Other	1	6	3	2	1	5
4/1/04-3/31/05 ALL	4/1/05-3/31/06 ALL	4/1/06-3/31/07 ALL		0-1MM	73 (4/1-9/30/06) 1-3MM	3-5MM	5-10MM	22 (10/1/06-3/31/07) 10-25MM	25MM & OVER
89	75	95	**NUMBER OF STATEMENTS**	10	11	13	16	27	18
%	%	%	**ASSETS**	%	%	%	%	%	%
25.4	25.3	24.1	Cash & Equivalents	30.1	12.3	21.8	28.4	21.5	29.6
16.2	16.4	20.0	Trade Receivables (net)	8.6	24.2	24.3	23.8	21.2	15.2
1.8	.8	.5	Inventory	.0	2.7	.0	.2	.5	.3
6.1	5.1	6.7	All Other Current	11.1	10.3	2.1	4.8	4.9	9.7
49.4	47.6	51.3	Total Current	49.8	49.6	48.2	57.3	48.1	54.7
37.8	38.1	34.1	Fixed Assets (net)	30.7	38.6	35.2	30.0	38.4	29.4
.1	.3	.4	Intangibles (net)	.0	.2	.3	.0	.7	.7
12.7	14.0	14.3	All Other Non-Current	19.6	11.6	16.3	12.7	12.8	15.2
100.0	100.0	100.0	Total	100.0	100.0	100.0	100.0	100.0	100.0
			LIABILITIES						
4.8	4.2	4.8	Notes Payable-Short Term	2.6	16.2	4.4	.8	4.0	4.3
1.3	1.5	1.5	Cur. Mat.-L.T.D.	.7	1.0	1.7	1.4	2.0	1.4
7.4	7.4	7.5	Trade Payables	8.9	3.4	4.6	10.7	8.1	7.6
.0	.1	.2	Income Taxes Payable	.0	.0	.9	.2	.0	.0
12.0	8.6	10.2	All Other Current	16.1	9.7	9.8	8.5	9.3	10.4
25.4	21.9	24.2	Total Current	28.3	30.3	21.3	21.6	23.3	23.8
14.4	13.8	15.3	Long-Term Debt	13.3	14.2	15.2	15.7	15.5	16.8
.0	.0	.1	Deferred Taxes	.0	.0	.0	.4	.1	.0
2.9	3.8	3.2	All Other Non-Current	1.1	.2	3.3	2.1	1.5	9.5
57.3	60.4	57.2	Net Worth	57.3	55.3	60.2	60.2	59.5	49.9
100.0	100.0	100.0	Total Liabilities & Net Worth	100.0	100.0	100.0	100.0	100.0	100.0
			INCOME DATA						
100.0	100.0	100.0	Net Sales	100.0	100.0	100.0	100.0	100.0	100.0
			Gross Profit						
97.2	95.5	94.2	Operating Expenses	89.4	94.3	95.1	90.8	96.2	96.4
2.8	4.5	5.8	Operating Profit	10.6	5.7	4.9	9.2	3.8	3.6
.1	1.0	.7	All Other Expenses (net)	6.3	.7	-.3	-.8	-.5	1.5
2.7	3.5	5.0	Profit Before Taxes	4.3	5.1	5.2	10.0	4.3	2.1
			RATIOS						
5.2	4.5	4.6	Current	3.6	7.9	5.0	4.8	4.6	5.1
2.1	2.4	2.2		1.4	1.8	2.4	3.3	2.2	1.8
1.1	1.1	1.2		1.1	.9	1.3	1.8	1.3	1.1
4.0	3.9	4.1	Quick	3.3	4.1	4.4	3.9	4.1	4.8
1.9	2.0	1.9		1.4	1.0	2.3	3.2	2.1	1.3
1.0	1.0	1.0		1.0	.6	1.3	1.8	1.2	1.0
0 UND	0 856.2	8 43.7	Sales/Receivables	0 UND	4 99.2	9 41.4	23 15.6	19 18.8	3 122.4
23 16.0	23 15.9	34 10.8		0 UND	15 24.0	31 11.7	39 9.4	37 9.8	26 13.9
40 9.1	44 8.4	53 6.9		29 12.7	40 9.1	48 7.6	57 6.4	58 6.3	50 7.3
			Cost of Sales/Inventory						
			Cost of Sales/Payables						
3.3	3.1	2.7	Sales/Working Capital	4.1	3.4	3.4	3.2	2.5	1.9
9.6	7.3	8.2		15.5	15.9	14.1	5.5	8.2	7.8
178.0	49.3	24.9		45.1	-78.2	24.6	9.9	19.9	114.0
16.8	9.0	9.1	EBIT/Interest				34.6	14.7	6.7
(54) 5.0	(46) 4.2	(62) 3.4				(11) 7.5	(19) 6.6	(12) 1.3	
.4	1.0	1.2					2.7	2.6	-1.9
			Net Profit + Depr., Dep., Amort./Cur. Mat. L/T/D						
.2	.2	.1	Fixed/Worth	.0	.1	.3	.0	.2	.1
.5	.6	.5		.2	.6	.7	.5	.5	.4
1.2	.9	1.0		1.0	2.4	.9	.8	1.3	1.3
.2	.3	.3	Debt/Worth	.1	.1	.2	.3	.2	.5
.7	.5	.6		1.0	.6	.6	.6	.5	1.0
1.8	1.5	1.6		2.5	1.9	1.9	1.0	1.6	1.8
16.4	14.4	19.3	% Profit Before Taxes/Tangible Net Worth	36.7	63.4	21.7	41.8	17.9	12.2
(88) 6.1	(73) 3.1	8.4		1.8	7.8	7.6	13.0	12.6	3.6
-6.2	-3.3	.7		-9.2	.3	-3.4	6.0	1.9	-5.2
9.6	7.9	11.7	% Profit Before Taxes/Total Assets	20.7	9.1	9.9	13.7	11.8	5.1
3.1	1.5	3.7		.4	3.0	3.6	8.1	5.3	.9
-2.7	-2.1	.1		-4.1	.0	-2.7	3.6	.8	-2.3
24.8	15.1	29.8	Sales/Net Fixed Assets	323.1	70.6	28.4	100.2	18.6	26.7
4.4	4.4	5.1		30.7	7.9	5.3	7.7	2.9	4.8
1.8	1.9	2.2		.6	1.2	1.9	2.9	1.9	2.3
2.7	2.3	2.2	Sales/Total Assets	2.5	4.8	3.2	2.6	1.9	1.7
1.5	1.4	1.4		1.4	1.9	1.8	1.9	1.2	1.4
.8	.7	.9		.2	.5	.9	1.2	1.0	.8
1.4	1.2	1.2	% Depr., Dep., Amort./Sales			1.4	.7	1.3	1.0
(73) 2.0	(65) 2.1	(82) 2.1			(11) 1.8	(15) 1.8	(26) 2.3	(16) 2.1	
3.3	3.5	3.5				3.2	3.4	3.7	3.2
3.0	1.2	4.7	% Officers', Directors' Owners' Comp/Sales						
(14) 9.2	(10) 6.9	(13) 11.8							
16.5	16.6	18.4							
1393363M	2300667M	2094685M	Net Sales ($)	6335M	20085M	52031M	125271M	394743M	1496220M
994816M	1962645M	1934357M	Total Assets ($)	25858M	26996M	51246M	86367M	359456M	1384434M

M = $ thousand　　　MM = $ million
See Pages 11 through 21 for Explanation of Ratios and Data

Current Data Sorted by Assets   Comparative Historical Data

0-500M	500M-2MM	2-10MM	10-50MM	50-100MM	100-250MM	Type of Statement	4/1/02-3/31/03 ALL	4/1/03-3/31/04 ALL
10	43	127	105	14	12	Unqualified	270	278
2	3	1				Reviewed	11	10
3	6	5	1		1	Compiled	13	40
5	4	5	5			Tax Returns	9	12
11	18	36	26	4	4	Other	89	115
	333 (4/1-9/30/06)		113 (10/1/06-3/31/07)					
31	74	174	132	18	17	**NUMBER OF STATEMENTS**	392	455
%	%	%	%	%	%	**ASSETS**	%	%
32.4	26.3	17.6	16.4	30.7	30.0	Cash & Equivalents	19.5	21.1
21.1	12.9	15.5	13.9	12.0	7.6	Trade Receivables (net)	18.9	16.4
1.9	2.4	2.3	1.9	5.6	4.9	Inventory	1.3	1.2
3.8	5.3	4.6	4.2	10.1	5.5	All Other Current	5.2	5.9
59.3	46.9	39.9	36.5	58.4	48.0	Total Current	44.8	44.7
33.9	40.5	45.3	43.0	21.2	26.9	Fixed Assets (net)	39.9	42.7
2.5	1.7	.7	1.1	.1	.4	Intangibles (net)	1.0	.6
4.5	10.8	14.0	19.4	20.3	24.7	All Other Non-Current	14.4	12.0
100.0	100.0	100.0	100.0	100.0	100.0	Total	100.0	100.0
						LIABILITIES		
10.2	2.5	3.0	2.1	.3	5.6	Notes Payable-Short Term	4.0	3.6
1.7	3.4	1.8	2.1	.7	1.5	Cur. Mat.-L.T.D.	1.7	1.9
9.2	8.3	6.2	5.1	2.8	3.7	Trade Payables	7.4	7.4
.0	.0	.0	.2	.0	.0	Income Taxes Payable	.1	.0
10.3	10.3	9.7	9.2	12.6	10.1	All Other Current	11.6	10.6
31.5	24.5	20.7	18.8	16.5	21.0	Total Current	24.8	23.5
20.1	18.2	21.3	22.1	14.2	20.4	Long-Term Debt	19.3	18.6
.0	.1	.1	.1	.0	.0	Deferred Taxes	.0	.0
1.9	2.0	2.0	3.3	3.2	8.7	All Other Non-Current	3.6	4.8
46.6	55.2	55.8	55.9	66.1	49.9	Net Worth	52.3	53.0
100.0	100.0	100.0	100.0	100.0	100.0	Total Liabilities & Net Worth	100.0	100.0
						INCOME DATA		
100.0	100.0	100.0	100.0	100.0	100.0	Net Sales	100.0	100.0
						Gross Profit		
94.2	91.5	93.7	93.0	97.8	93.9	Operating Expenses	95.8	95.2
5.8	8.5	6.3	7.0	2.2	6.1	Operating Profit	4.2	4.8
1.5	1.7	.7	2.6	-.2	-2.3	All Other Expenses (net)	2.0	1.8
4.2	6.7	5.5	4.4	2.4	8.4	Profit Before Taxes	2.2	3.0
						RATIOS		
6.6	7.0	3.9	3.6	9.6	5.6		4.3	4.3
1.9	2.4	2.1	1.7	4.7	3.9	Current	2.2	2.2
.8	1.1	1.4	1.0	1.9	1.1		1.2	1.1
3.3	6.1	3.3	3.1	7.1	4.7		3.6	3.6
1.5	1.9	1.7	1.4	2.3	2.3	Quick	1.7	1.7
.7	.9	1.1	.9	1.3	1.1		1.0	.9
0 UND	0 UND	6 62.0	9 41.2	2 147.8	1 321.2		9 41.0	5 79.2
12 31.5	16 23.2	27 13.8	28 13.0	33 10.9	27 13.7	Sales/Receivables	32 11.2	28 13.2
32 11.3	36 10.0	44 8.3	67 5.5	85 4.3	54 6.8		56 6.5	55 6.6
						Cost of Sales/Inventory		
						Cost of Sales/Payables		
4.6	3.1	3.8	2.9	.8	2.0		3.7	3.3
18.3	8.2	8.8	7.7	2.3	3.5	Sales/Working Capital	8.6	8.5
-83.8	112.4	25.4	768.0	8.4	5.7		34.5	58.0
7.9	6.9	7.9	7.5				6.6	7.7
(16) 2.9	(43) 3.3	(112) 2.2	(94) 2.0			EBIT/Interest	(249) 2.2	(287) 2.5
-.1	1.0	.8	.6				-1.8	-.3
						Net Profit + Depr., Dep., Amort./Cur. Mat. L/T/D		
.1	.2	.3	.3	.1	.1		.3	.3
.4	.7	.8	.8	.2	.4	Fixed/Worth	.7	.8
3.6	1.6	1.5	1.4	.8	1.4		1.4	1.6
.2	.2	.3	.3	.2	.3		.3	.3
.8	.6	.9	.8	.3	1.4	Debt/Worth	.8	.8
11.9	2.5	1.7	2.0	1.2	4.1		2.1	2.1
82.0	16.6	15.9	11.1	5.2	20.8		16.5	12.9
(27) 16.8	(68) 4.7	(173) 4.7	(127) 4.9	.3	6.8	% Profit Before Taxes/Tangible Net Worth	(377) 4.7	(438) 3.8
-10.9	-1.8	-1.3	-.6	-2.9	1.8		-6.4	-3.7
25.3	9.7	8.4	5.4	3.3	9.0		7.8	6.5
8.6	3.0	2.4	2.1	.2	2.5	% Profit Before Taxes/Total Assets	2.1	1.8
-5.6	-1.2	-.5	-.1	-1.5	.6		-3.4	-2.2
72.1	28.8	12.1	6.8	89.7	11.2		16.2	10.9
15.2	5.5	3.5	2.3	4.6		Sales/Net Fixed Assets	3.8	3.2
6.7	1.6	1.0	.9	1.6	1.3		1.6	1.2
4.9	2.6	2.7	1.5	1.1	1.2		2.6	2.3
3.6	1.8	1.2	.8	.6	.6	Sales/Total Assets	1.4	1.2
1.9	.8	.6	.4	.4	.3		.7	.6
.7	.9	1.1	1.0	.6	.8		1.1	1.4
(17) 1.0	(52) 1.5	(154) 2.2	(124) 2.7	(17) 1.7	(11) 1.9	% Depr., Dep., Amort./Sales	(343) 2.4	(384) 2.7
2.9	3.3	4.6	5.2	4.8	6.0		4.3	4.8
		3.9					1.8	2.1
	(18) 10.2					% Officers', Directors' Owners' Comp/Sales	(35) 9.2	(28) 8.8
		14.5					14.6	26.0
26113M	276509M	1371642M	3971962M	1135230M	3369107M	Net Sales ($)	7193031M	7501711M
7975M	92305M	874458M	3060540M	1318760M	2836666M	Total Assets ($)	6181029M	6691696M

Comparative Historical Data | Current Data Sorted by Sales

		Comparative Historical Data		Type of Statement	Current Data Sorted by Sales					
	279	262	311	Unqualified	25	50	36	67	69	64
	10	4	6	Reviewed	3	3				
	17	9	16	Compiled	4	5	1	1	1	4
	12	6	14	Tax Returns	6	8				
	105	186	99	Other	19	25	8	12	18	17
	4/1/04-3/31/05 ALL	4/1/05-3/31/06 ALL	4/1/06-3/31/07 ALL		333 (4/1-9/30/06)			113 (10/1/06-3/31/07)		
	423	467	446	**NUMBER OF STATEMENTS**	57	91	45	80	88	85
	0-1MM	1-3MM	3-5MM		0-1MM	1-3MM	3-5MM	5-10MM	10-25MM	25MM & OVER
	%	%	%	**ASSETS**	%	%	%	%	%	%
Cash & Equivalents	20.3	21.6	20.7		25.3	19.9	20.7	16.4	20.7	22.6
Trade Receivables (net)	15.4	14.7	14.5		10.5	7.3	11.1	14.2	23.8	17.6
Inventory	1.7	1.9	2.4		1.6	2.2	.9	2.5	1.5	4.8
All Other Current	3.1	6.0	4.8		2.5	3.9	3.6	6.9	5.1	5.6
Total Current	40.6	44.2	42.5		39.8	33.3	36.4	40.0	51.1	50.6
Fixed Assets (net)	43.6	38.6	41.4		48.5	48.7	46.7	42.6	32.8	33.8
Intangibles (net)	.7	1.3	1.1		1.4	1.3	.9	2.0	.4	.7
All Other Non-Current	15.1	15.9	15.1		10.4	16.8	16.0	15.5	15.7	14.9
Total	100.0	100.0	100.0		100.0	100.0	100.0	100.0	100.0	100.0
				LIABILITIES						
Notes Payable-Short Term	3.4	3.7	3.2		5.9	2.3	3.0	3.5	2.8	2.3
Cur. Mat.-L.T.D.	2.0	2.0	2.1		2.2	2.7	1.3	2.5	2.1	1.4
Trade Payables	6.3	6.8	6.2		3.1	5.1	6.5	5.0	8.0	8.7
Income Taxes Payable	.0	.0	.1		.0	.0	.0	.0	.2	.1
All Other Current	9.6	10.5	9.8		6.6	5.3	10.0	8.3	15.0	12.8
Total Current	21.4	23.0	21.4		17.8	15.3	20.8	19.3	28.1	25.5
Long-Term Debt	21.0	20.8	20.6		29.7	22.5	21.0	20.5	15.0	18.2
Deferred Taxes	.0	.0	.0		.0	.0	.0	.0	.2	.0
All Other Non-Current	3.3	3.6	2.7		1.1	1.9	1.9	3.4	1.7	5.4
Net Worth	54.3	52.6	55.3		51.4	60.3	56.3	56.8	55.0	50.9
Total Liabilties & Net Worth	100.0	100.0	100.0		100.0	100.0	100.0	100.0	100.0	100.0
				INCOME DATA						
Net Sales	100.0	100.0	100.0		100.0	100.0	100.0	100.0	100.0	100.0
Gross Profit										
Operating Expenses	94.3	93.4	93.4		87.1	89.4	93.9	95.1	96.5	96.6
Operating Profit	5.7	6.6	6.6		12.9	10.6	6.1	4.9	3.5	3.4
All Other Expenses (net)	1.6	1.7	1.3		3.9	2.8	2.1	-.2	-.3	.8
Profit Before Taxes	4.1	5.0	5.3		9.0	7.8	4.0	5.2	3.8	2.6
				RATIOS						
Current	4.5	4.8	4.8		7.8	7.3	3.9	3.5	3.5	4.2
	1.9	2.2	2.0		1.9	3.2	2.2	1.9	1.8	1.9
	1.1	1.2	1.2		.9	1.1	1.4	1.4	1.2	1.1
Quick	3.8	3.9	3.6		5.9	6.2	3.6	2.7	3.0	2.7
	1.7	1.8	1.6		1.8	2.2	2.0	1.4	1.6	1.6
	1.0	.8	1.0		.7	.7	1.1	1.0	1.0	1.0
Sales/Receivables	4 86.2	5 78.4	4 95.2		0 UND	0 999.8	12 29.3	9 42.7	15 23.6	7 50.1
	27 13.5	25 14.8	24 15.2		4 97.2	15 25.1	22 16.3	29 12.4	30 12.2	29 12.7
	47 7.8	48 7.6	48 7.6		40 9.1	35 10.3	48 7.6	52 7.0	62 5.8	46 7.9
Cost of Sales/Inventory										
Cost of Sales/Payables										
Sales/Working Capital	3.9	3.2	3.1		2.2	2.9	4.3	3.6	3.6	3.4
	9.3	7.2	8.0		5.2	5.5	7.5	8.4	8.4	9.4
	71.1	41.0	35.0		-54.0	106.4	22.0	21.3	36.5	54.4
EBIT/Interest	(278) 8.6	(286) 9.0	(281) 7.8		(30) 4.0	(59) 9.0	(32) 6.3	(52) 5.2	(53) 9.6	(55) 13.6
	2.2	2.5	2.4		2.0	2.4	2.7	2.2	1.9	3.1
	.1	.4	.8		-.1	.8	.8	.9	.5	1.0
Net Profit + Depr., Dep., Amort./Cur. Mat. L/T/D										
Fixed/Worth	.3	.2	.2		.1	.3	.3	.3	.2	.2
	.8	.7	.7		1.1	.8	.8	.7	.5	.7
	1.5	1.5	1.4		3.6	1.6	1.5	1.4	1.1	1.4
Debt/Worth	.3	.3	.2		.2	.1	.2	.3	.4	.3
	.8	.7	.8		.9	.6	.6	.8	.8	1.1
	1.9	2.1	1.9		4.2	1.9	1.7	2.1	1.4	2.2
% Profit Before Taxes/Tangible Net Worth	(408) 14.1	(446) 14.1	(430) 15.1		(52) 16.6	(86) 17.8	(42) 6.6	(79) 14.4	(87) 15.9	(84) 15.4
	3.9	4.7	4.8		5.2	6.2	.4	6.3	4.4	5.0
	-2.6	-2.2	-.9		-1.5	-.7	-2.6	.2	-1.0	.0
% Profit Before Taxes/Total Assets	6.5	7.5	7.5		9.2	9.2	4.4	8.0	7.5	6.4
	2.0	2.3	2.4		2.9	3.1	.0	2.9	2.1	2.6
	-1.1	-1.3	-.5		-1.0	-1.2	-1.9	.1	-.9	.0
Sales/Net Fixed Assets	13.0	18.4	14.7		27.5	9.2	13.3	10.2	21.7	23.4
	3.3	4.0	3.6		1.7	1.8	2.6	3.2	6.2	5.7
	1.1	1.4	1.1		.3	.6	.8	1.1	2.3	2.3
Sales/Total Assets	2.3	2.4	2.4		2.2	1.8	1.9	2.5	3.1	2.6
	1.1	1.1	1.1		.5	.7	1.0	1.1	1.6	1.5
	.5	.5	.5		.2	.4	.4	.6	.7	.8
% Depr., Dep., Amort./Sales	(366) 1.1	(401) .9	(375) 1.0		(34) 1.4	(74) 1.2	(41) 1.5	(71) 1.1	(81) .8	(74) .6
	2.3	2.0	2.1		5.1	3.5	2.5	2.5	1.4	1.5
	5.0	4.1	4.5		16.4	7.5	5.8	4.4	2.8	3.3
% Officers', Directors' Owners' Comp/Sales	(36) 2.9	(27) 2.4	(39) 6.4			(17) 6.7				
	9.0	8.0	11.8			12.0				
	24.8	13.7	16.5			13.0				
Net Sales ($)	5853075M	8662913M	10150563M		27394M	178485M	175481M	605250M	1353064M	7810889M
Total Assets ($)	5208157M	8032195M	8190704M		91455M	388783M	342534M	987687M	1354267M	5025978M

M = $ thousand   MM = $ million
See Pages 11 through 21 for Explanation of Ratios and Data

OTHER SERVICES—Civic and Social Organizations NAICS 813410 (SIC 8641, 8699)

Current Data Sorted by Assets | **Comparative Historical Data**

Type of Statement	0-500M	500M-2MM	2-10MM	10-50MM	50-100MM	100-250MM	4/1/02-3/31/03 ALL	4/1/03-3/31/04 ALL
Unqualified	9	38	96	97	17	9	172	170
Reviewed	3	6	4		1		11	7
Compiled	7	9	5	1			17	53
Tax Returns	12	9	5	1		1	22	23
Other	19	23	40	27	5	2	98	97
		265 (4/1-9/30/06)		181 (10/1/06-3/31/07)				
NUMBER OF STATEMENTS	50	85	150	126	23	12	320	350
ASSETS	%	%	%	%	%	%	%	%
Cash & Equivalents	37.3	23.6	17.6	18.4	19.4	16.5	23.3	23.0
Trade Receivables (net)	10.2	9.3	7.6	4.6	5.9	3.9	6.5	6.4
Inventory	2.3	2.8	1.1	.8	1.4	.3	1.3	2.0
All Other Current	5.1	3.1	3.6	3.0	4.7	3.0	3.4	5.5
Total Current	54.9	38.7	29.9	26.8	31.3	23.6	34.5	36.9
Fixed Assets (net)	35.9	52.3	56.4	53.2	43.4	40.9	52.4	49.7
Intangibles (net)	.3	.8	.4	.5	.2	.3	.6	.4
All Other Non-Current	8.8	8.2	13.3	19.5	25.0	35.2	12.5	13.1
Total	100.0	100.0	100.0	100.0	100.0	100.0	100.0	100.0
LIABILITIES								
Notes Payable-Short Term	11.2	4.4	2.4	2.6	.5	.7	3.4	3.0
Cur. Mat.-L.T.D.	3.7	2.3	1.9	1.4	1.3	2.0	2.5	2.3
Trade Payables	9.1	4.8	3.4	2.5	3.4	2.4	6.4	4.5
Income Taxes Payable	.0	.0	.1	.1	.0	.0	.1	.1
All Other Current	19.8	7.7	6.5	4.2	9.0	6.6	7.6	7.4
Total Current	43.8	19.2	14.2	10.8	14.1	11.8	20.0	17.4
Long-Term Debt	30.2	23.7	19.5	19.1	20.1	18.2	22.1	18.8
Deferred Taxes	.0	.0	.0	.0	.0	.0	.0	.0
All Other Non-Current	11.8	2.6	3.9	1.9	3.3	5.3	4.5	4.6
Net Worth	14.3	54.4	62.4	68.1	62.5	64.7	53.4	59.2
Total Liabilties & Net Worth	100.0	100.0	100.0	100.0	100.0	100.0	100.0	100.0
INCOME DATA								
Net Sales	100.0	100.0	100.0	100.0	100.0	100.0	100.0	100.0
Gross Profit								
Operating Expenses	98.1	94.9	94.0	90.3	95.9	80.2	94.9	94.4
Operating Profit	1.9	5.1	6.0	9.7	4.1	19.8	5.1	5.6
All Other Expenses (net)	1.7	2.6	1.6	.2	.1	-1.0	2.3	1.6
Profit Before Taxes	.2	2.6	4.4	9.5	4.0	20.8	2.8	4.1
RATIOS								
Current	8.8	6.1	6.4	5.9	3.3	4.7	5.0	6.5
	2.0	2.4	2.3	2.6	1.6	1.7	2.2	2.7
	.8	1.3	1.0	1.0	1.1	.4	1.0	1.1
Quick	7.1	5.6	5.4	5.4	2.9	4.2	4.3	5.0
	1.7	2.3	1.7	(125) 1.8	1.1	.7	1.7	1.9
	.7	1.1	.8	.8	.8	.2	.7	.7
Sales/Receivables	0 UND	0 UND	1 276.0	3 132.4	7 54.8	0 UND	0 UND	0 UND
	0 UND	8 44.6	14 26.2	12 29.3	24 15.3	2 199.2	9 42.4	9 38.5
	18 19.9	29 12.5	34 10.8	35 10.5	41 9.0	62 5.9	34 10.8	30 12.1
Cost of Sales/Inventory								
Cost of Sales/Payables								
Sales/Working Capital	4.4	3.2	2.8	1.6	2.6	1.8	2.8	2.4
	11.2	10.3	7.9	5.0	7.2	10.4	7.0	5.5
	-45.2	39.8	192.9	-484.8	125.9	-14.2	160.7	82.4
EBIT/Interest	6.1	3.7	5.3	11.5	3.8		5.2	6.5
	(21) 4.7	(54) 1.6	(94) 2.0	(88) 3.4	(15) 2.0		(199) 1.7	(206) 1.8
	.7	-1.1	-.4	1.0	.5		-1.5	-.8
Net Profit + Depr., Dep., Amort./Cur. Mat. L/T/D							11.0	5.5
							(13) 3.5	(11) 1.6
							.6	-.8
Fixed/Worth	.0	.4	.5	.4	.3	.1	.4	.3
	.8	.9	.9	.9	.6	.5	.9	.8
	2.3	1.8	1.6	1.2	1.1	1.4	1.5	1.4
Debt/Worth	.2	.3	.2	.2	.3	.2	.2	.2
	1.1	.7	.4	.4	.6	.4	.5	.4
	-7.3	2.5	1.4	.8	.9	.6	1.4	1.3
% Profit Before Taxes/Tangible Net Worth	22.2	15.5	8.6	10.7	5.1	19.1	9.4	11.4
	(37) 4.0	(79) 1.4	(146) 2.2	(125) 5.0	2.0	(11) 5.5	(301) 2.2	(331) 3.0
	-9.1	-5.2	-2.2	.3	-.6	.0	-3.7	-4.6
% Profit Before Taxes/Total Assets	10.4	9.0	5.7	6.9	3.4	17.4	6.0	6.8
	1.6	.7	1.3	3.2	1.0	4.5	1.4	1.7
	-7.0	-4.2	-1.4	.2	-.4	.4	-2.7	-3.2
Sales/Net Fixed Assets	UND	12.8	3.1	1.9	5.4	4.2	5.7	6.2
	12.6	2.2	1.2	.9	1.0	1.1	1.3	1.5
	2.3	.7	.6	.5	.7	.8	.7	.7
Sales/Total Assets	3.4	2.4	1.2	.7	.7	.7	1.3	1.2
	2.1	1.2	.7	.4	.5	.3	.7	.7
	1.2	.5	.4	.3	.3	.2	.4	.4
% Depr., Dep., Amort./Sales	1.1	1.2	2.0	3.1	1.7		2.5	2.5
	(20) 2.7	(61) 3.0	(129) 4.9	(111) 5.0	(19) 5.8		(246) 4.8	(267) 4.7
	7.1	6.8	7.5	8.4	8.7		7.8	7.5
% Officers', Directors' Owners' Comp/Sales			2.4	4.5			3.7	4.0
			(11) 7.4	(16) 15.6			(31) 10.2	(31) 10.5
			15.7	33.3			21.4	22.2
Net Sales ($)	26481M	175385M	675579M	1414532M	897509M	872411M	3363162M	3077906M
Total Assets ($)	12094M	108527M	777839M	2681350M	1523763M	1817548M	4266314M	4760208M

M = $ thousand   MM = $ million
See Pages 11 through 21 for Explanation of Ratios and Data

Comparative Historical Data / Current Data Sorted by Sales

			Type of Statement						
172	219	266	Unqualified	23	54	54	58	53	24
12	5	14	Reviewed	7	3	2	1		1
21	18	22	Compiled	15	4	1	1	1	
27	26	28	Tax Returns	21	4	2			1
96	154	116	Other	31	33	14	19	11	8
4/1/04-3/31/05 ALL	4/1/05-3/31/06 ALL	4/1/06-3/31/07 ALL		265 (4/1-9/30/06)			181 (10/1/06-3/31/07)		
				0-1MM	1-3MM	3-5MM	5-10MM	10-25MM	25MM & OVER
328	422	446	NUMBER OF STATEMENTS	97	98	73	79	65	34
%	%	%	ASSETS	%	%	%	%	%	%
27.1	25.3	21.3	Cash & Equivalents	23.9	22.7	22.6	18.4	16.8	22.1
6.2	7.5	7.2	Trade Receivables (net)	4.6	6.4	7.7	9.9	8.7	6.1
1.6	1.0	1.5	Inventory	1.5	2.2	.7	1.5	.7	2.4
3.8	4.8	3.5	All Other Current	2.6	3.9	3.2	4.0	3.0	6.0
38.6	38.6	33.4	Total Current	32.5	35.1	34.1	33.8	29.2	36.6
48.3	45.7	51.3	Fixed Assets (net)	58.1	50.0	51.8	48.7	49.8	43.7
.5	.7	.5	Intangibles (net)	.6	.4	.6	.5	.6	.2
12.6	15.0	14.8	All Other Non-Current	8.8	14.5	13.4	17.0	20.4	19.5
100.0	100.0	100.0	Total	100.0	100.0	100.0	100.0	100.0	100.0
			LIABILITIES						
4.3	3.0	3.7	Notes Payable-Short Term	6.7	2.4	3.2	3.1	3.5	1.7
1.8	2.6	2.0	Cur. Mat.-L.T.D.	2.6	2.9	.8	1.3	2.1	1.9
6.8	4.9	4.0	Trade Payables	4.3	3.5	3.3	4.2	4.7	4.1
.1	.1	.0	Income Taxes Payable	.0	.1	.0	.1	.1	.0
7.7	7.6	7.7	All Other Current	10.0	7.1	4.3	7.9	7.9	9.2
20.6	18.2	17.4	Total Current	23.5	16.0	11.7	16.5	18.3	17.0
17.5	24.4	21.4	Long-Term Debt	29.0	22.6	16.7	18.2	19.4	17.6
.0	.0	.0	Deferred Taxes	.0	.0	.0	.0	.0	.0
4.9	4.3	4.0	All Other Non-Current	5.3	4.6	2.9	2.9	3.7	4.0
57.0	53.1	57.2	Net Worth	42.1	56.8	68.8	62.4	58.6	61.4
100.0	100.0	100.0	Total Liabilities & Net Worth	100.0	100.0	100.0	100.0	100.0	100.0
			INCOME DATA						
100.0	100.0	100.0	Net Sales	100.0	100.0	100.0	100.0	100.0	100.0
			Gross Profit						
94.4	92.6	93.3	Operating Expenses	96.6	94.9	92.1	89.1	93.2	92.1
5.6	7.4	6.7	Operating Profit	3.4	5.1	7.9	10.9	6.8	7.9
1.1	1.7	1.2	All Other Expenses (net)	3.8	1.2	1.2	-.9	1.3	-.9
4.5	5.7	5.4	Profit Before Taxes	-.4	4.0	6.8	11.8	5.5	8.8
			RATIOS						
6.4	6.8	5.9	Current	10.0	7.4	7.7	4.5	3.8	3.8
2.4	2.7	2.3		2.7	2.5	3.6	2.0	1.3	2.1
1.0	1.2	1.0		.9	1.2	1.2	1.0	.9	1.2
5.4	5.2	5.2	Quick	8.7	5.9	7.3	3.8	3.4	3.0
1.9	2.1 (445)	1.8		2.3	2.2 (72)	2.7	1.6	1.2	1.3
.8	.9	.8		.8	1.1	1.0	.9	.7	.6
0 UND	1 587.6	0 936.6	Sales/Receivables	0 UND	0 UND	2 168.0	3 114.9	7 56.1	2 176.5
8 46.9	9 41.0	11 33.3		0 UND	9 39.3	12 30.7	15 24.7	19 18.9	15 24.2
27 13.3	36 10.1	33 11.1		15 23.7	28 12.9	33 11.0	35 10.5	44 8.3	40 9.1
			Cost of Sales/Inventory						
			Cost of Sales/Payables						
2.3	2.2	2.5	Sales/Working Capital	2.4	2.2	1.7	3.1	4.1	2.1
6.4	5.1	7.9		7.5	7.4	5.8	7.4	18.1	6.0
151.1	57.1	250.0		-47.3	38.2	39.9	165.4	-48.0	54.7
8.1	7.4	6.6	EBIT/Interest	5.0	3.9	4.9	16.0	7.8	17.4
(177) 1.6	(252) 2.3	(281) 2.3		(55) 1.3	(56) 2.1	(46) 1.4	(52) 4.5	(48) 2.9	(24) 3.7
-.4	-.5	.4		-.5	-1.3	.4	1.4	.8	-.1
		24.7	Net Profit + Depr., Dep., Amort./Cur. Mat. L/T/D						
	(10) 3.7								
		1.1							
.3	.2	.4	Fixed/Worth	.4	.3	.3	.4	.5	.3
.8	.8	.9		1.0	.8	.8	.8	.9	.7
1.5	1.4	1.5		2.1	1.5	1.3	1.2	1.6	1.1
.2	.2	.2	Debt/Worth	.3	.1	.2	.2	.3	.3
.5	.5	.5		.7	.3	.3	.5	.5	.5
1.4	1.2	1.4		4.1	1.7	.8	1.3	1.3	.8
11.4	10.6	11.1	% Profit Before Taxes/Tangible Net Worth	8.2	12.8	8.3	15.1	12.8	9.8
(311) 2.7	(396) 3.0	(421) 3.2		(85) .0	(90) 2.2	(76) 2.0	(64) 7.0	(33) 4.5	4.3
-3.0	-2.9	-1.5		-4.7	-3.3	-1.9	1.5	-.3	-.6
6.9	6.9	7.2	% Profit Before Taxes/Total Assets	4.9	6.2	5.5	8.3	8.2	6.4
1.5	2.0	1.9		.0	1.4	1.1	3.9	2.5	3.2
-1.9	-2.0	-1.3		-2.9	-2.9	-1.4	.6	-.2	-.2
10.9	13.2	5.2	Sales/Net Fixed Assets	6.1	7.0	4.0	6.6	5.5	5.0
1.4	1.3	1.2		.9	1.2	1.2	1.3	1.4	1.5
.7	.7	.6		.3	.6	.6	.7	.9	.8
1.3	1.3	1.3	Sales/Total Assets	1.8	1.3	1.5	1.2	1.3	1.1
.7	.6	.7		.5	.7	.7	.7	.7	.6
.4	.4	.3		.2	.3	.3	.4	.4	.5
2.0	1.8	1.9	% Depr., Dep., Amort./Sales	2.7	1.8	1.9	2.1	2.0	1.5
(253) 4.7	(317) 4.5	(349) 4.7		(56) 6.5	(75) 5.1	(66) 4.7	(67) 4.8	(59) 4.3	(26) 2.3
8.1	8.2	7.7		13.6	8.1	7.3	7.1	6.3	6.1
3.0	4.5	5.0	% Officers', Directors' Owners' Comp/Sales	5.9	7.4				
(28) 10.4	(38) 9.3	(42) 10.6		(11) 7.9	(11) 29.3				
27.8	26.6	32.4		13.2	42.8				
2626259M	4998434M	4061897M	Net Sales ($)	46033M	189465M	282018M	558790M	1021943M	1963648M
3704224M	7336199M	6921121M	Total Assets ($)	131654M	496539M	629287M	952793M	1753884M	2956964M

© RMA 2007

M = $ thousand   MM = $ million
See Pages 11 through 21 for Explanation of Ratios and Data

Current Data Sorted by Assets / Comparative Historical Data

Type of Statement	0-500M	500M-2MM	2-10MM	10-50MM	50-100MM	100-250MM		4/1/02-3/31/03 ALL	4/1/03-3/31/04 ALL
Unqualified	6	15	50	51	16	6		100	95
Reviewed	3	4	5	1				11	11
Compiled	6	1	1	1				10	29
Tax Returns	6	6	5					6	8
Other	13	22	27	15	3	3		43	58
		127 (4/1-9/30/06)			139 (10/1/06-3/31/07)				
	0-500M	500M-2MM	2-10MM	10-50MM	50-100MM	100-250MM	NUMBER OF STATEMENTS	170	201
	34	48	88	68	19	9			

	%	%	%	%	%	%	ASSETS	%	%
	32.0	50.2	37.5	37.9	37.4		Cash & Equivalents	32.0	31.3
	20.2	13.7	16.1	9.7	9.9		Trade Receivables (net)	15.1	13.7
	1.6	1.0	2.5	3.0	3.1		Inventory	1.8	2.2
	5.1	5.2	3.9	4.2	2.6		All Other Current	5.2	7.7
	58.9	70.1	59.9	54.8	53.0		Total Current	54.1	54.8
	24.1	18.6	25.0	24.8	21.0		Fixed Assets (net)	30.6	30.0
	3.9	.1	.7	2.6	.9		Intangibles (net)	.8	.7
	13.1	11.2	14.3	17.8	25.1		All Other Non-Current	14.5	14.4
	100.0	100.0	100.0	100.0	100.0		Total	100.0	100.0
							LIABILITIES		
	9.2	3.4	3.8	3.1	.7		Notes Payable-Short Term	3.9	5.7
	2.9	.9	1.2	1.8	1.2		Cur. Mat.-L.T.D.	2.2	3.0
	23.1	9.3	12.5	8.7	7.9		Trade Payables	13.7	10.2
	.2	.5	.3	.3	.0		Income Taxes Payable	.3	.1
	22.3	12.3	15.6	14.1	14.4		All Other Current	14.0	18.6
	57.6	26.4	33.4	28.0	24.2		Total Current	34.2	37.7
	21.2	19.8	9.6	12.2	10.5		Long-Term Debt	12.2	15.7
	.0	.1	.0	.3	.5		Deferred Taxes	.0	.4
	4.4	7.9	6.1	10.6	10.5		All Other Non-Current	6.9	7.7
	16.7	45.9	50.9	48.9	54.3		Net Worth	46.7	38.6
	100.0	100.0	100.0	100.0	100.0		Total Liabilities & Net Worth	100.0	100.0
							INCOME DATA		
	100.0	100.0	100.0	100.0	100.0		Net Sales	100.0	100.0
							Gross Profit		
	91.6	94.8	92.2	90.9	93.5		Operating Expenses	98.8	95.6
	8.4	5.2	7.8	9.1	6.5		Operating Profit	1.2	4.4
	1.2	1.5	-.1	.4	-3.1		All Other Expenses (net)	1.8	1.2
	7.2	3.7	7.8	8.7	9.7		Profit Before Taxes	-.6	3.2
							RATIOS		
	7.1	8.8	4.3	5.1	3.4		Current	4.2	4.2
	1.8	3.5	1.8	2.0	1.9			1.8	2.0
	.6	1.5	1.1	1.1	.9			1.1	1.1
	4.6	8.7	4.0	3.3	3.4		Quick	3.5	3.5
	1.6	3.0	1.7	1.7	1.7			1.5	1.5
	.6	1.3	1.0	.9	.7			.9	.8
	0 UND	2 206.1	5 68.1	7 50.8	5 77.0		Sales/Receivables	6 61.3	6 62.0
	12 31.6	15 24.9	22 16.5	27 13.6	15 24.1			19 19.1	17 21.2
	21 17.6	37 9.9	38 9.5	54 6.8	30 12.2			45 8.1	42 8.7
							Cost of Sales/Inventory		
							Cost of Sales/Payables		
	4.0	2.0	2.3	1.7	1.7		Sales/Working Capital	2.5	2.3
	21.2	4.4	6.2	3.8	3.3			6.3	5.9
	-44.8	22.5	38.2	30.8	-149.8			69.6	70.1
	11.3	6.2	21.3	19.5	22.8		EBIT/Interest	9.1	8.9
	(15) .8	(26) 1.9	(47) 8.3	(43) 7.2	(12) 6.9			(90) 1.7	(110) 2.2
	-10.2	-3.9	2.3	2.8	-9.7			-2.8	-.7
							Net Profit + Depr., Dep., Amort./Cur. Mat. L/T/D	4.4	(12) 3.4
									1.8
	.0	.0	.1	.1	.1		Fixed/Worth	.1	.1
	.4	.1	.4	.4	.3			.5	.6
	2.6	1.4	.8	.9	.8			1.2	1.3
	.3	.3	.4	.5	.4		Debt/Worth	.4	.5
	1.4	1.4	1.0	1.1	.8			1.1	1.1
	NM	5.9	2.1	2.3	1.8			2.9	3.5
	67.0	21.6	26.4	22.2	27.1		% Profit Before Taxes/Tangible Net Worth	14.1	15.4
	(26) 19.8	(43) 10.5	(83) 13.8	(65) 11.6	(18) 11.6			(159) 1.0	(179) 5.2
	-14.0	.4	3.3	6.0	3.4			-10.4	-1.8
	29.3	12.4	13.5	10.1	12.1		% Profit Before Taxes/Total Assets	5.8	7.0
	6.3	2.5	5.7	5.6	7.6			.2	2.1
	-7.7	.1	1.5	2.5	.0			-6.0	-1.8
	UND	134.3	44.4	18.0	19.6		Sales/Net Fixed Assets	20.5	42.2
	72.9	26.0	8.2	4.7	8.1			5.4	5.1
	5.4	4.2	2.6	2.4	4.0			1.9	1.9
	5.9	2.5	2.2	1.2	1.7		Sales/Total Assets	2.0	1.9
	3.2	1.5	1.3	.8	.8			1.1	1.1
	1.5	.8	.7	.5	.4			.6	.6
	.3	.5	.8	1.4	1.2		% Depr., Dep., Amort./Sales	1.3	1.3
	(10) 1.6	(36) 1.2	(75) 1.8	(58) 2.4	(18) 2.0			(133) 3.1	(149) 2.5
	2.4	2.3	2.7	3.7	3.7			4.7	4.7
			1.7				% Officers', Directors' Owners' Comp/Sales	5.8	2.9
		(15)	8.5					(14) 11.7	(14) 8.2
			17.2					14.9	21.1
	34538M	124147M	850309M	1927726M	2120130M	1258150M	Net Sales ($)	2700835M	2253741M
	8787M	57947M	445610M	1476255M	1395230M	1478705M	Total Assets ($)	2425037M	2221787M

M = $ thousand   MM = $ million
See Pages 11 through 21 for Explanation of Ratios and Data

Comparative Historical Data | Current Data Sorted by Sales

	4/1/04-3/31/05 ALL	4/1/05-3/31/06 ALL	4/1/06-3/31/07 ALL	Type of Statement	127 (4/1-9/30/06) 0-1MM	1-3MM	3-5MM	139 (10/1/06-3/31/07) 5-10MM	10-25MM	25MM & OVER
	99	121	144	Unqualified	9	23	14	23	37	38
	13	10	13	Reviewed	4	4	1		2	2
	13	8	9	Compiled	5	1	1	2		
	8	6	17	Tax Returns	4				1	
	48	69	83	Other	18	16	12	15	9	13
	181	214	266	NUMBER OF STATEMENTS	40	53	28	43	49	53
	%	%	%	**ASSETS**	%	%	%	%	%	%
	36.0	37.3	38.7	Cash & Equivalents	35.1	44.3	38.8	40.7	37.6	35.3
	14.5	11.1	13.9	Trade Receivables (net)	15.6	10.4	11.6	13.7	11.9	19.2
	1.3	1.9	2.2	Inventory	.8	1.3	.5	1.7	3.0	4.9
	4.7	5.2	4.3	All Other Current	7.9	3.9	4.9	2.0	4.2	3.8
	56.6	55.4	59.2	Total Current	59.4	60.0	55.8	58.1	56.6	63.2
	30.1	27.2	23.5	Fixed Assets (net)	25.4	25.1	28.0	24.2	23.3	17.9
	.7	2.1	1.5	Intangibles (net)	2.1	1.7	1.0	.5	2.0	1.4
	12.5	15.3	15.8	All Other Non-Current	13.1	13.2	15.2	17.2	18.1	17.6
	100.0	100.0	100.0	Total	100.0	100.0	100.0	100.0	100.0	100.0
				LIABILITIES						
	3.7	2.4	3.9	Notes Payable-Short Term	10.3	3.4	1.2	1.2	3.6	3.4
	2.4	2.5	1.5	Cur. Mat.-L.T.D.	1.2	2.1	.8	2.5	1.0	1.2
	11.2	9.8	11.7	Trade Payables	9.8	12.2	10.0	9.1	9.8	17.6
	.2	.2	.3	Income Taxes Payable	.0	.1	.7	.7	.2	.1
	17.2	15.2	15.3	All Other Current	22.6	11.4	14.6	14.7	13.5	16.3
	34.7	30.0	32.7	Total Current	43.9	29.3	27.2	28.2	28.1	38.6
	13.5	13.0	14.0	Long-Term Debt	22.4	18.7	15.5	10.5	10.4	8.2
	.2	.1	.1	Deferred Taxes	.0	.2	.0	.1	.2	.1
	7.2	8.8	7.7	All Other Non-Current	3.0	6.0	9.2	8.4	8.6	10.6
	44.4	48.0	45.5	Net Worth	30.6	45.7	48.1	52.9	52.6	42.6
	100.0	100.0	100.0	Total Liabilities & Net Worth	100.0	100.0	100.0	100.0	100.0	100.0
				INCOME DATA						
	100.0	100.0	100.0	Net Sales	100.0	100.0	100.0	100.0	100.0	100.0
				Gross Profit						
	93.1	92.4	92.3	Operating Expenses	88.7	90.2	94.8	94.0	91.7	95.0
	6.9	7.6	7.7	Operating Profit	11.3	9.8	5.2	6.0	8.3	5.0
	1.2	.8	.4	All Other Expenses (net)	3.1	3.2	-1.0	-1.8	-.5	-1.0
	5.7	6.9	7.3	Profit Before Taxes	8.2	6.5	6.1	7.8	8.8	6.0
				RATIOS						
	4.2	5.6	5.6	Current	8.6	10.4	5.2	5.7	5.0	2.6
	1.8	2.2	2.0		3.0	2.5	2.1	2.5	2.1	1.6
	1.1	1.1	1.1		1.0	1.1	1.2	1.2	1.1	1.1
	3.6	4.5	4.9	Quick	7.7	9.1	4.2	5.7	4.1	2.5
	1.6	1.9	1.8		2.7	2.3	2.0	2.2	1.8	1.5
	.9	.9	1.0		.8	1.0	1.1	1.1	.8	.8
	5 74.6	4 87.9	5 69.8	Sales/Receivables	0 UND	0 UND	5 76.1	6 59.1	9 39.2	13 28.6
	20 17.9	15 24.8	19 19.1		13 27.7	7 50.4	18 19.8	25 14.3	23 15.7	25 14.8
	42 8.7	39 9.3	38 9.5		33 10.9	25 14.3	38 9.7	41 8.8	46 7.9	41 8.8
				Cost of Sales/Inventory						
				Cost of Sales/Payables						
	2.5	2.1	2.2	Sales/Working Capital	1.2	2.0	2.5	2.2	2.0	2.7
	6.4	5.9	5.2		4.5	5.0	4.7	5.1	5.3	7.8
	118.8	43.7	42.7		NM	50.4	21.4	34.7	53.4	62.0
	12.4	15.8	17.7	EBIT/Interest	9.5	26.4	11.4	24.3	17.1	19.1
(88)	4.2	(121) 5.1	(148) 6.5		(16) 2.0	(28) 3.6	(18) 3.9	(26) 9.1	(25) 7.2	(35) 8.3
	.9	1.2	1.1		-14.4	-.1	.6	1.5	3.2	2.0
		7.5	16.9	Net Profit + Depr., Dep., Amort./Cur. Mat. L/T/D						
		(12) 2.6	(14) 8.5							
		1.5	3.3							
	.1	.1	.1	Fixed/Worth	.0	.0	.2	.1	.1	.1
	.5	.4	.3		.3	.3	.6	.4	.3	.5
	1.2	1.2	.9		3.3	1.1	1.7	.7	.7	.8
	.4	.4	.4	Debt/Worth	.2	.2	.4	.3	.4	.8
	1.1	.9	1.0		.9	1.0	1.1	.8	.8	1.3
	3.6	2.2	3.0		8.1	5.1	2.2	2.0	1.8	3.7
	22.1	25.8	24.7	% Profit Before Taxes/Tangible Net Worth	28.8	24.1	19.0	28.4	25.6	25.9
(166)	9.5	(200) 9.8	(244) 12.1		(34) 7.2	(46) 13.8	(26) 8.7	(41) 12.4	(48) 11.6	(49) 12.7
	1.0	1.2	3.1		-1.7	2.0	2.2	2.9	6.3	4.3
	9.6	9.3	12.7	% Profit Before Taxes/Total Assets	14.8	17.6	7.9	13.1	13.5	10.3
	4.2	4.8	5.5		2.3	5.3	2.7	6.0	7.1	5.6
	.2	.4	.8		-.9	.3	1.3	2.1	3.5	1.2
	43.9	34.3	46.2	Sales/Net Fixed Assets	UND	155.4	16.1	30.6	45.4	28.3
	6.1	7.3	8.9		14.5	15.0	6.3	5.1	9.7	11.7
	1.7	2.0	2.7		3.1	1.8	1.9	2.5	2.5	4.9
	2.0	1.9	2.1	Sales/Total Assets	1.9	2.8	2.1	1.7	1.9	2.6
	1.2	1.0	1.2		1.0	1.1	1.2	1.1	1.0	1.4
	.6	.6	.6		.4	.7	.7	.6	.6	.8
	1.0	1.1	.9	% Depr., Dep., Amort./Sales	.6	.9	1.0	1.1	1.0	.8
(139)	2.2	(172) 1.9	(205) 1.9		(21) 1.7	(35) 2.1	(27) 1.8	(35) 2.4	(42) 1.9	(45) 1.7
	3.9	3.3	3.0		2.5	3.6	2.6	2.9	3.4	3.3
	2.9	1.0	2.3	% Officers', Directors' Owners' Comp/Sales		2.0				
(21)	10.8	(27) 6.5	(36) 9.5			(13) 9.1				
	18.4	25.1	17.3			13.5				
	3685148M	3996407M	6315000M	Net Sales ($)	21475M	99743M	113999M	315783M	784655M	4979345M
	2145497M	3257526M	4862534M	Total Assets ($)	35195M	141996M	129409M	335732M	1073421M	3146781M

© RMA 2007

M = $ thousand   MM = $ million
See Pages 11 through 21 for Explanation of Ratios and Data

Current Data Sorted by Assets | **Comparative Historical Data**

	0-500M	500M-2MM	2-10MM	10-50MM	50-100MM	100-250MM	Type of Statement	ALL	ALL
	5	11	48	49	10	12	Unqualified	75	69
	1	2	3	2			Reviewed	2	5
		2	2	1			Compiled	7	26
	2	1	2				Tax Returns	1	4
	8	7	12	13	7	2	Other	35	33
		111 (4/1-9/30/06)			91 (10/1/06-3/31/07)			4/1/02-3/31/03	4/1/03-3/31/04
	0-500M	500M-2MM	2-10MM	10-50MM	50-100MM	100-250MM		ALL	ALL
	16	23	67	65	17	14	**NUMBER OF STATEMENTS**	120	137
	%	%	%	%	%	%	**ASSETS**	%	%
	56.8	31.8	37.7	36.7	38.4	26.6	Cash & Equivalents	31.7	32.2
	11.3	18.7	17.3	7.2	3.5	8.2	Trade Receivables (net)	9.0	8.6
	2.5	3.0	.6	1.2	.3	2.1	Inventory	2.0	1.2
	1.5	11.0	4.3	3.1	2.2	5.6	All Other Current	3.0	10.0
	72.1	64.5	59.9	48.2	44.3	42.4	Total Current	45.7	52.1
	15.2	26.5	24.9	27.8	24.5	22.8	Fixed Assets (net)	30.3	31.8
	3.9	1.7	1.5	2.1	.3	.8	Intangibles (net)	1.3	1.6
	8.8	7.3	13.7	22.0	31.0	34.1	All Other Non-Current	22.6	14.4
	100.0	100.0	100.0	100.0	100.0	100.0	Total	100.0	100.0
							LIABILITIES		
	9.2	4.0	2.0	.8	.2	.7	Notes Payable-Short Term	2.0	2.4
	.7	1.6	.7	.7	.3	.9	Cur. Mat.-L.T.D.	3.4	1.0
	10.3	5.9	10.3	8.5	11.9	5.9	Trade Payables	6.3	6.6
	.0	.0	.5	.6	.0	.2	Income Taxes Payable	.5	.2
	24.2	9.6	12.9	11.8	10.3	12.1	All Other Current	16.1	15.6
	44.5	21.1	26.3	22.8	22.8	19.7	Total Current	28.3	25.7
	11.3	10.2	12.0	13.6	11.0	16.4	Long-Term Debt	16.4	11.7
	.0	.0	.1	.3	.1	.1	Deferred Taxes	.4	.0
	8.9	9.1	9.9	10.4	11.0	6.0	All Other Non-Current	8.6	10.5
	35.9	59.5	51.7	52.9	55.2	57.8	Net Worth	46.3	52.0
	100.0	100.0	100.0	100.0	100.0	100.0	Total Liabilties & Net Worth	100.0	100.0
							INCOME DATA		
	100.0	100.0	100.0	100.0	100.0	100.0	Net Sales	100.0	100.0
							Gross Profit		
	94.7	95.6	92.8	93.9	93.5	94.6	Operating Expenses	97.7	93.6
	5.3	4.4	7.2	6.1	6.5	5.4	Operating Profit	2.3	6.4
	.4	.0	.2	-1.5	-1.6	-3.6	All Other Expenses (net)	3.2	.4
	4.9	4.3	7.0	7.6	8.2	9.1	Profit Before Taxes	-.9	6.0
							RATIOS		
	7.0	7.4	5.0	4.4	3.9	3.7		3.1	4.9
	3.0	4.3	2.3	2.3	1.9	2.4	Current	1.6	2.2
	.9	2.8	1.4	1.5	.9	.8		.9	1.1
	7.0	6.1	4.7	4.3	3.9	2.8		2.8	3.5
	3.0	3.6	2.3	2.0	1.8	1.3	Quick	1.4	1.7
	.8	2.3	1.2	1.0	.8	.7		.8	.8
	0 UND	0 UND	6 59.7	9 41.6	3 126.8	24 15.5		6 57.6	5 78.0
	4 83.4	14 26.3	15 24.2	17 21.5	9 41.3	37 9.9	Sales/Receivables	19 19.0	15 24.2
	23 15.9	47 7.8	46 8.0	34 10.7	27 13.5	55 6.6		34 10.7	34 10.6
							Cost of Sales/Inventory		
							Cost of Sales/Payables		
	2.7	1.8	2.5	2.2	2.3	1.5		3.0	2.0
	11.4	4.1	4.9	3.8	3.3	3.6	Sales/Working Capital	9.3	5.5
	-139.7	7.0	12.3	12.5	-41.9	-18.6		-89.9	38.1
			32.3	16.3				5.1	17.6
		(35) 5.8	(35) 6.3				EBIT/Interest	(67) 1.0	(78) 5.4
			2.3	2.1				-4.7	.4
							Net Profit + Depr., Dep., Amort./Cur. Mat. L/T/D		
	.0	.1	.1	.2	.1	.3		.2	.2
	.1	.2	.2	.5	.3	.5	Fixed/Worth	.6	.6
	NM	1.1	1.1	1.1	.8	.6		1.1	1.3
	.2	.3	.4	.4	.4	.6		.5	.4
	2.5	.6	.9	.8	.8	.7	Debt/Worth	.9	.9
	-5.5	1.9	2.0	1.7	2.3	1.0		1.8	1.9
	56.0	33.1	29.2	20.1	15.1	15.5		14.4	23.8
	(11) -3.2	(22) 3.5	(65) 9.8	(62) 9.8	13.6	9.5	% Profit Before Taxes/Tangible Net Worth	(115) -.2	(133) 6.3
	-48.6	-5.6	2.2	.5	8.3	4.3		-12.0	-1.5
	37.2	21.2	11.8	10.6	10.7	8.9		7.3	11.9
	-.8	2.0	5.8	5.6	7.7	5.3	% Profit Before Taxes/Total Assets	-.1	3.6
	-18.0	-9.3	.9	.5	3.2	2.5		-6.3	-.4
	UND	83.0	34.7	18.6	26.6	8.8		15.1	17.9
	127.2	20.1	18.2	4.8	3.2	2.7	Sales/Net Fixed Assets	3.9	4.5
	25.0	1.8	2.3	1.9	1.2	1.9		2.1	2.2
	6.4	3.0	2.4	1.2	1.1	.9		1.5	1.7
	2.8	1.3	1.2	.8	.7	.6	Sales/Total Assets	1.0	.9
	1.6	.8	.8	.6	.4	.4		.6	.6
		.4	1.2	1.5	1.7	1.6		1.8	1.5
	(19) 1.5	(51) 2.0	(60) 2.4	(14) 2.6	(10) 2.8		% Depr., Dep., Amort./Sales	(103) 2.9	(109) 2.6
		2.6	3.4	3.8	3.1	4.2		4.1	4.0
			2.3					5.3	8.4
		(11) 5.9					% Officers', Directors' Owners' Comp/Sales	(16) 14.8	(13) 15.5
			12.5					28.6	40.0
	12204M	54721M	552255M	1337241M	1219836M	1677739M	Net Sales ($)	3053712M	2409395M
	3499M	24807M	355135M	1442576M	1223402M	2384918M	Total Assets ($)	2894540M	2461146M

M = $ thousand   MM = $ million
See Pages 11 through 21 for Explanation of Ratios and Data

© RMA 2007

Comparative Historical Data | Current Data Sorted by Sales

Type of Statement									
	75	105	135	Unqualified	8	16	12	23	42	34
	4	6	8	Reviewed	1	1	1	2	1	2
	6	6	5	Compiled			2		1	
	3	5	5	Tax Returns	4			1	2	1
	28	50	49	Other	8	9	2	8	10	12

	4/1/04-3/31/05 ALL	4/1/05-3/31/06 ALL	4/1/06-3/31/07 ALL		0-1MM	1-3MM	3-5MM	5-10MM	10-25MM	25MM & OVER
					111 (4/1-9/30/06)			91 (10/1/06-3/31/07)		
NUMBER OF STATEMENTS	116	172	202		21	28	15	34	55	49
	%	%	%	**ASSETS**	%	%	%	%	%	%
	35.4	39.2	37.5	Cash & Equivalents	55.2	29.0	44.2	40.2	33.1	35.7
	12.4	10.0	12.0	Trade Receivables (net)	13.4	11.5	14.6	15.4	12.0	8.4
	2.6	1.2	1.3	Inventory	.0	3.9	.0	.8	1.1	1.2
	4.6	3.9	4.4	All Other Current	2.3	4.4	6.2	5.2	4.4	3.9
	55.1	54.4	55.1	Total Current	71.0	48.8	65.0	61.6	50.7	49.2
	29.8	27.4	25.1	Fixed Assets (net)	18.3	42.4	18.9	18.7	28.5	20.5
	.9	.7	1.8	Intangibles (net)	3.0	1.5	.1	1.7	1.8	1.8
	14.2	17.6	18.1	All Other Non-Current	7.7	7.3	16.0	18.0	19.0	28.5
	100.0	100.0	100.0	Total	100.0	100.0	100.0	100.0	100.0	100.0
				LIABILITIES						
	10.6	3.2	2.2	Notes Payable-Short Term	7.1	4.8	.0	.9	1.7	.6
	1.2	1.0	.9	Cur. Mat.-L.T.D.	.5	1.5	.7	.4	1.0	1.1
	9.1	8.1	9.0	Trade Payables	7.7	5.7	5.8	6.6	10.5	12.5
	.2	.4	.4	Income Taxes Payable	.0	.0	1.8	.1	.2	.7
	13.3	11.9	12.8	All Other Current	15.8	10.5	11.6	11.0	14.0	13.0
	34.3	24.6	25.3	Total Current	31.1	22.4	19.9	18.9	27.4	28.1
	13.2	10.6	12.5	Long-Term Debt	12.8	21.0	8.8	9.1	11.8	11.6
	.0	.1	.1	Deferred Taxes	.0	.0	.0	.0	.5	.1
	9.5	10.6	9.7	All Other Non-Current	8.9	4.2	4.0	14.6	8.6	13.0
	43.0	54.1	52.4	Net Worth	47.7	52.4	67.3	57.4	51.7	47.3
	100.0	100.0	100.0	Total Liabilities & Net Worth	100.0	100.0	100.0	100.0	100.0	100.0
				INCOME DATA						
	100.0	100.0	100.0	Net Sales	100.0	100.0	100.0	100.0	100.0	100.0
				Gross Profit						
	94.7	93.0	93.8	Operating Expenses	92.8	89.1	94.1	93.5	95.1	95.6
	5.3	7.0	6.2	Operating Profit	7.2	10.9	5.9	6.5	4.9	4.4
	-.3	-.8	-.8	All Other Expenses (net)	1.8	2.4	-.9	-1.8	-1.3	-2.3
	5.6	7.8	7.0	Profit Before Taxes	5.4	8.5	6.8	8.3	6.2	6.8
				RATIOS						
	4.2	4.9	5.0	Current	7.4	9.8	4.2	6.6	4.3	3.3
	2.2	2.5	2.5		3.5	3.0	2.6	3.5	2.1	1.9
	1.0	1.2	1.3		1.1	1.0	2.2	2.2	1.4	1.0
	3.8	4.4	4.6	Quick	7.4	7.9	4.2	6.6	4.3	3.0
	1.9	2.1	2.2		3.5	2.6	2.5	3.1	1.8	1.6
	.9	1.0	1.1		1.0	.8	2.0	2.2	1.0	.9
	3 136.6	5 77.7	5 74.1	Sales/Receivables	0 UND	1 323.6	4 96.1	7 51.3	5 68.6	9 40.2
	11 32.4	16 22.8	16 23.0		7 55.7	10 36.9	12 31.5	21 17.8	14 25.5	24 15.3
	39 9.4	36 10.3	39 9.4		38 9.7	33 11.2	62 5.9	48 7.6	40 9.1	36 10.2
				Cost of Sales/Inventory						
				Cost of Sales/Payables						
	2.5	2.1	2.2	Sales/Working Capital	1.7	2.9	1.6	1.8	2.4	2.3
	5.3	4.9	4.5		3.2	5.8	2.9	4.0	5.8	4.5
	-458.5	18.8	17.8		79.4	NM	4.5	9.0	21.0	-704.9
	22.5	29.7	23.0	EBIT/Interest		4.8		54.2	31.4	13.2
	(64) 5.0	(83) 6.1	(100) 5.8			(13) 2.3	(15)	(15) 16.9	(28) 6.9	(27) 5.0
	1.0	1.8	2.3			.8		6.4	2.4	2.8
			10.8	Net Profit + Depr., Dep., Amort./Cur. Mat. L/T/D						
		(11)	(11) 6.0							
			4.5							
	.1	.1	.1	Fixed/Worth	.0	.0	.1	.1	.1	.2
	.5	.3	.3		.1	.9	.1	.2	.4	.4
	1.7	.9	1.0		2.9	2.0	.4	.7	1.2	.8
	.4	.4	.4	Debt/Worth	.2	.3	.3	.3	.4	.6
	.8	.8	.8		.6	1.0	.5	.6	.8	1.0
	2.4	1.7	1.9		2.9	1.9	.8	1.6	1.7	2.4
	18.9	18.6	24.1	% Profit Before Taxes/Tangible Net Worth	27.5	27.7	20.3	36.5	28.5	15.0
	(108) 6.5	(167) 10.1	(191) 9.6		(18) -1.6	(25) 6.3	5.4	(51) 10.3	12.0	(48) 9.9
	.3	1.9	1.1		-40.5	-1.2	3.1	4.8	2.1	2.6
	9.0	9.9	11.8	% Profit Before Taxes/Total Assets	19.0	13.7	11.3	14.2	11.8	9.8
	3.5	4.9	5.5		1.0	2.0	4.1	6.7	6.8	5.4
	.1	.8	.4		-10.5	-1.4	2.0	3.6	.1	.8
	26.3	22.5	30.4	Sales/Net Fixed Assets	178.3	38.5	48.8	44.2	22.1	28.2
	6.4	5.2	8.8		67.0	3.3	22.0	18.4	5.2	6.6
	2.3	2.3	2.1		3.2	.9	2.6	3.6	1.8	2.1
	2.3	1.6	1.8	Sales/Total Assets	2.8	1.7	1.8	2.4	1.6	1.6
	1.1	1.0	1.0		1.3	.9	1.0	1.0	1.0	1.0
	.7	.6	.6		.7	.6	.5	.8	.7	.6
	1.1	1.5	1.2	% Depr., Dep., Amort./Sales	.3	1.2	1.2	1.0	1.4	1.3
	(96) 2.3	(142) 2.4	(161) 2.2		(14) 1.0	(19) 3.1	(11) 1.6	(27) 2.0	(49) 2.2	(41) 2.3
	3.8	3.8	3.3		5.2	4.6	3.1	2.5	3.5	3.1
	11.0	5.3	3.1	% Officers', Directors', Owners' Comp/Sales						
	(21) 16.7	(20) 11.9	(24) 6.9							
	30.9	23.7	22.4							
	3582057M	4871226M	4853996M	Net Sales ($)	11561M	52545M	61112M	255069M	868531M	3605178M
	3099961M	4729540M	5434337M	Total Assets ($)	15087M	72118M	72870M	245248M	1064260M	3964754M

M = $ thousand   MM = $ million
See Pages 11 through 21 for Explanation of Ratios and Data

Current Data Sorted by Assets   Comparative Historical Data

						Type of Statement		
	5	12	15	4	2	Unqualified	34	33
1	1					Reviewed		1
		1				Compiled	5	9
1	1	1				Tax Returns	3	
2	3	5	4	1	1	Other	22	22
	37 (4/1-9/30/06)		23 (10/1/06-3/31/07)				4/1/02-3/31/03 ALL	4/1/03-3/31/04 ALL
0-500M	500M-2MM	2-10MM	10-50MM	50-100MM	100-250MM			
4	10	19	19	5	3	NUMBER OF STATEMENTS	64	65
%	%	%	%	%	%	ASSETS	%	%
	52.9	33.8	39.5			Cash & Equivalents	37.5	39.2
	4.3	5.9	5.4			Trade Receivables (net)	4.9	4.7
	.2	.0	.0			Inventory	.4	.2
	1.1	3.4	3.3			All Other Current	1.7	9.3
	58.5	43.0	48.2			Total Current	44.5	53.3
	35.6	47.8	24.9			Fixed Assets (net)	39.0	37.5
	.0	.1	.0			Intangibles (net)	1.2	.2
	5.9	9.0	26.9			All Other Non-Current	15.3	8.9
	100.0	100.0	100.0			Total	100.0	100.0
						LIABILITIES		
	.4	1.2	.1			Notes Payable-Short Term	1.7	1.3
	3.4	4.5	.4			Cur. Mat.-L.T.D.	2.9	2.7
	2.4	3.7	2.3			Trade Payables	4.1	5.5
	.0	.0	.1			Income Taxes Payable	.1	.0
	4.6	14.1	5.7			All Other Current	7.1	9.0
	10.7	23.5	8.6			Total Current	16.0	18.5
	17.2	21.3	10.0			Long-Term Debt	19.6	17.1
	.0	.0	.2			Deferred Taxes	.0	.0
	4.5	2.1	4.1			All Other Non-Current	1.6	.7
	67.6	53.1	77.2			Net Worth	62.9	63.7
	100.0	100.0	100.0			Total Liabilties & Net Worth	100.0	100.0
						INCOME DATA		
	100.0	100.0	100.0			Net Sales	100.0	100.0
						Gross Profit		
	88.6	97.5	89.1			Operating Expenses	89.2	90.6
	11.4	2.5	10.9			Operating Profit	10.8	9.4
	3.9	.1	-1.8			All Other Expenses (net)	5.1	1.3
	7.5	2.4	12.6			Profit Before Taxes	5.6	8.1
						RATIOS		
	27.4	16.3	53.8				11.5	25.4
	7.1	4.5	5.9			Current	3.1	4.9
	2.4	1.3	2.8				1.3	1.5
	27.4	15.1	53.8				11.5	21.3
	7.1	4.5	5.9			Quick	3.0	4.8
	2.3	1.1	2.8				1.3	1.4
0 UND	0 UND	0 UND	4 84.2				0 UND	0 UND
0 UND	0 UND	0 UND	26 14.2			Sales/Receivables	0 UND	1 244.7
21 17.5	22 16.6	35 10.5					27 13.7	26 14.0
						Cost of Sales/Inventory		
						Cost of Sales/Payables		
	2.2	1.5	1.3				1.5	1.2
	3.8	3.6	2.5			Sales/Working Capital	6.0	3.3
	6.8	32.3	5.8				25.9	10.1
		3.9					13.1	5.8
		(11) .4				EBIT/Interest	(33) 2.1	(28) 2.1
		-.8					.3	.6
						Net Profit + Depr., Dep., Amort./Cur. Mat. L/T/D		
	.0	.6	.0				.1	.1
	.4	.8	.1			Fixed/Worth	.5	.7
	1.5	1.6	.8				1.4	1.2
	.2	.3	.0				.1	.1
	.4	.8	.3			Debt/Worth	.5	.4
	1.0	1.3	.5				1.5	1.4
	16.5	11.1	11.6				13.8	14.1
	7.1	(17) 8.3	6.1			% Profit Before Taxes/Tangible Net Worth	(61) 5.8	(61) 4.7
	2.3	-7.2	.1				-4.8	-2.9
	10.9	8.2	9.5				11.3	10.2
	4.8	4.2	5.4			% Profit Before Taxes/Total Assets	2.9	3.3
	.8	-2.8	.1				-2.5	-2.4
	63.1	5.7	406.1				13.0	19.9
	7.3	2.0	10.1			Sales/Net Fixed Assets	3.5	2.9
	1.0	.8	1.5				1.2	1.2
	2.3	1.4	1.2				1.4	1.4
	1.4	.9	.7			Sales/Total Assets	1.0	.9
	.5	.5	.2				.5	.5
		2.0	.7				1.4	1.3
	(15)	4.1	(14) 2.6			% Depr., Dep., Amort./Sales	(45) 2.9	(49) 3.2
		7.0	4.1				4.2	5.3
							6.6	6.8
						% Officers', Directors' Owners' Comp/Sales	(21) 23.3	(11) 13.0
							31.5	17.0
2165M	13562M	99635M	321155M	371235M	320879M	Net Sales ($)	1122726M	698922M
1143M	10873M	92030M	401170M	400549M	414977M	Total Assets ($)	835554M	751396M

M = $ thousand   MM = $ million
See Pages 11 through 21 for Explanation of Ratios and Data

Comparative Historical Data | Current Data Sorted by Sales

Hist 1	Hist 2	Hist 3	Type of Statement	0-1MM	1-3MM	3-5MM	5-10MM	10-25MM	25MM & OVER
26	36	38	Unqualified	2	7	3	8	8	10
4	1	2	Reviewed		2				
1	4	1	Compiled			1			
4	1	3	Tax Returns						
22	14	16	Other	3 4	5	3	1	2	1
4/1/04-3/31/05 ALL	4/1/05-3/31/06 ALL	4/1/06-3/31/07 ALL		37 (4/1-9/30/06)			23 (10/1/06-3/31/07)		
57	56	60	**NUMBER OF STATEMENTS**	9	14	7	9	10	11
%	%	%	**ASSETS**	%	%	%	%	%	%
40.7	44.1	39.8	Cash & Equivalents		43.7			38.3	38.8
4.9	4.4	5.1	Trade Receivables (net)		3.2			12.9	7.9
.1	.1	.0	Inventory		.1			.0	.1
6.4	5.5	4.0	All Other Current		2.6			1.2	13.9
52.1	54.1	48.9	Total Current		49.6			52.5	60.7
40.1	35.0	33.5	Fixed Assets (net)		36.9			30.7	17.1
.1	.2	.1	Intangibles (net)		.0			.1	.3
7.7	10.7	17.5	All Other Non-Current		13.5			16.6	21.9
100.0	100.0	100.0	Total		100.0			100.0	100.0
			LIABILITIES						
2.4	1.4	.6	Notes Payable-Short Term		1.2			.0	.9
2.1	2.3	2.2	Cur. Mat.-L.T.D.		2.5			6.5	.3
3.9	9.5	2.9	Trade Payables		2.9			4.4	5.8
.0	.0	.0	Income Taxes Payable		.0			.2	.0
7.9	5.9	9.0	All Other Current		3.5			16.7	12.6
16.2	19.1	14.9	Total Current		10.0			27.8	19.6
18.0	12.8	16.1	Long-Term Debt		13.7			10.7	8.1
.0	.0	.1	Deferred Taxes		.0			.0	.4
1.4	3.8	4.0	All Other Non-Current		3.8			6.2	8.5
64.5	64.2	65.0	Net Worth		72.4			55.3	63.5
100.0	100.0	100.0	Total Liabilties & Net Worth		100.0			100.0	100.0
			INCOME DATA						
100.0	100.0	100.0	Net Sales		100.0			100.0	100.0
			Gross Profit						
92.0	98.3	92.5	Operating Expenses		93.8			92.4	94.6
8.0	1.7	7.5	Operating Profit		6.2			7.6	5.4
2.9	-1.6	-.1	All Other Expenses (net)		-1.0			.6	-2.6
5.1	3.3	7.6	Profit Before Taxes		7.2			7.0	8.0
			RATIOS						
72.4	51.5	25.1			23.9			20.2	5.9
10.5	8.9	5.9	Current		5.3			2.3	2.8
1.6	2.6	2.2			2.4			1.1	2.2
70.7	51.3	25.1			23.5			20.2	5.9
7.6	8.4	5.3	Quick		5.1			2.1	2.6
1.4	2.6	1.9			2.2			1.1	1.7
0 UND	0 UND	0 UND		0 UND				8 44.5	10 37.1
0 UND	0 999.8	8 44.7	Sales/Receivables		0 UND			24 15.4	21 17.4
22 16.3	22 16.7	25 14.6			16 22.6			50 7.4	34 10.8
			Cost of Sales/Inventory						
			Cost of Sales/Payables						
1.1	1.4	1.5			2.7			1.4	2.1
3.0	2.8	3.5	Sales/Working Capital		3.8			5.2	3.2
8.9	7.0	6.6			7.2			NM	4.3
10.2	10.3	8.0							
(35) 3.5	(34) 2.0	(33) 2.5	EBIT/Interest						
-1.7	-2.8	-.2							
			Net Profit + Depr., Dep., Amort./Cur. Mat. L/T/D						
.1	.1	.0			.0			.0	.0
.7	.4	.5	Fixed/Worth		.4			.7	.3
1.1	1.0	1.3			1.0			1.6	.4
.1	.0	.2			.2			.2	.2
.5	.3	.5	Debt/Worth		.3			.5	.5
1.3	1.0	1.2			.6			5.4	1.5
10.6	13.5	12.5			16.5				29.3
(55) .9	(54) 6.0	(58) 6.2	% Profit Before Taxes/Tangible Net Worth		3.8				14.5
-7.0	-5.1	-2.4			-2.4				3.1
9.6	10.5	9.3			11.2			9.8	17.0
.8	5.3	3.7	% Profit Before Taxes/Total Assets		3.0			-.8	8.6
-5.1	-2.6	-1.9			-1.9			-5.9	1.5
14.7	23.2	47.9			132.1			145.6	26.1
2.5	4.0	4.2	Sales/Net Fixed Assets		10.1			4.1	9.0
1.1	1.6	1.3			.8			1.4	4.7
1.3	1.7	1.4			2.3			1.7	1.5
.7	1.0	.9	Sales/Total Assets		1.4			.8	1.2
.4	.6	.4			.3			.4	.9
1.8	.9	1.6			.8				.7
(45) 3.1	(46) 2.3	(46) 2.8	% Depr., Dep., Amort./Sales		(10) 3.7				(10) 1.4
4.9	3.6	4.6			7.3				1.9
6.2		7.7							
(12) 11.8		(10) 15.7	% Officers', Directors' Owners' Comp/Sales						
20.6		27.0							
2166936M	1072813M	1128631M	Net Sales ($)	4278M	28240M	27056M	62075M	168783M	838199M
1354964M	1114709M	1320742M	Total Assets ($)	16792M	61647M	49700M	111286M	308927M	772390M

M = $ thousand   MM = $ million
See Pages 11 through 21 for Explanation of Ratios and Data

Current Data Sorted by Assets

Comparative Historical Data

						Type of Statement		
16	22	56	57	11	9	Unqualified	115	125
7	2	2				Reviewed	6	10
5	2	9	1	1		Compiled	10	32
6	5	3				Tax Returns	6	11
38	16	23	22	7	3	Other	72	79
	149 (4/1-9/30/06)		174 (10/1/06-3/31/07)				4/1/02-3/31/03 ALL	4/1/03-3/31/04 ALL
0-500M	500M-2MM	2-10MM	10-50MM	50-100MM	100-250MM			
72	47	93	80	19	12	NUMBER OF STATEMENTS	209	257
%	%	%	%	%	%	ASSETS	%	%
54.1	38.2	23.6	27.0	23.8	31.8	Cash & Equivalents	23.5	28.4
8.9	11.7	7.7	6.8	7.1	7.0	Trade Receivables (net)	7.1	6.7
.1	1.4	2.8	1.3	.7	.5	Inventory	2.0	1.1
8.1	3.3	4.8	4.5	6.1	2.2	All Other Current	3.7	7.0
71.2	54.6	38.9	39.6	37.7	41.5	Total Current	36.3	43.3
15.1	31.2	47.4	43.5	40.8	29.4	Fixed Assets (net)	48.1	42.2
1.4	.1	.9	1.3	.1	1.1	Intangibles (net)	1.2	.9
12.2	14.0	12.8	15.6	21.4	27.9	All Other Non-Current	14.3	13.6
100.0	100.0	100.0	100.0	100.0	100.0	Total	100.0	100.0
						LIABILITIES		
9.8	7.5	2.6	1.4	1.5	9.4	Notes Payable-Short Term	6.0	4.2
3.8	2.4	2.0	.8	.8	.3	Cur. Mat.-L.T.D.	2.5	3.6
12.0	8.1	5.5	3.4	4.1	3.1	Trade Payables	5.7	5.0
.0	.4	.0	.1	.0	.1	Income Taxes Payable	.1	.1
20.3	12.6	9.8	8.7	15.9	7.0	All Other Current	9.0	10.7
46.0	31.0	20.0	14.5	22.3	19.8	Total Current	23.3	23.6
30.9	18.1	20.4	15.0	47.6	16.2	Long-Term Debt	19.4	19.7
.0	.0	.1	.2	.7	.6	Deferred Taxes	.1	.2
6.2	4.3	5.0	6.3	5.1	9.5	All Other Non-Current	7.2	5.2
16.9	46.7	54.5	64.1	24.3	53.9	Net Worth	50.1	51.3
100.0	100.0	100.0	100.0	100.0	100.0	Total Liabilities & Net Worth	100.0	100.0
						INCOME DATA		
100.0	100.0	100.0	100.0	100.0	100.0	Net Sales	100.0	100.0
						Gross Profit		
90.5	89.8	94.1	91.7	85.5	82.4	Operating Expenses	94.2	93.2
9.5	10.2	5.9	8.3	14.5	17.6	Operating Profit	5.8	6.8
4.0	4.0	2.3	.2	.9	-1.3	All Other Expenses (net)	3.0	1.8
5.5	6.2	3.6	8.1	13.6	18.8	Profit Before Taxes	2.8	5.0
						RATIOS		
4.7	7.2	6.1	6.7	3.3	3.5		4.4	5.2
2.0	2.3	2.1	2.9	1.7	2.0	Current	1.8	2.2
.8	.8	1.1	1.2	1.1	1.0		1.0	1.0
4.4	7.1	5.3	5.3	3.0	3.3		3.5	3.9
1.8	1.7	1.7	2.4	1.3	1.5	Quick	1.5	1.5
.7	.7	.7	1.1	.9	.8		.7	.7
0 UND	0 UND	2 193.9	4 87.7	8 46.5	8 45.7		3 136.1	1 354.0
2 180.3	6 57.4	11 32.5	15 23.6	21 17.3	35 10.5	Sales/Receivables	12 29.4	10 36.9
12 29.7	25 14.5	35 10.5	49 7.4	49 7.4	74 4.9		36 10.1	30 12.2
						Cost of Sales/Inventory		
						Cost of Sales/Payables		
3.1	1.8	2.5	1.5	2.4	1.2		2.7	2.3
6.7	6.8	8.3	3.4	4.4	5.3	Sales/Working Capital	7.1	5.8
-27.8	-23.0	84.5	22.1	18.6	NM		666.9	-146.6
12.0	14.9	7.8	10.0	57.7			5.3	9.8
(29) 3.8	(26) 6.2	(65) 1.2	(50) 2.9	(12) 10.3		EBIT/Interest	(126) 1.1	(146) 2.8
1.6	.1	-1.1	.7	4.3			-3.0	.6
						Net Profit + Depr., Dep., Amort./Cur. Mat. L/T/D	3.3	7.5
							(11) 2.4	(13) 3.2
							.2	.1
.0	.0	.3	.2	.0	.1		.4	.1
.0	.4	.7	.7	.8	.4	Fixed/Worth	.9	.8
.8	1.1	1.2	1.2	1.0	1.9		1.4	1.3
.2	.2	.2	.2	.3	.3		.2	.2
1.0	.9	.6	.4	.8	.7	Debt/Worth	.7	.7
UND	3.9	2.4	1.1	2.6	2.6		1.8	1.7
66.4	37.0	15.4	13.0	18.5	17.6		11.7	15.2
(54) 7.0	(41) 10.7	(87) 2.5	(78) 4.9	(18) 11.7	(11) 9.2	% Profit Before Taxes/Tangible Net Worth	(198) 1.2	(235) 5.3
-7.9	1.1	-4.2	-.4	3.3	5.4		-5.5	-1.4
32.8	16.5	8.2	7.2	8.7	8.4		5.4	8.7
6.5	5.4	1.3	3.3	4.3	4.8	% Profit Before Taxes/Total Assets	.3	2.2
-2.7	-1.2	-2.7	-.1	2.4	1.7		-3.8	-1.3
UND	UND	14.0	6.2	24.6	6.7		7.3	31.5
UND	11.6	1.6	1.9	1.0	3.8	Sales/Net Fixed Assets	1.5	2.2
31.4	2.3	.8	.6	.5	.7		.7	.8
3.4	1.9	1.4	.9	.7	.7		1.3	1.3
2.0	1.3	.7	.6	.6	.4	Sales/Total Assets	.7	.8
1.2	.6	.4	.3	.3	.3		.4	.5
.5	1.2	1.5	1.6	1.3			1.9	2.7
(11) 2.0	(22) 3.2	(81) 4.0	(68) 3.7	(14) 4.6		% Depr., Dep., Amort./Sales	(165) 4.4	(184) 4.9
10.4	7.0	7.3	8.5	7.9			8.9	8.2
		4.8					4.7	5.7
	(10) 13.9					% Officers', Directors' Owners' Comp/Sales	(18) 8.4	(43) 12.3
	26.9						17.2	31.4
38370M	84147M	524210M	1251869M	837177M	887839M	Net Sales ($)	2890269M	2917226M
15086M	53492M	439228M	1697291M	1284055M	1870405M	Total Assets ($)	4033363M	3878993M

Comparative Historical Data | | | | Current Data Sorted by Sales

			Type of Statement						
123	140	171	Unqualified	24	33	29	23	35	27
8	11	11	Reviewed	6	2	1	1	1	
11	6	18	Compiled	7	7	1	2	1	
8	8	14	Tax Returns	11	3				
66	113	109	Other	51	12	11	11	9	15
4/1/04-3/31/05 ALL	4/1/05-3/31/06 ALL	4/1/06-3/31/07 ALL		149 (4/1-9/30/06)		174 (10/1/06-3/31/07)			
				0-1MM	1-3MM	3-5MM	5-10MM	10-25MM	25MM & OVER
216	278	323	**NUMBER OF STATEMENTS**	99	57	42	37	46	42
%	%	%	**ASSETS**	%	%	%	%	%	%
29.8	32.7	33.7	Cash & Equivalents	43.7	27.7	29.7	28.4	28.3	32.7
6.7	7.5	8.3	Trade Receivables (net)	7.3	8.1	6.0	10.4	7.2	12.1
1.4	2.1	1.4	Inventory	.1	1.7	1.5	.6	4.0	2.1
3.1	5.0	5.2	All Other Current	5.2	6.2	6.0	2.4	6.9	4.1
41.0	47.3	48.6	Total Current	56.4	43.7	43.1	41.8	46.3	50.9
42.0	38.4	35.8	Fixed Assets (net)	28.8	43.3	39.6	39.2	38.8	32.4
.3	1.7	.9	Intangibles (net)	1.2	.1	.4	1.4	1.2	1.2
16.7	12.7	14.6	All Other Non-Current	13.6	12.9	16.8	17.7	13.7	15.5
100.0	100.0	100.0	Total	100.0	100.0	100.0	100.0	100.0	100.0
			LIABILITIES						
4.8	5.6	4.8	Notes Payable-Short Term	8.9	5.7	.7	4.0	.9	3.2
4.3	3.1	2.0	Cur. Mat.-L.T.D.	3.6	1.9	1.3	1.6	1.3	.6
7.8	5.5	6.6	Trade Payables	8.3	5.6	5.9	6.8	5.2	6.3
.2	.1	.1	Income Taxes Payable	.2	.0	.0	.0	.2	.0
9.9	10.0	12.5	All Other Current	13.0	11.4	9.1	13.8	12.9	14.9
27.0	24.1	26.2	Total Current	34.0	24.6	16.9	26.3	20.4	25.1
20.8	19.2	22.5	Long-Term Debt	30.4	20.0	22.1	11.5	12.3	28.6
.2	.1	.1	Deferred Taxes	.0	.0	.0	.1	.1	.6
7.2	7.8	5.7	All Other Non-Current	4.5	5.9	4.8	4.5	7.6	7.7
44.8	48.7	45.6	Net Worth	31.0	49.5	56.2	57.6	59.7	37.9
100.0	100.0	100.0	Total Liabilities & Net Worth	100.0	100.0	100.0	100.0	100.0	100.0
			INCOME DATA						
100.0	100.0	100.0	Net Sales	100.0	100.0	100.0	100.0	100.0	100.0
			Gross Profit						
93.8	92.9	91.1	Operating Expenses	91.5	90.6	90.6	85.8	94.3	92.9
6.2	7.1	8.9	Operating Profit	8.5	9.4	9.4	14.2	5.7	7.1
1.1	1.4	2.2	All Other Expenses (net)	3.6	6.8	.2	.2	.1	-1.2
5.0	5.8	6.7	Profit Before Taxes	4.9	2.6	9.3	14.1	5.6	8.3
			RATIOS						
4.7	6.0	5.6	Current	6.8	5.2	8.4	5.9	4.2	3.8
2.1	2.2	2.2		2.0	1.8	3.3	1.8	2.4	1.9
1.1	1.1	1.1		.8	.8	1.5	1.1	1.6	1.1
3.8	5.0	4.6	Quick	5.1	4.6	6.7	5.4	3.6	3.4
1.6	1.8	1.8		1.9	1.6	2.7	1.5	1.9	1.6
.8	.9	.8		.7	.7	1.2	.9	1.0	.9
1 600.3	2 191.5	0 841.1	Sales/Receivables	0 UND	3 129.0	2 213.4	6 62.7	4 95.6	8 48.6
9 41.6	9 38.8	10 37.3		0 994.0	14 26.8	9 42.1	29 12.6	11 32.5	22 16.4
28 13.0	35 10.5	35 10.5		15 24.8	35 10.3	28 13.1	63 5.8	36 10.2	39 9.4
			Cost of Sales/Inventory						
			Cost of Sales/Payables						
2.8	2.1	2.1	Sales/Working Capital	2.1	2.9	1.3	1.6	1.8	3.0
7.1	5.7	6.0		5.5	8.6	3.0	6.2	4.9	7.2
91.0	32.9	45.9		-17.1	-20.0	10.6	157.5	15.9	44.1
10.9	9.6	11.7	EBIT/Interest	6.9	8.7	15.8	12.9	14.2	13.0
(125) 2.2	(148) 2.6	(189) 3.1		(46) 2.4	(37) 1.2	(26) 4.1	(27) 4.1	(29) 3.8	(24) 5.8
-.9	-.4	.3		-.9	-1.7	.9	.9	.4	2.8
10.8			Net Profit + Depr., Dep., Amort./Cur. Mat. L/T/D						
(11) 4.4									
1.2									
.2	.1	.0	Fixed/Worth	.0	.1	.2	.2	.1	.1
.7	.7	.5		.0	.8	.6	.6	.6	.5
1.4	1.3	1.1		1.1	1.3	1.0	1.2	1.0	1.1
.3	.2	.2	Debt/Worth	.1	.3	.2	.2	.3	.4
.7	.6	.7		.9	.6	.5	.5	.6	.7
1.8	1.8	2.6		19.1	2.5	1.9	1.7	1.3	2.6
16.0	16.4	18.0	% Profit Before Taxes/Tangible Net Worth	30.1	15.3	14.2	17.5	17.9	18.1
(196) 4.7	(250) 4.8	(289) 6.1		(80) 3.2	(51) 3.0	(40) 6.6	(35) 4.8	(44) 5.0	(39) 12.4
-2.8	-1.6	-1.8		-5.2	-6.8	.9	-.4	-2.9	5.4
8.1	8.9	10.8	% Profit Before Taxes/Total Assets	21.0	9.2	8.2	11.2	9.9	9.1
2.3	2.9	3.3		2.0	1.4	3.7	2.5	3.7	5.4
-1.7	-1.5	-1.2		-2.4	-4.8	.3	-.1	-1.7	2.1
21.8	54.9	113.7	Sales/Net Fixed Assets	UND	103.4	11.9	10.2	18.2	27.3
2.7	3.5	4.2		UND	3.0	1.5	2.6	3.7	6.5
.7	.7	.9		.9	.9	.8	.7	1.0	1.6
1.8	1.5	1.8	Sales/Total Assets	2.1	1.8	1.2	1.3	1.6	1.8
.8	.8	.8		1.1	1.0	.5	.5	.8	.9
.5	.4	.4		.4	.6	.3	.4	.4	.6
1.4	1.8	1.5	% Depr., Dep., Amort./Sales	1.9	1.6	2.6	1.1	1.5	.7
(160) 3.6	(193) 4.1	(205) 3.8		(29) 8.6	(38) 4.3	(33) 4.8	(30) 3.7	(42) 2.5	(33) 1.8
8.2	8.9	8.1		16.3	8.1	7.2	8.7	5.3	6.2
5.7	5.6	4.5	% Officers', Directors' Owners' Comp/Sales	11.0					
(24) 10.7	(18) 11.6	(29) 12.9		(10) 21.4					
22.4	27.2	25.6		28.4					
4062105M	3895129M	3623612M	Net Sales ($)	40339M	104019M	171777M	262842M	726537M	2318098M
3603323M	5772881M	5359557M	Total Assets ($)	96283M	200461M	382522M	670847M	1152000M	2857444M

M = $ thousand   MM = $ million
See Pages 11 through 21 for Explanation of Ratios and Data

Current Data Sorted by Assets   Comparative Historical Data

							Type of Statement		
		2	2	4	4	2	Unqualified	19	21
	1	6	9	3	1		Reviewed	19	29
	1	2	3	1			Compiled	33	39
	19	8	8	1		1	Tax Returns	13	16
	3	10	19	10	3	1	Other	45	55
		22 (4/1-9/30/06)		102 (10/1/06-3/31/07)				4/1/02-3/31/03	4/1/03-3/31/04
	0-500M	500M-2MM	2-10MM	10-50MM	50-100MM	100-250MM		ALL	ALL
	24	28	41	19	9	3	NUMBER OF STATEMENTS	129	160
	%	%	%	%	%	%	ASSETS	%	%
	24.7	11.8	14.3	5.5			Cash & Equivalents	12.4	11.6
	6.9	22.2	19.3	23.5			Trade Receivables (net)	19.0	17.6
	11.7	15.1	13.3	10.2			Inventory	13.9	12.8
	11.5	5.2	8.3	1.9			All Other Current	4.5	5.4
	54.8	54.3	55.3	41.1			Total Current	49.9	47.4
	32.7	32.5	29.4	43.2			Fixed Assets (net)	38.2	39.0
	2.6	1.5	3.7	5.8			Intangibles (net)	3.6	2.5
	9.8	11.7	11.6	9.9			All Other Non-Current	8.3	11.1
	100.0	100.0	100.0	100.0			Total	100.0	100.0
							LIABILITIES		
	5.9	16.5	10.3	16.9			Notes Payable-Short Term	12.3	13.7
	4.1	1.6	4.0	2.3			Cur. Mat.-L.T.D.	4.9	4.5
	11.6	14.1	8.9	15.8			Trade Payables	8.0	8.7
	.1	.6	1.2	.5			Income Taxes Payable	.3	.9
	23.1	5.0	9.3	17.0			All Other Current	13.2	12.5
	44.8	37.8	33.8	52.4			Total Current	38.6	40.4
	24.3	26.1	24.3	14.8			Long-Term Debt	25.0	28.1
	.0	.0	.7	.5			Deferred Taxes	.3	.2
	2.6	2.1	2.9	5.4			All Other Non-Current	6.4	6.3
	28.4	34.0	38.4	27.0			Net Worth	29.6	25.0
	100.0	100.0	100.0	100.0			Total Liabilities & Net Worth	100.0	100.0
							INCOME DATA		
	100.0	100.0	100.0	100.0			Net Sales	100.0	100.0
							Gross Profit		
	87.7	78.7	80.6	87.5			Operating Expenses	87.8	83.9
	12.3	21.3	19.4	12.5			Operating Profit	12.2	16.1
	3.0	10.1	7.6	1.9			All Other Expenses (net)	5.8	3.6
	9.3	11.2	11.8	10.6			Profit Before Taxes	6.4	12.6
							RATIOS		
	2.3	3.6	4.0	1.4			Current	2.5	2.6
	1.6	1.5	1.9	1.1				1.3	1.2
	.8	1.0	1.1	.6				.7	.7
	1.4	3.5	3.6	1.2			Quick	1.6	1.7
	.8	1.1	.9	.6				.8	.7
	.3	.3	.5	.3				.3	.2
	0 UND	0 UND	0 UND	8 46.4			Sales/Receivables	0 UND	0 UND
	0 UND	1 511.1	23 15.7	33 11.0				15 24.0	15 23.8
	0 UND	45 8.1	44 8.2	58 6.3				46 8.0	54 6.8
							Cost of Sales/Inventory		
							Cost of Sales/Payables		
	18.2	3.7	2.8	9.4			Sales/Working Capital	6.4	5.1
	80.5	13.6	9.8	55.1				30.2	17.3
	-71.5	UND	79.7	-13.4				-19.1	-16.5
	6.8	6.6	15.4	9.2			EBIT/Interest	12.7	11.2
	(11) 1.1	(16) 1.5	(30) 5.5	(17) 4.7				(100) 3.7	(124) 4.4
	-2.0	-.1	-.9	1.3				1.1	1.6
							Net Profit + Depr., Dep., Amort./Cur. Mat. L/T/D	6.0	21.5
								(20) 2.7	(15) 5.5
								1.2	2.5
	.1	.2	.1	.4			Fixed/Worth	.2	.2
	.7	.7	.3	1.6				1.0	.9
	30.2	44.5	6.5	37.4				3.8	4.8
	.3	.6	.5	1.3			Debt/Worth	.8	.7
	1.0	1.7	1.9	4.3				1.9	1.7
	67.4	108.8	NM	64.8				7.7	12.5
	341.4	47.3	32.2	114.6			% Profit Before Taxes/Tangible Net Worth	53.3	44.7
	(20) 59.7	(23) 16.2	(31) 18.9	(16) 26.0				(108) 16.0	(127) 18.2
	9.8	.0	6.2	7.2				.0	3.2
	65.6	13.3	17.3	17.5			% Profit Before Taxes/Total Assets	18.5	16.9
	22.8	2.9	7.0	5.9				4.8	6.0
	-2.0	-1.8	.4	1.9				.0	1.2
	827.9	38.9	58.9	15.1			Sales/Net Fixed Assets	51.3	27.7
	13.2	11.0	13.0	6.4				9.9	6.7
	7.7	1.8	1.2	1.1				1.7	1.3
	13.6	3.7	3.1	2.7			Sales/Total Assets	3.8	3.3
	6.0	2.2	1.4	1.6				2.2	1.8
	2.8	.4	.4	.7				.7	.6
	.3	.2	.7	1.0			% Depr., Dep., Amort./Sales	1.0	1.1
	(13) 3.9	(23) 1.9	(33) 2.1	(16) 1.9				(100) 2.8	(124) 3.2
	7.2	5.0	5.0	9.3				11.4	9.2
	3.1		1.6				% Officers', Directors', Owners' Comp/Sales	2.5	1.3
	(12) 7.9		(11) 2.6					(31) 7.7	(41) 5.7
	25.4		10.5					17.3	9.4
	34115M	87308M	460419M	1483177M	740480M	1355442M	Net Sales ($)	2201516M	2327211M
	5434M	34185M	200632M	337325M	628909M	505679M	Total Assets ($)	1029188M	1290028M

M = $ thousand   MM = $ million

See Pages 11 through 21 for Explanation of Ratios and Data

Comparative Historical Data | Current Data Sorted by Sales

	4/1/04-3/31/05 ALL	4/1/05-3/31/06 ALL	4/1/06-3/31/07 ALL	Type of Statement	22 (4/1-9/30/06) 0-1MM	1-3MM	3-5MM	102 (10/1/06-3/31/07) 5-10MM	10-25MM	25MM & OVER
	14	13	14	Unqualified		2		4	2	6
	25	25	20	Reviewed	2	3	4	3	6	2
	32	19	7	Compiled	1	4		1	1	
	16	19	37	Tax Returns	15	12	7	6	3	
	58	56	46	Other	8	8	5	6	3	12
	145	132	124	**NUMBER OF STATEMENTS**	26	29	16	14	19	20
	%	%	%	**ASSETS**	%	%	%	%	%	%
	11.5	11.3	13.9	Cash & Equivalents	19.9	18.2	10.4	13.5	9.5	7.2
	19.2	18.0	17.8	Trade Receivables (net)	4.5	9.4	24.0	28.3	19.6	33.5
	10.9	10.6	12.8	Inventory	.4	9.7	31.5	5.8	20.2	16.5
	4.3	5.7	6.9	All Other Current	11.2	5.5	7.3	8.6	5.2	3.3
	45.9	45.5	51.4	Total Current	36.0	42.8	73.2	56.1	54.4	60.5
	36.5	39.7	33.0	Fixed Assets (net)	49.2	41.8	17.2	23.6	31.1	20.2
	4.3	4.6	4.8	Intangibles (net)	2.0	1.9	.5	8.9	4.8	13.0
	13.3	10.2	10.8	All Other Non-Current	12.8	13.5	9.2	11.4	9.7	6.4
	100.0	100.0	100.0	Total	100.0	100.0	100.0	100.0	100.0	100.0
				LIABILITIES						
	17.1	10.4	11.8	Notes Payable-Short Term	4.6	9.3	26.7	6.4	16.8	12.0
	3.7	3.7	3.2	Cur. Mat.-L.T.D.	1.9	3.7	5.8	5.4	2.6	1.2
	8.0	9.3	12.2	Trade Payables	1.6	12.7	13.6	11.1	14.2	23.1
	.7	.3	.7	Income Taxes Payable	.1	.0	.6	.4	2.9	.5
	12.1	9.8	12.1	All Other Current	18.7	5.6	3.8	9.3	12.7	21.1
	41.5	33.5	40.0	Total Current	27.0	31.3	50.5	32.7	49.2	57.9
	28.7	29.1	23.0	Long-Term Debt	34.2	15.1	28.8	33.2	23.9	7.4
	.4	.1	.3	Deferred Taxes	.8	.0	.1	.1	.2	.5
	6.4	2.8	3.4	All Other Non-Current	2.4	4.7	1.4	1.8	1.8	6.9
	23.1	34.5	33.2	Net Worth	35.6	48.9	19.2	32.2	25.0	27.3
	100.0	100.0	100.0	Total Liabilties & Net Worth	100.0	100.0	100.0	100.0	100.0	100.0
				INCOME DATA						
	100.0	100.0	100.0	Net Sales	100.0	100.0	100.0	100.0	100.0	100.0
				Gross Profit						
	82.0	79.8	83.4	Operating Expenses	57.6	81.4	95.3	92.0	94.0	94.3
	18.0	20.2	16.6	Operating Profit	42.4	18.6	4.7	8.0	6.0	5.7
	4.3	5.2	6.9	All Other Expenses (net)	23.8	2.4	3.8	3.8	2.1	.6
	13.7	15.0	9.7	Profit Before Taxes	18.5	16.2	.8	4.2	3.9	5.1
				RATIOS						
	2.6	3.3	2.7		5.3	5.3	5.7	2.5	1.6	1.4
	1.4	1.4	1.4	Current	1.4	2.1	1.8	1.8	1.1	1.2
	.9	.8	.9		.4	.9	1.1	1.1	.6	.9
	1.9	2.4	2.0		4.1	5.1	3.3	2.3	.8	1.1
	.9	.8	.8	Quick	.9	1.3	1.0	1.4	.5	.6
	.3	.4	.3		.1	.4	.1	.6	.2	.4
0	UND	0 UND	0 UND		0 UND	0 UND	0 UND	6 64.5	3 138.1	11 34.2
17	21.7	20 18.5	11 33.9	Sales/Receivables	0 UND	0 999.8	25 14.5	36 10.1	32 11.5	36 10.0
47	7.7	63 5.8	44 8.4		0 UND	32 11.6	77 4.7	47 7.8	63 5.8	58 6.3
				Cost of Sales/Inventory						
				Cost of Sales/Payables						
	7.3	6.3	6.8		1.1	4.1	2.9	7.0	8.5	14.6
	16.5	24.6	20.5	Sales/Working Capital	59.9	20.7	14.3	11.3	40.0	39.2
	-49.6	-37.1	-55.7		-5.0	-127.2	379.1	NM	-28.9	NM
	18.0	16.1	10.5			13.9	4.0	51.0	8.8	16.6
(113)	5.8	(104) 5.0	(84) 3.2	EBIT/Interest		(19) 5.3	(11) -.3	(12) 3.6	(15) 2.5	6.7
	1.9	2.0	.5			2.1	-5.3	.2	-1.7	2.6
	9.2	5.5	10.8							
(16)	6.1	(12) 3.3	(18) 4.6	Net Profit + Depr., Dep., Amort./Cur. Mat. L/T/D						
	1.9	1.2	1.6							
	.3	.3	.2		.4	.2	.0	.1	.3	.3
	1.0	1.2	.8	Fixed/Worth	1.3	.6	.2	.3	2.8	1.4
	5.2	4.3	15.3		UND	2.1	14.4	-2.7	-16.6	2.9
	.7	.9	.6		.5	.4	.7	.6	1.6	1.8
	1.9	2.3	2.2	Debt/Worth	2.0	.8	1.3	4.9	3.3	4.3
	7.8	9.1	61.8		UND	3.6	98.0	-4.0	-41.3	11.2
	47.5	65.9	64.5		77.0	50.3	260.1		42.2	109.9
(115)	22.3	(111) 27.4	(99) 22.3	% Profit Before Taxes/Tangible Net Worth	(20) 15.4	(27) 25.6	(14) 14.5		(14) 23.3	(16) 33.8
	5.9	10.1	5.8		3.4	5.8	-5.5		7.8	18.1
	17.7	17.7	20.2		27.0	28.6	16.6	27.8	11.7	20.4
	7.7	8.2	5.6	% Profit Before Taxes/Total Assets	3.6	14.0	.2	3.0	4.3	7.6
	2.4	2.8	.0		-.4	1.9	-3.1	-2.2	.6	4.1
	36.5	31.9	42.2		10.3	68.8	519.4	92.6	41.8	51.0
	9.0	7.3	12.3	Sales/Net Fixed Assets	1.0	9.1	31.3	27.0	14.8	15.0
	2.0	1.0	2.1		.2	1.5	9.5	8.9	3.1	11.6
	3.3	3.6	4.3		1.5	6.2	3.4	3.9	3.3	4.1
	2.0	1.6	2.0	Sales/Total Assets	.2	2.0	2.4	2.1	2.2	2.5
	.8	.5	.6		.1	.4	1.4	1.0		1.8
	1.0	1.2	.8		3.4	.5	.2	.4	.7	.6
(104)	2.7	(112) 2.7	(96) 2.1	% Depr., Dep., Amort./Sales	(18) 7.2	(20) 3.6	(13) 1.8	(11) 2.7	(17) 1.9	(17) 1.3
	8.4	7.9	5.5		24.2	6.5	3.5	5.0	3.5	1.8
	2.5	1.6	2.4		3.0					
(49)	6.7	(43) 3.9	(35) 3.3	% Officers', Directors' Owners' Comp/Sales	(10) 6.0					
	12.0	12.7	11.3		28.6					
	4361339M	2955651M	4160941M	Net Sales ($)	10195M	57909M	60455M	107603M	315950M	3608829M
	1625207M	1522251M	1712164M	Total Assets ($)	46270M	123913M	104382M	105542M	314976M	1017081M

M = $ thousand   MM = $ million
See Pages 11 through 21 for Explanation of Ratios and Data

PUBLIC ADMINISTRATION

Current Data Sorted by Assets

Comparative Historical Data

						Type of Statement		
2	4	9	23	11	4	Unqualified	26	20
						Reviewed		
	1					Compiled		1
	3					Tax Returns		
1	2	1	3	1		Other	6	7
	56 (4/1-9/30/06)		9 (10/1/06-3/31/07)				4/1/02-3/31/03	4/1/03-3/31/04
0-500M	500M-2MM	2-10MM	10-50MM	50-100MM	100-250MM		ALL	ALL
3	10	10	26	12	4	NUMBER OF STATEMENTS	32	28
%	%	%	%	%	%	ASSETS	%	%
	22.1	29.0	18.7	20.5		Cash & Equivalents	22.5	23.1
	13.9	7.4	10.0	13.0		Trade Receivables (net)	8.9	3.9
	12.0	.1	.3	1.6		Inventory	.4	.2
	7.6	4.6	3.0	1.5		All Other Current	8.2	8.0
	55.6	41.2	31.9	36.6		Total Current	40.0	35.2
	31.1	57.3	59.4	56.7		Fixed Assets (net)	49.5	54.5
	.0	.0	.2	1.0		Intangibles (net)	.1	.9
	13.3	1.5	8.5	5.7		All Other Non-Current	10.5	9.4
	100.0	100.0	100.0	100.0		Total	100.0	100.0
						LIABILITIES		
	6.6	.0	1.7	.3		Notes Payable-Short Term	.5	.2
	.3	1.0	2.2	1.3		Cur. Mat.-L.T.D.	1.0	1.0
	14.5	1.3	3.0	3.5		Trade Payables	2.0	2.2
	.0	.0	.0	.0		Income Taxes Payable	.0	.0
	10.6	2.2	3.3	2.5		All Other Current	6.9	3.5
	31.9	4.6	10.3	7.6		Total Current	10.4	6.9
	15.7	14.9	26.1	16.7		Long-Term Debt	14.8	27.1
	.0	.0	.0	.7		Deferred Taxes	.9	.0
	.4	7.6	6.0	26.5		All Other Non-Current	6.4	11.3
	52.0	72.9	57.5	48.5		Net Worth	67.5	54.7
	100.0	100.0	100.0	100.0		Total Liabilties & Net Worth	100.0	100.0
						INCOME DATA		
	100.0	100.0	100.0	100.0		Net Sales	100.0	100.0
						Gross Profit		
	80.6	83.0	85.8	82.0		Operating Expenses	93.7	98.6
	19.4	17.0	14.2	18.0		Operating Profit	6.3	1.4
	10.5	.2	-.2	5.1		All Other Expenses (net)	5.0	3.3
	8.8	16.8	14.4	12.9		Profit Before Taxes	1.3	-1.8
						RATIOS		
	5.0	19.3	6.0	6.4			8.7	6.8
	1.4	7.6	2.9	3.3		Current	4.4	4.4
	.9	2.5	1.9	1.9			2.6	2.8
	4.6	16.8	5.7	5.3			7.0	5.2
	1.2	7.2	2.4	2.9		Quick	4.1	3.2
	.3	2.3	1.5	1.6			2.1	2.3
0 UND	0 UND	9 UND	9 38.6	15 23.8			11 32.5	5 72.2
0 UND	9 39.6	45 8.2	49 7.5			Sales/Receivables	27 13.7	24 15.1
33 11.0	36 10.3	109 3.3	84 4.3				48 7.7	46 8.0
						Cost of Sales/Inventory		
						Cost of Sales/Payables		
	4.4	1.5	1.1	1.2			1.2	1.3
	6.9	2.3	3.2	3.5		Sales/Working Capital	2.0	2.4
	-77.2	5.3	7.6	5.7			5.6	3.3
			11.1	26.7			6.2	3.6
		(20)	5.5	(10) 6.2		EBIT/Interest	(20) 2.6	(16) .3
			2.4	.6			.9	-1.0
						Net Profit + Depr., Dep., Amort./Cur. Mat. L/T/D		
	.0	.0	.6	.9			.5	.7
	.2	1.0	1.1	1.1		Fixed/Worth	.7	1.0
	1.4	1.2	1.6	1.3			1.0	1.7
	.3	.2	.4	.3			.2	.2
	.9	.3	.7	.5		Debt/Worth	.3	.7
	4.3	.7	1.7	.9			1.0	1.6
	44.0	24.4	14.6	12.1		% Profit Before Taxes/Tangible Net Worth	7.9	4.2
	18.7	7.8	9.5	(11) 7.0			1.4	(27) -1.0
	6.1	.2	1.6	.1			-5.9	-6.9
	16.9	17.7	8.4	6.5		% Profit Before Taxes/Total Assets	4.7	3.2
	5.9	6.6	5.6	4.4			1.1	-.2
	4.0	.0	1.3	.8			-3.9	-3.0
	UND	UND	1.4	10.4			1.9	1.4
	46.2	.5	.6	.4		Sales/Net Fixed Assets	.5	.5
	.7	.3	.3	.3			.4	.3
	3.2	1.0	.7	.6			.8	1.1
	.9	.3	.4	.3		Sales/Total Assets	.3	.3
	.6	.2	.3	.2			.2	.2
			2.9				2.9	2.4
		(13)	6.1			% Depr., Dep., Amort./Sales	(15) 6.3	(12) 9.9
			15.5				13.3	24.3
						% Officers', Directors' Owners' Comp/Sales		
978M	30597M	36988M	382558M	682475M	324605M	Net Sales ($)	1087426M	297336M
902M	15042M	51418M	679068M	840240M	638213M	Total Assets ($)	1616264M	815213M

M = $ thousand   MM = $ million
See Pages 11 through 21 for Explanation of Ratios and Data

Comparative Historical Data | Current Data Sorted by Sales

				Type of Statement						
	23	37	53	Unqualified	5	5	4	12	13	14
		1		Reviewed						
		4	1	Compiled	1					
			3	Tax Returns	1	1	1			
	10	6	8	Other	3	1		2	1	1
	4/1/04-3/31/05	4/1/05-3/31/06	4/1/06-3/31/07			56 (4/1-9/30/06)			9 (10/1/06-3/31/07)	
	ALL	ALL	ALL		0-1MM	1-3MM	3-5MM	5-10MM	10-25MM	25MM & OVER
NUMBER OF STATEMENTS	33	48	65		10	7	5	14	14	15
	%	%	%	**ASSETS**	%	%	%	%	%	%
	34.6	31.6	21.2	Cash & Equivalents	21.7			20.4	23.8	19.4
	8.5	8.0	11.3	Trade Receivables (net)	17.4			11.1	11.5	12.0
	.8	.2	2.3	Inventory	.0			.2	.3	1.4
	6.1	6.9	3.4	All Other Current	.4			3.5	5.6	3.2
	50.0	46.7	38.2	Total Current	39.6			35.2	41.2	36.1
	38.9	44.2	53.9	Fixed Assets (net)	57.6			61.6	49.5	47.0
	.1	1.6	.3	Intangibles (net)	.0			.1	.7	.4
	10.9	7.5	7.6	All Other Non-Current	2.8			3.1	8.6	16.5
	100.0	100.0	100.0	Total	100.0			100.0	100.0	100.0
				LIABILITIES						
	.3	.7	1.8	Notes Payable-Short Term	.4			.4	3.2	.2
	1.5	2.0	1.4	Cur. Mat.-L.T.D.	.5			2.8	1.1	1.5
	2.9	4.8	4.5	Trade Payables	7.7			3.0	4.2	3.0
	.1	.1	.0	Income Taxes Payable	.0			.0	.0	.0
	5.5	9.0	4.1	All Other Current	2.4			4.5	4.4	4.5
	10.4	16.7	11.8	Total Current	11.1			10.7	12.9	9.1
	18.5	25.4	22.4	Long-Term Debt	29.4			26.6	14.5	23.5
	.0	.1	.1	Deferred Taxes	.0			.0	.6	.0
	15.8	8.7	11.5	All Other Non-Current	18.7			7.4	4.8	25.3
	55.3	49.1	54.3	Net Worth	40.8			55.3	67.2	42.1
	100.0	100.0	100.0	Total Liabilties & Net Worth	100.0			100.0	100.0	100.0
				INCOME DATA						
	100.0	100.0	100.0	Net Sales	100.0			100.0	100.0	100.0
				Gross Profit						
	90.7	88.1	84.2	Operating Expenses	72.2			81.1	85.8	91.3
	9.3	11.9	15.8	Operating Profit	27.8			18.9	14.2	8.7
	1.7	6.0	2.3	All Other Expenses (net)	10.1			1.4	1.1	1.2
	7.6	5.9	13.5	Profit Before Taxes	17.7			17.6	13.2	7.5
				RATIOS						
	8.9	7.9	8.1		34.0			6.0	11.5	4.1
	5.5	3.3	3.2	Current	3.9			2.4	3.8	3.0
	2.7	1.4	1.6		1.2			1.4	1.7	1.7
	7.5	5.2	8.1		34.0			5.7	10.7	4.1
	4.7	3.2	2.8	Quick	3.8			2.1	3.1	2.4
	1.7	1.3	1.4		.9			1.1	1.4	1.4
8	45.1	9 / 39.6	0 / 999.8		0 UND		18 / 20.2	1 / 332.9	8 / 47.7	
20	18.3	20 / 18.1	32 / 11.6	Sales/Receivables	0 UND		49 / 7.5	18 / 20.7	45 / 8.1	
59	6.2	53 / 6.9	69 / 5.3		46 / 8.0		124 / 2.9	55 / 6.7	57 / 6.4	
				Cost of Sales/Inventory						
				Cost of Sales/Payables						
	1.3	1.3	1.4		.8			1.4	1.0	2.1
	2.0	4.2	3.5	Sales/Working Capital	4.9			3.8	2.9	4.2
	4.9	14.4	6.9		NM			10.6	7.6	11.0
	14.5	6.0	14.2					11.6	11.2	48.3
(17)	3.5	(27) 2.3	(42) 6.2	EBIT/Interest	(11) 6.3		(10) 5.1	(10) 9.3		
	.9	.5	3.0					4.8	.6	3.0
				Net Profit + Depr., Dep., Amort./Cur. Mat. L/T/D						
	.0	.0	.2		.1			.6	.1	.0
	.8	1.0	1.0	Fixed/Worth	.9			1.2	.9	1.0
	1.1	1.7	1.3		1.4			1.6	1.1	1.6
	.2	.3	.3		.0			.4	.3	.5
	.5	.6	.6	Debt/Worth	.3			.9	.5	.7
	1.0	2.1	1.2		4.6			2.1	.7	1.5
	9.5	12.4	17.4	% Profit Before Taxes/Tangible				42.1	20.6	10.5
(29)	6.1	(43) 5.3	(63) 8.8	Net Worth			12.5	10.1	(14) 6.2	
	-.1	1.4	4.0					5.4	4.2	3.3
	7.2	6.8	8.2	% Profit Before Taxes/Total	9.1			16.8	8.8	6.2
	4.0	3.6	5.4	Assets	4.3			5.9	6.4	4.1
	-.1	.3	1.9		-1.4			2.4	2.6	.4
	UND	UND	42.7		UND			UND	UND	999.8
	1.6	1.1	.6	Sales/Net Fixed Assets	.4			.5	.6	1.1
	.4	.4	.3		.2			.3	.4	.6
	1.4	1.4	.9		.9			.6	1.2	1.1
	.6	.6	.4	Sales/Total Assets	.2			.4	.4	.6
	.3	.3	.3		.1			.2	.3	.3
	1.8	2.7	3.8							
(14)	4.6	(20) 5.8	(37) 9.6	% Depr., Dep., Amort./Sales						
	12.7	11.7	15.6							
				% Officers', Directors' Owners' Comp/Sales						
	533271M	2226776M	1458201M	Net Sales ($)	4958M	11860M	17658M	92481M	239387M	1091857M
	816342M	2252755M	2224883M	Total Assets ($)	18906M	27850M	66515M	278593M	558812M	1274207M

M = $ thousand   MM = $ million
See Pages 11 through 21 for Explanation of Ratios and Data

Current Data Sorted by Assets   Comparative Historical Data

1	2	6	12	5	3	Type of Statement	9	21
						Unqualified		
	1					Reviewed		
	1		1			Compiled		1
						Tax Returns		
	22 (4/1-9/30/06)		10 (10/1/06-3/31/07)			Other	6	1
							4/1/02- 3/31/03	4/1/03- 3/31/04
0-500M	500M-2MM	2-10MM	10-50MM	50-100MM	100-250MM		ALL	ALL
1	4	6	13	5	3	NUMBER OF STATEMENTS	15	23
%	%	%	%	%	%	**ASSETS**	%	%
			37.0			Cash & Equivalents	20.8	17.9
			3.8			Trade Receivables (net)	7.5	7.3
			.2			Inventory	.4	.3
			5.4			All Other Current	2.8	1.3
			46.4			Total Current	31.4	26.8
			47.0			Fixed Assets (net)	54.8	59.8
			.1			Intangibles (net)	.4	.1
			6.5			All Other Non-Current	13.6	13.3
			100.0			Total	100.0	100.0
						LIABILITIES		
			.0			Notes Payable-Short Term	.3	.3
			2.3			Cur. Mat.-L.T.D.	1.6	2.1
			1.9			Trade Payables	2.2	3.2
			2.5			Income Taxes Payable	.0	.0
			7.4			All Other Current	7.1	7.8
			14.2			Total Current	11.1	13.4
			31.2			Long-Term Debt	22.3	26.5
			.0			Deferred Taxes	.0	.0
			2.1			All Other Non-Current	1.0	3.9
			52.4			Net Worth	65.3	56.1
			100.0			Total Liabilities & Net Worth	100.0	100.0
						INCOME DATA		
			100.0			Net Sales	100.0	100.0
						Gross Profit		
			92.4			Operating Expenses	94.9	91.1
			7.6			Operating Profit	5.1	8.9
			-.4			All Other Expenses (net)	4.1	5.9
			8.1			Profit Before Taxes	1.0	3.1
						RATIOS		
			5.9				5.1	4.1
			3.7			Current	3.2	2.2
			2.4				1.5	1.3
			5.3				5.1	4.0
			3.6			Quick	2.1	2.0
			1.7				1.3	1.2
			0 UND				0 UND	14 25.8
			19 19.1			Sales/Receivables	22 16.9	37 9.9
			54 6.8				76 4.8	110 3.3
						Cost of Sales/Inventory		
						Cost of Sales/Payables		
			1.4				1.2	1.1
			3.0			Sales/Working Capital	3.5	3.7
			4.4				6.3	7.0
							2.7	3.7
						EBIT/Interest	(11) 1.4	(17) .9
							-2.0	-.8
						Net Profit + Depr., Dep., Amort./Cur. Mat. L/T/D		
			.0				.8	.8
			.9			Fixed/Worth	.9	1.1
			1.1				1.0	1.4
			.3				.3	.4
			.6			Debt/Worth	.4	.6
			.9				1.0	1.7
			11.2				4.2	9.1
			(12) 5.2			% Profit Before Taxes/Tangible Net Worth	.2	1.4
			1.6				-2.5	-2.6
			6.8				2.9	3.3
			4.0			% Profit Before Taxes/Total Assets	.1	.9
			1.1				-2.2	-1.6
			UND				.9	.8
			.8			Sales/Net Fixed Assets	.5	.5
			.5				.2	.2
			1.0				.6	.5
			.5			Sales/Total Assets	.2	.3
			.3				.2	.1
								1.8
						% Depr., Dep., Amort./Sales	(10)	6.8
								15.5
						% Officers', Directors' Owners' Comp/Sales		
814M	2512M	37802M	193459M	106566M	71364M	Net Sales ($)	146682M	169587M
253M	4842M	37854M	307580M	340643M	477908M	Total Assets ($)	492981M	722659M

M = $ thousand MM = $ million
See Pages 11 through 21 for Explanation of Ratios and Data

Comparative Historical Data | Current Data Sorted by Sales

			Type of Statement						
22	16	29	Unqualified	3	1	3	4	15	3
			Reviewed						
1	1	1	Compiled	1					
			Tax Returns						
3	3	2	Other	1				1	
4/1/04-3/31/05	4/1/05-3/31/06	4/1/06-3/31/07			22 (4/1-9/30/06)			10 (10/1/06-3/31/07)	
ALL	ALL	ALL		0-1MM	1-3MM	3-5MM	5-10MM	10-25MM	25MM & OVER
26	20	32	**NUMBER OF STATEMENTS**	5	1	3	4	16	3
%	%	%	**ASSETS**	%	%	%	%	%	%
30.5	37.1	36.0	Cash & Equivalents					23.8	
4.8	5.7	3.8	Trade Receivables (net)					5.0	
1.2	1.2	.4	Inventory					.2	
1.4	3.4	3.4	All Other Current					4.9	
37.9	47.5	43.6	Total Current					33.9	
52.5	48.0	48.4	Fixed Assets (net)					55.0	
.1	.1	1.2	Intangibles (net)					.2	
9.5	4.4	6.8	All Other Non-Current					10.8	
100.0	100.0	100.0	Total					100.0	
			LIABILITIES						
1.9	.2	2.7	Notes Payable-Short Term					.2	
1.2	1.6	3.0	Cur. Mat.-L.T.D.					3.1	
1.5	4.0	2.7	Trade Payables					4.1	
.0	.0	1.0	Income Taxes Payable					2.1	
7.5	9.5	6.7	All Other Current					3.8	
12.1	15.3	16.1	Total Current					13.2	
17.6	20.8	27.1	Long-Term Debt					21.4	
.0	.0	.0	Deferred Taxes					.0	
3.5	10.2	2.6	All Other Non-Current					2.6	
66.9	53.7	54.2	Net Worth					62.8	
100.0	100.0	100.0	Total Liabilities & Net Worth					100.0	
			INCOME DATA						
100.0	100.0	100.0	Net Sales					100.0	
			Gross Profit						
85.2	81.4	88.7	Operating Expenses					87.6	
14.8	18.6	11.3	Operating Profit					12.4	
3.9	6.1	-.5	All Other Expenses (net)					-.6	
10.9	12.6	11.8	Profit Before Taxes					13.0	
			RATIOS						
8.7	9.3	6.1						5.3	
5.4	5.3	3.5	Current					3.2	
1.7	1.8	1.6						1.5	
7.8	8.0	5.5						4.9	
3.8	4.8	3.2	Quick					2.8	
1.5	1.6	1.4						1.3	
8 45.1	4 89.6	0 UND						8 44.2	
23 16.0	17 21.7	14 25.5	Sales/Receivables					19 19.5	
58 6.3	38 9.5	44 8.3						44 8.3	
			Cost of Sales/Inventory						
			Cost of Sales/Payables						
1.0	.9	1.4						1.6	
2.3	1.3	2.5	Sales/Working Capital					3.3	
4.6	3.9	7.3						7.3	
5.5	7.7	7.4						20.3	
(20) 2.0	(13) 2.5	(23) 3.4	EBIT/Interest					(13) 5.1	
1.0	.6	1.8						3.0	
			Net Profit + Depr., Dep., Amort./Cur. Mat. L/T/D						
.0	.1	.1						.4	
.9	.9	.9	Fixed/Worth					.9	
1.4	1.7	1.3						1.2	
.2	.1	.3						.3	
.4	.5	.6	Debt/Worth					.5	
1.0	1.4	1.2						1.0	
8.0	11.1	11.9	% Profit Before Taxes/Tangible Net Worth					9.9	
3.3	(18) 2.4	(30) 6.3						6.3	
.0	-.4	2.0						2.7	
5.0	10.1	6.2	% Profit Before Taxes/Total Assets					5.2	
2.0	2.6	3.8						4.0	
.0	-.2	1.0						1.4	
UND	485.7	UND	Sales/Net Fixed Assets					5.9	
.4	.9	.8						.5	
.3	.3	.4						.3	
.8	1.0	.8	Sales/Total Assets					.8	
.3	.4	.4						.4	
.2	.2	.2						.2	
5.7	5.9	4.5	% Depr., Dep., Amort./Sales					4.5	
(12) 12.0	(10) 9.7	(20) 7.7						(11) 7.1	
16.9	20.3	14.0						14.7	
			% Officers', Directors' Owners' Comp/Sales						
552236M	948898M	412517M	Net Sales ($)	2914M	1251M	11264M	25008M	262125M	109955M
1512616M	876030M	1169080M	Total Assets ($)	7829M	944M	29391M	61386M	826023M	243507M

M = $ thousand   MM = $ million
See Pages 11 through 21 for Explanation of Ratios and Data

	Current Data Sorted by Assets						Comparative Historical Data	
Type of Statement							15	27
Unqualified								
Reviewed								
Compiled								
Tax Returns								
Other	1	1	8	6	6			
		21 (4/1-9/30/06)		11 (10/1/06-3/31/07)			7 4/1/02- 3/31/03 ALL	5 4/1/03- 3/31/04 ALL
			3	5	2			
	0-500M	500M-2MM	2-10MM	10-50MM	50-100MM	100-250MM		
		1	4	13	8	6		
NUMBER OF STATEMENTS							22	32
	%	%	%	%	%	%	%	%
ASSETS								
Cash & Equivalents				21.3			23.3	20.7
Trade Receivables (net)				14.6			8.9	1.8
Inventory				1.3			.5	.8
All Other Current				2.1			4.5	4.2
Total Current				39.3			37.2	27.5
Fixed Assets (net)				52.3			53.0	62.7
Intangibles (net)				.0			.5	.4
All Other Non-Current				8.4			9.3	9.5
Total				100.0			100.0	100.0
LIABILITIES								
Notes Payable-Short Term				.4			.2	1.0
Cur. Mat.-L.T.D.				3.0			1.1	1.2
Trade Payables				3.7			4.1	2.9
Income Taxes Payable				.0			.0	.0
All Other Current				6.9			9.7	10.7
Total Current				14.0			15.1	15.8
Long-Term Debt				21.8			8.9	13.5
Deferred Taxes				3.4			.0	.0
All Other Non-Current				8.0			1.7	2.2
Net Worth				52.9			74.3	68.4
Total Liabilties & Net Worth				100.0			100.0	100.0
INCOME DATA								
Net Sales				100.0			100.0	100.0
Gross Profit								
Operating Expenses				84.2			95.2	75.5
Operating Profit				15.8			4.8	24.5
All Other Expenses (net)				-.8			-1.2	1.0
Profit Before Taxes				16.6			6.0	23.6
RATIOS								
Current				6.3			5.1	3.1
				2.3			3.3	1.8
				1.6			1.7	.9
Quick				6.2			4.2	2.2
				1.9			3.0	1.5
				1.5			1.4	.7
Sales/Receivables		1	547.6				3 144.2	0 999.8
		35	10.5				20 18.1	1 300.4
		96	3.8				51 7.2	24 15.0
Cost of Sales/Inventory								
Cost of Sales/Payables								
Sales/Working Capital				1.8			1.7	4.0
				4.2			2.6	13.5
				15.1			5.3	-76.5
EBIT/Interest							16.3	46.8
							(12) 4.5	(18) 8.6
							1.5	2.1
Net Profit + Depr., Dep., Amort./Cur. Mat. L/T/D								
Fixed/Worth				.7			.6	.8
				1.1			.8	1.0
				1.3			1.0	1.3
Debt/Worth				.5			.1	.2
				.8			.3	.4
				1.3			.7	1.0
% Profit Before Taxes/Tangible Net Worth				113.3			14.2	133.2
			(12)	10.5			1.0	43.5
				4.1			-2.3	1.3
% Profit Before Taxes/Total Assets				50.2			6.5	90.5
				6.1			.7	26.0
				2.2			-2.0	.9
Sales/Net Fixed Assets				7.3			3.9	4.7
				1.9			.9	2.2
				.7			.6	.5
Sales/Total Assets				2.0			1.2	2.4
				1.2			.5	.9
				.4			.3	.4
% Depr., Dep., Amort./Sales							3.4	3.5
							(15) 5.4	(25) 5.2
							9.5	6.7
% Officers', Directors' Owners' Comp/Sales								
Net Sales ($)		1655M	7082M	442043M	383301M	316813M	581874M	1042194M
Total Assets ($)		1836M	21172M	368540M	535381M	916501M	943799M	1116997M

© RMA 2007

M = $ thousand   MM = $ million
See Pages 11 through 21 for Explanation of Ratios and Data

Comparative Historical Data				Current Data Sorted by Sales					

				Type of Statement						
25	22	22		Unqualified	1	1		3	5	12
1	2			Reviewed						
				Compiled						
				Tax Returns						
4	8	10		Other	2	1	1	2		4
4/1/04-	4/1/05-	4/1/06-				21 (4/1-9/30/06)		11 (10/1/06-3/31/07)		
3/31/05	3/31/06	3/31/07			0-1MM	1-3MM	3-5MM	5-10MM	10-25MM	25MM & OVER
ALL	ALL	ALL								
30	32	32		NUMBER OF STATEMENTS	3	2	1	3	7	16
%	%	%		ASSETS	%	%	%	%	%	%
25.8	27.5	24.0		Cash & Equivalents						21.8
3.4	4.1	10.7		Trade Receivables (net)						14.6
1.0	.5	1.1		Inventory						2.0
6.1	2.1	5.2		All Other Current						6.7
36.2	34.2	41.0		Total Current						45.2
60.8	61.1	53.9		Fixed Assets (net)						48.1
.4	.6	.0		Intangibles (net)						.0
2.7	4.1	5.0		All Other Non-Current						6.7
100.0	100.0	100.0		Total						100.0
				LIABILITIES						
1.2	.5	1.8		Notes Payable-Short Term						.3
2.6	2.7	2.6		Cur. Mat.-L.T.D.						2.8
4.4	2.2	4.4		Trade Payables						6.7
.0	.0	.9		Income Taxes Payable						.0
8.9	6.3	4.6		All Other Current						7.3
17.0	11.6	14.2		Total Current						17.0
19.0	31.5	24.8		Long-Term Debt						18.0
.0	.0	1.4		Deferred Taxes						2.7
3.7	1.0	6.1		All Other Non-Current						10.4
60.3	56.0	53.5		Net Worth						51.9
100.0	100.0	100.0		Total Liabilities & Net Worth						100.0
				INCOME DATA						
100.0	100.0	100.0		Net Sales						100.0
				Gross Profit						
75.3	82.0	80.2		Operating Expenses						82.2
24.7	18.0	19.8		Operating Profit						17.8
2.5	1.7	.2		All Other Expenses (net)						1.8
22.2	16.2	19.6		Profit Before Taxes						16.0
				RATIOS						
5.3	6.3	6.6								6.4
1.8	2.5	3.8		Current						2.6
.7	1.1	1.8								1.6
3.7	4.3	5.8								5.7
1.5	2.4	2.4		Quick						2.1
.6	1.0	1.7								1.2
0 844.3	1 697.7	10 38.2							1 699.1	
1 269.8	27 13.3	39 9.5		Sales/Receivables					41 8.9	
14 26.0	45 8.2	77 4.7							81 4.5	
				Cost of Sales/Inventory						
				Cost of Sales/Payables						
2.8	1.3	1.5								1.9
12.1	3.3	2.2		Sales/Working Capital						3.7
-29.0	32.1	5.5								17.1
35.5	16.8	12.5								15.2
(19) 19.6	(25) 4.6	(23) 5.5		EBIT/Interest					(10) 5.1	
7.0	2.0	2.6								3.0
				Net Profit + Depr., Dep., Amort./Cur. Mat. L/T/D						
.7	.8	.6								.2
1.0	1.2	1.1		Fixed/Worth						1.1
1.6	1.7	1.4								1.4
.3	.3	.5								.5
.5	1.0	.8		Debt/Worth						.8
1.5	1.5	1.3								1.6
116.7	36.0	23.5		% Profit Before Taxes/Tangible						114.1
45.9	(31) 7.3	(31) 9.0		Net Worth						15.0
2.8	1.5	3.9								2.5
68.9	13.6	10.4		% Profit Before Taxes/Total						29.8
20.4	4.1	4.5		Assets						5.6
1.8	1.0	2.1								1.8
4.6	3.1	4.5								111.6
1.8	.6	1.0		Sales/Net Fixed Assets						2.2
.7	.4	.3								1.0
2.5	1.3	1.3								1.7
1.5	.5	.5		Sales/Total Assets						1.2
.4	.3	.2								.7
3.3	3.4	4.6								4.1
(19) 4.8	(20) 6.6	(21) 5.7		% Depr., Dep., Amort./Sales					(11) 5.0	
5.4	10.6	16.7								6.7
				% Officers', Directors' Owners' Comp/Sales						
1824463M	929001M	1150894M		Net Sales ($)	2363M	3411M	4719M	25234M	116072M	999095M
1798915M	1528104M	1843430M		Total Assets ($)	18157M	15181M	3015M	99460M	484355M	1223262M

© RMA 2007

M = $ thousand   MM = $ million

See Pages 11 through 21 for Explanation of Ratios and Data

Current Data Sorted by Assets   Comparative Historical Data

Type of Statement

						Type of Statement		
		4	2	4	7		6	17
						Unqualified		
						Reviewed		
						Compiled		
						Tax Returns		
						Other		
	1	4	7	3	5		4	6
0-500M	18 (4/1-9/30/06) 500M-2MM	2-10MM	19 (10/1/06-3/31/07) 10-50MM	50-100MM	100-250MM		4/1/02-3/31/03 ALL	4/1/03-3/31/04 ALL
	1	8	9	7	12	**NUMBER OF STATEMENTS**	10	23

0-500M %	500M-2MM %	2-10MM %	10-50MM %	50-100MM %	100-250MM %		4/1/02-3/31/03 %	4/1/03-3/31/04 %
						ASSETS		
					18.1	Cash & Equivalents	25.3	15.0
					3.0	Trade Receivables (net)	1.5	9.6
					.3	Inventory	.8	2.8
					3.7	All Other Current	.7	4.7
					25.1	Total Current	28.4	32.1
					72.4	Fixed Assets (net)	69.6	60.7
					.5	Intangibles (net)	.3	1.3
					2.0	All Other Non-Current	1.7	5.9
					100.0	Total	100.0	100.0
						LIABILITIES		
					.0	Notes Payable-Short Term	1.0	4.8
					1.8	Cur. Mat.-L.T.D.	4.8	5.9
					1.0	Trade Payables	1.8	5.7
					.0	Income Taxes Payable	.0	.0
					13.4	All Other Current	9.4	8.2
					16.2	Total Current	17.0	24.5
					18.2	Long-Term Debt	20.3	21.9
					.0	Deferred Taxes	.0	.1
					.1	All Other Non-Current	1.3	1.9
					65.5	Net Worth	61.3	51.5
					100.0	Total Liabilties & Net Worth	100.0	100.0
						INCOME DATA		
					100.0	Net Sales	100.0	100.0
						Gross Profit		
					64.8	Operating Expenses	68.5	77.8
					35.2	Operating Profit	31.5	22.2
					1.0	All Other Expenses (net)	4.4	2.5
					34.1	Profit Before Taxes	27.1	19.6
						RATIOS		
					2.6		3.4	2.0
					1.5	Current	1.8	1.3
					.9		.9	1.0
					2.1		3.0	1.8
					1.3	Quick	1.8	.9
					.9		.7	.7
					1 438.6		0 UND	4 83.7
					4 94.9	Sales/Receivables	1 293.2	11 33.7
					8 48.0		19 19.2	29 12.5
						Cost of Sales/Inventory		
						Cost of Sales/Payables		
					8.1		4.9	5.0
					21.3	Sales/Working Capital	14.4	24.9
					-86.9		-79.2	-142.7
					685.9			24.8
					46.1	EBIT/Interest	(22)	5.9
					20.9			1.1
						Net Profit + Depr., Dep., Amort./Cur. Mat. L/T/D		
					1.0		.8	.8
					1.1	Fixed/Worth	1.4	1.1
					1.6		1.6	1.7
					.2		.3	.4
					.4	Debt/Worth	.6	1.0
					1.1		1.4	2.3
					175.8	% Profit Before Taxes/Tangible Net Worth	181.6	156.3
					95.7		78.1	28.4
					22.5		12.1	.2
					95.4	% Profit Before Taxes/Total Assets	98.3	59.9
					50.6		40.7	8.0
					18.3		5.1	.1
					3.0		3.0	5.3
					2.3	Sales/Net Fixed Assets	1.8	1.8
					1.3		.7	.9
					1.9		1.9	2.2
					1.7	Sales/Total Assets	1.5	1.2
					1.1		.6	.8
						% Depr., Dep., Amort./Sales		2.3
							(17) 4.8	4.8
								7.0
						% Officers', Directors' Owners' Comp/Sales		
	239M	163040M	456276M	1081766M	3452690M	Net Sales ($)	702798M	2253305M
	1669M	43636M	250228M	591185M	2054631M	Total Assets ($)	573640M	1877385M

© RMA 2007   M = $ thousand   MM = $ million
See Pages 11 through 21 for Explanation of Ratios and Data

(Left columns 0-500M, 500M-2MM, 2-10MM, 10-50MM, 50-100MM marked "DATA NOT AVAILABLE")

Comparative Historical Data   ## Current Data Sorted by Sales

			Type of Statement						
11	18	17	Unqualified				2	1	14
	1		Reviewed						
			Compiled						
			Tax Returns						
			Other						
6 4/1/04- 3/31/05 ALL	8 4/1/05- 3/31/06 ALL	20 4/1/06- 3/31/07 ALL		1 0-1MM	1 18 (4/1-9/30/06) 1-3MM	 3-5MM	2 19 (10/1/06-3/31/07) 5-10MM	4 10-25MM	12 25MM & OVER
17	27	37	NUMBER OF STATEMENTS	1	1		4	5	26
%	%	%	ASSETS	%	%	%	%	%	%
16.2	24.4	19.7	Cash & Equivalents	D					20.5
4.2	2.9	4.0	Trade Receivables (net)	A					4.2
1.7	.3	1.2	Inventory	T					1.2
2.6	3.1	3.0	All Other Current	A					3.6
24.7	30.7	28.0	Total Current						29.5
70.3	65.8	69.4	Fixed Assets (net)	N					68.5
3.1	1.4	.9	Intangibles (net)	O					.7
1.9	2.1	1.7	All Other Non-Current	T					1.3
100.0	100.0	100.0	Total						100.0
			LIABILITIES	A					
2.2	.7	1.0	Notes Payable-Short Term	V					1.3
4.4	3.0	1.6	Cur. Mat.-L.T.D.	A					1.9
2.7	2.0	2.7	Trade Payables	I					2.8
.0	.0	.0	Income Taxes Payable	L					.0
7.6	16.9	12.6	All Other Current	A					15.6
16.9	22.6	18.0	Total Current	B					21.6
29.1	23.4	22.1	Long-Term Debt	L					21.6
.0	.0	.0	Deferred Taxes	E					.0
2.3	1.0	2.6	All Other Non-Current						.1
51.6	52.9	57.2	Net Worth						56.8
100.0	100.0	100.0	Total Liabilties & Net Worth						100.0
			INCOME DATA						
100.0	100.0	100.0	Net Sales						100.0
			Gross Profit						
72.0	61.3	70.0	Operating Expenses						64.5
28.0	38.7	30.0	Operating Profit						35.5
2.3	2.1	3.8	All Other Expenses (net)						3.2
25.8	36.7	26.2	Profit Before Taxes						32.3
			RATIOS						
1.7	2.3	2.8							2.7
1.4	1.6	1.7	Current						1.6
1.0	.7	.9							.9
1.4	2.3	2.4							2.4
1.2	1.0	1.4	Quick						1.3
.8	.6	.9							.7
1 310.6	0 999.8	1 526.3						1	658.5
4 97.3	1 650.8	4 88.2	Sales/Receivables					3	110.2
19 19.0	5 67.1	9 41.0						6	57.5
			Cost of Sales/Inventory						
			Cost of Sales/Payables						
9.7	7.6	7.1							8.4
25.5	18.5	20.9	Sales/Working Capital						22.1
NM	-52.9	-120.6							-67.8
42.8	136.8	388.3							694.7
(15) 8.8	(21) 32.4	(29) 39.6	EBIT/Interest					(23)	43.9
3.9	12.0	7.7							12.5
			Net Profit + Depr., Dep., Amort./Cur. Mat. L/T/D						
1.1	.8	.9							.9
1.6	1.2	1.1	Fixed/Worth						1.1
2.5	2.6	1.7							1.6
.6	.1	.2							.2
1.1	.6	.4	Debt/Worth						.5
2.1	2.6	1.5							1.0
144.1	187.8	159.8	% Profit Before Taxes/Tangible						206.8
73.2 (25)	98.8 (35)	86.8	Net Worth					(25)	97.0
17.1	68.5	16.7							24.1
73.6	94.9	97.6	% Profit Before Taxes/Total						102.6
22.8	61.8	39.9	Assets						50.6
6.8	26.1	5.5							16.1
2.7	5.1	4.2							6.5
1.9	2.2	2.3	Sales/Net Fixed Assets						2.4
1.1	1.4	1.3							1.4
2.2	2.1	2.5							2.4
1.5	1.6	1.8	Sales/Total Assets						1.8
.9	1.0	.9							1.1
2.7	4.0	2.6							2.6
(13) 5.2	(16) 5.6	(27) 5.4	% Depr., Dep., Amort./Sales					(18)	5.5
6.3	7.8	6.5							6.4
			% Officers', Directors' Owners' Comp/Sales						
2409737M	3878651M	5154011M	Net Sales ($)	239M	2393M		24829M	79907M	5046643M
1805513M	2381788M	2941349M	Total Assets ($)	1669M	2872M		99429M	62564M	2774815M

M = $ thousand   MM = $ million
See Pages 11 through 21 for Explanation of Ratios and Data

Current Data Sorted by Assets   Comparative Historical Data

	0-500M	500M-2MM	2-10MM	10-50MM	50-100MM	100-250MM		4/1/02-3/31/03 ALL	4/1/03-3/31/04 ALL
Type of Statement		190 (4/1-9/30/06)		56 (10/1/06-3/31/07)					
Unqualified	2	13	40	68	36	35		194	157
Reviewed	1	2	2					3	2
Compiled			2	2	1			5	12
Tax Returns	2							1	2
Other		7	13	15	3	3		47	38
NUMBER OF STATEMENTS	5	22	57	84	40	38		250	211
ASSETS	%	%	%	%	%	%		%	%
Cash & Equivalents		45.6	28.3	27.7	24.8	22.3		25.6	30.7
Trade Receivables (net)		15.5	12.4	6.7	6.8	7.4		6.0	8.5
Inventory		.8	2.6	.6	.3	1.9		.6	.9
All Other Current		10.2	6.0	4.6	4.9	3.6		5.6	7.3
Total Current		72.0	49.3	39.5	36.8	35.2		37.8	47.3
Fixed Assets (net)		20.1	43.7	53.7	53.2	53.2		48.3	43.3
Intangibles (net)		.0	.0	.8	.3	.3		.4	.4
All Other Non-Current		7.8	7.0	5.9	9.7	11.4		13.5	8.9
Total		100.0	100.0	100.0	100.0	100.0		100.0	100.0
LIABILITIES									
Notes Payable-Short Term		12.7	2.4	.5	.2	2.2		2.1	2.4
Cur. Mat.-L.T.D.		1.1	1.8	2.1	1.5	1.9		1.0	1.6
Trade Payables		12.2	8.9	2.9	2.8	3.0		3.6	4.1
Income Taxes Payable		.8	.8	.5	.1	.6		.1	.0
All Other Current		9.5	5.9	8.6	6.8	4.5		6.0	8.3
Total Current		36.3	19.7	14.6	11.4	12.1		12.7	16.4
Long-Term Debt		5.5	21.6	22.6	21.8	32.5		20.0	18.9
Deferred Taxes		.0	.0	.0	.0	.0		.1	.1
All Other Non-Current		4.8	4.1	4.7	4.6	2.5		4.0	5.9
Net Worth		53.4	54.6	58.2	62.2	52.8		63.1	58.8
Total Liabilities & Net Worth		100.0	100.0	100.0	100.0	100.0		100.0	100.0
INCOME DATA									
Net Sales		100.0	100.0	100.0	100.0	100.0		100.0	100.0
Gross Profit									
Operating Expenses		95.1	88.6	87.6	88.6	87.5		91.7	89.7
Operating Profit		4.9	11.4	12.4	11.4	12.5		8.3	10.3
All Other Expenses (net)		-.4	1.9	2.2	2.0	1.8		4.0	3.4
Profit Before Taxes		5.3	9.5	10.2	9.4	10.7		4.3	6.8
RATIOS									
Current		7.8	6.4	7.7	7.2	5.0		8.0	8.2
		2.5	2.9	3.9	4.2	2.8		3.8	4.0
		1.6	1.5	1.6	2.3	1.9		1.7	1.6
Quick		6.1	5.5	6.4	6.2	4.8		6.0	7.3
		2.5	2.2	3.0	3.5	2.7		2.9 (210)	3.1
		1.4	1.3	1.3	1.8	1.6		1.3	1.3
Sales/Receivables		0 UND	1 279.9	4 90.3	14 25.8	9 39.8		4 84.3	0 972.3
		6 59.7	29 12.5	23 16.1	34 10.9	21 17.4		21 17.6	20 18.1
		41 9.0	45 8.0	45 8.1	50 7.3	55 6.6		41 8.8	52 7.0
Cost of Sales/Inventory									
Cost of Sales/Payables									
Sales/Working Capital		2.2	1.5	1.3	1.3	2.0		1.2	1.1
		6.4	4.3	2.5	1.9	3.4		2.6	2.4
		25.0	9.5	7.5	6.6	5.8		7.9	8.8
EBIT/Interest			7.6	11.1	7.3	12.6		5.7	7.1
			(38) 3.0	(59) 4.0	(29) 4.6	(32) 5.8		(177) 2.1	(115) 2.7
			1.2	1.7	1.6	1.5		-.1	.8
Net Profit + Depr., Dep., Amort./Cur. Mat. L/T/D									
Fixed/Worth		.0	.1	.5	.7	.7		.4	.0
		.1	.7	1.0	.9	1.1		.8	.8
		.6	1.3	1.3	1.2	1.7		1.1	1.2
Debt/Worth		.2	.3	.2	.2	.3		.2	.3
		.7	.7	.5	.5	.8		.5	.6
		1.3	2.2	1.2	1.1	2.2		.9	1.3
% Profit Before Taxes/Tangible Net Worth		23.4	22.8	13.4	11.1	15.4		6.4	11.2
		(21) 9.1	7.8	(81) 6.3	5.1	(36) 7.5		(246) 2.0	(206) 2.8
		-6.2	.6	.2	.4	2.8		-1.9	-.9
% Profit Before Taxes/Total Assets		15.1	8.9	7.3	5.4	8.0		3.8	5.7
		4.1	3.0	3.6	2.8	3.8		1.1	1.7
		-8.3	.4	.5	.3	1.4		-1.3	-.6
Sales/Net Fixed Assets		UND	91.5	2.8	1.2	2.0		11.9	UND
		525.5	2.8	.8	.5	.8		.6	1.0
		5.3	.5	.3	.3	.4		.3	.3
Sales/Total Assets		4.0	2.5	1.0	.6	.8		.9	1.4
		2.2	.6	.4	.3	.5		.4	.5
		1.1	.3	.2	.2	.3		.2	.2
% Depr., Dep., Amort./Sales			1.3	3.8	2.7	3.0		2.3	1.8
			(34) 4.2	(56) 7.5	(28) 7.1	(21) 7.3		(139) 6.1	(92) 5.6
			13.1	15.9	13.1	9.4		10.7	11.5
% Officers', Directors' Owners' Comp/Sales								3.1	1.2
						(24)		7.5	(21) 9.3
								19.5	22.2
Net Sales ($)	2355M	87010M	423874M	1941789M	2023068M	4602763M		6635311M	7072326M
Total Assets ($)	1602M	27812M	283072M	2160119M	2946665M	6193572M		11474737M	8741520M

© RMA 2007

M = $ thousand   MM = $ million

See Pages 11 through 21 for Explanation of Ratios and Data

Comparative Historical Data				Current Data Sorted by Sales					

			Type of Statement						
197	164	194	Unqualified	14	22	17	25	50	66
2	3	5	Reviewed	1	2	1		1	
1	4	4	Compiled			2	1	1	
1	1	2	Tax Returns	2					
41	42	41	Other	3	8	4	7	12	7
4/1/04-	4/1/05-	4/1/06-			190 (4/1-9/30/06)			56 (10/1/06-3/31/07)	
3/31/05	3/31/06	3/31/07		0-1MM	1-3MM	3-5MM	5-10MM	10-25MM	25MM & OVER
ALL	ALL	ALL							
241	214	246	NUMBER OF STATEMENTS	20	32	24	33	64	73
%	%	%	ASSETS	%	%	%	%	%	%
31.8	29.8	28.3	Cash & Equivalents	32.4	25.0	22.8	21.8	29.2	32.4
8.0	10.1	9.0	Trade Receivables (net)	4.9	3.5	8.0	12.1	10.0	10.7
.5	1.0	1.2	Inventory	.1	1.0	.2	.6	3.4	.3
5.4	5.4	5.3	All Other Current	6.2	3.3	4.9	9.0	3.4	6.1
45.8	46.2	43.8	Total Current	43.6	32.8	35.9	43.6	46.1	49.4
46.0	46.2	47.8	Fixed Assets (net)	44.8	62.6	56.7	45.2	45.1	42.7
.6	.7	.4	Intangibles (net)	.0	.3	.8	.5	.4	.3
7.6	6.9	8.0	All Other Non-Current	11.5	4.3	6.6	10.7	8.4	7.6
100.0	100.0	100.0	Total	100.0	100.0	100.0	100.0	100.0	100.0
			LIABILITIES						
1.2	1.9	2.3	Notes Payable-Short Term	1.7	1.7	.1	.7	6.9	.3
1.6	1.9	1.8	Cur. Mat.-L.T.D.	1.5	1.9	1.5	2.0	1.8	1.7
3.6	5.1	5.2	Trade Payables	3.3	2.0	3.1	8.8	6.6	5.0
.3	.4	.5	Income Taxes Payable	.2	.0	.0	.5	.7	.9
7.1	6.6	7.1	All Other Current	4.0	3.0	3.4	7.4	7.3	10.6
13.9	16.0	16.9	Total Current	10.6	8.8	8.1	19.3	23.3	18.5
20.7	19.8	21.8	Long-Term Debt	19.3	28.1	18.0	20.3	20.2	22.9
.0	.0	.0	Deferred Taxes	.0	.0	.0	.0	.0	.0
4.0	4.4	4.5	All Other Non-Current	10.6	1.3	8.6	1.4	2.9	5.6
61.4	59.8	56.0	Net Worth	59.5	61.8	65.4	59.0	53.6	53.0
100.0	100.0	100.0	Total Liabilities & Net Worth	100.0	100.0	100.0	100.0	100.0	100.0
			INCOME DATA						
100.0	100.0	100.0	Net Sales	100.0	100.0	100.0	100.0	100.0	100.0
			Gross Profit						
89.2	88.2	88.7	Operating Expenses	81.9	81.4	91.3	92.5	90.9	89.3
10.8	11.8	11.3	Operating Profit	18.1	18.6	8.7	7.5	9.1	10.7
3.4	4.0	1.8	All Other Expenses (net)	3.5	3.7	2.1	.2	.8	1.8
7.5	7.8	9.5	Profit Before Taxes	14.6	14.8	6.6	7.3	8.2	8.9
			RATIOS						
7.8	7.0	7.1		11.5	7.6	10.3	5.9	6.9	5.9
4.1	3.5	3.3	Current	3.7	4.1	5.4	2.4	3.1	3.2
1.9	1.7	1.7		2.0	1.7	2.3	1.4	1.6	1.9
7.6	6.4	6.1		10.5	7.2	9.7	4.7	5.7	5.3
3.5	3.0	2.7	Quick	3.5	3.5	4.9	1.8	2.7	2.8
1.7	1.3	1.4		1.7	1.3	1.6	1.1	1.3	1.6
2 149.7	5 74.9	4 82.6		0 UND	0 UND	11 33.5	5 72.4	6 62.9	9 39.9
23 16.0	27 13.7	25 14.8	Sales/Receivables	10 35.1	10 38.3	30 12.2	39 9.3	22 16.5	28 13.1
48 7.6	54 6.8	47 7.7		42 8.7	43 8.5	52 7.1	49 7.5	43 8.4	50 7.3
			Cost of Sales/Inventory						
			Cost of Sales/Payables						
1.3	1.3	1.4		.9	.9	.8	1.4	1.5	1.9
2.6	2.7	3.2	Sales/Working Capital	3.1	2.6	1.7	5.9	3.4	3.2
7.5	8.1	7.8		8.6	8.8	4.2	12.2	8.4	6.2
10.8	9.7	8.4		5.0	17.5	12.0	8.9	8.0	16.5
(161) 3.5	(138) 3.7	(168) 4.0	EBIT/Interest	(11) 3.1	(22) 2.4	(17) 4.1	(21) 2.6	(40) 3.9	(57) 5.5
1.0	1.1	1.5		.7	.0	.2	1.1	1.6	2.1
			Net Profit + Depr., Dep., Amort./Cur. Mat. L/T/D						
.0	.0	.2		.0	.7	.6	.3	.0	.0
.9	.9	.9	Fixed/Worth	.8	1.1	.8	.9	.9	1.0
1.3	1.2	1.3		1.1	2.1	1.5	1.3	1.1	1.3
.2	.2	.2		.2	.2	.2	.3	.2	.3
.5	.5	.6	Debt/Worth	.7	.6	.4	.6	.5	.7
1.1	1.3	1.4		1.7	1.6	1.1	1.4	1.4	1.5
13.0	10.6	15.1		21.5	14.7	8.8	16.3	14.6	18.6
(235) 4.1	(207) 4.0	(240) 6.8	% Profit Before Taxes/Tangible Net Worth	4.6	7.2	3.4	6.7	(62) 4.4	(69) 10.4
-.1	-.8	.7		-3.0	-.4	-2.0	.0	.2	2.9
7.4	6.8	7.8		12.6	9.0	6.2	7.4	7.5	9.0
2.5	2.5	3.3	% Profit Before Taxes/Total Assets	3.1	3.4	2.3	2.5	2.6	5.3
-.2	-.8	.3		-1.7	-.1	-1.0	.0	.0	1.9
525.1	UND	19.0		UND	1.5	4.7	26.3	44.2	UND
.9	.9	1.0	Sales/Net Fixed Assets	1.3	.5	.4	2.8	1.2	1.3
.4	.4	.4		.2	.2	.3	.4	.4	.6
1.2	1.2	1.4		1.3	.8	.6	3.0	1.4	1.5
.5	.5	.5	Sales/Total Assets	.3	.4	.3	.6	.5	.7
.2	.3	.3		.1	.1	.2	.2	.3	.4
3.3	3.3	1.8		1.5	3.2	4.3	.9	1.5	1.8
(105) 7.8	(106) 8.2	(151) 5.9	% Depr., Dep., Amort./Sales	(13) 11.6	(22) 7.5	(20) 7.7	(21) 7.6	(38) 7.0	(37) 3.6
17.2	16.4	12.6		19.7	19.6	16.7	12.1	12.8	7.5
2.4	5.8	3.5							2.8
(20) 6.8	(19) 12.7	(28) 14.9	% Officers', Directors' Owners' Comp/Sales					(12) 14.9	
18.8	16.6	31.5							35.6
5993637M	8387098M	9080859M	Net Sales ($)	11798M	55330M	96688M	238627M	1098661M	7579755M
9760796M	9173572M	11612842M	Total Assets ($)	45289M	228020M	404872M	582177M	2581254M	7771230M

M = $ thousand   MM = $ million
See Pages 11 through 21 for Explanation of Ratios and Data

	Current Data Sorted by Assets							Comparative Historical Data	
Type of Statement	0-500M	500M-2MM	2-10MM	10-50MM	50-100MM	100-250MM		11	23
Unqualified		10	11	4				11	23
Reviewed		2	4	3				6	6
Compiled	1	3	4					8	13
Tax Returns	3	6	2					9	16
Other	3	4	9					10	19
		33 (4/1-9/30/06)		36 (10/1/06-3/31/07)				4/1/02-3/31/03 ALL	4/1/03-3/31/04 ALL
NUMBER OF STATEMENTS	7	25	30	7				44	77
	%	%	%	%	%	%		%	%
ASSETS									
Cash & Equivalents		22.6	20.8					17.8	17.6
Trade Receivables (net)		17.0	4.5					12.7	11.7
Inventory		2.2	1.3					6.0	4.1
All Other Current		2.7	2.3					2.7	2.9
Total Current		44.6	28.9					39.3	36.3
Fixed Assets (net)		53.5	66.4					51.2	52.7
Intangibles (net)		.4	.3					3.6	3.2
All Other Non-Current		1.6	4.5					5.9	7.8
Total		100.0	100.0					100.0	100.0
LIABILITIES									
Notes Payable-Short Term		2.3	3.4					4.9	5.3
Cur. Mat.-L.T.D.		3.2	1.1					9.2	11.5
Trade Payables		7.0	.7					4.9	3.8
Income Taxes Payable		.0	.0					.2	.2
All Other Current		6.2	3.3					7.0	4.8
Total Current		18.7	8.5					26.2	25.5
Long-Term Debt		16.4	22.9					21.9	20.8
Deferred Taxes		.0	.0					.0	.0
All Other Non-Current		1.9	.8					3.4	3.5
Net Worth		63.0	67.8					48.5	50.2
Total Liabilities & Net Worth		100.0	100.0					100.0	100.0
INCOME DATA									
Net Sales		100.0	100.0					100.0	100.0
Gross Profit									
Operating Expenses		84.0	87.2					91.2	90.8
Operating Profit		16.0	12.8					8.8	9.2
All Other Expenses (net)		3.8	4.4					4.3	3.2
Profit Before Taxes		12.1	8.4					4.5	5.9
RATIOS									
Current		15.2	13.5					7.3	9.9
		3.9	6.4					3.1	2.3
		1.2	2.1					1.2	1.1
Quick		15.0	12.8					7.2	9.9
		3.4	6.1					2.7	2.0
		1.1	1.7					.8	.8
Sales/Receivables	0	UND	0	UND			0	UND	0 UND
	5	76.8	0	785.2			0	UND	0 UND
	59	6.1	11	34.5			38	9.7	40 9.1
Cost of Sales/Inventory									
Cost of Sales/Payables									
Sales/Working Capital		1.4	1.5					2.1	1.7
		2.4	2.5					4.8	6.5
		25.7	5.0					33.1	75.9
EBIT/Interest		7.9	6.3					7.6	7.5
	(17)	5.4	(21) 3.7				(33)	3.6	(58) 2.9
		1.6	.9					.3	-1.3
Net Profit + Depr., Dep., Amort./Cur. Mat. L/T/D									
Fixed/Worth		.4	.6					.7	.6
		.9	1.0					1.0	.9
		1.5	1.5					2.3	1.6
Debt/Worth		.1	.1					.3	.2
		.5	.4					.5	.5
		1.3	1.0					2.2	2.2
% Profit Before Taxes/Tangible Net Worth		21.7	10.1					14.4	11.8
		10.4	2.4				(40)	6.5	(69) 4.0
		2.9	.6					-2.8	-1.3
% Profit Before Taxes/Total Assets		10.4	8.6					9.5	7.9
		7.6	2.1					2.3	2.7
		1.9	.2					-3.5	-1.8
Sales/Net Fixed Assets		26.2	1.1					12.9	9.8
		.9	.6					.8	1.0
		.5	.3					.4	.4
Sales/Total Assets		1.6	.6					2.5	2.1
		.7	.3					.6	.5
		.3	.2					.3	.3
% Depr., Dep., Amort./Sales		2.2	6.1					2.8	2.2
	(20)	11.2	(17) 19.4				(27)	7.5	(41) 7.1
		25.1	29.1					25.2	17.7
% Officers', Directors' Owners' Comp/Sales								3.1	2.6
							(14)	5.1	(15) 4.7
								20.5	7.4
Net Sales ($)	3632M	39976M	79072M	119486M				90581M	169175M
Total Assets ($)	2465M	30099M	139655M	104694M				113018M	291172M

Note: Columns 50-100MM and 100-250MM are marked "DATA NOT AVAILABLE".

M = $ thousand   MM = $ million
See Pages 11 through 21 for Explanation of Ratios and Data

Comparative Historical Data | Current Data Sorted by Sales

			Type of Statement						
22	27	25	Unqualified	9	11	2		2	1
4	6	9	Reviewed	3	2		2	1	1
9	10	8	Compiled	4	3	1			
10	6	11	Tax Returns	7	2		2		
8	20	16	Other	3	11	1		1	
4/1/04-3/31/05 ALL	4/1/05-3/31/06 ALL	4/1/06-3/31/07 ALL		33 (4/1-9/30/06)			36 (10/1/06-3/31/07)		
				0-1MM	1-3MM	3-5MM	5-10MM	10-25MM	25MM & OVER
53	69	69	NUMBER OF STATEMENTS	26	29	4	4	4	2
%	%	%	ASSETS	%	%	%	%	%	%
24.8	24.1	22.2	Cash & Equivalents	23.3	25.4				
15.7	8.4	10.9	Trade Receivables (net)	2.1	10.4				
3.5	2.4	2.2	Inventory	.4	2.1				
3.8	3.4	2.4	All Other Current	.6	3.3				
47.8	38.4	37.7	Total Current	26.3	41.1				
46.2	56.8	58.1	Fixed Assets (net)	72.8	54.1				
1.4	.3	.3	Intangibles (net)	.4	.0				
4.5	4.5	3.9	All Other Non-Current	.5	4.8				
100.0	100.0	100.0	Total	100.0	100.0				
			LIABILITIES						
4.0	3.8	2.9	Notes Payable-Short Term	2.5	2.9				
17.5	3.3	2.5	Cur. Mat.-L.T.D.	3.4	1.4				
6.1	4.2	4.0	Trade Payables	2.8	2.2				
.0	.0	.0	Income Taxes Payable	.0	.0				
7.5	3.5	4.8	All Other Current	1.4	4.7				
35.2	14.9	14.2	Total Current	10.1	11.2				
17.8	22.6	21.2	Long-Term Debt	26.2	17.8				
.0	.0	.0	Deferred Taxes	.0	.0				
1.5	3.2	1.4	All Other Non-Current	.5	1.6				
45.5	59.3	63.3	Net Worth	63.2	69.4				
100.0	100.0	100.0	Total Liabilties & Net Worth	100.0	100.0				
			INCOME DATA						
100.0	100.0	100.0	Net Sales	100.0	100.0				
			Gross Profit						
86.2	85.6	86.2	Operating Expenses	81.9	86.7				
13.8	14.4	13.8	Operating Profit	18.1	13.3				
2.9	2.9	4.1	All Other Expenses (net)	7.7	2.6				
10.9	11.5	9.7	Profit Before Taxes	10.5	10.7				
			RATIOS						
10.3	14.3	11.7		10.8	18.0				
3.1	5.0	5.4	Current	3.7	8.4				
1.4	1.6	1.5		1.2	1.9				
10.3	12.9	11.6		9.8	16.3				
2.6	4.8	5.4	Quick	3.4	6.5				
1.2	1.4	1.2		1.0	1.6				
0 UND	0 UND	0 UND		0 UND	0 UND				
1 434.6	0 797.0	4 101.0	Sales/Receivables	0 UND	2 177.3				
41 8.9	14 25.8	34 10.7		7 50.6	61 6.0				
			Cost of Sales/Inventory						
			Cost of Sales/Payables						
1.7	1.4	1.4		1.1	1.3				
5.1	2.9	2.6	Sales/Working Capital	2.4	2.1				
15.1	11.8	11.4		20.5	5.6				
19.5	8.7	7.8		6.9	8.4				
(35) 3.6	(46) 4.5	(49) 4.4	EBIT/Interest	(17) 3.8	(22) 5.0				
.9	2.1	1.5		1.5	1.4				
			Net Profit + Depr., Dep., Amort./Cur. Mat. L/T/D						
.2	.4	.5		.8	.4				
.9	1.0	1.0	Fixed/Worth	1.1	.9				
1.8	1.6	1.4		1.8	1.2				
.2	.2	.2		.1	.1				
.8	.5	.5	Debt/Worth	.4	.3				
2.0	1.4	1.2		1.2	.9				
27.2	17.2	21.0	% Profit Before Taxes/Tangible Net Worth	10.1	16.2				
(50) 12.4	(68) 8.7	(68) 7.2		(25) 3.0	7.3				
-.3	2.1	1.4		1.2	1.5				
18.5	10.6	10.4	% Profit Before Taxes/Total Assets	7.7	10.4				
7.2	5.2	3.9		2.6	4.0				
-.2	.5	1.0		.5	1.1				
26.0	7.5	3.8		.8	7.2				
2.3	.7	.8	Sales/Net Fixed Assets	.4	.8				
.6	.3	.4		.2	.4				
2.6	1.8	1.1		.7	1.0				
.8	.5	.5	Sales/Total Assets	.3	.6				
.4	.2	.3		.2	.3				
1.8	4.2	2.8		13.5	4.9				
(37) 10.8	(46) 11.8	(45) 12.1	% Depr., Dep., Amort./Sales	(20) 22.7	(13) 10.3				
18.9	20.1	26.8		30.9	19.1				
1.2	3.4	2.5	% Officers', Directors' Owners' Comp/Sales						
(15) 3.8	(13) 8.0	(12) 4.1							
7.8	12.0	9.3							
231121M	299919M	242166M	Net Sales ($)	9760M	51650M	16574M	28076M	61078M	75028M
223080M	266354M	276913M	Total Assets ($)	35873M	125746M	32493M	8418M	44554M	29829M

M = $ thousand   MM = $ million
See Pages 11 through 21 for Explanation of Ratios and Data

Current Data Sorted by Assets | Comparative Historical Data

	0-500M	500M-2MM	2-10MM	10-50MM	50-100MM	100-250MM	Type of Statement	4/1/02-3/31/03 ALL	4/1/03-3/31/04 ALL
	1	5	20	32	17	8	Unqualified	40	75
		1	2				Reviewed		1
	1						Compiled	1	4
							Tax Returns		2
	1	3	6	5	1	2	Other	11	14
		88 (4/1-9/30/06)		17 (10/1/06-3/31/07)					
NUMBER OF STATEMENTS	3	9	28	37	18	10		52	96
	%	%	%	%	%	%	**ASSETS**	%	%
			26.9	20.4	31.2	15.0	Cash & Equivalents	24.0	26.0
			13.5	8.7	4.8	3.5	Trade Receivables (net)	13.1	11.5
			1.1	.1	.4	.1	Inventory	.2	.6
			5.4	4.1	2.1	2.7	All Other Current	8.7	6.1
			46.9	33.2	38.6	21.3	Total Current	46.0	44.2
			40.1	53.7	51.6	59.2	Fixed Assets (net)	34.8	47.1
			2.4	.2	.0	.0	Intangibles (net)	1.0	.5
			10.6	12.9	9.8	19.5	All Other Non-Current	18.1	8.3
			100.0	100.0	100.0	100.0	Total	100.0	100.0
							LIABILITIES		
			5.1	1.3	.4	.1	Notes Payable-Short Term	1.6	2.8
			5.4	3.0	1.5	3.2	Cur. Mat.-L.T.D.	1.3	1.8
			9.3	3.7	2.1	2.6	Trade Payables	4.0	6.5
			.0	.0	.0	.0	Income Taxes Payable	.0	.1
			9.7	6.6	7.6	8.3	All Other Current	13.0	9.5
			29.6	14.6	11.6	14.3	Total Current	20.1	20.6
			21.2	39.1	40.8	29.1	Long-Term Debt	16.9	27.2
			.1	.0	.0	.0	Deferred Taxes	.0	.0
			9.0	4.7	3.3	2.3	All Other Non-Current	6.0	4.5
			40.2	41.5	44.2	54.3	Net Worth	57.1	47.7
			100.0	100.0	100.0	100.0	Total Liabilities & Net Worth	100.0	100.0
							INCOME DATA		
			100.0	100.0	100.0	100.0	Net Sales	100.0	100.0
							Gross Profit		
			94.5	95.4	91.7	91.6	Operating Expenses	94.0	93.6
			5.5	4.6	8.3	8.4	Operating Profit	6.0	6.4
			2.8	1.2	.5	-.6	All Other Expenses (net)	2.4	2.3
			2.7	3.4	7.8	9.1	Profit Before Taxes	3.6	4.1
							RATIOS		
			3.4	5.5	8.0	3.9		4.9	5.4
			2.1	1.7	3.6	1.6	Current	2.6	2.1
			1.1	1.0	2.4	.8		1.4	1.3
			3.0	4.7	7.9	3.5		4.6	4.8
			2.0	1.7	3.2	1.3	Quick	2.1	1.8
			.8	.8	2.1	.6		1.3	1.0
		0 UND	2 192.3	0 UND	1 621.3			1 395.6	0 969.3
		9 40.2	9 39.5	10 36.2	11 34.0		Sales/Receivables	12 30.3	10 37.0
		50 7.3	45 8.1	40 9.0	28 12.8			36 10.2	39 9.4
							Cost of Sales/Inventory		
							Cost of Sales/Payables		
			4.8	3.5	1.3	5.4		2.8	3.1
			8.4	15.1	3.0	25.4	Sales/Working Capital	10.1	8.6
			188.2	-804.0	10.0	-89.7		23.0	37.6
			13.0	3.7	5.8			5.6	6.8
			(15) 1.5	(23) 1.5	(15) 3.1		EBIT/Interest	(19) 2.7	(45) 2.4
			-.4	-.1	.6			1.0	.6
							Net Profit + Depr., Dep., Amort./Cur. Mat. L/T/D		
			.3	.7	.7	.9		.0	.4
			.7	1.7	1.3	1.2	Fixed/Worth	.6	1.0
			2.1	2.9	2.4	1.7		.9	2.5
			.6	.5	.5	.4		.3	.3
			1.4	1.6	1.7	.8	Debt/Worth	.6	1.1
			4.2	4.2	2.7	1.8		1.7	3.7
			15.3	13.2	17.3	18.6		23.1	15.5
			(27) 5.0	(36) 6.0	10.0	8.3	% Profit Before Taxes/Tangible Net Worth	(49) 4.0	(90) 3.0
			-3.3	-1.0	.4	.1		-2.5	-6.6
			6.9	5.2	6.6	9.9		11.7	7.5
			2.3	2.8	2.8	5.1	% Profit Before Taxes/Total Assets	2.3	1.1
			-2.1	-1.0	.4	.2		-1.3	-3.4
			19.9	5.7	2.7	1.5		112.9	21.9
			6.3	1.9	1.3	1.2	Sales/Net Fixed Assets	3.0	2.3
			2.2	1.2	1.0	.9		1.1	1.0
			3.2	1.6	1.0	.9		2.7	2.3
			1.6	1.0	.8	.7	Sales/Total Assets	1.0	1.0
			1.2	.7	.6	.4		.6	.7
			1.0	1.1	1.4			.3	.2
			(26) 2.4	(23) 2.4	(14) 3.1		% Depr., Dep., Amort./Sales	(20) 1.9	(50) 2.1
			5.3	4.1	3.7			4.6	3.9
									3.4
							% Officers', Directors' Owners' Comp/Sales		(15) 6.2
									19.8
Net Sales ($)	4870M	36443M	502448M	1299387M	1001667M	1108019M		1775918M	3218058M
Total Assets ($)	514M	11104M	165859M	1066301M	1287740M	1642487M		1907641M	3445137M

© RMA 2007

M = $ thousand   MM = $ million

See Pages 11 through 21 for Explanation of Ratios and Data

Comparative Historical Data | Current Data Sorted by Sales

			Type of Statement						
43	55	83	Unqualified	4	4	5	6	22	42
2	1		Reviewed						
1	3	3	Compiled	1	1		1		
1	1	1	Tax Returns		1				
21	24	18	Other	1	3		4	2	8
4/1/04-3/31/05 ALL	4/1/05-3/31/06 ALL	4/1/06-3/31/07 ALL		88 (4/1-9/30/06)			17 (10/1/06-3/31/07)		
				0-1MM	1-3MM	3-5MM	5-10MM	10-25MM	25MM & OVER
68	84	105	**NUMBER OF STATEMENTS**	6	9	5	11	24	50
%	%	%	**ASSETS**	%	%	%	%	%	%
24.4	25.9	25.8	Cash & Equivalents				31.0	25.8	23.1
11.6	12.9	11.3	Trade Receivables (net)				19.8	13.3	8.2
1.6	3.0	.6	Inventory				1.8	.8	.2
7.1	5.9	3.7	All Other Current				1.8	5.1	4.7
44.6	47.7	41.5	Total Current				54.4	45.1	36.2
39.0	43.1	46.5	Fixed Assets (net)				30.2	40.8	55.1
1.8	1.6	.7	Intangibles (net)				6.0	.2	.1
14.6	7.6	11.2	All Other Non-Current				9.4	14.0	8.6
100.0	100.0	100.0	Total				100.0	100.0	100.0
			LIABILITIES						
1.2	1.6	2.8	Notes Payable-Short Term				5.9	2.7	1.2
2.0	2.8	3.1	Cur. Mat.-L.T.D.				1.7	4.9	2.8
8.6	6.5	6.2	Trade Payables				7.4	7.4	5.2
.0	.0	.0	Income Taxes Payable				.1	.0	.0
10.7	10.4	12.8	All Other Current				12.9	5.8	9.7
22.5	21.4	25.0	Total Current				27.9	20.8	19.0
18.9	23.5	29.7	Long-Term Debt				8.3	26.3	37.0
.0	.1	.0	Deferred Taxes				.2	.0	.0
5.8	4.4	5.2	All Other Non-Current				3.6	10.3	4.3
52.8	50.7	40.1	Net Worth				60.0	42.6	39.7
100.0	100.0	100.0	Total Liabilties & Net Worth				100.0	100.0	100.0
			INCOME DATA						
100.0	100.0	100.0	Net Sales				100.0	100.0	100.0
			Gross Profit						
96.0	94.1	94.4	Operating Expenses				96.8	95.9	94.8
4.0	5.9	5.6	Operating Profit				3.2	4.1	5.2
.8	.6	1.3	All Other Expenses (net)				1.8	-1.2	.9
3.2	5.3	4.3	Profit Before Taxes				1.4	5.3	4.3
			RATIOS						
3.6	5.9	5.1					4.6	5.7	4.8
2.1	2.4	2.2	Current				2.2	2.1	2.2
1.5	1.1	1.1					1.0	1.2	1.1
3.0	4.7	4.5					4.4	5.7	3.4
1.8	1.7	2.0	Quick				2.1	2.0	2.0
1.0	.9	.9					.9	.8	.9
3 135.2	1 372.3	1 508.5		12 29.5	2 160.9	0 UND			
17 22.0	13 27.6	10 36.3	Sales/Receivables	39 9.3	8 43.5	9 39.1			
42 8.7	48 7.7	45 8.1		52 7.0	48 7.7	27 13.5			
			Cost of Sales/Inventory						
			Cost of Sales/Payables						
3.3	3.5	3.7					3.9	3.0	3.7
6.8	8.1	9.8	Sales/Working Capital				6.6	8.5	12.0
19.4	103.6	116.1					-221.2	55.1	64.9
7.5	11.6	5.8						10.9	6.4
(38) 1.6	(54) 3.8	(67) 2.1	EBIT/Interest				(12) 1.5	(41) 3.1	
-.4	.9	.2					-1.0	.7	
			Net Profit + Depr., Dep., Amort./Cur. Mat. L/T/D						
.3	.2	.5					.1	.6	.8
.8	.9	1.0	Fixed/Worth				.4	.7	1.6
1.4	2.1	2.2					.8	1.8	2.6
.3	.3	.5					.3	.5	.8
.9	1.1	1.4	Debt/Worth				.5	1.1	1.7
2.3	2.4	3.4					1.3	3.1	3.6
19.4	29.0	16.2	% Profit Before Taxes/Tangible Net Worth				12.0	14.7	18.2
(65) 5.3	10.3	(100) 6.7					-.8	(23) 6.3	(49) 9.9
-3.5	.6	-.1					-11.7	1.4	.5
8.4	12.9	6.8	% Profit Before Taxes/Total Assets				6.9	6.0	7.7
2.6	4.0	2.8					-.7	3.3	3.2
-2.2	.4	-.5					-7.4	1.0	.3
18.5	20.7	10.4	Sales/Net Fixed Assets				556.6	11.0	5.1
3.9	3.8	2.2					9.5	3.4	1.6
1.5	1.4	1.2					1.3	1.4	1.1
2.1	2.6	2.1	Sales/Total Assets				3.4	2.2	1.7
1.0	1.4	1.0					1.6	1.4	.9
.5	.8	.7					.7	.7	.7
1.4	.7	1.0	% Depr., Dep., Amort./Sales					1.1	.5
(40) 2.5	(47) 1.9	(78) 2.6					(19)	2.5	(34) 2.6
4.5	3.1	3.8						4.0	3.6
	2.4	1.6	% Officers', Directors' Owners' Comp/Sales						1.6
	(17) 10.0	(18) 6.0						(13)	3.8
	19.3	14.3							10.8
2747760M	2832107M	3952834M	Net Sales ($)	3547M	19381M	21031M	84607M	431606M	3392662M
2175687M	2553986M	4174005M	Total Assets ($)	15856M	21312M	100569M	87416M	451709M	3497143M

M = $ thousand   MM = $ million
See Pages 11 through 21 for Explanation of Ratios and Data

Current Data Sorted by Assets

Comparative Historical Data

						Type of Statement		
2	1	10	4	2	3	Unqualified	5	10
	1	2				Reviewed	1	1
						Compiled		1
						Tax Returns		1
1		2	1	1	1	Other	6	7
	18 (4/1-9/30/06)			13 (10/1/06-3/31/07)			4/1/02-3/31/03	4/1/03-3/31/04
0-500M	500M-2MM	2-10MM	10-50MM	50-100MM	100-250MM		ALL	ALL
3	2	14	5	3	4	NUMBER OF STATEMENTS	12	20
%	%	%	%	%	%	**ASSETS**	%	%
		29.1				Cash & Equivalents	42.8	26.6
		24.5				Trade Receivables (net)	15.6	22.4
		.9				Inventory	.0	.2
		.6				All Other Current	9.6	12.7
		55.2				Total Current	67.9	61.9
		31.1				Fixed Assets (net)	27.4	33.4
		6.2				Intangibles (net)	.1	.2
		7.5				All Other Non-Current	4.6	4.5
		100.0				Total	100.0	100.0
						LIABILITIES		
		1.9				Notes Payable-Short Term	5.4	7.3
		3.1				Cur. Mat.-L.T.D.	.7	2.5
		3.9				Trade Payables	12.9	9.6
		.3				Income Taxes Payable	.2	.3
		15.8				All Other Current	20.3	19.1
		25.0				Total Current	39.5	38.7
		15.0				Long-Term Debt	11.8	16.4
		.2				Deferred Taxes	.0	.0
		1.1				All Other Non-Current	6.4	2.1
		58.7				Net Worth	42.2	42.7
		100.0				Total Liabilties & Net Worth	100.0	100.0
						INCOME DATA		
		100.0				Net Sales	100.0	100.0
						Gross Profit		
		93.6				Operating Expenses	93.7	95.5
		6.4				Operating Profit	6.3	4.5
		-.9				All Other Expenses (net)	.7	1.9
		7.3				Profit Before Taxes	5.6	2.6
						RATIOS		
		4.0					2.9	3.2
		2.5				Current	2.2	1.6
		1.3					1.2	1.0
		3.9					2.9	2.4
		2.4				Quick	1.5	1.4
		1.1					1.2	.8
	21	17.8					3	116.1	6	65.6
	48	7.6				Sales/Receivables	16	22.5	29	12.6
	56	6.6					40	9.0	52	7.1
						Cost of Sales/Inventory		
						Cost of Sales/Payables		
		2.3					4.8	7.4
		5.5				Sales/Working Capital	8.8	12.4
		19.7					43.4	-214.3
		12.7						18.1
	(10)	4.9				EBIT/Interest	(11)	5.7
		2.0						.5
						Net Profit + Depr., Dep., Amort./Cur. Mat. L/T/D		
		.3					.2	.3
		.7				Fixed/Worth	.7	.6
		1.2					1.7	1.5
		.4					.5	.4
		.8				Debt/Worth	1.4	1.7
		1.2					3.8	3.7
		25.6				% Profit Before Taxes/Tangible Net Worth	27.6	30.4
	(13)	8.0					(10)	8.9	(19)	4.8
		-.8					.6	-4.0
		13.1				% Profit Before Taxes/Total Assets	19.0	11.9
		5.1					5.7	2.8
		-.2					1.8	-2.3
		20.9				Sales/Net Fixed Assets	78.6	36.0
		5.9					7.1	16.0
		4.4					4.7	4.3
		2.7				Sales/Total Assets	3.6	4.5
		1.9					2.3	2.9
		1.2					1.7	1.6
		.7				% Depr., Dep., Amort./Sales		.5
	(13)	1.4					(14)	1.4
		2.5						1.8
						% Officers', Directors' Owners' Comp/Sales		
3172M	6359M	129035M	144363M	303320M	1317941M	Net Sales ($)	219400M	173245M
905M	2174M	70275M	85051M	192260M	798796M	Total Assets ($)	99688M	81335M

M = $ thousand   MM = $ million
See Pages 11 through 21 for Explanation of Ratios and Data

Comparative Historical Data / Current Data Sorted by Sales

				Type of Statement						
	23	18	22	Unqualified	1	2	1	6	6	6
	1	2	3	Reviewed		1		1		1
				Compiled						
	2			Tax Returns						
	3	5	6	Other	1		1	2		2
	4/1/04-3/31/05 ALL	4/1/05-3/31/06 ALL	4/1/06-3/31/07 ALL		0-1MM	18 (4/1-9/30/06) 1-3MM	3-5MM	13 (10/1/06-3/31/07) 5-10MM	10-25MM	25MM & OVER
	29	25	31	NUMBER OF STATEMENTS	2	3	2	9	6	9
	%	%	%	ASSETS	%	%	%	%	%	%
	26.7	27.8	33.2	Cash & Equivalents						
	23.5	24.2	19.3	Trade Receivables (net)						
	.2	1.4	.8	Inventory						
	7.3	12.1	2.3	All Other Current						
	57.6	65.5	55.6	Total Current						
	30.2	28.4	23.5	Fixed Assets (net)						
	.5	.1	5.0	Intangibles (net)						
	11.7	6.1	15.9	All Other Non-Current						
	100.0	100.0	100.0	Total						
				LIABILITIES						
	16.4	1.2	2.8	Notes Payable-Short Term						
	1.9	2.6	2.6	Cur. Mat.-L.T.D.						
	22.7	12.9	5.8	Trade Payables						
	.4	.2	.1	Income Taxes Payable						
	20.2	21.5	15.3	All Other Current						
	61.5	38.4	26.7	Total Current						
	10.0	9.4	16.8	Long-Term Debt						
	.0	.2	.1	Deferred Taxes						
	3.8	2.8	2.6	All Other Non-Current						
	24.7	49.1	53.9	Net Worth						
	100.0	100.0	100.0	Total Liabilties & Net Worth						
				INCOME DATA						
	100.0	100.0	100.0	Net Sales						
				Gross Profit						
	96.7	94.6	91.5	Operating Expenses						
	3.3	5.4	8.5	Operating Profit						
	-1.0	.2	-.2	All Other Expenses (net)						
	4.3	5.2	8.7	Profit Before Taxes						
				RATIOS						
	3.3	3.4	4.8							
	1.5	1.8	2.1	Current						
	1.0	1.0	1.3							
	2.9	3.1	4.5							
	1.4	1.6	1.8	Quick						
	.8	.7	1.2							
7	54.0	2 173.0	8 45.7	Sales/Receivables						
29	12.7	32 11.6	31 11.8							
58	6.3	50 7.3	53 6.9							
				Cost of Sales/Inventory						
				Cost of Sales/Payables						
	4.9	3.9	3.0							
	15.0	8.0	6.3	Sales/Working Capital						
	-279.2	-366.3	12.9							
	27.4	25.3	9.2							
(17)	5.7	(12) 11.0	(22) 5.7	EBIT/Interest						
	-1.9	.5	2.0							
				Net Profit + Depr., Dep., Amort./Cur. Mat. L/T/D						
	.2	.2	.2							
	.5	.8	.5	Fixed/Worth						
	1.4	1.5	.8							
	.5	.4	.4							
	1.2	.8	.9	Debt/Worth						
	2.1	4.2	2.7							
	23.9	25.2	29.9	% Profit Before Taxes/Tangible Net Worth						
(27)	10.7	15.0	(30) 13.3							
	-3.0	-1.2	-.4							
	11.5	10.3	14.6	% Profit Before Taxes/Total Assets						
	5.5	3.7	5.7							
	-2.5	.0	-.1							
	39.4	101.2	25.5	Sales/Net Fixed Assets						
	7.9	7.7	8.3							
	3.8	4.1	4.7							
	4.1	3.5	2.9							
	2.5	2.7	2.0	Sales/Total Assets						
	1.1	1.5	.9							
	.7	.7	.6							
(25)	1.3	(17) 1.4	(28) 1.3	% Depr., Dep., Amort./Sales						
	2.8	2.4	2.7							
				% Officers', Directors' Owners' Comp/Sales						
	1182964M	1386215M	1904190M	Net Sales ($)	1465M	5217M	7247M	64221M	90680M	1735360M
	397057M	541961M	1149461M	Total Assets ($)	6926M	1666M	8324M	105937M	215290M	811318M

M = $ thousand   MM = $ million
See Pages 11 through 21 for Explanation of Ratios and Data

Current Data Sorted by Assets | Comparative Historical Data

0-500M	500M-2MM	2-10MM	10-50MM	50-100MM	100-250MM	Type of Statement	4/1/02-3/31/03 ALL	4/1/03-3/31/04 ALL
1	2	14	14	4	4	Unqualified	40	40
	1	6	1			Reviewed	9	10
1	1	1	2			Compiled	7	8
3						Tax Returns	4	5
1	3	8	7	2		Other	23	25
		35 (4/1-9/30/06)		41 (10/1/06-3/31/07)				
6	7	29	24	6	4	NUMBER OF STATEMENTS	83	88
%	%	%	%	%	%	**ASSETS**	%	%
		11.4	17.6			Cash & Equivalents	13.4	13.2
		17.5	8.1			Trade Receivables (net)	15.2	16.4
		3.3	.7			Inventory	1.7	2.3
		1.2	3.6			All Other Current	2.3	1.7
		33.4	30.1			Total Current	32.6	33.7
		61.3	63.0			Fixed Assets (net)	53.7	52.1
		.9	.3			Intangibles (net)	4.3	5.8
		4.4	6.6			All Other Non-Current	9.3	8.4
		100.0	100.0			Total	100.0	100.0
						LIABILITIES		
		4.8	1.9			Notes Payable-Short Term	5.6	4.7
		3.0	3.1			Cur. Mat.-L.T.D.	5.7	3.9
		8.0	6.3			Trade Payables	7.7	7.1
		.1	.2			Income Taxes Payable	.1	.2
		6.8	5.5			All Other Current	6.9	9.1
		22.6	17.1			Total Current	26.0	25.0
		34.6	30.0			Long-Term Debt	25.0	29.5
		.0	.2			Deferred Taxes	.3	.8
		.9	2.2			All Other Non-Current	6.3	5.3
		41.8	50.6			Net Worth	42.4	39.4
		100.0	100.0			Total Liabilities & Net Worth	100.0	100.0
						INCOME DATA		
		100.0	100.0			Net Sales	100.0	100.0
						Gross Profit		
		87.9	85.3			Operating Expenses	90.1	88.8
		12.1	14.7			Operating Profit	9.9	11.2
		5.6	4.4			All Other Expenses (net)	3.2	4.1
		6.5	10.3			Profit Before Taxes	6.7	7.1
						RATIOS		
		4.8	5.2			Current	4.0	4.8
		2.0	1.8				1.5	1.6
		.9	1.1				.8	.9
		4.8	4.0			Quick	3.4	3.7
		1.8	1.5				1.3	1.5
		.6	1.0				.6	.8
		14 26.8	21 17.5			Sales/Receivables	25 14.7	28 13.0
		31 11.9	28 13.2				43 8.5	44 8.3
		62 5.9	52 7.0				64 5.7	72 5.0
						Cost of Sales/Inventory		
						Cost of Sales/Payables		
		1.7	2.2			Sales/Working Capital	1.5	2.1
		6.5	4.8				10.4	9.5
		-83.9	102.2				-13.9	-309.0
		12.0	5.6			EBIT/Interest	4.3	7.4
		(23) 2.9	(19) 2.5				(70) 2.4	(72) 3.4
		.5	1.3				1.2	1.3
						Net Profit + Depr., Dep.,	15.9	
						Amort./Cur. Mat. L/T/D	(11) 2.1	
							1.1	
		.8	1.1			Fixed/Worth	.8	.9
		1.3	1.3				1.4	1.4
		3.3	1.7				3.1	3.1
		.4	.5			Debt/Worth	.4	.5
		1.1	.8				1.4	1.5
		4.6	2.0				4.0	4.3
		57.4	12.2			% Profit Before Taxes/Tangible	23.3	34.2
		(24) 4.0	5.4			Net Worth	(71) 7.4	(73) 6.6
		-.5	.6				.6	.5
		17.2	4.6			% Profit Before Taxes/Total	7.6	9.9
		2.1	2.2			Assets	2.7	3.8
		-1.4	.5				.2	.1
		8.6	3.5			Sales/Net Fixed Assets	8.2	7.3
		.5	.4				1.2	1.7
		.2	.2				.3	.3
		2.9	1.5			Sales/Total Assets	2.0	1.9
		.4	.3				.5	.6
		.1	.2				.2	.2
		3.8	1.8			% Depr., Dep., Amort./Sales	4.6	4.2
		(25) 17.3	9.2				(71) 9.4	(73) 9.5
		24.6	18.7				17.7	17.4
						% Officers', Directors'	2.9	2.9
						Owners' Comp/Sales	(18) 6.9	(20) 3.7
							12.8	6.6
13031M	15068M	219281M	413319M	122971M	100812M	Net Sales ($)	1364670M	1585061M
1574M	8804M	167778M	471688M	404419M	695518M	Total Assets ($)	2586513M	2724641M

© RMA 2007   **M = $ thousand   MM = $ million**
See Pages 11 through 21 for Explanation of Ratios and Data

Comparative Historical Data   Current Data Sorted by Sales

			Type of Statement						
46	43	39	Unqualified	7	8	6	3	9	6
6	8	8	Reviewed	1	1		3	3	
5	4	5	Compiled		2		1	2	
3	4	3	Tax Returns			1	1		
23	35	21	Other	5	6	1	5	1	3
4/1/04-3/31/05 ALL	4/1/05-3/31/06 ALL	4/1/06-3/31/07 ALL		0-1MM	1-3MM 35 (4/1-9/30/06)	3-5MM	5-10MM	10-25MM 41 (10/1/06-3/31/07)	25MM & OVER
83	94	76	**NUMBER OF STATEMENTS**	14	17	8	13	15	9
%	%	%	**ASSETS**	%	%	%	%	%	%
12.3	12.0	14.2	Cash & Equivalents	14.5	10.0		14.1	13.0	
15.4	14.4	15.3	Trade Receivables (net)	10.4	13.3		18.8	16.5	
2.0	1.2	2.9	Inventory	.0	.2		3.7	3.5	
1.9	2.1	2.5	All Other Current	.1	3.4		.7	1.8	
31.6	29.6	34.8	Total Current	25.0	26.8		37.3	34.8	
56.6	59.9	55.1	Fixed Assets (net)	69.8	58.2		57.1	52.2	
2.7	2.8	2.0	Intangibles (net)	.8	5.9		.7	.7	
9.1	7.8	8.1	All Other Non-Current	4.5	9.0		5.0	12.3	
100.0	100.0	100.0	Total	100.0	100.0		100.0	100.0	
			LIABILITIES						
2.2	3.9	3.4	Notes Payable-Short Term	.2	2.9		6.2	4.9	
3.6	5.6	3.0	Cur. Mat.-L.T.D.	1.6	3.7		3.2	4.1	
7.0	5.9	7.5	Trade Payables	2.8	5.7		7.7	9.0	
.2	.0	.1	Income Taxes Payable	.0	.0		.0	.0	
4.4	6.9	6.4	All Other Current	3.2	4.4		9.7	8.0	
17.4	22.4	20.3	Total Current	7.8	16.7		26.8	25.9	
29.0	28.7	31.1	Long-Term Debt	37.2	41.8		35.2	27.5	
.5	.1	.1	Deferred Taxes	.0	.0		.0	.0	
4.1	3.3	1.7	All Other Non-Current	.1	1.0		3.1	1.4	
49.0	45.5	46.8	Net Worth	54.9	40.5		34.9	45.2	
100.0	100.0	100.0	Total Liabilities & Net Worth	100.0	100.0		100.0	100.0	
			INCOME DATA						
100.0	100.0	100.0	Net Sales	100.0	100.0		100.0	100.0	
			Gross Profit						
86.5	86.7	87.1	Operating Expenses	80.8	88.6		85.9	92.2	
13.5	13.3	12.9	Operating Profit	19.2	11.4		14.1	7.8	
3.3	4.4	3.3	All Other Expenses (net)	10.3	3.8		2.1	-.7	
10.2	8.9	9.5	Profit Before Taxes	8.9	7.6		12.0	8.5	
			RATIOS						
5.4	3.9	4.2		6.1	5.4		2.2	2.0	
2.5	2.1	1.9	Current	2.8	2.0		1.2	1.3	
1.2	1.0	1.1		1.2	1.3		.8	.9	
4.4	3.6	4.2		6.1	5.4		2.0	1.8	
2.1	1.7	1.4	Quick	2.8	1.5		1.0	1.1	
1.0	.9	.9		1.1	1.0		.8	.7	
29 12.7	18 20.6	21 17.5		0 UND	30 12.3		11 33.4	18 20.2	
45 8.1	38 9.7	33 11.1	Sales/Receivables	25 14.7	43 8.4		36 10.2	35 10.3	
62 5.9	56 6.6	58 6.3		36 10.1	67 5.5		74 4.9	58 6.3	
			Cost of Sales/Inventory						
			Cost of Sales/Payables						
1.3	1.3	2.3		1.1	1.6		6.5	3.2	
6.5	5.0	8.8	Sales/Working Capital	4.9	6.5		43.9	12.3	
27.9	NM	101.7		NM	22.0		-56.6	-37.9	
8.4	5.9	8.3			4.5		7.7	4.2	
(70) 2.9	(76) 2.8	(63) 2.9	EBIT/Interest		(13) 2.7		(11) 5.3	(14) 2.6	
1.2	1.2	1.1			.2		1.2	.9	
10.5			Net Profit + Depr., Dep.,						
(12) 1.9			Amort./Cur. Mat. L/T/D						
1.4									
.8	.8	.7		.6	1.1		.6	.9	
1.3	1.3	1.2	Fixed/Worth	1.3	1.6		1.3	1.2	
2.3	2.2	2.1		1.9	12.2		NM	1.7	
.3	.3	.4		.2	.4		.3	.6	
1.1	1.0	1.0	Debt/Worth	.6	1.4		1.7	1.5	
3.4	3.0	3.5		3.7	21.0		NM	2.5	
20.9	15.0	25.5	% Profit Before Taxes/Tangible	24.9	12.6		63.8	23.5	
(75) 6.3	(79) 5.4	(69) 5.7	Net Worth	(13) 4.2	(14) 3.5		(10) 25.5	6.0	
.3	1.5	.9		-.6	.7		3.4	.0	
6.5	6.0	10.5	% Profit Before Taxes/Total	18.2	5.0		17.2	6.9	
3.7	2.2	2.7	Assets	1.7	2.1		4.6	3.3	
-.1	.0	.1		-.6	-1.8		.9	.0	
8.2	5.8	11.0		4.5	5.0		22.1	4.4	
.5	.5	.7	Sales/Net Fixed Assets	.2	.4		1.5	2.1	
.2	.2	.2		.1	.2		.2	.3	
1.6	1.9	2.4		.9	1.4		3.4	1.9	
.3	.3	.4	Sales/Total Assets	.1	.3		1.1	1.0	
.1	.2	.1		.1	.1		.1	.2	
3.6	3.3	2.8		8.4	10.7		3.3	2.3	
(73) 10.7	(78) 13.2	(66) 11.4	% Depr., Dep., Amort./Sales	(12) 24.6	(14) 18.7		(12) 5.6	(14) 6.0	
20.0	22.9	21.6		27.5	22.6		18.8	19.7	
4.0	2.7	3.3	% Officers', Directors',						
(13) 6.7	(19) 5.1	(18) 5.9	Owners' Comp/Sales						
13.3	14.7	10.1							
1247198M	1258040M	884482M	Net Sales ($)	8267M	29166M	28355M	93509M	247410M	477775M
2937469M	2865089M	1749781M	Total Assets ($)	59970M	115174M	158004M	295164M	723226M	398243M

M = $ thousand   MM = $ million
See Pages 11 through 21 for Explanation of Ratios and Data

Current Data Sorted by Assets | Comparative Historical Data

	0-500M	500M-2MM	2-10MM	10-50MM	50-100MM	100-250MM		4/1/02-3/31/03 ALL	4/1/03-3/31/04 ALL
Type of Statement									
Unqualified	6	13	24	30	7	3		66	68
Reviewed			3						2
Compiled		1						1	4
Tax Returns	1		2					4	
Other	2	2	15	8	1	1		26	35
		77 (4/1-9/30/06)		42 (10/1/06-3/31/07)					
NUMBER OF STATEMENTS	9	16	44	38	8	4		97	109
	%	%	%	%	%	%		%	%
ASSETS									
Cash & Equivalents		28.6	15.3	14.6				14.0	13.3
Trade Receivables (net)		5.1	4.6	7.2				9.0	8.7
Inventory		2.4	3.9	2.7				2.2	3.1
All Other Current		2.9	6.1	4.9				5.0	4.5
Total Current		39.0	29.8	29.4				30.2	29.6
Fixed Assets (net)		47.4	48.0	55.1				49.9	51.1
Intangibles (net)		.8	1.4	.3				.5	.5
All Other Non-Current		12.8	20.7	15.3				19.4	18.8
Total		100.0	100.0	100.0				100.0	100.0
LIABILITIES									
Notes Payable-Short Term		1.2	5.1	2.6				4.5	4.2
Cur. Mat.-L.T.D.		2.1	2.8	1.7				1.9	3.9
Trade Payables		6.2	2.4	4.0				3.4	2.8
Income Taxes Payable		.1	.1	.0				.0	.1
All Other Current		8.5	4.5	4.7				7.4	7.8
Total Current		18.1	14.9	13.0				17.3	18.8
Long-Term Debt		37.7	25.7	28.2				27.4	26.8
Deferred Taxes		.0	.0	.0				.4	.7
All Other Non-Current		2.2	4.7	4.1				5.4	4.3
Net Worth		42.0	54.7	54.7				49.5	49.5
Total Liabilities & Net Worth		100.0	100.0	100.0				100.0	100.0
INCOME DATA									
Net Sales		100.0	100.0	100.0				100.0	100.0
Gross Profit									
Operating Expenses		82.5	89.0	98.6				86.8	88.4
Operating Profit		17.5	11.0	1.4				13.2	11.6
All Other Expenses (net)		6.0	3.8	-.3				6.1	3.8
Profit Before Taxes		11.5	7.3	1.7				7.2	7.8
RATIOS									
Current		5.9	5.8	5.3				5.4	4.6
		2.3	2.2	2.1				2.4	1.9
		.8	1.1	1.5				.8	1.0
Quick		4.9	4.0	4.9				3.9	3.1
		1.7	1.5	1.5				1.2	1.4
		.8	.6	.9				.6	.7
Sales/Receivables		0 UND	1 408.3	4 95.3				1 625.4	1 594.5
		2 208.3	6 60.8	9 38.6				12 31.5	16 22.2
		15 24.9	32 11.2	57 6.4				45 8.1	45 8.1
Cost of Sales/Inventory									
Cost of Sales/Payables									
Sales/Working Capital		3.4	1.5	2.5				1.9	2.4
		10.6	4.9	3.3				7.0	7.9
		-91.5	25.8	12.6				-22.2	NM
EBIT/Interest			11.9	5.0				5.3	8.9
			(32) 3.6	(31) 1.6				(57) 1.7	(68) 1.9
			1.0	-.6				.6	.2
Net Profit + Depr., Dep., Amort./Cur. Mat. L/T/D									
Fixed/Worth		.3	.4	.4				.2	.3
		.8	.9	1.0				1.0	.9
		5.2	1.8	1.9				1.7	2.0
Debt/Worth		.3	.3	.3				.3	.3
		1.4	.6	.7				1.0	.9
		5.9	2.3	2.2				3.0	4.0
% Profit Before Taxes/Tangible Net Worth		45.6	15.4	7.2				11.1	15.3
		(14) 11.5	(43) 6.2	1.4				(94) 3.2	(103) 5.4
		3.1	-.4	-3.5				-3.2	-.9
% Profit Before Taxes/Total Assets		15.2	6.9	4.4				4.3	5.8
		3.0	3.2	.5				1.3	1.6
		.2	-.7	-2.0				-1.3	-.8
Sales/Net Fixed Assets		22.5	3.6	2.7				5.1	4.2
		2.5	.9	.7				1.1	1.1
		.5	.4	.4				.5	.5
Sales/Total Assets		2.9	.7	.7				1.0	1.0
		1.5	.4	.5				.4	.4
		.4	.2	.3				.3	.2
% Depr., Dep., Amort./Sales		.7	2.1	2.7				1.4	1.5
		(11) 1.6	(38) 4.7	(36) 5.7				(75) 3.8	(88) 4.8
		15.3	10.4	11.8				8.9	10.5
% Officers', Directors' Owners' Comp/Sales									
Net Sales ($)	2678M	30514M	204788M	541473M	160740M	161611M		963925M	1253139M
Total Assets ($)	2511M	19258M	236549M	838989M	577348M	559448M		1980763M	2256381M

© RMA 2007

M = $ thousand   MM = $ million

See Pages 11 through 21 for Explanation of Ratios and Data

Comparative Historical Data

Current Data Sorted by Sales

			Type of Statement						
77	69	83	Unqualified	15	19	10	8	21	10
3	1	3	Reviewed	1	1		1		
3	2	1	Compiled	1					
2	3	3	Tax Returns	2	1				
27	42	29	Other	9	7	1	7	3	2
4/1/04- 3/31/05 ALL	4/1/05- 3/31/06 ALL	4/1/06- 3/31/07 ALL			77 (4/1-9/30/06)			42 (10/1/06-3/31/07)	
				0-1MM	1-3MM	3-5MM	5-10MM	10-25MM	25MM & OVER
112	117	119	**NUMBER OF STATEMENTS**	28	28	11	16	24	12
%	%	%	**ASSETS**	%	%	%	%	%	%
12.5	15.4	17.5	Cash & Equivalents	20.2	14.1	14.1	21.6	15.1	21.8
8.9	10.3	5.7	Trade Receivables (net)	4.7	3.2	3.3	5.2	5.7	16.5
2.0	2.7	2.9	Inventory	2.4	3.8	7.0	5.8	.1	.1
3.5	2.7	4.8	All Other Current	5.0	6.6	.8	4.9	5.5	2.3
26.9	31.0	30.9	Total Current	32.3	27.6	25.1	37.5	26.4	40.7
54.3	47.8	51.5	Fixed Assets (net)	50.7	52.8	48.9	48.2	55.5	49.1
.8	.5	.8	Intangibles (net)	.1	.1	2.0	3.2	.2	.4
18.0	20.7	16.8	All Other Non-Current	16.8	19.4	24.0	11.1	17.9	9.8
100.0	100.0	100.0	Total	100.0	100.0	100.0	100.0	100.0	100.0
			LIABILITIES						
4.2	5.9	3.8	Notes Payable-Short Term	7.9	3.3	3.6	3.8	1.1	1.1
2.2	2.1	2.2	Cur. Mat.-L.T.D.	2.0	3.2	.8	1.4	3.1	1.2
3.0	2.9	3.4	Trade Payables	1.5	4.6	2.0	1.8	4.3	6.1
.0	.0	.1	Income Taxes Payable	.0	.0	.0	.0	.0	.5
5.4	7.1	4.9	All Other Current	3.9	4.7	2.4	6.1	4.6	8.7
14.8	18.0	14.3	Total Current	15.3	15.8	8.7	13.2	13.1	17.7
31.8	33.7	33.5	Long-Term Debt	49.1	28.2	32.0	25.0	34.8	19.3
.6	.0	.0	Deferred Taxes	.0	.0	.0	.0	.0	.1
3.2	4.7	3.7	All Other Non-Current	5.4	1.9	5.4	.9	3.8	6.0
49.6	43.7	48.5	Net Worth	30.2	54.1	53.8	61.0	48.3	57.0
100.0	100.0	100.0	Total Liabilties & Net Worth	100.0	100.0	100.0	100.0	100.0	100.0
			INCOME DATA						
100.0	100.0	100.0	Net Sales	100.0	100.0	100.0	100.0	100.0	100.0
			Gross Profit						
88.8	87.5	90.7	Operating Expenses	85.4	86.5	89.0	97.8	96.6	93.1
11.2	12.5	9.3	Operating Profit	14.6	13.5	11.0	2.2	3.4	6.9
4.9	6.5	3.4	All Other Expenses (net)	9.9	1.8	10.3	-1.0	-.4	-.4
6.3	6.0	5.9	Profit Before Taxes	4.7	11.7	.8	3.3	3.8	7.3
			RATIOS						
3.9	4.2	5.7		7.8	6.1	4.4	5.4	4.8	6.7
2.0	2.1	2.2	Current	2.3	2.2	3.5	2.6	1.9	4.4
.9	1.1	1.2		.9	1.1	1.7	1.7	1.5	1.3
3.2	3.9	4.3		5.7	2.1	4.3	3.9	3.9	5.7
1.4	1.6	1.6	Quick	1.9	1.2	1.8	1.6	1.5	2.4
.6	.8	.8		.7	.4	1.0	.8	1.0	1.3
2 212.6	1 541.6	1 527.1		0 UND	0 UND	3 123.3	3 114.6	2 186.1	7 51.8
10 36.2	8 46.3	7 53.7	Sales/Receivables	1 365.3	5 71.5	7 54.7	13 28.0	8 45.4	13 27.6
42 8.7	53 6.9	35 10.4		24 15.3	30 12.0	39 9.3	41 8.8	49 7.4	49 7.5
			Cost of Sales/Inventory						
			Cost of Sales/Payables						
2.3	2.1	2.3		1.6	1.9	1.5	2.0	2.9	3.1
7.4	6.1	4.8	Sales/Working Capital	2.9	5.6	2.9	4.0	6.6	8.3
-57.8	62.0	22.3		NM	45.3	7.8	9.6	14.3	20.4
8.7	8.1	8.9		2.6	16.7		14.9	6.2	26.3
(78) 2.0	(74) 3.0	(84) 2.6	EBIT/Interest	(13) 1.0	(23) 3.5	(12) 1.6	(19) 2.5	(10) 10.6
.3	1.0	.7		.0	1.6		-1.7	1.5	3.2
			Net Profit + Depr., Dep., Amort./Cur. Mat. L/T/D						
.4	.2	.4		.5	.3	.3	.4	.7	.2
1.1	1.0	1.0	Fixed/Worth	1.4	1.1	.8	.8	1.2	.8
2.1	1.9	2.2		NM	2.0	1.0	1.7	2.0	1.2
.4	.4	.3		.2	.3	.2	.2	.4	.3
.9	1.2	.9	Debt/Worth	2.6	.7	.5	.5	1.0	.7
3.2	4.2	3.4		NM	2.6	9.1	1.5	3.4	2.2
12.2	15.7	13.2		15.3	16.5	18.0	14.5	12.1	13.4
(106) 3.4	(112) 5.4	(110) 5.0	% Profit Before Taxes/Tangible Net Worth	(21) 3.0	(27) 6.2	4.4	2.7	(23) 5.1	7.5
-2.8	-.5	-1.0		-3.6	.9	-34.1	-3.8	-2.1	2.5
5.0	5.8	6.7		5.7	6.6	6.7	10.0	5.6	10.1
1.0	1.7	2.1	% Profit Before Taxes/Total Assets	.3	2.4	.8	.9	2.1	4.2
-1.4	-.5	-.8		-1.8	.4	-3.3	-1.9	-.2	1.0
4.3	8.3	4.1		3.9	3.3	7.2	4.7	4.0	67.8
.8	1.3	.7	Sales/Net Fixed Assets	.7	.7	1.3	1.2	.9	1.4
.4	.4	.5		.3	.3	.4	.4	.6	.6
.7	.9	.9		.5	.7	.7	1.1	.9	4.8
.4	.4	.5	Sales/Total Assets	.4	.4	.4	.5	.6	.8
.2	.2	.2		.1	.2	.3	.3	.4	.4
1.4	1.6	2.3		4.0	1.5		1.9	1.9	.2
(95) 6.1	(92) 4.7	(102) 6.0	% Depr., Dep., Amort./Sales	(21) 14.0	(26) 6.3	(14) 4.2	(21) 3.4	5.0
12.2	11.1	12.1		22.0	11.3		15.5	8.5	7.4
6.7	4.0	4.4	% Officers', Directors' Owners' Comp/Sales						
(11) 15.0	(11) 12.7	(11) 17.4							
26.1	20.9	24.9							
1163137M	1645408M	1101804M	Net Sales ($)	13717M	53446M	41833M	102524M	363534M	526750M
2535777M	3096345M	2234103M	Total Assets ($)	67408M	146359M	184275M	251917M	836998M	747146M

© RMA 2007

M = $ thousand   MM = $ million
See Pages 11 through 21 for Explanation of Ratios and Data

Current Data Sorted by Assets | Comparative Historical Data

0-500M	500M-2MM	2-10MM	10-50MM	50-100MM	100-250MM	Type of Statement	4/1/02-3/31/03 ALL	4/1/03-3/31/04 ALL
3	13	22	22	8	6	Unqualified	38	35
	3	3	1	1		Reviewed	1	2
1		2				Compiled	2	7
						Tax Returns		
2	1	9	4		1	Other	20	20
	64 (4/1-9/30/06)		38 (10/1/06-3/31/07)					
6	17	36	27	9	7	**NUMBER OF STATEMENTS**	61	64
%	%	%	%	%	%	**ASSETS**	%	%
	22.1	15.5	15.1			Cash & Equivalents	18.2	14.9
	16.8	11.1	9.2			Trade Receivables (net)	10.1	11.2
	.0	2.9	.2			Inventory	.5	1.2
	.2	2.8	12.1			All Other Current	4.5	9.2
	39.1	32.4	36.6			Total Current	33.3	36.6
	44.7	43.9	29.5			Fixed Assets (net)	41.0	42.1
	.0	.8	.5			Intangibles (net)	2.3	1.4
	16.2	23.0	33.4			All Other Non-Current	23.3	19.9
	100.0	100.0	100.0			Total	100.0	100.0
						LIABILITIES		
	6.8	3.3	5.6			Notes Payable-Short Term	5.5	4.6
	2.3	5.0	2.8			Cur. Mat.-L.T.D.	3.1	3.4
	11.5	3.6	2.1			Trade Payables	3.8	3.6
	.0	.0	.0			Income Taxes Payable	.0	.0
	7.3	9.5	3.3			All Other Current	6.5	8.4
	27.7	21.5	13.8			Total Current	18.9	20.0
	42.5	37.5	34.3			Long-Term Debt	28.3	33.8
	.0	.0	.0			Deferred Taxes	.0	.0
	2.2	5.8	10.2			All Other Non-Current	5.2	3.3
	27.5	35.3	41.6			Net Worth	47.7	42.9
	100.0	100.0	100.0			Total Liabilities & Net Worth	100.0	100.0
						INCOME DATA		
	100.0	100.0	100.0			Net Sales	100.0	100.0
						Gross Profit		
	88.3	76.1	75.4			Operating Expenses	88.6	85.4
	11.7	23.9	24.6			Operating Profit	11.4	14.6
	3.8	11.4	11.7			All Other Expenses (net)	7.2	10.2
	8.0	12.5	12.8			Profit Before Taxes	4.2	4.4
						RATIOS		
	15.0	4.8	6.8				4.3	5.7
	1.1	1.2	2.4			Current	1.9	1.7
	.5	.6	1.2				.9	.7
	15.0	2.9	5.5				4.2	5.2
	1.1	1.0	.9			Quick	1.7	1.1
	.5	.3	.4				.4	.4
0 UND	0 UND		9 39.7				5 71.0	0 UND
1 385.0	7 49.2		40 9.2			Sales/Receivables	21 17.3	14 25.8
53 6.8	38 9.5		117 3.1				61 6.0	79 4.6
						Cost of Sales/Inventory		
						Cost of Sales/Payables		
	1.2	1.9	.4				1.4	1.2
	19.8	19.5	1.6			Sales/Working Capital	4.7	5.0
	-9.4	-8.7	27.4				-70.5	-11.6
	11.1	7.7	12.5				3.5	4.9
	(10) 3.3	(21) 3.8	(21) 2.6			EBIT/Interest	(40) 1.5	(42) 1.5
	1.5	1.2	1.2				-1.7	-2.4
						Net Profit + Depr., Dep., Amort./Cur. Mat. L/T/D		
	.1	.0	.0				.1	.1
	1.1	.9	.4			Fixed/Worth	.8	.9
	5.7	5.2	1.1				1.6	2.2
	.5	.3	.7				.5	.4
	1.2	1.5	1.5			Debt/Worth	.9	1.2
	NM	12.5	2.9				2.7	5.4
	14.3	18.4	13.9			% Profit Before Taxes/Tangible	10.9	14.9
	(13) 5.1	(31) 6.3	(26) 5.8			Net Worth	(56) 1.7	(57) 5.9
	.0	1.4	-.9				-4.0	-2.6
	7.9	6.4	5.5			% Profit Before Taxes/Total	3.6	5.0
	1.3	2.8	2.6			Assets	1.0	1.4
	.0	.2	-.5				-2.8	-1.3
	51.5	18.0	114.8				9.3	11.2
	3.3	1.1	1.4			Sales/Net Fixed Assets	1.1	1.1
	.3	.4	.3				.5	.4
	1.7	.7	.3				1.1	.6
	.6	.3	.2			Sales/Total Assets	.4	.3
	.2	.2	.1				.1	.1
	1.0	.7	.7				2.3	1.2
	(13) 2.4	(20) 3.2	(18) 5.0			% Depr., Dep., Amort./Sales	(46) 5.4	(47) 6.2
	9.7	6.7	8.2				9.6	11.5
						% Officers', Directors' Owners' Comp/Sales		
5700M	18349M	93547M	211758M	169517M	332666M	Net Sales ($)	816350M	348790M
1890M	18127M	176267M	684997M	675229M	1119183M	Total Assets ($)	1428417M	1159264M

M = $ thousand   MM = $ million
See Pages 11 through 21 for Explanation of Ratios and Data

Comparative Historical Data | Current Data Sorted by Sales

49	45	74	Type of Statement — Unqualified	16	22	12	11	5	8
1			Reviewed						
1	4	8	Compiled	5	1	1	1		
1	1	3	Tax Returns	3					
19	36	17	Other	5	5	1	3	1	2
4/1/04-3/31/05 ALL	4/1/05-3/31/06 ALL	4/1/06-3/31/07 ALL		64 (4/1-9/30/06) 0-1MM	1-3MM	3-5MM	38 (10/1/06-3/31/07) 5-10MM	10-25MM	25MM & OVER
71	86	102	**NUMBER OF STATEMENTS**	29	28	14	15	6	10
%	%	%	**ASSETS**	%	%	%	%	%	%
18.9	14.6	17.7	Cash & Equivalents	15.2	18.7	22.7	14.2		20.8
11.6	8.8	12.7	Trade Receivables (net)	14.6	11.6	12.1	9.7		10.0
1.2	1.4	2.0	Inventory	4.7	1.6	.0	1.5		.1
6.8	4.8	4.8	All Other Current	1.5	3.5	9.3	9.1		8.3
38.5	29.6	37.2	Total Current	36.0	35.4	44.1	34.5		39.3
41.3	45.5	37.1	Fixed Assets (net)	48.1	38.8	23.8	27.8		39.7
.6	1.4	.4	Intangibles (net)	.1	1.0	.2	.1		.2
19.5	23.5	25.2	All Other Non-Current	15.8	24.8	31.9	37.7		20.8
100.0	100.0	100.0	Total	100.0	100.0	100.0	100.0		100.0
			LIABILITIES						
3.7	5.4	3.9	Notes Payable-Short Term	4.8	2.0	6.5	1.0		6.8
2.8	4.1	3.4	Cur. Mat.-L.T.D.	1.7	4.9	4.8	2.7		3.9
2.6	3.4	5.0	Trade Payables	5.8	4.6	9.1	2.0		2.2
.1	.0	.0	Income Taxes Payable	.0	.0	.0	.1		.0
7.7	7.0	7.0	All Other Current	4.7	6.4	5.3	16.3		6.0
16.9	20.0	19.4	Total Current	17.1	17.8	25.6	22.2		18.9
33.6	30.5	36.7	Long-Term Debt	44.6	31.4	34.2	36.0		40.0
.1	.0	.0	Deferred Taxes	.0	.0	.0	.0		.0
4.4	5.1	5.4	All Other Non-Current	3.7	7.2	5.9	7.3		.6
45.1	44.4	38.5	Net Worth	34.6	43.7	34.2	34.5		40.5
100.0	100.0	100.0	Total Liabilities & Net Worth	100.0	100.0	100.0	100.0		100.0
			INCOME DATA						
100.0	100.0	100.0	Net Sales	100.0	100.0	100.0	100.0		100.0
			Gross Profit						
82.6	82.8	78.0	Operating Expenses	73.8	76.7	84.2	75.6		80.7
17.4	17.2	22.0	Operating Profit	26.2	23.3	15.8	24.4		19.3
8.9	8.5	9.4	All Other Expenses (net)	16.3	6.4	9.9	5.4		3.5
8.5	8.7	12.6	Profit Before Taxes	9.9	17.0	5.9	19.0		15.8
			RATIOS						
5.7	3.7	5.5	Current	14.8	7.2	16.3	4.6		3.9
2.6	1.8	1.9		1.8	1.8	1.9	2.6		2.7
.9	.8	.9		.3	.9	.2	1.2		1.1
5.7	2.9	4.3	Quick	14.8	6.7	13.4	3.1		3.4
1.8	1.1	1.3		1.0	1.2	.9	1.2		2.3
.5	.5	.5		.2	.4	.2	.7		.8
0 UND	0 UND	0 UND	Sales/Receivables	0 UND	0 UND	0 UND	0 UND		6 60.6
35 10.5	35 10.3	22 16.8		1 385.0	18 20.2	24 15.3	30 12.0		49 7.4
86 4.2	70 5.2	81 4.5		34 10.7	54 6.8	71 5.2	222 1.6		167 2.2
			Cost of Sales/Inventory						
			Cost of Sales/Payables						
1.0	1.1	.8	Sales/Working Capital	.7	.8	.7	.5		1.3
2.7	4.4	5.4		11.3	13.2	4.7	1.7		3.6
-35.1	-16.7	-32.3		-4.6	-49.2	-3.6	24.2		NM
7.4	5.9	8.0	EBIT/Interest	11.5	9.0	3.0	34.5		
(43) 3.1	(48) 2.2	(62) 3.0		(14) 3.0	(15) 6.2	(10) 1.7	(10) 3.4		
-.6	.1	1.2		1.2	2.9	.0	1.2		
			Net Profit + Depr., Dep., Amort./Cur. Mat. L/T/D						
.1	.2	.0	Fixed/Worth	.0	.0	.0	.0		.0
.8	1.0	.7		1.1	.5	.6	.1		.8
1.9	1.7	1.6		4.1	1.4	2.1	1.1		1.3
.4	.6	.5	Debt/Worth	.5	.3	.6	.4		.5
1.1	1.2	1.3		1.7	1.1	1.7	1.5		1.3
2.2	2.9	4.4		11.5	3.8	6.5	2.7		5.8
20.9	12.0	18.2	% Profit Before Taxes/Tangible Net Worth	15.1	22.7	11.9	20.6		
(66) 3.9	(83) 4.7	(92) 6.8		(25) 5.1	(25) 8.9	(13) 6.9	(14) 8.0		
-2.3	-1.5	.1		.1	.8	-.2	3.1		
7.6	3.8	6.6	% Profit Before Taxes/Total Assets	5.7	9.9	7.1	4.6		12.5
1.7	1.7	2.6		.9	4.0	1.6	2.6		5.2
-1.4	-1.0	.0		.1	.3	-1.8	1.1		-1.6
12.6	14.3	80.1	Sales/Net Fixed Assets	19.3	92.8	181.0	90.7		41.8
1.2	.7	2.2		.6	1.1	3.3	10.6		1.1
.3	.2	.4		.2	.4	.6	.3		.7
.8	.5	.6	Sales/Total Assets	.5	.9	1.5	.4		.7
.3	.2	.3		.2	.3	.4	.2		.5
.1	.1	.1		.1	.1	.2	.1		.3
2.0	.9	.8	% Depr., Dep., Amort./Sales	1.1	.8	1.7	.5		
(50) 4.4	(70) 3.8	(66) 2.8		(20) 3.0	(13) 1.6	(10) 5.3	(13) .9		
8.3	9.6	8.1		13.9	5.5	7.5	4.4		
			% Officers', Directors' Owners' Comp/Sales						
776355M	947081M	831537M	Net Sales ($)	14345M	50249M	53214M	105060M	93587M	515082M
1463681M	2191335M	2675693M	Total Assets ($)	83140M	247174M	256086M	758811M	210594M	1119888M

M = $ thousand   MM = $ million
See Pages 11 through 21 for Explanation of Ratios and Data

Current Data Sorted by Assets   Comparative Historical Data

0-500M	500M-2MM	2-10MM	10-50MM	50-100MM	100-250MM	Type of Statement	4/1/02-3/31/03 ALL	4/1/03-3/31/04 ALL
2	16	32	37	9	4	Unqualified	56	46
1			1		1	Reviewed	8	2
		3		1	1	Compiled	8	23
1						Tax Returns	3	6
5	1	10	12		2	Other	43	30
0-500M	102 (4/1-9/30/06) 500M-2MM	2-10MM	37 (10/1/06-3/31/07) 10-50MM	50-100MM	100-250MM			
8	18	45	50	10	8	NUMBER OF STATEMENTS	118	107
%	%	%	%	%	%	**ASSETS**	%	%
	36.9	27.8	13.1	13.3		Cash & Equivalents	15.6	16.4
	15.5	14.1	9.5	6.6		Trade Receivables (net)	10.7	12.8
	4.8	1.1	.9	.2		Inventory	5.0	5.3
	11.0	6.8	3.3	7.2		All Other Current	4.8	6.5
	68.3	49.8	26.8	27.3		Total Current	36.0	41.0
	19.9	27.4	45.8	50.0		Fixed Assets (net)	42.1	35.6
	.0	.8	2.6	5.2		Intangibles (net)	2.7	2.2
	11.8	22.0	24.8	17.6		All Other Non-Current	19.1	21.3
	100.0	100.0	100.0	100.0		Total	100.0	100.0
						LIABILITIES		
	4.1	4.0	1.4	.1		Notes Payable-Short Term	5.1	4.5
	1.7	1.4	2.4	1.4		Cur. Mat.-L.T.D.	3.4	2.4
	9.0	8.2	5.0	5.0		Trade Payables	6.5	4.0
	.0	.1	.0	.0		Income Taxes Payable	.3	.1
	11.1	8.4	5.8	7.6		All Other Current	6.3	7.5
	26.0	22.1	14.5	14.0		Total Current	21.6	18.5
	10.5	20.1	35.0	26.7		Long-Term Debt	28.6	26.2
	.0	.0	.0	.0		Deferred Taxes	.2	.1
	4.1	8.4	3.9	3.3		All Other Non-Current	3.1	4.7
	59.5	49.3	46.6	55.9		Net Worth	46.4	50.5
	100.0	100.0	100.0	100.0		Total Liabilities & Net Worth	100.0	100.0
						INCOME DATA		
	100.0	100.0	100.0	100.0		Net Sales	100.0	100.0
						Gross Profit		
	95.5	83.0	73.3	80.6		Operating Expenses	78.1	80.6
	4.5	17.0	26.7	19.4		Operating Profit	21.9	19.4
	-1.4	4.6	11.2	2.5		All Other Expenses (net)	7.6	8.0
	5.9	12.4	15.5	17.0		Profit Before Taxes	14.3	11.4
						RATIOS		
	4.9	3.6	5.0	4.5			3.8	6.1
	3.1	2.2	1.9	2.4		Current	1.9	2.7
	1.7	1.6	.8	1.3			1.1	1.2
	4.3	3.1	3.6	2.9			3.2	4.7
	2.0	1.8	1.4	1.9		Quick	(117) 1.4	2.1
	1.3	1.3	.6	.6			.8	.8
	0 UND	3 120.6	0 UND	0 UND			1 592.9	0 UND
	19 18.8	21 17.1	18 20.3	38 9.5		Sales/Receivables	21 17.3	16 22.9
	33 11.0	60 6.1	100 3.6	55 6.6			60 6.1	46 7.9
						Cost of Sales/Inventory		
						Cost of Sales/Payables		
	2.5	1.4	.9	1.2			1.6	1.3
	4.9	5.5	5.5	4.3		Sales/Working Capital	6.5	4.1
	12.7	17.3	-28.0	38.2			58.8	16.3
		19.1	5.7				6.0	9.6
	(21) 4.3		(26) 3.4			EBIT/Interest	(62) 3.3	(62) 3.4
		2.2	.6				.9	1.4
						Net Profit + Depr., Dep., Amort./Cur. Mat. L/T/D		
	.0	.1	.4	.8			.3	.1
	.1	.4	1.0	.9		Fixed/Worth	.9	.7
	.7	1.0	2.5	1.4			1.8	1.4
	.2	.4	.5	.4			.5	.4
	.6	1.1	1.5	.7		Debt/Worth	1.0	.8
	1.7	2.7	3.3	2.2			3.9	2.6
	31.8	24.6	19.2				21.1	28.4
	5.1	(44) 9.9	(48) 4.7			% Profit Before Taxes/Tangible Net Worth	(111) 7.0	(103) 9.7
	-3.2	2.2	-1.0				-.7	.8
	11.2	8.7	7.3	5.0			7.9	9.5
	2.5	4.6	2.5	2.3		% Profit Before Taxes/Total Assets	3.0	3.7
	-1.5	.8	-.3	-2.8			-.6	.5
	98.4	45.5	5.6	2.5			18.1	46.2
	22.3	9.3	.5	.6		Sales/Net Fixed Assets	1.5	2.7
	6.4	2.1	.2	.3			.2	.4
	3.2	1.8	.5	.6			1.2	1.9
	2.1	.7	.2	.4		Sales/Total Assets	.3	.3
	1.3	.2	.1	.1			.1	.1
	.6	.4	2.4				1.3	.9
	(13) 1.6	(31) 1.2	(39) 9.4			% Depr., Dep., Amort./Sales	(85) 3.2	(86) 3.3
	2.4	2.3	14.8				12.4	11.2
							2.7	1.0
						% Officers', Directors' Owners' Comp/Sales	(12) 3.9	(14) 5.3
							19.8	9.4
8038M	40303M	302384M	557862M	303659M	301029M	Net Sales ($)	1576745M	696019M
1994M	18321M	267671M	1088355M	683323M	1044771M	Total Assets ($)	2872566M	1422076M

M = $ thousand   MM = $ million
See Pages 11 through 21 for Explanation of Ratios and Data

Comparative Historical Data | Current Data Sorted by Sales

			Type of Statement						
56	66	100	Unqualified	15	23	12	22	16	12
3	3	3	Reviewed	1	1				1
14	7	5	Compiled	3		1	1		
3	2	1	Tax Returns		1				
29	34	30	Other	6	9	8		6	1
4/1/04-3/31/05 ALL	4/1/05-3/31/06 ALL	4/1/06-3/31/07 ALL		102 (4/1-9/30/06)			37 (10/1/06-3/31/07)		
				0-1MM	1-3MM	3-5MM	5-10MM	10-25MM	25MM & OVER
105	112	139	NUMBER OF STATEMENTS	25	34	21	23	22	14
%	%	%	ASSETS	%	%	%	%	%	%
18.8	18.9	22.2	Cash & Equivalents	26.2	24.6	16.2	15.5	24.2	25.9
10.7	10.6	12.7	Trade Receivables (net)	16.5	11.3	7.7	12.0	10.7	21.2
2.9	2.5	2.0	Inventory	.0	5.8	.3	.5	1.7	1.7
5.7	4.8	6.0	All Other Current	7.2	5.9	2.7	7.4	3.4	10.5
38.1	36.7	42.9	Total Current	49.9	47.7	26.9	35.4	39.9	59.3
40.5	41.0	35.2	Fixed Assets (net)	27.2	30.1	46.0	40.3	40.8	29.0
1.1	1.6	1.6	Intangibles (net)	.0	.0	3.3	3.6	.2	5.0
20.3	20.6	20.3	All Other Non-Current	22.9	22.2	23.9	20.7	19.1	6.7
100.0	100.0	100.0	Total	100.0	100.0	100.0	100.0	100.0	100.0
			LIABILITIES						
5.7	3.9	4.0	Notes Payable-Short Term	10.9	4.0	1.7	1.4	2.3	1.6
3.5	2.7	1.9	Cur. Mat.-L.T.D.	1.8	1.3	2.1	3.4	.8	2.6
5.6	4.9	6.8	Trade Payables	2.4	6.5	3.0	10.7	6.1	15.7
.1	.0	.0	Income Taxes Payable	.0	.1	.1	.0	.0	.0
7.1	7.8	8.0	All Other Current	9.8	7.3	8.4	3.1	8.3	13.2
21.9	19.3	20.7	Total Current	24.9	19.2	15.3	18.5	17.6	33.0
28.1	30.0	24.2	Long-Term Debt	22.7	24.6	38.4	28.0	18.1	7.7
.0	.0	.1	Deferred Taxes	.0	.0	.0	.0	.0	1.1
5.0	5.0	5.2	All Other Non-Current	5.2	5.4	1.5	7.2	5.4	6.4
45.0	45.6	49.9	Net Worth	47.1	50.8	44.8	46.2	58.9	51.8
100.0	100.0	100.0	Total Liabilties & Net Worth	100.0	100.0	100.0	100.0	100.0	100.0
			INCOME DATA						
100.0	100.0	100.0	Net Sales	100.0	100.0	100.0	100.0	100.0	100.0
			Gross Profit						
85.2	77.9	81.8	Operating Expenses	66.5	85.2	76.2	82.0	92.5	92.3
14.8	22.1	18.2	Operating Profit	33.5	14.8	23.8	18.0	7.5	7.7
5.8	9.7	5.8	All Other Expenses (net)	12.4	6.1	8.1	3.5	1.9	-.2
8.9	12.4	12.4	Profit Before Taxes	21.2	8.6	15.8	14.4	5.6	7.8
			RATIOS						
5.3	4.8	4.4		11.2	7.1	3.4	3.2	3.2	4.7
1.9	2.2	2.2	Current	2.9	2.8	2.2	1.9	2.0	2.2
1.0	1.1	1.3		1.2	1.3	1.4	1.3	1.4	1.2
3.9	4.1	3.2		7.1	6.2	2.9	2.8	2.5	4.0
1.5	1.7	1.8	Quick	1.9	1.7	1.9	1.7	1.8	1.8
.6	.7	1.0		.6	.7	1.2	1.1	.8	.7
0 UND	0 UND	1 330.7		0 UND	0 UND	18 20.1	1 330.7	4 85.5	4 83.5
19 18.8	15 24.4	23 15.8	Sales/Receivables	19 19.6	9 42.6	42 8.7	10 35.8	23 16.2	32 11.6
51 7.2	42 8.7	62 5.9		161 2.3	37 9.9	70 5.2	62 5.9	55 6.6	64 5.7
			Cost of Sales/Inventory						
			Cost of Sales/Payables						
1.9	1.2	1.7		.4	.8	1.6	3.4	1.3	3.5
5.8	5.5	5.2	Sales/Working Capital	2.3	4.9	3.8	5.7	6.2	7.6
186.4	43.1	19.6		24.8	21.2	18.2	17.5	30.8	32.7
6.8	8.3	10.4			19.9		6.1	20.5	
(65) 2.1	(52) 2.9	(66) 4.1	EBIT/Interest	(18) 4.3		(14) 3.5	(13) 4.2		
-.1	1.3	1.1			.9		.3	-.9	
			Net Profit + Depr., Dep., Amort./Cur. Mat. L/T/D						
.2	.1	.1		.0	.1	.4	.3	.3	.0
.9	.8	.7	Fixed/Worth	.1	.5	1.0	1.0	.7	.6
1.8	1.7	1.3		1.0	1.6	4.4	1.4	1.1	1.2
.4	.4	.4		.3	.3	.5	.9	.2	.2
1.1	1.1	1.1	Debt/Worth	1.1	.9	1.1	1.4	.6	1.3
2.7	3.4	2.6		3.5	2.6	4.8	2.0	1.7	3.0
18.6	15.1	21.7		12.1	13.7	21.8	29.4	16.0	41.2
(97) 8.1	(103) 6.6	(134) 6.8	% Profit Before Taxes/Tangible Net Worth	(23) 4.3	2.9	(20) 11.1	16.0	3.8	(12) 21.2
-.1	1.0	-.8		.7	-3.6	2.1	-1.6	-3.2	1.6
7.7	6.1	8.0		7.0	6.5	5.7	9.1	9.4	18.2
2.6	2.4	3.0	% Profit Before Taxes/Total Assets	1.7	1.5	3.5	5.8	3.0	8.2
-.8	.1	-.3		.6	-1.2	.7	-1.5	-1.5	-2.0
37.4	21.1	22.6		143.4	27.0	9.0	16.8	11.2	393.5
2.3	.9	3.2	Sales/Net Fixed Assets	17.4	6.4	1.7	1.1	2.7	15.6
.3	.2	.4		.2	.2	.2	.4	.3	.8
1.9	1.5	1.9		.6	2.1	1.0	1.5	2.3	3.4
.4	.3	.4	Sales/Total Assets	.1	.4	.3	.5	.6	1.8
.1	.1	.1		.1	.1	.1	.2	.2	.5
1.1	1.2	.9		.4	1.0	2.0	1.2	.9	
(75) 2.6	(83) 4.6	(96) 2.3	% Depr., Dep., Amort./Sales	(15) 1.1	(24) 2.2	(14) 5.9	(16) 4.9	(20) 2.4	
13.6	12.3	10.7		4.8	13.1	15.6	11.8	9.0	
4.4	4.5								
(14) 5.8	(14) 6.4		% Officers', Directors' Owners' Comp/Sales						
9.1	21.8								
968228M	1003407M	1513275M	Net Sales ($)	14722M	69682M	80247M	166757M	349971M	831896M
1333439M	2312040M	3104435M	Total Assets ($)	138672M	333701M	365052M	710519M	861271M	695220M

M = $ thousand   MM = $ million
See Pages 11 through 21 for Explanation of Ratios and Data

CONSTRUCTION— PERCENTAGE OF COMPLETION BASIS OF ACCOUNTING*

Current Data Sorted by Assets   Comparative Historical Data

0-1MM	1-10MM	10-50MM	50 & OVER	ALL	Type of Statement	4/1/02-3/31/03	4/1/03-3/31/04	4/1/04-3/31/05	4/1/05-3/31/06	4/1/06-3/31/07
	2	5	19	26	Unqualified	18	26	30	12	26
		3		3	Reviewed	8	7	4	1	3
1	14	5		20	Compiled	29	24	24	19	20
2	3			5	Tax Returns	5	8	11	2	5
4	13	15	8	40	Other	30	25	47	19	40
	16 (4/1-9/30/06)		78 (10/1/06-3/31/07)			ALL	ALL	ALL	ALL	ALL
0-1MM	1-10MM	10-50MM	50 & OVER	ALL	NUMBER OF STATEMENTS	90	90	116	53	94
7	32	28	27	94						
%	%	%	%	%	**ASSETS**	%	%	%	%	%
	13.3	9.7	10.0	11.8	Cash & Equivalents	8.8	8.2	9.3	8.3	11.8
	41.3	44.3	24.5	34.9	A/R - Progress Billings	30.7	28.3	29.6	37.4	34.9
	.0	.0	.1	.0	A/R - Current Retention	.5	.2	.2	1.0	.0
	5.7	3.6	12.7	7.5	Inventory	4.7	5.9	7.2	5.0	7.5
	.2	.4	.1	.2	Cost & Est. Earnings In Excess Billings	.2	.3	.3	.3	.2
	7.7	3.6	2.5	4.4	All Other Current	4.2	2.7	2.7	4.5	4.4
	68.3	61.7	49.8	58.8	Total Current	49.2	45.8	49.3	56.5	58.8
	26.4	30.2	34.1	30.1	Fixed Assets (net)	39.7	41.7	36.4	32.1	30.1
	.6	2.6	1.6	1.4	Joint Ventures & Investments	3.5	1.2	2.4	1.2	1.4
	.2	.8	8.7	3.5	Intangibles (net)	3.1	3.3	4.6	4.2	3.5
	4.6	4.7	5.8	6.2	All Other Non-Current	4.5	8.0	7.2	6.0	6.2
	100.0	100.0	100.0	100.0	Total	100.0	100.0	100.0	100.0	100.0
					LIABILITIES					
	11.5	10.0	2.4	8.6	Notes Payable-Short Term	10.3	8.3	9.5	9.8	8.6
	14.0	12.8	9.0	11.5	A/P - Trade	11.3	9.6	9.7	9.7	11.5
	.6	.0	.5	.3	A/P - Retention	.0	.6	.1	.1	.3
	.0	.9	.3	.4	Billings in Excess of Costs & Est. Earnings	.2	.1	.1	.1	.4
	.1	.8	.6	.5	Income Taxes Payable	.5	.2	.2	.2	.5
	2.2	1.8	1.7	2.0	Cur. Mat.-L/T/D	4.2	5.4	3.8	2.0	2.0
	9.0	9.7	8.8	8.7	All Other Current	6.3	6.8	6.7	7.2	8.7
	37.4	36.0	23.3	31.9	Total Current	32.8	31.0	30.0	29.0	31.9
	12.6	12.2	17.6	15.4	Long-Term Debt	19.3	18.3	19.5	16.3	15.4
	.1	.9	2.6	1.1	Deferred Taxes	.8	.9	1.3	1.3	1.1
	4.7	2.6	2.9	3.6	All Other Non-Current	5.5	7.1	3.7	2.9	3.6
	45.2	48.2	53.6	48.0	Net Worth	41.6	42.8	45.5	50.5	48.0
	100.0	100.0	100.0	100.0	Total Liabilities & Net Worth	100.0	100.0	100.0	100.0	100.0
					INCOME DATA					
	100.0	100.0	100.0	100.0	Contract Revenues	100.0	100.0	100.0	100.0	100.0
					Gross Profit					
	88.2	82.7	80.1	83.2	Operating Expenses	91.2	92.5	88.1	88.2	83.2
	11.8	17.3	19.9	16.8	Operating Profit	8.8	7.5	11.9	11.8	16.8
	2.0	.4	2.3	2.4	All Other Expenses (net)	2.4	3.0	2.8	1.7	2.4
	9.8	16.9	17.6	14.4	Profit Before Taxes	6.4	4.6	9.1	10.1	14.4
					RATIOS					
	3.0	3.1	3.1	3.1	Current	2.2	2.7	3.2	2.9	3.1
	1.9	1.7	2.2	2.0		1.6	1.5	1.6	1.8	2.0
	1.2	1.2	1.9	1.2		1.1	.9	.9	1.3	1.2
	7.9	28.0	3.6	6.7	Receivables/Payables	7.3	8.3	5.7	12.5	6.7
(30)	4.0	5.3	2.5	(90) 3.3		(86) 2.9	(85) 3.4	(109) 2.8	3.6	(90) 3.3
	1.8	1.5	1.8	1.7		1.4	1.6	1.8	2.0	1.7
51 7.2	45 8.2	58 6.3	46 8.0		Revenues/Receivables	42 8.6	39 9.3	47 7.8	60 6.1	46 8.0
67 5.5	64 5.7	74 4.9	66 5.6			65 5.6	61 5.9	64 5.7	86 4.2	66 5.6
85 4.3	101 3.6	102 3.6	88 4.1			93 3.9	83 4.4	87 4.2	109 3.3	88 4.1
					Cost of Revenues/Payables					
	4.1	4.8	3.1	3.7	Revenues/Working Capital	5.8	4.9	4.1	3.9	3.7
	7.1	10.5	4.5	6.9		11.4	13.4	10.6	6.3	6.9
	24.2	28.8	7.1	16.5		58.8	-82.1	-73.3	19.1	16.5
	17.7	37.2	30.2	23.7	EBIT/Interest	11.3	14.6	15.3	18.4	23.7
(31)	9.1	(27) 13.7	(26) 14.1	(88) 11.4		(83) 3.6	(81) 3.6	(107) 5.9	(50) 7.0	(88) 11.4
	2.7	6.3	6.4	4.6		1.2	.6	2.0	2.4	4.6
				20.7	Net Profit + Depr., Dep., Amort./Cur. Mat. L/T/D	6.4	4.2	5.9		20.7
			(11)	11.3		(14) 4.5	(11) 1.8	(17) 3.0	(11) 11.3	
				7.5		2.0	-.5	1.7		7.5
	.1	.1	.4	.2	Fixed/Worth	.4	.3	.3	.2	.2
	.4	.5	.8	.6		1.0	.9	.8	.8	.6
	.9	1.4	1.4	1.3		2.3	2.5	2.1	1.6	1.3
	.5	.4	.5	.4	Debt/Worth	.6	.5	.6	.6	.4
	1.0	1.1	1.1	1.0		1.5	1.4	1.4	1.0	1.0
	2.9	2.4	2.4	2.7		3.1	3.5	3.1	2.1	2.7
	58.6	80.4	63.8	64.4	% Profit Before Taxes/Tangible Net Worth	26.5	41.3	51.8	50.1	64.4
(31)	25.5	57.7	(26) 45.1	(90) 42.4		(79) 11.5	(81) 19.5	(108) 22.9	(51) 33.1	(90) 42.4
	15.0	30.4	24.9	23.4		3.7	1.3	5.7	2.4	23.4
	24.9	39.9	25.8	27.6	% Profit Before Taxes/Total Assets	12.8	15.5	16.8	23.3	27.6
	16.1	22.2	15.1	17.6		4.7	6.0	8.2	12.1	17.6
	1.8	14.7	10.8	8.0		.3	-.5	1.9	1.4	8.0
	1.1	.8	.5	.9	% Depr., Dep., Amort./Revenues	2.3	2.3	2.0	.6	.9
(20)	2.8	(20) 3.4	(10) 1.9	(53) 2.9		(67) 5.7	(62) 5.9	(87) 4.8	(39) 2.6	(53) 2.9
	6.3	6.0	2.9	5.8		9.0	11.6	12.5	6.9	5.8
	3.6			3.5	% Officers', Directors' Owners' Comp/Revenues	3.4	2.2	4.7	2.8	3.5
(15)	5.5		(24)	5.8		(31) 6.0	(23) 5.3	(35) 7.0	(21) 5.0	(24) 5.8
	9.5			10.8		10.0	11.5	12.6	11.0	10.8
2928M	130654M	642142M	27624933M	28400657M	Contract Revenues ($)	15895725M	14915619M	20792379M	5998666M	28400657M
6337M	78195M	396581M	40026603M	40507716M	Total Assets ($)	16226053M	16609814M	27462379M	7334030M	40507716M

© RMA 2007

M = $ thousand   MM = $ million

See Pages 11 through 21 for Explanation of Ratios and Data

Current Data Sorted by Assets　　　　　　　　　　**Comparative Historical Data**

0-1MM	1-10MM	10-50MM	50 & OVER	ALL	Type of Statement	4/1/02-3/31/03 ALL	4/1/03-3/31/04 ALL	4/1/04-3/31/05 ALL	4/1/05-3/31/06 ALL	4/1/06-3/31/07 ALL
	2	6	19	27	Unqualified	54	16	30	24	27
4	31	22	12	69	Reviewed	112	76	85	97	69
17	58	17	3	95	Compiled	181	108	124	116	95
43	132	17	10	202	Tax Returns	302	236	295	248	202
22	96	35	12	165	Other	193	80	152	157	165

72 (4/1-9/30/06)　　486 (10/1/06-3/31/07)

0-1MM	1-10MM	10-50MM	50 & OVER	ALL		02/03	03/04	04/05	05/06	06/07
86	319	97	56	558	**NUMBER OF STATEMENTS**	842	516	686	642	558
%	%	%	%	%	**ASSETS**	%	%	%	%	%
9.0	8.5	6.6	6.2	8.0	Cash & Equivalents	10.4	10.8	10.4	8.9	8.0
4.8	6.7	8.6	3.3	6.4	A/R - Progress Billings	8.2	8.9	9.3	6.9	6.4
.0	.7	.1	.4	.4	A/R - Current Retention	.6	.3	.4	.2	.4
52.4	51.8	61.1	62.8	54.6	Inventory	49.1	45.5	47.5	53.4	54.6
.2	2.0	3.5	3.4	2.2	Cost & Est. Earnings In Excess Billings	2.5	3.5	3.0	2.8	2.2
6.0	5.9	3.5	5.5	5.5	All Other Current	5.3	7.1	5.7	5.7	5.5
72.4	75.5	83.5	81.7	77.0	Total Current	76.1	76.0	76.2	78.0	77.0
18.8	12.5	6.0	7.2	11.8	Fixed Assets (net)	14.1	14.1	13.6	12.5	11.8
.6	3.0	2.5	.9	2.3	Joint Ventures & Investments	2.1	1.7	2.5	1.9	2.3
.4	.5	.4	1.2	.6	Intangibles (net)	.5	.9	.7	.6	.6
7.8	8.5	7.5	9.0	8.3	All Other Non-Current	7.2	7.3	7.0	7.1	8.3
100.0	100.0	100.0	100.0	100.0	Total	100.0	100.0	100.0	100.0	100.0
					LIABILITIES					
29.5	33.7	39.5	37.4	34.5	Notes Payable-Short Term	30.9	31.1	31.8	34.4	34.5
3.8	9.4	10.1	8.8	8.6	A/P - Trade	10.2	11.4	12.4	8.5	8.6
.0	.4	.1	.3	.3	A/P - Retention	.4	.4	.4	.4	.3
1.0	2.5	2.3	1.2	2.1	Billings in Excess of Costs & Est. Earnings	2.1	2.6	2.6	2.4	2.1
.0	.0	.1	.1	.0	Income Taxes Payable	.1	.1	.1	.3	.0
5.8	4.1	3.3	2.5	4.1	Cur. Mat.-L/T/D	4.8	6.0	4.6	3.7	4.1
12.9	10.2	8.0	6.7	9.9	All Other Current	9.2	11.3	9.3	10.4	9.9
53.1	60.4	63.4	56.9	59.4	Total Current	57.7	62.9	61.3	60.0	59.4
25.7	15.1	8.1	12.2	15.2	Long-Term Debt	12.8	13.4	13.7	15.0	15.2
.9	.1	.1	.1	.2	Deferred Taxes	.2	.1	.1	.1	.2
14.2	7.1	3.9	6.8	7.6	All Other Non-Current	6.5	6.7	8.4	6.3	7.6
6.0	17.3	24.5	24.1	17.5	Net Worth	22.8	16.9	16.5	18.6	17.5
100.0	100.0	100.0	100.0	100.0	Total Liabilities & Net Worth	100.0	100.0	100.0	100.0	100.0
					INCOME DATA					
100.0	100.0	100.0	100.0	100.0	Contract Revenues	100.0	100.0	100.0	100.0	100.0
24.5	20.0	18.7	20.0	20.5	Gross Profit	19.9	19.9	19.1	20.9	20.5
21.0	14.8	11.5	12.2	14.9	Operating Expenses	15.4	15.9	15.0	15.0	14.9
3.5	5.2	7.2	7.8	5.6	Operating Profit	4.5	4.0	4.1	5.9	5.6
3.1	1.3	.7	1.9	1.5	All Other Expenses (net)	.6	.6	.5	.6	1.5
.5	3.9	6.5	5.9	4.0	Profit Before Taxes	3.9	3.4	3.7	5.2	4.0
					RATIOS					
4.0	2.1	1.8	1.8	2.0	Current	2.1	1.9	1.8	2.0	2.0
1.2	1.3	1.2	1.3	1.3		1.3	1.2	1.2	1.2	1.3
1.0	1.0	1.1	1.1	1.0		1.0	1.0	1.0	1.0	1.0
14.0	1.3	1.0	.2	1.2	Receivables/Payables	1.3	1.4	1.3	1.4	1.2
(44) .0	(242) .1	(88) .1	(50) .1	(424) .1		(653) .1	(396) .1	(536) .2	(488) .1	(424) .1
.0	.0	.0	.0	.0		.0	.0	.0	.0	.0
0 UND	0 UND	0 UND	0 UND	0 UND	Revenues/Receivables	0 UND	0 UND	0 UND	0 UND	0 UND
0 UND	0 UND	0 999.8	1 625.6	0 UND		0 UND	0 UND	0 UND	0 UND	0 UND
0 UND	9 40.2	11 32.2	3 108.7	6 57.0		10 37.4	9 39.5	13 28.9	5 66.8	6 57.0
0 UND	0 UND	4 102.8	5 67.2	0 UND	Cost of Revenues/Payables	0 UND	0 UND	0 UND	0 UND	0 UND
0 UND	9 39.5	14 25.4	20 18.5	10 38.2		13 27.3	12 30.9	15 24.5	11 33.3	10 38.2
23 15.9	28 12.8	27 13.7	32 11.4	28 13.1		31 11.7	31 11.7	32 11.3	29 12.4	28 13.1
1.7	4.1	4.5	3.8	4.0	Revenues/Working Capital	5.9	6.5	5.9	4.5	4.0
17.9	15.4	10.2	7.0	13.0		15.0	18.0	18.0	14.4	13.0
-18.2	-64.2	35.7	20.6	UND		UND	-95.6	-110.3	-410.2	UND
4.9	11.2	28.8	11.9	13.4	EBIT/Interest	17.6	18.1	13.8	18.0	13.4
(54) 1.9	(264) 2.4	(85) 8.9	(45) 5.5	(448) 3.5		(661) 5.2	(406) 4.8	(518) 5.0	(516) 5.6	(448) 3.5
.2	1.0	2.8		1.2		1.4	1.2	1.6	1.7	1.2
	14.3			13.1	Net Profit + Depr., Dep., Amort./Cur. Mat. L/T/D	7.3	4.9	6.1	8.0	13.1
(12)	4.0		(22)	3.7		(76) 3.2	(54) 2.4	(48) 2.3	(27) -2.8	(22) 3.7
	1.0			1.2		.9	.7	.7	.9	1.2
.0	.0	.0	.0	.0	Fixed/Worth	.0	.1	.1	.0	.0
.2	.3	.1	.1	.2		.3	.3	.3	.2	.2
10.1	4.0	.4	.5	2.3		1.9	2.8	2.6	1.7	2.3
3.1	1.7	2.1	2.1	2.0	Debt/Worth	1.6	1.8	2.0	1.8	2.0
10.2	6.1	5.1	3.7	5.6		4.3	5.1	5.1	5.5	5.6
-24.6	45.0	10.6	7.3	31.0		21.6	36.3	33.0	26.9	31.0
82.0	83.7	67.9	63.4	74.4	% Profit Before Taxes/ Tangible Net Worth	83.1	78.5	80.4	84.6	74.4
(62) 11.0	(259) 29.0	(92) 40.6	(50) 35.4	(463) 34.0		(726) 37.9	(416) 35.5	(570) 37.7	(540) 39.6	(463) 34.0
-2.7	6.7	22.6	23.4	8.7		11.4	8.8	10.5	14.2	8.7
6.9	13.7	16.4	14.9	13.5	% Profit Before Taxes/ Total Assets	15.3	16.3	14.3	17.4	13.5
.6	3.8	7.8	9.5	4.5		6.7	5.4	5.8	6.8	4.5
-2.6	.2	3.2	3.7	.3		.8	.5	.9	1.3	.3
.9	.2	.1	.2	.2	% Depr., Dep., Amort./ Revenues	.3	.3	.3	.2	.2
(38) 1.8	(200) .5	(64) .3	(23) .3	(325) .5		(544) .6	(317) .6	(428) .6	(368) .6	(325) .5
7.5	1.1	.7	.6	1.2		1.4	1.6	1.5	1.3	1.2
3.7	1.6	.8	.5	1.6	% Officers', Directors' Owners' Comp/Revenues	1.8	1.8	1.4	1.6	1.6
(37) 7.5	(183) 3.2	(52) 1.7	(16) 2.8	(288) 3.2		(456) 3.5	(299) 3.7	(397) 3.1	(351) 3.1	(288) 3.2
11.8	5.7	3.4	4.9	6.2		7.0	6.7	6.1	5.8	6.2
46860M	1251709M	2156384M	135496895M	138951848M	Contract Revenues ($)	84992650M	21762072M	134263075M	94368836M	138951848M
82003M	1073026M	1815179M	74421403M	77391611M	Total Assets ($)	41985857M	9493032M	9684945M	57039347M	77391611M

M = $ thousand　　MM = $ million
See Pages 11 through 21 for Explanation of Ratios and Data

Current Data Sorted by Assets						Comparative Historical Data				

		1	2	3		Type of Statement					
	7	3		10		Unqualified	12	11	11	11	3
1	2			3		Reviewed	32	19	15	19	10
4	5			9		Compiled	20	13	9	7	3
1	6	6	1	14		Tax Returns	33	21	18	21	9
						Other	23	10	16	3	14
							4/1/02-	4/1/03-	4/1/04-	4/1/05-	4/1/06-
	4 (4/1-9/30/06)		35 (10/1/06-3/31/07)				3/31/03	3/31/04	3/31/05	3/31/06	3/31/07
0-1MM	1-10MM	10-50MM	50 & OVER	ALL			ALL	ALL	ALL	ALL	ALL
6	20	10	3	39		NUMBER OF STATEMENTS	120	74	69	61	39
%	%	%	%	%		ASSETS	%	%	%	%	%
	10.8	10.9		12.0		Cash & Equivalents	14.8	13.6	10.7	13.1	12.0
	29.6	32.4		28.9		A/R - Progress Billings	20.6	19.5	15.8	22.4	28.9
	.5	2.8		1.0		A/R - Current Retention	1.2	2.4	2.1	1.4	1.0
	28.8	17.8		22.0		Inventory	28.9	27.9	32.0	22.0	22.0
	3.4	11.0		5.3		Cost & Est. Earnings In Excess Billings	1.7	3.1	3.2	4.2	5.3
	6.3	3.1		9.4		All Other Current	8.4	7.6	9.2	12.6	9.4
	79.4	78.0		78.6		Total Current	75.5	74.0	72.9	75.8	78.6
	13.9	13.6		13.1		Fixed Assets (net)	15.4	16.8	15.9	14.0	13.1
	.9	2.0		3.3		Joint Ventures & Investments	1.6	1.4	3.4	2.0	3.3
	.0	3.5		.9		Intangibles (net)	.8	.1	.4	.3	.9
	5.8	2.8		4.1		All Other Non-Current	6.7	7.6	7.3	7.9	4.1
	100.0	100.0		100.0		Total	100.0	100.0	100.0	100.0	100.0
						LIABILITIES					
	19.2	27.8		20.2		Notes Payable-Short Term	20.7	14.5	20.8	24.0	20.2
	17.9	27.5		19.6		A/P - Trade	15.9	16.7	13.8	17.0	19.6
	.0	.4		.1		A/P - Retention	1.0	1.0	1.1	2.1	.1
	2.2	4.6		3.0		Billings in Excess of Costs & Est. Earnings	3.3	5.2	4.8	4.2	3.0
	.0	.1		.0		Income Taxes Payable	.4	.1	.0	.1	.0
	2.9	.2		2.8		Cur. Mat.-L/T/D	4.6	3.6	2.1	6.8	2.8
	5.2	3.1		6.4		All Other Current	11.9	9.7	7.3	10.2	6.4
	47.4	63.8		52.2		Total Current	57.9	50.8	50.0	64.5	52.2
	21.5	2.8		15.2		Long-Term Debt	10.2	17.4	16.6	12.0	15.2
	.5	.0		.3		Deferred Taxes	.2	.3	.6	.1	.3
	7.3	4.4		14.3		All Other Non-Current	3.2	5.2	3.9	4.1	14.3
	23.2	29.0		18.0		Net Worth	28.5	26.3	28.9	19.2	18.0
	100.0	100.0		100.0		Total Liabilities & Net Worth	100.0	100.0	100.0	100.0	100.0
						INCOME DATA					
	100.0	100.0		100.0		Contract Revenues	100.0	100.0	100.0	100.0	100.0
	19.4	14.7		19.7		Gross Profit	20.9	19.0	19.9	18.9	19.7
	14.4	10.2		14.7		Operating Expenses	15.7	15.3	13.1	13.2	14.7
	5.0	4.5		5.0		Operating Profit	5.2	3.7	6.8	5.8	5.0
	2.0	-.6		1.0		All Other Expenses (net)	.7	.5	1.3	.3	1.0
	3.0	5.2		3.9		Profit Before Taxes	4.5	3.2	5.5	5.5	3.9
						RATIOS					
	4.2	1.7		2.8			1.9	2.4	2.4	1.8	2.8
	1.5	1.4		1.5		Current	1.3	1.4	1.4	1.3	1.5
	1.3	1.1		1.1			1.0	1.1	1.1	1.0	1.1
	3.4			3.0			2.4	2.4	1.7	2.2	3.0
(17)	1.9		(33)	1.8		Receivables/Payables	(99) 1.1	(65) 1.2	(58) 1.0	(48) 1.1	(33) 1.8
	1.0			.7			.0	.1	.0	.2	.7
0	UND	0	UND	0 UND			0 UND	0 UND	0 UND	0 UND	0 UND
33	11.1	48	7.6	34 10.7		Revenues/Receivables	5 71.5	11 32.0	2 170.6	9 39.0	34 10.7
52	7.0	73	5.0	68 5.4			39 9.3	44 8.2	46 8.0	60 6.1	68 5.4
0	UND	8	46.7	5 67.3			0 751.3	7 50.7	7 52.3	1 619.3	5 67.3
24	15.2	42	8.6	24 15.2		Cost of Revenues/Payables	20 18.5	27 13.7	25 14.6	26 14.3	24 15.2
44	8.4	59	6.1	47 7.8			38 9.7	43 8.5	49 7.5	48 7.5	47 7.8
	3.8	8.1		5.1			7.4	5.7	5.7	8.5	5.1
	9.2	11.2		9.5		Revenues/Working Capital	14.3	11.8	13.0	19.4	9.5
	21.8	30.4		29.4			570.9	70.1	42.1	295.8	29.4
	9.6			12.0			36.2	32.0	40.4	43.4	12.0
(19)	2.0		(31)	4.8		EBIT/Interest	(94) 7.3	(60) 5.8	(53) 7.9	(58) 10.5	(31) 4.8
	.9			1.0			2.5	1.5	1.9	2.7	1.0
						Net Profit + Depr., Dep., Amort./Cur. Mat. L/T/D	7.3	5.8	7.5	16.4	
							(20) 2.2	(10) 2.2	(10) 1.4	(10) 9.3	
							1.1	1.0	-.9	2.4	
	.2	.0		.0			.1	.1	.0	.0	.0
	.4	.1		.3		Fixed/Worth	.3	.4	.2	.3	.3
	.8	1.1		.8			1.4	1.4	.9	1.1	.8
	1.4	1.7		1.4			1.3	1.2	1.5	1.3	1.4
	3.0	2.3		3.1		Debt/Worth	2.4	3.1	3.2	2.7	3.1
	38.1	6.1		14.7			12.1	8.6	5.1	10.8	14.7
	106.5	99.2		81.2			66.4	78.6	60.0	71.0	81.2
(17)	33.3	45.3	(35)	34.8		% Profit Before Taxes/ Tangible Net Worth	(110) 31.3	(69) 28.5	(65) 26.2	(53) 35.1	(35) 34.8
	1.1	4.7		4.9			12.2	4.3	8.4	13.1	4.9
	25.2	19.1		18.8			21.1	13.0	15.9	19.4	18.8
	3.9	12.4		7.9		% Profit Before Taxes/ Total Assets	7.4	5.6	5.4	9.4	7.9
	-.3	1.6		.1			2.4	1.2	1.6	1.3	.1
	.4			.2			.3	.3	.3	.3	.2
(13)	.6		(25)	.6		% Depr., Dep., Amort./ Revenues	(87) .5	(51) .5	(49) .5	(46) .6	(25) .6
	1.6			1.2			1.3	1.7	1.6	1.5	1.2
	.9			.9			1.5	1.5	.5	1.2	.9
(11)	3.0		(15)	2.9		% Officers', Directors' Owners' Comp/Revenues	(60) 2.9	(38) 2.6	(27) 2.0	(27) 2.5	(15) 2.9
	5.0			5.0			6.1	3.8	3.9	4.6	5.0
2908M	83703M	230207M	2995199M	3312017M		Contract Revenues ($)	11567776M	921274M	3400636M	174048525M	3312017M
1109M	40589M	158698M	4991677M	5192073M		Total Assets ($)	11236050M	639806M	3546286M	61759724M	5192073M

M = $ thousand   MM = $ million
See Pages 11 through 21 for Explanation of Ratios and Data

Current Data Sorted by Assets

Comparative Historical Data

0-1MM	1-10MM	10-50MM	50 & OVER	ALL	Type of Statement	4/1/02-3/31/03 ALL	4/1/03-3/31/04 ALL	4/1/04-3/31/05 ALL	4/1/05-3/31/06 ALL	4/1/06-3/31/07 ALL
1	1	2	5	8	Unqualified	4	4	15	6	8
1	1	2	3	7	Reviewed	4	8	30	9	7
1	7	10	2	20	Compiled	4	7	20	16	20
9	15	4	1	29	Tax Returns	2	13	43	29	29
3	6	6	8	23	Other	2	15	24	19	23
12 (4/1-9/30/06)		75 (10/1/06-3/31/07)								
15	29	24	19	87	NUMBER OF STATEMENTS	16	47	132	79	87
%	%	%	%	%	ASSETS	%	%	%	%	%
10.5	13.8	3.5	8.9	9.3	Cash & Equivalents	11.9	11.8	12.0	9.3	9.3
4.9	7.8	3.2	2.9	5.0	A/R - Progress Billings	16.0	12.9	12.7	5.9	5.0
.0	.0	.0	.0	.0	A/R - Current Retention	.1	.1	2.5	.2	.0
33.8	55.5	65.7	61.3	55.8	Inventory	23.5	44.2	44.7	53.7	55.8
.0	3.6	2.2	1.7	2.2	Cost & Est. Earnings In Excess Billings	1.7	2.7	2.6	2.3	2.2
8.8	4.3	5.0	6.9	5.8	All Other Current	10.8	7.0	4.1	11.1	5.8
58.0	85.0	79.6	81.7	78.1	Total Current	64.0	78.7	78.6	82.6	78.1
24.4	10.7	12.5	8.4	13.0	Fixed Assets (net)	19.8	12.5	13.2	9.6	13.0
.8	1.0	1.2	1.6	1.2	Joint Ventures & Investments	2.9	1.1	1.5	.5	1.2
.0	.2	.7	2.2	.8	Intangibles (net)	.0	1.0	.5	.9	.8
16.8	3.1	6.0	6.0	6.9	All Other Non-Current	13.3	6.8	6.3	6.4	6.9
100.0	100.0	100.0	100.0	100.0	Total	100.0	100.0	100.0	100.0	100.0
					LIABILITIES					
29.1	40.4	41.1	40.1	38.5	Notes Payable-Short Term	14.9	32.3	28.1	37.8	38.5
14.2	6.6	11.2	5.6	8.9	A/P - Trade	9.7	14.4	13.9	11.3	8.9
.0	1.4	.0	.0	.5	A/P - Retention	.0	.1	.2	.1	.5
.0	.6	.9	.2	.5	Billings in Excess of Costs & Est. Earnings	1.0	2.4	1.9	.6	.5
.0	.0	.1	.1	.0	Income Taxes Payable	.4	.1	.1	.0	.0
10.0	2.6	4.8	.5	4.0	Cur. Mat.-L/T/D	2.9	2.0	5.5	3.4	4.0
9.0	9.2	13.1	8.2	10.0	All Other Current	7.3	8.2	10.6	10.5	10.0
62.3	60.6	71.0	54.7	62.5	Total Current	36.2	59.5	60.2	63.8	62.5
16.3	11.3	9.8	11.1	11.7	Long-Term Debt	35.0	10.9	10.9	16.3	11.7
.0	.1	.0	.3	.1	Deferred Taxes	1.1	.1	.2	.1	.1
14.8	8.9	2.6	4.2	7.1	All Other Non-Current	6.3	5.1	6.1	7.5	7.1
6.5	19.1	16.6	29.7	18.5	Net Worth	21.4	24.4	22.5	12.3	18.5
100.0	100.0	100.0	100.0	100.0	Total Liabilities & Net Worth	100.0	100.0	100.0	100.0	100.0
					INCOME DATA					
100.0	100.0	100.0	100.0	100.0	Contract Revenues	100.0	100.0	100.0	100.0	100.0
30.2	13.6	15.8	19.7	18.4	Gross Profit	25.3	22.5	17.9	16.6	18.4
20.7	9.4	11.2	10.7	12.1	Operating Expenses	20.3	15.8	13.0	11.0	12.1
9.5	4.2	4.6	9.0	6.3	Operating Profit	5.0	6.8	4.9	5.6	6.3
4.1	.8	.7	.5	1.3	All Other Expenses (net)	1.8	.4	.6	1.1	1.3
5.4	3.5	3.9	8.5	5.0	Profit Before Taxes	3.2	6.3	4.4	4.5	5.0
					RATIOS					
3.0	2.6	1.6	1.6	1.7		3.5	1.5	1.8	1.8	1.7
.7	1.2	1.1	1.5	1.3	Current	1.5	1.2	1.3	1.2	1.3
.5	1.0	1.0	1.3	1.0		1.3	1.0	1.0	1.0	1.0
	1.3	.7	.6	.8		4.3	1.8	1.6	.9	.8
(18) .0	(22) .0	(18) .2	(63) .1		Receivables/Payables	(14) 1.4	(37) .4	(110) .6	(60) .0	(63) .1
.0	.0	.0	.0			.0	.0	.0	.0	.0
0 UND	0 UND	0 UND	0 999.8	0 UND		0 UND	0 UND	0 UND	0 UND	0 UND
0 UND	0 UND	0 999.8	3 124.9	0 UND	Revenues/Receivables	10 34.8	1 332.0	2 178.6	0 UND	0 UND
0 UND	3 126.6	6 57.6	8 46.7	6 62.8		68 5.4	24 15.1	31 11.9	2 208.1	6 62.8
0 UND	0 UND	6 63.3	9 42.7	0 UND		3 105.8	0 UND	1 329.3	0 UND	0 UND
0 UND	4 82.2	20 18.4	13 27.3	13 28.9	Cost of Revenues/Payables	20 18.4	18 20.1	19 19.1	8 45.0	13 28.9
50 7.3	21 17.1	40 9.2	27 13.5	28 13.0		62 5.8	39 9.5	40 9.2	24 15.4	28 13.0
1.7	3.5	3.3	2.8	3.3		3.9	5.8	6.7	6.3	3.3
-15.5	14.9	28.5	5.6	15.8	Revenues/Working Capital	8.6	15.3	12.2	11.8	15.8
-4.4	184.2	205.1	7.3	-47.8		12.4	72.0	209.8	59.2	-47.8
3.8	17.5	14.9	80.1	13.9		12.0	57.1	14.6	22.0	13.9
(13) 1.6	(23) 4.4	(21) 5.5	(13) 8.7	(70) 4.0	EBIT/Interest	(14) 2.5	(35) 4.5	(106) 5.3	(59) 6.1	(70) 4.0
.5	.9	1.2	1.7	1.0		.8	2.0	1.9	2.2	1.0
					Net Profit + Depr., Dep., Amort./Cur. Mat. L/T/D			5.3		
							(10) 2.9			
								-.5		
.2	.0	.1	.0	.0		.1	.1	.1	.0	.0
2.1	.3	.2	.1	.2	Fixed/Worth	.6	.2	.3	.2	.2
30.5	2.5	.7	.3	1.6		3.9	1.1	1.2	1.0	1.6
2.0	1.8	3.1	1.3	2.0		.9	2.3	1.5	2.5	2.0
4.4	8.2	7.4	2.8	4.9	Debt/Worth	3.8	4.2	3.8	5.1	4.9
44.9	NM	32.1	6.4	35.7		8.4	22.8	17.2	21.7	35.7
60.4	51.9	86.8	61.0	59.5		57.5	102.3	59.6	101.2	59.5
(12) 16.9	(22) 22.2	(23) 27.8	(18) 44.8	(75) 32.5	% Profit Before Taxes/ Tangible Net Worth	(15) 14.5	(41) 46.2	(115) 29.5	(69) 50.9	(75) 32.5
-16.6	5.2	1.5	20.8	5.5		-8.4	10.0	10.4	12.5	5.5
20.1	11.4	12.7	21.1	16.7		12.7	17.8	12.6	16.8	16.7
2.3	5.8	5.1	12.0	6.7	% Profit Before Taxes/ Total Assets	2.0	9.3	6.1	6.3	6.7
-2.2	-.1	.2	3.8	.3		-1.8	1.1	1.5	1.9	.3
	.3	.1	.1	.2		.4	.3	.3	.2	.2
(15) .4	(19) .3	(10) .1	(52) .4		% Depr., Dep., Amort./ Revenues	(13) 1.3	(26) .6	(91) .7	(47) .5	(52) .4
.9	.5	.5	.9			4.8	2.4	1.4	1.0	.9
	2.7	.9		1.1			.8	.8	1.1	1.1
(16) 3.8	(11) 1.1		(39) 3.0		% Officers', Directors' Owners' Comp/Revenues	(25) 2.2	(80) 2.3	(40) 2.8	(39) 3.0	
4.9	2.8		4.8			7.2	4.3	4.1	4.8	
8082M	97704M	486227M	45799463M	46391476M	Contract Revenues ($)	143460M	6287052M	30402694M	17168691M	46391476M
10510M	62621M	623603M	42100401M	42797135M	Total Assets ($)	172552M	5675309M	20356870M	5588958M	42797135M

M = $ thousand   MM = $ million
See Pages 11 through 21 for Explanation of Ratios and Data

Current Data Sorted by Assets					Type of Statement	Comparative Historical Data				
					Unqualified			1		
	4			4	Reviewed			3		4
1	4		1	6	Compiled	7	2	10		6
6	7		1	14	Tax Returns	6	6	22		14
4	7		1	12	Other	16	15	11		12
						5	14			
						4/1/02-	4/1/03-	4/1/04-	4/1/05-	4/1/06-
						3/31/03	3/31/04	3/31/05	3/31/06	3/31/07
5 (4/1-9/30/06)		31 (10/1/06-3/31/07)				ALL	ALL	ALL	ALL	ALL
0-1MM	1-10MM	10-50MM	50 & OVER	ALL						
11	22		3	36	NUMBER OF STATEMENTS	34	37	47		36
%	%	%	%	%	ASSETS	%	%	%	%	%
15.7	14.7			16.6	Cash & Equivalents	10.8	15.4	14.3		16.6
14.5	20.0			17.3	A/R - Progress Billings	22.5	21.3	12.9		17.3
.4	1.6			1.1	A/R - Current Retention	1.3	1.3	.4		1.1
13.2	13.1			14.9	Inventory	18.0	12.0	27.4		14.9
.0	1.8			1.3	Cost & Est. Earnings In Excess Billings	2.9	3.2	2.0		1.3
8.3	16.6			12.9	All Other Current	10.3	6.2	6.2		12.9
52.1	67.8			64.2	Total Current	65.8	59.3	63.3		64.2
33.0	19.2			22.9	Fixed Assets (net)	19.4	28.0	24.0		22.9
.0	2.0			1.2	Joint Ventures & Investments	4.0	2.3	3.2		1.2
4.1	3.0			3.1	Intangibles (net)	.4	2.6	3.0		3.1
10.9	8.0			8.6	All Other Non-Current	10.5	7.7	6.6		8.6
100.0	100.0			100.0	Total	100.0	100.0	100.0		100.0
					LIABILITIES					
5.4	13.8			10.4	Notes Payable-Short Term	18.3	19.6	25.6		10.4
8.2	14.6			12.0	A/P - Trade	12.8	12.8	8.2		12.0
9.7	.0			3.0	A/P - Retention	3.1	2.9	1.1		3.0
.6	4.6			3.2	Billings in Excess of Costs & Est. Earnings	1.9	2.2	1.6		3.2
.0	.0			.0	Income Taxes Payable	.2	.2	.2		.0
15.0	2.4			6.2	Cur. Mat.-L/T/D	7.7	7.5	7.1		6.2
4.0	10.4			8.8	All Other Current	7.0	9.8	7.9		8.8
42.9	45.9			43.7	Total Current	51.0	55.0	51.8		43.7
41.6	10.6			20.0	Long-Term Debt	17.0	16.0	22.4		20.0
.0	.1			.0	Deferred Taxes	.1	.4	.2		.0
26.4	3.6			10.3	All Other Non-Current	8.4	6.7	11.0		10.3
-10.8	39.9			26.0	Net Worth	23.4	21.9	14.6		26.0
100.0	100.0			100.0	Total Liabilties & Net Worth	100.0	100.0	100.0		100.0
					INCOME DATA					
100.0	100.0			100.0	Contract Revenues	100.0	100.0	100.0		100.0
33.8	29.6			30.3	Gross Profit	30.9	32.9	32.4		30.3
30.8	25.6			26.5	Operating Expenses	28.1	28.8	25.8		26.5
3.0	4.0			3.8	Operating Profit	2.9	4.1	6.6		3.8
.0	.5			.4	All Other Expenses (net)	.5	.3	.2		.4
3.0	3.5			3.4	Profit Before Taxes	2.3	3.9	6.4		3.4
					RATIOS					
4.6	3.2			3.9		2.4	1.9	3.6		3.9
2.6	1.6			1.6	Current	1.3	1.2	1.3		1.6
.3	1.2			.9		.9	.7	.8		.9
	5.0			5.1		2.7	3.0	4.0		5.1
(18)	1.3		(28)	1.4	Receivables/Payables	(25) 1.5	(28) 1.6	(38) .4	(28)	1.4
	.3			.3		.3	.3	.0		.3
0 UND	0 UND			0 UND		0 UND	0 UND	0 UND	0	UND
8 44.8	11 32.3		8 43.3		Revenues/Receivables	10 36.6	8 44.4	0 759.5	8	43.3
32 11.3	31 11.6		32 11.5			47 7.7	43 8.5	22 17.0	32	11.5
0 UND	0 UND			0 UND		0 UND	0 UND	0 999.0	0	UND
7 50.0	19 19.0		14 25.6		Cost of Revenues/Payables	15 23.8	18 20.8	10 37.8	14	25.6
20 18.5	38 9.6		31 11.6			39 9.4	36 10.0	28 13.1	31	11.6
5.6	9.5			8.8		4.8	11.8	7.0		8.8
17.5	16.7			17.5	Revenues/Working Capital	24.2	50.8	31.4		17.5
-9.4	NM			-61.6		-45.4	-18.9	-72.1		-61.6
	61.0			36.0		10.9	14.9	33.5		36.0
(21)	14.4		(30)	6.6	EBIT/Interest	(28) 6.1	(29) 4.0	(40) 9.7	(30)	6.6
	.6			.2		.4	-.8	1.9		.2
					Net Profit + Depr., Dep., Amort./Cur. Mat. L/T/D					
.1	.1			.0		.1	.1	.3		.0
6.3	.2			.3	Fixed/Worth	.3	.8	1.3		.3
-1.2	1.2			6.3		7.6	NM	33.4		6.3
3.7	.7			.8		1.0	1.0	1.6		.8
20.6	2.0			2.4	Debt/Worth	2.3	4.4	4.6		2.4
-3.6	3.3			19.6		64.2	NM	135.0		19.6
	86.9			85.2		45.6	96.3	223.3		85.2
(19)	39.0		(29)	41.7	% Profit Before Taxes/ Tangible Net Worth	(27) 11.8	(28) 24.3	(39) 77.1	(29)	41.7
	18.8			17.5		6.3	10.7	14.2		17.5
38.1	37.6			37.4		19.8	16.6	31.7		37.4
3.7	12.7			12.7	% Profit Before Taxes/ Total Assets	4.7	4.2	11.4		12.7
-4.5	-1.2			-.4		-.9	-2.2	1.5		-.4
	.3			.3		.2	.6	.4		.3
(11)	.5		(16)	1.2	% Depr., Dep., Amort./ Revenues	(23) .7	(20) 1.3	(36) 1.2	(16)	1.2
	1.9			2.3		2.3	2.7	2.4		2.3
	2.1			2.3		2.4	4.2	2.7		2.3
(10)	4.6		(15)	4.6	% Officers', Directors' Owners' Comp/Revenues	(26) 4.8	(21) 6.3	(29) 4.2	(15)	4.6
	6.0			8.7		10.5	9.8	7.5		8.7
7569M	78881M	5688247M	5774697M		Contract Revenues ($)	103126M	83363M	680567M		5774697M
3923M	24610M	1508836M	1537369M		Total Assets ($)	52693M	44816M	894192M		1537369M

© RMA 2007   M = $ thousand   MM = $ million
See Pages 11 through 21 for Explanation of Ratios and Data

Current Data Sorted by Assets | | | | | | | **Comparative Historical Data**

Current side column groups: **27 (4/1-9/30/06)** covers 0-1MM & 1-10MM; **93 (10/1/06-3/31/07)** covers 10-50MM, 50 & OVER, ALL.

0-1MM	1-10MM	10-50MM	50 & OVER	ALL		4/1/02-3/31/03 ALL	4/1/03-3/31/04 ALL	4/1/04-3/31/05 ALL	4/1/05-3/31/06 ALL	4/1/06-3/31/07 ALL
					Type of Statement					
	7	10	14	31	Unqualified	63	55	57	50	31
	26	15	7	48	Reviewed	105	58	65	63	48
1	9	1	1	11	Compiled	5	12	13	12	11
2	13	1		16	Tax Returns	16	11	21	13	16
	6	5	3	14	Other	25	14	28	21	14
3	61	32	24	120	**NUMBER OF STATEMENTS**	214	150	184	159	120
%	%	%	%	%	**ASSETS**	%	%	%	%	%
	17.8	17.1	17.4	17.4	Cash & Equivalents	20.8	20.7	16.8	17.4	17.4
	32.4	42.9	43.9	37.2	A/R - Progress Billings	38.8	36.6	38.5	40.0	37.2
	4.5	2.2	5.6	4.0	A/R - Current Retention	3.9	3.6	3.2	5.2	4.0
	7.0	5.6	2.3	6.4	Inventory	2.1	1.0	4.2	2.9	6.4
	3.7	6.0	6.2	4.7	Cost & Est. Earnings In Excess Billings	4.8	4.6	5.5	5.1	4.7
	4.3	5.8	8.0	5.6	All Other Current	5.9	8.2	4.6	6.5	5.6
	69.8	79.6	83.5	75.4	Total Current	76.4	74.6	72.7	77.0	75.4
	22.0	14.2	11.2	17.6	Fixed Assets (net)	15.0	16.5	17.7	15.6	17.6
	.8	.6	1.0	.8	Joint Ventures & Investments	1.1	1.7	1.2	1.2	.8
	1.1	.4	.2	.7	Intangibles (net)	.5	.9	.7	.5	.7
	6.4	5.2	4.2	5.5	All Other Non-Current	7.1	6.3	7.6	5.7	5.5
	100.0	100.0	100.0	100.0	Total	100.0	100.0	100.0	100.0	100.0
					LIABILITIES					
	9.5	3.4	2.4	7.0	Notes Payable-Short Term	7.6	5.6	5.9	5.3	7.0
	19.5	34.0	34.8	26.5	A/P - Trade	30.1	28.5	26.9	29.9	26.5
	.8	1.0	1.3	.9	A/P - Retention	1.8	2.6	1.8	2.1	.9
	5.2	10.8	12.9	8.1	Billings in Excess of Costs & Est. Earnings	8.1	6.6	6.1	8.5	8.1
	1.0	.1	.5	.6	Income Taxes Payable	.4	.3	.3	.3	.6
	4.4	3.4	1.2	3.4	Cur. Mat.-L/T/D	2.2	2.4	3.2	3.1	3.4
	8.6	10.5	9.9	9.2	All Other Current	8.9	7.4	7.7	7.2	9.2
	49.0	63.2	63.2	55.8	Total Current	59.0	53.3	52.0	56.4	55.8
	13.9	6.2	6.3	10.7	Long-Term Debt	7.1	8.8	10.5	9.1	10.7
	.7	.5	.5	.6	Deferred Taxes	.2	.5	.7	.5	.6
	3.5	3.6	1.9	3.4	All Other Non-Current	2.2	2.7	2.7	2.6	3.4
	32.8	26.5	28.1	29.5	Net Worth	31.5	34.7	34.0	31.3	29.5
	100.0	100.0	100.0	100.0	Total Liabilities & Net Worth	100.0	100.0	100.0	100.0	100.0
					INCOME DATA					
	100.0	100.0	100.0	100.0	Contract Revenues	100.0	100.0	100.0	100.0	100.0
	21.8	12.6	10.0	17.2	Gross Profit	15.4	15.3	15.8	15.7	17.2
	18.3	9.0	6.6	13.9	Operating Expenses	13.9	13.7	14.1	12.9	13.9
	3.4	3.6	3.4	3.3	Operating Profit	1.5	1.6	1.7	2.8	3.3
	-.1	-.2	-.1	-.1	All Other Expenses (net)	.3	.0	.0	.1	-.1
	3.5	3.8	3.5	3.4	Profit Before Taxes	1.2	1.5	1.6	2.7	3.4
					RATIOS					
	2.0	1.5	1.6	1.7	Current	1.7	2.0	1.8	1.8	1.7
	1.6	1.2	1.3	1.4		1.3	1.4	1.4	1.3	1.4
	1.1	1.1	1.2	1.1		1.1	1.1	1.2	1.1	1.1
	7.0	2.4	2.3	3.2	Receivables/Payables	2.2	2.0	2.6	2.4	3.2
	(56) 2.0	(31) 1.2	1.3	(113) 1.5		(207) 1.3	(146) 1.3	(176) 1.5	(152) 1.4	(113) 1.5
	1.2	.9	1.0	1.0		1.0	1.0	1.0	1.0	1.0
	13 27.9	25 14.4	43 8.6	23 15.7	Revenues/Receivables	33 11.1	27 13.7	29 12.7	31 11.7	23 15.7
	38 9.6	54 6.8	54 6.8	48 7.6		45 8.1	45 8.1	50 7.3	50 7.2	48 7.6
	79 4.6	81 4.5	70 5.2	74 4.9		66 5.6	70 5.3	70 5.2	72 5.0	74 4.9
	3 138.6	19 19.4	31 11.8	13 28.2	Cost of Revenues/Payables	22 16.3	21 17.4	17 21.9	18 19.8	13 28.2
	22 16.5	46 7.9	44 8.4	34 10.7		38 9.6	38 9.7	33 11.2	42 8.8	34 10.7
	53 6.9	63 5.8	60 6.1	57 6.4		55 6.6	59 6.2	58 6.3	62 5.9	57 6.4
	7.0	11.2	10.5	8.0	Revenues/Working Capital	9.4	7.2	8.8	9.5	8.0
	13.4	24.8	15.8	16.2		17.5	17.2	17.1	18.1	16.2
	61.6	51.1	24.0	37.6		47.5	44.2	33.7	39.6	37.6
	26.0	56.7	113.9	39.0	EBIT/Interest	17.3	27.3	28.4	32.2	39.0
	(57) 9.4	(27) 7.9	(22) 24.6	(109) 10.1		(167) 6.6	(116) 6.6	(145) 8.3	(121) 8.8	(109) 10.1
	1.4	4.0	7.8	2.9		1.3	.3	1.9	2.4	2.9
	4.3	7.2	37.4	5.4	Net Profit + Depr., Dep., Amort./Cur. Mat. L/T/D	10.8	9.2	6.7	6.6	5.4
	(17) 2.0	(12) 3.5	(10) 3.8	(39) 3.5		(70) 3.3	(39) 3.6	(50) 3.0	(42) 3.5	(39) 3.5
	.2	1.4	3.5	1.0		1.0	1.3	1.1	1.9	1.0
	.2	.3	.2	.2	Fixed/Worth	.1	.1	.2	.1	.2
	.4	.4	.3	.4		.3	.3	.4	.3	.4
	1.3	.8	.7	1.1		.6	.7	.8	.9	1.1
	.8	1.7	1.7	1.2	Debt/Worth	1.0	.9	1.1	1.1	1.2
	1.8	2.8	2.4	2.4		2.0	1.8	2.0	2.4	2.4
	4.9	7.5	5.2	6.2		3.8	4.8	4.0	5.2	6.2
	51.9	95.4	54.9	62.6	% Profit Before Taxes/Tangible Net Worth	35.4	32.3	35.0	46.4	62.6
	(53) 23.7	(31) 38.9	37.8	(109) 30.7		(196) 13.7	(138) 14.6	(171) 18.6	(147) 25.5	(109) 30.7
	9.4	13.7	24.0	11.5		1.9	.1	3.2	5.9	11.5
	16.4	20.5	18.0	17.7	% Profit Before Taxes/Total Assets	9.9	10.9	11.2	14.9	17.7
	6.9	8.8	8.3	7.7		4.1	3.6	5.4	6.1	7.7
	1.1	3.9	3.7	2.6		.5	-.9	.2	1.9	2.6
	.4	.3	.2	.3	% Depr., Dep., Amort./Revenues	.3	.4	.4	.3	.3
	(56) 1.0	.7	(18) .5	(108) .8		(191) .7	(117) .8	(158) .8	(128) .6	(108) .8
	2.1	1.2	.8	1.5		1.4	2.0	2.1	1.2	1.5
	2.1	.8		1.4	% Officers', Directors' Owners' Comp/Revenues	1.2	.9	.9	1.3	1.4
	(39) 3.3	(12) 1.8		(56) 2.8		(112) 2.0	(80) 1.7	(81) 2.2	(72) 2.3	(56) 2.8
	4.6	3.5		4.3		-4.4	4.5	2.1	4.3	
1157M	297787M	681936M	46813719M	47794599M	Contract Revenues ($)	5749700M	3685322M	7663195M	21101359M	47794599M
4662M	131414M	230704M	15813018M	16179798M	Total Assets ($)	2173121M	1282195M	3610277M	8905415M	16179798M

Current Data Sorted by Assets   **Comparative Historical Data**

Type of Statement	0-1MM	1-10MM	10-50MM	50 & OVER	ALL		4/1/02-3/31/03 ALL	4/1/03-3/31/04 ALL	4/1/04-3/31/05 ALL	4/1/05-3/31/06 ALL	4/1/06-3/31/07 ALL
Unqualified	2	13	50	33	98		124	96	119	138	98
Reviewed	2	90	72	7	171		225	156	214	206	171
Compiled		18	6	2	26		48	35	31	22	26
Tax Returns	5	20	5	1	31		49	36	40	34	31
Other	5	36	19	16	76		75	42	72	57	76
	76 (4/1-9/30/06)		326 (10/1/06-3/31/07)								
NUMBER OF STATEMENTS	14	177	152	59	402		521	365	476	457	402
ASSETS	%	%	%	%	%		%	%	%	%	%
Cash & Equivalents	17.6	19.1	23.7	22.4	21.3		19.1	19.3	19.6	21.1	21.3
A/R - Progress Billings	23.8	37.4	44.0	38.6	39.6		36.6	37.6	40.7	38.1	39.6
A/R - Current Retention	.0	1.9	3.4	5.0	2.8		2.8	3.5	4.0	4.3	2.8
Inventory	6.2	5.1	1.5	6.5	4.0		4.7	4.4	2.9	2.8	4.0
Cost & Est. Earnings In Excess of Billings	1.8	4.3	6.4	2.3	4.7		5.0	5.0	5.0	5.7	4.7
All Other Current	3.6	4.7	6.0	6.5	5.4		8.3	7.0	6.3	7.6	5.4
Total Current	53.0	72.4	84.9	81.4	77.8		76.4	76.8	78.4	79.6	77.8
Fixed Assets (net)	30.9	17.9	9.3	11.2	14.1		14.9	15.2	14.3	12.9	14.1
Joint Ventures & Investments	1.8	1.5	2.0	3.0	1.9		1.4	.9	1.3	2.3	1.9
Intangibles (net)	5.5	1.1	.1	.5	.8		.6	.6	.5	.4	.8
All Other Non-Current	8.8	7.1	3.7	3.9	5.4		6.7	6.6	5.5	4.8	5.4
Total	100.0	100.0	100.0	100.0	100.0		100.0	100.0	100.0	100.0	100.0
LIABILITIES											
Notes Payable-Short Term	31.3	9.8	2.7	2.2	6.8		9.2	9.7	7.4	6.0	6.8
A/P - Trade	17.1	25.4	34.1	37.7	30.2		29.3	29.4	31.5	31.4	30.2
A/P - Retention	.0	.6	2.2	4.4	1.8		1.6	2.0	2.6	2.8	1.8
Billings in Excess of Costs & Est. Earnings	3.0	5.5	9.5	9.9	7.6		7.0	6.7	7.3	8.8	7.6
Income Taxes Payable	2.9	.5	.4	.2	.5		.3	.3	.3	.4	.5
Cur. Mat.-L/T/D	2.5	2.9	1.3	.8	2.0		2.4	2.9	2.3	1.8	2.0
All Other Current	19.2	8.7	8.5	8.3	8.9		10.0	8.3	8.6	7.5	8.9
Total Current	75.8	53.5	58.8	63.5	57.7		59.7	59.3	59.9	58.7	57.7
Long-Term Debt	20.7	9.8	3.9	6.6	7.5		9.4	7.9	7.4	6.5	7.5
Deferred Taxes	.0	.8	.5	.1	.5		.6	.4	.5	.5	.5
All Other Non-Current	5.4	2.9	1.2	2.1	2.2		3.5	2.2	2.9	2.9	2.2
Net Worth	-2.0	32.9	35.6	27.7	32.0		26.8	30.1	29.3	31.4	32.0
Total Liabilities & Net Worth	100.0	100.0	100.0	100.0	100.0		100.0	100.0	100.0	100.0	100.0
INCOME DATA											
Contract Revenues	100.0	100.0	100.0	100.0	100.0		100.0	100.0	100.0	100.0	100.0
Gross Profit	41.0	21.0	12.6	11.5	17.2		15.9	16.1	16.7	14.6	17.2
Operating Expenses	36.6	16.3	9.0	6.9	12.9		13.6	14.7	14.6	12.1	12.9
Operating Profit	4.3	4.7	3.6	4.6	4.3		2.2	1.4	2.1	2.5	4.3
All Other Expenses (net)	2.0	.0	-.4	.0	-.1		.3	.1	-.1	-.1	-.1
Profit Before Taxes	2.4	4.7	4.0	4.6	4.4		2.0	1.3	2.2	2.6	4.4
RATIOS											
Current	2.3	2.1	1.7	1.5	1.9		1.8	1.8	1.8	1.7	1.9
	1.5	1.5	1.4	1.2	1.4		1.3	1.3	1.3	1.3	1.4
	.8	1.1	1.2	1.1	1.2		1.1	1.1	1.1	1.1	1.2
Receivables/Payables	UND	3.4	1.8	1.3	2.1		1.9	2.1	2.2	1.8	2.1
	(12) 2.4	(162) 1.6	(149) 1.3	(58) 1.1	(381) 1.3		(499) 1.3	(346) 1.3	(461) 1.3	(437) 1.2	(381) 1.3
	.6	.9	1.0	.9	.9		.8	.9	.9	.9	.9
Revenues/Receivables	0 UND	24 15.3	37 9.9	31 11.7	30 12.2		21 17.6	29 12.7	31 11.9	26 13.9	30 12.2
	25 14.5	43 8.5	53 6.8	52 7.0	49 7.4		45 8.1	47 7.8	50 7.3	49 7.4	49 7.4
	53 6.9	69 5.3	71 5.1	69 5.3	70 5.2		65 5.6	68 5.4	70 5.2	70 5.2	70 5.2
Cost of Revenues/Payables	0 UND	11 32.9	30 12.4	33 11.0	22 16.8		20 18.0	22 16.5	24 15.5	24 15.2	22 16.8
	34 10.8	32 11.3	44 8.2	55 6.7	40 9.2		38 9.5	40 9.0	42 8.8	43 8.5	40 9.2
	41 8.9	49 7.5	60 6.1	70 5.2	58 6.3		57 6.4	60 6.1	62 5.9	63 5.8	58 6.3
Revenues/Working Capital	7.0	7.0	8.8	11.3	8.3		9.4	8.4	9.5	8.4	8.3
	22.5	14.4	13.4	20.8	14.8		19.5	16.2	17.6	15.7	14.8
	-52.9	41.7	23.7	39.3	33.7		72.1	51.0	44.5	36.2	33.7
EBIT/Interest		23.5	69.0	96.4	47.2		15.8	21.0	25.8	40.9	47.2
		(150) 6.3	(111) 20.6	(44) 26.7	(312) 11.7		(409) 5.5	(285) 5.9	(366) 7.1	(353) 10.2	(312) 11.7
		1.7	5.6		6.5	3.2		1.2	.3	1.5	2.4	3.2
Net Profit + Depr., Dep., Amort./Cur. Mat. L/T/D		9.1	27.2		16.5		7.9	10.1	9.8	13.4	16.5
		(32) 3.4	(48) 7.7		(88) 5.5		(146) 3.3	(105) 2.7	(119) 3.2	(115) 3.7	(88) 5.5
		1.6	2.9		2.5		.9	.4	1.1	1.5	2.5
Fixed/Worth	.0	.1	.1	.1	.1		.1	.1	.1	.1	.1
	1.0	.3	.2	.2	.2		.3	.3	.3	.2	.2
	NM	.9	.4	.5	.6		.8	.8	.7	.6	.6
Debt/Worth	1.2	.8	1.2	1.4	1.1		1.2	1.1	1.2	1.2	1.1
	2.1	1.5	1.9	3.3	1.9		2.6	2.2	2.4	2.3	1.9
	-6.9	4.0	3.2	4.9	4.0		5.9	4.9	5.0	4.5	4.0
% Profit Before Taxes/Tangible Net Worth	90.7	62.5	53.3	51.0	54.2		41.0	33.4	37.6	42.7	54.2
	(10) 12.8	(162) 26.2	(150) 29.0	(58) 35.3	(380) 30.5		(482) 15.9	(334) 14.8	(441) 19.3	(432) 21.8	(380) 30.5
	-1.9	5.0	15.2	22.9	12.0		2.0	.9	2.2	5.8	12.0
% Profit Before Taxes/Total Assets	19.8	22.6	16.7	16.8	18.6		11.3	11.0	11.9	12.9	18.6
	3.9	10.6	9.8	8.2	9.5		4.1	3.8	4.7	5.6	9.5
	-3.9	1.7	4.4	4.7	3.2		.4	-.2	.6	1.4	3.2
% Depr., Dep., Amort./Revenues		.4	.2	.1	.2		.3	.3	.3	.2	.2
		(150) .8	(139) .4	(40) .2	(336) .5		(444) .6	(281) .7	(407) .6	(390) .5	(336) .5
		1.5	.8	.4	1.1		1.4	1.4	1.3	1.1	1.1
% Officers', Directors' Owners' Comp/Revenues		1.9	1.0	.3	1.3		1.3	1.5	1.2	1.1	1.3
		(111) 3.2	(78) 2.0	(16) .5	(211) 2.6		(265) 2.5	(202) 2.7	(251) 2.5	(227) 2.2	(211) 2.6
		5.2	3.6	1.0	4.6		4.7	5.3	4.4	4.1	4.6
Contract Revenues ($)	7511M	836446M	3285281M	64647350M	68776588M		35950833M	26791082M	85236886M	126575084M	68776588M
Total Assets ($)	9902M	332344M	1163151M	35687729M	37193126M		13236457M	8586482M	31052653M	57249591M	37193126M

M = $ thousand   MM = $ million
See Pages 11 through 21 for Explanation of Ratios and Data

Current Data Sorted by Assets   **Comparative Historical Data**

Current period counts: 25 (4/1-9/30/06), 83 (10/1/06-3/31/07)

0-1MM	1-10MM	10-50MM	50 & OVER	ALL	Type of Statement	4/1/02-3/31/03 ALL	4/1/03-3/31/04 ALL	4/1/04-3/31/05 ALL	4/1/05-3/31/06 ALL	4/1/06-3/31/07 ALL
1	8	16	2	27	Unqualified	48	34	28	32	27
	30	13	2	45	Reviewed	71	48	64	50	45
1	11			12	Compiled	19	16	13	21	12
2	7			9	Tax Returns	21	9	14	11	9
2	7	5	1	15	Other	20	16	16	16	15
6	63	34	5	108	**NUMBER OF STATEMENTS**	179	123	135	130	108
%	%	%	%	%		%	%	%	%	%
					ASSETS					
	16.6	18.7		17.1	Cash & Equivalents	13.6	14.1	17.9	14.8	17.1
	29.9	34.2		30.5	A/R - Progress Billings	30.1	32.1	29.4	31.2	30.5
	1.9	4.2		2.7	A/R - Current Retention	1.5	1.9	2.6	2.6	2.7
	3.5	1.2		2.7	Inventory	2.3	3.1	3.2	4.1	2.7
	3.7	5.0		3.9	Cost & Est. Earnings In Excess of Billings	3.1	3.1	3.3	3.8	3.9
	3.8	6.9		6.0	All Other Current	5.1	4.7	4.7	4.0	6.0
	59.4	70.2		63.0	Total Current	55.7	59.0	61.1	60.6	63.0
	34.5	25.7		31.5	Fixed Assets (net)	35.6	32.2	32.0	32.5	31.5
	1.2	.2		.8	Joint Ventures & Investments	1.7	.7	.6	1.4	.8
	.2	.1		.2	Intangibles (net)	1.4	1.4	.4	.5	.2
	4.7	3.7		4.6	All Other Non-Current	5.6	6.7	5.9	5.0	4.6
	100.0	100.0		100.0	Total	100.0	100.0	100.0	100.0	100.0
					LIABILITIES					
	9.2	5.3		9.6	Notes Payable-Short Term	7.9	8.6	6.6	5.9	9.6
	14.3	22.9		16.6	A/P - Trade	14.9	17.5	16.0	16.9	16.6
	.5	1.2		.8	A/P - Retention	.1	.5	.5	.5	.8
	3.4	7.8		5.1	Billings in Excess of Costs & Est. Earnings	2.9	3.0	3.6	3.7	5.1
	.1	.8		.3	Income Taxes Payable	.3	.4	.3	.6	.3
	5.5	4.4		5.5	Cur. Mat.-L/T/D	7.0	7.9	6.8	6.2	5.5
	4.4	7.9		6.9	All Other Current	6.1	6.5	5.4	6.7	6.9
	37.4	50.3		44.8	Total Current	39.2	44.4	39.2	40.5	44.8
	13.0	11.1		13.3	Long-Term Debt	19.2	17.8	16.0	14.4	13.3
	.8	1.2		.9	Deferred Taxes	1.3	1.3	1.3	1.3	.9
	3.6	3.3		4.7	All Other Non-Current	3.4	3.7	2.7	5.9	4.7
	45.2	34.1		36.3	Net Worth	36.9	32.8	40.8	37.8	36.3
	100.0	100.0		100.0	Total Liabilities & Net Worth	100.0	100.0	100.0	100.0	100.0
					INCOME DATA					
	100.0	100.0		100.0	Contract Revenues	100.0	100.0	100.0	100.0	100.0
	27.4	17.5		25.0	Gross Profit	28.8	27.6	27.7	27.9	25.0
	22.4	12.5		19.8	Operating Expenses	25.4	25.0	23.5	22.7	19.8
	5.0	5.0		5.2	Operating Profit	3.3	2.6	4.2	5.2	5.2
	.0	.1		.2	All Other Expenses (net)	.5	.8	.2	.0	.2
	5.0	4.9		5.0	Profit Before Taxes	2.8	1.8	4.1	5.2	5.0
					RATIOS					
	2.4	1.7		2.1		2.5	1.9	2.3	2.5	2.1
	1.6	1.4		1.5	Current	1.5	1.4	1.6	1.5	1.5
	1.2	1.1		1.1		1.1	1.1	1.2	1.2	1.1
	5.0	2.3		4.4		4.4	4.4	3.2	4.1	4.4
	(60) 2.2	1.7		(101) 1.9	Receivables/Payables	(172) 2.1	(122) 2.1	(128) 2.2	(122) 2.2	(101) 1.9
	1.1	1.1		1.2		1.3	1.3	1.4		1.2
	26 14.0	41 8.8		29 12.6		27 13.7	32 11.6	31 11.6	32 11.5	29 12.6
	48 7.6	61 5.9		54 6.8	Revenues/Receivables	51 7.2	55 6.6	53 6.9	56 6.5	54 6.8
	77 4.8	83 4.4		82 4.5		70 5.2	79 4.6	73 5.0	75 4.9	82 4.5
	11 33.9	29 12.7		12 29.9		12 30.3	14 25.5	16 23.4	13 28.2	12 29.9
	29 12.4	45 8.2		33 11.0	Cost of Revenues/Payables	30 12.3	35 10.5	34 10.8	30 12.4	33 11.0
	45 8.1	62 5.9		50 7.3		48 7.6	62 5.9	55 6.7	55 6.6	50 7.3
	4.7	7.4		6.5		6.2	6.6	6.2	5.7	6.5
	10.6	11.7		12.3	Revenues/Working Capital	12.2	13.3	11.1	12.0	12.3
	40.0	33.3		40.2		67.6	45.4	24.8	25.0	40.2
	16.7	25.6		19.2		9.9	13.7	18.2	18.7	19.2
	(58) 7.1	(33) 5.6		(101) 6.5	EBIT/Interest	(159) 3.3	(115) 3.5	(116) 5.1	(121) 6.1	(101) 6.5
	2.0	2.4		2.1		.6	.3	1.8	3.0	2.1
	3.3	5.3		3.9		6.0	3.5	3.8	4.4	3.9
	(15) 2.2	(19) 2.6		(38) 2.4	Net Profit + Depr., Dep., Amort./Cur. Mat. L/T/D	(71) 1.9	(40) 2.0	(52) 2.2	(47) 2.5	(38) 2.4
	.4	1.6		1.5		1.0	.9	1.1	1.4	1.5
	.3	.3		.3		.5	.4	.4	.4	.3
	.7	.8		.8	Fixed/Worth	.9	.8	.7	.7	.8
	1.5	1.2		1.5		1.7	1.7	1.4	1.3	1.5
	.6	1.3		.8		.7	.8	.7	.7	.8
	1.2	2.0		1.7	Debt/Worth	1.6	1.6	1.5	1.5	1.7
	2.4	3.5		3.3		3.6	3.4	2.7	2.9	3.3
	50.2	57.7		53.5		37.6	36.7	37.1	43.4	53.5
	(62) 22.5	22.4		(102) 23.8	% Profit Before Taxes/Tangible Net Worth	(166) 13.6	(110) 11.9	(128) 18.0	(121) 24.6	(102) 23.8
	5.2	9.2		7.9		2.1	-.2	2.3	8.3	7.9
	20.6	22.9		21.9		12.2	13.5	15.9	18.4	21.9
	11.1	6.0		9.7	% Profit Before Taxes/Total Assets	5.4	3.8	6.8	9.4	9.7
	2.0	1.8		2.0		.4	-2.4	.9	3.6	2.0
	2.1	1.3		1.6		2.0	2.2	2.0	1.4	1.6
	(59) 3.7	(33) 2.2		(103) 3.0	% Depr., Dep., Amort./Revenues	(158) 3.8	(99) 4.9	(117) 3.4	(120) 2.9	(103) 3.0
	5.4	3.3		4.8		6.7	6.9	5.5	5.1	4.8
	1.3	.9		1.0		1.8	1.4	1.2	1.5	1.0
	(36) 3.1	(15) 1.4		(56) 2.3	% Officers', Directors' Owners' Comp/Revenues	(89) 3.4	(65) 3.1	(79) 3.7	(68) 3.4	(56) 2.3
	4.7	2.5		4.0		7.0	7.4	7.2	5.8	4.0
3387M	293516M	755994M	486720M	1539617M	Contract Revenues ($)	2538233M	1212617M	1500993M	1883988M	1539617M
1172M	141585M	352039M	207643M	702439M	Total Assets ($)	1472019M	595632M	823974M	829236M	702439M

M = $ thousand   MM = $ million
See Pages 11 through 21 for Explanation of Ratios and Data

Current Data Sorted by Assets   Comparative Historical Data

0-1MM	1-10MM	10-50MM	50 & OVER	ALL	Type of Statement	4/1/02-3/31/03	4/1/03-3/31/04	4/1/04-3/31/05	4/1/05-3/31/06	4/1/06-3/31/07
2	2	2	13	19	Unqualified	14	10	16	4	19
1	16	6	2	25	Reviewed	26	17	25	19	25
5	13	4		22	Compiled	24	17	34	23	22
21	31	3	3	58	Tax Returns	53	51	100	60	58
12	24	7	2	45	Other	59	20	61	34	45
16 (4/1-9/30/06)		153 (10/1/06-3/31/07)				ALL	ALL	ALL	ALL	ALL
41	86	22	20	169	**NUMBER OF STATEMENTS**	176	115	236	140	169
%	%	%	%	%	**ASSETS**	%	%	%	%	%
7.6	5.2	8.0	6.5	6.3	Cash & Equivalents	7.9	6.4	7.8	7.8	6.3
.3	3.7	7.5	4.5	3.5	A/R - Progress Billings	4.8	3.3	3.8	2.7	3.5
2.4	.3	.1	.2	.8	A/R - Current Retention	.2	.7	.7	.6	.8
22.1	42.9	45.8	42.4	38.2	Inventory	34.0	45.3	40.0	47.8	38.2
.0	.1	.2	5.4	.7	Cost & Est. Earnings In Excess Billings	.3	1.8	1.1	.5	.7
8.2	5.0	4.5	1.5	5.3	All Other Current	4.8	4.0	4.0	6.3	5.3
40.6	57.1	66.0	60.6	54.7	Total Current	52.1	61.5	57.5	65.8	54.7
43.1	29.3	17.5	24.0	30.5	Fixed Assets (net)	32.5	28.4	24.6	21.1	30.5
3.5	3.5	2.3	3.4	3.3	Joint Ventures & Investments	5.6	3.1	4.4	3.4	3.3
.1	.3	.5	.3	.3	Intangibles (net)	.5	.4	.8	.3	.3
12.7	9.8	13.7	11.7	11.2	All Other Non-Current	9.3	6.6	12.7	9.5	11.2
100.0	100.0	100.0	100.0	100.0	Total	100.0	100.0	100.0	100.0	100.0
					LIABILITIES					
18.2	27.0	21.8	17.6	23.1	Notes Payable-Short Term	16.1	22.7	23.4	22.8	23.1
4.2	2.5	8.9	6.5	4.2	A/P - Trade	8.3	5.4	5.2	4.1	4.2
.7	1.1	.7	.0	.8	A/P - Retention	1.1	.4	.5	.0	.8
.0	.2	.7	1.0	.3	Billings in Excess of Costs & Est. Earnings	.5	.8	.3	.3	.3
.0	.1	.0	.0	.0	Income Taxes Payable	.1	.0	.1	.0	.0
3.3	1.4	2.1	4.8	2.3	Cur. Mat.-L/T/D	2.7	4.5	3.6	3.5	2.3
6.7	6.7	9.9	6.8	7.1	All Other Current	8.6	6.9	5.7	6.4	7.1
33.1	39.0	44.0	36.8	38.0	Total Current	37.3	40.7	38.8	37.0	38.0
35.3	30.6	22.6	30.3	30.6	Long-Term Debt	36.1	26.9	25.2	24.1	30.6
.0	.7	.6	.3	.4	Deferred Taxes	.2	.3	.1	.0	.4
13.9	9.7	21.5	4.7	11.7	All Other Non-Current	7.4	6.7	10.5	8.2	11.7
17.7	20.1	11.2	28.0	19.3	Net Worth	19.0	25.4	25.4	30.6	19.3
100.0	100.0	100.0	100.0	100.0	Total Liabilties & Net Worth	100.0	100.0	100.0	100.0	100.0
					INCOME DATA					
100.0	100.0	100.0	100.0	100.0	Contract Revenues	100.0	100.0	100.0	100.0	100.0
					Gross Profit					
80.5	81.3	84.5	88.3	82.4	Operating Expenses	82.6	86.6	84.3	86.4	82.4
19.5	18.7	15.5	11.7	17.6	Operating Profit	17.4	13.4	15.7	13.6	17.6
15.2	7.1	1.9	2.7	7.9	All Other Expenses (net)	6.0	5.4	3.7	2.2	7.9
4.3	11.5	13.6	9.0	9.7	Profit Before Taxes	11.3	8.0	12.0	11.4	9.7
					RATIOS					
4.2	6.5	4.4	3.3	4.5		3.4	4.4	3.6	5.1	4.5
1.1	1.5	1.7	1.5	1.5	Current	1.4	1.3	1.4	1.7	1.5
.3	.9	1.0	1.0	.8		.8	.8	.8	1.1	.8
8.5	2.5	1.5	1.3	1.7		1.3	1.0	1.8	2.0	1.7
(23) .0	(63) .0	(19) .3	(19) .1	(124) .1	Receivables/Payables	(141) .2	(79) .0	(168) .1	(99) .1	(124) .1
.0	.0	.0	.0	.0		.0	.0	.0	.0	.0
0 UND	0 UND	0 UND	0 UND	0 UND		0 UND	0 UND	0 UND	0 UND	0 UND
0 UND	0 UND	3 132.8	1 326.0	0 UND	Revenues/Receivables	1 580.5	0 UND	0 UND	0 UND	0 UND
0 UND	5 80.1	15 23.8	17 21.4	5 80.1		16 22.9	7 49.6	9 40.5	8 48.4	5 80.1
					Cost of Revenues/Payables					
.8	1.5	1.6	1.6	1.4		1.8	1.6	1.6	1.4	1.4
4.4	6.6	6.4	5.6	6.5	Revenues/Working Capital	8.5	6.8	7.3	4.5	6.5
-2.1	-200.4	-265.0	NM	-20.9		-11.5	-36.9	-18.9	38.9	-20.9
10.5	9.4	11.2	9.5	9.3		13.9	11.8	11.9	12.8	9.3
(19) 3.1	(62) 3.5	(17) 3.2	(17) 4.1	(115) 3.2	EBIT/Interest	(119) 4.1	(73) 3.4	(164) 5.1	(106) 3.3	(115) 3.2
.8	1.2	1.2	1.6	1.2		1.4	1.3	1.6	1.2	1.2
					Net Profit + Depr., Dep., Amort./Cur. Mat. L/T/D			2.6		
							(11) 1.6			
							1.0			
.0	.0	.0	.1	.0		.0	.0	.0	.0	.0
2.1	.8	.1	.4	.7	Fixed/Worth	.6	.5	.2	.2	.7
5.4	27.2	1.3	1.9	5.0		5.2	4.0	2.6	2.6	5.0
2.4	1.9	1.6	1.7	1.8		1.3	1.6	1.2	1.1	1.8
6.0	5.3	3.4	2.5	4.7	Debt/Worth	4.5	4.3	3.4	3.0	4.7
NM	110.5	7.5	5.0	33.4		18.5	21.0	13.5	8.9	33.4
38.6	93.0	66.0	27.8	63.0		61.6	65.9	66.2	73.8	63.0
(31) 14.2	(68) 35.4	(20) 35.0	17.5	(139) 24.6	% Profit Before Taxes/ Tangible Net Worth	(147) 24.2	(99) 31.0	(208) 30.4	(123) 28.9	(139) 24.6
-2.8	10.3	7.2	4.8	5.9		7.3	2.7	10.9	5.1	5.9
8.4	21.7	14.3	9.9	13.4		13.0	14.2	14.5	15.6	13.4
3.8	5.6	5.8	5.4	4.8	% Profit Before Taxes/ Total Assets	5.3	3.0	6.7	5.7	4.8
-2.0	.3	1.1	1.6	-.1		.9	.3	1.1	.8	-.1
2.1	.6	.2	.4	.5		.5	.3	.4	.3	.5
(22) 10.4	(50) 2.4	(16) .5	(11) 1.2	(99) 1.5	% Depr., Dep., Amort./ Revenues	(97) 1.8	(61) 1.4	(116) 1.5	(73) .9	(99) 1.5
24.6	10.0	2.3	1.3	9.7		8.0	8.6	6.0	4.3	9.7
	1.9			2.4		1.9	2.2	1.8	1.5	2.4
	(19) 2.6			(36) 4.5	% Officers', Directors' Owners' Comp/Revenues	(44) 4.6	(29) 3.4	(50) 3.6	(39) 4.2	(36) 4.5
	5.6			6.5		8.3	7.8	8.6	9.0	6.5
19031M	310593M	483282M	6051410M	6864316M	Contract Revenues ($)	26034757M	4611175M	29777983M	4880850M	6864316M
127976M	739599M	832613M	16178703M	17878891M	Total Assets ($)	30382699M	10784244M	32326306M	7348294M	17878891M

Current Data Sorted by Assets · **Comparative Historical Data**

0-1MM	1-10MM	10-50MM	50 & OVER	ALL		4/1/02-3/31/03 ALL	4/1/03-3/31/04 ALL	4/1/04-3/31/05 ALL	4/1/05-3/31/06 ALL	4/1/06-3/31/07 ALL
					Type of Statement					
1	10	34	23	68	Unqualified	137	78	88	96	68
	32	20	1	53	Reviewed	68	54	53	50	53
2	5	2		9	Compiled	19	12	11	5	9
3	4	1		8	Tax Returns	15	9	11	12	8
1	11	17	4	33	Other	27	21	37	19	33
\ 42 (4/1-9/30/06)		129 (10/1/06-3/31/07)								
7	62	74	28	171	**NUMBER OF STATEMENTS**	266	174	200	182	171
%	%	%	%	%	**ASSETS**	%	%	%	%	%
	16.2	15.4	20.1	16.1	Cash & Equivalents	16.1	14.0	14.2	14.1	16.1
	29.0	27.3	25.8	27.8	A/R - Progress Billings	25.8	25.5	30.5	28.6	27.8
	3.1	2.8	3.3	2.9	A/R - Current Retention	2.6	3.2	2.6	3.5	2.9
	4.9	4.3	3.6	4.3	Inventory	3.0	4.0	3.6	3.5	4.3
	2.6	5.3	3.2	3.9	Cost & Est. Earnings In Excess Billings	3.0	3.6	4.3	4.3	3.9
	2.6	4.1	3.1	3.6	All Other Current	5.6	5.3	4.3	3.8	3.6
	58.4	59.2	59.1	58.5	Total Current	56.1	55.5	59.5	57.9	58.5
	33.9	31.6	33.4	33.0	Fixed Assets (net)	36.4	34.7	33.8	33.3	33.0
	2.0	2.0	1.9	1.9	Joint Ventures & Investments	1.5	2.5	1.1	2.1	1.9
	1.4	.4	1.1	.9	Intangibles (net)	.4	.6	.4	.4	.9
	4.2	6.8	4.6	5.7	All Other Non-Current	5.5	6.6	5.3	6.3	5.7
	100.0	100.0	100.0	100.0	Total	100.0	100.0	100.0	100.0	100.0
					LIABILITIES					
	8.6	4.4	.9	6.0	Notes Payable-Short Term	7.1	7.5	6.7	6.6	6.0
	17.0	14.2	17.7	15.8	A/P - Trade	15.2	16.8	18.1	16.6	15.8
	.1	.8	1.2	.6	A/P - Retention	.6	.8	.4	.6	.6
	2.6	4.6	7.0	4.1	Billings in Excess of Costs & Est. Earnings	3.3	2.8	3.7	3.9	4.1
	.3	.9	.9	.6	Income Taxes Payable	.2	.3	.2	.5	.6
	5.6	4.7	2.9	4.8	Cur. Mat.-L/T/D	6.3	6.1	5.8	5.7	4.8
	4.5	8.2	6.1	7.7	All Other Current	7.8	6.6	5.1	6.3	7.7
	38.6	37.8	36.8	39.6	Total Current	40.5	40.8	40.0	40.3	39.6
	17.6	12.1	14.5	14.6	Long-Term Debt	15.8	15.2	16.3	14.9	14.6
	1.7	2.1	2.3	1.9	Deferred Taxes	1.4	1.4	2.0	1.6	1.9
	4.2	3.2	2.3	3.3	All Other Non-Current	3.0	3.2	2.7	2.5	3.3
	37.9	44.8	44.1	40.6	Net Worth	39.3	39.3	39.1	40.9	40.6
	100.0	100.0	100.0	100.0	Total Liabilities & Net Worth	100.0	100.0	100.0	100.0	100.0
					INCOME DATA					
	100.0	100.0	100.0	100.0	Contract Revenues	100.0	100.0	100.0	100.0	100.0
	23.5	18.4	14.7	20.6	Gross Profit	20.7	19.2	20.7	19.7	20.6
	19.7	12.4	9.1	15.6	Operating Expenses	18.3	16.9	17.3	15.8	15.6
	3.8	6.0	5.6	5.0	Operating Profit	2.4	2.3	3.4	3.9	5.0
	.0	-.1	.2	.1	All Other Expenses (net)	.4	.4	.2	.0	.1
	3.7	6.1	5.5	5.0	Profit Before Taxes	2.0	1.9	3.3	3.9	5.0
					RATIOS					
	2.3	2.0	2.0	2.0	Current	2.2	2.0	2.1	2.0	2.0
	1.5	1.6	1.6	1.6		1.4	1.4	1.5	1.5	1.6
	1.1	1.1	1.3	1.1		1.1	1.0	1.2	1.2	1.1
	6.5	3.3	2.5	3.5	Receivables/Payables	3.5	2.7	3.6	3.2	3.5
	(61) 2.2	2.1	1.4	(169) 2.0		(261) 1.9	(168) 1.6	(196) 1.9	(179) 1.8	(169) 2.0
	1.2	1.5	1.1	1.3		1.2	1.2	1.2	1.2	1.3
28 13.2	27 13.6	34 10.6	29 12.5		Revenues/Receivables	24 15.0	24 15.0	30 12.0	29 12.8	29 12.5
46 7.9	50 7.3	44 8.3	48 7.5			43 8.5	42 8.6	51 7.1	46 7.9	48 7.5
76 4.8	67 5.4	58 6.3	70 5.2			67 5.5	65 5.6	71 5.2	71 5.2	70 5.2
8 43.7	16 22.8	20 18.3	15 23.7		Cost of Revenues/Payables	13 28.1	15 24.9	14 26.4	16 22.1	15 23.7
28 13.2	31 11.8	29 12.6	30 12.2			28 13.2	30 12.2	32 11.5	29 12.5	30 12.2
52 7.0	42 8.8	46 8.0	45 8.1			45 8.0	50 7.4	52 7.0	45 8.1	45 8.1
	7.8	6.3	6.6	6.9	Revenues/Working Capital	6.8	8.4	6.7	7.2	6.9
	13.2	11.3	11.7	12.1		13.5	15.6	11.8	13.5	12.1
	41.6	27.0	18.7	35.4		58.4	281.5	35.7	36.2	35.4
	19.6	22.7	48.3	20.1	EBIT/Interest	10.7	10.5	17.9	13.5	20.1
	(56) 5.4	(69) 7.2	(25) 8.7	(155) 6.6		(240) 3.1	(159) 3.7	(186) 4.5	(167) 5.7	(155) 6.6
	1.8	4.1	3.7	3.1		1.1	1.5	1.8	2.2	3.1
	4.4	5.3	8.3	4.9	Net Profit + Depr., Dep., Amort./Cur. Mat. L/T/D	3.2	3.3	3.3	4.5	4.9
	(23) 2.0	(35) 2.4	(12) 3.4	(70) 2.4		(101) 1.7	(45) 1.6	(67) 1.7	(69) 2.1	(70) 2.4
	1.2	1.6	2.0	1.5		.8	.7	1.0	1.3	1.5
	.6	.4	.3	.4	Fixed/Worth	.5	.5	.4	.4	.4
	.8	.7	.7	.7		.8	.8	.8	.8	.7
	1.5	1.3	1.5	1.4		1.5	1.5	1.5	1.3	1.4
	.7	.7	1.0	.8	Debt/Worth	.7	.9	.8	.8	.8
	1.7	1.2	1.2	1.4		1.6	1.7	1.5	1.4	1.4
	4.1	2.5	1.9	2.6		3.1	3.4	3.2	2.7	2.6
	41.3	41.4	40.6	41.6	% Profit Before Taxes/Tangible Net Worth	25.6	26.0	34.7	30.5	41.6
	(57) 20.3	(73) 29.1	23.9	(164) 26.2		(259) 11.9	(168) 10.0	(188) 15.5	(176) 19.0	(164) 26.2
	9.8	12.4	12.7	11.2		1.9	2.9	4.5	5.9	11.2
	16.0	18.0	15.5	17.5	% Profit Before Taxes/Total Assets	9.7	9.7	13.0	12.8	17.5
	6.1	10.6	9.5	9.4		4.0	3.5	5.4	7.8	9.4
	2.8	6.1	4.6	4.2		.3	.7	1.4	2.1	4.2
	2.3	1.8	1.4	1.8	% Depr., Dep., Amort./Revenues	1.9	2.1	1.9	1.6	1.8
	(59) 3.3	(73) 2.8	(20) 2.8	(158) 3.0		(222) 3.6	(121) 3.3	(177) 3.1	(159) 3.1	(158) 3.0
	5.1	3.6	3.5	4.3		5.4	5.5	4.6	4.7	4.3
	1.9	1.2		1.3	% Officers', Directors' Owners' Comp/Revenues	1.5	1.5	1.3	1.3	1.3
	(34) 3.4	(33) 2.0		(76) 2.3		(122) 2.6	(83) 2.7	(96) 2.7	(88) 2.6	(76) 2.3
	6.4	3.9		4.7		5.4	5.0	5.4	4.7	4.7
3145M	334807M	1652603M	12569586M	14560141M	Contract Revenues ($)	22681338M	11940726M	7495493M	45851388M	14560141M
1934M	157644M	774604M	6714782M	7648964M	Total Assets ($)	8059789M	5430743M	3304900M	18173517M	7648964M

M = $ thousand   MM = $ million
See Pages 11 through 21 for Explanation of Ratios and Data

Current Data Sorted by Assets   Comparative Historical Data

0-1MM	1-10MM	10-50MM	50 & OVER	ALL	Type of Statement	ALL 4/1/02-3/31/03	ALL 4/1/03-3/31/04	ALL 4/1/04-3/31/05	ALL 4/1/05-3/31/06	ALL 4/1/06-3/31/07
	1	12	5	18	Unqualified	30	12	14	12	18
	13	1		14	Reviewed	21	12	15	17	14
	4	1		5	Compiled	11	5	4	6	5
3	3	1		7	Tax Returns	7	5	3	1	7
2	4			6	Other	10	11	4	6	6
	11 (4/1-9/30/06)		39 (10/1/06-3/31/07)							
5	25	15	5	50	NUMBER OF STATEMENTS	79	45	40	42	50
%	%	%	%	%	**ASSETS**	%	%	%	%	%
	12.1	14.5		13.0	Cash & Equivalents	11.9	18.4	13.8	14.2	13.0
	32.4	42.2		32.2	A/R - Progress Billings	27.1	27.8	29.6	27.7	32.2
	.2	2.0		.9	A/R - Current Retention	1.9	3.7	1.6	2.0	.9
	6.9	2.0		4.0	Inventory	4.2	5.2	2.2	4.6	4.0
	2.0	5.9		3.3	Cost & Est. Earnings In Excess Billings	3.7	3.1	4.6	4.9	3.3
	4.0	6.4		5.6	All Other Current	8.4	4.8	6.9	5.4	5.6
	57.6	73.0		59.0	Total Current	57.1	63.0	58.7	58.8	59.0
	35.6	23.0		32.1	Fixed Assets (net)	34.3	29.2	34.6	32.5	32.1
	.0	.5		.2	Joint Ventures & Investments	1.6	.5	.5	.6	.2
	1.5	.5		1.4	Intangibles (net)	2.2	1.4	.1	1.6	1.4
	5.3	3.0		7.3	All Other Non-Current	4.8	5.9	6.0	6.6	7.3
	100.0	100.0		100.0	Total	100.0	100.0	100.0	100.0	100.0
					LIABILITIES					
	4.7	5.0		7.3	Notes Payable-Short Term	8.8	7.0	6.6	11.5	7.3
	15.6	14.3		14.8	A/P - Trade	16.9	16.4	21.3	14.8	14.8
	.1	3.0		.9	A/P - Retention	.7	1.0	.3	.3	.9
	2.9	7.6		4.5	Billings in Excess of Costs & Est. Earnings	4.3	5.2	6.1	5.6	4.5
	.2	1.1		.4	Income Taxes Payable	.3	.6	.3	.3	.4
	8.0	3.8		6.8	Cur. Mat.-L/T/D	4.9	4.1	5.9	5.9	6.8
	11.0	8.0		10.0	All Other Current	7.4	7.7	5.0	7.6	10.0
	42.3	42.7		44.7	Total Current	43.4	42.0	45.5	46.1	44.7
	22.0	9.2		21.5	Long-Term Debt	22.0	17.5	13.1	14.5	21.5
	.1	1.9		.8	Deferred Taxes	1.2	1.2	1.7	1.0	.8
	6.8	1.2		4.7	All Other Non-Current	1.7	6.3	2.7	3.8	4.7
	28.8	44.9		28.3	Net Worth	31.7	33.1	37.0	34.5	28.3
	100.0	100.0		100.0	Total Liabilities & Net Worth	100.0	100.0	100.0	100.0	100.0
					INCOME DATA					
	100.0	100.0		100.0	Contract Revenues	100.0	100.0	100.0	100.0	100.0
	35.8	16.4		30.6	Gross Profit	25.8	23.2	21.7	24.6	30.6
	29.8	9.9		22.8	Operating Expenses	22.5	20.9	17.7	18.8	22.8
	6.1	6.4		7.9	Operating Profit	3.3	2.2	4.0	5.8	7.9
	.9	.2		.9	All Other Expenses (net)	1.2	1.0	.2	.7	.9
	5.2	6.2		7.0	Profit Before Taxes	2.1	1.2	3.8	5.1	7.0
					RATIOS					
	1.7	2.3		1.7	Current	1.9	2.1	1.9	1.8	1.7
	1.3	1.6		1.4		1.3	1.5	1.3	1.5	1.4
	1.1	1.3		1.1		1.0	1.1	1.0	1.1	1.1
	6.6	6.7		5.9	Receivables/Payables	3.9	4.3	2.7	3.6	5.9
	1.9	2.7	(47) 2.1			(76) 1.8	(43) 2.1	1.7	(39) 1.9	(47) 2.1
	1.3	1.3		1.3		1.2	1.3	1.1	.7	1.3
31 11.8	43 8.6		31 12.0		Revenues/Receivables	31 11.8	35 10.6	33 11.1	11 34.3	31 12.0
46 7.9	72 5.1		55 6.7			45 8.2	48 7.5	46 7.9	39 9.3	55 6.7
72 5.1	84 4.4		75 4.9			63 5.8	63 5.8	58 6.3	71 5.1	75 4.9
14 26.2	6 57.9		8 44.3		Cost of Revenues/Payables	15 24.9	18 19.9	18 20.0	9 39.6	8 44.3
29 12.5	27 13.5		29 12.5			32 11.5	33 11.2	30 12.0	27 13.5	29 12.5
58 6.3	37 9.8		49 7.4			51 7.2	46 7.9	46 7.9	52 7.0	49 7.4
	8.2	4.9		7.9	Revenues/Working Capital	8.7	6.7	8.7	7.6	7.9
	22.0	11.8		13.9		19.6	16.0	17.3	13.9	13.9
	41.4	14.7		41.1		300.5	71.3	-87.8	98.8	41.1
	9.5	47.9		20.6	EBIT/Interest	11.1	14.6	27.8	29.2	20.6
	3.9	(14) 19.8	(48) 7.0			(72) 3.6	(42) 4.0	(37) 7.9	(38) 7.2	(48) 7.0
	2.0	4.4		2.5		1.0	-.6	3.3	2.5	2.5
				16.9	Net Profit + Depr., Dep., Amort./Cur. Mat. L/T/D	3.8	8.9	10.3	13.3	16.9
			(17) 3.5			(22) 1.4	(12) 2.9	(14) 4.9	(10) 8.2	(17) 3.5
				1.0		.1	.9	1.3	2.5	1.0
	.6	.2		.3	Fixed/Worth	.4	.4	.5	.3	.3
	1.1	.4		.9		1.0	.8	.9	.7	.9
	2.6	1.2		1.9		2.6	2.2	1.6	1.5	1.9
	.9	.7		.9	Debt/Worth	1.1	1.2	1.0	.9	.9
	1.6	1.2		1.4		2.6	1.8	1.7	1.5	1.4
	8.6	1.9		5.5		6.8	5.8	2.7	3.0	5.5
	56.1	33.2		53.0	% Profit Before Taxes/Tangible Net Worth	36.3	37.0	49.6	55.0	53.0
	(21) 36.5	22.7	(43) 30.9			(71) 20.3	(41) 13.1	(37) 20.8	(37) 30.9	(43) 30.9
	9.2	14.5		9.5		1.6	-.2	6.2	12.1	9.5
	22.0	16.6		20.1	% Profit Before Taxes/Total Assets	12.6	12.7	16.3	22.6	20.1
	7.6	8.5		8.4		4.6	4.6	7.7	10.3	8.4
	3.6	5.9		3.9		.6	-3.3	2.2	5.3	3.9
	2.8	.7		1.4	% Depr., Dep., Amort./Revenues	.7	1.5	1.4	.9	1.4
	(24) 4.5	2.2	(47) 3.5			(63) 3.0	(31) 3.4	(35) 2.9	(38) 2.7	(47) 3.5
	8.1	3.5		5.2		9.2	5.7	5.8	5.9	5.2
	2.7			1.5	% Officers', Directors' Owners' Comp/Revenues	1.3	2.7	1.4	1.9	1.5
	(15) 4.4		(25) 4.0			(31) 3.5	(19) 4.8	(20) 3.1	(21) 3.2	(25) 4.0
	10.3			7.0		4.8	5.8	5.1	3.7	7.0
2711M	115785M	350484M	1657456M	2126436M	Contract Revenues ($)	7555027M	1855552M	437880M	589960M	2126436M
1378M	51607M	145258M	2093487M	2291730M	Total Assets ($)	5207717M	1116419M	174378M	255438M	2291730M

© RMA 2007   M = $ thousand   MM = $ million

See Pages 11 through 21 for Explanation of Ratios and Data

Current Data Sorted by Assets | **Comparative Historical Data**

	0-1MM	1-10MM	10-50MM	50 & OVER	ALL		4/1/02-3/31/03	4/1/03-3/31/04	4/1/04-3/31/05	4/1/05-3/31/06	4/1/06-3/31/07
Type of Statement											
Unqualified		2	2		4		11	8	6	16	4
Reviewed	2	11	10	1	24		37	28	36	44	24
Compiled	4	12	1	1	17		11	11	16	17	17
Tax Returns	6	12	1	1	20		20	14	25	21	20
Other	4	13	4	1	22		23	17	12	15	22
	15 (4/1-9/30/06)		72 (10/1/06-3/31/07)				ALL	ALL	ALL	ALL	ALL
NUMBER OF STATEMENTS	16	50	18	3	87		102	78	95	113	87
	%	%	%	%	%		%	%	%	%	%
ASSETS											
Cash & Equivalents	17.8	14.3	10.0		13.7		11.0	12.1	13.6	12.3	13.7
A/R - Progress Billings	20.3	35.3	39.8		33.6		33.7	33.1	35.1	37.8	33.6
A/R - Current Retention	.0	1.1	4.9		1.7		2.0	1.6	1.5	1.6	1.7
Inventory	2.8	1.9	3.8		2.6		1.7	2.5	1.6	3.1	2.6
Cost & Est. Earnings In Excess Billings	.0	.7	1.5		.8		2.0	2.3	1.9	2.4	.8
All Other Current	4.4	2.7	9.3		4.4		4.4	5.5	6.3	4.0	4.4
Total Current	45.3	56.1	69.3		56.6		54.8	57.1	60.0	61.3	56.6
Fixed Assets (net)	52.7	34.5	20.5		35.2		38.5	34.6	31.7	30.4	35.2
Joint Ventures & Investments	.0	.1	.2		.1		.5	.1	.6	.9	.1
Intangibles (net)	.0	1.1	3.4		1.4		.6	1.4	1.1	1.0	1.4
All Other Non-Current	2.1	8.2	6.6		6.7		5.5	6.7	6.6	6.5	6.7
Total	100.0	100.0	100.0		100.0		100.0	100.0	100.0	100.0	100.0
LIABILITIES											
Notes Payable-Short Term	12.8	7.9	8.8		8.9		7.3	8.4	9.7	9.5	8.9
A/P - Trade	11.5	17.4	18.5		16.5		16.9	17.9	17.4	16.7	16.5
A/P - Retention	.0	.7	.0		.4		.1	.1	.1	.2	.4
Billings in Excess of Costs & Est. Earnings	.0	1.2	5.3		2.3		2.3	3.1	2.6	2.5	2.3
Income Taxes Payable	2.1	.2	.8		.7		.4	.4	.2	.7	.7
Cur. Mat.-L/T/D	6.3	4.4	3.7		4.6		5.3	6.1	7.5	5.8	4.6
All Other Current	2.6	5.0	12.9		6.3		5.4	6.9	7.0	6.3	6.3
Total Current	35.3	36.7	49.9		39.7		37.7	42.9	44.5	41.6	39.7
Long-Term Debt	35.9	23.5	9.9		23.3		20.2	21.5	17.7	18.9	23.3
Deferred Taxes	.0	.9	.6		.6		1.0	.8	1.2	1.3	.6
All Other Non-Current	5.7	3.8	2.5		3.8		3.4	4.3	3.3	9.2	3.8
Net Worth	23.0	35.1	37.1		32.6		37.8	30.5	33.3	29.0	32.6
Total Liabilties & Net Worth	100.0	100.0	100.0		100.0		100.0	100.0	100.0	100.0	100.0
INCOME DATA											
Contract Revenues	100.0	100.0	100.0		100.0		100.0	100.0	100.0	100.0	100.0
Gross Profit	43.6	34.2	17.7		31.8		28.7	29.1	27.8	30.1	31.8
Operating Expenses	37.7	28.8	13.0		26.6		24.5	25.8	24.9	25.2	26.6
Operating Profit	5.9	5.3	4.7		5.3		4.3	3.3	3.0	4.9	5.3
All Other Expenses (net)	1.0	.8	.5		.9		.5	1.1	.4	.7	.9
Profit Before Taxes	4.9	4.5	4.2		4.4		3.8	2.2	2.6	4.2	4.4
RATIOS											
Current	3.0	3.6	1.7		2.8		2.3	2.0	2.4	2.4	2.8
	1.4	1.7	1.3		1.5		1.7	1.5	1.4	1.5	1.5
	.7	.9	1.1		.9		1.0	1.0	.9	1.1	.9
Receivables/Payables	UND	8.6	6.4		7.9		4.1	4.9	6.0	6.0	7.9
	(11) 3.5	(49) 2.9	2.4		(81) 2.9		(91) 2.2	(68) 1.9	(88) 2.5	(104) 2.7	(81) 2.9
	1.0	1.1	1.4		1.2		1.5	1.2	1.2	1.4	1.2
Revenues/Receivables	0 UND	15 23.8	30 12.0		19 19.2		28 12.8	19 19.3	22 16.3	30 12.2	19 19.2
	27 13.8	52 7.0	48 7.6		52 7.1		51 7.2	45 8.2	53 6.8	49 7.5	52 7.1
	71 5.1	81 4.5	83 4.4		81 4.5		72 5.1	77 4.8	77 4.7	80 4.6	81 4.5
Cost of Revenues/Payables	0 UND	6 56.7	11 32.3		4 96.1		11 32.9	9 38.6	8 48.2	10 37.1	4 96.1
	0 UND	21 17.3	29 12.7		22 16.9		27 13.7	26 14.3	23 16.2	25 14.8	22 16.9
	49 7.5	42 8.7	53 6.9		44 8.3		48 7.7	52 7.0	46 7.9	47 7.7	44 8.3
Revenues/Working Capital	12.8	6.4	7.2		6.9		7.5	8.8	7.3	6.8	6.9
	45.4	15.4	22.8		21.1		18.0	17.0	17.4	17.8	21.1
	-17.3	-82.9	45.1		-99.3		NM	-130.3	-172.8	71.5	-99.3
EBIT/Interest	6.7	20.1	21.4		13.4		10.5	14.9	10.9	15.9	13.4
	(13) 3.2	(47) 4.3	5.4		(81) 4.3		(93) 4.4	(74) 4.3	(84) 5.0	(106) 5.7	(81) 4.3
	-.6	1.0	3.1		1.2		1.1	1.5	1.4	1.9	1.2
Net Profit + Depr., Dep., Amort./Cur. Mat. L/T/D		9.8	9.8		9.8		4.3	3.2	4.1	5.1	9.8
		(12) 6.4	6.4		(20) 4.9		(31) 1.7	(18) 2.3	(26) 2.1	(31) 2.8	(20) 4.9
		1.0	1.0		1.4		1.0	1.5	.8	1.4	1.4
Fixed/Worth	1.2	.3	.3		.3		.4	.6	.4	.3	.3
	2.4	.8	.6		1.0		1.0	1.1	.9	.7	1.0
	NM	5.9	1.1		3.8		1.9	2.4	2.7	2.0	3.8
Debt/Worth	1.3	.4	1.3		.7		.8	1.1	.8	.9	.7
	3.2	1.6	2.5		2.2		1.4	2.0	2.1	1.9	2.2
	NM	7.6	3.9		5.9		4.5	5.9	6.1	4.4	5.9
% Profit Before Taxes/Tangible Net Worth	326.8	58.8	50.9		62.6		59.4	40.2	46.9	53.9	62.6
	(12) 48.1	(42) 28.5	(17) 34.3		(74) 30.7		(96) 21.0	(67) 21.0	(85) 17.3	(97) 24.3	(74) 30.7
	6.8	5.9	11.7		6.4		6.8	3.1	4.7	10.2	6.4
% Profit Before Taxes/Total Assets	29.9	22.1	21.0		20.9		17.4	13.9	14.3	17.6	20.9
	7.1	8.9	9.9		8.6		6.4	6.3	6.7	7.4	8.6
	-4.2	.7	3.5		1.0		1.3	.4	1.4	2.5	1.0
% Depr., Dep., Amort./Revenues	2.5	1.3	1.0		1.3		1.3	1.3	1.3	1.3	1.3
	(12) 5.4	(43) 2.5	(17) 1.5		(73) 2.5		(92) 2.9	(63) 2.9	(84) 2.3	(98) 2.4	(73) 2.5
	10.6	5.1	3.2		5.3		4.7	6.1	4.2	5.3	5.3
% Officers', Directors' Owners' Comp/Revenues		2.3	1.5		2.1		2.5	2.3	2.0	2.2	2.1
	(27) 5.0	(11) 2.0			(48) 4.5		(71) 3.9	(45) 3.9	(59) 4.0	(65) 4.2	(48) 4.5
		7.5	5.8		7.5		7.5	6.2	8.7	6.8	7.5
Contract Revenues ($)	8921M	196806M	323771M	771181M	1300679M		1084082M	768450M	575988M	10302438M	1300679M
Total Assets ($)	4285M	83154M	119543M	438719M	645701M		420024M	305668M	238053M	3498357M	645701M

© RMA 2007

M = $ thousand   MM = $ million
See Pages 11 through 21 for Explanation of Ratios and Data

Current Data Sorted by Assets   Comparative Historical Data

						Type of Statement					
	1	3	1	5		Unqualified	11	8	16	8	5
1	13	6		20		Reviewed	30	17	20	25	20
1	4	3		8		Compiled	13	6	11	9	8
1	1			2		Tax Returns	5	5	6	6	2
	1	3	2	6		Other	12	3	7	6	6

	8 (4/1-9/30/06)	33 (10/1/06-3/31/07)					4/1/02-3/31/03	4/1/03-3/31/04	4/1/04-3/31/05	4/1/05-3/31/06	4/1/06-3/31/07
	0-1MM	1-10MM	10-50MM	50 & OVER	ALL		ALL	ALL	ALL	ALL	ALL
	3	20	15	3	41	NUMBER OF STATEMENTS	71	39	60	54	41
	%	%	%	%	%	ASSETS	%	%	%	%	%
		7.8	12.3		10.8	Cash & Equivalents	12.7	9.9	9.4	12.6	10.8
		51.5	40.3		46.6	A/R - Progress Billings	43.7	43.2	44.6	43.2	46.6
		.3	2.3		1.2	A/R - Current Retention	1.6	2.3	2.2	2.2	1.2
		1.4	9.7		4.3	Inventory	2.8	4.3	2.6	5.8	4.3
		3.4	4.9		3.8	Cost & Est. Earnings In Excess Billings	4.9	5.2	5.3	3.9	3.8
		4.4	7.7		5.4	All Other Current	4.2	4.2	6.2	3.2	5.4
		68.7	77.1		72.0	Total Current	69.9	69.1	70.4	70.8	72.0
		26.0	16.1		22.1	Fixed Assets (net)	22.2	22.1	21.6	22.5	22.1
		.6	2.4		1.2	Joint Ventures & Investments	1.1	1.4	1.3	1.1	1.2
		.3	.3		.3	Intangibles (net)	.8	.4	1.0	.8	.3
		4.4	4.1		4.4	All Other Non-Current	6.0	7.0	5.7	4.8	4.4
		100.0	100.0		100.0	Total	100.0	100.0	100.0	100.0	100.0
						LIABILITIES					
		18.0	2.0		10.0	Notes Payable-Short Term	10.8	21.0	18.6	7.2	10.0
		15.5	16.0		16.9	A/P - Trade	13.7	20.7	16.5	17.1	16.9
		.0	.0		.0	A/P - Retention	1.0	.0	.9	.0	.0
		2.3	6.3		4.4	Billings in Excess of Costs & Est. Earnings	4.2	4.0	5.1	6.8	4.4
		.8	.6		.7	Income Taxes Payable	.3	.2	.4	.2	.7
		3.4	1.3		3.1	Cur. Mat.-L/T/D	2.5	3.0	2.1	3.1	3.1
		5.3	10.2		7.3	All Other Current	9.5	8.3	7.5	7.7	7.3
		45.4	36.4		42.4	Total Current	42.1	57.3	51.1	42.1	42.4
		9.1	5.5		9.1	Long-Term Debt	8.7	8.0	10.1	8.0	9.1
		.9	.1		.5	Deferred Taxes	.5	.3	.9	.6	.5
		2.2	3.4		2.3	All Other Non-Current	4.5	4.3	4.7	4.5	2.3
		42.5	54.7		45.7	Net Worth	44.3	30.0	33.1	44.8	45.7
		100.0	100.0		100.0	Total Liabilities & Net Worth	100.0	100.0	100.0	100.0	100.0
						INCOME DATA					
		100.0	100.0		100.0	Contract Revenues	100.0	100.0	100.0	100.0	100.0
		25.7	25.2		24.2	Gross Profit	22.0	16.4	19.8	26.5	24.2
		21.8	13.7		17.6	Operating Expenses	20.0	18.5	17.1	20.1	17.6
		3.9	11.6		6.7	Operating Profit	2.0	-2.1	2.7	6.4	6.7
		.5	.6		.7	All Other Expenses (net)	.3	.0	.0	.5	.7
		3.3	11.0		6.0	Profit Before Taxes	1.7	-2.0	2.7	5.9	6.0
						RATIOS					
		3.0	3.2		3.1		2.6	3.3	2.8	2.5	3.1
		1.7	2.4		2.1	Current	1.6	1.6	1.8	1.7	2.1
		1.1	1.4		1.2		1.2	1.2	1.3	1.3	1.2
		10.2	4.9		5.7		8.7	7.5	8.0	7.0	5.7
	(19)	4.2	2.4	(39)	3.0	Receivables/Payables	(70) 3.9	(38) 4.0	(59) 3.0	(51) 2.6	(39) 3.0
		1.9	1.5		1.5		2.1	1.8	1.9	2.0	1.5
	40 9.1	19 19.3		32 11.4		46 7.9	46 7.9	41 8.9	37 10.0	32 11.4
	64 5.7	54 6.7		57 6.4	Revenues/Receivables	71 5.1	65 5.6	67 5.4	58 6.3	57 6.4
	77 4.8	73 5.0		72 5.1		88 4.2	84 4.3	90 4.1	81 4.5	72 5.1
	10 36.1	16 23.1		12 30.6		10 35.4	9 40.0	12 30.5	11 31.9	12 30.6
	20 18.3	23 15.5		23 16.0	Cost of Revenues/Payables	21 17.4	18 20.3	27 13.5	24 15.4	23 16.0
	38 9.7	39 9.3		39 9.4		36 10.2	37 9.8	39 9.4	45 8.2	39 9.4
		5.6	3.8		5.3		5.2	5.6	5.6	6.2	5.3
		8.7	6.1		7.9	Revenues/Working Capital	8.3	9.3	8.8	9.8	7.9
		58.2	8.9		35.8		27.0	21.8	20.3	22.9	35.8
		12.6	73.6		57.6		8.0	9.0	25.2	28.5	57.6
		3.4	(13) 50.6	(38)	8.4	EBIT/Interest	(66) 3.1	(35) 1.6	(54) 4.5	(49) 7.7	(38) 8.4
		.7	10.1		1.4		-.3	-5.3	1.1	3.2	1.4
					8.9		7.9	5.1	11.0		8.9
			(13)	3.7	Net Profit + Depr., Dep.,	(19) 3.4	(10) 2.1	(20) 3.6	(13) 3.7
					1.8	Amort./Cur. Mat. L/T/D	1.6	.6	1.3		1.8
		.2	.1		.2		.2	.2	.1	.2	.2
		.6	.2		.4	Fixed/Worth	.5	.5	.5	.5	.4
		.9	.6		.8		1.0	.9	1.1	1.0	.8
		.8	.4		.5		.6	.6	.6	.6	.5
		1.3	.7		1.1	Debt/Worth	1.3	1.1	1.4	1.1	1.1
		3.0	1.7		2.7		2.6	3.2	2.5	2.7	2.7
		36.6	77.5		62.6		27.3	12.1	25.1	62.8	62.6
	(19)	8.8	(14) 50.5	(39)	26.4	% Profit Before Taxes/ Tangible Net Worth	(66) 11.5	(36) 2.5	(53) 12.5	(52) 28.2	(39) 26.4
		-2.0	21.6		3.3		-2.9	-25.5	1.5	9.9	3.3
		17.3	49.9		29.0		11.5	7.1	15.0	28.1	29.0
		3.3	27.7		10.1	% Profit Before Taxes/ Total Assets	3.5	.7	6.0	12.4	10.1
		-.7	9.3		1.9		-1.9	-13.5	.6	5.9	1.9
		.7	.5		.6		.5	.6	.4	.6	.6
	(19)	1.2	(14) .7	(37)	1.1	% Depr., Dep., Amort./ Revenues	(65) 1.2	(34) 1.2	(56) 1.2	(41) 1.3	(37) 1.1
		3.3	1.3		2.3		2.7	2.7	2.7	1.8	2.3
		2.9			1.8		2.5	2.2	1.9	1.8	1.8
	(10)	4.8	(22)	3.8	% Officers', Directors' Owners' Comp/Revenues	(39) 4.0	(27) 4.1	(25) 3.0	(25) 4.6	(22) 3.8
		5.9			5.9		7.2	6.3	5.5	7.5	5.9
2015M	107378M	355090M	469426M	933909M	Contract Revenues ($)	1063677M	276540M	1309714M	6590392M	933909M
358M	37075M	140618M	307707M	485758M	Total Assets ($)	494304M	115540M	592085M	3250279M	485758M

M = $ thousand   MM = $ million
See Pages 11 through 21 for Explanation of Ratios and Data

Current Data Sorted by Assets | **Comparative Historical Data**

0-1MM	1-10MM	10-50MM	50 & OVER	ALL		4/1/02-3/31/03 ALL	4/1/03-3/31/04 ALL	4/1/04-3/31/05 ALL	4/1/05-3/31/06 ALL	4/1/06-3/31/07 ALL
					Type of Statement					
		3		3	Unqualified	6	7	5	3	3
	25	5		30	Reviewed	32	23	26	36	30
4	4			8	Compiled	19	12	11	8	8
4	4			8	Tax Returns	18	15	15	18	8
	4			4	Other	10	7	9	9	4
12 (4/1-9/30/06)		41 (10/1/06-3/31/07)								
8	37	8		53	**NUMBER OF STATEMENTS**	85	64	66	74	53
%	%	%	%	%	**ASSETS**	%	%	%	%	%
	10.7			11.1	Cash & Equivalents	14.4	10.6	13.7	11.6	11.1
	46.8			41.4	A/R - Progress Billings	37.4	42.1	39.5	39.7	41.4
	5.6			5.6	A/R - Current Retention	1.7	4.8	4.4	4.6	5.6
	.8			1.0	Inventory	3.4	2.1	3.4	2.8	1.0
	4.1			3.5	Cost & Est. Earnings In Excess Billings	2.4	1.4	2.1	2.6	3.5
	3.9			5.0	All Other Current	7.1	4.4	5.3	4.1	5.0
	71.8			67.6	Total Current	66.3	65.4	68.3	65.5	67.6
	20.4			23.4	Fixed Assets (net)	24.9	28.5	23.6	26.3	23.4
	2.2			1.5	Joint Ventures & Investments	.5	.3	.2	.6	1.5
	.0			.0	Intangibles (net)	1.2	1.1	2.3	2.0	.0
	5.6			7.5	All Other Non-Current	7.2	4.8	5.6	5.7	7.5
	100.0			100.0	Total	100.0	100.0	100.0	100.0	100.0
					LIABILITIES					
	8.4			11.6	Notes Payable-Short Term	9.5	14.3	11.4	10.3	11.6
	15.7			15.5	A/P - Trade	14.7	15.8	15.8	16.3	15.5
	.0			.0	A/P - Retention	.0	.0	.0	.2	.0
	8.8			8.6	Billings in Excess of Costs & Est. Earnings	5.1	4.4	4.1	6.3	8.6
	.6			.4	Income Taxes Payable	.6	.2	.1	.7	.4
	2.9			3.1	Cur. Mat.-L/T/D	3.1	3.6	4.6	3.8	3.1
	9.2			8.7	All Other Current	10.4	9.7	6.8	7.7	8.7
	45.6			47.9	Total Current	43.4	48.0	42.8	45.3	47.9
	9.9			9.9	Long-Term Debt	13.0	21.0	13.6	13.9	9.9
	.7			.5	Deferred Taxes	1.0	.6	.7	.7	.5
	2.3			3.4	All Other Non-Current	5.5	4.7	2.0	3.4	3.4
	41.4			38.2	Net Worth	37.1	25.7	41.0	36.7	38.2
	100.0			100.0	Total Liabilities & Net Worth	100.0	100.0	100.0	100.0	100.0
					INCOME DATA					
	100.0			100.0	Contract Revenues	100.0	100.0	100.0	100.0	100.0
	22.6			25.3	Gross Profit	26.1	30.5	25.9	27.6	25.3
	18.5			20.8	Operating Expenses	22.9	27.1	21.9	23.2	20.8
	4.1			4.5	Operating Profit	3.3	3.4	3.9	4.4	4.5
	.2			.2	All Other Expenses (net)	.2	.3	.4	.0	.2
	3.9			4.4	Profit Before Taxes	3.0	3.1	3.6	4.4	4.4
					RATIOS					
	2.2			2.0		2.9	2.3	2.3	2.4	2.0
	1.6			1.6	Current	1.7	1.4	1.7	1.6	1.6
	1.3			1.2		1.1	.9	1.1	1.2	1.2
	8.5			8.1		6.1	6.1	6.1	6.0	8.1
	(35) 3.2			(50) 3.4	Receivables/Payables	(80) 3.1	(56) 4.0	(59) 3.3	(70) 3.4	(50) 3.4
	2.2			2.2		1.6	2.1	1.8	1.7	2.2
	(45) 8.1			(35) 10.6		(26) 14.1	(32) 11.3	(28) 13.1	(31) 11.7	(35) 10.6
	(73) 5.0			(63) 5.8	Revenues/Receivables	(51) 7.1	(61) 6.0	(58) 6.3	(58) 6.3	(63) 5.8
	(84) 4.3			(84) 4.3		(73) 5.0	(87) 4.2	(81) 4.5	(83) 4.4	(84) 4.3
	(10) 36.3			(6) 62.5		(8) 45.7	(8) 43.2	(10) 35.8	(11) 31.9	(6) 62.5
	(21) 17.4			(17) 21.7	Cost of Revenues/Payables	(20) 18.1	(20) 18.4	(20) 17.9	(21) 17.2	(17) 21.7
	(39) 9.4			(35) 10.5		(32) 11.3	(42) 8.6	(35) 10.5	(35) 10.4	(35) 10.5
	7.8			7.9		5.8	8.6	6.4	7.1	7.9
	10.2			10.5	Revenues/Working Capital	11.4	15.7	11.2	11.6	10.5
	23.6			42.5		81.5	-108.2	69.7	27.8	42.5
	17.3			18.8		17.2	9.2	16.0	18.8	18.8
	(33) 8.2			(46) 6.7	EBIT/Interest	(73) 6.0	(54) 3.9	(56) 5.0	(68) 5.4	(46) 6.7
	2.1			2.0		2.1	-.7	1.6	1.5	2.0
	9.6			9.2		16.8		5.1	6.7	9.2
	(13) 4.0			(14) 3.1	Net Profit + Depr., Dep., Amort./Cur. Mat. L/T/D	(18) 5.7		(11) 2.5	(18) 4.0	(14) 3.1
	1.7			1.4		1.3		1.8	2.1	1.4
	.2			.3		.2	.2	.2	.3	.3
	.4			.5	Fixed/Worth	.6	.6	.5	.5	.5
	.8			1.1		1.6	1.7	1.9	1.3	1.1
	.8			.9		.6	.9	.6	.7	.9
	1.7			1.7	Debt/Worth	1.2	1.8	1.2	1.2	1.7
	2.4			2.9		4.6	4.9	4.9	4.4	2.9
	56.8			59.0		42.5	52.8	43.4	66.3	59.0
	(36) 22.1			(50) 25.5	% Profit Before Taxes/Tangible Net Worth	(72) 16.9	(53) 24.3	(57) 23.7	(65) 21.3	(50) 25.5
	4.7			4.0		5.2	.5	6.2	5.7	4.0
	19.9			22.0		18.3	20.6	19.1	20.9	22.0
	7.7			7.9	% Profit Before Taxes/Total Assets	8.5	7.4	9.4	7.0	7.9
	2.1			1.4		.9	-1.8	1.3	1.3	1.4
	.8			.8		1.0	1.1	.9	1.1	.8
	(30) 1.4			(44) 1.4	% Depr., Dep., Amort./Revenues	(70) 2.1	(45) 2.1	(54) 1.7	(63) 2.0	(44) 1.4
	2.0			2.4		3.7	3.9	2.9	3.9	2.4
	2.2			2.5		3.0	3.5	2.5	1.9	2.5
	(21) 3.3			(30) 4.0	% Officers', Directors' Owners' Comp/Revenues	(56) 4.3	(42) 4.9	(45) 4.1	(51) 4.1	(30) 4.0
	5.7			8.0		8.3	8.3	9.0	6.7	8.0
4222M	181039M	113136M		298397M	Contract Revenues ($)	497165M	5086711M	406718M	414066M	298397M
1400M	69605M	39681M		110686M	Total Assets ($)	187526M	2113228M	147019M	171555M	110686M

(10-50MM and 50 & OVER current columns: DATA NOT AVAILABLE)

© RMA 2007

M = $ thousand   MM = $ million
See Pages 11 through 21 for Explanation of Ratios and Data

Current Data Sorted by Assets   Comparative Historical Data

				2	Type of Statement	5	2	2	3	2
	8	1 6	1	14	Unqualified / Reviewed	18	14	19	14	14
1	7		1	9	Compiled	9	4	3	4	9
	4		1	5	Tax Returns	12	6	8	6	5
3	6	1		10	Other	7	4	5	7	10
	11 (4/1-9/30/06)		29 (10/1/06-3/31/07)			4/1/02- 3/31/03	4/1/03- 3/31/04	4/1/04- 3/31/05	4/1/05- 3/31/06	4/1/06- 3/31/07
0-1MM	1-10MM	10-50MM	50 & OVER	ALL		ALL	ALL	ALL	ALL	ALL
4	25	8	3	40	NUMBER OF STATEMENTS	51	30	37	34	40
%	%	%	%	%	**ASSETS**	%	%	%	%	%
	12.6			12.4	Cash & Equivalents	12.1	11.7	10.7	15.4	12.4
	52.8			54.5	A/R - Progress Billings	45.8	47.4	51.0	45.6	54.5
	1.4			.9	A/R - Current Retention	1.9	1.8	1.8	3.3	.9
	8.8			8.9	Inventory	7.0	9.8	8.7	7.4	8.9
	3.0			2.8	Cost & Est. Earnings In Excess Billings	4.1	1.9	4.1	3.5	2.8
	3.6			2.9	All Other Current	3.8	1.7	2.5	3.4	2.9
	82.2			82.3	Total Current	74.7	74.4	78.8	78.6	82.3
	12.0			10.8	Fixed Assets (net)	18.9	16.4	14.9	15.8	10.8
	.2			1.4	Joint Ventures & Investments	.7	.1	.1	2.6	1.4
	.5			.3	Intangibles (net)	1.9	3.4	2.5	.2	.3
	5.0			5.2	All Other Non-Current	3.8	5.7	3.6	2.9	5.2
	100.0			100.0	Total	100.0	100.0	100.0	100.0	100.0
					LIABILITIES					
	12.5			9.9	Notes Payable-Short Term	9.0	7.2	7.6	10.3	9.9
	32.5			30.1	A/P - Trade	20.0	21.6	22.6	18.2	30.1
	.5			.3	A/P - Retention	.2	.0	.0	.0	.3
	3.2			5.9	Billings in Excess of Costs & Est. Earnings	3.3	4.5	4.9	5.5	5.9
	.1			.2	Income Taxes Payable	.1	.0	.5	.2	.2
	2.2			2.6	Cur. Mat.-L/T/D	3.3	3.2	1.8	2.4	2.6
	6.2			8.3	All Other Current	9.4	4.3	6.2	6.7	8.3
	57.1			57.3	Total Current	45.3	40.9	43.7	43.2	57.3
	10.4			8.1	Long-Term Debt	17.8	13.0	23.4	14.3	8.1
	.2			.1	Deferred Taxes	.7	.5	.3	.1	.1
	7.7			5.9	All Other Non-Current	8.5	1.2	12.7	9.0	5.9
	24.7			28.5	Net Worth	27.7	44.3	19.9	33.5	28.5
	100.0			100.0	Total Liabilities & Net Worth	100.0	100.0	100.0	100.0	100.0
					INCOME DATA					
	100.0			100.0	Contract Revenues	100.0	100.0	100.0	100.0	100.0
	27.3			28.0	Gross Profit	35.3	31.0	29.0	30.7	28.0
	25.6			25.1	Operating Expenses	29.4	25.7	27.4	27.3	25.1
	1.7			2.9	Operating Profit	5.9	5.3	1.6	3.5	2.9
	-.2			-.1	All Other Expenses (net)	.7	.5	.9	-.1	-.1
	1.8			3.0	Profit Before Taxes	5.2	4.9	.7	3.5	3.0
					RATIOS					
	1.6			1.6		2.5	3.0	2.9	3.3	1.6
	1.5			1.5	Current	1.8	1.9	1.7	2.1	1.5
	1.2			1.2		1.3	1.3	1.4	1.4	1.2
	2.7			3.2		4.0	4.1	4.2	4.6	3.2
	(24) 1.9		(39)	1.9	Receivables/Payables	(50) 2.8	(29) 2.2	(30) 2.4	3.6	(39) 1.9
	1.1			1.2		1.5	1.5	1.6	1.9	1.2
46	8.0		45	8.2		31 11.6	36 10.1	50 7.3	35 10.4	45 8.2
59	6.2		59	6.2	Revenues/Receivables	66 5.5	71 5.1	71 5.1	56 6.5	59 6.2
80	4.6		84	4.3		87 4.2	92 4.0	94 3.9	102 3.6	84 4.3
31	11.8		29	12.7		20 18.0	20 17.8	24 15.5	11 34.2	29 12.7
48	7.7		46	8.0	Cost of Revenues/Payables	30 12.3	34 10.8	40 9.2	30 12.2	46 8.0
64	5.7		61	6.0		49 7.4	59 6.1	53 6.9	44 8.3	61 6.0
	8.0			7.6		6.2	5.5	5.2	5.3	7.6
	12.8			12.9	Revenues/Working Capital	8.7	7.4	8.8	8.1	12.9
	25.0			28.4		14.9	14.3	13.3	17.2	28.4
	13.3			12.1		27.8	78.8	13.0	59.6	12.1
	(22) 3.8		(32)	3.9	EBIT/Interest	(45) 6.9	(28) 8.8	(32) 2.9	(29) 7.9	(32) 3.9
	.6			.8		3.0	2.0	-.2	4.1	.8
						12.8				
					Net Profit + Depr., Dep., Amort./Cur. Mat. L/T/D	(12) 3.1				
						1.0				
	.2			.1		.2	.2	.2	.1	.1
	.3			.3	Fixed/Worth	.4	.4	.3	.2	.3
	1.6			1.4		1.2	.5	1.7	.8	1.4
	1.5			1.5		.7	.9	.9	.4	1.5
	2.1			2.1	Debt/Worth	1.3	1.4	1.6	1.2	2.1
	11.0			7.5		4.2	2.7	6.8	3.6	7.5
	56.2			67.0		51.6	47.7	27.9	41.5	67.0
	(21) 17.1		(36)	19.0	% Profit Before Taxes/ Tangible Net Worth	(44) 30.7	(28) 19.6	(29) 9.6	(30) 12.3	(36) 19.0
	3.9			5.2		10.3	5.7	-2.0	5.6	5.2
	16.2			23.2		22.1	24.8	10.7	14.4	23.2
	3.5			4.0	% Profit Before Taxes/ Total Assets	8.8	7.9	2.4	7.2	4.0
	-1.7			-.9		4.6	2.3	-3.2	2.6	-.9
	.3			.2		.7	.7	.7	.5	.2
	(21) .8		(34)	.5	% Depr., Dep., Amort./ Revenues	(44) 1.1	(25) 1.0	(33) 1.1	(30) .7	(34) .5
	1.2			1.1		1.9	1.7	2.1	1.3	1.1
	2.5			2.4		2.7	2.8	2.3	1.8	2.4
	(19) 3.7		(29)	3.7	% Officers', Directors' Owners' Comp/Revenues	(30) 5.7	(21) 4.9	(27) 4.4	(25) 4.8	(29) 3.7
	5.3			7.3		12.4	9.8	9.2	8.5	7.3
2412M	109937M	179184M	1147306M	1438839M	Contract Revenues ($)	4923991M	146927M	167605M	588311M	1438839M
591M	33483M	58898M	278927M	371899M	Total Assets ($)	992970M	57073M	69600M	197809M	371899M

M = $ thousand   MM = $ million
See Pages 11 through 21 for Explanation of Ratios and Data

Current Data Sorted by Assets						Comparative Historical Data				
		11	1	12	**Type of Statement** Unqualified	9	4	7	10	12
1	29	11	1	42	Reviewed	61	37	51	48	42
1	11			12	Compiled	27	23	25	21	12
3	4	1		8	Tax Returns	21	5	16	10	8
3	11	3		17	Other	33	20	17	20	17
9 (4/1-9/30/06)		**82 (10/1/06-3/31/07)**				4/1/02- 3/31/03	4/1/03- 3/31/04	4/1/04- 3/31/05	4/1/05- 3/31/06	4/1/06- 3/31/07
0-1MM	1-10MM	10-50MM	50 & OVER	ALL		ALL	ALL	ALL	ALL	ALL
8	55	26	2	91	**NUMBER OF STATEMENTS**	151	89	116	109	91
%	%	%	%	%	**ASSETS**	%	%	%	%	%
	12.2	8.0		11.4	Cash & Equivalents	14.1	9.0	13.3	9.4	11.4
	48.2	49.0		46.5	A/R - Progress Billings	37.2	42.0	40.4	46.0	46.5
	1.6	6.1		2.7	A/R - Current Retention	1.1	1.7	1.8	1.8	2.7
	6.4	4.3		6.1	Inventory	5.9	5.4	7.7	6.6	6.1
	3.5	7.6		4.4	Cost & Est. Earnings In Excess Billings	3.9	5.3	4.5	5.4	4.4
	2.2	5.4		3.6	All Other Current	6.5	5.2	3.4	4.9	3.6
	74.2	80.5		74.7	Total Current	68.7	68.6	71.1	74.0	74.7
	19.1	12.4		17.7	Fixed Assets (net)	22.7	21.1	19.7	18.7	17.7
	.1	.1		.1	Joint Ventures & Investments	.5	.6	1.0	.3	.1
	2.0	1.5		1.7	Intangibles (net)	1.8	2.4	1.2	1.0	1.7
	4.6	5.6		5.8	All Other Non-Current	6.3	7.4	7.0	6.0	5.8
	100.0	100.0		100.0	Total	100.0	100.0	100.0	100.0	100.0
					LIABILITIES					
	7.5	6.9		8.7	Notes Payable-Short Term	12.4	11.9	11.2	9.4	8.7
	21.1	20.6		20.6	A/P - Trade	18.6	21.4	21.6	22.3	20.6
	.5	.0		.5	A/P - Retention	.2	.4	1.0	.6	.5
	5.4	11.5		6.7	Billings in Excess of Costs & Est. Earnings	3.4	4.4	4.2	4.8	6.7
	.1	.7		.4	Income Taxes Payable	.8	.2	.1	.2	.4
	3.6	2.4		3.4	Cur. Mat.-L/T/D	4.4	6.8	4.4	4.1	3.4
	5.8	14.0		8.5	All Other Current	11.2	7.7	8.0	6.9	8.5
	44.1	56.1		48.8	Total Current	51.1	52.8	50.5	48.4	48.8
	9.4	6.7		10.1	Long-Term Debt	11.1	12.2	13.1	12.9	10.1
	.5	.4		.4	Deferred Taxes	.6	.7	.6	.8	.4
	4.0	2.2		4.3	All Other Non-Current	3.4	3.0	3.5	5.3	4.3
	42.0	34.6		36.5	Net Worth	33.9	31.3	32.2	32.6	36.5
	100.0	100.0		100.0	Total Liabilties & Net Worth	100.0	100.0	100.0	100.0	100.0
					INCOME DATA					
	100.0	100.0		100.0	Contract Revenues	100.0	100.0	100.0	100.0	100.0
	31.4	23.1		29.6	Gross Profit	30.3	28.9	28.0	27.0	29.6
	26.2	17.5		23.7	Operating Expenses	27.7	25.4	24.9	23.5	23.7
	5.3	5.6		5.9	Operating Profit	2.6	3.6	3.1	3.6	5.9
	.0	.8		.1	All Other Expenses (net)	.7	.3	.1	.3	.1
	5.2	4.8		5.8	Profit Before Taxes	1.9	3.2	3.0	3.3	5.8
					RATIOS					
	3.4	1.7		2.4		2.1	1.8	2.1	2.1	2.4
	1.7	1.5		1.6	Current	1.4	1.4	1.5	1.5	1.6
	1.2	1.2		1.2		1.1	1.0	1.1	1.2	1.2
	4.7	4.5		4.5		4.6	3.9	3.6	4.0	4.5
	(54) 2.5	2.7	(90)	2.5	Receivables/Payables	(139) 2.2	(87) 2.6	(111) 2.1	(104) 2.3	(90) 2.5
	1.5	1.8		1.6		1.2	1.4	1.3	1.3	1.6
41	8.9	47 7.7	43	8.6		19 19.4	28 12.8	28 13.1	36 10.2	43 8.6
57	6.4	63 5.8	59	6.2	Revenues/Receivables	46 7.9	50 7.3	50 7.2	62 5.9	59 6.2
76	4.8	93 3.9	76	4.8		73 5.0	73 5.0	70 5.2	77 4.7	76 4.8
12	30.9	17 21.4	15	24.3		12 29.5	15 24.2	15 23.9	19 19.0	15 24.3
28	13.3	26 13.9	28	13.3	Cost of Revenues/Payables	27 13.6	27 13.6	26 13.9	33 11.0	28 13.3
52	7.1	44 8.3	51	7.2		48 7.5	53 6.9	52 7.1	55 6.7	51 7.2
	6.0	7.6		6.7		8.2	8.6	8.2	7.3	6.7
	10.4	15.4		12.3	Revenues/Working Capital	17.2	16.9	14.5	11.9	12.3
	21.1	24.1		26.3		76.9	NM	52.1	30.9	26.3
	21.0	33.5		22.7		14.9	11.3	14.7	14.7	22.7
	(50) 7.9	(24) 17.1	(82)	7.4	EBIT/Interest	(133) 4.1	(82) 4.0	(105) 5.7	(106) 6.5	(82) 7.4
	2.6	3.3		2.6		.4	.3	1.1	2.6	2.6
		15.5		13.2		5.3	8.2	6.9	5.7	13.2
		(11) 3.3	(20)	4.5	Net Profit + Depr., Dep., Amort./Cur. Mat. L/T/D	(42) 2.2	(21) 3.0	(39) 2.5	(33) 2.6	(20) 4.5
		1.4		1.8		.1	1.2	1.2	1.3	1.8
	.2	.2		.2		.3	.2	.2	.2	.2
	.4	.4		.4	Fixed/Worth	.5	.6	.5	.4	.4
	.9	.6		.9		1.2	1.5	1.2	1.3	.9
	.6	1.3		.9		.8	.9	.9	.9	.9
	1.6	1.9		1.8	Debt/Worth	1.8	1.7	1.9	1.6	1.8
	2.8	3.5		3.0		4.1	6.3	5.8	4.2	3.0
	49.4	53.5		53.7		38.2	50.0	59.4	45.7	53.7
	(51) 26.9	41.4	(83)	29.4	% Profit Before Taxes/ Tangible Net Worth	(134) 14.0	(75) 13.0	(104) 28.8	(96) 25.7	(83) 29.4
	8.9	19.2		11.3		-.1	-.7	2.2	7.6	11.3
	26.5	28.0		30.5		14.6	16.0	16.0	17.8	30.5
	9.6	11.5		9.8	% Profit Before Taxes/ Total Assets	5.0	4.7	6.1	7.9	9.8
	5.3	4.6		4.6		-1.7	-1.2	.2	2.9	4.6
	.6	.6		.6		.9	1.0	.6	.9	.6
	(43) 1.2	.9	(75)	1.0	% Depr., Dep., Amort./ Revenues	(133) 1.7	(71) 1.5	(103) 1.4	(95) 1.2	(75) 1.0
	2.6	1.2		2.2		2.8	2.7	2.2	1.9	2.2
	1.9	1.9		1.9		2.2	2.0	2.0	2.2	1.9
	(36) 3.4	(14) 2.7	(53)	3.1	% Officers', Directors' Owners' Comp/Revenues	(95) 4.4	(61) 4.0	(77) 3.4	(67) 3.2	(53) 3.1
	6.7	8.4		7.0		7.9	7.3	7.1	7.4	7.0
3342M	230761M	478765M	4668225M	5381093M	Contract Revenues ($)	10738454M	6891597M	696406M	5788234M	5381093M
991M	81961M	192231M	3532733M	3807916M	Total Assets ($)	3532983M	1534313M	246817M	3225718M	3807916M

M = $ thousand   MM = $ million
See Pages 11 through 21 for Explanation of Ratios and Data

Current Data Sorted by Assets | Comparative Historical Data

Type of Statement	42	42	42	33	31
Unqualified	42	42	42	33	31
Reviewed	154	138	165	140	115
Compiled	59	50	37	44	36
Tax Returns	46	43	57	49	43
Other	64	44	57	39	55

Current Data column groups:

	8	19	4	31
7	73	34	1	115
6	28	2		36
13	27	2	1	43
3	36	11	5	55

62 (4/1-9/30/06) | 218 (10/1/06-3/31/07)

0-1MM	1-10MM	10-50MM	50 & OVER	ALL		4/1/02-3/31/03 ALL	4/1/03-3/31/04 ALL	4/1/04-3/31/05 ALL	4/1/05-3/31/06 ALL	4/1/06-3/31/07 ALL
29	172	68	11	280	**NUMBER OF STATEMENTS**	365	317	358	305	280
%	%	%	%	%	**ASSETS**	%	%	%	%	%
14.5	12.8	10.8	10.4	12.4	Cash & Equivalents	13.3	11.2	12.0	11.6	12.4
38.7	45.3	54.0	61.7	47.4	A/R - Progress Billings	44.2	45.8	44.9	46.3	47.4
.1	1.3	3.9	1.0	1.8	A/R - Current Retention	1.6	1.7	1.9	2.3	1.8
7.5	7.8	5.3	4.9	7.1	Inventory	5.5	6.2	6.8	6.7	7.1
.6	4.1	6.2	1.7	4.2	Cost & Est. Earnings In Excess Billings	4.6	5.0	5.2	4.8	4.2
3.6	5.0	7.0	1.8	5.2	All Other Current	4.9	4.7	5.4	4.2	5.2
65.0	76.2	87.2	81.6	78.0	Total Current	74.1	74.5	76.2	76.0	78.0
22.7	16.4	9.1	12.7	15.1	Fixed Assets (net)	17.9	17.8	16.0	16.6	15.1
1.6	.7	.5	.0	.7	Joint Ventures & Investments	.5	.7	.7	1.0	.7
.7	1.4	.6	3.4	1.2	Intangibles (net)	1.2	1.7	1.3	1.4	1.2
10.1	5.3	2.6	2.3	5.0	All Other Non-Current	6.3	5.2	5.8	5.0	5.0
100.0	100.0	100.0	100.0	100.0	Total	100.0	100.0	100.0	100.0	100.0
					LIABILITIES					
20.3	12.1	9.1	6.9	12.0	Notes Payable-Short Term	13.9	13.1	14.7	11.4	12.0
16.4	20.0	23.0	21.8	20.5	A/P - Trade	18.8	19.6	22.5	20.4	20.5
.2	.1	.3	.0	.2	A/P - Retention	.1	.2	.2	.2	.2
1.4	4.0	11.8	9.8	5.8	Billings in Excess of Costs & Est. Earnings	5.1	5.7	4.7	5.5	5.8
.0	.2	.3	.0	.2	Income Taxes Payable	.3	.3	.3	.4	.2
3.3	2.5	1.8	2.3	2.4	Cur. Mat.-L/T/D	4.4	4.2	3.0	3.3	2.4
7.1	9.7	9.0	11.8	9.4	All Other Current	8.5	8.4	9.2	9.0	9.4
48.7	48.8	55.3	52.6	50.5	Total Current	51.1	52.1	54.4	50.2	50.5
25.5	11.5	5.5	9.4	11.4	Long-Term Debt	9.0	10.8	10.3	9.9	11.4
.0	.7	.6	.1	.6	Deferred Taxes	.7	.9	.5	.5	.6
4.1	3.3	5.3	3.3	3.9	All Other Non-Current	5.1	3.8	5.7	4.2	3.9
21.6	35.8	33.3	34.6	33.7	Net Worth	34.0	32.4	29.1	35.2	33.7
100.0	100.0	100.0	100.0	100.0	Total Liabilties & Net Worth	100.0	100.0	100.0	100.0	100.0
					INCOME DATA					
100.0	100.0	100.0	100.0	100.0	Contract Revenues	100.0	100.0	100.0	100.0	100.0
43.2	28.3	17.2	20.9	26.8	Gross Profit	27.9	26.6	27.8	26.9	26.8
40.9	23.5	13.1	17.3	22.5	Operating Expenses	26.2	24.3	25.1	22.9	22.5
2.3	4.8	4.1	3.5	4.3	Operating Profit	1.7	2.3	2.7	4.0	4.3
1.4	.4	.3	.9	.5	All Other Expenses (net)	.5	.5	.3	.1	.5
.9	4.4	3.8	2.6	3.8	Profit Before Taxes	1.2	1.8	2.4	3.9	3.8
					RATIOS					
2.4	2.8	2.3	3.0	2.6	Current	2.3	2.3	2.2	2.2	2.6
1.3	1.8	1.6	1.7	1.6		1.5	1.5	1.6	1.6	1.6
1.0	1.2	1.2	1.2	1.2		1.2	1.2	1.2	1.2	1.2
6.4	4.0	4.7	9.2	4.5	Receivables/Payables	4.6	4.5	3.8	4.3	4.5
(26) 2.9	(162) 2.4	(66) 2.8	3.8	(265) 2.5		(352) 2.8	(303) 2.8	(339) 2.5	(293) 2.6	(265) 2.5
1.3	1.6	1.8	1.7	1.7		1.9	1.8	1.6	1.8	1.7
23 16.0	36 10.1	58 6.3	51 7.2	40 9.0	Revenues/Receivables	40 9.2	40 9.2	38 9.5	41 9.0	40 9.0
42 8.7	58 6.2	73 5.0	65 5.6	61 6.0		56 6.5	61 5.9	59 6.2	62 5.9	61 6.0
64 5.7	79 4.6	95 3.9	78 4.7	81 4.5		78 4.7	84 4.3	82 4.5	85 4.3	81 4.5
6 61.5	15 23.8	20 18.6	10 36.4	15 23.8	Cost of Revenues/Payables	16 23.0	16 22.5	18 20.3	17 21.9	15 23.8
23 15.9	31 11.9	30 12.2	24 15.3	30 12.3		25 14.3	27 13.5	30 12.3	31 11.7	30 12.3
68 5.4	47 7.7	54 6.8	46 8.0	49 7.4		44 8.3	45 8.1	52 7.0	46 8.0	49 7.4
6.4	6.3	6.5	7.7	6.5	Revenues/Working Capital	6.5	6.6	6.9	6.7	6.5
46.2	9.3	9.7	10.4	9.8		11.6	11.5	11.6	10.6	9.8
280.6	19.1	16.9	22.9	22.7		29.4	28.8	28.6	25.9	22.7
7.3	20.5	15.4	65.2	19.0	EBIT/Interest	13.5	12.9	15.0	20.3	19.0
(23) 1.5	(156) 6.8	(60) 5.1	(10) 10.4	(249) 6.3		(315) 3.2	(288) 4.4	(311) 5.0	(258) 6.4	(249) 6.3
-.2	2.2	1.8	3.8	1.7		-.5	.7	1.0	1.8	1.7
	10.5	16.6		13.2	Net Profit + Depr., Dep., Amort./Cur. Mat. L/T/D	9.1	7.9	7.9	10.3	13.2
	(28) 4.1	(23) 6.3		(55) 5.0		(102) 3.0	(79) 2.3	(108) 2.6	(72) 3.7	(55) 5.0
	1.3	1.7		1.5		.7	.9	.5	1.9	1.5
.1	.2	.1	.2	.1	Fixed/Worth	.2	.2	.2	.2	.1
.8	.3	.2	.3	.3		.4	.4	.4	.3	.3
3.0	.8	.6	.6	.8		.9	1.0	1.0	.9	.8
1.1	.7	1.0	.9	.8	Debt/Worth	.8	.8	.8	.9	.8
2.8	1.6	2.1	1.8	1.8		1.5	1.8	1.7	1.7	1.8
10.0	4.0	4.7	4.8	4.6		3.7	4.4	5.0	4.3	4.6
134.4	56.8	57.4	51.9	57.4	% Profit Before Taxes/Tangible Net Worth	33.1	42.0	45.0	54.1	57.4
(23) 21.8	(152) 31.8	(63) 26.8	(10) 34.4	(248) 29.9		(326) 11.9	(279) 16.0	(312) 15.3	(272) 24.2	(248) 29.9
3.1	12.9	9.5	17.4	12.0		.3	1.2	1.3	5.8	12.0
19.4	21.9	19.6	19.5	21.0	% Profit Before Taxes/Total Assets	12.7	13.9	16.0	22.3	21.0
3.2	10.9	7.6	10.7	9.7		3.4	5.7	6.1	8.5	9.7
-6.5	3.7	1.5	5.9	2.1		-2.6	-.7	.1	1.8	2.1
1.2	.6	.3		.5	% Depr., Dep., Amort./Revenues	.6	.7	.7	.6	.5
(21) 1.7	(142) 1.1	(64) .5		(236) 1.0		(334) 1.3	(256) 1.3	(304) 1.2	(268) 1.1	(236) 1.0
3.5	1.8	1.0		1.6		2.3	2.3	1.9	1.8	1.6
5.3	2.6	1.2		2.1	% Officers', Directors' Owners' Comp/Revenues	2.8	2.0	2.2	2.6	2.1
(18) 10.2	(109) 4.1	(36) 1.7		(167) 4.2		(238) 5.3	(199) 3.7	(211) 4.7	(182) 4.5	(167) 4.2
19.8	7.2	4.8		7.3		8.5	7.2	8.1	8.4	7.3
14609M	733651M	1510980M	3757323M	6016563M	Contract Revenues ($)	31031225M	9379206M	21013196M	13065767M	6016563M
5394M	259767M	562947M	1165158M	1993266M	Total Assets ($)	11872857M	4698327M	6939259M	4378559M	1993266M

M = $ thousand   MM = $ million
See Pages 11 through 21 for Explanation of Ratios and Data

Current Data Sorted by Assets | **Comparative Historical Data**

0-1MM	1-10MM	10-50MM	50 & OVER	ALL	Type of Statement	4/1/02-3/31/03 ALL	4/1/03-3/31/04 ALL	4/1/04-3/31/05 ALL	4/1/05-3/31/06 ALL	4/1/06-3/31/07 ALL
	4	12	6	22	Unqualified	43	16	30	31	22
2	59	41	6	108	Reviewed	162	99	97	124	108
6	30	4	1	41	Compiled	101	47	58	47	41
12	28	2		42	Tax Returns	75	39	68	57	42
6	26	10	6	48	Other	82	39	50	61	48
66 (4/1-9/30/06)		195 (10/1/06-3/31/07)								
26	147	69	19	261	NUMBER OF STATEMENTS	463	240	303	320	261
%	%	%	%	%	ASSETS	%	%	%	%	%
19.3	11.7	7.8	11.6	11.4	Cash & Equivalents	12.0	11.7	11.5	12.9	11.4
20.6	41.8	50.9	50.1	42.7	A/R - Progress Billings	39.9	41.6	41.2	41.2	42.7
.0	2.3	4.4	2.6	2.6	A/R - Current Retention	2.2	2.5	1.9	1.9	2.6
8.1	11.0	5.5	4.3	8.8	Inventory	9.4	8.2	9.4	9.0	8.8
.0	3.2	6.2	6.2	3.9	Cost & Est. Earnings In Excess Billings	3.5	3.5	3.4	3.6	3.9
6.9	3.3	5.7	4.3	4.4	All Other Current	4.8	4.8	4.3	4.9	4.4
54.8	73.3	80.5	79.2	73.8	Total Current	71.7	72.4	71.7	73.5	73.8
32.8	18.2	12.1	10.9	17.5	Fixed Assets (net)	20.1	19.4	19.0	18.2	17.5
.1	.3	1.1	.6	.5	Joint Ventures & Investments	.8	.6	.6	.7	.5
2.1	1.6	.8	3.1	1.5	Intangibles (net)	1.1	1.5	1.9	1.7	1.5
10.2	6.6	5.4	6.3	6.6	All Other Non-Current	6.3	6.1	6.8	6.0	6.6
100.0	100.0	100.0	100.0	100.0	Total	100.0	100.0	100.0	100.0	100.0
					LIABILITIES					
19.6	10.4	5.8	6.2	9.8	Notes Payable-Short Term	10.5	11.9	13.3	11.3	9.8
17.6	22.2	26.8	24.4	23.1	A/P - Trade	22.3	21.3	22.6	22.5	23.1
.0	.1	.2		.1	A/P - Retention	.4	.2	.2	.4	.1
.1	4.3	10.4	10.8	6.0	Billings in Excess of Costs & Est. Earnings	4.8	5.5	4.7	4.7	6.0
.0	.2	.6	.4	.3	Income Taxes Payable	.4	.3	.3	.4	.3
5.0	4.0	2.5	2.9	3.6	Cur. Mat.-L/T/D	4.2	3.6	3.8	4.6	3.6
12.9	8.4	9.7	13.8	9.6	All Other Current	8.3	11.6	10.1	8.7	9.6
55.2	49.6	56.1	58.4	52.5	Total Current	51.0	54.3	55.1	52.5	52.5
28.0	14.2	6.4	5.3	12.9	Long-Term Debt	13.0	13.8	14.2	14.3	12.9
.0	.5	.6	.3	.5	Deferred Taxes	.5	.6	.3	.5	.5
16.2	5.1	2.7	1.4	5.3	All Other Non-Current	3.6	4.1	6.2	5.1	5.3
.6	30.5	34.3	34.6	28.9	Net Worth	31.8	27.1	24.3	27.6	28.9
100.0	100.0	100.0	100.0	100.0	Total Liabilities & Net Worth	100.0	100.0	100.0	100.0	100.0
					INCOME DATA					
100.0	100.0	100.0	100.0	100.0	Contract Revenues	100.0	100.0	100.0	100.0	100.0
43.2	30.1	18.2	19.4	27.5	Gross Profit	30.0	29.2	28.8	28.6	27.5
39.8	25.7	13.7	15.4	23.2	Operating Expenses	27.8	26.8	26.4	24.9	23.2
3.4	4.5	4.5	3.9	4.3	Operating Profit	2.3	2.4	2.3	3.6	4.3
1.4	.3	.2	.1	.4	All Other Expenses (net)	.5	.5	.4	.4	.4
2.0	4.1	4.3	3.9	4.0	Profit Before Taxes	1.8	1.9	1.9	3.2	4.0
					RATIOS					
2.1	2.2	1.9	1.6	2.0	Current	2.3	2.2	2.1	2.2	2.0
.9	1.5	1.4	1.4	1.4		1.5	1.4	1.4	1.4	1.4
.6	1.1	1.2	1.2	1.1		1.1	1.1	1.1	1.1	1.1
5.7	3.7	3.4	3.4	3.6	Receivables/Payables	3.4	3.6	3.2	3.5	3.6
(19) 1.4	(139) 2.2	2.2	2.3	(246) 2.2		(442) 2.1	(229) 2.3	(289) 2.1	(304) 2.1	(246) 2.2
.6	1.3	1.6	1.4	1.3		1.3	1.4	1.3	1.3	1.3
0 UND	27 13.5	56 6.5	50 7.3	30 12.3	Revenues/Receivables	28 13.0	32 11.5	27 13.5	29 12.8	30 12.3
15 23.7	49 7.5	69 5.3	70 5.2	56 6.6		50 7.3	52 7.0	48 7.6	49 7.5	56 6.6
37 10.0	68 5.4	85 4.3	89 4.1	76 4.8		74 5.0	74 4.9	71 5.2	73 5.0	76 4.8
0 UND	18 20.7	21 17.8	17 21.6	18 20.8	Cost of Revenues/Payables	18 20.6	18 20.1	19 19.3	19 18.9	18 20.8
24 15.2	33 11.1	34 10.7	38 9.5	33 11.1		31 11.9	30 12.3	30 12.1	30 12.1	33 11.1
51 7.1	48 7.6	50 7.3	50 7.4	49 7.4		51 7.2	47 7.8	48 7.6	45 8.1	49 7.4
9.4	6.9	8.6	8.6	7.7	Revenues/Working Capital	7.1	7.9	8.2	8.2	7.7
-107.9	14.6	13.9	12.9	15.2		14.7	14.0	16.5	15.1	15.2
-15.1	66.2	23.3	28.5	57.0		43.6	37.7	95.3	58.5	57.0
9.0	15.9	24.4	18.7	17.5	EBIT/Interest	14.5	17.2	17.8	18.2	17.5
(23) 2.6	(128) 4.5	(63) 10.2	(15) 8.3	(229) 6.1		(404) 4.2	(212) 5.3	(255) 4.3	(283) 5.2	(229) 6.1
-.2	1.3	4.3	3.6	1.7		.8	1.3	.7	2.0	1.7
	4.7	11.5		9.3	Net Profit + Depr., Dep., Amort./Cur. Mat. L/T/D	5.7	9.5	4.8	5.9	9.3
(34)	2.0	(22) 3.1		(61) 2.7		(146) 2.1	(62) 3.0	(76) 2.5	(78) 2.2	(61) 2.7
	.7	.7		1.0		.7	1.2	.8	.9	1.0
.2	.2	.2	.1	.2	Fixed/Worth	.2	.2	.2	.2	.2
1.9	.5	.3	.4	.5		.5	.5	.6	.5	.5
-1.8	1.2	.6	.7	1.2		1.3	1.5	1.6	1.5	1.2
1.4	.8	.9	1.4	.9	Debt/Worth	.8	.9	1.1	.9	.9
5.4	2.1	2.0	1.9	2.2		2.0	2.3	2.3	2.1	2.2
-4.4	5.0	4.0	4.3	5.2		5.0	5.2	6.4	6.7	5.2
184.6	61.6	51.8	46.2	58.2	% Profit Before Taxes/Tangible Net Worth	43.5	47.8	46.6	47.4	58.2
(15) 90.6	(126) 25.4	(65) 35.9	(18) 32.4	(224) 31.3		(413) 14.8	(206) 18.3	(251) 20.3	(271) 25.2	(224) 31.3
.0	4.7	13.9	21.0	6.9		.2	3.9	3.4	7.7	6.9
26.0	23.6	19.0	14.7	21.0	% Profit Before Taxes/Total Assets	14.4	15.3	15.2	16.8	21.0
4.3	7.6	11.0	11.3	9.7		5.0	5.7	5.7	8.1	9.7
-7.3	.9	5.3	4.3	1.2		-.8	.6	-.2	2.0	1.2
1.0	.8	.4	.3	.6	% Depr., Dep., Amort./Revenues	.8	.7	.6	.6	.6
(17) 2.0	(124) 1.3	(66) .7	(14) .5	(221) 1.0		(409) 1.5	(187) 1.2	(251) 1.2	(270) 1.1	(221) 1.0
3.2	2.0	1.1	.9	1.7		2.5	2.3	2.3	1.8	1.7
4.4	2.5	.9		1.9	% Officers', Directors' Owners' Comp/Revenues	2.5	2.3	2.3	1.9	1.9
(21) 8.9	(93) 4.3	(40) 1.8		(162) 3.8		(288) 4.5	(156) 4.5	(201) 4.1	(206) 4.3	(162) 3.8
12.4	7.3	3.2		7.3		8.8	7.6	7.6	7.4	7.3
16934M	619198M	1336134M	12562972M	14535238M	Contract Revenues ($)	19010216M	8652715M	6751057M	6604897M	14535238M
5546M	200595M	450998M	4422896M	5080035M	Total Assets ($)	10868176M	3419800M	1898955M	1717449M	5080035M

© RMA 2007

M = $ thousand   MM = $ million
See Pages 11 through 21 for Explanation of Ratios and Data

Current Data Sorted by Assets | Comparative Historical Data

Current Data date groupings: **20 (4/1-9/30/06)** covers 0-1MM & 1-10MM; **62 (10/1/06-3/31/07)** covers 10-50MM & 50 & OVER.

0-1MM	1-10MM	10-50MM	50 & OVER	ALL		4/1/02-3/31/03 ALL	4/1/03-3/31/04 ALL	4/1/04-3/31/05 ALL	4/1/05-3/31/06 ALL	4/1/06-3/31/07 ALL
					Type of Statement					
	3	6	2	11	Unqualified	16	9	12	13	11
	18	12	3	33	Reviewed	60	29	46	46	33
	7	1	2	10	Compiled	26	9	17	14	10
2	11	1		14	Tax Returns	17	14	14	17	14
1	11	2		14	Other	22	11	20	13	14
3	50	22	7	82	**NUMBER OF STATEMENTS**	141	72	109	103	82
%	%	%	%	%		%	%	%	%	%
					ASSETS					
	12.3	10.0		11.6	Cash & Equivalents	11.8	9.1	9.7	11.7	11.6
	51.8	61.3		52.7	A/R - Progress Billings	47.1	54.1	53.2	50.6	52.7
	2.1	2.7		2.0	A/R - Current Retention	1.5	3.7	2.3	3.1	2.0
	4.7	4.8		5.1	Inventory	4.2	4.8	5.9	5.9	5.1
	4.0	5.3		4.6	Cost & Est. Earnings In Excess Billings	4.0	3.7	4.1	4.6	4.6
	4.5	3.7		3.9	All Other Current	5.1	4.7	4.6	4.9	3.9
	79.4	87.7		80.0	Total Current	73.6	80.0	79.8	80.8	80.0
	11.5	9.7		12.5	Fixed Assets (net)	19.3	13.4	12.6	12.2	12.5
	.1	.2		.1	Joint Ventures & Investments	.5	.1	.3	.7	.1
	.8	.2		.6	Intangibles (net)	.5	1.4	1.8	.4	.6
	8.3	2.2		6.9	All Other Non-Current	6.1	5.0	5.5	5.8	6.9
	100.0	100.0		100.0	Total	100.0	100.0	100.0	100.0	100.0
					LIABILITIES					
	11.7	10.8		10.1	Notes Payable-Short Term	10.7	14.0	16.3	11.7	10.1
	16.3	15.4		15.2	A/P - Trade	15.1	20.5	16.8	15.1	15.2
	.0	.0		.1	A/P - Retention	.7	.2	.2	.3	.1
	3.6	10.5		5.4	Billings in Excess of Costs & Est. Earnings	4.0	4.6	6.0	6.3	5.4
	.2	.5		.2	Income Taxes Payable	.2	.3	.3	.4	.2
	1.9	1.0		1.9	Cur. Mat.-L/T/D	3.0	2.4	1.9	3.3	1.9
	9.8	12.9		11.7	All Other Current	10.3	11.2	10.8	9.5	11.7
	43.5	51.1		44.6	Total Current	43.9	53.1	52.3	46.7	44.6
	6.8	2.2		6.4	Long-Term Debt	10.2	9.4	10.3	8.4	6.4
	.8	.4		.6	Deferred Taxes	.8	.2	.7	.6	.6
	7.9	9.2		7.3	All Other Non-Current	4.2	5.6	5.9	4.3	7.3
	41.0	37.0		41.1	Net Worth	40.9	31.7	30.8	40.1	41.1
	100.0	100.0		100.0	Total Liabilties & Net Worth	100.0	100.0	100.0	100.0	100.0
					INCOME DATA					
	100.0	100.0		100.0	Contract Revenues	100.0	100.0	100.0	100.0	100.0
	23.6	19.0		23.7	Gross Profit	24.3	23.0	23.2	22.7	23.7
	20.3	15.5		19.4	Operating Expenses	21.3	19.4	21.0	18.5	19.4
	3.2	3.5		4.3	Operating Profit	3.1	3.5	2.2	4.2	4.3
	.2	.5		.2	All Other Expenses (net)	.1	.3	.3	.1	.2
	3.1	3.0		4.1	Profit Before Taxes	3.0	3.2	1.9	4.1	4.1
					RATIOS					
	3.0	2.3		2.9		2.9	2.6	2.5	2.6	2.9
	2.0	1.7		1.9	Current	1.9	1.6	1.6	1.7	1.9
	1.2	1.3		1.3		1.2	1.3	1.2	1.3	1.3
	9.5	6.0		7.8		7.3	6.3	6.8	7.4	7.8
	(49) 4.7	4.5		(79) 4.7	Receivables/Payables	(136) 3.9	3.5	(105) 3.8	(98) 4.2	(79) 4.7
	2.4	3.0		2.9		2.2	2.0	2.0	2.4	2.9
	35 10.5	52 7.0		40 9.1		37 9.8	47 7.7	40 9.1	51 7.1	40 9.1
	56 6.5	71 5.1		59 6.2	Revenues/Receivables	54 6.8	64 5.7	66 5.5	65 5.6	59 6.2
	75 4.9	98 3.7		77 4.7		79 4.6	83 4.4	86 4.3	80 4.6	77 4.7
	7 51.6	13 28.8		9 40.3		10 36.7	13 28.7	11 33.9	10 37.1	9 40.3
	15 24.6	20 18.1		16 22.5	Cost of Revenues/Payables	19 19.1	23 15.6	20 18.4	18 20.8	16 22.5
	25 14.5	30 12.1		27 13.4		33 11.0	43 8.6	36 10.0	33 11.2	27 13.4
	5.7	7.0		6.4		6.2	6.1	6.7	6.1	6.4
	10.8	9.8		10.0	Revenues/Working Capital	9.8	10.6	11.0	10.1	10.0
	23.8	11.9		20.0		30.2	23.7	28.1	17.8	20.0
	29.8	23.2		31.5		20.3	29.8	15.7	39.4	31.5
	(42) 11.8	(20) 10.2		(72) 12.0	EBIT/Interest	(119) 5.6	(61) 4.6	(93) 6.0	(91) 7.3	(72) 12.0
	1.3	3.7		1.9		1.7	.9	1.3	2.3	1.9
				31.1		4.6	4.3	5.6	23.2	31.1
				(14) 8.2	Net Profit + Depr., Dep., Amort./Cur. Mat. L/T/D	(43) 2.0	(16) 2.6	(29) 3.0	(24) 5.3	(14) 8.2
				3.7		.5	.5	.0	1.4	3.7
	.1	.1		.1		.1	.1	.1	.1	.1
	.2	.2		.2	Fixed/Worth	.3	.3	.3	.2	.2
	.6	.5		.6		1.0	.7	.9	.5	.6
	.5	.7		.5		.6	.8	1.0	.6	.5
	1.1	1.3		1.2	Debt/Worth	1.3	1.5	2.0	1.5	1.2
	3.0	3.3		2.7		3.0	3.9	7.7	3.1	2.7
	54.9	45.1		54.3		43.9	36.9	70.4	63.9	54.3
	(45) 23.8	(20) 31.2		(75) 32.6	% Profit Before Taxes/Tangible Net Worth	(133) 19.8	(63) 16.8	(98) 24.4	(98) 22.4	(75) 32.6
	4.8	6.1		6.7		5.5	4.2	3.2	4.3	6.7
	26.9	17.3		26.9		16.3	19.4	14.2	24.1	26.9
	9.0	10.8		13.1	% Profit Before Taxes/Total Assets	7.0	4.8	6.9	8.2	13.1
	.3	.8		1.2		1.8	.2	.3	1.8	1.2
	.4	.2		.3		.5	.5	.4	.4	.3
	(38) .8	.5		(66) .6	% Depr., Dep., Amort./Revenues	(123) 1.0	(51) .9	(88) .8	(89) .8	(66) .6
	1.2	.8		1.0		2.1	1.4	1.2	1.2	1.0
	2.6	1.1		2.2		2.2	2.1	1.8	1.5	2.2
	(35) 4.1	(12) 3.4		(51) 4.1	% Officers', Directors' Owners' Comp/Revenues	(85) 4.2	(51) 3.5	(67) 2.7	(64) 2.8	(51) 4.1
	7.0	6.9		7.1		8.9	6.8	7.0	6.8	7.1
866M	247191M	509798M	13806751M	14564606M	Contract Revenues ($)	1239190M	882236M	5588816M	1607305M	14564606M
946M	69495M	160205M	2108183M	2338829M	Total Assets ($)	439446M	296357M	1404011M	569994M	2338829M

M = $ thousand   MM = $ million
See Pages 11 through 21 for Explanation of Ratios and Data

Current Data Sorted by Assets | Comparative Historical Data

Type of Statement

0-1MM	1-10MM	10-50MM	50 & OVER	ALL	Type of Statement	4/1/02-3/31/03 ALL	4/1/03-3/31/04 ALL	4/1/04-3/31/05 ALL	4/1/05-3/31/06 ALL	4/1/06-3/31/07 ALL
	1	1		2	Unqualified	18	4	9	6	2
1	20	4		25	Reviewed	53	17	17	34	25
1	7		1	9	Compiled	37	11	14	6	9
4	3	1		8	Tax Returns	27	16	11	7	8
2	6		2	10	Other	29	7	7	7	10
	12 (4/1-9/30/06)		42 (10/1/06-3/31/07)							
8	37	8	1	54	**NUMBER OF STATEMENTS**	164	55	58	60	54

Assets

0-1MM %	1-10MM %	10-50MM %	50 & OVER %	ALL %	ASSETS	'02-'03 %	'03-'04 %	'04-'05 %	'05-'06 %	'06-'07 %
	13.8			12.4	Cash & Equivalents	13.9	14.5	16.6	13.8	12.4
	48.0			46.2	A/R - Progress Billings	37.0	40.0	40.9	48.0	46.2
	.9			1.9	A/R - Current Retention	.9	1.5	1.5	.8	1.9
	2.9			3.4	Inventory	4.5	1.1	1.3	2.3	3.4
	5.2			5.0	Cost & Est. Earnings In Excess Billings	4.4	2.8	3.7	4.9	5.0
	4.5			4.0	All Other Current	4.4	4.8	1.7	3.4	4.0
	75.3			72.8	Total Current	65.1	64.6	65.7	73.2	72.8
	15.7			17.8	Fixed Assets (net)	25.4	23.4	24.7	17.5	17.8
	1.0			.7	Joint Ventures & Investments	.5	.5	.4	1.8	.7
	.4			.3	Intangibles (net)	.6	.8	.3	.8	.3
	7.7			8.4	All Other Non-Current	8.3	10.7	8.9	6.7	8.4
	100.0			100.0	Total	100.0	100.0	100.0	100.0	100.0

Liabilities

0-1MM	1-10MM	10-50MM	50 & OVER	ALL	LIABILITIES	'02-'03	'03-'04	'04-'05	'05-'06	'06-'07
	13.8			15.5	Notes Payable-Short Term	15.0	12.2	19.9	15.9	15.5
	18.0			19.6	A/P - Trade	13.9	16.5	14.5	13.5	19.6
	.0			.0	A/P - Retention	.2	.0	.0	.0	.0
	3.4			3.3	Billings in Excess of Costs & Est. Earnings	2.4	2.1	1.3	2.1	3.3
	.6			.5	Income Taxes Payable	.6	.8	.5	.4	.5
	3.9			4.6	Cur. Mat.-L/T/D	6.2	4.1	4.7	2.6	4.6
	8.2			9.4	All Other Current	11.4	9.9	7.6	8.4	9.4
	48.1			52.9	Total Current	49.7	45.6	48.5	42.9	52.9
	7.8			13.0	Long-Term Debt	13.8	16.1	24.5	12.0	13.0
	.5			.4	Deferred Taxes	.8	.4	.4	.6	.4
	2.9			2.7	All Other Non-Current	6.0	6.1	4.4	5.7	2.7
	40.8			31.0	Net Worth	29.7	31.8	22.2	38.8	31.0
	100.0			100.0	Total Liabilities & Net Worth	100.0	100.0	100.0	100.0	100.0

Income Data

0-1MM	1-10MM	10-50MM	50 & OVER	ALL	INCOME DATA	'02-'03	'03-'04	'04-'05	'05-'06	'06-'07
	100.0			100.0	Contract Revenues	100.0	100.0	100.0	100.0	100.0
	26.7			30.6	Gross Profit	31.2	33.4	32.5	27.7	30.6
	22.8			25.9	Operating Expenses	29.0	29.9	30.1	23.9	25.9
	3.9			4.7	Operating Profit	2.2	3.6	2.4	3.8	4.7
	-.1			.1	All Other Expenses (net)	.6	.4	.3	.3	.1
	4.0			4.6	Profit Before Taxes	1.5	3.1	2.1	3.6	4.6

Ratios

0-1MM	1-10MM	10-50MM	50 & OVER	ALL	RATIOS	'02-'03	'03-'04	'04-'05	'05-'06	'06-'07
	2.3			2.5	Current	2.3	2.3	2.4	2.7	2.5
	1.8			1.7		1.5	1.5	1.5	1.8	1.7
	1.3			1.1		1.1	1.0	1.0	1.3	1.1
	7.7			7.6	Receivables/Payables	6.3	7.4	8.4	6.6	7.6
	(35) 3.4		(50) 3.6			(149) 3.8	(47) 3.5	(50) 3.7	(56) 3.9	(50) 3.6
	1.6			1.5		1.5	1.9	2.2	2.5	1.5
34	10.9	33	11.2		Revenues/Receivables	22 / 16.2	16 / 22.5	24 / 15.2	41 / 8.9	33 / 11.2
61	6.0	62	5.9			52 / 7.0	55 / 6.6	60 / 6.1	72 / 5.1	62 / 5.9
77	4.8	79	4.6			76 / 4.8	73 / 5.0	81 / 4.5	93 / 3.9	79 / 4.6
7	48.7	7	53.3		Cost of Revenues/Payables	8 / 44.7	2 / 176.0	3 / 127.1	10 / 37.1	7 / 53.3
20	17.8	21	17.5			20 / 18.1	24 / 15.5	23 / 16.0	21 / 17.3	21 / 17.5
37	9.8	38	9.5			38 / 9.7	40 / 9.0	40 / 9.1	36 / 10.0	38 / 9.5
	5.2			5.2	Revenues/Working Capital	7.6	7.5	5.7	5.4	5.2
	10.0			11.9		13.9	15.1	14.0	8.9	11.9
	25.3			225.6		51.5	999.8	-116.3	21.4	225.6
	19.2			19.2	EBIT/Interest	8.2	21.0	16.4	15.4	19.2
	(31) 5.6		(46) 4.9			(145) 2.8	(43) 7.0	(50) 3.9	(53) 3.8	(46) 4.9
	1.8			2.0		-.5	2.3	.2	1.7	2.0
				8.2	Net Profit + Depr., Dep., Amort./Cur. Mat. L/T/D	4.2	4.8	5.8	8.3	8.2
			(12) 2.6			(49) 1.9	(14) 2.0	(14) 1.2	(15) 2.7	(12) 2.6
				1.6		.8	.7	-.5	1.3	1.6
	.1			.1	Fixed/Worth	.3	.3	.2	.1	.1
	.3			.3		.5	.5	.5	.3	.3
	.7			1.1		1.6	1.6	1.6	.9	1.1
	.8			.7	Debt/Worth	.8	.7	.9	.7	.7
	1.1			1.3		1.6	2.0	1.9	1.3	1.3
	3.1			3.5		4.7	7.3	4.9	2.7	3.5
	55.1			55.2	% Profit Before Taxes/Tangible Net Worth	41.5	100.4	63.7	44.6	55.2
	(34) 12.9		(45) 20.7			(147) 12.9	(50) 23.6	(49) 11.3	(55) 23.6	(45) 20.7
	4.6			4.7		-2.9	7.6	-.5	8.0	4.7
	29.4			30.8	% Profit Before Taxes/Total Assets	13.2	20.5	22.6	16.5	30.8
	5.5			6.3		4.7	8.1	6.3	8.0	6.3
	1.6			1.9		-3.5	2.6	-.9	2.4	1.9
	.6			.6	% Depr., Dep., Amort./Revenues	.8	.8	.8	.7	.6
	(33) .9		(45) .9			(145) 1.6	(45) 1.2	(43) 2.3	(51) 1.0	(45) .9
	2.0			1.8		2.8	2.5	3.8	2.3	1.8
	1.4			1.9	% Officers', Directors' Owners' Comp/Revenues	2.9	3.2	2.4	2.6	1.9
	(19) 4.3		(29) 4.7			(104) 5.6	(38) 6.4	(39) 6.3	(33) 4.0	(29) 4.7
	7.6			9.1		9.2	11.7	11.0	7.2	9.1
4555M	161864M	103820M	5121862M	5392101M	Contract Revenues ($)	11473943M	241683M	231526M	11386706M	5392101M
1962M	60112M	37775M	623767M	723616M	Total Assets ($)	5734201M	87900M	90761M	3311040M	723616M

© RMA 2007

M = $ thousand   MM = $ million
See Pages 11 through 21 for Explanation of Ratios and Data

Current Data Sorted by Assets						Comparative Historical Data				
					Type of Statement					
		3		3	Unqualified			2	2	3
	6	4		10	Reviewed	19	11	10	12	10
1	4	2		7	Compiled	13	12	10	12	7
3	3			6	Tax Returns	5	10	12	2	6
1	6	1		8	Other	14	3	9	9	8
6 (4/1-9/30/06)		28 (10/1/06-3/31/07)				4/1/02-3/31/03	4/1/03-3/31/04	4/1/04-3/31/05	4/1/05-3/31/06	4/1/06-3/31/07
0-1MM	1-10MM	10-50MM	50 & OVER	ALL		ALL	ALL	ALL	ALL	ALL
5	19	10		34	NUMBER OF STATEMENTS	51	36	43	37	34
%	%	%	%	%	**ASSETS**	%	%	%	%	%
	7.9	4.6	DATA NOT AVAILABLE	6.6	Cash & Equivalents	9.9	13.4	11.7	7.4	6.6
	58.0	55.5		51.7	A/R - Progress Billings	50.5	41.9	51.5	50.6	51.7
	1.4	2.0		1.4	A/R - Current Retention	.9	.5	.9	.7	1.4
	10.8	6.9		11.5	Inventory	8.7	11.9	9.1	13.9	11.5
	2.3	9.6		4.1	Cost & Est. Earnings In Excess Billings	3.2	3.0	3.0	3.0	4.1
	2.4	6.8		3.6	All Other Current	5.6	3.1	4.1	3.1	3.6
	82.9	85.4		78.8	Total Current	78.8	73.9	80.4	78.7	78.8
	12.1	9.7		12.4	Fixed Assets (net)	12.8	16.0	12.4	14.0	12.4
	.0	.2		.1	Joint Ventures & Investments	.0	.2	.2	.0	.1
	.7	.0		1.9	Intangibles (net)	2.1	1.8	1.0	1.6	1.9
	4.3	4.6		6.8	All Other Non-Current	6.4	8.1	6.1	5.6	6.8
	100.0	100.0		100.0	Total	100.0	100.0	100.0	100.0	100.0
					LIABILITIES					
	16.5	17.8		28.6	Notes Payable-Short Term	20.9	10.3	22.6	16.6	28.6
	40.0	14.6		28.6	A/P - Trade	22.9	20.9	20.7	21.7	28.6
	.0	.1		.2	A/P - Retention	.9	.1	.1	.0	.2
	2.8	4.4		2.9	Billings in Excess of Costs & Est. Earnings	1.3	1.9	2.0	2.9	2.9
	.3	.5		.3	Income Taxes Payable	1.3	1.2	.9	.7	.3
	1.0	2.2		1.2	Cur. Mat.-L/T/D	3.9	1.8	2.2	3.6	1.2
	8.2	10.0		9.5	All Other Current	9.3	12.2	6.6	6.3	9.5
	68.8	49.5		71.3	Total Current	60.6	48.2	55.0	51.8	71.3
	13.4	12.4		13.0	Long-Term Debt	7.0	10.0	9.2	11.6	13.0
	.0	.8		.2	Deferred Taxes	.6	.2	.1	.0	.2
	1.4	2.0		1.4	All Other Non-Current	3.2	9.3	4.1	3.1	1.4
	16.4	35.3		14.0	Net Worth	28.7	32.3	31.6	33.5	14.0
	100.0	100.0		100.0	Total Liabilties & Net Worth	100.0	100.0	100.0	100.0	100.0
					INCOME DATA					
	100.0	100.0		100.0	Contract Revenues	100.0	100.0	100.0	100.0	100.0
	29.6	19.7		27.8	Gross Profit	26.7	28.9	29.6	25.9	27.8
	25.7	17.1		25.9	Operating Expenses	24.7	27.3	26.3	22.0	25.9
	3.9	2.7		1.9	Operating Profit	2.1	1.6	3.3	3.9	1.9
	.2	.6		.5	All Other Expenses (net)	.3	.3	.2	.6	.5
	3.7	2.0		1.4	Profit Before Taxes	1.8	1.3	3.1	3.4	1.4
					RATIOS					
	2.8	2.3		2.3		2.3	2.7	2.0	2.8	2.3
	1.5	1.6		1.4	Current	1.4	1.6	1.4	1.7	1.4
	.9	1.4		.9		1.1	1.2	1.2	1.1	.9
	10.3	UND		10.3		4.8	5.3	3.9	4.5	10.3
	2.6	3.9		(32) 2.8	Receivables/Payables	(49) 2.4	(35) 2.5	(41) 2.8	2.5	(32) 2.8
	1.2	2.5		1.6		1.7	1.1	1.6	1.4	1.6
	35 10.5	41 9.0		35 10.6		32 11.4	15 23.6	38 9.5	37 9.9	35 10.6
	53 6.9	55 6.6		47 7.8	Revenues/Receivables	58 6.3	43 8.4	58 6.3	50 7.3	47 7.8
	89 4.1	87 4.2		83 4.4		77 4.7	63 5.8	77 4.7	71 5.2	83 4.4
	13 27.2	0 UND		5 68.2		14 26.6	9 40.0	15 24.8	12 29.3	5 68.2
	38 9.7	21 17.7		29 12.6	Cost of Revenues/Payables	27 13.7	26 14.0	27 13.4	32 11.3	29 12.6
	44 8.4	31 11.6		42 8.7		41 8.8	41 8.8	41 8.9	54 6.8	42 8.7
	6.7	6.7		7.1		8.0	6.1	9.0	7.7	7.1
	10.1	11.9		15.5	Revenues/Working Capital	14.4	16.2	18.1	13.5	15.5
	-81.4	19.9		-77.0		46.4	39.5	39.1	60.3	-77.0
	15.2	12.8		8.3		12.9	21.6	15.7	13.2	8.3
	(16) 4.1	3.7		(31) 2.4	EBIT/Interest	(46) 3.7	(29) 4.6	(40) 5.4	(34) 6.3	(31) 2.4
	.5	.9		.1		1.0	1.8	.8	2.2	.1
						8.0	14.0	8.8	6.4	
					Net Profit + Depr., Dep., Amort./Cur. Mat. L/T/D	(18) 4.1	(10) 6.3	(13) 4.6	(11) 4.3	
						1.4	2.0	1.7	3.6	
	.1	.1		.1		.2	.2	.2	.1	.1
	.2	.3		.3	Fixed/Worth	.3	.3	.4	.3	.3
	-1.7	.6		-1.5		1.0	.8	.6	1.0	-1.5
	.5	1.1		.9		.7	1.0	1.2	.6	.9
	4.1	2.4		2.6	Debt/Worth	3.0	1.6	2.2	2.0	2.6
	-19.1	3.0		-17.9		8.0	4.9	8.4	10.0	-17.9
	39.9	34.4		35.7		49.1	49.9	59.8	90.0	35.7
	(14) 31.5	21.9		(25) 27.7	% Profit Before Taxes/ Tangible Net Worth	(41) 19.9	(32) 20.8	(40) 19.7	(33) 44.7	(25) 27.7
	-6.2	-2.4		-2.6		5.4	3.0	4.1	10.8	-2.6
	29.6	13.0		18.4		13.6	18.3	18.5	22.6	18.4
	11.2	7.4		5.1	% Profit Before Taxes/ Total Assets	5.4	7.3	6.4	11.6	5.1
	-.5	-.7		-4.0		.2	.0	-.3	2.9	-4.0
	.4	.2		.3		.5	.4	.7	.5	.3
	(10) .9	.5		(23) .7	% Depr., Dep., Amort./ Revenues	(46) 1.0	(32) .9	(35) 1.0	(29) .9	(23) .7
	1.9	.8		1.2		1.3	1.7	1.4	1.4	1.2
	2.3			2.4		2.6	3.1	3.3	2.5	2.4
	(14) 4.7			(22) 5.6	% Officers', Directors' Owners' Comp/Revenues	(38) 4.2	(27) 5.7	(33) 4.5	(24) 4.0	(22) 5.6
	7.8			9.6		6.5	9.0	5.9	5.3	9.6
3551M	68194M	176100M		247845M	Contract Revenues ($)	411493M	143003M	221033M	1341774M	247845M
977M	18402M	55925M		75304M	Total Assets ($)	129439M	37205M	67201M	261918M	75304M

M = $ thousand MM = $ million

See Pages 11 through 21 for Explanation of Ratios and Data

Current Data Sorted by Assets						Comparative Historical Data				
		7	26	5	38	Type of Statement — Unqualified	31	23	34	40	38
2	60	29		1	92	Reviewed	119	93	84	95	92
6	29				35	Compiled	42	39	29	37	35
7	16		3		26	Tax Returns	33	38	47	36	26
5	15	6	4		30	Other	49	31	44	46	30
46 (4/1-9/30/06)		175 (10/1/06-3/31/07)					4/1/02-3/31/03	4/1/03-3/31/04	4/1/04-3/31/05	4/1/05-3/31/06	4/1/06-3/31/07
0-1MM	1-10MM	10-50MM	50 & OVER	ALL			ALL	ALL	ALL	ALL	ALL
20	127	61	13	221		NUMBER OF STATEMENTS	274	224	238	254	221

0-1MM %	1-10MM %	10-50MM %	50 & OVER %	ALL %			%	%	%	%	%
9.0	8.1	8.5	11.1	8.5		ASSETS — Cash & Equivalents	8.0	9.3	10.7	9.6	8.5
15.5	31.3	30.8	24.5	29.3		A/R - Progress Billings	27.6	26.2	28.2	28.7	29.3
.1	.8	3.5	2.1	1.5		A/R - Current Retention	1.2	1.3	1.8	1.7	1.5
6.8	3.4	2.9	7.7	3.8		Inventory	1.8	2.0	2.8	3.6	3.8
1.2	2.4	2.8	2.2	2.4		Cost & Est. Earnings In Excess Billings	2.5	2.6	3.0	2.5	2.4
3.0	4.5	4.5	5.9	4.5		All Other Current	4.9	4.1	3.1	4.0	4.5
35.7	50.4	52.9	53.5	49.9		Total Current	46.0	45.5	49.6	50.0	49.9
60.9	43.4	42.7	35.3	44.3		Fixed Assets (net)	46.3	47.3	42.7	43.2	44.3
.0	.8	.5	2.6	.7		Joint Ventures & Investments	1.8	1.3	1.0	.5	.7
1.1	.5	.5	4.2	.8		Intangibles (net)	.5	.5	.7	1.1	.8
2.3	5.0	3.4	4.3	4.3		All Other Non-Current	5.4	5.4	5.9	5.2	4.3
100.0	100.0	100.0	100.0	100.0		Total	100.0	100.0	100.0	100.0	100.0
12.4	8.1	5.1	1.8	7.3		LIABILITIES — Notes Payable-Short Term	8.1	8.7	12.5	8.9	7.3
6.6	14.3	16.2	13.3	14.1		A/P - Trade	13.1	12.2	14.0	12.5	14.1
.0	.0	.3	1.2	.2		A/P - Retention	.4	.3	.4	.4	.2
.1	2.4	6.0	6.2	3.4		Billings in Excess of Costs & Est. Earnings	2.4	2.0	2.3	3.3	3.4
.0	.1	.5	.3	.2		Income Taxes Payable	.2	.3	.2	.3	.2
5.2	9.2	7.5	4.3	8.1		Cur. Mat.-L/T/D	9.0	9.4	8.3	7.9	8.1
5.1	5.4	4.8	8.2	5.3		All Other Current	4.8	6.9	5.4	7.0	5.3
29.5	39.6	40.5	35.4	38.6		Total Current	38.1	39.7	43.1	40.3	38.6
26.4	23.5	17.4	17.5	21.7		Long-Term Debt	20.7	24.2	21.8	23.4	21.7
1.4	1.2	1.5	.2	1.2		Deferred Taxes	1.4	.9	1.0	1.4	1.2
2.0	4.0	1.4	1.4	2.9		All Other Non-Current	3.5	9.0	4.5	2.7	2.9
40.7	31.8	39.2	45.5	35.5		Net Worth	36.3	26.1	29.6	32.2	35.5
100.0	100.0	100.0	100.0	100.0		Total Liabilities & Net Worth	100.0	100.0	100.0	100.0	100.0
100.0	100.0	100.0	100.0	100.0		INCOME DATA — Contract Revenues	100.0	100.0	100.0	100.0	100.0
54.8	32.0	20.5	22.3	30.3		Gross Profit	31.9	34.8	32.2	32.0	30.3
49.0	27.1	14.1	13.6	24.7		Operating Expenses	29.2	31.6	28.3	26.4	24.7
5.8	4.9	6.4	8.6	5.6		Operating Profit	2.7	3.2	4.0	5.6	5.6
1.6	.9	.5	.7	.8		All Other Expenses (net)	1.2	1.0	.6	.8	.8
4.2	4.1	5.9	8.0	4.8		Profit Before Taxes	1.5	2.2	3.3	4.8	4.8
3.7	1.8	1.6	2.3	1.8		RATIOS — Current	1.8	1.8	1.7	1.9	1.8
1.1	1.2	1.2	1.5	1.3		Current	1.2	1.2	1.3	1.3	1.3
.6	.9	1.0	1.2	1.0			.8	.9	.9	1.0	1.0
5.5	3.9	3.0	5.5	3.6		Receivables/Payables	4.3	4.4	3.7	4.6	3.6
(16) 1.9	(118) 2.4	(12) 2.0	2.8	(207) 2.2			(252) 2.4	(197) 2.3	(218) 2.5	(237) 2.5	(207) 2.2
.5	1.4	1.4	1.4	1.4			1.4	1.4	1.3	1.5	1.4
0 UND	28 12.8	40 9.0	22 16.4	31 11.6		Revenues/Receivables	28 13.1	23 15.9	27 13.6	32 11.2	31 11.6
24 15.4	53 6.9	59 6.2	43 7.0	53 7.0			46 7.9	48 7.6	54 6.8	53 6.9	53 7.0
51 7.1	76 4.8	85 4.3	56 6.5	77 4.7			73 5.0	74 4.9	75 4.9	76 4.8	77 4.7
0 UND	16 23.4	24 15.4	4 101.7	16 22.3		Cost of Revenues/Payables	12 31.2	7 49.6	15 24.0	13 27.1	16 22.3
27 13.6	31 11.6	33 11.0	21 17.8	31 11.8			26 14.0	28 12.9	29 12.8	29 12.4	31 11.8
88 4.2	50 7.2	49 7.5	44 8.2	50 7.4			48 7.6	46 7.9	54 6.7	47 7.8	50 7.4
5.5	8.7	9.0	7.2	8.6		Revenues/Working Capital	8.8	9.8	9.7	7.8	8.6
NM	19.7	18.4	12.8	18.7			24.7	27.9	21.5	20.8	18.7
-15.1	-72.7	127.3	NM	-119.1			-44.2	-52.5	-72.6	-122.3	-119.1
4.8	8.4	17.7	56.8	10.5		EBIT/Interest	7.4	7.3	9.1	10.6	10.5
(19) 2.3	(121) 3.1	(59) 6.7	(10) 10.5	(209) 4.3			(257) 2.5	(211) 2.8	(220) 3.3	(239) 4.3	(209) 4.3
.7	1.1	2.1	6.5	1.4			.3	.9	1.0	1.9	1.4
	3.8	3.8		4.0		Net Profit + Depr., Dep., Amort./Cur. Mat. L/T/D	3.0	2.2	2.5	2.4	4.0
	(39) 2.1	(22) 1.4		(63) 2.0			(88) 1.6	(50) 1.7	(65) 1.6	(76) 1.6	(63) 2.0
	1.0	.9		.9			.9	.8	1.1	1.0	.9
1.0	.7	.8	.4	.7		Fixed/Worth	.7	.9	.7	.7	.7
1.6	1.4	1.0	.8	1.2			1.2	1.3	1.2	1.3	1.2
2.9	2.5	1.6	1.5	2.3			2.3	3.1	2.3	2.3	2.3
.6	1.2	1.0	.9	1.1		Debt/Worth	.9	1.0	.9	1.0	1.1
1.3	2.2	1.7	1.3	1.8			1.7	2.0	1.9	2.0	1.8
3.9	4.0	2.6	2.1	3.3			4.0	5.6	4.7	4.3	3.3
44.1	59.6	51.6	61.8	51.6		% Profit Before Taxes/Tangible Net Worth	30.0	32.5	38.1	48.2	51.6
(19) 13.0	(116) 20.5	23.9	32.8	(209) 22.6			(252) 11.3	(196) 14.0	(211) 15.8	(229) 25.8	(209) 22.6
-1.2	1.3	9.1	18.7	3.9			-3.9	1.1	4.1	9.3	3.9
13.8	16.2	20.9	25.8	17.4		% Profit Before Taxes/Total Assets	10.4	11.8	13.6	16.5	17.4
5.3	6.8	9.8	14.0	8.2			3.7	4.9	5.9	8.1	8.2
-2.0	.2	2.8	8.0	1.3			-2.5	-.6	.1	2.4	1.3
2.9	3.7	2.5		3.0		% Depr., Dep., Amort./Revenues	3.4	3.6	3.1	2.8	3.0
(16) 8.0	(115) 5.6	(59) 4.9		(197) 5.4			(246) 5.8	(179) 7.3	(213) 5.7	(228) 5.3	(197) 5.4
10.3	9.1	7.0		8.3			9.2	10.3	8.6	8.6	8.3
6.3	2.3	1.0		2.2		% Officers', Directors' Owners' Comp/Revenues	2.1	2.0	1.5	1.8	2.2
(13) 9.8	(68) 3.2	(25) 2.1		(111) 3.2			(159) 4.4	(136) 4.1	(143) 3.9	(139) 3.7	(111) 3.2
16.2	5.3	3.3		6.2			6.6	6.3	6.6	7.1	6.6
11501M	540526M	1209269M	36362196M	38123492M		Contract Revenues ($)	10434312M	6629549M	81375646M	16894511M	38123492M
8566M	274071M	672979M	15242676M	16198292M		Total Assets ($)	3398247M	2795922M	36582058M	6504366M	16198292M

© RMA 2007

M = $ thousand   MM = $ million

See Pages 11 through 21 for Explanation of Ratios and Data

Current Data Sorted by Assets   Comparative Historical Data

	0-1MM	1-10MM	10-50MM	50 & OVER	ALL		4/1/02-3/31/03 ALL	4/1/03-3/31/04 ALL	4/1/04-3/31/05 ALL	4/1/05-3/31/06 ALL	4/1/06-3/31/07 ALL
Type of Statement											
Unqualified		2	5		7		8	8	7	20	7
Reviewed	3	29	13	2	47		64	74	43	49	47
Compiled	4	22	4	1	31		32	22	32	31	31
Tax Returns	12	15		1	28		37	44	39	31	28
Other	3	24	5	1	33		22	20	29	22	33
	23 (4/1-9/30/06)		123 (10/1/06-3/31/07)								
NUMBER OF STATEMENTS	22	92	27	5	146		163	168	150	153	146
	%	%	%	%	%		%	%	%	%	%
ASSETS											
Cash & Equivalents	25.3	11.2	12.4		13.5		12.0	11.2	11.8	12.0	13.5
A/R - Progress Billings	21.2	32.7	47.5		34.5		35.5	35.8	36.0	34.5	34.5
A/R - Current Retention	.0	.8	1.7		1.0		.6	.8	.6	1.7	1.0
Inventory	6.8	11.7	5.0		9.4		7.5	9.2	8.9	8.0	9.4
Cost & Est. Earnings In Excess Billings	.0	1.9	3.6		1.9		2.9	2.7	2.7	2.9	1.9
All Other Current	3.0	5.7	1.5		4.7		4.9	3.2	3.9	4.2	4.7
Total Current	56.4	64.0	71.7		65.0		63.4	62.8	63.9	63.5	65.0
Fixed Assets (net)	28.7	27.4	22.9		26.3		27.2	27.0	26.0	27.0	26.3
Joint Ventures & Investments	.0	.4	.3		.4		.1	.9	1.0	1.5	.4
Intangibles (net)	.9	2.6	.6		1.9		1.8	2.3	2.5	2.0	1.9
All Other Non-Current	14.1	5.6	4.5		6.5		7.5	7.0	6.5	6.1	6.5
Total	100.0	100.0	100.0		100.0		100.0	100.0	100.0	100.0	100.0
LIABILITIES											
Notes Payable-Short Term	46.9	12.8	10.1		17.2		11.4	13.5	15.3	11.2	17.2
A/P - Trade	10.6	15.6	18.6		16.1		17.8	18.7	17.8	18.7	16.1
A/P - Retention	.0	.3	.0		.2		.3	.5	.1	.2	.2
Billings in Excess of Costs & Est. Earnings	.2	1.3	8.3		2.6		3.5	3.4	3.7	3.3	2.6
Income Taxes Payable	.1	.1	.9		.2		.3	.2	.1	.2	..2
Cur. Mat.-L/T/D	14.4	4.5	3.6		5.7		5.2	6.9	4.8	4.6	5.7
All Other Current	10.7	9.1	8.3		9.2		7.3	7.2	11.2	10.3	9.2
Total Current	82.9	43.7	49.8		51.1		45.7	50.3	53.1	48.5	51.1
Long-Term Debt	21.3	18.2	12.4		17.4		15.6	22.1	23.8	19.5	17.4
Deferred Taxes	.0	.7	.9		.6		.8	.3	.4	.6	.6
All Other Non-Current	3.9	3.1	1.8		2.9		4.1	8.0	5.5	6.5	2.9
Net Worth	-8.1	34.2	35.1		27.9		33.9	19.2	17.2	24.9	27.9
Total Liabilities & Net Worth	100.0	100.0	100.0		100.0		100.0	100.0	100.0	100.0	100.0
INCOME DATA											
Contract Revenues	100.0	100.0	100.0		100.0		100.0	100.0	100.0	100.0	100.0
Gross Profit	50.6	33.7	19.7		33.1		33.3	32.6	34.4	31.4	33.1
Operating Expenses	45.1	28.7	15.3		28.2		29.5	29.7	32.0	27.3	28.2
Operating Profit	5.6	5.0	4.5		4.9		3.8	2.9	2.3	4.1	4.9
All Other Expenses (net)	.7	.7	.4		.6		1.1	.4	.7	.6	.6
Profit Before Taxes	4.9	4.4	4.1		4.3		2.8	2.5	1.7	3.5	4.3
RATIOS											
Current	2.5	2.5	1.6		2.2		2.1	2.1	2.0	2.3	2.2
	1.2	1.5	1.5		1.4		1.4	1.4	1.3	1.3	1.4
	.5	1.0	1.2		1.0		1.0	.9	.9	1.0	1.0
Receivables/Payables	14.9	5.0	4.3		5.0		4.8	4.1	4.8	4.2	5.0
	(15) 2.1	(88) 2.1	3.1		(135) 2.2		(149) 2.4	(150) 2.0	(135) 2.1	(141) 2.2	(135) 2.2
	1.1	1.0	1.9		1.2		1.2	1.2	1.1	1.3	1.2
Revenues/Receivables	0 UND	12 31.3	50 7.4		13 28.0		23 16.1	15 24.2	15 24.0	18 20.4	13 28.0
	13 27.1	37 9.9	70 5.2		40 9.2		47 7.8	42 8.7	41 8.8	48 7.6	40 9.2
	50 7.2	66 5.5	84 4.4		74 5.0		67 5.5	71 5.1	73 5.0	77 4.8	74 5.0
Cost of Revenues/Payables	0 UND	8 43.0	19 18.7		8 43.3		13 28.0	10 36.7	8 43.1	13 28.5	8 43.3
	3 145.0	23 15.9	29 12.7		24 15.3		27 13.4	22 16.2	25 14.6	26 14.1	24 15.3
	40 9.1	45 8.2	46 7.9		46 8.0		45 8.2	50 7.3	48 7.6	43 8.5	46 8.0
Revenues/Working Capital	11.0	7.3	8.0		8.2		7.2	8.6	8.6	7.6	8.2
	UND	15.5	15.2		16.5		17.5	18.0	19.6	15.7	16.5
	-21.0	-379.4	33.9		-666.6		232.9	-119.0	-45.5	NM	-666.6
EBIT/Interest	10.4	14.5	15.3		14.6		11.1	11.9	11.5	24.0	14.6
	(16) 3.8	(81) 4.7	(26) 6.9		(128) 5.3		(146) 3.5	(156) 3.5	(131) 2.9	(140) 4.8	(128) 5.3
	.2	1.0	2.6		1.3		1.1	.9	-.6	1.3	1.3
Net Profit + Depr., Dep., Amort./Cur. Mat. L/T/D		6.7	8.3		7.2		7.6	4.7	3.2	7.4	7.2
		(18) 2.1	(11) 3.2		(33) 2.4		(46) 2.6	(39) 2.6	(20) 2.4	(35) 2.5	(33) 2.4
		.9	2.1		.8		1.2	1.2	.8	1.7	.8
Fixed/Worth	.4	.2	.2		.2		.2	.3	.3	.3	.2
	1.6	.6	.7		.7		.7	.7	.8	.6	.7
	-10.0	2.4	1.5		2.0		1.6	9.5	UND	3.0	2.0
Debt/Worth	.6	.8	1.3		.9		.7	1.0	1.1	.8	.9
	3.5	1.8	1.9		1.9		1.8	2.3	3.0	2.1	1.9
	-8.4	5.4	3.4		5.5		5.7	20.0	-138.3	7.0	5.5
% Profit Before Taxes/Tangible Net Worth	814.3	77.0	66.7		79.1		53.4	51.7	53.3	54.2	79.1
	(15) 100.0	(82) 26.6	37.2		(129) 31.3		(145) 21.1	(131) 17.0	(112) 23.7	(124) 24.4	(129) 31.3
	15.4	6.4	16.0		7.9		2.0	3.3	2.4	5.6	7.9
% Profit Before Taxes/Total Assets	46.8	25.4	19.9		25.9		19.3	15.3	16.6	17.8	25.9
	9.7	10.3	11.3		10.3		6.2	4.6	5.2	7.6	10.3
	-9.3	1.5	6.1		1.5		.0	-.5	-4.0	.9	1.5
% Depr., Dep., Amort./Revenues	2.3	1.3	1.0		1.2		.6	1.0	.9	.8	1.2
	(16) 3.4	(67) 2.3	(26) 1.7		(112) 2.3		(137) 1.9	(125) 2.1	(111) 1.8	(129) 1.8	(112) 2.3
	7.1	3.2	3.0		3.3		4.1	4.1	3.1	3.4	3.3
% Officers', Directors' Owners' Comp/Revenues	5.9	2.8	1.2		2.7		2.5	2.4	2.2	2.5	2.7
	(14) 10.4	(62) 4.2	(16) 1.4		(95) 4.5		(110) 5.5	(103) 4.6	(77) 5.2	(95) 4.9	(95) 4.5
	29.3	6.3	2.9		7.2		10.3	8.0	8.8	7.5	7.2
Contract Revenues ($)	10454M	353384M	633203M	9673384M	10670425M		15884504M	922872M	2013858M	23002610M	10670425M
Total Assets ($)	3957M	131095M	239429M	3147810M	3522291M		6166968M	313457M	860211M	37988227M	3522291M

M = $ thousand   MM = $ million
See Pages 11 through 21 for Explanation of Ratios and Data

CONSTRUCTION
FINANCIAL MANAGEMENT
ASSOCIATION DATA

About the Construction Financial Management Association (CFMA) Data
Web site: www.cfma.org

Once again, we are delighted to include excerpts from *CFMA's 2007 Construction Industry Annual Financial Survey.* CFMA is **The Source and Resource for Construction Financial Professionals** and has more than 7,000 members in 89 chapters throughout the U.S.

The data presented are based on a survey sent to approximately 4,100 general members employed within U.S. construction firms, plus a small number of other U.S. contractors. Of the 905 total survey respondents, 92.5%, or 837 companies, provided detailed financial statement information, with 756 companies being included in the final participant population. Sixty-eight percent participated in the CFMA survey in 2006. The data submitted were compiled and analyzed by Moss Adams LLP in cooperation with CFMA. Moss Adams was not engaged to and did not audit or review this information and, accordingly, does not express an opinion or any other form of assurance on it.

Almost all companies (95.6%) included in the survey recognize contract revenue and profit in accordance with the percentage of completion method of accounting. Likewise, our Statement Studies contractor data primarily reflects only this method of accounting. It is entirely possible that some of the same contractor companies are included in both the CFMA and Statement Studies data presentations. The inclusion of the CFMA data has not affected our Statement Studies contractor composite data.

Fiscal year-end closing dates reflected in the CFMA survey range from 3/31/06 through 3/31/07. The CFMA data are most comparable to the RMA contractor data from 4/1/06 through 3/31/07 appearing in this edition.

The survey respondents were classified into three categories of construction based on the type of work performed. Classification was based on the level of contract volume reported for various NAIC codes. A contractor was included in a classification if at least one half of its annual contract revenue was attributable to that classification. CFMA categorized certain NAIC codes together. The classifications and NAIC codes included in each are as follows:

2002 North American Industry Classification (NAICS) Codes

RESIDENTIAL CONSTRUCTION:
- 236115 New Single-Family Housing Construction (Except Operative Builders)
- 236116 New Multifamily Housing Construction (Except Operative Builders)
- 236117 New Housing Operative Builders
- 236118 Residential Remodelers
- 236220 Commercial and Institutional Building Construction
- 236220 Commercial and Institutional Building Construction

GENERAL CONTRACTORS – COMMERCIAL & INDUSTRIAL:
- 236210 Industrial Building Construction
- 236220 Commercial and Institutional Building Construction

HEAVY & HIGHWAY, UTILITY CONSTRUCTION:
- 237110 Water and Sewer Line and Related Structures Construction
- 237120 Oil and Gas Pipeline and Related Structures Construction
- 237130 Power and Communication Line and Related Structures Construction
- 237310 Highway, Street, and Bridge Construction
- 237990 Other Heavy and Civil Engineering Construction
- 238910 Site Preparation Contractors
- 238990 All Other Specialty Trade Contractors

SPECIALTY TRADES:
- 238110 Poured Concrete Foundation and Structure Contractors
- 238120 Structural Steel and Precast Concrete Contractors
- 238130 Framing Contractors
- 238140 Masonry Contractors
- 238150 Glass and Glazing Contractors
- 238160 Roofing Contractors
- 238170 Siding Contractors
- 238190 Other Foundation, Structure, and Building Exterior Contractors
- 238210 Electrical Contractors
- 238220 Plumbing, Heating, and Air-Conditioning Contractors

- 238290 Other Building Equipment Contractors
- 238310 Drywall and Insulation Contractors
- 238320 Painting and Wall Covering Contractors
- 238330 Flooring Contractors
- 238340 Tile and Terrazzo Contractors
- 238350 Finish Carpentry Contractors
- 238390 Other Building Finishing Contractors
- 561621 Security Systems Services (except Locksmiths)
- 56291 Environmental Remediation Services

ARCHITECTURAL & ENGINEERING:
- 5413X Architectural, Engineering, and Related Services

CONSTRUCTION MATERIALS:
- 21231 Stone Mining and Quarrying
- 212321 Construction Sand and Gravel Mining
- 324121 Asphalt Paving Mixture and Block Manufacturing
- 32732 Ready-Mix Concrete Manufacturing
- 32733 Concrete Pipe, Brick, and Block Manufacturing
- 332322 Sheet Metal Work Manufacturing
- 3323X Architectural and Structural Metals Manufacturing
- 4233X Lumber and Other Construction Materials Wholesalers
- 4441 Building Material and Supplies Dealers
- 321214 Truss Manufacturing
- 321918 Other Millwork (including Flooring)

EQUIPMENT RENTAL:
- 53241 Construction Equipment Rental & Leasing

MAINTENANCE & REPAIRS:
- 81131 Repair and Maintenance-Machinery and Equipment
- 811412 Appliance Repair and Maintenance

REAL ESTATE SERVICES:
- 237210 Land Subdivision
- 53131 Real Estate Property Managers
- 53111 Lessors of Residential Buildings and Dwellings
- 53112 Lessors of Nonresidential Buildings

The CFMA financial data includes balance sheets, statements of earnings, and financial ratios. The balance sheets and statements of earning represent a weighted average of all companies included in each classification. Percentages are presented for each dollar amount in the financial statements. Due to rounding, the totals may not agree to the sum of various accounts. Such variations are few and insignificant.

The financial ratios are calculated from the composite balance sheets and statements of earning data. They are not averages of ratios for all companies included in the classification.

If you wish to purchase *CFMA's 2007 Construction Industry Annual Financial Survey* or have questions regarding the data, contact Brian Summers, Chief Operations Officer; Construction Financial Management Association, 29 Emmons Drive F-50, Princeton, NJ 08540; Phone 609-452-8000; Fax 609-452-0474; E-mail bsummers@cfma.org.

Interpretation of the
Construction Financial Management Association (CFMA) Data

CFMA's data should only be regarded as general information. It cannot be used to establish industry norms for a number of reasons, including the following:

(1) The financial statements used in the composite are not selected by any random or statistically reliable method. CFMA members voluntarily submitted financial data pertaining to themselves. Note that contractors' statements have no upper asset/sales limit.
(2) Many companies provide varied services; CFMA includes a contractor in a classification if at least one-half (1/2) of its annual contract revenue was completed within that classification.
(3) Some of the NAIC group samples may be rather small in relation to the total number of firms in a given industry category. A relatively small sample can increase the chances that some of our composites do not fully represent an industry group.
(4) There is the chance that an extreme statement can be present in a sample, causing a disproportionate influence on the industry composite. This is particularly true in a relatively small sample.
(5) Companies within the same industry may differ in their method of operations, which in turn can directly influence their financial statements. Since such differences affect financial data included in our sample, our composite calculations could be significantly affected.
(6) Other considerations that can result in variation among different companies engaged in the same general line of business are: different labor markets; geographical location; different accounting methods; quality of service rendered; sources and methods of financing; and terms of sale.

The use of CFMA's data may be helpful when considered with other methods of financial analysis. Nevertheless, RMA and CFMA do not recommend the use of CFMA's data to establish norms or parameters for a given industry or grouping, or the industry as a whole. Although CFMA believes that its data is accurate and representative within the confines of the aforementioned reasons, RMA and CFMA specifically make no representations regarding the accuracy of representativeness of the figures printed in this supplement of the RMA Annual Statement Studies.

All Companies
Composite

Balance Sheet

	2007 Participants		2006 Participants	
	Amount	Percent	Amount	Percent
Current assets:				
Cash and cash equivalents	$ 8,543,784	15.3 %	$ 6,160,799	14.2 %
Marketable securities and short-term investments	2,438,975	4.4	2,474,160	5.7
Receivables:				
Contract receivables currently due	20,608,340	36.9	17,103,492	39.4
Retainages on contracts	7,421,822	13.3	5,398,026	12.4
Unbilled work	692,231	1.2	476,039	1.1
Other receivables	884,894	1.6	652,942	1.5
Less allowance for doubtful accounts	(62,553)	(0.1)	(106,932)	(0.2)
Total receivables, net	29,544,733	52.9	23,523,568	54.1
Inventories	1,064,816	1.9	1,009,743	2.3
Costs and recognized earnings in excess of billings on uncompleted contracts	2,810,763	5.0	2,010,796	4.6
Investments in and advances to construction joint ventures	327,796	0.6	210,116	0.5
Income taxes:				
Current / refundable	17,827	0.0	17,424	0.0
Deferred	185,506	0.3	177,726	0.4
Other current assets	1,864,677	3.3	920,245	2.1
Total current assets	46,798,879	83.9	36,504,575	84.0
Property, plant and equipment	12,004,158	21.5	11,725,825	27.0
Less accumulated depreciation	(6,124,529)	(11.0)	(6,893,488)	(15.9)
Property, plant and equipment, net	5,879,630	10.5	4,832,337	11.1
Noncurrent assets:				
Long-term investments	986,432	1.8	568,319	1.3
Deferred income taxes	387,468	0.7	170,438	0.4
Other assets	1,756,975	3.1	1,387,616	3.2
Total noncurrent assets	3,130,874	5.6	2,126,373	4.9
Total assets	$ 55,809,383	100.0 %	$ 43,463,286	100.0 %

	2007 Participants		2006 Participants	
	Amount	Percent	Amount	Percent
Current liabilities:				
Current maturity on long-term debt	$ 705,386	1.3 %	$ 510,259	1.2 %
Notes payable and lines of credit	1,220,433	2.2	1,201,316	2.8
Accounts payable:				
Trade, including currently due to subcontractors	16,405,345	29.4	12,543,207	28.9
Subcontracts retainages	4,629,576	8.3	3,919,394	9.0
Other	727,460	1.3	371,276	0.9
Total accounts payable	21,762,382	39.0	16,833,876	38.7
Accrued expenses	3,758,727	6.7	2,895,331	6.7
Billings in excess of costs and recognized earnings on uncompleted contracts	6,963,332	12.5	5,670,833	13.0
Income taxes:				
Current	360,959	0.6	106,976	0.2
Deferred	42,805	0.1	22,335	0.1
Other current liabilities	703,622	1.3	542,160	1.2
Total current liabilities	35,517,646	63.6	27,783,086	63.9
Noncurrent liabilities				
Long-term debt, excluding current maturities	2,195,966	3.9	2,494,934	5.7
Deferred income taxes	1,123,834	2.0	161,511	0.4
Other	561,290	1.0	567,553	1.3
Total liabilities	39,398,737	70.6	31,007,084	71.3
Minority interests	68,680	0.1	87,856	0.2
Net worth:				
Common stock, par value	764,587	1.4	457,787	1.1
Preferred stock, stated value	90,764	0.2	118,346	0.3
Additional paid-in capital	1,880,067	3.4	2,308,018	5.3
Retained earnings	13,135,875	23.5	8,943,323	20.6
Treasury stock	(549,836)	(1.0)	(520,115)	(1.2)
Excess value of marketable securities	57,027	0.1	65,130	0.1
Other equity	963,482	1.7	995,855	2.3
Total net worth	16,341,966	29.3	12,368,346	28.5
Total liabilities and net worth	$ 55,809,383	100.0 %	$ 43,463,286	100.0 %

All Companies
Composite

Statement of Earnings

	2007 Participants		2006 Participants	
	Amount	Percent	Amount	Percent
Contract revenue	$ 154,696,293	98.0 %	$ 119,500,444	96.6 %
Other revenue	3,174,629	2.0	4,215,450	3.4
Total revenue	157,870,922	100.0	123,715,894	100.0
Contract cost	(139,283,761)	(88.2)	(109,859,426)	(88.8)
Other cost	(2,484,033)	(1.6)	(3,531,767)	(2.9)
Total cost	(141,767,794)	(89.8)	(113,391,193)	(91.7)
Gross profit	16,103,128	10.2	10,324,701	8.3
Selling, general and administrative expenses:				
Payroll	(5,442,878)	(3.4)	(3,553,973)	(2.9)
Professional fees	(228,907)	(0.1)	(269,317)	(0.2)
Sales and marketing costs	(582,300)	(0.4)	(309,283)	(0.2)
Technology costs	(184,584)	(0.1)	(204,837)	(0.2)
Administrative bonuses	(713,166)	(0.5)	(522,393)	(0.4)
Other	(4,870,600)	(3.1)	(2,763,495)	(2.2)
Total SG&A expenses	(12,022,435)	(7.6)	(7,623,299)	(6.2)
Income from operations	4,080,693	2.6	2,701,402	2.2
Interest income	416,777	0.3	241,939	0.2
Interest expense	(241,213)	(0.2)	(202,496)	(0.2)
Other income / (expense), net	31,999	0.0	185,080	0.1
Net earnings / (loss) before income taxes	4,288,256	2.7	2,925,926	2.4
Income tax (expense) / benefit	(628,886)	(0.4)	(306,576)	(0.2)
Net earnings	$ 3,659,370	2.3 %	$ 2,619,350	2.1 %
Average backlog	$ 123,121,158		$ 86,795,922	

Number of Participants

	Number
2007	756
2006	495

Financial Ratios

	2007 Participants		2006 Participants	
	Average	Median	Average	Median
Liquidity Ratios				
Current Ratio	1.3	1.4	1.3	1.4
Quick Ratio	1.1	1.2	1.2	1.2
Days of Cash	19.5	13.7	17.9	11.1
Working Capital Turnover	14.0	12.1	14.2	12.3
Profitability Ratios				
Return on Assets	7.7 %	8.8 %	6.7 %	6.4 %
Return on Equity	26.2 %	30.1 %	23.7 %	22.9 %
Times Interest Earned	18.8	13.9	15.4	12.3
Leverage Ratios				
Debt to Equity	2.4	2.2	2.5	2.3
Revenue to Equity	9.7	9.5	10.0	10.2
Asset Turnover	2.8	3.0	2.8	3.0
Fixed Asset Ratio	36.0 %	27.8 %	39.1 %	26.8 %
Equity to SG&A Expense	1.4	1.3	1.6	1.3
Underbillings to Equity	21.4 %	11.4 %	20.1 %	14.3 %
Backlog to Equity	7.5	5.7	7.0	4.5
Efficiency Ratios				
Backlog to Working Capital	10.9	8.0	10.0	6.1
Months in Backlog	9.4	7.2	8.4	5.9
Days in Accounts Receivable	48.9	53.6	51.4	53.2
Days in Inventory	2.7	2.9	3.2	2.0
Days in Accounts Payable	43.5	35.3	41.0	34.3
Operating Cycle	27.5	38.2	31.5	36.7

Note: Not all figures will appear to sum due to rounding.

Industrial & Nonresidential Contractors

Composite

Balance Sheet

	2007 Participants		2006 Participants	
	Amount	Percent	Amount	Percent
Current assets:		%	%	
Cash and cash equivalents	$ 15,160,904	17.9	$ 10,500,638	17.6
Marketable securities and short-term investments	5,118,510	6.1	5,501,887	9.2
Receivables:				
Contract receivables currently due	35,263,909	41.7	24,513,244	41.2
Retainages on contracts	12,019,960	14.2	8,830,755	14.8
Unbilled work	1,266,261	1.5	725,677	1.2
Other receivables	1,365,034	1.6	595,353	1.0
Less allowance for doubtful accounts	(47,284)	(0.1)	(50,195)	(0.1)
Total receivables, net	49,867,880	59.0	34,614,834	58.2
Inventories	103,536	0.1	84,601	0.1
Costs and recognized earnings in excess of billings on uncompleted contracts	3,097,355	3.7	1,952,833	3.3
Investments in and advances to construction joint ventures	574,176	0.7	337,767	0.6
Income taxes:				
Current / refundable	20,016	0.0	22,532	0.0
Deferred	246,423	0.3	202,932	0.3
Other current assets	2,823,319	3.3	1,277,853	2.1
Total current assets	77,012,121	91.1	54,495,878	91.6
Property, plant and equipment	7,968,420	9.4	6,590,576	11.1
Less accumulated depreciation	(4,256,267)	(5.0)	(3,718,290)	(6.2)
Property, plant and equipment, net	3,712,153	4.4	2,872,286	4.8
Noncurrent assets:				
Long-term investments	678,495	0.8	737,326	1.2
Deferred income taxes	369,443	0.4	134,152	0.2
Other assets	2,799,118	3.3	1,257,032	2.1
Total noncurrent assets	3,847,056	4.5	2,128,510	3.6
Total assets	$ 84,571,330	100.0 %	$ 59,496,673	100.0 %

	2007 Participants		2006 Participants	
	Amount	Percent	Amount	Percent
Current liabilities:		%	%	
Current maturity on long-term debt	$ 705,262	0.8	$ 199,748	0.3
Notes payable and lines of credit	286,128	0.3	892,596	1.5
Accounts payable:				
Trade, including currently due to subcontractors	32,662,616	38.6	22,248,894	37.4
Subcontracts retainages	12,030,939	14.2	9,050,823	15.2
Other	1,246,442	1.5	531,806	0.9
Total accounts payable	45,939,997	54.3	31,831,523	53.5
Accrued expenses	5,172,378	6.1	3,236,857	5.4
Billings in excess of costs and recognized earnings on uncompleted contracts	10,941,363	12.9	8,153,697	13.7
Income taxes:				
Current	555,279	0.7	49,181	0.1
Deferred	81,948	0.1	25,412	0.0
Other current liabilities	416,483	0.5	699,212	1.2
Total current liabilities	64,098,838	75.8	45,088,226	75.8
Noncurrent liabilities:				
Long-term debt, excluding current maturities	1,319,367	1.6	1,293,363	2.2
Deferred income taxes	183,290	0.2	91,205	0.2
Other	603,384	0.7	525,856	0.9
Total liabilities	66,204,878	78.3	46,998,650	79.0
Minority interests	58,632	0.1	125,914	0.2
Net worth:				
Common stock, par value	1,732,184	2.0	519,164	0.9
Preferred stock, stated value	186,287	0.2	264,938	0.4
Additional paid-in capital	2,930,962	3.5	1,003,846	1.7
Retained earnings	11,927,189	14.1	9,311,200	15.6
Treasury stock	(519,243)	(0.6)	(398,658)	(0.7)
Excess value of marketable securities	121,816	0.1	115,533	0.2
Other equity	1,928,625	2.3	1,556,087	2.6
Total net worth	18,307,820	21.6	12,372,110	20.8
Total liabilities and net worth	$ 84,571,330	100.0 %	$ 59,496,673	100.0 %

Industrial & Nonresidential Contractors

Composite

Statement of Earnings

	2007 Participants		2006 Participants	
	Amount	Percent	Amount	Percent
Contract revenue	$ 256,075,114	99.6 %	$ 183,914,787	98.7 %
Other revenue	992,393	0.4	2,359,568	1.3
Total revenue	257,067,507	100.0	186,274,355	100.0
Contract cost	(240,348,291)	(93.5)	(173,169,037)	(93.0)
Other cost	(532,957)	(0.2)	(2,003,609)	(1.1)
Total cost	(240,881,248)	(93.7)	(175,172,646)	(94.0)
Gross profit	16,186,260	6.3	11,101,709	6.0
Selling, general and administrative expenses:				
Payroll	(5,309,727)	(2.1)	(3,818,251)	(2.0)
Professional fees	(261,498)	(0.1)	(318,756)	(0.2)
Sales and marketing costs	(1,089,458)	(0.4)	(485,736)	(0.3)
Technology costs	(203,861)	(0.1)	(301,521)	(0.2)
Administrative bonuses	(971,217)	(0.4)	(537,095)	(0.3)
Other	(3,833,788)	(1.5)	(3,214,478)	(1.7)
Total SG&A expenses	(11,669,548)	(4.5)	(8,675,838)	(4.7)
Income from operations	4,516,711	1.8	2,425,872	1.3
Interest income	858,692	0.3	478,867	0.3
Interest expense	(104,122)	(0.0)	(96,856)	(0.1)
Other income / (expense), net	(70,560)	(0.0)	225,746	0.1
Net earnings / (loss) before income taxes	5,200,722	2.0	3,033,629	1.6
Income tax (expense) / benefit	(852,969)	(0.3)	(410,430)	(0.2)
Net earnings	$ 4,347,752	1.7 %	$ 2,623,199	1.4 %
Average backlog	$ 241,184,984		$ 128,556,658	

Number of Participants

	Number
2007	269
2006	185

Financial Ratios

	2007 Participants		2006 Participants	
	Average	Median	Average	Median
Liquidity Ratios				
Current Ratio	1.2	1.2	1.2	1.2
Quick Ratio	1.1	1.2	1.1	1.1
Days of Cash	21.2	19.7	20.3	16.6
Working Capital Turnover	19.9	18.3	19.8	19.0
Profitability Ratios				
Return on Assets	6.1 %	6.8 %	5.1 %	4.6 %
Return on Equity	28.4 %	30.5 %	24.5 %	22.4 %
Times Interest Earned	50.9	21.9	32.3	16.6
Leverage Ratios				
Debt to Equity	3.6	3.5	3.8	3.3
Revenue to Equity	14.0	16.5	15.1	15.4
Asset Turnover	3.0	3.5	3.1	3.4
Fixed Asset Ratio	20.3 %	17.4 %	23.2 %	17.5 %
Equity to SG&A Expense	1.6	1.3	1.4	1.3
Underbillings to Equity	23.8 %	11.9 %	21.6 %	13.1 %
Backlog to Equity	13.2	11.1	10.4	9.4
Efficiency Ratios				
Backlog to Working Capital	18.7	14.0	13.7	12.1
Months in Backlog	11.3	7.9	8.3	7.4
Days in Accounts Receivable	51.2	47.0	48.4	46.1
Days in Inventory	0.2	0.5	0.2	0.4
Days in Accounts Payable	50.7	44.7	46.8	41.6
Operating Cycle	21.9	26.5	22.1	26.0

Note: Not all figures will appear to sum due to rounding.

Heavy & Highway Contractors
Composite

Balance Sheet

Assets	2007 Participants Amount	Percent	2006 Participants Amount	Percent
Current assets:				
Cash and cash equivalents	$ 9,053,242	14.0 %	$ 7,057,507	15.0 %
Marketable securities and short-term investments	2,986,359	4.6	1,493,592	3.2
Receivables:				
Contract receivables currently due	17,751,168	27.5	13,378,005	28.5
Retainages on contracts	4,465,836	6.9	4,462,916	9.5
Unbilled work	1,036,582	1.6	646,070	1.4
Other receivables	1,288,178	2.0	893,599	1.9
Less allowance for doubtful accounts	(64,966)	(0.1)	(119,783)	(0.3)
Total receivables, net	24,476,798	37.9	19,260,808	41.0
Inventories	1,609,031	2.5	1,075,952	2.3
Costs and recognized earnings in excess of billings on uncompleted contracts	2,635,888	4.1	2,350,728	5.0
Investments in and advances to construction joint ventures	614,329	1.0	261,428	0.6
Income taxes:				
Current / refundable	23,496	0.0	18,794	0.0
Deferred	426,928	0.7	154,240	0.3
Other current assets	2,279,999	3.5	878,044	1.9
Total current assets	44,106,070	68.2	32,551,092	69.3
Property, plant and equipment	34,552,168	53.5	28,285,790	60.3
Less accumulated depreciation	(17,894,991)	(27.7)	(16,925,030)	(36.1)
Property, plant and equipment, net	16,657,177	25.8	11,360,760	24.2
Noncurrent assets:				
Long-term investments	836,193	1.3	327,687	0.7
Deferred income taxes	11,178	0.0	187,506	0.4
Other assets	3,022,151	4.7	2,517,844	5.4
Total noncurrent assets	3,869,523	6.0	3,033,036	6.5
Total assets	$ 64,632,770	100.0 %	$ 46,944,888	100.0 %

Liabilities and Net Worth	2007 Participants Amount	Percent	2006 Participants Amount	Percent
Current liabilities:				
Current maturity on long-term debt	$ 1,592,563	2.5 %	$ 1,266,814	2.7 %
Notes payable and lines of credit	821,528	1.3	499,259	1.1
Accounts payable:				
Trade, including currently due to subcontractors	12,572,430	19.5	9,479,005	20.2
Subcontracts retainages	1,142,000	1.8	985,615	2.1
Other	766,665	1.2	337,513	0.7
Total accounts payable	14,481,095	22.4	10,802,133	23.0
Accrued expenses	4,590,809	7.1	3,176,558	6.8
Billings in excess of costs and recognized earnings on uncompleted contracts	8,852,186	13.7	5,652,395	12.0
Income taxes:				
Current	136,288	0.2	100,599	0.2
Deferred	5,140	0.0	39,030	0.1
Other current liabilities	458,697	0.7	316,740	0.7
Total current liabilities	30,938,306	47.9	21,853,527	46.6
Noncurrent liabilities:				
Long-term debt, excluding current maturities	6,070,996	9.4	4,501,516	9.6
Deferred income taxes	548,226	0.8	338,143	0.7
Other	1,489,771	2.3	927,592	2.0
Total liabilities	39,047,300	60.4	27,620,777	58.8
Minority interests	196,805	0.3	67,858	0.1
Net worth:				
Common stock, par value	398,277	0.6	738,507	1.6
Preferred stock, stated value	40,597	0.1	15,152	0.0
Additional paid-in capital	2,766,505	4.3	3,377,716	7.2
Retained earnings	22,664,024	35.1	15,050,980	32.1
Treasury stock	(771,798)	(1.2)	(799,193)	(1.7)
Excess value of marketable securities	42,491	0.1	45,871	0.1
Other equity	248,569	0.4	817,222	1.7
Total net worth	25,388,665	39.3	19,256,253	41.0
Total liabilities and net worth	$ 64,632,770	100.0 %	$ 46,944,888	100.0 %

Heavy & Highway Contractors
Composite

Statement of Earnings

	2007 Participants		2006 Participants	
	Amount	Percent	Amount	Percent
Contract revenue	$ 140,808,865	94.5 %	$ 107,468,312	95.9 %
Other revenue	8,264,474	5.5	4,558,153	4.1
Total revenue	149,073,338	100.0	112,026,464	100.0
Contract cost	(126,395,504)	(84.8)	(98,375,737)	(87.5)
Other cost	(6,779,868)	(4.5)	(3,664,735)	(3.3)
To tal cost	(133,175,371)	(89.3)	(101,740,472)	(90.8)
Gross profit	15,897,967	10.7	10,285,992	9.2
Selling, general and administrative expenses:				
Payroll	(3,067,343)	(2.1)	(3,137,835)	(2.8)
Professional fees	(247,066)	(0.2)	(253,557)	(0.2)
Sales and marketing costs	(258,433)	(0.2)	(119,197)	(0.1)
Technology costs	(257,869)	(0.2)	(140,739)	(0.1)
Administrative bonuses	(602,257)	(0.4)	(397,644)	(0.4)
Other	(4,688,862)	(3.1)	(2,240,876)	(2.0)
Total SG&A expenses	(9,121,829)	(6.1)	(6,289,848)	(5.6)
Income from operations	6,776,138	4.5	3,996,144	3.6
Interest income	489,353	0.3	232,470	0.2
Interest expense	(434,994)	(0.3)	(300,329)	(0.3)
Other income / (expense), net	167,626	0.1	240,093	0.2
Net earnings / (loss) before income taxes	6,998,123	4.7	4,168,378	3.7
Income tax (expense) / benefit	(766,113)	(0.5)	(302,132)	(0.3)
Net earnings	$ 6,232,010	4.2 %	$ 3,666,246	3.5 %
Average backlog	$ 128,354,666		$ 101,672,124	

Number of Participants

	Number
2007	124
2006	99

Financial Ratios

	2007 Participants		2006 Participants	
	Average	Median	Average	Median
Liquidity Ratios				
Current Ratio	1.4	1.4	1.5	1.5
Quick Ratio	1.2	1.3	1.3	1.3
Days of Cash	21.9	16.0	22.7	16.5
Working Capital Turnover	11.3	11.4	10.5	10.0
Profitability Ratios				
Return on Assets	10.8 %	11.3 %	8.9 %	9.2 %
Return on Equity	27.6 %	30.3 %	21.6 %	21.5 %
Times Interest Earned	17.1	13.4	14.9	12.9
Leverage Ratios				
Debt to Equity	1.5	1.5	1.4	1.4
Revenue to Equity	5.9	6.6	5.8	5.4
Asset Turnover	2.3	2.4	2.4	2.3
Fixed Asset Ratio	65.6 %	62.8 %	59.0 %	57.9 %
Equity to SG&A Expense	2.8	2.2	3.1	2.5
Underbillings to Equity	14.5 %	8.9 %	15.6 %	7.7 %
Backlog to Equity	5.1	3.8	5.3	2.5
Efficiency Ratios				
Backlog to Working Capital	9.7	7.0	9.5	5.4
Months in Backlog	10.3	7.7	10.9	6.0
Days in Accounts Receivable	45.8	47.0	45.5	49.9
Days in Inventory	4.3	3.8	3.8	2.7
Days in Accounts Payable	36.1	31.2	34.7	28.9
Operating Cycle	36.0	39.8	37.2	42.0

Note: Not all figures will appear to sum due to rounding.

Specialty Trade Contractors
Composite

Balance Sheet

	2007 Participants		2006 Participants	
	Amount	Percent	Amount	Percent
Current assets:				
Cash and cash equivalents	$ 3,755,378	10.9 %	$ 1,522,161	6.3 %
Marketable securities and short-term investments	218,798	0.6	195,378	0.8
Receivables:				
Contract receivables currently due	12,169,083	35.4	12,238,313	50.9
Retainages on contracts	6,052,955	17.6	2,457,473	10.2
Unbilled work	151,784	0.4	166,523	0.7
Other receivables	376,282	1.1	325,137	1.4
Less allowance for doubtful accounts	(77,430)	(0.2)	(155,426)	(0.6)
Total receivables, net	18,672,674	54.3	15,032,020	62.6
Inventories	641,732	1.9	405,354	1.7
Costs and recognized earnings in excess of billings on uncompleted contracts	3,132,170	9.1	1,658,245	6.9
Investments in and advances to construction joint ventures	43,361	0.1	32,610	0.1
Income taxes:				
Current / refundable	16,559	0.0	12,603	0.1
Deferred	53,288	0.2	133,224	0.6
Other current assets	1,125,509	3.3	526,746	2.2
Total current assets	27,659,468	80.5	19,518,342	81.3
Property, plant and equipment	7,409,635	21.6	6,719,835	28.0
Less accumulated depreciation	(3,442,208)	(10.0)	(3,768,444)	(15.7)
Property, plant and equipment, net	3,967,428	11.5	2,951,391	12.3
Noncurrent assets:				
Long-term investments	1,568,244	4.6	580,520	2.4
Deferred income taxes	661,964	1.9	40,115	0.2
Other assets	518,206	1.5	931,742	3.9
Total noncurrent assets	2,748,415	8.0	1,552,378	6.5
Total assets	$ 34,375,310	100.0 %	$ 24,022,110	100.0 %

	2007 Participants		2006 Participants	
	Amount	Percent	Amount	Percent
Current liabilities:				
Current maturity on long-term debt	$ 347,203	1.0 %	$ 335,580	1.4 %
Notes payable and lines of credit	1,734,532	5.0	976,074	4.1
Accounts payable:				
Trade, including currently due to subcontractors	6,259,784	18.2	4,309,086	17.9
Subcontracts retainages	230,980	0.7	264,884	1.1
Other	345,952	1.0	227,625	0.9
Total accounts payable	6,836,715	19.9	4,801,595	20.0
Accrued expenses	2,823,114	8.2	2,525,757	10.5
Billings in excess of costs and recognized earnings on uncompleted contracts	3,799,814	11.1	3,549,630	14.8
Income taxes:				
Current	329,717	1.0	156,507	0.7
Deferred	28,353	0.1	13,214	0.1
Other current liabilities	1,190,453	3.5	517,148	2.2
Total current liabilities	17,089,901	49.7	12,875,505	53.6
Noncurrent liabilities				
Long-term debt, excluding current maturities	1,296,845	3.8	1,861,324	7.7
Deferred income taxes	2,486,798	7.2	84,885	0.4
Other	221,123	0.6	278,840	1.2
Total liabilities	21,094,668	61.4	15,100,552	62.9
Minority interests	28,825	0.1	29,983	0.1
Net worth:				
Common stock, par value	176,508	0.5	236,443	1.0
Preferred stock, stated value	41,847	0.1	39,022	0.2
Additional paid-in capital	847,020	2.5	3,127,698	13.2
Retained earnings	12,199,881	35.5	5,193,594	21.6
Treasury stock	(568,076)	(1.7)	(489,936)	(2.0)
Excess value of marketable securities	15,537	0.0	24,596	0.1
Other equity	539,100	1.6	715,158	3.0
Total net worth	13,251,817	38.6	8,891,575	37.0
Total liabilities and net worth	$ 34,375,310	100.0 %	$ 24,022,110	100.0 %

Specialty Trade Contractors

Composite

Statement of Earnings

	2007 Participants		2006 Participants	
	Amount	Percent	Amount	Percent
Contract revenue	$ 96,481,153	98.1 %	$ 61,769,481	93.8 %
Other revenue	1,826,142	1.9	4,049,975	6.2
Total revenue	98,307,295	100.0	65,819,456	100.0
Contract cost	(78,390,116)	(79.7)	(52,751,688)	(80.1)
Other cost	(1,353,269)	(1.4)	(3,129,659)	(4.8)
Total cost	(79,743,385)	(81.1)	(55,881,347)	(84.9)
Gross profit	18,563,911	18.9	9,938,109	15.1
Selling, general and administrative expenses:				
Payroll	(7,532,681)	(7.7)	(3,633,440)	(5.5)
Professional fees	(222,178)	(0.2)	(235,921)	(0.4)
Sales and marketing costs	(347,866)	(0.4)	(200,885)	(0.3)
Technology costs	(165,109)	(0.2)	(138,346)	(0.2)
Administrative bonuses	(649,064)	(0.7)	(563,314)	(0.9)
Other	(6,633,418)	(6.7)	(2,609,202)	(4.0)
Total SG&A expenses	(15,550,314)	(15.8)	(7,381,108)	(11.2)
Income from operations	3,013,596	3.1	2,557,001	3.9
Interest income	57,965	0.1	27,837	0.0
Interest expense	(282,532)	(0.3)	(184,521)	(0.3)
Other income / (expense), net	95,354	0.1	47,815	0.1
Net earnings / (loss) before income taxes	2,884,383	2.9	2,448,132	3.7
Income tax (expense) / benefit	(465,300)	(0.5)	(230,758)	(0.4)
Net earnings	$ 2,419,084	2.5 %	$ 2,217,374	3.4 %
Average backlog	$ 37,296,307		$ 34,815,759	

Number of Participants

	Number
2007	290
2006	176

Financial Ratios

	2007 Participants		2006 Participants	
	Average	Median	Average	Median
Liquidity Ratios				
Current Ratio	1.6	1.5	1.5	1.5
Quick Ratio	1.3	1.3	1.3	1.3
Days of Cash	13.8	77	8.3	4.6
Working Capital Turnover	9.3	9.3	9.9	9.9
Profitability Ratios				
Return on Assets	8.4 %	10.0 %	10.2 %	9.0 %
Return on Equity	21.8 %	28.9 %	27.5 %	27.9 %
Times Interest Earned	11.2	10.4	14.3	9.9
Leverage Ratios				
Debt to Equity	1.6	1.6	1.7	1.8
Revenue to Equity	7.4	7.8	7.4	8.9
Asset Turnover	2.9	2.9	2.7	2.9
Fixed Asset Ratio	29.9 %	26.2 %	33.2 %	25.3 %
Equity to SG&A Expense	0.9	1.0	1.2	1.0
Underbillings to Equity	24.8 %	13.2 %	20.5 %	20.3 %
Backlog to Equity	2.8	4.2	3.9	3.9
Efficiency Ratios				
Backlog to Working Capital	3.5	5.1	5.2	4.3
Months in Backlog	46	6.2	6.3	5.2
Days in Accounts Receivable	45.7	63.1	67.9	63.7
Days in Inventory	2.9	3.0	2.6	2.4
Days in Accounts Payable	29.8	27.7	29.2	28.4
Operating Cycle	32.5	48.1	49.6	45.0

Note: Not all figures will appear to sum due to rounding.

CFMA Comparative Financial Data

Balance Sheet
Most Recent Year-End

	All Companies		Industrial & Nonresidential		Heavy & Highway		Specialty Trade	
	Amount	Percent	Amount	Percent	Amount	Percent	Amount	Percent
Current assets:								
Cash and cash equivalents	$ 8,543,784	15.3 %	$ 15,160,904	17.9 %	$ 9,053,242	14.0 %	$ 3,755,378	10.9 %
Marketable securities and short-term investments	2,438,975	4.4	5,118,510	6.1	2,986,359	4.6	218,798	0.6
Receivables:								
Contract receivables currently due	20,608,340	36.9	35,263,909	41.7	17,751,168	27.5	12,169,083	35.4
Retainages on contracts	7,421,822	13.3	12,019,960	14.2	4,465,836	6.9	6,052,955	17.6
Unbilled work	692,231	1.2	1,266,261	1.5	1,036,582	1.6	151,784	0.4
Other receivables	884,894	1.6	1,365,034	1.6	1,288,178	2.0	376,282	1.1
Less allowance for doubtful accounts	(62,553)	(0.1)	(47,284)	(0.1)	(64,966)	(0.1)	(77,430)	(0.2)
Total receivables, net	29,544,733	52.9	49,867,880	59.0	24,476,798	37.9	18,672,674	54.3
Inventories	1,064,816	1.9	103,536	0.1	1,609,031	2.5	641,732	1.9
Costs and recognized earnings in excess of billings on uncompleted contracts	2,810,763	5.0	3,097,355	3.7	2,635,888	4.1	3,132,170	9.1
Investments in and advances to construction joint ventures	327,796	0.6	574,176	0.7	614,329	1.0	43,361	0.1
Income taxes:								
Current / refundable	17,827	0.0	20,016	0.0	23,496	0.0	16,559	0.0
Deferred	185,506	0.3	246,423	0.3	426,928	0.7	53,288	0.2
Other current assets	1,864,677	3.3	2,823,319	3.3	2,279,999	3.5	1,125,509	3.3
Total current assets	46,798,879	83.9	77,012,121	91.1	44,106,070	68.2	27,659,468	80.5
Property, plant and equipment	12,004,158	21.5	7,968,420	9.4	34,552,168	53.5	7,409,635	21.6
Less accumulated depreciation	(6,124,529)	(11.0)	(4,256,267)	(5.0)	(17,894,991)	(27.7)	(3,442,208)	(10.0)
Property, plant and equipment, net	5,879,630	10.5	3,712,153	4.4	16,657,177	25.8	3,967,428	11.5
Noncurrent assets:								
Long-term investments	986,432	1.8	678,495	0.8	836,193	1.3	1,568,244	4.6
Deferred income taxes	387,468	0.7	369,443	0.4	11,178	0.0	661,964	1.9
Other assets	1,756,975	3.1	2,799,118	3.3	3,022,151	4.7	518,206	1.5
Total noncurrent assets	3,130,874	5.6	3,847,056	4.5	3,869,523	6.0	2,748,415	8.0
Total assets	$ 55,809,383	100.0 %	$ 84,571,330	100.0 %	$ 64,632,770	100.0 %	$ 34,375,310	100.0 %

CFMA Comparative Financial Data

	All Companies		Industrial & Nonresidential		Heavy & Highway		Specialty Trade	
	Amount	Percent	Amount	Percent	Amount	Percent	Amount	Percent
Current liabilities:								
Current maturity on long-term debt	$ 705,386	1.3 %	$ 705,262	0.8 %	$ 1,592,563	2.5 %	$ 347,203	1.0 %
Notes payable and lines of credit	1,220,433	2.2	286,128	0.3	821,528	1.3	1,734,532	5.0
Accounts payable:								
Trade, including currently due								
to subcontractors	16,405,345	29.4	32,662,616	38.6	12,572,430	19.5	6,259,784	18.2
Subcontracts retainages	4,629,576	8.3	12,030,939	14.2	1,142,000	1.8	230,980	0.7
Other	727,460	1.3	1,246,442	1.5	766,665	1.2	345,952	1.0
Total accounts payable	21,762,382	39.0	45,939,997	54.3	14,461,095	22.4	6,836,715	19.9
Accrued expenses	3,758,727	6.7	5,172,378	6.1	4,550,809	7.1	2,823,114	8.2
Billings in excess of costs and recognized								
earnings on uncompleted contracts	6,963,332	12.5	10,941,363	12.9	8,852,186	13.7	3,799,814	11.1
Income taxes:								
Current	360,959	0.6	555,279	0.7	136,288	0.2	329,717	1.0
Deferred	42,805	0.1	81,948	0.1	5,140	0.0	28,353	0.1
Other current liabilities	703,622	1.3	416,483	0.5	458,697	0.7	1,190,453	3.5
Total current liabilities	35,517,646	63.6	64,098,838	75.8	30,938,306	47.9	17,089,901	49.7
Noncurrent liabilities								
Long-term debt, excluding current maturities	2,195,966	3.9	1,319,367	1.6	6,070,996	9.4	1,296,845	3.8
Deferred income taxes	1,123,834	2.0	183,290	0.2	548,226	0.8	2,486,798	7.2
Other	561,290	1.0	603,384	0.7	1,489,771	2.3	221,123	0.6
Total liabilities	39,398,737	70.6	66,204,878	78.3	39,047,300	60.4	21,094,668	61.4
Minority interests	68,680	0.1	58,632	0.1	196,805	0.3	28,825	0.1
Net worth:								
Common stock, par value	764,587	1.4	1,732,184	2.0	398,277	0.6	176,508	0.5
Preferred stock, stated value	90,764	0.2	186,287	0.2	40,597	0.1	41,847	0.1
Additional paid-in capital	1,880,067	3.4	2,930,962	3.5	2,766,505	4.3	847,020	2.5
Retained earnings	13,135,875	23.5	11,927,189	14.1	22,664,024	35.1	12,199,881	35.5
Treasury stock	(549,836)	(1.0)	(519,243)	(0.6)	(771,798)	(1.2)	(568,076)	(1.7)
Excess value of marketable securities	57,027	0.1	121,816	0.1	42,491	0.1	15,537	0.0
Other equity	963,482	1.7	1,928,625	2.3	248,569	0.4	539,100	1.6
Total net worth	16,341,966	29.3	18,307,820	21.6	25,383,665	39.3	13,251,817	38.6
Total liabilities and net worth	$ 55,809,383	100.0 %	$ 84,571,330	100.0 %	$ 64,632,770	100.0 %	$ 34,375,310	100.0 %

Note: Not all figures will appear to sum due to rounding.

CFMA Comparative Financial Data

Statement of Earnings
Most Recent Year End

	All Companies		Industrial & Nonresidential		Heavy & Highway		Specialty Trade	
	Amount	Percent	Amount	Percent	Amount	Percent	Amount	Percent
Contract revenue	$ 154,696,293	98.0 %	$ 256,075,114	99.6 %	$ 140,808,865	94.5 %	$ 96,481,153	98.1 %
Other revenue	3,174,629	2.0	992,393	0.4	8,264,474	5.5	1,826,142	1.9
Total revenue	157,870,922	100.0	257,067,507	100.0	149,073,338	100.0	98,307,295	100.0
Contract cost	(139,283,761)	(88.2)	(240,348,291)	(93.5)	(126,395,504)	(84.8)	(78,390,116)	(79.7)
Other cost	(2,484,033)	(1.6)	(532,957)	(0.2)	(6,779,868)	(4.5)	(1,353,269)	(1.4)
Total cost	(141,767,794)	(89.8)	(240,881,248)	(93.7)	(133,175,371)	(89.3)	(79,743,385)	(81.1)
Gross profit	16,103,128	10.2	16,186,260	6.3	15,897,967	10.7	18,563,911	18.9
Selling, general and administrative expenses:								
Payroll	(5,442,878)	(3.4)	(5,309,727)	(2.1)	(3,067,343)	(2.1)	(7,532,681)	(7.7)
Professional fees	(228,907)	(0.1)	(261,498)	(0.1)	(247,066)	(0.2)	(222,178)	(0.2)
Sales and marketing costs	(582,300)	(0.4)	(1,089,458)	(0.4)	(258,433)	(0.2)	(347,866)	(0.4)
Technology costs	(184,584)	(0.1)	(203,861)	(0.1)	(257,869)	(0.2)	(165,109)	(0.2)
Administrative bonuses	(713,166)	(0.5)	(971,217)	(0.4)	(602,257)	(0.4)	(649,064)	(0.7)
Other	(4,870,600)	(3.1)	(3,833,788)	(1.5)	(4,688,862)	(3.1)	(6,633,418)	(6.7)
Total SG&A expenses	(12,022,435)	(7.6)	(11,669,548)	(4.5)	(9,121,829)	(6.1)	(15,550,314)	(15.8)
Income from operations	4,080,693	2.6	4,516,711	1.8	6,776,138	4.5	3,013,596	3.1
Interest income	416,777	0.3	858,692	0.3	489,353	0.3	57,965	0.1
Interest expense	(241,213)	(0.2)	(104,122)	(0.0)	(434,994)	(0.3)	(282,532)	(0.3)
Other income / (expense), net	31,999	0.0	(70,560)	(0.0)	167,626	0.1	95,354	0.1
Net earnings / (loss) before income taxes	4,288,256	2.7	5,200,722	2.0	6,998,123	4.7	2,884,383	2.9
Income tax (expense) / benefit	(628,886)	(0.4)	(852,969)	(0.3)	(766,113)	(0.5)	(465,300)	(0.5)
Net earnings	$ 3,659,370	2.3 %	$ 4,347,752	1.7 %	$ 6,232,010	4.2 %	$ 2,419,084	2.5 %
Average backlog	$ 123,121,158		$ 241,184,984		$ 128,354,666		$ 37,296,307	

Number of Participants

	All Companies	Industrial & Nonresidential	Heavy & Highway	Specialty Trade
	Number	Number	Number	Number
2007	756	269	124	290
2006	495	185	99	176

CFMA Comparative Financial Data

Financial Ratios
Most Recent Year End

	All Companies		Industrial & Nonresidential		Heavy & Highway		Specialty Trade	
	Average	Median	Average	Median	Average	Median	Average	Median
Liquidity Ratios								
Current Ratio	1.3	1.4	1.2	1.2	1.4	1.4	1.6	1.5
Quick Ratio	1.1	1.2	1.1	1.2	1.2	1.3	1.3	1.3
Days of Cash	19.5	13.7	21.2	19.7	21.9	16.0	13.8	7.7
Working Capital Turnover	14.0	12.1	19.9	18.3	11.3	11.4	9.3	9.3
Profitability Ratios								
Return on Assets	7.7 %	8.8 %	6.1 %	6.8 %	10.8 %	11.3 %	8.4 %	10.0 %
Return on Equity	26.2 %	30.1 %	28.4 %	30.5 %	27.6 %	30.3 %	21.8 %	28.9 %
Times Interest Earned	18.8	13.9	50.9	21.9	17.1	13.4	11.2	10.4
Leverage Ratios								
Debt to Equity	2.4	2.2	3.6	3.5	1.5	1.5	1.6	1.6
Revenue to Equity	9.7	9.5	14.0	16.5	5.9	6.6	7.4	7.8
Asset Turnover	2.8	3.0	3.0	3.5	2.3	2.4	2.9	2.9
Fixed Asset Ratio	36.0 %	27.8 %	20.3 %	17.4 %	65.6 %	62.8 %	29.9 %	26.2 %
Equity to SG&A Expense	1.4	1.3	1.6	1.3	2.8	2.2	0.9	1.0
Underbillings to Equity	21.4 %	11.4 %	23.8 %	11.9 %	14.5 %	8.9 %	24.8 %	13.2 %
Backlog to Equity	7.5	5.7	13.2	11.1	5.1	3.8	2.8	4.2
Efficiency Ratios								
Backlog to Working Capital	10.9	8.0	18.7	14.0	9.7	7.0	3.5	5.1
Months in Backlog	9.4	7.2	11.3	7.9	10.3	7.7	4.6	6.2
Days in Accounts Receivable	48.9	53.6	51.2	47.0	45.8	47.0	45.7	63.1
Days in Inventory	2.7	2.9	0.2	0.5	4.3	3.8	2.9	3.0
Days in Accounts Payable	43.5	35.3	50.7	44.7	36.1	31.2	29.8	27.7
Operating Cycle	27.5	38.2	21.9	26.5	36.0	39.8	32.5	48.1

Note: Not all figures will appear to sum due to rounding.

TEXT—KEY WORD INDEX OF INDUSTRIES APPEARING IN THE STATEMENT STUDIES

STATEMENT STUDIES KEY WORD INDEX

A complete description of each industry category listed below begins on page 35.

STATEMENT STUDIES KEY WORD INDEX

A complete description of each industry category listed below begins on page 35.

STATEMENT STUDIES KEY WORD INDEX

A complete description of each industry category listed below begins on page 35.

STATEMENT STUDIES KEY WORD INDEX

A complete description of each industry category listed below begins on page 35.

STATEMENT STUDIES KEY WORD INDEX

A complete description of each industry category listed below begins on page 35.

RMA'S CREDIT & LENDING DICTIONARY

A

Absentee Owner: landlord who does not reside in his or her rental property.

Abstract of Title: condensed history of title to land and real property, consisting of ownership transfers and any conveyances or liens that may affect future ownership.

Acceleration Clause: provision in note or contract that allows holder to declare remaining balance due and payable immediately upon default in an obligation. Usual causes of default are failure to pay interest or principal installments in a timely manner, an adverse change in financing conditions, or failure to meet loan covenants.

Acceptance: drawee's signed agreement to honor draft as presented, which consists of signature alone, but will frequently be evidenced by drawee writing word "accepted," date it is payable, and signature. Sometimes called Trade Acceptance or Banker's Acceptance, depending upon function of acceptor.

Accommodation: 1. lending or extending credit to borrower. 2. loan or commitment to lend money.

Accord and Satisfaction: agreement between two or more persons or entities that satisfies or discharges obligation or settles claim or lawsuit. Generally involves disputed matter in which one party agrees to give and other party agrees to accept something in satisfaction different from, and usually less than, that originally asked for.

Account: 1. statement showing balance along with detailed explanation covering debits and credits. 2. right of payment for goods sold or leased or for services rendered on open account basis. 3. summarized record of financial transaction. 4. customer.

Accountant: person in charge of and skilled in the recording of financial transactions and maintenance of financial records.

Accounting: 1. theory and system of classifying, recording, summarizing, and auditing books of firm. 2. art of analyzing, interpreting, and reporting financial position and operating results of business.

Account Manager: 1. sometimes called Relationship Manager or Account Officer. 2. person responsible for overseeing all matters relating to a specific client or group of customers.

Account Number: unique identification number used to designate specific customer.

Accounts Payable: short-term liability representing amounts due trade creditors.

Accounts Payable Department: section of business office responsible for processing open account balances and paying amounts owed for goods and services purchased.

Accounts Receivable: money due to a business by its customers for goods sold or services performed on open account (or credit). Usually refers to short-term receivables.

Accounts Receivable Aging Report: report by customer that lists age of accounts receivable generally by 30-day intervals from invoice or due date. See also *Aging of Accounts Receivable*.

Accounts Receivable Financing: form of secured lending in which borrowings are typically limited to percentage of receivables pledged as collateral.

Accrual Accounting: basis of accounting in which expenses are recorded when incurred and revenues are recognized when earned, regardless of when cash is actually paid or received.

Accrue: 1. something gained, added, or accumulated, such as profit from a business transaction. 2. right to sue has become exercisable.

Accrued Expenses: short-term liabilities that represent expenses for goods used but not yet paid.

Accrued Income: income earned but not yet collected.

Accrued Interest: interest accumulated since last interest payment due date.

Accrued Liabilities: expenses or obligations for goods or services incurred but not yet paid.

ACH: see *Automated Clearinghouse*.

Acid Test: ratio between company's most liquid assets (generally, cash and accounts receivable) and current liabilities that represents the degree to which current liabilities can be paid with those assets.

Acknowledgment: 1. declaration making known receipt of something done or to be done; confirmation of receipt of order or of terms of contract. 2. statement of notary or other competent officer certifying that signature on document was personally signed by individual whose signature is affixed to instrument.

Acquisition: merger or taking over of controlling interest of one business by another.

Acquisition and Development Loan: loan made for the purpose of purchasing a property and completing all on-site improvements such as street layout, utility installation, and community area grading necessary to bring the site to a buildable state.

Acquittal: 1. release from obligation or contract. 2. to have accusation of crime dismissed by some formal legal procedure.

Active Account: 1. customer who makes frequent purchases. 2. bank account in which regular deposits or withdrawals are made.

Activity Charge: service charge imposed for check or deposit activity or any other maintenance charge.

Act of God: event that could not be prevented by reasonable foresight, is caused exclusively by forces and violence of nature, and is uninfluenced by human power (storm, flood, earthquake, or lightning).

Additional Dating: means of extending credit beyond normal sales terms, granted to induce buyers to place orders in advance of season or for other special reasons. See also *Advance Dating and Dating*.

Adjudication: judgment rendered by court, primarily used in bankruptcy proceedings.

Adjustable Interest Rate: interest rate on loan that may be adjusted up or down at specific intervals. Index used in determining adjusted interest rate and potential frequency of adjustments must be stated in loan documents.

Adjustable Rate Mortgage: loan is pursuant to an agreement executed at the inception of the loan that permits creditor to adjust interest rate from time to time based on a specific interest rate index.

Adjuster: person who deals with insured party to settle amount of loss, claim, or debt.

Adjustment: 1. settlement of disputed account. 2. change or concession in price or terms. 3. determining amount one is to receive in settlement of claim. 4. in accounting, entry made to correct or compensate for error or difference in account.

Adjustment Bureau: organization that supervises debt extensions and compromise arrangements or oversees orderly liquidation of troubled businesses for benefit of creditors.

Advance: 1. payment made before it is due. 2. disbursement of loan proceeds.

Advance Dating: additional time granted customers to pay for goods received and to earn available discounts. See also *Additional Dating and Dating*.

Advancement of Costs: prepayment of necessary legal expenses. Such charges, set by law, may be for commencement of suit and vary in different courts and states. Some items for which prepaid costs may be requested are filing fees, process serving, premiums on court bonds, trial fees, posting security for costs, entering judgment, recording abstract of judgment, issue execution, and discovery actions after judgment.

Advertising Allowance: promotional discount in price or payment given customers who share expense of advertising supplier's product.

Affidavit: voluntary written statement of facts pertaining to a transaction or event, signed under oath and witnessed by an authorized person.

Affiliate: business entity connected with another through common ownership or management, usually responsible for payment of its own obligations.

After-Acquired Property: security interest by which secured creditor automatically obtains interest in assets that debtor acquires after lien had been filed.

Agency: legal relationship between two parties in which one is authorized to act for another.

Agent: person legally authorized to act for another.

Agent Bank: formal designation that applies to a bank responsible for negotiating, structuring, and overseeing a loan or commitment to a borrower in which more than one bank is involved. See also *Lead Bank*.

Aggregate Balances: combined total of two or more demand deposit accounts, money markets, or time certificates of deposit. Term can also be applied to credit facility totals.

Aging of Accounts Receivable: accounting record of customer's receivables showing how long receivables have remained unpaid beyond regular terms of sale. Used as basis for advancing credit.

Agreement: a contract involving an offer and an acceptance between two or more parties, governing the terms of the contract and binding on the parties to the agreement (e.g., a loan agreement, security agreement, or guaranty).

AKA: see *Also Known As*.

Alert Action: a series of information services provided by credit reporting agencies; provides subscribers with listing of specific accounts on which unfavorable payment condition has recently been reported.

Allegation: statement of party to action, setting out what he or she intends to prove or contend.

ALLL: see *Allowance for Loan and Lease Losses*.

Allocation: sub-limit within a total credit facility that is to be used for a specific purpose.

Allonge: paper attached to a negotiable instrument for additional endorsements or other terms and conditions.

Allowance: accounting provision used to set aside amounts for depreciation, returns, or bad debts.

Allowance for Bad Debts: contra account against which uncollectible receivables are charged. See also *Bad Debt Reserve*.

Allowance for Loan and Lease Losses (ALLL): contra account, generally found on asset side of balance sheet as deduction from total loans outstanding; amount is intended to cover future losses of loans currently in the financial institution's portfolio. The ALLL should be adjusted monthly, concurrently with the generation of current financial statements.

Also Known As (AKA): sometimes used to designate a fictitious trade style or name.

ALTA Policy: an extended coverage title insurance policy that protects the lender against losses resulting from any defects in the title or claims against the property. The policy's coverage includes encroachments, mechanic's liens, and other matters that a physical inspection or inquiry of the parties would disclose.

Altered Check: check on which original entries have been changed (date, payee, or amount); financial institutions generally refuse to honor or pay checks that have been altered.

Amend: to correct, add to, or alter legal document.

Amicus Curiae: friend of court; uninvolved third party who intervenes in lawsuit, with court's permission, to introduce information or arguments in respect to the issue or principle of law to be decided.

Amortization: 1. reduction of loan by periodic principal payments. 2. decline in the book value of an intangible asset over the period owned.

Amortization Tables: calculation charts showing amounts required periodically to discharge debts over various periods of time and at different interest rates.

Amortize: 1. to write off the value of an intangible asset over the period owned. 2. to reduce or pay off debt or obligation by making periodic payments of principal.

Annual Percentage Rate (APR): annual cost of credit expressed as percentage; creditors are required under Federal Truth in Lending Act to disclose true annual interest on consumer loans, as well as the total dollar cost and other terms of loan.

Annual Report: yearly report detailing a company's comparative financial and organizational conditions.

Annuity: series of fixed periodic payments made at regular intervals.

Antecedent Credit Information: historical record of significant business information concerning individuals who are involved in ownership or management of business enterprise.

Anticipation: bridge loan made to a municipal or government borrower to cover expenses until revenue or tax proceeds are collected.

Appeal: complaint made to higher court by either plaintiff or defendant for court's review, correction, or reversal of lower court's decision.

Appearance: coming into court formally as plaintiff or defendant in lawsuit.

Appraisal: opinion of current value of real or personal property based upon cost of replacement, market, income, or fair value analysis.

Appreciation: increase in value of asset over its cost due to economic and other conditions. Property that increases in value as result of improvements or additions is not considered to have appreciated.

Appropriation: sum of money designated for a special purpose only.

APR: See *Annual Percentage Rate*.

Arbitration: submission for settlement of disputed matter, by nonjudicial means, to one or more impartial or disinterested third persons selected by disputants.

Arm's Length: business transaction between two or more parties that is open, sincere, and without personal influence, favoritism, or close relations.

Arrangement: plan for corporate reorganization for rescheduling or extension of time for payment of unsecured debts, such as an arrangement under Chapter 11 or 13 of the U. S. Bankruptcy Code.

Arrears: total or partial debt amounts that remain unpaid and past due.

Articles of Agreement: any written statement or contract, terms to which all parties consent.

Articles of Incorporation: formal papers that set forth pertinent data for formation of corporation and are filed with appropriate state agency.

Assess: 1. to fix rate or amount. 2. to set value of real and personal property, as for tax purposes.

Assessed Value: in the case of real property, value set by government agency for purpose of levying taxes.

Asset: 1. anything owned having monetary value. 2. item listed on left-hand side of balance sheet representing cash, or property, real or personal, belonging to an individual or company and convertible to cash.

Assigned Account: 1. account receivable pledged by borrower to factor or lender as security. 2. past-due customer whose account has been placed with collection agency.

Assigned Risk: insurance plan that provides coverage for risks rejected by regular markets and in which all licensed insurers are made to participate by various state laws.

Assignee: person to whom some rights, authority, or property is assigned.

Assignment: 1. written contract for transfer of one's title, legal rights, or property from one person to another. 2. in some states, form used to transfer claim to agency that undertakes collection of account for benefit of assigning creditor.

Assignment for the Benefit of Creditors: A liquidation technique in which an insolvent debtor goes out of business and an assignee facilitates the transfer of the insolvent debtor's estate for administration and payment of debts. Property transferred to assignee places such assets beyond control of debtor or reach of creditors.

Assignment of Claim: claim assigned to third party for collection.

Assignor: 1. one who transfers claim, right, or property. 2. individual, partnership, or corporation making assignment.

Assumed Liability: acknowledgment of responsibility for payment of obligation by third party.

At Sight: words used in negotiable instrument directing that payment be made upon presentation or demand.

Attached Account: legally frozen account on which payments have been suspended; release or disbursement of funds can be made only after court order.

Attachment: 1. legal writ or process by which debtor's property (or any interest therein) is seized and placed in custody of law. 2. Supplemental data provided as clarifying information to a document.

Attorney-in-Fact: private attorney who has written authorization to act for another. This authority is given by an instrument called power of attorney.

Attorney of Record: lawyer whose name must appear in permanent court records as person acting on behalf of party in legal matter.

Auction: public sale of property that is sold to highest bidder.

Audit: to examine a firm's records, accounts, or procedures for purpose of substantiating or verifying individual transactions or to confirm if assets and liabilities are properly accounted for, including income and expense items.

Audited Financial Statements: financial statements that have been examined by an independent certified public accountant to determine if the financial statements present fairly the financial position, results of operations, and cash flows in conformity with generally accepted accounting principles.

Auditor: person who deals with examination and verification of financial accounts and with making financial reports.

Auditor's Report: part of complete set of financial statements that explains degree of responsibility that independent accountant assumed for expressing an opinion on management's financial statements and assurance that is provided by said opinion.

Automated Cash Application: computerized procedures enabling payments to be quickly and automatically applied to accounts receivable.

Automated Clearinghouse (ACH): computer-based clearing and settlement facility for interchange of electronic debits and credits among financial institutions. ACH entries can be substituted for checks in recurring payments such as mortgages or in direct deposit distribution of federal and corporate benefits payments. Federal Reserve Banks furnish data processing services for most ACHs, although some are privately operated. Final settlement, or net settlement, of ACH transfers is made against reserve accounts at Federal Reserve Banks.

Available Balance: checking account balance that the customer actually may use; that is, current balance less deposits not yet cleared through the account.

Average Collected Balances: average dollar amount on deposit in checking accounts defined as the difference between ledger balance and deposit float, or those deposits posted to the account but having not yet cleared the financial institution upon which they are drawn. See also *Uncollected Funds*.

Average Collection Period: average number of days required to convert accounts receivable to cash.

Average Daily Balance: average amount of money that depositor keeps on deposit when calculated on a daily basis.

B

Backdating: predating document prior to date on which it was drawn.

Backlog: amount of revenue expected to be realized from work to be performed on uncompleted contracts, including new contractual agreements on which work has not begun.

Bad Check Laws: laws enacted in various states to encourage and facilitate lawful use of checks; statutes differ in various jurisdictions and are generally enforced according to state laws as well as local custom and usage.

Bad Debt: account receivable that proves uncollectible in normal course of business; full payment is doubtful.

Bad Debt Ratio: ratio of bad debt expense to sales, used as measure of quality of accounts receivable.

Bad Debt Reserve: reserve or provision for accounts receivables to be charged off company's books based on historical levels of bad debts or industry averages.

Balance: amount owed or unpaid on loan or credit transaction. Also called outstanding or unpaid balance.

Balance Due: total amount owed after applying debits and credits of account.

Balance Sheet: A financial statement listing the assets, liabilities, and owner's equity of a business entity or individual as of a specific date.

Balloon Payment: lump-sum payment of principal and sometimes accrued interest, usually due at end of term of installment loan in which periodic installments of principal and interest did not fully amortize loan.

Bank: financial institution chartered by state or federal government to transact financial business that includes receiving deposits, lending money, exchanging currencies, providing safekeeping, and investing money.

Bank Draft: sight or demand draft (order to pay) drawn by a bank (drawer) on its account at another bank (drawee).

Banker's Acceptance: draft or order to pay specified amount at specified time not to exceed 270 days, drawn on individuals, business firms, or financial institutions; draft becomes accepted when a financial institution formally acknowledges its obligation to honor such draft, usually by writing or stamping "Accepted" on face of instrument. When accepted in this manner, draft becomes liability of bank. See also *Draft and Time Draft*.

Bank Overdraft: check presented for collection for which there are not sufficient funds on deposit to make normal payment. Financial institution may honor such check, considering payment as loan to depositor for which the institution will usually collect interest or service charge.

Bankrupt: debtor who is unable to meet debt obligations as they become due or is insolvent and whose assets are administered for benefit of creditors.

Bankruptcy: Legal action taken under the U.S. Bankruptcy Code by or against an insolvent debtor who is unable to meet obligations as they become due. The bankrupt, if given discharge, is released from further liability of most debts listed as of the date of the bankruptcy filing.

• *Voluntary Bankruptcy:* any individual, partnership, corporation, estate, trust, or governmental unit may be afforded protection of debtor under U.S. Bankruptcy Code by filing petition. Exceptions: railroads, insurance or banking corporations, building and loan associations.

• *Involuntary Bankruptcy:* involuntary petition can be filed in bankruptcy court by three or more creditors or, if there are fewer than 12 creditors, by any one creditor. Petitioning creditors' claims must aggregate at least $5,000 in excess of value of any collateral of debtor. Involuntary cases may be filed against individuals, partnerships, or corporations other than farmers and nonprofit corporations and may be instituted under either Chapter 7 or Chapter 11 of the U.S. Bankruptcy Code. Involuntary petition must allege one of two grounds for relief: either that the debtor is generally not paying debts as they become due, or that the non-bankruptcy custodian, other than one appointed to enforce lien on less than substantially all of debtor's property, was appointed for, or took possession of, substantially all of debtor's property within 120 days of filing.

• *Chapter 7 Cases:* liquidation proceedings, formerly referred to as "straight bankruptcy," wherein nonexempt assets of debtor are converted to cash and proceeds distributed pro rata among creditors.

• *Chapter 9 Cases:* reorganization proceedings wherein municipality that is insolvent or unable to meet debts as they mature effects plan to adjust such debts.

• *Chapter 11 Cases:* reorganization proceedings available to all business enterprises; may be instituted either by debtor or creditor(s). For plan to be confirmed by court under Chapter 11, each class of creditors, as set forth in such plan, must accept plan or each class must receive at least that which it would receive on liquidation. Class of creditors has accepted plan when majority in number and two-thirds in dollar amount of those creditors actually voting approve it.

• *Chapter 12 Cases:* reorganization proceedings for agricultural concerns and small family-owned farms having debts under $1.5 million.

* *Chapter 13 Cases:* reorganization cases that may be instituted only by individuals with regular income who owe unsecured debts of less than $100,000 and secured debts of less than $350,000, other than stockbroker or commodity broker. For plan to be confirmed, it must provide for submission to trustee of all or any portion of debtor's future earnings as necessary for execution of plan, payment in full of all priority claims, and equal treatment of each member of class of creditors. While consent of unsecured creditors is not required, value of what they receive under plan may not be less than if debtor were liquidated.

Bankruptcy Judge: presiding judge of court in which bankruptcy cases are heard. (Formerly called Referee in Bankruptcy.) Duties of judge include supervising administrative details of bankrupt estates and ruling on all matters involving debtor-creditor problems.

Basis: 1. number of days used in calculating interest earned in investment or interest payable on bank loan. Also called accrual base. 2. original cost of asset plus capital improvements from which any taxable gains (or losses) are determined after deducting depreciation expenses.

Basis Point: 1/100th of a percent; 100 basis points equal 1%.

Bearer: negotiable item (check, note, bill, or draft) in which no payee is indicated or payee is shown as "cash" or "bearer." Item is payable to person in possession of it or to person who presents it for payment.

Bearer Paper: instrument that is made "payable to bearer." When negotiable instrument is endorsed in blank, it becomes bearer paper and can be transferred by delivery since it does not require endorsement.

Beneficiary: 1. person or organization named in will to inherit or receive property. 2. person or organization to whom insurance policy is payable. 3. person or organization for whose benefit trust is created.

Bid Bond: bond issued by surety on behalf of contractor that provides assurance to recipient of contractor's bid that if bid is accepted, contractor will execute contract and provide performance bond. Under bond, surety is obligated to pay recipient difference between contractor's bid and bid of next lowest responsible bidder if bid is accepted and contractor fails to execute contract or to provide performance bond.

Billing Cycle: number of days between payment due dates.

Bill of Costs: certified itemization of costs associated with lawsuit.

Bill of Lading: written instrument signed by common carrier or agent identifying freight and representing both receipt and contract for shipment. It must show name of consignee, description of goods, terms of carrier's contract, and directions for assigning to specific person at specific place. In form of negotiable instrument, it is evidence of holding title to goods being shipped.

Bill of Sale: written instrument evidencing transfer of title of specific personal property to buyer.

Binder: 1. written agreement that provides temporary legal protection pending issuance of final contract or policy. 2. temporary insurance contract; may be oral or written; also called cover note.

Blank Endorsement: endorser's writing on check, promissory note, or bill of exchange without indicating party to whom it is payable. Endorser merely signs his or her name, making the instrument "payable to bearer." Also called endorsement in blank.

Blanket Coverage: property coverage applicable to group of exposures (buildings, inventory, equipment, etc., combined or individually, at one or more locations), in single total amount of insurance; contrasts with Specific Coverage.

Blanket Mortgage: mortgage secured by two or more parcels of real property, frequently used by developers who acquire large tract of land for subdivision and resale to individual homeowners. Also called blanket trust deed.

Bond: contract issued by insurance or bonding company in support of principal's obligation to obligee. See also *Fidelity Bond and Surety Bond*.

Bonded Warehouse: federally approved warehouse under bond for strict observance of revenue laws; used for storing goods until duties are paid or property is otherwise released. Bonded warehouse assures owner of property that operators of warehouse are insured against loss by fraud and will keep proper inventory and accounting of goods in transit.

Bonding Company: company authorized to issue bid bonds, performance bonds, labor and materials bonds, or other types of surety bonds.

Book Value: 1. company's net worth calculated by adding total assets minus total liabilities. 2. value of asset (cost plus additions, less depreciation) shown on books or financial report of an entity.

Borrower's Certificate: A document required under a loan or other agreement to be submitted by the borrower or another designated party to certify the value of collateral and compliance with the terms of the agreement.

Bottom Line: (colloq.) final price, net profit, or end results.

Branch Banking: multioffice banking. Branch is any banking facility away from bank's main office that accepts deposits or makes loans. State laws strictly control opening of new banking offices by state-chartered banks, national banks, and thrift institutions.

Breach of Contract: failure to fulfill terms of contract, in part or whole.

Breach of Warranty: 1. failure to fully disclose information about condition of property or insured party. 2. failure to perform as promised.

Break-Even Analysis: A method of determining the number of units that must be sold at a given price to recover all fixed and variable costs.

Break-even Point: 1. point at which total sales are equal to total expenses. May be expressed in units or dollars. 2. amount received from sale that exactly equals amount of expense or cost.

Bridge Loan: loan that provides liquidity until defined event occurs that will generate cash, such as sale of noncurrent asset, replacement financing, or equity infusion.

Bulk Sales Acts: statutes designed to prevent defrauding of creditors through secret sale in bulk of merchant's goods. Most states require notice of proposed sale to all creditors.

Burden of Proof: 1. duty of producing sufficient evidence to prove position taken in lawsuit. 2. necessity of proving fact or facts as to truth of claim.

Business: 1. commercial, industrial, or mercantile activity engaged in by individual, partnership, corporation, or other form of organization for purpose of making, buying, or selling goods or services at profit. 2. occupation, profession, or trade.

Business Failure: 1. suspension of business resulting from insolvency or bankruptcy. 2. inability to fulfill normal business obligations.

Business Interruption Insurance: property insurance written to cover loss of profits and continuing expenses as result of shutdown by insured peril; exposure is classified as consequential loss. Also called earnings insurance.

Buyer's Market: market condition in which supply exceeds demand, which causes prices to decline.

Buy Out: to purchase at least a controlling percentage of a company's stock to take over its assets.

Bylaws: set of rules or regulations adopted to control internal affairs of organization.

C

C's of Credit: the "Five C's" of credit. A longstanding means of evaluating a customer by investigating Character, Collateral, Capacity, Conditions, and Capital.

Calendar Year: 12-month accounting period ending December 31.

Callable Loan: loan payable on demand.

Canceled Check: check that has been paid by a financial institution and on which the financial institution has imprinted evidence of payment so that it cannot be presented again.

Cancellation Clause: provision in contract or agreement allowing parties to rescind agreement under certain conditions.

Capacity: one of the "Five C's" of credit; a customer's ability to successfully absorb merchandise and to pay for the merchandise. Refers to customer's ability to produce sufficient cash so as to meet obligations when due.

Capital: 1. one of the "Five Cs" of credit; refers to financial resources the customer has at the time order is placed and those that he or she is likely to have when payment is due. 2. amount invested in business by owners or stockholders. 3. owner's equity in the business.

Cash: 1. money readily available for current expenditures; usually consists of cash on hand or money in a financial institution. 2. money equivalent, such as a check, paid at time of purchase. 3. any medium of exchange that the financial institution will accept at face value upon deposit.

Cash Basis Accounting: basis of accounting in which revenues and expenses are reported in the income statement when cash is received or paid out for the time period in which the revenues and expenses occur.

Cash Basis Loan: loan on which interest payments are recorded when collected from borrower. This is a loan in which the borrower has fallen behind on interest payments and is classified as a nonaccrual asset.

Cash Concentration and Disbursement (CCD): corporate electronic payment used in business-to-business and intracompany transfers of funds. Funds are cleared on overnight basis through nationwide automated clearinghouse network.

Cash Equivalents: accounting term for actual cash on hand and total of bank deposits.

Cash Flow: is based on an activity format, which classifies cash inflows and outflows in terms of operating, investing, and financing activities.

Cashier's Check: check drawn on financial institution's account, becoming direct obligation of the financial institution.

Cash Management Account: special type of deposit service that permits corporate customers to invest cash in demand deposit account until needed for operations.

Cash Surrender Value: in life insurance, amount payable under whole life policy when terminated by insured.

Casualty Insurance: coverage for automobile, liability, crime, boiler and machinery, health, bonds, aviation, workers' compensation, and other miscellaneous lines; contrasts with Property Insurance.

Certificate of Insurance: written statement issued by insurer indicating that insurance policy has been issued and showing details of coverage at time certificate was written; used as evidence of insurance.

Certified Check: depositor's check confirmed on its face as good by a financial institution and stamped "certified." It is then dated and signed by an authorized officer of the institution. Such check becomes an obligation of the financial institution, which guarantees that it is holding sufficient funds to cover payment of check on demand.

Certified Copy of Policy: document that provides evidence of insurance as of certain date; coverage may be terminated or changed after certification.

Certified Public Accountant (CPA): one who has been trained to do accounting and who has passed state test and received title of CPA; title certifies holder's qualification to practice accounting, audit, prepare reports, and analyze accounting information.

CGL: see *Comprehensive General Liability*.

Character: one of the "Five Cs" of credit; refers to evaluating qualities that would impel debtor to meet his or her obligations. Generally identified as customer's reputation, responsibility, integrity, and honesty.

Charge-Off: portion of principal balance of a loan or account receivable that an entity considers uncollectible; this amount may be partially or fully recovered in future. Also called a Write-Off.

Chart of Accounts: listing of all financial accounts or categories (usually numbered) into which business transactions are classified and recorded.

Chattel: item of tangible personal property, animate or inanimate, as distinguished from real property.

Chattel Mortgage: instrument of sale in which debtor transfers title in property to creditor as security for debt. Failure by debtor to comply with terms of contract may cause creditor's title in property to become absolute.

Check: order on a financial institution for payment of funds from depositor's account and payable on demand.

Claim: 1. action to recover payment, reimbursement, or compensation from entity legally liable for damage or injury.

Claimant: one who makes claim or asserts right.

Cleanup: period during which particular loan or entire borrowing has been paid off; out-of-debt period required under line of credit.

Clearinghouse: association of financial institutions or security dealers created to permit daily settlement and exchange of checks or delivery of stocks and other items between members in local geographic area.

Closed-End Credit: consumer installment loan made for predetermined amount, calling for periodic payments of principal and interest over specified period or term. Finance charge may be fixed or variable rate. Borrower does not have option of obtaining extra funds under original loan agreement. Contrasts with Open-End Credit.

Cloud on Title: outstanding claim or encumbrance on property that may impair owner's title.

Cognovit Note: form of promissory note or statement that allows creditor, in case of default by debtor, to enter judgment without trial. (Not recognized in all jurisdictions.)

Collateral: 1. one of the "Five C's" of credit; refers to real or personal property that may be available as security. 2. asset pledged by borrower in support of loan. See also *Secured Loan*.

Collateral Note: form of promissory note given for loan, pledging real or personal property as security for payment of debt.

Collectible: account capable of being collected.

Collection Agency: professional business service employed as agent to collect creditors' unpaid (past-due) accounts. Collection agency is usually compensated by receiving agreed upon contingent percentage of amount collected.

Collection Agency Report: report from collection agency that informs client of results of collection efforts, investigations, or recommendations.

Collection Charges: 1. fees charged by bank for collecting drafts, notes, coupons, or other instruments. 2. compensation paid to collection agency or attorney for collecting delinquent accounts.

Collection Item: 1. term for item received for collection that is to be credited to depositor's account after payment. Most financial institutions charge special (collection) fees for handling such items. 2. past due account assigned for collection.

Collection Period: number of days required for company's receivables to be collected and converted to cash.

Comaker: person who signs (and guarantees) note of another and by so doing promises to pay in full. See also *Cosigner*.

Commensurate: describes deposit balances that are in acceptable proportion to size of loan or commitment.

Commercial Debt: loan or obligation incurred for business purposes.

Commercial Law League of America (C.L.L.A.): national membership organization of commercial attorneys, commercial credit and collection agencies, credit insurance companies, and law list publishers. Objectives include setting standards for honorable dealings among members, improving the practice of commercial law, and promoting uniformity of legislation affecting commercial law.

Commercial Paper: short-term securities such as notes, drafts, bills of exchange, and other negotiable paper that arise out of commercial activity and become due on a definite maturity date.

Commercial Property: real estate used for business purposes or managed so as to produce income from rents and leases.

Commitment: agreement between a financial institution and borrower to make funds available under certain conditions for a specified period of time.

Commitment Fee: lender's charge for holding credit available, usually replaced with interest when funds are advanced, as in revolving credit. In business credit, a commitment fee is often charged for unused portion of line of credit.

Commitment Letter: letter from lender stating willingness to advance funds to named borrower, repayable at specified rate and time period, subject to escape clause(s) allowing lender to rescind agreement in event of materially adverse changes in borrower's financial condition.

Committee Approval: credit is approved by several people acting as group.

Common Law: body of law that was originated, developed, and administered in England.

Community Property: property shared by husband and wife, each having one-half interest in earnings of other; form of joint property ownership in some states.

Community Reinvestment Act of 1977 (CRA): federal law that requires mortgage lenders to demonstrate their commitment to home mortgage financing in economically disadvantaged areas. Prohibits redlining or credit allocation based on geographic region and requires lenders to file annual compliance statements.

Compensating Balance: demand deposit balance that must be maintained by borrower to compensate financial institution for loan accommodations and other services.

Compound Interest: interest calculated by adding accumulated interest to date to original principal. New balance becomes principal for additional interest calculations.

Comprehensive General Liability (CGL): policy form providing automatic coverage for all insured's business operations; may include auto exposures; newer form of CGL is called commercial general liability.

Concession: 1. granting of special privilege to digress from regular terms or previous conditions. 2. allowance or rebate from established price. 3. business enterprise operated under special permission.

Conditional Sales Contract: contract for sale of goods under which possession is delivered to buyer but title retained by seller until goods are paid for in full or until other conditions are met. In most states, conditional sales contracts have been replaced by security agreements having substantially the same definition under Uniform Commercial Code.

Conditions: one of the "Five C's" of credit; refers to general business environment and status of borrower's industry.

Confession of Judgment Note: note in which (after maturity) debtor permits attorney to appear in court and have judgment entered if payment is not made as agreed. Acceptance of note varies by state. See also *Cognovit Note*.

Confirmation: 1. supplier's written acknowledgment that he or she has accepted buyer's order. 2. customer's written verification of order previously placed. 3. proof verifying agreement or existence of assets and liabilities or claims against assets and liabilities.

Consent Judgment: judgment that debtor allows to be entered against him or her by motion filed with court.

Consideration: 1. element in contract without which contract is not binding. Contract is generally not valid without consideration. 2. reason for contracting parties to enter into contract. Act, promise, price, or motive for which agreement is entered into. 3. value given in exchange for benefit that is to be derived from contract. 4. compensation. Exchange of consideration is usually mutual, each party giving something up to other.

Consign: to send or forward goods to merchant, factor, or agent for sale with title retained by seller and with payment delayed, generally until sale is made.

Consignee: person or entity to which goods or property is consigned or shipped; ultimate recipient of shipment.

Consignment: arrangement under which consignor (seller) remains owner of property until such time as consignee (buyer) pays for goods; usually consignee pays consignor when goods are sold or holds proceeds of sale in trust for benefit of consignor.

Consignor: 1. one who delivers shipment or turns it over to carrier for transportation and delivery. 2. one who consigns goods to be sold without giving up title.

Consolidated Financial Statement: combined statement showing financial condition of parent corporation and its subsidiaries.

Consolidating Financial Statement: combined statement of subsidiary and parent companies that shows complete statement for each entity without netting intercompany transactions.

Construction Loan: interim financing for development and construction of real property, generally converted to long-term financing upon completion of construction.

Consumer Credit: debt incurred for personal, family, or household use.

Consumer Credit Protection Act (Truth in Lending Act of 1968): law that requires most lenders and those who extend consumer credit to disclose true credit costs. Act provides for limits on garnishment of wages, prohibits excessive interest, and makes available contents of consumer credit reports.

Consumer Sale Disclosure Statement: form required to be provided by creditor to customer, disclosing finance charge details as required under Consumer Credit Protection Act.

Contingent Fee: fee to be paid only in event of specific occurrence, usually successful results. Arrangement, for example, in which collection agency will receive stated percentage of any amounts recovered or in which lawyer will receive payment only if successful in prosecuting lawsuit.

Contingent Liability: liability in which a person(s) or business(es) is indirectly responsible for obligations of a third party. Such indirect liability is usually established by guaranty or endorsement, and the liability holder may turn to guarantors or endorsers for satisfaction of debt. See also *Endorsement and Guaranty*.

Contra Account: account that partially or wholly offsets another account or balance.

Contract: agreement between two or more entities or legally competent persons that creates, modifies, or destroys legal arrangement.

Controlled Disbursement: funds management technique in corporate cash management designed to maximize funds available for temporary investment in money market or for payment to trade creditors. Controls flow of checks through banking system to meet corporate investment and funds management requirements. Contrasts with delayed disbursement. See also *Federal Reserve Float and Treasury Workstation*.

Controller: person in business organization responsible for finances, internal auditing, and accounting systems in use in company's operations.

Conversion: process of consolidating or transferring data from one system to another.

Conveyance: 1. transfer of right, generally instrument transferring interest in real estate in form of deed. 2. transfer of property ownership (sometimes includes leases and mortgages) from one person or organization to another.

Copyright: intangible right granted to author or originator by federal government to solely and exclusively reproduce or publish specific literary, musical, or artistic work for certain number of years.

Corporate Reorganization: see *Bankruptcy*.

Corporate Veil: convention that corporate organization insulates organization's owners from liability for corporate activities.

Corporation: artificial person or legal entity organized under and treated by state laws, legally distinct from its shareholders and vested with capacity of continuous succession irrespective of changes in its ownership either in perpetuity or for limited term. It may be set up to contract, own, and discharge business within boundaries of powers granted it by its corporate charter.

Correspondent: organization or individual that carries on business relations or acts as agent with others in different cities or countries.

Cosigner: one of joint signers of loan documents. One who signs note of another as support for credit of the principal maker.

Cost of Funds: dollar cost of interest paid or accrued on funds acquired from various sources within bank and borrowed funds acquired from other financial institutions, including time deposits, advances at Federal Reserve discount window, federal funds purchased, and Eurodollar deposits. Financial institution may use internal cost of funds in pricing loans it makes.

Covenant: written agreement, convention, or promise between parties who pledge to do or not to do certain things or that stipulates truth of certain facts.

CPA: see *Certified Public Accountant*.

CRA: see *Community Reinvestment Act of 1977*.

Crash: sudden sharp decrease in business activity that can negatively affect stock market volumes and prices.

Credit: 1. privilege of buying goods and services, or for borrowing money in return for promise of future payment. 2. in bookkeeping, entry on ledger signifying cash payment, merchandise returned, or allowance to reduce debt. 3. accounting entry on right side of ledger sheet.

Credit Advisory Board (CAB): agency established by Financial Institutions Reform, Recovery, and Enforcement Act of 1989 "to monitor the credit standards and lending practices of insured depository institutions and the supervision of such standards and practices by the federal financial regulators" as well as to "ensure that insured depository institutions can meet the demands of a modern and globally competitive world." This board was granted permanent authorization by the Federal Deposit Insurance Corporation Improvement Act of 1991. Formerly known as Credit Standards Advisory Committee (CSAC).

Credit Analyst: person who evaluates the financial history and financial statements of credit applicants to assess creditworthiness. Analysts are trained to evaluate applicant's financial strength and to opine on the probability of full repayment, collateral adequacy, or whether a credit enhancement through a cosigner or guarantor is needed.

Credit Application: form completed by potential borrower and used by creditor to determine applicant's creditworthiness.

Credit Approval: decision to extend credit.

Credit Approval System: internal methods by which credit decisions are made.

Credit Bureau: agency that gathers information and provides its subscribers with credit reports on consumers.

Credit Checking: examining and analyzing creditworthiness of customer by contacting references, reviewing credit reports, etc.

Credit Department: department within a financial institution that performs operations and credit support functions for underwriting activities. May include maintenance of credit files, credit investigations, financial statement analysis and spreading, customers' accounts receivable audits, lender training, portfolio reporting, facilitation of credit meetings, etc.

Credit Enhancement: enhancement to creditworthiness of loans underlying asset-backed security or municipal bond, generally to get investment-grade rating from bond rating agency and to improve marketability of debt securities to investors. There are two general classifications of credit enhancements:

- third-party enhancement, in which third party pledges its own creditworthiness and guarantees repayment in form of standby letter of credit or commercial letter of credit issued by a financial institution, surety bond from insurance company, or special reserve fund managed by financial guaranty firm in exchange for fee.
- self-enhancement, which is generally done by issuer through over-collateralization-that is, pledging loans with book value greater than face value of bonds offered for sale.

Credit File: creditor's file that compiles information about customer, including correspondence, credit memorandums and analyses, credit ratings, a credit history, payment patterns, and credit inquiries.

Credit Granting: approval and extension of credit to a customer.

Credit Inquiry: request made by a financial institution or trade creditor concerning the responding bank's own customer.

Credit Insurance: life and health insurance issued in conjunction with borrowing by individuals; covers payments or unpaid balance when borrower is disabled or dies; in business, covers loss of receivables when debtor becomes insolvent.

Credit Interchange: exchange of credit information between individuals or groups.

Credit Interchange Bureau (CIB): 1. local bureaus offering members or subscribers credit reports usually based on recent ledger experiences. Generally refers to organized system of cooperating bureaus operated by regional credit associations. 2. credit agency that may limit its reporting to a particular trade.

Credit Investigation: inquiry made by a financial institution or trade creditor concerning subject that is not the responding financial institution's customer.

Credit Limit: maximum amount of credit made available to customer by specific creditor.

Credit Line: commitment by a financial institution to lend funds to a borrower up to a given amount over a specified future period under certain pre-established conditions. Normally reviewed annually.

Credit Management: function of planning, organizing, implementing, and supervising credit policies of a company.

Creditor: 1. one to whom debt is owed by another as a result of a financial transaction. 2. one who extends credit and to whom money is due.

Creditors' Committee: voluntary representative group of creditors that may examine affairs of insolvent debtor. Group will usually advise as to continuation of business, study accountant's and appraiser's reports, act as watchdog over operating business, make recommendations to appropriate groups or legal body so that creditors will realize largest settlement possible, and advise as to acceptability of settlement.

Creditors' Remedies: legal rights enabling creditors to collect delinquent debts owed them.

Credit Policy: company's written procedures for making credit decisions. Used to aid company in meeting its overall risk management objectives.

Credit Process Review: assessment of entire credit-granting process concerning specific financial institution loan portfolio(s).

Credit Rating: appraisal made by a financial institution or credit agency as to creditworthiness of a person or company. Such a report will include background on owners, estimate of financial strength and ability to pay when due, and company's payment record.

Credit Record: written history of how well a customer has handled debt repayment.

Credit Report: 1. report to aid management in reaching credit, sales, and financial decisions. 2. confidential report containing information obtained by mercantile agency that has investigated a company's background, credit history, financial strength, and payment record.

Credit Reporting Agency: company or trade interchange group that confidentially supplies subscribers or members with credit information and other relevant data as to a company's ability or likelihood to pay for goods and services purchased on credit.

Credit Research Foundation (CRF): education and research affiliate of National Association of Credit Management.

Credit Review: follow-up monitoring of loan or extension of credit by credit review officer or department, senior loan committee, auditor, or regulatory agency intended to determine whether loan was made in accordance with lender's written credit standards and policies and in compliance with banking regulations. Errors, omissions, concentrations, etc., if detected by credit review process, can then be corrected by lending officers, thus preventing deterioration in credit quality and possible loan losses. Also called loan review.

Credit Risk: 1. evaluation of a customer's ability or willingness to pay debts on time. 2. risk that a financial institution assumes when it makes an irrevocable payment on behalf of its customer against insufficient funds.

Credit Scoring: statistical model used to predict the creditworthiness of credit applicants. Credit scoring estimates repayment probability based on information in credit application and credit bureau report. The two main types of credit scoring are application scoring for new accounts and behavior scoring for accounts that have been activated and are carrying balances.

Credit Terms: stated and agreed on terms for debt repayment.

Credit Union: nonprofit cooperative financial organization chartered by state or federal government to provide financial services such as deposit and loan activities to a specific and limited group of people.

Creditworthy: term used to describe individual or entity deemed worthy of extension of credit.

CSAC: see *Credit Advisory Board*.

Current Assets: short-term assets of company, including cash, accounts receivable, temporary investments, and goods and materials in inventory.

Current Liabilities: short-term obligations due within one year, including current maturities of long-term debts.

Current Open Account: sale of goods or services for which customer does not pay for each purchase but rather is required to settle in full periodically or within specified time period after each transaction.

Current Ratio: total of current assets divided by total current liabilities; used as indication of a company's liquidity and ability to service current obligations.

D

D&B: see *Dun & Bradstreet, Inc.*

Dating (Terms): extension of credit terms beyond normal terms because of industry's seasonality or unusual circumstance.

Days Sales Outstanding (DSO): a calculation that expresses the average time in days that receivables are outstanding.

DBA: see *Doing Business As*.

DDA: see *Demand Deposit Account*.

Dealer Loan: see *Floor Plan*.

Debenture: unsecured, long-term indebtedness or corporate obligation.

Debit: entry on left side of accounting ledger.

Debit Card: magnetized plastic card that permits customers to withdraw cash from automatic teller machines and make purchases with charges deducted from funds on deposit at a predesignated account.

Debt: 1. specified amount of money, goods, or services that is owed from one to another, including not only obligation of debtor to pay but also right of creditor to receive and enforce payment. 2. financial obligation of debtor.

Debtor: person or entity indebted to or owing money to another.

Debtor in Possession (DIP): In a Chapter 11 bankruptcy, a debtor may continue to maintain possession of its assets and use them in normal business operations.

Debtor-in-Possession Financing: credit facilities extended to borrower who is reorganizing under Chapter 11 bankruptcy.

Debt Ratio: measure of firm's leverage position derived by dividing total debts by equity.

Debt Service: total interest and scheduled principal payments on debt due within given time frame.

Decision: judgment, decree, or verdict pronounced by court in determination of case.

Declarations Page: policy form containing data regarding insured, policy term, premium, type and amount of coverage, designation of forms and endorsements incorporated at time policy is issued, name of insurer, and countersignature of agent.

Deductible: portion of loss that is not insured; may be stated amount deducted from loss or percentage of loss or of value of property at time of loss.

Deduction: partial amount of payment that is withheld.

Deed: legal, written document used to transfer ownership of real property from one party to another.

Deed of Trust: legal document used in some states in lieu of mortgage. Title to real property passes from seller to trustee, who holds mortgaged property until mortgage has been fully paid and then releases title to borrower. Trustee is authorized to sell property if borrower defaults, paying amount of mortgage loan to lender and any remaining balance to former owner.

Defalcation: misappropriation of funds held in trust for another.

Defamation: injury to person's or entity's character, reputation, or good name by false and malicious statements (includes both libel and slander).

Default: to fail to meet obligation or terms of loan agreement such as payment of principal or interest.

Default Charge: legally agreed upon charge or penalty added to account when payment of debt is late or another event of default occurs under a loan agreement.

Defendant: person or entity defending or denying claim; party against which suit or charge has been filed in court of law. See also *Plaintiff*.

Defer: to postpone or delay action.

Deferred Payment Sale: selling on installment plan with payments delayed or postponed until future date.

Deficiency Judgment: decree requiring debtor to pay amount remaining due under defaulted contract after secured property has been liquidated.

Deficit: difference between receipts and expenses when expenses are greater.

Defraud: to deprive person of property by fraud, deceit, or artifice.

Defunct: business that has ceased to exist and is without assets; concern that has failed.

Delayed Disbursement: practice in cash management whereby a firm pays vendors and other corporations by disbursing payments from a financial institution in a remote city. Also called remote disbursement. Contrasts with controlled disbursement. See also *Federal Reserve Float*.

Delinquent: 1. past-due obligation; overdue and unpaid account. 2. to be in arrears in payment of debts, loans, taxes. 3. to have failed in duty or responsibility.

Demand Deposit Account (DDA): funds on deposit in checking account that are payable by a financial institution upon demand of depositor. See also *Time Deposit*.

Demand Draft: written order directing that payment be made, on sight, to a third party.

Demand Letter: correspondence sent by creditor, collection agency, or lawyer to debtor requesting payment of obligation by specific date.

Demand Loan: loan with no fixed due date and payable on demand by maker of loan; loan that can be "called" by lender at any time.

Demurrage: charge that is fixed by contract and payable by recipient of goods for detaining freight car or ship longer than agreed in order to load or unload. Purpose is remuneration to owner of vessel for earnings he or she was improperly caused to lose.

Deposit: 1. amount of money given as down payment for goods or as consideration for contract. 2. funds retained in customer's bank account.

Depreciation: decline in value of fixed assets, allocating purchase cost of an asset plus additions to value over its useful economic life as outlined by the Federal Tax Code.

Derivatives: broad family of financial instruments with characteristics of forward or option contracts.

Derogatory Account Information: adverse information on customers who have not paid accounts with other creditors according to payment terms, as reported to a credit bureau.

Directors and Officers Liability Insurance: legal liability coverage for wrongful acts including breach of duty but not fraud or dishonesty. Often known as E & O, or Errors and Omissions Insurance.

Disbursement: full or partial advancement of funds.

Discharge: 1. to cancel or release obligation. 2. to release debtor from all or most debts in bankruptcy.

Disclaimer Statement: notice disclaiming responsibility for accuracy, completeness, or timeliness of credit information. Most disclaimer statements urge recipients of the information not to rely unduly on it and stress the confidential nature of information being disclosed.

Discontinued Operations: operations of a segment of a company, usually a subsidiary whose activities represent a separate line of business that, although still operating, is the subject of a formal plan of disposal approved by management.

Discount: 1. interest deducted from face amount of note at time loan is made. 2. trade term used for reduction of invoice amount when payment has been made within specified terms.

Discounted Note: 1. borrowing arrangement in which interest is deducted from face amount of note before proceeds are advanced (see also *Note*). 2. term used when customer endorses note received from another party and presents it to a financial institution to obtain funds.

Dishonor: to fail to make payment of negotiable instrument on its due date.

Disintermediation: withdrawal of funds from interest-bearing deposit accounts when rates on competing financial instruments, such as money market mutual funds, stocks, and bonds, offer better returns.

Dismissal: court order or judgment disposing action, suit, or motion without trial.

Dispossess: legal action taken by landlord to put individual or business tenant out of his or her property.

Dissolution of Corporation: termination of entity's existence by law, expiration of charter, loss of all members, or failure to meet statutory level of members.

Distribution: one or more payments made to creditors who have approved claims filed in a bankruptcy proceeding, assignment for the benefit of creditors, or receivership.

Distributor: business engaged in the distribution or marketing of manufacturer's goods to customers or dealers. See also *Wholesaler*.

Dividend: 1. periodic distribution of cash or property to shareholders of corporation as return on their investment.

Document: any written instrument that records letters with figures or marks that may be used as evidence.

Documentary Evidence: any written record or inanimate object, as distinguished from oral evidence.

Documents of Title: Include bill of lading, dock warrant, dock receipt, warehouse receipt, order for the delivery of goods, and any other document that in the regular course of business or financing is treated as adequately evidencing that the person in possession of it is entitled to receive, hold, and dispose of the document and the goods it covers. To be a document of title, a document must purport to be issued by, or addressed to, a bailee and purport to cover goods in the bailee's possession that are either identified or are fungible portions of an identified mass.

Doing Business As (DBA): reference term placed before trade name under which business operates. Sometimes used as fictitious trade style acknowledging that name is not part of corporation title or registered trademark.

Domestic Corporation: company doing business in state in which it is incorporated.

Dormant Account: inactive deposit account in which there have been no deposits or withdrawals for a long period of time.

Doubtful Assets: assets that have all weaknesses inherent in substandard assets with added characteristic that weaknesses make collection or liquidation in full, on basis of currently existing facts, conditions, and values, highly questionable and improbable. Possibility of loss is extremely high. Because of cer-tain important and reasonably specific pending factors that may strengthen assets, classification as estimated loss is deferred until more exact status may be determined. Pending factors include proposed merger, acquisition, or liquidation procedures, capital injection, perfecting liens on additional collateral, and refinancing plans.

Downgrading: 1. lowering of assessment of customer's creditworthiness. 2. worsening the internally assigned credit quality rating of a loan or relationship in order to appropriately report risk.

Down Payment: up-front partial payment made to secure right to purchase goods.

Downstream Funding: funds borrowed by holding company for a subsidiary's use, generally to obtain more favorable rate; contrasts with Upstream Funding.

Draft: written order by one party (drawer) directing second party (drawee) to pay sum of money to third party (payee). See also *Banker's Acceptance, Letter of Credit, Sight Draft,* and *Time Draft.*

Drawee: person or entity that is expected to pay check or draft when instrument is presented for payment.

Drawer: party instructing drawee to pay someone else by writing or drawing check or draft. Also called maker or writer.

Drop Shipment: shipment of goods delivered directly from manufacturer to customer.

DSO: see *Days Sales Outstanding*.

Dual Banking: banking system in U.S., consisting of state banks, chartered and supervised by state banking departments, and national banks, chartered and regulated by Office of the Comptroller of the Currency.

Due Date: stated maturity date for debt obligation.

Due Diligence: 1. responsibility of an entity's directors and officers to act in a prudent manner in evaluating credit applications; in essence, using same degree of care that an ordinary person would use in making same analysis. 2. review that is made of a loan portfolio of a potential merger candidate by an acquiring institution.

Due Process of Law: law in its regular course of administration through courts as guaranteed by U.S. Constitution.

Dun: to repeatedly demand payment of debt; to be insistent in following debtor for payment.

Dun & Bradstreet, Inc. (D&B): international mercantile agency supplying information and credit ratings on all types of businesses.

Dun Letter: letter or notice sent by creditor requesting payment of past-due debt.

D-U-N-S Number: (Data Universal Numbering System) code developed by Dun & Bradstreet that identifies specific business name and location.

Durable Goods: goods that provide long-lasting qualities and continuing services.

Duress: unlawful constraint that forces person to do what he or she would not have done by choice.

Duty: 1. legal, moral, or ethical obligation. 2. tax collected on import or export of goods.

E

Earnest Money: money that one contracting party gives to another at the time of entering into the contract in order to bind the contract in good faith, and which will be forfeited if the purchaser fails to carry out the contract.

Earnings Report: 1. income statement showing a business's or individual's revenues and expenses for stated period of time.

Easement: right of owner of one parcel of land to use land of another for special purpose. Usually easement rights pass with land when it is sold.

Edge Act: banking legislation, passed in 1919, that allows national banks to conduct foreign lending operations through federal or state-chartered subsidiaries called Edge Act corporations. Such corporations can be chartered by other states and are allowed to own banks in foreign countries and to invest in foreign commercial and industrial firms.

EFT: see *Electronic Funds Transfer*.

Electronic Funds Transfer (EFT): computerized system enabling funds to be debited, credited, or transferred between financial institution accounts and vendors.

Embezzlement: fraudulent appropriation of one's property by person to whom it was entrusted.

Encumbrance: any right or interest in real or other property that diminishes the property's value and alters control of disposition.

Endorsement: 1. act of writing one's name on back of note, bill, check, or similar written instrument for payment of money; required on negotiable instrument to pass title properly to another. By signing such instrument, endorser becomes party to it and thereby liable, under certain conditions, for its payment. 2. change or addition to insurance policy, informally called rider.

Entrepreneur: person who plans, organizes, and runs operation of new business.

EOM Terms: Shipments during a month are invoiced in a single statement dated as of the last day of that month or the first day of the following month.

Equal Credit Opportunity Act of 1974: Federal Reserve Regulation B that prohibits creditors from discriminating against credit applicants on basis of age,

race, color, religion, national origin, sex, marital status, age, or receipt of public assistance.

Equitable Subordination: principles in section 510 (c) of U.S. Bankruptcy Code that permit bankruptcy court to subordinate, for purposes of distribution, all or part of creditor's claim against debtor's estate to claims of another creditor of that debtor after court has determined that first creditor has engaged in some form of wrongful conduct that has improved position relative to other creditors.

Equity: value of ownership, calculated by subtracting total liabilities from total assets.

Escheat: right of state to claim property or money if there is no legal claim made to it.

Escrow Account: deposit account to which access is restricted or limited by terms of written agreement entered into by three parties, including a financial institution.

Estate: any right, title, or interest that a person may have in lands or other personal property.

Estimate: amount of labor, materials, and other costs that a contractor anticipates for a project, as summarized in contractor's bid proposal for project.

Event of Default: a breach of an agreement between parties to a contract; a violation of one or more of the loan covenants as set forth in either the loan agreement, commitment letter, or promissory note.

Evergreen Revolving Credit: commitment to lend money that remains in effect unless lender takes specific action to terminate agreement; agreement may provide that, in event of termination, any outstanding amount will convert to term loan.

Exchange Rate: value of one country's currency to that of another country at a particular point in time.

Exclusive Sales Agreement: contractual arrangement, generally between a retailer and a manufacturer or wholesaler, giving retailer exclusive rights for sale of articles or services within a defined geographic area or through a defined distribution channel.

Execute: to complete and give validity to a legal document by signing, sealing, and delivering it.

Exempt: 1. to release, discharge, or waive from a liability to which others in the same general class are subject. 2. property not available for seizure.

Exemption: 1. immunity from general burden, tax, or charge. 2. legal right of debtor to hold portion of property free from claims or judgments.

Expense: cost or outlay of money used in business operating cycle.

Export-Import Bank: also called Ex-Im Bank. Provides guarantees of working capital loans for U.S. exporters; guarantees the repayment of loans or makes loans to foreign purchasers of U.S. goods and services. Ex-Im Bank also provides credit insurance that protects U.S. exporters against the risks of non-payment by foreign buyers for political or commercial reasons. Ex-Im Bank does not compete with commercial lenders, but assumes the risks they cannot accept.

F

Face Amount: indicated value of a financial instrument, as shown on its front.

Facility Fee: lender's charge for making a line of credit or other credit facility available to borrower (for example, a commitment fee).

Facsimile: exact copy of an original.

Factor: entity that purchases borrower's accounts receivable and may extend funds to borrower prior to collection of receivables.

Factoring: short-term financing from nonrecourse sale of accounts receivable to third party or factor. Factor assumes full risk of collection, including credit losses. Factoring is most common in the garment industry, but has been used in other industries as well. There are two basic types of factoring:
- discount factoring, in which factor pays discounted price for receivables before maturity date.
- maturity factoring, in which factor pays the client purchase price of factored accounts at maturity.

Fair Credit Billing Act of 1974 (FCBA): Federal Reserve Regulation Z details the provisions of this act by prescribing uniform methods of computing the cost of consumer credit, disclosure of credit terms, and procedures for resolving billing errors on certain kinds of credit accounts.

Fair Credit Reporting Act: federal legislation that regulates consumer credit reporting activities and gives consumer right to learn contents of his or her credit bureau file.

Fair Market Value: price that property would sell for between willing buyer and willing seller, neither of whom is obligated to effect transaction.

Fannie Mae: see *Federal National Mortgage Association*.

FASB: see *Financial Accounting Standards Board*.

FFB: see *Federal Financing Bank*.

FCBA: see *Fair Credit Billing Act of 1974*.

FDIC: see *Federal Deposit Insurance Corporation*.

FDICIA: see *Federal Deposit Insurance Corporation Improvement Act of 1991*.

Federal Deposit Insurance Corporation (FDIC): 1. federal agency that insures bank accounts for up to $100,000 at both commercial banks and thrifts through Bank Insurance Fund and Savings Association Fund. 2. federal regulator for state-chartered banks that are not members of Federal Reserve System.

Federal Deposit Insurance Corporation Improvement Act of 1991 (FDICIA): legislation that provides for recapitalization of Bank Insurance Fund and restructuring of financial services industry through:
- emphasis on more capital.
- government standards for lending, operations, and asset growth.
- quicker government seizure of struggling institutions.
- reduced liquidity options for all but the strongest banks.
- incentives for uninsured depositors to use only the largest and strongest banks.
- sharply increased regulatory costs and fees.
- easier rules for acquiring banks and thrifts.

Federal Financial Institutions Examination Council (FFIEC): interagency group of federal banking regulators formed in 1979 to maintain uniform standards for federal examination and supervision of federally insured depository institutions, bank holding companies, and savings and loan holding companies. Also runs schools for examiners employed by banks, thrifts, and credit union agencies. Council produces Uniform Bank Performance Report.

Federal Financing Bank (FFB): agency in U.S. Treasury established by Congress in 1973 to centralize borrowing by federal agencies. Instead of selling securities directly to financial markets, all but largest federal agencies raise capital by borrowing from U.S. Treasury through FFB. FFB makes loans at favorable rates to agencies that do not have ready access to credit markets; its debt is direct obligation of U.S. Treasury.

Federal Funds: unsecured advances of immediately available funds from excess balances in reserve accounts held at Federal Reserve Banks. Technically, these funds are not borrowings but purchases of immediately available funds. Banks advancing federal funds sell excess reserves; banks receiving federal funds buy excess reserves from selling banks. Federal funds sold are credit transactions on account of selling banks. See also *Federal Funds Rate*.

Federal Funds Rate: rate charged in interbank market for purchases of excess reserve balances. Rate of interest is key money market interest rate and correlates with rates on other short-term credit arrangements. Because the federal funds rate re-prices with each transaction, it is the most sensitive of money market rates and is watched carefully by the Federal Reserve Board.

Federal Home Loan Bank Board (FHLBB): federal agency established by Federal Home Loan Bank Act of 1932 to supervise reserve credit system, Federal Home Loan Bank System, for savings institutions. Board also acted as chartering agency and primary regulator of federal savings and loan associations under Home Owners Loan Act of 1933. Financial Institutions Reform, Recovery, and Enforcement Act of 1989 abolished board, transferring its powers in examination and supervision of federally chartered savings institutions to new agency, Office of Thrift Supervision, bureau of U.S. Treasury Department. Regulatory oversight of district Home Loan Banks was transferred to the five-member Federal Housing Finance Board.

Federal Home Loan Bank System: system of 11 regional banks established by Federal Home Loan Bank Act of 1932, acting as central credit system for savings and loan institutions. District Home Loan Banks make short-term credit advances to savings institutions, much like Federal Reserve System acts as lender of last resort to commercial banks. Each Home Loan Bank operates independently and has its own board of directors.

Federal Home Loan Mortgage Corporation (FHLMC): corporation authorized by Congress in 1970 as secondary market conduit for residential mortgages. Corporation purchases loans from mortgage originators and sells its own obligations and mortgage-backed bonds issued by Government National Mortgage Association to private investors, namely financial institution trust funds, insurance companies, pension funds, and thrift institutions. Also called Freddie Mac.

Federal Housing Administration (FHA): federal agency that insures residential mortgages. Created by National Housing Act of 1934, FHA is now part of Department of Housing and Urban Development. Both FHA and Department of Veterans Affairs have single-family mortgage programs to assist homebuyers who are unable to obtain financing from conventional mortgage lenders (banks, savings and loans, and other financial institutions).

Federal Housing Finance Board (FHFB): independent federal agency regulating credit advance activities of 11 Federal Home Loan Banks. This board, established by Financial Institutions Reform, Recovery, and Enforcement Act of 1989, has five members, including secretary of Housing and Urban Development, and four directors appointed by the President with Senate confirmation to serve seven-year terms. At least one director must represent the interests of community groups.

Federal National Mortgage Association (FNMA): federally chartered, stockholder-owned corporation that purchases residential mortgages insured or guaranteed by federal agencies, as well as conventional mortgages, in sec-

ondary mortgage market. Corporation raises capital to support its operations through collection of insurance and commitment fees, issuance of stock, and sale of debentures and notes. Also called Fannie Mae.

Federal Open Market Committee (FOMC): policy committee in Federal Reserve System that sets short-term monetary policy objectives for Fed. Committee is made up of seven governors of Federal Reserve Board, plus the presidents of six Federal Reserve Banks. President of Federal Reserve Bank of New York is permanent FOMC member. The other five slots are filled on rotating basis by presidents of other 11 Federal Reserve Banks. Committee carries out monetary objectives by instructing Open Market Desk at Federal Reserve Bank of New York to buy or sell government securities from special account, called open market account, at New York Fed.

Federal Reserve Board (FRB): U.S.'s central bank responsible for conduct of monetary policy; also oversees state-chartered banks that are members of Federal Reserve System, bank holding companies, and Edge Act corporations.

Federal Reserve Float: total amount of funds that Federal Reserve Banks, in their role as clearing agents, have credited to depositing institutions but have not charged to paying institutions.

Federal Reserve System: central bank of U.S. created by Federal Reserve Act of 1913. System consists of Board of Governors, made up of seven members, and a network of 12 Federal Reserve Banks and 25 branches throughout U.S. Board of Governors is responsible for setting monetary policy and reserve requirements. Board and banks share responsibility for setting the discount rate, the interest rate that depository institutions are charged for borrowing from Federal Reserve Banks.

Federal Trade Commission (FTC): federal regulatory agency that administers and enforces rules to prevent unfair business practices.

Fee Simple: estate in which owner is entitled to entire property and has unconditional power over its disposition.

FFIEC: see *Federal Financial Institutions Examination Council.*

FHA: see *Federal Housing Administration.*

FHLBB: see *Federal Home Loan Bank Board.*

FHLMC: see *Federal Home Loan Mortgage Corporation.*

Fictitious Name: pretend name used by firm in business transactions. Company is usually required to register this name with local authorities, along with true names and addresses of company's owners.

Fidelity Bond: contract issued by insurer to employer to cover loss caused by dishonest acts of employees; form of suretyship. Also called dishonesty insurance.

Fiduciary: person or entity acting in capacity of trustee for another.

Field Warehousing: method of using company's inventory to secure business loan. In leased and separate storage area of borrower's facility, goods act as security for loan and are released by custodian only upon lender's order.

FIFO: see *First-In First-Out.*

File: 1. organized folder containing accumulation of information and items retained for preservation or reference. 2. to deposit legal document with proper authority.

File Revision: routine gathering of credit information by credit grantor to update files on borrowers.

Filing Claims: 1. depositing of formal papers with proper public office and in manner and time frame prescribed by law in order to preserve creditor's rights. 2. method used to perfect security interest accomplished by recording in proper public office.

Finance Charges: total costs to an individual or business of obtaining credit, including interest and any fees.

Financial Analysis: evaluation by credit analyst of customer's financial situation to determine whether customer has ability to meet his or her obligations as they become due. Factors such as general condition of customer's industry, organizational structure, available collateral or guarantors, and past financial performance are considered.

Financial Accounting Standards Board (FASB): independent board responsible for establishing and interpreting generally accepted accounting principles, formed in 1973 to succeed and continue activities of Accounting Principles Board.

Financial Institutions Reform, Recovery, and Enforcement Act of 1989 (FIRREA): act signed into law on August 9, 1989, to provide funding and regulatory structure necessary to close several hundred insolvent savings associations and liquidate their assets, to consolidate federal insurance of banks and savings associations under direction of the Federal Deposit Insurance Corporation, to provide regulatory agencies with sweeping new enforcement powers, and to increase substantially civil and criminal penalties for violations of federal banking statutes and regulations. Act substantially alters relationship between savings institutions and regulators and imposes new requirements that must be observed in day-to-day operations of institutions.

Financial Position: standing of company, combining assets and liabilities as entered on balance sheet.

Financial Statements: reports consisting of individual's or company's balance sheet, income statement, and statement of cash flows, footnotes, and any supplemental schedules.

Financing Statement: form required to be completed by creditor and filed with appropriate county and state authorities in order to perfect creditor's security interest in collateral and to give public notice of such interest.

FIRREA: see *Financial Institutions Reform, Recovery, and Enforcement Act of 1989.*

First Deed of Trust: first recorded deed of trust that acts as first lien on property it describes.

First-In First-Out (FIFO): method of valuing inventory in which the first goods received are the first goods used or sold. Using this method, costs of inventory used to determine cost of goods sold are related to costs that were incurred first.

First Mortgage: mortgage on property that is superior to any others by fact of having been filed first.

Fiscal: anything involving financial matters or issues.

Fiscal Agent: person or organization serving as another's financial agent or representative.

Fiscal Year: fixed accounting year used as basis for annual financial reporting by business or government.

Five C's of Credit: method of evaluating potential borrower's creditworthiness based on five criteria: Capacity, Capital, Character, Collateral, and Conditions.

Fixed Assets: property used in normal course of business that is of a long-term nature, such as land, machinery, fixtures, and equipment.

Fixed-Rate Loan: loan with interest rate that does not vary over term of loan.

Fixture: that which is permanently attached or affixed to real property.

Flagging an Account: temporarily identifying an account for specific purpose or reason; may involve suspending activity.

Float: uncollected funds represented by checks deposited in one bank but not yet cleared through bank on which they are drawn.

Floating Interest Rate: loan interest rate that changes whenever the stated index rate, or base rate, changes.

Floating Lien: loan or credit facility secured by inventory or receivables. This type of security agreement gives lender interest in assets acquired by borrower after agreement, as well as those owned when agreement was made. When agreement covers proceeds from sales, lender also has recourse against cash collected from the payment of receivables.

Floor Plan: loan made to dealer for purchase of inventory acquired for resale and secured by that inventory, such as automobiles or appliances.

FNMA: see *Federal National Mortgage Association.*

FOB: see *Free on Board.*

FOB Point: point at which responsibility for freight charges begins and title passes. See also *Free on Board.*

FOMC: see *Federal Open Market Committee.*

Forbearance: Temporarily giving up the right to enforce a valid claim, in return for a promise. It is sufficient consideration to make a promise binding (for example, protracted payment arrangements or interest rate reduction in exchange for additional collateral or guarantors).

Forced Sale: 1. court-ordered sale of property, usually without owner's approval. 2. voluntary sale of goods or property to raise cash or to reduce inventory.

Foreclosure: legal termination of all of debtor's rights in property secured by mortgage after debtor has defaulted on obligation supported by such mortgage.

Foreign Corporation: corporation established under laws of a state other than that in which it is doing business.

Foreign Exchange: conversion of money of one country into its equivalent in currency of another country.

Foreign Item: check drawn on any financial institution other than the financial institution where it is presented for payment. Also called transit item.

Foreign Judgment: judgment obtained in state or country other than the one where the debtor now lives, is doing business, or has assets.

Forfeiture: penalty resulting in automatic loss of cash, property, or rights for not complying with legal terms of agreement.

Forgery: false making or material altering of any writing with intent to defraud.

Form 8K: report disclosing significant events potentially affecting corporation's financial condition or market value of its shares, required by Securities and Exchange Commission. Report is filed within 30 days after event (pending merger, amendment to corporate charter, charge to earnings for credit losses) took place and summarizes information that any reasonable investor would want to know before buying or selling securities.

Form 10K: annual financial report filed with Securities and Exchange Commission. Issuers of registered securities are required to file 10K, as are corporations with 500 or more shareholders or assets of $2 million and exchange-listed corporations. Report, which becomes public information once filed, summarizes key financial information, including sources and uses of funds by type of business, net pretax operating income, provision for income taxes and

credit losses, plus comparative financial statements for past two fiscal years. Summary of 10K report is included in annual report to stockholders.

Form 10Q: quarterly financial report filed by companies with listed securities and those corporations required to file annual 10K report with Securities and Exchange Commission. 10Q report, which does not have to be audited, summarizes key financial data on earnings and expenses and compares current financial information with data reported in same quarter of previous year.

Forwarding: referral or placement of out-of-town claims with attorney who then acts on behalf of creditor. In collection process, when authorized, agency may forward account to attorney for collection or suit.

Franchise: business agreement whereby one company allows another the right to conduct business under its name and/or distribute its products in exchange for royalties or another agreed upon method of payment.

Fraud: any act of deceit, omission, or commission used to deprive someone of right or property. Elements of fraud consist of intentional misrepresentation of fact, relied on by another to his or her detriment, that results in damages.

Fraudulent Conveyance: a transfer of property by a debtor, for the intent and purpose of defrauding creditors. Such property may be reached by the creditors through appropriate legal proceedings.

FRB: see *Federal Reserve Board.*

Freddie Mac: see *Federal Home Loan Mortgage Corporation.*

Free and Clear: 1. property with an unencumbered title. 2. title that is free of defects.

Free and Clear Delivery Receipt: delivery receipt signed by consignee completely absolving carrier from any claim for loss or damages.

Free Astray: freight shipment that has been lost. If it is carrier's fault and shipment is located, it is carrier's obligation to make delivery to original destination at no additional cost to shipper or consignee.

Free Demand Letter Service: pre-collection letter sent by collection agency to debtor, requesting that payment be made directly to creditor by given date. No charge is made for payments received within free demand period, but balances remaining unpaid are followed for collection by agency at its regular rates.

Free on Board (FOB): term identifying shipping point from which buyer assumes all responsibilities and costs for transportation.

Free Port: place where goods are imported or exported free of any duty.

Freight Forwarder: business that receives goods for transportation; services include consolidation of small freight shipments of less than carload, truckload, or container lots assembled for lower shipping rates.

Frozen Account: 1. account to which customer no longer has access. 2. account suspended by court order, violation of loan covenants, or checking account agreement, etc.

Frozen Assets: any assets that cannot be used by owner because of pending legal action.

FTC: see *Federal Trade Commission.*

Fund: cash or equivalents set aside for specific purpose.

Fund Accounting: fiscal and accounting entity with self-balancing set of accounts recording cash and other financial resources, together with all related liabilities and residual equities or balances, and changes therein, which are segregated for purpose of carrying on specific activities or obtaining certain objectives in accordance with special regulations, restrictions, or limitations.

Funded Debt: mortgages, bonds, debentures, notes, or other obligations with maturity of more than one year from statement date.

G

GAAP: see *Generally Accepted Accounting Principles.*

Garnishee: 1. person or entity that has possession of money or property belonging to defendant and is served with writ of garnishment to hold money or property for payment of defendant's debt to plaintiff. 2. one against whom garnishment has been served.

Garnishment: legal warning or procedure to one in possession of another's property not to allow owner access to such property as it will be used to satisfy judgment against owner.

General Contractor: contractor who enters into a contract with an owner for construction of a project and who takes full responsibility for its completion. Contractor may enter into subcontracts with various subcontractors for performance of specific parts or phases of project.

General Ledger: bookkeeping record comprising all assets, liabilities, proprietorship, revenue, and expense accounts. Entries for each account are posted, and balances are included for each entry.

Generally Accepted Accounting Principles (GAAP): conventions, rules, and procedures that define accepted accounting practices, including broad guidelines as well as detailed procedures. Financial Accounting Standards Board, an independent self-regulatory organization, is responsible for promulgating these principles.

General Obligation Debt: long-term debt or bond repaid from all otherwise unrestricted revenues, sales taxes, property taxes, license fees, property sales, rents, and so forth of municipality.

General Partner: participant in a business relationship who is personally liable, without limitation, for all partnership debts.

Ginnie Mae: see *Government National Mortgage Association.*

GNMA: see *Government National Mortgage Association.*

Going Concern: assumes that a business entity has a reasonable expectation of continuing in business and generating a profit for an indefinite period of time.

Goods on Approval: goods offered by seller to buyer with option of examining goods for specific period of time before deciding to purchase them.

Goodwill: 1. intangible assets of business consisting of its good reputation, valuable clientele, or desirable location that results in above normal earning power. 2. value or amount for which business could be sold above book value of its physical property and receivables.

Government National Mortgage Association (GNMA): corporation created by Congress that administers mortgage-backed securities program that channels new sources of funds into residential mortgages through sale of securities. Also called Ginnie Mae.

Grace Period: specified length of time beyond payment due date during which late fee will not be assessed.

Grantee: person to whom title in property is made.

Grantor: person who transfers title to property.

Gross Margin: gross profit as a percentage of sales.

Gross Profit: net sales less cost of sales.

Gross Sales: sales before returns and allowances; discounts are deducted to arrive at net sales.

Guarantor: person who agrees by execution of a contract to repay the debt of another if that person defaults.

Guaranty: separate agreement by which a party (or parties) other than debtor assumes responsibility for payment of obligation if principal debtor defaults or is subsequently unable to perform under the terms of the obligation.

Guardian: person who is legally responsible for the care and management of a minor or individual who is not mentally or legally competent (or of such person's property).

H

Hard Goods: durable consumer goods, usually including such items as major appliances and furniture, with relatively long, useful lives.

Heavy Industry: industry involved in manufacturing basic products such as metals, machinery, or other equipment.

Hidden Assets: assets not easily identified and either intentionally not disclosed or publicly reported at lower value than their true worth.

High Credit: largest amount of credit used by borrower during specified period of time.

Holder in Due Course: person who has taken negotiable instrument (check or note) for value, in good faith, and on assurance that it is complete and regular, not overdue or dishonored, and has no defect in ownership on part of previous holder or endorser.

Holding Company: company organized to hold and control stock in other companies.

Homestead Exemption: state's law allowing householder or head of family to exempt residence from attachment by creditors.

Housing and Urban Development, Department of: cabinet-level federal agency, founded in 1965, that promotes housing development in U.S. through direct loans, mortgage insurance, and guaranties. It houses Federal Housing Administration and Government National Mortgage Association.

HUD: see *Housing and Urban Development, Department of.*

Hypothecate: to pledge or assign property owned by one entity as security or collateral for loan to second entity.

Hypothecation: 1. offer of stocks, bonds, or other assets owned by party other than borrower as collateral for loan, without transferring title. Borrower retains possession but gives lender right to sell property in event of default by borrower. 2. pledging of negotiable securities to collateralize broker's margin loan. If broker pledges same securities to bank as collateral for broker's loan, process is referred to as re-hypothecation.

I

Immunity: condition of being exempt from duty that others are generally required to perform.

Import Letter of Credit: commercial letter of credit issued to finance import of goods.

Import Duty: government tax on imported items.

Impound: to seize or take into legal custody, usually at order of court. Cash, documents, or records may be impounded.

Inactive Account: account that has shown little or no activity over a substantial period of time.

Inactive Files: 1. accounts on which collection activity has been completed or suspended (claims either collected or found to be uncollectible) and on which no further work is being done. Also called closed or dead files. 2. stored records available for reference.

In Arrears: amounts due but not yet paid.

Income Property: real property acquired as investment and managed for profit.

Income Statement: summary of revenue and expenses covering a specified period.

Income Tax: tax levied by federal, state, or local governments on personal or business earnings.

Incorporation: formation of legal entity, with qualities of perpetual existence and succession.

Incumbrance: see *Encumbrance*.

Indebtedness: total amount of money or liabilities owed.

In Default: failing to abide by terms and conditions of note or loan agreement. This can include payments on interest or principal (or both) being past due.

Indemnity: 1. contract or assurance to reimburse another against anticipated loss, damage, or failure to fulfill obligation. 2. type of insurance that provides coverage for losses of this nature.

Indirect Liability: contingent liability such as a continuing guarantee.

Individual Signature: credit approved by one person on his or her own authority.

Indorsement: see *Endorsement*.

Industrial Consumer: purchaser who buys goods or services for business purposes.

Inquiry: request for credit information on a bank's customer.

Insider Loans: loans to directors and officers of bank, which must be reported to bank regulators under Financial Institutions Reform Act of 1978. Banking laws require that loans to insiders be made at substantially the same rate and credit terms as loans to other borrowers.

Insolvency: 1. inability to meet debts as they become due in ordinary course of business. 2. financial condition in which assets are not sufficient to satisfy liabilities.

Installment Sale: contract sale in which merchandise is purchased with down payment and balance is made in partial payments over agreed period of time.

Instrument: written formal or legal document.

In-Substance Foreclosure Assets: loans for which borrower is perceived to have little or no equity in the asset or project and the financial institution can reasonably anticipate proceeds for repayment only from the operation or sale of collateral.

Insufficient Funds: see *Non-sufficient Funds*.

Insurable Interest: interest such that loss or damage inflicts economic loss.

Insurable Value: maximum possible loss to which property is exposed; actual amount depends on basis of calculation per insurance policy.

Intangible Assets: nonmaterial assets of business that have no value in themselves but that represent value. Examples include trademarks, goodwill, patents, and copyrights.

Interchange: confidential exchange of credit information between individuals and trade groups.

Interchange Bureau: association organized to record and exchange or furnish confidential credit information about a member's payment experience and manner in which customers meet obligations.

Interchange Group: trade membership group within specific industry that meets regularly to exchange credit experiences and other confidential information.

Interchange Report: report usually obtained through credit interchange bureau showing recent credit experience as supplied by participating members.

Inter-creditor Agreement: document used when there is more than one lender involved in credit transaction to spell out each lender's rights and obligations.

Interest: 1. legally allowed or agreed upon compensation to lender for use of borrowed money. 2. any right in property but less than title to it.

Interest Bearing: term describing note or contract calling for payment of agreed interest.

Interest Only: loan term during which no principal repayments are made.

Interest Rate: cost of borrowing money expressed as an annualized percentage of the loan.

Internal Guidance Line of Credit: credit facility similar to a line of credit, but customer may or may not be advised of it; established for internal financial institution purposes, it provides financing for recurrent requests without referring each one to credit committee or other approval source.

International Consumer Credit Association: professional trade association of retail credit professionals. Association keeps members informed of latest developments in consumer credit and provides educational courses, seminars, textbooks, and other published material.

Intestate: dying without leaving valid will or any other specific instructions as to disposition of property.

Inventory: current assets of business that represent goods for sale, including raw materials, work in process, and finished goods.

Investigation: 1. gathering of credit information on a person or entity. 2. systematic research for information necessary for a business decision.

Investment: use of money for purpose of earning profit or return.

Investor: person or entity that puts money to use for capital appreciation or profit or to receive regular dividends.

Invoice: seller's descriptive, itemized billing for goods or services sold, showing date, terms, cost, purchase order number, method of shipment, and other identifying information.

Involuntary Bankruptcy: see *Bankruptcy*.

Itemized Statement: detailed listing of activity on account for particular period of time.

J

Jobber: see *Wholesaler*.

Joint Account: financial institution account shared or owned in name of two or more persons with full privileges available to each person.

Joint and Several: relative to liability, a term used when creditor has option of pursuing one or more signers of an agreement individually or all signers together.

Joint Tenancy with Rights of Survivorship: interest in property held by two or more persons that includes right of survivorship in which deceased person's interest passes to survivors. See also *Tenancy by Entirety*.

Joint Venture: business or undertaking entered into on one-time basis by two or more parties in which profits, losses, and control are shared.

Journal: account book of original entry in which all money receipts and expenses are chronologically recorded.

Judgment: court's determination of rights of parties to claim.

Judgment Creditor: one who has obtained judgment against debtor and can enforce it.

Judgment Debtor: one against whom judgment has been recovered but not satisfied.

Judgment Note: see *Cognovit Note*.

Judgment Lien: claim or encumbrance on property, allowed by law, usually against real estate of judgment debtor.

Judgment-Proof: term to describe judgment debtor from whom collection cannot be obtained or person who has no money or assets or has concealed or removed property subject to execution.

Judicial Sale: see *Forced Sale*.

Junior Mortgage: any mortgage filed after and subject to satisfaction of first mortgage.

Jurisdiction: 1. legal authority, power, capacity, and right of court to act. 2. geographic area within which court or government agency exercises power.

K

Keyperson Life Insurance: insurance policy written on owner or principal employee in which death benefits are payable to company.

Key Ratios: performance measures used to determine probable ability of business to operate profitably. Results are expressed in percentages that are then weighed against average percentages in each industry.

L

Landlord's Waiver: the relinquishment of a right(s) contained in a lease agreement by a lessor.

Last-In First-Out (LIFO): method of valuating inventory in which last goods received are the first ones sold. Using this method, inventory costs used to determine cost of goods sold are related to costs of inventory that were incurred last.

Late Charge: special legally agreed upon fee, charged by creditor, on any payment that is not made when due.

Lawful Money: legal tender for payment of all debts.

Law List: compiled publication of names and addresses of those in legal profession, often including court calendars, private investigators, and other information of interest to legal profession.

Lawsuit: suit, action, or cause instituted by one person against another in a court of law.

Lead Bank: financial institution that has the primary deposit or lending relationship in a multi-bank situation; usually in the context of shared credit and sometimes defined within an inter-creditor agreement. See also *Agent Bank*.

Leaseback: agreement by which one party sells property to another and, after completing sale, the first party rents it from second party.

Lease Contract: written agreement for which equipment or facilities can be obtained on rental payment basis for specified period of time.

Leased Department: section of department store not operated by store but by independent outside organization on contract or percentage-of-sales arrangement.

Leasehold: rights tenant holds in property as conferred by terms of lease.

Leasehold Improvement: permanent improvements made to rented property. Leasehold improvements are considered fixtures and depreciate over lease period.

Leasehold Interest: lessee's equity or ownership in leasehold improvements.

Lease-Purchase Agreement: contract providing for set amount of lease payments to be applied to purchase of property.

Ledger: in accounting, book of permanent records containing series of accounts to which debits and credits of transactions are posted from books of original entry.

Ledger Experience: trade experience reported by credit manager or interchange group. Such reports provide picture of account's paying habits, high credit, and terms of repayment.

Legal and Sovereign Risk: risk that government may intervene to affect bank's system or any participant of such system detrimentally.

Legal Composition: identification and description of lawful ownership or title to business entity.

Legal Entity: business organization that has capacity to make contract or agreement or assume obligation. Such organization may consist of individual proprietorship, partnership, corporation, or association.

Legal Right: natural right, right created by contract, and right created or recognized by law.

Legal Tender: any money that is recognized by law for payment of debt unless contract exists specifically calling for payment in another type of money.

Legal Title: document establishing right of ownership to property that is recognized and upheld by law.

Lender: one who extends funds to another with expectation of repayment with interest.

Lender's Loss Payable Endorsement: form attached to property insurance policies to cover lender's interest in what is insured; extends coverage to give lender protection beyond that in basic policy; language may be prescribed by banking industry, standard form prepared by insurance industry, or specified by lender. See also *Loss Payee Clause*.

Lessee: one to whom lease is given and therefore has right to use property in exchange for rental payments.

Lessor: owner who grants lease for use of property in return for rent.

Letter of Agreement: letter stating terms of agreement between addressor and addressee, usually prepared for signature by addressee as indication of acceptance of those terms as legally binding.

Letter of Credit: letter or document issued by bank on behalf of customer that is evidence of financial background of bank and ensures that payment will be made when proper documents confirm completion of related transaction. Such letters authorize drawing of sight or time drafts when certain terms and conditions are fulfilled. See also *Banker's Acceptance, Draft, Sight Draft, Standby Letter of Credit,* and *Time Draft*.

Letter of Intent: letter signifying intention to enter into formal agreement and usually setting forth general terms of such agreement.

Liable: duty or obligation enforceable by law.

Liabilities: indebtedness of an individual or entity.

Libel: written or published false and malicious statements about another that tend to defame or harm another's reputation.

LIBOR: see *London Interbank Offered Rate*.

Lien: legal right or encumbrance to secure payment performance on property pledged as collateral until the debt it secures is satisfied.

LIFO: see *Last-In First-Out*.

Limited Liability Company: legal entity that offers shareholders the same limitations on personal liability available to corporate shareholders. The owners of a limited liability company (LLC) have limited liability. They are not liable for the debts, liabilities, acts, or omissions of the company. Only their investment is at risk.

Limited Liability: legal exemption corporate stockholders or limited liability companies have from full financial responsibilities for debts of company.

Limited Partnership: partnership of one or more general partners who are personally, jointly, and separately responsible, with one or more special partners whose liabilities are limited to amount of investment.

Line of Credit: see *Credit Line*.

Liquid Assets: assets that can be readily converted into cash.

Liquidate: 1. to pay off or settle current obligation. 2. to sell off or convert assets into cash. 3. to dissolve business in order to raise cash for payment of debts.

Liquidation: process of dissolving a business, settling accounts, and paying off any claims or obligations; remaining cash is distributed to the owners of the business.

Liquidation Value: cash that can be realized from sale of assets in dissolving business, as distinct from its value as ongoing entity.

Liquidity: measure of quality and adequacy of current assets to meet current obligations as they come due.

Liquidity Ratio: company's most liquid assets (generally cash and accounts receivable) divided by current liabilities. Also called quick ratio.

List Price: generally advertised or posted price. Sometimes subject to trade or cash discounts.

Litigation: lawsuit brought to court for purpose of enforcing a right.

LLC: see *Limited Liability Company*.

Loan: money advanced to a borrower with agreement of repayment usually with interest within a specified period of time.

Loan Agreement: legal contract between a financial institution and a borrower that governs the terms and conditions for the life of a loan. Elements usually include description of loan, representations, and warranties reaffirming known facts about the borrower such as legal structure, affirmative and negative covenants, conditions that must be met before the loan is granted, delinquent payment penalties, and statement of remedies that the financial institution may take in event of default.

Loan Participation: sharing of loan(s) by a group of financial institutions that join together to make said loan(s), affording an opportunity to share the risk of a very large transaction. Arranged through correspondent banking networks in which smaller financial institutions buy a portion of an overall financing package. Participations are a convenient way for smaller financial institutions to book loans that would otherwise exceed their legal lending limits. Also called participation financing.

Loan Policy: principles that reflect a financial institution's credit culture, underwriting procedures, and overall approach to lending.

Loans Past Due: loans with interest or principal payments that are contractually past due a certain number of days.

Loan-to-Value Ratio (LTV): relationship, expressed as percent, between principal amount of loan and appraised value of the asset securing financing.

Loan Value: amount of money that can be borrowed against real or personal property.

Lockbox: regional financial institution depository used by corporations to obtain earlier receipt and collection of customer payments. Arrangement provides creditor with better control of accounts receivable and earlier availability of cash balances. Many large financial institutions offer lockbox processing as a cash management service to corporate customers. Lockboxes can be:
- retail, designed for remittance processing for consumer accounts.
- wholesale, in which payments from other entities are collected and submitted through depository transfer check or electronic debit into a concentration account for investment and disbursement as needed.

London Interbank Offered Rate (LIBOR): key rate index used in international lending. LIBOR is the rate at which major financial institutions in London are willing to lend Eurodollars to each other. This index is often used to determine interest rate charged to creditworthy borrowers.

Long-Arm Statutes: state statutes that allow state courts to exercise jurisdiction over nonresident persons or property outside their state's borders.

Long-Term Capital Gain (Loss): gain or loss realized from sale or exchange of capital asset held for longer than 12 months.

Long-Term Liabilities: all senior debt, including bonds, debentures, bank debt, mortgages, deferred portions of long term-debt, and capital lease obligations owed for longer than 12 months.

Loss: 1. circumstance in which expenses exceed revenues. 2. result if an asset is sold for less than its depreciated book value.

Loss Assets: assets considered uncollectible and of such little value that their continuance as realizable assets is not warranted.

Loss Leader: deliberate sale of product or service at or below cost in order to attract new customers.

Loss Payee Clause: provision in insurance policy or added by endorsement to cover lender/mortgagee's interest in property loss settlement. Provision is not as broad as lender's loss payable endorsement. Also called mortgagee clause and loss payable clause.

LTV: see *Loan-to-Value Ratio*.

Lump-sum Settlement: payment made in full with single, one-time payment.

M

Magnetic Ink Character Recognition (MICR): description of numbers and symbols that are printed in magnetic ink on documents for automated processing. Fully inscribed MICR line of information may include item's serial number, routing and transit number, check digit, account number, process control number, and amount.

Mail-Fraud Statute: federal law against using mails to defraud creditors by mailing false financial statements. Prosecution under mail-fraud statute must prove beyond reasonable doubt that:
- statement is false.
- statement was made with intention it should be relied on.
- it was made for the purpose of securing money or property.
- statement was delivered by mail.
- money or property was obtained by means of false statement.

Mailgram: telegraphic message transmitted electronically by Western Union and delivered by U.S. Postal Service.

Mail Teller: employee of a financial institution who receives mail deposits, checks them for accuracy, and returns stamped receipts for deposits to customers.

Majority Stockholder: person or entity that owns more than 50% of voting stock of a corporation, thereby having controlling interest.

Maker: one who signs or executes negotiable instrument.

Malpractice: professional misconduct with negligence.

Management: persons responsible for administering and carrying out policy of business or other organization.

Management Information System (MIS): established flow of information developed to keep managers informed of what is happening within their organization and to do it within a time frame that permits effective reaction when required. Efficient MIS helps managers make better decisions.

Management Report: statement in unaudited financial statements that says financials are representations of firm's management.

Manifest: shipping document that lists freight's origin, contents, value, destination, carrier, and other pertinent information for use at terminals or custom house.

Manufacturers Representative (Agent): independent, commissioned sales agent who represents several noncompeting manufacturers for sale of their products to related businesses within agreed, exclusive sales territory.

Marginal Account: borderline credit risk that does not have sufficient operating capital and from which payment may be delayed.

Markdown: price reduction of goods below normal selling price.

Market: 1. customer base for a company's goods or services. 2. securities exchange and its associated institutions.

Marketability: ease and rapidity with which product, service, or other asset can be sold or converted to cash.

Marketing: 1. activities necessary to facilitate the sale of goods or services through planned research, manufacturing, promotion, advertising, and distribution. 2. business promotion devoted to getting the maximum purchases of products or services by consumers.

Market Value: price that goods or property would bring in current market of willing buyers and sellers.

Markup: amount or percentage added to cost of goods to arrive at selling price.

Maturity Date: date when financial obligation, note, draft, bond, or instrument becomes due for payment.

Mechanic's Lien: enforceable claim, permitted by law in most states, securing payment to contractors, subcontractors, and suppliers of materials for work performed in constructing or repairing buildings. Lien attaches to real property, plus buildings and improvements situated on land, and remains in effect until workers have been paid in full or, in event of liquidation, gives contractor priority of lien ahead of other creditors.

Medium of Exchange: money or commodity accepted in payment or settlement of debt.

Memorandum (Consignment) Sale: sale of goods for which seller is not paid until retailer has sold merchandise. Seller retains title to such goods until retailer has sold merchandise and payment is made to retailer.

Mercantile Agency: organization that compiles credit and financial information and supplies subscribers or members with reports on applicants for credit; can also perform other functions such as collection of accounts or compiling of statistical trade information.

Merchandise Shortage: goods purchased but not included in shipment.

Merger: combining of two or more businesses to form a single organization.

Mezzanine Financing: 1. in corporate finance, leveraged buyout or restructuring financed through subordinated debt, such as preferred stock or convertible debentures. Transaction is financed by expanding equity, as opposed to debt. 2. second- or third-level financing of companies financed by venture capital. Senior to venture capital but junior to financial institution financing, it adds creditworthiness to firm. Generally used as intermediate-stage financing, preceding a company's initial public offering, it is considered less risky than start-up financing.

MICR: see *Magnetic Ink Character Recognition.*

Middle-of-Month (M.O.M.) Billing Term: billing system in which all shipments are charged on one invoice issued twice a month. For first half of month, credit period runs to the 25th and, for the second half, to the tenth of the following month.

MIS: see *Management Information System.*

Modified Accrual Accounting: basis of accounting in which expenditures are recognized when liability is incurred. Revenues are recognized when measurable and available. Exception is in debt service funds in which expenditures are recorded only when due.

M.O.M.: see *Middle-of-Month Billing Term.*

Money Judgment: court decision that adjudges payment of money rather than requiring act to be performed or property transferred.

Monitoring: service available through many credit reporting or interchange bureaus enabling subscribers to request that certain listed accounts be automatically monitored and reviewed and that updated reports be issued periodically.

Moratorium: 1. temporary extension or delay of normal period for payment of account. 2. Formal postponement during which debtor is permitted to delay payment of obligations.

Mortgage: debt instrument giving conditional ownership of asset to borrower, secured by the asset being financed. The instrument by which real estate is hypothecated as security for the repayment of a loan. Borrower gives lender a mortgage in exchange for the right to use property while mortgage is in effect and agrees to make regular payments of principal and interest. Mortgage lien is lender's security interest and is recorded in title documents in public land records. Lien is removed when debt is paid in full. Mortgage normally involves real estate and is considered long-term debt.

Mortgagee: lender who arranges mortgage financing, collects loan payments, and takes security interest in property financed.

Mortgagee Clause: provision in property policy, or added by endorsement, that extends protection, in limited manner, to mortgagee; not as broad as lender's loss payable endorsement.

Mortgagee Waiver: the relinquishment of right(s) contained in a mortgage by a mortgagee.

Mortgage Verification: request made by mortgagee to applicant's financial institution for information on applicant's accounts, as part of mortgagee's credit approval process.

Mortgagor: borrower in a mortgage contract who mortgages property in exchange for a loan.

Multinational Corporation: corporation whose operations are conducted on an international basis.

Multiple Signature Credit Approval: describes credit approval process in which credit is approved by two or more persons acting together.

Mutual Account Revision: routine exchange of credit information between two or more credit grantors that have extended credit to subject of inquiry.

N

NACM: see *National Association of Credit Management.*

National Association of Credit Management (NACM): national business organization of credit and financial professionals that promotes laws for sound credit, protects businesses against fraudulent debtors, improves the interchange of commercial credit information, develops credit practices, and provides education and certification programs for its members.

Negligence: failure to use reasonable care that an ordinarily prudent person would in like circumstances.

Negotiable: anything capable of being transferred by endorsement or delivery.

Negotiable Instrument: any written evidence of indebtedness, transferable by endorsement and delivery or by delivery only, that contains unconditional promise to pay specified sum on demand or at some fixed date.

Negotiate: to discuss, bargain, or work out plan of settlement, terms, or compromise in business transaction.

Net: amount left after necessary deductions have been made from gross amount.

Net Assets: sum of individual's or entity's total assets less total liabilities.

Net Earnings: total sales, less total operating, administrative, and overhead expenses, but before other expenses and income such as interest and dividends.

Net Income: amount of income remaining after deducting all expenses from total revenues.

Net Lease: agreement in which tenant assumes payment of other property expenses, such as taxes, maintenance, and insurance, in addition to rental payments.

Net Price: actual price paid after all discounts, allowances, and other authorized deductions have been taken.

Net Profit: income earned by business over specific period of time. Profit from transaction or sale, after deducting all costs, expenses, and miscellaneous reserves and adjustments from gross receipts.

Net Sales: total sales less returns, allowances, and discounts.

Net Working Capital: current assets less current liabilities; used as measure of a company's liquidity and indicates its ability to finance current operations.

Net Worth: total assets less total liabilities; reflects owners' net interest in company.

No Account: notation on rejected check when check writer does not have account at the financial institution on which check is drawn.

No Asset Case: insolvent or bankrupt estate with no assets available for payment of creditors' claims.

No Funds: notation on rejected check when check writer has account but not funds to cover check.

Nominal Balance: an account balance of less than $100.

Nominal Owner: person whose name appears on title to asset, but who has no interest in it.

Nonaccrual: loan on which a financial institution does not accrue interest; also known as a nonperforming loan.

Nonborrowing Account: banking relationship in which no extension of credit is involved.

Nonfinancial Information: facts used to evaluate a customer's creditworthiness; focuses on background and history rather than financial measures.

Nonpayment: failure or neglect to pay or discharge debt in accordance with terms of agreement.

Nonperforming Assets: total of earning assets listed as nonaccrual; formerly, earning assets acquired in foreclosure and through in-substance foreclosures.

Nonperforming Loans: amount of loans not meeting original terms of agreement, including renegotiated, restructured, and nonaccrual loans. Loans included in this total vary according to bank policy and regulation.

Nonprofit Corporation: organization specifically classified by the IRS as generally tax exempt and whose primary purpose for existence is to provide services of a charitable, fraternal, religious, social, or civic nature.

Nonrecource: inability of holder in due course to demand payment from endorser of debt instrument if party(ies) primarily liable fail to make payment.

Non-sufficient Funds (NSF): term used when collected demand deposit balances are less than the amount of the check being presented for payment and check is returned to payee's financial institution. See also *Overdraft*.

No Protest (N.P.): instructions given by one financial institution to another not to protest check or note when presented for payment. N.P. is usually stamped on instrument to avoid protest fee.

North American Industrial Classification System (NAICS): the Standard Industrial Classification (SIC) code is being replaced by the NAICS code. NAICS classifies establishments by their primary type of activity within a six-digit code. NAICS provides structural enhancements over SIC and identifies over 350 new industries. See also *SIC and Standard Industrial Classification*.

Notary Public: public officer authorized to administer oaths, attest and certify certain types of documents, and to take acknowledgements of conveyances.

Note: unconditional written promise by borrower to pay certain amount of money to lender on demand or at specified or determinable date. This instrument should meet all requirements of laws pertaining to negotiable instruments.

Notes Payable: liabilities represented by promissory notes, excluding trade debts, that are payable in future.

Notes Receivable: assets represented by promissory notes, excluding amounts due from customers for credit sales, to be collected in future.

Notice of Protest: formal statement that a certain bill of exchange, check, or promissory note was presented for payment or acceptance and that such payment or acceptance was not made. Such notice will also state that because instrument has been dishonored, maker, endorsers, or other parties to document will be held responsible for payment.

Novation: substitution of old contract for new one between same or different parties; substitution of new debtor or creditor for previous one, by mutual agreement.

NSF: see *Non-sufficient Funds*.

Nulla Bona: report made by sheriff when no assets are found within his or her jurisdiction on which to satisfy judgment against debtor.

O

Obligation: 1. law or duty binding parties to an agreement. 2. written promise to pay money or to do a specific thing.

Obligee: person or entity to which payment is due.

Obligor: person or entity required by contract to perform specific act.

Obsolescence: decline in perceived value of asset, frequently because of technological innovations, changes in an industry's processes, or changes required by law.

OCC: see *Office of the Comptroller of the Currency*.

Offer: proposal to make contract, usually presented by one party to another for acceptance.

Offering Basis: customer's loan requests considered individually on merits of each proposal.

Office of the Comptroller of the Currency (OCC): branch of the Treasury Department that regulates federally chartered banks.

Office of Thrift Supervision (OTS): branch of the Treasury Department that regulates state and federally chartered thrifts as well as those institutions in conservatorship.

Offset: amount allowed to be netted against another.

On Account: generally describes partial payment made toward settlement of unpaid balance.

On Account Payment: partial payment not intended as payment in full.

On Demand: debt instrument that is due and payable on presentation.

Open (Book) Account: credit extended without a formal written contract and represented on books and records of the seller as an unsecured account receivable for which payment is expected within a specified period after purchase.

Open-End Credit: consumer line of credit that may be added to, up to preset credit limit, or paid down at any time. Customer has option of paying off outstanding balance, without penalty, or making several installment payments. Contrasts with Closed-End Credit. Also called revolving credit or charge account credit.

Open Terms: selling on credit terms as opposed to having customer pay cash.

Operating Performance Ratios: financial measures designed to assist in evaluation of management performance.

Operating Statement: report of an individual's or entity's income and expenses for a specified period of time. See also *Income Statement*.

Operational Risk: risk concerning computer network failure due to system overload or other disruptions; also includes potential losses from fraud, malicious damage to data, and error.

Oral Contract: agreement that may or may not be written in whole or in part or signed but is legally enforceable.

Order: informal bill of exchange or letter or request identifying person to be paid.

Order for Relief: order issued by bankruptcy court judge upon filing of petition by debtor or filing of petition by creditors.

Order to Order: agreement for payment to be made for prior shipment before next delivery will be made.

OREO: see *Other Real Estate Owned*.

Other Real Estate Owned: real property usually taken as collateral and subsequently acquired through foreclosure, or by obtaining a deed in lieu of foreclosure, in satisfaction of the debts previously contracted. Real property formerly used as banking premises, or real property sold in a "covered transaction" as defined by banking regulations.

OTS: see *Office of Thrift Supervision*.

Outlet Store: retail operation where manufacturers' production overruns, discontinued merchandise, or irregular goods are sold at discount.

Out-of-Court Settlement: 1. settlement made by distressed debtor through direct negotiations with creditors or through creditors' committee; acceptance of such settlement is not obligatory to nonconsenting creditors. 2. agreement reached between opposing parties to settle pending lawsuit before matter has been decided by court.

Out-of-Pocket Expense: business expenses for which individual pays.

Out-of-Trust: an event occurring in floor plan financing where a borrower sells inventory securing the financial institution's loan and fails to promptly remit the proceeds to the financial institution in accordance with the loan agreement.

Outstanding: 1. amount of credit facility that is being used versus total amount made available. 2. unpaid or uncollected account.

Overdraft: negative account balance created when a check is paid when collected demand deposit balances are less than amount of check being presented for payment. See also *Non-sufficient Funds*.

Overdue: debt obligation on which payments are past due.

Overhead: selling and administrative business costs as contrasted with costs of goods sold.

Oversold: condition in which manufacturer or wholesaler finds itself after taking more orders than it can deliver within an agreed period of time.

Owed: debt that is due and payable.

Own: to have legal title to property.

Owner: person or entity that owns or has title to property.

Owner's Equity: mathematical difference between total assets and total liabilities that represents shareholders' equity or an individual's net worth.

Ownership: exclusive rights that one has to property, to exclusion of all others; having complete title to property.

Owner's Risk: term used in transportation contracts to exempt carrier from responsibility for loss or damage to goods.

P

Packing List: detailed listing of information on shipment's contents (enclosed for inspection with package).

Paid Direct: payment made by debtor directly to original creditor instead of to collection agency or attorney handling account for collection.

Paper Profit: unrealized income or gain on asset.

Paralegal: trained aide to attorney who handles various legal tasks.

Parent Company: an entity that holds controlling majority interest in subsidiaries.

Partial Payment: payment not in full for amount owed.

Participation: purchase or sale of a loan or credit facility among two or more financial institutions in which the acquiring institution (s) has no formal or direct role in establishing the terms and conditions binding the borrower. Participants do not participate in the document negotiation between the originating financial institution and the borrower.

Partnership: business arrangement in which two or more persons agree to engage, upon terms of mutual participation, in profits and losses.

Party: person concerned or taking part in a transaction or proceeding.

Past Due: payment or account that remains outstanding and unpaid after its agreed-upon payment or maturity date.

Pay: to satisfy, or make partial payments on, a debt obligation.

Payable: obligation that is due now or in future.

Payables: liabilities owed to trade creditors for purchase of supplies. Also called accounts payable.

Payee: person or entity named on a negotiable instrument as the one to whom the obligation is due.

Payer: party responsible for making payment as shown on check, note, or other type of negotiable instrument; also called maker or writer.

Payment: discharge, in whole or in part, of debt or performance of agreement.

Payment for Honor: payment of past-due obligation by someone else to save credit or reputation of person responsible for payment.

Payoff: receipt of payment in full on an obligation.

Penalty: 1. legal fine, forfeiture, or payment imposed for defaulting or violating terms of contract. 2. interest charge imposed for late payments that is permissible by law and imposed with customer's prior agreement or knowledge of seller's terms of sale.

Percentage Lease: lease of real property in which rental payments are based on percentage of retailer's sales.

Percentage of Completion: method of accounting commonly used by contractors and developers in which costs are related to percentage of job completion.

Perfection: with respect to security interests in personal property under Article 9 of the UCC, the action required to give the secured party rights in the collateral as against third parties with competing claims. In general, a security interest is not perfected until a properly executed financing statement has been recorded or the secured party is in the possession of the collateral, whichever applies as to that specific collateral type.

Performance: fulfillment of promise or agreement according to terms of contract or obligation.

Performance Bond: guaranty to project owner that the contractor will perform the work called for by the contract in accordance with the plans and specifications. Customarily issued by bonding and insurance companies, although financial institution letters of credit may be used.

Perjury: willfully and knowingly giving false testimony under oath.

Person: individual (natural person) or incorporated enterprise (artificial person) having certain legal rights and responsibilities.

Personal Check: check drawn by individual on his or her own bank account.

Personality: legal term for personal property or possessions that are not real estate.

Personally Liable: individual's responsibility for payment of obligation, generally used to refer to owner's or guarantor's responsibility.

Personal Property: movable or chattel property of any kind.

Petition: written application, made in contradiction to motion. Also used in some states in place of complaint.

Petition in Bankruptcy: document filed in court to declare bankruptcy. Petition can be either voluntary (filed by debtor) or involuntary (filed by creditors), depending on bankruptcy chapter rules.

Petty Cash: cash on hand or in designated bank account that is available for small, miscellaneous purchases.

Physical Inventory: inventory verification obtained by visual observation of items and itemization of quantities of goods on hand.

Piercing the Corporate Veil: legal action taken by creditor, when fraud or unjust enrichment may be involved, to hold principals of corporation (or other entities) liable for debts of corporation.

Plaintiff: person or entity that initiates legal action against another.

Plan of Arrangement: procedure in bankruptcy under Chapter 11 for debtor to restructure debts or rehabilitate by arriving at arrangement with creditors. See also *Bankruptcy, Chapter 11 Cases*.

Pledge: promise of personal property as security for performance of act, payment of debt, or satisfaction of obligation.

Points: 1. percentage fee charged to obtain a mortgage loan. 2. in shares of stock, one point equals $1.00.

Policy: 1. written statement by management that explains an organization's philosophy and approach to doing business. 2. written contract of insurance between insured and the insurance company.

Pooling Accounts: arrangement by a debtor listing all his or her debts with a debt management or pro-rating service with the understanding that the service will receive, as its fee, a portion of debtor's payments to his or her creditors and proportionately distribute the balance of payments to each creditor on a scheduled basis. Activities of such services may be covered by individual state statutes.

Postdated Check: check written for payment, effective at future date.

Power of Attorney: written document that authorizes one person to act as another's agent.

Preference: 1. right of a creditor to be paid before other creditors by virtue of having lien or collateral. 2. improperly paying or securing of one or more creditors, in whole or part, by an insolvent debtor to the exclusion of other creditors.

Preference Period: in bankruptcy, the 90-day period immediately preceding debtor entering into bankruptcy. If a creditor files new or additional liens against a debtor during this time, such claims may be disallowed by bankruptcy court.

Preferred Creditor: creditor whose account takes legal preference for payment over claims of others.

Prepaid Expenses: payment for goods or services not yet received.

Prepayment: payment of loan or debt before it actually becomes due.

Prime Contractor: contractor who enters into contract with the owner of the project for completion of all or portion of the project and takes full responsibility for its completion. See also *General Contractor*.

Prime Rate: an index or base rate published or publicly announced by a financial institution from time to time as the rate it is generally willing to give its most creditworthy customers.

Principal: 1. amount of money loaned or borrowed. 2. key decision maker or management of entity.

Priority: legal preferences that secured creditors have over general creditors in bankruptcy.

Priority Lien: lien recorded before other secured claims and payable ahead of other liens if liquidation of pledged collateral occurs. First mortgage has priority over second and third mortgages, known as junior liens. Secured creditor holding perfected security interest has priority over liens filed afterward.

Private Enterprise: business established to take economic risks for purpose of making profit.

Privilege: right that nature of debt gives to one debt holder over others.

Proceeds: actual amount of money given to or received from creditor after any deductions are made.

Profit: 1. amount of net income made by an entity in course of doing business. 2. increase in value of an asset over its depreciated book value at the time of sale.

Profit and Loss Statement (P & L): financial report of an individual's or entity's revenue and expenses for a given period of time. See also *Income Statement* and *Operating Statement*.

Pro Forma: projected financial statements.

Progress Payments: partial payments made on a long-term contract as it progresses. Required when a manufacturer or contractor cannot afford, or does not wish, to finance a project.

Projection: borrower's estimate of future performance over designated time period.

Promissory Note: written promise to make unconditional payment of specified amount on designated date, signed by maker.

Proof of Claim: creditor's formal document filed with court against estate of debtor if creditor is owed funds.

Proof of Loss: sworn statement filed by insured when making claim.

Property: something of value that is legally owned and in which person has exclusive and unrestricted right or interest.

Property Insurance: coverage that applies to loss caused by physical damage to property (buildings, contents, earnings, etc.) owned by insured.

Proposal: oral or written offer that, if accepted, constitutes a contract.

Proprietorship: single and exclusive ownership of a business by one person.

Pro Rata: share calculated in proportion to total amount.

Pro Rata Distribution: payment proportionate to uniform percentage of obligations to all creditors.

Protest: formal, written, notarized notice stating credit instrument has not been honored and that makers or endorsers will be held responsible for payment.

Prox.: see *Proximo*.

Proximo (Prox.): sales term used in invoices to mean next month after month of invoice. This term is sometimes used instead of EOM terms.

Proxy: written statement or power of attorney, authorizing an individual to act or speak for another.

Public Credit: debt incurred by government, federal and local, for a use that meet the needs of its citizens.

Purchase Money Lien: manufacturer's legal right to goods and products until the buyer makes payment. Under the Uniform Commercial Code, manufacturer's rights can take priority over lender's lien rights if both claim interest in same inventory. Lender may receive such priority if funds were provided to purchase asset, provided liens are filed within 20 days of borrower taking possession of collateral and noticing requirements have been met.

Purchase Money Mortgage: mortgage given by buyer to seller in lieu of cash, as partial payment on property.

Purchasing Power: value of money and its ability to buy goods and services in a given period.

Q

Qualified Acceptance: agreement to terms of contract only if certain conditions are meet. This constitutes counteroffer and rejection of original offer.

Qualified Endorsement: transfer of debt instrument to endorsee without recourse or liability to endorser.

Qualified Financial Statement: audit report issued by independent accountants that indicates restrictions on scope of audit performed, uncertainties, or disagreements with management.

Qualified Prospect: potential customer whose background and credit have been checked and approved.

Quantity Discount: price reduction extended to purchaser of a large volume of goods.

Quarterly Accounts Receivable Survey: index, compiled by Credit Research Foundation in affiliation with the National Association of Credit Management and published quarterly, that shows average days' sales outstanding for manufacturers and wholesalers.

Quick Assets: current assets that can be readily converted into cash (generally, accounts receivable).

Quick Assets Ratio: cash and cash equivalents plus trade receivables (net) divided by total current liabilities; used as measure of liquidity.

Quid Pro Quo: 1. giving of one valuable thing for another. 2. mutual consideration between parties to contract.

Quitclaim: to release or relinquish claim or title.

R

Rack Jobber: wholesale distributor who sells housewares and other convenience-type merchandise through retail stores and assumes responsibility for stocking and maintaining store's inventory.

Rate of Exchange: amount of one country's currency that can be bought with another country's currency at a particular point in time.

Rate of Interest: cost of borrowing money, usually expressed as annual percentage charge.

Rating: 1. assessment of borrower's financial strength and creditworthiness. 2. symbol used to denote borrower's creditworthiness.

Ratios: mathematical relationship between two or more things, used as indication of a company's financial strength relative to other companies of comparable size or in same industry.

Real Property: land and anything erected or growing on it or affixed to it.

Receivables: money due or collectible for goods sold, services performed, or money loaned. Also called accounts receivable.

Receivables Turnover: measurement of how effective a company is in collecting on its trade receivables.

Receiver: person appointed by the court to receive, take charge, and hold in trust a property in litigation or bankruptcy until a legal decision is made as to its disposition.

Receivership: 1. court action whereby money or property is placed under control, and administration of receiver is to be preserved for benefit of persons or creditors ultimately entitled to it. 2. procedure used to help a distressed debtor or to resolve a dispute.

Reclamation: 1. legal action by titleholder to recover property from another's possession. 2. process used to restore land to usable state.

Record: written account of act, transaction, or instrument drawn by proper legal authority that remains as permanent evidence.

Recourse: right of holder in due course to demand payment from anyone who endorsed instrument if original signer fails to pay.

Recovery: amount finally collected; amount of judgment.

Reference Check: contacting and interviewing business or professional associates of credit applicant to gain information about his or her creditworthiness.

References: names of trade suppliers or creditors provided by a customer to be used as a source of information about that customer.

Refer to Maker: term stamped by financial institution on a check to indicate its rejection.

Refinance: to reorganize existing debts by obtaining new debt that incorporates or pays off existing debts.

Register: book of factual public information, kept by a public official.

Regulation 9: regulation issued by the Comptroller of Currency allowing national banks to operate trust departments and act as fiduciaries. Under Regulation 9, a national bank is permitted to act as trustee, administrator, and registrar of stocks and bonds and engage in related activities, such as management of a collective investment fund, as long as these activities do not violate state legislation.

Regulation A: Federal Reserve Board regulation governing advances by Federal Reserve Banks to depository institutions at a Federal Reserve discount window. Credit advances are available to any bank or savings institution maintaining transaction accounts or non-personal time deposits. The Fed has two different programs for handling discount window borrowings:
- adjustment credit to meet temporary needs for funds when other sources are not available.
- extended credit, designed to assist financial institutions with longer-term needs for funds. This includes seasonal credit privileges extended to smaller financial institutions that do not have ready access to money market funds. Federal Reserve Banks may also extend emergency credit to financial institutions other than depository institutions in which failure to obtain credit would affect the economy adversely.

Regulation B: Federal Reserve regulation prohibiting discrimination against consumer credit applicants and establishing guidelines for collecting and evaluating credit information. Regulation B prohibits creditors from discriminating on the basis of age, sex, race, color, religion, national origin, marital status, or receipt of public assistance. Regulation B also requires creditors to give written notification of rejection, statement of applicant's rights under Equal Credit Opportunity Act of 1974, and statement listing reasons for rejection, or applicant has right to request reasons. If applicant is denied credit because of adverse information in credit bureau report, applicant is entitled to receive copy of bureau report at no cost. Creditors who furnish credit information when reporting information on married borrowers must report information in name of each spouse.

Regulation C: Federal Reserve regulation implementing Home Mortgage Disclosure Act of 1975, requiring depository institutions to make annual disclosure of location of certain residential loans to determine whether depository institutions are meeting credit needs of their local communities. Specifically exempted are institutions with assets of $10 million or less. Regulation C requires lenders of mortgages that are insured or guaranteed by a federal agency to disclose number and total dollar amount of mortgage loans originated or purchased in recent calendar year, itemized by census tract where property is located.

Regulation D: Federal Reserve regulation that sets uniform reserve requirements for depository financial institutions holding transaction accounts or non-personal time deposits. Reserves are maintained in form of vault cash or non-interest-bearing balance at a Federal Reserve Bank or at a correspondent bank.

Regulation E: Federal Reserve regulation that sets rules, liabilities, and procedures for electronic funds transfers (EFT) and establishes consumer protections using EFT systems. This regulation prescribes rules for solicitation and issuance of EFT debit cards, governs consumer liability for unauthorized transfers, and requires financial institutions to disclose annually terms and conditions of EFT services.

Regulation F: Federal Reserve regulation requiring state-chartered banks with 500 or more stockholders and at least $1 million in assets to file financial statements with the Board of Governors of the Federal Reserve System. In general, these state-chartered member banks must file registration statements, periodic financial statements, proxy statements, and various other disclosures of interest to investors. These regulations are substantially similar to those issued by Securities and Exchange Commission.

Regulation G: Federal Reserve regulation governing credit secured by margin securities extended or arranged by parties other than banks or broker/dealers. It requires lenders to register credit extensions of $200,000, secured by margin stock, or $500,000 in total credit, within 30 days after end of quarter.

Regulation H: Federal Reserve regulation defining membership requirements for state-chartered banks that become members of the Federal Reserve System. The regulation sets forth procedures as well as privileges and requirements for membership. The regulation also requires state-chartered banks acting as securities transfer agents to register with board.

Regulation I: Federal Reserve regulation requiring each member bank joining the Federal Reserve System to purchase stock in its Federal Reserve Bank equal to 6% of its capital and surplus. Federal Reserve Bank stock, which pays interest semiannually, is nontransferable and cannot be used as collateral. When bank increases or decreases its capital base, it must adjust its ownership of Federal Reserve stock accordingly.

Regulation J: Federal Reserve regulation providing legal framework for collection of checks and other cash items and net settlement of balances through Federal Reserve System. It specifies terms and conditions under which Federal Reserve Banks will receive checks for collection from depository institutions, presentment to paying banks, and return of unpaid items. It is supplemented by operating circulars issued by Federal Reserve Banks.

Regulation K: Federal Reserve regulation governing international banking operations by bank holding companies and foreign banks in the U.S. The regulation permits Edge Act corporations to engage in range of international banking and financial activities. It also permits U.S. banks to own up to 100% of non-financial companies located outside the U.S. Regulation K also imposes reserve requirements on Edge Act corporations, as specified in Regulation D, and limits interstate activities of foreign banks in the U.S.

Regulation L: Federal Reserve regulation prohibiting interlocking director arrangements in member banks or bank holding companies. Management official of state member bank or bank holding company may not act simultaneously as management official of another depository institution if both are not affiliated, are very large banks, or are located in same local area. Regulation L provides 10-year grandfather period for certain interlocks and allows some on exception basis, such as organizations owned by women or minority groups, newly chartered organizations, and in situations in which implementing regulation would endanger safety and soundness.

Regulation M: Federal Reserve regulation implementing consumer leasing provisions of Truth in Lending Act of 1968. It covers leases on personal property for more than four months for family, personal, or household use. It requires leasing companies to disclose in writing the cost of lease, including security deposit and monthly payments, taxes, and other payments, and in case of an open-end lease, whether a balloon payment may be applied. It also requires written disclosure of terms of lease, including insurance, guaranties, respon-

sibility for servicing property, and whether lessor has an option to buy property at lease termination.

Regulation N: Federal Reserve regulation governing transactions among Federal Reserve Banks and transactions involving Federal Reserve Banks and foreign banks and governments. This regulation gives the board responsibility for approving in advance negotiations or agreements by Federal Reserve Banks and foreign banks, bankers, and governments. The Federal Reserve Bank may, under direction of the Federal Open Market Committee, undertake negotiations, agreements, or facilitate open market transactions. Reserve Banks must report quarterly to the Board of Governors on accounts they maintain with foreign banks.

Regulation O: Federal Reserve regulation limiting amount of credit member banks may extend to their own executive officers. Regulation O also implements reporting requirements of Financial Institutions Regulatory and Interest Rate Control Act of 1978 and Garn-St. Germain Depository Institutions Act of 1982.

Regulation P: Federal Reserve regulation that sets minimum standards for security devices, such as bank vaults and currency handling equipment, including automated teller machines. Member bank must appoint security officer to develop and administer program to deter thefts and file the annual compliance statement with its Federal Reserve Bank.

Regulation Q: Federal Reserve regulation requiring depository institutions to state clearly terms for depositing and renewing time deposits and certificates of deposit and also any penalties for early withdrawal of savings accounts.

Regulation R: Federal Reserve regulation prohibiting individuals who are engaged in securities underwriting, sale, and distribution from serving as directors, officers, or employees of member banks. Regulation R specifically exempts those involved in government securities trading and general obligations of states and municipalities.

Regulation S: Federal Reserve regulation implementing section of Right to Financial Privacy Act of 1978 requiring government authorities to pay reasonable fees to financial institutions for financial records of individuals and small partnerships available to federal agencies in connection with government loan programs or Internal Revenue Service summons.

Regulation T: Federal Reserve regulation governing credit extensions by securities brokers and dealers, including all members of national securities exchanges. Brokers/dealers may not extend credit to their customers unless such loans are secured by margin securities-securities listed and traded on national securities exchange, mutual funds, and over-the-counter stock designated by Securities and Exchange Commission as eligible for trading in national market system. Generally, brokers/dealers may not extend credit on margin securities in excess of percentage of current market value permitted by board.

Regulation U: Federal Reserve regulation governing extensions of credit by banks for purchasing and carrying margin securities. Whenever lender makes loan secured by margin securities, bank must have customer execute purpose statement regardless of use of loan.

Regulation V: Federal Reserve regulation dealing with financing of contractors, subcontractors, and others involved in national defense work. The regulation spells out the authority granted to Federal Reserve Banks under the Defense Production Act of 1950 to assist federal departments and agencies in making and administering loan guaranties to defense-related contractors and sets maximum interest rates, guaranty fees, and commitment fees.

Regulation X: Federal Reserve regulation extending provisions of other securities-related regulations-Regulations G, T, and U-to foreign persons or organizations who obtain credit outside U.S. for purchase of U.S. Treasury securities.

Regulation Y: Federal Reserve regulation governing banking and nonbanking activities of bank holding companies and divestiture of impermissible nonbank activities. Regulation Y spells out procedures for forming bank holding company and procedures to be followed by bank holding companies acquiring voting shares in bank or nonbank companies. Regulation Y also lists those nonbank activities that are deemed closely related to banking and therefore permissible for bank holding companies.

Regulation Z: Federal Reserve regulation implementing consumer credit protections in the Truth in Lending Act of 1968. Major areas of regulation require lenders to:
- give borrowers written disclosure on essential credit terms, including cost of credit expressed as finance charge and annual percentage rate.
- respond to consumer complaints of billing errors on certain credit accounts within specified period.
- identify credit transactions on periodic statements of open-end credit accounts.
- provide certain rights regarding credit cards.
- inform customers of right of rescission in certain mortgage-related loans within specified period.
- comply with special requirements when advertising credit.

Regulation AA: Federal Reserve regulation establishing procedures for handling consumer complaints about alleged unfair or deceptive practices by a state member bank.

Regulation BB: Federal Reserve regulation implementing Community Reinvestment Act of 1977 (CRA). Banks are required to make available to public a statement indicating communities served, type of credit the lender is prepared to extend, and public comments to its CRA statement.

Regulation CC: Federal Reserve regulation implementing Expedited Funds Availability Act of 1987, setting endorsement standards on checks collected by depository financial institutions. Endorsement standard is designed to facilitate identification of endorsing bank and prompt return of unpaid checks. The regulation specifies funds availability schedules that banks must comply with and procedures for returning dishonored checks.

Release: to discharge debt or give up claim against party from whom it is due by party to whom it is due.

Remedy: legal means by which right is enforced or violation of right is prevented or compensated.

Rent: periodic payments made by tenant to owner in return for leasing land, building space, or equipment.

Reorganization: 1. voluntary or court-ordered change in capital structure of corporation in which all assets of an old corporation are transferred to a newly formed corporation. 2. restructuring of business entity, whether in or out of bankruptcy.

Replevin: legal action taken to recover possession of property unlawfully taken.

Repossess: action taken by creditor in which he or she takes possession of goods purchased under credit agreement or pledged as collateral if debtor defaults on terms of contract.

Rescind: to void contract from its inception. Result is that parties are restored to relative positions before contract was made.

Rescission: agreement by parties to contract that effects cancellation of contract.

Reserve: in accounting, funds set aside for specific purpose.

Reserve for Bad Debts: valuation account established for accounts receivable that may prove uncollectible.

Residence: place where person legally lives part or full time.

Residual Value: the estimated recoverable amount of a depreciable asset as of the time of its removal from service.

Resolution Trust Corporation (RTC): federal agency established in 1989 to oversee the savings and loan bailout.

Restraint of Trade: any action, by agreement or by combination, that tends to eliminate competition, artificially sets up prices, or results in monopoly.

Restrictive Endorsement: endorsement on negotiable instrument that limits any further negotiability, for example, "for deposit only" written on back of check.

Restructured Loan: loan on which a bank, for economic or legal reasons related to debtor's financial difficulties, grants concession to debtor that would not be considered otherwise.

Retailer: company that sells its product directly to end-user.

Retained Earnings: cumulative earnings and losses of company that remain undistributed to shareholders.

Retentions: amounts withheld by customer from total billings until contractor has satisfactorily completed project.

Retroactive: 1. effective as of past date. 2. having reference to prior time.

Return: rate of profit or earnings on sales or investment.

Return Items/Returned Checks: checks, drafts, or notes returned unpaid to originating bank by drawee bank so that originator can correct any errors or irregularities and may present items for collection again.

Revenue: 1. income from sales, interest, or dividends. 2. income from investment or wages.

Reviewed Financial Statements: business financial statements that are reviewed by independent accountants through inquiries of management and performance of analytical procedures on financials to provide limited assurance that no material modifications are necessary for statements to conform to generally accepted accounting principles. Independent accountants do not express opinion on review statements.

Revolving Charge: credit type that allows borrower to become indebted up to an approved credit limit, with no fixed maturity date. Finance costs are assessed monthly on unpaid balance, and periodic payments are required.

Revolving Credit: commitment under which funds can be borrowed, repaid, and re-borrowed during life of credit. Such credits have stated maturity date at which time borrower may have option of converting outstanding balance into term loan. See also *Evergreen Revolving Credit*.

Rider: any schedule or amendment attached to a contract or document that becomes part of it.

Right of Rescission: consumer's right as prescribed by Truth in Lending Act of 1968 to rescind certain credit and mortgage contracts within three days without penalty.

Right of Setoff: right of financial institution to apply borrower's funds on deposit to debt owed to the financial institution in event that payment on the debt is not made as agreed.

Risk-Based Capital: level of capital that bank is required to maintain; level is determined by relating capital to risk by type of asset.

RMA: see *Risk Management Association.*

RMA General Figure Ranges: dollar amount ranges established by RMA to ensure accuracy and consistency when exchanging credit information. There are four ranges: low, 1-1.9; moderate, 2-3.9; medium, 4-6.9; and high, 7-9.9. Ranges can be applied to any figure category. Sample figure categories are: nominal = under $100; 3 figures = from $100 to $999; 4 figures = from $1,000 to $9,999; 5 figures = from $10,000 to $99,999; and 6 figures = from $100,000 to $999,999. Information is reported, using both range description and figure category; for example, "average balances are in medium 4-figure range."

Risk Management Association (RMA): association of lending, credit, and risk management professionals. Originally, RMA was founded to facilitate the exchange of credit information. Today, RMA works continuously to improve practices of the financial services industry and to provide members with networking opportunities, training, research publications, and seminars.

Robinson-Patman Act: federal legislation prohibiting firms engaged in interstate commerce from charging different buyers different prices for the same goods unless there is difference in costs or the price does not restrict competition.

R.O.G. Dating: payment term that uses date customer is in receipt of goods as effective sale date.

Royalty: compensation made to another for use of his or her work.

RTC: see *Resolution Trust Corporation.*

Rule of 72: method commonly used to approximate time required for sum of money to double at given rate of interest. Rule of 72 is computed by dividing interest rate by 72.

Rule of 78s: mathematical formula used in computing interest rebated when borrower pays off loan before maturity. Rule of 78s is applied mostly to consumer loans in which finance charges were computed using add-on interest or discounted interest method of interest calculation. Also called sum of digits method.

S

Sale: agreement or contract that transfers title of goods or property from one person or entity to another for consideration.

Sale and Lease Back: arrangement whereby company sells goods with intent to lease those same goods from buyer.

Sale on Approval: purchase of goods conditioned on buyer approval of goods or retention of them beyond reasonable time.

Salvage Value: estimated worth of a depreciated asset at the end of its useful life.

Satisfaction: paying debt in full.

Satisfaction of Judgment: legal evidence that recorded judgment has been paid or settled and entered in court records.

Satisfaction Piece: legal evidence that debt has been paid in full or settled and that liens on collateral have been released.

SBA: see *Small Business Administration.*

Schedule: listing by account name or number of total sales, current sales, monies owing or paid, chargebacks, or credits. Also called aging schedule or trial balance.

Scheduled Liability: 1. in property insurance, listing of property-items or locations-covered. 2. in dishonesty insurance (fidelity bonding), listing of persons or positions covered.

Scheduled Payment: partial payments made at dates specified in credit agreement.

Schedules: in bankruptcy, lists showing debtor's property-location, quantity, and money value; names and addresses of creditors and their class; or names and addresses of stockholders of each class.

Scrap Value: worth of asset that is going to be destroyed or used for its components.

Seasonal Loans: loans used to finance cyclical buildup of current (working capital) assets until those assets can be converted to cash.

Second Lien: lien that can be honored only after first lien is satisfied.

Second Mortgage: mortgage secured by equity in property but one that cannot enforce payment until claims of first mortgage are satisfied.

Secret Partner: partner in business whose interest in partnership is not publicly known.

Secured Creditor: lender or other person whose claim is supported by taking collateral.

Secured Loan: loan supported by borrower's pledge of an asset such as marketable securities, accounts receivable, inventories, real estate, equipment, etc.

Secured Note: note that provides, upon default, certain pledged or mortgaged property that may be applied or sold in payment of debt.

Secured Party: 1. lender or other person to whom or in whose favor security interest has been given. Includes person to whom accounts or chattel paper have been sold. 2. trustee or agent representing holders of obligations issued under indenture of trust, equipment trust agreement, or the like.

Securities: 1. documents that evidence debt or property pledged in fulfillment of obligation. 2. evidence of indebtedness or right to participate in earnings and distribution of corporate, trust, and other property.

Security: guaranty or assets pledged that can be applied to loan or obligation.

Security Agreement: formally executed document that gives lender rights to property pledged by borrower in support of debt.

Security Interest: right that lender or lienholder obtains to debtor's goods as evidenced by security agreement.

Seller's Market: economic condition in which demand is greater than supply, and that typically causes prices to increase.

Sequestered Account: account that has been attached by court order with disbursements subject to court approval.

Service Business: firm that performs functions for its customers rather than sells goods.

Setoff: 1. defendant's counterdemand against plaintiff. 2. right of parties to contract to reduce debt owed to one party by netting it against amount owed by other. See also *Right of Setoff.*

Settle: 1. to mutually reach agreement for adjustment or liquidation of debt. 2. to negotiate payment of obligation or lawsuit for less than amount claimed.

Settlement: 1. adjustment or liquidation of accounts. 2. full and final payment of debt. See also *Out-of-Court Settlement.*

Shared National Credit (SNC): any loan originally $20 million or more that is shared at its inception by two or more financial institutions under a formal intercreditor or participation agreement or sold in part to one or more financial institutions with purchasing financial institution assuming its pro rata share of credit risk.

Shareholder: person or entity that legally owns stock in a corporation.

Sheriff's Sale: court-ordered sale of property to satisfy judgment, mortgage, lien, or other outstanding debt against debtor.

Sherman Antitrust Act: federal legislation aimed at prevention of business monopoly; act declares illegal every contract, combination, or conspiracy in restraint of normal trade.

Short-Term Liabilities: current debts that are due within one year.

Short-Term Loan: current debt obligation that matures within one year, evidenced by promissory note that spells out terms of agreement.

SIC: see *Standard Industrial Classification.*

Sight Draft: draft payable on demand when presented to drawee. See also *Draft, Letter of Credit,* and *Time Draft.*

Signal Action: notices that provide subscriber with list of accounts in which subscriber has interest and on which delinquent payments have been reported.

Signature Loan: unsecured loan backed only by borrower's signature on promissory note. No collateral is taken by lender. This loan is generally offered to individuals with good credit standing. Also called good faith loan or character loan.

Signature Verification: examination of signature on negotiable instrument to determine whether handwriting is genuine and whether person signing check is authorized to use account.

Simple Interest: interest calculated on outstanding principal amount of debt or investment only.

Single Proprietorship: ownership of company by one person.

Skip Tracing: process used to obtain information to locate debtor's whereabouts in order to collect payment on debts. Sources used include other creditors, friends, relatives, neighbors, directories, credit bureaus, court records, and other informants or references.

Slander: oral defamation of another's reputation.

Small Business Administration (SBA): federal agency whose function is to advise and assist small businesses; provides loan guaranties for small businesses, minorities, and veterans plus financial assistance to small businesses that have suffered catastrophes.

SNC: see *Shared National Credit.*

Soft Goods: nondurable consumer goods such as clothing and linen, having a short-term useful life.

Soldier's and Sailor's Relief Act: federal act, also passed by various states, under which right to legally enforce an obligation against a person is suspended during the period that person is in military service or for period thereafter.

Sole Owner: one with title to proprietorship.

Solvency: ability to pay one's debts in usual and ordinary course of business as they mature.

Special Material: made-to-order material or work done to customer's specifications that has no value to seller if order is canceled.

Special Mention Assets: as it relates to risk assessment of bank assets, assets that deserve management's close attention. If left uncorrected, these potential weaknesses may result in deterioration of repayment prospects for asset or in institution's credit position at some future date. Special mention assets are not adversely classified and do not expose institution to sufficient risk to warrant adverse classification.

Specific Coverage: property coverage on designated property or item. Contrasts with Blanket Coverage.

Specific Performance: court order directing party guilty of breach of contract to undertake complete performance of contractual obligation in instances in which damages would inadequately compensate injured party.

Speculation: investment made with hope of achieving large financial gain.

Speculator: one who makes risky investments for quick financial gain rather than long-term investment.

Stale Check: negotiable draft that has been held too long to be honored for payment; time varies from state to state.

Standard Industrial Classification (SIC): statistical classification standard underlying all establishment-based federal economic statistics classified by industry. SIC is used to promote comparability of establishment data describing various facets of the U.S. economy. Classification covers entire field of economic activities and defines industries in accordance with composition and structure of economy. It is revised periodically to reflect economy's changing industrial organization. See also *North American Industrial Classification System and NAICS.*

Standby Letter of Credit: type of letter of credit issued by bank that may be drawn on by payee only if party that makes letter of credit (drawer) defaults or does not perform according to terms of specific contract or agreement. See also *Letter of Credit.*

Statement: 1. itemized summary and accounting of charges, payments, and balance outstanding at close of billing period. 2. financial report.

Statement of Cash Flows: financial statement that shows cash receipts and disbursements for given period.

Statement of Changes in Owner's Equity: financial statement that reconciles changes in capital accounts (capital stock, paid in surplus, and retained earnings).

Statute: written law.

Statute of Frauds: law prohibiting filing of actions or suits against certain types of contracts unless the contracts are in writing.

Statute of Limitations: law that sets time frame for bringing action against another. Time frame varies according to nature of claim and jurisdiction.

Stay: act of arresting judicial proceeding by court order.

Stipulation: agreement between opposing attorneys in lawsuit, usually required to be in writing.

Stock: 1. merchandise or inventory on hand and available for sale. 2. certificate that indicates number of shares of ownership in corporation.

Stock Power: document executed in form of power of attorney by which owner of stock authorizes another party to sell or transfer stock.

Stop Payment Order: instructions given by depositor to a financial institution to dishonor, or not make payment on, a certain check.

Subchapter S: business concern chartered as corporation that is taxed as partnership. An S corporation has 35 or fewer shareholders and can use cash basis of accounting. Corporate gains (or losses) from operations are taxed to shareholders as individuals.

Subcontract: contract between prime contractor and another contractor or supplier to perform specified work or to supply specified materials in accordance with plans and specifications for project.

Subject: party on which credit information is requested.

Sublimit: specified, partial amount of credit facility that is designated for special use.

Subordination: 1. signed agreement acknowledging that one's claim or interest is inferior to another's. 2. act of agreeing to take secondary position.

Subpoena: process to demand person to appear in court and give testimony.

Subrogation: substitution of one creditor for another so that substituted creditor succeeds to rights, remedies, or proceeds of claim.

Subsidiary: business entity owned or controlled by another organization.

Substandard Assets: as it relates to risk assessment of bank assets, assets that are inadequately protected by current sound worth and paying capacity of obligor or of collateral pledged, if any. Assets so classified must have well-defined weakness or weaknesses that jeopardize liquidation of debt. They are characterized by distinct possibility that bank will sustain some loss if deficiencies are not corrected.

Summons: formal notice served on defendant stating that action has been instituted against him or her and requiring defendant to appear in court to answer it.

Supplementary Proceedings: statutory action requiring judgment debtor to appear in court to discover property against which action can be taken by creditor to enforce collection of judgment.

Supplier: business that sells goods, materials, or services to customers. Also called vendor.

Surety: one who agrees to be primarily liable with another and to fulfill another's obligations under terms of agreement.

Surety Bond: guaranty that payment or performance of some specific act will be completed under penalty or forfeiture of bond usually issued by a bonding company.

Suretyship: undertaking by person or entity to pay obligation of obligee in favor of principal when obligee defaults; such undertaking by individual is known as personal suretyship and by insurance company as corporate suretyship.

Suspense File: group of accounts, records, or other items held temporarily until final disposition is determined.

Swap: A financial derivative contract between two parties to exchange fixed-rate interest payments for floating-rate interest payments, or floating-rate interest payments on different bases (e.g., prime rate versus LIBOR), calculated on specific floating indices by reference to a notional principal amount for a specified term.

Sweep Account: type of cash management tool in which, when prearranged amount of cash accumulates in account, amount is automatically invested.

Swindle: 1. to obtain money or property by deceitful misrepresentation. 2. to cheat or fraudulently induce individual to give up his or her property willingly.

Swing Loan: see *Bridge Loan.*

Syndicate: temporary association of persons or firms formed to carry out business venture or project of mutual interest.

Syndication: project financing whereby commercial or investment bankers agree to advance portion of funding. Syndicator acts as investment manager, collecting loan origination fee or commitment fee from borrower and arranging for sale to other banks in group. Typically, syndicator keeps only a small portion of total financing. A syndicated loan differs from loan participation because syndicate members are known at outset to borrower. Syndication also separates lead bank from group of financial institutions that ultimately fund obligation.

T

Takeover: acquisition, seizure, control, or management of one business by another.

Tangible Assets: assets that can be weighed, measured, or counted, including cash, property, machinery, and buildings.

Tax: payments imposed by legislative authority for support of government and its functions.

Taxable Income: portion of individual's or entity's income that is subject to taxation.

Tax Avoidance: act of using legal deductions, exemptions, and tax code provisions to reduce taxes payable.

Tax Evasion: failure to report taxable income to avoid proper payment of taxes.

Tax Foreclosure: legal seizure and sale of property by authorized public official to satisfy unpaid taxes.

Tax Levy: legislative action by which tax is imposed.

Tax Lien: statutory claim by state or municipality against property of person owing taxes. Property may be sold to satisfy obligation or judgment filed against it.

Tax Sale: sale of property seized by governmental taxing body for nonpayment of taxes.

Tenancy by Entirety: ownership in property by husband and wife in which each becomes whole owner of the entire estate upon the other's death. See also *Joint Tenancy with Rights of Survivorship.*

Tenancy in Common: two or more persons who hold title to land or other property in undivided ownership.

Tender: 1. unconditional offer of money or performance to satisfy claim. 2. offer to buy stock to take control of company.

Term Loan: fixed-term business loan with a maturity of more than one year and with defined periodic payments, providing borrower with working capital to acquire assets or inventory or to finance plant and equipment.

Terms: conditions and requirements as set forth in sales proposal, contract, or promissory note.

Terms of Sale: mutually agreed upon conditions for transfer of title or ownership of goods or property.

Testimony: written or oral evidence given in court under oath.

Third Party: one who is not directly related to action between two parties but who may be affected by its outcome.

Third-Party Claim: demand made by person who is not party to action for delivery or possession of personal property, title to which is claimed by third party.

Time Deposit: 1. interest-bearing funds deposited in a financial institution for a specified period of time, such as certificates of deposit and savings accounts. 2. under Regulation D, deposit in which depositor is not permitted to make withdrawals within six days after date of deposit unless deposit is subject to early withdrawal penalty.

Time Draft: draft payable on fixed date or certain number of days after sight or date of draft. See also *Banker's Acceptance, Draft, Letter of Credit,* and *Sight Draft.*

Title: document that evidences legal ownership and possession of property.

Title Company: business that as contracted researches specific property's history through real estate records and issues policy to purchaser or lienholder guaranteeing that there are no known defects in title.

Title Insurance: a guarantee by a title insurance company that it will indemnify the insured, in a specific amount, against losses resulting from defects in the title to a property. The insured may be the owner of the property, that person's heirs and devises, or the lender and future assignees.

Title Search: to review history of property's ownership and any judgments or liens filed against it.

Tolling the Statute: act of debtor to freeze statute of limitations that extends period for creditor to legally enforce payment of account. Individual state laws and statutes apply.

Tort: violation of legal duty that results in injury or damage to another.

Trade Acceptance: draft, accepted by buyer, sent with shipment of goods, requiring customer to pay amount involved at specific date and place.

Trade Credit: accounts payable; credit extended from one company to another.

Trade Debts: liabilities due from one business to another for purchase of supplies, inventory, etc.

Trade-in: property accepted by seller as partial down payment on purchase of new item.

Trade Information: confidential exchange of payment history and credit information among suppliers.

Trademark: distinctive identifying mark, word, or logo of product or service; protected when registered with U.S. Patent Office.

Trade Name: name used by a company to identify itself in the course of business. Also known as Trade Style or Fictitious Name.

Trade Payment Record: summary of performance of company in meeting terms of its credit obligations.

Trade References: names of suppliers or business creditors with whom credit information on customer can be exchanged.

Treasury Workstation: microcomputer-based information management system that allows corporate treasurer to automate daily balance reporting of collected balances, to invest idle funds in short-term money market, and to disburse funds to trade creditors. Overall aim is improvement in productivity and eventual integration of funds management and corporate accounting systems, such as order entry and invoicing.

Trial Balance: listing of all account balances from general ledger used in preparing financial statements.

Truck Jobber: wholesale merchant who sells and delivers products from truck inventory at time of sale. Also called Wagon Distributor.

Trust: right to real or personal property that is held by one for benefit of another.

Trust Company: business that acts as fiduciary and agent, handling trusts, estates, and guardianships for individuals and businesses.

Trustee: one who holds or is entrusted with management of property or funds for benefit of another.

Trustee in Bankruptcy: person appointed by court or elected by creditors to manage bankrupt property and carry out responsibilities of trust in proceedings.

Trust Receipt: trust agreement (in receipt form) between a financial institution and borrower. It is temporarily substituted for possessory collateral securing creditor's loan so that creditor may release instruments, documents, or other property without releasing title to property. Borrower agrees to keep property (collateral), as well as any funds received from its sale, separate and distinct from borrower's own property and subject to repossession by the financial institution in event that he or she fails to comply with conditions specified in trust agreement.

Truth in Lending Act of 1968: See *Regulation Z.*

Turnkey: something that is constructed, supplied, or installed and fully ready as intended.

U

UCC: see *Uniform Commercial Code.*

Ultra Vires: unauthorized acts taken by corporation beyond powers conferred on it by corporate charter.

Umbrella Policy: in liability insurance, policy that applies excess coverage to primary or underlying contract; provides large limits and broad coverage or may cover only primary basis risks not otherwise insured.

Unaudited Financial Statement: financial statement or report based on figures that have not been verified by a qualified accountant.

Uncollected Funds: deposits not yet collected by a financial institution, such as checks that have not yet cleared.

Uncollectible Accounts: receivables or debts not capable of being settled or recovered.

Underwriter: 1. person who reviews application for insurance and decides whether or not to accept risk. 2. one who agrees to purchase entire issue of bonds or securities at end of certain period.

Undue Influence: improper or illegal pressure used to wrongfully take advantage of person or to influence his or her actions or decisions.

Unearned Discount: A term used to reflect a reduced price (from the face value of an invoice) taken by a buyer without the consent of the seller.

Unearned Income: income received in advance of being earned.

Unencumbered Property: property that has no legal defects in its title; a property free and clear of any liens or debts.

Unenforceable Claim: debt on which all collection efforts have failed.

Unfair Competition: any fraudulent or dishonest practice intended to harm or unfairly attract competitor's customers.

Uniform Commercial Code (UCC): comprehensive set of statutes created to provide uniformity in business laws in all states, as approved by National Conference of Commissioners on Uniform State Laws. Statutes can vary from state to state.

Unit Banking: banking system in several states that prohibits branching or operation of more than one full-service banking office by state-chartered or national banks. Limited branching laws encourage chartering of large numbers of small, independently owned state banks and large multi-bank holding companies that own numerous unit banks.

Unjust Enrichment: doctrine whereby one is not allowed to profit inequitably at another's expense.

Unsatisfied Judgment: recorded judgment that has not been released or discharged.

Unsecured Creditor: one who grants credit without taking collateral in support of it.

Unsecured Loan: loan made on strength of borrower's general financial condition. Contrasts with Secured Loan.

Upstream Funding: funds borrowed by a subsidiary of a holding company for holding company's use. Contrasts with Downstream Funding.

Usury: The rate of interest that exceeds the legal limit allowed to be charged for the use of another's money. Legal limit of interest for different types of loan transactions is established by state law.

V

Valuable Consideration: see *Consideration.*

Valuation: 1. the estimated or determined worth of something. 2. process of appraising or affixing value of something.

Value Received: phrase used in bill of exchange or promissory note to denote that lawful consideration has been given.

Variable Interest Rate: interest rate that fluctuates with changes in an identified base rate or index.

Vendor: trade supplier or service provider.

Venture Capital: capital invested or available for investment in the ownership element of a new enterprise.

Verdict: formal decision of judge or jury on matter submitted in trial.

Verification: 1. affidavit or statement under oath swearing to truth or accuracy of written document. 2. in accounting, confirmation of entries in books of account.

Verification of Deposit (VOD): formal request by creditor to debtor's bank for account balance information.

Vest: 1. to give immediate transfer of title to property. 2. to obtain absolute ownership.

VOD: see *Verification of Deposit.*

Void: having no legal force.

Voidable Contract: contract that is nullified as to party who committed invalid act but not with respect to other party, unless he or she agrees to treat it as such.

Voluntary Bankruptcy: bankruptcy initiated by debtor petitioning court to be declared bankrupt.

Voucher: 1. statement itemizing payment or receipt of money. 2. detachable portion of check that describes purpose for which check was issued.

W

Wage Assignment: agreement by borrower that permits creditor to collect certain portion of borrower's wages from employer in the event of a default.

Wage Garnishment: court order requiring that percentage of debtor's earnings be withheld by employer and paid directly to creditor.

Waiver: intentional or voluntary relinquishing of known legal right.

Warehouse Loans: loans made against warehouse receipts that are evidence of collateral for material stored in public warehouse.

Warehouse Receipt: receipt issued by person engaged in business of storing goods for hire. It is document of title that gives evidence that person in possession of warehouse receipt is entitled to receive, hold, and dispose of document and goods it covers. Warehouse receipt in turn obligates warehouser to keep goods safely and to redeliver them upon surrender of receipt, properly endorsed, and payment of storage charges.

Wholesaler: company whose primary function is as intermediary between manufacturer of goods and retailer or other wholesalers.

Will: legal declaration by person making disposition of property, effective only after death.

Windfall Profit: large, unexpected return or income.

Wire Fate: instructions to financial institution requesting confirmation by wire that out-of-town check, sent for collection, has been paid.

Without Exception: see *Free and Clear.*

Without Prejudice: legal term used in offer, motion, or suit to indicate that parties' rights or privileges involved remain intact and to allow new suit to be brought on same cause of action.

Without Recourse: term used in endorsing negotiable instrument excluding endorser from responsibility should obligation not be paid.

With Prejudice: legal term used for dismissal of lawsuit that bars any future action and that, if prosecuted to final adjudication, would have been adverse to plaintiff.

With Recourse: endorsement of negotiable instrument on which endorser remains responsible should obligation not be paid.

Working Capital: 1. current assets less current liabilities, used as measure of firm's liquidity. 2. funds available to finance company's current operations.

Working Papers: information or schedules used by accountant in preparing financial reports.

Work in Process (WIP): goods in act of being manufactured, but not yet finished and ready for sale, representing a portion of inventory.

Workout: problem loan on which the financial institution is working closely with borrower for repayment, restructuring, or modification because of noncompliance with loan covenants.

Wrap-Around Mortgage: A second or junior mortgage with a face value of both the amount it secures and the balance due under the first mortgage. Covenant contained within second mortgage used to induce sellers of commercial properties to sell to buyer who has small down payment, normally when interest rates are high.

Writ of Execution: 1. writ issued by court ordering sheriff to attach debtor's property to enforce payment of judgment.

Write-down: partial reduction in book value of asset as result of obsolescence or depreciation.

Write-off: see *Charge-off.*

Writ of Attachment: court order directing sheriff to seize property of debtor held as security for satisfaction of judgment.

Y

Yield: rate of return on investment.

Z

Zero Balance Account: a checking account (subordinate account) used for disbursing or collecting funds in which no balances are maintained. At the end of the processing day, funds are transferred from a master account or concentration account to cover activity in the subordinate account.

Zoning Ordinance: municipal regulation dividing land into districts and prescribing structural, architectural, and nature of use of buildings within these districts.

INDUSTRY DEFAULT PROBABILITIES AND CASH FLOW MEASURES— SAMPLE REPORT

AGRICULTURE—Wheat Farming NAICS 111140 (SIC 0111)

Current Data Sorted By Assets | **Type of Statement** | **Comparative Historical Data**

0-500M	500M-2MM	2-10MM	10-50MM	50-100MM	100-250MM	Type of Statement	4/1/01-3/31/02 ALL	4/1/02-3/31/03 ALL
	1	9	7	4	3	Unqualified	1	6
	2	7	5			Reviewed	1	6
	9	11	3			Compiled		12
8	11	4			1	Tax Returns	1	9
4	11	18	15	3	1	Other	3	11

Current period statement counts: 25 (4/1-9/30/05), 112 (10/1/05-3/31/06)

0-500M	500M-2MM	2-10MM	10-50MM	50-100MM	100-250MM	Sales Size / Number of Statements	4/1/01-3/31/02 ALL 6	4/1/02-3/31/03 ALL 44
12	34	49	30	7	5	Number of Statements	6	44

EXPECTED DEFAULT FREQUENCY (%)

0-500M	500M-2MM	2-10MM	10-50MM	50-100MM	100-250MM		4/1/01-3/31/02	4/1/02-3/31/03
.15	.21	.19	.20			Risk Calc EDF		.51
.25	.58 (29)	.38 (45)	.37 (28)			(1 yr)		1.16
1.32	1.13	.93	.87					3.24
A3 1.29	Baa2 2.02	A3 1.28	Baa1 1.41			Moodys EDF Rating (see note) — Risk Calc EDF (5 yr)		Baa3 4.27
Baa2 2.69	Ba1 4.57	Baa3 3.39	Baa2 2.52					Ba2 7.29
Ba2 6.03	Ba2 6.64	Ba1 5.38	Ba1 5.60					Ba3 11.68

CASH FLOW MEASURES (%)

0-500M	500M-2MM	2-10MM	10-50MM		4/1/01-3/31/02	4/1/02-3/31/03
				Cash from Trading/Sales		
13.1	18.6	12.8	22.5	Cash after Operations/Sales		17.3
8.1	8.4	5.5	5.4			4.6
2.4	.6	.3	.0			-.1
13.1	19.1	11.8	28.0	Net Cash after Operations/Sales		16.3
7.9	7.0	6.3	7.3			4.9
2.9	.7	-.1	1.3			-.2
9.6	10.9	4.7	10.2	Cash after Debt Amortization/Sales		6.1
1.0	2.7	.5	2.1			.2
-1.8	-.3	-3.4	-4.4			-5.6
22.8	10.2	3.5	7.7	Debt Service P&I Coverage		1.8
5.3 (11)	2.7 (30)	1.3 (46)	1.8 (26)			.9 (38)
.5	1.3	.0	.0			-.6
24.0	12.0	6.2	26.0	Interest Coverage (Operating Cash)		4.2
11.4 (11)	5.4 (30)	2.8 (46)	4.2 (23)			1.7 (38)
.5	2.0	.0	.0			-1.2
	12.6	12.5	33.8	Δ Inventory		25.0
	-6.2 (20)	2.4 (41)	4.5 (17)			2.8 (25)
	-35.3	-14.4	-14.0			-8.7
30.6	63.0	26.3	34.5	Δ Total Current Assets		52.5
2.8	10.9	-.9	11.3			6.1
-15.9	-23.4	-12.3	-8.7			-14.3
18.2	32.4	10.4	38.7	Δ Total Assets		32.3
-.4	8.0	2.2	19.3			6.1
-18.8	-8.8	-5.6	-1.2			-4.4
86.2	124.4	30.2	35.2	Δ Retained Earnings		29.0
26.4 (11)	32.1 (32)	8.0 (48)	11.1 (29)			3.1 (43)
-18.6	-.6	-5.4	-8.3			-9.7
27.7	36.4	15.9	25.3	Δ Net Sales		18.0
6.1	10.2	3.8	16.2			3.2
-24.4	-5.0	-2.4	-4.5			-6.6
				Δ Cost of Goods Sold		
158.3	184.8	46.3	58.4	Δ Profit before Int. & Taxes		131.5
67.9	45.8	5.9	13.5			5.3
9.4	-21.3	-41.0	-41.9			-41.3
-3.6	6.3	20.3	22.0	Δ Depr./Depl./Amort.		19.5
-35.0 (10)	-10.9 (29)	-3.8 (44)	9.4 (25)			.0 (41)
-79.0	-57.6	-17.3	-11.6			-25.9

RATIOS

0-500M	500M-2MM	2-10MM	10-50MM		4/1/01-3/31/02	4/1/02-3/31/03
62.5	51.1	21.1	17.4	Sustainable Growth Rate		13.9
18.8	4.1	6.2 (48)	1.0			4.3 (43)
-35.7	-19.2	-9.2	-12.7			-7.0
.2	.5	1.4	.0	Funded Debt/EBITDA		.7
1.0	1.8	4.2	1.2			4.4
3.0	4.6	7.8	7.7			8.4

0-500M	500M-2MM	2-10MM	10-50MM	50-100MM	100-250MM		4/1/01-3/31/02	4/1/02-3/31/03
10183M	128646M	537379M	939854M	632204M	2502199M	Net Sales ($)	103690M	1261287M
2875M	36020M	257891M	748596M	520460M	671806M	Total Assets ($)	44082M	569936M

M = $ thousand   MM = $ million

through 18 for explanation of ratios and data.

Note: The ratings are Moody's.edf rating (e.g. Ba1.edf) and not Moody's Investor Services Long-Term Bond Ratings.
If a number of statements appears for the Risk Calc EDF (1 yr), it also applies to the (5 yr).

AGRICULTURE—Wheat Farming NAICS 111140 (SIC 0111)

Comparative Historical Data			Type of Statement	Current Data Sorted By Sales					
2	13	24	Unqualified		1	3	2	8	10
6	8	14	Reviewed			2	3	6	3
9	14	23	Compiled	2	5	6	6	3	1
11	21	24	Tax Returns	7	8	3	5		1
12	33	52	Other	11	6	1	8	13	13
4/1/03 3/31/04 ALL	4/1/04 3/31/05 ALL	4/1/05 3/31/06 ALL		25 (4/1-9/30/05)		112 (10/1/05-3/31/06)			
40	89	137	Sales Size / Number of Statements	0-1MM 20	1-3MM 20	3-5MM 15	5-10MM 24	10-25MM 30	25MM & OVER 28
%	%	%	**EXPECTED DEFAULT FREQUENCY**	%	%	%	%	%	%
.58	.14	.17		.31	.15	.15	.27	.20	.15
1.16 (81)	.27 (126)	.37	Risk Calc EDF	(18) .57 (19)	.48 (13)	.62 (20)	.37 (29)	.33 (27)	.21
2.98	.86	.89	(1 yr)	1.60	1.14	1.39	.97	.70	.72
Ba1 5.52	.A3 1.18	A3 1.28	**Moodys EDF Rating** (see note) Risk Calc EDF (5 yr)	Baa2 2.93 A3	1.26 A3	1.17 Baa2	2.66 A3	1.24 A1	.85
Ba2 7.92	Baa2 2.65	Baa3 3.13		Baa3 4.19 Baa3	4.33 Ba1	4.97 Baa3	3.49 Baa2	2.40 Baa1	1.49
Ba3 12.23	Ba1 5.21	Ba1 5.72		Ba2 6.58 Ba2	6.50 Ba3	8.40 Ba2	6.42 Baa3	4.26 Baa3	3.97
%	%	%	**CASH FLOW MEASURES**	%	%	%	%	%	%
			Cash from Trading/Sales						
12.9	24.6	16.3	Cash after	84.2	16.0	25.0	11.8	9.8	11.9
4.8	6.6	6.7	Operations/Sales	25.6	9.5	3.1	6.1	5.9	4.5
.3	.6	.6		7.8	1.1	-2.3	1.6	.2	-2.5
12.6	23.2	17.3	Net Cash after	86.3	19.7	20.4	11.5	11.7	9.3
4.4	6.5	7.0	Operations/Sales	25.9	9.5	2.2	5.9	7.0	4.7
.5	1.1	1.0		7.0	2.1	-3.1	.8	2.1	-4.1
6.3	9.3	8.0	Cash after Debt	27.4	9.6	7.6	3.7	7.5	7.5
1.2	2.2	1.9	Amortization/Sales	6.3	2.0	.6	.3	2.9	2.2
-4.5	-4.0	-2.0		-4.3	-.4	-3.6	-1.6	-.3	-4.5
2.8	4.9	7.4	Debt Service	5.6	18.9	5.4	3.2	7.4	11.6
(34) 1.3 (81)	2.0 (125)	2.1	P&I Coverage	(18) 2.5 (18)	2.6 (21)	.8 (27)	2.1 (27)	1.8 (26)	2.5
.0	.2	.6		.6	1.1	-1.6	1.1	.0	-.4
7.0	8.8	12.2	Interest Coverage	5.6	18.9	9.1	10.0	21.6	22.9
(33) 2.5 (81)	3.3 (118)	3.9	(Operating Cash)	(18) 3.0 (18)	10.5 (21)	2.3 (27)	4.1 (27)	4.3 (19)	8.8
.2	.4	.5		1.1	1.2	-2.4	1.8	.0	.0
36.7	16.8	16.9	Δ Inventory		15.6	60.5	12.0	24.5	29.2
(24) 3.2 (60)	-1.1 (91)	3.0		(12) -2.3 (13)	7.4 (19)	2.4 (24)	-1.4 (18)	10.4	
-11.4	-22.5	-13.9			-27.7	-14.4	-17.8	-13.1	.0
27.6	21.4	34.7	Δ Total Current Assets	88.1	23.4	73.4	29.2	21.6	35.6
5.2	10.2	6.8		2.6	-4.0	31.0	1.5	9.1	10.4
-10.4	-11.4	-12.1		-19.1	-29.1	-7.8	-13.8	-8.2	-5.4
28.0	30.0	26.7	Δ Total Assets	9.1	27.9	59.6	19.3	17.3	37.3
4.8	7.9	6.0		-3.0	6.6	27.0	5.7	3.6	12.7
-3.1	-2.8	-5.8		-14.0	-5.2	-.6	-10.1	-4.1	-3.0
25.8	49.2	42.7	Δ Retained Earnings	116.4	50.0	39.2	48.1	31.9	50.4
(39) 3.4 (85)	10.3 (131)	16.2		25.7 (16)	27.1	14.5	6.3 (29)	15.2 (27)	21.8
-14.1	-9.8	-2.5		-4.7	-2.4	-2.3	-17.0	1.6	-7.1
21.6	28.2	25.9	Δ Net Sales	10.3	26.8	61.8	33.0	24.5	31.7
3.2	7.9	7.4		1.2	2.3	3.3	10.7	12.7	14.7
-7.8	.0	-2.4		-12.6	-8.8	-3.0	-2.0	.4	2.1
			Δ Cost of Goods Sold						
150.6	95.7	102.7	Δ Profit before	160.7	49.0	223.9	136.3	59.8	91.8
30.8 (88)	11.5	16.3	Int. & Taxes	36.2	14.3	5.1	15.9	11.7	34.4
-28.0	-26.9	-27.2		-17.4	-35.9	-30.4	-26.1	-43.4	-16.3
31.0	19.8	19.7	Δ Depr./Depl./Amort.	-5.1	.0	62.2	19.8	12.2	53.4
(34) 5.2 (71)	.0 (119)	-3.6		(16) -38.0 (19)	-13.8 (14)	4.7 (21)	.0 (25)	-4.8 (24)	14.5
-23.0	-12.6	-28.4		-100.0	-57.9	-12.0	-16.2	-20.1	-3.5
38.2	26.1	35.8	**RATIOS**	73.1	43.6	97.0	4.6	22.7	42.4
8.2 (87)	5.8 (136)	5.2	Sustainable Growth Rate	.4	4.9	11.0 (23)	-6.2	8.0	11.8
-.8	-2.6	-10.9		-28.6	-8.4	-2.2	-42.5	1.0	-8.8
1.3	.7	.4	Funded Debt/EBITDA	.6	.9	.1	1.4	.1	.1
3.4	3.4	2.3		4.5	1.7	1.9	3.5	1.6	1.7
7.3	6.6	6.5		7.1	4.6	6.2	9.2	4.6	7.5
593939M	1930153M	4750465M	Net Sales ($)	10433M	37704M	55139M	167816M	473209M	4006164M
433841M	1644466M	2237648M	Total Assets ($)	45306M	41772M	71763M	153656M	373482M	1551669M

M = $ thousand   MM = $ million

Note: The ratings are Moody's.edf rating (e.g. Ba1.edf) and not Moody's Investor Services Long-Term Bond Ratings. If a number of statements appears for the Risk Calc EDF (1 yr), it also applies to the (5 yr).

NOTES

NOTES

NOTES

NOTES